VideoHound's
GOLDEN
MOVIE
RETRIEVER

VideoHound's
GOLDEN
MOVIE
RETRIEVER

DETROIT • WASHINGTON, D.C. • LONDON

CREDITS

EDITORS:
Martin Connors
Julia Furtaw

CONTRIBUTING EDITORS:
Beth A. Fhaner
Christine Tomassini
Maria L. Sheler
Richard Lawson
Jan Klisz

PROGRAMMER:
Donald Dillaman

TYPESETTER:
Michael Boyd,
Atlis Publishing Services, Inc.

DESIGN SUPERVISOR:
Cynthia Baldwin

SFX AND COVER DESIGN:
Sheila Young Tomkowiak
Mary Krzewinski

PAGE DESIGN:
Kathleen Hourdakis

FRONTMATTER ATTENDANTS:
Barbara Yarrow
Todd Nessel

VIDEOHOUND'S PERSONAL ILLUSTRATOR:
Terry Colon

KEY GRIPS:
Mary Beth Trimper
Dorothy Maki
Evi Seoud
Mary Winterhalter Kelley

ASSISTANT TO MR. HOUND:
Jane P. Connors

CATERING:
Britt's Cafe

COSTUMES:
Dayton Hudson
K-Mart

RESEARCH:
Chuck Lewis

PUBLICITY HOUNDS:
Beth Dempsey
Jenny Sweetland

MARKETING MANAGER:
Lauri Taylor

A Cunning Canine Production

CONTENTS

INTRODUCTION • VI

USING VIDEOHOUND • IX

LASERDISC INDEX • 1

CAPTIONED INDEX • 15

FOREIGN FILM INDEX • 23

AWARDS INDEX • 35

ALTERNATE TITLES INDEX • 53

VIDEOS (A-Z) • 79

CATEGORY INDEX • 1023

KIBBLES INDEX • 1177

SERIES & PARTNERSHIPS INDEX • 1203

CAST INDEX • 1209

DIRECTOR INDEX • 1439

WRITER INDEX • 1505

COMPOSER INDEX • 1537

MUSIC VIDEO GUIDE • 1551

DISTRIBUTOR GUIDE • 1567

INTRODUCTION

We sat in the darkened Big Pooch viewing room, comparing notes after another day of watching the inspired, the competent, the strange, the disposable, and the near incoherent, consuming box after box of low-fat popcorn and scribbling notes, diligently assigning bones for quality and adjectives for effect. We had writer's block and hand cramps and our Slurpees had run dry. What is it about the movie review business that chews up so much talent? You meet enough ex-editors on the street, sleeping in doorways, pockets full of ticket stubs, you start to wonder about your own future. But we had a job to do.

We were tired from the endless video sessions, hour upon hour of movie marathons in which our emotions were exploited and our intelligence sometimes scorned. Dazed and temporarily confused, we wondered how Forrest Gump got into "Philadelphia" and why there were no angels in the outfield for "Little Big League." Suddenly the screen went blank and the television had a moment of brooding silence. We took advantage of the pause and decided to have a creative flash. "Let's do an index by scriptwriter with about 3,400 names," we said, "so you could look up a fellow like John Matewan Sayles and find he wrote a movie called 'Alligator.'" Or you could look up the life works of such writers as Joe Sliver Eszterhas, Quentin Natural Born Killer Tarantino, and Michael Jurassic Crichton." We were excited now. So we popped for another. "And let's have a composer index with more than 800 musical geniuses listed. With a quick glance, you can discover all the movies to which Marc Sleepless in Seattle Shaiman has lent his musical talent. Or look up the collected works of John Boom Boom Williams."

The creative buzz seemed nuclear, nearing cold fusion. But the big hound didn't seem to get it. He sat impassively at the end of the card table, paws tapping slowly on the cheap samsonite. You couldn't always read the big guy, even when he was jumping on you and slobbering on your clothes. Dogs were like that. A paw turned delicately down seemed a distinct possibility, but it was a likelihood we didn't want to consider. Somebody with a bright idea turned the lights on and we all blinked from the glare. The big hound scratched his ear and a smile began curling around the tip of his large nozella. You know, the snout. He let go with an enthusiastic howl and we knew we were home free. *VideoHound 1995* had its signature. We said a little prayer, sipped the last of the Slurpee, and went back to watching movies.

****

VideoHound 1995 comes your way with a number of key improvements and additions. A deluxe rest stop on the busy info highway, *VideoHound 1995* supplies billions and billions of details on video entertainment and dozens of convenient ways of unearthing the goods. The new, improved *VideoHound* includes nearly 1,500 new videos, three new indexes, expanded cast and category listings, and many other minor improvements (like the category *Wyatt Earp* in the Series Index). If you have a question about a film or you're looking for that hard-to-find video, *VideoHound 1995* can likely deliver the answer. As part of our quest to give you the best video guide $17.95 plus tax can buy (slightly more in Canada), we've also changed the cover, revised the title and copyright pages, updated the reader notes, and written entirely new acknowledgments. Yes, we have been busy.

Why so many new releases? Along with theatrical features released to video, the direct to video business is booming, creating more diversity at the corner video store and supplying you with more choices. Plus, cable and broadcast TV are contributing to the movie bonanza. Bigger than a dozen "Bridges of Madison County," *VideoHound* is the only video guide to comprehensively cover direct to video releases, while keeping a trained eye on the many more mainstream movies. In addition to new films on video, numerous older movies are finding their way onto video for the first time as studios continue to raid the vaults. Encompassing the known video universe, *VideoHound 1995* reviews these films as well. The task of selecting a video from more than 1,000 pages of reviews can be daunting; hence *VideoHound* provides you with a wide selection of indexes to narrow your search. We're continually devising new methods for you to find movie information. Sometimes it's not pretty. But it is our job.

A basic consideration for video selection is knowing who's in the cast, from the big stars to the supporting roles. A significant *VideoHound* improvement is the enlarged cast listings within the review section, providing you with a better idea of who's in a movie. These additions meant something had to give in the massive cast index. Pressed for space, we removed a bunch of well-intentioned but fairly obscure actors with but one film to their credit and replaced them with a number of better-known and busier actors. By

slimming the cast index a bit (still more than 13,000 full videographies and counting), we've managed to improve the *Hound's* overall portability by .00003% (take it to the beach! take it to the sauna! take it on vacation!) and believe that we can stand behind a limited guarantee (void in certain states) that for most of the next year, the binding will not explode in your hands as you casually page through, remarking once again upon the charm and precision of the prose.

Ever sing for your supper? New to *VideoHound 1995* is the song title index, a list of songs and the musicals in which they were performed. The index is a great little trivia trove, a trove being a valuable collection, a discovery, a treasure. So is the index a treasure of trivia? Why, yes, it's a rich repository of the memorable and forgettable which will afford hours of harmless fun, but will only slightly increase your intelligence. Humming something in the shower and wanna know the movie from which the song came? Check this index and shampoo in puzzlement no more. Should you refer to the index while in the shower, please note that the binding may become less permanent, and our extremely limited, void-in-certain-states guarantee no longer applies.

We've spent considerable time exploring the category index, removing or revising categories that annoyed us and adding 90 new lists we found amusing. For instance, *Buses*. Until "Speed," we hadn't really thought of buses. Now we can't get them out of our mind. Forrest Gump has the longest wait in Hollywood history for a bus. Mr. Gump recounts his entire life while waiting for a bus that he doesn't even need to catch. Everywhere we go, buses.

Waitresses seemed a natural, with "Frankie and Johnny" and "Untamed Heart" among a number of others. The slackers of *Generation X* deserved their own category ("Reality Bites," "Singles"). Then we had this killer breakthrough with *Killer*

Brains, Killer Cars, Killer Dreams, Killer Kats, Killer Pigs, and *Killer Rodents.* We felt less homicidal after venting those, segueing to *Party Hell* ("Slumber Party Massacre," anyone?).

Then we had fun with *Cave People* (Yabba dabba doo!) and *Capitol Capers* ("Dave"). *Genre Spoofs* seemed a natural, as did *Concert Films* (a bow to the age of Woodstock, now nearing the age of social security). *Lovers on the Lam* was inspired by a batch of movies where young men and women commit crimes in the spirit of togetherness: "Kalifornia," "Natural Born Killers," "Wild at Heart." Of course, don't forget the dating and random crime classic, "Bonnie and Clyde." *The Meaning of Life* was suggested by a film reviewer in our hometown who noted the recent spate of movies dealing with the spiritual side of things, including "Remains of the Day" and "Shadowlands." Speaking of Anthony Hopkins, the same reviewer, Judy Gerstel of the *Detroit Free Press*, also moved us to add *Repressed Men,* in which Hopkins is the pacesetter, with Hugh "Cary" Grant gaining ground quickly. To further enhance your browsing pleasure within the category index, we've also inserted *see* and *see also* references into the main of the index.

With this edition, we've added coverage of the CD-I format. Still in its infancy, CD-I is potentially a revolutionary step for the video business, as movies become available in a compact disc format offering all the advantages the music compact disc now offers—clarity, queuing ability, and minimal deterioration. The most significant problem with CD-I at the moment is disc storage. Video signals take up a lot of room, resulting in multiple disc sets for a single film. As the technologists figure out how to further compress the signal, the format could become very popular. The handful of flicks now available on CD-I are priced competitively with VHS, but you need a CD-I player and other gizmos to actually enjoy the view. For a list of films now available on CD-I, turn to the beginning of the Laser Disc/CD-I Index.

In our quest to make *VideoHound* even more useful, we've also added a black triangular symbol (in printing terms, a dingbat) to some listings in the category, kibbles, and series index. At first glance, that dingbat/symbol may look superfluous, an inexplicable whim of editors known for inexplicable whims. Stare a while however, and besides the wavy motion of the words on the page, you'll soon observe that the triangle indicates those movies rated three bones or above. Now you'll be able to separate the cream from the cheese and the crust from the wheat bread before turning back to the review section. The triangle survived a rigorous testing phase in which hundreds of dingbats were printed and discarded, lacking that certain something that makes a dingbat special. The little hand with the finger pointing? Been there, done that. The actual bones? Took up too much room. The asterisk? Not very original. All but the triangle, a simple but elegant geometric form, were found wanting.

As for the writer and composer indexes, we'll be burning a little midnight oil to expand and improve upon our start. In the meantime, please write to us with your ideas. We appreciate all of the cards and letters sent to us, even the ones in crayon, and urge you to continue communicating in the mode most suitable to your lifestyle (tearout card, fax, cellular phone, semaphore, telepathically). Creating each *VideoHound* is a cooperative act between readers and editors in which your suggestions become part of the grand *VideoHound* plan (make it better). We thank you for your ideas and for your continuing support.

USING VIDEOHOUND

ALPHABETIZATION

Titles are arranged on a word-by-word basis, including articles and prepositions. Leading articles (*A, An, The*) are ignored in English-language titles. The equivalent foreign articles are not ignored, however: *The Abyss* appears under "A" while *Les Miserables* appears under "L." **Other points to keep in mind:**

• Acronyms appear alphabetically as if regular words. For example *C.H.U.D.* is alphabetized as "Chud."
• Common abbreviations in titles file as if they are spelled out, so *St. Elmo's Fire* will be found under "Saint Elmo's Fire."
• Proper Names in titles are alphabetized beginning with the individual's first name; for instance, *Monty Python's The Meaning of Life* is under "M."
• Titles with numbers (*2001: A Space Odyssey*) are alphabetized as if the number was spelled out under the appropriate letter, in this case "Two Thousand One." When numeric titles gather in close proximity to each other (*2000 Year Old Man, 2001, 2069: A Sex Odyssey*), the titles will be arranged in a low (*2000*) to high (*2069*) numeric sequence.

INDEXES

LASERDISC/CD-I INDEX   Master list of more than 6,000 videos available in the laserdisc format, as well as a new list of CD-I movies.

ALTERNATE TITLE INDEX   A number of videos, particularly older or B-type releases, may have variant titles. More than 4,000 alternate titles that refer back to the primary titles as listed in the review section. The alternate titles are also noted within the review.

SONG TITLE INDEX   Alphabetic list of 4,700 songs performed during the course of a cinematic musical. Title of the movie in which the song was performed follows the song title.

CAST/DIRECTOR INDEX   The Cast Index provides full videographies of some 13,000 actors, while the Director Index lists the works of 6,000 directors. Although listed in a first name, last name sequence, the names are alphabetized by last name. Film titles, complete with initial year of release, are arranged in alphabetic order.

WRITER INDEX   Nearly 3,400 scriptwriters and script doctors are listed with their vital works. Names are arranged alphabetically by last name.

COMPOSER INDEX   Videographies of 800 composers, arrangers, and lyricists, are listed. Arranged alphabetically by last name.

CATEGORY INDEX   Nearly 500 terms ranging from the orthodox to slightly eccentric permit you to video sleuth from broad type to significant themes to signature scenes. The mix, arranged alphabetically by category, includes hundreds of traditional film genres and sub-genres as well as a feast of *VideoHound* exclusives. Integrated into the index are cross references, while preceding the index is a list of definitions. **Tipped triangle indicates a movie rated three bones or above.**

KIBBLES INDEX   Nearly 300 miscellaneous categories are presented, spanning the literary side of movie-making (adapted from a play, Hemingway on video) to key producers, to special effects masters to composers. Plus it provides lists of annual box-office winners (that are now on video) since 1939, classic movies, four-bone delights, trash films, modern Shakespeare, Disney fare, and of course, bottom of the barrel *Woof!* features, some of which are terrible enough to provide an amusing evening. A complete list of the categories precedes the index. **As in the Category Index, tipped triangles indicate quality views.**

SERIES INDEX   Nearly 70 concise listings of major movie series ranging from James Bond to National Lampoon to Godzilla to the *Raiders of the Lost Ark* to Dr. Seuss are presented. Recurring cinematic collaborations of note are also listed, including the Marx Brothers, Monty Python, Hope & Crosby, Abbott & Costello, and Turner & Douglas. The full list of series and film partners precedes the index. **Quality flicks get the triangular stamp of approval.**

AWARDS INDEX   The Awards Index lists 2,200 films honored by 12 national and international award bodies, representing some 90 categories of competition. This information is also contained in the review following the credits. **Only features available on video and reviewed in the main section are listed in this index; movies not yet released on video are not covered.**

As award-winning films find their way to video, they will be added to the review section and covered in this index. Awards listed include the American Academy Awards; Australia Film Institute; British Academy of Film and Television Arts; Cannes Film Festival; French Cesar; Canadian Genie; Golden Globe; Directors Guild of America; Edgar Allan Poe Awards; Independent Spirit; Montreal Film Festival; and the MTV Awards.

FOREIGN FILM INDEX   Here the *Hound* classifies 4,700 movies by the country/countries of record in which the feature was financed (and not necessarily filmed). Since the producers of a specific film may hail from more than one country, some videos will be listed under more than one country. The foreign codes also appear in the review immediately following the color or black and white designation. Tipped triangle following the title indicates three bone or above endeavor.

CAPTIONED INDEX   Lists more than 3,400 videos available with captioning for hearing impaired viewers provided by either the National Captioning Institute (Falls Church, VA) or the Caption Center (Los Angeles, CA).

MUSIC VIDEO GUIDE   Titles and distributor codes for more than 4,000 music videos and music performance recordings. Music videos are typically prefaced by the name of the artist for quick identification.

DISTRIBUTOR GUIDE   Each video review has at least one and as many as three distributor codes. In the reviews, these are located immediately before the critical rating at the bottom of the review. The full address and phone, toll-free, and fax numbers of the 340 distributors listed can be found in the Distributor Guide. A caution: a small number of distributors adhere to a nomadic life-style that includes frequent address changes. A tiny minority on the list in any given year will also go out of business. Up to three distributors are listed in order to give you more choice.

In the main section, those reviews with the code **OM** are on moratorium (distributed at one time, though not currently). Since a title enjoying such status was once distributed, it may well linger on your local video store shelf. When the distributor is not known, the code **NO** appears. For new releases to the theater that have not yet made it to video (but likely will in the coming year), the code **NYR** (not yet released) appears.

SAMPLE REVIEW

Each *VideoHound* review contains up to 18 items of information, ranging from the title to the review to awards received to the critical rating. Information of interest to the film buff or casual viewer includes precise length of the video, whether in color or black and white, availability in VHS or Beta formats (as well as laserdisc and CD-I), year first released, and list price. The review also contains information on colorized versions, alternate titles, sequels, remakes, sources of adaptations, songs (for most musicals), cast, and directors. Many reviews also identify writers, composers, and lyricists.

1 Aladdin 2 Boy meets princess, loses her, finds her, wins her from evil vizier and nasty parrot. Superb animation triumphs over average songs and storyline by capitalizing on Williams' talent for ad-lib with lightning speed genie changes, lots of celebrity spoofs, and even a few pokes at Disney itself. Adults will enjoy the 1,001 impersonations while kids will get a kick out of the big blue genie and the songs, three of which are the late Ashman's legacy. Kane and Salonga are responsible for the singing voices of Aladdin and Jasmine; Gottfried is a riot as the obnoxious parrot sidekick. Be forewarned: small children may be frightened by some of the scarier sequences.. **3** ♫ A Whole New World; Prince Ali; Friend Like Me; One Jump Ahead; Arabian Nights. **4** AKA: The Robin Williams Show.

5 1992 **6** (G) **7** 90m **8** *C* **9** *GB* **10** V: Robin Williams, Scott Weinger, Linda Larkin, Jonathan Freeman, Frank Welker, Gilbert Gottfried, Douglas Seale, Brad Kane, Lea Salonga **11** *D:* Ron Clements, John Musker **12** *W:* Ted Elliot, Terry Rossio **13** *M:* Alan Menken, Howard Ashman, Tim Rice **14** Academy Awards '92: Best Original Score, Best Song ("A Whole New World") Nominations: Best Sound, Best Sound Effects Editing, Best Song ("Friend Like Me"); MTV Movie Awards '93: Best Comedic Performance (Williams). **15** VHS **16** $24.95 **17** *DIS* **18** 🦴🦴🦴🦴

1 **Title**
2 **Description/review**
3 **Songs**
4 **Alternate title** (we made this up)
5 **Year released**
6 **MPAA Rating**
7 **Length**
8 **Black and white** (B) or **color** (C)
9 **Country produced in** (we made this up too)
10 **Cast** (V: indicates voiceovers; also includes cameos)
11 **Director**
12 **Writers**
13 **Composers/Lyricists**
14 **Awards** (Oscar nominations follow Academy Award winners)
15 **Format** (Beta, VHS, and/or LV-laserdisc)
16 **Price** (at highest retail level)
17 **Distributor code**
18 **One- to four-bone rating** (or *Woof!*)

The **LASERDISC/CD-I INDEX** includes 14 titles available in the new CD-I format and nearly 6,000 titles in the increasingly popular laserdisc format. Titles are arranged alphabetically.

CD-I

Apocalypse Now
Black Rain
Fatal Attraction
The Firm
A Hard Day's Night
The Hunt for Red October
Indecent Proposal
Naked Gun 2 1/2: The Smell of Fear
Patriot Games
Salt of the Earth
Sliver
Star Trek 6: The Undiscovered Country
Top Gun
White Christmas

Laserdisc

Abbott and Costello Meet Captain Kidd
Abbott and Costello Meet Frankenstein
Abbott and Costello Meet the Killer, Boris Karloff
The Abominable Dr. Phibes
About Last Night...
Above the Law
Abraham Lincoln
Absence of Malice
The Absent-Minded Professor
Absolute Beginners
Absolution
The Abyss
The Accidental Tourist
The Accused
Ace Ventura: Pet Detective
Aces: Iron Eagle 3
Aces Wild
Act of Piracy
Action Jackson
Actors and Sin
Adam's Rib
The Addams Family
Adios Amigo
Adventures in Babysitting
Adventures in Dinosaur City
The Adventures of Baron Munchausen

The Adventures of Buckaroo Banzai Across the Eighth Dimension
The Adventures of Captain Marvel
Adventures of Don Juan
Adventures of Eliza Fraser
The Adventures of Ford Fairlane
The Adventures of Huck Finn
The Adventures of Ichabod and Mr. Toad
The Adventures of Mark Twain
The Adventures of Milo & Otis
The Adventures of Robin Hood
The Adventures of the Wilderness Family
The Adventures of Tom Sawyer
The Adventurous Knights
Aelita: Queen of Mars
Affair in Trinidad
An Affair to Remember
The Affairs of Annabel
Afraid of the Dark
Africa Screams
An African Dream
The African Queen
After Dark, My Sweet
After Hours
Afterburn
Against All Flags
Against All Odds
The Age of Innocence
Agnes of God
The Agony and the Ecstasy
Air America
The Air Up There
Airborne
Airplane!
Airplane 2: The Sequel
Airport
Airport '77
Akira
Akira Kurosawa's Dreams
The Alamo
Alamo Bay
Alan & Naomi
Alexander Nevsky
Alexander the Great
Alice
Alice Adams

Alice Doesn't Live Here Anymore
Alice in Wonderland
Alien
Alien 3
Alien from L.A.
Alien Intruder
Alien Nation
Alienator
Aliens
Alive
Alive: 20 Years Later
All About Eve
All-American Murder
All Dogs Go to Heaven
All I Want for Christmas
All of Me
All Quiet on the Western Front
All That Jazz
All the King's Men
...All the Marbles
All the President's Men
All the Right Moves
All the Vermeers in New York
All You Need Is Cash
Allegheny Uprising
Allegro Non Troppo
Alligator 2: The Mutation
All's Fair
...Almost
Almost an Angel
Almost Blue
Almost Pregnant
Aloha Summer
Alpine Fire
Alsino and the Condor
Altered States
Alvin Purple
Always
Amadeus
Amazing Grace & Chuck
The Amazing Spider-Man
Amazing Stories
Amazon
Amazon Women on the Moon
Ambition
The Ambulance
The Ambushers
America at the Movies
The American Angels: Baptism of Blood
American Anthem
American Blue Note
American Boyfriends
American Eagle

American Flyers
The American Friend
American Friends
American Gigolo
American Gothic
American Graffiti
American Heart
An American in Paris
American Me
American Ninja 2: The Confrontation
American Ninja 3: Blood Hunt
American Ninja 4: The Annihilation
American Roulette
American Samurai
An American Tail
An American Tail: Fievel Goes West
An American Werewolf in London
The Americanization of Emily
The Amityville Horror
Amityville 2: The Possession
Amityville 3: The Demon
Amityville: A New Generation
The Amityville Curse
Amityville 1992: It's About Time
Among the Cinders
Amongst Friends
Amor Bandido
Amos and Andrew
The Amsterdam Kill
Amsterdamned
Anastasia
Anatomy of a Murder
Anchors Aweigh
And God Created Woman
And Justice for All
And Now for Something Completely Different
And the Ship Sails On
And Then There Were None
The Anderson Tapes
The Andersonville Trial
Andrei Rublev
Android
The Andromeda Strain
Andy and the Airwave Rangers
Andy Hardy Meets Debutante
Andy Warhol's Bad
Angel 3: The Final Chapter
Angel and the Badman

Angel Heart
Angel of Fury
Angel of H.E.A.T.
Angelo My Love
Angels Die Hard
Angels Over Broadway
Angels with Dirty Faces
Angie
Anguish
Animal Behavior
Animal Crackers
Animal Farm
Anna
Anna Karenina
Anne of Avonlea
Anne of Green Gables
Annie
Annie Hall
Another Chance
Another Country
Another 48 Hrs.
Another Stakeout
Another Time, Another Place
Another Woman
Another You
Any Man's Death
Any Which Way You Can
Apache Chief
Apache Rose
The Apartment
Apartment Zero
Apocalypse Now
The Appaloosa
The Applegates
Appointment with Death
Appointment with Fear
Apprentice to Murder
April Fool's Day
Arabian Nights
Arachnophobia
Arena
Armed and Dangerous
Armed Response
Army of Darkness
Around the World in 80 Days
Around the World in 80 Ways
The Arrival
Arrowhead
Arsenic and Old Lace
The Art of Dying
Arthur
Arthur 2: On the Rocks
Article 99
As You Like It
As You Were

Aspen Extreme
The Asphalt Jungle
Assassin
Assassination
Assassination of Trotsky
Assault and Matrimony
Asylum
At Close Range
At Play in the Fields of the Lord
At Sword's Point
At the Circus
Atlantic City
Attack of the 50 Foot Woman
Au Revoir Les Enfants
Auntie Lee's Meat Pies
Auntie Mame
Autobiography of a Princess
Autumn Sonata
Avalon
Avenging Angel
Avenging Force
Awakenings
The Awful Truth
Babar: The Movie
The Babe
Babes in Arms
Babes in Toyland
Babes on Broadway
Babette's Feast
Baby Boom
Baby It's You
Baby on Board
Baby, the Rain Must Fall
Baby...Secret of the Lost Legend
The Babysitter
The Bachelor and the Bobby-Soxer
Bachelor Mother
Bachelor Party
Back from Eternity
Back in Action
Back to Bataan
Back to School
Back to the Beach
Back to the Future
Back to the Future, Part 2
Back to the Future, Part 3
Backdraft
Backfire
Backstab
Backstreet Dreams
The Bad and the Beautiful
Bad Boy
Bad Boys
B.A.D. Cats
Bad Company
Bad Day at Black Rock
Bad Dreams
Bad Influence
Bad Jim
Bad Lieutenant
The Bad News Bears
The Bad News Bears Go to Japan
The Bad News Bears in Breaking Training
Bad Taste
Badge of the Assassin
Badlands
Bail Out
Baja Oklahoma
The Balcony
Ball of Fire
Ballad of Cable Hogue
Ballad of Gregorio Cortez
The Ballad of the Sad Cafe
Bambi
Bananas
Band of the Hand
The Band Wagon
Bang the Drum Slowly
The Bank Dick
The Banker
Barabbas

Barbarella
Barbarian Queen
The Barbarians
Barbarosa
Barbary Coast
Barefoot in the Park
Barfly
The Barkleys of Broadway
Barnum
The Barretts of Wimpole Street
Barry Lyndon
Bartleby
Basileus Quartet
Basket Case
Basket Case 2
Bat 21
The Bat Whispers
Bathing Beauty
Batman
*batteries not included
Battle Beyond the Stars
Battle Cry
The Battle of Algiers
Battle of Britain
Battle of the Bulge
Battleground
The Battleship Potemkin
Battlestar Galactica
Baxter
The Bay Boy
Beach Blanket Bingo
Beach Boys: An American Band
Beach Girls
Beaches
The Bear
The Beast from 20,000 Fathoms
Beastmaster
Beastmaster 2: Through the Portal of Time
The Beat
Beat Street
Beat the Devil
Beatlemania! The Movie
Beatrice
The Beautiful Blonde from Bashful Bend
Beautiful Dreamers
Beauty and the Beast
Beauty and the Beast: Once Upon a Time in New York
Bebe's Kids
Becket
Bed & Breakfast
Bedazzled
Bedford Incident
Bedknobs and Broomsticks
Bedlam
Bedroom Eyes
Bedroom Eyes 2
The Bedroom Window
Beethoven
Beethoven's Nephew
Beethoven's 2nd
Beetlejuice
Before Morning
The Beguiled
Being There
The Believers
Bell, Book and Candle
The Bellboy
Bells are Ringing
The Bells of St. Mary's
The Belly of an Architect
The Beloved Rogue
Ben
Ben-Hur
Beneath the Planet of the Apes
Beneath the 12-Mile Reef
Benji the Hunted
Benny & Joon
Berlin Blues
The Berlin Conspiracy

Berlin Express
Bert Rigby, You're a Fool
Best Buns on the Beach
Best Defense
Best Friends
The Best Little Whorehouse in Texas
Best of Comic Relief
The Best of John Candy on SCTV
Best of the Best
Best of the Best 2
The Best of Times
Best Seller
The Best Years of Our Lives
Betrayed
Betsy's Wedding
Better Off Dead
Betty Blue
Beulah Land
Beverly Hills Bodysnatchers
Beverly Hills Brats
Beverly Hills Cop
Beverly Hills Cop 2
Beverly Hills Madam
Beverly Hills 90210
Beware, My Lovely
Beyond Justice
Beyond the Door
Beyond the Door 3
Beyond the Stars
Beyond the Valley of the Dolls
Bhowani Junction
The Bible...In the Beginning
The Bicycle Thief
Big
Big Bad John
The Big Blue
Big Business
Big Chase
The Big Chill
Big Deadly Game
The Big Easy
Big Girls Don't Cry...They Get Even
Big Heat
The Big Hurt
Big Jake
Big Jim McLain
The Big Knife
The Big Man: Crossing the Line
Big Man on Campus
The Big Parade
The Big Picture
The Big Red One
Big Shots
The Big Sleep
The Big Slice
Big Steal
Big Street
Big Top Pee Wee
Big Town
Big Trouble
Big Trouble in Little China
Big Wednesday
Biggles
Bikini Summer
Bikini Summer 2
Bill & Ted's Excellent Adventure
Bill Cosby, Himself
A Bill of Divorcement
Billie
Billy Bathgate
Billy Budd
Billy Crystal: A Comic's Line
Billy Crystal: Don't Get Me Started
Billy Jack
Billy Rose's Jumbo
Biloxi Blues
Bingo
Bird
Bird on a Wire

The Bird with the Crystal Plumage
The Birds
Birdy
The Birth of a Nation
The Bishop's Wife
Bite the Bullet
Black and White in Color
Black Beauty
Black Caesar
The Black Cat
The Black Coin
Black Glove
The Black Hole
Black Magic
Black Moon Rising
Black Narcissus
Black Orpheus
The Black Pirate
Black Rain
Black Rainbow
Black Robe
The Black Room
The Black Stallion
The Black Stallion Returns
Black Sunday
Black Werewolf
Black Widow
Blackbeard the Pirate
Blackbeard's Ghost
Blackmail
Blackout
Blacula
Blade Runner
Blades
Blame It on Rio
Blank Check
Blaze
Blazing Guns
Blazing Saddles
Blind Date
Blind Fear
Blind Fools
Blind Fury
Blind Vision
Blindside
Blink
Blink of an Eye
Bliss
The Blob
Blood Alley
Blood & Concrete: A Love Story
Blood and Sand
Blood Games
Blood In...Blood Out: Bound by Honor
The Blood of Heroes
Blood on the Sun
Blood Red
Blood Relations
Blood Salvage
Blood Simple
Blood Warriors
Bloodhounds of Broadway
Bloodmatch
Bloodmoon
Bloodsport
Bloodstone: Subspecies 2
Bloody Mama
Blow Out
Blow-Up
Blowing Wild
Blown Away
The Blue and the Gray
Blue City
Blue Collar
Blue Hawaii
Blue Iguana
The Blue Lagoon
The Blue Max
Blue Steel
Blue Thunder
Blue Velvet
The Blues Brothers
Bob & Carol & Ted & Alice

Bob le Flambeur
Bob Roberts
Bobo
Bodies, Rest & Motion
Body and Soul
Body Bags
Body Chemistry
Body Chemistry 2: Voice of a Stranger
Body Chemistry 3: Point of Seduction
Body Double
Body Heat
Body Melt
Body of Evidence
Body Parts
Body Shot
The Body Snatcher
Body Snatchers
The Bodyguard
Boggy Creek II
Boiling Point
Bon Voyage!
Bon Voyage, Charlie Brown
Bonanza: The Return
The Bonfire of the Vanities
Bonnie & Clyde
The Boogey Man
Book of Love
Boomerang
The Boost
Bopha!
The Border
Border Devils
Border Rangers
Born Free
Born in East L.A.
Born Losers
Born of Fire
Born on the Fourth of July
Born to Be Bad
Born to Dance
Born Yesterday
The Borrower
The Bostonians
Bound for Glory
The Bounty
Bounty Tracker
Boxcar Bertha
Boxing Helena
A Boy and His Dog
A Boy Named Charlie Brown
The Boy Who Could Fly
The Boy Who Left Home to Find Out About the Shivers
The Boy with the Green Hair
Boyfriends & Girlfriends
The Boys from Brazil
The Boys in Company C
The Boys in the Band
The Boys Next Door
Boys Town
Boyz N the Hood
Braddock: Missing in Action 3
Brady's Escape
The Brain
Brain Donors
The Brain from Planet Arous
Brain Smasher...A Love Story
Brainstorm
Bram Stoker's Dracula
Branded
Brass
Brass Target
The Brave One
Brazil
Break of Hearts
Breaker Morant
Breakfast at Tiffany's
The Breakfast Club
Breakheart Pass
Breakin'
Breakin' 2: Electric Boogaloo
Breaking Away
Breaking In
Breaking the Rules

Breaking Up Is Hard to Do
Breakout
Breathless
Brewster McCloud
Brewster's Millions
Brian's Song
The Bride
The Bride of Frankenstein
Bride of Re-Animator
The Bride Wore Black
The Brides of Dracula
The Bridge of San Luis Rey
The Bridge on the River Kwai
A Bridge Too Far
The Bridges at Toko-Ri
Brigadoon
Bright Lights, Big City
Brighton Beach Memoirs
Bringing Up Baby
Broadcast News
Broadway Danny Rose
Broadway Melody of 1940
Broken Blossoms
Broken Lance
Bronco Billy
A Bronx Tale
The Brood
The Brotherhood
The Brotherhood of Satan
Brothers in Arms
Brubaker
Bruce Lee: Curse of the
    Dragon
The Brute Man
The Buccaneer
Buck Privates
Buck Rogers in the 25th
    Century
Bud and Lou
The Buddy Holly Story
Buddy's Song
Buffet Froid
Buffy the Vampire Slayer
Bugs & Daffy: The Wartime
    Cartoons
Bugs Bunny Superstar
Bugsy
Bugsy Malone
Bull Durham
Bulletproof
Bullfighter & the Lady
Bullies
Bullitt
Bullseye!
Bullshot Crummond
Bundle of Joy
Buona Sera, Mrs. Campbell
The 'Burbs
Burden of Dreams
Burglar
Buried Alive
Burke & Wills
The Burmese Harp
Burn!
Burndown
Burning Rage
Burning Secret
The Burns and Allen Show
Bury Me an Angel
Bus Stop
The Busby Berkeley Disc
Buster
Buster Keaton Rides Again/
    The Railrodder
Bustin' Loose
Butch Cassidy and the
    Sundance Kid
The Butcher's Wife
Butterfield 8
Butterfly
Buy & Cell
By Dawn's Early Light
By the Light of the Silvery
    Moon
Bye Bye Baby
Bye, Bye, Birdie

Bye Bye Brazil
Cabaret
Cabin Boy
Cabin in the Sky
The Cabinet of Dr. Caligari
Cactus Flower
Cactus in the Snow
Caddyshack
Caddyshack 2
Cadence
Cadillac Man
Cafe Romeo
The Cage
Caged Fear
Caged Fury
Caged in Paradiso
Cahill: United States Marshal
The Caine Mutiny
The Caine Mutiny Court
    Martial
Calamity Jane
Calendar Girl
California Suite
Caligula
Call Me
Call to Glory
Camelot
The Cameraman
Cameron's Closet
Camille Claudel
Campus Man
Can-Can
The Candidate
Candyman
Cannibal Women in the
    Avocado Jungle of Death
Cannonball Run
Cannonball Run 2
Can't Buy Me Love
Cape Fear
Capone
Capricorn One
Captain America
Captain Horatio Hornblower
Captain Ron
The Captive: The Longest
    Drive 2
Captured in Chinatown
Car 54, Where Are You?
Car Trouble
Caravaggio
Carbon Copy
The Cardinal
Career Opportunities
Carefree
Caribe
The Cariboo Trail
Carlito's Way
Carmen Jones
Carnal Knowledge
Carnival of Souls
Caroline?
Caroline at Midnight
Carousel
The Carpenter
Carrie
Cartel
Casablanca
Casanova
Casanova's Big Night
A Case for Murder
Case of the Baby Sitter
Casino Royale
Cassandra
Cast a Deadly Spell
Cast the First Stone
Casual Sex?
Casualties of War
Cat on a Hot Tin Roof
Cat People
Catch Me...If You Can
Catch-22
Catherine the Great
Cat's Eye
Cattle Queen of Montana
Caught in the Act

Cavalier of the West
Cave Girl
CB4: The Movie
Cellar Dweller
The Cemetery Club
Center of the Web
Certain Fury
Cesar
Cesar & Rosalie
Chain Reaction
Chained Heat
Chained Heat 2
Chameleon Street
The Champ
Champagne for Caesar
Champions
Chances Are
The Changeling
Chaplin
Chapter Two
The Charge of the Light
    Brigade
Chariots of Fire
Charlie Chan at the Opera
Charlie Chan at the Wax
    Museum
The Charlie Chan Collection
Charlie Chan in Paris
Charlie Chan in Rio
Charlie Chaplin: The Early
    Years, Vol. 1
Charlie Chaplin: The Early
    Years, Vol. 2
Charlie Chaplin: The Early
    Years, Vol. 3
Charlie Chaplin: The Early
    Years, Vol. 4
Charlotte's Web
Charly
The Chase
Chasers
Chattahoochee
Cheatin' Hearts
Check & Double Check
Checking Out
Cheech and Chong: Still
    Smokin'
Cheech and Chong's Next
    Movie
Cheech and Chong's Nice
    Dreams
Cheech and Chong's, The
    Corsican Brothers
Cheech and Chong's Up in
    Smoke
The Cheerleaders
Cheetah
Cherry 2000
Chicago Joe & the Showgirl
Children in the Crossfire
Children of a Lesser God
Children of Paradise
Children of the Corn
Children of the Damned
The Children's Hour
Child's Play
Child's Play 2
Child's Play 3
China Girl
China Sky
The China Syndrome
Chinatown
Chinese Connection
Chinese Roulette
The Chipmunk Adventure
Chisum
Chitty Chitty Bang Bang
Chocolat
The Chocolate War
Choose Me
Chopper Chicks in
    Zombietown
A Chorus Line
Christine
A Christmas Carol
Christmas in Connecticut

Christmas in July
A Christmas Story
Christopher Columbus: The
    Discovery
Christopher Strong
C.H.U.D.
C.H.U.D. 2: Bud the Chud
A Chump at Oxford
C.I.A.: Code Name Alexa
The Cincinnati Kid
Cinderella
Cinema Paradiso
Circuitry Man
Circus World
Citizen Cohn
Citizen Kane
City Heat
City Lights
City Limits
City of Hope
City of Joy
City Slickers
Claire's Knee
The Clan of the Cave Bear
Clara's Heart
Clarence Darrow
Clash by Night
Clash of the Titans
Class
Class Act
Class Action
Class of 1984
Class of 1999 2: The
    Substitute
Class of Nuke 'Em High, Part
    2: Subhumanoid Meltdown
Class Reunion
Clean and Sober
Cleopatra
Cliffhanger
A Climate for Killing
The Climb
Cloak and Dagger
Cloak & Dagger
The Clock
The Clockmaker
Clockwise
A Clockwork Orange
Close Encounters of the Third
    Kind
Closely Watched Trains
The Closer
Closet Land
Clouds Over Europe
Clown House
The Club
Club Paradise
Clue
Coal Miner's Daughter
Coast to Coast
Cobra
The Cobweb
The Coca-Cola Kid
Cocktail
The Cocoanuts
Cocoon
Cocoon: The Return
Code Name: Emerald
Code of Silence
Coffy
Cohen and Tate
Cold Feet
Cold Front
Cold Heaven
Cold Justice
Cold Turkey
Coldfire
The Collector
College
Collision Course
Colonel Redl
The Color of Money
The Color Purple
Colors
Coma
Comancheros

Combat Academy
Come Back Little Reba
Come Back, Little Sheba
Come Back to the Five &
    Dime Jimmy Dean, Jimmy
    Dean
Come See the Paradise
The Comedy of Terrors
The Comic
Coming Home
Coming to America
Commando
The Commitments
Common Threads: Stories
    from the Quilt
Communion
The Company of Wolves
The Competition
The Compleat Beatles
The Complete Showboat
Compromising Positions
The Comrades of Summer
Conan the Barbarian
Conan the Destroyer
Confidentially Yours
The Conformist
A Connecticut Yankee in King
    Arthur's Court
Conquest of the Planet of the
    Apes
Consenting Adults
Consuming Passions
Contempt
Continental Divide
The Conversation
Convicted
Convicts at Large
Coogan's Bluff
Cookie
Cool As Ice
Cool Blue
Cool Hand Luke
Cool Runnings
Cool World
Cooley High
Cop
Cop and a Half
Copacabana
Cornered
The Corsican Brothers
The Cosmic Eye
The Cotton Club
The Couch Trip
Counterforce
Country
Coupe de Ville
Courage Mountain
Courageous Avenger
The Courier
Court Jester
The Court Martial of Billy
    Mitchell
Cousin, Cousine
Cousins
Cover Girl
Cover-Up
The Covered Wagon
Cowboy
The Cowboys
Crack House
Crack-Up
Crackers
The Cranes are Flying
Crash and Burn
The Crawling Eye
The Crawling Hand
Crazy from the Heart
Crazy in Love
Crazy Moon
Crazy People
Creator
Creature
Creature from the Black
    Lagoon
The Creature Walks Among
    Us

Creeping

The Creeping Flesh
Creepozoids
Creepshow
Creepshow 2
Cria
Cries and Whispers
Crimes & Misdemeanors
Crimes of Passion
Crimes of the Heart
Criminal Law
Crimson Pirate
Crisscross
Critical Condition
Critters
Critters 2: The Main Course
Critters 4
Crocodile Dundee
Crocodile Dundee 2
Cromwell
Crooked Hearts
Crooked Trail
Cross Country
Cross Examination
Crossfire
The Crossing
Crossing Delancey
Crossing the Bridge
Crossing the Line
Crossroads
The Crowd
The Crush
Crusoe
Cry-Baby
Cry Freedom
Cry from the Mountain
A Cry in the Dark
The Crying Game
Cujo
Curfew
Curly Sue
The Curse
Curse 3: Blood Sacrifice
Curse 4: The Ultimate
    Sacrifice
Curse of the Cat People
Curse of the Demon
Cutter's Way
Cutting Class
The Cutting Edge
Cyborg
Cyborg 2
Cyborg Cop
Cyclone
Cyrano de Bergerac
Da
Dad
Daddy Long Legs
Daddy's Boys
Daddy's Dyin'...Who's Got the
    Will?
Daffy Duck's Movie: Fantastic
    Island
Daffy Duck's Quackbusters
Dakota
Damage
Dames
Damien: Omen 2
Damn the Defiant
Damn Yankees
A Damsel in Distress
Dance, Girl, Dance
Dance Macabre
Dance of the Damned
Dance with a Stranger
Dance with Death
Dancers
Dances with Wolves
Dandy in Aspic
Danger Zone
Dangerous
Dangerous Game
Dangerous Heart
Dangerous Liaisons
Dangerous Life
Dangerous Moves
Dangerous Pursuit

Dangerous When Wet
Danton
Darby O'Gill & the Little
    People
The Dark
Dark Age
The Dark Backward
Dark Before Dawn
The Dark Crystal
Dark Habits
Dark Passage
Dark Side of the Moon
Dark Star
Dark Tide
Dark Tower
Dark Victory
Dark Waters
The Dark Wind
Darkest Africa
Darkman
Darling
D.A.R.Y.L.
Das Boot
Date with an Angel
A Date with Judy
Dave
David and Bathsheba
David and Lisa
David Copperfield
Davy Crockett and the River
    Pirates
Dawn of the Dead
The Dawning
The Day After
A Day at the Races
Day of Atonement
Day of the Dead
The Day of the Dolphin
The Day of the Jackal
The Day of the Locust
Day of the Triffids
The Day the Earth Stood Still
Day Time Ended
Days of Heaven
Days of Thunder
Days of Wine and Roses
Dazed and Confused
D.C. Cab
The Dead
Dead Again
Dead Aim
Dead Alive
Dead Bang
Dead Calm
Dead End
Dead Heat
Dead Man Out
Dead Man's Revenge
Dead Men Don't Wear Plaid
Dead of Night
Dead of Winter
Dead On
Dead Poets Society
The Dead Pool
Dead Reckoning
Dead Ringers
Dead Space
Dead Zone
Deadbolt
Deadfall
Deadline
Deadlock
Deadly Bet
Deadly Companions
Deadly Dreams
Deadly Friend
Deadly Illusion
Deadly Possession
Deadly Rivals
The Deadly Trackers
Deadtime Stories
Deal of the Century
Dealers
Death Becomes Her
Death Before Dishonor
Death Dreams

Death Hunt
Death of a Salesman
Death of a Scoundrel
Death of an Angel
Death on the Nile
Death Ring
Death Warrant
Death Watch
Death Wish
Death Wish 2
Death Wish 3
Death Wish 4: The
    Crackdown
Death Wish 5: The Face of
    Death
Deathrow Gameshow
Deathstalker
Deathstalker 2: Duel of the
    Titans
Deathstalker 3
The Decameron
The Deceivers
December
Deceptions
Decline of Western Civilization
    1
Decoration Day
The Deep
Deep Cover
Deepstar Six
The Deer Hunter
Def by Temptation
Defending Your Life
Defense of the Realm
Defenseless
Deja Vu
The Delicate Delinquent
Delicatessen
Delirious
Deliverance
Delta Force
Delta Force 2: Operation
    Stranglehold
Delta Force 3: The Killing
    Game
Delusion
Demetrius and the Gladiators
Demolition Man
A Demon in My View
Demon Seed
Demon Wind
Demonic Toys
Demons
Demonstone
Denial: The Dark Side of
    Passion
Dennis the Menace
Dennis the Menace: Dinosaur
    Hunter
Descending Angel
Desert Bloom
The Desert Fox
Desert Hearts
Desert Kickboxer
Desert Phantom
Designing Woman
Desire and Hell at Sunset
    Motel
Desire Under the Elms
Desiree
Desk Set
Desperate Hours
Desperate Motives
Desperately Seeking Susan
Destination Moon
Destroyer
Destry Rides Again
The Detective
Detour
The Devil & Daniel Webster
The Devil at 4 O'Clock
Devil in the Flesh
Devil Monster
The Devil's Commandment
Devil's Rain
Devlin

Diabolique
Dial "M" for Murder
Diamond Head
Diamond Run
The Diamond Trap
Diamonds are Forever
Diane
Diary of a Chambermaid
Diary of a Hitman
Diary of a Lost Girl
The Diary of Anne Frank
Dick Tracy
Dick Tracy Returns
Dick Tracy vs. Crime Inc.
Die Hard
Die Hard 2: Die Harder
Die, Monster, Die!
Diggstown
Dillinger
Dim Sum: A Little Bit of Heart
Diner
Dinner at Eight
Diplomaniacs
Diplomatic Immunity
Dirt Bike Kid
Dirty Dancing
The Dirty Dozen
Dirty Harry
Dirty Mary Crazy Larry
Dirty Rotten Scoundrels
The Disappearance of
    Christina
The Discreet Charm of the
    Bourgeoisie
Disorderlies
Disorderly Orderly
Disorganized Crime
Distant Thunder
Distant Voices, Still Lives
The Distinguished Gentleman
Disturbed
Diva
The Dive
Divine Madness
Do or Die
Do the Right Thing
D.O.A.
Doc Hollywood
The Doctor
Dr. Alien
Dr. Caligari
Dr. Cyclops
Doctor Detroit
Doctor Dolittle
Doctor Duck's Super Secret
    All-Purpose Sauce
Dr. Giggles
Dr. Jekyll and Mr. Hyde
Dr. No
Dr. Strangelove, or: How I
    Learned to Stop Worrying
    and Love the Bomb
Doctor X
Doctor Zhivago
Dodge City
Dodsworth
Does This Mean We're
    Married?
Dog Day Afternoon
Dogfight
The Dogs of War
Doll Face
Dollar
Dollars
Dollman
The Dolls
A Doll's House
Dolly Dearest
Dominick & Eugene
Domino
Don Juan
Don Juan, My Love
Don Q., Son of Zorro
Dona Flor and Her Two
    Husbands
Dona Herlinda & Her Son

Donovan's Brain
Donovan's Reef
Don't Look Back
Don't Look Now
Don't Mess with My Sister!
Don't Tell Her It's Me
Don't Tell Mom the
    Babysitter's Dead
The Doors
The Doors: Soft Parade, a
    Retrospective
Doppelganger: The Evil Within
Double-Crossed
Double Exposure
Double Exposure: The Story
    of Margaret Bourke-White
Double Impact
Double Indemnity
Double Jeopardy
Double Trouble
Down Among the Z Men
Down and Out in Beverly Hills
Down Argentine Way
Down the Drain
Down to Earth
Downhill Racer
Downtown
Dracula
Dracula Blows His Cool
Dragnet
Dragon: The Bruce Lee Story
Dragonslayer
Dream a Little Dream
Dream Machine
The Dream Team
Dreams
Dreamscape
Dressed to Kill
The Dresser
Dressmaker
The Drifter
Drifting Weeds
Drive-In Massacre
Driving Force
Driving Me Crazy
Driving Miss Daisy
Drop Dead Fred
Drowning by Numbers
Drugstore Cowboy
Drums
Drums Along the Mohawk
A Dry White Season
The Duchess and the
    Dirtwater Fox
Duck Soup
DuckTales the Movie:
    Treasure of the Lost Lamp
Dudes
Duel of Hearts
The Duellists
Dumbo
Dune
Dune Warriors
The Dunera Boys
Dungeonmaster
Dynamite and Gold
The Eagle
Early Frost
An Early Frost
Earth Girls are Easy
Earth vs. the Flying Saucers
Earthquake
East of Eden
Easter Parade
Easy Living
Easy Money
Easy Rider
Easy Wheels
Eat a Bowl of Tea
Eating
Echo Park
Echoes of Paradise
Eddie and the Cruisers
Eddie and the Cruisers 2:
    Eddie Lives!
Eddie Macon's Run

Eddie Murphy "Delirious"
Eddie Murphy: Raw
The Eddy Duchin Story
Edge of Sanity
Educating Rita
Edward Scissorhands
Egg
Egg and I
The Egyptian
The Eiger Sanction
8 1/2
Eight Men Out
8 Million Ways to Die
18 Again!
84 Charing Cross Road
84 Charlie Mopic
Eijanaika
El Amor Brujo
El Cid
El Dorado
El Mariachi
Electra Glide in Blue
Electric Dreams
The Electric Horseman
Elena and Her Men
Eleni
Elephant Boy
The Elephant Man
Elmer Gantry
The Elusive Corporal
Elvira Madigan
Elvira, Mistress of the Dark
Elvis in Hollywood
Elvis Memories
Elvis on Tour
Elvis: One Night with You
Elvis: The Lost Performances
The Emerald Forest
Emissary
Emmanuelle in the Country
Emmanuelle, the Joys of a
    Woman
Emperor Jones
Empire of the Air: The Men
    Who Made Radio
Empire of the Sun
The Empire Strikes Back
Enchanted April
The Enchanted Cottage
The Enchanted Forest
Encounter at Raven's Gate
The End
End of the Line
Endless Descent
Endless Love
Endless Night
The Endless Summer
Enemies, a Love Story
Enemy Gold
Enemy Mine
The Enforcer
Enigma
Enormous Changes
Enrapture
Entangled
Enter the Dragon
Equinox
Equus
Eraserhead
Erik the Viking
Ernest Goes to Jail
Ernest Saves Christmas
The Errand Boy
Escape Artist
Escape from Alcatraz
Escape from New York
Escape from the Planet of the
    Apes
Escape to Witch Mountain
E.T.: The Extra-Terrestrial
Eternal Evil
Ethan Frome
Eve of Destruction
An Evening with Robin
    Williams
Evergreen

Eversmile New Jersey
Every Girl Should Be Married
Every Time We Say Goodbye
Every Which Way But Loose
Everybody Wins
Everybody's All American
Everybody's Dancin'
Everybody's Fine
Everything You Always
    Wanted to Know About
    Sex (But Were Afraid to
    Ask)
Evil Dead
Evil Dead 2: Dead by Dawn
Evil Spirits
The Evil That Men Do
Evil Under the Sun
The Ewok Adventure
The Ewoks: Battle for Endor
Ex-Mrs. Bradford
Excalibur
Excessive Force
Executive Action
Exodus
The Exorcist
The Exorcist 3
The Expendables
Experiment in Terror
The Experts
Explorers
Exquisite Corpses
Exterminator
Extreme Justice
Extreme Prejudice
Extremities
Eyes of Fire
Eyes of Laura Mars
Eyes of the Beholder
Eyes of the Panther
Eyewitness
F/X
F/X 2: The Deadly Art of
    Illusion
The Fable of the Beautiful
    Pigeon Fancier
The Fabulous Baker Boys
The Fabulous Dorseys
Fahrenheit 451
Fail-Safe
Fair Game
Faith
The Falcon and the Snowman
The Fall of the Roman Empire
The Fallen Idol
Falling Down
Falling from Grace
Falling in Love
False Identity
Fame
The Family
Family Business
Family Dog: Complete Series
A Family Matter
Family Plot
Family Viewing
The Fan
Fancy Pants
Fanny
Fanny and Alexander
Fantasia
Fantastic Voyage
Far and Away
Far from Home
Far from the Madding Crowd
Far North
A Far Off Place
Far Out Man
Faraway, So Close!
Farewell My Concubine
A Farewell to Arms
Farewell to the King
The Farmer Takes a Wife
Fast Food
Fast Forward
Fast Getaway
Fast Times at Ridgemont High

Fat Man and Little Boy
Fatal Attraction
Fatal Beauty
Fatal Instinct
Fatal Mission
Fatal Vision
Father
Father Hood
Father of the Bride
Fathers and Sons
Father's Little Dividend
A Father's Revenge
The Favor, the Watch, & the
    Very Big Fish
FBI Girl
The FBI Story
Fear
Fear City
The Fear Inside
Fear Strikes Out
Fearless
Fearless Tiger
The Fearless Vampire Killers
Feds
Fellini Satyricon
Fellini's Roma
Femme Fatale
Ferocious Female Freedom
    Fighters
Ferris Bueller's Day Off
Fever
A Few Good Men
Fiddler on the Roof
The Field
Field of Dreams
Field of Fire
Field of Honor
Fiend Without a Face
The Fiendish Plot of Dr. Fu
    Manchu
Fifth Avenue Girl
The Fifth Monkey
Fifty/Fifty
52 Pick-Up
55 Days at Peking
Fight for Us
Fighting Cowboy
The Final Alliance
Final Analysis
Final Approach
The Final Conflict
The Final Countdown
Final Notice
The Final Terror
A Fine Mess
The Finest Hour
Fingerprints Don't Lie
Finian's Rainbow
Fire Alarm
Fire and Ice
Fire and Rain
Fire Birds
Fire Down Below
Fire in the Sky
Firefall
Firefox
Firehawk
Firehead
Firepower
Firestarter
Firewalker
The Firing Line
The Firm
First Blood
First Born
The First Deadly Sin
First Men in the Moon
First Monday in October
First Name: Carmen
The First Power
A Fish Called Wanda
The Fisher King
F.I.S.T.
Fist Fighter
A Fistful of Dollars
A Fistful of Dynamite

Five Came Back
Five Easy Pieces
The Five Heartbeats
The 5000 Fingers of Dr. T
Five Weeks in a Balloon
The Flame & the Arrow
Flaming Signal
The Flamingo Kid
Flamingo Road
The Flash
Flashback
Flashdance
Flashpoint
Flat Top
Flatliners
Flesh and Blood
Flesh and Bone
Flesh Gordon
Fleshtone
Fletch
Fletch Lives
The Flight
A Flight of Rainbirds
Flight of the Eagle
Flight of the Innocent
Flight of the Intruder
Flight of the Navigator
The Flight of the Phoenix
Flight to Mars
Flight to Nowhere
Flirting
Florida Straits
Flower Drum Song
Flowers in the Attic
The Fly
The Fly 2
The Flying Deuces
Flying Leathernecks
Flying Tigers
FM
The Fog
Follies in Concert
Follow That Dream
Follow the Fleet
Food of the Gods: Part 2
Foolish Wives
Fools of Fortune
Footlight Parade
Footloose
For a Few Dollars More
For Better and For Worse
For Keeps
For Love or Money
For Me and My Gal
For Those About to Rock:
    Monsters in Moscow
For Your Eyes Only
The Forbidden Dance
Forbidden Games
Forbidden Planet
Forbidden Sun
Forbidden World
Force of Evil
Force 10 from Navarone
Forced March
Foreign Affairs
Foreign Correspondent
Forever Emmanuelle
Forever, Lulu
Forever Young
The Forgotten
The Forgotten One
A Forgotten Tune for the Flute
Fort Apache
Fort Apache, the Bronx
Fortress
The Fortune Cookie
The Forty-Ninth Parallel
42nd Street
48 Hrs.
Foul Play
The Four Feathers
Four for Texas
The 400 Blows
The Four Seasons

The 4D Man
1492: Conquest of Paradise
The 4th Man
The Fourth Protocol
Fourth Story
The Fourth War
Frame Up
Frances
Frankenhooker
Frankenstein
Frankenstein General Hospital
Frankenstein Meets the
    Wolfman
Frankenstein Unbound
Frankie and Johnny
Frantic
Fraternity Vacation
Frauds
Freaks
Freddy's Dead: The Final
    Nightmare
Free Grass
Free Ride
Free Willy
Freebie & the Bean
Freejack
Freeway
Freeze Frame
French Can-Can
The French Connection
French Connection 2
The French Lieutenant's
    Woman
Frenzy
Fresh Horses
The Freshman
Frida
Friday the 13th
Friday the 13th, Part 2
Friday the 13th, Part 3
Friday the 13th, Part 4: The
    Final Chapter
Friday the 13th, Part 5: A New
    Beginning
Friday the 13th, Part 6: Jason
    Lives
Friday the 13th, Part 7: The
    New Blood
Friday the 13th, Part 8: Jason
    Takes Manhattan
Fried Green Tomatoes
Friendly Persuasion
Friends, Lovers & Lunatics
Fright Night
Fright Night 2
The Fringe Dwellers
Frog
From Beyond
From Here to Eternity
From Hollywood to Deadwood
From Russia with Love
From the Earth to the Moon
From the Hip
From the Life of the
    Marionettes
From the Terrace
The Front
The Front Page
The Fugitive
Full Metal Jacket
Full Moon in Blue Water
Fuller Brush Man
Funeral in Berlin
The Funhouse
Funland
Funny About Love
Funny Face
Funny Farm
Funny Girl
Funny Lady
A Funny Thing Happened on
    the Way to the Forum
The Further Adventures of
    Tennessee Buck
Future Hunters
Future Kill

Future

Future Zone
G-Men vs. the Black Dragon
Gaby: A True Story
Galaxina
Galaxy of Terror
Gallipoli
The Gamble
The Gambler
The Gambler & the Lady
The Game
Game of Death
The Game of Love
Gamera, the Invincible
Gamera vs. Gaos
Gamera vs. Zigra
Gandhi
The Garbage Pail Kids Movie
The Garden of Allah
Garden of the Finzi-Continis
Gardens of Stone
Gas Food Lodging
Gas Pump Girls
Gaslight
The Gate
Gate 2
Gator Bait
Gator Bait 2: Cajun Justice
The Gauntlet
The Gay Divorcee
Gay Purr-ee
The General
General Spanky
Gentleman Jim
Gentleman's Agreement
Gentlemen Prefer Blondes
Genuine Risk
George's Island
Georgy Girl
Geronimo
Geronimo: An American
    Legend
Get Crazy
Get Out Your Handkerchiefs
Get That Man
The Getaway
Getting It Right
Ghost
The Ghost and Mrs. Muir
The Ghost Breakers
Ghost Chase
Ghost Dad
Ghost Fever
Ghost Story
Ghost Town
Ghostbusters
Ghostbusters 2
Ghosts Can't Do It
Ghoulies 2
G.I. Blues
G.I. Jane
Giant
Gidget
The Gig
Gigi
Gilda
Gimme Shelter
Ginger Ale Afternoon
The Girl Can't Help It
Girl Crazy
Girl from Calgary
The Girl in a Swing
A Girl in Every Port
The Girl Most Likely
A Girl to Kill for
Girlfriend from Hell
Girls Just Want to Have Fun
Girls Next Door
Give My Regards to Broad
    Street
The Gladiator
Gladiator
The Glass Bottom Boat
The Glass Key
The Glass Menagerie
Glass Tomb
Gleaming the Cube

Glen and Randa
Glengarry Glen Ross
The Glenn Miller Story
Glitch!
Gloria
Glory
Glory! Glory!
Go, Johnny Go!
Go Tell the Spartans
Go West
God Told Me To
The Goddess
The Godfather
The Godfather, Part 2
The Godfather, Part 3
God's Country
The Gods Must Be Crazy
The Gods Must Be Crazy 2
Godzilla, King of the Monsters
Godzilla 1985
Goin' South
Going Berserk
Going My Way
Going Places
Going Undercover
The Gold & Glory
Gold Diggers of 1933
Gold Diggers of 1935
The Gold Rush
Golden Age of Comedy
Golden Boy
The Golden Child
The Golden Coach
The Golden Seal
Golden Voyage of Sinbad
Goldfinger
Goldilocks & the Three Bears
Goliath Awaits
Gone with the Wind
Gonza the Spearman
Good Guys Wear Black
Good Morning, Babylon
Good Morning, Vietnam
The Good Mother
Good News
The Good Son
The Good, the Bad and the
    Ugly
The Good Wife
Goodbye Columbus
The Goodbye Girl
Goodbye, Mr. Chips
Goodbye, My Lady
Goodbye, New York
The Goodbye People
Goodfellas
The Goonies
Gorgo
The Gorgon
The Gorilla
Gorillas in the Mist
Gorky Park
The Gospel According to St.
    Matthew
Gotcha!
Gotham
Gothic
The Graduate
Graffiti Bridge
Grand Hotel
Grand Illusion
Grand Isle
Grand Prix
Grand Tour: Disaster in Time
Grandma's House
The Grapes of Wrath
The Grass is Greener
Grave of the Fireflies
Grave Secrets
Graveyard Shift
Grease
Grease 2
Great Balls of Fire
Great Bikini Off-Road
    Adventure
The Great Caruso

The Great Dictator
The Great Escape
Great Expectations
The Great Gatsby
The Great Lie
The Great McGinty
The Great Mouse Detective
Great Movie Stunts & the
    Making of Raiders of the
    Lost Ark
The Great Muppet Caper
The Great Outdoors
Great Race
The Great Train Robbery
The Great Waldo Pepper
A Great Wall
The Great Waltz
The Great Ziegfeld
The Greatest Show on Earth
The Greatest Story Ever Told
Greed
The Green Berets
Green Card
Green for Danger
Green Ice
Greetings
Gremlins
Gremlins 2: The New Batch
The Grey Fox
Greystoke: The Legend of
    Tarzan, Lord of the Apes
Griffith Biograph Program
The Grifters
Grim Prairie Tales
The Grim Reaper
Gross Anatomy
Grotesque
Ground Zero
Groundhog Day
Grumpy Old Men
Guadalcanal Diary
The Guardian
Guess Who's Coming to
    Dinner
Guilty as Charged
Guilty as Sin
Guilty by Suspicion
Gulliver's Travels
The Gumshoe Kid
Gun Fury
The Gun in Betty Lou's
    Handbag
Guncrazy
Gunfight at the O.K. Corral
The Gunfighter
The Gunfighters
Gunfire
Gung Ho
Gunga Din
The Gunrunner
Guns
Guns of Justice
The Guns of Navarone
Gus
Guys and Dolls
Gypsy
Hail Caesar
Hail Mary
Hair
Hairspray
Half Moon Street
The Hallelujah Trail
Halloween
Halloween 2: The Nightmare
    Isn't Over!
Halloween 3: Season of the
    Witch
Halloween 4: The Return of
    Michael Myers
Halloween 5: The Revenge of
    Michael Myers
Hamburger Hill
Hamburger...The Motion
    Picture
Hamlet
The Handmaid's Tale

Hang 'Em High
Hangfire
Hangin' with the Homeboys
Hanky Panky
Hannah and Her Sisters
Hanna's War
Hanoi Hilton
Hanover Street
Hans Christian Andersen
Hansel and Gretel
Hanussen
Happy Birthday to Me
The Happy Hooker
The Happy Hooker Goes
    Hollywood
Happy Hour
Happy Together
Hard Country
A Hard Day's Night
Hard Promises
Hard Target
Hard Times
Hard to Hold
Hard to Kill
The Hard Way
Hardbodies
Hardbodies 2
Hardcore
The Harder They Come
Hardware
Harem
Harlem Nights
Harley Davidson and the
    Marlboro Man
Harmagedon
Harold and Maude
Harper
Harry & Son
Harry and the Hendersons
Harry & Walter Go to New
    York
The Harvest
Harvey
The Harvey Girls
Hat Box Mystery
Hatari
Haunted Honeymoon
The Haunted Palace
Haunted Summer
The Haunting
Haunting of Sarah Hardy
Havana
Having It All
Having Wonderful Crime
Hawaii
Hawk the Slayer
Hawken's Breed
Hawks
The Hawks & the Sparrows
He Said, She Said
Head
Headhunter
Hear No Evil
Heart and Souls
Heart Condition
Heart Like a Wheel
Heart of Darkness
The Heart of Dixie
Heart of Midnight
Heart of the Stag
Heartaches
Heartbreak Hotel
The Heartbreak Kid
Heartbreak Ridge
Heartbreaker
Heartburn
Hearts of Fire
Hearts of the World
Heat
Heat and Sunlight
Heat of Desire
Heat Wave
Heathers
Heaven
Heaven and Earth
Heaven Can Wait

Heaven Help Us
Heaven is a Playground
Heaven's Gate
Heavy Petting
The Heiress
Hell Comes to Frogtown
Hell in the Pacific
Hell is for Heroes
Hellbound: Hellraiser 2
Hellfighters
Hellgate
Hellhole
Hello Again
Hello, Dolly!
Hello Mary Lou: Prom Night 2
Hellraiser
Hellraiser 3: Hell on Earth
Help!
Henry V
Henry & June
Henry: Portrait of a Serial
    Killer
Her Alibi
Herbie Rides Again
Hercules
Hercules Unchained
Here Comes Mr. Jordan
Here Comes the Groom
Here's Looking at You,
    Warner Bros.
Hero
Hero and the Terror
Hexed
Hey, Babu Riba
Hey There, It's Yogi Bear
Hi-Jacked
The Hidden
The Hidden 2
Hidden Agenda
The Hidden Fortress
Hidden Obsession
Hide and Go Shriek
Hider in the House
High & Low
High Anxiety
High Frequency
High Noon
High Plains Drifter
High Road to China
High Season
High Sierra
High Society
High Spirits
High Stakes
High Tide
Higher and Higher
The Highest Honor
Highlander
Highlander 2: The Quickening
Highpoint
Highway 13
The Hills Have Eyes
The Hindenburg
Hips, Hips, Hooray
His Majesty O'Keefe
History is Made at Night
History of the World: Part 1
The Hit
The Hit List
Hit the Deck
Hitcher
The Hitchhiker
Hitchhiker 2
Hitchhiker 3
Hitchhiker 4
The Hitchhiker's Guide to the
    Galaxy
The Hitman
Hobson's Choice
Hocus Pocus
Hoffa
The Holcroft Covenant
A Hole in the Head
Holiday
Holiday Affair
Holiday Inn

Holiday Rhythm
Hollywood Hot Tubs 2: Educating Crystal
Hollywood Outtakes & Rare Footage
Hollywood Shuffle
Hollywood Varieties
Hollywood Vice Sqaud
Hombre
Home Alone
Home Alone 2: Lost in New York
Home from the Hill
Home is Where the Hart is
Home Movies
A Home of Our Own
Home of the Brave
Homeboy
Homeboys
Homer and Eddie
Hometown Boy Makes Good
Homeward Bound: The Incredible Journey
Homework
Homicide
Honey, I Blew Up the Kid
Honey, I Shrunk the Kids
Honeymoon Academy
Honeymoon in Vegas
Honeymoon Killers
Honeysuckle Rose
Honkytonk Man
Hook
Hook, Line and Sinker
Hooper
Hoosiers
Hope and Glory
Hoppity Goes to Town
Hopscotch
The Horror Chamber of Dr. Faustus
The Horror of Dracula
Horror Planet
Horrors of Burke & Hare
Horse Feathers
Horseplayer
The Horse's Mouth
The Hostage Tower
Hostile Guns
Hostile Takeover
Hot Chocolate
Hot Pursuit
The Hot Rock
Hot Spot
Hot Stuff
Hot Target
Hot to Trot!
Hotel Colonial
The Hotel New Hampshire
The Hound of the Baskervilles
House
House 2: The Second Story
House 4: Home Deadly Home
House Calls
A House In The Hills
House of Cards
House of Dracula
House of Frankenstein
House of Games
The House of the Spirits
The House of Usher
House of Wax
The House on Carroll Street
House on Haunted Hill
The House on Sorority Row
House Party
House Party 2: The Pajama Jam
House Party 3
Houseboat
The Householder
The Housekeeper
Housesitter
How I Got into College
How I Won the War
How the West was Won

How to Get Ahead in Advertising
How to Marry a Millionaire
How to Murder Your Wife
How to Succeed in Business without Really Trying
How U Like Me Now?
Howard the Duck
Howard's End
The Howling
Howling 2: Your Sister is a Werewolf
Howling 3: The Marsupials
Howling 4: The Original Nightmare
Howling 5: The Rebirth
Howling 6: The Freaks
Huck and the King of Hearts
Huckleberry Finn
Hud
Hudson Hawk
Hugh Hefner: Once Upon a Time
The Human Comedy
The Human Shield
Humoresque
The Hunchback of Notre Dame
The Hunger
Hunk
The Hunt for Red October
The Hunt for the Night Stalker
The Hunter
Hunter in the Dark
Hunter's Blood
Hurricane
Husbands and Wives
Hush, Hush, Sweet Charlotte
Hussy
The Hustler
Hyper-Sapien: People from Another Star
Hysterical
I Am the Law
I Come in Peace
I Confess
I Could Go on Singing
I Died a Thousand Times
I Love Lucy
I Love N.Y.
I Love You Again
I Love You, Alice B. Toklas
I Love You to Death
I, Madman
I Married a Centerfold
I Married a Witch
I Married a Woman
I Never Sang For My Father
I Posed for Playboy
I Remember Mama
I Shot Billy the Kid
I Spit on Your Grave
I Vitelloni
I Walked with a Zombie
I Wanna Hold Your Hand
I Want to Live!
I Was a Teenage Zombie
Ice Pirates
Ice Station Zebra
Iceman
Identity Crisis
Idiot's Delight
Idolmaker
If...
If It's Tuesday, This Must Be Belgium
If Looks Could Kill
If You Could See What I Hear
Ike
Ikiru
I'll Cry Tomorrow
I'll Get You
Ilsa, Harem Keeper of the Oil Sheiks
Ilsa, She-Wolf of the SS
Ilsa, the Wicked Warden

I'm Dancing as Fast as I Can
I'm Gonna Git You Sucka
I'm the One You're Looking For
Imagemaker
Immediate Family
The Immortalizer
Impromptu
Improper Channels
Impulse
In Cold Blood
In Country
The In Crowd
In Harm's Way
The In-Laws
In Like Flint
In Love and War
In Name Only
In Person
In Praise of Older Women
In the Cold of the Night
In the Good Old Summertime
In the Heat of Passion
In the Heat of the Night
In the Line of Fire
In the Mood
In the Name of the Father
In the Navy
In the Soup
The Incident
Incident at Channel Q
The Incredible Hulk
The Incredible Hulk Returns
The Incredible Mr. Limpet
The Incredible Sarah
The Incredible Shrinking Man
The Incredible Shrinking Woman
Incubus
Indecency
The Indian Runner
Indian Summer
Indiana Jones and the Last Crusade
Indiana Jones and the Temple of Doom
Indio
Indochine
The Informer
Inherit the Wind
The Inner Circle
Inner Sanctum
Innerspace
Innocent Blood
An Innocent Man
Inside Daisy Clover
Inside Information
Inside Monkey Zetterland
Inside Moves
Inside the Third Reich
Insignificance
Interceptor
Interiors
Intermezzo
Internal Affairs
International House
The Interns
Intimate Power
Into the Fire
Into the Homeland
Into the Night
Into the Sun
Into the West
Into Thin Air
Intolerance
Intrigue
Intruder
Invader
Invaders from Mars
Invasion Earth: The Aliens Are Here!
Invasion of the Body Snatchers
Invasion U.S.A.
The Invisible Kid
The Invisible Man

The Invisible Ray
Irezumi
Irma La Douce
Iron & Silk
Iron Eagle
Iron Eagle 2
The Iron Mask
Iron Maze
The Iron Triangle
Iron Will
Ironweed
Irreconcilable Differences
Ishtar
The Island
Islands in the Stream
Isle of the Dead
Istanbul
It
It Came from Beneath the Sea
It Came from Hollywood
It Couldn't Happen Here
It Happened One Night
It Should Happen to You
It's A Gift
It's a Great Feeling
It's a Mad, Mad, Mad, Mad World
It's a Wonderful Life
It's Always Fair Weather
It's in the Bag
It's My Turn
Ivan the Terrible, Part 1
Ivan the Terrible, Part 2
I've Always Loved You
I've Heard the Mermaids Singing
Izzy & Moe
J. Edgar Hoover
Jabberwocky
Jack & the Beanstalk
Jack the Bear
Jack the Giant Killer
Jacknife
Jack's Back
Jacob's Ladder
The Jagged Edge
Jailhouse Rock
Jakarta
Jake Speed
James Dean Story
Jane Eyre
The January Man
Jason and the Argonauts
Jason Goes to Hell: The Final Friday
Jaws
Jaws 2
Jaws 3
Jaws: The Revenge
Jazz Singer
Jean de Florette
Jennifer 8
Jeremiah Johnson
The Jerk
Jesse James
Jesus Christ, Superstar
Jesus of Montreal
Jet Pilot
The Jetsons Meet the Flintstones
Jetsons: The Movie
The Jewel of the Nile
Jezebel
Jezebel's Kiss
JFK
The JFK Conspiracy
The Jigsaw Man
Jo Jo Dancer, Your Life is Calling
Joan of Arc
Joe
Joe Kidd
Joe Versus the Volcano
John & Yoko: A Love Story
John F. Kennedy
Johnny Angel

Johnny Be Good
Johnny Come Lately
Johnny Got His Gun
Johnny Guitar
Johnny Handsome
Johnny Stecchino
Jolson Sings Again
The Jolson Story
Josh and S.A.M.
Jour de Fete
Journey into Fear
Journey of Honor
Journey of Hope
The Journey of Natty Gann
Journey to the Center of the Earth
The Joy Luck Club
Joy of Living
Joy Sticks
Joyless Street
Ju Dou
Jubal
The Judge and the Assassin
Judgment at Nuremberg
Judgment in Berlin
Judgment Night
Judith of Bethulia
Judy Garland: The Golden Years at MGM
Jules and Jim
Julia
Julia and Julia
Juliet of the Spirits
Julius Caesar
Jumpin' at the Boneyard
Jumpin' Jack Flash
June Night
Jungle
The Jungle Book
Jungle Bride
Jungle Fever
Jungle Goddess
Jupiter's Darling
Jurassic Park
Just a Gigolo
Just Another Girl on the I.R.T.
Just One of the Girls
Just One of the Guys
K-9
Kafka
Kagemusha
Kalifornia
Kandyland
Kansas
Karate Cop
The Karate Kid
The Karate Kid: Part 2
The Karate Kid: Part 3
Katherine
Keaton's Cop
The Keep
Keep 'Em Flying
Keep the Change
Keeper of the City
Keeping Track
Keetje Tippei
Kelly's Heroes
Kentucky Fried Movie
Kentucky Jubilee
Kentucky Kernels
The Key
Key Largo
The Keys of the Kingdom
The KGB: The Secret War
Khartoum
Kickboxer
Kickboxer 2: The Road Back
Kickboxer 3: The Art of War
Kid
Kid from Brooklyn
Kid from Gower Gulch
Kid Galahad
Kidnapped
Kill Cruise
The Kill Reflex
Kill Slade

Killcrazy
The Killer Elite
Killer Instinct
Killer Klowns from Outer
  Space
Killer Tomatoes Eat France
The Killer's Edge
The Killing
A Killing Affair
The Killing Fields
Killing Floor
A Killing in a Small Town
The Killing Time
Killpoint
Kind Hearts and Coronets
Kindergarten Cop
The Kindred
The King and I
King Creole
King David
King Dinosaur
King Kong
King Kong Lives
King of Comedy
The King of Hearts
The King of Kings
King of New York
King of the Gypsies
King of the Hill
King of the Rocketmen
King Ralph
The King's Whore
Kinjite: Forbidden Subjects
Kismet
The Kiss
A Kiss Before Dying
Kiss Me a Killer
Kiss Me Deadly
Kiss Me Kate
Kiss Me, Stupid!
Kiss of the Spider Woman
Kiss Tomorrow Goodbye
The Kitchen Toto
Klute
Knife in the Water
Knight Moves
Knights of the Round Table
Knock on Any Door
Koyaanisqatsi
Kramer vs. Kramer
The Krays
Kriemhilde's Revenge
Kronos
Krull
Krush Groove
Kuffs
Kwaidan
La Bamba
L.A. Bounty
La Cage aux Folles
La Cage aux Folles 2
La Cage aux Folles 3: The
  Wedding
La Chienne
La Dolce Vita
La Lectrice
La Nuit de Varennes
La Passante
L.A. Story
La Strada
Labyrinth
Labyrinth of Passion
The Lacemaker
The Ladies' Man
Lady and the Tramp
Lady Beware
Lady Chatterley's Lover
The Lady Eve
Lady for a Day
The Lady from Shanghai
The Lady in Question
The Lady in White
Lady Jane
Lady Mobster
Lady on the Bus
Lady Sings the Blues

The Lady Vanishes
Ladyhawke
Ladykiller
L'Age D'Or
Laguna Heat
The Lair of the White Worm
Lake Consequence
Lambada
The Land Before Time
Land of the Pharaohs
Landslide
Lantern Hill
Laser Mission
Laserblast
Lassie, Come Home
Lassiter
Last Action Hero
The Last Boy Scout
Last Bullet
Last Dance
The Last Days of Chez Nous
The Last Detail
The Last Emperor
Last Exit to Brooklyn
The Last Fling
The Last Hit
The Last Hour
Last House on the Left
Last Hurrah
Last Light
The Last Metro
The Last of England
The Last of His Tribe
Last of the Clintons
The Last of the Finest
The Last of the Mohicans
Last of the Red Hot Lovers
The Last Picture Show
The Last Radio Station
Last Resort
The Last Riders
Last Rites
The Last Starfighter
Last Tango in Paris
The Last Temptation of Christ
The Last Time I Saw Paris
The Last Tycoon
The Last Unicorn
The Last Waltz
The Last Warrior
Late for Dinner
The Late Show
Latino
Lauderdale
Laura
The Lavender Hill Mob
L'Avventura
Law of Desire
Law of the Sea
The Lawnmower Man
Lawrence of Arabia
Le Boucher
Le Chat
Le Complot
Le Crabe Tambour
Le Grand Chemin
Le Mans
Leader of the Band
A League of Their Own
Lean on Me
Leap of Faith
Leather Jackets
Leatherface: The Texas
  Chainsaw Massacre 3
Leave It to the Marines
Leaving Normal
Legacy of Lies
Legal Eagles
Legend
The Legend of Hell House
The Legend of Hillbilly John
The Legend of Sleepy Hollow
The Legend of Wolf Mountain
Legion of Iron
The Lemon Drop Kid
The Lemon Sisters

Lena's Holiday
Leningrad Cowboys Go
  America
Lenny
Lensman
Leolo
Leonard Part 6
The Leopard Man
Leprechaun
Leprechaun 2
Les Biches
Les Comperes
Les Girls
Les Miserables
Less Than Zero
Let Him Have It
Let It Be
Let It Ride
L'Etat Sauvage
Lethal Weapon
Lethal Weapon 2
Lethal Weapon 3
Lethal Woman
Let's Dance
Let's Get Harry
The Letter
Letter to Brezhnev
A Letter to Three Wives
Leviathan
Liar's Edge
Libeled Lady
License to Drive
License to Kill
Liebestraum
The Life and Death of Colonel
  Blimp
Life & Times of Judge Roy
  Bean
Life is Sweet
Life Stinks
Life with Mikey
Lifeboat
Lifeforce
The Lift
The Light in the Jungle
Light of Day
Light Sleeper
Light Years
Lightning Bill
Lightning Over Water
Like Father, Like Son
Like Water for Chocolate
Lily in Love
Limelight
Limit Up
The Linguini Incident
The Lion Has Wings
The Lion in Winter
Lionheart
Lipstick
Liquid Sky
Listen to Me
Lisztomania
Little Annie Rooney
Little Big Man
Little Darlings
Little Dorrit, Film 1: Nobody's
  Fault
Little Dorrit, Film 2: Little
  Dorrit's Story
The Little Drummer Girl
The Little Foxes
The Little Girl Who Lives
  Down the Lane
The Little Mermaid
Little Monsters
Little Nemo: Adventures in
  Slumberland
A Little Night Music
Little Nikita
Little Ninjas
The Little Prince
The Little Princess
Little Red Riding Hood
A Little Romance
Little Shop of Horrors

Little Sweetheart
The Little Theatre of Jean
  Renoir
The Little Thief
Little Treasure
Little Vegas
Little Vera
Live and Let Die
The Living Daylights
Living Free
Loan Shark
Lobster Man from Mars
Local Hero
Logan's Run
Lola Montes
Lolita
London Kills Me
The Lone Runner
Lone Wolf McQuade
The Lonely Guy
The Lonely Lady
Lonesome Dove
Long Day's Journey into Night
Long Gone
The Long Goodbye
The Long, Long Trailer
The Long Riders
The Long Voyage Home
The Long Walk Home
The Longest Day
The Longest Drive
The Longest Yard
Look Back in Anger
Look Who's Laughing
Look Who's Talking
Look Who's Talking Now
Look Who's Talking, Too
Looker
Looking for Miracles
Looking for Mr. Goodbar
Loose Cannons
Lord of the Flies
The Lords of Discipline
The Lords of Flatbush
Lorenzo's Oil
Losin' It
Lost Angels
The Lost Boys
The Lost Continent
Lost Horizon
Lost in America
Lost in Yonkers
The Lost Patrol
Lost Squadron
The Lost Weekend
The Lost World
Love
Love Among the Ruins
Love and Death
Love and Hate: A Marriage
  Made in Hell
Love at First Bite
Love at Large
Love at Stake
The Love Bug
Love Crimes
Love Field
Love Finds Andy Hardy
Love from a Stranger
The Love Goddesses
Love Happy
Love is a Many-Splendored
  Thing
Love Letters
Love, Lies and Murder
Love Matters
Love Me or Leave Me
Love Meetings
Love or Money?
Love Potion 9
Love Story
Love with the Proper Stranger
The Loved One
Lovely to Look At
The Lover
Loverboy

Lovesick
Loving You
Lower Level
Lucky Luke: Daisy Town
Lucky Luke: The Ballad of the
  Daltons
Lucky Me
Lucky Stiff
Lucy and Desi: Before the
  Laughter
Lunatics: A Love Story
Lust for a Vampire
Lust for Life
Lust in the Dust
The Lusty Men
Luv
Lydia
M
M. Butterfly
Mac
Mac and Me
Macao
Macario
Macaroni
MacArthur
MacArthur's Children
Macbeth
Mack the Knife
MacKenna's Gold
Mad About You
Mad at the Moon
Mad Dog and Glory
Mad Max
Mad Max: Beyond
  Thunderdome
Mad Miss Manton
Madame Bovary
Madame Curie
Madame Sousatzka
Made in America
Made in Heaven
Made in USA
Mademoiselle Fifi
Madhouse
The Madwoman of Chaillot
Magdalene
Magic
The Magic Christian
The Magic Flute
Magic Kid
The Magic Voyage
Magical Mystery Tour
The Magician
The Magnificent Ambersons
The Magnificent Seven
Magnum Force
The Mahabharata
Mahogany
The Maid
Maid to Order
Major League
Major League 2
Making Mr. Right
The Making of a Legend:
  "Gone With the Wind"
The Makioka Sisters
Malarek
Malcolm
Malcolm X
Malone
The Maltese Falcon
Mama, There's a Man in Your
  Bed
The Mambo Kings
Mame
Man Bait
A Man Called Horse
A Man Called Sarge
Man Facing Southeast
A Man for All Seasons
Man from Cairo
The Man from Snowy River
Man from Utah
A Man in Love
The Man in the Gray Flannel
  Suit

The Man Inside
Man of a Thousand Faces
Man of Flowers
Man of La Mancha
Man on Fire
Man Outside
Man Trouble
The Man Who Came to Dinner
The Man Who Could Work Miracles
The Man Who Fell to Earth
The Man Who Knew Too Much
The Man Who Loved Women
The Man Who Shot Liberty Valance
The Man Who Would Be King
The Man with the Golden Gun
The Man with Two Brains
The Man Without a Face
The Manchurian Candidate
Mandingo
Manhattan
Manhattan Melodrama
Manhattan Murder Mystery
The Manhattan Project
Manhunt in the African Jungle
Manhunt of Mystery Island
Manhunter
Maniac Cop 2
The Manitou
Mannequin
Mannequin 2: On the Move
Manon of the Spring
Man's Best Friend
Marat/Sade
Marathon Man
March of the Wooden Soldiers
Marie Antoinette
Marius
Mark of Zorro
Marked for Death
Marked for Murder
Marked Woman
Marnie
Marooned
Married to It
Married to the Mob
The Marrying Man
Martial Law 2: Undercover
Martial Outlaw
Martians Go Home!
Martin
Marty
The Marx Brothers in a Nutshell
Mary of Scotland
Mary Poppins
M*A*S*H
M*A*S*H: Goodbye, Farewell & Amen
The Mask
Mask
Mask of the Dragon
Masks of Death
Masque of the Red Death
Masque of the Red Death/ Premature Burial
Masquerade
Mass Appeal
Massive Retaliation
The Master of Ballantrae
The Masters of Menace
Masters of the Universe
Matador
The Matchmaker
Matewan
Matinee
Maurice
Mausoleum
Max Dugan Returns
Max Headroom, the Original Story
Maxie
Maximum Force
Maximum Overdrive

Maximum Security
May Fools
May Wine
Maytime
McCabe & Mrs. Miller
The McConnell Story
McLintock!
McQ
McVicar
Me and Him
Me and the Kid
Mean Season
Mean Streets
Meatballs
Meatballs 2
The Mechanic
Mediterraneo
Meet John Doe
Meet Me in Las Vegas
Meet Me in St. Louis
Meet the Hollowheads
Meeting Venus
Mein Kampf
Melvin and Howard
Memoirs of an Invisible Man
Memorial Valley Massacre
Memories of Me
Memphis
Memphis Belle
Men are not Gods
Men at Work
Men Don't Leave
Men of Respect
Menace II Society
The Men's Club
Mercenary Fighters
Meridian: Kiss of the Beast
Mermaids
The Merry Widow
Messenger of Death
Metalstorm
The Meteor Man
Metropolis
Metropolitan
MGM: When the Lion Roars
Miami Blues
Miami Vice
Miami Vice 2: The Prodigal Son
Mickey's Christmas Carol
Micki & Maude
Midnight
Midnight Cabaret
A Midnight Clear
Midnight Cop
Midnight Cowboy
Midnight Crossing
Midnight Express
Midnight Run
Midway
The Mighty Ducks
Mighty Joe Young
The Mighty Quinn
The Milagro Beanfield War
Mildred Pierce
Miles from Home
Milky Way
The Milky Way
Millenium
Miller's Crossing
Million Dollar Haul
Million Dollar Mystery
Mindfield
Mindwarp
Ministry of Vengeance
Minnesota Clay
A Minor Miracle
The Miracle
Miracle Beach
Miracle in Milan
Miracle in Rome
Miracle in the Wilderness
Miracle Mile
Miracle of Our Lady of Fatima
Miracle on 34th Street
Miracles

The Mirror Crack'd
Mirror, Mirror
Mischief
Misery
The Misfits
Miss Firecracker
Ms. 45
Miss Right
Miss Sadie Thompson
Missing
Missing in Action
Missing in Action 2: The Beginning
The Mission
Mission Batangas
Mission Galactica: The Cylon Attack
Mission Manila
Mission of Justice
Mississippi Burning
Mississippi Masala
Mississippi Mermaid
Mrs. Miniver
Mrs. Soffel
Mr. Ace
Mr. & Mrs. Bridge
Mr. & Mrs. Smith
Mr. Arkadin
Mr. Baseball
Mr. Blandings Builds His Dream House
Mr. Deeds Goes to Town
Mr. Destiny
Mr. Hulot's Holiday
Mr. Jones
Mr. Lucky
Mr. Mom
Mr. North
Mr. Robinson Crusoe
Mr. Saturday Night
Mr. Skeffington
Mr. Smith Goes to Washington
Mr. Walkie Talkie
Mr. Wonderful
Mistress
Mo' Better Blues
Mo' Money
Mob Story
Mob War
Mobsters
Moby Dick
Model by Day
Modern Girls
Modern Romance
Modern Times
The Moderns
Mom
Mom and Dad Save the World
Mommie Dearest
Mon Oncle
Mona Lisa
Money for Nothing
The Money Pit
Money to Burn
Monkey Business
Monkey Shines
Monolith
Monsieur Hire
Monsieur Verdoux
The Monster Club
Monster High
Monster in a Box
The Monster Squad
Monterey Pop
A Month in the Country
Monty Python and the Holy Grail
Monty Python Live at the Hollywood Bowl
Monty Python's Flying Circus
Monty Python's Life of Brian
Monty Python's The Meaning of Life
Moon 44
Moon is Blue

Moon Over Parador
Moonfleet
Moonlighting
Moonraker
Moonrise
Moonstruck
Moontrap
More American Graffiti
More! Police Squad
The More the Merrier
Morgan!
Morgan Stewart's Coming Home
Morgan the Pirate
The Morning After
Morning Glory
Morocco
Mortal Sins
Mortal Thoughts
Mortuary Academy
Moscow Does Not Believe in Tears
Moscow on the Hudson
The Mosquito Coast
Motel Hell
Mother
Motor Patrol
Motown's Mustang
Moulin Rouge
The Mountain Men
Mountains of the Moon
Moving
Moving Violation
Moving Violations
Mozart: A Childhood Chronicle
Much Ado About Nothing
The Mummy
The Muppet Movie
The Muppets Take Manhattan
Murder by Death
Murder by Numbers
Murder, My Sweet
Murder on the Bayou
Murder on the Orient Express
Murder One
Murder Story
Murmur of the Heart
Murphy's Fault
Murphy's Law
Murphy's Romance
Muscle Beach Party
Music Box
The Music Lovers
The Music Man
The Music of Chance
The Music Teacher
Mutant
The Mutilator
Mutiny on the Bounty
My American Cousin
My Beautiful Laundrette
My Best Girl
My Bloody Valentine
My Blue Heaven
My Boyfriend's Back
My Chauffeur
My Darling Clementine
My Demon Lover
My Dinner with Andre
My Dog Shep
My Fair Lady
My Father the Hero
My Favorite Brunette
My Favorite Wife
My Favorite Year
My Girl
My Girl 2
My Heroes Have Always Been Cowboys
My Left Foot
My Life
My Life as a Dog
My Little Chickadee
My Little Girl
My Mom's a Werewolf

My Name is Ivan
My New Gun
My New Partner
My Night at Maud's
My Own Private Idaho
My Science Project
My Stepmother Is an Alien
My Tutor
My Wonderful Life
Mysterious Island
Mystery of the Wax Museum
Mystery Train
Mystic Pizza
Nadine
Nails
Naked
The Naked Gun: From the Files of Police Squad
Naked Gun 2 1/2: The Smell of Fear
Naked Jungle
Naked Kiss
The Naked Prey
The Name of the Rose
Napoleon
Narrow Margin
Nashville
Nasty Hero
Nate and Hayes
National Lampoon's Animal House
National Lampoon's Christmas Vacation
National Lampoon's Class Reunion
National Lampoon's European Vacation
National Lampoon's Loaded Weapon 1
National Lampoon's Vacation
National Velvet
Native Son
The Natural
Naughty Marietta
Navy SEALS
Nazarin
Near Dark
Near Misses
'Neath Canadian Skies
Necessary Roughness
Necromancer: Satan's Servant
Neighbors
Nemesis
The Neon Empire
Neptune's Daughter
Netherworld
Network
Nevada Smith
Never a Dull Moment
Never Cry Wolf
Never Give a Sucker an Even Break
Never on Tuesday
Never Say Never Again
Never So Few
Never Too Young to Die
The NeverEnding Story
The NeverEnding Story 2: Next Chapter
The New Adventures of Pippi Longstocking
The New Centurions
New Jack City
The New Kids
A New Life
New York, New York
New York Stories
News at Eleven
Newsfront
Next of Kin
Niagara
Nicholas and Alexandra
Night and the City
Night Angel
A Night at the Opera

Night

Night Breed
Night Caller from Outer Space
Night Eyes
Night Game
Night Games
A Night in the Life of Jimmy
  Reardon
Night Life
Night Life in Reno
'night, Mother
Night Nurse
Night of the Creeps
Night of the Cyclone
Night of the Demons
Night of the Demons 2
Night of the Fox
Night of the Generals
The Night of the Hunter
The Night of the Iguana
Night of the Laughing Dead
Night of the Living Dead
Night of the Sharks
Night of the Warrior
Night of the Wilding
Night on Earth
Night Patrol
The Night Porter
Night Shift
A Night to Remember
The Night Train to Kathmandu
Night Zoo
The Nightcomers
Nightflyers
Nighthawks
The Nightingale
Nightlife
A Nightmare on Elm Street
A Nightmare on Elm Street 2:
  Freddy's Revenge
A Nightmare on Elm Street 3:
  Dream Warriors
A Nightmare on Elm Street 4:
  Dream Master
A Nightmare on Elm Street 5:
  Dream Child
Nightwing
Nightwish
9 1/2 Ninjas
9 1/2 Weeks
Nine Lives of Fritz the Cat
9 to 5
976-EVIL
1900
1941
1969
1984
Ninja Turf
Ninotchka
The Ninth Configuration
No Escape, No Return
No Holds Barred
No Man of Her Own
No Man's Land
No Mercy
No Retreat, No Surrender
No Secrets
No Small Affair
No Time for Sergeants
No Way Out
Nobody's Fool
Nobody's Perfect
Nocturna
Nocturne
Noises Off
Nomads
None But the Brave
Norma Rae
North by Northwest
North Dallas Forty
North of the Border
North to Alaska
A Nos Amours
Nosferatu
Not Without My Daughter
Nothing But Trouble
Nothing in Common

Nothing Personal
Nothing Sacred
Notorious
Now and Forever
Now, Voyager
Nowhere to Run
The Nude Bomb
Nudo di Donna
Nuns on the Run
The Nun's Story
The Nutcracker Prince
Nuts
The Nutty Professor
Nyoka and the Tigermen
O Pioneers!
The Object of Beauty
The Obsessed
Obsessed
Obsession
The Occult Experience
Ocean's 11
Oceans of Fire
Octagon
Octopussy
The Odd Couple
Odd Man Out
The Odessa File
Of Human Bondage
Of Mice and Men
Off Beat
Off Limits
An Officer and a Gentleman
The Official Story
The Offspring
Oh, God!
Oh, God! You Devil
Oh, What a Night
Oklahoma!
Old Boyfriends
Old Explorers
Old Gringo
Old Yeller
Oldest Profession
Oliver!
Oliver Twist
Olivier, Olivier
The Omen
On a Clear Day You Can See
  Forever
On Dangerous Ground
On Deadly Ground
On Golden Pond
On Her Majesty's Secret
  Service
On Moonlight Bay
On the Beach
On the Town
On the Waterfront
Onassis
Once Around
Once Bitten
Once Upon a Forest
Once Upon a Honeymoon
Once Upon a Time in America
Once Upon a Time in the West
The One and Only, Genuine,
  Original Family Band
One Crazy Summer
One Day in the Life of Ivan
  Denisovich
One-Eyed Jacks
One False Move
One Flew Over the Cuckoo's
  Nest
One from the Heart
One Good Cop
One Magic Christmas
One Man Force
One Man Out
One More Saturday Night
One Night of Love
One, Two, Three
The Onion Field
Only One Night
Only the Lonely
Only the Strong

Only the Valiant
Only When I Laugh
Opera do Malandro
Operation Haylift
Operation Petticoat
The Opponent
Opportunity Knocks
The Opposite Sex
Options
Orca
Orchestra Wives
Ordeal by Innocence
Ordinary People
The Original Fabulous
  Adventures of Baron
  Munchausen
Orlando
Orphans
Orphans of the Storm
Oscar
Oscar's Greatest Moments:
  1971-1991
The Osterman Weekend
Otello
Othello
Other People's Money
The Other Side of Midnight
Our Daily Bread
Our Hospitality
Our Man Flint
Our Town
Out Cold
Out for Justice
Out of Africa
Out of Bounds
Out of Control
Out of Sight, Out of Her Mind
Out of the Blue
Out of the Body
Out of the Dark
Out of the Darkness
Out of the Past
Out of the Rain
The Out-of-Towners
Out on a Limb
The Outfit
Outland
The Outlaw
The Outlaw and His Wife
Outlaw Fury
Outlaw Gang
The Outlaw Josey Wales
Outrageous Fortune
The Outsiders
Over the Hill
Over the Top
Overboard
The Owl and the Pussycat
The Ox-Bow Incident
Oxford Blues
Pacific Heights
The Package
Paid to Kill
Paint It Black
Paint Your Wagon
The Painted Stallion
Pajama Game
Pajama Party
Pal Joey
Pale Blood
Pale Rider
The Paleface
The Palermo Connection
The Palm Beach Story
Palm Springs Weekend
Panic in Needle Park
Panic in the Streets
The Paper Chase
Paper Moon
A Paper Wedding
Paperhouse
Papillon
Parade
The Paradine Case
Paradise
Paradise Alley

Paramedics
Parasite
Pardon Mon Affaire
The Parent Trap
Parenthood
Parents
Paris, Texas
Paris Trout
Party Girl
Party Incorporated
Party Plane
Pascali's Island
Pass the Ammo
A Passage to India
Passenger 57
Passion Fish
Past Midnight
Pastime
Pat and Mike
Pat Garrett & Billy the Kid
Paternity
Paths of Glory
Patriot
Patti Rocks
Patton
Patty Hearst
Pauline at the Beach
The Pawnbroker
Payoff
Peacemaker
Peck's Bad Boy
Pecos Kid
Pee Wee's Big Adventure
Pee Wee's Playhouse
  Christmas Special
Peeping Tom
Peggy Sue Got Married
The Pelican Brief
Pelle the Conqueror
Pendulum
Penn and Teller Get Killed
Pennies From Heaven
Penny Serenade
Penthouse
The People Under the Stairs
People's Choice
Perfect
The Perfect Bride
Perfect Victims
The Perfect Weapon
Perfect Witness
A Perfect World
Perfectly Normal
Performance
The Perils of Gwendoline
Perils of the Darkest Jungle
Permanent Record
Personal Services
Personals
Pet Sematary
Pet Sematary 2
Pete Kelly's Blues
Pete Townshend: White City
Peter Pan
Peter's Friends
Pete's Dragon
Peyton Place
Phantasm
Phantasm II
Phantom of Liberty
Phantom of the Mall: Eric's
  Revenge
Phantom of the Opera
The Phantom of the Opera
Phantom of the Paradise
Phase 4
Philadelphia
The Philadelphia Experiment
Philadelphia Experiment 2
The Philadelphia Story
Physical Evidence
The Pick-Up Artist
The Pickle
Picnic
Picture of Dorian Gray
Pier 23

Pierrot le Fou
Pillow Talk
Pin
Pin-Up Girl
Ping Pong
Pink Cadillac
Pink Flamingos
Pink Floyd: The Wall
Pink Nights
The Pink Panther
The Pink Panther Strikes
  Again
Pinocchio
Pippin
Piranha 2: The Spawning
The Pirate
The Pirates of Penzance
The Pit & the Pendulum
Pitfall
P.K. and the Kid
A Place in the Sun
Places in the Heart
The Plainsman
Plan 9 from Outer Space
Planes, Trains & Automobiles
Planet of the Apes
Platoon
Platoon Leader
Play It Again, Sam
Play Misty for Me
The Player
Playing Away
Playing for Keeps
Playroom
Plaza Suite
Please Don't Eat the Daisies
Pleasure
Plenty
Pocketful of Miracles
Poetic Justice
The Point
Point Break
Point of Impact
Point of No Return
The Pointsman
The Polar Bear King
Police Academy
Police Academy 2: Their First
  Assignment
Police Academy 3: Back in
  Training
Police Academy 4: Citizens on
  Patrol
Police Academy 5:
  Assignment Miami Beach
Police Academy 6: City Under
  Siege
Police Court
Police Squad! Help Wanted!
Pollyanna
Poltergeist
Poltergeist 2: The Other Side
Poltergeist 3
Polyester
Popcorn
The Pope Must Diet
The Pope of Greenwich
  Village
Popeye
Pork Chop Hill
Porky's
Porky's 2: The Next Day
Porky's Revenge
Portfolio
The Portrait
Portrait of Jennie
The Poseidon Adventure
Posse
The Possessed
Postcards from the Edge
The Postman Always Rings
  Twice
The P.O.W. Escape
Power
The Power of One
Power, Passion & Murder

Prancer
Pray TV
Prayer for the Dying
Prayer of the Rollerboys
Predator
Predator 2
Prelude to a Kiss
The Presidio
Presumed Innocent
Pretty Baby
Pretty in Pink
Pretty Woman
Prettykill
Priceless Beauty
Prick Up Your Ears
Pride and Prejudice
The Pride of the Yankees
Primary Motive
Prime Evil
The Prince and the Pauper
The Prince and the Showgirl
Prince of Bel Air
Prince of Darkness
Prince of Pennsylvania
Prince of the City
The Prince of Tides
Princes in Exile
The Princess and the Pea
The Princess and the Pirate
The Princess Bride
Princess Tam Tam
The Principal
Prison
The Prisoner: Arrival
Prisoner in the Middle
Prisoner of Second Avenue
Prisoner of Zenda
Private Benjamin
The Private Eyes
Private Hell 36
Private Lessons
The Private Life of Henry VIII
Private Lives
A Private Matter
Private Resort
Private School
Private Wars
The Prizefighter and the Lady
Prizzi's Honor
Problem Child
Problem Child 2
The Prodigal
Prodigal Boxer: The Kick of
   Death
The Producers
The Professionals
Professionals
Project A-ko
Project: Alien
Project: Genesis
Project X
Prom Night
Prom Night 3: The Last Kiss
Promised a Miracle
Promised Land
Proof
Prospero's Books
Protector
Protocol
Prototype
Prototype X29A
Psych-Out
Psycho
Psycho 2
Psycho 3
Psycho 4: The Beginning
PT 109
Public Enemy
The Public Eye
Pulse
Pump Up the Volume
Pumping Iron
Pumping Iron 2: The Women
Pumpkinhead
Punchline
The Punisher

Punk Vacation
Puppet Master
Puppet Master 2
Puppet Master 3: Toulon's
   Revenge
The Puppetoon Movie
Pure Country
Pure Luck
Purgatory
Purple People Eater
Purple Rain
The Purple Rose of Cairo
The Pursuit of D.B. Cooper
Pygmalion
Python Wolf
Q & A
QB VII
Quackser Fortune Has a
   Cousin in the Bronx
Quadrophenia
Quality Street
Quatermass 2
Queen Christina
Queen Kelly
Queen of Hearts
The Queen of Spades
Queen of the Amazons
Queens Logic
Quest for Fire
Quest for the Mighty Sword
Quick Change
Quick, Let's Get Married
Quicksand: No Escape
Quicksilver
Quiet Cool
The Quiet Earth
The Quiet Man
Quiet Thunder
Quigley Down Under
Quo Vadis
Rabbit Test
Rabid Grannies
Race for Life
Race for Your Life, Charlie
   Brown
Rachel and the Stranger
Rachel River
Racing with the Moon
The Racket
Rad
Radar Men from the Moon
Radar Secret Service
Radio Days
Radio Flyer
Radioactive Dreams
Rage and Honor
A Rage in Harlem
Raggedy Man
Raging Bull
Ragtime
Raiders of the Lost Ark
Railroaded
The Railway Station Man
The Rain Killer
Rain Man
Rainbow
The Rainbow
The Rainmaker
Raintree County
Raise the Red Lantern
Raise the Titanic
A Raisin in the Sun
Raising Arizona
Raising Cain
Rambling Rose
Rambo: First Blood, Part 2
Rambo 3
Ran
Rancho Notorious
Rangeland Empire
Rapid Fire
The Rapture
Rapunzel
Rascal Dazzle
Rashomon
Ratings Game

The Raven
Raw Courage
Raw Deal
Raw Justice
Raw Nerve
Rawhead Rex
Rawhide Romance
The Razor's Edge
The Re-Animator
The Real Buddy Holly Story
Real Bullets
Real Genius
The Real McCoy
Real Men
Reality Bites
Rear Window
Reason to Die
Rebecca
Rebecca of Sunnybrook Farm
Rebel
Rebel Storm
Rebel Without a Cause
Reckless
Recruits
The Red and the White
The Red Balloon
Red Balloon/White Mane
Red Beard
Red Blooded American Girl
Red Dawn
Red Desert
Red Headed Stranger
Red Heat
Red Kiss
The Red Menace
The Red Pony
Red River
Red Rock Outlaw
Red Rock West
Red Scorpion
Red Shoe Diaries
Red Shoe Diaries 2: Double
   Dare
Red Shoe Diaries 3: Another
   Woman's Lipstick
The Red Shoes
Red Sonja
Red Surf
Red Tent
Red, White & Busted
Reds
The Ref
The Reflecting Skin
Reform School Girls
Regarding Henry
Reilly: Ace of Spies
The Reincarnation of Peter
   Proud
The Rejuvenator
Relentless
Relentless 2: Dead On
The Reluctant Debutante
The Remains of the Day
Rembrandt
Remo Williams: The
   Adventure Begins
Remote Control
Rendez-vous
Renegade Girl
Renegades
Rent-A-Cop
Rented Lips
Repentance
Repo Man
Repossessed
Requiem for Dominic
The Rescue
The Rescuers
The Rescuers Down Under
Reservoir Dogs
The Restless Breed
Retribution
Return
Return of Captain Invincible
Return of Frank James
The Return of Martin Guerre

The Return of Spinal Tap
The Return of Swamp Thing
Return of the Dragon
Return of the Fly
Return of the Jedi
Return of the Killer Tomatoes
Return of the Living Dead
Return of the Living Dead 2
Return of the Living Dead 3
The Return of the Musketeers
Return of the Pink Panther
Return of the Vampire
Return to Oz
Return to Snowy River
Return to the Blue Lagoon
Return to Two Moon Junction
Reunion
Revenge
Revenge of the Creature
Revenge of the Nerds
Revenge of the Nerds 2:
   Nerds in Paradise
Revenge of the Pink Panther
Revenge of the Red Baron
Reversal of Fortune
Revolution
Rhapsody in Blue
Rhinestone
Rich and Famous
Rich and Strange
Rich Girl
Rich in Love
Richard III
Ricochet
Ride in the Whirlwind
Ride the High Country
Riders of the Storm
Riding Speed
Riding the Edge
Riff Raff
The Right Stuff
Rikky and Pete
Rikyu
Rimfire
Ring of Fire
Ring of Steel
Ringside
Rio Grande
Rio Lobo
The Rise and Fall of Legs
   Diamond
Rising Sun
Risky Business
Rita, Sue & Bob Too
The Ritz
The River
River of Death
River of No Return
The River Rat
A River Runs Through It
River's Edge
Road House
The Road to Hong Kong
The Road to Morocco
The Road to Singapore
The Road to Utopia
The Road to Zanzibar
The Road Warrior
Roads to the South
Roadside Prophets
Roaring City
Roaring Roads
The Roaring Twenties
The Robe
Robin and Marian
Robin and the Seven Hoods
Robin Hood
Robin Hood: Prince of Thieves
Robinson Crusoe of Clipper
   Island
Robinson Crusoe on Mars
RoboCop
RoboCop 2
Robot Jox
Robot Monster
Robot Wars

Rocco and His Brothers
Rock-a-Doodle
Rock & Rule
Rock 'n' Roll High School
   Forever
The Rocketeer
Rocketship X-M
Rockula
Rockwell: A Legend of the
   Wild West
Rocky
Rocky 2
Rocky 3
Rocky 4
Rocky 5
The Rocky Horror Picture
   Show
Rodan
Roe vs. Wade
Roger & Me
Rollerball
Rollercoaster
Rolling Home
Rolling Thunder
Rolling Vengeance
Roman Holiday
Romance on the High Seas
Romance with a Double Bass
Romancing the Stone
Rome Adventure
Romeo and Juliet
Romeo Is Bleeding
Romero
Rooftops
The Rookie
Room Service
A Room with a View
Rooster Cogburn
Rope
Rosalie Goes Shopping
The Rosary Murders
The Rose
The Rose Garden
Rose Marie
The Rose Tattoo
Rosebud Beach Hotel
Rosemary's Baby
Rosencrantz & Guildenstern
   Are Dead
Rough Cut
Round Midnight
Round Trip to Heaven
The Rousters
Rover Dangerfield
Roxanne
Royal Wedding
R.S.V.P.
Rubin & Ed
Ruby
Rude Awakening
Rudolph the Red-Nosed
   Reindeer
Rudy
The Rules of the Game
The Ruling Class
Rumble Fish
The Rumor Mill
Rumpelstiltskin
Run
Run of the Arrow
Runaway
Runaway Train
The Runestone
Running Away
Running Brave
The Running Man
Running Mates
Running on Empty
Running Out of Luck
Running Scared
Rush Week
The Russia House
Russkies
Rustler's Paradise
Rustler's Rhapsody
Ruthless People

Ryan's Daughter
Sabotage
Saboteur
Sabrina
The Sacrifice
Sadie Thompson
Sagebrush Trail
Sahara
Saigon Commandos
The Sailor Who Fell from Grace with the Sea
St. Elmo's Fire
The Saint of Fort Washington
Salaam Bombay!
Salem's Lot
Salome's Last Dance
Salsa
Salt of the Earth
Salvador
Same Time, Next Year
Sammy & Rosie Get Laid
Samson and Delilah
Samurai 1: Musashi Miyamoto
Samurai 2: Duel at Ichijoji Temple
Samurai 3: Duel at Ganryu Island
San Francisco
The Sand Pebbles
The Sandlot
Sands of Iwo Jima
Sanjuro
Santa Claus is Coming to Town
Santa Claus: The Movie
Santa Sangre
Saps at Sea
Sarafina!
Sarah, Plain and Tall
Satisfaction
Saturday Night Fever
Saturn 3
Savage Beach
Savage Drums
Savage Streets
Savannah Smiles
Save Me
Save the Tiger
Saving Grace
Sawdust & Tinsel
Say Anything
Say Yes!
Scandal
Scandal in a Small Town
Scandalous
Scanner Cop
Scanners
Scanners 2: The New Order
Scanners 3: The Takeover
Scaramouche
Scared Stiff
Scarface
The Scarlet Pimpernel
The Scars of Dracula
Scavengers
Scenes from a Mall
Scenes from the Class Struggle in Beverly Hills
Scenes from the Goldmine
Scent of a Woman
Schindler's List
School Daze
School Ties
Scorchers
Scorpion
Scotland Yard Inspector
Scream for Help
Screen Test
Scrooge
Scrooged
Sea Chase
The Sea Hawk
Sea of Love
Search and Destroy
The Searchers
Second Chance

Second Chorus
Second Sight
Secret Admirer
The Secret Agent
The Secret Garden
Secret Honor
The Secret Life of Walter Mitty
The Secret of My Success
The Secret of NIMH
The Secret Policeman's Other Ball
Secret Policeman's Private Parts
The Seduction of Joe Tynan
See No Evil
See No Evil, Hear No Evil
See You in the Morning
Seems Like Old Times
Seize the Day
Self-Defense
Semi-Tough
The Sender
Separate But Equal
Separate Ways
September
September Affair
Sgt. Pepper's Lonely Hearts Club Band
Serial
The Serpent and the Rainbow
The Serpent of Death
Serpico
Sesame Street Presents: Follow That Bird
The Set-Up
Seven Beauties
Seven Brides for Seven Brothers
Seven Days in May
Seven Faces of Dr. Lao
Seven Hours to Judgment
The Seven Percent Solution
Seven Samurai
The Seven-Ups
The Seven Year Itch
1776
The Seventh Coin
The Seventh Seal
The Seventh Sign
The Seventh Victim
The Seventh Voyage of Sinbad
Sex and the Single Girl
sex, lies and videotape
Sex on the Run
Sexual Response
The Shadow Man
Shadow of a Doubt
Shadow of Chikara
Shadow of China
Shadow of the Wolf
Shadowhunter
Shadows and Fog
Shadows in the Storm
Shadowzone
Shag: The Movie
The Shaggy Dog
Shakedown
Shaker Run
Shakes the Clown
The Shakiest Gun in the West
Shall We Dance
Shame
Shampoo
Shamus
Shane
The Shanghai Gesture
Shanghai Surprise
Sharky's Machine
Shattered
She-Devil
She Done Him Wrong
She Wore a Yellow Ribbon
Sheena

Shelley Duvall's Bedtime Stories
The Sheltering Sky
Shenandoah
Shep Comes Home
Sherlock Holmes and the Secret Weapon
Sherlock Holmes Faces Death
Sherlock Holmes: The Voice of Terror
She's Back
She's Having a Baby
She's Out of Control
The Shining
Ship of Fools
Shipwrecked
Shirley Valentine
Shock Corridor
Shock 'Em Dead
A Shock to the System
Shocker
The Shoes of the Fisherman
Shogun
Shogun Assassin
Shoot the Moon
Shoot the Piano Player
Shoot to Kill
Shootfighter: Fight to the Death
The Shooting
Shooting Elizabeth
The Shootist
The Shop Around the Corner
The Shop on Main Street
Short Circuit
Short Circuit 2
Short Cuts
Short Time
A Shot in the Dark
Shout
Shout at the Devil
Show Boat
Show Business
A Show of Force
Showdown
Showdown in Little Tokyo
The Shrieking
The Shrimp on the Barbie
Shy People
Sibling Rivalry
The Sicilian
Sid & Nancy
Side Out
Sidekicks
The Siege of Firebase Gloria
Siegfried
Siesta
Signs of Life
The Silence
Silence Like Glass
The Silence of the Lambs
Silent Movie
Silent Night, Deadly Night
Silent Night, Deadly Night 2
Silent Night, Deadly Night 3: Better Watch Out!
Silent Night, Deadly Night 4: Initiation
The Silent Partner
Silent Rage
Silent Running
Silent Tongue
The Silk Road
Silk Stockings
Silkwood
Silver Bandit
Silver Bullet
The Silver Streak
Silverado
Simba
Simple Men
Sinatra
Sinbad and the Eye of the Tiger
Sinbad of the Seven Seas
Sinbad the Sailor

Since You Went Away
Sincerely Charlotte
Sincerely Yours
Sinful Life
Sing
Singin' in the Rain
Single White Female
Singles
Sins of Jezebel
Sirocco
Sister Act
Sister Act 2: Back in the Habit
Sister Kenny
Sister, Sister
The Sisterhood
Six Degrees of Separation
Six Weeks
Sixteen Candles
'68
Sizzle Beach U.S.A.
Skeeter
Skeleton Coast
Sketch Artist
Ski Patrol
Ski School
Skin Art
Skin Deep
Sky High
Sky Liner
Skyline
Slamdance
Slammer Girls
Slap Shot
Slapstick of Another Kind
Slaughter
Slaughter of the Innocents
Slaughterhouse Five
Slave Girls from Beyond Infinity
Slaves of New York
Sleepaway Camp 3: Teenage Wasteland
Sleeper
Sleeping Beauty
The Sleeping Car
Sleeping with the Enemy
Sleepless in Seattle
Sleepwalk
Sleepwalkers
Sleuth
Slipping into Darkness
Slipstream
Sliver
The Slugger's Wife
Slugs
Slumber Party '57
Slumber Party Massacre 2
Small Change
Small Sacrifices
Smash Palace
Smile
Smiles of a Summer Night
Smithereens
Smokescreen
Smokey and the Bandit
Smokey and the Bandit, Part 2
Smokey and the Bandit, Part 3
Smooth Talk
Sneakers
Sniper
Snoopy, Come Home
Snow White and the Seven Dwarfs
So Dear to My Heart
So I Married an Axe Murderer
Soapdish
S.O.B.
Social Error
Sodom and Gomorrah
Solar Crisis
Solarbabies
Solaris
Soldier of Orange
A Soldier's Story

Solomon and Sheba
Some Came Running
Some Kind of Hero
Some Kind of Wonderful
Some Like It Hot
Somebody Has to Shoot the Picture
Someone Behind the Door
Someone to Love
Someone to Watch Over Me
Something Special
Something to Sing About
Something Wicked This Way Comes
Something Wild
Sometimes They Come Back
Somewhere in Time
Sommersby
Son of Dracula
Son of Frankenstein
Son of Kong
The Son of Monte Cristo
Son of Paleface
Son of the Morning Star
Son of the Pink Panther
Son of the Sheik
The Song of Bernadette
Song of the Islands
A Song to Remember
Songwriter
Sonny Boy
Sons of Katie Elder
Sophie's Choice
Sorcerer
Sorority Babes in the Slimeball Bowl-A-Rama
Sorry, Wrong Number
S.O.S. Coast Guard
Soul Man
Soultaker
The Sound of Music
Sounder
Sourdough
South Central
South of Reno
South Pacific
Southern Comfort
Souvenir
Soylent Green
Space: 1999
Spaceballs
SpaceCamp
Spaced Invaders
Spacehunter: Adventures in the Forbidden Zone
Spaceways
The Spanish Main
Sparrows
Spartacus
The Spawning
Speaking Parts
A Special Day
Spectre of the Rose
Speed Zone
Spellbound
Spellcaster
Spetters
Spiders
Spies
Spies, Lies and Naked Thighs
Spies Like Us
Spike of Bensonhurst
The Spiral Staircase
Spirit of '76
Spirit of the Beehive
Spirit of the Eagle
The Spirit of West Point
Spite Marriage
Splash
Splendor in the Grass
Split Decisions
Splitting Heirs
The Spoilers
Spontaneous Combustion
Spookies
Spring Break

Springtime in the Rockies
Spy
Spy in Black
The Spy Who Came in from the Cold
The Spy Who Loved Me
Square Dance
Square Dance Jubilee
The Squeeze
Squeeze Play
Squirm
Stacking
Stage Door Canteen
Stage Fright
Stage Struck
Stagecoach
Stakeout
Stalag 17
Stalin
Stalking Danger
Stand and Deliver
Stand By Me
Stanley and Iris
Star!
The Star Chamber
Star Crash
Star 80
A Star is Born
Star of Midnight
Star Quest
Star Slammer
Star Trek: The Motion Picture
Star Trek 2: The Wrath of Khan
Star Trek 3: The Search for Spock
Star Trek 4: The Voyage Home
Star Trek 5: The Final Frontier
Star Trek: The Cage
Star Trek the Next Generation: Encounter at Farpoint
Star Wars
Starchaser: The Legend of Orin
Stardust Memories
Starlight Hotel
Starman
Stars and Bars
Starting Over
State of Emergency
State of Grace
State of Siege
State of the Union
State of Things
Static
Stay Awake
Stay Hungry
Stay Tuned
Staying Alive
Staying Together
Steal the Sky
Stealing Heaven
Stealing Home
Steamboat Bill, Jr.
Steel
Steel and Lace
Steel Dawn
The Steel Helmet
Steel Magnolias
Steele Justice
Steele's Law
Stella
Stella Dallas
Step Lively
The Stepfather
Stepfather 2: Make Room for Daddy
Stepfather 3: Father's Day
Stephen King's Golden Years
Stephen King's It
Stephen King's The Tommyknockers
Steppenwolf
Stepping Out

The Sterile Cuckoo
Steve Martin Live
Stewardess School
Stick
Sticky Fingers
Still of the Night
The Sting
The Sting 2
Stir Crazy
A Stolen Face
Stone Cold
The Stone Killer
Stop Making Sense
Stop! or My Mom Will Shoot
Stop That Cab
Stormy Monday
Stormy Weather
Story of Adele H.
The Story of Boys & Girls
The Story of O
The Story of O, Part 2
The Story of Qui Ju
The Story of Vernon and Irene Castle
Storyville
Stranded
The Strange Affair of Uncle Harry
Strange Brew
Strange Invaders
The Strange Love of Martha Ivers
A Stranger Among Us
The Stranger and the Gunfighter
Stranger on the Third Floor
Stranger than Paradise
Strangers
Strangers on a Train
Strapless
Strategic Air Command
Straw Dogs
Strays
Streamers
Street Asylum
Street Crimes
Street Hunter
Street Knight
Street Smart
Street Soldiers
A Streetcar Named Desire
Streets of Fire
Streets of Gold
Streetwalkin'
Streetwise
Strictly Ballroom
Strike a Pose
Strike It Rich
Strike Up the Band
Striking Distance
Stripes
Stroke of Midnight
Strong Man
Student Bodies
A Study in Terror
Stuff Stephanie in the Incinerator
The Stunt Man
Subspecies
Suburban Commando
Suburbia
Subway
Success is the Best Revenge
Sucker Money
Sudden Death
Sudden Impact
Suddenly, Last Summer
Suds
Sugar Cane Alley
Sugar Hill
The Sugarland Express
The Suicide Club
Sullivan's Travels
Summer
Summer and Smoke
Summer Camp Nightmare

Summer Heat
Summer Lovers
Summer of '42
The Summer of Miss Forbes
A Summer Place
Summer Rental
Summer School
Summer Stock
Summer's Games
Summertime
Sunday, Bloody Sunday
Sunday in the Park with George
Sundown Riders
The Sundowners
Sunset
Sunset Boulevard
Sunset Strip
The Sunshine Boys
Super Force
Super Mario Bros.
Supergirl
Superman: The Movie
Superman 2
Superman 3
Superman 4: The Quest for Peace
Support Your Local Sheriff
The Sure Thing
Surf Ninjas
Surrender
The Survivalist
Survivor
Survivors
Susan Slept Here
Suspect
Suspicion
Suspiria
Swamp Thing
The Swan
Swashbuckler
Swedenhielms
Sweeney Todd: The Demon Barber of Fleet Street
Sweet Bird of Youth
Sweet Charity
Sweet Country
Sweet Dreams
Sweet Hearts Dance
Sweet Liberty
Sweet Smell of Success
Sweet Talker
Sweethearts
Sweetie
Swept Away...
Swimmer
Swimming to Cambodia
The Swindle
Swing Kids
Swing Shift
Swing Time
The Swiss Family Robinson
Switch
Switching Channels
Swoon
The Sword & the Rose
Sword & the Sorcerer
The Sword in the Stone
The Swordsman
Sylvester
Sylvia Scarlett
T Bone N Weasel
T-Men
Table for Five
Taffin
Tai-Pan
Tailspin: Behind the Korean Airline Tragedy
Take Me Out to the Ball Game
Take the Money and Run
Take Two
Taken Away
Taking Care of Business
The Taking of Beverly Hills
The Taking of Flight 847: The Uli Derickson Story

The Tale of the Frog Prince
Talent for the Game
Tales from the Crypt
Tales from the Darkside
Tales from the Darkside: The Movie
Tales of Robin Hood
Tales of the Unexpected
Talk of the Town
Talk Radio
The Tall Guy
Tall in the Saddle
Tall Lie
Tall Story
Tall Texan
Talons of the Eagle
The Taming of the Shrew
Tampopo
Tango and Cash
Tank
Tanner '88
Tap
Tapeheads
Taras Bulba
Target
Tartuffe
Tarzan and His Mate
Tarzan, the Ape Man
A Taste for Killing
Tatie Danielle
Taxi Driver
A Taxing Woman
A Taxing Woman's Return
TC 2000
Tea and Sympathy
The Teacher
Teachers
The Teahouse of the August Moon
Teamster Boss: The Jackie Presser Story
Teen Wolf
Teenage Mutant Ninja Turtles: The Movie
Teenage Mutant Ninja Turtles 3
The Telephone
Tell Them Willie Boy Is Here
The Temp
The Tempest
10
The Ten Commandments
Ten Days That Shook the World
Ten Little Indians
10 Rillington Place
Ten to Midnight
Ten Wanted Men
Tender Mercies
The Tender Trap
The Tenth Man
Tequila Sunrise
Terminal Bliss
Terminal Exposure
Terminal Force
The Terminator
Terminator 2: Judgment Day
Terms of Endearment
Terror by Night
Terror in Beverly Hills
Terror in the Swamp
Terror Street
Terror Train
Tess
Testament
Tex
The Texas Chainsaw Massacre
Texas Chainsaw Massacre, Part 2
Texas Guns
Texasville
Thank Your Lucky Stars
That Hamilton Woman
That Night
That Obscure Object of Desire

That Sinking Feeling
That Summer of White Roses
That Touch of Mink
That Was Then...This Is Now
That'll Be the Day
That's Dancing!
That's Entertainment
That's Entertainment, Part 2
That's Life!
That's Singing: The Best of Broadway
Theatre of Blood
Thelma & Louise
Them!
There's No Business Like Show Business
There's Nothing Out There
These Three
They All Laughed
They Came to Cordura
They Got Me Covered
They Live
They Live by Night
They Made Me a Criminal
They Never Come Back
They Shoot Horses, Don't They?
They Were So Young
They Won't Believe Me
Thief
The Thief of Baghdad
Thief of Baghdad
Thief of Hearts
Thieves of Fortune
The Thin Blue Line
The Thin Man
The Thing
The Thing Called Love
Things Change
The Things of Life
Think Big
Third Degree Burn
The Third Man
Third Solution
'38: Vienna Before the Fall
The 39 Steps
This Boy's Life
This Could Be the Night
This Gun for Hire
This is Spinal Tap
This Island Earth
This Land is Mine
This Property is Condemned
Thompson's Last Run
Thoroughly Modern Millie
Those Magnificent Men in Their Flying Machines
Thousand Pieces of Gold
Thousands Cheer
Three Amigos
The Three Caballeros
Three Days of the Condor
Three Days to a Kill
The Three Faces of Eve
Three for the Road
Three Fugitives
The 317th Platoon
Three Legionnaires
Three Men and a Baby
Three Men and a Cradle
Three Men and a Little Lady
The Three Musketeers
3 Ninjas
Three O'Clock High
Three of Hearts
The Three Penny Opera
3:10 to Yuma
The Three Worlds of Gulliver
Throne of Blood
Throw Momma from the Train
Thumbelina
Thumbelina
Thunder & Mud
Thunder in Paradise
Thunder in the Pines
Thunderball
Thunderbolt & Lightfoot

Thunderground

Thunderground
Thunderheart
Thursday's Game
THX 1138
Ticks
Tie Me Up! Tie Me Down!
Tiger Claws
Tiger Warsaw
A Tiger's Tale
Tightrope
The Tigress
Till Marriage Do Us Part
Till the Clouds Roll By
Till the End of Time
Tillie's Punctured Romance
Time After Time
Time Bandits
The Time Guardian
The Time Machine
A Time of Destiny
Time of the Gypsies
Time Runner
A Time to Die
Time to Kill
Timebomb
Timerider
Times of Harvey Milk
Tin Men
Tiny Toon Adventures: How I
    Spent My Vacation
To Be or Not to Be
To Catch a Killer
To Catch a Thief
To Die for
To Die Standing
To Have & Have Not
To Joy
To Kill a Mockingbird
To Kill a Priest
To Live & Die in L.A.
To the Death
Toast of New York
Tobor the Great
Toby McTeague
Togetherness
Tokyo Joe
Tokyo Olympiad
Tokyo Pop
Toll of the Desert
Tom, Dick, and Harry
Tom Jones
Tom Sawyer
Tom Thumb
Tomb of Ligeia
Tombstone
Tomcat: Dangerous Desires
Tommy
Too Many Girls
Too Much Sun
Tootsie
Top Gun
Top Hat
Top Secret!
Topaz
Topaze
Topper Returns
Tora! Tora! Tora!
Torch Song
Torch Song Trilogy
Torchlight
Torn Curtain
Torrents of Spring
Torture Garden
Total Exposure
Total Recall
Touch and Go
Touch of Evil
Tough Assignment
Tough Guys
Tough Guys Don't Dance
Tour of Duty
Tourist Trap
Tous les Matins du Monde
The Towering Inferno
The Toxic Avenger
The Toxic Avenger, Part 2

The Toy
Toy Soldiers
Traces of Red
Trading Hearts
Trading Places
Trail of Terror
Trail of the Mounties
Trail of the Pink Panther
Train Robbers
Train to Tombstone
Trancers
Trancers 2: The Return of
    Jack Deth
Trancers 3: Deth Lives
Transformations
Transmutations
Transylvania 6-5000
Trap on Cougar Mountain
Trapeze
Trapper County War
Travels with My Aunt
Treasure Island
Treasure of Monte Cristo
Treasure of the Sierra Madre
A Tree Grows in Brooklyn
The Tree of Wooden Clogs
Tremors
Trespass
Tribute
Tricks of the Trade
Trinity is Still My Name
The Trip to Bountiful
Tripods: The White Mountains
Tripwire
Triumph of the Spirit
Troll
Tron
Troop Beverly Hills
Tropical Snow
Trouble Bound
Trouble in Mind
The Trouble with Angels
The Trouble with Harry
True Believer
True Blood
True Colors
True Confessions
True Grit
True Love
True Romance
True Stories
Trust
Trust Me
Truth or Dare
Truth or Die
Tucker: The Man and His
    Dream
Tuff Turf
Tumbleweeds
Tune in Tomorrow
Tunes of Glory
The Tunnel
The Tunnel of Love
The Turn of the Screw
Turner and Hooch
Turtle Diary
Tusks
The Tuttles of Tahiti
Twelve Angry Men
Twelve Chairs
Twelve O'Clock High
12:01
20 Million Miles to Earth
20,000 Leagues Under the
    Sea
Twenty-One
Twice Dead
Twice in a Lifetime
Twilight of the Cockroaches
The Twilight Zone
Twilight Zone: The Movie
Twilight's Last Gleaming
Twin Peaks
Twin Peaks: Fire Walk with
    Me
Twins

Twisted Obsession
Twister
Two Evil Eyes
Two for the Road
Two for the Seesaw
Two Girls and a Sailor
The Two Jakes
Two Minute Warning
Two Moon Junction
Two of a Kind
Two Rode Together
2001: A Space Odyssey
2010: The Year We Make
    Contact
Two Weeks in Another Town
Tycoon
Ugetsu
UHF
Ulysses
Ulzana's Raid
Umberto D
Un Coeur en Hiver
The Unbearable Lightness of
    Being
The Unbelievable Truth
The Unborn
Uncaged
Uncle Buck
Uncommon Valor
The Undefeated
Under Capricorn
Under Fire
Under Siege
Under Suspicion
Under the Biltmore Clock
Under the Boardwalk
Under the Cherry Moon
Under the Earth
Under the Gun
Under the Volcano
Undercover Blues
Undersea Kingdom
Understudy: The Graveyard
    Shift 2
Underwater
Unfaithfully Yours
The Unforgiven
Unforgiven
The Unholy
Unholy Four
The Unholy Three
The Uninvited
Uninvited
Union City
Universal Soldier
Unlawful Entry
The Unnamable
The Unnamable 2: The
    Statement of Randolph
    Carter
Unnatural Causes
Unsettled Land
The Unsinkable Molly Brown
Untamed Heart
Until The End of The World
The Untouchables
Up Periscope
Up the Creek
Up Your Alley
Uranus
Urban Cowboy
Urusei Yatsura Movie 2:
    Beautiful Dreamer
Urusei Yatsura Movie 4: Lum
    the Forever
Used Cars
Used People
Utilities
Vagabond
Valentino Returns
Valley Girl
The Valley of Gwangi
Valley of the Lawless
Valmont
Vamp
Vampire's Kiss

Vanishing Point
Varieties on Parade
The Velvet Vampire
Vengeance
Vengeance Is Mine
Vera Cruz
The Verdict
Verne Miller
Vertigo
A Very Old Man with
    Enormous Wings
V.I. Warshawski
Vice Academy
Vice Squad
Vice Versa
Victim of Love
Victor/Victoria
Videodrome
Vietnam, Texas
A View to a Kill
The Vikings
Village of the Damned
Vincent & Theo
Vincent, Francois, Paul and
    the Others
Vincent: The Life and Death of
    Vincent van Gogh
The Vineyard
The Violent Men
Violets Are Blue
Virgin High
Virgin Queen of St. Francis
    High
Virgin Sacrifice
Vision Quest
The Visitors
Vital Signs
Viva Las Vegas
Viva Villa!
Viva Zapata!
Volere Volare
Volunteers
Von Ryan's Express
Voyage to the Bottom of the
    Sea
Voyager
Wackiest Ship in the Army
Wacko
Wages of Fear
Wagon Master
Wait Until Dark
Waiting for the Light
A Walk in the Sun
Walker: Texas Ranger: One
    Riot, One Ranger
Walking Tall
Walking Tall: Part 2
Walking Tall: The Final
    Chapter
Wall Street
The Wannsee Conference
Wanted Dead or Alive
War and Peace
War Lover
War of the Robots
The War of the Roses
The War of the Worlds
War Party
The War Room
The War Wagon
WarGames
Warlords
Warm Nights on a Slow-
    Moving Train
Warm Summer Rain
The Warrior & the Sorceress
Warrior Queen
The Warriors
The Wash
Watchers
Watchers 2
The Waterdance
Waterland
Waterloo Bridge
Watermelon Man
Wavelength

Waxwork
The Way We Were
Wayne's World
We All Loved Each Other So
    Much
We the Living
We Think the World of You
Wedding Band
A Wedding in Galilee
Wedding Rehearsal
Weeds
Weekend at Bernie's 2
Weekend Pass
Weird Science
Welcome Home
Welcome Home, Roxy
    Carmichael
Welcome to Spring Break
We're No Angels
We're Talkin' Serious Money
West of Zanzibar
West Side Story
Western Pacific Agent
The Westerner
Westworld
The Whales of August
What About Bob?
What Comes Around
What Ever Happened to Baby
    Jane?
What Have I Done to Deserve
    This?
What Price Hollywood?
What's Love Got to Do With
    It?
What's New Pussycat?
What's Up, Tiger Lily?
Wheels of Fire
When a Stranger Calls
When a Stranger Calls Back
When Comedy was King
When Dinosaurs Ruled the
    Earth
When Harry Met Sally
When Nature Calls
When the Whales Came
When the Wind Blows
When Worlds Collide
Where Angels Fear to Tread
Where Eagles Dare
Where the Boys Are
Where the Day Takes You
Where the Heart Is
Where the North Begins
Where's Poppa?
While the City Sleeps
A Whisper to a Scream
Whispers
Whispers in the Dark
The Whistle Blower
White Christmas
The White Dawn
White Fang
White Gorilla
White Heat
White Hot
White Hunter, Black Heart
White Light
White Line Fever
White Mane
White Mischief
White Nights
White Palace
White Sands
White Water Summer
Who Am I This Time?
Who Framed Roger Rabbit?
Who'll Stop the Rain?
Wholly Moses!
The Whoopee Boys
Who's Afraid of Virginia
    Woolf?
Who's Harry Crumb?
Who's That Girl?
Why Me?
Wide Sargasso Sea

Wild at Heart
The Wild Bunch
Wild Geese
Wild Gypsies
Wild in the Streets
The Wild Life
The Wild One
Wild Orchid
The Wild Pair
Wild Rovers
Wild Strawberries
Wild Thing
Wild Zone
Wildcard
Wildcats
Wilder Napalm
Wildest Dreams
Wildfire
Will Penny
Willard
Willie & Phil
The Willies
Willow
Willy Wonka & the Chocolate
  Factory
Winchester '73
Wind
The Wind and the Lion
The Window
Windy City
Wings
Wings of Danger
Wings of Desire
Winners Take All
Winning
The Winning Team
Winter Kills
Winter People
Wired
Wisdom
Wish You Were Here
Witchboard
Witchboard 2: The Devil's
  Doorway
Witchcraft
Witchcraft 2: The Temptress
Witchcraft 4: Virgin Heart
The Witches
The Witches of Eastwick
WitchTrap
Withnail and I
Without a Clue
Without Honors
Without Reservations
Witness
Witness for the Prosecution
The Wiz
The Wizard
The Wizard of Loneliness
The Wizard of Oz
The Wizard of Speed and
  Time
Wizards
The Wolf Man
Wolfen
The Wolves
Woman Condemned
The Woman in Green
The Woman in Red
A Woman Named Jackie
Woman of Desire
A Woman of Distinction
Woman of the Year
A Woman's Tale
The Women
Women & Men: In Love There
  Are No Rules
Women & Men: Stories of
  Seduction
Women in Love
Women on the Verge of a
  Nervous Breakdown
The Wonderful World of the
  Brothers Grimm
Wonderland
Woodstock

The Word
Working Girl
The World According to Garp
A World Apart
World Gone Wild
The World of Henry Orient
The World of Suzie Wong
World's Greatest Lover
Worth Winning
The Wraith
Wrangler
The Wreck of the Mary Deare
Wrestling Ernest Hemingway
Write to Kill
The Wrong Guys
Wrong is Right
The Wrong Man
Wuthering Heights
X: The Man with X-Ray Eyes
Xanadu
Xtro
Xtro 2: The Second Encounter
The Yakuza
Yankee Doodle Dandy
Yanks
The Year My Voice Broke
The Year of Living
  Dangerously
Year of the Comet
Year of the Dragon
Year of the Gun
Year of the Quiet Sun
The Yearling
Yellow Submarine
Yellowbeard
Yentl
Yes, Giorgio
Yojimbo
Yor, the Hunter from the
  Future
You Can't Hurry Love
You Can't Take It with You
You Only Live Twice
You Were Never Lovelier
You'll Never Get Rich
Young and Innocent
Young Doctors in Love
Young Einstein
Young Frankenstein
Young Guns
Young Guns 2
Young Lady Chatterly 2
The Young Lions
Young Man with a Horn
Young Mr. Lincoln
Young Nurses in Love
Young Sherlock Holmes
Youngblood
Yours, Mine & Ours
Z
Zabriskie Point
Zandalee
Zapped!
Zapped Again
Zardoz
Zebrahead
Zelig
Zelly & Me
Zentropa
Zeppelin
Ziegfeld Follies
Ziegfeld Girl
Zipperface
Zombie
Zombies of the Stratosphere
Zombies on Broadway
Zoot Suit
Zora Is My Name!
Zorba the Greek
Zorro's Black Whip
Zorro's Fighting Legion
Zou Zou
Zulu
Zulu Dawn

CAPTIONED INDEX

The **CAPTIONED INDEX** identifies 3,400 videos available with captioning for hearing-impaired viewers provided by either the National Captioning Institute (Falls Church, VA) or the Caption Center (Los Angeles, CA). Titles are arranged alphabetically.

Abbott and Costello Go to Mars
Abbott and Costello in the Foreign Legion
Abbott and Costello Meet the Keystone Kops
Above the Law
The Abyss
Acceptable Risks
Accidental Meeting
The Accidental Tourist
The Accused
Ace Ventura: Pet Detective
Act of Vengeance
Action Jackson
Adam
The Addams Family
Addams Family Values
Adrift
The Adventurers
Adventures in Babysitting
Adventures in Dinosaur City
Adventures in Spying
The Adventures of Baron Munchausen
The Adventures of Buckaroo Banzai Across the Eighth Dimension
The Adventures of Ford Fairlane
The Adventures of Huck Finn
The Adventures of Milo & Otis
The Adventures of Robin Hood
The Adventures of Sherlock Holmes
An Affair in Mind
An Affair to Remember
Afraid of the Dark
After Dark, My Sweet
After Hours
After Midnight
After Pilkington
After the Shock
Afterburn
Against All Odds
The Age of Innocence
Age Old Friends
Agnes of God
Air America
Air Force
The Air Up There
Airborne
Aladdin

Aladdin and His Wonderful Lamp
The Alamo
Alamo Bay
The Alamo: Thirteen Days to Glory
Alfredo, Alfredo
Ali Baba and the Forty Thieves
Alias Billy the Kid
Alice
Alice in Wonderland
Alien 3
Alien Intruder
Alien Nation
Aliens
Alive
Alive: 20 Years Later
All-American Murder
All Creatures Great and Small
All That Jazz
All Dogs Go to Heaven
All the Kind Strangers
All the Right Moves
All Through the Night
Allan Quartermain and the Lost City of Gold
Allegheny Uprising
All's Fair
Almost an Angel
Almost Partners
Almost Pregnant
Almost You
Always
Amazing Grace & Chuck
The Amazing Spider-Man
Ambition
The Ambulance
The American Angels: Baptism of Blood
American Anthem
American Dreamer
American Flyers
American Ninja
American Ninja 2: The Confrontation
American Samurai
American Shaolin: King of the Kickboxers 2
An American Story
An American Summer
An American Tail
An American Tail: Fievel Goes West
Amityville: A New Generation

Amityville 1992: It's About Time
Amongst Friends
Amore!
Amos and Andrew
Anchors Aweigh
And a Nightingale Sang
And the Band Played On
And You Thought Your Parents Were Weird!
Andy Hardy Meets Debutante
Angel of Fury
Angie
Anguish
Animal Instincts
Anna
Anne of Avonlea
Anne of Green Gables
Annie
Annie Oakley
Another 48 Hrs.
Another Stakeout
Another Thin Man
Another Time, Another Place
Another Woman
Another You
Antarctica
Antonia and Jane
Apache Uprising
A.P.E.X.
The Apple Dumpling Gang
The Applegates
Appointment with Death
Apprentice to Murder
April Fool's Day
Arabian Nights
Arachnophobia
Arcade
Are You Lonesome Tonight
Arena
Armed and Dangerous
Armed for Action
Army of Darkness
Around the World in 80 Days
Arrivederci, Baby!
Arrowhead
Arsenic and Old Lace
Arthur
Arthur 2: On the Rocks
Article 99
Artists and Models
Ash Wednesday
Aspen Extreme
Assassination
The Assassination Bureau

Assault and Matrimony
Assault at West Point: The Court-Martial of Johnson Whittaker
Assault on a Queen
At Close Range
At Play in the Fields of the Lord
The Atomic City
The Attic: The Hiding of Anne Frank
Avalon
Avenging Angel
Avenging Force
Awakenings
The Babe
Babe Ruth Story
Baby Boom
The Baby Doll Murders
Baby It's You
Baby of the Bride
Baby on Board
Baby, Take a Bow
Babycakes
Bachelor in Paradise
Bachelor Party
Back Home
Back in Action
Back to Bataan
Back to School
Back to the Beach
Back to the Future
Back to the Future, Part 2
Back to the Future, Part 3
Backdraft
Backfield in Motion
Backstab
Backtrack
The Bad and the Beautiful
Bad Behavior
Bad Channels
Bad Dreams
Bad Lieutenant
Bad Medicine
Bagdad Cafe
The Ballad of Little Jo
The Ballad of the Sad Cafe
Bambi
Bandolero!
Barbarian and the Geisha
Barbarians at the Gate
Bare Essentials
Barfly
The Baron and the Kid
Based on an Untrue Story

Basic Instinct
Basket Case 2
Basket Case 3: The Progeny
The Bastard
Bat 21
Batman
Batman: Mask of the Phantasm
Batman Returns
Battle Circus
Battle Cry
Battle for the Planet of the Apes
Battle of Britain
Battle of the Bulge
Battleground
Battling for Baby
The Bay Boy
Beach Boys: An American Band
The Bear
The Beast
The Beast with Five Fingers
Beastmaster 2: Through the Portal of Time
Beat the Devil
The Beautiful Blonde from Bashful Bend
Beautiful Dreamers
Beauty and the Beast
Bebe's Kids
Becoming Colette
Bed & Breakfast
The Bedroom Window
Beer
Beethoven
Beethoven Lives Upstairs
Beethoven's 2nd
Beetlejuice
Being There
The Believers
Belizaire the Cajun
The Bells of St. Mary's
Ben-Hur
Beneath the Planet of the Apes
Benefit of the Doubt
Benji the Hunted
Benny & Joon
Bernard and the Genie
Bert Rigby, You're a Fool
Best Defense
Best of Comic Relief
Best of Eddie Murphy
Best of the Best 2

The Best of the Two Ronnies
The Best of Times
Betrayed
Betsy's Wedding
Better Off Dead
Betty Blue
The Beverly Hillbillies
Beverly Hills Brats
Beverly Hills Cop
Beverly Hills Cop 2
Beyond Darkness
Beyond Justice
Beyond the Door
Beyond the Door 3
Beyond Therapy
The Big Blue
Big Business
The Big Chill
The Big Easy
Big Girls Don't Cry...They Get
    Even
Big Jake
Big Jim McLain
The Big Picture
Big Shots
The Big Sky
The Big Stampede
Big Top Pee Wee
Big Trail
Big Trouble in Little China
Biggles
The Bikini Car Wash
    Company
The Bikini Car Wash
    Company 2
Bill & Ted's Bogus Journey
Bill & Ted's Excellent
    Adventure
Bill Cosby, Himself
A Bill of Divorcement
Billy Bathgate
Billy Crystal: Midnight Train to
    Moscow
Billy the Kid
Bingo
Bird
Bird on a Wire
Birdy
Bitter Harvest
Black Ice
Black Magic
Black Magic Woman
Black Moon Rising
Black Rain
Black Rainbow
The Black Stallion
The Black Stallion Returns
Black Widow
Blackboard Jungle
Blackmail
Blame It on the Bellboy
Blank Check
Blaze
Bleak House
Blessed Event
Blind Fury
Blind Man's Bluff
Blind Spot
Blind Vision
Blind Witness
Blink
Blink of an Eye
The Bliss of Mrs. Blossom
The Blob
Blood Alley
Blood and Roses
Blood Games
Blood In...Blood Out: Bound
    by Honor
The Blood of Heroes
Blood Simple
Blood Warriors
Bloodfist 2
Bloodhounds of Broadway
Bloodlust: Subspecies 3
Bloodsport

Bloodstone: Subspecies 2
Bloodsucking Pharoahs of
    Pittsburgh
Blossoms in the Dust
Blown Away
Blue
The Blue Bird
Blue Chips
Blue City
Blue De Ville
Blue Ice
Blue Iguana
Blue Steel
Blue Thunder
Blue Velvet
The Blue Yonder
Bob Roberts
Bodies, Rest & Motion
Body Bags
Body Chemistry 2: Voice of a
    Stranger
Body Double
The Body in the Library
Body Language
Body of Evidence
Body of Influence
Body Parts
Body Snatchers
Body Waves
The Bodyguard
Boeing Boeing
Bonanza: The Return
The Bonfire of the Vanities
Book of Love
Boom Town
Boomerang
Bopha!
Border Radio
Border Shootout
Borderline
Boris and Natasha: The Movie
Born on the Fourth of July
Born to Ride
Born Yesterday
The Borrowers
The Boss' Wife
The Boston Strangler
Bounty Tracker
Boxing Helena
Boy in Blue
A Boy Named Charlie Brown
The Boy Who Could Fly
The Boy Who Loved Trolls
Boys Town
Boyz N the Hood
Braddock: Missing in Action 3
The Brain
Brain Damage
Brain Donors
Brain Smasher...A Love Story
Bram Stoker's Dracula
Branded
The Bravados
Brazil
The Breakfast Club
Breakheart Pass
Breaking In
Breaking the Rules
Breath of Scandal
Breathing Fire
Brewster's Millions
Brian's Song
The Bride
Bride of Re-Animator
The Bride Wore Red
Brideshead Revisited
Bridge to Silence
Bridge to Terabithia
A Bridge Too Far
A Brief History of Time
Bright Angel
Bright Eyes
Bright Lights, Big City
Brighton Beach Memoirs
Broadcast News
Broadway Bound

Broadway Melody of 1938
Broken Angel
Broken Arrow
The Broken Chain
Broken Lance
A Bronx Tale
The Brother from Another
    Planet
The Brotherhood of the Rose
Brotherly Love
Bruce Lee: The Legend
The Buccaneer
Buckskin
The Buddy Holly Story
The Buddy System
Buddy's Song
Buffalo Bill
Buford's Beach Bunnies
Bugsy
Bull Durham
The Bulldozer Brigade
Bullies
A Bunny's Tale
Bureau of Missing Persons
Burglar
Burke & Wills
The Burning Bed
The Burns and Allen Show
Business as Usual
Busted Up
Buster
But Not for Me
The Butcher's Wife
By the Sword
Cabaret
Cabin Boy
The Cabin in the Cotton
Caddyshack 2
Cadence
Cadillac Man
Cafe Romeo
The Cage
The Caine Mutiny
The Caine Mutiny Court
    Martial
Calendar Girl
Call of the Rockies
Call of the Wild
Came a Hot Friday
Camelot
Can-Can
Can She Bake a Cherry Pie?
Candleshoe
Candyman
Cannibal Women in the
    Avocado Jungle of Death
Cannonball Run 2
Can't Buy Me Love
The Canterville Ghost
Cape Fear
Capone
Captain Blood
Captain January
Captain Ron
Captive Hearts
The Captive: The Longest
    Drive 2
Captive Wild Woman
Car 54, Where Are You?
The Care Bears Movie
The Care Bears Movie 2: A
    New Generation
Career
Career Opportunities
Careful, He Might Hear You
The Cariboo Trail
Carlito's Way
Caroline?
Carousel
Carrie
Casablanca
Casanova
A Case for Murder
Casey at the Bat
Cast a Deadly Spell
Cast a Giant Shadow

Castaway
Castle in the Desert
Casualties of War
Catch Me...If You Can
Catch the Heat
Cat's Eye
Caught in the Act
Caught in the Draft
CB4: The Movie
The Cemetery Club
Chained Heat 2
Chains of Gold
The Chair
Champion
Champions
Chances Are
Chantilly Lace
Chaplin
Chapter Two
The Charge of the Light
    Brigade
Charles & Diana: A Palace
    Divided
A Charlie Brown Christmas
Charlie Brown's All-Stars
Charlie Chan at the Opera
Charlie Chan at the Wax
    Museum
Charlie Chan in Paris
Charlie Chan in Rio
Charlie Chan's Secret
The Chase
Chasers
Chato's Land
Cheatin' Hearts
Cheetah
Cherry 2000
Chicago Joe & the Showgirl
Child of Darkness, Child of
    Light
Children of a Lesser God
Children of the Corn 2: The
    Final Sacrifice
The Children of Times Square
Children's Carol
The Children's Hour
Child's Play
Child's Play 2
Child's Play 3
China Beach
The China Lake Murders
China O'Brien
China O'Brien 2
The China Syndrome
China White
Chinatown
The Chinatown Murders: Man
    Against the Mob
Chinese Web
The Chipmunk Adventure
Chitty Chitty Bang Bang
The Chocolate War
Chopper Chicks in
    Zombietown
A Chorus Line
Christabel
Christine
The Christmas Coal Mine
    Miracle
Christmas in Connecticut
The Christmas Wife
A Christmas Without Snow
Christopher Columbus: The
    Discovery
Chrome and Hot Leather
Chrome Soldiers
The Chronicles of Narnia
Chuka
Cinderella
The Circus
The Cisco Kid
Citizen Cohn
Citizen Kane
City Boy
City Heat
City of Hope

City Slickers
The Civil War, Episode 1: The
    Cause—1861
The Civil War, Episode 2: A
    Very Bloody Affair—1862
The Civil War, Episode 3:
    Forever Free—1862
The Civil War, Episode 4:
    Simply Murder—1863
The Civil War, Episode 5: The
    Universe of Battle—1863
The Civil War, Episode 6:
    Valley of the Shadow of
    Death—1864
The Civil War, Episode 7:
    Most Hallowed Ground—
    1864
The Civil War, Episode 8: War
    is All Hell—1865
The Civil War, Episode 9: The
    Better Angels of Our
    Nature—1865
The Clan of the Cave Bear
Clara's Heart
Clarence
Class Action
The Class of Miss MacMichael
Class of 1999 2: The
    Substitute
Class of Nuke 'Em High, Part
    2: Subhumanoid Meltdown
Clean and Sober
Cliffhanger
A Climate for Killing
Cloak & Dagger
Clockwise
A Clockwork Orange
Close Encounters of the Third
    Kind
Closet Land
Clown House
Club Paradise
Clue
Cobra
The Coca-Cola Kid
Cocktail
Cocoon
Cocoon: The Return
Code Name: Emerald
Codename: Icarus
Cohen and Tate
Cold Feet
Cold Heaven
Cold Sweat
College Swing
Collision Course
The Color Purple
Colors
The Comancheros
Come Back Little Reba
Come Back, Little Sheba
Come Blow Your Horn
Come See the Paradise
The Comfort of Strangers
Comin' Round the Mountain
Coming Home
Coming Out of the Ice
Coming to America
Commando
The Commitments
Committed
Common Bonds
Common Threads: Stories
    from the Quilt
The Company of Wolves
Compromising Positions
Comrades in Arms
The Comrades of Summer
Conagher
Conan the Barbarian
Conan the Destroyer
Confessions of a Serial Killer
Conquest of Space
Conquest of the Planet of the
    Apes
Conrack

Consenting Adults
The Cook, the Thief, His Wife & Her Lover
Cookie
Cool As Ice
Cool Blue
Cool Change
Cool Runnings
Cool World
Cop
Cop and a Half
Copper Canyon
The Cotton Club
The Couch Trip
The Counterfeit Traitor
Coupe de Ville
Courage
Courage Mountain
The Court Martial of Jackie Robinson
Cousins
The Cover Girl Murders
Cover-Up
Covergirl
Crash and Burn
The Crawlers
Crazy from the Heart
Crazy in Love
Crazy Moon
Crazy People
Creature
The Creature Walks Among Us
Creepshow
Creepshow 2
Crime of Passion
Crimes & Misdemeanors
Crimes of Passion
Crimes of the Heart
Crimewave
Criminal Justice
Crisscross
Critical Condition
Critters 2: The Main Course
Critters 3
Critters 4
Crocodile Dundee
Crocodile Dundee 2
Crooked Hearts
The Crossing
Crossing Delancey
Crossing the Bridge
Crossroads
The Crucifer of Blood
The Crush
Cry-Baby
A Cry in the Dark
A Cry in the Night
A Cry in the Wild
The Crying Game
Cthulhu Mansion
Cult of the Cobra
Curly Sue
Curly Top
The Curse
Curse 3: Blood Sacrifice
Curse 4: The Ultimate Sacrifice
Curse of the Pink Panther
The Cutting Edge
Cyborg 2
Cyborg Cop
Da
Dad
Daddy Long Legs
Daddy's Dyin'...Who's Got the Will?
Daffy Duck's Quackbusters
Dakota
Damage
Damn Yankees
Damned River
Dance with a Stranger
Dance with Death
Dancers
Dances with Wolves

The Dancing Princesses
Danger: Diabolik
Dangerous Game
Dangerous Heart
Dangerous Liaisons
A Dangerous Man: Lawrence after Arabia
Dangerous Pursuit
A Dangerous Woman
Dangerously Close
Danielle Steel's Changes
Danielle Steel's ''Daddy''
Danielle Steel's Kaleidoscope
Daring Dobermans
Dario Argento's Trauma
The Dark
Dark Corner
The Dark Half
Dark Night of the Scarecrow
Dark Victory
The Dark Wind
Darkman
D.A.R.Y.L.
A Date with Judy
Dave
David and Bathsheba
David Copperfield
Davy Crockett, King of the Wild Frontier
A Day in October
Day of Atonement
Day One
Days of Thunder
Dazed and Confused
D.C. Cab
The Dead
Dead Again
Dead Alive
Dead Calm
Dead Connection
Dead End Drive-In
Dead Heat
Dead in the Water
Dead Man's Revenge
Dead of Winter
Dead On
Dead on the Money
The Dead Pool
Dead Reckoning
Dead Silence
Dead Wrong
Dead Wrong: The John Evans Story
Dead Zone
Deadfall
Deadlock
Deadly Conspiracy
Deadly Currents
Deadly Desire
Deadly Exposure
Deadly Friend
Deadly Game
Deadly Illusion
The Deadly Mantis
Deadly Rivals
Deadly Surveillance
The Deadly Trackers
Dear America: Letters Home from Vietnam
Dear Brigitte
Death Becomes Her
Death Before Dishonor
Death of a Salesman
Death of a Soldier
Death Wish 4: The Crackdown
Death Wish 5: The Face of Death
Deathfight
Deceived
December
Deception
Deceptions
Decline of Western Civilization 2: The Metal Years

Decoration Day
Deep Cover
Deep Red
Defending Your Life
Defense of the Realm
Defenseless
The Defiant Ones
The Delicate Delinquent
Delicatessen
Delirious
Delta Force
Delta Force 2: Operation Stranglehold
Delta Heat
Demetrius and the Gladiators
Demolition Man
A Demon in My View
Demonic Toys
Denial: The Dark Side of Passion
Dennis the Menace
Dennis the Menace: Dinosaur Hunter
The Denver & Rio Grande
Descending Angel
Desert Kickboxer
Desire and Hell at Sunset Motel
Desire Under the Elms
Desiree
Desk Set
Desperate Characters
Desperate Hours
Detonator
The Devil's Daughter
The Devil's Disciple
The Diamond Trap
Diamond's Edge
Diana: Her True Story
Diary of a Hitman
The Diary of Anne Frank
Dick Tracy
Die Hard
Die Hard 2: Die Harder
Diggstown
Dimples
Diplomatic Immunity
Dirt Bike Kid
Dirty Dancing
The Dirty Dozen: The Next Mission
Dirty Rotten Scoundrels
Dirty Work
The Disappearance of Christina
Dishonored
Disorderlies
Disorganized Crime
Distant Thunder
The Distinguished Gentleman
The Dive
Dive Bomber
Diving In
Do the Right Thing
D.O.A.
The Doberman Gang
Doc Hollywood
The Doctor
Dr. Alien
Doctor Dolittle
Dr. Giggles
Doctor Mordrid: Master of the Unknown
Dr. No
Doctor Who and the Daleks
Doctor Who: Day of the Daleks
Doctor Who: Pyramids of Mars
Doctor Who: Revenge of the Cybermen
Doctor Who: Robots of Death
Doctor Who: Spearhead from Space
Doctor Who: Terror of the Zygons

Doctor Who: The Ark in Space
Doctor Who: The Brain of Morbius
Doctor Who: The Five Doctors
Doctor Who: The Seeds of Death
Doctor Who: The Talons of Weng-Chiang
Doctor Who: The Time Warrior
Doctor Zhivago
Dodge City
Dog Day Afternoon
Dog Pound Shuffle
Doin' Time on Planet Earth
The Dollmaker
Dollman
Dollman vs Demonic Toys
Dolly Dearest
Dominick & Eugene
Don't Tell Her It's Me
Don't Tell Mom the Babysitter's Dead
The Doors
The Doors: Soft Parade, a Retrospective
Doppelganger: The Evil Within
Double-Crossed
Double Impact
The Double Life of Veronique
The Double O Kid
Double Vision
The Dove
Down & Dirty
Down Argentine Way
Down by Law
Downtown
Dracula Blows His Cool
Dracula's Daughter
Dracula's Widow
Dragnet
Dragon: The Bruce Lee Story
Dragonard
Dragonworld
Dream a Little Dream
Dream Chasers
The Dream Team
Dressed to Kill
The Dresser
The Driver
Driving Miss Daisy
Drop Dead Fred
Drums Along the Mohawk
A Dry White Season
DuckTales the Movie: Treasure of the Lost Lamp
Duel at Diablo
Duel of Hearts
Dumbo
Dune
Duplicates
Dust Devil
Dutch
Dying to Remember
Dying Young
Earth Girls are Easy
East of Eden
Eat a Bowl of Tea
Eat the Peach
Eating
Ed and His Dead Mother
Eddie and the Cruisers
Eddie Murphy: Raw
The Eddy Duchin Story
Edge of Darkness
Edge of Sanity
Educating Rita
Edward Scissorhands
The Efficiency Expert
The Egyptian
Eight Men Out
8 Million Ways to Die
18 Again!
El Diablo
Eleni
Elephant Walk

11 Harrowhouse
The Eliminators
Elvira, Mistress of the Dark
Elvis and Me
Elvis: The Lost Performances
The Emerald Forest
The Emperor's New Clothes
Empire of the Air: The Men Who Made Radio
Empire of the Sun
The Empire Strikes Back
Employees' Entrance
Enchanted April
The Enchantress
Encino Man
Encounter at Raven's Gate
The End of Innocence
End of the Line
End of the Road
The Endless Game
Enemies, a Love Story
Enemy Mine
Enemy Territory
Entangled
Enter the Dragon
Equinox
Equinox Flower
Erik the Viking
Ernest Goes to Jail
The Ernest Green Story
Ernest Scared Stupid
Escape from Fort Bravo
Escape from Planet Earth
Escape from the Planet of the Apes
Escape Me Never
E.T.: The Extra-Terrestrial
Ethan Frome
Eve of Destruction
Every Breath
Everybody Wins
Everybody's All American
Everybody's Fine
Evil Clutch
The Evil That Men Do
The Ewok Adventure
The Ewoks: Battle for Endor
Ex-Lady
Excessive Force
Executive Suite
Exodus
The Exorcist 3
The Experts
Explorers
Exposure
Extreme Justice
Extremities
Eye on the Sparrow
Eyes of Julia Deep
Eyes of Laura Mars
Eyes of the Beholder
F/X
F/X 2: The Deadly Art of Illusion
Fade to Black
Fail-Safe
Faith
The Falcon and the Snowman
Fallen Angels 1
Fallen Angels 2
Fallen Champ: The Untold Story of Mike Tyson
Falling Down
Falling from Grace
Falling in Love
False Arrest
Family Business
Family Dog: Complete Series
Fancy Pants
Fanny and Alexander
Fantasia
Far and Away
Far North
A Far Off Place
Faraway, So Close!
Farewell to the King

The Farmer Takes a Wife
Fast Forward
Fastest Gun Alive
Fat Man and Little Boy
Fatal Attraction
Fatal Beauty
Fatal Charm
Fatal Exposure
Fatal Instinct
Fatal Mission
Father Goose
Father Hood
Father of the Bride
Fatso
The Favor, the Watch, & the Very Big Fish
Fawlty Towers
Fear, Anxiety and Depression
The Fear Inside
Fear Strikes Out
Fearless
Fearless Tiger
Feds
Felix the Cat: The Movie
Female
Femme Fatale
Fergie & Andrew: Behind Palace Doors
Ferris Bueller's Day Off
Fever
Fever Pitch
A Few Good Men
Fiddler on the Roof
Field of Dreams
Fifty/Fifty
52 Pick-Up
The Fig Tree
The Fighting Kentuckian
Fighting Seabees
The Final Alliance
Final Analysis
Final Approach
Final Notice
Final Round
Final Verdict
Final Warning
Finders Keepers
A Fine Mess
Fine Things
The Finest Hour
The Finishing Touch
Fire and Ice
Fire and Rain
Fire Birds
Fire in the Sky
The Fire Next Time
Firefall
The Firefly
Firepower
Firestarter
Firewalker
The Firm
First Born
The First Power
A Fish Called Wanda
The Fisher King
Fist of Honor
A Fistful of Dollars
The Five Heartbeats
The Five Pennies
The Flamingo Kid
Flamingo Road
The Flash
The Flash 2: Revenge of the Trickster
Flashback
Flashdance
Flatliners
Flesh and Bone
Fletch
Fletch Lives
Flight of the Intruder
The Flight of the Phoenix
Flim-Flam Man
Flipper
Flirting

Florida Straits
Flowers in the Attic
The Fly
Flying Tigers
Folks!
Footlight Serenade
Footloose
For a Few Dollars More
For Love or Money
For Me and My Gal
For Richer, For Poorer
For the Boys
For the First Time
Forbidden
The Forbidden Dance
Foreign Correspondent
Forever Female
Forever James Dean
Forever Young
The Forgotten
Forgotten Prisoners
Forsaking All Others
Fortress
Four Eyes and Six Guns
Four for Texas
1492: Conquest of Paradise
The Fourth War
The Fox and the Hound
Foxes
Foxfire
Frame Up
Framed
Frankenhooker
Frankenstein
Frankenstein and the Monster from Hell
Frankenstein Unbound
Frankenweenie
Frankie and Johnny
Frantic
Fraternity Vacation
Freaky Friday
Freddy's Dead: The Final Nightmare
Free Willy
Freeway
Freeze Frame
French Connection 2
The French Lesson
Fresh Horses
The Freshman
Friday the 13th
Friday the 13th, Part 4: The Final Chapter
Friday the 13th, Part 5: A New Beginning
Friday the 13th, Part 6: Jason Lives
Friday the 13th, Part 7: The New Blood
Friday the 13th, Part 8: Jason Takes Manhattan
Fried Green Tomatoes
Friendly Fire
Friendly Persuasion
Friends
A Friendship in Vienna
Fright Night
Frog
From Beyond
From Hollywood to Deadwood
From "Star Wars" to "Jedi": The Making of a Saga
From the Hip
Frozen Assets
The Fugitive
Fulfillment
Full Exposure: The Sex Tape Scandals
Full Metal Jacket
Funny About Love
The Funny Farm
Funny Farm
Future Cop
The Gamble

The Gambler Returns: The Luck of the Draw
Garbo Talks
Gardens of Stone
Gas Food Lodging
Gate 2
Gator Bait 2: Cajun Justice
The Gauntlet
Gay Purr-ee
The Geisha Boy
Gentleman Jim
George Washington
George Washington: The Forging of a Nation
Geronimo: An American Legend
Get Smart, Again!
The Getaway
Getting Physical
Getting Up and Going Home
Gettysburg
Ghost
The Ghost and Mrs. Muir
The Ghost Breakers
Ghost Dad
Ghost in the Machine
The Ghost of Frankenstein
Ghostbusters
Ghostbusters 2
Ghosts Can't Do It
Giant
Giants of Rome
The Gift of Love
The Gig
Gilda
The Girl from Missouri
The Girl Who Spelled Freedom
Girls Just Want to Have Fun
Give My Regards to Broad Street
The Gladiator
Gladiator
Gleaming the Cube
Glengarry Glen Ross
Glory
Glory Years
God Bless the Child
The Godfather 1902-1959: The Complete Epic
The Godfather, Part 3
The Gods Must Be Crazy
The Gods Must Be Crazy 2
Godzilla vs. Biollante
Going Bananas
Going Under
The Golden Child
Golden Earrings
Golden Voyage of Sinbad
Goldfinger
Goldilocks & the Three Bears
Gone with the Wind
The Good Father
Good Morning, Vietnam
The Good Mother
The Good Son
The Goodbye Bird
Goodbye, Miss 4th of July
Goodbye, Mr. Chips
The Goodbye People
Goodfellas
The Goonies
Gor
Gordon's War
The Gorgeous Hussy
The Gospel According to Vic
Gotcha!
The Graduate
Graffiti Bridge
Grand Canyon
Grand Hotel
Grand Isle
Grand Prix
Grand Tour: Disaster in Time
Grandview U.S.A.
The Grapes of Wrath

Grave Secrets: The Legacy of Hilltop Drive
Graveyard Shift
Great American Traffic Jam
Great Balls of Fire
Great Bank Hoax
Great Bikini Off-Road Adventure
The Great Escape
Great Expectations
The Great Gatsby
The Great Moment
The Great Mouse Detective
The Great Outdoors
The Great White Hope
The Greatest Story Ever Told
The Green Berets
Green Card
Green Ice
Gremlins
Gremlins 2: The New Batch
Greystoke: The Legend of Tarzan, Lord of the Apes
The Grifters
Gross Anatomy
Groundhog Day
Grumpy Old Men
Gryphon
The Guardian
The Guardsman
Guess Who's Coming to Dinner
Guilty as Charged
Guilty as Sin
Guilty by Suspicion
Guilty of Innocence
Gun Glory
The Gun in Betty Lou's Handbag
Guncrazy
Gung Ho
Guys and Dolls
Gypsy
Gypsy Angels
Hadley's Rebellion
Hail the Conquering Hero
The Hairdresser's Husband
Hairspray
Half a Sixpence
Half Moon Street
Halloween 4: The Return of Michael Myers
Halloween 5: The Revenge of Michael Myers
Hamburger...The Motion Picture
Hamlet
The Hand that Rocks the Cradle
The Handmaid's Tale
Hangin' with the Homeboys
Hanky Panky
Hannah and Her Sisters
Hannie Caulder
Hanoi Hilton
Hansel and Gretel
Happy Anniversary 007: 25 Years of James Bond
Hard Hunted
Hard Promises
Hard Target
Hard to Hold
Hard to Kill
The Hard Way
Hardbodies
Hardware
Harlem Nights
Harley Davidson and the Marlboro Man
Harry and the Hendersons
Harry and Tonto
The Harvest
Haunted Gold
Haunting of Sarah Hardy
Havana
Hawks

He Said, She Said
Heads
Hear My Song
Hear No Evil
Heart and Souls
The Heart is a Lonely Hunter
Heart Like a Wheel
Heart of Darkness
The Heart of Dixie
Heartbreak Hotel
Heartbreak Ridge
Heartburn
Hearts of Darkness: A Filmmaker's Apocalypse
Hearts of Fire
Heat
The Heat of the Day
Heat Wave
Heathers
Heaven and Earth
Heaven Can Wait
Heaven is a Playground
Hector's Bunyip
Heidi
Hell is for Heroes
Hellbound: Hellraiser 2
Heller in Pink Tights
Hellhole
Hello Again
Hello, Dolly!
Hello Mary Lou: Prom Night 2
Hellraiser
Hellraiser 3: Hell on Earth
Helter Skelter
Henry V
Henry & June
Her Alibi
Hercules
Here Come the Girls
Here Come the Littles: The Movie
Here Comes the Groom
Hero
A Hero Ain't Nothin' But a Sandwich
Heroes for Sale
He's Your Dog, Charlie Brown!
Hexed
Hey There, It's Yogi Bear
The Hidden
The Hidden 2
Hidden Agenda
Hidden Obsession
Hiding Out
High Anxiety
High Heels
High Noon
High Spirits
Highlander
Highlander 2: The Quickening
Highway to Hell
The Hindenburg
Hired to Kill
History of the World: Part 1
Hit!
The Hit List
Hit the Dutchman
Hitcher
Hitler's Daughter
Hitz
Hobson's Choice
Hocus Pocus
Hoffa
The Holcroft Covenant
Hold Your Man
Hollywood Boulevard 2
Home Alone
Home Alone 2: Lost in New York
A Home of Our Own
Homecoming: A Christmas Story
Hometown Boy Makes Good
Homewrecker
Homicide

Honey, I Blew Up the Kid
Honey, I Shrunk the Kids
Honeymoon Academy
Honeymoon in Vegas
Honeymooners Hidden Episodes, Vol. 1
Honor and Glory
Hook
Hooper
Hoosiers
Hope and Glory
The Horse Soldiers
Horseplayer
The Hospital
Hostage
Hostages
Hostile Guns
Hot Dog...The Movie!
Hot Millions
Hot Shots!
Hot Shots! Part Deux
Hot Spot
Hot to Trot!
Hotel Imperial
Hotel Room
Houdini
The Hound of the Baskervilles
House
House 2: The Second Story
House 4: Home Deadly Home
A House In The Hills
House of Cards
House of Dracula
House of Fear
House of Horrors
House of Strangers
The House of the Spirits
The House on Carroll Street
House on Haunted Hill
The House on Skull Mountain
House Party 2: The Pajama Jam
House Party 3
Household Saints
The Housekeeper
Housekeeping
Housesitter
How I Got into College
How to Be a Perfect Person in Just Three Days
How to Murder Your Wife
How U Like Me Now?
Howard the Duck
Howard's End
Huckleberry Finn
The Hucksters
Hudson Hawk
The Human Shield
The Hunt for Red October
Hunter's Blood
Hurricane Smith
Husbands and Lovers
Husbands and Wives
Hush, Hush, Sweet Charlotte
The Hustler
I Come in Peace
I Don't Buy Kisses Anymore
I Live My Life
I Live with Me Dad
I Love You to Death
I Posed for Playboy
I Wake Up Screaming
I Wanna Hold Your Hand
Ice
If Looks Could Kill
I'll Take Sweden
Illegally Yours
Illicit Behavior
Illusions
Immediate Family
Immortal Sergeant
Impulse
In a Moment of Passion
In a Stranger's Hand
The In Crowd
In Harm's Way

In Search of a Golden Sky
In Search of the Castaways
In the Cold of the Night
In the Line of Duty: Ambush in Waco
In the Line of Fire
In the Mood
In the Name of the Father
In the Navy
In the Soup
The Incident
An Inconvenient Woman
The Incredible Mr. Limpet
Indecency
Indecent Proposal
The Indian Runner
Indian Summer
Indiana Jones and the Last Crusade
Indiana Jones and the Temple of Doom
Indio
Indiscreet
Indochine
The Inner Circle
Inner Sanctum
Innerspace
Innocent Blood
An Innocent Man
Innocent Prey
Instant Justice
Instant Karma
Interceptor
Internal Affairs
Internecine Project
Intersection
Intimate Power
Intimate Stranger
Into the Night
Into the Sun
Into the West
Intruder
Intruders
Invaders from Mars
Invasion of Privacy
Invasion of the Body Snatchers
Invisible Agent
The Invisible Man's Revenge
Invisible: The Chronicles of Benjamin Knight
The Invisible Woman
Invitation to a Gunfighter
Irma La Douce
Iron Eagle
Iron Warrior
Iron Will
Ironclads
Ironheart
Ironweed
Irreconcilable Differences
Is Paris Burning?
Ishtar
Island of Lost Souls
Island of Terror
It Came From Outer Space
It Came Upon a Midnight Clear
It Happened One Night
It Started in Naples
It Takes Two
The Italian Job
It's a Wonderful Life
Ivory Hunters
Jack & the Beanstalk
Jack the Bear
Jacknife
Jack's Back
Jacob's Ladder
The Jagged Edge
Jailbait
Jake Speed
Jane Eyre
The January Man
Jason Goes to Hell: The Final Friday

Jaws: The Revenge
The Jayhawkers
Jeeves & Wooster: Jeeves' Arrival
Jennifer 8
Jericho Fever
Jersey Girl
Jesse
Jet Pilot
Jetsons: The Movie
The Jewel of the Nile
JFK
JFK: Reckless Youth
Jo Jo Dancer, Your Life is Calling
Joey Breaker
Johnny Appleseed
Johnny Be Good
Johnny Dangerously
Johnny Handsome
Johnny Suede
The Josephine Baker Story
Josh and S.A.M.
Joshua Then and Now
Journey of Honor
Journey to the Center of the Earth
The Joy Luck Club
Judgment
Judgment Night
Juggernaut
Juice
Julia and Julia
Jumpin' Jack Flash
Jumping Jacks
June Bride
The Jungle Book
Jungle Fever
Jurassic Park
Just Around the Corner
Just for You
Just One of the Guys
Just the Way You Are
Justine
K-9
K-9000
Kafka
Kalifornia
Karate Cop
The Karate Kid
The Karate Kid: Part 2
The Karate Kid: Part 3
Keep 'Em Flying
Keep the Change
Keeper of the City
Keeping Track
Key Exchange
The Keys of the Kingdom
Kickboxer 3: The Art of War
Kid
Kid Colter
Kid Galahad
The Kid Who Loved Christmas
Kidco
Kidnapped
Kill Cruise
Kill Me Again
Killer Fish
Killer Image
Killer Instinct
Killer Klowns from Outer Space
Killer Tomatoes Strike Back
Killing at Hell's Gate
The Killing Beach
The Killing Fields
Killing Hour
A Killing in a Small Town
The Killing of a Chinese Bookie
Kindergarten Cop
The King and I
King David
King Kong
King Kong Lives
King of New York

King of the Hill
The King of the Kickboxers
King of the Wind
King Ralph
Kings Row
The King's Whore
Kismet
A Kiss Before Dying
Kiss Me Deadly
Kiss of Death
Kiss of the Spider Woman
Kiss Shot
The Kissing Place
The Kitchen Toto
The Klansman
Knight Moves
Knights
Knights & Emeralds
Kramer vs. Kramer
The Krays
Krull
Krush Groove
K2: The Ultimate High
Kuffs
La Balance
La Bamba
L.A. Law
L.A. Story
Labyrinth
The Ladies' Man
Ladies of the Chorus
Ladies They Talk About
Lady by Choice
Lady Dragon
Lady Dragon 2
The Lady in White
Lady Jane
Lady Killer
Lady Mobster
Ladybugs
Ladyhawke
Ladykiller
Ladykillers
Lake Consequence
Lambada
The Land Before Time
Land of the Pharaohs
The Land Unknown
Landslide
Lantern Hill
Laser Mission
Last Action Hero
The Last Boy Scout
The Last Days of Chez Nous
The Last Days of Patton
Last Days of Pompeii
The Last Dragon
The Last Emperor
The Last Hit
The Last Hunt
Last Light
The Last of His Tribe
The Last of Mrs. Cheyney
The Last of the Finest
The Last Picture Show
Last Plane Out
Last Rites
The Last Safari
Last Song
The Last Unicorn
The Last Voyage
The Last Waltz
The Late Show
Latino
The Laughing Policeman
Laurel Avenue
The Law and Jake Wade
The Lawnmower Man
Lawrence of Arabia
Le Mans
A League of Their Own
Lean on Me
Leap of Faith
Leather Jackets
Leave 'Em Laughing
Leaving Normal

The Leech Woman
Legacy of Lies
Legal Eagles
Legend
Legend of Billie Jean
The Legend of Hell House
The Legend of Sleepy Hollow
The Legend of Wolf Mountain
The Lemon Sisters
Lenny
Leonard Part 6
Leprechaun 2
Less Than Zero
Let Freedom Ring
Let It Ride
Lethal Lolita—Amy Fisher: My Story
Lethal Weapon
Lethal Weapon 2
Lethal Weapon 3
Let's Dance
Let's Get Harry
Let's Make it Legal
Letter to Brezhnev
Leviathan
Liberty & Bash
License to Kill
Lies
Lies Before Kisses
Life is Sweet
A Life of Sin
Life Stinks
Life with Mikey
Lifeboat
The Lighthorsemen
The Lightning Incident
Lightning: The White Stallion
The Lightship
Li'l Abner
Lili
Lilies of the Field
Limit Up
Linda
The Linguini Incident
Link
Lionheart
Lisa
Listen to Me
Little Big Man
The Little Colonel
Little Dorrit, Film 1: Nobody's Fault
Little Dorrit, Film 2: Little Dorrit's Story
The Little Drummer Girl
Little Lord Fauntleroy
Little Man Tate
The Little Match Girl
The Little Mermaid
Little Miss Broadway
Little Miss Millions
Little Monsters
Little Nikita
The Little Princess
Little Red Riding Hood
Little Shop of Horrors
Little Treasure
Little Women
The Littlest Rebel
Live Wire
Livin' Large
The Living Daylights
Local Hero
Lock Up
London Kills Me
Lone Justice
Lonely in America
Lonesome Dove
The Long Day Closes
The Long Gray Line
The Long, Hot Summer
The Long, Long Trailer
The Long Walk Home
Look Who's Talking
Look Who's Talking Now
Look Who's Talking, Too

Lookalike

The Lookalike
Looker
Looking for Miracles
Loose Cannons
Lord of the Flies
Lorenzo's Oil
Lorna Doone
Lost Angels
The Lost Boys
The Lost Capone
Lost in America
Lost in Yonkers
The Lost World
Love Among the Ruins
Love and Bullets
Love at Large
The Love Bug
Love, Cheat & Steal
Love Field
Love Finds Andy Hardy
Love Hurts
A Love in Germany
Love in the Afternoon
Love is a Many-Splendored
  Thing
Love Kills
Love, Lies and Murder
Love Matters
Love Me or Leave Me
Love or Money?
Love Potion #9
Love with the Proper Stranger
Lovelines
The Lover
Loverboy
Lower Level
Lucas
Lucy and Desi: Before the
  Laughter
Lust in the Dust
M. Butterfly
Ma and Pa Kettle
Ma and Pa Kettle at the Fair
Ma and Pa Kettle Back On the
  Farm
Ma and Pa Kettle Go to Town
Mac
Mac and Me
Macaroni
Mad at the Moon
Mad Dog and Glory
The Mad Ghoul
Mad Max: Beyond
  Thunderdome
Madam Satan
Made for Each Other
Made in America
Made in Heaven
Madhouse
Magic Kid
The Magnificent Ambersons
The Maid
Major League
Major League 2
Malcolm X
Malibu Bikini Shop
Malice
Malone
The Maltese Falcon
The Mambo Kings
A Man and a Woman
A Man Called Horse
A Man Called Peter
A Man for All Seasons
Man from Monterey
The Man I Love
The Man in the Gray Flannel
  Suit
The Man in the Iron Mask
The Man in the Moon
Man Made Monster
Man of the West
Man Trouble
The Man Upstairs
The Man Who Loved Women

The Man Who Shot Liberty
  Valance
The Man Who Would Be King
The Man with One Red Shoe
The Man Without a Face
The Manchurian Candidate
Mandroid
Manhattan Murder Mystery
Manhunter
Maniac Cop 2
Maniac Cop 3
Mannequin
Man's Best Friend
Mansfield Park
Map of the Human Heart
Marie
Marked for Death
Marked Woman
Maroc 7
Married to It
Married to the Mob
The Marrying Man
Martial Law 2: Undercover
Martial Outlaw
Martin's Day
Marty
Mary Poppins
Mascara
Mask
Masquerade
Mass Appeal
Masters of the Universe
The Matchmaker
Matewan
Matinee
Matters of the Heart
Maurice
Max and Helen
Max Headroom, the Original
  Story
Max Maven's Mindgames
May Wine
McBain
The McConnell Story
McQ
Me and Him
Me and the Kid
Mean Streets
Meatballs
Meatballs 2
Meatballs 4
Mediterraneo
Meet Danny Wilson
Meet the Hollowheads
Melody in Love
Memoirs of an Invisible Man
Memories of Me
Memphis
Memphis Belle
Men at Work
Men Don't Leave
Men of Respect
Menace II Society
Meridian: Kiss of the Beast
Mermaids
Merton of the Movies
Messenger of Death
The Meteor Man
Miami Blues
Micki & Maude
A Midnight Clear
The Mighty Ducks
The Mighty Pawns
Mikey
Mildred Pierce
Miles from Home
Millenium
Miller's Crossing
Million Dollar Mystery
Millions
Milo & Otis
Mindwalk: A Film for
  Passionate Thinkers
Mindwarp
Miracle Down Under
Miracle Mile

Miracle on 34th Street
Mirrors
Mischief
Misery
Mishima: A Life in Four
  Chapters
Miss Firecracker
Miss Rose White
The Mission
Mission of Justice
Mississippi Burning
Mississippi Masala
Mrs. Doubtfire
Mrs. Soffel
Mr. & Mrs. Bridge
Mr. Baseball
Mr. Billion
Mr. Corbett's Ghost
Mr. Destiny
Mr. Frost
Mr. Hobbs Takes a Vacation
Mister Johnson
Mr. Jones
Mr. Love
Mr. Lucky
Mr. Mom
Mr. Music
Mr. Nanny
Mr. North
Mr. Saturday Night
Mr. Wonderful
Mistress
Misty
Mo' Better Blues
Mobsters
Moby Dick
Model by Day
Modern Love
The Mole People
Mom
Mom and Dad Save the World
Money for Nothing
The Money Pit
Monkey Shines
Monolith
The Monolith Monsters
Monsieur Beaucaire
The Monster and the Girl
Monster in a Box
Monster in the Closet
Monster on the Campus
Montana
Monte Carlo
Monte Walsh
Monty Python Live at the
  Hollywood Bowl
Monty Python's Life of Brian
Monty Python's Parrot Sketch
  Not Included
Moon 44
Moon Over Miami
Moonlighting
Moonraker
Moonstruck
More American Graffiti
Morituri
The Morning After
Mortal Passions
Mortal Sins
Mortal Thoughts
Moscow on the Hudson
The Mosquito Coast
Mother Goose Rock 'n'
  Rhyme
The Mountain
Mountains of the Moon
Moving
Moving Violations
Much Ado About Nothing
The Mummy's Curse
The Mummy's Ghost
The Mummy's Hand
The Mummy's Tomb
Munchie
The Muppet Christmas Carol
The Muppets Take Manhattan

Murder by Moonlight
Murder in New Hampshire:
  The Pamela Smart Story
A Murder is Announced
Murder 101
Murder Ordained
Murder Over New York
Murderers Among Us: The
  Simon Wiesenthal Story
Murderous Vision
Murders in the Rue Morgue
Murphy's Law
Murphy's Romance
The Music Man
The Music of Chance
My Beautiful Laundrette
My Best Friend Is a Vampire
My Blue Heaven
My Boyfriend's Back
My Cousin Vinny
My Darlin' Clementine
My Darling Clementine
My Fair Lady
My Father is Coming
My Father the Hero
My Favorite Blonde
My Friend Irma
My Geisha
My Girl
My Girl 2
My Grandpa is a Vampire
My Heroes Have Always Been
  Cowboys
My Left Foot
My Life
My Little Pony: The Movie
My Man Adam
My New Gun
My Own Private Idaho
My Samurai
My Stepmother Is an Alien
Mysterious Island
Mystery Date
Mystic Pizza
Nadine
Nails
The Naked Country
The Naked Edge
The Naked Gun: From the
  Files of Police Squad
Naked Gun 2 1/2: The Smell
  of Fear
Naked Lunch
The Naked Maja
The Name of the Rose
Narrow Margin
National Lampoon's
  Christmas Vacation
National Lampoon's European
  Vacation
National Velvet
Native Son
Nativity
The Natural
Navy SEALS
Necessary Roughness
Needful Things
Nemesis
Neon City
Neptune Factor
Neptune's Daughter
Nervous Ticks
Netherworld
Never Forget
Never on Tuesday
Never Say Never Again
Never Too Young to Die
The NeverEnding Story
The NeverEnding Story 2:
  Next Chapter
The New Adventures of Pippi
  Longstocking
The New Kids
A New Kind of Love
A New Life
New Year's Day

New York, New York
Newsies
Next of Kin
Next Stop, Greenwich Village
Night and the City
The Night Before
Night Breed
Night Eyes 2
A Night in Heaven
A Night in the Life of Jimmy
  Reardon
'night, Mother
Night of Dark Shadows
Night of the Comet
Night of the Creeps
Night of the Cyclone
Night of the Demons 2
The Night of the Following
  Day
Night Patrol
Night Rhythms
The Night They Raided
  Minsky's
The Night Train to Kathmandu
The Night Walker
Nighthawks
The Nightingale
The Nightmare Before
  Christmas
A Nightmare on Elm Street
A Nightmare on Elm Street 2:
  Freddy's Revenge
A Nightmare on Elm Street 3:
  Dream Warriors
A Nightmare on Elm Street 4:
  Dream Master
A Nightmare on Elm Street 5:
  Dream Child
Nightmare on the 13th Floor
Nijinsky
9 1/2 Ninjas
976-EVIL
976-EVIL 2: The Astral Factor
1918
1969
90 Days
Ninja the Battalion
Ninja Vengeance
No Escape, No Return
No Holds Barred
No Man's Land
No Retreat, No Surrender 3:
  Blood Brothers
No Small Affair
No Time for Sergeants
Nobody's Fool
Nobody's Perfect
None But the Brave
North to Alaska
Not as a Stranger
Not Quite Human
Not Quite Human 2
Not Without My Daughter
Nothing But Trouble
Nothing in Common
Notorious
Nowhere to Hide
Nowhere to Run
The Nutcracker Prince
Nuts
O Pioneers!
The Object of Beauty
O.C. and Stiggs
The Odessa File
Of Mice and Men
Off Limits
Official Denial
Oh, God! You Devil
Oh, Heavenly Dog!
Oh, What a Night
Oklahoma!
The Old Curiosity Shop
Old Gringo
Old Yeller
Oliver!
Oliver Twist

Ollie Hopnoodle's Haven of Bliss
Omar Khayyam
Omen 4: The Awakening
On Borrowed Time
On Deadly Ground
On the Line
On the Waterfront
Onassis
Once Around
Once Bitten
Once Upon a Crime
Once Upon a Forest
Once Upon a Time in America
One Against the Wind
One Crazy Summer
One Deadly Summer
One False Move
One Good Cop
One Magic Christmas
One Man's War
One More Saturday Night
Only the Strong
Only You
Opening Night
Opera do Malandro
Operation C.I.A.
Operation Crossbow
Operation Petticoat
Opportunity Knocks
Orchestra Wives
The Organization
Original Intent
Orlando
Orphans
Orpheus Descending
Oscar
Oscar's Greatest Moments: 1971-1991
Other People's Money
Our Little Girl
Our Modern Maidens
Out for Blood
Out of Africa
Out of Bounds
Out of the Dark
Out on a Limb
The Outfit
Outland
Outlaw of Gor
Outrageous Fortune
Over the Hill
Over the Top
Overboard
The Ox-Bow Incident
Oxford Blues
Pacific Heights
The Package
Pair of Aces
Pajama Game
Pale Rider
The Palermo Connection
The Pamela Principle
Panic in the Streets
Papa's Delicate Condition
A Paper Wedding
The Paradine Case
Paradise
Paradise Motel
Parasite
Pardners
The Parent Trap
Parenthood
Paris Blues
Paris, Texas
Paris Trout
The Park is Mine
Parting Glances
The Party
A Passage to India
Passed Away
Passenger 57
Passion Fish
Past Midnight
Pat and Mike
Paths of Glory

Patriot Games
Paul and Michelle
The Pawnbroker
Payback
Payoff
The Pearl of Death
Pecos Bill
Pee Wee's Big Adventure
Pee Wee's Playhouse Festival of Fun
Peggy Sue Got Married
The Pelican Brief
Penalty Phase
Penitentiary 3
Penn and Teller Get Killed
The Penthouse
The People Under the Stairs
Perfect
The Perfect Bride
Perfect Family
Perfect Harmony
A Perfect Little Murder
The Perfect Marriage
The Perfect Weapon
A Perfect World
Permanent Record
Personal Property
Personals
Pet Sematary
Pet Sematary 2
Peter Pan
Peter's Friends
Pete's Dragon
Peyton Place
The Phantom of the Opera
Phantom of the Ritz
Phar Lap
Philadelphia
Philadelphia Experiment 2
Phobia
Phone Call from a Stranger
Physical Evidence
The Piano
The Pick-Up Artist
The Pickle
The Pied Piper of Hamelin
Pin-Up Girl
Pink Cadillac
Pinocchio
Pistol: The Birth of a Legend
The Pit & the Pendulum
Pittsburgh
Places in the Heart
The Plague
The Plague Dogs
Plain Clothes
Planes, Trains & Automobiles
Planet of the Apes
Platinum Blonde
Platoon
The Player
Playing for Keeps
Playroom
Pocketful of Miracles
A Pocketful of Rye
Poetic Justice
Point Blank
Point Break
Point of Impact
Point of No Return
Poker Alice
Police Academy
Police Academy 2: Their First Assignment
Police Academy 3: Back in Training
Police Academy 4: Citizens on Patrol
Police Academy 5: Assignment Miami Beach
Police Academy 6: City Under Siege
Pollyanna
Poltergeist 2: The Other Side
Poltergeist 3
A Poor Little Rich Girl

The Poor Little Rich Girl
The Pope Must Diet
Pork Chop Hill
Porky's Revenge
The Portrait
Portrait of Jennie
Posse
The Possession of Joel Delaney
Postcards from the Edge
The Postman Always Rings Twice
Power
The Power of One
Prancer
Prayer for the Dying
Praying Mantis
Predator
Predator 2
Prehysteria
Prelude to a Kiss
The Preppie Murder
President's Target
The Presidio
Pressure Point
Presumed Innocent
Pretty in Pink
Pretty Woman
Prey of the Chameleon
Priceless Beauty
Pride and Prejudice
Pride of Jesse Hallum
The Pride of the Yankees
Prime Cut
The Prime of Miss Jean Brodie
Prime Target
Primo Baby
The Prince of Tides
Princes in Exile
The Princess and the Pea
The Princess Bride
The Princess Who Never Laughed
Prison
Prison Stories: Women on the Inside
Private Investigations
Private Lives
A Private Matter
Private Wars
Prizzi's Honor
Problem Child
Problem Child 2
The Program
Programmed to Kill
Project: Shadowchaser
Project X
Prom Night 4: Deliver Us From Evil
Promised a Miracle
Proof
Protector
Protocol
Prototype X29A
Proud Men
Psychic
Psycho 3
Pucker Up and Bark Like a Dog
Pulse
Pump Up the Volume
Pumping Iron 2: The Women
Pumpkinhead
Punchline
The Punisher
Puppet Master
Puppet Master 2
Puppet Master 3: Toulon's Revenge
Puppet Master 4
Pure Country
Pure Luck
Purple Rain
The Purple Rose of Cairo
Pursuit

Pursuit to Algiers
Puss 'n Boots
Q & A
Quarterback Princess
The Queen of Mean
Queens Logic
The Quest
Question of Faith
Quick Change
Quicksand: No Escape
Quicksilver
The Quiet Earth
The Quiet Man
Quigley Down Under
The Quiller Memorandum
Quo Vadis
Race with the Devil
The Racers
The Rachel Papers
Racing with the Moon
Rad
Radio Flyer
Rafferty & the Gold Dust Twins
Rage and Honor
A Rage in Harlem
Raggedy Ann and Andy: A Musical Adventure
Raiders of the Lost Ark
Raiders of the Sun
The Railway Station Man
Rain Man
The Rainmaker
Raise the Red Lantern
A Raisin in the Sun
Raising Arizona
Raising Cain
Rambo: First Blood, Part 2
Rampage
Ran
Rancho Deluxe
Rap Master Ronnie
Rapid Fire
Rapunzel
Ratboy
Ratings Game
Raw Deal
Raw Justice
The Razor's Edge
Real Genius
The Real McCoy
Real Men
Reality Bites
Rebecca
Rebecca of Sunnybrook Farm
Rebel
Rebel Without a Cause
The Rebels
Red Garters
Red Headed Stranger
Red Line 7000
Red River
Red Rock West
Red Shoe Diaries
Red Shoe Diaries 2: Double Dare
Red Shoe Diaries 3: Another Woman's Lipstick
Red Shoe Diaries 4: Auto Erotica
The Red Shoes
Red Sonja
Red Wind
Reds
The Ref
Reform School Girl
Regarding Henry
Relentless
Relentless 3
The Remains of the Day
Remote
Renegades
Rent-A-Cop
Repossessed
The Rescue
The Rescuers

The Rescuers Down Under
Reservoir Dogs
The Restless Breed
Return of Frank James
The Return of Jafar
Return of Superfly
The Return of Swamp Thing
Return of the Bad Men
Return of the Dragon
Return of the Jedi
Return of the Killer Tomatoes
Return of the Living Dead 2
Return of the Living Dead 3
The Return of the Musketeers
Return to Lonesome Dove
Return to Peyton Place
Return to Salem's Lot
Return to the Blue Lagoon
Return to the Lost World
Return to Two Moon Junction
Reuben, Reuben
Reunion
Revenge of the Creature
Revenge of the Nerds
Revenge of the Nerds 2: Nerds in Paradise
Reversal of Fortune
Revolution
Revolver
Rhinestone
Rich Girl
Rich in Love
Ricochet
Ride Him, Cowboy
Ride the Wild Surf
Riding the Edge
Riff Raff
The Right Stuff
Rikky and Pete
Ring of Fire
Ring of Fire 2: Blood and Steel
Ring of Steel
Ring of the Musketeers
Rio Grande
Rio Lobo
Rip van Winkle
Ripping Yarns
Rising Son
Rising Sun
The Ritz
The River
River of Death
River of Diamonds
The River Rat
A River Runs Through It
River's Edge
Roadside Prophets
The Roaring Twenties
Robin Hood
Robin Hood: Men in Tights
Robin Hood: Prince of Thieves
Robin Hood...The Legend: Herne's Son
Robin Hood...The Legend: Robin Hood and the Sorcerer
Robin Hood...The Legend: The Swords of Wayland
Robin Hood...The Legend: The Time of the Wolf
Robinson Crusoe & the Tiger
RoboCop
RoboCop 2
RoboCop 3
Robot Jox
Robot Wars
Rock 'n' Roll High School
Rock 'n' Roll High School Forever
Rocket Gibraltar
The Rocketeer
Rockula
Rockwell: A Legend of the Wild West
Rocky 4
Rocky 5

The Rocky Horror Picture Show
Roe vs. Wade
Roger & Me
Romancing the Stone
Romantic Comedy
Rome Adventure
Romeo Is Bleeding
Romero
The Rookie
Rookie of the Year
A Room with a View
The Rosary Murders
The Rose
The Rose and the Jackal
The Rose Tattoo
Rosencrantz & Guildenstern Are Dead
Rough Night in Jericho
Round Midnight
Round Numbers
Round Trip to Heaven
The Rounders
Roxanne
Rubdown
Ruby
Ruby in Paradise
Rudolph the Red-Nosed Reindeer
Rudy
Rudyard Kipling's Classic Stories
Rumpelstiltskin
Run
Runaway
Runaway Father
Runaway Train
The Runestone
The Runner Stumbles
Running Away
Running Cool
Running Delilah
Running Mates
Running on Empty
Running Scared
The Russia House
The Russians are Coming, the Russians are Coming
Russkies
Rustler's Rhapsody
Sacred Ground
St. Elmo's Fire
The Saint of Fort Washington
Salvador
Samantha
Samaritan: The Mitch Snyder Story
San Antonio
The Sandlot
Sands of Iwo Jima
Santa Claus is Coming to Town
Santa Claus: The Movie
Santa Sangre
Sarafina!
Sarah, Plain and Tall
Satan's Princess
Satisfaction
Save Me
Saving Grace
Say Anything
Scanner Cop
Scanners 2: The New Order
Scanners 3: The Takeover
The Scarlet & the Black
Scarlet Claw
Scarlet Empress
Scenes from a Mall
Scent of a Woman
School Daze
School Ties
Scissors
Scrooge
Scrooged
Scruples
Sea of Love

Sea Wolves
The Search for Bridey Murphy
Searching for Bobby Fischer
Second Sight
Second Victory
The Secret
The Secret Diary of Sigmund Freud
Secret Games
Secret Games 2: The Escort
The Secret Garden
The Secret of My Success
The Secret of NIMH
Secret Places
Secret Weapon
See No Evil, Hear No Evil
See You in the Morning
Seedpeople
The Seekers
Sense & Sensibility
The Sensuous Nurse
Separate But Equal
September
September 30, 1955
The Serpent of Death
Servants of Twilight
Sesame Street Presents: Follow That Bird
Seven Minutes in Heaven
Seven Thieves
The Seven-Ups
The Seventh Sign
Sex and the Single Girl
Sex Crimes
sex, lies and videotape
Sexual Response
Shadey
Shadow Force
Shadow of the Wolf
Shadowhunter
Shadowlands
Shadows and Fog
Shadowzone
Shampoo
Shattered
Shattered Vows
She-Devil
Sheena
The Shell Seekers
Shelley Duvall's Bedtime Stories
The Sheltering Sky
Sherlock Holmes and the Secret Weapon
Sherlock Holmes Faces Death
Sherlock Holmes in Washington
Sherlock Holmes: The Voice of Terror
She's a Good Skate, Charlie Brown
She's Gotta Have It
She's Having a Baby
She's Out of Control
The Shining
The Shining Hour
Shining Through
Ship of Fools
Shipwrecked
Shirley Valentine
A Shock to the System
Shock Treatment
Shocker
Shoot to Kill
Shootfighter: Fight to the Death
The Shop Around the Corner
Short Circuit
Short Circuit 2
Short Cuts
Short Time
Shout
A Show of Force
Showdown
Showdown at Williams Creek
Showdown in Little Tokyo

The Shrimp on the Barbie
Shy People
Sibling Rivalry
Sid & Nancy
Side By Side
Side Out
Sidekicks
Siesta
The Sign of Four
Silas Marner
Silence Like Glass
The Silence of the Lambs
The Silencer
Silent Motive
Silent Tongue
Silent Victim
Silver Bullet
Silver River
The Silver Stallion: King of the Wild Brumbies
Silverado
Simple Men
Sinatra
Since You Went Away
Sincerely Charlotte
Singin' in the Rain
Single White Female
Singles
Sins of Desire
The Sins of Dorian Gray
Sister Act
Sister Act 2: Back in the Habit
The Sisters
Six Degrees of Separation
Sketch Artist
Ski Patrol
Ski School
Skier's Dream
Skin Art
The Skull
Sky Pirates
Skylark
Skyscraper Souls
Slamdance
Slaughter of the Innocents
Sleeper
Sleeping Beauty
Sleeping with the Enemy
Sleepless in Seattle
Sleepwalkers
The Slender Thread
Sliver
Slow Burn
The Slugger's Wife
Slumber Party Massacre 2
Smokescreen
A Smoky Mountain Christmas
Smooth Talker
SnakeEater 2: The Drug Buster
SnakeEater 3: His Law
Sneakers
Sniper
Snoopy, Come Home
Snow Kill
The Snow Queen
Snow White and the Seven Dwarfs
Snow White and the Three Stooges
So I Married an Axe Murderer
Soapdish
Society
Sodom and Gomorrah
Solar Crisis
Solarbabies
The Soldier
Soldier in the Rain
Soldier of Fortune
Soldier's Fortune
A Soldier's Story
A Soldier's Tale
Some Kind of Wonderful
Some Like It Hot
Somebody Has to Shoot the Picture

Somebody Up There Likes Me
Someone to Love
Someone to Watch Over Me
Something Wild
Sometimes They Come Back
Somewhere in Sonora
Sommersby
Son-in-Law
Son of Ali Baba
Son of the Morning Star
Son of the Pink Panther
Song of the Islands
Songwriter
Sorcerer
Sorority Girl
Sorry, Wrong Number
Soul Man
The Sound of Music
Sounder
Sourdough
South Central
South Pacific
Souvenir
Spaceballs
Spaced Invaders
Spacehunter: Adventures in the Forbidden Zone
Spartacus
The Spellbinder
Spellbound
Spellcaster
Spider Woman
Spiderman: The Deadly Dust
Spies Like Us
Spirit of '76
Spirits
Split Decisions
Split Second
Splitting Heirs
Springtime in the Rockies
Spy
The Spy Who Came in from the Cold
Spymaker: The Secret Life of Ian Fleming
The Squeeze
Stakeout
Stalin
Stand and Deliver
Stand By Me
Stand Up and Cheer
Stanley and Iris
Stanley and Livingstone
Star!
Star Spangled Girl
Star Trek: The Motion Picture
Star Trek 2: The Wrath of Khan
Star Trek 3: The Search for Spock
Star Trek 4: The Voyage Home
Star Trek 5: The Final Frontier
Star Trek 6: The Undiscovered Country
Star Trek the Next Generation: Encounter at Farpoint
Star Trek 25th Anniversary Special
Star Wars
Stark
Starman
Stars and Bars
Stars and Stripes Forever
Stars in My Crown
State Fair
State of Grace
Stay Tuned
Staying Alive
Steal the Sky
Stealing Home
Steaming
Steel and Lace
Steel Magnolias
Steele Justice

Stella
The Stepfather
Stepfather 3: Father's Day
Stephen King's Golden Years
Stephen King's The Stand
Stephen King's The Tommyknockers
Stepmonster
Stepping Out
Stick
Still Not Quite Human
The Sting
Stolen Hours
The Stone Boy
Stone Cold
The Stooge
Stop! or My Mom Will Shoot
Storm
Storm and Sorrow
Stormy Monday
Stormy Weather
The Story of Robin Hood & His Merrie Men
The Story of Ruth
Storyville
Stowaway
Straight Talk
Straight to Hell
Stranded
Strange Interlude
The Stranger
A Stranger Among Us
The Stranger and the Gunfighter
Stranger than Paradise
Strangers
Strangers in Good Company
Strays
Street Knight
Street Smart
A Streetcar Named Desire
Streets of Fire
Strictly Ballroom
Strike a Pose
Striking Distance
Stripes
The Stuff
Subspecies
The Substitute
Suburban Commando
Subway
Sudden Impact
Sudie & Simpson
Sugar Hill
Summer and Smoke
Summer Camp Nightmare
Summer of '42
Summer Rental
Summer School
A Summer Story
A Summer to Remember
Sun Valley Serenade
Sunset
Sunset Grill
Sunset Heat
Sunstroke
Super Mario Bros.
Superfly T.N.T.
Superman 4: The Quest for Peace
The Supernaturals
Support Your Local Gunfighter
Support Your Local Sheriff
The Sure Thing
Surf Nazis Must Die
Surf Ninjas
Surrender
Survival Quest
Survivors
Susan and God
Susannah of the Mounties
Suspiria
Suzy
Sweet Hearts Dance
Sweet Killing

Sweet Liberty
Sweet Lies
Sweet Poison
Sweet Revenge
Sweet Talker
Swimming to Cambodia
Swing Kids
Switch
Switching Channels
Swoon
The Sword in the Stone
Sword of Gideon
Sylvester
Sylvia
Tagget
Tai-Pan
Tainted Blood
Take This Job & Shove It
Taken Away
Taking Care of Business
The Taking of Beverly Hills
A Tale of Springtime
The Tale of the Frog Prince
A Tale of Two Cities
Talent for the Game
Tales from Avonlea, Vol. 1: The Journey Begins
Tales from the Crypt, Vol. 3
Tales from the Darkside: The Movie
Tales from the Gimli Hospital
Tales That Witness Madness
Talk to Me
Talkin' Dirty After Dark
Talons of the Eagle
Tango and Cash
Tank
Tap
Tarantula
Target
Target: Favorite Son
A Taste for Killing
TC 2000
Tea and Sympathy
Teachers
Teamster Boss: The Jackie Presser Story
Teen Wolf
Teen Wolf Too
Teenage Mutant Ninja Turtles: The Movie
Teenage Mutant Ninja Turtles 2: The Secret of the Ooze
Telegraph Trail
The Telephone
The Temp
The Ten Million Dollar Getaway
The Tenth Man
Tequila Sunrise
Terminal Bliss
Terminator 2: Judgment Day
Termini Station
Terms of Endearment
Terror by Night
Terror Stalks the Class Reunion
The Terrorists
Test Tube Teens from the Year 2000
Testament
The Texas Chainsaw Massacre
Texas Chainsaw Massacre, Part 2
Texasville
Thanksgiving Story
That Certain Woman
That Night
That Summer of White Roses
That Was Then...This Is Now
That's Life!
Thelma & Louise
There Goes the Neighborhood
There's No Business Like Show Business

Thief of Hearts
The Thin Blue Line
The Thing Called Love
Things Change
Third Degree Burn
This Boy's Life
This is My Life
This Property is Condemned
The Thorn Birds
Those Daring Young Men in Their Jaunty Jalopies
Thousand Pieces of Gold
Three Amigos
Three Daring Daughters
Three Days of the Condor
Three Days to a Kill
Three Fugitives
Three Men of Heat
The Three Little Pigs
The Three Lives of Thomasina
Three Men and a Baby
Three Men and a Little Lady
Three Men on a Horse
The Three Musketeers
3 Ninjas
Three of a Kind
Three Violent People
Throw Momma from the Train
Thumbelina
Thunder and Lightning
Ticks
Tiger Claws
A Tiger's Tale
Tightrope
The Tigress
Till There was You
Time Runner
Time to Kill
Timebomb
Tin Men
Tiny Toon Adventures: How I Spent My Vacation
To Be or Not to Be
To Be the Best
To Dance with the White Dog
To Die for 2
To Live & Die in L.A.
To Sleep with Anger
To the Death
Tokyo Pop
Tom and Jerry: The Movie
Tombstone
Tomcat: Dangerous Desires
Tomorrow's Child
Too Hot to Handle
Tootsie
Top Gun
Top Secret!
Topaze
Torch Song Trilogy
Total Exposure
Total Recall
Toto le Heros
Touch and Go
Tough Guys Don't Dance
Tourist Trap
The Towering Inferno
The Toxic Avenger, Part 2
Toy Soldiers
Toys in the Attic
Traces of Red
The Tracker
Tracks
Trading Places
Trail of the Pink Panther
Trancers
Trancers 2: The Return of Jack Deth
Trancers 3: Deth Lives
Trancers 4: Jack of Swords
Transylvania 6-5000
Treacherous Crossing
Treasure Island
A Tree Grows in Brooklyn
Tremors
Trial and Error

Tribute to a Bad Man
Trick or Treat
The Trip to Bountiful
TripleCross
Troll 2
Troop Beverly Hills
Tropical Snow
Trouble Bound
Trouble in Mind
True Believer
True Colors
True Identity
True Love
True Romance
True Stories
Trust
Truth or Dare
Truth or Die
Tucker: The Man and His Dream
Tuff Turf
Tune in Tomorrow
Turk 182!
The Turn of the Screw
Turtle Diary
Twelve Angry Men
12:01
Twenty Bucks
Twenty Dollar Star
20,000 Leagues Under the Sea
24 Hours to Midnight
29th Street
Twice in a Lifetime
Twin Peaks
Twin Peaks: Fire Walk with Me
Two for the Seesaw
The Two Jakes
Two Kinds of Love
Two of a Kind
2010: The Year We Make Contact
Two Weeks in Another Town
UHF
Ulterior Motives
Ultimate Desires
Ulzana's Raid
The Unbearable Lightness of Being
Uncommon Valor
Undeclared War
The Undefeated
Under Siege
Under Suspicion
Under the Cherry Moon
Undercover
Undercover Blues
Unfaithfully Yours
Unforgiven
Uninvited
Universal Soldier
Unlawful Entry
The Unnamable 2: The Statement of Randolph Carter
Untamed Heart
Until September
Until The End of The World
Until They Sail
The Untouchables
Used People
Utu
The Vagrant
Valdez is Coming
Valmont
Vamp
Vampire at Midnight
The Vanishing
A Very Brady Christmas
V.I. Warshawski
Vibes
Vice Versa
Victim of Beauty
Victory
Video Americana

Vietnam War Story 1
Vietnam War Story 2
A View to a Kill
The Vindicator
Violence at Noon
Violets Are Blue
The Virgin Queen
Vision Quest
Vital Signs
Voyage of Terror: The Achille Lauro Affair
Voyage to the Bottom of the Sea
Wager of Love
Wagon Master
Wait Until Spring, Bandini
Waiting for the Light
Waiting for the Moon
Walker: Texas Ranger: One Riot, One Ranger
Wall Street
A Waltz Through the Hills
Wanted Dead or Alive
War of the Gargantuas
The War of the Roses
War Party
The War Room
WarGames
Warlock
Warning Sign
The Waterdance
Waterloo
Waterloo Bridge
Waxwork 2: Lost in Time
Way Out West
Wayne's World 2
Web of Deceit
Wee Willie Winkie
Weekend at Bernie's 2
Weep No More My Lady
Weird Science
Welcome Home, Roxy Carmichael
Welcome to L.A.
We're No Angels
We're Not Married
West Side Story
Western Union
Westward the Women
Wetherby
Whale for the Killing
What Comes Around
What Ever Happened to Baby Jane?
What the Moon Saw
What's Eating Gilbert Grape
What's Love Got to Do With It?
When a Stranger Calls Back
When Harry Met Sally
When Ladies Meet
When the Time Comes
When the Whales Came
Where Angels Fear to Tread
Where Angels Go, Trouble Follows
Where Are the Children?
Where Love Has Gone
Where Sleeping Dogs Lie
Where the Boys Are '84
Where the Day Takes You
Where the Heart Is
Where the Red Fern Grows: Part 2
Where the River Runs Black
Where's Poppa?
Which Way Home
Whispers in the Dark
The Whistle Blower
White Christmas
White Fang
White Heat
White Hunter, Black Heart
White Lie
White Nights
White of the Eye

White Palace
White Sands
Who Has Seen the Wind?
Who is Killing the Great Chefs of Europe?
Who Shot Pat?
Whore
Who's Harry Crumb?
Who's That Girl?
Who's the Man?
Why Me?
Wide Sargasso Sea
The Wilby Conspiracy
Wild at Heart
Wild Cactus
Wild Hearts Can't Be Broken
The Wild Life
The Wild One
Wild Orchid
Wild Orchid 2: Two Shades of Blue
Wild Palms
Wildcats
Wilder Napalm
Wildfire
Wildflower
Will Penny
Willow
Willy Wonka & the Chocolate Factory
Wind
The Winds of War
Windy City
Wings of Fame
Winner Takes All
Winners Take All
The Winning Team
Winter Meeting
Winter People
Wisdom
Wise Guys
Witchboard 2: The Devil's Doorway
Witchcraft 4: Virgin Heart
The Witches
The Witches of Eastwick
Without a Clue
Witness
The Wizard
The Wizard of Loneliness
The Wizard of Oz
The Wizard of Speed and Time
Wizards
The Wolf at the Door
A Woman, Her Men and Her Futon
The Woman in Green
Woman of Desire
A Woman Under the Influence
A Woman's Tale
Wombling Free
Women & Men: In Love There Are No Rules
Women & Men: Stories of Seduction
Woodstock
Woof!
Words by Heart
Workin' for Peanuts
Working Girl
The World According to Garp
A World Apart
The World of Henry Orient
World War III
Worth Winning
The Wreck of the Mary Deare
Wrestling Ernest Hemingway
Writer's Block
The Wrong Guys
The Wrong Man
Yankee Doodle Dandy
Yanks
The Year of Living Dangerously
Year of the Comet

Year

Year of the Dragon
Yentl
You Can't Take It with You
Young Catherine
The Young Detectives on
   Wheels
Young Einstein
Young Frankenstein
Young Guns
Young Guns 2
Young Mr. Lincoln
Young Sherlock Holmes
Yours, Mine & Ours
Zandalee
Zebrahead
Zelly & Me
Zentropa
Zeppelin
Zoo Radio
Zorro, the Gay Blade
Zulu

FOREIGN FILM INDEX

The **FOREIGN FILM INDEX** classifies nearly 4,700 movies by the country of record in which they were produced, and not necessarily filmed. Since the feature may have been financed or produced by more than one country, some videos will appear with more than one country of origin. The codes appear in the review immediately following the color or black and white designation near the top of the review.

Key to Country Origination Tags

AL Algerian	**CH** Chinese	**GR** Greek	**LI** Lithuanian	**SA** South African
AR Argentinean	**CZ** Czech	**HK** Hong Kong	**MX** Mexican	**SP** Spanish
AT Austrian	**DK** Danish	**HU** Hungarian	**NZ** New Zealand	**SW** Swedish
AU Australian	**NL** Dutch	**IN** Indian	**NI** Nicaraguan	**SI** Swiss
BE Belgian	**PH** Filipino	**IR** Irish	**NO** Norwegian	**TU** Turkish
BR Brazilian	**FI** Finnish	**IS** Israeli	**PL** Polish	**TW** Taiwanese
GB British	**FR** French	**IT** Italian	**PT** Portuguese	**YU** Yugoslavian
CA Canadian	**GE** German	**JP** Japanese	**RU** Russian	

Algerian

The Battle of Algiers▶

Argentinean

Camila▶
The Curious Dr. Humpp
The Devil's Possessed
The Enchanted Forest
Eversmile New Jersey
Far Away and Long Ago
Fridays of Eternity
Funny, Dirty Little War
La Boca del Lobo
Made in Argentina
Man Facing Southeast▶
Miss Mary
The Official Story▶
The Stranger▶
Tango Bar
Time for Revenge
Times to Come▶
Two to Tango
Veronico Cruz

Australian

ABC's of Love & Sex,
    Australia Style
Air Hawk
Alice to Nowhere
Alison's Birthday
All the Rivers Run
...Almost
Alvin Purple
Alvin Rides Again
American Roulette
Anzacs: The War Down
    Under▶
Archer's Adventure
Around the World in 80 Ways
Attack Force Z
Backlash
Barnaby and Me
Barry McKenzie Holds His
    Own
Between Wars
Black Robe▶
Bliss▶
Blood Money
Bloodmoon
Blue Fin
Body Melt
Breaker Morant▶

Breakfast in Paris
Burke & Wills
Cactus
Caddie
Camel Boy
Careful, He Might Hear You▶
Carry Me Back
The Cars That Ate Paris▶
The City's Edge
Clowning Around
Clowning Around 2
The Club▶
The Coca-Cola Kid▶
Color Me Dead
Contagion
Crocodile Dundee▶
The Crossing
A Cry in the Dark▶
Dangerous Summer
Dark Age
Dark Forces
Dead Calm▶
Dead Easy
Dead End Drive-In
Deadly Possession
Death of a Soldier
Demonstrator
The Devil's Playground▶
Dogs in Space
Don's Party▶
The Dreaming
The Dunera Boys▶
Dusty
Earthling
Echo Park
Echoes of Paradise
The Efficiency Expert
The Empty Beach
Endplay
Escape 2000
Eureka Stockade
The Everlasting Secret Family
Fantasy Man
Fast Talking
Father
Fatty Finn
The Fire in the Stone
Fists of Blood
Flirting▶
For Love Alone
Fortress
Forty Thousand Horsemen
Fran
Frenchman's Farm
The Fringe Dwellers

Gallagher's Travels
Gallipoli▶
Georgia
The Getting of Wisdom
The Good Wife
Grendel, Grendel, Grendel
Ground Zero▶
Hard Knocks
Heatwave▶
Heaven Tonight
High Rolling in a Hot Corvette
High Tide▶
The Highest Honor
Howling 3: The Marsupials
I Live with Me Dad
An Indecent Obsession
Inn of the Damned
Innocent Prey
The Irishman
Kangaroo▶
The Killing Beach
Killing of Angel Street
Kitty and the Bagman
Lady Stay Dead
The Last Bastion
The Last Days of Chez Nous
The Last Wave▶
The Lighthorsemen▶
Lonely Hearts▶
Long John Silver
The Long Weekend
Mad Dog Morgan
Mad Max: Beyond
    Thunderdome
Magee and the Lady
Malcolm
The Man from Snowy River
Man of Flowers
The Mango Tree
Mesmerized
Midnight Dancer
Miracle Down Under
Money Movers
Monkey Grip▶
Moving Targets
My Brilliant Career▶
My First Wife
The Naked Country
Nevil Shute's The Far Country
Newsfront▶
Next of Kin
No Room to Run
Norman Loves Rose
Now and Forever
The Odd Angry Shot

Overlanders▶
Palm Beach
Panic Station
Patrick
Phar Lap
The Piano▶
Picnic at Hanging Rock▶
Plumber
Poor Girl, A Ghost Story
Prince and the Great Race
Prisoner Cell Block H
Prisoners of the Sun▶
Proof▶
Puberty Blues
Puzzle
Queen of the Road
The Quest
Quigley Down Under
Razorback
Rebel
Return of Captain Invincible
Return to Snowy River▶
Ride a Wild Pony▶
The Right Hand Man
Rikky and Pete
Road Games
Romper Stomper
Run, Rebecca, Run
Runaway Island, Part 1
Runaway Island, Part 2
Runaway Island, Part 3
Runaway Island, Part 4
Sara Dane
Savage Attraction
Second Time Lucky
Shame
Silver City
The Silver Stallion: King of the
    Wild Brumbies
Sirens▶
Sky Pirates
Smuggler's Cove
Squizzy Taylor
Starstruck
Strangers
Strictly Ballroom▶
Summer City
Sunday Too Far Away▶
Survivor
Sweet Talker
Sweetie▶
The Tale of Ruby Rose▶
Tearaway
A Test of Love
Three's Trouble

Thundering Forest
Tim
Torn Allegiance
Touch & Go
A Town Like Alice
Travelling North
Treasure of the Yankee
    Zephyr
Typhoon Treasure
Under Capricorn
Vincent: The Life and Death of
    Vincent van Gogh▶
The Wacky World of Wills &
    Burke
Walk into Hell
Warm Nights on a Slow-
    Moving Train
Waterfront
We of the Never Never▶
Who Killed Baby Azaria?
Wide Sargasso Sea
The Wild Duck
Windrider
The Winds of Jarrah
The Winter of Our Dreams
A Woman's Tale▶
A Yank in Australia
The Year My Voice Broke▶
The Year of Living
    Dangerously▶
Young Einstein

Austrian

The Hands of Orlac
Heidi▶
Time Troopers

Belgian

Between Heaven and Earth
Daughters of Darkness▶
The Devil's Nightmare
Dust▶
Les Rendez-vous D'Anna
Man Bites Dog
Mascara
The Music Teacher
Night and Day▶
One Sings, the Other Doesn't
Rabid Grannies
Toute Une Nuit▶
A Wedding in Galilee▶

Brazilian

Amor Bandido
At Midnight, I'll Take Your Soul
Awakenings of the Beast
Black God & White Devil
Black Orpheus▶
Bye Bye Brazil
The Dolphin
Dona Flor and Her Two Husbands▶
Earth Entranced
Gabriela
Hallucinations of a Deranged Mind
The Hour of the Star▶
I Love You
Killer Fish
Kiss of the Spider Woman▶
Lady on the Bus
Luzia
Opera do Malandro
Pixote▶
Quilombo
The Story of Fausta
Strange World of Coffin Joe
Subway to the Stars
Via Appia
Women in Fury
Xica▶

British

Abdulla the Great
Abigail's Party
The Abominable Dr. Phibes▶
Above Us the Waves▶
Absolute Beginners
Absolution
Accident
Accused
Across the Bridge
Action for Slander
The Adventurers
Adventures of a Private Eye
Adventures of a Taxi Driver
The Adventures of Sadie
The Adventures of Sherlock Holmes: Hound of the Baskervilles
The Adventures of Tartu
An Affair in Mind
The Affair of the Pink Pearl
After Darkness
After Julius
After Pilkington
After the Fox
Afterward
Alamut Ambush
Alfie▶
Alias John Preston
Alice▶
Alice's Adventures in Wonderland
Alien Women
All Creatures Great and Small▶
American Friends
American Roulette
And Nothing But the Truth
And Now for Something Completely Different▶
And Now the Screaming Starts
And Soon the Darkness
Angel with the Trumpet
Anna Karenina
Another Country
Another Time, Another Place
Another Time, Another Place▶
Antonia and Jane
Apartment Zero▶
Appointment with Crime
Aria

Armistead Maupin's Tales of the City
The Arsenal Stadium Mystery
As You Like It
The Asphyx▶
The Assassination Bureau▶
Assassination of Trotsky
The Assassination Run
Assault
Assault on Agathon
Asylum
At the Earth's Core
The Atomic Man
The Baby and the Battleship
Baby Love
Bachelor of Hearts
Backbeat▶
Bad Behavior
Ballad in Blue
The Ballad of the Sad Cafe
Ballet Shoes
Bananas Boat
Battle Beneath the Earth
Battle Hell
The Battle of the Sexes▶
The Bawdy Adventures of Tom Jones
Beachcomber▶
Beast in the Cellar
Beast of Morocco
Beat Girl
Bedazzled▶
The Belles of St. Trinian's▶
Bellman and True
The Belly of an Architect▶
Benny Hill's Crazy World
Bernard and the Genie
Best Enemies
The Best of the Two Ronnies
Betrayal
Bewitched
The Big Man: Crossing the Line▶
Big Zapper
Biggles
Billy Budd▶
Billy Liar▶
The Bitch
Bitter Sweet
Black Beauty
The Black Cat
Black Eyes
Black Limelight
Black Narcissus▶
Black Werewolf
Blackmail▶
Blackout
Blake's Seven
Blat
Bleak House
The Bliss of Mrs. Blossom▶
Blithe Spirit▶
Blockhouse
Blonde Blackmailer
Blood Beast Terror
Blood Island
Blood of the Vampire
The Blood on Satan's Claw▶
Bloodbath at the House of Death
The Bloodsuckers
Blow-Up▶
Blue Blood
The Blue Lamp▶
Blue Money
Blue Murder at St. Trinian's▶
Bobo
The Body in the Library
The Body Vanished
Bonnie Prince Charlie
The Borrowers▶
The Boy Friend▶
The Brain
Brazil▶
Breaking Glass
The Bretts▶

The Brides of Dracula
Brideshead Revisited▶
The Bridge on the River Kwai▶
A Bridge Too Far
Brief Encounter▶
Bright Smiler
Brighton Rock▶
Brimstone & Treacle▶
Britannia Hospital
Broken Melody
Brothers in Law
The Browning Version▶
Buddy's Song
Bugsy Malone
Bulldog Drummond at Bay
Bulldog Jack▶
Bullshot
Burn Witch, Burn!▶
Burning Secret
Buster
Butler's Dilemma
Butterflies
Butterfly Ball
Caesar and Cleopatra
Call Him Mr. Shatter
Calling Paul Temple
Candles at Nine
A Canterbury Tale▶
Captain Horatio Hornblower▶
Captain Kronos: Vampire Hunter▶
Captain's Paradise▶
The Captain's Table
Captive Heart▶
Car Trouble
Caravaggio▶
Carlton Browne of the F.O.
Carrington, V.C.▶
Carry On Admiral
Carry On at Your Convenience
Carry On Behind
Carry On Cleo
Carry On Cowboy
Carry On Dick
Carry On Doctor▶
Carry On Emmanuelle
Carry On England
Carry On Nurse
Carry On 'Round the Bend
Carry On Screaming
The Case of the Frightened Lady
The Case of the Missing Lady
The Case of the Mukkinese Battle Horn
The Cassandra Crossing
Cast a Dark Shadow▶
The Castle of Fu Manchu
The Cat and the Canary
Catch Me a Spy
Catherine the Great
The Chalk Garden▶
Chamber of Horrors
Champagne
Champions
The Charge of the Light Brigade
Chariots of Fire▶
Charlie Grant's War
The Charmer
Chicago Joe & the Showgirl
The Children
Children of Rage
Children of the Damned
Children of the Full Moon
Chinese Boxes
Chitty Chitty Bang Bang
Choice of Weapons
A Chorus of Disapproval
Christabel
Christian the Lion
A Christmas Carol▶
Christopher Columbus
The Chronicles of Narnia

Circle of Iron
Circle of Power
Circus of Fear
Circus of Horrors
The Citadel▶
City Boy▶
City of Joy
Clash of the Titans
The Class of Miss MacMichael
The Clergyman's Daughter
Clockwise
A Clockwork Orange▶
Codename: Icarus
Cold War Killers
The Collector▶
The Comeback
Comfort and Joy▶
Coming Through
Coming Up Roses
Conduct Unbecoming
The Confessional
The Conqueror Worm▶
Conspiracy of Hearts▶
Conspirator
Consuming Passions
The Cook, the Thief, His Wife & Her Lover▶
Cool Mikado
Corridors of Blood
Cottage to Let
The Count of Monte Cristo
Counterblast
The Courageous Mr. Penn
The Courtesans of Bombay▶
The Courtney Affair
The Crackler
The Crawling Eye
The Creeping Flesh
Crimes at the Dark House▶
The Crimes of Stephen Hawke
The Crimson Cult
Crimson Pirate▶
Cromwell
Crooks & Coronets
Crow Hollow
Crucible of Horror
Cruel Sea▶
A Cry from the Streets
Cry of the Banshee
Cry Terror
Cry, the Beloved Country▶
Cul de Sac▶
The Curse of Frankenstein
Curse of the Demon▶
The Curse of the Werewolf
Curtain Up
Cyrano de Bergerac
Daleks—Invasion Earth 2150 A.D.
Dam Busters▶
Damage▶
Damn the Defiant▶
Dance with a Stranger▶
Dandy in Aspic
Danger Man
Danger UXB
A Dangerous Man: Lawrence after Arabia
Dangerous Moonlight▶
Dante's Inferno: Life of Dante Gabriel Rossetti
The Dark Angel▶
Dark Journey▶
Dark of the Sun
Dark Places
Darling▶
The Dawning
A Day in the Death of Joe Egg▶
The Day Will Dawn▶
The Dead▶
Dead Lucky
Dead of Night▶
The Deadly Game
Deadly Recruits

Deadly Strangers
Dealers
Dear Murderer
Death Goes to School
The Death of Adolf Hitler
Death on the Nile
Death Ship
Decameron Nights
The Deceivers
A Dedicated Man
Deep End▶
Deep in the Heart
Defense of the Realm▶
Deja Vu
The Demi-Paradise▶
Demon Barber of Fleet Street
Demons of the Mind
Department Store
The Deputy Drummer
The Destructors
The Detective▶
Devil Doll
Devil Girl from Mars
Devil on Horseback
The Devils▶
The Devil's Disciple▶
The Devil's Undead
Diamonds are Forever▶
Dick Barton, Special Agent
Dick Barton Strikes Back
Die! Die! My Darling!
Die, Monster, Die!
Die Screaming, Marianne
Digby, the Biggest Dog in the World
Dinner at the Ritz
Disciple of Death
Distant Voices, Still Lives▶
The Divorce of Lady X▶
The Doctor and the Devils
Doctor at Large
Doctor at Sea
Doctor Blood's Coffin
Doctor in Distress
Doctor in the House▶
Dr. Jekyll and Sister Hyde
Dr. No▶
Doctor Phibes Rises Again
Dr. Strangelove, or: How I Learned to Stop Worrying and Love the Bomb▶
Dr. Syn
Dr. Terror's House of Horrors
Doctor Who: An Unearthly Child
Doctor Who and the Daleks
Doctor Who: Cybermen—The Early Years
Doctor Who: Daleks Invasion of Earth 2150 A.D.
Doctor Who: Day of the Daleks
Doctor Who: Death to the Daleks
Doctor Who: Earthshock
Doctor Who: Mawdryn Undead
Doctor Who: Pyramids of Mars
Doctor Who: Revenge of the Cybermen
Doctor Who: Robots of Death
Doctor Who: Shada
Doctor Who: Spearhead from Space
Doctor Who: Terror of the Zygons
Doctor Who: The Ark in Space
Doctor Who: The Brain of Morbius
Doctor Who: The Caves of Androzani
Doctor Who: The Curse of Fenric
Doctor Who: The Deadly Assassin

Doctor Who: The Five Doctors
Doctor Who: The Hartnell Years
Doctor Who: The Keeper of Traken
Doctor Who: The Masque of Mandragora
Doctor Who: The Mind Robber
Doctor Who: The Pertwee Years
Doctor Who: The Seeds of Death
Doctor Who: The Sontaran Experiment/The Genesis of the Daleks
Doctor Who: The Talons of Weng-Chiang
Doctor Who: The Three Doctors
Doctor Who: The Time Warrior
Doctor Who: The Tom Baker Years
Doctor Who: The Troughton Years
Doctor Who: The Twin Dilemma
Doctor Who: The War Games
Doctor Who: Tomb of the Cyberman
The Dogs of War
Don't Hang Up
Don't Open Till Christmas
Doomwatch
Down Among the Z Men
Dracula Has Risen from the Grave
The Draughtsman's Contract▶
Dreamchild▶
Dreaming Lips
Dressed for Death
Dressmaker
Drowning by Numbers▶
Drums
Dual Alibi
Duel of Hearts
The Duellists▶
The Dummy Talks
Dust to Dust
Dutch Girls
Dutchman▶
Dynasty of Fear
Eagle's Wing
East of Elephant Rock
Easy Virtue
Eat the Rich
Ebony Tower
Edge of Darkness
Edge of Sanity
Edge of the World▶
Educating Rita▶
Edward II
The Electronic Monster
Elephant Boy▶
11 Harrowhouse▶
The Elusive Pimpernel
Embassy
Empire State
Enchanted April
Encore▶
The Endless Game
Endless Night
An Englishman Abroad▶
Enigma
The Entertainer▶
Erik the Viking
Escapade▶
Escape from El Diablo
Escape to Athena
Eureka!
Evergreen
The Evil Mind
The Evil of Frankenstein
Evil Under the Sun

The Executioner
Experience Preferred... But Not Essential
Eye Witness
Fall and Rise of Reginald Perrin 1▶
Fall and Rise of Reginald Perrin 2▶
The Fall of the House of Usher
The Fallen Idol▶
Fame is the Spur
Family Life
Fanny Hill
Far from the Madding Crowd▶
Farewell, My Lovely▶
The Farmer's Wife
Fatal Confinement
The Favor, the Watch, & the Very Big Fish
Fawlty Towers
The Fearless Vampire Killers▶
Feet Foremost
The Field▶
The Fiend
The Fiendish Plot of Dr. Fu Manchu
The Fifth Musketeer
The Final Option
The Final Programme
Finessing the King
Fire and Sword
Fire Down Below
Fire Maidens from Outer Space
Fire Over England▶
First Men in the Moon
Five Golden Dragons
Five Miles to Midnight
Flambards
Flame Over India▶
Flame to the Phoenix
The Flame Trees of Thika▶
Flesh and Blood Show
Flight from Singapore
Follow That Camel
Fools of Fortune
Footlight Frenzy
For Your Eyes Only▶
Forbidden Passion: The Oscar Wilde Movie
Foreign Body
The Foreman Went to France
Forever Young
Fortunes of War▶
The Forty-Ninth Parallel▶
Four Days in July
The Four Feathers▶
Four Sided Triangle
Four Weddings and a Funeral▶
The Fourth Protocol▶
The Franchise Affair
The Freakmaker
Freddie as F.R.O.7
The French Lesson
Frenzy
Frenzy▶
Frieda
Friends
Fright
Frightmare
From Beyond the Grave
From Russia with Love▶
Frozen Alive
Full Circle
Funny Money
The Gambler & the Lady
Game for Vultures
The Gamma People
Gandhi▶
Gangway
Gaslight▶
The Gay Lady
Genevieve▶
Georgy Girl▶

Getting It Right
The Ghost Camera
The Ghost Goes West▶
Ghost in the Noonday Sun
Ghost Ship
The Ghost Train
The Ghoul
The Gift Horse
The Gilded Cage
A Girl in a Million
The Girl in the Picture
The Girl on a Motorcycle
Girly
Give My Regards to Broad Street
The Go-Between▶
The Golden Salamander
Goldfinger▶
The Good Father▶
Gorgo
The Gorgon
The Gospel According to Vic
Great Expectations▶
Great Expectations
Great Expectations
Great McGonagall
The Great St. Trinian's Train Robbery
The Great Train Robbery▶
The Greed of William Hart
Greek Street
Green for Danger
Green Grow the Rushes
Green Ice
The Green Man▶
Gregory's Girl▶
Grown Ups
Gulag
Gulliver's Travels
Gumshoe
Guns at Batasi
Hail Mary
Hamlet▶
Hamlet
The Hand
The Hand▶
A Handful of Dust▶
The Hands of Orlac
Hands of the Ripper
The Happiest Days of Your Life▶
Happy Since I Met You▶
A Hard Day's Night▶
Harry Black and the Tiger
The Haunted Strangler
Haunted: The Ferryman
The Hawk
Hawks
Hear My Song▶
Heart's Desire
Heat and Dust▶
Heat Wave
Heavens Above▶
Hedda
Hellbound: Hellraiser 2
The Hellfire Club
Hellraiser
Hennessy
Henry V▶
Hi-Di-Hi
The Hidden Room▶
High Command
High Hopes▶
High Season
The Hit
The Hitchhiker's Guide to the Galaxy
Hobson's Choice▶
The Holcroft Covenant
Hope and Glory▶
Horror Hospital
Horror Hotel
The Horror of Dracula▶
The Horror of Frankenstein
Horror Planet
The Horse's Mouth▶

Hot Millions▶
Hotel du Lac
Hotel Paradiso
Hotel Reserve▶
The Hound of the Baskervilles▶
The Hound of the Baskervilles
Hour of Decision
The House in Marsh Road
The House of Eliott
The House of Lurking Death
House of Mystery
The House of 1000 Dolls
The House of the Arrow▶
House of Whipcord
House on Marsh Road
The House that Dripped Blood
The House that Vanished
How I Learned to Love Women
How I Won the War
How Many Miles to Babylon?
How to Get Ahead in Advertising▶
Howard's End▶
Hue and Cry▶
Hullabaloo Over Georgie & Bonnie's Pictures
The Human Factor
The Human Monster
Hussy
Hysteria
I Am a Camera▶
I, Claudius, Vol. 1: A Touch of Murder/Family Affairs
I Don't Want to Be Born
I Know Where I'm Going▶
I Live in Grosvenor Square
I See a Dark Stranger▶
I Stand Condemned
I Want What I Want
If...▶
If I Were Rich
The Impossible Spy▶
Impulse
In Celebration▶
In Search of the Castaways▶
In the Name of the Father▶
In the Shadow of Kilimanjaro
In Which We Serve▶
Inheritance▶
The Innocent
Innocents in Paris
Inserts
Inside Out
Insignificance▶
Inspector Hornleigh
Instant Justice
International Velvet
Internecine Project
Interrupted Journey
Intimate Contact▶
Invasion
Invasion of the Body Stealers
The Ipcress File▶
The Iron Duke
Island of Desire
Island of Terror▶
Island of the Burning Doomed
It Couldn't Happen Here
It Takes a Thief
The Italian Job
It's Love Again
Jabberwocky
Jack the Ripper
Jamaica Inn
Jane & the Lost City
Jane Eyre▶
Jason and the Argonauts▶
Java Head▶
Jeeves & Wooster: Jeeves' Arrival
Jericho
The Jewel in the Crown
The Jigsaw Man
Johnny Frenchman

Johnny Nobody
Joseph Andrews
Journey to the Far Side of the Sun▶
Jubilee
Jude the Obscure
Juggernaut▶
Julius Caesar
Just William's Luck
The Key
The Key Man
Killer Fish
The Killing Fields▶
Killing Heat
Kind Hearts and Coronets▶
A Kind of Loving▶
A King in New York
King Lear▶
The King of Hearts▶
King of the Damned
King Solomon's Treasure
Kings and Desperate Men
The King's Rhapsody
Kipperbang
Kipps▶
The Kitchen Toto▶
The Knack▶
Knight Without Armour▶
Knights & Emeralds
The Krays▶
Krull
Lady Caroline Lamb
Lady Chatterley's Lover
Lady in Distress
Lady Jane▶
Lady of the Lake
The Lady Vanishes▶
The Lady Vanishes
Ladykillers▶
The Lair of the White Worm▶
Land of Fury
Land of the Minotaur
The Land That Time Forgot
The Last Days of Dolwyn
Last Holiday▶
The Last of England▶
Last Reunion
Late Extra
The Lavender Hill Mob▶
Lawrence of Arabia▶
The League of Gentlemen▶
Leather Boys
The Legacy
Legend
Legend of the Werewolf
Leon the Pig Farmer
Les Carabiniers▶
Let Him Have It▶
Let's Make Up
Letter to Brezhnev▶
Letters to an Unknown Lover
License to Kill▶
Lies
The Life and Death of Colonel Blimp▶
Life is Sweet▶
Lillie▶
Lily of Killarney
The Limping Man
Link
Lion of the Desert▶
Lisztomania
Little Dorrit, Film 1: Nobody's Fault▶
Little Dorrit, Film 2: Little Dorrit's Story▶
The Little Match Girl
The Little Prince
The Little Princess
Live and Let Die
The Living Dead
Local Hero▶
Lola
Lolita▶
London Kills Me
London Melody

The Loneliness of the Long Distance Runner▶
The Lonely Passion of Judith Hearne▶
Long Ago Tomorrow
The Long Dark Hall
The Long Day Closes▶
The Long Good Friday▶
Look Back in Anger▶
The Looking Glass War
Loophole
Loose Connections
Loot...Give Me Money, Honey!
Lord of the Flies▶
Lorna Doone
The Lost Language of Cranes▶
Love and Bullets
The Love Factor
Love for Lydia▶
Love from a Stranger
Love on the Dole▶
Lucky Jim
The Lunatic
Lust for a Vampire
Mad Death
Made in Heaven
Mademoiselle
Madhouse
Madhouse Mansion
The Magic Christian▶
Magical Mystery Tour
The Mahabharata
Major Barbara▶
Make Me an Offer
Make Mine Mink▶
The Making of The Hitchhiker's Guide to the Galaxy
A Man About the House
Man Bait
A Man for All Seasons▶
Man Friday
The Man in Grey▶
The Man in the Mist
The Man in the White Suit▶
Man of Evil
Man on the Run
The Man Outside
The Man Who Fell to Earth▶
Man Who Had Power Over Women
The Man Who Haunted Himself
The Man Who Knew Too Much▶
The Man Who Lived Again
The Man Who Never Was▶
The Man with the Golden Gun
Mandy▶
Mania
Maniac
Mansfield Park
The Manxman
Marat/Sade▶
March or Die
Maria's Child
The Mark▶
Mark of the Devil
Mark of the Devil 2
The Mark of the Hawk▶
The Marquise
A Married Man
Masque of the Red Death▶
A Matter of WHO
Maurice▶
Max and Helen
Max Headroom, the Original Story
The Maze▶
The McGuffin
McVicar
The Medusa Touch
Meet Sexton Blake
Melody
Men are not Gods

Men of Sherwood Forest
Men of Two Worlds
The Merchant of Venice▶
Merlin of the Crystal Cave
Merry Christmas, Mr. Lawrence▶
A Midsummer Night's Dream
The Mill on the Floss
Mimi
Mine Own Executioner▶
The Miniver Story
The Miracle
The Mirror Crack'd
The Misadventures of Mr. Wilt
The Missionary
Mr. Arkadin▶
Mr. Love
Mohammed: Messenger of God
Mona Lisa▶
The Monster Club
A Month in the Country▶
Monty Python and the Holy Grail▶
Monty Python Live at the Hollywood Bowl▶
Monty Python Meets Beyond the Fringe
Monty Python's Flying Circus
Monty Python's Life of Brian▶
Monty Python's The Meaning of Life▶
The Moon Stallion
Moonlight Sonata
Moonlighting▶
The Moonraker
Moonraker!
Morgan!
Morons from Outer Space
The Mouse That Roared▶
Much Ado About Nothing▶
The Mummy▶
The Muppet Movie▶
Murder▶
Murder at the Baskervilles
Murder by Moonlight
Murder in the Footlights
Murder in the Old Red Barn
A Murder is Announced
Murder of a Moderate Man
Murder on the Campus
Murder on the Orient Express▶
Murders at Lynch Cross
Murphy's War
The Music Lovers
My Friend Walter
My Son, the Vampire
Mysterious Island▶
Naked▶
The Naked Edge
The Naked Truth
Nancy Astor
Nasty Habits
Ned Kelly
Negatives
Never Let Go
Never Too Late to Mend
Next Victim
Nice Girl Like Me
Nicholas Nickleby▶
Night Ambush
Night and the City▶
Night Beat
Night Birds
Night Caller from Outer Space
The Night Has Eyes
Night of the Laughing Dead
Night Train to Munich▶
The Night Visitor
Night Watch
The Nightcomers
Nine Days a Queen▶
1984▶
99 Women

No Comebacks
No Love for Johnnie▶
No Surrender▶
No Trace
Norman Conquest
The Norman Conquests, Part 1: Table Manners▶
The Norman Conquests, Part 2: Living Together▶
The Norman Conquests, Part 3: Round and Round the Garden▶
Northanger Abbey
Nothing But the Night
Number 1 of the Secret Service
Nuts in May
O Lucky Man!▶
The Oblong Box
The Obsessed
Octopussy
The Odd Job
Odd Man Out▶
The Odessa File
Of Human Bondage
The Offence▶
Office Romances
Oh, Alfie
Oh, Mr. Porter
O.H.M.S.
The Old Curiosity Shop
Old Mother Riley's Ghosts
Old Spanish Custom
Oliver!▶
Oliver Twist▶
Oliver Twist
On Approval▶
On Her Majesty's Secret Service▶
One Day in the Life of Ivan Denisovich▶
One-Eyed Soldiers
One of Our Aircraft Is Missing▶
One Wish Too Many
Only Two Can Play▶
Open All Hours
Order of the Black Eagle
Orlando▶
Out of Season
Overture
Paid to Kill
Paper Marriage
Paper Mask
Paper Tiger
Paperhouse▶
Party! Party!
Pascali's Island▶
A Passage to India▶
The Passing of the Third Floor Back
Passport to Pimlico
Paul and Michelle
The People That Time Forgot
A Perfect Spy
Performance▶
Permission To Kill
Personal Services
The Persuaders
Peter's Friends
Phantom Fiend
The Phantom Light
Philby, Burgess and MacLean: Spy Scandal of the Century
The Pickwick Papers
Pictures
Piece of Cake
Pimpernel Smith
Pink Floyd: The Wall
The Pink Panther▶
The Pink Panther Strikes Again▶
Pink Strings and Sealing Wax
Playing Away
A Pocketful of Rye
Poldark▶

The Pope Must Diet
Porridge
Portrait of a Lady
Postmark for Danger
Postmark for Danger/ Quicksand
Power
Power Play
Prick Up Your Ears▶
Pride and Prejudice
Priest of Love
The Prime of Miss Jean Brodie▶
Prime Suspect▶
Prime Suspect 2▶
The Prince and the Pauper
The Princess and the Goblin
The Prisoner▶
The Prisoner: Arrival
A Private Function
Private Life of Don Juan
The Private Life of Henry VIII▶
The Private Life of Sherlock Holmes▶
The Private Secretary
Privates on Parade
Promise Her Anything
The Promoter▶
Providence▶
Psychomania
Psychopath
Pulp
Puppet on a Chain
The Pure Hell of St. Trinian's
Pursuit of the Graf Spee
Pygmalion▶
Quadrophenia▶
Quartet▶
Quatermass 2▶
Quatermass Conclusion
The Quatermass Experiment▶
Queen of Hearts▶
The Queen of Spades▶
Quest for Love
A Question of Attribution
Race for Life
Railway Children▶
The Rainbow▶
Rattle of a Simple Man
Reach for the Sky
The Red Shoes▶
Redneck
Reilly: Ace of Spies▶
The Remains of the Day▶
Rembrandt▶
Rentadick
Repulsion▶
The Return of the Musketeers
Return of the Soldier▶
Reunion▶
Revenge
Revolution
Rhodes
Rich and Strange
Richard III▶
Richard's Things
The Riddle of the Sands
Riff Raff▶
The Ring
Ring of Bright Water▶
Ripping Yarns
Rising Damp
Rita, Sue & Bob Too▶
Road to 1984
Roadhouse Girl
Robbery
Robbery Under Arms
Robin and Marian
Robin Hood: The Movie
Robin Hood...The Legend: Herne's Son
Robin Hood...The Legend: Robin Hood and the Sorcerer
Robin Hood...The Legend: The Swords of Wayland

Robin Hood...The Legend: The Time of the Wolf
Roboman
The Rocking Horse Winner
Rogue's Yarn
Romance with a Double Bass▶
Romantic Englishwoman▶
Romeo and Juliet▶
Room at the Top▶
Room to Let
A Room with a View▶
The Ruling Class▶
Rumpole of the Bailey
Rumpole of the Bailey: Rumpole's Return▶
The Runaway Bus
Running Blind
Ryan's Daughter
Saigon: Year of the Cat
Sailing Along
The Sailor Who Fell from Grace with the Sea
The Saint
Salaam Bombay!▶
The Salamander
Sammy & Rosie Get Laid▶
Sanders of the River▶
Sapphire▶
The Satanic Rites of Dracula
Saturn 3
Savage Messiah▶
Say Hello to Yesterday
Scandal▶
The Scarlet Pimpernel▶
The Scars of Dracula
School for Scandal
Scotland Yard Inspector
Scott of the Antarctic
Scream and Scream Again
Scream of Fear▶
Scrooge▶
Scrooge
Scrubbers
Scum▶
Sea Devils
Sea Wolves
Seance on a Wet Afternoon▶
Seaside Swingers
Sebastian
Second Best Secret Agent in the Whole Wide World
Second Chance
The Secret Adversary
The Secret Agent▶
The Secret Four
The Secret Garden
The Secret of the Loch
Secret Places
The Secret Policeman's Other Ball▶
Secret Policeman's Private Parts
Secrets
The Sender
Sense & Sensibility
A Sense of Freedom▶
The Servant▶
The 7 Brothers Meet Dracula
The Seventh Veil▶
Sexton Blake and the Hooded Terror
Shadey
The Shadow
The Shadow Man
Shadowlands▶
Shaka Zulu▶
Shattered
The Shell Seekers
Sherlock Holmes and the Incident at Victoria Falls
Sherlock Holmes: The Master Blackmailer
Shirley Valentine▶
The Shooting Party▶
A Shot in the Dark

The Shout▶
Shout at the Devil▶
Sidewalks of London▶
The Sign of Four
Silas Marner▶
The Silent Enemy
The Silent Mr. Sherlock
  Holmes
The Silent Passenger
Silent Scream
Simba▶
Sinbad and the Eye of the
  Tiger
Singleton's Pluck▶
Sirens▶
Sister Dora
Six Wives of Henry VIII▶
Skin Game
Slayground
Slipstream
The Smallest Show on Earth▶
The Snake Woman
Someone at the Door
Song of Freedom
S.O.S. Pacific
Space: 1999
Space: 1999—Alien Attack▶
The Spaniard's Curse
Spellbound
Spiral Staircase
Spitfire▶
Split Second
Spy in Black▶
Spy of Napoleon
The Spy Who Loved Me
Spy with a Cold Nose
Spymaker: The Secret Life of
  Ian Fleming
Stage Fright▶
The Stars Look Down▶
Starship
The Statue
Staying On
Stealing Heaven
Steaming
Stevie
A Stolen Face
Storm in a Teacup
Stormy Monday
Strange Awakening
The Strange Case of the End
  of Civilization as We Know
  It
Stranger in Town
Straw Dogs▶
The Stud
A Study in Terror▶
Subterfuge
Success is the Best Revenge
Sudden Terror
A Summer Story▶
Sunday, Bloody Sunday▶
Supergirl
Supergrass
Suspended Alibi
Svengali
Sweeney Todd: The Demon
  Barber of Fleet Street
Sweet William▶
Sword of Lancelot
Sword of Sherwood Forest
Sword of the Valiant
Taffin
Tale of a Vampire
A Tale of Two Cities▶
Tales from the Crypt▶
Tales of Beatrix Potter▶
Tales That Witness Madness
A Taste of Honey▶
Taste the Blood of Dracula
Tears in the Rain
The Tell-Tale Heart
The Temptress
Ten Little Indians
10 Rillington Place▶
Terronauts

The Terror
Terror Ship
The Terrornauts
Tess▶
That Sinking Feeling▶
Theatre of Blood▶
There's a Girl in My Soup
Things Happen at Night
Things to Come▶
Think Dirty
Thirteenth Day of Christmas
30 Is a Dangerous Age,
  Cynthia
The Thirty-Nine Steps
The 39 Steps▶
This Happy Breed▶
This Lightning Always Strikes
  Twice
This Sporting Life▶
Those Daring Young Men in
  Their Jaunty Jalopies
Those Fantastic Flying Fools
Those Glory, Glory Days
Those Magnificent Men in
  Their Flying Machines▶
Threads▶
Three of a Kind
Three Stops to Murder
The Three Weird Sisters
Thunder in the City▶
Thunderball
Tiger Bay▶
Time Bandits
Time for Murder
Time Lock
Tintorera...Tiger Shark
To See Such Fun
To Sir, with Love
Tom Brown's School Days
Tom Brown's School Days▶
Tom Jones▶
Tom Thumb▶
Tomb of Ligeia▶
Tomb of the Undead
Too Many Crooks
Torture Garden
Touch Me Not
Tough Guy
Tower of Evil
Tower of Terror
A Town Called Hell
Traffik▶
Transatlantic Tunnel
Transmutations
Trap
Treasure Island
Treasure of Monte Cristo
Triple Cross▶
Triple Echo
The Triumph of Sherlock
  Holmes
Truth About Women
Tunes of Glory▶
Turtle Diary▶
21 Days
Two-Way Stretch
The Unbreakable Alibi
The Uncanny
Under Capricorn
Under Milk Wood
Under Suspicion
Under the Red Robe
The Unearthly Stranger
Uneasy Terms
Unexplained Laughter
Unholy Four
Unicorn
Unmasked Part 25
Unmasking the Idol
The Unstoppable Man
Unsuitable Job for a Woman
Up the Creek
Utz

Valentino
Valley of the Eagles
Vampire Circus
The Vampire Lovers
The Vampyr
Vampyres
Vault of Horror
Vendetta for the Saint
Venom
Venus in Furs
Veronico Cruz
A Very British Coup▶
The Very Edge
The Vicious Circle
Victim▶
A View to a Kill
Village of the Damned▶
The V.I.P.'s▶
The Virgin and the Gypsy
The Virgin Soldiers
The Virgin Witch
The Vision
A Voyage' Round My Father▶
Wagner: The Complete Epic
Wagner: The Movie
Waltz of the Toreadors▶
War Lover
The Warriors
Water
Water Babies
Watership Down
The Way Out
We Dive at Dawn▶
We Think the World of You▶
Wellington: The Duel Scandal
Wetherby▶
What a Carve-Up!
What's Good for the Goose
When Dinosaurs Ruled the
  Earth
When the Whales Came
When the Wind Blows▶
When Thief Meets Thief
Where Angels Fear to Tread▶
Where the Bullets Fly
While I Live
Whiskey Galore▶
The Whistle Blower▶
Whistle Down the Wind▶
White Fire
Whoops Apocalypse
Who's Who
The Wicked Lady
Wild Geese
Wild Geese 2
Windom's Way▶
Winner Takes All
The Winslow Boy▶
Winter Flight
Wish You Were Here▶
Withnail and I▶
Without a Clue
Woman in Black
Wombling Free
Women in Love▶
Wonderland▶
Wonderwall: The Movie
A World Apart▶
The World is Full of Married
  Men
The World of Suzie Wong
The World Owes Me a Living
The Wreck of the Mary Deare
The Wrong Arm of the Law▶
The Wrong Box▶
Wuthering Heights
Xtro
A Year in Provence▶
Yellow Submarine▶
Yesterday's Hero
You Only Live Twice
Young and Innocent▶
The Young Ones
Young Winston▶
Yuri Nosenko, KGB
A Zed & Two Noughts▶

Zeppelin

Canadian

Abducted
The Adjuster
The Agency
American Boyfriends
The Amityville Curse
And Then You Die▶
Angel Square
Angela
Anne of Avonlea▶
Anne of Green Gables▶
The Apprenticeship of Duddy
  Kravitz▶
Atlantic City▶
Babar: The Movie
The Bay Boy
Beautiful Dreamers
Being at Home with Claude
The Best of the Kids in the
  Hall
The Best of the Monsters
Beyond the Silhouette
The Big Crimewave
Big Meat Eater
Black Christmas
Black Robe▶
Blades of Courage
Blood Relations
Blood Relatives
The Bloody Brood
Boy in Blue
Breaking All the Rules
The Brood
Buffalo Jump▶
Bullies
Busted Up
By Design
Bye Bye Blues▶
Cafe Romeo
Candy Mountain
Cathy's Curse
The Changeling
Christina
Circle of Two
City Boy▶
City on Fire
Class of 1984
Clearcut
Close to Home
Cold Comfort
Concrete Angels
Confidential
Cordelia
Covergirl
Cross Country
Curtains
Dan Candy's Law
Dancing in the Dark
Daughter of Death
Dead Ringers▶
Death Ship
Death Weekend
Deathdream
The Decline of the American
  Empire▶
Deranged▶
Dirty Tricks
Disappearance
Distant Thunder
Dr. Bethune▶
Dog Pound Shuffle▶
The Dog Who Stopped the
  War
A Doll's House▶
Double Identity
The Double Negative
Drying Up the Streets
Eddie and the Cruisers 2:
  Eddie Lives!
Eliza's Horoscope
Family Viewing▶
Fatal Attraction

Fight for Your Life
Final Assignment
Find the Lady
Fish Hawk
Friends, Lovers & Lunatics
Full Circle
Funeral Home
The Funny Farm
Gas
The Girl in Blue
Girls on the Road
Glory Enough for All: The
  Discovery of Insulin
The Godsend
Going Berserk
Goldenrod
The Grey Fox▶
The Groundstar Conspiracy▶
The Gunfighters
The Gunrunner
Happy Birthday to Me
Harry Tracy
Heartaches▶
Heaven on Earth
Heavenly Bodies
High Ballin'
High Country
Highpoint
Hockey Night
Hog Wild
The Housekeeper
Humongous
Iceman▶
If You Could See What I Hear
In Celebration▶
In Praise of Older Women
In Trouble
Incubus
Into the Fire
Iron Eagle 2
I've Heard the Mermaids
  Singing▶
Jesus of Montreal▶
John and the Missus
Joshua Then and Now▶
Journey
Journey into Fear
Keeper
The Kidnapping of the
  President
Killing 'em Softly
King Solomon's Treasure
Ladies of the Lotus
Lantern Hill
Last Chase
Leolo
Les Bons Debarras
Lies My Father Told Me▶
The Little Girl Who Lives
  Down the Lane
Loose Screws
Lost
Lost in the Barrens
Love Songs
Loyalties
A Man, a Woman, and a Bank
The Man Inside
Maria Chapdelaine
Martin's Day
Masala
The Mask
Mazes and Monsters
Meatballs
Melanie
Middle Age Crazy
Mindfield
Mon Oncle Antoine▶
Murder by Decree▶
Murder by Phone
My American Cousin▶
My Bloody Valentine
My Pleasure Is My Business
My Side of the Mountain
My Twentieth Century▶
'Neath Canadian Skies
Next of Kin

Night Breed
Night Zoo
Nikki, the Wild Dog of the
    North
90 Days▶
North of the Border
Northern Extremes
The Nutcracker Prince
The Odyssey of the Pacific
Oedipus Rex
Of Unknown Origin
Oh, What a Night
One Night Stand
One Plus One
Outrageous!▶
Outside Chance of Maximillian
    Glick
Palais Royale
Pandemonium
A Paper Wedding▶
Paperback Hero
Phobia
Pick-Up Summer
Playgirl Killer
Porky's
Porky's 2: The Next Day
Porky's Revenge
Power Play
Princes in Exile
Prom Night
Psycho Girls
The Pyx▶
Quiet Day In Belfast▶
Rabid
Red Blooded American Girl
The Reincarnate
Reno and the Doc
Rituals
Roadkill
Rock 'n' Roll Nightmare
Salmonberries
The Savage Woman
Scanners
Scanners 2: The New Order
Seizure
Shoot
Showdown at Williams Creek
Silence of the North
The Silent Partner▶
Slipstream
Spacehunter: Adventures in
    the Forbidden Zone
Spasms
Speaking Parts▶
Spirit Rider▶
Spring Fever
Starship Invasions
Storm
Straight for the Heart
Strangers in Good Company▶
Surrogate
Tales from Avonlea, Vol. 1:
    The Journey Begins▶
Termini Station
They Came from Within
32 Short Films About Glenn
    Gould▶
Threshold
Trap
Tribute
Tulips
Unfinished Business
Utilities
Videodrome
The Vindicator
Virgin Queen of St. Francis
    High
Visiting Hours
The War Boy
Wedding in White
Where the Spirit Lives
A Whisper to a Scream
Whispering City▶
Why Shoot the Teacher▶
Wild Horse Hank
The Woman Inside

Xtro 2: The Second Encounter
Your Ticket Is No Longer Valid

Cantonese
Naked Killer

Chinese
The Armour of God
A Better Tomorrow
A Better Tomorrow, Part 2
Breaking with Old Ideas
China, My Sorrow
Chinese Connection
The Go-Masters▶
The Horse Thief▶
Jackie Chan's Police Force
Ju Dou▶
Lai Shi: China's Last Eunuch
Life on a String
Mission Kiss and Kill
Paper Marriage
Raise the Red Lantern▶
Red Sorghum▶
Return of the Dragon
The Silk Road
Slaughter in San Francisco
Song of the Exile
The Story of Qui Ju▶
Thousand Mile Escort
Yellow Earth

Columbian
Maria

Czech
All My Good Countrymen
Closely Watched Trains▶
Death is Called Engelchen▶
Diamonds of the Night▶
Ecstasy
The Firemen's Ball▶
Larks on a String▶
Loves of a Blonde▶
New Pastures
On the Comet▶
The Original Fabulous
    Adventures of Baron
    Munchausen
A Prayer for Katarina
    Horovitzova▶
The Report on the Party and
    the Guests▶
The Shop on Main Street▶
Sweet Light in a Dark Room▶
Tereza▶
Transport from Paradise

Danish
Babette's Feast▶
Day of Wrath▶
The Element of Crime
Emma's Shadow▶
Friends Forever▶
Gertrud▶
Hunger
Kiss Daddy Goodnight
Ladies on the Rocks
Leaves from Satan's Book
Memories of a Marriage▶
The Night Visitor
Ordet▶
Pelle the Conqueror▶
Twist & Shout▶
The Wolf at the Door
A World of Strangers▶
You Are Not Alone

Dutch
Amsterdamned

Army Brats
The Assault▶
Broken Mirrors
Cold Blood
Dear Boys
Egg
Fatal Error
A Flight of Rainbirds
The 4th Man▶
In for Treatment▶
Keetje Tippei
The Lift
The Man Inside
On Top of the Whale
The Pointsman
Question of Silence▶
Rembrandt—1669
Soldier of Orange▶
Spetters
To Play or To Die
Turkish Delights
The Vanishing▶

Filipino
Beast of the Yellow Night
Beyond Atlantis
Blind Rage
Brides of the Beast
Caged Fury
Circle of Fear
The Deadly and the Beautiful
Devil Woman
Horror of the Blood Monsters
Night of the Cobra Woman
Once Before I Die
Perfumed Nightmare▶
Raw Force
Stickfighter
Stryker
Terror is a Man
The Thirsty Dead
Turumba▶
Twilight People
The Vampire Hookers
The Vampire People

Finnish
Ariel▶
The Day the Earth Froze
Leningrad Cowboys Go
    America
The Match Factory Girl▶

French
A Nous la Liberte▶
Act of Aggression
Adorable Julia
After the Fall of New York
Akermania, Vol. 1▶
Alberto Express
Ali Baba and the 40 Thieves▶
Alice in Wonderland
Alphaville▶
The American Friend▶
And God Created Woman
And Hope to Die
And Now My Love
Andy Warhol's Dracula▶
Andy Warhol's Frankenstein
Angele▶
Another Man, Another Chance
As If It Were Raining
Assassination of Trotsky
The Associate
Atlantic City▶
Attack of the Robots
Au Revoir Les Enfants▶
The Avenger
Babar: The Movie
Babette's Feast▶
Back to the Wall
The Baker's Wife▶

Band of Outsiders
Bandits
Barjo
Basileus Quartet▶
The Battle of Austerlitz
The Battle of El Alamein
Baxter
The Bear▶
Beatrice▶
Beau Pere▶
Beauty and the Beast▶
Beethoven
Beethoven's Nephew
Bernadette
The Best Way
Betty Blue▶
Between Heaven and Earth
The Big Grab
Bilitis
Bim/Dream of the Wild Horses
Bizarre Bizarre▶
Black and White in Color▶
Black Orpheus▶
Black Tights
Blood and Black Lace
The Blood of Others
Blue Country
Blue Jeans
Bluebeard▶
Bob le Flambeur▶
Bonjour Tristesse▶
Borsalino▶
Boudu Saved from
    Drowning▶
Boy Meets Girl▶
Boyfriends & Girlfriends
The Brain
Breathless▶
The Bride Is Much Too
    Beautiful
The Bride Wore Black▶
Buffet Froid▶
By the Blood of Others▶
Caged Women
Camille Claudel▶
Candy Mountain
Captain Blackjack
Carnival in Flanders▶
Cartouche▶
Castle of Blood
Castle of the Living Dead
Cat and Mouse▶
The Cat o' Nine Tails
Catch Me a Spy
Catherine & Co.
Cathy's Curse
Cesar▶
Cesar & Rosalie▶
Charles et Lucie▶
Charlie Bravo
Children of Paradise▶
Chloe in the Afternoon▶
Choice of Arms
Christ Stopped at Eboli▶
Circle of Love
Circonstances Attenuantes
Circus Angel▶
City of Joy
Claire's Knee▶
Cleo from 5 to 7▶
The Clockmaker▶
Cobra
A Coeur Joie
Cold Sweat
Comment Ca Va?
Confidentially Yours▶
The Conformist▶
Conquest of Mycene
Contempt▶
Conversation Piece▶
Coup de Grace
Coup de Torchon▶
Cousin, Cousine▶
The Cousins▶
Crainquebille▶
Crazy for Love

The Crazy Ray▶
The Crime of Monsieur
    Lange▶
Cross My Heart
The Cry of the Owl
Cyrano de Bergerac▶
Daddy Nostalgia▶
Damage▶
Dangerous Liaisons
Danton▶
Daughters of Darkness▶
The Day and the Hour
Day for Night▶
A Day in the Country▶
The Day the Sky Exploded
The Daydreamer
Deadly Sting
The Deadly Trap
Death Watch▶
The Decameron▶
Delicatessen▶
Delusions of Grandeur
Devil in the Flesh▶
The Devil's Commandment
The Diabolical Dr. Z
Diabolically Yours
Diabolique▶
Diary of a Chambermaid▶
Diary of a Country Priest▶
Dirty Dishes▶
Dirty Hands
The Discreet Charm of the
    Bourgeoisie▶
Diva▶
Dr. Bethune▶
Dog Day
Donkey Skin▶
Dos Cruces en Danger Pass▶
Double Agents
Double Identity
The Double Life of Veronique
Dracula & Son
Dressmaker
Duke of the Derby
Dust▶
The Earrings of Madame
    De...▶
Edith & Marcel
The Eighties
The Elegant Criminal
Elena and Her Men▶
Elle Voit des Nains Partout
Elsa, Elsa
Emmanuelle
Emmanuelle 4
Emmanuelle 5
Emmanuelle & Joanna
Emmanuelle in Bangkok
Emmanuelle in Soho
Emmanuelle in the Country
Emmanuelle on Taboo Island
Emmanuelle, the Joys of a
    Woman
Empty Canvas
End of Desire
Enigma
Entr'acte
Entre-Nous▶
Erendira
Erotic Escape
Et La Tenoresse?...Bordel!
Eternal Return
The Eyes, the Mouth
Fahrenheit 451▶
Fanny▶
Fantastic Planet▶
Fatal Fix
The Favor, the Watch, & the
    Very Big Fish
Fellini's Roma
Femmes de Paris
Fernandel the Dressmaker
Field of Honor
The Fire Within▶
First Name: Carmen▶
Forbidden Games▶

Four Adventures of Reinette and Mirabelle►
Four Bags Full
The 400 Blows►
France/Tour/Detour/Deux/ Enfants►
Frantic►
Franz
French Can-Can►
The French Detective►
The French Touch
The French Way
From Hell to Victory
Full Moon in Paris
The Game is Over
Gervaise►
Get Out Your Handkerchiefs►
The Gift
Girl in His Pocket
A Girl on Her Own
Godard/Truffaut Shorts
Godson►
Going Places►
The Golden Coach►
Goliath and the Dragon
Grain of Sand►
Grand Illusion►
The Great War
The Green Room►
Hail Mary
The Hairdresser's Husband►
The Hands of Orlac
Hanna K.
Happy New Year►
Harem
Harvest►
Head of the Family
Head Over Heels►
Heart of a Nation►
Heat of Desire
Hercules Against the Moon Men
Here and Elsewhere
High Heels
Hiroshima, Mon Amour►
The Holes
Holiday Hotel
Honor Among Thieves
The Horror Chamber of Dr. Faustus►
The Horse of Pride
Hothead
Howling 2: Your Sister is a Werewolf
I Killed Rasputin
I Love All of You
I Sent a Letter to My Love►
Icy Breasts►
In the Realm of the Senses►
Indochine►
Infernal Trio
The Invaders
Investigation
Invitation au Voyage
Is Paris Burning?►
Istanbul
It Happened in the Park
It Means That to Me
Italian Straw Hat►
J'Accuse►
Jacko & Lise
Jacquot
Jailbird's Vacation
Je Tu Il Elle
Jean de Florette►
Jenny Lamour
Jesus of Montreal►
Josepha►
Jour de Fete►
Journey Beneath the Desert
Journey to the Lost City
The Joy of Knowledge
Judex
The Judge and the Assassin►
Jules and Jim►
Jupiter's Thigh

Just Another Pretty Face
Kapo►
The Killing Game
The King of Hearts►
The Klutz
La Balance►
La Belle Noiseuse►
La Bete Humaine►
La Boum
La Cage aux Folles►
La Cage aux Folles 2
La Cage aux Folles 3: The Wedding
La Chartreuse de Parme
La Chevre►
La Chienne►
La Chute de la Maison Usher►
La Discrete►
La Femme Nikita►
La Grande Vadrouille►
La Lectrice
La Marseillaise►
La Merveilleuse Visite
La Nuit de Varennes►
La Passante►
La Petite Sirene►
La Ronde►
La Rupture
La Symphonie Pastorale►
La Truite►
La Vengeance d'une Femme►
The Lacemaker►
Lady Chatterley's Lover
Lady L
L'Age D'Or►
Landscape in the Mist►
L'Anne Sainte
L'Annee des Meduses►
L'Argent►
The Last Metro►
Last Tango in Paris►
The Last Winters
Last Year at Marienbad►
L'Atalante►
Le Bal►
Le Beau Mariage►
Le Beau Serge►
Le Bonheur
Le Boucher►
Le Bourgeois Gentilhomme
Le Cas du Dr. Laurent►
Le Cavaleur
Le Chat►
Le Complot►
Le Corbeau►
Le Crabe Tambour►
Le Dernier Combat►
Le Doulos►
Le Gendarme de Saint-Tropez
Le Gentleman D'Epsom
Le Grand Chemin►
Le Joli Mai
Le Jour Se Leve►
Le Magnifique
Le Million►
Le Petit Amour►
Le Plaisir►
Le Repos du Guerrier
Le Secret►
Le Sex Shop►
L'Ecole Buisoniere
Leon Morin, Priest
Leonor
Les Assassins de L'Ordre
Les Aventuriers
Les Biches►
Les Carabiniers►
Les Comperes►
Les Enfants Terrible►
Les Grandes Gueules
Les Miserables►
Les Mistons►
Les Nuits Fauves►
Les Rendez-vous D'Anna
Les Violons du Bal►
Les Visiteurs du Soir►

L'Etat Sauvage►
Letters from My Windmill►
Letters to an Unknown Lover
L'Homme Blesse►
License to Kill
Life and Nothing But►
Life Is a Long Quiet River►
Liliom
The Little Thief►
Little World of Don Camillo►
L'Odeur des Fauves►
Lola►
Lola Montes►
Loulou►
Love and the Frenchwoman►
A Love in Germany
Love on the Run►
Love Songs
Love Without Pity
The Lover►
The Lovers►
Lovers Like Us
The Loves of Hercules
The Lower Depths►
Lucky Luciano
Lumiere
Madame Bovary►
Madame Rosa►
Mademoiselle
The Mahabharata
Maids of Wilko
Make Room for Tomorrow►
Mama Dracula
Mama, There's a Man in Your Bed►
A Man and a Woman►
A Man and a Woman: 20 Years Later
Man from Nowhere
A Man in Love►
The Man in the Raincoat
Man in the Silk Hat
Man on Fire
The Man Who Loved Women►
Manon of the Spring►
Maria Chapdelaine►
Maria Chapdelaine
Marius►
A Married Woman►
Marry Me, Marry Me►
Martin Luther
Masculine Feminine►
Max, Mon Amour
May Fools►
Melodie en Sous-Sol
Menage►
The Milky Way►
Mill of the Stone Women
Minnesota Clay
Mississippi Mermaid►
Mr. Hulot's Holiday►
Mr. Peek-A-Boo
Modigliani
Mon Oncle►
Mon Oncle D'Amerique►
The Mongols
The Monocle
Monsieur Hire►
Monsieur Vincent►
Moon in the Gutter
Morgan the Pirate
Mouchette►
Murder at 45 R.P.M.
Muriel►
Murmur of the Heart►
My Best Friend's Girl►
My Father's Glory►
My Life to Live►
My Mother's Castle►
My New Partner
My Night at Maud's►
My Other Husband
The Mystery of Alexina
Nais►
The Name of the Rose

Nana►
Napoleon►
Napoleon
Next Summer►
Next Year If All Goes Well
Night and Day►
Night Flight from Moscow
1900►
No Fear, No Die
No Problem
A Nos Amours►
Nous N'Irons Plus au Bois
Nouvelle Vague
Numero Deux
The Nun
Oasis of the Zombies
An Occurrence at Owl Creek Bridge►
Oldest Profession
Olivier, Olivier►
One Deadly Summer►
One Sings, the Other Doesn't
One Wild Moment
One Woman or Two
The Outside Man
Overseas: Three Women with Man Trouble►
Pain in the A—►
Panique►
Pantaloons
Parade►
Pardon Mon Affaire►
Pardon Mon Affaire, Too!
Paris Belongs to Us►
Paris, Texas►
The Passion of Joan of Arc►
Passion of Love►
Pattes Blanches
Paul and Michelle
Pauline at the Beach►
The Peking Blond
Pepe Le Moko►
Peppermint Soda►
Peril►
The Perils of Gwendoline
The Perverse Countess
Petit Con
Phaedra
Phantom of Liberty►
Pickpocket►
Picnic on the Grass►
Pierrot le Fou►
The Plague
Planets Against Us
Playtime►
Poil de Carotte
Police
Possession
Pouvoir Intime
Princess Academy
Princess Tam Tam►
Prix de Beaute►
Prize of Peril
A Propos de Nice►
The Proud Ones
The Purple Taxi
Quartet►
Quatorze Juliet
Quest for Fire►
Qui Etes Vous, Mr. Sorge?
Ramparts of Clay►
Ran►
Rape of Love►
The Rape of the Sabines
The Rascals
Ravishing Idiot
The Red and the Black►
The Red Balloon►
Red Balloon/Occurrence at Owl Creek Bridge►
Red Kiss►
Red Sun
Rendez-Moi Ma Peau
Rendez-vous►
The Respectful Prostitute
The Return of Dr. Mabuse

The Return of Martin Guerre►
The Return of the Musketeers
Return of the Tall Blond Man With One Black Shoe
Reunion►
Ricco
Rider on the Rain►
Rififi►
The Rise of Louis XIV►
The River►
Road to Salina►
Roads to the South
Robert et Robert►
Round Midnight►
The Sacrifice►
Salut l'Artiste►
Samson and the 7 Miracles of the World
Sand and Blood
Sans Soleil►
Scene of the Crime►
Scoumoune
Secret Agent Super Dragon
Seven Deadly Sins►
The Sheep Has Five Legs
Sheer Madness►
Shoot the Piano Player►
A Simple Story►
Sincerely Charlotte►
Six Fois Deux/Sur et Sous la Communication►
Six in Paris
The Slap
Small Change►
Smiling Madame Beudet/The Seashell and the Clergyman►
Soft and Hard
The Soft Skin►
Sois Belle et Tais-Toi
Soldat Duroc...Ca Va Etre Ta Fete!
Son of Samson
The Sorrow and the Pity►
Soviet Spy
Special Police
Spirits of the Dead►
Spoiled Children
Sputnik
State of Siege►
Stay As You Are
Stolen Kisses►
Stormy Waters
The Story of a Love Story
Story of Adele H.►
The Story of Women►
Subway
Sugar Cane Alley►
Summer►
A Sunday in the Country►
Sundays & Cybele►
Swann in Love
Swashbuckler
Sweet Ecstasy
Swimming Pool
Sylvia and the Phantom►
Sympathy for the Devil
A Tale of Springtime
The Tall Blond Man with One Black Shoe►
Tamango
Tartuffe
Tatie Danielle►
Tchao Pantin►
Ten Days Wonder
The Tenant►
Terror of Rome Against the Son of Hercules
Tess►
The Testament of Dr. Cordelier►
The Testament of Orpheus►
That Man from Rio
That Naughty Girl
There Goes Barder
Therese►

French

The Things of Life▶
36 Fillete▶
This Man Must Die▶
This Special Friendship
This Sweet Sickness
The 317th Platoon▶
Three Men and a Cradle▶
Tiger of the Seven Seas
Time Out for Love
Toni▶
Too Beautiful for You
Too Pretty to Be Honest
Too Shy to Try
Topaze▶
Toto le Heros▶
Tournament
Tous les Matins du Monde▶
Toute Une Nuit▶
The Trial▶
Tricheurs
Triple Cross▶
Tristana▶
Trois Couleurs: Blanc▶
Trois Couleurs: Bleu▶
Trois Couleurs: Rouge▶
12 Plus 1▶
Twist
Two English Girls▶
Two of Us▶
Umbrellas of Cherbourg▶
Un Chien Andalou▶
Un Coeur en Hiver
Uncle Tom's Cabin
Under Satan's Sun▶
Under the Roofs of Paris▶
Une Jeunesse▶
Uranus▶
Utopia
Vagabond▶
The Valley Obscured by the
   Clouds
Van Gogh▶
The Vanishing▶
A Very Curious Girl
A Very Private Affair
Vincent, Francois, Paul and
   the Others▶
Violette▶
Viva Maria!
Volpone▶
Voulez-Vous Danser Avec
   Moi?
Voyage en Balloon
Voyage-Suprise▶
Voyager▶
Wages of Fear▶
The Wanderer
We Will Not Enter the Forest▶
Web of the Spider
Wedding in Blood▶
A Wedding in Galilee▶
Weekend▶
Well-Digger's Daughter▶
Where the Hot Wind Blows
Where the Sky Begins
Widow Couderc▶
The Wild Child▶
Window Shopping
Without Warning
The Wolf at the Door
A Woman is a Woman▶
The Woman Next Door▶
Woman Times Seven
The Women
The Wonders of Aladdin
The Would-Be Gentleman
Yesterday, Today and
   Tomorrow▶
Your Turn Darling
Z▶
Zazie dans le Metro▶
Zero for Conduct▶
Zero for Conduct/Taris/A
   Propos de Nice
Zombie Lake
Zou Zou

German

Aguirre, the Wrath of God▶
Ali: Fear Eats the Soul▶
The American Friend▶
The American Soldier
Among the Cinders
Andy Warhol's Frankenstein
Angry Harvest▶
Anita, Dances of Vice
The Avenger
Backstairs
Bagdad Cafe▶
Baron Munchausen▶
Battleforce
The Berlin Affair
Berlin Alexanderplatz▶
The Bitter Tears of Petra von
   Kant
The Black Abbot
Black Beauty
A Black Veil for Lisa
Blood and Black Lace
The Blue Angel▶
The Blue Hour
The Blue Light▶
The Blum Affair
Boarding School
The Brain
The Cabinet of Dr. Caligari▶
The Captain from Koepenick
The Castle▶
The Castle of Fu Manchu
The Cat o' Nine Tails
The Catamount Killing
Cave of the Living Dead
Celeste▶
Charm of La Boheme
The Children
Chinese Boxes
Chinese Roulette
Christiane F.▶
Circus of Fear
Club Extinction
Code Name Alpha
Codename: Wildgeese
Colonel Redl▶
Commandos
The Conformist▶
Congress Dances
The Cop & the Girl
Count Dracula
Coup de Grace
Creature with the Blue Hand
Crimes of Dr. Mabuse▶
Curse of the Yellow Snake
The Damned
Dandelions
Das Boot▶
Das Testament des Dr.
   Mabuse▶
Daughter of Death
Daughters of Darkness▶
David▶
Dead Eyes of London
Deadline
Deadly Game
Death Watch▶
The Decameron▶
Deep End▶
Despair▶
Deutschland im Jahre Null▶
The Devil in Silk
Diary of a Lost Girl▶
Die Grosse Freiheit Nr. 7
Dr. Mabuse the Gambler▶
Dr. Mabuse vs. Scotland Yard
Door with the Seven Locks
Dorian Gray
Drachenfutter▶
Dracula vs. Frankenstein
Effi Briest▶
Erendira
Europa, Europa▶
Every Man for Himself & God
   Against All▶

Fabulous Adventures of
   Baron Munchausen
Faraway, So Close!
Faust▶
Fight for Gold
First Love
First Spaceship on Venus▶
Fitzcarraldo▶
Flatfoot
For Your Love Only
Forger of London
Forget Mozart
Fortune's Fool
Fox and His Friends▶
F.P. 1
F.P. 1 Doesn't Answer
Frankenstein '80
Frozen Alive
Full Hearts & Empty Pockets
Geheimakte WB1
Germany in Autumn
The Goalie's Anxiety at the
   Penalty Kick▶
Gods of the Plague▶
Goetz von Berlichingen
The Golem▶
Hanussen▶
The Head
Heart of Glass▶
Heidi▶
Homecoming▶
Horrors of Spider Island
The House of 1000 Dolls
Hunted!
The Indian Scarf
The Inheritors
Inn on the River
The Innocent
Invisible Adversaries
The Invisible Dr. Mabuse▶
Journey to the Lost City
Joyless Street▶
Jud Suess▶
The Jumper
Jungle Warriors
Just a Gigolo
Kameradschaft▶
Kamikaze '89▶
King, Queen, Knave▶
Kings of the Road—In the
   Course of Time▶
Knife in the Head
Kolberg
Kriemhilde's Revenge▶
La Passante▶
The Lacemaker▶
The Last Five Days
The Last Laugh▶
The Last Tomahawk
Les Miserables▶
Les Rendez-vous D'Anna
Let It Rock
Lethal Obsession
The Lost Honor of Katharina
   Blum▶
The Lost One
A Love in Germany
M▶
The Mad Executioners
Maedchen in Uniform▶
Malou
The Man Inside
A Man Like Eva▶
Mark of the Devil
Mark of the Devil 2
The Marriage of Maria Braun▶
Master Touch
Me and Him
Men...▶
Menschenfrauen
Metropolis▶
Mission Stardust
Mr. Superinvisible
The Monster of London City
Moon 44

Mother Kusters Goes to
   Heaven▶
Mozart: A Childhood
   Chronicle▶
My Father is Coming
The Mysterious Magician
Naked in the Night
The Name of the Rose
The Nasty Girl▶
Night Flight from Moscow
1900▶
99 Women
No Survivors, Please
Nosferatu▶
Oldest Profession
One Arabian Night▶
The Oppermann Family
An Orphan Boy of Vienna
Othello
Out of Order
Pandora's Box▶
Paris, Texas▶
Passion
The Pedestrian▶
The Phantom of Soho
Possession
The Practice of Love
The Princess and the
   Swineherd
Q Ships
Querelle
Requiem for Dominic▶
The Return of Dr. Mabuse
Reunion▶
The Revolt of Job▶
Roboman
Rosa Luxemburg
Rosalie Goes Shopping▶
Sacred Mountain/White
   Flame▶
Salmonberries
Savage Attraction
The Scarlet Letter▶
Schnelles Geld
The Scorpion Woman
Secret Agent Super Dragon
Secret of the Black Trunk
Secrets of a Soul
The Seducers
Seduction: The Cruel Woman
The Serpent's Egg
Shattered▶
Sheer Madness▶
Sherlock Holmes and the
   Deadly Necklace
Shocking Asia
Siegfried▶
Singing the Blues in Red▶
Slavers
Spiders▶
Spies▶
Spring Symphony
The Squeaker
State of Things▶
The Stationmaster's Wife
The Strange Countess
Stranger than Paradise▶
Strangler of Blackmoor Castle
Strangler of the Tower
The Street
Stroszek▶
Student of Prague▶
A Study in Terror▶
Sugarbaby▶
Swann in Love
Swiss Conspiracy
Symphony in the Mountains
Taxi zum Klo▶
Teenage Wolfpack
They Were So Young
'38: Vienna Before the Fall
The Thousand Eyes of Dr.
   Mabuse
The Three Penny Opera▶
Tiefland
The Tin Drum▶

Tonio Kroger
The Torture Chamber of Dr.
   Sadism
Tower of Screaming Virgins
Traenen in Florenz
Triumph of the Will
Tromba, the Tiger Man
Uncle Tom's Cabin
Utz
The Vampire Happening
Vampyr▶
Variety▶
Veronika Voss▶
Via Appia
Voyager▶
The Wannsee Conference▶
Warning Shadows▶
Waxworks▶
Web of the Spider
The Werewolf vs. the Vampire
   Woman
Westfront 1918▶
Where the Green Ants Dream
The White Rose▶
Why Does Herr R. Run
   Amok?
Wings of Desire▶
A Woman in Flames▶
Woman in the Moon
Woyzeck▶
The Wrong Move
Year of the Quiet Sun▶
Zentropa

Greek

The Brave Bunch
A Dream of Passion
Emmanuelle's Daughter
The Enchantress
Girl in Black
Iphigenia
Landscape in the Mist▶
A Matter of Dignity
The Mediterranean in Flames
Never on Sunday▶
Phaedra
Restless
Stella
Torpedo Attack
Young Aphrodites

Hong Kong

The Amsterdam Connection
The Amsterdam Kill
The Blazing Ninja
Clash of the Ninja
Crack Shadow Boxers
Empire of Spiritual Ninja
Farewell My Concubine
Goliathon
Hard-Boiled
Infra-Man
Just Like Weather▶
The Killer▶
Ninja Champion
Ninja Destroyer
Ninja Exterminators
Ninja Fantasy
Ninja Hunt
The Reincarnation of Golden
   Lotus▶
Rouge

Hungarian

Adoption▶
After the Revolution
Almanac of Fall
Another Way▶
Bad Guys
Brady's Escape
Cat's Play
Cold Days

Colonel Redl▶
Father▶
The Fifth Seal
Flowers of Reverie
The Girl▶
Hanussen▶
A Happy New Year!
A Hungarian Fairy Tale▶
Hungarian Rhapsody▶
Lily in Love
The Little Valentino
Love▶
Love Film
Mephisto▶
The Midas Touch
My Twentieth Century▶
Nice Neighbor▶
Nobody's Daughter
Oh, Bloody Life!
The Princess and the Goblin
The Red and the White▶
Red Earth
The Revolt of Job▶
Riddance▶
The Round Up
Sinbad
Stand Off
Sunday Daughters▶
Time Stands Still▶
Wagner: The Complete Epic
Wagner: The Movie

Indian

The Adversary
Aparajito▶
Bombay Talkie
Company Limited
Days and Nights in the Forest
Deadly Thief
The Deceivers
Devi▶
Distant Thunder▶
The Home and the World▶
The Householder
Mere Jeevan Saathi
Pather Panchali▶
Salaam Bombay!▶
Spices▶
Two Daughters▶
The World of Apu▶

Irish

Broth of a Boy
Cal▶
The Commitments▶
The Courier
The Crying Game▶
Danny Boy▶
Eat the Peach
In the Name of the Father▶
Into the West▶
Men of Ireland
My Left Foot▶
Paddy
Playboy of the Western World
Quackser Fortune Has a
  Cousin in the Bronx▶
The Snapper▶

Israeli

Beyond the Walls
Children of Rage
Cup Final
Dead End Street
Diamonds
Double Edge
Drifting
Eagles Attack at Dawn
Echoes of Conflict
Escape to the Sun
Goodbye, New York
Hill 24 Doesn't Answer▶

The House on Chelouche
  Street
I Don't Give a Damn
Intimate Story
Iron Eagle 2
Justine
Kuni Lemel in Tel Aviv
The Last Winter
Late Summer Blues
Madame Rosa▶
Madman
My Michael▶
Noa at Seventeen▶
Sallah▶
They Were Ten
Unsettled Land
The Wooden Gun

Italian

Accatone!▶
Ace High
Acqua e Sapone
Adios, Hombre
After the Fall of New York
After the Fox
Aladdin
Alfredo, Alfredo
Alien Contamination
All Screwed Up▶
All the Way, Boys
Allegro Non Troppo▶
Allonsanfan▶
Almost Human
Alone Against Rome
Amarcord▶
Amore▶
And the Ship Sails On▶
Andy Warhol's Dracula▶
Andy Warhol's Frankenstein
An Angel for Satan
Angel in a Taxi
Any Gun Can Play
Arabian Nights▶
Arena
Assassination of Trotsky
Assault on Agathon
Assignment Outer Space
Assunta Spina
Atlas in the Land of the
  Cyclops
Atom Age Vampire
Ator the Fighting Eagle
Augustine of Hippo▶
Autopsy
The Avenger
Ay, Carmela!▶
The Bacchantes
Bad Man's River
Bandits of Orgosolo
Barbarian Queen
Barbarian Queen 2: The
  Empress Strikes Back
The Barbarians
Basileus Quartet▶
The Battle of Algiers▶
The Battle of Austerlitz
The Battle of El Alamein
Battle of the Commandos
Battle of the Worlds
Beauty on the Beach
Before the Revolution
Belle Starr
Bellissima▶
Bellissimo: Images of the
  Italian Cinema
The Belly of an Architect▶
The Berlin Affair
Beyond Obsession
Beyond the Door
Beyond the Door 2
Beyond the Law
The Bible...In the Beginning▶
The Bicycle Thief▶
Big Boss

Big Deal on Madonna Street▶
The Bird with the Crystal
  Plumage
Bitter Rice▶
Bix
Bizarre
The Black Cat
Black Cat
The Black Cobra
Black Lemons
The Black Maid
The Black Pirate▶
The Black Pirate
Black Sabbath▶
Black Sunday▶
A Black Veil for Lisa
Blaise Pascal▶
Blastfighter
Blood and Black Lace
Blood Brothers
Blood Feud
Blood Ties
The Bloody Pit of Horror
Blow-Up▶
Boccaccio '70
Body Moves
The Boldest Job in the West
Boomerang
Boot Hill
The Boss Is Served
Bullet for Sandoval
A Bullet for the General
Buried Alive
Burn!▶
Bye Bye Baby
Cabiria
Cafe Express
Caged Women
Caligula
Cambio de Cara
Camorra: The Naples
  Connection
The Canterbury Tales
Carthage in Flames
Cartouche▶
Casanova '70
Castle of Blood
The Castle of Fu Manchu
Castle of the Living Dead
The Cat o' Nine Tails
Catch as Catch Can
Catherine & Co.
The Cheaters
The Children Are Watching
  Us▶
Chino
Christ Stopped at Eboli▶
The Christmas That Almost
  Wasn't
The Church▶
Cinema Paradiso▶
City of the Walking Dead
City of Women
The Clowns▶
Cobra
Code Name Alpha
Codename: Wildgeese
Cold Steel for Tortuga
Cold Sweat
Collector's Item▶
Colossus and the Amazon
  Queen
Commandos
Condemned to Hell
Confessions of a Police
  Captain
The Conformist▶
Conquest
Conquest of Mycene
Contempt▶
Contraband
Control
Conversation Piece▶
Coriolanus, Man without a
  Country

Corleone
Corrupt▶
Cosmos: War of the Planets
Could It Happen Here?
Count Dracula
Counter Punch
Creepers
Crime Busters
The Cry of the Owl
The Damned
Danger: Diabolik
Dangerous Liaisons
Dangerous Obsession
Dark Eyes▶
Daughters of Darkness▶
Day of the Cobra
The Day the Sky Exploded
Deadly Impact
Deadly Revenge
The Deadly Trap
Death in Venice▶
Death Rage
The Decameron▶
Delta Force Commando 2
Demons
Demons 2
Devil in the Flesh
Devil of the Desert Against the
  Son of Hercules
Devilfish
Devil's Crude
The Devil's Daughter
The Devil's Nightmare
Dial Help
Diary of Forbidden Dreams▶
Divine Nymph
Divorce—Italian Style▶
Doctor Butcher M.D.
Domino
Dorian Gray
Down & Dirty▶
Dracula vs. Frankenstein
Driver's Seat
Duel of Champions
The Easy Life▶
The Eclipse▶
8 1/2▶
1860
Emerald Jungle
Empty Canvas
Era Notte a Roma▶
Ernesto
Everybody's Fine
Evil Clutch
Evil's Commandment
Exterminators of the Year
  3000
Eyeball
Eyes Behind the Stars
The Eyes, the Mouth
Fabiola▶
The Family
The Family▶
Fangs of the Living Dead
Fear in the City
Fellini Satyricon▶
Fellini's Roma
Fifth Day of Peace
Fiorile▶
A Fistful of Dollars▶
A Fistful of Dynamite▶
Five for Hell
Flatfoot
Flight of the Innocent
The Flowers of St. Francis▶
For a Few Dollars More
Forever Mary▶
Four Ways Out
Foxtrap
Frankenstein '80
Full Hearts & Empty Pockets
The Fury of Hercules
Gangsters
Garden of the Finzi-Continis▶

Garringo
Generale Della Rovere▶
The Ghost
The Giant of Marathon
The Giant of Metropolis
Giants of Rome
The Giants of Thessaly
Ginger & Fred▶
Gladiator of Rome
Gladiators 7
Go for It
The Gold of Naples▶
Goliath Against the Giants
Goliath and the Barbarians
Goliath and the Dragon
Goliath and the Sins of
  Babylon
The Good, the Bad and the
  Ugly▶
Goodnight, Michelangelo
The Gospel According to St.
  Matthew▶
The Grand Duel
Graveyard Shift
Great Adventure
The Great War
The Grim Reaper▶
Grim Reaper
Gun Fight at Red Sands
Gunfire
The Hanging Woman
Happy New Year▶
Hatchet for the Honeymoon
The Hawks & the Sparrows
Head of the Family
Hearts & Armour
Hell Commandos
Hellbenders
Henry IV
Hercules
Hercules 2
Hercules Against the Moon
  Men
Hercules and the Captive
  Women
Hercules and the Princess of
  Troy
Hercules in the Haunted World
Hercules, Prisoner of Evil
Hercules Unchained
Hero of Rome
Herod the Great
High Frequency
His Name was King
Homo Eroticus/Man of the
  Year
Honey
Honor Among Thieves
The Horrible Dr. Hichcock
Hotel Colonial
The House by the Cemetery
House on the Edge of the
  Park
How Funny Can Sex Be?
Howling 2: Your Sister is a
  Werewolf
The Human Factor
Hundra
Husband Hunting
I Hate Blondes
I Killed Rasputin
I Vitelloni▶
The Icicle Thief▶
Il Bell'Antonio
Il Grido
Il Sorpasso
Immortal Bachelor
Indiscretion of an American
  Wife
Infernal Trio
Inferno
The Inheritance
The Innocent▶
The Inquiry
Intermezzo▶
Intervista▶

Italian

The Invaders
Invasion of the Flesh Hunters
The Invincible Gladiator
The Invisible Dead
Island Monster
Johnny Stecchino▶
A Joke of Destiny, Lying in
   Wait Around the Corner
   Like a Bandit
Journey Beneath the Desert
Journey to the Lost City
Joyful Laughter
Judex
Juliet of the Spirits▶
Kaos▶
Kapo▶
Kidnap Syndicate
Kill, Baby, Kill▶
La Cicada
La Dolce Vita▶
La Grande Bourgeoise
La Notte Brava
La Nuit de Varennes▶
La Signora di Tutti▶
La Strada▶
La Terra Trema▶
La Vie Continue
Lady Caroline Lamb
Lady Frankenstein
Lady L
Lady of the Evening
The Lady Without Camelias
Landscape in the Mist▶
The Last Days of Pompeii
The Last Emperor▶
The Last Hunter
The Last Man on Earth
Last Tango in Paris▶
The Last Tomahawk
Last Year at Marienbad▶
L'Avventura▶
Le Bal▶
The Legend of Blood Castle
The Legend of the Wolf
   Woman
Leon Morin, Priest
Leonor
Les Carabiniers▶
Les Miserables
Life of Verdi
Lightning Bolt
Linchamiento
The Lion of Thebes▶
Lisa and the Devil
Little World of Don Camillo▶
Lobster for Breakfast
Lola
Love and Anarchy▶
Love in the City▶
Love Meetings
Lovers and Liars
Loves & Times of
   Scaramouche
The Loves of Hercules
Lucky Luciano
L'Udienza
Lunatics & Lovers
Lure of the Sila
Macaroni
Maciste in Hell
The Mad Butcher
Malicious
A Man Called Rage
Man from Cairo
Man from Deep River
Man of Legend
The Man Who Wagged His
   Tail
Man with a Cross
Manhattan Baby
Manhunt
Marauder
Marriage Italian Style▶
Master Touch
Mean Frank and Crazy Tony
Medea

Mediterraneo▶
Medusa Against the Son of
   Hercules
Messalina vs. the Son of
   Hercules
The Messiah▶
Miami Cops
Miami Horror
Mill of the Stone Women
Millions
Minnesota Clay
A Minute to Pray, A Second to
   Die
The Miracle▶
Miracle in Milan▶
Mission Stardust
Mississippi Mermaid▶
Mister Mean
Mr. Superinvisible
Mole Men Against the Son of
   Hercules
Mondo Cane
Mondo Cane 2
The Mongols
Moon in the Gutter
Morgan the Pirate
Moving Target
Muriel▶
My Wonderful Life
The Name of the Rose
Nana
Navajo Joe
Nefertiti, Queen of the Nile
The New Gladiators
New Mafia Boss
New York Ripper
The Night After Halloween
The Night Evelyn Came Out of
   the Grave
Night Flight from Moscow
A Night Full of Rain
The Night of the Shooting
   Stars▶
Night of the Zombies
The Night Porter
Nightmare Castle
Nights of Cabiria▶
1900▶
1990: The Bronx Warriors
99 Women
Nudo di Donna▶
Odds and Evens
Oedipus Rex▶
Oldest Profession
Once Upon a Time in the
   West▶
Open City▶
Open Doors▶
The Opponent
Orgy of the Vampires
Ossessione▶
Otello▶
Other Hell
Padre Padrone▶
Pain in the A—▶
Paisan▶
Palombella Rossa
Panic Button
Paranoia
Pardon My Trunk
Partner▶
The Passenger▶
Passion of Love▶
Passionate Thief
Peddlin' in Society
Phantom of Death
Phenomenal and the Treasure
   of Tutankamen
Pieces
Pierrot le Fou▶
Planet of the Vampires
Planet on the Prowl
Planets Against Us
Pool Hustlers
Porcile
Private Affairs

The Puma Man
Quo Vadis
The Rape of the Sabines
The Red Desert▶
Red Sun
Redneck
Regina
The Return of Dr. Mabuse
Revenge of the Dead
Revolt of the Barbarians
Ricco
Rocco and His Brothers▶
Roland the Mighty
Romeo and Juliet
Romeo and Juliet▶
The Roof
Rorret▶
Rough Justice
Rush
The Ruthless Four
Sacrilege
Salammbo
Salo, or the 120 Days of
   Sodom
Samson
Samson Against the Sheik
Samson and His Mighty
   Challenge
Samson and the 7 Miracles of
   the World
Santa Sangre▶
Sardinia Kidnapped
Satanik
Savage Island
The Scalawag Bunch
Scenes from a Murder
The Scent of a Woman
The Scorpion's Tail
Secret Agent 00
Secret Agent Super Dragon
Seduced and Abandoned▶
Seduction of Mimi▶
Senso▶
The Sensuous Nurse
Seven Beauties▶
Seven Deadly Sins▶
Seven Deaths in the Cat's Eye
Seven Doors of Death
Sex with a Smile
The She-Beast
Shoeshine▶
Shoot Loud, Louder, I Don't
   Understand!
Sicilian Connection
Sinbad of the Seven Seas
Sins of Rome
The Slaughter of the Vampires
Slave of the Cannibal God
The Sleazy Uncle
Smugglers
Sodom and Gomorrah
Son of Captain Blood
Son of Samson
Sonny and Jed
Sonny Boy
Sotto, Sotto
Spaghetti House
A Special Day▶
The Spider's Stratagem▶
Spirits of the Dead▶
The Squeeze
Star Crash
Stateline Motel
The Station
The Story of Boys & Girls▶
Stranger in Paso Bravo
Stromboli
Submission
Summer Affair
Summer Night
Summer Night with Greek
   Profile, Almond Eyes &
   Scent of Basil
Superargo
Suspiria▶
Swept Away...▶

The Swindle
The Sword of El Cid
The Taming of the Shrew▶
The Tempter
Tentacles
10th Victim▶
Teorema
Teresa Venerdi▶
Terror Creatures from the
   Grave
Terror of Rome Against the
   Son of Hercules
Terror of the Steppes
That Man from Rio
They Call Me Trinity
Thief of Baghdad
Third Solution
Three Brothers▶
Throne of Fire
Thunder Warrior 2
Tiger of the Seven Seas
Tigers in Lipstick
Till Marriage Do Us Part
Time of Indifference
Time Out for Love
'Tis a Pity She's a Whore
To Forget Venice
Together
Torso
Torture Chamber of Baron
   Blood
The Tragedy of a Ridiculous
   Man
Tramplers
The Tree of Wooden Clogs▶
Trinity is Still My Name
Tristana▶
Triumph of the Son of
   Hercules
12 Plus 1▶
Twitch of the Death Nerve
Two Evil Eyes
Two Nights with Cleopatra
2020 Texas Gladiators
Two Women▶
Tyrant of Lydia Against the
   Son of Hercules
Ulysses
Umberto D▶
Uncle Tom's Cabin
Unsane
Ursus in the Valley of the
   Lions
Utz
Vanina Vanini▶
Variety Lights▶
Venus Against the Son of
   Hercules
Verdi
A Very Old Man with
   Enormous Wings
Viking Massacre
Violent Breed
Violent Professionals
The Virgin of Nuremberg
Viva Maria!
Volere Volare
War Bus Commando
War Victims
The Warning
Warriors of the Wasteland
Watch Me When I Kill
Waterloo
We All Loved Each Other So
   Much▶
We the Living
Web of the Spider
Wedding in Blood▶
Weekend▶
Werewolf in a Girl's Dormitory
When Women Had Tails
When Women Lost Their Tails
Where the Hot Wind Blows
Where's Piccone▶
White Nights▶
Wifemistress

Wild, Wild Planet
The Witch
A Woman of Rome
Woman Times Seven
Women in Cell Block 7
Women's Prison Massacre
The Wonders of Aladdin
Yesterday, Today and
   Tomorrow▶
Yor, the Hunter from the
   Future
Zombie

Japanese

An Actor's Revenge
The Adventures of Milo &
   Otis▶
Akira
Akira Kurosawa's Dreams
Antarctica
Arcadia of My Youth
Attack of the Mushroom
   People
Attack Squadron
An Autumn Afternoon▶
Baby Cart 1: Lend a
   Child...Lend an Arm
Baby Cart 4: Heart of a
   Parent...Heart of a Child
Baby Cart at the River Styx
Baby Cart to Hades
The Bad Sleep Well▶
The Ballad of Narayama▶
The Battle of the Japan Sea
Being Two Isn't Easy
Black Lizard
Black Magic Terror
Black Rain▶
Body Snatcher from Hell
The Burmese Harp▶
The Bushido Blade
The Castle of Cagliostro
The Crucified Lovers▶
The Cruel Story of Youth▶
The Dagger of Kamui
Dagora, the Space Monster
The Day and the Hour
Demon City Shinjuku
Dersu Uzala▶
Destroy All Monsters
Destroy All Planets
Dodes 'ka-den▶
Double Suicide▶
Drifting Weeds▶
Drunken Angel▶
Early Summer▶
Eijanaika▶
The Empire of Passion▶
Equinox Flower
Face of Another
The Family Game▶
Fires on the Plain▶
Forest of Little Bear
47 Ronin, Part 1▶
47 Ronin, Part 2▶
Fugitive Alien
The Funeral▶
The Gambling Samurai
Gamera, the Invincible
Gamera vs. Barugon
Gamera vs. Gaos
Gamera vs. Guiron
Gamera vs. Zigra
Gappa the Trifibian Monster
Gate of Hell▶
A Geisha▶
Ghidrah the Three Headed
   Monster
The Ghost of Yotsuya
The Go-Masters▶
Godzilla, King of the Monsters
Godzilla 1985
Godzilla on Monster Island
Godzilla Raids Again

Godzilla vs. Biollante
Godzilla vs. Megalon
Godzilla vs. Monster Zero
Godzilla vs. Mothra
Godzilla vs. the Cosmic
   Monster
Godzilla vs. the Sea Monster
Godzilla vs. the Smog
   Monster
Godzilla's Revenge
Golden Demon
Gonza the Spearman
Gorath
Grave of the Fireflies▶
The Green Slime
GUY: Awakening of the Devil
H-Man
Half Human
Harmagedon
Heaven & Earth▶
The Hidden Fortress▶
High & Low▶
Himatsuri▶
Hiroshima, Mon Amour▶
Human Beasts
The Human Condition: A
   Soldier's Prayer▶
The Human Condition: No
   Greater Love▶
The Human Condition: Road
   to Eternity▶
The Human Vapor
Hunter in the Dark
I Live in Fear▶
Ikiru▶
The Imperial Japanese Empire
Imperial Navy
In the Realm of the Senses▶
The Insect Woman▶
Irezumi▶
The Island▶
Kagemusha▶
Kamikaze
King Kong Versus Godzilla
Kojiro▶
Kwaidan▶
Late Chrysanthemums
Late Spring▶
Lensman
Life of Oharu▶
Love and Faith▶
The Lower Depths▶
MacArthur's Children▶
The Makioka Sisters▶
The Manster
The Men Who Tread on the
   Tiger's Tail
Merry Christmas, Mr.
   Lawrence▶
Mistress▶
Mother▶
Mothra▶
Murder in the Doll House
My Neighbor Totoro
The Mysterians
No Regrets for Our Youth▶
Nomugi Pass
Odd Obsession
Okoge
One-Eyed Swordsman
Onibaba▶
Osaka Elegy
Otaku no Video
Phoenix
Planet Busters
The Pornographers▶
Port Arthur
Princess Yang Kwei Fei▶
The Professional: Golgo 13
Project A-ko
Project A-ko 2: Plot of the
   Daitokuji Financial Group
Project A-ko 3: Cinderella
   Rhapsody
Proof of the Man
Ran▶

Rashomon▶
Red Beard▶
Red Lion
Revenge of a Kabuki Actor
Rhapsody in August
Rikisha-Man▶
Rikyu▶
Rodan
Saga of the Vagabond
Samurai 1: Musashi
   Miyamoto▶
Samurai 2: Duel at Ichijoji
   Temple▶
Samurai 3: Duel at Ganryu
   Island▶
Samurai Reincarnation
Sandakan No. 8▶
Sanjuro▶
Sanshiro Sugata▶
Sansho the Bailiff▶
Sea Prince and the Fire Child
The Secret of the Telegian
Seven Samurai▶
She and He
Shin Heike Monogatari▶
Shinobi Ninja
Shiokari Pass
Shogun Assassin
The Silk Road
Sisters of Gion▶
Snow Country
Son of Godzilla
Starvengers
Station
The Story of the Late
   Chrysanthemum▶
Stray Dog▶
Street of Shame▶
Summer Vacation: 1999
The Sun's Burial▶
Sword of Doom▶
Sword of Fury II
Swords of Death
Tampopo▶
Tattooed Hit Man
A Taxing Woman▶
A Taxing Woman's Return▶
Terror Beneath the Sea
Terror of Mechagodzilla
Tetsuo: The Iron Man
Throne of Blood▶
Tidal Wave
Time of the Apes
Tokyo Decadence
Tokyo Olympiad
Tokyo Story▶
Toward the Terra
Twenty-Four Eyes▶
Twilight of the Cockroaches
Ugetsu▶
Urotsukidoji 1: Legend of the
   Overfiend
Urotsukidoji 2: Legend of the
   Demon Womb
Urusei Yatsura Movie 1: Only
   You
Urusei Yatsura Movie 2:
   Beautiful Dreamer
Urusei Yatsura Movie 3:
   Remember My Love
Urusei Yatsura Movie 4: Lum
   the Forever
Urusei Yatsura Movie 6:
   Always My Darling
Utamaro and His Five Women
Varan the Unbelievable
Vengeance Is Mine▶
Violence at Noon▶
Virus
War in Space
War of the Gargantuas
Warning from Space
What's Up, Tiger Lily?▶
When a Woman Ascends the
   Stairs
The White Sheik▶

A Wind Named Amnesia
The Wolves▶
Woman in the Dunes▶
X from Outer Space
Yog, Monster from Space
Yojimbo▶
Zatoichi: Master Ichi and a
   Chest of Gold
Zatoichi: The Blind
   Swordsman and the Chess
   Expert
Zatoichi: The Blind
   Swordsman and the
   Fugitives
Zatoichi: The Blind
   Swordsman's Vengeance
Zatoichi: The Life and Opinion
   of Masseur Ichi
Zatoichi vs. Yojimbo▶
Zatoichi: Zatoichi's Flashing
   Sword
Zeram
Zero Pilot

Lithuanian

Adomas Nori Buti Zmogumi
Velnio Nuotaka

Mexican

Amenaza Nuclear
Anita de Montemar
Arizona
Attack of the Mayan Mummy
Bellas de Noche
Black Pit of Dr. M
The Bloody Vampire
The Brainiac
Bring Me the Vampire
By Hook or Crook
Cabeza de Vaca▶
Caches de Oro
Calacan▶
Camelia
Children of Sanchez
Conexion Mexico
Conquest
The Craving
Creature of the Walking Dead
The Criminal Life of
   Archibaldo de la Cruz▶
Crossfire
The Curse of the Aztec
   Mummy
The Curse of the Crying
   Woman
Curse of the Devil
Curse of the Stone Hand
Dance of Death
Despedida de Casada
Diamante, Oro y Amor
Dona Herlinda & Her Son
Dos Esposas en Mi Cama
Dos Postolas Gemelas
El Ametralladora
El Aviador Fenomeno
El Aviso Inoportuno
El Bruto
El Ceniciento
El Ciclon
El Cuarto Chino
El Derecho de Comer
El Forastero Vengador
El Fugitivo
El Gallo de Oro
El Gavilan Pollero
El Gendarme Desconocido
El Hombre Contra el Mundo
El Hombre de la Furia
El Libro de Piedra
El Penon de las Animas
El Profesor Hippie
El Rey
El Robo al Tren Correo

El Sabor de la Venganza
El Tesoro de Chucho el Roto
El Zorro Blanco
El Zorro Vengador
Emiliano Zapata
Emilio Varela vs. Camelia La
   Texana
Erendira
The Exterminating Angel▶
Face of the Screaming
   Werewolf
The Fear Chamber
Fearmaker
Fever Mounts at El Pao
Flor Silvestre
Foxtrot
Frontera Sin Ley
Genie of Darkness
Gente Violenta
The Great Madcap
Guitarras Lloren Guitarras
Guns for Dollars
The Illusion Travels by
   Streetcar▶
Invasion of the Vampires
Invasion of the Zombies
Jungle Warriors
Justicia para los Mexicanos
La Bella Lola
La Carcel de Laredo
La Casa de Madame Lulu
La Chamuscada
La Choca
La Corona de un Campeon
La Diosa Arrodillada
La Fuerza Inutil
La Fuga del Rojo
La Generala
La Hifa Sin Padre
La Justicia Tiene Doce Anos
La Mansion de la Locura
La Marchanta
La Mentira
La Montana del Diablo
La Trinchera
La Venganza del Rojo
Lagrimas de Amor
Like Water for Chocolate▶
The Living Coffin
The Living Head
Los Amores de Marieta
Los Apuros de Dos Gallos
Los Asesinos
Los Caciques
Los Cacos
Los Caifanes
Los Dos Hermanos
Los Hermanos Centella
Los Hermanos Diablo
Los Olvidados▶
Los Sheriffs de la Frontera
Los Tres Amores de Losa
Los Tres Calaveras
Los Vampiros de Coyacan
Macario
The Man and the Monster
Manos Torpes
Marcados por el Destino
Maria Candelaria
Mariachis
Mexican Bus Ride
Mision Suicida
The Monster Demolisher
Murderer in the Hotel
Musico, Poeta y Loco
Narda or The Summer
Nazarin▶
The Neighborhood Thief
Neutron and the Black Mask
Neutron vs. the Amazing Dr.
   Caronte
Neutron vs. the Death Robots
Neutron vs. the Maniac
The New Invisible Man
Ni Chana Ni Juana
Nido de Aguilas

Night of a Thousand Cats
Night of the Bloody Apes
Nosotros
Orlak, the Hell of Frankenstein
Pancho Villa Returns
Para Servir a Usted
Patsy, Mi Amor
The Pearl▶
The Robot vs. the Aztec
   Mummy
Samson in the Wax Museum
Samson vs. the Vampire
   Women
Santa Claus
Santa Sangre▶
Savage!
Semaforo en Rojo
Sexo Y Crimen
Siempre Hay una Primera Vez
Simon Blanco
Sin Salida
The Sinister Invasion
Sisters of Satan
The Snake People
Somos Novios
Soy un Golfo
Spiritism
Susana▶
Swamp of the Lost Monster
Tacos al Carbon
Target Eagle
Temporada Salvaje
Thor el Conquistador
Tintorera...Tiger Shark
Torero
The Treasure of the Amazon
Triumphs of a Man Called
   Horse
The Vampire
The Vampire's Coffin
Viridiana▶
Viva Chihuahua (Long Live
   Chihuahua)
Vivo o Muerto
Warlock Moon
Witches' Mountain
The Witch's Mirror
A Woman Without Love▶
World of the Vampires
Wrestling Women vs. the
   Aztec Ape
Wrestling Women vs. the
   Aztec Mummy
Wuthering Heights
Y Donde Esta el Muerto?
   (And... Where Is the Dead)
Yanco
The Young One

New Zealand

Among the Cinders
An Angel at My Table▶
Bad Blood
Bad Taste▶
Beyond Reasonable Doubt
The Bridge to Nowhere
Came a Hot Friday
Crush
Dangerous Orphans
Dark of the Night
Dead Alive
Goodbye Pork Pie
Heart of the Stag
Hot Target
Iris
Mesmerized
Nate and Hayes
The Navigator▶
Never Say Die
Nutcase
The Quiet Earth▶
Second Time Lucky
Shaker Run
The Silent One

New

Sleeping Dogs
Smash Palace
Starlight Hotel
Sylvia
Tearaway
Treasure of the Yankee
   Zephyr
Utu▶
Vigil▶
Wild Horses

Nicaraguan

Alsino and the Condor▶

Norwegian

Edvard Munch
One Day in the Life of Ivan
   Denisovich▶
Pathfinder▶
Shipwrecked

Polish

Ashes and Diamonds▶
Baritone
Border Street
A Brivele der Mamen▶
Casimir the Great
Colonel Wolodyjowski
The Conductor
Danton▶
Deja Vu
Der Purimshpiler
Dr. Judym
The Double Life of Veronique
The Dybbuk▶
Enigma Secret
Fever▶
First Spaceship on Venus▶
Foul Play
A Generation▶
Greta▶
Hands Up▶
Hero of the Year
In an Old Manor House
In Desert and Wilderness
The Interrogation▶
Kanal▶
Karate Polish Style
Knife in the Water▶
Korczak▶
Land of Promise
Leper
Maids of Wilko
Mamele
Man of Iron▶
Man of Marble▶
Moonlighting▶
Mother of Kings
Nights and Days
No End
Paper Marriage
The Peasants
Pharaoh
The Singing Blacksmith
The Structure of Crystals
Train to Hollywood▶
Trois Couleurs: Blanc▶
Trois Couleurs: Rouge▶
The Unapproachable
W Hour
Without Love
A Woman and a Woman
Year of the Quiet Sun▶
Yidl Mitn Fidl

Portuguese

Black Orpheus▶
In the White City▶
Life is Beautiful
Return of the Evil Dead
Tombs of the Blind Dead

Romanian

The Oak

Russian

Adomas Nori Buti Zmogumi
Aelita: Queen of Mars
Alexander Nevsky▶
The Amphibian Man
Andrei Rublev▶
Arsenal▶
Ashik Kerib▶
Autumn Marathon
Ballad of a Soldier▶
Baltic Deputy▶
The Battleship Potemkin▶
Bed and Sofa▶
Burglar▶
Chapayev▶
The Cigarette Girl of
   Mosselprom
Close to Eden
The Color of Pomegranates▶
Come and See▶
Commissar▶
The Cranes are Flying▶
Crime and Punishment
The Day the Earth Froze
Dersu Uzala▶
Don Quixote▶
Early Russian Cinema, Vol. 1:
   Beginnings
Early Russian Cinema, Vol. 2:
   Folklore & Legend
Early Russian Cinema, Vol. 3:
   Starewicz's Fantasies
Early Russian Cinema, Vol. 4:
   Provincial Variations
Early Russian Cinema, Vol. 5:
   Chardynin's Pushkin
Early Russian Cinema, Vol. 6:
   Class Distinctions
Early Russian Cinema, Vol. 7:
   Evgenii Bauer
Early Russian Cinema, Vol. 8:
   Iakov Protazanov
Early Russian Cinema, Vol. 9:
   High Society
Early Russian Cinema, Vol.
   10: The End of an Era
Earth▶
A Forgotten Tune for the
   Flute▶
Freedom is Paradise▶
Freeze-Die-Come to Life▶
Fury is a Woman▶
The General Line▶
The Girl with the Hat Box
Guerilla Brigade
Happiness
Incident at Map-Grid 36-80
The Inspector General
Ivan the Terrible, Part 1▶
Ivan the Terrible, Part 2▶
Jazzman▶
Kindergarten▶
Kino Pravda/Enthusiasm
The Lady with the Dog▶
The Legend of Suram
   Fortress
Little Vera▶
The Magic Voyage of Sinbad
The Man with a Movie
   Camera▶
The Mirror▶
Moscow Does Not Believe in
   Tears▶
Mother▶
My Apprenticeship▶
My Childhood▶
My Name is Ivan▶
My Universities▶
No Greater Love
Oblomov▶
The Overcoat▶

The Patriots▶
Peter the First: Part 1
Peter the First: Part 2
Planet Burg
Private Life
Que Viva Mexico▶
Rasputin▶
Repentance▶
Shadows of Forgotten
   Ancestors▶
The Shooting Party
Sideburns
A Slave of Love▶
Solaris
Solo Voyage: The Revenge
Stalker▶
Storm Over Asia▶
Strike▶
A Summer to Remember▶
Sword & the Dragon
Taxi Blues▶
Tchaikovsky
Ten Days That Shook the
   World▶
The Theme▶
The Tsar's Bride▶
An Unfinished Piece for a
   Player Piano▶
War and Peace▶
Waterloo
Zvenigora▶

South African

African Rage
City of Blood
Deadly Passion
Emissary
The Evil Below
House of the Living Dead
Kill Slade
Place of Weeping
Stay Awake

Spanish

Anguish
Any Gun Can Play
Attack of the Robots
Autopsy of a Ghost
Ay, Carmela!▶
Bad Man's River
Belle Epoque▶
Benjamin Argumedo
Bestia Nocturna
Between Heaven and Earth
Black Beauty
The Black Pirate
The Blood Spattered Bride
Blood Wedding▶
Brandy Sheriff
Bromas S.A.
Brujo Luna
Bullet for Sandoval
Cabeza de Vaca▶
Cada Noche un Amor
Camila▶
Cancion en el Alma
Carmen▶
The Castle of Fu Manchu
Cauldron of Blood
Chimes at Midnight▶
The Christmas Kid
The City and the Dogs▶
City of the Walking Dead
Como Dos Gotas de Agua
Conquest
Count Dracula
Cria▶
The Criminal Life of
   Archibaldo de la Cruz▶
Curse of the Devil
Danzon▶
Dark Habits
Dawn of the Pirates

Demons in the Garden▶
Departamento Compartido
Desde el Abismo
Desperados
Details of a Duel: A Question
   of Honor
The Devil's Possessed
The Diabolical Dr. Z
Dias de Ilusion
Dr. Jekyll and the Wolfman
Dr. Orloff's Monster
Don Juan, My Love▶
Don Quixote▶
Don Segundo Sombra
Donde Duermen
   Dos...Duermen Tres
Dos Chicas de Revista
Dracula vs. Frankenstein
Dracula's Great Love
Duel of Champions
Duelo en el Dorado
El Barbaro
El Cochecito▶
El Condor
El Cristo de los Milagros
El Diputado▶
El Muerto
El Norte▶
El Super▶
El: This Strange Passion▶
Endless Descent
Escape from El Diablo
Esposa y Amante
Esta Noche Cena Pancho
Exorcism's Daughter
Expertos en Pinchazos
The Exterminating Angel▶
Exterminators of the Year
   3000
The Fable of the Beautiful
   Pigeon Fancier
Fangs of the Living Dead
Fin de Fiesta
Fotografo de Senoras
Frida
From Hell to Victory
Frontera
Fuerte Perdido
Furia Pasional
The Fury of the Wolfman
The Garden of Delights▶
Garringo
Gladiators 7
Goliath Against the Giants
Gran Valor en la Facultad de
   Medicina
Grandes Amigos
Graveyard of Horror
Great Adventure
The Green Wall▶
Half of Heaven▶
The Hanging Woman
Hatchet for the Honeymoon
Hellbenders
High Heels▶
The Holy Innocents▶
Honey
Horror Express
Horror of the Zombies
Horror Rises from the Tomb
The House of 1000 Dolls
House of Psychotic Women
Human Beasts
The Hunt▶
I'm the One You're Looking
   For
In a Glass Cage
In Memoriam
Inquisition
The Invincible Gladiator
It Happened at Nightmare Inn
Jamon, Jamon
Johnny Barrows, El Malo
Jornada de Muerte
Kashmiri Run
King of Kong Island

La Hija del General
La Hora 24
La Ley del Revolver
La Nueva Cigarra
La Virgen de Guadalupe
Labyrinth of Passion
Last Day of the War
The Last Supper▶
Law of Desire▶
The Legend of Blood Castle
Leonor
Letters from the Park▶
Lightning Bolt
The Lion's Share
Lovers: A True Story▶
Mama Turns a Hundred▶
Man of Legend
The Man Who Wagged His
   Tail
Marianela
Matador
Mayalunta
Miracle in Rome
Mission Stardust
Mr. Superinvisible
The Mummy's Revenge
Murder Mansion
Navajo Joe
The Nest
Night of the Death Cult
Night of the Howling Beast
Night of the Zombies
99 Women
Oasis of the Zombies
On the Line
Orgy of the Vampires
Padre Nuestro
Pancho Villa
Passion for Power
Pepi, Luci, Bom and Other
   Girls on the Heap
Pieces
Pistoleros Asesinos
The Plague
Princess Cinderella
Pulsebeat
Red Sun
Remolina de Pasiones
Return of the Evil Dead
The Return of the Musketeers
Ricco
The Rue Morgue Massacres
The Saga of the Draculas
Satanik
Savage Island
The Scarlet Letter▶
The Scorpion's Tail
The Screaming Dead
The Sea Serpent
Sex is Crazy
Skyline▶
Son of Captain Blood
Sound of Horror
Spirit of the Beehive▶
The Stilts▶
Stormquest
The Summer of Miss Forbes
Superargo
Supersonic Man
The Sword of El Cid
Target Eagle
That Obscure Object of
   Desire▶
Tie Me Up! Tie Me Down!
Tombs of the Blind Dead
A Town Called Hell
Treasure of the Four Crowns
Tristana▶
Una Vez en la Vida
Under the Earth▶
The Uprising▶
Ursus in the Valley of the
   Lions
Vengeance of the Zombies
A Very Old Man with
   Enormous Wings

Virgin Among the Living Dead
Viridiana▶
Web of Deception
The Werewolf vs. the Vampire
    Woman
When the Screaming Stops
A Witch Without a Broom
Women on the Verge of a
    Nervous Breakdown▶
Yellow Hair & the Fortress of
    Gold
Zombie Lake

Swedish

The Adventures of Picasso
After the Rehearsal▶
The Assignment
The Atonement of Gosta
    Berling▶
Autumn Sonata▶
The Best Intentions▶
Brink of Life
The Count of the Old Town
Cries and Whispers▶
The Devil's Eye
Devil's Wanton
The Doll
Dollar
Dreams
Elvira Madigan▶
The Emigrants▶
Face to Face▶
Fanny and Alexander▶
Flight of the Eagle
From the Life of the
    Marionettes▶
Good Evening, Mr.
    Wallenberg
Gorilla
The Great Adventure▶
Hour of the Wolf▶
House of Angels
I Am Curious (Yellow)
Inga
The Inside Man
Intermezzo▶
Invasion of the Animal People
Istanbul
June Night
Killing Heat
Lesson in Love
The Magic Flute▶
The Magician▶
The Match Factory Girl▶
Miss Julie
Monika
Montenegro▶
The Mozart Brothers▶
My Life as a Dog▶
The New Land▶
Night Is My Future
Ninja Mission
Only One Night
The Outlaw and His Wife
The Ox
The Passion of Anna▶
Pelle the Conqueror▶
Persona▶
The Phantom Chariot
Pippi Goes on Board
Pippi in the South Seas
Pippi Longstocking
Pippi on the Run
Port of Call▶
The Sacrifice▶
Sawdust & Tinsel▶
Scenes from a Marriage▶
Secrets of Women▶
The Seventh Seal▶
The Shame▶
The Silence▶
Smiles of a Summer Night▶
Sofie
Summer Interlude▶

Swedenhielms
Thomas Graal's Best Film▶
Three Strange Loves▶
Through a Glass Darkly▶
To Joy▶
Torment▶
The Touch
Treasure of Arne
Unmarried Mothers
The Virgin Spring▶
The Visitors
Walpurgis Night▶
Wardogs
Wild Strawberries▶
The Winter Light▶
Witchcraft Through the Ages▶
A Woman's Face▶

Swiss

After Darkness
Alpine Fire
Big Bluff
The Boat is Full▶
Candy Mountain
The Castle▶
Chimes at Midnight▶
Dangerous Moves▶
Drachenfutter▶
A Dream of Passion
First Love
Foxtrot
Hail Mary
Heidi
In the White City▶
Jonah Who Will Be 25 in the
    Year 2000▶
Journey of Hope▶
King Lear
The Lacemaker▶
Night and Day▶
Nouvelle Vague
The Pedestrian▶
Trois Couleurs: Blanc▶
Trois Couleurs: Rouge▶

Taiwanese

The Association
The Outcasts▶
The Wedding Banquet▶

Turkish

Baba▶
The Horse▶
Istanbul
The Wall▶
Yol▶

Vietnamese

The Scent of Green Papaya▶

Yugoslavian

The Battle of Austerlitz
Battle of Neretva
Battleforce
Cave of the Living Dead
Guns of War
Hey, Babu Riba
Innocence Unprotected
Kapo▶
The Love Affair, or The Case
    of the Missing Switchboard
    Operator▶
Man is Not a Bird
One-Eyed Soldiers
Operation Cross Eagles
Romance of a Horsethief
The She-Beast
Son of Samson
Stealing Heaven
Sweet Movie

Time of the Gypsies▶
Tito and Me▶
Track of the Vampire
Uncle Tom's Cabin
Ward Six
When Father was Away on
    Business▶

AWARDS INDEX

The **AWARDS INDEX** lists 2,200 films honored by 12 national and international award bodies, representing some 90 categories of competition. This information is also contained in the review following the credits. **Only features available on video and reviewed in the main section are listed in this index; movies not yet released on video are not covered.** As award-winning films find their way to video, they will be added to the review section and covered in this index. The awards covered include:

American Academy Awards
Australia Film Institute
British Academy of Film
and Television Arts
Cannes Film Festival

French Cesar
Canadian Genie
Golden Globe
Directors Guild of America
Edgar Allan Poe Awards

Independent Spirit
Montreal Film Festival
MTV Movie Awards

ACADEMY AWARDS

ACTOR

1928
Emil Jannings
Last Command

1930
George Arliss
Disraeli

1931
Lionel Barrymore
A Free Soul

1932
Wallace Beery
The Champ
Fredric March
Dr. Jekyll and Mr. Hyde

1933
Charles Laughton
The Private Life of Henry VIII

1934
Clark Gable
It Happened One Night

1935
Victor McLaglen
The Informer

1936
Paul Muni
The Story of Louis Pasteur

1937
Spencer Tracy
Captains Courageous

1938
Spencer Tracy
Boys Town

1939
Robert Donat
Goodbye, Mr. Chips

1940
James Stewart
The Philadelphia Story

1941
Gary Cooper
Sergeant York

1942
James Cagney
Yankee Doodle Dandy

1943
Paul Lukas
Watch on the Rhine

1944
Bing Crosby
Going My Way

1945
Ray Milland
The Lost Weekend

1946
Fredric March
The Best Years of Our Lives

1947
Ronald Colman
A Double Life

1948
Laurence Olivier
Hamlet

1949
Broderick Crawford
All the King's Men

1950
Jose Ferrer
Cyrano de Bergerac

1951
Humphrey Bogart
The African Queen

1952
Gary Cooper
High Noon

1953
William Holden
Stalag 17

1954
Marlon Brando
On the Waterfront

1955
Ernest Borgnine
Marty

1956
Yul Brynner
The King and I

1957
Alec Guinness
The Bridge on the River Kwai

1958
David Niven
Separate Tables

1959
Charlton Heston
Ben-Hur

1960
Burt Lancaster
Elmer Gantry

1961
Maximilian Schell
Judgment at Nuremberg

1962
Gregory Peck
To Kill a Mockingbird

1963
Sidney Poitier
Lilies of the Field

1964
Rex Harrison
My Fair Lady

1965
Lee Marvin
Cat Ballou

1966
Paul Scofield
A Man for All Seasons

1967
Rod Steiger
In the Heat of the Night

1968
Cliff Robertson
Charly

1969
John Wayne
True Grit

1970
George C. Scott
Patton

1971
Gene Hackman
The French Connection

1972
Marlon Brando
The Godfather

1973
Jack Lemmon
Save the Tiger

1974
Art Carney
Harry and Tonto

1975
Jack Nicholson
One Flew Over the Cuckoo's Nest

1976
Peter Finch
Network

1977
Richard Dreyfuss
The Goodbye Girl

1978
Jon Voight
Coming Home

1979
Dustin Hoffman
Kramer vs. Kramer

1980
Robert De Niro
Raging Bull

1981
Henry Fonda
On Golden Pond

1982
Ben Kingsley
Gandhi

1983
Robert Duvall
Tender Mercies

1984
F. Murray Abraham
Amadeus

1985
William Hurt
Kiss of the Spider Woman

1986
Paul Newman
The Color of Money

1987
Michael Douglas
Wall Street

1988
Dustin Hoffman
Rain Man

1989
Daniel Day-Lewis
My Left Foot

1990
Jeremy Irons
Reversal of Fortune

1991
Anthony Hopkins
The Silence of the Lambs

1992
Al Pacino
Scent of a Woman

1993
Tom Hanks
Philadelphia

ACTOR— SUPPORTING

1936
Walter Brennan
Come and Get It

1937
Joseph Schildkraut
The Life of Emile Zola

1939
Thomas Mitchell
Stagecoach

1940
Walter Brennan
The Westerner

1941
Donald Crisp
How Green was My Valley

1942
Van Heflin
Johnny Eager

ACTOR—
SUPPORTING
▶cont.

1943
Charles Coburn
The More the Merrier

1944
Barry Fitzgerald
Going My Way

1945
James Dunn
A Tree Grows in Brooklyn

1946
Harold Russell
The Best Years of Our Lives

1947
Edmund Gwenn
Miracle on 34th Street

1948
Walter Huston
Treasure of the Sierra Madre

1949
Dean Jagger
Twelve O'Clock High

1950
George Sanders
All About Eve

1951
Karl Malden
A Streetcar Named Desire

1952
Anthony Quinn
Viva Zapata!

1953
Frank Sinatra
From Here to Eternity

1954
Edmond O'Brien
The Barefoot Contessa

1955
Jack Lemmon
Mister Roberts

1956
Anthony Quinn
Lust for Life

1957
Red Buttons
Sayonara

1958
Burl Ives
Big Country

1959
Hugh Griffith
Ben-Hur

1960
Peter Ustinov
Spartacus

1961
George Chakiris
West Side Story

1962
Ed Begley, Sr.
Sweet Bird of Youth

1963
Melvyn Douglas
Hud

1964
Peter Ustinov
Topkapi

1965
Martin Balsam
A Thousand Clowns

1966
Walter Matthau
The Fortune Cookie

1967
George Kennedy
Cool Hand Luke

1969
Gig Young
They Shoot Horses, Don't They?

1970
John Mills
Ryan's Daughter

1971
Ben Johnson
The Last Picture Show

1972
Joel Grey
Cabaret

1973
John Houseman
The Paper Chase

1974
Robert De Niro
The Godfather, Part 2

1975
George Burns
The Sunshine Boys

1976
Jason Robards, Jr.
All the President's Men

1977
Jason Robards, Jr.
Julia

1978
Christopher Walken
The Deer Hunter

1979
Melvyn Douglas
Being There

1980
Timothy Hutton
Ordinary People

1981
John Gielgud
Arthur

1982
Louis Gossett, Jr.
An Officer and a Gentleman

1983
Jack Nicholson
Terms of Endearment

1984
Haing S. Ngor
The Killing Fields

1985
Don Ameche
Cocoon

1986
Michael Caine
Hannah and Her Sisters

1987
Sean Connery
The Untouchables

1988
Kevin Kline
A Fish Called Wanda

1989
Denzel Washington
Glory

1990
Joe Pesci
Goodfellas

1991
Jack Palance
City Slickers

1992
Gene Hackman
Unforgiven

1993
Tommy Lee Jones
The Fugitive

ACTRESS

1928
Janet Gaynor
Sunrise

1929
Mary Pickford
Coquette

1930
Norma Shearer
The Divorcee

1931
Marie Dressler
Min & Bill

1932
Helen Hayes
The Sin of Madelon Claudet

1933
Katharine Hepburn
Morning Glory

1934
Claudette Colbert
It Happened One Night

1935
Bette Davis
Dangerous

1936
Luise Rainer
The Great Ziegfeld

1937
Luise Rainer
The Good Earth

1938
Bette Davis
Jezebel

1939
Vivien Leigh
Gone with the Wind

1940
Ginger Rogers
Kitty Foyle

1941
Joan Fontaine
Suspicion

1942
Greer Garson
Mrs. Miniver

1943
Jennifer Jones
The Song of Bernadette

1944
Ingrid Bergman
Gaslight

1945
Joan Crawford
Mildred Pierce

1947
Loretta Young
The Farmer's Daughter

1948
Jane Wyman
Johnny Belinda

1949
Olivia de Havilland
The Heiress

1950
Judy Holliday
Born Yesterday

1951
Vivien Leigh
A Streetcar Named Desire

1952
Shirley Booth
Come Back, Little Sheba

1953
Audrey Hepburn
Roman Holiday

1954
Grace Kelly
Country Girl

1955
Anna Magnani
The Rose Tattoo

1956
Ingrid Bergman
Anastasia

1957
Joanne Woodward
The Three Faces of Eve

1958
Susan Hayward
I Want to Live!

1959
Simone Signoret
Room at the Top

1960
Elizabeth Taylor
Butterfield 8

1961
Sophia Loren
Two Women

1962
Anne Bancroft
The Miracle Worker

1963
Patricia Neal
Hud

1964
Julie Andrews
Mary Poppins

1965
Julie Christie
Darling

1966
Elizabeth Taylor
Who's Afraid of Virginia Woolf?

1967
Katharine Hepburn
Guess Who's Coming to Dinner

1968
Barbra Streisand
Funny Girl
Katharine Hepburn
The Lion in Winter

1969
Dame Maggie Smith
The Prime of Miss Jean Brodie

1970
Glenda Jackson
Women in Love

1971
Jane Fonda
Klute

1972
Liza Minnelli
Cabaret

1973
Glenda Jackson
A Touch of Class

1974
Ellen Burstyn
Alice Doesn't Live Here Anymore

1975
Louise Fletcher
One Flew Over the Cuckoo's Nest

1976
Faye Dunaway
Network

1977
Diane Keaton
Annie Hall

1978
Jane Fonda
Coming Home

1979
Sally Field
Norma Rae

1980
Sissy Spacek
Coal Miner's Daughter

1981
Katharine Hepburn
On Golden Pond

1982
Meryl Streep
Sophie's Choice

1983
Shirley MacLaine
Terms of Endearment

1984
Sally Field
Places in the Heart

1985
Geraldine Page
The Trip to Bountiful

1986
Marlee Matlin
Children of a Lesser God

1987
Cher
Moonstruck

1988
Jodie Foster
The Accused

1989
Jessica Tandy
Driving Miss Daisy

1990
Kathy Bates
Misery

1991
Jodie Foster
The Silence of the Lambs

1992
Emma Thompson
Howard's End

1993
Holly Hunter
The Piano

ACTRESS—SUPPORTING

1936
Gale Sondergaard
Anthony Adverse

1938
Fay Bainter
Jezebel

1939
Hattie McDaniel
Gone with the Wind

1940
Jane Darwell
The Grapes of Wrath

1941
Mary Astor
The Great Lie

1942
Teresa Wright
Mrs. Miniver

1944
Ethel Barrymore
None But the Lonely Heart

1945
Anne Revere
National Velvet

1946
Anne Baxter
The Razor's Edge

1947
Celeste Holm
Gentleman's Agreement

1948
Claire Trevor
Key Largo

1949
Mercedes McCambridge
All the King's Men

1950
Josephine Hull
Harvey

1951
Kim Hunter
A Streetcar Named Desire

1952
Gloria Grahame
The Bad and the Beautiful

1953
Donna Reed
From Here to Eternity

1954
Eva Marie Saint
On the Waterfront

1955
Jo Van Fleet
East of Eden

1956
Dorothy Malone
Written on the Wind

1957
Miyoshi Umeki
Sayonara

1958
Wendy Hiller
Separate Tables

1959
Shelley Winters
The Diary of Anne Frank

1960
Shirley Jones
Elmer Gantry

1961
Rita Moreno
West Side Story

1962
Patty Duke
The Miracle Worker

1963
Margaret Rutherford
The V.I.P.'s

1964
Lila Kedrova
Zorba the Greek

1965
Shelley Winters
A Patch of Blue

1966
Sandy Dennis
Who's Afraid of Virginia Woolf?

1967
Estelle Parsons
Bonnie & Clyde

1968
Ruth Gordon
Rosemary's Baby

1969
Goldie Hawn
Cactus Flower

1970
Helen Hayes
Airport

1971
Cloris Leachman
The Last Picture Show

1972
Eileen Heckart
Butterflies Are Free

1973
Tatum O'Neal
Paper Moon

1974
Ingrid Bergman
Murder on the Orient Express

1975
Lee Grant
Shampoo

1976
Beatrice Straight
Network

1977
Vanessa Redgrave
Julia

1978
Dame Maggie Smith
California Suite

1979
Meryl Streep
Kramer vs. Kramer

1980
Mary Steenburgen
Melvin and Howard

1981
Maureen Stapleton
Reds

1982
Jessica Lange
Tootsie

1983
Linda Hunt
The Year of Living Dangerously

1984
Peggy Ashcroft
A Passage to India

1985
Anjelica Huston
Prizzi's Honor

1986
Dianne Wiest
Hannah and Her Sisters

1987
Olympia Dukakis
Moonstruck

1988
Geena Davis
The Accidental Tourist

1989
Brenda Fricker
My Left Foot

1990
Whoopi Goldberg
Ghost

1991
Mercedes Ruehl
The Fisher King

1992
Marisa Tomei
My Cousin Vinny

1993
Anna Paquin
The Piano

ART DIRECTION

1946
Anna and the King of Siam

1957
Sayonara

1958
Gigi

1967
Camelot

1968
Oliver!

1969
Hello, Dolly!

1970
Patton

1971
Nicholas and Alexandra

1972
Cabaret

1973
The Sting

1974
The Godfather, Part 2

1975
Barry Lyndon

1976
All the President's Men

1977
Star Wars

1978
Heaven Can Wait

1979
All That Jazz

1980
Tess

1981
Raiders of the Lost Ark

1982
Gandhi

1983
Fanny and Alexander

1984
Amadeus

1985
Out of Africa

1986
A Room with a View

1987
The Last Emperor

1988
Dangerous Liaisons

1989
Batman

1990
Dick Tracy

1991
Bugsy

1992
Howard's End

1993
Schindler's List

ART DIRECTION (B & W)

1947
Great Expectations

1948
Hamlet

1949
The Heiress

1950
Sunset Boulevard

1951
A Streetcar Named Desire

1952
The Bad and the Beautiful

1953
Julius Caesar

1954
On the Waterfront

1955
The Rose Tattoo

1956
Somebody Up There Likes Me

1959
The Diary of Anne Frank

1960
The Apartment

1961
The Hustler

1962
To Kill a Mockingbird

1964
Zorba the Greek

1965
Ship of Fools

1966
Who's Afraid of Virginia Woolf?

ART DIRECTION (COLOR)

1947
Black Narcissus

1948
The Red Shoes

1949
Little Women

1950
Samson and Delilah

1951
An American in Paris

1952
Moulin Rouge

1953
The Robe

1954
20,000 Leagues Under the Sea

1955
Picnic

1956
The King and I

1959
Ben-Hur

1960
Spartacus

1961
West Side Story

1962
Lawrence of Arabia

1963
Cleopatra

1964
My Fair Lady

1965
Doctor Zhivago

1966
Fantastic Voyage

CINEMATOGRAPHY

1928
Sunrise

1931
Tabu: A Story of the South Seas

1932
Lee Garmes
Shanghai Express

1933
A Farewell to Arms

1934
Cleopatra

1935
A Midsummer Night's Dream

1936
Anthony Adverse

1937
The Good Earth

1967
Bonnie & Clyde

1968
Romeo and Juliet

1969
Butch Cassidy and the Sundance Kid

1970
Ryan's Daughter

1971
Fiddler on the Roof

1972
Cabaret

1973
Cries and Whispers

1974
The Towering Inferno

1975
Barry Lyndon

1976
Bound for Glory

1977
Close Encounters of the Third Kind

1978
Days of Heaven

1979
Apocalypse Now

1980
Tess

1981
Reds

1982
Gandhi

1983
Fanny and Alexander

1984
The Killing Fields

1985
Out of Africa

1986
The Mission

1987
The Last Emperor

1988
Mississippi Burning

1989
Glory

1990
Dances with Wolves

1991
JFK

1992
A River Runs Through It

1993
Schindler's List

CINEMATOGRAPHY (B & W)

1939
Wuthering Heights

1940
Rebecca

1941
How Green was My Valley

1942
Mrs. Miniver

1943
The Song of Bernadette

1944
Laura

1945
Picture of Dorian Gray

1946
Anna and the King of Siam

1947
Great Expectations

1948
The Naked City

1949
Battleground

1950
The Third Man

1951
A Place in the Sun

1952
The Bad and the Beautiful

1953
From Here to Eternity

1954
On the Waterfront

1955
The Rose Tattoo

1956
Somebody Up There Likes Me

1958
The Defiant Ones

1959
The Diary of Anne Frank

1961
The Hustler

1962
The Longest Day

1963
Hud

1964
Zorba the Greek

1965
Ship of Fools

1966
Who's Afraid of Virginia Woolf?

CINEMATOGRAPHY (COLOR)

1939
Gone with the Wind

1941
Blood and Sand

1943
Phantom of the Opera

1944
Wilson

1946
The Yearling

1947
Black Narcissus

1948
Joan of Arc

1949
She Wore a Yellow Ribbon

1950
King Solomon's Mines

1951
An American in Paris

1952
The Quiet Man

1953
Shane

1954
Three Coins in the Fountain

1955
To Catch a Thief

1956
Around the World in 80 Days

1957
The Bridge on the River Kwai

1958
Gigi

1959
Ben-Hur

1960
Spartacus

1961
West Side Story

1962
Lawrence of Arabia

1963
Cleopatra

1964
My Fair Lady

1965
Doctor Zhivago

1966
A Man for All Seasons

COSTUME DESIGN

1948
Joan of Arc

1957
Les Girls

1958
Gigi

1967
Camelot

1968
Romeo and Juliet

1969
Anne of the Thousand Days

1970
Cromwell

1971
Nicholas and Alexandra

1972
Travels with My Aunt

1973
The Sting

1974
The Great Gatsby

1975
Barry Lyndon

1977
Star Wars

1978
Death on the Nile

1979
All That Jazz

1980
Tess

1981
Chariots of Fire

1982
Gandhi

1983
Fanny and Alexander

1984
Amadeus

1985
Ran

1986
A Room with a View

1987
The Last Emperor

1988
Dangerous Liaisons

1989
Henry V

1990
Cyrano de Bergerac

1991
Bugsy

1992
Bram Stoker's Dracula

1993
The Age of Innocence

COSTUME DESIGN (B & W)

1948
Hamlet

1949
The Heiress

1951
A Place in the Sun

1952
The Bad and the Beautiful

1953
Roman Holiday

1954
Sabrina

1955
I'll Cry Tomorrow

1959
Some Like It Hot

1961
La Dolce Vita

1963
8 1/2

1964
The Night of the Iguana

1965
Darling

1966
Who's Afraid of Virginia Woolf?

COSTUME DESIGN (COLOR)

1949
Adventures of Don Juan

1950
Samson and Delilah

1951
An American in Paris

1952
Moulin Rouge

1953
The Robe

1954
Gate of Hell

1955
Love is a Many-Splendored Thing

1956
The King and I

1959
Ben-Hur

1960
Spartacus

1961
West Side Story

1962
The Wonderful World of the Brothers Grimm

1963
Cleopatra

1964
My Fair Lady

1965
Doctor Zhivago

1966
A Man for All Seasons

DIRECTOR

1930
Lewis Milestone
All Quiet on the Western Front

1933
Frank Lloyd
Cavalcade

1934
Frank Capra
It Happened One Night

1935
John Ford
The Informer

1936
Frank Capra
Mr. Deeds Goes to Town

1937
Leo McCarey
The Awful Truth

1938
Frank Capra
You Can't Take It with You

1939
Victor Fleming
Gone with the Wind

1940
John Ford
The Grapes of Wrath

1941
John Ford
How Green was My Valley

1942
William Wyler
Mrs. Miniver

1943
Michael Curtiz
Casablanca

1944
Leo McCarey
Going My Way

1945
Billy Wilder
The Lost Weekend

1946
William Wyler
The Best Years of Our Lives

1947
Elia Kazan
Gentleman's Agreement

1948
John Huston
Treasure of the Sierra Madre

1949
Joseph L. Mankiewicz
A Letter to Three Wives

1950
Joseph L. Mankiewicz
All About Eve

1951
George Stevens
A Place in the Sun

1952
John Ford
The Quiet Man

1953
Fred Zinneman
From Here to Eternity

1954
Elia Kazan
On the Waterfront

1955
Delbert Mann
Marty

1956
George Stevens
Giant

1957
David Lean
The Bridge on the River Kwai

1958
Vincente Minnelli
Gigi

1959
William Wyler
Ben-Hur

1960
Billy Wilder
The Apartment

1961
Robert Wise
West Side Story

1962
David Lean
Lawrence of Arabia

1963
Tony Richardson
Tom Jones

1964
George Cukor
My Fair Lady

1965
Robert Wise
The Sound of Music

1966
Fred Zinneman
A Man for All Seasons

1967
Mike Nichols
The Graduate

1968
Carol Reed
Oliver!

1969
John Schlesinger
Midnight Cowboy

1970
Franklin J. Schaffner
Patton

1971
William Friedkin
The French Connection

1972
Bob Fosse
Cabaret

1973
George Roy Hill
The Sting

1974
Francis Ford Coppola
The Godfather, Part 2

1975
Milos Forman
One Flew Over the Cuckoo's Nest

1976
John G. Avildsen
Rocky

1977
Woody Allen
Annie Hall

1978
Michael Cimino
The Deer Hunter

1979
Robert Benton
Kramer vs. Kramer

1980
Robert Redford
Ordinary People

1981
Warren Beatty
Reds

1982
Richard Attenborough
Gandhi

1983
James L. Brooks
Terms of Endearment

1984
Milos Forman
Amadeus

1985
Sydney Pollack
Out of Africa

1986
Oliver Stone
Platoon

1987
Bernardo Bertolucci
The Last Emperor

1988
Barry Levinson
Rain Man

1989
Oliver Stone
Born on the Fourth of July

1990
Kevin Costner
Dances with Wolves

1991
Jonathan Demme
The Silence of the Lambs

1992
Clint Eastwood
Unforgiven

1993
Steven Spielberg
Schindler's List

FILM

1927
Wings

1929
Broadway Melody

1930
All Quiet on the Western Front

1931
Cimarron

1932
Grand Hotel

1933
Cavalcade

1934
It Happened One Night

1935
Mutiny on the Bounty

1936
The Great Ziegfeld

1937
The Life of Emile Zola

1938
You Can't Take It with You

1939
Gone with the Wind

1940
Rebecca

1941
How Green was My Valley

1942
Mrs. Miniver

1943
Casablanca

1944
Going My Way

1945
The Lost Weekend

1946
The Best Years of Our Lives

1947
Gentleman's Agreement

1948
Hamlet

1949
All the King's Men

1950
All About Eve

1951
An American in Paris

1952
The Greatest Show on Earth

1953
From Here to Eternity

1954
On the Waterfront

1955
Marty

1956
Around the World in 80 Days

1957
The Bridge on the River Kwai

1958
Gigi

1959
Ben-Hur

1960
The Apartment

1961
West Side Story

1962
Lawrence of Arabia

1963
Tom Jones

1964
My Fair Lady

1965
The Sound of Music

1966
A Man for All Seasons

1967
In the Heat of the Night

1968
Oliver!

1969
Midnight Cowboy

1970
Patton

1971
The French Connection

1972
The Godfather

1973
The Sting

1974
The Godfather, Part 2

1975
One Flew Over the Cuckoo's Nest

1976
Rocky

1977
Annie Hall

1978
The Deer Hunter

1979
Kramer vs. Kramer

1980
Ordinary People

1981
Chariots of Fire

1982
Gandhi

1983
Terms of Endearment

1984
Amadeus

1985
Out of Africa

1986
Platoon

1987
The Last Emperor

1988
Rain Man

1989
Driving Miss Daisy

1990
Dances with Wolves

1991
The Silence of the Lambs

1992
Unforgiven

1993
Schindler's List

FEATURE DOCUMENTARY

1942
Prelude to War

1954
Vanishing Prairie

1961
The Sky Above, the Mud Below

1970
Woodstock

1971
The Hellstrom Chronicle

1972
Marjoe

1975
The Man Who Skied Down Everest

1976
Harlan County, U.S.A.

1983
Times of Harvey Milk

1989
Common Threads: Stories from the Quilt

FILM EDITING

1935
A Midsummer Night's Dream

1936
Anthony Adverse

1937
Lost Horizon

FILM EDITING
▶cont.

1938
The Adventures of Robin Hood

1939
Gone with the Wind

1941
Sergeant York

1942
The Pride of the Yankees

1943
Air Force

1944
Wilson

1945
National Velvet

1946
The Best Years of Our Lives

1947
Body and Soul

1948
The Naked City

1949
Champion

1950
King Solomon's Mines

1951
A Place in the Sun

1952
High Noon

1953
From Here to Eternity

1954
On the Waterfront

1955
Picnic

1956
Around the World in 80 Days

1957
The Bridge on the River Kwai

1958
Gigi

1959
Ben-Hur

1960
The Apartment

1961
West Side Story

1962
Lawrence of Arabia

1963
How the West was Won

1964
Mary Poppins

1965
The Sound of Music

1966
Grand Prix

1967
In the Heat of the Night

1968
Bullitt

1969
Z

1970
Patton

1971
The French Connection

1972
Cabaret

1973
The Sting

1974
The Towering Inferno

1975
Jaws

1976
Rocky

1977
Star Wars

1978
The Deer Hunter

1979
All That Jazz

1980
Raging Bull

1981
Raiders of the Lost Ark

1982
Gandhi

1983
The Right Stuff

1984
The Killing Fields

1985
Witness

1986
Platoon

1987
The Last Emperor

1988
Who Framed Roger Rabbit?

1989
Born on the Fourth of July

1990
Dances with Wolves

1991
JFK

1992
Unforgiven

1993
Schindler's List

FILM—FOREIGN LANGUAGE

1949
The Bicycle Thief

1951
Rashomon

1952
Forbidden Games

1954
Gate of Hell

1955
Samurai 1: Musashi Miyamoto

1956
La Strada

1957
Nights of Cabiria

1958
Mon Oncle

1959
Black Orpheus

1960
The Virgin Spring

1961
Through a Glass Darkly

1962
Sundays & Cybele

1963
8 1/2

1964
Yesterday, Today and Tomorrow

1965
The Shop on Main Street

1966
A Man and a Woman

1967
Closely Watched Trains

1968
War and Peace

1969
Z

1971
Garden of the Finzi-Continis

1972
The Discreet Charm of the Bourgeoisie

1973
Day for Night

1974
Amarcord

1975
Dersu Uzala

1976
Black and White in Color

1977
Madame Rosa

1978
Get Out Your Handkerchiefs

1979
The Tin Drum

1980
Moscow Does Not Believe in Tears

1981
Mephisto

1983
Fanny and Alexander

1984
Dangerous Moves

1985
The Official Story

1986
The Assault

1987
Babette's Feast

1988
Pelle the Conqueror

1989
Cinema Paradiso

1990
Journey of Hope

1991
Mediterraneo

1992
Indochine

1993
Belle Epoque

MAKEUP

1981
An American Werewolf in London

1982
Quest for Fire

1984
Amadeus

1985
Mask

1986
The Fly

1987
Harry and the Hendersons

1988
Beetlejuice

1989
Driving Miss Daisy

1990
Dick Tracy

1991
Terminator 2: Judgment Day

1992
Bram Stoker's Dracula

1993
Mrs. Doubtfire

MUSIC

1934
One Night of Love

1935
The Informer

1936
Anthony Adverse

1938
The Adventures of Robin Hood
Alexander's Ragtime Band

1939
Stagecoach
The Wizard of Oz

1940
Pinocchio
Tin Pan Alley

1941
Dumbo

1942
Now, Voyager
Yankee Doodle Dandy

1943
The Song of Bernadette
This is the Army

1944
Cover Girl
Since You Went Away

1945
Anchors Aweigh
Spellbound

1946
The Best Years of Our Lives
The Jolson Story

1947
A Double Life

1948
Easter Parade
The Red Shoes

1949
The Heiress
On the Town

1950
Sunset Boulevard

1951
An American in Paris
A Place in the Sun

1952
High Noon

1953
Lili

1954
Seven Brides for Seven Brothers

1955
Love is a Many-Splendored Thing
Oklahoma!

1956
Around the World in 80 Days
The King and I

1957
The Bridge on the River Kwai

1958
Gigi

1959
Ben-Hur

1960
Exodus
Song Without End

1961
Breakfast at Tiffany's
West Side Story

1962
Lawrence of Arabia
The Music Man

1963
Irma La Douce
Tom Jones

1964
Mary Poppins
My Fair Lady

1965
Doctor Zhivago
The Sound of Music

1966
Born Free
A Funny Thing Happened on the Way to the Forum

1967
Camelot
Thoroughly Modern Millie

1968
The Lion in Winter
Oliver!

1969
Butch Cassidy and the Sundance Kid
Hello, Dolly!

1970
Let It Be
Love Story
1971
Fiddler on the Roof
Summer of '42
1972
Cabaret
1973
The Sting
The Way We Were
1974
The Godfather, Part 2
The Great Gatsby
1975
Barry Lyndon
Jaws
1976
Bound for Glory
The Omen
1977
A Little Night Music
Star Wars
1978
The Buddy Holly Story
Midnight Express
1979
All That Jazz
A Little Romance
1980
Fame
1981
Chariots of Fire
1982
E.T.: The Extra-Terrestrial
Victor/Victoria
1983
The Right Stuff
Yentl
1984
A Passage to India
Purple Rain
1985
Out of Africa
1986
Round Midnight
1987
The Last Emperor
1988
The Milagro Beanfield War
1989
The Little Mermaid
1990
Dances with Wolves
1991
Beauty and the Beast
1992
Aladdin
1993
Schindler's List

SONG

1934
"The Continental"
The Gay Divorcee
1936
"The Way You Look Tonight"
Swing Time

1939
"Over the Rainbow"
The Wizard of Oz
1940
"When You Wish Upon a Star"
Pinocchio
1941
"The Last Time I Saw Paris"
Lady Be Good
1942
"White Christmas"
Holiday Inn
1943
"You'll Never Know"
Hello, Frisco, Hello
1944
"Swinging on a Star"
Going My Way
1945
"It Might as Well Be Spring"
State Fair
1946
"On the Atchison, Topeka and Santa Fe"
The Harvey Girls
1948
"Buttons and Bows"
The Paleface
1949
"Baby It's Cold Outside"
Neptune's Daughter
1951
"In the Cool, Cool, Cool of the Evening"
Here Comes the Groom
1952
"High Noon (Do Not Forsake Me, Oh My Darlin')"
High Noon
1953
"Secret Love"
Calamity Jane
1954
"Three Coins in the Fountain"
Three Coins in the Fountain
1955
"Love Is a Many-Splendored Thing"
Love is a Many-Splendored Thing
1956
"Whatever Will Be, Will Be (Que Sera, Sera)"
The Man Who Knew Too Much
1958
"Gigi"
Gigi
1959
"High Hopes"
A Hole in the Head
1960
"Never on Sunday"
Never on Sunday
1961
"Moon River"
Breakfast at Tiffany's

1962
"Days of Wine and Roses"
Days of Wine and Roses
1963
"Call Me Irresponsible"
Papa's Delicate Condition
1964
"Chim Chim Cher-ee"
Mary Poppins
1965
"The Shadow of Your Smile"
The Sandpiper
1966
"Born Free"
Born Free
1967
"Talk to the Animals"
Doctor Dolittle
1968
"Windmills of Your Mind"
Thomas Crown Affair
1969
"Raindrops Keep Fallin' on My Head"
Butch Cassidy and the Sundance Kid
1970
"For All We Know"
Lovers and Other Strangers
1971
"Theme from Shaft"
Shaft
1972
"The Morning After"
The Poseidon Adventure
1973
"The Way We Were"
The Way We Were
1974
"We May Never Love Like This Again"
The Towering Inferno
1975
"I'm Easy"
Nashville
1976
"Evergreen"
A Star is Born
1977
"You Light Up My Life"
You Light Up My Life
1978
"Last Dance"
Thank God It's Friday
1979
"It Goes Like It Goes"
Norma Rae
1980
"Fame"
Fame
1981
"Arthur's Theme"
Arthur
1982
"Up Where We Belong"
An Officer and a Gentleman

1983
"Flashdance...What a Feeling"
Flashdance
1984
"I Just Called to Say I Love You"
The Woman in Red
1985
"Say You, Say Me"
White Nights
1986
"Take My Breath Away"
Top Gun
1987
"(I've Had) the Time of My Life"
Dirty Dancing
1988
"Let the River Run"
Working Girl
1989
"Under the Sea"
The Little Mermaid
1990
"Sooner or Later"
Dick Tracy
1991
"Beauty and the Beast"
Beauty and the Beast
1992
"A Whole New World"
Aladdin
1993
"Streets of Philadelphia"
Philadelphia

SOUND

1933
A Farewell to Arms
1934
One Night of Love
1935
Naughty Marietta
1936
San Francisco
1937
Hurricane
1938
The Cowboy and the Lady
1940
Strike Up the Band
1941
That Hamilton Woman
1942
Yankee Doodle Dandy
1943
This Land is Mine
1944
Wilson
1945
The Bells of St. Mary's
1946
The Jolson Story
1947
The Bishop's Wife
1948
The Snake Pit
1949
Twelve O'Clock High

1950
All About Eve
1951
The Great Caruso
1953
From Here to Eternity
1954
The Glenn Miller Story
1955
Oklahoma!
1956
The King and I
1957
Sayonara
1958
South Pacific
1959
Ben-Hur
1960
The Alamo
1961
West Side Story
1962
Lawrence of Arabia
1963
How the West was Won
1964
My Fair Lady
1965
The Sound of Music
1966
Grand Prix
1967
In the Heat of the Night
1968
Oliver!
1969
Hello, Dolly!
1970
Patton
1971
Fiddler on the Roof
1972
Cabaret
1973
The Exorcist
1974
Earthquake
1975
Jaws
1976
All the President's Men
1977
Star Wars
1978
The Deer Hunter
1979
Apocalypse Now
1980
The Empire Strikes Back
1981
Raiders of the Lost Ark
1982
E.T.: The Extra-Terrestrial
1983
The Right Stuff
1984
Amadeus

SOUND ▶cont.

1985
Out of Africa

1986
Platoon

1987
The Last Emperor

1988
Bird

1989
Glory

1990
Dances with Wolves

1991
Terminator 2: Judgment Day

1992
The Last of the Mohicans

1993
Jurassic Park

WRITING

1931
Cimarron

1932
The Champ

1933
Little Women

1934
It Happened One Night

1935
The Informer

1936
The Story of Louis Pasteur

1937
The Life of Emile Zola
A Star is Born

1938
Boys Town
Pygmalion

1939
Gone with the Wind
Mr. Smith Goes to Washington

1940
The Great McGinty
The Philadelphia Story

1941
Citizen Kane
Here Comes Mr. Jordan

1942
Mrs. Miniver
Woman of the Year

1943
Casablanca
The Human Comedy

1944
Going My Way
Wilson

1945
The Lost Weekend

1946
The Best Years of Our Lives
The Seventh Veil

1947
The Bachelor and the Bobby-Soxer
Miracle on 34th Street

1948
The Search
Treasure of the Sierra Madre

1949
Battleground
Joseph L. Mankiewicz
A Letter to Three Wives
The Stratton Story

1950
All About Eve
Panic in the Streets
Sunset Boulevard

1951
An American in Paris
A Place in the Sun

1952
The Bad and the Beautiful
The Greatest Show on Earth
The Lavender Hill Mob

1953
From Here to Eternity
Roman Holiday

1954
Broken Lance
Country Girl
On the Waterfront

1955
Love Me or Leave Me
Marty

1956
Around the World in 80 Days
The Brave One
The Red Balloon

1957
The Bridge on the River Kwai
Designing Woman

1958
The Defiant Ones
Gigi

1959
Pillow Talk
Room at the Top

1960
The Apartment
Elmer Gantry

1961
Judgment at Nuremberg
Splendor in the Grass

1962
Divorce—Italian Style
To Kill a Mockingbird

1963
How the West was Won
Tom Jones

1964
Becket
Father Goose

1965
Darling
Doctor Zhivago

1966
A Man and a Woman
A Man for All Seasons

1967
Guess Who's Coming to Dinner

1968
The Lion in Winter
The Producers

1969
Butch Cassidy and the Sundance Kid
Midnight Cowboy

1970
M*A*S*H
Patton

1971
The French Connection
The Hospital

1972
The Candidate
The Godfather

1973
The Exorcist
The Sting

1974
Chinatown
The Godfather, Part 2

1975
Dog Day Afternoon
One Flew Over the Cuckoo's Nest

1976
All the President's Men
Network

1977
Annie Hall
Julia

1978
Coming Home
Midnight Express

1979
Breaking Away
Kramer vs. Kramer

1980
Melvin and Howard
Ordinary People

1981
Chariots of Fire
On Golden Pond

1982
Gandhi
Missing

1983
Tender Mercies
Terms of Endearment

1984
Amadeus
Places in the Heart

1985
Out of Africa
Witness

1986
Hannah and Her Sisters
A Room with a View

1987
The Last Emperor
Moonstruck

1988
Dangerous Liaisons
Rain Man

1989
Dead Poets Society
Driving Miss Daisy

1990
Dances with Wolves
Ghost

1991
The Silence of the Lambs
Thelma & Louise

1992
The Crying Game
Howard's End

1993
The Piano
Schindler's List

AUSTRALIAN FILM INSTITUTE

ACTOR

1974
Jack Thompson
Sunday Too Far Away

1975
John Meillon
Fourth Wish

1976
Nick Tate
The Devil's Playground
Simon Burke
The Devil's Playground

1978
Bill Hunter
Newsfront

1979
Mel Gibson
Tim

1980
Jack Thompson
Breaker Morant

1981
Mel Gibson
Gallipoli

1983
Norman Kaye
Man of Flowers

1984
John Hargreaves
My First Wife

1986
Colin Friels
Malcolm

1987
Leo McKern
Travelling North

1988
Sam Neill
A Cry in the Dark

1990
Max von Sydow
Father

1991
Hugo Weaving
Proof

1992
Russell Crowe
Romper Stomper

1993
Harvey Keitel
The Piano

ACTOR—SUPPORTING

1991
Russell Crowe
Proof

1992
Barry Otto
Strictly Ballroom

ACTRESS

1977
Pat Bishop
Don's Party

1980
Tracey Mann
Hard Knocks

1981
Judy Davis
The Winter of Our Dreams

1982
Noni Hazlehurst
Monkey Grip

1983
Wendy Hughes
Careful, He Might Hear You

1985
Noni Hazlehurst
Fran

1986
Judy Davis
Kangaroo

1987
Judy Davis
High Tide

1988
Meryl Streep
A Cry in the Dark

1990
Julia Blake
Father

1991
Sheila Florence
A Woman's Tale

1992
Lisa Harrow
The Last Days of Chez Nous

1993
Holly Hunter
The Piano

ACTRESS—SUPPORTING

1992
Pat Thomsen
Strictly Ballroom

CINEMATOGRAPHY

1992
Black Robe

1993
The Piano

COSTUME DESIGN

1992
Strictly Ballroom

1993
The Piano

DIRECTOR

1991
Jocelyn Moorhouse
Proof

1992
Baz Luhrmann
Strictly Ballroom

1993
Jane Campion
The Piano

FILM

1974
Sunday Too Far Away

1976
The Devil's Playground

1978
Newsfront

1979
My Brilliant Career

1980
Breaker Morant

1981
Gallipoli

1982
Lonely Hearts

1983
Careful, He Might Hear You

1985
Bliss

1986
Malcolm

1987
The Year My Voice Broke

1988
The Navigator

1990
Flirting

1991
Proof

1992
Strictly Ballroom

1993
The Piano

FILM EDITING

1991
Proof

1993
The Piano

MUSIC

1992
Romper Stomper

1993
The Piano

SOUND

1992
Romper Stomper

1993
The Piano

WRITING

1991
Proof

1992
Strictly Ballroom

1993
The Piano

BRITISH ACADEMY OF FILM AND TELEVISION ARTS

ACTOR

1952
Marlon Brando
Viva Zapata!

1953
Marlon Brando
Julius Caesar
John Gielgud
Julius Caesar

1954
Kenneth More
Doctor in the House
Marlon Brando
On the Waterfront

1955
Ernest Borgnine
Marty
Laurence Olivier
Richard III

1956
Francois Perier
Gervaise

1957
Alec Guinness
The Bridge on the River Kwai
Henry Fonda
Twelve Angry Men

1958
Sidney Poitier
The Defiant Ones
Trevor Howard
The Key

1959
Peter Sellers
I'm All Right Jack
Jack Lemmon
Some Like It Hot

1960
Jack Lemmon
The Apartment

1961
Paul Newman
The Hustler
Peter Finch
No Love for Johnnie

1962
Burt Lancaster
Birdman of Alcatraz
Peter O'Toole
Lawrence of Arabia

1963
Marcello Mastroianni
Divorce—Italian Style
Dirk Bogarde
The Servant

1964
Richard Attenborough
Seance on a Wet Afternoon
Marcello Mastroianni
Yesterday, Today and Tomorrow

1965
Lee Marvin
Cat Ballou
Dirk Bogarde
Darling

1966
Rod Steiger
The Pawnbroker
Richard Burton
Who's Afraid of Virginia Woolf?

1967
Rod Steiger
In the Heat of the Night
Paul Scofield
A Man for All Seasons

1968
Spencer Tracy
Guess Who's Coming to Dinner

1969
Dustin Hoffman
Midnight Cowboy

1970
Robert Redford
Butch Cassidy and the Sundance Kid

1971
Peter Finch
Sunday, Bloody Sunday

1972
Gene Hackman
The French Connection

1973
Walter Matthau
Pete 'n' Tillie

1974
Jack Nicholson
Chinatown
Jack Nicholson
The Last Detail

1975
Al Pacino
Dog Day Afternoon

1976
Jack Nicholson
One Flew Over the Cuckoo's Nest

1977
Peter Finch
Network

1978
Richard Dreyfuss
The Goodbye Girl

1979
Jack Lemmon
The China Syndrome

1980
John Hurt
The Elephant Man

1981
Burt Lancaster
Atlantic City

1982
Ben Kingsley
Gandhi

1983
Michael Caine
Educating Rita
Dustin Hoffman
Tootsie

1984
Haing S. Ngor
The Killing Fields

1985
William Hurt
Kiss of the Spider Woman

1986
Bob Hoskins
Mona Lisa

1987
Sean Connery
The Name of the Rose

1988
John Cleese
A Fish Called Wanda

1989
Daniel Day-Lewis
My Left Foot

1990
Philippe Noiret
Cinema Paradiso

1992
Anthony Hopkins
The Silence of the Lambs

1993
Robert Downey, Jr.
Chaplin

1994
Anthony Hopkins
The Remains of the Day

ACTOR— SUPPORTING

1971
Edward Fox
The Go-Between

1972
Ben Johnson
The Last Picture Show

1973
Arthur Lowe
O Lucky Man!

1974
John Gielgud
Murder on the Orient Express

1975
Fred Astaire
The Towering Inferno

1976
Brad Dourif
One Flew Over the Cuckoo's Nest

1977
Edward Fox
A Bridge Too Far

1978
John Hurt
Midnight Express

1979
Robert Duvall
Apocalypse Now

1981
Ian Holm
Chariots of Fire

1982
Jack Nicholson
Reds

1983
Denholm Elliott
Trading Places

1984
Denholm Elliott
A Private Function

1985
Denholm Elliott
Defense of the Realm

1986
Ray McAnally
The Mission

1987
Daniel Auteuil
Jean de Florette

1988
Michael Palin
A Fish Called Wanda

1989
Ray McAnally
My Left Foot

1990
Salvatore Cascio
Cinema Paradiso

1992
Alan Rickman
Robin Hood: Prince of Thieves

1993
Gene Hackman
Unforgiven

1994
Ralph Fiennes
Schindler's List

ACTRESS

1952
Vivien Leigh
A Streetcar Named Desire

1953
Leslie Caron
Lili
Audrey Hepburn
Roman Holiday

1955
Katie Johnson
Ladykillers
Betsy Blair
Marty

1956
Anna Magnani
The Rose Tattoo

1958
Simone Signoret
Room at the Top

1959
Shirley MacLaine
Ask Any Girl
Audrey Hepburn
The Nun's Story

ACTRESS ▶cont.

1960
Shirley MacLaine
The Apartment

1961
Sophia Loren
Two Women

1962
Anne Bancroft
The Miracle Worker

1963
Patricia Neal
Hud
Rachel Roberts
This Sporting Life

1964
Audrey Hepburn
Charade

1965
Julie Christie
Darling
Patricia Neal
In Harm's Way

1966
Elizabeth Taylor
Who's Afraid of Virginia Woolf?

1967
Anouk Aimee
A Man and a Woman

1968
Katharine Hepburn
Guess Who's Coming to Dinner

1969
Dame Maggie Smith
The Prime of Miss Jean Brodie

1970
Katharine Ross
Butch Cassidy and the Sundance Kid

1971
Glenda Jackson
Sunday, Bloody Sunday

1972
Liza Minnelli
Cabaret

1973
Delphine Seyrig
The Discreet Charm of the Bourgeoisie

1974
Joanne Woodward
Summer Wishes, Winter Dreams

1975
Ellen Burstyn
Alice Doesn't Live Here Anymore

1976
Louise Fletcher
One Flew Over the Cuckoo's Nest

1977
Diane Keaton
Annie Hall

1978
Jane Fonda
Julia

1979
Jane Fonda
The China Syndrome

1980
Judy Davis
My Brilliant Career

1981
Meryl Streep
The French Lieutenant's Woman

1982
Katharine Hepburn
On Golden Pond

1983
Julie Walters
Educating Rita

1984
Dame Maggie Smith
A Private Function

1985
Peggy Ashcroft
A Passage to India

1986
Dame Maggie Smith
A Room with a View

1987
Anne Bancroft
84 Charing Cross Road

1988
Dame Maggie Smith
The Lonely Passion of Judith Hearne

1989
Pauline Collins
Shirley Valentine

1990
Jessica Tandy
Driving Miss Daisy

1992
Jodie Foster
The Silence of the Lambs

1993
Emma Thompson
Howard's End

1994
Holly Hunter
The Piano

ACTRESS— SUPPORTING

1961
Dora Bryan
A Taste of Honey

1969
Celia Johnson
The Prime of Miss Jean Brodie

1970
Susannah York
They Shoot Horses, Don't They?

1971
Margaret Leighton
The Go-Between

1972
Cloris Leachman
The Last Picture Show

1973
Valentina Cortese
Day for Night

1974
Ingrid Bergman
Murder on the Orient Express

1975
Diane Ladd
Alice Doesn't Live Here Anymore

1976
Jodie Foster
Taxi Driver

1977
Jenny Agutter
Equus

1978
Geraldine Page
Interiors
Vanessa Redgrave
Julia

1979
Rachel Roberts
Yanks

1982
Rohini Hattangady
Gandhi
Maureen Stapleton
Reds

1983
Jamie Lee Curtis
Trading Places

1984
Liz Smith
A Private Function

1985
Rosanna Arquette
Desperately Seeking Susan

1986
Judi Dench
A Room with a View

1987
Susan Wooldridge
Hope and Glory

1988
Judi Dench
A Handful of Dust

1989
Michelle Pfeiffer
Dangerous Liaisons

1990
Whoopi Goldberg
Ghost

1992
Kate Nelligan
Frankie and Johnny

1993
Miranda Richardson
Damage

1994
Miriam Margolyes
The Age of Innocence

DIRECTOR

1955
Laurence Olivier
Richard III

1968
Mike Nichols
The Graduate

1969
John Schlesinger
Midnight Cowboy

1970
George Roy Hill
Butch Cassidy and the Sundance Kid

1971
John Schlesinger
Sunday, Bloody Sunday

1972
Bob Fosse
Cabaret

1973
Francois Truffaut
Day for Night

1974
Roman Polanski
Chinatown

1975
Stanley Kubrick
Barry Lyndon

1976
Milos Forman
One Flew Over the Cuckoo's Nest

1977
Woody Allen
Annie Hall

1978
Alan Parker
Midnight Express

1979
Francis Ford Coppola
Apocalypse Now

1980
Akira Kurosawa
Kagemusha

1981
Louis Malle
Atlantic City

1982
Richard Attenborough
Gandhi

1983
Bill Forsyth
Local Hero

1984
Wim Wenders
Paris, Texas

1986
Woody Allen
Hannah and Her Sisters

1987
Oliver Stone
Platoon

1988
Louis Malle
Au Revoir Les Enfants

1989
Kenneth Branagh
Henry V

1990
Martin Scorsese
Goodfellas

1992
Alan Parker
The Commitments

1993
Clint Eastwood
Unforgiven

1994
Steven Spielberg
Schindler's List

FILM

1947
The Best Years of Our Lives
Odd Man Out

1948
The Fallen Idol
Hamlet

1949
The Bicycle Thief
The Third Man

1950
All About Eve
The Blue Lamp

1951
La Ronde
The Lavender Hill Mob

1953
Forbidden Games
Genevieve

1954
Hobson's Choice
Wages of Fear

1955
Richard III

1956
Gervaise
Reach for the Sky

1957
The Bridge on the River Kwai

1958
Room at the Top

1959
Ben-Hur
Sapphire

1960
The Apartment

1961
Ballad of a Soldier
The Hustler
A Taste of Honey

1962
Lawrence of Arabia

1963
Tom Jones

1964
Dr. Strangelove, or: How I Learned to Stop Worrying and Love the Bomb

1965
The Ipcress File
My Fair Lady

1966
The Spy Who Came in from the Cold
Who's Afraid of Virginia Woolf?

1967
A Man for All Seasons

1968
The Graduate

1969
Midnight Cowboy

1970
Butch Cassidy and the Sundance Kid

1971
Sunday, Bloody Sunday

1972
Cabaret

1973
Day for Night

1975
Alice Doesn't Live Here Anymore

1976
One Flew Over the Cuckoo's Nest

1977
Annie Hall

1978
Julia

1979
Manhattan

1980
The Elephant Man

1981
Chariots of Fire

1982
Gandhi

1983
Educating Rita

1984
The Killing Fields

1985
The Purple Rose of Cairo

1986
A Room with a View

1987
Hope and Glory
Jean de Florette

1988
The Last Emperor

1989
Dead Poets Society

1990
Goodfellas

1992
The Commitments

1993
Unforgiven

1994
Schindler's List
Shadowlands

CANNES

ACTOR

1946
Ray Milland
The Lost Weekend

1949
Edward G. Robinson
House of Strangers

1951
Michael Redgrave
The Browning Version

1952
Marlon Brando
Viva Zapata!

1953
Charles Vanel
Wages of Fear

1955
Spencer Tracy
Bad Day at Black Rock

1958
Paul Newman
The Long, Hot Summer

1961
Anthony Perkins
Goodbye Again

1962
Murray Melvin
A Taste of Honey

1963
Richard Harris
This Sporting Life

1964
Saro Urzi
Seduced and Abandoned

1965
Terence Stamp
The Collector

1966
Per Oscarsson
Hunger

1969
Jean-Louis Trintignant
Z

1971
Riccardo Cucciolla
Sacco & Vanzetti

1973
Giancarlo Giannini
Love and Anarchy

1974
Jack Nicholson
The Last Detail

1978
Jon Voight
Coming Home

1979
Jack Lemmon
The China Syndrome

1981
Ugo Tognazzi
The Tragedy of a Ridiculous Man

1982
Jack Lemmon
Missing

1984
Alfredo Landa
The Holy Innocents
Francesco Rabal
The Holy Innocents

1985
William Hurt
Kiss of the Spider Woman

1986
Michel Blanc
Menage
Bob Hoskins
Mona Lisa

1987
Marcello Mastroianni
Dark Eyes

1988
Forest Whitaker
Bird

1989
James Spader
sex, lies and videotape

1990
Gerard Depardieu
Cyrano de Bergerac

1991
John Turturro
Barton Fink

1992
Tim Robbins
The Player

1993
David Thewlis
Naked

ACTRESS

1946
Michele Morgan
La Symphonie Pastorale

1951
Bette Davis
All About Eve

1952
Lee Grant
Detective Story

1953
Shirley Booth
Come Back, Little Sheba

1956
Susan Hayward
I'll Cry Tomorrow

1957
Giulietta Masina
Nights of Cabiria

1958
Eva Dahlbeck
Brink of Life
Bibi Andersson
Brink of Life
Ingrid Thulin
Brink of Life

1959
Simone Signoret
Room at the Top

1960
Melina Mercouri
Never on Sunday

1961
Sophia Loren
Two Women

1962
Katharine Hepburn
Long Day's Journey into Night
Rita Tushingham
A Taste of Honey

1965
Samantha Eggar
The Collector

1966
Vanessa Redgrave
Morgan!

1967
Pia Degermark
Elvira Madigan

1969
Vanessa Redgrave
Isadora

1971
Kitty Winn
Panic in Needle Park

1973
Joanne Woodward
The Effect of Gamma Rays on Man-in-the-Moon Marigolds

1974
Marie-Jose Nat
Les Violons du Bal

1975
Valerie Perrine
Lenny

1976
Dominique Sanda
The Inheritance

1978
Jill Clayburgh
An Unmarried Woman
Isabelle Huppert
Violette

1979
Sally Field
Norma Rae

1981
Isabelle Adjani
Quartet

1982
Jadwiga Jankowska Cieslak
Another Way

1984
Helen Mirren
Cal

1985
Cher
Mask
Norma Aleandro
The Official Story

1986
Barbara Sukowa
Rosa Luxemburg

1987
Barbara Hershey
Shy People

1988
Barbara Hershey
A World Apart
Jodhi May
A World Apart
Linda Mvusi
A World Apart

1989
Meryl Streep
A Cry in the Dark

1991
Irene Jacob
The Double Life of Veronique

1992
Pernilla August
The Best Intentions

1993
Holly Hunter
The Piano

DIRECTOR

1951
Luis Bunuel
Los Olvidados

1955
Jules Dassin
Rififi

1957
Robert Bresson
A Man Escaped

1958
Ingmar Bergman
Brink of Life

1959
Francois Truffaut
The 400 Blows

1969
Vojtech Jasny
All My Good Countrymen

1976
Ettore Scola
Down & Dirty

1978
Nagisa Oshima
The Empire of Passion

1979
Terence Malick
Days of Heaven

1982
Werner Herzog
Fitzcarraldo

1983
Robert Bresson
L'Argent

1984
Bertrand Tavernier
A Sunday in the Country

1985
Andre Techine
Rendez-vous

1986
Martin Scorsese
After Hours

1989
Emir Kusturica
Time of the Gypsies

1990
Pavel Lounguine
Taxi Blues

1991
Joel Coen
Barton Fink

1992
Robert Altman
The Player

1993
Mike Leigh
Naked

FILM

1946
The Lost Weekend

1949
The Third Man

1951
Los Olvidados
Miracle in Milan
Miss Julie

1952
Othello
White Mane

1953
Wages of Fear

1954
Gate of Hell

1955
Marty

1957
Friendly Persuasion

1958
The Cranes are Flying

1959
Black Orpheus

FILM ▶cont.

1960
La Dolce Vita

1961
Viridiana

1964
Umbrellas of Cherbourg

1966
A Man and a Woman

1967
Blow-Up
Dutchman

1969
If...

1970
M*A*S*H

1971
The Go-Between

1973
Scarecrow

1974
The Conversation

1976
Taxi Driver

1977
Padre Padrone

1978
*The Tree of Wooden
Clogs*

1979
Apocalypse Now
The Tin Drum

1980
All That Jazz
Kagemusha

1981
Man of Iron

1982
Missing
Yol

1983
The Ballad of Narayama

1984
Paris, Texas

1985
Dance with a Stranger
*When Father was Away
on Business*

1986
The Mission

1987
Under Satan's Sun

1988
Pelle the Conqueror

1989
sex, lies and videotape

1990
*Overseas: Three Women
with Man Trouble*
Wild at Heart

1991
Barton Fink

1992
The Best Intentions
My New Gun

1993
Farewell My Concubine
The Piano

1994
Pulp Fiction

CESAR

ACTOR

1978
Jean Rochefort
Le Crabe Tambour

1979
Michel Serrault
La Cage aux Folles

1981
Gerard Depardieu
The Last Metro

1983
Philippe Leotard
La Balance

1984
Coluche
Tchao Pantin

1986
Christopher Lambert
Subway

1987
Daniel Auteuil
Jean de Florette

1988
Richard Bohringer
Le Grand Chemin

1990
Philippe Noiret
Life and Nothing But

1991
Gerard Depardieu
Cyrano de Bergerac

1992
Jacques Dutronc
Van Gogh

ACTOR—
SUPPORTING

1977
Claude Brasseur
Pardon Mon Affaire

1978
Jacques Dufilho
Le Crabe Tambour

1979
Jacques Villeret
Robert et Robert

1980
Jean Bouise
Hothead

1984
Richard Anconina
Tchao Pantin

1986
Michel Boujenah
Three Men and a Cradle

1989
Patrick Chesnais
La Lectrice

1991
Jacques Weber
Cyrano de Bergerac

1993
Andre Dussollier
Un Coeur en Hiver

ACTRESS

1978
Simone Signoret
Madame Rosa

1981
Catherine Deneuve
The Last Metro

1982
Isabelle Adjani
Possession

1983
Nathalie Baye
La Balance

1984
Isabelle Adjani
One Deadly Summer

1985
Sabine Azema
A Sunday in the Country

1986
Sandrine Bonnaire
Vagabond

1988
Anemone
Le Grand Chemin

1989
Isabelle Adjani
Camille Claudel

1990
Carol Bouquet
Too Beautiful for You

1991
Anne Parillaud
La Femme Nikita

1993
Catherine Deneuve
Indochine

1994
Juliette Binoche
Trois Couleurs: Bleu

ACTRESS—
SUPPORTING

1976
Marie-France Pisier
Cousin, Cousine

1979
Stephane Audran
Violette

1984
Suzanne Flon
One Deadly Summer

1987
Emmanuelle Beart
Jean de Florette

1989
Helene Vincent
Life Is a Long Quiet River

1991
Dominique Blanc
May Fools

1993
Dominique Blanc
Indochine

DIRECTOR

1978
Alain Resnais
Providence

1980
Roman Polanski
Tess

1981
Francois Truffaut
The Last Metro

1983
Andrzej Wajda
Danton

1984
Ettore Scola
Le Bal

1986
Michel DeVille
Peril

1987
Alain Cavalier
Therese

1988
Louis Malle
Au Revoir Les Enfants

1990
Bertrand Blier
Too Beautiful for You

1991
Jean-Paul Rappeneau
Cyrano de Bergerac

1992
Alain Corneau
Tous les Matins du Monde

1993
Claude Sautet
Un Coeur en Hiver

FILM

1978
Providence

1980
Tess

1981
The Last Metro

1983
La Balance

1984
Le Bal

1986
Three Men and a Cradle

1987
Therese

1988
Au Revoir Les Enfants

1989
Camille Claudel

1990
Too Beautiful for You

1991
Cyrano de Bergerac

1992
Tous les Matins du Monde

1993
Les Nuits Fauves

CANADIAN
GENIE

ACTOR

1980
Christopher Plummer
Murder by Decree

1982
Nick Mancuso
Ticket to Heaven

1983
Donald Sutherland
Threshold

1984
Eric Fryer
The Terry Fox Story

1986
John Wildman
My American Cousin

1987
Gordon Pinsent
John and the Missus

1988
Roger Le Bel
Night Zoo

1989
Jeremy Irons
Dead Ringers

1990
Remy Girard
Jesus of Montreal

ACTOR—
SUPPORTING

1981
German Houde
Les Bons Debarras

1982
Saul Rubinek
Ticket to Heaven

1983
R.H. Thomson
*If You Could See What I
Hear*

1984
Michael Zelniker
The Terry Fox Story

1985
Alan Scarfe
The Bay Boy

1986
Alan Arkin
Joshua Then and Now

1987
Gabriel Arcand
*The Decline of the
American Empire*

1988
German Houde
Night Zoo

1990
Remy Girard
Jesus of Montreal

ACTRESS

1980
Kate Lynch
Meatballs

1981
Marie Tifo
Les Bons Debarras

1982
Margot Kidder
Heartaches

1983
Rae Dawn Chong
Quest for Fire

1986
Margaret Langrick
My American Cousin

1987
Martha Henry
Dancing in the Dark

1988
Sheila McCarthy
I've Heard the Mermaids Singing

1990
Rebecca Jenkins
Bye Bye Blues

ACTRESS—SUPPORTING

1980
Genevieve Bujold
Murder by Decree

1981
Kate Reid
Atlantic City

1983
Jackie Burroughs
The Grey Fox

1986
Linda Sorensen
Joshua Then and Now

1987
Louise Portal
The Decline of the American Empire

1988
Paule Baillargeon
I've Heard the Mermaids Singing

1989
Colleen Dewhurst
Obsessed

1990
Robyn Stevan
Bye Bye Blues

1992
Monique Mercure
Naked Lunch

CINEMATOGRAPHY

1993
32 Short Films About Glenn Gould

DIRECTOR

1980
Bob (Benjamin) Clark
Murder by Decree

1981
Francis Mankiewicz
Les Bons Debarras

1983
Phillip Borsos
The Grey Fox

1984
Bob (Benjamin) Clark
A Christmas Story
David Cronenberg
Videodrome

1986
Sandy Wilson
My American Cousin

1987
Denys Arcand
The Decline of the American Empire

1988
Jean-Claude Lauzon
Night Zoo

1989
David Cronenberg
Dead Ringers

1990
Denys Arcand
Jesus of Montreal

1992
David Cronenberg
Naked Lunch

1993
Francois Girard
32 Short Films About Glenn Gould

FILM

1980
The Changeling

1981
Les Bons Debarras

1982
Ticket to Heaven

1983
The Grey Fox

1984
The Terry Fox Story

1985
The Bay Boy

1986
My American Cousin

1987
The Decline of the American Empire

1988
Night Zoo

1989
Dead Ringers

1990
Jesus of Montreal

1992
Naked Lunch

1993
32 Short Films About Glenn Gould

FILM EDITING

1993
32 Short Films About Glenn Gould

GOLDEN GLOBE AWARDS

ACTOR—DRAMA

1944
Paul Lukas
Watch on the Rhine

1945
Alexander Knox
Wilson

1946
Ray Milland
The Lost Weekend

1947
Gregory Peck
The Yearling

1948
Ronald Colman
A Double Life

1949
Laurence Olivier
Hamlet

1950
Broderick Crawford
All the King's Men

1951
Jose Ferrer
Cyrano de Bergerac

1953
Gary Cooper
High Noon

1955
Marlon Brando
On the Waterfront

1956
Ernest Borgnine
Marty

1957
Kirk Douglas
Lust for Life

1958
Alec Guinness
The Bridge on the River Kwai

1959
David Niven
Separate Tables

1960
Anthony (Tony) Franciosa
Career

1961
Burt Lancaster
Elmer Gantry

1962
Maximilian Schell
Judgment at Nuremberg

1963
Gregory Peck
To Kill a Mockingbird

1964
Sidney Poitier
Lilies of the Field

1965
Peter O'Toole
Becket

1966
Omar Sharif
Doctor Zhivago

1967
Paul Scofield
A Man for All Seasons

1968
Rod Steiger
In the Heat of the Night

1969
Peter O'Toole
The Lion in Winter

1970
John Wayne
True Grit

1971
George C. Scott
Patton

1972
Gene Hackman
The French Connection

1973
Marlon Brando
The Godfather

1974
Al Pacino
Serpico

1975
Jack Nicholson
Chinatown

1976
Jack Nicholson
One Flew Over the Cuckoo's Nest

1977
Peter Finch
Network

1978
Richard Burton
Equus

1979
Jon Voight
Coming Home

1980
Dustin Hoffman
Kramer vs. Kramer

1981
Robert De Niro
Raging Bull

1982
Henry Fonda
On Golden Pond

1983
Ben Kingsley
Gandhi
Robert Duvall
Tender Mercies

1984
Tom Courtenay
The Dresser

1985
F. Murray Abraham
Amadeus

1986
Jon Voight
Runaway Train

1987
Bob Hoskins
Mona Lisa

1988
Michael Douglas
Wall Street

1989
Dustin Hoffman
Rain Man

1990
Tom Cruise
Born on the Fourth of July

1991
Jeremy Irons
Reversal of Fortune

1992
Nick Nolte
The Prince of Tides

1993
Al Pacino
Scent of a Woman

1994
Tom Hanks
Philadelphia

ACTOR—MUSICAL/COMEDY

1951
Fred Astaire
Three Little Words

1953
Donald O'Connor
Singin' in the Rain

1954
David Niven
Moon is Blue

1955
James Mason
A Star is Born

1956
Tom Ewell
The Seven Year Itch

1957
Cantinflas
Around the World in 80 Days

1958
Frank Sinatra
Pal Joey

1960
Jack Lemmon
Some Like It Hot

1961
Jack Lemmon
The Apartment

1962
Glenn Ford
Pocketful of Miracles

1963
Marcello Mastroianni
Divorce—Italian Style

1965
Rex Harrison
My Fair Lady

1966
Lee Marvin
Cat Ballou

1967
Alan Arkin
The Russians are Coming, the Russians are Coming

1968
Richard Harris
Camelot

1969
Ron Moody
Oliver!

ACTOR— MUSICAL/ COMEDY ▶cont.

1970
Peter O'Toole
Goodbye, Mr. Chips

1971
Albert Finney
Scrooge

1972
Chaim Topol
Fiddler on the Roof

1974
George Segal
A Touch of Class

1975
Art Carney
Harry and Tonto

1976
Walter Matthau
The Sunshine Boys

1977
Kris Kristofferson
A Star is Born

1978
Richard Dreyfuss
The Goodbye Girl

1979
Warren Beatty
Heaven Can Wait

1980
Peter Sellers
Being There

1981
Ray Sharkey
Idolmaker

1982
Dudley Moore
Arthur

1983
Dustin Hoffman
Tootsie

1984
Michael Caine
Educating Rita

1985
Dudley Moore
Micki & Maude

1986
Jack Nicholson
Prizzi's Honor

1987
Paul Hogan
Crocodile Dundee

1988
Robin Williams
Good Morning, Vietnam

1989
Tom Hanks
Big

1990
Morgan Freeman
Driving Miss Daisy

1991
Gerard Depardieu
Green Card

1992
Robin Williams
The Fisher King

1993
Tim Robbins
The Player

1994
Robin Williams
Mrs. Doubtfire

ACTOR— SUPPORTING

1945
Barry Fitzgerald
Going My Way

1947
Clifton Webb
The Razor's Edge

1948
Edmund Gwenn
Miracle on 34th Street

1949
Walter Huston
Treasure of the Sierra Madre

1950
James Whitmore
Battleground

1952
Peter Ustinov
Quo Vadis

1954
Frank Sinatra
From Here to Eternity

1955
Edmond O'Brien
The Barefoot Contessa

1957
Earl Holliman
The Rainmaker

1958
Red Buttons
Sayonara

1959
Burl Ives
Big Country

1960
Stephen Boyd
Ben-Hur

1961
Sal Mineo
Exodus

1962
George Chakiris
West Side Story

1963
Omar Sharif
Lawrence of Arabia

1964
John Huston
The Cardinal

1965
Edmond O'Brien
Seven Days in May

1966
Oskar Werner
The Spy Who Came in from the Cold

1967
Richard Attenborough
The Sand Pebbles

1968
David Attenborough
Doctor Dolittle

1970
Gig Young
They Shoot Horses, Don't They?

1971
John Mills
Ryan's Daughter

1972
Ben Johnson
The Last Picture Show

1973
Joel Grey
Cabaret

1974
John Houseman
The Paper Chase

1975
Fred Astaire
The Towering Inferno

1976
Richard Benjamin
The Sunshine Boys

1977
Laurence Olivier
Marathon Man

1978
Peter Firth
Equus

1979
John Hurt
Midnight Express

1980
Robert Duvall
Apocalypse Now
Melvyn Douglas
Being There

1981
Timothy Hutton
Ordinary People

1982
John Gielgud
Arthur

1983
Louis Gossett, Jr.
An Officer and a Gentleman

1984
Jack Nicholson
Terms of Endearment

1985
Haing S. Ngor
The Killing Fields

1986
Klaus Maria Brandauer
Out of Africa

1987
Tom Berenger
Platoon

1988
Sean Connery
The Untouchables

1989
Martin Landau
Tucker: The Man and His Dream

1990
Denzel Washington
Glory

1991
Bruce Davison
Longtime Companion

1992
Jack Palance
City Slickers

1993
Gene Hackman
Unforgiven

1994
Tommy Lee Jones
The Fugitive

ACTRESS— DRAMA

1944
Jennifer Jones
The Song of Bernadette

1945
Ingrid Bergman
Gaslight

1946
Ingrid Bergman
The Bells of St. Mary's

1947
Rosalind Russell
Sister Kenny

1949
Jane Wyman
Johnny Belinda

1950
Olivia de Havilland
The Heiress

1951
Gloria Swanson
Sunset Boulevard

1953
Shirley Booth
Come Back, Little Sheba

1954
Audrey Hepburn
Roman Holiday

1955
Grace Kelly
Country Girl

1956
Anna Magnani
The Rose Tattoo

1957
Ingrid Bergman
Anastasia

1958
Joanne Woodward
The Three Faces of Eve

1959
Susan Hayward
I Want to Live!

1960
Elizabeth Taylor
Suddenly, Last Summer

1961
Greer Garson
Sunrise at Campobello

1962
Geraldine Page
Summer and Smoke

1963
Geraldine Page
Sweet Bird of Youth

1966
Samantha Eggar
The Collector

1967
Anouk Aimee
A Man and a Woman

1969
Joanne Woodward
Rachel, Rachel

1970
Genevieve Bujold
Anne of the Thousand Days

1971
Ali MacGraw
Love Story

1972
Jane Fonda
Klute

1974
Marsha Mason
Cinderella Liberty

1975
Gena Rowlands
A Woman Under the Influence

1976
Louise Fletcher
One Flew Over the Cuckoo's Nest

1977
Faye Dunaway
Network

1978
Jane Fonda
Julia

1979
Jane Fonda
Coming Home

1980
Sally Field
Norma Rae

1981
Mary Tyler Moore
Ordinary People

1982
Meryl Streep
The French Lieutenant's Woman

1983
Meryl Streep
Sophie's Choice

1984
Shirley MacLaine
Terms of Endearment

1985
Sally Field
Places in the Heart

1986
Whoopi Goldberg
The Color Purple

1987
Marlee Matlin
Children of a Lesser God

1988
Sally Kirkland
Anna
Sigourney Weaver
Gorillas in the Mist

1989
Jodie Foster
The Accused
Shirley MacLaine
Madame Sousatzka

1990
Michelle Pfeiffer
The Fabulous Baker Boys

1991
Kathy Bates
Misery

1992
Jodie Foster
The Silence of the Lambs

1993
Emma Thompson
Howard's End

1994
Debra Winger
A Dangerous Woman
Holly Hunter
The Piano

ACTRESS— MUSICAL/COMEDY

1951
Judy Holliday
Born Yesterday

1955
Judy Garland
A Star is Born

1956
Jean Simmons
Guys and Dolls

1957
Deborah Kerr
The King and I

1958
Kay Kendall
Les Girls

1959
Rosalind Russell
Auntie Mame

1960
Marilyn Monroe
Some Like It Hot

1961
Shirley MacLaine
The Apartment

1963
Rosalind Russell
Gypsy

1964
Shirley MacLaine
Irma La Douce

1965
Julie Andrews
Mary Poppins

1966
Julie Andrews
The Sound of Music

1967
Lynn Redgrave
Georgy Girl

1968
Anne Bancroft
The Graduate

1969
Barbra Streisand
Funny Girl

1971
Carrie Snodgress
Diary of a Mad Housewife

1972
Twiggy
The Boy Friend

1973
Liza Minnelli
Cabaret

1974
Glenda Jackson
A Touch of Class

1975
Raquel Welch
The Three Musketeers

1976
Ann-Margret
Tommy

1977
Barbra Streisand
A Star is Born

1978
Diane Keaton
Annie Hall
Marsha Mason
The Goodbye Girl

1979
Dame Maggie Smith
California Suite
Ellen Burstyn
Same Time, Next Year

1980
Bette Midler
The Rose

1981
Sissy Spacek
Coal Miner's Daughter

1982
Bernadette Peters
Pennies From Heaven

1983
Julie Andrews
Victor/Victoria

1984
Julie Walters
Educating Rita

1985
Kathleen Turner
Romancing the Stone

1986
Kathleen Turner
Prizzi's Honor

1987
Sissy Spacek
Crimes of the Heart

1988
Cher
Moonstruck

1989
Melanie Griffith
Working Girl

1990
Jessica Tandy
Driving Miss Daisy

1991
Julia Roberts
Pretty Woman

1992
Bette Midler
For the Boys

1993
Miranda Richardson
Enchanted April

1994
Angela Bassett
What's Love Got to Do With It?

ACTRESS— SUPPORTING

1945
Agnes Moorehead
Mrs. Parkington

1946
Angela Lansbury
Picture of Dorian Gray

1947
Anne Baxter
The Razor's Edge

1948
Celeste Holm
Gentleman's Agreement

1949
Ellen Corby
I Remember Mama

1950
Mercedes McCambridge
All the King's Men

1951
Josephine Hull
Harvey

1952
Kim Hunter
A Streetcar Named Desire

1953
Katy Jurado
High Noon

1954
Grace Kelly
Mogambo

1956
Marisa Pavan
The Rose Tattoo

1957
Eileen Heckart
The Bad Seed

1958
Elsa Lanchester
Witness for the Prosecution

1959
Hermione Gingold
Gigi

1960
Susan Kohner
Imitation of Life

1961
Janet Leigh
Psycho

1962
Rita Moreno
West Side Story

1963
Angela Lansbury
The Manchurian Candidate

1964
Margaret Rutherford
The V.I.P.'s

1965
Agnes Moorehead
Hush, Hush, Sweet Charlotte

1966
Ruth Gordon
Inside Daisy Clover

1967
Jocelyn Lagarde
Hawaii

1968
Carol Channing
Thoroughly Modern Millie

1969
Ruth Gordon
Rosemary's Baby

1970
Goldie Hawn
Cactus Flower

1971
Maureen Stapleton
Airport
Karen Black
Five Easy Pieces

1972
Ann-Margret
Carnal Knowledge

1973
Shelley Winters
The Poseidon Adventure

1974
Linda Blair
The Exorcist

1975
Karen Black
The Great Gatsby

1976
Brenda Vaccaro
Once is Not Enough

1977
Katharine Ross
Voyage of the Damned

1978
Vanessa Redgrave
Julia

1979
Dyan Cannon
Heaven Can Wait

1980
Meryl Streep
Kramer vs. Kramer

1981
Mary Steenburgen
Melvin and Howard

1982
Joan Hackett
Only When I Laugh

1983
Jessica Lange
Tootsie

1984
Cher
Silkwood

1985
Peggy Ashcroft
A Passage to India

1986
Meg Tilly
Agnes of God

1987
Dame Maggie Smith
A Room with a View

1988
Olympia Dukakis
Moonstruck

1989
Sigourney Weaver
Working Girl

1990
Julia Roberts
Steel Magnolias

1991
Whoopi Goldberg
Ghost

1992
Mercedes Ruehl
The Fisher King

1993
Joan Plowright
Enchanted April

1994
Winona Ryder
The Age of Innocence

BEST FILM— DRAMA

1944
The Song of Bernadette

1945
Going My Way

1946
The Lost Weekend

1947
The Best Years of Our Lives

1948
Gentleman's Agreement

1949
Johnny Belinda
Treasure of the Sierra Madre

1950
All the King's Men

1951
Sunset Boulevard

1952
A Place in the Sun

1953
The Greatest Show on Earth

1954
The Robe

1955
On the Waterfront

1956
East of Eden

1957
Around the World in 80 Days

1958
The Bridge on the River Kwai

1959
The Defiant Ones

1960
Ben-Hur

1961
Spartacus

1962
The Guns of Navarone

1963
Lawrence of Arabia

1964
The Cardinal

1965
Becket

1966
Doctor Zhivago

1967
A Man for All Seasons

GOLDEN GLOBE AWARDS

BEST FILM— DRAMA ▶cont.

1968
In the Heat of the Night

1969
The Lion in Winter

1970
Anne of the Thousand Days

1971
Love Story

1972
The French Connection

1973
The Godfather

1974
The Exorcist

1975
Chinatown

1976
One Flew Over the Cuckoo's Nest

1977
Rocky

1978
The Turning Point

1979
Midnight Express

1980
Kramer vs. Kramer

1981
Ordinary People

1982
On Golden Pond

1983
E.T.: The Extra-Terrestrial

1984
Terms of Endearment

1985
Amadeus

1986
Out of Africa

1987
Platoon

1988
The Last Emperor

1989
Rain Man

1990
Born on the Fourth of July

1991
Dances with Wolves

1992
Bugsy

1993
Scent of a Woman

1994
Schindler's List

BEST FILM— MUSICAL/COMEDY

1952
An American in Paris

1955
Carmen Jones

1956
Guys and Dolls

1957
The King and I

1958
Les Girls

1959
Gigi

1960
Some Like It Hot

1961
The Apartment
Song Without End

1962
West Side Story

1963
The Music Man
That Touch of Mink

1964
Tom Jones

1965
My Fair Lady

1966
The Sound of Music

1967
The Russians are Coming, the Russians are Coming

1968
The Graduate

1969
Oliver!

1971
*M*A*S*H*

1972
Fiddler on the Roof

1973
Cabaret

1974
American Graffiti

1975
The Longest Yard

1976
The Sunshine Boys

1977
A Star is Born

1978
The Goodbye Girl

1979
Heaven Can Wait

1980
Breaking Away

1981
Coal Miner's Daughter

1982
Arthur

1983
Tootsie

1984
Yentl

1985
Romancing the Stone

1986
Prizzi's Honor

1987
Hannah and Her Sisters

1988
Hope and Glory

1989
Working Girl

1990
Driving Miss Daisy

1991
Green Card

1992
Beauty and the Beast

1993
The Player

1994
Mrs. Doubtfire

DIRECTOR

1944
Henry King
The Song of Bernadette

1945
Leo McCarey
Going My Way

1946
Billy Wilder
The Lost Weekend

1947
Frank Capra
It's a Wonderful Life

1948
Elia Kazan
Gentleman's Agreement

1949
John Huston
Treasure of the Sierra Madre

1950
Robert Rossen
All the King's Men

1951
Billy Wilder
Sunset Boulevard

1953
Cecil B. DeMille
The Greatest Show on Earth

1955
Elia Kazan
On the Waterfront

1956
Joshua Logan
Picnic

1957
Elia Kazan
Baby Doll

1958
David Lean
The Bridge on the River Kwai

1959
Vincente Minnelli
Gigi

1960
William Wyler
Ben-Hur

1962
Stanley Kramer
Judgment at Nuremberg

1963
David Lean
Lawrence of Arabia

1965
George Cukor
My Fair Lady

1966
David Lean
Doctor Zhivago

1967
Fred Zinneman
A Man for All Seasons

1968
Mike Nichols
The Graduate

1969
Paul Newman
Rachel, Rachel

1970
Charles Jarrott
Anne of the Thousand Days

1971
Arthur Hiller
Love Story

1972
William Friedkin
The French Connection

1973
Francis Ford Coppola
The Godfather

1974
William Friedkin
The Exorcist

1975
Roman Polanski
Chinatown

1976
Milos Forman
One Flew Over the Cuckoo's Nest

1977
Sidney Lumet
Network

1978
Herbert Ross
The Turning Point

1979
Michael Cimino
The Deer Hunter

1980
Francis Ford Coppola
Apocalypse Now

1981
Robert Redford
Ordinary People

1982
Warren Beatty
Reds

1983
Richard Attenborough
Gandhi

1984
Barbra Streisand
Yentl

1985
Milos Forman
Amadeus

1986
John Huston
Prizzi's Honor

1987
Oliver Stone
Platoon

1988
Bernardo Bertolucci
The Last Emperor

1966
David Lean
Doctor Zhivago

1989
Clint Eastwood
Bird

1990
Oliver Stone
Born on the Fourth of July

1991
Kevin Costner
Dances with Wolves

1992
Oliver Stone
JFK

1993
Clint Eastwood
Unforgiven

1994
Steven Spielberg
Schindler's List

MUSIC

1948
Life with Father

1949
The Red Shoes

1950
The Inspector General

1951
Sunset Boulevard

1952
September Affair

1953
High Noon

1960
On the Beach

1961
The Alamo

1962
The Guns of Navarone

1963
To Kill a Mockingbird

1965
The Fall of the Roman Empire

1966
Doctor Zhivago

1967
Hawaii

1968
Camelot

1969
The Shoes of the Fisherman

1970
Butch Cassidy and the Sundance Kid

1971
Love Story

1972
Shaft

1973
The Godfather

1974
Jonathan Livingston Seagull

1975
The Little Prince

1976
Jaws

1977
A Star is Born

1978
Star Wars

1979
Midnight Express

1980
Apocalypse Now

1981
The Stunt Man

1983
E.T.: The Extra-Terrestrial

1984
Flashdance

1985
A Passage to India

1986
Out of Africa

1987
The Mission

1988
The Last Emperor

1989
Gorillas in the Mist

1990
The Little Mermaid

1991
The Sheltering Sky

1993
Aladdin

1994
Heaven and Earth

SONG

1965
"Circus World"
Circus World

1968
"If Ever I Should Leave You"
Camelot

1969
"Windmills of Your Mind"
Thomas Crown Affair

1970
"Jean"
The Prime of Miss Jean Brodie

1971
"Whistling Away the Dark"
Darling Lili

1972
"Life Is What You Make It"
Kotch

1973
"Ben"
Ben

1974
"The Way We Were"
The Way We Were

1975
"I Feel Love"
Benji

1976
"I'm Easy"
Nashville

1977
"Evergreen"
A Star is Born

1978
"You Light Up My Life"
You Light Up My Life

1980
"The Rose"
The Rose

1981
"Fame"
Fame

1982
"Arthur's Theme"
Arthur

1983
"Up Where We Belong"
An Officer and a Gentleman

1984
"Flashdance...What a Feeling"
Flashdance

1985
"I Just Called to Say I Love You"
The Woman in Red

1986
"Say You, Say Me"
White Nights

1987
"Take My Breath Away"
Top Gun

1988
"(I've Had) the Time of My Life"
Dirty Dancing

1989
"Let the River Run"
Working Girl

1990
"Under the Sea"
The Little Mermaid

1991
"Blaze of Glory"
Young Guns 2

1993
"A Whole New World"
Aladdin

1994
"Streets of Philadelphia"
Philadelphia

WRITING

1948
Miracle on 34th Street

1949
The Search

1950
Battleground

1951
All About Eve

1953
Five Fingers

1954
Lili

1955
Sabrina

1966
Doctor Zhivago

1967
A Man for All Seasons

1968
In the Heat of the Night

1969
Charly

1970
Anne of the Thousand Days

1971
Love Story

1972
The Hospital

1973
The Godfather

1974
The Exorcist

1975
Chinatown

1976
One Flew Over the Cuckoo's Nest

1977
Network

1978
The Goodbye Girl

1979
Midnight Express

1980
Kramer vs. Kramer

1981
The Ninth Configuration

1982
On Golden Pond

1983
Gandhi

1984
Terms of Endearment

1985
Amadeus

1986
The Purple Rose of Cairo

1987
The Mission

1988
The Last Emperor

1989
Running on Empty

1990
Born on the Fourth of July

1991
Dances with Wolves

1994
Schindler's List

DIRECTORS GUILD OF AMERICA

DIRECTOR

1948
Joseph L. Mankiewicz
A Letter to Three Wives

1949
Carol Reed
The Third Man

1950
Joseph L. Mankiewicz
All About Eve

1951
George Stevens
A Place in the Sun

1952
John Ford
The Quiet Man

1953
Fred Zinneman
From Here to Eternity

1954
Elia Kazan
On the Waterfront
Billy Wilder
Sabrina

1955
Delbert Mann
Marty

1956
George Stevens
Giant

1957
David Lean
The Bridge on the River Kwai

1958
Vincente Minnelli
Gigi

1959
William Wyler
Ben-Hur

1960
Billy Wilder
The Apartment

1961
Robert Wise
West Side Story
Jerome Robbins
West Side Story

1962
David Lean
Lawrence of Arabia

1963
Tony Richardson
Tom Jones

1964
George Cukor
My Fair Lady

1965
Robert Wise
The Sound of Music

1966
Fred Zinneman
A Man for All Seasons

1967
Mike Nichols
The Graduate

1968
Anthony Harvey
The Lion in Winter

1969
John Schlesinger
Midnight Cowboy

1970
Charles Jarrott
Anne of the Thousand Days
Franklin J. Schaffner
Patton

1971
William Friedkin
The French Connection

1972
Francis Ford Coppola
The Godfather

1973
George Roy Hill
The Sting

1974
Francis Ford Coppola
The Godfather, Part 2

1975
Milos Forman
One Flew Over the Cuckoo's Nest

1976
John G. Avildsen
Rocky

1977
Woody Allen
Annie Hall

1978
Michael Cimino
The Deer Hunter

1979
Robert Benton
Kramer vs. Kramer

1980
Robert Redford
Ordinary People

1981
Warren Beatty
Reds

1982
Richard Attenborough
Gandhi

1983
James L. Brooks
Terms of Endearment

1984
Milos Forman
Amadeus

1985
Steven Spielberg
The Color Purple

1986
Oliver Stone
Platoon

1987
Bernardo Bertolucci
The Last Emperor

1988
Barry Levinson
Rain Man

1989
Oliver Stone
Born on the Fourth of July

1990
Kevin Costner
Dances with Wolves

1991
Jonathan Demme
The Silence of the Lambs

1992
Clint Eastwood
Unforgiven

1993
Steven Spielberg
Schindler's List

DIRECTOR ▶*cont.*

INDEPENDENT SPIRIT AWARDS

ACTOR

1986
M. Emmet Walsh
Blood Simple

1987
James Woods
Salvador

1988
Dennis Quaid
The Big Easy

1989
Edward James Olmos
Stand and Deliver

1990
Matt Dillon
Drugstore Cowboy

1991
Danny Glover
To Sleep with Anger

1992
River Phoenix
My Own Private Idaho

1993
Harvey Keitel
Bad Lieutenant

1994
Jeff Bridges
American Heart

ACTOR— SUPPORTING

1988
Morgan Freeman
Street Smart

1989
Lou Diamond Phillips
Stand and Deliver

1990
Max Perlich
Drugstore Cowboy

1991
Bruce Davison
Longtime Companion

1992
David Strathairn
City of Hope

1993
Steve Buscemi
Reservoir Dogs

ACTRESS

1986
Geraldine Page
The Trip to Bountiful

1987
Isabella Rossellini
Blue Velvet

1988
Sally Kirkland
Anna

1989
Jodie Foster
Five Corners

1990
Andie MacDowell
sex, lies and videotape

1991
Anjelica Huston
The Grifters

1992
Judy Davis
Impromptu

1993
Fairuza Balk
Gas Food Lodging

1994
Ashley Judd
Ruby in Paradise

ACTRESS— SUPPORTING

1988
Anjelica Huston
The Dead

1989
Rosana De Soto
Stand and Deliver

1990
Laura San Giacomo
sex, lies and videotape

1991
Sheryl Lee Ralph
To Sleep with Anger

1992
Diane Ladd
Rambling Rose

1993
Alfre Woodard
Passion Fish

CINEMATOGRAPHY

1986
Trouble in Mind

1987
Platoon

1988
Matewan

1989
The Unbearable Lightness of Being

1990
Drugstore Cowboy

1991
Wild at Heart

1992
Kafka

1993
Night on Earth

DIRECTOR

1986
Martin Scorsese
After Hours
Joel Coen
Blood Simple

1987
Oliver Stone
Platoon

1988
John Huston
The Dead

1989
Ramon Menendez
Stand and Deliver

1990
Steven Soderberg
sex, lies and videotape

1991
Charles Burnett
To Sleep with Anger

1992
Martha Coolidge
Rambling Rose

1993
Carl Franklin
One False Move

1994
Robert Altman
Short Cuts

FILM

1986
After Hours

1987
Platoon

1988
River's Edge

1989
Stand and Deliver

1990
sex, lies and videotape

1991
The Grifters

1992
Rambling Rose

1993
The Player

1994
Short Cuts

FIRST FEATURE

1988
Dirty Dancing

1989
Mystic Pizza

1990
Heathers

1991
Metropolitan

1992
Straight Out of Brooklyn

1993
The Waterdance

1994
El Mariachi

MUSIC

1993
Twin Peaks: Fire Walk with Me

WRITING

1986
The Trip to Bountiful

1987
Platoon

1988
River's Edge

1989
Stand and Deliver

1990
Drugstore Cowboy

1991
To Sleep with Anger

1992
My Own Private Idaho

1993
The Waterdance

1994
Short Cuts

MONTREAL WORLD FILM FESTIVAL

ACTOR

1979
Giuliano Gemma
Corleone

1980
Robert Duvall
The Great Santini

1983
Gerard Depardieu
Danton

1985
Armin Mueller-Stahl
Angry Harvest

1987
Leo McKern
Travelling North

1989
Daniel Day-Lewis
My Left Foot

ACTOR— SUPPORTING

1986
Dennis Hopper
Blue Velvet

ACTRESS

1978
Glenda Jackson
Stevie

1988
Udvaros Dorottya
Oh, Bloody Life!

DIRECTOR

1992
Maurizio Nichetti
Volere Volare

FILM

1980
The Stunt Man

1982
Brimstone & Treacle
Time for Revenge

1983
The Go-Masters

1988
La Lectrice

1989
Freedom is Paradise

MTV MOVIE AWARDS

ACTION SEQUENCE

1992
Terminator 2: Judgment Day

1993
Lethal Weapon 3

1994
The Fugitive

ACTOR

1992
Arnold Schwarzenegger
Terminator 2: Judgment Day

1993
Denzel Washington
Malcolm X

1994
Tom Hanks
Philadelphia

ACTRESS

1992
Linda Hamilton
Terminator 2: Judgment Day

1993
Sharon Stone
Basic Instinct

1994
Janet Jackson
Poetic Justice

BREAKTHROUGH PERFORMANCE

1992
Edward Furlong
Terminator 2: Judgment Day

1993
Marisa Tomei
My Cousin Vinny

1994
Alicia Silverstone
The Crush

COMEDIC PERFORMANCE

1992
Billy Crystal
City Slickers

1993
Robin Williams
Aladdin

1994
Robin Williams
Mrs. Doubtfire

FILM

1992
Terminator 2: Judgment Day

1993
A Few Good Men

1994
Menace II Society

KISS

1992
Macaulay Culkin/Anna Chlumsky
My Girl

1993
Christian Slater/Marisa Tomei
Untamed Heart

1994
Demi Moore/Woody Harrelson
Indecent Proposal

MOST DESIRABLE FEMALE

1992
Linda Hamilton
Terminator 2: Judgment Day

1993
Sharon Stone
Basic Instinct

1994
Janet Jackson
Poetic Justice

MOST DESIRABLE MALE

1992
Keanu Reeves
Point Break

1993
Christian Slater
Untamed Heart

1994
William Baldwin
Sliver

NEW FILMMAKER

1992
John Singleton
Boyz N the Hood

1993
Carl Franklin
One False Move

1994
Steven Zaillian
Searching for Bobby Fischer

ON-SCREEN DUO

1992
Mike Myers/Dana Carvey
Wayne's World

1993
Mel Gibson/Danny Glover
Lethal Weapon 3

1994
Harrison Ford/Tommy Lee Jones
The Fugitive

SONG

1992
"(Everything I Do) I Do for You"
Robin Hood: Prince of Thieves

1993
"I Will Always Love You"
The Bodyguard

1994
"Will You Be There"
Free Willy

VILLAIN

1992
Rebecca DeMornay
The Hand that Rocks the Cradle

1993
Jennifer Jason Leigh
Single White Female

1994
Alicia Silverstone
The Crush

The **SONG TITLE INDEX** lists 4,700 songs from major movie musicals. Arranged alphabetically, each song title is referenced to the movie in which it appears.

The A-stairable Rag See You'll Never Get Rich (1941)

A-Tisket-A-Tasket See Two Girls and a Sailor (1944)

Aba Daba Honeymoon See Two Weeks with Love (1950)

About A Quarter To Nine See The Jolson Story (1946)

About a Quarter to Nine See Jolson Sings Again (1949)

Above the Stars See The Wonderful World of the Brothers Grimm (1962)

Abraham See White Christmas (1954)

Abraham, Abraham See Holiday Inn (1942)

Absolute Beginners See Absolute Beginners (1986)

Absolute Perfection See Back to the Beach (1987)

Accidents Will Happen See Mr. Music (1950)

The Acid Queen See Tommy (1975)

Action See Breakin' 2: Electric Boogaloo (1984)

Adam and Eve See Spinout (1966)

Adelaide's Lament See Guys and Dolls (1955)

Adios See The Glenn Miller Story (1954)

Afraid to Fall in Love See Summer Holiday (1948)

African Etude See The Road to Zanzibar (1941)

After All This Time See Swing Parade of 1946 (1946)

After Dark See Thank God It's Friday (1978)

After Sundown See Going Hollywood (1933)

After the Ball See The Jolson Story (1946)

After the Ball See Show Boat (1936)

After the Ball See Show Boat (1951)

After the Ball See Strike Up the Band (1940)

After the Party See How to Stuff a Wild Bikini (1965)

After Today See Doctor Dolittle (1967)

After You Get What You Want You Don't Want It See There's No Business Like Show Business (1954)

After You've Gone See All That Jazz (1979)

After You've Gone See For Me and My Gal (1942)

After You've Gone See Jolson Sings Again (1949)

Ah Che a Voi Perdoni Iddio See A Damsel in Distress (1937)

Ah, Love See Meet Me in St. Louis (1944)

Ah-Oom See The Wonderful World of the Brothers Grimm (1962)

Ah Still Suits Me See Show Boat (1936)

Ah, Sweet Mystery of Life See Naughty Marietta (1935)

Ah, the Moon is Here See Footlight Parade (1933)

Ah Yes, I Remember It Well See Gigi (1958)

Ain't Got a Dime to My Name See The Road to Morocco (1942)

Ain't Misbehavin' See Stormy Weather (1943)

Ain't Nature Grand See Dangerous When Wet (1953)

Ain't There Anyone Here For Love? See Gentlemen Prefer Blondes (1953)

Ain't We Got Fun See By the Light of the Silvery Moon (1953)

Ain't We Got Fun See I'll See You in My Dreams (1951)

Air des Bijoux See San Francisco (1936)

Alabamy Bound See Show Business (1944)

Albany Bound See The Great American Broadcast (1941)

Aldonza See Man of La Mancha (1972)

Alexander's Ragtime Band See Alexander's Ragtime Band (1938)

Alexander's Ragtime Band See There's No Business Like Show Business (1954)

Ali Baba Be My Baby See Here Come the Girls (1953)

Alice in Wonderland See Alice in Wonderland (1951)

Alive and Kicking See Best Foot Forward (1943)

All About Love See Bundle of Joy (1956)

All Alone See Alexander's Ragtime Band (1938)

All Alone Monday See Three Little Words (1950)

The All-American Swing See My Lucky Star (1938)

All 'Er Nuthin' See Oklahoma! (1955)

All God's Chillun Got Rhythm See A Day at the Races (1937)

All Hail, Danville High See Summer Holiday (1948)

All Hallow's Eve See Meet Me in St. Louis (1944)

All I Do Is Dream of You See The Affairs of Dobie Gillis (1953)

All I Do Is Dream Of You See The Boy Friend (1971)

All I Do Is Dream of You See Broadway Melody of 1936 (1935)

All I Do is Dream of You See Singin' in the Rain (1952)

All I Need is the Girl See Gypsy (1962)

All I Need Is the Girl See Gypsy (1993)

All I Owe Iowa See State Fair (1945)

All I Want Is You See Seaside Swingers (1965)

All I Want to Do Play the Drums See Follow the Leader (1944)

All In Fun See Broadway Rhythm (1944)

All In The Cause Of Economy See Half a Sixpence (1967)

All My Loving See A Hard Day's Night (1964)

All of a Sudden My Heart Sings See Anchors Aweigh (1945)

All Of Me See Lady Sings the Blues (1972)

All of Me See Meet Danny Wilson (1952)

All of You See Silk Stockings (1957)

All Out for Freedom See Up in Arms (1944)

All Over the World See Xanadu (1980)

All That I Am See Spinout (1966)

All the Colors of the Rainbow See The Girl Most Likely (1957)

All the Things You Are See Because You're Mine (1952)

All the Things You Are See Broadway Rhythm (1944)

All the Things You Are See Till the Clouds Roll By (1946)

All Together Now See Yellow Submarine (1968)

All You Can Eat See Krush Groove (1985)

All You Need is Love See Yellow Submarine (1968)

Allegro Appassionato, Opus 10 See Three Daring Daughters (1948)

Alleluia See The Sound of Music (1965)

Alma Mater See Three Daring Daughters (1948)

Almost See The Trouble with Girls (and How To Get Into It) (1969)

Almost in Love See Live a Little, Love a Little (1968)

Almost Like Being in Love See Brigadoon (1954)

Almost Paradise See Footloose (1984)

Aloha Oe See Hawaii Calls (1938)

Aloha Oe See I Married an Angel (1942)

Alone at a Drive-In Movie *See* Grease (1978)

Alone With You *See* Rebecca of Sunnybrook Farm (1938)

Along *See* How to Stuff a Wild Bikini (1965)

Always True To You Darling In My Fashion *See* Kiss Me Kate (1953)

Am I Blue? *See* Funny Lady (1975)

Am I Ready *See* Spinout (1966)

Amazed and Confused *See* Jazz Singer (1980)

The Amazing Journey *See* Tommy (1975)

America *See* Jazz Singer (1980)

America *See* Let Freedom Ring (1939)

America *See* West Side Story (1961)

America I Love You *See* Tin Pan Alley (1940)

American Boy *See* Stage Door Canteen (1943)

American Eagles *See* This is the Army (1943)

An American in Paris *See* An American in Paris (1951)

An American in Paris (instrumental) *See* Rhapsody in Blue (1945)

American Patrol *See* The Glenn Miller Story (1954)

Among the Young *See* Pajama Party (1964)

Amor *See* Broadway Rhythm (1944)

Anatevka *See* Fiddler on the Roof (1971)

Anchors Aweigh (instrumental) *See* In the Navy (1941)

And... *See* A Chorus Line (1985)

And Dreams Remain *See* Holiday in Mexico (1946)

And I Love Her *See* A Hard Day's Night (1964)

And the Sky Smiled *See* Goodbye, Mr. Chips (1969)

And Then You Kissed Me *See* Step Lively (1944)

And There You Are *See* I Love Melvin (1953)

And This Is My Beloved *See* Kismet (1955)

Angel *See* Yolanda and the Thief (1945)

Anges Purs *See* I Married an Angel (1942)

Anitra's Dance *See* A Song is Born (1948)

Annabella *See* Zis Boom Bah (1942)

Annabella's Bustle *See* Girl Rush (1944)

Anniversary Song *See* Jolson Sings Again (1949)

The Anniversary Song *See* The Jolson Story (1946)

Another Girl *See* Help! (1965)

Antoinette and Anatole *See* Naughty Marietta (1935)

Antonio *See* The Heat's On (1943)

Anvil Chorus *See* Maytime (1937)

Anvil Chorus *See* A Song is Born (1948)

Any Bonds Today *See* Holiday Inn (1942)

Any Gal From Texas *See* The French Line (1954)

Any Old Iron *See* The Boy Friend (1971)

Any Old Love *See* Something to Sing About (1936)

Anyone Can Tell I Love You *See* Ladies of the Chorus (1949)

Anything Can Happen in New York *See* Babes on Broadway (1941)

Anything Goes *See* Night and Day (1946)

Anywhere *See* Tonight and Every Night (1945)

Anywhere I Wander *See* Hans Christian Andersen (1952)

Apalachicola, Florida *See* The Road to Rio (1947)

Applause, Applause *See* Give a Girl a Break (1953)

Appreciation *See* Viva Las Vegas (1963)

April Showers *See* Jolson Sings Again (1949)

April Showers *See* The Jolson Story (1946)

Arabian Nights *See* Aladdin (1992)

Arabian Nights *See* The Return of Jafar (1994)

Are We Dancing? *See* The Happiest Millionaire (1967)

Are You a Beautiful Dream? *See* Two Tickets to Broadway (1951)

Are You Kidding? *See* Footlight Serenade (1942)

Are You My Love? *See* Dancing Pirate (1936)

Argentine Moon *See* Rogue of the Rio Grande (1930)

The Army's Made a Man Out of Me *See* This is the Army (1943)

The Arnaz Jam *See* Holiday in Havana (1949)

The Arrest *See* Jesus Christ, Superstar (1973)

Arrivederci Roma *See* The Seven Hills of Rome (1958)

An Artist's Life *See* The Great Waltz (1938)

Art's Blues *See* The Fabulous Dorseys (1947)

Arye With His Bass *See* Yidl Mitn Fidl (1936)

As Long As He Needs Me *See* Oliver! (1968)

As Long As I Have You *See* King Creole (1958)

As Long As There's Music *See* Step Lively (1944)

As Long As We Believe *See* Fast Forward (1984)

As Soon As They See Eileen *See* My Sister Eileen (1955)

As We Go Along *See* Head (1968)

Ascot Gavotte *See* My Fair Lady (1964)

Ask the Madame *See* Step Lively (1944)

At A Georgia Camp Meeting *See* Show Boat (1936)

At A Georgia Camp Meeting *See* Stormy Weather (1943)

At Christmas Time *See* Song of Norway (1970)

At Last *See* Orchestra Wives (1942)

At Sundown *See* The Fabulous Dorseys (1947)

At Sundown *See* Glorifying the American Girl (1930)

At Sundown *See* Love Me or Leave Me (1955)

At the Ballet *See* A Chorus Line (1985)

At the Codfish Ball *See* Captain January (1936)

At the Crossroads *See* Doctor Dolittle (1967)

At the Gates of the Emerald City *See* The Wizard of Oz (1939)

Atmosphere *See* My Sister Eileen (1955)

Au Revoir *See* Rebecca of Sunnybrook Farm (1938)

Auf Wiedersehn *See* Deep in My Heart (1954)

Auld Lang Syne *See* Little Miss Broadway (1938)

Aunt Polly's Soliloquy *See* Tom Sawyer (1973)

Avalon *See* The Jolson Story (1946)

Avalon *See* New York, New York (1977)

Ave Maria *See* Fantasia (1940)

Ave Maria *See* For the First Time (1959)

Ave Maria *See* Girl of the Golden West (1938)

Ave Maria *See* Going My Way (1944)

Ave Maria *See* The Great Caruso (1951)

Ave Maria *See* Holiday in Mexico (1946)

Ave Maria *See* It's a Date (1940)

Ave Maria *See* The Jolson Story (1946)

Ave Maria *See* Stage Door Canteen (1943)

Ave Verum Corpus *See* Amadeus (1984)

Ay, Ay, Ay *See* Escape to Paradise (1939)

Babalu *See* Two Girls and a Sailor (1944)

The Babbitt and the Bromide *See* Ziegfeld Follies (1946)

Babes in Arms *See* Babes in Arms (1939)

Babes on Broadway *See* Babes on Broadway (1941)

Baby Come Out of the Clouds *See* Duchess of Idaho (1950)

Baby Doll *See* The Belle of New York (1952)

Baby Face *See* Glorifying the American Girl (1930)

Baby Face *See* Jolson Sings Again (1949)

Baby Face *See* Thoroughly Modern Millie (1967)

Baby, I Don't Care *See* Jailhouse Rock (1957)

Baby, It's Cold Outside *See* Neptune's Daughter (1949)

Baby Jane and the Newsboys *See* Gypsy (1962)

Baby, Let Me Take You Dreaming *See* Court Jester (1956)

Baby Take a Bow *See* Stand Up and Cheer (1934)

Baby You Knock Me Out *See* It's Always Fair Weather (1955)

Baby, You'll Never Be Sorry *See* Two Tickets to Broadway (1951)

Bach Boogie *See* A Song is Born (1948)

Bachelor's Dinner Song *See* The Belle of New York (1952)

Back, Back, Back to Baltimore *See* Look for the Silver Lining (1949)

Back Home Again in Indiana *See* Roberta (1935)

Back in My Baby's Arms *See* Coal Miner's Daughter (1980)

Back in My Shell *See* One Night in the Tropics (1940)

Back in the Saddle Again *See* Melody Ranch (1940)

Back In Your Own Backyard *See* Jolson Sings Again (1949)

Back to Back *See* Second Fiddle (1939)

The Bad Humor Man *See* You'll Find Out (1940)

Bad Man *See* FM (1978)

Baia *See* The Three Caballeros (1945)

Bal Petit Bal *See* New Faces of 1952 (1954)

Balboa *See* The Girl Most Likely (1957)

Bali Boogie *See* Wonder Man (1945)

Bali Ha'i *See* South Pacific (1958)

Ballade In A Flat, Opus 47 *See* A Song to Remember (1945)

Ballet in Jive *See* Hollywood Canteen (1944)

Ballin' the Jack *See* For Me and My Gal (1942)

Ballroom Dancing *See* Give My Regards to Broad Street (1984)

Baltimore Oriole *See* The Stork Club (1945)

Banana *See* King Creole (1958)

Bang! Bang! *See* Robin and the Seven Hoods (1964)

Baptize the Beat *See* Beat Street (1984)

Barbary Coast *See* Girl Crazy (1943)

The Barber's Ball *See* Yankee Doodle Dandy (1942)

Barber's Song *See* Man of La Mancha (1972)

Basin Street Blues *See* The Glenn Miller Story (1954)

Basin Street Blues *See* Stormy Weather (1943)

The Bat *See* The Great Waltz (1938)

Battle Cry *See* Sweet Rosie O'Grady (1943)

Battle Hymn of the Republic *See* The Five Pennies (1959)

The Battle Hymn of the Republic *See* Stars and Stripes Forever (1952)

Baubles, Bangles, and Beads *See* Kismet (1955)

Bavarian Drinking Song *See* For the First Time (1959)

Bayou Trouble Tree *See* New Moon (1940)

Be a Boy Again *See* Song of Norway (1970)

Be a Clown *See* The Pirate (1948)

Be a Lion *See* The Wiz (1978)

Be Back Soon *See* Oliver! (1968)

Be Careful, It's My Heart *See* Holiday Inn (1942)

The Be-Gat *See* Finian's Rainbow (1968)

Be Happy *See* The Little Prince (1974)

Be My Little Baby Bumble Bee *See* By the Light of the Silvery Moon (1953)

Be My Love *See* Because You're Mine (1952)

Be My Love *See* The Toast of New Orleans (1950)

Be Optimistic *See* Little Miss Broadway (1938)

Be Our Guest *See* Beauty and the Beast (1991)

Be Prepared *See* The Lion King (1994)

Beach Ball *See* Pajama Party (1964)

Beach Blanket Bingo *See* Beach Blanket Bingo (1965)

Beach Party *See* Beach Party (1963)

Beach Shack *See* Spinout (1966)

Beale Street Blues *See* Stormy Weather (1943)

Beat Out Dat Rhythm on a Drum *See* Carmen Jones (1954)

Beat Street Breakdown *See* Beat Street (1984)

Beat Street Strut *See* Beat Street (1984)

Beautiful Changes *See* Glorifying the American Girl (1930)

The Beautiful Day *See* Scrooge (1970)

Beautiful Dreamer *See* Harmony Lane (1935)

Beautiful Face, Have a Heart *See* Funny Lady (1975)

Beautiful Faces Need Beautiful Clothes *See* Easter Parade (1948)

Beautiful Girl *See* Going Hollywood (1933)

Beautiful Girl *See* Singin' in the Rain (1952)

Beautiful Lady *See* Two Weeks with Love (1950)

The Beautiful People of Denver *See* The Unsinkable Molly Brown (1964)

Beautiful Spring *See* Easy to Love (1953)

Beautiful Things *See* Doctor Dolittle (1967)

Beauty and the Beast *See* Beauty and the Beast (1991)

Beauty School Dropout *See* Grease (1978)

Because *See* The Great Caruso (1951)

Because *See* Sgt. Pepper's Lonely Hearts Club Band (1978)

Because of You *See* Girls! Girls! Girls! (1962)

Because You're Mine *See* Because You're Mine (1952)

Because You're You *See* Bikini Beach (1964)

Bed of Ashes *See* Knights of the City (1985)

Bedelia *See* Hello, Frisco, Hello (1943)

The Bee *See* Hollywood Canteen (1944)

Been a Long Day *See* How to Succeed in Business without Really Trying (1967)

Before the Parade Passes By *See* Hello, Dolly! (1969)

Begin the Beguine *See* Broadway Melody of 1940 (1940)

Begin the Beguine *See* Night and Day (1946)

Beginner's Luck *See* Frankie and Johnny (1965)

Beginner's Luck *See* Shall We Dance (1937)

Being for the Benefit of Mr. Kite *See* Sgt. Pepper's Lonely Hearts Club Band (1978)

Being in Love *See* The Music Man (1962)

Believe in Yourself *See* The Wiz (1978)

Bell Song *See* I Dream Too Much (1935)

Bella Notte *See* Lady and the Tramp (1955)

Belle *See* Beauty and the Beast (1991)

Belly Up to the Bar, Boys *See* The Unsinkable Molly Brown (1964)

Beloved *See* The Student Prince (1954)

A Bench in the Park *See* King of Jazz (1930)

Berceuse In D Flat, Opus 57 *See* A Song to Remember (1945)

Berry Me Not *See* Panama Hattie (1942)

Besame Mucho *See* Club Havana (1946)

Beside the Rio Tonto *See* Ride 'Em Cowboy (1942)

Best Things *See* Paint Your Wagon (1969)

The Best Things Happen While You're Dancing *See* White Christmas (1954)

The Best Things in Life Are Free *See* Good News (1947)

Betrothal Hymn *See* Song of Norway (1970)

Better Be Ready *See* How to Stuff a Wild Bikini (1965)

Better Git It In Your Soul (The Hot and the Cool) *See* Absolute Beginners (1986)

Better Luck Next Time *See* Easter Parade (1948)

Better Than a Dream *See* Bells are Ringing (1960)

Between You and Me *See* Broadway Melody of 1940 (1940)

Beware *See* Call Out the Marines (1942)

Bewitched, Bothered and Bewildered *See* Pal Joey (1957)

Beyond the Bend *See* It Happened at the World's Fair (1963)

Bibbidy-Bobbidi-Boo *See* Cinderella (1950)

Bidin' My Time *See* Girl Crazy (1943)

Bidin' My Time *See* The Glenn Miller Story (1954)

Big Boots *See* G.I. Blues (1960)

Big Chief Hole in the Ground *See* Two Tickets to Broadway (1951)

Big Love, Big Heartache *See* Roustabout (1964)

Big Stuff *See* Dixie Jamboree (1944)

Bikini Drag *See* Bikini Beach (1964)

Bill *See* The Man I Love (1946)

Bill *See* Show Boat (1936)

Bill *See* Show Boat (1951)

Bill Bailey, Won't You Please Come Home? *See* Paradise, Hawaiian Style (1966)

Billie *See* Yankee Doodle Dandy (1942)

Billy-A-Dick *See* For the Boys (1991)

Billy Boy *See* So Dear to My Heart (1949)

Bim, Bam, Boom *See* Bathing Beauty (1944)

Bindin' My Time *See* Rhapsody in Blue (1945)

The Binge *See* It's Always Fair Weather (1955)

Birds of a Feather *See* The Road to Zanzibar (1941)

Black Bottom *See* A Star is Born (1954)

The Black Hills of Dakota *See* Calamity Jane (1953)

A Blarney from Killarney *See* The Naughty Nineties (1945)

Bless Your Beautiful Hide *See* Seven Brides for Seven Brothers (1954)

Blind Barnabas *See* A Song is Born (1948)

Blind Date *See* Funny Lady (1975)

Blood Money *See* Jesus Christ, Superstar (1973)

Bloody Mary *See* South Pacific (1958)

Bluddle-Uddle-Um-Dum *See* Snow White and the Seven Dwarfs (1937)

Blue Bell *See* The Jolson Story (1946)

The Blue Danube *See* The Great Waltz (1938)

The Blue Danube *See* That Girl from Paris (1936)

Blue Jay Way *See* Magical Mystery Tour (1967)

Blue Jean Polka *See* Summer Stock (1950)

Blue Monday Blues *See* Rhapsody in Blue (1945)

Blue Moon *See* At the Circus (1939)

Blue Moon *See* Grease (1978)

Blue Moon *See* New York, New York (1977)

Blue Moon *See* This Could Be the Night (1957)

Blue Moon of Kentucky *See* Sweet Dreams (1985)

Blue Skies *See* Alexander's Ragtime Band (1938)

Blue Skies *See* Glorifying the American Girl (1930)

Blue Skies *See* Jazz Singer (1927)

Blue Skies *See* White Christmas (1954)

Blue Skies, Grey Skies *See* Yankee Doodle Dandy (1942)

Blue Suede Shoes *See* G.I. Blues (1960)

Bluebells of Broadway *See* Lucky Me (1954)

Bluebird *See* Nashville (1975)

Blues in the Night *See* Thank Your Lucky Stars (1943)

Bobby's Dream *See* New York, New York (1977)

Boccherini's Minuet in Boogie *See* Higher and Higher (1944)

Body and Soul *See* The Man I Love (1946)

Body Rock *See* Body Rock (1984)

Bojangles of Harlem *See* Swing Time (1936)

Bolero in the Jungle *See* George White's Scandals (1945)

Bombshell From Brooklyn *See* Stage Door Canteen (1943)

Bongo Rock *See* Absolute Beginners (1986)

Bonjour Paris *See* Funny Face (1957)

Boogie Barcarolle *See* You'll Never Get Rich (1941)

Boogie Stop Shuffle (The Rough and the Smooth) *See* Absolute Beginners (1986)

Boogie Woogie Conga *See* Four Jacks and a Jill (1941)

Boom Biddy Boom Boom *See* The Toast of New Orleans (1950)

Bored *See* Kismet (1955)

Born to Hand-Jive *See* Grease (1978)

Born to Love *See* Rappin' (1985)

Bosom Buddies *See* Mame (1974)

Boston Beguine *See* New Faces of 1952 (1954)

Bounce *See* Knights of the City (1985)

Bouncin' the Blues *See* The Barkleys of Broadway (1949)

Bouquet and Lace *See* George White's Scandals (1945)

The Bowery *See* Stars and Stripes Forever (1952)

Boy For Sale *See* Oliver! (1968)

The Boy Friend *See* The Boy Friend (1971)

The Boy Friend *See* Broadway Melody (1929)

The Boy I Left Behind *See* Tonight and Every Night (1945)

A Boy Like Me, A Girl Like You *See* Girls! Girls! Girls! (1962)

A Boy Like That *See* West Side Story (1961)

A Boy Needs a Girl *See* Muscle Beach Party (1964)

The Boy Next Door *See* Meet Me in St. Louis (1944)

Boy, What Love Has Done to Me *See* Girl Crazy (1943)

Brand New Day *See* The Wiz (1978)

Brass Buttons and Epaulets *See* Just Around the Corner (1938)

Brazil *See* The Road to Rio (1947)

Brazilian Boogie *See* Broadway Rhythm (1944)

Breakers Revenge *See* Beat Street (1984)

Breakin...There's No Stopping Us *See* Breakin' (1984)

Breakout *See* Staying Alive (1983)

The Breeze Kissed Your Hair *See* The Cat and the Fiddle (1934)

Brigadoon *See* Brigadoon (1954)

Brighten the Corner *See* Meet Me in St. Louis (1944)

Bring on Those Beautiful Girls *See* Ziegfeld Follies (1946)

Bring on Those Wonderful Men *See* Ziegfeld Follies (1946)

Broadway Babies *See* Broadway Melody (1929)

Broadway, Broadway *See* Gypsy (1962)

Broadway Melody *See* Broadway Melody (1929)

Broadway Melody *See* Broadway Melody of 1936 (1935)

Broadway Melody *See* Singin' in the Rain (1952)

Broadway Rhythm *See* Babes in Arms (1939)

Broadway Rhythm *See* Broadway Melody of 1936 (1935)

Broadway Rhythm *See* Broadway Melody of 1938 (1937)

Broadway Rhythm *See* Presenting Lily Mars (1943)

Broadway Rhythm *See* Singin' in the Rain (1952)

Broadway Serenade for the Lonely Heart *See* Broadway Serenade (1939)

Broadway's Gone Hillbilly *See* Stand Up and Cheer (1934)

Brodny *See* The Inspector General (1949)

Broken Melody *See* Fashions of 1934 (1934)

Bronco Busters *See* Girl Crazy (1943)

Brooklyn *See* The West Point Story (1950)

The Brotherhood of Man *See* How to Succeed in Business without Really Trying (1967)

Brush Up Your Shakespeare *See* Kiss Me Kate (1953)

Buckle Down, Winsocki *See* Best Foot Forward (1943)

Buckskin Beauty *See* Pardners (1956)

Buenas Noches, Buenos Aires *See* On an Island with You (1948)

Bugle Call Rag *See* New York, New York (1977)

Bugle Call Rag *See* Stage Door Canteen (1943)

Build A Little Home *See* Roman Scandals (1933)

The Bullfighter Was A Lady *See* Fun in Acapulco (1963)

Bullfrog *See* Night and Day (1946)

Bumper Found a Grand *See* Hallelujah, I'm a Bum (1933)

Bundle of Joy *See* Bundle of Joy (1956)

Burlington Bertie from Bow *See* Star! (1968)

Busy Doin' Nothin' *See* A Connecticut Yankee in King Arthur's Court (1949)

But Beautiful *See* The Road to Rio (1947)

But Definitely *See* The Poor Little Rich Girl (1936)

But, Mr. Adams *See* 1776 (1972)

But Not For Me *See* Girl Crazy (1943)

But the World Goes 'Round *See* New York, New York (1977)

But What of Truth *See* I Married an Angel (1942)

But Where Are You? *See* Follow the Fleet (1936)

Buy a Bar of Barry's *See* The Poor Little Rich Girl (1936)

By A Waterfall *See* Footlight Parade (1933)

By Damn *See* Marco (1973)

By Madame Fuelle *See* The French Line (1954)

By Myself *See* The Band Wagon (1953)

By Strauss *See* An American in Paris (1951)

By The Beautiful Sea *See* For Me and My Gal (1942)

By the Beautiful Sea *See* The Story of Vernon and Irene Castle (1939)

By the Kissing Rock *See* The West Point Story (1950)

By the Light of the Silvery Moon *See* By the Light of the Silvery Moon (1953)

By the Light of the Silvery Moon *See* Hello, Frisco, Hello (1943)

By the Light of the Silvery Moon *See* The Jolson Story (1946)

By the Light of the Silvery Moon *See* The Story of Vernon and Irene Castle (1939)

By the Light of the Silvery Moon *See* Two Weeks with Love (1950)

By the Waters of Minnetonka *See* Bathing Beauty (1944)

Bye, Bye Baby *See* Gentlemen Prefer Blondes (1953)

Bye Bye Birdie *See* Bye, Bye, Birdie (1963)

Bye Bye Blackbird *See* Pete Kelly's Blues (1955)

Bye Bye Love *See* All That Jazz (1979)

Bye-Yum Pum Pum *See* The Happiest Millionaire (1967)

C-A-T Spells Cat *See* Daddy Long Legs (1955)

Ca C'est L'Amour *See* Les Girls (1957)

Cabaret *See* Cabaret (1972)

Cabin in the Sky *See* Cabin in the Sky (1943)

The Caissons Go Rolling Along *See* The Heat's On (1943)

Caldonia *See* Look Out Sister (1948)

Caledonia *See* Swing Parade of 1946 (1946)

California, Here I Come *See* Jolson Sings Again (1949)

California, Here I Come *See* The Jolson Story (1946)

California, Here I Come *See* Rose of Washington Square (1939)

California Sun *See* Back to the Beach (1987)

Call Me *See* Rappin' (1985)

Call of the Canyon *See* Melody Ranch (1940)

The Call of the Sea *See* Tea for Two (1950)

Call Out the Marines *See* Call Out the Marines (1942)

The Call to Arms *See* That Girl from Paris (1936)

Camellia *See* The Rose (1979)

Camelot *See* Camelot (1967)

Camptown Races *See* Girl of the Golden West (1938)

Can-Can *See* The Merry Widow (1952)

Can I Go On Not Knowing *See* The Wiz (1978)

Can You Dig It *See* Head (1968)

Can You Feel It *See* Knights of the City (1985)

Can You Feel My Heart Beat *See* Thunder Alley (1985)

Can You Feel the Love Tonight *See* The Lion King (1994)

Can You Picture That? *See* The Muppet Movie (1979)

Can You Rock It Like This *See* Krush Groove (1985)

Can You Spell Schenectady? *See* The Farmer Takes a Wife (1953)

Canadian Capers *See* My Dream is Yours (1949)

Candlelight and Wine *See* Around the World (1943)

Can't Buy Me Love *See* A Hard Day's Night (1964)

Can't Help Lovin' Dat Man *See* Show Boat (1936)

Can't Help Lovin' Dat Man *See* Show Boat (1951)

Can't Help Lovin' Dat Man *See* Till the Clouds Roll By (1946)

Can't Look Back *See* Thunder Alley (1985)

Can't Stop Talking *See* Let's Dance (1950)

Can't Stop the Street *See* Krush Groove (1985)

Can't We Be Friends? *See* Young Man with a Horn (1950)

Can't You Hear Me Callin', Caroline? *See* Look for the Silver Lining (1949)

Cape Dance *See* Ship Ahoy (1942)

Cap'n Andy's Ballyhoo *See* Show Boat (1936)

Capri, Capri *See* For the First Time (1959)

Caprice Viennoise *See* I Married an Angel (1942)

Captain Custard *See* The Road to Singapore (1940)

Captain Walker Didn't Come Home *See* Tommy (1975)

Cara Nome *See* That Midnight Kiss (1949)

Cara Nome *See* They Shall Have Music (1939)

The Carioca *See* Flying Down to Rio (1933)

The Carioca *See* I'll See You in My Dreams (1951)

Carlotta, You Gotta Be Mine *See* Latin Lovers (1953)

Carmita *See* Rogue of the Rio Grande (1930)

Carnival of Venice *See* The Five Pennies (1959)

Carny Town *See* Roustabout (1964)

Caro Nome *See* I Dream Too Much (1935)

Caro Nome *See* Maytime (1937)

Carolina In The Morning *See* I'll See You in My Dreams (1951)

Carolina in the Morning *See* Jolson Sings Again (1949)

Carolina in the Morning *See* Look for the Silver Lining (1949)

Carousel Ballet *See* Carousel (1956)

Carousel Waltz *See* Carousel (1956)

Carry Me Back to Old Virginny *See* Maytime (1937)

Carry That Weight *See* Sgt. Pepper's Lonely Hearts Club Band (1978)

Casta Diva *See* They Shall Have Music (1939)

Castles in the Air *See* Two Girls and a Sailor (1944)

Catch a Ride *See* Back to the Beach (1987)

'Cause We All Got Cake *See* Too Many Girls (1940)

Cavaquinho *See* The Road to Rio (1947)

Celeste Aida *See* The Great Caruso (1951)

Celeste Aida *See* That Midnight Kiss (1949)

C'est Manifique *See* Can-Can (1960)

C'est Moi *See* Camelot (1967)

C'est Si Bon *See* New Faces of 1952 (1954)

Cha Bomm Pa Pa *See* Nancy Goes to Rio (1950)

Chacun le Sait *See* Athena (1954)

Challenge Dance *See* Give a Girl a Break (1953)

Change of Habit *See* Change of Habit (1969)

Change Partners *See* Carefree (1938)

Chanson Boheme *See* I Married an Angel (1942)

Chansonette *See* Naughty Marietta (1935)

Chantilly Lace *See* The Buddy Holly Story (1978)

Charles Atlas Song *See* The Rocky Horror Picture Show (1975)

Charleston *See* Tea for Two (1950)

The Charm of You *See* Anchors Aweigh (1945)

Charmaine *See* Thoroughly Modern Millie (1967)

Charmaine *See* Two Girls and a Sailor (1944)

Chattanooga Choo Choo *See* The Glenn Miller Story (1954)

Chattanooga Choo Choo *See* Springtime in the Rockies (1942)

Chattanooga Choo Choo *See* Sun Valley Serenade (1941)

Chava Ballet *See* Fiddler on the Roof (1971)

Che Gelida Manina! *See* The Great Caruso (1951)

Cheek to Cheek *See* Top Hat (1935)

Cheer Up, Charlie See Willy Wonka & the Chocolate Factory (1971)

Chemical Reaction See Silk Stockings (1957)

Chesay See Frankie and Johnny (1965)

Chi Me Frena See Maytime (1937)

Chicago See In the Good Old Summertime (1949)

Chicago Illinois See Victor/Victoria (1982)

Chicago Style See The Road to Bali (1953)

Chicken Soup See The Three Musketeers (1939)

Chico-Chico See Doll Face (1946)

Chim Chim Cheree See Mary Poppins (1964)

Chin Up! Cheerio! Carry On! See Babes on Broadway (1941)

China Boy See The Stork Club (1945)

Chinatown, My Chinatown See Jolson Sings Again (1949)

Chinatown, My Chinatown See The Seven Little Foys (1955)

Chitty Chitty Bang Bang See Chitty Chitty Bang Bang (1968)

Chop Suey See Flower Drum Song (1961)

Chorale for Brass, Piano, and Bongo (instrumental) See The Road to Bali (1953)

Choreography See White Christmas (1954)

Christmas See Tommy (1975)

A Christmas Carol See Scrooge (1970)

Christmas Children See Scrooge (1970)

Christmas is Coming See The Christmas That Almost Wasn't (1966)

Christmas Land See The Wonderful World of the Brothers Grimm (1962)

Christmas Story See On Moonlight Bay (1951)

The Christmas That Almost Wasn't See The Christmas That Almost Wasn't (1966)

Chu-Chi Face See Chitty Chitty Bang Bang (1968)

A Cigarette, Sweet Music and You See DuBarry Was a Lady (1943)

Cinderella See Cinderella (1950)

Cinderella's Fella See Going Hollywood (1933)

Cindy Lou McWilliams See Sing Your Worries Away (1942)

The Circle of Life See The Lion King (1994)

Circle Sky See Head (1968)

A Circus Must Be Different in a Ziegfeld Show See The Great Ziegfeld (1936)

Circus on Parade See Billy Rose's Jumbo (1962)

Ciri-Biri-Bin See One Night of Love (1934)

Ciribiribee See Hit the Deck (1955)

The City Gates are Open See The Wizard of Oz (1939)

Clambake See Clambake (1967)

Clap Hands, Here Comes Charley See Funny Lady (1975)

Clap Yo' Hands See Funny Face (1957)

Clap Yo' Hands See Rhapsody in Blue (1945)

Clean Up Your Own Back Yard See The Trouble with Girls (and How To Get Into It) (1969)

Cleopatterer See Till the Clouds Roll By (1946)

The Climb See Viva Las Vegas (1963)

Climb Every Mountain See The Sound of Music (1965)

Close (instrumental) See Rosalie (1938)

Closer and Closer and Closer See The Little Prince (1974)

The Closer You Are See Two Tickets to Broadway (1951)

The Closest to Love See Body Rock (1984)

The Clouds Will Soon Roll By See Pennies From Heaven (1981)

Coal Miner's Daughter See Coal Miner's Daughter (1980)

A Cockeyed Optimist See South Pacific (1958)

Coconut Milk See Pagan Love Song (1950)

Coffee Break See How to Succeed in Business without Really Trying (1967)

Coffee Time See Yolanda and the Thief (1945)

Cokctails for Two See Murder at the Vanities (1934)

Cold As Ice See FM (1978)

College Swing See College Swing (1938)

Colorado Is My Home See The Unsinkable Molly Brown (1964)

Colors See Rappin' (1985)

Columbia, The Gem of the Ocean See Maytime (1937)

Come Along See Frankie and Johnny (1965)

Come Along With Me See Can-Can (1960)

Come and Get Your Happiness See Rebecca of Sunnybrook Farm (1938)

Come Back to Me See On a Clear Day You Can See Forever (1970)

Come Boys, Let's All Be Gay, Boys See The Student Prince (1954)

Come Dance With Me See The Seven Hills of Rome (1958)

Come Drink to the Girl That You Love See Lottery Bride (1930)

Come, Josephine in My Flying Machine See The Story of Vernon and Irene Castle (1939)

Come On, Everybody See Viva Las Vegas (1963)

Come On Papa See Three Little Words (1950)

Come Out, Come Out, Wherever You Are See Step Lively (1944)

Come Out, Come Out Wherever you Are See The Wizard of Oz (1939)

Come Prima See For the First Time (1959)

Come Rain or Come Shine See For the Boys (1991)

Come To Me See Indiscreet (1931)

Come To My Arms See Latin Lovers (1953)

Come Together See Sgt. Pepper's Lonely Hearts Club Band (1978)

Come Up to My Place See On the Town (1949)

Comedy Ballet See The Seven Little Foys (1955)

Comment Allez-Vous See The French Line (1954)

The Company Way See How to Succeed in Business without Really Trying (1967)

Concert No. 27 for Pianoforte and Orchestra in B Flat Major See Amadeus (1984)

A Concerto for Clarinet and Orchestra in A Major See Amadeus (1984)

Concerto for Index Finger See Two Girls and a Sailor (1944)

Concerto in E Minor for Violin and Orchestra See They Shall Have Music (1939)

Concerto in F See Rhapsody in Blue (1945)

Concerto in F (3rd Movement) See An American in Paris (1951)

Confidence See Clambake (1967)

Conga See My Sister Eileen (1955)

The Conga See Too Many Girls (1940)

Consider Yourself See Oliver! (1968)

Consolation in D Flat See Song Without End (1960)

Constantly See The Road to Morocco (1942)

Contagious See Knights of the City (1985)

The Continental See The Gay Divorcee (1934)

Cool See West Side Story (1961)

Cool Napoli See Absolute Beginners (1986)

Copacobana See Holiday in Havana (1949)

Copper Colored Gal See The Cotton Club (1984)

Coquette See Easy to Love (1953)

The Cornfields See The Wizard of Oz (1939)

Cosi, Cosa See Everybody Sing (1938)

The Cossack Dance See Fantasia (1940)

Cotton Blossom See Show Boat (1936)

Cotton Candy Land See It Happened at the World's Fair (1963)

Cotton Club Stomp See The Cotton Club (1984)

Could We Start Again, Please? See Jesus Christ, Superstar (1973)

Could You Pass in Love See My Lucky Star (1938)

Could You Use Me? See Girl Crazy (1943)

Count Your Blessings Instead of Sheep See White Christmas (1954)

Country Waltz See Thunder Alley (1985)

The Country's in the Very Best of Hands See Li'l Abner (1959)

County Fair See So Dear to My Heart (1949)

A Couple of Swells See Easter Parade (1948)

Courtroom See Rappin' (1985)

Cousin Kevin See Tommy (1975)

Cover Girl See Cover Girl (1944)

Cow Boogie See Ride 'Em Cowboy (1942)

A Cowboy Has to Yodel in the Morning See Song of Nevada (1944)

Cowboy Santa See Girl in Gold Boots (1969)

Crackly Corn Flakes See Rebecca of Sunnybrook Farm (1938)

Crawfish See King Creole (1958)

Crazy See Sweet Dreams (1985)

Crazy For You See Ladies of the Chorus (1949)

Crazy Horse See The Girl Most Likely (1957)

Crazy Rhythm See The Cotton Club (1984)

Crazy Rhythm See Tea for Two (1950)

Crazy World See Victor/Victoria (1982)

Crippled Cow See A Star is Born (1976)

Cross My Heart and Hope to Die See Girl Happy (1965)

Crossing the Border See Songwriter (1984)

Crucifixion See Jesus Christ, Superstar (1973)

Cruella de Vil See 101 Dalmations (1961)

Cry and You Cry Alone See Tonight and Every Night (1945)

Cry of the City See Knights of the City (1985)

The Crystal Candelabra See The Cat and the Fiddle (1934)

Cuanto La Gusto See A Date with Judy (1948)

The Cuban Overture See Rhapsody in Blue (1945)

Cuban Rhapsody See Romance on the High Seas (1948)

Cuddle Up a Little Closer See On Moonlight Bay (1951)

Cuddle Up a Little Closer See The Story of Vernon and Irene Castle (1939)

Cuddlesome Baby See Dance of Life (1929)

The Curse of an Aching Heart See Rose of Washington Square (1939)

The Curse of an Aching Heart See Show Business (1944)

Curves See Fast Forward (1984)

The Cycle Set See Beach Blanket Bingo (1965)

Daddy Long Legs See Daddy Long Legs (1955)

Daddy-O See A Song is Born (1948)

Daddy Was a Minstrel Man *See* Babes in Arms (1939)

Daddy Wouldn't Buy Me a Bow-Wow *See* Evergreen (1934)

Daddy's Song *See* Head (1968)

Dainty June and Her Farmboys *See* Gypsy (1962)

Daisy Chain *See* Mrs. Brown, You've Got a Lovely Daughter (1968)

Dalmation Plantation *See* 101 Dalmations (1961)

Dames *See* Dames (1934)

Dammed For All Time *See* Jesus Christ, Superstar (1973)

Dance 10, Looks 3 *See* A Chorus Line (1985)

Dance All Night *See* Thank God It's Friday (1978)

Dance at the Gym *See* West Side Story (1961)

Dance of the Hours *See* Fantasia (1940)

Dance Teach/Down Street Rap *See* Knights of the City (1985)

Dance Your Cares Away *See* New Moon (1940)

Dancing *See* Hello, Dolly! (1969)

Dancing *See* Xanadu (1980)

Dancing Dildos *See* The First Nudie Musical (1975)

Dancing in the Dark *See* The Band Wagon (1953)

Dancing in the Sheets *See* Footloose (1984)

Dancing on the Ceiling *See* Evergreen (1934)

Danger, Danger *See* Thunder Alley (1985)

Danny Boy *See* Little Nellie Kelly (1940)

Dardanella *See* Two Girls and a Sailor (1944)

Dark is the Night *See* Rich, Young and Pretty (1951)

The Darktown Strutters' Ball *See* The Story of Vernon and Irene Castle (1939)

Darling Lili *See* Darling Lili (1970)

Dat, Dot, Dah *See* Stormy Weather (1943)

Datin' *See* Paradise, Hawaiian Style (1966)

Dat's Love *See* Carmen Jones (1954)

The Daughter of Rosie O'Grady *See* Show Business (1944)

Daughters of Triton *See* The Little Mermaid (1989)

The Day After Forever *See* Going My Way (1944)

The Day I Looked Jesus in the Eye *See* Nashville (1975)

A Day in New York *See* On the Town (1949)

A Day in the Life *See* Sgt. Pepper's Lonely Hearts Club Band (1978)

A Day in the Life *See* Yellow Submarine (1968)

De Camptown Races *See* Harmony Lane (1935)

De Camptown Races *See* Stormy Weather (1943)

The Deadwood Stage (Whip-Crack-Away!) *See* Calamity Jane (1953)

Dear, Dear *See* Evergreen (1934)

Dear June *See* Hallelujah, I'm a Bum (1933)

Dear Little Boy *See* Star! (1968)

Dear Mr. Gable (You Made Me Love You) *See* Broadway Melody of 1938 (1937)

Dearly Beloved *See* You Were Never Lovelier (1942)

Deceived *See* Tommy (1975)

December the 25th *See* Scrooge (1970)

Dee-Are-A-Gee-O-En (Dragon) *See* The Wonderful World of the Brothers Grimm (1962)

Deep Freeze Dinah *See* Everybody's Dancin' (1950)

Deep in My Heart *See* The Student Prince (1954)

Deep In the Heart of Texas *See* Rich, Young and Pretty (1951)

Delicious *See* Rhapsody in Blue (1945)

Delightfully Dangerous *See* Delightfully Dangerous (1945)

Delirious Escape *See* The Wizard of Oz (1939)

Deliver *See* Body Rock (1984)

Dengozo *See* Look for the Silver Lining (1949)

Dere's a Cafe on de Corner *See* Carmen Jones (1954)

Dere's Yellow Gold on de Trees (De Banana) *See* The Opposite Sex (1956)

The Desert Song *See* Deep in My Heart (1954)

The Desert Song *See* The Desert Song (1953)

Desire *See* Here Come the Girls (1953)

Destiny Waltz *See* The Story of Vernon and Irene Castle (1939)

Detroit *See* The Happiest Millionaire (1967)

Deutschland Uber Alles *See* Stage Door Canteen (1943)

Devils and Seducers *See* Staying Alive (1983)

The Devonshire Regiment *See* Royal Wedding (1951)

Diamonds Are A Girl's Best Friend *See* Gentlemen Prefer Blondes (1953)

The Dickey Bird Song *See* Three Daring Daughters (1948)

Did I Get Stinkin' at the Savoy? *See* Panama Hattie (1942)

Did You Ever Have the Feeling? *See* Two Girls and a Sailor (1944)

Did You Ever See A Dream Walking? *See* Pennies From Heaven (1981)

Didja Ever *See* Easy to Love (1953)

Didya Ever *See* G.I. Blues (1960)

Dig-Dig-Dig For Your Dinner *See* Summer Stock (1950)

Dig You Later *See* Doll Face (1946)

Digga Digga Doo *See* Stormy Weather (1943)

Dinah *See* Rose Marie (1936)

Ding Dong the Witch is Dead *See* The Wizard of Oz (1939)

Dirty, Dirty Feeling *See* Tickle Me (1965)

Dirty Hands, Dirty Face *See* Jazz Singer (1927)

Dis Flower *See* Carmen Jones (1954)

Disco Queen *See* Thank God It's Friday (1978)

Disgustingly Rich *See* Higher and Higher (1944)

Dissertation on the State of Bliss *See* Country Girl (1954)

Dites-Moi *See* South Pacific (1958)

Dixiana *See* Dixiana (1930)

Dixie *See* Stars and Stripes Forever (1952)

Dixie-Anna *See* Dimples (1936)

Dixie Showboat *See* Dixie Jamboree (1944)

Dixieland Rock *See* King Creole (1958)

Do *See* Girl Crazy (1943)

Do Do Do *See* Tea for Two (1950)

Do, Do, Do *See* Star! (1968)

Do I Love You *See* For Me and My Gal (1942)

Do I Love You *See* Night and Day (1946)

Do I Love You, Do I? *See* DuBarry Was a Lady (1943)

Do It Again *See* FM (1978)

Do It Again *See* Thoroughly Modern Millie (1967)

Do It the Hard Way *See* Pal Joey (1957)

Do It Yourself *See* Bells are Ringing (1960)

Do Not Disturb *See* Girl Happy (1965)

Do Nothing Till You Hear from Me *See* New York, New York (1977)

Do Re Mi *See* The Sound of Music (1965)

Do the Clam *See* Girl Happy (1965)

Do You Feel Alright? *See* Thunder Alley (1985)

Do You Love Me? *See* Fiddler on the Roof (1971)

Do You Think It's All Right *See* Tommy (1975)

Do You Want It Right Now? *See* Fast Forward (1984)

Do You Want the Real Thing? *See* Thank God It's Friday (1978)

Do You Want to Laugh or Cry? *See* Girl in Gold Boots (1969)

Doctor Dolittle *See* Doctor Dolittle (1967)

Doctor, Lawyer, Indian Chief *See* The Stork Club (1945)

Dodge *See* Rappin' (1985)

Dog Song *See* On an Island with You (1948)

Dogs and Cats *See* Thunder Alley (1985)

Dogs in the Yard *See* Fame (1980)

A Dog's Life *See* Paradise, Hawaiian Style (1966)

Doin' the Best I Can *See* G.I. Blues (1960)

Doin' the Grizzly Bear *See* Hello, Frisco, Hello (1943)

Dolce Far Niente *See* The Unsinkable Molly Brown (1964)

Doll on a Music Box *See* Chitty Chitty Bang Bang (1968)

The Doll Shop *See* For Me and My Gal (1942)

The Donkey Serenade *See* The Firefly (1937)

Don't Ask Me Not to Sing *See* Roberta (1935)

Don't Ask Me Why *See* King Creole (1958)

Don't Ask Us Not To Sing *See* The Cat and the Fiddle (1934)

Don't Be a Do-Badder *See* Robin and the Seven Hoods (1964)

Don't Be That Way *See* The Benny Goodman Story (1955)

Don't Be That Way *See* New York, New York (1977)

Don't Blame Me *See* New York, New York (1977)

Don't Burn the Candle at Both Ends *See* Look Out Sister (1948)

Don't Carry Tales Out of School *See* Pin-Up Girl (1944)

Don't Ever Leave Me *See* Sweet Adeline (1935)

Don't Explain *See* Lady Sings the Blues (1972)

Don't Fence Me In *See* Hollywood Canteen (1944)

Don't Fence Me In *See* Night and Day (1946)

Don't Get Around Much Anymore *See* New York, New York (1977)

Don't Leave Me Daddy *See* For Me and My Gal (1942)

Don't Leave Me Now *See* Jailhouse Rock (1957)

Don't Let It Bother You *See* The Gay Divorcee (1934)

Don't Let This Night Get Away *See* Jupiter's Darling (1955)

Don't Look Now But My Heart Is Showing *See* One Touch of Venus (1948)

Don't Marry Me *See* Flower Drum Song (1961)

Don't Mention Love To Me *See* In Person (1935)

Don't Nobody Bring Me Bad News *See* The Wiz (1978)

Don't Rain On My Parade *See* Funny Girl (1968)

Don't Sit Under the Apple Tree with Anyone Else But Me *See* Private Buckaroo (1942)

Don't Stop Now *See* Beach Party (1963)

Don't Take That Rag Off'n the Bush *See* Li'l Abner (1959)

Don't Think it Ain't Been Charming *See* You'll Find Out (1940)

Don't Walk Away *See* Xanadu (1980)

Don't Worry About the Mule *See* Swing Parade of 1946 (1946)

Don't Worry Island *See* Stage Door Canteen (1943)

Don't You Dog Me *See* Krush Groove (1985)

Doodle-Ee-Doo *See* Around the World (1943)

Dorothy's Rescue *See* The Wizard of Oz (1939)

Dorsey Concerto *See* The Fabulous Dorseys (1947)

Down Among the Sheltering Palms *See* That Midnight Kiss (1949)

Down Argentina Way *See* Down Argentine Way (1940)

Down at the Old Bull and Bush *See* Star! (1968)

Down on Melody Farms *See* Everybody Sing (1938)

Down to Her Socks *See* Songwriter (1984)

Down to Lovetown *See* Thank God It's Friday (1978)

Down to the River *See* Nashville (1975)

Down Where The Trade Winds Blow *See* Hawaii Calls (1938)

Dream *See* Daddy Long Legs (1955)

Dream Dancing *See* This Could be the Night (1957)

Dream Dancing *See* You'll Never Get Rich (1941)

A Dream Is a Wish Your Heart Makes *See* Cinderella (1950)

The Dreamer *See* Thank Your Lucky Stars (1943)

Drink, Drink, Drink *See* The Student Prince (1954)

Drinking Song *See* Paradise Island (1930)

The Drinking Song *See* Ziegfeld Follies (1946)

Drivin' Blues *See* Thunder Alley (1985)

Drop Me Off in Harlem *See* The Cotton Club (1984)

Drop That Name *See* Bells are Ringing (1960)

Drum Crazy *See* Easter Parade (1948)

Drums of the Islands *See* Paradise, Hawaiian Style (1966)

Du und Du *See* The Great Waltz (1938)

DuBarry Was a Lady *See* DuBarry Was a Lady (1943)

The Dubbing *See* Man of La Mancha (1972)

Dues *See* Nashville (1975)

Dulcinea *See* Man of La Mancha (1972)

Dustin' The Stars *See* Mad About Money (1930)

Dusty Road *See* Let Freedom Ring (1939)

The Dwarfs' Yodel Song *See* Snow White and the Seven Dwarfs (1937)

D'ya Love Me? *See* Sunny (1941)

E Lucevan Le Steele *See* The Great Caruso (1951)

An Earful of Music *See* Kid Millions (1934)

Early Bird *See* Captain January (1936)

Earth Boy *See* Girls! Girls! Girls! (1962)

Earthbound *See* The Seven Hills of Rome (1958)

Ease on Down the Road *See* The Wiz (1978)

Easter Parade *See* Alexander's Ragtime Band (1938)

Easter Parade *See* Easter Parade (1948)

Easter Parade *See* Holiday Inn (1942)

Easy Come, Easy Go *See* Easy Come, Easy Go (1967)

Easy Rider *See* She Done Him Wrong (1933)

Easy Street *See* Annie (1982)

Easy to Love *See* Born to Dance (1936)

Easy to Love *See* Easy to Love (1953)

Easy to Love *See* Night and Day (1946)

Ebony Rhapsody *See* Murder at the Vanities (1934)

Eddie's Teddy *See* The Rocky Horror Picture Show (1975)

Edelweiss *See* The Sound of Music (1965)

Edge of Reality *See* Live a Little, Love a Little (1968)

The Egg *See* 1776 (1972)

E.H.S. *See* George White's Scandals (1945)

El Capitan *See* Stars and Stripes Forever (1952)

El Toro *See* Fun in Acapulco (1963)

Eleanor Rigby *See* Give My Regards to Broad Street (1984)

Eleanor Rigby *See* Yellow Submarine (1968)

Electric Boogaloo *See* Breakin' 2: Electric Boogaloo (1984)

Elegance *See* Hello, Dolly! (1969)

Elegua *See* Crossover Dreams (1985)

Eli Eli *See* The Jolson Story (1946)

The Embassy Waltz *See* My Fair Lady (1964)

Embraceable You *See* An American in Paris (1951)

Embraceable You *See* Girl Crazy (1943)

Embraceable You *See* Rhapsody in Blue (1945)

Emerald City Ballet *See* The Wiz (1978)

End of the Trail *See* Melody Trail (1935)

End of the Yellow Brick Road *See* The Wiz (1978)

Enesco's "Rumanian Rhapsody" *See* Three Daring Daughters (1948)

English March *See* The Firefly (1937)

Entr'acte *See* Half a Sixpence (1967)

Entrance of Lucy James *See* Born to Dance (1936)

Estrellita *See* They Shall Have Music (1939)

Estrellita *See* Two Girls and a Sailor (1944)

Etiquette *See* Pagan Love Song (1950)

Etude In A Flat, Opus 25, No. 1 (partial) *See* A Song to Remember (1945)

Etude In C Minor, Opus 10, No. 12 *See* A Song to Remember (1945)

Etude in E, Opus 10, No. 3 *See* A Song to Remember (1945)

Evergreen *See* A Star is Born (1976)

Every Baby Nees a Da Da Daddy *See* Ladies of the Chorus (1949)

Every Little Movement Has a Meaning All Its Own *See* The Jolson Story (1946)

Every Little Movement Has a Meaning All Its Own *See* On Moonlight Bay (1951)

Every Little Movement Has a Meaning All Its Own *See* Presenting Lily Mars (1943)

Every Lover Must Meet His Fate *See* Sweethearts (1938)

Every Now and Then *See* The Great Gabbo (1929)

Everybody Come Aboard *See* Frankie and Johnny (1965)

Everybody Loves My Baby *See* Love Me or Leave Me (1955)

Everybody Rejoice *See* The Wiz (1978)

Everybody Sing *See* Broadway Melody of 1938 (1937)

Everybody Step *See* Alexander's Ragtime Band (1938)

Everybody's Doin' It *See* Alexander's Ragtime Band (1938)

Everybody's Doin' It *See* Easter Parade (1948)

Everybody's Doin' It *See* The Fabulous Dorseys (1947)

Everything *See* A Star is Born (1976)

Everything I Have Is Yours *See* Dancing Lady (1933)

Everything I Touch Turns to Gold *See* Girl in Gold Boots (1969)

Everything Old is New Again *See* All That Jazz (1979)

Everything's Alright *See* Jesus Christ, Superstar (1973)

Everything's Coming Up Roses *See* Gypsy (1962)

Everything's Coming Up Roses *See* Gypsy (1993)

Everything's Up to Date in Kansas City *See* Oklahoma! (1955)

Evil Lies *See* The Rose (1979)

Ev'ry Night at Seven *See* Royal Wedding (1951)

Ev'ry Time *See* Best Foot Forward (1943)

Experience *See* The Road to Rio (1947)

Eye of the Storm *See* Songwriter (1984)

The Eyes of Texas Are Upon You *See* Viva Las Vegas (1963)

Eyesight to the Blind *See* Tommy (1975)

Fabulous Places *See* Doctor Dolittle (1967)

The Fair *See* Meet Me in St. Louis (1944)

A Fair Story by the Fireside *See* Song O' My Heart (1929)

The Fall *See* Xanadu (1980)

Falling in Love Again *See* The Blue Angel (1930)

Fame *See* Fame (1980)

A Family Man *See* Marco (1973)

Fan Tan Fanny *See* Flower Drum Song (1961)

Fancy Forgetting *See* The Boy Friend (1971)

Fancy Pants *See* Fancy Pants (1950)

Fantasia Mexican *See* Fiesta (1947)

Fantasie Impromptu, Opus 66 *See* A Song to Remember (1945)

Fantasy on Themes From "Rigoletto" *See* Song Without End (1960)

Far From Over *See* Staying Alive (1983)

Far from the Home I Love *See* Fiddler on the Roof (1971)

The Farmer and the Cowman *See* Oklahoma! (1955)

Farmer in the Dell *See* Let's Sing Again (1936)

Farver Chris'mas *See* Scrooge (1970)

Fascinatin' Rhythm *See* Rhapsody in Blue (1945)

Fascinating Rhythm *See* Girl Crazy (1943)

Fascinating Rhythm *See* Lady Be Good (1941)

Fascination *See* Follies Girl (1943)

Fast Forward *See* Fast Forward (1984)

Fat Boys *See* Krush Groove (1985)

Fat, Fat Fatima *See* Deep in My Heart (1954)

Fate *See* Kismet (1955)

Fated to Be Mated *See* Silk Stockings (1957)

Faust *See* Phantom of the Paradise (1974)

F.D.R. Jones *See* Babes on Broadway (1941)

Feed the Birds *See* Mary Poppins (1964)

Feel the Spin *See* Krush Groove (1985)

Feeling High *See* Hollywood Party (1934)

The Feeling That We HAve *See* The Wiz (1978)

Feels Like the First Time *See* FM (1978)

A Fella With an Umbrella *See* Easter Parade (1948)

The Fellow I'd Follow *See* Small Town Girl (1953)

Fiddle About *See* Tommy (1975)

Fidelity Feduciary Bank *See* Mary Poppins (1964)

Fifi *See* Dangerous When Wet (1953)

'51 is Going to Be A Good Year *See* Tommy (1975)

Fill The World With Love *See* Goodbye, Mr. Chips (1969)

Final Attraction *See* Songwriter (1984)

Finale *See* Rappin' (1985)

Finale *See* Thank Your Lucky Stars (1943)

Finch's Frolic *See* How to Succeed in Business without Really Trying (1967)

Find My Way *See* Thank God It's Friday (1978)

Fine and Dandy *See* Lullaby of Broadway (1951)

Fine, Fine, Fine *See* Small Town Girl (1953)

A Fine Romance *See* Swing Time (1936)

A Fine Romance *See* Till the Clouds Roll By (1946)

Fire *See* Knights of the City (1985)

Fire Down Below *See* The Rose (1979)

First Love Never Dies *See* Rappin' (1985)

The First Nudie Musical *See* The First Nudie Musical (1975)

The First Thing You Know *See* Paint Your Wagon (1969)

Fit as a Fiddle *See* Singin' in the Rain (1952)

Five Foot Two *See* Love Me or Leave Me (1955)

Five Foot Two, Eyes of Blue *See* Strike Up the Band (1940)

The Five Pennies *See* The Five Pennies (1959)

Fixing a Hole *See* Sgt. Pepper's Lonely Hearts Club Band (1978)

Flame in the Fire *See* Rappin' (1985)

Flash *See* Two Girls and a Sailor (1944)

Flash, Bang, Wallop! *See* Half a Sixpence (1967)

Flashdance...What a Feeling *See* Flashdance (1983)

Fleur de Paris *See* Le Bal (1982)

Fleurette *See* Three Daring Daughters (1948)

A Flight of Fancy *See* Just for You (1952)

Flight of the Bumble Bee *See* Stage Door Canteen (1943)

Flip the Dip *See* New York, New York (1977)

Flippity Flop *See* Dance of Life (1929)

The Flower Market *See* My Fair Lady (1964)

Flower Song *See* Les Girls (1957)

Floyd's Theme *See* Thank God It's Friday (1978)

Fly Boy *See* Beach Blanket Bingo (1965)

Fly Like An Eagle *See* FM (1978)

Flyin' Home *See* A Song is Born (1948)

Flying *See* Knights of the City (1985)

Flying Down to Rio *See* Flying Down to Rio (1933)

Flying Saucers *See* Yes, Sir, Mr. Bones (1951)

FM *See* FM (1978)

FM Reprise *See* FM (1978)

A Foggy Day in Londontown *See* A Damsel in Distress (1937)

Follow in My Footsteps *See* Broadway Melody of 1938 (1937)

Follow Me *See* Camelot (1967)

Follow the Fold *See* Guys and Dolls (1955)

Follow the Yellow Brick Road *See* The Wizard of Oz (1939)

Follow Your Leader *See* How to Stuff a Wild Bikini (1965)

Food, Glorious Food *See* Oliver! (1968)

The Fool on the Hill *See* Magical Mystery Tour (1967)

Foolin' Around *See* Sweet Dreams (1985)

Foolish Tears *See* Everybody's Dancin' (1950)

Football *See* Good News (1947)

Footloose *See* Footloose (1984)

For All We Know *See* New York, New York (1977)

For Me and My Gal *See* For Me and My Gal (1942)

For Me and My Gal *See* Jolson Sings Again (1949)

For the Sake of the Children *See* Nashville (1975)

For What? *See* The Road to Rio (1947)

For You *See* Girl in Gold Boots (1969)

For Your Country and My Country *See* Alexander's Ragtime Band (1938)

Forbidden Fruit *See* Star! (1968)

Fort Lauderdale Chamber of Commerce *See* Girl Happy (1965)

Fortuosity *See* The Happiest Millionaire (1967)

Forty-five Minutes to Broadway *See* Yankee Doodle Dandy (1942)

Forty-Second Street *See* 42nd Street (1933)

Frankfurt Special *See* G.I. Blues (1960)

Frankie and Johnny *See* Frankie and Johnny (1965)

Frankie and Johnny *See* Meet Me in Las Vegas (1956)

Frankie and Johnny *See* She Done Him Wrong (1933)

Frantic Situation *See* Beat Street (1984)

Freddie and His Fiddle *See* Song of Norway (1970)

Freddie Get Ready *See* My Dream is Yours (1949)

Freddy My Love *See* Grease (1978)

Free to be Free *See* Rose Marie (1954)

Freebootin' *See* Tom Sawyer (1973)

The French Lesson *See* Good News (1947)

The French Line *See* The French Line (1954)

Fresh as a Daisy *See* Panama Hattie (1942)

Friend Like Me *See* Aladdin (1992)

Friendly Star *See* Summer Stock (1950)

Friendship *See* DuBarry Was a Lady (1943)

Frog's Legs So Fine *See* The Muppet Movie (1979)

From Here to Eternity *See* Thank God It's Friday (1978)

From the Heart *See* Love Songs (1985)

From This Day On *See* Brigadoon (1954)

From This Moment On *See* Kiss Me Kate (1953)

FU12 *See* Rappin' (1985)

Fugue for Tinhorns *See* Guys and Dolls (1955)

Fun in Acapulco *See* Fun in Acapulco (1963)

Funiculi Funicula *See* Let Freedom Ring (1939)

Funny Face *See* Funny Face (1957)

Funny Girl *See* Funny Girl (1968)

The Ga-Ga Bird *See* The Great Gabbo (1929)

Gallivantin' Around *See* Show Boat (1936)

The Game *See* Rappin' (1985)

Game Over *See* New York, New York (1977)

The Gardner's Daughter *See* Frankie and Johnny (1965)

Gary, Indiana *See* The Music Man (1962)

Gaston's Soliloquy *See* Gigi (1958)

Gay Parisienne *See* The Desert Song (1953)

Gay Peree *See* Victor/Victoria (1982)

Gee, But It's Great to Meet a Friend from Your Own Home Town *See* Hello, Frisco, Hello (1943)

Gee, I Wish I Was Back in the Army *See* White Christmas (1954)

Gee, Officer Krupke *See* West Side Story (1961)

Geechy Joe *See* Stormy Weather (1943)

The General Jumped At Dawn *See* Hollywood Canteen (1944)

Get Back *See* Sgt. Pepper's Lonely Hearts Club Band (1978)

Get Happy *See* Summer Stock (1950)

Get Happy *See* Young Man with a Horn (1950)

Get Me a Taxi *See* DuBarry Was a Lady (1943)

Get Me To The Church on Time *See* My Fair Lady (1964)

Get On Board *See* Dimples (1936)

Get Thee Behind Me, Satan *See* Follow the Fleet (1936)

Get Your Police Gazette *See* Sweet Rosie O'Grady (1943)

Gethsemane *See* Jesus Christ, Superstar (1973)

Gettin' Corns For My Country *See* Hollywood Canteen (1944)

Getting Better *See* Sgt. Pepper's Lonely Hearts Club Band (1978)

Getting To Know You *See* The King and I (1956)

G.I. Blues *See* G.I. Blues (1960)

Giannina Mia *See* The Firefly (1937)

Gigi *See* Gigi (1958)

Gimme a Pigfoot and a Bottle of Beer *See* Lady Sings the Blues (1972)

Gimme Back My Heart *See* Thunder Alley (1985)

Gimme Some Skin *See* In the Navy (1941)

The Girl at the Ironing Board *See* Dames (1934)

The Girl Gets Around *See* Footloose (1984)

Girl Happy *See* Girl Happy (1965)

The Girl Hunt *See* The Band Wagon (1953)

The Girl I Love to Leave Behind *See* Stage Door Canteen (1943)

The Girl I Never Loved *See* Clambake (1967)

The Girl In No Man's Land *See* Darling Lili (1970)

The Girl Most Likely *See* The Girl Most Likely (1957)

A Girl Named Mary and a Boy Named Bill *See* The Stooge (1951)

A Girl Needs a Boy *See* Muscle Beach Party (1964)

The Girl Next Door *See* Athena (1954)

The Girl on the Magazine Cover *See* Easter Parade (1948)

The Girl on the Police Gazette *See* On the Avenue (1937)

The Girl With the Yaller Shoes *See* Meet Me in Las Vegas (1956)

A Girlfriend of a Boyfriend of Mine *See* Whoopee! (1930)

Girls Are Here To Stay *See* Here Come the Girls (1953)

The Girls at Maxim's *See* The Merry Widow (1934)

Girls, Girls, Girls *See* Girls! Girls! Girls! (1962)

Girls, Girls, Girls *See* The Merry Widow (1934)

Girls, Girls, Girls *See* The Merry Widow (1952)

A Girls Needs a Boy *See* Seaside Swingers (1965)

Give a Little Whistle *See* Pinocchio (1940)

Give Her Lovin' *See* How to Stuff a Wild Bikini (1965)

Give Me a Band and My Baby *See* My Sister Eileen (1955)

Give Me a Break *See* Can't Stop the Music (1980)

Give Me My Saddle *See* Ride 'Em Cowboy (1942)

Give Me the Simple Life *See* Let's Make Love (1960)

Give My Regards to Broadway *See* Broadway Melody (1929)

Give My Regards to Broadway *See* The Great American Broadcast (1941)

Give My Regards to Broadway *See* Jolson Sings Again (1949)

Give My Regards to Broadway *See* Yankee Doodle Dandy (1942)

Give the Girl a Break *See* Give a Girl a Break (1953)

Glad to Have You Aboard *See* Skirts Ahoy! (1952)

Glinda's Theme *See* The Wiz (1978)

Gloria *See* Flashdance (1983)

Glow, Little Glow Worm *See* The Story of Vernon and Irene Castle (1939)

Go Back to the City Again *See* Melody Ranch (1940)

Go To Sleep *See* On a Clear Day You Can See Forever (1970)

Go to the Mirror *See* Tommy (1975)

God Bless America *See* This is the Army (1943)

God Bless the Child *See* Lady Sings the Blues (1972)

God's Country *See* Babes in Arms (1939)

Goin' Co'tin *See* Seven Brides for Seven Brothers (1954)

Goin' North *See* Thank Your Lucky Stars (1943)

Going Hollywood *See* Going Hollywood (1933)

Going My Way *See* Going My Way (1944)

Going to the Country Fair *See* Sweet Rosie O'Grady (1943)

Gold Fever *See* Paint Your Wagon (1969)

Golden Days *See* The Student Prince (1954)

Golden Helmet of Mambrino *See* Man of La Mancha (1972)

Golden Slumbers *See* Sgt. Pepper's Lonely Hearts Club Band (1978)

The Goldwyn Stomp *See* A Song is Born (1948)

Golly Gee *See* Rappin' (1985)

Good Day, Sunshine *See* Give My Regards to Broad Street (1984)

Good For Baby *See* Crossover Dreams (1985)

Good Ground *See* Way Down South (1939)

A Good Man Is Hard to Find *See* Meet Danny Wilson (1952)

Good Morning *See* Babes in Arms (1939)

Good Morning *See* Singin' in the Rain (1952)

Good Morning, Good Morning *See* Sgt. Pepper's Lonely Hearts Club Band (1978)

Good Morning Heartache *See* Lady Sings the Blues (1972)

Good Neighbors *See* Panama Hattie (1942)

Good News *See* Good News (1947)

Good News Tomorrow *See* Zis Boom Bah (1942)

Good Night, Good Neighbor *See* Thank Your Lucky Stars (1943)

Good Night, My Love *See* Stowaway (1936)

Good Night Sleep Tight *See* The Five Pennies (1959)

Good Times *See* Songwriter (1984)

The Good Times *See* Beach Blanket Bingo (1965)

Goodbye Broadway, Hello France *See* For Me and My Gal (1942)

Goodbye Broadway, Hello France *See* Tin Pan Alley (1940)

Goodbye, Eddie, Goodbye *See* Phantom of the Paradise (1974)

Goodbye Girls *See* Deep in My Heart (1954)

Goodbye My Lady Love *See* Meet Me in St. Louis (1944)

Goodbye, My Lady Love *See* Show Boat (1936)

Goodbye, Old Girl *See* Damn Yankees (1958)

Goodnight Ladies *See* The Music Man (1962)

Goodnight, My Someone *See* The Music Man (1962)

Goodnight Now *See* Spotlight Scandals (1943)

Goodnight Sweetheart *See* Holiday in Mexico (1946)

Goodtime Charlie *See* The Road to Utopia (1946)

The Gospel of No Name City *See* Paint Your Wagon (1969)

Gossip *See* Gigi (1958)

Got a Lot of Livin' To Do *See* Loving You (1957)

Got a New Lease on Life *See* In Person (1935)

Got to Get You Into My Life *See* Sgt. Pepper's Lonely Hearts Club Band (1978)

Gotta Have Me Go With You *See* A Star is Born (1954)

Gotta Stop That Man *See* How to Succeed in Business without Really Trying (1967)

Granada *See* Because You're Mine (1952)

Granada *See* Two Girls and a Sailor (1944)

Grand March *See* For the First Time (1959)

Grand Old Ivy *See* How to Succeed in Business without Really Trying (1967)

Grant Avenue *See* Flower Drum Song (1961)

Gratification *See* Tom Sawyer (1973)

Grease *See* Grease (1978)

Greased Lightnin' *See* Grease (1978)

The Great American Broadcast *See* The Great American Broadcast (1941)

Great Balls of Fire *See* Absolute Beginners (1986)

Great Big Town *See* Pal Joey (1957)

The Great Come and Get It Day *See* Finian's Rainbow (1968)

Great Day *See* Funny Lady (1975)

Great News in the Making *See* Around the World (1943)

Green Eyes *See* The Fabulous Dorseys (1947)

Green Grass and High Tides *See* FM (1978)

Guadalajara *See* Fun in Acapulco (1963)

Guadeamas Igitur *See* A Song is Born (1948)

Guenevere *See* Camelot (1967)

Guiding Star *See* Dixiana (1930)

Guys and Dolls *See* Guys and Dolls (1955)

The Gypsy Drinking Song *See* The Inspector General (1949)

Gypsy Rhapsody *See* The Wonderful World of the Brothers Grimm (1962)

A Gypsy Told Me *See* Happy Landing (1938)

Ha! Cha Cha *See* The Cat and the Fiddle (1934)

Habanera *See* Going My Way (1944)

Habanera *See* One Night of Love (1934)

Hail, Hail, the Gang's All Here *See* Panama Hattie (1942)

Hail to the Chief *See* Stars and Stripes Forever (1952)

Hakuna Matata *See* The Lion King (1994)

Half a Sixpence *See* Half a Sixpence (1967)

Hallelujah *See* Hit the Deck (1955)

Hallelujah, I'm A Bum *See* Hallelujah, I'm a Bum (1933)

Hancock's Half Hour *See* Absolute Beginners (1986)

Hand Me Down That Can O' Beans *See* Paint Your Wagon (1969)

Hands Across the Border *See* Call Out the Marines (1942)

Hang On To Me *See* Lady Be Good (1941)

Hannibal, Mo. *See* Tom Sawyer (1973)

Hannibal's Victory March *See* Jupiter's Darling (1955)

The Happiest Day of My Life *See* Royal Wedding (1951)

Happiness *See* Scrooge (1970)

Happiness Bound *See* Hit the Ice (1943)

Happiness Is Just a Thing Called Joe *See* Cabin in the Sky (1943)

Happiness Is Just a Thing Called Joe *See* I'll Cry Tomorrow (1955)

Happiness Pie *See* The Old Curiosity Shop (1975)

Happy Birthday *See* Three Daring Daughters (1948)

Happy Birthday to You *See* Little Miss Broadway (1938)

Happy Easter *See* Easter Parade (1948)

Happy Ending *See* It Happened at the World's Fair (1963)

Happy Ending *See* Rebecca of Sunnybrook Farm (1938)

Happy Endings *See* New York, New York (1977)

Happy Feet *See* King of Jazz (1930)

Happy Harvest *See* Summer Stock (1950)

Happy Holidays *See* Holiday Inn (1942)

Happy Hunting Horn *See* Pal Joey (1957)

Happy Street *See* Muscle Beach Party (1964)

Happy Talk *See* South Pacific (1958)

Happy Times *See* The Inspector General (1949)

A Hard Day's Night *See* A Hard Day's Night (1964)

Hard-Headed Woman *See* King Creole (1958)

Hard Knocks *See* Roustabout (1964)

Hard Luck *See* Frankie and Johnny (1965)

Hardrock *See* Fast Forward (1984)

Harlem Nocturne *See* Le Bal (1982)

Harlem On The Prairie *See* Harlem on the Prairie (1938)

Harrigan *See* Yankee Doodle Dandy (1942)

The Harum Scarum Baron of the Harmonium *See* Song of Nevada (1944)

Has Anybody Here Seen Kelly *See* Hello, Frisco, Hello (1943)

Has Anybody Seen Our Ship? *See* Star! (1968)

The Hat My Father Wore on St. Patrick's Day *See* Take Me Out to the Ball Game (1949)

Hats Off *See* Hats Off (1937)

Hattie from Panama *See* Panama Hattie (1942)

Have You Ever Been Blue? *See* Absolute Beginners (1986)

Have Yourself a Merry Little Christmas *See* Meet Me in St. Louis (1944)

Having It All *See* Absolute Beginners (1986)

Hawaii Calls *See* Hawaii Calls (1938)

Hawaiian War Chant *See* It's a Date (1940)

Hazoy *See* New York, New York (1977)

He Ain't Got Rhythm *See* On the Avenue (1937)

He Isn't You *See* On a Clear Day You Can See Forever (1970)

He Loves and She Loves *See* Funny Face (1957)

He Needs Me *See* Pete Kelly's Blues (1955)

He Plays the Violin *See* 1776 (1972)

He Was a Dandy *See* Dimples (1936)

He Who Loves and Runs Away *See* The Firefly (1937)

Heart *See* Damn Yankees (1958)

The Heart of a Gentle Woman *See* Nashville (1975)

Heart of the Beat *See* Breakin' (1984)

A Heart That's Free *See* San Francisco (1936)

A Heart That's Free *See* Two Weeks with Love (1950)

Heart to Heart *See* Thunder Alley (1985)

Heat Doesn't Bother Me *See* Absolute Beginners (1986)

Heat Wave *See* Alexander's Ragtime Band (1938)

Heat Wave *See* White Christmas (1954)

Heather on the Hill *See* Brigadoon (1954)

Heaven? *See* Manhattan Merry-Go-Round (1937)

Heaven In Your Arms *See* It's Love Again (1936)

Heaven On Their Minds *See* Jesus Christ, Superstar (1973)

Heaven Will Protect the Working Girl *See* Sweet Rosie O'Grady (1943)

Heavenly Days *See* Here Come the Girls (1953)

Heavenly Happy *See* Summer Stock (1950)

A Heavenly Party *See* Joy of Living (1938)

Heigh Ho *See* Snow White and the Seven Dwarfs (1937)

Heigh Ho Everybody *See* Vagabond Lover (1929)

Heigh-Ho! The Gang's All Here *See* Dancing Lady (1933)

Hell Hath No Fury *See* Meet Me in Las Vegas (1956)

The Hell of It *See* Phantom of the Paradise (1974)

Hellacious Acres *See* A Star is Born (1976)

Hello *See* Hollywood Party (1934)

Hello Again *See* Jazz Singer (1980)

Hello Dolly *See* Hello, Dolly! (1969)

Hello, Frisco, Hello *See* Hello, Frisco, Hello (1943)

Hello, Frisco, Hello *See* The Story of Vernon and Irene Castle (1939)

Hello, Hello, Who's Your Lady Friend? *See* The Story of Vernon and Irene Castle (1939)

Hello, Mi Amigo *See* The Heat's On (1943)

Hello, Michelle *See* Girl in Gold Boots (1969)

Hello Twelve, Hello Thirteen, Hello Love *See* A Chorus Line (1985)

Hello, Young Lovers *See* The King and I (1956)

Help! *See* Help! (1965)

Helping Out Friends *See* Never Steal Anything Small (1959)

Her Is *See* Pajama Game (1957)

Here Am I *See* Sweet Adeline (1935)

Here Comes Heaven Again *See* Doll Face (1946)

Here Comes the Bride *See* Absolute Beginners (1986)

Here Comes the Sun *See* Sgt. Pepper's Lonely Hearts Club Band (1978)

Here, Pussy, Pussy *See* The Goldwyn Follies (1938)

Here's to the Girls *See* Ziegfeld Follies (1946)

Here's to the Old Days *See* Dixiana (1930)

Here's What I'm Here For *See* A Star is Born (1954)

Hernando's Highway *See* Pajama Game (1957)

Herod's Song *See* Jesus Christ, Superstar (1973)

Heroes in the Fall *See* Too Many Girls (1940)

He's a Lady's Man *See* Good News (1947)

He's a Tramp *See* Lady and the Tramp (1955)

He's Got a Secret Weapon *See* Around the World (1943)

He's Just Crazy For Me *See* Just for You (1952)

He's My Friend *See* The Unsinkable Molly Brown (1964)

He's Not the Marrying Kind *See* Melody Cruise (1932)

He's the Wizard *See* The Wiz (1978)

He's Your Uncle, Not Your Dad *See* Speedway (1968)

Hey Babe Hey *See* Born to Dance (1936)

Hey, Big Spender *See* Sweet Charity (1969)

Hey, Bulldog *See* Yellow Submarine (1968)

Hey Butcher *See* I Married an Angel (1942)

Hey, Hey, Hey *See* Clambake (1967)

Hey Little Schoolgirl *See* Absolute Beginners (1986)

Hey There *See* Pajama Game (1957)

Hey, What Did the Bluebird Say? *See* Dimples (1936)

Hey, What's Your Name *See* Kid from Brooklyn (1946)

Hey Young Fella *See* Dancing Lady (1933)

Hi-De-Ho *See* Hi-De-Ho (1935)

Hi-Diddle-Dee-Dee (An Actor's Life For Me) *See* Pinocchio (1940)

Hi Ho Little Dogies *See* Song of Nevada (1944)

Hieraten *See* Cabaret (1972)

High and Low *See* The Band Wagon (1953)

High and Low *See* Lottery Bride (1930)

High Flyin' *See* Broadway Serenade (1939)

High Hopes *See* Lucky Me (1954)

High on the List *See* Mr. Music (1950)

High Society Calypso *See* High Society (1956)

Hilda Matilda *See* Skirts Ahoy! (1952)

Hill of Dreams *See* Song of Norway (1970)

His Love Makes Me Beautiful *See* Funny Girl (1968)

History of the Beat *See* Daddy Long Legs (1955)

Hoe Down *See* Babes on Broadway (1941)

Hola E Pae *See* I Dood It (1943)

Hold Me Close to You *See* Skirts Ahoy! (1952)

Hold Me in Your Arms *See* Young at Heart (1954)

Hold On, Little Doggie, Hold On *See* Melody Trail (1935)

Hold Tight *See* New York, New York (1977)

Hold Your Man *See* Dancing Lady (1933)

Holding Out for a Hero *See* Footloose (1984)

Holiday in Havana *See* Holiday in Havana (1949)

Holiday in Mexico *See* Holiday in Mexico (1946)

Holiday Inn *See* Holiday Inn (1942)

Holiday Inn *See* Mrs. Brown, You've Got a Lovely Daughter (1968)

Holly Rock *See* Krush Groove (1985)

Hollywood *See* FM (1978)

Hollywood Party *See* Hollywood Party (1934)

Home Cookin' *See* Fancy Pants (1950)

Home Is Where The Heart Is *See* Kid Galahad (1962)

Home Sweet Home *See* Let Freedom Ring (1939)

Honestly Sincere *See* Bye, Bye, Birdie (1963)

Honey *See* Nashville (1975)

Honey Bun *See* South Pacific (1958)

Honey in the Honeycomb *See* Cabin in the Sky (1943)

Honey, What Ya Doin' Tonight *See* The First Nudie Musical (1975)

Honeymoon Hotel *See* Footlight Parade (1933)

Honeysuckle Rose *See* New York, New York (1977)

Honeysuckle Rose *See* Tin Pan Alley (1940)

Honolulu *See* Honolulu (1939)

Hooray for Captain Spaulding *See* Three Little Words (1950)

Hoots Mon *See* The Road to Bali (1953)

Hope We Never Change *See* Staying Alive (1983)

Hopelessly Devoted To You *See* Grease (1978)

Hora Staccato *See* Bathing Beauty (1944)

Hora Staccato *See* They Shall Have Music (1939)

Horatio's Narration *See* Jupiter's Darling (1955)

The Horrible One *See* Meet Me in St. Louis (1944)

Hosanna *See* Jesus Christ, Superstar (1973)

Hot and Happy *See* Happy Landing (1938)

Hot Chocolate Soldiers *See* Hollywood Party (1934)

Hot Dog *See* Loving You (1957)

Hot Lunch Jam *See* Fame (1980)

Hotcha Cornia *See* Thank Your Lucky Stars (1943)

Hound Dog *See* Grease (1978)

House of Sand *See* Paradise, Hawaiian Style (1966)

The House of Singing Bamboo *See* Pagan Love Song (1950)

A House That Has Everything *See* Clambake (1967)

How About a Cheer for the Navy *See* This is the Army (1943)

How About Us? *See* How to Stuff a Wild Bikini (1965)

How About You? *See* Babes on Broadway (1941)

How About You? *See* Royal Wedding (1951)

How Are Things in Glocca Morra? *See* Finian's Rainbow (1968)

How Can I Thank You *See* Little Miss Broadway (1938)

How Can Love Survive? *See* The Sound of Music (1965)

How Can You Believe Me When I Said I Love You When You Know I've Been A Liar All My Life? *See* Royal Wedding (1951)

How Come? *See* Tom Sawyer (1973)

How Deep is the Ocean *See* Meet Danny Wilson (1952)

How Deep Is Your Love? *See* Saturday Night Fever (1977)

How Did You Get Out of My Dreams? *See* George White's Scandals (1945)

How D'ja Like to Love Me? *See* College Swing (1938)

How Do You Do *See* Fast Forward (1984)

How Do You Fall in Love *See* Sing Your Worries Away (1942)

How Do You Feel About Foolin' Around? *See* Songwriter (1984)

How Do You Like Your Eggs in the Morning? *See* Rich, Young and Pretty (1951)

How Do You Solve A Problem Like Maria? *See* The Sound of Music (1965)

How I Love Her *See* The Night They Raided Minsky's (1969)

How Long Did I Dream? *See* Playmates (1941)

How Long Has This Been Going On? *See* Funny Face (1957)

How Lovely to be a Woman *See* Bye, Bye, Birdie (1963)

How Lucky Can You Get? *See* Funny Lady (1975)

How Sweet You Are *See* Thank Your Lucky Stars (1943)

How To Handle a Woman *See* Camelot (1967)

How to Stuff a Wild Bikini *See* How to Stuff a Wild Bikini (1965)

How To Succeed in Business Without Really Trying *See* How to Succeed in Business without Really Trying (1967)

How Would You Like To Be *See* It Happened at the World's Fair (1963)

How Ya Gonna Keep 'Em Down on the Farm? *See* For Me and My Gal (1942)

Howdy Neighbor *See* Summer Stock (1950)

Howja Like to Spoon with Me? *See* Till the Clouds Roll By (1946)

Hula Ba Lua *See* In the Navy (1941)

Human Race *See* Love Songs (1985)

Humoresque Number 7 in G Flat *See* The Great Ziegfeld (1936)

Humpty Dumpty Heart *See* Playmates (1941)

A Hundred Million Miracles *See* Flower Drum Song (1961)

Hungarian Fantasy *See* Song Without End (1960)

Hungarian Fantasy *See* Three Daring Daughters (1948)

The Hurdy Gurdy Man *See* Melody Trail (1935)

Hurry, It's Lovely Up Here *See* On a Clear Day You Can See Forever (1970)

Hushabye Mountain *See* Chitty Chitty Bang Bang (1968)

Hustle Bustle *See* The Christmas That Almost Wasn't (1966)

Hustlin' News Gal *See* This Could Be the Night (1957)

The Hyacinth *See* Let's Dance (1950)

A Hymn to Him *See* My Fair Lady (1964)

Hymn To The Sun *See* Honolulu (1939)

I Ain't Down Yet *See* The Unsinkable Molly Brown (1964)

(I Ain't Help to That Step) But I'll Dig It *See* Second Chorus (1940)

I Am Going to Like It Here *See* Flower Drum Song (1961)

I Am My Ideal *See* Beach Blanket Bingo (1965)

I am the Captain *See* Broadway Melody of 1940 (1940)

I Am With You Now *See* Love Songs (1985)

I Begged Her *See* Anchors Aweigh (1945)

I Believe in Love *See* A Star is Born (1976)

I Believe in This Country *See* The Happiest Millionaire (1967)

I Believe In You *See* How to Succeed in Business without Really Trying (1967)

I Cain't Say No *See* Oklahoma! (1955)

I Can Always Find a Little Sunshine at the YMCA *See* Alexander's Ragtime Band (1938)

I Can Do That *See* A Chorus Line (1985)

I Can Do Without Broadway, But Can Broadway Do Without Me? *See* On an Island with You (1948)

I Can See You *See* Rich, Young and Pretty (1951)

I Can't Be Bothered Now *See* A Damsel in Distress (1937)

I Can't Believe That You're In Love With Me *See* Thoroughly Modern Millie (1967)

I Can't Get You Out of My Mind *See* The Naughty Nineties (1945)

I Can't Give You Anything But Love, Baby *See* Stormy Weather (1943)

I Can't Live Without My Radio *See* Krush Groove (1985)

I Can't Tell a Lie *See* Holiday Inn (1942)

I Caught a Code In My Dose *See* Funny Lady (1975)

I Concentrate on You *See* Broadway Melody of 1940 (1940)

I Could Be Happy *See* The Boy Friend (1971)

I Could Have Danced all Night *See* My Fair Lady (1964)

I Could Write a Book *See* Pal Joey (1957)

I Couldn't Sleep a Wink Last Night *See* Higher and Higher (1944)

I Cried for You *See* Babes in Arms (1939)

I Cried for You *See* Bathing Beauty (1944)

I Cried for You *See* Lady Sings the Blues (1972)

I Didn't Know What Time It Was *See* Pal Joey (1957)

I Didn't Know What Time It Was *See* Too Many Girls (1940)

I Don't Believe A Word Of It *See* Half a Sixpence (1967)

I Don't Care *See* In the Good Old Summertime (1949)

I Don't Care If the Sun Don't Shine *See* Scared Stiff (1953)

I Don't Have to Hide Anymore *See* The First Nudie Musical (1975)

I Don't Know How To Love Him *See* Jesus Christ, Superstar (1973)

I Don't Know If I Found It in You *See* Nashville (1975)

I Don't Know What I Want *See* The Girl Most Likely (1957)

I Don't Need Anything But You *See* Annie (1982)

I Don't Wanna Be Tied *See* Girls! Girls! Girls! (1962)

I Don't Want To *See* Girls! Girls! Girls! (1962)

I Dream Too Much *See* I Dream Too Much (1935)

I Dreamed I Dwelt in Marble Halls *See* The Glenn Miller Story (1954)

I Dreamt I Dwelt in Marble Halls *See* Maytime (1937)

I Enjoy Being a Girl *See* Flower Drum Song (1961)

I Fall in Love Too Easily *See* Anchors Aweigh (1945)

I Fall In Love With You Every Day *See* College Swing (1938)

I Fall to Pieces *See* Sweet Dreams (1985)

I Feel Like I'm Not Out of Bed Yet *See* On the Town (1949)

I Feel Pessimistic *See* Good News (1947)

I Feel Pretty *See* West Side Story (1961)

I Feel That I'v Known You Forever *See* Tickle Me (1965)

I Feel You Near Me *See* Song O' My Heart (1929)

I Found a Million Dollar Baby In a Five and Ten Cent Store *See* Funny Lady (1975)

I Get a Funny Feeling *See* Skirts Ahoy! (1952)

I Get a Kick Out of You *See* Night and Day (1946)

I Give My Heart to You, Oo-ooh *See* The Naughty Nineties (1945)

I Got A Gal Named Nettie *See* Hi-De-Ho (1935)

I Got a Woman *See* Ballad in Blue (1966)

I Got It Bad *See* This Could Be the Night (1957)

I Got Love *See* I Dream Too Much (1935)

I Got Lucky *See* Kid Galahad (1962)

I Got Out of Bed on the Right Side *See* Dangerous When Wet (1953)

I Got Plenty O'Nuttin' *See* Rhapsody in Blue (1945)

I Got Rhythm *See* An American in Paris (1951)

I Got Rhythm *See* Girl Crazy (1943)

I Got Rhythm *See* Rhapsody in Blue (1945)

I Gotta Say I Love You Cause I Can't Tell A Lie *See* Holiday Inn (1942)

I Guess I'll Have to Change My Plan *See* The Band Wagon (1953)

I Had the Craziest Dream *See* Springtime in the Rockies (1942)

I Had To Kiss You *See* Latin Lovers (1953)

I Hate Men *See* Kiss Me Kate (1953)

I Hate Men *See* Kiss Me Kate (1953)

I Hate People *See* Scrooge (1970)

I Have A Dream *See* Jupiter's Darling (1955)

I Have a Heart *See* West Side Story (1961)

I Have Confidence In Me *See* The Sound of Music (1965)

I Have Dreamed *See* The King and I (1956)

I Have the Love *See* Rose Marie (1954)

I Have the Room Above Her *See* Show Boat (1936)

I Haven't A Thing to Wear *See* Four Jacks and a Jill (1941)

I Haven't Got a Thing to Sell *See* Copacabana (1947)

I Haven't Got a Thing to Wear *See* Never Steal Anything Small (1959)

I Hear the Birdies Sing *See* Footlight Serenade (1942)

I Hear You Calling Me *See* Song O' My Heart (1929)

I Hope I Get It *See* A Chorus Line (1985)

I Just Can't Wait to Be King *See* The Lion King (1994)

I Knew Your Father's Son *See* Follies Girl (1943)

I Know, I Know, I Know *See* That Midnight Kiss (1949)

I Know That You Know *See* Hit the Deck (1955)

I Know That You Know *See* Tea for Two (1950)

I Know What I Am *See* Half a Sixpence (1967)

I Know Why *See* The Glenn Miller Story (1954)

I Know Why and So Do You *See* Sun Valley Serenade (1941)

I Know You Remember *See* The Duke is the Tops (1938)

I Left My Hat in Haiti *See* Royal Wedding (1951)

I Left My Heart at the Stage Door Canteen *See* This is the Army (1943)

I Like a Guy What Takes His Time *See* She Done Him Wrong (1933)

I Like a Military Tune *See* Iceland (1942)

I Like Him/I Like Her *See* Funny Lady (1975)

I Like Life *See* Scrooge (1970)

I Like Men *See* Dangerous When Wet (1953)

I Like Myself *See* It's Always Fair Weather (1955)

I Like to Be Love by You *See* Springtime in the Rockies (1942)

I Lost My Sugar in Salt Lake City *See* Stormy Weather (1943)

I Love a Piano *See* Easter Parade (1948)

I Love An Old-Fashioned Song *See* Kid from Brooklyn (1946)

I Love Louisa *See* The Band Wagon (1953)

I Love Paris *See* Can-Can (1960)

I Love Rock 'n Roll *See* Flashdance (1983)

I Love the South *See* Private Buckaroo (1942)

I Love the Way You Say Goodnight *See* Lullaby of Broadway (1951)

I Love Those Men *See* Neptune's Daughter (1949)

I Love To Cry at Weddings *See* Sweet Charity (1969)

I Love to Go Swimmin' with Wimmin *See* Deep in My Heart (1954)

I Love to Laugh *See* Mary Poppins (1964)

I Love to Rhyme *See* The Goldwyn Follies (1938)

I Love To Walk in the Rain *See* Just Around the Corner (1938)

I Love You *See* Song of Norway (1970)

I Love You *See* Vagabond Lover (1929)

I Love You, Samantha *See* High Society (1956)

I Love You So Much *See* Three Little Words (1950)

I Love You to Death *See* Can't Stop the Music (1980)

I Love You Too Much *See* Staying Alive (1983)

I Loved You Once in Silence *See* Camelot (1967)

I Married An Angel *See* I Married an Angel (1942)

I May be Wrong *See* Young Man with a Horn (1950)

I May Never Fall in Love with You *See* The Unsinkable Molly Brown (1964)

I Met a Girl *See* Bells are Ringing (1960)

I Met Her at a Party *See* Melody Cruise (1932)

I Might Fall Back On You *See* Show Boat (1951)

I Must Have You *See* Sunny Skies (1930)

I Need Air *See* The Little Prince (1974)

I Need Somebody to Lean On *See* Viva Las Vegas (1963)

I **Need You** See Help! (1965)

I **Never Felt Better** See Athena (1954)

I **Never Felt This Way Before** See Bundle of Joy (1956)

I **Never Get Enough** See Nashville (1975)

I **Never Knew** See I'll See You in My Dreams (1951)

I **Never Knew Heaven Could Speak** See Rose of Washington Square (1939)

I **Never Met a Rose** See The Little Prince (1974)

I **Never Trust A Woman** See Jupiter's Darling (1955)

I **Only Have Eyes For You** See Dames (1934)

I **Only Have Eyes For You** See Jolson Sings Again (1949)

I **Only Have Eyes For You** See Tea for Two (1950)

I **Only Have Eyes for You** See Young Man with a Horn (1950)

I **Owe You** See Manhattan Merry-Go-Round (1937)

I **Poured My Heart Into Song** See Second Fiddle (1939)

I **Refuse to Rock 'n Roll** See Meet Me in Las Vegas (1956)

I **Saw You First** See Higher and Higher (1944)

I **Shook** See Everybody's Dancin' (1950)

I **Should Care** See Thrill of a Romance (1945)

I **Should Have Known Better** See A Hard Day's Night (1964)

I **Sing the Body Electric** See Fame (1980)

I **Slipped, I Stumbled, I Fell** See Wild in the Country (1961)

I **Speak to the Stars** See Lucky Me (1954)

I **Still See Elisa** See Paint Your Wagon (1969)

I **Take to You** See The Great American Broadcast (1941)

I **Talk To the Trees** See Paint Your Wagon (1969)

I **Think I Like You** See Doctor Dolittle (1967)

I **Think I'm Going To Like It Here** See Fun in Acapulco (1963)

I **Think I'm Gonna Like It Here** See Annie (1982)

I **Think Of You** See Holiday in Mexico (1946)

I **Think You Think** See Beach Blanket Bingo (1965)

I **Think You're the Sweetest Kid I've Ever Known** See Summer Holiday (1948)

I **Told A Lie** See Follies Girl (1943)

I **Used to be Colorblind** See Carefree (1938)

I **Wake Up in the Morning** See George White's Scandals (1945)

I **Walk With God** See The Student Prince (1954)

I **Wanna Be a Dancin' Man** See The Belle of New York (1952)

I **Wanna Be Free** See Jailhouse Rock (1957)

I **Wanna Be Loved By You** See Three Little Words (1950)

I **Wanna Be Your Man** See A Hard Day's Night (1964)

I **Wanna Dance** See Thank God It's Friday (1978)

I **Wanna Go To the Zoo** See Stowaway (1936)

I **Wanna Swing** See Everybody Sing (1938)

I **Wanna Wander** See I Love Melvin (1953)

I **Want A Girl Just Like the Girl That Married Dear Old Dad** See The Jolson Story (1946)

I **Want a Girl (Just Like the Girl Who Married Dear Old Dad)** See Show Business (1944)

I **Want to be a Drummer in the Band** See George White's Scandals (1945)

I **Want to be a Minstrel Man** See Kid Millions (1934)

I **Want to Be a Minstrel Man** See Yes, Sir, Mr. Bones (1951)

I **Want to Be Bad** See Pennies From Heaven (1981)

I **Want to be Happy** See Tea for Two (1950)

I **Want to Go Back to Michigan** See Easter Parade (1948)

I **Want You (She's So Heavy)** See Sgt. Pepper's Lonely Hearts Club Band (1978)

I **Want You to Be My Girl** See Krush Groove (1985)

I **Was Born in Virginia** See Yankee Doodle Dandy (1942)

I **Was Doing Alright** See The Goldwyn Follies (1938)

I **Was Drunk Last Night** See Meet Me in St. Louis (1944)

I **Watch the Love Parade** See The Cat and the Fiddle (1934)

I **Whistle a Happy Tune** See The King and I (1956)

I **Wish I Had A Girl** See I'll See You in My Dreams (1951)

I **Wish It Could Be Otherwise** See Li'l Abner (1959)

I **Wonder What the King is Doing Tonight** See Camelot (1967)

I **Wonder What's Become of Sally** See Night and Day (1946)

I **Won't Dance** See Lovely to Look At (1952)

I **Won't Dance** See Roberta (1935)

I **Won't Dance** See Till the Clouds Roll By (1946)

I **Won't Give It Away** See Knights of the City (1985)

Ice Cold Katie See Thank Your Lucky Stars (1943)

Ice Cream Fantasy See Kid Millions (1934)

Ich Liebe Dich See For the First Time (1959)

I'd **Do Anything** See Oliver! (1968)

Id' **Know You Anywhere** See You'll Find Out (1940)

I'd **Leave My Happy Home for You** See The Naughty Nineties (1945)

I'd **Like to Make You Happy** See Good News (1947)

I'd **Like to Set You to Music** See Hit the Ice (1943)

I'd **Love a Home in the Mountains** See Melody Trail (1935)

I'd **Rather Be Blue Over You** See Funny Girl (1968)

I'd **Rather Lead a Band** See Follow the Fleet (1936)

Ida, Sweet as Apple Cider See Broadway Rhythm (1944)

If A Girl Isn't Pretty See Funny Girl (1968)

If All the World Were Paper See Little Miss Broadway (1938)

If Ever I Would Leave You See Camelot (1967)

If He Walked Into My Life See Mame (1974)

If I Could Be With You See The Man I Love (1946)

If I Didn't Care See The Great American Broadcast (1941)

If I Fell See A Hard Day's Night (1964)

If I Give in to You See Evergreen (1934)

If I Had a Dozen Hearts See The Stork Club (1945)

If I Had a Million Dollars See Transatlantic Merry-Go-Round (1934)

If I Had My Druthers See Li'l Abner (1959)

If I Love Again See Funny Lady (1975)

If I Loved You See Carousel (1956)

If I Only Had a Brain/a Heart/the Nerve See The Wizard of Oz (1939)

If I Ruled the World See Krush Groove (1985)

If I Were a Bell See Guys and Dolls (1955)

If I Were a Rich Man See Fiddler on the Roof (1971)

If I Were an Artist See Surf Party (1964)

If I Were the King of the Forest See The Wizard of Oz (1939)

If I Were You See On an Island with You (1948)

If It's a Dream See Dixie Jamboree (1944)

If Mama Was Married See Gypsy (1962)

If Mother Could Only See Us Now See Girl Rush (1944)

If My Friends Could See Me Now See Sweet Charity (1969)

If The Rain's Got To Fall See Half a Sixpence (1967)

If This Be Slav'ry See Jupiter's Darling (1955)

If This Isn't Love See Finian's Rainbow (1968)

If Widows are Rich See The Merry Widow (1934)

If You Believe Me See There's No Business Like Show Business (1954)

If You Can Dream See Meet Me in Las Vegas (1956)

If You Could See Her See Cabaret (1972)

If You Don't Mind See The Music Man (1962)

If You Feel Like Singing, Sing See Summer Stock (1950)

If You Haven't Got Love See Indiscreet (1931)

If You Knew Susie See The Great Ziegfeld (1936)

If You Knew Susie See If You Knew Susie (1948)

If You Stub Your Toe on the Moon See A Connecticut Yankee in King Arthur's Court (1949)

If You Think I Don't Need You See Viva Las Vegas (1963)

If You Want the Rainbow, You Must Have the Rain See Funny Lady (1975)

If You Were the Only Girl in the World See By the Light of the Silvery Moon (1953)

If You Were the Only Girl in the World See Vagabond Lover (1929)

If You're Not Kissing Me See Good News (1947)

If'n I Was God See Tom Sawyer (1973)

Il Bacio See Broadway Melody of 1940 (1940)

I'll **Always Be Irish** See The Happiest Millionaire (1967)

I'll **Be Back** See Spinout (1966)

I'll **Be Hard to Handle** See Lovely to Look At (1952)

I'll **Be Hard to Handle** See Roberta (1935)

I'll **Be Lucky With You** See Just Around the Corner (1938)

I'll **Be Marching to a Love Song** See Footlight Serenade (1942)

I'll **Be Marching to a Love Song** See Pin-Up Girl (1944)

I'll **Be Reminded of You** See Vagabond Lover (1929)

I'll **Be True to You** See Yankee Doodle Dandy (1942)

I'll **Begin Again** See Scrooge (1970)

I'll **Build a Broadway For You** See Little Miss Broadway (1938)

I'll **Build a Stairway to Paradise** See An American in Paris (1951)

I'll **Capture Your Heart** See Holiday Inn (1942)

I'll **Do Anything for You** See Panama Hattie (1942)

I'll **Do It Again** See Hallelujah, I'm a Bum (1933)

I'll **Follow the Trail** See Lottery Bride (1930)

I'll **Forget You** See By the Light of the Silvery Moon (1953)

I'll **Get By** See A Star is Born (1954)

I'll **Give You Three Guesses** See Darling Lili (1970)

I'll **Go Home With Bonnie Jean** See Brigadoon (1954)

I'll **Know** See Guys and Dolls (1955)

I'll **Never Be Jealous Again** See Pajama Game (1957)

I'll **Never Love You** See The Toast of New Orleans (1950)

I'll Never Say Never Again *See* The Fabulous Dorseys (1947)

I'll Never Say No to You *See* The Unsinkable Molly Brown (1964)

I'll Never Stop Loving You *See* Love Me or Leave Me (1955)

I'll Remember April *See* Ride 'Em Cowboy (1942)

I'll See You Again *See* Bitter Sweet (1940)

I'll See You In My Dreams *See* I'll See You in My Dreams (1951)

I'll Si-Si Ya In Bahia *See* Just for You (1952)

I'll Still Belong to You *See* Whoopee! (1930)

I'll String Along with You *See* My Dream is Yours (1949)

I'll Take Love *See* Easy Come, Easy Go (1967)

I'll Take Romance *See* Holiday in Havana (1949)

I'll Take Romance *See* Jolson Sings Again (1949)

I'll Take Tallulah *See* Ship Ahoy (1942)

I'll Take the High Note *See* Bathing Beauty (1944)

I'll Tell the Man in the Street *See* I Married an Angel (1942)

Ill Wind *See* The Cotton Club (1984)

I'm a Big Success with You *See* Take It Big (1944)

I'm a Brass Band *See* Sweet Charity (1969)

I'm a Honky-Tonk Girl *See* Coal Miner's Daughter (1980)

I'm a Mean Old Lion *See* The Wiz (1978)

I'm a Singing Juggler *See* Can't Stop the Music (1980)

I'm a Square in the Social Circle *See* The Stork Club (1945)

I'm a Yankee Doodle Dandy *See* The Seven Little Foys (1955)

I'm Alive *See* Xanadu (1980)

I'm Always Chasing Rainbows *See* Ziegfeld Girl (1941)

I'm an Ordinary Man *See* My Fair Lady (1964)

I'm Bad *See* The Christmas That Almost Wasn't (1966)

I'm Easy *See* Nashville (1975)

I'm Falling In Love Tonight *See* It Happened at the World's Fair (1963)

I'm Falling in Love with Someone *See* Naughty Marietta (1935)

I'm Feeling Like a Million *See* Broadway Melody of 1938 (1937)

I'm Forever Blowing Bubbles *See* On Moonlight Bay (1951)

I'm Free *See* Footloose (1984)

I'm Free *See* Tommy (1975)

I'm Gettin' Tired So I Can Sleep *See* This is the Army (1943)

I'm Getting Sentimental Over You *See* DuBarry Was a Lady (1943)

I'm Getting Sentimental Over You *See* Keep 'Em Flying (1941)

I'm Getting Sentimental Over You *See* New York, New York (1977)

I'm Getting Sentimental Over You *See* A Song is Born (1948)

I'm Glad I'm Not Young Anymore *See* Gigi (1958)

I'm Going Back *See* Bells are Ringing (1960)

I'm Going Back There Someday *See* The Muppet Movie (1979)

I'm Going Home *See* The Rocky Horror Picture Show (1975)

I'm Going Shopping With You *See* Gold Diggers of 1935 (1935)

I'm Going to Maxim's *See* The Merry Widow (1952)

I'm Gonna Live Till I Die *See* This Could Be the Night (1957)

I'm Gonna Meet My Mary *See* A Date with Judy (1948)

I'm Gonna Wash That Man Right Out of My Hair *See* South Pacific (1958)

I'm Great *See* My Sister Eileen (1955)

I'm Hans Christian Andersen *See* Hans Christian Andersen (1952)

I'm Happy Just To Dance With You *See* A Hard Day's Night (1964)

I'm Here Again *See* Thank God It's Friday (1978)

I'm in Good Shape For the Shape I'm In *See* Four Jacks and a Jill (1941)

I'm in Love *See* Romance on the High Seas (1948)

I'm in Love Again *See* Night and Day (1946)

I'm In Love With a Wonderful Guy *See* South Pacific (1958)

I'm in Love with Miss Logan *See* New Faces of 1952 (1954)

I'm In Love With Vienna *See* The Great Waltz (1938)

I'm in Love With You *See* The Great Gabbo (1929)

I'm Just a Vagabond Lover *See* Glorifying the American Girl (1930)

I'm Just a Vagabond Lover *See* Vagabond Lover (1929)

I'm Just Wild About Harry *See* Babes in Arms (1939)

I'm Just Wild About Harry *See* Jolson Sings Again (1949)

I'm Just Wild About Harry *See* Rose of Washington Square (1939)

I'm Late *See* Alice in Wonderland (1951)

I'm Laughing *See* Stand Up and Cheer (1934)

I'm Laughing Ickey *See* The Great Gabbo (1929)

I'm Like A Fish Out Of Water *See* Hit the Ice (1943)

I'm Looking for the Boy with the Wistful Eyes *See* Keep 'Em Flying (1941)

I'm Looking Out for Me *See* The Return of Jafar (1994)

I'm Looking Over a Four-Leaf Clover *See* Jolson Sings Again (1949)

I'm Never Gonna Give You Up *See* Staying Alive (1983)

I'm Not at All in Love *See* Pajama Game (1957)

I'm Not Myself Today *See* Just Around the Corner (1938)

I'm Not Talking To You *See* Half a Sixpence (1967)

I'm Old Fashioned *See* You Were Never Lovelier (1942)

I'm Olga from the Volga *See* Thin Ice (1937)

I'm On My Way *See* Paint Your Wagon (1969)

I'm On Your Side *See* The Little Prince (1974)

I'm Only Teasin' *See* Delightfully Dangerous (1945)

I'm Only Thinking of Him *See* Man of La Mancha (1972)

I'm Past My Prime *See* Li'l Abner (1959)

I'm Putting All My Eggs In One Basket *See* Follow the Fleet (1936)

I'm Sitting On Top of the World *See* The Jolson Story (1946)

I'm Sitting on Top of the World *See* Love Me or Leave Me (1955)

I'm Sitting on Top of the World *See* Thoroughly Modern Millie (1967)

I'm Sorry for Myself *See* Second Fiddle (1939)

I'm Sorry I Made You Cry *See* Rose of Washington Square (1939)

I'm Sorry, I Want a Ferrari *See* Never Steal Anything Small (1959)

I'm Sorta Kinda Glad I Met You *See* Swing It, Professor (1937)

I'm Stepping Out With a Memory Tonight *See* Footlight Serenade (1942)

I'm Still Crazy About You *See* Footlight Serenade (1942)

I'm the Boy Next Door *See* How to Stuff a Wild Bikini (1965)

I'm the Echo *See* I Dream Too Much (1935)

I'm the Greatest Father of Them All *See* The Seven Little Foys (1955)

I'm The Greatest Star *See* Funny Girl (1968)

I'm Through with Love *See* The Affairs of Dobie Gillis (1953)

I'm Through With Love *See* I'll See You in My Dreams (1951)

I'm Tired *See* The Seven Little Foys (1955)

I'm Unlucky at Gambling *See* Night and Day (1946)

I'm Wishing *See* Snow White and the Seven Dwarfs (1937)

I'm Your Pal *See* Scared Stiff (1953)

I'm Yours *See* Second Chorus (1940)

I'm Yours *See* The Stooge (1951)

I'm Yours *See* Tickle Me (1965)

Imagine *See* Athena (1954)

Imitation Routine *See* The Seven Hills of Rome (1958)

The Impossible Dream *See* Man of La Mancha (1972)

Impressions in a Harlem Flat *See* The Cat and the Fiddle (1934)

In a Kingdom of Our Own *See* Yankee Doodle Dandy (1942)

In A Moment of Madness *See* Two Girls and a Sailor (1944)

In a Shower of Stars *See* Delightfully Dangerous (1945)

In My Garden of Joy *See* Star! (1968)

In My Life *See* For the Boys (1991)

In My Way *See* Wild in the Country (1961)

In My Wildest Dreams *See* Dangerous When Wet (1953)

In Other Words *See* Broadway Rhythm (1944)

In Our Little Den of Iniquity *See* Pal Joey (1957)

In Our United State *See* Give a Girl a Break (1953)

In the Gloaming *See* Dance of Life (1929)

In the Good Old Summertime *See* In the Good Old Summertime (1949)

In the Hall of the Mountain King *See* Song of Norway (1970)

In the Mood *See* The Glenn Miller Story (1954)

In the Mood *See* Le Bal (1982)

In the Mood *See* Sun Valley Serenade (1941)

In the Shade of the Old Apple Tree *See* The Stork Club (1945)

In the Shade of the Old Apple Tree *See* The Wizard of Oz (1939)

In the Still of the Night *See* Night and Day (1946)

In the Still of the Night *See* Rosalie (1938)

In the Valley Where the Evening Sun Goes Down *See* The Harvey Girls (1946)

Inamorata *See* Artists and Models (1955)

The Inch Worm *See* Hans Christian Andersen (1952)

Incurably Romantic *See* Let's Make Love (1960)

Indian Love Call *See* One Night of Love (1934)

Indian Love Call *See* Rose Marie (1936)

Indian Love Call *See* Rose Marie (1954)

Indubitably Me *See* Seaside Swingers (1965)

Inka Dinka Doo *See* Two Girls and a Sailor (1944)

The Inspector General *See* The Inspector General (1949)

Into the Forest of the Wild Beast *See* The Wizard of Oz (1939)

Iowa Stubborn *See* The Music Man (1962)

Ireland, Mother Ireland *See* Song O' My Heart (1929)

Is Anybody There? *See* 1776 (1972)

Is It Love? (Or The Gypsy in Me) *See* Presenting Lily Mars (1943)

Is It OK If I Call You Mine? *See* Fame (1980)

Is It True What They Say About Dixie? *See* Jolson Sings Again (1949)

Is That Good? *See* Moon Over Miami (1941)

Is This What Feeling Gets? *See* The Wiz (1978)

Is Your Rent Paid Up in Heaven? *See* Yes, Sir, Mr. Bones (1951)

Isn't It Better *See* Funny Lady (1975)

Isn't It Kinda Fun? *See* State Fair (1945)

Isn't It Kinda Fun? *See* State Fair (1962)

Isn't This A Lovely Day *See* Top Hat (1935)

Isn't This a Night For Love *See* Melody Cruise (1932)

Isn't This a Silly Song? *See* Snow White and the Seven Dwarfs (1937)

Isn't This Better *See* Funny Lady (1975)

It *See* Deep in My Heart (1954)

It All Depends on You *See* Love Me or Leave Me (1955)

It Began In Yucatan *See* Two Tickets to Broadway (1951)

It Could Only Happen in Brooklyn *See* The West Point Story (1950)

It Doesn't Cost a Dime to Dream *See* The Lemon Drop Kid (1951)

It Don't Worry Me *See* Nashville (1975)

It Feels So Right *See* Tickle Me (1965)

It Had To Be You *See* I'll See You in My Dreams (1951)

It Had to Be You *See* Show Business (1944)

It Happened in Kaloha *See* It's a Date (1940)

It Happened in Monterey *See* King of Jazz (1930)

It Happened in Sun Valley *See* Sun Valley Serenade (1941)

It Happens Every Time *See* Give a Girl a Break (1953)

It Just Happened to Happen *See* Sing Your Worries Away (1942)

It Makes No Difference When You're In the Army *See* Zis Boom Bah (1942)

It Might as Well Be Spring *See* State Fair (1945)

It Might as Well Be Spring *See* State Fair (1962)

It Must Be June *See* 42nd Street (1933)

It Only Happens When I Dance With You *See* Easter Parade (1948)

It Only Hurts When I Cry *See* Beach Blanket Bingo (1965)

It Only Takes a Moment *See* Hello, Dolly! (1969)

It Really Was No Miracle *See* The Wizard of Oz (1939)

It Takes a Woman *See* Hello, Dolly! (1969)

It Takes Love to Make a Home *See* Never Steal Anything Small (1959)

It Was Great When It All Began *See* The Rocky Horror Picture Show (1975)

It Was Just One of Those Things *See* Night and Day (1946)

It Was Just One of Those Things *See* Panama Hattie (1942)

It Was Sweet of You *See* Transatlantic Merry-Go-Round (1934)

It Won't Be Long 'til Christmas *See* The Happiest Millionaire (1967)

Italian Calypso *See* The Seven Hills of Rome (1958)

Italian Street Song *See* Broadway Serenade (1939)

Italian Street Song *See* Holiday in Mexico (1946)

Italian Street Song *See* Naughty Marietta (1935)

Itching for a 'Scratch *See* Rappin' (1985)

It's A Blue World *See* Jolson Sings Again (1949)

It's a Bore *See* Gigi (1958)

It's A Boy *See* Tommy (1975)

It's a Fine Life *See* Oliver! (1968)

It's a Grand Night for Singing *See* State Fair (1945)

It's a Grand Night for Singing *See* State Fair (1962)

It's a Great Big World *See* The Harvey Girls (1946)

It's a Great Day For the Irish *See* Little Nellie Kelly (1940)

It's a Hat *See* The Little Prince (1974)

(It's a) Long, Lonely Highway *See* Tickle Me (1965)

It's A Long Way to Tipperary *See* For Me and My Gal (1942)

It's A Long Way to Tipperary *See* The Story of Vernon and Irene Castle (1939)

It's a Most Unusual Day *See* A Date with Judy (1948)

It's A New World *See* A Star is Born (1954)

It's a Nice Face *See* Sweet Charity (1969)

It's a Perfect Relationship *See* Bells are Ringing (1960)

It's a Simple Little System *See* Bells are Ringing (1960)

It's a Wonderful World *See* New York, New York (1977)

It's a Wonderful World *See* Roustabout (1964)

It's All In a Lifetime *See* The Great American Broadcast (1941)

It's All Over But the Shouting *See* Rosalie (1938)

It's All Right With Me *See* Can-Can (1960)

It's All the Same *See* Man of La Mancha (1972)

It's All Too Much *See* Yellow Submarine (1968)

It's Always You *See* The Road to Zanzibar (1941)

It's Anybody's Spring *See* The Road to Utopia (1946)

It's Bigger Than You and Me *See* My Sister Eileen (1955)

It's Carnival Time *See* Roustabout (1964)

It's Delightful to be Married *See* The Great Ziegfeld (1936)

It's Fate, Baby, It's Fate *See* Take Me Out to the Ball Game (1949)

It's Independence Day *See* Summer Holiday (1948)

It's Like That *See* Krush Groove (1985)

It's Love Again *See* It's Love Again (1936)

It's Love, Love, Love *See* Song of Nevada (1944)

It's Magic *See* Romance on the High Seas (1948)

It's Mine, It's Yours *See* Country Girl (1954)

It's Never Too Late to Fall in Love *See* The Boy Friend (1971)

It's Nice To Be Out in the Morning *See* Mrs. Brown, You've Got a Lovely Daughter (1968)

It's Only a Paper Moon *See* Funny Lady (1975)

It's Our Home Town *See* Summer Holiday (1948)

It's Raining on Prom Night *See* Grease (1978)

It's Round Up Time in Reno *See* Manhattan Merry-Go-Round (1937)

It's Serious *See* Thank God It's Friday (1978)

It's So Easy *See* The Buddy Holly Story (1978)

It's That Kind of Day *See* Pajama Party (1964)

It's the Hard Knock Life *See* Annie (1982)

It's the Little Things in Texas *See* State Fair (1962)

It's The Only Way to Travel *See* The Road to Hong Kong (1962)

It's Today *See* Mame (1974)

It's Tulip Time in Holland *See* Hello, Frisco, Hello (1943)

It's Whatcha Do With Watcha Got *See* So Dear to My Heart (1949)

It's You *See* The Music Man (1962)

It's You or No One *See* Romance on the High Seas (1948)

I've a Strange New Rhythm in My Heart *See* Rosalie (1938)

I've Already Started *See* The Unsinkable Molly Brown (1964)

I've Been Working On the Railroad *See* Let Freedom Ring (1939)

I've Come To Wive It Wealthily In Padua *See* Kiss Me Kate (1953)

I've Got a Bone To Pick With You *See* The Great American Broadcast (1941)

I've Got a Crush on You *See* Meet Danny Wilson (1952)

I've Got a Date With a Dream *See* My Lucky Star (1938)

I've Got a Date with Judy *See* A Date with Judy (1948)

I've Got a Feelin' You're Foolin' *See* Singin' in the Rain (1952)

I've Got a Feeling You're Fooling *See* Broadway Melody of 1936 (1935)

I've Got a Gal in Kalamazoo *See* Orchestra Wives (1942)

I've Got a Girl in Every Port *See* Hello, Frisco, Hello (1943)

I've Got a Girl In Every Port *See* Paradise Island (1930)

I've Got a Golden Ticket *See* Willy Wonka & the Chocolate Factory (1971)

I've Got a Lot in Common With You *See* The Sky's the Limit (1943)

I've Got a One-Track Mind *See* You'll Find Out (1940)

I've Got My Eye on You *See* Broadway Melody of 1940 (1940)

I've Got My Love to Keep Me Warm *See* On the Avenue (1937)

I've Got No Strings *See* Pinocchio (1940)

I've Got to Find About My Baby *See* Girl Happy (1965)

I've Got To Get Back To New York *See* Hallelujah, I'm a Bum (1933)

I've Got To Hear That Beat *See* Small Town Girl (1953)

I've Got to Sing a Torch Song *See* Gold Diggers of 1933 (1933)

I've Got You All To Myself *See* Moon Over Miami (1941)

I've Got You Under My Skin *See* Born to Dance (1936)

I've Got You Under My Skin *See* Night and Day (1946)

I've Grown Accustomed to Her Face *See* My Fair Lady (1964)

I've Had My Moments *See* Hollywood Party (1934)

I've Learned to Smile Again See Zis Boom Bah (1942)

I've Never Seen Anything Like It See Doctor Dolittle (1967)

I've Still Got My Health See Panama Hattie (1942)

I've Written A Letter to Daddy See The Rose (1979)

Ja-da See Rose of Washington Square (1939)

Jack and the Beanstalk See Let's Dance (1950)

Jailhouse Rap See Knights of the City (1985)

Jailhouse Rock See Jailhouse Rock (1957)

Jalousie See Anchors Aweigh (1945)

Jamaica Sky See Back to the Beach (1987)

Japanese Sandman See Thoroughly Modern Millie (1967)

Jazz Baby See Thoroughly Modern Millie (1967)

Jazza, Jazza Doo Do See Deep in My Heart (1954)

Je Veux Vivre See Three Daring Daughters (1948)

Je Vous Amie See Copacabana (1947)

Jeepers, Creepers See My Dream is Yours (1949)

Jenny See Star! (1968)

Jericho See I Dood It (1943)

Jerusalem See Jazz Singer (1980)

Jesus Christ, Superstar See Jesus Christ, Superstar (1973)

Jet Song See West Side Story (1961)

The Jewish Wedding Song See Thoroughly Modern Millie (1967)

Jezebel See The Seven Hills of Rome (1958)

Jimmy See Thoroughly Modern Millie (1967)

Jimmy's Girl See Girl in Gold Boots (1969)

Jingle Bells See The Five Pennies (1959)

Jingle Bells See Look for the Silver Lining (1949)

The Jitter Bug See The Cotton Club (1984)

Jitterbug Bite See Dance, Girl, Dance (1940)

The Jockey on the Carousel See I Dream Too Much (1935)

John Heggerstrom See Song of Norway (1970)

John 19 See Jesus Christ, Superstar (1973)

Johnny Get Your Gun Again See Private Buckaroo (1942)

Join the Navy See Hit the Deck (1955)

Jolly Holliday See Mary Poppins (1964)

The Jolly Tar and the Milkmaid See A Damsel in Distress (1937)

Josephine See Silk Stockings (1957)

Joshua Fit De Battle O' Jericho See A Song is Born (1948)

Josie See Kid from Brooklyn (1946)

Jubilation T. Cornpone See Li'l Abner (1959)

Judaline See A Date with Judy (1948)

Judas's Death See Jesus Christ, Superstar (1973)

Judy Awakens See The Pirate (1948)

Judy, Part 2 See Crossover Dreams (1985)

Jump Jim Crow See Maytime (1937)

Jumpin' Jive See Stormy Weather (1943)

June Bride See Seven Brides for Seven Brothers (1954)

June is Bustin' Out All Over See Carousel (1956)

The Jungle See Body Rock (1984)

Jungle Red See The Opposite Sex (1956)

Just a Little Fond Affection See Swing Parade of 1946 (1946)

Just a Memory See Look for the Silver Lining (1949)

Just a Stranger in Town See The Heat's On (1943)

Just an Echo in the Valley See Going Hollywood (1933)

Just Another Dream See Paradise Island (1930)

Just Another Pretty Boy See Thunder Alley (1985)

Just Around the Corner See Just Around the Corner (1938)

Just Blew in From the Windy City See Calamity Jane (1953)

Just by Your Example See Evergreen (1934)

Just For a Day See Song O' My Heart (1929)

Just for You See Just for You (1952)

Just for You See Rose Marie (1936)

Just Forget About Love See The Return of Jafar (1994)

Just Imagine See Good News (1947)

Just in Time See Bells are Ringing (1960)

Just Leave Everything to Me See Hello, Dolly! (1969)

Just Let Me Look At You See Joy of Living (1938)

Just One More Chance See The Stooge (1951)

Just One of Those Things See Can-Can (1960)

Just One of Those Things See Lullaby of Broadway (1951)

Just One of Those Things See Night and Day (1946)

Just The Way You Are See FM (1978)

Just You, Just Me See New York, New York (1977)

Just You Wait, 'Enry 'Iggins See My Fair Lady (1964)

Justine See A Swingin' Summer (1965)

K-K-K-Katy See Tin Pan Alley (1940)

Kaigoon See The Road to Singapore (1940)

Kalua See Till the Clouds Roll By (1946)

Kanine Krunchies Kommercial See 101 Dalmations (1961)

Kansas City See Oklahoma! (1955)

Katie Went to Haiti See DuBarry Was a Lady (1943)

Keep A'Goin' See Nashville (1975)

Keep On Doin' What You're Doin' See Hips, Hips, Hooray (1934)

Keep On Rockin' See The Rose (1979)

Keep Romance Alive See Hips, Hips, Hooray (1934)

Keep the Flag A-Flying See Follies Girl (1943)

Keep Young and Beautiful See Roman Scandals (1933)

Keeping Myself For You See Hit the Deck (1955)

The Key To My Kingdom See FM (1978)

Kids See Bye, Bye, Birdie (1963)

Kids Get All the Breaks See The Christmas That Almost Wasn't (1966)

Killer See Rappin' (1985)

Killer Blow See Absolute Beginners (1986)

Kindergarten Congo See Moon Over Miami (1941)

King Chanticleer See By the Light of the Silvery Moon (1953)

King Chanticleer See Hello, Frisco, Hello (1943)

King Cotton See Stars and Stripes Forever (1952)

King Creole See King Creole (1958)

King of Jam See Vogues of 1938 (1937)

King of Jazzmania See Dance of Life (1929)

King of Rock See Krush Groove (1985)

King of the Whole Wide World See Kid Galahad (1962)

The King's New Clothes See Hans Christian Andersen (1952)

A Kiss in the Dark See Look for the Silver Lining (1949)

Kiss Me Kate See Kiss Me Kate (1953)

A Kiss Or Two See Hit the Deck (1955)

The Kiss Polka See Sun Valley Serenade (1941)

Kiss the Girl See The Little Mermaid (1989)

Kitty My Love See Song O' My Heart (1929)

Kol Nidre See Jazz Singer (1927)

Kold Krush See Krush Groove (1985)

Krush Groovin' See Krush Groove (1985)

K.T. Country See Thunder Alley (1985)

Kulebiaka See Presenting Lily Mars (1943)

Kurtis Blow Rap See Knights of the City (1985)

La Bamba See Fiesta (1947)

La Belle Fille D'amour See The Happiest Millionaire (1967)

La Bumba Rhumba See Panama Hattie (1942)

La Campanella See Song Without End (1960)

La Donna e Mobile See For the First Time (1959)

La Donna e Mobile See Let's Sing Again (1936)

La Donna e Mobile See Maytime (1937)

La Donne a Mobile See The Great Caruso (1951)

La Fatal Pietra See The Great Caruso (1951)

La Habanera See Les Girls (1957)

La La Lu See Lady and the Tramp (1955)

La Luna Enamorada See Fiesta (1947)

La Marseillaise See Le Bal (1982)

La Serenata See The Goldwyn Follies (1938)

La Traviata See Ziegfeld Follies (1946)

La Vie en Rose See Le Bal (1982)

Ladies In Waiting See Les Girls (1957)

Ladies of the Bath See DuBarry Was a Lady (1943)

Ladies of the Chorus See Ladies of the Chorus (1949)

Ladies of the Chorus See This is the Army (1943)

Ladies of the Dance See Dance of Life (1929)

Lady Alcohol See Rappin' (1985)

Lady Be Good See Rhapsody in Blue (1945)

The Lady from the Bayou See Hit the Deck (1955)

The Lady Is a Tramp See Pal Joey (1957)

Lady, Lady, Lady See Flashdance (1983)

A Lady Loved a Soldier See Dixiana (1930)

A Lady Loves See I Love Melvin (1953)

The Lady Loves Me See Viva Las Vegas (1963)

Lady Sings the Blues See Lady Sings the Blues (1972)

L'Amour Toujours, Tonight For Sure See Rich, Young and Pretty (1951)

The Land Around Us See Country Girl (1954)

Land On Your Feet See Footlight Serenade (1942)

The Land Where the Good Songs Go See Till the Clouds Roll By (1946)

Landlords and Tenants See Absolute Beginners (1986)

Largo See Song Without End (1960)

Largo Al Factotum See Maytime (1937)

Largo al Factotum See Broadway Melody of 1938 (1937)

Last Call For Love See Ship Ahoy (1942)

Last Dance See Thank God It's Friday (1978)

The Last Rose of Summer See Maytime (1937)

The Last Supper See Jesus Christ, Superstar (1973)

The Last Time I Saw Paris See Lady Be Good (1941)

The Last Time I Saw Paris See Till the Clouds Roll By (1946)

Lavender Blue (Dilly Dilly) See So Dear to My Heart (1949)

Lazy See Holiday Inn (1942)

Lazy Breezes *See* Paradise Island (1930)

Le Jazz Hot *See* Victor/Victoria (1982)

The Leader Doesn't Like Music *See* Honolulu (1939)

Leadville Johnny Brown (Soliloquy) *See* The Unsinkable Molly Brown (1964)

Learn to Croon *See* Jolson Sings Again (1949)

Leave It to Jane *See* Till the Clouds Roll By (1946)

Leave It to Me *See* Love Songs (1985)

Leave Us Leap *See* George White's Scandals (1945)

Lee-Ah-Loo *See* Because You're Mine (1952)

The Lees of Old Virginia *See* 1776 (1972)

Leg of Mutton *See* Deep in My Heart (1954)

Lemon and Lime *See* Mrs. Brown, You've Got a Lovely Daughter (1968)

Leo-Leo *See* Hit the Deck (1955)

Les Filles de Cadiz *See* Broadway Serenade (1939)

Les Filles de Cadiz *See* Holiday in Mexico (1946)

Les Filles de Cadiz *See* Maytime (1937)

Les Girls *See* Les Girls (1957)

Les Poissons *See* The Little Mermaid (1989)

Les Preludes *See* Song Without End (1960)

Lesbian Butch Dyke *See* The First Nudie Musical (1975)

Let a Little Love Come In *See* The Belle of New York (1952)

Let 'Em Eat Cake *See* The First Nudie Musical (1975)

Let Me Be the One *See* Nashville (1975)

Let Me Call You Sweetheart *See* The Rose (1979)

Let Me Dance For You *See* A Chorus Line (1985)

Let Me Entertain You *See* Gypsy (1962)

Let Me Sing *See* White Christmas (1954)

Let Me Sing and I'm Happy *See* Jolson Sings Again (1949)

Let Me Sing and I'm Happy *See* The Jolson Story (1946)

Let the Music Play *See* Knights of the City (1985)

Let the Worry Bird Worry For You *See* Two Tickets to Broadway (1951)

Let Us Pray *See* Change of Habit (1969)

Let Your Body Rock *See* Body Rock (1984)

Let Yourself Go *See* Follow the Fleet (1936)

Let's Be Buddies *See* Panama Hattie (1942)

Let's Begin *See* Roberta (1935)

Let's Bring New Glory to Old Glory *See* Iceland (1942)

Let's Call the Whole Thing Off *See* Shall We Dance (1937)

Let's Choo Choo to Idaho *See* Duchess of Idaho (1950)

Let's Do A Little Dreaming *See* Let's Go Collegiate (1941)

Let's Do It *See* Can-Can (1960)

Let's Do It *See* Night and Day (1946)

Let's Do the Copacabana *See* Copacabana (1947)

Let's Drive Out To The Drive-In *See* Harvest Melody (1943)

Let's Face the Music and Dance *See* Follow the Fleet (1936)

Let's Face the Music and Dance *See* Le Bal (1982)

Let's Face the Music and Dance *See* Pennies From Heaven (1981)

Let's Go Bavarian *See* Dancing Lady (1933)

Let's Go Fly a Kite *See* Mary Poppins (1964)

Let's Go to the Movies *See* Annie (1982)

Let's Have a Drink On It *See* The Happiest Millionaire (1967)

Let's Have Another *See* Hats Off (1937)

Let's Have Another Cup of Coffee *See* There's No Business Like Show Business (1954)

Let's Hear It For Me *See* Funny Lady (1975)

Let's Hear it for the Boy *See* Footloose (1984)

Let's K-nock K-nees *See* The Gay Divorcee (1934)

Let's Keep 'Em Flying *See* Keep 'Em Flying (1941)

Let's Kiss and Make Up *See* Funny Face (1957)

Let's Make A Deal *See* Thank God It's Friday (1978)

Let's Make Comparisons *See* Two Tickets to Broadway (1951)

Let's Make Love *See* Let's Make Love (1960)

Let's Misbehave *See* Pennies From Heaven (1981)

Let's Not Be Sensible *See* The Road to Hong Kong (1962)

Let's Say It With Firecrackers *See* Holiday Inn (1942)

Let's Sing Again *See* Let's Sing Again (1936)

Let's Start the New Year Right *See* Holiday Inn (1942)

The Letter *See* Mame (1974)

Liberation *See* Can't Stop the Music (1980)

Liberation Agitato *See* The Wiz (1978)

Libiamo Ne' Lieti Calici *See* Ziegfeld Follies (1946)

Libra Timbero *See* Crossover Dreams (1985)

Lida Rose/Will I Ever Tell You? *See* The Music Man (1962)

Lido Shuffle *See* FM (1978)

Liebestod *See* Holiday in Mexico (1946)

Liebestod *See* Maytime (1937)

Liebestraum *See* Girl of the Golden West (1938)

Liebestraum *See* Song Without End (1960)

Liebestraum *See* Three Daring Daughters (1948)

Life as It Really Is *See* Man of La Mancha (1972)

Life At Last *See* Phantom of the Paradise (1974)

Life Can Be Beautiful *See* Take It Big (1944)

Life Goes On *See* Staying Alive (1983)

Life Has Its Funny Little Ups And Downs *See* I Love Melvin (1953)

The Life I Lead *See* Mary Poppins (1964)

Life In The Fast Lane *See* FM (1978)

Life Is Just a Bowl of Cherries *See* Pennies From Heaven (1981)

Life is Just a Bowl of Cherries *See* George White's Scandals (1945)

Life is So Precious *See* Mr. Music (1950)

The Life Of An Elephant *See* Jupiter's Darling (1955)

Life Upon the Wicked Stage *See* Show Boat (1951)

Life's Been Good To Me *See* FM (1978)

Life's Full of Consequence *See* Cabin in the Sky (1943)

Light Cavalry *See* Stars and Stripes Forever (1952)

The Light Cavalry Overture *See* Strike Up the Band (1940)

The Light of My Life *See* Call Out the Marines (1942)

The Lights and the Smiles *See* The First Nudie Musical (1975)

Like Animals *See* Doctor Dolittle (1967)

Like the Fella Once Said *See* You'll Find Out (1940)

Li'l Black Sheep *See* Cabin in the Sky (1943)

The Lilac Tree *See* Spotlight Scandals (1943)

Limehouse Blues *See* Star! (1968)

Limehouse Blues *See* Young Man with a Horn (1950)

Limehouse Blues *See* Ziegfeld Follies (1946)

Linda Brown *See* Stormy Weather (1943)

Lions and Tigers and Bears *See* The Wizard of Oz (1939)

Listening To You *See* Tommy (1975)

Little Annie Rooney *See* Sweet Rosie O'Grady (1943)

Little Bird, Little Bird *See* Man of La Mancha (1972)

The Little Birds *See* Darling Lili (1970)

Little Boy Blue *See* Song O' My Heart (1929)

A Little Brains, a Little Talent *See* Damn Yankees (1958)

Little Brown Jug *See* The Glenn Miller Story (1954)

Little Brown Jug *See* Meet Me in St. Louis (1944)

Little Brown Jug *See* The Story of Vernon and Irene Castle (1939)

Little Cat *See* Absolute Beginners (1986)

Little Egypt *See* Roustabout (1964)

Little Girl Blue *See* Billy Rose's Jumbo (1962)

Little Girls *See* Annie (1982)

A Little Gossip *See* Man of La Mancha (1972)

The Little House *See* Song of Norway (1970)

A Little Kiss Each Morning *See* Vagabond Lover (1929)

Little Lamb *See* Gypsy (1962)

A Little Less Conversation *See* Live a Little, Love a Little (1968)

Little Lost Tune *See* Mad About Money (1930)

A Little More of Your Armor *See* Latin Lovers (1953)

Little Nellie Kelly *See* Yankee Doodle Dandy (1942)

Little Old Lady From Baltimore *See* Hi-De-Ho (1935)

Little Old Rhythm *See* Hats Off (1937)

Little One *See* High Society (1956)

Little Prince (From Who Knows Where) *See* The Little Prince (1974)

Live and Let Live *See* Can-Can (1960)

Live and Love Tonight *See* Murder at the Vanities (1934)

The Live Oak Tree *See* Just for You (1952)

Living High *See* Footlight Serenade (1942)

Livingston Saturday Night *See* FM (1978)

Liza *See* George White's Scandals (1945)

Liza *See* I'll See You in My Dreams (1951)

Liza *See* The Jolson Story (1946)

Liza *See* The Man I Love (1946)

Liza *See* Rhapsody in Blue (1945)

Liz's Theme *See* Crossover Dreams (1985)

Loch Lomond *See* Bathing Beauty (1944)

Loch Lomond *See* It's a Date (1940)

Lolita *See* The Seven Hills of Rome (1958)

London is London *See* Goodbye, Mr. Chips (1969)

London Town *See* Happy Go Lovely (1951)

Lonely Feet *See* Sweet Adeline (1935)

The Lonely Goatherd *See* The Sound of Music (1965)

Lonely Heart *See* The Inspector General (1949)

Lonely Man *See* Wild in the Country (1961)

Lonely Night *See* Thrill of a Romance (1945)

Lonesome Cowboy *See* Loving You (1957)

Lonesome Man *See* Girl in Gold Boots (1969)

Lonesome Man Blues *See* Meet Danny Wilson (1952)

Lonesome Polecat Lament *See* Seven Brides for Seven Brothers (1954)

Long Ago and Far Away *See* Cover Girl (1944)

Long Ago and Far Away *See* Till the Clouds Roll By (1946)

Long Ago Last Night *See* The Great American Broadcast (1941)

The Long and Winding Road *See* Give My Regards to Broad Street (1984)

The Long and Winding Road *See* Sgt. Pepper's Lonely Hearts Club Band (1978)

Long Before I Knew You *See* The West Point Story (1950)

Long Live the Night *See* The Desert Song (1953)

Long Title: Do I Have To Do This All Over Again *See* Head (1968)

Longhair Jam Session *See* A Song is Born (1948)

Look at Me, I'm Sandra Dee *See* Grease (1978)

Look for the Silver Lining *See* The Great Ziegfeld (1936)

Look for the Silver Lining *See* Look for the Silver Lining (1949)

Look for the Silver Lining *See* Till the Clouds Roll By (1946)

Look Out *See* Too Many Girls (1940)

Look Out Broadway *See* Frankie and Johnny (1965)

Look Out! I'm Romantic *See* Easy to Love (1953)

Look To the Rainbow *See* Finian's Rainbow (1968)

Look What You've Done To Me *See* Let's Go Collegiate (1941)

Lookin for the Lost Chord *See* Melody Trail (1935)

Lord I You Can't Come Send One Angel Down *See* Way Down South (1939)

The Lord's Prayer *See* Because You're Mine (1952)

The Lord's Prayer *See* Stage Door Canteen (1943)

Lose That Long Face *See* A Star is Born (1954)

Lost Inside of You *See* A Star is Born (1976)

A Lot of Livin' to Do *See* Bye, Bye, Birdie (1963)

Loughi Sereni E Cari *See* Song O' My Heart (1929)

Louise *See* Jazz Singer (1980)

Louise *See* The Stooge (1951)

Louisiana *See* Way Down South (1939)

Louisiana Hayride *See* The Band Wagon (1953)

Love *See* Ziegfeld Follies (1946)

Love and Learn *See* Take It Big (1944)

Love and Learn *See* That Girl from Paris (1936)

Love at First Sight *See* Love at First Sight (1976)

A Love Bizarre *See* Krush Groove (1985)

Love Boat *See* Broadway Melody (1929)

Love Can Change the Stars *See* Athena (1954)

Love Finds a Way *See* My Dream is Yours (1949)

Love For Sale *See* Night and Day (1946)

Love Goes Up and Down *See* Knights of the City (1985)

Love Has the Longest Memory *See* The Old Curiosity Shop (1975)

Love is a Many Splendored Thing *See* Grease (1978)

Love Is All *See* It's a Date (1940)

Love Is For Loves *See* Kid Galahad (1962)

Love Is Good for Anything That Ails You *See* Pennies From Heaven (1981)

Love Is Here To Stay *See* An American in Paris (1951)

Love is Here to Stay *See* The Goldwyn Follies (1938)

Love Is Like a Firefly *See* The Firefly (1937)

Love Is Like This *See* Nancy Goes to Rio (1950)

Love is Only Love *See* Hello, Dolly! (1969)

Love is the Time *See* Northwest Outpost (1947)

Love Isn't Born, It's Made *See* Thank Your Lucky Stars (1943)

A Love Like Ours *See* Two Girls and a Sailor (1944)

Love Look Away *See* Flower Drum Song (1961)

The Love Machine *See* Easy Come, Easy Go (1967)

Love Masterpiece *See* Thank God It's Friday (1978)

Love Me *See* The Stork Club (1945)

Love Me Love My Pekinese *See* Born to Dance (1936)

Love Me or Leave Me *See* I'll See You in My Dreams (1951)

Love Me or Leave Me *See* Love Me or Leave Me (1955)

Love Me, Please *See* Seaside Swingers (1965)

Love Me Tender *See* FM (1978)

Love Me With a Feeling *See* The Rose (1979)

The Love Nest *See* Yankee Doodle Dandy (1942)

Love Never Went to College *See* Too Many Girls (1940)

Love of My Life *See* The Pirate (1948)

Love on the Rocks *See* Jazz Singer (1980)

Love Serenade *See* Let Freedom Ring (1939)

Love Triangle *See* Krush Groove (1985)

Love Walked In *See* The Goldwyn Follies (1938)

Love Walked In *See* Rhapsody in Blue (1945)

Love with All the Trimmings *See* On a Clear Day You Can See Forever (1970)

Love Ya *See* On Moonlight Bay (1951)

Love You Dearly *See* Lucky Me (1954)

Love, You Didn't Do Right By Me *See* White Christmas (1954)

The Loveliest Night of the Year *See* The Great Caruso (1951)

Loveliness and Love *See* Moon Over Miami (1941)

Lovely Lady in White *See* One in a Million (1936)

Lovely Lonely Man *See* Chitty Chitty Bang Bang (1968)

Lovely One *See* Murder at the Vanities (1934)

Lovely One *See* Vogues of 1938 (1937)

Lovely to Look At *See* Lovely to Look At (1952)

Lovely to Look At *See* Roberta (1935)

A Lovely Way To Spend An Evening *See* Higher and Higher (1944)

Lover Come Back *See* New Moon (1940)

Lover, Come Back to Me *See* Deep in My Heart (1954)

Lover Doll *See* King Creole (1958)

Lover Man (Oh Where Can You Be?) *See* Lady Sings the Blues (1972)

Lover's Knot *See* Iceland (1942)

Love's a Secret Weapon *See* Bikini Beach (1964)

Lovesick Blues *See* Sweet Dreams (1985)

Lovin', Livin', and Givin' *See* Thank God It's Friday (1978)

Loving You *See* Loving You (1957)

Loving You *See* Mame (1974)

Loving You *See* Something to Sing About (1936)

Luck Be a Lady *See* Guys and Dolls (1955)

Lucky Bird *See* Hit the Deck (1955)

Lucky Charm *See* Meet Me in Las Vegas (1956)

Lucky in Love *See* Good News (1947)

Lucky Me *See* Lucky Me (1954)

Lucky Song *See* Artists and Models (1955)

Lucy in the Sky With Diamonds *See* Sgt. Pepper's Lonely Hearts Club Band (1978)

Lucy in the Sky With Diamonds *See* Yellow Submarine (1968)

Lullaby *See* Let's Sing Again (1936)

Lullaby in Blue *See* Bundle of Joy (1956)

Lullaby of Broadway *See* Gold Diggers of 1935 (1935)

Lullaby of Broadway *See* Lullaby of Broadway (1951)

Lullaby of Broadway *See* Young Man with a Horn (1950)

Lullaby of the Lord *See* Small Town Girl (1953)

The Lusty Month of May *See* Camelot (1967)

Lydia the Tattooed Lady *See* At the Circus (1939)

Ma Blushin' Rose *See* Jolson Sings Again (1949)

Ma Blushin' Rose *See* The Jolson Story (1946)

Ma Blushin' Rosie *See* The Naughty Nineties (1945)

Ma, I Miss Your Apple Pie *See* Private Buckaroo (1942)

The Machine Gun Song *See* Stage Door Canteen (1943)

Macho Man *See* Can't Stop the Music (1980)

Mack the Black *See* The Pirate (1948)

Macushia *See* Hawaii Calls (1938)

Madame Crematon *See* Ziegfeld Follies (1946)

Madame, I Love Your Crepes Suzettes *See* DuBarry Was a Lady (1943)

Made For Each Other *See* Holiday in Havana (1949)

Mademoiselle From Armentieres *See* For Me and My Gal (1942)

Madison Avenue *See* How to Stuff a Wild Bikini (1965)

Magic *See* Xanadu (1980)

Magic is the Moonlight *See* Bathing Beauty (1944)

Magic is the Moonlight *See* Nancy Goes to Rio (1950)

Magic Night *See* Can't Stop the Music (1980)

Magic Smoke Chords *See* The Wizard of Oz (1939)

Magical Mystery Tour *See* Magical Mystery Tour (1967)

Main Street *See* On the Town (1949)

Make a Wish *See* Make a Wish (1937)

Make Believe *See* Show Boat (1936)

Make Believe *See* Show Boat (1951)

Make Believe *See* Till the Clouds Roll By (1946)

Make 'Em Laugh *See* Singin' in the Rain (1952)

Make It Another Old Fashioned *See* Panama Hattie (1942)

Make Way For Tomorrow *See* Cover Girl (1944)

Makin' Whoopee *See* The Great Ziegfeld (1936)

Makin' Whoopee! *See* I'll See You in My Dreams (1951)

Makin' Whoopee *See* Show Business (1944)

Makin' Whoopee *See* Whoopee! (1930)

The Maladjusted Jester *See* Court Jester (1956)

Mama I Wanna Make Rhythm *See* Manhattan Merry-Go-Round (1937)

Mama, Look Sharp *See* 1776 (1972)

Mama Mia Che Vo Sape *See* That Midnight Kiss (1949)

Mama Yo Quiero *See* Babes on Broadway (1941)

Mama Yo Quiero *See* Down Argentine Way (1940)

Mama Yo Quiero *See* Scared Stiff (1953)

Mamba Combo *See* This Could Be the Night (1957)

Mame *See* Mame (1974)

A Man Chases a Girl Until She Catches Him *See* There's No Business Like Show Business (1954)

A Man Has Dreams *See* Mary Poppins (1964)

The Man I Love See Lady Sings the Blues (1972)

The Man I Love See The Man I Love (1946)

The Man I Love See New York, New York (1977)

The Man I Love See Rhapsody in Blue (1945)

The Man I Love See Young Man with a Horn (1950)

The Man in the Moon See Mame (1974)

Man of La Mancha See Man of La Mancha (1972)

The Man Who Owns Broadway See Yankee Doodle Dandy (1942)

The Man With the Big Felt Hat See Never a Dull Moment (1950)

Mandy See Kid Millions (1934)

Mandy See This is the Army (1943)

Mandy See White Christmas (1954)

Manhattan See Two Tickets to Broadway (1951)

Manhattan Downbeat See The Barkleys of Broadway (1949)

Manhattan Merry-Go-Round See Manhattan Merry-Go-Round (1937)

Manhattan Serenade See Broadway Rhythm (1944)

Manhunt See Flashdance (1983)

A Man's Gotta Be What He's Born To Be See Tom Sawyer (1973)

Many a New Day See Oklahoma! (1955)

M'Appari See The Great Caruso (1951)

March, March See It's Always Fair Weather (1955)

March of the Meanies See Yellow Submarine (1968)

March of the Munchkins See The Wiz (1978)

March of the Musketeers See The Great Ziegfeld (1936)

March of the Siamese Children See The King and I (1956)

March of the Winkies See The Wizard of Oz (1939)

Marche Funebre See Funny Face (1957)

Marching Through Berlin See Stage Door Canteen (1943)

Marguerita See Fun in Acapulco (1963)

Maria See West Side Story (1961)

Maria Inez See Week-End In Havana (1941)

Marian, the Librarian See The Music Man (1962)

Marianne See New Moon (1940)

Marie See Alexander's Ragtime Band (1938)

Marie See The Fabulous Dorseys (1947)

Marijuana See Murder at the Vanities (1934)

The Marseillaise See New Moon (1940)

Mary's a Grand Old Name See The Seven Little Foys (1955)

Mary's a Grand Old Name See Yankee Doodle Dandy (1942)

Masie, My Pretty Daisy See She Done Him Wrong (1933)

The Mast See The Pirate (1948)

Matchmaker, Matchmaker See Fiddler on the Roof (1971)

Matrimonial Stomp See Li'l Abner (1959)

Mattinata See The Great Caruso (1951)

Maxim's See The Merry Widow (1934)

Maxixe Dengozo See The Story of Vernon and Irene Castle (1939)

Maxwell's Silver Hammer See Sgt. Pepper's Lonely Hearts Club Band (1978)

May I Present the Girl See I Married an Angel (1942)

Maybe See Annie (1982)

Maybe This Time See Cabaret (1972)

Maytime Finale See Maytime (1937)

Mazurka See Maytime (1937)

Mazurka In B Flat, Opus 7, No. 1 See A Song to Remember (1945)

Me and My Shadow See Funny Lady (1975)

Me 'N You 'N the Moon See Pardners (1956)

Me Ol' Bam-Boo See Chitty Chitty Bang Bang (1968)

Mean Green Mother From Outer Space See Little Shop of Horrors (1986)

Mean Mister Mustard See Sgt. Pepper's Lonely Hearts Club Band (1978)

Mean to Me See Lady Sings the Blues (1972)

Mean to Me See Love Me or Leave Me (1955)

Mean Woman Blues See Loving You (1957)

The Meanest Girl in Town See Girl Happy (1965)

Meco's Theme See Thank God It's Friday (1978)

The Medicine Show See The Inspector General (1949)

Meet Me In St. Louis See Meet Me in St. Louis (1944)

Meet Me Tonight In Dreamland See In the Good Old Summertime (1949)

Mein Herr See Cabaret (1972)

Melancholy Rhapsody See Young Man with a Horn (1950)

Melinda See On a Clear Day You Can See Forever (1970)

Melody See They Shall Have Music (1939)

Melody in 4-F See Up in Arms (1944)

Melody of Laughter See The Merry Widow (1934)

Melody Ranch See Melody Ranch (1940)

Memories See I'll See You in My Dreams (1951)

Memories Are Made of This See The Seven Hills of Rome (1958)

Memories of You See The Benny Goodman Story (1955)

Memphis See Nashville (1975)

Memphis Bill See Yes, Sir, Mr. Bones (1951)

Mem'ry Island See Summer Stock (1950)

Men See Lucky Me (1954)

Mephisto Waltz See Song Without End (1960)

Merecumbe See Crossover Dreams (1985)

Merry Christmas See In the Good Old Summertime (1949)

The Merry-Go-Runaround See The Road to Bali (1953)

The Merry Old Land of Oz See The Wizard of Oz (1939)

The Merry Widow Waltz See The Merry Widow (1934)

The Merry Widow Waltz See The Merry Widow (1952)

A Message from the Man in the Moon See A Day at the Races (1937)

Mexico See Fun in Acapulco (1963)

Michelle See Le Bal (1982)

Midnight in Memphis See The Rose (1979)

Midsummer's Eve See Song of Norway (1970)

The Mightiest Matador See Dance of Life (1929)

Milady See Mr. Music (1950)

Military Man See The Poor Little Rich Girl (1936)

Military Polka See The West Point Story (1950)

Milkman Keep Those Bottles Quiet See Broadway Rhythm (1944)

Milkshake See Can't Stop the Music (1980)

A Million Miles Away Behind the Door See Paint Your Wagon (1969)

Mimi From Tahiti See Rhythm Parade (1943)

Mind if I Make Love to You? See High Society (1956)

Mine See Rhapsody in Blue (1945)

Minnie from Trinidad See Ziegfeld Girl (1941)

Minnie Shimmy See Girl in Gold Boots (1969)

Minnie the Moocher See The Cotton Club (1984)

The Minstrel Show See White Christmas (1954)

Miracle Cure See Tommy (1975)

Miracle of Miracles See Fiddler on the Roof (1971)

Miriano See Fiesta (1947)

Miserer See Maytime (1937)

Mis'ry's Comin' Around See Show Boat (1936)

Miss Otis Regrets See Night and Day (1946)

Miss Turnstiles Ballet See On the Town (1949)

Miss U.S.A. See Deep in My Heart (1954)

Mission Number See Whoopee! (1930)

Mississippi Mud See King of Jazz (1930)

Missouri Waltz See The Story of Vernon and Irene Castle (1939)

Mrs. Brown, You've Got a Lovely Daughter See Mrs. Brown, You've Got a Lovely Daughter (1968)

Mr. & Mrs. See Deep in My Heart (1954)

Mr. and Mrs. Hoofer at Home See Three Little Words (1950)

Mr. & Mrs. Sippi See Dixiana (1930)

Mister Booze See Robin and the Seven Hoods (1964)

Mr. Gallagher & Mr. Shean See Ziegfeld Girl (1941)

Mr. Goldstone, I Love You See Gypsy (1962)

Mr. Goldstone, I Love You See Gypsy (1993)

Mr. Music See Mr. Music (1950)

Mr. Snow See Carousel (1956)

Mockin' Bird See A Song is Born (1948)

A Moke from Shamokin See Around the World (1943)

Molasses to Rum See 1776 (1972)

Mollie O'Donahue See Sweet Adeline (1935)

Molly Malone See Yankee Doodle Dandy (1942)

Moments Like This See College Swing (1938)

Mon Ami Pierrot See Naughty Marietta (1935)

Money Greases the Wheel See Las Vegas Hillbillys (1966)

Money, Money See Cabaret (1972)

Money To Burn See Half a Sixpence (1967)

Monotonous See New Faces of 1952 (1954)

The Mooch See The Cotton Club (1984)

Mood Indigo See The Cotton Club (1984)

Moody Girl See Staying Alive (1983)

The Moon and the Willow Tree See The Road to Singapore (1940)

Moon Face See That Girl from Paris (1936)

Moon Over Miami See Moon Over Miami (1941)

Moon Over Monte Carlo See Transatlantic Merry-Go-Round (1934)

Moonflowers See The Road to Bali (1953)

Mooning See Grease (1978)

Moonlight and Roses See Tin Pan Alley (1940)

Moonlight Bay See Tin Pan Alley (1940)

Moonlight Becomes You See The Road to Morocco (1942)

Moonlight Serenade See The Glenn Miller Story (1954)

The Moonlight Waltz See One in a Million (1936)

More I Cannot Wish You See Guys and Dolls (1955)

More Than A Feeling See FM (1978)

More Than a Woman *See* Saturday Night Fever (1977)

More Than Just a Friend *See* State Fair (1962)

More Than You Know *See* Funny Lady (1975)

More Than You Know *See* Hit the Deck (1955)

Morning Hymn *See* The Sound of Music (1965)

Morning Star *See* Dance, Girl, Dance (1940)

The Most Beautiful Girl in the World *See* Billy Rose's Jumbo (1962)

The Most Beautiful Thing in My Life *See* Mrs. Brown, You've Got a Lovely Daughter (1968)

The Most Exciting Night *See* Lovely to Look At (1952)

A Most Important Affair *See* Higher and Higher (1944)

Mother, I Still Have You *See* Jazz Singer (1927)

Mother, What Do I Do Now? *See* Dance, Girl, Dance (1940)

The Mountie Who Never Got His Man *See* Rose Marie (1954)

The Mounties *See* Rose Marie (1936)

The Mounties *See* Rose Marie (1954)

Movin Right Along *See* The Muppet Movie (1979)

Mozart's "Piano Sonata No. 11 in A" *See* Three Daring Daughters (1948)

Mulligatawny *See* A Date with Judy (1948)

Munchkinland *See* The Wizard of Oz (1939)

Muscle Beach Party *See* Muscle Beach Party (1964)

Muscle Bustle *See* Muscle Beach Party (1964)

Musetta's Waltz *See* It's a Date (1940)

Musetta's Waltz *See* Nancy Goes to Rio (1950)

The Music and the Mirror *See* A Chorus Line (1985)

The Music Goes 'Round and Around *See* The Five Pennies (1959)

The Music Goes 'Round and Around *See* Holiday in Mexico (1946)

Music in My Heart *See* Make a Wish (1937)

Music Is Better Than Words *See* It's Always Fair Weather (1955)

Music Makes Me *See* Flying Down to Rio (1933)

The Music Stopped *See* Higher and Higher (1944)

Musical Contract *See* Broadway Serenade (1939)

Muskrat Ramble *See* A Song is Born (1948)

Must Be Love *See* Sunny Skies (1930)

My Baby Just Cares for Me *See* Whoopee! (1930)

My Baby's Cookin' in Another Man's Pan *See* Nashville (1975)

My Best Girl *See* Mame (1974)

My Blue Heaven *See* Good News (1947)

My Blue Heaven *See* Love Me or Leave Me (1955)

My Bluebirds are Singing the Blues *See* International House (1933)

My Brooklyn Love Song *See* If You Knew Susie (1948)

My Buddy *See* I'll See You in My Dreams (1951)

My Campfire Dreams *See* Make a Wish (1937)

My Dancing Lady *See* Dancing Lady (1933)

My Dream is Yours *See* My Dream is Yours (1949)

My Favorite Things *See* The Sound of Music (1965)

My First Love *See* Muscle Beach Party (1964)

My First Promise *See* Best Foot Forward (1943)

My Flaming Heart *See* Small Town Girl (1953)

My Friend the Doctor *See* Doctor Dolittle (1967)

My Funny Valentine *See* Pal Joey (1957)

My Gal Sal *See* Jazz Singer (1927)

My Gal Sal *See* Melody Ranch (1940)

My Gaucho *See* Small Town Girl (1953)

My Girl Back Home *See* South Pacific (1958)

My Heart Beats Faster *See* Neptune's Daughter (1949)

My Heart Belongs to Daddy *See* Let's Make Love (1960)

My Heart Belongs to Daddy *See* Night and Day (1946)

My Heart Knows a Lovely Song *See* Court Jester (1956)

My Heart Tells Me *See* Sweet Rosie O'Grady (1943)

My Heart Was Doing a Bolero *See* Copacabana (1947)

My Hero *See* Two Weeks with Love (1950)

My, How the Time Goes By *See* If You Knew Susie (1948)

My Idaho Home *See* Nashville (1975)

My Joe *See* Carmen Jones (1954)

My Kind of Town *See* Robin and the Seven Hoods (1964)

My Lady *See* The Three Musketeers (1939)

My Mammy *See* Absolute Beginners (1986)

My Mammy *See* Jazz Singer (1927)

My Mammy *See* Jolson Sings Again (1949)

My Mammy *See* The Jolson Story (1946)

My Mammy *See* Rose of Washington Square (1939)

My Man *See* Funny Girl (1968)

My Man *See* The Great Ziegfeld (1936)

My Man *See* Lady Sings the Blues (1972)

My Man *See* Rose of Washington Square (1939)

My Melancholy Baby *See* A Star is Born (1954)

My Mother Told Me *See* Two Girls and a Sailor (1944)

My, My, Ain't That Somethin'? *See* Stormy Weather (1943)

My Nephew From Nice *See* That Girl from Paris (1936)

My Northern Lights *See* Lottery Bride (1930)

My One Ambition is You *See* Dixiana (1930)

My One and Only *See* Rhapsody in Blue (1945)

My One and Only Highland Fling *See* The Barkleys of Broadway (1949)

My Pal Bumper *See* Hallelujah, I'm a Bum (1933)

My Part of Town *See* Knights of the City (1985)

My Personal Property *See* Sweet Charity (1969)

My Prayer For Tonight *See* Melody Trail (1935)

My Rival *See* Viva Las Vegas (1963)

My Romance *See* Billy Rose's Jumbo (1962)

My Sam *See* Sweet Rosie O'Grady (1943)

My Secret *See* Krush Groove (1985)

My Secret Love Affair *See* Thin Ice (1937)

My Shining Hour *See* The Sky's the Limit (1943)

My Ship *See* Star! (1968)

My Sunny Tennessee *See* Three Little Words (1950)

My Sweetie *See* This is the Army (1943)

My Swiss Hillbilly *See* Thin Ice (1937)

My Time of Day *See* Guys and Dolls (1955)

My Walking Stick *See* Alexander's Ragtime Band (1938)

My Week *See* One Touch of Venus (1948)

My White Knight *See* The Music Man (1962)

My Wonderful One Let's Dance *See* Two Girls and a Sailor (1944)

Mynah Bird *See* Delightfully Dangerous (1945)

Mystery *See* Fast Forward (1984)

'N' Everything *See* Star! (1968)

Nagasaki *See* My Dream is Yours (1949)

The Naked and the Dead *See* Absolute Beginners (1986)

The Name of the Song is Prune *See* The Christmas That Almost Wasn't (1966)

Namely You *See* Li'l Abner (1959)

Nancy Goes to Rio *See* Nancy Goes to Rio (1950)

The Nango *See* Week-End In Havana (1941)

Napoleonic Waltz *See* Maytime (1937)

Napoli *See* Absolute Beginners (1986)

Napoli *See* Lottery Bride (1930)

Naughty But Nice *See* The Belle of New York (1952)

The Navy Waltz *See* Skirts Ahoy! (1952)

Nearer and Dearer *See* Northwest Outpost (1947)

The Nearness of You *See* Girls! Girls! Girls! (1962)

Neath the Southern Moon *See* Naughty Marietta (1935)

'Neath the Yellow Moon In Old Tahiti *See* Rhythm Parade (1943)

A Needle in a Haystack *See* The Gay Divorcee (1934)

Nellie is a Darling *See* Little Nellie Kelly (1940)

Nellie Kelly I Love You *See* Little Nellie Kelly (1940)

Never *See* Footloose (1984)

Never Before *See* The Muppet Movie (1979)

Never Gonna Dance *See* Swing Time (1936)

Never Let Me Go *See* Girls! Girls! Girls! (1962)

Never Look Back *See* Love Me or Leave Me (1955)

Never Say Yes *See* Spinout (1966)

Never So Beautiful *See* Here Come the Girls (1953)

Never Steal Anything Small *See* Never Steal Anything Small (1959)

Never Till Now *See* The Seven Hills of Rome (1958)

Never Was There Such a Perfect Day *See* Everybody Sing (1938)

Nevertheless *See* Three Little Words (1950)

New Love *See* Beach Blanket Bingo (1965)

A New Love is Old *See* The Cat and the Fiddle (1934)

New Moon Over Nevada *See* Song of Nevada (1944)

New Orleans *See* King Creole (1958)

A New Pair of Shoes *See* Broadway Melody of 1938 (1937)

The New Step *See* The Great Gabbo (1929)

New Sun in the Sky *See* The Band Wagon (1953)

New York, New York *See* New York, New York (1977)

New York, New York *See* On the Town (1949)

Nice Work If You Can Get It *See* An American in Paris (1951)

Nice Work If You Can Get It *See* A Damsel in Distress (1937)

Night and Day *See* The Gay Divorcee (1934)

Night and Day *See* Night and Day (1946)

Night and You *See* Latin Lovers (1953)

The Night Before *See* Help! (1965)

Night Fever *See* Saturday Night Fever (1977)

Night in Tunisia *See* New York, New York (1977)

The Night is Filled With Music *See* Carefree (1938)

Night Moves *See* FM (1978)

Night of My Nights *See* Kismet (1955)

Night on Bald Mountain *See* Fantasia (1940)

Night on Bald Mountain *See* The Wizard of Oz (1939)

Night Rider *See* Tickle Me (1965)

The Night They Invented Champagne *See* Gigi (1958)

The Night They Raided Minsky's *See* The Night They Raided Minsky's (1969)

The Night Was Made for Love *See* The Cat and the Fiddle (1934)

The Night We Said Goodbye *See* The Rose (1979)

Nights of Gladness *See* The Story of Vernon and Irene Castle (1939)

Nina *See* The Pirate (1948)

99 1/2 *See* Breakin' (1984)

Nitro *See* A Swingin' Summer (1965)

Niun Mi Tema *See* For the First Time (1959)

No Man In The House *See* Follies Girl (1943)

No Matter How You Slice It, It's Still Salome *See* DuBarry Was a Lady (1943)

No Matter What Happens *See* Yentl (1983)

No More Lonely Nights *See* Give My Regards to Broad Street (1984)

No More Love *See* Roman Scandals (1933)

No More Weeping *See* New Moon (1940)

No, No, Nanette *See* Tea for Two (1950)

No, No, No *See* Dixie Jamboree (1944)

No No Nora *See* I'll See You in My Dreams (1951)

No Strings *See* Top Hat (1935)

No Time to Argue *See* Broadway Serenade (1939)

No Two People *See* Hans Christian Andersen (1952)

No Values *See* Give My Regards to Broad Street (1984)

No Wonder *See* Yentl (1983)

No You, No Me *See* Thank Your Lucky Stars (1943)

Nobles Seigneurs *See* Maytime (1937)

Nobody *See* The Seven Little Foys (1955)

Nobody *See* Strike Up the Band (1940)

Nobody Know De Trouble I See *See* Way Down South (1939)

Nobody Knows the Trouble I've Seen *See* Private Buckaroo (1942)

Nobody Said It Was Going To Be Easy *See* Songwriter (1984)

Nobody's Sweetheart *See* I'll See You in My Dreams (1951)

Nobody's Sweetheart *See* Stormy Weather (1943)

Nocturn In E Flat, Opus 9, No. 2 *See* A Song to Remember (1945)

Nocturne In C Minor, Opus 48, No. 1 *See* A Song to Remember (1945)

None But the Lonely Heart *See* One Night of Love (1934)

Nora Malone *See* The Naughty Nineties (1945)

Not Again *See* The Pirate (1948)

Not Since Ninevah *See* Kismet (1955)

Not Such a Bad Boy *See* Give My Regards to Broad Street (1984)

Nothing *See* A Chorus Line (1985)

Nothing In the World (Quite Like a Friend) *See* The Return of Jafar (1994)

Nothing is Impossible *See* Give a Girl a Break (1953)

Nothing to do But Wait *See* The Christmas That Almost Wasn't (1966)

Now, Ain't That Somethin'—Caw Blimey *See* Seaside Swingers (1965)

Now and Then *See* Follow the Leader (1944)

Now! Baby, Now *See* The Opposite Sex (1956)

Now I Know *See* Up in Arms (1944)

Now is the Month of Maying *See* Maytime (1937)

Now It Can Be Told *See* Alexander's Ragtime Band (1938)

Now Watch Me Dance *See* The Wiz (1978)

Now You Has Jazz *See* High Society (1956)

Now You've Met the Angel *See* I Married an Angel (1942)

Nowhere Man *See* Sgt. Pepper's Lonely Hearts Club Band (1978)

Nowhere Man *See* Yellow Submarine (1968)

Nowhere to Run *See* Thunder Alley (1985)

Number 39 in E Flat Major *See* Amadeus (1984)

Number 40 in G Minor *See* Amadeus (1984)

Number 41 in C Major *See* Amadeus (1984)

Numi, Pieta *See* The Great Caruso (1951)

The Nutcracker Suite *See* Fantasia (1940)

O, Du Mein Holder Abendstern *See* Maytime (1937)

O Paradiso *See* The Great Caruso (1951)

O Solo Mio *See* For the First Time (1959)

The Object of My Affection *See* The Fabulous Dorseys (1947)

Oblivious *See* Everybody's Dancin' (1950)

O'Brien to Ryan to Goldberg *See* Take Me Out to the Ball Game (1949)

The Oceana Roll *See* Two Weeks with Love (1950)

Of All Things *See* Duchess of Idaho (1950)

Off the Record *See* Yankee Doodle Dandy (1942)

Oh, Boy *See* The Buddy Holly Story (1978)

Oh, Brother *See* Swing Parade of 1946 (1946)

Oh By Jingo *See* Skirts Ahoy! (1952)

Oh Darling *See* Sgt. Pepper's Lonely Hearts Club Band (1978)

Oh Frenchy *See* For Me and My Gal (1942)

Oh Gee! Oh Joy! *See* Look for the Silver Lining (1949)

Oh, Genevieve *See* A Song is Born (1948)

Oh, How I Hate to Get Up In the Morning *See* Alexander's Ragtime Band (1938)

Oh, How I Hate to Get Up in the Morning *See* This is the Army (1943)

Oh, It's a Lovely War *See* Star! (1968)

Oh Johnny *See* Spotlight Scandals (1943)

Oh, Johnny, Oh *See* For Me and My Gal (1942)

Oh Lady Be Good *See* Lady Be Good (1941)

Oh Lady Be Good *See* Rhapsody in Blue (1945)

Oh Leo, It's Love *See* Transatlantic Merry-Go-Round (1934)

Oh Me Oh Mi-Am-Mi *See* Moon Over Miami (1941)

Oh Me, Oh My *See* Tea for Two (1950)

Oh Mister Man Up in the Moon *See* Dimples (1936)

Oh Mon Amour *See* For the First Time (1959)

Oh My Goodness *See* The Poor Little Rich Girl (1936)

Oh Sing, Sweet Nightingale *See* Cinderella (1950)

Oh So Beautiful *See* Mad About Money (1930)

Oh! Susanna *See* Harmony Lane (1935)

Oh, Them Dudes *See* Let's Dance (1950)

Oh, What a Beautiful Morning *See* Oklahoma! (1955)

Oh Where is the Groom? *See* Sweet Rosie O'Grady (1943)

Oh You Beautiful Doll *See* Broadway Rhythm (1944)

Oh, You Beautiful Doll *See* For Me and My Gal (1942)

Oh, You Beautiful Doll *See* The Story of Vernon and Irene Castle (1939)

Oh You Wonderful Girl *See* Yankee Doodle Dandy (1942)

Okay Toots *See* Kid Millions (1934)

Oklahoma *See* Oklahoma! (1955)

Ol' Dan Patch *See* So Dear to My Heart (1949)

Ol' Man River *See* The Great Ziegfeld (1936)

Ol' Man River *See* Show Boat (1936)

Ol' Man River *See* Show Boat (1951)

Ol' Man River *See* Till the Clouds Roll By (1946)

An Old-Fashioned Garden *See* Night and Day (1946)

An Old-Fashioned Melody *See* Swing It, Professor (1937)

An Old-Fashioned Tune is Always New *See* Second Fiddle (1939)

Old Folks at Home *See* Harmony Lane (1935)

The Old Man *See* White Christmas (1954)

Old Man Mississippi *See* Nashville (1975)

Old Man Rip *See* Make a Wish (1937)

The Old Piano Roll Blues *See* Rich, Young and Pretty (1951)

The Old School Bell *See* College Swing (1938)

Old Souls *See* Phantom of the Paradise (1974)

An Old Straw Hat *See* Rebecca of Sunnybrook Farm (1938)

The Oldest Established *See* Guys and Dolls (1955)

The Olive Tree *See* Kismet (1955)

Oliver *See* Oliver! (1968)

Ombre Ma Full *See* New Moon (1940)

On a Clear Day, You Can See Forever *See* On a Clear Day You Can See Forever (1970)

On a Sunday Afternoon *See* Broadway Melody of 1936 (1935)

On a Sunday Afternoon *See* The Naughty Nineties (1945)

On an Island with You *See* On an Island with You (1948)

On Blue Venetian Waters *See* A Day at the Races (1937)

On Broadway *See* All That Jazz (1979)

On How To Be Lovely *See* Funny Face (1957)

On Moonlight Bay *See* On Moonlight Bay (1951)

On Moonlight Bay *See* Ship Ahoy (1942)

On Parade *See* Sweethearts (1938)

On the 10:10 *See* Just for You (1952)

On the Atchison, Topeka and the Santa Fe *See* The Harvey Girls (1946)

On the Banks of the Wabash *See* The Jolson Story (1946)

On the Bumpy Road to Love *See* Listen, Darling (1938)

On the Castle Wall *See* The Wizard of Oz (1939)

On the Erie Canal *See* The Farmer Takes a Wife (1953)

On the Good Ship Lollipop/When I'm With You/Animal Crackers medley *See* Rebecca of Sunnybrook Farm (1938)

On the Prairie *See* Melody Trail (1935)

On the Road to Zanzibar *See* The Road to Zanzibar (1941)

On the Robert E. Lee *See* Jazz Singer (1980)

On the Street Where You Live *See* My Fair Lady (1964)

On the Sunny Side of the Street *See* Swing Parade of 1946 (1946)

On the Town *See* On the Town (1949)

On to Combat *See* DuBarry Was a Lady (1943)

On With the Motley *See* The Great Ziegfeld (1936)

Once-a-Year Day *See* Pajama Game (1957)

Once Again Right Away *See* New York, New York (1977)

Once and For Always *See* A Connecticut Yankee in King Arthur's Court (1949)

Once In a While *See* New York, New York (1977)

Once in the Highlands *See* Brigadoon (1954)

Once More the Blue and White *See* Mr. Music (1950)

Once to Every Heart *See* Hollywood Canteen (1944)

Once Too Often *See* Pin-Up Girl (1944)

Once Upon a Song *See* Delightfully Dangerous (1945)

Once Upon A Time *See* It's Always Fair Weather (1955)

Once You Find Your Guy *See* Never a Dull Moment (1950)

One *See* A Chorus Line (1985)

One Alone *See* Deep in My Heart (1954)

One Alone *See* The Desert Song (1953)

One Boy *See* Bye, Bye, Birdie (1963)

One Broken Heart For Sale *See* It Happened at the World's Fair (1963)

One Day When We Were Young *See* The Great Waltz (1938)

One Fine Day (Une Bel Di) *See* The Great Ziegfeld (1936)

One Flower *See* The Desert Song (1953)

One For My Baby *See* The Sky's the Limit (1943)

One for My Baby *See* Young at Heart (1954)

One Good Time, One Good Place *See* Girl in Gold Boots (1969)

One Hand, One Heart *See* West Side Story (1961)

The One I Love *See* Everybody Sing (1938)

The One I Love Belongs To Somebody Else *See* I'll See You in My Dreams (1951)

One, I Love You *See* Nashville (1975)

One in a Million *See* One in a Million (1936)

One Jump Ahead *See* Aladdin (1992)

One Kiss *See* New Moon (1940)

One Last Kiss *See* Bye, Bye, Birdie (1963)

One Look at You *See* Broadway Serenade (1939)

One Moment Alone *See* The Cat and the Fiddle (1934)

One More Dance *See* Till the Clouds Roll By (1946)

One More Day *See* Jailhouse Rock (1957)

One More Mile to Go *See* Northwest Outpost (1947)

One More Moment *See* Love Songs (1985)

One Never Knows, Does One *See* Stowaway (1936)

One Night of Love *See* One Night of Love (1934)

One O'Clock Jump *See* I Dood It (1943)

One Song *See* Snow White and the Seven Dwarfs (1937)

One Thing Leads to Another *See* Body Rock (1984)

One Track Heart *See* Roustabout (1964)

One-Two-Three *See* Happy Go Lovely (1951)

One's On the Way *See* Coal Miner's Daughter (1980)

Only a Northern Song *See* Yellow Submarine (1968)

Only Make Believe *See* Show Boat (1936)

Only When You're In My Arms *See* The Story of Vernon and Irene Castle (1939)

Only You *See* The Great Waltz (1938)

Only You *See* Le Bal (1982)

Onward Onward *See* The Inspector General (1949)

Ooh, She's Done It Again *See* Mrs. Brown, You've Got a Lovely Daughter (1968)

Oom-Pah-Pah *See* Oliver! (1968)

Oompa-Loompa-Doompa-Dee-Doo *See* Willy Wonka & the Chocolate Factory (1971)

Oops *See* The Belle of New York (1952)

Open a New Window *See* Mame (1974)

Open Your Eyes *See* Royal Wedding (1951)

Opening Concerto—The Life of the Wife of the Sailor *See* Song of Norway (1970)

Opening Night *See* Lovely to Look At (1952)

Opera Number *See* Wonder Man (1945)

The Opposite Sex *See* The Opposite Sex (1956)

Optimistic Voices *See* The Wizard of Oz (1939)

Opus One *See* New York, New York (1977)

Or Was It Spring *See* Duchess of Idaho (1950)

Orchids in the Moonlight *See* Flying Down to Rio (1933)

Orgasm *See* The First Nudie Musical (1975)

Ortchi Chornya *See* Wonder Man (1945)

Os Pintinhos No Perreiro *See* George White's Scandals (1945)

The Other Generation *See* Flower Drum Song (1961)

Our Big Love Scene *See* Going Hollywood (1933)

Our Love Is Here to Stay *See* Lady Sings the Blues (1972)

Our State Fair *See* State Fair (1945)

Our State Fair *See* State Fair (1962)

Out Here On My Own *See* Fame (1980)

Out of My Dreams *See* Oklahoma! (1955)

Out of Sight, Out of Mind *See* In Person (1935)

Out of the Blue *See* Something to Sing About (1936)

Out of This World *See* Kiss Me Kate (1953)

Out to Lunch *See* A Swingin' Summer (1965)

Outer Spaceways Inc. *See* Sun Ra & His Intergalactic Solar Arkestra: Space is the Place (1974)

Over and Over Again *See* Billy Rose's Jumbo (1962)

Over at the Frankenstein Place *See* The Rocky Horror Picture Show (1975)

Over My Shoulder *See* Evergreen (1934)

Over Night *See* Thin Ice (1937)

Over the Bannister *See* Meet Me in St. Louis (1944)

Over the Rainbow *See* The Glenn Miller Story (1954)

Over the Waves *See* The Great Caruso (1951)

Over the Waves *See* Strike Up the Band (1940)

Over There *See* Yankee Doodle Dandy (1942)

The Owl and the Bobcat *See* Naughty Marietta (1935)

Pack Up Your Sins and Go to the Devil *See* Alexander's Ragtime Band (1938)

Pack Up Your Troubles *See* For Me and My Gal (1942)

Pack Up Your Troubles In Your Old Kit Bag *See* On Moonlight Bay (1951)

Paddy Me Lad *See* Song O' My Heart (1929)

Pagan Love Song *See* Pagan Love Song (1950)

Page's Aria *See* Maytime (1937)

Pagliacci *See* Two Tickets to Broadway (1951)

A Pair of Blue Eyes *See* Song O' My Heart (1929)

The Pajama Game *See* Pajama Game (1957)

Pajama Party *See* Pajama Party (1964)

Pan American Jubilee *See* Springtime in the Rockies (1942)

Papa, Can You Hear Me *See* Yentl (1983)

Papa-Oom-Mow-Mow *See* Back to the Beach (1987)

Paper Doll *See* Two Girls and a Sailor (1944)

Parade of the Glorified Girls *See* The Great Ziegfeld (1936)

Parade of the Wooden Soldiers *See* Rebecca of Sunnybrook Farm (1938)

Paradise *See* The Five Pennies (1959)

Paradise, Hawaiian Style *See* Paradise, Hawaiian Style (1966)

Pardners *See* Pardners (1956)

Pardon Me, Madame *See* Rose Marie (1936)

Paris *See* Rich, Young and Pretty (1951)

Paris Loves Lovers *See* Silk Stockings (1957)

Parisian Pierrot *See* Star! (1968)

Parisian Pretties *See* Lucky Me (1954)

The Parisians *See* Gigi (1958)

Part of Your World *See* The Little Mermaid (1989)

Party *See* Loving You (1957)

The Party's Over *See* Bells are Ringing (1960)

Pass That Peace Pipe *See* Good News (1947)

Passacaglia In C Minor *See* Song Without End (1960)

Passepied *See* Three Daring Daughters (1948)

Pastoral Symphony *See* Fantasia (1940)

Pat Sez He *See* Let Freedom Ring (1939)

Pathetique Symphony *See* Song Without End (1960)

Peace *See* Here Come the Girls (1953)

Peace on Earth *See* Lady and the Tramp (1955)

Peanut Vendor *See* A Star is Born (1954)

Pearl of the Persian Sea *See* On the Town (1949)

Pearly Shells *See* Surf Party (1964)

Peggy Sue *See* The Buddy Holly Story (1978)

Pelican Falls High *See* Two Tickets to Broadway (1951)

Pennies From Heaven *See* Pennies From Heaven (1981)

Pennsylvania 6-5000 *See* The Glenn Miller Story (1954)

Penny Arcade *See* The Night They Raided Minsky's (1969)

Penny Candy *See* New Faces of 1952 (1954)

Penny the Poo *See* A Swingin' Summer (1965)

People *See* Funny Girl (1968)

People Like You and Me *See* Orchestra Wives (1942)

People Will Say We're in Love *See* Oklahoma! (1955)

Pepperland *See* Yellow Submarine (1968)

Pepperland Laid Waste *See* Yellow Submarine (1968)

The Perfect Boy *See* How to Stuff a Wild Bikini (1965)

Perfect Gentleman *See* The Night They Raided Minsky's (1969)

A Perfect Love *See* The Opposite Sex (1956)

The Perfect Nanny *See* Mary Poppins (1964)

Perpetual Motion *See* Mad About Money (1930)

Personality *See* The Road to Utopia (1946)

Perversion *See* The First Nudie Musical (1975)

Pet Me, Poppa *See* Guys and Dolls (1955)

Pete Kelly's Blues *See* Pete Kelly's Blues (1955)

Peter's Denial *See* Jesus Christ, Superstar (1973)

Petticoat Army *See* Rhythm Parade (1943)

Pettin' in the Park *See* Gold Diggers of 1933 (1933)

Petunia See Frankie and Johnny (1965)

The Phantom's Theme (Beauty and the Beast) See Phantom of the Paradise (1974)

The Physician See Star! (1968)

Piano Concerto in B-flat Minor See The Barkleys of Broadway (1949)

Piano Concerto in F See An American in Paris (1951)

Piano Concerto No. 1 See Song Without End (1960)

Piano Dance See Let's Dance (1950)

The Piano Lesson See The Music Man (1962)

Piccadilly See Star! (1968)

The Piccolino See Top Hat (1935)

Piccolo Pete See Vagabond Lover (1929)

Pick a Little See The Music Man (1962)

Pick a Pocket or Two See Oliver! (1968)

Pick Up the Pace See Krush Groove (1985)

Pick Yourself Up See Swing Time (1936)

Picture Me Without You See Dimples (1936)

Piddle, Twiddle and Resolve See 1776 (1972)

A Piece of Sky See Yentl (1983)

Pig Foot Pete See Keep 'Em Flying (1941)

Pilate and Christ See Jesus Christ, Superstar (1973)

Pilate's Dream See Jesus Christ, Superstar (1973)

Pilgrim's Chorus See Song Without End (1960)

Pinball Wizard See Tommy (1975)

Pineapple Picker See For the First Time (1959)

Pirouette See Look for the Silver Lining (1949)

Planet Schmanet See The Rocky Horror Picture Show (1975)

Plant You Now, Dig You Later See Pal Joey (1957)

Plantons la Vigne See Maytime (1937)

Play a Simple Melody See There's No Business Like Show Business (1954)

Play That Barbershop Chord See In the Good Old Summertime (1949)

Play Us a Polka, Dot See Sweet Adeline (1935)

Please Don't Go See Krush Groove (1985)

Please Don't Monkey With Broadway See Broadway Melody of 1940 (1940)

Please Don't Say No, Say Maybe See Thrill of a Romance (1945)

Please Don't Stop Loving Me See Frankie and Johnny (1965)

Please Don't Talk About Me When I'm Gone See Lullaby of Broadway (1951)

Plenty to Be Thankful For See Holiday Inn (1942)

Plymouth University Song See My Lucky Star (1938)

Pocketful of Rainbows See G.I. Blues (1960)

A Poem Set to Music See Springtime in the Rockies (1942)

Poison Ivy League See Roustabout (1964)

Polka See Till the Clouds Roll By (1946)

Polonaise in A Flat Major See Holiday in Mexico (1946)

Polonaise In A Flat, Opus 53 (partial) See A Song to Remember (1945)

Polythene Pam See Sgt. Pepper's Lonely Hearts Club Band (1978)

Poor Andre See The French Line (1954)

Poor Butterfly See Thoroughly Modern Millie (1967)

Poor Jerusalem See Jesus Christ, Superstar (1973)

Poor John See Cover Girl (1944)

Poor Jud Is Dead See Oklahoma! (1955)

Poor Little Me, I'm on K.P. See This is the Army (1943)

Poor Little Pierette See The Boy Friend (1971)

Poor Mr. Chisholm See Second Chorus (1940)

Poor Pierrot See The Cat and the Fiddle (1934)

Poor, Poor, Pitiful Me See FM (1978)

Poor Unfortunate Souls See The Little Mermaid (1989)

Poor You See Ship Ahoy (1942)

Poppies See The Wizard of Oz (1939)

Poppy Girls See The Wiz (1978)

Pore Jud See Oklahoma! (1955)

The Porpoise Song See Head (1968)

Portland Fancy See Summer Stock (1950)

Posh See Chitty Chitty Bang Bang (1968)

Pottawatomie See Too Many Girls (1940)

Prayer See Naughty Marietta (1935)

Pre-Historic Man See On the Town (1949)

Preludium See The Sound of Music (1965)

Pretty as a Picture See Sweethearts (1938)

Pretty Baby See Broadway Rhythm (1944)

Pretty Baby See I'll See You in My Dreams (1951)

Pretty Baby See Rose of Washington Square (1939)

Pretty Baby See Young Man with a Horn (1950)

Pretty Girl See Fast Forward (1984)

A Pretty Girl Is Like a Melody See Alexander's Ragtime Band (1938)

A Pretty Girl is Like a Melody See The Great Ziegfeld (1936)

A Pretty Girl is Like a Melody See There's No Business Like Show Business (1954)

A Pretty Girl Milking Her Cow See Little Nellie Kelly (1940)

Prince Ali See Aladdin (1992)

Private Buckaroo See Private Buckaroo (1942)

Prologue See West Side Story (1961)

Promise Me Anything See Beach Party (1963)

A Proper Gentleman See Half a Sixpence (1967)

The Psalm See Man of La Mancha (1972)

Psychic Flash See Love Songs (1985)

Pump It Up/Let's Get Funky See Krush Groove (1985)

Puppet On a String See Girl Happy (1965)

Pure Imagination See Willy Wonka & the Chocolate Factory (1971)

Put a Tax on Love See Roman Scandals (1933)

Put 'Em Back the Way They Wuz See Li'l Abner (1959)

Put 'Em in a Box, Tie 'Em with a Ribbon, and Throw 'Em in the Deep Blue Sea See Romance on the High Seas (1948)

Put It In Reverse See Harvest Melody (1943)

Put It There, Pal See The Road to Utopia (1946)

Put Me to the Test See Cover Girl (1944)

Put Me to the Test See A Damsel in Distress (1937)

Put on a Happy Face See Bye, Bye, Birdie (1963)

Put On Your Sunday Clothes See Hello, Dolly! (1969)

Put the Blame on Me See Tickle Me (1965)

Put Your Arms Around Me Honey See In the Good Old Summertime (1949)

Put Your Trust in the Moon See Zis Boom Bah (1942)

A Puzzlement See The King and I (1956)

Quainty Dainty Me See Everybody Sing (1938)

Que Chica? See Playmates (1941)

Queen Bee See A Star is Born (1976)

Queen of the Jungle See The Great Ziegfeld (1936)

Queenie Wahine's Papaya See Paradise, Hawaiian Style (1966)

Questa o Quella See The Seven Hills of Rome (1958)

Quick Sands See Stage Door Canteen (1943)

Quiet Life See Absolute Beginners (1986)

Quilp See The Old Curiosity Shop (1975)

Quintet See West Side Story (1961)

A Quintet For Strings in E Flat See Amadeus (1984)

The Race Is On See Half a Sixpence (1967)

Racing with the Clock See Pajama Game (1957)

Radiotron See Breakin' 2: Electric Boogaloo (1984)

Ragamuffin Romeo See King of Jazz (1930)

Ragtime Cowboy Joe See Hello, Frisco, Hello (1943)

Ragtime Violin See Alexander's Ragtime Band (1938)

Ragtime Violin See Easter Parade (1948)

Rain Dance Ballet See Finian's Rainbow (1968)

The Rain in Spain See My Fair Lady (1964)

The Rainbow Connection See The Muppet Movie (1979)

Rainbow Valley See Girl Rush (1944)

Raindrops on a Drum See Northwest Outpost (1947)

A Rainy Sunday See Hi-De-Ho (1935)

Rakoczy March See Song Without End (1960)

Rang Tang Tang See Stormy Weather (1943)

Rap Tap on Wood See Born to Dance (1936)

Rappin' See Rappin' (1985)

Ready to Groove See A Swingin' Summer (1965)

Ready, Willing and Able See Young at Heart (1954)

A Real Nice Clambake See Carousel (1956)

Rebola a Bola See Week-End In Havana (1941)

Red Blues See Silk Stockings (1957)

Red Hot and Beautiful See Doll Face (1946)

Red Hot Roadster See A Swingin' Summer (1965)

Red Light See Fame (1980)

Red Robins, Bob Whites and Blue Birds See Pin-Up Girl (1944)

Redskin Rhumba See A Song is Born (1948)

Reefer Man See International House (1933)

Rehearsal Ballet See Meet Me in Las Vegas (1956)

Reincarnation See Hollywood Party (1934)

Relax See It Happened at the World's Fair (1963)

Remember See Alexander's Ragtime Band (1938)

Remember My Forgotten Man See Gold Diggers of 1933 (1933)

Remember When See 101 Dalmations (1961)

Remind Me See One Night in the Tropics (1940)

The Restless Age See Spotlight Scandals (1943)

Return to Sender See Girls! Girls! Girls! (1962)

Reverie See Maytime (1937)

Reviewing the Situation See Oliver! (1968)

Revolutionary Etude See That Midnight Kiss (1949)

Revolutionary March See The Great Waltz (1938)

Rhapsody in Blue See The Great Ziegfeld (1936)

Rhapsody in Blue See King of Jazz (1930)

Rhapsody in Blue See Rhapsody in Blue (1945)

Rhumba Boogie See Everybody's Dancin' (1950)

Rhumba Rumbero See Holiday in Havana (1949)

A Rhyme and a Reason See Song of Norway (1970)

Rhythm Cocktail See Stormy Weather (1943)

Rhythm of Life See Sweet Charity (1969)

Rhythm of the Islands See It's a Date (1940)

Rhythm of the Rio *See* Escape to Paradise (1939)

Ribbons and Wrappings *See* Song of Norway (1970)

Ribbons Down My Back *See* Hello, Dolly! (1969)

Rich Man's Frug *See* Sweet Charity (1969)

Richer Than A Millionaire *See* Swing It, Professor (1937)

Ridin' For A Fall *See* Thank Your Lucky Stars (1943)

Riding the Rainbow *See* Kid Galahad (1962)

The Riff Song *See* The Desert Song (1953)

The Right Girl for Me *See* Take Me Out to the Ball Game (1949)

Right or Wrong *See* Something to Sing About (1936)

The Right Place For A Girl *See* Rose Marie (1954)

The Right Somebody to Love *See* Captain January (1936)

The Ring *See* The Pirate (1948)

Ring Dem Bells *See* The Cotton Club (1984)

Rio Rita *See* The Great Ziegfeld (1936)

Riot City *See* Absolute Beginners (1986)

The Rite of Spring *See* Fantasia (1940)

Ritual Fire Dance *See* Three Daring Daughters (1948)

Ritual Fire Dance *See* Two Girls and a Sailor (1944)

The Ritz Roll 'n Rock *See* Silk Stockings (1957)

River Song *See* Tom Sawyer (1973)

Rivera *See* The Boy Friend (1971)

Road to Morocco *See* The Road to Morocco (1942)

Road to Paradise *See* Maytime (1937)

The Road to Paradise *See* Deep in My Heart (1954)

Rock-A-Bye Your Baby With a Dixie Melody *See* The Jolson Story (1946)

Rock-A-Bye Your Baby with a Dixie Melody *See* Rose of Washington Square (1939)

Rock and Roll *See* Transatlantic Merry-Go-Round (1934)

Rock and Roll Tumbleweed *See* The Opposite Sex (1956)

Rock Around the Ollie Vee *See* The Buddy Holly Story (1978)

Rock Baby Rock *See* Absolute Beginners (1986)

Rock Island *See* The Music Man (1962)

Rock 'n' Reelin' *See* Ride 'Em Cowboy (1942)

Rock 'n' Roll Is Here To Stay *See* Grease (1978)

Rock 'n' Roll Party Queen *See* Grease (1978)

Rockabye Your Baby *See* Jolson Sings Again (1949)

Rocking at the 21's *See* Absolute Beginners (1986)

Rodeo Rose *See* Melody Ranch (1940)

Rodrigo Bay *See* Absolute Beginners (1986)

Roller Skate Rag *See* Funny Girl (1968)

Rolling Down the River *See* The Naughty Nineties (1945)

Rolling Home *See* Born to Dance (1936)

Rolling Stone *See* Nashville (1975)

Romance *See* The Desert Song (1953)

Romance and Rhumba *See* Week-End In Havana (1941)

Romance In The Rain *See* Harlem on the Prairie (1938)

Rome Wasn't Built in a Day *See* Roman Scandals (1933)

Romeo and Juliet *See* The Goldwyn Follies (1938)

Romeo and Juliet *See* Thank God It's Friday (1978)

Romeo Jones *See* Seaside Swingers (1965)

Romeo Smith and Juliet Jones *See* Playmates (1941)

Romeria Vasca *See* Fiesta (1947)

Rondo Capriccioso *See* Song Without End (1960)

Rondo Capriccioso *See* They Shall Have Music (1939)

A Rookie and His Rhythm *See* Stage Door Canteen (1943)

Room Enuff for Us *See* Li'l Abner (1959)

A Room in Bloomsbury *See* The Boy Friend (1971)

Rosalie *See* Night and Day (1946)

Rosalie *See* Rosalie (1938)

The Rose *See* The Rose (1979)

Rose Marie *See* Rose Marie (1936)

Rose Marie *See* Rose Marie (1954)

The Rose of Tralee *See* Song O' My Heart (1929)

Rose of Washington Square *See* Rose of Washington Square (1939)

Rose of Washington Square *See* Thoroughly Modern Millie (1967)

Rose Room *See* The Story of Vernon and Irene Castle (1939)

Rosemary *See* How to Succeed in Business without Really Trying (1967)

Rose's Cafe *See* Nashville (1975)

The Roses of Success *See* Chitty Chitty Bang Bang (1968)

Rose's Turn *See* Gypsy (1962)

Rose's Turn *See* Gypsy (1993)

Rosie *See* Bye, Bye, Birdie (1963)

Rosie, My Little Posie *See* The Naughty Nineties (1945)

Round She Whirls *See* Lottery Bride (1930)

Roustabout *See* Roustabout (1964)

Route 66 *See* Three Daring Daughters (1948)

Row, Row, Row *See* The Story of Vernon and Irene Castle (1939)

Row, Row, Row *See* Two Weeks with Love (1950)

Rubberneckin' *See* Change of Habit (1969)

Rumble *See* West Side Story (1961)

Run Little Rainrop Run *See* Springtime in the Rockies (1942)

Run, Run, Run *See* Romance on the High Seas (1948)

Runnin' Wild *See* The Fabulous Dorseys (1947)

Runnin' Wild *See* Muscle Beach Party (1964)

Russian Dance *See* The Merry Widow (1934)

Russian Easter Hymn *See* Northwest Outpost (1947)

Sabbath Prayer *See* Fiddler on the Roof (1971)

The Sabre Dance *See* The Barkleys of Broadway (1949)

The Sadder But Wiser Girl *See* The Music Man (1962)

Sadie, Sadie *See* Funny Girl (1968)

Safety in Numbers *See* The Boy Friend (1971)

Sagebrush Lullaby *See* Never a Dull Moment (1950)

A Sailor's Life For Me *See* In the Navy (1941)

A Sailor's Not a Sailor *See* There's No Business Like Show Business (1954)

St. Bridget *See* Mame (1974)

St. Louis Blues *See* Rose Marie (1936)

St. Louis Blues March *See* The Glenn Miller Story (1954)

Sally, My Dear Sally *See* Sing Your Worries Away (1942)

Sally Simpson *See* Tommy (1975)

Salome *See* DuBarry Was a Lady (1943)

Sam and Delilah *See* Girl Crazy (1943)

Sam, the Accordion Man *See* Dance of Life (1929)

Sam the Old Accordian Man *See* Glorifying the American Girl (1930)

Sam, the Old Accordian Man *See* Love Me or Leave Me (1955)

Samantha *See* Can't Stop the Music (1980)

San Antonio Rose *See* Sweet Dreams (1985)

San Domingo *See* Scared Stiff (1953)

San Francisco *See* Hello, Frisco, Hello (1943)

San Francisco *See* I'll See You in My Dreams (1951)

San Francisco *See* San Francisco (1936)

Sand Castles *See* Paradise, Hawaiian Style (1966)

Sands of Time *See* Kismet (1955)

Sandy *See* Grease (1978)

Santa Baby *See* New Faces of 1952 (1954)

Santa Claus *See* The Christmas That Almost Wasn't (1966)

Santa Lucia *See* Absolute Beginners (1986)

Santa Lucia *See* Maytime (1937)

Santa Lucia *See* That Midnight Kiss (1949)

The Satellites are Spinning *See* Sun Ra & His Intergalactic Solar Arkestra: Space is the Place (1974)

Satin and Silk *See* Silk Stockings (1957)

Saturday Afternoon Before The Game *See* I Love Melvin (1953)

Saudades *See* Lady Be Good (1941)

Sawdust, Spangles and Dreams *See* Billy Rose's Jumbo (1962)

Say A Prayer For Me Tonight *See* Gigi (1958)

Say It With Music *See* Alexander's Ragtime Band (1938)

Scandals *See* George White's Scandals (1945)

Scherzo In B Flat Minor *See* A Song to Remember (1945)

Schooldays *See* Goodbye, Mr. Chips (1969)

Schubert's Serenade *See* Thrill of a Romance (1945)

Science Fiction Double Feature *See* The Rocky Horror Picture Show (1975)

Scorpio *See* Absolute Beginners (1986)

Scratch My Back (Then I'll Scratch Yours) *See* Paradise, Hawaiian Style (1966)

Sea of Holes *See* Yellow Submarine (1968)

Sea of Monsters *See* Yellow Submarine (1968)

The Sea of the Moon *See* Pagan Love Song (1950)

Sea of Time *See* Yellow Submarine (1968)

Sea Wall *See* The Pirate (1948)

Seal It With A Kiss *See* That Girl from Paris (1936)

The Search is Through *See* Country Girl (1954)

Second Hand Rose *See* Funny Girl (1968)

Second Time Around *See* Seaside Swingers (1965)

Secret Love *See* Calamity Jane (1953)

Secret Surfin' Spot *See* Beach Party (1963)

A Secretary Is Not A Toy *See* How to Succeed in Business without Really Trying (1967)

Seduce Me Tonight *See* Flashdance (1983)

See Me, Feel Me *See* Tommy (1975)

See the Circus *See* Here Come the Girls (1953)

See the Phantoms *See* Scrooge (1970)

Seeing's Believing *See* The Belle of New York (1952)

Selling Out *See* Absolute Beginners (1986)

Sempre Libera *See* Maytime (1937)

Sempre Libera *See* One Night of Love (1934)

Sempre Libera *See* San Francisco (1936)

Senorita *See* Girl of the Golden West (1938)

Sensation *See* Tommy (1975)

Sentimental Lady *See* FM (1978)

Serafin *See* The Pirate (1948)

Serenade *See* Deep in My Heart (1954)

Serenade *See* The Student Prince (1954)

Serenade in Blue *See* Orchestra Wives (1942)

Serenade To a Fish *See* The Goldwyn Follies (1938)

The Servant's Chorus *See* My Fair Lady (1964)

Seven and a Half Cents *See* Pajama Game (1957)

Seven Hills of Rome *See* The Seven Hills of Rome (1958)

Seven Lonely Days *See* Sweet Dreams (1985)

Seventeen *See* Broadway Rhythm (1944)

Seventy-six Trombones *See* The Music Man (1962)

Sextet *See* One Night of Love (1934)

Sextet from Lucia di Lammermoor *See* The Great Caruso (1951)

Sgt. Pepper's Lonely Hearts Club Band *See* Sgt. Pepper's Lonely Hearts Club Band (1978)

Sgt. Pepper's Lonely Hearts Club Band *See* Yellow Submarine (1968)

Shadow Waltz *See* Gold Diggers of 1933 (1933)

Shadows on the Moon *See* Girl of the Golden West (1938)

Shadows on the Moon Reprise *See* Girl of the Golden West (1938)

The Shady Dame from Seville *See* Victor/Victoria (1982)

Shady Lady *See* Best Foot Forward (1943)

Shaking the Blues Away *See* Easter Parade (1948)

Shaking the Blues Away *See* Love Me or Leave Me (1955)

Shall We Dance? *See* The King and I (1956)

Shall We Dance *See* Shall We Dance (1937)

Shall We Gather at the Rhythm? *See* Follies Girl (1943)

Shampoo Commercial *See* A Star is Born (1954)

Shanghai Lil *See* Footlight Parade (1933)

A Shanty in Old Shanty Town *See* Lullaby of Broadway (1951)

Sharpshooter *See* Body Rock (1984)

She Came Through the Bathroom Window *See* Sgt. Pepper's Lonely Hearts Club Band (1978)

She Didn't Say 'Yes' *See* The Cat and the Fiddle (1934)

She Didn't Say Yes *See* Till the Clouds Roll By (1946)

She Loves You *See* A Hard Day's Night (1964)

The Sheik of Araby *See* Tin Pan Alley (1940)

She's a Follies Girl *See* The Great Ziegfeld (1936)

She's Funny That Way *See* Meet Danny Wilson (1952)

She's Got You *See* Sweet Dreams (1985)

She's Leaving Home *See* Sgt. Pepper's Lonely Hearts Club Band (1978)

She's Mine, All Mine *See* Three Little Words (1950)

She's Not Thinking of Me *See* Gigi (1958)

She's On It *See* Krush Groove (1985)

She's Too Far Above Me *See* Half a Sixpence (1967)

She's Way Up Thar *See* Stand Up and Cheer (1934)

Shine *See* Cabin in the Sky (1943)

Shine On Harvest Moon *See* I'll See You in My Dreams (1951)

Shine On Harvest Moon *See* Look for the Silver Lining (1949)

Shine On Harvest Moon *See* Nancy Goes to Rio (1950)

Shine on Harvest Moon *See* The Great Ziegfeld (1936)

A Shine On Your Shoes *See* The Band Wagon (1953)

Ship Ahoy *See* Naughty Marietta (1935)

Ship Ahoy *See* Ship Ahoy (1942)

Shipoopi *See* The Music Man (1962)

Shoeless Joe From Hannibal Mo *See* Damn Yankees (1958)

Shoes *See* New Moon (1940)

Shoes With Wings On *See* The Barkleys of Broadway (1949)

Shootin' the Works for Uncle Sam *See* You'll Never Get Rich (1941)

Shopping Around *See* G.I. Blues (1960)

Shorty George *See* You Were Never Lovelier (1942)

Should I? *See* Singin' in the Rain (1952)

Shoulder to Shoulder *See* Lottery Bride (1930)

Shout It Out *See* Frankie and Johnny (1965)

Show Me *See* My Fair Lady (1964)

The Show Must Go On *See* Cover Girl (1944)

The Show Must Go On *See* Everybody Sing (1938)

Showboat Medley *See* Till the Clouds Roll By (1946)

The Showboat's Comin' to Town *See* The Naughty Nineties (1945)

Showdown *See* Breakin' (1984)

Showdown *See* Fast Forward (1984)

Shuffle Blues *See* Le Bal (1982)

Shuffle Off to Buffalo *See* 42nd Street (1933)

Siamese Cat Song *See* Lady and the Tramp (1955)

Siberia *See* Silk Stockings (1957)

Sidewalks of New York *See* Maytime (1937)

Sign of Love *See* Back to the Beach (1987)

Silent Night *See* Going My Way (1944)

Silk Stockings *See* Silk Stockings (1957)

Silly Love Songs *See* Give My Regards to Broad Street (1984)

Silver Bells *See* The Lemon Drop Kid (1951)

Silver Threads Among the Gold *See* She Done Him Wrong (1933)

Simon Zealotes *See* Jesus Christ, Superstar (1973)

The Simple Joys of Maidenhood *See* Camelot (1967)

Sin *See* Girl in Gold Boots (1969)

Sin Fe *See* Crossover Dreams (1985)

Since I Kissed My Baby Goodbye *See* You'll Never Get Rich (1941)

Since You've Gone *See* Nashville (1975)

Sincere *See* The Music Man (1962)

Sing a Rainbow *See* Pete Kelly's Blues (1955)

Sing a Song *See* Nashville (1975)

Sing Before Breakfast *See* Broadway Melody of 1936 (1935)

Sing Me a Song That Sells *See* Let's Make Love (1960)

Sing of Spring *See* A Damsel in Distress (1937)

Sing, Sing, Sing *See* The Benny Goodman Story (1955)

Sing to Your Senorita *See* Down Argentine Way (1940)

Sing, You Children *See* Easy Come, Easy Go (1967)

Sing You Sinners *See* I'll Cry Tomorrow (1955)

Sing Your Worries Away *See* Sing Your Worries Away (1942)

Singin' in the Rain *See* Singin' in the Rain (1952)

Singing in the Rain *See* Little Nellie Kelly (1940)

Singing in the Sun *See* Pagan Love Song (1950)

Singlefoot Serenade *See* Duchess of Idaho (1950)

Sister Suffragette *See* Mary Poppins (1964)

Sisters *See* White Christmas (1954)

Sit Down John *See* 1776 (1972)

Sit Down, You're Rocking the Boat *See* Guys and Dolls (1955)

Sittin' on a Backyard Fence *See* Footlight Parade (1933)

Situation Wise *See* It's Always Fair Weather (1955)

Six Jerks in a Jeep *See* Private Buckaroo (1942)

Six Months Out of Every Year *See* Damn Yankees (1958)

Sixteen, Going on Seventeen *See* The Sound of Music (1965)

Skip to My Lou *See* Meet Me in St. Louis (1944)

Skirts Ahoy! *See* Skirts Ahoy! (1952)

Slap Polka *See* Hit the Ice (1943)

Slap That Bass *See* Shall We Dance (1937)

Sleep, Baby, Sleep in Your Jeep *See* Stage Door Canteen (1943)

Sleep Lagoon *See* Absolute Beginners (1986)

Sleeping Beauty Ballet *See* Meet Me in Las Vegas (1956)

Sleepy Lagoon *See* DuBarry Was a Lady (1943)

Slide Some Oil to Me *See* The Wiz (1978)

Slipped Disc *See* The Benny Goodman Story (1955)

Slow Ride *See* FM (1978)

Slowly but Surely *See* Tickle Me (1965)

Sluefoot *See* Daddy Long Legs (1955)

Slumming on Park Avenue *See* On the Avenue (1937)

The Small House of Uncle Thomas *See* The King and I (1956)

Small Talk *See* Pajama Game (1957)

Small Towns Are Smile Towns *See* Small Town Girl (1953)

Small World *See* Gypsy (1962)

Smash the Mirror *See* Tommy (1975)

Smile Away Each Rainy Day *See* Darling Lili (1970)

Smiles *See* For Me and My Gal (1942)

Smoke Gets in Your Eyes *See* Lovely to Look At (1952)

Smoke Gets in Your Eyes *See* Roberta (1935)

Smoke Gets in Your Eyes *See* Till the Clouds Roll By (1946)

Smorgasbord *See* Spinout (1966)

Snack Attack *See* Rappin' (1985)

Snookey Ookums *See* Easter Parade (1948)

Snooks *See* Everybody Sing (1938)

Snow *See* White Christmas (1954)

So Am I *See* Lady Be Good (1941)

So Dear To My Heart *See* So Dear to My Heart (1949)

So In Love *See* Kiss Me Kate (1953)

So In Love *See* Wonder Man (1945)

So Long, Dearie *See* Hello, Dolly! (1969)

So Long, Farewell *See* The Sound of Music (1965)

So Long, Honey Lamb *See* Funny Lady (1975)

So Long Mary *See* Yankee Doodle Dandy (1942)

So-Long, Oo-Long *See* Three Little Words (1950)

So Long Sarah Jane *See* I Dood It (1943)

So Near and Yet So Far *See* You'll Never Get Rich (1941)

So the Bluebirds and the Blackbirds Got Together *See* King of Jazz (1930)

So This Is Love *See* Cinderella (1950)

So What? *See* Absolute Beginners (1986)

So You Wanted to See the Wizard *See* The Wiz (1978)

Sobbin' Women *See* Seven Brides for Seven Brothers (1954)

Softly as in a Morning Sunrise *See* New Moon (1940)

Softly, as in a Morning Sunrise *See* Deep in My Heart (1954)

Sold My Soul To Rock 'n' Roll *See* The Rose (1979)

Soldier's Chorus *See* Maytime (1937)

Soldiers of Fortune *See* Girl of the Golden West (1938)

Soldiers of Fortune Reprise *See* Girl of the Golden West (1938)

Solid Potato Salad *See* Broadway Rhythm (1944)

Soliloquies *See* South Pacific (1958)

Soliloquy *See* Carousel (1956)

Soliloquy For Three Heads *See* The Inspector General (1949)

Solitary Seminole *See* Moon Over Miami (1941)

The Solitary Wanderer *See* Song of Norway (1970)

Solvejg's Song—Norwegian National Anthem *See* Song of Norway (1970)

Sombody Loves Me *See* Pete Kelly's Blues (1955)

Some Day My Prince Will Come *See* Snow White and the Seven Dwarfs (1937)

Some Enchanted Evening *See* South Pacific (1958)

Some Fun Now *See* Little Shop of Horrors (1986)

Some Like You *See* My Dream is Yours (1949)

Some of These Days *See* All That Jazz (1979)

Some of These Days *See* Broadway Melody of 1938 (1937)

Some of These Days *See* Rose Marie (1936)

Some Other Time *See* Step Lively (1944)

Some People *See* Gypsy (1962)

Some People *See* Gypsy (1993)

Somebody Loves Me *See* Broadway Rhythm (1944)

Somebody Loves Me *See* Lullaby of Broadway (1951)

Somebody Loves Me *See* Rhapsody in Blue (1945)

Somebody Super Like You *See* Phantom of the Paradise (1974)

Somebody's Eyes *See* Footloose (1984)

Somebody's Walkin' In My Dreams *See* Doll Face (1946)

Someday I'll Find You *See* Star! (1968)

Someday Soon *See* Bundle of Joy (1956)

Someone Belonging to Someone *See* Staying Alive (1983)

Someone Loves You After All *See* The Great Ziegfeld (1936)

Someone to Love *See* Follies Girl (1943)

Someone to Love *See* Holiday in Mexico (1946)

Someone To Watch Over Me *See* Rhapsody in Blue (1945)

Someone to Watch Over Me *See* Star! (1968)

Someone to Watch Over Me *See* Young at Heart (1954)

Somethin' Real Special *See* The Farmer Takes a Wife (1953)

Something Better *See* The Muppet Movie (1979)

Something Good *See* The Sound of Music (1965)

Something in Your Smile *See* Doctor Dolittle (1967)

Something Sort of Grandish *See* Finian's Rainbow (1968)

Something There *See* Beauty and the Beast (1991)

Something to Remember You By *See* The Band Wagon (1953)

Something to Sing About *See* Something to Sing About (1936)

Something Wonderful *See* The King and I (1956)

Something's Coming *See* West Side Story (1961)

Something's Got To Give *See* Daddy Long Legs (1955)

Sometimes I Feel Like a Motherless Child *See* Way Down South (1939)

Sometimes I'm Happy *See* Hit the Deck (1955)

Sometimes in the Night *See* Thunder Alley (1985)

Somewhere *See* The Old Curiosity Shop (1975)

Somewhere *See* West Side Story (1961)

Somewhere Over the Rainbow *See* The Wizard of Oz (1939)

Somewhere There's Someone *See* A Star is Born (1954)

The Son of a Gun Who Pick on Uncle Sam *See* Panama Hattie (1942)

Sonata In B Minor *See* Song Without End (1960)

The Song Angels Sing *See* Because You're Mine (1952)

A Song is Born *See* A Song is Born (1948)

Song O' My Heart *See* Song O' My Heart (1929)

Song of Freedom *See* Holiday Inn (1942)

Song of India *See* New York, New York (1977)

The Song of Norway *See* Song of Norway (1970)

Song of the Bandoleros *See* Rogue of the Rio Grande (1930)

Song of the Bayou *See* The Toast of New Orleans (1950)

Song of the Dawn *See* King of Jazz (1930)

Song of the Enchilada Man *See* Scared Stiff (1953)

Song of the King *See* The King and I (1956)

Song of the Metronome *See* Second Fiddle (1939)

Song of the Musketeers *See* The Three Musketeers (1939)

The Song of the Setting Sun *See* Whoopee! (1930)

Song of the Shrimp *See* Girls! Girls! Girls! (1962)

Songs of Life *See* Jazz Singer (1980)

Songwriter *See* Songwriter (1984)

Sonny Boy *See* Jolson Sings Again (1949)

Soon as I Get Home *See* The Wiz (1978)

Sophistication *See* Can't Stop the Music (1980)

The Sorcerer's Apprentice *See* Fantasia (1940)

A Sorry Phoney *See* The Wiz (1978)

The Sound of Music *See* The Sound of Music (1965)

The Sound of the City *See* Can't Stop the Music (1980)

Sourwood Mountain *See* So Dear to My Heart (1949)

South America, Take It Away *See* New York, New York (1977)

South American Way *See* Down Argentine Way (1940)

Southland *See* Yes, Sir, Mr. Bones (1951)

Spaghetti *See* Marco (1973)

The Spaniard Who Blighted My Life *See* The Jolson Story (1946)

Spanish Lies *See* A Star is Born (1976)

Sparks *See* Tommy (1975)

Speak Low *See* One Touch of Venus (1948)

Special to Me *See* Phantom of the Paradise (1974)

Specialization *See* Let's Make Love (1960)

Speed Lovers *See* The Speed Lovers (1968)

Speedway *See* Speedway (1968)

Spic and Spanish *See* Too Many Girls (1940)

Spin a Little Web of Dreams *See* Fashions of 1934 (1934)

The Sping *See* Panama Hattie (1942)

Spinout *See* Spinout (1966)

A Spoonful of Sugar *See* Mary Poppins (1964)

The Sport of Kings *See* The Old Curiosity Shop (1975)

Spozalizio *See* Song Without End (1960)

Spring Again *See* The Goldwyn Follies (1938)

Spring Fever *See* Girl Happy (1965)

Spring is Here *See* I Married an Angel (1942)

Spring Love Is in the Air *See* Rosalie (1938)

Spring, Spring, Spring *See* Seven Brides for Seven Brothers (1954)

Springtide, Opus 43, no. 6 *See* Three Daring Daughters (1948)

Stairway to the Stars *See* The Glenn Miller Story (1954)

Stand Up and Cheer *See* Stand Up and Cheer (1934)

Stand Up and Fight *See* Carmen Jones (1954)

The Stanley Steamer *See* Summer Holiday (1948)

Star! *See* Star! (1968)

Star Eyes *See* I Dood It (1943)

Starlight, Starbright *See* In the Navy (1941)

Stars and Stripes Forever *See* Stars and Stripes Forever (1952)

Startin' Tonight *See* Girl Happy (1965)

Stay Awake *See* Mary Poppins (1964)

Stay on the Right Side, Sister *See* Love Me or Leave Me (1955)

Stay Out of the Kitchen *See* Yes, Sir, Mr. Bones (1951)

Stay With Me *See* The Rose (1979)

Staying Alive *See* Saturday Night Fever (1977)

Steadfast, Loyal and True *See* King Creole (1958)

Stealin' Apples *See* A Song is Born (1948)

Steam Heat *See* Pajama Game (1957)

Step in Time *See* Mary Poppins (1964)

Step Up and Take a Bow *See* At the Circus (1939)

Steppin' Out With My Baby *See* Easter Parade (1948)

Stereophonic Sound *See* Silk Stockings (1957)

Stetson *See* Whoopee! (1930)

Stick-To-It-Ivity *See* So Dear to My Heart (1949)

Stiff Upper Lip *See* A Damsel in Distress (1937)

Stillman's Gym *See* It's Always Fair Weather (1955)

Stop, Look, Listen *See* Spinout (1966)

Stop Where You Are *See* Paradise, Hawaiian Style (1966)

Stormy Weather *See* Stormy Weather (1943)

Stormy Weather *See* Swing Parade of 1946 (1946)

Story of the Very Merry Widow *See* Pin-Up Girl (1944)

Stout Hearted Men *See* New Moon (1940)

Stouthearted Men *See* Deep in My Heart (1954)

Strange Fruit *See* Lady Sings the Blues (1972)

Strange Music *See* Song of Norway (1970)

Strange Thing, Mystifying *See* Jesus Christ, Superstar (1973)

Strange Things *See* Girl in Gold Boots (1969)

Stranger in a Strange Land *See* Beat Street (1984)

Stranger in Paradise *See* Kismet (1955)

Stranger in Paris *See* New Moon (1940)

Stranger Things Have Happened *See* Copacabana (1947)

Straw Hat Song *See* Holiday in Havana (1949)

Strawberry Fields Forever *See* Sgt. Pepper's Lonely Hearts Club Band (1978)

Street People *See* Breakin' (1984)

Street Singer *See* Maytime (1937)

Strengthen the Dwelling *See* The Happiest Millionaire (1967)

Strictly on the Corny Side *See* A Date with Judy (1948)

Strictly U.S.A. *See* Take Me Out to the Ball Game (1949)

Strike Up the Band *See* Strike Up the Band (1940)

Strike Up the Band, Here Comes a Sailor *See* Hello, Frisco, Hello (1943)

String of Pearls *See* The Glenn Miller Story (1954)

Student Drinking Song *See* Maytime (1937)

Students Are We *See* Good News (1947)

Stuff Like That There *See* For the Boys (1991)

Stuffed Animal *See* Pajama Party (1964)

Stumbling *See* Thoroughly Modern Millie (1967)

Style *See* Robin and the Seven Hoods (1964)

(Such an) Easy Question *See* Tickle Me (1965)

Suddenly *See* Xanadu (1980)

Sue Me *See* Guys and Dolls (1955)

Sugar *See* Pete Kelly's Blues (1955)

Summer In St. Louis *See* Meet Me in St. Louis (1944)

Summer Is Icumen In *See* Maytime (1937)

Summer Love *See* Jazz Singer (1980)

Summer Nights *See* Grease (1978)

Summer Serenade *See* Sweethearts (1938)

Summertime *See* Rhapsody in Blue (1945)

Summertime in Heidelberg *See* The Student Prince (1954)

Sun Showers *See* Broadway Melody of 1938 (1937)

Sun, Sun, Sun, Sun, Sun *See* Back to the Beach (1987)

Sunday *See* Flower Drum Song (1961)

Sunday Jumps *See* Royal Wedding (1951)

Sunday, Monday, and Always *See* Take It Big (1944)

Sunday, Monday, or Always? *See* The Road to Utopia (1946)

Sunflower Song *See* Kid from Brooklyn (1946)

Sunny *See* Sunny (1941)

Sunny *See* Till the Clouds Roll By (1946)

Sunny Days *See* Sunny Skies (1930)

Sunrise, Sunset *See* Fiddler on the Roof (1971)

Super-Heroes *See* The Rocky Horror Picture Show (1975)

Supercalifragilisticexpialidocious *See* Mary Poppins (1964)

Superstition Song *See* Lucky Me (1954)

Sur La Plage *See* The Boy Friend (1971)

Sure Thing *See* Cover Girl (1944)

Surfer's Holiday *See* Muscle Beach Party (1964)

Surfin' and a-Swingin' *See* Beach Party (1963)

Surfin' Bird *See* Back to the Beach (1987)

Surfin' Woodie *See* Muscle Beach Party (1964)

Surprise, Surprise *See* A Chorus Line (1985)

Surrender *See* Thunder Alley (1985)

Surrey with the Fringe on Top *See* Oklahoma! (1955)

Suspended in Time *See* Xanadu (1980)

The Swan *See* Funny Girl (1968)

Swanee *See* Jolson Sings Again (1949)

Swanee *See* The Jolson Story (1946)

Swanee *See* Rhapsody in Blue (1945)

Swanee *See* A Star is Born (1954)

Swanee River *See* Harmony Lane (1935)

Sweet 16 *See* Let's Go Collegiate (1941)

Sweet and Lovely *See* Two Girls and a Sailor (1944)

Sweet Charity *See* Sweet Charity (1969)

Sweet Cider Time *See* Hello, Frisco, Hello (1943)

Sweet Dreams *See* Sweet Dreams (1985)

Sweet Dreams of You *See* Coal Miner's Daughter (1980)

Sweet Dreams, Sweetheart *See* Hollywood Canteen (1944)

Sweet Ices, Papayas, Berry Man *See* The Pirate (1948)

Sweet Potato Piper *See* The Road to Singapore (1940)

Sweet Rosie O'Grady *See* Dance of Life (1929)

Sweet Rosie O'Grady *See* Sweet Rosie O'Grady (1943)

Sweet Sue *See* Rhythm Parade (1943)

Sweet Sue *See* Second Chorus (1940)

Sweet Transvestite *See* The Rocky Horror Picture Show (1975)

Sweethearts *See* The Great Caruso (1951)

Sweethearts *See* Sweethearts (1938)

Sweethearts *See* Three Daring Daughters (1948)

Sweethearts of America *See* Presenting Lily Mars (1943)

Swing Concerto *See* Second Chorus (1940)

Swing Low Sweet Chariot *See* Dimples (1936)

Swing Low, Sweet Chariot *See* Everybody Sing (1938)

Swing Low, Sweet Chariot *See* Nashville (1975)

Swing Me an Old-Fashioned Song *See* Little Miss Broadway (1938)

Swing, Mr. Mendelssohn, Swing *See* Everybody Sing (1938)

Swing the Jinx Away *See* I Dood It (1943)

Swing Trot *See* The Barkleys of Broadway (1949)

Swingin' Down the Lane *See* I'll See You in My Dreams (1951)

Swingin' On a Star *See* Going My Way (1944)

Swingin' the Jinx Away *See* Born to Dance (1936)

Switching It Off *See* Absolute Beginners (1986)

S'Wonderful *See* An American in Paris (1951)

S'Wonderful *See* Funny Face (1957)

S'Wonderful *See* Rhapsody in Blue (1945)

The Sword of Damocles *See* The Rocky Horror Picture Show (1975)

Sympathy *See* The Firefly (1937)

Syncopated Walk *See* The Story of Vernon and Irene Castle (1939)

Tahiti *See* Pagan Love Song (1950)

T'Ain't Nobody's Business If I Do *See* Lady Sings the Blues (1972)

Tait Song *See* Good News (1947)

Take a Memo to the Moon *See* Lucky Me (1954)

Take Back Your Mink *See* Guys and Dolls (1955)

Take Him *See* Pal Joey (1957)

Take It Big *See* Take It Big (1944)

Take it Easy *See* Two Girls and a Sailor (1944)

Take Me Back to New York Town *See* The Story of Vernon and Irene Castle (1939)

Take Me Out to the Ball Game *See* Take Me Out to the Ball Game (1949)

Take Me To Broadway *See* Small Town Girl (1953)

Take Me To The Fair *See* It Happened at the World's Fair (1963)

Take Ten Terrific Girls But Only 9 Costumes *See* The Night They Raided Minsky's (1969)

Taking a Chance on Love *See* Cabin in the Sky (1943)

Taking a Chance on Love *See* I Dood It (1943)

Taking a Chance on Love *See* New York, New York (1977)

Taking a Chance on Love *See* This Could Be the Night (1957)

Taking Miss Mary to the Ball *See* On an Island with You (1948)

Tales of Vienna Woods *See* The Great Waltz (1938)

Taliostro's Dance *See* DuBarry Was a Lady (1943)

Talk to the Animals *See* Doctor Dolittle (1967)

Tampico *See* Ship Ahoy (1942)

Tapedeck in His Tractor (The Cowboy Song) *See* Nashville (1975)

The Tapioca *See* Thoroughly Modern Millie (1967)

Tarantella *See* That Girl from Paris (1936)

Taste *See* Fast Forward (1984)

Tchaikovsky's "Fourth Symphony" *See* Three Daring Daughters (1948)

Tea Cup *See* International House (1933)

Tea For Two *See* Tea for Two (1950)

Team Work *See* Body Rock (1984)

Teamwork *See* The Road to Hong Kong (1962)

A Tear, a Kiss, a Smile *See* Dixiana (1930)

Tears On My Pillow *See* Grease (1978)

Ted Ain't Dead *See* Absolute Beginners (1986)

Teddy Bear *See* Loving You (1957)

Teddy Bears Picnic *See* Absolute Beginners (1986)

The Telephone Hour *See* Bye, Bye, Birdie (1963)

Tell Me *See* For Me and My Gal (1942)

Tell Me Why *See* A Hard Day's Night (1964)

Tell Me Why Nights Are Lonely *See* On Moonlight Bay (1951)

Tell Me With Your Eyes *See* Northwest Outpost (1947)

The Temple *See* Jesus Christ, Superstar (1973)

Tempo of the Trail *See* Spotlight Scandals (1943)

Temptation *See* A Date with Judy (1948)

Temptation *See* Going Hollywood (1933)

Temptation *See* The Seven Hills of Rome (1958)

Ten Cents a Dance *See* Love Me or Leave Me (1955)

Ten Pins in the Sky *See* Listen, Darling (1938)

Ten Thousand Cattle Straying *See* Let Freedom Ring (1939)

Ten Thousand Sheep *See* The West Point Story (1950)

Ten Year Montage *See* It's Always Fair Weather (1955)

Tender Love *See* Krush Groove (1985)

The Tender Trap *See* This Could Be the Night (1957)

A Tender Word Will Mend It All *See* Swing Parade of 1946 (1946)

Tenderly *See* Harvest Melody (1943)

Tess's Torch Song *See* Up in Arms (1944)

Tevye's Dream *See* Fiddler on the Roof (1971)

Tex Yeux *See* Rose Marie (1936)

Texas Tommy *See* The Story of Vernon and Irene Castle (1939)

Thank God It's Friday *See* Thank God It's Friday (1978)

Thank Heaven For Little Girls *See* Gigi (1958)

Thank Heaven For You *See* International House (1933)

Thank You For the Use of the Hall *See* Little Miss Broadway (1938)

Thank You Very Much *See* Scrooge (1970)

Thank Your Lucky Stars *See* Thank Your Lucky Stars (1943)

Thank Your Lucky Stars and Stripes *See* Playmates (1941)

Thanks A Lot But No Thanks *See* It's Always Fair Weather (1955)

Thanks to the Rolling Sea *See* Girls! Girls! Girls! (1962)

That Ain't Right *See* Stormy Weather (1943)

That International Rag *See* Alexander's Ragtime Band (1938)

That Lucky Fellow *See* Broadway Rhythm (1944)

That Old Black Magic *See* Meet Danny Wilson (1952)

That Old Devil Moon *See* Finian's Rainbow (1968)

That Old Feeling *See* Vogues of 1938 (1937)

That Terrific Rainbow *See* Pal Joey (1957)

That What the Well-Dressed Man in Harlem Will Wear *See* This is the Army (1943)

That'll Be the Day *See* The Buddy Holly Story (1978)

That's All There Is, Folks *See* On the Town (1949)

That's Entertainment *See* The Band Wagon (1953)

That's For Me *See* State Fair (1945)

That's for Me *See* State Fair (1962)

That's Him *See* One Touch of Venus (1948)

That's How I Need You *See* Two Weeks with Love (1950)

That's Motivation *See* Absolute Beginners (1986)

That's the Best of All *See* Cover Girl (1944)

That's The Hawaiian In Me *See* Hawaii Calls (1938)

That's the Moon My Son *See* Private Buckaroo (1942)

That's the Rhythm of the Day *See* Dancing Lady (1933)

That's What I Call a Healthy Girl *See* How to Stuff a Wild Bikini (1965)

That's What I Want For Christmas *See* Stowaway (1936)

That's What Love Is *See* Surf Party (1964)

That's What Rainy Day is For *See* Easy to Love (1953)

That's What You Jolly Well Get *See* Thank Your Lucky Stars (1943)

Theatre Lobby Number *See* Up in Arms (1944)

Them There Eyes *See* Lady Sings the Blues (1972)

The Theme From the Wonderful World of the Brothers Grimm *See* The Wonderful World of the Brothers Grimm (1962)

Then We Are Decided *See* Jesus Christ, Superstar (1973)

Then You May Take Me to the Fair *See* Camelot (1967)

Then You'll Be Home *See* Mr. Music (1950)

Then You'll Remember Me *See* Song O' My Heart (1929)

There Ain't Nothing Like a Song *See* Speedway (1968)

There Are Those *See* The Happiest Millionaire (1967)

There Are Worse Things I Could Do *See* Grease (1978)

There Comes a Time *See* I Married an Angel (1942)

There Goes My Heart *See* The Heat's On (1943)

There Goes That Guitar *See* The Heat's On (1943)

There Goes the Ball Game *See* New York, New York (1977)

There Has to Be a Reason *See* Pajama Party (1964)

There Is Nothing Like a Dame *See* South Pacific (1958)

There Must Be Someone Waiting For Me *See* Glorifying the American Girl (1930)

There Once Was a Man *See* Pajama Game (1957)

There Will Never Be Another You *See* Iceland (1942)

There'll Be Some Changes Made *See* All That Jazz (1979)

There'll Come A Time *See* The Great Waltz (1938)

There's a Brand New Day on the Horizon *See* Roustabout (1964)

There's a Coach Comin' In *See* Paint Your Wagon (1969)

There's A Doctor *See* Tommy (1975)

There's a King of Hush *See* Mrs. Brown, You've Got a Lovely Daughter (1968)

There's a Rainbow Round My Shoulder *See* The Jolson Story (1946)

There's a Rising Moon For Every Falling Star *See* Young at Heart (1954)

There's a Small Hotel *See* Pal Joey (1957)

There's Beauty Everywhere *See* Ziegfeld Follies (1946)

There's Danger in Your Eyes, Cherie *See* Rich, Young and Pretty (1951)

There's Gonna Be a Party Tonight *See* The Seven Hills of Rome (1958)

There's Gotta Be Something Better Than This *See* Sweet Charity (1969)

(There's) No Room To Rhumba (In A Sports Car) *See* Fun in Acapulco (1963)

There's No Tomorrow *See* Two Tickets to Broadway (1951)

There's No Two Ways About Love *See* Stormy Weather (1943)

There's Nothing Like Love *See* My Sister Eileen (1955)

There's Something About an Empty Chair *See* Damn Yankees (1958)

They All Laughed *See* Shall We Dance (1937)

They Call Me Wicked Lola *See* The Blue Angel (1930)

They Call the Wind Maria *See* Paint Your Wagon (1969)

They Can't Take That Away From Me *See* The Barkleys of Broadway (1949)

They Can't Take That Away From Me *See* Shall We Dance (1937)

They Chopped Down the Old Apple Tree *See* Around the World (1943)

They Didn't Believe Me *See* That Midnight Kiss (1949)

They Didn't Believe Me *See* Till the Clouds Roll By (1946)

They Go Wild, Simply Wild Over Me *See* For Me and My Gal (1942)

They Obviously Want Me to Sing *See* The Lemon Drop Kid (1951)

They Remind Me Too Much Of You *See* It Happened at the World's Fair (1963)

They'll Never Outfox the Fox *See* Court Jester (1956)

They're Either Too Young or Too Old *See* Thank Your Lucky Stars (1943)

They're Wearing 'Em Higher in Hawaii *See* Show Business (1944)

Things Are Looking Up *See* A Damsel in Distress (1937)

Think Pink *See* Funny Face (1957)

Thinking of You *See* DuBarry Was a Lady (1943)

Thinking of You *See* Three Little Words (1950)

This Boy *See* A Hard Day's Night (1964)

This Can't Be Love *See* Billy Rose's Jumbo (1962)

This Could Be the Night *See* Beat Street (1984)

This Could Be The Night *See* This Could Be the Night (1957)

This Heart is Mine *See* Ziegfeld Follies (1946)

This Is A Happy Little Ditty *See* Just Around the Corner (1938)

This Is Living *See* Kid Galahad (1962)

This Is My Heaven *See* Paradise, Hawaiian Style (1966)

This Is My World *See* Half a Sixpence (1967)

This Is One of Those Moments *See* Yentl (1983)

This Is Our Last Night Together *See* Stand Up and Cheer (1934)

This is the Army, Mr. Jones *See* This is the Army (1943)

This is the Day for Love *See* Yolanda and the Thief (1945)

This is the Hour *See* Melody Cruise (1932)

This Is the Life *See* Alexander's Ragtime Band (1938)

This Isn't Heaven *See* State Fair (1962)

This Jesus Must Die *See* Jesus Christ, Superstar (1973)

This Looks Familiar *See* The Muppet Movie (1979)

This May Be the Night *See* My Lucky Star (1938)

This Must Be Heaven *See* Love Songs (1985)

This Nearly Was Mine *See* South Pacific (1958)

This Night Was Made For Dreaming *See* Honolulu (1939)

This Time is the Last Time *See* This is the Army (1943)

This Time of Year *See* Finian's Rainbow (1968)

This Year's Kisses *See* On the Avenue (1937)

Thoity Poiple Boids *See* Follies Girl (1943)

Thoroughly Modern Millie *See* Thoroughly Modern Millie (1967)

Those Endearing Young Charms *See* The Affairs of Dobie Gillis (1953)

Those Magic Changes *See* Grease (1978)

Those Were the Good Old Days *See* Damn Yankees (1958)

Threatening Witch *See* The Wizard of Oz (1939)

Three Blind Mice *See* Holiday in Mexico (1946)

Three Blind Mice *See* Rose Marie (1936)

The Three B's (Barrelhouse, Boogie Woogie, and the Blues) *See* Best Foot Forward (1943)

The Three Caballeros *See* The Three Caballeros (1945)

Three Little Sisters *See* Private Buckaroo (1942)

Three Little Words *See* Three Little Words (1950)

Three Men on a Date *See* Best Foot Forward (1943)

Three O'Clock in the Morning *See* Presenting Lily Mars (1943)

Three O'Clock in the Morning *See* That Midnight Kiss (1949)

Three There Were *See* Song of Norway (1970)

The Thrill of a New Romance See Two Girls and a Sailor (1944)

The Thrill of a Romance See Thrill of a Romance (1945)

Through Your Eyes to Your Heart See Delightfully Dangerous (1945)

Thumbelina See Hans Christian Andersen (1952)

Thunder Alley See Thunder Alley (1985)

Tibetan Jam See Breakin' (1984)

Tic Tac Do Meu Coracao See Springtime in the Rockies (1942)

Tic, Tic, Tic See My Dream is Yours (1949)

Ticket To Ride See Help! (1965)

Tico Tico See Club Havana (1946)

Tico Tico See Copacabana (1947)

Tico-Tico See Bathing Beauty (1944)

The Tight Rope See The Pirate (1948)

Till My Love Comes Back to Me See Young at Heart (1954)

Till the Clouds Roll By See Till the Clouds Roll By (1946)

Till Then See 1776 (1972)

Till There Way You See The Music Man (1962)

Till We Meet Again See For Me and My Gal (1942)

Till We Meet Again See On Moonlight Bay (1951)

Time Alone Will Tell See Pin-Up Girl (1944)

Time and Time Again See Nancy Goes to Rio (1950)

Time Changes Everything See Broadway Serenade (1939)

Time For Christmas See The Christmas That Almost Wasn't (1966)

The Time For Parting See It's Always Fair Weather (1955)

Time for Tea See New Faces of 1952 (1954)

Time On My Hands See Look for the Silver Lining (1949)

The Time Warp See The Rocky Horror Picture Show (1975)

Tina Lina See The Toast of New Orleans (1950)

Tinkle, Tinkle, Tinkle See Evergreen (1934)

Tira Lira La See I Married an Angel (1942)

Tired of It All See Hips, Hips, Hooray (1934)

'Tis the Last Rose of Summer See The Great Caruso (1951)

Tis the Last Rose of Summer See One Night of Love (1934)

A Tisket, A Tasket See Ride 'Em Cowboy (1942)

T.K. and Jessie Rap See Knights of the City (1985)

To Count Palaffi See I Married an Angel (1942)

To Life See Fiddler on the Roof (1971)

To Love or Not to Love See Rosalie (1938)

To Me See The Fabulous Dorseys (1947)

To See You See The Road to Bali (1953)

To the Inn We're Marching See The Student Prince (1954)

The Toast of New Orleans See The Toast of New Orleans (1950)

Toccata & Fugue in D See Fantasia (1940)

Today I Love Everybody See The Farmer Takes a Wife (1953)

Today I'm A Debutante See Higher and Higher (1944)

Today It Rained Champagne See Tommy (1975)

Today, Tomorrow and Forever See Viva Las Vegas (1963)

Todos Vuelven See Crossover Dreams (1985)

Together See Keep 'Em Flying (1941)

Together, Wherever We Go See Gypsy (1993)

Tom, Dick, or Harry See Kiss Me Kate (1953)

Tom Sawyer See Tom Sawyer (1973)

Tom, Tom the Piper's Son See Presenting Lily Mars (1943)

Tommy Can You Hear Me? See Tommy (1975)

Tommy's Holiday Camp See Tommy (1975)

Tomorrow See Annie (1982)

Tomorrow Belongs to Me See Cabaret (1972)

Tomorrow is Another Day See A Day at the Races (1937)

Tomorrow Night See Yentl (1983)

Tonight See West Side Story (1961)

Tonight and Every Night See Tonight and Every Night (1945)

Tonight Is So Right For Love See G.I. Blues (1960)

Tonight Will Teach Me to Forget See The Merry Widow (1934)

Too Bad See Silk Stockings (1957)

Too Darn Hot See Kiss Me Kate (1953)

Too Late Now See Royal Wedding (1951)

Too Marvelous for Words See Young Man with a Horn (1950)

Too Much Mustard See The Story of Vernon and Irene Castle (1939)

Too-ra-loo-ra-loo-ra See Going My Way (1944)

Too Romantic See The Road to Singapore (1940)

Toot Sweet See Chitty Chitty Bang Bang (1968)

Toot Toot Tootsie Goodbye See The Jolson Story (1946)

Toot Toot Tootsie Goodbye See Rose of Washington Square (1939)

Toot, Toot, Tootsie Goodbye See I'll See You in My Dreams (1951)

Toot, Toot, Tootsie Goodbye See Jazz Singer (1927)

Toot, Toot, Tootsie Goodbye See Jolson Sings Again (1949)

Tootin' My Own Horn See Rhythm Parade (1943)

Top Hat White Tie and Tails See Le Bal (1982)

Top Hat, White Tie and Tails See Top Hat (1935)

Toreador Song See Broadway Melody of 1938 (1937)

Torna a Surriento See The Great Caruso (1951)

Torpedo Joe See Melody Ranch (1940)

Totem Tom Tom See Rose Marie (1936)

Totem Tom Tom See Rose Marie (1954)

Toto's Chase See The Wizard of Oz (1939)

Touch-a Touch-a Touch-a Touch Me See The Rocky Horror Picture Show (1975)

The Touch of Your Hand See Lovely to Look At (1952)

The Touch of Your Hand See Roberta (1935)

A Toujours See Gigi (1958)

The Tourist Trade See Romance on the High Seas (1948)

Tra-La-La See An American in Paris (1951)

Tra-La-La See Escape to Paradise (1939)

Tradition See Fiddler on the Roof (1971)

Tramp, Tramp, Tramp See Naughty Marietta (1935)

Trapped in a Stairway See Thank God It's Friday (1978)

Treat Him Nicely See Beach Party (1963)

Treat Me Nice See Jailhouse Rock (1957)

Treat Me Rough See Girl Crazy (1943)

Tres Jolie Waltz See The Story of Vernon and Irene Castle (1939)

Trial Before Pilate See Jesus Christ, Superstar (1973)

Triplets See The Band Wagon (1953)

Trolley Song See Meet Me in St. Louis (1944)

Tropical Magic See Week-End In Havana (1941)

Trouble See King Creole (1958)

Trouble See The Music Man (1962)

Trouble in the U.S.A. See Nashville (1975)

The Trouble with Women See One Touch of Venus (1948)

Troubles of the World See New Moon (1940)

Truckin See The Cotton Club (1984)

True Blue Lou See Dance of Life (1929)

True Love See High Society (1956)

Truly Scrumptious See Chitty Chitty Bang Bang (1968)

Trumpet Blues See Bathing Beauty (1944)

Trumpet Boogie See This Could Be the Night (1957)

Truthful Parson Brown See Broadway Melody (1929)

Try to Forget See The Cat and the Fiddle (1934)

Try To See It My Way See Dames (1934)

Tu Carino (Carmen's Theme) See Beat Street (1984)

Tulip Time See The Great Ziegfeld (1936)

Tumblin' Tumbleweeds See Hollywood Canteen (1944)

Tunnel of Love See Let's Dance (1950)

Turkey in the Straw See Stars and Stripes Forever (1952)

Turn on the Old Music Box See Pinocchio (1940)

Turn On the Red Hot Heat (Burn the Blues Away) See Vogues of 1938 (1937)

Turtles, Berries and Gumbo See King Creole (1958)

Tutti Frutti See Le Bal (1982)

Tuxedo Junction See The Glenn Miller Story (1954)

'Twas Not So Long Ago See Sweet Adeline (1935)

A Twinkle in Your Eye See I Married an Angel (1942)

Twinkle, Twinkle, Little Star See Hats Off (1937)

Twixt Myself and Me See A Connecticut Yankee in King Arthur's Court (1949)

Two Blind Loves See At the Circus (1939)

Two Dreams Met See Down Argentine Way (1940)

Two Hundred Years See Nashville (1975)

Two Ladies See Cabaret (1972)

Two Little Bluebirds See Sunny (1941)

A (Two) Little Girl(s) From Little Rock See Gentlemen Prefer Blondes (1953)

Two Little Girls in Blue See Sweet Rosie O'Grady (1943)

Two Lost Souls See Damn Yankees (1958)

Two Lovers Met in the Night See Romance on the High Seas (1948)

Two O'Clock Jump See Best Foot Forward (1943)

Two of a Kind See Rappin' (1985)

Two Soliloquies See South Pacific (1958)

Two Strong Men See Lottery Bride (1930)

A Typical Day See Li'l Abner (1959)

The Ugly Duckling See Hans Christian Andersen (1952)

Ukelele Lady See I'll See You in My Dreams (1951)

Un Bel Di See Broadway Serenade (1939)

Un bel di See One Night of Love (1934)

Un Sospiro See Song Without End (1960)

Una Furtiva Lacrima See That Midnight Kiss (1949)

Una Voce Poco Fa See That Girl from Paris (1936)

Uncle Tom's Cabin *See* The Naughty Nineties (1945)

Under the Anheuser Bush *See* Meet Me in St. Louis (1944)

Under the Bamboo Tree *See* Meet Me in St. Louis (1944)

Under the Gun *See* Songwriter (1984)

Under the Sea *See* The Little Mermaid (1989)

Underture *See* Tommy (1975)

Une Dame Noble Et Sage *See* Maytime (1937)

Unnecessary Town *See* Li'l Abner (1959)

Up In the Clouds *See* Three Little Words (1950)

Up Where the People Are *See* The Unsinkable Molly Brown (1964)

Upholstery *See* Phantom of the Paradise (1974)

Us Girls *See* Beat Street (1984)

Uskadara *See* New Faces of 1952 (1954)

V-J Stomp *See* New York, New York (1977)

Va Va Voom *See* Absolute Beginners (1986)

Vagabond King Waltz *See* I'll Cry Tomorrow (1955)

Valentine Candy *See* The Happiest Millionaire (1967)

Valse In A Flat, Opus 34, No. 1 *See* A Song to Remember (1945)

Valse in D Flat (Minute Waltz) *See* A Song to Remember (1945)

Valse Oubliee *See* Song Without End (1960)

The Vamp *See* Rose of Washington Square (1939)

Vanishing Point *See* Body Rock (1984)

Variations on "I Got Rhythm" (instrumental) *See* Rhapsody in Blue (1945)

Varsity Drag *See* Good News (1947)

The Vegetarian *See* Doctor Dolittle (1967)

Venezia *See* Athena (1954)

Venezia e Napoli *See* Song Without End (1960)

A Very Merry Un-Birthday *See* Alice in Wonderland (1951)

The Very Thought of You *See* Young Man with a Horn (1950)

Vesti La Giubba *See* For the First Time (1959)

Vesti la Giubba *See* The Great Caruso (1951)

Vilia *See* The Merry Widow (1934)

Vino, Dinero y Amor *See* Fun in Acapulco (1963)

Virginia Ham and Eggs *See* Maytime (1937)

Viva Las Vegas *See* Viva Las Vegas (1963)

Vive L'Amour *See* Thrill of a Romance (1945)

Vive l'Opera *See* Maytime (1937)

Vocalize *See* Athena (1954)

Voices of Spring *See* The Great Waltz (1938)

Voila *See* The Three Musketeers (1939)

Volare *See* Absolute Beginners (1986)

Voodoo Moon *See* Hollywood Canteen (1944)

Vote for Autry *See* Melody Ranch (1940)

Wailing *See* New Moon (1940)

Wait and See *See* The Harvey Girls (1946)

Wait For Me *See* The Night They Raided Minsky's (1969)

Wait Till the Sun Shines Nellie *See* In the Good Old Summertime (1949)

Wait Till the Sun Shines Nellie *See* Rhythm Parade (1943)

Wait Till You See Paris *See* The French Line (1954)

Waitin' at the Gate for Katy *See* The Fabulous Dorseys (1947)

Waitin' For My Dearie *See* Brigadoon (1954)

Waitin' for the Robert E. Lee *See* The Story of Vernon and Irene Castle (1939)

Waiting at the Church *See* Sweet Rosie O'Grady (1943)

Waiting for the Robert E. Lee *See* Babes on Broadway (1941)

Waiting for the Robert E. Lee *See* Jazz Singer (1927)

Waiting for the Robert E. Lee *See* The Jolson Story (1946)

Wake Up Jacob *See* Ride 'Em Cowboy (1942)

Waking Up *See* Staying Alive (1983)

Walk Through the World *See* Goodbye, Mr. Chips (1969)

Walkin Down Broadway *See* Strike Up the Band (1940)

Walking After Midnight *See* Sweet Dreams (1985)

Walking Arm in Arm With Jim *See* Girl Rush (1944)

Walking the Dog *See* Shall We Dance (1937)

Walls *See* Marco (1973)

The Walls Have Ears *See* Girls! Girls! Girls! (1962)

Walter Winchell Rhumba *See* Holiday in Mexico (1946)

Walter's Gavotte *See* Hello, Dolly! (1969)

Waltz In C Sharp Minor, Opus 64, No. 2 *See* A Song to Remember (1945)

Waltz in D Flat, Opus 64, No. 1 *See* They Shall Have Music (1939)

Waltz in Swing Time *See* Swing Time (1936)

Waltz Serenade *See* Anchors Aweigh (1945)

Wandrin' Star *See* Paint Your Wagon (1969)

Wanna Find a Boy *See* Sunny Skies (1930)

Wanna Sing Like an Angel *See* Lucky Me (1954)

Wanting You *See* New Moon (1940)

Warm Hands, Cold Heart *See* Duchess of Idaho (1950)

Warmer Than a Whisper *See* The Road to Hong Kong (1962)

The Warmest Baby in the Bunch *See* Yankee Doodle Dandy (1942)

Wash Your Neck With a Cake of Peck's *See* The Poor Little Rich Girl (1936)

Washington Post *See* Stars and Stripes Forever (1952)

Washington Post March *See* Show Boat (1936)

Wasn't I There? *See* Mr. Music (1950)

Watch Closely Now *See* A Star is Born (1976)

Watch Your Footwork *See* The Happiest Millionaire (1967)

Water Nymph *See* The Goldwyn Follies (1938)

Watusi *See* Sun Ra & His Intergalactic Solar Arkestra: Space is the Place (1974)

Way Down Yonder in New Orleans *See* The Story of Vernon and Irene Castle (1939)

The Way He Makes Me Feel *See* Yentl (1983)

The Way They Do It in Paris *See* New Moon (1940)

The Way You Look Tonight *See* Swing Time (1936)

We Can Dance *See* Love Songs (1985)

(We Dance) So Close to the Fire *See* Staying Alive (1983)

We Don't Want The Bacon *See* For Me and My Gal (1942)

We Go Together *See* Grease (1978)

We Got Annie *See* Annie (1982)

We Gotta Keep Up With the Joneses *See* The Girl Most Likely (1957)

We Hate to Leave *See* Anchors Aweigh (1945)

We Have Never Met As Of Yet *See* I Love Melvin (1953)

We Kiss in a Shadow *See* The King and I (1956)

We Meet in the Funniest Places *See* Stage Door Canteen (1943)

We Mustn't Say Goodbye *See* Stage Door Canteen (1943)

We Need a Little Christmas *See* Mame (1974)

We Never Dream the Same Dream Twice *See* Melody Ranch (1940)

We Never Talk Much *See* Rich, Young and Pretty (1951)

We Open in Venice *See* Kiss Me Kate (1953)

We Saw the Sea *See* Follow the Fleet (1936)

We Should Be Together *See* Little Miss Broadway (1938)

We Were So Young *See* Sweet Adeline (1935)

We Will Fight *See* Skirts Ahoy! (1952)

We Will Rock You *See* FM (1978)

Weary *See* Northwest Outpost (1947)

Weary Blues *See* Summer Holiday (1948)

The Web of Love *See* The Great Gabbo (1929)

We'd Like to Go On A Trip *See* Lullaby of Broadway (1951)

Wedding Cake Walk *See* You'll Never Get Rich (1941)

Wedding Celebration *See* Fiddler on the Roof (1971)

Wedding Dance *See* Brigadoon (1954)

Wedding in the Spring *See* You Were Never Lovelier (1942)

The Wedding of the Painted Doll *See* Broadway Melody (1929)

Wedding of the Painted Doll *See* Singin' in the Rain (1952)

Wedding Samba *See* On an Island with You (1948)

Wedding Song *See* The Rocky Horror Picture Show (1975)

A Weekend in Havana *See* Week-End In Havana (1941)

A Weekend in the Country *See* The Barkleys of Broadway (1949)

Welcome *See* Tommy (1975)

Welcome, Burleigh *See* Kid from Brooklyn (1946)

Welcome Egghead *See* Daddy Long Legs (1955)

Welcome to My Dreams *See* The Road to Utopia (1946)

A Welcome Toast *See* Song of Norway (1970)

Well All Right *See* The Buddy Holly Story (1978)

We'll Be Together, Mama *See* Girls! Girls! Girls! (1962)

Well, Did You Evah *See* DuBarry Was a Lady (1943)

Well, Did You Evah? *See* High Society (1956)

Well, I'll Be Switched *See* The French Line (1954)

We'll Make Hay While the Sun Shines *See* Going Hollywood (1933)

The Wells Fargo Wagon *See* The Music Man (1962)

We're Back in Circulation Again *See* One in a Million (1936)

We're Coming in Loaded *See* Girls! Girls! Girls! (1962)

We're Doing it for the Natives in Jamaica *See* The Farmer Takes a Wife (1953)

We're Having a Baby *See* Hollywood Canteen (1944)

We're in Business *See* The Farmer Takes a Wife (1953)

We're in the Money *See* Gold Diggers of 1933 (1933)

We're In The Navy *See* In the Navy (1941)

We're Living the Life We Love *See* If You Knew Susie (1948)

We're Not Gonna Take It *See* Tommy (1975)

We're Off to See the Wizard *See* The Wizard of Oz (1939)

We're On Our Way to France *See* Alexander's Ragtime Band (1938)

We're On Our Way to France *See* This is the Army (1943)

We're On the Road to Hong Kong *See* The Road to Hong Kong (1962)

We're Out of the Red *See* Stand Up and Cheer (1934)

We're Staying Home Tonight *See* Thank Your Lucky Stars (1943)

Were Thine That Special Face *See* Kiss Me Kate (1953)

We've Come to Copa *See* Copacabana (1947)

We've Got a Job to Do *See* Private Buckaroo (1942)

Whad Do I Care for a Dame? *See* Pal Joey (1957)

What a Little Moonlight Can Do *See* Lady Sings the Blues (1972)

What a Lot of Flowers *See* Goodbye, Mr. Chips (1969)

What A Lovely Day For A Wedding *See* Royal Wedding (1951)

What a Rumba Does to Romance *See* College Swing (1938)

What About the Boy? *See* Tommy (1975)

What Are Children Like When They're Fast Asleep? *See* The Christmas That Almost Wasn't (1966)

What Are Cowboys Made Of? *See* Melody Ranch (1940)

What Are We Going to Do? *See* Song of Nevada (1944)

What Are You Doin' the Rest of Your Life *See* Hollywood Canteen (1944)

What Are You Going to Do to Help the Boys? *See* For Me and My Gal (1942)

What Can I Do For You? *See* Moon Over Miami (1941)

What Can I Say After I Say I'm Sorry? *See* Pete Kelly's Blues (1955)

What Can You Do With a General *See* White Christmas (1954)

What Did I Have That I Don't Have? *See* On a Clear Day You Can See Forever (1970)

What Did Romeo Say to Juliet? *See* College Swing (1938)

What Do I Do Now? (Gooch's Sont) *See* Mame (1974)

What Do I Want With Money? *See* If You Knew Susie (1948)

What Do the Simple Folk Do? *See* Camelot (1967)

What Do You Think I Am? *See* Broadway Rhythm (1944)

What Do You Want With Money? *See* Hallelujah, I'm a Bum (1933)

What Does an English Girl Think of a Yank *See* Tonight and Every Night (1945)

What Does He Look Like? *See* This is the Army (1943)

What Every Woman Lives For *See* Frankie and Johnny (1965)

What Good is a Gal Without a Guy? *See* Skirts Ahoy! (1952)

What I Did for Love *See* A Chorus Line (1985)

What I Wouldn't Do For That Man *See* Glorifying the American Girl (1930)

What is a Circus *See* Billy Rose's Jumbo (1962)

What Is This That I Feel? *See* The French Line (1954)

What Is This Thing Called Love *See* Night and Day (1946)

What Makes a WAVE? *See* Skirts Ahoy! (1952)

What Makes the Sun Set? *See* Anchors Aweigh (1945)

What Shall I Do with Today? *See* Goodbye, Mr. Chips (1969)

What Shouldn't Happen to a Dog *See* The Old Curiosity Shop (1975)

What Would I Do If I Could Feel? *See* The Wiz (1978)

What'd I Say? *See* Ballad in Blue (1966)

What'd I Say *See* Viva Las Vegas (1963)

Whatever Happened to Saturday Night *See* The Rocky Horror Picture Show (1975)

Whatever Lola Wants *See* Damn Yankees (1958)

What'll I Do? *See* Alexander's Ragtime Band (1938)

What's Cookin *See* Seaside Swingers (1965)

What's Good About Goodnight *See* Joy of Living (1938)

What's She Really Like? *See* G.I. Blues (1960)

What's So Good About Morning? *See* Bundle of Joy (1956)

What's The Buzz? *See* Jesus Christ, Superstar (1973)

What's the Use of Wond'rin *See* Carousel (1956)

What's Wrong With That? *See* The Happiest Millionaire (1967)

Wheels of Love *See* Girl in Gold Boots (1969)

Wheels on My Heels *See* Roustabout (1964)

When a Felon Needs a Friend *See* The Old Curiosity Shop (1975)

When a Maid Comes Knocking at Your Heart *See* The Firefly (1937)

When A Man Has a Daughter *See* The Happiest Millionaire (1967)

When A Man Loves a Woman *See* The Rose (1979)

When I Am Older *See* Goodbye, Mr. Chips (1969)

When I Close My Door *See* The Farmer Takes a Wife (1953)

When I Grow Too Old to Dream *See* Deep in My Heart (1954)

When I Look at You *See* Presenting Lily Mars (1943)

When I Look in Your Eyes *See* Doctor Dolittle (1967)

When I Love, I Love *See* Week-End In Havana (1941)

When I Marry Mister Snow *See* Carousel (1956)

When I Was Younger *See* Goodbye, Mr. Chips (1969)

When I.C.U. *See* Breakin' 2: Electric Boogaloo (1984)

When I'm 64 *See* Sgt. Pepper's Lonely Hearts Club Band (1978)

When I'm Not Near the Girl I Love *See* Finian's Rainbow (1968)

When I'm Out With the Belle of New York *See* The Belle of New York (1952)

When I'm Sixty Four *See* Yellow Submarine (1968)

When I'm with You *See* The Poor Little Rich Girl (1936)

When Irish Eyes Are Smiling *See* Let Freedom Ring (1939)

When Is Sometime? *See* A Connecticut Yankee in King Arthur's Court (1949)

When It's Cactus Time in Arizona *See* Girl Crazy (1943)

When Johnny Comes Marching Home *See* For Me and My Gal (1942)

When Love Comes Swingin' *See* How to Stuff a Wild Bikini (1965)

When Love Goes Wrong *See* Gentlemen Prefer Blondes (1953)

When My Ship Comes In *See* Kid Millions (1934)

When Somebody Thinks You're Wonderful *See* Scared Stiff (1953)

When Television Comes *See* Ziegfeld Follies (1946)

When the Children Are Asleep *See* Carousel (1956)

When the Idle Poor Become the Idle Rich *See* Finian's Rainbow (1968)

When the Midnight Choo-Choo Leaves for Alabam' *See* Alexander's Ragtime Band (1938)

When the Midnight Choo-Choo Leaves for Alabam *See* Easter Parade (1948)

When the Midnight Choo-Choo Leaves for Alabam *See* There's No Business Like Show Business (1954)

When The Red Red Robin Comes Bob Bob Bobbin' Along *See* I'll Cry Tomorrow (1955)

When the Red Red Robin Comes Bob Bob Bobbin' Along *See* Jolson Sings Again (1949)

When the Saints Go Marching In *See* The Five Pennies (1959)

When the Saints Go Marching In *See* Frankie and Johnny (1965)

When the Saints Go Marching In *See* The Seven Hills of Rome (1958)

When the Wine Is Full of Fire *See* The Firefly (1937)

When We Wed *See* Song of Norway (1970)

When Winter Comes *See* Second Fiddle (1939)

When You and I Were Young, Maggie *See* The Fabulous Dorseys (1947)

When You Love Someone *See* Here Come the Girls (1953)

When You Were a Smile on Your Mother's Lips and a Twinkle in Your Father's Eye *See* Dames (1934)

When You Were Sweet Sixteen *See* The Jolson Story (1946)

When You Were Sweet Sixteen *See* Little Miss Broadway (1938)

When You Wish Upon a Star *See* Pinocchio (1940)

When You Wore A Tulip *See* For Me and My Gal (1942)

When You Wore a Tulip *See* Hello, Frisco, Hello (1943)

When You're Dancing the Waltz *See* Dancing Pirate (1936)

When You're In Love *See* Seven Brides for Seven Brothers (1954)

When You're Smiling *See* Meet Danny Wilson (1952)

When You've Got a Little Springtime in Your Heart *See* Evergreen (1934)

Whenever You're Away From Me *See* Xanadu (1980)

Where Am I Going? *See* Sweet Charity (1969)

Where Are the Words? *See* Doctor Dolittle (1967)

Where Did I Go Wrong? *See* Pajama Party (1964)

Where Did My Childhood Go *See* Goodbye, Mr. Chips (1969)

Where Did You Get That Girl? *See* Three Little Words (1950)

Where Did You Learn To Dance? *See* I Love Melvin (1953)

Where Do They Come From Now *See* Murder at the Vanities (1934)

Where Do We Come From? *See* Girls! Girls! Girls! (1962)

Where Do We Go From Here? *See* For Me and My Gal (1942)

Where Does Love Begin? *See* Step Lively (1944)

Where Else But Here *See* Let Freedom Ring (1939)

Where Have You Been All My Life? *See* Hats Off (1937)

Where Is a Man *See* The First Nudie Musical (1975)

Where Is It Written *See* Yentl (1983)

Where Is Love? *See* Oliver! (1968)

Where Is The Life That Late I Led? *See* Kiss Me Kate (1953)

Where or When *See* Babes in Arms (1939)

Where There's Love *See* Three Daring Daughters (1948)

Where There's Music *See* Presenting Lily Mars (1943)

Where You Are *See* The Great American Broadcast (1941)

Where's the Mate For Me? *See* Show Boat (1936)

Wherever You Are *See* Four Jacks and a Jill (1941)

While Strolling in the Park One Day *See* Show Business (1944)

While They Were Dancing Around *See* The Story of Vernon and Irene Castle (1939)

Whip-Poor-Will *See* Look for the Silver Lining (1949)

Whistle While You Work *See* Snow White and the Seven Dwarfs (1937)

Whistling Away the Dark *See* Darling Lili (1970)

A Whistling Tune *See* Kid Galahad (1962)

White Christmas *See* Holiday Inn (1942)

White Christmas *See* White Christmas (1954)

The White Keys and the Black Keys *See* The Heat's On (1943)

Who? *See* Sunny (1941)

Who? *See* Till the Clouds Roll By (1946)

Who Are We to Say *See* Girl of the Golden West (1938)

Who Are We to Say Reprise *See* Girl of the Golden West (1938)

Who Killed Vaudeville? *See* George White's Scandals (1945)

Who Knows? *See* Rosalie (1938)

Who Needs Money? *See* Clambake (1967)

Who Wants to Be a Millionaire? *See* High Society (1956)

Who Will Be With You When I'm Far Away? *See* Two Girls and a Sailor (1944)

Who Will Buy? *See* Oliver! (1968)

A Whole New World *See* Aladdin (1992)

Who'll Buy My Memories *See* Songwriter (1984)

Whoop-Ti-Ay *See* Paint Your Wagon (1969)

Who's Afraid of Love *See* One in a Million (1936)

Who's Complaining? *See* Cover Girl (1944)

Who's Got the Pain *See* Damn Yankees (1958)

Who's Sorry Now? *See* Three Little Words (1950)

Who's Your Little Whozis? *See* The Stooge (1951)

Whose Side Are You On? *See* The Rose (1979)

Why Am I Blue *See* Show Business (1944)

Why Am I So Gone (About That Gal?) *See* Les Girls (1957)

Why Are We Here? (Blue Danube) *See* It's Always Fair Weather (1955)

Why? Because *See* Everybody Sing (1938)

Why Can't Every Day Be Christmas? *See* The Christmas That Almost Wasn't (1966)

Why Can't I? *See* Billy Rose's Jumbo (1962)

Why Can't the English? *See* My Fair Lady (1964)

Why Can't You Behave *See* Kiss Me Kate (1953)

Why Do I Love You *See* Show Boat (1936)

Why Do I Love You? *See* Show Boat (1951)

Why Do They Always Pick On Me? *See* Hello, Frisco, Hello (1943)

Why Do You Want to Break My Heart? *See* Body Rock (1984)

Why Don't You Do Right? *See* Stage Door Canteen (1943)

Why Fight the Feeling? *See* Let's Dance (1950)

Why is Love So Crazy *See* Pagan Love Song (1950)

Why Is the Desert (Lovely to See)? *See* The Little Prince (1974)

Why Must There Be an Opening Song? *See* Step Lively (1944)

Why, Oh Why *See* Hit the Deck (1955)

Why Should I Care? *See* Rosalie (1938)

Why Was I Born *See* The Man I Love (1946)

Why Was I Born? *See* Sweet Adeline (1935)

Why Was I Born? *See* Till the Clouds Roll By (1946)

Why You Pretend *See* Artists and Models (1955)

Wild in the Country *See* Wild in the Country (1961)

Wild Rose *See* Look for the Silver Lining (1949)

The Wild Wild West *See* The Harvey Girls (1946)

Wilkommen *See* Cabaret (1972)

Will Someone Ever Look at Me That Way? *See* Yentl (1983)

Will You Marry Me *See* Yolanda and the Thief (1945)

Will You Remember *See* Deep in My Heart (1954)

Will You Remember? *See* Maytime (1937) .

William Tell Overture *See* Maytime (1937)

Willing and Eager *See* State Fair (1962)

Willy Wonka, the Candy Man *See* Willy Wonka & the Chocolate Factory (1971)

The Wind in the Trees *See* Girl of the Golden West (1938)

The Wind! The Wind! *See* Pardners (1956)

The Winning End *See* Staying Alive (1983)

Wish I May *See* Best Foot Forward (1943)

Wishing *See* George White's Scandals (1945)

The Wishing Waltz *See* Sweet Rosie O'Grady (1943)

The Witch's Castle *See* The Wizard of Oz (1939)

With A Kiss *See* The French Line (1954)

With a Little Bit of Luck *See* My Fair Lady (1964)

With a Little Help From My Friends *See* Sgt. Pepper's Lonely Hearts Club Band (1978)

With a Smile and a Song *See* Snow White and the Seven Dwarfs (1937)

With a Song in My Heart *See* Young Man with a Horn (1950)

With My Eyes Wide Open I'm Dreaming *See* The Stooge (1951)

With My Head in the Clouds *See* This is the Army (1943)

With One More Look At You *See* A Star is Born (1976)

With Plenty of Money and You *See* My Dream is Yours (1949)

With The Sun Warm Upon Me *See* The Farmer Takes a Wife (1953)

Without Love *See* Silk Stockings (1957)

Without You *See* My Fair Lady (1964)

The Wiz *See* The Wiz (1978)

Wolf Call *See* Girl Happy (1965)

A Woman in Love *See* Guys and Dolls (1955)

Woman in the Moon *See* A Star is Born (1976)

The Woman In You *See* Staying Alive (1983)

A Woman's Kiss *See* The Firefly (1937)

Wonder Why *See* Rich, Young and Pretty (1951)

Wonderful Copenhagen *See* Hans Christian Andersen (1952)

Wonderful Guy *See* South Pacific (1958)

Wonderful, Wonderful Day *See* Seven Brides for Seven Brothers (1954)

Wonderful World *See* Live a Little, Love a Little (1968)

Won't You Charleston With Me? *See* The Boy Friend (1971)

Won't You Come Play With Me? *See* The Great Ziegfeld (1936)

Wooden Heart *See* G.I. Blues (1960)

Wooden Shoes *See* Sweethearts (1938)

Wooly Bully *See* Back to the Beach (1987)

The Words Are in My Heart *See* Gold Diggers of 1935 (1935)

The Work Song *See* Cinderella (1950)

The World is for the Young *See* Mrs. Brown, You've Got a Lovely Daughter (1968)

A World Of Our Own *See* It Happened at the World's Fair (1963)

Worry About Tomorrow *See* Bundle of Joy (1956)

The Worry Song *See* Anchors Aweigh (1945)

Would You *See* Singin' in the Rain (1952)

Would You? *See* The Road to Utopia (1946)

Would You? *See* San Francisco (1936)

Would You, Could You *See* Happy Go Lovely (1951)

Would You Like to Be the Love of My Life? *See* Second Chorus (1940)

Wouldn't It Be Funny *See* Mr. Music (1950)

Wouldn't It Be Lovely? *See* My Fair Lady (1964)

Write Your Own Songs *See* Songwriter (1984)

Wrong to Dream *See* Song of Norway (1970)

Wunderbar *See* Kiss Me Kate (1953)

Xanadu *See* Xanadu (1980)

Yahrzeit *See* Jazz Singer (1927)

The Yam *See* Carefree (1938)

The Yama Yama Man *See* The Story of Vernon and Irene Castle (1939)

Yama Yama Man *See* Look for the Silver Lining (1949)

Yankee Doodle Blues *See* Rhapsody in Blue (1945)

The Yankee Doodle Boy *See* Yankee Doodle Dandy (1942)

Yankee Doodle Dandy *See* Pin-Up Girl (1944)

Yankee Doodle Dandy *See* Yankee Doodle Dandy (1942)

The Yellow Rose of Texas *See* Viva Las Vegas (1963)

Yellow Submarine *See* Yellow Submarine (1968)

Yes, I Do *See* Nashville (1975)

Yes, Indeedy *See* Take Me Out to the Ball Game (1949)

Yes Sir, That's My Baby *See* I'll See You in My Dreams (1951)

Yes, Yes *See* Pennies From Heaven (1981)

Yesterday *See* Give My Regards to Broad Street (1984)

Yesterdays *See* Lovely to Look At (1952)

Yesterdays *See* Roberta (1935)

Yesterdays *See* Till the Clouds Roll By (1946)

Yiddle on Your Fiddle *See* The Great Ziegfeld (1936)

Yiddle With His Fiddle See Yidl Mitn Fidl (1936)

Yipsee-I-O See Nancy Goes to Rio (1950)

Yiri Yiri Bon See Crossover Dreams (1985)

Y.M.C.A. See Can't Stop the Music (1980)

Yo Te Amo Mucho—And That's That See Holiday in Mexico (1946)

Yoga is as Yoga Goes See Easy Come, Easy Go (1967)

Yolanda See Yolanda and the Thief (1945)

Yonny and his Oompah See Happy Landing (1938)

You See The Great Ziegfeld (1936)

You Ain't Right with the Lord See Dixie Jamboree (1944)

You Ain't Woman Enough to Take My Man See Coal Miner's Daughter (1980)

You and I See Goodbye, Mr. Chips (1969)

You and I See Meet Me in St. Louis (1944)

You and Me See Victor/Victoria (1982)

You and Your Kiss See One Night in the Tropics (1940)

You Appeal to Me See Happy Landing (1938)

You Are Beautiful See Flower Drum Song (1961)

You Are Love See Show Boat (1936)

You Are Love See Show Boat (1951)

You Are My Lucky Star See Babes in Arms (1939)

You Are My Lucky Star See The Boy Friend (1971)

You Are My Lucky Star See Broadway Melody of 1936 (1935)

You Are My Lucky Star See New York, New York (1977)

You Are My Lucky Star See Singin' in the Rain (1952)

You Are My Lucky Star See Three Little Words (1950)

You Are My Sunshine See DuBarry Was a Lady (1943)

You are the Most Precious Thing in My Life See Thank God It's Friday (1978)

You Are The Music to the Words in my Heart See Happy Landing (1938)

You Are Too Beautiful See Hallelujah, I'm a Bum (1933)

You Are Woman, I Am Man See Funny Girl (1968)

You Baby Baby See Jazz Singer (1980)

You Belong in a Love Song See Higher and Higher (1944)

You Brought a New Kind of Love to Me See New York, New York (1977)

You Can Always Tell a Lady by the Company She Keeps See Thank God It's Friday (1978)

You Can Always Tell A Yank See Hollywood Canteen (1944)

You Can Count on Me See On the Town (1949)

You Can Do It See Knights of the City (1985)

You Can Do No Wrong See The Pirate (1948)

You Can Do No Wrong See The Pirate (1948)

You Can't Do Wrong Doin' Right See Duchess of Idaho (1950)

You Can't Do Wrong Doing Right See The Affairs of Dobie Gillis (1953)

You Can't Say No In Acapulco See Fun in Acapulco (1963)

You Can't Say No to a Soldier See Iceland (1942)

You Can't Win See The Wiz (1978)

You Could Have Knocked Me Over With A Feather See Harvest Melody (1943)

You Couldn't Be Cuter See Joy of Living (1938)

You Dear See Two Girls and a Sailor (1944)

You Did It See My Fair Lady (1964)

You Do Something to Me See Because You're Mine (1952)

You Do Something to Me See Can-Can (1960)

You Do Something to Me See Night and Day (1946)

You Don't Have To Know the Language See The Road to Rio (1947)

The You Don't Want To Play With Me Blues See The Boy Friend (1971)

You Excite Me See Tonight and Every Night (1945)

You Go Your Way and I'll Go Crazy See Four Jacks and a Jill (1941)

You Got Class See Here Come the Girls (1953)

You Gotta Come Down See Girl in Gold Boots (1969)

You Gotta Have a Gimmick See Gypsy (1962)

(You Gotta Have) Heart See Damn Yankees (1958)

You Gotta Pull Strings See The Great Ziegfeld (1936)

You Gotta S-M-I-L-E to Be H-A-P-P-Y See Stowaway (1936)

You Gotta Stop See Easy Come, Easy Go (1967)

You Hit the Spot See Scared Stiff (1953)

You Look So Familiar See Artists and Models (1955)

You Love Me See The West Point Story (1950)

You Lucky People You See The Road to Zanzibar (1941)

You Made Me Love You See Jolson Sings Again (1949)

You Made Me Love You See The Jolson Story (1946)

You Made Me Love You See Love Me or Leave Me (1955)

You Made Me Love You See Private Buckaroo (1942)

You Made Me Love You See Three Daring Daughters (1948)

You May Not Remember See Show Business (1944)

You Must Have Been a Beautiful Baby See My Dream is Yours (1949)

You, My Love See Young at Heart (1954)

You Never Give Me Your Money See Sgt. Pepper's Lonely Hearts Club Band (1978)

You Never Looked So Beautiful See The Great Ziegfeld (1936)

You Never Looked So Beautiful See Ziegfeld Girl (1941)

You Rat, You See The Night They Raided Minsky's (1969)

You Say the Sweetest Things, Baby See Tin Pan Alley (1940)

You Started Something See Moon Over Miami (1941)

You Stepped Out of a Dream See Ziegfeld Girl (1941)

You Talk Just Like My Maw See Carmen Jones (1954)

You Took Advantage of me See A Star is Born (1954)

You Two See Chitty Chitty Bang Bang (1968)

You Were Meant For Me See Broadway Melody (1929)

You Were Meant For Me See Singin' in the Rain (1952)

You Were Never Lovelier See You Were Never Lovelier (1942)

You Will Remember Vienna See Deep in My Heart (1954)

You With the Crazy Eyes See Let's Make Love (1960)

You, Wonderful You See Summer Stock (1950)

You Won't Forget Me See Duchess of Idaho (1950)

You'd Be Hard to Replace See The Barkleys of Broadway (1949)

You'd Be Surprised See There's No Business Like Show Business (1954)

You'll Never Change Him See Beach Blanket Bingo (1965)

You'll Never Get Away From Me See Gypsy (1962)

You'll Never Get Away From Me See Gypsy (1993)

You'll Never Know See Hello, Frisco, Hello (1943)

You'll Never Know See Lady Be Good (1941)

You'll Never Walk Alone See Carousel (1956)

Young and Beautiful See Jailhouse Rock (1957)

Young and Healthy See 42nd Street (1933)

Young at Heart See Young at Heart (1954)

Young Dreams See King Creole (1958)

The Young Man with a Horn See Two Girls and a Sailor (1944)

Young Man with a Horn See The Opposite Sex (1956)

Younger Than Springtime See South Pacific (1958)

Your Broadway and My Broadway See Broadway Melody of 1938 (1937)

Your Cheatin' Heart See Sweet Dreams (1985)

Your Country and My Country See This is the Army (1943)

Your Day Begins Tonight See Little Shop of Horrors (1986)

Your Dream is the Same as My Dream See One Night in the Tropics (1940)

Your Eyes Have Told Me So See By the Light of the Silvery Moon (1953)

Your Eyes Have Told Me So See I'll See You in My Dreams (1951)

Your Good Will Ambassador See Darling Lili (1970)

Your Head on My Shoulder See Kid Millions (1934)

Your Land and My Land See Deep in My Heart (1954)

Your Mother Should Know See Magical Mystery Tour (1967)

Your Smiling Face See FM (1978)

You're a Child See The Little Prince (1974)

You're a Grand Old Flag See Yankee Doodle Dandy (1942)

You're A Lucky Fellow, Mr. Smith (instrumental) See In the Navy (1941)

You're a Natural See College Swing (1938)

You're a Queer One, Julie Jordan See Carousel (1956)

You're a Sweetheart See Meet Danny Wilson (1952)

You're a Wonderful Girl See Yankee Doodle Dandy (1942)

You're All the World to Me See Royal Wedding (1951)

You're an Angel See Lottery Bride (1930)

You're Awful See On the Town (1949)

You're Blind See Krush Groove (1985)

You're Dangerous See The Road to Zanzibar (1941)

You're Dependable See Lullaby of Broadway (1951)

You're Devastating See Lovely to Look At (1952)

You're Devasting See Roberta (1935)

You're Drafted See Rhythm Parade (1943)

You're Getting to Be a Habit With Me See 42nd Street (1933)

You're Getting to Be a Habit With Me *See* Lullaby of Broadway (1951)

You're Gonna Lose That Girl *See* Help! (1965)

You're Here and I'm Here *See* The Story of Vernon and Irene Castle (1939)

You're Just Too, Too *See* Les Girls (1957)

You're Laughing at Me *See* On the Avenue (1937)

You're Lookin' at Country *See* Coal Miner's Daughter (1980)

You're Lucky *See* Best Foot Forward (1943)

You're My Little Pin Up Girl *See* Pin-Up Girl (1944)

You're Nearer *See* Too Many Girls (1940)

You're Never Fully Dressed Without a Smile *See* Annie (1982)

You're Never Too Old *See* Ladies of the Chorus (1949)

You're Not the Only One *See* Knights of the City (1985)

You're Off To See The World *See* In the Navy (1941)

You're On Your Own *See* Higher and Higher (1944)

You're Only Second Rate *See* The Return of Jafar (1994)

You're Out of the Woods *See* The Wizard of Oz (1939)

You're Perfect In Every Department *See* Bundle of Joy (1956)

You're Pretty Terrific Yourself *See* Stage Door Canteen (1943)

You're Sensational *See* High Society (1956)

You're So Easy To Dance With *See* Holiday Inn (1942)

You're the Cause Of It All *See* Kid from Brooklyn (1946)

You're the One That I Want *See* Grease (1978)

You're the Reason I Feel Like Dancing *See* Thank God It's Friday (1978)

You're the Top *See* Night and Day (1946)

You're Words, My Music *See* Lady Be Good (1941)

Yours and Mine *See* Broadway Melody of 1938 (1937)

Yours, Yours, Yours *See* 1776 (1972)

You've Changed *See* Lady Sings the Blues (1972)

You've Got Me This Way *See* You'll Find Out (1940)

You've Got That Thing *See* Night and Day (1946)

You've Got To Be Carefully Taught *See* South Pacific (1958)

You've Got To Hide Your Love Away *See* Help! (1965)

You've Gotta Eat Your Spinach, Baby *See* The Poor Little Rich Girl (1936)

You've Gotta Have a Gimmick *See* Gypsy (1993)

You...You... *See* Scrooge (1970)

Yubla *See* Lottery Bride (1930)

Zana Zaranda *See* Call Out the Marines (1942)

Ziguener *See* Bitter Sweet (1940)

Zilch's Hats *See* Hats Off (1937)

Zing A Little Zong *See* Just for You (1952)

Zing! Went the Strings of My Heart *See* Listen, Darling (1938)

Zing! Went the Strings Of My Heart *See* Lullaby of Broadway (1951)

Zip *See* Pal Joey (1957)

Zis Boom Bah *See* Zis Boom Bah (1942)

Zombie Stomp *See* Horror of Party Beach (1964)

ALTERNATE TITLES INDEX

The **ALTERNATE TITLE INDEX** lists over 3,600 variant titles for movies, including foreign titles. Titles are listed in alphabetical order followed by a cross-reference to the appropriate title as listed in the main video review section.

A-009 Missione Hong Kong *See* Code Name Alpha (1967)

Abar, the First Black Superman *See* In Your Face (1977)

Abbott and Costello in the Navy *See* In the Navy (1941)

Abbott and Costello Meet the Ghosts *See* Abbott and Costello Meet Frankenstein (1948)

ABC Murders *See* The Alphabet Murders (1965)

Abdullah's Harem *See* Abdulla the Great (1956)

Abismos de Pasion *See* Wuthering Heights (1953)

Absent-Minded *See* The Daydreamer (1975)

Absinthe *See* Madame X (1966)

The Accused *See* The Mark of the Hawk (1957)

Ace *See* The Great Santini (1980)

Act of Violence *See* Deadline Assault (1990)

Adam Wants to Be a Man *See* Adomas Nori Buti Zmogumi (1959)

Addict *See* Born to Win (1971)

Addio, Fratello, Crudele *See* 'Tis a Pity She's a Whore (1973)

Adorable Idiot *See* Ravishing Idiot (1964)

The Adventure *See* L'Avventura (1960)

Adventure for Two *See* The Demi-Paradise (1943)

The Adventure of Lyle Swan *See* Timerider (1983)

Adventures at Rugby *See* Tom Brown's School Days (1940)

The Adventures of Chatran *See* The Adventures of Milo & Otis (1989)

The Adventures of Hercules *See* Hercules 2 (1985)

The Adventures of Jack London *See* Jack London (1944)

The Adventures of the Great Mouse Detective *See* The Great Mouse Detective (1986)

The Adventuress *See* I See a Dark Stranger (1946)

Aerobicide *See* Killer Workout (1986)

An Affair of the Heart *See* Body and Soul (1947)

An Affair of the Heart *See* The Love Affair, or The Case of the Missing Switchboard Operator (1967)

African Fury *See* Cry, the Beloved Country (1951)

After Jenny Died *See* Revenge (1971)

Afurika Monogatari *See* Green Horizon (1983)

Against All Odds *See* Kiss and Kill (1968)

Agatha Christie's Endless Night *See* Endless Night (1971)

Agatha Christie's Ten Little Indians *See* Ten Little Indians (1989)

The Age of Beauty *See* Belle Epoque (1992)

Age of Gold *See* L'Age D'Or (1930)

Agent 38-24-36 *See* Ravishing Idiot (1964)

The Agitators *See* The Fix (1984)

Agoniya *See* Rasputin (1985)

Agostino di Ippona *See* Augustine of Hippo (1972)

Aimez-Vous Brahms *See* Goodbye Again (1961)

Airport '79 *See* The Concorde: Airport '79 (1979)

Akage *See* Red Lion (1969)

Akahige *See* Red Beard (1965)

Al Di La Della Legge *See* Beyond the Law (1968)

Al-Ris-Alah *See* Mohammed: Messenger of God (1977)

Alem Da Paixao *See* Happily Ever After (1986)

Alfie Darling *See* Oh, Alfie (1975)

Alfred Hitchcock's Bon Voyage & Aventure Malgache *See* Aventure Malgache (1944)

Alfred Hitchcock's Bon Voyage & Aventure Malgache *See* Bon Voyage (1944)

Ali Baba et les Quarante Voleurs *See* Ali Baba and the 40 Thieves (1954)

Alias Bulldog Drummond *See* Bulldog Jack (1935)

Alien P.I. *See* Alien Private Eye (1987)

Alien Terror *See* The Sinister Invasion (1968)

Alien Thunder *See* Dan Candy's Law (1973)

Alien Within *See* Evil Spawn (1987)

The Alien's Return *See* The Return (1980)

Alistair MacLean's Death Train *See* Detonator (1993)

Alive by Night *See* Evil Spawn (1987)

All Good Citizens *See* All My Good Countrymen (1968)

All in Place *See* All Screwed Up (1974)

All Night Long *See* Toute Une Nuit (1982)

All That Money Can Buy *See* The Devil & Daniel Webster (1941)

All the Mornings of the World *See* Tous les Matins du Monde (1992)

All This and Glamour Too *See* Vogues of 1938 (1937)

All Weekend Lovers *See* The Killing Game (1967)

Alley of Nightmares *See* She-Freak (1967)

Almost Human *See* Shock Waves (1977)

Alone Together *See* Crisscross (1992)

Alphaville, a Strange Case of Lenny Caution *See* Alphaville (1965)

Alphaville, Une etrange Aventure de Lenny Caution *See* Alphaville (1965)

Alter Ego *See* Murder by the Book (1987)

Amanti d'Oltretomba *See* Nightmare Castle (1965)

Amateur Hour *See* I Was a Teenage TV Terrorist (1987)

The Amazing Quest of Ernest Bliss *See* Amazing Adventure (1937)

Amazon Women *See* Gold of the Amazon Women (1979)

Amazonia: The Catherine Miles Story *See* White Slave (1986)

American Nightmares *See* Combat Shock (1984)

American Rickshaw *See* American Tiger (1989)

American Warrior *See* American Ninja (1985)

The American Way *See* Riders of the Storm (1988)

Amerikaner Shadkhn *See* American Matchmaker (1940)

Ami de Mon Ami *See* Boyfriends & Girlfriends (1988)

Amityville 3D *See* Amityville 3: The Demon (1983)

The Amityville Horror: The Evil Escapes, Part 4 *See* Amityville 4 (1989)

Amok *See* Schizo (1977)

The Amorous General *See* Waltz of the Toreadors (1962)

The Amorous Sex *See* Sweet Beat (1962)

Amour de Poche *See* Girl in His Pocket (1962)

Amy Fisher: My Story *See* Lethal Lolita—Amy Fisher: My Story (1992)

And Comes the Dawn...But Colored Red *See* Web of the Spider (1970)

And Once Upon a Love *See* Fantasies (1973)

And Then There Were None *See* Ten Little Indians (1975)

And Woman...Was Created *See* And God Created Woman (1957)

Anderson's Angels *See* Chesty Anderson USN (1976)

Andrews' Raiders See The Great Locomotive Chase (1956)

Andy Colby's Incredibly Awesome Adventure See Andy and the Airwave Rangers (1989)

Angel in Red See Uncaged (1991)

Angel of Vengeance See Ms. 45 (1981)

Angel of Vengeance See WarCat (1988)

An Angel Passed Over Brooklyn See The Man Who Wagged His Tail (1957)

Angel Street See Gaslight (1939)

Angels for Kicks See Wild Riders (1971)

Anglagard See House of Angels (1992)

Animal House See National Lampoon's Animal House (1978)

Anita—Tanze des Lasters See Anita, Dances of Vice (1987)

Anne of Green Gables: The Sequel See Anne of Avonlea (1987)

Annie's Coming Out See A Test of Love (1984)

The Antichrist See The Tempter (1974)

L'Anticristo See The Tempter (1974)

Antinea, l'Amante Della Citta Sepolta See Journey Beneath the Desert (1961)

The Anxious Years See Dark Journey (1937)

Any Number Can Win See Melodie en Sous-Sol (1963)

Anyone for Venice? See The Honey Pot (1967)

Anything for Love See 11 Harrowhouse (1974)

Apocalipsis Canibal See Night of the Zombies (1983)

Apu Sansat See The World of Apu (1959)

Apur Sansar See The World of Apu (1959)

The Aqua Sex See The Mermaids of Tiburon (1962)

Arctic Heat See Born American (1986)

Are You Dying Young Man? See Beast in the Cellar (1970)

The Arena See Naked Warriors (1973)

Arizona Ripper See Terror at London Bridge (1985)

Armored Attack See The North Star (1943)

Army Mystery See Criminals Within (1941)

Arthur the King See Merlin and the Sword (1985)

Artist Nude Secrets See Artist's Studio Secrets (1964)

Ascenseur Pour L'Echafaud See Frantic (1958)

Ascent to Heaven See Mexican Bus Ride (1951)

Ashanti See Ashanti, Land of No Mercy (1979)

The Assassination Team See Wardogs (1987)

Assault Force See ffolkes (1980)

Assault on Paradise See Maniac (1977)

Assignment: Istanbul See The Castle of Fu Manchu (1968)

Assignment: Kill Castro See The Mercenaries (1980)

Asylum Erotica See Slaughter Hotel (1971)

Asylum of the Insane See Flesh and Blood Show (1973)

At First Sight See Love at First Sight (1976)

At the Villa Rose See House of Mystery (1941)

Atlantic City U.S.A. See Atlantic City (1981)

Atlas Against the Cyclops See Atlas in the Land of the Cyclops (1961)

Atoll K See Utopia (1951)

Atomic Rocketship See Flash Gordon: Rocketship (1936)

Ator the Invincible See Blade Master (1984)

Attack of the Monsters See Gamera vs. Guiron (1969)

Attack of the Phantoms See KISS Meets the Phantom of the Park (1978)

Attack of the Rebel Girls See Assault of the Rebel Girls (1959)

Attention! Une Femme Peut en Cacher une Autre See My Other Husband (1985)

Aura See The Witch (1966)

Austerlitz See The Battle of Austerlitz (1960)

The Avengers See The Day Will Dawn (1942)

Avenging Godfather See Avenging Disco Godfather (1976)

L'Aventure Sauvage See Trap (1966)

A.W.O.L. See Lionheart (1990)

Az en XX. Szazadom See My Twentieth Century (1990)

Babes in Toyland See March of the Wooden Soldiers (1934)

The Baby Vanishes See Broadway Limited (1941)

Bachelor Girl Apartment See Any Wednesday (1966)

Bachelor Knight See The Bachelor and the Bobby-Soxer (1947)

Backwoods Massacre See Midnight (1981)

Bad Girl See Teenage Bad Girl (1959)

Bad Girls See Delinquent School Girls (1984)

Bad Man of Harlem See Harlem on the Prairie (1938)

The Bailiff See Sansho the Bailiff (1954)

Baisers Voles See Stolen Kisses (1968)

The Baited Trap See The Trap (1959)

Bakushu See Early Summer (1951)

The Banana Monster See Schlock (1973)

Bande a Part See Band of Outsiders (1964)

The Bandit See Crossfire (1967)

Banditi a Orgosolo See Bandits of Orgosolo (1961)

Bang Bang See Bang Bang Kid (1967)

Bangiku See Late Chrysanthemums (1954)

The Bank Detective See The Bank Dick (1940)

Banner in the Sky See Third Man on the Mountain (1959)

The Bar Sinister See It's a Dog's Life (1955)

Barbados Quest See Murder on Approval (1956)

Barbarella, Queen of the Galaxy See Barbarella (1968)

The Barbarians and Co. See The Barbarians (1987)

The Barbaric Beast of Boggy Creek, Part II See Boggy Creek II (1983)

Bargain Basement See Department Store (1935)

Baron Blood See Torture Chamber of Baron Blood (1972)

Batman: The Animated Movie See Batman: Mask of the Phantasm (1993)

Batmen of Africa See Darkest Africa (1936)

Battle Beyond the Stars See The Green Slime (1968)

The Battle for Anzio See Anzio (1968)

Battle of the Astros See Godzilla vs. Monster Zero (1968)

The Battle of the Mareth Line See Battleforce (1978)

The Battle of the River Plate See Pursuit of the Graf Spee (1957)

Battle Stripe See The Men (1950)

Battletruck See Warlords of the 21st Century (1982)

The Battling Bellhop See Kid Galahad (1937)

Battling Hoofer See Something to Sing About (1936)

Bawang Bie Ji See Farewell My Concubine (1993)

Bay of Blood See Twitch of the Death Nerve (1971)

Bayou See Poor White Trash (1957)

Be Beautiful but Shut Up See Just Another Pretty Face (1958)

Be My Valentine, Or Else... See Hospital Massacre (1981)

Be Roringen See The Touch (1971)

The Bear Hunt See Bare Hunt (1963)

The Beast Must Die See Black Werewolf (1975)

The Beast of War See The Beast (1988)

Beasts See Twilight People (1972)

Beatlemania See Beatlemania! The Movie (1981)

Beatsville See The Rebel Set (1959)

Beautiful But Dangerous See She Couldn't Say No (1952)

Beautiful But Deadly See The Don is Dead (1973)

A Beautiful Place to Kill See Paranoia (1969)

Beethoven's Great Love See Beethoven (1936)

Beggars' Opera See The Threepenny Opera (1931)

The Beginners See The First Time (1969)

The Beginners Three See The First Time (1969)

Behind Enemy Lines See The P.O.W. Escape (1986)

Behind Locked Doors See Human Gorilla (1948)

Behind the Iron Mask See The Fifth Musketeer (1979)

Bells See Murder by Phone (1982)

The Beloved See Restless (1972)

Berry Gordy's The Last Dragon See The Last Dragon (1985)

Bethune, The Making of a Hero See Dr. Bethune (1990)

Between Us See Entre-Nous (1983)

Beware! The Blob See Son of Blob (1972)

Bewitching Scatterbrain See Ravishing Idiot (1964)

The Beyond See Seven Doors of Death (1982)

Beyond Obsession See Beyond the Door (1975)

Beyond the Fog See Tower of Evil (1972)

Beyond the Living See Hospital of Terror (1978)

Beyond the Living Dead See The Hanging Woman (1972)

Beyond the Rising Moon See Star Quest (1989)

Bez Konca See No End (1984)

The Big Bankroll See The King of the Roaring '20s: The Story of Arnold Rothstein (1961)

The Big Boss See Fists of Fury (1973)

The Big Day See Jour de Fete (1948)

Big Deal at Dodge City See A Big Hand for the Little Lady (1966)

Big Duel in the North See Godzilla vs. the Sea Monster (1966)

Big Enough and Old Enough See Savages from Hell (1968)

The Big Heart See Miracle on 34th Street (1947)

The Big Lobby See Rosebud Beach Hotel (1985)

The Big Payoff See Win, Place, or Steal (1972)

Big Time Operators See The Smallest Show on Earth (1957)

The Biggest Right on Earth See Ghidrah the Three Headed Monster (1965)

Biggles: Adventures in Time See Biggles (1985)

Bijo to Ekitainigen See H-Man (1959)

Bikini Genie See Wildest Dreams (1990)

Billy the Kid's Fighting Pals See Trigger Men (1941)

Birds of Prey See Beaks: The Movie (1987)

Birthmark See The Omen (1976)

Birumano Tategoto See The Burmese Harp (1956)

The Bitch See La Chienne (1931)

Bittere Ernte See Angry Harvest (1985)

Black Angels See Black Bikers from Hell (1970)

Black Arrow Strikes See Black Arrow (1948)

The Black Book See Reign of Terror (1949)

The Black Bounty Killer See Boss (1974)

The Black Buccaneer See The Black Pirate (1926)

Black Flowers for the Bride See Something for Everyone (1970)

Black Frankenstein See Blackenstein (1973)

Black Gauntlet See Black Starlet (1974)

Black Jack See Captain Blackjack (1951)

Black Love, White Love See Sweet Love, Bitter (1967)

Black Rider See Joshua (1976)

Blade of Steel See The Far Pavilions (1984)

Blake Edwards' Son of the Pink Panther See Son of the Pink Panther (1993)

Blast-Off See Those Fantastic Flying Fools (1967)

Blazing Arrows See Fighting Caravans (1931)

Blazing Magnums See Strange Shadows in an Empty Room (1976)

Bless 'Em All See The Act (1982)

Blind Alley See Perfect Strangers (1984)

The Blind Dead See Tombs of the Blind Dead (1972)

Blind Man's Bluff See Cauldron of Blood (1967)

Blind Terror See See No Evil (1971)

Blonde Bombshell See Bombshell (1933)

The Blonde From Peking See The Peking Blond (1968)

A Blonde in Love See Loves of a Blonde (1965)

Blondie Has Servant Trouble See Blondie Has Trouble (1940)

Blood and Sand See Sand and Blood (1987)

Blood Bath See Track of the Vampire (1966)

Blood Beast from Outer Space See Night Caller from Outer Space (1966)

Blood Brides See Hatchet for the Honeymoon (1970)

The Blood Brother See Texas Pioneers (1932)

Blood Castle See The Blood Spattered Bride (1972)

Blood Ceremony See The Legend of Blood Castle (1972)

Blood Couple See Black Vampire (1973)

Blood Creature See Terror is a Man (1959)

The Blood Crowd See The McMasters (1970)

The Blood Cult of Shangri-La See The Thirsty Dead (1974)

Blood Demon See The Torture Chamber of Dr. Sadism (1969)

Blood Doctor See Mad Doctor of Blood Island (1969)

The Blood Drinkers See The Vampire People (1966)

Blood Feast See Night of a Thousand Cats (1972)

Blood Fiend See Theatre of Death (1967)

Blood for Dracula See Andy Warhol's Dracula (1974)

Blood Hunger See Vampyres (1974)

Blood is My Heritage See Blood of Dracula (1957)

Blood Mad See The Glove (1978)

Blood Money See The Killer's Edge (1990)

Blood Moon See The Werewolf vs. the Vampire Woman (1970)

Blood Oath See Prisoners of the Sun (1991)

Blood of Frankenstein See Dracula vs. Frankenstein (1971)

Blood of Fu Manchu See Kiss and Kill (1968)

Blood of the Man Devil See House of the Black Death (1965)

Blood of the Undead See Schizo (1977)

Blood On His Lips See Hideous Sun Demon (1959)

The Blood Seekers See Cain's Cutthroats (1971)

Blood Splash See Nightmare (1982)

The Blood Suckers See Alien Massacre (1967)

The Blood Suckers See Dr. Terror's House of Horrors (1965)

Blood Thirst See Salem's Lot (1979)

Bloodline See Sidney Sheldon's Bloodline (1979)

Bloodsilver See Beyond the Law (1968)

The Bloody Bushido Blade See The Bushido Blade (1980)

Bloody Pom Poms See Cheerleader Camp (1988)

Bloomfield See The Hero (1971)

Blue See Trois Couleurs: Bleu (1993)

Blue and the Gold See The Annapolis Story (1955)

Blue Heat See The Last of the Finest (1990)

Blue Manhattan See Hi, Mom! (1970)

Blue Sierra See Courage of Lassie (1946)

Blues for Lovers See Ballad in Blue (1966)

Blues La-Chofesh Ha-Godol See Late Summer Blues (1987)

Blunt See The 4th Man (1979)

The Boat See Das Boot (1981)

Bodas de Sangre See Blood Wedding (1981)

The Body Stealers See Invasion of the Body Stealers (1969)

Bogus Bandits See The Devil's Brother (1933)

The Bold Cavalier See The Bold Caballero (1936)

Bolero: An Adventure in Ecstasy See Bolero (1984)

Bombsight Stolen See Cottage to Let (1941)

The Border See Frontera (19??)

Border Heat See Deadly Stranger (1988)

Born Natturunnar See Children of Nature (1992)

Born to Kill See Cockfighter (1974)

Bosambo See Sanders of the River (1935)

Boss Nigger See Boss (1974)

Boudu Sauve des Eaux See Boudu Saved from Drowning (1932)

Bound by Honor See Blood In...Blood Out: Bound by Honor (1993)

Bourbon St. Shadows See The Invisible Avenger (1958)

A Bout de Souffle See Breathless (1959)

The Boxer See Counter Punch (1971)

The Boyfriend School See Don't Tell Her It's Me (1990)

Boyichi and the Supermonster See Gamera vs. Gaos (1967)

The Boys from Brooklyn See Bela Lugosi Meets a Brooklyn Gorilla (1952)

The Brain Machine See Mind Warp (1972)

The Brainsnatchers See The Man Who Lived Again (1936)

Brainwash See Circle of Power (1983)

Branded See Bad Boy (1939)

Brandy Ashore See Green Grow the Rushes (1951)

The Brave and the Beautiful See The Magnificent Matador (1955)

The Brave Young Men of Weinberg See Up the Academy (1980)

Break In See Loophole (1983)

Breakdance See Breakin' (1984)

Breakdance 2: Electric Boogaloo See Breakin' 2: Electric Boogaloo (1984)

The Breakup See La Rupture (1970)

Brenn, Hexe, Brenn See Mark of the Devil (1969)

Brennendes Geheimnis See Burning Secret (1989)

Bride of the Atom See Bride of the Monster (1956)

The Bride of the Lake See Lily of Killarney (1934)

Brides of Blood See Brides of the Beast (1968)

Bridge Across Time See Terror at London Bridge (1985)

Broken Hearts and Noses See Crimewave (1985)

Bronenosets Potemkin See The Battleship Potemkin (1925)

Bronx Warriors See 1990: The Bronx Warriors (1983)

Brothel 8 See Sandakan No. 8 (1974)

Brotherhood of the Yakuza See The Yakuza (1975)

Bruce Brown's The Endless Summer 2 See The Endless Summer 2 (1994)

Bruce Lee's Game of Death See Game of Death (1979)

The Brute See El Bruto (1952)

Brutti, Sporchi, e Cattivi See Down & Dirty (1976)

Buck Rogers See Destination Saturn (1939)

Buckaroo Banzai See The Adventures of Buckaroo Banzai Across the Eighth Dimension (1984)

Bud Abbott and Lou Costello in Hollywood See Abbott and Costello in Hollywood (1945)

Build My Gallows High See Out of the Past (1947)

A Bullet from God See God's Gun (1975)

Bullfighter See Torero (1956)

Bump in the Night See The Final Terror (1983)

The Bunny Caper See Games Girls Play (1975)

Burn Out See Journey into Fear (1974)

Burn, Witch, Burn See Mark of the Devil (1969)

Burning Cross See The Klansman (1974)

Burning Hearts See Kolberg (1945)

The Burning Man See Dangerous Summer (1982)

The Butcher See Le Boucher (1969)

The Butcher See Psycho from Texas (1983)

Butcher Baker (Nightmare Maker) See Night Warning (1982)

The Butterfly Revolution See Summer Camp Nightmare (1986)

Bvongiorno, Elefante See Pardon My Trunk (1952)

By Hook or By Crook See I Dood It (1943)

By Rocket to the Moon See Woman in the Moon (1929)

Cabiria See Nights of Cabiria (1957)

Caccia Ai Violenti See One Step to Hell (1968)

Caccia alla Volpe See After the Fox (1966)

Cactus Jack See The Villain (1979)

Cafe of the Seven Sinners See Seven Sinners (1940)

The Cage See My Sister, My Love (1978)

Caged Females See Caged Heat (1974)

Caged Heart See L'Addition (1985)

Cain's Way See Cain's Cutthroats (1971)

Calhoun See Nightstick (1987)

The California Dolls See ...All the Marbles (1981)

California Holiday See Spinout (1966)

California Hot Wax See The Bikini Car Wash Company (1990)

California in 1878 See Fighting Thru (1930)

California Man See Encino Man (1992)

The Californian *See* The Gentleman from California (1937)

Call Harry Crown *See* 99 & 44/100 Dead (1974)

Call it Murder *See* Midnight (1934)

Call of the Savage *See* Savage Fury (1933)

Call the Cops *See* Find the Lady (1975)

The Calling *See* Murder by Phone (1982)

Calling Northside 777 *See* Call Northside 777 (1948)

Campanadas a Medianoche *See* Chimes at Midnight (1967)

Camper John *See* Gentle Savage (1973)

Campsite Massacre *See* The Final Terror (1983)

Canicule *See* Dog Day (1983)

Cannibal Orgy, or the Maddest Story Ever Told *See* Spider Baby (1964)

Cannibals in the City *See* Invasion of the Flesh Hunters (1982)

Cannibals in the Streets *See* Invasion of the Flesh Hunters (1982)

Capitaine Morgan *See* Morgan the Pirate (1960)

Captain Mephisto and the Transformation Machine *See* Manhunt of Mystery Island (1945)

Captain Midnight *See* On the Air Live with Captain Midnight (1979)

Captain Yankee *See* Jungle Raiders (1985)

Captive Women 3: Sweet Sugar *See* Sweet Sugar (1972)

Caravans West *See* Wagon Wheels (1934)

The Card *See* The Promoter (1952)

Cardigan's Last Case *See* State's Attorney (1931)

Carnage *See* Twitch of the Death Nerve (1971)

Carnival of Fools *See* Death Wish Club (1983)

Carnival of Thieves *See* Caper of the Golden Bulls (1967)

Carquake *See* Cannonball (1976)

The Cars That Eat People *See* The Cars That Ate Paris (1974)

Cartagine in Fiamme *See* Carthage in Flames (1960)

Cartes sur Table *See* Attack of the Robots (1966)

Carthage en Flammes *See* Carthage in Flames (1960)

The Case of Jonathan Drew *See* The Lodger (1926)

The Case of the Hillside Stranglers *See* The Hillside Strangler (1989)

Case of the Missing Switchboard Operator *See* The Love Affair, or The Case of the Missing Switchboard Operator (1967)

Cash *See* If I Were Rich (1933)

Cassanova and Co. *See* Sex on the Run (1978)

Castle in the Sky *See* Yidl Mitn Fidl (1936)

Castle of Doom *See* Vampyr (1931)

Castle of Terror *See* Castle of Blood (1964)

Castle of Terror *See* The Virgin of Nuremberg (1965)

The Castle of the Spider's Web *See* Throne of Blood (1957)

Castle of the Walking Dead *See* The Torture Chamber of Dr. Sadism (1969)

The Cat *See* Le Chat (1975)

C.A.T. Squad *See* Stalking Danger (1986)

C.A.T. Squad: Python Wolf *See* Python Wolf (1988)

Catchfire *See* Backtrack (1989)

Catholic Boys *See* Heaven Help Us (1985)

Cathy Tippel *See* Keetje Tippei (1975)

Cauchemares *See* Cathy's Curse (1977)

Cavalleria Commandos *See* Cavalry Command (1963)

The Cave Dwellers *See* One Million B.C. (1940)

Cave Man *See* One Million B.C. (1940)

Cavegirl *See* Cave Girl (1985)

C.C. & Company *See* Chrome Hearts (1970)

Cell Block Girls *See* Women's Prison Escape (19??)

Cemetary Girls *See* The Vampire Hookers (1978)

Cemetary Girls *See* The Velvet Vampire (1971)

Cento Dollari D'Odio *See* Uncle Tom's Cabin (1969)

Ceremonia Sangrienta *See* The Legend of Blood Castle (1972)

A Certain Mr. Scratch *See* The Devil & Daniel Webster (1941)

Cet Obscur Objet Du Desir *See* That Obscure Object of Desire (1977)

Chaingang Girls *See* Sweet Sugar (1972)

The Challenge *See* It Takes a Thief (1959)

Chamber of Fear *See* The Fear Chamber (1968)

Champ d'Honneur *See* Field of Honor (1987)

Champion Charlie *See* The Champion/His New Job (1915)

A Change of Face *See* Cambio de Cara (1971)

Changes *See* Danielle Steel's Changes (1991)

Chaos-Kaos *See* Kaos (1985)

Charterhouse at Parma *See* La Chartreuse de Parme (1948)

Chastnaya Zhizn *See* Private Life (1982)

The Chautauqua *See* The Trouble with Girls (and How To Get Into It) (1969)

Che? *See* Diary of Forbidden Dreams (1973)

Cheaters *See* Tricheurs (1984)

Chernobyl: The Final Warning *See* Final Warning (1990)

Chevy Van *See* The Van (1977)

The Chief Wants No Survivors *See* No Survivors, Please (1963)

Chikamatsu Monogatari *See* The Crucified Lovers (1954)

Chikyu Boelgun *See* The Mysterians (1958)

The Child *See* Kill and Go Hide (1976)

Child of Satan *See* To the Devil, A Daughter (1976)

Child of the Night *See* What the Peeper Saw (1972)

Childish Things *See* Confessions of Tom Harris (1972)

China 9, Liberty 37 *See* Gunfire (1978)

Chinchero *See* The Last Movie (1971)

The Chinese Room *See* El Cuarto Chino (1971)

Christmas Evil *See* Terror in Toyland (1985)

A Christmas Memory *See* ABC Stage 67: Truman Capote's A Christmas Memory (1966)

The Christmas Tree *See* When Wolves Cry (1969)

Christmas Vacation *See* National Lampoon's Christmas Vacation (1989)

Chuck Norris vs. the Karate Cop *See* Slaughter in San Francisco (1981)

Ciao! Manhattan *See* Edie in Ciao! Manhattan (1972)

Cica Tomina Koliba *See* Uncle Tom's Cabin (1969)

The Circle *See* The Vicious Circle (1957)

The Circle *See* Woman in Brown (1948)

Citadel of Crime *See* Wheel of Fortune (1941)

Citizen's Band *See* FM (1978)

The City Jungle *See* The Young Philadelphians (1959)

The City of the Dead *See* Horror Hotel (1960)

City of the Living Dead *See* Gates of Hell (1983)

The Clairvoyant *See* The Evil Mind (1934)

The Clairvoyant *See* Killing Hour (1984)

The Clansman *See* The Birth of a Nation (1915)

Class of '86 *See* National Lampoon's Class of '86 (1986)

Class Reunion *See* National Lampoon's Class Reunion (1982)

Claude *See* Two of Us (1968)

Clean Slate *See* Coup de Torchon (1981)

Cleo de 5 a 7 *See* Cleo from 5 to 7 (1961)

Clickety Clack *See* Dodes 'ka-den (1970)

Clinton & Nadine *See* Blood Money: The Story of Clinton and Nadine (1988)

The Closest of Kin *See* All the Lovin' Kinfolk (1989)

Club Dead *See* Terror at Red Wolf Inn (1972)

Coast of Terror *See* Summer City (1977)

Coastwatcher *See* The Last Warrior (1989)

Cobweb Castle *See* Throne of Blood (1957)

Code Name: Operation Crossbow *See* Operation Crossbow (1965)

Code Name: Trixie *See* The Crazies (1973)

Code 645 *See* G-Men Never Forget (1948)

Codename: The Soldier *See* The Soldier (1982)

Coffin of Terror *See* Castle of Blood (1964)

Colin Nutley's House of Angels *See* House of Angels (1992)

Collision Course *See* The Bamboo Saucer (1968)

Colonel Blimp *See* The Life and Death of Colonel Blimp (1943)

Colorado Ranger *See* Guns of Justice (1950)

Come Back to Me *See* Doll Face (1946)

Come Dance with Me *See* Voulez-Vous Danser Avec Moi? (1959)

Come 'n' Get It *See* Lunch Wagon (1981)

Coming Attractions *See* Loose Shoes (1980)

Comizi d'Amore *See* Love Meetings (1964)

Communion *See* Alice Sweet Alice (1976)

Como Agua para Chocolate *See* Like Water for Chocolate (1993)

The Company of Strangers *See* Strangers in Good Company (1991)

Computer Killers *See* Horror Hospital (1973)

The Con Man *See* The Con Artists (1980)

Concerto *See* I've Always Loved You (1946)

Confession *See* Repentance (1987)

The Confession *See* Quick, Let's Get Married (1971)

Confessions of A Peeping John *See* Hi, Mom! (1970)

Confidential Report *See* Mr. Arkadin (1955)

The Conflict *See* Catholics (1973)

The Conspiracy *See* Le Complot (1973)

Contamination *See* Alien Contamination (1981)

Continuavamo A Chiamarlo Trinita *See* Trinity is Still My Name (1975)

Convention City *See* Sons of the Desert (1933)

Coonskin *See* Streetfight (1975)

Cop Killers *See* Corrupt (1984)

Cop Tips Waitress $2 Million *See* It Could Happen to You (1994)

A Corps Perdu *See* Straight for the Heart (1988)

The Corpse *See* Crucible of Horror (1969)

A Corpse Hangs in the Web *See* Horrors of Spider Island (1959)

The Cosmic Man Appears in Tokyo *See* Warning from Space (1956)

Cosmo 2000: Planet Without a Name *See* Cosmos: War of the Planets (1980)

Count Dracula and His Vampire Bride *See* The Satanic Rites of Dracula (1973)

Count Dracula's Great Love *See* Dracula's Great Love (1972)

Country Music *See* Las Vegas Hillbillys (1966)

Country Music Daughter *See* Nashville Girl (1976)

Coup de Foudre *See* Entre-Nous (1983)

Coup de Tete *See* Hothead (1978)

Courage *See* Raw Courage (1984)

The Courage of Kavik, the Wolf Dog *See* Kavik the Wolf Dog (1984)

Court Martial *See* Carrington, V.C. (1954)

The Courtneys of Curzon Street *See* The Courtney Affair (1947)

Crack *See* Strike Force (1975)

Cradle of Crime *See* Dead End (1937)

Crash of Silence *See* Mandy (1953)

The Crawling Monster *See* Creeping Terror (1964)

Crazy for You *See* Vision Quest (1985)

Crazy Horse *See* Friends, Lovers & Lunatics (1989)

Crazy House *See* Night of the Laughing Dead (1975)

Crazy Jack and the Boy *See* Silence (1973)

Crazy Streets *See* Forever, Lulu (1987)

Created to Kill *See* Embryo (1976)

The Creature Wasn't Nice *See* Spaceship (1981)

Creatures *See* From Beyond the Grave (1973)

Creatures of the Prehistoric Planet *See* Horror of the Blood Monsters (1970)

Creatures of the Red Planet *See* Horror of the Blood Monsters (1970)

The Creature's Revenge *See* Brain of Blood (1971)

The Creeper *See* Dark Side of Midnight (1986)

The Creeper *See* Rituals (1979)

The Creepers *See* Assault (1970)

The Creepers *See* Island of Terror (1966)

The Creeping Unknown *See* The Quatermass Experiment (1956)

Creeps *See* Bloody Birthday (1980)

Cria Cuervos *See* Cria (1976)

The Cricket *See* La Cicada (1983)

Crime Boss *See* New Mafia Boss (1972)

Crime et Chatiment *See* Crime and Punishment (1935)

Crimes in the Wax Museum *See* Nightmare in Wax (1969)

Crimes, Inc. *See* Gangs, Inc. (1941)

The Crimes of Dr. Mabuse *See* Testament of Dr. Mabuse (1962)

The Criminal *See* The Concrete Jungle (1982)

The Crimson Altar *See* The Crimson Cult (1968)

Crimson Executioner *See* The Bloody Pit of Horror (1965)

The Crimson Ghost *See* Cyclotrode "X" (1946)

Crooks in Clover *See* Penthouse (1933)

Crossed Swords *See* The Prince and the Pauper (1978)

Crossing the Line *See* The Big Man: Crossing the Line (1991)

The Crown Caper *See* Thomas Crown Affair (1968)

Cruel Swamp *See* Swamp Women (1955)

The Cry *See* Il Grido (1957)

Crying Out Loud *See* Cotton Queen (1937)

Crypt of Dark Secrets *See* Mardi Gras Massacre (1978)

C.S. Lewis Through the Shadowlands *See* Shadowlands (1985)

Csillagosok, Katonak *See* The Red and the White (1968)

Cuba Crossing *See* The Mercenaries (1980)

Cuban Rebel Girls *See* Assault of the Rebel Girls (1959)

Cult of the Dead *See* The Snake People (1968)

Cupid in the Rough *See* Aggie Appleby, Maker of Men (1933)

Curley and His Gang in the Haunted Mansion *See* Who Killed Doc Robbin? (1948)

Curse of Dark Shadows *See* Night of Dark Shadows (1971)

The Curse of Demon Mountain *See* Shadow of Chikara (1977)

The Curse of Dracula *See* Return of Dracula (1958)

Curse of Melissa *See* The Touch of Satan (1970)

Curse of the Blood-Ghouls *See* The Slaughter of the Vampires (1962)

Curse of the Crimson Altar *See* The Crimson Cult (1968)

Curse of the Dragon *See* Bruce Lee: Curse of the Dragon (1993)

Curse of the Living Dead *See* Kill, Baby, Kill (1966)

Curse of the Mushroom People *See* Attack of the Mushroom People (1963)

Curses of the Ghouls *See* The Slaughter of the Vampires (1962)

Cutter and Bone *See* Cutter's Way (1981)

Cybele *See* Sundays & Cybele (1962)

Czlowiek z Zelaza *See* Man of Iron (1981)

Da Bancarella a Bancarotta *See* Peddlin' in Society (1947)

Daddy *See* Danielle Steel's "Daddy" (1992)

Daddy's Deadly Darling *See* Pigs (1973)

Dagboek Van Een Oude Dwaas *See* Diary of a Mad Old Man (1988)

Dagora *See* Dagora, the Space Monster (1965)

Dai Koesu Yongkari *See* Yongkari Monster of the Deep (1967)

Daibosatsu Toge *See* Sword of Doom (1967)

Daikaiju Baran *See* Varan the Unbelievable (1961)

Daikaiju Gamera *See* Gamera, the Invincible (1966)

Daikyoju Gappa *See* Gappa the Trifibian Monster (1967)

Dalle Ardenne All'Inferno *See* Dirty Heroes (1971)

Dance of the Dwarfs *See* Jungle Heat (1984)

Dance of the Vampires *See* The Fearless Vampire Killers (1967)

Danger Rides the Range *See* Three Texas Steers (1939)

Dangerous Charter *See* Creeping Terror (1964)

Dangerous Female *See* The Maltese Falcon (1931)

A Dangerous Friend *See* The Todd Killings (1971)

Dangerous Love Affairs *See* Dangerous Liaisons (1960)

Danielle Steel's Fine Things *See* Fine Things (1990)

Danny Travis *See* The Last Word (1980)

Dans la Ville Blanche *See* In the White City (1983)

Dans les Griffes du Maniaque *See* The Diabolical Dr. Z (1965)

Danza Macabra *See* Castle of Blood (1964)

Daoma Zei *See* The Horse Thief (1987)

Dark Angel *See* I Come in Peace (1990)

The Dark Avenger *See* The Warriors (1955)

Dark Eyes *See* Demon Rage (1982)

Dark Eyes of London *See* Dead Eyes of London (1961)

Dark Eyes of London *See* The Human Monster (1939)

Dark Sands *See* Jericho (1938)

D'Artagnan *See* The Three Musketeers (1916)

Das Bildnes des Dorian Gray *See* Dorian Gray (1970)

Das Blaue Licht *See* The Blue Light (1932)

Das Phantom von Soho *See* The Phantom of Soho (1964)

Das Schlangenei *See* The Serpent's Egg (1978)

Das Schloss *See* The Castle (1968)

Das Ungeheuer von London City *See* The Monster of London City (1964)

Dashiell Hammett's The Dain Curse *See* The Dain Curse (1978)

The Daughter of Frankenstein *See* Lady Frankenstein (1972)

David Lynch's Hotel Room *See* Hotel Room (1993)

Day of the Woman *See* I Spit on Your Grave (1977)

The Day the Hot Line Got Hot *See* The Hot Line (1969)

The Day the Screaming Stopped *See* The Comeback (1977)

The Day They Gave the Babies Away *See* All Mine to Give (1956)

Daybreak *See* Le Jour Se Leve (1939)

De Aanslag *See* The Assault (1986)

De la Part des Copains *See* Cold Sweat (1974)

De Sable et de Sang *See* Sand and Blood (1987)

De Stilte Rond Christine M *See* Question of Silence (1983)

De Wisselwachter *See* The Pointsman (1986)

Dead Aim *See* Born in America (1990)

Dead Kids *See* Strange Behavior (1981)

Dead of Night *See* Deathdream (1972)

Dead on Course *See* Wings of Danger (1952)

Dead or Alive *See* A Minute to Pray, A Second to Die (1967)

Dead or Alive *See* The Tracker (1988)

Dead People *See* Messiah of Evil (1974)

Deadly Companion *See* The Double Negative (1980)

Deadly Desire *See* Maybe I'll Be Home in the Spring (1970)

Deadly Desires *See* Home for the Holidays (1972)

Deadly Encounter *See* The Meal (1975)

Deadly is the Female *See* Gun Crazy (1949)

The Deadly Rays From Mars *See* Flash Gordon: Mars Attacks the World (1938)

Deadly Rivals *See* Rivals (1972)

Deadly Sting *See* Evil Spawn (1987)

The Deadly Three *See* Enter the Dragon (1973)

The Deadly Tower *See* Sniper (1975)

Deadly Treasure of the Piranha *See* Killer Fish (1979)

Dear Inspector *See* Dear Detective (1978)

Death and the Green Slime *See* The Green Slime (1968)

Death Bite *See* Spasms (1982)

Death Collector *See* Family Enforcer (1976)

Death Corps *See* Shock Waves (1977)

Death Dimension *See* Kill Factor (19??)

Death From Outer Space *See* The Day the Sky Exploded (1957)

Death Game *See* Seducers (1977)

Death House *See* Silent Night, Bloody Night (1973)

Death of a Hooker *See* Who Killed Mary What's 'Er Name? (1971)

Death of Her Innocence *See* Our Time (1974)

Death Ride to Osaka *See* Girls of the White Orchid (1985)

Death Scream *See* The Deadly Trap (1971)

Death Train *See* Detonator (1993)

Death Trap *See* Eaten Alive (1976)

Death Vengeance *See* Fighting Back (1982)

The Death Wheelers *See* Psychomania (1973)

Deathstalker 3: The Warriors From Hell *See* Deathstalker 3 (1989)

Debajo del Mundo *See* Under the Earth (1986)

The Debt *See* Veronico Cruz (1987)

Decoy for Terror *See* Playgirl Killer (1966)

Dedee *See* Dedee d'Anvers (1949)

Delta Pi *See* Mugsy's Girls (1985)

Dem Khann's Zindl *See* The Cantor's Son (1937)

Demanty Noci *See* Diamonds of the Night (1964)

Dementia *See* Daughter of Horror (1955)

Demon *See* God Told Me To (1976)

The Demon *See* Onibaba (1964)

Demon Master *See* Craze (1974)

The Demon Planet *See* Planet of the Vampires (1965)

Demoni *See* Demons (1986)

Demonios En El Jardin *See* Demons in the Garden (1982)

The Deputy *See* El Diputado (1978)

Der Amerikanische Soldat *See* The American Soldier (1970)

Der Blaue Engel *See* The Blue Angel (1930)

Der Chef Wuenscht Keine Zeugen *See* No Survivors, Please (1963)

Der Fluch Der Gruenen Augen *See* Cave of the Living Dead (1965)

Der Fussgaenger *See* The Pedestrian (1973)

Der Hauptmann von Koepenick *See* The Captain from Koepenick (1956)

Der Henker Von London *See* The Mad Executioners (1965)

Der Himmel Uber Berlin *See* Wings of Desire (1988)

Der Joker *See* Lethal Obsession (1987)

Der Kongress Tanzt *See* Congress Dances (1931)

Der Letzte Mann *See* The Last Laugh (1924)

Der Morder Dimitri Karamasoff *See* The Brothers Karamazov (1958)

Der Prozess *See* The Trial (1963)

Der Schweigende Stern *See* First Spaceship on Venus (1960)

Der Toderspringer *See* The Jumper (1985)

Der Verlone *See* The Lost One (1951)

Der Vilner Shtot Khazn *See* Overture to Glory (1940)

Deranged *See* Idaho Transfer (1973)

Des Enfants Gates *See* Spoiled Children (1977)

The Deserter *See* Ride to Glory (1971)

Desperate Siege *See* Rawhide (1950)

The Destroyers *See* Devastator (1985)

Destruction, Inc. *See* Just for the Hell of It (1968)

Det Sjunde Inseglet *See* The Seventh Seal (1956)

Det Stora Aventyret *See* The Great Adventure (1953)

Detective Geronimo *See* The Mad Bomber (1972)

The Detective Kid *See* The Gumshoe Kid (1989)

Deutschland im Herbst *See* Germany in Autumn (1978)

The Devil Walks at Midnight *See* The Devil's Nightmare (1971)

The Devil Within Her *See* I Don't Want to Be Born (1975)

The Devil Woman *See* Onibaba (1964)

The Devil's Bride *See* Velnio Nuotaka (1975)

Devil's Doll *See* The Devil's Hand (1961)

The Devil's Envoys *See* Les Visiteurs du Soir (1942)

Devil's Express *See* Gang Wars (1975)

The Devil's Men *See* Land of the Minotaur (1977)

The Devil's Mountain *See* La Montana del Diablo (1987)

Devil's Odds *See* The Wild Pair (1987)

The Devil's Plot *See* Counterblast (1948)

The Devil's Undead *See* Nothing But the Night (1972)

The Devil's Weed *See* Wild Weed (1949)

The Diabolical Dr. Mabuse *See* The Thousand Eyes of Dr. Mabuse (1960)

Diabolik *See* Danger: Diabolik (1968)

Diaboliquement Votre *See* Diabolically Yours (1967)

Dial 999 *See* The Way Out (1956)

Diamond Alley *See* Little Ladies of the Night (1977)

Diamond Earrings *See* The Earrings of Madame De... (1954)

Diamond Skulls *See* Dark Obsession (1990)

Diamonds and Crime *See* Hi Diddle Diddle (1943)

Diario Segreto Di Un Carcere Femminele *See* Women in Cell Block 7 (1977)

Diary of Oharu *See* Life of Oharu (1952)

Dick Tracy Meets Karloff *See* Dick Tracy Meets Gruesome (1947)

Dick Tracy's Amazing Adventure *See* Dick Tracy Meets Gruesome (1947)

Die, Beautiful Marianne *See* Die Screaming, Marianne (1973)

Die Bitteren Traenen der Petra von Kant *See* The Bitter Tears of Petra von Kant (1972)

Die Blechtrommel *See* The Tin Drum (1979)

Die Buechse Der Pandora *See* Pandora's Box (1928)

Die Dreigroschenoper *See* The Three Penny Opera (1962)

Die Dreigroschenoper *See* The Threepenny Opera (1931)

Die Ehe Der Maria Braun *See* The Marriage of Maria Braun (1979)

Die Flambierte Frau *See* A Woman in Flames (1984)

Die Folterkammer des Dr. Fu Manchu *See* The Castle of Fu Manchu (1968)

Die Holle von Macao *See* The Corrupt Ones (1967)

Die Holle von Manitoba *See* A Place Called Glory (1966)

Die Nibelungen *See* Kriemhilde's Revenge (1924)

Die Regenschirme Von Cherbourg *See* Umbrellas of Cherbourg (1964)

Die Schlangengrube und das Pendel *See* The Torture Chamber of Dr. Sadism (1969)

Die Sehns Ucht Der Veronika Voss *See* Veronika Voss (1982)

Die Toten Augen von London *See* Dead Eyes of London (1961)

Die Unsichtbaren Krallen des Dr. Mabuse *See* The Invisible Dr. Mabuse (1962)

Die Verlorene Ehre Der Katharina Blum *See* The Lost Honor of Katharina Blum (1975)

Die Xue Shuang Xiong *See* The Killer (1990)

Dio Mio, Come Sono Caduta in Basso *See* Till Marriage Do Us Part (1974)

A Dirty Knight's Work *See* Choice of Weapons (1976)

Dirty Mary *See* A Very Curious Girl (1969)

Disaster at Valdez *See* Dead Ahead: The Exxon Valdez Disaster (1992)

Disco Godfather *See* Avenging Disco Godfather (1976)

The Discreet *See* La Discrete (1990)

Disney's Blank Check *See* Blank Check (1993)

Distant Cousins *See* Desperate Motives (1992)

Dites-Lui Que Je L'Aime *See* This Sweet Sickness (1977)

Divine Obsession *See* Dangerous Obsession (1988)

Divorzio All'Italiana *See* Divorce—Italian Style (1962)

Djavulens Oga *See* The Devil's Eye (1960)

Do You Want to Dance with Me? *See* Voulez-Vous Danser Avec Moi? (1959)

Docteur M. *See* Club Extinction (1989)

Docteur Popaul *See* High Heels (1972)

Dr. Black and Mr. White *See* Dr. Black, Mr. Hyde (1976)

The Doctor from Seven Dials *See* Corridors of Blood (1958)

Doctor Gore *See* The Body Shop (1972)

Dr. Jekyll y el Hombre Lobo *See* Dr. Jekyll and the Wolfman (1971)

Dr. Maniac *See* The Man Who Lived Again (1936)

Doctor Maniac *See* House of the Living Dead (1973)

Doctor of Doom *See* Wrestling Women vs. the Aztec Ape (1962)

Dr. Terror's Gallery of Horrors *See* Alien Massacre (1967)

Doctors Wear Scarlet *See* The Bloodsuckers (1970)

A Dog, a Mouse, and a Sputnik *See* Sputnik (1961)

Dog Soldiers *See* Who'll Stop the Rain? (1978)

Doin' It *See* The First Time (1969)

Doin' It *See* First Time (1982)

Doing Life *See* Truth or Die (1986)

Doing Time *See* Porridge (1991)

Doktor Mabuse der Spieler *See* Dr. Mabuse the Gambler (1922)

Dolwyn *See* The Last Days of Dolwyn (1949)

Dom Za Vesanje *See* Time of the Gypsies (1990)

The Domino Killings *See* The Domino Principle (1977)

Don Juan *See* Private Life of Don Juan (1934)

Don Juan, Mi Querido Fantasma *See* Don Juan, My Love (1990)

Dona Flor e Seus Dois Maridos *See* Dona Flor and Her Two Husbands (1978)

Dona Herlinda y Su Hijo *See* Dona Herlinda & Her Son (1986)

Don't Fence Me In *See* Western Double Feature 4: Rogers & Evans (194?)

Don't Look Now, We've Been Shot At *See* La Grande Vadrouille (1966)

The Doomsday Machine *See* Escape from Planet Earth (1967)

The Door With Seven Locks *See* Chamber of Horrors (1940)

Doppelganger *See* Journey to the Far Side of the Sun (1969)

The Double *See* Kagemusha (1980)

Double Down *See* Stacy's Knights (1983)

Double Hit *See* The Arab Conspiracy (1976)

Double Possession *See* Black Vampire (1973)

Double Trouble *See* No Deposit, No Return (1976)

Douce Violence *See* Sweet Ecstasy (1962)

Down Went McGinty *See* The Great McGinty (1940)

Dracula *See* Bram Stoker's Dracula (1992)

Dracula *See* The Horror of Dracula (1958)

Dracula Contra Frankenstein *See* Dracula vs. Frankenstein (1971)

Dracula in the Castle of Blood *See* Web of the Spider (1970)

Dracula Pere et Fils *See* Dracula & Son (1976)

Dracula Saga *See* The Saga of the Draculas (1972)

Dracula: The Bloodline Continues... *See* The Saga of the Draculas (1972)

Dracula vs. Frankenstein *See* The Screaming Dead (1972)

Dracula's Castle *See* Blood of Dracula's Castle (1969)

Dracula's Dog *See* Zoltan...Hound of Dracula (1977)

Dracula's Virgin Lovers *See* Dracula's Great Love (1972)

Dragon Chow *See* Drachenfutter (1987)

Dragon Lady *See* G.I. Executioner (1971)

Dragonfly *See* One Summer Love (1976)

Dragon's Food *See* Drachenfutter (1987)

Draws *See* American Tickler (1976)

The Dreaded Persuasion *See* The Narcotics Story (1958)

Dream Slayer *See* Blood Song (1982)

Dreams *See* Akira Kurosawa's Dreams (1990)

Dreamworld *See* Covergirl (1983)

Dripping Deep Red *See* Deep Red: Hatchet Murders (1975)

Drivers to Hell *See* Wild Ones on Wheels (1962)

Drole de Drama *See* Bizarre Bizarre (1939)

The Drum *See* Drums (1938)

Du Rififi Chez les Hommes *See* Rififi (1954)

Duck, You Sucker *See* A Fistful of Dynamite (1972)

The Duckweed Story *See* Drifting Weeds (1959)

Due Notti Con Cleopatra *See* Two Nights with Cleopatra (1954)

Due Occhi Diabolici *See* Two Evil Eyes (1990)

Duel of the Gargantuas *See* War of the Gargantuas (1970)

Duello Nel Texas *See* Gun Fight at Red Sands (1963)

Dumb Dicks *See* Detective School Dropouts (1985)

Dungeons and Dragons *See* Mazes and Monsters (1982)

Duvar *See* The Wall (1983)

Dynamite Women *See* The Great Texas Dynamite Chase (1976)

Dyrygent *See* The Conductor (1980)

Each Man For Himself *See* The Ruthless Four (1970)

Each One For Himself *See* The Ruthless Four (1970)

Eagle's Nest *See* Nido de Aguilas (1976)

Earth Defense Forces *See* The Mysterians (1958)

The Earth Will Tremble *See* La Terra Trema (1948)

East Connection *See* Conexion Oriental (1970)

East of Shanghai *See* Rich and Strange (1932)

East of the Bowery *See* Follow the Leader (1944)

East of the Rising Sun *See* Malaya (1949)

Easy Go *See* Free and Easy (1930)

Eaten Alive by Cannibals *See* Emerald Jungle (1980)

Ebirah, Terror of the Deep *See* Godzilla vs. the Sea Monster (1966)

Eboli *See* Christ Stopped at Eboli (1979)

Edgar Allan Poe's Conqueror Worm *See* The Conqueror Worm (1968)

Edgar Allen Poe's The Oblong Box *See* The Oblong Box (1969)

The Edge of Hell *See* Rock 'n' Roll Nightmare (1985)

Edipo Re *See* Oedipus Rex (1967)

Ein Mann wie Eva *See* A Man Like Eva (1983)

Ein Toter Hing im Netz *See* Horrors of Spider Island (1959)

Eine Liebe in Deutschland *See* A Love in Germany (1984)

Einer Frisst den Anderen *See* Dog Eat Dog (1964)

Ekstase *See* Ecstasy (1933)

El Ataud Del Coffin *See* The Vampire's Coffin (1958)

El Ataud Del Vampiro *See* The Vampire's Coffin (1958)

El Buque Maldito *See* Horror of the Zombies (1974)

El Cazador de la Muerte *See* Deathstalker (1983)

El Cobra *See* The Cobra (1968)

El Coleccionista de Cadaveres *See* Cauldron of Blood (1967)

El Dedo En El Gatillo *See* Finger on the Trigger (1965)

El Espiritu de la Colmena *See* Spirit of the Beehive (1973)

El Grito de la Muerte *See* The Living Coffin (1958)

El la Nave Va *See* And the Ship Sails On (1983)

El Mas Fabulosi Golpe del Far West *See* The Boldest Job in the West (1971)

El Pirata Negro *See* The Black Pirate (1965)

El Rapto de las Sabinas *See* The Rape of the Sabines (1961)

El Retorno de la Walpurgis *See* Curse of the Devil (1973)

El Robot Humano *See* The Robot vs. the Aztec Mummy (1959)

El Rublo de las dos Caras *See* The Hot Line (1969)

El Sonido de la Muerte *See* Sound of Horror (1964)

El Tesoro del Amazones *See* The Treasure of the Amazon (1984)

El Verano de la Senora Forbes *See* The Summer of Miss Forbes (1988)

Electric Boogaloo "Breakin' 2" *See* Breakin' 2: Electric Boogaloo (1984)

The Electric Monster *See* The Electronic Monster (1957)

Elena et les Hommes *See* Elena and Her Men (1956)

Elevator to the Gallows *See* Frantic (1958)

Emergency Landing *See* Robot Pilot (1941)

Emil Und Die Detektive *See* Emil and the Detective (1964)

Emma Mae *See* Black Sister's Revenge (1976)

The Emperor of Peru *See* The Odyssey of the Pacific (1982)

Empire of Passion *See* In the Realm of Passion (1980)

The Empress Yang Kwei Fei *See* Princess Yang Kwei Fei (1955)

En Effeuillant la Marguerite *See* Mademoiselle Striptease (1957)

En Enda Natt *See* Only One Night (1942)

En Kvinnas Ansikte *See* A Woman's Face (1938)

En Lekiton i Karlek *See* Lesson in Love (1954)

The Enchanted Island *See* La Isla Encantada (1984)

End of the Rainbow *See* Northwest Outpost (1947)

End of the World *See* Panic in the Year Zero! (1962)

End of the World (in Our Usual Bed in a Night Full of Rain) *See* A Night Full of Rain (1978)

Enemies of the Public *See* Public Enemy (1931)

Enemy from Space *See* Quatermass 2 (1957)

Enemy Round-Up *See* Hillbilly Blitzkrieg (1942)

The Enigma of Kaspar Hauser *See* Every Man for Himself & God Against All (1975)

Enormous Changes at the Last Minute *See* Enormous Changes (1983)

Enormous Changes at the Last Minute *See* Trumps (1988)

Ensayo de un Crimen *See* The Criminal Life of Archibaldo de la Cruz (1955)

Entebbe: Operation Thunderbolt *See* Operation Thunderbolt (1977)

Entre Tinieblas *See* Dark Habits (1984)

Episoda Del Mare *See* La Terra Trema (1948)

Ercole al Centro Della Terra *See* Hercules in the Haunted World (1964)

Ercole Alla Conquista di Atlantide *See* Hercules and the Captive Women (1963)

Ercole Contro Molock *See* Conquest of Mycene (1963)

Ercole e la Regina di Lidia *See* Hercules Unchained (1959)

Erik the Conqueror *See* The Invaders (1963)

Ernest Hemingway's the Killers *See* The Killers (1964)

Escapade *See* Utopia (1951)

Escape from the Dark *See* The Littlest Horse Thieves (1976)

Escape If You Can *See* St. Benny the Dip (1951)

The Escape of Megagodzilla *See* Terror of Mechagodzilla (1978)

Escape Route *See* I'll Get You (1953)

Escape to Freedom *See* Judgment in Berlin (1988)

Escapement *See* The Electronic Monster (1957)

Escort Girl *See* Half Moon Street (1986)

Espiritismo *See* Spiritism (1961)

Et Dieu Crea la Femme *See* And God Created Woman (1957)

Et Mourir de Plaisir *See* Blood and Roses (1961)

Etat de Siege *See* State of Siege (1973)

European Vacation *See* National Lampoon's European Vacation (1985)

Every Day's a Holiday *See* Seaside Swingers (1965)

Every Home Should Have One *See* Think Dirty (1970)

Every Man For Himself *See* The Ruthless Four (1970)

Every Night a New Lover *See* Cada Noche un Amor (1975)

Every Woman's Man *See* The Prizefighter and the Lady (1933)

Everybody's Cheering *See* Take Me Out to the Ball Game (1949)

Evil Dead 3 *See* Army of Darkness (1992)

Evil in the Swamp *See* All the Kind Strangers (1974)

Ewiger Walzer *See* The Eternal Waltz (1954)

Except For Me and Thee *See* Friendly Persuasion (1956)

Expedition Moon *See* Rocketship X-M (1950)

Exploring the Kinsey Report *See* One Plus One (1961)

Expose *See* The House on Straw Hill (1976)

Extase *See* Ecstasy (1933)

Extenuating Circumstances *See* Circonstances Attenuantes (1936)

Extreme Close-Up *See* Sex Through a Window (1972)

An Eye for an Eye *See* Psychopath (1973)

An Eye for an Eye *See* Talion (1966)

Eyes of Hell *See* The Mask (1961)

Eyes Without a Face *See* The Horror Chamber of Dr. Faustus (1959)

Eyewitness *See* Sudden Terror (1970)

Fabula de la Bella Palomera *See* The Fable of the Beautiful Pigeon Fancier (1988)

The Fabulous Baron Munchausen *See* The Original Fabulous Adventures of Baron Munchausen (1961)

Face of a Stranger *See* The Promise (1978)

Face the Music *See* Black Glove (1954)

The Faceless Monsters *See* Nightmare Castle (1965)

Fakebook *See* American Blue Note (1989)

Falcon's Gold *See* Robbers of the Sacred Mountain (1983)

Fall Break *See* The Mutilator (1985)

The Fall Guy *See* What's Up Front (1963)

The Fall of the House of Usher *See* La Chute de la Maison Usher (1928)

False Face *See* Scalpel (1976)

False Faces *See* Let 'Em Have It (1935)

Falstaff *See* Chimes at Midnight (1967)

Fanatic *See* Die! Die! My Darling! (1965)

The Fanatic *See* The Last Horror Film (1982)

Fangelse *See* Devil's Wanton (1949)

Fanny by Gaslight *See* Man of Evil (1948)

Fanny Och Alexander *See* Fanny and Alexander (1983)

Fan's Video *See* Otaku no Video (1991)

The Far Country *See* Nevil Shute's The Far Country (1985)

Farewell, Friend *See* Honor Among Thieves (1968)

Farewell, My Love *See* Murder, My Sweet (1944)

The Farm *See* The Curse (1987)

Farm Girl *See* The Farmer's Other Daughter (1965)

Farm of the Year *See* Miles from Home (1988)

Fashions *See* Fashions of 1934 (1934)

Fast Fortune *See* 11 Harrowhouse (1974)

Fatal Assassin *See* African Rage (1978)

Fatal Woman *See* Femme Fatale (1990)

The Father *See* Baba (1973)

Father & Son: Dangerous Relations *See* Dangerous Relations (1993)

Father Brown *See* The Detective (1954)

Father Damien: The Leper Priest *See* Damien: The Leper Priest (1980)

The Father Kino Story *See* Mission to Glory (1980)

Father Master *See* Padre Padrone (1977)

Father, Son and the Mistress *See* For Richer, For Poorer (1992)

Faustrecht der Freiheit *See* Fox and His Friends (1975)

Fear *See* Night Creature (1979)

The Fear *See* Gates of Hell (1983)

Fear Eats the Soul *See* Ali: Fear Eats the Soul (1974)

Fear in the City of the Living Dead *See* Gates of Hell (1983)

Fear in the Night *See* Dynasty of Fear (1972)

Feast of Flesh *See* Blood Feast (1963)

Federico Fellini's 8 1/2 *See* 8 1/2 (1963)

Federico Fellini's Intervista *See* Intervista (1987)

Feel the Heat *See* Catch the Heat (1987)

Female *See* The Violent Years (1956)

The Female Butcher *See* The Legend of Blood Castle (1972)

A Few Days in the Life of I.I. Oblomov *See* Oblomov (1981)

The Fiend with the Atomic Brain *See* Blood of Ghastly Horror (1972)

The Fiend with the Electronic Brain *See* Blood of Ghastly Horror (1972)

Fiendish Ghouls *See* Mania (1960)

Fierce *See* Fighting Mad (1977)

The Fifth Chair *See* It's in the Bag (1945)

The Fighting Phantom *See* The Mysterious Rider (1933)

The Fighting Pimpernel *See* The Elusive Pimpernel (1950)

The Fighting Seventh *See* Little Big Horn (1951)

Film d'Amore et d'Anarchia *See* Love and Anarchy (1973)

Filofax *See* Taking Care of Business (1990)

The Final Crash *See* Steelyard Blues (1973)

Finally, Sunday *See* Confidentially Yours (1983)

Fine and Dandy *See* The West Point Story (1950)

Fire Festival *See* Himatsuri (1985)

Fire in Eden *See* Tusks (1989)

The First and the Last *See* 21 Days (1937)

The First Great Train Robbery *See* The Great Train Robbery (1979)

The First Hello *See* High Country (1981)

The First of the Few *See* Spitfire (1942)

The First Rebel *See* Allegheny Uprising (1939)

The First Time *See* The Fighter (1952)

First Woman Into Space *See* Space Monster (1964)

A Fist Full of Chopsticks *See* They Call Me Bruce? (1982)

Fist of Fury *See* Chinese Connection (1973)

Fist Right of Freedom *See* Fox and His Friends (1975)

Five Bloody Days to Tombstone *See* Gun Riders (1969)

Five Bloody Graves *See* Gun Riders (1969)

Five Day Lover *See* Time Out for Love (1961)

Five Days *See* Paid to Kill (1954)

Five Minutes to Live *See* Door to Door Maniac (1961)

Five Women Around Utamaro *See* Utamaro and His Five Women (1946)

Flash Gordon's Trip to Mars *See* Flash Gordon: Mars Attacks the World (1938)

Flatbed Annie *See* Flatbed Annie and Sweetiepie: Lady Truckers (1979)

The Flesh and the Fiends *See* Mania (1960)

The Flesh Creatures *See* Horror of the Blood Monsters (1970)

Flesh Creatures of the Red Planet *See* Horror of the Blood Monsters (1970)

Flesh for Frankenstein *See* Andy Warhol's Frankenstein (1974)

The Flight *See* The Taking of Flight 847: The Uli Derickson Story (1988)

The Flight of the White Stallions *See* The Miracle of the White Stallions (1963)

Flipper and the Pirates *See* Flipper's New Adventure (1964)

Floating Weeds *See* Drifting Weeds (1959)

Flying Aces *See* The Flying Deuces (1939)

Fog *See* A Study in Terror (1966)

Folies Bourgeoises *See* Twist (1976)

The Folks at Red Wolf Inn *See* Terror at Red Wolf Inn (1972)

Follow That Bird *See* Sesame Street Presents: Follow That Bird (1985)

Follow the Hunter *See* Fangs of the Wild (1954)

Follow Your Dreams *See* Independence Day (1983)

Fontane Effi Briest *See* Effi Briest (1974)

For a Few Bullets More *See* Any Gun Can Play (1967)

For Better or For Worse *See* Honeymoon Academy (1990)

For Love or Money *See* If I Were Rich (1933)

For Men Only *See* Tall Lie (1953)

For We Too Do Not Forgive *See* Death is Called Engelchen (1963)

Forbidden Alliance *See* The Barretts of Wimpole Street (1934)

Forbidden Love *See* Freaks (1932)

Forbidden Paradise *See* Hurricane (1979)

Forbidden Passions *See* The Sensuous Teenager (1970)

Forbidden Son *See* Bulldance (1988)

The Forbin Project *See* Colossus: The Forbin Project (1970)

Forbrydelsens Element *See* The Element of Crime (1984)

Ford Fairlane *See* The Adventures of Ford Fairlane (1990)

The Forest Primeval *See* The Final Terror (1983)

Forgotten Prisoners: The Amnesty Files *See* Forgotten Prisoners (1990)

The Forsyte Saga *See* That Forsyte Woman (1950)

Fort Lost *See* Fuerte Perdido (1978)

Fortune in Diamonds *See* The Adventurers (1951)

47 Samurai *See* 47 Ronin, Part 1 (1942)

Forward March *See* Doughboys (1930)

The Four Just Men *See* The Secret Four (1940)

A Fourth for Marriage *See* What's Up Front (1963)

4...3...2...1...Morte *See* Mission Stardust (1968)

F.P. 1 Antwortet Nicht *See* F.P. 1 Doesn't Answer (1933)

Fra Diavolo *See* The Devil's Brother (1933)

Frage 7 *See* Question 7 (1963)

Francis *See* Francis the Talking Mule (1949)

Frankenstein '88 *See* The Vindicator (1985)

Frankenstein Meets the Spacemen *See* Frankenstein Meets the Space Monster (1965)

Frasier the Lovable Lion *See* Frasier the Sensuous Lion (1973)

Fraternally Yours *See* Sons of the Desert (1933)

The Freak From Suckweasel Mountain *See* Geek Maggot Bingo (1983)

Free to Live *See* Holiday (1938)

Frenzy *See* Torment (1944)

Freylekhe Kabtsonim *See* The Jolly Paupers (1938)

The Fright *See* Visiting Hours (1982)

The Frightened Lady *See* The Case of the Frightened Lady (1939)

Frightmare 2 *See* Frightmare (1974)

Friz Freleng's Looney Looney Looney Bugs Bunny Movie *See* Looney Looney Looney Bugs Bunny Movie (1981)

The Frog Prince *See* The French Lesson (1986)

From a Whisper to a Scream *See* The Offspring (1987)

From Broadway to Cheyenne *See* Broadway to Cheyenne (1932)

From the Mixed-Up Files of Mrs. Basil E. Frankweiler *See* The Hideaways (1973)

Fruhlingssinfonie *See* Spring Symphony (1986)

The Fruit Machine *See* Wonderland (1988)

Fukkatsu no Hi *See* Virus (1982)

The Fulfillment of Mary Gray *See* Fulfillment (1989)

The Fun House *See* Last House on Dead End Street (1977)

Fun Loving *See* Quackser Fortune Has a Cousin in the Bronx (1970)

Fuoco Fatuo *See* The Fire Within (1964)

Furankenshutain No Kaijusanda Tai Gailah *See* War of the Gargantuas (1970)

The Further Adventures of Ma and Pa Kettle *See* Ma and Pa Kettle (1949)

Fury of Samson *See* The Fury of Hercules (1961)

Fury of the Succubus *See* Demon Rage (1982)

Fury of the Vikings *See* The Invaders (1963)

Future Cop *See* Trancers (1985)

Gallery of Horror *See* Alien Massacre (1967)

Gambara vs. Barugon *See* Gamera vs. Barugon (1966)

Gamblin' Man *See* Cockfighter (1974)

Game of Survival *See* Tenement (1985)

Gamera *See* Gamera, the Invincible (1966)

Gamera Tai Barugon *See* Gamera vs. Barugon (1966)

Gamera Tai Gaos *See* Gamera vs. Gaos (1967)

Gamera Tai Guiron *See* Gamera vs. Guiron (1969)

Gamera Tai Shinkai Kaiju Jigara *See* Gamera vs. Zigra (1971)

Gamera vs. Gyaos *See* Gamera vs. Gaos (1967)

Gamera vs. the Deep Sea Monster Zigra *See* Gamera vs. Zigra (1971)

Gamma Sango Uchu Daisakusen *See* The Green Slime (1968)

Gamma 693 *See* The Chilling (1989)

Gamma 693 *See* Night of the Zombies (1981)

Gammera *See* Gamera, the Invincible (1966)

Gang War *See* Odd Man Out (1947)

Gangs of Sonora *See* Western Double Feature 6: Rogers & Trigger (1950)

Ganja and Hess *See* Black Vampire (1973)

The Gardener *See* Seeds of Evil (1976)

The Gargon Terror *See* Teenagers from Outer Space (1959)

Garou Garou le Passe Muraille *See* Mr. Peek-A-Boo (1950)

Gas-s-s-s... or, It May Become Necessary to Destroy the World in Order to Save It *See* Gas-s-s-s! (1970)

Gasu Ningen Daiichigo *See* The Human Vapor (1968)

A Gathering of Old Men *See* Murder on the Bayou (1991)

Gatto Rossi In Un Labirinto Do Vetro *See* Eyeball (1978)

The Gay Divorce *See* The Gay Divorcee (1934)

The Gay Mrs. Trexel *See* Susan and God (1940)

Gebroken Spiegels *See* Broken Mirrors (1985)

Geheimecode Wildganse *See* Codename: Wildgeese (1984)

Georgia's Friends *See* Four Friends (1981)

Gestapo *See* Night Train to Munich (1940)

Get Down and Boogie *See* Darktown Strutters (1974)

Get Well Soon *See* Visiting Hours (1982)

Getting Even *See* Utilities (1983)

Gharbar *See* The Householder (1963)

Ghare Baire *See* The Home and the World (1984)

Ghidora, The Three-Headed Monster *See* Ghidrah the Three Headed Monster (1965)

Ghidorah Sandai Kaiju Chikyu Saidai No Kessan *See* Ghidrah the Three Headed Monster (1965)

Ghidrah *See* Ghidrah the Three Headed Monster (1965)

The Ghost Creeps *See* Boys of the City (1940)

The Ghost of John Holling *See* Mystery Liner (1934)

The Ghost Steps Out *See* The Time of Their Lives (1946)

Ghost Story *See* Madhouse Mansion (1974)

The Ghoul in School *See* Werewolf in a Girl's Dormitory (1961)

The Giant Leeches *See* Attack of the Giant Leeches (1959)

Gigantis, the Fire Monster *See* Godzilla Raids Again (1959)

Gilbert Grape *See* What's Eating Gilbert Grape (1993)

Gill Woman *See* Voyage to the Planet of Prehistoric Women (1968)

Gill Women of Venus *See* Voyage to the Planet of Prehistoric Women (1968)

Gingerbread House *See* Who Slew Auntie Roo? (1971)

Gion Bayashi *See* A Geisha (1953)

Gion Festival Music *See* A Geisha (1953)

Girl in Pawn *See* Little Miss Marker (1934)

Girl in the Moon *See* Woman in the Moon (1929)

Girl in the Park *See* Sanctuary of Fear (1979)

Girl in the Street *See* London Melody (1937)

The Girl Was Young *See* Young and Innocent (1937)

Girls For Rent *See* I Spit on Your Corpse (1974)

Girls in Uniform *See* Maedchen in Uniform (1931)

Giro City *See* And Nothing But the Truth (1982)

Giu la Testa *See* A Fistful of Dynamite (1972)

Giulietta Degli Spiriti *See* Juliet of the Spirits (1965)

Gladiatorerna *See* The Gladiators (1970)

The Glass Cage *See* Glass Tomb (1955)

Gli Indifferenti *See* Time of Indifference (1964)

Gli Invasori *See* The Invaders (1963)

Glorious Sacrifice *See* The Glory Trail (1936)

Glory at Sea *See* The Gift Horse (1952)

The Glove: Lethal Terminator *See* The Glove (1978)

Glump *See* Please Don't Eat My Mother (1972)

G'mar Giviya *See* Cup Final (1992)

Gnaw: Food of the Gods 2 *See* Food of the Gods: Part 2 (1988)

Go and See *See* Come and See (1985)

The Goat *See* La Chevre (1981)

Godzilla Fights the Giant Moth *See* Godzilla vs. Mothra (1964)

Godzilla Versus the Bionic Monster *See* Godzilla vs. the Cosmic Monster (1974)

Godzilla vs. Gigan *See* Godzilla on Monster Island (1972)

Godzilla vs. Hedora *See* Godzilla vs. the Smog Monster (1972)

Godzilla vs. Mechagodzilla *See* Godzilla vs. the Cosmic Monster (1974)

Godzilla vs. the Giant Moth *See* Godzilla vs. Mothra (1964)

Godzilla vs. the Thing *See* Godzilla vs. Mothra (1964)

Godzilla's Counter Attack *See* Godzilla Raids Again (1959)

Going Ape *See* Where's Poppa? (1970)

Gojira *See* Godzilla, King of the Monsters (1956)

Gojira no Musuko *See* Son of Godzilla (1966)

Gojira Tai Hedora *See* Godzilla vs. the Smog Monster (1972)

Gojira Tai Megaro *See* Godzilla vs. Megalon (1976)

Gojira Tai Meka-Gojira *See* Godzilla vs. the Cosmic Monster (1974)

Goke, Body Snatcher from Hell *See* Body Snatcher from Hell (1969)

Goke the Vampire *See* Body Snatcher from Hell (1969)

Gokiburi *See* Twilight of the Cockroaches (1990)

Golden Hands of Kurigal *See* Federal Agents vs. Underworld, Inc. (1949)

The Golden Heist *See* Inside Out (1975)

The Golden Hour *See* Pot O' Gold (1941)

Golden Ivory *See* White Huntress (1957)

The Golden Rooster *See* El Gallo de Oro (1965)

The Golden Trail *See* Riders of the Whistling Skull (1937)

Goliat Contra Los Gigantes *See* Goliath Against the Giants (1963)

Goliath and the Giants *See* Goliath Against the Giants (1963)

Goliath and the Golden City *See* Samson and the 7 Miracles of the World (1962)

Goliath Contro I Giganti *See* Goliath Against the Giants (1963)

Gomar the Human Gorilla *See* Night of the Bloody Apes (1968)

Good Luck, Miss Wyckoff *See* The Shaming (1971)

A Good Marriage *See* Le Beau Mariage (1982)

Good Morning Babilonia *See* Good Morning, Babylon (1987)

A Good Time, A Bad Girl *See* Good Time with a Bad Girl (1967)

Good to Go *See* Short Fuse (1988)

Goodbye Bruce Lee: His Last Game of Death *See* Game of Death (1979)

Goodbye, Children *See* Au Revoir Les Enfants (1987)

Goodbye Gemini *See* Twinsanity (1970)

Goodbye to the Hill *See* Paddy (1970)

Gordon il Pirata Nero *See* The Black Pirate (1926)

Gorilla *See* Nabonga (1944)

Gosta Berling's Saga *See* The Atonement of Gosta Berling (1924)

Gotter der Pest *See* Gods of the Plague (1969)

Gran Amore del Conde Dracula *See* Dracula's Great Love (1972)

The Grand Highway *See* Le Grand Chemin (1987)

The Grass is Singing *See* Killing Heat (1984)

The Grasshopper *See* The Passing of Evil (1970)

Grave Desires *See* Brides of the Beast (1968)

Grave Robbers from Outer Space *See* Plan 9 from Outer Space (1956)

Graveyard Tramps *See* Invasion of the Bee Girls (1973)

The Great Adventure *See* The Adventurers (1951)

Great American Bugs Bunny-Road Runner Chase *See* The Bugs Bunny/Road Runner Movie (1979)

The Great Balloon Adventure *See* Olly Olly Oxen Free (1978)

The Great Day *See* A Special Day (1977)

Great Friends *See* Grandes Amigos (197?)

The Great Georgia Bank Hoax *See* Great Bank Hoax (1978)

The Great Lester Boggs *See* Hootch Country Boys (1975)

The Great Manhunt *See* The Doolins of Oklahoma (1949)

Great Monster Yongkari *See* Yongkari Monster of the Deep (1967)

The Great Schnozzle *See* Palooka (1934)

The Great Spy Mission *See* Operation Crossbow (1965)

The Great Wall is a Great Wall *See* A Great Wall (1986)

The Greatest Battle *See* Battleforce (1978)

The Greatest Battle on Earth *See* Ghidrah the Three Headed Monster (1965)

The Greatest Love *See* Europa '51 (1952)

The Greeks Had a Word for Them *See* Three Broadway Girls (1932)

Green Monkey *See* Blue Monkey (1987)

The Green Ray *See* Summer (1986)

Greta the Mad Butcher *See* Ilsa, the Wicked Warden (1978)

Grey Matter *See* Mind Warp (1972)

Gridlock *See* Great American Traffic Jam (1980)

Grijpstra and de Gier *See* Fatal Error (1983)

Grine Felder *See* Green Fields (1937)

Gringo *See* Gun Fight at Red Sands (1963)

The Grip of the Strangler *See* The Haunted Strangler (1958)

Gruner Felder *See* Green Fields (1937)

Gruppo di Famiglia in un Interno *See* Conversation Piece (1975)

Guardian of the Wilderness *See* Mountain Man (1977)

Gun Man from Bodie *See* Gunman from Bodie (1941)

Gun Moll *See* Jigsaw (1949)

Guney's The Wall *See* The Wall (1983)

Gunpoint *See* At Gunpoint (1955)

Guns in the Afternoon *See* Ride the High Country (1962)

Guns, Sin and Bathtub Gin *See* Lady in Red (1979)

Gwendoline *See* The Perils of Gwendoline (1984)

Gycklarnas Afton *See* Sawdust & Tinsel (1953)

Haakon Haakonsen *See* Shipwrecked (1990)

Hab Og Karlighed *See* Twist & Shout (1984)

Habricha el Hashemesh *See* Escape to the Sun (1972)

Hadaka No Shima *See* The Island (1961)

Hail to the Chief *See* Hail (1973)

Half Slave, Half Free 2 *See* Charlotte Forten's Mission: Experiment in Freedom (1985)

Hallelujah, I'm a Tramp *See* Hallelujah, I'm a Bum (1933)

Hallucination Generation *See* Hallucination (1967)

Ham Ham *See* Jamon, Jamon (1993)

Ha'Matarah Tiran *See* Sinai Commandos (1968)

The Hammond Mystery *See* The Undying Monster (1942)

Hand of Night *See* Beast of Morocco (1966)

Handgun *See* Deep in the Heart (1983)

Handle With Care *See* Citizens Band (1977)

Hands of a Killer *See* Planets Against Us (1961)

The Hands of Orlac *See* Mad Love (1935)

Hands of the Strangler *See* The Hands of Orlac (1960)

Handsome Serge *See* Le Beau Serge (1958)

The Hangover *See* The Female Jungle (1956)

Hans Christian Andersen's Thumbelina *See* Thumbelina (1994)

Happiness *See* Le Bonheur (1965)

Happy Go Lucky *See* Hallelujah, I'm a Bum (1933)

Happy Mother's Day, Love, George *See* Run, Stranger, Run (1973)

The Happy New Year Caper *See* Happy New Year (1974)

Happy Times *See* The Inspector General (1949)

Hard Driver *See* The Last American Hero (1973)

Hard Stick *See* A Real American Hero (1978)

The Hardcore Life *See* Hardcore (1979)

Harem Holiday *See* Harum Scarum (1965)

Harlem Hot Shot *See* The Black King (1932)

Harlequin *See* Dark Forces (1983)

Harold Robbins' The Betsy *See* The Betsy (1978)

Harp of Burma *See* The Burmese Harp (1956)

Harry Black *See* Harry Black and the Tiger (1958)

Harry Tracy—Desperado *See* Harry Tracy (1983)

Harry's Machine *See* Hollywood Harry (1986)

The Hatchet Murders *See* Deep Red: Hatchet Murders (1975)

The Haunted and the Hunted *See* Dementia 13 (1963)

The Haunting of Hamilton High *See* Hello Mary Lou: Prom Night 2 (1987)

The Haunting of Julia *See* Full Circle (1977)

Haus Der Tausend Freuden *See* The House of 1000 Dolls (1967)

Haxan *See* Witchcraft Through the Ages (1922)

He Lived to Kill *See* Night of Terror (1933)

He Loved an Actress *See* Mad About Money (1930)

He or She *See* Glen or Glenda (1953)

He, She or It *See* The Doll (1962)

Head On *See* Fatal Attraction (1980)

Head Over Heels *See* Chilly Scenes of Winter (1979)

The Head That Wouldn't Die *See* The Brain That Wouldn't Die (1963)

A Heart in Winter *See* Un Coeur en Hiver (1993)

The Heart of New York *See* Hallelujah, I'm a Bum (1933)

Hearts and Minds *See* Master Touch (1974)

Heartstone *See* Demonstone (1989)

Heavenly Pursuits *See* The Gospel According to Vic (1987)

Hector Servadac's Ark *See* On the Comet (1968)

The Heir to Genghis Khan *See* Storm Over Asia (1928)

The Heist *See* Dollars (1971)

Heldorado *See* Helldorado (1946)

Hell Bent for Glory *See* Lafayette Escadrille (1958)

Hell in Normandy *See* Special Forces (1968)

Hell of the Living Dead *See* Night of the Zombies (1983)

Hell to Macao *See* The Corrupt Ones (1967)

Hellborn *See* The Sinister Urge (1960)

Hellcamp *See* Opposing Force (1987)

Hellfire on Ice, Part 2: Escape from Hell *See* Escape from Hell (1989)

Hello Elephant *See* Pardon My Trunk (1952)

Hellraiser 2 *See* Hellbound: Hellraiser 2 (1988)

Her Mad Night *See* Held for Murder (1932)

Hercules and the Conquest of Atlantis *See* Hercules and the Captive Women (1963)

Hercules and the Haunted Women *See* Hercules and the Captive Women (1963)

Hercules and the Hydra *See* The Loves of Hercules (1960)

Hercules Goes Bananas *See* Hercules in New York (1970)

Hercules: The Movie *See* Hercules in New York (1970)

Here Come the Tigers *See* Manny's Orphans (1978)

Here Is a Man *See* The Devil & Daniel Webster (1941)

Here Lies Love *See* Second Woman (1951)

Here We Go Again *See* Pride of the Bowery (1941)

The Hero of Pine Ridge *See* Yodelin' Kid From Pine Ridge (1937)

Heroes Die Hard *See* Mr. Kingstreet's War (1971)

Herzbube *See* King, Queen, Knave (1972)

The Heterosexuals *See* Les Biches (1968)

Hets *See* Torment (1944)

Hex *See* The Shrieking (1973)

Hidden Face *See* Jail Bait (1954)

The Hidden Room of 1,000 Horrors *See* The Tell-Tale Heart (1962)

Hidden Vision *See* Night Eyes (1990)

Hide and Shriek *See* American Gothic (1988)

High Rolling *See* High Rolling in a Hot Corvette (1977)

The Highest Bidder *See* Woman Hunt (1972)

Highway to Hell *See* Running Hot (1983)

Him *See* Only You (1994)

The Hindu *See* Sabaka (1955)

His Other Woman *See* Desk Set (1957)

Histoires Extraordinaires *See* Spirits of the Dead (1968)

History of a Great Love *See* Historia de un Gran Amor (1957)

Hitler's Gold *See* Inside Out (1975)

Hitman *See* American Commandos (1984)

HMS Defiant *See* Damn the Defiant (1962)

Hol Volt, Hol Nem Volt *See* A Hungarian Fairy Tale (1987)

Holiday *See* Jour de Fete (1948)

Hollow Point *See* The Wild Pair (1987)

Hollow Triumph *See* The Scar (1948)

Hollyweird *See* Flicks (1985)

Hollywood Cowboy *See* Hearts of the West (1975)

Hollywood Hoodlum *See* Hollywood Mystery (1934)

The Hollywood Strangler *See* Don't Answer the Phone (1980)

Hollywood Stunt Man *See* Movie Stuntmen (1953)

Hollywood Thrillmakers *See* Movie Stuntmen (1953)

Holocaust 2000 *See* The Chosen (1977)

Holy Terror *See* Alice Sweet Alice (1976)

Hombre Mirando Al Sudeste *See* Man Facing Southeast (1986)

Home Front *See* Morgan Stewart's Coming Home (1987)

Home In Oklahoma *See* Big Show (1937)

Home is Where the Heart Is *See* Square Dance (1987)

Home on the Range *See* Western Double Feature 2: Wayne & Hale (198?)

L'Homme du Minnesota *See* Minnesota Clay (1965)

L'Homme Qui Aimait les Femmes *See* The Man Who Loved Women (1977)

Honeymoon in Bali *See* My Love For Yours (1939)

Honeymoon of Fear *See* Dynasty of Fear (1972)

The Honeymooners: The Lost Episodes *See* Honeymooners Hidden Episodes, Vol. 1 (1953)

The Honorary Consul *See* Beyond the Limit (1983)

Hoodlum Girls *See* Youth Aflame (1959)

The Hooker Cult Murders *See* The Pyx (1973)

Hopalong Cassidy Enters *See* Hopalong Cassidy (1935)

The Hopeless Ones *See* The Round Up (1966)

A Hora Da Estrela *See* The Hour of the Star (1985)

The Horrible House on the Hill *See* Devil Times Five (1974)

The Horrible Mill Women *See* Mill of the Stone Women (1960)

Horror Castle *See* The Virgin of Nuremberg (1965)

Horror Convention *See* Nightmare in Blood (1975)

Horror Creatures of the Prehistoric Planet *See* Horror of the Blood Monsters (1970)

Horror High *See* Twisted Brain (1974)

Horror Hotel Massacre *See* Eaten Alive (1976)

Horror in the Midnight Sun *See* Invasion of the Animal People (1962)

Horror Maniacs *See* The Greed of William Hart (1948)

Horror of the Stone Women *See* Mill of the Stone Women (1960)

Horror on Snape Island *See* Tower of Evil (1972)

Horse, My Horse *See* The Horse (1982)

A Horse Named Comanche *See* Tonka (1958)

Horsie *See* Queen for a Day (1951)

Hostage *See* Savage Attraction (1983)

Hostage: Dallas *See* Getting Even (1986)

Hostage: The Christine Maresch Story *See* Savage Attraction (1983)

Hot and Cold *See* Weekend at Bernie's (1989)

Hot Car Girl *See* Hot Rod Girl (1956)

Hot Lead *See* Run of the Arrow (1956)

The Hot One *See* Corvette Summer (1978)

Hot Seat *See* The Chair (1987)

Hot Spot *See* I Wake Up Screaming (1941)

Hot Sweat *See* Keetje Tippel (1975)

The Houghland Murder Case *See* Murder by Television (1935)

The Hounds of Zaroff *See* The Most Dangerous Game (1932)

Hour of Glory *See* The Small Back Room (1949)

House 3 *See* The Horror Show (1989)

House by the Lake *See* Death Weekend (1976)

House in Nightmare Park *See* Night of the Laughing Dead (1975)

House of Crazies *See* Asylum (1972)

House of Doom *See* The Black Cat (1934)

House of Evil *See* Dance of Death (1968)

House of Evil *See* The House on Sorority Row (1983)

The House of Exorcism *See* Lisa and the Devil (1975)

House of Fear *See* Fearmaker (1989)

House of Insane Women *See* Exorcism's Daughter (1974)

House of Mortal Sin *See* The Confessional (1975)

House of Mystery *See* Night Monster (1942)

House of Pleasure *See* Le Plaisir (1952)

House of Terror *See* Face of the Screaming Werewolf (1959)

House of the Dark Stairway *See* A Blade in the Dark (1983)

House of Usher *See* The Fall of the House of Usher (1960)

The House Where Death Lives *See* Delusion (1984)

The House Where Hell Froze Over *See* Keep My Grave Open (1980)

House Without Windows *See* Seven Alone (1975)

How Is It Going? *See* Comment Ca Va? (1976)

How Long Can You Fall? *See* Till Marriage Do Us Part (1974)

How Sleep the Brave *See* Once Upon a Time in Vietnam (198?)

How to Irritate People *See* John Cleese on How to Irritate People (1968)

How To Steal a Diamond in Four Easy Lessons *See* The Hot Rock (1970)

Huang Tudi *See* Yellow Earth (1989)

Huggers *See* Crazy Moon (1987)

The Human Beast *See* La Bete Humaine (1938)

The Human Tornado *See* Dolemite 2: Human Tornado (1976)

Hunchback *See* The Hunchback of Notre Dame (1982)

Hungry Pets *See* Please Don't Eat My Mother (1972)

Hungry Wives *See* Season of the Witch (1973)

Hunt to Kill *See* The White Buffalo (1977)

The Hunted *See* Touch Me Not (1974)

Hunter of the Apocalypse *See* The Last Hunter (1980)

Hunters Are For Killing *See* Hard Frame (1970)

Hustler Squad *See* The Doll Squad (1973)

I Accuse *See* J'Accuse (1937)

I Am a Fugitive From the Chain Gang *See* I Am a Fugitive from a Chain Gang (1932)

I Bambini Ci Guardano *See* The Children Are Watching Us (1944)

I Became a Criminal *See* They Made Me a Criminal (1939)

I Call First *See* Who's That Knocking at My Door? (1968)

I Changed My Sex *See* Glen or Glenda (1953)

I Cinque Della Vendetta *See* Five Giants from Texas (1966)

I Coltelli Del Vendicatore *See* Viking Massacre (197?)

I Corpi Presentano Tracce Di Violenza Carnale *See* Torso (1973)

I Crossed the Line *See* The Black Klansman (1966)

I Giorni Dell'Inferno *See* Days of Hell (1984)

I Hate Your Guts *See* Shame (1961)

I Have a New Master *See* Passion for Life (1948)

I Have Lived *See* After Midnight (1933)

I Led Two Lives *See* Glen or Glenda (1953)

I Love to Kill *See* Impulse (1974)

I Married Too Young *See* Married Too Young (1962)

I Nuovi Barbari *See* Warriors of the Wasteland (1983)

I Pianeti Contro di Noi *See* Planets Against Us (1961)

I Skiachtra *See* The Enchantress (1985)

I Tre Volti della Paura *See* Black Sabbath (1964)

I, Vampiri *See* The Devil's Commandment (1956)

I Want Her Dead *See* W (1974)

I Was a Teenage Boy *See* Something Special (1986)

I You She He *See* Je Tu Il Elle (1974)

Ich und Er *See* Me and Him (1989)

Ici et Ailleurs *See* Here and Elsewhere (197?)

Identikit *See* Driver's Seat (1973)

Idi i Smotri *See* Come and See (1985)

Ieri, Oggi E Domani *See* Yesterday, Today and Tomorrow (1964)

If He Hollers, Let Him Go *See* Dead Right (1968)

If You Can't Say It, Just See It *See* Whore (1991)

If You Feel Like Singing *See* Summer Stock (1950)

Ike: The War Years *See* Ike (1979)

Il Bidone *See* The Swindle (1955)

Il Buco *See* Night Watch (1972)

Il Castello de Morti Vivi *See* Castle of the Living Dead (1964)

Il Cobra *See* The Cobra (1968)

Il Conformista *See* The Conformist (1971)

Il Crudeli *See* Hellbenders (1967)

Il Diario di una Cameriera *See* Diary of a Chambermaid (1964)

Il Diavolo in Corpo *See* Devil in the Flesh (1987)

Il Dio Chiamato a Dorian *See* Dorian Gray (1970)

Il Disprezzo *See* Contempt (1964)

Il Figlio del Capitano Blood *See* Son of Captain Blood (1962)

Il Fiume Del Grande Caimano *See* The Great Alligator (1981)

Il Generale Della-Rovere *See* Generale Della Rovere (1960)

Il Giardino Del Finzi-Contini *See* Garden of the Finzi-Continis (1971)

Il Gigante Di Metropolis *See* The Giant of Metropolis (1961)

Il Giorno e L'Ora *See* The Day and the Hour (1963)

Il Gladiatore Di Roma *See* Gladiator of Rome (1963)

Il Gladiatore Invincible *See* The Invincible Gladiator (1963)

Il Ladro Di Bagdad *See* Thief of Baghdad (1961)

Il Lago di Satana *See* The She-Beast (1965)

Il Mio Nome e Nessuno *See* My Name is Nobody (1974)

Il Mondo Di Yor *See* Yor, the Hunter from the Future (1983)

Il Montagna di Dio Cannibale *See* Slave of the Cannibal God (1979)

Il Mulino Delle Donne di Pietra *See* Mill of the Stone Women (1960)

Il Natale Che Quasi Non Fu *See* The Christmas That Almost Wasn't (1966)

Il Pianeta Degli Uomini Spenti *See* Battle of the Worlds (1961)

Il Portiere de Notte *See* The Night Porter (1974)

Il Processo *See* The Trial (1963)

Il Re Dei Criminali *See* Superargo (1967)

Il Roso Segmo Della Pollias *See* Hatchet for the Honeymoon (1970)

Il Sicario *See* The Hit Man (1961)

Il Sigillo de Pechino *See* The Corrupt Ones (1967)

Il Terror Dei Baraberi *See* Goliath and the Barbarians (1960)

Il Tigre *See* Tiger and the Pussycat (1967)

Il Treno *See* The Train (1965)

Il Vangelo Secondo Matteo *See* The Gospel According to St. Matthew (1964)

Ill Met By Moonlight *See* Night Ambush (1957)

Illicit Interlude *See* Summer Interlude (1950)

Ilsa, the Absolute Power *See* Ilsa, the Wicked Warden (1978)

Ilya Mourometz *See* Sword & the Dragon (1956)

Im Stahlnetz Des Dr. Mabuse *See* The Return of Dr. Mabuse (1961)

Immediate Disaster *See* The Stranger from Venus (1954)

The Important Story of Alcoholism *See* One Too Many (1951)

Impossible Object *See* The Story of a Love Story (1973)

In Bed with Madonna *See* Truth or Dare (1991)

In Love *See* Falling in Love Again (1980)

In Love and Engaged *See* Somos Novios (1968)

In Old Oklahoma *See* War of the Wildcats (1943)

In the Devil's Garden *See* Assault (1970)

In the Grip of the Spider *See* Web of the Spider (1970)

In the Woods *See* Rashomon (1951)

In Weiter Ferne, So Nah! *See* Faraway, So Close! (1993)

Incense For the Damned *See* The Bloodsuckers (1970)

Incident at Victoria Falls *See* Sherlock Holmes and the Incident at Victoria Falls (1991)

The Incredible Invasion *See* The Sinister Invasion (1968)

The Incredible Praying Mantis *See* The Deadly Mantis (1957)

The Incredible Torture Show *See* Bloodsucking Freaks (1975)

The Incredibly Strange Creatures *See* Incredibly Strange Creatures Who Stopped Living and Became Mixed-Up Zombies (1963)

Indian Love Call *See* Rose Marie (1936)

Indiscretion *See* Christmas in Connecticut (1945)

Indiscretion *See* Indiscretion of an American Wife (1954)

The Infernal Idol *See* Craze (1974)

The Infra Superman *See* Infra-Man (1976)

Inn of the Frightened People *See* Revenge (1971)

Innocence is Bliss *See* Miss Grant Takes Richmond (1949)

The Innocent and the Damned *See* Girls' Town (1959)

The Insect *See* The Insect Woman (1963)

Inseminoid *See* Horror Planet (1980)

L'Insoumis *See* Fight for Us (1989)

Interlude *See* Intermezzo (1936)

Intermezzo: A Love Story *See* Intermezzo (1939)

The Intruder *See* Shame (1961)

The Invader *See* Old Spanish Custom (1936)

The Invaders *See* The Forty-Ninth Parallel (1941)

Invasion Earth 2150 A.D. *See* Daleks—Invasion Earth 2150 A.D. (1966)

Invasion Force *See* Hangar 18 (1980)

Invasion of Planet X *See* Godzilla vs. Monster Zero (1968)

Invasion of the Astro-Monsters *See* Godzilla vs. Monster Zero (1968)

Invasion of the Astros *See* Godzilla vs. Monster Zero (1968)

Invasion of the Flying Saucers *See* Earth vs. the Flying Saucers (1956)

Invasion of the Zombies *See* Horror of Party Beach (1964)

An Investigation of Murder *See* The Laughing Policeman (1974)

The Invisible Creature *See* House on Marsh Road (1960)

The Invisible Horror *See* The Invisible Dr. Mabuse (1962)

Iron Hand *See* Goetz von Berlichingen (1980)

The Iron Hand *See* Chinese Connection (1973)

The Iron Kiss *See* Naked Kiss (1964)

Irving Berlin's Alexander's Ragtime Band *See* Alexander's Ragtime Band (1938)

Irving Berlin's Second Fiddle *See* Second Fiddle (1939)

Island of Monte Cristo *See* Sword of Venus (1953)

Island of the Burning Damned *See* Island of the Burning Doomed (1967)

Island of the Fishmen *See* Screamers (1980)

Island of the Living Horror *See* Brides of the Beast (1968)

Isle of Lost Women *See* 99 Women (1969)

Isle of the Living Dead *See* The Snake People (1968)

Isle of the Snake People *See* The Snake People (1968)

Isn't Life A Bitch? *See* La Chienne (1931)

Istanbul, Keep Your Eyes Open *See* Istanbul (1990)

It Comes Up Murder *See* The Honey Pot (1967)

It Happened at Lakewood Manor *See* Ants (1977)

It Happened in Paris *See* The Lady in Question (1940)

It Happened One Summer *See* State Fair (1945)

It Hurts Only When I Laugh *See* Only When I Laugh (1981)

It Lives By Night *See* The Bat People (1974)

It Only Take Five Minutes *See* Five Minutes to Love (1963)

It Stalked the Ocean Floor *See* Monster from the Ocean Floor (1954)

It! The Vampire From Beyond Space *See* It! The Terror from Beyond Space (1958)

It Won't Rub Off, Baby *See* Sweet Love, Bitter (1967)

The Italian Connection *See* Hired to Kill (1973)

The Italian Connection *See* Manhunt (1973)

It's Hot in Hell *See* Un Singe en Hiver (1962)

It's Hot in Paradise *See* Horrors of Spider Island (1959)

It's My Life *See* My Life to Live (1962)

It's Only Money *See* Double Dynamite (1951)

Ivan's Childhood *See* My Name is Ivan (1962)

Jack Kerouac's America *See* Kerouac (1984)

Jack London's Klondike Fever *See* Klondike Fever (1979)

Jackals *See* American Justice (1986)

Jackie Chan's Police Story *See* Jackie Chan's Police Force (1985)

Jack's Wife *See* Season of the Witch (1973)

Jacqueline Susann's Once is Not Enough *See* Once is Not Enough (1975)

Jacquot de Nantes *See* Jacquot (1991)

Jail Birds *See* Pardon Us (1931)

Jailbirds' Vacation *See* Les Grandes Gueules (1965)

James Clavell's Shogun *See* Shogun (1980)

Japan Sinks *See* Tidal Wave (1975)

Jatszani Kell *See* Lily in Love (1985)

Jaws 3-D *See* Jaws 3 (1983)

Jayne Mansfield: A Symbol of the '50s *See* The Jayne Mansfield Story (1980)

J.C. *See* Iron Horsemen (1971)

Je Vous Salue Marie *See* Hail Mary (1985)

Jean de Florette 2 *See* Manon of the Spring (1987)

Jeder Fur Sich Und Gott Gegen Alle *See* Every Man for Himself & God Against All (1975)

Jennie *See* Portrait of Jennie (1948)

Jennifer (The Snake Goddess) *See* Jennifer (1978)

The Jester *See* Der Purimshpiler (1937)

Jesus de Montreal *See* Jesus of Montreal (1989)

Jeu de Massacre *See* The Killing Game (1967)

Jew Suss *See* Power (1934)

The Jewish Jester *See* Der Purimshpiler (1937)

The Jezebels *See* Switchblade Sisters (1975)

Jigokumen *See* Gate of Hell (1954)

Jim Buck *See* Portrait of a Hitman (1977)

Job Lazadasa *See* The Revolt of Job (1984)

Joe Palooka *See* Palooka (1934)

John Carpenter Presents Body Bags *See* Body Bags (1993)

John le Carre's A Perfect Spy *See* A Perfect Spy (1988)

Johnnie Mae Gibson: FBI *See* Johnnie Gibson F.B.I. (1987)

Johnny Vagabond *See* Johnny Come Lately (1943)

Johnny Zombie *See* My Boyfriend's Back (1993)

A Joke of Destiny *See* A Joke of Destiny, Lying in Wait Around the Corner Like a Bandit (1984)

Joker's Wild *See* Body Trouble (1992)

Jonas—Qui Aura 25 Ans en l'an 2000 *See* Jonah Who Will Be 25 in the Year 2000 (1976)

Joseph Sold by His Brothers *See* Joseph & His Brethren (1960)

Journey into Autumn *See* Dreams (1955)

J.R. *See* Who's That Knocking at My Door? (1968)

A Judgement in Stone *See* The Housekeeper (1986)

Jules et Jim *See* Jules and Jim (1962)

Jules Verne's Rocket to the Moon *See* Those Fantastic Flying Fools (1967)

Julie Darling *See* Daughter of Death (1982)

July Pork Bellies *See* For Pete's Sake (1974)

Jumbo *See* Billy Rose's Jumbo (1962)

Jungfrukallan *See* The Virgin Spring (1959)

Jungle Gold *See* Perils of the Darkest Jungle (1944)

Jungle Woman *See* Nabonga (1944)

Juninatten *See* June Night (1940)

Just Another Day at the Races *See* Win, Place, or Steal (1972)

Just Ask for Diamond *See* Diamond's Edge (1988)

Just in Time *See* Only You (1994)

Justice Rides Again *See* Destry Rides Again (1939)

Kaiju Daisenso *See* Godzilla vs. Monster Zero (1968)

Kaiju Soshingeki *See* Destroy All Monsters (1968)

Kaitei Daisenso *See* Terror Beneath the Sea (1966)

Kakushi Toride No San Akunin *See* The Hidden Fortress (1958)

Kaleidoscope *See* Danielle Steel's Kaleidoscope (1992)

Kamakazi *See* Attack Squadron (197?)

Karamazov *See* The Brothers Karamazov (1958)

Katie's Passion *See* Keetje Tippel (1975)

The Kent Chronicles *See* The Bastard (1978)

Kettle Creek *See* Mountain Justice (1930)

The Key *See* Odd Obsession (1960)

Key West Crossing *See* The Mercenaries (1980)

KGOD *See* Pray TV (1980)

Kid Auto Races at Venice *See* Kid's Auto Race/ Mabel's Married Life (1915)

The Kidnap of Mary Lou *See* Almost Human (1979)

Kill Castro *See* The Mercenaries (1980)

Killbots *See* Chopping Mall (1986)

Killer Bait *See* Too Late for Tears (1949)

Killer Bats *See* The Devil Bat (1941)

The Killer Behind the Mask *See* Savage Weekend (1980)

Killer Grizzly *See* Grizzly (1976)

Killer of Killers *See* The Mechanic (1972)

Killer With a Label *See* One Too Many (1951)

The Killers *See* Pigs (1973)

Killers of the Wild *See* Children of the Wild (1937)

Kimono No Kiroku *See* I Live in Fear (1955)

Kin Folk *See* All the Lovin' Kinfolk (1989)

Kinfolk *See* All the Lovin' Kinfolk (1989)

King Cobra *See* Jaws of Satan (1981)

King Gun *See* The Gatling Gun (1972)

King Kong Tai Godzilla *See* King Kong Versus Godzilla (1963)

King Oedipus *See* Oedipus Rex (1957)

King of Africa *See* One Step to Hell (1968)

The King of Criminals *See* Superargo (1967)

King of the Jungleland *See* Darkest Africa (1936)

Kings Ransom *See* Devastator (1985)

Kisenga, Man of Africa *See* Men of Two Worlds (1946)

A Kiss from Eddie *See* The Arousers (1970)

Kiss My Butterfly *See* I Love You, Alice B. Toklas (1968)

KKK *See* The Klansman (1974)

The Knack...and How to Get It *See* The Knack (1965)

The Kneeling Goddess *See* La Diosa Arrodillada (1947)

Knives of the Avenger *See* Viking Massacre (197?)

The Knock-Out Cop *See* Flatfoot (1978)

Koks I Kulissen *See* Ladies on the Rocks (1983)

Komissar *See* Commissar (1968)

Koneko Monogatari *See* The Adventures of Milo & Otis (1989)

Konjiki Yasha *See* Golden Demon (1953)

Kootenai Brown *See* Showdown at Williams Creek (1991)

Kopek and Broom *See* Find the Lady (1975)

Krasnaya Palatka *See* Red Tent (1969)

Kronos *See* Captain Kronos: Vampire Hunter (1974)

Kumonosujo, Kumonosu-djo *See* Throne of Blood (1957)

Kung Fu Master *See* Le Petit Amour (1987)

Kunisada Chuji *See* The Gambling Samurai (1960)

Kuroi Ame *See* Black Rain (1988)

Kvinn odrom *See* Dreams (1955)

Kvinnors Vantan *See* Secrets of Women (1952)

Kyuketsuki Gokemidoro *See* Body Snatcher from Hell (1969)

La Banda J.&S. Cronaca Criminale del Far West *See* Sonny and Jed (1973)

La Belle et Laete *See* Beauty and the Beast (1946)

La Bestia Uccide a Sangue Freddo *See* Slaughter Hotel (1971)

La Cabeza Viviente *See* The Living Head (1959)

La Camara Del Terror *See* The Fear Chamber (1968)

La Casa Con La Scala Nel Bulo *See* A Blade in the Dark (1983)

La Casa Del Terror *See* Face of the Screaming Werewolf (1959)

La Casa Dell' Exorcismo *See* Lisa and the Devil (1975)

La Casa Embrujada *See* The Curse of the Crying Woman (1961)

La Casa Nel Parco *See* House on the Edge of the Park (1984)

La Case de L'Oncle Tom *See* Uncle Tom's Cabin (1969)

La Caza *See* The Hunt (1967)

La Chambre Verte *See* The Green Room (1978)

La Chiesa *See* The Church (1990)

La Ciociara *See* Two Women (1961)

La Ciudad y los Perros *See* The City and the Dogs (1985)

La Commare Secca *See* The Grim Reaper (1962)

La Comtesse Perverse *See* The Perverse Countess (1973)

La Decima Vittima *See* 10th Victim (1965)

La Dentelliere *See* The Lacemaker (1977)

La Diagonale du Fou *See* Dangerous Moves (1984)

La Dixieme Victime *See* 10th Victim (1965)

La Donna E Donna *See* A Woman is a Woman (1960)

La Double Vie de Veronique *See* The Double Life of Veronique (1991)

La Dueda Interna *See* Veronico Cruz (1987)

La Famiglia *See* The Family (1987)

La Femme d'a Cote *See* The Woman Next Door (1981)

La Femme De Mon Pote *See* My Best Friend's Girl (1984)

La Femme du Boulanger *See* The Baker's Wife (1933)

La Femme Mariee *See* A Married Woman (1965)

La Fiancee du Pirate *See* A Very Curious Girl (1969)

La Figlia di Frankenstein *See* Lady Frankenstein (1972)

La Fille Du Puisatier *See* Well-Digger's Daughter (1946)

La Folie des Grandeurs *See* Delusions of Grandeur (1976)

La Francaise et L'Amour *See* Love and the Frenchwoman (1960)

La Furia Di Ercole *See* The Fury of Hercules (1961)

La Gloire de Mon Pere *See* My Father's Glory (1991)

La Grande Guerre *See* The Great War (1959)

La Grieta *See* Endless Descent (1990)

La Historia Oficial *See* The Official Story (1985)

La Horripilante Bestia Humana *See* Night of the Bloody Apes (1968)

La Illusion en Travnia *See* The Illusion Travels by Streetcar (1953)

La Invasion de Los Vampiros *See* Invasion of the Vampires (1961)

La Isla Del Tersoro *See* Treasure Island (1972)

La Joven *See* The Young One (1961)

La Kermesse Heroique *See* Carnival in Flanders (1935)

La Legge *See* Where the Hot Wind Blows (1959)

La Ley del Deseo *See* Law of Desire (1986)

La Linea Del Cielo *See* Skyline (1984)

La Loi *See* Where the Hot Wind Blows (1959)

La Lune Dans le Caniveau *See* Moon in the Gutter (1983)

La Mala Ordina *See* Manhunt (1973)

La Maldicion de a Llorona *See* The Curse of the Crying Woman (1961)

La Maldicion de la Momia Azteca *See* The Curse of the Aztec Mummy (1959)

La Marca del Muerto *See* Creature of the Walking Dead (1960)

La Mariee Etait en Noir *See* The Bride Wore Black (1968)

La Mitad del Cielo *See* Half of Heaven (1986)

La Momia Azteca Contra el Robot Humano *See* The Robot vs. the Aztec Mummy (1959)

La Morte Vestita di Dollar *See* Dog Eat Dog (1964)

La Morte Viene Dalla Spazio *See* The Day the Sky Exploded (1957)

La Motocyclette *See* The Girl on a Motorcycle (1968)

La Muerte Viviente *See* The Snake People (1968)

La Nipote del Vampiro *See* Fangs of the Living Dead (1968)

La Noche de Los Mil Gatos *See* Night of a Thousand Cats (1972)

La Noche dell Terror Ciego *See* Tombs of the Blind Dead (1972)

La Noia: L'Ennui Et Sa Diversion, L'Erotisme *See* Empty Canvas (1964)

La Notte Che Evelyn Usca Dalla Tomba *See* The Night Evelyn Came Out of the Grave (1971)

La Novia Esangentada *See* The Blood Spattered Bride (1972)

La Nuit Americaine *See* Day for Night (1973)

La Nuit de Generaux *See* Night of the Generals (1967)

La Nuit Des Espions *See* Double Agents (1959)

La Passante du Sans Souci *See* La Passante (1983)

La Passion Beatrice *See* Beatrice (1988)

La Permission *See* The Story of a Three Day Pass (1968)

La Planete Sauvage *See* Fantastic Planet (1973)

La Poupee *See* The Doll (1962)

La Prise de Pouvoir Par Louis XIV *See* The Rise of Louis XIV (1966)

La Romana *See* A Woman of Rome (1956)

La Ruee Des Vikings *See* The Invaders (1963)

La Secta de los Tughs *See* Dawn of the Pirates (19??)

La Spada del Cid *See* The Sword of El Cid (1962)

La Spina Dorsale del Diavolo *See* Ride to Glory (1971)

L.A. Streetfighters *See* Ninja Turf (1986)

La Strega in Amore *See* The Witch (1966)

La Tatiche de Ercole *See* Hercules (1958)

La Tragedia di un Uomo Ridicolo *See* The Tragedy of a Ridiculous Man (1981)

La Vendetta De Ercole *See* Goliath and the Dragon (1961)

La Vergine de Norimberga *See* The Virgin of Nuremberg (1965)

La Victoire en Chantant *See* Black and White in Color (1976)

La Vie Devant Soi *See* Madame Rosa (1977)

La Vie est Rien d'Autre *See* Life and Nothing But (1989)

La Vie Est Une Longue Fleuve Tranquille *See* Life Is a Long Quiet River (1988)

La Vie Privee *See* A Very Private Affair (1962)

Laberinto de Pasiones *See* Labyrinth of Passion (1982)

Labyrinth *See* A Reflection of Fear (1972)

Ladri di Biciclette *See* The Bicycle Thief (1948)

Ladri di Saponette *See* The Icicle Thief (1989)

Lady Beware *See* 13th Guest (1932)

The Lady Dances *See* The Merry Widow (1934)

The Lady Dracula *See* Lemora, Lady Dracula (1973)

Lady Hamilton *See* That Hamilton Woman (1941)

Lady in the Fog *See* Scotland Yard Inspector (1952)

Lady Jane Grey *See* Nine Days a Queen (1934)

The Lady Killers *See* Ladykillers (1955)

Lady of Deceit *See* Born to Kill (1947)

Lady of the Shadows *See* The Terror (1963)

L'Albero Degli Zoccoli *See* The Tree of Wooden Clogs (1978)

L'Amant de Lady Chatterley *See* Lady Chatterley's Lover (1955)

The Lament of the Path *See* Pather Panchali (1954)

L'Amour en Fuite *See* Love on the Run (1978)

The Lamp *See* The Outing (1987)

Lancelot and Guinevere *See* Sword of Lancelot (1963)

Landru *See* Bluebeard (1963)

The Lane Frost Story *See* 8 Seconds (1994)

L'Anee Derniere a Marienbad *See* Last Year at Marienbad (1961)

Larceny Lane *See* Blonde Crazy (1931)

Larsen, Wolf of the Seven Seas *See* The Legend of the Sea Wolf (1958)

Las Vegas Strip War *See* The Vegas Strip Wars (1984)

Lashou Shentan *See* Hard-Boiled (1992)

Lasky Jedne Plavovlasky *See* Loves of a Blonde (1965)

L'Associe *See* The Associate (1982)

The Last Adventure *See* Les Aventuriers (1977)

The Last Adventurers *See* Down to the Sea in Ships (1922)

The Last Battle *See* Le Dernier Combat (1984)

Last Chance For a Born Loser *See* Stateline Motel (1975)

The Last Days of Man on Earth *See* The Final Programme (1973)

The Last Days of Sodom and Gomorrah *See* Sodom and Gomorrah (1962)

The Last Elephant *See* Ivory Hunters (1990)

The Last Frontier *See* Savage Wilderness (1955)

The Last Great Treasure *See* Mother Lode (1982)

Last House on the Left, Part 2 *See* Twitch of the Death Nerve (1971)

Last Message From Saigon *See* Operation C.I.A. (1965)

Last of the Cowboys *See* Great Smokey Roadblock (1976)

The Last Page *See* Man Bait (1952)

Last Rites *See* Dracula's Last Rites (1979)

The Last Victim *See* Forced Entry (1975)

The Last Warrior *See* The Final Executioner (1983)

The Last Will of Dr. Mabuse *See* Testament of Dr. Mabuse (1943)

The Late Edwina Black *See* The Obsessed (1951)

Latin Love *See* Greek Street (1930)

Latin Quarter *See* Frenzy (1946)

Laughterhouse *See* Singleton's Pluck (1984)

The Law *See* Where the Hot Wind Blows (1959)

Law Breakers *See* Les Assassins de L'Ordre (1971)

The Law of the Gun *See* La Ley del Revolver (1978)

Lazy Bones *See* Hallelujah, I'm a Bum (1933)

Le Blonde de Pekin *See* The Peking Blond (1968)

Le Caporal Epingle *See* The Elusive Corporal (1962)

Le Carrosse D'Or *See* The Golden Coach (1952)

Le Cerveau *See* The Brain (1969)

Le Charme Discret de la Bourgeoisie *See* The Discreet Charm of the Bourgeoisie (1972)

Le Chateau de Ma Mere *See* My Mother's Castle (1991)

Le Cheval D'Orgeuil *See* The Horse of Pride (1980)

Le Cri du Hibou *See* The Cry of the Owl (1992)

Le Crime de Monsieur Lange *See* The Crime of Monsieur Lange (1936)

Le Danger Vient de l'Escape *See* The Day the Sky Exploded (1957)

Le Declin De L'Empire Americain *See* The Decline of the American Empire (1986)

Le Dejeuner Sur l'Herbe *See* Picnic on the Grass (1959)

Le Dernier Metro *See* The Last Metro (1980)

Le Desert des Tartares *See* The Desert of the Tartars (1976)

Le Diable au Corps *See* Devil in the Flesh (1946)

Le Distrait *See* The Daydreamer (1975)

Le Fantome de la Liberte *See* Phantom of Liberty (1968)

Le Feu Follet *See* The Fire Within (1964)

Le Geant de la Vallee Das Rois *See* Son of Samson (1962)

Le Gentleman D'epsom *See* Duke of the Derby (1962)

Le Grand Bleu *See* The Big Blue (1988)

Le Grand Blond Avec Une Chassure Noire *See* The Tall Blond Man with One Black Shoe (1972)

Le Grand Meaulnes *See* The Wanderer (1967)

Le Jour et L'Heure *See* The Day and the Hour (1963)

Le Journal d'un Cure de Campagne *See* Diary of a Country Priest (1950)

Le Journal d'une Femme de Chambre *See* Diary of a Chambermaid (1964)

Le Juge et L'assassin *See* The Judge and the Assassin (1975)

Le Locataire *See* The Tenant (1976)

Le Maitre de Musique *See* The Music Teacher (1988)

Le Mepris *See* Contempt (1964)

Le Meraviglie Di Aladino *See* The Wonders of Aladdin (1961)

Le Mur *See* The Wall (1983)

Le Neveu de Beethoven *See* Beethoven's Nephew (1988)

Le Nottie de Cabiria *See* Nights of Cabiria (1957)

Le Pays Bleu *See* Blue Country (1977)

Le Peau Douce *See* The Soft Skin (1964)

Le Petit Monde de Don Camillo *See* Little World of Don Camillo (1951)

Le Plus Vieux Metier du Monde *See* Oldest Profession (1967)

Le Proces *See* The Trial (1963)

Le Rayon Vert *See* Summer (1986)

Le Regle du Jeu *See* The Rules of the Game (1939)

Le Roi de Coeur *See* The King of Hearts (1966)

Le Rouble a Deux Faces *See* The Hot Line (1969)

Le Rouge aux Levres *See* Daughters of Darkness (1971)

Le Rouge et le Noir *See* The Red and the Black (1957)

Le Salaire De La Peur *See* Wages of Fear (1955)

Le Sang d'un Poete *See* The Blood of a Poet (1930)

le Sant de l'Ange *See* Cobra (1971)

Le Sauvage *See* Lovers Like Us (1975)

Le Train *See* The Train (1965)

Le Trou *See* Night Watch (1972)

Le Vieil Homme Et L'Enfant *See* Two of Us (1968)

Le Voleur De Bagdad *See* Thief of Baghdad (1961)

Leader of the Pack *See* Unholy Rollers (1972)

L'eclisse *See* The Eclipse (1966)

L'Ecole Buissonniere *See* Passion for Life (1948)

Legacy of Blood *See* Blood Legacy (1973)

The Legacy of Maggie Walsh *See* The Legacy (1979)

The Legend *See* James Dean (1976)

Legend in Leotards *See* Return of Captain Invincible (1983)

Legend of Cougar Canyon *See* The Secret of Navajo Cave (1976)

The Legend of Gosta Berling *See* The Atonement of Gosta Berling (1924)

The Legend of Machine Gun Kelly *See* Melvin Purvis: G-Man (1974)

Legend of the Bayou *See* Eaten Alive (1976)

Legend of the Seven Golden Vampires *See* The 7 Brothers Meet Dracula (1973)

Legend of Witch Hollow *See* The Witchmaker (1969)

Legenda Del Rudio Malese *See* Jungle Raiders (1985)

Legenda Suramskoi Kreposti *See* The Legend of Suram Fortress (1985)

The Legendary Curse of Lemora *See* Lemora, Lady Dracula (1973)

Legion of the Damned *See* Battle of the Commandos (1971)

L'Enfant Sauvage *See* The Wild Child (1970)

Leona Helmsley: The Queen of Mean *See* The Queen of Mean (1990)

Lepassager de la Pluie *See* Rider on the Rain (1970)

L'Eredita Ferramonti *See* The Inheritance (1976)

Les Amities Particulieres *See* This Special Friendship (1967)

Les Bas Fonds *See* The Lower Depths (1936)

Les Choses De La Vie *See* The Things of Life (1970)

Les Corrompus *See* The Corrupt Ones (1967)

Les Cousins *See* The Cousins (1959)

Les Deux Anglaises et le Continent *See* Two English Girls (1972)

Les Deux Rivales *See* Time of Indifference (1964)

Les Diabolique *See* Diabolique (1955)

Les Dimanches de Ville d'Arvay *See* Sundays & Cybele (1962)

Les Enfants du Paradise *See* Children of Paradise (1944)

Les Felins *See* Joy House (1964)

Les Femmes *See* The Women (1969)

Les Gaspards *See* The Holes (1972)

Les Grandes Gueules *See* Jailbird's Vacation (1965)

Les Grandes Personnes *See* Time Out for Love (1961)

Les innocents aux Mains Sales *See* Dirty Hands (1976)

Les Jeux Interdits *See* Forbidden Games (1952)

Les Liaisons Dangereuses *See* Dangerous Liaisons (1960)

Les Liens de Sang *See* Blood Relatives (1977)

Les Louves *See* Letters to an Unknown Lover (1984)

Les Mille Et Une Nuits *See* The Wonders of Aladdin (1961)

Les Mongols *See* The Mongols (1960)

Les Noces de Papier *See* A Paper Wedding (1989)

Les Nuits De La Pleine *See* Full Moon in Paris (1984)

Les Orgueilleux See The Proud Ones (1953)

Les Parapluies De Cherbourg See Umbrellas of Cherbourg (1964)

Les Quartre Cents Coups See The 400 Blows (1959)

Les Ripoux See My New Partner (1984)

Les Somnambules See Mon Oncle D'Amerique (1980)

Les Vacances de Monsieur Hulot See Mr. Hulot's Holiday (1953)

Les Valseuses See Going Places (1974)

Les Yeux Noirs See Dark Eyes (1987)

Les Yeux Sans Visage See The Horror Chamber of Dr. Faustus (1959)

Lesbian Twins See The Virgin Witch (1970)

L'Ete Meurtrier See One Deadly Summer (1983)

L'Ete Prochain See Next Summer (1984)

L'Eternel Retour See Eternal Return (1943)

Lethal See The KGB: The Secret War (1986)

A Letter to Mama See A Brivele der Mamen (1938)

A Letter to Mother See A Brivele der Mamen (1938)

Letyat Zhuravit See The Cranes are Flying (1957)

L'Evangile Selon Saint-Matthieu See The Gospel According to St. Matthew (1964)

L'Histoire d'Adele H. See Story of Adele H. (1975)

L'Homme de Rio See That Man from Rio (1964)

L'Hypothese du Tableau Vole See The Hypothesis of the Stolen Painting (1978)

Libido See The Sensuous Teenager (1970)

Licensed to Kill See Second Best Secret Agent in the Whole Wide World (1965)

The Life and Adventures of Nicholas Nickleby See Nicholas Nickleby (1946)

The Life and Loves of Beethoven See Beethoven (1936)

Life at Stake See The Key Man (1957)

Life in the Food Chain See Age Isn't Everything (1991)

Life of Brian See Monty Python's Life of Brian (1979)

The Life of Jack London See Jack London (1944)

The Light Fantastic See Love is Better Than Ever (1952)

Lights of Variety See Variety Lights (1951)

Like a Crow on a June Bug See Sixteen (1972)

Like Father, Like Son See The Executioner (1978)

Like Two Drops of Water See Como Dos Gotas de Agua (197?)

Lila See Mantis in Lace (1968)

Lilacs in the Spring See Let's Make Up (1955)

L'Inafferrabile Invincible See Mr. Superinvisible (1973)

Lincoln See Gore Vidal's Lincoln (1988)

L'Innocente See The Innocent (1976)

The Lion's Den See La Boca del Lobo (1989)

L'Isola Degli Uomini Pesce See Screamers (1980)

The Little Martyr See The Children Are Watching Us (1944)

The Little Mermaid See La Petite Sirene (1980)

Little Mother See Mamele (1938)

Little Pal See Healer (1936)

The Little Sister See The Tender Age (1984)

Live a Little, Steal a Lot See Murph the Surf (1975)

Live to Love See The Devil's Hand (1961)

The Liver Eaters See Spider Baby (1964)

Ljubarni Slucaj See The Love Affair, or The Case of the Missing Switchboard Operator (1967)

Lo Chiamavano Trinita See They Call Me Trinity (1972)

Lo Que Vendra See Times to Come (1981)

Lo Sbarco di Anzio See Anzio (1968)

Lo Scatenato See Catch as Catch Can (1968)

Lo Sceicco Bianco See The White Sheik (1952)

Lo Spettro See The Ghost (1963)

Lo Strano Vizio Della Signora Wardh See The Next Victim (1971)

Lo Zio Indegno See The Sleazy Uncle (1989)

Loaded Weapon 1 See National Lampoon's Loaded Weapon 1 (1993)

Lock Your Doors See The Ape Man (1943)

The Lodger: A Case of London Fog See The Lodger (1926)

L'Oeuvre au Noir See The Abyss (1989)

The Lone Troubador See Two-Gun Troubador (1937)

The Lonely Hearts Killers See Honeymoon Killers (1970)

Lonely Man See Gun Riders (1969)

The Loner See Ruckus (1981)

The Long Arm See The Third Key (1957)

The Long, Dark Night See The Pack (1977)

Long John Silver Returns to Treasure Island See Long John Silver (1953)

The Long Ride See Brady's Escape (1984)

The Long Shot See African Rage (1978)

Look Down and Die See Steel (1980)

Loonies On Broadway See Zombies on Broadway (1944)

Loose Joints See Flicks (1985)

The Loot See The Bloody Tattoo (19??)

Looters See Trespass (1992)

L'Opera De Quat'Sous See The Threepenny Opera (1931)

Lords of Treason See Secret Honor (1985)

L'Oro Di Napoli See The Gold of Naples (1954)

L'Orribile Segreto Del Dr. Hichcock See The Horrible Dr. Hichcock (1962)

Los Ambiciosos See Fever Mounts at El Pao (1959)

Los Despiadados See Hellbenders (1967)

Los Ojos Azules de la Muneca Rota See House of Psychotic Women (1973)

Los Santos Inocentes See The Holy Innocents (1984)

Los Tigres del Desierto See The Desert Tigers (19??)

Loser Take All See Strike It Rich (1990)

The Lost Glory of Troy See The Avenger (1962)

The Lost Illusion See The Fallen Idol (1949)

Lost Women See Mesa of Lost Women (1952)

Lost Women of Zarpa See Mesa of Lost Women (1952)

The Loudest Whisper See The Children's Hour (1961)

Louis L'Amour's Conagher See Conagher (1991)

Louis L'Amour's "The Shadow Riders" See The Shadow Riders (1982)

Love and Hate: The Story of Colin and Joanne Thatcher See Love and Hate: A Marriage Made in Hell (1990)

The Love Cage See Joy House (1964)

Love Eternal See Eternal Return (1943)

The Love Factor See Alien Women (1969)

Love in Las Vegas See Viva Las Vegas (1963)

Love is Blind See Love at First Sight (1976)

The Love Maniac See Blood of Ghastly Horror (1972)

Love Trap See Curse of the Black Widow (1977)

Love You to Death See Deadly Illusion (1987)

Lover of the Great Bear See Smugglers (1975)

Lover, Wife See Wifemistress (1979)

Lovers From Beyond the Tomb See Nightmare Castle (1965)

Lovers Must Learn See Rome Adventure (1962)

The Lovers of Montparnasse See Modigliani (1958)

Loves of a Scoundrel See Death of a Scoundrel (1956)

The Loves of Isadora See Isadora (1968)

The Loyal 47 Ronin See 47 Ronin, Part 1 (1942)

L'Ucello dalle Piume di Cristallo See The Bird with the Crystal Plumage (1970)

Luci Del Varieta See Variety Lights (1951)

The Lucifer Project See Barracuda (1978)

Lucky Boots See Gun Play (1936)

Lucky 13 See Running Hot (1983)

The Lullaby See The Sin of Madelon Claudet (1931)

L'Ultimo Uomo Della Terra See The Last Man on Earth (1964)

Lunch on the Grass See Picnic on the Grass (1959)

Lunch Wagon Girls See Lunch Wagon (1981)

L'Une Chante L'Autre Pas See One Sings, the Other Doesn't (1977)

L'Uomo Dalle Due Ombre See Cold Sweat (1974)

L'Uomo di Rio See That Man from Rio (1964)

Lust of the Vampires See The Devil's Commandment (1956)

Lusty Night in Rome See La Notte Brava (1959)

Lycanthropus See Werewolf in a Girl's Dormitory (1961)

Lynching See Linchamiento (1968)

M. Hire See Monsieur Hire (1989)

Ma Nuit Chez Maud See My Night at Maud's (1969)

Macabra See Demonoid, Messenger of Death (1981)

Macabre Serenade See Dance of Death (1968)

Maccheroni See Macaroni (1985)

Maciste Alla Corte Del Gran Khan See Samson and the 7 Miracles of the World (1962)

Maciste at the Court of the Great Khan See Samson and the 7 Miracles of the World (1962)

Maciste la Regina di Samar See Hercules Against the Moon Men (1964)

Maciste, L'Eroe Piu Grande Del Mondo See Goliath and the Sins of Babylon (1964)

Maciste Nella Terra dei Ciclopi See Atlas in the Land of the Cyclops (1961)

Mad Dog See Mad Dog Morgan (1976)

The Mad Hatter See Breakfast in Hollywood (1946)

Mad Magazine's Up the Academy See Up the Academy (1980)

Mad Trapper of the Yukon See Challenge To Be Free (1976)

Mad Wednesday See The Sin of Harold Diddlebock (1947)

Madagascar Landing See Aventure Malgache (1944)

Madame De See The Earrings of Madame De... (1954)

Madame Frankenstein See Lady Frankenstein (1972)

Mademoiselle France See Reunion in France (1942)

Madmen of Mandoras See They Saved Hitler's Brain (1964)

Madonna Truth or Dare *See* Truth or Dare (1991)

Mafia Junction *See* Super Bitch (1989)

The Mafu Cage *See* My Sister, My Love (1978)

The Magnificent Seven *See* Seven Samurai (1954)

The Magnificent Showman *See* Circus World (1964)

Making It *See* Going Places (1974)

Mako: The Jaws of Death *See* Jaws of Death (1976)

Malenka, the Vampire *See* Fangs of the Living Dead (1968)

Malenkaya Vera *See* Little Vera (1988)

Malice in Wonderland *See* The Rumor Mill (1986)

Malizia *See* Malicious (1974)

Man and His Mate *See* One Million B.C. (1940)

A Man Betrayed *See* Wheel of Fortune (1941)

Man-Eater *See* Shark! (1968)

The Man From C.O.T.T.O.N., Purlie Victorious *See* Gone are the Days (1963)

Man from Music Mountain *See* Texas Legionnaires (1943)

The Man From Nevada *See* The Nevadan (1950)

Man in a Cocked Hat *See* Carlton Browne of the F.O. (1959)

A Man in Mommy's Bed *See* With Six You Get Eggroll (1968)

The Man in Possession *See* Personal Property (1937)

Man in the Middle *See* 48 Hours to Live (1960)

Man Looking Southeast *See* Man Facing Southeast (1986)

Man of Bronze *See* Jim Thorpe: All American (1951)

Man of Fury *See* El Hombre de la Furia (1965)

Man of the Frontier *See* Red River Valley (1936)

Man of the Hour *See* Colonel Effingham's Raid (1945)

Man on the Move *See* Jigsaw (1971)

The Man Who Changed His Mind *See* The Man Who Lived Again (1936)

The Man Who Watched Trains Go By *See* Paris Express (1953)

The Man With The Deadly Lens *See* Wrong is Right (1982)

The Man with the Synthetic Brain *See* Blood of Ghastly Horror (1972)

The Man With the X-Ray Eyes *See* X: The Man with X-Ray Eyes (1963)

The Man with the Yellow Eyes *See* Planets Against Us (1961)

The Man with Thirty Sons *See* The Magnificent Yankee (1950)

Manhattan Project: The Deadly Game *See* The Manhattan Project (1986)

The Maniacs Are Loose *See* The Thrill Killers (1965)

Manon des Sources *See* Manon of the Spring (1987)

The Manster—Half Man, Half Monster *See* The Manster (1959)

Marching Along *See* Stars and Stripes Forever (1952)

Margaret Bourke-White *See* Double Exposure: The Story of Margaret Bourke-White (1989)

Maria Marten *See* Murder in the Old Red Barn (1936)

Marie *See* Maria (1971)

Marie Walewska *See* Conquest (1937)

Marijuana the Devil's Weed *See* Wild Weed (1949)

Marijuana: The Devil's Weed *See* Marihuana (1936)

Marilyn *See* Roadhouse Girl (1953)

Marine Issue *See* Instant Justice (1986)

Mark of Terror *See* Drums of Jeopardy (1931)

Mark of the Avenger *See* The Mysterious Rider (1938)

Mark of the Claw *See* Dick Tracy's Dilemma (1947)

Mark of the Vampire *See* The Vampire (1957)

Mark Twain *See* The Adventures of Mark Twain (1985)

Married in Haste *See* Consolation Marriage (1931)

Mars Invades Puerto Rico *See* Frankenstein Meets the Space Monster (1965)

The Marseille Contract *See* The Destructors (1974)

Marusa No Onna *See* A Taxing Woman (1987)

Marusa No Onna II *See* A Taxing Woman's Return (1988)

The Marvelous Visit *See* La Merveilleuse Visite (1974)

The Marx Brothers at the Circus *See* At the Circus (1939)

Masculin Feminin *See* Masculine Feminine (1966)

Mask of Dust *See* Race for Life (1955)

Mask of Fury *See* First Yank into Tokyo (1945)

Massacre at Fort Holman *See* A Reason to Live, A Reason to Die (1973)

Massacre Hill *See* Eureka Stockade (1949)

Massacre Mafia Style *See* The Executioner (1978)

The Master *See* Master Ninja (1978)

Master Dolorosa *See* The Torture of Silence (1917)

Master of Lassie *See* The Hills of Home (1948)

Matango *See* Attack of the Mushroom People (1963)

The Mating of the Sabine Women *See* The Rape of the Sabines (1961)

Matt Riker *See* Mutant Hunt (1987)

Mauri *See* Big Mo (1973)

Max, My Love *See* Max, Mon Amour (1986)

The Mayfair Bank Caper *See* The Big Scam (1979)

Mazel Tov Ou le Mariage *See* Marry Me, Marry Me (1969)

McKlusky *See* White Lightning (1973)

The McMasters...Tougher Than the West Itself *See* The McMasters (1970)

Meachorei Hasoragim *See* Beyond the Walls (1984)

The Medicine Hat Stallion *See* Peter Lundy and the Medicine Hat Stallion (1977)

Meet Miss Marple *See* Murder She Said (1962)

Meet the Applegates *See* The Applegates (1989)

Meet Whiplash Willie *See* The Fortune Cookie (1966)

The Meetings of Anna *See* Les Rendez-vous D'Anna (1978)

Mekagojira No Gyakushu *See* Terror of Mechagodzilla (1978)

Melody of Youth *See* They Shall Have Music (1939)

Men in Tights *See* Robin Hood: Men in Tights (1993)

Men of Steel *See* Steel (1980)

The Mercenaries *See* Dark of the Sun (1968)

Mery per Sempre *See* Forever Mary (1989)

The Message *See* Mohammed: Messenger of God (1977)

Messer Im Kopf *See* Knife in the Head (1978)

Metempsycose *See* Tomb of Torture (1965)

Meurtre en 45 Tours *See* Murder at 45 R.P.M. (1965)

Mi Revolver es la Ley *See* Colt is My Law (19??)

Mickey Spillane's Margin for Murder *See* Margin for Murder (1981)

Microscopia *See* Fantastic Voyage (1966)

Midnight at Madame Tussaud's *See* Midnight at the Wax Museum (1936)

Midnight Heat *See* Sunset Heat (1992)

The Mighty Ducks 2 *See* D2: The Mighty Ducks (1994)

The Mighty Peking Man *See* Goliathon (1979)

The Mighty Thunder *See* Tundra (1936)

The Mighty Ursus *See* Ursus in the Valley of the Lions (1962)

Mignonne *See* Your Turn Darling (1963)

Mikan No Taikyoku *See* The Go-Masters (1982)

Mike Leigh's Naked *See* Naked (1993)

Mikres Aphrodites *See* Young Aphrodites (1963)

Milagro en Roma *See* Miracle in Rome (1988)

Milczaca Gwiazda *See* First Spaceship on Venus (1960)

Mile a Minute Love *See* Roaring Speedboats (1937)

Milou en Mai *See* May Fools (1990)

Milou in May *See* May Fools (1990)

Mind Games *See* The Agency (1981)

Mindwarp: An Infinity of Terror *See* Galaxy of Terror (1981)

The Miracle of Fatima *See* Miracle of Our Lady of Fatima (1952)

Miracle of Life *See* Our Daily Bread (1934)

Miracolo a Milano *See* Miracle in Milan (1951)

Miss Europe *See* Prix de Beaute (1930)

Miss Muette *See* The Diabolical Dr. Z (1965)

Mr. Ashton was Indiscreet *See* The Senator was Indiscreet (1947)

Mr. Bug Goes to Town *See* Hoppity Goes to Town (1941)

Mr. Celebrity *See* Turf Boy (1942)

Mr. Fox of Venice *See* The Honey Pot (1967)

Mr. Invisible *See* Mr. Superinvisible (1973)

Mr. Quilp *See* The Old Curiosity Shop (1975)

Mr. Sebastian *See* Sebastian (1968)

Mister V *See* Pimpernel Smith (1942)

Mr. Wrong *See* Dark of the Night (1985)

Misterios del Ultratumba *See* Black Pit of Dr. M (1947)

Mit Eva Fing Die Sunde An *See* The Bellboy and the Playgirls (1962)

Mitt Liv Som Hund *See* My Life as a Dog (1985)

The Model Killer *See* The Hollywood Strangler Meets the Skid Row Slasher (1979)

Model Massacre *See* Color Me Blood Red (1964)

A Modern Bluebeard *See* Boom in the Moon (1946)

A Modern Hero *See* Knute Rockne: All American (1940)

Modigliani of Montparnasse *See* Modigliani (1958)

Mogliamante *See* Wifemistress (1979)

The Mogul *See* Ratings Game (1984)

Molly Louvain *See* The Strange Love of Molly Louvain (1932)

Mondo Pazzo *See* Mondo Cane 2 (1964)

A Monkey in Winter *See* Un Singe en Hiver (1962)

Monkey Shines: An Experiment in Fear *See* Monkey Shines (1988)

Monsieur Hulot's Holiday *See* Mr. Hulot's Holiday (1953)

Monster *See* Humanoids from the Deep (1980)

The Monster Baran *See* Varan the Unbelievable (1961)

Monster from a Prehistoric Planet *See* Gappa the Trifibian Monster (1967)

Monster Maker *See* Monster from the Ocean Floor (1954)

Monster of Monsters *See* Ghidrah the Three Headed Monster (1965)

Monster of Terror *See* Die, Monster, Die! (1965)

The Monster Show *See* Freaks (1932)

The Monster Walked *See* The Monster Walks (1932)

The Monster with Green Eyes *See* Planets Against Us (1961)

Monster Yongkari *See* Yongkari Monster of the Deep (1967)

Monster Zero *See* Godzilla vs. Monster Zero (1968)

The Monsters Are Loose *See* The Thrill Killers (1965)

Monsters From the Moon *See* Robot Monster (1953)

Monsters from the Unknown Planet *See* Terror of Mechagodzilla (1978)

Monstrosity *See* The Atomic Brain (1964)

Montana Justice *See* Man from Montana (1941)

Monte Carlo or Bust *See* Those Daring Young Men in Their Jaunty Jalopies (1969)

Montenegro—Or Pigs and Pearls *See* Montenegro (1981)

Montparnasse 19 *See* Modigliani (1958)

Morgan: A Suitable Case for Treatment *See* Morgan! (1966)

Morgan il Pirata *See* Morgan the Pirate (1960)

Morgen Grauen *See* Time Troopers (1989)

The Mormon Peril *See* Trapped by the Mormons (1922)

Morning Terror *See* Time Troopers (1989)

Mortal Sins *See* Dangerous Obsession (1988)

Morte a Venezia *See* Death in Venice (1971)

Morton of the Mounted *See* Timber Terrors (1935)

Moscow Distrusts Tears *See* Moscow Does Not Believe in Tears (1980)

Moscow Nights *See* I Stand Condemned (1936)

Moskwa Sljesam Nje Jerit *See* Moscow Does Not Believe in Tears (1980)

Mosura Tai Goira *See* Godzilla vs. Mothra (1964)

Motel *See* Pink Motel (1982)

Motel Vacancy *See* Talking Walls (1985)

Mother Goose A Go-Go *See* The Unkissed Bride (1966)

Mother Riley Meets the Vampire *See* My Son, the Vampire (1952)

Mothra vs. Godzilla *See* Godzilla vs. Mothra (1964)

Mountain of Cannibal Gods *See* Slave of the Cannibal God (1979)

Movie Struck *See* Pick a Star (1937)

The Moving Target *See* Harper (1966)

Mud *See* The Stick-Up (1977)

Mujeres al Borde de un Ataque de Nervios *See* Women on the Verge of a Nervous Breakdown (1988)

Mumsy, Nanny, Sonny, and Girly *See* Girly (1970)

Munkbrogreven *See* The Count of the Old Town (1934)

Murder by Mail *See* Schizoid (1980)

Murder by Proxy *See* Blackout (1954)

The Murder in Thorton Square *See* Gaslight (1944)

Murder, Inc. *See* The Enforcer (1951)

Murder on Diamond Row *See* The Squeaker (1937)

Murder One *See* Death Sentence (1974)

The Murderer Dmitri Karamazov *See* The Brothers Karamazov (1958)

Muriel, Or the Time of Return *See* Muriel (1963)

Muriel, Ou le Temps d'Un Retour *See* Muriel (1963)

The Murri Affair *See* La Grande Bourgeoise (1974)

Music in Darkness *See* Night Is My Future (1947)

Mussolini: The Decline and Fall of Il Duce *See* Mussolini & I (1985)

Mutant *See* Forbidden World (1982)

The Mutation *See* The Freakmaker (1973)

Mutations *See* The Freakmaker (1973)

The Mutilator *See* The Dark (1979)

Mutter Kusters Fahrt Zum Himmel *See* Mother Kusters Goes to Heaven (1976)

My Brother, the Outlaw *See* My Outlaw Brother (1951)

My Crazy Life *See* Mi Vida Loca (1994)

My Darling Shiksa *See* Over the Brooklyn Bridge (1983)

My Father, My Master *See* Padre Padrone (1977)

My Favourite Year *See* My Favorite Year (1982)

My Girlfriend's Boyfriend *See* Boyfriends & Girlfriends (1988)

My Gun is Jammed *See* Bare Hunt (1963)

My Hero *See* A Southern Yankee (1948)

My Love Letters *See* Love Letters (1983)

My Name is John *See* The Legend of Hillbilly John (1973)

My Night with Maud *See* My Night at Maud's (1969)

My Son Alone *See* American Empire (1942)

My Summer Story *See* It Runs in the Family (1994)

My Teenage Daughter *See* Teenage Bad Girl (1959)

My Uncle *See* Mon Oncle (1958)

My Uncle, Mr. Hulot *See* Mon Oncle (1958)

Mystere Alexina *See* The Mystery of Alexina (1986)

Mysterious Invader *See* The Astounding She-Monster (1958)

The Mysterious Satellite *See* Warning from Space (1956)

The Mystery of Kaspar Hauser *See* Every Man for Himself & God Against All (1975)

Mystery of the Black Jungle *See* The Black Devils of Kali (1955)

The Mystery of the Marie Celeste *See* The Mystery of the Mary Celeste (1937)

Mystique *See* Circle of Power (1983)

Na Komete *See* On the Comet (1968)

Nagooa *See* Drifting (1982)

The Naked Goddess *See* The Devil's Hand (1961)

Naked Island *See* The Island (1961)

The Naked Night *See* Sawdust & Tinsel (1953)

Naked Space *See* Spaceship (1981)

The Naked Temptress *See* The Naked Witch (1964)

Naked Under Leather *See* The Girl on a Motorcycle (1968)

The Naked Weekend *See* Circle of Power (1983)

Naked Youth *See* The Cruel Story of Youth (1960)

Nankai No Kai Ketto *See* Godzilla vs. the Sea Monster (1966)

Nara Livet *See* Brink of Life (1957)

Narayama-Bushi-Ko *See* The Ballad of Narayama (1983)

Nathaniel Hawthorne's "Twice Told Tales" *See* Twice-Told Tales (1963)

Nattvardsgaesterna *See* The Winter Light (1962)

Nature's Mistakes *See* Freaks (1932)

The Navy Steps Out *See* A Girl, a Guy and a Gob (1941)

Neat and Tidy *See* Adventures Beyond Belief (1987)

Necromancy *See* The Witching (1972)

Ned Kelly, Outlaw *See* Ned Kelly (1970)

Neil Simon's Biloxi Blues *See* Biloxi Blues (1988)

Neil Simon's Brighton Beach Memoirs *See* Brighton Beach Memoirs (1986)

Neil Simon's Broadway Bound *See* Broadway Bound (1992)

Neil Simon's Lost in Yonkers *See* Lost in Yonkers (1993)

Neil Simon's The Slugger's Wife *See* The Slugger's Wife (1985)

Nella Stretta M Orsa Del Ragno *See* Web of the Spider (1970)

The Neptune Disaster *See* Neptune Factor (1973)

Neskolko Dnei iz Zhizni I.I. Oblomov *See* Oblomov (1981)

Nevada Heat *See* Fake Out (1982)

Never Cry Devil *See* Night Visitor (1989)

Never Give an Inch *See* Sometimes a Great Notion (1971)

The New Adventures of Don Juan *See* Adventures of Don Juan (1949)

New Adventures of Tarzan *See* Tarzan and the Green Goddess (1938)

The New Barbarians *See* Warriors of the Wasteland (1983)

New Girl in Town *See* Nashville Girl (1976)

New Wave *See* Nouvelle Vague (1990)

New Wine *See* Melody Master (1941)

The Newcomers *See* The Wild Country (1971)

The Next Man *See* The Arab Conspiracy (1976)

Night Beauties *See* Bellas de Noche (19??)

The Night Caller *See* Night Caller from Outer Space (1966)

Night Comes Too Soon *See* The Ghost of Rashmon Hall (1947)

Night Encounter *See* Double Agents (1959)

Night Hair Child *See* What the Peeper Saw (1972)

Night Legs *See* Fright (1971)

The Night of San Lorenzo *See* The Night of the Shooting Stars (1982)

Night of the Beast *See* House of the Black Death (1965)

Night of the Big Heat *See* Island of the Burning Doomed (1967)

Night of the Bloodsuckers *See* The Vampire Hookers (1978)

Night of the Claw *See* Island Claw (1980)

Night of the Dark Full Moon *See* Silent Night, Bloody Night (1973)

Night of the Demon *See* Curse of the Demon (1957)

Night of the Demon *See* The Touch of Satan (1970)

Night of the Doomed *See* Nightmare Castle (1965)

Night of the Eagle *See* Burn Witch, Burn! (1962)

Night of the Flesh Eaters *See* Night of the Living Dead (1968)

Night of the Seagulls *See* Night of the Death Cult (1975)

Night of the Silicates *See* Island of Terror (1966)

Night of the Wehrmacht Zombies *See* Night of the Zombies (1981)

Night Shadows *See* Mutant (1983)

The Night They Invented Striptease *See* The Night They Raided Minsky's (1969)

Night Train *See* Night Train to Munich (1940)

Night Walk *See* Deathdream (1972)

Nightingale See The Young Nurses (1973)

A Nightingale Sang in Berkeley Square See The Big Scam (1979)

Nightmare See City of the Walking Dead (1983)

Nightmare See Nightmare in Badham County (1976)

Nightmare at Shadow Woods See Blood Rage (1987)

Nightmare City See City of the Walking Dead (1983)

Nightmare House See Scream, Baby, Scream (1969)

Nightmare Island See The Slayer (1982)

Nightmare Maker See Night Warning (1982)

Nightmare on Elm Street 6: Freddy's Dead See Freddy's Dead: The Final Nightmare (1991)

Nightriders See Western Double Feature 2: Wayne & Hale (198?)

Nights in a Harem See Son of Sinbad (1955)

Nijushi No Hitomi See Twenty-Four Eyes (1954)

1990 I Guerrieri del Bronx See 1990: The Bronx Warriors (1983)

1999—Nen No Natsu Yasumi See Summer Vacation: 1999 (1988)

Ningen No Joken See The Human Condition: Road to Eternity (1959)

Ninja Dragons See Magic Kid (1992)

Nippon Chiubotsu See Tidal Wave (1975)

Nippon Konchuki See The Insect Woman (1963)

No Greater Love See The Human Condition: Road to Eternity (1959)

No Knife See The Frisco Kid (1979)

No Man's Land See No Man's Range (1935)

No Place Like Homicide See What a Carve-Up! (1962)

The No-Tell Hotel See Rosebud Beach Hotel (1985)

Nobi See Fires on the Plain (1959)

Noce in Galilee See A Wedding in Galilee (1987)

Nocturna, Granddaughter of Dracula See Nocturna (1979)

Norman Rockwell's Breaking Home Ties See Breaking Home Ties (1987)

North Sea Hijack See ffolkes (1980)

The Northfield Cemetery Massacre See Northville Cemetery Massacre (1976)

Northwest Frontier See Flame Over India (1960)

Nosferatu, A Symphony of Horror See Nosferatu (1922)

Nosferatu, A Symphony of Terror See Nosferatu (1922)

Nosferatu, Eine Symphonie des Grauens See Nosferatu (1922)

Nosferatu, The Vampire See Nosferatu (1922)

Not Against the Flesh See Vampyr (1931)

Not Wanted See Streets of Sin (1949)

Nothing in Order See All Screwed Up (1974)

Nowhere to Hide See Fatal Chase (1977)

Noz w Wodzie See Knife in the Water (1962)

Nuclear Run See Chain Reaction (1980)

Nuclear Terror See Golden Rendezvous (1977)

Nude In His Pocket See Girl in His Pocket (1962)

Nuit et Jour See Night and Day (1991)

Number Two See Numero Deux (1975)

Numbered Days See Cycle Psycho (19??)

Nuovo Cinema Paradiso See Cinema Paradiso (1988)

Nurse Sherri See Hospital of Terror (1978)

The Nutcracker See George Balanchine's The Nutcracker (1993)

Nybyggarna See The New Land (1973)

Nyoka and the Lost Secrets of Hippocrates See Nyoka and the Tigermen (1942)

Obch Od Na Korze See The Shop on Main Street (1965)

Obsession See The Hidden Room (1949)

Occhi Senza Volto See The Horror Chamber of Dr. Faustus (1959)

Oci Ciornie See Dark Eyes (1987)

October See Ten Days That Shook the World (1927)

Odio le Bionde See I Hate Blondes (1983)

Office Party See Hostile Takeover (1988)

The Official History See The Official Story (1985)

The Official Version See The Official Story (1985)

Oh, Charlie See Hold That Ghost (1941)

Okasan See Mother (1952)

The Old and the New See The General Line (1929)

The Old Corral See Song of the Gringo (1936)

Old Greatheart See Way Back Home (1932)

Old Heidelberg See The Student Prince in Old Heidelberg (1927)

The Old Man and the Boy See Two of Us (1968)

Old Mother Riley Meets the Vampire See My Son, the Vampire (1952)

Old Shatterhand See Apaches Last Battle (1964)

Olelkezo Tekintetek See Another Way (1982)

Omar Mukhtar See Lion of the Desert (1981)

The Omen 3 See The Final Conflict (1981)

On the Great White Trail See Renfrew on the Great White Trail (1938)

On the Road Again See Honeysuckle Rose (1980)

Once Upon a Texas Train See Texas Guns (1990)

One Born Every Minute See Flim-Flam Man (1967)

One Cup of Coffee See Pastime (1991)

One For All See The President's Mystery (1936)

One for Sorrow, Two for Joy See Signs of Life (1989)

One Horse Town See Small Town Girl (1953)

One Hundred Percent Pure See The Girl from Missouri (1934)

One-Man Mutiny See The Court Martial of Billy Mitchell (1955)

One Plus One See Sympathy for the Devil (1970)

Onkel Toms Hutte See Uncle Tom's Cabin (1969)

Only the French Can! See French Can-Can (1955)

Onna Ga Kaidan O Agaru Toki See When a Woman Ascends the Stairs (1960)

Operacione Paura See Kill, Baby, Kill (1966)

Operation Cicero See Five Fingers (1952)

Operation Kid Brother See Secret Agent 00 (1967)

Operation Overthrow See Power Play (1981)

Operation Serpent See Fer-De-Lance (1974)

Operation Undercover See Report to the Commissioner (1974)

Operazione Goldman See Lightning Bolt (1967)

Opium Connection See The Poppy is also a Flower (1966)

The Oracle See The Horse's Mouth (1958)

Orazi e Curiazi See Duel of Champions (1961)

Orca—Killer Whale See Orca (1977)

Order of Death See Corrupt (1984)

Orfeu Negro See Black Orpheus (1958)

Orgasmo See Paranoia (1969)

Orkobefogadas See Adoption (1975)

Orlak, El Inflerno de Frankenstein See Orlak, the Hell of Frankenstein (1960)

Orphee See Orpheus (1949)

Oru Kaiju Daishingeki See Godzilla's Revenge (1969)

Osenny Marafon See Autumn Marathon (1979)

Other People's Business See Way Back Home (1932)

The Other Side of Paradise See Foxtrot (1976)

Otto E Mezzo See 8 1/2 (1963)

Our Daily Bread See City Girl (1930)

Our Girl Friday See The Adventures of Sadie (1955)

Ourselves Alone See River of Unrest (1937)

Out of Rosenheim See Bagdad Cafe (1988)

Out of the Darkness See Night Creature (1979)

Out of the Darkness See Teenage Caveman (1958)

Out of the Night See Strange Illusion (1945)

Out of the Shadow See Murder on the Campus (1952)

Out on Probation See Daddy-O (1959)

The Outcry See Il Grido (1957)

Outer Reach See Spaced Out (1980)

Outlaw Gun See A Minute to Pray, A Second to Die (1967)

Outside In See Red, White & Busted (1975)

The Outsider See Fatal Error (1983)

Outsider in Amsterdam See Fatal Error (1983)

The Outsiders See Band of Outsiders (1964)

Over Her Dead Body See Enid is Sleeping (1990)

The Pace That Kills See Cocaine Fiends (1936)

Panga See Curse 3: Blood Sacrifice (1990)

Panic See Panique (1947)

Panic at Lakewood Manor See Ants (1977)

Panic on the Trans-Siberian Express See Horror Express (1972)

Panico en el Transiberiano See Horror Express (1972)

Panny z Wilka See Maids of Wilko (1979)

Paper Bullets See Gangs, Inc. (1941)

The Parasite Murders See They Came from Within (1975)

Pardon Me, Your Teeth are in My Neck See The Fearless Vampire Killers (1967)

Paris Brule-T-Il? See Is Paris Burning? (1968)

Paris Does Strange Things See Elena and Her Men (1956)

Paris is Ours See Paris Belongs to Us (1960)

Paris Nous Appartient See Paris Belongs to Us (1960)

Paris Qui Dort See The Crazy Ray (1922)

Paris vu Par See Six in Paris (1968)

Park Plaza See Norman Conquest (1953)

Paroxismus See Venus in Furs (1970)

Parts: The Clonus Horror See The Clonus Horror (1979)

Party Girls See Party Incorporated (1989)

Pasqualino Settebellezze See Seven Beauties (1976)

Pasqualino: Seven Beauties See Seven Beauties (1976)

Passages from "Finnegans Wake" See Finnegan's Wake (1963)

Passages from James Joyce's "Finnegans Wake" See Finnegan's Wake (1963)

The Passerby See La Passante (1983)

The Passion Flower Hotel See Boarding School (1983)

Passion Play See Love Letters (1983)

Passione d'Amore See Passion of Love (1982)

Passions See The Passing of Evil (1970)

Passport to Shame *See* Room 43 (1958)

The Patsy *See* L'Addition (1985)

Patterns of Power *See* Patterns (1956)

Patton: A Salute to a Rebel *See* Patton (1970)

Patton—Lust for Glory *See* Patton (1970)

Pauline a la Plage *See* Pauline at the Beach (1983)

Paura Nella Citta Dei Morti Viventi *See* Gates of Hell (1983)

The Peace Game *See* The Gladiators (1970)

Peacemaker *See* The Ambassador (1984)

Peau d'Ane *See* Donkey Skin (1970)

The Peking Medallion *See* The Corrupt Ones (1967)

Penn of Pennsylvania *See* The Courageous Mr. Penn (1941)

People Toys *See* Devil Times Five (1974)

People's Enemy *See* Prison Train (1938)

Pepi, Luci, Bom y Otras Chicas del Monton *See* Pepi, Luci, Bom and Other Girls on the Heap (1980)

Percy's Progress *See* It's Not the Size That Counts (1974)

Peril en la Demeure *See* Peril (1985)

Perils from Planet Mongo *See* Flash Gordon: Rocketship (1936)

The Perils of Gwendoline in the Land of the Yik-Yak *See* The Perils of Gwendoline (1984)

Perils of Nyoka *See* Nyoka and the Tigermen (1942)

Persecution *See* The Graveyard (1974)

Persecution and Assassination of Jean-Paul Marat as Performed by the Inmates of the Asylum of Charenton Under the Direction of the Marquis De Sade *See* Marat/Sade (1966)

Perseus the Invincible *See* Medusa Against the Son of Hercules (1962)

Peter Rabbit and Tales of Beatrix Potter *See* Tales of Beatrix Potter (1971)

Petersen *See* Jock Petersen (1974)

Petroleum Girls *See* Legend of Frenchie King (1971)

Phantom Fiend *See* The Return of Dr. Mabuse (1961)

The Phantom of Terror *See* The Bird with the Crystal Plumage (1970)

Phantom of the Air *See* The Phantom Broadcast (1933)

Phantom of the Plains *See* Western Double Feature 7: Wild Bill & Crabbe (1945)

The Phantom Ship *See* The Mystery of the Mary Celeste (1937)

Phar Lap: Heart of a Nation *See* Phar Lap (1984)

Phenomena *See* Creepers (1985)

Philo Vance Returns *See* Infamous Crimes (1947)

Phoebe *See* Zelly & Me (1988)

The Phoenix *See* War of the Wizards (1981)

Pickup on 101 *See* Where the Eagle Flies (1972)

Pigsty *See* Porcile (1969)

Pilgrimage to Rome *See* L'Anne Sainte (1978)

The Pilot *See* Danger in the Skies (1979)

Pinball Pick-Up *See* Pick-Up Summer (1979)

Pinball Summer *See* Pick-Up Summer (1979)

Pioneers *See* Pioneer Woman (1973)

Pippi Langstrump Pa de Sju Haven *See* Pippi in the South Seas (1974)

Piranha 2: Flying Killers *See* Piranha 2: The Spawning (1982)

Pirate's Fiancee *See* A Very Curious Girl (1969)

Pirate's Harbor *See* Haunted Harbor (1944)

The Pizza Connection *See* The Sicilian Connection (1985)

The Plains of Heaven *See* Panic Station (1982)

Planet of Horrors *See* Galaxy of Terror (1981)

Planet of the Lifeless Men *See* Battle of the Worlds (1961)

The Plants Are Watching *See* The Kirlian Witness (1978)

Players *See* The Club (1981)

Playgirl Gang *See* Switchblade Sisters (1975)

The Playgirls and the Bellboy *See* The Bellboy and the Playgirls (1962)

Playing for Keeps *See* Lily in Love (1985)

Please! Mr. Balzac *See* Mademoiselle Striptease (1957)

Plein Sud *See* Heat of Desire (1984)

Pluck of the Irish *See* Great Guy (1936)

Pocomania *See* The Devil's Daughter (1939)

Poe's Tales of Terror *See* Tales of Terror (1962)

Poisoned by Love: The Kern County Murders *See* Murder So Sweet (1993)

Pokayaniye *See* Repentance (1987)

Police Connection *See* The Mad Bomber (1972)

Police Force *See* Jackie Chan's Police Force (1985)

The Police Story *See* Jackie Chan's Police Force (1985)

Poncomania *See* The Devil's Daughter (1939)

Pony Express *See* Peter Lundy and the Medicine Hat Stallion (1977)

Pookie *See* The Sterile Cuckoo (1969)

Poor Albert and Little Annie *See* I Dismember Mama (1974)

The Poor Outlaws *See* The Round Up (1966)

The Pope Must Die *See* The Pope Must Diet (1991)

Popiol i Diament *See* Ashes and Diamonds (1958)

Poppies Are Also Flowers *See* The Poppy is also a Flower (1966)

Porte Aperte *See* Open Doors (1989)

Portrait of a Woman, Nude *See* Nudo di Donna (1983)

Portrait of Alison *See* Postmark for Danger (1956)

Portrait of Maria *See* Maria Candelaria (1946)

Potemkin *See* The Battleship Potemkin (1925)

Practice Makes Perfect *See* Le Cavaleur (1978)

Prairie Outlaws *See* Wild West (1946)

Prairie Rustlers *See* Western Double Feature 7: Wild Bill & Crabbe (1945)

Pratidwandi *See* The Adversary (1971)

The Prehistoric Sound *See* Sound of Horror (1964)

Prehistoric World *See* Teenage Caveman (1958)

Prenom: Carmen *See* First Name: Carmen (1983)

Preparez Vous Mouchoirs *See* Get Out Your Handkerchiefs (1978)

Preppies *See* Making the Grade (1984)

The President's Women *See* Foreplay (1975)

Pride of Kentucky *See* The Story of Seabiscuit (1949)

Priority Red One *See* Delta Force Commando 2 (1990)

Prison *See* Devil's Wanton (1949)

The Prisoner *See* Cold Room (1984)

The Private Life of Paul Joseph Goebbels *See* Enemy of Women (1944)

The Private Lives of Elizabeth and Essex *See* Elizabeth, the Queen (1968)

Private Snuffy Smith *See* Snuffy Smith, Yard Bird (1942)

The Private Wore Skirts *See* Never Wave at a WAC (1952)

Profession: Reporter *See* The Passenger (1975)

The Profile of Terror *See* The Sadist (1963)

Profumo di Donna *See* The Scent of a Woman (1975)

Profundo Rosso *See* Deep Red: Hatchet Murders (1975)

Prom Night 2 *See* Hello Mary Lou: Prom Night 2 (1987)

Promise Her Anything *See* Promises! Promises! (1963)

A Proposito Luciano *See* Lucky Luciano (1974)

The Protectors, Book One *See* Angel of H.E.A.T. (1982)

Proud, Damned, and Dead *See* The Proud and the Damned (1972)

Przesluchanie *See* The Interrogation (1982)

Psycho a Go Go! *See* Blood of Ghastly Horror (1972)

Psycho-Circus *See* Circus of Fear (1967)

Psycho Killers *See* Mania (1960)

Psycho Puppet *See* Delirium (1977)

Psycho Sisters *See* The Sibling (1972)

Psychotic *See* Driver's Seat (1973)

Ptang, Yang, Kipperbang *See* Kipperbang (1982)

Public Be Damned *See* The World Gone Mad (1933)

The Public Be Hanged *See* The World Gone Mad (1933)

Puo Una Morta Rivivere Per Amore? *See* Venus in Furs (1970)

The Purim Player *See* Der Purimshpiler (1937)

Purple Death from Outer Space *See* Flash Gordon Conquers the Universe (1940)

The Purple Riders *See* Purple Vigilantes (1938)

Pursuit *See* Apache Blood (1975)

Q Planes *See* Clouds Over Europe (1939)

Quai des Orfevres *See* Jenny Lamour (1947)

Quando De Donne Avevando La Coda *See* When Women Had Tails (1970)

Que He Hecho Yo Para Merecer Esto! *See* What Have I Done to Deserve This? (1985)

Que La Bete Meure *See* This Man Must Die (1970)

Queen of Blood *See* Planet of Blood (1966)

Queen of Broadway *See* Kid Dynamite (1943)

Queen of the Cannibals *See* Doctor Butcher M.D. (1980)

Queen of the Gorillas *See* The Bride & the Beast (1958)

The Queen's Husband *See* The Royal Bed (1931)

Quei Temerari Sulle Loro Pazze, Scatenate, Scalcinate Carriole *See* Those Daring Young Men in Their Jaunty Jalopies (1969)

Quella Villa Accanto Al Cimitero *See* The House by the Cemetery (1983)

Quelqu' Un Derriere la Porte *See* Someone Behind the Door (1971)

Quemimada! *See* Burn! (1970)

The Quest *See* The Longest Drive (1976)

Quien Sabe? *See* A Bullet for the General (1968)

A Quiet Little Neighborhood, A Perfect Little Murder *See* A Perfect Little Murder (1990)

A Quiet Place to Kill *See* Paranoia (1969)

Quoi De Neuf, Pussycat? *See* What's New Pussycat? (1965)

Race for the Yankee Zephyr *See* Treasure of the Yankee Zephyr (1983)

The Radical *See* Katherine (1975)

Radio Ranch *See* The Phantom Empire (1935)

Radon *See* Rodan (1956)

Radon the Flying Monster *See* Rodan (1956)

Rafferty and the Highway Hustlers See Rafferty & the Gold Dust Twins (1975)

Rage See Rabid (1977)

Rage of the Buccaneers See The Black Pirate (1926)

Ragged Angels See They Shall Have Music (1939)

The Raging Moon See Long Ago Tomorrow (1971)

Raging Waters See The Green Promise (1949)

Rags to Riches See Callie and Son (1981)

Raiders of the Doomed Kingdom See After the Fall of Saigon (1988)

Rainbow on the River See It Happened in New Orleans (1936)

Raise Ravens See Cria (1976)

Ramblin' Man See The Concrete Cowboys (1979)

Ramrodders See The Ramrodder (1969)

Ransom See Maniac (1977)

The Rape of Richard Beck See Broken Badge (1985)

Rape Squad See Act of Vengeance (1974)

Rasputin: The Mad Monk See Rasputin and the Empress (1932)

The Rats See Deadly Eyes (1982)

The Raven See Le Corbeau (1943)

RE: Lucky Luciano See Lucky Luciano (1974)

The Reader See La Lectrice (1988)

The Rebel See The Bushwackers (1952)

Rebel of the Road See Hot Rod (1979)

Rebel with a Cause See The Loneliness of the Long Distance Runner (1962)

Rece do Gory See Hands Up (1981)

Record of a Living Being See I Live in Fear (1955)

Red See Trois Couleurs: Rouge (1994)

Red Dragon See Code Name Alpha (1967)

Red Dragon See Manhunter (1986)

The Red Hangman See The Bloody Pit of Horror (1965)

The Red Head See Poil de Carotte (1931)

Red Hot Tires See Racing Luck (1935)

Red Hot Wheels See To Please a Lady (1950)

Red on Red See Scarred (1984)

The Red Tide See Blood Tide (1982)

Redneck County See Hooch Country Boys (1975)

The Refugee See Three Faces West (1940)

Rehearsal for a Crime See The Criminal Life of Archibaldo de la Cruz (1955)

Rejuvenatrix See The Rejuvenator (1988)

The Remarkable Mr. Kipps See Kipps (1941)

Remembrance of Love See Holocaust Survivors...Remembrance of Love (1983)

Remorques See Stormy Waters (1941)

Renegade Girls See Caged Heat (1974)

Renfrew of the Royal Mounted on the Great White Trail See Renfrew on the Great White Trail (1938)

Reprieved See Sing Sing Nights (1935)

Requiem fur Dominic See Requiem for Dominic (1991)

The Rescue See Let's Get Harry (1987)

The Resurrection Syndicate See Nothing But the Night (1972)

Retaliator See Programmed to Kill (1986)

Retik, the Moon Menace See Radar Men from the Moon (1952)

Return from the Past See Alien Massacre (1967)

The Return of Maxwell Smart See The Nude Bomb (1980)

The Return of Mr. H. See They Saved Hitler's Brain (1964)

Return of the Blind Dead See Return of the Evil Dead (1975)

The Return of the Giant Monsters See Gamera vs. Gaos (1967)

Return of the Living Dead See Messiah of Evil (1974)

Return of the Magnificent Seven See Return of the Seven (1966)

Return of the Zombies See The Hanging Woman (1972)

Reunion See Reunion in France (1942)

Revenge See Blood Feud (1979)

The Revenge of Dracula See Dracula vs. Frankenstein (1971)

The Revenge of Milady See The Four Musketeers (1975)

The Revenge of the Blood Beast See The She-Beast (1965)

Revenge of the Dead See Night of the Ghouls (1959)

Revenge of the Innocents See South Bronx Heroes (1985)

Revenge of the Living Dead See Children Shouldn't Play with Dead Things (1972)

Revenge of the Screaming Dead See Messiah of Evil (1974)

Revenge Squad See Hit & Run (1982)

Rhodes of Africa See Rhodes (1936)

Rhosyn A Rhith See Coming Up Roses (1987)

Rhythm on the Ranch See Rootin' Tootin' Rhythm (1938)

Rich, Young, and Deadly See Platinum High School (1960)

Riches and Romance See Amazing Adventure (1937)

Richie See The Death of Richie (1976)

Ride a Dark Horse See Man & Boy (1971)

Riders See Guerilla Brigade (1939)

Riffraff See Riff Raff (1935)

The Right to Eat See El Derecho de Comer (1987)

Ripped Off See Counter Punch (1971)

Risate de Gioia See Passionate Thief (1960)

The Rise of Catherine the Great See Catherine the Great (1934)

The Rise of Helga See Susan Lenox: Her Fall and Rise (1931)

Rising to Fame See Susan Lenox: Her Fall and Rise (1931)

Riso Amaro See Bitter Rice (1949)

Rites of Summer See White Water Summer (1987)

The Road See La Strada (1954)

Road to Avonlea See Tales from Avonlea, Vol. 1: The Journey Begins (1990)

Road to Frisco See They Drive by Night (1940)

Roaring Timber See Come and Get It (1936)

Rob Roy See Rob Roy—The Highland Rogue (1953)

Robinson Crusoeland See Utopia (1951)

Rocco et Ses Freres See Rocco and His Brothers (1960)

Rocket to the Moon See Cat Women of the Moon (1953)

Rocky Mountain Mystery See The Fighting Westerner (1935)

Roger Corman's Frankenstein Unbound See Frankenstein Unbound (1990)

Roma See Fellini's Roma (1972)

Roma, Citta Aperta See Open City (1945)

Romance and Riches See Amazing Adventure (1937)

Romance da Empregada See The Story of Fausta (1988)

Romauld et Juliet See Mama, There's a Man in Your Bed (1989)

Rome, Open City See Open City (1945)

Romeo in Pyjamas See Parlor, Bedroom and Bath (1931)

Romeo, Julia a Tma See Sweet Light in a Dark Room (1960)

Romeo, Juliet and Darkness See Sweet Light in a Dark Room (1960)

Rommel—Desert Fox See The Desert Fox (1951)

Rona Jaffe's Mazes and Monsters See Mazes and Monsters (1982)

The Rook See Something for Everyone (1970)

Rookies See Buck Privates (1941)

Rookies Come Home See Buck Privates Come Home (1947)

The Rose and the Sword See Flesh and Blood (1985)

Rosemary's Killer See The Prowler (1981)

The Rotten Apple See Five Minutes to Love (1963)

Rouge Baiser See Red Kiss (1985)

Rough Company See The Violent Men (1955)

Ruby Cairo See Deception (1992)

Rudyard Kipling's Jungle Book See The Jungle Book (1942)

Rue Cases Negres See Sugar Cane Alley (1983)

Rumpo Kid See Carry On Cowboy (1966)

Run, Simon, Run See Savage Run (1970)

The Runaways See South Bronx Heroes (1985)

Russicum See Third Solution (1989)

Rustler's Roundup See Rustler's Hideout (1944)

The Rutles See All You Need Is Cash (1978)

The Saboteur See Morituri (1965)

Saboteur: Code Name Morituri See Morituri (1965)

The Sabre and the Arrow See Last of the Comanches (1952)

Sabrina Fair See Sabrina (1954)

Sacco e Vanzetti See Sacco & Vanzetti (1971)

Sadko See The Magic Voyage of Sinbad (1952)

The Saga of Dracula See The Saga of the Draculas (1972)

The Saga of Gosta Berling See The Atonement of Gosta Berling (1924)

The Saga of the Road See Pather Panchali (1954)

Saikaku Ichidai Onna See Life of Oharu (1952)

St. Martin's Lane See Sidewalks of London (1940)

Sakima and the Masked Marvel See The Masked Marvel (1943)

Salerno Beachhead See A Walk in the Sun (1946)

The Salute of the Jugger See The Blood of Heroes (1989)

Salvation! Have You Said Your Prayers Today? See Salvation! (1987)

Sam Cooper's Gold See The Ruthless Four (1970)

Sam Marlowe, Private Eye See The Man with Bogart's Face (1980)

Sanda Tai Gailah See War of the Gargantuas (1970)

Sandakan House 8 See Sandakan No. 8 (1974)

The Sandpit Generals See Defiant (1970)

Sans Toit Ni Loi See Vagabond (1985)

Sansho Dayu See Sansho the Bailiff (1954)

Santa Claus Defeats the Aliens See Santa Claus Conquers the Martians (1964)

Santo en el Museo de Cera *See* Samson in the Wax Museum (1963)

Santo in the Wax Museum *See* Samson in the Wax Museum (1963)

Satanic Mechanic *See* Perfect Killer (1977)

Satan's Claw *See* The Blood on Satan's Claw (1971)

Satan's Daughters *See* Vampyres (1974)

Satan's Dog *See* Play Dead (1981)

Satan's Mistress *See* Demon Rage (1982)

Satan's Satellites *See* Zombies of the Stratosphere (1952)

Satan's Skin *See* The Blood on Satan's Claw (1971)

Satellite of Blood *See* First Man into Space (1959)

Satin Vengeance *See* Naked Vengeance (1985)

Saturday Island *See* Island of Desire (1952)

Satyricon *See* Fellini Satyricon (1969)

Saul e David *See* Saul and David (1968)

The Savage *See* Lovers Like Us (1975)

Savage Apocalypse *See* Invasion of the Flesh Hunters (1982)

Savage Beasts *See* The Wild Beasts (1985)

Savage Nights *See* Les Nuits Fauves (1992)

Savage Season *See* Temporada Salvaje (1987)

The Savage State *See* L'Etat Sauvage (1978)

Sayat Nova *See* The Color of Pomegranates (1969)

Scaramouche *See* Loves & Times of Scaramouche (1976)

Scared Stiff *See* Treasure of Fear (1945)

The Scaremaker *See* Girls Night Out (1983)

Scarface: The Shame of a Nation *See* Scarface (1931)

Scarlet Buccaneer *See* Swashbuckler (1976)

The Scarlet Buccaneer *See* Swashbuckler (1984)

Scherben *See* Shattered (1921)

Schloss Vogelod *See* The Haunted Castle (1921)

The School That Ate My Brain *See* Zombie High (1987)

The Scotland Yard Mystery *See* The Living Dead (1936)

Scoundrel in White *See* High Heels (1972)

Scream *See* The Night God Screamed (198?)

Scream and Die *See* The House that Vanished (1973)

Scream Free! *See* Free Grass (1969)

Screwface *See* Marked for Death (1990)

Scrooge *See* A Christmas Carol (1951)

Scum of the Earth *See* Poor White Trash 2 (1975)

Search for the Mother Lode *See* Mother Lode (1982)

Searchers of the Voodoo Mountain *See* Warriors of the Apocalypse (1985)

Season of Dreams *See* Stacking (1987)

Second Chances *See* Probation (1932)

The Second Coming *See* Messiah of Evil (1974)

Seconds to Live *See* Viva Knievel (1977)

Secret File: Hollywood *See* Secret File of Hollywood (1962)

Secret Honor: A Political Myth *See* Secret Honor (1985)

Secret Honor: The Last Testament of Richard M. Nixon *See* Secret Honor (1985)

The Secret of Dr. Mabuse *See* The Thousand Eyes of Dr. Mabuse (1960)

The Secret of Dorian Gray *See* Dorian Gray (1970)

Secret Paper WB1 *See* Geheimakte WB1 (1942)

The Secret Stranger *See* Rough Riding Rangers (1935)

Secret Weapon *See* Sherlock Holmes and the Secret Weapon (1942)

Secrets of the Red Bedroom *See* Secret Weapons (1985)

Sedotta e Abbandonata *See* Seduced and Abandoned (1964)

The Seductress *See* The Teacher (1974)

Seed of Innocence *See* Teen Mothers (1980)

Seed of Terror *See* Grave of the Vampire (1972)

The Seekers *See* Land of Fury (1955)

Seishun Zanoku Monogatari *See* The Cruel Story of Youth (1960)

Sengoku Gunto-Den *See* Saga of the Vagabond (1959)

Sensations *See* Sensations of 1945 (1944)

Sensuous Vampires *See* The Vampire Hookers (1978)

Separate Beds *See* The Wheeler Dealers (1963)

Sept Fois Femme *See* Woman Times Seven (1967)

Sergeant Steiner *See* Breakthrough (1978)

The Serpent *See* Night Flight from Moscow (1973)

Seryozha *See* A Summer to Remember (1961)

Sette Volte Donna *See* Woman Times Seven (1967)

Seven Bad Men *See* Rage at Dawn (1955)

Seven Different Ways *See* Quick, Let's Get Married (1971)

Seven Graves for Rogan *See* Time to Die (1983)

Seven Sisters *See* The House on Sorority Row (1983)

Sex Play *See* Games Girls Play (1975)

The Sex Racketeers *See* Man of Violence (1971)

The Shadow Versus the Thousand Eyes of Dr. Mabuse *See* The Thousand Eyes of Dr. Mabuse (1960)

The Shadow Warrior *See* Kagemusha (1980)

Shadows in an Empty Room *See* Strange Shadows in an Empty Room (1976)

Shadows of Our Ancestors *See* Shadows of Forgotten Ancestors (1964)

Shadows of Our Forgotten Ancestors *See* Shadows of Forgotten Ancestors (1964)

Shadows of the Peacock *See* Echoes of Paradise (1986)

Shalimar *See* Deadly Thief (1978)

Shame of the Sabine Women *See* The Rape of the Sabines (1961)

Shark Reef *See* She Gods of Shark Reef (1956)

Shatter *See* Call Him Mr. Shatter (1974)

Shatterhand *See* Apaches Last Battle (1964)

She Devil *See* Drums O'Voodoo (1934)

She Drives Me Crazy *See* Friends, Lovers & Lunatics (1989)

She Got What She Asked For *See* Yesterday, Today and Tomorrow (1964)

She Knew No Other Way *See* Last Resort (1986)

She Monster of the Night *See* Frankenstein's Daughter (1958)

She Shoulda Said No *See* Wild Weed (1949)

Sheba *See* The Graveyard (1974)

She'll Be Sweet *See* Magee and the Lady (1978)

Shenanigans *See* Great Bank Hoax (1978)

Sheriff of Wichita *See* Western Double Feature 4: Rogers & Evans (194?)

Sherlock Holmes *See* The Adventures of Sherlock Holmes (1939)

Sherlock Holmes and the Scarlet Claw *See* Scarlet Claw (1944)

Sherlock Holmes and the Spider Woman *See* Spider Woman (1944)

Sherlock Holmes and the Woman in Green *See* The Woman in Green (1945)

Sherlock Holmes Grosster Fall *See* A Study in Terror (1966)

Sherlock Holmes Und Das Halsband des Todes *See* Sherlock Holmes and the Deadly Necklace (1962)

Shichinin No Samurai *See* Seven Samurai (1954)

Shinju Ten No Amijima *See* Double Suicide (1969)

The Ship was Loaded *See* Carry On Admiral (1957)

Shivers *See* They Came from Within (1975)

Shock *See* Beyond the Door 2 (1979)

Shocked *See* Mesmerized (1984)

Shogun Island *See* Raw Force (1981)

Shoot the Pianist *See* Shoot the Piano Player (1962)

The Shop on High Street *See* The Shop on Main Street (1965)

The Shuttered Room *See* Blood Island (1968)

Sidney Sheldon's Windmills of the Gods *See* Windmills of the Gods (1988)

Siegfried's Death *See* Siegfried (1924)

Siegfrieds Tod *See* Siegfried (1924)

Signe Charlotte *See* Sincerely Charlotte (1986)

Significant Other *See* When a Man Loves a Woman (1994)

The Silent Flute *See* Circle of Iron (1978)

Silent Night, Evil Night *See* Black Christmas (1975)

The Silent One *See* El Callao (197?)

Silken Skin *See* The Soft Skin (1964)

Silver Blaze *See* Murder at the Baskervilles (1937)

Silver Devil *See* Wild Horse (1931)

The Sin *See* The Shaming (1971)

Sinai Commandos: The Story of the Six Day War *See* Sinai Commandos (1968)

The Singing Musketeer *See* The Three Musketeers (1939)

Sinister House *See* Who Killed Doc Robbin? (1948)

Sisters *See* Some Girls (1988)

Sitting Bull's History Lesson *See* Buffalo Bill & the Indians (1976)

The Sixth of June *See* D-Day, the Sixth of June (1956)

Skatel *See* Blades of Courage (1988)

Ski Lift to Death *See* Snowblind (1978)

Skipper *See* The Todd Killings (1971)

Skyggen Af Emma *See* Emma's Shadow (1988)

The Slammer *See* Short Eyes (1979)

The Slasher *See* Cosh Boy (1961)

Slasher in the House *See* Home Sweet Home (1980)

The Slaughterers *See* Invasion of the Flesh Hunters (1982)

Slave Girls *See* Prehistoric Women (1950)

Slaves of the Invisible Monster *See* The Invisible Monster (1950)

Slay It Again, Sam *See* Codename: Foxfire (1985)

Slip Slide Adventures *See* Water Babies (1979)

Small Town Massacre *See* Strange Behavior (1981)

Smart Alec *See* Movie Maker (1986)

Smokey and the Bandit Ride Again *See* Smokey and the Bandit, Part 2 (1980)

Smorgasbord *See* Cracking Up (1983)

Smultron-Stallet *See* Wild Strawberries (1957)

Snake Eyes *See* Dangerous Game (1993)

Snow White and the Three Clowns *See* Snow White and the Three Stooges (1961)

Snuffy Smith *See* Snuffy Smith, Yard Bird (1942)

So Evil, My Sister See The Sibling (1972)

Sodome et Gomorrhe See Sodom and Gomorrah (1962)

Soldier Duroc See Soldat Duroc...Ca Va Etre Ta Fete! (196?)

Soldier in Skirts See Triple Echo (1977)

The Soldier Who Declared Peace See Tribes (1970)

The Soldiers See Les Carabiniers (1963)

Solomon Northrup's Odyssey See Half Slave, Half Free (1985)

Sombra, the Spider Woman See The Black Widow (1947)

Some Like it Cool See Sex on the Run (1978)

Someone is Killing the Great Chefs of Europe See Who is Killing the Great Chefs of Europe? (1978)

Someone's Killing the World's Greatest Models See She's Dressed to Kill (1979)

Something is Out There See Day of the Animals (1977)

Something Like the Truth See The Offence (1973)

Something to Hide See Shattered (1972)

Something Waits in the Dark See Screamers (1980)

Somewhere in France See The Foreman Went to France (1942)

Sommarlek See Summer Interlude (1950)

Sommarnattens Leende See Smiles of a Summer Night (1955)

Son of My Life See Hijazo de Mi Vidaza (197?)

Song from the Heart See Cancion en el Alma (19??)

The Song of the Road See Pather Panchali (1954)

Song of the Sierra See Springtime in the Sierras (1947)

Sons of the Legion See Sons of the Desert (1933)

Sons of the Musketeers See At Sword's Point (1951)

Sophie's Place See Crooks & Coronets (1969)

Soul See Earth (1930)

Sound From a Million Years Ago See Sound of Horror (1964)

Sound of Fury See Try and Get Me (1950)

Soup to Nuts See Waitress (1981)

Sous le Soleil de Satan See Under Satan's Sun (1987)

Sous les Toits de Paris See Under the Roofs of Paris (1929)

South of Panama See Panama Menace (1941)

South Sea Woman See Pearl of the South Pacific (1955)

Southwest to Sonora See The Appaloosa (1966)

Space 2074 See Star Quest (1989)

The Space Amoeba See Yog, Monster from Space (1971)

Space Avenger See Alien Space Avenger (1991)

Space Invasion from Lapland See Invasion of the Animal People (1962)

Space Invasion of Lapland See Invasion of the Animal People (1962)

Space Men See Assignment Outer Space (1961)

Space Men Appear in Tokyo See Warning from Space (1956)

Space Mission of the Lost Planet See Horror of the Blood Monsters (1970)

Space Monster Dagora See Dagora, the Space Monster (1965)

Space Mutants See Planet of the Vampires (1965)

Space Soldiers See Flash Gordon: Rocketship (1936)

Spaceship to the Unknown See Flash Gordon: Rocketship (1936)

Spara Forte, Piu Forte...Non Capisco See Shoot Loud, Louder, I Don't Understand! (1966)

The Specter of Freedom See Phantom of Liberty (1968)

Speed Brent Wins See Breed of the Border (1933)

The Spell of Amy Nugent See Spellbound (1941)

Spell of the Hypnotist See Fright (1956)

Spettri See Specters (1987)

The Spider See Earth vs. the Spider (1958)

Spider Baby, or the Maddest Story Ever Told See Spider Baby (1964)

Spider-Man See The Amazing Spider-Man (1977)

Spies-A-Go-Go See Nasty Rabbit (1964)

Spies, Lies, and Alibis See Code Name: Chaos (1990)

Spinal Tap See This is Spinal Tap (1984)

Spione See Spies (1928)

Spirit of Tattoo See Irezumi (1983)

Spirit of the Dead See The Asphyx (1972)

Spirit of the People See Abe Lincoln in Illinois (1940)

The Spiritualist See The Amazing Mr. X (1948)

Spivs See I Vitelloni (1953)

The Split See The Manster (1959)

The Spooky Movie Show See The Mask (1961)

Spoorloos See The Vanishing (1988)

Spot See Dog Pound Shuffle (1975)

Spymaker See Spymaker: The Secret Life of Ian Fleming (1990)

Squadron of Doom See Ace Drummond (1936)

Stacey and Her Gangbusters See Stacey (1973)

Stakeout 2 See Another Stakeout (1993)

The Stand See Stephen King's The Stand (1994)

Stand and Deliver See Bowery Blitzkrieg (1941)

Stand Easy See Goon Movie (1953)

Stanno Tutti Bene See Everybody's Fine (1990)

Star Child See Space Raiders (1983)

Stardust See Mad About Money (1930)

Starlight Slaughter See Eaten Alive (1976)

The Statutory Affair See Lola (1969)

Stella Star See Star Crash (1978)

Stephen King's Graveyard Shift See Graveyard Shift (1990)

Stephen King's Silver Bullet See Silver Bullet (1985)

Stephen King's Sleepwalkers See Sleepwalkers (1992)

Still Smokin' See Cheech and Chong: Still Smokin' (1983)

Storia de Ragazzi e di Ragazze See The Story of Boys & Girls (1991)

Stormy Crossing See Black Tide (1956)

Story of a Marriage See On Valentine's Day (1986)

The Story of an Artist's Studio Secrets See Artist's Studio Secrets (1964)

The Story of Gosta Berling See The Atonement of Gosta Berling (1924)

The Story of Joseph and His Brethren See Joseph & His Brethren (1962)

The Story of Robin Hood See The Story of Robin Hood & His Merrie Men (1952)

A Story of the Cruelties of Youth See The Cruel Story of Youth (1960)

The Story Without A Name See Without Warning (1952)

Straight Jacket See Dark Sanity (1982)

Straight on Till Morning See Dressed for Death (1974)

Strange Adventure See Wayne Murder Case (1938)

The Strange Adventure of David Gray See Vampyr (1931)

The Strange Case of Madeleine See Madeleine (1950)

Strange Deception See The Accused (1948)

Strange Incident See The Ox-Bow Incident (1943)

Strange Interval See Strange Interlude (1932)

Strange Journey See Fantastic Voyage (1966)

The Strange Ones See Les Enfants Terrible (1950)

The Strange World of Planet X See The Cosmic Monsters (1958)

The Stranger See Shame (1961)

Stranger in Our House See Summer of Fear (1978)

Stranger in the House See Black Christmas (1975)

A Stranger Walked In See Love from a Stranger (1947)

Strangler's Morgue See The Crimes of Stephen Hawke (1936)

Street Gang See Vigilante (1983)

Street Legal See The Last of the Finest (1990)

Street Love See Scarred (1984)

Street of Shadows See The Shadow Man (1953)

Streets of New York See The Abe Lincoln of Ninth Avenue (1939)

Strictly Confidential See Broadway Bill (1934)

Strictly for Pleasure See Perfect Furlough (1959)

Striking Back See Search and Destroy (1981)

Strip Poker See The Big Switch (1970)

Striptease Lady See Lady of Burlesque (1943)

Struktura Krysztalu See The Structure of Crystals (1969)

The Stu Erwin Show See The Trouble with Father (1950)

Subida Al Cielo See Mexican Bus Ride (1951)

The Submersion of Japan See Tidal Wave (1975)

Subspecies 2 See Bloodstone: Subspecies 2 (1993)

Subspecies 3 See Bloodlust: Subspecies 3 (1993)

Succubus See The Devil's Nightmare (1971)

Such Men are Dangerous See The Racers (1955)

Suicide Run See Too Late the Hero (1970)

Suicide Squadron See Dangerous Moonlight (1941)

A Suitable Case for Treatment See Morgan! (1966)

The Sullivans See The Fighting Sullivans (1942)

Summer Madness See Summertime (1955)

Summer of Innocence See Big Wednesday (1978)

Summer with Monika See Monika (1952)

Summerplay See Summer Interlude (1950)

Summertime Killer See Ricco (1974)

Sumurun See One Arabian Night (1921)

The Sun Demon See Hideous Sun Demon (1959)

Suna No Onna See Woman in the Dunes (1964)

Sunburst See Slashed Dreams (1974)

Sunless See Sans Soleil (1982)

Sunrise—A Song of Two Humans See Sunrise (1927)

Sunset of a Clown See Sawdust & Tinsel (1953)

Super Dragon See Secret Agent Super Dragon (1966)

Super Fly T.N.T. See Superfly T.N.T. (1973)

The Super Inframan See Infra-Man (1976)

Superargo the Giant See Superargo (1967)

Superfantagenio See Aladdin (1986)

Superman and the Strange People *See* Superman & the Mole Men (1951)

Supersnooper *See* Super Fuzz (1981)

Surf 2: The End of the Trilogy *See* Surf 2 (1984)

Surf Warriors *See* Surf Ninjas (1993)

Suspected Alibi *See* Suspended Alibi (1956)

Swamp Diamonds *See* Swamp Women (1955)

Sweeney Todd: The Demon Barber of Fleet Street *See* Demon Barber of Fleet Street (1936)

Sweet Candy *See* Candy Stripe Nurses (1974)

Sweet Dirty Tony *See* The Mercenaries (1980)

Sweet Kill *See* The Arousers (1970)

Sweet Revenge *See* Code of Honor (1984)

Sweet Smell of Woman *See* The Scent of a Woman (1975)

Sweet Violence *See* Sweet Ecstasy (1962)

Swept Away...By an Unusual Destiny in the Blue Sea of August *See* Swept Away... (1975)

Swing It Buddy *See* Swing It, Professor (1937)

Swing, Teacher, Swing *See* College Swing (1938)

Switchboard Operator *See* The Love Affair, or The Case of the Missing Switchboard Operator (1967)

Swords of Blood *See* Cartouche (1962)

Sylvia and the Ghost *See* Sylvia and the Phantom (1945)

Symphony of Love *See* Ecstasy (1933)

Szegenylegenyek Nehezeletuck *See* The Round Up (1966)

T & A Academy *See* H.O.T.S. (1979)

T & A Academy 2 *See* Gimme an F (1985)

Tacones Lejanos *See* High Heels (1991)

Tainted Money *See* Show Them No Mercy (1935)

A Tale of Africa *See* Green Horizon (1983)

Tale of the Cock *See* Confessions of Tom Harris (1972)

A Talent for Loving *See* Gun Crazy (1969)

Tales from the Crypt II *See* Vault of Horror (1973)

Tales of the City *See* Armistead Maupin's Tales of the City (1993)

Tangled Trails *See* Sands of Sacrifice (1921)

Tanner: A Political Fable *See* Tanner '88 (1988)

Target: Embassy *See* Embassy (1972)

Target in the Sun *See* The Man Who Would Not Die (1975)

Target of an Assassin *See* African Rage (1978)

Tartu *See* The Adventures of Tartu (1943)

Taste of Fear *See* Scream of Fear (1961)

Tears in Florence *See* Traenen in Florenz (1984)

Teen Kanya *See* Two Daughters (1961)

Teenage Monster *See* Meteor Monster (1957)

The Teenage Psycho Meets Bloody Mary *See* Incredibly Strange Creatures Who Stopped Living and Became Mixed-Up Zombies (1963)

Tell It To the Marines *See* Here Come the Marines (1952)

Tell Your Children *See* Reefer Madness (1938)

Tema *See* The Theme (1979)

Tempo di Uccidere *See* Time to Kill (1989)

Tendre Poulet *See* Dear Detective (1978)

Tenebrae *See* Unsane (1982)

Tengoku To Jigoku *See* High & Low (1962)

Tenue de Soiree *See* Menage (1986)

Terminal Station Indiscretion *See* Indiscretion of an American Wife (1954)

Terminus Station *See* Indiscretion of an American Wife (1954)

Terra em Transe *See* Earth Entranced (1966)

Terreur dans l'Espace *See* Planet of the Vampires (1965)

Terror Castle *See* The Virgin of Nuremberg (1965)

Terror Eyes *See* Night School (1981)

Terror From the Sun *See* Hideous Sun Demon (1959)

Terror Hospital *See* Hospital of Terror (1978)

Terror House *See* The Night Has Eyes (1942)

Terror House *See* Terror at Red Wolf Inn (1972)

Terror in Space *See* Planet of the Vampires (1965)

Terror in the Midnight Sun *See* Invasion of the Animal People (1962)

Terror of Sheba *See* The Graveyard (1974)

The Terror Strikes *See* The War of the Colossal Beast (1958)

Terror under the House *See* Revenge (1971)

Texas Desperadoes *See* Drift Fence (1936)

Texas in Flames *See* She Came to the Valley (1977)

Texas Road Agent *See* Road Agent (1926)

Texas Serenade *See* Old Corral (1936)

Teyve der Milkhiker *See* Tevye (1939)

That Man Mr. Jones *See* Fuller Brush Man (1948)

That Others May Live *See* Border Street (1948)

That They May Live *See* J'Accuse (1937)

That's the Way of the World *See* Shining Star (1975)

Therese Und Isabell *See* Therese & Isabelle (1968)

These Foolish Things *See* Daddy Nostalgia (1990)

They Call Me Hallelujah *See* Guns for Dollars (1973)

They Don't Wear Pajamas at Rosie's *See* The First Time (1969)

They Loved Life *See* Kanal (1956)

They Made Me a Fugitive *See* They Made Me a Criminal (1939)

They Passed This Way *See* Four Faces West (1948)

They're Coming to Get You *See* Dracula vs. Frankenstein (1971)

Thin Air *See* Invasion of the Body Stealers (1969)

The Thing From Another World *See* The Thing (1951)

Thirst *See* Three Strange Loves (1949)

The Thirteen Chairs *See* 12 Plus 1 (1970)

The Thirty-Sixth Chamber *See* Master Killer (1984)

Thomas Crown and Company *See* Thomas Crown Affair (1968)

Thoroughbred *See* Run for the Roses (1978)

Those Were the Happy Times *See* Star! (1968)

Thou Shall Not Kill *See* Avenging Conscience (1914)

Thou Shalt Honour Thy Wife *See* Master of the House (1925)

Three Bad Men in the Hidden Fortress *See* The Hidden Fortress (1958)

Three Colors: Blue *See* Trois Couleurs: Bleu (1993)

Three Colors: Red *See* Trois Couleurs: Rouge (1994)

Three Colors: White *See* Trois Couleurs: Blanc (1994)

Three Crazy Legionnaires *See* Three Legionnaires (1937)

Three For the Money *See* Win, Place, or Steal (1972)

Three Rascals in the Hidden Fortress *See* The Hidden Fortress (1958)

The Three Skeletons *See* Los Tres Calaveras (1964)

Three Steps to the Gallows *See* White Fire (1953)

The Threepenny Opera *See* Mack the Knife (1989)

Through the Looking Glass *See* The Velvet Vampire (1971)

Thunder *See* Thunder Warrior (1985)

Thunder Mountain *See* Shadow of Chikara (1977)

Thunder on the Trail *See* Thundering Trail (1951)

Thursday the 12th *See* Pandemonium (1982)

Tidal Wave *See* Portrait of Jennie (1948)

Tierra Bru Tal *See* Savage Guns (1968)

The Tiger *See* Tiger Warsaw (1987)

Tiger in the Sky *See* The McConnell Story (1955)

Tiger of Bengal *See* Journey to the Lost City (1958)

The Tiger Woman *See* Perils of the Darkest Jungle (1944)

Tigers Don't Cry *See* African Rage (1978)

Tight Little Island *See* Whiskey Galore (1948)

Til Dawn Do Us Part *See* Dressed for Death (1974)

Tim Burton's The Nightmare Before Christmas *See* The Nightmare Before Christmas (1993)

Timber Tramps *See* The Big Push (1975)

Time Flyers *See* The Blue Yonder (1986)

A Time For Caring *See* Generation (1969)

The Time of Return *See* Muriel (1963)

Time Raiders *See* Warriors of the Apocalypse (1985)

Time Trap *See* The Time Travelers (1964)

Time Warp Terror *See* Bloody New Year (1987)

Timeslip *See* The Atomic Man (1956)

Tini Zabutykh Predkiv *See* Shadows of Forgotten Ancestors (1964)

Tintorera *See* Tintorera...Tiger Shark (1978)

Tintorera...Bloody Waters *See* Tintorera...Tiger Shark (1978)

Tirez sur le Pianiste *See* Shoot the Piano Player (1962)

Titan Find *See* Creature (1985)

To Be a Man *See* Cry of Battle (1963)

To Catch a Spy *See* Catch Me a Spy (1971)

To Elvis, With Love *See* Touched by Love (1980)

To Have and to Hold *See* When a Man Loves a Woman (1994)

To Live *See* Ikiru (1952)

To Love a Vampire *See* Lust for a Vampire (1971)

Today We Live *See* The Day and the Hour (1963)

A Toi De Faire *See* Your Turn Darling (1963)

Tomb of the Cat *See* Tomb of Ligeia (1964)

Tomb of the Living Dead *See* Mad Doctor of Blood Island (1969)

The Tommyknockers *See* Stephen King's The Tommyknockers (1993)

Too Many Chefs *See* Who is Killing the Great Chefs of Europe? (1978)

Topio Stin Omichli *See* Landscape in the Mist (1988)

Torture Zone *See* The Fear Chamber (1968)

Toto the Hero *See* Toto le Heros (1991)

The Touch of Melissa *See* The Touch of Satan (1970)

Tower of Terror *See* Assault (1970)

Tower of Terror *See* Hard to Die (1990)

A Town Called Bastard *See* A Town Called Hell (1972)

The Town That Cried Terror *See* Maniac (1977)

T.R. Sloane *See* Death Ray 2000 (1981)

Trail of the Royal Mounted *See* Mystery Trooper (1932)

Train of Terror *See* Terror Train (1980)

Train 2419 *See* The Return of Casey Jones (1934)

Traitement de Choc *See* Shock Treatment (1981)

Transport Z Raje *See* Transport from Paradise (1965)

The Transvestite *See* Glen or Glenda (1953)

Tras el Cristal *See* In a Glass Cage (1986)

Trauma *See* Dario Argento's Trauma (1993)

Travels with Anita *See* Lovers and Liars (1981)

The Tree of Hands *See* Innocent Victim (1990)

Tree of Liberty *See* The Howards of Virginia (1940)

Trial by Combat *See* Choice of Weapons (1976)

Trigger, Jr. *See* Western Double Feature 6: Rogers & Trigger (1950)

A Trip with Anita *See* Lovers and Liars (1981)

Triple Trouble *See* Kentucky Kernels (1934)

Tristan and Isolde *See* Lovespell (1979)

Trois Hommes et un Couffin *See* Three Men and a Cradle (1985)

The Trollenberg Terror *See* The Crawling Eye (1958)

Tromba *See* Tromba, the Tiger Man (1952)

Trop Belle Pour Toi *See* Too Beautiful for You (1988)

Trop Jolie pour Etre Honette *See* Too Pretty to Be Honest (1972)

Tropicana *See* The Heat's On (1943)

Trottie True *See* The Gay Lady (1949)

Trouble at 16 *See* Platinum High School (1960)

Trouble Chaser *See* Li'l Abner (1940)

The Troubles of Two Roosters *See* Los Apuros de Dos Gallos (1969)

The Trout *See* La Truite (1983)

Truman Capote's A Christmas Memory *See* ABC Stage 67: Truman Capote's A Christmas Memory (1966)

Truman Capote's The Glass House *See* The Glass House (1972)

Try and Find It *See* Hi Diddle Diddle (1943)

Tsarskaya Nevesta *See* The Tsar's Bride (1966)

Tsubaki Sanjuro *See* Sanjuro (1962)

Tsvet Granata *See* The Color of Pomegranates (1969)

Tudor Rose *See* Nine Days a Queen (1934)

Tueur de Ch icago *See* Scarface Mob (1962)

Tulitkkutehtaan Tytto *See* The Match Factory Girl (1990)

The Tunnel *See* Transatlantic Tunnel (1935)

Turkey Shoot *See* Escape 2000 (1981)

Turtle Beach *See* The Killing Beach (1992)

Twelve Miles Out *See* Second Woman (1951)

Twenty-One Days Together *See* 21 Days (1937)

Twice Bitten *See* The Vampire Hookers (1978)

Twilight of the Dead *See* Gates of Hell (1983)

Twinkle, Twinkle, Killer Kane *See* The Ninth Configuration (1979)

Twinky *See* Lola (1969)

The Twisted Road *See* They Live by Night (1949)

2 Cries in the Night *See* Funeral Home (1982)

Two Minds for Murder *See* Someone Behind the Door (1971)

Two Weeks in September *See* A Coeur Joie (1967)

Tystnaden *See* The Silence (1963)

U-238 and the Witch Doctor *See* Jungle Drums of Africa (1953)

Uccellacci e Uccellini *See* The Hawks & the Sparrows (1967)

Uccidero Un Uomo *See* This Man Must Die (1970)

Uchu Daikaiju Dogora *See* Dagora, the Space Monster (1965)

Uchudai Dogora *See* Dagora, the Space Monster (1965)

Uchujin Tokyo Ni Arawaru *See* Warning from Space (1956)

Ugetsu Monogatari *See* Ugetsu (1953)

Ukigusa *See* Drifting Weeds (1959)

Ulica Graniczna *See* Border Street (1948)

Ulisse *See* Ulysses (1955)

The Ultimate Chase *See* The Ultimate Thrill (1974)

Ultimate Desires *See* Beyond the Silhouette (1990)

The Ultimate Solution of Grace Quigley *See* Grace Quigley (1984)

Ultimi Giorni di Pompeii *See* The Last Days of Pompeii (1960)

The Umbrella Woman *See* The Good Wife (1986)

Un Amour De Swann *See* Swann in Love (1984)

Un Amour En Allemagne *See* A Love in Germany (1984)

Un Angelo e Sceso a Brooklyn *See* The Man Who Wagged His Tail (1957)

Un Arma de Dos Filos *See* Shark! (1968)

Un Autre Homme, Une Autre Chance *See* Another Man, Another Chance (1977)

Un Chapeau de Paille d'Italie *See* Italian Straw Hat (1927)

Un Complicato Intrigo Di Donne, Vicoli E Delitti *See* Camorra: The Naples Connection (1985)

Un Condamne a Mort s'est Echappe *See* A Man Escaped (1957)

Un, Deux, Trois, Quatrel *See* Black Tights (1960)

Un Dimanche a la Campagne *See* A Sunday in the Country (1984)

Un Elephant a Trompe Enormement *See* Pardon Mon Affaire (1976)

Un Grand Amour de Beethoven *See* Beethoven (1936)

Un Homme Amoureux *See* A Man in Love (1987)

Un Homme Est Mort *See* The Outside Man (1973)

Un Homme et Un Femme *See* A Man and a Woman (1966)

Un Homme Et Une Femme: Vingt Ans Deja *See* A Man and a Woman: 20 Years Later (1986)

Un Minuto Per Pregare, Un Istante Per Morire *See* A Minute to Pray, A Second to Die (1967)

Un Senor Muy Viejo Con Unas Alas Enormes *See* A Very Old Man with Enormous Wings (1988)

Un Trem Para as Estrelas *See* Subway to the Stars (1987)

Un Uomo da Rispettare *See* Master Touch (1974)

Un Zoo, La Nuit *See* Night Zoo (1987)

Una Bruja Sin Escoba *See* A Witch Without a Broom (1968)

Una Giornata Speciale *See* A Special Day (1977)

Una Hacka Para la Luna de Miel *See* Hatchet for the Honeymoon (1970)

Una Ragione Per Vivere e Una Per Morire *See* A Reason to Live, A Reason to Die (1973)

Unakrsna Vatra *See* Operation Cross Eagles (1969)

Uncle Harry *See* The Strange Affair of Uncle Harry (1945)

Uncle Silas *See* Inheritance (1947)

Unconventional Linda *See* Holiday (1938)

Under California Skies *See* Under California Stars (1948)

Under the Clock *See* The Clock (1945)

Under the Sun of Satan *See* Under Satan's Sun (1987)

Underground *See* The Lower Depths (1936)

An Underwater Odyssey *See* Neptune Factor (1973)

Underworld *See* Transmutations (1985)

Underworld After Dark *See* Big Town After Dark (1947)

Une Femme Est Une Femme *See* A Woman is a Woman (1960)

Une Femme ou Deux *See* One Woman or Two (1985)

Une Histoire Simple *See* A Simple Story (1979)

Une Partie de Campagne *See* A Day in the Country (1946)

Ungus of Terror *See* Attack of the Mushroom People (1963)

Unknown Satellite Over Tokyo *See* Warning from Space (1956)

Untel Pere et Fils *See* Heart of a Nation (1943)

The Unvanquished *See* Aparajito (1958)

Uomo Dalla Pelle Dura *See* Counter Punch (1971)

Up in the Cellar *See* Three in the Cellar (1970)

Up the Chastity Belt *See* Naughty Knights (1971)

The Upstate Murders *See* Savage Weekend (1980)

Urga *See* Close to Eden (1990)

Ursus *See* Ursus in the Valley of the Lions (1962)

The Usual Unidentified Thieves *See* Big Deal on Madonna Street (1958)

Utamaro O Meguru Gonin No Onna *See* Utamaro and His Five Women (1946)

Utvandrarna *See* The Emigrants (1972)

Vacation *See* National Lampoon's Vacation (1983)

Vagabond Violinist *See* Broken Melody (1934)

Valborgmassoafton *See* Walpurgis Night (1941)

The Valdez Horses *See* Chino (1975)

Valdez the Half Breed *See* Chino (1975)

Valley of Fear *See* Sherlock Holmes and the Deadly Necklace (1962)

Valley of the Swords *See* The Castilian (1963)

The Vampire *See* Vampyr (1931)

The Vampire and the Robot *See* My Son, the Vampire (1952)

The Vampire-Beast Craves Blood *See* Blood Beast Terror (1967)

Vampire Men of the Lost Planet *See* Horror of the Blood Monsters (1970)

Vampire Over London *See* My Son, the Vampire (1952)

Vampire's Night Orgy *See* Orgy of the Vampires (1973)

Vampyr, Der Traum Des David Gray *See* Vampyr (1931)

Vampyr, Ou L'Etrang e Aventure De David Gray *See* Vampyr (1931)

Vampyres, Daughters of Dracula *See* Vampyres (1974)

Vasectomy *See* Vasectomy: A Delicate Matter (1986)

The Veil *See* Haunts (1977)

Velvet House *See* Crucible of Horror (1969)

Vendetta: Secrets of a Mafia Bride *See* A Family Matter (1991)

Vengeance *See* The Brain (1962)

Vengeance: The Story of Tony Cimo *See* Vengeance (1989)

Venus in Peltz *See* Venus in Furs (1970)

The Venusian *See* The Stranger from Venus (1954)

Vessel of Wrath *See* Beachcomber (1938)

The Veteran *See* Deathdream (1972)

The Vicious Circle *See* Woman in Brown (1948)

Victims of the Beyond *See* Sucker Money (1934)

Vindicator See Wheels of Fire (1984)

Violence et Passion See Conversation Piece (1975)

Violent Journey See The Fool Killer (1965)

Violent Midnight See Psychomania (1963)

Violent Rage See Fearmaker (1989)

Violent Streets See Thief (1981)

The Violet See La Violetera (1971)

Violette Noziere See Violette (1978)

Virgin Hunters See Test Tube Teens from the Year 2000 (1993)

The Virtuous Tramps See The Devil's Brother (1933)

Virus See Invasion of the Flesh Hunters (1982)

Viskingar Och Rop See Cries and Whispers (1972)

Vita Privata See A Very Private Affair (1962)

Vitelloni See I Vitelloni (1953)

Vivement Dimanche! See Confidentially Yours (1983)

Viviamo Oggi See The Day and the Hour (1963)

Vivre Savie See My Life to Live (1962)

The Vixen See The Women (1969)

Vogues See Vogues of 1938 (1937)

Voodoo Blood Bath See I Eat Your Skin (1964)

Vortex See Day Time Ended (1980)

Voyage Beyond the Sun See Space Monster (1964)

Voyage to a Prehistoric Planet See Voyage to the Prehistoric Planet (1965)

Vredens Dag See Day of Wrath (1943)

Vzlomschik See Burglar (1987)

Wages of Fear See Sorcerer (1977)

Waiting Women See Secrets of Women (1952)

The Waltons: The Children's Carol See Children's Carol (1980)

The Wandering Kid See Urotsukidoji 1: Legend of the Overfiend (1993)

Wannseekonferenz See The Wannsee Conference (1984)

Want a Ride, Little Girl? See Impulse (1974)

Wanted Women See Jessie's Girls (1975)

The Wanton Contessa See Senso (1954)

War Between the Planets See Planet on the Prowl (1965)

War Games See Suppose They Gave a War and Nobody Came? (1970)

The War of the Monsters See Gamera vs. Barugon (1966)

War of the Planets See Cosmos: War of the Planets (1980)

War Shock See Battle Shock (1956)

Ward 13 See Hospital Massacre (1981)

Warlock See Skullduggery (1979)

The Warm-Blooded Spy See Ravishing Idiot (1964)

Warrior's Rest See Le Repos du Guerrier (1962)

Warum Lauft Herr R Amok? See Why Does Herr R. Run Amok? (1969)

Washington, B.C. See Hail (1973)

Water Cyborgs See Terror Beneath the Sea (1966)

The Watts Monster See Dr. Black, Mr. Hyde (1976)

The Way Ahead See Immortal Battalion (1944)

The Way of Life See They Call It Sin (1932)

Ways of Love See The Miracle (1948)

We See Nosotros (1944)

We Will All Meet in Paradise See Pardon Mon Affaire, Too! (1977)

Wedding Bells See Royal Wedding (1951)

Wedding Breakfast See The Catered Affair (1956)

Wednesday's Child See Family Life (1971)

Weekend Babysitter See Weekend with the Babysitter (1970)

Welcome Home Brother Charles See Soul Vengeance (1975)

The Well-Made Marriage See Le Beau Mariage (1982)

Wendy Cracked a Walnut See ...Almost (1990)

We're In the Army Now See Pack Up Your Troubles (1932)

The Werewolf and the Yeti See Night of the Howling Beast (1975)

What? See Diary of Forbidden Dreams (1973)

What a Man See Never Give a Sucker an Even Break (1941)

What Changed Charley Farthing See Bananas Boat (1978)

What Lola Wants See Damn Yankees (1958)

The Wheelchair See El Cochecito (1960)

Wheels of Terror See The Misfit Brigade (1987)

When Knighthood Was in Flower See The Sword & the Rose (1953)

When Michael Calls See Shattered Silence (1971)

When the Girls Meet the Boys See Girl Crazy (1943)

When Youth Conspires See Old Swimmin' Hole (1940)

Where the Hell's the Gold? See Dynamite and Gold (1988)

Where the River Bends See Bend of the River (1952)

While Plucking the Daisy See Mademoiselle Striptease (1957)

White See Trois Couleurs: Blanc (1994)

White Paws See Pattes Blanches (1949)

White Trash on Moonshine Mountain See Moonshine Mountain (1964)

A White White Boy See The Mirror (1975)

Who? See Roboman (1975)

Who Dares Wins See The Final Option (1982)

Who Fears the Devil See The Legend of Hillbilly John (1973)

Who is Killing the Stuntman See Stunts (1977)

Who Murdered Joy Morgan? See Killjoy (1981)

Who Shot Patakango? See Who Shot Pat? (1992)

Whoever Slew Auntie Roo? See Who Slew Auntie Roo? (1971)

Why Not? See Eijanaika (1981)

The Widow and the Gigolo See Roman Spring of Mrs. Stone (1961)

Wild Beds See Tigers in Lipstick (1980)

Wild Drifters See Cockfighter (1974)

Wild Flower See Fiorile (1993)

Wild Flower See Flor Silvestre (1958)

Wild For Kicks See Beat Girl (1960)

Wild Geese See Mistress (1953)

Wild Horses of Fire See Shadows of Forgotten Ancestors (1964)

The Wild Pack See Defiant (1970)

The Wild Side See Suburbia (1983)

Wild Youth See Naked Youth (1959)

Wildcat See Great Scout & Cathouse Thursday (1976)

Wilderness Family, Part 2 See Further Adventures of the Wilderness Family, Part 2 (1977)

Willy Milly See Something Special (1986)

Wilt See The Misadventures of Mr. Wilt (1990)

The Wind Bloweth Where it Listeth See A Man Escaped (1957)

A Window in London See Lady in Distress (1939)

A Window to the Sky See The Other Side of the Mountain (1975)

Wings of the Apache See Fire Birds (1990)

Winter Rates See Out of Season (1975)

The Wistful Widow See The Wistful Widow of Wagon Gap (1947)

The Witch See Superstition (1982)

Witch Doctor See Men of Two Worlds (1946)

Witchfinder General See The Conqueror Worm (1968)

Witchkill See The Witchmaker (1969)

Witch's Curse See Maciste in Hell (1960)

The Witch's Horsemen See Los Jinetes de la Bruja (1976)

With Words and Music See The Girl Said No (1937)

Wit's End See G.I. Executioner (1971)

The Wizard of Mars See Horrors of the Red Planet (1964)

Wo Die Grunen Ameisen Traumen See Where the Green Ants Dream (1984)

Wolf Larsen See The Legend of the Sea Wolf (1958)

Woman Alone See Sabotage (1936)

A Woman Destroyed See Smash-Up: The Story of a Woman (1947)

The Woman in His House See The Animal Kingdom (1932)

Woman of Antwerp See Dedee d'Anvers (1949)

Woman of Dolwyn See The Last Days of Dolwyn (1949)

Woman of Osaka See Osaka Elegy (1936)

Woman of Summer See The Stripper (1963)

Woman of the Dunes See Woman in the Dunes (1964)

A Woman's Devotion See Battle Shock (1956)

A Woman's Revenge See La Vengeance d'une Femme (1989)

Women in Cages See The Big Doll House (1971)

Women in Prison See Ladies They Talk About (1933)

Women of Nazi Germany See Hitler (1962)

Women's Penitentiary 4 See Caged Women (1984)

Women's Penitentiary I See The Big Doll House (1971)

Women's Penitentiary II See The Big Bird Cage (1972)

Wonder Women See The Deadly and the Beautiful (1973)

The Word See Ordet (1955)

The World and His Wife See State of the Union (1948)

The World of Yor See Yor, the Hunter from the Future (1983)

The Worlds of Gulliver See The Three Worlds of Gulliver (1959)

Worthy Deceivers See Big Bluff (1955)

The Wounded Man See L'Homme Blesse (1983)

Wrong Bet See Lionheart (1990)

The Wrong Kind of Girl See Bus Stop (1956)

X See X: The Man with X-Ray Eyes (1963)

X-Ray See Hospital Massacre (1981)

Xiyan See The Wedding Banquet (1993)

Xochimilco See Maria Candelaria (1946)

The XYZ Murders See Crimewave (1985)

Yangtse Incidents See Battle Hell (1956)

A Yank In London See I Live in Grosvenor Square (1946)

A Yankee in King Arthur's Court See A Connecticut Yankee in King Arthur's Court (1949)

Yanzhi Kou *See* Rouge (1987)

The Year of the Jellyfish *See* L'Annee des Meduses (1986)

Yellow Hair and the Pecos Kid *See* Yellow Hair & the Fortress of Gold (1984)

Yiddle with a Fiddle *See* Yidl Mitn Fidl (1936)

Yingxiong Bense *See* A Better Tomorrow (1986)

Yokihi *See* Princess Yang Kwei Fei (1955)

Yosei Gorasu *See* Gorath (1964)

You Better Watch Out *See* Terror in Toyland (1985)

You Can't Steal Love *See* Murph the Surf (1975)

You Don't Need Pajamas at Rosie's *See* The First Time (1969)

The Young and the Damned *See* Los Olvidados (1950)

The Young and the Immortal *See* The Sinister Urge (1960)

The Young and the Passionate *See* I Vitelloni (1953)

Young Commandos *See* Delta Force 3: The Killing Game (1991)

The Young Cycle Girls *See* Cycle Vixens (1979)

Young Dracula *See* Andy Warhol's Dracula (1974)

Young Dracula *See* Son of Dracula (1943)

Young Hearts *See* Promised Land (1988)

Young Hellions *See* High School Confidential (1958)

Young Invaders *See* Darby's Rangers (1958)

The Young Ladies of Wilko *See* Maids of Wilko (1979)

Young Scarface *See* Brighton Rock (1947)

The Youngest Spy *See* My Name is Ivan (1962)

Your Past Is Showing *See* The Naked Truth (1958)

Your Red Wagon *See* They Live by Night (1949)

Your Witness *See* Eye Witness (1949)

Youth Takes a Hand *See* Behind Prison Walls (1943)

Yukinojo Henge *See* An Actor's Revenge (1963)

Zabudnite na Mozarta *See* Forget Mozart (1985)

Zamri Oumi Voskresni *See* Freeze-Die-Come to Life (1990)

Zato Ichi To Yojimbo *See* Zatoichi vs. Yojimbo (1970)

Zatoichi Meets Yojimbo *See* Zatoichi vs. Yojimbo (1970)

Zayn Vaybs Lubovnik *See* His Wife's Lover (1931)

Zazie in the Subway *See* Zazie dans le Metro (1961)

Zazie in the Underground *See* Zazie dans le Metro (1961)

Zee & Co. *See* X, Y & Zee (1972)

Zeisters *See* Fat Guy Goes Nutzoid (1986)

Zemlya *See* Earth (1930)

Zerkalo *See* The Mirror (1975)

Zero de Conduit *See* Zero for Conduct (1933)

Zeta One *See* Alien Women (1969)

Ziemia Obiecana *See* Land of Promise (1974)

Zombie *See* I Eat Your Skin (1964)

Zombie Creeping Flesh *See* Night of the Zombies (1983)

Zombie Flesh Eaters *See* Zombie (1980)

Zombies *See* I Eat Your Skin (1964)

Zormba *See* Zorba the Greek (1964)

Z.P.G. *See* Zero Population Growth (1972)

Zuckerbaby *See* Sugarbaby (1985)

VIDEOHOUND'S GOLDEN MOVIE RETRIEVER

A Nous la Liberte Two tramps encounter industrialization and automation, making one into a wealthy leader, the other into a nature-loving iconoclast. A poignant, fantastical masterpiece by Clair, made before he migrated to Hollywood. Though the view of automation may be dated, it influenced such films as Chaplin's "Modern Times." In French with English subtitles.
1931 87m/B *FR* Henri Marchand, Raymond Cordy, Rolla France, Paul Olivier, Jacques Shelly, Andre Michaud; *D:* Rene Clair; *W:* Rene Clair. Academy Awards '32 Nominations: Best Interior Decoration; National Board of Review Awards '32: 5 Best Foreign Films of the Year. **VHS, Beta, 8mm** $49.95 *ING, NOS, MRV* ✂✂✂✂

Aaron Loves Angela Puerto Rican girl falls in love with a black teen amidst the harsh realities of the Harlem ghetto. "Romeo and Juliet" meets "West Side Story" in a cliched comedy drama.
1975 (R) 99m/C Kevin Hooks, Irene Cara, Moses Gunn, Robert Hooks, Jose Feliciano; *D:* Gordon Parks Jr.; *M:* Jose Feliciano. **VHS, Beta** $59.95 *COL* ✂✂

Abbott and Costello Go to Mars Poor parody of sci-fi films finds the frantic duo aboard a rocket ship and accidentally heading off into outer space. They don't land on Mars, but Venus, which is populated by lots of pretty women and no men. Even this duo looks good to the ladies. Cheapie production and uninspired buffoonery.
1953 77m/B Bud Abbott, Lou Costello, Mari Blanchard, Robert Paige, Martha Hyer, Horace McMahon, Jack Kruschen, Anita Ekberg; *D:* Charles Lamont; *W:* John Grant, D.D. Beauchamp. **VHS** $14.98 *MCA* ✂½

Abbott and Costello in Hollywood Bud and Lou appear as a barber and porter of a high class tonsorial parlor in Hollywood. A rather sarcastic look at backstage Hollywood, Abbott & Costello style. Ball makes a guest appearance. *AKA:* Bud Abbott and Lou Costello In Hollywood.
1945 111m/B Bud Abbott, Lou Costello, Frances Rafferty, Warner Anderson, Lucille Ball; *D:* Sylvan Simon. **VHS, Beta** $19.98 *MGM, CCB* ✂✂

Abbott and Costello in the Foreign Legion Fight promoters Jonesy and Max trail their runaway fighter to Algiers where they're tricked into joining the French Foreign Legion. They have to cope with a sadistic sargeant, a sexy spy, and still find their man. Most amusement comes from Lou's wild desert mirages.
1950 80m/B Bud Abbott, Lou Costello, Walter Slezak, Patricia Medina, Douglass Dumbrille, Leon Belasco, Marc Lawrence, Tor Johnson; *D:* Charles Lamont; *W:* John Grant, Martin Ragaway, Leonard Stern. **VHS** $14.95 *MCA* ✂✂½

Abbott and Costello Meet Captain Kidd With pirates led by Captain Kidd on their trail, Abbott and Costello follow a treasure map. Bland A&C swashbuckler spoof with a disinterested Laughton impersonating the Kidd. One of the duo's few color films.
1952 70m/C Bud Abbott, Lou Costello, Charles Laughton, Hillary Brooke, Fran Warren, Bill Shirley, Leif Erickson; *D:* Charles Lamont. **VHS, Beta** $29.95 *NOS, VCI* ✂✂

Abbott and Costello Meet Dr. Jekyll and Mr. Hyde Abbott and Costello take on evil Dr. Jekyll, who has transformed himself into Mr. Hyde, and is terrorizing London. A lame attempt at recapturing the success of "Abbott and Costello Meet Frankenstein."
1952 77m/B Bud Abbott, Lou Costello, Boris Karloff, Craig Stevens, Helen Westcott, Reginald Denny; *D:* Charles Lamont. **VHS, Beta** $14.95 *MCA* ✂✂

Abbott and Costello Meet Frankenstein Big-budget A&C classic is one of their best efforts and was rewarded handsomely at the box office. Two unsuspecting baggage clerks deliver a crate containing the last but not quite dead remains of Dracula and Dr. Frankenstein's monster to a wax museum. The fiends are revived, wreaking havoc with the clerks. Chaney makes a special appearance to warn the boys that trouble looms. Last film to use the Universal creature pioneered by Karloff in 1931. *AKA:* Abbott and Costello Meet the Ghosts.
1948 83m/B Bud Abbott, Lou Costello, Lon Chaney Jr., Bela Lugosi, Glenn Strange, Lenore Aubert, Jane Randolph; *D:* Charles T. Barton; *V:* Vincent Price. **VHS, Beta** $14.95 *MCA* ✂✂✂

Abbott & Costello Meet the Invisible Man Abbott and Costello play newly-graduated detectives who take on the murder case of a boxer (Franz) accused of killing his manager. Using a serum that makes people invisible, the boxer helps Costello in a prizefight that will frame the real killers, who killed the manager because the boxer refused to throw a fight. Great special effects and hilarious gags make this one of the best from the crazy duo.
1951 82m/B Bud Abbott, Lou Costello, Nancy Guild, Adele Jergens, Sheldon Leonard, William Frawley, Gavin Muir, Arthur Franz; *D:* Charles Lamont. **VHS** $14.95 *MCA* ✂✂✂

Abbott and Costello Meet the Keystone Kops It's 1912 and the boys are bilked into buying a fake movie studio by a clever con man. When they find out they've been tricked, the duo head to Hollywood to track him down and find out the crook is trying to cheat Sennett's film company. Sennett himself trained A&C and the new Keystone Kops in their recreations of his silent screen routines. Good final chase sequence but the earlier work is tired.
1954 79m/B Bud Abbott, Lou Costello, Fred Clark, Lynn Bari, Mack Sennett, Maxie "Slapsie" Rosenbloom, Frank Wilcox, Harold Goodwin; *D:* Charles Lamont; *W:* John Grant; *M:* Henry Mancini. **VHS** $14.98 *MCA* ✂✂½

Abbott and Costello Meet the Killer, Boris Karloff Unremarkable Abbott and Costello murder mystery. Karloff plays a psychic who tries to frame Lou for murder. Pleasant enough but not one of their best.
1949 84m/B Bud Abbott, Lou Costello, Boris Karloff, Lenore Aubert, Gar Moore, Donna Martell, Alan Mowbray, James Flavin, Roland Winters; *D:* Charles T. Barton. **VHS, Beta** $9.95 *MCA* ✂✂

Abbott & Costello Meet the Mummy Okay comedy from the duo has them stranded in Egypt with a valuable medallion which will lead to secret treasure and the mummy who guards the tomb. The last of the films the twosome made for Universal.
1955 90m/B Bud Abbott, Lou Costello, Marie Windsor, Michael Ansara, Dan Seymour, Kurt Katch, Richard Deacon, Mel Welles, Edwin Parker; *D:* Charles Lamont; *W:* John Grant. **VHS** $14.98 *MCA, FCT* ✂✂½

Abbott and Costello Scrapbook Rare glimpses of the comedy duo from screen tests, previews, and flubs.

197? 60m/B Bud Abbott, Lou Costello. **VHS, Beta $29.95** DVT 𝄂𝄂½

ABC Stage 67: Truman Capote's A Christmas Memory
A television drama special narrated by Capote about his remembered childhood experience of baking dozens of fruitcakes for friends at Christmas with his elderly distant cousin, Miss Sook Faulk (Page). She is quiet, lovely and true in this sensitive portrait of why we give and what we have to be thankful for. Adapted from a Capote short story by Capote and Eleanor Perry. *AKA:* Truman Capote's A Christmas Memory; A Christmas Memory. **1966 51m/B** Geraldine Page, Donnie Melvin; *D:* Frank Perry. **VHS, Beta, 8mm $24.99** MOV, VYY 𝄂𝄂½

ABC's of Love & Sex, Australia Style
An Australian-made sex-education parody.
1986 87m/C *AU* Brigittia Almsrom, Rettima Borer, Ian Broadbent. **VHS, Beta $19.95** ACA 𝄂

Abducted
A woman jogger is abducted by a crazed mountain man in the Canadian Rockies. Weird and unbelievably tedious film is nevertheless highlighted by some spectacular wilderness footage of the Vancouver area, a travelogue bonus for those in the mood.
1986 (PG) 87m/C *CA* Dan Haggerty, Roberta Weiss, Lawrence King Phillips; *D:* Boon Collins. **VHS, Beta $79.95** PSM 𝄂½

Abduction
Exploitative account of the Patty Hearst kidnapping, loosely adapted from the Harrison James novel written before the kidnapping. A young woman from a wealthy capitalist family is kidnapped by black radicals and held for an unusual ransom. Oh, and she tangles with lesbians, too.
1975 (R) 100m/C Judith-Marie Bergan, David Pendleton, Gregory Rozakis, Leif Erickson, Dorothy Malone, Lawrence Tierney; *D:* Joseph Zito. **VHS, Beta $59.95** MED 𝄂½

The Abduction of Allison Tate
Rich developer takes land belonging to a group of Native Americans. Three young tribe members retaliate by kidnapping the developer's daughter. But when their plans go awry and one of the trio is killed, Allison finds herself sympathizing more with them than with her father's ambitions.
1992 (R) 95m/C Leslie Hope, Bernie White; *D:* Paul Leder. **VHS $79.95** MNC 𝄂½

The Abduction of Kari Swenson
An account of the true-life (it really happened) kidnapping of Olympic biathalon hopeful Swensen by a pair of mischievous Montana mountain men with matrimony in mind. The movie details the abduction of Swenson by the scruffy father and son duo and the massive manhunt. As the put-upon Kari, Pollan exceeds script expectations in this made-for-television exercise in stress avoidance.
1987 100m/C Joe Don Baker, M. Emmet Walsh, Ronny Cox, Michael Bowen, Geoffrey Blake, Dorothy Fielding, Tracy Pollan; *D:* Stephen Gyllenhaal. **VHS $79.95** VMK 𝄂½

Abduction of St. Anne
An almost interesting made-for-television mystical thriller about a detective and a bishop trying to track down a gangster's daughter, who may have nifty supernatural healing powers the Church would be very interested in having documented.
1975 78m/C Robert Wagner, E.G. Marshall, William Windom, Lloyd Nolan; *D:* Harry Falk; *M:* George Duning. **VHS, Beta $49.95** WOV, GKK 𝄂

The Abductors
Caffaro's super-agent takes on international white slavery, a worthy target for any exploitation effort. While the novelty is a tough and intelligent on-screen heroine, sufficient sleaze and violence bring it all down to the proper level of swampland video. Sequel to the never-to-be-forgotten "Ginger."
1972 (R) 90m/C Cheri Caffaro, William Grannell, Richard Smedley, Patrick Wright, Jennifer Brooks; *D:* Don Schain. **VHS, Beta $39.95** MON 𝄂

Abdulla the Great
A dissolute Middle Eastern monarch falls for a model, who spurns him for an army officer. While distracted by these royal shenanigans, the king is blissfully unaware of his subjects' disaffection—until they revolt. Dares to lampoon Egypt's dead King Farouk, going against conventional Hollywood wisdom ("Farouk in film is box office poison"). *AKA:* Abdullah's Harem.
1956 89m/C *GB* Gregory Ratoff, Kay Kendall, Sydney Chaplin; *D:* Gregory Ratoff. **VHS, Beta $24.95** VYY 𝄂𝄂

Abe Lincoln in Illinois
Massey considered this not only his finest film but a part he was "born to play." Correct on both counts, this Hollywood biography follows Lincoln from his log cabin days to his departure for the White House. The Lincoln-Douglass debate scene and Massey's post-presidential election farewell to the citizens of Illinois are nothing short of brilliant. Written by Sherwood from his Pulitzer-Prize winning play. Contrasted with the well-known "Young Mr. Lincoln" (Henry Fonda), its relative anonymity is perplexing. *AKA:* Spirit of the People.
1940 110m/B Raymond Massey, Gene Lockhart, Ruth Gordon, Mary Howard, Dorothy Tree, Harvey Stephens, Minor Watson, Alan Baxter, Howard da Silva, Maurice Murphy, Clem Bevans, Herbert Rudley; *D:* John Cromwell; *W:* Robert Sherwood. **VHS, Beta $19.95** MED, RKO, TTC 𝄂𝄂𝄂𝄂

The Abe Lincoln of Ninth Avenue
All-American tale of a poor young man making good in New York. His role model is Abraham Lincoln. Cooper is exceptional, supported by effective performances by the rest of the cast. *AKA:* Streets of New York.
1939 68m/B Jackie Cooper, Martin Spelling, Marjorie Reynolds, Dick Purcell, George Cleveland, George Irving; *D:* William Nigh. **VHS, Beta, 8mm $24.95** VYY 𝄂𝄂½

Abigail's Party
Steadman plays the hostess for a very ill-fated dinner party, especially when she realizes her husband has just died on her new carpet.
1977 105m/C *GB* Alison Steadman; *D:* Mike Leigh. **VHS $79.95** WBF, BTV 𝄂𝄂

Abilene Town
In a post-Civil War Kansas town far from the freeway, Scott is the tough marshall trying to calm the conflict between cattlemen and homesteaders. He also finds time to participate in a romantic triangle with dance hall vixen Dvorak and heart-of-gold Fleming. Snappy pace keeps it interesting. Based on a novel by Ernest Haycox.
1946 90m/B Randolph Scott, Ann Dvorak, Edgar Buchanan, Rhonda Fleming, Lloyd Bridges; *D:* Edwin L. Marin. **VHS, Beta $9.95** CNG, MRV, NOS 𝄂𝄂𝄂

The Abominable Dr. Phibes
After being disfigured in a freak car accident that killed his wife, an evil genius decides that the members of a surgical team let his wife die and shall each perish by a different biblical plague. High camp with the veteran cast in top form.
1971 (PG) 90m/C *GB* Vincent Price, Joseph Cotten, Hugh Griffith, Terry-Thomas, Virginia North, Susan Travers, Alex Scott, Caroline Munro; *D:* Robert Fuest. **VHS, Beta $14.98** VES, LIV, ORI 𝄂𝄂𝄂

The Abomination
After a 5,000-year-old creature possesses him during a nightmare, a boy goes on an eye-gouging frenzy. Only the audience gets hurt.
1988 (R) 100m/C Van Connery, Victoria Chaney, Gaye Bottoms, Suzy Meyer, Jude Johnson, Blue Thompson, Scott Davis; *D:* Max Raven. **VHS, Beta** DMP 𝄂

About Last Night...
Semi-realistic comedy-drama which explores the ups and downs of one couple's relationship. Mostly quality performances, especially Perkins and Belushi as friends of the young lovers. Based on David Mamet's play "Sexual Perversity in Chicago," but considerably softened so that more people would buy tickets at the box office, the film acts as a historical view of contemporary mating rituals before the onset of the AIDS crisis.
1986 (R) 113m/C Rob Lowe, Demi Moore, Elizabeth Perkins, James Belushi, George DiCenzo, Robin Thomas, Michael Alldredge; *D:* Edward Zwick; *W:* Tim Kazurinsky, Denise DeClue; *M:* Miles Goodman. **VHS, Beta $14.95** COL 𝄂𝄂𝄂

Above and Beyond
Good performance by Taylor as Col. Paul Tibbets, the man who piloted the Enola Gay, which dropped the atomic bomb on Hiroshima. Focuses on the secrecy of the mission and the strain this puts on Tibbets marriage. Exciting action sequences of the mission itself.
1953 122m/B Robert Taylor, Eleanor Parker, James Whitmore, Larry Keating, Larry Gates, Robert Burton, Jim Backus; *D:* Melvin Frank, Norman Panama; *W:* Norman Panama, Beirne Lay Jr., Frank Panama. **VHS $19.98** MGM 𝄂𝄂𝄂

Above Suspicion
MacMurray and Crawford are American honeymooners (poor Fred!) asked to assist an international intelligence organization. They engage the Nazis in a tense battle of wits. Well-made and engaging.
1943 91m/B Joan Crawford, Fred MacMurray, Conrad Veidt, Basil Rathbone, Reginald Owen; *D:* Richard Thorpe. **VHS $19.98** MGM 𝄂𝄂𝄂

Above the Law
In his debut, Seagal does his wooden best to portray a tough Chicago police detective planning an enormous drug bust of one of the biggest felons in the state. Unfortunately, the FBI has ordered him to back off and find another bust. The reasons are almost as complex as Seagal's character, and like most details of the flick, stupid. However, people don't watch these movies for the acting or the plot, but for the fight scenes, which are well-choreographed and violent. Watch it with someone you love.
1988 (R) 99m/C Steven Seagal, Pam Grier, Henry Silva, Sharon Stone, Ron Dean, Daniel Faraldo; *D:* Andrew Davis; *W:* Steven Pressfield. **VHS, Beta, 8mm $19.95** WAR, TLF 𝄂𝄂

Above the Rim
Vulgar, violent hoopster drama about a fiercely competitive inner-city playground game. Kyle-Lee Watson (Martin), a self-involved high school star raised by a saintly single mom (Pinkins), is torn between the lure of the streets and his college recruiting chances. His odds aren't made any easier by homeboy hustler Birdie (Shakur), who wants to improve his chances of making money on the local games by making sure Watson plays for his team. Energetic b-ball

sequences, strong performances lose impact amid formulaic melodrama and the usual obscenities. Debut for director Pollack.
1994 (R) 96m/C Duane Martin, Tupac Shakur, Leon, Marlon Wayans, Tonya Pinkins, Bernie Mac; *D:* Jeff Pollack; *W:* Jeff Pollack, Barry Michael Cooper; *M:* Marcus Miller. **VHS** NYR ✗✗½

Above Us the Waves During WWII, the British navy immobilizes a huge German battleship off the coast of Norway. Effectively dramatizes the British naval preparations for what seemed a suicidal mission: using midget submarines to plant underwater explosives on the hull of the German vessel and detonating them before the Germans could detect the danger.
1956 92m/C *GB* John Mills, John Gregson, Donald Sinden, James Robertson Justice, Michael Medwin, James Kenney, O.E. Hasse, William Russell, Thomas Heathcote, Lee Patterson, Theodore Bikel, Lyndon Brook, Anthony Newley; *D:* Ralph Thomas. **VHS** REP ✗✗✗

Abraham Lincoln Griffith's first talking movie takes Abraham Lincoln from his birth through his assassination. This restored version includes the original slavery sequences which were believed to be lost, but obviously were not. Musical score included.
1930 97m/B Walter Huston, Una Merkel, Kay Hammond, E. Allen Warren, Hobart Bosworth, Fred Warren, Henry B. Walthall, Russell Simpson; *D:* D.W. Griffith. **VHS, Beta $19.95** NOS, MRV, CCB ✗✗½

Abraxas: Guardian of the Universe Good space cop versus bad space cop with an ecological twist. Good-guy Abraxas (Ventura) has the task of stopping planets from destroying their environments and fighting senseless wars. His ex-partner Secundas (Ole-Thorsen) has his own mission, seeking an anti-life power which could destroy the universe. They decide to fight it out, using Earth as the battleground. Also available in an edited PG-13 version.
1990 (R) 90m/C Jesse Ventura, Sven Ole-Thorsen; *Cameos:* James Belushi. **VHS $89.95** PSM ✗✗½

Abroad with Two Yanks Two Marine buddies on furlough exhibit slapstick tendencies while competing for the same girl. Along the way a big chase ensues with the two soldiers in drag. Typical wartime shenanigans likely to incite only weak chuckling or inspired snoozing.
1944 81m/B William Bendix, Dennis O'Keefe, Helen Walker, John Loder, George Cleveland, Janet Lambert, James Flavin, Arthur Hunnicutt; *D:* Allan Dwan. **VHS, Beta $12.95** LIV ✗✗

Absence of Malice High-minded story about the harm that the news media can inflict. Field is the earnest reporter who, after being fed some facts by an unscrupulous federal investigator, writes a story implicating Newman in a murder he didn't commit. Field hides behind journalistic confidentiality privilege to put off the outraged Newman, who loses a friend to suicide during the debacle. Interesting performances by Field and Newman.
1981 (PG) 116m/C Paul Newman, Sally Field, Bob Balaban, Melinda Dillon, Luther Adler, Barry Primus, Josef Sommer, John Harkins, Don Hood, Wilford Brimley; *D:* Sydney Pollack; *W:* Kurt Luedtke; *M:* Dave Grusin. **VHS, Beta $14.95** COL ✗✗½

The Absent-Minded Professor Classic dumb Disney fantasy of the era. A professor accidentally invents an anti-gravity substance called flubber, causing inanimate objects and people to become airborne. Great sequence of the losing school basket-ball team taking advantage of flubber during a game. MacMurray is convincing as the absent-minded genius in this newly colored version. Followed by "Son of Flubber."
1961 97m/C Fred MacMurray, Nancy Olson, Keenan Wynn, Tommy Kirk, Leon Ames, Ed Wynn; *D:* Robert Stevenson. **VHS, Beta $19.99** DIS, BTV ✗✗✗½

Absolute Beginners Fervently stylish camp musical exploring the lives of British teenagers in the 1950s who never quite gets untracked, although MTV video moments fill out a spare plot line. Based on a novel by Colin MacInnes. ♫Absolute Beginners; That's Motivation; Volare; Killer Blow; Have You Ever Been Blue?; Quiet Life; Having It All; Selling Out; Va Va Voom; The Naked and the Dead; Better Git It In Your Soul (The Hot and the Cool); Boogie Stop Shuffle (The Rough and the Smooth); Rodrigo Bay; Riot City; Ted Ain't Dead; Napoli; Cool Napoli; Little Cat; Landlords and Tenants; Santa Lucia; So What?; Hey Little Schoolgirl; Rock Baby Rock; Scorpio; Switching It Off; Hancock's Half Hour; Here Comes the Bride; My Mammy; Sleep Lagoon; Teddy Bears Picnic; Rocking at the 21's; Bongo Rock; Great Balls of Fire; Heat Doesn't Bother Me.
1986 (PG) 107m/C *GB* David Bowie, Ray Davies, James Fox, Eddie O'Connell, Patsy Kensit, Anita Morris, Sade Adu; *D:* Julien Temple; *W:* Richard Burridge, Don MacPherson. **VHS, Beta $79.95** HBO ✗✗

Absolution Two English boys trapped in a Catholic boarding school conspire to drive a tyrannical priest over the edge of sanity. As a result, bad things (including murder) occur. Burton is interesting in sadistic character study. Not released in the U.S. until 1988 following Burton's death, maybe due to something written in the will.
1981 (R) 105m/C *GB* Richard Burton, Dominic Guard, Dai Bradley, Andrew Keir, Billy Connolly, Willoughby Gray; *D:* Anthony Page. **VHS, Beta $9.95** SIM, TWE, FCT ✗✗

The Abyss Underwater sci-fi adventure about a team of oil-drilling divers pressed into service by the navy to locate and disarm an inoperative nuclear submarine. A high-tech thriller with fab footage underwater and pulsating score. The laserdisc version contains 27 extra minutes of footage. *AKA:* L'Oeuvre au clair.
1989 (PG-13) 140m/C Ed Harris, Mary Elizabeth Mastrantonio, Todd Graff, Michael Biehn, John Bedford Lloyd, J.C. Quinn, Leo Burmester, Kidd Brewer Jr., Kimberly Scott, Adam Nelson, George Robert Kirk, Chris Elliott, Jimmie Ray Weeks; *D:* James Cameron; *W:* James Cameron; *M:* Alan Silvestri. Academy Awards '89: Best Visual Effects; Nominations: Best Cinematography, Best Sound. **VHS, Beta $14.98** FXV ✗✗✗

Accatone! Accatone (Citti), a failure as a pimp, tries his luck as a thief. Hailed as a return to Italian neo-realism, this is a gritty, despairing, and dark look at the lives of the street people of Rome. Pasolini's first outing, adapted by the director from his novel, "A Violent Life." Pasolini served as mentor to Bernardo Bertolucci, listed in the credits as an assistant director.
1961 116m/B *IT* Franco Citti, Franca Pasut, Roberto Scaringelli, Adele Cambria, Paolo Guidi, Silvana Corsini; *D:* Pier Paolo Pasolini. **VHS $29.95** WBF, APD, ING ✗✗✗

Acceptable Risks Toxic disaster strikes when a plant manager is ordered to cut costs and sacrifice safety at the Citichem plant. Predictable plot stars Dennehy as the plant manager who risks all and fights politicians to reinstate the safety standards. Meanwhile, Tyson is the city manager who tries to warn the town of a possible chemical accident that could have devastating effects on the community. Made for television drama that shamelessly preys on audience fears.
1986 (R) 97m/C Brian Dennehy, Cicely Tyson, Kenneth McMillan, Christine Ebersole, Beah Richards, Richard Gilliland; *D:* Rick Wallace. **VHS, Beta $79.95** PSM ✗✗

Access Code Government agents attempt to uncover a private organization that has gained control of nuclear weapons for the purpose of world domination. A ragged patchwork of disconnected scenes meant to test the virtue of patience.
1984 90m/C Martin Landau, Michael Ansara, MacDonald Carey; *D:* Mark Sobel. **VHS, Beta $79.95** PSM ✗

Accident A tangled web of guilt, remorse, humor and thwarted sexuality is unravelled against the background of the English countryside in this complex story of an Oxford love triangle. An inside view of English repression at the university level adapted for the screen by Pinter from the novel by Nicholas Mosley. Long-winded but occasionally engrossing character study with interesting performances.
1967 100m/C *GB* Dirk Bogarde, Michael York, Stanley Baker, Jacqueline Sassard, Delphine Seyrig, Alexander Knox, Vivien Merchant, Freddie Jones, Harold Pinter; *D:* Joseph Losey; *W:* Harold Pinter. **VHS, Beta** NO ✗✗½

Accident Skate for your life. A hockey game turns into a nightmare when the roof over the arena collapses under the weight of too much ice and snow. One of the few hockey disaster films.
1983 104m/C Terence Kelly, Fiona Reid, Frank Perry; *D:* Donald Brittain. **VHS, Beta $59.95** TWE ✗½

Accidental Meeting A female version of "Strangers on a Train." Two women meet because of an auto accident and wind up talking about their lives. The main topic is man trouble and both "jokingly" plot to murder each other's man. Only, one woman does the deed and the other soon finds herself on the murderess' hit list.
1993 (R) 91m/C Linda Gray, Linda Purl, Leigh McCloskey, David Hayward, Ernie Lively, Kent McCord; *D:* Michael Zinberg; *W:* Pete Best, Christopher Horner. **VHS, Beta** PAR ✗✗½

The Accidental Tourist A bittersweet and subtle story, adapted faithfully from Anne Tyler's novel, of an introverted, grieving man who learns to love again after meeting an unconventional woman. After his son's death and subsequent separation from wife Turner, Macon Leary (Hurt) avoids emotional confrontation, burying himself in routines with the aid of his obsessive-compulsive siblings. Kooky dog-trainer Muriel Pritchett (an exuberant Davis) wins his attention, but not without struggle. Hurt effectively uses small gestures to describe Macon's emotional journey, while Davis grabs hearts with her open performance. Outstanding supporting cast.
1988 (PG) 121m/C William Hurt, Geena Davis, Kathleen Turner, Ed Begley Jr., David Ogden Stiers, Bill Pullman, Amy Wright; *D:* Lawrence Kasdan; *W:* Lawrence Kasdan; *M:* John Williams. Academy Awards '88: Best Supporting Actress (Davis); Nominations: Best Adapted Screenplay, Best Picture, Best Original Score; New York Film Critics Awards '88: Best Film. **VHS, Beta, 8mm $19.98** WAR, BTV ✗✗✗½

Accidents A scientist discovers that his invention has been stolen and is going to be used to cause worldwide havoc. He becomes concerned and spends the remainder

of the movie trying to relieve himself of anxiety.
1989 (R) 90m/C Edward Albert, Leigh Taylor-Young, Jon Cypher; **D:** Gideon Amir. **VHS, Beta** $79.75 *TWE ⅛*

Accomplice Plodding whodunit with Arlen as a shy, bookish private eye hired by his old flame to locate her missing husband. His investigations uncover several murders and long after the viewers have put 2 + 2 together, the P.I. smells a rat. The missing husband was a ruse to divert him from the real scam-a bank heist. Painfully low-level excitement.
1946 66m/B Richard Arlen, Veda Ann Borg, Tom Dugan, Francis Ford; **D:** Walter Colmes. **VHS** $19.95 *NOS ⅛*

Accused Married dancers Fairbanks and Del Rio are working in a Parisian revue when the show's sultry leading lady (Desmond) makes a pass at Fairbanks. Though he's turned her down, through a series of misunderstandings Del Rio believes the worst and the two women get into a vicious argument. When the star is found dead guess who gets the blame? Del Rio is lovely, Desmond is spiteful, and Fairbanks serves as a fine object of two women's affections.
1936 83m/B *GB* Douglas Fairbanks Jr., Dolores Del Rio, Florence Desmond, Basil Sydney, Athole Stewart, Esme Percy, Googie Withers, Cecil Humphreys; **D:** Thornton Freeland. **VHS** *HCV ⅛½*

The Accused Young is cast against character in this story of a college professor who is assaulted by one of her students and kills him in self-defense. A courtroom drama ensues, where Young is defended by the dead man's guardian. Film noir with nice ensemble performance. *AKA:* Strange Deception.
1948 101m/B Loretta Young, Robert Cummings, Wendell Corey, Sam Jaffe, Douglas Dick, Sara Allgood, Ann Doran; **D:** William Dieterle. **VHS, Beta** $89.95 *PAR ⅛⅛*

The Accused Provocative treatment of a true story involving a young woman gang raped in a bar while onlookers cheer. McGillis is the assistant district attorney who takes on the case and must contend with the victim's questionable past and a powerful lawyer hired by a wealthy defendant's parents. As the victim with a past, Foster gives an Oscar-winning performance that won raves for its strength and complexity.
1988 (R) 110m/C Jodie Foster, Kelly McGillis, Bernie Coulson, Leo Rossi, Ann Hearn, Carmen Argenziano, Steve Antin, Tom O'Brien, Peter Van Norden, Woody Brown; **D:** Jonathan Kaplan; **W:** Tom Topor; **M:** Brad Fiedel. **VHS, Beta, 8mm** $14.95 *PAR, FCT, BTV ⅛*

Ace Crawford, Private Eye Bumbling private eye struggles with confusing murder and somehow manages to solve the case.
19?? 71m/C Tim Conway, Billy Barty, Bill Henderson. **VHS** *MCG ⅛⅛*

Ace Drummond The complete 13-chapter serial about a murder organization that tries to stop several countries from forming a worldwide clipper ship air service and government troubleshooter Ace Drummond who's out to stop them. *AKA:* Squadron of Doom.
1936 260m/B John "Dusty" King, Jean Rogers, Noah Beery Jr.; **D:** Ford Beebe. **VHS, Beta** $24.95 *GPV, HHT, VCN ⅛⅛*

Ace High Spaghetti western about a ruthless outlaw named Cat Stevens trying to save himself from the noose. Patterned after the famous Sergio Leone-Clint Eastwood westerns, with less of a budget and more camp tendencies.
1968 120m/C *IT* Eli Wallach, Terence Hill, Bud Spencer, Brock Peters, Kevin McCarthy; **D:** Giuseppe Colizzi. **VHS, Beta** $14.95 *PAR, FCT ⅛½*

Ace of Aces An American sculptor is reviled, particularly by his girlfriend, when he does not join fellows in enlisting in what becomes WWI. Out to prove he's not lacking testosterone, he becomes a pilot in France, but is embittered by his experiences. Dated but well-acted war melodrama.
1933 77m/B Richard Dix, Elizabeth Allan, Theodore Newton, Ralph Bellamy, Joseph Sawyer, Frank Conroy, William Cagney; **D:** J. Walter Ruben. **VHS, Beta** $19.98 *TTC ⅛⅛*

Ace of Hearts A seedy story about a rich guy in the South Pacific who pays heavily to have himself killed.
1985 90m/C Mickey Rooney, Chris Robinson, Pilar Velasquez. **VHS, Beta** $39.95 *VCD ⅛*

Ace Ventura: Pet Detective Shamelessly silly comedy casts human cartoon Carrey, he of the rubber limbs and spasmodic facial muscles, as Ace, the guy who'll find missing pets, big or small. When the Miami Dolphins' mascot Snowflake is kidnapped, he abandons his search for an albino pigeon to save the lost dolphin just in time for the Super Bowl. This is brain candy, running full throttle with juvenile humor, some charm, and the hyper-energetic Carrey, not to mention Young as the police chief with a secret. Critically trashed box office smash catapulted Carrey into nearly instant stardom after seven seasons as the geeky white guy on "In Living Color."
1993 (PG-13) 87m/C Jim Carrey, Dan Marino, Courteney Cox, Sean Young, Tone Loc; **D:** Tom Shadyac; **W:** Jim Carrey, Tom Shadyac, Jack Bernstein; **M:** Ira Newborn. **VHS, 8mm** $24.96 *WAR ⅛*

Aces and Eights Standard western detailing the final days of Wild Bill Hickok, who was holding aces and eights when shot in the back (he never did finish the game). McCoy does his usual best as the sanitized Billy.
1936 62m/B Tim McCoy, Jimmy Aubrey, Luana Walters, Wheeler Oakman, Earle Hodgins, Frank Glennon; **D:** Sam Newfield. **VHS** $19.95 *NOS, DVT, RXM ⅛⅛*

Aces: Iron Eagle 3 Colonel "Chappy" Sinclair returns once again in this air adventure. He's been keeping busy flying in air shows when he stumbles across the nefarious activities of a Peruvian drug baron working out of a remote village. Sinclair recruits a team of maverick air circus pilots and they "borrow" a fleet of WWII vintage aircraft to raid the village, coming up against a fellow Air Force officer who turns out to be another villain. Lots of action and a stalwart cast.
1992 (R) 98m/C Louis Gossett Jr., Rachel McLish, Paul Freeman, Horst Buchholz, Christopher Cazenove, Sonny Chiba, Fred Dalton Thompson, Mitchell Ryan, Robert Estes, J.E. Freeman; **D:** John Glen. **VHS** $19.95 *COL ⅛⅛*

Aces Wild Another poker title. Outlaws menace an honest newspaper until the lawmen show up and send them on their way.
1937 62m/B Harry Carey Sr., Gertrude Messinger, Edward Cassidy, Roger Williams; **D:** Harry Fraser. **VHS, Beta** *NO ⅛½*

The Acid Eaters Straight-laced desk jockeys spend their weekends exploring the realm of the senses. Includes nudity.
1967 62m/C Buck Kartalian, Pat Barringer; **D:** B. Ron Elliott; **W:** B. Ron Elliott, Carl Monson; **M:** Billy Allen. **VHS** $23.00 *SMW, TPV ⅛*

Acorn People An unemployed teacher takes a summer job at a camp for handicapped children and learns sensitivity. Made-for-television weeper adapted by Tewkesbury from the book by Ron Jones.
1982 97m/C Ted Bessell, Cloris Leachman, LeVar Burton, Dolph Sweet, Cheryl Anderson; **D:** Joan Tewkesbury. **VHS, Beta** *TLF ⅛⅛*

Acqua e Sapone A young innocent model goes to Rome under the watchful eyes of an appointed priest-chaperon, but finds love, fun and other sinful things. Sudsy/romantic comedy.
1983 (PG) 100m/C *IT* Carlo Verdone, Natasha Hovey, Florinda Bolkan, Elena Bolkan; **D:** Carlo Verdone. **VHS, Beta** $59.95 *ING ⅛½*

Across 110th Street Gritty, violent cop thriller in the blaxploitation genre. Both the Mafia and the cops hunt down three black hoods who, in a display of extremely bad judgement, knocked over a mob-controlled bank while disguised as police. Lots of bullets create buckets of blood. Filmed on location in Harlem.
1972 (R) 102m/C Anthony Quinn, Yaphet Kotto, Anthony (Tony) Franciosa, Paul Benjamin, Ed Bernard, Antonio Fargas, Tim O'Connor, Lewis Gilbert, Richard Ward; **D:** Barry Shear. **VHS, Beta** $14.95 *MGM, FOX ⅛⅛*

Across the Bridge A man on the run from Scotland Yard for stealing a fortune flees to Mexico, in the process killing a man and assuming his identity. An ironic twist and his love for a dog seal his final destiny. Steiger's psychological study as the fugitive is compelling. Based on a novel by Graham Greene.
1957 103m/B *GB* Rod Steiger, David Knight, Marla Landi, Noel William, Bernard Lee; **D:** Ken Annakin. **VHS, Beta** *LCA ⅛⅛½*

Across the Great Divide Two orphans must cross the rugged snow-covered Rocky Mountains in 1876 in order to claim their inheritance—a 400-acre plot of land in Salem, Oregon. Pleasant coming-of-age tale with majestic scenery.
1976 (G) 102m/C Robert F. Logan, George Flower, Heather Rattray, Mark Hall; **D:** Stewart Raffill; **W:** Stewart Raffill; **M:** Angelo Badalamenti. **VHS, Beta** $9.98 *MED, VTR ⅛⅛½*

Across the Pacific Classic Bogie/Huston vehicle made on the heels of "The Maltese Falcon." Bogie is an American Army officer booted out of the service on false charges of treason. When no other military will accept him, he sails to China (via the Panama Canal) to offer his services to Chiang Kai-Shek. On board, he meets a variety of seedy characters who plan to blow up the canal. Huston again capitalizes on the counterpoint between the rotundly acerbic Greenstreet, who plays a spy, and stiff-lipped Bogart, who's wooing Astor. Great Bogie moments and fine direction make this an adventure classic. When he departed for the service just prior to filming the final scenes, Huston turned over direction to Vincent Sherman. Also available colorized.
1942 97m/B Humphrey Bogart, Mary Astor, Sydney Greenstreet, Charles Halton, Victor Sen Yung, Roland Got, Keye Luke, Richard Loo; **D:** John Huston. **VHS** $19.98 *MGM, FCT ⅛⅛⅛½*

Across the Plains Predictable oater about two brothers who are raised separately after their parents are murdered by outlaws. One is brought up by Indians, the other by the outlaws responsible for wiping out the folks, who tell the boy that Indians did in his ma and pa. Eventually the brothers meet and fight. Odds favor the good one winning, aided by Indian pals.

1939 59m/B Jack Randall, Frank Yaconelli, Joyce Bryant, Hal Price, Dennis Moore, Glenn Strange, Bud Osborne; *D:* Spencer Gordon Bennet. **VHS, Beta** $19.95 *NOS, GPV, DVT* ✗ ½

Across the Tracks Two brothers, one a juvie-home rebel, the other a straight-A jock, are at odds when the black sheep is pressured into selling drugs. In an attempt to save his brother from a life of crime, the saintly one convinces his brother to join him on the school track team, and the brothers are forced to face off in a big meet. Fairly realistic good guy/bad guy who's really a good guy teen drama. Also available in an "R" rated version.
1989 (PG-13) 101m/C Rick Schroder, Brad Pitt, Carrie Snodgress; *D:* Sandy Tung; *W:* Sandy Tung; *M:* Joel Goldsmith. **VHS** $19.95 *ACA* ✗✗

Across the Wide Missouri Pioneer epic stars Gable as a rugged fur trapper who marries an Indian woman (Marques) so he can trap beaver pelts on her people's rich land. On the journey to the Indian territory however, the trapper truly falls in love with his bride. Superior historical drama is marred slightly by the use of narration (provided by Howard Keel). Look for lively performances from Menjou as a French tippler and Naish as the quirky Indian Chief. Beautiful scenery filmed in the spectacular Rocky Mountains.
1951 78m/C Clark Gable, Ricardo Montalban, John Hodiak, Adolphe Menjou, Maria Elena Marques, J. Carroll Naish, Jack Holt, Alan Napier; *D:* William A. Wellman. **VHS, Beta** $19.98 *MGM, CCB* ✗✗ ½

The Act A muddled satire about political double dealing and union corruption further muddled by a twangy musical score manufactured by folksy Sebastian. *AKA:* Bless 'Em All.
1982 (R) 90m/C Jill St. John, Eddie Albert, Pat Hingle, Robert Ginty, Sarah Langenfeld, Nicolas Surovy; *D:* Sig Shore; *M:* John Sebastian. **VHS, Beta** $69.95 *VES* ✗✗

Act of Aggression When a Parisian man finds his wife and daughter murdered at a summer resort, he takes the law into his own hands, with predictable results.
1973 (R) 100m/C *FR* Jean-Louis Trintignant, Catherine Deneuve, Claude Brasseur. **VHS, Beta** $59.95 *FCT* ✗✗

Act of Passion: The Lost Honor of Kathryn Beck A woman meets a man at a party and has the proverbial one-night stand. Her privacy is shattered when she discovers that he's a terrorist under surveillance by the police and press. Strong performances by Thomas and Kristofferson help turn this into an interesting American television remake of the German "Lost Honor of Katharina Blum," based loosely on a novel by Heinrich Boll.
1983 100m/C Marlo Thomas, Kris Kristofferson, George Dzundza, Jon DeVries; *D:* Simon Langton. **VHS, Beta** $69.95 *VMK* ✗✗ ½

Act of Piracy A bankrupt contractor reunites with his estranged wife to track down the brutal terrorists who have kidnapped their son.
1989 (R) 105m/C Ray Sharkey, Gary Busey. **VHS, Beta** $89.98 *WAR* ✗ ½

Act of Vengeance A group of women band together to hunt down and exact revenge on the man who raped them. Exploitative action-filled thriller. *AKA:* Rape Squad.
1974 (R) 90m/C Jo Ann Harris, Peter Brown, Jennifer Lee, Lisa Moore, Connie Strickland, Pat Estrin; *D:* Bob Kelljan. **VHS, Beta** $19.99 *HBO* ✗✗

Act of Vengeance Drama about Jock Yablonski, a United Mine Workers official who challenged the president, Tony Boyle. Made for cable, based on fact, showing the events that led up to the murder of Yablonski and his family. Intriguing story lacking cinematic drive.
1986 97m/C Charles Bronson, Ellen Burstyn, Wilford Brimley, Hoyt Axton, Robert Schenkkan, Ellen Barkin, Keanu Reeves; *D:* John MacKenzie; *W:* Scott Spencer. **VHS,** *NO* ✗✗ ½

Acting on Impulse Impulsive, troublemaking movie star (Fiorentino) becomes a murder suspect when her producer is killed. This doesn't slow her down. She checks into a hotel with a major party attitude and manages to seduce a conservative businessman (Howell) and his junior exec (Allen) into helping her forget her troubles. And then the businessman's fiance turns up dead. Any connection? Made for cable television.
1993 (R) 94m/C Linda Fiorentino, C. Thomas Howell, Nancy Allen, Adam Ant. **VHS** $89.95 *ACA* ✗✗

Action for Slander A British army officer sporting the typical stiff upper lip is accused of cheating during a card game, and the slander mars his reputation until the case is taken to court. Dryly earnest and honest in its depiction of class differences in pre-war England. Based on a novel by Mary Borden.
1938 84m/B *GB* Clive Brook, Ann Todd, Margaretta Scott, Ronald Squire, Francis L. Sullivan, Felix Aylmer, Googie Withers; *D:* Tim Whelan. **VHS, Beta, 8mm** $24.95 *VYY* ✗✗ ½

Action in Arabia A newsman uncovers a Nazi plot to turn the Arabs against the Allies while investigating a colleague's murder in Damascus. The desert teems with spies, double agents, and sheiks as suave Sanders goes about his investigative business. Quintessential wartime B-movie.
1944 75m/B George Sanders, Virginia Bruce, Lenore Aubert, Gene Lockhart, Robert Armstrong, H.B. Warner, Alan Napier, Michael Ansara; *D:* Leonide Moguy. **VHS, Beta** $19.98 *RKO, TTC* ✗✗

Action in the North Atlantic Massey and Bogart are the captain and first mate of a Merchant Marine vessel running the lone supply route to the Soviet Union. Eventually they wind up locking horns with a Nazi U-boat. Plenty of action and strenuous flag waving in this propagandorama. Gordon fans won't want to miss her as Massey's wife. Also available colorized.
1943 126m/B Humphrey Bogart, Raymond Massey, Alan Hale, Julie Bishop, Ruth Gordon, Sam Levene, Dane Clark; *D:* Lloyd Bacon. **VHS** $19.98 *MGM, FCT* ✗✗

Action Jackson Power-hungry auto tycoon Nelson tries to frame rebellious black police sergeant Weathers for murder. Being a graduate of Harvard and a tough guy, the cop doesn't go for it. Nelson eats up the screen as the heavy with no redeeming qualities, while Weathers is tongue-in-cheek as the resourceful good guy who keeps running afoul of the law in spite of his best efforts. Lots of action, violence, and a few sexy women help cover the plot's lack of common sense.
1988 (R) 96m/C Carl Weathers, Vanity, Craig T. Nelson, Sharon Stone; *D:* Craig R. Baxley; *W:* Robert Reneau; *M:* Herbie Hancock, Michael Kamen. **VHS, Beta** $19.98 *LHV, WAR* ✗✗

Action U.S.A. A young woman witnesses the murder of her boyfriend by gangsters, who then pursue her to make sure she will never tell what she saw. Throughout Texas she rambles with the mob sniffing at her heels, grateful for the opportunity to

participate in numerous stunts and car crashes.
1989 90m/C Barri Murphy, Greg Cummins, William Knight, William Smith, Cameron Mitchell; *D:* John Stewart; *W:* David Reskin. **VHS, Beta** $79.95 *IMP* ✗ ½

Actor: The Paul Muni Story Musical biography of Paul Muni, from his beginnings as a traveling actor in Hungary to his New York theatre and movie career.
1978 105m/C Herschel Bernardi, Georgia Brown, Harold Gould. **VHS, Beta** $39.95 *LIV* ✗✗

Actors and Sin Two-part film casting a critical eye toward actors and Hollywood. "Actor's Blood" is the melodramatic story of Shakespearean actor Robinson and his unhappy actress daughter. She commits suicide and he sets out to prove it was murder. Heavy going. Lighter and more entertaining is "Woman of Sin," which relates a Hollywood satire involving a theatrical agent and his newest client, a precocious nine-year-old.
1952 82m/B Edward G. Robinson, Eddie Albert, Marsha Hunt, Alan Reed, Dan O'Herlihy, Tracey Roberts; *D:* Lee Games, Ben Hecht. **VHS** $19.95 *COL, HEG* ✗✗ ½

An Actor's Revenge In the early 19th century, a female impersonator in a Kabuki troupe takes revenge on the three men who killed his parents. Fascinating study of opposites—male/female, stage/life, love/hate. In Japanese with English subtitles. *AKA:* Yukinojo Henge.
1963 110m/C *JP* Kazuo Hasegawa, Fujiko Yamamoto, Ayako Wakao, Ganjiro Nakamura; *D:* Kon Ichikawa; *W:* Teinosuke Kinugasa, Daisuke Ito, Natto Wada; *M:* Yashushi Akutagawa. **VHS** $79.95 *NYF, ING* ✗✗

Adam Television docu-drama based on a tragic, true story. John and Reve Williams (Travanti and Williams) desperately search for their 6-year-old son abducted during an outing. During their long search and struggle, they lobby Congress for use of the FBI's crime computer. Eventually their efforts led to the creation of the Missing Children's Bureau. Sensitive, compelling performances by Travanti and Williams as the agonized, courageous parents.
1983 100m/C Daniel J. Travanti, JoBeth Williams, Martha Scott, Richard Masur, Paul Regina, Mason Adams; *D:* Michael Tuchner. **VHS, Beta** *NO* ✗✗✗ ½

Adam at 6 A.M. Douglas is a young college professor who decides to spend a summer laboring in Missouri, where life, he thinks, is simpler. Of course, he learns that life in the boonies has its own set of problems, but unfortunately it takes him the entire movie before he catches the drift.
1970 (PG) 100m/C Michael Douglas, Lee Purcell, Joe Don Baker, Charles Aidman, Marge Redmond, Louise Latham, Grayson Hall, Dana Elcar, Meg Foster, Richard Derr, Anne Gwynne; *D:* Robert Scheerer. **VHS, Beta** $59.98 *FOX* ✗✗

Adam Had Four Sons Satisfying character study involving the typical turn-of-the-century family nearly consumed by love, jealousy, and hatred. In the early part of the century, a goodly governess (Bergman in her second U.S. film) watches sympathetically over four sons of an American businessman after their mother dies. Economic necessity separates Bergman from the family for several years. Upon her return, she tangles with scheming bride-to-be Hayward, a bad girl intent on dividing and conquering the family before walking down the aisle with one of the sons. Based on a novel by Charles Bonner.

1941 81m/B Ingrid Bergman, Warner Baxter, Susan Hayward, Fay Wray, Richard Denning, June Lockhart, Robert Shaw; *D:* Gregory Ratoff. **VHS, Beta $59.95** *COL* ♫♫½

Adam's Rib Classic war between the sexes cast Tracy and Hepburn as married attorneys on opposite sides of the courtroom in the trial of blonde bombshell Holliday, charged with attempted murder of the lover of her philandering husband. The battle in the courtroom soon takes its toll at home as the couple is increasingly unable to leave their work at the office. Sharp, snappy dialogue by Gordon and Kanin with superb direction by Cukor. Perhaps the best of the nine movies pairing Tracy and Hepburn. Also available colorized.
1950 101m/B Spencer Tracy, Katharine Hepburn, Judy Holliday, Tom Ewell, David Wayne, Jean Hagen, Hope Emerson, Polly Moran, Marvin Kaplan, Paula Raymond, Tommy Noonan; *D:* George Cukor; *W:* Garson Kanin, Ruth Gordon; *M:* Miklos Rozsa. **VHS, Beta $19.95** *MGM, VYG, HMV* ♫♫♫♫

The Addams Family The positively ooky family, based on the characters created by cartoonist Charles Addams, appear in the original, uncut television episodes. Two episodes per tape. This volume includes ''The Addams Family Goes to School'' and ''Morticia and the Psychiatrist.''
1964 50m/B John Astin, Carolyn Jones, Jackie Coogan, Ted Cassidy, Blossom Rock, Ken Weatherwax, Lisa Loring, Felix Silla. **VHS $9.95** *WOV, MOV* ♫♫♫♫

The Addams Family Everybody's favorite family of ghouls hits the big screen, but something is lost in the translation. An imposter claiming to be long-lost Uncle Fester (Lloyd), who says he was in the Bermuda Triangle for 25 years, shows up at the Addams' home to complete a dastardly deed—raid the family's immense fortune. Although Fester's plan is foiled, a series of plot twists highlight the ghoulish family's eccentricities. Darkly humorous but eventually disappointing: Julia, Huston, and Ricci are great in their roles and the sets look good, but the plot is thin. Much closer to the original comic strip by Charles Addams than the popular TV show ever was.
1991 (PG-13) 102m/C Anjelica Huston, Raul Julia, Christopher Lloyd, Dan Hedaya, Elizabeth Wilson, Judith Malina, Carel Struycken, Dana Ivey, Paul Benedict, Christina Ricci, Jimmy Workman, Christopher Hart, John Franklin; *Cameos:* Marc Shaiman; *D:* Barry Sonnenfeld; *W:* Larry Thompson, Caroline Thompson; *M:* Marc Shaiman. **VHS, Beta $14.95** *PAR* ♫♫

Addams Family Values The creepy Addams' are back, but this time they leave the dark confines of the mansion to meet the ''real'' world. New baby Pubert causes homicidal jealousy in sibs Wednesday and Pugsley, causing Mom and Dad to hire a gold-digging, serial-killing nanny (Cusack) with designs on Uncle Fester to watch over the tot. A step above its predecessor, chock full of black humor, sub-plots, and one-liners. Cusack fits right in with an outrageously over the top performance and Ricci nearly steals the show again as the deadpan Wednesday.
1993 (PG-13) 93m/C Anjelica Huston, Raul Julia, Christopher Lloyd, Joan Cusack, Carol Kane, Christina Ricci, Jimmy Workman, Kaitlyn Hooper, Kristen Hooper, Carel Struycken, David Krumholtz, Christopher Hart, Dana Ivey, Peter MacNicol, Christine Baranski, Mercedes McNab; *D:* Barry Sonnenfeld; *W:* Paul Rudnick; *M:* Marc Shaiman. **VHS, Beta** *PAR* ♫♫½

Adios Amigo Offbeat western comedy has ad-libbing Pryor hustling as a perennially inept con man. Script and direction (both provided by Williamson) are not up to Pryor's level, although excessive violence and vulgarity are avoided in a boring attempt to provide good clean family fare.
1975 (PG) 87m/C Fred Williamson, Richard Pryor, Thalmus Rasulala, James Brown, Robert Philip, Mike Henry; *D:* Fred Williamson; *W:* Fred Williamson. **VHS $9.95** *SIM, VMK* ♫♫

Adios Gringo Routine oater in which a young rancher is swindled in a cattle deal and forced to kill in self defense.
1965 ?m/C Montgomery Wood, Evelyn Stewart. **VHS $16.95** *SNC* ♫½

Adios, Hombre An innocent man who was imprisoned for murder escapes from prison and seeks revenge. You'll be saying adios as well.
1968 90m/C *IT* Craig Hill, Giulia Rubini; *D:* Mario Caiano. **VHS, Beta $49.95** *UNI* ♫

The Adjuster Critics either loved or hated this strange film. Insurance adjuster Noah Render's clients look to him for all sorts of comfort, so much so that his own identity becomes a blurred reflection of their tragedies. Wife Hera is a film censor who secretly tapes the pornographic videos she watches at work. Their carefully organized lives are invaded by Bubba and Mimi, a wealthy couple who pass themselves off as filmmakers who want to use the Render house as a movie set. They are instead looking to involve the Renders in their latest and most elaborate erotic fantasy. Lots of symbolism, but little substance.
1991 (R) 102m/C *CA* Elias Koteas, Arsinee Khanjian, Maury Chaykin, Gabrielle Rose, David Hemblen, Jennifer Dale, Don McKellar, Raoul Trujillo; *D:* Atom Egoyan; *W:* Atom Egoyan; *M:* Mychael Danna. **VHS $79.98** *ORI* ♫♫

The Admiral Was a Lady Four ex-GIs try to get by in life without going to work. Hendrix walks into their lives as a winning ex-Wave gifted with a knack for repartee who is disgusted by their collective lack of ambition. Nevertheless, she is pursued by the zany quartet with predictable results.
1950 87m/B Edmond O'Brien, Wanda Hendrix, Rudy Vallee, Steve Brodie; *D:* Albert Rogell. **VHS, Beta $14.98** *NOS, FRH, VHE* ♫♫

Adomas Nori Buti Zmogumi Soviet Lithuanian feature in its original form, with dialogue in Lithuanian. A young worker scrapes together money for a ticket to Buenos Aires, but the money is stolen by the manager of the travel office. *AKA:* Adam Wants to Be a Man.
1959 90m/B *RU LI D:* V. Zhalakyavichus. **VHS** *IHF* ♫♫

Adoption The third of Meszaros's trilogy, involving a middle-aged Hungarian woman who longs for a child and instead forms a deep friendship with a 19-year-old orphan. In Hungarian with English subtitles. *AKA:* Orkobefogadas.
1975 89m/B *HU D:* Marta Meszaros. **VHS, Beta $69.95** *KIV, ING* ♫♫♫

The Adorable Cheat A low-budget, late-silent melodrama about a young woman who tries to get involved in the family business, despite her father's refusal of her help. Once in the business, she finds love.
1928 76m/B Lila Lee, Cornelius Keefe, Burr McIntosh; *D:* Burton King. **VHS, Beta, 8mm $16.95** *GPV, VYY* ♫♫

Adorable Julia When an actress takes on a lover many years younger than herself, the laughs begin to fly in this sex comedy based on W. Somerset Maugham's novel.

1962 97m/C *FR* Lilli Palmer, Charles Boyer; *D:* Alfred Weidenmann. **VHS $29.95** *FCT, VEC* ♫♫

Adrift Yet another couple-in-terror-from-psychos-on-the-high-seas flick. Katie and Guy Nast (Jackson and Welsh) are on an anniversary sailing adventure intended to shore up their shaky marriage. They discover a boat adrift with two survivors (Greenwood and Rowan) who have a suspicious story but they help them nonetheless. Big mistake. Made for television.
1993 92m/C Kate Jackson, Kenneth Welsh, Bruce Greenwood, Kelly Rowan; *D:* Christian Duguay. **VHS $89.95** *WOV* ♫♫½

The Adultress When a husband and wife cannot satisfy their desire to have a family, they hire a young man to help them in this dumb made-for-television melodrama.
1977 (R) 85m/C Tyne Daly, Eric (Hans Gudegast) Braeden, Gregory Morton; *D:* Norbert Meisel. **VHS, Beta** *NO* ♫

Adventure Gable's first postwar film has him as a roughneck sailor romancing a shy and reserved librarian (Garson). Dull and disappointing—both stars deserve better. However, there is a touching scene of Gable with newborn child that might be of interest to some. Based on the novel by Clyde Brion Davis.
1945 130m/B Clark Gable, Greer Garson, Joan Blondell, Thomas Mitchell, Tom Tully, John Qualen, Richard Haydn, Lina Romay; *D:* Victor Fleming; *W:* Vincent Lawrence, Frederick Hazlitt Brennan. **VHS $19.98** *MGM* ♫♫

Adventure Island En route to Australia, a small ship stops at a remote island for supplies. The crew is greeted by a crazed, tyrannical leader who makes their lives difficult. Dull low-budget remake of 1937's ''Ebb Tide.''
1947 66m/C Rory Calhoun, Rhonda Fleming, Paul Kelly, John Abbott; *D:* Peter Stewart. **VHS, Beta $16.95** *SNC* ♫½

Adventure of the Action Hunters A dying sailor leaves a tourist couple a message leading to a treasure, and they vie for it along with gangsters, mercenaries and other unsavory types.
1987 (PG) 81m/C Ronald Hunter, Sean Murphy, Joe Cimino; *D:* Lee Bonner. **VHS, Beta** *NO* ♫

The Adventurer An escaped convict saves two wealthy women from death. They mistake him for a gallant sportsman and bring him home. Early Chaplin silent with music track.
1917 20m/B Charlie Chaplin, Charles Halton; *D:* Charlie Chaplin. **VHS, Beta** *CAB* ♫♫½

The Adventurers At the turn of the century, two Boers and an English officer set out to recover stolen jewels hidden in the jungles of South Africa. On the way, greed and anger take their toll a la ''The Treasure of Sierra Madre,'' only on a less convincing scale. *AKA:* Fortune in Diamonds; The Great Adventure.
1951 82m/B *GB* Dennis Price, Jack Hawkins, Siobhan McKenna, Peter Hammond, Bernard Lee; *D:* David MacDonald. **VHS, Beta $19.95** *NOS* ♫♫

The Adventurers Sleazy Harold Robbins novel retains its trashy aura on film. Unfortunately, this turkey is also long and boring. Set in South America, it tells the tale of a rich playboy who uses and destroys everyone who crosses his path. His vileness results from having seen his mother murdered by outlaws, but his obsession is to avenge his father's murder. Blood, gore, revolutions, and exploitive sex follow him everywhere. Watch and be amazed at the big-name stars who signed on for this one.

1970 (R) 171m/C Candice Bergen, Olivia de Havilland, Bekim Fehmiu, Charles Aznavour, Alan Badel, Ernest Borgnine, Leigh Taylor-Young, Fernando Rey, Thommy Berggren, John Ireland, Sydney Tafler, Rossano Brazzi, Anna Moffo, Christian Roberts, Yorgo Voyagis, Angela Scoular, Yolande Donlan, Ferdinand "Ferdy" Mayne, Jaclyn Smith, Peter Graves, Roberta Haynes; **D:** Lewis Gilbert. VHS $29.95 *PAR Woof!*

Adventures Beyond Belief
An irreverent motorcyclist is chased across Europe for a murder he didn't commit. Firmly within the boundaries of belief. **AKA:** Neat and Tidy.
1987 95m/C Elke Sommer, Jill Whitlow, Graham Stark, Stella Stevens, Larry Storch, Thick Wilson, Skyler Cole, Edie Adams, John Astin; **D:** Marcus Thompson. VHS, Beta *NO ⅛*

Adventures in Babysitting
Pleasant comedy has its moments when a babysitter and her charges leave peaceful suburbia for downtown Chicago to rescue a friend in trouble. After a flat tire strands them on the freeway, trouble takes on a new meaning. Shue is charming as the hapless sitter, unexpectedly dateless, who finds herself doing a lot more than just watching the kids. Ludicrous at times, but still fun to watch.
1987 (PG-13) 102m/C Elisabeth Shue, Keith Coogan, Maia Brewton, Anthony Rapp, Calvin Levels, Vincent D'Onofrio, Penelope Ann Miller, George Newbern, John Ford Noonan, Lolita David, Albert Collins; **D:** Chris Columbus; **W:** David Simkins; **M:** Michael Kamen. VHS, Beta, 8mm $89.95 *TOU ⅞½*

Adventures in Dinosaur City
Expect to see lots of movies riding on the coattails of the dino mania sweeping the land. Some will be good, others will not. "Adventures" falls into the latter category. Modern-day pre-teen siblings are transported back in time to the stone age. There they meet their favorite TV characters (they're dinosaurs) and help them solve prehistoric crimes. Family film may amuse kids, but adults should stick to "Jurassic Park."
1992 (PG) 88m/C Omri Katz, Shawn Hoffman, Tiffanie Poston, Pete Koch, Megan Hughes, Tony Doyle, Mimi Maynard; **D:** Brett Thompson; **W:** Willie Baronet, Lisa Morton; **M:** Fredric Teetsel. VHS $89.98 *REP ⅞*

Adventures in Spying
Brian McNichols is just trying to enjoy his summer vacation when he discovers that a notorious drug lord is living in his neighborhood. After realizing there is a reward for his capture, he enlists the help of his friend (Schoelen) to get the man's picture for the police. Action-packed film is geared towards the junior high set, but relies too heavily on coincidence and other plot connivances to compete with espionage flicks directed at an older market.
1992 (PG-13) 92m/C Jill Schoelen, Bernie Coulson, Seymour Cassel, G. Gordon Liddy, Michael Emil; **D:** Hil Covington; **W:** Hil Covington; **M:** James Stemple. VHS $89.95 *NLC ⅞*

The Adventures of a Gnome Named Gnorm
Silly cop caper finds LAPD detective Casey (Hall) stuck with a very strange new partner—a bark-wearing gnome named Gnorm. The two team up to go after a diamond smuggling ring. The special-effects creature may hold the kiddies interest.
1993 (PG) 86m/C VHS $94.99 *PGV ⅞½*

Adventures of a Private Eye
A self-mocking British detective farce about an inept private eye who takes his time tracking down a beautiful girl's blackmailer, bedding down with all the women he meets along the way.

1987 96m/C *GB* Christopher Neil, Suzy Kendall, Irene Handl; **D:** Stanley Long. VHS, Beta $29.95 *ACA ⅛*

Adventures of a Taxi Driver
Cabbie finds sex, crime, sex, adventure and sex on the road in this off-duty comedy.
1976 89m/C *GB* Barry Evans, Judy Geeson, Adrienne Posta, Diana Dors, Liz Fraser; **D:** Stanley Long. VHS, Beta $29.95 *ACA Woof!*

The Adventures of Baron Munchausen
From the director of "Time Bandits," "Brazil," and "The Fisher King" comes an ambitious, imaginative, chaotic, and under-appreciated marvel based on the tall (and often confused) tales of the Baron. Munchausen encounters the King of the Moon, Venus, and other odd and fascinating characters during what might be described as an circular narrative in which flashbacks dovetail into the present and place is never quite what it seems. Wonderful special effects and visually stunning sets occasionally dwarf the actors and prove what Gilliam can do with a big budget.
1989 (PG) 126m/C John Neville, Eric Idle, Sarah Polley, Valentina Cortese, Oliver Reed, Uma Thurman, Sting, Jonathan Pryce, Bill Paterson, Peter Jeffrey, Alison Steadman, Charles McKeown, Dennis Winston, Jack Purvis; **Cameos:** Robin Williams; **D:** Terry Gilliam; **W:** Terry Gilliam; **M:** Michael Kamen. VHS, Beta, 8mm $19.95 *COL, CRC ⅞⅞½*

The Adventures of Buckaroo Banzai Across the Eighth Dimension
A man of many talents, Buckaroo Banzai (Weller) travels through the eighth dimension in a jet-propelled Ford Fiesta to battle Planet 10 aliens led by the evil Lithgow. Buckaroo incorporates his vast knowledge of medicine, science, music, racing, and foreign relations to his advantage. Offbeat and often humorous cult sci-fi trip. **AKA:** Buckaroo Banzai.
1984 (PG) 100m/C Peter Weller, Ellen Barkin, Jeff Goldblum, Christopher Lloyd, John Lithgow, Lewis Smith, Rosalind Cash, Robert Ito, Pepe Serna, Vincent Schiavelli, Dan Hedaya, Yakov Smirnoff, Jamie Lee Curtis; **D:** W.D. Richter; **M:** Michael Boddicker. VHS, Beta $9.99 *VES, LIV ⅞⅞⅞*

The Adventures of Bullwhip Griffin
A rowdy, family-oriented comedy-adventure set during the California Gold Rush. Light Disney farce catches Russell at the tail end of his teenage star days. Pleshette and McDowall embark upon an ocean trip from Boston to San Francisco to find her brother, Russell, who's out west digging for gold. Assorted comedic adventures take place.
1966 110m/C Roddy McDowall, Suzanne Pleshette, Karl Malden, Harry Guardino; **D:** James Neilson. VHS, Beta $69.95 *DIS ⅞⅞½*

Adventures of Captain Fabian
When the captain of the "China Sea" learns that a beautiful woman has been falsely imprisoned, he comes to her rescue. Not one of Flynn's better swashbucklers, with typically low-quality Republic production.
1951 100m/B Errol Flynn, Vincent Price, Agnes Moorehead, Micheline Presle; **D:** William Marshall. VHS, Beta $39.95 *NO ⅛½*

The Adventures of Captain Marvel
A 12-episode cliff-hanging serial based on the comic book character. Details the adventures of klutzy Billy Batson, who transforms into superhero Captain Marvel by speaking the magic word, "Shazam!"
1941 240m/B Tom Tyler, Frank "Junior" Coghlan, Louise Currie; **D:** William Witney. VHS $29.95 *VCN, REP, MLB ⅞⅛½*

Adventures of Don Juan
Flynn's last spectacular epic features elegant costuming and loads of action. Don Juan saves Queen Margaret from her evil first minister. He then swashbuckles his way across Spain and England in an effort to win her heart. Grand, large-scale fun and adventure with Flynn at his self-mocking best. Special laserdisc edition includes the original trailer. **AKA:** The New Adventures of Don Juan.
1949 111m/C Errol Flynn, Viveca Lindfors, Robert Douglas, Romney Brent, Alan Hale, Raymond Burr, Aubrey Mather, Ann Rutherford; **D:** Vincent Sherman. Academy Awards '49: Best Costume Design (Color); Nominations: Best Art Direction/Set Decoration (Color). VHS, Beta $19.98 *MGM, MLB ⅞⅞½*

Adventures of Eliza Fraser
A young shipwrecked couple move from bawdy pleasures to cannibalism after being captured by aborigines.
1976 114m/C Susannah York, Trevor Howard, Leon Lissek, Abigail, Noel Ferrier, Carole Skinner; **D:** Tim Burstall. VHS, Beta $19.95 *NWV ⅞½*

The Adventures of Ford Fairlane
The Diceman plays an unusual detective specializing in rock 'n' roll cases. When a heavy metal singer dies on stage, he takes the case in his own inimitable fashion, pursuing buxom gals, sleazy record executives and even his ex-wife. Not surprisingly, many of his stand-up bits are worked into the movie. Clay, the ever-so-controversial comic in his first (and likely last) starring role haplessly sneers his way through this rock 'n roll dud of a comedy thriller. A quick effort to cash in on Clay's fading star. Forget about it. **AKA:** Ford Fairlane.
1990 (R) 101m/C Andrew Dice Clay, Wayne Newton, Priscilla Presley, Morris Day, Lauren Holly, Maddie Corman, Gilbert Gottfried, David Patrick Kelly, Brandon Call, Robert Englund, Ed O'Neill, Sheila E, Kari Wuhrer, Tone Loc; **D:** Renny Harlin; **W:** David Arnott, Daniel Waters. VHS, Beta $19.98 *FXV Woof!*

The Adventures of Frank and Jesse James
The bad brothers of the Wild West are trying to make good for rip-offs committed in their names, so they're hoping to hit pay-dirt with a silver mine. A 13-episode serial on two cassettes.
1948 180m/B Steve Darrell, Clayton Moore, Noel Neill, Stanley Andrews. VHS $29.98 *REP, MOV Woof!*

The Adventures of Frontier Fremont
A rough and tumble story of a man who leaves the city, grows a beard, and makes the wilderness his home (and the animals his friends). Mountain life, that's the life for me. Almost indistinguishable from Haggerty's "Grizzly Adams," with the usual redeeming panoramic shots of majestic mountains.
1975 95m/C Dan Haggerty, Denver Pyle; **D:** Richard Friedenberg. VHS, Beta $41.00 *VCI ⅛½*

The Adventures of Gallant Bess
The time-honored story of a rodeo man torn between his girl and his talented horse (the Bess of the title).
1948 73m/C Cameron Mitchell, Audrey Long, Fuzzy Knight, James Millican; **D:** Lew Landers. VHS *VEC, HEG ⅛*

The Adventures of Hairbreadth Harry
Three short spoofs of the early melodramas cranked out by the movie industry. Includes "Sawdust Baby," "Fearless Harry," and "Rudolph's Revenge."
192? 65m/B Billy West. VHS, Beta *GPV ⅞⅞*

The Adventures of Huck Finn
Decent Disney attempt at adapting an American favorite by Mark Twain. Mischievious Huck and runaway slave Jim travel down the muddy Mississippi, working on life and friendship and getting into all sorts of adventures in the pre-Civil War era. Fast-paced and amusing with good performances by Wood (in the title role) and Broadway trained Vance (as Jim). Racial epithets and minstrel show dialect have been eliminated in this version. Some material, including Jim's close call with a lynch mob and Huck's drunken, brutal father may be too strong for immature children.
1993 (PG) 108m/C Elijah Wood, Courtney B. Vance, Robbie Coltrane, Jason Robards Jr., Ron Perlman, Dana Ivey, Anne Heche, James Gammon, Paxton Whitehead, Tom Aldredge, Curtis Armstrong, Mary Louise Wilson, Frances Conroy; **D:** Stephen Sommers; **W:** Stephen Sommers; **M:** Bill Conti. **VHS, Beta $39.99** *DIS, BTV* 🐾🐾🐾

The Adventures of Huckleberry
Finn Mark Twain's classic story about a boy who runs away and travels down the Mississippi on a raft, accompanied by a runaway slave, is done over in MGM-style. Rooney is understated as Huck (quite a feat), while the production occasionally floats aimlessly down the Mississippi. An entertaining follow-up to "The Adventures of Tom Sawyer."
1939 89m/B Mickey Rooney, Lynne Carver, Rex Ingram, William Frawley, Walter Connolly; **D:** Richard Thorpe. **VHS, Beta $19.98** *MGM, HMV* 🐾🐾🐾

The Adventures of Huckleberry
Finn A lively adaptation of the Twain saga in which Huck and runaway slave Jim raft down the Mississipi in search of freedom and adventure. Miscasting of Hodges as Huck hampers the proceedings, but Randall shines as the treacherous King. Strong supporting cast includes Keaton as a lion-tamer and boxing champ Moore as Jim.
1960 107m/C Tony Randall, Eddie Hodges, Archie Moore, Patty McCormack, Neville Brand, Mickey Shaughnessy, Judy Canova, Andy Devine, Sherry Jackson, Buster Keaton, Finlay Currie, Josephine Hutchinson, Parley Baer, John Carradine, Royal Dano, Sterling Holloway, Harry Dean Stanton; **D:** Michael Curtiz. **VHS, Beta $19.98** *MGM, FCT* 🐾🐾½

The Adventures of Huckleberry
Finn The classic adventure by Mark Twain of an orphan boy and a runaway slave done again as a TV movie and starring F-Troop. Lacks the production values of earlier versions.
1978 100m/C Forrest Tucker, Larry Storch, Kurt Ida, Mike Mazurki, Brock Peters; **D:** Jack B. Hively. **VHS, Beta** *NO* 🐾🐾

The Adventures of Huckleberry
Finn An adaptation of the Mark Twain story about the adventures encountered by Huckleberry Finn and a runaway slave as they travel down the Mississippi River. Top-notch cast makes this an entertaining version. Originally made for television in a much longer version for PBS's "American Playhouse."
1985 121m/C Sada Thompson, Lillian Gish, Richard Kiley, Jim Dale, Barnard Hughes, Patrick Day, Frederic Forrest, Geraldine Page, Butterfly McQueen, Samm-Art Williams; **D:** Peter Hunt. **VHS, Beta $19.95** *MCA* 🐾🐾½

The Adventures of Ichabod and
Mr. Toad Disney's wonderfully animated versions of Kenneth Grahame's "The Wind in the Willows" and "The Legend of Sleepy Hollow" by Washington Irving. Rathbone narrates the story of Mr. Toad, who suffers from arrogance and eventually must defend himself in court after being charged with driving a stolen vehicle (Disney did take liberties with the story). Crosby provides all the voices for "Ichabod," which features one of the all-time great animated sequences— Ichabod riding in a frenzy through the forest while being pursued by the headless horseman. A treat for all ages.
1949 68m/C D: Clyde Geronomi, James Algar; **V:** Jack Kinney, Bing Crosby. **VHS** *DIS, WTA* 🐾🐾🐾½

Adventures of Kit Carson
Television western, which ran from 1951-1955, set in the 1880s about the famed frontiersman who kept the peace with the help of Mexican sidekick El Toro. Two episodes per tape.
1951 50m/C Bill Williams, John Hamilton, Bill Diamond. **VHS, Beta $19.99** *MOV, MVC* 🐾🐾🐾

The Adventures of Marco Polo
Lavish Hollywood production based on the exploits of 13th-century Venetian explorer Marco Polo (Cooper). He becomes the first white man to record his visit to the Eastern court of Kublai Khan, where he falls for a beautiful princess also desired by the evil Rathbone. Lots of action, though its hard to picture the laconic Cooper in the title role.
1938 100m/B Gary Cooper, Sigrid Gurie, Basil Rathbone, Ernest Truex, George Barbier, Binnie Barnes, Alan Hale, H.B. Warner; **D:** Archie Mayo; **M:** Robert Sherwood. **VHS $19.98** *FCT* 🐾🐾½

The Adventures of Mark Twain
March stars as Mark Twain, the nom de plume of Samuel Clemens, the beloved humorist and writer. His travels and adventures along the Mississippi and on to the California gold rush would later result in the books and stories which would make him so well-known. March attains a quiet nobility as he goes from young man to old sage, along with Smith, who plays Olivia, Twain's beloved wife.
1944 130m/B Fredric March, Alexis Smith, Donald Crisp, Alan Hale, Sir C. Aubrey Smith, John Carradine, William Henry, Robert Barratt, Walter Hampden, Percy Kilbride; **D:** Irving Rapper; **W:** Alan LeMay, Harry Chandlee. **VHS, Beta $19.98** *MGM, FCT, BTV* 🐾🐾🐾

The Adventures of Mark Twain A
clay-animated fantasy based on, and radically departing from, the life and work of Mark Twain. Story begins with Twain flying into outer space in a blimp with stowaways Huck Finn, Tom Sawyer and Becky Thatcher and takes off from there. Above average entertainment for kids and their folks. *AKA:* Mark Twain.
1985 (G) 86m/C D: Will Vinton; **W:** Susan Shadburne; **V:** James Whitmore, Chris Ritchie, Gary Krug, Michele Mariana. **VHS, Beta** *BAR* 🐾🐾🐾

The Adventures of Milo & Otis
Delightful Japanese children's film about a farm-dwelling dog and cat and their odyssey after the cat is accidentally swept away on a river. Notable since no humans appear in the film. A record-breaking success in its homeland. Well received by U.S. children. Narrated by Moore. *AKA:* Koneko Monogatari; The Adventures of Chatran.
1989 (G) 89m/C JP D: Masanori Hata; **W:** Mark Saltzman; **M:** Michael Boddicker. **VHS, Beta $19.95** *COL, RDG, HMV* 🐾🐾🐾

The Adventures of Nellie Bly
Made for television "Classics Illustrated" story of Nellie Bly, a strong-willed female reporter doing her best to expose wrongdoings in the late 19th century. A decent performance by Purl is overshadowed by the general lack of direction.
1981 100m/C Linda Purl, Gene Barry, John Randolph, Raymond Buktenica, J.D. Cannon, Elayne Heilveil, Cliff Osmond; **D:** Henning Schellerup. **VHS, Beta** *NO* 🐾

Adventures of Ozzie & Harriet
Each volume in this 12-set series contains 4 episodes of the Nelsons' hit TV show from 1953-1964. Vol. 1 features 17-year-old Mary Tyler Moore doing the commercials. Vol. 2 features Mamie Van Doren as the housemother of Ricky's fraternity (some housemother!). The program was the prototype of family sitcoms. Original commercials included. Tapes are available for purchase individually.
195? 56m/B Ozzie Nelson, Harriet Hilliard Nelson, Ricky Nelson, David Nelson; **D:** Ozzie Nelson. **VHS $19.99** *MOV* 🐾

The Adventures of Picasso A
Swedish satire on the life of Picasso, dubbed in English. Don't look for art or facts here, or, for that matter, many laughs.
1980 88m/C SW Gosta Ekman, Lena Nyman, Hans Alfredson, Margareta Krook, Bernard Cribbins, Wilfrid Brambell; **D:** Tage Danielsson. **VHS, Beta** *NO* 🐾

Adventures of Red Ryder The thrills
of the rugged West are presented in this twelve-episode serial. Based on the then-famous comic strip character.
1940 240m/B Donald (Don "Red") Barry, Noah Beery Sr.; **D:** William Witney. **VHS, Beta $80.00** *VCN, MLB* 🐾

The Adventures of Rex & Rinty
An adventure serial in 12 chapters, featuring Rin-Tin-Tin, Jr.
1935 156m/B Kane Richmond, Harry Woods, Smiley Burnette; **D:** Ford Beebe, B. Reeves Eason. **VHS, Beta $49.95** *NOS, VCN, DVT* 🐾🐾

The Adventures of Rin Tin Tin
Chronicles the adventures of that crime-fighting dog, Rin-Tin-Tin.
1947 65m/B Rin Tin Tin, Robert (Bobby) Blake. **VHS $9.99** *CCB* 🐾🐾½

The Adventures of Robin Hood
Rollicking Technicolor tale of the legendary outlaw, regarded as the swashbuckler standard-bearer. The justice-minded Saxon knight battles the Normans, outwits evil Prince John, and gallantly romances Maid Marian. Grand castle sets and lush forest photography display ample evidence of the huge (in 1938) budget of $2 million plus. Just entering his prime, Flynn enthusiastically performed most of his own stunts, including intricate sword play and advanced tree and wall climbing. His Robin brims with charm and bravura, the enthusiastic protector of poor Saxons everywhere and the undeclared king of Sherwood forest. The rest of the cast likewise attacks with zest: de Havilland, a cold but eventually sympathetic Maid Marian; Rains' dastardly Prince John (the predecessor to Alan Rickman's over-the-top spin as the Sheriff in Costner's remake); and Rathbone's conniving Sir Guy to Robin's band of very merry men. Based on various Robin Hood legends as well as Sir Walter Scott's "Ivanhoe" and the opera "Robin Hood" by De Koven-Smith. Also available in letter-box format.
1938 102m/C Errol Flynn, Olivia de Havilland, Basil Rathbone, Alan Hale, Una O'Connor, Claude Rains, Patric Knowles, Eugene Pallette, Herbert Mundin, Melville Cooper, Ian Hunter, Montagu Love; **D:** Michael Curtiz; **W:** Norman Reilly, Seton I. Miller; **M:** Erich Wolfgang Korngold. Academy Awards '38: Best Film Editing, Best Interior Decoration, Best Original Score; Nominations: Best Picture. **VHS, Beta $19.98** *MGM, FOX, CRC* 🐾🐾🐾🐾

The Adventures of Robin Hood
Filmed on location in England and starring Greene as the legendary outlaw/hero, with Pleasance as the evil Prince John. Two episodes per tape. Volume 1 features "The Highlander" and "Tables Turned." Additional episodes are available.
1955 60m/C Richard Greene, Donald Pleasence. VHS, Beta $19.95 *MVC, MOV* 🎬🎬🎬🎬

The Adventures of Sadie Collins is stranded on a desert island with three men, two of whom continuously chase her around. Naturally, she falls for the guy who ignores her. Obvious sex comedy which plays on Collins' scantily-clad physical assets. Based on the novel "The Cautious Amorist" by Norman Lindsay. *AKA:* Our Girl Friday.
1955 87m/C *GB* Joan Collins, George Cole, Kenneth More, Robertson Hare, Hermione Gingold, Walter Fitzgerald; *D:* Noel Langley; *W:* Noel Langley. VHS *NO* 🎬🎬½

The Adventures of Sherlock Holmes The immortal Sherlock Holmes and his assistant Dr. Watson conflict with Scotland Yard as they both race to stop arch-criminal Professor Moriarty. The Yard is put to shame as Holmes, a mere amateur sleuth, uses his brilliant deductive reasoning to save the damsel in distress and to stop Moriarty from stealing the Crown Jewels. Second in the series and the last of Rathbone's appearances as the brilliant detective. *AKA:* Sherlock Holmes.
1939 83m/B Basil Rathbone, Nigel Bruce, Ida Lupino, George Zucco, E.E. Clive, Mary Gordon; *D:* Alfred Werker. VHS, Beta $14.95 *FOX* 🎬🎬½

The Adventures of Sherlock Holmes: Hound of the Baskervilles Holmes tackles the mysterious and long-lived curse of the Baskervilles. Made for British television. Fine acting, detailed production. A pleasure.
1989 120m/C *GB* Jeremy Brett, Edward Hardwicke. VHS $39.95 *MPI* 🎬🎬½

The Adventures of Sherlock Holmes' Smarter Brother The unknown brother of the famous Sherlock Holmes takes on some of his brother's more disposable excess cases and makes some hilarious moves. Moments of engaging farce borrowed from the Mel Brooks school of parody (and parts of the Brooks ensemble as well).
1978 (PG) 91m/C Gene Wilder, Madeline Kahn, Marty Feldman, Dom DeLuise, Leo McKern, Roy Kinnear, John Le Mesurier, Douglas Wilmer, Thorley Walters; *D:* Gene Wilder; *W:* Gene Wilder. VHS, Beta *FOX* 🎬🎬🎬

Adventures of Smilin' Jack WWII flying ace Smilin' Jack Martin comes to life in this action-packed serial. Character from the Zack Moseley comic strip about air force fighting over China.
1943 90m/B Tom Brown, Sidney Toler; *D:* Ray Taylor. VHS, Beta $26.95 *SNC, NOS, VAN* 🎬🎬🎬

The Adventures of Tartu A British secret agent, sent to blow up a Nazi poison gas factory in Czechoslovakia, poses as a Romanian. One of Donat's lesser films, in the style of "The 39 Steps." *AKA:* Tartu.
1943 103m/C *GB* Robert Donat, Valerie Hobson, Glynis Johns; *D:* Harold Bucquet. VHS, Beta $19.95 *HHT, VCN, TIM* 🎬🎬½

The Adventures of Tarzan The screen's first Tarzan in an exciting jungle thriller. Silent.
1921 153m/B Elmo Lincoln. VHS, Beta $27.95 *VYY, GVV* 🎬🎬

The Adventures of the Flying Cadets Early aerial war adventure serial in thirteen complete chapters.
1944 169m/B Johnny Downs, Regis Toomey; *D:* Ray Taylor, Lewis D. Collins. VHS, Beta $39.95 *VYY, VCN, NOS* 🎬½

The Adventures of the Little Rascals Six classic "Our Gang" comedies featuring the Little Rascals. Each short is presented in its original form.
193? 100m/B VHS *REP* 🎬½

The Adventures of the Masked Phantom The adventures of the Masked Phantom.
1938 56m/B Monte Rawlins, Betty Burgess, Larry Mason, Sonny Lamont, Jack Ingram; *D:* Charles Abbott. VHS, Beta $19.95 *NOS, VYY, RXM* 🎬½

The Adventures of the Wilderness Family The story of a modern-day pioneer family who becomes bored with the troubles of city life and heads for life in the wilderness. There, they find trouble in paradise. Family-oriented adventure offering pleasant scenery. Followed by "The Wilderness Family, Part 2."
1976 (G) 100m/C Robert F. Logan, Susan Damante Shaw; *D:* Stewart Raffill; *W:* Stewart Raffill. VHS, Beta $9.98 *MED, VTR* 🎬🎬

The Adventures of Tom Sawyer The vintage Hollywood adaptation of the Mark Twain classic, with art direction by William Cameron Menzies. Not a major effort from the Selznick studio, but quite detailed and the best Tom so far.
1938 91m/C Tommy Kelly, Walter Brennan, Victor Jory, May Robson, Victor Kilian, Jackie Moran, Donald Meek, Anne Gillis, Marcia Mae Jones, Clara Blandick, Margaret Hamilton; *D:* Norman Taurog; *M:* Max Steiner. VHS, Beta $14.98 *FOX, FCT, MLB* 🎬🎬🎬

The Adventures of Tom Sawyer Tom Sawyer is a mischievous Missouri boy who gets into all kinds of trouble in this white-washed, made for TV adaptation of the Mark Twain classic.
1973 76m/C Jane Wyatt, Buddy Ebsen, Vic Morrow, Jim McGiver, Josh Albee, Jeff Tyler. VHS, Beta $39.95 *MCA* 🎬🎬

The Adventurous Knights An athlete learns he is the heir to a Transylvanian throne.
1935 60m/B David Sharpe, Mary Kornman, Mickey Daniels, Gertrude Messinger; *D:* Edward Roberts. VHS, Beta *NO* Woof!

The Adversary A young man must quit college because of his father's death. He struggles to find employment in Calcutta but his hardships are magnified by the impersonal society. In Bengali with English subtitles. *AKA:* Pratidwandi.
1971 110m/C *IN D:* Satyajit Ray; *W:* Satyajit Ray. VHS $39.95 *FCT* 🎬🎬½

Advise and Consent An interesting political melodrama with a fascinating cast, based upon Allen Drury's novel. The President chooses a candidate for the Secretary of State position which divides the Senate and causes the suicide of a senator. Controversial in its time, though somewhat turgid today. Laughton's last film.
1962 139m/C Don Murray, Charles Laughton, Henry Fonda, Walter Pidgeon, Lew Ayres, Burgess Meredith, Gene Tierney, Franchot Tone, Paul Ford, George Grizzard, Betty White, Peter Lawford, Edward Andrews; *D:* Otto Preminger; *W:* Wendell Mayes. VHS, Beta $19.98 *WAR, KAR, VTR* 🎬🎬🎬

Aelita: Queen of Mars Though the title had blockbuster potential, "Aelita" is a little-known silent Soviet sci-fi flick destined to remain little known. After building a rocket to fly to Mars, a Russian engineer finds its no Martian holiday on the fourth planet from the sun, with the Martians in the midst of a revolution. Silent, with a piano score.
1924 113m/B *RU D:* Iakov Protazanov. VHS $29.95 *KIV, FCT, SNC* 🎬🎬

The Affair Songwriter/polio victim Wood falls in love for the first time with attorney Wagner. Delicate situation handled well by a fine cast in this television movie.
1973 74m/C Natalie Wood, Robert Wagner, Bruce Davison, Kent Smith, Frances Reid, Pat Harrington; *D:* Gilbert Cates. VHS, Beta *NO* 🎬🎬🎬

An Affair in Mind British television movie about a professional writer who falls in love with a beautiful woman who tries to convince him to assist her in murderering her husband.
1989 88m/C *GB* Amanda Donohoe, Stephen Dillon, Matthew Marsh, Kean-Laurent Cochot; *D:* Michael Baker. VHS, Beta $19.98 *FOX* 🎬🎬

Affair in Trinidad Fun in the tropics as nightclub singer Hayworth enlists the help of brother-in-law Ford to find her husband's murderer. The trail leads to international thieves and espionage in a romantic thriller that reunites the stars of "Gilda." Hayworth sings (with Jo Ann Greer's voice) "I've Been Kissed Before."
1952 98m/B Rita Hayworth, Glenn Ford, Alexander Scourby, Torin Thatcher, Valerie Bettis, Steve Geray; *D:* Vincent Sherman. VHS $19.95 *COL, CCB* 🎬🎬

The Affair of the Pink Pearl The husband-and-wife private investigation team of Tommy and Tuppence must find within 24 hours the culprit who stole a valuable pink pearl. Based on the Agatha Christie series of short stories. Made for British television.
1984 60m/C James Warwick, Francesca Annis. VHS, Beta $14.95 *TPV* 🎬½

An Affair to Remember McCarey remakes his own "Love Affair," with less success. A nightclub singer and wealthy bachelor discover love on an ocean liner, and agree to meet six months later on top of the Empire State Building in NYC to see if their feelings are the same. Major weepie requires lots of tissues and was gathering dust on store shelves until "Sleepless in Seattle" used it as a plot device. Yet another remake is expected late in 1994 starring Warren Beatty and Annette Bening.
1957 115m/C Cary Grant, Deborah Kerr, Richard Denning, Cathleen Nesbitt, Neva Patterson, Robert Q. Lewis, Fortuna Bonanova, Matt Moore, Nora Marlowe, Sarah Selby; *D:* Leo McCarey; *W:* Leo McCarey, Delmer Daves; *M:* Hugo Friedhofer. VHS, Beta $19.98 *FOX* 🎬🎬½

The Affairs of Annabel The first of the popular series of Annabel pictures Lucy made in the late 1930s. Appealing adolescent is zoomed to movie stardom by her press agent's stunts. A behind-the-scenes satire on Hollywood, stars, and agents.
1938 68m/B Lucille Ball, Jack Oakie, Ruth Donnelly, Fritz Feld, Bradley Page; *D:* Ben Stoloff. VHS, Beta $29.95 *CCB, RKO, IME* 🎬🎬½

The Affairs of Dobie Gillis Light musical-comedy about a group of college kids and their carefree antics. Complete with big-band tunes, dance numbers, and plenty of collegiate shenanigans, this '50s classic inspired a hit TV series, "The Many Loves of Dobie Gillis." ♫I'm Through with Love; All I Do Is Dream of You; You Can't Do Wrong

Doing Right; Those Endearing Young Charms.
1953 72m/B Debbie Reynolds, Bobby Van, Barbara Ruick, Bob Fosse, Lurene Tuttle, Hans Conried, Charles Lane; **D:** Don Weis; **W:** Max Shulman. VHS **$19.98** MGM ⅊⅊½

Afraid of the Dark Convoluted psycho-thriller from a child's point of view. Young Lucas is fearful for his blind mother. It seems a vicious slasher has been attacking blind women and Lucas' father, a policeman, has yet to apprehend the criminal. But...Lucas it seems has a problem with reality. With his fantasies and realities mixed, all the people in his life also play entirely different roles. Characters are so detached and unreal that a viewer is prevented from a clear understanding of anything that may, or may not, be going on. Directorial debut of Peploe.
1992 (R) 91m/C Ben Keyworth, James Fox, Fanny Ardant, Paul McGann, Clare Holman, Robert Stephens; **D:** Mark Peploe. VHS **$89.95** COL, NLC ⅊⅊

Africa Screams Abbott and Costello go on an African safari in possession of a secret map. Unheralded independent A&C film is actually quite good in the stupid vein, with lots of jungle slapstick, generally good production values and a supporting cast of familiar comedy faces.
1949 79m/B Lou Costello, Bud Abbott, Shemp Howard, Hillary Brooke, Joe Besser, Clyde Beatty; **D:** Charles T. Barton. VHS, Beta **$9.95** KAR, MRV, CNG ⅊⅊½

Africa Texas Style An East African rancher hires an American cowboy and his Navajo sidekick to help run his wild game ranch. Decent family adventure which served as the pilot for the short-lived TV series "Cowboy in Africa." Features lots of wildlife footage and a cameo appearance by Hayley Mills.
1967 109m/C Hugh O'Brian, John Mills, Nigel Green, Tom Nardini; **Cameos:** Hayley Mills; **D:** Andrew Marton; **M:** Malcolm Arnold. VHS **$19.98** REP ⅊⅊

An African Dream A period tale about a black man and a white woman fighting against repression in South Africa.
1990 (PG) 94m/C Kitty Aldridge, John Kani, Dominic Jephcott, John Carson, Richard Haines, Joy Stewart Spence; **D:** John Smallcombe. VHS, Beta **$14.95** HMD, IME, FCT ⅊½

African Journey A moving, cross-cultural drama of friendship. A young black American goes to Africa for the summer to be with his divorced father who is working in the diamond mines. There he meets a young black African like himself; they overcome cultural clashes and learn respect for one another. Beautiful scenery, filmed in Africa. Part of the "Wonderworks" series.
1989 174m/C Jason Blicker, Pedzisai Sithole. VHS **$79.95** PME, HMV, BTV ⅊½

The African Queen After bible-thumping spinster Hepburn's missionary brother is killed in WWI Africa, hard-drinking, dissolute steamer captain Bogart offers her safe passage. Not satisfied with sanctuary, she persuades him to destroy a German gunboat blocking the British advance. The two spend most of their time battling aquatic obstacles and each other, rather than the Germans. Time alone on a African river turns mistrust and aversion to love, a transition effectively counterpointed by the continuing suspense of their daring mission. Classic war of the sexes script adapted from C.S. Forester's novel makes wonderful use of natural dialogue and humor. Shot on location in Africa.

1951 105m/C Humphrey Bogart, Katharine Hepburn, Robert Morley, Theodore Bikel, Peter Bull, Walter Gotell; **D:** John Huston; **W:** John Huston, James Agee. Academy Awards '51: Best Actor (Bogart); Nominations: Best Actress (Hepburn), Best Director (Huston), Best Screenplay. VHS, Beta **$59.98** FOX, FCT, TLF ⅊⅊⅊⅊

African Rage Little known release about an aging male nurse (yes, Quinn) who discovers he's dying of an incurable disease. With nothing left to lose, he plans the kidnapping of an African leader, hoping that the ransom will support his family. Meanwhile, another man is plotting the same leader's death. Decent performances help move along the improbable plot. **AKA:** Tigers Don't Cry; The Long Shot; Target of an Assassin; Fatal Assassin.
1978 90m/C SA Anthony Quinn, John Phillip Law, Simon Sabela, Ken Gampu, Marius Weyers, Sandra Prinsloo; **D:** Peter Collinson. VHS, Beta **$9.95** MPI ⅊⅊

Afrita Hanen A rare Egyptian fantasy starring former Mid-Eastern actor, Farrid El Atrache. In Arabic with titles.
1947 97m/B Farrid El Atrache. VHS, Beta **$39.95** FCT ⅊⅊⅊

After Dark, My Sweet A troubled young man in search of a little truth ends up entangled in a kidnapping scheme. Muddled direction is overcome by above average performances and gritty realism. Based on the novel by Jim Thompson.
1990 (R) 114m/C Jason Patric, Rachel Ward, Bruce Dern, George Dickerson, James Cotton, Corey Carrier, Rocky Giordani; **D:** James Foley; **W:** Robert Redlin, James Foley; **M:** Maurice Jarre. VHS **$89.95** LIV ⅊⅊⅊

After Darkness Slow-moving psycho-suspenser about a man obsessed with trying to remedy his twin brother's schizophrenia.
1985 104m/C SI GB John Hurt, Julian Sands, Victoria Abril, Pamela Salem; **D:** Dominique Othenin-Girard. VHS, Beta **$19.95** CEL ⅊

After Hours An absurd, edgy black comedy that's filled with novel twists and turns and often more disturbing than funny. An isolated uptown New York yuppie (Dunne) takes a late night stroll downtown and meets a sexy woman in an all-night coffee shop. From there he wanders through a series of threatening and surreal misadventures, leading to his pursuit by a vigilante mob stirred by ice cream dealer O'Hara. Something like "Blue Velvet" with more Catholicism and farce. Or similar to "Something Wild" without the high school reunion. Great cameos from the large supporting cast, including Cheech and Chong as burglars. A dark view of a small hell-hole in the Big Apple.
1985 (R) 97m/C Griffin Dunne, Rosanna Arquette, John Heard, Teri Garr, Catherine O'Hara, Verna Bloom, Linda Fiorentino, Dick Miller, Bronson Pinchot; **Cameos:** Richard "Cheech" Marin, Thomas Chong; **D:** Martin Scorsese. VHS, Beta **$19.98** WAR, KIV ⅊⅊⅊½

After Julius Twenty years after Julius Grace's death, his memory still hovers over his wife's and daughters' lives. British soap opera moves with glacier-like speed. Adapted from the book by Elizabeth Jane Howard.
1978 150m/C GB Faith Brook, John Carson, Cyd Hayman; **D:** John Glenister. VHS NO ⅊⅊

After Midnight An aspiring playwright tries to get his work produced, only to meet with dead ends. Eventually, he hooks up with a talented young actress with whom he finds romance and success. **AKA:** I Have Lived.
1933 69m/B Alan Dinehart, Anita Page, Allen Vincent, Greta Gustafson; **D:** Richard Thorpe. VHS, Beta **$16.95** SNC ⅊

After Midnight Suspended in a central story about an unorthodox professor who preys upon the deepest fears of his students, a trio of terror tales come to life. From the writers of "The Fly II" and "Nightmare on Elm Street, Part IV." Some chills, few thrills.
1989 90m/C Marg Helgenberger, Marc McClure, Alan Rosenberg, Pamela Segall, Nadine Van Der Velde, Ramy Zada, Jillian McWhirter, Billy Ray Sharkey; **D:** Jim Wheat. VHS, Beta **$89.98** FOX, MGM ⅊⅊

After Pilkington British television thriller about an uptight Oxford professor who runs into his bewitching childhood sweetheart after many years. She persuades him to help search for a missing archaeologist.
1988 100m/C GB Bob Peck, Miranda Richardson, Barry Foster; **D:** Christopher Morahan. VHS, Beta **$19.98** FOX ⅊⅊

After the Fall of New York Dim-witted post-apocalyptic tale set in New York after the fall of the "Big Bomb." A man, driven to search for the last normal woman, has reason to believe she is frozen alive and kept in the heart of the city. His mission: locate her, thaw her, engage in extremely limited foreplay with her, and repopulate the planet. A poorly dubbed dating allegory.
1985 (R) 95m/C IT FR Michael Sopkiw, Valentine Monnier, Anna Kanakis, Roman Geer, Edmund Purdom, George Eastman; **D:** Martin Dolman. VHS, Beta **$79.98** VES, LIV Woof!

After the Fall of Saigon Soldiers in Vietnam go on a killing rampage. Dubbed; country of origin isn't known. **AKA:** Raiders of the Doomed Kingdom.
1988 100m/C Danny Aswatep, Peter Ramwa, Rayak Ramnate, Krao Spartacus. VHS, Beta NO ⅊

After the Fox Sellers is a con artist posing as a film director to carry out a bizarre plan to steal gold from Rome. Features occasional backhand slaps at Hollywood, with Mature turning in a memorable performance as the has-been actor starring in Sellers' movie. Though the screenplay was co-written by Neil Simon, the laughs are marginal. **AKA:** Caccia alla Volpe.
1966 103m/C GB IT Peter Sellers, Victor Mature, Martin Balsam, Britt Ekland; **D:** Vittorio De Sica; **W:** Neil Simon; **M:** Burt Bacharach. VHS, Beta **$14.95** MGM, FOX ⅊⅊

After the Promise During the Depression, a poor carpenter tries to regain custody of his four sons following the death of his wife. Maudlin television melodrama based on a true story.
1987 100m/C Mark Harmon, Diana Scarwid, Rosemary Dunsmore, Donnelly Rhodes, Mark Hildreth, Trey Ames, Richard Billingsley; **D:** David Greene; **M:** Ralph Burns. VHS **$19.95** STE, NWV ⅊⅊

After the Rehearsal Two actresses, one young, the other at the end of her career, challenge their director with love and abuse. Each questions his right to use them on stage and off. A thoughtful discussion of the meaning and reason for art originally made for Swedish television. Swedish with English subtitles.
1984 (R) 72m/C SW Erland Josephson, Ingrid Thulin, Lena Olin; **D:** Ingmar Bergman; **W:** Ingmar Bergman. VHS, Beta **$59.98** COL, ING ⅊⅊⅊

After the Revolution A struggling novelist decides to write his next book from the viewpoint of his cat. In Hungarian with English subtitles.
1990 82m/C HU **D:** Andras Szirtes. VHS **$59.95** FCT ⅊⅊

After the Shock Documentary-like dramatization of the San Francisco-Oakland earthquake of October, 1989 and, of course, its aftermath. Incorporates actual footage of the disaster. Made for cable.
1990 (PG) 92m/C Yaphet Kotto, Rue McClanahan, Jack Scalia, Scott Valentine; *D:* Gary Sherman; *W:* Gary Sherman. VHS, Beta $79.95 *PAR* ✶✶

After the Thin Man Second in a series of six "Thin Man" films, this one finds Nick, Nora and Asta, the lovable terrier, seeking out a murderer from Nora's own blue-blooded relatives. Fast-paced mystery with a witty script and the popular Powell/Loy charm. Sequel to "The Thin Man," followed by "Another Thin Man."
1936 113m/B William Powell, Myrna Loy, James Stewart, Elissa Landi, Joseph Calleia, Jessie Ralph, Alan Marshal; *D:* Woodbridge S. Van Dyke. VHS, Beta $19.98 *MGM* ✶✶✶

Afterburn When Ted, her Air Force pilot husband, is killed in a crash of his F-16 fighter, Janet Harduvel learns the official explanation is pilot error. Convinced that something was wrong with his plane, Janet sets out to investigate, and eventually sue, military contractor General Dynamics. Dern turns in a great performance as the tough widow determined to clear her husband's name. Based on a true story; made for cable television.
1992 (R) 103m/C Laura Dern, Robert Loggia, Vincent Spano, Michael Rooker, Andy Romano; *D:* Robert Markowitz. VHS $89.99 *HBO, FCT* ✶✶✶

Aftermath Three astronauts return to Earth and are shocked to discover that the planet has been ravaged by a nuclear war. Quickly they make new plans.
1985 96m/C Steve Barnett, Larry Latham; *D:* Ted V. Mikels. VHS, Beta $9.99 *PSM* ✶½

Aftershock A beautiful alien and a mysterious stranger battle the Earth's repressive, evil government.
1988 (R) 90m/C Jay Roberts Jr., Elizabeth Kaitan, Chris Mitchum, Richard Lynch, John Saxon, Russ Tamblyn, Michael Berryman, Chris De Rose, Chuck Jeffreys; *D:* Frank Harris. VHS, Beta $79.95 *PSM* ✶½

Afterward Made-for-British-television horror story about a family that moves into a supposedly haunted house with deadly results.
1985 60m/C GB Michael J. Shannon, Kay Harper, John Grillo. VHS, Beta $59.95 *PSM* ✶

Against A Crooked Sky A young boy sets out with an elderly trapper to find his sister, who was captured by the Indians. Similiar story to "The Searchers," but no masterpiece.
1975 (G) 89m/C Richard Boone, Stewart Peterson, Clint Ritchie, Geoffrey Land, Jewel Blanch; *D:* Earl Bellamy. VHS, Beta $14.98 *LIV, VES* ✶✶

Against All Flags An enjoyable Flynn swashbuckler about a British soldier slashing his way through the Spanish fleet at the turn of the 18th century. Though the story has been told before, tight direction and good performances win out. O'Hara is a tarty eyeful as a hot-tempered pirate moll.
1952 81m/C Errol Flynn, Maureen O'Hara, Anthony Quinn, Mildred Natwick; *D:* George Sherman. VHS, Beta $14.95 *BAR, MCA* ✶✶✶

Against All Odds An interesting love triangle evolves when an ex-football player, played by Bridges, travels to Mexico to find his good friend's girlfriend. Contains complicated plot, numerous double crosses, sensual love scenes, and a chase scene along

Sunset Boulevard. As the good friend sans conscience, Woods stars. A remake of 1947's "Out of the Past."
1984 (R) 122m/C Jeff Bridges, Rachel Ward, James Woods, Alex Karras, Jane Greer, Richard Widmark, Dorian Harewood, Swoosie Kurtz, Bill McKinney, Saul Rubinek; *D:* Taylor Hackford; *M:* Michel Colombier, Larry Carlton. VHS, Beta, 8mm $12.95 *COL* ✶✶½

Against the Drunken Cat Paws A blind young martial arts student seeks to regain her sight and avenge the death of her father.
1975 94m/C Chia Ling, Ou-Yang Ksiek. VHS, Beta $39.95 *UNI* ✶

Against the Wind A motley crew is trained for a mission into Nazi Germany to blow up records and rescue a prisoner. The first half of the film focuses on the group's training, but despite its intensity they win only a pyrrhic victory. A well-done production with solid performances from the cast.
1948 96m/B Robert Beatty, Jack Warner, Simone Signoret, Gordon Jackson, Paul Dupuis, Peter Illing; *D:* Charles Crichton. VHS $19.95 *NOS, VEC* ✶✶½

Agatha A speculative period drama about Agatha Christie's still unexplained disappearance in 1926, and a fictional American reporter's efforts to find her. Beautiful but lackluster mystery. Unfortunately, Hoffman and Redgrave generate few sparks.
1979 (PG) 98m/C Dustin Hoffman, Vanessa Redgrave, Timothy Dalton, Helen Morse, Tony Britton, Timothy West, Celia Gregory; *D:* Michael Apted. VHS, Beta $64.95 *WAR* ✶✶½

Age Isn't Everything An appalling clumsy comedy about a recent college graduate who abruptly becomes an old man while retaining his youthful exterior. He looks the same, but walks slowly and talks with a thick Yiddish accent, get it? The cast just marks time until an inexplicable ending. *AKA:* Life in the Food Chain.
1991 (R) 91m/C Jonathan Silverman, Robert Prosky, Rita Moreno, Paul Sorvino, Rita Karin, Robert Cicchini, Brian Williams, Dee Hoty; *Cameos:* Dr. Joyce Brothers, Bella Abzug; *W:* Douglas Katz. VHS $89.99 *VES* ✶

The Age of Innocence Magnificently lavish adaptation of Edith Wharton's novel of passion thwarted by convention is visually stunning, but don't expect action since these people kill with a word or gesture. Lead performances are strong though perhaps miscast, with Ryder an exception. Outwardly docile and conventional, she nevertheless holds on to her husband with steely manipulation. Woodward's narration of Wharton's observations helps sort out what goes on behind the proper facades. Although slow, see this one for the beautiful period authenticity, thanks to Scorsese, who obviously labored over the small details. He shows up as a photographer; his parents appear in a scene on a train.
1993 (PG) 138m/C Daniel Day-Lewis, Michelle Pfeiffer, Winona Ryder, Richard E. Grant, Alec McCowen, Miriam Margolyes, Sian Phillips, Geraldine Chaplin, Stuart Wilson, Mary Beth Hurt, Michael Gough, Alexis Smith, Jonathan Pryce, Robert Sean Leonard; *Cameos:* Martin Scorsese; *D:* Martin Scorsese; *W:* Jay Cocks, Martin Scorsese; *M:* Elmer Bernstein. Academy Awards '93: Best Costume Design; Nominations: Best Adapted Screenplay, Best Art Direction/Set Decoration, Best Supporting Actress (Ryder); Directors Guild of America Awards '93: Best Director (Scorsese); Golden Globe Awards '94: Best Actress—Drama (Pfeiffer), Best Director (Scorsese), Best Film—Drama; British Academy Awards '94: Best Supporting Actress (Margolyes); Golden Globe Awards '94: Best Supporting Actress (Ryder); National Board of

Review Awards '93: Best Director (Scorsese), Best Supporting Actress (Ryder). VHS, 8mm *COL* ✶✶✶

Age Old Friends Crusty octogenarian Cronyn must choose. His daughter (played by real-life offspring Tandy) wants him to move out of a retirement home and into her house. But he's struggling to keep neighbor and increasingly senile friend Gardenia from slipping into "zombieland." An emotional treat with two fine actors deploying dignity and wit in the battle against old age. Originally adapted for HBO from the Broadway play, "A Month of Sundays" by Bob Larbey.
1989 89m/C Vincent Gardenia, Hume Cronyn, Tandy Cronyn, Esther Rolle, Michelle Scarabelli; *D:* Allen Kroeker. VHS, Beta $79.99 *HBO* ✶✶✶½

The Agency An advertising agency attempts to manipulate public behavior and opinion through the use of subliminal advertising. A good premise is bogged down by a dull script and plodding performances by all concerned. Based on a Paul Gottlieb novel. *AKA:* Mind Games.
1981 (R) 94m/C *CA* Robert Mitchum, Lee Majors, Valerie Perrine, Saul Rubinek, Alexandra Stewart, George Kaczender; *D:* George Kaczender; *M:* Lewis Furey. VHS, Beta $69.95 *VES, MTX, VTR* ✶✶

Agent on Ice Hockey team is stalked by lawyers. No, wait. An ex-CIA agent is stalked for cover-up purposes by the agency and the mob. One slippery fellow.
1986 (R) 96m/C Tom Ormeny, Clifford David, Louis Pastore, Matt Craven; *D:* Clark Worswick. VHS, Beta $19.95-*STE, NWV* ✶✶

Aggie Appleby, Maker of Men A wimpy society boy transforms himself into a tough guy, all for the love of a dame. Based on a play by Joseph O. Kesserling. Very slight comedy. *AKA:* Cupid in the Rough.
1933 73m/B Charles Farrell, Wynne Gibson, William Gargan, ZaSu Pitts; *D:* Mark Sandrich. VHS $19.98 *FCT* ✶½

Agnes of God Stage to screen translation of John Pielmeier's play loses something in the translation. Coarse chain-smoking psychiatrist Fonda is sent to a convent to investigate whether young nun Tilly is fit to stand trial. Seems that the nun may have given birth to and then strangled her baby, although she denies ever having sexual relations and knows nothing about an infant. Naive Tilly is frightened by probing Fonda, while worldly mother-superior Bancroft is distrusting. Melodramatic stew of Catholicism, religious fervor, and science features generally good performances, although Fonda often seems to be acting (maybe it's the cigarettes).
1985 (PG-13) 99m/C Jane Fonda, Anne Bancroft, Meg Tilly, Anne Pitoniak, Winston Reckert, Gratien Gelinas; *D:* Norman Jewison; *W:* John Pielmeier; *M:* Georges Delerue. Academy Awards '85 Nominations: Best Actress (Bancroft), Best Supporting Actress (Tilly), Best Original Score; Golden Globe Awards '86: Best Supporting Actress (Tilly). VHS, Beta $12.95 *COL* ✶✶

The Agony and the Ecstasy Big-budget (for 1965 anyway at $12 million) adaptation of the Irving Stone book recounts the conflict between Michelangelo and Pope Julius II after His Holiness directs the artist to paint the Sistine Chapel. Follow the tortured artist through his unpredictable creative process and the hours (it seems literal due to movie length) of painting flat on his back. Heston exudes quiet strength in his sincere interpretation of the genius artist, while Harrison has a fling as the Pope. Slow script is not up to the generally good performances.

Disappointing at the box office, but worth a look on the small screen for the sets alone. **1965 136m/C** Charlton Heston, Rex Harrison, Harry Andrews, Diane Cilento, Alberto Lupo, Adolfo Celi; **D:** Carol Reed; **W:** Philip Dunne; **M:** Jerry Goldsmith. **VHS, Beta $19.98** FOX, IGP 🎬🎬½

Agony of Love An unhappy homemaker rents a nearby apartment to live out her wildest fantasies and bring some excitement into her otherwise dull life. **1966 ?m/C VHS $20** SMW, TPV 🎬🎬½

Aguirre, the Wrath of God Herzog at his best, combining brilliant poetic images and an intense narrative dealing with power, irony, and death. Spanish conquistadors in 1590 search for the mythical city of gold in Peru. Instead, they descend into the hell of the jungle. Kinski is fabulous as Aquirre, succumbing to insanity while leading a continually diminishing crew in this compelling, extraordinary drama shot in the jungles of South America. Both English- and German-language versions available. **1972 94m/C** GE Klaus Kinski, Ruy Guerra, Del Negro, Helena Rojo, Cecilia Rivera, Peter Berling, Danny Ades; **D:** Werner Herzog; **W:** Werner Herzog. **VHS $59.95** NYF, APD, ING 🎬🎬🎬½

Ah, Wilderness! Delightful tale of a teen boy coming of age in small town America. Watch for the hilarious high school graduation scene. Based on the play by Eugene O'Neill. Remade in 1948 as "Summer Holiday," a musical with Mickey Rooney in the lead. **1935 101m/B** Wallace Beery, Lionel Barrymore, Aline MacMahon, Eric Linden, Cecilia Parker, Spring Byington, Mickey Rooney, Charley Grapewin, Frank Albertson; **D:** Clarence Brown. **VHS $19.98** MGM, BTV 🎬🎬🎬½

Ain't No Way Back Two hunters stumble upon a feudin' bunch of moonshiners and must leave their city ways behind if they plan to survive. **1989 90m/C VHS, Beta** NO 🎬

Air America It's the Vietnam War and the CIA is operating a secret drug smuggling operation in Southeast Asia to finance the effort. Flyboys Gibson and Downey drop opium and glib lines all over Laos. Big-budget Gibson vehicle with sufficient action but lacking much of a story, which was adapted from a book by Christopher Robbins. **1990 (R) 113m/C** Mel Gibson, Robert Downey Jr., Marshall Bell, Nancy Travis, David Marshall Grant, Tim Thomerson, Lane Smith; **D:** Roger Spottiswoode; **W:** Richard Rush. **VHS, Beta $19.95** LIV, IME 🎬🎬

Air Force One of the finest of the WWII movies, Hawks' exciting classic has worn well through the years, in spite of the Japanese propaganda. It follows the hazardous exploits of a Boeing B-17 bomber crew who fight over Pearl Harbor, Manila, and the Coral Sea. Extremely realistic dogfight sequences and powerful, introspective real guy interfacing by the ensemble cast are masterfully combined by Hawks. **1943 124m/B** John Garfield, John Ridgely, Gig Young, Arthur Kennedy, Charles Drake, Harry Carey Sr., George Tobias; **D:** Howard Hawks. Academy Awards '43: Best Film Editing; Nominations: Best Black and White Cinematography, Best Original Screenplay. **VHS** FOX 🎬🎬🎬½

Air Hawk Australian made for TV release details the adventures of an outback pilot involved with stolen diamonds. **1984 90m/C** AU Eric Oldfield, Louise Howitt, Ellie MacLure, David Robson, David Baker; **D:** David Baker. **VHS, Beta $59.95** VCD 🎬

Air Raid Wardens Laurel & Hardy play a couple of small-town failures who become the local air raid wardens during WWII. They even manage to make a mess of this but redeem themselves when they overhear a spy plot and save the town's munitions factory from a German spy ring. A so-so effort from the comic duo. **1943 67m/B** Stan Laurel, Oliver Hardy, Edgar Kennedy, Jacqueline White, Stephen McNally, Russell Hicks, Howard Freeman, Donald Meek, Henry O'Neill; **D:** Edward Sedgwick. **VHS $19.98** MGM 🎬🎬

The Air Up There Assistant basketball coach Jimmy Dolan (Bacon) heads to the African village of Winabi to recruit talented (and tall) Saleh (Maina) to play b-ball in the U.S. But Saleh is next in line to be the tribe's king and doesn't want to leave. Stupid American in foreign country learning from the natives story is lighthearted, but relies heavily on formula—and borders on the stereotypical, though climatic game is a lot of fun. **1994 (PG) 108m/C** Kevin Bacon, Charles Gitona Maina, Sean McCann, Dennis Patrick; **D:** Paul Michael Glaser; **W:** Max Apple; **M:** David Newman. **VHS** HPH 🎬🎬

Airborne Cool California rollerblade dude gets transplanted to Cincinnati for a school year, and has to prove himself when those good ol' midwestern boys come after him. Nothing short of a skate vehicle appealing largely, if not solely, to the high school contingent. **1993 (PG) 91m/C** Shane McDermott, Seth Green, Brittney Powell, Edie McClurg, Pat O'Brien; **D:** Rob Bowman; **W:** Bill Apablasa; **M:** Stewart Copeland. **VHS, Beta** WAR 🎬½

Airheads "Wayne's World" meets "Dog Day Afternoon." Silly farce has three metal heads (Buscemi, Fraser, Sadler) holding a radio station hostage in order to get their demo tape played. Events snowball and they receive instant fame. Cast and crew rich with subversive comedic talents, including Sandler and Farley from "Saturday Night Live." Soundtrack authenticity supplied by White Zombie and The Galatic Cowboys. **1994 (PG-13) ?m/C** Brendan Fraser, Steve Buscemi, Adam Sandler, Chris Farley, Michael McKean, Judd Nelson, Joe Mantegna, Michael Richards, Ernie Hudson, Amy Locane, Nina Siemaszko, John Melendez; **D:** Michael Lehmann; **W:** Rich Wilkes; **M:** Carter Burwell. **VHS** NYR 🎬🎬½

Airplane! Classic lampoon of disaster flicks is stupid but funny and launched a bevy wanna-be spoofs. A former pilot who's lost both his girl (she's the attendant) and his nerve takes over the controls of a jet when the crew is hit with food poisoning. The passengers become increasingly crazed and ground support more surreal as our hero struggles to land the plane. Clever, fast-paced, and very funny parody mangles every Hollywood cliche within reach. The gags are so furiously paced that when one bombs it's hardly noticeable. Launched Nielsen's second career as a comic actor. And it ain't over till it's over: don't miss the amusing final credits. Followed by "Airplane 2: The Sequel." **1980 (PG) 88m/C** Robert Hays, Julie Hagerty, Lloyd Bridges, Peter Graves, Robert Stack, Leslie Nielsen, Stephen Stucker, Ethel Merman; **Cameos:** Kareem Abdul-Jabbar, Barbara Billingsley; **D:** Jerry Zucker, Jim Abrahams, David Zucker; **W:** Jerry Zucker, Jim Abrahams, David Zucker; **M:** Elmer Bernstein. **VHS, Beta, 8mm $14.95** PAR 🎬🎬🎬½

Airplane 2: The Sequel Not a Zucker, Abrahams and Zucker effort, and sorely missing their slapstick and script finesse. The first passenger space shuttle has taken off for the moon and there's a mad bomber on board. Given the number of jokes mugging, it's more of a loveboat in space than a fitting sequel to "Airplane." Nonetheless, some funny laughs and gags. **1982 (PG) 84m/C** Robert Hays, Julie Hagerty, Lloyd Bridges, Raymond Burr, Peter Graves, William Shatner, Sonny Bono, Chuck Connors, Chad Everett, Stephen Stucker, Rip Torn, Ken Finkleman, Sandahl Bergman; **D:** Ken Finkleman; **M:** Elmer Bernstein. **VHS, Beta $14.95** PAR 🎬🎬

Airport Old-fashioned disaster thriller built around an all-star cast, fairly moronic script, and an unavoidable accident during the flight of a passenger airliner. A box-office hit that paved the way for many lesser disaster flicks (including its many sequels) detailing the reactions of the passengers and crew as they cope with impending doom. Considered to be the best of the "Airport" series; adapted from the Arthur Hailey novel. **1970 137m/C** Dean Martin, Burt Lancaster, Jean Seberg, Jacqueline Bisset, George Kennedy, Helen Hayes, Van Heflin, Maureen Stapleton, Barry Nelson, Lloyd Nolan; **D:** George Seaton; **W:** George Seaton. Academy Awards '70: Best Supporting Actress (Stapleton); Nominations: Best Adapted Screenplay, Best Art Direction/Set Decoration, Best Cinematography, Best Costume Design, Best Film Editing, Best Picture, Best Sound, Best Supporting Actress (Stapleton), Best Original Score; Golden Globe Awards '71: Best Supporting Actress (Stapleton). **VHS, Beta $14.98** MCA, BTV 🎬🎬🎬

Airport '75 After a mid-air collision, a jumbo 747 is left pilotless. Airline attendant Black must fly da plane. She does her cross-eyed best in this absurd sequel to "Airport" built around a lesser "all-star cast." Safe on the ground, Heston tries to talk the airline hostess/pilot into landing, while the impatient Kennedy continues to grouse as leader of the foam-ready ground crew. A slick, insincere attempt to find box office magic again (which unfortunately worked, leading to two more sequels). **1975 (PG) 107m/C** Charlton Heston, Karen Black, George Kennedy, Gloria Swanson, Helen Reddy, Sid Caesar, Efrem Zimbalist Jr., Susan Clark, Dana Andrews, Linda Blair, Myrna Loy; **D:** Jack Smight. **VHS, Beta $59.95** GKK 🎬🎬

Airport '77 Billionaire Stewart fills his converted passenger jet with priceless art and sets off to Palm Beach for a museum opening, joined by an uninvited gang of hijackers. Twist to this in-flight disaster is that the bad time in the air occurs underwater, a novel (and some might say, desperate) twist to the old panic in the plane we're all gonna die formula. With a cast of familiar faces, some of them stars and some of them just familiar faces, this is yet another sequel to "Airport" and another box-office success, leading to the last of the tired series in 1979. **1977 (PG) 114m/C** Jack Lemmon, James Stewart, Lee Grant, Brenda Vaccaro, Joseph Cotten, Olivia de Havilland, Darren McGavin, Christopher Lee, George Kennedy, Kathleen Quinlan; **D:** Jack Smight. **VHS, Beta $14.98** MCA 🎬🎬

Akermania, Vol. 1 This compilation of director Akerman's shorter works includes "I'm Hungry, I'm Cold," the story of two Belgian girls on the loose in Paris, and "Saute Ma Ville," Akerman's first film. Both are in French with English subtitles. Also included is "Hotel Monterey," a silent experimental film.

1992 89m/C *FR* Maria De Medeiros, Pascale Salkin, Chantal Akerman; *D:* Chantal Akerman. VHS $59.95 *WAC, ING* 🎬🎬

Akira Secret government experiments on children with ESP go awry, resulting in an atomic bomb drop on Tokyo. The city in turn builds itself up into a Megalopolis and the experiments continue. Animated; in Japanese with English subtitles or dubbed. **1989** 124m/C *JP D:* Katsuhiro Otomo. VHS $29.95 *WTA, STP, ING* 🎬🎬

Akira Kurosawa's Dreams An anthological lesson regarding the simultaneous loss of humanity and nature that threatens us all from the renowned Japanese director. Although the startling and memorable imagery is still present, Kurosawa's lessons are strangely trite and consequently lack the power that is normally associated with his work. Watch for Scorsese as Van Gogh. With English subtitles. *AKA:* Dreams. **1990** (PG) 120m/C *JP* Akira Terao, Mitsuko Baisho, Meiko Harada, Chishu Ryu, Hisashi Igawa, Mitsunori Isaki, Toshihiko Nakano, Yoshitaka Zushi, Toshie Negishi, Martin Scorsese; *D:* Akira Kurosawa; *W:* Akira Kurosawa; *M:* Shinichiro Ikebe. VHS $89.95 *ING, WAR, FCT* 🎬🎬½

Al Capone Film noir character study of one of the most colorful gangsters of the Roaring Twenties. Sort of an underworld "How to Succeed in Business." Steiger chews scenes and bullets as they fly by, providing the performance of his career. Plenty of gangland violence and mayhem and splendid cinematography keep the fast-paced period piece sailing. **1959** 104m/C Rod Steiger, Fay Spain, Murvyn Vye, Nehemiah Persoff, Martin Balsam, James Gregory, Joe De Santis; *D:* Richard Wilson. VHS, Beta $14.98 *FOX, FCT* 🎬🎬🎬

Alabama's Ghost Musician steals a dead master magician's secrets, incurring the wrath of the paranormal underworld. **1972** 96m/C Christopher Brooks, E. Kerrigan Prescott; *D:* Fredric Hobbs. VHS, Beta $29.95 *LIV* 🎬½

Aladdin A comedic Italian modernization of the Aladdin fable. *AKA:* Superfantagenio. **1986** (PG) 97m/C *IT* Bud Spencer, Luca Venantini, Janet Agren, Julian Voloshin, Umberto Raho; *D:* Bruno Corbucci. VHS, Beta $9.95 *MED* 🎬

Aladdin Boy meets princess, loses her, finds her, wins her from evil vizier and nasty parrot. Superb animation triumphs over average songs and storyline by capitalizing on Williams' talent for ad-lib with lightning speed genie changes, lots of celebrity spoofs, and even a few pokes at Disney itself. Adults will enjoy the 1,001 impersonations while kids will get a kick out of the big blue genie and the songs, three of which are the late Ashman's legacy. Kane and Salonga are responsible for the singing voices of Aladdin and Jasmine; Gottfried is a riot as the obnoxious parrot sidekick. Be forewarned: small children may be frightened by some of the scarier sequences. ♫A Whole New World; Prince Ali; Friend Like Me; One Jump Ahead; Arabian Nights. **1992** (G) 90m/C *D:* Ron Clements, John Musker; *W:* Ron Clements, John Musker, Ted Elliot, Terry Rossio; *M:* Alan Menken, Howard Ashman, Tim Rice; *V:* Robin Williams, Scott Weinger, Linda Larkin, Jonathan Freeman, Frank Welker, Gilbert Gottfried, Douglas Seale, Brad Kane, Lea Salonga. Academy Awards '92: Best Song ("A Whole New World"), Best Original Score; Nominations: Best Song ("Friend Like Me"), Best Sound, Best Sound Effects Editing; Golden Globe Awards '93: Best Song ("A Whole New World"), Best Score; MTV Movie Awards

'93: Best Comedic Performance (Williams). VHS, Beta $24.99 *DIS, BTV, WTA* 🎬🎬½

Aladdin and His Wonderful Lamp The story of Aladdin, a young man who finds a magical oil lamp when he is trapped in a tiny cave. From the "Faerie Tale Theatre" series and director of "Beetlejuice" and "Batman" Tim Burton. **1984** 60m/C Valerie Bertinelli, Robert Carradine, Leonard Nimoy, James Earl Jones; *D:* Tim Burton. VHS, Beta $14.98 *KUI, FOX, FCT* 🎬🎬½

Alakazam the Great! A Japanese animated film about an arrogant monkey who is sent on a mission to learn about life. **1961** 84m/C *D:* Lee Kresel; *V:* Frankie Avalon, Dodie Stevens, Jonathan Winters, Arnold Stang, Sterling Holloway. VHS $14.95 *CNG* 🎬🎬½

The Alamo Old-fashioned patriotic battle epic recounts the real events of the 1836 fight for independence in Texas. The usual band of diverse and contentious personalities, including Wayne as a coonskin-capped Davy Crockett, defend a small fort against a very big Mexican raiding party outside of San Antonio. Before meeting mythic death, they fight with each other, learn the meaning of life, and ultimately come to respect each other. Just to make it more entertaining, Avalon sings. Big-budget production features an impeccable musical score by Tiomkin and an impressive 7,000 extras for the Mexican army alone. Wayne reportedly received directorial assistance from John Ford, particularly during the big massacre finale. **1960** 161m/C John Wayne, Richard Widmark, Laurence Harvey, Frankie Avalon, Richard Boone, Carlos Arruza, Chill Wills, Veda Ann Borg; *D:* John Wayne; *M:* Dimitri Tiomkin. Academy Awards '60: Best Sound; Nominations: Best Color Cinematography, Best Film Editing, Best Picture, Best Song ("The Green Leaves of Summer"), Best Supporting Actor (Wills), Best Original Score; Golden Globe Awards '61: Best Score. VHS, Beta $19.98 *MGM, FOX, TLF* 🎬🎬🎬

Alamo Bay A slow-moving but sincere tale of contemporary racism. An angry Vietnam veteran and his red-neck buddies feel threatened by Vietnamese refugees who want to go into the fishing business. Set in Texas, filled with Texas-sized characters, and based on a true Texas story, as interpreted by the French Malle. **1985** 99m/C Ed Harris, Ho Nguyen, Amy Madigan, Donald Moffatt, Cynthia Carle, Truyen V. Tran, Rudy Young; *D:* Louis Malle; *W:* Alice Arlen; *M:* Ry Cooder. VHS, Beta $79.95 *COL* 🎬🎬½

The Alamo: Thirteen Days to Glory The legendary Davy Crockett (Keith), Colonel William Travis (Baldwin), and Jim Bowie (Arness) overcome personal differences to unite against the Mexican Army, vowing to hold down the fort or die. It takes a true Texan to fully appreciate the merits of this rather pedestrian retelling of a familiar story, but the battle scenes are pretty heady (although they lose some of their froth on the small screen). If nothing else, the ever-versatile Julia is worth seeing as Santa Anna in this made-for-TV rendering of J. Lon Tinkle's "Thirteen Days to Glory." You may not want to remember the Alamo this way. **1987** 180m/C James Arness, Lorne Greene, Alec Baldwin, Brian Keith, Raul Julia; *D:* Peter Werner; *M:* Peter Bernstein. VHS, Beta $24.98 *FRH* 🎬🎬

Alamut Ambush A federal agent is stalked by assassins, and decides to hunt them in return. Sequel to "Cold War Killer." **1986** 94m/C *GB* Terence Stamp, Michael Culver; *D:* Ken Grieve. VHS, Beta *NO* 🎬

Alan & Naomi In 1944, 14-year-old Alan Silverman is more concerned with his Brooklyn stickball team than the war raging across Europe. This changes when his upstairs neighbor offers refuge to a French-Jewish mother and her young daughter and he is asked to befriend the girl. Naomi witnessed the brutal death of her father by the Nazis and retreated into a world of her own. Together the two build a sweet, if unlikely, friendship. Fine performances save this average coming of age tale. Based on the novel by Myron Levoy. **1992** (PG) 95m/C Lukas Haas, Vanessa Zaoui, Michael Gross, Amy Aquino, Kevin Connolly, Zohra Lampert; *D:* Sterling Van Wagenen; *W:* Jordan Horowitz; *M:* Dick Hyman. VHS $89.95 *COL* 🎬🎬½

The Alaska Wilderness Adventure The tale of a family struggling for survival in the Arctic wilderness. Baby, it's cold out there. **1978** 90m/C VHS, Beta *NO* 🎬🎬

Alberto Express Black comedy explores the debts children owe their parents—literally. Alberto's family has a peculiar tradition. It seems that now he's married and about to become a father, he's expected to pay back every cent spent on his own upbringing. Cash poor (and panicky) Alberto hops a train from Paris to Rome and frantically tries to raise the necessary cash by preying, in a series of increasingly bizarre ways, on his fellow passengers before he faces his father once again. In French and Italian with English subtitles. **1992** 90m/C *FR* Sergio Castellitto, Nino Manfredi, Marie Trintignant, Jeanne Moreau, Michel Aumont, Dominique Pinon, Marco Messeri, Eugenia Marruzzo; *D:* Arthur Joffe; *W:* Arthur Joffe. VHS $89.95 *FXL* 🎬🎬½

Albino Albino chief leads African terrorists to murder white settlers, one of whom is an ex-policeman's fiancee. So the ex-cop pursues the bad guys, who are fairly easy to identify (just look for the big group hanging with the albino). Danning, Lee, and Howard only briefly show faces and collect checks. **1976** (R) 85m/C Christopher Lee, Trevor Howard, Sybil Danning, Horst Frank, James Faulkner; *D:* Jurgen Goslar. VHS, Beta $54.95 *MED* Woof!

The Alchemist See humans transformed into murderous zombies! A bewitched man seeks revenge upon the evil magician who placed a curse on him, causing him to live like an animal. Painfully routine, with a few chills along the way. Amonte is an alias for Charles Band. Filmed in 1981 and released four years later. **1981** (R) 86m/C Robert Ginty, Lucinda Dooling, John Sanderford, Viola Kate Stimpson, Bob Glaudini; *D:* James Amonte; *M:* Richard Band. VHS, Beta $79.98 *VES, LIV* Woof!

Alex in Wonderland A semi-autobiographical and satirical look at Hollywood from the standpoint of a young director who's trying to follow up his recent hit (in real life, "Bob & Carol & Ted & Alice") with a picture of some integrity that will keep the mass audience away. The confused plot provides obvious parallels to Fellini (who appears in a cameo) and some sharp, often bitter insights into the Hollywood of the early '60s. Strong performances by Sutherland and Burstyn compensate somewhat for the patience-trying self-indulgent arty whining of the script.

1970 (R) 109m/C Donald Sutherland, Ellen Burstyn, Jeanne Moreau, Paul Mazursky; *Cameos:* Federico Fellini; *D:* Paul Mazursky; *W:* Larry Tucker, Paul Mazursky. VHS, Beta $19.98 *MGM, FCT* ♫♫ ½

Alexander Nevsky A story of the invasion of Russia in 1241 by the Teutonic Knights of Germany and the defense of the region by good old Prince Nevsky. Eisenstein's first completed project in nearly ten years, it was widely regarded as an artistic disappointment upon release and as pro-war propaganda for the looming conflict with the Nazis. Fabulous Prokofiev score illuminates the classic battle scenes, which used thousands of Russian army regulars. Dubbed in English.
1938 107m/B *RU* Nikolai Cherkassov, N.P. Okholopkov, Al Abrikossov; *D:* Sergei Eisenstein; *M:* Sergei Prokofiev. VHS, Beta, 8mm $24.95 *VYY, MRV, NOS* ♫♫♫ ½

Alexander the Great A lavish epic about the legendary Greek conqueror of the fourth century B.C., which provides Burton a rare chance at an adventure role. Here we find Alexander is the product of a dysfunctional royal family who hopes to create an idealized world modeled after Greek culture to make up for the love he lacks from daddy. This he does by conquering everything before dying at the age of 33. The great cast helps to overcome the sluggish pacing of the spectacle, while numerous battle scenes featuring loads of spears and arrows are staged effectively.
1955 135m/C Richard Burton, Fredric March, Claire Bloom, Harry Andrews, Peter Cushing, Danielle Darrieux, Helmut Dantine; *D:* Robert Rossen. VHS, Beta $19.98 *MGM, FCT* ♫♫ ½

Alexander: The Other Side of Dawn Tired made-for-television sequel to the television movie "Dawn: Portrait of a Teenage Runaway." A young man turns to prostitution to support himself on the street of Los Angeles.
1977 100m/C Leigh McCloskey, Eve Plumb, Earl Holliman, Juliet Mills, Jean Hagen, Loni Chapman; *D:* John Erman. VHS *MOV* ♫♫

Alexander's Ragtime Band Energetic musical that spans 1915 to 1938 and has Power and Ameche battling for Faye's affections. Power is a society nabob who takes up ragtime. He puts together a band, naming the group after a piece of music (hence the title), and finds a singer (Faye). Ameche is a struggling composer who brings a Broadway producer to listen to their performance. Faye gets an offer to star in a show and becomes an overnight success. Over the years the trio win and lose success, marry and divorce, and finally end up happy. Corny but charming. ♫Alexander's Ragtime Band; All Alone; Blue Skies; Easter Parade; Everybody's Doin' It; Everybody Step; For Your Country and My Country; Heat Wave; I Can Always Find a Little Sunshine at the YMCA; Marie; My Walking Stick; Now It Can Be Told; Oh, How I Hate to Get Up In the Morning; Pack Up Your Sins and Go to the Devil; A Pretty Girl Is Like a Melody; Ragtime Violin; Remember; Say It With Music; That International Rag; This Is the Life; We're On Our Way to France; What'll I Do?; When the Midnight Choo-Choo Leaves for Alabam'. *AKA:* Irving Berlin's Alexander's Ragtime Band.
1938 105m/B Tyrone Power, Alice Faye, Don Ameche, Ethel Merman, Jack Haley, Jean Hersholt, Helen Westley, John Carradine, Paul Hurst, Joe King, Ruth Terry; *D:* Henry King; *W:* Kathryn Scola, Lamar Trotti; *M:* Irving Berlin, Irving Berlin. Academy Awards '38: Best Score; Nominations: Best Film Editing, Best Interior

Decoration, Best Picture, Best Song ("Now It Can Be Told"), Best Writing. VHS $19.98 *FXV* ♫♫♫

Alfie What's it all about, Alfie? Caine, in his first starring role, plays the British playboy out of control in mod London. Alfie is a despicable, unscrupulous and vile sort of guy who uses woman after woman to fulfill his basic needs and then casts them aside until...tragedy strikes. Though this box office hit was seen as a sophisticated take on current sexual mores upon release, it now seems a dated but engaging comedy, notable chiefly for its performances. From the play by Bill Naughton. The title song "Alfie", sung by Dionne Warwick, was a top ten hit.
1966 (PG) 113m/C *GB* Michael Caine, Shelley Winters, Millicent Martin, Vivien Merchant, Julia Asher; *D:* Lewis Gilbert. Academy Awards '66 Nominations: Best Actor (Caine), Best Adapted Screenplay, Best Picture, Best Song ("Alfie"), Best Supporting Actress (Merchant); Golden Globe Awards '67: Best Foreign Film; National Board of Review Awards '66: 10 Best Films of the Year, Best Supporting Actress (Merchant). VHS, Beta $59.95 *PAR* ♫♫♫

Alfredo, Alfredo Hoffman plays a mild-mannered bank clerk who regrets marrying a sexy woman. Lightweight domestic comedy. In Italian with English subtitles (Hoffman's voice was dubbed).
1972 (R) 97m/C *IT* Dustin Hoffman, Stefania Sandrelli, Carla Gravina, Clara Colosimo, Daniela Patella, Dulio Del Prete; *D:* Pietro Germi. VHS *PAR* ♫♫

Algiers Nearly a scene-for-scene Americanized remake of the 1937 French "Pepe Le Moko" about a beautiful rich girl (Lamarr) who meets and falls in love with a notorious thief (Boyer), then a leading sex symbol). Pursued by French police and hiding in the underworld-controlled Casbah, Boyer meets up with Lamarr in a tragically fated romance done in the best tradition of Hollywood. Boyer provides a measured performance as Le Moko, while Lamarr is appropriately sultry in her American film debut (which made her a star). Later remade as the semi-musical "Casbah."
1938 96m/B Charles Boyer, Hedy Lamarr, Sigrid Gurie, Gene Lockhart, Joseph Calleia, Alan Hale; *D:* John Cromwell. VHS, Beta $9.95 *CNG, MRV, NOS* ♫♫♫

Ali Baba and the Forty Thieves Ali Baba and his gang of thieves do battle against Hulogn Khan, leader of the Mongols, to save Baghdad and its citizens from ruin and death.
1943 87m/C Jon Hall, Turhan Bey, Maria Montez, Andy Devine, Kurt Katch, Frank Puglia, Fortuna Bonanova, Moroni Olsen, Scotty Beckett; *D:* Arthur Lubin; *W:* Edmund Hartmann. VHS $14.98 *MCA, FCT* ♫♫ ½

Ali Baba and the 40 Thieves French adaptation of the popular novel "A Thousand and One Nights." Servant boy Ali Baba discovers the magic cave holding the stolen treasure of Abdul and his 40 thieves. Shot on location in Morocco. Also available dubbed. *AKA:* Ali Baba et les Quarante Voleurs.
1954 92m/C *FR* Samia Gamal, Dieter Borsche, Henri Vilbert; *D:* Jacques Becker; *W:* Jacques Becker. VHS $59.95 *FRA, FCT* ♫♫♫

Ali: Fear Eats the Soul A widow cleaning woman in her sixties has a love affair with a Moroccan man 30 years her junior. To no one's surprise, both encounter racism and moral hypocrisy in West Germany. Serious melodrama from Fassbinder, who wrote it and appears as the squirmy son-in-law. In German with English subtitles. *AKA:* Fear Eats the Soul.

1974 68m/C *GE* Brigitte Mira, El Hedi Ben Salem, Irm Hermann; *D:* Rainer Werner Fassbinder. VHS $79.95 *NYF, FCT, ING* ♫♫♫

Alias Billy the Kid Western adventure with Carson posing as a famous outlaw to find out who's behind the scam involving the Denton City cattle trade.
1946 54m/B Sunset Carson. VHS $9.98 *REP* ♫♫

Alias John Law The Good Guy fights for oil rights against the bad guys. Confused program western with an especially convoluted plot.
1935 54m/B Bob Steele; *D:* Robert North Bradbury. VHS, Beta *NO* ♫

Alias John Preston Yet another one of those pseudo-psychological to sleep perchance to dream movies. Lee plays a man haunted by dreams in which he's a murderer, and soon starts to question whether his dreams might not imitate life. It's been done before, it's been done since, and it's been done better.
1956 66m/B *GB* Betta St. John, Alexander Knox, Christopher Lee, Sandra Dorne, Patrick Holt, Betty Ann Davies, John Longden, Bill Fraser, John Stuart; *D:* David MacDonald. VHS $19.98 *SNC* ♫ ½

Alice A twist on the "Alice in Wonderland" tale. Alice witnesses an attempted murder, faints, and awakens in a weird, yet strangely familiar environment. Adapted from the stage production.
1986 80m/C Sophie Barjae, Susannah York, Jean-Pierre Cassel, Paul Nicholas. VHS, Beta $59.95 *LHV, WAR* ♫♫

Alice An acclaimed surreal version of Lewis Carroll's already surreal "Alice in Wonderland," with the emphasis on Carroll's obsessiveness. Utilizing animated puppets and a live actor for Alice, Czech director Svankmajer injects grotesque images and black comedy into Wonderland. Not for the kids.
1988 84m/C *GB* Kristina Kohoutova; *D:* Jan Svankmajer. VHS $490.00 *ICA, WTA, ING* ♫♫♫ ½

Alice Farrow is "Alice," a woman plagued with doubts about her lifestyle, her religion, and her happiness. Her perfect children, husband, and apartment don't prevent her backaches, and she turns to an Oriental "herbalist" for aid. She finds his methods unusual and the results of the treatments surprising. Lightweight fairytale of Yuppiedom gone awry. Fine performances, but superficial and pointed story that may leave the viewer looking for more. (Perhaps that's Allen's point.) Farewell performance from character actor Luke, unbilled cameo from Judith Ivey, and first time out for Dylan O'Sullivan Farrow, adopted daughter of Allen and Farrow, as Kate.
1990 (PG-13) 106m/C Mia Farrow, William Hurt, Joe Mantegna, Keye Luke, Alec Baldwin, Cybill Shepherd, Blythe Danner, Gwen Verdon, Bernadette Peters, Judy Davis, Patrick O'Neal, Julie Kavner, Caroline Aaron, Holland Taylor, Robin Bartlett, David Spielberg, Bob Balaban, Dylan O'Sullivan Farrow, Elle Macpherson; *D:* Woody Allen; *W:* Woody Allen. Academy Awards '90 Nominations: Best Original Screenplay; National Board of Review Awards '90: Best Actress (Farrow). VHS, Beta $92.98 *ORI, FCT* ♫♫♫

Alice Adams Based on the classic Booth Tarkington novel about a poor girl from a small Midwestern town who falls in love with a man from the upper level of society. She tries desperately to fit in and nearly alienates her family and friends. The sets may be dated, but the insight on human behavior is timeless.

1935 99m/B Katharine Hepburn, Fred MacMurray, Evelyn Venable, Hattie McDaniel, Fred Stone; *D:* George Stevens. Academy Awards '35 Nominations: Best Actress (Hepburn), Best Picture; National Board of Review Awards '35: 10 Best Films of the Year. **VHS, Beta** $14.98 *CCB, MED, NOS* 🎞🎞½

Alice Doesn't Live Here Anymore
Scorcese marries road opera with pseudo-feminist semi-realistic melodrama and produces uneven but interesting results. When a Alice's husband dies suddenly, leaving her with their eleven-year-old son, she leaves for California, but finds herself stranded in Phoenix, down to her last few bucks. There she lands a job as a waitress in a diner where she meets kindly rancher Kristofferson. Notable for its female point of view, it was also the basis for the once popular TV show "Alice." Burstyn and Ladd lend key performances, while Kristofferson is typically wooden.
1974 (PG) 105m/C Ellen Burstyn, Kris Kristofferson, Diane Ladd, Jodie Foster, Harvey Keitel, Vic Tayback, Billy Green Bush; *D:* Martin Scorsese; *W:* Robert Getchell. Academy Awards '74: Best Actress (Burstyn); Nominations: Best Original Screenplay, Best Supporting Actress (Ladd); British Academy Awards '75: Best Actress (Burstyn), Best Film, Best Supporting Actress (Ladd). **VHS, Beta** $19.98 *WAR, FCT, BTV* 🎞🎞½

Alice in the Cities
American and German culture are compared and contrasted in this early Wenders road work about a German journalist in the USA on assignment who suddenly finds himself custodian of a worldly nine-year-old girl abandoned by her mother. Together they return to Germany and search for the girl's grandmother. Along the way they learn about each other, with many distinctive and graceful Wenders moments.
1974 110m/B Ruediger Vogler, Yella Rottlaender, Elisabeth Kreuzer, Edda Kochi; *D:* Wim Wenders; *W:* Wim Wenders. **VHS, Beta** $29.95 *FCT, APD, GLV* 🎞🎞🎞

Alice in Wonderland
Another version of the Lewis Carroll classic which combines the usage of Lou Bunin's puppets and live action to tell the story. Released independently to cash in on the success of the Disney version. Takes a more adult approach to the story and is worth viewing on its own merits.
1950 83m/C *FR* Carol Marsh, Stephen Murray, Pamela Brown, Felix Aylmer, Ernest Milton; *D:* Dallas Bower. **VHS, Beta** $39.95 *MON, WTA* 🎞🎞½

Alice in Wonderland
Classic Disney dream version of Lewis Carroll's famous children's story about a girl who falls down a rabbit hole into a magical world populated by strange creatures. Beautifully animated with some startling images, but served with a strange dispassion warmed by a fine batch of songs. Wynn's Mad Hatter and Holloway's Cheshire Cat are among the treats in store. 🎵Alice in Wonderland; I'm Late; A Very Merry Un-Birthday.
1951 (G) 75m/C *D:* Clyde Geronimi; *V:* Kathryn Beaumont, Ed Wynn, Sterling Holloway, Jerry Colonna, Hamilton Luske, Wilfred Jackson. **VHS, Beta** $24.99 *DIS, FCT, KUI* 🎞🎞🎞

Alice in Wonderland
Musical version of the Lewis Carroll's classic tale performed by the Children's Theatre Company and School.
1982 81m/C Annie Enneking, Solvieg Olsen, Wendy Lehr, Jason McLean, Gary Briggle, Elizabeth Fink. **VHS, Beta** $39.95 *MCA* 🎞🎞½

Alice Sweet Alice
Mediocre, gory who-killed-her, best remembered as the debut of Shields (in a small role). *AKA:* Holy Terror; Communion.
1976 (R) 112m/C Brooke Shields, Linda Miller, Paula Sheppard; *D:* Alfred Sole. **VHS, Beta** $29.95 *REP, MRV, BTV* 🎞½

Alice Through the Looking Glass
Based on Lewis Carroll's classic adventure. Follows the further adventures of young Alice. After a chess piece comes to life, it convinces Alice that excitement and adventure lie through the looking glass.
1966 72m/C Judi Rolin, Ricardo Montalban, Nanette Fabray, Robert Coote, Agnes Moorehead, Jack Palance, Jimmy Durante, Tom Smothers, Roy Castle, Richard Denning; *D:* Alan Handley. **VHS, Beta** $14.98 *SUE, CNG, KAR* 🎞½

Alice to Nowhere
Concerns a running argument in the Outback over a fortune in gems unknowingly carried by a young woman. Made for Australian television and based on a novel by Evan Green.
1986 210m/C *AU* Rosie Jones, Steve Jacobs, John Waters, Ruth Cracknell; *D:* John Power. **VHS, Beta** $59.95 *PAR* 🎞🎞

Alice's Adventures in Wonderland
Musical adaptation of Lewis Carroll's timeless fantasy of a young girl who meets new friends when she falls into a rabbit hole.
1972 96m/C *GB* Fiona Fullerton, Michael Crawford, Ralph Richardson, Flora Robson, Peter Sellers, Robert Helpmann, Dudley Moore, Michael Jayston, Spike Milligan, Michael Hordern; *D:* William Sterling; *W:* William Sterling; *M:* John Barry. **VHS, Beta** *VES* 🎞🎞

Alice's Restaurant
Based on the popular and funny 20-minute Arlo Guthrie song "Alice's Restaurant Massacre" about a Flower Child during the Last Big War who gets hassled for littering, man. Step back in time and study the issues of the hippie era, including avoiding the draft, dropping out of college, and dealing with the local pigs. Sort of a modern movie in the cinematic ambling genre, in that nothing really happens.
1969 (PG) 111m/C Arlo Guthrie, James Broderick, Pat Quinn, Geoff Outlaw; *D:* Arthur Penn. **VHS, Beta** $19.95 *MVD, MGM* 🎞🎞½

Alien
Terse direction, stunning sets and special effects, and a well-seasoned cast save this from being another "Slimy monster from Outerspace" story. Instead it's a grisly rollercoaster of suspense and fear (and a huge box office hit). Intergalactic freighter's crew is invaded by an unstoppable carnivorous alien intent on picking off the crew one by one. While the cast mostly bitches and banters while awaiting the horror of their imminent departure, Weaver is exceptional as Ripley, a self-reliant survivor who goes toe to toe with the Big Ugly. Futuristic, in the belly of the beast visual design creates a vivid sense of claustrophobic doom enhanced further by the ominous score. Oscar-winning special effects include the classic baby alien busting out of the crew guy's chest routine, a rib-splitting ten on the gore meter. Successfully followed by "Aliens" and "Alien 3."
1979 (R) 116m/C Tom Skerritt, Sigourney Weaver, Veronica Cartwright, Yaphet Kotto, Harry Dean Stanton, Ian Holm, John Hurt; *D:* Ridley Scott; *W:* Dan O'Bannon; *M:* Jerry Goldsmith. Academy Awards '79: Best Visual Effects; Nominations: Best Art Direction/Set Decoration. **VHS, Beta** $19.98 *FOX* 🎞🎞🎞½

Alien 3
Picks up where "Aliens" left off as Ripley crash lands on Fiorina 161, a planet that serves as a penal colony for 25 celibate but horny men who smell bad. Ripley is forced to shave her head because of the planet's lice problem, and she sets out to survive on the cold, unfriendly planet until a rescue ship can come for her. Fending off sexual advances from the men, Ripley soon discovers she wasn't the only survivor of the crash—the alien survived too and has somehow implanted her with an alien of her own. Dark and disturbing, filled with religious allegories, and a universe removed from the two earlier Aliens. Intended as the final installment of the series.
1992 (R) 135m/C Sigourney Weaver, Charles S. Dutton, Charles Dance, Paul McGann, Brian Glover, Ralph Brown, Danny Webb, Christopher John Fields, Holt McCallany, Lance Henriksen; *D:* David Fincher; *M:* Elliot Goldenthal. **VHS** *FXV* 🎞🎞

Alien Contamination
Tale of two astronauts who return to Earth from an expedition on Mars carrying some deadly bacterial eggs. Controlled by a Martian intent on conquering the world, the eggs squirt a gloppy juice that makes people explode on contact (a special effect). A cheap and sloppy attempt to cash in on the success of "Alien." Dubbed. *AKA:* Contamination.
1981 (R) 90m/C *IT* Ian McCulloch, Louise Monroe, Martin Mase, Samuel Rauch, Lisa Hahn; *D:* Lewis (Luigi Cozzi) Coates; *W:* Lewis (Luigi Cozzi) Coates. **VHS, Beta** *NO* Woof!

Alien Dead
The teenage victims of a bizarre meteor crash reincarnate as flesh-eating ghouls anxious for a new supply of human food in this extremely low-budget sleep inducer.
1985 (R) 87m/C Buster Crabbe, Linda Lewis, Ray Roberts; *D:* Fred Olen Ray. **VHS, Beta** $19.95 *ACA, GHV* 🎞

The Alien Factor
Another low-budget crazed critter from outerspace dispatch, this one featuring multiple aliens, one of whom is good, who have the misfortune of crash landing near Baltimore. The grotesque extra-terrestrials jolt a small town out of its sleepy state by wreaking havoc (except for the good one, of course). Decent special effects.
1978 (PG) 82m/C Don Leifert, Tom Griffith, Mary Mertens, Dick Dyszel; *D:* Donald M. Dohler. **VHS, Beta** $59.95 *VCI* 🎞½

Alien from L.A.
Awesomely inept comedy about a California girl who unwittingly stumbles onto the famed continent of Atlantis and can't find a yogurt stand. Weakly plotted and acted and filmed. Like, really.
1987 (PG) 88m/C Kathy Ireland, Thom Mathews, Don Michael Paul, Linda Kerridge, William R. Moses; *D:* Albert Pyun; *W:* Albert Pyun. **VHS, Beta** $79.95 *MED* Woof!

Alien Intruder
What happens when an evil demon appears before the soldiers of the future in the guise of a beautiful woman? Futuristic trash B-movie emerges from the depths.
1993 (R) 90m/C Billy Dee Williams, Tracy Scoggins, Maxwell Caulfield; *D:* Ricardo Jacques Gale. **VHS** $89.95 *PMH* 🎞🎞

Alien Massacre
One of the worst films of all time—five short horror stories about zombies and vampires. Goes by many names—stinks all of them. *AKA:* Dr. Terror's Gallery of Horrors; Return from the Past; The Blood Suckers; Gallery of Horror.
1967 90m/C Lon Chaney Jr., John Carradine, Rochelle Hudson, Roger Gentry, Mitch Evans; *D:* David L. Hewitt. **VHS, Beta** $19.95 *ACA, MRV* Woof!

Alien Nation
A few hundred thousand alien workers land accidentally on Earth and slowly become part of its society, although widely discriminated against. One of the "newcomers" teams with a surly and bigoted human cop to solve a racially motivated

murder. An inconsistent and occasionally transparent script looks at race conflicts and includes some humorous parallels with contemporary American life. Basis for the television series. Producer Hurd was also the force behind "The Terminator" and "Aliens."
1988 (R) 89m/C James Caan, Mandy Patinkin, Terence Stamp, Kevyn Major Howard, Peter Jason, Jeff Kober, Leslie Bevins; **D:** Graham Baker; **M:** Rockne S. O'Bannon; **M:** Curt Sobel. **VHS, Beta $19.98** FOX ♂♂½

Alien Predators Three friends encounter a malevolent alien in this dull reworking of the plot of "The Andromeda Strain" with laughable special effects tossed in for those outwitted by the script.
1980 (R) 92m/C Dennis Christopher, Martin Hewitt, Lynn-Holly Johnson, Luis Prendes; **D:** Deran Sarafian. **VHS, Beta $79.95** VTR Woof!

Alien Prey Two lesbians are making love when they are unexpectedly devoured by a hungry and indiscreet alien. No safe sex there. Graphic sex, violence, and cannibalism abound. Interesting twist to the old eat 'em and leave 'em genre.
1983 (R) 85m/C Barry Stokes, Sally Faulkner; **D:** Norman J. Warren. **VHS, Beta** NO ♂½

Alien Private Eye An extraterrestrial detective searches Los Angeles for a missing magic disk while investigating an intergalactic crime ring. **AKA:** Alien P.I.
1987 90m/C Nikki Fastinetti; **D:** Nik Rubenfeld. **VHS** NO ♂♂

Alien Seed Aliens kidnap a woman and impregnate her. Estrada is the government scientist hot on her trail. (How far could a woman carrying alien offspring wander?)
1989 88m/C Erik Estrada, Heidi Paine, Steven Blade; **D:** Bob James. **VHS $79.95** AIP ♂

Alien Space Avenger A spaceship piloted by four alien convicts crash lands in New York City. Stalked by an intergalactic bounty hunter whose job is to kill them, the aliens attack and hide inside human bodies to avoid discovery. It's a race against time as the preservation of the human race depends on the avenger's ability to seek and destroy the alien invaders. Bland ripoff of "Aliens" is reminiscent of old-time "B" sci-fi flicks, with more gore and violence. Shot with the old 3-strip Technicolor method. **AKA:** Space Avenger.
1991 88m/C Robert Prichard, Mike McClerie, Charity Staley, Gina Mastrogiacomo, Kick Fairbanks Fogg, Angela Nicholas, Marty Roberts, James Gillis; **D:** Richard W. Haines; **W:** Richard W. Haines, Linwood Sawyer; **M:** Richard Fiocca. **VHS $89.95** AIP ♂♂

Alien Warrior An extraterrestrial fights a street pimp to save a crime-ridden Earth neighborhood. Low-brain rip-off of Superman.
1985 (R) 92m/C Brett Clark, Pamela Saunders; **D:** Edward Hunt. **VHS, Beta $79.98** VES, LIV Woof!

Alien Women A soft-core British science fiction yarn about scantily clad alien babes and the special agent who's trying to uncover their secret. It's all very sketchy, silly and campy, though pleasantly cast with plenty of lovely British actresses. **AKA:** Zeta One; The Love Factor.
1969 (R) 86m/C GB James Robertson Justice, Charles Hawtrey, Robin Hawdon, Anna Gael, Brigitte Skay, Dawn Addams, Valerie Leon, Yutte Stensgaard, Wendy Lingham, Rita Webb, Caroline Hawkins; **D:** Michael Cort. **VHS, Beta $59.95** PSM, SNC ♂

Alienator In the improbable future, an unstoppable android killer is sent after an intergalactic villain. An intentional "Terminator" rip-off.
1989 (R) 93m/C Jan-Michael Vincent, John Phillip Law, Ross Hagen, Dyana Ortelli, Dawn Wildsmith, P.J. Soles, Teagan Clive, Robert Clarke, Leo Gordon, Robert Quarry, Fox Harris, Hoke Howell, Jay Richardson; **D:** Fred Olen Ray. **VHS, Beta $79.95** PSM ♂

Aliens The bitch is back, some 50 years later. Popular sequel to "Alien" amounts to non-stop, ravaging combat in space. Contact with a colony on another planet has mysteriously stopped. Fresh from deep space sleep, Ripley and a slew of pulsar-equipped Marines return to confront the mother alien at her nest, which is also inhabited by a whole bunch of the nasty critters spewing for a fight. Something's gotta give, and the Oscar-winning special effects are especially inventive (and messy) in the alien demise department. Dimension (acting biz talk) is given to our hero Ripley, as she discovers maternal instincts lurking within her space suit while looking after a young girl, the lone survivor of the colony. Tension-filled gore blaster. Followed by "Aliens 3."
1986 (R) 138m/C Sigourney Weaver, Michael Biehn, Lance Henriksen, Bill Paxton, Paul Reiser, Carrie Henn, Jenette Goldstein; **D:** James Cameron; **W:** Walter Hill; **M:** James Horner. Academy Awards '86: Best Sound Effects Editing, Best Visual Effects; Nominations: Best Actress (Weaver), Best Art Direction/Set Decoration, Best Film Editing, Best Sound, Best Original Score. **VHS, Beta $19.98** FOX ♂♂♂½

Aliens Are Coming A spaceship crash lands on Earth, and its devious denizens begin invading human bodies. TV movie that's a dull echo of "Invasion of the Body Snatchers."
1980 100m/C Tom Mason, Melinda Fee, Max Gail, Eric (Hans Gudegast) Braeden, Matthew Laborteaux; **D:** Harvey Hart; **M:** William Goldstein. **VHS, Beta $9.95** WOV, GKK ♂½

Aliens from Spaceship Earth Are strange, celestial forces invading our universe? If they are, is man prepared to defend his planet against threatening aliens of unknown strength? Lame docudrama featuring the Hurdy Gurdy man himself, Donovan.
1977 107m/C Donovan, Lynda Day George; **D:** Don Como. **VHS, Beta $59.95** GEM ♂½

Alison's Birthday A teenage girl learns that some of her family and friends are Satan worshipers at a terrifying birthday party. Meanwhile, the ghost of her dad hovers about, asking for more lines.
1979 99m/C AU Joanne Samuel, Lou Brown, Bunny Brooke; **D:** Ian Coughlan. **VHS, Beta** NO ♂♂

Alive Recounts the true-life survival story of a group of Uruguayan rugby players in 1972. After their plane crashes in the remote, snowy Andes (in a spectacular sequence) they're forced to turn to cannibalism during a 10-week struggle to stay alive. Marshall doesn't focus on the gruesome idea, choosing instead to focus on all aspects of their desperate quest for survival. The special effects are stunning, but other parts of the film are never fully realized, including the final scene. Based on the nonfiction book by Piers Paul Read.
1993 (R) 127m/C Ethan Hawke, Vincent Spano, Josh Hamilton, Bruce Ramsay, John Haymes Newton, David Kriegel, Kevin Breznahan, Sam Behrens, Illeana Douglas, Jack Noseworthy, Christian Meoli, Jake Carpenter; **Cameos:** John Malkovich; **D:** Frank Marshall; **W:** John Patrick Shanley; **M:** James Newton Howard. **VHS, Beta $19.99** TOU ♂♂½

Alive: 20 Years Later With the release of the big-screen fictional version comes this follow-up documentary with the survivors of the 1972 mountain plane crash telling their own story.
1993 51m/C Jill Fullerton-Smith. **VHS, Beta $39.95** TOU ♂♂½

All About Eve One of the wittiest (and most cynical) flicks of all time follows aspiring young actress Baxter as she ingratiates herself with a prominent group of theater people so she can become a Broadway star without the usual years of work. The not-so-innocent babe becomes secretary to aging star Davis and ruthlessly uses everyone in her climb to the top, much to Davis' initial disbelief and eventual displeasure. Satirical, darkly funny view of the theater world features exceptional work by Davis, Sanders, and Ritter. Based on "The Wisdom of Eve" by Mary Orr. Later staged as the musical "Applause."
1950 138m/B Bette Davis, Anne Baxter, George Sanders, Celeste Holm, Gary Merrill, Thelma Ritter, Marilyn Monroe, Hugh Marlowe, Gregory Ratoff, Eddie Fisher; **D:** Joseph L. Mankiewicz; **W:** Joseph L. Mankiewicz. Academy Awards '50: Best Director (Mankiewicz), Best Picture, Best Screenplay, Best Sound, Best Supporting Actor (Sanders); Nominations: Best Film Editing; Academy Awards '50: Best Actress (Baxter), Best Actress (Davis), Best Art Direction/Set Decoration (B & W), Best Black and White Cinematography, Best Supporting Actress (Holm, Ritter), Best Original Score; Cannes Film Festival '51: Best Actress (Davis); Directors Guild of America Awards '50: Best Director (Mankiewicz); Golden Globe Awards '51: Best Screenplay; National Board of Review Awards '50: 10 Best Films of the Year; New York Film Critics Awards '50: Best Actress (Davis), Best Director (Mankiewicz), Best Film. **VHS, Beta $19.98** FOX, BTV, HMV ♂♂♂♂

All-American Murder A rebellious young man is enrolled in a typical, all-American college for one last shot at mainstream life. Things start out okay, as he meets an attractive young coed. Hours later, he finds himself accused of her grisly murder. The youth is then given 24 hours to prove his innocence by a canny homicide detective. Average performances highlight this film, which isn't able to rise above the mediocre.
1991 (R) 94m/C Christopher Walken, Charlie Schlatter, Josie Bisset, Joanna Cassidy, Richard Kind, Woody Watson, J.C. Quinn, Amy Davis; **D:** Anson Williams; **W:** Barry Sandler. **VHS, Beta $89.95** PSM ♂♂

All Creatures Great and Small Taken from James Herriot's best selling novels, this is a delightful, quiet drama of a veterinarian's apprentice in rural England. Fine performance by Hopkins. Followed by "All Things Bright and Beautiful" and a popular British television series.
1974 92m/C GB Simon Ward, Anthony Hopkins, Lisa Harrow, Brian Stirner, Freddie Jones, T.P. McKenna; **D:** Claude Whatham. **VHS, Beta $29.97** RDG, FOX, HMV ♂♂♂

All Dogs Go to Heaven Somewhat heavy-handed animated musical (Reynolds sings) about a gangster dog who is killed by his partner in business. On the way to Heaven, he discovers how to get back to Earth to seek his revenge. When he returns to Earth, he is taken in by a little girl and learns about something he missed in life the first time around: Love. Expertly animated, but the plot may not keep the grown-ups engrossed, and the kids may notice its lack of charm.

1989 (G) 85m/C **D:** Don Bluth; **W:** Don Bluth, David A. Weiss; **M:** Ralph Burns; **V:** Burt Reynolds, Judith Barsi, Dom DeLuise, Vic Tayback, Charles Nelson Reilly, Melba Moore, Candy Devine, Loni Anderson. **VHS, Beta, 8mm** $14.95 *MGM, RDG, WTA* 𝚺𝚺

All Fall Down A young man (de Wilde) idolizes his callous older brother (Beatty) until a tragedy forces him to grow up. Saint plays the older woman taken in by the brothers' family, who is seduced and abandoned. When she finds herself pregnant and alone, she commits suicide causing the younger brother, who loved her from afar, to vow to kill his older sibling. A well-acted melodrama. Also available colorized.
1962 111m/B Eva Marie Saint, Brandon de Wilde, Warren Beatty, Karl Malden, Angela Lansbury, Constance Ford, Barbara Baxley; **D:** John Frankenheimer; **W:** William Inge. **VHS** $19.98 *MGM* 𝚺𝚺½

All God's Children Made for television drama about the controversial forced busing issue and two families who must face it. Top-notch cast is occasionally mislead by meandering script attempting to stay true to a sensitive issue.
1980 100m/C Richard Widmark, Ned Beatty, Ossie Davis, Ruby Dee, Mariclare Costello, George Spell, Trish Van Devere, Ken Swofford; **D:** Jerry Thorpe; **M:** Billy Goldenberg. **VHS, Beta** NO 𝚺𝚺½

All I Want for Christmas Low-budget, sappy holiday tale of a young girl (Birch) who wants to reunite her divorced parents. Determined to fulfill her Christmas wish, Hallie seeks out the Santa Claus at Macy's department store to tell him the one thing she truly wants for Christmas. Birch is charming as are Bacall as her grandmother and Neilsen as Santa but the story is too squishy and bland to be believable.
1991 (G) 92m/C Thora Birch, Leslie Nielsen, Lauren Bacall, Jamey Sheridan, Harley Jane Kozak, Ethan Randall, Kevin Nealon, Andrea Martin; **D:** Robert Lieberman; **W:** Richard Kramer, Thom Eberhardt, Gail Parent; **M:** Neal Israel, Bruce Broughton. **VHS** $19.95 *PAR* 𝚺𝚺

All in a Night's Work The founder of a one-man publishing empire is found dead with a smile on his face. His nephew inherits the business and finds himself caught in a series of big and small business misunderstandings. He's also falling in love with the woman he suspects was responsible for his uncle's grin. Nicely paced sex and business comedy with warm performances.
1961 94m/C Dean Martin, Shirley MacLaine, Cliff Robertson, Charlie Ruggles; **D:** Joseph Anthony; **W:** Sidney Sheldon. **VHS, Beta** $19.95 *STE, FOX* 𝚺𝚺½

All Mine to Give Sad saga of a Scottish family of eight who braved frontier hardships, epidemics, and death in the Wisconsin wilderness more than a century ago. Midway through, mom and dad die, leaving the oldest child struggling to keep the family together. A strange, though often effective, combination of pioneer adventures and tearjerking moments that avoids becoming hopelessly soapy due to fine performances. Unless you're pretty weathered, you'll need some hankies. Based on the reminiscences of Dale and Katherine Eunson as detailed in a "Cosmopolitan" magazine article. **AKA:** The Day They Gave the Babies Away.
1956 102m/C Glynis Johns, Cameron Mitchell, Rex Thompson, Patty McCormack, Ernest Truex, Hope Emerson, Alan Hale Jr., Royal Dano, Reta Shaw, Rita Johnson, Ellen Corby, Jon Provost; **D:** Allen Reisner; **M:** Max Steiner. **VHS, Beta** $15.95 *VCI* 𝚺𝚺½

All My Good Countrymen A lyrical, funny film about the eccentric denizens of a small Moravian village soon after the socialization of Czechoslovakia in 1948. Completed during the Soviet invasion of 1968 and immediately banned. In Czech with English subtitles. **AKA:** All Good Citizens.
1968 115m/C CZ Vladimir Mensik, Radoslav Brozobohaty, Pavel Pavlovsky; **D:** Vojtech Jasny. Cannes Film Festival Nominations: cs 69: Best Film; Cannes Film Festival '69: Best Director (Jasny). **VHS, Beta** $59.95 *FCT, AUD* 𝚺𝚺½

All My Sons A wealthy family is distraught when their eldest son is listed as missing-in-action during WWII. They must cope with guilt, as well as grief, because the father's business reaped profits from the war. Adapted for television from the acclaimed Arthur Miller play.
1986 122m/C James Whitmore, Aidan Quinn, Joan Allen, Michael Learned; **D:** John Power. **VHS, Beta** $39.95 *MCA* 𝚺𝚺𝚺

All Night Long Offbeat middle-age crisis comedy about a burned-out and newly demoted drugstore executive in L.A. who leaves his wife, takes up with his fourth cousin by marriage, and begins a humorous rebellion, becoming an extremely freelance inventor while joining the drifters, weirdos and thieves of the night. An obscure, sometimes uneven little gem with Hackman in top form and an appealing supporting performance by Streisand. Highlighted by delightful malapropisms and sataric inversion of the usual cliches.
1981 (R) 100m/C Gene Hackman, Barbra Streisand, Diane Ladd, Dennis Quaid, Kevin Dobson, William Daniels; **D:** Jean-Claude Tramont; **W:** W.D. Richter. **VHS, Beta** $14.95 *GKK* 𝚺𝚺𝚺

All Night Long/Smile Please Two classic comedies by the most overlooked of the great silent clowns, both produced by slapstick progenitor Mack Sennett.
1924 66m/B Harry Langdon, Natalie Kingston, Jack Cooper, Alberta Vaughn. **VHS, Beta** $24.95 *VYY* 𝚺𝚺𝚺

All of Me A wealthy woman (Tomlin) dies and her guru accidentally transfers her soul to the right side of the lawyer's body, a modern version of existential hell. Lawyer Martin indulges in some funny slapstick as he discovers that his late client is waging an internal war for control of his body. Flat and cliched at times, but redeemed by the inspired clowning of Martin and witty Martin/Tomlin repartee. Based on the novel "Me Too" by Ed Davis.
1984 (PG) 93m/C Steve Martin, Lily Tomlin, Victoria Tennant, Madolyn Smith, Richard Libertini, Dana Elcar, Selma Diamond; **D:** Carl Reiner; **W:** Phil Alden Robinson. **VHS, Beta** $19.98 *HBO, FCT* 𝚺𝚺½

All Over Town Two vaudevillians with a trained seal find themselves involved in a murder when they are kidnapped by a gang of thugs. A lesser Olsen and Johnson comedy with scattered funny moments.
1937 52m/B Ole Olsen, Chic Johnson, Mary Howard, Franklin Pangborn, James Finlayson; **D:** James W. Horne; **W:** Murray Schisgal. **VHS, Beta** $19.95 *NOS, MRV, VYY* 𝚺𝚺½

All Quiet on the Western Front Extraordinary and realistic anti-war epic based on the novel by Erich Maria Remarque. Seven patriotic German youths go together from school to the battlefields of WWI. They experience the horrors of war first-hand, stuck in the trenches and facing gradual extermination. Centers on experiences of one of the young men, Paul Baumer, who changes from enthusiastic war endorser to battle-weary veteran in an emotionally exact performance by Ayres. Boasts a gigantic budget (for the time) of $1.25 million, and features more than 2,000 extras swarming about battlefields set up on ranchland in California. Relentless anti-war message is emotionally draining and startling with both graphic shots and haunting visual poetry. Extremely controversial in the U.S. and Germany upon release, the original version was 140 minutes long (some versions are available with restored footage) and featured ZaSu Pitts as Ayres mother (later reshot with Mercer replacing her). Remarque, who had fought and been wounded on the Western Front, was eventually forced to leave Germany for the U.S. due to the film's ongoing controversy.
1930 103m/B Lew Ayres, Louis Wolheim, John Wray, Slim Summerville, Russell Gleason, Raymond Griffith, Ben Alexander, Beryl Mercer; **D:** Lewis Milestone. Academy Awards '30: Best Director (Milestone), Best Picture; Nominations: Best Cinematography, Best Writing; National Board of Review Awards '30: 10 Best Films of the Year. **VHS, Beta** $19.95 *MCA, FCT, GLV* 𝚺𝚺𝚺𝚺

All Quiet on the Western Front A big-budget television remake of the 1930 masterpiece starring John Boy. Sensitive German youth Thomas plunges excitedly into WWI and discovers its terror and degradation. Nowhere near the original's quality.
1979 150m/C Richard Thomas, Ernest Borgnine, Donald Pleasence, Patricia Neal; **D:** Delbert Mann. **VHS, Beta** $14.95 *FOX, FCT* 𝚺𝚺½

All Screwed Up A group of young immigrants come to Milan and try to adjust to city life; they soon find that everything is in its place, but nothing is in order. Wertmuller in a lighter vein than usual. **AKA:** All in Place; Nothing in Order.
1974 104m/C IT Luigi Diberti, Lina Polito; **D:** Lina Wertmuller; **W:** Lina Wertmuller. **VHS, Beta** *FOX* 𝚺𝚺𝚺

All That Jazz Fosse's autobiographical portrait with Scheider fully occupying his best role as the obsessed, pill-popping, chain-smoking choreographer/director dancing simultaneously with love and death. But even while dying, he creates some great dancing. Vivid and imaginative with exact editing, and an eerie footnote to Fosse's similar death almost ten years later. Egocentric and self-indulgent for sure, but that's entertainment. ♫On Broadway; Everything Old is New Again; After You've Gone; There'll Be Some Changes Made; Some of These Days; Bye Bye Love.
1979 (R) 120m/C Roy Scheider, Jessica Lange, Ann Reinking, Leland Palmer, Cliff Gorman, Ben Vereen, Erzebet Foldi, John Lithgow, Wallace Shawn, Sandahl Bergman, Nicole Fosse, Keith Gordon, Ben Masters, Theresa Merritt; **D:** Bob Fosse; **M:** Ralph Burns. Academy Awards '79: Best Art Direction/Set Decoration, Best Costume Design, Best Film Editing, Best Original Score; Nominations: Best Actor (Scheider), Best Cinematography, Best Director (Fosse), Best Original Screenplay, Best Picture; Cannes Film Festival '80: Best Film. **VHS, Beta** $19.98 *FOX, FCT* 𝚺𝚺𝚺½

All the Brothers Were Valiant Brothers Taylor and Granger are New England whaling captains but Granger decides to treasure hunt instead. He finds a priceless cache of black pearls on an island but angers the locals who regard the gems as sacred. When Taylor rescues him, Granger promptly turns his brother's crew into mutineers in order to return to the island and retrieve his prize. Lots of brawling and there's an incidental love story with Blyth desired by both men (she's married Taylor and just happens

to be aboard). Last role for Stone. Based on the novel by Ben Ames Williams.
1953 101m/C Robert Taylor, Stewart Granger, Ann Blyth, Betta St. John, Keenan Wynn, James Whitmore, Kurt Kasznar, Lewis Stone, Robert Burton, Peter Whitney, John Lupton, Billie Dove; *D:* Richard Thorpe; *W:* Harry Brown; *M:* Miklos Rozsa. **VHS $19.98** MGM ⅋⅋½

All the Kind Strangers Traveling photographer Keach picks up a young hitch-hiker and takes him to the boy's home. He discovers six other children there who want him as a father, his alternative being death. He and ''Mother'' Eggar plot their escape from the dangerous orphans. Made-for-tele-vision thriller short on suspense. *AKA:* Evil in the Swamp.
1974 72m/C Stacy Keach, Robby Benson, John Savage, Samantha Eggar; *D:* Burt Kennedy. **VHS, Beta $59.98** FOX ⅋⅋

All the King's Men Grim and graphic classic set in the Depression follows the rise of a Louisiana farm-boy from angry and honest political hopeful to powerful but cor-rupt governor. Loosely based on the life (and death) of Huey Long and told by a newsman who's followed his career (Ireland). Willy Stark (Crawford, in his break-through role) is the politician who, while appearing to im-prove the state, rules dictatorially, betraying friends and constituents and proving once again that power corrupts. In her first major role, McCambridge delivers a powerful per-formance as the cunning political aide. Po-tent morality play based on the Robert Penn Warren book.
1949 109m/B Broderick Crawford, Mercedes McCambridge, John Ireland, Joanne Dru, John Derek, Anne Seymour, Sheppard Strudwick; *D:* Robert Rossen; *W:* Robert Rossen. Academy Awards '49: Best Actor (Crawford), Best Picture, Best Supporting Actress (McCambridge); Nominations: Best Director (Rossen), Best Film Editing, Best Screenplay, Best Supporting Actor (Ireland); New York Film Critics Awards '49: Best Actor (Crawford), Best Film. **VHS, Beta $19.95** COL, BTV ⅋⅋⅋

All the Lovin' Kinfolk Two recent Hillbilly High graduates decide to take on the big city, but find themselves in dire situations. For those with time to kill. *AKA:* Kin Folk; Kinfolk; The Closest of Kin.
1989 (R) 80m/C Mady Maguire, Jay Scott, Anne Ryan, John Denis, Donna Young; *D:* John Hayes. **VHS** NO ⅋

...All the Marbles A manager of two beautiful lady wrestlers has dreams of going to the top. Aldrich's last film, and an atypical one, with awkward pacing and a thin veil of sex exploitation. Falk provides needed grace and humor as the seedy manager, with Young contributing his usual competent bit as a hustling promoter dabbling in criminal activity. One of the few tag-team women wrestling pictures, it builds to a rousing finale match in the ''Rocky'' tradition, although the shift in tone and mounting cliches effectively body slam the intent. *AKA:* The California Dolls.
1981 (R) 113m/C Peter Falk, Burt Young, Richard Jaeckel, Vicki Frederick; *D:* Robert Aldrich. **VHS, Beta** MGM, OM ⅋⅋

All the President's Men True story of the Watergate break-in that led to the political scandal of the decade, based on the best-selling book by Washington Post report-ers Bob Woodward and Carl Bernstein. Intriguing, terse thriller is a nail-biter even though the ending is no secret. Expertly paced by Pakula with standout performances by Hoffman and Redford as the reporters who slowly uncover and connect the seem-ingly isolated facts that ultimately lead to

criminal indictments of the Nixon Administra-tion. Deep Throat Holbrook and Robards as executive editor Ben Bradlee lend authentici-ty to the endeavor, a realistical portrayal of the stop and go of journalistic investigations.
1976 (PG) 135m/C Robert Redford, Dustin Hoffman, Jason Robards Jr., Martin Balsam, Jane Alexander, Hal Holbrook, F. Murray Abraham, Stephen Collins, Lindsay Crouse; *D:* Alan J. Pakula; *W:* William Goldman. Academy Awards '76: Best Adapted Screenplay, Best Art Direction/Set Decoration, Best Sound, Best Supporting Actor (Robards), Best Film Editing, Best Picture, Best Supporting Actress (Alexander); New York Film Critics Awards '76: Best Director (Pakula), Best Film, Best Supporting Actor (Robards). **VHS, Beta $19.98** WAR, BTV ⅋⅋⅋½

All the Right Moves Cruise is the high school football hero hoping for a scholarship so he can vacate pronto the dying Pennsyl-vania mill town where he grew up. At least he thinks that's what he wants to do. Further mixing up his own mixed feelings are his pushy, ambitious coach (Nelson, doing what he does best), his understanding dad (Cioffi) and supportive girlfriend (Thompson, in a notable early role). Strong performances push the relatively cliched melodrama into field goal range. Cinematographer Chap-man's directorial debut.
1983 (R) 90m/C Tom Cruise, Lea Thompson, Craig T. Nelson, Christopher Penn; *D:* Michael Chapman; *W:* Michael Kane. **VHS, Beta $14.98** FOX, FXV ⅋⅋½

All the Rivers Run First made-for-ca-ble miniseries. A young Australian girl spends her inheritance on a river boat and becomes the first female river captain in Australian history. Directed by George Miller of ''Man from Snowy River'' fame. Four parts.
1984 400m/C *AU* Sigrid Thornton, John Waters, Diane Craig, Charles Tingwell, Gus Mercurio; *D:* George Miller, Pina Amenta. **VHS $79.95** HBO ⅋⅋½

All the Vermeers in New York A stressed-out Wall Street broker flees to the soothing recesses of the Metropolitan Muse-um's Vermeer Room. There he meets a beautiful, manipulative French actress dreaming of success in Manhattan. Amidst the opulent art world of New York, the two pursue their relationship to an ultimately tragic end. Jost offers an inside look at the collision of commerce and art and the corrupt underside of New York in this elegant con-temporary film.
1991 87m/C Emmanuelle Chaulet, Stephen Lack, Grace Phillips, Katherine Bean, Laurel Lee Kiefer, Gracie Mansion, Gordon Joseph Weiss, Roger Ruffin; *D:* Jon Jost; *W:* Jon Jost. **VHS $24.98** WAC, ING ⅋⅋⅋½

All the Way, Boys Two inept adven-turers crash-land a plane in the Andes in the hope of discovering slapstick, but find none. ''Trinity'' cast up to no good.
1973 (PG) 105m/C *IT* Terence Hill, Bud Spencer, Cyril Cusack, Michel Antoine; *D:* Giuseppe Colizzi. **VHS, Beta $59.98** SUE ⅋½

All the Young Men Fairly powerful men-uniting-in-battle story with an interesting cast, highlighted by Poitier in an early role. A tiny marine squadron overrun by the Chinese in the Korean War attempts to resist the numerous attackers. In their spare time, the men confront racial prejudice when a black man (guess who) takes command.
1960 86m/B Alan Ladd, Sidney Poitier, James Darren, Glenn Corbett, Mort Sahl; *D:* Hall Bartlett; *W:* Hall Bartlett. **VHS, Beta $14.99** COL ⅋⅋⅋

All This and Heaven Too When a governess arrives at a Parisian aristocrat's home in the 1840s, she causes jealous tension between the husband and his wife. The wife is soon found murdered. Based on Rachel Field's best-seller.
1940 141m/B Charles Boyer, Bette Davis, Barbara O'Neil, Virginia Weidler, Jeffrey Lynn, Helen Westley, Henry Daniell, Harry Davenport; *D:* Anatole Litvak. **VHS, Beta $19.95** MGM ⅋⅋⅋

All Through the Night A very funny spy spoof as well as a thrilling crime story with Bogart playing a gambler who takes on a Nazi spy ring. Features memorable double-talk and a great auction scene that inspired the one with Cary Grant in ''North by North-west.'' Suspense builds throughout the film as Lorre appears in a sinister role as Pepi and Veidt gives a fine performance as the spymaster.
1942 107m/B Humphrey Bogart, Conrad Veidt, Karen Verne, Jane Darwell, Frank McHugh, Peter Lorre, Judith Anderson, William Demarest, Jackie Gleason, Phil Silvers, Barton MacLane, Martin Kosleck; *D:* Vincent Sherman. **VHS $19.98** MGM ⅋⅋⅋

All Tied Up Ladies man Brian (Galligan) thinks he's found true love with Linda (Hatch-er) but that doesn't mean he's stopped seeing other women. And when Linda finds out, she breaks it off. So Brian goes over to her house to work things out and gets tied up—literally—by Linda and her girlfriends. Talk about teaching a guy a lesson.
1992 (R) 90m/C Zach Galligan, Teri Hatcher, Tracy Griffith, Lara Harris; *D:* John Mark Robinson; *W:* Robert Madero, I. Markie Lane; *M:* Bernardo Bonazzi. **VHS $89.95** COL ⅋⅋½

All You Need Is Cash ''The Rutles'' star in this parody of The Beatles' legend, from the early days of the ''Pre-Fab Four'' in Liverpool to their worldwide success. A marvelous pseudo-documentary, originally shown on NBC-TV and with various SNL alumni (including Weiss), that captures the development of the Beatles and '60s rock with devastating effect. Served as the inspi-ration for ''This Is Spinal Tap.'' *AKA:* The Rutles.
1978 70m/C Eric Idle, Neil Innes, Rikki Fataar, Dan Aykroyd, Gilda Radner, John Belushi, George Harrison, Paul Simon, Mick Jagger, John Halsey; *D:* Eric Idle, Gary Weis. **VHS, Beta $14.95** MVD, MLT ⅋⅋⅋

Allan Quartermain and the Lost City of Gold While trying to find his brother, Quartermain discovers a lost African civilization, in this weak adaptation of an H. Rider Haggard adventure. An ostensible se-quel to the equally shallow ''King Solomon's Mines.''
1986 (PG) 100m/C Richard Chamberlain, Sharon Stone, James Earl Jones; *D:* Gary Nelson; *W:* Gene Quintano, Lee Reynolds. **VHS, Beta $9.99** FHE, MED, VTR ⅋½

Allegheny Uprising Set in 1759, the story of a frontiersman who clashes with a British military commander in order to stop the sale of firearms to Indians. The stars of ''Stagecoach'' are back on board in this lesser effort. Also available colorized. *AKA:* The First Rebel.
1939 81m/B John Wayne, Claire Trevor, George Sanders, Brian Donlevy, Chill Wills, Moroni Olsen; *D:* William A. Seiter. **VHS, Beta $14.98** RKO, CCB, TTC ⅋⅋½

Allegro Non Troppo An energetic and bold collection of animated skits set to classical music in this Italian version of Disney's ''Fantasia.'' Watch for the evolution of life set to Ravel's Bolero, or better yet, watch the whole darn movie. Features Ni-

chetti (often referred to as the Italian Woody Allen, particularly by people in Italy) who went on to write, direct, and star (he may have sold concessions in the lobby as well) in "The Icicle Thief."
1976 (PG) 75m/C *IT* Maurizio Nichetti; *D:* Bruno Bozzetto. **VHS $29.95** *BMG, IME, ING* ✂✂✂

Alley Cat Woman uses martial arts to fight back against a street gang that attacked her.
1984 (R) 82m/C Karin Mani, Robert Torti, Brit Helfer, Michael Wayne, Jon Greene; *D:* Edward Victor. **VHS, Beta $69.98** *VES, LIV* ✂

Alligator Dumped down a toilet 12 long years ago, lonely alligator Ramon resides in the city sewers, quietly eating and sleeping. In addition to feasting on the occasional stray human, Ramon devours the animal remains of a chemical plant's experiment involving growth hormones and eventually begins to swell at an enormous rate. Nothing seems to satisfy Ramon's ever-widening appetite: not all the people or all the buildings in the whole town, but he keeps trying, much to the regret of the guilt-ridden cop and lovely scientist who get to know each other while trying to nab the gator. Mediocre special effects are only a distraction in this witty eco-monster take.
1980 (R) 94m/C Robert Forster, Lewis Teague, Jack Carter, Henry Silva, Robin Riker, Dean Jagger; *D:* Lewis Teague; *W:* John Sayles, Frank Ray Perilli. **VHS, Beta $14.98** *LIV* ✂✂✂

Alligator 2: The Mutation Not a sequel to 1980's surprisingly good "Alligator," but a bland rehash with a decent cast. Once again a toxic alligator grows to enormous size and menaces a community. A Donald-Trump-like villain and pro wrestlers (!) bring this up to date, but it's all on the level of a TV disaster movie; even the PG-13 rating is a bit too harsh.
1990 (PG-13) 92m/C Steve Railsback, Dee Wallace Stone, Joseph Bologna, Woody Brown, Bill Daily, Brock Peters. **VHS $19.98** *COL, NLC* ✂✂

Alligator Alley When two young divers witness a major drug deal, they become entangled in a web of danger they never expected.
1972 92m/C Steve Alaimo, John Davis Chandler, Willie Pastrano, Jeremy Slate, Cece Stone; *D:* William Grefe. **VHS, Beta $79.95** *PSM* ✂

Alligator Eyes Stranger wearing trouble like a cheap perfume enters the midst of a vacationing trio of New Yorkers. Their vulnerabilities are exposed by a young hitchhiker sporting a slinky polka dot ensemble and way cool sunglasses who insinuates herself into their vacation plans (not to mention their private lives), before the three realize she's blind and full of manipulative and vindictive tricks, thanks to the usual brutal childhood. Psycho-sexo-logical thriller has some fine performances and a promising beginning, before fizzling into celluloid cotton candy.
1990 (R) 101m/C Annabelle Larsen, Roger Kabler, Mary McLain, Allen McCullough, John MacKay; *D:* John Feldman; *W:* John Feldman; *M:* Sheila Silver. **VHS $19.95** *ACA* ✂✂½

The Allnighter A college coed searches through the hypersexed beach-party milieu of her senior year for Mr. Right. Bangle Hoffs is directed by her mom, to no avail.
1987 (PG-13) 95m/C Susanna Hoffs, John Terlesky, Joan Cusack, Michael Ontkean; *D:* Tamar Simon Hoffs; *M:* Charles Bernstein. **VHS, Beta $79.95** *MCA* ✂

Allonsanfan Early Taviani, in which a disillusioned Jacobin aristocrat in 1816, after Napoleon has fallen, struggles with his revolutionary ideals and his accustomed lifestyle. Exciting score. In Italian with English subtitles.
1973 115m/C *IT* Marcello Mastroianni, Laura Betti, Renato de Carmine, Lea Massari, Mimsy Farmer, Claudio Cassinelli; *D:* Paolo Taviani; *M:* Ennio Morricone. **VHS, Beta $29.95** *FCT, WBF, ING* ✂✂½

All's Fair Silly and predictable comedy about executives who take on their spouses at weekend war games. An unfortunate waste of a good cast.
1989 89m/C George Segal, Sally Kellerman, Robert Carradine, Jennifer Edwards, Jane Kaczmarek, John Kapelos, Lou Ferrigno; *D:* Rocky Lane. **VHS, Beta $79.95** *MED* ✂

Almanac of Fall Set in a claustrophic apartment, where the occupants reveal all their deepest hositilies, fears, and obsessions. In Hungarian with English subtitles.
19?? 119m/C *HU* Hedi Temessy, Erika Bodnar, Miklos B. Szekely, Pal Hetenyi, Janos Dersi; *D:* Bela Tarr; *W:* Bela Tarr. **VHS $59.95** *FCT* ✂✂

Almos' a Man Richard Wright's story of a black teenage farm worker in the late 1930's who must endure the pains of growing up. From the "American Short Story" series.
1978 (G) 51m/C Madge Sinclair, Robert Dogui, LeVar Burton. **VHS, Beta $24.95** *MON, MTI, KAR* ✂✂

...Almost Arquette plays a curiously giddy bookworm with a vivid imagination. When her husband disappears on their anniversary, the man of her dreams shows up to sweep her off her feet. Is he real or is he simply another daydream? Almost a good time. *AKA:* Wendy Cracked a Walnut.
1990 (PG) 87m/C *AU* Rosanna Arquette, Bruce Spence; *D:* Michael Pattinson. **VHS** *NO* ✂✂

Almost an Angel Another in a recent spat of angels and ghosts assigned back to earth by the head office. A life-long criminal (Hogan) commits a heroic act and finds himself a probationary angel returned to earth to gain permanent angel status. He befriends a wheelchair-bound man, falls in love with the guy's sister, and helps her out at a center for potential juvenile delinquents. Melodramatic and hokey in places, relying too much on Hogan's crocodilian charisma.
1990 (PG) 98m/C Paul Hogan, Linda Kozlowski, Elias Koteas, Doreen Lang, Charlton Heston; *D:* John Cornell; *W:* Paul Hogan. **VHS $14.95** *PAR* ✂½

Almost Angels Two boys romp in Austria as members of the Vienna Boys Choir. Lesser sentimental Disney effort that stars the actual members of the Choir; not much of a draw for today's Nintendo-jaded young viewers.
1962 85m/C Vincent Winter, Peter Weck, Hans Holt; *D:* Steve Previn. **VHS, Beta $69.95** *DIS* ✂✂

Almost Blue A gigantic, slow-moving, movie cliche. Madsen is a sulky, hard-living sax player going off the deep end because of his wife's death. Walden is the good woman who comes along to save him from himself. Tenor saxman Ernie Watts doubles for Madsen. Do yourself a favor—skip the movie and listen to some good jazz instead.
1993 (R) 98m/C Michael Madsen, Lynette Walden, Garrett Morris, Gale Mayron, Yaphet Kotto; *D:* Keoni Waxman. **VHS $89.98** *LIV* ✂½

Almost Human An Italian Mafia gorefest about a second-class don who kidnaps a businessman's daughter, and then has trouble trying to collect a ransom. For aficionados of Italian Mafia gorefests only (check your weapons at the door). *AKA:* The Kidnap of Mary Lou.
1979 (R) 90m/C *IT* Henry Silva, Tomas Milian, Laura Belli; *D:* Umberto Lenzi; *M:* Ennio Morricone. **VHS, Beta $79.95** *PSM* Woof!

Almost Partners Grandpa's ashes are in trouble. His urn and remains have been stolen. Fortunately, his teenage granddaughter and a detective are on the case. From the PBS "Wonderworks" television series.
1987 58m/C Paul Sorvino, Royana Black, Mary Wickes; *D:* Alan Kingsberg. **VHS $29.95** *PME, HMV, FCT* Woof!

An Almost Perfect Affair Taxing romantic comedy about an ambitious independent American filmmaker who, after finishing a movie about an executed murderer, travels to the Cannes festival and proceeds to fall in love or lust with the wife of an Italian producer. Numerous inside jokes and capable performances nearly overcome script lethargy.
1979 (PG) 92m/C Keith Carradine, Monica Vitti, Raf Vallone, Christian de Sica, Dick Anthony Williams; *D:* Michael Ritchie; *M:* Georges Delerue. **VHS, Beta $59.95** *PAR* ✂✂

Almost Pregnant Linda Anderson (Roberts) desperately wants a baby, but her husband, Charlie (Conaway) is unable to get her pregnant. Dead set against artificial insemination, Linda decides to take a lover. Charlie doesn't want to lose her, so he goes along with her idea. Linda falls in love with the new guy; discovers he's had a vasectomy and takes yet another lover while continuing to see the other two guys. Hilarious complications abound in her outrageous quest for a baby. An unrated version containing explicit scenes is also available.
1991 (R) 90m/C Tanya Roberts, Jeff Conaway, Joan Severance, Dom DeLuise; *D:* Michael DeLuise; *W:* Fred Stroppel. **VHS $19.95** *COL* ✂✂½

Almost Royal Family All kinds of problems arise when a family inherits an island on the St. Lawrence River embargoed by the United States and Canada.
1984 52m/C Sarah Jessica Parker, John Femia. **VHS, Beta $39.95** *WAR* ✂

Almost You Normal marital conflicts and uncertainties grow exponentially when a wealthy New York City thirty-something couple hires a lovely young nurse to help care for the wife after a car accident. An unsentimental marital comedy with a good cast that still misses.
1985 (R) 91m/C Brooke Adams, Griffin Dunne, Karen Young, Marty Watt, Christine Estabrook, Josh Mostel, Laura Dean, Dana Delany, Miguel Pinero, Joe Silver, Suzzy Roche, Spalding Gray; *D:* Adam Brooks; *M:* Jonathan Elias. **VHS, Beta $79.98** *FOX* ✂✂

Aloha, Bobby and Rose A mechanic and his girlfriend in L.A. become accidentally involved in an attempted robbery and murder and go on the run for Mexico, of course. Semi-satisfying drama in the surf, with fine location photography.
1974 (PG) 90m/C Paul LeMat, Dianne Hull, Robert Carradine, Tim McIntire, Edward James Olmos, Leigh French; *D:* Floyd Mutrux. **VHS, Beta $49.95** *ACA* ✂✂½

Aloha Summer Six surfing teenagers of various ethnic backgrounds learn of love and life in 1959 Hawaii while riding the big wave of impending adulthood, with a splash of Kung Fu thrown in for good measure. Sensitive and bland.

1988 (PG) 97m/C Chris Makepeace, Lorie Griffin, Don Michael Paul, Sho Kosugi, Yuji Okumoto, Tia Carrere; *D:* Tommy Lee Wallace. **VHS, Beta** $19.98 *WAR, LHV ⅃⅃*

Alone Against Rome A muscle-bound warrior takes on the forces of Rome to avenge himself against a scornful woman. 1962 100m/B *IT* Lang Jeffries, Rossana Podesta, Phillippe LeRoy; *D:* Herbert Wise. **VHS, Beta** $16.95 *SNC ⅃½*

Alone in the Dark Slash and dash horror attempt featuring four escaped patients from a mental hospital who decide that they must kill their doctor because they don't like him. Conveniently, a city-wide blackout provides the opportunity, as the good doctor defends home and family against the aging stars intent on chewing up as much scenery as possible. 1982 (R) 92m/C Jack Palance, Donald Pleasence, Martin Landau, Dwight Schultz; *D:* Jack Sholder. **VHS, Beta** $19.95 *NLC, COL ⅃⅃*

Alone in the Neon Jungle A glamorous big-city police captain is assigned to clean up the most corrupt precinct in town. Pleshette is untypically cast but still manages to make her role believable in a serviceable TV cop drama with more dialogue than action. 1987 90m/C Suzanne Pleshette, Danny Aiello, Georg Stanford Brown, Frank Converse, Joe Morton; *D:* Georg Stanford Brown. **VHS** $19.95 *COL, NLC ⅃⅃*

Alone in the T-Shirt Zone A maniacal T-shirt designer lands in a mental institution. 1986 81m/C Michael Barrack, Taylor Gilbert, Bill Barron. **VHS, Beta** $19.95 *STE, NWV ⅃*

Along Came Jones Cowboy Cooper, who can't handle a gun and is saddled with grumpy sidekick Demarest, is the victim of mistaken identity as both the good guys and the bad guys pursue him thinking he is a vicious killer. Young is the woman who rides to his defense. Offbeat and charming western parody based on a novel by Alan le May. 1945 93m/B Gary Cooper, Loretta Young, Dan Duryea, William Demarest; *D:* Stuart Heisler; *W:* Nunnally Johnson. **VHS, Beta** $19.98 *MGM, FCT ⅃⅃⅃*

Along the Great Divide A U.S. marshal and his deputy battle pursuing vigilantes and the untamed frontier to bring a falsely accused murderer to trial (and of course, find the real bad guy). Douglas' first western has the usual horse opera cliches supported by excellent cinematography. 1951 88m/B Kirk Douglas, John Agar, Walter Brennan, Virginia Mayo; *D:* Raoul Walsh. **VHS, Beta** $19.98 *WAR, TLF ⅃⅃*

Along the Sundown Trail Standard western escapades as cowboy G-men round up the villains. 1942 59m/B William Boyd, Art Davis, Lee Powell, Julie Duncan, Kermit Maynard, Charles "Blackie" King; *D:* Sam Newfield. **VHS, Beta** $11.95 *GPV, VCN ⅃*

Alpha Beta A stage production set to film studying the break-up of a marriage, where all the husband and wife have in common is the children. Finney and Roberts efficiently carry the load. 1973 70m/C Albert Finney, Rachel Roberts; *D:* Anthony Page. **VHS, Beta** NO *⅃⅃½*

The Alpha Incident Time-worn doomsday drama about an alien organism with the potential to destroy all living things. Government works hard to cover up.

1976 (PG) 86m/C Ralph Meeker, Stafford Morgan, John Goff, Carol Irene Newell, John Alderman; *D:* Bill Rebane. **VHS, Beta** $9.95 *MED ⅃½*

Alphabet City A drug kingpin who runs New York's Lower East Side has decided to turn over a new leaf, but first he must survive his last night as a criminal while figuring out a way to pay off his large debts. Very stylish and moody, but light on content and plot. 1984 (R) 85m/C Vincent Spano, Michael Winslow, Kate Vernon, Jami Gertz, Zohra Lampert, Ray Serra, Kenny Marino, Daniel Jordano, Miguel Pinero; *D:* Amos Poe; *W:* Amos Poe. **VHS, Beta** $79.98 *FOX ⅃⅃*

The Alphabet Murders Picture this: Randall playing Agatha Christie's famous Belgian sleuth, Hercule Poirot, and Rutherford—in a cameo—as Miss Marple. As if that wouldn't be enough to make Dame Agatha roll over in her grave, there's plenty of cloying wisecracking and slapsticking throughout. An adaptation of ''The ABC Murders'' in which Poirot stalks a literate killer who snuffs out his victims in alphabetical order. Hardly a must-see, unless you're hellbent on viewing the entire Randall opus. *AKA:* ABC Murders. 1965 90m/B Tony Randall, Anita Ekberg, Robert Morley, Maurice Denham, Guy Rolfe, Sheila Allen; *Cameos:* Margaret Rutherford; *D:* Frank Tashlin. **VHS, Beta** $19.98 *MGM, FCT ⅃⅃*

Alphaville Engaging and inimitable Godard attempt at science fiction mystery. P.I. Lemmy Caution searches for a scientist in a city (Paris as you've never seen it before) run by robots and overseen by a dictator. The futuristic techno-conformist society must be upended so that Caution may save the scientist as well as nonconformists everywhere. In French with subtitles. *AKA:* Alphaville, a Strange Case of Lenny Caution; Alphaville, Une etrange Aventure de Lenny Caution. 1965 100m/B *FR* Eddie Constantine, Anna Karina, Akim Tamiroff; *D:* Jean-Luc Godard; *W:* Jean-Luc Godard. **VHS, Beta** $24.95 *NOS, SNC, MRV ⅃⅃⅃*

Alpine Fire Coming of age story about an adolescent girl and her deaf-mute brother living an isolated life in the Swiss Alps. When life on the mountain overwhelms them, they turn to each other for love. Sharply observed with a naturalistic style, elevating the proceedings above mere voyeurism. 1989 (R) 119m/C *SI* Thomas Knock, Johanna Lier, Dorothea Moritz, Rolf Illig; *D:* Fredi M. Murer. **VHS, Beta** $79.98 *VES, LIV ⅃⅃½*

Alsino and the Condor An acclaimed Nicaraguan drama about a young boy, caught in war-torn Nicaragua between the Somoza government and the Sandinista rebels, who dreams of flying above the human strife. In Spanish with English subtitles. 1982 (R) 89m/C *NI* Dean Stockwell, Alan Esquivel; *D:* Miguel Littin. **VHS, Beta** $29.95 *FCT, ING, TPV ⅃⅃⅃*

Altered States Obsessed with the task of discovering the inner man, Hurt's ambitious researcher ignores his family while consuming hallucinogenic drugs and floating in an immersion tank. He gets too deep inside, slipping way back through the evolutionary order and becoming a menace in the process. Confusing script based upon Chayefsky's (alias Sidney Aaron) confusing novel is supported by great special effects and the usual self-indulgent and provocative Russell direction. Chayefsky eventually washed his hands of the project after artistic differences with the producers. Others who departed from the film include initial director William Penn and special effects genius John Dyks-

tra (relieved ably by Bran Ferren). Hurt's a solemn hoot in his first starring role. 1980 (R) 103m/C William Hurt, Blair Brown, Bob Balaban, Charles Haid, Dori Brenner, Drew Barrymore; *D:* Ken Russell; *W:* Paddy Chayefsky. **VHS, Beta** $14.95 *WAR ⅃⅃⅃*

Alternative A female magazine editor finds herself unmarried and quite pregnant. She is caught in a tug-of-war between the baby's father and her current lover. Dated liberated woman and career snoozer. 1976 90m/C Wendy Hughes, Peter Adams, Mary Mackie, Carla Hoogeveen, Tony Bonner. **VHS, Beta** NO *⅃⅃*

Alvarez Kelly Offbeat western with Holden as the Mexican-Irish Kelly who has just sold a herd of cattle to the North during the Civil War. Confederate officer Widmark kidnaps Holden in an effort to have the cattle redirected to the South. Aided by the traditional women in the midst of men intent on double-crossing each other, a fierce hatred develops between the two, erupting into violence. Sleepy performance by Holden is countered by an intensive Widmark. Based on a true Civil War incident, the script occasionally wanders far afield with the cattle, who cleverly heighten the excitement by stampeding. 1966 109m/C William Holden, Richard Widmark, Janice Rule, Patrick O'Neal, Harry Carey Jr.; *D:* Edward Dmytryk. **VHS, Beta** $14.95 *COL, GKK ⅃⅃½*

Alvin Purple Pedestrian comedy about a Mr. Purple, an ordinary Aussie who sells waterbeds and is for some reason constantly being pursued by throngs of sexually insatiable women. Fortunately, he too enjoys sex, even though complications abound. Sexual situations, double entendres, and a script that aims for cleverness (but rarely attains it) somehow made the lust romp a hit in its native Australia, while worldwide it helped establish a market for Down Under cinema. Shot in Melbourne, and followed by ''Alvin Rides Again.'' 1973 (R) 97m/C *AU* Graeme Blundell, George Whaley, Ellie MacLure, Jacki Weaver; *D:* Tim Burstall; *W:* Alan Finney, Alan Hopgood, Tim Burstall. **VHS, Beta** $19.95 *NWV ⅃½*

Alvin Rides Again The sexually insatiable Alvin Purple is asked to impersonate an American gangster who was accidentally killed. Another Aussie sex farce from the original writers, who conspire to create a decent sequel to ''Alvin Purple,'' with much of the same cast and crew. 1974 89m/C *AU* Graeme Blundell, Alan Finney, Brionny Behets, Frank Thring, Jeff Ashby, Robin Copping; *D:* David Bilcock; *W:* Tim Burstall, Alan Finney, Alan Hopgood. **VHS, Beta** $19.95 *NWV ⅃⅃*

Always Jaglom fictionally documents his own divorce and reconciliation with Patrice Townsend: set in the director's home and starring his friends and family, the film provides comic insight into the dynamics of married/about-to-be-married and used-to-be-married relationships. Set at a Fourth of July barbecue, this bittersweet romantic comedy is a veritable feast for Jaglom fans, but not everyone will find the director's free-form narrative to their taste. 1985 (R) 105m/C Henry Jaglom, Patrice Townsend, Bob Rafelson, Melissa Leo, Andre Gregory, Michael Emil, Joanna Frank, Alan Rachins, Jonathan Kaufer; *D:* Henry Jaglom; *W:* Henry Jaglom. **VHS, Beta** $79.98 *VES, LIV ⅃⅃⅃*

Always A hotshot pilot (Dreyfuss) meets a fiery end and finds that his spirit is destined to become a guardian angel to the greenhorn fire-fighting flyboy (Johnson) who steals his

girl's heart. Warm remake of "A Guy Named Joe," one of Spielberg's favorite movies. Sparks between Dreyfuss and Hunter eventually ignite, but Goodman delivers the most heat. Hepburn makes an appearance as the angel who guides Dreyfuss. An old-fashioned tree-burner romance that includes actual footage of the 1988 Yellowstone fire.
1989 (PG) 123m/C Holly Hunter, Richard Dreyfuss, John Goodman, Audrey Hepburn, Brad Johnson, Marg Helgenberger, Keith David, Roberts Blossom; *D:* Steven Spielberg; *W:* Jerry Belson; *M:* John Williams. **VHS, Beta $19.95** MCA, FCT *♪♪*½

Amadeus Entertaining adaptation by Shaffer of his play about the intense rivalry between 18th century composers Antonio Salieri and Wolfgang Amadeus Mozart. Abraham's Salieri is a man who desires greatness but is tortured by envy and sorrow. His worst attacks of angst occur when he comes into contact with Hulce's Mozart, an immature, boorish genius who, despite his gifts, remains unaffected and delighted by the beauty he creates while irking the hell out of everyone around him. Terrific period piece filmed on location in Prague; excellent musical score, beautiful sets, nifty billowy costumes, and realistic American accents for the 18th century Europeans. ♫Concert No. 27 for Pianoforte and Orchestra in B Flat Major; Ave Verum Corpus; A Quintet For Strings in E Flat; A Concerto for Clarinet and Orchestra in A Major; Number 39 in E Flat Major; Number 40 in G Minor; Number 41 in C Major.
1984 (PG) 158m/C F. Murray Abraham, Tom Hulce, Elizabeth Berridge, Simon Callow, Roy Dotrice, Christine Ebersole, Jeffrey Jones, Kenny L. Baker, Cynthia Nixon, Vincent Schiavelli; *D:* Milos Forman; *W:* Peter Shaffer. Academy Awards '84: Best Actor (Abraham), Best Adapted Screenplay, Best Art Direction/Set Decoration, Best Costume Design, Best Director (Forman), Best Makeup, Best Picture, Best Sound; Nominations: Best Actor (Hulce), Best Cinematography, Best Film Editing; Cesar Awards '85: Best Foreign Film; Directors Guild of America Awards '84: Best Director (Forman); Golden Globe Awards '85: Best Actor—Drama (Abraham), Best Director (Forman), Best Film—Drama, Best Screenplay. **VHS, Beta $14.98** REP, GLV, BTV *♪♪♪*½

Amarcord Semi-autobiographical Fellini fantasy which takes place in the village of Rimini, his birthplace. Focusing on the young Zanin's impressions of his town's colorful slices of life, Fellini takes aim at facism, family life, and religion in 1930's Italy. Visually ripe, delivering a generous, occasionally uneven mix of satire, burlesque, drama, and tragicomedic lyricism. Considered by people in the know as one of Fellini's best films and the topic of meaningful discussions among art film students everywhere.
1974 (R) 124m/C *IT* Magali Noel, Bruno Zanin, Pupella Maggio, Armando Brancia, Tonino Guerra; *D:* Federico Fellini; *W:* Federico Fellini, Tonino Guerra. Academy Awards '74: Best Foreign Language Film; Nominations: Best Director (Fellini), Best Original Screenplay; National Board of Review Awards '74: 5 Best Foreign Films of the Year; New York Film Critics Awards '74: Best Director (Fellini), Best Film. **VHS, Beta** APD *♪♪♪*½

The Amateur Computer technologist for the CIA dives into a plot of international intrigue behind the Iron Curtain when he investigates the death of his girlfriend, murdered by terrorists. Confused and ultimately disappointing spy drama cursed with a wooden script written by Littell, based on his novel.
1982 (R) 112m/C John Savage, Christopher Plummer, Marthe Keller, Arthur Hill, Ed Lauter; *D:* Charles Jarrott. **VHS, Beta $59.98** FOX *♪*½

Amateur Night Sloppy musical comedy about the backstage bickering occuring during the amateur night at a famous nightclub.
1985 91m/C Geoffrey Deuel, Dennis Cole, Allen Kirk. **VHS, Beta $69.98** VES, LIV *♪*

Amazing Adventure A millionaire wins a bet when he rises from a chauffeur's position to the executive board room without using his wealth. Though not particularly amazing, lightweight English comedy has Grant working hard to charm over and above the demands of the dated formula, a performance he undertook during a vacation from Hollywood. Adapted from a novel by E. Phillips Oppenheim. *AKA:* Romance and Riches; The Amazing Quest of Ernest Bliss; Riches and Romance.
1937 63m/C Cary Grant, Mary Brian, Henry Kendall, Leon M. Lion, Ralph Richardson; *D:* Alfred Zeisler. **VHS, Beta $19.95** NOS, BAR, DVT *♪♪*

The Amazing Colossal Man A standard '50s sci-fi film about atomic radiation. Colonel Manning is exposed to massive doses of plutonium when an experiment backfires (literally). The former good-guy grows to seventy feet and starts taking out his anger on a helpless Las Vegas. Can anything stop his murderous rampages? Followed by "War of the Colossal Beast."
1957 79m/B Glenn Langan, Cathy Downs, William Hudson, James Seay, Russ Bender, Lyn Osborn; *D:* Bert I. Gordon. **VHS $9.95** COL, FUS *♪♪*

The Amazing Dobermans Family-oriented pooch performance piece featuring Astaire in one of his lesser roles. Ex-con man Astaire and his five trained Dobermans assist an undercover agent in foiling a small-time criminal's gambling and extortion racket. The last in a series that includes "The Daring Dobermans" and "The Doberman Gang."
1976 (G) 96m/C Fred Astaire, Barbara Eden, James Franciscus, Jack Carter, Billy Barty; *D:* Byron Ross Chudnow. **VHS, Beta $9.95** MED *♪♪*

Amazing Grace Some righteous mothers led by Moms Mabley go up against corrupt city politics in this extremely dated comedy that was cast with a sense of the absurd.
1974 99m/C Moms Mabley, Slappy White, Moses Gunn, Rosalind Cash, Dolph Sweet, Butterfly McQueen, Stepin Fetchit; *D:* Stan Lathan. **VHS** NO *♪♪*

Amazing Grace & Chuck Perhaps the only anti-war/sports fantasy ever made. After a visit to a Minuteman missile site in Montana, 12-year-old Little Leaguer Chuck learns of the dangers of nuclear arms. He begins a protest by refusing to play until the nations come to a peace agreement. In a sudden surge of social conscience, athletes worldwide put down their equipment and join in droves, starting with pro-basketball star Amazing Grace Smith (Denver Nugget English). Capra-like fantasy has good intentions but ultimately lacks two key elements: coherency and plausibility.
1987 (PG) 115m/C Jamie Lee Curtis, Gregory Peck, William L. Petersen, Joshua Zuehlke, Alex English; *D:* Mike Newell; *M:* Elmer Bernstein. **VHS, Beta $19.99** HBO *♪♪*

The Amazing Howard Hughes Reveals the full story of the legendary millionaire's life and career, from daring test pilot to inventor to Hollywood film producer to isolated wealthy paranoiac with a germ phobia. Lingers on the rich guy with big problems theme. Big-budget, made for television drama with a nice performance by Jones.

1977 119m/C Tommy Lee Jones, Ed Flanders, James Hampton, Tovah Feldshuh, Lee Purcell; *D:* William A. Graham. **VHS, Beta $19.95** FCT *♪♪*½

Amazing Mr. Blunden Solid kidvid about two youngsters aided by a ghost who travel back in time to save the lives of two murdered children. Adapted by Jeffries from Antonia Barber's novel, "The Ghosts."
1972 (G) 100m/C Laurence Naismith, Lynne Frederick, Garry Miller, Marc Granger, Rosalyn London, Diana Dors; *D:* Lionel Jeffries; *M:* Elmer Bernstein. **VHS, Beta $19.95** MED *♪♪*½

The Amazing Mr. X When a woman's husband dies, she tries to contact him via a spiritualist. Things are not as they seem however, and the medium may just be part of an intricate scheme to defraud the woman. *AKA:* The Spiritualist.
1948 79m/B Turhan Bey, Lynn Bari, Cathy O'Donnell, Richard Carlson, Donald Curtis, Virginia Gregg; *D:* Bernard Vorhaus. **VHS, Beta $19.95** NOS, SNC, RXM *♪♪*½

The Amazing Spider-Man The Marvel Comics superhero's unique powers are put to the test when he comes to the rescue of the government by preventing an evil scientist from blackmailing the government for big bucks. The wall-walking web-slinger has his origins probed (a grad student bit by a radioactive spider develops super-human powers) in his live-action debut, which was made for television and led to a short-lived series. *AKA:* Spider-Man.
1977 94m/C Nicholas Hammond, David White, Lisa Eilbacher, Michael Pataki; *D:* E.W. Swackhamer. **VHS, Beta $24.98** FOX, IME *♪♪*

Amazing Stories From the Steven Spielberg produced television series. "The Mission" sees a WWII tail gunner trapped in an unusual predicament. In "The Wedding Ring," a man gives his wife a strange ring and bizarre situations ensue. Additional episodes available.
1985 70m/C Kevin Costner, Casey Siemaszko, Kiefer Sutherland, Danny DeVito, Rhea Perlman; *D:* Danny DeVito, Steven Spielberg. **VHS $19.98** MCA, FCT, MOV *♪♪*

The Amazing Transparent Man A mad scientist makes a crook invisible in order to steal the radioactive materials he needs. The crook decides to rob banks instead. Shot at the Texas State Fair for that elusive futuristic look. For Ulmer fans only.
1960 58m/B Douglas Kennedy, Marguerite Chapman, James Griffith, Ivan Triesault; *D:* Edgar G. Ulmer. **VHS $16.95** NOS, SNC Woof!

The Amazing Transplant A sleaze-bag psycho has a "love enhancing" transplant, much to the pleasure of his sexual partners. Much to their and our dismay, however, he then kills them and bores us.
1970 90m/C Juan Fernandez, Linda Southern; *D:* Doris Wishman. **VHS, Beta $24.95** TPV Woof!

Amazon An adventure movie filmed in the Brazilian rainforest with an environmental message. A businessman being chased by the police in the Amazon jungle is rescued by a bush pilot who dreams of mining the Amazon's riches. A Brazilian woman enters the picture and persuades the businessman to help save the rainforest. Portions of the proceeds from the sale of this film go to the Rainforest Action Network.
1990 90m/C Kari Vaananen, Robert Davi, Rae Dawn Chong; *D:* Mika Kaurismaki. **VHS $89.98** LIV *♪♪*

Amazon Jail Scantily clad women go over the wall and promptly get caught by devil worshiping men in the jungle. They should have known better. Redeemed only by lingerie selection.
1985 94m/C Elisabeth Hartmann, Mauricio Do Valle, Sondra Graffi; D: Oswald De Oliveira. VHS, Beta NO &

Amazon Women on the Moon A plotless, irreverent media spoof, depicting the programming of a slipshod television station as it crams weird commercials and shorts around a comical '50s science fiction film. Inconsistent, occasionally funny anthology hangs together very loosely. Produced by Landis, with the usual amount of in-joke cameos and allusions to his other works of art.
1987 (R) 85m/C Rosanna Arquette, Steve Guttenberg, Steve Allen, B.B. King, Michelle Pfeiffer, Arsenio Hall, Andrew Dice Clay, Howard Hesseman, Lou Jacobi, Carrie Fisher, Griffin Dunne, Sybil Danning, Henny Youngman, Monique Gabrielle, Paul Bartel, Kelly Preston; D: John Landis, Joe Dante, Carl Gottlieb, Peter Horton, Robert Weiss. VHS, Beta $14.98 MCA &&

The Amazons Goofy made for television drama about a beautiful doctor who discovers an underground organization of Amazon-descended women bent on taking over the world or at least making life hard for men while investigating a Congressman's mysterious death.
1984 100m/C Tamara Dobson, Jack Scalia, Stella Stevens, Madeleine Stowe, Jennifer Warren; D: Paul Michael Glaser. VHS, Beta NO &½

Amazons Tall, strong women who occasionally wander around nude search for a magical talisman that will overthrow an evil magician.
1986 (R) 76m/C Windsor Taylor Randolph, Penelope Reed, Joseph Whipp, Willie Nelson, Danitza Kingsley; D: Alex Sessa. VHS, Beta $79.95 MGM &

The Ambassador An American ambassador (Mitchum) is sent to the Middle East to try to solve the area's deep political problems. He quickly becomes the target of terrorist attacks, and is blamed for the nation's unrest. To make matters worse, his wife is having an affair with a PLO leader. The President ignores him, forcing the ambassador to fend for himself. Talk about your bad days. Hudson's last feature. Based on Elmore Leonard's "52 Pickup," and remade a year later under its own title. AKA: Peacemaker.
1984 97m/C Robert Mitchum, Ellen Burstyn, Rock Hudson, Fabio Testi, Donald Pleasence; D: J. Lee Thompson. VHS, Beta $79.95 MGM &&½

Ambassador Bill An Oklahoma rancher is appointed ambassador to a country in revolt. Rogers, of course, saves the day with his rustic witticisms. Based on the story "Ambassador from the United States" by Vincent Sheean.
1931 68m/B Will Rogers, Marguerite Churchill, Greta Nissen; D: Sam Taylor. VHS $19.98 FOX, FCT &&

The Ambassador's Daughter The Parisian adventures of an American ambassador's daughter De Havilland and soldier Forsythe, who, unaware of her position, falls in love with her. Faltering comedy is supported by an expert cast (although nearly 40, De Havilland is charming as the young woman) with especially good performances from Menjou and Loy.
1956 102m/C Olivia de Havilland, John Forsythe, Myrna Loy, Adolphe Menjou, Edward Arnold, Francis Lederer, Tommy Noonan, Minor Watson; D: Norman Krasna; W: Norman Krasna. VHS, MOV &&

Amber Waves Credible made for television drama about a generation-gap conflict between a Midwestern farmer (Weaver) and an irresponsible male model (Russell) who has coasted through life on con and charm.
1982 98m/C Dennis Weaver, Kurt Russell; D: Joseph Sargent. VHS, Beta TLF &&½

Ambition Scriptwriter/star Phillips gets a bone for chutzpah by taking an unsavory lead role; his character torments a paroled psycho so that the killer will kill again and inspire a true-crime bestseller. The plot looks good on paper, but onscreen it's padded and unconvincing.
1991 (R) 99m/C Lou Diamond Phillips, Clancy Brown, Cecilia Peck, Richard Bradford, Willard Pugh, Grace Zabriskie, Katherine Armstrong, John Cullum, Haing S. Ngor; D: Scott Goldstein; W: Lou Diamond Phillips; M: Leonard Rosenman. VHS, Beta $92.98 FXV, MED, VTR &½

The Ambulance A New York cartoonist witnesses a mysterious ambulance at work and decides to investigate. His probings uncover a plot to sell the bodies of dying diabetics. A surprisingly good no-money feature from low-budget king Cohen. Includes an appearance by Marvel Comics' Stan Lee as himself.
1990 (R) 95m/C Eric Roberts, James Earl Jones, Megan Gallagher, Richard Bright, Janine Turner, Eric (Hans Gudegast) Braeden, Red Buttons, Laurene Landon, Jill Gatsby, Nicholas Chinlund; D: Larry Cohen; W: Larry Cohen. VHS, COL, EPC &&½

Ambush at Tomahawk Gap Three released prisoners go in search of hidden loot and tempers rise when the goods don't turn up. Then the Apaches show up.
1953 73m/C John Hodiak, John Derek, David Brian, Maria Elena Marques, Ray Teal; D: Fred F. Sears. VHS, Beta GKK &&

The Ambush Murders True story of a stalwart white attorney defending a black activist accused of killing two cops. Not the compelling television it could be, but still enjoyable. From Ben Bradlee, Jr.'s novel.
1982 100m/C James Brolin, Dorian Harewood, Alfre Woodard, Louis Giambalvo, John McLiam, Teddy Wilson, Antonio Fargas, Amy Madigan; D: Steven Hilliard Stern. VHS, Beta $49.95 FRH, LIV &&½

Ambush Trail Stranger-in-town Steele metes out justice to help local ranchers while sidekick Saylor leaves 'em laughing.
1946 60m/B Bob Steele, Syd Saylor, I. Stanford Jolley, Lorraine Miller, Charles "Blackie" King, Kermit Maynard; D: Harry Fraser. VHS $19.95 NOS, GPV &&

The Ambushers Martin's third Matt Helm farce finds him handling a puzzling case involving the first United States spacecraft. When the craft is hijacked with Rule on board, it's Matt to the rescue, regaining control before unfriendly forces can take it back to Earth. Tired formula seems to have worn Martin out while the remainder of the cast goes to camp. Followed by "The Wrecking Crew."
1967 102m/C Dean Martin, Janice Rule, James Gregory, Albert Salmi, Senta Berger; D: Henry Levin. VHS, Beta $14.95 COL Woof!

Amenaza Nuclear A Mexican farce about two idiots who try to stop mysterious Chinamen from stealing nuclear arms.
19?? 106m/C MX Emeterio Y. Felipes, Lydia Zamora, Ki Jeong Lee. VHS, Beta $59.95 MAD &

America New York cable station receives worldwide fame when their signal bounces off of the moon. Uninspired piece of fluff from otherwise talented director Downey.
1986 (R) 83m/C Zack Norman, Tammy Grimes, Michael J. Pollard, Monroe Arnold, Richard Belzer, Liz Torres, Howard Thomashefsky, Laura Ashton, Robert Downey Jr.; D: Robert Downey. VHS NO &½

America at the Movies Scenes from more than 80 of the finest American motion pictures fly by in an effort to tell the story of the cinema and provide a portrait of America as it has been seen on screen for half a century. Scenes from "The Birth of a Nation," "Citizen Kane," "Dr. Strangelove," "East of Eden," "The French Connection," and "From Here to Eternity," are among the many included. Some black and white scenes; produced by the American Film Institute.
1976 116m/C John Wayne, Orson Welles, Peter Sellers, James Dean, Gene Hackman, Burt Lancaster, Julie Harris, Deborah Kerr, Al Pacino, Robert De Niro. VHS, Beta $59.95 COL, IME &&½

America First A group of seven travelers try to build an "Eden" with the inhabitants of an Appalachian hollow.
1970 90m/C Michael Kennedy, Walter Keller, Pat Estrin, Lois McGuire. VHS, Beta NO &½

America/The Fall of Babylon A double feature containing abridged versions; in "America," a Boston patriot and the daughter of an aristocratic Virginia Tory fall in love during the Revolutionary War; "The Fall of Babylon" is one of the stories in D.W. Griffith's "Intolerance." Silent.
1924 56m/B Neil Hamilton, Lionel Barrymore, Constance Talmadge, Elmer Clifton, Alfred Paget. VHS, Beta $29.98 CCB &&

America 3000 Hundreds of years in the holocaust-torn future, men rebel against a brutal, overpowering race of women, with predictable results.
1986 (PG-13) 94m/C Chuck Wagner, Laurene Landon; D: David Engelbach. VHS, Beta $79.95 MGM &

The American Angels: Baptism of Blood Three beautiful young women, each with a personal dream, strive to make it in the world of professional wrestling. Hackneyed plot devices, but those simply watching for the wrestling scenes won't be disappointed.
1989 (R) 99m/C Jan MacKenzie, Tray Loren, Mimi Lesseos, Trudy Adams, Patricia Cavoti, Susan Sexton, Jean Kirkland, Jeff Lundy, Lee Marshall; D: Beverly Sebastian, Ferd Sebastian. VHS, Beta $79.95 PAR &

American Anthem A young gymnast must choose between family responsibilities or the parallel bars. Olympic gymnast Gaylord makes his movie debut but doesn't get the gold. Good fare for young tumblers, but that's about it. Followed by two of the films' music videos and tape-ads featuring Max Headroom.
1986 (PG-13) 100m/C Mitch Gaylord, Janet Jones, Michelle Phillips, Michael Pataki; D: Albert Magnoli. VHS, Beta $19.98 LHV, WAR &

American Aristocracy A silent comic romp in which Fairbanks, an old moneyed dandy, wreaks havoc on an island resort whose clientele is composed of the nouveau well-to-do.
1917 52m/B Douglas Fairbanks Sr., Jewel Carmen, Albert Parker; D: Lloyd Ingraham. VHS, Beta $16.95 GPV &&½

American Autobahn A low-budget independent actioner about a journalist who discovers an underworld weapons ring that hits the highway in pursuit of him.
1984 90m/C Jan Jalenak, Michael von der Goltz, Jim Jarmusch; **D:** Andre Degas. **VHS, Beta** *NO* 🎬½

American Blue Note Loosely plotted, bittersweet account of a struggling jazz quartet in the early 1960s, as its leader (MacNicol) must decide if their fruitless tours of sleazy bars and weddings are still worth it. The debut of director Toporoff. **AKA:** Fakebook.
1989 (PG-13) 96m/C Peter MacNicol, Carl Capotorto, Tim Guinee, Bill Christopher-Myers, Jonathan Walker, Charlotte d'Amboise, Louis Guss, Zohra Lampert, Trini Alvarado, Sam Behrens; **D:** Ralph Toporoff; **W:** Gilbert Girion, Larry Schanker. **VHS $89.95** *COL, BTV* 🎬🎬

American Born Murder Inc. returns to the dismay of one idealist who embarks on a battle he doesn't intend to lose. The mob had better look out.
1989 Joey Travolta, Andrew Zeller; **D:** Raymond Martino; **W:** Raymond Martino. **VHS** *PMH* 🎬½

American Boyfriends An ostensible sequel to "My American Cousin," in which two Canadian girls go to California and discover innocent romance and friendship.
1989 (PG-13) 90m/C *CA* Margaret Langrick, John Wildman, Jason Blicker, Lisa Repo Martell; **D:** Sandy Wilson; **W:** Sandy Wilson. **VHS, Beta $79.95** *LIV* 🎬🎬

An American Christmas Carol Charles Dickens' classic story is retold with limited charm in a made for television effort. This time a greedy American financier (Winkler) learns about the true meaning of Christmas.
1979 98m/C Henry Winkler, David Wayne, Dorian Harewood; **D:** Eric Till; **M:** Hagood Hardy. **VHS, Beta $12.98** *VES, LIV* 🎬🎬

American Commandos An ex-Green Beret slaughters the junkies who killed his son and raped his wife, and then joins his old buddies for a secret, Rambo-esque mission in Vietnam providing a tired rehash of Vietnam movie cliches. **AKA:** Hitman.
1984 (R) 96m/C Chris Mitchum, John Phillip Law, Franco Guerrero; **D:** Bobby Suarez. **VHS, Beta $79.98** *LIV* 🎬

American Dream A midwestern family leaves the suburbs and moves into a Chicago inner-city neighborhood. Good TV-movie pilot for the short-lived series that was Emmy nominated for direction and writing.
1981 90m/C Stephen Macht, Karen Carlson, John Karlen, Andrea Smith, John Malkovich, John McIntire; **D:** Mel Damski. **VHS, Beta $29.95** *UNI* 🎬🎬🎬

American Dreamer A housewife wins a trip to Paris as a prize from a mystery writing contest. Silly from a blow on the head, she begins living the fictional life of her favorite literary adventure. Sporadic comedy with a good cast wandering about courtesy of a clumsy screenplay.
1984 (PG) 105m/C JoBeth Williams, Tom Conti, Giancarlo Giannini, Coral Browne, James Staley; **D:** Rick Rosenthal; **M:** Lewis Furey. **VHS, Beta $19.98** *FOX* 🎬🎬

American Eagle A veteran goes crazy and seeks sadistic, bloody revenge on his war buddies. Now his war buddies are the only ones who can stop him.
1990 (R) 92m/C Asher Brauner, Robert F. Lyons, Vernon Wells, Kai Baker; **D:** Robert J. Smawley. **VHS $89.95** *VMK* 🎬½

American Empire Two Civil War heroes struggle to build a cattle empire in Texas and are hampered by rustlers, one of whom was their partner. A fine, veteran cast and a tight script keep things moving, including the cattle. **AKA:** My Son Alone.
1942 82m/B Preston Foster, Richard Dix, Frances Gifford, Leo Carrillo; **D:** William McGann. **VHS, Beta $16.95** *NOS, MRV, DVT* 🎬🎬½

American Fabulous The posthumously released autobiography of an eccentric homosexual who lived life in the fast lane. Jeffrey Strouth performs his monologue from the back seat of a 1957 Cadillac, where the images of small-town America are seen to contrast sharply with his flamboyant style. His grotesque and candid recollections include his alcoholic Elvis-impersonator father, a stint as a teenage prostitute, drag queen friends, and drug addiction in New York. Strouth puts a comic twist on even the most brutal of his memories. He died of AIDS at the age of 33 in 1992.
1992 105m/C Jeffrey Strouth; **D:** Reno Dakota; **W:** Jeffrey Strouth. **VHS $59.95** *FRV, ICA* 🎬🎬½

American Flyers Two competitive brothers train for a grueling three-day bicycle race in Colorado while tangling with personal drama, including the spector that one of them may have inherited dad's tendency for cerebral aneurisms and is sure to drop dead during a bike race soon. Written by bike movie specialist Teisch ("Breaking Away") with a lot of the usual cliches (the last bike ride, battling bros, eventual understanding), which are gracefully overridden by fine bike-racing photography. Interesting performances, especially Chong as a patient girlfriend and Amos as the trainer.
1985 (PG-13) 113m/C Kevin Costner, David Marshall Grant, Rae Dawn Chong, Alexandra Paul, John Amos, Janice Rule, Robert Townsend, Jennifer Grey, Luca Bercovici; **D:** John Badham; **W:** Steve Tesich; **M:** Lee Ritenour, Greg Mathieson. **VHS, Beta $19.98** *WAR* 🎬🎬

The American Friend Tribute to the American gangster film helped introduce Wenders to American moviegoers. Young Hamburg picture framer thinks he has a terminal disease and is set up by American expatriate Hopper to become a hired assassin in West Germany. The lure is a promise of quick money that the supposedly dying man can then leave his wife and child. After the first assasination, the two bond. Hopper is the typical Wenders protagonist, a strange man in a strange land looking for a connection. Great, creepy thriller adapted from Patricia Highsmith's novel "Ripley's Game." Fuller and Ray (better known as directors) appear briefly as gangsters.
1977 127m/C *FR GE* Bruno Ganz, Dennis Hopper, Elisabeth Kreuzer, Gerard Blain, Jean Eustache, Samuel Fuller, Nicholas Ray, Wim Wenders; **D:** Wim Wenders; **W:** Wim Wenders. Cannes Film Festival Nominations: cs '77: Best Film; National Board of Review Awards '77: 5 Best Foreign Films of the Year. **VHS, Beta $29.95** *FCT, GLV, ING* 🎬🎬🎬½

American Friends Genteel story masquerades as high comedy. Palin is a fussy middle-aged Oxford classics tutor. On a holiday he meets American Hartley (Booth) and her adopted daughter, Elinor (Alvarado). Both women are immensely attracted to the don (for reasons that are unclear) and follow him back to Oxford, where he's engaged in a battle of succession with his rival Molina. Dismal screenplay lacks logic and urgency, making it difficult to care about the story or the characters. Script is said to have been inspired by an incident in the life of Palin's

great-grandfather. If this sounds like your cup of tea, save your time and watch a Merchant Ivory film instead.
1991 (PG) 95m/C *GB* Michael Palin, Connie Booth, Trini Alvarado, Alfred Molina; **D:** Tristan Powell; **W:** Michael Palin, Tristam Powell; **M:** Georges Delerue. **VHS $92.95** *VMK, FCT* 🎬🎬

The American Gangster Documentary look at the beginnings of organized crime and the rise of the gangster in American society. Includes vintage film and photographs. Profiles include Bugsy Siegel, Al Capone, John Dillinger, Pretty Boy Floyd, and Lucky Luciano.
1992 45m/C **VHS $14.95** *COL* 🎬🎬

American Gigolo A Los Angeles loner who sexually services the rich women of Beverly Hills becomes involved with the wife of a California state senator and is then framed for a murder he did not commit. A highly stylized but empty view of seamy low lives marred by a contrived plot, with decent romp in the hay readiness displayed by Gere.
1979 (R) 117m/C Richard Gere, Lauren Hutton, Hector Elizondo, Paul Schrader; **D:** Paul Schrader; **W:** Paul Schrader. **VHS, Beta $59.95** *PAR* 🎬🎬

American Gothic Three couples headed for a vacation are instead stranded on an island and captured by a demented family headed by Steiger and De Carlo, a scary enough proposition in itself. Even worse, Ma and Pa have three middle-aged moronic offspring who still dress as children and are intent on killing the thwarted vacationers (who are none too bright themselves) one by bloody one. A stultifying career low for all involved. **AKA:** Hide and Shriek.
1988 (R) 89m/C Rod Steiger, Yvonne De Carlo, Michael J. Pollard, Sarah Torgov, Fiona Hutchinson; **D:** John Hough. **VHS, Beta $89.95** *VMK* Woof!

American Graffiti Atmospheric, episodic look at growing up in the innocence of America before the Kennedy assassination and the Vietnam War. It all takes place on one hectic but typical night in the life of a group of recent California high school grads unsure of what the next big step in life is. So they spend their time cruising, listening to Wolfman Jack, and meeting at the drive-in. Slice of '60s life boasts a prudent script, great set design, authentic soundtrack, and consistently fine performances by the young cast. Catapulted Dreyfuss, Ford, and Somers to stardom, branded Lucas a hot directorial commodity with enough leverage to launch "Star Wars," and steered Howard and Williams towards continued age-of-innocence nirvana on "Happy Days."
1973 (PG) 112m/C Richard Dreyfuss, Ron Howard, Cindy Williams, MacKenzie Phillips, Paul LeMat, Charles Martin Smith, Suzanne Somers, Candy Clark, Harrison Ford, Bo Hopkins, Joe Spano, Kathleen Quinlan, Wolfman Jack; **D:** George Lucas; **W:** George Lucas, Gloria Katz, Willard Huyck. Academy Awards '73 Nominations: Best Director (Lucas), Best Film Editing, Best Picture, Best Story & Screenplay, Best Supporting Actress (Clark); Golden Globe Awards '74: Best Film—Musical/Comedy. **VHS, Beta $14.95** *MCA, FCT* 🎬🎬🎬½

American Heart Jack (Bridges) is a suspicious ex-con, newly released from prison, with few prospects and little hope. He also has a teenaged son, Nick (Furlong), he barely remembers but who desperately wants to have his father back in his life. Jack is reluctantly persuaded to let Nick stay with him in his cheap hotel where Nick befriends fellow resident, Molly, a teenage hooker, and other castoff street kids. Suberb performances by both male leads—Furlong, both yearning and frustrated as he pursues his dream of having a family, and Bridges as the tough parolee, unwilling to open his heart. Hardboiled, poignant, and powerful. **1992 (R) 114m/C** Jeff Bridges, Edward Furlong, Lucinda Jenney, Tracey Kapisky, Don Harvey, Margaret Welsh; *D:* Martin Bell; *W:* Peter Silverman; *M:* James Newton Howard. Independent Spirit Aw Nominations: rds '94: Best Cinematography, Best First Feature, Best Supporting Actor (Furlong), Best Supporting Actress (Jenney); Independent Spirit Awards '94: Best Actor (Bridges). **VHS $92.98** *LIV, BTV* 🐾🐾½

An American in Paris Lavish, imaginative musical features a sweeping score, and knockout choreography by Kelly. Ex-G.I. Kelly stays on in Paris after the war to study painting, supported in his efforts by rich American Foch, who hopes to acquire a little extra attention. But Kelly loves the lovely Caron, unfortunately engaged to an older gent. Highlight is an astonishing 17-minute ballet which holds the record for longest movie dance number—and one of the most expensive, pegged at over half a million for a month of filming. For his efforts, the dance king won a special Oscar citation. While it sure looks like Paris, most of it was filmed in MGM studios. ♫S'Wonderful; I Got Rhythm; Embraceable You; Love Is Here To Stay; Tra-La-La; I'll Build a Stairway to Paradise; Nice Work If You Can Get It; By Strauss; Concerto in F (3rd Movement); An American in Paris; Piano Concerto in F. **1951 113m/C** Gene Kelly, Leslie Caron, Oscar Levant, Nina Foch, Georges Guetary; *D:* Vincente Minnelli; *W:* Alan Jay Lerner; *M:* George Gershwin, Ira Gershwin. Academy Awards '51: Best Art Direction/Set Decoration (Color), Best Color Cinematography, Best Costume Design (Color), Best Picture, Best Story & Screenplay, Best Score; Nominations: Best Director (Minnelli), Best Film Editing; Golden Globe Awards '52: Best Film—Musical/Comedy; National Board of Review Awards '51: 10 Best Films of the Year. **VHS, Beta, 8mm $19.98** *MGM, TLF, BTV* 🐾🐾🐾🐾

American Justice Two cops, one of whom looks suspiciously like a Simon of "Simon and Simon" fight political corruption and white slavery near the Mexican border. The chief white slaver bears a full resemblance to the other Simon. Sufficient action but less than original. *AKA:* Jackals. **1986 (R) 96m/C** Jameson Parker, Gerald McRaney, Wilford Brimley, Jack Lucarelli; *D:* Gary Grillo. **VHS, Beta $79.98** *LIV* 🐾🐾

American Kickboxer 1 Barrett stars as B.J. Quinn, a down on his luck kickboxing champion who spends much of his time onscreen aimlessly wandering (apparently searching for the meaning of his life.) Lackluster script and performances will make this one trying—even for kickboxing fans. Barrett is Chuck Norris' former workout partner, bu t there isn't enough action often enough for him to show off his formidable skills. **1991 (R) 93m/C** John Barrett, Keith Vitali, Brad Morris, Terry Norton, Ted Leplat; *D:* Frans Nel; *W:* Emil Kolbe; *M:* Frank Becker. **VHS, Beta $89.99** *CAN* 🐾½

American Matchmaker Nat Silver decides to go into the matchmaking business, after his own marriages fail miserably, hoping to experience happiness vicariously. However, he soon begins to realize that one of his clients is a better match for him than the man he chose for her. In Yiddish with English subtitles. *AKA:* Amerikaner Shadkhn. **1940 87m/B** Leo Fuchs, Judith Abarbanel. **VHS $69.95** *ERG* 🐾🐾½

American Me Violent and brutal depiction of more than thirty years of gang wars and drugs in East Los Angeles. Santana founded a street as a teenager, but has spent the last 18 years in prison, where he's the boss of the so-called Mexican Mafia, which oversees the drugs, scams, murders, and violence that are an everyday fact of prison life. Released from Folsom, Santana goes back to his old neighborhood and attempts to distance himself from his old life but finds his gang ties are stronger than any other alliance. Unsparing and desolate directorial debut from Olmos. **1992 (R) 119m/C** Edward James Olmos, William Forsythe, Pepe Serna, Danny De La Paz, Evelina Fernandez, Sal Lopez, Daniel Villarreal, Cary-Hiroyuki Tagawa; *D:* Edward James Olmos; *W:* Floyd Mutrux, Desmond Nakano; *M:* Dennis Lambert. **VHS $19.98** *MCA* 🐾🐾🐾

American Nightmare Young man searches for his missing sister against a background of pornography, drug peddling, and prostitution in the slums of a city. The usual titillating squalid urban drama. **1981 85m/C** Lawrence S. Day, Lora Staley, Lenore Zann, Michael Ironside, Alexandra Paul; *D:* Don McBrearty. **VHS, Beta $54.95** *MED* 🐾½

American Ninja American Dudikoff is G.I. Joe, a martial-arts expert stationed in the Philippines who alienates most everyone around him (he's a rebel). Deadly black-belt war begins with Joe confronting the army which is selling stolen weapons to the South American black market. Aided by one faithful pal, Joe uses his head-kicking martial arts skills to stop hundreds of ninja combatants working for the corrupt arms dealer. In his spare time he romances the base chief's daughter. Efficient rib-crunching chop-socky action wrapped in no-brainer plot and performed by nonactors. Cannon epic mercilessly followed by at least three sequels. *AKA:* American Warrior. **1985 (R) 96m/C** Michael Dudikoff, Guich Koock, Judie Aronson, Steve James; *D:* Sam Firstenberg; *M:* George S. Clinton. **VHS, Beta $14.95** *MGM* 🐾🐾

American Ninja 2: The Confrontation Soldiers Dudikoff and James are back again using their martial arts skills (in lieu of any acting) to take on a Caribbean drug-lord. Apparently he has been kidnapping Marines and taking them to his island, where he genetically alters them to become fanatical ninja assassins eager to do his dirty work. The script hardly gets in the way of the rib-crunching action, but is an improvement upon Ninja Number One. **1987 (R) 90m/C** Michael Dudikoff, Steve James, Larry Poindexter, James Conway; *D:* Sam Firstenberg; *W:* Gary Conway, James Booth. **VHS, Beta $19.95** *MED, VTR* 🐾

American Ninja 3: Blood Hunt Second sequel in the American Ninja series. Bradley replaces Dudikoff as the martial arts good guy fighting the martial arts bad guys on a Caribbean island. He's pursued by ex-evangelist Marjoe, who wants to inject him with a nasty virus before unloading the germs to bad buys worldwide. Less ninjutsu; more uninspired martial arts. **1989 (R) 90m/C** David Bradley, Steve James, Marjoe Gortner, Michele Chan, Calvin Jung; *D:* Cedric Sundstrom; *W:* Paul DeMielche, Gary Conway; *M:* George S. Clinton. **VHS, Beta $14.95** *MGM, CAN* Woof!

American Ninja 4: The Annihilation Dudikoff returns after noticeable absence in last sequel. He should have stayed away from #4—its a rehash of tired ideas that never gets off the ground.

Forget this and see "American Ninja 2: The Confrontation," the best of this series. **1991 (R) 99m/C** Michael Dudikoff, David Bradley, James Booth, Dwayne Alexandre, Robin Stille, Ken Gampu; *D:* Cedric Sundstrom; *W:* David Geeves; *M:* Nicolaas Tenbroek. **VHS, Beta $89.99** *CAN* Woof!

American Pluck Before he can inherit anything, a playboy millionaire's son must go out into the world and prove he can make his own way. He meets a beautiful princess, who is pursued by a villainous count. Walsh, as the dashing hero, was the younger brother of director Raoul. Silent with original organ music. **1925 91m/B** George Walsh, Wanda Hawley, Frank Leigh, Sidney De Grey; *D:* Richard Stanton. **VHS, Beta, 8mm $24.95** *VYY* 🐾🐾

American Roulette Garcia is the exiled president of a Latin American country living in London in this thin political thriller. A plot riddled with weaknesses and poor direction make this potentially interesting film dull and lifeless. **1988 (R) 102m/C** *GB AU* Andy Garcia, Kitty Aldridge, Robert Stephens, Al Matthews, Susannah York; *D:* Maurice Hatton; *M:* Michael Gibbs. **VHS** *NO* 🐾

American Samurai Drew is the adopted son of a Japanese samurai, who gives him the family's sacred sword. This gesture angers his stepbrother who gets involved with Japanese gangsters and illegal live-blade fighting, and who also vows revenge on this American upstart. Lots of sword play to go with the chop-socky action. **1992 (R) 89m/C** David Bradley, Mark Dacascos, John Fujioka, Valarie Trapp; *D:* Sam Firstenberg; *W:* John Corcoran. **VHS $89.99** *WAR, PMS, CAN* 🐾½

The American Scream An innocent family vacationing in the mountains stumbles on to a satanic cult. And that can really ruin a vacation. **198? 85m/C** Jennifer Darling, Pons Marr, Blackie Cammett, Kimberly Kramer, Jean Sapienza, Kevin Kaye, Matt Borlenghi, James Cooper; *D:* Mitchell Linden. **VHS, Beta $59.95** *GHV* 🐾½

American Shaolin: King of the Kickboxers 2 When Drew gets his butt kicked in a karate tournament he decides to head to China and learn some fight-winning moves from a group of warrior monks. **1992 (PG-13) 103m/C** Reese Madigan, Trent Bushy, Daniel Dae Kim, Billy Chang, Cliff Lenderman, Zhang Shi Yen, Kim Chan, Alice Zhang Hung; *D:* Lucas Lowe. **VHS $89.95** *ACA* 🐾½

The American Soldier Fassbinder's homage to the American gangster film tells the story of Ricky, a charismatic hit man. Ricky always wears a gun in a shoulder holster, sports a fedora and a white double-breasted suit, and drinks Scotch straight from the bottle. He also carries out his assigned murders with complete efficiency and no emotion. In German with English subtitles. *AKA:* Der Amerikanische Soldat. **1970 80m/C** *GE* Karl Scheydt, Elga Sorbas, Jan George; *D:* Rainer Werner Fassbinder; *W:* Rainer Werner Fassbinder; *M:* Peer Raben. **VHS $79.95** *NYF, ING* 🐾🐾½

An American Story Earnest but predictable story based on an actual incident. Six WWII vets return to their small Texas town as heroes. But when they find a corrupt mayor and a brutal sheriff running things they decide to campaign to unseat the local politicos, in spite of some dire warnings. Meade (Johnson), their commanding officer in Europe, is the designated leader in the plan but his ambitious wife and father-in-law want

him to align himself with the status quo instead. Hallmark Hall of Fame production is enjoyable and better than most made for TV movies, but fails to reach the heights of many other HHF offerings.
1992 (PG) 97m/C Brad Johnson, Kathleen Quinlan, Tom Sizemore, Josef Sommer, Patricia Clarkson, Lisa Blount, G.W. Bailey, John M. Jackson; **D:** John Gray; **W:** John Gray. VHS $89.98 REP �️✂️½

An American Summer A Chicago kid spends a summer with his aunt in beach-rich Los Angeles in this coming-of-age tale filled with '90s teen idols.
1990 100m/C Brian Austin Green, Joanna Kerns, Michael Landes. VHS NO ✂️✂️

An American Tail While emigrating to New York in the 1880s, a young Russian mouse (Fievel) is separated from his family. He matures as he learns to live on the Big Apple's dirty boulevards. The bad guys are of course cats. Excellent animation and a high-minded (though sentimental and stereotypical) plot keep it interesting for adults. Produced by Spielberg and the first big hit for the Bluth factory, a collection of expatriate Disney artists. Knowing better than to let a money-making mouse tale languish, Bluth followed with "An American Tale: Fievel Goes West."
1986 (G) 81m/C D: Don Bluth; **M:** James Horner; **V:** Dom DeLuise, Madeline Kahn, Phillip Glasser, Christopher Plummer, Nehemiah Persoff, Will Ryan, John Finnegan, Cathianne Blore. VHS, Beta $24.98 MCA, WTA, APD ✂️✂️½

An American Tail: Fievel Goes West Fievel and the Mousekewitz family continue their pursuit of the American dream by heading West, where the intrepid mouse seeks to become a famous lawman while his sister looks to make it big as a dance hall singer. The score is performed by the London Symphony Orchestra. Unfortunately released at the same time as "Beauty and the Beast," "Fievel Goes West" suffers from comparison. Worthwhile viewing for the whole family, but it won't ever reach the heights of "B&B." The laser edition is letter-boxed and features chapter stops.
1991 (G) 75m/C D: Phil Nibbelink, Simon Wells; **W:** Flint Dille; **M:** James Horner; **V:** John Cleese, Dom DeLuise, Phillip Glasser, Amy Irving, Jon Lovitz, Cathy Cavadini, Nehemiah Persoff, Erica Yohn, James Stewart. VHS, Beta $24.98 MCA, WTA ✂️✂️

American Tickler A thigh-slappin' (or is it head-whacking?) series of satirical pastiches in the grand style of "Kentucky Fried Movie," only more sophomoric. A tasteless collection of yearning to be funny sketches about American institutions. **AKA:** Draws.
1976 (R) 77m/C W.P. Dremak, Joan Sumner, Marlow Ferguson, Jeff Alin; **D:** Chuck Vincent. VHS, Beta $59.95 GEM ✂️✂️

American Tiger The collegiate hero of "American Tiger" is, like so many college students, framed for murder, and he applies himself to clearing his sullied name. Somewhere during this process, he finds himself in the middle of a battle between good and evil on a football field. About what you'd expect from a supernatural kung-fu teen-action drama. **AKA:** American Rickshaw.
1989 (R) 93m/C Mitch Gaylord, Donald Pleasence, Daniel Greene, Victoria Prouty; **D:** Martin Dolman. VHS $19.95 ACA ✂️✂️

An American Werewolf in London Strange, darkly humorous version of the classic man-into-wolf horror tale became a cult hit, but never clicked with most American critics. Two American college students (Naughton and Dunne) backpacking through England are viciously attacked by a werewolf one foggy night. Dunne is killed, but keeps appearing (in progressively decomposed form) before the seriously wounded Naughton, warning him of impending werewolfdom when the moon is full; Dunne advises suicide. Seat-jumping horror and gore, highlighted by intensive metamorphosis sequences orchestrated by Rick Baker, are offset by wry humor, though the shifts in tone don't always work. Great moon songs permeate the soundtrack, including CCR's "Bad Moon Rising" and Van Morrison's "Moondance."
1981 (R) 97m/C David Naughton, Griffin Dunne, Jenny Agutter, Frank Oz, Brian Glover, David Schofield; **D:** John Landis; **W:** John Landis; **M:** Elmer Bernstein. VHS, Beta $14.98 LIV, VES ✂️✂️✂️

Americana A troubled Vietnam vet tries to restore himself by rebuilding a merry-go-round in a small midwestern town, while dealing with opposition from the local residents. Offbeat, often effective post-Nam editorial that was produced and directed in 1973 by Carradine and then shelved. Hershey and Carradine were a couple back then.
1981 (PG) 90m/C David Carradine, Barbara Hershey, Bruce Carradine, John Blythe Barrymore Jr., Michael Greene; **D:** David Carradine; **W:** Richard Carr. VHS, Beta $69.98 VES, LIV ✂️✂️½

The Americanization of Emily A happy-go-lucky American naval officer (Garner) with no appetite for war discovers to his horror that he may be slated to become the first casualty of the Normandy invasion as part of a military PR effort in this black comedy-romance. Meanwhile, he spreads the charisma in an effort to woo and uplift Emily (Andrews), a depressed English woman who has suffered the loss of her husband, father, and brother during the war. A cynical, often funny look at military maneuvers and cultural drift that was adapted by Paddy Chayefsky from William Bradford Huie's novel. Also available colorized.
1964 117m/B James Garner, Julie Andrews, Melvyn Douglas, James Coburn, Joyce Grenfell, Keenan Wynn, Judy Carne, Liz Fraser, Edward Binns; **D:** Arthur Hiller; **W:** Paddy Chayefsky. VHS $19.95 MGM ✂️✂️✂️

The Americano Ever-suave Fairbanks frees a South American politician locked in a dungeon, returns him to political success, and captures the heart of his beautiful daughter. Based on Eugene P. Lyle, Jr.'s "Blaze Derringer."
1917 58m/B Douglas Fairbanks Sr., Alma Rubens, Spottiswoode Aitken, Lillian Langdon, Carl Stockade, Tom Wilson; **D:** John Emerson. VHS, Beta $16.95 GPV ✂️✂️½

Americano A cowboy travelling to Brazil with a shipment of Brahma bulls discovers the rancher he's delivering them to has been murdered. An odd amalgam of western cliches and a South American setting.
1955 85m/C Glenn Ford, Frank Lovejoy, Abbe Lane, Cesar Romero; **D:** William Castle. VHS $19.98 REP ✂️✂️

The Americano/Variety The two silent classics in abridged form: "The Americano," (1917) about a soldier-of-fortune who aids a revolt-ridden Caribbean country, and "Variety," (1925) a classic German masterpiece about the career of a trapeze artist.
1925 54m/B Douglas Fairbanks Sr., Emil Jannings; **D:** John Emerson, E.A. Dupont. VHS, Beta $39.95 CCB ✂️✂️

America's Deadliest Home Video Camp spoof about America's obsession with videotaping everything in sight. Video enthusiast Doug is taken hostage by the Clint Dryer gang who want him to tape their crime spree. Every aspect is only seen through the lens of the video camera.
1992 87m/C Danny Bonaduce, Mick Wynhoff, Mollena Williams, Melora Walters; **D:** Jack Perez; **W:** Jack Perez. VHS $39.95 FCT ✂️✂️

Americathon It is the year 1998 and the United States is almost bankrupt, so President Chet Roosevelt decides to stage a telethon to keep the country from going broke. Interesting satiric premise with a diverse cast, but a poor script and slack pacing spoil all the fun. The soundtrack features music by The Beach Boys and Elvis Costello while the narration is by George Carlin.
1979 (PG) 85m/C Peter Riegert, John Ritter, Nancy Morgan, Harvey Korman, Fred Willard, Meatloaf, Elvis Costello, Chief Dan George, Howard Hesseman, Jay Leno; **Cameos:** Tommy Lasorda, Peter Marshall; **D:** Neal Israel; **W:** Monica Johnson. VHS, Beta $59.95 LHV, WAR Woof!

Amin: The Rise and Fall Excessively violent and ultimately pointless dramatization of Idi Amin's eight-year reign of terror in Uganda, which resulted in the deaths of a half million people and the near ruin of a nation.
1982 101m/C Joseph Olita, Geoffrey Keen; **D:** Sharad Patel. VHS, Beta $59.95 EMI Woof!

The Amityville Horror Sometimes a house is not a home. Ineffective chiller that became a box-office biggie, based on a supposedly real-life occurrence in Amityville, Long Island. The Lutz family moves into the house of their dreams only to find it full of nightmares. Once the scene of a grisly mass murder, the house takes on a devilish attitude, plunging the family into supernatural terror. Pipes and walls ooze icky stuff, flies manifest in the strangest places, and doors mysteriously slam while exorcist Steiger staggers from room to room in scene-chewing prayer. Based on the Jay Anson book and followed by a number of sequels.
1979 (R) 117m/C James Brolin, Margot Kidder, Rod Steiger, Don Stroud, Murray Hamilton, Helen Shaver, Amy Wright; **D:** Stuart Rosenberg; **W:** Sandor Stern. VHS, Beta WAR, OM ✂️✂️

Amityville 2: The Possession More of a prequel than a sequel to "The Amityville Horror" (1979). Relates the story of the house's early years as a haven for demonic forces intent on driving a father to beat the kids, a mother to prayer, and a brother to lust after his sister (before he murders them all). Young etc. portray an obnoxious family that you're actually glad to see wasted by the possessed son. A stupid, clumsy attempt to cash in on the success of the first film, which was also stupid and clumsy but could at least claim novelty in the bad housing development genre. Followed by "Amityville III: The Demon" in 1983.
1982 (R) 110m/C James Olson, Burt Young, Andrew Prine, Moses Gunn, Rutanya Alda; **D:** Damiano Damiani; **M:** Howard Blake. VHS, Beta $9.98 SUE Woof!

Amityville 3: The Demon America's worst real-estate value dupes another funky buyer. The infamous Amityville house is once again restless with terror and gore, though supported with even less plot than the usual smidgin. Cynical reporter Roberts moves in while trying to get to the bottom of the story by way of the basement. Courtesy of 3-D technology, monsters sprang at theater patrons but the video version is strictly two-dimensional, forcing the viewer to press his or her face directly onto the television screen

in order to derive similar effect. *AKA:* Amityville 3-D.
1983 (R) 98m/C Tony Roberts, Tess Harper, Robert Joy, Candy Clark, John Beal, Leora Dana, John Harkins, Lori Loughlin, Meg Ryan; *D:* Richard Fleischer; *W:* David Ambrose; *M:* Howard Blake. VHS, Beta $79.98 *VES, LIV* ♂♂½

Amityville 4 It's an unusual case of house-to-house transference as the horror from Amityville continues, now lodged in a Californian residence. The usual good house gone bad story has the place creating a lot of unusual creaks and rattles before deciding to use its inherited powers to attack and possess a little girl. Special effects from Richard Stutsman ("The Lost Boys" and "Jaws"). Made for television. *AKA:* The Amityville Horror: The Evil Escapes, Part 4.
1989 (R) 95m/C Patty Duke, Jane Wyatt, Norman Lloyd, Frederic Lehne, Brandy Gold; *D:* Sandor Stern; *M:* Rick Conrad. VHS $89.95 *VMK* ♂♂½

Amityville: A New Generation And the bad sequels just go on and on and on. Terry is a young photographer who's given an old mirror by a crazy homeless man (tell me why he took it). He shares a loft with three friends and all begin experiencing vivid and terrifying dreams of murder. Seems the mirror is tied to Amityville and its evil legacy and Terry is the designated inheritor.
1993 (R) 92m/C Ross Partridge, Julia Nickson-Soul, David Naughton, Richard Roundtree, Terry O'Quinn; *D:* John Murlowski; *W:* Christopher DeFaria, Antonio Toro. VHS $92.98 *REP* ♂♂½

The Amityville Curse The possessed house is yet again purchased by a pathetically uninformed family. The usual ghostly shenanigans occur with low-budget regularity in this fifth film in the series. Never released theatrically, for good reason.
1990 (R) 91m/C *CA* Kim Coates, Dawna Wightman, Helen Hughes, David Stein, Anthony Dean Rubes, Cassandra Gava, Jan Rubes; *D:* Tom Berry. VHS $9.99 *STE, VMK* Woof!

Amityville 1992: It's About Time Time is of the essence in the sixth installment of the Amityville flicks. A vintage clock (from Amityville, of course), causes creepy goings-on in a family's house. Actually a halfway decent horror film with high-grade special effects, and much, much better than previous Amityville sequels, which isn't saying much.
1992 (R) 95m/C Stephen Macht, Shawn Weatherly, Megan Ward, Damon Martin, Nita Talbot, Dick Miller; *D:* Tony Randel. VHS $14.98 *REP* ♂♂

Among the Cinders Sometimes interesting coming of age drama about a sixteen-year-old New Zealand boy who runs away to his grandfather's farm to forget about his friend's accidental death. At the farm, he meets an older woman and compromises his virtue.
1983 103m/C *GE NZ* Paul O'Shea, Derek Hardwick, Rebecca Gibney, Yvonne Lawley, Amanda Jones; *D:* Rolf Haedrich. VHS, Beta $9.95 *NWV, STE* ♂♂

Amongst Friends Three boyhood buddies, Trevor (McGaw), Billy (Lindsey), and Andy (Parlavecchio), from a nice Long Island neighborhood turn to crime out of boredom. Trevor gets busted and goes to prison for two years. Upon getting out, he finds his old cronies still share the taste for crime and general aimlessness but also still want that one big score. Trevor finally agrees to join Andy and Billy in a drug deal but the jealous Billy, who wants Trevor's old girlfriend Laura (Sorvino), plans a double-cross that will affect them all. Filled with cutting attacks on the society that spawns aimless youth. Debut of then 26-year-old writer/director Weiss.
1993 (R) 88m/C Patrick McGaw, Steve Parlavecchio, Joseph Lindsey, Mira Sorvino, David Stepkin, Michael Artura; *D:* Rob Weiss; *W:* Rob Weiss; *M:* Mick Jones. VHS *COL* ♂♂

Amor Bandido When cab drivers in Rio are turning up dead, a young prostitute is torn between her detective father and her prime suspect boyfriend. Drama based on a true story. In Portuguese with English subtitles.
1979 95m/C *BR* Paulo Gracindo, Cristina Ache, Paulo Guarniero; *D:* Bruno Barreto. VHS $79.95 *FXL, IME, ING* ♂♂½

Amore Rossellini's tribute to actress Magnani consists of the short films "The Human Voice" and "The Miracle." In "The Human Voice," Magnani is shown alone, speaking to her lover on the telephone. Based on Jean Cocteau's one-act drama. In "The Miracle," she is a simple peasant girl who believes her illegitimate child is acutally the new Messiah. In Italian with English subtitles.
1948 78m/B *IT* Anna Magnani; *D:* Roberto Rossellini. VHS $59.95 *FCT, ING, CVC* ♂♂♂

Amore! Wealthy investment banker Saul Schwartz (Scalia) hates his job, his wife, and his life. The only way he loses himself is by watching movies starring Italian matinee idol Rudolfo Carbonera (Hamilton). So Saul gets divorced and decides to change his life—by going to Hollywood and becoming an actor like his debonair idol. With the help of some newfound friends he transforms himself into suave leading man material (under the name of Salvatore Guiliano III) but promptly winds up falling for a writer (Ireland), who couldn't care less.
1993 (PG-13) 93m/C Jack Scalia, Kathy Ireland, Elliott Gould, George Hamilton, Brenda Epperson, James Doohan, Katherine Helmond, Betsy Russell, Norm Crosby, Frank Gorshin; *D:* Lorenzo Doumani; *W:* Lorenzo Doumani. VHS $89.95 *PMH* ♂♂½

The Amorous Adventures of Moll Flanders An amusing romp set in 18th century England focusing on a poor orphan girl who seeks wealth. Moll plots to get ahead through an advantageous series of romances and marriages. Her plan is ruined when she falls in love and she turns out to be a wanted highwayman, landing her in prison. Not surprisingly, love (and money) conquers all. Based on the novel by Daniel Defoe. Novak tries in this female derivative of "Tom Jones," but this period piece isn't her style.
1965 126m/C Kim Novak, Richard Johnson, Angela Lansbury, Vittorio De Sica, Leo McKern, George Sanders, Lilli Palmer; *D:* Terence Young; *M:* John Addison. VHS $19.95 *PAR* ♂♂

Amos Douglas is Amos, an aging baseball coach confined most reluctantly to a nursing home. He's disturbed by recent suspicious events there, his concern causing him to take on Montgomery, the staunch head nurse. Well-acted drama produced by Douglas's son Peter, offering an echo of "One Flew Over the Cuckoo's Nest," which Dad starred in on Broadway and son Michael helped produced as a movie classic.
1985 100m/C Kirk Douglas, Elizabeth Montgomery, Dorothy McGuire, Noriyuki "Pat" Morita, James Sloyan, Ray Walston; *D:* Michael Tuchner; *M:* Georges Delerue. VHS *NO* ♂♂½

Amos and Andrew Embarrassing attempt at comedy stops short of endorsing the stereotypes it tries to parody. Prizewinning African-American author Andrew Sterling (Jackson) is seen moving into a house on an island previously reserved for the uptight white, and the neighbors call the cops, assuming he's a thief. Chief of police (Coleman) eagerly gets into the act, then exploits drifter Amos (Cage) in a cover-up attempt when he realizes his mistake. Talented cast can't overcome lame jokes and transparent plot that serves as an opportunity to bring black and white together for a "see how much we have in common" bonding session.
1993 (PG-13) 96m/C Nicolas Cage, Samuel L. Jackson, Michael Lerner, Margaret Colin, Giancarlo Esposito, Dabney Coleman, Bob Balaban, Aimee Graham, Brad Dourif, Chelcie Ross, Jodi Long; *D:* E. Max Frye; *W:* E. Max Frye; *M:* Richard Gibbs. VHS $19.95 *COL, IME, NLC* ♂♂½

The Amphibian Man What does a scientist do once he's created a young man with gills? Plunge him in the real world of aqua pura to experience life and love, albeit underwater. Trouble is, the protagonist, who's come to be known as the Sea Devil, takes a dive for a young pretty he's snatched from the jaws of death. A 60's Soviet sci-fi romance originally seen on American television.
1961 96m/C *RU* K. Korieniev, M. Virzinskaya; *D:* Y. Kasancki. VHS $19.98 *SNC* ♂♂

The Amsterdam Connection Film company acts as a cover for prostitution and drug smuggling, with the girls acting as international couriers.
197? 90m/C *HK* Chen Shing, Kid Sherrif, Yeung Sze, Jason Pai Piu, Fang Mui San; *D:* Fang Mui San, Lo Ke. VHS, Beta *NO* ♂

The Amsterdam Kill A washed-up ex-agent of the U.S. Drug Enforcement Agency is hired by a desperate U.S. Drug Enforcement Agency to hunt down the kingpin of a narcotics syndicate in Hong Kong. Tedious pace with occasional spells of violence fails to awaken somnambulent Mitchum. Shot on location in Hong Kong.
1978 (R) 93m/C *HK* Robert Mitchum, Richard Egan, Keye Luke, Leslie Nielsen, Bradford Dillman; *D:* Robert Clouse. VHS, Beta $9.95 *GKK* ♂♂

Amsterdamned A crime thriller taking place on the canals of Amsterdam featuring a serial skindiver killer who surfaces periodically to slash and splash. A steely detective fishes for clues. Dubbed.
1988 (R) 114m/C *NL* Monique Van De Ven, Huub Stapel; *D:* Dick Maas. VHS, Beta $89.98 *VES, LIV* ♂♂

Amy Set in the early 1900s, the story follows the experiences of a woman after she leaves her well-to-do husband to teach at a school for the deaf and blind. Eventually she organizes a football game between the handicapped kids and the other children in the neighborhood. Good Disney family fare.
1981 (G) 100m/C Jenny Agutter, Barry Newman, Kathleen Nolan, Margaret O'Brien, Nanette Fabray, Chris Robinson, Lou Fant; *D:* Vincent McEveety. VHS, Beta $69.95 *DIS* ♂♂½

The Amy Fisher Story Amy Fisher wishes she looked this good. Perhaps if she did, she could be acting in made-for-television movies like Barrymore instead of providing fodder for them. The ABC account draws from a variety of sources to dramatize the relationship between Amy and her married, ahem, friend, and Amy's subsequent attack on his wife. Although it tries not to take sides, it does include some pretty hot sex scenes which could be why this docudrama garnered the highest ratings of the three network productions released on TV. See also: "Casualties of Love: The 'Long Island Lolita' Story" and "Lethal Lolita—Amy Fisher: My Story."

1993 96m/C Drew Barrymore, Anthony John Denison, Harley Jane Kozak, Tom Mason, Laurie Paton, Ken Pogue, Linda Darlow; **D:** Andy Tennant; **W:** Janet Brownell. **VHS $89.98** *ABC* 🎬🎬

Anastasia Bergman won her second Oscar, and deservedly so, for her classic portrayal of the amnesia victim chosen by Russian expatriate Brynner to impersonate Anastasia, the last surviving member of the Romanoff dynasty. As such, she becomes part of a scam to collect millions of rubles deposited in a foreign bank by her supposed father, the now-dead Czar. But is she just impersonating the princess? Brynner as the scheming White General and Hayes as the Grand Duchess who needs to be convinced turn in fine performances as well. Based on Marcelle Maurette's play.
1956 105m/C Ingrid Bergman, Yul Brynner, Helen Hayes, Akim Tamiroff; **D:** Anatole Litvak; **W:** Arthur Laurents. Academy Awards '56: Best Actress (Bergman); Nominations: Best Original Score; Golden Globe Awards '57: Best Actress—Drama (Bergman). **VHS** *TCF* 🎬🎬🎬½

Anastasia: The Mystery of Anna Irving stars as Anna Anderson, a woman who claimed to be the Grand Duchess Anastasia, the sole surviving daughter of Russian Czar Nicholas II. A powerful epic reliving her experience of royalty, flight from execution, and struggle to retain her heritage. The story of Anastasia remains as one of the greatest dramatic mysteries of the 20th century. Adapted from the book "Anastasia: The Riddle of Anna Anderson" by Peter Kurth; originally broadcast on cable television.
1986 190m/C Amy Irving, Olivia de Havilland, Jan Niklas, Nicolas Surovy, Susan Lucci, Elke Sommer, Edward Fox, Claire Bloom, Omar Sharif, Rex Harrison; **D:** Marvin J. Chomsky; **W:** Jim Goldman. **VHS $79.95** *CAF, PBS, FUS* 🎬🎬½

Anatomy of a Murder Considered by many to be the best courtroom drama ever made. Small-town lawyer in northern Michigan faces an explosive case as he defends an army officer who has killed a man he suspects was his philandering wife's rapist. Realistic, cynical portrayal of the court system isn't especially concerned with guilt or innocence, focusing instead on the interplay between the various courtroom characters. Classic performance by Stewart as the down home but brilliant defense lawyer who matches wits with Scott, the sophisticated prosecutor; terse and clever direction by Preminger. Though tame by today's standards, the language used in the courtroom was controversial. Filmed in upper Michigan; based on the bestseller by judge Robert Traver.
1959 161m/B James Stewart, George C. Scott, Arthur O'Connell, Ben Gazzara, Lee Remick, Eve Arden, Orson Bean, Kathryn Grant, Murray Hamilton, Joseph Welch; *Cameos:* Duke Ellington; **D:** Otto Preminger; **W:** Wendell Mayes; **M:** Duke Ellington. Academy Awards '59 Nominations: Best Actor (Stewart), Best Adapted Screenplay, Best Black and White Cinematography, Best Film Editing, Best Picture, Best Supporting Actor (O'Connell, Scott); National Board of Review Awards '59: 10 Best Films of the Year; New York Film Critics Awards '59: Best Actor (Stewart). **VHS, Beta $19.95** *COL* 🎬🎬🎬🎬

Anatomy of a Psycho A man plans to avenge his gas chambered brother by committing mass murder. Very cheaply and poorly produced.
1961 75m/B Ronnie Burns, Pamela Lincoln, Darrell Howe, Russ Bender; **D:** Brooke L. Peters. **VHS, Beta $16.95** *SNC* 🎬

Anatomy of a Seduction Television formula melodrama of a middle-aged divorcee's affair with her son's best friend. Age knows no boundaries when it comes to television lust.
1979 100m/C Susan Flannery, Jameson Parker, Rita Moreno, Ed Nelson, Michael Le Clair; **D:** Steven Hilliard Stern; **M:** Hagood Hardy. **VHS, 8mm $79.99** *HBO* 🎬🎬

Anatomy of Terror A made for television drama about an army vet going bonkers (what? really?) and revealing espionage secrets in his home life.
1974 73m/C Paul Burke, Polly Bergen, Dinsdale Landen, Basil Henson. **VHS, Beta $29.95** *LIV* 🎬

Anchors Aweigh Snappy big-budget (for then) musical about two horny sailors, one a girl-happy dancer and the other a shy singer. While on leave in Hollywood they return a lost urchin to his sister. The four of them try to infiltrate a movie studio to win an audition for the girl from maestro Iturbi. Kelly's famous dance with Jerry the cartoon Mouse (of "Tom and Jerry" fame) is the second instance of combining live action and animation. The young and handsome Sinatra's easy crooning and Grayson's near operatic soprano are blessed with music and lyrics by Styne and Cahn. Lots of fun, with conductor-pianist Iturbi contributing and Hollywood-style Little Mexico also in the brew. 🎵We Hate to Leave; I Fall in Love Too Easily; The Charm of You; The Worry Song; Jalousie; All of a Sudden My Heart Sings; I Begged Her; What Makes the Sun Set?; Waltz Serenade.
1945 139m/C Frank Sinatra, Gene Kelly, Kathryn Grayson, Jose Iturbi, Sharon McManus, Dean Stockwell, Carlos Ramirez, Pamela Britton; **D:** George Sidney; **M:** Jules Styne, Sammy Cahn. Academy Awards '45: Best Score; Nominations: Best Actor (Kelly), Best Color Cinematography, Best Picture, Best Song ("I Fall in Love Too Easily"). **VHS, Beta $19.98** *MGM* 🎬🎬🎬

And a Nightingale Sang WWII England is the scene of this sweet romance, a sad and humorous tale of a woman who gives everything for the war effort. Stunning recreation of the final days of the Blitzkreig. Originally produced for Masterpiece Theatre.
1991 90m/C Joan Plowright, Tom Watt, Phyllis Logan, John Woodvine. **VHS $19.95** *PBS, FUS* 🎬🎬½

And Baby Makes Six An unexpected pregnancy creates new challenges for a couple with grown children. Dewhurst is excellent as usual. Made for television. Followed by "Baby Comes Home."
1979 100m/C Colleen Dewhurst, Warren Oates, Maggie Cooper, Mildred Dunnock, Timothy Hutton, Allyn Ann McLerie; **D:** Waris Hussein; **W:** Shelley List. **VHS, 8mm** *NO* 🎬🎬½

And God Created Woman Launching pad for Bardot's career as a sex siren, as she flits across the screen in a succession of scanty outfits and hangs out at the St. Tropez beach in what is euphemistically known as a swimsuit while turning up the heat for the males always in attendance. The plot concerns an 18-year-old nymphomaniac who is given a home by a local family with three handsome young sons. A cutting-edge sex film in its time that was boffo at the box office. In French with English subtitles. *AKA:* And Woman...Was Created; Et Dieu Crea la Femme.
1957 (PG) 93m/C FR Brigitte Bardot, Curt Jurgens, Jean-Louis Trintignant, Christian Marquand; **D:** Roger Vadim; **W:** Roger Vadim. **VHS, Beta** *NO* 🎬🎬½

And God Created Woman Loose, dull remake by Vadim of his own 1957 softcore favorite about a free-spirited woman dodging men and the law while yearning for rock and roll stardom. DeMornay is a prisoner who hopes to marry one of the local hunks (Spano) so she can be paroled. They marry, she strips, he frets, while political hopeful Langella smacks his lips in anticipation. Available in an unrated 100-minute version.
1988 (R) 98m/C Rebecca DeMornay, Vincent Spano, Frank Langella, Donovan Leitch, Judith Chapman, Thelma Houston; **D:** Roger Vadim; **M:** Tom Chase, Steve Rucker. **VHS, Beta $89.98** *VES, LIV* 🎬½

And God Said to Cain Another Biblically titled western from the prolific Kinski, about a put-upon gunman who must fight for his life.
196? 95m/C Klaus Kinski. **VHS, Beta $29.95** *UNI* 🎬

And Hope to Die Moody, muddled crime drama with a good cast about a fleeing Frenchman who joins a gang of hardened criminals in Canada. They go ahead with their plans to kidnap a retarded girl even though she is already dead. Standard caper film is enhanced by arty camera work and some unusual directorial touches.
1972 95m/C FR Robert Ryan, Jean-Louis Trintignant, Aldo Ray, Tisa Farrow; **D:** Rene Clement. **VHS, Beta** *NO* 🎬🎬½

And I Alone Survived Made-for-television adaptation of the true story of a woman who survives a leisure-plane crash in the Sierra Nevadas and her struggle to get to the village below. Brown does her best to elevate the proceedings above the usual I-hope-I-don't-die cliches.
1978 90m/C Blair Brown, David Ackroyd, Vera Miles, G.D. Spradlin; **D:** William A. Graham. **VHS, Beta $79.95** *PSM* 🎬🎬

And Justice for All Earnest attorney Pacino questions the law and battles for justice in and out of the courtroom. He's hired to defend a detested judge from a rape charge, while dealing with a lost-soul caseload of eccentric and tragedy-prone clients. Overly melodramatic, an odd mix of satire, cynicism, and seemingly sincere drama that hits with a club when a stick will do. Jewison aims for black surrealism, permitting both Pacino and Warden (as a judge losing his sanity) to veer into histrionics, to the detriment of what is essentially a gripping behind-the-scenes story. Excellent cast creates sparks, including Lahti in her film debut. And Baltimore never looked lovelier.
1979 (R) 120m/C Al Pacino, Jack Warden, Christine Lahti, Thomas G. Waites, Craig T. Nelson, John Forsythe, Lee Strasberg; **D:** Norman Jewison; **W:** Barry Levinson, Valerie Curtin; **M:** Dave Grusin. **VHS, Beta, 8mm $14.95** *COL* 🎬🎬½

And Nothing But the Truth A multinational corporation is out to ruin the investigative television report team trying to do a story on the company. *AKA:* Giro City.
1982 90m/C GB Glenda Jackson, Jon Finch, Kenneth Colley, James Donnelly; **D:** Karl Francis. **VHS, Beta** *NO* 🎬🎬½

And Now for Something Completely Different A compilation of skits from BBC-television's "Monty Python's Flying Circus" featuring Monty Python's own weird, hilarious brand of humor. Sketches include "The Upper Class Twit of the Year Race," "Hell's Grannies" and "The Townswomen's Guild Reconstruction of Pearl Harbour." A great introduction to Python for the uninitiated, or a chance for the converted to see their favorite sketches again.

1972 (PG) 89m/C *GB* John Cleese, Michael Palin, Eric Idle, Graham Chapman, Terry Gilliam, Terry Jones; **D:** Ian McNaughton; **W:** John Cleese, Michael Palin, Graham Chapman, Terry Gilliam, Terry Jones. **VHS, Beta $19.95** COL, TVC 🎬🎬🎬

And Now Miguel Plodding tale of a young boy who wants to take over as head shepherd of his family's flock. Filmed in New Mexico, but the over-long outdoor shots make it drag a bit in spite of Cardi's competent performance.
1966 95m/C Pat Cardi, Michael Ansara, Guy Stockwell, Clu Gulager, Joe De Santis, Pilar Del Rey, Buck Taylor; **D:** James B. Clark. **VHS $24.95** NOS 🎬🎬

And Now My Love A French couple endeavor to maintain their romance despite interfering socio-economic factors—she's a millionaire and he's an ex-con filmmaker. Keller plays three roles spanning three generations, as Lelouch invests autobiographical details to invent a highly stylized, openly sentimental view of French folks in love with love. Along the way he comments on social mores and changing attitudes through the years. Dubbed in English.
1974 (PG) 121m/C *FR* Marthe Keller, Andre Dussollier, Carla Gravina; **D:** Claude Lelouch; **W:** Claude Lelouch. **VHS, Beta $19.95** COL, ING, SUE 🎬🎬

And Now the Screaming Starts The young bride-to-be of the lord of a British manor house is greeted by bloody faces at the window, a severed hand, and five corpses. Then Cushing shows up to investigate. Good-looking, sleek production with genuine chills.
1973 (R) 87m/C *GB* Peter Cushing, Herbert Lom, Patrick Magee, Ian Ogilvy, Stephanie Beacham, Geoffrey Whitehead, Guy Rolfe; **D:** Roy Ward Baker. **VHS, Beta $79.95** PSM, MED 🎬🎬½

And Soon the Darkness One of two vacationing young nurses disappears in France where a teenager was once murdered and the search is on. Predictable, ineffective suspenser.
1970 (PG) 94m/C *GB* Pamela Franklin, Michele Dotrice, Sandor Eles, John Nettelton, Claire Kelly, Hanna-Marie Pravda; **D:** Robert Fuest; **W:** Brian Clemens. **VHS, Beta $59.99** HBO 🎬🎬

And the Band Played On Randy Shilts' monumental, and controversial, 1987 book on the AIDS epidemic comes to television in an equally controversial made for cable movie. Details the intricate medical research undertaken by doctors in France and the U.S. who fought to isolate and identify the mystery virus despite governmental neglect, red tape, clashing egos, and lack of funding. Various aspects of gay life are shown objectively, without sensationalizing. Celebrity cameos are somewhat distracting though most acquit themselves well. The script went through numerous rewrites; director Spottiswoode reportedly objected to HBO interference at the editing stage.
1993 (PG-13) 140m/C Matthew Modine, Alan Alda, Ian McKellan, Lily Tomlin, Glenne Headly, Richard Masur, Saul Rubinek, Charles Martin Smith, Patrick Bauchau, Nathalie Baye, Christian Clemenson; *Cameos:* Richard Gere, David Clennon, Phil Collins, Alex Courtney, David Dukes, David Marshall Grant, Ronald Guttman, Anjelica Huston, Ken Jenkins, Richard Jenkins, Tchéky Karyo, Swoosie Kurtz, Jack Laufer, Steve Martin, Dakin Matthews, Peter McRobbie, Lawrence Monoson, B.D. Wong, Donal Logue, Jeffrey Nordling, Stephen Spinella; **D:** Roger Spottiswoode; **W:** Arnold Schulman; **M:** Carter Burwell. **VHS $49.99** HBO 🎬🎬🎬

And the Children Shall Lead A young black girl is moved by the coming of the civil rights movement to her small Mississippi town. Part of the "Wonderworks" series.
1985 60m/C Danny Glover, LeVar Burton, Pam Potillo, Denise Nicholas, Andrew Prine; **D:** Michael Pressman. **VHS $29.95** PME, PTB, HMV 🎬🎬🎬

And the Ship Sails On On the eve of WWI, a group of devoted opera lovers take a luxury cruise to pay their respects to a recently deceased opera diva. Also on board is a group of fleeing Serbo-Croation freedom fighters. A charming and absurd autumnal homage-to-life by Fellini shot entirely in the studio. *AKA:* El la Nave Va.
1983 (PG) 130m/C *IT* Freddie Jones, Barbara Jefford, Janet Suzman, Peter Cellier; **D:** Federico Fellini; **W:** Federico Fellini, Tonino Guerra. **VHS, Beta $59.95** COL, APD, ING 🎬🎬🎬

And Then There Were None An all-star cast makes up the ten colorful guests invited to a secluded estate in England by a mysterious host. What the invitations do not say, however, is the reason they have been specifically chosen to visit—to be murdered, one by one. Cat and mouse classic based on Agatha Christie's book with an entertaining mix of suspense and black comedy. Remade in 1966 and again in 1975 as "Ten Little Indians," but lacking the force and gloss of the original.
1945 97m/C Louis Hayward, Barry Fitzgerald, Walter Huston, Roland Young, Sir C. Aubrey Smith, Judith Anderson, Mischa Auer, June Duprez; **D:** Rene Clair. **VHS, Beta $19.95** NOS, VCI 🎬🎬🎬½

And Then You Die An intense crime drama about a Canadian drug lord who amasses a fortune from the cocaine and marijuana trade. His empire is threatened as the Mafia, Hell's Angels, and the police try to bring him down.
1988 (R) 115m/C *CA* Kenneth Welsh, R.H. Thomson, Wayne Robson, Tom Harvey, George Bloomfield, Graeme Campbell; **D:** Francis Mankiewicz. **VHS, Beta $79.95** VMK 🎬🎬🎬

And You Thought Your Parents Were Weird! A pair of introverted, whiz kid brothers invent a lovable robot to provide fatherly guidance as well as companionship for their widowed mother. Surprisingly charming, sentimental film is only slightly hampered by low-budget special effects.
1991 (PG) 92m/C Marcia Strassman, Joshua Miller, Edan Gross, John Quade, Sam Behrens, Susan Gibney, Gustav Vintas, Eric Walker; **D:** Tony Cookson; **W:** Tony Cookson; **M:** Randall Miller; **V:** Alan Thicke, Richard Libertini. **VHS $92.95** VMK 🎬🎬½

The Anderson Tapes Newly released from prison, an ex-con assembles his professional pals and plans the million-dollar robbery of an entire luxury apartment house on NYC's upper east side. Of course, he's unaware that a hoard of law men from federal, state, and local agencies are recording their activities for a wide variety of reasons, though none of the surveillance is coordinated and it has nothing to do with the planned robbery. Based on the novel by Lawrence Sanders, the intricate caper is effectively shaped by Lumet, who skillfully integrates broad satire with suspense. Shot on location in New York City. Walken is The Kid, his first major role.
1971 (PG) 100m/C Sean Connery, Dyan Cannon, Martin Balsam, Christopher Walken, Alan King, Ralph Meeker, Garrett Morris, Margaret Hamilton; **D:** Sidney Lumet; **W:** Frank Pierson; **M:** Quincy Jones. **VHS, Beta $9.95** GKK, COL 🎬🎬🎬

The Andersonville Trial Details the atrocities experienced by captured Union soldiers who were held in the Confederacy's notorious Andersonville prison during the American Civil War. Provides an interesting account of the war-crimes trial of the Georgia camp's officials, under whom more than 14,000 prisoners died. Moving, remarkable television drama based on the Pulitzer-honored book by MacKinlay Kantor.
1970 150m/C Martin Sheen, William Shatner, Buddy Ebsen, Jack Cassidy, Richard Basehart, Cameron Mitchell; **D:** George C. Scott. **VHS, Beta $59.95** LIV 🎬🎬🎬½

Andre More human-animal interaction from the man from snowy river. True story of a seal with an inclination to swim hundreds of miles every summer to visit the family in Maine that saved his life. Sort of a "Free Willy" in reverse with an appealing smaller sea mammal.
1994 (G) ?m/C Keith Carradine, Tina Majorino, Chelsea Field, Keith Szarabajka, Shane Meier; **D:** George Miller; **W:** Dana Baratta. **VHS** NYR 🎬🎬½

Andrei Rublev A 15th-century Russian icon painter must decide whether to record history or participate in it as Tartar invaders make life miserable. During the black and white portion, he becomes involved in a peasant uprising, killing a man in the process. After a bout of pessimism and a vow of silence, he goes forth to create artistic beauty as the screen correspondingly blazes with color. A brilliant historical drama censored by Soviet authorities until 1971. In Russian with English subtitles.
1966 185m/C *RU* Anatoli Solonitzin, Ivan Lapikov, Nikolai Grinko, Nikolai Sergueiev; **D:** Andrei Tarkovsky; **W:** Andrei Tarkovsky, Andrej Mikhalkov-Kontchalovsky. **VHS $79.95** FXL, NOS, FCT 🎬🎬🎬½

Androcles and the Lion Stage-bound Hollywood version of the George Bernard Shaw story about a tailor in Imperial Rome who saves Christians from a hungry lion he had previously befriended. Sharp dialogue and a plot that's relatively (within the bounds of Hollywood) faithful help a great play become a semi-satisfying cinematic morsel. Harpo Marx was originally cast as Androcles, but was fired by producer Howard Hughes three weeks into the shooting.
1952 105m/B Jean Simmons, Alan Young, Victor Mature, Robert Newton, Maurice Evans; **D:** Chester Erskine. **VHS, Beta $19.95** COL, SUE 🎬🎬½

Android When an android who has been assisting a quirky scientist in space learns that he is about to be permanently retired, he starts to take matters into his own synthetic hands. Combines science fiction, suspense and cloned romance. A must for Kinski fans.
1982 (PG) 80m/C Klaus Kinski, Don Opper, Brie Howard; **D:** Aaron Lipstadt. **VHS, Beta $69.95** MED 🎬🎬½

The Andromeda Strain A satellite falls back to earth carrying a deadly bacteria that must be identified in time to save the population from extermination. The tension inherent in the bestselling Michael Crichton novel is talked down by a boring cast. Also available in letter-box format.
1971 (G) 131m/C Arthur Hill, David Wayne, James Olson, Kate Reid, Paula Kelly; **D:** Robert Wise. **VHS, Beta $59.95** MCA 🎬🎬½

Andy and the Airwave Rangers Andy is whisked into the TV!! He finds adventure and excitement—car chases, intergalactic battles, and cartoons. *AKA:* Andy Colby's Incredibly Awesome Adventure.

1989 75m/C Dianne Kay, Vince Edwards, Bo Svenson, Richard Thomas, Erik Estrada; *D:* Deborah Brock. **VHS** $79.95 *COL* ♫♫

Andy Griffith Show
Life in Mayberry with smalltown sheriff Andy (Griffith), inept deputy Barney Fife (Knotts), Andy's son Opie (Howard), Aunt Bee (Bavier) and all the other townsfolk in the first of the rural comedy series. Two episodes: "Barney's Sidecar" and "The Darlings Are Coming." Additional episodes are available.
1960 52m/B Andy Griffith, Don Knotts, Ron Howard, Jim Nabors, Francis Bavier, George Lindsey, Howard McNear, Hal Smith, Howard Morris. **VHS, Beta** *MOV* ♫♫

Andy Hardy Gets Spring Fever
Andy falls for a beautiful acting teacher, and then goes into a funk when he finds she's engaged. Judge Hardy and the gang help heal the big wound in his heart. A lesser entry (and the seventh) from the popular series.
1939 88m/B Mickey Rooney, Lewis Stone, Ann Rutherford, Fay Holden, Cecilia Parker, Sara Haden, Helen Gilbert; *D:* Woodbridge S. Van Dyke. **VHS, Beta** $19.95 *MGM* ♫♫

Andy Hardy Meets Debutante
Seems like there should be an article in that title. Garland's second entry in series, wherein Andy meets and falls foolishly for glamorous debutante Lewis with Betsy's help while family is on visit to New York. Judy/Betsy sings "I'm Nobody's Baby" and "Singing in Rain." Also available with "Love Finds Andy Hardy" on laser disc.
1940 86m/B Mickey Rooney, Judy Garland, Lewis Stone, Ann Rutherford, Fay Holden, Sara Haden, Cecilia Parker, Diana Lewis, Tom Neal; *D:* George B. Seitz. **VHS, Beta** $19.95 *MGM* ♫♫½

Andy Hardy's Double Life
In this entertaining installment from the Andy Hardy series, Andy proposes marriage to two girls at the same time and gets in quite a pickle when they both accept. Williams makes an early screen splash.
1942 91m/B Mickey Rooney, Lewis Stone, Ann Rutherford, Fay Holden, Sara Haden, Cecilia Parker, Esther Williams, William Lundigan, Susan Peters, Robert (Bobby) Blake; *D:* George B. Seitz. **VHS, Beta** $19.95 *MGM, MLB* ♫♫½

Andy Hardy's Private Secretary
After Andy fails his high school finals he gets help from a sympathetic faculty member. As the secretary, Grayson makes a good first impression in one of her early screen appearances. The Hardy series was often used as a training ground for new MGM talent.
1941 101m/B Mickey Rooney, Kathryn Grayson, Lewis Stone, Fay Holden, Ian Hunter, Gene Reynolds, Sara Haden; *D:* George B. Seitz. **VHS, Beta** $19.95 *MGM* ♫♫

Andy Warhol's Bad
In the John Waters' school of "crime is beauty," a Queens housewife struggles to make appointments for both her home electrolysis clinic and her all-female murder-for-hire operation, which specializes in children and pets (who are thrown out of windows and knived, respectively). Her life is further complicated by a boarder (King) who's awaiting the go-ahead for his own assignment, an autistic child unwanted by his mother. One of Warhol's more professional-appearing films, and very funny if your tastes run to the tasteless.
1977 (R) 100m/C Perry King, Carroll Baker, Susan Tyrrell, Stefania Cassini; *D:* Jed Johnson. **VHS, Beta** $59.95 *SUE, MLB* ♫♫♫

Andy Warhol's Dracula
Sex and camp humor, as well as a large dose of blood, highlight Warhol's treatment of the tale. As Dracula can only subsist on the blood of pure, untouched maidens ("were-gins"), gardener Dallesandro rises to the occasion in order to make as many women as he can ineligible for Drac's purposes. Very reminiscent of Warhol's "Frankenstein," but with a bit more spoofery. Look for Roman Polanski in a cameo peek as a pub patron. *AKA:* Blood for Dracula; Young Dracula.
1974 (R) 106m/C *IT FR* Udo Kier, Arno Juergling, Maxine McKendry, Joe Dallesandro, Vittorio De Sica; *Cameos:* Roman Polanski; *D:* Paul Morrissey; *W:* Paul Morrissey. **VHS, Beta** $79.95 *TRI, GEM, ING* ♫♫♫

Andy Warhol's Frankenstein
A most outrageous parody of Frankenstein, featuring plenty of gore, sex, and bad taste in general. Baron von Frankenstein (Kier) derives sexual satisfaction from his corpses (he delivers a particularly thought-provoking philosphy on life as he lustfully fondles a gall bladder; his wife seeks her pleasure from the monster himself (Dallesandro). Originally made in 3-D, this is one of Warhol's campiest outings. *AKA:* Flesh for Frankenstein.
1974 (R) 95m/C *GE FR IT* Udo Kier, Dalia di Lazzaro, Monique Van Vooren, Joe Dallesandro; *D:* Paul Morrissey; *W:* Paul Morrissey. **VHS, Beta** $79.95 *TRI, MLB* ♫♫½

Angel
Low-budget leerer about a 15-year-old honor student who attends an expensive Los Angeles private school during the day and by night becomes Angel, a streetwise prostitute making a living amid the slime and sleaze of Hollywood Boulevard. But wait, all is not perfect. A psycho is following her, looking for an opportunity.
1984 (R) 94m/C Donna Wilkes, Cliff Gorman, Susan Tyrrell, Dick Shawn, Rory Calhoun, John Diehl, Elaine Giftos, Ross Hagen; *D:* Robert Vincent O'Neil. **VHS, Beta** $19.95 *STE* ♫½

Angel 3: The Final Chapter
Former hooker Angel hits the streets to save her newly discovered sister from a life of prostitution. Trashy sequel with a better cast to tepid "Avenging Angel," which was the inept 1985 follow-up to 1984's tasteless "Angel."
1988 (R) 100m/C Maud Adams, Mitzi Kapture, Richard Roundtree, Mark Blankfield, Kin Shriner, Tawny Fere, Toni Basil; *D:* Tom De Simone. **VHS, Beta** $19.95 *STE, NWV, IME Woof!*

Angel and the Badman
When notorious gunslinger Wayne is wounded during a shoot-out, a pacifist family takes him in and nurses him back to health. While he's recuperating, the daughter in the family (Russell) falls for him. She begs him not to return to his previous life. But Wayne, though smitten, thinks that a Duke's gotta do what a Duke's gotta do. And that means finding the dirty outlaw (Cabot) who killed his pa. Predictable but nicely done, with a good cast and script. Wayne provides one of his better performances (and also produced).
1947 100m/B John Wayne, Gail Russell, Irene Rich, Harry Carey Sr., Bruce Cabot; *D:* James Edward Grant; *W:* James Edward Grant. **VHS** $19.98 *REP, CNG, MRV* ♫♫½

An Angel at My Table
New Zealand television mini-series chronicling the life of Janet Frame, New Zealand's premiere writer/poet. At once whimsical and tragic, the film tells of how a mischievous, free-spirited young girl was wrongly placed in a mental institution for eight years, yet was ultimately able to cultivate her incredible storytelling gifts, achieving success, fame and happiness. Adapted from three of Frame's novels: "To the Is-land," "An Angel at My Table," and "The Envoy From Mirror City." Highly acclaimed the world over, winner of over 20 major international awards.
1989 (R) 157m/C *NZ* Kerry Fox, Alexia Keogh, Karen Fergusson, Iris Churn, K.J. Wilson, Martyn Sanderson; *D:* Jane Campion; *W:* Laura Jones. **VHS** $19.95 *COL, ING, NLC* ♫♫♫♫

Angel Baby
A mute girl struggles to redefine her faith when she is cured by preacher, but then sees him fail with others. Fine performances all around, notably Reynolds in his screen debut, with cinematography by Haskell Wexler. Adapted from "Jenny Angel" by Elsie Oaks Barber.
1961 97m/B George Hamilton, Salome Jens, Mercedes McCambridge, Joan Blondell, Henry Jones, Burt Reynolds; *D:* Paul Wendkos, Hubert Cornfield. **VHS** *NO* ♫♫½

Angel City
A Florida labor camp is the setting for this made-for-TV drama. A family of rural West Virginia migrant workers find themselves trapped inside the camp and exploited by the boss-man. Adapted from Patricia Smith's book.
1980 90m/C Ralph Waite, Paul Winfield, Jennifer Warren, Jennifer Jason Leigh, Mitchell Ryan; *D:* Philip Leacock; *W:* James Lee Barrett. **VHS** $59.95 *XVC* ♫♫½

Angel City
An experimental parody of film mysteries where a detective investigates the nature of visual truth in and about Hollywood.
1984 75m/C Bob Glaudini; *D:* Jon Jost. **VHS, Beta** *FCT* ♫♫

An Angel for Satan
Steele plays a dual role in her last major, Italian horror film. She gives a strong performance as a woman obsessed by the spirit of a statue. In Italian with no subtitles.
1966 ?m/C *IT* Barbara Steele, Anthony Steffen. **VHS** $16.95 *SNC* ♫½

Angel Heart
Exotic, controversial look at murder, voodoo cults, and sex in 1955 New Orleans. Bonet defiantly sheds her image as a young innocent (no more Cosby Show for you, young lady). Rourke is slimy as marginal NYC private eye Angel, hired by the devilish De Niro to track a missing big band singer who violated a "contract." His investigation leads him to the bizarre world of the occult in New Orleans, where the blood drips to a different beat. Visually stimulating, with a provocative sex scene between Bonet and Rourke, captured in both R-rated and unrated versions. Adapted by Parker from "Falling Angel" by William Hjortsberg.
1987 (R) 112m/C Mickey Rourke, Robert De Niro, Lisa Bonet, Charlotte Rampling, Michael Higgins, Charles Gordone, Kathleen Wilhoite, Stocker Fountelieu, Brownie McGhee; *D:* Alan Parker; *W:* Alan Parker; *M:* Trevor Jones. **VHS, Beta** $14.95 *LIV, FCT* ♫♫½

Angel in a Taxi
A six-year-old boy in an orphanage decides to choose his own mother, a beautiful ballerina he sees in a magazine, when an ugly couple try to adopt him. Italian film dubbed in English.
1959 89m/B *IT* Wera Cecova, Ettore Manni, Vittorio De Sica, Marietto, Gabriel Ferzetti. **VHS, Beta, 8mm** $24.95 *VYY, FCT* ♫½

Angel of Death
A small mercenary band of Nazi hunters attempt to track down Josef Mengele in South America. Stupid entry in the minor "let's find the darn Nazi before he really causes trouble" genre. Director Franco is also known as A. Frank Drew White.
1986 (R) 92m/C Chris Mitchum, Fernando Rey, Susan Andrews; *D:* Jess (Jesus) Franco. **VHS, Beta** $19.95 *STE, NWV Woof!*

Angel of Destruction
Undercover cop is assigned to protect controversial rock star from psycho fan. Cop gets killed and cop's sister decides to go after the killer.

1994 (R) 80m/C Maria Ford, Charlie Spradling; *D:* Charles Philip Moore. **VHS** *NHO* 🎬½

Angel of Fury Rothrock plays the head of security of a computer corporation who must battle terrorists after the company's top-secret computer. And there's no one she can trust. Lots of martial arts action with the competent Rothrock.
1993 (R) 91m/C Cynthia Rothrock, Christopher Barnes, Peter O'Brien; *D:* Ackyl Anwary. **VHS $92.95** *IMP* 🎬🎬½

Angel of H.E.A.T. Porn-star Chambers is Angel, a female super-agent on a mission to save the world from total destruction. Sex and spies abound with trashy nonchalance. *AKA:* The Protectors, Book One.
1982 (R) 90m/C Marilyn Chambers, Mary Woronov, Steve Johnson; *D:* Helen Sanford, Myrl A. Schreibman. **VHS, Beta $69.95** *VES Woof!*

Angel on My Shoulder A murdered convict makes a deal with the Devil (Rains) and returns to earth for revenge as a respected judge who's been thinning Hell's waiting list. Occupying the good judge, the murderous Muni has significant problems adjusting. Amusing fantasy with Muni in a rare and successful comic role. Co-written by Segall, who scripted "Here Comes Mr. Jordan," in which Rains played an angel. Remade in 1980.
1946 101m/b Paul Muni, Claude Rains, Anne Baxter, Onslow Stevens; *D:* Archie Mayo; *W:* Harry Segall. **VHS, Beta $9.95** *CNG, MRV, NOS* 🎬🎬🎬

Angel on My Shoulder A small-time hood wrongfully executed for murder comes back as district attorney. He owes the devil, but he's finding it tough to be evil enough to repay his debt. Okay television remake of the better 1946 film starring Paul Muni.
1980 96m/C Peter Strauss, Richard Kiley, Barbara Hershey, Janis Paige; *D:* John Berry. **VHS, Beta $69.98** *SUE* 🎬🎬

Angel Square A Canadian production from the director of the acclaimed "Bye Bye Blues." When the father of a neighborhood boy is brutally attacked, the community bands together to search for the culprit.
1992 106m/C *CA* Ned Beatty; *D:* Anne Wheeler. **VHS** *NO* 🎬🎬

Angel Town A foreign exchange student, who happens to be a champion kick-boxer, is forced into combat with LA street gangs.
1989 (R) 90m/C Olivier Gruner, Theresa Saldana, Frank Aragon, Tony Valentino, Peter Kwong, Mike Moroff; *D:* Eric Karson. **VHS, Beta $89.95** *IMP* 🎬

Angel with the Trumpet Depressing character study of a woman who marries to please her family, rather than herself. When the Gestapo finds out about her Jewish ancestry, she must make the most important decision of her life.
1950 98m/B *GB* Eileen Herlie, Basil Sydney, Norman Wooland, Maria Schell, Olga Edwards, Oskar Werner, Anthony Bushell, Wilfrid Hyde-White; *D:* Anthony Bushell. **VHS $24.95** *NOS* 🎬🎬

Angela Twisted love story about a young man (Railsback) who jumps the bones of an older woman, unaware that she is the mother he's been separated from for 23 long years. Seems that way back when, the boy was kidnapped by crime boss Huston from mom Loren, an ex-prostitute, who then turned in the boy's dad, who was something of a criminal. Mom thought son was dead, dad vowed revenge from prison, and son went about his unwitting business. It all comes together insipidly, at the expense of the cast and viewer.

1977 91m/C *CA* Sophia Loren, Steve Railsback, John Huston, John Vernon; *D:* Boris Sagal; *M:* Henry Mancini. **VHS, Beta $69.98** *SUE, SIM* 🎬

Angele A lovely, naive country girl is lured to the city by a cunning pimp who knows that she wants to escape her oppressive father. With her illegitimate baby, she's discovered in a whorehouse and taken in disgrace back home to dad, who promptly locks her in the barn. One special guy, however, appreciates her purity and plots to rescue her. What he lacks in material resources he makes up for in character. An overlong but moving story of lost innocence and intolerance. In French with English subtitles. Based on the novel "Un de Baumugnes" by Jean Giono.
1934 130m/B *FR* Orane Demazis, Fernandel, Henri Puopon, Edouard Delmont; *D:* Marcel Pagnol. **VHS $59.95** *INT, ING* 🎬🎬🎬

Angelo My Love Compassionate docudrama about New York's modern gypsy community. Follows the adventures of 12-year-old Angelo Evans, the streetwise son of a fortune teller, who, with a fresh view, explores the ups and downs of his family's life. Duvall financed the effort and cast nonprofessional actors in this charming tale of reality and fairy-tale.
1983 (R) 91m/C Angelo Evans, Michael Evans, Steve "Patalay" Tsiginoff, Cathy Kitchen, Millie Tsiginoff; *D:* Robert Duvall; *M:* Michael Kamen. **VHS, Beta $59.95** *COL* 🎬🎬🎬

Angel's Brigade Seven models get together to stop a big drug operation. Drive-in vigilante movie fare fit for a rainy night.
1979 (PG) 97m/C Jack Palance, Peter Lawford, Jim Backus, Arthur Godfrey; *D:* Greydon Clark; *W:* Greydon Clark. **VHS, Beta $19.98** *LIV* 🎬🎬

Angels Die Hard Novel biker story with the cyclists as the good guys intent on helping a town during a mining disaster. Grizzly Adams makes an early film appearance.
1984 (R) 86m/C Tom Baker, R.G. Armstrong, Dan Haggerty, William Smith; *D:* Richard Compton. **VHS, Beta $19.95** *STE, NWV* 🎬🎬

Angels from Hell Early application in the nutso 'Nam returnee genre. Disillusioned Vietnam veteran forms a massive biker gang for the sole purpose of wreaking havoc upon the Man, the Establishment and anyone else responsible for sending him off to war. The big gang invades a town, with predictably bloody results. Sort of a follow-up to "Hell's Angels on Wheels."
1968 86m/C Tom Stern, Arlene Martel, Ted Markland, Stephen Oliver, Paul Bertoya, James Murphy, Jack Starrett, Pepper Martin, Luana Talltree; *D:* Bruce Kessler. **VHS** *NO* 🎬

Angels Hard as They Come Opposing Hell's Angels leaders clash in a hippie-populated ghost town. A semi-satiric spoof of the biker genre's cliches features an early Glenn appearance and Busey's film debut.
1971 (R) 86m/C Gary Busey, Scott Glenn, James Inglehart, Gary Littlejohn, Sharon Peckinpah; *D:* Joe Viola; *W:* Jonathan Demme. **VHS, Beta $24.98** *SUE* 🎬🎬

Angels in the Outfield Enjoyable comedy fantasy about the lowly Pittsburgh Pirates who get a little celestial help in their race for the pennant. Great performances all around, especially Douglas as the gruff manager of the losing baseball team. Based on a story by Richard Conlin.
1951 102m/C Paul Douglas, Janet Leigh, Keenan Wynn, Donna Corcoran, Lewis Stone, Spring Byington, Bruce (Herman Brix) Bennett, Marvin Kaplan, Ellen Corby, Jeff Richards; *D:* Clarence Brown; *W:* Dorothy Kingsley, George Wells. **VHS $19.98** *MGM* 🎬🎬🎬

Angels in the Outfield Remake of the 1951 fantasy about a lowly baseball team who, along with some heavenly animated help find themselves on a winning streak. The new lineup includes Glover as manager of the hapless California Angels, Danza as a washed-up pitcher, and Lloyd as captain of the celestial spirits. Gordon-Levitt plays the foster child who believes he'll get his family back together if the Angels win the pennant. Familar ground still yields good, heartfelt family fare. Oakland A's third baseman Carney Lansford served as technical advisor, molding actors into fair semblance of baseball team.
1994 (PG) ?m/C Danny Glover, Tony Danza, Christopher Lloyd, Brenda Fricker, Ben Johnson, Joseph Gordon-Levitt, Jay O. Sanders; *D:* William Dear; *W:* Holly Goldberg Sloan. **VHS** 🎬🎬½

Angels of the City What's a girl got to do to join a sorority? A house prank turns vicious when two coeds take a walk on the wild side and accidentally observe a murder, making them the next targets. Credible exploitation effort, if that's not an oxymoron.
1989 90m/C Lawrence Hilton-Jacobs, Cynthia Cheston, Kelly Galindo, Sandy Gershman; *D:* Lawrence Hilton-Jacobs; *W:* Lawrence Hilton-Jacobs, Raymond Martino. **VHS, Beta $29.95** *PMH* 🎬🎬

Angels One Five A worm's-eye view of British air power in WWII. What little "excitement" there is, is generated by flashing lights, plotting maps and status boards. Hawkins and Denison are the only bright spots.
1954 97m/B Jack Hawkins, Michael Denison, Dulcie Gray, John Gregson, Cyril Raymond, Veronica Hurst, Harold Goodwin, Geoffrey Keen, Vida Hope. **VHS $19.95** *NOS* 🎬🎬

Angels Over Broadway Slick, fast-paced black comedy about con man Fairbanks, who plans to hustle suicidal thief Qualen during a poker game, but has a change of heart. With the help of call-girl Hayworth and drunken playwright Mitchell, he helps Qualen turn his life around. Ahead of its time with an offbeat morality, but a delight in the '90s.
1940 80m/B Douglas Fairbanks Jr., Rita Hayworth, Thomas Mitchell, John Qualen, George Watts; *D:* Ben Hecht, Lee Garmes. **VHS, Beta $19.95** *FCT, COL* 🎬🎬🎬

Angels' Wild Women From the man who brought you "Dracula vs. Frankenstein" comes an amalgamation of hippies, motorcycle dudes, evil desert gurus and precious little plot.
1972 85m/C Kent Taylor, Regina Carrol, Ross Hagen, Maggie Bemby, Vicki Volante; *D:* Al Adamson. **VHS** *NO Woof!*

Angels with Dirty Faces Rousing classic with memorable Cagney twitches and the famous long walk from the cell to the chair. Two young hoods grow up on NYC's lower East Side with diverse results—one enters the priesthood and the other opts for crime and prison. Upon release from the pen, famed gangster Cagney sets up shop in the old neighborhood, where Father O'Brien tries to keep a group of young toughs (the Dead End Kids) from following in his footsteps. Bogart's his unscrupulous lawyer and Bancroft a crime boss intent on double-crossing Cagney. Reportedly they were blasting real bullets during the big shootout, no doubt helping Cagney's intensity. Adapted from a story by Rowland Brown.

1938 97m/B James Cagney, Pat O'Brien, Humphrey Bogart, Ann Sheridan, George Bancroft, Billy Halop, Leo Gorcey, Huntz Hall, Bobby Jordan, Dan Jesse, Gabriel Dell, J. Frank Burke, William Tracy, Bernard Punsley; *D:* Michael Curtiz; *W:* John Wexley, Warren Duff; *M:* Max Steiner. **VHS, Beta $19.98** MGM, FOX, MLB 𝆏𝆏𝆏

Angie Brassy Angie finds herself pregnant and unmarried. Tired of the advice and criticism she receives from her close knit neighborhood she strikes out of Brooklyn to find a new life for herself. Average "woman's movie" wrought with messages of pregnancy, childbirth, friendship, love, and family has far too much going on and relies too heavily on formula soap. Davis, in what could have been a juicy (read "Oscar") role is strong, but her performance is drowned by all the melodrama. Madonna was originally cast as Angie, but was bounced when the filming of "Snake Eyes" conflicted. Adapted from the book "Angie, I Says" by Avra Wing. **1994** (R) 108m/C Geena Davis, Aida Turturro, Stephen Rea, Philip Bosco, James Gandolfini, Jenny O'Hara; *D:* Martha Coolidge; *W:* Todd Graff. **VHS** HPH 𝆏𝆏

AngKor: Cambodia Express An American journalist travels back to Vietnam to search for his long lost love. **1981** 96m/C Robert Walker Jr., Christopher George; *D:* Lek Kitiparaporn. **VHS, Beta $69.98** VES, LIV 𝆏

Angry Harvest During the WWII German occupation of Poland, a gentile farmer shelters a young Jewish woman on the run, and a serious, ultimately interdependent relationship forms. Acclaimed; Holland's first film since her native Poland's martial law imposition made her an exile to Sweden. In German with English subtitles. Contains nudity and violence. *AKA:* Bittere Ernte. **1985** 102m/C GE Armin Mueller-Stahl, Elisabeth Trissenaar, Wojciech Pszoniak, Margit Carstensen, Kurt Raab, Kathe Jaenicke, Hans Beerhenke, Isa Haller; *D:* Agnieszka Holland; *W:* Agnieszka Holland. Academy Awards '85 Nominations: Best Foreign Language Film; Montreal World Film Festival '85: Best Actor (Mueller-Stahl). **VHS, Beta $69.95** FCT, GLV, ING 𝆏𝆏𝆏

Angry Joe Bass Contemporary Native American Joe Bass faces government officials who continually usurp his fishing rights. Something like "Billy Jack" without the intelligence. **1976** 82m/C Henry Bal, Molly Mershon; *D:* Thomas G. Reeves. **VHS, Beta** NO 𝆏

The Angry Red Planet An unintentionally amusing sci-fi adventure about astronauts on Mars fighting off aliens and giant, ship-swallowing amoebas. Filmed using bizarre "Cinemagic" process, which turns almost everything pink. Wild effects have earned the film cult status. **1959** 83m/C Gerald Mohr, Les Tremayne, Jack Kruschen; *D:* Ib Melchior. **VHS, Beta $19.95** HBO 𝆏𝆏

Anguish Well-done horror thriller about a lunatic who, inspired to duplicate the actions of an eyeball-obsessed killer in a popular film, murders a movie audience as they watch the movie. Violence and gore abound. **1988** (R) 85m/C SP Zelda Rubinstein, Michael Lerner, Talia Paul, Clara Pastor; *D:* Bigas Luna; *W:* Bigas Luna; *M:* J.M. Pagan. **VHS, Beta $79.98** FOX 𝆏𝆏½

Animal Behavior An animal researcher and a music professor fall in love on a college campus. Bowen's (she actually released it under the alias Riley H. Anne) comedy was filmed in 1985 and edited/shelved for over 4 years, with good reason. **1989** (PG) 79m/C Karen Allen, Armand Assante, Holly Hunter, Josh Mostel, Richard Libertini; *D:* Jenny Bowen; *W:* Susan Rice; *M:* Cliff Eidelman. **VHS, Beta $89.99** HBO 𝆏

Animal Called Man Two crooked buddies join a big western gang in pillaging a small town and get in too deep. **1987** 83m/C Vassilli Karis, Craig Hill. **VHS, Beta $59.95** TWE 𝆏

Animal Crackers The second and possibly the funniest of the thirteen Marx Brothers films, "Animal Crackers" is a screen classic. Groucho is a guest at the house of wealthy matron Margaret Dumont and he, along with Zeppo, Chico, and Harpo, destroy the tranquility of the estate. Complete with the Harry Ruby music score—including Groucho's "Hooray for Captain Spaulding" with more quotable lines than any other Marx Brothers film: "One morning I shot an elephant in my pajamas. How he got into my pajamas, I'll never know." Based on a play by George S. Kaufman. **1930** (G) 98m/B Groucho Marx, Chico Marx, Harpo Marx, Zeppo Marx, Lillian Roth, Margaret Dumont, Louis Sorin, Hal Thompson, Richard Greig; *D:* Victor Neerman; *W:* Morrie Ryskind. **VHS, Beta $14.98** MCA, FCT 𝆏𝆏𝆏½

Animal Farm An animated version of George Orwell's classic political satire about a barnyard full of animals who parallel the growth of totalitarian dictatorships. Not entirely successful, but probably best translation of Orwell to film. **1955** 73m/C *D:* John Halas, Joy Batchelor. **VHS, Beta, 8mm $24.95** VYY, KUI, VTR 𝆏𝆏𝆏

Animal Instincts A woman takes a prescription drug that makes her a nymphomaniac, and her police officer husband discovers that he's turned on by videotaping her in bed with other men and women. One of the many in her constant stream of lovers is a politician whose campaign is based on shutting down all the town's sex clubs. Another in the string of sexual thrillers riding on the coattails of "Basic Instinct." **1992** (R) 94m/C Maxwell Caulfield, Jan-Michael Vincent, Mitch Gaylord, Shannon Whirry, Delia Sheppard, John Saxon, David Carradine; *D:* Alexander Gregory Hippolyte. **VHS $89.95** ACA 𝆏𝆏

The Animal Kingdom A romantic triangle develops when Howard, married to Loy, has an affair with Harding. The problem is Harding acts more like a wife and Loy a mistress. Intelligently written and directed, with a marvelous performance from veteran character actor Gargan. *AKA:* The Woman in His House. **1932** 95m/B Ann Harding, Leslie Howard, Myrna Loy, Neil Hamilton, William Gargan, Henry Stephenson, Ilka Chase; *D:* Edward H. Griffith; *W:* Horace Jackson. **VHS $29.95** RKO, FCT, HEG 𝆏𝆏𝆏

Anita, Dances of Vice German avant-garde film celebrates Anita Berber, the "most scandalous woman in 1920s Berlin." Berber was openly bisexual, used drugs, and danced nude in public. In von Praunheim's film, she rises from the dead and creates yet more scandal. *AKA:* Anita—Tanze des Lasters. **1987** 85m/C GE Lotti Huber, Ina Blum, Mikhail Honesseau; *D:* Rosa von Praunheim. **VHS, Beta $49.95** ICA, GLV, ING 𝆏𝆏

Anita de Montemar A man is torn between his wife and his child-bearing girlfriend. **196?** 127m/C MX Amparo Rivelles, Fernando Soler. **VHS, Beta $59.95** UNI 𝆏

The Ann Jillian Story Jillian stars as herself in this television melodrama recounting her battle with breast cancer. Several musical numbers are included. **1988** 96m/C Ann Jillian, Tony LoBianco, Viveca Lindfors, Leighton Bewley; *D:* Corey Allen. **VHS, Beta** NO 𝆏½

Ann Vickers A dashing young army captain wins over the heart of a dedicated social worker. Okay adaptation of a Sinclair Lewis novel, with Dunne suffering more than usual. **1933** 76m/B Irene Dunne, Walter Huston, Bruce Cabot, Conrad Nagel, Edna May Oliver; *D:* John Cromwell. **VHS, Beta $19.98** RKO, TTC 𝆏𝆏½

Anna Age, envy, and the theatrical world receive their due in an uneven but engrossing drama about aging Czech film star Anna, making a sad living in New York doing commercials and trying for off-Broadway roles. She takes in Krystyna, a young Czech peasant girl who eventually rockets to model stardom. Modern, strongly acted "All About Eve" with a story partially based on a real Polish actress. Kirkland drew quite a bit of flak for shamelessly self-promoting for the Oscar. She still lost. **1987** (PG-13) 101m/C Sally Kirkland, Paulina Porizkova, Robert Fields, Stefan Schnabel, Larry Pine, Ruth Maleczech; *D:* Yurek Bogayevicz; *W:* Agnieszka Holland; *M:* Greg Hawkes. Academy Awards '87 Nominations: Best Actress (Kirkland); Golden Globe Awards '88: Best Actress—Drama (Kirkland); Independent Spirit Awards '88: Best Actress (Kirkland). **VHS, Beta $79.98** VES, LIV 𝆏𝆏𝆏

Anna and the King of Siam Splendid adaptation, from the book by Margaret Landon, about the true life adventures of 33-year-old English widow Anna Leonowens. In 1862 Anna and her son travelled to the exotic kingdom of Siam to educate the harem and children of the king. Dunne is splendid as the strong-willed governess as is Harrison (in his first American film) as the authoritarian eastern ruler. Remade as the musical "The King and I." **1946** 128m/B Irene Dunne, Rex Harrison, Linda Darnell, Lee J. Cobb, Gale Sondergaard, Mikhail Rasumny, Dennis Hoey, Richard Lyon, John Abbott; *D:* John Cromwell; *W:* Sally Benson, Talbot Jennings; *M:* Bernard Wheeler, William Darling. **VHS $19.98** FXV 𝆏𝆏𝆏½

Anna Christie Silent production of Eugene O'Neill's play that even he liked. A young girl is sent away by her father, a seaman, and finds her way to Chicago, where she becomes a prostitute. Later she visits her father's barge and falls for a sailor. She shares her past life story, hoping they will understand. This film was acclaimed when it was released, and still remains a touching work of art. Remade in 1930. **1923** 75m/B Blanche Sweet, George F. Marion Sr., William Russell, Eugenie Besserer, Chester Conklin, George Siegmann, Victor Potel, Fred Kohler Jr.; *D:* John Wray. **VHS, Beta $34.95** GPV, FCT 𝆏𝆏𝆏½

Anna Christie Garbo is the ex-prostitute who finds love with sailor Bickford. Bickford is unaware of his lover's tarnished past and she does her best to keep it that way. Garbo's first sound film was advertised with the slogan "Garbo Talks!" Adapted from the classic Eugene O'Neill play, the film is a slow but rewarding romantic drama. **1930** 90m/B Greta Garbo, Marie Dressler, Charles Bickford, George F. Marion Sr.; *D:* Clarence Brown. **VHS, Beta $19.98** MGM 𝆏𝆏½

Anna Karenina Cinematic Tolstoy with Garbo as the sad, moody Anna willing to give up everything to be near Varonsky (March), the cavalry officer she's obsessed with. A classic Garbo vehicle with March and Rathbone providing excellent support. Interestingly, a remake of the Garbo and John Gilbert silent, "Love."
1935 85m/B Greta Garbo, Fredric March, Freddie Bartholomew, Maureen O'Sullivan, May Robson, Basil Rathbone, Reginald Owen, Reginald Denny; **D:** Clarence Brown. **VHS, Beta** $19.98 NOS, MGM, HEG *&&*½

Anna Karenina Stiff version of Tolstoy's passionate story of illicit love between a married woman and a military officer. In spite of exquisite costumes, Leigh and Richardson as leads, still tedious.
1948 123m/C *GB* Vivien Leigh, Ralph Richardson, Kieron Moore; **D:** Julien Duvivier. **VHS** $39.95 GKK, FCT, MRV *&&*½

Anna Karenina Made for television version of Tolstoy's novel of betrayal, intrigue, and forbidden love. Anna, defying all social practices of the time, falls into the arms of a dashing count. Features an excellent performance from Paul "A Man For All Seasons" Scofield.
1985 (PG) 96m/C Jacqueline Bisset, Christopher Reeve, Paul Scofield, Ian Ogilvy, Anna Massey, Judi Bowker; **D:** Simon Langton. **VHS, Beta** $89.95 VES *&&*½

Anna to the Infinite Power Sci fi based on the book of the same name follows a young gal with telepathic powers. When the girl discovers that she has sisters as the result of a strange scientific experiment, she sets out to find them, drawing on her own inner strength.
1984 101m/C Dina Merrill, Martha Byrne, Mark Patton; **D:** Robert Wiemer. **VHS, Beta** $59.95 COL *&&*½

Annabel Takes a Tour/Maid's Night Out A delightful comedy double feature. In "Annabel Takes a Tour," a fading movie star falls in love with a writer while on a tour to boost her career, and in "Maids Night Out," an heiress and a millionaire fall in love.
1938 131m/B Lucille Ball, Jack Oakie, Ruth Donnelly, Joan Fontaine, Allan "Rocky" Lane, Hedda Hopper, Alice White; **D:** Lew Landers. **VHS, Beta** $34.95 RKO, MLB, TTC *&&*½

Annapolis Life's in the pink for two guys at the U.S. naval academy until jealousy rears its loathsome head when they fall for the same gal. Just when it's beginning to look like love and honor is an either-or proposition, the lovelorn rivals find that although love transcends all, a guy's gotta do what a guy's gotta do, even if it means sticking up for his romantic nemesis. Lots of sub-par male bonding.
1928 63m/B Johnny Mack Brown, Hugh Allan, Hobart Bosworth, William "Billy" Bakewell, Charlotte Walker, Jeanette Loff; **D:** Christy Cabanne. **VHS, Beta** $19.95 GPV, FCT *&*

The Annapolis Story Cliche-ridden WWII drama about two naval cadets romancing the same lucky girl. Low-rent time for director Siegel which wastes a decent cast. *AKA:* Blue and the Gold.
1955 81m/C John Derek, Kevin McCarthy, Diana Lynn, Pat Dooley, L.Q. Jones; **D:** Don Siegel. **VHS, Beta** $19.98 FOX *&*½

Anne of Avonlea Equally excellent mini-series sequel to "Anne of Green Gables" in which the romantic heroine grows up and discovers romance. The same cast returns and Sullivan continues his tradition of lavish filming on Prince Edward Island and

beautiful costumes. Based on the characters from L.M. Montgomery's classic novels "Anne of Avonlea," "Anne of the Island," and "Anne of Windy Poplars." CBC, PBS, and Disney worked together on this Wonder-Works production. On two tapes. *AKA:* Anne of Green Gables: The Sequel.
1987 224m/C *CA* Megan Follows, Colleen Dewhurst, Wendy Hiller, Frank Converse, Patricia Hamilton, Schuyler Grant, Jonathan Crombie, Rosemary Dunsmore; **D:** Kevin Sullivan; **W:** Kevin Sullivan; **M:** Hagood Hardy. **VHS, Beta** $29.95 KUI, BVV, DIS *&&&*½

Anne of Green Gables A lonely Canadian couple adopts an orphan who keeps them on their toes with her animated imagination, and wins a permanent place in their hearts. Warm (but loose) adaptation of Lucy Maud Montgomery's popular novel is entertaining although 1985 remake is far superior. Followed by "Anne of Windy Poplars."
1934 79m/B Anne Shirley, Tom Brown, O.P. Heggie; **D:** George Nichols. **VHS, Beta** $19.98 RKO, TTC *&&&*

Anne of Green Gables Splendid production of the famous Lucy Maud Montgomery classic about a young orphan girl growing to young adulthood with the help of a crusty brother and sister duo. The characters come to life under Sullivan's direction, and the movie is enhanced by the beautiful Prince Edward Island scenery and wonderful costumes. One of the few instances where an adaptation lives up to (if not exceeds) the quality of the original novel. A WonderWorks presentation that was made with the cooperation of the Disney channel, CBC, and PBS. Followed by "Anne of Avonlea." On two tapes.
1985 197m/C *CA* Megan Follows, Colleen Dewhurst, Richard Farnsworth, Patricia Hamilton, Schuyler Grant, Jonathan Crombie, Marilyn Lightstone, Charmion King, Rosemary Radcliffe, Jackie Burroughs; **D:** Kevin Sullivan; **W:** Kevin Sullivan, Joe Weisenfeld; **M:** Hagood Hardy. **VHS, Beta** $29.95 KUI, BVV, IGP *&&&*½

Anne of the Thousand Days Lavish re-telling of the life and loves of Henry the VIII. Henry tosses aside his current wife for the young and devastatingly beautiful Anne Boleyn. Burton's performance of the amoral king garnered him an Oscar nomination. Watch for Elizabeth Taylor as a masked courtesan at the costume ball.
1969 (PG) 145m/C Richard Burton, Genevieve Bujold, Irene Papas, Anthony Quayle, John Colicos, Michael Hordern; **D:** Hal B. Wallis; **M:** Georges Delerue. Academy Awards '69: Best Costume Design; Nominations: Best Actor (Burton), Best Actress (Bujold), Best Adapted Screenplay, Best Art Direction/Set Decoration, Best Cinematography, Best Picture, Best Sound, Best Supporting Actor (Quayle), Best Original Score; Directors Guild of America Awards '70: Best Director (Jarrott); Golden Globe Awards '70: Best Actress—Drama (Bujold), Best Director (Jarrott), Best Film—Drama, Best Screenplay. **VHS** $59.95 MCA *&&&*½

Annie Stagy big-budget adaption of the Broadway musical, which was an adaptation of the comic strip. A major financial disaster upon release, still it's an entertaining enterprise curiously directed by Huston and and engagingly acted by Finney and Quinn. ♫Tomorrow; It's the Hard Knock Life; Maybe; I Think I'm Gonna Like It Here; Little Girls; We Got Annie; Let's Go to the Movies; You're Never Fully Dressed Without a Smile; Easy Street; I Don't Need Anything But You.
1982 (PG) 128m/C Aileen Quinn, Carol Burnett, Albert Finney, Bernadette Peters, Ann Reinking, Tim Curry; **D:** John Huston; **M:** Ralph Burns. **VHS, Beta, 8mm** $14.95 COL, FCT, MLT *&&*

Annie Hall Acclaimed coming-of-cinematic-age film for Allen is based in part on his own life. His love affair with Hall/Keaton is chronicled as an episodic, wistful comedy commenting on family, love, loneliness, communicating, maturity, driving, city life, careers, and various other topics. Abounds with classic scenes, including future star Goldblum and his mantra at a cocktail party; Allen and the lobster pot; and Allen, Keaton, a bathroom, a tennis racket, and a spider. The film operates on many levels, as does Keaton's wardrobe, which started a major fashion trend. Don't blink or you'll miss several future stars in bit parts. Expertly shot by Gordon Willis.
1977 (PG) 94m/C Woody Allen, Diane Keaton, Tony Roberts, Paul Simon, Shelley Duvall, Carol Kane, Colleen Dewhurst, Christopher Walken, Janet Margolin, John Glover, Jeff Goldblum, Sigourney Weaver, Marshall McLuhan, Beverly D'Angelo, Shelley Hack; **D:** Woody Allen; **W:** Woody Allen, Marshall Brickman. Academy Awards '77: Best Actress (Keaton), Best Director (Allen), Best Original Screenplay, Best Picture; Nominations: Best Actor (Allen); British Academy Awards '77: Best Actress (Keaton), Best Director (Allen), Best Film; Directors Guild of America Awards '77: Best Director (Allen); Golden Globe Awards '78: Best Actress—Musical/Comedy (Keaton); National Board of Review Awards '77: 10 Best Films of the Year, Best Actress (Keaton); National Society of Film Critics Awards '77: Best Actress (Keaton), Best Film. **VHS, Beta** $14.95 MGM, FOX, VYG *&&&&*

Annie Oakley Energetic biographical drama based on the life and legend of sharpshooter Annie Oakley and her on-off relationship with Wild Bill Hickok. Stanwyck makes a great Oakley. Later musicalized as "Annie Get Your Gun."
1935 90m/B Barbara Stanwyck, Preston Foster, Melvyn Douglas, Pert Kelton, Andy Clyde; **D:** George Stevens. **VHS, Beta** $19.98 RKO, MED, NOS *&&&*

Annie Oakley This biography of the acclaimed shooting star covers her career from age 15 to retirement, including some actual silent footage of Miss Oakley filmed by Thomas Edison in 1923. Made for television. From the "Tall Tales & Legends" series by Shelly Duvall.
1985 52m/C Jamie Lee Curtis, Cliff DeYoung, Brian Dennehy; **D:** Michael Lindsay-Hogg. **VHS, Beta** $19.98 FOX *&&&*

The Annihilators A group of Vietnam vets band together in an extremely violent manner to protect their small town from a gang of thugs.
1985 (R) 87m/C Gerrit Graham, Lawrence Hilton-Jacobs, Paul Koslo, Christopher Stone, Andy Wood, Sid Conrad, Dennis Redfield; **D:** Charles E. Sellier. **VHS, Beta** $9.95 NWV, STE Woof!

Another Chance Girl-crazy bachelor is returned from heaven for a second chance and has to choose between a "bad" girl and a "good" girl. What a choice!
1988 (R) 99m/C Bruce Greenwood, Frank Annese, Jeff East, Anne Ramsey, Barbara Edwards; **D:** Jerry Vint. **VHS** $9.98 REP *&&*

Another Country Julian Mitchell's adaptation of his play about the true story of two English boarding school friends who wind up as spies for the Soviet Union. Based on the lives of Guy Burgess and Donald MacLean, whose youth is rather fancifully depicted in this loving recreation of 1930s English life. Although the film is inferior to the award-winning play, director Kanievska manages to transform a piece into a solid film, and Everett's performance as Burgess is outstanding.

1984 90m/C GB Rupert Everett, Colin Firth, Michael Jenn, Robert Addie, Anna Massey, Betsy Brantley, Rupert Wainwright, Cary Elwes; D: Marek Kanievska. VHS, Beta $24.98 SUE 🐾🐾½

Another 48 Hrs. Continuing chemistry between Nolte and Murphy is one of the few worthwhile items in this stodgy rehash. Any innovation by Murphy seems lost, the story is redundant of any other cop thriller, and violence and car chases abound. Pointlessly energetic and occasionally fun for only the true devotee.
1990 (R) 98m/C Eddie Murphy, Nick Nolte, Brion James, Kevin Tighe, Bernie Casey, David Anthony Marshall, Ed O'Ross; D: Walter Hill; W: Jeb Stuart; M: James Horner. VHS, Beta, 8mm $14.95 PAR 🐾½

Another Man, Another Chance Remake of Lelouch's "A Man and a Woman," set in the turn-of-the-century American West, pales by comparison to the original. Slow-moving tale casts widow Bujold and widower Caan as lovers. AKA: Un Autre Homme, Une Autre Chance.
1977 (PG) 132m/C FR James Caan, Genevieve Bujold, Francis Huster, Jennifer Warren, Susan Tyrrell; D: Claude Lelouch; W: Claude Lelouch. VHS, Beta NO 🐾🐾

Another Pair of Aces: Three of a Kind Nelson and Kristofferson team up to clear the name of Taylor, a Texas Ranger accused of murder. Made for television; some scenes deemed too racy for TV were added to the video version. Sequel to "A Pair of Aces."
1991 93m/C Willie Nelson, Kris Kristofferson, Joan Severance, Rip Torn, Dan Kamin, Ken Farmer; D: Bill Bixby. VHS $89.95 VMK 🐾🐾🐾

Another Stakeout Sequel six years after the original finds Dreyfuss and Estevez partnered again for another stakeout, this time to keep an eye on Moriarty, a reluctant witness against the Mob. The two spying detectives find themselves in an upscale neighborhood where blending in is a hard thing to do. O'Donnell is a breath of fresh air as a wisecracking assistant district attorney. Stowe briefly reprises her role as Dreyfuss' girlfriend. Writer Kouf reportedly had difficulty penning the script, surprising since there isn't much new here. AKA: Stakeout 2.
1993 (PG-13) 109m/C Richard Dreyfuss, Emilio Estevez, Rosie O'Donnell, Cathy Moriarty, Madeleine Stowe, John Rubinstein, Marcia Strassman, Dennis Farina, Miguel Ferrer; D: John Badham; W: Jim Kouf. VHS $96.83 TOU 🐾🐾½

Another Thin Man Powell and Loy team up for the third in the delightful "Thin Man" series. Slightly weaker series entry takes its time, but has both Powell and Loy providing stylish performances. Nick Jr. is also introduced as the newest member of the sleuthing team. Sequel to "After the Thin Man;" followed by "Shadow of the Thin Man."
1939 105m/B William Powell, Myrna Loy, Virginia Grey, Otto Kruger, Sir C. Aubrey Smith, Ruth Hussey; D: Woodbridge S. Van Dyke. VHS $24.95 MGM 🐾🐾½

Another Time, Another Place Sappy melodrama about an American journalist who suffers an emotional meltdown when her married British lover is killed during WWII. So she heads for Cornwall to console the widow and family.
1958 98m/B GB Lana Turner, Barry Sullivan, Glynis Johns, Sean Connery, Terrence Langdon; D: Lewis Allen. VHS, Beta $19.95 BAR, PAR 🐾🐾

Another Time, Another Place Bored young Scottish housewife married to an older fella falls in love with an Italian prisoner-of-war who works on her farm during WWII. Occasionally quirky, always finely crafted view of wartime Britain and the little-known life of POWs in England.
1983 (R) 101m/C GB Phyllis Logan, Giovanni Mauriello, Gian Luca Favilla, Paul Young, Tom Watson; D: Michael Radford. VHS, Beta $24.98 SUE 🐾🐾🐾

Another Way The director of 1971's much-lauded "Love" sets this politically charged love story in Hungary in 1958. Opening with a view of a female corpse, the story flashes backward to look at the woman's journalistic career and her relationship with a women colleague. Candid love scenes between women in Hungary of 1958, considered a cinematic novelty in many places outside Hungary. In Hungarian with English subtitles. AKA: Olelkezo Tekintetek.
1982 100m/C HU Jadwiga Jankowska Cieslak, Grazyna Szapolowska, Josef Kroner, Hernadi Judit, Andorai Peter; D: Karoly Makk. Cannes Film Festival Nominations: cs 82: Best Film; Cannes Film Festival '82: Best Actress (Cieslak). VHS, Beta $59.95 EVD, FCT, ING 🐾🐾🐾

Another Woman The study of an intellectual woman whose life is changed when she begins to eavesdrop. What she hears provokes her to examine every relationship in her life, finding things quite different than she had believed. Heavy going, with Rowlands effective as a woman coping with an entirely new vision of herself. Farrow plays the catalyst. Although Allen's comedies are more popular than his dramas, this one deserves a look.
1988 (PG) 81m/C Gena Rowlands, Gene Hackman, Mia Farrow, Ian Holm, Betty Buckley, Martha Plimpton, Blythe Danner, Harris Yulin, Sandy Dennis, David Ogden Stiers, John Houseman, Philip Bosco, Frances Conroy, Kenneth Welsh, Michael Kirby; D: Woody Allen; W: Woody Allen. VHS, Beta $14.98 ORI 🐾🐾🐾

Another You Con man Wilder takes pathological liar Pryor under his care and decides to use his talents to his fullest advantage. Posing as successful businessmen, the duo initiate a scam so complicated that they may end up being double-crossed or worse yet, dead! Can the pair see their plan through without losing their lives? Sad to see how far these two gifted comedians have fallen. Their collaboration is tired and the movie generally dreadful.
1991 (R) 98m/C Richard Pryor, Gene Wilder, Mercedes Ruehl, Vanessa Williams, Stephen Lang, Kevin Pollak; D: Maurice Phillips. VHS, 8mm $19.95 COL 🐾

Antarctica Due to unfortunate circumstances, a group of scientists must leave their pack of huskies behind on a frozen glacier in the Antarctic. The film focuses on the dogs' subsequent struggle for survival. Dubbed.
1984 112m/C JP Ken Takakura, Masako Natsume, Keiko Oginome; D: Koreyoshi Kurahara; M: Vangelis. VHS, Beta $59.98 FOX 🐾🐾

Anthony Adverse March is a young man in the 19th century who searches for manhood across America and Mexico. He grows slowly as he battles foes, struggles against adversity and returns home to find his lover in this romantic swashbuckler. A star-studded cast, lush costuming, and an energetic musical score. Highly acclaimed in its time, but now seems dated. Based on the novel by Hervey Allen.

1936 141m/B Fredric March, Olivia de Havilland, Anita Louise, Gale Sondergaard, Claude Rains, Louis Hayward, Scotty Beckett; D: Mervyn LeRoy. Academy Awards '36: Best Cinematography, Best Film Editing, Best Supporting Actress (Sondergaard), Best Score; Nominations: Best Interior Decoration, Best Picture. VHS, Beta $19.98 MGM, BTV, FHE 🐾🐾½

Antonia and Jane Enjoyable film tells the story of a longstanding, heavily tested friendship between two women. From the very beginning, they are a study in contrasts—Jane as rather plain, frumpy, and insecure; Antonia as glamorous, elegant, and successful. Both believe that each other's lives are more interesting and exciting than their own. Kidron, who directed this smart witty comedy for British television, offers an honest look into the often complex world of adult friendships.
1991 (R) 75m/C GB Imelda Staunton, Saskia Reeves, Patricia Leventon, Alfred Hoffman, Maria Charles, John Bennett, Richard Hope, Alfred Marks, Lila Kaye, Bill Nighy, Brenda Bruce; D: Beeban Kidron; W: Marcy Kahan; M: Rachel Portman. VHS, Beta PAR 🐾🐾🐾

Antonio A Texas millionaire on the run from his wife and her divorce lawyer alights in a small Chilean village and turns it upside down.
1973 89m/C Larry Hagman, Trini Lopez, Noemi Guerrero, Pedro Becker; D: Claudio Guzman. VHS, Beta HEG 🐾🐾

Antonio Das Mortes Antonio is a savage mercenary hired to kill rebels against the Brazilian government. Belatedly he realizes he sympathizes with the targets and turns his guns the other way for an incredible shootout finale. A visually lavish political polemic, espousing revolutionary guerrilla action within the format of a South American western. In Portuguese with English subtitles.
1968 100m/C Mauricio Do Valle, Odete Lara; D: Glauce Rocha; W: Glauce Rocha. VHS $59.95 ING 🐾🐾½

Antony and Cleopatra Heston wrote, directed, and starred in this long, dry adaptation of the Shakespeare play that centers on the torrid romance between Mark Antony and Cleopatra.
1973 (PG) 150m/C Charlton Heston, Hildegarde Neff, Fernando Rey, Eric Porter; D: Charlton Heston. VHS, Beta $24.98 SUE 🐾🐾

Ants A mad bug parable for the planet-obsessed 90s. Insecticide-infected ants turn militant and check into a local hotel to vent their chemically induced foul mood on the unsuspecting clientele. The guest register includes a gaggle of celebrities who probably wish they'd signed on the Love Boat instead. Made for television (an ant farm would probably be just too horrible on the big screen). AKA: Panic at Lakewood Manor; It Happened at Lakewood Manor.
1977 100m/C Suzanne Somers, Robert Foxworth, Myrna Loy, Lynda Day George, Gerald Gordon, Bernie Casey, Barry Van Dyke, Karen Lamm, Anita Gillette, Moosie Drier, Steve Franken, Brian Dennehy, Bruce French, Stacy Keach, Rene Enriquez, James Storm; D: Robert Scheerer. VHS, Beta LIV 🐾½

Any Gun Can Play Typical spaghetti western. Three men (banker, thief, and bounty hunter) compete for a treasure of gold while wandering about the Spanish countryside. AKA: For a Few Bullets More.
1967 103m/C IT SP Edd Byrnes, Gilbert Roland, George Hilton, Kareen O'Hara, Pedro Sanchez, Gerard Herter; D: Enzo G. Castellari. VHS HHE 🐾

Any Man's Death Savage is a globe-trotting reporter on the trail of a worldwide conspiracy who accidentally uncovers a Nazi war criminal in Africa. Well-meaning but confused tale.
1990 (R) 105m/C John Savage, William Hickey, Mia Sara, Ernest Borgnine, Michael Lerner; *D:* Tom Clegg. **VHS, Beta** *PSM &&*

Any Number Can Play Fast-moving drama about an ailing gambler who faces a series of crises. Gable gives a commanding performance as the noble dice-roller. Based on the novel by Edward Harris Heath.
1949 102m/B Clark Gable, Alexis Smith, Wendell Corey, Audrey Totter, Frank Morgan, Mary Astor, Lewis Stone, Barry Sullivan; *D:* Mervyn LeRoy; *W:* Richard Brooks. **VHS $19.98** *MGM &&½*

Any Wednesday Okay sex farce about powerful industrialist Robards' use of his mistress's apartment as a tax write-off. When a young company executive learns of the "company" apartment, he meets Robards' nonchalant wife for a tryst of their own. Based on Muriel Resnik's Broadway play; similar to the 1960 "The Apartment." *AKA:* Bachelor Girl Apartment.
1966 110m/C Jane Fonda, Jason Robards Jr., Dean Jones, Rosemary Murphy; *D:* Robert Ellis Miller; *W:* Julius J. Epstein, Philip C. Epstein; *M:* George Duning. **VHS, Beta $19.98** *WAR &&½*

Any Which Way You Can Bad brawler Philo Beddoe and his buddy Clyde, the orangutan, are back again in the sequel to "Every Which Way But Loose." This time Philo is tempted to take part in a big bout for a large cash prize. Clyde steals scenes, brightening up the no-brainer story.
1980 (PG) 116m/C Clint Eastwood, Sondra Locke, Ruth Gordon, Harry Guardino; *D:* Buddy Van Horn. **VHS, Beta $19.98** *WAR &&*

Anything for a Thrill Two kids save a cameraman's career, make friends with a millionairess, and foil some crooks.
1937 59m/B Frankie Darro, Kane Richmond; *D:* S.A. Grandi. **VHS $24.95** *NOS, DVT, HEG &*

Anzacs: The War Down Under Well-made Australian TV miniseries about the Australian & New Zealand Army Corps during WWI. Follows the men from the time they enlist to the campaigns in Gallipoli and France.
1985 165m/C *AU* Paul Hogan, Andrew Clarke, Jon Blake, Megan Williams; *D:* George Miller. **VHS, Beta $19.95** *CEL &&&*

Anzio The historic Allied invasion of Italy during WWII as seen through the eyes of American war correspondent Mitchum. Fine cast waits endlessly to leave the beach, though big battle scenes are effectively rendered. Based on the book by Wynford Vaughan Thomas. *AKA:* The Battle for Anzio; Lo Sbarco di Anzio.
1968 117m/C Robert Mitchum, Peter Falk, Arthur Kennedy, Robert Ryan, Earl Holliman, Mark Damon, Reni Santoni, Patrick Magee; *D:* Edward Dmytryk. **VHS, Beta** *NO &*

Apache Lancaster is the only Indian in Geronimo's outfit who refuses to surrender in this chronicle of a bitter battle between the Indians and the U.S. cavalry in the struggle for the West. First western for Aldrich is a thoughtful piece for its time that had the original tragic ending reshot (against Aldrich's wishes) to make it more happy. Adapted from "Bronco Apache" by Paul I. Wellman.
1954 91m/C Burt Lancaster, John McIntire, Jean Peters; *D:* Robert Aldrich. **VHS, Beta $19.98** *MGM, FOX, FCT &&½*

Apache Blood An Indian Brave, the lone survivor of an Indian massacre by the U.S. Army, squares off with a calvary scout in the forbidding desert. *AKA:* Pursuit.
1975 (R) 92m/C Ray Danton, DeWitt Lee, Troy Nabors, Diane Taylor, Eva Kovacs, Jason Clark; *D:* Thomas Quillen. **VHS $19.99** *PSM &½*

Apache Chief Two Apache tribe leaders, one good, the other evil clash. Ultimately, and perhaps predictably, they face each other in hand-to-hand combat and peace prevails.
1950 60m/B Alan Curtis, Tom Neal, Russell Hayden, Carol Thurston; *D:* Frank McDonald. **VHS, Beta** *NO &*

Apache Kid's Escape The Apache Kid leads the cavalry on a wild chase across the plains in this saga of the old west.
1930 60m/B Jack Perrin, Buzz Barton. **VHS, Beta $19.95** *NOS, DVT, RXM &*

Apache Rose Gambling boat owner plots to gain control of oil found on Vegas Ranch. Roy and Dale oppose the idea. First of the series in color; the original, unedited version of the film.
1947 75m/B Roy Rogers, Dale Evans, Olin Howland, George Meeker; *D:* William Witney. **VHS, Beta $9.99** *FOX, NOS, VCN &&*

Apache Uprising A standard western with Calhoun as the lawman up against gunfighters and stagecoach robbers as well as the usual Indians.
1966 60m/C Rory Calhoun, Corinne Calvet, DeForest Kelley, John Russell, Lon Chaney Jr., Gene Evans, Richard Arlen, Robert Harris, Arthur Hunnicutt, Jean Parker, Johnny Mack Brown; *D:* R.G. Springsteen. **VHS** *PAR &½*

Apache Woman Bridges stars as a government agent sent to investigate some crimes committed by a group of Apache Indians. As he tries to calm the townspeople, Bridges discovers that the group is made up of white people led by an educated half-breed. He instigates the help of the half-breed's sister (and also Bridges' love interest) to stop the gang. Some good action, but lots of dull spots.
1955 82m/C Lloyd Bridges, Joan Taylor, Lance Fuller, Morgan Jones, Paul Birch, Jonathan Haze, Paul Dubov, Lou Place; *D:* Roger Corman. **VHS $19.95** *COL, FCT &½*

Apaches Last Battle A boundary scout discovers the ward of an Apache chief has been framed for murder by a cavalry officer who wants to start an Indian war in this exciting Euro western. *AKA:* Old Shatterhand; Shatterhand.
1964 ?m/C Lex Barker, Guy Madison, Pierre Brice. **VHS $16.95** *SNC, VTR &&*

Aparajito The second of the Apu trilogy, about a boy growing up in India, after "Pather Panchali," and before "The World of Apu." Apu is brought to Benares and his education seriously begins. The work of a master; in Bengali with English subtitles. *AKA:* The Unvanquished.
1958 108m/B *IN* Pinaki Sen Gupta, Karuna Banerjee, Kanu Banerjee, Ramani Sen Gupta; *D:* Satyajit Ray. **VHS, Beta $29.95** *FCT, MRV, TIM &&&½*

The Apartment A lowly insurance clerk tries to climb the corporate ladder by "loaning" his apartment out to executives having affairs. Problems arise, however, when he unwittingly falls for the most recent girlfriend of the boss. Highly acclaimed social satire.
1960 125m/B Jack Lemmon, Shirley MacLaine, Fred MacMurray, Ray Walston, Jack Kruschen, Joan Shawlee, Edie Adams, Hope Holiday, David Lewis; *D:* Billy Wilder; *W:* I.A.L. Diamond, Billy Wilder. Academy Awards '60: Best Art Direction/

Set Decoration (B & W), Best Director (Wilder), Best Film Editing, Best Picture, Best Story & Screenplay; Nominations: Best Actor (Lemmon), Best Actress (MacLaine), Best Black and White Cinematography, Best Sound, Best Supporting Actor (Kruschen); British Academy Awards '60: Best Actor (Lemmon), Best Actress (MacLaine), Best Film; Directors Guild of America Awards '60: Best Director (Wilder); Golden Globe Awards '61: Best Actor—Musical/Comedy (Lemmon), Best Actress—Musical/Comedy (MacLaine), Best Film—Musical/Comedy; National Board of Review Awards '60: 10 Best Films of the Year; New York Film Critics Awards '60: Best Director (Wilder), Best Film. **VHS, Beta $19.98** *MGM, BTV &&&½*

Apartment Zero A decidedly weird, deranged psychological drama about the parasite/host-type relationship between two roommates in downtown Buenos Aires: one, an obsessive British movie nut, the other, a sexually mesmerizing stud who turns out to be a cold-blooded psycho.
1988 (R) 124m/C *GB* Hart Bochner, Colin Firth, Fabrizio Bentivoglio, Liz Smith; *D:* Martin Donovan; *W:* Martin Donovan, David Koepp. **VHS, Beta $14.95** *ACA, FCT, IME &&&½*

The Ape When his daughter dies of a crippling disease, Karloff becomes fixated with the mission to cure paralysis. Obviously distraught, he begins donning the hide of an escaped circus ape whose spinal fluid is the key to the serum. Hide-bedecked, he slays unknowing townspeople to tap them of their spinal fluid and cure his latest patient.
1940 62m/B Boris Karloff, Maris Wrixon, Henry Hall, Gertrude Hoffman; *D:* William Nigh. **VHS, Beta $19.95** *NOS, SNC, VYY &&*

A*P*E* A*P*E* is thirty-six feet tall and ten tons of animal fury who destroys anything that comes between him and the actress he loves. Cheap rip-off of Kong.
1976 (PG) 87m/C Rod Arrants, Joanna DeVarona, Alex Nicol; *D:* Paul Leder. **VHS, Beta $19.95** *NWV Woof!*

The Ape Man With the aid of a secret potion, a scientist turns himself into a murderous ape. The only way to regain his human side is to ingest human spinal fluid. Undoubtedly inspired by Boris Karloff's 1940 film, "The Ape." *AKA:* Lock Your Doors.
1943 64m/B Wallace Ford, Bela Lugosi; *D:* William Beaudine. **VHS, Beta $19.95** *NOS, MRV, SNC &&*

A.P.E.X. Nicholas Sinclair (Keats), a researcher from 2073, time travels back to 1973 to retrieve a faulty robot probe called A.P.E.X. (Advanced Prototype Extermination Unit). Unwittingly he has been infected with a mysterious virus and when he returns it's to a version of his own time where humans are dying from the virus and robots are sent to eradicate the few survivors. It also seems Sinclair is now a guerilla in an anti-robot army. Yes, it sounds like "The Terminator" but the action moves and though the budget is limited the special effects are still impressive.
1994 (R) 103m/C Richard Keats, Mitch Cox, Lisa Ann Russell, Marcus Aurelius, Adam Lawson; *D:* Phillip J. Roth; *W:* Phillip J. Roth, Ronald Schmidt; *M:* Jim Goodwin. **VHS** *REP &&*

Apocalipsis Joe A lonely gunfighter looks to kick an evil criminal out of a small town.
1965 90m/C Eduardo Fajardo, Mary Paz Pondal, Fernando Ceruli, Fernando Bilbao. **VHS, Beta $34.90** *MAD &&½*

Apocalypse Now Coppola's $40 million epic vision of the Vietnam War was inspired by Joseph Conrad's novella "Heart of Darkness," and continues to be the subject of debate. Disillusioned Army captain Sheen travels upriver into Cambodia to assassinate overweight renegade colonel Brando. His trip is punctuated by surrealistic battles and a terrifying descent into a land where human rationality seems to have slipped away. Considered by some to be the definitive picture of war in its overall depiction of chaos and primal bloodletting; by others, over-wrought and unrealistic. May not translate as well to the small screen, yet worth seeing if for nothing more than Duvall's ten minutes of scenery chewing as a battle-obsessed major ("I love the smell of napalm in the morning!"), a study in manic machismo. Stunning photography by Vittorio Storaro, awe-inspiring battle scenes, and effective soundtrack montage. Both Sheen and Coppola suffered emotional breakdowns during the prolonged filming, and that's a very young Fishburne in his major film debut. Available in widescreen format on laserdisc and in a remastered version in letterbox on VHS with a remixed soundtrack that features Dolby Surround stereo. In 1991 a documentary detailing the making of the film, "Hearts of Darkness: A Filmmaker's Apocalypse," was released. **1979 (R) 153m/C** Marlon Brando, Martin Sheen, Robert Duvall, Frederic Forrest, Sam Bottoms, Scott Glenn, Albert Hall, Laurence "Larry" Fishburne, Harrison Ford, G.D. Spradlin, Dennis Hopper, Colleen Camp, Tom Mason; *D:* Francis Ford Coppola; *W:* Francis Ford Coppola, John Milius; *M:* Carmine Coppola. Academy Awards '79: Best Cinematography, Best Sound; Nominations: Best Adapted Screenplay, Best Art Direction/Set Decoration, Best Director (Coppola), Best Film Editing, Best Picture, Best Supporting Actor (Duvall); British Academy Awards '79: Best Director (Coppola), Best Supporting Actor (Duvall); Golden Globe Awards '80: Best Director (Coppola), Best Supporting Actor (Duvall), Best Score; National Board of Review Awards '79: 10 Best Films of the Year; National Society of Film Critics Awards '79: Best Supporting Actor (Forrest). **VHS, Beta, CDV $29.95** *PAR* 🐾🐾🐾🐾

Apology A psychotic killer stalks Warren, an experimental artist, in Manhattan while a detective stalks the killer. Made for cable, so expect a little more sex and violence than network TV movies. Written by Medhoff, author of "Children of a Lesser God." **1986 98m/C** Lesley Ann Warren, Peter Weller, John Glover, George Loros, Jimmie Ray Weeks, Christopher North, Harvey Fierstein; *D:* Robert Bierman; *W:* Mark Medoff; *M:* Maurice Jarre. **VHS $19.95** *HBO* 🐾🐾

The Appaloosa A lamenting loner who decides to begin anew by breeding Appaloosas is ripped off by a desperate woman who steals his horse in order to get away from her abusive amour. Brando falls in love with the girl and the two amazingly survive a wealth of obstacles in their battle against Mexican bandits. *AKA:* Southwest to Sonora. **1966 99m/C** Marlon Brando, Anjanette Comer, John Saxon; *D:* Sidney J. Furie; *W:* James Bridges. **VHS, Beta $14.95** *MCA* 🐾🐾½

Applause Morgan plays a down-and-out burlesque star trying to protect her fresh from the convent daughter. Definitely dated, but a marvelous performance by Morgan. Film buffs will appreciate this early talkie. **1929 78m/B** Helen Morgan, Joan Peers, Fuller Mellish Jr., Henry Wadsworth, Dorothy Cumming; *D:* Rouben Mamoulian. **VHS** *PAR* 🐾🐾🐾

The Apple Futuristic musical filmed in Berlin that features a young, innocent, folk-singing couple who nearly become victims of the evil, glitzy record producer who tries to recruit the couple into a life of sex and drugs. **1980 (PG) 90m/C** Catherine Mary Stewart, Alan Love, Grace Kennedy, Joss Ackland; *D:* Menahem Golan. **VHS, Beta** *NO* 🐾½

The Apple Dumpling Gang Three frisky kids strike it rich and trigger the wildest bank robbery in the gold-mad West. Unmistakably Disney, a familial subplot and a wacky duo are provided. Mediocre yet superior to its sequel, "The Apple Dumpling Gang Rides Again." **1975 (G) 100m/C** Bill Bixby, Susan Clark, Don Knotts, Tim Conway, David Wayne, Slim Pickens, Harry Morgan; *D:* Norman Tokar; *M:* Buddy Baker. **VHS, Beta $19.99** *DIS* 🐾🐾

The Apple Dumpling Gang Rides Again Two lovable hombres terrorize the West in their bungling attempt to go straight. Fans of Conway or Knotts may appreciate this sequel to Disney's "The Apple Dumpling Gang." **1979 (G) 88m/C** Tim Conway, Don Knotts, Tim Matheson, Kenneth Mars, Harry Morgan, Jack Elam; *D:* Vincent McEveety; *M:* Buddy Baker. **VHS, Beta $69.95** *DIS* 🐾🐾

The Applegates Ecologically correct Amazonian beetles are more than a little miffed about the slash-and-burn tactics in their home and decide to establish a kinder, gentler habitat. Bug Begley and his brood transform themselves into average Americans, but then don't want to leave their decadent life: even insects aren't immune to the lure of sex, drugs, and cable shopping networks. Imaginative, often quite funny one-joke flick should've been shorter. Fits quite well as a double feature with Lehmann's earlier "Heathers." *AKA:* Meet the Applegates. **1989 (R) 90m/C** Ed Begley Jr., Stockard Channing, Dabney Coleman, Cami Cooper, Bobby Jacoby, Glenn Shadix, Susan Barnes, Adam Biesk, Savannah Smith Boucher; *D:* Michael Lehmann; *W:* Michael Lehmann, Redbeard Simmons. **VHS, Beta $89.98** *MED, FOX, VTR* 🐾🐾½

The Appointment A supernatural force enters the bodies and minds of people and suddenly everyone begins going crazy. **1982 90m/C** Edward Woodward, Jane Merrow; *D:* Lindsey C. Vickers. **VHS, Beta, 8mm** *NO Woof!*

Appointment in Honduras An adventurer goes on a dangerous trek through the Central American jungles to deliver funds to the Honduran President. **1953 79m/C** Glenn Ford, Ann Sheridan, Zachary Scott; *D:* Jacques Tourneur. **VHS, Beta** *NO* 🐾🐾

Appointment with Crime After serving a prison sentence, an ex-con sets out to avenge himself against the colleagues who double crossed him. Well done, highlighted by superior characterizations. Based on the story by Michael Leighton. **1945 91m/B** *GB* William Hartnell, Raymond Lovell, Robert Beatty, Herbert Lom, Joyce Howard, Alan Wheatley, Cyril Smith; *D:* John Harlow; *W:* John Harlow. **VHS, Beta $16.95** *SNC* 🐾🐾½

Appointment with Death Disappointing Agatha Christie mystery with Hercule Poirot solving the murder of a shrewish widow in 1937 Palestine. **1988 (PG) 103m/C** Peter Ustinov, Lauren Bacall, Carrie Fisher, John Gielgud, Piper Laurie, Hayley Mills, Jenny Seagrove, David Soul; *D:* Michael Winner; *W:* Anthony Shaffer, Michael Winner; *M:* Pino Donaggio. **VHS, Beta $19.98** *WAR, FCT* 🐾½

Appointment with Fear A tough detective investigates a murder and all of the clues lead him into a comatose asylum inmate. **1985 (R) 95m/C** Michael Wyle, Michelle Little, Garrick Dowhen; *D:* Alan Smithee. **VHS, Beta $14.95** *LIV* 🐾

Apprentice to Murder A small Pennsylvania Dutch town is shaken by a series of murders, thought to be associated with a bizarre local mystic and healer. Based on a true story, sort of. **1988 (PG-13) 97m/C** Donald Sutherland, Mia Sara, Chad Lowe, Eddie Jones; *D:* Ralph L. Thomas; *W:* Allan Scott. **VHS, Beta $19.95** *STE, NWV, HHE* 🐾🐾

The Apprenticeship of Duddy Kravitz Young Jewish man in Montreal circa 1948 is driven by an insatiable need to be the "somebody" everyone has always told him he will be. A series of get-rich-quick schemes backfire in different ways, and he becomes most successful at driving people away. Young Dreyfuss is at his best. Made in Canada with thoughtful detail, and great cameo performances. Script by Richler, from his novel. **1974 (PG) 121m/C** *CA* Richard Dreyfuss, Randy Quaid, Denholm Elliott, Jack Warden, Micheline Lanctot, Joe Silver; *D:* Ted Kotcheff; *W:* Mordecai Richler, Lionel Chetwynd. Academy Awards '74 Nominations: Best Adapted Screenplay; Berlin International Film Festival '74: Golden Berlin Bear. **VHS, Beta $14.95** *PAR* 🐾🐾🐾½

April Fool A man makes a fortune in the umbrella business and then discovers his daughter has fallen in love with the son of a nouveaux riche neighbor, resulting in all sorts of complications. **1926 63m/B** Alexander Carr, Mary Alden, Raymond Keane, Snitz Edwards; *D:* Nat Ross; *W:* Zion Myer. **VHS $14.95** *GPV* 🐾🐾½

April Fools A bored stockbroker falls in love with a beautiful woman who turns out to be married to his boss. **1969 (PG) 95m/C** Jack Lemmon, Catherine Deneuve, Sally Kellerman, Peter Lawford, Charles Boyer, Myrna Loy, Harvey Korman; *D:* Stuart Rosenberg; *M:* Marvin Hamlisch. **VHS, Beta $19.98** *FOX* 🐾🐾

April Fool's Day Rich girl Foreman invites eight college friends to spend the April Fool's weekend with her at her family's isolated island mansion. Everyone is subjected to an endless series of practical jokes when things apparently turn deadly and several of the kids begin disappearing. Lame spoof of "Friday the 13th" and other teenagers-in-peril slasher films. **1986 (R) 90m/C** Deborah Foreman, Jay Baker, Pat Barlow, Lloyd Berry, Deborah Goodrich, Ken Olandt, Griffin O'Neal, Tom Heaton, Mike Nomad, Leah K. Pinsent, Clayton Rohner, Amy Steel, Thomas F. Wilson; *D:* Fred Walton; *W:* Danilo Bach; *M:* Charles Bernstein. **VHS, Beta $19.95** *PAR* 🐾

April In Paris Dynamite Jackson (Day), a chorus girl accidentally sent by the State Department to perform in Paris, meets S. Winthrop Putnam (Bolger), a timid fellow trapped in an unpleasant marriage. They eventually sing and dance their way to warm feelings as they begin a lifelong romance and live happily ever after. **1952 100m/C** Doris Day, Ray Bolger, Claude Dauphin, Eve Miller, George Givot, Paul Harvey; *D:* David Butler; *W:* Jack Rose, Melville Shavelson. **VHS $19.98** *WAR, CCB, MVD* 🐾🐾

The Arab Conspiracy Sharpe plays a hit-woman conspiring with assassins from all over the world to kill Arab leaders. One problem—she falls in love with Saudi Arabian ambassador Connery who tries to gain peace with Palestine. *AKA:* The Next Man; Double Hit. **1976 (R) 108m/C** Sean Connery, Cornelia Sharpe, Albert Paulsen, Adolfo Celi, Charles Cioffi; *D:* Richard Sarafian; *W:* Alan R. Trustman; *M:* Michael Kamen. **VHS $9.95** *SIM, QVD, VTR* 🐾🐾

Arabesque A college professor is drawn into international espionage by a beautiful woman and a plot to assassinate an Arab prince. Stylish and fast moving. From the novel "The Cipher" by Gordon Votler.
1966 105m/C Gregory Peck, Sophia Loren, George Coulouris; **D:** Stanley Donen; **M:** Henry Mancini. **VHS, Beta $14.95** *MCA, FCT* ✍✍½

Arabian Nights Two brothers fight for the throne of Turkey and the affection of the sultry dancing girl Scheherazade. Enchanting costumes and lavish sets augment the fantasy atmosphere.
1942 87m/C Jon Hall, Maria Montez, Sabu, Leif Erickson, Edgar Barrier, Richard Lane, Turhan Bey; **D:** John Rawlins; **W:** Michael Hogan. **VHS $14.98** *MCA, FCT* ✍✍

Arabian Nights The third of Pasolini's epic, explicit adaptations of classic portmanteau, featuring ten of the old Scheherazade favorites adorned by beautiful photography, explicit sex scenes and homoeroticism. In Italian with English subtitles; available dubbed.
1974 130m/C Ninetto Davoli, Franco Merli, Ines Pellegrini, Luigina Rocchi; **D:** Pier Paolo Pasolini; **M:** Ennio Morricone. **VHS, Beta $11.95** *WBF, ING, APD* ✍✍✍

Arachnophobia Big-budget big-bug horror story has a few funny moments as lots and lots of spiders wreak havoc in a white picket fence community somewhere off the beaten track. Lethal South American spider makes a trek to sunny California, meets up with local spiders, and rapidly multiplies. Utterly arachnophobic (read: totally scared of spiders) town doctor Daniels pairs with gung-ho exterminator Goodman to try and track down the culprits. The script's a bit yawn-inspiring but the cast and effects will keep you from dozing off. Directorial debut for Marshall, a longtime friend and producer for Spielberg.
1990 (PG-13) 109m/C Jeff Daniels, John Goodman, Harley Jane Kozak, Julian Sands, Roy Brocksmith, Stuart Pankin, Brian McNamara, Mark L. Taylor, Henry Jones, Peter Jason, James Handy; **D:** Frank Marshall; **W:** Wesley Strick, Don Jakoby; **M:** Trevor Jones. **VHS, Beta $14.99** *HPH* ✍✍½

Arcade All the kids in town are desperate to play the new virtual reality game Arcade, only the game is just a little too real. Seems it can transport you into another world with its stunning graphics and sound effects but you really put your life on the line. Only Alex (Ward) worries when kids start to disappear and she decides to battle the game for their lives.
1993 (R) 85m/C Megan Ward, Peter Billingsley, John de Lancie, Sharon Farrell, Seth Green, Humberto Ortiz, Jonathan Fuller, Norbert Weisser; **D:** Albert Pyun; **W:** David S. Goyer; **M:** Alan Howarth. **VHS, Beta** *PAR* ✍½

Arcadia of My Youth In the 30th century the evil Illumidus Empire has conquered Earth and only the heroic Captain Harlock and his friends can battle their tyranny. Based on Matsumoto Leiji's comic book series. Draws parallels to the post-WWII occupation of Japan. Animated; in Japanese with English subtitles.
1982 130m/C *JP* **VHS $39.95** *ANI, WTA* ✍½

Arch of Triumph In Paris, an Austrian refugee doctor falls in love just before the Nazis enter the city. Big-budget box-office loser featuring fine cast but sluggish pace. Based on the Erich Maria Remarque novel and remade for television.

1948 120m/B Ingrid Bergman, Charles Boyer, Charles Laughton, Louis Calhern; **D:** Lewis Milestone; **W:** Harry Brown, Lewis Milestone. **VHS $129.98** *REP* ✍✍✍

Arch of Triumph A refugee doctor falls in love with a mystery woman as the Nazis enter Paris. Made for television remake of the 1948 film.
1985 95m/C Anthony Hopkins, Lesley-Anne Down, Donald Pleasence, Frank Finlay; **D:** Waris Hussein; **W:** Charles Israel; **M:** Georges Delerue. **VHS $19.95** *FCT* ✍✍½

Archer: The Fugitive from the Empire A young warrior battles the forces of evil in this television movie. Lots of strange names to learn even if you already know who's going to win the final battle.
1981 97m/C Lane Caudell, Belinda Bauer, George Kennedy, Victor Campos, Kabir Bedi, George Innes, Marc Alaimo, Allen Rich, John Hancock, Priscilla Pointer, Richard Dix, Sharon Barr; **D:** Nick Corea. **VHS, Beta $39.95** *MCA* ✍

Archer's Adventure An Australian family film based on a true story. A horsetrainer's young apprentice delivers a prize racehorse to Melbourne, through 600 miles of tough frontier, devious bush rangers, and disaster.
1985 120m/C *AU* Brett Climo; **D:** Denny Lawrence. **VHS, Beta $14.95** *NWV, STE* ✍½

Are Parents People? Lighthearted silent comedy about a young girl's successful attempts to reunite her feuding parents. It all begins as she runs away and spends the night in the office of a doctor she has grown to like. After a frantic night of searching, her parents are reunited through their love for her.
1925 60m/B Betty Bronson, Adolphe Menjou, Florence Vidor. **VHS $16.95** *GPV, PAR* ✍✍

Are You in the House Alone? Made for television adaptation of Richard Peck's award-winning novel. Story of a high school coed who becomes the target of a terror campaign.
1978 100m/C Blythe Danner, Kathleen Beller, Tony Bill, Scott Colomby; **D:** Walter Grauman; **M:** Charles Bernstein. **VHS, Beta $49.95** *WOV, GKK* ✍✍

Are You Lonesome Tonight Suspense thriller casts Seymour as a wealthy socialite who discovers her husband is having an affair with a phone-sex girl. His sudden and mysterious disapppearance forces her to hire a private detective (Stevenson) to track him down, with only the taped conversations as clues. Average made for cable television fare.
1992 (PG-13) 91m/C Jane Seymour, Parker Stevenson, Beth Broderick, Joel Brooks, Robert Pine; **D:** E.W. Swackhamer; **W:** Wesley Moore. **VHS, Beta $19.95** *PAR* ✍✍½

Arena Remember old boxing melodramas about good-natured palookas, slimy opponents, gangsters and dames? This puts those cliches in a garish sci-fi setting, with handsome Steve Armstrong battling ETs and the astro-mob to be the first human pugilistic champ in decades. A really cute idea (from the screenwriters of "The Rocketeer"), but it conks out at the halfway point. Worth a look for buffs.
1988 (PG-13) 97m/C *IT* Paul Satterfield, Claudia Christian, Hamilton Camp, Marc Alaimo, Armin Shimerman, Shari Shattuck, Jack Carter; **D:** Peter Manoogian; **W:** Danny Bilson, Paul DeMeo; **M:** Richard Band. **VHS $14.95** *COL* ✍✍

Aria Ten directors were given carte blanche to interpret ten arias from well-known operas. Henry and D'Angelo star in Julian Temple's rendition of Verdi's "Rigoletto." In Fonda's film debut, she and her lover travel

to Las Vegas and eventually kill themselves in the bathtub, just like "Romeo & Juliet." Jarman's piece (a highlight) shows an aged operatic star at her last performance remembering an early love affair. "I Pagliacci" is the one aria in which the director took his interpretation in a straightforward manner.
1988 (R) 90m/C *GB* Theresa Russell, Anita Morris, Bridget Fonda, Beverly D'Angelo, Buck Henry, John Hurt; **D:** Ken Russell, Charles Sturridge, Robert Altman, Bill Bryden, Jean-Luc Godard, Bruce Beresford, Nicolas Roeg, Franc Roddam, Derek Jarman, Julien Temple. **VHS, Beta $29.95** *ACA, FCT* ✍✍

Ariel Refreshing, offbeat Finnish comedy by highly praised newcomer Kaurismaki. Hoping to find work in Southern Finland, an out-of-work miner from Northern Finland (Pajala) jets off in his white Cadillac convertible given to him in a cafe by a friend, who promptly shoots himself. There's no linear progression toward a happy ending, although antiheroic subject does find employment and romances a meter maid. Mostly, though, he's one of those it's hell being me guys who wouldn't have any luck if it weren't for bad luck. Strange slice-of-life sporting film noir tendencies, although essentially anti-stylistic.
1989 74m/C *FI* Susanna Haavisto, Turo Pajala, Matti Pellonpaa; **D:** Aki Kaurismaki; **W:** Aki Kaurismaki. **VHS $79.95** *KIV, FCT, ING* ✍✍✍

Arizona Arthur is a hellion in wild 1860 Tucson who falls for the wandering Holden. He's headed for California and she can't keep him in town so Arthur throws herself into business by establishing a freight line. Only warring Apaches try to burn her out and Holden rides in to save the day (with the calvary and a stampeding cattle herd). Holden's first western is lively but long.
1940 121m/B Jean Arthur, William Holden, Warren William, Porter Hall, Paul Harvey, George Chandler, Regis Toomey, Edgar Buchanan; **D:** Wesley Ruggles; **W:** Claude Binyon; **M:** Victor Young. **VHS $14.95** *COL* ✍✍½

Arizona A group of illegal aliens struggle for survival after they cross the border into the harsh desert.
1986 94m/C *MX* Roberto "Flaco" Guzman, Juan Valentin. **VHS, Beta** *MED* ✍½

Arizona Badman There is a bad man in Arizona, and he must be gotten rid of.
1942 60m/B Reb Russell; **D:** S. Roy Luby. **VHS, Beta $19.95** *NOS, DVT* ✍½

Arizona Bound Mesa City is infested with a villain and our "Rough Rider" trio must rid the town of him.
1941 57m/B Buck Jones, Tim McCoy, Raymond Hatton, Dennis Moore, Luana Walters; **D:** Spencer Gordon Bennet. **VHS, Beta $19.95** *NOS, VCN, DVT* ✍

Arizona Bushwackers Routine western that has Confederate spy Keel taking job as sheriff in small Arizona town. Once there, he has to straighten out a few bad guys who have been selling weapons to the Apaches. Notable for presence of old western-movie veterans Ireland, Donlevy, Brady, and MacLane. Based on a story by Steve Fisher.
1967 87m/C Howard Keel, Yvonne De Carlo, John Ireland, Marilyn Maxwell, Scott Brady, Brian Donlevy, Barton MacLane; **D:** Lesley Selander. **VHS $14.95** *PAR* ✍✍

Arizona Cowboy An ex-G.I., now the rodeo's big attraction, gets involved in a robbery.
1949 57m/B Rex Allen, Gordon Jones, Roy Barcroft; **D:** R.G. Springsteen. **VHS, Beta $29.95** *DVT* ✍

Arizona Days Cowboys join a minstrel group and rescue the show when a group of toughs try to break it up.
1937 56m/B Tex Ritter, Eleanor Stewart, Syd Saylor, Snub Pollard; **D:** John English. **VHS, Beta** $19.95 *NOS, VCI, VDM* ℤℤ½

Arizona Gangbusters Below-average oater has real-life cowboy McCoy fighting city hall in order to fight other baddies.
1940 57m/B Tim McCoy, Pauline Hadden, Forrest Taylor, Julian Rivero, Curly Dresden; **D:** Peter Stewart. **VHS** $19.95 *DVT, HEG* ℤ

Arizona Gunfighter A young cowhand seeks revenge against the man who murdered his father in this western.
1937 60m/B Bob Steele, Ted Adams; **D:** Sam Newfield. **VHS, Beta** $19.95 *NOS, DVT* ℤ

Arizona Heat A violent cop is teamed up with a tough, but tender female cop in this all-too-familiar tale of two cops chasing a cop killer.
1987 (R) 91m/C Michael Parks, Denise Crosby, Hugh Farrington; **D:** John G. Thomas. **VHS** $79.98 *REP* ℤℤ

Arizona Kid Another sagebrush saga featuring Roy in singin' and fightin' action.
1939 54m/B Roy Rogers; **D:** Horace Carpenter. **VHS, Beta** $9.99 *NOS, DVT, TIM* ℤ

Arizona Mahoney Weird mixture of circus adventure and serious western doesn't work too well. Confused film with farfetched reasons for having the paths of circus performers and cowboys cross. Based on a Zane Grey novel.
1936 58m/B Joe Cook, Robert Cummings, June Martel, Marjorie Gateson, John Miljan, James Mason; **D:** James Hogan; **W:** Robert Yost, Stuart Anthony. **VHS** $19.99 *MOV* ℤ

Arizona Raiders Arizona rangers hunt down killers who have been terrorizing the territory.
1965 88m/C Audie Murphy, Buster Crabbe, Gloria Talbott; **D:** William Whitney. **VHS, Beta** $19.95 *NOS, VCI, VCN* ℤℤ

Arizona Roundup Good vs. bad amid tumbleweed, bleached-white chaps, bloodless shoot-outs and happy endings.
1942 54m/B Tom Keene, Sugar Dawn, Jack Ingram; **D:** Robert Tansey. **VHS, Beta** $19.95 *NOS, VDM* ℤℤ½

Arizona Stagecoach The Range Busters set out to bust a notorious, guiltless, devil-may-care outlaw gang.
1942 58m/B Ray Corrigan, Max Terhune, Kermit Maynard, Charles "Blackie" King, John "Dusty" King; **D:** S. Roy Luby. **VHS, Beta** $19.95 *NOS* ℤ

Arizona Terror Our hero is on a quest for vengeance, seeking the posse that killed his partner.
1931 64m/B Ken Maynard. **VHS, Beta** *VCN* ℤ½

Arizona Whirlwind Our intrepid heroes must battle torrents of gunfire in order to prevent a stage hold-up in this western saga.
1944 59m/B Ken Maynard, Hoot Gibson, Bob Steele. **VHS, Beta** $19.95 *NOS, DVT* ℤ

Ark of the Sun God Another adventurer battles the Nazis and nutsies for a 2000-year-old ark buried in the Sahara.
1982 95m/C David Warbeck, John Steiner, Susie Sudlow, Alan Collins, Riccardo Palacio; **D:** Anthony M. (Antonio Margheriti) Dawson. **VHS, Beta** $59.95 *TWE* ℤ

Armed and Dangerous Candy and Levy are incompetent security guards assigned to a do-nothing job. Things get spiced up when a mobster tries to run a crime ring under their nose. Candy catches on and winds up in a full-fledged chase. Not as funny

as it sounds, though occasionally has moments of genuine comedy.
1986 (PG-13) 88m/C John Candy, Eugene Levy, Kenneth McMillan, Brion James, Robert Loggia, Meg Ryan, Don Stroud, Jonathan Banks, Steve Railsback, Bruce Kirby, Tony Burton, Larry Hankin, Judy Landers, David Wohl; **D:** Mark L. Lester; **W:** Harold Ramis, Peter Torokvei, James Keach, Brian Grazer. **VHS, Beta** $14.95 *COL* ℤℤ

Armed for Action Routine action thriller casts Estevez as Sgt. Phil Towers who gets more than he bargained for when his prisoner, Mafia hitman David Montel, escapes while en route from New York to Los Angeles. When he finally catches up with them, Towers leads a small army of locals on a brutal assault.
1992 88m/C Joe Estevez, Rocky Patterson, Barri Murphy, David Harrod, J. Scott Guy; **D:** Shane Spaulding. **VHS** $89.95 *AIP* ℤ

Armed Response Carradine leads a group of mercenaries in a battle against Chinatown mobsters. They race to locate a priceless jade statue before it can fall into the wrong hands.
1986 (R) 86m/C David Carradine, Lee Van Cleef, Mako, Lois Hamilton, Ross Hagen, Brent Huff; **D:** Fred Olen Ray. **VHS, Beta** *NO* ℤℤ

Armistead Maupin's Tales of the City Carefree '70s San Francisco is the setting for the interconnected stories of the inhabitants of 28 Barbary Lane. There's mysterious landlady Mrs. Madrigal (Dukakis); free-spirit Mona Ramsey (Webb); her gay roomie, Michael "Mouse" Tolliver (D'Amico); hetero lawyer-turned-waiter Brian (Gross); nerdy, secretive Norman (DeSantis); and the naively sweet Mary Ann Singleton (Linney). Definite time-warp factor in this pre-AIDS depiction of sex and drugs, but also the timeless search for love and happiness. Maupin first wrote the stories as an ongoing serial for the *San Francisco Chronicle* and they were later turned into 6 novels. Made for British TV. **AKA:** Tales of the City.
1993 360m/C *GB* Olympia Dukakis, Donald Moffatt, Chloe Webb, Laura Linney, Marcus D'Amico, Paul Gross, Stanley DeSantis, William Campbell, Cynda Williams, Barbara Garrick, Thomas Gibson, Nina Foch, Paul Dooley, Belita Morena; *Cameos:* Karen Black, Edie Adams, Michael Jeter, Ian McKellan, Rod Steiger, Paul Bartel; **D:** Alastair Reid; **W:** Richard Kramer. **VHS** $59.95 *PGV* ℤℤ½

Armored Car Robbery Talman and his buddies plot to rob an armored car but are foiled by McGraw and his crimefighters. Surprisingly good B-crime drama.
1950 68m/B Charles McGraw, Adele Jergens, William Talman, Steve Brodie; **D:** Richard Fleischer. **VHS** *RKO* ℤℤ

Armored Command A beautiful German spy infiltrates an American outpost during the Battle of the Bulge. Tepid WWII fare made too long after the fact.
1961 105m/B Burt Reynolds, Tina Louise, Howard Keel, Earl Holliman, Warner Anderson, Carleton Young; **D:** Byron Haskin. **VHS, Beta** $19.98 *FOX, TLF* ℤ½

The Armour of God Chan plays an adventurous thief who steals and sells pieces of a prized medieval armour set to collectors. When a criminal gang kidnaps his girl to get the entire set, Chan must come up with some spectacular saves of both the armour and the girl. In Cantonese with English subtitles.
1986 100m/C *CH* Jackie Chan; **D:** Jackie Chan. **VHS** $49.95 *FCT* ℤ

Army Brats In this Dutch film a military family goes bloodily and comically to war with itself. Even in a welfare state, parents can't control their wee ones.

1984 105m/C *NL* Akkemay, Frank Schaafsma, Peter Faber; **D:** Ruud Van Hemert. **VHS, Beta** $59.95 *WAR* ℤ½

Army of Darkness Campbell returns for a third "Evil Dead" round as the square-jawed, none too bright hero, Ash in this comic book extravaganza. He finds himself hurled back to the 14th-century through the powers of an evil book. There he romances a babe, fights an army of skeletons, and generally causes all those Dark Age knights a lot of grief, as he tries to get back to his own time. Raimi's technical exuberance is apparent and, as usual, the horror is graphic but still tongue-in-cheek. **AKA:** Evil Dead 3.
1992 (R) 77m/C Bruce Campbell, Embeth Davidtz, Marcus Gilbert, Ian Abercrombie, Richard Grove, Michael Earl Reid, Tim Quill, Patricia Tallman, Theodore Raimi, Ivan Raimi; *Cameos:* Bridget Fonda; **D:** Sam Raimi; **W:** Ivan Raimi, Sam Raimi; **M:** Danny Elfman, Joseph Lo Duca. **VHS, Beta** $19.98 *MCA, FCT* ℤℤℤ

Arnold Outrageous black comedy involving a woman who marries a cadaver to gain his large inheritance. Lots of bizarre and creative deaths in this horror spoof. Unusual wedding scene is a must-see.
1973 (PG) 96m/C Stella Stevens, Roddy McDowall, Elsa Lanchester, Victor Buono, Bernard Fox, Farley Granger, Shani Wallis; **D:** Georg Fenady; **M:** George Duning. **VHS, Beta** *LIV* ℤℤ½

Around the World Kyser leads a USO-like tour to entertain troops. Interesting only in a historical sense. ♫Doodle-Ee-Doo; He's Got a Secret Weapon; Candlelight and Wine; Great News in the Making; They Chopped Down the Old Apple Tree; A Moke from Shamokin.
1943 80m/B Kay Kyser, Ish Kabibble, Ginny Simms, Joan Davis, Mischa Auer; **D:** Allan Dwan. **VHS, Beta** $19.98 *TTC* ℤ½

Around the World in 80 Days Niven is the unflappable Victorian Englishman who wagers that he can circumnavigate the earth in four-score days. With his faithful manservant Cantinflas they set off on a spectacular journey. A perpetual favorite providing ample entertainment. Star-gazers will particularly enjoy the more than 40 cameo appearances by many of Hollywood's biggest names. Adapted from the novel by Jules Verne.
1956 (G) 178m/C David Niven, Shirley MacLaine, Cantinflas, Robert Newton, Charles Boyer, Joe E. Brown, Martine Carol, John Carradine, Charles Coburn, Ronald Colman; *Cameos:* Melville Cooper, Noel Coward, Andy Devine, Reginald Denny, Fernandel, Marlene Dietrich, Hermione Gingold, Cedric Hardwicke, Trevor Howard, Glynis Johns, Buster Keaton, Evelyn Keyes, Peter Lorre, Mike Mazurki, Victor McLaglen, John Mills, Robert Morley, Jack Oakie, George Raft, Cesar Romero, Gilbert Roland, Red Skelton, Frank Sinatra, Ava Gardner; **D:** Michael Anderson Sr.; **W:** James Poe, John Farrow, S.J. Perelman; **M:** Victor Young. Academy Awards '56: Best Adapted Screenplay, Best Color Cinematography, Best Film Editing, Best Picture, Best Original Score; Nominations: Best Art Direction/Set Decoration (Color), Best Costume Design (Color), Best Director (Anderson); Golden Globe Awards '57: Best Actor—Musical/Comedy (Cantinflas), Best Film—Drama; National Board of Review Awards '56: 10 Best Films of the Year; New York Film Critics Awards '56: Best Film. **VHS, Beta** $29.98 *WAR, BTV, HMV* ℤℤ

Around the World in 80 Ways Sometimes clever, sometimes crude Australian comedy about an aging man rescued from a nursing home and taken on a phony trip around the world by his sons. Odd, but genuinely funny at times.

1986 (R) 90m/C *AU* Philip Quast, Alan Penney, Diana Davidson, Kelly Dingwall, Gosia Dobrowolska; *D:* Stephen MacLean; *W:* Stephen MacLean, Paul Leadon; *M:* Chris Neal. **VHS** $19.98 *SUE, NLC, WTA* ♂♂½

Around the World Under the Sea
Bunch of men and one woman scientist plunge under the ocean in an experiment to predict earthquakes. They plant earthquake detectors along the ocean floor and discover the causes of tidal waves. They have men-women battles. They see big sea critters.
1965 111m/C David McCallum, Shirley Eaton, Gary Merrill, Keenan Wynn, Brian Kelly, Lloyd Bridges; *D:* Andrew Marton. **VHS, Beta** $59.95 *MGM* ♂♂

Aroused
Hollister is an apparently dedicated policeman who commits a number of blunders in the pursuit of a serial killer, including leaving his wife with the sociopath while he cavorts with the prostitute assigned to his protection. Director Holden's psycho-thriller was gorily ahead of its time. Includes heart-stopping castration sequence.
1966 78m/B Janine Lenon, Steve Hollister, Fleurette Carter, Joanna Mills, Tony Palladino, Ted Gelanza; *D:* Anton Holden. **VHS** $23.00 *SMW, TPV* ♂

The Arousers
Cult item starring hunk Hunter as a handsome California psycho. Tab travels the coast searching for a woman he is able to make love to; those who fail to arouse him come to tragic, climactic ends. Definitely underground and moderately interesting. *AKA:* Sweet Kill; A Kiss from Eddie.
1970 (R) 85m/C Tab Hunter, Nadyne Turney, Roberta Collins, Isabel Jewell, John Aprea, Angel Fox; *D:* Curtis Hanson. **VHS, Beta** $24.98 *SUE* ♂♂½

The Arrangement
Veteran advertising executive Douglas attempts suicide and then sets out to search for the meaning of life. Along the way he attempts to patch up his "arrangements" with his wife, his mistress and his father. Forced, slow, and self-conscious, though well acted. Adapted by Kazan from the director's own novel.
1969 (R) 126m/C Kirk Douglas, Faye Dunaway, Deborah Kerr, Richard Boone, Hume Cronyn, Elia Kazan; *D:* Elia Kazan; *M:* David Amram. **VHS, Beta** $59.95 *WAR* ♂½

Arrest Bulldog Drummond
Captain Drummond is accused of killing the inventor of a futuristic detonator machine and must track down the real killers. Part of the "Bulldog Drummond" series.
1938 57m/B John Howard, Heather Angel, George Zucco, H.B. Warner, E.E. Clive, Reginald Denny, John Sutton; *D:* James Hogan. **VHS, Beta** $16.95 *PAR, RXM, SNC* ♂♂

The Arrival
An never-seen alien parasite turns an old man into a vampiric young stud after female blood. Plot and characterization never do arrive. Horror director Stuart Gordon cameos as a hairy biker.
1990 (R) 107m/C John Saxon, Joseph Culp, Robert Sampson, Michael J. Pollard; *Cameos:* David Schmoeller; *D:* David Schmoeller; *W:* David Schmoeller; *M:* Richard Band. **VHS** $19.95 *PSM* ♂

Arrivederci, Baby!
An unfunny sex comedy with Curtis as a modern Bluebeard who weds rich women and kills them for their money. His last mate plans to turn the tables and kill him first.
1966 100m/C Tony Curtis, Rosanna Schiaffino, Lionel Jeffries, Zsa Zsa Gabor, Nancy Kwan, Fenella Fielding, Anna Quayle, Warren Mitchell, Mischa Auer; *D:* Ken Hughes; *W:* Ken Hughes. **VHS** *PAR* ♂

Arrowhead
A long-running argument between a tough Cavalry scout and an Apache chief pits the cowboys against the Indians in this western fantasy. The personal battles that become all-out wars turn back to fist-fights before the matter is finally settled.
1953 105m/C Charlton Heston, Jack Palance, Katy Jurado, Brian Keith, Milburn Stone; *D:* Charles Marquis Warren. **VHS, Beta** $14.95 *PAR* ♂♂½

Arrowsmith
A small-town medical researcher battles his conscience as he juggles his selfish and unselfish motivations for the work he does. He travels to the West Indies to confront the issues of his life and come to terms with himself once and for all. A talented cast takes their time. Based on the classic Sinclair Lewis novel. Two edited versions available (99 and 89 minutes), both of which delete much of Loy.
1931 95m/B Ronald Colman, Helen Hayes, Myrna Loy; *D:* John Ford. **VHS, Beta** $19.98 *SUE* ♂♂½

Arsenal
Classic Russian propagandist drama about strikes affecting the Russian home front during WWI, marking Dovshenko's first great achievement in the realm of Eisenstein and Pudovkin. Silent.
1929 70m/B *RU* Semyon Svashenko; *D:* Alexander Dovzhenko. **VHS, Beta** $24.95 *NOS, MRV, IHF* ♂♂♂

The Arsenal Stadium Mystery
Inspector Banks of Scotland Yard tracks down the killer of a football star in this clever but unassuming murder mystery.
1939 85m/B *GB* Leslie Banks, Greta Gynt, Ian MacLean, Liane Linden, Anthony Bushell, Esmond Knight; *D:* Thorold Dickinson. **VHS** $16.95 *SNC* ♂♂½

Arsenic and Old Lace
Set-bound but energetic adaptation of the classic Joseph Kesselring play. Easy-going drama critic Grant is caught in a sticky situation when he learns of his aunts' favorite pastime. Apparently the kind, sweet, lonely spinsters lure gentlemen to the house and serve them elderberry wine with a touch of arsenic, then they bury the bodies in the cellar—a cellar which also serves as the Panama Canal for Grant's cousin (who thinks he's Theodore Roosevelt). Massey and Lorre excel in their sinister roles. One of the best madcap black comedies of all time—a must-see. Shot in 1941 and released a wee bit later. Available colorized.
1944 158m/B Cary Grant, Josephine Hull, Jean Adair, Raymond Massey, Jack Carson, Priscilla Lane, John Alexander, Edward Everett Horton, John Ridgely, James Gleason, Peter Lorre; *D:* Frank Capra; *W:* Julius J. Epstein, Philip C. Epstein. **VHS, Beta** $19.95 *MGM, VYG, FOX* ♂♂♂½

The Art of Crime
A gypsy/detective is drawn into a homicide case when one of his fellow antique dealers is charged with murder. Maintains an atmospheric edge over others of the crime art genre. A pilot for a prospective television series based on the novel "Gypsy in Amber."
1975 72m/C Ron Leibman, Jose Ferrer, David Hedison, Jill Clayburgh; *D:* Richard Irving; *W:* Bill Davidson, Martin Smith. **VHS** *MOV* ♂♂½

The Art of Dying
A loony videophile decides to start staging productions of his all-time favorite scenes. Trouble is, his idea of a fabulous film moment calls for lots of blood and bile as he lures teenage runaways to his casting couch. Director Hauser stars as the cop who's none too impressed with the cinematic remakes, while cult favorite Pollard is his partner. If you like a little atmosphere and psychological depth in your slashers, you'll find this to be the stuff that populates film noir nightmares.
1990 90m/C Wings Hauser, Michael J. Pollard, Sarah Douglas, Kathleen Kinmont, Sydney Lassick; *D:* Wings Hauser. **VHS** $19.95 *PMH* ♂♂♂

Arthur
Spoiled, alcoholic billionaire Moore stands to lose everything he owns when he falls in love with a waitress. He must choose between wealth and a planned marriage, or poverty and love. Surprisingly funny, with an Oscar for Gielgud as Moore's valet, and great performance from Minnelli. Arguably the best role Moore's ever had, and he makes the most of it, taking the one-joke premise to a nomination for Oscar actor.
1981 (PG) 97m/C Dudley Moore, Liza Minnelli, John Gielgud, Geraldine Fitzgerald, Stephen Elliott, Jill Eikenberry, Lou Jacobi; *D:* Steve Gordon; *M:* Burt Bacharach. **Academy Awards '81:** Best Song ("Arthur's Theme"), Best Supporting Actor (Gielgud); **Nominations:** Best Actor (Moore), Best Original Screenplay. **VHS, Beta, 8mm** $19.98 *WAR, FCT, BTV* ♂♂♂

Arthur 2: On the Rocks
When Arthur finally marries his sweetheart, it may not be "happily ever after" because the father of the girl he didn't marry is out for revenge. When Arthur discovers that he is suddenly penniless, a bit of laughter is the cure for the blues and also serves well when the liquor runs out. A disappointing sequel with few laughs.
1988 (PG) 113m/C Dudley Moore, Liza Minnelli, John Gielgud, Geraldine Fitzgerald, Stephen Elliott, Ted Ross, Barney Martin, Jack Gilford; *D:* Bud Yorkin; *M:* Burt Bacharach. **VHS, Beta, 8mm** $14.95 *WAR, FCT* ♂½

Arthur's Hallowed Ground
A cricket field caretaker battles the board of directors over the fate of his favorite plot of sod.
1984 75m/C Jimmy Jewel, Jean Bolt, Michael Elphick; *D:* Freddie Young. **VHS, Beta** $59.95 *MGM* ♂

Article 99
Doctors in a Kansas City Veteran's Administration hospital try to heal patients while putting up with bureaucratic red tape and a stingy administrator. When rogue physician Sturgess (Liotta) is dismissed, the patients hold a siege. Sort of son of "M.A.S.H." (Big Daddy Sutherland did Hawkeye) that gets its title from a fictional rule that says veterans can be treated only for conditions related to military service. Erstwhile cast labors to combine comedic and dramatic intentions of script.
1992 (R) 100m/C Ray Liotta, Kiefer Sutherland, Forest Whitaker, Lea Thompson, John C. McGinley, John Mahoney, Keith David, Kathy Baker, Eli Wallach, Noble Willingham, Julie Bovasso, Troy Evans, Lynne Thigpen, Jeffrey Tambor, Rutanya Alda; *D:* Howard Deutch; *M:* Danny Elfman. **VHS** $92.98 *ORI* ♂♂

Artists and Models
Martin is a struggling comic book artist and Lewis his idiot roommate. The pair become mixed up in both romance and intrigue when Lewis begins talking in his sleep about spys and such. One of the duo's more pleasant cinematic outings. ♪Inamorata; Lucky Song; You Look So Familiar; Why You Pretend.
1955 109m/C Dean Martin, Jerry Lewis, Shirley MacLaine, Dorothy Malone, Eddie Mayehoff, Eva Gabor, Anita Ekberg, George Winslow, Jack Elam, Herbert Rudley, Nick Castle; *D:* Frank Tashlin; *W:* Don McGuire. **VHS** $14.95 *PAR, MLB* ♂♂½

Artist's Studio Secrets
An artist from Greenwich Village only gets aroused by clothed models, so his wife jealously arranges for him to only work with nude women. *AKA:* The Story of an Artist's Studio Secrets; Artist Nude Secrets.

1964 78m/B VHS, Beta $19.95 *VDM, TPV* 🎞️

As If It Were Raining Constantine gets involved in an embezzlement scheme in Spain in this espionage thriller.
1963 85m/C *FR* Eddie Constantine, Henri Cogan, Elisa Montes, Jose Nieto, Silvia Solar; *D:* Jose Monter. VHS $16.95 *SNC* 🎞️🎞️

As Is Two gay New Yorkers deal with a troubled romance and AIDS. A cable television adaptation from the William M. Hoffman play.
1985 86m/C Jonathan Hadary, Robert Carradine; *D:* Michael Lindsay-Hogg. VHS, Beta $19.98 *LHV, WAR* 🎞️½

As Summers Die Louisiana attorney Glenn fights in the late 1950s to protect the rights of a black family, against the wishes of a powerful local clan. Glenn finds support in surprising places, though. From Winston Groom's acclaimed novel. A cable television movie.
1986 100m/C Scott Glenn, Jamie Lee Curtis, Penny Fuller, Bette Davis, John Randolph, Beah Richards, Ron O'Neal, John McIntire; *D:* Jean-Claude Tramont. VHS, Beta $14.95 *CNG* 🎞️🎞️

As You Desire Me Garbo plays an amnesia victim who returns to a husband she doesn't even remember after an abusive relationship with a novelist. An interesting, if not down-right bizarre movie, due to the pairing of the great Garbo and the intriguing von Stroheim. An adaption of Luigi Pirandello's play.
1932 71m/B Greta Garbo, Melvyn Douglas, Erich von Stroheim, Owen Moore, Hedda Hopper; *D:* George Fitzmaurice. VHS, Beta $19.98 *MGM, FCT* 🎞️🎞️🎞️

As You Like It A Duke's banished daughter poses as a man to win the attentions of one of her father's attendants in this highly stylized Shakespearean comedy adapted by J.M. Barrie and Robert Cullen. Early Shakespearean Olivier.
1936 96m/B *GB* Elisabeth Bergner, Laurence Olivier, Henry Ainley, Felix Aylmer; *D:* Paul Czinner; *W:* J.M. Barrie, Robert Cullen. VHS, Beta $19.95 *NOS, MRV, VYY* 🎞️🎞️½

As You Were A girl with a photographic memory enlists in the Army, becoming both a nuisance and comedic victim to her sergeant.
1951 57m/B Joseph Sawyer, William Tracy, Sondra Rogers, Joan Vohs. VHS, Beta *NO* 🎞️

As Young As You Feel A 65-year-old man is forced to retire from his job. He poses as the head of the conglomerate and convinces them to repeal their retirement policy. He then gains national publicity when he makes a speech about the dignity of man. Watch for Monroe as the boss's secretary. Fine comic performances enhance the script; based on a story by Chayefsky.
1951 77m/C Monty Woolley, Thelma Ritter, David Wayne, Jean Peters, Constance Bennett, Marilyn Monroe, Allyn Joslyn, Albert Dekker, Clinton Sundberg, Minor Watson; *D:* Harmon Jones; *W:* Paddy Chayefsky. VHS $14.98 *FXV* 🎞️🎞️🎞️

Ash Wednesday Taylor endures the pain of cosmetic surgery in an effort to rescue her floundering union with Fonda. Another undistinguished performance by Liz. Fonda is especially slimy as the philandering husband, but only appears in the latter stages of the film.
1973 (R) 99m/C Elizabeth Taylor, Henry Fonda, Helmut Berger, Keith Baxter, Margaret Blye, Maurice Teynac, Monique Van Vooren; *D:* Larry Peerce; *M:* Maurice Jarre. VHS $14.95 *PAR, FCT, CCB* 🎞️

Ashanti, Land of No Mercy Caine of the week movie with Michael portraying a doctor acting as a missionary in South Africa who finds himself alone in a battle to rescue his wife from a band of slave traders. The chase spans many Middle Eastern countries and begins to look bleak for our man. Talented cast and promising plot are undone by slow pace. Based on the novel "Ebano" by Alberto Vasquez-Figueroa. *AKA:* Ashanti.
1979 117m/C Michael Caine, Omar Sharif, Peter Ustinov, Rex Harrison, William Holden, Beverly Johnson; *D:* Richard Fleischer. VHS, Beta $19.98 *TWE* 🎞️🎞️

Ashes and Diamonds In the closing days of WWII, a Polish resistance fighter assassinates the wrong man, tries to find love with the right women, and questions the meaning of struggle. A seminal Eastern European masterpiece that defined a generation of pre-solidarity Poles. Available in Polish with English subtitles or dubbed into English. The last installment of the trilogy that includes "A Generation" and "Kanal" and based on a novel by Jerzy Andrzewski. *AKA:* Popiol i Diament.
1958 105m/B *PL* Zbigniew Cybulski, Eva Krzyzewska, Adam Pawlikowski, Bogumil Kobiela, Waclaw Zastrzezynski; *D:* Andrzej Wajda. VHS, Beta $24.95 *ING, SUE, MRV* 🎞️🎞️🎞️½

Ashes and Embers A black Vietnam vet in Los Angeles has trouble fitting into society, eventually running afoul of the police. Ethiopian-born director Gerima endows vital subject matter with a properly alienated mood.
1982 120m/C John Anderson, Evelyn Blackwell; *D:* Haile Gerima. VHS $59.95 *FCT* 🎞️🎞️

Ashik Kerib Ashik Kerib is a wandering minstrel who is rejected by a rich merchant as his daughter's suitor. He then journeys for 1,000 days trying to earn enough money to marry his beloved. Along the way he's imprisoned by an evil sultan and rides a flying horse, among other adventures. Wonderful use of exotic makeup and costumes highlight this Arabian Nights tale. Adapted from a story by Mikhail Lermontov. Paradjanov's last film. In Russian with English subtitles.
1988 75m/C *RU* Yiur Mgoyan, Veronkia Metonidze, Levan Natroshvili, Sofiko Chiaureli; *D:* Dodo Abashidze, Sergei Paradjanov; *W:* Giya Badridze; *M:* Djavashir Kuliev. VHS $59.95 *KIV, FCT* 🎞️🎞️🎞️

Ask Any Girl Lighthearted fluff about a small-town girl who moves to Manhattan. MacLaine plays the bright Meg who gets a job at an ad agency and decides to set her sights on marrying her boss (Young). She asks his older brother's (Niven) help in her quest and the inevitable happens.
1959 101m/C Shirley MacLaine, David Niven, Gig Young, Rod Taylor, Jim Backus, Claire Kelly, Elisabeth Fraser; *D:* Charles Walters. VHS $19.98 *MGM, MOV* 🎞️½

Aspen Extreme Former Aspen ski instructor writes and directs a movie on (what else?) ski instructors in (where?) Aspen! Long on ski shots and short on plot, this movie never leaves the bunny hill. Two Detroiters leave Motown for Snowtown to pursue a life on the slopes. T.J (Gross) soon has his hands full with two beautiful women (Polo and Hughes) who encourage his dream of becoming a writer. His friend Dexter (Berg), however, acquires a few bad habits, and the whole movie just goes downhill from there.

1993 (PG-13) 128m/C Paul Gross, Peter Berg, Finola Hughes, Teri Polo, Martin Kemp, Nicolette Scorsese, William Russ; *D:* Patrick Hasburgh; *W:* Patrick Hasburgh; *M:* Michael Convertino. VHS, Beta $94.95 *HPH, BVV* 🎞️

The Asphalt Jungle An aging criminal emerges from his forced retirement (prison) and assembles the old gang for one final heist. A very realistic storyline and a superb cast make this one of the best crime films ever made. Highly acclaimed; based on the work of W.R. Burnett.
1950 112m/B Sterling Hayden, Louis Calhern, Jean Hagen, James Whitmore, Sam Jaffe, John McIntire, Marc Lawrence, Barry Kelley, Anthony Caruso, Teresa Celli, Marilyn Monroe; *D:* John Huston; *W:* Ben Maddow; *M:* Miklos Rozsa. Academy Awards '50 Nominations: Best Black and White Cinematography, Best Director (Huston), Best Screenplay, Best Supporting Actor (Jaffe); Edgar Allan Poe Awards '50: Best Screenplay; National Board of Review Awards '50: 10 Best Films of the Year, Best Director (Huston). VHS, Beta $19.98 *MGM, VYG* 🎞️🎞️🎞️

The Asphyx Nineteenth century doctor Stephens is studying death when he discovers The Asphyx, an aura that surrounds a person just before they die. Stephens delves deeper into his research and finds the keys to immortality. However, his irresponsibility in unleashing the obscure supernatural power on the world brings a swarm of unforeseen and irreversible troubles. High-class sci fi. *AKA:* Spirit of the Dead.
1972 (PG) 98m/C *GB* Robert Stephens, Robert Powell, Jane Lapotaire, Alex Scott, Ralph Arliss, Fiona Walker, John Lawrence; *D:* Peter Newbrook. VHS, Beta $19.95 *VCI, MED* 🎞️🎞️🎞️

Assassin Athletic karate fighter poses as an underworld figure and infiltrates the largest gang in Japan where he is hired as a hit man.
1979 86m/C Sonny Chiba. VHS, Beta $59.98 *FOX* 🎞️

Assassin Made for TV drama about a mad scientist who creates a bionic killer for a bizarre plot to take over the world. He programs the cyborg to assassinate the President and other key people to help carry out his plan. A retired CIA operative emerges to stop the scientist by trying to destroy the robot.
1986 (PG-13) 94m/C Robert Conrad, Karen Austin, Richard Young, Jonathan Banks, Robert Webber; *D:* Sandor Stern. VHS, Beta $29.95 *ACA* 🎞️🎞️

Assassin Fairly lame thriller about a CIA agent protecting a Senator who falls under suspicion when his charge is shot by an assassin. In investigating the killing the agent discovers the usual governmental conspiracy.
1989 (R) 92m/C Steve Railsback, Nicholas Guest, Xander Berkeley, Elpidia Carrillo; *D:* Jon Hess. VHS, Beta $79.99 *HBO* 🎞️🎞️

Assassin of Youth Girl is introduced to marijuana and soon becomes involved in "the thrills of wild parties," and the horrors of the "killer weed." Camp diversion.
1935 70m/B Luana Walters, Arthur Gardner; *D:* Elmer Clifton. VHS, Beta $16.95 *SNC, NOS, VDM* 🎞️½

Assassination A serious threat has been made to First Lady Ireland and no one is taking it lightly. Secret Service agent Bronson has been called as Ireland's personal bodyguard and suddenly they are both the target of terrorist attacks. Strangely though, the attacks seem to be directed from inside the White House. Bronson as you've seen him many times before.

1987 (R) 93m/C Charles Bronson, Jill Ireland, Stephen Elliott, Michael Ansara; **D:** Peter Hunt. **VHS, Beta** $9.98 *MED, VTR* ♫

The Assassination Bureau Set in Victorian-era London, this amusing farce concerns a society of international assassins lead by the charming Reed. Rigg is an intrepid reporter who pays Reed to have his own organization try to kill him. Reed in turn will try to get them first. A cross-European chase ends in a battle aboard a Zepplin. Tongue-in-cheek whimsy with a fine cast. Based on a short story by Jack London. 1969 106m/C *GB* Oliver Reed, Diana Rigg, Telly Savalas, Curt Jurgens, Philippe Noiret, Warren Mitchell, Beryl Reid, Clive Revill, Kenneth Griffith, Vernon Dobtcheff, Annabella Incontrera; **D:** Basil Dearden. **VHS** *PAR* ♫♫♫

Assassination of Trotsky Middling attempt to dramatize the last days of the Russian Revolutionary leader in Mexico before he's done in with an ice pick. 1972 113m/C *FR GB IT* Richard Burton, Alain Delon, Romy Schneider, Valentina Cortese, Jean Desailly; **D:** Joseph Losey. **VHS, Beta** $19.98 *REP, FCT, ING* ♫♫

The Assassination Run A retired British spy is involved against his will in an intricate plot of terrorism, counter-terrorism and espionage. 1984 111m/C *GB* Malcolm Stoddard, Mary Tamm; **D:** Ken Hannam. **VHS, Beta** $19.98 *FOX* ♫

Assault Violent sex murders in a girl's school have the police baffled. The school's pretty art teacher offers to act as bait in order to catch the murderer. *AKA:* In the Devil's Garden; Tower of Terror; The Creepers. 1970 89m/C *GB* Suzy Kendall, Frank Finlay, Freddie Jones, James Laurenson, Lesley-Anne Down, Tony Beckley; **D:** Sidney Hayers. **VHS, Beta** $59.95 *SUE* ♫½

The Assault Powerful and disturbing drama about a Dutch boy who witnesses the arbitrary murder of his family by Nazis. The memory tortures him and leaves him empty as he matures. Years later he meets other victims and also the perpetrators of the incident, each of them changed forever by it. Thought-provoking consideration of WWII and the horrors of living in Nazi Germany from many points of view. Based on a novel by Harry Mulisch. Dutch language dubbed into English. *AKA:* De Aanslag. 1986 (PG) 149m/C *NL* Derek De Lint, Marc Van Uchelen, Monique Van De Ven; **D:** Fons Rademakers. **VHS, Beta** $19.98 *MGM, ING, SWC* ♫♫♫½

Assault and Matrimony Real-life married people Tucker and Eikenberry play a married couple fighting tooth and nail. Lots of slapstick and general nonsense. Television film based on James Anderson's novel. 1987 100m/C John Hillerman, Michelle Phillips, Joe Cortese, Michael Tucker, Jill Eikenberry; **D:** James Frawley. **VHS, Beta** $89.95 *VMK* ♫½

Assault at West Point: The Court-Martial of Johnson Whittaker In 1880, Johnson C. Whittaker, a black West Point cadet, is found beaten, mutilated, and tied to his bed. Instead of seeking his attackers, the Academy sets up a court martial to expel Whittaker, claiming he faked his own attack. Clashes also ignite within Whittaker's defense counsel—white abolitionist lawyer Chamberlain, whose own racism is thinly disguised, and black lawyer Greener, who originally encouraged Whittaker to enroll at the Point. Interesting case but a shallow production. Based on a

true story and adapted from the book by John Marszalek. Made for television. 1994 (PG-13) 98m/C Seth Gilliam, Samuel L. Jackson, Sam Waterston, John Glover, Al Freeman Jr.; **D:** Harry Moses; **W:** Harry Moses; **M:** Terence Blanchard. **VHS** *REP* ♫♫½

Assault of the Killer Bimbos Five foolish girls manage to seduce, then kill, a town's criminal element. 1987 90m/C Karen Nielsen, Debi Thibeault, Lisa Schmidt, Simone; **D:** Gorman Bechard; **W:** Ted V. Mikels. **Beta** *NO* ♫½

Assault of the Party Nerds Nerds throw a wild party to try and attract new members to their fraternity, while a jock frat plots against them. Sound familiar? Little more than a ripoff of "Revenge of the Nerds" made especially for video. 1989 (R) 82m/C Linnea Quigley, Troy Donahue, Richard Gabai, C. Paul Demsey, Marc Silverberg, Robert Mann, Richard Rifkin, Deborah Roush; **D:** Richard Gabai. **VHS, Beta** $79.95 *PSM* ♫

Assault of the Rebel Girls A reporter gets involved with smuggling in Castro's Cuba. Flynn's last film, saving the worst for last. *AKA:* Cuban Rebel Girls; Attack of the Rebel Girls. 1959 66m/B Errol Flynn, Beverly Aadland, John McKay, Jackie Jackler, Marie Edmund; **D:** Barry Mahon; **W:** Errol Flynn. **VHS, Beta** $59.95 *MED* ♫½

Assault on a Queen Stupid Sinatra vehicle about a group of con men who plot together to rob the Queen Mary on one of her trips. Their attack vessel is a renovated WWII German U-boat. The producers tried to capitalize on the popularity of "Ocean's Eleven," but they didn't even come close. Based on a novel by Jack Finney. 1966 106m/C Frank Sinatra, Virna Lisi, Anthony (Tony) Franciosa, Richard Conte, Reginald Denny; **D:** Jack Donohue; **W:** Rod Serling. **VHS** $14.95 *PAR* ♫

Assault on Agathon Amid the scenic Greek isles, an "executed" WWII guerilla leader returns to lead a revolution, and bloodshed and bombings ensue. 1975 (PG) 95m/C *GB IT* Nina Van Pallandt, Marianne Faithfull, John Woodvine, Nico Minardos; **D:** Laslo Benedek. **VHS, Beta** $59.95 *GEM, MRV, PSM* ♫♫

Assault on Precinct 13 Urban horror invades LA. A sleepy police station in Los Angeles is suddenly under siege from a violent youth gang. Paranoia abounds as the police are attacked from all sides and can see no way out. Carpenter's musical score adds much to the setting of this unique police exploitation story that somehow stands as Carpenter's adaptation of Howard Hawks' "Rio Bravo." Semi-acclaimed and very gripping. 1976 91m/C Austin Stoker, Darwin Joston, Martin West, Tony Burton, Nancy Loomis, Kim Richards, Henry Brandon; **D:** John Carpenter; **W:** John Carpenter; **M:** John Carpenter. **VHS, Beta** $54.95 *MED* ♫♫♫

Assault with a Deadly Weapon When the police budget is cutback, crime runs rampant in an unnamed American city. 1982 86m/C Sandra Foley, Richard Holliday, Lamont Jackson; **D:** Arthur Kennedy. **VHS, Beta** $39.95 *LIV* ♫

The Assignment The assassination of a high-ranking officer in an uneasy Latin American nation spurs violence and political instability. A Swedish diplomat is assigned the tremendous task of restoring peace and stability between the political factions. 1978 92m/C *SW* Christopher Plummer, Thomas Hellberg, Carolyn Seymour, Fernando Rey; **D:** Mats Arehn. **VHS, Beta** $19.95 *NWV* ♫♫

Assignment Outer Space A giant spaceship with bytes for brains is on a collision course with Earth. A team of astronauts is sent to save the world from certain peril. Seems they take the task lightly, though, and their mission (and hence the plot) revolves more around saving sexy sultress Farinon from certain celibacy. If you're into stultifying Italian space operas with a gratuitous sex sub-plot then look up this assignment, but don't say we didn't warn you. Narrated by Jack Wallace; director Margheriti is also known as Anthony Dawson, not to be confused with the actor of the same name. *AKA:* Space Men. 1961 79m/B *IT* Rik von Nutter, Gabriella Farinon, Archie Savage, Dave Montresor, Alan Dijon; **D:** Anthony M. (Antonio Margheriti) Dawson. **VHS** $19.98 *NOS, SNC* ♫

Assignment Skybolt When terrorists get their hands on a hydrogen bomb, a special mission is detached to stop them before they start WWIII. 198? 109m/C **D:** Greg Tallas. **VHS, Beta** $19.99 *BFV* ♫½

The Assisi Underground True but boringly told story of how the Catholic Church helped to save several hundred Italian Jews from being executed by the Nazis during the 1943 German occupation of Italy. Edited from 178 minutes, a good-will gesture from the producers. 1984 115m/C James Mason, Ben Cross, Maximilian Schell, Irene Papas; **D:** Alexander Ramati; **M:** Pino Donaggio. **VHS, Beta** $79.95 *MGM, IGP* ♫

The Associate A French farce about a penniless financial consultant who invents a fictitious partner in order to get his business rolling. English subtitles. *AKA:* L'Associe. 1982 (R) 93m/C *FR* Michel Serrault, Claudine Auger, Catherine Alric, Julien Pardot; **D:** Rene Gainville; **W:** Jean-Claude Carriere. **VHS, Beta** $39.98 *SUE* ♫♫

The Association A man and a woman go undercover to bust an international white slavery ring. 198? 92m/C *TW* Carter Huang, Angela Mao; **D:** Cheung Wo Chang. **VHS, Beta** *NO* ♫½

Assunta Spina A very early, very rare Italian epic about ancient Rome, the prototype for the Italian silent epics to come. 1915 70m/B *IT* **VHS, Beta** $39.98 *FCT* ♫♫

The Astounding She-Monster How can you not love a movie with a title like this? A bad script and snail-paced plot are a good start. A geologist wanting only to be left alone with his rocks survives a brush with the kidnappers of a wealthy heiress only to happen upon an alien spacecraft that's crashed nearby. At the helm is a very tall, high-heeled fem-alien in an obligatory skin-tight space outfit. Excellent, our rock jock thinks, but it seems she kills with the slightest touch. For connoisseurs of truly bad movies. *AKA:* Mysterious Invader. 1958 60m/B Robert Clarke, Kenne Duncan, Marilyn Harvey, Jeanne Tatum, Shirley Kilpatrick, Ewing Miles Brown; **D:** Ronnie Ashcroft. **VHS** $19.98 *SNC, MRV, CNM* Woof!

The Astro-Zombies A contender as one of the worst movies of all time. Carradine plays a mad scientist creating zombies who eat people's guts. Cult favorite Satana stars. Co-written and co-produced by Rogers of "M*A*S*H" fame. 1967 83m/C Tura Satana, Wendell Corey, John Carradine, Tom Pace, Joan Patrick, Rafael Campos; **D:** Ted V. Mikels; **W:** Ted V. Mikels, Wayne Rogers. **VHS, Beta** $49.95 *VCI* Woof!

Asylum Four strange and chilling stories weave together in this film. A murderer's victim seeks retribution. A tailor seems to be collecting his bills. A man who makes voodoo dolls...only to become one later on. A woman plagued by a double. A doctor visiting the asylum tells each tale. Horrifying and grotesque, not as humorless as American horror films. *AKA:* House of Crazies.
1972 (PG) 100m/C *GB* Peter Cushing, Herbert Lom, Britt Ekland, Barbara Parkins, Patrick Magee, Barry Morse; *D:* Roy Ward Baker. **VHS, Beta $9.99** *STE, PSM, MED* 🎬🎬½

Asylum of Satan A beautiful concert pianist is savagely tortured by a madman in the Asylum of Satan. Filmed on location in Louisville, Kentucky.
1972 87m/C Charles Kissinger, Carla Borelli, Nick Jolly, Sherry Steiner; *D:* William Girdler; *W:* William Girdler. **VHS, Beta $19.95** *VCI* 🎬

At Close Range Based on the true story of Bruce Johnston Sr. and Jr. in Brandywine River Valley, Pennsylvania. Father, Walken, tempts his teen-aged son, Penn, into pursuing criminal activities with talk of excitement and high living. Penn soon learns that his father is extremely dangerous and a bit unstable, but he's still fascinated by his wealth and power. Sometimes overbearing and depressing, but good acting and fancy camera work. A young cast of stars includes Masterson as the girl Penn tries to impress. Features Madonna's "Live to Tell."
1986 (R) 115m/C Sean Penn, Christopher Walken, Christopher Penn, Mary Stuart Masterson, Crispin Glover, Kiefer Sutherland, Candy Clark, Tracy Walter, Millie Perkins, Alan Autry, David Strathairn, Eileen Ryan; *D:* James Foley; *W:* Nicholas Kazan; *M:* Patrick Leonard. **VHS, Beta $79.98** *VES, LIV* 🎬🎬🎬

At Gunpoint A store owner becomes the town hero when, by accident, he shoots and kills a bank robber. *AKA:* Gunpoint.
1955 81m/C Fred MacMurray, Dorothy Malone, John Qualen, Walter Brennan; *D:* Alfred Werker. **VHS, Beta $39.95** *REP, HHE* 🎬🎬

At Gunpoint A no-account bank robber spends his six year stint in the slammer plotting his revenge. Having gone thoroughly stircrazy, the vengeful criminal stalks the lawman who put him away, like so many vengeful criminals before him. Run of the mill addition to big list of bad-guy-hunting-for-revenge flicks.
1990 90m/C Frank Kanig, Tain Bodkin, Scott Claflin; *D:* Steven Harris; *W:* Steven Harris. **VHS $79.95** *CAF* 🎬½

At Midnight, I'll Take Your Soul South American import about an evil graved-igger named Coffin Joe (Marins), who wanders the streets of his hometown in order to meet a desirable woman. His mission is to sire a son to continue his legacy. A study in psycho-sexual horror, this makes "Apocalypse Now" look like a beach party. In Spanish with English subtitles.
1963 ?m/B *BR* Jose Mojica Marins; *D:* Jose Mojica Marins. **VHS $20.00** *SMW, FCT, TPV* 🎬

At Play in the Fields of the Lord A thoughtful epic that never quite lives up to its own self-importance—or length. Two yankee missionary couples try to evangelize a fearsome tribe of Brazilian rain-forest dwellers. One of the Christian families suffers a crisis of faith that's well-acted but not as powerful as a co-plot regarding a modern American Indian (Berenger) who joins the jungle natives with calamitous results. Based on the novel by Peter Matthiessen.
1991 (R) 186m/C Tom Berenger, Aidan Quinn, Kathy Bates, John Lithgow, Daryl Hannah, Tom Waits, Stenio Garcia, Nelson Xavier, Jose Dumont, Niilo Kivirinta; *D:* Hector Babenco; *W:* Hector Babenco, Jean-Claude Carriere; *M:* Zbigniew Preisner. **VHS, Beta $19.98** *MCA* 🎬🎬🎬

At Sword's Point Adventure tale based on Alexandre Dumas' "The Three Musketeers," wherein the sons of the musketeers vie to save their queen from the evil plots of Duke Douglas. *AKA:* Sons of the Musketeers.
1951 81m/C Cornel Wilde, Maureen O'Hara, Robert Douglas, Dan O'Herlihy, Alan Hale Jr., Blanche Yurka; *D:* Lewis Allen. **VHS, Beta $19.95** *MED, TTC, FCT* 🎬🎬

At the Circus Marx Brothers invade the circus to save it from bankruptcy and cause their usual comic insanity, though they've done it better before. Beginning of the end for the Marxes, a step down in quality from their classic work, though frequently darn funny. 🎵Lydia the Tattooed Lady; Step Up and Take a Bow; Two Blind Loves; Blue Moon. *AKA:* The Marx Brothers at the Circus.
1939 87m/B Groucho Marx, Chico Marx, Harpo Marx, Margaret Dumont, Kenny L. Baker, Florence Rice, Eve Arden, Nat Pendleton, Fritz Feld; *D:* Edward Buzzell. **VHS, Beta $19.95** *MGM* 🎬🎬½

At the Earth's Core A Victorian scientist invents a giant burrowing machine, which he and his crew use to dig deeply into the Earth. To their surprise, they discover a lost world of subhuman creatures and prehistoric monsters. Based on Edgar Rice Burrough's novels.
1976 (PG) 90m/C *GB* Doug McClure, Peter Cushing, Caroline Munro; *D:* Kevin Connor. **VHS, Beta** *WAR, OM* 🎬🎬

At War with the Army Serviceable comedy from Martin and Lewis in their first starring appearance, as the recruits get mixed up in all kinds of wild situations at their army base. Based on the play by James Allardice.
1950 93m/B Dean Martin, Jerry Lewis, Polly Bergen, Mike Kellin; *D:* Hal Walker. **VHS, Beta $24.95** *NOS, MRV, CAB* 🎬🎬

Atalia Relates the love between Atalia, a war widow, and the younger man she loves. The problem stems from the fact that she lives in a Kibbutz, and the lifestyle contradicts sharply from that of her beliefs in love, forcing her to eventually make a momentous decision.
1985 90m/C Michal Bat-Adam, Yftach Katzur, Dan Toren; *D:* Akiva Tevet. **VHS $79.95** *ERG* 🎬🎬

Athena Two sisters (Powell and Reynolds) from an eccentric, health-faddist family fall in love with their opposites. Purdom is the stuffy Boston lawyer who goes off with Powell and Reynolds entices a TV crooner (Damone). Routine romance with routine songs. Reeves, who would become a star as a movie muscleman, appears in a brief role. 🎵Love Can Change the Stars; The Girl Next Door; Imagine; Venezia; Chacun le Sait; I Never Felt Better; Vocalize.
1954 96m/C Jane Powell, Debbie Reynolds, Edmund Purdom, Vic Damone, Louis Calhern, Evelyn Varden, Linda Christian, Virginia Gibson, Nancy Kilgas, Dolores Starr, Jane Fischer, Cecile Rogers, Steve Reeves; *D:* Richard Thorpe; *W:* William Ludwig, Leonard Spigelgass; *M:* Hugh Martin, Ralph Blane. **VHS $19.98** *MGM* 🎬🎬½

Atlantic City A small-time, aging Mafia hood falls in love with a young clam bar waitress, and they share the spoils of a big score against the backdrop of Atlantic City. Wonderful character study that becomes something more, a piercing declaration about a city's transformation and the effect on the people who live there. Lancaster, in a sterling performance, personifies the city, both of them fading with time. *AKA:* Atlantic City U.S.A.
1981 (R) 104m/C *FR CA* Burt Lancaster, Susan Sarandon, Kate Reid, Michel Piccoli, Hollis McLaren; *D:* Louis Malle. Academy Awards '81 Nominations: Best Actor (Lancaster), Best Actress (Sarandon), Best Director (Malle), Best Original Screenplay, Best Picture; British Academy Awards '81: Best Actor (Lancaster), Best Director (Malle); National Society of Film Critics Awards '81: Best Film. **VHS, Beta $14.95** *PAR* 🎬🎬🎬½

Atlantis, the Lost Continent If anything could sink the fabled lost continent of Atlantis it's this cheap fantasy flick. A greek sailor saves a princess and takes her back to her Atlantis home where he's promptly enslaved by the island's evil ruler. But this hero won't put up with any nonsense so he leads his fellow slaves in a revolt and gains his freedom before sinking both evil ruler and island (using atomic power no less!).
1961 90m/C Anthony Hall, Joyce Taylor, John Dall, Bill Smith, Edward Platt, Frank De Kova; *D:* George Pal. **VHS $14.98** *MGM, FCT* 🎬

Atlas The mighty Atlas takes on massive armies, one of which includes director Corman, in a bid to win the hand of a princess. About as cheap as they come, although it is one of the few Sword & Sandal epics that isn't dubbed.
1960 84m/C Michael Forest, Frank Wolff, Barboura Morris, Walter Maslow; *D:* Roger Corman; *W:* Charles B. Griffith. **VHS $19.95** *DVT, SNC, HEG* 🎬

Atlas in the Land of the Cyclops Atlas takes on a hideous one-eyed monster to save a baby from an evil queen. Not a divorce custody drama. *AKA:* Atlas Against the Cyclops; Maciste Nella Terra dei Ciclopi.
1961 100m/C *IT* Mitchell Gordon, Chelo Alonso, Vira Silenti; *D:* Antonio Leonuiola. **VHS $19.98** *SNC* Woof!

Atom Age Vampire Mad scientist doing research on Japanese nuclear bomb victims falls in love with a woman disfigured in an auto crash. To remove her scars, he treats her with a formula derived from the glands of freshly killed women. English dubbed. Not among the best of its kind (a low-rent district if ever there was one), but entertaining in a mischievous, boy-is-this-a-stupid-film sort of way.
1961 71m/B *IT* Alberto Lupo, Susanne Loret, Sergio Fantoni; *D:* Albert Magnoli. **VHS, Beta $16.95** *SNC, NOS, VYY* Woof!

Atomic Attack Nuclear bomb is dropped on New York City and a family living 50 miles away must escape. Gentlemen, start your engines.
1950 50m/B Walter Matthau. **VHS $29.95** *IHF* 🎬

The Atomic Brain An old woman hires a doctor to transplant her brain into the body of a beautiful young girl. Of the three girls who are abducted, two become homicidal zombies and the third starts to act catty when she is given a feline brain. A must-see for bad-brain movie fans. *AKA:* Monstrosity.
1964 72m/B Frank Gerstle, Erika Peters, Judy Bamber, Marjorie Eaton, Frank Fowler, Margie Fisco; *D:* Joseph Mascelli. **VHS $19.98** *NOS, SNC* Woof!

The Atomic Cafe A chillingly humorous compilation of newsreels and government films of the 1940's and 1950's that show America's preoccupation with the A-Bomb. Some sequences are in black and white.

Includes the infamous training film "Duck and Cover," which tells us what to do in the event of an actual bombing.
1982 92m/C D: Kevin Rafferty. **VHS, Beta** NO ♂♂♂

The Atomic City Barry plays a nuclear physicist at Los Alamos whose son is kidnapped by terrorists who want his bomb-making formulas. The bad guys hide out in the nearby mountains which at least makes for some pleasant scenery in this average thriller.
1952 84m/B Gene Barry, Lee Aaker, Michael Moore, Lydia Clarke, Nancy Gates, Milburn Stone; **D:** Jerry Hopper. **VHS** PAR ♂♂½

The Atomic Kid A man survives an atomic blast because of a peanut butter sandwich he was eating. As a result, he himself becomes radioactive and discovers that he has acquired some strange new powers which get him into what pass for hilarious predicaments.
1954 86m/B Mickey Rooney, Robert Strauss, Elaine Davis, Bill Goodwin; **D:** Leslie Martinson; **W:** Blake Edwards. **VHS $19.98** REP ♂♂½

The Atomic Man Owing to radioactive experimentation, a scientist exists for a short time in the future. Once there, both good and evil forces want to use him for their own purposes. **AKA:** Timeslip.
1956 78m/B GB Gene Nelson, Faith Domergue, Joseph Tomelty, Peter Arne; **D:** Ken Hughes. **VHS $16.95** NOS, SNC ♂½

Atomic Submarine Futuristic sci fi plots government agents against alien invaders. The battle, however, takes place in the ocean beneath the Arctic and is headed by an atomic-powered submarine clashing with a special alien underwater saucer. We all live on the atomic submarine: fun for devotees.
1959 80m/C Arthur Franz, Dick Foran, Bob Steele, Brett Halsey, Joi Lansing; **D:** Spencer Gordon Bennet. **VHS, Beta $39.95** SNC ♂♂

The Atonement of Gosta Berling A priest, forced to leave the priesthood because of his drinking, falls in love with a young married woman. Garbo shines in the first role which brought her critical acclaim; Hanson's performance also makes this a memorable drama. Adapted from the novel by Selma Lagerlof. **AKA:** Gosta Berling's Saga; The Legend of Gosta Berling; The Story of Gosta Berling; The Saga of Gosta Berling.
1924 91m/B SW Lars Hanson, Greta Garbo, Ellen Cederstrom, Mona Martenson, Jenny Hasselquist, Gerda Lundequist; **D:** Mauritz Stiller. **VHS** VYY, MRV, DVT ♂♂♂

Ator the Fighting Eagle Styled after "Conan The Barbarian" this mythical action fantasy stars O'Keeffe as Ator, son of Thorn. Ator must put an end to the tragic Dynasty of the Spiders, thereby fulfilling the legend of his family at the expense of the viewer. Goofy low-budget sword and sandal stuff. Followed by "The Blade Master."
1983 (PG) 98m/C IT Miles O'Keeffe, Sabrina Siani, Ritza Brown, Edmund Purdom, Laura Gemser; **D:** David Hill. **VHS, Beta** NO Woof!

Attack Force Z An elite corps of Australian military is Force Z. Volunteers are chosen for a dangerous mission: find the plane that crashed somewhere in the South Pacific and rescue the defecting Japanese government official on board, all before the end of WWII and the feature. Talented cast is effectively directed in low-key adventure featuring young Gibson.
1984 84m/C AU Sam Neill, Chris Haywood, Mel Gibson, John Phillip Law, John Waters; **D:** Tim Burstall. **VHS, Beta $19.99** MCG, MTX ♂♂

Attack of the Beast Creatures The survivors of a wrecked ocean liner are stranded on a desert island overrun by savage creatures. This makes them anxious.
1985 82m/C Robert Nolfi, Robert Langyel, Julia Rust, Lisa Pak; **D:** Michael Stanley. **VHS, Beta** NO Woof!

Attack of the 50 Foot Woman A beautiful, abused housewife has a frightening encounter with a giant alien, causing her to grow to an enormous height. Then she goes looking for hubby. Perhaps the all-time classic '50s sci fi, a truly fun movie highlighted by the sexy, 50-foot Hayes in a giant bikini. Has intriguing psychological depth and social commentary done in a suitably cheezy manner. Also available with "House on Haunted Hill" on laser disc.
1958 72m/B Allison Hayes, William Hudson, Roy Gordon; **D:** Nathan Hertz. **VHS, Beta $14.98** FOX, FCT ♂♂½

Attack of the 50 Ft. Woman Campy remake of the 1958 sci-fi cult classic features the statuesque Hannah in the title role. Nancy's a put-upon hausfrau with zero self-esteem thanks to her domineering father (Windom) and loutish hubby (Baldwin). They should have been sweet to her because after an encounter with a flying saucer Nancy starts to grow...and grow...and grow. And then she decides to get some revenge. Made for television.
1993 90m/C Daryl Hannah, Daniel Baldwin, William Windom, Frances Fisher, Cristi Conaway, Paul Benedict, Lewis Arquette, Xander Berkeley, Hamilton Camp, Richard Edson, Victoria Haas, O'Neal Compton; **D:** Christopher Guest; **W:** Joseph Dougherty; **M:** Nicholas Pike. **VHS** HBO ♂♂½

Attack of the Giant Leeches Cheapo Corman fare about giant leeches in a murky swamp who suddenly decide to make human flesh their new food supply. Perturbed inn keeper plays along by forcing his wife and lover into the murk. Leeches frolic. Sometimes tedious, sometimes chilling, always low budget and slimy. Although the special effects aren't top notch, this might be a fine choice for a late night scare/laugh. **AKA:** The Giant Leeches.
1959 62m/B Ken Clarke, Yvette Vickers, Gene Roth, Bruno Ve Sota; **D:** Bernard L. Kowalski. **VHS $14.95** VYY, SNC, NOS ♂

Attack of the Killer Refrigerator Chiller featuring a group of sleazy college students having a wild party. In the process, they abuse a hapless refrigerator. Fed up, the vengeful appliance goes on a rampage of murder and destruction. Certain to make you view kitchen appliances in a new light. Planned sequels in the newfound kitchen-utility horror genre include "Refrigerator II: Brutally Defrosted" and "Bloody, Bloody Coffee Maker."
1990 ?m/C VHS BFA Woof!

Attack of the Killer Tomatoes Candidate for worst film ever made, deliberate category. Horror spoof that defined "low budget" stars several thousand ordinary tomatoes that suddenly turn savage and begin attacking people. No sci-fi cliche remains untouched in this dumb parody. A few musical numbers are performed in lieu of an actual plot. Followed by "Return of the Killer Tomatoes."
1977 (PG) 87m/C D: John DeBello. **VHS, Beta $19.95** MED Woof!

Attack of the Mayan Mummy A greedy doctor gets his patient to channel her former self so that she can show him where to find an ancient tomb that is filled with treasure. Good idea.
1963 77m/B MX Richard Webb, Nina Knight, Norman Burton, Steve Conte; **D:** Jerry Warren. **VHS $16.95** NOS, LOO, SNC Woof!

Attack of the Mushroom People Secluded island is the site where people eating mysterious mushrooms have been turning into oversized, killer 'shrooms' themselves. Trouble is, the only witness to this madness has gone insane. Will anyone believe him before it's too late? **AKA:** Matango; Ungus of Terror; Curse of the Mushroom People.
1963 70m/B JP Akira Kubo, Kenji Sahara, Yoshio Tsuchiya, Hiroshi Koizumi; **D:** Inoshiro Honda. **VHS $20.00** SMW ♂♂

Attack of the Robots Silly spy spoof about powerful government officials who are being killed off by a mad scientist's robots. Interpol agent Lemmy Caution comes to the rescue. **AKA:** Cartes sur Table.
1966 88m/B FR SP Eddie Constantine, Fernando Rey; **D:** Jess (Jesus) Franco; **W:** Jean-Claude Carriere. **VHS, Beta $24.95** VYY ♂½

Attack of the Swamp Creature A deranged scientist transforms himself into a swamp critter and terrorizes a small town.
1975 96m/C Frank Crowell, David Robertson; **D:** Arnold Stevens. **VHS, Beta $29.95** LIV Woof!

Attack Squadron Story of Japan's suicidal WWII pilots. **AKA:** Kamakazi.
197? 105m/C JP **VHS, Beta** NO ♂½

The Attic Psycho-drama about an overbearing invalid father and his insecure and unmarried daughter. The girl learns to escape her unhappy life by hiding in the attic. Not horrifying, but a clear analytical look into the game of control.
1980 (R) 92m/C Carrie Snodgress, Ray Milland, Rosemary Murphy, Ruth Cox, Francis Bay, Marjorie Eaton; **D:** George Edwards. **VHS, Beta $59.95** FOX, MON ♂♂½

The Attic: The Hiding of Anne Frank Steenburgen is wonderful in the true story of Miep Gies, the Dutch woman who hid Otto Frank, her employer, and his family from the Nazis. Unusual because it is told from Gies' perspective, rather than from the more familiar Anne Frank story. Based on Gies' book, "Anne Frank Remembered." Made for television.
1988 95m/C Mary Steenburgen, Paul Scofield, Huub Stapel, Eleanor Bron, Miriam Karlin, Lisa Jacobs, Ronald Pickup; **D:** John Erman; **W:** William Hanley; **M:** Richard Rodney Bennett. **VHS $79.95** CAF ♂♂½

Attica Tense made for television depiction of the infamous Attica prison takeover in 1971 and the subsequent bloodbath as state troops were called in. Although edited due to the searing commentary by Rockefeller, it remains powerful and thought-provoking. Adapted from the Tom Wicker bestseller "A Time to Die."
1980 97m/C George Grizzard, Charles Durning, Anthony Zerbe, Roger E. Mosley; **D:** Marvin J. Chomsky. **VHS, Beta $9.98** SUE, NLC ♂♂♂

Au Revoir Les Enfants During the Nazi occupation of France in the 1940s, the headmaster of a Catholic boarding school hides three Jewish boys among the other students by altering their names and identities. Two of the students, Julien (Manesse) and Jean (Fejto), form a friendship that ends tragically when Jean and the other boys are discovered and taken away by the Gestapo. Compelling and emotionally wrenching com-

ing of age tale based on an incident from director Malle's childhood is considered to be his best film to date and quite possibly the best he will ever make. In French with English subtitles. Other 1987 movies with similar themes are "Hope and Glory" and "Empire of the Sun." *AKA:* Goodbye, Children.
1987 (PG) 104m/C *FR* Gaspard Manesse, Raphael Fejto, Francine Racette, Stanislas Carre de Malberg, Philippe Morier-Genoud, Francois Berleand, Peter Fitz, Francois Negret, Irene Jacob; *D:* Louis Malle; *W:* Louis Malle; *M:* Franz Schubert, Camille Saint-Saens. Academy Awards '87 Nominations: Best Foreign Language Film, Best Original Screenplay; British Academy Awards '88: Best Director (Malle); Cesar Awards '88: Best Director (Malle), Best Film; Los Angeles Film Critics Association Awards '87: Best Foreign Film; Venice Film Festival '87: Best Film. **VHS, Beta $19.98** ING, ORI, FCT *IIII*

Audrey Rose Parents of a young girl are terrified when their darling daughter is having dreadful dreams. Mysterious friend Hopkins cements their fears when he declares that his dead daughter has been reincarnated in their child. The nightmares continue suggesting that none other than Lucifer could be at work. Good cast is hampered by slow-moving take-off on "The Exorcist" with a weak staged ending. Adapted by DeFelitta from his novel.
1977 (PG) 113m/C Marsha Mason, Anthony Hopkins, John Beck, John Hillerman; *D:* Robert Wise; *W:* Frank DeFelitta. **VHS, Beta $14.95** MGM *II*

Augustine of Hippo One of Rossellini's later historical epics, depicting the last years of St. Augustine and how they exemplify the growing conflicts between Church and State, Christian ethic and societal necessity. In Italian with subtitles. *AKA:* Agostino di Ippona.
1972 120m/C *IT D:* Roberto Rossellini. **VHS, Beta $59.95** FCT *III*

Auntie Entertainer must dress and act like his madam aunt who has died, in order to fool her former employees in a house of prostitution.
1980 (R) 85m/C VHS, Beta NO Woof!

Auntie Lee's Meat Pies Auntie Lee's meat pie business is booming thanks to her five beautiful nieces. They help keep their aunt supplied with the secret ingredient—gorgeous young men! Four Playboy Playmates are featured in this cannibalistic horror comedy.
1992 (R) 100m/C Karen Black, Noriyuki "Pat" Morita, Pat Paulsen, Huntz Hall, Michael Berryman, David Parry, Stephen Quadros; *D:* Joseph F. Robertson. **VHS $79.95** COL *I 1/2*

Auntie Mame A young boy is brought up by his only surviving relative—flamboyant and eccentric Auntie Mame. Mame is positive that "life is a banquet and most poor suckers are starving to death." Based on the Patrick Dennis novel about his life with "Auntie Mame." Part of the "A Night at the Movies" series, this tape simulates a 1958 movie evening, with a Road Runner cartoon, "Hook, Line and Stinker," a newsreel and coming attractions for "No Time for Sergeants" and "Chase a Crooked Shadow."
1958 161m/C Rosalind Russell, Patric Knowles, Roger Smith, Peggy Cass, Forrest Tucker, Coral Browne; *D:* Morton DaCosta; *W:* Betty Comden, Adolph Green. Academy Awards '58 Nominations: Best Actress (Russell), Best Art Direction/Set Decoration, Best Color Cinematography, Best Film Editing, Best Picture, Best Supporting Actress (Cass); Golden Globe Awards '59: Best Actress—Musical/Comedy (Russell). **VHS, Beta $19.95** WAR *III*

The Aurora Encounter Aliens surreptitiously infiltrate a small town in 1897, and spread benevolence everywhere. Family fare.
1985 (PG) 90m/C Jack Elam, Peter Brown, Carol Bagdasarian, Dottie West, George "Spanky" McFarland; *D:* Jim McCullough. **VHS, Beta $14.95** NWV, STE, HHE *II*

Author! Author! Sweet, likable comedy about playwright Pacino who is about to taste success with his first big hit. Suddenly his wife walks out, leaving him to care for her four children and his own son. His views shift as he begins to worry about, among other things, who will watch the obnoxious kids on opening night.
1982 (PG) 100m/C Al Pacino, Tuesday Weld, Dyan Cannon, Alan King, Andre Gregory; *D:* Arthur Hiller; *W:* Israel Horovitz; *M:* Dave Grusin. **VHS, Beta $14.98** FOX *II 1/2*

Autobiography of a Princess A brief character study shot by Merchant-Ivory in six days. An East Indian princess, living in self-enforced exile in London, invites her father's former tutor to tea. They watch old movie footage of royal India together and dream of a happier past.
1975 59m/C James Mason, Madhur Jaffrey; *D:* James Ivory; *W:* Ruth Prawer Jhabvala. **VHS $29.95** FCT, ING, LUM *II*

The Autobiography of Miss Jane Pittman The history of blacks in the South is seen through the eyes of a 110-year-old former slave. From the Civil War through the Civil Rights movement, Miss Pittman relates every piece of black history, allowing the viewer to experience the injustices. Tyson is spectacular in moving, highly acclaimed television drama. Received nine Emmy awards; adapted by Tracy Keenan Wynn from the novel by Ernest J. Gaines.
1974 110m/C Cicely Tyson, Odetta, Joseph Tremice, Richard Dysart, Michael Murphy, Katherine Helmond; *D:* John Korty. **VHS, Beta** PSM *III 1/2*

Autopsy Rash of unexplainable, spontaneous suicides cause a college student to become emotionally upset.
1978 (R) 89m/C *IT* Mimsy Farmer, Barry Primus, Angela Goodwin, Ray Lovelock; *D:* Armando Crispino; *M:* Ennio Morricone. **VHS, Beta $19.95** MPI, PSM *I 1/2*

Autopsy A young gold-digger and a millionaire marry, and then cheat on each other, provoking blackmail and murder.
197? 90m/C Fernando Rey, Gloria Grahame, Christian Hay. **VHS, Beta** NO *I*

Autopsy A war correspondent in Vietnam discovers the gruesome secret behind the doctors' autopsy methods at a military hospital.
1986 90m/C VHS, Beta NO *I*

Autopsy of a Ghost Comedy/horror film stars Rathbone as a ghost and Mitchell as a mad scientist. Notable as Rathbone's last screen appearance. In Spanish with no subtitles.
1967 ?m/C *SP* Basil Rathbone, John Carradine, Cameron Mitchell. **VHS $16.95** SNC *I 1/2*

An Autumn Afternoon Ozu's final film is a beautiful expression of his talent. In postwar Tokyo, an aging widower loses his only daughter to marriage and begins a life of loneliness. A heart-wrenching tale of relationships and loss. In Japanese with English subtitles.
1962 112m/C *JP* Chishu Ryu, Shima Iwashita, Shin-Ichiro Mikami, Mariko Okada, Keiji Sada; *D:* Yasujiro Ozu; *W:* Yasujiro Ozu. **VHS $69.95** NYF, ING *IIII 1/2*

Autumn Born Young heiress is abducted by her guardian and imprisoned while she's taught to obey his will. Ill-fated ex-Playmate Dorothy Stratton's first film.
1979 (R) 76m/C Dorothy Stratton. **VHS, Beta $39.95** MON *I 1/2*

Autumn Leaves Crawford plays a middle-aged typist grasping at her last chance for love. She marries a younger man who's been romancing her, then finds him more and more unstable and violent. Weak story material that could turn melodramatic and tawdry, but doesn't because of Crawford's strength.
1956 108m/B Cliff Robertson, Joan Crawford, Vera Miles, Lorne Greene; *D:* Robert Aldrich. **VHS, Beta $9.95** GKK *II 1/2*

Autumn Marathon To say that this is one of the better Russian movies of the past three decades is sort of faint praise, given the state of Soviet cinema. Written by playwright Volodin, it's just another paint-by-number version of the philandering man who's really an OK Joe who loves his kids comedy. In Russian with English subtitles. *AKA:* Osenny Marafon.
1979 100m/C *RU* Oleg Basilashvili, Natalia Gundareva, Marina Neyelova; *D:* Georgi Daniela; *W:* Alexander Volodin. **VHS $59.95** KIV, AUD *II 1/2*

Autumn Sonata Nordic family strife as famed concert pianist Bergman is reunited with a daughter she has not seen in years. Bergman's other daughter suffers from a degenerative nerve disease and had been institutionalized until her sister brought her home. Now the three women settle old scores, and balance the needs of their family. Excellent performance by Bergman in her last film.
1978 97m/C *SW* Ingrid Bergman, Liv Ullmann, Halvar Bjork, Lena Nyman, Gunnar Bjornstrand; *D:* Ingmar Bergman; *W:* Ingrid Bergman. Academy Awards '78 Nominations: Best Actress (Bergman), Best Original Screenplay; Golden Globe Awards '79: Best Foreign Film; National Board of Review Awards '78: 5 Best Foreign Films of the Year, Best Actress (Bergman), Best Director (Bergman); National Society of Film Critics Awards '78: Best Actress (Bergman). **VHS, Beta** FOX *III*

Avalanche Disasterama as vacationers at a new winter ski resort find themselves at the mercy of a monster avalanche leaving a so-called path of terror and destruction in its wake. Talented cast is buried by weak material, producing a snow-bound adventure yawn.
1978 (PG) 91m/C Rock Hudson, Mia Farrow, Robert Forster, Rick Moses; *D:* Corey Allen. **VHS, Beta $9.98** SUE *I 1/2*

Avalanche Express Marvin is a CIA agent who uses a defector (Shaw) to lure a scientist (Schell), specializing in biological warfare, aboard a European train. Marvin wants to eliminate Schell but all plans go awry when the snow begins to fall. Ineffective thriller. Director Robson's and actor Shaw's last film—much of Shaw's dialogue was dubbed due his death before the film's soundtrack was completed. Based on a novel by Colin Forbes.
1979 (PG) 89m/C Lee Marvin, Robert Shaw, Maximilian Schell, Linda Evans, Mike Connors, Joe Namath, Horst Buchholz, David Hess; *D:* Mark Robson; *W:* Abraham Polonsky. **VHS $19.98** WAR *I*

Avalon Powerful but quiet portrait of the break-up of the family unit as seen from the perspective of a Russian family settled in Baltimore at the close of WWII. Initally, the family is unified in their goals, ideologies and social lives. Gradually, all of this disinte-

grates; members move to the suburbs and television replaces conversation at holiday gatherings. Levinson based his film on experiences within his own family of Russian Jewish immigrants.
1990 (PG) 126m/C Armin Mueller-Stahl, Aidan Quinn, Elizabeth Perkins, Joan Plowright, Lou Jacobi, Leo Fuchs, Eve Gordon, Kevin Pollak, Israel Rubinek, Elijah Wood, Grant Gelt, Bernard Hiller; **D:** Barry Levinson; **W:** Barry Levinson; **M:** Randy Newman. **VHS, Beta, 8mm $19.95** *COL, FCT* ꒰꒰꒰

Avanti! Stuffy businessman Wendell Armbruster (Lemmon) heads to Italy to claim his father's body when the old man dies while on vacation. Then he discovers dad has been visiting his mistress lo these many years. While trying to get through mountains of red tape, Wendell finds himself romancing the woman's daughter (Mills). Too long but still amusing.
1972 (R) 144m/C Jack Lemmon, Juliet Mills, Clive Revill, Edward Andrews, Gianfranco Barra, Franco Angrisano; **D:** Billy Wilder; **W:** I.A.L. Diamond, Billy Wilder. **VHS $19.98** *MCA* ꒰꒰½

Avenged A vigilante saga of no special merit. Crude thugs violate and kill a young girl. Acquitted as a result of a slip in the arrest, they hit the streets again, thinking they are home free. However, the victim's brother shows up demanding they pay dearly for what they have done. His technique of penance is indeed outside the law.
19?? 90m/C VHS *NO* ꒰꒰

The Avenger The story of a criminal who cuts off the heads of people and mails them off makes for a shocker. Graphic violence will appeal to those who like a good mail-order gorefest and are not employed by the post office.
1960 102m/B *GE* Ingrid van Bergen, Heinz Drache, Ina Duscha, Mario Litto, Klaus Kinski; **D:** Karl Anton. **VHS $16.95** *SNC* ꒰꒰½

The Avenger This time muscleman Reeves plays Aeneas and leads the Trojans in battle against the Greeks. Its supposedly an adaptation of "The Aeneid" by Virgil. **AKA:** The Lost Glory of Troy.
1962 108m/C *FR IT* Steve Reeves, Giacomo "Jack" Rossi-Stuart, Carla Marlier, Gianno Garko, Liana Orfei; **D:** Giorgio Rivalta. **VHS $19.95** *SNC, NOS, VYY* ꒰

Avenging Angel Law student Molly "Angel" Stewart is back on the streets to retaliate against the men who killed the policeman who saved her from a life of prostitution. Worthless sequel to 1984's "Angel," exploiting the original's exploitative intent. Followed listlessly by "Angel III: The Final Chapter."
1985 (R) 94m/C Betsy Russell, Rory Calhoun, Susan Tyrrell, Ossie Davis, Barry Pearl, Ross Hagen, Karin Mani, Robert Tessier; **D:** Robert Vincent O'Neil. **VHS, Beta $14.95** *NWV, STE* Woof!

Avenging Conscience An early eerie horror film, based on tales of Edgar Allan Poe. D.W. Griffith's first large-scale feature. Silent. **AKA:** Thou Shall Not Kill.
1914 78m/B Henry B. Walthall, Blanche Sweet; **D:** D.W. Griffith. **VHS, Beta $19.95** *GPV, VYY, LSV* ꒰꒰

Avenging Disco Godfather Moore parodies the "Godfather" and martial arts movies. **AKA:** Avenging Godfather; Disco Godfather.
1976 (R) 99m/C Rudy Ray Moore, Lady Reed, Carol Speed, Jimmy Lynch; **D:** Rudy Ray Moore. **VHS, Beta $29.95** *XVC* ꒰½

Avenging Force Okay actioner about retired CIA agent Dudikoff returning to the force to help colleague James run for political office. A group of right-wing terrorists called "Pentangle" threatens James, so Dudikoff adds his name to their wanted list. Conflict leads to a forest manhunt where the avenging force does its avenging.
1986 (R) 104m/C Michael Dudikoff, Steve James, John P. Ryan; **D:** Sam Firstenberg; **W:** Mercer Ellington; **M:** George S. Clinton. **VHS, Beta $19.95** *MED, VTR* ꒰꒰

The Avenging Hand Leaden suspense story about a hotel filled with thieves all searching for stolen loot.
1943 56m/B Noah Beery Jr., Kathleen Kelly, Louis Borell, James Harcourt, Charles Oliver, Reginald Long; **D:** Victor Hanbury. **VHS** *HCV* ꒰½

Aventure Malgache Hitchcock worked with the Moliere Players on this propaganda piece about the French Resistance. He based this story on the experiences of the actor Clarousse. Working for the Resistance in occupied Madagascar Clarousse is betrayed and sent to prison by the Vichy government. Rescued by the British he returns to resume his work. In French with English subtitles. **AKA:** Madagascar Landing; Alfred Hitchcock's Bon Voyage & Aventure Malgache.
1944 31m/B **D:** Alfred Hitchcock. **VHS** *MIL* ꒰½

The Average Woman Gritty journalist consults plain Jane for "Modern Woman" story and finds a major rewrite in order when he falls with a thud for Miss Jane.
1924 52m/B Pauline Garon, David Powell, Burr McIntosh, Harrison Ford, De Sacia Mooers; **D:** William Cabanne. **VHS, Beta $14.95** *GPV, GVV* ꒰꒰

The Aviator Pilot Reeve, haunted by the memory of a fatal crash, tries to find a new line of work. Large sums of money persuade him to transport spoiled Arquette to Washington. When the biplane crashes in the mountain wilderness, the two fall in love between scavenging for food and fighting wild animals. From the director of "Man From Snowy River."
1985 (PG) 98m/C Christopher Reeve, Rosanna Arquette, Jack Warden, Tyne Daly, Marcia Strassman, Sam Wanamaker, Scott Wilson; **D:** George Miller; **W:** Marc Norman. **VHS, Beta $14.95** *MGM* ꒰꒰

The Awakening An archeologist discovers the tomb of a murderous queen, but upon opening the coffin, the mummy's spirit is transferred to his baby daughter, born at that instant. They call that bad luck.
1980 (R) 101m/C Charlton Heston, Susannah York, Stephanie Zimbalist; **D:** Mike Newell; **W:** Allan Scott; **M:** Claude Bolling. **VHS, Beta $19.95** *WAR* ꒰½

Awakening of Candra Based on a real 1975 incident, a young couple honeymooning in the mountains is assaulted by a lunatic fisherman. The psycho kills the husband and rapes the girl, then he brainwashes poor Candra into thinking it was all an accident. Intense subject matter should be horrifying, but falls short of the mark in this television flop.
1981 96m/C Blanche Baker, Cliff DeYoung, Richard Jaeckel; **D:** Paul Wendkos. **VHS, Beta $59.95** *GEM* Woof!

Awakenings Marshall's first dramatic effort is based on the true story of Dr. Oliver Sacks, from his book of the same title. It details his experimentation with the drug L-dopa which inspired the "awakening" of a number of catatonic patients, some of whom had "sleeping" for as long as thirty years.

Occasionally over-sentimental, but still providing a poignant look at both the patients—who find themselves confronted with lost opportunities and faded youth—and at Sacks, who must watch their exquisite suffering as they slip away. De Niro's performance as the youngest of the group is heart-rending, while Williams offers a subdued, moving performance as the doctor.
1990 (PG-13) 120m/C Robin Williams, Robert De Niro, John Heard, Julie Kavner, Penelope Ann Miller, Max von Sydow, Anne Meara; **D:** Penny Marshall; **W:** Steven Zaillian; **M:** Randy Newman. **VHS, Beta, 8mm $19.95** *COL, FCT* ꒰꒰꒰½

Awakenings of the Beast Documents the protracted sufferings of an LSD drug user who is beset with hallucinatory visions and is prone to fits of frenzied violence. In Spanish with English subtitles.
1968 ?m/C *BR* Jose Mojica Marins; **D:** Jose Mojica Marins. **VHS $20.00** *SMW, FCT* ꒰

Away All Boats The true story of one Captain Hawks, who led a crew of misfits to victory in WWII Pacific aboard transport USS Belinda. Battle scenes are well done; look for early (and brief) appearance by young Clint Eastwood.
1956 114m/B Jeff Chandler, George Nader, Richard Boone, Julie Adams, Keith Andes, Lex Barker; **D:** Joseph Pevney. **VHS, Beta $19.95** *MCA* ꒰꒰½

The Awful Dr. Orlof Set in a bygone era, Dr. Orlof (Vernon) is a retired prison physician who needs unblemished skin to remedy the horrible disfigurement of his daughter Melissa (Lorys), ravaged by fire. He abducts promising young women candidates with the help of his blind zombie henchman Morpho (Valle), who simply cannot be trusted with a scalpel. After several surgical mishaps, they kidnap the perfect specimen, a woman who bears an uncanny resemblance to Melissa. Unfortunately, she is engaged to suspicious police Inspector Tanner (San Martin). French version with English subtitles that includes more explicit gore is also available.
1962 86m/B Howard Vernon, Diana Lorys, Frank Wolff, Riccardo Valle, Conrado San Martin; **D:** Jess (Jesus) Franco; **M:** Pagan Angel, Ramirez Angel. **VHS $23.00** *SMW, VSM, TPV* ꒰

The Awful Truth Classic screwball comedy. Young couple discards their marriage made in heaven and go their separate ways in search of happiness. Meticulously sabotaging each others' new relationships, they discover they really were made for each other. First on-screen pairing for Grant and Dunne: Grant is at his most charming with dead-on comic timing while Dunne is brilliant as his needling ex. The scene where Dunne poses as Grant's prodigal fan-dancing sister who pays a surprise cocktail-hour visit to the family of his stuffy, upper-class bride-to-be is among the most memorable screwball vignettes of all time. And don't miss the custody battle they have over the family dog (Asta of "The Thin Man" fame). Based on Arthur Richman's play. Preceded by 1925 and 1929 versions; remade in 1953 as "Let's Do it Again."
1937 92m/B Irene Dunne, Cary Grant, Ralph Bellamy, Alexander D'Arcy, Cecil Cunningham, Molly Lamont, Esther Dale, Joyce Compton, Robert Allen, Robert Warwick, Mary Forbes; **D:** Leo McCarey; **W:** Vina Delmar. Academy Awards '37: Best Director (McCarey); Nominations: Best Actress (Dunne), Best Film Editing, Best Picture, Best Screenplay, Best Supporting Actor (Bellamy). **VHS, Beta $19.95** *MLB, BTV, COL* ꒰꒰꒰꒰

Ay, Carmela! During the Spanish Civil War, two vaudevillians with strong anti-Franco views are captured by Franco forces and sentenced to execution. They are reprieved when a theater-loving Lieutenant offers to spare their lives if they will entertain the troops. Clever and entertaining farce, with poignant undertones.
1990 105m/C *SP IT* Carmen Maura, Andres Pajares, Gabino Diego, Maurizio De Razza, Miguel Rellan, Edward Zentara, Jose Sancho, Antonio Fuentes; *D:* Carlos Saura; *W:* Rafael Azcona. VHS $89.98 *HBO, ING* 🎬🎬🎬

Baba A poor boatman agrees to be the fall guy in a murder in exchange for the actual murderer supporting his family. But after 24 years in prison, the boatman finds all his sacrificing has been in vain. His daughter has become a prostitute and his son is working as one of the murderer's henchman. In Turkish with English subtitles. *AKA:* The Father.
1973 95m/C *TU D:* Yilmaz Guney. VHS $39.95 *FCT, HEG* 🎬🎬🎬

Babar: The Movie The lovable Babar, king of the elephants, must devise a plan to outwit an angry hoard of attacking rhinos. Based on the characters of Jean and Laurent de Brunhoff.
1988 (G) 75m/C *CA FR D:* Alan Bunce; *W:* Alan Bunce; *V:* Gavin Magrath, Gordon Pinsent, Sarah Polley, Chris Wiggins, Elizabeth Hanna. VHS, Beta, 8mm $24.95 *FHE, IME, WTA* 🎬🎬½

Babe! A fine television movie about the life of one of America's most famous woman athletes, Babe Didrickson. Adapted by Joanna Lee from Didrickson's autobiography, "The Life I've Led." The movie was nominated for Outstanding Special of 1975-76 and Clark won an Emmy for her work.
1975 120m/C Susan Clark, Alex Karras, Slim Pickens, Jeanette Nolan, Ellen Geer, Ford Rainey; *D:* Buzz Kulik; *M:* Jerry Goldsmith. VHS NO 🎬🎬🎬½

The Babe Follows the life of legendary baseball player Babe Ruth, portrayed as a sloppy drunkard whose appetites for food, drink, and sex were as large as he was. Alvarado and McGillis do well as the Babe's first and second wives, but this is Goodman's show from start to finish. He's excellent as Ruth, and looks the part, but his fine performance can't make up for a lackluster script filled with holes.
1992 (PG) 115m/C John Goodman, Kelly McGillis, Trini Alvarado, Bruce Boxleitner, Peter Donat, J.C. Quinn, Richard Tyson, James Cromwell, Joe Ragno, Bernard Kates, Michael McGrady, Stephen Caffrey; *D:* Arthur Hiller; *W:* John Fusco; *M:* Elmer Bernstein. VHS $19.98 *MCA* 🎬🎬½

Babe Ruth Story An overly sentimental biography about the famed baseball slugger. Bendix is miscast as the Bambino, but the actual film clips of the Babe are of interest. A movie to be watched during those infrequent bouts of sloppy baseball mysticism.
1948 107m/B William Bendix, Claire Trevor, Charles Bickford, William Frawley, Sam Levene, Gertrude Niesen; *D:* Roy Del Ruth. VHS, Beta $19.98 *FOX* 🎬🎬

Babes in Arms The children of several vaudeville performers team up to put on a show to raise money for their financially impoverished parents. Loosely adapted from the Rodgers and Hart Broadway musical of the same name; features some of their songs as well as new additions. ♫Babes in Arms; I Cried for You; Good Morning; You Are My Lucky Star; Broadway Rhythm; Where or When; Daddy Was a Minstrel Man; I'm Just Wild About Harry; God's Country.
1939 91m/B Judy Garland, Mickey Rooney, Charles Winninger, Guy Kibbee, June Preisser; *D:* Busby Berkeley; *M:* Richard Rodgers, Lorenz Hart. VHS, Beta $19.98 *MGM* 🎬🎬½

Babes in Toyland A lavish Disney production of Victor Herbert's timeless operetta, with Toyland being menaced by the evil Barnaby and his Bogeymen. Yes, Annette had a life after Mickey Mouse and before the peanut butter commercials. Somewhat charming, although the roles of the lovers seem a stretch for both Funicello and Kirk. But the flick does sport an amusing turn by Wynn.
1961 105m/C Annette Funicello, Ray Bolger, Tommy Sands, Ed Wynn, Tommy Kirk; *D:* Jack Donohue. VHS $14.99 *DIS* 🎬🎬

Babes in Toyland Young girl must save Toyland from the clutches of the evil Barnaby and his monster minions. Bland TV remake of the classic doesn't approach the original.
1986 96m/C Drew Barrymore, Noriyuki "Pat" Morita, Richard Mulligan, Eileen Brennan, Keanu Reeves, Jill Schoelen, Googy Gress; *D:* Clive Donner; *M:* Leslie Bricusse. VHS $9.98 *ORI* 🎬½

Babes on Broadway Mickey and Judy put on a show to raise money for a settlement house. Nearly the best of the Garland-Rooney series, with imaginative numbers staged by Berkeley. ♫Babes on Broadway; Anything Can Happen in New York; How About You?; Hoe Down; Chin Up! Cheerio! Carry On!; Mama Yo Quiero; F.D.R. Jones; Waiting for the Robert E. Lee.
1941 118m/B Mickey Rooney, Judy Garland, Fay Bainter, Richard Quine, Virginia Weidler, Ray Macdonald, Busby Berkeley; *D:* Busby Berkeley. VHS, Beta $19.98 *MGM* 🎬🎬½

Babette's Feast A simple, moving pageant-of-life fable. A group of religiously zealous villagers are taught love and forgiveness through a lavish banquet prepared by one of their housemaids, who turns out to be a world-class chef. Adapted from a tale by Isak Dinesen. In French and Danish with English subtitles.
1987 102m/C *DK FR* Stephane Audran, Bibi Andersson, Bodil Kjer, Birgitte Federspiel, Jean-Philippe LaFont, Ebbe Rode, Jarl Kulle; *D:* Gabriel Axel. VHS, Beta $19.98 *ORI, FCT, APD* 🎬🎬🎬½

The Baby Bizarre story of a social worker who resorts to swinging an ax to cut the apron strings of "baby," a retarded man-child, from his over-protective and insane (bad combination) mother and sisters. Low-budget production looks and feels like a low-budget production, but any movie featuring a grown man wandering about in diapers can't be all bad.
1972 (PG) 85m/C Anjanette Comer, Ruth Roman, Marianna Hill, Suzanne Zenor, David Manzy, Michael Pataki; *D:* Ted Post. VHS, Beta NO 🎬🎬

The Baby and the Battleship The old baby out of (on the?) water plot. While on liberty in Italy, a sailor, after a series of complications, becomes custodian of a baby and attempts to hide the tyke aboard his battleship (hence the title). More complications ensue. Some funny moments. Great cast.
1956 96m/C *GB* John Mills, Richard Attenborough, Andre Morell, Bryan Forbes, Lisa Gastoni, Michael Hordern, Lionel Jeffries, Gordon Jackson, John Le Mesurier; *D:* Jay Lewis. VHS $19.95 *NOS, MOV, VEC* 🎬🎬½

Baby Boom When a hard-charging female executive becomes the reluctant mother of a baby girl (a gift from a long-lost relative), she adjusts with great difficulty to motherhood and life outside the rat race and New York City (and Sam Shepard as the love interest). A fairly harmless collection of cliches bolstered by Keaton's usual nervous performance as a power-suited yuppie ad queen saddled with a noncareer-enhancing baby, moving from manic yuppie ad maven to jelly-packing Vermont store-owner/mom. To best appreciate flick, see it with a bevy of five- and six-year-olds (a good age for applauding the havoc that a baby creates).
1987 (PG) 103m/C Diane Keaton, Sam Shepard, Harold Ramis, Sam Wanamaker, James Spader, Pat Hingle, Mary Gross, Victoria Jackson, Paxton Whitehead, Annie Golden, Dori Brenner, Robin Bartlett, Christopher Noth, Britt Leach; *D:* Charles Shyer; *W:* Charles Shyer, Nancy Meyers; *M:* Bill Conti. VHS, Beta $14.95 *MGM, FCT, FOX* 🎬🎬½

Baby Cart 1: Lend a Child...Lend an Arm First in a series of six from the sword-wielding samurai genre. Chronicles the events leading up to a samurai warrior's (Wakayama) expulsion from his native village along with his infant son (Tomikawa). Father's intense rivalry with the evil Shogun whom he was ousted by becomes an epic struggle of good vs. evil. The adorable little "Lone Cub" provides an effective counterpoint for Dad's sideline excursion into a local brothel. In Japanese with English subtitles in a letterbox format.
1972 83m/C *JP* Tomisaburo Wakayama, Akihiro Tomikawa; *D:* Kenji Misumi. VHS $27.90 *VSM* 🎬

Baby Cart 4: Heart of a Parent...Heart of a Child Fourth in a series of six. A man (Wakayama) pushes his son (Tomikawa) across Japan in a baby cart loaded with deadly accessories including built-in guns and switchblades. Copious amounts of bloodshed. In Japanese with English subtitles in a letterbox format.
1972 80m/C *JP* Tomisaburo Wakayama, Akihiro Tomikawa; *D:* Buichi Sato. VHS $27.90 *VSM* 🎬

Baby Cart at the River Styx Second of six films in the "Kozure Ohkami" ("Sword of Vengeance") series about a man who wheels his motherless infant through the Chinese countryside in a baby cart armed with secret weapons, plotting his revenge on the warlord who expelled him. This one features the intro of Sayka and her fellow female assassins. Subtitled in English.
1972 80m/C *JP* Tomisaburo Wakayama, Akihiro Tomikawa; *D:* Kenji Misumi. VHS $27.90 *VSM* 🎬

Baby Cart to Hades The third "Kozure Ohkami" ("Sword of Vengeance") film once again finds samurai Itto Ogami and his son Diagoro embroiled in a power struggle between a regional landlord and a governor in feudal Japan. Subtitled in English.
1972 88m/C *JP* Tomisaburo Wakayama, Akihiro Tomikawa; *D:* Kenji Misumi. VHS $27.90 *VSM* 🎬

Baby Doll Suggestive sex at its best, revolving around the love of cotton in Mississippi. Nubile Baker is married to slow-witted Malden, who runs a cotton gin. His torching of Wallach's cotton gin begins a cycle of sexual innuendo and tension, brought to exhilarating life on screen, without a single filmed kiss. Performers and sets ooze during the steamy exhibition, which was considered highly erotic when released. Excellent performances from entire cast, with expert pacing by director Kazan. Screenplay is based on Tennessee Williams' "27 Wagons Full of Cotton."
1956 115m/B Eli Wallach, Carroll Baker, Karl Malden, Mildred Dunnock, Rip Torn; *D:* Elia Kazan; *W:* Tennessee Williams. Academy Awards '56 Nominations: Best Actress (Baker), Best Adapted Screenplay, Best Black and White

Cinematography, Best Supporting Actress (Dunnock); Golden Globe Awards '57: Best Director (Kazan). **VHS, Beta $19.98** *WAR, FCT* ♫♫♫

The Baby Doll Murders Someone in L.A. is killing beautiful young women and then leaving a broken baby doll at the scene of the crime. The gruesome murderer manages to elude everyone, until Detective Benz discovers a link between the victims and a pattern begins to form. He also discovers that his partner's wife is going to be the next victim unless he can stop this ruthless serial killer from striking again.
1992 (R) 90m/C Jeff Kober, Melanie Smith, John Saxon, Tom Hodges; **D:** Paul Leder; **W:** Paul Leder. **VHS $89.98** *REP* ♫♫

Baby Face A small town girl moves to the city when her father dies. There she gets a job at a bank and sleeps her way to the top of the business world, discarding used men left and right. The Hays Office was extremely upset with the then risque material and forced Warner to trim the first cut.
1933 70m/B Barbara Stanwyck, George Brent, Donald Cook, John Wayne, Henry Kolker, Margaret Lindsay, Douglass Dumbrille, James Murray; **D:** Alfred E. Green. **VHS, Beta $19.98** *MGM, FCT* ♫♫

Baby Face Harry Langdon Two silent shorts by the limpid-eyed comedian: "Saturday Afternoon" (1926), and "Lucky Stars" (1925).
1926 60m/B Harry Langdon, Alice Ward, Natalie Kingston, Vernon Dent, Harry Edwards; **D:** Harry Edwards; **W:** Frank Capra, Arthur Ripley. **VHS, Beta, 8mm $19.95** *VYY* ♫♫½

Baby Face Morgan Poor comedy about gangsters who attempt to take advantage of the FBI's preoccupation with saboteurs and spies by muscling in on an insurance firm.
1942 60m/B Mary Carlisle, Richard Cromwell, Robert Armstrong, Chick Chandler, Charles Judels, Warren Hymer, Vince Barnett, Ralf Harolde; **D:** Arthur Dreifuss. **VHS $16.95** *SNC* ♫♫

Baby Girl Scott Hurt and Lithgow play the parents of an extremely premature infant who is being kept alive by technology. They make a heartrending decision and then must battle doctors and the system to let their daughter die with dignity. Made for television.
1987 97m/C John Lithgow, Mary Beth Hurt, Linda Kelsey, John Korty. **VHS $59.98** *LIV* ♫♫½

Baby It's You In New Jersey in the '60s, the relationship between a smart, attractive Jewish girl who yearns to be an actress and a street-smart Catholic Italian boy puzzles their family and friends. It all works due to Arquette's strong acting and Sayles' script, which explores adolescent dreams, the transition to adulthood, class differences, and the late 1960s with insight and humor. Interesting period soundtrack (Woolly Bully and, for some reason, Bruce Springsteen) helps propel the film, a commercial job which helped finance Sayles' more independent ventures.
1982 (R) 105m/C Rosanna Arquette, Vincent Spano, Jack Davidson, Joanna Merlin, Nick Ferrari, Leora Dana, Robert Downey Jr., Tracy Pollan, Matthew Modine; **D:** John Sayles; **W:** John Sayles. **VHS, Beta $79.95** *PAR* ♫♫♫

Baby Love A softcore fluff-fest about a trollop seducing a doctor's family. The doctor may or may not be her father. Hayden tantalizes the doctor, the doctor's son, and the doctor's wife, as well as the neighbors, leaving only those in adjoining communities untouched. Based on the novel by Tina Chad Christian.

1969 (R) 98m/C *GB* Ann Lynn, Keith Barron, Linda Hayden, Derek Lamden, Diana Dors, Patience Collier; **D:** Alastair Reid. **VHS, Beta $59.95** *NLC* Woof!

Baby Love Nerds get revenge against the freshmen who run the local frat house.
1983 80m/C VHS, Beta $59.95 *MGM* Woof!

The Baby Maker A couple who cannot have children because the wife is sterile decides to hire a woman to have a child for them. However, the relationship between the husband and the surrogate progresses beyond what either of them wanted. Hershey stars as the free-love surrogate mama (just before she underwent the supreme 60s transformation into Barbara Seagull) and Bridges makes his directorial debut. Flick is interesting as a combo critique/exploitation of those wild and groovy 1960s.
1970 (R) 109m/C Barbara Hershey, Collin Wilcox-Horne, Sam Groom, Scott Glenn, Jeannie Berlin; **D:** James Bridges; **W:** James Bridges. **VHS $59.95** *WAR* ♫♫

Baby of the Bride Follow-up to "Children of the Bride," has McClanahan settling into wedded bliss with younger husband Shackleford when she discovers she's pregnant. Not only is she unsure about wanting to be a mom again at her age but then grown—and single—daughter McNichol announces she is also pregnant. The sheer silliness of this made-for-television fare makes it fun to watch.
1991 93m/C Rue McClanahan, Ted Shackleford, Kristy McNichol, John Wesley Shipp, Anne Bobby, Conor O'Farrell; **D:** Bill Bixby; **W:** Bart Baker. **VHS $89.98** *TTC* ♫♫½

Baby on Board Kane plays the wife of a Mafia bookkeeper who is accidentally killed in a gangland murder. Out for revenge, she tracks her husband's killer to JFK airport with her four-year old daughter in tow. Just as she pulls the loaded gun from her purse and takes aim, a pickpocket snatches her purse, accidentally firing the gun. Now she's on the run and she jumps into the first cab she can find, driven by Reinhold. New York City is turned upside down as mother, daughter, and cabbie try to elude the mob in this funny but predictable comedy.
1992 (PG) 90m/C Carol Kane, Judge Reinhold, Geza Kovacs, Errol Slue, Alex Stapley, Holly Stapley; **D:** Francis Schaeffer. **VHS, Beta $89.95** *PSM* ♫♫

Baby Snakes: The Complete Version Concert footage of Zappa is interspersed with clay animation by Bruce Bickford.
1979 166m/C Frank Zappa, Joey Psychotic, Ron Delsener, Donna U. Wanna; **D:** Frank Zappa. **VHS, Beta $79.95** *MVD, MPI* ♫♫

Baby, Take a Bow Temple's first starring role. As a cheerful Pollyanna-type she helps her father, falsely accused of theft, by finding the true thief.
1934 76m/B Shirley Temple, James Dunn, Claire Trevor, Alan Dinehart; **D:** Harry Lachman. **VHS, Beta $19.98** *FOX* ♫♫

Baby, the Rain Must Fall A rockabilly singer, paroled from prison after serving time for a knifing, returns home to his wife and daughter, but his outbursts of violence make the reunion difficult. Unsentimental with realistic performances, but script is weak (although written by Foote, based on his play, "The Traveling Lady"). Theme song was a Top 40 hit.
1964 100m/B Steve McQueen, Lee Remick, Don Murray; **D:** Robert Mulligan; **W:** Horton Foote Jr.; **M:** Elmer Bernstein. **VHS, Beta $9.95** *COL, MOV* ♫♫

Babycakes A marshmellow romance between an overweight mortuary attendant who decides to follow her heart when she falls for a hunky ice skater. Can she make him appreciate her inner beauty instead of just her not-the-normal-beauty-standard outward appearance? (Happy ending guaranteed.) A made for television remake of the darker German film "Sugarbaby."
1989 94m/C Ricki Lake, Craig Sheffer, Paul Benedict, Betty Buckley, John Karlen, Nada Despotovich; **D:** Paul Schneider. **VHS $89.98** *TTC* ♫♫½

The Babylon Story from "Intolerance" Lavishly produced vignette from Griffith's film "Intolerance" as it was released on its own in 1919, in order to recoup the studio losses incurred by that grandest of cinematic follies. Silent with organ score, tinted color.
1916 25m/C Constance Talmadge, Alfred Paget; **D:** D.W. Griffith. **VHS, Beta $19.95** *VYY* ♫♫♫½

Baby's Day Out Poor man's "Home Alone" refits tired Hughes formula using little tiny baby for original spin. Adorable Baby Bink crawls his way onto the city streets, much to his frantic mother's dismay, and unwittingly outsmarts his would-be kidnappers. As in HA I and II, the bad guys fall victim to all sorts of cataclysmic Looney Tunes violence. Small kids will get a kick out of this one. Particular problem for the moviemakers was that the nine-month old Worton twins were past the year mark by the end of the shoot, a world of difference in infantdom. Blue screens and out-of-sequence shooting were used to overcome the developmental gap.
1994 (PG) 98m/C Adam Worton, Jacob Worton, Joe Mantegna, Lara Flynn Boyle, Joe Pantoliano, Fred Dalton Thompson, John Neville, Brian Haley, Matthew Glave; **D:** Patrick Read Johnson; **W:** John Hughes; **M:** Bruce Broughton. **VHS** *NYR* ♫♫½

Baby...Secret of the Lost Legend A sportswriter and his paleontologist wife risk their lives to reunite a hatching brontosaurus with its mother in the African jungle. Although this Disney film is not lewd in any sense, beware of several scenes displaying frontal nudity and some violence.
1985 (PG) 95m/C William Katt, Sean Young, Patrick McGoohan, Julian Fellowes; **D:** B.W.L. Norton. **VHS, Beta $79.95** *TOU* ♫♫

The Babysitter A family hires the mysterious but ingratiating Johanna (Zimbalist) as live-in help without checking on her references (who'd all checked out). The babysitter is the answer to all their problems—Mom's an alcoholic, Dad's a workaholic, and their daughter's just plain maladjusted—but once Johanna's gained their trust (or, in Dad's case, lust), she sets out to manipulate and exploit the family for her own psychotic purposes. Houseman plays the nosy neighbor who's on to her evil plan. Fair made-for-TV treatment of a common suspense plot.
1980 96m/C William Shatner, Patty Duke, Stephanie Zimbalist, Quinn Cummings, John Houseman, David Wallace; **D:** Peter Medak. **VHS, Beta** *NO* ♫♫

The Bacchantes Poorly dubbed account of a ballerina, her life and loves. Based on the play by Euripides.
1963 100m/B *IT* Taina Elg, Pierre Brice, Alessandra Panaro, Alberto Lupo, Akim Tamiroff; **D:** Giorgio Ferroni. **VHS $39.95** *FCT* ♫♫

The Bachelor Beautiful, seductive period drama about a shy and solitary physician who is forced into a new life when a family tragedy changes everything he once took for granted. Richardson and Carradine give brilliant performances in this provocative story of one man's sexual awakening. Based on a novel by Arthur Schnitzler.

1993 105m/C Keith Carradine, Miranda Richardson, Mari Torocsik, Max von Sydow, Kristin Scott Thomas, Sarah-Jane Fenton, Franco Diogene; *D:* Roberto Faenza; *W:* Roberto Faenza, Ennio de Concini, Hugh Fleetwood; *M:* Ennio Morricone. VHS **$89.95** TRI 🎬🎬🎬

The Bachelor and the Bobby-Soxer Playboy Grant is brought before Judge Loy for disturbing the peace and sentenced to court her teen-age sister Temple. Cruel and unusual punishment? Maybe, but the wise Judge hopes that the dates will help Temple over her crush on handsome Grant. Instead, Loy and Grant fall for each other. **AKA:** Bachelor Knight.

1947 95m/B Cary Grant, Myrna Loy, Shirley Temple, Rudy Vallee, Harry Davenport, Ray Collins, Veda Ann Borg; *D:* Irving Reis; *W:* Sidney Sheldon. VHS, **Beta $14.98** CCB, MED, RKO 🎬🎬🎬

Bachelor Apartment Once at the leading edge of the bachelor on the loose genre, this one's hopelessly dated. The scandalous womanizing of a wealthy thirties Lothario just doesn't have the same impact on the men just don't understand generation. Nevertheless, as vintage if-the-walls-could-talk fluff, it's good for a giggle.

1931 77m/B Lowell Sherman, Irene Dunne, Norman Kerry, Claudia Dell, Noel Francis, Charles Coleman; *D:* Lowell Sherman. VHS **$19.98** TTC, FCT 🎬🎬½

Bachelor Bait A marriage license clerk who's tired of just handing out licenses opens a matrimonial service for men.

1934 75m/B Stuart Erwin, Rochelle Hudson, Pert Kelton, Richard "Skeets" Gallagher. VHS, **Beta** CCB 🎬½

Bachelor in Paradise Silly tale starring Hope as a writer of books to the lovelorn who decides to do firsthand research on the sexual goings-on of a suburban California community. All the married ladies find him charming (much to their husbands disgust) and the lone single woman, Turner, isn't single by the end of the movie.

1969 109m/C Bob Hope, Lana Turner, Janis Paige, Jim Hutton, Paula Prentiss, Don Porter, Virginia Grey, Agnes Moorehead, John McGiver; *D:* Jack Arnold; *W:* Hal Kanter, Valentine Davies, Hal Kanter; *M:* Henry Mancini. VHS **$19.98** MGM, FCT 🎬🎬½

Bachelor Mother A single salesgirl causes a scandal when she finds an abandoned baby and is convinced by her boss to adopt the child. Smart, witty comedy with nice performance by Rogers.

1939 82m/B Ginger Rogers, David Niven, Charles Coburn; *D:* Garson Kanin. VHS, **Beta $19.98** CCB, MED, FCT 🎬🎬🎬

Bachelor of Hearts Sophomoric British comedy set at Cambridge University, with a German exchange student whose difficulty with English brings him to date several women in one evening. Notable for horror fans as the debut of femme fright fave Barbara Steele.

1958 94m/C GB Hardy Kruger, Sylvia Syms, Ronald Lewis; *D:* Wolf Rilla; *W:* Frederic Raphael. VHS **$19.95** NOS 🎬½

Bachelor Party He's silly, cute, and poor. She's intelligent, beautiful, and rich. It must be a marriage made in heaven, because no one in their right mind would put these two together. All is basically well, except that her parents hate him and his friends dislike her. Things are calm until right before the big event, when bride-to-be Kitaen objects to

Hank's traditional pre-nuptial partying. Light and semi-entertaining with scattered laughs.

1984 (R) 105m/C Tom Hanks, Tawny Kitaen, Adrian Zmed, George Grizzard, Robert Prescott, William Tepper, Wendie Jo Sperber, Barry Diamond, Michael Dudikoff, Deborah Harmon, John Bloom, Toni Alessandra, Monique Gabrielle, Angela Aames, Rosanne Katon; *D:* Neal Israel; *W:* Pat Proft; *M:* Robert Folk. VHS, **Beta $14.98** FXV, FOX 🎬🎬

Back Door to Heaven Traces the path of a young boy who is born into a poor family and the reasons for his turning to a life of crime. A grim and powerful drama with many convincing performances.

1939 85m/B Wallace Ford, Aline MacMahon, Stuart Erwin, Patricia Ellis, Kent Smith, Van Heflin, Jimmy Lydon; *D:* William K. Howard. VHS **$19.95** NOS, MOV 🎬🎬🎬½

Back from Eternity Eleven survivors of a plane crash are stranded in a headhunter region of South America's jungle. Remake of "Five Came Back" (1939), which was also directed by Farrow.

1956 97m/B Robert Ryan, Rod Steiger, Anita Ekberg, Phyllis Kirk, Keith Andes, Gene Barry; *D:* John Farrow. VHS, **Beta $19.95** VCI 🎬🎬

Back Home A family reunion movie with pure Disney sentiment. A 12-year-old English girl, who has been living in America during WWII, is reunited with her family in postwar England. Made for cable television.

1990 103m/C Hayley Carr, Hayley Mills, Jean Anderson, Rupert Frazer, Brenda Bruce, Adam Stevenson, George Clark; *D:* Piers Haggard. VHS DIS 🎬🎬½

Back in Action Veteran LA detective Rossi (Piper) is out to bust the ruthless drug gang who gunned down his partner. But he's got company—martial-arts expert Billy (Blanks) whose young sister has fallen prey to the same gang. So the two action junkies reluctantly team up to cause some major damage.

1994 (R) 93m/C Roddy Piper, Billy Blanks, Bobbie Phillips, Matt Birman, Nigel Bennett, Damon D'Oliveira, Kai Soremekun; *D:* Steve DiMarco; *W:* Karl Schiffman. VHS MCA 🎬½

Back in the USSR Danger follows two lovers caught up in the Moscow underworld. When young American touring Russia unwittingly gets involved with a beautiful art thief. Lots of fast-paced action in an otherwise muddled film. The first American film shot entirely on location in Moscow.

1992 (R) 87m/C Frank Whaley, Natalia Negoda, Roman Polanski, Claudia Robinson, Dey Young, Andrew Divoff, Brian Blessed, Ravil Issyanov; *D:* Deran Sarafian. VHS **$19.98** FXV 🎬½

Back Roads Southern hooker meets a down-on-his-luck boxer and both head out for a better life in California, finding love along the way. Ritter road trip lacks any comedic rhythm and survives on Field and Jones working to entertain.

1981 (R) 94m/C Sally Field; Tommy Lee Jones, David Keith; *D:* Martin Ritt; *W:* Gary De Vore. VHS, **Beta $69.98** FOX 🎬½

Back Street The forbidden affair between a married man and a beautiful fashion designer carries on through many anxious years to a tragic end. The lavish third film version of the Fanny Hurst novel.

1961 107m/C Susan Hayward, John Gavin, Vera Miles; *D:* David Miller. VHS, **Beta $14.98** MCA, MLB 🎬🎬

Back to Back A beautiful young vigilante embarks on a rampage to clear her family's name and make her town's redneck crooks pay for their crimes. Never released in theaters.

1990 (R) 95m/C Bill Paxton, Todd Field, Apollonia, Luke Askew, Ben Johnson, David Michael-Standing, Susan Anspach, Sal Landi; *D:* John Kincade. VHS, **Beta $79.95** MGM 🎬

Back to Bataan Colonel forms guerrilla army to raid Japanese in the Philippines and to help Americans landing on Leyte. Also available in a colorized version.

1945 95m/B John Wayne, Anthony Quinn, Beulah Bondi, Fely Franquelli, Richard Loo, Philip Ahn, Lawrence Tierney; *D:* Edward Dmytryk. VHS, **Beta $19.98** TTC 🎬🎬½

Back to Hannibal: The Return of Tom Sawyer and Huckleberry Finn Mark Twain's characters Tom Sawyer and Huckleberry Finn are reunited as adults to solve a murder mystery. Tom is a lawyer, Finn a newspaper man, and it's Becky Thatcher's husband who's been murdered. Did a freed slave really commit the crime? Made for television.

1990 92m/C Raphael Sbarge, Mitchell Anderson, Megan Follows, William Windom, Ned Beatty, Paul Winfield; *D:* Paul Krasny. VHS **$19.99** DIS 🎬🎬½

Back to School Dangerfield plays an obnoxious millionaire who enrolls in college to help his wimpy son, Gordon, achieve campus stardom. His motto seems to be "if you can't buy it, it can't be had." At first, his antics embarrass his shy son, but soon everyone is clamoring to be seen with the pair as Gordon develops his own self confidence.

1986 (PG-13) 96m/C Rodney Dangerfield, Keith Gordon, Robert Downey Jr., Sally Kellerman, Burt Young, Paxton Whitehead, Adrienne Barbeau, M. Emmet Walsh, Severn Darden, Ned Beatty, Sam Kinison, Kurt Vonnegut Jr., Robert Picardo, Terry Farrell, Edie McClurg, Jason Hervey; *D:* Alan Metter; *W:* Will Aldis, Steven Kampmann, Harold Ramis, Peter Torokvei, Steven Kampmann; *M:* Danny Elfman. VHS, **Beta $19.98** HBO 🎬🎬½

Back to the Beach Frankie and Annette return to the beach as self-parodying, middle-aged parents with rebellious kids, and the usual run of sun-bleached, lover's tiff comedy ensues. Plenty of songs and guest appearances from television past. Tries to bring back that surf, sun, and sand feel of the orignal "Beach Party" movies, but fails. ♫Absolute Perfection; California Sun; Catch a Ride; Jamaica Sky; Papa-Oom-Mow-Mow; Sign of Love; Sun, Sun, Sun, Sun, Sun; Surfin' Bird; Wooly Bully.

1987 (PG) 92m/C Frankie Avalon, Annette Funicello, Connie Stevens, Jerry Mathers, Bob Denver, Barbara Billingsley, Tony Dow, Paul (Pee Wee Herman) Reubens, Edd Byrnes, Dick Dale, Don Adams, Lori Loughlin; *D:* Lyndall Hobbs; *M:* Stephen Dorff. VHS, **Beta $19.95** PAR 🎬½

Back to the Future When neighborhood mad scientist Doc Brown constructs a time machine from a DeLorean, his youthful companion Marty accidentally transports himself to 1955. There, Marty must do everything he can to bring his parents together, elude the local bully, and get back...to the future. Solid fast-paced entertainment is even better due to Lloyd's inspired performance as the loony Doc while Fox is perfect as the boy completely out of his element. Soundtrack features Huey Lewis and the News. Followed by two sequels.

1985 (PG) 116m/C Michael J. Fox, Christopher Lloyd, Lea Thompson, Crispin Glover, Wendie Jo Sperber, Marc McClure, Thomas F. Wilson, James Tolkan, Casey Siemaszko, Billy Zane, George DiCenzo, Courtney Gains, Claudia Wells, Jason Hervey, Harry Waters Jr., Maia Brewton, J.J. Cohen; *Cameos:* Huey Lewis; *D:* Robert Zemeckis; *W:* Robert Zemeckis, Bob Gale; *M:* Alan Silvestri. Academy Awards '85 Nominations:

Best Original Screenplay, Best Song ("The Power of Love"), Best Sound; People's Choice Awards '86: Best Film. **VHS, Beta $19.95** MCA, FCT, TLF ♂♂♂

Back to the Future, Part 2 Taking up exactly where Part 1 left off, Doc Brown and Marty time-hop into the future (2015 to be exact) to save Marty's kids, then find themselves returning to 1955 to retrieve a sports almanac that causes havoc for the McFly family. Clever editing allows for Marty Part 2 to see Marty Part 1 at the school dance. Most of the cast returns, although Glover appears only in cuts from the original and Shue steps in as girlfriend Jennifer. Not up to the original, but still satisfying. Cliffhanger ending sets up Part 3, which was shot simultaneously with this.
1989 (PG) 107m/C Michael J. Fox, Christopher Lloyd, Lea Thompson, Thomas F. Wilson, Harry Waters Jr., Charles Fleischer, Joe Flaherty, Elisabeth Shue, James Tolkan, Casey Siemaszko, Jeffrey Weissman, Flea, Billy Zane, J.J. Cohen, Darlene Vogel, Jason Scott Lee, Crispin Glover, Ricky Dean Logan; *D:* Robert Zemeckis; *W:* Robert Zemeckis, Bob Gale; *M:* Alan Silvestri. **VHS, Beta $19.95** MCA ♂♂½

Back to the Future, Part 3 Picks up where Part 2 climaxed a la cliffhanger. Stuck in 1955, time-traveling hero Marty frantically searches for Doc Part 1 so he can return to 1985. Instead, he finds himself in the Wild West circa 1885, trying to save Doc's life. Plot is related to earlier BTTFs, so first time viewers might be confused. For those who've seen previous incarnations, the clever interconnections are really nifty. Nearly matches the original for excitement and offers some snazzy new special effects. Supposedly the last installment, though don't be surprised if another sequel follows. The complete trilogy is available as a boxed set.
1990 (PG) 118m/C Michael J. Fox, Christopher Lloyd, Mary Steenburgen, Thomas F. Wilson, Lea Thompson, Elisabeth Shue, Matt Clark, Richard Dysart, Pat Buttram, Harry Carey Jr., Dub Taylor, James Tolkan, Marc McClure, Wendie Jo Sperber, J.J. Cohen, Ricky Dean Logan; *D:* Robert Zemeckis; *W:* Jeffrey Weissman; *M:* Alan Silvestri. **VHS, Beta $19.95** MCA ♂♂♂

Back to the Wall Moreau is an adulturous wife whose web of deceit results in a suspenseful tale of murder and blackmail.
1956 94m/B *FR* Jeanne Moreau, Gerard Oury, Claire Maurier; *D:* Edouard Molinaro. **VHS $29.95** FCT, ING ♂♂

Backbeat Explores the Beatles' early days between '60 and '62, when they were playing Hamburg's underground music scene. Storyline driven by the triangle of John Lennon, his best friend and orginal bass player, Stu Sutcliff, more painter than musician, and the woman Stu left the band for, Astrid Kirchherr, the photographer who came up with the band's signature look. Hart's dead-on as Lennon, playing him a second time (check out "The Hours and Times"). Energetic, enjoyable debut for director Softley is best when the music takes center stage. Produced by Don Was, it captures the Fab Four's early bar band sound with a "supergroup" comprised of alternative rockers from current hot bands.
1994 (R) 100m/C *GB* Stephen Dorff, Sheryl Lee, Ian Hart, Gary Bakewell, Chris O'Neill, Scot Williams, Kai Wiesinger, Jennifer Ehle; *D:* Iain Softley; *W:* Michael Thomas, Stephen Ward, Iain Softley; *M:* Don Was. **VHS** NYR ♂♂♂

Backdraft High action story of Chicago firemen has some of the most stupendous incendiary special effects ever filmed. But then there's that plot, B-movie hokum about

a mystery arsonist torching strategic parts of the community with the finesse of an expert and a brother-against-brother conflict. Straight-forward performances from most of the cast in spite of the weak storyline. Writer Widen wrote from experience—he used to be a fireman; real-life Chicago firefighters were reportedly very happy with the realistic and intense fire scenes. Forget the plot and just watch the fires. Also available in a letterboxed version.
1991 (R) 135m/C Kurt Russell, William Baldwin, Robert De Niro, Donald Sutherland, Jennifer Jason Leigh, Scott Glenn, Rebecca DeMornay, Jason Gedrick, J.T. Walsh, Tony Mockus Sr., Clint Howard, David Crosby; *D:* Ron Howard; *W:* Gregory Widen; *M:* Hans Zimmer. **VHS, Beta $19.98** MCA ♂♂½

Backfield in Motion Silly but harmless comedy about a widowed mom who tries to get closer to her high-schooler son by organizing a mother-son football game. But it's the boys' football coach who really wants to get close—to mom. Made for television movie debut of both Arnolds.
1991 95m/C Roseanne (Barr) Arnold, Tom Arnold, Colleen Camp, Conchata Ferrell, Johnny Galecki, Kevin Scannell; *D:* Richard Michaels. **VHS, Beta** TTC ♂♂½

Backfire If you're gonna rob a bank, you shouldn't let anyone hear you plan it, and if you're not gonna rob a bank, you shouldn't let anyone hear you plan one. This vintage "Lightning" Carson crime western has Carson and friend suspected of bank robbery because someone heard them planning one. The sheriff follows their every footstep as they search for the real perpetrators.
1922 56m/B Jack Hoxie, George Sowards, Lew Meehan, Florence Gilbert; *D:* Alvin J. Neitz. **VHS, Beta $9.95** GPV ♂♂

Backfire A mysterious stranger enters the lives of a disturbed 'Nam vet and his discontented wife, setting a pattern of murder and double-cross in motion.
1988 (R) 90m/C Karen Allen, Keith Carradine, Jeff Fahey, Bernie Casey, Dinah Manoff, Dean Paul Martin; *D:* Gilbert Cates. **VHS, Beta $29.95** VMK ♂♂

Background to Danger A suspenseful WWII actioner about American agent Raft who travels to Turkey to receive secret documents from the soon-to-be-murdered Massen. Greenstreet is the Nazi master spy who also wants the documents as do Russian spies, Lorre and Marshall. Somewhat confusing plot but fast-paced. Based on the thriller "Uncommon Danger" by Eric Ambler. This film was Warner Brothers' follow-up to "Casablanca" with Raft in the Bogie role he had turned down in that cinema classic.
1943 80m/B George Raft, Sydney Greenstreet, Peter Lorre, Brenda Marshall, Osa Massen, Turhan Bey, Kurt Katch, Raoul Walsh. **VHS $19.98** MGM, MOV ♂♂♂

Backlash An aborigine barmaid is raped. When her assailant turns up dead, she's charged with murder and winds up in the custody of two police officers on a trip across the outback. Holes in the plot undermine this interesting, although graphic, drama with racial overtones.
1986 (R) 88m/C *AU* David Argue, Gia Carides, Lydia Miller, Brian Syron, Anne Smith; *D:* Bill Bennett; *W:* Bill Bennett; *M:* Michael Atkinson, Michael Spicer. **VHS, Beta $79.95** MCG ♂♂½

Backstab A spellbinding tale of work, lust, and murder. Architect Brolin finds himself unable to get over the death of his wife, until a seductive and mysterious woman helps him over his grief. They spend the night together, engulfed in passion, but in the

morning he wakes to find himself sleeping with the corpse of his boss. Only the first twist in this intriguing thriller.
1990 (R) 91m/C James Brolin, Meg Foster, Isabelle Truchon; *D:* Jim Kaufman. **VHS $89.98** MED, VTR ♂♂½

Backstairs An obscure German silent film about urban degradation and familial strife.
1921 44m/B *GE* Henny Porten, Fritz Kortner, William Dieterle; *D:* Leopold Jessner. **VHS, Beta $39.95** ING, NOS, DVT ♂♂♂

Backstreet Dreams The young parents of an autistic child find themselves torn apart due to their feelings of guilt. The father has an affair with a specialist hired to help the boy, causing further strife. Interesting story possibilities never get far.
1990 (R) 104m/C Brooke Shields, Jason O'Malley, Sherilyn Fenn, Tony Fields, Burt Young, Anthony (Tony) Franciosa, Nick Cassavetes, Ray "Boom Boom" Mancini; *D:* Rupert Hitzig; *M:* Bill Conti. **VHS $79.98** VMK ♂♂

Backtrack Foster co-stars in this thriller about an artist who accidentally witnesses a mob hit. The mob puts a hitman (Hopper) on her trail, and after studying her background and listening to audio tapes she recorded, he finds himself falling in love. Originally intended for a theatrical release, it hit the European screens in a different cut as "Catchfire;" Hopper restored his original version and it was released on cable TV in the U.S . *AKA:* Catchfire.
1989 (R) 102m/C Dennis Hopper, Jodie Foster, Dean Stockwell, Vincent Price, John Turturro, Fred Ward, G. Anthony Sirico, Julie Adams, Frank Gio, Sy Richardson, Helena Kallianiotes, Bob Dylan; *Cameos:* Charlie Sheen, Joe Pesci; *D:* Dennis Hopper; *M:* Michel Colombier. **VHS $19.98** LIV ♂♂♂

Backwoods Two campers wish they had never encountered a mountain man when he begins to stalk them with murder in mind.
1987 (R) 90m/C Jack O'Hara, Dick Kreusser, Brad Armacot; *D:* Dean Crow. **VHS, Beta** NO ♂♂♂

The Bad and the Beautiful The story of a Hollywood producer, told from the eyes of an actress, a writer, and a director. Featuring what some consider Turner's best performance ever. Winner of five Oscars, a splendid drama.
1952 118m/B Kirk Douglas, Lana Turner, Dick Powell, Gloria Grahame, Barry Sullivan, Walter Pidgeon, Gilbert Roland; *D:* Vincente Minnelli. Academy Awards '52: Best Art Direction/Set Decoration (B & W), Best Black and White Cinematography, Best Costume Design (B & W), Best Screenplay, Best Supporting Actress (Grahame); Nominations: Best Actor (Douglas). **VHS $19.98** MGM, BTV ♂♂♂♂

Bad Attitude Leon is a narcotics officer on a mission to restore his badge after his careless pistol work gets him booted off the force. The quick-tempered cop relentlessly pursues druglord Finque with the help of an open-minded preacher (De Veaux) and his sexy, streetwise assistant (Lim).
1993 (R) 87m/C Leon, Gina Lim, Nathaniel DeVeaux, Susan Finque; *D:* Bill Cummings. **VHS $69.95** XVC ♂♂

Bad Behavior Unscripted character-driven drama. Gerry and Ellie McAllister are an Irish couple living in North London. He's tired of working for the local planning commission, she's bored being just a mum at home, and both are still a little uneasy living in England. When they decide to remodel the family bath, the unexpected problems lead to an emotional shakeup. Don't expect a lot of drama, the film works only if you accept the decency of

the characters and the small moments of recognizable daily life. Director Blair wrote a basic script outline and had the actors improvise their dialogue, in character, over a long rehearsal period to develop their roles.
1992 (R) 103m/C *GB* Stephen Rea, Sinead Cusack, Philip Jackson, Clare Higgins, Phil Daniels, Saira Todd; *D:* Les Blair. **VHS $94.95** *VMK* ♪♪½

Bad Blood The true story of Stan Graham, who went on a killing spree in the New Zealand bush when his farm was foreclosed and his life ruined.
1987 104m/C *NZ* Jack Thompson, Carol Burns, Dennis Lill; *D:* Mike Newell. **VHS, Beta $29.95** *ACA* ♪♪

Bad Boy A country boy goes to the big city, and succumbs to urban evils and temptations, but is eventually saved by motherly love. *AKA:* Branded.
1939 60m/B Johnny Downs, Helen MacKellar, Rosalind Keith, Holmes Herbert; *D:* Kurt Neumann. **VHS, Beta NO** ♪½

Bad Boys When a gang member's little brother is killed in a rumble, the teen responsible (Penn, who else?) goes to a reformatory, where he quickly (though somewhat reluctantly) takes charge. Meanwhile, on the outside, his rival attacks Penn's girlfriend (Sheedy, in her feature film debut) in retaliation, is incarcerated, and ends up vying with Penn for control of the cell block. Backed into a corner by their mutual hatred and escalating peer pressure, the two are pushed over the brink into a final and shattering confrontation. Not as violent as it could be, to its credit; attempts to communicate a message.
1983 123m/C Sean Penn, Esai Morales, Reni Santoni, Jim Moody, Eric Gurry, Ally Sheedy, Clancy Brown; *D:* Rick Rosenthal; *M:* Bill Conti. **VHS, Beta NO** ♪♪♪

Bad Bunch A white liberal living in Watts tries to befriend a ruthless black street gang, but is unsuccessful.
1976 82m/C Greydon Clark, Tom Johnigam, Pamela Corbett, Jacqulin Cole, Aldo Ray, Jock Mahoney; *D:* Greydon Clark. **VHS, Beta $59.95** *VCI* ♪

B.A.D. Cats Two members of a police burglary auto detail team chase after a group of car thieves who are planning a million-dollar gold heist.
1980 74m/C Asher Brauner, Michelle Pfeiffer, Vic Morrow, Jimmie Walker, Steve Hanks, LaWanda Page; *D:* Bernard L. Kowalski. **VHS, Beta $59.95** *LHV* ♪

Bad Channels Radio goes awry when female listeners of station KDUL are shrunk and put into specimen jars by a way-out disc jockey and a visiting alien, who plans to take the women back to his planet. Mildly amusing comedy features ex-MTV VJ Quinn and score by Blue Oyster Cult. Also available with Spanish subtitles.
1992 (R) 88m/C Paul Hipp, Martha Quinn, Aaron Lustig, Ian Patrick Williams, Charlie Spradling; *D:* Ted Nicolaou; *W:* Jackson Barr; *M:* Blue Oyster Cult. **VHS, Beta** *PAR* ♪♪

Bad Charleston Charlie Dud of a gangster comedy with terrible acting. A comedy?
1973 (PG) 91m/C Ross Hagen, John Carradine; *D:* Ivan Nagy. **VHS NO** *Woof!*

Bad Company Thoughtful study of two very different Civil War draft dodgers roaming the Western frontier and eventually turning to a fruitless life of crime. Both the cast and script are wonderful in an entertaining film that hasn't been given the attention it's due.

1972 (PG) 94m/C Jeff Bridges, Barry Brown, Jim Davis, John Savage; *D:* Robert Benton; *W:* David Newman. **VHS, Beta $14.95** *PAR* ♪♪♪½

Bad Day at Black Rock Story of a one-armed man uncovering a secret in a Western town. Wonderful performances from all concerned, especially Borgnine. Fine photography, shot using the new Cinemascope technique. Based on the novel by Howard Breslin.
1954 81m/C Spencer Tracy, Robert Ryan, Anne Francis, Dean Jagger, Walter Brennan, John Ericson, Ernest Borgnine, Lee Marvin; *D:* John Sturges. Academy Awards '54 Nominations: Best Actor (Tracy), Best Director (Sturges); Cannes Film Festival '55: Best Actor (Tracy). **VHS $19.98** *MGM, VYG, CRC* ♪♪♪½

Bad Dreams The only surviving member of a suicidal religious cult from the '60s awakens in 1988 from a coma. She is pursued by the living-dead cult leader, who seeks to ensure that she lives up (so to speak) to the cult's pact. Blood begins flowing as her fellow therapy group members begin dying, but the only bad dreams you'd get from this flick would be over the money lost on the video rental.
1988 (R) 84m/C Bruce Abbott, Jennifer Rubin, Richard Lynch, Harris Yulin, Dean Cameron, Elizabeth Daily, Susan Ruttan, Charles Fleischer; *D:* Andrew Fleming; *W:* Andrew Fleming, Steven E. de Souza; *M:* Jay Michael Ferguson. **VHS, Beta $89.98** *FOX* ♪½

Bad Georgia Road A New Yorker inherits a moonshine operation from her uncle, and fights off the syndicate for its profits.
1977 (R) 85m/C Gary Lockwood, Carol Lynley, Royal Dano, John Wheeler, John Kerry; *D:* John Broderick. **VHS, Beta $49.95** *VCI* ♪½

Bad Girls Latest in the current western craze turns the tables as women take their turns being the gunslingers. Four hooker chums hastily flee town after one kills a nasty customer—only to find the bank where their cash was stashed was robbed by baddies Loggia and Russo. Wearing stylish duds and with each hair perfectly in place the beauties manage to recover their loot. Unexciting script leaves a lot to be desired, but a strong performance from Stowe makes this nearly worthwhile. Lots of off-set drama with original director Tamra Davis fired, and the actresses reportedly having a less-than-bonding experience.
1994 (R) 99m/C Andie MacDowell, Madeleine Stowe, Mary Stuart Masterson, Drew Barrymore, James Russo, Dermot Mulroney, Robert Loggia, James LeGros; *D:* Jonathan Kaplan; *W:* Ken Friedman, Yolande Finch; *M:* Jerry Goldsmith. **VHS** *NYR* ♪♪½

Bad Girls Do Cry Unbelievably bad exploitation film. Idiotic plot with long scenes of girls stripping down to their undies. Although an American film, the voice track was dubbed in later.
1954 ?m/C Bill Page, Misty Ayers, Heather English, Ben Frommer. **VHS $16.95** *SNC, TPV Woof!*

Bad Girls Dormitory At the New York Female Juvenile Reformatory, suicide seems a painless and welcome escape. Utilizes standard genre identifiers, including rape, drugs, soapy showers, bad docs, and desperate young women trapped in a web of frustration and desire. Cheap and mindless titillation.
1984 (R) 95m/C Carey Zuris, Teresa Farley; *D:* Tim Kincaid. **VHS, Beta $49.95** *AHV* ♪♪

Bad Girls from Mars "B" movie sleaze-o-rama in which everyone is murdered, either before, after, or during sex, just like in real life. When the director of the film within this film hires an actress who is, shall we say, popular, to be the heroine of his latest sci-fier, the fun, slim as it is, begins.
1990 (R) 86m/C Edy Williams, Brinke Stevens, Jay Richardson, Oliver Darrow; *D:* Fred Olen Ray; *W:* Sherman Scott, Mark Thomas McGee. **VHS $89.95** *VMK Woof!*

Bad Girls Go to Hell From the sultana of sleaze, Wishman, comes this winning entry into Joe Bob Briggs' "Sleaziest Movies in the History of the World" series. A ditsy-but-sexy housewife accidentally commits murder and what follows is a plethora of perversion involving hirsute men and gender-bending women who are hell-bent on showing her how hot it is where bad girls go.
1965 98m/B *D:* Doris Wishman; *W:* Doris Wishman. **VHS $19.98** *SVI Woof!*

Bad Girls in the Movies A compilation of film clips depicting sleazy, criminal, female characters from women's prison films and other seedy sub-genres.
1986 56m/C David Carradine, Gene Autry, Yvonne De Carlo. **VHS, Beta $19.98** *LIV* ♪

Bad Guys A goulash western about the outlaw days of Hungary in the 1860s. A gang of bandits terrorizes the Transdanubian countryside. In Hungarian with English subtitles. For those seeking the Eastern European Wild West experience.
1979 93m/C *HU* Janos Derzsi, Djoko Rosic, Mari Kiss, Gyorgy Dorner, Laszlo Szabo, Miklos Benedek; *D:* Gyorgy Szomjas. **VHS $69.95** *EVD, FCT, ING* ♪♪

Bad Guys An inane comedy about two ridiculous policemen who decide to take the wrestling world by storm after being kicked off the police force. Featuring scenes with many of the world's most popular wrestlers.
1986 (PG) 86m/C Adam Baldwin, Mike Jolly, Michelle Nicastro, Ruth Buzzi, James Booth, Gene LeBell, Norman Burton; *D:* Joel Silberg; *M:* William Goldstein. **VHS $79.95** *LIV* ♪

Bad Influence A lackluster effort in the evil-doppelganger school of psychological mystery, where a befuddled young executive (Spader) is led into the seamier side of life by a mysterious stranger (Lowe).
1990 (R) 99m/C Rob Lowe, James Spader, Lisa Zane, Christian Clemenson, Kathleen Wilhoite; *D:* Curtis Hanson; *M:* Trevor Jones. **VHS, Beta $14.95** *COL* ♪½

Bad Jim A cowpoke buys Billy the Kid's horse and, upon riding it, becomes an incorrigible outlaw himself. First feature film for Hollywood legend Clark Gable's son.
1989 (PG) 110m/C James Brolin, Richard Roundtree, John Clark Gable, Harry Carey Jr., Ty Hardin, Pepe Serna, Rory Calhoun; *D:* Clyde Ware. **VHS, Beta $79.95** *COL* ♪½

Bad Lands A small cowboy posse finds themselves trapped with a band of Apache Indians in the Arizona desert. A remake of "The Lost Patrol."
1939 70m/B Robert Barratt, Guinn Williams, Douglas Walton, Andy Clyde, Addison Richards, Robert Coote, Paul Hurst, Noah Beery Jr.; *D:* Lew Landers. **VHS, Beta $19.98** *TTC* ♪♪½

Bad Lieutenant Social chaos and degeneration characterize story as well as nameless loner lieutenant Keitel, who is as corrupt as they come. Assigned to a case involving a raped nun, he's confronted by his own lagging Catholic beliefs and the need for saving grace. From cult filmmaker Ferrara ("Ms. 45") and filled with violence, drugs, and grotesque sexual situations. Tense,

over-the-top, urban drama is not intended for seekers of the subtle. Rent it with "Reservoir Dogs" and prepare yourself for a long tense evening of top-rated Keitel and screen-splitting violence. "R" rated version is also available at 91 minutes.
1992 (NC-17) 98m/C Harvey Keitel, Brian McElroy, Frankie Acciario, Peggy Gormley, Stella Keitel, Victor Argo, Paul Calderone, Leonard Thomas, Frankie Thorn; **D:** Abel Ferrara; **W:** Zoe Tamerlaine Lund, Abel Ferrara; **M:** Joe Delia. **VHS $19.98** *LIV, FCT ✶✶✶*

Bad Man of Deadwood A man-with-a-past joins a circus as a sharp-shooter, and is threatened with disclosure.
1941 54m/B Roy Rogers, George "Gabby" Hayes. **VHS, Beta $24.95** *DVT, NOS, RXM ✶*

Bad Manners When an orphan is adopted by a wealthy but entirely selfish couple, a group of his orphan friends try to free him from his new home and lifestyle.
1984 (R) 85m/C Martin Mull, Karen Black, Anne DeSalvo, Murphy Dunne, Pamela Segall, Edy Williams, Susan Ruttan, Richard Deacon; **D:** Bobby Houston. **VHS, Beta $19.95** *STE ✶*

Bad Man's River A Mexican revolutionary leader hires a gang of outlaws to blow up an arsenal used by the Mexican Army.
1972 92m/C *IT SP* Lee Van Cleef, James Mason, Gina Lollobrigida; **D:** Gene Martin; **W:** Philip Yordan. **VHS, Beta** *NO ✶✶*

Bad Medicine A youth who doesn't want to be a doctor is accepted by a highly questionable Latin American school of medicine. Remember that it was for medical students like these that the U.S. liberated Grenada.
1985 (PG-13) 97m/C Steve Guttenberg, Alan Arkin, Julie Hagerty, Bill Macy, Curtis Armstrong, Julie Kavner, Joe Grifasi, Robert Romanus, Taylor Negron, Gilbert Gottfried; **D:** Harvey Miller. **VHS, Beta $79.98** *FOX* Woof!

Bad Men of the Border Routine oater has Kirby posing as a bandit in order to infiltrate an outlaw band passing counterfeit money. He rounds up the bad guys and finds time to romance Armida too.
1945 56m/B Kirby Grant, Fuzzy Knight, Armida, John Eldridge, Francis McDonald; **D:** Wallace Fox; **W:** Adele Buffington. **VHS $19.99** *MOV ✶½*

The Bad News Bears Family comedy about a misfit Little League team that gets whipped into shape by a cranky, sloppy, beer-drinking coach who recruits a female pitcher. O'Neal and Matthau are top-notch. The kids' language is rather adult, and very titillating for younger viewers. Spawned two sequels and a television series.
1976 (PG) 102m/C Walter Matthau, Tatum O'Neal, Vic Morrow, Joyce Van Patten, Jackie Earle Haley; **D:** Michael Ritchie. **VHS, Beta, 8mm $14.95** *PAR ✶✶✶*

The Bad News Bears Go to Japan The second sequel, in which the famed Little League team goes to the Little League World Series in Tokyo. Comic adventure features Curtis as a talent agent out to exploit the team's fame.
1978 (PG) 102m/C Tony Curtis, Jackie Earle Haley, Tomisaburo Wakayama, George Wyner; **D:** John Berry. **VHS, Beta $19.95** *PAR ✶*

The Bad News Bears in Breaking Training With a chance to take on the Houston Toros for a shot at the little league baseball Japanese champs, the Bears devise a way to get to Texas to play at the famed Astrodome. Disappointing sequel to "The Bad News Bears"; followed by "The Bad News Bears Go to Japan" (1978).

1977 (PG) 105m/C William Devane, Clifton James, Jackie Earle Haley, Jimmy Baio; **D:** Michael Pressman; **W:** Paul Brickman. **VHS, Beta $14.95** *PAR ✶✶½*

Bad Ronald No, not a political biography of Ronald Reagan... Fascinating thriller about a disturbed teenager who kills a friend after being harassed repeatedly. The plot thickens after the boy's mother dies, and he is forced to hide out in a secret room when an unsuspecting family with three daughters moves into his house. The story is accurately recreated from the novel by John Holbrook Vance.
1974 78m/C Scott Jacoby, Pippa Scott, John Larch, Dabney Coleman, Kim Hunter, John Fiedler; **D:** Buzz Kulik. **VHS $49.95** *LIV ✶✶✶*

The Bad Seed A mother makes the tortuous discovery that her cherubic eight-year-old daughter harbors an innate desire to kill. Based on Maxwell Anderson's powerful Broadway stage play. Remade for television in 1985.
1956 129m/B Patty McCormack, Nancy Kelly, Eileen Heckart, Henry Jones, Evelyn Varden, Paul Fix; **D:** Mervyn LeRoy. Academy Awards '56 Nominations: Best Actress (Kelly), Best Black and White Cinematography, Best Supporting Actress (Heckart, McCormack); Golden Globe Awards '57: Best Supporting Actress (Heckart). **VHS, Beta $59.95** *WAR ✶✶½*

The Bad Seed Television remake of the movie with the same name. Story about a sadistic little child who kills for her own evil purposes. Acting is not up to par with previous version.
1985 100m/C Blair Brown, Lynn Redgrave, David Carradine, Richard Kiley, David Ogden Stiers, Carrie Wells; **D:** Paul Wendkos. **VHS $59.95** *NO ✶✶*

The Bad Sleep Well Japanese variation of the 1940 Warner Brothers crime dramas. A tale about corruption in the corporate world as seen through the eyes of a rising executive.
1960 135m/B *JP* Toshiro Mifune, Masayuki Kato, Masayuki Mori, Takashi Shimura, Akira Nishimura; **D:** Akira Kurosawa. **VHS, Beta** *COL, APD, ING ✶✶✶½*

Bad Taste A definite pleaser for the person who enjoys watching starving aliens devour the average, everyday human being. Alien fast-food manufacturers come to earth in hopes of harvesting all of mankind. The earth's fate lies in the hands of the government who must stop these rampaging creatures before the whole human race is gobbled up. Terrific make-up jobs on the aliens add the final touch to this gory, yet humorous cult horror flick.
1988 90m/C *NZ* Peter Jackson, Pete O'Herne, Mike Minett, Terry Potter, Craig Smith, Doug Wren, Dean Lawrie; **D:** Peter Jackson. **VHS $19.95** *FCT ✶✶✶*

Badge of the Assassin A television movie based on the true story of a New York assistant DA who directed a campaign to catch a pair of cop-killers from the '70s.
1985 96m/C James Woods, Yaphet Kotto, Alex Rocco, David Harris, Pam Grier, Steven Keats, Richard Bradford, Rae Dawn Chong; **D:** Mel Damski. **VHS, Beta $29.95** *VMK ✶✶*

Badge 373 In the vein of "The French Connection," a New York cop is suspended and decides to battle crime his own way.
1973 (R) 116m/C Robert Duvall, Verna Bloom, Eddie Egan; **D:** Howard W. Koch. **VHS, Beta $14.95** *PAR ✶½*

The Badlanders A western remake of the crime drama "The Asphalt Jungle." Ladd and Borgnine plan a gold robbery against Smith, who cheated them out of their share

in a gold mine. Cross and double-cross follow the partners as does romance.
1958 85m/C Alan Ladd, Ernest Borgnine, Kent Smith, Katy Jurado, Claire Kelly, Nehemiah Persoff, Adam Williams; **D:** Delmer Daves. **VHS $19.98** *MGM ✶✶✶*

Badlands Based loosely on the Charlie Starkweather murders of the 1950s, this impressive debut by director Malick recounts a slow-thinking, unhinged misfit's killing spree across the midwestern plains, accompanied by a starry-eyed 15-year-old school-girl. Sheen and Spacek are a disturbingly numb, apathetic, and icy duo.
1974 (PG) 94m/C Martin Sheen, Sissy Spacek, Warren Oates; **D:** Terence Malick; **W:** Terence Malick. **VHS, Beta $39.98** *WAR ✶✶✶½*

Badman's Territory A straight-shooting marshal has to deal with such notorious outlaws as the James and Dalton boys in a territory outside of government control.
1946 79m/B Randolph Scott, Ann Richards, George "Gabby" Hayes, Steve Brodie; **D:** Tim Whelan. **VHS, Beta $19.98** *RKO ✶✶✶*

Badmen of Nevada Badmen roam Nevada in the early days before law and order.
1933 57m/B Kent Taylor, Gail Patrick. **VHS, Beta $29.95** *VCN ✶½*

Baffled Nimoy is a race car driver who has visions of people in danger. He must convince an ESP expert (Hampshire) of the credibility of his vision, and then try to save the lives of the people seen with his sixth sense. Made for television.
1972 90m/C Leonard Nimoy, Susan Hampshire, Vera Miles, Rachel Roberts, Jewel Blanch, Christopher Benjamin; **D:** Philip Leacock. **VHS** *FOX ✶✶½*

Bagdad Cafe A large German woman, played by Sagebrecht, finds herself stranded in the Mojave desert after her husband dumps her on the side of the highway. She encounters a rundown cafe where she becomes involved with the off-beat residents. A hilarious story in which the strange people and the absurdity of their situations are treated kindly and not made to seem ridiculous. Spawned a short-lived TV series with Whoopi Goldberg. *AKA:* Out of Rosenheim.
1988 (PG) 91m/C *GE* Marianne Sagebrecht, CCH Pounder, Jack Palance, Christine Kaufmann, Monica Calhoun, Darron Flagg; **D:** Percy Adlon; **W:** Percy Adlon; **M:** Bob Telson. Academy Awards '88 Nominations: Best Song ("Calling You"); Cesar Awards '89: Best Foreign Film. **VHS, Beta $14.98** *FCT, VTR ✶✶✶*

Bahama Passage Trite story of one lady's efforts to win the affection of a macho Bahamas stud.
1942 83m/C Madeleine Carroll, Sterling Hayden, Flora Robson, Leo G. Carroll; **D:** Edward H. Griffith. **VHS** *PAR, MLB ✶✶½*

Bail Jumper A story of love and commitment against incredible odds; some of which happen to be a swarm of locusts, a tornado, and falling meteorites. Joe and Elaine are small-time hoods escaping their dreary lives in Murky Springs Missouri by heading for that great bastion of idyllism and idealism—New York City. But even as the world starts to crumble around them, get the message that love prevails.
1989 96m/C Eszter Balint, B.J. Spalding, Tony Askin, Joie Lee; **D:** Christian Faber. **VHS, Beta $79.95** *FXL ✶*

Bail Out Three bounty hunters, armed to the teeth, run a car-trashing police gauntlet so they may capture a valuable crook.
1990 (R) 88m/C David Hasselhoff, Linda Blair, John Vernon, Tom Rosales, Charlie Brill; **D:** Max Kleven. **VHS, Beta $89.98** *VES, LIV ✶*

Bail Out at 43,000 Movie about the lifestyles and love affairs of your average, everyday parachutist.
1957 80m/B John Payne, Karen Steele, Paul Kelly; *D:* Francis D. Lyon; *W:* Paul Monash. **VHS** *MGM &&*

Baja Oklahoma A made-for-cable-television film about a country barmaid with dreams of being a country singer. Songs by Willie Nelson, Emmylou Harris and Billy Vera.
1987 97m/C Lesley Ann Warren, Peter Coyote, Swoosie Kurtz, Willie Nelson, Julia Roberts; *D:* Bobby Roth; *W:* Bobby Roth. **VHS, Beta $19.98** *WAR, LHV &*

Baker's Hawk A young boy befriends a red-tailed hawk and learns the meaning of family and caring.
1976 98m/C Clint Walker, Diane Baker, Burl Ives; *D:* Lyman Dayton. **VHS, Beta $39.95** *BPG, HHE &&*

The Baker's Wife There's a new baker in town, and he brings with him to the small French village an array of tantalizing breads, as well as a discontented wife. When she runs off with a shepherd, her loyal and naive husband refuses to acknowledge her infidelity; however, in his loneliness, the baker can't bake, so the townspeople scheme to bring his wife back. Panned as overly cute Marcel Pagnol peasant glorification, and hailed as a visual poem full of wit; you decide. In French with subtitles. Also available for French students without subtitles; a French script booklet is also available. *AKA:* La Femme du Boulanger.
1933 101m/B *FR* Raimu, Ginette LeClerc, Charles Moulton, Charpin, Robert Vattier; *D:* Marcel Pagnol. **VHS, Beta $39.95** *INT, MRV, DVT &&& ½*

Bakery/Grocery Clerk A package of shorts featuring crazy comedian Larry Semon, getting tangled up in mayhem and molasses. Silent with piano score.
1921 55m/B Larry Semon, Oliver Hardy, Lucille Carlisle; *D:* Larry Semon. **VHS, Beta $19.98** *CCB &&*

Balalaika Rather dull operetta about the Russian revolution with Eddy playing a Russian prince. Eddy masquerades as a member of the proletariat in order to romance Massey, who was expected to become the next Garbo. Didn't happen, though. Eddy's rendition of "Stille Nacht" ("Silent Night") is highlight of film. Based on the operetta by Eric Maschwitz, George Ponford, and Bernard Gruen.
1939 102m/B Nelson Eddy, Ilona Massey, Charlie Ruggles, Frank Morgan, Lionel Atwill, Sir C. Aubrey Smith, Joyce Compton; *D:* Reinhold Schunzel; *W:* Leon Gordon, Charles Bennett, Jacques Deval. **VHS $19.98** *MGM &&*

Balboa Set on sun-baked Balboa Island, this is a melodramatic tale of high-class power, jealousy, and intrigue. Never-aired pilot for a television mini-series, in the nighttime soap tradition (even features Steve Kanaly from TV's "Dallas"). Special appearance by Cassandra Peterson, also known as horror hostess Elvira; and if that interests you, look for Sonny Bono, as well.
1982 92m/C Tony Curtis, Carol Lynley, Chuck Connors, Sonny Bono, Steve Kanaly, Jennifer Chase, Lupita Ferrer, Martine Beswick, Henry Jones, Cassandra Peterson; *D:* James Polakof. **VHS, Beta $69.98** *VES, LIV* Woof!

The Balcony A film version of the great Jean Genet play about a surreal brothel, located in an unnamed, revolution-torn city, where its powerful patrons act out their fantasies. Scathing and rude.

1963 87m/B Peter Falk, Shelley Winters, Lee Grant, Kent Smith, Peter Brocco, Ruby Dee, Jeff Corey, Leonard Nimoy, Joyce Jameson; *D:* Joseph Strick. **VHS, Beta $29.95** *MFV, ING &&&*

Balkan Express A crew of unlikely slobs become heroes in war-ravaged Europe.
1983 102m/C VHS, Beta $19.95 *STE, NWV & ½*

Ball of Fire A gang moll hides out with a group of mundane professors, trying to avoid her loathsome boyfriend. The professors are busy compiling an encyclopedia and Stanwyck helps them with their section on slang in the English language. Cooper has his hands full when he falls for this damsel in distress and must fight the gangsters to keep her. Stanwyck takes a personal liking to naive Cooper and resolves to teach him more than just slang.
1941 111m/B Gary Cooper, Barbara Stanwyck, Dana Andrews, Gene Krupa, Oscar Homolka, Dan Duryea, S.Z. Sakall, Henry Travers; *D:* Howard Hawks; *W:* Billy Wilder, Charles Brackett. **VHS, Beta $19.98** *SUE &&&*

Ballad in Blue Real life story of Ray Charles and a blind child. Tearjerker also includes some of Charles' hit songs. ♫I Got a Woman; What'd I Say?. *AKA:* Blues for Lovers.
1966 89m/B *GB* Ray Charles, Tom Bell, Mary Peach, Dawn Addams, Piers Bishop, Betty McDowall; *D:* Paul Henreid. **VHS, Beta $39.95** *LIV &&*

Ballad of a Gunfighter A feud between two outlaws reaches the boiling point when they both fall in love with the same woman.
1964 84m/C Marty Robbins, Bob Barron, Joyce Redd, Nestor Paiva, Laurette Luez; *D:* Bill Ward. **VHS, Beta $9.99** *FHE, PSM &*

Ballad of a Soldier As a reward for demolishing two German tanks, a nineteen-year-old Russian soldier receives a six-day pass so he can see his mother; however, he meets another woman. Well directed and photographed, while avoiding propaganda.
1960 88m/B *RU* Vladimir Ivashov, Shanna Prokhorenko; *D:* Grigori Chukrai. Academy Awards '61 Nominations: Best Story & Screenplay; British Academy Awards '61: Best Film. **VHS, Beta $24.95** *VYY, NOS, HHT &&& ½*

Ballad of Cable Hogue A prospector, who had been left to die in the desert by his double-crossing partners, finds a waterhole. A surprise awaits his former friends when they visit the remote well. Not the usual violent Peckinpah horse drama, but a tongue-in-cheek comedy romance mixed with tragedy. Obviously offbeat and worth a peek.
1970 (R) 122m/C Jason Robards Jr., Stella Stevens, David Warner, L.Q. Jones, Strother Martin, Slim Pickens; *D:* Sam Peckinpah; *M:* Jerry Goldsmith. **VHS, Beta $19.98** *WAR &&&*

Ballad of Gregorio Cortez Tragic story based on one of the most famous manhunts in Texas history. A Mexican cowhand kills a Texas sheriff in self-defense and tries to elude the law, all because of a misunderstanding of the Spanish language. Olmos turns in a fine performance as Cortez.
1983 (PG) 105m/C Edward James Olmos, James Gammon, Tom Bower, Alan Vint, Barry Corbin, Rosana De Soto, Bruce McGill, Brion James, Pepe Serna, William Sanderson; *D:* Robert M. Young; *W:* Robert M. Young. **VHS, Beta $14.98** *SUE, ING, NLC &&&*

The Ballad of Little Jo Inspired by a true story set during the 1866 gold rush. Easterner Josephine Monaghan is cast out of her wealthy family after she has a baby out of wedlock. Heading west, she passes her-

self off as a man—Little Jo—in an attempt to forestall harrasssment. Solemn and overly-earnest attempt by Greenwald to demystify the old west and bring a feminist viewpoint to a familiar saga.
1993 (R) 110m/C Suzy Amis, Bo Hopkins, Ian McKellan, Carrie Snodgress, David Chung, Rene Auberjonois, Heather Graham, Anthony Heald, Sam Robards, Ruth Maleczech; *D:* Maggie Greenwald; *W:* Maggie Greenwald; *M:* David Mansfield. **VHS** *COL && ½*

The Ballad of Narayama Director Imamura's subtle and vastly moving story takes place a vague century ago. In compliance with village law designed to control population among the poverty-stricken peasants, a healthy seventy-year-old woman must submit to solitary starvation atop a nearby mountain. We follow her as she sets into motion the final influence she will have in the lives of her children and grandchildren, a situation described with detachment and without imposing a tragic perspective. In Japanese with English subtitles. *AKA:* Narayama-Bushi-Ko.
1983 129m/C *JP* Ken Ogata, Sumiko Sakamoto, Takejo Aki, Tonpei Hidari, Shoichi Ozawa; *D:* Shohei Imamura; *W:* Shohei Imamura. **VHS $59.95** *HMV, FCT &&&&*

The Ballad of Paul Bunyan The good-humored, legendary American giant is pitted against a powerful lumber camp boss who likes to pick on the little guy.
1972 30m/C *D:* Arthur Rankin Jr., Jules Bass. **VHS $6.95** *STE, PSM &&&&*

The Ballad of the Sad Cafe Unusual love story set in a small Southern town during the Depression. The everday lives of its townspeople are suddenly transformed when a distant relation of the town's outcast (Redgrave) unexpectedly shows up. A moving story that tries to portray both sides of love and its power to enhance and destroy simultaneously. Emotion never seems to come to life in a movie that's nice to watch, but is ultimately disappointing. Adapted from the play by Edward Albee, which was based on the critically acclaimed novella by Carson McCullers. A British/U.S. co-production.
1991 (PG-13) 100m/C *GB* Vanessa Redgrave, Keith Carradine, Cork Hubbert, Rod Steiger, Austin Pendleton, Beth Dixon, Lanny Flaherty, Mert Hatfield, Earl Hindman, Anne Pitoniak; *D:* Simon Callow; *W:* Michael Hirst; *M:* Richard Robbins. **VHS** *NO && ½*

Ballbuster Cops take on gangs in an all-out high-stakes battle to win back the streets.
19?? 100m/C Ivan Rogers, Bonnie Paine, W. Randolph Galvin, Bill Shirk, Brenda Banet; *D:* Eddie Beverly Jr.; *W:* Eddie Beverly Jr. **VHS $39.95** *XVC && ½*

Ballet Shoes The classic children's tale of three sisters living a very sheltered life with their guardian Sylvia, who is working to support all four of them. A story of hope and possibilities. From the BBC Television network.
19?? 120m/C *GB* **VHS $29.95** *BFS, HMV &&*

The Balloonatic/One Week "The Balloonatic" (1923) features Keaton in several misadventures. In "One Week" (1920), Keaton and his new bride, Seely, receive a new home as a wedding gift—the kind you have to assemble yourself. Silent.
1923 48m/B Buster Keaton, Phyllis Haver, Sybil Seely; *D:* Buster Keaton. **VHS, Beta $17.95** *CCB &&*

Baltic Deputy An early forerunner of Soviet historic realism, where an aging intellectual deals with post-revolution Soviet life. In Russian with subtitles.

1937 95m/B RU Nikolai Cherkassov; D: Yosif Heifitz. VHS, Beta $35.95 FCT, IHF 🎬🎬🎬 ½

The Baltimore Bullet Two men make their living traveling through the country as pool hustlers, bilking would-be pool sharks. Features ten of the greatest pool players in the world.
1980 (PG) 103m/C James Coburn, Omar Sharif, Bruce Boxleitner, Ronee Blakley, Jack O'Halloran; D: Robert Ellis Miller; W: Robert Vincent O'Neil. VHS, Beta $9.98 SUE, NLC 🎬🎬

Bambi A true Disney classic, detailing the often harsh education of a newborn deer and his friends in the forest. Proves that Disney animation was—and still is—the best to be found. Thumper still steals the show and the music is delightful, including "Let's Sing a Gay Little Spring Song," "Love is a Song," "Little April Shower," "The Thumper Song," and "Twitterpated." Stands as one of the greatest children's films of all time; a genuine perennial from generation to generation. Based very loosely on the book by Felix Salten.
1942 (G) 69m/C D: David Hand; W: Larry Morey; M: Frank Churchill, Edward Plumb; V: Bobby Stewart, Peter Behn, Stan Alexander, Cammie King, Donnie Dunagan, Hardie Albright, John Sutherland, Tim Davis, Sam Edwards, Sterling Holloway, Anne Gillis, Perce Pearce. VHS, Beta $26.99 DIS, APD, RDG 🎬🎬🎬

The Bamboo Saucer Russian and American scientists race to find a U.F.O. in Red China. AKA: Collision Course.
1968 103m/C Dan Duryea, John Ericson, Lois Nettleton, Nan Leslie; D: Frank Telford. VHS $19.98 REP 🎬 ½

Bananas Intermittently hilarious pre-"Annie Hall" Allen fare is full of the director's signature angst-ridden philosophical comedy. A frustrated product tester from New York runs off to South America, where he volunteers his support to the revolutionary force of a shaky Latin-American dictatorship and winds up the leader. Don't miss cameos by Stallone and Garfield. Witty score contributes much.
1971 (PG) 82m/C Woody Allen, Louise Lasser, Carlos Montalban, Howard Cosell, Charlotte Rae, Conrad Bain; Cameos: Sylvester Stallone, Allen (Gooritz) Garfield; D: Woody Allen; W: Woody Allen; M: Marvin Hamlisch. VHS, Beta $14.95 MGM, FCT, FOX 🎬🎬🎬

Bananas Boat A captain takes a man and his daughter away from the collapsing government of their banana republic. The cast and director take a few risks but fail in this would-be comedy. AKA: What Changed Charley Farthing.
1978 91m/C GB Doug McClure, Hayley Mills, Lionel Jeffries, Dilys Hamlett, Warren Mitchell; D: Sidney Hayers. VHS $79.95 VCI Woof!

Band of Angels Orphaned Amantha (De Carlo) learns she has African-American blood and since it's the pre-Civil War era she promptly winds up on the auction block. She becomes both the property and the mistress of mysterious New Orleans landowner Hamish Bond (Gable). Then the Civil War comes along bringing threats and revelations. De Carlo looks properly sultry but this is a weak attempt at costume drama. Based on the novel by Robert Penn Warren.
1957 127m/C Clark Gable, Yvonne De Carlo, Sidney Poitier, Efrem Zimbalist Jr., Rex Reason, Patric Knowles, Torin Thatcher, Andrea King, Ray Teal; D: Raoul Walsh; W: John Twist, Ivan Goff; M: Max Steiner. VHS $29.99 WAR, MOV 🎬🎬 ½

Band of Outsiders A woman hires a pair of petty criminals to rip off her aunt; Godard vehicle for exposing self-reflexive comments on modern film culture. In French with English subtitles. AKA: Bande a Part; The Outsiders.
1964 97m/B FR Sami Frey, Anna Karina, Claude Brasseur, Louisa Colpeyn; D: Jean-Luc Godard; W: Jean-Luc Godard. VHS, Beta $49.95 ING, NOS, MRV 🎬🎬 ½

Band of the Hand A "Miami Vice" type melodrama about five convicts who are trained to become an unstoppable police unit. The first feature film by Glaser, last seen as Starsky in "Starsky & Hutch."
1986 (R) 109m/C Stephen Lang, Michael Carmine, Lauren Holly, Leon Robinson; D: Paul Michael Glaser; W: Jack Baran, Leo Garen. VHS, Beta NO 🎬

The Band Wagon A Hollywood song-and-dance man finds trouble when he is persuaded to star in a Broadway musical. Charisse has been called Astaire's most perfect partner, perhaps by those who haven't seen Rogers. ♫That's Entertainment; Dancing in the Dark; By Myself; A Shine On Your Shoes; Something to Remember You By; High and Low; I Love Louisa; New Sun in the Sky; I Guess I'll Have to Change My Plan; Louisiana Hayride; Triplets; The Girl Hunt.
1953 112m/C Fred Astaire, Cyd Charisse, Oscar Levant, Nanette Fabray, Jack Buchanan, Bobby Watson; D: Vincente Minnelli; M: Arthur Schwartz, Jason James Richter. VHS, Beta $19.98 MGM, FCT 🎬🎬🎬

Bandera Bandits An escaped convict, while evading a ruthless sheriff, marries a young girl and together they romp off into the sunset.
197? 98m/C Telly Savalas, Susan George. VHS, Beta $59.95 TWE Woof!

Bandit King of Texas A varmit is swindling unsuspecting settlers in a land scheme and then robbing and murdering them when they go to visit their supposed property. Rocky and friends come to the rescue.
1949 60m/B Allan "Rocky" Lane, Eddy Waller, Helene Stanley, Robert Bice, Harry Lauter, Jim Nolan, John Hamilton, Lane Bradford; D: Fred Brannon; W: Olive Cooper. VHS $11.95 GPV 🎬🎬 ½

Bandit Queen Spanish girl forms a band to stop seizure of Spanish possessions by lawless Californians.
1951 71m/B Barbara Britton, Willard Parker, Philip Reed, Jack Perrin; D: William Berke. VHS, Beta RXM 🎬 ½

Bandits Three cowboys team up with a band of Mexican outlaws to fight a Mexican traitor.
1973 83m/C Robert Conrad, Jan-Michael Vincent, Roy Jenson; D: Robert Conrad, Alfredo Zacharias. VHS, Beta $19.95 UNI 🎬 ½

Bandits Simon Verini (Yanne), a sophisticated fence, is given the loot from a 10 million dollar Cartier heist to exchange for cash by Mozart (Bruel) the leader of the thieves. But two of Mozart's gang want to keep the jewels instead and kidnap Verini's wife as ransom. She's killed, even after he returns the goods, and Verini is then framed for the theft and spends 10 years in prison. He's sent his daughter Marie-Sophie to a Swiss boarding school and upon his release works to both establish a relationship with her and to find those responsible for his wife's death. Director Lelouch's wife portrays the adult Marie-Sophie. In French with English subtitles.

1986 98m/C FR Jean Yanne, Marie-Sophie L(elouch), Patrick Bruel, Charles Gerard, Corinne Marchand, Christine Barbelivien; D: Claude Lelouch; W: Pierre Uytterhoeven, Claude Lelouch. VHS $89.95 FXL, FCT 🎬🎬 ½

Bandits of Orgosolo An acclaimed, patient drama about a Sardinian shepherd who shelters a band of thieves from the police. When one of the cops is killed the shepherd panics and flees into the hills for survival. Dubbed in English. AKA: Banditi a Orgosolo.
1961 98m/B IT Michele Cossu, Peppeddu Cuccu; D: Vittorio de Seta. VHS, Beta $24.95 NOS, FCT, VYY 🎬🎬 ½

Bandolero! In Texas, Stewart and Martin are two fugitive brothers who run into trouble with their Mexican counterparts.
1968 (PG) 106m/C James Stewart, Raquel Welch, Dean Martin, George Kennedy, Will Geer, Harry Carey Jr., Andrew Prine; D: Andrew V. McLaglen; M: Jerry Goldsmith. VHS, Beta $19.98 FOX 🎬🎬 ½

Bang Bang Kid A western spoof about a klutzy gunfighter defending a town from outlaws. AKA: Bang Bang.
1967 (G) 78m/C Tom Bosley, Guy Madison, Sandra Milo; D: Stanley Prager. VHS, Beta NO 🎬🎬

Bang the Drum Slowly The original television adaptation of a Mark Harris novel about baseball. A ball player stricken by a terminal illness strikes an unlikely friendship with a teammate. Interesting role for an actor (Newman) who claims to have been driven to acting by running away from the sporting goods business.
1956 60m/B Paul Newman, George Peppard, Albert Salmi. VHS $14.95 NOS, WKV 🎬🎬

Bang the Drum Slowly The touching story of a major league catcher who discovers that he is dying of Hodgkins disease and wants to play just one more season. De Niro is the weakening baseball player and Moriarty is the friend who helps him see it through. Based on a novel by Mark Harris.
1973 (PG) 97m/C Robert De Niro, Michael Moriarty, Vincent Gardenia, Phil Foster, Ann Wedgeworth, Heather MacRae, Selma Diamond, Danny Aiello; D: John Hancock. Academy Awards '73 Nominations: Best Supporting Actor (Gardenia); National Board of Review Awards '73: 10 Best Films of the Year; New York Film Critics Awards '73: Best Supporting Actor (De Niro). VHS, Beta $14.95 PAR, FCT 🎬🎬🎬

The Bank Dick Fields wrote the screenplay (using an alias) and stars in this zany comedy about a man who accidentally trips a bank robber and winds up as a guard. Fields' last major role is a classic, a worthy end to his great career. Side two of the laserdisc is in CAV format, which allows single frame access to the frenetic cops and robbers chase sequence. AKA: The Bank Detective.
1940 73m/B W.C. Fields, Cora Witherspoon, Una Merkel, Evelyn Del Rio, Jack Norton, Jessie Ralph, Franklin Pangborn, Shemp Howard, Grady Sutton, Russell Hicks, Richard Purcell, Reed Hadley; D: Eddie Cline; W: W.C. Fields, Mahatma Kane Jeeves. VHS, Beta $14.98 MCA 🎬🎬🎬🎬

Bank Shot Hilarious comedy about a criminal who plans to rob a bank by stealing the entire building. Based on the novel by Donald Westlake, and the sequel to "The Hot Rock."
1974 83m/C George C. Scott, Joanna Cassidy, Sorrell Booke, G. Wood, Clifton James, Bob Balaban, Bibi Osterwald; D: Gower Champion; W: Wendell Mayes. VHS NO 🎬🎬🎬

The Banker A cop, played by Forster, suspects a wealthy, highly influential banker of brutal serial killings.
1989 (R) 90m/C Robert Forster, Jeff Conaway, Leif Garrett, Duncan Regehr, Shanna Reed, Deborah Richter, Richard Roundtree, Teri Weigel, E.J. Peaker; **D:** William Webb. **VHS, Beta** NO ⅛⅛

Banzai Runner A cop whose brother was killed in an exclusive desert-highway race decides to avenge by joining the race himself.
1986 88m/C Dean Stockwell, John Shepherd, Charles Dierkop; **D:** John G. Thomas; **M:** Joel Goldsmith. **VHS, Beta $19.95** VMK ⅛⅛

Bar-20 Stage hold-ups and jewel robberies abound in this Hopalong Cassidy western.
1943 54m/B George Reeves, Douglas Fowley, William Boyd, Andy Clyde, Robert Mitchum, Victor Jory; **D:** Lesley Selander. **VHS, Beta $19.95** NOS, MRV, GVV ⅛½

Barabbas Barabbas, a thief and murderer, is freed by Pontius Pilate in place of Jesus. He is haunted by this event for the rest of his life. Excellent acting, little melodrama, lavish production make for fine viewing. Based on the novel by Lagerkvist.
1962 144m/C Anthony Quinn, Silvana Mangano, Arthur Kennedy, Jack Palance, Ernest Borgnine, Katy Jurado; **D:** Richard Fleischer. **VHS, Beta $59.95** COL ⅛⅛½

Barbarella Based on the popular French sci-fi comic strip drawn by Jean-Claude Forest, this cult classic details the bizarre adventures of a space nymphette (Fonda) encountering fantastic creatures and super beings. You'll see sides of Fonda you never saw before (not even in the workout videos). Notorious in its day; rather silly, dated camp now. Don't miss the elbow-sex scene. Terry Southern contributed to the script. **AKA:** Barbarella, Queen of the Galaxy.
1968 (PG) 98m/C Jane Fonda, John Phillip Law, David Hemmings, Marcel Marceau, Anita Pallenberg, Milo O'Shea; **D:** Roger Vadim; **W:** Terry Southern; **M:** Charles Fox. **VHS, Beta $19.98** FUS, PAR ⅛⅛½

Barbarian and the Geisha The first US diplomat in Japan undergoes culture shock as well as a passionate love affair with a geisha, circa 1856.
1958 104m/C John Wayne, Eiko Ando, Sam Jaffe, So Yamamura; **D:** John Huston; **M:** Hugo Friedhofer. **VHS, Beta $19.98** FOX ⅛⅛

Barbarian Queen Female warriors led by beauteous babe seek revenge for the capture of their men in this sword-and-sorcery epic. Low-budget rip-off "Conan the Barbarian" is laughable. Also available in an unrated version. Followed by "Barbarian Queen 2: The Empress Strikes Back."
1985 (R) 71m/C IT Lana Clarkson, Frank Zagarino, Katt Shea Ruben, Dawn Dunlap, Susana Traverso; **D:** Hector Olivera. **VHS, Beta $29.98** VES, LIV ⅛

Barbarian Queen 2: The Empress Strikes Back Apparently one movie wasn't enough to tell the beautiful Princess Athalia's story. This time she fights her evil brother Ankaris. He throws her in prison, she escapes, joins a band of female rebels, and leads them into battle. No better than the first attempt.
1989 (R) 87m/C IT Lana Clarkson, Greg Wrangler, Rebecca Wood, Elizabeth Jaegen, Roger Cundy; **D:** Joe Finley. **VHS $89.98** LIV ⅛

The Barbarians Two bodybuilder siblings in animal skins battle wizards and warlords in this dumb-but-fun U.S./Italian co-production. **AKA:** The Barbarians and Co.

1987 (R) 88m/C IT David Paul, Peter Paul, Richard Lynch, Eva LaRue, Virginia Bryant, Sheeba Alahani, Michael Berryman; **D:** Ruggero Deodato; **M:** Pino Donaggio. **VHS, Beta $19.95** MED, VTR ⅛

Barbarians at the Gate In the "greed is good" financial climate of the 80's, this made-for-cable movie chronicles the $25 billion dollar battle in 1988 for RJR Nabisco, which at the time was working on developing a "smokeless cigarette." Garner is CEO F. Ross Johnson, who is confident that their "smokeless cigarette" will boost the stock's value—until he gets the test-marketing results. Unwilling to risk the product's failure, Johnson decides to buy the company and is challenged by master dealer Kravis (Pryce). Fascinating social commentary on the nastiest mega-deal in history. Based on the book by Bryan Burrough and John Helyar.
1993 (R) 107m/C James Garner, Jonathan Pryce, Peter Riegert, Joanna Cassidy, Fred Dalton Thompson, Leilani Sarelle Ferrer, Matt Clark, Jeffrey DeMunn; **D:** Glenn Jordan; **W:** Larry Gelbart; **M:** Richard Gibbs. **VHS $92.99** HBO, FCT, BTV ⅛⅛⅛½

Barbarosa Offbeat western about an aging, legendary outlaw constantly on the lam who reluctantly befriends a naive farmboy and teaches him survival skills. Nelson and Busey are a great team, solidly directed. Lovely Rio Grande scenery.
1982 (PG) 90m/C Willie Nelson, Gilbert Roland, Gary Busey, Isela Vega; **D:** Fred Schepisi. **VHS, Beta $19.95** FOX ⅛⅛⅛

Barbary Coast A ruthless club owner tries to win the love of a young girl by building her into a star attraction during San Francisco's gold rush days.
1935 90m/B Edward G. Robinson, Walter Brennan, Brian Donlevy, Joel McCrea, Donald Meek, David Niven, Miriam Hopkins; **D:** Howard Hawks. **VHS, Beta** NO ⅛⅛⅛

The Barbary Coast A turn-of-the-century detective sleuths the streets of San Francisco in this average made-for-television movie.
1974 100m/C William Shatner, Dennis Cole, Lynda Day George, John Vernon, Charles Aidman, Michael Ansara, Neville Brand, Bill Bixby; **D:** Bill Bixby. **VHS** SUE, ORI ⅛⅛

The Barber Shop Fields portrays the bumbling, carefree barber Cornelius O'Hare, purveyor of village gossip and problem solver. Havoc begins when a gangster enters the shop and demands that Cornelius change his appearance.
1933 21m/B W.C. Fields, Elise Cavanna, Harry Watson, Dagmar Oakland, Frank Yaconelli. **VHS, Beta $24.98** CCB ⅛⅛

Barcelona Serious Ted (Nichols) is an American sales rep, posted to Barcelona, who can't quite get into the city's pleasure-loving rhythm. This is not a problem for Ted's cousin Fred (Eigeman), an obnoxious naval officer, with whom Ted had had a rivalry dating back to their boyhood. In the 1980s, the two must also deal with an anti-Americanism, which leads both to violence and romantic developments. Tart dialogue, thoughtful performances, and exotic locales prove enticing in low-budget sleeper that effectively mixes drama and dry comedy. Watch for Eigeman in Tom Cruise's uniform from "A Few Good Men."
1994 100m/C Taylor Nichols, Christopher Eigeman, Tushka Bergen, Mira Sorvino, Pep Munne, Francis Creighton, Thomas Gibson, Jack Gilpin, Nuria Badia, Hellena Schmied; **D:** Whit Stillman; **W:** Whit Stillman; **M:** Tom Judson, Mark Suozzo. **VHS** NYR ⅛⅛⅛

The Barcelona Kill When a journalist and her boyfriend get in too deep with the Barcelona mob, their troubles begin.
1977 86m/C Linda Hayden, John Astin, Simon Andrew, Maximo Valverde; **D:** Jose Antonio De La Loma. **VHS, Beta** NO ⅛½

Bare Essentials Made for TV yuppie Club Med nightmare in which a high-strung couple from New York find themselves marooned on a desert isle with only two other inhabitants. With no cellular telephoning ability and an absence of large-ticket consumer goods to purchase, the two turn their reluctant sights on each other, focusing on the bare essentials, as it were. Great soul-searching scenes for the inarticulate.
1991 (PG) 94m/C Gregory Harrison, Lisa Hartman, Mark Linn-Baker, Charlotte Lewis; **D:** Martha Coolidge. **VHS $89.98** REP ⅛

Bare Hunt Detective Max T. Unimportant is dragged into the underground world of prospective nude actresses in this supposedly funny "nudie." **AKA:** My Gun is Jammed; The Bear Hunt.
1963 69m/B **VHS, Beta $19.95** VDM, TPV ⅛

Bare Knees A woman causes a scandal in her family when she arrives at her sister's birthday party with bare knees, cigarettes, and other flapper items. The quintessential flapper movie.
1928 61m/B Virginia Lee Corbin, Donald Keith, Jane Winton, Johnnie Walker, Forrest Stanley, Maude Fulton; **D:** Erle C. Kenton. **VHS, Beta $17.95** GPV ⅛⅛

Bare Knuckles The adventures of a low-rent bounty hunter.
1977 (R) 90m/C Robert Viharo, Sherry Jackson, Michael Heit, Gloria Hendry, John Daniels; **D:** Don Edmunds. **VHS, Beta $59.95** TWE ⅛

The Barefoot Contessa The story, told in flashback, of a Spanish dancer's rise to Hollywood stardom, as witnessed by a cynical director. Shallow Hollywood self-examination.
1954 128m/C Ava Gardner, Humphrey Bogart, Edmond O'Brien, Valentina Cortese, Rossano Brazzi; **D:** Joseph L. Mankiewicz; **W:** Joseph L. Mankiewicz. Academy Awards '54: Best Supporting Actor (O'Brien); Nominations: Best Story & Screenplay; Golden Globe Awards '55: Best Supporting Actor (O'Brien). **VHS, Beta $19.98** MGM, FOX, FCT ⅛⅛⅛

The Barefoot Executive A mailroom boy who works for a national television network finds a chimpanzee that can pick hit shows in this Disney family comedy.
1971 92m/C Kurt Russell, John Ritter, Harry Morgan, Wally Cox, Heather North; **D:** Robert Butler. **VHS, Beta** DIS, OM ⅛⅛

Barefoot in Athens Television presentation from "George Schaefer's Showcase Theatre" chronicles the last years of the philosopher Socrates who, barefoot and unkempt, an embarrassment to his wife, and a dangerous critic to the corrupt Athenian leaders, nevertheless believes that democracy and truth are all-important in his city.
1966 76m/C Peter Ustinov, Geraldine Page, Anthony Quayle; **D:** George Schaefer. **VHS, Beta** FHS ⅛⅛

Barefoot in the Park Neil Simon's Broadway hit translates well to screen. A newly wedded bride (Fonda) tries to get her husband (Redford, reprising his Broadway role) to loosen up and be as free-spirited as she is.
1967 106m/C Robert Redford, Jane Fonda, Charles Boyer, Mildred Natwick; **D:** Gene Saks; **W:** Neil Simon. **VHS, Beta $14.95** PAR ⅛⅛⅛

Barfly Bukowski's semi-autobiographical screenplay is the story of a talented writer who chooses to spend his time as a lonely barfly, hiding his literary abilities behind glasses of liquor. Dunaway's character is right on target as the fellow alcoholic.
1987 (R) 100m/C Mickey Rourke, Faye Dunaway, Alice Krige, Frank Stallone, J.C. Quinn, Jack Nance; *D:* Barbet Schroeder; *W:* Charles Bukowski. **VHS, Beta, 8mm $19.98** *WAR, FCT ✺✺✺*

The Bargain Hart's first feature, in which he portrays a bandit desperately trying to go straight. Original titles with musical score.
1915 50m/B William S. Hart. **VHS, Beta $19.95** *NOS, GPV, DVT ✺½*

Baritone Concerned Polish drama about a prominent opera singer who promises to deliver a grand concert upon returning to his small town, only to lose his voice just before the show is to start. Proof positive that the opera ain't over 'til the fat lady sings.
1985 100m/C *PL* Zbigniew Zapassiewicz; *D:* Janusz Zaorski. **VHS $49.95** *FCT ✺✺*

Barjo In a bland and isolated French suburb lives willful housewife Fanfan (Bouchet) with her older businessman husband Charles (Bohringer) and her eccentric twin brother Barjo (Girardot). Barjo is obsessed with lists and extraterrestrials and his sister's affair with their next-door neighbor, which he likes to spy on. Her husband naturally begins to go crazy. Deadpan satire based on the novel "Confessions of a Crap Artist" by Philip K. Dick. The post-WWII American setting of the novel makes a decidedly uneasy transistion to contemporary French life. In French with English subtitles.
1993 85m/C *FR* Anne Brochet, Hippolyte Girardot, Richard Bohringer, Consuelo de Haviland, Renaud Danner, Nathalie Boutefeu; *D:* Jerome Boivin; *W:* Jerome Boivin, Jacques Audiard; *M:* Hughes LeBars. **VHS $89.98** *FXL ✺✺*

The Barkleys of Broadway The famous dancing team's last film together; they play a quarreling husband/wife showbiz team. ♫They Can't Take That Away From Me; The Sabre Dance; Swing Trot; Manhattan Downbeat; A Weekend in the Country; My One and Only Highland Fling; You'd Be Hard to Replace; Bouncin' the Blues; Shoes With Wings On; Piano Concerto in B-flat Minor.
1949 109m/C Fred Astaire, Ginger Rogers, Gale Robbins, Oscar Levant, Jacques Francois, Billie Burke; *D:* Charles Walters; *W:* Adolph Green, Betty Comden; *M:* Harry Warren, Ira Gershwin. **VHS, Beta $19.98** *MGM ✺✺✺*

Barn of the Naked Dead Prine plays a sicko who tortures women while his radioactive monster dad terrorizes the Nevada desert. Rudolph's first film, directed under the pseudonym Gerald Comier. Also on video as "Terror Circus" and "Nightmare Circus."
1973 86m/C Andrew Prine, Manuella Thiess, Sherry Alberoni, Gylian Roland, Al Cormier, Jennifer Ashley; *D:* Alan Rudolph. **VHS** *NO Woof!*

Barnaby and Me Australian star Barnaby the Koala Bear joins an international con-man in this romantic adventure. The mob is chasing the con-man when he meets and falls for a lovely young woman and her daughter.
1977 90m/C *AU* Sid Caesar, Juliet Mills, Sally Boyden; *D:* Norman Panama. **VHS, Beta $14.95** *ACA ✺✺*

Barnum P.T. Barnum's life is focused upon in this biography about the man who helped to form "The Greatest Show On Earth."
1986 100m/C Burt Lancaster, Hanna Schygulla, Jenny Lind, John Roney; *D:* Lee Philips. **VHS, Beta $29.95** *ACA ✺✺½*

The Baron Vengeance is the name of the game when an underworld boss gets stiffed on a deal. Fast-paced no-brainer street drama.
1988 88m/C Calvin Lockhart, Charles McGregor, Joan Blondell, Richard Lynch, Marlene Clark; *D:* Philip Fently. **VHS** *NO ✺½*

The Baron and the Kid A pool shark finds out that his opponent at a charity exhibition game is his long-lost son. Based on Johnny Cash's song. Made for TV.
1984 100m/C Johnny Cash, Darren McGavin, June Carter Cash, Richard Roundtree; *D:* Gary Nelson; *M:* Brad Fiedel. **VHS, Beta $59.98** *FOX ✺*

Baron Munchausen The German film studio UFA celebrated its 25th anniversary with this lavish version of the Baron Munchausen legend, starring a cast of top-name German performers at the height of the Third Reich. Filmed in Agfacolor; available in English subtitled or dubbed versions.
1943 120m/C *GE* Hans Albers, Kaethe Kaack, Hermann Speelmanns, Leo Slezak; *D:* Josef von Baky. **VHS, Beta $59.95** *ING, VCD, GLV ✺✺✺*

Baron of Arizona Land office clerk almost succeeds in convincing the U.S. that he owned the state of Arizona.
1951 99m/B Vincent Price, Ellen Drew, Beulah Bondi, Reed Hadley, Vladimir Sokoloff; *D:* Samuel Fuller; *W:* Samuel Fuller. **VHS, Beta** *RXM ✺✺✺*

Barracuda Lots of innocent swimmers are being eaten by crazed killer barracudas.
AKA: The Lucifer Project.
1978 (R) 90m/C Wayne Crawford, Jason Evers, Roberta Leighton; *D:* Harry Kerwin. **VHS, Beta** *NO Woof!*

The Barretts of Wimpole Street The moving, almost disturbing, account of poetess Elizabeth Barrett, an invalid confined to her bed, with only her poetry and her dog to keep her company. She is wooed by poet Robert Browning, in whose arms she finds true happiness and a miraculous recovery. Multi-faceted drama expertly played by all.
AKA: Forbidden Alliance.
1934 110m/B Fredric March, Norma Shearer, Charles Laughton, Maureen O'Sullivan, Katherine Alexander, Una O'Connor, Ian Wolfe; *D:* Sidney Franklin. **VHS $19.98** *MGM, CCB ✺✺✺*

Barry Lyndon Ravishing adaptation of the classic Thackeray novel about the adventures of an Irish gambler moving from innocence to self-destructive arrogance in the aristocracy of 18th Century England. Visually opulent. Kubrick received excellent performances from all his actors, and a stunning display of history, but the end result still overwhelms. O'Neal has seldom been better.
1975 (PG) 185m/C Ryan O'Neal, Marisa Berenson, Patrick Magee, Hardy Kruger, Guy Hamilton; *D:* Stanley Kubrick. Academy Awards '75: Best Art Direction/Set Decoration, Best Cinematography, Best Costume Design, Best Original Score; Nominations: Best Adapted Screenplay, Best Director (Kubrick), Best Picture; British Academy Awards '75: Best Director (Kubrick); National Board of Review Awards '75: 10 Best Films of the Year, Best Director (Kubrick). **VHS, Beta $29.95** *WAR ✺✺✺½*

Barry McKenzie Holds His Own In this sequel to "The Adventures of Barry McKenzie," we find that after a young man's aunt is mistaken for the Queen of England, two emissaries of Count Plasma of Transylvania kidnap her to use as a Plasma tourist attraction. Based on the 'Private Eye' comic strip, this crude Australian film is as disappointing as the first of the Barry McKenzie stories.
1974 93m/C *AU* Barry Humphries, Barry Crocker, Donald Pleasence; *D:* Bruce Beresford; *W:* Barry Humphries, Bruce Beresford. **VHS, Beta** *NO ✺✺*

Bartleby A new version of the classic Herman Melville short story. McEnery is Bartleby the clerk, who refuses to leave his job even after he's fired; Scofield is his frustrated boss.
1970 79m/C Paul Scofield, John McEnery, Colin Jeavons, Thorley Walters; *D:* Anthony Friedman. **VHS $29.95** *WST ✺✺½*

Barton Fink This eerie comic nightmare comes laden with awards (including the Palme D'Or from Cannes) but only really works if you care about the time and place. Fink is a trendy New York playwright staying in a seedy Hollywood hotel in the 1940s, straining to write a simple B-movie script. Macabre events, both real and imagined, compound his writer's block. Superb set design from Dennis Gassner complements an unforgettable cast of grotesques.
1991 (R) 116m/C John Turturro, John Goodman, Judy Davis, Michael Lerner, John Mahoney, Tony Shalhoub, Jon Polito, Steve Buscemi, David Warrilow, Richard Portnow, Christopher Murney; *D:* Joel Coen; *W:* Joel Coen, Ethan Coen; *M:* Carter Burwell. Academy Awards '91 Nominations: Best Art Direction/Set Decoration, Best Costume Design, Best Supporting Actor (Lerner); Cannes Film Festival '91: Best Actor (Turturro), Best Director (Coen), Best Film; Los Angeles Film Critics Association Awards '91: Best Supporting Actor (Lerner); New York Film Critics Awards '91: Best Supporting Actress (Davis). **VHS $19.98** *FXV, CCB ✺✺✺*

Based on an Untrue Story Campy spoof of popular "true story" television docudramas in which powerful Satin Chau (Fairchild), a perfume mogul, loses her sense of smell. Satin leaves her mentor Varda (Cannon) to discovery herself but finds that only her two separated-at-birth sisters, Velour (Lake) and Corduroy (Jackson), hold the secrets to the past. It's hard to spoof a genre that's become a cliche but this television movie does its best.
1993 90m/C Morgan Fairchild, Dyan Cannon, Victoria Jackson, Ricki Lake, Harvey Korman, Robert Goulet, Dan Hedaya; *D:* Jim Drake. **VHS** *FXV ✺✺½*

The Bashful Bachelor Yokel joker Abner trades his delivery car for a race horse, hoping to win a big race.
1942 78m/B Chester Lauck, Norris Goff, ZaSu Pitts, Grady Sutton, Louise Currie, Irving Bacon, Earle Hodgins, Benny Rubin; *D:* Malcolm St. Clair. **VHS $24.95** *NOS, RXM ✺✺*

Basic Instinct Controversial thriller had tongues wagging months before its theatrical release. Burnt-out detective Douglas falls for beautiful, manipulative murder suspect Stone, perfectly cast as a bisexual ice queen who may or may not have done the deed. Noted for highly erotic sex scenes and an expensive (3 million bucks) script; ultimately the predictable plot is disappointing. Gay activists tried to interrupt filming because they objected to the depiction of Stone's character but only succeeded in generating more free publicity. The American release was edited to avoid an "NC-17" rating, but an uncut, unrated video version is also available.
1992 (R) 123m/C Michael Douglas, Sharon Stone, George Dzundza, Jeanne Tripplehorn, Denis Arndt, Leilani Sarelle Ferrer, Bruce A. Young, Chelcie Ross, Dorothy Malone, Wayne Knight, Stephen Tobolowsky; *D:* Paul Verhoeven; *W:* Joe Eszterhas; *M:* Jerry Goldsmith. Academy Awards '92 Nominations: Best Film Editing, Best

Original Score; MTV Movie Awards '93: Best Actress (Stone), Most Desirable Female (Stone). **VHS, Beta** $49.98 *LIV, PMS* 🎬🎬½

Basic Training Three sexy ladies wiggle into the Pentagon in their efforts to clean up the government.
1986 (R) 85m/C Ann Dusenberry, Rhonda Shear, Angela Aames, Walter Gotell; *D:* Andrew Sugarman. **VHS, Beta** $79.98 *LIV, VES Woof!*

Basileus Quartet The replacement for a violinist in a well-established quartet creates emotional havoc. Beautiful music, excellent and evocative photography.
1982 118m/C *FR IT* Pierre Malet, Hector Alterio, Omero Antonutti, Michel Vitold, Alain Cuny, Gabriel Ferzetti, Elisabeth Kreuzer; *D:* Fabio Carpi. **VHS** $29.95 *TPV* 🎬🎬🎬

Basket Case A gory horror film about a pair of Siamese twins—one normal, the other gruesomely deformed. The pair is surgically separated at birth, and the evil disfigured twin is tossed in the garbage. Fraternal ties being what they are, the normal brother retrieves his twin—essentially a head atop shoulders—and totes him around in a basket (he ain't heavy). Together they begin twisted and deadly revenge, with the brother-in-a-basket in charge. Very entertaining, if you like this sort of thing. Followed by two sequels, if you just can't get enough.
1982 89m/C Kevin Van Hentenryck, Terri Susan Smith, Beverly Bonner; *D:* Frank Henenlotter. **VHS, Beta** $19.95 *MED* 🎬🎬🎬

Basket Case 2 Surgically separated teenage mutant brothers Duane and Belial are back! This time they've found happiness in a "special" family—until they're plagued by the paparazzi. Higher production values make this sequel slicker than its low-budget predecessor, but it somehow lacks the same charm.
1990 (R) 90m/C Kevin Van Hentenryck, Annie Ross, Kathryn Meisle, Heather Rattray, Jason Evers, Ted Sorel, Matt Mitler; *D:* Frank Henenlotter; *W:* Frank Henenlotter; *M:* Joe Renzetti. **VHS, Beta** $9.99 *STE, IME, SGE* 🎬🎬½

Basket Case 3: The Progeny In this sequel to the cult horror hits "Basket Case" and "Basket Case 2," Belial is back and this time he's about to discover the perils of parenthood as the mutant Mrs. Belial delivers a litter of bouncing mini-monsters. Everything is fine until the police kidnap the little creatures and chaos breaks out as Belial goes on a shocking rampage in his newly created mechanical body. Weird special effects make this a cult favorite for fans of the truly outrageous.
1992 (R) 90m/C Annie Ross, Kevin Van Hentenryck, Gil Roper, Tina Louise Hilbert, Dan Biggers, Jim O'Doherty; *D:* Frank Henenlotter; *W:* Robert Martin, Frank Henenlotter; *M:* Joe Renzetti. **VHS** $19.98 *MCA, SGE* 🎬🎬½

The Bastard Dashing (but alas, illegitimate) nobleman roams Europe on futile, Roots-like search, then settles for America during the Revolutionary War in this long-winded television adaptation of John Jakes' equally cumbersome bestseller (part of his popular Bicentennial series). Stevens stars, along with many supporting performers merely keeping active. Followed by "The Rebels" and "The Seekers." *AKA:* The Kent Chronicles.
1978 189m/C Andrew Stevens, Tom Bosley, Kim Cattrall, Buddy Ebsen, Lorne Greene, Olivia Hussey, Cameron Mitchell, Harry Morgan, Patricia Neal, Eleanor Parker, Donald Pleasence, William Shatner, Barry Sullivan, Noah Beery Jr., William Daniels, Keenan Wynn; *D:* Lee H. Katzin; *M:* John Addison. **VHS** $29.98 *MCA* 🎬🎬½

The Bat A bat-obsessed killer stalks the halls of a spooky mansion in this early film version of the Mary Roberts Rinehart novel.
1926 81m/B Andre de Beranger, Charles Herzinger, Emily Fitzroy, Louise Fazenda, Arthur Houseman, Robert McKim, Jack Pickford, Jewel Carmen; *D:* Roland West; *W:* Roland West. **VHS, Beta** $16.95 *SNC, FUS* 🎬🎬🎬

The Bat A great plot centering around a murderer called the Bat, who kills hapless victims by ripping out their throats when he isn't busy searching for a million dollars worth of securities stashed in the old house he is living in. Adapted from the novel by Mary Roberts Rinehart.
1959 80m/B Vincent Price, Agnes Moorehead, Gavin Gordon, John Sutton, Lenita Lane, Darla Hood; *D:* Crane Wilbur. **VHS, Beta** $16.95 *NOS, SNC, DVT* 🎬🎬

The Bat People Less-than-gripping horror flick in which Dr. John Bech is bitten by a bat while on his honeymoon. He then becomes a sadistic bat creature, compelled to kill anyone who stumbles across his path. The gory special effects make for a great movie if you've ever been bitten by that sort of thing. *AKA:* It Lives By Night.
1974 (R) 95m/C Stewart Moss, Marianne McAndrew, Michael Pataki, Paul Carr; *D:* Jerry Jameson. **VHS, Beta** $14.95 *HBO* 🎬

Bat 21 Hackman, an American officer, is stranded in the wilds of Vietnam alone after his plane is shot down. He must rely on himself and Glover, with whom he has radio contact, to get him out. Glover and Hackman give solid performances in this otherwise average film.
1988 (R) 112m/C Gene Hackman, Danny Glover, Jerry Reed, David Marshall Grant, Clayton Rohner, Erich Anderson, Joe Dorsey; *D:* Peter Markle; *W:* Marc Norman. **VHS, Beta** $19.98 *MED, VTR* 🎬🎬

The Bat Whispers A masked madman is stalking the halls of a creepy mansion; eerie tale that culminates in an appeal to the audience to keep the plot under wraps. Unusually crafted film for its early era. Comic mystery based on the novel and play by Mary Roberts Rinehart and Avery Hopwood.
1930 82m/B Chester Morris, Chance Ward, Richard Tucker, Wilson Benge, DeWitt Jennings, Una Merkel, Spencer Charters; *D:* Roland West; *W:* Roland West. **VHS** $24.95 *NOS, DVT, MLB* 🎬🎬½

Bataan A rugged war-time combat drama following the true story of a small platoon in the Philippines endeavoring to blow up a pivotal Japanese bridge. Also available in a colorized version.
1943 115m/B Robert Taylor, George Murphy, Thomas Mitchell, Desi Arnaz Sr., Lee Bowman, Lloyd Nolan, Robert Walker; *D:* Tay Garnett. **VHS, Beta** $59.95 *MGM, TLF* 🎬🎬½

Bathing Beauty This musical stars Skelton as a pop music composer with the hots for college swim teacher Williams. Rathbone is a music executive who sees the romance as a threat to Skelton's career and to his own profit margin. Full of aquatic ballet, Skelton's shtick, and wonderful original melodies. The first film in which Williams received star billing. ♫ I Cried for You; Bim, Bam, Boom; Tico-Tico; I'll Take the High Note; Loch Lomond; By the Waters of Minnetonka; Magic is the Moonlight; Trumpet Blues; Hora Staccato.
1944 101m/C Red Skelton, Esther Williams, Basil Rathbone, Bill Goodwin, Jean Porter, Carlos Ramirez, Donald Meek, Ethel Smith, Helen Forrest; *D:* George Sidney; *M:* Xavier Cugat. **VHS** $19.98 *MGM, TTC, FCT* 🎬🎬½

Batman Holy television camp, Batman! Will the caped crusader win the Bat-tle against the combined forces of the Joker, the Riddler, the Penguin, and Catwoman? Will Batman and Robin save the United World Security Council from dehydration? Will the Bat genius ever figure out that Russian journalist Miss Kitka and Catwoman are one and the same? Biff! Thwack! Socko! Not to be confused with the Michael Keaton version of the Dark Knight, this is the pot-bellied Adam West Batman, teeming with Bat satire and made especially for the big screen.
1966 104m/C Burt Ward, Adam West, Burgess Meredith, Cesar Romero, Frank Gorshin, Lee Meriwether; *D:* Leslie Martinson. **VHS, Beta** $19.98 *FOX* 🎬🎬½

Batman The blockbuster fantasy epic that renewed Hollywood's faith in media blitzing. The Caped Crusader is back in Gotham City, where even the criminals are afraid to walk the streets alone. There's a new breed of criminal in Gotham, led by the infamous Joker. Their random attacks via acid-based make-up are just the beginning. Keaton is surprisingly good as the dual personality hero though Nicholson steals the show. Marvelously designed and shot. Much better on the big screen. Followed in 1992 by "Batman Returns."
1989 (PG-13) 126m/C Michael Keaton, Jack Nicholson, Kim Basinger, Robert Wuhl, Tracy Walter, Billy Dee Williams, Pat Hingle, Michael Gough, Jack Palance, Jerry Hall; *D:* Tim Burton; *W:* Sam Hamm, Warren Skaaren; *M:* Danny Elfman, Prince. **VHS, Beta, 8mm** $19.98 *FOX, WAR* 🎬🎬🎬½

Batman: Mask of the Phantasm Based on the Fox television series with the animated Batman fending off old enemy the Joker, new enemy the Phantasm, and dreaming of his lost first love. Cartoon film noir set in the 1940's but filled with '90s sarcasm. Complicated storyline with a stylish dark look may be lost on the kiddies but adults will stay awake. *AKA:* Batman: The Animated Movie.
1993 (PG) 77m/C *D:* Eric Radomski, Bruce W. Timm; *W:* Michael Reaves, Alan Burnett, Paul Dini, Martin Pako; *M:* Shirley Walker; *V:* Kevin Conroy, Dana Delany, Mark Hamill, Stacy Keach, Hart Bochner, Abe Vigoda, Efrem Zimbalist Jr., Dick Miller. **VHS** $19.96 *WAR* 🎬🎬🎬

Batman Returns More of the same from director Burton, with Batman more of a supporting role overshadowed by provocative villains. DeVito is the cruely misshapen Penguin who seeks to rule over Gotham City; Pfeiffer is the exotic and dangerous Catwoman— who has more than a passing purrsonal interest in Batman; Walken is the maniacal tycoon Max Shreck. Pfeiffer fares best in her wickedly sexy role and second-skin costume (complete with bullwhip). Plot is secondary to special effects and nightmarish settings. Despite a big budget, this grandiose sequel is of the love it or leave it variety.
1992 (PG-13) 126m/C Michael Keaton, Danny DeVito, Michelle Pfeiffer, Christopher Walken, Michael Gough, Michael Murphy, Cristi Conaway, Pat Hingle, Vincent Schiavelli, Jan Hooks, Paul (Pee Wee Herman) Reubens, Andrew Bryniarski; *D:* Tim Burton; *W:* Daniel Waters; *M:* Danny Elfman. **VHS** $19.98 *WAR* 🎬🎬½

*batteries not included As a real estate developer fights to demolish a New York tenement, the five remaining residents are aided by tiny metal visitors from outer space in their struggle to save their home. Each resident gains a renewed sense of life in this sentimental, wholesome family film produced by Spielberg. Cronyn and Tandy keep the schmaltz from getting out of hand. Neat little space critters. **1987 (PG) 107m/C** Hume Cronyn, Jessica Tandy, Frank McRae, Michael Carmine, Elizabeth Pena, Dennis Boutsikaris; *D:* Matthew Robbins; *W:* Matthew Robbins, Brad Bird, Brent Maddock, S.S. Wilson; *M:* James Horner. **VHS, Beta $19.95** MCA *♂♂½*

Battle Beneath the Earth The commies try to undermine democracy once again when American scientists discover a Chinese plot to invade the U.S. via a series of underground tunnels. Perhaps a tad jingoistic. **1968 112m/C** *GB* Kerwin Mathews, Peter Arne, Viviane Ventura, Robert Ayres; *D:* Montgomery Tully. **VHS, Beta $59.95** MGM *♂♂*

Battle Beyond the Stars The planet Akir must be defended against alien rapscallions in this intergalactic Corman creation. Sayles authored the screenplay and co-authored the story on which it was based. **1980 (PG) 105m/C** Richard Thomas, Robert Vaughn, George Peppard, Sybil Danning, Sam Jaffe, John Saxon, Darlanne Fluegel; *D:* Jimmy T. Murakami; *W:* John Sayles; *M:* James Horner. **VHS, Beta $19.98** VES, LIV *♂♂½*

Battle Beyond the Sun Former Russian movie "Nebo Zowet" is Americanized. Everyone is trying to send a mission to Mars. Roger Corman was the producer, Thomas Colchart is a pseudonym for Francis Ford Coppola. **1963 75m/C** Edd Perry, Arla Powell, Bruce Hunter, Andy Stewart; *D:* Francis Ford Coppola; *M:* Les Baxter. **VHS $16.95** NOS, SNC *♂♂*

Battle Circus Sappy drama casts Bogart as a surgeon at a M*A*S*H unit during the Korean War. Allyson is a combat nurse who finds love amongst the harsh reality of a war zone. Bogart was badly miscast and his performance proves it. Weak script and uninspired performances don't help this depressing story. **1953 90m/B** Humphrey Bogart, June Allyson, Keenan Wynn, Robert Keith, William Campbell; *D:* Richard Brooks; *W:* Richard Brooks. **VHS $19.98** MGM *♂½*

Battle Cry A group of U.S. Marines train, romance, and enter battle in WWII. Based on the novel by Leon Uris. Part of the "A Night at the Movies" series, this tape simulates a 1955 movie evening, with a cartoon, "Speedy Gonzales," a newsreel, and coming attractions for "Mr. Roberts" and "East of Eden." **1955 169m/C** Van Heflin, Aldo Ray, Mona Freeman, Tab Hunter, Dorothy Malone, Anne Francis, James Whitmore, Raymond Massey; *D:* Raoul Walsh. **VHS, Beta $69.95** WAR *♂♂♂*

Battle for the Planet of the Apes A tribe of human atomic bomb mutations are out to make life miserable for the peaceful ape tribe. The story is told primarily in flashback with the opening and closing sequences taking place in the year 2670 A.D. Final chapter in the five-movie simian saga. **1973 (G) 96m/C** Roddy McDowall, Lew Ayres, John Huston, Paul Williams, Claude Akins, Severn Darden, Natalie Trundy; *D:* J. Lee Thompson. **VHS, Beta $19.98** FOX *♂♂*

Battle Hell The true story of how a British ship was attacked by the Chinese Peoples Liberation Army on the Yangtze River in 1949. *AKA:* Yangtse Incidents. **1956 112m/B** *GB* Richard Todd, Akim Tamiroff, Keye Luke; *D:* Michael Anderson Sr. **VHS, Beta** NO *♂♂*

The Battle of Algiers Famous, powerful, award-winning film depicting the uprisings against French Colonial rule in 1954 Algiers. A seminal documentary-style film

which makes most political films seem ineffectual by comparison in its use of nonprofessional actors, gritty photography, realistic violence, and a boldly propagandistic sense of social outrage. **1966 123m/B** *AL IT* Yacef Saadi, Jean Martin, Brahim Haggiag, Tommaso Neri, Samia Kerbash, Fawzia el Kader, Michele Kerbash, Mohamed Ben Kassen; *D:* Gillo Pontecorvo; *W:* Franco Solinas; *M:* Ennio Morricone. Academy Awards '66 Nominations: Best Foreign Language Film; Academy Awards '68: Best Director (Pontecorvo), Best Story & Screenplay; Venice Film Festival '66: Best Film. **VHS, Beta $29.95** ING, IHF, TPV *♂♂♂½*

The Battle of Austerlitz Ambitious but numbing costume drama about the events leading up to the epic battle between Napoleon and the overwhelming forces of the Czar and the Austrian Emperor at Austerlitz. Napoleon won. Film has been drastically cut from original 166 minute release. Watch director Gance's silent version, "Napoleon," for a truly epic experience. *AKA:* Austerlitz. **1960 (PG) 123m/C** *FR IT YU* Claudia Cardinale, Martine Carol, Leslie Caron, Vittorio De Sica, Jean Marais, Ettore Manni, Jack Palance, Orson Welles; *D:* Abel Gance. **VHS $69.95** LIV, TPV *♂♂*

The Battle of Blood Island Two G.I.s, one Christian and one Jewish, face death at the hands of the Japanese during WWII. Still, they bicker incessantly before finally pulling together to save themselves. **1960 64m/B** Richard Devon, Ron Kennedy; *D:* Joel Rapp. **VHS, Beta $16.95** NOS, SNC *♂*

Battle of Britain A powerful retelling of the most dramatic aerial combat battle of WWII, showing how the understaffed Royal Air Force held off the might of the German Luftwaffe. **1969 (G) 132m/C** Michael Caine, Laurence Olivier, Trevor Howard, Kenneth More, Christopher Plummer, Robert Shaw, Susannah York, Ralph Richardson, Curt Jurgens, Michael Redgrave, Nigel Patrick, Edward Fox; *D:* Guy Hamilton. **VHS, Beta $19.98** MGM, FOX *♂♂½*

Battle of China A look at the people, culture, and industry of China, and Japan's total commitment to conquer the country during WWII, through authentic newsreel footage. **1944 67m/B** *D:* Frank Capra. **VHS, Beta $19.98** MPI, MRV, HHT *♂♂½*

The Battle of El Alamein Action filled movie about the alliance of Italy and Germany in a war against the British, set in a North African desert in the year 1942. **1968 105m/C** *IT FR* Frederick Stafford, Ettore Manni, Robert Hossein, Michael Rennie, George Hilton, Ira Furstenberg; *D:* Calvin Jackson Padget. **VHS, Beta $14.95** CNG, MRV, GEM *♂♂*

Battle of Elderbush Gulch An ancient pioneering western short famous for innocently employing the now-established cliches of bad guy, good guy, and helpless frontier heroine. One of Gish's first films. **1913 22m/B** Lillian Gish; *D:* D.W. Griffith. **VHS, Beta $29.95** VCN, PYR, GVV *♂♂*

Battle of Neretva During WWII, Yugoslav partisans are facing German and Italian troops and local Chetniks as they battle for freedom. Big budget war film lost continuity with U.S. cut. **1969 106m/C** *YU* Yul Brynner, Curt Jurgens, Orson Welles, Hardy Kruger, Franco Nero, Sergei Bondarchuk; *D:* Veljko Bulajic. **VHS $39.98** ING, REP *♂♂*

The Battle of Russia Hitler's forces are victorious in Moscow and Leningrad but are thoroughly defeated at the battle of Stalingrad. Authentic newsreel footage.

1944 83m/B *D:* Frank Capra. **VHS, Beta $19.98** HHT, MRV, CCB *♂♂*

The Battle of San Pietro John Huston's powerful documentary about the famous battle in Italy's Liri Valley, stressing the number of losses sustained in taking this military objective. The film was almost suppressed by the U.S. government, because it was considered to be too strong for general release. **1944 43m/B** John Huston. **VHS, Beta $19.98** IHF, WFV, FUS *♂♂*

Battle of the Bulge A recreation of the famous offensive by Nazi Panzer troops on the Belgian front during 1944-45, an assault that could have changed the course of WWII. **1965 141m/C** Henry Fonda, Robert Shaw, Robert Ryan, Dana Andrews, Telly Savalas, Ty Hardin, Pier Angeli, George Montgomery, Charles Bronson; *D:* Ken Annakin; *W:* Philip Yordan. **VHS, Beta $59.95** WAR *♂♂*

Battle of the Bullies A made-for-television special about an unsalvageable nerd who plots a high-tech revenge upon a slew of high school bullies. **1985 45m/C** Manny Jacobs, Christopher Barnes, Sarah Inglis. **VHS, Beta $19.95** NWV Woof!

Battle of the Commandos A tough Army colonel leads a group of convicts on a dangerous mission to destroy a German-built cannon before it's used against the Allied Forces. *AKA:* Legion of the Damned. **1971 94m/C** *IT* Jack Palance, Curt Jurgens, Thomas Hunter, Robert Hunter; *D:* Umberto Lenzi. **VHS $39.98** REP *♂*

Battle of the Eagles Follows the true adventures of the "Partisan Squadron," the courageous airmen known as the "Knights of the Sky" during WWII in Yugoslavia. **1981 102m/C** Bekim Fehmiu, George Taylor, Gloria Samara, Frank Phillips; *D:* Tom Raymonth. **VHS, Beta** NO *♂½*

The Battle of the Japan Sea A Japanese epic, dubbed in English, centering around the historic WWII battle between Japan and Russia. **1970 (G) 120m/C** *JP* Toshiro Mifune. **VHS, Beta $69.95** VCD *♂♂*

The Battle of the Sexes Sophisticated British comedy has mild-mannered Sellers trying to prevent a business takeover by the brash American Cummings. A good supporting cast and the impeccable Sellers make this one unique. Adapted from the James Thurber short story "The Catbird Seat." **1960 88m/B** *GB* Peter Sellers, Robert Morley, Constance Cummings, James B. Clark; *D:* Charles Crichton. **VHS, Beta** MRV *♂♂♂*

Battle of the Worlds Typical low-budget science fiction. A scientist tries to stop an alien planet from destroying the Earth. Even an aging Rains can't help this one. Poorly dubbed in English. *AKA:* Il Pianeta Degli Uomini Spenti; Planet of the Lifeless Men. **1961 84m/C** *IT* Claude Rains, Maya Brent, Bill Carter, Marina Orsini, Jacqueline Derval; *D:* Anthony M. (Antonio Margheretti) Dawson. **VHS $16.95** SNC, MRV *♂*

Battle of Valiant Thundering hordes of invading barbarians trample the splendor of ancient Rome beneath their grimy sandals. **1963 90m/C** Gordon Mitchell, Ursula Davis, Massimo Serato; *D:* John Gentil. **VHS, Beta** NO *♂*

Battle Shock Painter is accused of murdering a cantina waitress while on his honeymoon in Mexico. *AKA:* A Woman's Devotion; War Shock.

1956 88m/C Ralph Meeker, Janice Rule, Paul Henreid; *D:* Paul Henreid; *M:* Les Baxter. **VHS** $39.95 *REP* 🎬½

Battleforce Exciting battle scenes lose their power in the confusion of this mixed-up WWII film about Rommel's last days. Dubbed sequences, news-reel vignettes and surprise performances by big name stars are incomprehensibly glued together. *AKA:* The Battle of the Mareth Line; The Greatest Battle.
1978 97m/C *GE YU* Henry Fonda, Stacy Keach, Helmut Berger, Samantha Eggar, Giuliano Gemma, John Huston; *D:* Umberto Lenzi. **VHS, Beta** $9.99 *QVD, TLF* 🎬

Battleground A tightly-conceived post-WWII character drama, following a platoon of American soldiers through the Battle of the Bulge. Available in a Colorized version.
1949 118m/B Van Johnson, John Hodiak, James Whitmore, George Murphy, Ricardo Montalban, Marshall Thompson, Jerome Courtland, Don Taylor, Bruce Cowling, Leon Ames, Douglas Fowley, Richard Jaeckel, Scotty Beckett; *D:* William A. Wellman; *W:* Robert Pirosh. Academy Awards '49: Best Black and White Cinematography, Best Story & Screenplay; Nominations: Best Director (Wellman), Best Film Editing, Best Picture, Best Supporting Actor (Whitmore); Golden Globe Awards '50: Best Screenplay, Best Supporting Actor (Whitmore). **VHS, Beta** $19.98 *MGM* 🎬🎬🎬

The Battleship Potemkin Eisenstein's best work documents mutiny aboard the Russian battleship Potemkin in 1905 which led to a civilian uprising against the Czar in Odessa, and the resulting crackdown by troops loyal to the Czar. Beautiful cinematography, especially the use of montage sequences, changed filmmaking. In particular, a horrifying sequence depicting the slaughter of civilians on an Odessa beach by soldiers coming down the stairs leading to it is exceptional; many movies pay homage to this scene including "The Untouchables" and "Love and Death." Viewers should overlook obvious Marxist overtones and see this film for what it is: a masterpiece. *AKA:* Potemkin; Bronenosets Potemkin.
1925 71m/B *RU* Alexander Antonov, Vladimir Barsky, Grigori Alexandrov, Mikhail Gomorov, Sergei Eisenstein; *D:* Sergei Eisenstein. **VHS, Beta** $19.98 *REP, MRV, NOS* 🎬🎬🎬🎬

Battlestar Galactica Plot episode of the sci-fi television series which was later released in the theaters. The crew of the spaceship Galactica must battle their robot enemies in an attempt to reach Earth. Contains special effects designed by John "Star Wars" Dykstra. Individual episodes of the series are also available.
1978 (PG) 125m/C Lorne Greene, Dirk Benedict, Karen Jensen, Jane Seymour, Patrick Macnee, Terry Carter, John Colicos, Richard A. Colla, Laurette Spang, Richard Hatch; *D:* Richard A. Colla. **VHS, Beta** $14.98 *MCA, MOV* 🎬🎬½

Battling Bunyon A wily youngster becomes a comedy boxer for profit, and eventually gets fed up and battles the champ. Silent.
1924 71m/B Chester Conklin, Wesley Barry, Mollie Malone, Jackie Fields. **VHS, Beta** $16.95 *GPV, VYY* 🎬🎬½

Battling Butler Rich young Keaton tries to impress a young lady by impersonating a boxer. All goes well until he has to fight the real thing. Mostly charming if uneven; one of Keaton's more unusual efforts, thought to be somewhat autobiographical. Silent.
1926 70m/B Buster Keaton, Sally O'Neil, Snitz Edwards, Francis McDonald, Mary O'Brien, Tom Wilson, Walter James; *D:* Buster Keaton. **VHS** *NO* 🎬🎬½

Battling for Baby It's the war of the Grandmas. New mother Katherine decides to return to work and both her mother and mother-in-law want to look after the little tyke. Silly made-for-TV fluff.
1992 93m/C Courteney Cox, Suzanne Pleshette, Debbie Reynolds, John Terlesky, Doug McClure, Leigh Lawson, Mary Jo Catlett; *D:* Art Wolff; *W:* Walter Lockwood, Nancy Silvers. **VHS** $89.98 *TTC* 🎬🎬

Battling Marshal Fast-moving action western starring Carson.
1948 52m/B Sunset Carson, Lee Roberts; *D:* Oliver Drake. **VHS, Beta** $29.95 *VCN* 🎬½

Battling Orioles The once scrappy baseball team is now a bunch of grumpy old men, that is until Glenn whips them into shape. Silent.
1924 7m/B Glenn Tryon, Blanche Mehaffey; *D:* Hal Roach. **VHS, Beta, 8mm** $35.95 *GVV* 🎬½

Battling Outlaws Western featuring American cowboy Bob Steele.
1947 64m/B Bob Steele. **VHS, Beta** $19.95 *NOS, VCN* 🎬½

Battling with Buffalo Bill Twelve episodes of the vintage serial concerning the exploits of the legendary Indian fighter.
1931 180m/B Tom Tyler, Rex Bell, Franklin Farnum. **VHS, Beta** $29.95 *VCN* 🎬½

The Bawdy Adventures of Tom Jones An exploitive extension of the Fielding novel about the philandering English lad, with plenty of soft-core skin and lewdness.
1976 (R) 89m/C *GB* Joan Collins, Trevor Howard, Terry-Thomas, Arthur Lowe; *Murray Melvin; D:* Cliff Owen. **VHS, Beta** $59.95 *MCA* 🎬½

Baxter A bull terrier lives his life with three different sets of masters. He examines all of humankind's worst faults and the viewer quickly realizes that Baxter's life depends on his refusal to obey like a good dog should. Based on the novel by Ken Greenhall. Funny, sometimes erotic, quirky comedy. In French with English subtitles.
1989 82m/C *FR* Lisa Delamare, Jean Mercure, Jacques Spiesser, Catherine Ferran, Jean-Paul Roussillon, Sabrina Leurquin; *D:* Jerome Boivin; *W:* Jerome Boivin, Jacques Audiard; *M:* Marc Hillman, Patrick Roffe. **VHS** $89.95 *FXL, PMS* 🎬🎬½

The Bay Boy Set in the 1930s in Nova Scotia, this period piece captures the coming-of-age of a rural teenage boy. Young Sutherland's adolescent angst becomes a more difficult struggle when he witnesses a murder, and is tormented by the secret.
1985 (R) 107m/C *CA* Liv Ullmann, Kiefer Sutherland, Peter Donat, Matthieu Carriere, Joe MacPherson, Isabelle Mejias, Alan Scarfe, Chris Wiggins, Leah K. Pinsent; *D:* Daniel Petrie; *M:* Claude Bolling. **VHS, Beta** $79.98 *ORI* 🎬🎬½

Bayou Romance Painter inherits a Louisiana plantation, moves in, and falls in love with a young gypsy.
1986 90m/C Annie Potts, Michael Ansara, Barbara Horan. **Beta** $14.95 *PSM* 🎬

Be My Valentine, Charlie Brown The Peanuts gang endures the follies of the heart on St. Valentine's Day. Animated.
1975 30m/C *D:* Phil Roman. **VHS, Beta** $9.98 *MED, VTR, WTA* 🎬

Beach Blanket Bingo Fifth entry in the "Beach Party" series (after "Pajama Party") is by far the best and has achieved near-cult status. Both Funicello and Avalon are back, but this time a very young Evans catches Avalon's eye. Throw in a mermaid, some moon-doggies, skydiving, sizzling beach parties, and plenty of nostalgic golly-

gee-whiz fun and you have the classic '60s beach movie. Totally implausible, but that's half the fun when the sun-worshiping teens become involved in a kidnapping and occasionally break into song. Followed by "How to Stuff a Wild Bikini." 🎵Beach Blanket Bingo; The Cycle Set; Fly Boy; The Good Times; I Am My Ideal; I Think You Think; It Only Hurts When I Cry; New Love; You'll Never Change Him.
1965 96m/C Frankie Avalon, Annette Funicello, Linda Evans, Don Rickles, Buster Keaton, Paul Lynde, Harvey Lembeck, Deborah Walley, John Ashley, Jody McCrea, Marta Kristen, Timothy Carey, Earl Wilson, Bobbi Shaw; *D:* William Asher; *W:* Sher Townsend, Leo Townsend; *M:* Les Baxter. **VHS, Beta** *NO* 🎬🎬🎬

Beach Boys: An American Band An in-depth look at the lives and music of the Beach Boys with a soundtrack that features over forty of their songs.
1985 (PG-13) 103m/C Brian Wilson, Carl Wilson, Dennis Wilson, Mike Love, Al Jardine, Bruce Johnson; *D:* Malcolm Leo. **VHS, Beta** $29.95 *MVD, LIV, VES* 🎬🎬

Beach Girls Three voluptuous coeds intend to re-educate a bookish young man and the owner of a beach house.
1982 (R) 91m/C Debra Blee, Val Kline, Jeana Tomasina, Adam Roarke; *D:* Patrice Townsend. **VHS, Beta** $39.95 *PAR* 🎬

The Beach Girls and the Monster Here's one on the cutting edge of genre bending: while it meticulously maintains the philosophical depth and production values of sixties beach bimbo fare, it manages to graft successfuly with the heinous critter from the sea genre to produce a hybrid horror with acres o'flesh.
1965 70m/B Jon Hall, Sue Casey, Walker Edmiston; *D:* Jon Hall; *M:* Frank Sinatra Jr. **VHS** $19.98 *SNC* 🎬

Beach House In this boring comedy, adolescents frolic on the beach, get inebriated, and listen to rock 'n' roll.
1982 76m/C Kathy McNeil, Richard Duggan, Ileana Seidel, John Cosola, Spence Waugh, Paul Anderson, John A. Gallagher. **VHS, Beta** *NO* 🎬

Beach Party Started the "Beach Party" series with the classic Funicello/Avalon combo. Scientist Cummings studying the mating habits of teenagers intrudes on a group of surfers, beach bums, and bikers, to his lasting regret. Typical beach party bingo, with sand, swimsuits, singing, dancing, and bare minimum in way of a plot. Followed by "Muscle Beach Party." 🎵Beach Party; Don't Stop Now; Promise Me Anything; Secret Surfin' Spot; Surfin' and a-Swingin'; Treat Him Nicely.
1963 101m/C Frankie Avalon, Annette Funicello, Harvey Lembeck, Robert Cummings, Dorothy Malone, Morey Amsterdam, Jody McCrea, John Ashley, Candy Johnson, Dolores Wells, Yvette Vickers, Eva Six; *D:* William Asher; *W:* Lou Rusoff; *M:* Les Baxter. **VHS, Beta** *NO* 🎬🎬

Beachcomber Comedy set in the Dutch East Indies about a shiftless beachcomber (Laughton) who falls in love with a missionary's prim sister (Lanchester), as she attempts to reform him. The real-life couple of Laughton and Lanchester are their usual pleasure to watch. Remade in 1954. Story by W. Somerset Maugham. *AKA:* Vessel of Wrath.
1938 88m/B *GB* Charles Laughton, Elsa Lanchester, Robert Newton, Tyrone Guthrie; *D:* Erich Pommer. **VHS, Beta** $19.95 *NOS, MRV, DVT* 🎬🎬🎬

Beaches Based on the novel by Iris Rainer Dart about two girls whose friendship survived the test of time. The friendship is renewed once more when one of the now middle-aged women learns that she is dying slowly of a fatal disease.
1988 (PG-13) 123m/C Bette Midler, Barbara Hershey, John Heard, Spalding Gray, Lainie Kazan, James Read; *D:* Garry Marshall; *W:* Mary Agnes Donoghue; *M:* Georges Delerue. **VHS, Beta, 8mm $19.99** *TOU, JCF ♪♪♪ 1/2*

Beaks: The Movie Two television reporters try to figure out why birds of prey are suddenly attacking humans. Owes nothing to Hitchcock's "The Birds." *AKA:* Birds of Prey.
1987 (R) 86m/C Christopher Atkins, Michelle Johnson; *D:* Rene Cardona Jr. **VHS, Beta $14.95** *LIV* Woof!

The Bear Breathtaking, effortlessly entertaining family film about an orphaned bear cub tagging after a grown male and dealing with hunters. The narrative is essentially from the cub's point of view, with very little dialogue. A huge money-maker in Europe. Based on a novel by James Oliver Curwood.
1989 (PG) 92m/C *FR* Jack Wallace, Tcheky Karyo, Andre Lacombe; *D:* Jean-Jacques Annaud; *W:* Gerard Brach, Michael Kane; *M:* Bill Conti. **VHS, Beta $14.95** *COL, RDG, HMV ♪♪♪*

Bear Island Group of secret agents cleverly disguising themselves as U.N. weather researchers converge upon Bear Island in search of a Nazi U-Boat. Looks like rain.
1980 (PG) 118m/C Donald Sutherland, Richard Widmark, Barbara Parkins, Vanessa Redgrave, Christopher Lee, Lloyd Bridges; *D:* Don Sharp. **VHS, Beta $19.95** *STE ♪ 1/2*

The Bears & I A young Vietnam vet helps Indians regain their land rights while raising three bear cubs. Beautiful photography in this Disney production.
1974 (G) 89m/C Patrick Wayne, Chief Dan George, Andrew Duggan, Michael Ansara; *D:* Bernard McEveety; *M:* Buddy Baker. **VHS $69.95** *DIS ♪♪*

The Beast Violent and cliche-driven war drama notable for its novel twist: wild Russian tank officer becomes lost in the Afghanistan wilderness while being tracked by Afghan rebels with revenge in mind. Filmed in the Israel desert and adapted by William Mastrosimone from his play. *AKA:* The Beast of War.
1988 (R) 93m/C George Dzundza, Jason Patric, Steven Bauer, Stephen Baldwin, Don Harvey, Kabir Bedi, Erik Avari, Haim Gerafi; *D:* Kevin Reynolds; *W:* William Mastrosimone; *M:* Mark Isham. **VHS, Beta $89.95** *COL ♪♪ 1/2*

The Beast from Haunted Cave Gold thieves hiding in a wilderness cabin encounter a spiderlike monster. Surprisingly good performances from Sinatra (Frank's nephew) and Carol. Produced by Gene Corman, Roger's brother.
1960 64m/B Michael Forest, Sheila Carol, Frank Wolff, Richard Sinatra, Wally Campo; *D:* Monte Hellman; *W:* Charles B. Griffith. **VHS $19.98** *DVT, MRV, SNC ♪♪*

The Beast from 20,000 Fathoms Atomic testing defrosts a giant dinosaur in the Arctic; the hungry monster proceeds onwards to its former breeding ground, now New York City. Oft-imitated saurian-on-the-loose formula is still fun, brought to life by Ray Harryhausen special effects. Based loosely on the Ray Bradbury story "The Foghorn."

1953 80m/B Paul Christian, Paula Raymond, Cecil Kellaway, Kenneth Tobey, Donald Woods, Lee Van Cleef, Steve Brodie, Mary Hill; *D:* Eugene Lourie. **VHS, Beta $19.95** *WAR, FCT, MLB ♪♪ 1/2*

Beast in the Cellar Every family has something to hide, and in the case of two spinster sisters, it's their murderous inhuman brother, whom they keep chained in the cellar. Like all brothers, however, the "beast" rebels against his sisters' bossiness and escapes to terrorize their peaceful English countryside. The sisters' (Reid and Robson) performances aren't bad, but rest of effort is fairly disappointing. *AKA:* Are You Dying Young Man?.
1970 (R) 85m/C *GB* Beryl Reid, Flora Robson, T.P. McKenna; *D:* James Kelly. **VHS, Beta** *NO ♪ 1/2*

Beast of Morocco Interesting vampire film about a Morrocan vampire princess who sets her sights on seducing a noted archaeologist. Of course his girlfriend ends up being abducted by the vampire's servant. *AKA:* Hand of Night.
1966 ?m/C *GB* William Sylvester, Alizia Gur, Terence de Marney. **VHS $16.95** *SNC ♪♪*

Beast of the Yellow Night A dying soldier sells his soul to Satan at the close of WWII. Years later, existing without aging, he periodically turns into a cannibal monster. Although the first half is tedious, the monster turns things around when he finally shows up. Decent gore effects.
1970 (R) 87m/C *PH* John Ashley, Mary Wilcox, Eddie Garcia, Vic Diaz; *D:* Eddie Romero. **VHS, Beta $19.95** *NOS, VCI, INC* Woof!

The Beast of Yucca Flats A really cheap, quasi-nuclear protest film. A Russian scientist is chased by communist agents into a nuclear testing area and is caught in an atomic blast. As a result, he turns into a club-weilding monster. Voice over narration is used in lieu of dialogue as that process proved too expensive.
1961 53m/B Tor Johnson, Douglas Mellor, Larry Aten, Barbara Francis; *D:* Coleman Francis; *W:* Coleman Francis. **VHS $12.95** *SNC, CNM, MLB* Woof!

The Beast that Killed Women Colonists at a sunny Florida nudist camp have their beach party interrupted by an escaped gorilla. Director Mahon, in his first color effort, stretches this panicky moment into an hour of fleshy fun and games.
1965 60m/C *D:* Barry Mahon. **VHS $24.95** *SMW, TPV ♪♪ 1/2*

The Beast with Five Fingers After a pianist mysteriously dies and leaves his fortune to his private nurse, the occupants of his villa are terrorized by a creature that turns out to be the pianist's hand which was severed by his personal secretary (Lorre). Lorre is also terrorized by hallucinations of the hand, and no matter what he does to stop it (nail it to a desk, throw it in the fire, etc.), nothing can keep the hand from carrying out its mission. A creepy thriller with inventive shots of the severed hand.
1946 88m/B Robert Alda, Andrea King, Peter Lorre, Victor Francen, J. Carroll Naish, Charles Dingle; *D:* Robert Florey. **VHS $19.98** *MGM ♪♪ 1/2*

The Beast Within Young woman has the misfortune of being raped by an unseen creature in a Mississippi swamp. Seventeen years later, her son conceived from that hellish union begins to act quite strange, developing a penchant for shedding his skin before turning into an insect-like critter with a cannibalistic appetite. First film to use the air

"bladder" type of prosthetic make-up popularized in later, and generally better, horror films. Contains some choice cuts in photo editing: the juxtaposition of hamburger and human "dead meat" is witty. Based on Edward Levy's 1981 novel.
1982 (R) 98m/C Ronny Cox, Bibi Besch, L.Q. Jones, Paul Clemens, Don Gordon; *D:* Philippe Mora; *W:* Tom Holland; *M:* Les Baxter. **VHS, Beta $14.95** *MGM ♪♪*

Beastmaster Adventure set in a wild and primitive world. The Beastmaster is involved in a life-and-death struggle with overwhelming forces of evil. Campy neanderthal flesh flick.
1982 (PG) 119m/C Marc Singer, Tanya Roberts, Rip Torn, John Amos, Josh Milrad, Billy Jacoby; *D:* Don A. Coscarelli. **VHS, Beta $19.98** *MGM ♪♪*

Beastmaster 2: Through the Portal of Time This time the laughs are intentional as the Beastmaster follows an evil monarch through a dimensional gate to modern-day L.A., where the shopping is better for both trendy clothes and weapons. Fun for genre fans, with a behind-the-scenes featurette on the tape.
1991 (PG-13) 107m/C Marc Singer, Kari Wuhrer, Sarah Douglas, Wings Hauser, James Avery, Robert Fieldsteel, Arthur Malet, Robert Z'Dar, Michael Berryman; *D:* Sylvio Tabet; *M:* Robert Folk. **VHS $14.98** *REP ♪ 1/2*

Beasts A young couple's plans for a romantic weekend in the Rockies are slightly changed when the pair are savagely attacked by wild beasts.
1983 92m/C Tom Babson, Kathy Christopher, Vern Potter. **VHS, Beta $49.95** *PSM ♪*

The Beat Unrealistic film about a bookish new kid who intercedes in the tension between two rival street gangs, changing their lives in his literary way.
1988 101m/C John Savage, Kara Glover, Paul Dillon, David Jacobson, William McNamara; *D:* Peter Mones; *M:* Carter Burwell. **VHS, Beta $79.98** *LIV, VES ♪*

Beat Girl An architect's rebellious teenage daughter sinks to the bottom and gets involved in murder along the way. *AKA:* Wild For Kicks.
1960 85m/B *GB* David Farrar, Noelle Adam, Christopher Lee, Gillian Hills, Shirley Anne Field, Oliver Reed; *D:* Edmond T. Greville; *M:* John Barry. **VHS $29.95** *SNC, FCT, HEG ♪♪*

Beat Street Intended as a quick cash-in on the break dancing trend, this essentially plotless musical features kids trying to break into local show biz with their rapping and dancing skills. Features the music of Afrika Bambaata and the Soul Sonic Force, Grand Master Melle Mel and the Furious Five, and others. ♪Beat Street Breakdown; Baptize the Beat; Stranger in a Strange Land; Beat Street Strut; Us Girls; This Could Be the Night; Breakers Revenge; Tu Carino (Carmen's Theme); Frantic Situation.
1984 (PG) 106m/C Rae Dawn Chong, Leon Grant, Saundra Santiago, Guy Davis, Jon Chardiet, Duane Jones, Kadeem Hardison; *D:* Stan Lathan. **VHS, Beta $79.98** *VES, LIV ♪♪ 1/2*

Beat the Devil Each person on a slow boat to Africa has a scheme to beat the other passengers to the uranium-rich land that they all hope to claim. An unusual black comedy which didn't fare well when released, but over the years has come to be the epitome of spy-spoofs.
1953 89m/C Humphrey Bogart, Gina Lollobrigida, Peter Lorre, Robert Morley, Jennifer Jones; *D:* John Huston. **VHS, Beta $9.95** *CNG, MRV, NOS ♪♪♪*

Beatlemania! The Movie Boring look at the Fab Four. Not the real Beatles, but impersonators who do a very inadequate job. Based on the equally disappointing stage show. *AKA:* Beatlemania.
1981 86m/C Mitch Weissman, Ralph Castelli, David Leon, Tom Teeley; *D:* Joseph Manduke. VHS, Beta *IME* ⅟

The Beatniks Story about the dark secrets of the beat generation in which a man is promised fame and fortune by an agent, but his dreams are dashed when his friend commits murder. A big waste of time.
1960 78m/B Tony Travis, Peter Breck, Karen Kadler, Joyce Terry; *D:* Paul Frees. VHS **$16.95** *SNC, TPV* ⅟

Beatrice In France during the Middle Ages, a barbaric soldier of the Hundred Years' War returns to his estate that his daughter has maintained, only to brutalize and abuse her. In French with English subtitles. *AKA:* La Passion Beatrice.
1988 (R) 132m/C *FR* Julie Delpy, Barnard Pierre Donnadieu, Nils Tavernier; *D:* Bertrand Tavernier; *W:* Colo Tavernieu O'Hagan. VHS, Beta *NO* ⅟⅟⅟½

Beau Brummel The famous silent adaptation of the Clyde Fitch play about an ambitious English dandy's rise and fall.
1924 80m/B John Barrymore, Mary Astor, Willard Louis, Irene Rich, Carmel Myers, Alec B. Francis, William Humphreys; *D:* Harry Beaumont. VHS, Beta **$19.95** *NOS, HHT, VYY* ⅟⅟½

Beau Brummel Lavish production casts Granger in the role of the rags-to-riches dandy and chief adviser to the Prince of Wales. Born into a life of poverty, George Bryan Brummel uses wit and intelligence to meet the vain Prince and ingratiate himself to the future king (George IV). He also manages to catch the eye of Taylor, who falls in love with him. Outstanding period piece cinematography, sets, and costumes. Shot on location in England's beautiful countryside, many of the interior shots are from a 15th-century mansion, Ockwell Manor, located near Windsor Castle. Remake of the 1924 silent film starring John Barrymore. Based on the play by Clyde Fitch.
1954 113m/C Stewart Granger, Elizabeth Taylor, Peter Ustinov, Robert Morley, James Donald, James Hayter, Rosemary Harris, Paul Rogers, Noel Willman, Peter Dyneley, Charles Carson; *D:* Curtis Bernhardt; *W:* Karl Tunberg. VHS **$19.98** *MGM* ⅟⅟⅟

Beau Geste The classic Hollywood adventure film based on the Percival Christopher Wren story about three brothers who join the Foreign Legion after nobly claiming responsibility for a jewel theft they didn't commit. Once enlisted, they must face desert wars and the most despicable commanding officer ever, before clearing their family name. A rousing, much-copied epic.
1939 114m/B Gary Cooper, Ray Milland, Robert Preston, Brian Donlevy, Donald O'Connor, J. Carroll Naish, Susan Hayward, James Stephenson; *D:* William A. Wellman. VHS, Beta **$29.95** *MCA* ⅟⅟⅟½

Beau Pere Bittersweet satiric romp from Blier about the war zone of modern romance, wherein a 30-year-old widower falls madly in love with his 14-year-old stepdaughter. Sharp-edged and daring. In French with subtitles.
1981 125m/C *FR* Patrick Dewaere, Nathalie Baye, Ariel Besse, Maurice Ronet; *D:* Bertrand Blier. VHS, Beta **$59.95** *MED, ING* ⅟⅟⅟

Beau Revel Critically acclaimed romantic drama of the silent era. A passionate dancing girl played by Vidor, one of the twenties' more prolific romantic leads (and erstwhile wife of director King Vidor) is the object of romantic interest of a father and son, which leaves the threesome lovelorn, suicidal, and emotionally scarred. You might recognize Stone from his later role as Judge Hardy in the MGM "Hardy Family" series.
1921 70m/B Lewis Stone, Florence Vidor, Lloyd Hughes, Katherine Kirkham, William Conklin; *D:* John Wray. VHS, Beta **$24.95** *GPV, FCT* ⅟⅟⅟½

The Beautiful Blonde from Bashful Bend Charming comedy-western gets better with age. Grable is the pistol packing mama mistaken for the new school teacher. Fun performances by all, especially Herbert.
1949 77m/C Betty Grable, Cesar Romero, Rudy Vallee, Olga San Juan, Hugh Herbert, Porter Hall, Sterling Holloway, El Brendel; *D:* Preston Sturges. VHS **$19.98** *FOX* ⅟⅟½

Beautiful Dreamers Maurice Bucke is a young Canadian physician who runs the London Insane Asylum. After a chance meeting with poet Walt Whitman, both men discover their mutual outrage for current treatment of the mentally ill. However, Bucke persuades Whitman to visit his asylum in order to try Whitman's theory of human compassion on the asylum's inmates. However, Bucke runs into opposition from the local townspeople, scandalized by Whitman's radical reputation. Fairly humdrum with a larger-than-life performance by Torn as Whitman. Based on Whitman's visit to Canada in 1880.
1992 (PG-13) 108m/C *CA* Rip Torn, Colm Feore, Wendel Meldrum, Sheila McCarthy, Colin Fox; *D:* John Kent Harrison; *W:* John Kent Harrison. VHS **$9.95** *HMD, FCT* ⅟½

Beauty and the Beast The classic medieval fairy tale is brought to life on the big screen for the first time. Beauty takes the place of her father after he is sentenced to die by the horrible Beast and falls in love with him. Cocteau uses the story's themes and famous set-pieces to create a cohesive and captivating surreal hymn to romantic love that is still the definitive version of B&B. In French with subtitles. *AKA:* La Belle et Laete.
1946 90m/B *FR* Jean Marais, Josette Day, Marcel Andre, Mila Parely, Nane Germon, Michel Auclair, Georges Auric; *D:* Jean Cocteau. VHS, Beta **$19.95** *ING, SUE, MLB* ⅟⅟⅟⅟

Beauty and the Beast From "Faerie Tale Theatre" comes the story of a Beauty who befriends a Beast and learns a lesson about physical appearance and true love.
1983 60m/C Susan Sarandon, Susan Sarandon, Klaus Kinski, Anjelica Huston, Klaus Kinski, Stephen Elliott; *D:* Roger Vadim. VHS, Beta **$12.95** *WTA, FOX, FCT* ⅟⅟⅟⅟

Beauty and the Beast Wonderful Disney musical combines superb animation, splendid characters, and lively songs about a beautiful girl, Belle, and the fearsome and disagreeable Beast. Supporting cast includes the castle servants (a delightful bunch of household objects). Notable as the first animated feature to be nominated for the Best Picture Oscar. Destined to become a classic. The deluxe video version features a work-in-progress rough film cut, a compact disc of the soundtrack, a lithograph depicting a scene from the film, and an illustrated book. ♫Beauty and the Beast; Belle; Something There; Be Our Guest.
1991 (G) 84m/C *D:* Kirk Wise, Gary Trousdale; *M:* Alan Menken, Howard Ashman; *V:* Paige O'Hara, Robby Benson, Rex Everhart, Richard White, Jesse Corti, Angela Lansbury, Jerry Orbach, David Ogden Stiers, Bradley Michael Pierce, Jo Anne Worley, Kimmy Robertson. Academy Awards '91: Best Song ("Beauty and the Beast"), Best Score; Nominations: Best Picture, Best Song ("Belle", "Be Our Guest"), Best Sound; Golden Globe Awards '92: Best Film—Musical/Comedy. VHS **$24.99** *DIS, OM* ⅟⅟⅟⅟

Beauty and the Beast: Once Upon a Time in New York When socialite attorney Catherine Chandler is brutally attacked in New York, Vincent, a mysterious man/beast, rescues and befriends her, taking her to his fantastical subterranean world. Pilot for the popular television series. Additional episodes are available.
1987 48m/C Ron Perlman, Linda Hamilton, Roy Dotrice, Ray Wise. VHS **$14.98** *REP, MOV* ⅟⅟⅟⅟

Beauty for the Asking It sounds like a workable Lucille Ball vehicle—a beautician develops a bestselling skin cream—and even the title sounds like something you'd like to love Lucy in. But somehow the numerous plot implausibilities managed to get by the story's five writers, and the idea of a jilted woman making millions while being financed by her ex's wife just doesn't fly (perhaps it was an idea ahead of its time). Die-hard Lucy fans may find this interesting.
1939 68m/B Lucille Ball, Patric Knowles, Donald Woods, Frieda Inescort, Frances Mercer; *D:* B.P. Fineman. VHS **$19.98** *TTC, FCT* ⅟

Beauty on the Beach A comedy about a mad psychologist, his bizarre experiments with women, and his eventual descent into insanity. In Italian with English subtitles.
196? 90m/C *IT* Valeria Fabrizi. VHS, Beta *NO* ⅟

Bebe's Kids When ladies' man Robin falls for the lovely Jamika, he gets some unexpected surprises when he takes her out on a first date to an amusement park—and she brings along four kids. Animated comedy takes some funny pot-shots at both black and white culture and Disneyland. The children are amusing, especially baby PeeWee, a tot with chronically dirty diapers and Tone Loc's gravelly voice. Based on characters created by the late comedian Robin Harris. The video includes the seven-minute animated short "Itsy Bitsy Spider."
1992 (PG-13) 74m/C *D:* Bruce Smith; *W:* Reginald Hudlin; *M:* John Barnes; *V:* Faizon Love, Vanessa Bell Calloway, Wayne Collins, Jonell Green, Marques Houston, Tone Loc, Nell Carter, Myra J. VHS, Beta **$14.95** *PAR, WTA* ⅟⅟½

Because of the Cats Police inspector uncovers an evil cult within his seaside village while investigating a bizarre rape and burglary.
1974 90m/C Bryan Marshall, Alexandra Stewart, Alex Van Rooyen, Sylvia Kristel, Sebastian Graham Jones; *D:* Fons Rademakers. VHS, Beta **$49.95** *PSM* ⅟½

Because You're Mine Lanza plays an opera star who is drafted and falls in love with Morrow, his top sergeant's sister. Plenty of singing—maybe too much at times, but Lanza's fans will enjoy it nonetheless. ♫All the Things You Are; Because You're Mine; Be My Love; Granada; Lee-Ah-Loo; The Lord's Prayer; The Song Angels Sing; You Do Something to Me.
1952 103m/C Mario Lanza, James Whitmore, Doretta Morrow, Dean Miller, Paula Corday, Jeff Donnell, Spring Byington; *D:* Alexander Hall. VHS **$19.98** *MGM* ⅟⅟

Becket Adaptation of Jean Anouilh's play about the tumultuous friendship between Henry II of England and the Archbishop of Canterbury Thomas Becket. Becket views his position in the church of little relation to the sexual and emotional needs of a man, until he becomes archbishop. His growing concern for religion and his shrinking need of Henry as friend and confidant eventually cause the demise of the friendship and the resulting tragedy. Flawless acting from every cast member, and finely detailed artistic direction make up for the occasional slow moment.

1964 148m/C Richard Burton, Peter O'Toole, John Gielgud, Donald Wolfit; *D:* Peter Glenville; *W:* Edward Anhalt. Academy Awards '64: Best Adapted Screenplay; Nominations: Best Actor (Burton), Best Actor (O'Toole), Best Art Direction/Set Decoration (Color), Best Color Cinematography, Best Costume Design (Color), Best Director (Glenville), Best Film Editing, Best Picture, Best Sound, Best Supporting Actor (Gielgud), Best Original Score; Golden Globe Awards '65: Best Actor—Drama (O'Toole), Best Film—Drama; National Board of Review Awards '64: 10 Best Films of the Year. **VHS, Beta $59.95** *MPI, VCI, TVC* 🎬🎬🎬

Becky Sharp This premiere Technicolor film tells the story of Becky Sharp, a wicked woman who finally performs one good deed.

1935 83m/C Miriam Hopkins, Frances Dee, Cedric Hardwicke, Billie Burke, Nigel Bruce, Pat Nixon; *D:* Rouben Mamoulian. **VHS, Beta $19.95** *NOS, MRV, HEG* 🎬🎬½

Becoming Colette Tedious flashbacking bio of French writer Colette, from her innocent days in the country to her (bad) marriage to writer/publisher Willy and on and on to her own growing career as a writer. She begins writing stories, using an alter-ego character, Claudine, which detail her sexual escapades. Lots of naked flesh but little passion. A postscript notes that Colette wrote "Gigi" and was the first woman to receive the French Legion of Honor.

1992 (R) 97m/C Mathilda May, Klaus Maria Brandauer, Virginia Madsen, Paul Rhys, Jean-Pierre Aumont, John van Dreelen, Lucienne Hamon; *D:* Danny Huston; *W:* Ruth Graham; *M:* John Scott. **VHS $89.95** *ACA* 🎬🎬

Bed & Breakfast Three generations of women lead quiet lives while running a failing Nantucket bed and breakfast. When a mystery man washes up on their beach, he charms them all, but it seems that he has a past that could endanger everyone. Lightweight final role for Dewhurst, though she provides some sparks as the strong and loving matriarch. Gentle romantic comedy skims the surface, but is still enjoyable.

1992 (PG-13) 97m/C Roger Moore, Talia Shire, Colleen Dewhurst, Nina Siemaszko, Ford Rainey, Stephen Root, Jamie Walters, Victor Slezak; *D:* Robert Ellis Miller; *W:* Cindy Myers; *M:* David Shire. **VHS $9.95** *HMD* 🎬🎬½

Bed and Sofa Adultery, abortion, and women's rights are brought about by a housing shortage which forces a man to move in with a married friend. Famous, ground-breaking Russian silent.

1927 73m/B *RU* Nikolai Batalov, Vladimar Fogel; *D:* Abram Room. **VHS, Beta $49.95** *ING, IHF* 🎬🎬🎬½

Bedazzled In the process of hanging himself, Stanley, a short-order cook is approached by the devil with an offer: seven wishes in exchange for his soul. Each of Stanley's wishes is granted with surprising consequences. Cult comedy is a sometimes uneven, but thoroughly entertaining and funny retelling of the Faustian story.

1968 (PG) 107m/C *GB* Dudley Moore, Peter Cook, Eleanor Bron, Michael Bates, Raquel Welch; *D:* Stanley Donen; *W:* Peter Cook. **VHS, Beta** *FOX* 🎬🎬

Bedford Incident The U.S.S. Bedford discovers an unidentified submarine in North Atlantic waters. The Bedford's commander drives his crew to the point of exhaustion as they find themselves the center of a fateful controversy.

1965 102m/B Richard Widmark, Sidney Poitier, James MacArthur, Martin Balsam, Wally Cox, Donald Sutherland, Eric Portman; *D:* James B. Harris. **VHS, Beta $14.95** *COL, IME* 🎬🎬½

Bedknobs and Broomsticks A novice witch and three cockney waifs ride a magic bedstead and stop the Nazis from invading England during WWII. Celebrated for its animated art.

1971 (G) 117m/C Angela Lansbury, Roddy McDowall, David Tomlinson, Bruce Forsyth, Sam Jaffe; *D:* Robert Stevenson. Academy Awards '71: Best Visual Effects; Nominations: Best Art Direction/Set Decoration, Best Costume Design, Best Song ("The Age of Not Believing"), Best Original Score. **VHS, Beta $24.99** *DIS, WTA* 🎬🎬½

Bedlam Creeper set in the famed asylum in 18th-century London. A woman, wrongfully committed, tries to stop the evil doings of the chief (Karloff) of Bedlam, and endangers herself. Fine horror film co-written by producer Lewton.

1945 79m/B Jason Robards Sr., Ian Wolfe, Glenn Vernon, Boris Karloff, Anna Lee, Billy House, Richard Fraser; *D:* Mark Robson. **VHS, Beta $19.95** *TTC, MED, FCT* 🎬🎬🎬

Bedroom Eyes A successful businessman becomes a voyeur by returning nightly to a beautiful woman's window, until she is killed and he is the prime suspect. Part comic, part disappointing thriller.

1986 (R) 90m/C Kenneth Gilman, Dayle Haddon, Christine Cattall; *D:* William Fruet. **VHS, Beta $29.95** *FOX* 🎬¼

Bedroom Eyes 2 After discovering his wife has had an affair, a stockbroker takes a lover. When she turns up dead, he and his wife become murder suspects. Provides some suspenseful moments.

1989 (R) 85m/C Wings Hauser, Kathy Shower, Linda Blair, Jane Hamilton, Jennifer Delora; *D:* Chuck Vincent. **VHS $89.95** *VMK, IME* 🎬🎬

The Bedroom Window Guttenberg is having an illicit affair with his boss' wife (Huppert), who witnesses an assault on another woman (McGovern) from the bedroom window. To keep the affair secret Guttenberg reports the crime, but since it is secondhand, the account is flawed and he becomes a suspect. Semi-tight thriller reminiscent of Hitchcock mysteries isn't always believable, but is otherwise interesting.

1987 (R) 113m/C Steve Guttenberg, Elizabeth McGovern, Isabelle Huppert, Wallace Shawn, Paul Shenar, Carl Lumbly, Frederick Coffin, Brad Greenquist; *D:* Curtis Hanson; *W:* Curtis Hanson; *M:* Patrick Gleeson, Michael Shrieve, Felix Mendelessohn. **VHS, Beta $9.99** *FHE, VES, LIV* 🎬🎬½

Bedtime for Bonzo A professor adopts a chimp to prove that environment, not hereditary, determines a child's future. Fun, lighthearted comedy that stars a future president. Followed by "Bonzo Goes to College."

1951 83m/B Ronald Reagan, Diana Lynn, Walter Slezak, Jesse White, Bonzo the Chimp; *D:* Fred de Cordova. **VHS, Beta $14.95** *MCA, FCT* 🎬🎬

Bedtime Story Two con artists attempt to fleece an apparently wealthy woman and each other on the French Riviera. Re-made in 1988 as "Dirty Rotten Scoundrels." One of Brando's thankfully few forays into comedy.

1963 99m/C Marlon Brando, David Niven, Shirley Jones, Dody Goodman, Marie Windsor; *D:* Ralph Levy. **VHS, Beta $14.98** *MCA* 🎬🎬

Beer A female advertising executive devises a dangerous sexist campaign for a cheap beer, and both the beer and its nickname become nationwide obsessions. Not especially amusing.

1985 (R) 83m/C Loretta Swit, Rip Torn, Dick Shawn, David Alan Grier, William Russ, Kenneth Mars, Peter Michael Goetz; *D:* Patrick Kelly; *M:* Bill Conti. **VHS, Beta** *NO* 🎬

The Bees Sting of a poor movie is painful. A strain of bees have ransacked South America and are threatening the rest of the world. The buzz is that no one is safe. Cheap rip-off of "The Swarm," which is saying something.

1978 (PG) 93m/C John Saxon, John Carradine, Angel Tompkins, Claudio Brook, Alicia Encinas; *D:* Alfredo Zacharias. **VHS, Beta $29.98** *WAR* Woof!

Beethoven Startling biography of the musical genius, filled with opulent, impressionistic visuals. *AKA:* Beethoven's Great Love; The Life and Loves of Beethoven; Un Grand Amour de Beethoven.

1936 116m/B *FR* Harry Baur, Jean-Louis Barrault, Marcel Dalio; *W:* Abel Gance. **VHS $59.95** *CVC, ING, TPV* Woof!

Beethoven Adorable St. Bernard puppy escapes from dognappers and wanders into the home of the Newtons, who, over dad's objections, adopt him. Beethoven grows into a huge, slobbering dog who sorely tries dad's patience. To make matters worse, two sets of villains also wreak havoc on the Newton's lives. Evil veterinarian Dr. Varnick plots to steal Beethoven for lab experiments, and yuppie couple Brad and Brie plot to take over the family business. Enjoyable cast, particularly Grodin as dad and Chris as Beethoven enable this movie to please more than the milk and cookies set. Followed by "Beethoven's 2nd."

1992 (PG) 89m/C Charles Grodin, Bonnie Hunt, Dean Jones, Oliver Platt, Stanley Tucci, Nicholle Tom, Christopher Castile, Sarah Rose Karr, David Duchovny, Patricia Heaton, Laurel Cronin; *D:* Brian Levant; *W:* John Hughes, Amy Holden Jones. **VHS $19.98** *MCA, FCT* 🎬🎬½

Beethoven Lives Upstairs In 19th century Vienna 10 year-old Christoph's life is turned upside-down when the family's eccentric new tenant turns out to be composer Ludwig Van Beethoven. In time, Christoph comes to appreciate the beauty of the music and the tragedy of the composer's deafness. Features more than 25 excerpts of Beethoven's works.

1992 52m/C Neil Munro, Illya Woloshyn, Fiona Reid, Paul Soles, Sheila McCarthy, Albert Schultz; *D:* David Devine; *W:* Heather Conkie. **VHS $19.98** *BMG, MVD* 🎬🎬½

Beethoven's Nephew A tepid pseudo-historical farce about Beethoven's strange obsession with his only nephew. Directed by erstwhile Warhol collaborator Morrissey. *AKA:* Le Neveu de Beethoven.

1988 103m/C *FR* Wolfgang Reichmann, Ditmar Prinz, Jane Birkin, Nathalie Baye; *D:* Paul Morrissey; *W:* Paul Morrissey. **VHS, Beta $9.99** *NWV, STE* 🎬½

Beethoven's 2nd Sequel has awwww factor going for it as new daddy Beethoven slobbers over four adorable and appealing St. Bernard pups and his new love Missy. Same basic evil subplot as the first, with wicked kidnappers replacing evil vet. During the upheaval, the Newtons take care of the little yapping troublemakers, providing the backdrop for endless puppy mischief and exasperation on Grodin's part. Silly subplots and too many human moments tend to drag, but the kids will find the laughs (albeit stupid ones).

1993 (PG) 87m/C Charles Grodin, Bonnie Hunt, Nicholle Tom, Christopher Castile, Sarah Rose Karr, Debi Mazar, Christopher Penn, Ashley Hamilton; *D:* Rod Daniel; *M:* Len Blum; *M:* Randy Edelman. **VHS $24.98** *MCA* 🎬🎬½

Beetlejuice The after-life is confusing for a pair of ultra-nice novice ghosts who are faced with chasing an obnoxious family of post-modern art lovers who move into their house. Then they hear of a poltergeist who promises to rid the house of all trespassers for a price. Things go from bad to impossible when the maniacal Keaton (as the demonic "Betelgeuse") works his magic. The calypso scene is priceless. A cheesy, funny, surreal farce of life after death with inventive set designs popping continual surprises. Ryder is striking as the misunderstood teen with a death complex, while O'Hara is hilarious as the yuppie art poseur.
1988 (PG) 92m/C Michael Keaton, Geena Davis, Alec Baldwin, Sylvia Sidney, Catherine O'Hara, Winona Ryder, Jeffrey Jones, Dick Cavett; **D:** Tim Burton; **W:** Michael McDowell, Warren Skaaren; **M:** Danny Elfman. **VHS, Beta, 8mm $19.98** *WAR, FCT, TLF* 🎬🎬🎬½

Before I Hang When a doctor invents a youth serum from the blood of a murderer, he'll stop at nothing to keep his secret. Karloff himself stands the test of time, and is satisfying as the mad scientist, giving this horror flick its appeal.
1940 60m/B Boris Karloff, Evelyn Keyes, Bruce (Herman Brix) Bennett, Edward Van Sloan; **D:** Nick Grinde. **VHS, Beta $59.95** *COL* 🎬🎬

Before Morning Police officer poses as a blackmailer to find out which of the two women in the murder victim's life are guilty.
1933 68m/B Leo Carrillo, Lora Baxter, Taylor Holmes. **VHS, Beta** *NO* 🎬½

Before the Revolution One of Bertolucci's first films. Love and politics are mixed when a young man who is dabbling in communism is also flirting with his young aunt. Striking and powerful film that has yet to lose its effect despite the times.
1965 115m/C *IT* Francesco Barilli, Adrianna Asti, Alain Midgette, Morando Morandini, Domenico Alpi; **D:** Bernardo Bertolucci; **W:** Bernardo Bertolucci; **M:** Ennio Morricone. **VHS $59.95** *NYF, ING* 🎬🎬

Beggars in Ermine A handicapped, impoverished man organizes all the beggars in the world into a successful corporation. Unusual performance from Atwill.
1934 70m/B Lionel Atwill, Henry B. Walthall, Betty Furness, Jameson Thomas, James Bush, Astrid Allwyn, George "Gabby" Hayes; **D:** Phil Rosen. **VHS, Beta $14.95** *VYY, SNC* 🎬½

Beginning of the End Produced the same year as "The Deadly Mantis," Gordon's effort adds to 1957's harvest of bugs on a rampage "B"-graders. Giant, radiation-spawned grasshoppers attack Chicago causing Graves to come to the rescue. Easily the best giant grasshopper movie ever made.
1957 73m/B Peggy Castle, Peter Graves, Morris Ankrum, Richard Benedict, James Seay; **D:** Bert I. Gordon. **VHS** *VTR* 🎬½

The Beguiled During the Civil War a wounded Union soldier is taken in by the women at a girl's school in the South. He manages to seduce both a student and a teacher, and jealousy and revenge ensue. Decidedly weird psychological melodrama from action vets Siegel and Eastwood.
1970 (R) 109m/C Clint Eastwood, Geraldine Page, Elizabeth Hartman; **D:** Don Siegel. **VHS, Beta $14.98** *MCA* 🎬🎬🎬

Behave Yourself! A married couple adopts a dog who may be the key for a million-dollar hijacking setup by a gang of hoodlums.
1952 81m/B Shelley Winters, Farley Granger, William Demarest, Lon Chaney Jr., Hans Conried, Elisha Cook Jr., Francis L. Sullivan; **D:** George Beck. **VHS, Beta $15.95** *NOS, VCI* 🎬½

Behind Enemy Lines Special Forces soldier goes on a special mission to eliminate a possible Nazi spy. Made for television.
1985 (R) 83m/C Hal Holbrook, Ray Sharkey, David McCallum, Tom Isbell, Anne Twomey, Robert Patrick; **D:** Sheldon Larry. **VHS, Beta $79.95** *MED* 🎬½

Behind Locked Doors A journalist fakes mental illness to have himself committed to an asylum, where he believes a crooked judge is in hiding. A superior "B" mystery/suspense feature, with some tense moments.
1948 61m/B Lucille Bremer, Richard Carlson, Tor Johnson, Douglas Fowley, Herbert Heyes, Ralf Harolde; **D:** Budd Boetticher. **VHS $19.95** *VDM* 🎬🎬½

Behind Office Doors Astor stars as the secretarial "power behind the throne" in this look at who really wields power in an office. Her boss takes her for granted until things go wrong.
1931 82m/B Mary Astor, Robert Ames, Ricardo Cortez, Charles Sellon; **D:** Melville Brown. **VHS $19.95** *NOS, HEG* 🎬🎬

Behind Prison Walls A steel tycoon and his son are sent to prison, and the son tries to convert his dad to socialism. A fun, light hearted film, the last for veteran Tully. **AKA:** Youth Takes a Hand.
1943 64m/B Alan Baxter, Gertrude Michael, Tully Marshall, Edwin Maxwell, Jacqueline Dalya, Matt Willis; **D:** Steve Sekely. **VHS $16.95** *SNC* 🎬🎬

Behind the Front Two friends tumble in and out of trouble in this comic Army film. One of the most profitable films of the late twenties.
1926 60m/B Wallace Beery, Raymond Hatton, Richard Arlen, Mary Brian, Chester Conklin; **D:** Edward Sutherland. **VHS** *GPV* 🎬🎬½

Behind the Mask Lamont Cranston, better known as do-gooder "The Shadow," finds himself accused of murdering a blackmailing newspaper reporter. Based on the radio serial.
1937 68m/C Kane Richmond, Barbara Reed, George Chandler, Dorothea Kent, Robert Shayne, June Clyde; **D:** Phil Karlson. **VHS $16.95** *GPV, ADL* 🎬🎬½

Behind the Rising Sun A Japanese publisher's political views clash with those of his American-educated son in 1930s Japan. Well done despite pre-war propaganda themes.
1943 88m/B Tom Neal, J. Carroll Naish, Robert Ryan, Mike Mazurki, Margo, Gloria Holden, Don Douglas; **D:** Edward Dmytryk. **VHS, Beta $19.98** *RKO* 🎬🎬

Behold a Pale Horse A Spanish police captain attempts to dupe Peck into believing that his mother is dying and he must visit her on her deathbed. Loyalist Spaniard Peck becomes privy to the plot against him, but goes to Spain anyway in this post Spanish Civil War film.
1964 118m/B Gregory Peck, Anthony Quinn, Omar Sharif, Mildred Dunnock; **D:** Fred Zinneman; **M:** Maurice Jarre. **VHS, Beta $9.95** *GKK* 🎬🎬

The Being People in Idaho are terrorized by a freak who became abnormal after radiation was disposed in the local dump. Another dull monster-created-by-nuclear-waste non-event. Of limited interest is Buzzi. However, you'd be more entertained (read: amused) by Troma's "The Toxic Avenger," which takes itself much (much!) less seriously.
1983 (R) 82m/C Ruth Buzzi, Martin Landau, Jose Ferrer; **D:** Jackie Kong. **VHS, Beta** *NO* 🎬

Being at Home with Claude Yves is a 22-year-old Montreal hustler being interrogated by a nameless inspector (Dupuis) for the murder of his lover, Claude (Pichette). Yves has admitted his guilt but the inspector wants to reconstruct the event and determine a motive. Lots of black-and-white flashbacks as Yves dwells on his work and his psychologically love-death relationship with Claude. Rather pretentious and long-winded. Based on the play by Rene-Daniel DuBois. In French with English subtitles.
1992 86m/C *CA* Roy Dupuis, Jacques Godin, Jean-Francois Pichette, Gaston Lepage; **D:** Johanne Boisvert; **W:** Jean Boudin. **VHS $89.95** *ACA, FCT* 🎬🎬

Being Human Ambitious comedy drama from idiosyncratic Forsyth promises more than it delivers, and shackles Williams in the process. Williams is Hector, a regular guy continuously reincarnated throughout the milennia. He plays a caveman, a Roman slave, a Middle Ages nomad, a crew member on a 17th century new world voyage, and a modern New Yorker in separate vignettes that echo and/or extend the main themes of family, identity, and random fate. But Williams manages to emerge from each sketch as nothing more than an unassuming everyman who never learns his lesson. One of Williams' periodic chancy ventures away from his comedic roots occasionally strikes gold, but often seems overly restrained.
1994 (PG-13) 125m/C Robin Williams, John Turturro, Anna Galiena, Vincent D'Onofrio, Hector Elizondo, Lorraine Bracco, Lindsay Crouse, Kelly Hunter, William H. Macy, Grace Mahlaba, Theresa Russell, Charles Miller, Helen Miller; **D:** Bill Forsyth; **W:** Bill Forsyth; **M:** Michael Gibbs. **VHS** *NYR* 🎬🎬½

Being There A feeble-minded gardener, whose entire knowledge of life comes from watching television, is sent out into the real world when his employer dies. Equipped with his prize possession, his remote control unit, the gardener unwittingly enters the world of politics and is welcomed as a mysterious sage. Sellers is wonderful in this satiric treat adapted by Jerzy Kosinski from his novel.
1979 (PG) 130m/C Peter Sellers, Shirley MacLaine, Melvyn Douglas, Jack Warden, Richard Dysart, Richard Basehart; **D:** Hal Ashby. Academy Awards '79: Best Supporting Actor (Douglas); Nominations: Best Actor (Sellers); Cannes Film Festival '80: Best Film; Golden Globe Awards '80: Best Actor—Musical/Comedy (Sellers), Best Supporting Actor (Douglas); National Board of Review Awards '79: 10 Best Films of the Year, Best Actor (Sellers). **VHS, Beta $19.98** *FOX, FCT, WAR* 🎬🎬🎬½

Being Two Isn't Easy Director Ichikawa shows the world through the eyes of a two-year-old as a young couple struggle to raise their son. In Japanese with English subtitles.
1962 88m/C *JP* Fujiko Yamamoto, Eiji Funakoshi; **D:** Kon Ichikawa. **VHS $29.95** *HMV, FCT* 🎬🎬

Bela Lugosi Meets a Brooklyn Gorilla Two men who look like Dean Martin and Jerry Lewis (but aren't) get lost in the jungle, where they meet mad scientist Lugosi. Worse than it sounds. Real Jerry sued for unflattering imitation. **AKA:** The Boys from Brooklyn.
1952 74m/B Bela Lugosi, Duke Mitchell, Sammy Petrillo; **D:** William Beaudine. **VHS, Beta $19.95** *NOS, SNC, AOV* Woof!

Bela Lugosi Scrapbook A compilation of Lugosi appearances, outtakes, flubs, and trailers.
197? 60m/B Bela Lugosi. **VHS, Beta $29.95** *DVT, RXM* 🎬½

B

Belfast Assassin A British anti-terrorist agent goes undercover in Ireland to find an IRA assassin who shot a British cabinet minister.
1984 130m/C Derek Thompson, Ray Lonnen. VHS, Beta $49.95 PSM ℐℐ

The Believers Tense horror mystery set in New York city about a series of gruesome, unexplained murders. A widowed police psychologist investigating the deaths unwittingly discovers a powerful Santeria cult that believes in the sacrifice of children. Without warning he is drawn into the circle of the ''Believers'' and must free himself before his own son is the next sacrifice. Gripping (and grim), unrelenting horror.
1987 (R) 114m/C Martin Sheen, Helen Shaver, Malick Bowens, Harris Yulin, Robert Loggia, Jimmy Smits, Richard Masur, Harley Cross, Elizabeth Wilson, Lee Richardson, Britt Leach; D: John Schlesinger; W: Mark Frost; M: J. Peter Robinson. VHS, Beta $19.99 HBO ℐℐ½

Belizaire the Cajun 19th-century Louisiana love story. White prejudice against the Cajuns is rampant and violent, but that doesn't stop sexy faith healer Assante from falling in love with the inaccessible Cajun wife (Youngs) of a rich local. Made with care on a tight budget. Worthwhile, though uneven.
1986 (PG) 103m/C Armand Assante, Gail Youngs, Will Patton, Stephen McHattie, Michael Schoeffling, Robert Duvall, Nancy Barrett; D: Glen Pitre; W: Glen Pitre; M: Michael Doucet. VHS, Beta $79.98 FOX ℐℐ½

Bell, Book and Candle A young witch makes up her mind to refrain from using her powers. When an interesting man moves into her building, she forgets her decision and enchants him with a love spell.
1958 106m/C James Stewart, Kim Novak, Jack Lemmon, Elsa Lanchester, Ernie Kovacs, Hermione Gingold; D: Richard Quine; W: Daniel Taradash; M: George Duning. VHS, Beta $19.95 COL, FCT, MLB ℐℐ½

Bell Diamond A study by the experimental filmmaker of a Vietnam vet surviving in a bankrupt mining town. Created without a script using non-professional actors.
1981 96m/C D: Jon Jost. VHS, Beta FCT ℐℐ

Bell from Hell A tale of insanity and revenge, wherein a young man, institutionalized since his mother's death, plots to kill his aunt and three cousins.
1974 80m/C Viveca Lindfors, Renaud Verley, Alfredo Mayo; D: Claudio Guerin Hill. VHS, Beta $49.95 UNI ℐℐ

The Bell Jar Based on poet Sylvia Plath's acclaimed semi-autobiographical novel, this is the story of a young woman who becomes the victim of mental illness. Not for the easily depressed and a disjointed and disappointing adaptation of Plath's work.
1979 (R) 113m/C Marilyn Hassett, Julie Harris, Barbara Barrie, Anne Bancroft, Robert Klein, Anne Jackson; D: Larry Peerce. VHS, Beta $29.98 VES ℐ½

Bell Ringer of Antigua Inspirational story by Royer, one of Hollywood's pioneering women. Shot on location in Guatemala.
1946 ?m/C D: Fanchon Royer; W: Fanchon Royer. VHS $15.95 LOO ℐℐ

Bellamy Murderous madman massacres masseuses, and Bellamy is the cop out to get him.
1980 92m/C John Stanton, Timothy Elston, Sally Conabere; D: Colin Eggleston, Pina Amenta. VHS, Beta NO ℐℐ

Bellas de Noche A Mexican pimp gets in trouble with the mob. In Spanish. *AKA:* Night Beauties.

19?? 110m/C MX MX Jorge Rivero, Lalo El Mimo, Rafael Inclan, Sasha Montenegro. VHS, Beta $53.95 MAD ℐ

The Bellboy Lewis makes his directorial debut in this plotless but clever outing. He also stars as the eponymous character, a bellboy at Miami's Fountainbleau Hotel. Cameos from Berle and Winchell are highlights.
1960 72m/B Jerry Lewis, Alex Gerry, Bob Clayton, Sonny Sands; *Cameos:* Milton Berle, Walter Winchell; D: Jerry Lewis; W: Jerry Lewis. VHS, Beta $59.95 LIV ℐℐ½

The Bellboy and the Playgirls Early Coppola effort adds new film footage to a 1958 German movie. Stars Playboy playmate June ''The Body'' Wilkinson, with other centerfolds of the time. *AKA:* The Playgirls and the Bellboy; Mit Eva Fing Die Sunde An.
1962 93m/C June Wilkinson; D: Francis Ford Coppola; W: Francis Ford Coppola. VHS NO Woof!

Belle Epoque Young army deserter Fernando (Sanz) embarks on a personal voyage of discovery and meets Manolo (Gomez), an eccentric old man, and father to four beautiful daughters. Fernando can't believe his luck—and the sisters share his interest, resulting in an amusing round of musical beds. Lighthearted romp set in 1930's Spain with a terrific screenplay that tastefully handles the material without stooping to the obvious leering possibilities. In addition to Oscar, won 9 Spanish Goyas, including best picture, director, actress (Gil), and screenplay. In Spanish with English subtitles. *AKA:* The Age of Beauty.
1992 (R) 108m/C SP Jorge Sanz, Fernando Gomez, Ariadna Gil, Maribel Verdu, Penelope Cruz, Miriam Diaz-Aroca, Mary Carmen Ramirez, Michel Galabru, Gabino Diego; D: Fernando Trueba; W: Rafael Azcona. VHS NYR ℐℐℐ

The Belle of New York A turn-of-the-century bachelor falls in love with a Salvation Army missionary in this standard musical. ♫Naughty But Nice; Baby Doll; Oops; I Wanna Be a Dancin' Man; Seeing's Believing; Bachelor's Dinner Song; When I'm Out With the Belle of New York; Let a Little Love Come In.
1952 82m/C Fred Astaire, Vera-Ellen, Marjorie Main, Keenan Wynn, Alice Pearce, Gale Robbins, Clinton Sundberg; D: Charles Walters. VHS, Beta $19.98 MGM, FHE ℐℐ

Belle of the Nineties West struts as a 1890s singer who gets involved with a boxer. Her trademark sexual innuendos were already being censored but such lines as ''It's better to be looked over than overlooked,'' done in West style, get the point across.
1934 73m/B Mae West, Roger Pryor, Johnny Mack Brown, John Miljan, Katherine DeMille, Harry Woods, Edward Gargan; D: Leo McCarey; W: Mae West. VHS $14.98 MCA, BTV ℐℐ½

Belle Starr The career of Wild West outlaw Belle Starr is chronicled in this strange western pastiche about lawlessness and sexual agression. Wertmuller directed under the pseudonym Nathan Wich. Dubbed in English.
1979 90m/C IT Elsa Martinelli, Robert Wood, George Eastman, Dan Harrison; D: Lina Wertmuller. VHS, Beta $59.95 FCT ℐ½

The Belles of St. Trinian's Sim is priceless in a dual role as the eccentric headmistress of a chaotic, bankrupt girls' school and her bookie twin brother who scheme the school into financial security. The first in a series of movies based on a popular British cartoon by Ronald Searles about a girls' school and its mischievous students.

Followed by ''Blue Murder at St. Trinian's,'' ''The Pure Hell of St. Trinian's,'' and ''The Great St. Trinian's Train Robbery.''
1953 86m/B GB Alastair Sim, Joyce Grenfell, Hermione Baddeley, George Cole, Eric Pohlmann, Renee Houston, Beryl Reid; D: Frank Launder; M: Malcolm Arnold. VHS, Beta $39.95 HMV ℐℐℐ

Bellhop/The Noon Whistle Two comedic shorts back to back, separately featuring the famous comics Laurel and Hardy.
1922 46m/B Stan Laurel, Oliver Hardy. VHS, Beta $49.95 CCB ℐℐℐ

Bellissima A woman living in an Italian tenement has unrealistic goals for her plain but endearing daughter when a famous director begins casting a role designed for a child. The mother's maternal fury and collision with reality highlight a poignant film. English subtitles.
1951 130m/B IT Anna Magnani; D: Luchino Visconti; W: Luchino Visconti, Cesare Zavattini, Francesco Rosi, Suso Cecchi D'Amico. VHS $49.95 CIG, APD ℐℐℐ

Bellissimo: Images of the Italian Cinema A panoramic film history of Italian cinema, featuring film clips, behind-the-scenes footage and interviews with the industry's leading figures. Clips from ''Open City,'' ''Divorce Italian Style,'' ''8 1/2,'' and ''Seven Beauties'' are included. In English, and Italian with subtitles.
1987 110m/C IT Sophia Loren, Marcello Mastroianni, Bernardo Bertolucci, Dino de Laurentiis, Marco Ferreri, Roberto Rossellini, Vittorio De Sica, Pier Paolo Pasolini, Franco Zeffirelli, Federico Fellini, Lina Wertmuller, Monica Vitti, Giancarlo Giannini, Toto, Anna Magnani; D: Gianfranco Mingozzi. VHS, Beta $29.95 WBF, FCT, ING ℐℐℐ

Bellman and True Rewarding, but sometimes tedious character study of a mild mannered computer whiz who teams with a gang of bank robbers. Fine performances, especially subtle dangerous gang characters.
1988 (R) 112m/C GB Bernard Hill, Kieran O'Brien, Richard Hope, Frances Tomelty, Derek Newark, John Kavanagh, Ken Bones; D: Richard Loncraine. VHS, Beta $14.95 MGM, CAN, VES ℐℐ½

Bells are Ringing A girl who works for a telephone answering service can't help but take an interest in the lives of the clients, especially a playwright with an inferiority complex. Based on Adolph Green and Betty Comden's Broadway musical. Special letter-boxed edition along with the original trailer available on laserdisc format. ♫Just in Time; The Party's Over; It's a Perfect Relationship; Do It Yourself; It's a Simple Little System; Better Than a Dream; I Met a Girl; Drop That Name; I'm Going Back.
1960 126m/C Judy Holliday, Dean Martin, Fred Clark, Eddie Foy Jr., Jean Stapleton; D: Vincente Minnelli; W: Betty Comden, Adolph Green. VHS, Beta $19.98 MGM ℐℐ½

Bells of Coronado Rogers and Evans team up to expose the murderer of a profitable uranium mine. A gang of smugglers trying to trade the ore to foreign powers is thwarted. The usual thin storyline, but filled with action and riding stunts.
1950 67m/B Roy Rogers, Dale Evans, Pat Brady, Grant Withers; D: William Witney. VHS $12.98 REP ℐℐ

Bells of Death A young martial arts student infiltrates the gang that killed his family and kidnapped his sister, finishing them off one by one.
1990 91m/C Chun Ping, Chang Yi, Chao Hsin Yen; D: Yueh Fung. VHS $14.95 HMD ℐ½

Bells of Rosarita Roy helps foil an evil plan to swindle Evans out of the circus she inherited. All-star western cast under the big top.
1945 54m/B Roy Rogers, Dale Evans, George "Gabby" Hayes, Sunset Carson, Adele Mara, Grant Withers, Roy Barcroft, Addison Richards; **D:** Frank McDonald. VHS, Beta $19.95 *NOS, MRV, VCN ♂♂½*

The Bells of St. Mary's An easy-going priest finds himself in a subtle battle of wits with the Mother Superior over how the children of St. Mary's school should be raised. It's the sequel to "Going My Way." Songs include the title tune and "Aren't You Glad You're You?" Also available in a colorized version.
1945 126m/B Bing Crosby, Ingrid Bergman, Henry Travers; **D:** Leo McCarey. Academy Awards '45: Best Sound; Nominations: Best Actress (Bergman); Academy Awards '45: Best Actor (Crosby), Best Director (McCarey), Best Film Editing, Best Picture, Best Song ("Aren't You Glad You're You"), Best Original Score; Golden Globe Awards '46: Best Actress—Drama (Bergman); New York Film Critics Awards '45: Best Actress (Bergman). VHS, Beta $39.98 *REP, IGP ♂♂♂½*

Bells of San Angelo Roy foils thieves' attempts to steal a girl's inherited ranch.
1947 54m/C Roy Rogers, Dale Evans; **D:** William Witney. VHS, Beta $19.95 *NOS, DVT, TIM ♂*

Bells of San Fernando An Irish seaman wanders into California during early Spanish rule and confronts a cruel overseer in this lackluster Western drama. Scripted by "Cisco Kid" Renaldo.
1947 75m/B Donald Woods, Gloria Warren, Byron Foulger; **D:** Terry Morse; **W:** Jack DeWitt, Duncan Renaldo. VHS $19.99 *MOV ♂*

The Belly of an Architect A thespian feast for the larger-than-life Dennehy as blustering American architect whose personal life and health both crumble as he obsessively readies an exhibition in Rome. A multi-tiered, carefully composed tragicomedy from the ideosyncratic filmmaker Greenaway, probably his most accessible work for general audiences.
1991 (R) 119m/C *GB IT* Brian Dennehy, Chloe Webb, Lambert Wilson; **D:** Peter Greenaway; **W:** Peter Greenaway. VHS *NO ♂♂♂½*

Beloved Enemy A romantic tragedy set in Civil War-torn Ireland in the 1920s. A rebel leader and a proper English lady struggle to overcome the war's interference with their burgeoning relationship.
1936 86m/B David Niven, Merle Oberon, Brian Aherne, Karen Morley, Donald Crisp; **D:** H.C. Potter. VHS, Beta $19.95 *NOS, CAB ♂♂½*

The Beloved Rogue Crosland—who gained a reputation for innovation, having directed "Don Juan" the previous year (noted for the debut of synchronized music), and "The Jazz Singer" the following year (noted for the first talkie bits)—mounted this well-designed and special effect-laden medieval costumer. Barrymore is in high profile as a swashbuckling caricature of French poet Francois Villon, who battles mightily (and verbally) with Louis XI (played by Veidt, in his first US film). Marked by the excesses typical of Barrymore's prestige days, it flouts history, taking generous poetic license when the facts ain't fab enough. In short, it's great entertainment.
1927 110m/B John Barrymore, Conrad Veidt, Marceline Day, Henry Victor, Mack Swain, Slim Summerville; **D:** Alan Crosland. VHS, Beta $27.95 *GPV, FCT, VYG ♂♂♂*

Below the Belt Almost interesting tale of street-smart woman from New York City who becomes part of the blue-collar "circus" of lady wrestlers. Ex-wrestling champ Burke plays herself.
1980 98m/C Regina Baff, Mildred Burke, John C. Becher; **D:** Robert Fowler. VHS, Beta $59.99 *TPV ♂♂*

Below the Border The Rough Riders go undercover to straighten out some cattle rustlers.
1942 57m/B Buck Jones, Tim McCoy, Raymond Hatton, Linda Brent, Roy Barcroft, Charles "Blackie" King; **D:** Howard Bretherton. VHS, Beta $9.99 *NOS, DVT, VDM ♂½*

Below the Deadline A man framed for embezzlement is set free and allowed to clear his name by a sympathetic detective.
1929 79m/B Frank Leigh, Barbara Worth, Arthur Rankin, Walter Merrill; **D:** J.P. McGowan. VHS $16.95 *SNC, VYY ♂♂*

The Belstone Fox Orphaned fox goes into hiding, and is hunted by the hound he has befriended and his former owner.
1973 103m/C Eric Porter, Rachel Roberts, Jeremy Kemp; **D:** James Hill. VHS, Beta *SUE ♂♂*

Ben Sequel to "Willard" finds police Detective Kirtland still on the hunt for a killer rat pack led by Ben, king of the rodents. Title song by young Michael Jackson hit the top of the charts.
1972 (PG) 95m/C Joseph Campanella, Lee Montgomery, Arthur O'Connell, Rosemary Murphy, Meredith Baxter Birney; **D:** Phil Karlson. Academy Awards '72 Nominations: Best Song ("Ben"); Golden Globe Awards '73: Best Song ("Ben"). VHS, Beta $14.95 *PSM, PAR ♂½*

Ben-Hur Second film version of the renowned story of Jewish and Christian divisiveness in the time of Jesus. Battle scenes and chariot races still look good, in spite of age. Problems lingered on the set and at a cost of over $4,000,000 it was the most expensive film of its time and took years to finish. A hit at the box office, it still stands as the all-time silent classic. In 1931, a shortened version was released. Based on the novel by Lewis Wallace.
1926 148m/B Ramon Novarro, Francis X. Bushman, May McAvoy, Betty Bronson, Claire McDowell, Carmel Myers, Nigel de Brulier, Ferdinand P. Earle; **D:** Fred Niblo. VHS, Beta $29.95 *MGM ♂♂♂♂*

Ben-Hur The third film version of the Lew Wallace classic stars Heston in the role of a Palestinian Jew battling the Roman empire at the time of Christ. Won a record 11 Oscars. The breathtaking chariot race is still one of the best screen races today. Perhaps one of the greatest pictures of all time. Also available in letterbox format.
1959 212m/C Charlton Heston, Jack Hawkins, Stephen Boyd, Haya Harareet, Hugh Griffith, Martha Scott, Sam Jaffe, Cathy O'Donnell, Finlay Currie, Karl Tunberg; **D:** William Wyler; **M:** Miklos Rozsa. Academy Awards '59: Best Actor (Heston), Best Art Direction/Set Decoration (Color), Best Color Cinematography, Best Costume Design (Color), Best Director (Wyler), Best Film Editing, Best Picture, Best Sound, Best Special Effects, Best Supporting Actor (Griffith), Best Original Score; Nominations: Best Adapted Screenplay; British Academy Awards '59: Best Film; Directors Guild of America Awards '59: Best Director (Wyler); Golden Globe Awards '60: Best Director (Wyler), Best Film—Drama, Best Supporting Actor (Boyd). VHS, Beta $29.98 *MGM, APD, BTV ♂♂♂♂*

Ben Turpin: An Eye for an Eye Two silent Ben Turpin comedies: "He Looked Crooked, or Why Ben Bolted" (1917) and "Ten Dollars or Ten Days" (1924).

1924 77m/B Ben Turpin, Harry Gribbon. VHS, Beta, 8mm $24.95 *VYY ♂♂♂♂*

Bend of the River A haunted, hardened guide leads a wagon train through Oregon territory, pitting himself against Indians, the wilderness and a former comrade-turned-hijacker. **AKA:** Where the River Bends.
1952 91m/C James Stewart, Arthur Kennedy, Rock Hudson, Harry Morgan, Royal Dano; **D:** Anthony Mann. VHS, Beta $14.98 *MCA ♂♂♂*

Beneath Arizona Skies/Paradise Canyon A package of John Wayne westerns filled with lots of rumble tumble action.
1935 109m/B John Wayne. VHS, Beta $19.95 *REP ♂½*

Beneath the Planet of the Apes In the first sequel, another Earth astronaut passes through the same warp and follows the same paths as Taylor, through Ape City and to the ruins of bomb-blasted New York's subway system, where warhead-worshipping human mutants are found. The strain of sequelling shows instantly, and gets worse through the next three films; followed by "Escape from the Planet of the Apes."
1970 (G) 108m/C Charlton Heston, James Franciscus, Kim Hunter, Maurice Evans, James Gregory, Natalie Trundy, Jeff Corey, Linda Harrison, Victor Buono; **D:** Ted Post. VHS, Beta $19.98 *FOX, FUS ♂♂½*

Beneath the 12-Mile Reef Two rival groups of divers compete for sponge beds off the Florida coast. Lightweight entertainment notable for underwater photography and early Cinemascope production, as well as Moore in a bathing suit.
1953 102m/C Robert Wagner, Terry Moore, Gilbert Roland, Richard Boone, Peter Graves, J. Carroll Naish; **D:** Robert D. Webb. VHS, Beta $19.95 *NOS, FCT, GEM ♂♂*

Beneath the Valley of the Ultra-Vixens Sex comedy retread directed by the man with an obsession for big. Scripted by Roger Ebert, who also scripted the cult classic "Beyond the Valley of the Dolls." Explicit nudity.
1979 90m/C Francesca "Kitten" Natavidad, Ann Marie, Ken Kerr, Stuart Lancaster; **D:** Russ Meyer; **W:** Roger Ebert. VHS $89.95 *RMF ♂*

Benefit of the Doubt Ex-con Sutherland, released from prison after 22 years, attempts to repaint his family a la Norman Rockwell. Grown-up daughter Irving, who testified against him in her mother's murder, wants to put a crimp in those plans since daddy's new vision of family fondness frankly makes her stomach turn. Aside from the sexual shenanigans, and the haunting Monument Valley backdrop, an extended chase scene would seem to be the film's only hope of salvation. Unfortunately, it fails to deliver, being both implausible and boring. Based on a story by Michael Lieber.
1993 (R) 92m/C Donald Sutherland, Amy Irving, Christopher McDonald, Rider Strong, Graham Greene, Theodore Bikel, Gisele Kovach, Ferdinand "Ferdy" Mayne; **D:** Jonathan Heap; **W:** Jeffrey Polman, Christopher Keyser; **M:** Hummie Mann. VHS, Beta *PAR ♂♂*

The Beniker Gang Five orphans, supported by the eldest who writes a syndicated advice column, work together as a family. A made-for-television film.
1983 (G) 87m/C Andrew McCarthy, Jennie Dundas, Danny Pintauro, Charlie Fields; **D:** Ken Kwapis. VHS, Beta $59.95 *WAR ♂♂½*

Benjamin Argumedo A true story of the struggle to survive a revolution, and what a person has to endure after it is over.

1978 97m/C *SP* Antonio Aguilar, Flor Silvestre, Jose Galvez, Irma Lozano; *D:* Mario Hernandez. **VHS, Beta** NO 🐾🐾

Benji In the loveable mutt's first feature-length movie, he falls in love with a female named Tiffany, and saves two young children from kidnappers. Kiddie classic that was a box office hit when first released. Followed by "For the Love of Benji."
1974 (G) 87m/C Benji, Peter Breck, Christopher Connelly, Patsy Garrett, Deborah Walley, Cynthia Smith; *D:* Joe Camp. Academy Awards '74 Nominations: Best Song ("Benji's Theme (I Feel Love)"); Golden Globe Awards '75: Best Song ("I Feel Love"). **VHS, Beta** $19.99 VES, FCT, APD 🐾🐾🐾

Benji the Hunted The heroic canine, shipwrecked off the Oregon coast, discovers a litter of orphaned cougar cubs, and battles terrain and predators to bring them to safety.
1987 (G) 89m/C Benji, Red Steagall, Frank Inn; *D:* Joe Camp. **VHS, Beta** $19.99 DIS 🐾½

Benji's Very Own Christmas Story Benji and his friends go on a magic trip and meet Kris Kringle and learn how Christmas is celebrated around the world. Also included: "The Phenomenon of Benji," a documentary about Benji's odyssey from the animal shelter to international stardom.
1983 60m/C **VHS, Beta** $14.99 BFV 🐾🐾

Benny & Joon Depending on your tolerance for cute eccentrics and whimsy this will either charm you with sweetness or send you into sugar shock. Masterson is Joon, a mentally disturbed young woman who paints and has a habit of setting fires. She lives with overprotective brother Benny (Quinn). Sam (Depp) is the outsider who charms Joon, a dyslexic loner who impersonates his heroes Charlie Chaplin and Buster Keaton with eery accuracy. Depp is particularly fine with the physical demands of his role, but the film's easy dismissal of Joon's mental illness is a serious flaw. The laserdisc version is letter-boxed.
1993 (PG) 98m/C Johnny Depp, Mary Stuart Masterson, Aidan Quinn, Julianne Moore, Oliver Platt, CCH Pounder, Dan Hedaya, Joe Grifasi, William H. Macy, Eileen Ryan; *D:* Jeremiah S. Chechik; *W:* Barry Berman; *M:* Rachel Portman. **VHS, Beta** $19.98 MGM 🐾🐾½

The Benny Goodman Story The life and music of Swing Era bandleader Benny Goodman is recounted in this popular bio-pic. Covering Benny's career from his child prodigy days to his monumental 1938 Carnegie Hall Jazz Concert, the movie's soggy plot machinations are redeemed by a non-stop music track featuring the real Benny and an all-star lineup. ♫Don't Be That Way; Memories of You; Sing, Sing, Sing; Slipped Disc.
1955 116m/C Steve Allen, Donna Reed, Gene Krupa, Lionel Hampton, Kid Ory, Ben Pollack, Harry James, Stan Getz, Teddy Wilson, Martha Tilton; *D:* Valentine Davies; *M:* Henry Mancini. **VHS, Beta** $19.95 MCA, FCT 🐾🐾

Benny Hill's Crazy World The British comedian delivers some of his best material with the help of "Hill's Angels."
1974 55m/C *GB* Benny Hill. **VHS, Beta** $19.99 HBO 🐾🐾

Beretta's Island When Interpol operative Beretta comes out of retirement to track his friend's killer, the chase leads him back to his homeland of Sardinia, which has been overrun by drugs.
1992 (R) 97m/C Franco Columbu, Ken Kercheval; *Cameos:* Arnold Schwarzenegger. **VHS** $89.98 LIV 🐾🐾

Bergonzi Hand Drama about two art scoundrels who are astonished when an immigrant admits to painting a forged "Bergonzi."
1970 62m/C Keith Mitchell, Gordon Jackson, Martin Miller. **VHS, Beta** $24.95 VYY 🐾

The Berlin Affair A sordid tale from "The Night Porter" director about a Japanese woman seducing various parties in pre-WWII Germany.
1985 (R) 97m/C *IT GE* Mio Takaki, Gudrun Landgrebe, Kevin McNally; *D:* Liliana Cavani; *M:* Pino Donaggio. **VHS, Beta** $79.95 MGM, ING 🐾½

Berlin Alexanderplatz Fassbinder's 15 1/2-hour epic follows the life, death, and resurrection of Franz Biberkof, a former transit worker who has just finished a lengthy prison term and must learn to adjust in the harsh social atmosphere of Berlin in the 1920s. Melodramatic parable with Biblical overtones considered by some to be a masterpiece. Based on the novel by Alfred Doblin; originally aired as a miniseries on German television. On eight tapes.
1980 930m/C *GE* Gunter Lamprecht, Hanna Schygulla, Barbara Sukowa, Gottfried John, Elisabeth Trissenaar, Brigitte Mira, Karin Baal, Ivan Desny; *D:* Rainer Werner Fassbinder. **VHS, Beta** $400.00 FCT, MGM 🐾🐾🐾🐾

Berlin Blues A nightclub singer is torn between two men.
1989 (PG-13) 90m/C Julia Migenes-Johnson, Keith Baxter; *D:* Richardo Franco. **VHS** $79.95 CAN 🐾🐾½

The Berlin Conspiracy Espionage/action potboiler does an imaginative job of setting its action against the fall of the Berlin Wall and the end of the Cold War. A CIA agent forms a shaky alliance with his East German spymaster rival to prevent germ warfare technology from falling into terrorist hands.
1991 (R) 83m/C Marc Singer, Mary Crosby, Stephen Davies, Richard Leparmentier, Terence Henry; *D:* Terence H. Winkless. **VHS** $89.95 COL 🐾🐾

Berlin Express Battle of wits ensues between the Allies and the Nazis who are seeking to keep Germans divided in post-WWII Germany. Espionage and intrigue factor heavily.
1948 86m/B Robert Ryan, Merle Oberon, Paul Lukas, Charles Korvin; *D:* Jacques Tourneur. **VHS, Beta** $19.95 MED, TTC, FCT 🐾🐾🐾

Berlin Tunnel 21 Based on the novel by Donald Lindquist, five American soldiers attempt a daring Cold War rescue of a beautiful German girl. The plan is to construct a tunnel under the Berlin Wall. A better-than-average film that was made for television.
1981 150m/C Richard Thomas, Jose Ferrer, Horst Buchholz; *D:* Richard Michaels. **VHS, Beta** NO 🐾½

Bernadette A French-made version of the legend of St. Bernadette, who endured persecution after claiming to have seen the Virgin Mary. Beautiful in its simplicity, but overly long.
1990 120m/C *FR* Sydney Penny, Roland LeSaffre, Michele Simonnet, Bernard Dheran, Arlette Didier; *D:* Jean Delannoy. **VHS, Beta** IGP 🐾🐾½

Bernard and the Genie It seems Bernard Bottle is not going to have a happy Christmas—he's been fired from his job and his girlfriend has left him. But things take a turn for the better when he discovers an antique lamp and its resident Genie. But with the Genie granting his every wish, Bernard's sudden wealth is causing some suspicions among both his greedy ex-employer and the police. Meanwhile, the Genie discovers the delights of modern-day England and poses as a department store Santa to truly fulfill a child's Christmas wish. Amusing family fare.
199? (G) 70m/C *GB* Alan Cumming, Lenny Henry, Rowan Atkinson; *D:* Paul Weiland. **VHS** $19.98 FOX, BTV 🐾🐾½

Berserk! A seedy traveling circus is beset by a series of murders. Not heralded as one of Crawford's best pieces.
1967 95m/C Joan Crawford, Diana Dors, Judy Geeson, Ty Hardin; *D:* James O'Connolly. **VHS, Beta** $19.95 COL 🐾½

Berserker Six camping college students are attacked by a bloodthirsty psychotic out of a Nordic myth, who takes the shape of a badder-than-the-average bear.
1987 (R) 85m/C Joseph Alan Johnson, Valerie Sheldon, Greg Dawson; *D:* Jef Richard. **VHS, Beta** $9.99 PSM 🐾🐾

Bert Rigby, You're a Fool A star-struck British coal miner finds his way to Hollywood singing old showtunes, only to be rebuffed by a cynical industry. Available with Spanish subtitles.
1989 (R) 94m/C Robert Lindsay, Robbie Coltrane, Jackie Gayle, Bruno Kirby, Cathryn Bradshaw, Corbin Bernsen, Anne Bancroft; *D:* Carl Reiner; *W:* Carl Reiner; *M:* Ralph Burns. **VHS, Beta** $14.95 WAR, MVD 🐾🐾½

Besame Intrigue, espionage, and romance get mixed together in this movie.
1987 101m/C Sara Montiel, Maurice Ronet, Franco Fabrizi. **VHS, Beta** $53.95 MAD 🐾🐾

Best Buns on the Beach Sexploitation movie about 10 beautiful girls in a bikini contest, that ends up with them going topless. Ridiculous plot, for mature (??) audiences.
1987 60m/C **VHS** $29.95 IME Woof!

The Best Christmas Pageant Ever The meanest kids in town just decided to participate in the town's Christmas pageant and something special happens when the curtain finally goes up.
1986 60m/C Dennis Weaver, Karen Grassle. **VHS** $19.95 RHV Woof!

Best Defense A U.S. Army tank operator is sent to Kuwait to test a new state-of-the-art tank in a combat situation. Although the cast is popular, the movie as a whole is not funny and the story frequently is hard to follow.
1984 (R) 94m/C Dudley Moore, Eddie Murphy, Kate Capshaw, George Dzundza, Helen Shaver; *D:* Willard Huyck; *W:* Willard Huyck, Gloria Katz. **VHS, Beta** $14.95 PAR 🐾

Best Enemies An English film about a man suffering the trials of the 1960s, including Vietnam, and how it affects his relationships with his friends and wife.
1986 96m/C *GB* Sigrid Thornton, Paul Williams, Judy Morris, Brandon Burke; *D:* David Baker. **VHS, Beta** $29.95 ACA 🐾½

Best Foot Forward Vintage musical about a movie star who agrees to accompany a young cadet to a military ball. Based on the popular Broadway show. The film debuts of Walker, Allyson, and DeHaven. ♫Buckle Down, Winsocki; The Three B's (Barrelhouse, Boogie Woogie, and the Blues); Alive and Kicking; Two O'Clock Jump; Ev'ry Time; Three Men on a Date; Wish I May; Shady Lady; My First Promise; You're Lucky.
1943 95m/C Lucille Ball, June Allyson, Tommy Dix, Nancy Walker, Virginia Weidler, Gloria De Haven, William Gaxton, Harry James; *D:* Edward Buzzell. **VHS, Beta** $19.98 MGM 🐾🐾½

Best Friends A pair of screenwriters decide to marry after years of living and working together. Story based on the lives of screenwriters Barry Levinson and Valerie Curtin.
1982 (PG) 109m/C Goldie Hawn, Burt Reynolds, Jessica Tandy, Barnard Hughes, Audra Lindley, Keenan Wynn, Ron Silver; *D:* Norman Jewison; *W:* Valerie Curtin, Barry Levinson. VHS, Beta $14.95 *WAR ♫♫*

The Best Intentions Ingmar Bergman wrote the screenplay chronicling the early years of the stormy relationship of his parents. Set in Sweden at the turn of the century, the film focuses on the class differences that divide his mother and father, while portrayal of little Bergy is limited to a bundle under his mother's maternity dress. Inspired performances and directing illuminates the emotionally complex relationship, revealing truths about the universal human condition along the way. Six-hour version was shot for television in Europe and Japan. Director August and actress August met and married during filming. In Swedish with English subtitles.
1992 182m/C *SW* Samuel Froler, Pernilla August, Max von Sydow, Ghita Norby, Mona Malm, Lena Endre, Bjorn Kjellman; *D:* Bille August; *W:* Ingmar Bergman. VHS $89.98 *ACA, FCT ♫♫♫*

Best Kept Secrets A feisty woman discovers corruption and blackmail in the police department where her husband is an officer.
1988 104m/C Patty Duke, Frederic Forrest, Peter Coyote; *D:* Jerrold Freedman. VHS, Beta $79.95 *VMK ♫♫*

Best Legs in the 8th Grade A handsome attorney bumps into the gorgeous homeroom angel who had ignored his nebbishly dull countenance in grade school. Lightweight made for TV comedy.
1984 60m/C Tim Matheson, James Belushi, Annette O'Toole, Kathryn Harrold; *D:* Tom Patchett. VHS, Beta *NO ♫♫*

The Best Little Girl in the World Exceptional made for TV tale of an apparently perfect teenager suffering from anorexia. Slow starvation is her only cry for help. Fine performances from Durning and Saint.
1981 96m/C Charles Durning, Eva Marie Saint, Jennifer Jason Leigh, Melanie Mayron, Viveca Lindfors, Jason Miller, David Spielberg, Lisa Pelikan, Ally Sheedy; *D:* Sam O'Steen; *M:* Billy Goldenberg. VHS, Beta *NO ♫♫*

The Best Little Whorehouse in Texas Parton is the buxom owner of The Chicken Ranch, a house of ill-repute that may be closed down unless Sheriff-boyfriend Reynolds can think of a way out. Strong performances don't quite make up for the erratically comic script. Based on the long-running Broadway musical, in turn based on a story by Larry McMurtry. Available in a letterboxed edition on laserdisc.
1982 (R) 115m/C Dolly Parton, Burt Reynolds, Dom DeLuise, Charles Durning, Jim Nabors, Lois Nettleton; *D:* Colin Higgins. VHS, Beta $14.98 *MCA, FCT ♫♫*

The Best Man An incisive, darkly satiric political tract, based on Gore Vidal's play, about two presidential contenders who vie for the endorsement of the aging ex-president, and trample political ethics in the process.
1964 104m/B Henry Fonda, Cliff Robertson, Lee Tracy, Margaret Leighton, Edie Adams, Kevin McCarthy, Ann Sothern, Gene Raymond, Shelley Berman, Mahalia Jackson; *D:* Franklin J. Schaffner; *W:* Gore Vidal. VHS, Beta $19.98 *MGM ♫♫♫½*

The Best of Abbott & Costello Live A compilation of vintage live-television routines by the duo, naturally including "Who's on First," along with their other celebrated bits.
1954 58m/B Bud Abbott, Lou Costello, George Raft, Charles Laughton. VHS, Beta $19.88 *WAR ♫♫♫½*

The Best of Bogart A two-cassette gift pack of the Bogie classics "The Maltese Falcon" and "Casablanca."
1943 204m/B Humphrey Bogart, Ingrid Bergman, Mary Astor, Sydney Greenstreet. VHS, Beta $39.95 *MGM ♫♫♫*

Best of Bugs Bunny & Friends This collection includes classics from great cartoon stars Bugs Bunny, Daffy Duck, Tweetie Pie and Porky Pig. Includes "Duck Soup to Nuts," "A Feud There Was" and "Tweetie Pie."
1940 53m/C *D:* Friz Freleng, Chuck Jones, Robert McKimson. VHS, Beta *MGM ♫♫♫*

The Best of Chaplin Three Chaplin comedies when he worked with Mutual. Includes "The Rink," "One A.M.," and "The Floorwalker."
1918 60m/B Charlie Chaplin; *D:* Charlie Chaplin. VHS $59.95 *MVC, VRS ♫♫♫*

Best of Comic Relief All-star comedic array of stand-up acts was taped "live" in concert to raise money for America's homeless and released on cable television.
1986 120m/C Whoopi Goldberg, Robin Williams, Billy Crystal, Carl Reiner, Harold Ramis, Martin Short, Jerry Lewis, Howie Mandel, Eugene Levy, Steve Allen, Doc Severinsen, Sid Caesar, John Candy, George Carlin. VHS, Beta $39.95 *LHV, WAR ♫♫♫*

Best of Comic Relief '90 More than 40 stars make this two hours a real treat, and the hosts aren't so bad themselves: Whoopi Goldberg, Billy Crystal and Robin Williams. Proceeds from this event, and subsequent tape sales go to Comic Relief, Inc. to benefit the homeless in America. Stars include: Bobcat Goldthwait, Elayne Boosler, George Carlin, Louis Anderson, Dennis Miller, The Simpsons.
1990 120m/C *Performed by:* Bob(cat) Goldthwait, Elayne Boosler, George Carlin, Louie Anderson, Dennis Miller. VHS, Beta $29.95 *RHI ♫♫♫*

Best of Eddie Murphy A compilation of Murphy's funniest bits from his three seasons on "Saturday Night Live," including appearances as Stevie Wonder, Buckwheat, Bill Cosby and Little Richard.
1989 78m/C Eddie Murphy, Joe Piscopo, Robin Duke, Tim Kazurinsky, Mary Gross, Gary Kroeger, Brad Hall, Julia Louis-Dreyfus. VHS, Beta $14.95 *PAR ♫♫½*

Best of Ernie Kovacs A compilation of some of the best moments from Ernie Kovacs' television programs that features such memorable characters as Percy Dovetonsils and the Nairobi Trio.
1956 60m/B Ernie Kovacs, Edie Adams, Ernie Hatrak, Bill Wendell, Peter Hanley. VHS, Beta $19.95 *WST, DVT, TVC ♫♫½*

The Best of John Candy on SCTV Some of Candy's most memorable characters, including Johnny LaRue, Yosh Schmenge, and the grown up Theodore "Beaver" Cleaver, are featured on this compilation of his years on SCTV (Second City Television).
198? 62m/C John Candy, Eugene Levy, Rick Moranis, Catherine O'Hara, Harold Ramis, Martin Short. VHS $14.95 *COL ♫♫½*

The Best of Soap: Jessica's Wonderful Life From the camp TV sitcom comes this take-off on "It's a Wonderful Life." Jessica Tate (Helmond) finds herself at the stairway to heaven, pleading with an angel (Arthur) to return to aid her very dysfunctional family.
197? 70m/C Katherine Helmond, Beatrice Arthur, Robert Mandan, Cathryn Damon, Richard Mulligan, Billy Crystal. VHS $14.95 *REP ♫½*

The Best of Soap: Who Killed Peter? From the outrageous comedy TV series, featuring the eccentric and rich Tate family and the equally eccentric, but working-class, Campbell family. When Jessica Tate (Helmond) is convicted of murdering her tennis pro, brother-in-law Burt (Mulligan) decides to investigate. Crystal gained attention as gay son Jodie Dallas.
1977 72m/C Katherine Helmond, Richard Mulligan, Diana Canova, Robert Urich, Robert Mandan, Ted Wass, Billy Crystal, Robert Guillaume. VHS $14.95 *REP ♫½*

Best of the Badmen A whole bunch of outlaws, although seemingly quite nice, are brought together by an ex-Union general who is being framed. Too much talk, not enough action.
1950 84m/B Robert Ryan, Claire Trevor, Jack Buetel, Robert Preston, Walter Brennan, Bruce Cabot, John Archer, Lawrence Tierney; *D:* William D. Russell. VHS, Beta $19.98 *TTC ♫♫½*

Best of the Best An interracial kick-boxing team strives to win a world championship.
1989 (PG-13) 95m/C Eric Roberts, Sally Kirkland, Christopher Penn, Phillip Rhee, James Earl Jones, John P. Ryan, John Dye, David Agresta, Tom Everett, Louise Fletcher, Simon Rhee; *D:* Robert Radler. VHS, Beta $14.95 *COL ♫½*

Best of the Best 2 The Coliseum is a notorious martial-arts venue owned by the champion fighter Brackus and his manager Weldon. No rules death matches are the norm and when their friend is killed Tommy and Alex set up a grudge match with Brackus.
1993 (R) 100m/C Eric Roberts, Phillip Rhee, Christopher Penn, Ralph Moeller, Wayne Newton, Edan Gross, Sonny Landham, Meg Foster, Simon Rhee, Claire Stansfield, Betty Carvalho; *D:* Robert Radler; *W:* John Allen Nelson, Max Strom; *M:* David Michael Frank. VHS $19.98 *FXV ♫½*

The Best of the Kenny Everett Video Show Scenes from the popular British late-night television show combining new wave rock music, outrageous dancing and innovative video special effects.
1981 104m/C Kenny Everett. VHS, Beta *NO ♫½*

The Best of the Kids in the Hall Features some of the best clips from the hot Canadian comedy ensemble "The Kids in the Hall." Executive producer Lorne Michaels is best known for producing "Saturday Night Live."
1993 120m/C *CA* Dave Foley, Bruce McCulloch, Kevin McDonald, Mark McKinney, Scott Thompson. VHS $59.95 *COL ♫½*

The Best of the Monsters The Canadian comedy team offers a televised look at movie monsters. There is also plenty of political humor mixed in, which might be difficult or elusive for Americans.
196? 45m/B *CA* Wayne & Shuster. VHS, Beta $24.95 *NOS, DVT ♫♫*

The Best of the Two Ronnies A selection of skits from the well-loved BBC comedy series.

197? 45m/C *GB* Ronnie Barker, Ronnie Corbett. VHS, Beta **$14.98** FOX ℐ½

The Best of Times Slim story of two grown men who attempt to redress the failures of the past by reenacting a football game they lost in high school due to a single flubbed pass. With this cast, it should have been better.
1986 (PG) 105m/C Robin Williams, Kurt Russell, M. Emmet Walsh, Pamela Reed, Holly Palance, Donald Moffatt, Margaret Whitton, Kirk Cameron; **D:** Roger Spottiswoode; **W:** Ron Shelton. VHS, Beta, 8mm **$14.98** SUE, NLC ℐℐ

Best of W.C. Fields Three of W.C. Field's Mack Sennett shorts are presented in their complete, uncut form: "The Dentist," "The Fatal Glass of Beer," and "The Golf Specialist."
1933 58m/B W.C. Fields, Elise Cavanna. VHS **$19.95** REP ℐℐ

Best Revenge Two aging hippies engage in a Moroccan drug deal in order to free a kidnapped friend from a sleazy gangster. They get caught by the police, but escape, searching for the engineers of the frame-up.
1983 (R) 92m/C John Heard, Levon Helm, Alberta Watson, John Rhys-Davies, Moses Znaimer; **D:** John Trent; **M:** Keith Emerson. VHS, Beta **$59.95** LHV, WAR ℐℐ

Best Seller An interesting, subtext-laden thriller about a cop/bestselling author with writer's block, and the strange symbiotic relationship he forms with a slick hired killer, who wants his own story written. Dennehy is convincing as the jaded cop, and is paired well with the psychotic Woods.
1987 (R) 112m/C James Woods, Brian Dennehy, Victoria Tennant, Paul Shenar, Seymour Cassel, Allison Balson, George Coe, Anne Pitoniak; **D:** John Flynn; **W:** Larry Cohen; **M:** Jay Michael Ferguson. VHS, Beta **$14.98** VES ℐℐℐ

The Best Way Two summer camp counselors discover they might be gay and desirous of each other. Miller's first film; in French with English subtitles.
1982 85m/C *FR* Patrick Dewaere, Patrick Bouchitey, Christine Pascal, Claude Pieplu; **D:** Claude Miller. VHS, Beta **$79.95** FCT ℐℐ½

The Best Years of Our Lives Three WWII vets return home to try to pick up the threads of their lives. A film that represented a large chunk of American society and helped it readjust to the modern post-war ambience is now considered an American classic. Supporting actor Russell, an actual veteran, holds a record for winning two Oscars for a single role. In addition to his Best Supporting Actor award, Russell was given a special Oscar for bringing home and courage to fellow veterans. Based on the novella by MacKinley Kantor. Remade for television as "Returning Home" in 1975.
1946 170m/B Fredric March, Myrna Loy, Teresa Wright, Dana Andrews, Virginia Mayo, Harold Russell, Hoagy Carmichael, Gladys George, Roman Bohnen, Steve Cochran, Charles Halton; **D:** William Wyler; **W:** Robert Sherwood; **M:** Hugo Friedhofer. Academy Awards '46: Best Actor (March), Best Director (Wyler), Best Film Editing, Best Picture, Best Screenplay, Best Supporting Actor (Russell), Best Original Score; Nominations: Best Sound; British Academy Awards '47: Best Film; Golden Globe Awards '47: Best Film—Drama; National Board of Review Awards '46: 10 Best Films of the Year, Best Director (Wyler). VHS, Beta **$14.98** HBO, SUE, FCT ℐℐℐℐ

Bestia Nocturna A psychopath stalks the freeways, mutilating his victims. He is hunted by one man, who relies on his wits to hunt the madman.

1986 93m/C *SP* Raymundo Capetillo, Laura Flores, Eric Del Castillo, Roberto Canedo; **D:** Humberto Martinez Mijares. VHS, Beta **$79.95** MED, PMS ℐℐ

Bethune The life story of a Canadian doctor who started a practice in Communist China.
1977 88m/C Donald Sutherland, Kate Nelligan, David Gardner, James Hong; **D:** Eric Till. VHS, Beta **$59.95** TWE ℐℐ½

Betrayal Psycho-thriller pits an unhappy widow against her seemingly innocent hired companion. Seems this girl has a boyfriend who has a plan to murder the lonely lady for her money. Routine and predictable.
1974 78m/C Amanda Blake, Dick Haymes, Tisha Sterling, Sam Groom; **D:** Gordon Hessler; **M:** Ernest Gold. VHS **$79.95** JEF ℐ

Betrayal Telefilm based on the book by Lucy Freeman and Julie Roy about a historic malpractice case involving a psychiatrist and one of his female patients. The doctor convinced the female patient that sex with him would serve as therapy.
1978 95m/C Lesley Ann Warren, Rip Torn, Ron Silver, Richard Masur, Stephen Elliott, John Hillerman, Peggy Ann Garner; **D:** Paul Wendkos. VHS, Beta NO ℐℐ½

Betrayal An unusual adult drama, beginning at the end of a seven-year adulterous affair and working its way back in time to finally end at the start of the betrayal of a husband by his wife and his best friend. Kingsley and Irons make Pinter's adaptation of his own play work.
1983 (R) 95m/C *GB* Ben Kingsley, Patricia Hodge, Jeremy Irons; **D:** David Jones; **W:** Harold Pinter. VHS, Beta **$59.98** FOX ℐℐ½

Betrayal from the East A carnival barker saves the Panama Canal from the vicious Japanese war machine in this rather silly wartime drama.
1944 82m/B Lee Tracy, Nancy Kelly, Richard Loo, Abner Biberman, Regis Toomey, Philip Ahn, Addison Richards, Sen Yung, Drew Pearson; **D:** William Berke. VHS, Beta **$19.98** TTC ℐℐ

Betrayal of the Dove Slater stars as a divorced woman set-up on a blind date by best friend Le Brock. Zane is the dashing doctor who sweeps Slater off her feet but things are never quite what they seem. He may not be Mr. Right and the best friend has her own hidden agenda.
1992 (R) 93m/C Helen Slater, Kelly Le Brock, Billy Zane, Alan Thicke, Harvey Korman, Stuart Pankin, David Lander; **D:** Strathford Hamilton; **W:** Robby Benson. VHS **$89.95** PSM ℐℐ

Betrayed Bombshell Turner and strongman Gable star in this story of WWII intrigue. Suspected of being a Nazi informer, Turner is sent back to Holland for a last chance at redemption. Her cover as a sultry nightclub performer has the Nazis drooling and ogling (can you spell h-o-t?), but her act may be blown by an informant. Can luscious Lana get out of this one intact?
1954 107m/C Clark Gable, Lana Turner, Victor Mature, Louis Calhern, O.E. Hasse, Wilfrid Hyde-White, Ian Carmichael, Niall MacGinnis, Nora Swinburne, Roland Culver; **D:** Gottfried Reinhardt. VHS, Beta **$19.98** MGM, CCB ℐℐℐ

Betrayed A rabid political film, dealing with an implausible FBI agent infiltrating a white supremacist organization via her love affair with a handsome farmer who turns out to be a murderous racist. Winger is memorable in her role as the FBI agent, despite the film's limitations, and admirers of Costa-Gavras's directorial work and political stances will want to see how the director botched this one.

1988 (R) 112m/C Tom Berenger, Debra Winger, John Mahoney, John Heard, Albert Hall; **D:** Constantin Costa-Gavras; **W:** Joe Eszterhas. VHS, Beta **$14.95** MGM ℐℐ

A Betrayed Man Extremely rare 30's independent film.
1936 ?m/C John Hughes, Smiley Burnette. VHS **$15.95** LOO ℐℐ

The Betsy A story of romance, money, power, and mystery centering around the wealthy Hardeman family and their automobile manufacturing business. Loosely patterned after the life of Henry Ford as portrayed in the Harold Robbins' pulp-tome. Olivier is the redeeming feature. **AKA:** Harold Robbins' The Betsy.
1978 (R) 132m/C Laurence Olivier, Kathleen Beller, Robert Duvall, Lesley-Anne Down, Edward Herrmann, Tommy Lee Jones, Katharine Ross, Jane Alexander; **D:** Daniel Petrie; **W:** William Bast, Walter Bernstein; **M:** John Barry. VHS, Beta **$59.98** FOX ℐℐ

Betsy's Wedding Betsy wants a simple wedding, but her father has other, grander ideas. Then there's the problem of paying for it, which Dad tries to take care of that in a not-so-typical manner. Alda at his hilarious best.
1990 (R) 94m/C Alan Alda, Joey Bishop, Madeline Kahn, Molly Ringwald, Catherine O'Hara, Joe Pesci, Ally Sheedy, Burt Young, Anthony LaPaglia, Julie Bovasso, Nicholas Coster, Bibi Besch, Dylan Walsh; **D:** Alan Alda; **W:** Alan Alda; **M:** Bruce Broughton. VHS, Beta **$89.95** TOU ℐℐ½

Better Late Than Never Fun television tale of senior citizens in revolt at an old-age home. Fine characters portrayed by some of the best in the business.
1979 100m/C Harold Gould, Tyne Daly, Strother Martin, Harry Morgan, Victor Buono, George Gobel, Lou Jacobi, Donald Pleasence, Larry Storch; **D:** Richard Crenna; **M:** Charles Fox. VHS **$59.98** FOX ℐℐ

Better Late Than Never Two penniless old fools vie for the acceptance of a bratty 10-year-old millionairess, who must choose one as her guardian. Niven's last film.
1983 95m/C David Niven, Art Carney, Dame Maggie Smith, Kimberly Partridge, Catherine Hicks, Melissa Prophet; **D:** Bryan Forbes. VHS, Beta **$59.98** FOX ℐ½

Better Off Dead A compulsive teenager's girlfriend leaves him and he decides to end it all. After several abortive attempts, he decides instead to out-ski his ex-girlfriend's obnoxious new boyfriend. Uneven but funny.
1985 (PG) 97m/C John Cusack, Curtis Armstrong, Diane Franklin, Kim Darby, David Ogden Stiers, Dan Schneider, Amanda Wyss, Taylor Negron, Vincent Schiavelli, Demian Slade, Scooter Stevens; **D:** Steve Holland; **W:** Steve Holland; **M:** Rupert Hine. VHS, Beta **$79.98** FOX ℐℐ½

A Better Tomorrow Gangster movie with the requisite bloodletting and male bonding. Film captured a big box-office. In Cantonese with English subtitles. **AKA:** Yingxiong Bense.
1986 95m/C *CH* Chow Yung Fat, Leslie Cheung, Ti Lung; **D:** John Woo. VHS **$39.95** FCT ℐ½

A Better Tomorrow, Part 2 A smooth-talking gangster, who was killed in Part I, returns in Part II as the dead man's twin brother (unmentioned in Part I). He teams up with a cop and a reformed gangster to fight the forces of evil. In Cantonese with English subtitles.
1988 100m/C *CH* Chow Yung Fat, Leslie Cheung; **D:** John Woo. VHS **$39.95** FCT ℐ½

Betty Blue A vivid, intensely erotic film about two young French lovers and how their inordinately strong passion for each other destroys them, leading to poverty, violence, and insanity. English subtitles. From the director of "Diva." Based on the novel "37.2 Le Matin" by Philippe Djian.
1986 (R) 121m/C *FR* Beatrice Dalle, Jean-Hughes Anglade, Gerard Darmon, Consuelo de Haviland, Clementine Celarie, Jacques Mathou, Vincent Lindon; *D:* Jean-Jacques Beineix; *W:* Jean-Jacques Beineix; *M:* Gabriel Yared. **VHS, Beta $79.98** *FOX, ING* 🎭🎭🎭

Between Fighting Men The orphaned daughter of a shepherd is adopted by the cowpoke who caused her father's death. The cowpoke's sons fall in love with, and compete for, the love of the girl.
1932 62m/B Ken Maynard, Ruth Hall, Josephine Dunn, Wallace MacDonald; *D:* Forrest Sheldon. **VHS $19.95** *NOS, DVT* 🎭½

Between Friends Two women with only their respective divorces in common, meet and become fast friends. The rapport between Burnett and Taylor makes for a touching drama. Adapted for cable television from the book "Nobody Makes Me Cry," by Shelley List, one of the producers.
1983 105m/C Elizabeth Taylor, Carol Burnett; *D:* Lou Antonio; *M:* James Horner. **VHS, Beta $69.95** *VES* 🎭🎭½

Between God, the Devil & a Winchester Violent western with plenty of shooting and dust. Lots of cowboys are hot on the trail of some stolen loot from a church but apparently God isn't on their side since the majority bite the dust and become a snack for the vultures.
1972 98m/C Gilbert Roland, Richard Harrison; *D:* Dario Silvester. **VHS, Beta $49.95** *UNI* 🎭

Between Heaven and Earth Maria (Maura) is an ambitious television journalist, prone to surreal dreams, who becomes pregnant after a one-night stand. After witnessing a violent protest, Maria becomes convinced that she can communicate with her unborn baby and that the child is unwilling to be born into such a violent world. So Maria must try to convince her baby otherwise. In French with English subtitles.
1993 80m/C *BE FR SP* Carmen Maura, Jean-Pierre Cassel, Didier Bezace, Samuel Mussen, Andre Delvaux; *D:* Marion Hansel; *W:* Marion Hansel. **VHS $79.95** *FCT* 🎭🎭

Between Heaven and Hell Prejudiced Southern gentleman Wagner finds how wrong his misconceptions are, as he attempts to survive WWII on a Pacific Island. Ebsen is exceptional, making this rather simplistic story a meaningful classic.
1956 94m/C Robert Wagner, Terry Moore, Broderick Crawford, Buddy Ebsen, Robert Keith, Brad Dexter, Mark Damon, Kenneth Clark, Harvey Lembeck, Frank Gorshin, Scatman Crothers; *D:* Richard Fleischer. **VHS $14.98** *FXV* 🎭🎭🎭

Between Men A father kills a man he believes killed his son and flees. Later in life, the son meets his father. For father and son, this causes some major concern.
1935 59m/B Johnny Mack Brown, Beth Marion, William Farnum, Earl Dwire, Lloyd Ingraham, Milburn Morante, William S. Hart; *D:* Robert North Bradbury. **VHS, Beta $19.95** *NOS, DVT, GPV* 🎭🎭

Between the Lines A witty, wonderfully realized ensemble comedy about the staff of a radical post-'60s newspaper always on the brink of folding, and its eventual sell-out.

1977 (R) 101m/C John Heard, Lindsay Crouse, Jeff Goldblum, Jill Eikenberry, Stephen Collins, Lewis J. Stadlen, Michael J. Pollard, Marilu Henner, Bruno Kirby; *D:* Joan Micklin Silver; *M:* Michael Kamen. **VHS, Beta $69.95** *VES* 🎭🎭🎭½

Between Two Women A television movie about a wife's rocky relationship with her bossy mother-in-law, until the latter has a stroke and needs care. Dewhurst won an Emmy for her portrayal of the mother-in-law.
1986 95m/C Farrah Fawcett, Michael Nouri, Colleen Dewhurst, Danny Corkill; *D:* Willis Goldbeck. **VHS, Beta $19.98** *WAR* 🎭🎭

Between Wars Young doctor in Australia's Medical Corps encounters conflict when he tries to introduce Freud's principles into his work.
1974 97m/C *AU* Corin Redgrave, Arthur Dignam, Judy Morris, Patricia Leehy, Gunter Meisner; *D:* Michael Thornhill. **VHS, Beta** *NO* 🎭🎭

Beulah Land A television mini-series about 45 years in the lives of a Southern family, through the Civil War. Based on the novels "Beulah Land" and "Look Away, Beulah Land" by Lonnie Coleman.
1980 267m/C Lesley Ann Warren, Michael Sarrazin, Don Johnson, Meredith Baxter Birney, Dorian Harewood, Eddie Albert, Hope Lange, Paul Rudd; *D:* Virgil W. Vogel, Harry Falk. **VHS, Beta $29.95** *COL, TVC* 🎭

The Beverly Hillbillies The successful sitcom series, which ran from 1962-1971, features Jed Clampett and his Ozark clan striking oil, getting rich, and heading for the good life in California. Two episodes per tape.
1962 51m/B Buddy Ebsen, Irene Ryan, Donna Douglas, Max Baer Sr., Nancy Kulp, Raymond Bailey, Phil Silvers; *Cameos:* John Wayne. **VHS $12.98** *FXV, MOV* 🎭½

The Beverly Hillbillies Big-screen transfer of the long-running TV show may appeal to fans. Ozark mountaineer Jed Clampett discovers oil, becomes an instant billionaire, and packs his backwoods clan off to the good life in California. Minimal plot finds dim-bulb nephew Jethro and daughter Elly May looking for a bride for Jed. Not that any of it matters. Everyone does fine by their impersonations, particularly Varney as the good-hearted Jed and Leachman as stubborn Granny. Ebsen, the original Jed, reprises another of his TV roles, detective Barnaby Jones. And yes, the familiar strains of the "Ballad of Jed Clampett" by Jerry Scoggins starts this one off, too.
1993 (PG) 93m/C Jim Varney, Erika Eleniak, Diedrich Bader, Cloris Leachman, Dabney Coleman, Lily Tomlin, Lea Thompson, Rob Schneider, Linda Carlson, Penny Fuller, Kevin Connolly; *Cameos:* Buddy Ebsen, Zsa Zsa Gabor, Dolly Parton; *D:* Penelope Spheeris; *W:* Larry Konner, Mark Rosenthal, Jim Fisher, Jim Staahl; *M:* Lalo Schifrin. **VHS** *FXV* 🎭🎭½

Beverly Hills Bodysnatchers A mad scientist and a greedy mortician plot to get rich, but their plan backfires when they bring a Mafia godfather back to life and he terrorizes Beverly Hills.
1989 (R) 85m/C Vic Tayback, Frank Gorshin, Brooke Bundy, Seth Jaffe, Art Metrano; *D:* Jon Mostow. **VHS $39.95** *IME* 🎭½

Beverly Hills Brats A spoiled, rich Hollywood brat hires a loser to kidnap him, in order to gain his parents' attention, only to have both of them kidnapped by real crooks.
1989 (PG-13) 90m/C Martin Sheen, Burt Young, Peter Billingsley, Terry Moore; *D:* Dimitri Sotirakis; *M:* Barry Goldberg. **VHS, Beta $89.95** *LIV, IME, VTR* 🎭

Beverly Hills Cop When a close friend of smooth-talking Detroit cop Axle Foley is brutally murdered in L.A., he traces the murderer to the posh streets of Beverly Hills. There he must stay on his toes to keep one step ahead of the killer and two steps ahead of the law. Better than average Murphy vehicle.
1984 (R) 105m/C Eddie Murphy, Judge Reinhold, John Ashton, Lisa Eilbacher, Ronny Cox, Steven Berkoff, James Russo, Jonathan Banks, Stephen Elliott, Bronson Pinchot, Paul Reiser; *W:* Damon Wayans, Rick Overton; *D:* Martin Brest; *W:* Danilo Bach, Dan Petrie Jr.; *M:* Harold Faltermeyer. Academy Awards '84 Nominations: Best Original Screenplay; People's Choice Awards '85: Best Film. **VHS, Beta, 8mm $14.95** *PAR* 🎭🎭½

Beverly Hills Cop 2 The highly successful sequel to the first profitable comedy, with essentially the same plot, this time deals with Foley infiltrating a band of international munitions smugglers.
1987 (R) 103m/C Eddie Murphy, Judge Reinhold, Juergen Prochnow, Ronny Cox, John Ashton, Brigitte Nielsen, Allen (Gooritz) Garfield, Paul Reiser, Dean Stockwell; *D:* Tony Scott; *W:* Larry Ferguson, Warren Skaaren; *M:* Harold Faltermeyer. **VHS, Beta, 8mm $14.95** *PAR* 🎭½

Beverly Hills Cop 3 Yes, Detroit cop Axel Foley (Murphy) just happens to find another case that takes him back to his friends on the Beverly Hills PD. This time he uncovers a criminal network fronting WonderWorld, an amusement park with a squeaky-clean image. Fast-paced action, lots of gunplay, and Eddie wisecracks his way through the slow spots. Reinhold returns as the still impossibly naive Rosewood, with Bronson briefly reprising his role as Serge of the undeterminable accent. Critically panned box office disappointment relies too heavily on formula and is another disappointing followup.
1994 (R) 109m/C Eddie Murphy, Judge Reinhold, Hector Elizondo, Timothy Carhart, Stephen McHattie, Theresa Randle, John Saxon, Alan Young, Bronson Pinchot; *Cameos:* Al Green, Gil Hill; *D:* John Landis; *W:* Steven E. de Souza; *M:* Nile Rodgers. **VHS** *NYR* 🎭½

Beverly Hills Knockouts A bevy of beautiful boxers pummel each other with both fists.
1989 60m/C **VHS, Beta $39.95** *CEL* 🎭½

Beverly Hills Madam In this routine plot, a stable of elite call girls struggle with their lifestyle and their madam, played by Dunaway. Made for television.
1986 (PG-13) 97m/C Faye Dunaway, Louis Jourdan, Donna Dixon, Robin Givens, Marshall Colt, Melody Anderson, Terry Farrell; *D:* Harvey Hart. **VHS, Beta $59.98** *ORI* 🎭

Beverly Hills 90210 In the pilot episode for the immensely popular series, the world is introduced to the exciting teens who wander the halls of West Beverly High. Join Brandon and Brenda Walsh as they move from Minneapolis to Beverly Hills and experience all the trials and tribulations that come with the new zip code. Includes 25 minutes of previously unseen footage.
1990 90m/C Jason Priestly, Shannen Doherty, Jennie Garth, Brian Austin Green, Tori Spelling, Ian Ziering, Gabrielle Carteris. **VHS $19.99** *WOV, MOV* 🎭

Beverly Hills 90210: The Graduation The 1993 end-of-the-season episode of the hit TV series finds the group finally getting out of Beverly Hills High. As they graduate the friends share plans for the summer (and the future) and you'll see lots of flashbacks as well as their final graduation

prank. Includes interviews with the cast and music videos from the series soundtrack.
1993 90m/C Jason Priestly, Shannen Doherty, Luke Perry, Jennie Garth, Brian Austin Green, Tori Spelling, Ian Ziering, Gabrielle Carteris. **VHS $14.98** *WOV* 🐾

Beverly Hills Vamp A madame and her girls are really female vampires with a penchant for hot-blooded men.
1988 (R) 88m/C Britt Ekland, Eddie Deezen, Debra Lamb; **D:** Fred Olen Ray. **VHS, Beta $79.95** *VMK* 🐾🐾

Beware A black singer saves a college from bankruptcy and makes off with the gym teacher. The photography may be a bit harsh, but the all-black cast made this a pioneering but impressive film.
1946 64m/B Louis Jordan, Frank Wilson, Emory Richardson, Valerie Black, Milton Woods; **D:** Bud Pollard. **VHS $24.95** *NOS, RXM* 🐾🐾½

Beware, My Lovely Taut chiller. Lonely widow Lupino hires a new handy-man. He's great with screen doors and storm windows, but has a problem with sharp tools. Intense and gripping with fine performances.
1952 77m/B Ida Lupino, Robert Ryan, Taylor Holmes, O.Z. Whitehead, Barbara Whiting, Dee Pollock; **D:** Harry Horner. **VHS $19.98** *REP* 🐾🐾½

Beware of Pity A crippled baroness thinks she's found true love with a military officer, but it turns out his marriage proposal grew out of pity for her, not passion. A quality but somber British-made historical drama, based on a novel by Stefan Zweig.
1946 105m/B Lilli Palmer, Albert Lieven, Cedric Hardwicke, Gladys Cooper, Ernest Thesiger, Freda Jackson; **D:** Maurice Elvey. **VHS $19.95** *NOS* 🐾🐾½

Bewitched A made-for-British-television horror story about an elderly couple ostensibly plagued by the witch-like conniving of a dead woman.
1985 60m/C *GB* Eileen Atkins, Alfred Lynch; **D:** Edmund Oboler. **VHS, Beta $59.95** *PSM* 🐾🐾½

Beyond a Reasonable Doubt In order to get a behind-the-scenes glimpse at the judicial system, a man plays the guilty party to a murder. Alas, when he tries to vindicate himself, he is the victim of his own folly. Not as interesting as it sounds on paper.
1956 80m/B Dana Andrews, Joan Fontaine, Sidney Blackmer, Philip Bourneuf, Barbara Nichols, Sheppard Strudwick, Arthur Franz, Edward Binns; **D:** Fritz Lang. **VHS** *NO* 🐾🐾

Beyond Atlantis An ancient underwater tribe is discovered when it kidnaps land-lubbin' women with which to mate.
1973 (PG) 91m/C *PH* John Ashley, Patrick Wayne, George Nader; **D:** Eddie Romero. **VHS, Beta $49.95** *VCI* Woof!

Beyond Darkness When Peter and his family move into their New England home they are immediately beset by some unknown terror. With the help of Father George, Peter learns his house was built upon the graves of twenty witches burned for heresy. The witches have decided to seek revenge by kidnapping Peter's young son and sacrificing him to an evil demon. Can Peter destroy the evil spirits before they destroy his son?
1992 (R) 111m/C Gene Le Brock, David Brandon, Barbara Bingham, Michael Stephenson, Stephen Brown; **D:** Clyde Anderson. **VHS $89.95** *IMP* 🐾½

Beyond Dream's Door A young, All-American college student's childhood nightmares come back to haunt him, making dreams a horrifying reality.

1988 86m/C Nick Baldasare, Rick Kesler, Susan Pinsky, Norm Singer; **D:** Jay Woelfel. **VHS, Beta** *NO* 🐾

Beyond Erotica After being cut out of his father's will, a sadistic young man takes out his rage on his mother and a peasant girl.
1979 90m/C David Hemmings, Alida Valli, Andrea Rau. **VHS $59.95** *PSM* 🐾

Beyond Evil Relatively dimwitted newlywed couple moves into an old island mansion despite rumors that the house is haunted. Sure enough, wife George becomes possessed by the vengeful spirit of a woman murdered 200 years earlier, and a reign of pointless terror begins. Poor rip-off of hybrid Amityville/Exorcist paranormality.
1980 (R) 98m/C John Saxon, Lynda Day George, Michael Dante, Mario Milano; **D:** Herb Freed; **W:** Herb Freed; **M:** Pino Donaggio. **VHS, Beta $49.95** *MED* Woof!

Beyond Fear Compelling drama about a man forced to aid a gang in robbery while they hold his wife and son captive.
1975 92m/C Michael Boquet. **VHS, Beta $49.95** *PSM* 🐾🐾½

Beyond Fear Tipper Taylor (Lesseos) is a wilderness tour guide who's also a martial arts expert. This is going to come in handy when her tour group is stalked by two men who are after a videotape innocently filmed by someone in Tipper's group. It seems the tape shows the men committing a murder.
1993 (R) 84m/C Mimi Lesseos. **VHS $89.95** *MNC* 🐾🐾½

Beyond Innocence A 17-year-old lusts after a mature married woman. Ostensibly based on Raymond Radiguet's "Devil in the Flesh."
1987 87m/C Keith Smith, Katia Caballero, John Morris; **D:** Scott Murray. **VHS, Beta** *NO* 🐾

Beyond Justice High action-adventure with the prolific Hauer starring as an ex-CIA agent who is hired to rescue the kidnapped son of a beautiful executive.
1992 (PG-13) 113m/C Rutger Hauer, Carol Alt, Omar Sharif, Elliott Gould. **VHS $9.99** *VMK* 🐾🐾

Beyond Obsession The strange relationship between a political prisioner, his daughter, and her obsession with a mysterious American is provocatively explored.
1982 116m/C *IT* Marcello Mastroianni, Elenora Giorgi, Tom Berenger, Michel Piccoli; **D:** Liliana Cavani. **VHS $19.95** *FCT* 🐾🐾

Beyond Reason A psychologist uses unorthodox methods by treating the criminally insane with dignity and respect.
1977 88m/C Telly Savalas, Laura Johnson, Diana Muldaur, Marvin Laird, Priscilla Barnes; **D:** Telly Savalas. **VHS, Beta $59.95** *MED* 🐾

Beyond Reasonable Doubt Chilling true-life murder mystery which shattered the peaceful quiet of a small New Zealand town and eventually divided the country. An innocent farmer (Hargreaves) was convicted of a grisly double murder based on evidence planted by a local cop (Hemmings, in a superb role). It wasn't until Yallop's book questioned the facts of the case that it was reopened. Yallop also wrote the screenplay.
1980 127m/C *NZ* David Hemmings, John Hargreaves, Martyn Sanderson, Grant Tilly, Diana Rowan, Ian Watkin; **D:** John Laing; **W:** David Yallop. **VHS, Beta** *NO* 🐾🐾½

Beyond the Bermuda Triangle Unfortunate and flat television flick. Businessman MacMurray, now retired, doesn't have enough to do. He begins an investigation of the mysterious geometric island area when his friends and fiancee disappear. Silly.

1975 78m/C Fred MacMurray, Sam Groom, Donna Mills, Suzanne Reed, Dana Plato, Woody Woodbury; **D:** William A. Graham. **VHS** *NO* 🐾½

Beyond the Call of Duty Renegade U.S. Army Commander Len Jordan (Vincent) is after a particularly deadly Vietcong enemy. Aided by the head of a special forces naval unit he tracks his quarry through the notorious Mekong River Delta. But Jordan's mission may be hindered, both personally and professionally, by a beautiful American journalist after a hot story.
1992 (R) 92m/C Jan-Michael Vincent, Eb Lottimer, Jillian McWhirter; **D:** Cirio H. Santiago. **VHS $89.98** *NHO* 🐾½

Beyond the Carribean Bizarre jungle thriller featuring voodoo and native crucifixion. Also known as "Manhunters of the Carribean."
1932 ?m/B Andre Roosevelt. **VHS $16.95** *SNC* 🐾🐾

Beyond the Door San Francisco woman finds herself pregnant with a demonic child. One of the first "Exorcist" ripoffs; skip this one and go right to the sequel, "Beyond the Door 2." In Italian; dubbed. **AKA:** Beyond Obsession.
1975 (R) 97m/C *IT* Juliet Mills, Richard Johnson, David Colin Jr.; **D:** Oliver Hellman. **VHS, Beta $54.95** *MED, COL* Woof!

Beyond the Door 2 Better treatment of the possession theme, but this time the door is to the home of a new family: Colin (from the original) plays a boy possessed by his dead father, who seeks revenge on his widow and her new husband. Director Bava's last feature. **AKA:** Shock.
1979 (R) 90m/C *IT* John Steiner, Daria Nicolodi, David Colin Jr., Ivan Rassimov; **D:** Mario Bava; **W:** Lamberto Bava, Franco Barbieri. **VHS, Beta $59.95** *MED* 🐾🐾½

Beyond the Door 3 Fool American students in Yugoslavia board a hellish locomotive which speeds them toward a satanic ritual. Demonic disaster-movie stuff (with poor miniatures) isn't as effective as the on-location filming; Serbian scenery and crazed peasants impart an eerie pagan aura. What this has to do with earlier "Beyond the Door" movies only the marketing boys can say. Some dialogue in Serbo-Croat with English subtitles.
1991 (R) 94m/C Mary Kohnert, Sarah Conway Ciminera, William Geiger, Renee Rancourt, Alex Vitale, Victoria Zinny, Savina Gersak, Bo Svenson; **D:** Jeff Kwitny. **VHS $89.95** *COL* Woof!

Beyond the Forest Camp diva Davis, in her last role for Warner Bros., really turns on the histrionics as a big-city gal married to a small-town guy (Cotten) and bored out of her mind. Although the most memorable line, "What a dump," has become larger-than-life, the film itself is rather small and muddled (interestingly, Vidor directed "The Fountainhead" the same year.) A trashy melodrama full of ennui, envy, unwanted pregnancy, and murder, it's decidedly high on camp and low on art.
1949 96m/B Bette Davis, Joseph Cotten, David Brian, Ruth Roman, Minor Watson, Regis Toomey; **D:** King Vidor. **VHS $19.95** *MGM, FCT* 🐾½

Beyond the Law Spaghetti western with Van Cleef as the too smart bad guy. He becomes sheriff, picks up the stack of silver at the depot, and disappears. Humorous and clever, with fine location photography. **AKA:** Bloodsilver; Al Di La Della Legge.

1968 91m/C *IT* Lee Van Cleef, Antonio Sabato, Lionel Stander, Bud Spencer, Gordon Mitchell, Ann Smyrner; *D:* Giorgio Stegani. **VHS $19.95** *IMP, QVD* ♫♫

Beyond the Limit The story of an intense and darkly ominous love triangle which takes place in the South American coastal city of Corrientes. Based on Graham Greene's novel "The Honorary Consul." *AKA:* The Honorary Consul.
1983 (R) 103m/C Michael Caine, Richard Gere, Bob Hoskins, Elpidia Carrillo; *D:* John MacKenzie; *W:* Christopher Hampton. **VHS, Beta $59.95** *PAR* ♫♫½

Beyond the Next Mountain A missionary in China attempts to convert all those he meets. Thin plot and marginal acting will likely make viewers fall asleep.
1987 (PG) 97m/C Alberto Isaac, Jon Lormer, Bennett Ohta, Richard Lineback, Edward Ashley, Barry Foster; *D:* James F. Collier, Rolf Forsberg. **VHS, Beta $79.95** *VCI, VGD* ♫

Beyond the Poseidon Adventure A sequel to the 1972 film in which salvage teams and ruthless looting vandals compete for access to the sunken ocean liner. Sinking ships should be abandoned.
1979 (PG) 115m/C Michael Caine, Sally Field, Telly Savalas, Peter Boyle, Jack Warden, Slim Pickens, Shirley Knight, Shirley Jones, Karl Malden, Mark Harmon; *D:* Irwin Allen. **VHS, Beta $19.98** *WAR* ♫

Beyond the Rockies Keene and a group of cowboys battle cattle rustlers in this action-packed sagebrush saga. Solid script with good direction by Allen.
1932 55m/B Tom Keene, Rochelle Hudson, Ernie Adams, Julian Rivero, Hank Bell, Tom London; *D:* Fred Allen; *W:* John P. McCarthy. **VHS $19.99** *MOV* ♫♫½

Beyond the Silhouette It starts out as another sleazy video sex thriller, as the lawyer heroine discovers her sensuality and poses a lot in her underclothes. Then in the third act it become a hyper-paranoid political-conspiracy assassination-o-rama. Pretty weird junk. *AKA:* Ultimate Desires.
1990 90m/C *CA* Tracy Scoggins, Marc Singer, Brion James; *D:* Lloyd A. Simandl. **VHS, Beta** *NO* ♫

Beyond the Stars A sci-fi adventure directed by the author of "Cocoon," wherein a whiz-kid investigates the NASA cover-up of a deadly accident that occurred on the moon during the Apollo 11 landing. Unfortunately, the interesting cast can't make up for the script.
1989 94m/C Martin Sheen, Christian Slater, Olivia D'Abo, F. Murray Abraham, Robert Foxworth, Sharon Stone; *D:* David Saperstein. **VHS, Beta $89.95** *LIV* ♫

Beyond the Time Barrier Air Force test pilot gets more than he bargained for when his high speed plane carries him into the future. There he sees the ravages of an upcoming plague, to which he must return.
1960 75m/B Robert Clarke, Darlene Tompkins, Arianne Arden, Vladimir Sokoloff; *D:* Edgar G. Ulmer. **VHS, Beta $16.95** *SNC, CNM* ♫♫½

Beyond the Valley of the Dolls Sleazy, spirited non-sequel to "Valley of the Dolls." Meyer ("Faster, Pussycat! Kill! Kill!") directed this Hollywood parody ("BVD," as it came to be known) about an all-girl rock combo and their search for stardom. Labeled the first "exploitation horror camp musical"—how can you pass that up? Screenplay by film critic Ebert, from an original story by Ebert and Meyer. Mondo trasho.
1970 (NC-17) 109m/C Edy Williams, Dolly Reed; *D:* Russ Meyer; *W:* Roger Ebert. **VHS, Beta $19.98** *FXV, BTV* ♫♫½

Beyond the Walls The opposing factions of a hellish Israeli prison unite to beat the system. Brutal with good characterizations. Available in both subtitled and dubbed versions. *AKA:* Meachorei Hasoragim.
1984 (R) 104m/C *IS* Arnon Zadok, Muhamad Bakri; *D:* Uri Barbash. Academy Awards '84 Nominations: Best Foreign Language Film; Venice Film Festival '85: Best Film. **VHS, Beta $79.95** *WAR, ING* ♫♫½

Beyond Therapy A satire on modern psychotherapy, from the play by Christopher Durang, about a confused, crazily neurotic couple and their respective, and not any saner, analysts. Unfortunately, comes off as disjointed and confused.
1986 (R) 93m/C Jeff Goldblum, Tom Conti, Julie Hagerty, Glenda Jackson, Christopher Guest; *D:* Robert Altman; *W:* Robert Altman. **VHS, Beta $19.95** *STE, NWV* ♫½

Beyond Tomorrow Young romance is guided from the spirit world during the Christmas season, as two "ghosts" come back to help young lovers.
1940 84m/B Richard Carlson, Sir C. Aubrey Smith, Jean Parker, Charles Winninger, Harry Carey Sr., Maria Ouspenskaya, Rod La Rocque; *D:* Edward Sutherland. **VHS, Beta $16.95** *SNC, NOS, DVT* ♫♫

Bhowani Junction A half-Indian, half-English woman is torn between her country and the British officer she loves in post-colonial India. Great cinematography. Based on a book by John Masters.
1956 110m/C Ava Gardner, Stewart Granger, Bill Travers, Abraham Sofaer, Francis Matthews, Marne Maitland, Peter Illing, Edward Chapman, Freda Jackson, Lionel Jeffries; *D:* George Cukor. **VHS $19.98** *MGM* ♫♫

The Bible...In the Beginning The book of Genesis is dramatized, including the stories of Adam and Eve, Cain and Abel, and Noah and the flood.
1966 155m/C *IT* George C. Scott, Richard Harris, Stephen Boyd, John Huston, Peter O'Toole, Franco Nero, Ava Gardner; *D:* John Huston. **VHS, Beta $29.98** *FOX* ♫♫♫

The Bicycle Thief A world classic and indisputable masterpiece about an Italian workman who finds a job, only to have the bike he needs for work stolen; he and his son search Rome for it. A simple story that seems to contain the whole of human experience, and the masterpiece of Italian neorealism. Based on the book by Luigi Bartolini. In Italian with English subtitles. *AKA:* Ladri di Biciclette.
1948 90m/B *IT* Lamberto Maggiorani, Lianella Carell, Enzo Staiola, Elena Altieri, Vittorio Antonucci, Gino Saltamerenda, Fausto Guerzoni; *D:* Vittorio De Sica; *W:* Cesare Zavattini. Academy Awards '49: Best Foreign Language Film; Nominations: Best Screenplay; British Academy Awards '49: Best Film; Golden Globe Awards '50: Best Foreign Film; National Board of Review Awards '49: 5 Best Foreign Films of the Year, Best Director (De Sica). **VHS, Beta $69.95** *ING, NOS, MRV* ♫♫♫♫

Big A 13-year-old boy makes a wish at a carnival fortune-teller to be "big." When he wakes up the next morning he finds that he suddenly won't fit into his clothes and his mother doesn't recognize him. Until he finds a cure, he must learn to live in the adult world—complete with job, apartment, and romance. Perkins is wonderful as a warming cynic while Hanks is totally believable as the little boy inside a man's body. Marshall directs with authority and the whole thing clicks from the beginning.

1988 (PG) 98m/C Tom Hanks, Elizabeth Perkins, John Heard, Robert Loggia, Jared Rushton, David Moscow, Jon Lovitz, Mercedes Ruehl; *D:* Penny Marshall; *W:* Gary Ross. Academy Awards '88 Nominations: Best Actor (Hanks), Best Original Screenplay; Golden Globe Awards '89: Best Actor—Musical/Comedy (Hanks); People's Choice Awards '89: Best Film—Musical/Comedy. **VHS, Beta $19.98** *FOX, HMV* ♫♫♫

Big Bad John Some good ol' boys ride around in trucks as they get into a variety of shootouts. The soundtrack includes music by Willie Nelson, The Charlie Daniels Band, and others.
1990 (PG-13) 91m/C Jimmy Dean, Ned Beatty, Jack Elam, Bo Hopkins, Romy Windsor, Doug English. **VHS, Beta** *IME* ♫

Big Bad Mama Tough and sexy machine-gun toting mother moves her two nubile daughters out of Texas during the Depression, and they all turn to robbing banks as a means of support while creating sharp testosterone increases among the local men. "Wild Palm" Dickinson has notable nude scene with Captain Kirk. "Big Bad Mama 2" arrived some 13 years later.
1974 (R) 83m/C Angie Dickinson, William Shatner, Tom Skerritt, Susan Sennett, Robbie Lee, Sally Kirkland, Noble Willingham, Royal Dano, Dick Miller; *D:* Steve Carver; *W:* William W. Norton Sr. **VHS, Beta $39.98** *NO* ♫♫½

Big Bad Mama 2 Belated Depression-era sequel to the 1974 Roger Corman gangster film, where the pistol-packin' matriarch battles a crooked politician with the help of her two daughters.
1987 (R) 85m/C Angie Dickinson, Robert Culp, Danielle Brisebois, Julie McCullough; *D:* Jim Wynorski; *W:* Jim Wynorski, R.J. Robertson. **VHS, Beta $14.95** *MGM* ♫½

The Big Bet High school sex comedy about a guy who is challenged by the school bully to get the gorgeous new girl into bed. Energetic romp is for adults.
1985 (R) 90m/C Sylvia Kristel, Kimberly Evenson, Ron Thomas; *D:* Bert I. Gordon. **VHS, Beta** *NO* ♫

The Big Bird Cage Prison spoof sequel to "The Big Doll House." Horny females incarcerated in a rural jail decide to defy their homosexual guards and plan an escape. They are aided by revolutionaries led by a Brooklynese expatriate and his lover. *AKA:* Women's Penitentiary II.
1972 (R) 93m/C Pam Grier, Sid Haig, Anitra Ford, Candice Roman, Teda Bracci, Carol Speed, Karen McKevic; *D:* Jack Hill. **VHS, Beta $39.98** *WAR* ♫♫

The Big Blue Vapid, semi-true tale about competing free-divers, who descend deep into the big blue without the aid of any kind of breathing apparatus. Arquette is the ditz who makes them come up for air. *AKA:* Le Grand Bleu.
1988 (PG) 122m/C Rosanna Arquette, Jean Reno, Jean-Marc Barr, Paul Shenar, Sergio Castellitto, Marc Duret, Griffin Dunne; *D:* Luc Besson; *W:* Luc Besson; *M:* Bill Conti. **VHS, Beta $89.95** *COL* ♫½

Big Bluff Disappointing result from an interesting premise; fatally ill woman finds love, but when she surprisingly recovers, her new husband decides to help her back along the path to death. Uneven and melodramatic. *AKA:* Worthy Deceivers.
1955 70m/B *SI* John Bromfield, Martha Vickers, Robert Hutton, Rosemary Bowie; *D:* W. Lee Wilder. **VHS $19.99** *NOS, MOV, HEG* ♫♫

Big Boss A hoodlum climbs to the top of a crime syndicate. An Italian film previously titled "Mr. Scarface."

1977 (R) 90m/C *IT* Jack Palance, Edmund Purdom, Al Cliver, Harry Baer, Gisela Hahn. Beta *NO* 𝄞½

The Big Brawl Chicago gangster recruits a martial arts expert to fight in a free-for-all match in Texas.
1980 (R) 95m/C Jackie Chan, Jose Ferrer, Mako, Rosalind Chao; *D:* Robert Clouse. VHS, Beta $19.98 *WAR* 𝄞½

The Big Bus The wild adventures of the world's first nuclear-powered bus as it makes its maiden voyage from New York to Denver. Clumsy disaster-movie parody.
1976 (PG) 88m/C Joseph Bologna, Stockard Channing, Ned Beatty, Ruth Gordon, Larry Hagman, John Beck, Jose Ferrer, Lynn Redgrave, Sally Kellerman, Stuart Margolin, Richard Mulligan, Howard Hesseman, Richard B. Shull; *D:* James Frawley. VHS, Beta $49.95 *PAR* 𝄞𝄞

Big Business Strained high-concept comedy about two sets of identical twins, each played by Tomlin and Midler, mismatched at birth by a near-sighted country nurse. The city set of twins intends to buy out the factory where the country set of twins work. So the country twins march up to the big city to stop the sale and destruction of their beloved home. Both set of twins stay in the Plaza Hotel and zany consequences ensue. Essentially a one-joke outing with some funny moments, but talented comediennes Midler and Tomlin are somewhat wasted. Great technical effects.
1988 (PG) 98m/C Bette Midler, Lily Tomlin, Fred Ward, Edward Herrmann, Michele Placido, Barry Primus, Michael Gross, Mary Gross, Daniel Gerroll, Roy Brocksmith; *D:* Jim Abrahams. VHS, Beta, 8mm $89.95 *TOU* 𝄞𝄞

Big Business Girl Less than remarkable comedy starring Young as a corporate climber who must dodge her boss' advances and save her troubled marriage when her jazz singer husband is called away to perform in Paris. Based on a story by Patricia Reilly and Harold N. Swanson.
1931 72m/B Loretta Young, Frank Albertson, Ricardo Cortez, Joan Blondell, Dorothy Christy; *D:* William Seiler; *W:* Robert Lord. VHS $19.98 *MGM* 𝄞𝄞

The Big Bust Out Several female convicts escape from prison only to be sold into slavery and face additional torture. Nothing redeeming about this exploitative film.
1973 (R) 75m/C Vonetta McGee, Monica Taylor, Linda Fox, Karen Carter, Gordon Mitchell; *D:* Karen Carter. VHS, Beta $24.98 *SUE* Woof!

Big Calibre A rancher is inches away from being lynched for his dad's murder before he is found to be innocent.
1935 59m/B Bob Steele, Bill Quinn, Earl Dwire, Peggy Campbell, John Elliott, Georgia O'Dell; *D:* Robert North Bradbury. VHS, Beta $12.95 *SNC, DVT, HEG* 𝄞

The Big Cat Mountain valley in Utah is ravaged by a cougar, while two ranchers fuss and feud. Big cat, bickering, help make okay adventure.
1949 75m/C Lon McCallister, Peggy Ann Garner, Preston Foster, Forrest Tucker; *D:* Phil Karlson. VHS, Beta $19.95 *NOS, MRV, DVT* 𝄞𝄞

The Big Chase A rookie cop chases down a mob of payroll thieves in this early action film.
1954 60m/B Glenn Langan, Adele Jergens, Lon Chaney Jr., Jim Davis. VHS, Beta *NO* 𝄞

The Big Chill Seven former '60s radicals, now coming upon middle age and middle class affluence, reunite on the occasion of an eighth friend's suicide and use the occasion to re-examine their past relationships and commitments. A beautifully acted, immensely enjoyable ballad to both the counter-culture and its Yuppie descendants. Great period music. Kevin Costner is the dead man whose scenes never made it to the big screen.
1983 (R) 108m/C Tom Berenger, Glenn Close, Jeff Goldblum, William Hurt, Kevin Kline, Mary Kay Place, Meg Tilly, JoBeth Williams; *D:* Lawrence Kasdan; *W:* Lawrence Kasdan. VHS, Beta, 8mm $14.95 *COL, VYG, CRC* 𝄞𝄞𝄞½

Big Combo A gangster's ex-girlfriend helps a cop to smash a crime syndicate. Focuses on the relationship between Wilde's cop and the gangster Conte in an effective film noir, with some scenes of torture that were ahead of their time.
1955 87m/B Cornel Wilde, Richard Conte, Jean Wallace, Brian Donlevy, Earl Holliman, Lee Van Cleef, Helen Walker; *D:* Joseph H. Lewis; *W:* Philip Yordan. VHS, Beta $19.95 *PSM* 𝄞𝄞𝄞

Big Country Ex-sea captain Peck heads west to marry fiance Baker and live on her father's (Bickford) ranch. Peck immediately clashes with ranch foreman Heston and finds out there's a vicious feud with neighbor Ives. Then Peck decides he and Baker aren't meant to be and he falls for schoolmarm Simmons instead. Its too long but if you like sprawling western sagas, this one has its moments.
1958 (R) 168m/C Gregory Peck, Charlton Heston, Burl Ives, Jean Simmons, Carroll Baker, Chuck Connors; *D:* William Wyler. Academy Awards '58: Best Supporting Actor (Ives); Nominations: Best Original Score; Golden Globe Awards '59: Best Supporting Actor (Ives). VHS, Beta $29.98 *MGM, BTV* 𝄞𝄞½

The Big Crimewave A cast of unknowns in a comedy about a loner who takes a bus to Kansas City (Kansas City?) to become a screenwriter, with comic adventures along the way. A feast of jabs at genre films.
1986 80m/C *CA* John Paizs, Eva Covacs, Darrel Baran; *D:* John Paizs. VHS, Beta *HHE* 𝄞𝄞

Big Deadly Game A vacationing American gets caught up in a complicated espionage plot by helping a mysterious wartime buddy.
1954 63m/B Lloyd Bridges, Simone Silva, Finlay Currie. VHS, Beta *NO* 𝄞½

Big Deal on Madonna Street A band of inept crooks plan to make themselves very rich when they attempt to rob a jewelry store. Their elaborate plans cause numerous (and hilarious) disasters. In Italian with English subtitles. Remade as "Crackers." *AKA:* The Usual Unidentified Thieves.
1958 90m/B *IT* Marcello Mastroianni, Vittorio Gassman, Toto, Claudia Cardinale; *D:* Mario Monicelli. VHS, Beta $29.95 *ING, CVC, MRV* 𝄞𝄞𝄞½

The Big Dis An interracial comedy about a young black soldier on a weekend pass who's looking for a willing sexual partner. His confidence is shattered when 12 possibilities turn him down. Feature debut of Eriksen and O'Brien.
1989 88m/B *D:* Gordon Eriksen, John O'Brien. VHS $59.95 *FCT, ICA* 𝄞𝄞

The Big Doll House Roger Corman-produced prison drama about a group of tormented female convicts who decide to break out. Features vintage Grier, and a caliber of women's-prison sleaziness that isn't equalled in today's films. *AKA:* Women's Penitentiary I; Women in Cages.
1971 (R) 93m/C Judy Brown, Roberta Collins, Pam Grier, Brooke Mills, Pat Woodell, Sid Haig, Christianne Schmidtmer, Kathryn Loder; *D:* Jack Hill; *M:* Les Baxter. VHS, Beta $24.98 *SUE, NLC* 𝄞

The Big Easy A terrific thriller. A slick New Orleans detective uncovers a heroin-based mob war while romancing the uptight assistant DA who's investigating corruption on the police force. An easy, Cajun-flavored mystery, a fast-moving action-comedy, a very sexy romance, and a serious exploration of the dynamics of corruption.
1987 (R) 101m/C Dennis Quaid, Ellen Barkin, Ned Beatty, John Goodman, Ebbe Roe Smith, Charles Ludlum, Lisa Jane Persky, Tom O'Brien, Grace Zabriskie; *D:* Jim McBride; *W:* Dan Petrie Jr.; *M:* Brad Fiedel. VHS, Beta $14.99 *HBO, FCT* 𝄞𝄞𝄞

The Big Fix Private investigator Moses Wine finds himself in an ironic situation: searching for a fugitive alongside whom he'd protested in the 60s. Based on a Roger Simen novel.
1978 (PG) 108m/C Richard Dreyfuss, Susan Anspach, Bonnie Bedelia, John Lithgow, F. Murray Abraham, Fritz Weaver, Mandy Patinkin; *D:* Jeremy Paul Kagan; *M:* Bill Conti. VHS, Beta $59.95 *MCA* 𝄞𝄞𝄞

Big Foot Even genre devotees will be disappointed with this one. Sasquatch, who has procreation on his mind, searches rather half-heartedly for a human mate. A horror flick that forgot to include the horror.
1972 92m/C Chris Mitchum, Joi Lansing, John Carradine, John Mitchum; *D:* Bob Slatzer. VHS, Beta *NO* Woof!

The Big Gag An international group of comedians travel the world and pull gags on people. Lame.
1987 (R) 84m/C VHS, Beta $79.95 *TWE, HHE* 𝄞

Big Girls Don't Cry...They Get Even A teenage girl decides to run away from home after she's driven crazy by her eccentric new stepfamily. Comic confusion ensues as various family members set out to find her. Hackneyed script and annoying characters hinder this comedy.
1992 (PG) 98m/C Hillary Wolf, Griffin Dunne, Margaret Whitton, David Strathairn, Ben Savage, Adrienne Shelly, Patricia Kalember; *D:* Joan Micklin Silver. VHS *COL, NLC* 𝄞½

The Big Grab A dark big caper thriller about a couple of aging French thugs determined to rip off a casino at Cannes. In French with English subtitles. Also called "Any Number Can Win."
1963 118m/B *FR* Jean Gabin, Alain Delon, Viviane Romance, Maurice Biraud, Carla Marlier; *D:* Henri Verneuil. VHS, Beta $19.95 *FCT* 𝄞𝄞½

A Big Hand for the Little Lady Fonda and Woodward, playing two West-headed country bumpkins, get involved in a card game in Laredo against high rollers Robards and McCarthy. Fonda risks their savings, finds himself stuck with a losing hand, and has a bit of heart trouble; that's where the little lady comes in. Fine performances and a nifty twist ending don't entirely compensate for the overly-padded script (which evolved from a 48-minute TV play drafted by Sydney Carroll). *AKA:* Big Deal at Dodge City.
1966 95m/C Henry Fonda, Joanne Woodward, Jason Robards Jr., Charles Bickford, Burgess Meredith, Kevin McCarthy; *D:* Fielder Cook. VHS, Beta $59.95 *WAR, FCT* 𝄞𝄞𝄞

The Big Hangover Odd story about a man whose allergy to alcohol makes him drunk at the most inopportune moments. Johnson stars as the attorney with the peculiar problem and Taylor plays the boss' daughter who helps him overcome the allergy. Good supporting cast can't help this otherwise boring and predictable film.

1950 82m/B Van Johnson, Elizabeth Taylor, Percy Waram, Fay Holden, Leon Ames, Edgar Buchanan, Selena Royle, Gene Lockhart; **D:** Norman Krasna; **W:** Norman Krasna. VHS $19.98 MGM 🎥🎥

Big Heat When detective Ford's wife (played by Jocelyn Brando, sister of Marlon) is killed in an explosion meant for him, he pursues the gangsters behind it and uncovers a police scandal. His appetite is whetted after this discovery and he pursues the criminals even more vigorously with the help of gangster moll Gloria Grahame. Definitive film noir.
1953 90m/B Glenn Ford, Lee Marvin, Gloria Grahame, Jocelyn Brando, Alexander Scourby, Carolyn Jones; **D:** Fritz Lang. VHS, Beta $59.95 COL 🎥🎥🎥½

The Big House Prison melodrama at its best follows top con Beery as he plans a big breakout—and is betrayed. Life in the pen is depicted as brutal and futile, with sadistic guards and a hapless warden. Spawned numerous imitators.
1930 80m/B Wallace Beery, Chester Morris, Robert Montgomery, Lewis Stone, Leila Hyams, George F. Marion Sr., Karl Dane, DeWitt Jennings; **D:** George Hill; **W:** Francis Marion. VHS $19.98 MGM 🎥🎥🎥

The Big Hurt A reporter investigating a bizarre double murder discovers a secret government agency involved in torture and mind-control.
1987 (R) 90m/C David Bradshaw, Lian Lunson, Simon Chilvers, Nick Wateres; **D:** Barry Peak. VHS, Beta NO 🎥½

Big Jake An aging Texas cattle man who has outlived his time swings into action when outlaws kidnap his grandson and wound his son. He returns to his estranged family to help them in the search for Little Jake. O'Hara is once again paired up with Wayne and the chemistry is still there.
1971 (PG) 90m/C John Wayne, Richard Boone, Maureen O'Hara, Patrick Wayne, Chris Mitchum, Bobby Vinton; **D:** George Sherman; **M:** Elmer Bernstein. VHS, Beta $19.98 FOX 🎥🎥

Big Jim McLain Wayne and Arness are federal agents working on behalf of the House Un-American Activities Committee to eliminate communist terrorism in Hawaii. And there's a suspicious psychiatrist, too: Wayne falls for a babe whose boss is a shrink who doesn't quite seem on the level. Definitely not a highpoint in the Duke's career.
1952 90m/C John Wayne, Nancy Olson, James Arness, Veda Ann Borg; **D:** Edward Ludwig. VHS $19.98 WAR, FCT 🎥🎥

The Big Knife Palance plays a Hollywood superstar who refuses to renew his studio contract, which enrages studio boss Steiger. It seems Steiger knows a very damaging secret about the star and is willing to go to any lengths to have Palance re-sign or wind up destroying himself. A ruthless, emotional look at fame and power, with excellent performances by all. Based on the play by Clifford Odets.
1955 113m/B Jack Palance, Rod Steiger, Ida Lupino, Shelley Winters, Wendell Corey, Jean Hagen, Ilka Chase, Everett Sloane, Wesley Addy, Paul Langton; **D:** Robert Aldrich. $34.98 FCT 🎥🎥🎥

The Big Lift Two G.I.'s assigned to the Berlin airlift ally themselves in counter-intelligence when they discover that their mutual girlfriend is a spy.
1950 119m/B Montgomery Clift, Paul Douglas, Cornell Borchers, Bruni Lobel, O.E. Hasse; **D:** George Seaton. VHS, Beta $19.95 NOS, MRV, DVT 🎥🎥½

The Big Man: Crossing the Line Neeson shines as a down on his luck Scottish miner who loses his job during a union strike. Desperate for cash and unable to resolve his bitterness at being unable to support his family, he's enticed by a Glasgow hood to fight in an illegal bare-knuckled boxing match. What follows is an overlong and extremely brutal fight. Good performances from a talented cast overcome a rather preachy script that doesn't disguise its contempt for the Thatcher government, but also allows a glimpse into the tough times that many Brits suffered during the '80s. Based on the novel by William McIlvanney. **AKA:** Crossing the Line.
1991 (R) 93m/C GB Liam Neeson, Joanne Whalley-Kilmer, Ian Bannen, Billy Connolly, Hugh Grant, Maurice Roeves, Rob Affleck; **D:** David Leland; **W:** Don MacPherson; **M:** Ennio Morricone. VHS $89.95 COL 🎥🎥🎥

Big Man on Campus A modern-day Quasimodo makes his home in an affluent university's belltower. Of course he falls in love with one of the pretty young co-eds and races out of his tower only to be captured by the psychology department. Really, really bad.
1989 (PG-13) 102m/C Tom Skerritt, Corey Parker, Allan Katz, Cindy Williams, Melora Hardin, Jessica Harper; **D:** Jeremy Paul Kagan. VHS, Beta $33.96 VES 🎥

Big Meat Eater A musical gore-comedy about extraterrestrials using radioactive butcher's discards for ship fuel. Deliberate camp that is so bad its funny!
1985 81m/C CA George Dawson, Big Miller, Andrew Gillies; **D:** Chris Windsor. VHS, Beta $49.95 MED 🎥🎥

Big Mo True story of the friendship that developed between Cincinnati Royals basketball stars Maurice Stokes and Jack Twyman after a strange paralysis hit Stokes. **AKA:** Mauri.
1973 (G) 110m/C Bernie Casey, Bo Svenson, Stephanie Edwards, Janet MacLachlan; **D:** Daniel Mann. VHS, Beta $69.95 VES 🎥🎥

Big Mouth A dopey fisherman gets ahold of a treasure map and is pursued by cops and gangsters. Standard Lewis fare, with the requisite infantile histrionics; must be French to appreciate.
1967 107m/C Jerry Lewis, Jeannine Riley, Harold J. Stone, Charlie Callas, Buddy Lester, Susan Bay; **D:** Jerry Lewis; **W:** Jerry Lewis. VHS, Beta $49.98 COL 🎥

Big News Based on the play "For Two Cents" by George S. Brooks, this early talkie uses sound to great advantage. Fired for going after a gangster who's a big advertiser (Hardy), reporter Armstrong nevertheless keeps after the crook. When the intrepid reporter pushes too far, murder enters the picture.
1929 75m/B Robert Armstrong, Carole Lombard, Tom Kennedy, Warner Richmond, Wade Boteler, Sam Hardy, Lew Ayres; **D:** Gregory La Cava. VHS $19.95 NOS 🎥🎥

The Big Parade Wonderful WWI silent, considered to be one of the best war flicks of all time. Gilbert and Adoree are exceptional as lovers torn apart by the conflict. Interesting and thoughtful picture of the trauma and trouble brought to men and their loved ones in wartime. Battle scenes are compelling and intense; Vidor's masterpiece.
1925 141m/B John Gilbert, Renee Adoree, Hobart Bosworth, Claire McDowell, Claire Adams, Karl Dane, Tom O'Brien; **D:** King Vidor. VHS $29.95 MGM 🎥🎥🎥🎥

The Big Picture A hilarious, overlooked comedy by and starring a variety of Second City/National Lampoon alumni, about a young filmmaker who is contracted by a big studio, only to see his vision trampled by formula-minded producers, crazed agents, hungry starlets, and every other variety of Hollywood predator.
1989 (PG-13) 95m/C Kevin Bacon, Jennifer Jason Leigh, Martin Short, Michael McKean, Emily Longstreth, J.T. Walsh, Eddie Albert, Richard Belzer, John Cleese, June Lockhart, Stephen Collins, Roddy McDowall, Kim Miyori, Teri Hatcher, Dan Schneider, Jason Gould, Tracy Brooks Swope; **D:** Christopher Guest; **W:** Christopher Guest, Michael McKean, Michael Varhol; **M:** David Nichtern. VHS, Beta $89.95 COL 🎥🎥½

The Big Push Motley bunch of Alaskan lumberjacks get together to save a poor widow's logging camp from a pair of greedy mill owners. **AKA:** Timber Tramps.
1975 (PG) 98m/C Joseph Cotten, Claude Akins, Cesar Romero, Tab Hunter, Roosevelt Grier, Leon Ames, Stubby Kaye, Patricia Medina; **D:** Tay Garnett. VHS, Beta $59.95 GEM 🎥½

Big Red Set amid the spectacular beauty of Canada's Quebec Province, an orphan boy protects a dog which later saves him from a mountain lion.
1962 89m/C Walter Pidgeon, Gilles Payant; **D:** Norman Tokar. VHS, Beta $69.95 DIS 🎥🎥½

The Big Red One Fuller's harrowing, intense semi-autobiographical account of the U.S. Army's famous First Infantry Division in WWII, the "Big Red One." A rifle squad composed of four very young men, led by the grizzled Marvin, cut a fiery path of conquest from the landing in North Africa to the liberation of the concentration camp at Falkenau, Czechoslovakia. In part a tale of lost innocence, the film scores highest by bringing the raw terror of war down to the individual level.
1980 (PG) 113m/C Lee Marvin, Robert Carradine, Mark Hamill, Stephane Audran; **D:** Samuel Fuller; **W:** Samuel Fuller. VHS, Beta $19.98 FOX, WAR 🎥🎥🎥½

The Big Scam Criminal mastermind Niven recruits ex-con Jordan to pull off a massive bank heist. **AKA:** A Nightingale Sang in Berkeley Square; The Mayfair Bank Caper.
1979 102m/C Richard Jordan, David Niven, Oliver Tobias, Elke Sommer, Gloria Grahame, Hugh Griffith, Richard Johnson; **D:** Ralph Thomas. VHS $9.95 SIM 🎥🎥½

Big Score When a policeman is falsely accused and dismissed from the Chicago Police Department, he goes after the men who really stole the money from a drug bust. Script was originally intended to be a Dirty Harry flick; too bad it wasn't.
1983 (R) 88m/C Fred Williamson, John Saxon, Richard Roundtree, Nancy Wilson, Ed Lauter, Ron Dean, D'Urville Martin, Michael Dante, Joe Spinell; **D:** Fred Williamson. VHS, Beta $69.95 VES 🎥

Big Shots Two kids, one naive and white, the other black and streetwise, search for a stolen watch.
1987 (PG-13) 91m/C Ricky Busker, Darius McCrary, Robert Joy, Paul Winfield, Robert Prosky, Jerzy Skolimowski; **D:** Robert Mandel; **W:** Joe Eszterhas; **M:** Bruce Broughton. VHS, Beta $19.98 LHV, WAR 🎥

Big Show A western adventure about the making of a western adventure. Autry jangles spurs aplenty in duel role. **AKA:** Home In Oklahoma.
1937 54m/B Gene Autry, Smiley Burnette; **D:** Mack V. Wright. VHS, Beta $19.95 NOS, VCN, VDM 🎥🎥

The Big Sky It's 1830, and a rowdy band of fur trappers embark upon a back breaking expedition up the uncharted Missouri River. Based on the A.B. Guthrie Jr. novel, it's an effortlessly enjoyable and level-headed Hawksian American myth, with a streak of gentle gallows humor. Also available colorized.
1952 122m/C Kirk Douglas, Dewey Martin, Arthur Hunnicutt, Elizabeth Threatt, Buddy Baer, Steve Geray, Jim Davis; **D:** Howard Hawks. **VHS, Beta $14.98** RKO, FCT, TTC ΩΩΩ

The Big Sleep Private eye Philip Marlowe, hired to protect a young woman from her own indiscretions, falls in love with her older sister while uncovering murders galore. A dense, chaotic thriller that succeeded in defining and setting a standard for its genre. The very best Raymond Chandler on film combining a witty script with great performances, especially from Bogart and Bacall.
1946 114m/B Humphrey Bogart, Lauren Bacall, John Ridgely, Martha Vickers, Louis Jean Heydt, Regis Toomey, Peggy Knudsen, Dorothy Malone, Bob Steele, Elisha Cook Jr.; **D:** Howard Hawks; **W:** William Faulkner, Jules Furthman, Leigh Brackett; **M:** Max Steiner. **VHS, Beta $19.98** MGM, FOX, TLF ΩΩΩΩ

The Big Sleep A tired remake of the Raymond Chandler potboiler about exhausted Los Angeles private dick Marlowe and his problems in protecting a wild young heiress from her own decadence and mob connections. Mitchum appears to need a rest.
1978 (R) 99m/C Robert Mitchum, Sarah Miles, Richard Boone, Candy Clark, Edward Fox, Joan Collins, John Mills, James Stewart, Oliver Reed, Harry Andrews, James Donald, Colin Blakely, Richard Todd; **D:** Michael Winner; **W:** Michael Winner. **VHS, Beta $19.98** COL ΩΩ

The Big Slice Two would-be crime novelists want to improve their fiction. One masquerades as a cop, the other as a crook, and they infiltrate the underworld from both ends. Clever comedy premise, but vaudeville-level jokes fall flat.
1990 (R) 86m/C Casey Siemaszko, Leslie Hope, Justin Louis, Heather Locklear, Kenneth Welsh, Nicholas Campbell, Henry Ramer; **D:** John Bradshaw; **W:** John Bradshaw; **M:** Mychael Danna, Jeff Danna. **VHS $19.95** ACA Ω½

The Big Sombrero Autry takes a stand against the marriage between an unsuspecting, wealthy Mexican girl and the fortune-seeking bridegroom who wants her land.
1949 77m/C Gene Autry, Elena Verdugo, Steve Dunne, George Lewis; **D:** Frank McDonald. **VHS $39.98** NO ΩΩ

Big Stakes Extremely rare Western feature that has a Texas cowboy falling for a Mexican senorita. Plenty of action as complications ensue.
1922 ?m/B VHS GVV Ω

The Big Stampede Twenty-five year old Wayne stars in this action-packed Western that was a remake of "Land Beyond the Law" from Ken Maynard's silent. Based on a story by Marion Jackson.
1932 63m/B John Wayne, Noah Beery Sr., Luis Alberni, Berton Churchill, Paul Hurst, Lafe McKee, Frank Ellis, Hank Bell; **D:** Tenny Wright; **W:** Kurt Kempler. **VHS, Beta $19.98** MGM, GPV ΩΩ

Big Steal An Army officer recovers a missing payroll and captures the thieves after a tumultuous chase through Mexico.
1949 72m/B Robert Mitchum, William Bendix, Jane Greer, Ramon Novarro, Patric Knowles; **D:** Don Siegel. **VHS, Beta** MED ΩΩΩ

Big Store Late Marx Brothers in which they are detectives in a large metropolitan department store, foiling a hostile takeover and preventing a murder. Their last MGM effort, with some good moments between the Tony Martin song numbers which include "If It's You" and the immortal "Tenement Symphony." Groucho also leads the "Sing While You Sell" number.
1941 96m/B Groucho Marx, Harpo Marx, Chico Marx, Tony Martin, Margaret Dumont, Virginia Grey, Virginia O'Brien; **D:** Charles Riesner. **VHS, Beta $19.95** MGM, CCB ΩΩ½

Big Street A timid busboy, in love with a disinterested nightclub singer, gets to prove his devotion when she is crippled in a fall. Based on a Damon Runyon story, "Little Pinks."
1942 88m/B Henry Fonda, Lucille Ball, Agnes Moorehead, Louise Beavers, Barton MacLane, Eugene Pallette, Ozzie Nelson; **D:** Irving Reis. **VHS, Beta $19.95** MED, RKO, TTC ΩΩ½

The Big Sweat Maybe you've heard this one before: a man who has been framed by the mob escapes from prison and heads for Mexico. But first, he's got to get past the mobsters and police who are hot on his trail. And maybe you've seen some of it before: some of the same stock footage appears in Lommel's "Cold Heat." Not surprisingly, this one bypassed theaters and went straight to video.
1990 85m/C Robert Z'Dar, Steve Molone, Kevin McBride, William Roebuck, Cheri Caspari, David Rushing, Joanne Watkins, Ken Letner; **D:** Ulli Lommel; **W:** Max Bolt; **M:** John Massari. **VHS $14.95** AIP Ω

The Big Switch Gambler is framed for murder and becomes embroiled in a plot to reinstate an old gangster kingpin. **AKA:** Strip Poker.
1970 (R) 68m/C Sebastian Breaks, Virginia Wetherell, Erika Raffael; **D:** Pete Walker. **VHS, Beta $59.95** MON Ω½

Big Top Pee Wee Pee Wee's second feature film following the success of "Pee Wee's Big Adventure." This time Pee Wee owns a farm, has a girlfriend (!) and lives the good life until a weird storm blows a traveling circus onto his property. Cute, but not the manic hilarity the first one was.
1988 (PG) 86m/C Paul (Pee Wee Herman) Reubens, Kris Kristofferson, Susan Tyrrell, Penelope Ann Miller; **D:** Randal Kleiser; **W:** Paul (Pee Wee Herman) Reubens; **M:** Danny Elfman. **VHS, Beta, 8mm $14.95** PAR ΩΩ

Big Town A newspaper is saved by a new editor who brings integrity to the once scandalous paper. The editor and his reporters also solve a series of murders. Some action, but weak dialogue and direction hold it back. Based on the radio program of the same name. Also known as "Guilty Assignment."
1947 59m/B Philip Reed, Hillary Brooke, Robert Lowery, Byron Barr, Veda Ann Borg, Nana Bryant, Charles Arnt; **D:** William C. Thomas. **VHS $16.95** SNC Ω

Big Town A farmboy, lucky with dice, hits Chicago to claim his fortune where he meets floozies, criminals, and other streetlife. Look for Lane's strip number.
1987 (R) 109m/C Matt Dillon, Diane Lane, Tommy Lee Jones, Bruce Dern, Tom Skerritt, Lee Grant, Suzy Amis; **D:** Ben Bolt. **VHS, Beta $89.98** VES, LIV ΩΩ

Big Town After Dark Daring journalists search for the bottom-line story on a gang of criminals. They find themselves caught behind the firing lines when the sun goes down. Slightly better than average thriller. **AKA:** Underworld After Dark.
1947 69m/B Philip Reed, Hillary Brooke, Richard Travis, Anne Gillis; **D:** William C. Thomas. **VHS $16.95** NOS, SNC, RXM ΩΩ

Big Trail This pioneering effort in wide-screen cinematography was Wayne's first feature film. A wagon train on the Oregon trail encounters Indians, buffalo, tough terrain, and romantic problems.
1930 110m/B John Wayne, Marguerite Churchill, El Brendel, Tully Marshall, Tyrone Power Sr., Ward Bond, Helen Parrish; **D:** Raoul Walsh. **VHS, Beta $19.98** FOX ΩΩΩ

Big Trees A ruthless lumberman attempts a takeover of the California Redwood Timberlands that are owned by a group of peaceful homesteaders.
1952 89m/C Kirk Douglas, Patrice Wymore, Eve Miller, Alan Hale Jr., Edgar Buchanan; **D:** Felix Feist. **VHS, Beta $19.95** NOS, MRV, DVT ΩΩΩ

Big Trouble An insurance broker endeavors to send his three sons to Yale by conspiring with a crazy couple in a fraud scheme that goes awry in every possible manner. Look for the cameo by screenwriter Bergman as Warren Bogle.
1986 (R) 93m/C Alan Arkin, Peter Falk, Beverly D'Angelo, Charles Durning, Robert Stack, Paul Dooley, Valerie Curtin, Richard Libertini; **Cameos:** Andrew Bergman; **D:** John Cassavetes; **W:** Andrew Bergman; **M:** Bill Conti. **VHS, Beta $19.95** COL ΩΩ

Big Trouble in Little China A trucker plunges beneath the streets of San Francisco's Chinatown to battle an army of spirits. An uproarious comic-book-film parody with plenty of action and a keen sense of sophomoric sarcasm.
1986 (PG-13) 99m/C Kurt Russell, Suzze Pai, Dennis Dun, Kim Cattrall, James Hong, Victor Wong, Kate Burton; **D:** John Carpenter; **W:** Gary Goldman, W.D. Richter; **M:** John Carpenter, Alan Howarth. **VHS, Beta $14.98** FXV, FOX ΩΩ½

Big Valley The western television series's two feature-length episodes: "Explosion," and "Legend of a General."
1968 90m/C Richard Long, Linda Evans, Barbara Stanwyck, Lee Majors. **VHS, Beta** NO ΩΩ½

Big Wednesday Three California surfers from the early sixties get back together after the Vietnam war to reminisce about the good old days and take on the big wave. **AKA:** Summer of Innocence.
1978 (PG) 120m/C Jan-Michael Vincent, Gary Busey, William Katt, Lee Purcell, Patti D'Arbanville; **D:** John Milius; **W:** John Milius. **VHS, Beta $59.95** WAR ΩΩ½

The Big Wheel Old story retold fairly well. Rooney is young son determined to travel in his father's tracks as a race car driver, even when dad buys the farm on the oval. Good acting and direction keep this a cut above average.
1949 92m/B Mickey Rooney, Thomas Mitchell, Spring Byington, Mary Hatcher, Allen Jenkins, Michael O'Shea; **D:** Edward Ludwig. **VHS** GPV, VCI ΩΩ½

Big Zapper Violent P.I. Marlowe and masochistic assistant Rock work together in this British comic strip film.
1973 94m/C GB Linda Marlowe, Gary Hope, Sean Hewitt, Richard Monette, Penny Irving; **D:** Lindsay Shonteff. **VHS** VCD Ω½

The Bigamist Have you heard the one about the traveling salesman in this movie? He has one wife in Los Angeles, another in San Francisco, and they inevitably find out about each other. A maudlin soap opera with a do-it-yourself ending, only shows why bigamy was done better as farce in the later "Micki and Maude."
1953 79m/B Edmond O'Brien, Joan Fontaine, Ida Lupino, Edmund Gwenn, Jane Darwell, Kenneth Tobey; **D:** Ida Lupino. **VHS $19.98** DVT, NOS, HEG ΩΩ

B

Biggles Time-travel fantasy in which a young businessman from present-day New York City is inexplicably transferred into the identity of a 1917 WWI flying ace. He suddenly finds himself aboard a fighter plane over Europe during WWI. *AKA:* Biggles: Adventures in Time.
1985 (PG) 100m/C *GB* Neil Dickson, Alex Hyde-White, Peter Cushing; *D:* John Hough. VHS, Beta $19.95 *STE, NWV* 🦴🦴

Bikers, Blondes, and Blood A montage of the sleaze genre's greatest moments including a clip from Jayne Mansfield's "Single Room Furnished." Suitable for dorm keggers, frat parties or any other venue where the audience has supplementary amusements available. Some clips in black and white.
1993 90m/B VHS $23.00 *SMW, TPV* 🦴🦴

Bikini Beach Surfing teenagers of the "Beach Party" series follow up "Muscle Beach Party" with a third fling at the beach and welcome a visitor, British recording star "Potato Bug" (Avalon in a campy dual role). But, golly gee, wealthy Wynn wants to turn their sandy, surfin' shores into a retirement community. What to do? Sing a few songs, dance in your bathing suits, and have fun. Classic early '60s nostalgia is better than the first two efforts; followed by "Pajama Party." 🎵Because You're You; Love's a Secret Weapon; Bikini Drag.
1964 100m/C Annette Funicello, Frankie Avalon, Martha Hyer, Harvey Lembeck, Don Rickles, Stevie Wonder, John Ashley, Keenan Wynn, Jody McCrea, Candy Johnson, Danielle Aubry, Meredith MacRae, Dolores Wells, Donna Loren, Timothy Carey; *D:* William Asher; *W:* William Asher, Leo Townsend, Robert Dillon; *M:* Les Baxter. VHS, Beta $9.98 *SUE* 🦴🦴½

The Bikini Car Wash Company Babes in bikinis in Los Angeles. A young man is running his uncle's carwash when he meets a business major who persuades him to let her take over the business for a cut of the profits. She decides that a good gimmick would be to dress all the female employees in the tiniest bikinis possible. The story is of course secondary to the amount of flesh on display. Also available in an unrated version. *AKA:* California Hot Wax.
1990 (R) 87m/C Joe Dusic, Neriah Napaul, Suzanne Browne, Kristie Ducati; *D:* Ed Hansen. VHS $89.95 *IMP* Woof!

The Bikini Car Wash Company 2 Entrepreneur Melissa and the other lovely ladies of the Bikini Car Wash Co. find themselves a big success, so much so that a greedy businessman wants to buy them out. In order to get money to fight the takeover, the ladies take to the airwaves of a cable-access station. Their new business adventure involves selling sexy lingerie which means the flesh quotient is as great as ever. An unrated version is also available.
1992 (R) ?m/C Kristie Ducati, Suzanne Browne, Neriah Napaul, Rikki Brando, Greg Raye, Larry De Russy; *D:* Gary Orona; *W:* Bart B. Gustis; *M:* Michael Smith. VHS $89.95 *IMP* 🦴

Bikini Island Beautiful swimsuit models gather on a remote tropical island for a big photo shoot, each vying to be the next cover girl of the hottest swimsuit magazine. Before long, scantily clad lovelies are turning up dead and full out madness ensues. Will the mystery be solved before they run out of models, or will the magazine have no choice but to grace its cover with a bikinied cadaver? Low-budget trash that has few, if any, redeeming qualities.
1991 (R) 85m/C Holly Floria, Alicia Anne, Jackson Robinson, Shannon Stiles, Cyndi Pass, Sherry Johnson; *D:* Anthony Markes; *W:* Emerson Bixby; *M:* Marc David Deeker. VHS, Beta $19.95 *PSM* 🦴

Bikini Summer Laughs, music, and skin are the order of the day as two nutty guys and a few beautiful girls form an unlikely friendship on the beach. Konop was Julia Robert's "Pretty Woman" body double. Sort of the 90's version of the old 60's Frankie and Annette beach parties.
1991 90m/C David Millburn, Melinda Armstrong, Jason Clow, Shelley Michelle, Alex Smith, Kent Lipham, Kelly Konop, Carmen Santa Maria; *D:* Robert Veze; *W:* Robert Veze, Nick Stone; *M:* John Gonzalez. VHS $29.95 *PMH* 🦴½

Bikini Summer 2 An eccentric family decides to stage a bikini contest to raise money to help the homeless.
1992 (R) 94m/C Jeff Conaway, Jessica Hahn, Melinda Armstrong, Avalon Anders; *D:* Jeff Conaway; *M:* Jim Halfpenny. VHS $19.95 *PMH* 🦴

Bilitis A young girl from a private girls' school is initiated into the pleasures of sex and the unexpected demands of love. One of director Hamilton's exploitative meditations on nudity.
1977 (R) 95m/C *FR* Patti D'Arbanville, Bernard Giraudeau, Mona Kristensen; *D:* David Hamilton. VHS, Beta $54.95 *MED* 🦴½

Bill A made-for-television movie based on a true story about a mentally retarded man who sets out to live independently after 44 years in an institution. Rooney gives an affecting performance as Bill and Quaid is strong as the filmmaker who befriends him. Awarded Emmys for Rooney's performance and the well written script. Followed by "Bill: On His Own."
1981 97m/C Mickey Rooney, Dennis Quaid, Largo Woodruff, Harry Goz; *D:* Anthony Page. VHS, Beta $59.95 *LIV* 🦴🦴🦴

Bill and Coo An unusual love story with a villian and hero using an all bird cast.
1947 61m/C *D:* Dean Riesner. VHS, Beta, 8mm $19.95 *VYY, MRV, NOS* 🦴🦴

Bill & Ted's Bogus Journey Big-budget sequel to B & T's first movie has better special effects but about the same quota of laughs. Slain by lookalike robot duplicates from the future, the airhead heroes pass through heaven and hell before tricking the Grim Reaper into bringing them back for a second duel with their heinous terminators. Most excellent closing-credit montage. Non-fans still won't think much of it.
1991 (PG) 98m/C Keanu Reeves, Alex Winter, William Sadler, Joss Ackland, Pam Grier, George Carlin, Amy Stock-Poynton, Hal Landon Jr., Annette Azcuy, Sarah Trigger, Chelcie Ross, Taj Mahal, Roy Brocksmith, William Shatner; *D:* Pete Hewitt; *W:* Chris Matheson, Edward Solomon; *M:* David Newman. VHS $14.98 *ORI* 🦴🦴

Bill & Ted's Excellent Adventure Excellent premise: when the entire future of the world rests on whether or not two '80s dudes pass their history final, Rufus comes to the rescue in his time-travelling telephone booth. Bill and Ted share an adventure through time as they meet and get to know some of history's most important figures.
1989 (PG) 105m/C Keanu Reeves, Alex Winter, George Carlin, Bernie Casey, Dan Shor, Robert Barron, Amy Stock-Poynton, Ted Steedman, Ted Steedman, Rod Loomis, Al Leong, Tony Camilieri; *D:* Stephen Herek; *W:* Chris Matheson, Edward Solomon; *M:* David Newman. VHS, Beta, 8mm $14.95 *COL, SUE, NLC* 🦴🦴½

Bill Cosby, Himself Cosby shares his hilarious observations on marriage, drugs, alcohol, dentists, child-bearing and child-rearing in this performance. Recorded at Toronto's Hamilton Place Performing Arts Center.
1981 (PG) 104m/C Bill Cosby; *D:* Bill Cosby. VHS, Beta $19.98 *FOX* 🦴🦴½

Bill Murray Live from the Second City Prior to his "Saturday Night Live" stardom, Murray performs a few of his comedy acts with his Second City pals.
197? 60m/C Bill Murray, Tim Kazurinsky, Mary Gross, George Wendt, Danny Breen. VHS, Beta $19.98 *TWE* 🦴🦴½

A Bill of Divorcement Hepburn's screen debut, as the daughter of a shell-shocked WWI vet, who requires her care after her mother decides to divorce him. Creaky early talker.
1932 76m/B John Barrymore, Katharine Hepburn, Billie Burke, Henry Stephenson, David Manners, Paul Cavanagh, Elizabeth Patterson; *D:* George Cukor. VHS, Beta $39.98 *FOX* 🦴🦴

Bill: On His Own Rooney is again exceptional in this sequel to the Emmy-winning TV movie "Bill." After 44 years in an institution, a mentally retarded man copes more and more successfully with the outside world. Fine supporting cast and direction control the melodramatic potential.
1983 100m/C Mickey Rooney, Helen Hunt, Teresa Wright, Dennis Quaid, Largo Woodruff, Paul Leiber, Harry Goz; *D:* Anthony Page. VHS $59.95 *LIV* 🦴🦴🦴

Billie Duke stars as a tomboy athlete who puts the boys' track team to shame. Some amusing but very predictable situations, plus a few songs from Miss Duke. Based on Ronald Alexander's play "Time Out for Ginger."
1965 86m/C Patty Duke, Jim Backus, Jane Greer, Warren Berlinger, Billy DeWolfe, Charles Lane, Dick Sargent, Susan Seaforth Hayes, Ted Bessell, Richard Deacon; *D:* Don Weis; *W:* Ronald Alexander. VHS, Beta $19.98 *MGM* 🦴½

The Billion Dollar Hobo Poor, unsuspecting heir of a multimillion dollar fortune must duplicate his benefactor's experience as a hobo during the Depression in order to collect his inheritance. Slow-moving family stuff.
1978 (G) 96m/C Tim Conway, Will Geer, Eric Weston, Sydney Lassick; *D:* Stuart E. McGowan. VHS, Beta $59.98 *FOX* 🦴½

A Billion for Boris Boris' TV gives a sneak preview of the future and Boris plans to make some money off of it. Zany comedy in the vein of "Let It Ride."
1990 89m/C Lee Grant, Tim Kazurinsky; *W:* Mary Rogers. VHS, Beta $79.95 *IMP* 🦴🦴½

Billionaire Boys Club Chilling look at greed in the '80s. Nelson plays Joe Hunt, who gets together with a group of rich, preppie friends to manipulate investments in the commodities markets. When a slick con man (Silver) gets in their way he's murdered to keep their schemes intact. Based on a true story and adapted from the book by Sue Horton. Originally shown on television in two parts, the video version is considerably pared down.
1987 94m/C Judd Nelson, Frederic Lehne, Brian McNamara, Raphael Sbarge, John Stockwell, Barry Tubb, Stan Shaw, Jill Schoelen, Ron Silver, James Sloyan, James Karen; *D:* Marvin J. Chomsky. VHS $79.98 *LIV* 🦴½

Billy Bathgate Uneven but well acted drama set in 1935 New York. A street-wise young man dreams getting ahead during the Depression means gaining the attention of mobster Dutch Schultz and joining his gang.

As Billy becomes the confidant of the racketeer he learns the criminal life is filled with suspicion and violence; in order to stay alive he must rely on every trick he's learned. Willis has a small role as a rival mobster who gets fitted for cement overshoes. Kidman does well as Dutch's girlfriend with Hill fine as the gang's number man. Based on the novel by E.L. Doctorow.
1991 (R) 107m/C Dustin Hoffman, Nicole Kidman, Loren Dean, Bruce Willis, Steven Hill, Steve Buscemi, Stanley Tucci, Tim Jerome, Billy Jaye, Katherine Houghton, Mike Starr, John Costelloe, Moira Kelly; **D:** Robert Benton; **W:** Tom Stoppard; **M:** Mark Isham. **VHS, Beta $92.95** TOU *♫♫♫*

Billy Budd The classic Melville good-evil allegory adapted to film, dealing with a British warship in the late 1700s, and its struggle between evil master-at-arms and innocent shipmate. Stamp's screen debut as the naive Billy who is tried for the murder of the sadistic first mate. Well directed and acted.
1962 123m/B *GB* Terence Stamp, Peter Ustinov, Robert Ryan, Melvyn Douglas, Paul Rogers, John Neville, Ronald Lewis, David McCallum, John Meillon; **D:** Peter Ustinov; **W:** Peter Ustinov, Robert Rossen. **VHS, Beta $59.98** FOX *♫♫♫*

Billy Crystal: A Comic's Line Comedian Billy Crystal performs a one-man show, highlighting spoofs, of rock videos and other stand-up comics.
1983 59m/C Billy Crystal. **VHS, Beta $19.95** PAR *♫♫*

Billy Crystal: Don't Get Me Started Crystal hosts a comedy television special featuring his standard routines from "Saturday Night Live" and numerous guest stars.
1986 60m/C Billy Crystal, Sammy Davis Jr., Eugene Levy, Christopher Guest, Rob Reiner. **VHS, Beta $14.95** VES, LIV *♫♫♫*

Billy Crystal: Midnight Train to Moscow Recorded live at Moscow's Pushkin Theatre, Crystal travels to Russia, his ancestral home, and shows that comedy is an international language. A breakthrough in Glasnost.
1989 72m/C Billy Crystal; **D:** Paul Flaherty. **VHS $19.98** HBO *♫♫♫*

Billy Galvin A bullheaded ironworker tries to straighten out the turbulent relationship he has with his rebellious son.
1986 (PG) 95m/C Karl Malden, Lenny Von Dohlen, Joyce Van Patten, Toni Kalem, Keith Szarabajka, Alan North, Paul Guilfoyle, Barton Heyman; **D:** John Gray; **W:** John Gray; **M:** Joel Rosenbaum. **VHS, Beta $79.95** LIV, VES *♫♫½*

Billy Jack On an Arizona Indian reservation, a half-breed ex-Green Beret with pugnacious martial arts skills (Laughlin) stands between a rural town and a school for runaways. Laughlin stars with his real-life wife Taylor. Features the then-hit song "One Tin Soldier," sung by Coven. The movie and its marketing by Laughlin inspired a "Billy Jack" cult phenomenon. A Spanish-dubbed version of this film is also available. Followed by a sequel in 1974, "Trail of Billy Jack," which bombed.
1971 (PG) 112m/C Tom Laughlin, Delores Taylor, Clark Howat; **D:** Tom Laughlin; **W:** Tom Laughlin. **VHS, Beta $14.95** WAR *♫♫*

Billy Liar A young Englishman dreams of escaping from his working class family and dead-end job as an undertaker's assistant. Parallels James Thurber's story, "The Secret Life of Walter Mitty."
1963 94m/B *GB* Tom Courtenay, Julie Christie, Finlay Currie; **D:** John Schlesinger; **M:** Richard Rodney Bennett. **VHS, Beta** NO *♫♫♫*

Billy: Portrait of a Street Kid A ghetto youngster tries pry himself up and out of his bleak surroundings through education, but complications arise when he gets his girlfriend pregnant.
1977 96m/C LeVar Burton, Tina Andrews, Ossie Davis, Michael Constantine; **D:** Steven Gethers. **VHS, Beta $34.95** WOV *♫♫*

Billy Rose's Jumbo Better-than-average update of the circus picture. Durante and Raye are terrific, as are the Rodgers and Hart songs. Fun, with lively production numbers in the inimitable Berkeley style. ♫Over and Over Again; Circus on Parade; Why Can't I?; This Can't Be Love; The Most Beautiful Girl in the World; My Romance; Little Girl Blue; What is a Circus; Sawdust, Spangles and Dreams. **AKA:** Jumbo.
1962 125m/C Doris Day, Stephen Boyd, Jimmy Durante, Martha Raye, Dean Jagger; **D:** Charles Walters; **W:** Sidney Sheldon. **VHS $19.98** MGM *♫♫♫*

Billy the Kid Billy Bonney joins up with a group of outlaws in a Southwest town where he bumps into his old friend Jim Sherwood, now the marshal. Attempting to change his ways, he falls back into the life of a bandit when an outlaw friend is murdered. Although an entertaining western, the story bears no resemblance to the actual last days of Billy the Kid. Based on a story by Howard Emmett Rogers and Bradbury Foote, suggested by the book "The Saga of Billy the Kid" by Walter Noble Burns.
1941 94m/C Robert Taylor, Brian Donlevy, Ian Hunter, Mary Howard, Gene Lockhart, Lon Chaney Jr., Guinn Williams, Cy Kendall, Henry O'Neill, Ted Adams, Frank Puglia, Mitchell Lewis, Dick Curtis, Grant Withers, Joe Yule, Eddie Dunn, Kermit Maynard, Chill Wills, Olive Blakeney, Carl Pitti; **D:** David Miller; **W:** Gene Fowler; **M:** David Snell. **VHS $19.98** MGM *♫♫½*

Billy the Kid in Texas The famed outlaw takes on trouble and makes sure the Texans never forget that he has been there.
1940 52m/B Bob Steele. **VHS, Beta $19.95** NOS, VCN *♫½*

Billy the Kid Returns While trying to clean up a town of its criminal element, Rogers is mistaken for the legendary Billy. Complications ensue.
1938 60m/B Roy Rogers, George "Gabby" Hayes, Smiley Burnette, Lynn (Mary Hart) Roberts; **D:** Joseph Kane. **VHS, Beta $19.95** NOS, HHT, VCN *♫½*

Billy the Kid Trapped Billy and his partner are rescued from hanging by an outlaw band.
1942 59m/B Buster Crabbe, Al "Fuzzy" St. John, Bud McTaggart, Anne Jeffreys, Glenn Strange; **D:** Sherman Scott. **VHS $19.95** NOS, MRV, DVT *♫½*

Billy the Kid Versus Dracula The title says it all. Dracula travels to the Old West, anxious to put the bite on a pretty lady ranch owner. Her fiance, the legendary outlaw Billy the Kid, steps in to save his girl from becoming a vampire herself. A Carradine camp classic.
1966 95m/C Chuck Courtney, John Carradine, Melinda Plowman, Walter Janovitz, Harry Carey Jr., Roy Barcroft, Virginia Christine, Bing Russell; **D:** William Beaudine. **VHS, Beta $19.95** NOS, SUE, VYY *♫♫*

Billyboy Coming of age film with the world of boxing as background. Excellent fight scenes.
1979 94m/C Duane Bobrick, Kim Braden. **VHS, Beta** BFV *♫♫*

Biloxi Blues Eugene Morris Jerome has been drafted and sent to boot camp in Biloxi, Mississippi where he encounters a troubled drill sergeant, hostile recruits, and a skillful prostitute. Walken is the drill sergeant from hell. Some good laughs from the ever-wry Broderick. A sequel to Neil Simon's "Brighton Beach Memoirs" and adapted by Simon from his play. Followed by "Broadway Bound." **AKA:** Neil Simon's Biloxi Blues.
1988 (PG-13) 105m/C Matthew Broderick, Christopher Walken, Casey Siemaszko, Matt Mulern, Corey Parker, Penelope Ann Miller, Michael Dolan, Park Overall; **D:** Mike Nichols; **W:** Neil Simon; **M:** Georges Delerue. **VHS, Beta $14.95** MCA *♫♫½*

Bim/Dream of the Wild Horses Two famous French shorts, the first of which is dubbed into English.
1952 110m/B *FR* **VHS, Beta $39.95** ING, DVT, GVV *♫♫½*

Bimini Code Two female adventurers accept a dangerous mission where they wind up on Bimini Island in a showdown with the mysterious Madame X.
1984 95m/C Vickie Benson, Krista Richardson, Frank Alexander, Rosanna Simanaitis; **D:** Barry Clark. **VHS, Beta $49.95** PSM *♫*

Bingo Mediocre spoof of hero-dog movies. The heroic title mutt roams from Denver to Green Bay in search of his absent-minded master, with numerous absurd adventures en route. Some cute moments, but sometimes Bingo is just lame-o. Good family fare.
1991 (PG) 90m/C Cindy Williams, David Rasche, Robert J. Steinmiller Jr., David French, Kurt Fuller, Joe Guzaldo, Glenn Shadix; **D:** Matthew Robbins; **W:** Jim Strain; **M:** Richard Gibbs. **VHS $19.95** COL *♫♫½*

Bingo Inferno A short narrative film about a precocious kid who connives to break his mother of a compulsive Bingo addiction.
1987 13m/C Beta NO *♫♫½*

Bingo Long Traveling All-Stars & Motor Kings Set in 1939, this film follows the comedic adventures of a lively group of black ball players who have defected from the old Negro National League. The All-Stars travel the country challenging local white teams.
1976 (PG) 111m/C Billy Dee Williams, James Earl Jones, Richard Pryor, Stan Shaw; **D:** John Badham; **W:** Matthew Robbins; **M:** William Goldstein. **VHS, Beta $49.95** MCA, FCT *♫♫♫*

Bio Hazard A toxic monster needs human flesh to survive and consequently goes on a rampage.
1985 (R) 84m/C Angelique Pettyjohn, Carroll Borland, Richard Hench; **D:** Fred Olen Ray. **VHS, Beta $39.98** MTX *♫*

The Bionic Woman Sky-diving accident leaves tennis pro Jaimie Somers crippled and near death. Her bionic buddy, Steve Austin, gets his friends to rebuild her and make her better than she was before. The pilot for the television series.
1975 96m/C Lindsay Wagner, Lee Majors, Richard Anderson, Alan Oppenheimer; **D:** Richard Moder. **VHS, Beta $39.95** MCA *♫♫*

The Birch Interval A chronicle of a young Amish girl growing up and experiencing adult passions and fears when she visits her kin in their isolated Pennsylvania community.
1978 (PG) 104m/C Eddie Albert, Rip Torn, Ann Wedgeworth; **D:** Delbert Mann; **W:** Joanna Crawford. **VHS, Beta $9.95** MED *♫♫*

Bird The richly-textured, though sadly one-sided biography of jazz sax great Charlie Parker, from his rise to stardom to his premature death via extended heroin use. A remarkably assured, deeply imagined film from Eastwood that never really shows the Bird's genius of creation. The soundtrack features Parker's own solos re-mastered from original recordings.
1988 (R) 160m/C Forest Whitaker, Diane Venora, Michael Zelniker, Samuel E. Wright, Keith David, Michael McGuire, James Handy, Damon Whitaker, Morgan Nagler; **D:** Clint Eastwood; **W:** Joel Oliansky; **M:** Lennie Niehaus. **VHS, Beta $19.98** *MVD, WAR, FCT ✗✗✗*

Bird of Paradise An exotic South Seas romance in which an adventurer is cast onto a remote Polynesian island when his yacht haphazardly sails into a coral reef. There he becomes enamored of an exotic island girl, and nature seems to disapprove.
1932 80m/B Joel McCrea, Dolores Del Rio, Lon Chaney Jr.; **D:** King Vidor. **VHS, Beta, 8mm $19.95** *NOS, MRV, VYY ✗✗½*

Bird on a Wire After suddenly being forced to emerge from a prolonged period under the Witness Protection Program, an ex-hood and his ex-girlfriend are pursued by old enemies.
1990 (PG-13) 110m/C Mel Gibson, Goldie Hawn, David Carradine, Bill Duke, Stephen Tobolowsky; **D:** John Badham; **W:** David Seltzer. **VHS, Beta $19.98** *MCA ✗✗*

The Bird with the Crystal Plumage An American writer living in Rome witnesses a murder. He becomes involved in the mystery when the alleged murderer is cleared because the woman believed to be his next victim is shown to be a psychopathic murderer. Vintage Argento mayhem. **AKA:** L'Ucello dalle Plume di Cristallo; The Phantom of Terror.
1970 (PG) 98m/C *IT* Tony Musante, Suzy Kendall, Eva Renzi; **D:** Dario Argento; **W:** Dario Argento; **M:** Ennio Morricone. **VHS, Beta $19.95** *VCI, MRV ✗✗*

Birdman of Alcatraz Robert Stroud, convicted of two murders and sentenced to life imprisonment on the Island, becomes an internationally accepted authority on birds. Lovingly told, with stunning performance from Lancaster, and exceptionally fine work from the supporting cast. The confinement of Stroud's prison cell makes the film seem claustrophobic and tedious at times, just as the imprisonment must have been. Ritter played Stroud's mother, who never stops trying to get him out of prison.
1962 143m/B Burt Lancaster, Karl Malden, Thelma Ritter, Betty Field, Neville Brand, Edmond O'Brien, Hugh Marlowe, Telly Savalas; **D:** John Frankenheimer; **M:** Elmer Bernstein. Academy Awards '62 Nominations: Best Actor (Lancaster), Best Black and White Cinematography, Best Supporting Actor (Savalas), Best Supporting Actress (Ritter); British Academy Awards '62: Best Actor (Lancaster). **VHS $19.98** *COL, FCT ✗✗✗*

The Birds Hitchcock attempted to top the success of "Psycho" with this terrifying tale of Man versus Nature, in which Nature alights, one by one, on the trees of Bodega Bay to stage a bloody act of revenge upon the civilized world. Only Hitchcock can twist the harmless into the horrific while avoiding the ridiculous; this is perhaps his most brutal film, and one of the cinema's purest, horrifying portraits of apocalypse. Based on a short story by Daphne Du Maurier; screenplay by novelist Evan Hunter (aka Ed McBain).
1963 120m/C Rod Taylor, Tippi Hedren, Jessica Tandy, Veronica Cartwright, Suzanne Pleshette; **D:** Alfred Hitchcock. **VHS, Beta $19.95** *MCA ✗✗✗½*

Birds & the Bees A millionaire falls in love with an alluring card shark, and then calls it all off when he learns of her profession, only to fall in love with her again when she disguises herself. A remake - and poor shade - of Preston Sturge's 1941 classic "The Lady Eve."
1956 94m/C Mitzi Gaynor, David Niven, George Gobel, Reginald Gardiner, Hans Conried; **D:** Norman Taurog; **W:** Sidney Sheldon. **VHS, Beta $19.95** *BAR ✗✗*

Birds of Paradise Three attractive women who inherit a yacht travel to the Florida Keys to find romance.
1984 (R) 90m/C **VHS, Beta** *NO Woof!*

Birds of Prey Made-for-television action film pits an ex-WWII army pilot against a group of kidnapping thieves in an airborne chopper chase.
1972 81m/C David Janssen, Ralph Meeker, Elayne Heilveil; **D:** William A. Graham. **VHS, Beta $49.95** *PSM ✗*

Birds of Prey A tough urban cop stalks a breed of cold, ruthless assassins in a large city. In HiFi.
1985 90m/C **VHS, Beta $19.95** *STE, NWV ✗*

Birdy An adaptation of the William Wharton novel about two Philadelphia youths, one with normal interests, the other obsessed with birds, and their eventual involvement in the Vietnam War, wrecking one physically and the other mentally. A hypnotic, evocative film, with a compelling Peter Gabriel soundtrack.
1984 (R) 120m/C Matthew Modine, Nicolas Cage, John Harkins, Sandy Baron, Karen Young, Bruno Kirby; **D:** Alan Parker; **M:** Peter Gabriel. **VHS, Beta $79.95** *COL ✗✗✗½*

Birgitt Haas Must Be Killed A ruthless secret agent (Noiret) plots to murder a German female terrorist and make it appear that her boyfriend was the killer. Never quite hits the mark, despite novel premise and strong cast.
1983 105m/C Philippe Noiret, Jean Rochefort, Elisabeth Kreuzer; **D:** Laurent Heynemann. **VHS, Beta $39.95** *GLV ✗✗½*

The Birth of a Nation Lavish Civil War epic in which Griffith virtually invented the basics of film grammar. Gish and Walthall have some of the most moving scenes ever filmed and the masterful battle choreography brought the art of cinematography to new heights. Griffith's positive attitude toward the KKK notwithstanding, this was the first feature length silent, and it brought credibility to an entire industry. Based on the play "The Clansman" and the book "The Leopard's Spots" by Thomas Dixon, it is still a rouser, and of great historical interest. Silent with music score. Also available in a 124 minute version. **AKA:** The Clansman.
1915 175m/B Lillian Gish, Mae Marsh, Henry B. Walthall, Ron Harron, Wallace Reid, Joseph Henabery, Donald Crisp, Raoul Walsh, Erich von Stroheim, Eugene Pallette; **D:** D.W. Griffith. **VHS $39.95** *VYY, MRV, REP ✗✗✗✗*

Birthday Boy A cable comedy about a buffoonish salesman's 30th birthday, on which he takes an ill-fated business trip. Written by Belushi.
1985 33m/C James Belushi; **D:** Claude Conrad; **W:** James Belushi. **VHS, Beta $29.98** *VES, LIV ✗✗*

The Bishop's Wife An angel comes down to earth at Christmas to help a young bishop, his wife and his parishioners. Excellent performances by the cast make this an entertaining outing.
1947 109m/B Cary Grant, Loretta Young, David Niven, Monty Woolley, Elsa Lanchester, James Gleason, Gladys Cooper, Regis Toomey; **D:** Henry Koster. Academy Awards '47: Best Sound; Nominations: Best Director (Koster), Best Film Editing, Best Picture, Best Original Score. **VHS, Beta $14.98** *HBO, SUE, FCT ✗✗✗*

The Bitch High-camp follies are the rule in this lustful continuation of "The Stud" as it follows the erotic adventures of a beautiful divorcee playing sex games for high stakes on the international playgrounds of high society. A collaborative effort by the sisters Collins: written by Jackie, with sister Joan well cast in the title role.
1978 (R) 90m/C *GB* Joan Collins, Kenneth Haigh, Michael Coby, Ian Hendry, Carolyn Seymour, Sue Lloyd, John Ratzenberger; **D:** Gerry O'Hara. **VHS, Beta** *NO Woof!*

Bite the Bullet Moralistic western tells of a grueling 600-mile horse race where the participants reluctantly develop respect for one another. Unheralded upon release and shot in convincing epic style by Harry Stradling. Excellent cast.
1975 (PG) 131m/C Gene Hackman, James Coburn, Candice Bergen, Dabney Coleman, Jan-Michael Vincent, Ben Johnson, Ian Bannen, Paul Stewart, Sally Kirkland; **D:** Richard Brooks; **W:** Richard Brooks. **VHS, Beta $12.95** *COL ✗✗✗½*

Bits and Pieces Crazed mutilating killer strikes fear in the hearts of the city dwellers.
1977 86m/C **VHS, Beta $59.95** *TWE ✗*

Bitter Harvest Emmy-nominated made-for-television movie concerning a dairy farmer frantically trying to discover what is mysteriously killing off his herd. Howard is excellent as the farmer battling the bureaucracy to find the truth. Based on a true story.
1981 98m/C Ron Howard, Art Carney, Tarah Nutter, Richard Dysart, Barry Corbin, Jim Haynie, David Knell; **D:** Roger Young. **VHS, Beta $14.95** *FRH, LIV ✗✗✗*

Bitter Harvest Rubin and Kensit are the femme fatales who turn their considerable wiles on the innocent Baldwin. He's more than happy to be their lover but does he want to be their victim as well?
1993 (R) 98m/C Stephen Baldwin, Patsy Kensit, Jennifer Rubin, Adam Baldwin, M. Emmet Walsh; **D:** Duane Clark; **W:** Randall Fontana. **VHS $92.95** *PSM ✗✗*

Bitter Moon Polanski effort looks promising, but ultimately disappoints. Bored British couple (Grant and Scott Thomas) meet up with sexual deviants (Coyote and Seigner, aka Mrs. Polanski) on a cruise and learn that passion and cruelty often share the same path to destruction. Masquerades as high class art, but whenever substance is lacking expect a silly, kinky sex scene. Needless to say, there isn't much substance, so erotic mischief abounds. Scott Thomas manages to hold her own, but Coyote is almost embarrassingly over the top. Based on the Pascal Bruckner novel "Lunes de Fiel."
1992 (R) 135m/C Peter Coyote, Emmanuelle Seigner, Hugh Grant, Kristin Scott Thomas, Victor Banerjee; **Cameos:** Stockard Channing; **D:** Roman Polanski; **W:** Roman Polanski, Gerard Brach, John Brownjohn; **M:** Vangelis. **VHS** *NYR ✗½*

Bitter Rice Mangano became a star with her sultry performance about survival in postwar Italy. She scrapes by, working in the rice fields of the Po Valley, loved by the down-to-earth Vallone, who provides her

B

with little excitement. Gassman is the rotten-to-the-core thief who meets up with Mangano while he's running from the police. He mistreats her, she steals his money and betrays her friends, and both destroy each other. In Italian with English subtitles. *AKA:* Riso Amaro.
1949 96m/C *IT* Silvana Mangano, Vittorio Gassman, Raf Vallone; *D:* Guiseppe de Santis. **VHS $29.95** *FCT* ⅢⅢⅢ

Bitter Sweet Tragic tale of a woman who finally marries the man she loves, only to find that he is a compulsive gambler. Written by Coward, adapted from his operetta.
1933 76m/B *GB* Anna Neagle, Fernand Graavey, Esme Percy, Clifford Heatherly, Hugh Williams; *D:* Herbert Wilcox; *W:* Noel Coward. **VHS $19.95** *NOS, MRV, DVT* ⅢⅢ½

Bitter Sweet The second version of the Noel Coward operetta, about young romance in 1875 Vienna. Creaky and overrated, but the lush Technicolor and Coward standards help to compensate. 🎵Ziguener; I'll See You Again.
1940 94m/C Jeanette MacDonald, Nelson Eddy, George Sanders, Felix Bressart, Ian Hunter, Sig Rumann, Herman Bing, Fay Holden, Curt Bois, Edward Ashley; *D:* Woodbridge S. Van Dyke; *W:* Lesser Samuels, Noel Coward. **VHS, Beta $19.98** *MGM* ⅢⅢ

The Bitter Tea of General Yen Stanwyck arrives in Shanghai to marry a missionary (Gordon) during the threatening days of China's civil war. Unexpectedly swept into the arms of an infamous warlord (Asher), she becomes fascinated, although his attempts to seduce her fail. She even remains with him while his enemies close in. Exotic and poetic, if melodramatic by today's standards. The interracial aspects were considered very daring for their time. Adapted from the book by Grace Zaring Stone.
1933 89m/B Barbara Stanwyck, Nils Asther, Gavin Gordon, Walter Connolly, Lucien Littlefield, Toschia Mori, Richard Loo, Clara Blandick; *D:* Frank Capra; *W:* Edward Paramore. **VHS $19.95** *COL, FCT, BTV* ⅢⅢⅢ

The Bitter Tears of Petra von Kant Dark German story of lesbian love, the fashion world, obsession and anger. Claustrophobic settings and slow pace may frustrate some viewers. In German with English subtitles. *AKA:* Die Bitteren Traenen der Petra von Kant.
1972 124m/C *GE* Margit Carstensen, Hanna Schygulla, Irm Hermann, Eva Mattes; *D:* Rainer Werner Fassbinder. **VHS $79.95** *NYF, FCT, ING* ⅢⅢ

Bittersweet Love Two young people fall in love and marry, only to have the bride's mother and the groom's father confess a 30-year-old affair, disclosing that the two newlyweds are actually half-siblings.
1976 (PG) 92m/C Lana Turner, Robert Lansing, Celeste Holm, Robert Alda, Meredith Baxter Birney; *D:* David Miller. **VHS, Beta $59.98** *SUE* Ⅲ½

Bix Based on the brief life of legendary Jazz Age cornetist Leon Bix Beiderbecke, who died at age 28. Story unfolds in flashbacks, through friend Joe Venuti memories of the dissipated genius and the music he created with Hoagy Carmichael, Pee Wee Russell, Paul Whiteman, and others.
1990 100m/C *IT* Bryant Weeks, Emile Levisetti, Mark Collver, Sally Groth; *D:* Pupi Avati; *W:* Pupi Avati, Antonio Avati, Lino Patruno. **VHS $59.95** *RHP* ⅢⅢ

Bizarre When a wife escapes her perverse, psychologically threatening marriage, she finds her husband still haunts her literally and figuratively, and plots psychological revenge. Dubbed.
1987 93m/C *IT* Florence Guerin, Luciano Bartoli, Robert Egon Spechtenhauser, Stefano Sabelli. **VHS, Beta $79.95** *PSM* Ⅲ

Bizarre Bizarre A mystery writer is accused of murder and disappears, only to return in disguise to try to clear his name. Along the way, a number of French comedians are introduced with a revue of comedy-farce sketches that include slapstick, burlesque, black humor, and comedy of the absurd. In French with English subtitles. *AKA:* Drole de Drama.
1939 90m/B *FR* Louis Jouvet, Michel Simon, Francoise Rosay; *D:* Marcel Carne. **VHS, Beta $24.95** *NOS, HHT, FST* ⅢⅢⅢ

The Black Abbot A mysterious black-hooded figure is seen entering a ruined Abbey tower that leads to a country house with buried treasure. Based on an Edgar Wallace story.
1963 95m/C *GE* Joachim Fuchsberger, Dieter Borsche, Gritt Bottcher, Eva Scholtz, Franz Gottlieb; *D:* Franz Gottlieb. **VHS $16.95** *SNC* ⅢⅢ

Black and White as Day and Night A man's talent for the game of chess becomes a destructive obsession. In German with English subtitles.
1963 ?m/C Bruno Ganz. **VHS $16.95** *SNC* ⅢⅢ

Black and White in Color An award-winning satire about a French soldier at an African outpost, who, upon hearing the news of the beginning of WWI, takes it upon himself to attack a neighboring German fort. Calamity ensues. In French, with English subtitles. *AKA:* La Victoire en Chantant.
1976 (PG) 90m/C *FR* Jean Carmet, Jacques Dufilho, Catherine Rouvel, Jacques Spiesser, Dora Doll, Jacques Perrin; *D:* Jean-Jacques Annaud; *W:* George Conchon, Jean-Jacques Annaud. **VHS, Beta $39.98** *LHV, WAR, ING* ⅢⅢⅢ

Black Arrow Original adventure film of the famous Robert Louis Stevenson novel. Upon return from 16th century's War of the Roses, a young man must avenge his father's murder by following a trail of clues in the form of black arrows. Well made and fun. *AKA:* Black Arrow Strikes.
1948 76m/B Louis Hayward, Janet Blair, George Macready, Edgar Buchanan, Paul Cavanagh; *D:* Gordon Douglas. **VHS, Beta $69.95** *DIS* ⅢⅢⅢ

The Black Arrow Exiled bowman returns to England to avenge the injustices of a villainous nobleman. Made-for-cable version of the Robert Louis Stevenson medieval romp is not as well done as the 1948 adaptation.
1984 93m/C Oliver Reed, Benedict Taylor, Georgia Slowe, Stephen Chase, Donald Pleasence; *D:* John Hough. **VHS, Beta $69.95** *DIS* ⅢⅢ

Black Beauty In this adaptation of Anna Sewell's familiar novel, a young girl develops a kindred relationship with an extraordinary horse.
1946 74m/B Mona Freeman, Richard Denning, Evelyn Ankers; *D:* Max Nosseck. **VHS, Beta $9.99** *CCB, MED, VTR* ⅢⅢ

Black Beauty International remake of the classic horse story by Anna Sewell.
1971 (G) 105m/C *GB GE SP* Mark Lester, Walter Slezak; *D:* James Hill. **VHS, Beta $14.95** *PAR, FCT* ⅢⅢ

Black Beauty Remake of the classic Anna Sewell children's novel about an oft-sold horse whose life has its shares of ups and downs. Timeless tale still brings children and adults to tears. Six-year-old quarterhorse named Justin gives a nuanced portrayal as the Black Beauty, recalling Olivier in "Hamlet." Directorial debut of "Secret Garden" screenwriter Thompson.
1994 (G) ?m/C Andrew Knott, Sean Bean, David Thewlis, Jim Carter, Alun Armstrong, Eleanor Bron, Peter Cook, Peter Davison, John McEnery, Nicholas Jones; *D:* Caroline Thompson; *W:* Caroline Thompson. **VHS** *NYR* ⅢⅢⅢ

Black Beauty/Courage of Black Beauty Two feature-length films based on Anna Sewell's novel about the love of a child for a black stallion. "Black Beauty" was first released in 1946; "Courage of Black Beauty" in 1957. Excellent for children who love horses, of course.
1957 145m/C Mona Freeman, Johnny Crawford; *D:* Max Nosseck, Harold Schuster. **VHS, Beta $12.95** *MED* Ⅲ

Black Belt Jones Martial arts expert fights the mob to save a school of self-defense in Los Angeles' Watts district.
1974 (R) 87m/C Jim Kelly, Gloria Hendry, Scatman Crothers; *D:* Robert Clouse. **VHS, Beta $14.95** *WAR* Ⅲ

Black Bikers from Hell Black gang-members infiltrate and wreak havoc on their rivals. Who can stop these brutal young men? Cast with real bikers and biker chicks. *AKA:* Black Angels.
1970 (R) 87m/C King John III, Des Roberts, Linda Jackson, James Whitworth, James Young-El, Clancy Syrko, Beverly Gardner; *D:* Lawrence Merrick; *W:* Lawrence Merrick. **VHS, Beta $59.95** *TPV, JEF* Ⅲ½

Black Bird In this satiric "sequel" to "The Maltese Falcon," detective Sam Spade, Jr. searches for the mysterious black falcon statuette that caused his father such trouble. Features appearances by Elisha Cook Jr. and Lee Patrick, who starred in the 1941 classic "The Maltese Falcon" with Humphrey Bogart.
1975 (PG) 98m/C George Segal, Stephane Audran, Lionel Stander, Lee Patrick, Elisha Cook Jr., Connie Kreski; *D:* David Giler. **VHS, Beta $9.95** *GKK* Ⅲ

Black Box Affair An American secret agent must find a black box lost in a B-52 plane crash before it falls into the wrong hands.
1966 95m/C Craig Hill, Teresa Gimpera, Luis Martin, Jorge Rigaud. **VHS, Beta** *NO* Ⅲ½

Black Brigade Pryor and Williams star in this low budget movie as leaders of an all-black outfit assigned to a suicide mission behind Nazi lines during WWII. Their force wreaks havoc and earns them the respect of military higher-ups. Lots of action and climactic finish.
1969 90m/C Richard Pryor, Billy Dee Williams, Stephen Boyd. **VHS** *QVD* ⅢⅢ

Black Caesar A small-time hood climbs the ladder to be the head of a Harlem crime syndicate. Music by James Brown. Followed by the sequel "Hell Up in Harlem."
1973 (R) 92m/C Fred Williamson, Julius W. Harris, Val Avery, Art Lund, Gloria Hendry; *D:* Larry Cohen; *M:* James Brown. **VHS, Beta $9.98** *ORI* ⅢⅢ

The Black Cat "First of the Boris and Bela pairings stands up well years after release. Polished and taut, with fine sets and interesting acting. Confrontation between architect and devil worshipper acts as plot, with strange twists. Worth a look. Also

available with "The Raven" (1935) on Laser Disc. *AKA:* House of Doom.
1934 65m/B Boris Karloff, Bela Lugosi, David Manners, Jacqueline Wells, Lucille Lund, Henry Armetta; *D:* Edgar G. Ulmer. VHS $9.95 *MED, MLB, MCA* 🎞🎞🎞½

The Black Cat Spaghetti splatter-meister Fulci, best known for his unabashed ripoffs "Zombie" and "Gates of Hell," tones down the gore this time in a vaguely Poe-ish tale of a medium with some marbles loose (Magee) whose kitty provides the temporary habitat for spirits its master calls up. The dreary English village setting and the downright myopic camerawork add up to an oppressive viewing experience.
1981 92m/C *IT GB* Patrick Magee, Mimsy Farmer, David Warbeck, Al Cliver, Dagmar Lassander; *D:* Lucio Fulci; *W:* Lucio Fulci; *M:* Pino Donaggio. VHS $14.98 *MED, RHI* Woof!

Black Cat Filmmakers find lots of action in a haunted house. Chock full of references to the works of spaghetti horror dons Mario Bava and Dario Argento.
1990 ?m/C *IT* Caroline Munro, Brett Halsey; *D:* Lewis (Luigi Cozzi) Coates; *W:* Lewis (Luigi Cozzi) Coates. VHS, Beta *COL* 🎞½

Black Christmas A college sorority is besieged by an axe-murderer over the holidays. *AKA:* Silent Night, Evil Night; Stranger in the House.
1975 (R) 98m/C *CA* Olivia Hussey, Keir Dullea, Margot Kidder, John Saxon; *D:* Bob (Benjamin) Clark. VHS, Beta $19.98 *WAR* 🎞🎞½

Black Cobra A lesbian exacts revenge for her lover's snake-bite murder by trapping the guilty party with his own snakes.
1983 97m/C Laura Gemser, Jack Palance. VHS, Beta $79.95 *GEM* Woof!

The Black Cobra After photographing a psychopath in the process of killing someone, a beautiful photographer seeks the help of a tough police sergeant to protect her. The leader of the Black Cobras gang gives chase.
1987 90m/C *IT* Fred Williamson, Karl Landgren, Eva Grimaldi. VHS, Beta $79.95 *TWE* Woof!

Black Cobra 2 A mismatched team of investigators tracks a notorious terrorist. They find him holding a school full of children as hostage.
1989 95m/C Fred Williamson. VHS $14.95 *HMD* 🎞🎞

Black Cobra 3: The Manila Connection Interpol turns to police lieutenant Robert Malone (Williamson) when a team of high-tech weapons thieves threatens the world. Malone attacks like a cyclone on the terrorists' jungle haven. They won't know what hit 'em!
1990 (R) 92m/C Fred Williamson, Forry Smith, Debra Ward; *D:* Don Edwards. VHS $14.95 *HMD* 🎞½

The Black Coin A 15-episode adventure serial about a cursed silver piece from the Middle Ages and the ill luck that has followed its possessors through the years.
1936 316m/B Ralph Graves, Ruth Mix, Dave O'Brien, Matthew Betz. VHS, Beta $39.95 *VYY, NOS, MLB* 🎞½

Black Devil Doll from Hell This shot-on-video movie deals with a nasty little voodoo doll that likes to kill its owners.
1984 70m/C Shirley Jones, Rickey Roach, Marie Sainvilvs; *D:* Chester Turner. VHS, Beta $49.95 *HHT* 🎞

The Black Devils of Kali Adventurers in the Indian jungle discover a lost race of idol-worshipping primitives. Racist garbage produced near the end of Republic Pictures'

existence. Based on a novel by Emillio Salgari. *AKA:* Mystery of the Black Jungle.
1955 72m/B Lex Barker, Jane Maxwell, Luigi Tosi, Paul Muller; *D:* Ralph Murphy. VHS $16.95 *SNC, MLB* 🎞

Black Dragon Young farm boy moves to the city and teams up with an undercover narcotics agent to infiltrate and destroy the underworld syndicate.
1974 (R) 93m/C Ron Van Cliff, Jorge Estraga, Nancy Veronica. VHS $54.95 *SUN* 🎞

The Black Dragons Weird and fairly stupid war drama involving sabotage by the Japanese. Lugosi is the plastic surgeon who deftly cuts and pastes Japanese face parts to permit agents to pass as Americans. Also available colorized.
1942 62m/B Bela Lugosi, Joan Barclay, George Pembroke, Clayton Moore; *D:* William Nigh. VHS, Beta $19.95 *VYY, MRV, SNC* 🎞

Black Dragon's Revenge The Black Dragon arrives in Hong Kong to investigate the death of a great kung fu master.
1975 90m/C Ron Van Cliff, Charles Bonet, Jason Rai Pow. VHS $52.95 *SUN* 🎞

Black Eagle Pre-Glasnost, anti-Soviet tale of two high-kicking spies. CIA and KGB agents race to recover innovative equipment in the Mediterranean.
1988 (R) 93m/C Bruce Doran, Jean-Claude Van Damme, Sho Kosugi; *D:* Eric Karson. VHS, Beta *NO* 🎞🎞

Black Eliminator A black cop struggles to stop a maniacal secret agent who plans to destroy the world.
197? 84m/C Jim Kelly, George Lazenby, Harold Sakata, Bob Minos, Patch MacKenzie, Aldo Ray. VHS, Beta *NO* 🎞

Black Eyes A lowly waiter, working in a Moscow restaurant, manages to overhear a number of stock tips from the wealthy patrons and makes a tidy pile of rubles to improve his daughter's life. The daughter already thinks he's a successful businessman and is disillusioned when she discovers dad's true profession. All comes out right in the end.
1939 72m/B *GB* Otto Kruger, Mary Maguire, Walter Rilla, John Wood, Marie Wright; *D:* Herbert Brenon. VHS *HCV* 🎞½

Black Force Brothers who fight crime with violent actions, are called for assistance in the recovery of an African artifact. Originally known as "Force Four."
1975 82m/C Malachi Lee, Warhawk Tanzania, Owen Watson, Judie Soriano; *D:* Michael Fink. VHS, Beta *NO* 🎞

Black Force 2 The brothers are back on the scene in another violent, cartilage-shattering adventure.
1978 90m/C Terry Carter, James B. Sikking. VHS *NO* 🎞🎞

Black Fury A coal miner's efforts to protest working conditions earn him a beating by the company goons who also kill his friend. He draws national attention to this brutal plight of the workers when he barricades himself inside the mine. Muri's carefully detailed performance adds authenticity to this powerful drama, but it proved too depressing to command a big box office.
1935 95m/B Paul Muni, Barton MacLane, Henry O'Neill, John Qualen, J. Carroll Naish; *D:* Michael Curtiz. VHS, Beta $59.95 *FOX* 🎞🎞🎞

Black Gestapo A black-exploitation film about a vigilante army taking over a Los Angeles ghetto, first to help residents, but later to abuse them. Extremely violent.

1975 (R) 89m/C Rod Perry, Charles Robinson, Phil Hoover, Ed Gross. VHS, Beta $59.95 *UNI* Woof!

Black Glove A trumpet star defends himself against charges of murdering a Spanish singer by tracking down the real killer. *AKA:* Face the Music.
1954 84m/B Alex Nicol, Eleanor Summerfield. VHS, Beta $19.95 *NOS* 🎞

Black God & White Devil Another Brazilian socio-political commentary by Rocha, an oft-incendiary filmmaker whose left-leaning works are steeped in mysticism, obscure folklore, and powerful images. An impoverished man transforms from a religious zealot to a bandit, his tale underscored by conflict between poor masses and wealthy landowners.
1964 102m/C *BR* *D:* Glauce Rocha. VHS $59.95 *FST* 🎞🎞

Black Godfather The grueling story of a hood clawing his way to the top of a drug-selling mob. Features an all-black cast.
1974 (R) 90m/C Rod Perry, Damu King, Don Chastain, Jimmy Witherspoon, Diane Summerfield; *D:* John Evans. VHS, Beta *NO* 🎞

Black Gold Oil field suspense thriller by "B" movie king Hopton.
1936 ?m/B Frankie Darro, Leroy Mason; *D:* Russell Hopton. VHS $16.95 *SNC, VYY* 🎞🎞

The Black Hand Kelly plays well against character in this atmospheric turn-of-the-century thriller. The evil society of the Black Hand murders his father, and he seeks revenge. Well made drama.
1950 93m/B Gene Kelly, J. Carroll Naish, Teresa Celli, Marc Lawrence, Frank Puglia; *D:* Richard Thorpe. VHS *NO* 🎞🎞🎞

Black Hand Unemployed Italian immigrant is drawn into a web of murder and betrayal after he is attacked by an Irish gang.
1976 90m/C Lionel Stander, Mike Placido. VHS, Beta *NO* 🎞½

Black Hills Dull oater with Dean and his sidekick Ates out to avenge the murder of a struggling ranch owner.
1948 60m/B Eddie Dean, Roscoe Ates, Shirley Patterson, Terry Frost, Nina Bara, Bill Fawcett; *D:* Ray Taylor. VHS $19.99 *MOV* 🎞

The Black Hole A high-tech, computerized Disney space adventure dealing with a mad genius who attempts to pilot his craft directly into a black hole. Except for the top quality special effects, a pretty creaky vehicle.
1979 (G) 97m/C Maximilian Schell, Anthony Perkins, Ernest Borgnine, Yvette Mimieux, Joseph Bottoms, Robert Forster; *D:* Gary Nelson; *M:* John Barry. VHS, Beta *DIS, OM* 🎞½

Black Ice After an affair with a popular politician ends violently, Vanessa (Pacula) realizes her boss set up his death—and she's next in line. She finds the nearest taxi and offers the driver plenty of cash if he can quickly get her out of the country. It's going to be the ride of her life. Also available in an unrated version.
1992 (R) 90m/C Michael Nouri, Michael Ironside, Joanna Pacula; *D:* Neill Fearnley. VHS, Beta $89.95 *PSM* 🎞🎞

The Black King Prejudiced propaganda based on the life of Marcus Garvey, black leader of the '20s, who advocated black superiority and a return to Africa. A black con man takes advantage of fellow blacks by organizing a phony back-to-Africa movement, enriching himself in the process. When one man's girlfriend deserts him for the bogus leader, the jilted one blows the whistle. *AKA:* Harlem Hot Shot.

1932 70m/B A.B. Comethiere, Vivian Baber, Knolly Mitchell, Dan Michaels, Mike Jackson; *D:* Bud Pollard. **VHS $24.95** *FCT, BTV, HEG* ♫ ½

The Black Klansman A black man masquerades as a white extremist in order to infiltrate the KKK and avenge his daughter's murder. In the interest of racial harmony, he seduces the Klan leader's daughter. As bad as it sounds. *AKA:* I Crossed the Line.
1966 88m/B Richard Gilden, Rima Kutner, Harry Lovejoy; *D:* Ted V. Mikels. **VHS, Beta $39.95** *UNI* ♫

The Black Lash Two lawmen go undercover to break a silver hijacking gang.
1952 55m/B Lash LaRue, Al "Fuzzy" St. John, Peggy Stewart, Kermit Maynard; *D:* Ron Ormond. **VHS, Beta $19.95** *NOS, DVT, GPV* ♫

Black Lemons While in prison, a convict is stalked by the Mafia because of what he knows. He eventually spills the beans to the cops, putting himself in unavoidable jeopardy.
198? 93m/C *IT* Peter Carsten, Antonio Sabato, Florinda Bolkan; *D:* Camillo Bazzoni. **VHS, Beta $59.95** *UNI* ♫

Black Like Me Based on John Howard Griffin's successful book about how Griffin turned his skin black with a drug and traveled the South to experience prejudice firsthand. Neither the production nor the direction enhance the material.
1964 107m/B James Whitmore, Roscoe Lee Browne, Will Geer, Walter Mason, John Marriott, Clifton James, Dan Priest; *D:* Carl Lerner. **VHS, Beta $19.95** *RHI, UND, PTB* ♫ ½

Black Limelight Massey plays a fugitive from justice and Marion the loyal wife who clears her husband of the murder of his mistress. Distracting lead performance by Marion who insists on shouting her lines. Based on the play by Gordon Sherry.
1938 60m/B *GB* Raymond Massey, Joan Marion, Walter Hudd, Henry Oscar, Dan Tobin; *D:* Paul Stein; *W:* Walter Summers. **VHS $19.95** *DVT* ♫ ½

Black Lizard A camp spectacle set in the Japanese underworld. The Lizard is the glamorous queen of Tokyo crime who plots to steal a famous diamond by first kidnapping the owner's daughter. Complications arise when she falls for a detective. The Lizard is played by female impersonator Maruyama. Mishima, who wrote the original drama and the screenplay, has a cameo as an embalmed corpse. Style is all. In Japanese with English subtitles.
1968 112m/C *JP* Akihiro Maruyama, Isao Kimura; *Cameos:* Yukio Mishima; *D:* Kinji Fukasaku; *W:* Yukio Mishima. **VHS $79.95** *CCN, ING* ♫♫

Black Magic Cagliostro the magician becomes involved in a plot to supply a double for Marie Antoinette.
1949 105m/B Orson Welles, Akim Tamiroff, Nancy Guild, Raymond Burr; *D:* Gregory Ratoff; *W:* Charles Bennett. **VHS, Beta $12.95** *MED* ♫♫ ½

Black Magic Insomniac Alex, haunted by the nightly appearances of his dead cousin Ross, goes to Ross' hometown to see if he can find a way to make the apparition disappear. On the way, he runs into his cousin's ex-girlfriend Lilian and falls in love. Problem is, Lilian's a witch, maybe. Lightweight made for cable TV fare.
1992 (PG-13) 94m/C Rachel Ward, Judge Reinhold, Brion James, Anthony LaPaglia; *D:* Daniel Taplitz; *W:* Daniel Taplitz. **VHS $89.98** *MCA* ♫♫ ½

Black Magic Terror Jilted by her lover, the old queen of black magic has everybody under her spell. Trouble starts, however, when she turns her back on one of her subjects.
1979 85m/C *JP* Suzanna, W.D. Mochtar, Alan Nuary; *D:* L. Sudjio. **VHS, Beta $59.95** *TWE* ♫

Black Magic Woman An art gallery owner has an affair with a beautiful and exotic woman but starts to get cold feet when he's plagued by inexplicable phenomena. Seems that black magic woman has put a voodoo spell on him. Listless companion to director Warren's "Blood Spell" that gives away the ending, has a wretched script, and poor acting.
1991 (R) 91m/C Mark Hamill, Amanda Wyss, Apollonia, Abadah Viera, Larry Hankin, Victor Rivers, Bonnie Ebson; *D:* Deryn Warren; *W:* Gerry Daly; *M:* Randy Miller. **VHS $89.95** *VMK Woof!*

The Black Maid A scantily-clad, sassy black maid cleans, cooks, cusses and drives her racist employer to the brink of insanity.
1974 90m/C *IT* **VHS, Beta** *NO Woof!*

The Black Marble A beautiful policewoman is paired with a policeman who drinks too much, is divorced, and is ready to retire. Surrounded by urban craziness and corruption, they eventually fall in love. Based on the Joseph Wambaugh novel.
1979 (PG) 110m/C Paula Prentiss, Harry Dean Stanton, Robert Foxworth, James Woods, Michael Dudikoff, Barbara Babcock, John Hancock, Judy Landers, Anne Ramsey, Christopher Lloyd; *D:* Harold Becker; *M:* Maurice Jarre. **VHS, Beta $9.98** *SUE, NLC* ♫♫♫

Black Market Rustlers The Range Busters are at it again. This time they break up a cattle rustling syndicate.
1943 60m/B Ray Corrigan, Dennis Moore, Max Terhune; *D:* S. Roy Luby. **VHS, Beta $19.95** *VCN, VDM, RXM* ♫ ½

Black Moon Rising Based on an idea by John Carpenter ("Halloween"), this film deals with the theft of a new jet-powered car and its involvement in an FBI investigation. Solid performances and steady action enhance this routine effort.
1986 (R) 100m/C Tommy Lee Jones, Linda Hamilton, Richard Jaeckel, Robert Vaughn; *D:* Harley Cokliss; *W:* John Carpenter. **VHS, Beta $19.95** *STE, NWV* ♫♫ ½

Black Narcissus A group of Anglican nuns attempting to found a hospital and school in the Himalayas confront native distrust and human frailties amid beautiful scenery. Adapted from the novel by Rumer Godden. Stunning cinematography. Crucial scenes were cut from the American release by censors.
1947 101m/C *GB* Deborah Kerr, David Farrar, Sabu, Jean Simmons, Kathleen Byron, Flora Robson, Esmond Knight; *D:* Michael Powell, Emeric Pressburger. **VHS, Beta $29.95** *VYG, MLB* ♫♫♫ ½

Black Oak Conspiracy Based on a true story, this film deals with a mining company conspiracy discovered by an inquisitive stuntman.
1977 (R) 92m/C Jesse Vint, Karen Carlson, Albert Salmi, Seymour Cassel, Robert F. Lyons; *D:* Bob Kelljan. **VHS, Beta $59.98** *NLC* ♫♫

Black Orchid A businessman and a crook's widow fall in love and try to persuade their children it can work out.
1959 96m/B Sophia Loren, Anthony Quinn, Ina Balin, Mark Richmond, Jimmie Baird; *D:* Martin Ritt; *W:* Joseph Stefano. **VHS, Beta $14.95** *PAR* ♫♫ ½

Black Orpheus The legend of Orpheus and Eurydice unfolds against the colorful background of the carnival in Rio de Janeiro. In the black section of the city, Orpheus is a street-car conductor and Eurydice, a country girl fleeing from a man sworn to kill her. Dancing, incredible music, and black magic add to the beauty of this film. Based on the play "Orfeu da Conceica." In Portuguese with English subtitles or dubbed. *AKA:* Orfeu Negro.
1958 103m/C *BR FR PT* Breno Mello, Marpessa Dawn, Lea Garcia, Fausto Guerzoni, Lourdes De Oliveira; *D:* Marcel Camus; *M:* Antonio Carlos Jobim, Luis Bonfa. **VHS, Beta $29.95** *CVC, FOX, VYG* ♫♫♫ ½

Black Panther True story of psychokiller Donald Neilson, who murdered heiress Lesley Whittle in England in the 1970s.
1977 90m/C Donald Sumpter, Debbie Farrington; *D:* Ian Merrick. **VHS, Beta $69.95** *VES, LIV* ♫ ½

The Black Pirate A shipwrecked mariner vows revenge on the pirates who destroyed his father's ship. Quintessential Fairbanks, this film features astounding athletic feats and exciting swordplay. Silent film with music score. Also available in color. *AKA:* Rage of the Buccaneers; The Black Buccaneer; Gordon il Pirata Nero.
1926 122m/B *IT* Douglas Fairbanks Sr., Donald Crisp, Billie Dove; *D:* Albert Parker. **VHS, Beta $19.95** *VYY, MRV, REP* ♫♫♫

The Black Pirate Italian pirate yarn dubbed into Spanish. *AKA:* El Pirata Negro.
1965 82m/C *SP IT* George Hilton, Claude Dantes, Tony Kendall. **VHS, Beta** *NO* ♫

Black Pit of Dr. M The ghost of a doctor who has been unjustly executed for murder seeks revenge on employees of an insane asylum. The horror is not just confined to the asylum. *AKA:* Misterios del Ultratumba.
1947 90m/B *MX* Gaston Santos, Rafael Bertrand, Mapita Cortes; *D:* Fernando Mendez; *W:* Raymond Obon. **VHS, Beta $39.95** *MAD, SMW* ♫

Black Rain Erstwhile Ozu assistant Imamura directs this powerful portrait of a post-Hiroshima family five years after the bombing. Tanaka plays a young woman who, having been caught in a shower of black rain (radioactive fallout) on an ill-timed visit to Hiroshima, returns to her village to find herself ostracized by her peers and no longer considered marriage-worthy. Winner of numerous awards (including five Japanese Academy Awards). In Japanese with English subtitles. *AKA:* Kuroi Ame.
1988 123m/B *JP* Kazuo Kitamura, Yoshiko Tanaka, Etsuko Ichihara, Shoichi Ozawa, Norihei Miki; *D:* Shohei Imamura. **VHS $79.95** *FXL, FCT, ING* ♫♫♫

Black Rain Douglas portrays a ruthless American cop chasing a Japanese murder suspect through gang-controlled Tokyo. Loads of action and stunning visuals from the man who brought you "Blade Runner."
1989 (R) 125m/C Michael Douglas, Andy Garcia, Kate Capshaw, Ken Takakura, Yusaku Matsuda, John Spencer, Shigeru Koyama; *D:* Ridley Scott; *W:* Craig Bolotin, Warren Lewis; *M:* Hans Zimmer. **VHS, Beta, 8mm, CDV $14.95** *PAR* ♫♫ ½

Black Rainbow Surprisingly good thriller that's relatively unknown, haunted by a menacing mood. Robards and Arquette are a father/daughter duo who perform clairvoyance scams at carnival sideshows. Suddenly, without warning, Arquette's former cons become real: she sees murder victims—before their demise. Quirky sleeper filmed on location in North Carolina.

1991 (R) 103m/C Rosanna Arquette, Jason Robards Jr., Tom Hulce, Ron Rosenthal, John Bennes, Linda Pierce, Mark Joy; **D:** Mike Hodges; **W:** Mike Hodges. **VHS, Beta** $19.98 *VTR, FXV, MED ♪♪♪*

The Black Raven An action film that combines several plots into one. The Black Raven is an inn that sees more excitement than any other—not the least of which is murder!
1943 64m/B George Zucco, Wanda McKay, Glenn Strange, I. Stanford Jolley; **D:** Sam Newfield. **VHS, Beta** $16.95 *SNC, MLB, RXM ♪♪½*

Black Robe In 1634 a young Jesuit priest journeys across the North American wilderness to bring the word of God to Canada's Huron Indians. The winter journey is brutal and perilous and he begins to question his mission after seeing the strength of the Indian's native ways. Stunning cinematography, a good script, and fine acting combine to make this superb. Portrays the Indians in a realistic manner, the only flaw being that Beresford portrays the white culture with very few redeeming qualities and as the only reason for the Indian's downfall. Moore adapted his own novel for the screen. Winner of six Canadian Genie awards in 1991.
1991 (R) 101m/C AU CA Lothaire Bluteau, Aden Young, Sandrine Holt, August Schellenberg, Tantoo Cardinal, Billy Two Rivers, Lawrence Bayne, Harrison Liu; **D:** Bruce Beresford; **W:** Brian Moore; **M:** Georges Delerue. **VHS** $94.95 *VMK, ING ♪♪♪½*

The Black Room As an evil count lures victims into his castle of terror, the count's twin brother returns to fulfill an ancient prophecy. Karloff is wonderful in his dual role as the twin brothers.
1935 70m/B Boris Karloff, Marian Marsh, Robert Allen, Katherine DeMille, John Buckler, Thurston Hall; **D:** Roy William Neill. **Beta** $9.95 *GKK, MLB ♪♪♪*

The Black Room Couples are lured to a mysterious mansion where a brother and his sister promise to satisfy their sexual desires.
1982 (R) 90m/C Linnea Quigley, Stephen Knight, Cassandra Gaviola, Jim Stathis; **D:** Norman Thaddeus Vane. **VHS, Beta** $69.95 *VES, LIV ♪*

Black Roses A disgusting band of rockers shows up in a small town, and the local kids start turning into monsters. Coincidence?
1988 (R) 90m/C Carmine Appice, Sal Viviano, Carla Ferrigno, Julie Adams, Ken Swofford, John Martin; **D:** John Fasano. **VHS, Beta** $79.95 *IMP ♪*

Black Sabbath An omnibus horror film with three parts, climaxing with Karloff as a Wurdalak, a vampire who must kill those he loves. Also available with "Black Sunday" on Laser Disc. **AKA:** I Tre Volti della Paura.
1964 99m/C IT Boris Karloff, Jacqueline Pierreux, Michele Mercier, Lidia Alfonsi, Susy Anderson, Mark Damon, Rika Dialina; **D:** Mario Bava. **VHS, Beta** $16.95 *SNC, HBO ♪♪♪*

Black Samurai When his girlfriend is held hostage, a martial arts warrior will stop at nothing to destroy the organization that abducted her.
1977 (R) 84m/C Jim Kelly; **D:** Al Adamson. **VHS, Beta** *NO ♪*

The Black Scorpion Two geologists in Mexico unearth a nest of giant scorpions living in a dead volcano. Eventually one of the oversized arachnids escapes to wreak havoc on Mexico City.
1957 85m/B Richard Denning, Mara Corday, Carlos Rivas; **D:** Edward Ludwig. **VHS** $19.98 *WAR, MLB, FRG ♪♪½*

Black Shampoo A black hairdresser on the Sunset Strip fights the mob with a chainsaw.
1976 90m/C John Daniels, Tanya Boyd, Joe Ortiz; **D:** Greydon Clark. **VHS, Beta** $59.95 *VCI Woof!*

Black Sister's Revenge Poorly selected video title mars this intelligent drama about a young black woman's struggle to adjust to the big city after growing up in the deep South. **AKA:** Emma Mae.
1976 100m/C Jerri Hayes, Ernest Williams II, Charles D. Brook III, Eddie Allen; **D:** Jamaa Fanaka; **W:** Jamaa Fanaka. **VHS, Beta** $59.95 *UNI ♪♪*

The Black Six Six black Vietnam veterans are out to punish the white gang who killed the brother of one of the black men.
1974 (R) 91m/C Gene Washington, Carl Eller, Lem Barney, Mercury Morris, Joe "Mean Joe" Greene, Willie Lanier, Rosalind Miles, John Isenbarger, Ben Davidson, Maury Wills; **D:** Matt Cimber. **VHS, Beta** $49.90 *UNI ♪*

The Black Stallion A young boy and a wild Arabian Stallion are the only survivors of a shipwreck, and they develop a deep affection for each other. When rescued, they begin training for an important race. Exceptionally beautiful first half. Rooney plays a horse trainer, again. Great for adults and kids.
1979 (PG) 120m/C Kelly Reno, Mickey Rooney, Teri Garr, Clarence Muse; **D:** Carroll Ballard; **W:** Bill Wittliff, Melissa Mathison, Jeanne Rosenberg; **M:** Carmine Coppola. Academy Awards '79: Best Sound Effects Editing; Nominations: Best Film Editing, Best Supporting Actor (Rooney). **VHS, Beta** $19.98 *MGM, FOX, TLF ♪♪♪*

The Black Stallion Returns Sequel to "The Black Stallion" follows the adventures of young Alec as he travels to the Sahara to search for his beautiful horse, which was stolen by an Arab chieftain. Unfortunately lacks much of the charm that was present in the first film. Adapted from the stories by Walt Farley.
1983 (PG) 103m/C Kelly Reno, Teri Garr, Vincent Spano; **D:** Robert Dalva; **M:** Georges Delerue. **VHS, Beta** $19.98 *FOX ♪♪½*

Black Starlet A girl from the projects of Chicago travels to Hollywood in search of fame. She winds her way through a world of sleaze and drugs in order to make it to the top. **AKA:** Black Gauntlet.
1974 (R) 90m/C Juanita Brown, Eric Mason, Rockne Tarkington, Damu King, Diane Holden; **D:** Chris Munger. **VHS** $59.95 *GEM ♪½*

Black Sunday Executed one hundred years previously, a witch returns with her vampire servant to do the bidding of Satan. A must see for horror fans; firsts for Steele as star and Bava as director. Also available with "Black Sabbath" on Laser Disc.
1960 83m/B IT Barbara Steele, John Richardson, Ivo Garrani, Andrea Checchi, Arturo Dominici; **D:** Mario Bava. **VHS** $19.98 *SNC, MRV, MOV ♪♪♪*

Black Sunday An Arab terrorist group plots to steal the Goodyear Blimp and load it with explosives. Their intent is to explode it over a Miami Super Bowl game to assassinate the U.S. president and to kill all the fans. Based on Thomas Harris' novel.
1977 (R) 143m/C Robert Shaw, Bruce Dern, Marthe Keller, Fritz Weaver, Steven Keats, Michael Gazzo, William Daniels; **D:** John Frankenheimer; **W:** Ernest Lehman; **M:** John Williams. **VHS, Beta** $24.95 *PAR ♪♪½*

Black Terrorist Terrorists take over a ranch and slay the inhabitants. They keep a young boy alive and the mother tries to rescue him.

1985 81m/C Allan Granville, Vera Jones; **D:** Neil Hetherington. **VHS, Beta** *NO ♪♪½*

Black Tide Suspicions arise that a drowning may have actually been a murder. **AKA:** Stormy Crossing.
1956 ?m/C John Ireland, Derek Bond. **VHS** $16.95 *SNC, VYY ♪♪*

Black Tights Chevalier introduces four stories told in dance by Roland Petit's Ballet de Paris company: "The Diamond Crusher," "Cyrano de Bergerac," "A Merry Mourning," and "Carmen." A keeper for dance fans. Shearer's Roxanne in "Cyrano" was her last performance before retirement. **AKA:** Un, Deux, Trois, Quatre!.
1960 120m/C FR Cyd Charisse, Zizi Jeanmarie, Moira Shearer, Dirk Sanders, Roland Petit; **D:** Terence Young. **VHS, Beta** $24.95 *VYY, NOS, VAI ♪♪½*

Black Tower An interesting murder mystery telling the story of a desperately impoverished medical student.
1950 54m/B Peter Cookson, Warren William, Anne Gwynne, Charles Calvert. **VHS, Beta** $24.95 *VYY ♪♪*

Black Vampire Jones plays a professor of African studies who is turned into a vampire by another vampire. He then marries the villain's ex-wife, played by Clark, a veteran of Russ Meyer films. Not much of a story but the acting is actually quite good and there are some creepy moments thanks mainly to an interesting score. **AKA:** Blood Couple; Ganja and Hess; Double Possession.
1973 (R) 83m/C Duane Jones, Marlene Clark, Bill Gunn, Sam Waymon, Leonard Jackson, Candece Tarpley, Mabel King; **D:** Bill Gunn; **W:** Bill Gunn. **VHS, Beta** $9.95 *GEM ♪½*

A Black Veil for Lisa A man attempts to exact revenge upon his unfaithful wife, but things go horribly awry.
1968 87m/C IT GE John Mills, Lucianna Paluzzi, Robert Hoffman; **D:** Massimo Dallamano. **VHS** *REP ♪♪*

Black Venus A soft-core epic, starring the former Miss Bahamas, Josephine Jacqueline Jones, about the 18th-century French aristocracy. Laughably based upon the stories of Balzac. European film dubbed in English.
1983 (R) 80m/C Josephine Jacqueline Jones, Emiliano Redondo; **D:** Claude Mulot. **VHS, Beta** $79.95 *MGM Woof!*

Black Water Gold Television movie about a search for sunken Spanish gold.
1969 75m/C Ricardo Montalban, Keir Dullea, Lana Wood, Bradford Dillman, France Nuyen; **D:** Alan Landsburg. **VHS** *NO ♪♪½*

Black Werewolf A millionaire sportsman invites a group of men and women connected with bizarre deaths or the eating of human flesh to spend the cycle of a full moon at his isolated lodge. **AKA:** The Beast Must Die.
1975 (PG) 93m/C GB Peter Cushing, Calvin Lockhart, Charles Gray, Anton Diffring; **D:** Paul Annett. **VHS, Beta** $9.95 *MED, PSM ♪♪*

The Black Widow A fortune-teller plots to steal scientific secrets and take over the world. Serial in thirteen episodes. **AKA:** Sombra, the Spider Woman.
1947 164m/B Bruce Edwards, Carol Forman, Anthony Warde; **D:** Spencer Gordon Bennet. **VHS** $19.98 *VCN, REP, MLB ♪♪*

Black Widow A federal agent pursues a beautiful murderess who marries rich men and then kills them, making the deaths look natural. The agent herself becomes involved in the final seduction. The two women are enticing and the locations picturesque.

1987 (R) 101m/C Debra Winger, Theresa Russell, Sami Frey, Nicol Williamson, Terry O'Quinn, Dennis Hopper, D.W. Moffett, Lois Smith, Mary Woronov, Rutanya Alda, James Hong, Diane Ladd; *Cameos:* David Mamet; *D:* Bob Rafelson; *W:* Ronald Bass; *M:* Michael Small. VHS, Beta $19.98 *FOX* 🎞🎞🎞

The Black Windmill An English spy is caught between his service and the kidnapping of his family by rival spies.
1974 (PG) 102m/C Michael Caine, Donald Pleasence, Delphine Seyrig, Clive Revill, Janet Suzman, John Vernon; *D:* Don Siegel. VHS, Beta $59.95 *MCA* 🎞🎞½

Blackbeard the Pirate The 18th-century buccaneer is given the full-blooded, Hollywood treatment.
1952 99m/C Robert Newton, Linda Darnell, Keith Andes, William Bendix, Richard Egan; *D:* Raoul Walsh. VHS, Beta $19.98 *RKO, TTC* 🎞🎞

Blackbeard's Ghost Disney comedy in which the famed 18th-century pirate's spirit (Ustinov) summoned to wreak havoc in order to prevent an old family home from being turned into a casino.
1967 107m/C Peter Ustinov, Dean Jones, Suzanne Pleshette, Elsa Lanchester, Richard Deacon; *D:* Robert Stevenson. VHS, Beta $14.99 *DIS* 🎞🎞

Blackbelt 2: Fatal Force A man seeks to avenge his brother's murder by going after his killers.
1993 (R) ?m/C Blake Bahner, Roxanne Baird, Michael Vlastas. VHS $89.98 *NHO* 🎞½

Blackboard Jungle Well-remembered urban drama about an idealistic teacher in a slum area who fights doggedly to connect with his unruly students. Bill Hailey's "Rock Around the Clock" over the opening credits was the first use of rock music in a mainstream feature film. Based on Evan Hunter novel.
1955 101m/B Glenn Ford, Anne Francis, Louis Calhern, Sidney Poitier, Vic Morrow, Richard Kiley, Margaret Hayes, John Hoyt, Warner Anderson; *D:* Richard Brooks; *W:* Richard Brooks. VHS, Beta $19.95 *MGM* 🎞🎞🎞½

Blackenstein Doctor into nouveau experimentation restores a man's arms and legs. But a jealous assistant gives our man a bogus injection, causing him to become "Blackenstein," a large African American with chip on hulking shoulder who enjoys killing people and otherwise causing big trouble. Ripe blaxploitation. *AKA:* Black Frankenstein.
1973 (R) 87m/C John Hart, Ivory Stone, Andrea King, Liz Renay, Joe DiSue; *D:* William A. Levey. VHS, Beta $29.95 *MED* Woof!

Blackjack Las Vegas is the scene for action and excitement as the mob puts the hit on tough guy William Smith.
1978 (R) 104m/C William Smith, Tony Burton, Paris Earl, Damu King, Diane Summerfield, Angela May; *D:* John Evans. VHS *TPV* 🎞🎞

Blackmail This first sound film for Great Britain and director Hitchcock features an early visualization of some typical Hitchcockian themes. The story follows the police investigation of a murder, and a detective's attempts to keep his girlfriend from being involved. Look for Hitchcock's screen cameo. Made as a silent, this was reworked to become a talkie.
1929 86m/B *GB* Anny Ondra, John Longdon, Sara Allgood, Charles Paton, Cyril Ritchard; *Cameos:* Alfred Hitchcock; *D:* Alfred Hitchcock; *W:* Charles Bennett, Alfred Hitchcock. VHS, Beta $9.98 *REP, MRV, NOS* 🎞🎞🎞

Blackmail Familiar story is given new life in this suspenseful movie originally made for cable TV. Blakely is a lonely woman who succumbs to Midkiff's attentions. She doesn't suspect that he's conning her with the help of his lover, Toussaint. Engaging thriller adapted from a short story by Bill Crenshaw.
1991 (R) 87m/C Susan Blakely, Dale Midkiff, Beth Toussaint, John Saxon, Mac Davis; *D:* Ruben Preuss. VHS, Beta *PAR* 🎞🎞🎞

Blackout Blind man recovers his sight and finds that the brother of his girlfriend, once thought dead, is actually alive and well and running a smuggling ring. Routine.
1950 73m/B *GB* Maxwell Reed, Dinah Sheridan, Patric Doonan, Eric Pohlmann; *D:* Robert S. Baker. VHS, Beta $16.95 *SNC* 🎞½

Blackout A drunken private eye is offered a murder case, and is subsequently framed for the crime. *AKA:* Murder by Proxy.
1954 87m/B Dane Clark, Belinda Lee, Betty Ann Davies; *D:* Terence Fisher. VHS, Beta $89.98 *MLB* 🎞🎞

Blackout Four killers terrorize an office building during the 1977 New York electrical blackout. Soon the police enter, confront them, and the fun starts. Comic touches provide some relief from the violence here.
1978 (R) 86m/C Jim Mitchum, Robert Carradine, Ray Milland, June Allyson, Jean-Pierre Aumont, Belinda J. Montgomery; *D:* Eddy Matalon; *W:* Joseph Stefano. VHS, Beta $59.95 *NLC* 🎞🎞

Blackout Made-for-cable-TV thriller. An aging police chief suspects a disfigured amnesiac is responsible for past killings, in spite of the fact that he now leads a subdued family life.
1985 99m/C Richard Widmark, Keith Carradine, Kathleen Quinlan, Michael Beck, Gerald Hiken; *D:* Douglas Hickox; *W:* David Ambrose. VHS, Beta $79.95 *MED* 🎞🎞½

Blackout Strange memories from childhood come back to her as a woman fights for her life.
1988 (R) 91m/C Carol Lynley, Gail O'Grady, Michael Keys Hall, Joseph Gian, Joanna Miles; *D:* Doug Adams. VHS, Beta *NO* 🎞🎞

The Blacksmith/The Balloonatic Two Buster Keaton shorts: "The Blacksmith" (1922) features Buster as the local blacksmith's apprentice who suddenly finds himself in charge. "The Balloonatic" (1923) presents Buster trapped in a runaway hot air balloon. Both films include music score.
1923 57m/B Buster Keaton, Virginia Fox, Phyllis Haver; *D:* Buster Keaton. VHS, Beta $24.95 *VYY* 🎞🎞

The Blacksmith/The Cops "The Blacksmith" is a burlesque of Longfellow's famous poem "The Village Blacksmith." In "Cops" Buster tries a new business venture to win his girl's hand. Chaos ensues. Silent comedy at its most adroit.
1922 38m/B Buster Keaton, Virginia Fox. VHS, Beta $19.95 *CCB* 🎞🎞

Blacula The African Prince Mamuwalde stalks the streets of Los Angeles trying to satisfy his insatiable desire for blood. Mildly successful melding of blaxploitation and horror that spawned a sequel, "Scream, Blacula, Scream."
1972 (PG) 92m/C William Marshall, Thalmus Rasulala, Denise Nicholas, Vonetta McGee; *D:* William Crain. VHS, Beta $9.98 *ORI* 🎞🎞

Blade An honest cop challenges a dirty cover-up in killer-stalked New York.
1972 (PG) 79m/C Steve Landesburg, John Schuck, Kathryn Walker; *D:* Ernie Pintoff. VHS, Beta $59.95 *GEM, MRV* 🎞🎞

Blade in Hong Kong Made-for-TV action outing. Investigator travels to Hong Kong, finds trouble and romance in the underbelly of the city. Pilot for un-sold series.
1985 100m/C Terry Lester, Keye Luke, Mike Preston, Jean-Marie Hon, Leslie Nielsen, Nancy Kwan, Anthony Newley, Ellen Regan; *D:* Reza Badiyi. VHS *NO* 🎞🎞½

A Blade in the Dark A young man composing a score for a horror film moves into a secluded villa and is inspired and haunted by the mysterious murder he witnesses. *AKA:* La Casa Con La Scala Nel Buio; House of the Dark Stairway.
1983 99m/C Andrea Occhipinti, Anny Papa; *D:* Lamberto Bava. VHS, Beta $69.98 *VES, LIV* 🎞🎞

Blade Master In this sequel to "Ator the Fighting Eagle," O'Keeffe as Ator is back as the Blade Master. Ator defends his people and his family name in a battle against the "Geometric Nucleus": a primitive bomb. His quest leads him and his small band of men to the castle of knowledge. *AKA:* Ator the Invincible.
1984 (PG) 92m/C Miles O'Keeffe, Lisa Foster; *D:* David Hills. VHS, Beta $19.95 *MED* 🎞½

Blade of the Ripper A madman armed with a razor slashes his way through the lovelies of the international jet set.
1984 90m/C George Hilton, Edwige Fenech. VHS, Beta *NO* Woof!

Blade Runner Los Angeles, the 29th century. World-weary cop tracks down a handful of renegade "replicants" (synthetically produced human slaves who, with only days left of life, search madly for some way to extend their prescribed lifetimes). Moody, beautifully photographed, dark thriller with sets from an architect's dream. Based on "Do Androids Dream of Electric Sheep" by Philip K. Dick. Laser edition features restored footage, information about special effects, and production sketches. Director's cut, released at 117 minutes, removes Ford's narration and the last scene of the film, which Scott considered too "up," and inserts several short scenes, including a dream sequence.
1982 (R) 122m/C Harrison Ford, Rutger Hauer, Sean Young, Daryl Hannah, M. Emmet Walsh, Edward James Olmos, Joe Turkel, Brion James, Joanna Cassidy; *D:* Ridley Scott; *W:* Hampton Fancher, David Peoples. VHS, Beta, 8mm $9.95 *COL, WAR, SUP* 🎞🎞½

Blades Another junk heap from Troma, dealing with the efforts of three golfers who try to stop a maniacal power mower that's been grinding duffers with regularity.
1989 (R) 101m/C Robert North, Jeremy Whelan, Victoria Scott, Jon McBride. VHS, Beta $79.98 *MED, VTR* 🎞

Blades of Courage A made-for-television biography of Olympic skater Lori Larouche. Choreographed by Debbi Wilkes. *AKA:* Skate!.
1988 98m/C *CA* Lynn Nightingale, Christianne Hirt, Colm Feore, Rosemary Dunsmore; *D:* Randy Bradshaw. VHS, Beta $29.95 *ACA* 🎞🎞

Bladestorm Ultra-cheapo fantasy/warrior rehash.
1986 87m/C VHS, Beta *NO* 🎞

Blaise Pascal Another of Rossellini's later historical portraits, detailing the life and times of the 17th-century philosopher, seen as a man whose scientific ideas conflicted with his own religious beliefs. Made for Italian television. In Italian with subtitles.
1971 131m/C *IT* *D:* Roberto Rossellini. VHS, Beta $79.95 *FCT* 🎞🎞🎞½

Blake of Scotland Yard Blake, the former Scotland Yard inspector, battles against a villain who has constructed a murderous death ray.
1936 70m/B Ralph Byrd, Herbert Rawlinson, Joan Barclay, Lloyd Hughes; *D:* Robert F. Hill. VHS, Beta $24.95 *VYY, DVT, VCN* 🎬🎬½

Blake's Seven Freedom-fighter Blake and his crew battle against a totalitarian super-power in this futuristic space adventure series from Great Britain. Created by Terry Nation of "Doctor Who" fame. Each volume contains two episodes and is available individually.
1978 105m/C *GB* Gareth Thomas, Sally Knyvette, Paul Darrow, Michael Keating, David Jackson, Jan Chappell; *D:* Michael E. Briant, Vere Lorrimer. VHS $24.98 *BFS, TVC, MOV* 🎬🎬½

Blame It on Rio A middle-aged man has a ridiculous fling with his best friend's daughter while on vacation with them in Rio de Janeiro. Caine and Johnson are amusing, but the script is somewhat weak. Remake of the French film "One Wild Moment."
1984 (R) 90m/C Michael Caine, Joseph Bologna, Demi Moore, Michelle Johnson, Valerie Harper; *D:* Stanley Donen; *W:* Charlie Peters, Larry Gelbart. VHS, Beta $29.95 *VES, LIV* 🎬🎬

Blame It on the Bellboy Wild farce set in Venice about a hotel bellboy who confuses three similarly named visitors—sending the wrong ones to meet corporate bigwigs, date women, or even kill. The brisk pace loses it towards the end and devolves into chase scenes.
1992 (PG-13) 79m/C Dudley Moore, Bryan Brown, Richard Griffiths, Andreas Katsulas, Patsy Kensit, Alison Steadman, Bronson Pinchot, Lindsay Anderson, Penelope Wilton; *D:* Mark Herman; *W:* Mark Herman; *M:* Trevor Jones. VHS, Beta $94.95 *HPH* 🎬🎬½

Blame It on the Night A rock star gets to take care of the military cadet son he never knew after the boy's mother suddenly dies. Mick Jagger helped write the story. Available in VHS and Beta Hi-Fi.
1984 (PG-13) 85m/C Nick Mancuso, Byron Thames, Leslie Ackerman, Billy Preston, Merry Clayton; *D:* Gene Taft. VHS, Beta $79.98 *FOX* 🎬🎬

Blank Check Parents may want to verify the whereabouts of their checkbooks after this one. 11-year-old Preston receives a blank check from a mobster on the run, cashes it for a million bucks, and goes on a spending orgy under an assumed name. Where are his parents? Apparently they don't have a problem with a shadowy benefactor taking their son under his wing. Sound familiar? And who thought it would be a good idea to have the little twerp mooning after a comely bank teller? Formula aside, this blatant rip-off of "Home Alone" tries to throw in an ending moral but probably won't fool the kids either. *AKA:* Disney's Blank Check.
1993 (PG) 93m/C Brian Bonsall, Miguel Ferrer, Michael Lerner, Tone Loc, Rick Ducommun, Karen Duffy; *D:* Rupert Wainwright; *W:* Colby Carr, Blake Snyder; *M:* Nicholas Pike. VHS *DIS* 🎬

Blankman Self-appointed superhero (Wayans), who makes up in creativity what he lacks in superpowers, fights crime in his underwear and a cape made from his grandmother's bathrobe. Life is simple, until an ambitious TV reporter (Givens) finds out about him. Silly one-joke premise is carried a little too far; didn't similar "Meteor Man" crash? Gifted comedian Wayans tries but can't make this guy fly.

1994 ?m/C Damon Wayans, Robin Givens, David Alan Grier, Jason Alexander, Jon Polito; *D:* Mike Binder; *W:* Damon Wayans, J.F. Lawton. VHS *NYR* 🎬🎬

The Blasphemer A well-crafted, engrossing drama about misfortune that befalls someone who disobeys one of the sacred Commandments. Silent music score.
1921 89m/B VHS, Beta $24.95 *VYY* 🎬🎬

Blast-Off Girls A scuzzball promoter sets out to avenge himself for being blacklisted by the rock 'n' roll industry. He discovers a fresh group, but without corporate backing he can only pay them with groovy clothes and mini-skirted girls. Trouble ensues when they unexpectedly hit the charts and want real money.
1967 83m/C Ray Sager, Dan Conway; *D:* Herschell Gordon Lewis. VHS $19.99 *MOV, SMW* 🎬

Blastfighter After local hoodlums kill his daughter, an ex-con cop goes on a spree of violence and revenge. Director Bava uses the pseudonym "John Old, Jr.," as his father Mario Bava occasionally credited himself as John Old. Italian film shot in Atlanta.
1985 (R) 93m/C *IT* Michael Sopkiw, Valerie Blake, George Eastman; *D:* Lamberto Bava. VHS, Beta $69.95 *VES, LIV* Woof!

Blat A gangster of Italian-Russian descent tries to pull a sting on merry old England's financial world in this comedy. Made for British television.
19?? 90m/C *GB* Robert Hardy, Adrienne Corri, Alfred Molina. VHS $49.95 *FCT* 🎬½

Blaze The true story of Louisiana governor Earl Long who became involved with a stripper, Blaze Starr, causing a political scandal of major proportions. Robust, good-humored bio-pic featuring a fine character turn by Newman.
1989 (R) 117m/C Paul Newman, Lolita Davidovich, Jerry Hardin, Robert Wuhl, Gailard Sartain, Jeffrey DeMunn, Richard Jenkins, Garland Bunting; *D:* Ron Shelton; *W:* Ron Shelton. VHS, Beta $89.95 *TOU* 🎬🎬½

Blazing Guns A marshal, masquerading inexplicably as a tenderfoot, enters a lawless town and is immediately hired as a deputy.
1950 54m/B Raymond Hatton, Russell Hayden, Fuzzy Knight, Betty Adams. VHS, Beta $19.95 *NOS, HEG* 🎬

The Blazing Ninja Deadly kung-fu senses-dulling mind-paralyzing experience about master of some martial art versus student of same.
19?? 86m/C *HK* Philip Cheung, Sony Tanaka, Ronny Lee, Tim Chen, Sandy Peng, Godfrey Ho; *D:* Godfrey Ho; *W:* Szeto On. VHS $14.98 *VTR* Woof!

Blazing Saddles Wild, wacky spoof by Brooks of every cliche in the western film genre. Little is Black Bart, a convict offered a reprieve if he will become a sheriff and clean up a nasty frontier town; the previous recipients of this honor have all swiftly ended up in shallow graves. A crazy, silly film with a cast full of loveable loonies including comedy greats Wilder, Kahn, and Korman. Watch for the Count Basie Orchestra. A group writing effort, based on an original story by Bergman. Was the most-viewed movie in its first year of release on HBO cable.
1974 (R) 90m/C Cleavon Little, Harvey Korman, Madeline Kahn, Gene Wilder, Mel Brooks, John Hillerman, Alex Karras, Dom DeLuise, Liam Dunn; *D:* Mel Brooks, Alan Uger; *W:* Mel Brooks, Norman Steinberg, Andrew Bergman, Richard Pryor, Alan Uger; *M:* John Morris. VHS, Beta $14.95 *WAR* 🎬🎬🎬½

Blazing Stewardesses The Hound salutes the distributor for truth in advertising, as they stamped this as one of the world's worst videos. Lusty, busty stewardesses relax at a western guest ranch under siege from hooded riders and the aging gags of the Ritz Brothers.
1975 (R) 95m/C Yvonne De Carlo, Bob Livingston, Donald (Don "Red") Barry, Regina Carrol; *Cameos:* The Ritz Brothers; *D:* Al Adamson. VHS *NO Woof!*

Bleak House The British television mini-series adaptation of the Charles Dickens tome about an interminable lawsuit and the decadent, criminal ruling class of 19th-century England. On three tapes.
1985 391m/C *GB* Denholm Elliott, Diana Rigg, Philip Franks, Peter Vaughan, T.P. McKenna, Charles Drake; *D:* Ross Devenish. VHS, Beta $29.98 *FOX, SIG, TVC* 🎬🎬½

Bless the Beasts and Children A group of six teenage boys at a summer camp attempt to save a herd of buffalo from slaughter at a national preserve. Treacly Kramer backwater. Based on the novel by Glendon Swarthout.
1971 (PG) 109m/C Billy Mumy, Barry Robins, Miles Chapin, Darel Glaser, Bob Kramer, Ken Swofford, Jesse White; *D:* Stanley Kramer. VHS, Beta $14.95 *COL* 🎬🎬½

Blessed Event Fast-moving, entertaining film about a Broadway gossip columnist with a poison pen. Tracy has the role of a lifetime as a Walter Winchell prototype who thinks no one is exempt from his juicy column. Powell makes film debut as a crooner after a brief career as a band singer. Based on a play by Manuel Seff and Forrest Wilson.
1932 77m/B Lee Tracy, Mary Brian, Dick Powell, Allen Jenkins, Ruth Donnelly, Emma Dunn, Walter Miller, Tom Dugan, Isabel Jewell; *D:* Roy Del Ruth; *W:* Howard J. Green. VHS $19.98 *MGM* 🎬🎬🎬

Blind Ambition Television mini-series docu-drama traces the career of John Dean, special counsel to President Richard M. Nixon. Focuses on his fractured personal life and touches on virtually all of the Watergate headlines.
1982 95m/C Martin Sheen, Rip Torn. VHS, Beta *TLF* 🎬🎬½

Blind Date Blind man agrees to have a visual computer implanted in his brain in order to help the police track down a psychopathic killer. Violent scenes may be disturbing to some.
1984 (R) 100m/C Joseph Bottoms, Kirstie Alley, Keir Dullea, James Daughton, Lana Clarkson, Marina Sirtis; *D:* Nico Mastorakis; *W:* Nico Mastorakis. VHS, Beta $79.95 *VES, LIV* 🎬½

Blind Date A blind date between a workaholic yuppie and a beautiful blonde starts off well, but when she drinks too much at dinner, things get out of hand. In addition to embarrassing her date and destroying the restaurant, she has a jealous ex-boyfriend who must be dealt with.
1987 (PG-13) 95m/C Kim Basinger, Bruce Willis, John Larroquette, William Daniels, George Coe, Mark Blum, Phil Hartman, Stephanie Faracy, Alice Hirson, Graham Stark; *D:* Blake Edwards. VHS, Beta $14.95 *COL* 🎬🎬

Blind Faith Action and adventure take a turn for the horrific when several men find themselves in captivity.
1989 (R) ?m/C Eric Gunn, Kevin Yon, Lynne Browne; *D:* Dean Wilson; *W:* Dean Wilson. VHS *HHE* 🎬

Blind Fear A blind woman is stalked by three killers in an abandoned country inn.

1989 (R) 98m/C Shelley Hack, Jack Langedijk, Kim Coates, Jan Rubes, Heidi von Palleske; **D:** Tom Berry. **VHS, Beta** $29.95 ACA 🐾½

Blind Fists of Bruce A rich, idle young man learns the techniques of kung fu from a former warrior.
197? 92m/C Bruce Li; **D:** Kam Bo. **VHS, Beta** NO 🐾½

Blind Fools A scathing indictment of children neglected by ambitious parents.
1940 66m/B Herbert Rawlinson, Claire Whitney, Russell Hicks, Miriam Battista. **VHS, Beta** NO 🐾½

Blind Fury A blind Vietnam vet enlists the aid of a Zen master and a sharpshooter to tackle the Mafia. Hauer works well in the lead, but unfortunately, the movie doesn't.
1990 (R) 86m/C Rutger Hauer, Terry O'Quinn, Brandon Call, Lisa Blount, Randall "Tex" Cobb, Noble Willingham, Meg Foster, Sho Kosugi, Nick Cassavetes, Charles Cooper, Rick Overton; **D:** Phillip Noyce; **W:** Charles Robert Carner; **M:** J. Peter Robinson. **VHS, Beta** $14.95 COL. FCT 🐾🐾½

Blind Husbands An Austrian officer is attracted to the pretty wife of a dull surgeon. Controversial in its day, this lurid, sumptuous melodrama instigated many stubborn Hollywood myths, including the stereotype of the brusque, jodhpur-clad Prussian officer. This was von Stroheim's first outing as director.
1919 98m/C Erich von Stroheim, Fay Wray; **D:** Erich von Stroheim. **VHS, Beta** $24.95 VYY, GVV 🐾🐾🐾½

Blind Justice An innocent man is identified as a rapist, and the accusation ruins his life. Made for television.
1986 94m/C Tim Matheson, Lisa Eichhorn, Mimi Kuzyk, Philip Charles MacKenzie, Tom Atkins; **D:** Rod Holcomb; **M:** Miles Goodman. **VHS, Beta** $59.98 FOX 🐾🐾

Blind Man's Bluff A blind professor is accused of murdering his neighbor, but as he tries to solve the mystery, evidence points to his ex-girlfriend who may have framed him for the murder. Surprisingly suspenseful made for cable TV movie is hampered by a stock Hollywood ending.
1991 (PG-13) 86m/C Robert Urich, Lisa Eilbacher, Patricia Clarkson, Ken Pogue, Ron Perlman; **D:** James Quinn; **W:** Joel Gross. **VHS, Beta** PAR 🐾½

Blind Rage When the United States government transports $15 million to the Philippines, five blind kung fu masters want a piece of the action.
1978 (R) 81m/C PH D'Urville Martin, Leo Fong, Tony Ferrer, Dick Adair, Darnell Garcia, Leila Hermosa, Fred Williamson; **D:** Efren C. Pinon. **VHS, Beta** $59.95 MGM 🐾

Blind Side DeMornay and Silver are a married couple whose Mexican vacation turns into trouble when they get into a hit-and-run accident which they don't report. Back home, they're frightened by the sudden appearance of Hauer, who's also just back from Mexico. They think he's after blackmail but he's really just a run-of-the-mill psycho intrigued by DeMornay, who at least keeps her character in control. Silver and Hauer have a great time chewing scenery. Made for cable television. Also available in an unrated version which run 98 minutes.
1993 (R) 92m/C Rebecca DeMornay, Ron Silver, Rutger Hauer; **D:** Geoff Murphy. **VHS** $79.99 HBO 🐾½

Blind Spot Okay family drama which works because of the performances and not the script. Woodward stars as Nell Harrington, a take-charge U.S. Representative long married to Simon (Weaver). Her troubled,

pregnant daughter Phoebe (Linney) is married to Nell's aide Charlie (Diamond). Charlie is killed and Phoebe injured in a car crash but the real tragedy is when Nell discovers what caused the accident—drugs—and that her daughter is a cocaine addict. Lots of suffering. Made for television.
1993 99m/C Joanne Woodward, Laura Linney, Fritz Weaver, Reed Edward Diamond, Cynthia Martells, Patti Yasutake, Patti D'Arbanville; **D:** Michael Toshiyuki Uno; **W:** Nina Shengold; **M:** Patrick Williams. **VHS** REP 🐾🐾½

Blind Vengeance A man whose son was murdered by white supremacists decides to take his own special revenge when they are acquitted by the local jury. But this isn't your usual bloodbath, instead he plays psychological games with the men, waiting for them to break. Made for cable television.
1990 (R) 93m/C Gerald McRaney, Marg Helgenberger, Thalmus Rasulala, Lane Smith, Don Hood, Grand Bush; **D:** Lee Philips; **W:** Henri Simoun, Curt Allen. **VHS** $79.95 MCA 🐾🐾½

Blind Vision Von Dohlen stars as William Dalton, a mail clerk who is in love with his beautiful neighbor Leanne (Shelton). Suffering from extreme shyness, Dalton can only spy on her through a telephoto lens. Things start to get complicated for him when one of Leanne's boyfriends turns up dead outside her apartment. Soon afterwards, their landlady and a local police detective uncover a shocking sexual secret that forces Dalton into a deadly game of obsession and desire.
1991 92m/C Lenny Von Dohlen, Deborah Shelton, Ned Beatty, Robert Vaughn, Louise Fletcher; **D:** Shuki Levy. **VHS** $89.95 WOV 🐾½

Blind Witness Routine story about a blind woman who's the only witness to her husband's murder during a robbery. Made for television.
1989 92m/C Victoria Principal, Paul LeMat, Stephen Macht, Matt Clark, Tim Choate; **D:** Richard A. Colla. **VHS** $89.95 WOV 🐾🐾½

Blinded by the Light Young woman tries to save her brother from attachment to a quasi-religious cult, The Light of Salvation. Real-life brother and sister McNichol team up in this made-for-television drama, one of the earlier examinations of cult behavior.
1982 90m/C Kristy McNichol, Jimmy McNichol, Anne Jackson, Michael McGuire; **D:** John Alonzo. **VHS, Beta** TLF 🐾🐾

Blindfold: Acts of Obsession Madeline's (Doherty) marriage is boring so she consults therapist Jennings (Nelson). He suggests a number of sexual fantasies Madeline plays out with hubby Woods only to have murder enter the picture. Then Madeline's older sister Chris (Alfonso) is assigned to investigate and lets out lots of family secrets. Shannen in the buff, murder, infidelity, deception, and sex. An unrated version is also available.
1994 (R) 93m/C Shannen Doherty, Judd Nelson, Michael Woods, Kristian Alfonso, Shell Danielson, Drew Snyder; **D:** Lawrence L. Simeone; **W:** Lawrence L. Simeone; **M:** Shuki Levy. **VHS** $92.95 AVE 🐾

Blindside A surveillance hobbyist who owns a motel spies on his tenants until a murder involves him in a big-scale drug war.
1988 (R) 98m/C Harvey Keitel, Lori Hallier, Lolita David, Alan Fawcett, Michael Rudder; **D:** Paul Lynch. **VHS, Beta** $14.98 NLC 🐾🐾

Blink Recent corneal transplants allow blind musician Emma (Stowe) to regain her sight, but until they "settle" what she sees may not register in her mind immediately, a phenomenon the script dubs "retroactive vision." This poses a problem for Chicago cop Quinn when he falls for Emma—the only one who

can recognize a sadistic killer. Average thriller has been done better before, but adds two attractive leads, enough suspense, and a unique twist to the typical woman-in-jeopardy tale to keep things interesting. The distorted images in Stowe's blurry vision were created by computer. Stowe also learned fiddle for her place as the fictional member of the real-life Irish-American band, The Drovers.
1993 (R) 106m/C Madeleine Stowe, Aidan Quinn, Laurie Metcalf, James Remar, Bruce A. Young, Peter Friedman, Paul Dillon, Michael Kirkpatrick; **D:** Michael Apted; **W:** Dana Stevens; **M:** Brad Fiedel. **VHS** COL 🐾🐾½

Blink of an Eye Special agent Sam Browning (Pare) must use his psychic powers and military skills against the terrorists who have kidnapped the CIA director's daughter.
1992 (R) 90m/C Michael Pare. **VHS** $89.95 VMK 🐾½

Bliss A savage, surreal Australian comedy about an advertising executive who dies suddenly for a few minutes, and upon his awakening he finds the world maniacally, bizarrely changed. Based on the Peter Carey novel, and one of the most inspired absurdist films of the decade.
1985 (R) 112m/C AU Barry Otto, Lynette Curran, Helen Jones; **D:** Ray Lawrence; **W:** Peter Carey. **VHS, Beta** $19.95 NWV, STE 🐾🐾🐾½

The Bliss of Mrs. Blossom Three's a crowd in this light-hearted romp through the machinations of a brassiere manufacturer (Attenborough) and his neglected wife (MacLaine). Mrs. Blossom finds sewing machine repairman Booth so appetizing that she hides him in the attic of the Blossom home. He reads books and redecorates, until, several plot twists later, Attenborough discovers the truth. Witty and wise, with fine supporting cast and excellent pacing.
1968 93m/C GB Shirley MacLaine, Richard Attenborough, James Booth, Freddie Jones, John Cleese; **D:** Joseph McGrath. **VHS** $14.95 PAR, MOV 🐾🐾🐾

Blithe Spirit Charming and funny adaptation of Coward's famed stage play. A man remarries and finds his long-dead wife is unhappy enough about it to come back and haunt him. Clever supporting cast, with Rutherford exceptional as the medium. Received Oscar for its Special Effects.
1945 96m/C GB Rex Harrison, Constance Cummings, Kay Hammond, Margaret Rutherford, Hugh Wakefield, Joyce Carey; **D:** David Lean. **VHS** MLB 🐾🐾🐾½

The Blob Sci fi thriller about a small town's fight against a slimy jello invader from space. Slightly rebellious McQueen (in his first starring role) redeems himself when he saves the town with quick action. Low-budget, horror/teen-fantasy became a camp classic. Other names considered included "The Glob," "The Glob that Girdled the Globe," "The Meteorite Monster," "The Molten Meteorite," and "The Night of the Creeping Dead." Followed by a worthless sequel in 1972, "Son of Blob" and a worthwhile remake in 1988. Laserdisc contains an additional fifteen minutes of McQueen interviews and the trailers for both the original and the 1988 remake.
1958 83m/C Steve McQueen, Aneta Corseaut, Olin Howland, Earl Rowe; **D:** Irvin S. Yeaworth Jr. **VHS, Beta** $19.95 COL, GEM, VYG 🐾🐾½

The Blob A hi-tech remake of the 1958 camp classic about a small town beset by a fast-growing, man-eating mound of glop shot into space by scientists, irradiated into an unnatural being, and then returned to earth.

Well-developed characters make this an excellent tribute to the first film.
1988 (R) 92m/C Kevin Dillon, Candy Clark, Joe Seneca, Shawnee Smith, Donovan Leitch, Jeffrey DeMunn, Ricky Paull Goldin; *D:* Chuck Russell; *W:* Frank Darabont, Chuck Russell. **VHS, Beta** $89.95 COL ♂♂♂

Block-heads Twenty years after the end of WWI, soldier Stan is found, still in his foxhole, and brought back to America, where he moves in with old pal Ollie. Also includes a 1934 Charley Chase short "I'll Take Vanilla."
1938 75m/B Stan Laurel, Oliver Hardy, Billy Gilbert, Patricia Ellis, James Finlayson, Charley Chase; *D:* John Blystone. **VHS, Beta** $19.95 CCB, MLB ♂♂♂

Blockhouse Four men are entombed in a subterranean stronghold for six years after the D-Day invasion of Normandy. Encourages claustrophobic feeling in viewer. Based on Jean Paul Cleberts' novel "Le Blockhaus."
1973 88m/C *GB* Peter Sellers, Charles Aznavour, Per Oscarsson, Peter Vaughan, Leon Lissek, Alfred Lynch, Jeremy Kemp; *D:* Clive Rees. **VHS, Beta** No Woof!

Blonde Blackmailer Boring story about an innocent man who serves time for the murder of a female blackmailer. When he's released, he searches for the real killer.
1958 69m/B *GB* Richard Arlen, Susan Shaw, Vincent Ball, Constance Leigh; *D:* Charles Deane; *W:* Charles Deane. **VHS** RXM ♂

Blonde Cobra/The Doctor's Dream Here are two short films by Ken Jacobs: Underground film star Jack Smith reminisces about his career in "Blonde Cobra" and a country doctor saves the life of a little girl in "Doctor's Dream."
1984 57m/C **VHS, Beta** No ♂

Blonde Crazy A charming grifter hooks up with a gorgeous blonde as he works the territory of a big wheel criminal. Escapist fare, with fun performances from Cagney and Blondell. *AKA:* Larceny Lane.
1931 81m/B James Cagney, Joan Blondell, Louis Calhern, Ray Milland, Nat Pendleton; *D:* Roy Del Ruth. **VHS** $19.98 MGM ♂♂½

Blonde in Black Leather A bored Italian housewife takes up with a leather-clad lady biker, and together they cavort about.
1977 88m/C Claudia Cardinale, Monica Vitti; *D:* Carlo DiPalma. **VHS, Beta** $59.95 NLC ♂♂½

Blonde Savage Charting African territories, an adventurer encounters a white jungle queen swinging amongst the vines. Essentially a cheap, distaff "Tarzan."
1947 62m/B Leif Erickson, Gale Sherwood, Veda Ann Borg, Douglass Dumbrille, Frank Jenks, Matt Willis, Ernest Whitman; *D:* Steve Sekely. **VHS, Beta** $16.95 SNC ♂

Blonde Venus A German cafe singer marries an Englishman, but their marriage hits the skids when he contracts radiation poisoning and she gets a nightclub job to pay the bills. Sternberg's and Dietrich's fourth film together, and characteristically beautiful, though terribly strange. Dietrich's cabaret number "Hot Voodoo," in a gorilla suit and blonde afro, attains new heights in early Hollywood surrealism.
1932 94m/B Marlene Dietrich, Herbert Marshall, Cary Grant, Dickie Moore, Hattie McDaniel, Sidney Toler; *D:* Josef von Sternberg. **VHS, Beta** $14.98 MCA ♂♂♂½

Blondie Chic Young's famous comic strip debuted on the big screen with Singleton in the title role, Lake as the bumbling Dagwood, and Simms as Baby Dumpling (son Alexander, when he grows up). The couple are about to celebrate their 5th wedding anniver-

sary when Dagwood loses his job and Blondie suspects him of infidelity. The series eventually contained 28 films.
1938 68m/B Penny Singleton, Arthur Lake, Larry Simms, Gene Lockhart, Ann Doran, Jonathan Hale, Gordon Oliver, Stanley Andrews; *D:* Frank Strayer; *W:* Richard Flournoy **VHS** $19.99 MOV ♂♂½

Blondie Has Trouble Mr. Dithers has a property he just can't sell because of rumors that the house is haunted. So he offers to let the Bumsteads stay in it to prove that the rumors are false. The Bumsteads also find the creepy mansion comes complete with two equally creepy servants. 6th film in the series. *AKA:* Blondie Has Servant Trouble.
1940 70m/B Penny Singleton, Arthur Lake, Larry Simms, Danny Mummert, Jonathan Hale, Arthur Hohl, Esther Dale, Irving Bacon; *D:* Frank Strayer; *W:* Richard Flournoy. **VHS** $19.99 MOV ♂♂½

Blondie Hits the Jackpot Dagwood is fired for the umpteenth time after he makes a mistake in a construction deal and tries frantically to get his job back. Meanwhile, Blondie wins the big prize on a radio quiz show. The 26th film in the series.
1949 66m/B Penny Singleton, Arthur Lake, Larry Simms, Marjorie Kent, Jerome Cowan, Lloyd Corrigan, Danny Mummert, James Flavin; *D:* Edward L. Bernds; *W:* Jack Henley. **VHS** $19.99 MOV ♂½

Blondie in Society A weak entry (the ninth) in the comedic series. Dagwood brings home a pedigreed Great Dane and Blondie decides to enter the pooch in the local dog show. Then an important client of Dagwood's decides he wants the dog.
1941 77m/B Penny Singleton, Arthur Lake, Larry Simms, William Frawley, Edgar Kennedy, Jonathan Hale, Danny Mummert, Chick Chandler; *D:* Frank Strayer; *W:* Karen De Wolf. **VHS** $19.99 MOV ♂½

Blondie Knows Best Dagwood impersonates his boss, Mr. Dithers, and causes all sorts of problems. Howard, one of the Three Stooges, has a cameo as a myopic process-server. The 18th film in the series.
1946 66m/B Penny Singleton, Arthur Lake, Larry Simms, Marjorie Kent, Jonathan Hale, Steve Geray, Jerome Cowan, Danny Mummert; *Cameos:* Shemp Howard; *D:* Abby Berlin; *W:* Edward L. Bernds, Al Martin. **VHS** $19.99 MOV ♂½

Blondie Takes a Vacation Third in the series of fluff films adapted from Chic Young's comic strip. After the Bumstead family is snubbed at a snobby mountain resort they move to a friendlier nearby hotel where they try to help out the owners who are in danger of losing their investment. Baby Dumpling does his bit by unleashing a skunk in the ventilation system of the competing hotel.
1939 68m/B Penny Singleton, Arthur Lake, Larry Simms, Danny Mummert, Donald Meek, Donald MacBride, Thomas Ross, Robert Wilcox, Irving Bacon; *D:* Frank Strayer; *W:* Richard Flournoy. **VHS** $19.99 MOV ♂♂½

Blondie's Blessed Event Cookie is born, causing even more chaos in the Bumstead household. Meanwhile, Dagwood gets into trouble at work when he hires a cynical playwright to write an important speech for him. 11th entry in series.
1942 69m/B Penny Singleton, Arthur Lake, Larry Simms, Norma Jean Wayne, Jonathan Hale, Danny Mummert, Hans Conried, Irving Bacon, Stanley Brown, Mary Wickes, Paul Harvey, Arthur O'Connell; *D:* Frank Strayer; *W:* Richard Flournoy, Karen De Wolf, Connie Leo. **VHS** $19.99 MOV ♂♂½

Blood Alley A seasoned Merchant Marine captain takes on a cargo of refugee Chinese to smuggle through enemy territory. Middling, mid-career Wayne vehicle.
1955 115m/C John Wayne, Lauren Bacall, Paul Fix, Joy Kim, Berry Kroeger, Mike Mazurki, Anita Ekberg; *D:* William A. Wellman. **VHS, Beta** $19.98 WAR, FCT ♂♂

Blood and Black Lace Beautiful models are being brutally murdered and an inspector is assigned to the case, but not before more gruesome killings occur. Bava is, as usual, violent and suspenseful. Horror fans will enjoy this flick.
1964 90m/C *IT FR GE* Cameron Mitchell, Eva Bartok, Mary Arden; *D:* Mario Bava. **VHS, Beta** $59.95 MED ♂

Blood & Concrete: A Love Story Bizarre, violent and stylish film-noir spoof, definitely not for all tastes. The innocent hero gets drawn into a maelstrom of intrigue over a killer aphrodisiac drug. Beals, an addicted punk rocker, gets to perform a few songs.
1990 (R) 97m/C Billy Zane, Jennifer Beals, Darren McGavin; *D:* Jeff Reiner; *W:* Jeff Reiner. **VHS** $89.95 COL ♂♂

Blood and Guns Romance, revenge, and action abound in post-revolutionary Mexico.
1979 (R) 96m/C Orson Welles, Tomas Milian, John Steiner; *D:* Giulio Petroni. **VHS, Beta** MRV ♂½

Blood and Roses A girl who is obsessed with her family's vampire background becomes possessed by a vampire and commits numerous murders. The photography is good, but the plot is hazy and only effective in certain parts. Based on the book "Carmilla" by Sheridan LeFanu. Later remade as "The Vampire Lovers" and "The Blood-Spattered Bride." *AKA:* Et Mourir de Plaisir.
1961 74m/C Mel Ferrer, Elsa Martinelli, Annette Vadim, Marc Allegret; *D:* Roger Vadim; *W:* Roger Vadim. **VHS** PAR ♂♂

Blood and Sand Vintage romance based on Vincente Blasco Ibanez's novel about the tragic rise and fall of a matador, and the women in his life. The film that made Valentino a star. Remade in 1941. Silent.
1922 87m/B Rudolph Valentino, Nita Naldi, Lila Lee, Walter Long; *D:* Fred Niblo. **VHS, Beta** $19.95 REP, NOS, CAB ♂♂♂

Blood and Sand Director Mamoulian "painted" this picture in the new technicolor technique, which makes it a veritable explosion of color and spectacle. Power is the matador who becomes famous and then falls when he is torn between two women, forsaking his first love, bullfighting. Based on the novel "Sangre y Arena" by Vicente Blasco Ibanez. This movie catapulted Hayworth to stardom, primarily for her dancing, but also for her sexiness and seductiveness (and of course, her acting). Remake of the 1922 silent classic; remade again in 1989.
1941 123m/C Tyrone Power, Linda Darnell, Rita Hayworth, Alla Nazimova, Anthony Quinn, J. Carroll Naish, John Carradine, George Reeves; *D:* Rouben Mamoulian; *W:* Jo Swerling; *M:* Alfred Newman. Academy Awards '41: Best Color Cinematography; Nominations: Best Interior Decoration. **VHS, Beta** $19.98 FXV ♂♂♂

Blood and Sand A bullfighter on the verge of super-stardom risks it all when he falls under the spell of a sexy, seductive woman. Will she destroy his one opportunity for fame? Interesting for people who actually enjoy watching the "sport" of bullfighting. Originally made in 1922 and remade in 1941.

1989 (R) 96m/C Christopher Rydell, Sharon Stone, Ana Torrent, Jose-Luis De Villalonga, Simon Andrew; **D:** Javier Elorrieta. VHS **$89.95** *VMK* 🎞🎞

Blood and Sand/Son of the Sheik A double feature containing two abridged versions; in "Blood and Sand," an idolized matador meets another woman just before his wedding; in "Son of the Sheik," a man believes he has been betrayed by a dancing girl, and he abducts her to seek revenge. Silent.
1926 56m/B Rudolph Valentino, Lila Lee, Vilma Banky. VHS, Beta **$29.98** *CCB* 🎞🎞

Blood and Steel The railroad tycoon's daughter and the construction foreman wind up together on an exciting train ride. Silent.
1925 ?m/B Helen Holmes, William Desmond; **D:** J.P. McGowan. VHS, Beta, 8mm **$55.95** *GVV* 🎞🎞

Blood at Sundown Routine oater where man returns home after the Civil War to find his wife kidnapped by a group of Mexican outlaws who have also taken over his village.
19?? 92m/C Giuliano Gemma, Hally Hamond, Nieves Navarro, Antonio Casas, Fernando Sancho, Pajarito, George Martin; **D:** Duccio Tessari. VHS, Beta **$19.95** *IMP* 🎞½

Blood Beach A group of teenagers are devoured by menacing sand, which keeps people from getting to the water by swallowing them whole. Weak parody with some humorous moments; more silly than scary.
1981 (R) 92m/C David Huffman, Marianna Hill, John Saxon, Burt Young, Otis Young; **D:** Jeffrey Bloom. VHS, Beta **$54.95** *MED* Woof!

Blood Beast Terror An entomologist transforms his own daughter into a Deathshead Moth and she proceeds to terrorize and drink innocent victims' blood. **AKA:** The Vampire-Beast Craves Blood.
1967 81m/C *GB* Peter Cushing, Robert Flemyng, Wanda Ventham; **D:** Vernon Sewell. VHS, Beta **$39.98** *MON* 🎞½

Blood Bride A lonely young woman finally finds happiness with her new husband but her world comes crashing about her with soul-mangling ferocity when she discovers he is actually a bloodthirsty maniac.
19?? 90m/C Ellen Barber, Philip English. VHS, Beta *NO* 🎞½

Blood Brothers A young man who dreams of becoming a lawyer is disturbed when he discovers that his family has mafia ties.
1974 (R) 148m/C *IT* Claudia Cardinale, Franco Nero, Lina Polito; **D:** Pasquale Squitieri. VHS, Beta *NO* 🎞🎞

Blood Brothers James Grizzly Adams, who lives in the mountains of the American wilderness, relives the story of how he met his Indian blood brother, Nakuma. Beautiful scenery.
1977 50m/C Dan Haggerty. VHS, Beta **$14.98** *MCG* 🎞🎞

Blood Clan Based on the true story of Katy Bane, daughter of notorious Scottish cult leader, Sawney Bane, in whose lair were found the remains of over 1000 killed and cannibalized followers. When found, Bane's entire family was sentenced to death with the exception of Katy, who left to make a new start in Canada. When a rash of mysterious deaths break out in Katy's new home, she must defend herself from rumors that her father's murderous cult is resurfacing.
1991 (R) 91m/C Gordon Pinsent, Michelle Little, Robert Wisden; **D:** Charles Wilkinson. VHS **$29.95** *MNC, FXL* 🎞½

Blood Cult A bizarre series of murder-mutilations take place on a small midwestern campus. Contains graphic violence that is not for the squeamish. This film was created especially for the home video market.
1985 92m/C Chuck Ellis, Julie Andelman, Jim Vance, Joe Hardt; **D:** Christopher Lewis. VHS, Beta **$24.95** *VCI* 🎞

Blood Debts A father is out for revenge after he saves his daughter from some hunters who raped her and also killed her boyfriend.
1983 91m/C Richard Harrison, Mike Manty, Jim Gaines, Anne Jackson, Anne Milhench; **D:** Teddy Page. VHS, Beta *NO* 🎞

Blood Diner Two spirit-possessed, diner-owning brothers kill countless young girls for demonic rituals, and serve their corpses as gourmet food in their restaurant. Some funny moments mixed in with the requisite gore. Cult potential.
1987 88m/C Rick Burks, Carl Crew; **D:** Jackie Kong. VHS, Beta **$19.98** *VES, LIV* Woof!

Blood Feast The first of Lewis' gore-fests, in which a demented caterer butchers hapless young women to splice them together in order to bring back an Egyptian goddess. Dated, campy, and gross; reportedly shot in four days (it shows). **AKA:** Feast of Flesh.
1963 70m/C Connie Mason, Thomas Wood, Malcolm Arnold; **D:** Herschell Gordon Lewis. VHS, Beta **$29.95** *RHI, SVI* 🎞

Blood Feud In Italy preceding Europe's entry into WWII, a young widow is in mourning over the brutal murder of her husband by the Sicilian Mafia. In the meantime she must contend with the rivalry between Mastroianni as a lawyer and Giannini as a small-time crook both vying for her affections. Dubbed. **AKA:** Revenge.
1979 (R) 112m/C *IT* Sophia Loren, Marcello Mastroianni, Giancarlo Giannini; **D:** Lina Wertmuller; **W:** Lina Wertmuller. VHS, Beta **$59.95** *FOX* 🎞🎞

Blood for a Silver Dollar Action-filled western, littered with murder, revenge and romance.
1966 98m/C Montgomery Wood, Evelyn Stewart. VHS, Beta **$24.95** *VYY* 🎞½

Blood Freak An absolutely insane anti-drug, Christian splatter film. A Floridian biker is introduced to drugs by a young woman and eventually turns into a poultry-monster who drinks the blood of junkies. Narrated by a chain smoker who has a coughing fit. Don't miss it.
1972 86m/C Steve Hawkes, Dana Culliver, Randy Grinter Jr., Tina Anderson, Heather Hughes; **D:** Steve Hawkes, Brad Grinter. VHS, Beta *NO* Woof!

Blood Frenzy Psychologist's patients take a therapeutic trip to the desert. The sun and heat take their toll, and everyone gets violent. This kind of therapy we don't need, and the movie's a waste, as well. Made for video. Loring was Wednesday on TV's "The Addams Family."
1987 90m/C John Montero, Lisa Loring, Hank Garrett, Wendy MacDonald; **D:** Hal Freeman. VHS, Beta *NO* 🎞

Blood Games Buxom baseball team bats 1000 against the home team and the winning babes find out just how poor losers can be. Diamonds aren't always a girl's best friend.
1990 (R) 90m/C Gregory Cummings, Laura Albert, Shelly Abblett, Luke Shay, Ross Hagen; **D:** Tanya Rosenberg. VHS **$79.95** *COL* Woof!

Blood Hook A self-parodying teenage-slasher film about kids running into a backwoods fishing tournament while on vacation, complete with ghouls, cannibalism and grotesquerie.
1986 85m/C Mark Jacobs, Lisa Todd, Patrick Danz; **D:** James Mallon. VHS, Beta **$14.95** *PSM, PAR* 🎞½

Blood In...Blood Out: Bound by Honor Three-hour epic about Chicano gang culture focuses on three buddies whose lives evolve into a drug-addicted artist, a narc, and a prison regular. Written by acclaimed poet Baca, the film touches on issues such as poverty, racism, drugs, and violence as they pertain to Hispanic life. Unfortunately, the extreme violence (shootings, stabbings, and garrotings) completely overwhelms the rest of the story. Contains profanity, nudity, and sexual innuendo. Based on a story by Ross Thomas. **AKA:** Bound by Honor.
1993 (R) 180m/C Damian Chapa, Jesse Borrego, Benjamin Bratt, Enrique Castillo, Victor Rivers, Delroy Lindo, Tom Towles; **D:** Taylor Hackford; **W:** Floyd Mutrux, Jimmy Santiago Baca, Jeremy Iacone; **M:** Bill Conti. VHS, Beta **$96.03** *HPH, BVV, TOU* 🎞🎞

Blood Island A couple inherit an old house on a remote New England island where the woman grew up. They discover that this old house needs more than a paint job to make it livable; seems there's something evil in them there walls. Based on an H.P. Lovecraft story. Greene, who's best known for later directing "Godspell," and the solid cast fail to animate the inert script. **AKA:** The Shuttered Room.
1968 100m/C *GB* Gig Young, Carol Lynley, Oliver Reed, Flora Robson; **D:** David Greene. VHS **$29.98** *ACE* 🎞🎞

Blood Lake A psychotic killer stalks teenagers, to the detriment of all.
1987 90m/C VHS **$19.95** *VCI* Woof!

Blood Legacy Four heirs must survive a night in a lonely country estate to collect their money; what do you think happens? Average treatment of the haunted house theme. **AKA:** Legacy of Blood.
1973 (R) 77m/C John Carradine, John Russell, Faith Domergue, Merry Anders; **D:** Carl Monson. VHS, Beta **$14.95** *CNG, MRV, GEM* 🎞🎞

Blood Lust Dr. Jekyll returns to London to wreak havoc upon the human race.
198? 90m/C VHS, Beta *NO* 🎞

Blood Mania A retired surgeon's daughter decides to murder her father to collect her inheritance prematurely, but soon learns that crime doesn't pay as well as medicine. Low-budget, low-interest flick.
1970 (R) 90m/C Peter Carpenter, Maria de Aragon, Alex Rocco; **D:** Robert Vincent O'Neil. VHS, Beta **$19.95** *VCI* 🎞

Blood Money A dying ex-criminal returns to Australia to redeem his name and die with dignity.
1980 (PG) 64m/C *AU* Bryan Brown, John Flaus, Chrissie James; **D:** Christopher Fitchett. VHS, Beta *NO* 🎞½

Blood Money: The Story of Clinton and Nadine A confusing action/thriller with a good cast. Garcia is a small-time exotic bird smuggler whose gun-running brother has been murdered. He uses high-class hooker Barkin to get close to his brother's contacts, who turn out to be running guns to the Nicaraguan contras and involved in a dangerous government conspiracy. Made for cable television. **AKA:** Clinton & Nadine.

1988 95m/C Andy Garcia, Ellen Barkin, Morgan Freeman; **D:** Jerry Schatzberg. **VHS, Beta** $79.95 FCT ⬥⬥½

The Blood of a Poet Cocteau's first film, a practically formless piece of poetic cinema, detailing all manner of surreal events occurring in the instant a chimney falls. In French with English subtitles. **AKA:** Le Sang d'un Poete.
1930 55m/B Jean Cocteau; **D:** Jean Cocteau. **VHS, Beta** $19.95 VYY, MRV, HHT ⬥⬥½

Blood of Dracula They don't make 1950s rock'n'roll girls' school vampire movies like this anymore, for which we may be grateful. Hypnotism, an amulet, and a greasepaint makeup job turn a shy female student into a bloodsucker. **AKA:** Blood is My Heritage.
1957 71m/B Sandra Harrison, Louise Lewis, Gail Ganley, Jerry Blaine, Heather Ames, Malcolm Atterbury; **D:** Herbert L. Strock. **VHS** $9.95 COL, MLB ⬥½

Blood of Dracula's Castle Couple inherit an allegedly deserted castle but upon moving in, discover Mr. and Mrs. Dracula have settled there. The vampires keep young women chained in the dungeon for continual blood supply. Also present are a hunchback and a werewolf. Awesome Adamson production is highlighted by the presence of the gorgeous Volante. Early cinematography effort by the renowned Laslo Kovacs. **AKA:** Dracula's Castle.
1969 84m/C John Carradine, Alexander D'Arcy, Paula Raymond, Ray Young, Vicki Volante, Robert Dix, John Cardos; **D:** Jean Hewitt, Al Adamson. **VHS, Beta** $29.95 VCI ⬥

Blood of Ghastly Horror A young man thinks he has a new lease on life when he is the happy recipient of a brain transplant, but his dreams are destroyed when he evolves into a rampaging killer. This movie is so awful it hides behind numerous but rather creative aliases. **AKA:** The Fiend with the Atomic Brain; Psycho a Go Go!; The Love Maniac; The Man with the Synthetic Brain; The Fiend with the Electronic Brain.
1972 87m/C John Carradine, Kent Taylor, Tommy Kirk, Regina Carrol; **D:** Al Adamson. **VHS** $14.95 MOV Woof!

The Blood of Heroes A post-apocalyptic action flick detailing the adventures of a battered team of ''juggers,'' warriors who challenge small village teams to a brutal sport (involving dogs' heads on sticks) that's a cross between jousting and football. **AKA:** The Salute of the Jugger.
1989 (R) 97m/C Rutger Hauer, Joan Chen, Vincent D'Onofrio, Anna Katarina; **D:** David Peoples; **W:** David Peoples; **M:** Todd Boekelheide. **VHS, Beta** $89.99 HBO ⬥⬥

Blood of Jesus A sinful husband accidentally shoots his newly-baptized wife, causing an uproar in their rural town. Williams later starred as Andy on the ''Amos 'n' Andy'' television series.
1941 50m/C Spencer Williams Jr., Kathryn Craviness; **D:** Spencer Williams Jr.; **W:** Spencer Williams Jr. **VHS** $34.95 FCT, HEG, BTV ⬥⬥

The Blood of Others A driveling adaptation of the Simone de Beauvoir novel about a young French woman at the outbreak of WWII torn between her absent boyfriend in the Resistance and a kind, wealthy German. Made for French television, it stars Jodie Foster and Michael Ontkean as the Gallic pair.
1984 130m/C FR Jodie Foster, Sam Neill, Michael Ontkean, Stephane Audran, Lambert Wilson, John Vernon, Kate Reid, Jean-Pierre Aumont; **D:** Claude Chabrol; **W:** Brian Moore. **VHS, Beta** $9.99 PSM ⬥

Blood of the Vampire A Transylvanian doctor is executed for being a vampire and his hunchbacked assistant brings him back to life.
1958 84m/C GB Donald Wolfit, Vincent Ball, Barbara Shelley, Victor Maddern; **D:** Henry Cass; **W:** Jimmy Sangster. **VHS, Beta** $59.95 MPI, MLB ⬥½

The Blood on Satan's Claw Graphic tale centering on the Devil himself. Townspeople in an English village circa 1670 find the spirit of Satan taking over their children, who begin to practice witchcraft. Well made with lots of attention to period details. Not for the faint-hearted. **AKA:** Satan's Skin; Satan's Claw.
1971 90m/C GB Patrick Wymark, Linda Hayden, Barry Andrews, Michele Dotrice; **D:** Piers Haggard. **VHS, Beta** $14.95 MGM, FCT ⬥⬥⬥

Blood on the Badge Illegal arms have been stolen from a military arsenal and fall into the hands of Libyan Nationalists who begin a terrorist campaign. Detective Neal Farrow is assigned to stop them.
19?? 92m/C Ramon Estevez, David Harrod, Rocky Patterson, Desiree Laforge, Dean Nolen, Melissa Deleon, Todd Everett; **D:** Bret McCormick. **VHS** $89.95 AIP ⬥½

Blood on the Moon Well-acted film about a cowboy's involvement in a friend's underhanded schemes. Based on a Luke Short novel, this dark film revolves around a western land dispute between cattlemen and homesteaders.
1948 88m/B Robert Mitchum, Robert Preston, Walter Brennan, Barbara Bel Geddes; **D:** Robert Wise. **VHS, Beta** $19.95 MED, TTC ⬥⬥½

Blood on the Mountain After escaping from prison, Jim plots revenge against his accomplice, only to kill an innocent man instead.
1988 71m/C Stracker Edwards, Tim Jones, Paula Preston, Cliff Turknett, Rich Jury; **D:** Donald W. Thompson. **VHS** MIV ⬥

Blood on the Sun Newspaperman in Japan uncovers plans for world dominance as propaganda, violence, and intrigue combine in this action-adventure. Also available colorized.
1945 98m/B James Cagney, Sylvia Sidney, Robert Armstrong, Wallace Ford; **D:** Frank Lloyd; **M:** Miklos Rozsa. **VHS** $19.95 NOS, MRV, HHT ⬥⬥

Blood Orgy of the She-Devils Exploitative gore nonsense about female demons, beautiful witches, and satanic worship. Some movies waste all their creative efforts on their titles.
1974 (PG) 73m/C Lila Zaborin, Tom Pace, Leslie McRae, Ray Myles. **VHS, Beta** NO Woof!

Blood Rage A maniacal twin goes on a murderous rampage through his brother's neighborhood. AKA ''Nightmare at Shadow Woods.'' Only for die-hard ''Mary Hartman'' fans. **AKA:** Nightmare at Shadow Woods.
1987 (R) 87m/C Louise Lasser, Mike Soper; **D:** John Grissmer; **M:** Richard Einhorn. **VHS, Beta** $79.95 PSM Woof!

Blood Red In 1895 Northern California, an Italian immigrant and his family give bloody battle to a powerful industrialist who wants their land in wine-growing country. Watch for the scenes involving veteran Roberts and his then-newcomer sister, pretty woman Julia.
1988 91m/C Eric Roberts, Dennis Hopper, Giancarlo Giannini, Burt Young, Carlin Glynn, Lara Harris, Susan Anspach, Julia Roberts, Elias Koteas, Frank Campanella, Aldo Ray, Horton Foote Jr.; **D:** Peter Masterson. **VHS, Beta, 8mm** $14.95 COL, SUE ⬥½

Blood Relations A woman is introduced to her fiance's family only to find out that they, as well as her fiance, are murdering, perverted weirdos competing for an inheritance.
1987 (R) 88m/C CA Jan Rubes, Ray Walston, Lydie Denier, Kevin Hicks, Lynne Adams; **D:** Graeme Campbell. **VHS, Beta** $19.98 SUE, NLC ⬥½

Blood Relatives Langlois admits she saw her brother kill her cousin, with whom he had been carrying on an incestuous relationship. But the discovery of the dead girl's diary by police inspector Sutherland reveals many more layers of intrigue than were initially evident. Based on a novel by Ed McBain. The French actors have been dubbed into English. **AKA:** Les Liens de Sang.
1977 94m/C CA Lisa Langlois, Donald Sutherland, Stephane Audran, David Hemmings, Donald Pleasence, Laurent Malet, Micheline Lanctot, Aude Landry; **D:** Claude Chabrol; **W:** Claude Chabrol. **VHS** CIC ⬥

Blood Ring When Sue's boxer husband goes missing she enlists old friend Max to help find him. They uncover a gambling ring run by drug lords where the kickboxing matches are to the death. Naturally, Max decides to use his expert kickboxing skills to get a violent revenge.
1993 90m/C Dale ''Apollo'' Cook, Andrea Lamatsch, Don Nakaya Neilsen, Steve Tartalia; **D:** Irvin Johnson; **W:** Ron Davies VHS $89.95 AIP ⬥½

Blood Salvage A crazy junkman kidnaps beautiful girls, selling their organs to the highest bidder. He meets his match when a potential target refuses to become a victim in spite of her wheelchair. Interesting plot twists keep this Grade B thriller above average.
1990 (R) 90m/C Evander Holyfield, Lori Birdsong, Danny Nelson, John Saxon, Ray Walston; **D:** Tucker Johnson. **VHS, Beta** TTC ⬥

Blood Screams Nosy people drop in on an old town in Mexico and attempt to uncover the secrets hidden there, but bizarre entities throw out the unwelcome mat and terrorize them. Lots of blood and screaming.
1988 75m/C Ran Sands, James Garnett. **VHS, Beta** $19.98 WAR Woof!

Blood Simple A jealous husband hires a sleazy private eye to murder his adulterous wife and her lover. A dark, intricate, morbid morality tale that deviates imaginatively from the standard murder mystery thriller. First film scripted by the Cohen brothers.
1985 (R) 96m/C John Getz, M. Emmet Walsh, Dan Hedaya, Frances McDormand; **D:** Joel Coen; **W:** Ethan Coen, Joel Coen; **M:** Carter Burwell. **VHS, Beta** $79.95 MCA ⬥⬥⬥½

Blood Sisters Sorority babes intend to spend a giggle-strewn night in a haunted house but end up decapitated, butchered, and cannibalized.
1986 (R) 85m/C Amy Brentano, Marla MacHart, Brigete Cossu, Randy Mooers; **D:** Roberta Findlay. **VHS, Beta** $14.95 COL Woof!

Blood Song A patient (yester-decade teen throb Frankie Avalon) escapes into the night from a mental institution after murdering an attendant. He takes his only possession with him, a carved wooden flute. A young woman sees him burying his latest victim, and now he's on a hunt to play his ''blood song'' for her. Pretty bad, but fun to see Avalon play a less-than-squeaky-clean role. **AKA:** Dream Slayer.
1982 90m/C Frankie Avalon, Donna Wilkes, Richard Jaeckel, Dane Clark, Antoinette Bower; **D:** Alan J. Levi. **VHS, Beta** NO ⬥

The Blood Spattered Bride Newlywed couple honeymoon in a remote castle in southern Spain. They are visited by a mysterious young woman who begins to influence the bride in the ways of lesbian bloodsucking. Okay '70s Euro-eroti-horror based on LeFanu's "Carmilla." *AKA:* Blood Castle; La Novia Esangentada.
1972 82m/C *SP* Simon Andrew, Maribel Martin, Alexandra Bastedo, Dean Selmier, Rosa Ma Rodriguez, Montserrat Julio; *D:* Vicente Aranda. **VHS, Beta $59.95** *MPI* ♂

Blood Thirst Obscure horror film about a woman who stays young by indulging in ritual killings and strange experiments.
1965 ?m/C Robert Winston, Yvonne Nielson. **VHS $16.95** *SNC* ♂

Blood Tide A disgusting, flesh-eating monster disrupts a couple's vacation in the Greek isles. Beautiful scenery, good cast, bad movie. *AKA:* The Red Tide.
1982 (R) 82m/C James Earl Jones, Jose Ferrer; *W:* Nico Mastorakis. **VHS, Beta** *NO* ♂

Blood Ties An American naval engineer in Sicily gets involved with the Mob in order to save his father's life.
1987 98m/C *IT* Brad Davis, Tony LoBianco, Vincent Spano, Barbara DeRossi, Maria Conchita Alonso; *D:* Giacomo Battiato. **VHS, Beta $69.95** *TWE* ♂ ½

Blood Ties Reporter Harry Martin belongs to an unusual family—modern-day vampires (who prefer to be known as Carpathian-Americans). But they have an age-old problem with a band of fanatical vampire hunters. This time around you'll root for the bloodsuckers. Made for television.
1992 90m/C Harley Venton, Patrick Bauchau, Kim Johnston-Ulrich, Michelle Johnson, Jason London, Bo Hopkins, Grace Zabriskie; *D:* Jim McBride; *W:* Richard Shapiro. **VHS** *NHO* ♂♂ ½

Blood Tracks A woman kills her abusive husband, then hides out in the mountains with her kids until they turn into cannibalistic savages. Years later, people show up to shoot a music video. Blood runs in buckets.
1986 82m/C Jeff Harding, Michael Fitzpatrick, Naomi Kaneda; *D:* Mike Jackson. **Beta** *NO* ♂ ½

Blood Vows: The Story of a Mafia Wife TV's Laura Ingalls (Gilbert) leaps from the prairie to modern-day mafia in this warped Cinderella story. She meets the man of her dreams, whom she slowly finds is her worst nightmare as she becomes trapped within the confines of her new-found "family." Made for television soaper is way over the top in terms of melodrama.
1987 100m/C Melissa Gilbert, Joe Penny, Eileen Brennan, Talia Shire, Anthony (Tony) Franciosa; *D:* Paul Wendkos; *M:* William Goldstein. **VHS $39.95** *FRH* ♂♂

Blood Voyage A crewman aboard a pleasure yacht must find out who is killing off his passengers one by one.
1977 (R) 80m/C Jonathon Lippe, Laurie Rose, Midori, Mara Modair; *D:* Frank Mitchell. **VHS, Beta $59.95** *MON* Woof!

Blood Warriors An ex-Marine finds out a old buddy is leading a private army of mercenaries. When he refuses to join up their friendship turns violent.
1993 93m/C David Bradley, Frank Zagarino; *D:* Sam Firstenberg. **VHS $94.95** *IMP, IME* ♂ ½

Blood Wedding A wonderfully passionate dance film from Saura and choreographed by Gades, based on the play by famed author Federico Garcia Lorca. A young bride runs off with her married lover on her wedding day and her jilted husband comes after them. If you like flamenco, there

are two more: "Carmen" and "El Amor Brujo." In Spanish with English subtitles. *AKA:* Bodas de Sangre.
1981 71m/C *SP* Antonio Gades, Christina Hoyos, Marisol, Carmen Villena; *D:* Carlos Saura. **VHS, Beta $24.95** *XVC, CTH, MED* ♂♂♂

Bloodbath Drugs, sex and terrorism—Dennis Hopper is typecast as an American degenerate who, along with his expatriate friends, is persecuted by local religious cults who need sacrifices.
19?? 89m/C Dennis Hopper, Carroll Baker, Richard Todd, Faith Brook, Win Wells; *D:* Silvio Narizzano. **VHS, Beta $79.94** *GHV, HHE* ♂♂♂

Bloodbath at the House of Death Price and his compatriots fight a team of mad scientists in this parody of popular horror films. Fun to see Price spoofing his own genre; die-hard horror camp fans will be satisfied. Best line: "Wanna fork?"
1985 92m/C *GB* Kenny Everett, Pamela Stephenson, Vincent Price, Gareth Hunt; *D:* Ray Cameron. **VHS, Beta $59.95** *MED* ♂♂

Bloodbath in Psycho Town A film crew is marked for death by a hooded man when it enters a remote little village.
1989 (R) 87m/C Ron Arragon, Donna Baltron, Dave Elliott; *D:* Allessandro DeGaetano; *W:* Allessandro DeGaetano. **VHS** *NO* ♂

Bloodbeat A supernatural being terrorizes a family as they gather at their country home to celebrate Christmas.
1985 84m/C Helen Benton, Terry Brown, Claudia Peyton; *D:* Fabrice A. Zaphiratos. **VHS, Beta $59.98** *TWE* ♂

Bloodbrothers Portrayal of working-class Italian men's lives—if that's possible without the benefit of Italian writers, producers, or director. Still, lots of cussing and general intensity, as Gere's character struggles between staying in the family construction business and doing what he wants to do—work with children. Re-cut for television and re-titled "A Father's Love."
1978 (R) 120m/C Richard Gere, Paul Sorvino, Tony LoBianco, Kenneth McMillan, Marilu Henner, Danny Aiello, Lelia Goldoni, Yvonne Wilder; *D:* Robert Mulligan; *M:* Elmer Bernstein. **VHS $19.98** *WAR* ♂♂ ½

Bloodfight Exciting kick-boxing and martial arts tournament turns sour when champ offends the sense of honor of the master. Now the champ must battle the master, and only one will remain standing!
1990 (PG-13) ?m/C Bolo Yeung. **VHS $19.95** *IMP* ♂

Bloodfist A kickboxer tears through Manila searching for his brother's killer. A Roger Corman production.
1989 (R) 85m/C Don "The Dragon" Wilson, Rob Kaman, Billy Blanks, Kris Aguilar, Riley Bowman, Michael Shaner; *D:* Terence H. Winkless. **VHS, Beta $14.95** *MGM* ♂♂

Bloodfist 2 Six of the world's toughest martial artists find themselves kidnapped and forced to do the bidding of the evil Su. The mysterious recluse stages a series of incredible fights between the experts and his own army of drugged warriors.
1990 (R) 85m/C Don "The Dragon" Wilson, Maurice Smith, James Warring, Timothy Baker, Richard Hill, Rina Reyes; *D:* Andy Blumenthal. **VHS, Beta $14.95** *MGM* ♂♂ ½

Bloodfist 3: Forced to Fight Just as long as nobody's forced to watch, real-life world champion kickboxer Wilson thrashes his way through another showdown-at-the-arena plot. Better-than-average fight choreography.

1992 (R) 90m/C Don "The Dragon" Wilson, Richard Roundtree, Laura Stockman, Richard Paul, Rick Dean, Peter "Sugarfoot" Cunningham; *D:* Oley Sassone; *M:* Nigel Holton. **VHS $89.98** *NHO* ♂ ½

Bloodfist 4: Die Trying To rescue his daughter, a fighter must do battle with the FBI, the CIA, and an international arms cartel.
1992 (R) 86m/C Don "The Dragon" Wilson, Catya Sassoon, Amanda Wyss, James Tolkan, Liz Torres; *D:* Paul Ziller. **VHS** *NHO* ♂ ½

Bloodfist 5: Human Target When undercover FBI agent Jim Roth (Wilson) attempts to unravel an international arms deal he's found out and left for dead. He comes to with no memory only to find himself caught between the arms dealers and the FBI, who think he's turned double-agent. Both sides want Roth dead.
1993 (R) ?m/C Don "The Dragon" Wilson, Denice Duff, Yuji Okumoto, Don Stark, Danny Lopez, Steve James, Michael Yama; *D:* Jeff Yonis; *W:* Jeff Yonis. **VHS** *NHO* ♂ ½

Bloodhounds of Broadway A musical tribute to Damon Runyon, detailing the cliched adventures of an assortment of jazz-age crooks, flappers, chanteuses, and losers.
1989 (PG) 90m/C Madonna, Rutger Hauer, Randy Quaid, Matt Dillon, Jennifer Grey, Julie Hagerty, Esai Morales, Anita Morris, Josef Sommer, William S. Burroughs, Ethan Phillips, Stephen McHattie, Dinah Manoff, Googy Gress, Tony Azito, Tony Longo, Madeleine Potter; *D:* Howard Brookner; *W:* Howard Brookner, Colman DeKay; *M:* Jonathan Sheffer. **VHS, Beta $19.95** *COL* ♂♂ ½

Bloodlink A well-to-do doctor has a recurring nightmare about killing an elderly woman. This prompts him to explore his past, discovering that he was separated at birth from a twin brother. Naturally, only by searching frantically for his long-lost sibling can the good doctor hope to solve the mystery of the recurring nightmare. A somnolent tale indeed.
1986 (R) 98m/C Michael Moriarty, Penelope Milford, Geraldine Fitzgerald, Cameron Mitchell, Sarah Langenfeld; *D:* Alberto De Martino. **VHS, Beta $24.95** *SUE, VTR* ♂ ½

Bloodlust More teenagers fall prey to yet another mad scientist, who stores their dead bodies in glass tanks. Low-budget ripoff of "The Most Dangerous Game" and other such films. A must for Mike Brady (Robert Reed) fans though.
1959 89m/B Wilton Graff, June Kennedy, Robert Reed, Lilyan Chauvin; *D:* Ralph Brooke; *W:* Ralph Brooke. **VHS $16.95** *SNC, NOS* ♂

Bloodlust: Subspecies 3 Equally gory followup to "Bloodstone: Subspecies 2." Sadistic vampire Radu is still battling for Michelle's soul, this time against Michelle's sister Becky, aided by his disgusting Mummy and the demonic Subspecies. Castle Vladislas is awash is blood and Becky discovers more than Michelle's fate is at risk. *AKA:* Subspecies 3.
1993 (R) 83m/C Anders Hove, Kevin Blair, Denice Duff, Pamela Gordon, Ion Haiduc, Michael DellaFemina; *D:* Ted Nicolaou; *W:* Ted Nicolaou. **VHS, Beta** *PAR* ♂ ½

Bloodmatch A whodunit, martial-arts-style: the "sleuth" kidnaps all the suspects in a corruption case and kickboxes each to death until somebody confesses. Not exactly Agatha Christie, and artsy camera moves fail to exploit the fancy footwork.
1991 (R) 85m/C Thom Mathews, Michel Qissi, Benny "The Jet" Urquidez, Marianne Taylor, Hope Marie Carlton, Dale Jacoby, Thunder Wolf, Vincent Klyn, Peter "Sugarfoot" Cunningham,

Hector Pena; **D:** Albert Pyun; **W:** K. Mannah; **M:** Tony Riparetti. VHS $19.98 HBO ♂

Bloodmoon The setting is Australia but the sleazy story's all too familiar: an insane killer employs knives and other sharp objects to prevent sex-crazed students from getting past third base.
1990 104m/C **AU** Leon Lissek, Christine Amor, Ian Patrick Williams, Helen Thomson, Hazel Howson, Craig Cronin, Anya Molina; **D:** Alec Mills; **W:** Richard Brennan; **M:** Briany May. VHS, Beta $14.98 LIV Woof!

Bloodshed A psychotic harbors a girl's dead body, and systematically kills anyone who discovers his secret.
1983 (R) 88m/C Laslo Papas, Beverly Ross; **D:** Richard Cassidy. VHS, Beta NO ♂

Bloodspell A student with an evil power unleashes it on those who cross his path.
1987 (R) 87m/C Anthony Jenkins, Aaron Teich, Alexandra Kennedy, John Reno; **D:** Deryn Warren. VHS, Beta $79.98 MCG ♂

Bloodsport American soldier Van Damme endeavors to win the deadly Kumite, an outlawed martial arts competition in Hong Kong. Lots of kick-boxing action and the sound of bones cracking.
1988 (R) 92m/C Jean-Claude Van Damme, Leah Ayres, Roy Chiao, Donald Gibb, Bolo Yeung, Norman Burton, Forest Whitaker; **D:** Newton Arnold. VHS, Beta $19.98 WAR, TLF ♂♂½

Bloodstalkers Two vacationers in Florida meet up with a band of slaughtering, swamp-based lunatics.
1976 91m/C Kenny Miller, Celea Ann Cole, Jerry Albert; **D:** Robert W. Morgan. VHS, Beta $39.95 VMK Woof!

Bloodstone A couple honeymooning in the Middle East unexpectedly become involved in a jewel heist when they discover a valuable ruby amongst their luggage. Nonstop action and humor.
1988 (PG-13) 90m/C Charlie Brill, Christopher Neame, Jack Kehler, Brett Stimely; **D:** Dwight Little; **W:** Nico Mastorakis. VHS, Beta $79.98 MCG ♂♂

Bloodstone: Subspecies 2 A gory sequel to "Subspecies" finds Radu the vampire pursuing the luscious Michelle. Radu gets some help from his ghoulish mother and yucky demonic spawn. Filmed on location in Romania. **AKA:** Subspecies 2.
1993 (R) 107m/C Anders Hove, Denice Duff, Kevin Blair, Michael Denish, Pamela Gordon, Ion Haiduc; **D:** Ted Nicolaou; **W:** Ted Nicolaou. VHS PAR ♂♂½

The Bloodsuckers A British horror tale set on a Greek Island. An Oxford don is seduced into an ancient vampire cult. Director Michael Burrowes replaces Hartford-Davis in the credits due to a dispute over post-production editing. **AKA:** Incense For the Damned; Doctors Wear Scarlet.
1970 90m/C **GB** Patrick Macnee, Peter Cushing, Patrick Mower, Edward Woodward; **D:** Robert Hartford-Davis. VHS, Beta $19.98 SNC ♂♂

Bloodsuckers from Outer Space Via an alien invasion, Texas farmers becoming bloodsucking zombies.
1983 80m/C Thom Meyer, Laura Ellis, Billie Keller, Kim Braden; **D:** Glenn Coburn. VHS, Beta $19.98 LHV, WAR Woof!

Bloodsucking Freaks Virtually plotless Troma gagfest full of torture, cannibalistic dwarfs, and similar debaucheries, all played out on a Soho Grand Guignol stage (horror shows that allegedly contained real torture and death). Features "The Caged Sexoids," if that tells you anything (a cage of naked cannibal women tended by a dwarf). Not to mention the woman who has her brain

sucked out through a straw. Filmed in "Ghoulovision" and originally rated X. Intolerable for most. **AKA:** The Incredible Torture Show.
1975 (R) 89m/C Seamus O'Brian, Niles McMaster; **D:** Joel M. Reed. VHS, Beta $59.98 VES Woof!

Bloodsucking Pharoahs of Pittsburgh Pittsburgh is plagued by crazed cannibals who think eternal life is in Pennsylvania. Two detectives on the case are mystified.
1990 (R) 89m/C Jake Dengel, Joe Sharkey, Suzanne Fletcher, Beverly Penberthy, Shawn Elliott, Pat Logan, Jane Hamilton; **D:** Alan Smithee; **W:** Dean Tschetter. VHS, Beta $79.95 PAR, FCT Woof!

Bloody Avenger A trio of detectives search for a murderer in the streets of Philadelphia.
198? 100m/C Jack Palance, George Eastman, Jenny Tamburi; **D:** Al Bradley. VHS, Beta $59.95 VMK ♂

Bloody Birthday Three youngsters, bound together by their eerie birth during an eclipse (you know what that means), kill everyone around them that ever gave them problems. Typical "and the fun continues" ending; standard fare. **AKA:** Creeps.
1980 (R) 92m/C Susan Strasberg, Jose Ferrer, Lori Lethin, Melinda Cordell, Joe Penny, Ellen Geer, Julie Brown, Michael Dudikoff, Billy Jacoby; **D:** Edward Hunt. VHS, Beta $9.99 PSM ♂½

The Bloody Brood Really bad flick about a drug-dealing beatnik gang who commit nasty crimes, like feeding messenger boys hamburgers filled with ground glass. Yuck.
1959 80m/C **CA** Jack Betts, Barbara Lord, Peter Falk, Robert Christie; **D:** Julian Hoffman. VHS $16.95 SNC, TPV Woof!

Bloody Che Contra Follows rebel leader trying to flee the Bolivian mountains and the threat of government forces and chronicles the danger he and his men encounter.
19?? 89m/C John Ireland, Francesco Rabal. VHS, Beta NO ♂

The Bloody Fight Two young people learn the cost of courage and the high price of justice when they avenge a murderer.
19?? 90m/C Alan Tang, Yu In Yin, Tan Chin, Pai Ying, Lui Ran In; **D:** N.G. Tien Tsu. VHS, Beta NO ♂

Bloody Mama Corman's violent, trashy story of the infamous Barker Gang of the 30s, led by the bloodthirsty and sex-crazed Ma Barker (Winters, can't you just picture it?) and backed by her four perverted sons. De Niro is the space cadet sibling, Walden the homosexual ex-con, Stroud the sadistic mama lover, and Kimbrough the lady killer. They're joined by Walden's prison lover, Dern, who also has a thing for Ma Barker. Winters is a riot in this perverse stew of crime, violence, and, of course, sentimental blood bonding (the family that slays together, stays together). First of the Corman-produced (and sometimes directed) mama movies, followed by "Big Bad Mama" and "Crazy Mama."
1970 90m/C Shelley Winters, Robert De Niro, Don Stroud, Pat Hingle, Bruce Dern, Diane Varsi, Robert Walden, Clinton Kimbrough, Scatman Crothers; **D:** Roger Corman. VHS, Beta $69.95 VES, LIV ♂♂½

Bloody Moon Tourists are being brutally attacked and murdered during a small Spanish village's Festival of the Moon.

1983 84m/C Olivia Pascal, Christopher Brugger; **D:** Jess (Jesus) Franco. VHS, Beta $59.95 TWE Woof!

Bloody New Year Corpses stalk the living as a group of teens happen upon an impromptu New Year's Eve party on a deserted island. Auld acquaintance shouldn't be forgot, just this flick. **AKA:** Time Warp Terror.
1987 (R) 90m/C **D:** Norman J. Warren. VHS, Beta $29.95 ACA ♂

The Bloody Pit of Horror While wife Jayne Mansfield was in Italy filming "Primitive Love," bodybuilder Hargitay starred in this sado-horror epic. He owns a castle that is visited by a group of models for a special shoot. While in the dungeon, Hargitay becomes possessed by the castle's former owner, a sadist, and begins torturing the models. Supposedly based on the writings of the Marquis de Sade. **AKA:** Crimson Executioner; The Red Hangman.
1965 87m/B **IT** Mickey Hargitay, Louise Barrett, Walter Brandi, Moa Thai, Ralph Zucker, Albert Gordon; **D:** Max (Massimo Pupillo) Hunter. VHS $19.98 SNC ♂½

The Bloody Tattoo A suspicious woman has a map tattooed on her body telling where a treasure is buried. The robbers who drew the map are now looking for her so they can find the treasure. A story full of killing and greed. **AKA:** The Loot.
19?? 90m/C Ko Fay, David Keung, Tsui Siu Keung, Lily Lee. VHS $49.95 OCE ♂½

Bloody Trail A Union soldier who chooses the recently pummeled South as the venue for postwar R-and-R is, for some reason, pursued by Confederates. And his good ol' boy pursuers don't have a sudden change of heart when he teams up with a former slave. Lots of violence and nudity; little plot and entertainment.
1972 91m/C Paul Harper, Rance Howard, John Mitchum; **D:** Richard Robinson. VHS $19.95 ACA ♂

The Bloody Vampire Atmospheric and chilling Mexican vampire film. Sequel to "Invasion of the Vampires."
1962 ?m/C **MX** Carlos Agosti. VHS $16.95 SNC ♂½

Bloody Wednesday It's sanity checkout time when a hotel caretaker is driven mad by tormentors...or is he driving himself mad? What is it about vacant hotels that make men lose their minds? If you can remove "The Shining" from yours, this flick's worthwhile.
1987 89m/C Raymond Elmendorf, Pamela Baker, Navarre Perry; **D:** Mark Gilhuis; **W:** Philip Yordan; **M:** Al Sendry. VHS, Beta $79.95 PSM ♂♂½

Blossoms in the Dust The true story of Edna Gladney is told as she starts the Texas Children's Home and Aid Society of Fort Worth. Major league Garson tear-jerker.
1941 100m/B Greer Garson, Walter Pidgeon, Felix Bressart, Marsha Hunt, Fay Holden, Samuel S. Hinds, Kathleen Howard; **D:** Mervyn LeRoy. Academy Awards '41: Best Interior Decoration; Nominations: Best Actress (Garson), Best Color Cinematography, Best Picture. VHS, Beta $19.98 MGM ♂♂

The Blot A story about a poorly paid professor and his family, whose lifestyle contrasts with that of an affluent neighbor, a butcher.
1921 55m/B Louis Calhern, Claire Windsor; **D:** Lois Weber. VHS, Beta $19.95 GPV, GVV, DVT ♂♂

Blow Out When a prominent senator is killed in a car crash, a sound effects engineer becomes involved in political intrigue as he tries to expose a conspiracy with the evidence he has gathered. An intricate mystery and homage to Antonioni's ''Blow-Up.''
1981 (R) 108m/C John Travolta, Nancy Allen, John Lithgow, Dennis Franz; **D:** Brian DePalma; **W:** Brian DePalma; **M:** Pino Donaggio. **VHS, Beta** WAR, OM 🎭🎭🎭

Blow-Up A young London photographer takes some pictures of a couple in the park and finds out he may have recorded evidence of a murder. Though marred by badly dated 1960s modishness, this is Antonioni's most accessible film, a sophisticated treatise on perception and the film-consumer-as-voyeur, brilliantly assembled and wrought.
1966 111m/C GB IT David Hemmings, Vanessa Redgrave, Sarah Miles, Jane Birkin, Veruschka; **D:** Michelangelo Antonioni; **W:** Tonino Guerra, Michelangelo Antonioni; **M:** Herbie Hancock. Academy Awards '66 Nominations: Best Director (Antonioni), Best Story & Screenplay; Cannes Film Festival '67: Best Film; National Society of Film Critics Awards '66: Best Director (Antonioni), Best Film. **VHS, Beta** $19.98 MGM, VYG, FCT 🎭🎭🎭½

Blowing Wild Filmed in Mexico, this Quinn-Stanwyck-Cooper love triangle, set in the early thirties, speaks of lust and vengeance, rashness and greed. Stanwyck, married to oil tycoon Quinn, lusts after one-time lover wildcatter Cooper.
1954 92m/B Gary Cooper, Barbara Stanwyck, Anthony Quinn, Ruth Roman, Ward Bond; **D:** Hugo Fregonese; **W:** Philip Yordan. **VHS** $19.98 REP, FCT 🎭½

Blown Away A mafia wife goes up against her husband in order to retrieve her kidnapped child.
1990 (R) 92m/C Loni Anderson, John Heard, James Naughton; **D:** Michael Miller. **VHS, Beta** $29.95 ACA 🎭

Blown Away Boston Irish bomb-squad cop Jimmy Dove (Bridges) is after former compatriot Ryan Gaerity (Jones), an Irish radical who's taken his bombing expertise onto Jimmy's new turf. Meanwhile, Jimmy wants to keep his unsavory past from unsuspecting wife Amis. Real life dad Lloyd plays Jeff's uncle. Expect suspense as everyday objects become lethal in Gaerity's knowledgeable hands. The final explosion was more than even the special effects coordinator desired—windows were unintentionally blown out in nearby buildings. New ground for Bridges who isn't known for action roles; Jones is hot after his Oscar win for ''The Fugitive.''
1994 (R) 121m/C Jeff Bridges, Tommy Lee Jones, Suzy Amis, Lloyd Bridges, Forest Whitaker; **D:** Stephen Hopkins; **W:** Joe Batteer, John Rice. **VHS** NYR 🎭🎭🎭

Blown Away Haim and Feldman are brothers working at a ski resort where Haim falls for rich teenager Eggert. She's a young femme fatale who manages to get Haim all hot and bothered but she's actually using the unsuspecting dupe in a murder plot. Also available in an unrated version at 93 minutes.
1992 (R) 91m/C Nicole Eggert, Corey Haim, Corey Feldman. **VHS** $89.98 LIV 🎭½

Blue A dull western about an American boy (Stamp) raised by Mexicans who doesn't trust another living soul until he finds himself face to face with his former gang, led by his adoptive father (Montalban).
1968 113m/C Terence Stamp, Joanna Pettet, Karl Malden, Ricardo Montalban, Joe De Santis, Sally Kirkland; **D:** Silvio Narizzano; **M:** Manos Hadjidakis. **VHS** PAR 🎭

Blue Meditation/memoir of director Jarman's deteriorating AIDS condition consists of narration and a soundtrack set against an unvaried blue screen. Jarman ponders the associations with the color blue (sky, ocean, blindness, heaven, eternity) and his own physical problems, alternately expressed with dreamy vagueness or incendiary contempt. Limited in appeal, depending highly on boredom tolerance and ability to suspend visual expectations.
1993 (R) 76m/C **D:** Derek Jarman; **W:** Derek Jarman; **M:** Simon Fisher Turner. **VHS** NYR 🎭🎭

The Blue and the Gray Epic television mini-series about love and hate inflamed by the Civil War. Keach plays a Pinkerton's secret service agent in this loosely based historical romance. The uncut version is available on three cassettes; the 295 minute version is on two cassettes.
1985 398m/C Gregory Peck, Lloyd Bridges, Colleen Dewhurst, Stacy Keach, John Hammond, Sterling Hayden, Warren Oates; **D:** Andrew V. McLaglen; **M:** Bruce Broughton. **VHS, Beta** $34.95 COL, TVC, FCT 🎭🎭

The Blue Angel Tale of a man stripped of his dignity. A film classic filled with sensuality and decay, which made Dietrich a European star and led to her discovery in Hollywood. When a repressed professor (Jannings) goes to a nightclub hoping to catch some of his students in the wrong, he's taken by Lola, the sultry singer portrayed by Dietrich. After spending the night with her, losing his job, and then marrying her, he goes on tour with the troupe, peddling indiscreet photos of his wife. Versions were shot in both German and English, with the German version sporting English subtitles. 🎵 Falling in Love Again; They Call Me Wicked Lola. **AKA:** Der Blaue Engel.
1930 90m/B GE Marlene Dietrich, Emil Jannings, Kurt Gerron, Rosa Valetti, Hans Albers; **D:** Josef von Sternberg; **W:** Robert Lieberman, Karl Vollmoller, Carl Zuckmayer; **M:** Karl Vollmoller. **VHS, Beta, 8mm** $24.95 NOS, FCT, BAR 🎭🎭🎭🎭

The Blue Bird A weird, dark fantasy about two children who search for the blue bird of happiness in various fantasy lands, but find it eventually at home. Overlooked and impressively fatalistic.
1940 98m/C Shirley Temple, Gale Sondergaard, John Russell, Eddie Collins, Nigel Bruce, Jessie Ralph, Spring Byington, Sybil Jason; **D:** Walter Lang. **VHS, Beta** $19.98 FOX, MLB 🎭🎭🎭

Blue Blazes Rawden Hart plays a lumberjack who gains control of a local saloon after shooting its villainous proprietor.
1918 ?m/B William S. Hart. **VHS, Beta, 8mm** $18.95 GPV, GVV 🎭🎭🎭

Blue Blood A demonic butler inflicts nightmares upon a family to gain possession of its mansion.
1973 90m/C GB Oliver Reed, Derek Jacobi, Fiona Lewis; **D:** Andrew Sinclair. **VHS, Beta** NO 🎭

Blue Canadian Rockies Autry's employer sends him to Canada to discourage his daughter from marrying a fortune hunter. The daughter has turned the place into a dude ranch and wild game preserve. When Autry arrives, he encounters some mysterious killings.
1952 58m/B Gene Autry, Pat Buttram, Gail Davis, Ross Ford, Tom London; **D:** George Archainbaud. **VHS, Beta** $39.95 CCB 🎭½

Blue Chips Nolte does Bobby Knight in this saga of Western U basketball coach Pete Bell, suffering through his first losing season. What follows is a tug of war between rich alumni who want to win at any cost and his ethics as he recruits for a new season. Larger than life hoopster O'Neal's film debut. McDonnell and Woodard are merely afterthoughts, but look for cameos from many real life b-ballers, including Dick Vitale and Larry Bird. Average script is bolstered by exciting game footage, shot during real games for authenticity.
1994 (PG-13) 108m/C Nick Nolte, Shaquille O'Neal, Mary McDonnell, Ed O'Neill, J.T. Walsh, Alfre Woodard; **Cameos:** Larry Bird, Bobby Knight, Rick Pitino; **D:** William Friedkin; **W:** Ron Shelton; **M:** Nile Rodgers, Jeff Beck, Jed Leiber. **VHS, Beta** PAR 🎭🎭½

Blue City A young man returns to his Florida hometown to find his father murdered, and subsequently vows to solve and avenge the matter. Based on a Ross Mac-Donald thriller.
1986 (R) 83m/C Judd Nelson, Ally Sheedy, Paul Winfield, Anita Morris, David Caruso, Julie Carmen, Scott Wilson; **D:** Michelle Manning; **W:** Walter Hill, Lukas Heller; **M:** Ry Cooder. **VHS, Beta** $14.95 PAR 🎭½

Blue Collar An auto assembly line worker, tired of the poverty of his life, hatches a plan to rob his own union. A study of the working class and the robbing of the human spirit.
1978 (R) 114m/C Richard Pryor, Harvey Keitel, Yaphet Kotto, Ed Begley Jr.; **D:** Paul Schrader; **W:** Paul Schrader, Leonard Schrader; **M:** Jack Nitzsche. **VHS, Beta** $69.95 MCA, FCT 🎭🎭🎭

Blue Country A joyful romantic comedy about a pair of free souls who leave their stagnant lives behind to seek out a more idyllic existence. Subtitled in English. **AKA:** Le Pays Bleu.
1977 (PG) 104m/C FR Brigitte Fossey, Jacques Sernas. **VHS, Beta** $59.95 COL 🎭🎭½

Blue De Ville Two young women buy a '59 Cadillac and journey from St. Louis to New Mexico, having adventures on the way. The rambling, free-spirited movie was a pilot for a prospective series that never set sail—but when ''Thelma & Louise'' hit big this superficially similar item was hauled out on video.
1986 (PG) 96m/C Jennifer Runyon, Kimberly Pistone, Mark Thomas Miller, Alan Autry, Robert Prescott; **D:** Jim Johnston. **VHS** $89.98 VMK 🎭🎭

Blue Desert Cox is strong in her performance as Lisa Roberts, a comic book artist who leaves New York City for small town Arizona life after surviving a traumatic rape. Once there, she's befriended by Sheffer and Sweeney, a local cop. Battersby does a good job of keeping the suspense level high (in his directorial debut) as Cox finds that there's danger in small towns, too. Fine performances keep this slightly above average.
1991 (R) 98m/C D.B. Sweeney, Courteney Cox, Craig Sheffer, Philip Baker Hall, Sandy Ward; **D:** Bradley Battersby; **W:** Bradley Battersby; **M:** Jerry Goldsmith. **VHS** $19.95 ACA 🎭🎭🎭

Blue Fin When their tuna boat is shipwrecked, and the crew disabled, a young boy and his father learn lessons of love and courage as the son tries to save the ship.
1978 (PG) 93m/C AU Hardy Kruger, Greg Rowe; **D:** Carl Schultz. **VHS, Beta** $59.98 SUE 🎭

Blue Fire Lady The heartwarming story of a young girl and her love of horses which endures even her father's disapproval. Good family fare.
1978 96m/C Cathryn Harrison, Mark Holden, Peter Cummins. **VHS, Beta** $19.95 MED 🎭🎭

Blue Hawaii A soldier, returning to his Hawaiian home, defies his parents by taking a job with a tourist agency. Presley sings "Can't Help Falling in Love." For Elvis fans.
1962 101m/C Elvis Presley, Angela Lansbury, Joan Blackman, Roland Winters, Iris Adrian, John Archer, Steve Brodie; *D:* Norman Taurog; *W:* Hal Kanter. **VHS, Beta $14.98** *FOX, MVD* 🎬🎬

Blue Heaven A couple struggles through problems with their marriage and alcohol abuse.
1984 100m/C Leslie Denniston, James Eckhouse; *D:* Kathleen Dowdey. **VHS, Beta $69.95** *VES, LIV* 🎬

The Blue Hour Theo is a Berlin hustler whose business is so good he can pick his clients. Marie, his next-door neighbor, lives with her boyfriend Paul until he just walks out one day. Marie is shattered and refuses to leave her apartment until Theo takes an interest in her plight. Just when it seems that the improbable couple could find true love, Paul comes back. In German with English subtitles.
1991 87m/C *GE* Andreas Herder, Dina Leipzig, Cyrill Rey-Coquais; *D:* Marcel Gisler. **VHS $39.95** *WBF, FCT* 🎬🎬

Blue Ice Harry Anders (Caine) is an ex-spy with an eye for the ladies and a loyalty to his friends. When his friends start winding up dead, Harry decides to investigate—a very dangerous decision, especially when a mysterious woman (Young) takes an interest. Made for cable television.
1992 (R) 96m/C Michael Caine, Sean Young, Ian Bannen; *D:* Russell Mulcahy; *W:* Ron Hutchinson; *M:* Michael Kamen. **VHS** *HBO* 🎬🎬½

Blue Iguana An inept bounty hunter travels south of the border to recover millions from a crooked South American bank, and meets up with sexy women, murderous thugs, and corruption.
1988 (R) 88m/C Dylan McDermott, Jessica Harper, James Russo, Dean Stockwell, Pamela Gidley, Tovah Feldshuh; *D:* John Lafia. **VHS, Beta $89.95** *PAR* 🎬🎬

Blue Jeans A young French boy experiences sexual awakening and humiliation in a British school. In French with English subtitles.
1978 80m/C *FR D:* Hugues des Roziers. **VHS, Beta $29.95** *FCT* 🎬🎬½

Blue Jeans and Dynamite A stuntman is hired to lift the "Golden Mask of the Duct Tomb" and is followed on land, water, and air. Great chase scenes and action-filled finale.
1987 90m/C Robert Vaughn, Simon Andrew, Katia Kristine. **VHS** *NO* 🎬🎬

The Blue Knight Kennedy brings energy and care to this basically standard story. Policeman waiting for retirement searches for his partner's killer. Unexceptional treatment made palatable by actors. Made for television movie.
1975 72m/C George Kennedy, Alex Rocco, Glynn Turman, Verna Bloom, Michael Margotta, Seth Arnold; *D:* J. Lee Thompson. **VHS $49.95** *LIV* 🎬🎬½

The Blue Lagoon Useless remake of 1949 film of the same name. An adolescent boy and girl marooned on a desert isle discover love (read: sex) without the restraints of society. Not too explicit, but nonetheless intellectually offensive. Gorgeous photography of island paradise is wasted on this Shields vehicle.
1980 (R) 105m/C Brooke Shields, Christopher Atkins, Leo McKern, William Daniels; *D:* Randal Kleiser. **VHS, Beta $84.95** *COL* Woof!

The Blue Lamp Action-adventure fans familiar with the hoary plot where a cop must avenge the wrongful death of his partner will appreciate this suspenseful British detective effort. It's one of the very first in the genre to explore buddy cop revenge in a very British sort of way. Also sports a concluding chase scene which has stood the test of time. Led to the long-running British TV series "Dixon of Dock Green."
1949 84m/B *GB* Dirk Bogarde, Jimmy Hanley, Jack Warner, Bernard Lee, Robert Flemyng, Patric Doonan, Bruce Seton, Frederick Piper, Betty Ann Davies, Peggy Evans; *D:* Basil Dearden. **VHS $29.95** *FCT* 🎬🎬🎬

The Blue Light Fairy tale love story, based on an Italian fable about a mysterious woman, thought to be a witch, and a painter. Riefenstahl's first film which brought her to the attention of Adolf Hitler, who requested she make films glorifying the Nazi Party. In German with English subtitles. *AKA:* Das Blaue Licht.
1932 77m/B *GE* Leni Riefenstahl, Matthias Wieman, Max Holsboer; *D:* Leni Riefenstahl; *W:* Leni Riefenstahl. **VHS, Beta $19.95** *VYY, MRV, FCT* 🎬🎬🎬

The Blue Lightning Investigator Elliott travels to Australia to retrieve the priceless Blue Lightening gem. He must fight the crime lord in his Aussie encampment. Nice scenery, but unexceptional television story.
1986 95m/C Sam Elliott, Rebecca Gilling, Robert Culp, John Meillon, Robert Coleby, Max Phipps; *D:* Lee Philips. **VHS $39.95** *FRH* 🎬🎬½

The Blue Max During WWI a young German, fresh out of aviation training school, competes for the coveted "Blue Max" flying award with other members of a squadron of seasoned flyers from aristocratic backgrounds. Based on a novel by Jack D. Hunter.
1966 155m/C George Peppard, James Mason, Ursula Andress; *D:* John Guillermin; *M:* Jerry Goldsmith. **VHS, Beta $29.98** *FOX* 🎬🎬½

Blue Money A wild, comedic caper film about a cab-driving nightclub impressionist who absconds with a briefcase packed with cash and is pursued by everyone, even the I.R.A. Originally made for British television.
1984 82m/C *GB* Tim Curry, Dabby Bishop, Billy Connolly, Frances Tomelty; *D:* Colin Bucksey. **VHS, Beta** *NO* 🎬🎬

Blue Monkey A mysterious alien plant impregnates a man, who gives birth to a huge, man-eating insect larva. It subsequently grows up into a giant bug, and roams around a quarantined hospital looking for patients to eat. What made you think it had anything to do with monkeys? *AKA:* Green Monkey.
1987 (R) 97m/C Steve Railsback, Susan Anspach, Gwynyth Walsh, John Vernon, Joe Flaherty; *D:* William Fruet. **VHS, Beta $79.95** *COL* 🎬

Blue Movies A couple of jerks try their hand at making porn films with predictable results.
1988 (R) 92m/C Larry Linville, Lucinda Crosby, Steve Levitt, Darien Mathias, Larry Poindexter; *D:* Paul Koval. **VHS, Beta $29.95** *ACA* Woof!

Blue Murder at St. Trinian's The second of the madcap British comedy series (based on cartoons by Ronald Searle) about an incredibly ferocious pack of schoolgirls. This time they travel to the European continent and make life miserable for a jewel thief. Highlight: fantasy sequence in ancient Rome showing the girls thrown to the lions—and scaring the lions.

1956 86m/B *GB* Joyce Grenfell, Terry-Thomas, George Cole, Alastair Sim, Lionel Jeffries, Thorley Walters; *D:* Frank Launder; *M:* Malcolm Arnold. **VHS $24.95** *VYY, VDM, FUS* 🎬🎬

Blue Paradise A depiction of Adam and Eve as they peruse the primal landscape and each other.
1986 90m/C Mark Gregory, Andrea Goldman. **VHS, Beta $59.95** *TWE, MLB* Woof!

Blue Ribbon Babes A filmed record of a female athletic competition in Florida, featuring wet T-shirt contests, mud wrestling, and powder-puff boxing.
1986 60m/C VHS, Beta $24.95 *AHV* Woof!

Blue Skies Again Spunky young woman determined to play major league baseball locks horns with the chauvinistic owner and the gruff manager of her favorite team.
1983 (PG) 91m/C Robyn Barto, Harry Hamlin, Mimi Rogers, Kenneth McMillan, Dana Elcar, Andy Garcia; *D:* Richard Michaels. **VHS, Beta $69.95** *WAR* 🎬½

Blue Steel A young Wayne saves a town from financial ruin by leading the citizens to a gold strike. Also available with "Man From Utah" on Laser Disc.
1934 59m/B John Wayne, George "Gabby" Hayes; *D:* Robert North Bradbury. **VHS, Beta $8.95** *CNG, NOS, MRV* 🎬

Blue Steel Director Bigelow's much-heralded, proto-feminist cop thriller. A serious female rookie's gun falls into the hands of a Wall Street psycho who begins a killing spree. Action film made silly with over-anxious sub-text and patriarchy-directed rage.
1990 (R) 102m/C Jamie Lee Curtis, Ron Silver, Clancy Brown, Louise Fletcher, Philip Bosco, Elizabeth Pena, Tom Sizemore; *D:* Kathryn Bigelow; *W:* Eric Red; *M:* Brad Fiedel. **VHS, Beta, 8mm $14.95** *MGM* 🎬🎬

Blue Sunshine A certain brand of L.S.D. called Blue Sunshine starts to make its victims go insane.
1978 (R) 94m/C Zalman King, Deborah Winters, Mark Goddard, Robert Walden, Charles Siebert, Ann Cooper, Ray Young, Alice Ghostley; *D:* Jeff Lieberman; *W:* Jeff Lieberman. **VHS, Beta $69.95** *VES* 🎬🎬½

Blue Thunder Police helicopter pilot Scheider is chosen to test an experimental high-tech chopper that can see through walls, record a whisper, and level a city block. Seems anti-terrorist supercopter is needed to ensure security during 1984 Olympics. Bothered by Vietnam flashbacks, Scheider then battles wacky McDowell in the skies over L.A. High-techy police drama with satisfying aerial combat scenes nearly crashes with storyline.
1983 (R) 110m/C Roy Scheider, Daniel Stern, Malcolm McDowell, Candy Clark, Warren Oates; *D:* John Badham; *W:* Dan O'Bannon, Don Jakoby. **VHS, Beta $12.95** *COL* 🎬🎬½

Blue Tornado An eerie bright light, emitted from a mountain, makes supersonic jets disappear into thin air. A beautiful researcher and a cocky pilot set out to solve the mystery. Better-than-average aerial sequences don't make up for goofy story and ludicrous dialogue.
1990 (PG-13) 96m/C Dirk Benedict, Patsy Kensit, Ted McGinley, David Warner; *D:* Tony B. Dobb. **VHS $89.95** *VMK* 🎬

Blue Velvet Disturbing, unique exploration of the dark side of American suburbia, involving an innocent college youth who discovers a severed ear in an empty lot, and is thrust into a turmoil of depravity, murder, and sexual deviance. Brutal, grotesque, and unmistakably Lynch; an immaculately made, fiercely imagined film that is unlike any other.

Mood is enhanced by the Badalamenti soundtrack. Graced by splashes of Lynchian humor, most notably the movie's lumber theme. Hopper is riveting as the chief sadistic nutcase and Twin Peaks' MacLachlan is a study in loss of innocence. Cinematography by Frederick Elmes.
1986 (R) 121m/C Kyle MacLachlan, Isabella Rossellini, Dennis Hopper, Laura Dern, Hope Lange, Jack Nance, Dean Stockwell, George Dickerson, Brad Dourif; *D:* David Lynch; *W:* David Lynch; *M:* Angelo Badalamenti. Academy Awards '86 Nominations: Best Director (Lynch); Independent Spirit Awards '87: Best Actress (Rossellini); Montreal World Film Festival '86: Best Supporting Actor (Hopper); National Society of Film Critics Awards '86: Best Director (Lynch), Best Film, Best Supporting Actor (Hopper). **VHS, Beta $19.98** *WAR* 𝄞𝄞𝄞

The Blue Yonder In this made-for-video feature, a young boy travels back in time to meet the grandfather he never knew, risking historical integrity. *AKA:* Time Flyers.
1986 89m/C Art Carney, Peter Coyote, Huckleberry Fox; *D:* Mark Rosman. **VHS, Beta $69.95** *DIS* 𝄞

Bluebeard Tormented painter with a psychopathic urge to strangle his models is the basis for this effective, low-budget film. One of Carradine's best vehicles.
1944 73m/B John Carradine, Jean Parker, Nils Asther; *D:* Edgar G. Ulmer. **VHS, Beta $19.95** *NOS, MRV, SNC* 𝄞𝄞½

Bluebeard French biography of Henri-Desire Landru, who seduced and murdered eleven women and was subsequently beheaded. Dubbed into English. *AKA:* Landru.
1963 108m/C *FR* Charles Denner, Danielle Darrieux, Michele Morgan, Hildegarde Neff; *D:* Claude Chabrol. **VHS, Beta $59.98** *NLC* 𝄞𝄞𝄞

Bluebeard Lady killer Burton knocks off series of beautiful wives in soporific remake of the infamous story.
1972 (R) 128m/C Richard Burton, Raquel Welch, Joey Heatherton, Nathalie Delon, Virna Lisi, Sybil Danning; *D:* Edward Dmytryk; *M:* Ennio Morricone. **VHS $59.95** *LIV* 𝄞½

Blueberry Hill While her mother struggles with the grief over husband's death, a young girl learns in a small town learns about life, music, and her late father from a jazz singer. Good soundtrack.
1988 (R) 93m/C Jennifer Rubin, Carrie Snodgress, Margaret Avery; *D:* Strathford Hamilton. **VHS, Beta $79.98** *FOX* 𝄞½

The Blues Brothers As an excuse to run rampant on the city of Chicago, Jake and Elwood Blues attempt to raise $5,000 for their childhood orphanage by putting their old band back together. Good music, and lots of cameos.
1980 (R) 133m/C John Belushi, Dan Aykroyd, James Brown, Cab Calloway, Ray Charles, Henry Gibson, Aretha Franklin, Carrie Fisher, John Candy; *Cameos:* Frank Oz, Steven Spielberg, Twiggy, Paul (Pee Wee Herman) Reubens, Steve Lawrence, John Lee Hooker; *D:* John Landis; *W:* Dan Aykroyd, John Landis. **VHS, Beta $19.95** *MCA* 𝄞𝄞½

Blues Busters Another entry in the "Bowery Boys" series. When Sach emerges from a tonsillectomy with the velvety voice of a crooner, Slip cashes in by turning Louie's Sweet Shop into a nightclub, the better to showcase his buddy's talents. Sach's singing voice provided by John Lorenz.
1950 68m/B Leo Gorcey, Huntz Hall, Adele Jergens, Gabriel Dell, Craig Stevens, Phyllis Coates, Bernard Gorcey, David Gorcey; *D:* William Beaudine. **VHS $14.98** *WAR* 𝄞𝄞½

Bluffing It A made-for-television movie about an older man who has been disguising his illiteracy for years.
1987 120m/C Dennis Weaver, Janet Carroll, Michelle Little, Robert Sean Leonard, Cleavant Derricks, Victoria Wauchope; *D:* James Sadwith; *M:* Brad Fiedel. **VHS** *NO* 𝄞𝄞

The Blum Affair In post-WWI Germany, a Jewish man is framed for the murder of an accountant and uncovers in his capture and prosecution a rat's nest of corruption and anti-Semitism. In German with English subtitles.
1948 109m/B *GE* Hans-Christian Blech, Gisela Trowe, Kurt Ehrhardt, Paul Bildt, Klaus Becker; *D:* Erich Engel. **VHS, Beta $24.95** *NOS, FCT, APD* 𝄞𝄞

Blume in Love An ironic comedy/drama about a man who falls hopelessly in love with his ex-wife who divorced him for cheating on her while they were married.
1973 (R) 115m/C George Segal, Susan Anspach, Kris Kristofferson, Shelley Winters, Marsha Mason; *D:* Paul Mazursky; *W:* Paul Mazursky; *M:* Bill Conti. **VHS, Beta $19.98** *WAR* 𝄞𝄞𝄞

BMX Bandits Three adventurous Aussie teens put their BMX skills to the test when they witness a crime and are pursued by the criminals. Much big air.
1983 92m/C Nicole Kidman, David Argue, John Ley, Angelo D'Angelo; *D:* Brian Trenchard-Smith; *W:* Patrick Edgeworth. **VHS $79.95** *IMP* 𝄞𝄞

Boarding House Residents of a boardinghouse discover sinister doings in the basement. It does not occur to any of them to move to another house.
1983 (R) 90m/C Hank Adly, Kalassu, Alexandra Day; *D:* John Wintergate. **VHS, Beta** *MRV* 𝄞

Boarding School Basic teen sex comedy about students at a proper Swiss boarding school for girls who devise a plan to seduce the boys at a nearby school by posing as prostitutes. Kinski stars as the American girl who masterminds the caper. *AKA:* The Passion Flower Hotel.
1983 (R) 100m/C *GE* Nastassia Kinski; *D:* Andre Farwagi. **VHS, Beta $69.95** *VES, LIV* 𝄞𝄞

Boardinghouse Blues A showbiz musical centered around a boarding house with tenant troubles. It's an excuse for popular black entertainers of the day to perform, including Lucky Millinder, Bull Moose Jackson, Una Mae Carlisle, and Stumpy and Stumpy.
1948 90m/C Dusty Fletcher, Moms Mabley; *D:* Josh Binney. **VHS $34.95** *FCT, RXM* 𝄞𝄞

The Boat is Full A group of refugees pose as a family in order to escape from Nazi Germany as they seek asylum in Switzerland. Available in German with English subtitles or dubbed into English.
1981 104m/C *SI* Tina Engel, Curt Bois, Renate Steiger, Mathias Gnaedinger; *D:* Markus Imhoof. Academy Awards '81 Nominations: Best Foreign Language Film; Berlin International Film Festival '81: Best Director (Imhoof). **VHS, Beta $34.95** *SUE, GLV, JCF* 𝄞𝄞𝄞

The Boatniks An accident-prone Coast Guard ensign finds himself in charge of the "Times Square" of waterways: Newport Harbor. Adding to his already "titanic" problems is a gang of ocean-going jewel thieves who won't give up the ship!
1970 (G) 99m/C Robert Morse, Stefanie Powers, Phil Silvers, Norman Fell, Wally Cox, Don Ameche; *D:* Norman Tokar. **VHS, Beta $69.95** *DIS* 𝄞𝄞½

Bob & Carol & Ted & Alice Two California couples have attended a trendy therapy session and, in an attempt to be more in touch with sexuality, resort to applauding one another's extramarital affairs and swinging. Wacky and well-written, this is a farce on free love and psycho-speak. Mazursky's directorial debut.
1969 (R) 104m/C Natalie Wood, Robert Culp, Dyan Cannon, Elliott Gould; *D:* Paul Mazursky; *W:* Paul Mazursky, Larry Tucker; *M:* Quincy Jones. **VHS, Beta $9.95** *GKK* 𝄞𝄞½

Bob le Flambeur Wonderful film noir of a compulsive gambler who decides to take a final fling by robbing the casino at Deauville. In French, subtitled in English. English title is "Bob the Gambler."
1955 106m/B *FR* Roger Duchesne, Isabel Corey, Daniel Cauchy; *D:* Jean-Pierre Melville. **VHS, Beta $59.95** *COL, ING, CVC* 𝄞𝄞𝄞

Bob Roberts Pseudo-documentary satire about a 1990 Pennsylvania senatorial race between Robbins' right-wing folk singer/entrepreneur versus Vidal's aging liberal incumbent. Roberts seems like a gee-whiz kinda guy but he'll stop at nothing to get elected and he knows a lot about political dirty tricks and, even more important, manipulating the media to get what he wants. Robbins directorial debut turned out to be very timely in view of the 1992 presidential campaign. Features a number of cameos. Line to remember: "Vote first. Ask questions later."
1992 (R) 105m/C Tim Robbins, Giancarlo Esposito, Ray Wise, Rebecca Jenkins, Harry J. Lennix, John Ottavino, Robert Stanton, Alan Rickman, Gore Vidal, Brian Doyle-Murray, Anita Gillette, David Strathairn; *Cameos:* Susan Sarandon, James Spader, John Cusack, Fred Ward, Pamela Reed; *D:* Tim Robbins; *W:* Tim Robbins; *M:* David Robbins. **VHS $19.98** *LIV, BTV* 𝄞𝄞𝄞

Bobbie Jo and the Outlaw Wonderwoman Carter is a bored carhop who yearns to be a country singer. She becomes involved with Marjoe, who fancies himself as a contemporary Billy the Kid. Together, they do their Bonnie and Clyde thing, to a significantly lesser dramatic effect than the original, though a glut of violence keeps the bodies dropping.
1976 (R) 89m/C Lynda Carter, Marjoe Gortner, Jesse Vint; *D:* Mark L. Lester. **VHS, Beta $69.98** *VES, LIV* 𝄞½

Bobby Deerfield Cold-blooded Grand Prix driver comes face to face with death each time he races, but finally learns the meaning of life when he falls in love with a critically ill woman. Even with race cars, soap opera stalls.
1977 (PG) 124m/C Al Pacino, Marthe Keller, Anny Duperey, Romolo Valli; *D:* Sydney Pollack; *W:* Alvin Sargent; *M:* Dave Grusin. **VHS, Beta $14.95** *WAR* 𝄞𝄞

Bobo Lousy bullfighter tries to lure a gorgeous woman into romance. Filmed in Spain and Italy.
1967 103m/C *GB* Peter Sellers, Britt Ekland, Rossano Brazzi, Adolfo Celi; *D:* Robert Parrish. **VHS, Beta $19.98** *WAR, FCT* 𝄞½

Boccaccio '70 Three short bawdy/comedy/pageant-of-life films inspired by "The Decameron," each pertaining to ironically twisted sexual politics in middle class life. A fourth story, "Renzo and Luciana," by Mario Monichelli, has been cut. Dubbed.
1962 145m/C *IT* Anita Ekberg, Romy Schneider, Tomas Milian, Sophia Loren; *D:* Vittorio De Sica, Luchino Visconti, Federico Fellini; *W:* Federico Fellini. **VHS, Beta** *FCT, MLB* 𝄞𝄞

Bodies, Rest & Motion Stagnant twentysomething movie in which four young people basically do nothing in the sun-baked town of Enfield, Arizona. Similar to the movie "Singles," but without the Seattle grunge scene. The title's reference to Newton is fitting: "A body in rest or motion remains in that state unless acted upon by an outside force." Appealing cast is wasted in listless film that's content to just drift along. Based on the play by Roger Hedden.
1993 (R) 94m/C Phoebe Cates, Bridget Fonda, Tim Roth, Eric Stoltz, Scott Johnson, Scott Frederick; **D:** Michael Steinberg; **W:** Roger Hedden; **M:** Michael Convertino. VHS $95.95 *NLC, BTV* 🎬🎬

Body and Soul The first screen appearance of Robeson has him cast in a dual role as a conniving preacher and his good brother. The preacher preys on the heroine, making her life a misery. Objections by censors to the preacher's character caused him to be redeemed and become worthy of the heroine's love.
1924 ?m/B Paul Robeson, Julia Theresa Russell, Mercedes Gilbert; **D:** Oscar Micheaux. VHS $29.95 *FCT* 🎬🎬

Body and Soul A young boxer fights his way unscrupulously to the top. Vintage '40s boxing film that defines the genre. Remade in 1981. *AKA:* An Affair of the Heart.
1947 104m/B John Garfield, Lilli Palmer, Hazel Brooks, Anne Revere, William Conrad, Canada Lee; **D:** Robert Rossen; **W:** Abraham Polonsky. Academy Awards '47: Best Film Editing; Nominations: Best Actor (Garfield), Best Original Screenplay. VHS $14.98 *REP* 🎬🎬🎬½

Body & Soul Interesting remake of 1947 gem about a boxer who loses his perspective in the world of fame, fast cars, and women.
1981 (R) 109m/C Leon Isaac Kennedy, Jayne Kennedy, Peter Lawford, Muhammad Ali, Perry Lang; **D:** George Bowers. VHS, Beta $19.95 *MGM* 🎬🎬½

Body Bags Three gory, though humorous, made for cable horror stories hosted by horrormeister Carpenter as your friendly local coroner. "The Gas Station" finds the young female overnight attendant menaced by a psycho. "Hair" is about a balding yuppie who'll do anything for a full head of hair. Then he meets the sinister Dr. Lock and his magical new-hair growth treatment. The grisly "Eye" concerns a ballplayer who loses the aforementioned appendage and finds that his transplanted eyeball, taken from an executed serial killer, is subject to ghastly visions. Several fellow horror directors have cameos. *AKA:* John Carpenter Presents Body Bags.
1993 (R) 95m/C Alex Datcher, Robert Carradine, Stacy Keach, David Warner, Mark Hamill, Twiggy, John Agar, Deborah Harry, Sheena Easton, David Naughton, John Carpenter; *Cameos:* Wes Craven, Sam Raimi, Roger Corman, Tobe Hooper; **D:** Tobe Hooper, John Carpenter; **W:** Billy Brown, Dan Angel; **M:** John Carpenter, Jim Lang. VHS *REP* 🎬🎬½

Body Beat Wild jazz and rock dancers are integrated into a previously classical ballet academy. While the students become fast friends, the teachers break off into two rival factions.
1988 (PG) 90m/C Tony Fields, Galyn Gorg, Scott Grossman, Eliska Krupka. VHS, Beta $29.95 *VMK* 🎬🎬

The Body Beneath A living-dead ghoul survives on the blood of innocents and is still preying on victims today.
1970 85m/C Gavin Reed, Jackie Skarvellis, Susan Heard, Colin Gordon; **D:** Andy Milligan. VHS, Beta *NO* Woof!

Body Chemistry A married sexual-behavior researcher starts up a passionate affair with his lab partner. When he tries to end the relationship, his female associate becomes psychotic. You've seen it all before in "Fatal Attraction." And you'll see it again in "Body Chemistry 2."
1990 (R) 84m/C Marc Singer, Mary Crosby, Lisa Pescia, Joseph Campanella, David Kagen; **D:** Kristine Peterson; **W:** Jackson Barr. VHS, Beta $19.95 *COL* 🎬

Body Chemistry 2: Voice of a Stranger An ex-cop (Harrison) obsessed with violent sex gets involved with a talk-radio psychologist (Pescia) whose advice could prove deadly in this erotic sequel.
1991 (R) 84m/C Gregory Harrison, Lisa Pescia, Morton Downey Jr., Robin Riker; **D:** Adam Simon. VHS $19.95 *COL* 🎬½

Body Chemistry 3: Point of Seduction TV producer Alan Clay (Stevens) finds himself caught in a business and sexual triangle when he okays the making of a movie about the life of a TV sex therapist (Shattuck). Seems the lady's lovers have a nasty habit of getting murdered which doesn't prevent Clay from getting personally involved. His actress wife (Fairchild), who wants to star in the movie, is not pleased. Lives up to its title.
1993 (R) 90m/C Andrew Stevens, Morgan Fairchild, Shari Shattuck; **D:** Jim Wynorski. VHS *NHO* 🎬🎬

Body Count A weird and wealthy family will stop at nothing, including murder and cannibalism, to enhance their fortune. Rather than bodies, count the minutes 'til the movie's over. Also titled "The 11th Commandment."
1987 90m/C Marilyn Hassett, Dick Sargent, Steven Ford, Greg Mullavey, Thomas Ryan, Bernie White; **D:** Paul Leder. VHS, Beta $79.98 *MCG* 🎬½

Body Double A voyeuristic unemployed actor peeps on a neighbor's nightly disrobing and sees more than he wants to. A grisly murder leads him into an obsessive quest through the world of pornographic films.
1984 (R) 114m/C Craig Wasson, Melanie Griffith, Greg Henry, Deborah Shelton, Guy Boyd, Dennis Franz, David Haskell, Rebecca Stanley, Barbara Crampton; **D:** Brian DePalma; **W:** Brian DePalma; **M:** Pino Donaggio. VHS, Beta $14.95 *COL* 🎬🎬🎬

Body Heat During a Florida heat wave, a none-too-bright lawyer becomes involved in a steamy love affair with a mysterious woman and then in a plot to kill her husband. Hurt and Turner (in her film debut) became stars under Kasdan's direction (the three would reunite for "The Accidental Tourist"). Hot love scenes supplement a twisting mystery with a surprise ending. Rourke's arsonist and Danson's soft shoe shouldn't be missed.
1981 (R) 113m/C William Hurt, Kathleen Turner, Richard Crenna, Ted Danson, Mickey Rourke; **D:** Lawrence Kasdan; **W:** Lawrence Kasdan; **M:** John Barry. VHS, Beta $19.98 *WAR* 🎬🎬🎬½

The Body in the Library A British television-produced Miss Marple mystery, based on Agatha Christie's 1942 novel, involving the septuagenarian detective investigating the murder of a young woman in a wealthy British mansion.
1987 155m/C *GB* Joan Hickson; **D:** Silvio Narizzano. VHS, Beta $29.98 *FOX, HMV* 🎬½

Body Language A successful businesswoman, with a man problem, hires a super secretary with answers to all life's questions—and a deadly agenda all her own.
1992 (R) 93m/C Heather Locklear, Linda Purl, Edward Albert, James Acheson; **D:** Arthur Seidelman; **W:** Dan Gurskis, Brian Ross. VHS, Beta *PAR* 🎬🎬

Body Melt When a crazed doctor unleashes an experimental drug on an unsuspecting town, the residents begin to literally melt away.
1993 82m/C *AU* Gerard Kennedy, Andrew Daddo, Ian Smith, Vincent Gil, Regina Gaigalas; **D:** Philip Brophy; **W:** Philip Brophy; **M:** Philip Brophy. VHS $89.95 *PSM* 🎬🎬½

Body Moves Romantic entanglements heat up the competition when two couples enter a steamy dance contest. Not apt to move you.
1990 (PG-13) 98m/C *IT* Kirk Rivera, Steve Messina, Dianne Granger, Linsley Allen, Philip Spruce, Nicole Kolman, Susan Gardner; **D:** Gerry Lively; **W:** Daniel Steel. VHS, Beta $89.95 *PSM* 🎬🎬

Body of Evidence Bad movie with pretensions takes "Basic Instinct" a step further. Instead of an ice pick and sex, sex itself is used as the weapon in a murder trial featuring Madonna as the defendant, Dafoe as her lawyer, and Mantegna as the prosecutor. The plot is, of course, secondary to the S&M sex scenes with Dafoe which feature hot wax and broken glass. Madonna's lack of performance is the least of the film's problems since everyone seems to have forgotten any acting talent they possess. Director Edel fails to direct—the film even looks bad. "Body" was the subject of another NC-17 ratings flap but this film shouldn't be seen by anybody. An unrated version is also available.
1992 (R) 99m/C Madonna, Willem Dafoe, Joe Mantegna, Anne Archer, Michael Forest, Charles Hallahan, Mark Rolston, Richard Riehle, Julianne Moore, Frank Langella, Juergen Prochnow, Stan Shaw; **D:** Uli Edel; **W:** Brad Mirman; **M:** Graeme Revell. VHS, Beta $19.98 *MGM* Woof!

Body of Influence A Beverly Hills psychiatrist gets overly involved with a beautiful female patient. But she not only wants his love—she wants his life. Also available in an unrated version.
1993 (R) 96m/C Nick Cassavetes, Shannon Whirry, Sandahl Bergman, Don Swayze, Anna Karin, Catherine Parks, Diana Barton, Richard Roundtree; **D:** Andrew Garroni; **W:** David Schreiber. VHS $89.95 *ACA* 🎬🎬

Body Parts For fans of the demented dismemberer niche. Body Parts, a sleazy skin club, loses some of its star talent when the strippers start turning up in cameo video appearances. Seems there's a psycho killer on the loose who videotapes the dismemberment of his stripper-victims. The police decide they've got to meet this guy when he sends them a sample of his work.
1990 90m/C Teri Lee, Dick Monda, Johnny Mandel. VHS *NO* 🎬

Body Parts A crime psychologist loses his arm in an auto accident and receives a transplant from an executed murderer. Does the limb have an evil will or is it its own? Poorly paced horror goes off the deep end in gore with its third act. Based on the novel "Choice Cuts" by French writers Pierre Boileau and Thomas Narcejac, whose work inspired some of the greatest suspense films.
1991 (R) 88m/C Jeff Fahey, Kim Delaney, Lindsay Duncan, Peter Murnik, Brad Dourif, Zakes Mokae, Johnny Walsh, Paul Benevictor; **D:** Eric Red; **W:** Eric Red, Norman Snider, Larry Gross; **M:** Loek Dikker. VHS, Beta $14.95 *PAR* 🎬🎬

Body Rock Brooklyn breakdancer Lamas deserts his buddies to work at a chic Manhattan nightclub. Watching Lamas as the emcee/breakdancing fool is a hoot. ♫Body Rock; Team Work; Why Do You Want to Break My Heart?; One Thing Leads to Another; Let Your Body Rock; Vanishing Point; Sharpshooter; The Jungle; Deliver; The Closest to Love.
1984 (PG-13) 93m/C Lorenzo Lamas, Vicki Frederick, Cameron Dye, Michelle Nicastro, Ray Sharkey, Grace Zabriskie, Carole Ita White; *D:* Marcelo Epstein. **VHS, Beta $19.95** *STE* Woof!

The Body Shop Unorthodox love story in which a man decides to patch up his relationship with his dead wife by piecing together her dismembered body. For lovers only. Under "Doctor Gore" title the film includes an intro by horror director Herschell Gordon Lewis. *AKA:* Doctor Gore.
1972 91m/C Pat Patterson, Jenny Driggers, Roy Mehaffey, Linda Faile, Candy Furr; *D:* Pat Patterson. **VHS** *VCI* Woof!

Body Shot Celebrity shutterbug Mickey Dane (Patrick) is fingered in the murder of a rock star after it turns out he did a kinky layout for a look-alike. When police find out he had an obsession for the dead woman, he employs his photographic expertise in the search for the real killer. Effective tension-builder with fast-paced chases through the seamy side of Los Angeles.
1993 (R) 98m/C Robert Patrick, Michelle Johnson; *D:* Dimitri Logothetis. **VHS $89.95** *TRI* ♫♫½

Body Slam A small-time talent monger hits it big with a rock and roll/ professional wrestling tour. Piper's debut; contains some violence and strong language.
1987 (PG) 100m/C Roddy Piper, Captain Lou Albano, Dirk Benedict, Tanya Roberts, Billy Barty, Charles Nelson Reilly, John Astin, Wild Samoan, Tonga Kid, Barry Gordon; *D:* Hal Needham; *M:* John D'Andrea. **VHS, Beta $19.98** *SUE, NLC* ♫½

The Body Snatcher Based on Robert Louis Stevenson's story about a grave robber who supplies corpses to research scientists. Set in Edinburgh in the 19th century, this Lewton production is superior. One of Karloff's best vehicles.
1945 77m/B Edith Atwater, Russell Wade, Rita Corday, Boris Karloff, Bela Lugosi, Henry Daniell; *D:* Robert Wise. **VHS, Beta $19.95** *MED, RKO, TTC* ♫♫♫½

Body Snatcher from Hell An airliner passes through a mysterious cloud and crashes in a desert. One by one, the passengers are turned into vampires. Some interesting special effects. *AKA:* Goke, Body Snatcher from Hell; Goke the Vampire; Kyuketsuki Gokemidoro.
1969 84m/C *JP* Hideo Ko, Teruo Yoshida, Tomomi Sato, Eizo Kitamura, Masay Takahashi, Cathy Horlan, Kazuo Kato, Yuko Kusunoki; *D:* Hajime Sato. **VHS $16.95** *SNC* ♫½

Body Snatchers Yet another version of "Invasion of the Body Snatchers." An innocent family arrive at an Army base which turns out to be infested with pod people. This time around the heroine is angst-ridden teenager Marti (Anwar) and the pods have something to do with a mysterious toxic spill. The 1978 remake was well done; this so-so version takes advantage of the advances in special effects (particularly in Anwar's bathtub scene) and sound technology but is slow-paced with few jolts of terror.
1993 (R) 87m/C Gabrielle Anwar, Meg Tilly, Terry Kinney, Forest Whitaker, Billy Wirth, R. Lee Ermey; *D:* Abel Ferrara; *W:* Stuart Gordon, Dennis Paoli, Nicholas St. John; *M:* Joe Delia. **VHS** *WAR* ♫♫

Body Trouble After being attacked by sharks while vacationing in the Caribbean, a man washes ashore in Miami and then somehow makes his way to New York City. There he meets Vera Vin Rouge and her friends Cinnamon, Spice, Paprika, and Johnny Zero, a gangster. Zero decides he doesn't like the man, so he chases him back to the Caribbean. Supposedly this all happens in only one day. Hmmm... *AKA:* Joker's Wild.
1992 (R) 98m/C Dick Van Patten, Priscilla Barnes, Frank Gorshin, James Hong, Marty Rackham, Michael Unger, Jonathan Soloman, Brit Helfer, Leigh Clark, Patricia Cardell, Richie Barathy; *D:* Bill Milling; *W:* Bill Milling. **VHS $89.95** *TRI* ♫½

The Body Vanished Murder mystery featuring a corpse that disappears from the scene of the crime.
1939 ?m/C *GB* Lewis Wilson, Frances Dubay, Dana Wilson. **VHS $16.95** *SNC* ♫♫

Body Waves Beach comedy starring Calvert as a teenager who bets his father that he can raise money on his own. In typical teen movie fashion, he invents a sex cream that drives boys and girls wild. Brain candy featuring lots of skimpy bikinis.
1992 (R) 80m/C Bill Calvert, Leah Lail, Larry Linville, Dick Miller, Jim Wise; *D:* P.J. Pesce. **VHS $89.98** *NHO* ♫½

The Bodyguard The Yakuza, Japan's mafia, and New York's big crime families face off in this martial arts extravaganza.
1976 (R) 89m/C Sonny Chiba, Aaron Banks, Bill Louie, Judy Lee; *D:* Maurice Sarli. **VHS, Beta $29.95** *MED* ♫½

The Bodyguard Buttoned-down, ex-Secret Service agent turned private bodyguard reluctantly takes on a wildly successful singer/actress as a client. Houston, in her acting debut as the over-indulged diva, doesn't have to stretch too far but acquits herself well. Costner has really bad hair day but easily portrays the tightly wound Frank. Critically trashed, a box office smash, and too long. Originally scripted by producer Kasdan over a decade ago, with Steve McQueen in mind. Predictable romantic melodrama is kept moving by the occasional sharp dialog and a few action pieces. Songs include the smash hit "I Will Always Love You," written and originally performed by Dolly Parton.
1992 (R) 130m/C Kevin Costner, Whitney Houston, Gary Kemp, Bill Cobbs, Ralph Waite, Tomas Arana, Michele Lamar Richards, Mike Starr, Christopher Birt, DeVaughn Nixon, Charles Keating, Robert Wuhl; *Cameos:* Debbie Reynolds; *D:* Mick Jackson; *W:* Lawrence Kasdan. Academy Awards '92 Nominations: Best Song ("I Have Nothing"), Best Song ("Run to You"); MTV Movie Awards '93: Best Song ("I Will Always Love You"). **VHS $19.98** *WAR, BTV* ♫♫

Boeing Boeing A dated but still amusing sex farce about a bachelor newspaperman (Curtis) in Paris, his three stewardess girlfriends, and the elaborate plots he resorts to in trying to keep them from finding out about each other. When the new Boeing jet makes air travel faster all Curtis' schemes may come crashing down. Ritter is fun as the exasperated housekeeper and Lewis amazingly subdued as Curtis' business rival.
1965 102m/C Tony Curtis, Jerry Lewis, Dany Saval, Christianne Schmidtmer, Suzanna Leigh, Thelma Ritter; *D:* John Rich; *W:* Edward Anhalt. **VHS $14.95** *PAR* ♫♫½

Bog Boggy beast from the Arctic north awakens to eat people. Scientists mount an anti-monster offensive.
1984 (PG) 90m/C Gloria De Haven, Marshall Thompson, Leo Gordon, Aldo Ray. **VHS, Beta $49.95** *PSM* ♫

Boggy Creek II The continuing saga of the eight-foot-tall, 300 pound monster from Texarkana. Third in a series of low-budget movies including "The Legend of Boggy Creek" and "Return to Boggy Creek." *AKA:* The Barbaric Beast of Boggy Creek, Part II.
1983 (PG) 93m/C Charles B. Pierce, Cindy Butler, Serene Hedin; *D:* Charles B. Pierce; *W:* Charles B. Pierce. **VHS, Beta $59.95** *MED* ♫½

Bogie: The Last Hero Television biography of Humphrey Bogart, populated by almost-lookalikes who can almost act.
1980 100m/C Kevin J. O'Connor, Kathryn Harrold, Ann Wedgeworth, Patricia Barry, Alfred Ryder, Donald May, Richard Dysart, Arthur Franz; *D:* Vincent Sherman; *M:* Charles Bernstein. **VHS, Beta $14.95** *FRH* ♫½

Bohemian Girl The last of Laurel and Hardy's comic operettas finds them as guardians of a young orphan (Hood, famous for her roles in the Our Gang comedies), whom no one realizes is actually a kidnapped princess.
1936 74m/B Stan Laurel, Oliver Hardy, Mae Busch, Darla Hood, Jacqueline Wells, Thelma Todd, James Finlayson; *D:* James W. Horne. **VHS, Beta $19.95** *MED, CCB* ♫♫♫

Boiling Point Lawman proves once again that justice always triumphs.
1932 67m/B Hoot Gibson. **VHS, Beta $19.95** *NOS, VCI, DVT* ♫½

Boiling Point Darkly-flavored action drama delves into the personalities of its two main characters before setting up a final confrontation. Treasury agent Jimmy Mercer (Snipes) is trying to solve his partner's murder, relentlessly pursuing the murderers in cold and methodical fashion. Sleazy Red Diamond (Hopper), just out of prison, owes the mob and has one week to pay them back. Lawman and crook both come home to women, (Davidovich and Perrine) graduates of the Hollywood school of female martyrdom, selflessly supportive of their men. Grim but cliched. Adapted from the Gerald Petievich novel "Money Men."
1993 (R) 93m/C Wesley Snipes, Dennis Hopper, Lolita Davidovich, Viggo Mortensen, Dan Hedaya, Valerie Perrine, Seymour Cassel, Jonathan Banks, Tony LoBianco, Christine Elise, James Tolkan, Paul Gleason; *D:* James B. Harris; *W:* James B. Harris; *M:* Cory Lerios, John D'Andrea. **VHS, Beta $19.98** *WAR* ♫♫½

The Bold Caballero Rebel chieftain Zorro overthrows oppressive Spanish rule in the days of early California. *AKA:* The Bold Cavalier.
1936 69m/B Bob Livingston, Heather Angel, Sig Rumann, Robert Warwick; *D:* Wills Root. **VHS, Beta $19.95** *NOS, VDM, VCN* ♫½

The Boldest Job in the West Italian western about bankrobbers who meet to divide their spoils. Problem is, the guys with the loot don't show. Dubbed in English. *AKA:* El Mas Fabulosi Golpe del Far West.
1971 200m/C *IT* Mark Edwards, Frank Sancho, Carmen Sevilla; *D:* Joseph Loman. **VHS, Beta** *NO* ♫

Bolero Beginning in 1936, this international epic traces the lives of four families across three continents and five decades, highlighting the music and dance that is central to their lives.

1982 173m/C James Caan, Geraldine Chaplin, Robert Hossein, Nicole Garcia, Jacques Villeret; *D:* Claude Lelouch; *W:* Claude Lelouch. **VHS, Beta** $19.95 VES ✰✰½

Bolero What sounds like a wet dream come true is really just a good snooze: Bo Derek plays a beautiful young woman who goes on a trip around the world in hopes of losing her virginity; in Spain, she meets a bullfighter who's willing to oblige. Too bad Bo cannot act as good as she looks. *AKA:* Bolero: An Adventure in Ecstasy.
1984 (R) 106m/C Bo Derek, George Kennedy, Andrea Occhipinti, Anna Obregon, Olivia D'Abo; *D:* John Derek; *W:* John Derek; *M:* Peter Bernstein. **VHS, Beta** $19.95 LIV Woof!

Bomb at 10:10 An American pilot escapes from a German POW camp and plots to assassinate a camp commandant.
1967 87m/C George Montgomery, Rada Popovic, Peter Banicevic; *D:* Charles Damic. **VHS, Beta** $14.95 GEM ✰✰

Bombardier A group of cadet bombardiers discover the realities of war on raids over Japan during WWII. Also available colorized.
1943 99m/B Pat O'Brien, Randolph Scott, Robert Ryan, Eddie Albert, Anne Shirley, Barton MacLane; *D:* Richard Wallace. **VHS, Beta** $14.98 RKO, TTC ✰✰½

Bombay Talkie A bored British writer (Kendal) heads to India to gather "experiences" and becomes involved with an Indian movie actor (Kapoor). Early clash-of-cultures film from Merchant Ivory has it's dull spots; the behind-the-scenes look at the Indian film industry is more interesting than the romance.
1970 (PG) 110m/C IN Jennifer Kendal, Shashi Kapoor, Zia Mohyeddi, Aparna Sen; *D:* James Ivory; *W:* Ruth Prawer Jhabvala. **VHS, Beta** $29.95 ING, SUE, NLC ✰✰½

Bombs Away! An atomic bomb is mistakenly shipped to a seedy war surplus store in Seattle, and causes much chicanery.
1986 90m/C Michael Huddleston, Pat McCormick; *D:* Bruce Wilson. **VHS, Beta** $14.95 COL, NLC ✰

Bombshell Wry insightful comedy into the Hollywood of the 1930s. Harlow plays a naive young actress manipulated by her adoring press agent. He thwarts her plans until she finally notices and begins to fall in love with him. Brilliant satire with Harlow turning in perhaps the best performance of her short career. *AKA:* Blonde Bombshell.
1933 96m/B Jean Harlow, Lee Tracy, Pat O'Brien, Una Merkel, Sir C. Aubrey Smith, Franchot Tone; *D:* Victor Fleming. **VHS, Beta** $19.98 MGM, BTV, FCT ✰✰✰

Bon Voyage One of director Hitchcock's short propaganda pieces filmed as a tribute to the French Resistance. In London an RAF pilot is interrogated by the Free French about his escape from France. He was aided by a Polish agent who was actually working for the Gestapo to learn about the Resistance's movements. Flashbacks show the pilot's adventures from the spy's point-of-view. In French with English subtitles. *AKA:* Alfred Hitchcock's Bon Voyage & Aventure Malgache.
1944 26m/B John Blythe; *D:* Alfred Hitchcock. **VHS** $39.95 MIL ✰✰✰

Bon Voyage! A family's long-awaited European "dream" vacation turns into a series of comic misadventures in this very Disney, very family, very predictable comedy.
1962 131m/C Fred MacMurray, Jane Wyman, Deborah Walley, Michael Callan, Tommy Kirk, Jessie Royce Landis; *D:* James Neilson. **VHS, Beta** $69.95 DIS ✰½

Bon Voyage, Charlie Brown The "Peanuts" comic strip group becomes exchange students in Europe, led by Charlie Brown, Linus, Peppermint Patty, Marcie, and the irrepressible beagle, Snoopy.
1980 (G) 76m/C *D:* Bill Melendez; *W:* Charles M. Schulz. **VHS, Beta** $14.95 PAR, WTA ✰✰✰

Bonanza This western series about the Cartwright clan and their Ponderosa ranch ran on TV from 1959-1973, second only to "Gunsmoke." Additional episodes available. In "The Pure Truth" Hoss escapes from jail after being unjustly accused of robbing the bank. An eccentric recluse comes to his aid.
1964 50m/C Lorne Greene, Pernell Roberts, Dan Blocker, Michael Landon, Glenda Farrell. **VHS** $14.98 REP, MOV ✰✰✰

Bonanza: The Return In 1905, the children of various members of the Cartwright clan work to see the Ponderosa is safe from an unscrupulous businessman. Lame update of the classic family western series. Made for television.
1993 (PG) 96m/C Michael Landon Jr., Dirk Blocker, Emily Warfield, Alistair MacDougall, Brian Leckner, Dean Stockwell, Ben Johnson, Richard Roundtree, Linda Gray, Jack Elam. **VHS** $92.95 VMK ✰✰

The Bone Yard A weird mortuary is the setting for strange goings on when a murder is investigated.
1990 (R) 98m/C Ed Nelson, Deborah Rose, Norman Fell, Jim Eustermann, Denise Young, Willie Stratford Jr., Phyllis Diller; *D:* James Cummins; *W:* James Cummins. **VHS, Beta** $19.95 PSM ✰

The Bonfire of the Vanities If you liked Tom Wolfe's viciously satirical novel, chances are you won't like this version. If you didn't read the book, you probably still won't like it. Miscast and stripped of the book's gutsy look inside its characters, the film's sole attribute is Vilmos Zsigmond's photography. Hanks is all wrong as wealthy Wall Street trader Sherman McCoy who, lost in the back streets of the Bronx, panics and accidentally kills a young black kid. Willis' drunken journalist/narrator, Griffith's mistress, and Freeman's righteous judge are all awkward and thinly written. If you're still awake, look for F. Murray Abraham's cameo as the Bronx D.A.
1990 (R) 126m/C Tom Hanks, Melanie Griffith, Bruce Willis, Morgan Freeman, Alan King, Kim Cattrall, Saul Rubinek, Clifton James, Donald Moffatt, Richard Libertini, Andre Gregory, Robert Stephens; *Cameos:* F. Murray Abraham; *D:* Brian DePalma; *W:* Michael Cristofer; *M:* Dave Grusin. **VHS, Beta, 8mm** $19.98 WAR, FCT ✰½

Bonjour Tristesse An amoral French girl conspires to break up her playboy father's upcoming marriage to her stuffy godmother in order to maintain her decadent freedom. Preminger attempted, unsuccessfully, to use this soaper to catapult Seberg to stardom. Based on the novel by Francoise Sagan.
1957 94m/C FR Deborah Kerr, David Niven, Jean Seberg, Mylene Demongeot, Geoffrey Horne, Walter Chiari, Jean Kent; *D:* Otto Preminger; *W:* Arthur Laurents. **VHS, Beta** $69.95 COL ✰✰✰

Bonnie & Clyde Based on the biographies of the violent careers of Bonnie Parker and Clyde Barrow, who roamed the Southwest robbing banks. In the Depression era, when any job, even an illegal one, was cherished, money, greed, and power created an unending cycle of violence and fury. Highly controversial and influential, with pronounced bloodshed that spurred mainstream cinematic proliferation. Established Dunaway as a star; produced by Beatty in one of his best performances.
1967 111m/C Warren Beatty, Faye Dunaway, Michael J. Pollard, Gene Hackman, Estelle Parsons; *D:* Arthur Penn; *W:* David Newman, Robert Benton. Academy Awards '67: Best Cinematography, Best Supporting Actress (Parsons); Nominations: Best Actor (Beatty), Best Actor (Hackman, Pollard), Best Actress (Dunaway), Best Director (Penn), Best Picture, Best Story & Screenplay; Academy Awards '67: Best Costume Design. **VHS, Beta** $19.98 WAR, BTV ✰✰✰½

Bonnie Prince Charlie Historical epic opening in 1745 and romanticizing the title pretender to the British throne, who united Scottish clans in a doomed campaign against King George. Talky and rather slow-moving except for stirring battle scenes. A notorious box-office flop in its native Britain, where the original running time was 140 minutes.
1948 135m/C GB David Niven, Margaret Leighton, Judy Campbell, Jack Hawkins, Morland Graham, Finlay Currie, Elwyn Brook-Jones, John Laurie; *D:* Anthony Kimmins. **VHS** $19.95 NOS ✰✰

Bonnie Scotland Laurel & Hardy accidentally join an India-bound Scottish regiment. Laughs aplenty.
1935 81m/B Stan Laurel, Oliver Hardy, James Finlayson, Daphne Pollard, June Lang; *D:* James W. Horne. **VHS, Beta** $19.98 MGM, MLB ✰✰½

Bonnie's Kids Two sisters become involved in murder, sex, and stolen money.
1973 (R) 107m/C Tiffany Bolling, Robin Mattson, Scott Brady, Alex Rocco; *D:* Arthur Marks. **VHS, Beta** NO ✰½

The Boogey Man Through the reflection in a mirror, a girl witnesses her brother murder their mother's lover. Twenty years later this memory still haunts her; the mirror is now broken, revealing its special powers. Who will be next? Murder menagerie; see footage from this flick mirrored in "The Boogey Man 2."
1980 (R) 93m/C John Carradine, Suzanna Love, Ron James; *D:* Ulli Lommel. **VHS, Beta** $59.95 VCI, HHE ✰✰

Boogey Man 2 The story continues; same footage, new director but with Lommel, the director of the original "Boogey Man," co-writing the script and appearing in the film.
1983 90m/C John Carradine, Suzanna Love, Shannah Hall, Ulli Lommel, Sholto Von Douglas; *D:* Bruce Starr. **VHS, Beta** $29.95 VHE, VTR Woof!

Book of Love "Zany" hijinks as a teenager struggles with friendship, girls, and those all-important hormones when he moves to a new neighborhood in the mid-50's. Average rehash of every 50's movie and TV show cliche in existence. Surprise! There's a classic rock 'n' roll soundtrack. Adapted by Kotzwinkle from his novel "Jack in the Box."
1991 (PG-13) 88m/C Chris Young, Keith Coogan, Aeryk Egan, Josie Bisset, Tricia Leigh Fisher, Danny Nucci, Michael McKean, John Cameron Mitchell, Lewis Arquette; *D:* Robert Shaye; *W:* William Kotzwinkle; *M:* Stanley Clarke. **VHS, 8mm** $19.95 COL ✰✰

Boom in the Moon Keaton fares poorly in this sci-fi comedy. He's trapped on a space ship to the moon. Poor production, with uneven direction and acting. *AKA:* A Modern Bluebeard.
1946 83m/C Buster Keaton, Angel Garasa, Virginia Serret, Fernando Soto, Luis Barreiro; *D:* Jaime Salvador. **VHS** NO Woof!

Boom Town A lively vintage comedy/drama/romance about two oil-drilling buddies competing amid romantic mix-ups and fortunes gained and lost.
1940 120m/B Clark Gable, Spencer Tracy, Claudette Colbert, Hedy Lamarr, Frank Morgan, Lionel Atwill, Chill Wills, Curt Bois; **D:** Jack Conway. **VHS, Beta $19.98** MGM, CCB ✂️✂️½

Boomerang A father rescues his wrongly convicted son from prison. Dubbed.
1976 101m/C IT Alain Delon, Carla Gravina, Dora Doll; **D:** Jose Giovanni. **VHS, Beta $59.95** UNI ✂️½

Boomerang Successful, womanizing marketing exec for a cosmetics company (Murphy) meets his match when he falls for a colleague (Givens) who is as vain and sexually predatory as he is. She treats him the way he treats women (as a sex object), and he's shocked into the arms of a nice girl (Berry). Although it's refreshing to see this sexual role reversal, the typical Murphy-style humor is in play with sexist jokes and a couple of vulgar female characters. Grier and Lawrence are great as Murphy's best friends. Blaustein and Sheffield are the same guys who wrote Murphy's "Coming to America."
1992 (R) 118m/C Eddie Murphy, Halle Berry, Robin Givens, David Alan Grier, Martin Lawrence, Grace Jones, Geoffrey Holder, Eartha Kitt, Chris Rock, Tisha Campbell, John Witherspoon, Melvin Van Peebles; **D:** Reginald Hudlin; **W:** Barry W. Blaustein, David Sheffield. **VHS, Beta $19.95** PAR ✂️✂️

The Boost A feverish, messy melodrama about a young couple's spiraling decline from yuppie-ish wealth in a haze of cocaine abuse.
1988 (R) 95m/C James Woods, Sean Young, John Kapelos, Steven Hill, Kelle Kerr, John Rothman, Amanda Blake, Grace Zabriskie; **D:** Harold Becker; **W:** Darryl Ponicsan. **VHS, Beta $19.95** HBO ✂️½

Boot Hill Two guys mess with western baddies and wild women in spaghetti oater.
1969 (PG) 97m/C IT Terence Hill, Bud Spencer, Woody Strode, Victor Buono, Lionel Stander; **D:** Giuseppe Colizzi. **VHS, Beta** NO ✂️½

Boot Hill Bandits "Crash" Corrigan fights on the side of right in this classic western as he helps corral Wells Fargo bandits.
1942 58m/B Ray Corrigan, John "Dusty" King, Max Terhune, Jean Brooks, John Merton, Glenn Strange; **D:** S. Roy Luby. **VHS $19.95** NOS, HEG ✂️½

Boothill Brigade Former footballer Brown rides to the rescue when criminals steal land from homesteaders.
1937 58m/B Johnny Mack Brown, Claire Rochelle, Dick Curtis, Horace Murphy, Frank LaRue, Edward Cassidy, Bobby Nelson, Frank Ball, Steve Clark; **D:** Sam Newfield. **VHS $19.95** NOS, MRV ✂️

Bootleg A detective is on a case that leads to crooked politics and espionage.
1989 82m/C Ray Meagher; **D:** John Prescott. **VHS $79.95** AIP ✂️

Boots & Saddles A young English lord wants to sell the ranch he has inherited but Autry is determined to make him a real Westerner.
1937 54m/B Gene Autry, Judith Allen, Smiley Burnette; **D:** Joseph Kane. **VHS, Beta $19.95** NOS, MRV, VYY ✂️½

Boots Malone An old down-on-his-luck gambling addict and a young, rich kid fascinated by the sordid atmosphere of the racetrack stumble upon one another and form a symbiotic relationship. All goes well for while, but there'd be no movie unless a collection of obstacles suddenly threatens

their success, friendship, and even their lives. A rather melodramatic buddy tale, but Holden and Stewart hold interest.
1952 103m/C William Holden, John Stewart, Ed Begley Sr., Harry Morgan, Whit Bissell; **D:** William Dieterle; **M:** Elmer Bernstein. **VHS** GKK ✂️✂️½

Boots of Destiny Cheap western with Maynard and his sidekick Barnett on the lam and coming to the aid of ranch owner Dell. Based on a story by E. Morton Hough.
1937 59m/B Ken Maynard, Claudia Dell, Vince Barnett, Edward Cassidy, Martin Garralaga; **D:** Arthur Rosson; **W:** Arthur Rosson. **VHS $19.99** MOV ✂️

Bopha! Father-son strife set against the anti-apartheid movement in the Senior township police officer Mikah takes pride in his peaceful community, particularly in light of the growing unrest in the other townships. Son Zweli has become an activist and wife Rosie must be the family peacemaker. Then a prominent freedom movement member is arrested and two officers of the secret police make their sinister appearance. Well-acted; directorial debut of Freeman. Adapted from the play by Percy Mtwa, although the hopeful ending has been changed in the movie. The title, a Zulu word, stands for arrest or detention. Filmed on location in Zimbabwe.
1993 (PG-13) 121m/C Danny Glover, Maynard Eziashi, Alfre Woodard, Malcolm McDowell, Marius Weyers, Malick Bowens, Robin Smith, Michael Chinyamurindi, Christopher John Hall, Grace Mahlaba; **D:** Morgan Freeman; **W:** Brian Bird, John Wierick; **M:** James Horner. **VHS, Beta** PAR ✂️✂️✂️

Bordello A made-for-television western spoof about cowboys and shady ladies.
1979 90m/C Chuck Connors, Michael Conrad, John Ireland, Isela Vega, George Rivero. **VHS, Beta $79.95** PSM ✂️

The Border A border guard faces corruption and violence within his department and tests his own sense of decency when the infant of a poor Mexican girl is kidnapped. Excellent cast, fine cinematography, unusual Nicholson performance.
1982 (R) 107m/C Jack Nicholson, Harvey Keitel, Valerie Perrine, Warren Oates, Elpidia Carrillo; **D:** Tony Richardson; **W:** Deric Washburn, Walon Green; **M:** Ry Cooder. **VHS, Beta $14.98** MCA ✂️✂️✂️

Border Badmen It's just another tired old western, even if it does appropriate the classic mystery-thriller plot; following the reading of a siler baron's will, someone starts killing off the relatives.
1945 59m/B Buster Crabbe, Lorraine Miller, Charles "Blackie" King, Ray Bennett, Archie Hall, Budd Buster, Bud Osborne; **D:** Sam Newfield. **VHS, Beta** GPV, MRV ✂️½

Border Bandits Plodding oater has Brown going after the bad guys. Not only is it a dirty job, but apparently pretty boring.
1946 57m/B Johnny Mack Brown, Raymond Hatton, John Merton, Frank LaRue, Steve Clark, Charles Stevens, Bud Osborne; **D:** Lambert Hillyer. **VHS $19.95** DVT, HEG ✂️

Border Caballero Western star McCoy and lady cowpoke January shoot out the skies in this lackluster McCoy vehicle. Based on a story by Norman S. Hall.
1936 57m/B Tim McCoy, Lois January, Ralph Byrd, Ted Adams; **D:** Sam Newfield; **W:** Joseph O'Donnell. **VHS $19.99** MOV ✂️½

Border Devils A boy is pursued by a ruthless gang of outlaws, until he is saved by the good guys.
1932 60m/B Harry Carey Sr., Art Mix, George "Gabby" Hayes; **D:** William Nigh. **VHS, Beta** NO ✂️

Border Feud LaRue endeavors to prevent someone who, by instigating a family feud, will claim large gold mine rights.
1947 54m/B Lash LaRue, Al "Fuzzy" St. John, Bob Duncan; **D:** Ray Taylor. **VHS, Beta $12.95** COL ✂️

Border Law Jones plays a heroic Texas Ranger who goes undercover to find the man who killed his brother. One of Jones' finest outings and far better than most B westerns.
1931 62m/B Buck Jones, Lupita Tova, James Mason, Frank Rice, Glenn Strange; **D:** Louis King; **W:** Stuart Anthony. **VHS $19.99** MOV, GVV ✂️✂️½

The Border Legion Sappy retelling of Grey's novel about an outlaw sacrificing himself for a pair of young lovers. This time Rogers is the outlaw with a heart of gold. Originally filmed in 1930 with Jack Holt, Richard Arlen, and Fay Wray.
1940 58m/B Roy Rogers, George "Gabby" Hayes, Carol Hughes, Joseph Sawyer, Maude Eburne, Jay Novello; **D:** Joseph Kane; **W:** Olive Cooper, Louis Stevens. **VHS $19.99** MOV ✂️½

Border Patrol Another installment in the Hopalong Cassidy series. This time there's a villainous owner of a silvermine to reckon with. A man so low he's abducting hapless Mexicans as they cross the border, forcing them to work his mines. Hoppy is saddled with the task of persuading him that the town ain't big enough for the both of them. Robert Mitchum makes his perfectly-forgettable film debut as one of the bad guys. Not one of the best in the series, but plenty of action.
1943 63m/B William Boyd, Andy Clyde, Jay Kirby, Russell Simpson, Claudia Drake, George Reeves, Duncan Renaldo; **D:** Lesley Selander. **VHS $19.95** NOS ✂️✂️

Border Phantom Steele (whom you might recognize as Canino in "The Big Sleep"), takes on a suave Chinese businessman who heads a mail order business: seems he's smuggling mail-order brides from Mexico in this vintage "B"-grade horse opera.
1937 60m/B Bob Steele, Harley Wood, Don Barclay, Karl Hackett, Horace Murphy, Miki Morita; **D:** S. Roy Luby. **VHS $19.99** NOS, MRV, VTR ✂️✂️

Border Radio A rock singer decides to steal a car and try to outrun some tough thugs hot on his trail.
1988 88m/C Chris D, Luana Anders; **D:** Allison Anders, Kurt Voss; **W:** Allison Anders, Kurt Voss. **VHS $19.95** FCT Woof!

Border Rangers A man joins the Rangers in order to avenge the murders of his brother and sister-in-law.
1950 57m/B Robert Lowery, Donald (Don "Red") Barry, Lyle Talbot, Pamela Blake; **D:** William Berke. **VHS, Beta** NO ✂️

Border Romance Three Americans have their horses stolen by bandits while riding through Mexico. Trouble with the locals follows in this early sound western.
1930 58m/B Don Terry, Armida, Marjorie Kane. **VHS, Beta $19.95** VYY ✂️½

Border Roundup The "Lone Rider" uncovers a gang of thieving crooks.
1941 57m/B George Houston, Al "Fuzzy" St. John, Dennis Moore; **D:** Sam Newfield. **VHS, Beta $19.95** VDM ✂️

Border Saddlemates A U.S. government agent becomes involved in a crooked deal when he is asked to doctor Canadian silver foxes.
1952 67m/B Rex Allen. **VHS, Beta $29.95** DVT ✂️

B

Border Shootout A trigger-happy sheriff battles a rich young cattle rustler.
1990 (PG) 110m/C Glenn Ford, Charlene Tilton, Jeff Kaake, Michael Horse, Russell Todd, Cody Glenn, Sergio Calderon, Michael Ansara; *D:* C.T. McIntyre. VHS, Beta $79.98 TTC ✗✗

Border Street This film shows how a group of Polish Jews fought off the German occupation forces in the Warsaw ghetto. In Polish with English subtitles. *AKA:* Ulica Graniczna; That Others May Live.
1948 110m/B PL VHS, Beta $39.95 IHF ✗✗½

Border Vengeance Reb is a member of a family of outlaws. He aims to improve himself and steer his family to the straight and narrow trail.
1935 45m/B Reb Russell, Mary Jane Carey, Kenneth MacDonald, Hank Bell, Glenn Strange, Norman Feusier, Charles ''Slim'' Whitaker; *D:* Ray Heinz. VHS $10.95 GPV ✗✗½

Border Vigilantes Hoppy and pals try to rid a town of outlaws that even the vigilantes can't run off. The big surprise comes when they find out who the leader of the outlaws is.
1941 61m/B William Boyd, Russell Hayden, Andy Clyde, Victor Jory, Morris Ankrum, Frances Gifford, Ethel Wales, Hal Taliaferro; *D:* Derwin Abrahams. VHS $19.95 NOS ✗✗

Borderline MacMurray and Trevor play undercover agents trying to infiltrate a Mexican drug ring. With their real identities hidden, they fall for each other and make a run for the border. Although the leads work well together, they're hindered by an occasionally confusing script. Unfortunately, director Seiter never decides whether the material is of a comedic or dramatic nature.
1950 88m/B Fred MacMurray, Claire Trevor, Raymond Burr, Roy Roberts, Jose Torvay, Morris Ankrum, Charles Lane, Don Diamond, Nacho Galindo, Pepe Hern, Richard Irving; *D:* William A. Seiter. VHS HEG ✗✗

Borderline Bronson is a border patrol guard in pursuit of a murderer in this action flick. Meanwhile, he gets caught up in trying to help an illegal alien and her young child.
1980 (PG) 106m/C Charles Bronson, Wilford Brimley, Bruno Kirby, Benito Morales, Ed Harris, Kenneth McMillan; *D:* Jerrold Freedman. VHS, Beta $59.98 FOX ✗✗

Bordertown Gunfighters A cowboy breaks up a vicious lottery racket and falls in love in the process.
1943 56m/B Wild Bill Elliott, Anne Jeffreys. VHS, Beta $29.95 DVT ✗½

Boris and Natasha: The Movie The two inept spies from the classic television cartoon ''The Adventures of Rocky and Bullwinkle'' star in this mediocre live-action comedy. These nogoodniks are sent by ''Fearless Leader'' to America and encounter the usual misadventures. For true fun watch the original animated versions. Never released theatrically, it aired for the first time on cable television.
1992 (PG) 88m/C Sally Kellerman, Dave Thomas, Paxton Whitehead, Andrea Martin, Alex Rocco, Larry Cedar, Arye Gross, Christopher Neame, Anthony Newley; *Cameos:* John Candy, John Travolta, Charles Martin Smith; *D:* Charles Martin Smith. VHS $19.95 ACA, NLC ✗½

B.O.R.N. Hagen uncovers an underground network of doctors who kill people and sell the body parts and organs.
1988 (R) 90m/C Ross Hagen, P.J. Soles, William Smith, Hoke Howell, Russ Tamblyn, Amanda Blake, Clint Howard, Rance Howard, Debra Lamb; *D:* Ross Hagen. VHS, Beta $79.95 PSM ✗½

Born Again This is the filmed adaptation of Charles Colson's biography of why he became a born again Christian.
1978 110m/C Dean Jones, Anne Francis, Dana Andrews, George Brent; *D:* Irving Rapper; *M:* Les Baxter. VHS, Beta $59.98 SUE ✗½

Born American Pre-Glasnost flick about teenagers vacationing in Finland who ''accidentally'' cross the Russian border. There they battle the Red Plague. Melodramatic and heavily politicized. Original release banned in Finland. *AKA:* Arctic Heat.
1986 (R) 95m/C Mike Norris, Steve Durham, David Coburn, Thalmus Rasulala, Albert Salmi; *D:* Renny Harlin. VHS, Beta NO ✗

Born Beautiful Made for TV. Beautiful young women come to New York, hoping to strike it rich in the world of modeling. At the same time, a still beautiful, but older and overexposed model comes to grips with a change in her career. Well-told, but sugarcoated.
1982 100m/C Erin Gray, Ed Marinaro, Polly Bergen, Lori Singer, Ellen Barber, Judith Barcroft, Michael Higgins; *D:* Harvey Hart; *M:* Brad Fiedel. VHS WAR ✗✗½

Born Free The touching story of a game warden in Kenya and his wife raising Elsa the orphaned lion cub. When the cub reaches maturity, they work to return her to life in the wild. Great family entertainment based on Joy Adamson's book. Theme song became a hit.
1966 95m/C Virginia McKenna, Bill Travers; *D:* James Hill; *M:* John Barry. VHS, Beta $14.95 COL, HMV ✗✗✗

Born in America A young orphan is adopted by an undertaker. The boy grows up enveloped by his guardian's business and, when things are slow, works to bring in business himself. *AKA:* Dead Aim.
1990 90m/C James Westerfield, Glen Lee, Virgil Frye, Venetia Vianello; *D:* Jose Antonio Bolanos. VHS NO ✗

Born in East L.A. Marin brings his Bruce Springsteen-parody song to life as he plays a mistakenly deported illegal alien who struggles to return to the U.S. Surprisingly resolute effort by the usually self-exploiting Mexican-American. Stern is the American expatriate who helps him get back and Lopez is the love interest who stalls him.
1987 (R) 85m/C Richard ''Cheech'' Marin, Daniel Stern, Paul Rodriguez, Jan-Michael Vincent, Kamala Lopez, Tony Plana, Vic Trevino, A. Martinez; *D:* Richard ''Cheech'' Marin. VHS, Beta $14.95 MCA, FCT ✗✗

Born in Flames An acclaimed futuristic feminist film about women who band together in an effort to gain control of the state owned media.
1983 90m/C *D:* Lizzie Borden. VHS ICA ✗

Born Innocent As if ''The Exorcist'' weren't bad enough, Blair is back for more abuse-on-film, this time as a 14-year-old runaway from a dysfunctional family who lands in a reform school for girls. There, she must struggle to be as brutal as her peers in order to survive. Fairly tame by today's standards, but controversial at its made-for-TV premiere, chiefly due to a rape scene involving a broom handle. First trip up the river for Blair.
1974 92m/C Linda Blair, Joanna Miles, Kim Hunter, Richard Jaeckel; *D:* Donald Wrye. VHS, Beta NO ✗½

Born Invincible A Kung Fu master avenges the kick-death of a student by randomly kick-killing suspects.
1976 90m/C Lo Lieh, Carter Wong, Nancy Yan; *D:* Joseph Kuo. VHS, Beta $59.95 GEM ✗

Born Killer Teenagers in the woods meet up with murderous escaped convicts.
1989 90m/C Francine Lapensee, Fritz Matthews, Ted Prior, Adam Tucker; *D:* Kimberly Casey. VHS, Beta $14.95 AIP ✗½

Born Losers The original ''Billy Jack'' film in which the Indian martial arts expert takes on a group of incorrigible bikers bothering some California babes and runs afoul of the law. Classic drive-in fare.
1967 (PG) 112m/C Tom Laughlin, Elizabeth James, Jeremy Slate, William Wellman Jr., Robert Tessier, Jane Russell; *D:* Tom Laughlin; *W:* Tom Laughlin. VHS, Beta $59.95 VES, LIV ✗✗

Born of Fire A flutist investigating his father's death seeks the Master Musician; his search leads him to the volcanic (and supernatural) mountains of Turkey.
1987 (R) 84m/C Peter Firth, Susan Crowley, Stephan Kalipha; *D:* Jamil Dehlavi. VHS, Beta $79.95 VMK ✗½

Born on the Fourth of July A riveting meditation on American life affected by the Vietnam War, based on the real-life, bestselling experiences of Ron Kovic, though some facts are subtly changed. The film follows him as he develops from a naive recruit to an angry, wheelchair-bound paraplegic to an active antiwar protestor. Well-acted and generally lauded; Kovic co-wrote the screenplay and appears as a war veteran in the opening parade sequence.
1989 (R) 145m/C Tom Cruise, Kyra Sedgwick, Raymond J. Barry, Jerry Levine, Tom Berenger, Willem Dafoe, Frank Whaley, John Getz, Caroline Kava, Bryan Larkin, Abbie Hoffman, Stephen Baldwin, Josh Evans; *D:* Oliver Stone; *W:* Oliver Stone; *M:* John Williams. Academy Awards '89: Best Director (Stone), Best Film Editing; Nominations: Best Actor (Cruise), Best Adapted Screenplay, Best Cinematography, Best Picture, Best Sound, Best Original Score; Directors Guild of America Awards '89: Best Director (Stone); Golden Globe Awards '90: Best Actor—Drama (Cruise), Best Director (Stone), Best Film—Drama, Best Screenplay. VHS, Beta, 8mm $14.95 MCA, FCT, BTV ✗✗✗½

Born to Be Bad Fontaine, an opportunistic woman who was b-b-born to be b-b-bad, attempts to steal a wealthy business man away from his wife while carrying on an affair with a novelist. Ray's direction (he's best known for ''Rebel Without a Cause,'' filmed five years later) prevents the film from succumbing to standard Hollywood formula.
1950 93m/B Joan Fontaine, Robert Ryan, Zachary Scott, Joan Leslie, Mel Ferrer; *D:* Nicholas Ray. VHS, Beta $19.98 TTC ✗✗½

Born to Be Wild A pair of truck drivers are commissioned to deliver a shipment of dynamite. The dynamite will be used to destroy a dam, preventing the surrounding land from falling into the hands of unscrupulous land barons. Good action picture thanks to the cast.
1938 66m/B Ralph Byrd, Doris Weston, Ward Bond, Robert Emmett Keane, Bentley Hewlett, Charles Williams; *D:* Joseph Kane. VHS, Beta $16.95 SNC, RXM ✗✗

Born to Boogie A concert, a chronicle, and a tribute, ''Born To Boogie'' is about Marc Bolan and his band T. Rex. The film, which features concert footage from a 1972 concert at the Wembley Empire Pool in London, chronicles the glitter rock era and the next wave of British rock and roll, and pays tribute to Bolan, who died in 1977 just as he was starting a comeback. Ringo Starr and Elton John join T. Rex in the studio for ''Children of the Revolution'' and ''Tutti-Frutti'' as well as a psychedelic soiree where

Bolan plays acoustic versions of his hits. This film was never released in the United States. **1972 75m/C** Marc Bolan, Elton John, Ringo Starr; *D:* Ringo Starr. **VHS $29.98** *MPI, MVD* 🎬🎬

Born to Dance A quintessential MGM 1930s dance musical, wherein a beautiful dancer gets a sailor and a big break in a show. Great songs by Cole Porter sung in a less than great manner by a gangly Stewart. Powell's first starring vehicle. 🎵Love Me Love My Pekinese; I've Got You Under My Skin; Hey Babe Hey; Easy to Love; Rolling Home; Rap Tap on Wood; Entrance of Lucy James; Swingin' the Jinx Away.
1936 108m/B Eleanor Powell, James Stewart, Virginia Bruce, Una Merkel, Frances Langford, Sid Silvers, Raymond Walburn, Reginald Gardiner, Buddy Ebsen; *D:* Roy Del Ruth; *M:* Cole Porter, Cole Porter. **VHS, Beta $19.98** *MGM, MLB* 🎬🎬½

Born to Kill A ruthless killer marries a girl for her money. Minor tough-as-nails film noir exemplifying Tierney's stone-faced human-devil film persona. *AKA:* Lady of Deceit.
1947 92m/B Lawrence Tierney, Claire Trevor, Walter Slezak, Elisha Cook Jr.; *D:* Robert Wise. **VHS, Beta $19.98** *TTC* 🎬🎬🎬

Born to Race In the world of competitive auto racing, a beautiful engineer is kidnapped for her new controversial engine design.
1988 (R) 95m/C Joseph Bottoms, George Kennedy, Marc Singer, Marla Heasly; *D:* James Fargo. **VHS, Beta $79.98** *FOX* 🎬🎬

Born to Ride A biker rebel joins the Army prior to WWII in order to escape a prison term after a good ol' boy brush with the law. He shuns Army discipline, but proves himself in action as the leader of a scout troup for the Army's motorcycle calvary brigade. Available with Spanish subtitles.
1991 (PG) 88m/C John Stamos, John Stockwell, Teri Polo, Kris Kamm; *D:* Graham Baker. **VHS, Beta $19.98** *WAR* 🎬🎬

Born to Run A young Australian boy dreams of restoring his grandfather's run-down horse farm to its former glory. Filmed on location.
1977 87m/C VHS, Beta $69.95 *DVT* 🎬🎬

Born to Run Nicky Donatello (Grieco) is a Brooklyn street drag racer who gets mixed up with the mob while trying to rescue his no-account brother. But he still finds time to fall for an uptown model who also happens to be the mobster's girlfriend. Made for television.
1993 97m/C Richard Grieco, Jay Acovone, Shelli Lether, Christian Campbell, Brent Stait, Martin Cummins, Wren Roberts, Joe Cortese; *D:* Albert Magnoli; *W:* Randall Badat. **VHS** *FXV* 🎬🎬½

Born to Win A New York hairdresser with an expensive drug habit struggles through life in this well made comedy drama. Excellent acting from fine cast, well-paced, and interestingly photographed. Not well received when first released, but worth a look. *AKA:* Addict.
1971 (R) 90m/C George Segal, Karen Black, Paula Prentiss, Hector Elizondo, Robert De Niro, Jay Fletcher; *D:* Ivan Passer. **VHS $9.99** *OVD, MGM* 🎬🎬½

Born Yesterday Ambitious junk dealer Harry Brock is in love with smart but uneducated Billie Dawn. He hires newspaperman Paul Verrall to teach her the finer points of etiquette. During their sessions, they fall in love and Billie realizes how she has been used by Brock. She retaliates against him and gets to deliver that now-famous line: "Do me a favor, drop dead." Based on the Broadway play.

1950 103m/B Judy Holliday, Broderick Crawford, William Holden; *D:* George Cukor. Academy Awards '50: Best Actress (Holliday); Nominations: Best Costume Design (B & W), Best Director (Cukor), Best Picture, Best Screenplay; Golden Globe Awards '51: Best Actress—Musical/Comedy (Holliday). **VHS, Beta $19.95** *COL, FCT, BTV* 🎬🎬🎬½

Born Yesterday Remake of the 1950 classic suffers in comparison, particularly Griffith, who has the thankless task of surpassing (or even meeting) Judy Holliday's Oscar-winning mark as not-so-dumb blonde Billie Dawn. Her intellectual inadequacies are glaring when she hits the political world of D.C. with obnoxious tycoon boyfriend Goodman. To save face, he hooks her up with a journalist (Johnson) willing to coach her in Savvy 101, a la Eliza Doolittle. What worked well in post-WWII America seems sadly outdated today; stick with the original.
1993 (PG) 102m/C Melanie Griffith, John Goodman, Don Johnson, Edward Herrmann, Max Perlich, Fred Dalton Thompson, Nora Dunn, Benjamin C. Bradlee, Sally Quinn, Michael Ensign, William Frankfather, Celeste Yarnall, Meg Wittner; *D:* Luis Mandoki; *W:* Douglas McGrath; *M:* George Fenton. **VHS, Beta $94.95** *BVV, HPH* 🎬🎬

The Borrower An exiled unstable mutant insect alien serial killer (you know the type) must switch heads with human beings regularly to survive. This colorful, garish gorefest has humor and attitude, but never develops behind the basic grossout situation.
1989 (R) 97m/C Rae Dawn Chong, Don Gordon, Antonio Fargas, Tom Towles; *D:* John McNaughton. **VHS $19.98** *WAR, CAN* 🎬🎬

The Borrowers Excellent made for television adaptation of the May Norton childrens classics "The Borrowers" and "The Borrowers Afield." This miniature family (about mouse-size) live beneath the floorboards of an English house and borrow what they need to survive from the normal-sized human inhabitants. Problems come when the teeny family are discovered and must make their way to a new home. Sweet and humorous. On two cassettes.
1993 199m/C *GB* Ian Holm, Penelope Wilton, Rebecca Callard; *D:* John Henderson. **VHS $59.98** *TTC* 🎬🎬🎬

Borsalino Delon and Belmondo are partners in crime in this seriocomic film about gang warfare in 1930's Marseilles. The costumes, settings, and music perfectly capture the mood of the period. Followed by a sequel "Borsalino and Co." Based on "The Bandits of Marseilles" by Eugene Saccomano.
1970 (R) 124m/C *FR* Jean-Paul Belmondo, Alain Delon, Michel Bouquet, Catherine Rouvel, Francoise Christophe, Corinne Marchand; *D:* Jacques Deray; *W:* Jacques Deray, Claude Sautet, Jean-Claude Carriere; *M:* Claude Bolling. **VHS $19.95** *PAR* 🎬🎬🎬

Boss Blaxploitation western parody with Williamson and Martin as a couple of bounty hunters tearing apart a town to find a fugitive. Relatively non-violent. *AKA:* The Black Bounty Killer; Boss Nigger.
1974 (PG) 87m/C Fred Williamson, D'Urville Martin, R.G. Armstrong, William Smith, Carmen Hayworth, Barbara Leigh; *D:* Jack Arnold; *W:* Fred Williamson. **VHS** *NO* 🎬½

Boss Cowboy A cowboy shows who wears the chaps in his family when he kidnaps his girlfriend to prevent her from moving East.
1935 51m/B Buddy Roosevelt, Frances Morris, Sam Pierce, Fay McKenzie, Lafe McKee; *D:* Victor Adamson. **VHS, Beta** *NO* 🎬

Boss Foreman A languorous, entwining comedy of errors about a construction foreman and his misadventures with the mob.
1939 58m/B Henry Armetta. **VHS, Beta $19.95** *VYY Woof!*

The Boss Is Served A mother (Berger) and three daughters, racked with debt, are forced to take in boarders. The lascivious man and teenage son want to be more than just boarders to the lovely Berger. In Italian with English subtitles.
1967 95m/C *IT* Senta Berger, Maurizio Arena, Bruno Zamin. **VHS, Beta** *NO* 🎬🎬

Boss of Big Town Gangsters try to infiltrate the milk industry in this standard crime drama.
1943 65m/B John Litel, Florence Rice, H.B. Warner, Jean Brooks, John Miljan, Mary Gordon, John Maxwell; *D:* Arthur Dreifuss. **VHS, Beta $16.95** *SNC, RXM* 🎬🎬

Boss of Bullion City A crooked sheriff is exposed by Brown and sidekick Knight in this sagebrush saga. Based on a story by Arthur St. Claire.
1941 61m/B Johnny Mack Brown, Fuzzy Knight, Maria Montez, Earle Hodgins, Harry Woods; *D:* Ray Taylor; *W:* Victor McLeod, Arthur St. Claire. **VHS $19.99** *MOV* 🎬½

Boss of Rawhide The Texas Rangers fight for law and order in the old west despite odds against them.
1944 60m/B Dave O'Brien, James Newill. **VHS, Beta $19.95** *NOS, DVT* 🎬

Boss' Son Worthwhile coming-of-age tale about a young man who learns more than he bargained for about life when he goes to work for his father in the family carpet business. Dad feels he should work his way up through the ranks and makes him a delivery man. The young man meets reality head on and must deal with the injustices of the world around him. Independently filmed by director/writer Roth.
1979 97m/C Rita Moreno, James Darren, Asher Brauner, Rudy Solari, Henry Sanders, Richie Havens, Piper Laurie, Elena Verdugo; *D:* Bobby Roth; *W:* Bobby Roth. **VHS, Beta $69.95** *VES, LIV* 🎬🎬

The Boss' Wife A young stockbroker attempts to fix what's wrong with his life by maneuvering sexually with the boss' wife, and complications set in.
1986 (R) 83m/C Daniel Stern, Arielle Dombasle, Christopher Plummer, Martin Mull, Melanie Mayron, Lou Jacobi; *D:* Ziggy Steinberg; *M:* Bill Conti. **VHS, Beta $79.98** *FOX* 🎬🎬

The Boston Strangler Based on Gerold Frank's bestselling factual book about the deranged killer who terrorized Boston for about a year and a half. Traces events from first killing to prosecution. Curtis, going against type, is compelling in title role.
1968 116m/C Tony Curtis, Henry Fonda, George Kennedy, Murray Hamilton, Mike Kellin, George Voskovec, William Hickey, James Brolin, Hurd Hatfield, William Marshall, Jeff Corey, Sally Kellerman; *D:* Richard Fleischer; *W:* Edward Anhalt. **VHS, Beta $19.98** *FOX* 🎬🎬½

The Bostonians A faith healer's daughter is forced to choose between the affections of a militant suffragette and a young lawyer in 19th Century Boston. Based on Henry James' classic novel.
1984 (PG) 120m/C Christopher Reeve, Vanessa Redgrave, Madeleine Potter, Jessica Tandy, Nancy Marchand, Wesley Addy, Linda Hunt, Wallace Shawn; *D:* James Ivory; *W:* Ruth Prawer Jhabvala. **VHS, Beta $79.98** *VES, LIV* 🎬🎬½

Botany Bay A rousing costumer about a convict ship in the 1700s that, after a trying voyage, lands in Australia, wherein a framed doctor conquers the local plague. From the novel by Charles Nordoff.
1953 99m/C Alan Ladd, James Mason, Patricia Medina, Cedric Hardwicke; *D:* John Farrow. **VHS, Beta $19.95** *BAR* ♫♫

Bottoms Up Three nymphomaniacs seduce a virginal mechanic and turn him into an insatiable womanizer. Skin aplenty.
1987 90m/C Adam Janas, Sparky Abbrams, Kathleen Johnson. **VHS, Beta $9.99** *PSM* Woof!

Boudu Saved from Drowning A suicidal tramp completely disrupts the wealthy household of the man that saves him from drowning. A gentle but sardonic farce from the master filmmaker. Remade in 1986 as "Down and Out In Beverly Hills." **AKA:** Boudu Sauve des Eaux.
1932 87m/B *FR* Michel Simon, Charles Grandval, Jean Daste; *D:* Jean Renoir. **VHS, Beta $59.95** *INT, MRV, DVT* ♫♫♫ ½

Boulevard Nights A young Latino man tries to escape his neighborhood's street-gang violence, while his older brother is sucked into it. Music by Schifrin, known for the "Mission: Impossible" theme.
1979 (R) 102m/C Richard Yniguez, Danny De La Paz, Marta DuBois, Carmen Zapata, Victor Millan; *D:* Michael Pressman; *M:* Lalo Schifrin. **VHS, Beta $19.98** *WAR* ♫♫

Boulevard of Broken Dreams Successful Hollywood screenwriter Tom Garfield (Waters) returns to his native Australia to figure out how his life got so screwed up. His estranged wife is living with someone else and his daughter barely remembers him. Affecting look at personal priorities versus success.
1994 (PG-13) 95m/C John Waters, Kim Gyngell. **VHS $92.95** *ACA* ♫♫

Bound and Gagged: A Love Story For some reason, Elizabeth (Saltarelli), who is desperate for a husband, thinks that she might increase her chances of finding one if she kidnaps her friend Leslie (Allen) and goes on a weird wild goose chase through Minnesota with the hostage and her hopeless partner-in-crime, Cliff (Denton). Go figure.
1993 (R) 96m/C Ginger Lynn Allen, Karen Black, Chris Denton, Elizabeth Saltarelli, Mary Ella Ross, Chris Mulkey; *D:* Daniel Appleby; *W:* Daniel Appleby; *M:* William Murphy. **VHS $89.95** *TRI* ♫

Bound for Glory The award-winning biography of American folk singer Woody Guthrie set against the backdrop of the Depression. Superb portrayal of the spirit and feelings of the period featuring many of his songs encased in the incidents that inspired them. Haskell Wexler's award-winning camera work is superbly expressive.
1976 (PG) 149m/C David Carradine, Ronny Cox, Melinda Dillon, Randy Quaid; *D:* Hal Ashby; *W:* Robert Getchell. Academy Awards '76: Best Adapted Score, Best Cinematography; Nominations: Best Adapted Screenplay, Best Costume Design, Best Film Editing, Best Picture; Cannes Film Festival '77: Best Film; National Board of Review Awards '76: Best Actor (Carradine). **VHS, Beta $19.98** *MGM* ♫♫♫ ½

The Bounty A new version of "Mutiny on the Bounty," with emphasis on a more realistic relationship between Fletcher Christian and Captain Bligh—and a more sympathetic portrayal of the captain, too. The sensuality of Christian's relationship with a Tahitian beauty also receives greater importance.

1984 (PG) 130m/C Mel Gibson, Anthony Hopkins, Laurence Olivier, Edward Fox, Daniel Day-Lewis, Bernard Hill, Philip Davis, Liam Neeson; *D:* Roger Donaldson; *W:* Robert Bolt. **VHS, Beta $29.98** *VES, LIV* ♫♫♫

Bounty Hunters A man hunts down his friend's killer.
1989 (R) 91m/C Robert Ginty, Bo Hopkins, Loeta Waterdown; *D:* Robert Ginty. **VHS, Beta $79.95** *AIP* ♫♫

The Bounty Man A bounty hunter brings an outlaw in, robbing him of his freedom and his girlfriend.
1972 74m/C Clint Walker, Richard Basehart, Margot Kidder, Arthur Hunnicutt, John Ericson, Gene Evans; *D:* John Llewellyn Moxey. **VHS, Beta $19.98** *FOX* ♫♫

Bounty Tracker Johnny Damone (Lamas) is a bounty-hunter in pursuit of the killer-for-hire who murdered his brother. This personal vendetta leads to an action-packed martial arts showdown between Johnny and his cold-blooded prey.
1993 (R) 90m/C Lorenzo Lamas, Matthias Hues. **VHS $89.98** *REP* ♫ ½

Bouquet of Barbed Wire Overlong soaper revolves around a weathly family and their hidden secrets: incest and infidelity. On three tapes.
1976 330m/C Frank Finlay, Susan Penhaligon, Deborah Grant, Sheila Allen, James Aubrey; *D:* Tom Wharmby. **VHS** *NO* ♫ ½

The Bourne Identity Chamberlain stars as an amnesiac trying to piece together the fragments of his memory. Is he U.S. espionage agent Jason Bourne or an international terrorist? Aided by Smith (the kidnap victim who falls in love with her captor), the two traverse Europe trying to escape the spy network out to assassinate the mystery man who knows too little. Exciting adaptation of the Robert Ludlum thriller. Originally a two-part television miniseries.
1988 185m/C Richard Chamberlain, Jaclyn Smith, Denholm Elliott, Anthony Quayle, Donald Moffatt, Yorgo Voyagis; *D:* Roger Young; *W:* Carol Sobieski. **VHS $79.99** *WAR, BTV* ♫♫♫

Bowery at Midnight Lugosi plays a man who recycles criminals into zombies that commit crimes for his benefit. Bela and an intense mood can't quite save this pic.
1942 60m/B Bela Lugosi, Tom Neal, Dave O'Brien, Wanda McKay; *D:* Wallace Fox. **VHS, Beta $19.95** *NOS, MRV, SNC* ♫ ½

Bowery at Midnight/Dick Tracy vs. Cueball On one tape, the vintage Lugosi grade-C thriller about zombies in the Bowery, and a standard Dick Tracy entry.
1942 125m/B Bela Lugosi, Morgan Conway, Dick Wessel, Skelton Knaggs. **VHS, Beta** *AOV* ♫ ½

Bowery Blitzkrieg This lesser "East Side Kids" entry has Gorcey opting to enter the boxing ring rather than turn to crime. Needs more Huntz. **AKA:** Stand and Deliver.
1941 62m/B Leo Gorcey, Huntz Hall, Bobby Jordan, Warren Hull, Charlotte Henry, Keye Luke; *D:* Wallace Fox. **VHS $19.95** *NOS, VEC, HEG* ♫

Bowery Buckaroos The Bowery Boys take their act West in search of gold, meeting up with the usual amounts of goofy characters and hilarious misunderstandings.
1947 66m/B Leo Gorcey, Huntz Hall, Bobby Jordan, Gabriel Dell, Billy Benedict, David Gorcey, Julie Briggs, Bernard Gorcey, Chief Yowlachie, Iron Eyes Cody; *D:* William Beaudine. **VHS $14.98** *WAR* ♫♫

Boxcar Bertha Scorsese's vivid portrayal of the South during the 1930s' Depression casts Hershey as a woman who winds up in cahoots with an anti-establishment train robber. Based on the book "Sister of the Road" by Boxcar Bertha Thomson.
1972 (R) 90m/C Barbara Hershey, David Carradine, John Carradine; *D:* Martin Scorsese. **VHS, Beta $69.95** *VES, LIV* ♫♫ ½

Boxcar Blues Bird (Coufos) is a down and out fighter who decides to fight "The Man" (Ventura), a bare knuckle fighter who enjoys beating his opponents to death. On the way to the fight, in New Orleans, he meets up with his girl Casey (Langrick), along with some other shady characters, including a truck driving preacher.
1990 96m/C Paul Coufos, Margaret Langrick, Jesse Ventura, M. Emmet Walsh, Donny Lalonde; *D:* Damian Lee. **VHS $79.95** *VHE, VTR* ♫

The Boxer and Death A new-wave Czech film about a boxer in a Nazi concentration camp who interests the boxing-obsessed commandant in a match. In Czech with subtitles.
1963 120m/B Stefan Kvietik; *D:* Peter Solan. **VHS, Beta $24.95** *NOS, FCT, DVT* ♫♫♫

Boxing Helena Highly publicized as the film that cost Basinger almost $9 million in damages, the debut of director/writer Jennifer Lynch (daughter of David) explores the dark side of relationships between men and women. Sands is Dr. Nick Cavanaugh, a surgeon who becomes dangerously obsessed with the beautiful, yet unattainable Helena (Fenn). When she is hit by a car near his home, he performs emergency surgery and amputates her arms and legs, forcing her to be dependent on him. Metaphorically a situation, albeit an extreme one, that mirrors the power struggle in any sexual relationship. Problematic in some aspects, although equally fascinating as it is disturbing.
1993 (R) 107m/C Julian Sands, Sherilyn Fenn, Bill Paxton, Kurtwood Smith, Betsy Clark, Nicolette Scorsese, Art Garfunkel; *D:* Jennifer Lynch; *W:* Jennifer Lynch; *M:* Graeme Revell. **VHS** *ORI* ♫♫

A Boy and His Dog In the post-holocaust world of 2024, a young man (Johnson) and his telepathic canine (McIntire supplies narration of the dog's thoughts) cohort search for food and sex. They happen upon a community that drafts Johnson to repopulate their largely impotent race; Johnson is at first ready, willing, and able, until he discovers the mechanical methods they mean to employ. Based on a short story by Harlan Ellison. The dog was played by the late Tiger of "The Brady Bunch."
1975 (R) 87m/C Don Johnson, Suzanne Benton, Jason Robards Jr., Charles McGraw, Alvy Moore; *D:* L.Q. Jones; *V:* Tim McIntire. **VHS, Beta $9.99** *CCB, MED, MRV* ♫♫ ½

Boy, Did I Get a Wrong Number! A real estate agent gets more than he bargained for when he accidentally dials a wrong number. Zany comedy persists as Hope gets entangled in the life of sexy starlet Sommer.
1966 100m/C Bob Hope, Phyllis Diller, Marjorie Lord, Elke Sommer, Cesare Danova; *D:* George Marshall. **VHS, Beta $19.98** *MGM, FCT* ♫

The Boy Friend Russell pays tribute to the Busby Berkeley Hollywood musical. Lots of charming dance numbers and clever parody of plot lines in this adaptation of Sandy Wilson's stage play. Fun! ♫The Boy Friend; I Could Be Happy; Won't You Charleston With Me?; Fancy Forgetting; Sur La Plage; A Room in Bloomsbury; Safety in Numbers; It's

Never Too Late to Fall in Love; Poor Little Pierette; Rivera; The You Don't Want To Play With Me Blues; All I Do Is Dream Of You; You Are My Lucky Star; Any Old Iron.
1971 (G) 135m/C *GB* Twiggy, Christopher Gable, Moyra Fraser, Max Adrian, Vladek Sheybal, Georgina Hale, Tommy Tune; *D:* Ken Russell; *W:* Ken Russell. VHS **$19.95** MGM 🎬🎬🎬

The Boy God Rocco here describes his trials and everyday shenanigans; he the young demi-God, battling evil on a fantasy land.
1986 100m/C Nino Muhlach; *D:* Erastheo J. Navda. VHS, **Beta $39.95** VCD 🎬

Boy in Blue A "Rocky"-esque biography of Canadian speed-rower Ned Hanlan, who set aside lackluster pursuits to turn to rowing.
1986 (R) 97m/C *CA* Nicolas Cage, Christopher Plummer, David Naughton; *D:* Charles Jarrott. VHS, **Beta $79.98** FOX 🎬½

The Boy in the Plastic Bubble Well-made, sensitive television drama about a young man born with immunity deficiencies who must grow up in a specially controlled plastic environment. Travolta is endearing as the boy in the bubble.
1976 100m/C John Travolta, Robert Reed, Glynnis O'Connor, Diana Hyland, Ralph Bellamy, Anne Ramsey; *D:* Randal Kleiser. VHS, **Beta $59.95** PSM 🎬🎬½

Boy Meets Girl Cagney and O'Brien play screenwriters whose every film is a variation on the boy meets girl theme. Trouble is they're running out of ideas and their scripts get increasingly outlandish. A fading cowboy actor is supposed to star in the duo's next film—if they can ever settle down to work. Then they get the idea to feature their friend Wilson's baby in the movie—and guess who becomes a new star. Good satire on moviemaking and movie moguls, which made fine use of the Warner studio back lots, sound stages, and offices. Based on the play by Bella and Samuel Spewack who also wrote the screenplay.
1938 86m/B James Cagney, Pat O'Brien, Ralph Bellamy, Dick Foran, Marie Wilson, Frank McHugh, Bruce Lester, Ronald Reagan, Penny Singleton, James Stephenson; *D:* Lloyd Bacon; *W:* Bella Spewack, Samuel Spewack. VHS **$19.98** MGM, FCT 🎬🎬🎬

Boy Meets Girl A French Holden Caulfield type character cruises the seamier side of Paris in this acclaimed film. Carax's directoral debut at age 22. In French with English subtitles.
1984 100m/B *FR* Denis Lavant, Mireille Perrier; *D:* Leo Carax. VHS **$49.95** FCT, MGM 🎬🎬🎬

A Boy Named Charlie Brown Charlie Brown enters the National Spelling Bee in New York and makes the final rounds with one other contestant. Based on Charles Schultz's popular comic strip characters from "Peanuts." Music by the Vince Guaraldi trio is, as always, a treat.
1970 86m/C *D:* Bill Melendez; *W:* Charles M. Schulz; *M:* Vince Guaraldi, Rod McKuen. VHS, **Beta $14.98** FOX, WTA 🎬🎬🎬

Boy of Two Worlds Because he is of a lineage foreign to his late father's town, a boy is exiled to the life of a junior Robinson Crusoe.
1970 (G) 103m/C Jimmy Sternman, Edvin Adolphson; *D:* Astrid Henning Jensen. VHS, **Beta $29.95** GEM 🎬½

Boy Takes Girl A little girl finds it hard adjusting to life on a farming cooperative during a summer recess.

1983 93m/C Gabi Eldor, Hillel Neeman, Dina Limon; *D:* Michal Bat-Adam. VHS, **Beta $59.95** MGM 🎬½

Boy! What a Girl Moore (in drag) is mistaken for a woman, and is fought over by a couple of suitors.
1945 60m/B Tim Moore, Duke Williams, Sheila Guyse, Beth Mays, Elwood Smith; *D:* Arthur Leonard. VHS, **Beta $34.95** FCT, GVV, DVT 🎬🎬

The Boy Who Could Fly After a plane crash kills his parents, a boy withdraws into a fantasy land where he can fly. The young daughter of a troubled family makes friends with him and the fantasy becomes real. A sweet film for children, charming though melancholy for adults, too. Fine cast, including Savage, Dewhurst, and Bedelia keep this from becoming sappy.
1986 (PG) 120m/C Lucy Deakins, Jay Underwood, Bonnie Bedelia, Colleen Dewhurst, Fred Savage, Fred Gwynne, Louise Fletcher, Jason Priestly; *D:* Nick Castle; *W:* Nick Castle; *M:* Bruce Broughton. VHS, **Beta $14.95** WAR, LHV 🎬🎬🎬

The Boy Who Left Home to Find Out About the Shivers From "Faerie Tale Theatre" comes this tale about a boy who learns about fear.
1981 60m/C Peter MacNicol, Christopher Lee, Vincent Price; *D:* Graeme Clifford. VHS, **Beta $14.98** KUI, FOX 🎬🎬🎬

The Boy Who Loved Trolls Paul's fantastic dreams come true when he meets Ofoeti, a real, live troll. The only problem is Ofeoti only has a day to live, and Paul must find a way to save him. Aired on PBS as part of the "Wonderworks" series.
1984 58m/C Sam Waterston, Susan Anton, Matt Dill; *D:* Harvey Laidman. VHS **$29.95** PME, HMV, FCT 🎬🎬

The Boy with the Green Hair When he hears that his parents were killed in an air raid, a boy's hair turns green. The narrow-minded members of his community suddenly want nothing to do with him and he becomes an outcast. Thought-provoking social commentary.
1948 82m/C Pat O'Brien, Robert Ryan, Barbara Hale, Dean Stockwell; *D:* Joseph Losey. VHS, **Beta $29.95** IME 🎬🎬🎬

Boyfriends & Girlfriends Another one of Rohmer's "Comedies and Proverbs," in which two girls with boyfriends fade in and out of interest with each, casually reshuffling their relationships. Typical, endless-talks-at-cafes Rohmer, the most happily consistent of the aging French New Wave. In French with subtitles. *AKA:* My Girlfriend's Boyfriend; Ami de Mon Ami.
1988 (PG) 102m/C *FR* Emmanuelle Chaulet, Sophie Renoir, Eric Viellard, Francois-Eric Gendron; *D:* Eric Rohmer; *W:* Eric Rohmer. VHS, **Beta $14.98** ORI, ING 🎬🎬½

The Boys from Brazil Based on Ira Levin's novel, a thriller about Dr. Josef Mengele endeavoring to reconstitute the Nazi movement from his Brazilian sanctuary by cloning a brood of boys from Hitler's genes.
1978 (R) 123m/C Gregory Peck, James Mason, Laurence Olivier, Uta Hagen, Steve Guttenberg, Denholm Elliott, Lilli Palmer; *D:* Franklin J. Schaffner; *W:* Heywood Gould; *M:* Jerry Goldsmith. Academy Awards '78 Nominations: Best Actor (Olivier), Best Film Editing, Best Original Score; National Board of Review Awards '78: Best Actor (Olivier). VHS, **Beta $59.98** FOX 🎬🎬½

The Boys in Company C A frank, hard-hitting drama about five naive young men involved in the Vietnam War.

1977 (R) 127m/C Stan Shaw, Andrew Stevens, James Canning, Michael Lembeck, Craig Wasson; *D:* Sidney J. Furie; *W:* Sidney J. Furie. VHS, **Beta $59.95** COL 🎬🎬

The Boys in the Band A group of gay friends get together one night for a birthday party. A simple premise with a compelling depiction of friendship, expectations, and lifestyle. One of the first serious cinematic presentations to deal with the subject of homosexuality. The film was adapted from Mart Crowley's play using the original cast.
1970 (R) 120m/C Frederick Combs, Cliff Gorman, Laurence Luckinbill, Kenneth Nelson, Leonard Frey; *D:* William Friedkin. VHS, **Beta $59.98** FOX 🎬🎬½

The Boys Next Door Two California lads kill and go nuts during a weekend in Los Angeles. Sheen overacts as a budding psychotic, not an easy thing to do. Apparently is trying to show what a particular lifestyle can lead to. Violent.
1985 (R) 90m/C Maxwell Caulfield, Charlie Sheen, Christopher McDonald, Hank Garrett, Patti D'Arbanville, Moon Zappa; *D:* Penelope Spheeris; *W:* Glen Morgan, James Wong; *M:* George S. Clinton. VHS, **Beta $19.95** STE, NWV 🎬🎬½

Boy's Night Out Amusing comedy about four businessmen who desperately want to escape the suburban doldrums by setting up an apartment equipped with plaything Novak. Little do they know, but Novak is a sociology student studying the American male, and they are merely her guinea pigs in an experiment beyond their control. Blair, Page, and Gabor provide comic relief. Based on a story by Marvin Worth and Arne Sultan.
1962 113m/C Kim Novak, James Garner, Tony Randall, Howard Duff, Janet Blair, Patti Page, Jessie Royce Landis, Oscar Homolka, Zsa Zsa Gabor; *D:* Michael Gordon; *W:* Ira Wallach. VHS **$19.98** MGM 🎬🎬

Boys of the City The East Side Kids run amuck in an eerie mansion while trying to solve the murder of a judge. *AKA:* The Ghost Creeps.
1940 63m/B Leo Gorcey, Bobby Jordan; *D:* Joseph H. Lewis. VHS, **Beta $24.95** NOS, SNC, DVT 🎬🎬

Boy's Reformatory Brothers are framed. One takes the rap, goes to the title institution, breaks out, and hunts the real bad guys. Creaky and antiquated.
1939 62m/B Frankie Darro, Grant Withers, David Durand, Warren McCollum; *D:* Howard Bretherton. VHS **$15.95** NOS, LOO 🎬½

Boys Town Righteous portrayal of Father Flanagan and the creation of Boys Town, home for juvenile soon-to-be-ex-delinquents.
1938 93m/B Spencer Tracy, Mickey Rooney, Henry Hull, Gene Reynolds, Sidney Miller, Frankie Thomas Jr.; *D:* Norman Taurog. Academy Awards '38: Best Actor (Tracy), Best Original Screenplay; Nominations: Best Director (Taurog), Best Picture, Best Screenplay. VHS, **Beta $19.98** MGM, BTV, IGP 🎬🎬🎬½

Boyz N the Hood Singleton's debut as a writer and director is an astonishing picture of young black men, four high school students with different backgrounds, aims, and abilities trying to survive Los Angeles gangs and bigotry. Excellent acting throughout, with special nods to Fishburne and Gooding, Jr. Violent outbreaks outside theaters where this ran only proves the urgency of its passionately nonviolent, pro-family message. Hopefully those viewers scared off at the time will give this a chance in the safety of their VCRs. Singleton was the youngest director ever nominated for an Oscar. The

B

laserdisc version includes two extra scenes and an interview with Singleton.

1991 (R) 112m/C Laurence "Larry" Fishburne, Ice Cube, Cuba Gooding Jr., Nia Long, Morris Chestnut, Tyra Ferrell, Angela Bassett; *D:* John Singleton; *W:* John Singleton; *M:* Stanley Clarke. Academy Awards '91 Nominations: Best Director (Singleton), Best Original Screenplay; Chicago Film Critics Awards '91: Most Promising Actor (Ice Cube); MTV Movie Awards '92: Best New Filmmaker Award (Singleton); National Board of Review Awards '91: 10 Best Films of the Year. **VHS, Beta, 8mm $19.95** COL, CRC, FCT 𝄞𝄞𝄞 ½

Braddock: Missing in Action 3 The battle-scarred, high-kicking 'Nam vet battles his way into the jungles once more, this time to rescue his long-lost Vietnamese family. A family effort, Chuck co-wrote the script; his brother directed.

1988 (R) 104m/C Chuck Norris, Aki Aleong, Roland Harrah III; *D:* Aaron Norris; *W:* Chuck Norris. **VHS, Beta $9.98** MED, CCB, VTR 𝄞

The Brady Bunch, Vol. 1 Four episodes from tv's grooviest family. "The Honeymoon" premiere episode tells how Mike and his 3 boys get hitched to Carol and her 3 girls. "Dear Libby" finds the kids worried about the newlyweds after reading an advice column letter. "Alice Doesn't Live Here Any More" finds housekeeper Alice worried she's not needed. Marica tries to win Mike the "Father of the Year" award. Additional episodes available.

1969 120m/C Robert Reed, Florence Henderson, Ann B. Davis, Maureen McCormick, Barry Williams, Eve Plumb, Christopher Knight, Michael Lookinland, Susan Olsen. **VHS** CMB 𝄞

Brady's Escape American WWII pilot is shot down in the Hungarian countryside and befriended by Hungarian csikos (cowboys) in this made-for-cable television movie. *AKA:* The Long Ride.

1984 92m/C HU John Savage, Kelly Reno; *D:* Pal Gabor. **VHS, Beta $9.95** CAF 𝄞 ½

The Brain A scientist learns that a mind isn't always a terrible thing to waste when he finds himself being manipulated by the brain of a dead man he's trying to keep alive. Remake of "Donovan's Brain" (1953). *AKA:* Vengeance.

1962 83m/B GB GE Anne Heywood, Peter Van Eyck, Bernard Lee, Cecil Parker, Jack MacGowran; *D:* Freddie Francis. **VHS, Beta $19.95** NOS, SNC 𝄞𝄞 ½

The Brain Run of the mill comedy caper has Niven planning to heist millions from a NATO train. The caper begins when lots of other crooks decide to rob the same train. The cast holds this one together. *AKA:* Le Cerveau.

1969 (G) 100m/C FR David Niven, Jean-Paul Belmondo, Bourvil, Eli Wallach, Silvia Monti, Fernand Valois; *D:* Gerard Oury; *M:* Georges Delerue. **VHS** PAR 𝄞𝄞

The Brain Dr. Blake, host of a popular TV talk-show, is in league with a power-hungry alien brain. Viewers of his show kill themselves and others in the midst of many special effects. The ratings go down.

1988 (R) 94m/C Tom Breznahan, Cyndy Preston, David Gale; *D:* Edward Hunt. **VHS, Beta $14.95** LIV 𝄞 ½

Brain Damage A tongue-in-bloody-cheek farce about a brain-sucking parasite. The parasite in question, Aylmer, addicts our dubious hero to the euphoria induced by the blue liquid the parasite injects into his brain, paving the way for the bloody mayhem that follows. Poor shadow of Henenlotter's far-superior "Basket Case." In fact, it even includes an inside-joke cameo by Van Hen-

tenryck, reprising his "Basket Case" character; look for him on the subway.

1988 (R) 89m/C Rick Herbst, Gordon MacDonald, Jennifer Lowry; *Cameos:* Kevin Van Hentenryck; *D:* Frank Henenlotter. **VHS, Beta $14.95** PAR 𝄞𝄞

Brain Dead Low-budget but brilliantly assembled puzzle-film about a brain surgeon who agrees to perform experimental surgery on a psychotic to retrieve some corporately valuable data—his first mistake, which begins a seemingly endless cycle of nightmares and identity alterations. A mind-blowing sci-fi feast from ex-"Twilight Zone" writer Charles Beaumont.

1989 (R) 85m/C Bill Pullman, Bill Paxton, Bud Cort, Patricia Charbonneau, Nicholas Pryor, George Kennedy; *D:* Adam Simon. **VHS, Beta $14.95** MGM 𝄞𝄞𝄞 ½

Brain Donors Goofy, uneven film starring Turturro as a sleazy lawyer trying to take over the Oglethorpe Ballet Company by sweet-talking its aged patronness. He is helped by two eccentric friends, and together the three crack a lot of bad but witty jokes. The film culminates into a hilarious ballet scene featuring someone giving CPR to the ballerina playing the dying swan, an actor in a duck suit, duck hunters, and a pack of hounds. This trio reminds us of second-rate Marx Brothers (or the Three Stooges) but the movie has enough funny moments to be worth a watch.

1992 (PG) 79m/C John Turturro, Bob Nelson, Mel Smith, Nancy Marchand, John Savident, George de la Pena, Juli Donald, Spike Alexander, Teri Copley; *D:* Dennis Dugan; *W:* Pat Proft; *M:* Ira Newborn. **VHS, Beta $14.95** PAR 𝄞𝄞 ½

The Brain Eaters A strange ship from inside the Earth invades a small town, and hairy monsters promptly attach themselves to people's necks in a daring bid to control the planet. The imaginative story compensates somewhat for the cheap special effects. Watch for Nimoy before he grew pointed ears.

1958 60m/B Edwin Nelson, Alan Frost, Jack Hill, Joanna Lee, Jody Fair, Leonard Nimoy; *D:* Bruno Ve Sota. **VHS $9.95** NOS, CNM 𝄞𝄞

The Brain from Planet Arous Lassie meets Alien when an evil alien brain appropriates the body of a scientist in order to take over planet Earth. His plans are thwarted, however, by a good alien brain that likewise inhabits the body of the scientist's dog. High camp and misdemeanors.

1957 80m/B John Agar, Joyce Meadows, Robert Fuller, Henry Travis; *D:* Nathan Juran. **VHS, Beta $19.95** RHI, SNC, CNM 𝄞

Brain of Blood Deals with a scientist who transplants the brain of a politician into the body of a deformed idiot. The change is minimal. *AKA:* The Creature's Revenge.

1971 107m/C Kent Taylor, John Bloom, Regina Carrol, Angelo Rossitto, Grant Williams, Reed Hadley, Vicki Volante, Zandor Vorkov; *D:* Al Adamson. **VHS, Beta** NO Woof!

Brain Smasher...A Love Story A bouncer and a super model become the targets of a gang of killer ninjas who want the mysterious blood-red lotus the model's been given. Of course they do. What's the lovely Hatcher doing in such a stupid movie?

1993 (PG-13) 88m/C Andrew Dice Clay, Teri Hatcher; *D:* Albert Pyun. **VHS $92.95** VMK 𝄞

The Brain That Wouldn't Die Love is a many-splattered thing when a brilliant surgeon keeps the decapitated head of his fiancee alive after an auto accident while he searches for a suitably stacked body onto which to transplant the head. Absurd and

satiric (head talks so much that Doc tapes her/its mouth shut) adding up to major entry in trash film genre; much of the gore was slashed for the video, however. *AKA:* The Head That Wouldn't Die.

1963 92m/B Herb Evers, Virginia Leith, Adele Lamont; *D:* Joseph Green. **VHS, Beta $19.98** SNC, MRV, FCT 𝄞𝄞 ½

The Brainiac Sorcerer sentenced for black magic returns to strike dark deeds upon the descendants of those who judged him. He turns himself into a hideous monster, feeding on his victims' brains and blood. Yuck.

1961 75m/B MX Abel Salazar, Ariadne Welter, Mauricio Garces, Rosa Maria Gallardo. **VHS, Beta $54.95** SNC, MRV, HHT 𝄞 ½

Brainscan Teenage loner takes a trip in virtual reality and finds that murder is the first stop. Furlong ("Terminator 2") is the troubled youth whose voyage is led by Smith as Trickster, the Freddy Krueger meets David Bowie tour guide from virtual hell. Langella turns in a straight performance as a local cop hot on the trail. Hard-core horror fans will be disappointed by the lack of on-screen violence, and special effects buffs won't see anything new. Lame effort tries to appeal to a wide audience and is bland as a result. The end is left wide open, so expect a sequel or two or three.

1994 (R) 95m/C Edward Furlong, Frank Langella, T. Ryder Smith, David Hemblen, Amy Hargreaves, Jamie Marsh, Victor Ertmanis; *D:* John Flynn; *W:* Andrew Kevin Walker; *M:* George S. Clinton. **VHS** NYR 𝄞

Brainstorm Husband-and-wife scientist team invents headphones that can record dreams, thoughts, and fantasies (VCR-style) and then allow other people to experience them by playing back the tape. Their marriage begins to crumble as the husband becomes more and more obsessed with pushing the limits of the technology; things get worse when the government wants to exploit their discovery. Special effects and interesting camerawork punctuate this sci-fi flick. Wood's last film; in fact, she died before production was completed.

1983 (PG) 106m/C Natalie Wood, Christopher Walken, Cliff Robertson, Louise Fletcher; *D:* Douglas Trumbull; *W:* Bruce Joel Rubin; *M:* James Horner. **VHS, Beta $14.95** MGM 𝄞𝄞 ½

Brainwaves A young woman has disturbing flashbacks after her brain is electrically revived following a car accident. Curtis is the demented doctor who jump-starts her.

1982 (R) 83m/C Suzanna Love, Tony Curtis, Keir Dullea, Vera Miles; *D:* Ulli Lommel; *W:* Ulli Lommel. **VHS, Beta $24.98** SUE 𝄞

Bram Stoker's Dracula Coppola's highly charged view of the vampire classic is visually stunning, heavy on eroticism and violence, and weak in plot and performance. Oldman, in a number of amazing transformations, portrays the deadly bloodsucker as a lonely soul determined to reunite with his lost love, the innocent Ryder. Hopkins cheerfully chews the scenery as nemesis Van Helsing, newcomer Frost is fetching, Reeves is lightweight, and Ryder goes way over the top. Musician Waits is great as bug-eating madman Renfield. Filmed entirely on soundstages with beautiful costumes and some amazing visual effects and sets. Laserdisc includes "The Making of Bram Stoker's Dracula." *AKA:* Dracula.

1992 (R) 128m/C Gary Oldman, Winona Ryder, Anthony Hopkins, Keanu Reeves, Richard E. Grant, Cary Elwes, Bill Campbell, Sadie Frost, Tom Waits; *D:* Francis Ford Coppola; *W:* Jim V. Hart. Academy Awards '92: Best Costume Design, Best Makeup, Best Sound Effects

Editing; Nominations: Best Art Direction/Set Decoration. **VHS, Beta, 8mm** $19.95 COL ♂♂

The Bramble Bush Guy (Burton) is a doctor who returns to his New England hometown to care for a dying friend, Larry (Drake). Unfortunately, Guy falls for Larry's wife Mar (Rush) and they have an affair. When Guy pulls the plug on his friend's suffering, suspicious townspeople (who of course know what's going on) wonder just how "merciful" the doctor was really being and he's tried for murder. Tawdry "Peyton Place"-ish soap opera based on the novel by Charles Mergendahl.
1960 104m/C Richard Burton, Barbara Rush, Tom Drake, Jack Carson, Angie Dickinson, James Dunn, Henry Jones, Frank Conroy, Carl Benton Reid; **D:** Daniel Petrie; **W:** Philip Yordan. **VHS** $29.99 WAR ♂♂½

Brand New Life A childless couple in their 40s are unexpectedly confronted by the wife's first pregnancy. Both have careers and well-ordered lives that promise to be disrupted.
1972 74m/C Cloris Leachman, Martin Balsam, Wilfrid Hyde-White, Mildred Dunnock; **D:** Sam O'Steen; **M:** Billy Goldenberg. **VHS, Beta** LCA ♂

Brand of Fear Crooning cowpoke Wakely puts down his guitar long enough to chase rustlers off the land of an innocent lady in this average oater.
1949 56m/B Jimmy Wakely, Dub Taylor, Gail Davis, Tom London; **D:** Oliver Drake; **W:** Basil Dickey. **VHS** $19.99 MOV ♂½

Brand of Hate A good cowboy rustles up a gang of rustlers.
1934 61m/B Bob Steele, George "Gabby" Hayes, Lucille Browne, James Flavin; **D:** Lewis Collins. **VHS, Beta** $19.95 NOS, RXM ♂

Brand of the Outlaws A cowboy becomes an unwitting aid to rustlers in this early western.
1936 56m/B Bob Steele, Margaret Marquis, Virginia True Boardman, Jack Rockwell; **D:** Robert North Bradbury. **VHS, Beta** $19.95 NOS, DVT ♂

Branded Ladd (pre-"Shane") impersonates the long-gone son of rich rancher Bickford, with unusual results. Nicely balanced action and love scenes make this old Max Brand story a better-than-average western. Filmed in Technicolor.
1950 95m/C Alan Ladd, Mona Freeman, Charles Bickford, Joseph Calleia, Milburn Stone; **D:** Rudolph Mate. **VHS** $14.95 PAR ♂♂½

Branded a Coward A man whose parents were killed seeks revenge via his trusty six-shooters.
1935 56m/B Johnny Mack Brown, Billie Seward, Yakima Canutt; **D:** Sam Newfield. **VHS, Beta** $19.95 NOS, DVT ♂

Branded Men A couple of oddballs become mixed up in a number of zany, western-type adventures.
1931 60m/B Ken Maynard, June Clyde, Irving Bacon, Billy Bletcher, Charles "Blackie" King, Donald Keith; **D:** Phil Rosen. **VHS** $19.95 NOS ♂♂

Brandy Sheriff A former outlaw tries to make up for the time he lost in prison. In Spanish.
1978 90m/C SP Alex Nicol, Maria Contrera, Antonio Casas. **VHS, Beta** $59.95 HHT ♂½

Brannigan The Duke stars in the somewhat unfamiliar role of a rough and tumble Chicago police officer. He travels across the Atlantic to arrest a racketeer who has fled the States rather than face a grand jury indictment. Humor and action abound.

1975 (PG) 111m/C John Wayne, John Vernon, Mel Ferrer, Daniel Pilon, James Booth, Ralph Meeker, Lesley-Anne Down, Richard Attenborough; **D:** Douglas Hickox; **W:** Michael Butler, William W. Norton Sr. **VHS, Beta** $19.98 MGM, FOX ♂♂½

Brass First post-Archie Bunker role for O'Connor, who plods through this average police drama at a snail's pace, dragging everything else down with him. Made-for-TV pilot for a series that never aired.
1985 (PG) 94m/C Carroll O'Connor, Lois Nettleton, Jimmie Baird, Paul Shenar, Vincent Gardenia, Anita Gillette; **D:** Corey Allen. **VHS** $19.98 ORI ♂½

Brass Target Hypothetical thriller about a plot to kill George Patton in the closing days of WWII for the sake of $250 million in Nazi gold stolen by his staff. Interesting cast can't find story.
1978 (PG) 111m/C Sophia Loren, George Kennedy, Max von Sydow, John Cassavetes, Patrick McGoohan, Robert Vaughn, Bruce Davison, Edward Herrmann, Ed Bishop; **D:** John Hough. **VHS, Beta** $59.95 MGM ♂½

The Bravados A rough, distressing Western revenge tale, wherein a man is driven to find the four men who murdered his wife. In tracking the perpetrators, Peck realizes that he has been corrupted by his vengeance.
1958 98m/C Gregory Peck, Stephen Boyd, Joan Collins, Albert Salmi, Henry Silva, Lee Van Cleef, George Voskovec, Barry Coe; **D:** Henry King; **W:** Philip Yordan. **VHS, Beta** $39.98 FOX ♂♂♂

The Brave Bunch A courageous Greek soldier tries to save his men and country during WWII.
1970 110m/C GR Peter Funk, John Miller; **D:** Dacosta Carayan. **VHS, Beta** $39.95 LIV ♂½

The Brave One A love story between a Spanish boy and the bull who saves his life. The animal is later carted off to the bull ring. Award-winning screenplay by the then-blacklisted Trumbo, as "Robert Rich."
1956 100m/C Michael Ray, Rodolpho Moyos, Joi Lansing; **D:** Irving Rapper; **W:** Dalton Trumbo. Academy Awards '56: Best Original Screenplay; Nominations: Best Film Editing. **VHS, Beta** $49.95 VCI ♂♂♂

Braveheart When a Native American adapts to the white man's world, he alienates his own people. He eventually chooses to renounce his love for a white woman, and returns to lead his people. Silent.
1925 ?m/B Rod La Rocque; **D:** Alan Hale. **VHS, Beta, 8mm** $55.95 GVV ♂♂♂

Brazil The acclaimed nightmare comedy about an Everyman trying to survive in a surreal paper-choked bureaucratic society. There are copious references to "1984" and "The Trial," fantastic mergings of glorious fantasy and stark reality, and astounding visual design.
1985 (R) 131m/C GB Jonathan Pryce, Robert De Niro, Michael Palin, Katherine Helmond, Kim Greist, Bob Hoskins, Ian Holm, Peter Vaughan, Ian Richardson; **D:** Terry Gilliam; **W:** Terry Gilliam, Tom Stoppard; **M:** Michael Kamen. Academy Awards '85 Nominations: Best Art Direction/Set Decoration, Best Original Screenplay; Los Angeles Film Critics Association Awards '85: Best Film. **VHS, Beta** $19.95 MCA, FCT ♂♂♂½

Break of Hearts Hepburn marries Boyer, who becomes an alcoholic, and then more troubles arise. Very soapy, but well-made.
1935 78m/B Katharine Hepburn, Charles Boyer, Jean Hersholt, John Beal, Sam Hardy; **D:** Phillip Moeller. **VHS, Beta** $19.98 TTC ♂♂½

Breakdown A boxer is set up by his girlfriend's father to take the rap for a murder. Lackluster effort.
1953 76m/B Ann Richards, William Bishop, Anne Gwynne, Sheldon Leonard, Wally Cassell, Richard Benedict; **D:** Edmond Angelo. **VHS, Beta** $16.95 NOS, SNC ♂

Breaker! Breaker! Convoy of angry truck drivers launch an assault on the corrupt and sadistic locals of a small Texas town. Goofy entry in "mad or sex-crazed trucker armed with a CB radio" genre.
1977 (PG) 86m/C Chuck Norris, George Murdock; **D:** Don Hulette. **VHS, Beta** $9.98 SUE ♂

Breaker Morant In 1901 South Africa, three Australian soldiers are put on trial for avenging the murder of several prisoners. Based on a true story which was then turned into a play by Kenneth Ross, this riveting, popular antiwar statement and courtroom drama heralded Australia's film renaissance. Rich performances by Woodward and Waters.
1980 (PG) 107m/C AU Edward Woodward, Jack Thompson, John Waters, Bryan Brown; **D:** Bruce Beresford; **W:** Jonathon Hardy, David Stevens, Bruce Beresford. Academy Awards '80 Nominations: Best Adapted Screenplay; Cannes Film Festival '80: Best Film; Australian Film Institute '80: Best Actor (Thompson), Best Film. **VHS, Beta, 8mm** $9.99 CCB, COL, HMV ♂♂♂½

Breakfast at Tiffany's Truman Capote's amusing story of an endearingly eccentric New York City playgirl and her shaky romance with a young writer. Hepburn lends Holly Golightly just the right combination of naivete and worldly wisdom with a dash of melancholy. A wonderfully offbeat romance.
1961 114m/C Audrey Hepburn, George Peppard, Patricia Neal, Buddy Ebsen, Mickey Rooney, Martin Balsam, John McGiver; **D:** Blake Edwards; **W:** George Axelrod; **M:** Henry Mancini. Academy Awards '61: Best Song ("Moon River"), Best Original Score; Nominations: Best Actress (Hepburn), Best Adapted Screenplay, Best Art Direction/Set Decoration (Color). **VHS, Beta, 8mm** $14.95 PAR, FCT ♂♂♂½

The Breakfast Club Five students from different cliques at a Chicago suburban high school spend a day together in detention. Rather well done teenage culture study; these characters delve a little deeper than the standard adult view of adolescent stereotypes. One of John Hughes' best movies. Soundtrack features Simple Minds and Wang Chung.
1985 (R) 97m/C Ally Sheedy, Molly Ringwald, Judd Nelson, Emilio Estevez, Anthony Michael Hall, Paul Gleason, John Kapelos; **D:** John Hughes; **W:** John Hughes; **M:** Gary Chang, Keith Forsey. **VHS, Beta** $19.95 MCA, FCT ♂♂♂

Breakfast in Hollywood Movie about the popular morning radio show of the 1940s hosted by Tom Breneman, a coast-to-coast coffee klatch. **AKA:** The Mad Hatter.
1946 93m/B Tom Breneman, Bonita Granville, Eddie Ryan, Beulah Bondi, Billie Burke, ZaSu Pitts, Hedda Hopper, Spike Jones; **D:** Harold Schuster. **VHS, Beta** $29.95 NO ♂½

Breakfast in Paris Two American professionals in Paris, both crushed from past failures in the love department, find each other.
1981 85m/C AU Rod Mullinar, Barbara Parkins, Jack Lenoir; **D:** John Lamond. **VHS, Beta** $19.95 STE, NWV ♂½

Breakheart Pass A governor, his female companion, a band of cavalrymen, and a mysterious man travel on a train through the mountains of Idaho in 1870. The mystery man turns out to be a murderer. Based on a novel by Alistair MacLean.

B

1976 (PG) 92m/C Charles Bronson, Ben Johnson, Richard Crenna, Jill Ireland, Charles Durning, Ed Lauter, Archie Moore; *D:* Tom Gries; *M:* Jerry Goldsmith. VHS, Beta $19.98 *MGM, FOX* 🎬🎬

Breakin' Dance phenomenon break dancing along with the hit songs that accompanied the fad. ♫Tibetan Jam; Heart of the Beat; Breakin...There's No Stopping Us; Street People; Showdown; 99 1/2. *AKA:* Breakdance.
1984 (PG) 87m/C Lucinda Dickey, Adolfo "Shabba Doo" Quinones, Michael "Boogaloo Shrimp" Chambers, Ben Lokey, Christopher McDonald, Phineas Newborn III; *D:* Joel Silberg. VHS, Beta $79.95 *MGM* 🎬

Breakin' 2: Electric Boogaloo Breakdancers hold a benefit concert to preserve an urban community center. ♫Electric Boogaloo; Radiotron; Action; When I.C.U. *AKA:* Breakdance 2: Electric Boogaloo; Electric Boogaloo "Breakin' 2".
1984 (PG) 94m/C Lucinda Dickey, Adolfo "Shabba Doo" Quinones, Michael "Boogaloo Shrimp" Chambers, Susie Bono; *D:* Sam Firstenberg. VHS, Beta $79.95 *MGM* 🎬

Breakin' Through The choreographer of a troubled Broadway-bound musical decides to energize his shows with a troupe of street dancers.
1984 73m/C Ben Vereen, Donna McKechnie, Reid Shelton; *D:* Peter Medak. VHS, Beta $69.95 *DIS* 🎬

Breaking All the Rules Comedy about two teenage lovers who find themselves embroiled in a slapdash jewel robbery at an amusement park during the last day of summer break.
1985 (R) 91m/C *CA* Carolyn Dunn, Carl Marotte, Thor Bishopric, Rachel Hayward; *D:* James Orr; *W:* James Orr. VHS, Beta $14.95 *NWV, STE* 🎬½

Breaking Away A light-hearted coming-of-age drama about a high school graduate's addiction to bicycle racing, whose dreams are tested against the realities of a crucial race. An honest, open look at present Americana with tremendous insight into the minds of average youth; shot on location at Indiana University. Great bike-racing photography. Quaid, Barrie, and Christopher give exceptional performances. Basis for television series.
1979 (PG) 100m/C Dennis Christopher, Dennis Quaid, Daniel Stern, Jackie Earle Haley, Barbara Barrie, Paul Dooley, Amy Wright; *D:* Peter Yates; *W:* Steve Tesich. Academy Awards '79: Best Original Screenplay; Nominations: Best Director (Yates), Best Picture, Best Supporting Actress (Barrie), Best Original Score; Golden Globe Awards '80: Best Film—Musical/Comedy; National Board of Review Awards '79: 10 Best Films of the Year, Best Supporting Actor (Dooley). VHS, Beta $59.98 *FOX, HMV* 🎬🎬🎬½

Breaking Glass A "New Wave" musical that gives an insight into the punk record business and at the same time tells of the rags-to-riches life of a punk rock star.
1980 (PG) 94m/C *GB* Hazel O'Connor, Phil Daniels, Jon Finch, Jonathan Pryce; *D:* Brian Gibson. VHS, Beta $49.95 *PAR* 🎬🎬½

Breaking Home Ties Norman Rockwell's illustration is the basis for this coming of age story set in a small Texas town. A young man is eager to be off to college and lessen his family ties but his mother's serious illness may prevent both. Good performances help overcome the sentimentality. Originally made for television. *AKA:* Norman Rockwell's Breaking Home Ties.
1987 95m/C Jason Robards Jr., Eva Marie Saint, Doug McKeon, Claire Trevor, Erin Gray; *D:* John Wilder; *W:* John Wilder. VHS $79.95 *CAF* 🎬🎬½

Breaking In A semi-acclaimed comedy about a professional thief who takes a young amateur under his wing and shows him the ropes. Under-estimated Reynolds is especially charming. Witty and innovative script, with intelligent direction from Forsyth.
1989 (R) 95m/C Burt Reynolds, Casey Siemaszko, Sheila Kelley, Lorraine Toussaint, Albert Salmi, Harry Carey Jr., Maury Chaykin, Stephen Tobolowsky, David Frishberg; *D:* Bill Forsyth; *W:* John Sayles; *M:* Michael Gibbs. VHS, Beta $14.95 *HBO, WAR* 🎬🎬🎬

Breaking Loose A surfer is on the run from a vicious motorcycle gang that kidnapped his girlfriend, but turns to fight eventually, board in hand.
1990 (R) 88m/C Peter Phelps, Vince Martin, Abigail, David Ngcombujarra; *D:* Rod Hay. VHS $14.95 *HMD* 🎬🎬

Breaking the Ice Unlikely mixture of Mennonites and a big city ice skating show. Young man leaves the farm to get a job singing at the rink. Musical numbers abound with backing by Victor Young and his Orchestra.
1938 79m/B Bobby Breen, Charlie Ruggles, Dolores Costello, Billy Gilbert, Margaret Hamilton. VHS, Beta $19.95 *NOS, VYY, DVT* 🎬🎬

Breaking the Rules Predicatable buddy-road movie with a tearjerking premise and comedic overtones. Rob, Gene, and Phil were best buds growing up in Cleveland but young adulthood has separated them. They are reunited by Phil, who is dying of leukemia, and whose last wish is a cross-country road trip to California so he can appear as a contestant on "Jeopardy." Along the way they meet brassy waitress Mary, who impulsively decides to join them and winds up bringing the trio's shaky friendship back together. Potts does well as the big-haired, big-hearted Mary but the actors must work hard to maintain any dignity given the story's melodrama.
1992 (PG-13) 100m/C Jason Bateman, C. Thomas Howell, Jonathan Silverman, Annie Potts, Kent Bateman, Shawn Phelan; *D:* Neal Israel; *W:* Paul Shapiro; *M:* David Kitay. VHS $92.99 *HBO* 🎬🎬½

Breaking Up A woman fights to rediscover her personal identity after her fifteen-year marriage crumbles. Made for television. Emmy nominated.
1978 90m/C Lee Remick, Granville Van Dusen, David Stambaugh; *D:* Delbert Mann. VHS, Beta *TLF* 🎬🎬½

Breaking Up Is Hard to Do Six men leave their wives and shack up together on Malibu for a summer of partying and introspection. Made for television; edited down from its original 201 minute length.
1979 96m/C Billy Crystal, Bonnie Franklin, Ted Bessell, Jeff Conaway, Tony Musante, Robert Conrad, Trish Stewart, David Ogden Stiers, George Gaynes; *D:* Lou Antonio. VHS, Beta $9.99 *VMK, STE* 🎬

Breaking with Old Ideas A film made in the waning years of Mao's Cultural Revolution about the construction of a college of workers. In Chinese with subtitles.
1975 126m/C *CH D:* Li Wen-Hua. VHS, Beta $39.95 *FCT* 🎬🎬

Breakout The wife of a man imprisoned in Mexico hires a Texas bush pilot (Bronson) to help her husband (Duvall) escape.
1975 (PG) 96m/C Charles Bronson, Jill Ireland, Robert Duvall, John Huston, Sheree North, Randy Quaid; *D:* Tom Gries; *M:* Jerry Goldsmith. VHS, Beta $64.95 *COL* 🎬🎬

Breakthrough German soldier, broken at the end of WWII, sets out to negotiate with the Allies. Average at best. *AKA:* Sergeant Steiner.
1978 (PG) 96m/C Richard Burton, Robert Mitchum, Rod Steiger, Michael Parks, Curt Jurgens; *D:* Andrew V. McLaglen. VHS, Beta $9.95 *WOV* 🎬🎬

Breath of Scandal An American diplomat in Vienna rescues a princess when she is thrown off a horse; he falls for her like a ton o' bricks. Viennese politics complicate things. Based on a play by Molnar.
1960 98m/C Sophia Loren, John Gavin, Maurice Chevalier, Angela Lansbury; *D:* Michael Curtiz. VHS *PAR, BAR* 🎬🎬

Breathing Fire A Vietnamese teenager and his American brother find out their ex-GI father is behind an armed bank robbery and murder. They join together to protect the only eyewitness—a young girl—against the ruthless gang of criminals and their own father. Lots of kickboxing action for martial arts fans.
1991 (R) 86m/C Bolo Yeung, Jonathan Ke Quan, Jerry Trimble; *D:* Lou Kennedy. VHS $89.98 *IMP* 🎬🎬

Breathless Godard's first feature catapulted him to the vanguard of French filmmakers. A carefree Parisian crook, who emulates Humphrey Bogart, falls in love with an American girl with tragic results. Wonderful scenes of Parisian life. Established Godard's Brechtian, experimental style. Belmondo's film debut. Mistitled "Breathless" for American release, the film's French title actually means "Out of Breath"; however, the fast-paced, erratic musical score leaves you breathless. French with English subtitles. Remade with Richard Gere in 1983 with far less intensity. *AKA:* A Bout de Souffle.
1959 90m/B *FR* Jean-Paul Belmondo, Jean Seberg, Daniel Boulanger, Jean-Pierre Melville, Liliane Robin; *D:* Jean-Luc Godard; *W:* Jean-Luc Godard. VHS, Beta $24.95 *NOS, MRV, CVC* 🎬🎬🎬🎬

Breathless Car thief turned cop killer has a torrid love affair with a French student studying in Los Angeles as the police slowly close in. Glossy, smarmy remake of the Godard classic that concentrates on the thin plot rather than any attempt at revitalizing the film syntax.
1983 (R) 105m/C Richard Gere, Valerie Kaprisky, Art Metrano, John P. Ryan, Lisa Jane Persky; *D:* Jim McBride; *W:* Jim McBride, L.M. Kit Carson; *M:* Jack Nitzsche. VHS, Beta $29.98 *VES* 🎬🎬

A Breed Apart An on-going battle over a rare eagle's eggs strikes sparks between a reclusive conservationist and a scheming adventurer hired by a billionaire collector.
1984 (R) 95m/C Kathleen Turner, Rutger Hauer, Powers Boothe, Donald Pleasence, Brion James, John Dennis Johnston; *D:* Philippe Mora. VHS, Beta $14.95 *HMD* 🎬🎬

Breed of the Border Tough-fisted cowboys must take the law into their own hands.
1933 60m/B Bob Steele, Marion Byron, George "Gabby" Hayes, Ernie Adams; *D:* Robert North Bradbury. VHS, Beta $19.95 *NOS, DVT* 🎬

Brenda Starr Amateurish adaptation of the comic strip by Dale Messick. Shields stars as girl reporter Brenda Starr, who is once again risking her life to get the scoop. She finds herself in the jungles of South America searching for a mad scientist who is creating a rocket fuel that could destroy the world. The most entertaining thing about this film is the costumes designed by Bob Mackie.

1986 (PG) 94m/C Brooke Shields, Timothy Dalton, Tony Peck, Diana Scarwid, Nestor Serrano, Jeffrey Tambor, June Gable, Charles Durning, Eddie Albert, Henry Gibson, Ed Nelson; **D:** Robert Ellis Miller; **W:** James David Buchanan. VHS COL ✗

The Bretts Amusing two-part British miniseries follows the egos and eccentricities of the British theatrical dynasty, the Bretts. Part 1 is set in the '20s and introduces the family heads, Charles (Rodway) and Lydia (Murray), who enjoy performing off-stage almost as well as they enjoy performing on. Also introduced are their five children and loyal (if opinionated) servants. Part 2 follows the family into the 30s with son Edwin (Yelland) having become a film star, actress daughter Martha (Lang) falling for a politician, and son Tom (Winter) continuing to write his gloomy social dramas. Each part is on 6 cassettes. 1988 600m/C GB Barbara Murray, Norman Rodway, David Yelland, Belinda Lang, George Winter, Janet Maw, Tim Wylton, Bert Parnaby, Lysette Anthony, Clive Francis, Frank Middlemass, John Castle, Hugh Fraser, Patrick Ryecart, Sally Cookson, Billy Boyle; **W:** Rosemary Anne Sisson. VHS $129.95 SIG ✗✗✗

Brewster McCloud Altman's first picture after M*A*S*H reunites much of the cast and combines fantasy, black comedy, and satire in the story of a young man whose head is in the clouds or at least in the upper reaches of the Houston Astrodome. Brewster (Cort) lives covertly in the Dome and dreams of flying. He also has a guardian angel (Kellerman) who watches over him and may actually be killing people who give him a hard time. Murphy is a cop obsessed with catching the killer. And there's a circus allegory as well. Hard to figure what it all means and offbeat as they come, but for certain tastes, exquisite. 1970 (R) 101m/C Bud Cort, Sally Kellerman, Shelley Duvall, Michael Murphy, William Windom, Rene Auberjonois, Stacy Keach, John Schuck, Margaret Hamilton; **D:** Robert Altman. VHS, Beta $19.98 MGM ✗✗✗½

Brewster's Millions If Brewster, an ex-GI, can spend a million dollars in one year, he will inherit a substantially greater fortune. Originally a 1902 novel, this is the fifth of seven film adaptations. 1945 79m/B Dennis O'Keefe, June Havoc, Eddie Anderson, Helen Walker, Gail Patrick, Mischa Auer; **D:** Allan Dwan. VHS, Beta $19.95 MED ✗✗½

Brewster's Millions An aging minor league baseball player must spend 30 million dollars in order to collect an inheritance of 300 million dollars. He may find that money can't buy happiness. Seventh remake of the story. 1985 (PG) 101m/C Richard Pryor, John Candy, Lonette McKee, Stephen Collins, Jerry Orbach, Pat Hingle, Tovah Feldshuh, Hume Cronyn, Rick Moranis; **D:** Walter Hill; **W:** Herschel Weingrod, Timothy Harris; **M:** Ry Cooder. VHS, Beta $19.95 MCA ✗½

Brian's Song The story of the unique relationship between Gale Sayers, the Chicago Bears' star running back, and his teammate Brian Piccolo. The friendship between the Bears' first interracial roommates ended suddenly when Brian Piccolo lost his life to cancer. Made for television. Incredibly well-received in its time. 1971 (G) 74m/C James Caan, Billy Dee Williams, Jack Warden, Shelley Fabares, Judy Pace; **D:** Buzz Kulik. VHS, Beta $64.95 COL ✗✗✗✗

The Bride Re-telling of "The Bride of Frankenstein." Sting's Dr. Frankenstein has much more success in creating his second monster (Beals). She's pretty and intelligent and he may even be falling in love with her. When she begins to gain too much independence, though, the awful truth about her origins comes out. Fans of the two leads will want to see this one, but for a true classic see Elsa Lanchester's bride. 1985 (PG-13) 118m/C Sting, Jennifer Beals, Anthony Higgins, David Rappaport, Geraldine Page, Clancy Brown, Phil Daniels, Veruschka; **D:** Franc Roddam; **M:** Maurice Jarre. VHS, Beta $9.95 FOX ✗½

The Bride & the Beast While on an African safari honeymoon, a big game hunter's new bride is carried off by a gorilla. Ludicrous jungle tale. **AKA:** Queen of the Gorillas. 1958 78m/B Charlotte Austin, Lance Fuller, William Justine; **D:** Adrian Weiss; **W:** Edward D. Wood Jr.; **M:** Les Baxter. VHS, Beta AOV Woof!

The Bride Came C.O.D. Rough'n'tough pilot Cagney is hired by a rich Texas oil man to prevent his daughter (the one with the Bette Davis eyes) from marrying cheesy bandleader Carson. The payoff: $10 per pound if she's delivered unwed. What a surprise when Cagney faces the timeworn dilemma of having to choose between love and money. A contemporary issue of "Time" magazine trumpeted: "Screen's most talented tough guy rough-houses one of screen's best dramatic actresses." That tells you right there it's a romantic comedy. Cagney and Davis—a likely pairing, you'd think—are essentially fish out of water, bothered and bewildered by a weak script. 1941 92m/B Bette Davis, James Cagney, Stuart Erwin, Jack Carson, George Tobias, Eugene Pallette, William Frawley; **D:** William Keighley; **W:** Julius J. Epstein, Philip C. Epstein. VHS $19.95 MGM, FCT ✗✗

The Bride Is Much Too Beautiful Bardot, playing a French farm girl, becomes a renowned model. Dubbed. 1958 90m/C FR Brigitte Bardot, Louis Jourdan, Micheline Presle, Marcel Amont; **D:** Fred Surin. VHS, Beta $29.95 NOS, FCT, HEG ✗✗½

The Bride of Frankenstein The classic sequel to the classic original in which Dr. F. seeks to build a mate for his monster. More humor than the first, but also more pathos, including the monster's famous but short-lived friendship with a blind hermit. Lanchester plays both the bride and Mary Shelley in the opening sequence. 1935 75m/B Boris Karloff, Elsa Lanchester, Ernest Thesiger, Colin Clive, Una O'Connor, Valerie Hobson, Dwight Frye, John Carradine, E.E. Clive, O.P. Heggie, Gavin Gordon, Douglas Walton; **D:** James Whale. VHS, Beta $14.95 MCA, MLB ✗✗✗✗

Bride of Killer Nerd Harold Kunkel, left over from the original "Killer Nerd," finds his opposite sex nirvana in the person of Thelma, also a nerd in mind, body, and soul. They relentlessly pursue revenge on the rockers who humiliate them at a campus beer bash. 1991 75m/C Toby Radloff, Wayne A. Harold, Heidi Lohr; **D:** Mark Steven Bosko. VHS TEM ✗

Bride of Re-Animator Herbert West is back, and this time he not only re-animates life but creates life—sexy female life—in this sequel to the immensely popular "Re-Animator." High camp and blood curdling gore make this a standout in the sequel parade. Available in a R-rated version as well.

1989 99m/C Bruce Abbott, Claude Earl Jones, Fabiana Udenio, Jeffrey Combs, Kathleen Kinmont, David Gale; **D:** Brian Yuzna; **M:** Richard Band. VHS, Beta $89.95 LIV ✗✗½

Bride of the Gorilla Burr travels to the jungle where he finds a wife, a plantation, and a curse in this African twist on the werewolf legend. Chaney is the local policeman on his trail. Burr's physical changes are fun to watch. 1951 76m/B Raymond Burr, Barbara Payton, Lon Chaney Jr., Tom Conway, Paul Cavanagh; **D:** Robert Siodmak; **W:** Robert Siodmak. VHS $16.95 NOS, MRV, SNC ✗✗

Bride of the Monster Lugosi stars as a mad scientist trying to create a race of giants. Classic Woodian badness. **AKA:** Bride of the Atom. 1956 70m/B Bela Lugosi, Tor Johnson, Loretta King, Tony McCoy; **D:** Edward D. Wood Jr. VHS, Beta $19.95 NOS, SNC, VYY Woof!

The Bride Walks Out Newlywed crisis: a woman with rich taste learns how to adjust to living on her husband's poor salary, but not before she samples the life of the wealthy. Interesting in a sociological sort of way. 1936 81m/B Barbara Stanwyck, Gene Raymond, Robert Young, Ned Sparks, Willie Best, Helen Broderick, Hattie McDaniel; **D:** Leigh Jason. VHS, Beta $19.98 RKO, TTC ✗✗

The Bride Wore Black Truffaut's homage to Hitchcock, complete with Bernard Herrmann score. A young woman exacts brutal revenge on the five men who accidentally killed her husband. Excellent cinematography from Raoul Coutard. **AKA:** La Mariee Etait en Noir. 1968 107m/C FR Jeanne Moreau, Claude Rich, Jean-Claude Brialy, Michel Bouquet, Michael Lonsdale; **D:** Francois Truffaut; **M:** Bernard Herrmann. VHS $19.98 MGM, MLB, ING ✗✗✗

The Bride Wore Red Crawford stars as a cabaret singer who masquerades as a socialite in an attempt to break into the upper crust. When a wealthy aristocrat invites her to spend two weeks at a posh resort in Tyrol, Crawford plays her part to the hilt, managing to charm both a rich gentleman and the village postman. Typical "love conquers all" melodrama. 1937 103m/B Joan Crawford, Franchot Tone, Robert Young, Billie Burke, Reginald Owen, Lynne Carver, George Zucco; **D:** Dorothy Arzner. VHS $19.98 MGM ✗✗

The Brides of Dracula A young French woman unknowingly frees a vampire. He wreaks havoc, sucking blood and creating more of the undead to carry out his evil deeds. One of the better Hammer vampire films. 1960 86m/C GB Peter Cushing, Martita Hunt, Yvonne Monlaur, Freda Jackson, David Peel, Mona Washbourne; **D:** Terence Fisher. VHS $14.98 MCA, FCT ✗✗½

Brides of the Beast Filipino radiation monsters get their jollies by eating beautiful young naked women. Newly arrived research scientist and his bride oppose this custom. First in a series of "Blood Island" horrors. **AKA:** Brides of Blood; Grave Desires; Island of the Living Horror. 1968 85m/C PH John Ashley, Kent Taylor, Beverly Hills, Eva Darren, Mario Montenegro; **D:** Eddie Romero, Gerardo (Gerry) De Leon. VHS, Beta NO Woof!

The Brides Wore Blood Four prospective brides are mysteriously murdered, but one is brought back to life and becomes a vampire's mate. 1984 86m/C VHS, Beta NO Woof!

Brideshead Revisited The acclaimed British miniseries based on the Evelyn Waugh classic about an Edwardian young man who falls under the spell of a wealthy aristocratic family and struggles to retain his integrity and values. On six tapes.
1981 540m/C *GB* Jeremy Irons, Anthony Andrews, Diana Quick, Laurence Olivier, John Gielgud, Claire Bloom, Stephane Audran, Mona Washbourne, John Le Mesurier; *D:* Charles Sturridge, Michael Lindsay-Hogg. VHS, Beta $99.99 MOV, FUS, FCT 𝖅𝖅𝖅

The Bridge at Remagen Based on the true story of allied attempts to capture a vital bridge before retreating German troops destroy it. For war-film buffs.
1969 (PG) 115m/C George Segal, Robert Vaughn, Ben Gazzara, Bradford Dillman, E.G. Marshall; *D:* John Guillermin; *W:* William Roberts; *M:* Elmer Bernstein. VHS, Beta NO 𝖅𝖅½

The Bridge of San Luis Rey A priest investigates the famous bridge collapse in Lima, Peru that left five people dead. Based upon the novel by Thornton Wilder.
1944 89m/B Lynn Bari, Francis Lederer, Louis Calhern, Akim Tamiroff, Donald Woods, Alla Nazimova, Blanche Yurka; *D:* Rowland V. Lee. VHS, Beta $19.95 NWV, IME 𝖅𝖅𝖅

The Bridge on the River Kwai Award-winning adaptation of the Pierre Bouelle novel about the battle of wills between a Japanese POW camp commander and a British colonel over the construction of a rail bridge, and the parallel efforts by escaped prisoner Holden to destroy it. Holden's role was originally cast for Cary Grant. Memorable too for whistling "Colonel Bogey March." Because the writers were blacklisted, Boulle (who spoke no English) was credited as screenwriter.
1957 161m/C *GB* William Holden, Alec Guinness, Jack Hawkins, Sessue Hayakawa, James Donald, Geoffrey Horne, Andre Morell, Ann Sears; *D:* David Lean; *W:* Michael Wilson, Carl Foreman; *M:* Malcolm Arnold. Academy Awards '57: Best Actor (Guinness), Best Adapted Screenplay, Best Color Cinematography, Best Director (Lean), Best Film Editing, Best Picture, Best Original Score; Nominations: Best Supporting Actor (Hayakawa); British Academy Awards '57: Best Actor (Guinness), Best Film; Directors Guild of America Awards '57: Best Director (Lean); Golden Globe Awards '58: Best Actor—Drama (Guinness), Best Director (Lean), Best Film—Drama; National Board of Review Awards '57: 10 Best Films of the Year, Best Director (Lean), Best Supporting Actor (Hayakawa). VHS, Beta $19.95 COL, BTV, HMV 𝖅𝖅𝖅𝖅

Bridge to Hell A group of allied P.O.W.s try to make their way to the American front during WWII in Yugoslavia. A heavily guarded bridge occupied by Nazi troops stands between them and freedom. A special introduction by Michael Dudikoff doing martial arts.
1987 94m/C Jeff Connors, Francis Ferre, Andy Forrest, Paky Valente; *D:* Umberto Lenzi. VHS $59.95 CAN 𝖅½

The Bridge to Nowhere Five city kids go hunting and back-packing in the New Zealand wilderness, and are hunted by a maniacal backwoodsman.
1986 82m/C *NZ* Bruno Lawrence, Alison Routledge, Margaret Umbers, Philip Gordon; *D:* Ian Mune. VHS, Beta $19.98 NLC 𝖅𝖅

Bridge to Silence A young hearing-impaired mother's life begins to crumble following the death of her husband in a car crash. Her mother tries to get custody of her daughter and a friend applies romantic pressure. Made for TV melodrama features Matlin in her first television speaking role.
1989 95m/C Marlee Matlin, Lee Remick, Josef Sommer, Michael O'Keefe, Allison Silva, Candice Brecker; *D:* Karen Arthur. VHS $59.95 FRH 𝖅𝖅

Bridge to Terabithia An imaginative girl and a young boy learn the joys of friendship in a magic make-believe kingdom called Terabithia. Adapted from the novel by Katherine Paterson. Originally aired by PBS for the "Wonderworks" television series.
1985 58m/C Annette O'Toole, Julian Coutts, Julie Beaulieu; *D:* Eric Till. VHS $29.95 PME, HMV, FCT 𝖅𝖅

A Bridge Too Far A meticulous recreation of one of the most disastrous battles of WWII, the Allied defeat at Arnhem in 1944. Misinformation, adverse conditions, and overconfidence combined to prevent the Allies from capturing six bridges that connected Holland to the German border.
1977 (PG) 175m/C *GB* Sean Connery, Robert Redford, James Caan, Michael Caine, Elliott Gould, Gene Hackman, Laurence Olivier, Ryan O'Neal, Liv Ullmann, Dirk Bogarde, Hardy Kruger, Arthur Hill, Edward Fox, Anthony Hopkins; *D:* Richard Attenborough; *W:* William Goldman; *M:* John Addison. VHS, Beta $29.98 MGM, FOX 𝖅𝖅

The Bridges at Toko-Ri Based on the James A. Michener novel, the rousing war-epic about a lawyer being summoned by the Navy to fly bombing missions during the Korean War. A powerful anti-war statement.
1955 103m/C William Holden, Grace Kelly, Fredric March, Mickey Rooney, Robert Strauss, Earl Holliman, Keiko Awaji, Charles McGraw; *D:* Mark Robson; *W:* Valentine Davis. Academy Awards '55: Best Special Effects; Nominations: Best Film Editing. VHS, Beta $14.95 PAR 𝖅𝖅𝖅½

Brief Encounter Based on Noel Coward's "Still Life" from "Tonight at 8:30," two middle-aged, middle-class people become involved in a short and bittersweet romance in WWII England. Intensely romantic, underscored with Rachmaninoff's Second Piano Concerto.
1946 86m/B *GB* Celia Johnson, Trevor Howard, Stanley Holloway, Cyril Raymond, Joyce Carey; *D:* David Lean; *W:* Noel Coward. Academy Awards '46 Nominations: Best Actress (Johnson), Best Director (Lean), Best Screenplay; National Board of Review Awards '46: 10 Best Films of the Year; New York Film Critics Awards '46: Best Actress (Johnson). VHS, Beta $19.95 PAR, ING, HMV 𝖅𝖅𝖅𝖅

A Brief History of Time A stunning documentary about physicist Stephen Hawking, the author of the popular book "Brief History of Time." Crippled by Lou Gehrig's Disease, Hawking narrates the film in the computer-synthesized voice he uses to speak. Interviews with family, friends, and colleagues, bring Hawking's scientific theories to light.
1992 (G) 85m/C Stephen Hawking; *D:* Errol Morris; *W:* Stephen Hawking; *M:* Philip Glass. VHS, Beta $19.95 PAR, BTV, WSH 𝖅𝖅𝖅

The Brig A film by Jonas Mekas documenting the Living Theatre's infamous performance of Kenneth H. Brown's experimental play. Designed by Julian Beck.
1964 65m/B Adolfas Mekas, Jim Anderson, Warren Finnerty, Henry Howard, Tom Lillard, James Tiroff, Gene Lipton; *D:* John Mekas. VHS, Beta $29.95 MFV, FCT, TPV 𝖅𝖅𝖅

Brigadoon The story of a magical, 18th century Scottish village which awakens once every 100 years and the two modern-day vacationers who stumble upon it. Main highlight is the Lerner and Loewe score. ♫Brigadoon; Almost Like Being in Love; I'll Go Home With Bonnie Jean; Wedding Dance; From This Day On; Heather on the Hill; Waitin' For My Dearie; Once in the Highlands.
1954 108m/C Gene Kelly, Van Johnson, Cyd Charisse; *D:* Vincente Minnelli; *M:* Frederick Loewe, Alan Jay Lerner. VHS, Beta, 8mm $19.98 MGM, TLF 𝖅𝖅𝖅

Bright Angel Road movie pairs an unconventional team: George wants to visit his aunt to see if she's heard from his mother who ran off with another man; Luey is a free-spirit trying to free her brother from jail. Good performances by Mulroney, Taylor, & Pullman. Ford adapted two of his short stories, "Childern" and "Great Falls" for the gritty and uncompromising script of life in the modern west.
1991 (R) 94m/C Dermot Mulroney, Lili Taylor, Sam Shepard, Valerie Perrine, Burt Young, Bill Pullman, Benjamin Bratt, Mary Kay Place, Delroy Lindo, Kevin Tighe, Sheila McCarthy; *D:* Michael Fields; *W:* Richard Ford; *M:* Chris Young. VHS $92.99 HBO 𝖅𝖅½

Bright Eyes Shirley Temple stars as an adorable orphan caught between foster parents. Submitted for an MPAA rating when the video was released. Also available colorized.
1934 (PG) 84m/B Shirley Temple, James Dunn, Lois Wilson, Jane Withers, Judith Allen; *D:* David Butler. VHS, Beta $14.98 FOX, MLT 𝖅𝖅

Bright Lights, Big City Based on Jay McInerney's popular novel, Fox plays a contemporary yuppie working in Manhattan as a magazine journalist. As his world begins to fall apart, he embarks on an endless cycle of drugs and nightlife. Fox is poorly cast, and his character is hard to care for as he becomes more and more dissolute. Although McInerney wrote his own screenplay, the intellectual abstractness of the novel can't be captured on film.
1988 (R) 110m/C Michael J. Fox, Kiefer Sutherland, Phoebe Cates, Frances Sternhagen, Swoosie Kurtz, Tracy Pollan, Jason Robards Jr., John Houseman, Dianne Wiest, Charlie Schlatter, William Hickey; *D:* James Bridges. VHS, Beta $14.95 MGM 𝖅𝖅

Bright Smiler A made-for-British-television mystery about a writer who retires to her favorite spa and falls into the hands of a malevolent masseuse.
1985 60m/C *GB* Janet Suzman. VHS, Beta $59.95 PSM 𝖅½

Brighton Beach Memoirs The film adaptation of the popular (and semiautobiographical) Neil Simon play. Poignant comedy/drama about a young Jewish boy's coming of age in Depression-era Brooklyn. Followed by "Biloxi Blues" and "Broadway Bound." *AKA:* Neil Simon's Brighton Beach Memoirs.
1986 (PG-13) 108m/C Blythe Danner, Bob Dishy, Judith Ivey, Jonathan Silverman, Brian Drillinger, Stacey Glick, Lisa Waltz, Jason Alexander; *D:* Gene Saks; *W:* Neil Simon; *M:* Michael Small. VHS, Beta $19.95 MCA, FCT 𝖅𝖅½

Brighton Rock Sterling performances highlight this seamy look at the British underworld. Attenborough is Pinkie Brown, a small-time hood who ends up committing murder. He manipulates a waitress to get himself off the hook, but things don't go exactly as he plans. Based on the novel by Graham Greene. *AKA:* Young Scarface.
1947 92m/B *GB* Richard Attenborough, Hermione Baddeley, William Hartnell, Carol Marsh, Nigel Stock, Wylie Watson, Alan Wheatley, George Carney, Reginald Purdell; *D:* John Boulting. VHS DVT, HEG 𝖅𝖅𝖅

Brighton Strangler An actor who plays a murderer assumes the role of the strangler after suffering from a concussion. Decent psychodrama.
1945 67m/B John Loder, June Duprez, Miles Mander; *D:* Max Nosseck. **VHS, Beta $34.95** *RKO* ✶✶

The Brighton Strangler/Before Dawn A mystery double feature: In "The Brighton Strangler," an actor takes his part too seriously as he murders Londoners at night; in "Before Dawn" a brilliant scientist turns to a life of murderous crime.
1945 128m/B John Loder, June Duprez, Miles Mander, Stuart Oland, Dorothy Wilson. **VHS, Beta $39.95** *RKO, TTC* ✶✶

Brighty of the Grand Canyon The spunky donkey Brighty roams across the Grand Canyon in search of adventure. He finds friendship with a gold-digging old prospector who hits pay dirt.
1967 90m/C Joseph Cotten, Pat Conway, Dick Foran, Karl Swenson; *D:* Norman Foster. **VHS, Beta $24.95** *AHV, KAR* ✶ 1/2

Brimstone & Treacle Weird, obsessive psychodrama in which a young rogue (who may or may not be an actual agent of the Devil) infiltrates the home of a staid British family caring for their comatose adult daughter.
1982 (R) 85m/C *GB* Sting, Denholm Elliott, Joan Plowright, Suzanna Hamilton; *D:* Richard Loncraine; *W:* Dennis Potter. **VHS, Beta $14.95** *MGM* ✶✶✶

Bring Me the Head of Alfredo Garcia Peckinpah falters in this poorly paced outing. American piano player on tour in Mexico finds himself entwined with a gang of bloodthirsty bounty hunters. Bloody and confused.
1974 (R) 112m/C Warren Oates, Isela Vega, Gig Young, Robert Webber, Helmut Dantine, Emilio Fernandez, Kris Kristofferson; *D:* Sam Peckinpah. **VHS $59.95** *MGM* ✶✶

Bring Me the Vampire A wealthy baron must endure a night of terror in order to receive an inheritance.
1961 100m/B *MX* Maria Eugenia San Martin, Hector Godoy, Joaquin Vargas. **VHS $16.95** *SNC, MOV* ✶

Bringing Up Baby The quintessential screwball comedy, featuring Hepburn as a giddy socialite with a "baby" leopard, and Grant as the unwitting object of her affections. One ridiculous situation after another add up to high speed fun. Hepburn looks lovely, the supporting actors are in fine form, and director Hawks manages the perfect balance of control and mayhem. From a story by Hagar Wilde, who helped Nichols with the screenplay. Also available in a colorized version.
1938 103m/B Katharine Hepburn, Cary Grant, May Robson, Charlie Ruggles, Walter Catlett, Fritz Feld, Jonathan Hale, Barry Fitzgerald, Ward Bond; *D:* Howard Hawks; *W:* Dudley Nichols. **VHS, Beta $14.98** *TTC, HMV, BTV* ✶✶✶✶

Brink of Life Three pregnant women in a hospital maternity ward await the impending births with mixed feelings. Early Bergman; in Swedish with English subtitles. *AKA:* Nara Livet.
1957 82m/B *SW* Eva Dahlbeck, Bibi Andersson, Ingrid Thulin, Babro Ornas, Max von Sydow, Erland Josephson, Gunnar Sjoberg; *D:* Ingmar Bergman. **VHS, Beta $24.95** *VYY, ING* ✶✶ 1/2

Brink's Job Recreates the "crime of the century," Tony Pino's heist of 2.7 million dollars from a Brink's truck. The action picks up five days before the statute of limitations is about to run out.

1978 (PG) 103m/C Peter Falk, Peter Boyle, Warren Oates, Gena Rowlands, Paul Sorvino, Sheldon Leonard, Allen (Gooritz) Garfield; *D:* William Friedkin; *W:* Walon Green; *M:* Richard Rodney Bennett. **VHS, Beta $59.95** *MCA* ✶✶✶

Britannia Hospital This is a portrait of a hospital at its most chaotic: the staff threatens to strike, demonstrators surround the hospital, a nosey BBC reporter pursues an anxious professor, and the eagerly-anticipated royal visit degenerates into a total shambles.
1982 (R) 111m/C *GB* Malcolm McDowell, Leonard Rossiter, Graham Crowden, Joan Plowright, Mark Hamill, Alan Bates; *D:* Lindsay Anderson. **VHS, Beta** *NO* ✶✶ 1/2

British Intelligence Silly American-made film about British espionage. Boris Karloff plays a butler (who is also a spy) trapped by an agent who visits the home of a British bureaucrat. Half-baked story that doesn't hold up.
1940 62m/B Boris Karloff, Margaret Lindsay, Maris Wrixon, Holmes Herbert, Leonard Mudie, Bruce Lester; *D:* Terry Morse. **VHS $16.95** *NOS, SNC, MLB* ✶ 1/2

A Brivele der Mamen A Jewish mother does her best to hold her fragile family together, in spite of the ravages of war and poverty. Her travails take her and her family from the Polish Ukraine to New York City. In Yiddish with English subtitles. *AKA:* A Letter to Mother; A Letter to Mama.
1938 90m/C *PL* Berta Gersten, Lucy Gerhman, Misha Gerhman, Edmund Zayenda; *D:* Joseph Green. **VHS, Beta $79.95** *ERG, ING* ✶✶✶

Broadcast News The acclaimed, witty analysis of network news shows, dealing with the three-way romance between a driven career-woman producer, an ace nebbish reporter and a brainless, popular on-screen anchorman. Incisive and funny, though often simply idealistic.
1987 (R) 132m/C William Hurt, Albert Brooks, Holly Hunter, Jack Nicholson, Joan Cusack, Robert Prosky, Lois Chiles, Gennie James; *Cameos:* John Cusack; *D:* James L. Brooks; *W:* James L. Brooks; *M:* Bill Conti, Michael Gore. Academy Awards '87 Nominations: Best Actor (Hurt), Best Actress (Hunter), Best Cinematography, Best Film Editing, Best Original Screenplay, Best Picture, Best Supporting Actor (Brooks); National Board of Review Awards '87: 10 Best Films of the Year, Best Actress (Hunter). **VHS, Beta $19.98** *FOX* ✶✶✶ 1/2

Broadway Bill A man decides to abandon his nagging wife and his job in her family's business for the questionable pleasures of owning a racehorse known as Broadway Bill. This racetrack comedy was also remade by Frank Capra in 1951 as "Riding High." *AKA:* Strictly Confidential.
1934 90m/C Warner Baxter, Myrna Loy, Walter Connolly, Helen Vinson, Margaret Hamilton, Frankie Darro; *D:* Frank Capra. **VHS** *NO* ✶✶✶

Broadway Bound The final film in Simon's trilogy (preceded by "Brighton Beach Memoirs" and "Biloxi Blues"). This time the playwright's alter ego, Eugene Morris Jerome, is ready to leave Brooklyn for good, hoping to make it as a comedy writer for a radio show. Meanwhile, his mother decides what to do about her unfaithful father. Made for television. *AKA:* Neil Simon's Broadway Bound.
1992 90m/C Jonathan Silverman, Anne Bancroft, Jerry Orbach, Corey Parker, Hume Cronyn, Michele Lee, Jonathan Silverman; *D:* Paul Bogart; *W:* Neil Simon. **VHS** *ABC* ✶✶ 1/2

Broadway Danny Rose One of Woody Allen's best films, a hilarious, heart-rending anecdotal comedy about a third-rate talent agent involved in one of his client's

infidelities. The film magically unfolds as show business veterans swap Danny Rose stories at a delicatessen. Allen's Danny Rose is pathetically lovable.
1984 (PG) 85m/B Woody Allen, Mia Farrow, Nick Apollo Forte, Sandy Baron, Milton Berle, Howard Cosell; *D:* Woody Allen; *W:* Woody Allen. **VHS, Beta $19.98** *VES* ✶✶✶ 1/2

The Broadway Drifter A silent Jazz Age drama about a playboy who repents his decadent ways by opening a girls' health school. Complications ensue.
1927 90m/B George Walsh, Dorothy Hall, Bigelow Cooper, Arthur Donaldson; *D:* Bernard McEveety. **VHS, Beta, 8mm $24.95** *VYY* ✶✶

Broadway Limited Three aspiring actors head for the Great White Way with a baby to use as a prop. Thinking the baby kidnapped, the police make things tough for the trio. McLaglen was wasted on this one, which was apparently made to show off the considerable assets of Woodworth. *AKA:* The Baby Vanishes.
1941 75m/B Victor McLaglen, Marjorie Woodworth, Dennis O'Keefe, Patsy Kelly, ZaSu Pitts, Leonid Kinskey, George E. Stone; *D:* Gordon Douglas. **VHS $19.95** *NOS* ✶✶

Broadway Melody Early musical in which two sisters hope for fame on Broadway, and encounter a wily song and dance man who traps both their hearts. Dated, but still charming, with a lovely score. Considered the great granddaddy of all MGM musicals; followed by three more melodies in 1935, 1937, and 1940. ♫Broadway Melody; Give My Regards to Broadway; Truthful Parson Brown; The Wedding of the Painted Doll; The Boy Friend; You Were Meant For Me; Love Boat; Broadway Babies.
1929 104m/B Bessie Love, Anita Page, Charles King, Jed Prouty, Kenneth Thomson, Edward Dillon, Mary Doran; *D:* Harry Beaumont; *M:* Nacio Herb Brown, Arthur Freed. Academy Awards '29: Best Picture; Nominations: Best Actress (Love), Best Director (Beaumont). **VHS, Beta $19.98** *MGM, BTV* ✶✶ 1/2

Broadway Melody of 1936 Exceptional musical comedy with delightful performances from Taylor and Powell. Benny is a headline-hungry columnist who tries to entrap Taylor by using Powell. ♫Broadway Melody; Broadway Rhythm; You Are My Lucky Star; I've Got a Feeling You're Fooling; All I Do Is Dream of You; Sing Before Breakfast; On a Sunday Afternoon.
1935 110m/B Jack Benny, Eleanor Powell, Robert Taylor, Una Merkel, Sid Silvers, Buddy Ebsen; *D:* Roy Del Ruth; *M:* Nacio Herb Brown, Arthur Freed. **VHS, Beta $19.98** *MGM, MLB, CCB* ✶✶✶

Broadway Melody of 1938 Third entry in the melody series lacks the sparkle of "Broadway Melody of 1936" despite the all-star cast. Lots of singing and dancing without much charm. Two bright spots: a young Garland singing the now famous "Dear Mr. Gable" and the always lovely Powell's dance numbers. ♫Broadway Rhythm; Dear Mr. Gable (You Made Me Love You); A New Pair of Shoes; Yours and Mine; I'm Feeling Like a Million; Everybody Sing; Follow in My Footsteps; Your Broadway and My Broadway; Sun Showers; Some of These Days; Toreador Song; Largo al Factotum.
1937 110m/B Eleanor Powell, Sophie Tucker, George Murphy, Judy Garland, Robert Taylor, Buddy Ebsen; *D:* Roy Del Ruth; *M:* Nacio Herb Brown, Arthur Freed. **VHS, Beta $19.98** *MGM* ✶✶ 1/2

Broadway Melody of 1940 The last entry in the melody series features the only screen teaming of Astaire and Powell. The flimsy plot is just an excuse for a potent series of Cole Porter musical numbers. ♫ I Concentrate on You; I've Got My Eye on You; Begin the Beguine; I am the Captain; Please Don't Monkey With Broadway; Between You and Me; Il Bacio.
1940 103m/B Fred Astaire, Eleanor Powell, George Murphy, Frank Morgan, Ian Hunter; *D:* Norman Taurog. **VHS, Beta $19.98** *MGM, TTC, FCT* ♫♫ ½

Broadway Rhythm A too-long look at Broadway behind-the-scenes. Murphy plays a Broadway producer who hopes to land a Hollywood star for his new show. She rejects his offer in favor of a show being produced by his father. Just a chance to showcase a number of popular vaudeville acts, songs, and the music of Tommy Dorsey and his orchestra. ♫ All the Things You Are; That Lucky Fellow; In Other Words; Seventeen; All In Fun; Brazilian Boogie; What Do You Think I Am?; Somebody Loves Me; Milkman Keep Those Bottles Quiet; Solid Potato Salad; Manhattan Serenade; Pretty Baby; Oh You Beautiful Doll; Amor; Ida, Sweet as Apple Cider.
1944 111m/C George Murphy, Ginny Simms, Charles Winninger, Gloria De Haven, Nancy Walker, Ben Blue, Lena Horne, Eddie Anderson; *D:* Roy Del Ruth; *W:* Dorothy Kingsley, Harry Clork. **VHS $19.98** *MGM* ♫♫ ½

Broadway Serenade Melodramatic musical in which a songwriter (Ayres) and his wife, singer MacDonald, make career choices that destroy their marriage. ♫ Broadway Serenade for the Lonely Heart; High Flyin'; One Look at You; Time Changes Everything; Un Bel Di; No Time to Argue; Italian Street Song; Les Filles de Cadiz; Musical Contract.
1939 114m/B Jeanette MacDonald, Lew Ayres, Ian Hunter, Frank Morgan, Wally Vernon, Rita Johnson, Virginia Grey, William Gargan; *D:* Robert Z. Leonard; *W:* Charles Lederer. **VHS $19.98** *MGM* ♫♫ ½

Broadway to Cheyenne A group of big city gangsters try to take over a small western town but are opposed by heroic cowboys. *AKA:* From Broadway to Cheyenne.
1932 53m/B Rex Bell, George "Gabby" Hayes, Marceline Day, Robert Ellis, Alan Bridge, Matthew Betz; *D:* Harry Fraser. **VHS, Beta $9.95** *GPV, RXM, VDM* ♫

Broken Angel Jamie seemed to be such a nice girl, with good looks and great grades—and membership in a notorious street gang. When Jamie disappears, her family discovers her secret activities and dad tries to find his wayward little girl. Melodramatic made for television goo.
1988 94m/C William Shatner, Susan Blakely, Erika Eleniak, Roxann Biggs; *D:* Richard T. Heffron. **VHS $14.95** *MGM* ♫ ½

Broken Arrow A U.S. scout befriends Cochise and the Apaches, and helps settlers and Indians live in peace together in the 1870s. Acclaimed as the first Hollywood film to side with the Indians, and for Chandler's portrayal of Cochise.
1950 93m/C James Stewart, Jeff Chandler, Will Geer, Debra Paget, Basil Ruysdael, Arthur Hunnicutt, Jay Silverheels; *D:* Delmer Daves. **VHS, Beta $19.98** *FOX* ♫♫ ½

Broken Badge Crenna stars as a macho, chauvinistic cop whose attitude towards rape victims changes dramatically after he himself is raped by a couple of thugs.

Excellent TV movie. *AKA:* The Rape of Richard Beck.
1985 100m/C Richard Crenna, Meredith Baxter Birney, Pat Hingle, Frances Lee McCain, Cotter Smith, George Dzundza, Joanna Kerns; *D:* Karen Arthur; *W:* James G. Hirsch. **VHS $9.95** *SIM, VTR* ♫♫♫

Broken Blossoms One of Griffith's most widely acclaimed films, photographed by Billy Bitzer, about a young Chinaman in London's squalid Limehouse district hoping to spread the peaceful philosophy of his Eastern religion. He befriends a pitiful street waif who is mistreated by her brutal father, resulting in tragedy. Silent. Revised edition contains introduction from Gish and a newly-recorded score.
1919 102m/B Lillian Gish, Richard Barthelmess, Donald Crisp; *D:* D.W. Griffith. **VHS, Beta $19.95** *NOS, MRV, HHT* ♫♫♫ ½

The Broken Chain In the mid 18th-century Joseph Brant (Schweig), a member of the Mohawk tribe, is sent away to be educated by the British. When he returns, his loyalties are divided between his Native American roots and his English mentor, Sir William Johnson (Brosnan). His boyhood friend Lohaheo (White Shirt) disdains Joseph's white man ways, leading to tragic consequences. Historical background features the French and Indian Wars, the splintering of the Iroquois Confederacy, and the coming of the American Revolution. Filmed on location in Virginia. Made for television.
1993 93m/C Eric Schweig, Wes Studi, Buffy Saint Marie, Pierce Brosnan, J.C. White Shirt, Floyd "Red Crow" Westerman, Graham Greene, Elaine Bilstad, Kim Snyder; *D:* Lamont Johnson; *W:* Earl W. Wallace; *M:* Charles Fox. **VHS** *TTC* ♫♫ ½

Broken Hearts of Broadway Stories of heartbreak and success along the Great White Way.
1923 85m/B Colleen Moore, John Walker, Alice Lake, Tully Marshall, Creighton Hale; *D:* Irving Cummings. **VHS $19.95** *GPV* ♫♫

Broken Lance Western remake of "House of Strangers" that details the dissolution of a despotic cattle baron's family. Beautifully photographed.
1954 96m/C Spencer Tracy, Richard Widmark, Robert Wagner, Jean Peters, Katy Jurado, Earl Holliman, Hugh O'Brian, E.G. Marshall; *D:* Edward Dmytryk; *W:* Philip Yordan. Academy Awards '54: Best Story; Nominations: Best Supporting Actress (Jurado). **VHS, Beta $39.98** *FOX* ♫♫♫ ½

The Broken Mask A doctor performs remarkable plastic surgery on a patient, but when the patient becomes attracted to his sweetheart, he throws the Hippocratic oath to the wind, and his patient's spiffy new look has got to go. A ground-breaker amid plastic surgery-gone-amok pieces.
1928 58m/B Cullen Landis, Barbara Bedford, Wheeler Oakman, James Marcus; *D:* James Hogan. **VHS, Beta $19.95** *GPV, FCT* ♫♫

Broken Melody An opera singer sent to prison by mistake must escape in order to return to the woman of his dreams. *AKA:* Vagabond Violinist.
1934 62m/B John Garrick, Margot Grahame, Merle Oberon, Austin Trevor, Charles Carson, Harry Terry; *D:* Bernard Vorhaus. **VHS $29.95** *FCT* ♫ ½

Broken Mirrors A disturbing film which intertwines two stories of violence against women: prostitutes go about their daily business in Amsterdam, while a twisted serial killer who imprisons, photographs, and ultimately destroys his victims, draws near. An

independently made chiller with staunch feminist agenda. *AKA:* Gebroken Spiegels.
1985 110m/C *NL* Lineke Rijsman, Henriette Tol, Edda Barends, Eddie Brugman, Coby Stunnenberg; *D:* Morleen Gorris; *W:* Morleen Gorris. *ICA* ♫♫ ½

Broken Strings All-black musical in which a concert violinist must come to terms with himself after an auto accident limits the use of his left hand.
1940 50m/B Clarence Muse, Sybil Lewis, William Washington, Matthew "Stymie" Beard; *D:* Bernard B. Ray. **VHS, Beta $19.95** *VYY, NOS, VCN* ♫

Broken Trust Erica inherits her fabulously wealthy uncle's estate but she has problems knowing who to trust now that she has all this money. Seems her husband is greedy and her sister resentful but just how far will they go to get what Erica has?
1993 85m/C Kimberly Foster, Nick Cassavetes, Kathryn Harris, Don Swayze, Edward Albert, Wendy MacDonald; *D:* Rafael Portillo. **VHS $89.95** *MNC* ♫♫

Bromas S.A. A group of teenagers get into a bunch of funny situations.
1987 104m/C *SP* Mauricio Garces, Gloria Marin, Manuel Valdez, Hermanos King. **VHS, Beta $54.95** *MAD* ♫♫

Bronco Billy Eastwood stars as a New Jersey shoe clerk who decides to fulfill his dream of being a cowboy hero by becoming the proprietor of a rag-tag wild west show. Locke's one-note performance as a spoiled rich girl who joins up is a problem and the film's charm is as ragged as the acts. Good if you want to see Eastwood in something other than a shoot-'em-up.
1980 (PG) 117m/C Clint Eastwood, Sondra Locke, Bill McKinney, Scatman Crothers, Sam Bottoms, Geoffrey Lewis, Dan Vadis, Sierra Pecheur; *D:* Clint Eastwood; *M:* Stephen Dorff. **VHS, Beta $19.98** *WAR, TLF, RXM* ♫♫ ½

Bronson Lee, Champion Kung-fu and karate highlight this action adventure.
1978 (PG) 81m/C Tadashi Yamashita. **VHS, Beta $19.98** *NO* ♫

Bronson's Revenge Two frontier soldiers face constant danger as they attempt to transport death row prisoners, a large quantity of gold, and a stranded woman across the Rocky Mountains territory.
1979 (R) 90m/C Robert Hundar, Roy Hill, Emma Cohen. **VHS $52.95** *SUN* ♫ ½

The Bronx Executioner Android, robot, and human interests clash in futuristic Manhattan and all martial arts hell breaks loose. Special introduction by martial arts star Michael Dudikoff.
1986 88m/C Rob Robinson, Margie Newton, Chuck Valenti, Gabriel Gori; *D:* Bob Collins. **VHS, Beta $59.95** *CAN* ♫

A Bronx Tale Vivid snapshot of a young Italian-American boy growing up in the '60s among neighborhood small-time wiseguys. As a 9-year-old Calogero witnesses mobster Sonny kill a man but doesn't rat to the police, so Sonny takes the kid under his wing. His upright bus-driving father Lorenzo doesn't approve but the kid is drawn to Sonny's apparent glamor and power. At 17, he's gotten both an education in school and on the streets but he needs to make a choice. Good period detail and excellent performances. Palminteri shows both Sonny's charisma and violence and De Niro handles the less-showy father role with finesse. Based on Palminteri's one-man play; De Niro's directorial debut.

1993 (R) 122m/C Robert De Niro, Chazz Palminteri, Lillo Brancato, Frank Capra, Taral Hicks, Kathrine Narducci, Clem Caserta, Alfred Sauchelli Jr., Frank Pietrangolare; *Cameos:* Joe Pesci; *D:* Robert De Niro; *W:* Chazz Palminteri. VHS *HBO* ♂♂♂

The Bronx War Rival gangs take to the streets in this film from the director of "Hangin' with the Homeboys." A malicious gang leader tricks his gang into going to war over a girl he wants. Very violent; an unrated version available.
1990 (R) 91m/C Joseph P. Vasquez, Fabio Urena, Charmaine Cruz, Andre Brown, Marlene Forte, Francis Colon, Miguel Sierra, Kim West; *D:* Joseph P. Vasquez. VHS $19.95 *ACA* ♂♂

Bronze Buckaroo Horse opera in which a cowpoke seeks revenge for his pa's death. Commendable performances from the all-black cast and crew.
1939 57m/B Herbert Jeffries, Artie Young, Rellie Hardin, Spencer Williams Jr., Clarence Brooks, F.E. Miller; *D:* Richard C. Kahn; *W:* Richard C. Kahn. VHS $24.95 *NOS, MRV, TPV* ♂♂

The Brood Cronenberg's inimitable biological nightmares, involving an experimentally malformed woman who gives birth to murderous demon-children that kill every time she gets angry. Extremely graphic. Not for all tastes.
1979 (R) 92m/C *CA* Samantha Eggar, Oliver Reed; *D:* David Cronenberg; *W:* David Cronenberg. VHS, Beta $19.98 *SUE* ♂♂½

Broth of a Boy A hungry British producer decides to film a birthday party of the oldest man in the world. The old Irishman wants a portion of the profits. Well made and thought provoking.
1959 77m/B *IR* Barry Fitzgerald, Harry Brogan, Tony Wright, June Thorburn, Eddie Golden; *D:* George Pollock. VHS $19.95 *NOS, HEG, FCT* ♂♂½

The Brother from Another Planet An black alien escapes from his home planet and winds up in Harlem, where he's pursued by two alien bounty hunters. Independently made morality fable by John Sayles before he hit the big time; features Sayles in a cameo as an alien bounty hunter.
1984 109m/C Joe Morton, Dee Dee Bridgewater, Ren Woods, Steve James, Maggie Renzi, David Strathairn; *Cameos:* John Sayles; *D:* John Sayles; *W:* John Sayles; *M:* Mason Daring. VHS, Beta $19.98 *FOX, FCT* ♂♂♂

Brother Future T.J., a black, streetsmart city kid who thinks school and helping others is all a waste of time gets knocked out in a car accident. As he's lying unconscious, he is transported back in time to a slave auction block in the Old South. There the displaced urbanite is forced to work on a cotton plantation, and watch the stirrings of a slave revolt. T.J. sees the light and realizes how much opportunity he's been wasting in his own life. He comes to just a few moments later, but worlds away from who he was before. Part of the "Wonderworks" series.
1991 110m/C Phill Lewis, Frank Converse, Carl Lumbly, Vonetta McGee. VHS $29.95 *PME, HMV, BTV* ♂♂♂

Brother John An early look at racial tensions and labor problems. An angel goes back to his hometown in Alabama to see how things are going.
1970 (PG) 94m/C Sidney Poitier, Will Geer, Bradford Dillman, Beverly Todd, Paul Winfield; *D:* James Goldstone; *M:* Quincy Jones. VHS, Beta $14.95 *COL, FCT* ♂♂♂

Brother Orchid Mobster puts a henchman in charge of his gang while he vacations in Europe. Upon his return, he is deposed and wounded in an assassination attempt.

Hiding out in a monastary, he plots to regain control of the gang, leading to fish outta water episodes and a change in his outlook on life. Fine cast fans through farce intelligently.
1940 87m/B Edward G. Robinson, Humphrey Bogart, Ann Sothern, Donald Crisp, Ralph Bellamy, Allen Jenkins, Charles D. Brown, Cecil Kellaway; *D:* Lloyd Bacon. VHS, Beta $19.98 *MGM, CCB* ♂♂♂

Brother Sun, Sister Moon Post-'60s costume epic depicting the trials of St. Francis of Assisi as he evaluates his beliefs in Catholicism.
1973 (PG) 120m/C Graham Faulkner, Judi Bowker, Alec Guinness, Leigh Lawson, Kenneth Cranham, Lee Montague, Valentina Cortese; *D:* Franco Zeffirelli; *M:* Donovan. VHS, Beta $14.95 *PAR, APD, TVC* ♂♂½

The Brotherhood Two hot-headed brothers in a Mafia syndicate clash over old vs. new methods and the changing of the Family's guard.
1968 96m/C Kirk Douglas, Alex Cord, Irene Papas, Luther Adler, Susan Strasberg, Murray Hamilton; *D:* Martin Ritt; *W:* Lalo Schifrin. VHS, Beta $14.95 *PAR* ♂♂½

Brotherhood of Death Three black Vietnam veterans return to their southern hometown to get even with the Klansmen who slaughtered all of the townspeople.
1976 (R) 85m/C Roy Jefferson, Larry Jones, Mike Bass, Le Tari, Haskell V. Anderson; *D:* Bill Berry. VHS, Beta $59.95 *MPI* ♂½

Brotherhood of Justice Young men form a secret organization to rid their neighborhood of drug dealers and violence. As their power grows, their propriety weakens, until all are afraid of the "Brotherhood of Justice." Exciting made-for-television feature.
1986 97m/C Keanu Reeves, Kiefer Sutherland, Billy Zane, Joe Spano, Darren Dalton, Evan Mirand, Don Michael Paul; *D:* Charles Braverman; *M:* Brad Fiedel. VHS $89.95 *VMK, STE* ♂♂

The Brotherhood of Satan In an isolated southern town, a satanic coven persuades children to join in their devil-may-care attitude. Worthwhile.
1971 (PG) 92m/C Strother Martin, L.Q. Jones, Charles Bateman, Anna Capri, Charles Robinson, Alvy Moore, Geri Reischl; *D:* Bernard McEveety. VHS, Beta $9.95 *GKK, IME* ♂♂½

The Brotherhood of the Rose Too many twists and turns mar the otherwise mediocre plot of this murky adaption of a book by David (First Blood) Morrell. Strauss and Morse are the C.I.A. agents marked for death and running for their lives after uncovering their boss's (Mitchum) plot of world domination. Though almost every scene takes place in a different country, the movie was in fact filmed entirely in New Zealand. Convoluted and frustratingly difficult to follow.
1989 (PG-13) 103m/C Robert Mitchum, Peter Strauss, Connie Sellecca, James B. Sikking, David Morse, M. Emmet Walsh, James Hong; *D:* Marvin J. Chomsky. VHS $89.95 *VMK* ♂½

Brotherly Love Good twin/bad twin made-for-TV mystery about an escaped psychopath who's out to get his businessman twin brother (Hirsch in both roles).
1985 94m/C Judd Hirsch, Karen Carlson, George Dzundza, Barry Primus, Lori Lethin; *D:* Jeff Bleckner. VHS, Beta $59.98 *FOX* ♂½

Brothers in Arms Savage mountainmen have developed a weird religion that requires them to hunt down and mercilessly massacre human prey.

1988 (R) 95m/C Todd Allen, Jack Starrett, Dedee Pfeiffer; *D:* George J. Bloom III. VHS $79.95 *REP* ♂♂

Brothers in Law Wry British humor in this tale of a rookie lawyer up against a veteran judge who forces him to sink or swim.
1957 94m/B *GB* Richard Attenborough, Ian Carmichael, Terry-Thomas, Miles Malleson, John Le Mesurier; *D:* Roy Boulting. VHS $19.95 *NOS* ♂♂½

The Brothers Karamazov Hollywood adaptation of the classic novel by Dostoyevsky, in which four 19th-Century Russian brothers struggle with their desires for the same beautiful woman and with the father who brutalizes them. Incredible performances from every cast member, especially Cobb. Long and extremely intense, with fine direction from Brooks. Marilyn Monroe tried desperately to get Schell's part. *AKA:* Karamazov; The Murderer Dmitri Karamazov; Der Morder Dimitri Karamasoff.
1958 147m/C Yul Brynner, Claire Bloom, Lee J. Cobb, William Shatner, Maria Schell, Richard Basehart; *D:* Richard Brooks; *W:* Richard Brooks. VHS, Beta $24.95 *MGM, ING* ♂♂♂

Brother's Keeper Filmmakers Berlinger and Sinofsky document the story of the eccentric and reclusive Ward brothers, four bachelor dairy farmers who shared the same two-room shack for more than 60 years in rural New York. When Bill Ward dies, brother Delbert is accused of murder and goes to trial. The film covers a year's span in preparation for the trial and how the media attention changed the Ward's lives.
1992 104m/C *D:* Joe Berlinger, Bruce Sinofsky. VHS $89.95 *FXL, BTV* ♂♂♂

Brothers Lionheart The Lion brothers fight for life, love and liberty during the Middle Ages.
1985 (G) 120m/C Staffan Gotestam, Lars Soderdahl, Allan Edwall; *D:* Olle Hellbron. VHS, Beta *NO* ♂♂½

Brothers of the West Cowboy saves his brothers from being lynched by proving the guilt of the real outlaws.
1937 56m/B Tom Tyler, Bob Terry, Lois Wilde, Dorothy Short. VHS, Beta $19.95 *NOS, VCN, DVT* ♂½

Brothers O'Toole The misadventures of a pair of slick drifters who, by chance, ride into a broken-down mining town in the 1890s.
1973 94m/C John Astin, Steve Carlson, Pat Carroll, Hans Conried, Lee Meriwether; *D:* Richard Erdman. VHS, Beta $49.95 *VCI* ♂♂

The Browning Version A lonely, unemotional classics instructor at a British boarding school realizes his failure as a teacher and as a husband. From the play by Terrence Rattigan.
1951 89m/B *GB* Michael Redgrave, Jean Kent, Nigel Patrick, Wilfrid Hyde-White, Bill Travers; *D:* Anthony Asquith. VHS, Beta $39.95 *HMV, MOV, FUS* ♂♂♂½

Brubaker A sanctimonious drama about a reform warden who risks his life to replace brutality and corruption with humanity and integrity in a state prison farm. Powerful prison drama.
1980 (R) 131m/C Robert Redford, Jane Alexander, Yaphet Kotto, Murray Hamilton, David Keith, Morgan Freeman, Matt Clark, M. Emmet Walsh, Everett McGill; *D:* Stuart Rosenberg; *W:* W.D. Richter, Arthur Ross. VHS, Beta $19.98 *FOX* ♂♂♂

Bruce Lee: Curse of the Dragon A behind the scenes look at the continuing mystery surrounding the life and untimely death of the martial arts superstar who died in 1973 at the age of 32. Highlights the spectacular fight sequences from Lee's movies as well as footage from his funeral and an interview with his son Brandon Lee, whose own death in 1993 raised further comment about a Lee family curse. *AKA:* The Curse of the Dragon.
1993 90m/C VHS, Beta $79.99 WAR, BTV &&&

Bruce Lee Fights Back From the Grave Bruce Lee returns from the grave to fight the Black Angel of Death with his feet and to wreak vengeance on the evil ones who brought about his untimely demise.
1976 (R) 97m/C Deborah Chaplin, Anthony Bronson; *D:* Umberto Lenzi. VHS, Beta $49.95 MED &

Bruce Lee: The Legend Tribute to the king of karate films features rare footage and interviews with many of the star's closest friends.
1984 88m/C Bruce Lee, Steve McQueen, James Coburn. VHS, Beta $19.98 FOX &

Bruce Lee's Ways of Kung Fu Copious head-kicking film in honor of the long-dead star. Brings together the best from Shaolin: White Crane, Wu-Deng, Dragon-Fist, Kwun-Lun, Eagle Claws, Tiger, and Leopard in a fight against the Dragon.
198? 87m/C Bruce Lei, Philip Cheung, Pearl Lin. VHS, Beta $39.95 UNI &

Bruce Le's Greatest Revenge Bruce Le, one e. Kung-fu action and martial arts fighting occur when a martial arts student gets involved in a clash between Chinese and a discriminatory European Club.
1980 (R) 94m/C Bruce Le. VHS, Beta $24.95 GEM &

Bruce Li in New Guinea Bruce Li, i, not ee. The tribe of a remote island worships the legendary Snake Pearl. Two masters of Kung-fu visit the isle and discover they must defend the daughter of the murdered chief against a cruel wizard.
1980 (PG) 98m/C Bruce Li, Ho Chung Dao, Chen Sing; *D:* C.Y. Yang. VHS, Beta $19.95 OCE, GEM, MRV &

Bruce Li the Invincible Cheng, the Kung-Fu killer, is pursued by the vengeance-minded Bruce.
1980 93m/C Bruce Li, Ho Chung Dao, Chen Sing. VHS $19.95 OCE, MRV, GEM &

Bruce the Superhero Chop-socky action as the coattails-riding Bruce Le takes on the Black Dragon Society.
1979 88m/C Bruce Le. VHS, Beta $19.99 BFV, MRV &

Bruce's Deadly Fingers Bruce Lee kept a book of deadly finger techniques for kung fu killing. When a vicious gangster kidnaps the Master's ex-girlfriend, one of his followers must rescue her and maintain the book's integrity.
1980 90m/C Bruce Le, Lo Lieh, Chan Wai, Nora Miao, Rose Marie, Yuen Man Chi, Chang Leih, Young Zee, Wuk Ma No Hans. VHS, Beta $24.95 GEM &

Bruce's Fists of Vengeance Le and Lee guard master Bruce Lee's kicking secrets from an evil adversary.
1984 87m/C Bruce Le, Jack Lee, Ken Watanabe, Romano Kristoff, Don Gordon. VHS, Beta $57.95 GEM &

Brujo Luna Evil ritualists kill and eat innocent people. Lots of blood and gore—not for the faint of heart. In Spanish.

197? 90m/C SP Laurie Walters, Joe Spano. VHS, Beta $29.95 UNI Woof!

Brussels Transit The story of a Yiddish family's arrival and adjustment to the new world of Brussels, Belgium, after WWII. In Yiddish with English subtitles.
1980 80m/B *D:* Samy Szlingerbaum. VHS $69.95 ING &&&

Brutal Glory Set in New York City in 1918 and based on the true story of the boxer known as "The Real McCoy." Fascinating and detailed history of a period, a champion, and the man who made it happen.
1989 96m/C Robert Vaughn, Timothy Brantley, Leah K. Pinsent; *D:* Koos Roets. VHS NO &&

The Brute Man A young man who had been disfigured by his school mates goes out on a trail of revenge. Hatton is convincing in the title role, as in real life he was afflicted with acromegaly, an ailment that produces an enlargment of the bones in the face, hands, and feet.
1946 62m/B Rondo Hatton, Tom Neal, Jane Adams; *D:* Jean Yarborough. VHS, Beta $14.95 AOV, MLB, COL &&

The Buccaneer A swashbuckling version of the adventures of pirate Jean LaFitte and his association with President Andrew Jackson during the War of 1812. Remake of Cecille B. DeMille's 1938 production.
1958 121m/C Yul Brynner, Charlton Heston, Claire Bloom, Inger Stevens, Charles Boyer, Henry Hull, E.G. Marshall, Lorne Greene; *D:* Anthony Quinn; *M:* Elmer Bernstein. VHS, Beta $14.95 BAR, FCT, RXM &&

Buck and the Preacher A trail guide and a con man preacher join forces to help a wagon train of former slaves who are seeking to homestead out West. Poitier's debut as a director.
1972 (PG) 102m/C Sidney Poitier, Harry Belafonte, Ruby Dee, Cameron Mitchell, Denny Miller; *D:* Sidney Poitier. VHS, Beta $14.95 COL &&½

Buck Privates Abbott and Costello star as two dim-witted tie salesmen, running from the law, who become buck privates during WWII. The duo's first great success, and the film that established the formula for each subsequent film. *AKA:* Rookies.
1941 84m/B Bud Abbott, Lou Costello, Shemp Howard, Lee Norman, Alan Curtis, The Andrews Sisters; *D:* Arthur Lubin. VHS, Beta $14.95 MCA &&½

Buck Privates Come Home Abbott and Costello return to their "Buck Privates" roles as two soldiers trying to adjust to civilian life after the war. They also try to help a French girl sneak into the United States. Funny antics culminate into a wild chase scene. *AKA:* Rookies Come Home.
1947 77m/B Bud Abbott, Lou Costello, Tom Brown, Joan Shawlee, Nat Pendleton, Beverly Simmons, Don Beddoe, Don Porter, Donald MacBride; *D:* Charles T. Barton. VHS $14.98 MCA &&

Buck Rogers Conquers the Universe The story of Buck Rogers, written by Phil Nolan in 1928, was the first science fiction story done in the modern super-hero space genre. Many of the "inventions" seen in this movie have actually come into existence—spaceships, ray guns (lasers), anti-gravity belts—a testament to Nolan's almost psychic farsightedness.
1939 91m/B Buster Crabbe, Constance Moore, Jackie Moran; *D:* Ford Beebe, Saul Goodkind. VHS, Beta $29.95 FOX &&

Buck Rogers in the 25th Century An American astronaut, preserved in space for 500 years, is brought back to life by a young Draconian flagship. Outer space adventures begin when he is accused of being a spy from Earth. Based on the classic movie serial. Made for TV movie that began the popular series. Additional series episodes are available.
1979 (PG) 90m/C Gil Gerard, Pamela Hensley, Erin Gray, Henry Silva; *D:* Daniel Haller. VHS, Beta $14.98 MCA, MOV &&

A Bucket of Blood Cult favorite Dick Miller stars as a sculptor with a peculiar "talent" for lifelike artwork. Corman fans will see thematic similarities to his subsequent work, "Little Shop of Horrors" (1960). "Bucket of Blood" was made in just five days, while "Little Shop of Horrors" was made in a record breaking two days. Corman horror/spoof noted for its excellent beatnik atmosphere.
1959 66m/B Dick Miller, Barboura Morris, Antony Carbone, Julian Burton, Ed Nelson, Bert Convy; *D:* Roger Corman. VHS, Beta $19.95 NOS, RHI, SNC &&&

Buckeye and Blue A hero turned outlaw, his 14 year-old female sidekick, and a gang known as the McCoys are all on the lam from the law in this western adventure.
1987 (PG) 94m/C Robin Lively, Jeffery Osterhage, Rick Gibbs, Will Hannah, Kenneth Jensen, Patrick Johnston, Stuart Rogers, Michael Horse; *D:* J.C. Compton. VHS, Beta $29.95 ACA &½

Buckskin Slowmoving western about a marshall protecting townspeople from a greedy, land-grabbing cattle baron.
1968 98m/C Barry Sullivan, Wendell Corey, Joan Caulfield, Lon Chaney Jr., John Russell, Barbara Hale, Barton MacLane, Bill Williams; *D:* Michael Moore. VHS PAR &½

Buckskin Frontier Story is built around Western railroad construction and cattle empires in the 1860s. Cobb tries to stop the railroad from coming through by hiring Jory to do his dirty work.
1943 75m/B Richard Dix, Jane Wyatt, Lee J. Cobb, Albert Dekker, Victor Jory, Lola Lane, Max Baer Sr.; *D:* Lesley Selander. VHS, Beta $9.95 NOS, MRV, GPV &½

Bucktown A black man who reopens his murdered brother's bar fights off police corruption and racism in a Southern town.
1975 (R) 95m/C Fred Williamson, Pam Grier, Bernie Hamilton, Thalmus Rasulala, Art Lund; *D:* Arthur Marks. VHS, Beta $59.98 ORI &½

Bud and Lou Comedy/drama recounts Abbott & Costello's rise in Hollywood. While the story, based on the book by Bob Thomas, is interesting, the two funnymen in the leads can't pull off the old classic skits.
1978 98m/C Harvey Korman, Buddy Hackett, Michele Lee, Arte Johnson, Robert Reed; *D:* Robert C. Thompson. VHS, Beta $29.95 JTC &½

Buddha Assassinator Young Kung-Fu enthusiast challenges a Ming dynasty lord to a duel to the death.
1982 93m/C Hwang Jang Lee, Mang Hai, Lung Fei, Chien Yueh Sheng. VHS, Beta $59.95 WVE &

Buddy Buddy A professional hitman's well-ordered arrangement to knock off a state's witness keeps being interrupted by the suicide attempts of a man in the next hotel room.
1981 (R) 96m/C Jack Lemmon, Walter Matthau, Paula Prentiss, Klaus Kinski; *D:* Billy Wilder; *W:* Billy Wilder, I.A.L. Diamond. VHS, Beta $19.98 MGM &&½

The Buddy Holly Story An acclaimed biography of the famed 1950s pop star, spanning the years from his meteoric career's beginnings in Lubbock to his tragic early death in the now famous plane crash. Busey performs Holly's hits himself. ♫Rock Around the Ollie Vee; That'll Be the Day; Oh, Boy; It's So Easy; Well All Right; Chantilly Lace; Peggy Sue.
1978 (PG) 113m/C Gary Busey, Don Stroud, Charles Martin Smith, Conrad Janis, William Jordan; **D:** Steve Rash; **M:** Joe Renzetti. Academy Awards '78: Best Adapted Score; Nominations: Best Actor (Busey), Best Sound; National Society of Film Critics Awards '78: Best Actor (Busey). **VHS, Beta $19.95** COL ⊘⊘⊘½

The Buddy System A tale of contemporary love and the modern myths that outline the boundaries between lovers and friends.
1983 (PG) 110m/C Richard Dreyfuss, Susan Sarandon, Jean Stapleton, Nancy Allen, Wil Wheaton, Ed Winter, Keene Curtis; **D:** Glenn Jordan; **W:** Mary Agnes Donoghue. **VHS $59.98** FOX ⊘⊘

Buddy's Song A '60s coming of age tale, only in this case it's the father and not the son who needs to grow up. Dad (Daltrey) is more interested in hanging out with his no-account musician friends than in looking after his family. Although he's not above meddling in his teenage son's musical career, which could be the success his father's never was. Based on the novel by Nigel Hinton who also did the screenplay. British teen idol Hawkes (in his film debut) had a top ten hit song from the film with "The One and Only."
1991 (R) 106m/C GB Roger Daltrey, Chesney Hawkes; **W:** Nigel Hinton. **VHS $89.95** VMK, BTV ⊘⊘

Buffalo Bill A light, fictionalized account of the life and career of Bill Cody, from frontier hunter to showman.
1944 89m/C Joel McCrea, Maureen O'Hara, Linda Darnell, Thomas Mitchell, Edgar Buchanan, Anthony Quinn, Moroni Olsen, Sidney Blackmer; **D:** William A. Wellman. **VHS, Beta $39.98** FOX ⊘⊘

Buffalo Bill & the Indians A perennially underrated Robert Altman historical pastiche, portraying the famous Wild West character as a charlatan and shameless exemplar of encroaching imperialism. Great all-star cast amid Altman's signature mise-en-scene chaos. **AKA:** Sitting Bull's History Lesson.
1976 (PG) 135m/C Paul Newman, Geraldine Chaplin, Joel Grey, Will Sampson, Harvey Keitel, Burt Lancaster, Kevin McCarthy; **D:** Robert Altman; **W:** Robert Altman, Alan Rudolph; **M:** Richard Baskin. **VHS, Beta $19.98** FOX ⊘⊘⊘

Buffalo Bill Rides Again With an Indian uprising on the horizon, Buffalo Bill is called in. Mr. Bill finds land swindlers pitting natives against ranchers, but there's precious little action or interest here.
1947 68m/C Richard Arlen, Jennifer Holt, Edward Cassidy, Edmund Cobb, Charles Stevens; **D:** Bernard B. Ray. **VHS, Beta** GPV ⊘½

Buffalo Jump An independent woman, working as a lounge singer in Toronto, returns to her home in Alberta when her father dies. To her surprise he has left her the family ranch and, to the surprise of everyone else, she decides to stay and run it. She hires a good-looking local man to help her out and they both discover that they want more than a working relationship. However, the fireworks really start when he proposes a marriage of convenience. Engaging performances and beautiful scenery help raise this romantic tale of opposites above the average.
1990 97m/C CA Wendy Crewson, Paul Gross, Marion Gilsenan, Kyra Harper, Victoria Snow; **D:** Eric Till. **VHS $19.95** ACA ⊘⊘⊘

Buffalo Rider An adventure film depicting the real-life experiences of C.J. "Buffalo" Jones who worked to save the American buffalo from extinction.
1978 90m/C Rick Guinn, John Freeman, Pricilla Lauris, George Sager, Rich Scheeland; **D:** George Lauris. **VHS, Beta** NO ⊘½

Buffalo Stampede Our heroes are involved in a plot to round up buffalo to sell for meat.
1933 60m/B Randolph Scott, Buster Crabbe, Harry Carey Sr., Noah Beery Sr., Raymond Hatton. **VHS, Beta $19.95** NOS, VCN, MRV ⊘

Buffet Froid Surreal black comedy about a group of bungling murderers. First rate acting and directing makes this film a hilarious treat. From the director of "Menage." In French with English subtitles.
1979 95m/C FR Gerard Depardieu, Bernard Blier, Jean Carmet, Genevieve Page, Denise Gence, Carol Bouquet, Jean Benguigui, Michel Serrault; **D:** Bertrand Blier. **VHS $59.95** INT, ING, TPV ⊘⊘⊘½

Buffy the Vampire Slayer Funny, near-camp teen genre spoof. Buffy is a typical mall gal concerned with shopping and cheerleading, until the mysterious Sutherland proclaims it her destiny to slay the vampires who have suddenly infested Los Angeles. Like, really. Buffy requires some convincing, but eventually takes up the challenge, fighting off the vamps and their seductive leader Hauer, aided by perpetual guy-in-distress Perry. "Pee Wee" Reubens is unrecognizable and terribly amusing as the vampire king's sinister henchman, engaging in one of the longer death scenes of film history. Check out Cassandra (Wagner), Natalie Wood's daughter.
1992 (PG-13) 98m/C Kristy Swanson, Donald Sutherland, Luke Perry, Paul (Pee Wee Herman) Reubens, Rutger Hauer, Michele Abrams, Randall Batinkoff, Hilary Swank, Paris Vaughan, David Arquette, Candy Clark, Natasha Gregson Wagner; **D:** Fran Rubel Kazui; **W:** Joss Whedon; **M:** Carter Burwell. **VHS $19.98** FXV, PMS ⊘⊘⊘

Buford's Beach Bunnies Harry Buford has made a fortune selling barbecued rabbit sandwiches served by the sexiest waitresses around. Harry wants to leave the business to his son Jeeter—if Jeeter can overcome his overwhelming fear of women. So three of Harry's waitresses decide to show Jeeter a very good time. Lots of pretty girls in not much clothing.
1992 (R) 90m/C Jim Hanks, Rikki Brando, Monique Parent, Amy Page, Barrett Cooper, Ina Rogers, Charley Rossman, David Robinson; **D:** Mark Pirro; **W:** Mark Pirro. **VHS $89.95** IMP ⊘

Bug The city of Riverside is threatened with destruction after a massive earth tremor unleashes a super-race of ten-inch mega-cockroaches that belch fire, eat raw meat, and are virtually impervious to Raid. Produced by gimmick-king William Castle, who wanted to install windshield wiper-like devices under theatre seats that would brush against the patrons' feet as the cockroaches crawled across the screen; unfortunately, the idea was squashed flat.
1975 (PG) 100m/C Bradford Dillman, Joanna Miles, William Castle; **D:** Jeannot Szwarc; **M:** Charles Fox. **VHS, Beta $19.95** PAR Woof!

Bugles in the Afternoon Life in the army during Custer's last days, within a love triangle, revenge and the Little Big Horn for added spice.
1952 85m/C Ray Milland, Hugh Marlowe, Helena Carter, Forrest Tucker, Barton MacLane, George Reeves; **D:** Roy Rowland. **VHS $14.95** REP, FCT ⊘⊘

Bugs & Daffy: The Wartime Cartoons A compilation of Daffy and Bugs classics made during WWII, often dominated by propaganda and Axis-baiting.
1945 120m/C **D:** Robert McKimson, Chuck Jones, Friz Freleng. **VHS, Beta $19.95** MGM, WTA ⊘⊘

Bugs Bunny: Hollywood Legend Six episodes featuring the wascally wabbit, including "Hair-Raising Hare," "A Hare Grows in Manhattan," and "Herr Meets Hare."
1990 60m/C **V:** Mel Blanc. **VHS $12.98** MGM, FCT, WTA ⊘⊘

The Bugs Bunny/Road Runner Movie A compilation of classic Warner Brothers cartoons, starring Bugs Bunny, Daffy Duck, Elmer Fudd, the Road Runner, Wile E. Coyote, Porky Pig, and Pepe Le Pew, including some all-new animated sequences. Also available with Spanish dubbing. **AKA:** Great American Bugs Bunny-Road Runner Chase.
1979 (G) 98m/C **D:** Chuck Jones, Phil Monroe; **V:** Mel Blanc. **VHS, Beta $14.95** WAR, WTA, APD ⊘⊘

Bugs Bunny Superstar A collection of nine animated classics starring everybody's favorite "wascally wabbitt." Includes fascinating interviews and behind the scenes moments featuring the men and women who brought Bugs to life.
1975 (G) 91m/C **D:** Larry Jackson, Bob Clampett, Tex Avery, Friz Freleng; **V:** Mel Blanc. **VHS $19.95** MGM, WTA ⊘⊘

Bugs Bunny's Comedy Classics A collection of classic wabbit tales including "Easter Yeggs," "Racketeer Rabbit," "The Hair-Brained Hypnotist," "Acrobatty Rabbit," "Falling Hare," and "Haredevil Hare."
1988 60m/C **V:** Mel Blanc. **VHS $12.98** MGM, FCT, WTA ⊘⊘

Bugs Bunny's 3rd Movie: 1,001 Rabbit Tales A compilation of old and new classic cartoons featuring Bugs, Daffy, Sylvester, Porky, Elmer, Tweety, Speedy Gonzalez and Yosemite Sam.
1982 (G) 74m/C **D:** Chuck Jones, Robert McKimson, Friz Freleng. **VHS, Beta $14.95** WAR, FCT, WTA ⊘⊘

Bugsy Beatty is Benjamin "Bugsy" Siegel, the 40s gangster who built the Flamingo Hotel in Las Vegas when it was still a virtual desert, before it became a gambling mecca. Bening is perfect as Bugsy's moll, Virginia Hill, who inspired him to carry out his dream of building the Flamingo (which was her nickname). Beatty and Bening heat up the screen and their off-screen relationship was no different. Fans anticipated their seemingly imminent marriage almost as much as the release of this movie. Almost nothing mars this film which Toback adapted from a novel by Dean Jennings, "We Only Kill Each Other: The Life and Bad Times of Bugsy Siegel."
1991 (R) 135m/C Warren Beatty, Annette Bening, Harvey Keitel, Ben Kingsley, Elliott Gould, Joe Mantegna, Richard Sarafian, Bebe Neuwirth, Wendy Phillips, Robert Beltran, Bill Graham, Lewis Van Bergen, Debrah Farentino; **D:** Barry Levinson; **W:** James Toback; **M:** Ennio Morricone. Academy Awards '91: Best Art Direction/Set Decoration, Best Costume Design; Nominations: Best Actor (Beatty), Best Cinematography, Best Director (Levinson), Best Original Screenplay, Best Picture, Best Supporting Actor (Keitel, Kingsley), Best Original Score; Chicago Film Critics Awards '91: Best

Supporting Actor (Keitel); Golden Globe Awards '92: Best Film—Drama; Los Angeles Film Critics Association Awards '91: Best Director (Levinson), Best Film; National Board of Review Awards '91: 10 Best Films of the Year, Best Actor (Beatty). **VHS, Beta, 8mm** $19.95 *COL* 🐾🐾🐾½

Bugsy Malone Delightful musical features an all-children's cast highlighting this spoof of 1930s' gangster movies.
1976 (G) 94m/C *GB* Jodie Foster, Scott Baio, Florrie Augger, John Cassisi, Martin Lev; *D:* Alan Parker; *W:* Alan Parker; *M:* Paul Williams. **VHS, Beta** $14.95 *PAR* 🐾🐾½

Bull Durham Lovable American romantic comedy, dealing with a very minor minorleague team and three of its current constituents: an aging baseball groupie that beds one player each season; a cocky, foolish new pitcher; and the older, weary catcher brought in to wise the rookie up. The scene in which Sarandon tries poetry out on the banal rookie is a hoot. Highly acclaimed, the film sears with Sarandon and Costner's love scenes.
1988 (R) 107m/C Kevin Costner, Susan Sarandon, Tim Robbins, Trey Wilson, Robert Wuhl, Jenny Robertson; *D:* Ron Shelton; *W:* Ron Shelton; *M:* Michael Convertino. **VHS, Beta** $19.98 *ORI, HMV* 🐾🐾🐾½

Bull of the West Cattlemen battle for land in the wide open spaces of the old West.
1989 90m/C Charles Bronson, Lee J. Cobb, Brian Keith, George Kennedy, DeForest Kelley, Doug McClure. **VHS** *NO* 🐾½

Bulldance At a gymnastic school in Crete, a girl's obsession with Greek mythological ritual leads to murder. *AKA:* Forbidden Son.
1988 105m/C Lauren Hutton, Cliff DeYoung, Renee Estevez; *D:* Zelda Barron. **VHS, Beta** *ACA* 🐾

Bulldog Courage Young man is out to avenge his father's murder.
1935 66m/B Tim McCoy, Lois January, Joan Woodbury, John Elliott; *D:* Sam Newfield. **VHS, Beta** $19.95 *NOS, VCN, DVT* 🐾

Bulldog Drummond The Bulldog Drummond character, created by "Sapper" (Herman Cyril McNeile), underwent a number of different incarnations from 20s silents through the 40s, and even occasionally in the 50s and 60s. A suave ex-British officer (a precursor to the glib shaken-not-stirred gentleman-spy variety), Bulldog has been played by the likes of Colman, Ralph Richardson, and Tom Conway, among others. In this, the first installment in the long-standing series, a WWI vet, bored with civilian life, is enlisted by a beautiful woman to help her father in various adventures.
1929 85m/B Ronald Colman, Joan Bennett, Montagu Love; *D:* F. Richard Jones. **VHS, Beta** $19.98 *SUE, RXM* 🐾🐾½

Bulldog Drummond at Bay Drummond searches for a group of foreign agents who are trying to steal the plans for a top-secret warplane. Poor British entry to the "Bulldog Drummond" series.
1937 63m/B *GB* John Lodge, Dorothy Mackaill, Victor Jory, Claud Allister, Hugh Miller; *D:* Norman Lee. **VHS** $16.95 *SNC* 🐾

Bulldog Drummond Comes Back Drummond, aided by Colonel Nielson, rescues his fiancee from the hands of desperate kidnappers.
1937 119m/B John Howard, John Barrymore, Louise Campbell, Reginald Denny, Guy Standing; *D:* Louis King. **VHS, Beta** $16.95 *SNC, NOS, DVT* 🐾

Bulldog Drummond Escapes Drummond, aided by his side-kick and valet, rescues a beautiful girl from spies. He then falls in love with her.

1937 67m/B Ray Milland, Heather Angel, Reginald Denny, Guy Standing, Porter Hall, E.E. Clive; *D:* James Hogan. **VHS, Beta** $16.95 *SNC, NOS, VYY* 🐾🐾

Bulldog Drummond in Africa/ Arrest Bulldog Drummond Two mid-series Bulldog Drummond films, with two new villains.
1938 115m/B John Howard, H.B. Warner, George Zucco. **VHS, Beta** $19.98 *SUE, RXM* 🐾🐾

Bulldog Drummond's Bride Ace detective Bulldog Drummond has to interrupt his honeymoon in order to pursue a gang of bank robbers across France and England. The last of the Bulldog Drummond film series.
1939 69m/B John Howard, Heather Angel, H.B. Warner, E.E. Clive, Reginald Denny, Eduardo Ciannelli; *D:* James Hogan. **VHS, Beta** *DVT, MRV, RXM* 🐾🐾

Bulldog Drummond's Peril Murder and robbery drag the adventurous Drummond away from his wedding and he pursues the villains until they are behind bars. One in the film series.
1938 77m/B John Barrymore, John Howard, Louise Campbell, Reginald Denny, E.E. Clive, Porter Hall; *D:* James Hogan. **VHS, Beta** $16.95 *SNC, CAB, RXM* 🐾

Bulldog Drummond's Revenge Bulldog's "Revenge" was made during the series' heyday and was the second to star Howard as Drummond; Barrymore revels in the character of Inspector Neilson of Scotland Yard, and Denny is Algy. In this typically fast-paced installment, suave sleuth Drummond stalks the master criminal responsible for stealing the formula to an explosive.
1937 55m/B John Howard, John Barrymore, Reginald Denny, Louise Campbell, Frank Puglia, Nydia Westman, Lucien Littlefield; *D:* Louis King. **VHS, Beta** $16.95 *SNC, MOV* 🐾

Bulldog Drummond's Revenge/ Bulldog Drummond's Peril Once again, Bulldog Drummond becomes entangled with diamond counterfeiters, secret explosives, and other crime and criminals. Two episodes in a series.
1938 118m/B John Howard, John Barrymore, Louise Campbell, Reginald Denny, E.E. Clive, Porter Hall. **VHS, Beta** $19.98 *SUE* 🐾🐾½

Bulldog Drummond's Secret Police The 15th Drummond film, adapted from Herman Cyril McNeile's famed detective novels featuring a million-pound treasure stashed in the Drummond manor and the murderous endeavors to retrieve it.
1939 54m/B John Howard, Heather Angel, H.B. Warner, Reginald Denny, E.E. Clive, Leo G. Carroll; *D:* James Hogan. **VHS, Beta** $16.95 *SNC, VYY, RXM* 🐾

Bulldog Edition Two newspapers engage in an all-out feud to be number one in the city, even going so far as to employ gangsters for purposes of sabotage.
1936 57m/B Ray Walker, Evelyn Knapp, Regis Toomey, Cy Kendall, Billy Newell, Oscar Apfel, Betty Compson, Robert Warwick; *D:* Charles Lamont. **VHS, Beta** $16.95 *SNC* 🐾

Bulldog Jack Fine entry in the series has Drummond's colleague battling it out with Richardson, the leader of gang of jewel thieves. *AKA:* Alias Bulldog Drummond.
1935 62m/B *GB* Fay Wray, Jack Hulbert, Claude Hulbert, Ralph Richardson, Paul Graetz, Gibb McLaughlin; *D:* Walter Forde. **VHS, Beta** $16.95 *NOS, SNC* 🐾🐾

The Bulldozer Brigade Young friends fight city hall in an effort to save their secret wooded playground from land developers.
1985 86m/C **VHS** $39.98 *FHE, BTV* 🐾🐾½

Bullet Code It's quick-shooting shenanigans when O'Brien chases a pack of angry rustlers off his neighbor's land.
1940 56m/B George O'Brien, Virginia Vale, Howard Hickman, Harry Woods, Charles "Slim" Whitaker; *D:* David Howard; *W:* Doris Schroeder. **VHS** $19.99 *MOV* 🐾🐾

Bullet for Sandoval An ex-Confederate renegade loots and pillages the north Mexican countryside on his way to murder the grandfather of the woman he loves.
1970 96m/C *SP IT* Ernest Borgnine, George Hilton; *D:* Julio Buchs. **VHS, Beta** $19.95 *VCI* 🐾🐾

A Bullet for the General An American mercenary joins with rebel forces during the Mexican Revolution. *AKA:* Quien Sabe?.
1968 95m/C *IT* Martine Beswick, Lou Castel, Gian Marie Volonte, Klaus Kinski; *D:* Damiano Damiani. **VHS, Beta** $14.95 *COL, NLC* 🐾

A Bullet Is Waiting A diligent sheriff finally catches his man only to be trapped in a blinding snowstorm with the hardened criminal.
1954 83m/C Jean Simmons, Rory Calhoun, Stephen McNally, Brian Aherne; *D:* John Farrow. **VHS, Beta** *GKK* 🐾🐾

Bulletproof An unstoppable ex-CIA agent battles to retrieve a high-tech nuclear tank from terrorist hands.
1988 (R) 93m/C Gary Busey, Darlanne Fluegel, Henry Silva, Thalmus Rasulala, L.Q. Jones, R.G. Armstrong, Rene Enriquez; *D:* Steve Carver. **VHS, Beta** $14.95 *COL* 🐾

Bullets or Ballots Tough New York cop goes undercover to join the mob in order to get the goods on them. Old-fashioned danger and intrigue follow, making for some action-packed thrills.
1938 82m/B Edward G. Robinson, Humphrey Bogart, Barton MacLane, Joan Blondell, Frank McHugh, Louise Beavers; *D:* William Keighley. **VHS, Beta** $19.98 *MGM, CCB* 🐾🐾🐾

Bullfighter & the Lady An American goes to Mexico to learn the fine art of bullfighting in order to impress a beautiful woman.
1950 87m/B Robert Stack, Gilbert Roland, Virginia Grey, Katy Jurado; *D:* Budd Boetticher. **VHS** $19.98 *REP* 🐾🐾½

Bullfighters Stan and Ollie are in hot pursuit of a dangerous criminal which leads them to Mexico where Stan winds up in a bull ring.
1945 61m/B Stan Laurel, Oliver Hardy, Margo Woode, Richard Lane; *D:* Malcolm St. Clair. **VHS, Beta** $29.98 *FOX, MLB* 🐾🐾

Bullies A woodland-transplanted young man decides to fight back against an ornery mountain clan who have raped his mother, tortured his father, and beat up his girlfriend. Brutal and unpalatable.
1986 (R) 96m/C *CA* Janet-Laine Green, Dehl Berti, Stephen Hunter, Jonathan Crombie, Olivia D'Abo; *D:* Paul Lynch. **VHS, Beta** $79.95 *MCA* Woof!

Bullitt A detective assigned to protect a star witness for 48 hours senses danger; his worst fears are confirmed when his charge is murdered. Based on the novel, "Mute Witness" by Robert L. Pike, and featuring one of filmdom's most famous car chases.
1968 (PG) 105m/C Steve McQueen, Robert Vaughn, Jacqueline Bisset, Don Gordon, Robert Duvall, Norman Fell, Simon Oakland; *D:* Peter Yates; *W:* Alan R. Trustman. Academy Awards '68: Best Film Editing; Nominations: Best Sound; Edgar Allan Poe Awards '68: Best Screenplay. **VHS, Beta** $19.98 *WAR* 🐾🐾🐾

Bullseye! Knockabout farce is a letdown considering the talents involved. Shady scientists (Moore and Caine) pursue/are pursued by lookalike con-artists (Caine and Moore), who are pursued in turn by international agents. Full of inside jokes and celebrity cameos, but nothing exceptional.
1990 (PG-13) 95m/C Michael Caine, Roger Moore, Sally Kirkland, Patsy Kensit, Jenny Seagrove, John Cleese; *Cameos:* Lee Patterson, Deborah Barrymore, Mark Burns, Debra Lang, Lynn Nesbitt, Steffanie Pitt, Alexandra Pigg; *D:* Michael Winner; *M:* John Du Prez. VHS **$89.95** COL 🐾½

Bullshot Zany English satire sends up the legendary Bulldog Drummond. In the face of mad professors, hapless heroines, devilish Huns and deadly enemies, our intrepid hero remains distinctly British.
1983 (PG) 84m/C *GB* Alan Shearman, Diz White, Ron House, Frances Tomelty, Michael Aldridge, Ron Pember, Christopher Good; *D:* Dick Clement; *M:* John Du Prez. VHS, Beta NO 🐾🐾½

Bullshot Crummond The Low Moan Spectacular comedy troupe performs this satire that trashes oldtime adventure serials.
1984 90m/C VHS, Beta **$39.95** RKO, TTC 🐾🐾½

Bullwhip A man falsely accused of murder saves himself from the hangman's noose by agreeing to a shotgun wedding.
1958 80m/C Guy Madison, Rhonda Fleming, James Griffith, Peter Adams; *D:* Harmon Jones. VHS **$19.98** REP 🐾🐾

Bummer Rock band's wild party turns into tragedy when the bass player goes too far with two groupies. It's a bad scene, man.
1973 (R) 90m/C Kipp Whitman, Dennis Burkley, Carol Speed, Connie Strickland; *D:* William Allen Castleman. VHS, Beta NO Woof!

Bums Sergeant Andrew Holloman is a military officer in search of his long lost brother. It turns out his brother was homeless and is now dead at the hands of a skid row killer. Holloman recruits a platoon of other homeless people to help him track the killer but what he discovers is a multimillion conspiracy behind the murders.
1993 94m/C Christopher McDonald, Haskell Phillips, Dawn Evans; *D:* Andy Galler; *W:* Pat Allee, Ben Hurst. VHS **$89.95** MNC 🐾🐾

Bunco Two policemen working for the Los Angeles Police Department's Bunco Squad discover a college for con artists complete with tape-recorded lessons and on-the-job training.
1983 60m/C Tom Selleck, Robert Urich, Donna Mills, Will Geer, Arte Johnson, Alan Feinstein. VHS, Beta **$59.95** LHV, WAR 🐾

Bundle of Joy Salesgirl who saves an infant from falling off the steps of a foundling home is mistaken for the child's mother. Remake of 1939's "Bachelor Mother." ♫Bundle of Joy; I Never Felt This Way Before; Lullaby in Blue; Worry About Tomorrow; All About Love; Someday Soon; What's So Good About Morning?; You're Perfect In Every Department.
1956 98m/C Debbie Reynolds, Eddie Fisher, Adolphe Menjou; *D:* Norman Taurog. VHS, Beta **$19.95** VCI 🐾🐾½

A Bunny's Tale The story of Gloria Steinem's undercover journey into the Playboy Club as a fledgling journalist. It is here that she discovered her dedication as a feminist. Based on the book by Steinem.
1985 97m/C Kirstie Alley, Cotter Smith, Deborah Van Valkenburgh, Joanna Kerns, Delta Burke, Diana Scarwid; *D:* Karen Arthur. VHS, Beta **$79.95** PSM 🐾🐾

Buona Sera, Mrs. Campbell The lovely Lollobridgida and some fast-paced plot moves are the main highlights of this comedy. Mrs. Campbell convinced her three American WWII lovers that each of them had fathered her daughter. All three have supported mother and child through the years, unbeknowst to each other and their wives. When their 20-year reunion brings them back to Italy, Mrs. Campbell must do some fast-thinking and some quick-stepping to keep everyone happy.
1968 113m/C Gina Lollobrigida, Shelley Winters, Phil Silvers, Peter Lawford, Telly Savalas, Lee Grant, Janet Margolin, Marian Moses; *D:* Melvin Frank. VHS **$19.98** MGM 🐾🐾½

The 'Burbs A tepid satire about suburbanites suspecting their creepy new neighbors of murderous activities. Well-designed and sharp, but light on story.
1989 (PG) 101m/C Tom Hanks, Carrie Fisher, Rick Ducommun, Corey Feldman, Brother Theodore, Bruce Dern, Gale Gordon, Courtney Gains; *D:* Joe Dante; *M:* Jerry Goldsmith. VHS, Beta **$14.95** MCA, CCB 🐾½

Burden of Dreams The landmark documentary chronicling the berserk circumstances behind the scenes of Werner Herzog's epic "Fitzcarraldo." Stuck in the Peruvian jungles, the film crew was subjected to every disaster imaginable while executing Herzog's vision, including disease, horrendous accident, warring local tribes and the megalomaniacal director himself. Considered better than "Fitzcarraldo," although both films discuss a man's obsession.
1982 94m/C Klaus Kinski, Mick Jagger, Jason Robards Jr., Werner Herzog; *D:* Les Blank. VHS, Beta **$59.95** TPV, FFM, BTV 🐾½

Bureau of Missing Persons Comedy-drama about big-city bureau of missing persons, in which the hardened Stone is in charge. O'Brien plays a tough cop who is transferred to the bureau and Davis stars as the mystery woman with whom he gets involved. Although fast-paced and intriguing, the film is somewhat confusing and never stays in one direction for very long.
1933 75m/B Bette Davis, Lewis Stone, Pat O'Brien, Glenda Farrell, Allen Jenkins, Ruth Donnelly, Hugh Herbert; *D:* Roy Del Ruth. VHS **$19.98** MGM 🐾½

Burgess, Philby, and MacLean: Spy Scandal of the Century An intriguing, true spy story about three double agents who were able to infiltrate British Intelligence and pass on U.S. atomic secrets to the Soviet Union. Originally aired on PBS.
1986 83m/C VHS, Beta MTI 🐾🐾½

Burglar Not to be confused with the Whoopi Goldberg vehicle, this Russian film relates a story no less American than apple pie and teenage angst. Senka and would-be punk star Kostya are two neglected and disaffected brothers whose father is a drunken womanizer best known for absentee paternalism. When Howmuch, a serious heavy metalloid, pressures Kostya to steal a synthesizer, brother Senka steps in to steal the Community Center's property himself. In Russian with English subtitles, the solid performances hold their own against the heavy musical content. *AKA:* Vzlomschik.
1987 89m/C *RU* Konstantin Kinchev, Oleg Yelykomov; *D:* Valery Orgorodnikov. VHS **$59.95** FCT, KIV 🐾🐾🐾

Burglar A cat burglar moves to the right side of the law when she tries to solve a murder case. Whoopi's always a treat, but this movie's best forgotten; fans of Whoopi should watch "Jumpin' Jack Flash" again

instead. Co-star Bob "Bobcat" Goldthwaite elevates the comedic level a bit.
1987 (R) 103m/C Whoopi Goldberg, Bob(cat) Goldthwait, Lesley Ann Warren, John Goodman, G.W. Bailey, James Handy, Anne DeSalvo; *D:* Hugh Wilson; *W:* Hugh Wilson. VHS, Beta **$19.98** WAR, KIV 🐾🐾

Burial Ground A classically grisly splatter film in which the hungry dead rise and proceed to kill the weekend denizens of an isolated aristocratic mansion.
1985 85m/C Karen Well, Peter Bark; *D:* Andrew Bianchi. VHS, Beta **$79.95** VES, LIV 🐾

Buried Alive A man is sent to prison on trumped up charges. Only the prison nurse believes he is innocent as a crooked politician strives to keep him behind bars.
1939 74m/B Beverly Roberts, Robert Wilcox, George Pembroke, Ted Osborn, Paul McVey, Alden Chase; *D:* Victor Halperin. Beta **$16.95** NOS, MRV, LOO 🐾

Buried Alive Director d'Amato reaps his finest gore-fest to date, incorporating the well-established taxidermist gone loony motif in his repertoire of appalling bad taste. Not for the squeamish, this bloodier-than-thou spaghetti spooker is chock full of necrophilia, cannibalism, and more.
1981 90m/C *IT* Kieran Canter, Cinzia Monreale, Franca Stoppi; *D:* Joe D'Amato. VHS NO 🐾🐾

Buried Alive Once Ravenscroft Hall was an asylum for the incurably insane. Now, the isolated mansion is a school for troubled teenage girls, run by a charismatic psychiatrist. Captivated by his charm, a young woman joins the staff. Soon, she is tormented by nightmare visions of the long-dead victims of a nameless killer. When the students begin to disappear, she realizes he still lives...and she may be his next victim. Carradine's last role.
1989 (R) 97m/C Robert Vaughn, Donald Pleasence, Karen Witter, John Carradine, Ginger Lynn Allen; *D:* Gerard Kikione. VHS **$14.95** COL 🐾🐾

Buried Alive One of the many horror flicks entitled "Buried Alive," this one is not bad, injecting a bit of levity into the time-worn genre. Schemestress Leigh and her paramour poison her husband. Or so they think, only to discover that he's not quite dead. Made for cable.
1990 (PG-13) 93m/C Tim Matheson, Jennifer Jason Leigh, William Atherton, Hoyt Axton; *D:* Frank Darabont; *W:* Mark Patrick Carducci; *M:* Michel Colombier. VHS **$79.95** MCA 🐾🐾½

Burke & Wills A lush, big-budgeted true story of the two men who first crossed Australia on foot, and explored its central region. Popular Australian film.
1985 (PG-13) 120m/C *AU* Jack Thompson, Nigel Havers, Greta Scacchi, Ralph Cotterill, Drew Forsythe, Chris Haywood, Matthew Fargher; *D:* Graeme Clifford; *W:* Michael Thomas; *M:* Peter Sculthorpe. VHS, Beta **$19.98** NLC, ING 🐾🐾½

Burlesque of Carmen A silent pastiche of the Bizet opera, with Charlie as Don Schmose. Interesting early work.
1916 30m/B Charlie Chaplin, Ben Turpin, Edna Purviance; *D:* Charlie Chaplin. VHS, Beta **$19.95** NOS, DVT, HEG 🐾🐾

The Burmese Harp At the end of WWII, a Japanese soldier is spiritually traumatized and becomes obsessed with burying the masses of war casualties. A searing, acclaimed anti-war statement, in Japanese with English subtitles. Remade by Ichikawa in 1985. *AKA:* Harp of Burma; Birumano Tategoto.

1956 115m/B *JP* Shoji Yasui, Rentaro Mikuni, Tatsuya Mihashi, Tanie Kitabayashi, Yunosuke Ito; *D:* Kon Ichikawa. VHS, **Beta** $29.95 *CVC, ING, APD* 🎬🎬🎬

Burn! An Italian-made indictment of imperialist control by guerrilla-filmmaker Pontecorvo, depicting the efforts of a 19th century British ambassador to put down a slave revolt on a Portuguese-run Caribbean island. Great Brando performance. *AKA:* Quemimada!.
1970 (PG) 112m/C *IT* Marlon Brando, Evarist Marquez, Renato Salvatori; *D:* Gillo Pontecorvo; *M:* Ennio Morricone. VHS, **Beta** $19.98 *MGM, VYG, CRC* 🎬🎬🎬 ½

Burn 'Em Up Barnes Twelve episodes each depicting the adventures of "Burn 'Em Up" Barnes, a racer, and his buddy, Bobbie.
1934 40m/B Frankie Darro, Lola Lane, Jack Mulhall. VHS, **Beta** $26.95 *SNC, NOS, VCN* 🎬🎬🎬 ½

Burn Witch, Burn! A college professor proudly finds himself rapidly rising in his profession. His pride turns to horror though when he discovers that his success is not due to his own abilities, but to the efforts of his witchcraft practicing wife. Excellent, atmospheric horror with a genuinely suspenseful climax. *AKA:* Night of the Eagle.
1962 87m/B *GB* Peter Wyngarde, Janet Blair, Margaret Johnston, Anthony Nicholls, Colin Gordon, Kathleen Byron, Reginald Beckwith, Jessica Dunning; *D:* Sidney Hayers; *W:* Richard Matheson. VHS $18.00 *FRG* 🎬🎬🎬

Burndown Victims of a serial killer in a town with a large nuclear reactor are themselves radioactive, which leads the Police Chief and a beautiful reporter to the truth and the hidden conspiracy.
1989 (R) 97m/C Cathy Moriarty, Peter Firth; *D:* James Allen. VHS, **Beta** *NO* 🎬

The Burning Story of macabre revenge set in the dark woods of a seemingly innocent summer camp.
1982 (R) 90m/C Brian Matthews, Leah Ayres, Holly Hunter, Jason Alexander; *D:* Tony Maylam. VHS, **Beta** *NO* 🎬

The Burning Bed A made for television dramatic expose (based on a true story) about wife-beating. Fawcett garnered accolades for her performance as the battered wife who couldn't take it anymore. Highly acclaimed and Emmy-nominated.
1985 95m/C Farrah Fawcett, Paul LeMat, Penelope Milford, Richard Masur; *D:* Robert Greenwald. VHS, **Beta** $79.98 *FOX* 🎬🎬🎬 ½

The Burning Court Unusual horror film involving occultism, possession, and family curses. Dubbed into English. Based on a story by John Dickson Carr.
1962 ?m/C Nadja Tiller, Jean-Claude Brialy, Edith Scob. VHS $16.95 *SNC* 🎬 ½

The Burning Hills Unexceptional cow flick based on a Louis L'Amour novel. Hunter hides from cattle thieves in a barn and, eventually, in the arms of a half-breed Mexican girl (Wood). Tedious and unsurprising.
1956 94m/C Tab Hunter, Natalie Wood, Skip Homeier, Eduard Franz; *D:* Stuart Heisler. VHS $29.99 *WAR, MLB* 🎬 ½

Burning Rage A blazing, abandoned coal mine threatens to wreak havoc in the Appalachians. The government sends geologist Mandrell to help prevent a disaster. Made for television.
1984 100m/C Barbara Mandrell, Tom Wopat, Bert Remsen, John Pleshette, Carol Kane, Eddie Albert; *D:* Gilbert Cates. VHS *VTR* 🎬

Burning Secret After WWI, a widow in Austria (Dunaway) meets a baron (Brandauer) who has befriended her son. Mutual seduction ensues but the sparks don't fly. Adapted from Stefan Zweig story. *AKA:* Brennendes Geheimnis.
1989 (PG) 107m/C *GB* Faye Dunaway, Klaus Maria Brandauer, Ian Richardson, David Eberts; *D:* Andrew Birkin; *W:* Andrew Birkin. VHS, **Beta** $89.98 *VES, IME, LIV* 🎬🎬

Burning Vengeance A DEA agent enters the deadly world of drugs and single-handedly annihilates the drug smugglers and destroys their kingpin.
1989 120m/C VHS, **Beta** *AIP* 🎬🎬

The Burns and Allen Show George and Gracie's classic vaudeville routines are a highlight of this sitcom series, with George the perpetually harried husband to the scatterbrained Gracie. Additional episodes are available.
1950 115m/B Gracie Allen, George Burns. VHS, **Beta** *SHO, COL, MOV* 🎬🎬

Burnt Offerings A family rents an old mansion for the summer and they become affected by evil forces that possess the house. Based on the novel by Robert Marasco.
1976 (PG) 116m/C Oliver Reed, Karen Black, Bette Davis, Burgess Meredith; *D:* Dan Curtis. VHS, **Beta** $14.95 *MGM* 🎬🎬

Bury Me an Angel A female biker sets out to seek revenge against the men who killed her brother.
1971 85m/C Dixie Peabody, Terry Mace, Clyde Ventura, Dan Haggerty, Stephen Whittaker, Gary Littlejohn; *D:* Barbara Peeters. VHS, **Beta** $19.95 *STE, NWV, HHT* 🎬

Bury Me Not On the Lone Prairie When his brother is murdered in cold blood by claim jumpers, mining engineer Brown goes to avenge the dead. Based on a story by Sherman Lowe.
1941 57m/B Johnny Mack Brown, Fuzzy Knight, Nell O'Day, Frank O'Connor, Kermit Maynard; *D:* Ray Taylor; *W:* Sherman Lowe, Victor McLeod. VHS $19.99 *MOV* 🎬🎬

The Bus Is Coming A love story entwined with the problems of blacks in a small town.
1972 95m/C Mike Sims, Stephanie Faulkner, Morgan Jones; *D:* Horace Jackson. VHS, **Beta** *NO* 🎬🎬

Bus Stop Murray plays a naive cowboy who falls in love with Monroe, a barroom singer, and decides to marry her without her permission. Considered by many to be the finest performance by Marilyn Monroe; she sings "That Old Black Magic" in this one. Very funny with good performances by all. Based on the William Inge play. *AKA:* The Wrong Kind of Girl.
1956 96m/C Marilyn Monroe, Arthur O'Connell, Hope Lange, Don Murray, Betty Field, Casey Adams, Hans Conried, Eileen Heckart; *D:* Joshua Logan; *W:* George Axelrod. Academy Awards '56 Nominations: Best Supporting Actor (Murray); National Board of Review Awards '56: 10 Best Films of the Year. VHS, **Beta** $14.98 *FOX* 🎬🎬🎬

The Busby Berkeley Disc A collection of the innovative dance director's work at Warner Bros. studio covering 1933-37. Berkeley was known for his elaborate production numbers, beautiful women, military precision, and kaleidoscopic patterns in such films as "42nd Street," "Footlight Parade," and the "Gold Diggers" series.
1992 176m/B $39.98 *MGM* 🎬🎬🎬

Bush Mama A hallucinatory film about a black woman on welfare trying to care for her daughter in a Los Angeles ghetto. Street violence varies with fantasy scenes in a loose narrative filled with flashbacks.
1976 100m/C *D:* Haile Gerima. VHS $59.95 *FCT* 🎬🎬

The Bushbaby The young Brooks is given a tiny bushbaby while visiting Africa with her father. Because of her pet she misses her ship home and finds herself with former servant Gossett, who agrees to take her to a family friend. Unfortunately, the authorities think he's kidnapped the girl and the two, along with the trouble-causing pet, are pursued by the police. Simple-minded kiddie fare.
1970 100m/C Margaret Brooks, Louis Gossett Jr., Donald Houston, Laurence Naismith, Marne Maitland, Geoffrey Bayldon, Jack Gwillim; *D:* John Trent. VHS $14.98 *MGM, FCT* 🎬 ½

The Busher All-American pitcher's romance is interrupted by a gratuitous Mr. Moneybags. Minor-league conflict with little real hardball.
1919 54m/B Charles Ray, Colleen Moore, John Gilbert. VHS, **Beta** $19.95 *GPV, FCT, GVV* 🎬 ½

The Bushido Blade An action-packed samurai thriller of adventure and betrayal set in medieval Japan. *AKA:* The Bloody Bushido Blade.
1980 92m/C *JP* Richard Boone, James Earl Jones, Frank Converse; *D:* Tom Kotani. VHS, **Beta** *NO* 🎬🎬 ½

The Bushwackers Ireland plays a veteran of the Confederate army who wishes only to put his violent past behind him. He is forced to reconsider his vow when old-west bullies threaten his family. *AKA:* The Rebel.
1952 70m/B Dorothy Malone, John Ireland, Wayne Morris, Lawrence Tierney, Jack Elam, Lon Chaney Sr., Myrna Dell; *D:* Rod Amateau. VHS $16.95 *NOS, LOO, SNC* 🎬 ½

Business as Usual A meek boutique manager in Liverpool defends a sexually harassed employee, is fired, fights back, and creates a national furor over her rights as a woman.
1988 (PG) 89m/C Glenda Jackson, Cathy Tyson, John Thaw; *D:* Lezli-Ann Barrett. VHS, **Beta** $19.98 *WAR* 🎬🎬

Busted Up A young, hard-luck urban street-fighter battles for the sake of his family and neighborhood against local crimelords.
1986 (R) 93m/C *CA* Irene Cara, Paul Coufos, Tony Rosato, Stan Shaw, Gordon Judges; *D:* Conrad Palmisano. VHS, **Beta** $79.95 *MCA* 🎬

Buster The story of Buster Edwards, the one suspect in the 1963 Great Train Robbery who evaded being captured by police. Collins makes his screen debut as one of Britain's most infamous criminals. Collins also performs on the film's soundtrack, spawning two hit singles, "Two Hearts" and "Groovy Kind of Love."
1988 (R) 102m/C *GB* Phil Collins, Julie Walters, Larry Lamb, Stephanie Lawrence, Ellen Beaven, Michael Atwell, Ralph Brown, Christopher Ellison, Sheila Hancock, Martin Jarvis, Anthony Quayle; *D:* David Green; *M:* Anne Dudley. VHS, **Beta** $89.95 *HBO* 🎬🎬 ½

Buster and Billie Tragedy ensues when a popular high school student falls in love with the class tramp in rural Georgia in 1948. Serious, decently appointed period teen drama.
1974 (R) 100m/C Jan-Michael Vincent, Joan Goodfellow, Clifton James, Pamela Sue Martin, Robert Englund; *D:* Daniel Petrie. VHS, **Beta** $59.95 *COL* 🎬 ½

Buster Keaton Festival, Vol. 1 A collection of three Keaton silent shorts from 1921-1922: "Paleface," "The Blacksmith" and "Cops." All shorts have a newly composed musical score.
1922 55m/B Buster Keaton. **VHS, Beta $19.95** VDM *I* 1/2

Buster Keaton Festival, Vol. 2 Three rare silent shorts featuring the great comic: "The Boat," "Frozen North," and "Electric House."
1923 55m/B Buster Keaton. **VHS, Beta $19.95** VDM *I* 1/2

Buster Keaton Festival, Vol. 3 Three more rare silent shorts with Keaton: "Daydreams," "The Balloonatic," and "The Garage," also featuring Fatty Arbuckle.
1920 54m/B Buster Keaton. **VHS, Beta $19.95** VDM *I* 1/2

Buster Keaton Rides Again/The Railrodder "The Railrodder" is a silent comedy short that returns Buster Keaton to the type of slapstick he made famous in his legendary 1920's films. "Buster Keaton Rides Again" (in black-and-white) is a documentary-style look at Keaton filmed during the making of "The Railrodder." Besides scenes of Keaton at work, there is also a capsule rundown of his career.
1965 81m/C Buster Keaton. **VHS, Beta $29.95** GPV *I* 1/2

Buster Keaton: The Golden Years Features three classic Buster Keaton silent shorts; "The Pale Face," "Daydreams," and "The Blacksmith," all from 1921.
1921 60m/B Buster Keaton. **VHS, Beta $29.95** DVT, HEG *I* 1/2

Buster Keaton: The Great Stone Face Program from the Rohauer Collection contains footage of Buster Keaton in "Fatty at Coney Island," "Cops," "Balloonatics," "Day Dreams," and "The General."
1968 60m/B Buster Keaton. **VHS, Beta $57.95** MAS *I* 1/2

Bustin' Loose A fast-talking ex-con reluctantly drives a bus load of misplaced kids and their keeper cross-country.
1981 (R) 94m/C Richard Pryor, Cicely Tyson, Robert Christian, George Coe, Bill Quinn; **D:** Oz Scott; **W:** Richard Pryor. **VHS, Beta $14.95** MCA *III*

Busting Gould and Blake play a pair of slightly off-the-wall L.A. cops. The pair are forced "to bust" local addicts and prostitutes instead of the real crime bosses because much of the police department is on the take. Plenty of comedy and action as well as highly realistic drama.
1974 (R) 92m/C Elliott Gould, Robert (Bobby) Blake, Allen (Gooritz) Garfield, Antonio Fargas, Michael Lerner, Sid Haig, Cornelia Sharpe; **D:** Peter Hyams; **W:** Peter Hyams; **M:** Billy Goldenberg. **VHS $14.95** MGM, MCA *II* 1/2

But Not for Me Gable stars as a middled-aged entertainment executive who thinks he can forestall maturity by carrying on with his youthful secretary.
1959 105m/B Clark Gable, Carroll Baker, Lilli Palmer, Lee J. Cobb, Barry Coe, Thomas Gomez, Charles Lane; **D:** Walter Lang; **W:** John Michael Hayes. **VHS $14.95** PAR *III* 1/2

But Where Is Daniel Wax? At a class reunion, a doctor and a popular singing star reminisce about their youth and Daniel Wax, their one-time hero. Hebrew with English subtitles.
1974 95m/C Lior Yaeni, Michael Lipkin, Esther Zevko; **D:** Avram Heffner. **VHS, Beta $79.95** ERG, ING *II*

Butch and Sundance: The Early Days Traces the origins of the famous outlaw duo. It contains the requisite shootouts, hold-ups, and escapes. A "prequel" to "Butch Cassidy and the Sundance Kid."
1979 (PG) 111m/C Tom Berenger, William Katt, John Schuck, Jeff Corey, Jill Eikenberry, Brian Dennehy, Peter Weller; **D:** Richard Lester. **VHS, Beta $19.98** FOX *II* 1/2

Butch Cassidy and the Sundance Kid Two legendary outlaws at the turn of the century take it on the lam with a beautiful, willing ex-school teacher. With a clever script, humanly fallible characters, and warm, witty dialogue, this film was destined to become a box-office classic. Featured the hit song, "Raindrops Keep Falling on My Head" and renewed the buddy film industry, as Newman and Redford trade insult for insult. Look for the great scene where Newman takes on giant Ted Cassidy in a fist fight.
1969 (PG) 110m/C Paul Newman, Robert Redford, Katharine Ross, Jeff Corey, Strother Martin, Cloris Leachman, Kenneth Mars, Ted Cassidy, Henry Jones, George Furth, Sam Elliott; **D:** George Roy Hill; **W:** William Goldman; **M:** Burt Bacharach. Academy Awards '69: Best Cinematography, Best Song ("Raindrops Keep Fallin' on My Head"), Best Story & Screenplay, Best Original Score; Nominations: Best Director (Hill), Best Picture, Best Sound; British Academy Awards '70: Best Actor (Redford), Best Actress (Ross), Best Director (Hill), Best Film; Golden Globe Awards '70: Best Score. **VHS, Beta $19.98** FOX, TLF *IIII*

The Butcher's Wife Charming tale of a young psychic (Moore) who brings romance to a Greenwich Village neighborhood that never quite gets off the ground. Moore stars as the clairvoyant whose mystical powers bring magic into the lives of everyone around her, including the local psychiatrist (Daniels), who falls under her spell. Talented cast is virtually wasted with a script that is lightweight; excepting Steenburgen and Dzundza who shine.
1991 (PG-13) 107m/C Demi Moore, Jeff Daniels, George Dzundza, Frances McDormand, Margaret Colin, Mary Steenburgen, Max Perlich, Miriam Margolyes, Christopher Durang, Diane Salinger; **D:** Terry Hughes; **W:** Ezra Litwack, Marjorie Schwartz; **M:** Michael Gore. **VHS, Beta $14.95** PAR *II*

Butler's Dilemma A jewel thief and a playboy both claim the identity of a butler who never existed, with humorous results.
1943 75m/B GB Richard Hearne, Francis L. Sullivan, Hermione Gingold, Ian Fleming. **VHS, Beta $24.95** VYY *II*

Butterfield 8 A seedy film of the John O'Hara novel about a prostitute that wants to go straight and settle down. Taylor won an Oscar, perhaps because she was ill and had lost in the two previous years in more deserving roles.
1960 108m/C Elizabeth Taylor, Laurence Harvey, Eddie Fisher, Dina Merrill, Mildred Dunnock, Betty Field, Susan Oliver, Kay Medford; **D:** Daniel Mann; **W:** John Michael Hayes, Charles Schnee. Academy Awards '60: Best Actress (Taylor); Nominations: Best Color Cinematography. **VHS, Beta $19.98** MGM, BTV *III*

Butterflies Ria, a middle-aged housewife with two lazy sons, is beginning to feel her age, and like a butterfly, feeling like she has too much to do and not enough time. Then Leonard appears in her life—divorced, lonely and romantic. Made for British television.
1975 60m/C GB **VHS $29.95** BFS *III*

Butterflies Are Free Fast-paced humor surrounds the Broadway play brought to the big screen. Blind youth Albert is determined to be self-sufficient. A next-door-neighbor actress helps him gain independence from his over-protective mother (Heckart).
1972 (PG) 109m/C Goldie Hawn, Edward Albert, Eileen Heckart, Michael Glaser; **D:** Milton Katselas. Academy Awards '72: Best Supporting Actress (Heckart); Nominations: Best Cinematography, Best Sound. **VHS, Beta $9.95** GKK *III*

Butterfly Based on James M. Cain's novel about an amoral young woman (Pia, who'd you think?) who uses her beauty and sensual appetite to manipulate the men in her life, including her father. Set in Nevada of the 1930s, father and daughter are drawn into a daring and forbidden love affair by their lust and desperation.
1982 (R) 105m/C Pia Zadora, Stacy Keach, Orson Welles, Edward Albert, James Franciscus, Lois Nettleton, Stuart Whitman, June Lockhart; **D:** Matt Cimber; **M:** Ennio Morricone. **VHS, Beta $79.95** VES, LIV *I* 1/2

Butterfly Affair Beautiful singer, involved in a scheme to smuggle two million dollars worth of gems, plots to double-cross her partners in crime.
1971 (PG) 75m/C Claudia Cardinale, Henri Charriere, Stanley Baker; **D:** Jean Herman. **VHS, Beta** NO *I* 1/2

Butterfly Ball Retelling of the 19th century classic combines the rock music of Roger Glover, live action and animation by Halas and Batchelor. Only for the brain-cell depressed.
1976 85m/C GB Twiggy, Ian Gillian, David Coverdale; **D:** Tony Klinger. **VHS, Beta** NO *I*

Buy & Cell A stockbroker attempts to set up a business while serving a prison sentence. An assortment of amusing inmates doesn't help matters much. Fans of Malcolm McDowell will enjoy his performance as the shady warden.
1989 (R) 95m/C Robert Carradine, Michael Winslow, Malcolm McDowell, Ben Vereen, Lise Cutter, Randall "Tex" Cobb, Roddy Piper; **D:** Robert Boris. **VHS $19.95** STE, NWV *I* 1/2

Buying Time Two teenagers are arrested when they try to pry their money away from a dishonest bookie, and the police use their connections to solve a drug-related murder.
1989 (R) 97m/C Dean Stockwell, Jeff Schultz, Michael Rudder, Dean De Santis, Leslie Toth, Laura Cruickshank; **D:** Mitchell Gabourie. **VHS, Beta $79.95** FOX *I*

Buzzy Rides the Range Average "B" western with a kid saving the day.
1940 ?m/C Robert "Buzzy" Henry, Dave O'Brien. **VHS $15.95** LOO *II*

By Dawn's Early Light Made-for-cable-TV thriller about two Air Force pilots who must decide whether or not to drop the bombs that would begin WWIII.
1989 100m/C Powers Boothe, Rebecca DeMornay, James Earl Jones, Martin Landau, Rip Torn, Darren McGavin; **M:** Trevor Jones. **VHS, Beta $89.99** HBO *II*

By Design Two cohabiting women want to have a baby, so they embark on a search for the perfect stud. Not one of Astin's better performances.
1982 (R) 90m/C CA Patty Duke, Sara Botsford; **D:** Claude Jutra. **VHS, Beta** NO *I*

By Hook or Crook Zany Mexican comedy/mystery featuring the "Super-Mexican" detective solving a series of high-society murders.

1985 94m/C *MX* Rafael Inclan, Maribel Guardia; *D:* Julio Ruiz Llaneza. VHS, Beta $72.95 *MED* ♪

By Love Possessed Can a seemingly typical, quiet, New England town stay quiet when Lana Turner is your neighbor? Vintage romantic melodrama about an attorney who is drawn into an affair when he realizes his home life is not all it could be.
1961 115m/C Lana Turner, Efrem Zimbalist Jr., Jason Robards Jr., George Hamilton, Thomas Mitchell; *D:* John Sturges; *M:* Elmer Bernstein. VHS $14.95 *MGM* ♪♪½

By the Blood of Others In a small French town, a psycho holds two women hostage in a farmhouse, and the townspeople try to figure out a solution without getting anyone killed. In French with English subtitles.
1973 90m/C *FR* Mariangela Melato; *D:* Marc Simenon. VHS, Beta $59.95 *FCT* ♪♪♪

By the Light of the Silvery Moon The equally old-fashioned sequel to "On Moonlight Bay" finds Day engaged to MacRae, who's just returned from Army service in WWI. He wants to postpone their marriage until he gets financially secure and the waiting causes some jealous misunderstandings (naturally resolved by movie's end). Based on Booth Tarkington's "Penrod" stories. ♫By the Light of the Silvery Moon; I'll Forget You; Your Eyes Have Told Me So; Be My Little Baby Bumble Bee; If You Were the Only Girl in the World; Ain't We Got Fun; King Chanticleer.
1953 101m/C Doris Day, Gordon MacRae, Leon Ames, Billy Gray, Rosemary DeCamp, Mary Wickes, Russell Arms, Maria Palmer; *D:* David Butler; *W:* Robert O'Brien, Irving Elinson; *M:* Max Steiner. VHS $19.98 *WAR, MVD* ♪♪½

By the Sword Maximilian Suba (Abraham) is a one-time fencing whiz who has spent the last 25 years in prison for the murder of his mentor during a fencing match. Upon his release, Suba heads back to his old fencing grounds to see what's become of the murdered man's now-grown son and discovers Alexander (Roberts) is as ruthless and ambitious as Suba once was. Incoherent plot leaves both actors and viewers in the dark.
1993 (R) 91m/C F. Murray Abraham, Eric Roberts, Mia Sara, Christopher Rydell; *D:* Jeremy Paul Kagan; *W:* John McDonald, James Donadio; *M:* Bill Conti. VHS *COL* ♪½

Bye Bye Baby Two luscious young women cavort amid lusty Italian men on various Mediterranean beaches.
1988 (R) 80m/C *IT* Carol Alt, Brigitte Nielsen, Jason Connery, Luca Barbareschi; *D:* Enrico Oldoini; *M:* Manuel De Sica. VHS, Beta $79.95 *PSM, PAR* ♪

Bye, Bye, Birdie Energized and sweet film version of the Broadway musical about a teen rock and roll idol (Pearson doing Elvis) coming to a small town to see one of his fans before he leaves for the army. The film that made Ann-Margret a star. ♫Bye Bye Birdie; The Telephone Hour; How Lovely to be a Woman; Honestly Sincere; One Boy; Put on a Happy Face; Kids; One Last Kiss; A Lot of Livin' to Do; Rosie.
1963 112m/C Dick Van Dyke, Janet Leigh, Ann-Margret, Paul Lynde, Bobby Rydell, Maureen Stapleton, Ed Sullivan, Trudi Ames; *D:* George Sidney. VHS, Beta $19.95 *COL* ♪♪♪

Bye Bye Blues The lives of the Cooper family are disrupted when the husband is called to service during WWII and is then taken prisoner by the Japanese. In need of money, wife Daisy (Jenkins) joins a local swing band and begins charming all who watch her, especially the band's trombone player (Reilly). A sweet-spirited tale of love, loyalty, and the search for inner strength. Jenkins gives a strong performance as the shy wife who becomes an independent woman during her husband's absence.
1989 (PG) 110m/C *CA* Rebecca Jenkins, Michael Ontkean, Luke Reilly, Stuart Margolin, Robyn Stevan, Kate Reid, Wayne Robson; *D:* Anne Wheeler; *W:* Anne Wheeler; *M:* George Blondheim. VHS $29.95 *MNC* ♪♪½

Bye Bye Brazil A changing Brazil is seen through the eyes of four wandering gypsy minstrels participating in a tent show traveling throughout the country. Lots of Brazilian charm. In Portuguese with English subtitles.
1979 115m/C *BR* Jose Wilker, Betty Faria, Fabio Junior, Zaira Zambello; *D:* Carlos Diegues; *W:* Carlos Diegues. VHS, Beta $79.95 *FXL, ING, TPV* ♪♪½

The C-Man Customs agent Jagger finds work isn't so dull after all. Murder and theft on an international scale make for a busy week as he follows jewel smugglers from Paris to New York. Docu-style though routine crime story.
1949 75m/B Dean Jagger, John Carradine, Harry Landers, Rene Paul; *D:* Joseph Lerner. VHS $16.95 *SNC* ♪♪

Cabaret Hitler is rising to power, racism and anti-Semitism are growing, and the best place to hide from it all is the cabaret. With dancing girls, androgynous master of ceremonies Grey and American expatriate and singer Minnelli, you can laugh and drink and pretend tomorrow will never come. Minnelli does just that. Face to face with the increasing horrors of Nazism, she persists in the belief that the "show must go on." Based on the John Kander's hit Broadway musical (taken from the Christopher Isherwood stories), the film is impressive, with excellent direction and cinematography. ♫Cabaret; Wilkommen; Mein Herr; Maybe This Time; Two Ladies; Money, Money; Hieraten; Tomorrow Belongs to Me; If You Could See Her.
1972 (PG) 119m/C Liza Minnelli, Joel Grey, Michael York, Marisa Berenson; *D:* Bob Fosse; *W:* Jay Presson Allen; *M:* Ralph Burns. Academy Awards '72: Best Actress (Minnelli), Best Art Direction/Set Decoration, Best Cinematography, Best Director (Fosse), Best Film Editing, Best Sound, Best Supporting Actor (Grey), Best Score; Nominations: Best Adapted Screenplay, Best Picture; British Academy Awards '72: Best Actress (Minnelli), Best Director (Fosse), Best Film; Golden Globe Awards '73: Best Actress—Musical/Comedy (Minnelli), Best Film—Musical/Comedy, Best Supporting Actor (Grey). VHS, Beta $19.98 *FOX, BTV, CCB* ♪♪♪½

Cabeza de Vaca In 1528, a Spanish expedition shipwrecks in unknown territory off the Florida coast. Cabeza de Vaca is captured by the Iguase Indian tribe and made a slave to their shaman. He's later freed, but leaves with respect for their culture. Spanish soldiers find him and want his help in capturing the natives, but he is outraged by their cruelty and must confront his own people. Strong visual style easily brings the audience deeply into this uncharted world. Based on Cabeza de Vaca's book "Naufragios." Director Echevarria's feature film debut.
1990 (R) 111m/C *MX SP* Juan Diego, Daniel Gimenez Cacho, Roberto Sosa, Carlos Castanon, Gerardo Villarreal, Roberto Cobo, Jose Flores, Ramon Barragan; *D:* Nicolas Echevarria; *W:* Guillermo Sheridan, Nicolas Echevarria; *M:* Mario Lavista. VHS $89.98 *NHO, FCT* ♪♪♪

Cabin Boy Obnoxious "fancy lad" Elliott mistakenly boards the wrong boat and becomes the new cabin boy for a ridiculous bunch of mean, smelly sailors. Fish out of water saga is so bad it's—bad, a blundering attempt at parody that's just plain stupid. Surprisingly produced by Tim Burton, this effort will disappoint even diehard Burton and Elliott fans. Look for real life dad Bob as the lad's dad; good friend Letterman appears briefly as nasty "Old Salt," but uses the alias Earl Hofert in the final credits. As usual, the acerbic Letterman gets the best line, one that viewers will understand all too well: "Man, oh, man do I hate them fancy lads."
1994 (PG-13) 80m/C Chris Elliott, Ann Magnuson, Ritch Brinkley, James Gammon, Brian Doyle-Murray, Russ Tamblyn, Brion James, Ricki Lake, Bob Elliott; *Cameos:* David Letterman; *D:* Adam Resnick; *W:* Adam Resnick; *M:* Steve Bartek. VHS *TOU* Woof!

The Cabin in the Cotton Davis stars as a rich, ruthless Southern belle in this dated melodrama about sharecroppers. Barthelmess is cast as a poor sharecropper who is almost brought to ruin when he falls for the sexy Southern vamp. Contains Davis's most famous line, "Ah'd love t'kiss you, but ah jes washed mah hair."
1932 77m/B Bette Davis, Richard Barthelmess, Dorothy Jordan, Henry B. Walthall, Tully Marshall; *D:* Michael Curtiz; *W:* Paul Green. VHS $19.98 *MGM* ♪♪½

Cabin in the Sky A poor woman fights to keep her husband's soul out of the devil's clutches. Based on a Broadway show and featuring an all-Black cast. Lively dance numbers and a musical score with contributions from Duke Ellington. Minnelli's first feature film. ♫Cabin in the Sky; Happiness Is Just a Thing Called Joe; Taking a Chance on Love; Life's Full of Consequence; Li'l Black Sheep; Shine; Honey in the Honeycomb.
1943 99m/C Ethel Waters, Eddie Anderson, Lena Horne, Rex Ingram, Louis Armstrong, Duke Ellington; *D:* Vincente Minnelli; *M:* Duke Ellington, Harold Arlen, E.Y. Harburg. VHS, Beta $19.98 *MGM, MLB, FHE* ♪♪♪

The Cabinet of Dr. Caligari A pioneering film in the most extreme expressionistic style about a hypnotist in a carnival and a girl-snatching somnambulist. Highly influential in its approach to lighting, composition, design and acting. Much imitated. Silent.
1919 52m/B *GE* Conrad Veidt, Werner Krauss, Lil Dagover; *D:* Robert Wiene. VHS, Beta $11.95 *SNC, REP, MRV* ♪♪♪

Cabiria The pioneering Italian epic about a Roman and a slave girl having a love affair in Rome during the Second Punic War. Immense sets and set-pieces; an important influence on Griffith and DeMille. Silent.
1914 123m/B *IT D:* Giovanni Pastrone. VHS, Beta, 8mm $39.95 *KIV, FCT, ING* ♪♪½

Cabo Blanco A bartender and a variety of other characters, including an ex-Nazi and a French woman searching for her lover, assemble in Peru after WWII. Nazi Robards controls police chief Rey, while American Bronson runs the local watering hole and eyes French woman Sanda. Hey, this sounds familiar. Everyone shares a common interest: finding a missing treasure of gold, lost in a ship wreck. Remaking "Casablanca" via "The Treasure of Sierra Madre" is never easy.
1981 (R) 87m/C Charles Bronson, Jason Robards Jr., Dominique Sanda, Fernando Rey, Gilbert Roland, Simon MacCorkindale; *D:* J. Lee Thompson; *M:* Jerry Goldsmith. VHS, Beta $59.95 *MED* ♪♪

Caches de Oro A routine arrest turns into the bloodiest case of a federal judge's career.
19?? 90m/C MX Alvaro Zermeno, Fernando Casanova, Tony Bravo, Patsy Pepping. **VHS, Beta $79.95** MED *√√*

Cactus Melodrama about a young French woman, separated from her husband, who faces the reality of losing her sight after a car accident. She experiences a growing relationship with a blind man and contemplates the thought of risky surgery which may improve her eyesight or cause complete blindness. Countering all that blindness and tangled romance is a camera that pans lush Australian landscapes and humorously focuses on the small telling details of daily life.
1986 95m/C AU Isabelle Huppert, Robert Menzies, Monica Maughan, Sheila Florence, Norman Kaye, Banduk Marika; **D:** Paul Cox; **W:** Norman Kaye, Paul Cox, Bob Ellis; **M:** Giovanni Pergolese, Yannis Markopolous, Elsa Davis. **VHS, Beta $19.98** LHV *√√*

Cactus Flower Good cast doesn't quite suffice to make this adaptation of a Broadway hit work. A middle-aged bachelor dentist gets involved with a kookie mistress, refusing to admit his real love for his prim and proper receptionist. Hawn's big leap to stardom.
1969 (PG) 103m/C Walter Matthau, Goldie Hawn, Ingrid Bergman, Jack Weston, Rick Lenz; **D:** Gene Saks; **M:** Quincy Jones. **VHS, Beta $14.95** COL *√√*

Cactus in the Snow A virginal Army private serving during the Vietnam War era tries to find sex on a 72-hour leave and instead discovers love. Some guys have all the luck. Melodrama never grabs where it ought to.
1972 90m/C Richard Thomas, Mary Layne, Lucille Benson; **D:** Martin Zweiback. **VHS, Beta** NO *√√½*

Cada Noche un Amor A singer is deceived into working as a harem girl for rich Arabs. **AKA:** Every Night a New Lover.
1975 90m/C SP Sara Montiel, Fernando Graney. **VHS, Beta** MAD *√*

Caddie Based on an autobiographical story of a woman who leaves her unfaithful husband in 1930s Australia. Struggling to raise her two children, she works as a waitress in a bar where she finds romance with one of the regulars. Average script bolstered by Morse's performance.
1981 107m/C AU Helen Morse, Jack Thompson; **D:** Donald Crombie. **VHS, Beta** NO *√√½*

The Caddy Lewis plays frantic caddy prone to slapstick against Martin's smooth professional golfer with a bent toward singing. Mostly a series of Martin and Lewis sketches that frequently land in the rough. Introduces several songs, including a couple Martin and Lewis rendition of "That's Amore." Look for cameos by a host of professional golfers.
1953 95m/C Dean Martin, Jerry Lewis, Donna Reed, Barbara Bates, Joseph Calleia, Marshall Thompson, Fred Clark; **Cameos:** Ben Hogan, Sam Snead, Byron Nelson, Julius Boros, Jimmy Thomson, Harry E. Cooper; **D:** Norman Taurog. **VHS, Beta $14.95** PAR *√√*

Caddyshack Inspired performances by Murray and Dangerfield drive this sublimely moronic comedy onto the green. The action takes place at Bushwood Country Club, where caddy O'Keefe is bucking to win the club's college scholarship. Characters involved in various sophomoric set pieces include obnoxious club president Knight, a playboy who is too laid back to keep his score (Chase), a loud, vulgar, and extremely

rich golfer (Dangerfield), and Murray as a filthy gopher-hunting groundskeeper. Occasional dry moments are followed by scenes of pure (and tasteless) anarchy, so watch with someone immature. Does for golf what "Major League" tried to do for baseball.
1980 (R) 99m/C Chevy Chase, Rodney Dangerfield, Ted Knight, Michael O'Keefe, Bill Murray, Sarah Holcomb, Brian Doyle-Murray; **D:** Harold Ramis; **W:** Brian Doyle-Murray, Doug Kenney, Harold Ramis. **VHS, Beta $19.98** WAR *√√√½*

Caddyshack 2 Obligatory sequel to "Caddyshack," minus Bill Murray who wisely avoided further encroachment of gopher holes and director Ramis who opted for the screenwriting chore. Mason is the star of the show as a crude self-made millionaire who tangles with the snobs at the country club. Although it occasionally earns a side-splitting chuckle, "Shack 2" has significantly fewer guffaws than the original, proving once again that funny guys are always undone by lousy scripts and weak direction.
1988 (PG) 103m/C Jackie Mason, Chevy Chase, Dan Aykroyd, Dyan Cannon, Robert Stack, Dina Merrill, Randy Quaid, Jessica Lundy, Jonathan Silverman, Chynna Phillips; **D:** Allan Arkush; **W:** Harold Ramis, Peter Torokvei. **VHS, Beta, 8mm $19.98** WAR *√√*

Cadence The directorial debut of actor Martin Sheen, this fitful melodrama stars son Charlie as an unruly trooper on a 1960s army base. Placed in an all-black stockade for punishment, he bonds with his brother prisoners by defying the hardcase sergeant (played by Sheen the elder). Characters and situations are intriguing but not rendered effectively. Based on the novel "Count a Lonely Cadence" by Gordon Weaver.
1989 (PG-13) 97m/C Charlie Sheen, Martin Sheen, Laurence "Larry" Fishburne, Michael Beach, Ramon Estevez; **D:** Martin Sheen; **M:** Georges Delerue. **VHS $14.98** REP *√√*

Cadillac Girls Page is a self-destructive teenager who is arrested for car theft. To avoid jail, Page is placed in her single mom's custody and moves to her family's straitlaced hometown in Nova Scotia. Mom isn't exactly good at parenting and Page's adolescent anger extends to putting the moves on mom's potential new beau.
1993 99m/C Jennifer Dale, Gregory Harrison, Mia Kirshner. **VHS $89.95** MNC *√½*

Cadillac Man Williams is the quintessential low-life car salesman in this rather disjointed comedy. A lesser comedic talent might have stalled and been abandoned, but Williams manages to drive away despite the flat script and direction. One storyline follows his attempt to sell 12 cars in 12 days or lose his job, while another follows his confrontation with a gun-toting, mad-as-hell cuckolded husband. Williams and Robbins are often close to being funny in a hyperkinetic way, but the situations are dumb enough to rob most of the scenes of their comedy. Watch for a movie-stealing bit by the spunky waitress at the local Chinese restaurant.
1990 (R) 95m/C Robin Williams, Tim Robbins, Pamela Reed, Fran Drescher, Zack Norman, Annabella Sciorra, Lori Petty, Paul Guilfoyle; **D:** Roger Donaldson; **W:** Ken Friedman. **VHS, Beta $9.98** ORI *√√*

Caesar and Cleopatra Based on the classic George Bernard Shaw play. Caesar meets the beautiful Cleopatra in ancient Egypt and helps her gain control of her life. Remains surprisingly true to Shaw's adaptation, unlike many other historical films of the same era.

1946 135m/C GB Claude Rains, Vivien Leigh, Stewart Granger, Flora Robson, Francis L. Sullivan, Cecil Parker; **D:** Gabriel Pascal. **VHS, Beta** NO *√√½*

Cafe Express A con artist (he sells coffee illegally aboard an Italian train) stays one step ahead of the law as he raises money to help his ailing son. As in "Bread and Chocolate," Manfredi is again the put-upon working class hero comedically attempting to find a better way of life in this bittersweet tale.
1983 90m/C IT Nino Manfredi, Gigi Reder, Adolfo Celi, Vittorio Mezzogiorno; **D:** Nanni Loy. **VHS, Beta** NO *√√½*

Cafe Romeo Tale of twenty-something friendships forged in the neighborhood coffeehouse of a heavily Italian community. Lia (Stewart) is a waitress who dreams of becoming a fashion designer, but her marriage to a small time hood holds her back. Crombie, her cousin by marriage, is a dental student confused about his future, but very much in love with Lia. Quiet movie boasts average script that's helped along by strong performances. Originally broadcast on Canadian TV.
1991 (R) 93m/C CA Catherine Mary Stewart, Jonathan Crombie; **D:** Rex Bromfield. **VHS $89.98** REP *√*

The Cage Gangsters enlist a brain-damaged Vietnam vet played by Ferrigno to participate in illegal "cage fights," enclosed wrestling matches fought to the death. Crude and annoying.
1989 (R) 101m/C Lou Ferrigno, Reb Brown, Michael Dante, Mike Moroff, Marilyn Tokuda, James Shigeta, Al Ruscio; **D:** Hugh Kelley. **VHS, Beta $14.98** ORI *√*

The Cage Sent to prison for murdering his girlfriend, Jive has no idea what the pen has in store for him. The inmates stage a mock trial, the defendant is found guilty and the sentence is too horrible to imagine. From a stage play by the San Quentin Drama Workshop and co-starring Hayes, author of "Midnight Express."
1990 90m/C Rick Cluchey, William 'Hayes; **D:** Rick Cluchey; **W:** Rick Cluchey. **VHS, Beta** NO *√√√*

Caged Fear Young Krissie (Cloke) is mistakenly put behind bars in a brutal, high-security prison for a shootout caused by her outlaw husband Tommy (Keith) during their honeymoon. Tommy comes up with an outrageous scheme to rescue her. Not quite as bad as it sounds, but close.
1992 (R) 94m/C David Keith, Deborah May, Ray Sharkey, Loretta Devine, Karen Black, Kristen Cloke; **D:** Bobby Houston; **W:** Bobby Houston. **VHS $89.95** NLC *√½*

Caged Fury American women being held captive in Southeast Asia are brainwashed into becoming walking time bombs. Yes, that dame's gonna blow. Made in the Philippines with the best of intentions.
1980 (R) 90m/C PH Bernadette Williams, Taffee O'Connell, Jennifer Laine; **D:** Cirio H. Santiago. **VHS, Beta** NO *√*

Caged Fury Two Los Angeles women allegedly commit sexual crimes and are sent to prison. Cheap, exploitive women's prison rehash.
1990 85m/C Erik Estrada, Richie Barathy, Roxanna Michaels, Paul Smith, James Hong, Greg Cummins; **D:** Bill Milling. **VHS, Beta $79.95** COL *√*

Caged Heat Low-budget babes-behind-bars film touted as the best sexploitation film of the day. Demme's directorial debut is a genre-altering installment in Roger Corman's

formulaic cellblock Cinderella cycle. Recycled plot—innocent woman is put behind bars, where she loses some of her innocence—boasts an updated treatment. These babes may wear hot pants and gratuitously bare their midriffs, but they're not brainless bimbos. They're strong individuals who work together to liberate themselves. Reached cult status. Cult diva Steele returned to the big screen after six years to play the wheel-chair-ridden prison warden, written specifically for her. *AKA:* Renegade Girls; Caged Females.
1974 (R) 83m/C Juanita Brown, Erica Gavin, Roberta Collins, Barbara Steele, Ella Reid, Cheryl "Rainbeaux" Smith; *D:* Jonathan Demme; *W:* Jonathan Demme. VHS *SUE, NWV* ⅛⅛

Caged in Paradiso A convicted criminal and his wife are dumped onto a remote prisoner's isle to live out their lives. When Cara loses contact with her husband, she must fend for herself. Survival tale boringly told.
1989 (R) 90m/C Irene Cara; *D:* Michael Snyder. VHS, Beta $79.95 *VMK, IME* ⅛ ½

Caged Terror Two urbanites hit the countryside for a weekend and meet a band of crazy rapists who ravage the wife and set the husband raging with bloodthirsty revenge. Squalid stroll through the ruins.
1972 76m/C Percy Harkness, Elizabeth Suzuki, Leon Morenzie. VHS, Beta $59.95 *NWV Woof!*

Caged Women Undercover journalist enters a women's prison and gets the usual eyeful. *AKA:* Women's Penitentiary 4.
1984 (R) 97m/C *FR IT* Laura Gemser, Gabriele Tinti, Lorraine De Selle, Maria Romano; *D:* Vincent Dawn. VHS, Beta $69.95 *VES, LIV, PHX* ⅛

Cahill: United States Marshal The aging Duke in one of his lesser moments, portraying a marshal who comes to the aid of his sons. The boys are mixed up with a gang of outlaws, proving that no matter how good a parent you are, sometimes the kids just lean toward the wayward. Turns out, though, that the boys harbor a grudge against the old man due to years of workaholic neglect. Will Duke see the error of his ways and reconcile with the delinquent boys? Will he catch the outlaw leader? Will he go on to star in other Duke vehicles?
1973 (PG) 103m/C John Wayne, Gary Grimes, George Kennedy, Neville Brand, Marie Windsor, Harry Carey Jr.; *D:* Andrew V. McLaglen; *M:* Elmer Bernstein. VHS, Beta $19.98 *WAR, TLF* ⅛⅛

The Caine Mutiny A group of naval officers revolt against a captain they consider mentally unfit. Bogart is masterful as Captain Queeg, obsessed with cleanliness while onboard and later a study in mental meltdown during the court-martial of a crew member who participated in the mutiny. Based on the Pulitzer-winning novel by Herman Wouk, the drama takes a close look at the pressure-filled life aboard ship during WWII.
1954 125m/C Humphrey Bogart, Jose Ferrer, Van Johnson, Fred MacMurray, Lee Marvin, Claude Akins, E.G. Marshall, Robert Francis, May Wynn, Tom Tully; *D:* Edward Dmytryk; *W:* Stanley Roberts; *M:* Max Steiner. VHS, Beta, 8mm $19.95 *COL, HMV* ⅛⅛⅛⅛

The Caine Mutiny Court Martial A young lieutenant is up for a court-martial after taking control of the U.S.S. Caine in the midst of a typhoon. In order to save him, his lawyer must discredit the paranoid Commander Queeg. As the events of the mutiny unfold, it becomes clear that Queeg's obsession with discipline had become a threat to everyone aboard. Good performances, particularly by Bogosian as the lawyer. Based on

the Pulitzer Prize-winning novel by Herman Wouk. Made for television.
1988 (PG) 100m/C Jeff Daniels, Eric Bogosian, Brad Davis, Peter Gallagher, Michael Murphy, Kevin J. O'Connor, Daniel H. Jenkins; *D:* Robert Altman. VHS $89.95 *VMK* ⅛⅛⅛

Cain's Cutthroats A former Confederate army captain and a bounty hunting preacher team up to settle the score with soldiers on a gang-raping, murdering spree. *AKA:* Cain's Way; The Blood Seekers.
1971 (R) 87m/C Scott Brady, John Carradine, Robert Dix. VHS, Beta $19.95 *GHV* ⅛

Cairo War correspondent Young lands in Cairo where he is supposed to pass along classified information to a Nazi spy posing as a Brit. He meets and falls in love with American movie queen thought to be enemy agent (MacDonald) and a race across the desert follows when Young is trapped in a pyramid. Catchy tunes can't save this cheesy WWII spy spoof that marked the end of MacDonald's MGM contract.
1942 101m/B Jeanette MacDonald, Robert Young, Ethel Waters, Reginald Owen, Grant Mitchell, Lionel Atwill, Eduardo Ciannelli, Mitchell Lewis; *D:* Woodbridge S. Van Dyke; *W:* John McClain; *M:* Herbert Stothart. VHS $19.98 *MGM* ⅛⅛

Cajon Pass A group of trains challenges the terrain attempting to go through Cajon Pass into Los Angeles.
1988 60m/C VHS, Beta $49.95 *VRL* ⅛⅛

Cal A young Catholic man is recruited into the Irish Republican Army. He falls in love with an older Protestant widow, whose husband, a policeman, he helped kill, acting as the get-away driver for his fellow Republicans. Thoughtful and tragic, with excellent performances; set in Northern Ireland.
1984 (R) 104m/C *IR* Helen Mirren, John Lynch, Donal McCann, Kitty Gibson, Ray McAnally, John Kavanagh; *D:* Pat O'Connor; *W:* Bernard MacLaverty; *M:* Mark Knopfler. Cannes Film Festival Nominations: cs 84: Best Film; Cannes Film Festival '84: Best Actress (Mirren). VHS, Beta $19.98 *WAR, FCT, ING* ⅛⅛⅛

Calacan A non-human settlement filled with culture and tradition fears only the living in this family musical.
1979 ?m/C *MX* Mauro Mendonca, Sylvia Guevara, Dora Montiel. VHS, Beta *NO* ⅛⅛⅛

Calamity Jane In one of her best Warner musicals, Day stars as the rip-snortin', gun-totin' Calamity Jane of Western lore, in an on-again, off-again romance with Wild Bill Hickok. ♫Secret Love; Just Blew in From the Windy City; The Black Hills of Dakota; The Deadwood Stage (Whip-Crack-Away!).
1953 101m/C Doris Day, Howard Keel, Allyn Ann McLerie; *D:* David Butler; *M:* Sammy Fain, Paul Francis Webster. Academy Awards '53: Best Song ("Secret Love"); Nominations: Best Sound, Best Original Score. VHS, Beta $19.98 *WAR, FCT* ⅛⅛⅛

Calamity Jane A made-for-television biography of the famous lady crack shot. Alexander is cast as the tough-as-nails woman who considered herself on a par with any man.
1982 96m/C Jane Alexander, Frederic Forrest, Ken Kercheval, Talia Balsam, David Hemmings; *D:* James Goldstone. VHS, Beta $19.98 *FOX* ⅛⅛ ½

Calendar Girl In 1962 three high-school best friends borrow a convertible and travel from their Nevada homes to Hollywood to meet their pinup idol, Marilyn Monroe. Roy's (Priestley) a rebel, Ned's (Olds, in his film debut) sensitive, and Scott's (O'Connell) just a nice guy. They stay with Roy's Uncle Harvey (Pantoliano), an aspiring actor, and

work to meet their dream girl. Which they finally do, in a notably weak sequence which fits in with this notably uninspired film. The three actors at least have enough comradery to make realistic buddies—one of the few true touches in the film.
1993 (PG-13) 86m/C Jason Priestly, Gabriel Olds, Jerry O'Connell, Joe Pantoliano, Stephen Tobolowsky, Kurt Fuller, Steve Railsback, Emily Warfield, Stephanie Anderson; *Cameos:* Chubby Checker; *D:* John Whitesell; *W:* Paul Shapiro; *M:* Hans Zimmer. VHS, 8mm COL ⅛⅛ ½

Calendar Girl Murders Minor mystery about the murder of some girlie magazine pinups. Made for television.
1984 104m/C Robert Culp, Tom Skerritt, Barbara Parkins, Sharon Stone; *D:* William A. Graham; *M:* Brad Fiedel. VHS *EDV* ⅛⅛ ½

California Casanova Mirthless, semi-musical farce about a nerdy stagehand learning to be a great lover to win a beautiful singer's heart who's being blackmailed by a cruel gangster. Nice cast; nobody's home.
1989 (R) 94m/C Jerry Orbach, Audrey Landers, Tyrone Power Jr., Bryan Genesse, Ken Kercheval, Ted Davis, Joyce Blair; *D:* Nathaniel Christian; *W:* Nathaniel Christian. VHS $19.95 *ACA Woof!*

California Dreaming Nerdy young man heads west to California where he tries to fit in with the local beach crowd. Reminiscent of the popular beach movies of the '60s.
1979 (R) 93m/C Dennis Christopher, Tanya Roberts, Glynnis O'Connor, John Calvin, Seymour Cassel; *D:* John Hancock. VHS, Beta $69.95 *VES, LIV* ⅛⅛

California Girls Radio station stages a beauty contest and three sexy ladies prove to be tough competition. Features women in little swimsuits, minimal plot, and a soundtrack by the Police, Kool & the Gang, Blondie, Queen, and 10cc.
1984 83m/C Al Music, Mary McKinley, Alicia Allen, Lantz Douglas, Barbara Parks; *D:* Rick Wallace. VHS, Beta *NO* ⅛

California Gold Rush Hays portrays young aspiring writer, Bret Harte, who, in search of adventure in 1849, arrives in Sutter's Fort and takes on a job at the local sawmill. When gold is found, Sutter's Fort is soon overrun with fortune hunters whose greed, violence and corruption threaten to tear apart the peaceful community. Made for television.
1981 100m/C Robert Hays, John Dehner, Dan Haggerty, Ken Curtis; *D:* Jack B. Hively. VHS, Beta *NO* ⅛⅛

California Joe California is being eyed by Confederate sympathizers and also by their leader, who wants it for his own plans. Enter California Joe, a Union officer in disguise, who will save the day. Standard western.
1943 55m/B Donald (Don "Red") Barry, Lynn Merrick, Helen Talbot. VHS, Beta $24.95 *DVT* ⅛

California Straight Ahead Denny—whose niche in the twenties was silent action comedies, and who had teamed with director Pollard earlier in the decade to produce "The Leatherpushers" series—stars in this silent actioner which features a cross-country road trip, zoo animals-on-a-rampage, and a car-racing conclusion (sounds like an action formula ahead of its time). Audiences didn't realize until the talkies that the All-American manly man was in fact played by a Brit. For those who revel in trivia, Denny appeared in the 1961 "Batman."
1925 77m/B Reginald Denny, Gertrude Olmsted, Tom Wilson, Lucille Ward, John Steppling; *D:* Harry Pollard. VHS, Beta $24.95 *GPV, FCT* ⅛⅛

California Suite The posh Beverly Hills Hotel is the setting for four unrelated Neil Simon skits, ranging from a battling husband and wife to feuding friends. Simonized dialogue is crisp and funny.
1978 (PG) 103m/C Alan Alda, Michael Caine, Bill Cosby, Jane Fonda, Walter Matthau, Richard Pryor, Dame Maggie Smith, Elaine May; *D:* Herbert Ross; *W:* Neil Simon; *M:* Claude Bolling. Academy Awards '78: Best Supporting Actress (Smith); Nominations: Best Adapted Screenplay, Best Art Direction/Set Decoration; Golden Globe Awards '79: Best Actress—Musical/Comedy (Smith). **VHS, Beta $14.95** *COL* 🎞🎞🎞

Caligari's Cure Palazzolo's first film is a satiric, non-narrative stab at his Catholic upbringing via German expressionism and modern performance art.
1982 70m/C *D:* Tom Palazzolo. **VHS, Beta** *FCT* 🎞🎞

Caligula Infamous, expensive, extremely graphic, and sexually explicit adaptation of the life of the mad Roman emperor, Caligula. Scenes of decapitation, necrophilia, rape, bestiality, and sadomasochism abound. Biggest question is why Gielgud, O'Toole, and McDowell lent their talents to this monumentally abhorred film (not to mention Gore Vidal on the writing end, who didn't want the credit). Adult magazine publisher Bob Guccione coproduced and didn't particularly want to release it. Also available in a censored, "R" rated version.
1980 143m/C *IT* Malcolm McDowell, John Gielgud, Peter O'Toole, Helen Mirren; *D:* Tinto Brass; *W:* Gore Vidal. **VHS, Beta $79.95** *VES, HHE* Woof!

Call Him Mr. Shatter A hired killer stalks a tottering Third World president and becomes embroiled in international political intrigue. *AKA:* Shatter.
1974 (R) 90m/C *GB* Stuart Whitman, Peter Cushing, Anton Diffring; *D:* Michael Carreras. **VHS, Beta $59.98** *NLC* 🎞

Call Me Psycho-drama about a lusty young woman who responds positively to an obscene telephone caller until she witnesses him murder another person. Doubt creeps into the relationship.
1988 (R) 98m/C Patricia Charbonneau, Patti D'Arbanville, Sam Freed, Boyd Gaines, Stephen McHattie; *D:* Sollace Mitchell. **VHS, Beta $79.98** *VES* 🎞🎞

Call Me Bwana Pure cornpone with Hope as a bumbling explorer sent with CIA agent Adams to track down a lost American space capsule in deepest Africa. Enemy agents Ekberg and Jeffries try to make things difficult.
1963 103m/C Bob Hope, Edie Adams, Anita Ekberg, Lionel Jeffries, Percy Herbert, Paul Carpenter, Orlando Martins; *D:* Gordon Douglas; *W:* Nate Monaster, Johanna Harwood. **VHS $19.98** *MGM, FCT* 🎞 ½

Call Northside 777 Chicago reporter Stewart finds himself in the crux of a decade-old murder investigation when he follows up a newspaper ad offering $5,000 for any information leading to the arrest and conviction of a police murderer. The cunning reporter discovers police coverups and missing evidence pointing to an imprisoned man's innocence. Powerful performance from Stewart directs this docu-drama based on the real-life story of Chicago's Joe Majczek, unjustly imprisoned for eleven years for a murder he didn't commit, and the Pulitzer Prize winning reporter Jim McGuire who, through a clever investigation, found enough evidence to have the case re-opened. *AKA:* Calling Northside 777.

1948 111m/B James Stewart, Richard Conte, Lee J. Cobb, Helen Walker, Betty Garde, Moroni Olsen, E.G. Marshall, Howard Smith, John McIntire, Paul Harvey, George Tyne, Michael Chapin, Addison Richards, Richard Rober, Eddie Dunn, Charles Lane, Walter Greaza, William Post Jr., George Melford, Charles Miller, Lionel Stander, Jonathan Hale; *D:* Henry Hathaway; *M:* Alfred Newman. **VHS $19.99** *FXV* 🎞🎞🎞 ½

Call of the Canyon A crooked agent for a local meat packer won't pay a fair price, so Gene goes off to talk to the head man to set him straight.
1942 71m/B Gene Autry, Smiley Burnette, Ruth Terry, Thurston Hall, Pat Brady; *D:* Joseph Santley. **VHS, Beta $29.98** *CCB, VCN, GPV* 🎞 ½

Call of the Forest Bobby makes friends with a beautiful wild black stallion which is captured and tamed by his father. The father has found a goldmine, also desired by a villain, and Bobby and his horse must come to his father's aid. Black Diamond (the horse) has the best role.
1949 74m/B Robert Lowery, Ken Curtis, Martha Sherrill, Chief Thundercloud, Charles Hughes; *D:* John F. Link. **VHS $19.95** *NOS, DVT, VYY* 🎞 ½

Call of the Rockies Action-packed oater in which Carson and Burnette ride across country to save Placer City's mine from crooked townsmen.
1944 54m/B Sunset Carson, Smiley Burnette. **VHS $9.98** *REP* 🎞🎞

Call of the Wild Jack London's famous story about a man whose survival depends upon his knowledge of the Alaskan wilderness almost comes to life. Filmed in Finland.
1972 (PG) 105m/C Charlton Heston, Michele Mercier, George Eastman; *D:* Ken Annakin. **VHS, Beta $14.95** *KUI, SIM, MPI* 🎞🎞

Call of the Wild Another of Jack London's survival tales is dramatized for television. John Thornton (Schroder) is a rich greenhorn seeking adventure during the 1897 Klondike gold rush. Buck is a German shepherd, sold as a sled dog, who finds adventures of his own in the frozen North until man and dog are united to search for a legendary gold mine. The book is more exciting but the film is more violent. Filmed on location in British Columbia.
1993 97m/C Rick Schroder, Gordon Tootoosis, Mia Sara, Duncan Fraser, Richard Newman, Brent Stait. **VHS $89.95** *CAF* 🎞🎞 ½

Call Out the Marines A group of army buddies re-enlist to break up a spy ring. Two of the guys fall in love with the same girl, not realizing that she's one of the spies. McLaglen and Lowe's last comedy together. Mediocre outing isn't redeemed by below average musical numbers. 🎵Call Out the Marines; Zana Zaranda; The Light of My Life; Beware; Hands Across the Border.
1942 67m/B Robert Smith, Frank Ryan, Victor McLaglen, Binnie Barnes, Paul Kelly, Edmund Lowe, Franklin Pangborn; *D:* Frank Ryan. **VHS, Beta $34.95** *RKO* 🎞🎞

Call to Glory Pilot for the critically praised television series. An Air Force pilot and his family face turbulent times during the Cuban missile crisis.
1984 96m/C Craig T. Nelson, Cindy Pickett, Gabriel Damon, Keenan Wynn, Elisabeth Shue, G.D. Spradlin. **VHS, Beta $14.95** *PAR* 🎞🎞 ½

The Caller A strange man enters the house of a lone woman and sets off a long night of suspense and an almost longer evening of inept movie-making.
1987 90m/C Malcolm McDowell, Madolyn Smith; *D:* Arthur Seidelman; *M:* Richard Band. **VHS, Beta $89.95** *TWE* 🎞

Callie and Son Details the sordid story of a waitress who works her way up to become a Dallas socialite and her obsessive relationship with her illegitimate son. Also known as "Rags to Riches." *AKA:* Rags to Riches.
1981 97m/C Lindsay Wagner, Dabney Coleman, Jameson Parker, Andrew Prine, James Sloyan, Michelle Pfeiffer; *D:* Waris Hussein; *M:* Billy Goldenberg. **VHS, VHS, Beta $19.98** *WAR* 🎞🎞

Calling Paul Temple The wealthy patients of a nerve doctor have been dying and a detective is called in to investigate.
1948 92m/B *GB* John Bentley, Dinah Sheridan, Margaretta Scott, Abraham Sofaer, Celia Lipton, Alan Wheatley, Wally Patch; *D:* Maclean Rogers. **VHS, Beta $16.95** *SNC* 🎞 ½

Calling Wild Bill Elliott The crooked territorial governor is exposed by hero Elliott and sidekick Hayes and justice is restored in this typical B-western. Elliott's first film for Republic; he went on to star in 16 Red Ryder films as well as other westerns for the studio.
1943 55m/B Wild Bill Elliott, George "Gabby" Hayes, Herbert Heyes, Anne Jeffreys, Fred Kohler Jr., Roy Barcroft, Yakima Canutt; *D:* Spencer Gordon Bennet. **VHS $9.98** *REP* 🎞 ½

Cambio de Cara Two reporters investigate corporate corruption. Dubbed into Spanish. *AKA:* A Change of Face.
1971 90m/C *IT* Adolfo Celi, Geraldine Hooper. **VHS, Beta** *NO* 🎞

Came a Hot Friday Two cheap conmen arrive in a 1949 southern New Zealand town, run various scams and pursue women.
1985 (PG) 101m/C *NZ* Peter Bland, Philip Gordon, Billy T. James; *D:* Ian Mune. **VHS, Beta $19.98** *NLC* 🎞🎞

Camel Boy True story of a young Arabian boy who befriends a camel and their treacherous trek across the desert.
1984 78m/C *AU D:* Yoram Gross. **VHS, Beta $69.95** *VES, LIV, WTA* 🎞 ½

Camelia After much emotional pain, beautiful Camelia learns to love again from the young, warmhearted Rafael. But her new love will not protect her from fate.
19?? 108m/B *MX* Maria Felix, Jorge Mistral. **VHS, Beta $54.95** *MED* 🎞🎞

Camelot The long-running Lerner and Loewe Broadway musical about King Arthur, Guinevere, and Lancelot was adapted from T.H. White's book, "The Once and Future King." Redgrave and Nero have chemistry as the illicit lovers, Harris is strong as the king struggling to hold together his dream, but muddled direction undermines the effort. Laserdisc edition contains 28 minutes of previously edited footage, trailers and backstage info. 🎵I Wonder What the King is Doing Tonight; The Simple Joys of Maidenhood; Camelot; C'est Moi; The Lusty Month of May; Follow Me; How To Handle a Woman; Then You May Take Me to the Fair; If Ever I Would Leave You; What Do the Simple Folk Do?; I Loved You Once in Silence; Guenevere.
1967 150m/C Richard Harris, Vanessa Redgrave, David Hemmings, Franco Nero, Lionel Jeffries; *D:* Joshua Logan; *M:* Frederick Loewe, Alan Jay Lerner. Academy Awards '67: Best Art Direction/Set Decoration, Best Costume Design, Best Score; Nominations: Best Cinematography, Best Sound; Golden Globe Awards '68: Best Actor—Musical/Comedy (Harris), Best Song ("If Ever I Should Leave You"), Best Score. **VHS, Beta $29.98** *WAR, RDG, HMV* 🎞🎞

The Cameraman After moving to MGM, Keaton made his first feature with a major studio, giving up the artistic control he had enjoyed in his previous films. Spared from

C

the vilification of studio politics (not the case with later Keaton films) "The Cameraman" enjoyed both critical and popular success. Keaton's inept tintype portrait-maker has a heart that pitter-patters for an MGM office girl. He hopes to impress her by joining the ranks of the newsreel photographers. Fortuitously poised to grab a photo scoop on a Chinese tong war, he is forced to return empty-handed when an organ-grinder's monkey absconds with his firsthand footage. Silent with a musical score.
1928 78m/B Buster Keaton, Marceline Day, Harold Goodwin, Harry Gribbon, Sidney Bracy, Edward Brophy, Vernon Dent, William Irving; **D:** Edward Sedgwick. VHS $29.95 MGM, FCT ♦♦♦♦

Cameron's Closet Every child's nightmare comes true. A young boy is convinced that a monster lives in his closet due to his perverse father's psychological tortures. Only this time the monster is real!
1989 (R) 86m/C Cotter Smith, Mel Harris, Scott Curtis, Chuck McCann, Leigh McCloskey, Kim Lankford, Tab Hunter; **D:** Armand Mastroianni. VHS $14.95 COL ♦♦1/2

Camila The true story of the tragic romance between an Argentinean socialite and a Jesuit priest in 1847. The two lovers escape to a small provincial village where they live together as man and wife. Eventually they are recognized and condemned to death. Available in Spanish with English subtitles or dubbed into English.
1984 121m/C AR SP Susu Pecoraro, Imanol Arias, Hector Alterio, Elena Tasisto; **D:** Maria-Luisa Bemberg. VHS, Beta $19.95 COL, SUE, AUD ♦♦♦

Camilla Elderly Tandy's a former violinist fleeing from her son. Striking out from Georgia, she hooks up with frustrated musician Fonda, who's driving an old Volkswagen to Toronto. Sort of a May-December female-bonding road trip with lots of conversation and comic asides. Lack of stereotyping and fairly novel twist on the road movie keep this one on the highway.
1994 ?m/C Jessica Tandy, Bridget Fonda, Graham Greene, Howie Mandel, Hume Cronyn, Elias Koteas, Maury Chaykin; **D:** Deepa Mehta; **W:** Paul Quarrington. VHS NYR ♦♦♦

Camille The classic Alexandre Dumas story about a dying French courtesan falling in love with a shallow young nobleman. A clean, romantic adaptation that somehow escapes the cliches and stands as one of the most telling monuments to Garbo's unique magic and presence on film.
1936 108m/B Greta Garbo, Robert Taylor, Lionel Barrymore, Henry Daniell, Elizabeth Allan, Rex O'Malley, Lenore Ulric, Laura Hope Crews; **D:** George Cukor. Academy Awards '37 Nominations: Best Actress (Garbo); National Board of Review Awards '37: 10 Best Films of the Year; New York Film Critics Awards '36: Best Actress (Garbo). VHS, Beta $24.95 MGM ♦♦♦1/2

Camille Claudel A lushly romantic version of the art world at the turn of the century, when art was exploding in new forms and independence for women was unheard of. Sculptor Claudel's tragic love for art, Auguste Rodin (for whom she modeled), and independence clash, costing her sanity. Very long, it requires an attentive and thoughtful viewing. In French with English subtitles.
1989 (R) 149m/C FR Isabelle Adjani, Gerard Depardieu, Laurent Grevill, Alain Cuny, Madeleine Robinson, Katrine Boorman; **D:** Bruno Nuytten; **W:** Bruno Nuytten, Marilyn Goldin; **M:** Gabriel Yared. Academy Awards '89 Nominations: Best Actress (Adjani), Best Foreign Language Film;

Cesar Awards '89: Best Actress (Adjani), Best Film. VHS, Beta $19.98 ORI, IME, ING ♦♦♦

Camorra: The Naples Connection A prostitute and an American drug dealer find themselves embroiled in the murders of Neapolitan Mafia heads. Violent, overblown, minor Wertmuller. **AKA:** Un Complicato Intrigo Di Donne, Vicoli E Delitti.
1985 (R) 94m/C IT Harvey Keitel, Angela Molina, Lorraine Bracco, Francesco Rabal; **D:** Lina Wertmuller; **W:** Lina Wertmuller. VHS, Beta $79.95 MGM ♦♦

Camp Classics #1 Five corny classics spanning four decades make up this collection: "Mystery of the Leaping Fish" with Douglas Fairbanks, "Foreign Press Awards," "Musical Beauty Shop," "Edsel Commercial," and "Nixon's Checkers Speech."
195? 80m/B Douglas Fairbanks Sr. VHS, Beta $37.00 WFV ♦♦

Camp Cucamonga: How I Spent My Summer Vacation Zany antics at summer camp abound when Camp Cucamonga's owner mistakes the new handyman for the camp inspector. Well known stars from TV's "Cheers," "The Jeffersons," "The Wonder Years," and "The Love Boat" are featured in this silly made for television flick.
1990 100m/C John Ratzenberger, Sherman Hemsley, Josh Saviano, Danica McKellar, Chad Allen, Dorothy Lyman, Lauren Tewes, G. Gordon Liddy; **D:** Roger Duchonwny. VHS $9.99 GKK ♦

Camp Double Feature Two cautionary anti-pot films, now universally recognized as high camp: "Reefer Madness" and "Marihuana." Both are available individually on video.
1939 120m/B Harley Wood, Hugh McArthur, Paul Ellis, Dave O'Brien, Dorothy Short. VHS, Beta $34.95 JEF ♦

Camp Nowhere Video fodder for the juniors in the household as kids turn tables on parents. Instead of trudging off to summer camp for the umpteenth time, a group of upscale kids create their own with the help of laid-off drama teacher Lloyd, who must first con their parents into believing that Camp Nowhere is legit. What follows is that very special summer camp in the Hollywood tradition with lots of junk food, video games galore, and of course, no rules. Camp beserko formula good for a few laughs.
1994 (PG) ?m/C Christopher Lloyd, Wendy Makkena, M. Emmet Walsh, Peter Scolari, Peter Onorati, Ray Baker, Kate Mulgrew, Jonathan Jackson, Romy Walthall, Maryedith Burrell, Tom Wilson, Nathan Cavaleri, Andrew Keegan, Melody Kay; **D:** Jonathan Prince; **W:** Andrew Kurtzman, Eliot Wald. VHS NYR ♦♦

Campaign in Poland This documentary chronicles the German invasion of Poland during WWII.
1940 80m/B VHS, Beta $29.95 NOS, DVT, HEG ♦♦

The Campus Corpse Young man stumbles into deadly college frat hazing and discovers he and rest of cast are utterly devoid of acting ability.
1977 (PG) 92m/C Charles Martin Smith, Jeff East, Brad Davis; **D:** Douglas Curtis. VHS, Beta $69.95 VES ♦

Campus Knights If you're a serious student of the campus caper film, this is one of the earliest (though not one of the best) of the genre (if such a distinction can be made). The story involves twin brothers—one a tweedy high-browed professor, the other a bon vivant man about town—who wreak fraternal chaos on the quads.

1929 70m/B Raymond McKee, Shirley Palmer, Marie Quillen, Jean Laverty, Sybil Grove; **D:** Albert Kelly. VHS, Beta $24.95 GPV, FCT ♦

Campus Man An entrepreneurial college student markets a beefcake calendar featuring his best friend, until the calendar's sales threaten his friend's amateur athletic status.
1987 (PG) 94m/C John Dye, Steve Lyon, Kim Delaney, Miles O'Keeffe, Morgan Fairchild, Kathleen Wilhoite; **D:** Ron Casden; **M:** James Newton Howard. VHS, Beta $14.95 PAR ♦

Can-Can Lackluster screen adaptation of the Cole Porter musical bears little resemblance to the stage version. MacLaine is a cafe owner who goes to court to try and get the "Can-Can," a dance considered risque in gay Paree at the end of the nineteenth century, made legal. Love interest Sinatra happens to be a lawyer. ♫C'est Manifique; Let's Do It; I Love Paris; You Do Something to Me; It's All Right With Me; Live and Let Live; Come Along With Me; Just One of Those Things.
1960 131m/C Frank Sinatra, Shirley MacLaine, Maurice Chevalier, Louis Jourdan, Juliet Prowse, Marcel Dalio, Leon Belasco; **D:** Walter Lang. VHS, Beta $19.98 FOX, FCT ♦♦

Can I Do It...Till I Need Glasses? More to the point, can you stay awake till the end? Prurient juvenile junk. Brief Williams footage was grafted to this mess during 15 minutes of Mork fame.
1977 72m/C Robin Williams, Roger Behr, Debra Klose, Moose Carlson, Walter Olkewicz; **D:** I. Robert Levy. VHS, Beta $19.95 MED Woof!

Can She Bake a Cherry Pie? Two offbeat characters meet and fall in love in an odd sort of way. Slow-moving and talky but somewhat rewarding. One of Black's better performances.
1983 90m/C Karen Black, Michael Emil, Michael Margotta, Frances Fisher, Martin Frydberg; **D:** Henry Jaglom; **W:** Henry Jaglom. VHS, Beta $39.95 PAR, FCT ♦♦

Can You Feel Me Dancing? Family-happy lightweight entertainment coproduced by Kent Bateman and starring Bateman progeny Jason and Justine as brother and sister, a novel premise that only a father could love. A blind independence-impaired teenager tries to liberate herself from her overbearing family, and finds the secret to conquering her fears and to standing up for herself when she falls in love. Written by spouse-team Steven and J. Miyoko Hensley.
1985 95m/C Jason Bateman, Justine Bateman; **W:** Steven Hensley, J. Miyoko Hensley. VHS $79.95 MNC ♦♦

Can You Hear the Laughter? The Story of Freddie Prinze Heartstring tugging biography of the late Puerto Rican comedian whose troubled life lead to suicide in spite of his apparent success. He was most noted for his starring role in "Chico and the Man."
1979 100m/C Ira Angustain, Kevin Hooks, Randee Heller, Devon Ericson, Julie Carmen, Stephen Elliott; **D:** Burt Brinckerhoff. VHS, Beta $79.95 GEM ♦♦

Canadian Bacon Feature film debut for Moore, who irritated many with "Roger and Me" was inspired by the Persian Gulf War. Title refers to the military code name for a campaign to whip up anti-Canadian hysteria and justify a U.S. invasion of its neighbor to the north. Evil political advisor Pollak convinces well-meaning but inept President Alda that it's just the thing to get the presidential popularity up and those defense industries humming. Ugly Americans abound, at expense of polite Canadians, heh? Bipartisan

satire was filmed in Toronto, which is shown to good advantage. Candy in one of last roles is the superpatriotic sheriff of Niagara Falls, New York.
1994 ?m/C Alan Alda, Kevin Pollak, John Candy, Rhea Perlman, Rip Torn, Bill Nunn, Kevin J. O'Connor, Steven Wright, G.D. Spradlin; *Cameos:* Michael Moore; *D:* Michael Moore; *W:* Michael Moore; *M:* Elmer Bernstein. **VHS** *NYR* ♫♫½

Canadian Mounties Vs. Atomic Invaders Mountie Don Roberts and undercover agent Kay Conway chase foreign agents and face natural disasters (avalanches and reindeer stampedes) to keep atomic missiles away from Canada and the U.S. Part of "The Cliffhanger Serials" series. 12 chapters.
1953 169m/B William Henry, Susan Morrow, Arthur Space. **VHS** $29.98 *REP, MQV* ♫♫½

Cancel My Reservation New York talk show host Hope sets out for a vacation on an Arizona ranch, but winds up in trouble due to a mysterious corpse, a rich rancher, and an enigmatic mystic. Even more muddled than it sounds. Based on the novel "Broken Gun" by Louis L'Amour, with pointless cameos by Crosby, Wayne, and Wilson.
1972 (G) 99m/C Bob Hope, Eva Marie Saint, Ralph Bellamy, Anne Archer, Forrest Tucker, Keenan Wynn, Flip Wilson, Noriyuki "Pat" Morita, Chief Dan George; *Cameos:* John Wayne, Bing Crosby, Doodles Weaver; *D:* Paul Bogart; *W:* Arthur Marx. **VHS, Beta** $14.95 *COL, FCT* ♫

Cancion en el Alma A talented boy singer is stuck in a greedy custody battle over his potential revenues in the wide world of Puerto Rican entertainment. *AKA:* Song from the Heart.
19?? 70m/C *SP* Luis Fernando Ramirez, Claudia Osuna. **VHS, Beta** *NO* ♫½

The Candidate Realistic, satirical look at politics and political campaigning. A young, idealistic lawyer is talked into trying for the Senate seat and learns the truth about running for office. Ritchie's other efforts include "Downhill Racer" and "Bad News Bears."
1972 (PG) 105m/C Robert Redford, Peter Boyle, Don Porter, Allen (Gooritz) Garfield, Karen Carlson, Melvyn Douglas, Michael Lerner; *D:* Michael Ritchie; *W:* Jeremy Larner. Academy Awards '72: Best Story & Screenplay; Nominations: Best Sound; National Board of Review Awards '72: 10 Best Films of the Year. **VHS, Beta** $19.98 *WAR* ♫♫♫

Candles at Nine An innocent showgirl must spend a month in her late uncle's creepy mansion in order to inherit it, much to the malevolent chagrin of the rest of the family who want the place and the loot for themselves. Uninspired.
1944 84m/B *GB* Jessie Matthews, John Stuart, Reginald Purdell; *D:* John Harlow. **VHS, Beta** $16.95 *SNC, VYY, MLB* ♫½

Candleshoe A Los Angeles street urchin poses as an English matron's long lost granddaughter in order to steal a fortune hidden in Candleshoe, her country estate, where Niven butlers. Somewhat slapstichky Disney fare.
1978 (G) 101m/C Vivian Pickles, Helen Hayes, David Niven, Jodie Foster, Leo McKern; *D:* Norman Tokar. **VHS, Beta** $19.99 *DIS* ♫♫

Candy Mountain Guitar playin' O'Connor roadtrips across America and Canada in search of a legendary guitar maker Yulin. Occasional interest derives from musician cameos from the likes of Buster Poindexter, Dr. John and Redbone.

1987 (R) 90m/C *FR SI CA* Kevin J. O'Connor, Harris Yulin, Tom Waits, Bulle Ogier, Roberts Blossom; *Cameos:* David Johansen, Leon Redbone, Joe Strummer, Dr. John, Rita MacNeil, Laurie Metcalf; *D:* Robert Frank; *W:* Rudy Wurlitzer. **VHS** $14.98 *REP, FCT* ♫♫

Candy Stripe Nurses Even hard-core Roger Corman fans might find his final installment in the nursing comedy pentad to be a lethargic exercise in gratuitous "sexual situations." Bet those uniforms don't meet hospital standards. The previous films in the series are: "The Student Nurses," "Private Duty Nurses," "Night Call Nurses," and "The Young Nurses." *AKA:* Sweet Candy.
1974 80m/C Candice Rialson, Robin Mattson, Maria Rojo, Kimberly Hyde, Dick Miller, Stanley Ralph Ross, Monte Landis, Tom Baker; *D:* Allan Holleb. **VHS, Beta** $59.95 *SUE* ♫

Candy Tangerine Man Respectable businessman leads a double life as loving father and LA pimp.
1975 88m/C John Daniels, Tom Hankerson, Eli Haines, Marva Farmer, George Flower; *D:* Matt Cimber. **VHS, Beta** $49.95 *UNI* ♫

Candyman This terrifying tale from horror maven Clive Barker is an effective combination of American gothic, academia, and urban squalor. A search for dissertation material leads graduate student Helen Lyle (Madsen) into gang-infested housing. There she encounters the urban myth of Candyman, the son of a former slave who was lynched and is now back with a hook and a vendetta. Filled with the appropriate amount of yucky stuff, yet successfully employs subtle scare tactics and plausible characters.
1992 (R) 98m/C Virginia Madsen, Tony Todd, Xander Berkeley, Kasi Lemmons, Vanessa Williams, DeJuan Guy, Michael Culkin, Gilbert Lewis, Stanley DeSantis; *D:* Bernard Rose; *W:* Bernard Rose; *M:* Philip Glass. **VHS, Beta, 8mm** *COL* ♫♫

Cannery Row Baseball has-been Nolte lives anonymously among the downtrodden in the seemy part of town and carries on with working girl girlfriend Winger. Based on John Steinbeck's "Cannery Row" and "Sweet Thursday."
1982 (PG) 120m/C Nick Nolte, Debra Winger, Audra Lindley, M. Emmet Walsh, Frank McRae, James Keane, Sunshine Parker; *D:* David S. Ward; *W:* David S. Ward; *M:* Jack Nitzsche. **VHS, Beta** $19.98 *MGM* ♫♫½

Cannibal Campout Crazed orphans with eating disorders make square meal of coed babes getting back to nature.
1988 89m/C Carrie Lindell, Richard Marcus, Amy Chludzinski, Jon McBride; *D:* Jon McBride, Tom Fisher. **VHS, Beta** *DMP* ♫

Cannibal Women in the Avocado Jungle of Death Tongue-in-cheek cult classic features erstwhile playmate Tweed as feminist anthropologist who searches with ditzy student and mucho macho male guide for lost tribe of cannibal women who dine on their mates. Lawton directed under the alias "J.D. Athens."
1989 (PG-13) 90m/C Shannon Tweed, Adrienne Barbeau, Karen Mistal, Barry Primus, Bill Maher; *D:* J.F. Lawton; *W:* J.F. Lawton. **VHS, Beta** $79.95 *PAR* ♫♫½

Cannon Ball/Eyes Have It Conklin stars in "The Cannon Ball" (1915), as an explosives expert in the Boom Powder Factory. "The Eyes Have It" (1928), stars Turpin involved in another misunderstanding with wife and mother-in-law. Silent.
1915 41m/B Chester Conklin, Ben Turpin, Georgia O'Dell, Helen Gilmore, Jack Lipson. **VHS, Beta** $19.98 *CCB* ♫♫½

Cannon Movie Tales: Red Riding Hood Bright re-telling of the little girl in red and that nasty wolf.
1989 (G) 84m/C Craig T. Nelson, Isabella Rossellini; *D:* Adam Brooks. **VHS** *WAR* ♫♫½

Cannon Movie Tales: Sleeping Beauty Fairchild stars in this version of the sleeping princess and the evil witch.
1989 (G) 90m/C Morgan Fairchild, Tracy Welch, Nicholas Clay, Sylvia Miles, Kenny L. Baker, David Holliday; *D:* David Irving. **VHS** *WAR* ♫♫½

Cannon Movie Tales: Snow White The incomparable Rigg stars in this witty retelling of the beautiful girl and her seven little friends.
1989 85m/C Diana Rigg, Sarah Peterson, Billy Barty; *D:* Michael Berz. **VHS** *WAR* ♫♫♫

Cannon Movie Tales: The Emperor's New Clothes Caesar stars in this version of vain despot and the crafty tailors.
1989 85m/C Sid Caesar, Robert Morse, Clive Revill; *D:* David Irving. **VHS** *WAR* ♫♫½

Cannonball Assorted ruthless people leave patches of rubber across the country competing for grand prize in less than legal auto race. Not top drawer New World but nonetheless a cult fave. Inferior to Bartel's previous cult classic, "Death Race 2000." Most interesting for plethora of cult cameos, including Scorsese, Dante, and grandmaster Corman. *AKA:* Carquake.
1976 (PG) 93m/C David Carradine, Bill McKinney, Veronica Hamel, Gerrit Graham, Robert Carradine, Sylvester Stallone, Jonathan Kaplan; *Cameos:* Martin Scorsese, Roger Corman, Joe Dante; *D:* Paul Bartel. **VHS, Beta** *NO* ♫♫

Cannonball/Dizzy Heights and Daring Hearts Two classic comedies featuring Conklin, the Keystone Kops, and wacky aeroplanes from the irrepressible Sennett.
1916 71m/B Chester Conklin; *D:* Mack Sennett. **VHS, Beta** $29.95 *VYY* ♫♫

Cannonball Run So many stars, so little plot. Reynolds and sidekick DeLuise disguise themselves as paramedics to foil cops while they compete in cross-country Cannonball race. Shows no sign of having been directed by an ex-stuntman. One of 1981's top grossers—go figure. Followed by equally languid sequel "Cannonball Run II."
1981 (PG) 95m/C Burt Reynolds, Farrah Fawcett, Roger Moore, Dom DeLuise, Dean Martin, Sammy Davis Jr., Jack Elam, Adrienne Barbeau, Peter Fonda, Molly Picon, Bert Convy, Jamie Farr; *D:* Hal Needham. **VHS, Beta** $29.98 *VES* ♫½

Cannonball Run 2 More mindless cross-country movie spinning with gratuitous star cameos. Director Needham apparently subscribes to the two wrongs make a right school of sequels.
1984 (PG) 109m/C Burt Reynolds, Dom DeLuise, Jamie Farr, Marilu Henner, Shirley MacLaine, Jim Nabors, Frank Sinatra, Sammy Davis Jr., Dean Martin, Telly Savalas, Susan Anton, Catherine Bach, Jack Elam, Sid Caesar, Ricardo Montalban, Charles Nelson Reilly; *Cameos:* Henry Silva, Tim Conway, Don Knotts, Molly Picon; *D:* Hal Needham; *M:* Stephen Dorff. **VHS, Beta** $19.98 *WAR* ♫

The Canon Operation An ostensibly true story about Korean War espionage.
1983 90m/C **VHS, Beta** $59.95 *VCD* ♫

Can't Buy Me Love Unpopular high school nerd Dempsey buys a month of dates with teen babe Peterson for $1000 in order to win friends and influence people. Previously known as "Boy Rents Girl."

1987 (PG-13) 94m/C Patrick Dempsey, Amanda Peterson, Dennis Dugan, Courtney Gains; D: Steve Rash; M: Robert Folk. VHS, Beta $19.99 TOU ♫½

Can't Stop the Music Retired model invites friends from Greenwich Village to a party to help the career of her roommate, an aspiring composer. Disco inferno that nearly reaches heights of surreal ineptness. Put it in a time capsule and let the people of the future decide what the heck was going on in the seventies. Features two of the top hits by the Village People. ♫Y.M.C.A.; Macho Man; Give Me a Break; The Sound of the City; Samantha; I'm a Singing Juggler; Sophistication; Liberation; I Love You to Death; Magic Night; Milkshake.
1980 (PG) 120m/C Valerie Perrine, Bruce Jenner, Steve Guttenberg, Paul Sand, Leigh Taylor-Young, Village People; D: Nancy Walker. VHS, Beta $14.98 REP Woof!

A Canterbury Tale Writer-director team Powell and Pressburger have loosely modeled a retelling of Chaucer's famous tale of a pilgrimage to the cathedral in Canterbury. Set in Nazi-threatened Britain in 1944, the story follows the pilgrimage of three Brits and an American GI to the eponymous cathedral. Strange, effective, worth looking at. The 95-minute American version, with added footage of Kim Hunter, is inferior to the 124-minute original.
1944 124m/B GB Eric Portman, Sheila Sim, Dennis Price, Esmond Knight, Charles Hawtrey, Hay Petrie; D: Michael Powell, Emeric Pressburger. VHS $39.95 HMV ♫♫♫

The Canterbury Tales Four Chaucer tales, most notably "The Merchant's Tale" and "The Wife of Bath," are recounted by travelers, with director Pasolini as the bawdy poet. Deemed obscene by the Italian courts, it's the second entry in Pasolini's medieval "Trilogy of Life," preceded by "The Decameron" and followed by "The Arabian Nights." In Italian with English subtitles.
1971 109m/C IT Laura Betti, Ninetto Davoli, Pier Paolo Pasolini, Hugh Griffith, Josephine Chaplin, Michael Balfour, Jenny Runacre; D: Pier Paolo Pasolini. VHS, Beta $79.95 WBF, ING, APD ♫♫

The Canterville Ghost Laughton, a 300-year old ghost with a yellow streak, is sentenced to spook a castle until he proves he's not afraid of his own shadow. American troops stay at the castle during WWII, and, as luck would have it, soldier Young is distantly related to spunky young keeper of the castle O'Brien, ghost Laughton's descendant. Once Young is acquainted with his cowardly ancestor, he begins to fear a congenital yellow streak, and both struggle to be brave despite themselves. Vaguely derived from an Oscar Wilde tale.
1944 95m/B Charles Laughton, Robert Young, Margaret O'Brien, William Gargan, Reginald Owen, Rags Ragland, Una O'Connor, Peter Lawford, Mike Mazurki; D: Jules Dassin. VHS, Beta $19.98 MGM ♫♫½

The Canterville Ghost During a family's vacation in an old English manor, they run into a ghost who is doomed to haunt the place until he can overcome his fears. Problems start when the family tries to scare him away. From the "Wonderworks" family movie series.
1991 58m/C Richard Kiley, Mary Wickes. VHS $14.95 PME, FCT ♫♫½

Cantonen Iron Kung Fu The ten tigers of Quon Tung perfect martial arts skills known as Cantonen Iron Kung Fu.
197? 90m/C Liang Jia Ren; D: Li Chao. VHS, Beta $54.95 WVE ♫

The Cantor's Son Real-life story based on Moishe Oysher's life, vaguely influenced by Jolson's "Jazz Singer." Runaway Oysher joins troupe of performers as a youth, travels to the shores of America, and finds fame once his beautiful voice is discovered. Returning to his mother country to celebrate his parents' golden anniversary, he encounters his childhood sweetheart and falls in love, but another woman is written into the plot to complicate matters. Poorly acted, laughable staging. In Yiddish with English subtitles. AKA: Dem Khann's Zindl.
1937 90m/B Judith Abarbanel, Florence Weiss, Moishe Oysher, Isadore Cashier; D: Ilya Motyleff. VHS, Beta $79.95 ERG, ING, HEG ♫½

Canvas: The Fine Art of Crime A ruthless, underhanded art gallery owner recruits a desperate young artist into his art stealing schemes. The artist learns how to steal, but decides he wants out after his burglary partner has a brush with death. The gallery owner, however, wants one last job completed.
1992 (R) 94m/C Gary Busey, John Rhys-Davies, Vittorio Rossi, Nick Cavaiola, Cary Lawrence; D: Alain Zaloum. VHS $89.98 LIV ♫♫

Cape Fear Former prosecutor turned small-town lawyer Peck and his family are plagued by the sadistic attentions of criminal Mitchum, who just finished a six year sabbatical at the state pen courtesy of prosecutor Peck. Taut and creepy; Mitchum's a consummate psychopath. Based on (and far superior to) John MacDonald's "The Executioners." Don't pass this one up in favor of the Scorsese remake.
1961 106m/B Gregory Peck, Robert Mitchum, Polly Bergen, Martin Balsam, Telly Savalas, Jack Kruschen; D: J. Lee Thompson. VHS, Beta $19.95 MCA ♫♫♫½

Cape Fear Scorsese takes on this terrifying tale of brutality and manipulation (previously filmed in 1961) and cranks it up a notch as a paroled convict haunts the lawyer who put him away. Great cast, a rollercoaster of suspense. Note the cameos by Mitchum, Peck, and Balsam, stars of the first version. Original source material was "The Executioners" by John D. MacDonald. Breath-taking rollercoaster of a film. Bernstein adapted the original score by Bernard Herrmann.
1991 (R) 128m/C Robert De Niro, Nick Nolte, Jessica Lange, Juliette Lewis, Joe Don Baker, Illeana Douglas, Fred Dalton Thompson; Cameos: Robert Mitchum, Gregory Peck, Martin Balsam; D: Martin Scorsese; W: Wesley Strick; M: Bernard Herrmann. Academy Awards '91 Nominations: Best Actor (De Niro), Best Supporting Actress (Lewis); Chicago Film Critics Awards '91: Most Promising Actress (Lewis). VHS $19.98 MCA ♫♫♫

Caper of the Golden Bulls Former bank robber Boyd is blackmailed into joining a group of safecrackers who plan to assault the Royal Bank of Spain during the annual Santa Maria bull run. More like siesta of the golden bulls. AKA: Carnival of Thieves.
1967 104m/C Stephen Boyd, Yvette Mimieux, Giovanna Ralli, Walter Slezak, Vito Scotti; D: Russel Rouse. VHS, Beta $59.98 NLC ♫

Capone This is the story of the gangster after Elliot Ness put him in a Chicago jail. That didn't stop Capone from running his crime empire until a single FBI agent worked to sent the crime boss to Alcatraz, where his power would be useless. Exuberant performances from Sharkey and Carradine. Made for television.
1989 (R) 96m/C Ray Sharkey, Keith Carradine, Debrah Farentino. VHS $89.95 VMK ♫♫½

Capricorn One Astronauts Brolin, Simpson and Waterston follow Mission Controller Holbrook's instructions to fake a Mars landing on a fabricated soundstage when their ship is discovered to be defective. When they find out they're supposed to expire in outer space so that the NASA scam won't become public knowledge, they flee to the desert, while reporter Gould sniffs out the cover up.
1978 (R) 123m/C Elliott Gould, James Brolin, Brenda Vaccaro, O.J. Simpson, Hal Holbrook, Sam Waterston, Karen Black, Telly Savalas; D: Peter Hyams; W: Peter Hyams; M: Jerry Goldsmith. VHS, Beta $59.98 FOX ♫♫♫

Captain America Captain America battles a mad scientist in this fifteen-episode serial based on the comic book character.
1944 240m/B Dick Purcell, Adrian Booth, Lionel Atwill; D: John English; W: Elmer Clifton. VHS, Beta $109.95 VCN, MLB, VTR ♫♫

Captain America Marvel Comic character steps into feature film and flounders. The patriotic superhero son of WWII hero fights bad guy with contraband nuclear weapon. Made for television. Followed the same year with "Captain America II: Death Too Soon."
1979 98m/C Reb Brown, Len Birman, Heather Menzies, Steve Forrest, Robin Mattson, Joseph Ruskin, Michael McManus; D: Rod Holcomb. VHS, Beta $14.98 MCA ♫½

Captain America Based on the Marvel Comics superhero. It's 1941 and Steve Rogers has just been recruited to join a top secret experimental government program after flunking his army physical. Injected with a serum, Steve becomes super strong, fast, and smart but is matched in all three by an evil Nazi counterpart, Red Skull. The two battle to a WWII standstill and while Red Skull goes on with his evil plots, the next 40 years finds Captain America fast frozen in the Alaskan tundra. Finally, our hero is thawed in time to do a final battle with his evil nemesis. This one is ridiculous even by comic book standards but it may amuse the kids.
1989 (PG-13) 103m/C Matt Salinger, Scott Paulin, Ronny Cox, Ned Beatty, Darren McGavin, Melinda Dillon; D: Albert Pyun; W: Stephen Tolkin. VHS $19.95 COL ♫½

Captain America 2: Death Too Soon Terrorists hit America where it hurts, threatening to use age accelerating drug. Sequelized superhero fights chronic crow lines and series dies slow, painful death. Made for television.
1979 98m/C Reb Brown, Connie Sellecca, Len Birman, Christopher Lee, Katherine Justice, Lana Wood, Christopher Carey; D: Ivan Nagy. VHS, Beta $14.98 MCA ♫

Captain Apache Union intelligence officer Van Cleef investigates murder of Indian commissioner and discovers fake Indian war landscam. As clever as the title.
1971 95m/C Lee Van Cleef, Carroll Baker, Stuart Whitman; D: Alexander Singer; W: Philip Yordan. VHS, Beta $19.95 MRV, PSM ♫

Captain Blackjack All star cast craps out in wannabe thriller about drug smuggling on the French Riviera. Social butterfly Moorehead directs drug traffic, detective Marshall undercovers as doctor, and Sanders looks bored in a British sort of way. AKA: Black Jack.
1951 90m/B FR George Sanders, Herbert Marshall, Agnes Moorehead, Patricia Roc, Marcel Dalio; D: Julien Duvivier. VHS VEC ♫

Captain Blood Sabatini adventure story launched then unknown 26-year old Flynn and 19-year old De Havilland to fame in perhaps the best pirate story ever. Exiled into slavery by a tyrannical governor, Irish physician Peter Blood is forced into piracy but ultimately earns a pardon for his swashbuckling ways. Love interest De Havilland would go on to appear in seven more features with Flynn, who took the part Robert Donat declined for health reasons. Cleverly budgeted using ship shots from silents, and miniature sets when possible. First original film score by composer Korngold. Also available colorized.

1935 120m/B Errol Flynn, Olivia de Havilland, Basil Rathbone, J. Carroll Naish, Guy Kibbee, Lionel Atwill; **D:** Michael Curtiz. **VHS, Beta $19.98** *MGM, FCT, MLB* ♫♫♫ ½

Captain Caution Young girl throws caution to the wind when dad dies during the War of 1812, assisting young Mature to take over the old man's ship to do battle with the British. Watch for then unknown sailor Ladd.

1940 84m/B Victor Mature, Louise Platt, Bruce Cabot, Alan Ladd, Robert Barratt, Vivienne Osborne; **D:** Richard Wallace. **VHS, Beta** *MED* ♫♫

The Captain from Koepenick Popular true life comedy about a Berlin cobbler in 1906 who rebels against military bureaucracy by impersonating a Prussian officer and wreaking havoc on his town, arresting authorities and capturing soldiers, only to enjoy folk herodom when his ruse is discovered. Remake of Richard Oswald's 1931 classic. In German with subtitles. *AKA:* Der Hauptmann von Koepenick.

1956 93m/B *GE* Heinz Ruehmann, Hannelore Schroth, Martin Held, Erich Schellow; **D:** Helmut Kaeutner. **VHS, Beta $24.95** *NOS, FCT* ♫♫ ½

Captain Horatio Hornblower A colorful drama about the life and loves of the British sea captain during the Napoleonic wars. Peck is rather out of his element as the courageous, swashbuckling hero (Errol Flynn was originally cast) but there's enough fast-paced derring-do to make this a satisfying saga. Based on the novel by C.S. Forester.

1951 117m/C *GB* Gregory Peck, Virginia Mayo, Robert Beatty, Denis O'Dea, Christopher Lee; **D:** Raoul Walsh; **W:** Ivan Goff. **VHS, Beta $19.98** *WAR* ♫♫♫

Captain January Crusty old lighthouse keeper rescues little orphan girl with curly hair from drowning and everyone breaks into cutsey song and dance, interrupted only when the authorities try to separate the two. ♫At the Codfish Ball; Early Bird; The Right Somebody to Love.

1936 74m/B Shirley Temple, Guy Kibbee, Buddy Ebsen, Slim Summerville, Jane Darwell, June Lang, George Irving, Si Jenks; **D:** David Butler. **VHS, Beta $19.98** *FOX* ♫♫ ½

Captain Kidd Laughton huffs and puffs and searches for treasure on the high seas, finds himself held captive with rest of cast in anemic swashbuckler.

1945 83m/B Charles Laughton, John Carradine, Randolph Scott, Reginald Owen, Gilbert Roland, Barbara Britton, John Qualen, Sheldon Leonard; **D:** Rowland V. Lee. **VHS, Beta $9.95** *CNG, MRV, NOS* ♫♫

Captain Kronos: Vampire Hunter Captain Kronos fences thirsty foes in Hammer horror hybrid. Artsy, atmospheric and atypical, it's written and directed with tongue firmly in cheek by Clemens, who penned many an "Avengers" episode. *AKA:* Kronos.

1974 (R) 91m/C *GB* Horst Janson, John Carson, Caroline Munro, Ian Hendry, Shane Briant, Wanda Ventham; **D:** Brian Clemens; **W:** Brian Clemens. **VHS, Beta $44.95** *PAR* ♫♫♫

Captain Newman, M.D. Three army guys visit stiff shrink Peck during the final months of WWII in VA ward for the mentally disturbed. Much guilt and agonizing, with

comic relief courtesy of Curtis. Peck is sub par, the direction flounders and there's something unsettling about quicksilver shifts from pathos to parody. Nonetheless touching with fine performance from Darin as guilt ridden hero. Based on the novel by Leo Rosten.

1963 126m/C Gregory Peck, Bobby Darin, Tony Curtis, Angie Dickinson, Eddie Albert, James Gregory, Jane Withers, Larry Storch, Robert Duvall; **D:** David Miller. **VHS, Beta $59.95** *MCA* ♫♫ ½

Captain Ron Harried couple Short and Place inherit a large boat and, with their two smart-mouthed kids, go to the Caribbean to sail the boat back to the U.S. Of course they know nothing about sailing, so they hire Captain Ron (Russell), a one-eyed, Long John Silver-talking boat captain. From there, numerous mishaps occur. Amusing sounding premise sinks like a stone. Russell looks great in his teeny-weeny bikini, and the scenery is beautiful, but that's about it.

1992 (PG-13) 104m/C Kurt Russell, Martin Short, Mary Kay Place, Meadow Sisto, Benjamin Salisbury; **D:** Thom Eberhardt; **W:** Thom Eberhardt. **VHS, Beta $94.95** *TOU* ♫ ½

Captain Scarlett Formulaic swashbuckler has nobleman Greene and highway guy Young fighting nasty French Royalists who've been putting the pressure on impecunious peasants. Runaway Spanish damsel in distress courtesy of Amar. Most novel aspect of the production is that the post-Napoleon French terrain has that vaguely south of the border feel.

1953 75m/C Richard Greene, Leonora Amar, Isobel Del Puerto, Nedrick Young, Manolo Fabregas; **D:** Thomas Carr. **VHS, Beta $19.95** *NOS, MRV, GEM* ♫ ½

Captain Sinbad Captain Sinbad must destroy the evil El Kerim, but first he must tackle a many-headed ogre, man-eating fish and crocodiles, a large fist clad in a spiked glove, an invisible monster, and more. To kill the villain, Sinbad must destroy his heart, which is kept in a tower with no entrance. A huge, witty, epic production with lots of special effects. This one is fun.

1963 85m/C Guy Williams, Heidi Bruhl, Pedro Armendariz Sr., Abraham Sofaer, Bernie Hamilton, Helmut Schneider; **D:** Byron Haskin. **VHS** *MGM* ♫♫ ½

Captain Swagger A man on the brink of thievery experiences some changes that keep him on the right side of the law.

1925 50m/B Rod La Rocque, Sue Carol, Richard Tucker, Victor Potel, Ullrich Haupt; **D:** Edward H. Griffith. **VHS, Beta $14.95** *GPV* ♫ ½

Captains Courageous Rich brat Bartholomew takes a dip sans life jacket while leaning over an ocean liner railing to relieve himself of the half dozen ice cream sodas imprudently consumed at sea. Picked up by a Portugese fishing boat, he at first treats his mandatory three month voyage as an unscheduled cab ride, but eventually, through a deepening friendship with crewman Tracy, develops a hitherto unhearalded work ethic. The boy's filial bond with Tracy, of course, requires that the seaman meet with watery disaster. Based on the Rudyard Kipling novel. Director Fleming went on to "Gone With the Wind" and "The Wizard of Oz."

1937 116m/B Spencer Tracy, Lionel Barrymore, Freddie Bartholomew, Mickey Rooney, Melvyn Douglas, Charley Grapewin, John Carradine, Bobby Watson, Jack LaRue; **D:** Victor Fleming. Academy Awards '37: Best Actor (Tracy); Nominations: Best Film Editing, Best Picture, Best Screenplay; National Board of Review Awards '37: 10 Best Films of the Year. **VHS, Beta $19.98** *MGM, BMV, BTV* ♫♫♫

Captains of the Clouds Unabashedly patriotic film starring Cagney as a daredevil, independent Canadian bush pilot who makes his own flying rules. When WWII begins he joins the Royal Canadian Air Force but washes out when he can't follow orders. However, he finds a way to prove himself a hero as a civilian pilot ferrying a bomber to England. Cagney's first Technicolor film.

1942 113m/C James Cagney, Dennis (Stanley Morner) Morgan, Brenda Marshall, Alan Hale, George Tobias, Reginald Gardiner, Reginald Denny, Russell Arms, Paul Cavanagh, Charles Halton; **D:** Michael Curtiz. **VHS $19.95** *MGM, FCT* ♫♫ ½

Captain's Paradise Golden Fleece captain Guinness chugs between wives in Gibraltar and North Africa, much to the adulation of chief officer Goldner. While Gibraltar little woman Johnson is homegrown homebody, little woman de Carlo is paint the town red type, allowing Guinness to have cake and eat it too, it seems, except that he's inconveniently positioned in front of a firing squad at movie's start.

1953 89m/B *GB* Alec Guinness, Yvonne De Carlo, Celia Johnson, Miles Malleson, Nicholas Phipps, Ferdinand "Ferdy" Mayne, Sebastian Cabot; **D:** Anthony Kimmins; **M:** Malcolm Arnold. **VHS, Beta $19.98** *FCT* ♫♫ ½

The Captain's Table Former cargo vessel captain Gregson is given luxury liner to command, and fails to revise his cargo captain style to fit new crew and clientele. British cast saves unremarkable script from mediocrity.

1960 90m/C *GB* John Gregson, Peggy Cummins, Donald Sinden, Nadia Gray; **D:** Jack Lee. **VHS $19.95** *PAR* ♫♫

Captive Spoiled heiress is kidnapped by terrorist trio and brainwashed into anti-establishment Hearst-like creature.

1987 (R) 98m/C Oliver Reed, Irina Brook, Xavier DeLuc, Hiro Arai; **D:** Paul Mayersberg. **VHS, Beta** *VTR* ♫ ½

Captive Heart Czech soldier Redgrave assumes the identity of a dead British officer in order to evade Nazis in WWII. Captured and imprisoned in camp reserved for British POWs, his stalagmates think they smell a spy, but he manages to convince them he's an OK Joe. Meanwhile, he's been writing letters home to the little missus, which means he's got a little explaining to do when he's released from prison. Especially fine Redgrave performance.

1947 86m/B *GB* Michael Redgrave, Basil Radford, Jack Warner, Jimmy Hanley, Rachel Kempson, Mervyn Johns; **D:** Basil Dearden. **VHS, Beta $19.95** *NOS, DVT, VEC* ♫♫♫

Captive Hearts Well frayed story holds cast captive in sushi romance. Two American flyers are shot down and taken prisoner in isolated Japanese mountain village, and one is shot by Cupid's arrow.

1987 (PG) 97m/C Noriyuki "Pat" Morita, Michael Sarrazin, Chris Makepeace; **D:** Paul Almond. **VHS, Beta $14.95** *MGM, FOX* ♫

Captive Planet Bargain basement FX and really atrocious acting hold audience captive in routine earth on the verge of obliteration yarn.

1978 95m/C Sharon Baker, Chris Auram, Anthony Newcastle; **D:** Al Bradley. **VHS, Beta** *NO* ♫

Captive Rage South American general Reed hijacks planeful of girlies to encourage US to release his son, who's in trouble because he swaps money for white powder. Violence lives up to title, all else disappoints.

1988 (R) 99m/C Oliver Reed, Robert Vaughn, Claudia Udy; *D:* Cedric Sundstrom. **VHS, Beta** $79.99 *MCG* ♫

The Captive: The Longest Drive 2
Matheson and Russell play two recently reunited brothers in search of their sister, whom they believe is still a captive of the Cheyenne Indians who also raised Russell. Along the way the two come to the aid of a pioneer woman and her young son. This western was actually a brief television series known as "The Quest," and is a continuation of the pilot episode released on video as "The Longest Drive."
1976 (PG-13) 80m/C Kurt Russell, Tim Matheson. **VHS** $89.95 *VMK* ♫♫

Captive Wild Woman
Mad scientist Dr. Sgimund Walters (Carradine) transforms an ape into the beautiful Paula Depress (Aquanetta), who promptly joins the circus as a mysterious animal trainer. Unfortunately, she falls in love with fellow trainer Fred (Stone), who already has a gal, bringing back the beast in the pretty Paula. Sequelled by "Jungle Captive" and "Jungle Woman."
1943 61m/B Acquanetta, John Carradine, Milburn Stone, Evelyn Ankers, Lloyd Corrigan, Vince Barnett, Paul Fix; *D:* Edward Dmytryk; *W:* Griffin Jay, Henry Sucher. **VHS** $14.98 *MCA* ♫♫½

The Capture
Above-average story told in flashback has Ayres hiding out in Mexico because he thought he killed an innocent man. He seeks out the widow to question her about him and they wind up marrying. When he finds the real culprit, the man is killed and the evidence points to Ayres. Ayres and Wright are great, as is the native Mexican musical score.
1950 67m/B Lew Ayres, Teresa Wright, Victor Jory, Jacqueline White, Jimmy Hunt, Duncan Renaldo, William "Billy" Bakewell; *D:* John Sturges. **VHS** $19.95 *NOS* ♫♫♫

The Capture of Bigfoot
Barefoot monster tracks footprints around town after 25 years of peace, and evil businessman attempts to capture creature for personal gain.
1979 (PG) 92m/C Stafford Morgan, Katherine Hopkins, Richard Kennedy, Otis Young, George Flower, John Goff; *D:* Bill Rebane. **VHS, Beta** $29.95 *AHV* ♫

The Capture of Grizzly Adams
Framed for murder, Adams and his ever-faithful companion Ben the bear must not only clear his name but outwit a band of outlaws who are holding his young daughter captive. Made for television.
1982 96m/C Dan Haggerty, Chuck Connors, June Lockhart, Kim Darby, Noah Beery Jr., Keenan Wynn. **VHS** $89.95 *WOV* ♫½

Captured in Chinatown
Dog chases bad guys in Chinatown. Bow wow.
1935 53m/B Marion Shilling, Charles Delaney, Philo McCullough, Robert Ellis; *D:* Elmer Clifton. **VHS, Beta** $12.95 *SNC* ♫

Car Crash
Organized crime hits stock car racing head on to produce crashing bore.
19?? 103m/C Joey Travolta, Anna Obregon, Vittorio Mezzogiorno. **VHS** *NO* ♫

Car 54, Where Are You?
The first situation comedy about police officers ran on television from 1961-1963. Join offbeat New York cops Gunther Toody and Francis Muldoon of the beleaguered 53rd Precinct. Each cassette contains two episodes. Eight cassettes.
1961 50m/B Fred Gwynne, Joe E. Ross, Nipsey Russell, Al Lewis; *D:* Stanley Prager, Nat Hiken. **VHS** $14.95 *REP, FCT, MOV* ♫

Car 54, Where Are You?
Exceedingly lame remake of the exceedingly lame television series, which ran for only two seasons, 1961-63. This time, Toody (Johansen) and Muldoon (McGinley) are protecting a mafia stool pigeon (Piven), while vampy Velma Velour (Drescher) sets her sights on Muldoon. Not many laughs and a waste of a talented cast. Sat on the shelf at Orion for three years (with good reason).
1994 (PG-13) 89m/C David Johansen, Fran Drescher, Rosie O'Donnell, John C. McGinley, Nipsey Russell, Al Lewis, Daniel Baldwin, Jeremy Piven; *D:* Bill Fishman; *W:* Ebbe Roe Smith, Erik Tarloff, Peter McCarthy, Peter Crabbe; *M:* Bernie Worrell, Pray For Rain. **VHS** *ORI* ♫

Car Trouble
Young English husband buys new Jaguar and wife's not so minor car trouble causes major marital trouble. Funnybone-tickling pairing of Walters and Charleson.
1986 (R) 93m/C *GB* Julie Walters, Ian Charleson; *D:* David Green; *M:* Meatloaf. **VHS, Beta** $79.95 *MCG* ♫♫

Car Wash
L.A. carwash provides a soap-opera setting for disjointed comic bits about owners of dirty cars and people who hose them down for a living. Econo budget and lite plot, but serious comic talent. A sort of disco carwash version of "Grand Hotel."
1976 (PG) 97m/C Franklin Ajaye, Sully Boyer, Richard Brestoff, George Carlin, Richard Pryor, Melanie Mayron, Ivan Dixon, Antonio Fargas; *D:* Michael A. Schultz; *W:* Joel Schumacher. **VHS, Beta** $14.98 *MCA, FCT* ♫♫½

Caravaggio
Controversial biography of the late Renaissance painter famous for his bisexuality, fondness for prostitute models, violence and depravity. Photography by Gabriel Beristain reproduces the artist's visual style.
1986 97m/C *GB* Nigel Terry, Sean Bean, Tilda Swinton; *D:* Derek Jarman; *W:* Derek Jarman. **VHS, Beta** $79.95 *TPV, FCT, ING* ♫♫♫

Caravan to Vaccares
French Duke hires young American to sneak Eastern European scientist into the States, and little suspense ensues. Based on Alistair MacLean novel.
1974 (PG) 98m/C David Birney, Charlotte Rampling; *D:* Geoffrey Reeve. **VHS, Beta** $69.95 *MED* ♫

The Caravan Trail
A cowboy becomes marshal in order to bring to justice those who have stolen land and murdered his friend. This was shot in color, which was rare for the 1940s.
1946 53m/C Eddie Dean, Lash LaRue, Emmett Lynn, Jean Carlin, Charles "Blackie" King, Robert Barron, Lloyd Ingraham, Bud Osborne; *D:* Robert Emmett. **VHS** $19.95 *NOS, RXM, HEG* ♫♫

Carbon Copy
Successful white executive has life turned inside out when his seventeen-year old illegitimate son, who happens to be black, decides it's time to look up dear old dad. Typical comedy-with-a-moral.
1981 (PG) 92m/C George Segal, Susan St. James, Jack Warden, Paul Winfield, Dick Martin, Vicky Dawson, Tom Poston, Denzel Washington; *D:* Michael A. Schultz; *W:* Stanley Shapiro; *M:* Bill Conti. **VHS, Beta** $9.95 *COL, SUE* ♫♫

Cardiac Arrest
Lunatic eviscerates victims in trolley town. They left their hearts in San Francisco.
1974 (PG) 95m/C Garry Goodrow, Mike Chan, Max Gail; *D:* Murray Mintz. **VHS, Beta** $69.95 *MED* ♫

The Cardinal
Priestly young Tryon rises through ecclesiastical ranks to become Cardinal, struggling through a plethora of tests of faith, none so taxing as the test of the audience's patience. Had Preminger excised some sixty minutes of footage, he might have had a compelling portrait of faith under fire, but as it stands, the cleric's life is epic confusion. Fine acting, even from Tryon, who later went on to bookish fame, and from Huston who's normally on the other side of the camera. McNamara's final performance. Based on the Henry Morton Robinson novel.
1963 175m/C Tom Tryon, Carol Lynley, Dorothy Gish, Maggie McNamara, Cecil Kellaway, John Huston, John Saxon, Burgess Meredith; *D:* Otto Preminger. Academy Awards '63 Nominations: Best Art Direction/Set Decoration (Color), Best Color Cinematography, Best Director (Preminger), Best Film Editing, Best Supporting Actor (Huston); Golden Globe Awards '64: Best Film—Drama, Best Supporting Actor (Huston). **VHS, Beta** $29.98 *WAR, IME, VTR* ♫♫½

The Care Bears Movie
The Care Bears leave their cloud home in Care-a-lot to try and teach earthlings how to share their feelings of love and caring for each other.
1984 (G) 75m/C *D:* Arna Selznick; *V:* Mickey Rooney, Georgia Engel, Harry Dean Stanton. **VHS, Beta** $14.95 *LIV, VES, VTR* ♫

The Care Bears Movie 2: A New Generation
Sequel to the sweet adventures of the animated bear family and their new offspring.
1986 (G) 77m/C *D:* Dale Schott; *V:* Maxine Miller, Pam Hyatt, Hadley Key. **VHS, Beta** $14.95 *COL, WTA* ♫

Career
An overwrought, depressing drama about the trials and tribulations of an actor trying to make it on Broadway. He'll try anything to succeed. Good direction, but so-so acting.
1959 105m/B Dean Martin, Anthony (Tony) Franciosa, Shirley MacLaine, Carolyn Jones, Joan Blackman, Robert Middleton, Donna Douglas; *D:* Joseph Anthony. Academy Awards '59 Nominations: Best Art Direction/Set Decoration (B & W), Best Black and White Cinematography, Best Costume Design (B & W); Golden Globe Awards '60: Best Actor—Drama (Franciosa). **VHS** *PAR* ♫♫½

Career Opportunities
"Home Alone" clone for teenagers from John Hughes' factory. Whaley is an unsuccessful con-artist who finally gets a job as the night janitor of the local department store. He fools around at company expense until he finds the town's beauty (Connelly) asleep in a dressing room. The pair then play make-believe until its time to thwart some small-time thieves. Unexciting and unrealistic in the worst way; no wonder Candy isn't billed—he probably didn't want to be.
1991 (PG-13) 83m/C Frank Whaley, Jennifer Connelly, Dermot Mulroney, Kieran Mulroney, John M. Jackson, Jenny O'Hara, Noble Willingham, Barry Corbin, Denise Galik, William Forsythe; *Cameos:* John Candy; *D:* Bryan Gordon; *W:* John Hughes; *M:* Thomas Newman. **VHS** $19.95 *MCA* ♫½

Carefree
Dizzy radio singer Rogers can't make up her mind about beau Bellamy, so he sends her to analyst Astaire. Seems she can't even dream a little dream until shrink Astaire prescribes that she ingest some funny food, which causes her to dream she's in love with the Fredman. Au contraire, says he, it's a Freudian thing, and he hypnotically suggests that she really loves Bellamy. The two line up to march down the aisle together, and Fred stops dancing just long enough to realize he's in love with Ginger. A screwball comedy with music. ♫I Used to be Color-blind; The Night is Filled With Music; Change Partners; The Yam.
1938 83m/B Fred Astaire, Ginger Rogers, Ralph Bellamy, Jack Carson, Franklin Pangborn, Hattie McDaniel; *D:* Mark Sandrich; *M:* Irving Berlin. **VHS, Beta** $14.98 *TTC, RKO, MED* ♫♫♫

Careful Butler-in-training Neale courts Neville in an alpine mountain village where silence is golden, or at least being quiet will lessen the chance of an avalanche. Dig a little deeper and you find incest, repression and other nasty things. Highly individualistic black comedy parodies German Expressionism and Freudian psychology to the point of absurdity, dealing with snow, sex, sleep, spirits, and obsessive/compulsive personality disorders. Third film from Canadian cult director Maddin is awash in vivid primary colors when it suits the scene's mood and employs between-scenes titles in a homage to cinematic antiquity.
1994 100m/C Kyle McCulloch, Gosia Dobrowolska, Jackie Burroughs, Sarah Neville, Brent Neale, Paul Cox, Victor Cowie, Michael O'Sullivan, Vince Rimmer, Katya Gardner; **D:** Guy Maddin; **W:** Guy Maddin, George Toles; **M:** John McCulloch. **VHS** *NYR* 𝒵𝒵

Careful, He Might Hear You Abandoned by his father, six-year-old P.S. becomes a pawn between his dead mother's two sisters, one working class and the other wealthy, and his worldview is further overturned by the sudden reappearance of his prodigal father. Set in Depression-era Australia, Schultz's vision is touching and keenly observed, and manages a sort of child's eye sense of proportion. Based on a novel by Sumner Locke Elliott.
1984 (PG) 113m/C *AU* Nicholas Gledhill, Wendy Hughes, Robyn Nevin, John Hargreaves; **D:** Carl Schultz. **VHS, Beta $59.98** *FOX* 𝒵𝒵𝒵

Caribe Caribbean travelogue masquerades as spy thriller. Arms smuggling goes awry, and neither voodoo nor bikinied blondes can prevent audience from dozing. Never released theatrically.
1987 96m/C John Savage, Kara Glover, Stephen McHattie, Sam Malkin; **D:** Michael Kennedy. **VHS, Beta $79.98** *LIV, VES* 𝒵 1/2

The Cariboo Trail Two prospecting men seek their fortune in British Columbia, the golden West of Canada in the 1890s. But they find themselves opposed by a ruthless rancher and claim-jumpers. Actually filmed in Colorado with excellent cinematography and solid performances from some big names, it's still a run-of-the-mill entry. Made the same year that the Gabby Hayes' show first aired.
1950 80m/C Angela Douglas, Randolph Scott, George "Gabby" Hayes, Bill Williams, Victor Jory; **D:** Gerald Thomas, Edwin L. Marin. **VHS** *FRH, IME* 𝒵𝒵

Carlito's Way Puerto Rican crime czar Carlito Brigante (Pacino) has just gotten out of jail and wants to go straight. But his drug underworld cohorts don't believe he can do it. Penn (barely recognizable) is great as a sleazy coked-out lawyer who's way out of his league. Remarkably subdued violence given DePalma's previous rep—it's effective without being gratuitous, especially the final shootout set in Grand Central Station. Pacino's performance is equally subdued, with controlled tension and lots of eye contact rather than grandiose emotions. Based on the novels "Carlito's Way" and "After Hours" by Edwin Torres. Pacino and DePalma previously teamed up for "Scarface."
1993 (R) 145m/C Al Pacino, Sean Penn, Penelope Ann Miller, Luis Guzman, John Leguizamo, Ingrid Rogers, James Rebhorn, Viggo Mortensen, Jorge Porcel, Joseph Siravo, Adrian Pasdar; **D:** Brian DePalma; **W:** David Koepp; **M:** Patrick Doyle. **VHS** *MCA* 𝒵𝒵𝒵

Carlton Browne of the F.O. Bumbling Brit diplomat Thomas visits tiny Pacific island of Gallardia, forgotten by the mother country for some fifty years, to insure tenuous international agreement after the island's king dies. Not sterling Sellers but some shining moments. **AKA:** Man in a Cocked Hat.
1959 88m/C *GB* Peter Sellers, Terry-Thomas, Lucianna Paluzzi, Ian Bannen; **D:** Roy Boulting, Jeffrey Dell; **M:** John Addison. **VHS, Beta $19.98** *FCT* 𝒵𝒵 1/2

Carmen Choreographer casts Carmen and finds life imitates art when he falls under the spell of the hotblooded Latin siren. Bizet's opera lends itself to erotically charged flamenco context. Well acted, impressive scenes including cigarette girls' dance fight and romance between Carmen and Don Jose. In Spanish with English subtitles.
1983 (R) 99m/C *SP* Antonio Gades, Laura Del Sol, Paco DeLucia, Christina Hoyos; **D:** Carlos Saura. **VHS, Beta $29.98** *CTH, MED, ING* 𝒵𝒵𝒵

Carmen Jones Bizet's tale of fickle femme fatale Carmen heads South with an all black cast and new lyrics by Hammerstein II. Soldier Belafonte falls big time for factory working belle Dandridge during the war, and runs off with miss thang after he kills his C.O. and quits the army. Tired of prettyboy Belafonte, Dandridge's eye wanders upon prize pugilist Escamillo, inspiring ex-soldier beau to wring her throaty little neck. Film debuts of Carroll and Peters. More than a little racist undertone to the direction. Actors' singing is dubbed. ♫Dat's Love; Dere's a Cafe on de Corner; Beat Out Dat Rhythm on a Drum; You Talk Just Like My Maw; Stand Up and Fight; Dis Flower; My Joe.
1954 105m/C Dorothy Dandridge, Harry Belafonte, Pearl Bailey, Roy Glenn, Diahann Carroll, Brock Peters; **D:** Otto Preminger. Academy Awards '54 Nominations: Best Actress (Dandridge), Best Original Score; Golden Globe Awards '55: Best Film—Musical/Comedy. **VHS** *MLB* 𝒵𝒵𝒵

Carmilla An adaptation of the Sheridan Le Fanu lesbian vampire tale. From Shelley Duvall's cable television series "Nightmare Classics."
1989 60m/C Meg Tilly, Ione Skye, Roddy McDowall, Roy Dotrice; **D:** Gabrielle Beaumont. **VHS, Beta $59.95** *NO* 𝒵𝒵𝒵

Carnage Hungry house consumes inhabitants.
1984 91m/C Leslie Den Dooven, Michael Chiodo, Deeann Veeder; **D:** Andy Milligan. **VHS, Beta $49.95** *MED* 𝒵

Carnal Crimes Well-acted upscale softcore trash about a sensuous woman, ignored by her middle-aged lawyer husband and drawn to a young stud photographer with a shady past and S&M tendencies. Available in a sexy unrated version also.
1991 (R) 103m/C Martin Hewitt, Linda Carol, Rich Crater, Alex Kubik, Yvette Stefens, Paula Trickey; **D:** Alexander Gregory Hippolyte; **W:** Jon Robert Samsel; **M:** Matthew Ross, Jeff Fishman. **VHS** *NO* 𝒵 1/2

Carnal Knowledge Carnal knowledge of the me generation. Three decades in the sex-saturated lives of college buddies Nicholson and Garfunkel, chronicled through girlfriends, affairs and marriages. Controversial upon release, it's not a flattering anatomy of Y chromosome carriers. Originally written as a play. Kane's debut.
1971 (R) 96m/C Jack Nicholson, Candice Bergen, Art Garfunkel, Ann-Margret, Rita Moreno, Carol Kane; **D:** Mike Nichols; **W:** Jules Feiffer. Academy Awards '71 Nominations: Best Supporting Actress (Ann-Margret); Golden Globe Awards '72: Best Supporting Actress (Ann-

Margret). **VHS, Beta, 8mm $14.98** *SUE, COL, FOX* 𝒵𝒵𝒵

Carnival in Flanders When Spanish invaders enter a small 17th century Flemish village they discover all the men have disappeared. So it's up to the women to save the town from destruction—and they decide to do it by seducing the invaders. Classic French costume farce with a witty script and fine performances. In French with English subtitles. **AKA:** La Kermesse Heroique.
1935 90m/B *FR* Francoise Rosay, Louis Jouvet, Jean Murat, Andre Aleme, Micheline Cheirel; **D:** Jacques Feyder. **VHS, Beta $39.95** *HTV, MRV, HHT* 𝒵𝒵𝒵 1/2

Carnival Lady Silver spooner Vincent is scheduled to tie the knot until little lady-to-be discovers he's a bit out of pocket after the stock market takes a wee dip. Jilted and impecunious, he heads for the big top, where he horns in on the high diver's turf, and it's all downhill from there.
1933 66m/B Patricia "Boots" Mallory, A. Vincent. **VHS, Beta $29.95** *VCN* 𝒵

Carnival of Blood Boring talky scenes punctuated by Coney Island murder mayhem followed by more boring talky scenes. Young's debut, not released for five years. The question's not why they delayed release, but why they bothered at all. A carnival of cliches.
1971 (PG) 80m/C Earle Edgerton, Judith Resnick, Martin Barlosky, John Harris, Burt Young; **W:** Leonard Kirtman. **VHS, Beta** *NO* 𝒵

Carnival of Souls Cult-followed zero budget zombie opera has young Hilligoss and girlfriends take wrong turn off bridge into river. Mysteriously unscathed, Hilligoss rents room and takes job as church organist, but she keeps running into dancing dead people, led by director Harvey. Spooky, very spooky. Laserdisc version offers restored picture quality and a refined audio track, as well as introductory feature on the movie's background.
1962 80m/B Candace Hilligoss, Sidney Berger, Frances Feist, Stan Levitt, Art Ellison, Herk Harvey; **D:** Herk Harvey. **VHS, Beta $19.99** *MRV, SNC, NOS* 𝒵𝒵𝒵

Carnival Rock Story of love triangular in seedy nightclub. Club owner Stewart loves chanteuse Cabot who loves card playin' Hutton. Who cares? Maybe hard-core Corman devotees. Good tunes from the Platters, the Blockbusters, Bob Luman and David Houston.
1957 80m/B Susan Cabot, Brian Hutton, David J. Stewart, Dick Miller; **D:** Roger Corman. **VHS, Beta $9.95** *RHI, AOV, FCT* 𝒵 1/2

Carnival Story Yet another melodramatic cliche about love triangular under the big top. German girl joins American-owned carnival and two guys start acting out unbecoming territorial behavior. Filmed in Germany.
1954 94m/C Anne Baxter, Steve Cochran, Lyle Bettger, George Nader; **D:** Kurt Neumann. **VHS, Beta $19.95** *NOS, GEM, DVT* 𝒵 1/2

The Carnivores The flesh-eaters of the animal kingdom—bears, lions, tigers, and others—and their survival instincts are the focus of this nature documentary.
1983 90m/C VHS, Beta $69.95 *DIS* 𝒵𝒵

Carnosaur Straight from the Corman film factory, this exploitive quickie about dinosaurs harkens back to '50s-style monster epics. Predictable plot with extremely cheap effects. Genetic scientist Dr. Jane Tiptree (Ladd) is hatching diabolic experiments with chickens when things go awry. The experiments result in a bunch of lethal prehistoric

C

creatures wrecking havoc among the community.
1993 (R) 82m/C Diane Ladd, Raphael Sbarge, Jennifer Runyon, Harrison Page, Clint Howard, Ned Bellamy; *D:* Adam Simon; *W:* Adam Simon; *M:* Nigel Holton. VHS **$91.50** *NHO &&&*

Carny Hothead carnival bozo Busey and peacemaker Robertson experience friendship difficulties when runaway Foster rolls in hay with one and then other. Originally conceived as a documentary by "Derby" filmmaker Kaylor, it's a candid, unsavory, behind-the-scenes anatomy. Co-written by "The Band" member Robertson.
1980 (R) 102m/C Gary Busey, Robbie Robertson, Jodie Foster, Meg Foster, Kenneth McMillan, Elisha Cook Jr., Craig Wasson; *D:* Robert Kaylor; *W:* Robbie Robertson. VHS, Beta **$19.98** *FOX, WAR &&&*

Carolina Skeletons As a child in a small southern town Gossett, Jr. watched as his brother was accused of a vicious double murder and quickly tried and executed. Thirty years later, the ex-Green Beret returns home to find the real killer and clear his brother's name. But there are those in the town who will do anything to stop their secrets from being revealed.
1992 (R) 94m/C Louis Gossett Jr., Bruce Dern, Melissa Leo, Paul Robeling, G.D. Spradlin, Bill Cobbs, Henderson Forsythe, Clifton James; *D:* John Erman; *W:* Tracy Keenan Wynn; *M:* John Morris. VHS *TRI &&*

Caroline? A wealthy young woman is presumed dead in a plane crash. Now 15 years later a stranger appears at the family home claiming to be Caroline—and wanting her inheritance. Is it possible that what she says is true or is it all an elaborate ruse? An especially good performance by Zimbalist. Made for television as a "Hallmark Hall of Fame" presentation. Based on the novel "Father's Arcane Daughter" by E.L. Konigsburg.
1990 (PG) 100m/C Stephanie Zimbalist, Pamela Reed, George Grizzard, Dorothy McGuire, Patricia Neal, Shawn Phelan, Jenny Jacobs; *D:* Joseph Sargent; *M:* Charles Bernstein. VHS **$14.98** *REP &&&*

Caroline at Midnight After a reporter's former girlfriend, Caroline, dies in a mysterious auto accident he winds up falling for her girlfriend Victoria. Then he discovers both women are connected to drug-dealing cops. Good cast in this atmospheric erotic thriller with plenty of puzzles.
1993 (R) 92m/C Clayton Rohner, Mia Sara, Timothy Daly, Judd Nelson, Virginia Madsen, Zach Galligan; *D:* Scott McGinnis. VHS *NHO &&*

Carousel Much-loved Rodgers & Hammerstein musical based on Ferenc Molnar's play "Liliom" (filmed by Fritz Lang in 1935) about a swaggering carnival barker (MacRae) who tries to change his life after he falls in love with a good woman. Killed while attempting to foil a robbery he was supposed to help commit, he begs his heavenly hosts for the chance to return to the mortal realm just long enough to set things straight with his teenage daughter. Now indisputably a classic, the film lost $2 million when it was released. ♫If I Loved You; Soliloquy; You'll Never Walk Alone; What's the Use of Wond'rin; When I Marry Mister Snow; When the Children Are Asleep; A Real Nice Clambake; Carousel Ballet; Carousel Waltz; You're a Queer One, Julie Jordan; Mr. Snow; June is Bustin' Out All Over.
1956 128m/C Gordon MacRae, Shirley Jones, Cameron Mitchell, Gene Lockhart, Barbara Ruick, Robert Rounseville, Richard Deacon, Tor Johnson; *D:* Henry King; *M:* Richard Rodgers,

Oscar Hammerstein. VHS, Beta **$19.98** *FOX, RDG, HMV &&&*

The Carpathian Eagle Police wonder why murdered victims have hearts ripped out while audience wonders what weird title has to do with anything. Routine evisceration fest, part of Elvira's Thriller Video.
1981 60m/C Suzanne Danielle, Sian Phillips, Pierce Brosnan, Anthony Valentine; *D:* Francis Megahy. VHS, Beta **$29.95** *LIV &*

The Carpenter Post-nervous breakdown woman receives nightly visits from guy who builds stuff with wood. Very scary stuff. Also available in slightly longer unrated version.
1989 (R) 85m/C Wings Hauser, Lynne Adams, Pierce Lenoir, Barbara Ann Jones; *D:* David Wellington. VHS **$89.98** *REP &*

Carpet of Horror The city of London is terrorized by a small ball emitting poison gas in this schlock horror film. Death results when the ball is rolled into the living rooms of intended victims.
1964 ?m/C Joachim Berger, Carl Lange, Karin Dor. VHS **$16.95** *SNC &&*

The Carpetbaggers Uncannily Howard Hughesian Peppard wallows in wealth and women in Hollywood in the 1920s and 1930s. Spayed version of the Harold Robbins novel. Ladd's final appearance. Followed by the prequel "Nevada Smith." Introduced by Joan Collins.
1964 (PG) 150m/C George Peppard, Carroll Baker, Alan Ladd, Elizabeth Ashley, Lew Ayres, Martha Hyer, Martin Balsam, Robert Cummings, Archie Moore, Audrey Totter; *D:* Edward Dmytryk; *W:* John Michael Hayes; *M:* Elmer Bernstein. VHS, Beta **$14.95** *PAR &&*

Carrie In a part turned down by Cary Grant, Olivier plays a married American who self destructs as the woman he loves scales the heights to fame and fortune. The manager of a posh epicurean mecca, Olivier deserts wife Hopkins and steals big bucks from his boss to head east with paramour Jones, a country bumpkin transplanted to Chicago. Once en route to thespian fame in the Big Apple, Jones abandons her erstwhile beau, who crumbles pathetically. Adapted from Theodore Dreiser's "Sister Carrie," it's mega melodrama, but the performances are above reproach.
1952 118m/B Laurence Olivier, Jennifer Jones, Miriam Hopkins, Eddie Albert, Basil Ruysdael, Ray Teal, Barry Kelley, Sara Berner, William Reynolds, Mary Murphy, Charles Halton; *D:* William Wyler. VHS, Beta **$19.98** *PAR, FCT &&&*

Carrie Overprotected by religious fanatic mother Laurie and mocked by the in-crowd, shy, withdrawn high school girl Carrie White is asked to the prom. Realizing she's been made the butt of a joke, she unleashes her considerable telekinetic talents. Travolta, Allen, and Irving are teenagers who get what they deserve. Based on the Stephen King novel. Laserdisc version features the original movie trailer, an interview with screenwriter Lawrence D. Cohen, publicity shots, a study of De Palma's film-making techniques, and commentary by film expert Laurent Bouzereau.
1976 (R) 98m/C Sissy Spacek, Piper Laurie, John Travolta, William Katt, Amy Irving, Nancy Allen, Edie McClurg, Betty Buckley; *D:* Brian DePalma; *M:* Pino Donaggio. VHS, Beta **$14.95** *MGM, FOX, CRC &&&*

The Carrier Smalltown Sleepy Rock is ideal family-raising turf until plague mysteriously blights inhabitants, and townspeople are out to exterminate all potential carriers. Silverman is standout as local spiritual leader; well orchestrated crowd scenes. Best

park your IQ before watching. Filmed on location in Manchester, Michigan.
1987 (R) 99m/C Gregory Fortescue, Steve Dixon, Paul Silverman; *D:* Nathan J. White. VHS, Beta *NO &&*

Carrington, V.C. British army major Niven is brought up for a court-martial on embezzlement charges because he arranges, without official permission, to be reimbursed for money owed to him. A former war hero, he decides to defend himself in court, and, once an affair comes to light, his vindictive wife joins the opposition. Good cast, superlative Niven performance. *AKA:* Court Martial.
1954 100m/B *GB* David Niven, Margaret Leighton, Noelle Middleton, Laurence Naismith; *D:* Anthony Asquith. VHS, Beta **$39.95** *MON &&&*

Carry Me Back Two brothers carry dead dad back to Australian ranch in order to inherit mucho dinero.
1982 93m/C *AU* Grant Tilly, Kelly Johnson. VHS, Beta **$39.95** *LIV &½*

Carry On Admiral Weak British comedy about two friends who get drunk and decide it would be fun to switch identities. One has an easy job as a public relations exec but the other is supposedly the captain of a ship. His lack of sea knowledge causes wacky catastrophes. Unrelated to the "Carry On" series of comedies. *AKA:* The Ship was Loaded.
1957 85m/B *GB* David Tomlinson, Brian Reece, Peggy Cummins, Eunice Gayson, A.E. Matthews, Lionel Murton, Joan Sims; *D:* Val Guest; *W:* Val Guest. VHS **$19.98** *FUS &½*

Carry On at Your Convenience Low-brow humor in and around a toilet factory.
1971 86m/C *GB* Sidney James, Kenneth Williams, Charles Hawtrey, Joan Sims, Kenneth Cope; *D:* Gerald Thomas. VHS, Beta **$19.95** *NO &½*

Carry On Behind "Carry On" crew heads for archeological dig and find themselves sharing site with holiday caravan.
1975 95m/C *GB* Sidney James, Kenneth Williams, Elke Sommer, Joan Sims; *D:* Gerald Thomas. VHS, Beta **$59.98** *SUE &&*

Carry On Cleo "Carry On" spoof of Shakespeare's "Antony and Cleopatra."
1965 91m/C *GB* Sidney James, Amanda Barrie, Kenneth Williams, Kenneth Connor, Jim Dale, Charles Hawtrey, Joan Sims; *D:* Gerald Thomas. VHS, Beta *NO &&½*

Carry On Cowboy "Carry On" western parody of "High Noon." *AKA:* Rumpo Kid.
1966 91m/C *GB* Sidney James, Kenneth Williams, Jim Dale. VHS, Beta *NO &&*

Carry On Cruising "Carry On" gang attacks sailing world with low humor and raunchiness.
1962 89m/C Sidney James, Kenneth Williams, Liz Fraser; *D:* Gerald Thomas. VHS, Beta *NO &*

Carry On Dick What made the seemingly endless "Carry On" series of super-low-budget British farces such a hit is a mystery not to be solved. Low production values, scripts that peter out midway, and manifest humor don't normally a classic make; and yet the gang has its following. "Dick," a detective movie spoof, was preceded by some twenty-odd carryings on; suffice it to say that the series, which began in 1958 with "Carry on Sergeant," has not improved with age in subsequent incarnations.
1975 95m/C *GB* Sidney James, Joan Sims; *D:* Gerald Thomas. VHS *NO &&*

Carry On Doctor British series continues as characters of questionable competence join the medical profession. Hospital staff gets caught in battle over secret weight loss formula.
1968 95m/C *GB* Frankie Howerd, Kenneth Williams, Jim Dale, Barbara Windsor; *D:* Gerald Thomas. VHS $19.95 *PAR ♂♂♂*

Carry On Emmanuelle Bedroom diplomat Emmanuelle enters international politics by taking on foreign legion. Part of the British "Carry On" series.
1978 104m/C *GB* Suzanne Danielle, Kenneth O'Connor, Kenneth Williams, Beryl Reid; *D:* Gerald Thomas. VHS, Beta NO *♂*

Carry On England Mercifully, the gang didn't carry on much beyond this entry, in which a WWII antiaircraft fleet captain bumbles through the usual pranks and imbroglios.
1976 89m/C *GB* Kenneth Connor, Patrick Mower, Judy Geeson; *D:* Gerald Thomas. VHS NO *♂♂*

Carry On Nurse Men's ward in a British hospital declares war on nurses and the rest of the hospital. The second of the "Carry On" series.
1959 86m/B *GB* Shirley Eaton, Kenneth Connor, Hattie Jacques, Wilfrid Hyde-White; *D:* Gerald Thomas. VHS, Beta $19.95 *NOS, VYY, VDM ♂♂*

Carry On 'Round the Bend Williams, who played in the original ("Carry On Sergeant"), and Carry On regulars (charpeimugged James and ever-zaftig Jacques), go 'round the bend in yet another installment of the British spoof.
1972 89m/C *GB* Sidney James, Kenneth Williams, Hattie Jacques; *D:* Gerald Thomas. VHS NO *♂♂½*

Carry On Screaming "Carry On" does horror. A pair of goofy detectives trail monsters suspected in kidnapping.
1966 97m/C *GB* Harry H. Corbett, Kenneth Williams, Fenella Fielding, Joan Sims, Charles Hawtrey, Jim Dale, Angela Douglas, Jon Pertwee; *D:* Gerald Thomas. VHS $19.98 *MOV ♂♂*

The Cars That Ate Paris Parasitic town in the Parisian (Australia) outback preys on car and body parts generated by deliberate car accidents inflicted by wreck-driving wreckless youths. Weir's first film released internationally, about a small Australian town that survives economically via deliberately contriving car accidents and selling the wrecks' scrap parts. A broad, bitter black comedy with some horror touches. *AKA:* The Cars That Eat People.
1974 (PG) 91m/C *AU* Terry Camilleri, Kevin Miles, John Meillon, Melissa Jaffe; *D:* Peter Weir; *W:* Peter Weir. VHS, Beta $19.95 *COL ♂♂♂*

Carson City Kid Typical western which has Rogers trying to exact revenge on the man who killed his brother.
1940 54m/B Roy Rogers. VHS, Beta $19.95 *NOS, VCN, MED ♂½*

Cartel O'Keeffe, "B" actor extraordinaire, plays the wrong man to pick on in this rancid dope opera. Hounded by drug lord Stroud and framed for murder, pilot O'Keeffe decides the syndicate has gone too doggone far when they kill his sister. Exploitive and otherwise very bad.
1990 (R) 106m/C Miles O'Keeffe. VHS *IME Woof!*

Carthage in Flames A graphic portrayal of the destruction of ancient Carthage in a blood and guts battle for domination of the known world. A tender love story is a welcome aside in this colorful Italian-made epic. *AKA:* Cartagine in Fiamme; Carthage en Flammes.
1960 96m/C *IT* Anne Heywood, Jose Suarez, Pierre Brasseur; *D:* Carmine Gallone. VHS, Beta NO *♂♂*

Cartier Affair A beautiful television actress unwittingly falls in love with the man who wants to steal her jewels. Collins designed her own wardrobe. Made for television.
1984 120m/C Joan Collins, David Hasselhoff, Telly Savalas, Ed Lauter, Joe La Due; *D:* Rod Holcomb. VHS, Beta $39.98 *LHV, WAR ♂*

Cartouche A swashbuckling action-comedy set in 18th-century France. Belmondo plays a charming thief who takes over a Paris gang, aided by the lovely Cardinale. When he is captured, she sacrifices her life to save him and Belmondo and his cohorts vow to have their revenge. Based on a French legend and a well-acted combination of tragedy, action, and farce. In French with English subtitles. *AKA:* Swords of Blood.
1962 115m/C *FR IT* Jean-Paul Belmondo, Claudia Cardinale, Odile Versois, Philippe Lemaire; *D:* Philippe de Broca; *M:* Georges Delerue. VHS $29.95 *FCT, HTV ♂♂♂*

Carve Her Name with Pride The true story of Violette Szabo who at age nineteen became a secret agent with the French Resistance in WWII.
1958 119m/B Virginia McKenna, Paul Scofield. VHS, Beta *LCA ♂♂½*

The Cary Grant Collection Three of Cary Grant's most memorable films: "Father Goose," Oscar-winning script; "Indiscreet" (w/ Ingrid Bergman); and "Operation Petticoat" (Tony Curtis and Grant are quite a team in this military comedy! Some great gags.)
1990 336m/C Cary Grant, Ingrid Bergman, Leslie Caron, Trevor Howard, Tony Curtis, Dina Merrill, Gavin MacLeod, Madlyn Rhue; *D:* Ralph Nelson, Stanley Donen, Blake Edwards. VHS, Beta $59.95 *REP ♂♂½*

Casablanca Can you see George Raft as Rick? Jack Warner did, but producer Hal Wallis wanted Bogart. Considered by many to be the best film ever made and one of the most quoted movies of all time, it rocketed Bogart from gangster roles to romantic leads as he and Bergman (who never looked lovelier) sizzle on screen. Bogart runs a gin joint in Morocco during the Nazi occupation, and meets up with Bergman, an old flame, but romance and politics do not mix, especially in Nazi-occupied French Morocco. Greenstreet, Lorre, and Rains all create memorable characters, as does Wilson, the piano player to whom Bergman says the oft-misquoted, "Play it, Sam." Without a doubt, the best closing scene ever written; it was scripted on the fly during the end of shooting, and actually shot several ways. See it in the original black and white. Laserdisc edition features restored imaging and sound and commentary by film historian Ronald Haver about the production, the play it was based on, and the famed evolution of the screenplay on audio track two. 50th Anniversary Edition contains a restored and remastered print, the original 1942 theatrical trailer, a film documentary narrated by Lauren Bacall, and a booklet.
1942 (PG) 102m/B Humphrey Bogart, Ingrid Bergman, Paul Henreid, Claude Rains, Peter Lorre, Sydney Greenstreet, Conrad Veidt, S.Z. Sakall, Dooley Wilson, Marcel Dalio, John Qualen, Helmut Dantine; *D:* Michael Curtiz; *W:* Julius J. Epstein, Philip C. Epstein, Howard Koch; *M:* Max Steiner. Academy Awards '43: Best Director (Curtiz), Best Picture, Best Screenplay; Nominations: Best Actor (Bogart),

Best Black and White Cinematography, Best Film Editing, Best Supporting Actor (Rains), Best Original Score; National Board of Review Awards '45: 10 Best Films of the Year. VHS, Beta, 8mm $19.98 *MGM, FOX, VYG ♂♂♂♂*

Casablanca Express Nazi commandos hijack Churchill's train in this action-adventure drama.
1989 90m/C Glenn Ford, Donald Pleasence, Jason Connery; *D:* Sergio Martino. VHS, Beta NO *♂*

Casanova A comedic romp through the bedrooms of 18th-century Europe with Chamberlain as the legendary lover. Lots of lovely ladies and hammy performances. Made for television.
1987 (PG-13) 122m/C Richard Chamberlain, Faye Dunaway, Sylvia Kristel, Ornella Muti, Hanna Schygulla, Sophie Ward, Frank Finlay, Kenneth Colley; *D:* Simon Langton; *W:* George MacDonald Fraser. VHS, Beta $89.98 *TTC ♂♂*

Casanova Brown Lighthearted comedy about a shy English professor (Cooper) who learns that his recent ex-wife (Wright) has had a baby (guess whose). When Cooper learns Wright has decided to give their daughter up for adoption he kidnaps the tyke and attempts fatherhood in a hotel room. When Wright finds out where he is, the twosome (who have really been in love all along) decide to remarry and be a family. Cooper, with baby and surrounded by diapers, makes a comedic sight. Based on the play "The Little Accident" by Floyd Dell and Thomas Mitchell.
1944 94m/B Gary Cooper, Teresa Wright, Frank Morgan, Anita Louise, Patricia Collinge, Edmund Breon, Jill Esmond, Emory Parnell, Isobel Elsom, Mary Treen, Halliwell Hobbes; *D:* Sam Wood; *W:* Nunnally Johnson; *M:* Arthur Lange. VHS, Beta $19.98 *MGM, FCT ♂♂½*

Casanova '70 Mastroianni plays a handsome soldier who has a knack for enticing liberated women in this comic rendition of the much-cinematized legendary yarn. Trouble is, he's in the mood only when he believes that he's in imminent danger. In Italian with English subtitles.
1965 113m/C *IT* Marcello Mastroianni, Virna Lisi, Michele Mercier, Guido Alberti, Margaret Lee, Bernard Blier, Liana Orfei; *D:* Mario Monicelli; *W:* Tonino Guerra. VHS *FOX ♂♂½*

Casanova's Big Night Classic slapstick comedy stars Hope masquerading as Casanova to determine the nature of Fontaine's intentions in marrying the real Casanova. The all-star cast provides one hilarious scene after another in this dated film. Price has a cameo as the "real" Casanova. Based on a story by Aubrey Wisberg.
1954 85m/C Bob Hope, Joan Fontaine, Audrey Dalton, Basil Rathbone, Hugh Marlowe, Vincent Price, John Carradine, Raymond Burr; *D:* Norman Z. McLeod; *W:* Hal Kanter, Edmund Hartmann. VHS $14.95 *PAR, CCB ♂♂½*

A Case for Murder Jack Hammet has just become the youngest full partner ever at his Chicago law firm, with a knack for winning impossible cases. His next one's a beaut. Seems an envious colleague has gotten himself murdered and his estranged wife is the prime suspect. Jack decides to work with newly-arrived lawyer Kate Weldon but as the two become personally involved, Kate begins to question Jack's ethics. Seems the evidence is more than a little shady and Jack isn't telling all.
1993 (R) 94m/C Peter Berg, Jennifer Grey, Belinda Bauer; *D:* Duncan Gibbins; *W:* Duncan Gibbins, Pablo F. Fenjves. VHS $89.98 *MCA ♂♂½*

A Case of Deadly Force Based on the true story of a black man wrongfully killed by Boston's Tactical Police Force who mistook him for a robber. The police investigation calls it self-defense but the family and the attorney they hire fight to change the verdict. Excellent cast, great dramatic story. Originally made for television.
1986 95m/C Richard Crenna, John Shea, Lorraine Toussaint, Frank McCarthy, Tom Isbell; *D:* Michael Miller. VHS $79.95 *CAF* ♩♩♩

A Case of Libel A made for television dramatization based on attorney Louis Nizer's account of Quentin Reynolds' libel suit against columnist Westbrook Pegler.
1983 90m/C Daniel J. Travanti, Ed Asner; *D:* Eric Till. VHS, Beta $59.95 *LIV* ♩♩½

Case of the Baby Sitter A private eye investigates jewel thieves posing as nobility.
1947 40m/B Tom Neal, Allen Jenkins, Pamela Blake. VHS, Beta $16.95 *SNC* ♩

The Case of the Frightened Lady A homicidal family does its collective best to keep its dark past a secret in order to collect some inheritance money. Watch, if you're still awake, for the surprise ending. *AKA:* The Frightened Lady.
1939 80m/B *GB* Marius Goring, Helen Haye, Penelope Dudley Ward, Felix Aylmer, Patrick Barr; *D:* George King. VHS, Beta $16.95 *SNC* ♩

The Case of the Lucky Legs Yes, there was a Perry Mason before Raymond Burr. Erle Stanley Gardner's sleuthing litigator's first appearance was 1934's "The Case of the Howling Dog," which initiated Warner Bros' "A"-grade (but soon-to-be "B"-grade) series. More akin to Nick Charles than to Gardner's character or to his later TV incarnation, the "Lucky Legs" Perry is a high-living, interminably hungover tippler who winces and wisecracks as he unravels the case of the corpse of a crooked con man. William, who left shortly after the series was downgraded to "B" status, plays the esquire; Tobin plays his smart-mouthed secretary, and Ellis is the tomato suspected of murder.
1935 76m/B Warren William, Genevieve Tobin, Patricia Ellis, Lyle Talbot, Allen Jenkins, Barton MacLane, Peggy Shannon, Porter Hall; *D:* Archie Mayo. VHS, Beta $16.95 *SNC, RXM* ♩♩½

The Case of the Missing Lady A famous Arctic explorer asks Tommy and Tuppence to find his missing fiancee. Based on the Christie story.
1983 51m/C *GB* Francesca Annis, James Warwick. VHS, Beta $14.95 *TPV* ♩½

The Case of the Mukkinese Battle Horn The cast of Britain's "The Goon Show" takes over in a zany, slapdash featurette-length mystery spoof.
1956 27m/C *GB* Peter Sellers, Spike Milligan, Dick Emery. VHS, Beta, 8mm $14.95 *VYY* ♩♩

Casey at the Bat From Shelley Duvall's made for cable television "Tall Tales and Legends" series, in which the immortal poem is brought to life. Rousing comedy for the whole family.
1985 52m/C Bill Macy, Hamilton Camp, Elliott Gould, Carol Kane, Howard Cosell; *D:* David Steinberg. VHS, Beta $19.98 *FOX* ♩♩

Casey Jones and Fury (Brave Stallion) An episode from each of these early adventure series.
1957 60m/B Alan Hale Jr., Peter Graves. VHS, Beta $24.95 *NOS, DVT* ♩♩

Casey's Shadow The eight-year-old son of an impoverished horse trainer raises a quarter horse and enters it in the world's richest horse race.
1978 (PG) 116m/C Walter Matthau, Alexis Smith, Robert Webber, Murray Hamilton; *D:* Martin Ritt. VHS, Beta $19.95 *COL* ♩♩

Cash McCall McCall (Garner) is a corporate raider who just loves making money. But problems come in when he falls for the lovely daughter (Wood) of his latest takeover target, failing businessman Jagger. Based on the novel by Cameron Hawley.
1960 116m/C James Garner, Natalie Wood, Dean Jagger, Nina Foch, E.G. Marshall, Henry Jones, Otto Kruger, Roland Winters, Parley Baer, Dabbs Greer; *D:* Joseph Pevney; *W:* Lenore Coffee, Marion Hargrove. VHS $29.99 *WAR* ♩♩½

Casimir the Great A dramatized biography of the popular ruler who was instrumental in Poland's development during the period of transition between ancient and modern times. Presented in two segments. In Polish with English subtitles.
19?? ?m/C *PL* Krzysztof Chamiec, Wladyslaw Hanoza. VHS $69.95 *FCT* ♩♩½

Casino A made-for-television thriller about back-stabbings and ritzy romance aboard a high-priced gambling liner.
1980 100m/C Mike Connors, Lynda Day George, Bo Hopkins, Gary Burghoff, Joseph Cotten, Robert Reed, Barry Sullivan; *D:* Don Chaffey. VHS, Beta $79.95 *PSM* ♩½

Casino Royale The product of five directors, three writers and a mismatched cast of dozens, this virtually plotless spoof of James Bond films can stand as one of the low-water marks for 1960s comedy. And yet, there are some marvelous bits within, scenes of bizarre hilarity. Welles and Sellers literally couldn't stand the sight of one another, and their scenes together were filmed separately, with stand-ins.
1967 130m/C David Niven, Woody Allen, Peter Sellers, Ursula Andress, Orson Welles, Deborah Kerr, Peter O'Toole, Jean-Paul Belmondo, Charles Boyer, Joanna Pettet, John Huston, William Holden, George Raft; *D:* John Huston, Ken Hughes, Robert Parrish, Val Guest, Joseph McGrath; *M:* Burt Bacharach. VHS, Beta $19.95 *MRV, COL* ♩

Cass Disenchanted filmmaker returns home to Australia to experiment with alternative lifestyles.
1978 90m/C Michelle Fawden, John Waters, Judy Morris, Peter Carroll. VHS, Beta *NO* ♩

Cass Timberlane Scandalous story of a May-December romance set in a small Midwestern town. Tracy stars as Cass Timberlane, a widowed judge who falls for a voluptuous young girl from the wrong side of the tracks (Turner). They marry and experience problems when she is shunned by his snobbish friends. Good performances, especially from the supporting cast, dominate this fairly predictable film. Based on the novel by Sinclair Lewis.
1947 119m/B Spencer Tracy, Lana Turner, Zachary Scott, Tom Drake, Mary Astor, Albert Dekker, Margaret Lindsay, John Litel, Mona Barrie, Josephine Hutchinson, Rose Hobart, Selena Royle; *Cameos:* Walter Pidgeon; *D:* George Sidney; *W:* Donald Ogden Stewart. VHS $19.98 *MGM* ♩♩½

Cassandra A fragile young woman has dreams that foretell the future—specifically, a series of grisly murders.
1987 (R) 94m/C Shane Briant, Brionny Behets, Tessa Humphries, Kit Taylor, Lee James; *D:* Colin Eggleston. VHS, Beta *VTR* ♩

The Cassandra Crossing A terrorist with the plague causes havoc on a transcontinental luxury train. Turgid adventure filmed in France and Italy.
1976 (R) 129m/C *GB* Sophia Loren, Richard Harris, Ava Gardner, Burt Lancaster, Martin Sheen, Ingrid Thulin, Lee Strasberg, John Phillip Law, Lionel Stander, O.J. Simpson, Ann Turkel, Alida Valli; *D:* George P. Cosmatos; *W:* Tom Mankiewicz; *M:* Jerry Goldsmith. VHS, Beta *FOX* ♩½

Cassie Follows the rise of Cassie, a successful country and western singer, and documents all her trials along the way.
1987 (R) 75m/C Marilyn Chambers; *D:* Godfrey Daniels. VHS, Beta *NO* ♩

Cast a Dark Shadow Bogarde is the charmer who decides to reap his reward by marrying and murdering elderly women for their fortunes. But Bogarde meets his match when he plots against his latest intended (Lockwood). Tidy thriller with effective performances. Based on the play "Murder Mistaken" by Janet Green.
1955 82m/B *GB* Dirk Bogarde, Margaret Lockwood, Mona Washbourne, Kay Walsh, Kathleen Harrison, Robert Flemyng, Walter Hudd; *D:* Lewis Gilbert; *W:* John Cresswell. VHS $29.95 *FCT* ♩♩♩

Cast a Deadly Spell A bubbly, flavorful witch's brew of private-eye and horror cliches, set in a fantasy version of 1948 Los Angeles where sorcery and voodoo abound, but gumshoe Harry P. Lovecraft uses street smarts instead of magic to track down a stolen Necronomicon—and if you know what that is you'll want to watch. Wild creatures and f/x wizardry complement this made-for-cable-TV trick and treat.
1991 (R) 93m/C Fred Ward, David Warner, Julianne Moore, Clancy Brown, Alexandra Powers; *D:* Martin Campbell; *W:* Joseph Dougherty, Dave Edison. VHS $89.99 *HBO* ♩♩♩

Cast a Giant Shadow Follows the career of Col. David "Mickey" Marcus, an American Jew and WWII hero who helped turn Israel's army into a formidable fighting force during the 1947-48 struggle for independence.
1966 142m/C Kirk Douglas, Senta Berger, Angie Dickinson, John Wayne, James Donald, Chaim Topol, Frank Sinatra, Yul Brynner; *D:* Melville Shavelson; *W:* Melville Shavelson; *M:* Elmer Bernstein. VHS, Beta $19.98 *MGM, FCT* ♩♩

Cast the First Stone Made for TV soaper based on the true story of a former nun who becomes a small town schoolteacher. After being raped, Diane Martin discovers she's pregnant and when she decides to keep the baby the school board dismisses her. The plot centers around her fight to regain her job and dignity—while trying to convince everybody that she doesn't deserve to lose her job simply because she is an unwed mother. Eikenberry gives a strong performance, but it can't carry this lackluster film.
1989 94m/C Jill Eikenberry, Richard Masur, Joe Spano, Lew Ayres, Holly Palance; *D:* John Korty. VHS $59.95 *COL* ♩♩

Castaway Based on the factual account by Lucy Irvine. The story of Michael Wilmington, who placed an ad for a young woman to spend a year on a Pacific atoll with him, and the battle of the sexes that followed.
1987 (R) 118m/C Oliver Reed, Amanda Donohoe, Tony Rickards, Georgina Hale, Frances Barber, Todd Rippon; *D:* Nicolas Roeg; *W:* Allan Scott; *M:* Stanley Myers. VHS, Beta $19.98 *WAR* ♩♩½

The Castaway Cowboy A shanghaied cowboy becomes partners with a widow when she turns her Hawaiian potato farm into a cattle ranch. Good, clean "family fare."
1974 (G) 91m/C James Garner, Robert Culp, Vera Miles; **D:** Vincent McEveety. **VHS, Beta** DIS, OM 🐾🐾

The Castilian Some very odd casting in this historical tale of heroism and swordplay about a Spanish nobleman who leads his followers against the invading Moors and their evil king (Crawford). Based on a 13th century poem. **AKA:** Valley of the Swords.
1963 128m/C Cesar Romero, Broderick Crawford, Alida Valli, Frankie Avalon, Espartaco Santoni, Fernando Rey, Jorge Rigaud; **D:** Javier Seto; **W:** Sidney Pink. **VHS $19.98** WAR, HBO, FCT 🐾🐾½

Casting Call Eighteen would-be Hollywood starlets undress and cavort for the camera, in hopes of getting real film work.
1988 60m/C VHS, Beta $19.95 AHV 🐾🐾½

The Castle A man is summoned by the seemingly invisible occupants of a castle to their village. All his efforts to meet with those inhabiting the castle are futile and the task gradually becomes his obsession. Both wonderfully acted and shot, this is a well-executed adaptation of Franz Kafka's novel. **AKA:** Das Schloss.
1968 90m/C GE SI Maximilian Schell, Cordula Trantow, Trudik Daniel, Helmut Qualtinger; **D:** Rudolf Noelte. **VHS, Beta** NO 🐾🐾🐾

Castle in the Desert Charlie Chan investigates murder and other strange goings-on in a spooky old castle. One of the last in the series.
1942 62m/B Sidney Toler, Arleen Whelan, Richard Derr, Douglass Dumbrille, Henry Daniell, Victor Sen Yung; **D:** Harry Lachman. **VHS $19.98** FOX 🐾🐾½

Castle of Blood Staying overnight in a haunted castle, a poet is forced to deal with a number of creepy encounters. Cult favorite Steele enhances this atmospheric chiller. Dubbed in English. **AKA:** Castle of Terror; Coffin of Terror; Danza Macabra.
1964 85m/B IT FR Barbara Steele, George Riviere, Margrete Robsahm, Henry Kruger, Montgomery Glenn, Sylvia Sorente; **D:** Anthony M. (Antonio Margheriti) Dawson. **VHS $16.95** SNC 🐾🐾

The Castle of Cagliostro An animated Japanese adventure tale featuring a hero named Wolf, who's a thief. Wolf infiltrates the suspicious country of Cagliostro, whose one industry is conterfeiting money, and winds up rescuing a princess. Lots of violence to go with the action. In Japanese with English subtitles.
1980 100m/C JP VHS **$29.95** WTA, STP 🐾🐾

Castle of Evil Group of heirs gathers on a deserted isle to hear the reading of the will of your basic mad scientist. One by one, they fall victim to a humanoid created by the loony doc in his own image. Inspired moments of unintentional fun.
1966 81m/C Scott Brady, Virginia Mayo, Lisa Gaye, David Brian, Hugh Marlowe, William Thourlby, Shelly Morrison; **D:** Francis D. Lyon. **VHS $14.98** REP, FCT Woof!

The Castle of Fu Manchu The final chapter in a series starring Lee as the wicked doctor. This time, Lee has developed a gadget which will put the earth into a deep freeze, and at his mercy. To fine tune this contraption, he enlists the help of a gifted scientist by abducting him. However, the helper/hostage has a bad ticker, so Lee must abduct a heart surgeon to save his life, and thus, the freezer project. Most critics felt this was the weakest installment in the series. **AKA:** Assignment: Istanbul; Die Folterkammer des Dr. Fu Manchu.
1968 (PG) 92m/C GE SP IT GB Christopher Lee, Richard Greene, H. Marion Crawford, Tsai Chin, Gunther Stoll, Rosalba (Sara Bay) Neri, Maria Perschy; **D:** Jess (Jesus) Franco. **VHS $19.95** MRV 🐾

Castle of the Creeping Flesh A surgeon's daughter is brutally murdered. Vowing to bring her back he begins ripping out the organs of innocent people and transplanting them into her body. Has the dubious honor of being one of the few movies to sport actual open heart surgery footage. So bad it's...just bad.
1968 85m/C Adrian Hoven, Janine Reynaud, Howard Vernon; **D:** Percy G. Parker. **VHS, Beta** NO Woof!

Castle of the Living Dead Evil Count Drago's hobbies include mummifying a traveling circus group visiting his castle. Lee is as evil as ever, but be sure to look for Sutherland's screen debut. In a dual role, he plays not only the bumbling inspector, but also a witch, in drag. **AKA:** Il Castello de Morti Vivi.
1964 90m/B IT FR Christopher Lee, Gaia Germani, Phillipe LeRoy, Jacques Stanislawsky, Donald Sutherland; **D:** Herbert Wise. **VHS $16.95** SNC, MRV 🐾🐾

Casual Sex? Two young women, looking for love and commitment, take a vacation at a posh resort where they are confronted by men with nothing on their minds but sex, be it casual or the more formal black-tie variety. Supposedly an examination of safe sex in a lightly comedic vein, though the comic is too light and the morality too limp. Adapted from the play by Wendy Goldman and Judy Toll.
1988 (R) 87m/C Lea Thompson, Victoria Jackson, Stephen Shellan, Jerry Levine, Mary Gross, Andrew Dice Clay; **D:** Genevieve Robert. **VHS, Beta $19.95** MCA 🐾½

Casualties of Love: The "Long Island Lolita" Story Told from the Buttafuoco's point of view, Amy Fisher was nothing but a wacko fatally attracted teenager who misunderstood Joey's harmless flirtations and deliberately went after his wife with a gun. The Buttafuocos received $300,000 from CBS to tell their side of the story which features Milano, who resembles Amy not in the least, as the lead. One of three competing network television versions of the sordid tale. See also: "The Amy Fisher Story" and "Lethal Lolita—Amy Fisher: My Story."
1993 (PG-13) 94m/C Jack Scalia, Alyssa Milano, Phyllis Lyons, Jack Kehler, Michael Bowen, J.E. Freeman, Nicky Corello, Lawrence Tierney, Peter Van Norden, Anne DeSalvo; **D:** John Herzfeld; **W:** John Herzfeld. **VHS $59.95** COL 🐾🐾

Casualties of War A Vietnam war morality play about army private Fox in the bush who refuses to let his fellow soldiers and commanding sergeant (Penn) skirt responsibility for the rape and murder of a native woman. Fox achieves his dramatic breakthrough. Based on the true story by Daniel Lang.
1989 (R) 120m/C Sean Penn, Michael J. Fox, Don Harvey, Thuy Thu Le, John Leguizamo, Sam Robards, John Reilly, Erik King; **D:** Brian DePalma; **W:** David Rabe; **M:** Ennio Morricone. **VHS, Beta, 8mm $14.95** COL 🐾🐾🐾

A Casualty of War Made-for-TV adaptation of Frederic Forsyth's thriller about modern-day arms smuggling (Libya to Ireland) and espionage. Well-acted, with the exception of Hack.
1990 (R) 96m/C Shelley Hack, David Threlfall, Richard Hope, Alan Howard, Clarke Peters; **D:** Tom Clegg; **W:** Frederick Forsyth. **VHS** NO 🐾🐾½

The Cat A boy and a tamed mountain lion become friends on the run from a murderous poacher.
1966 95m/C Peggy Ann Garner, Roger Perry, Barry Coe; **D:** Ellis Kadisan. **VHS, Beta $14.95** COL, NLC 🐾

Cat and Mouse A very unorthodox police inspector is assigned to investigate a millionaire's mysterious death. Who done it? French dialogue with English subtitles.
1978 (PG) 107m/C FR Michele Morgan, Serge Reggiani, Jean-Pierre Aumont; **D:** Claude Lelouch. **VHS, Beta $59.95** COL 🐾🐾🐾½

The Cat and the Canary A great silent film about the ghost of a madman that wanders nightly through the corridors of an old house. Remade twice, once in 1939 and again in 1979.
1927 70m/B Laura La Plante, Creighton Hale, Tully Marshall, Gertrude Astor; **D:** Paul Leni. **VHS, Beta $19.95** NOS, MRV, VYY 🐾🐾🐾

The Cat and the Canary A stormy night, a gloomy mansion, and a mysterious will combine to create an atmosphere for murder. An entertaining remake of the 1927 silent film.
1979 (PG) 96m/C GB Carol Lynley, Michael Callan, Wendy Hiller, Olivia Hussey, Daniel Massey, Honor Blackman, Edward Fox, Wilfrid Hyde-White; **D:** Radley Metzger. **VHS, Beta** COL, OM 🐾🐾

The Cat and the Fiddle Lovely Jerome Kern-Oscar Hammerstein operetta in which Novarro plays a struggling composer who forces his affections on MacDonald. She sings in response to his romantic proposals. The final sequence is in color. ♫The Night Was Made for Love; She Didn't Say 'Yes'; A New Love is Old; Try to Forget; One Moment Alone; Don't Ask Us Not To Sing; I Watch the Love Parade; The Breeze Kissed Your Hair; Impressions in a Harlem Flat; Poor Pierrot; The Crystal Candelabra; Ha! Cha. Cha.
1934 90m/B Ramon Novarro, Jeanette MacDonald, Frank Morgan, Charles Butterworth. **VHS $19.98** MGM 🐾🐾🐾

Cat Ballou At the turn of the century, a schoolmarm turns outlaw with the help of a drunken gunman. Marvin played Kid Shelleen and his silver-nosed evil twin Tim Strawn in this cheery spoof of westerns. Cole and Kaye sing the narration in a one of a kind Greek chorus.
1965 96m/C Jane Fonda, Lee Marvin, Michael Callan, Dwayne Hickman, Reginald Denny, Nat King Cole, Stubby Kaye; **D:** Elliot Silverstein; **W:** Frank Pierson. Academy Awards '65: Best Actor (Marvin); Nominations: Best Adapted Screenplay, Best Film Editing, Best Song ("The Ballad of Cat Ballou"), Best Original Score; Berlin International Film Festival '65: Best Actor (Marvin); British Academy Awards '65: Best Actor (Marvin); Golden Globe Awards '66: Best Actor—Musical/Comedy (Marvin); National Board of Review Awards '65: 10 Best Films of the Year, Best Actor (Marvin). **VHS, Beta $14.95** COL, BTV 🐾🐾🐾½

Cat Chaser Weller walks listlessly through the role of an ex-soldier in Miami who has an affair with the wife of an exiled—but still lethal—military dictator. Surpisingly low-key, sometimes effective thriller that saves its energy for sex scenes, also available in a less steamy, 90-minute "R" rated version. Based on an Elmore Leonard novel.
1990 97m/C Kelly McGillis, Peter Weller, Charles Durning, Frederic Forrest, Tomas Milian, Juan Fernandez; **D:** Abel Ferrara; **W:** Elmore Leonard; **M:** Chick Corea. **VHS $89.98** VES 🐾🐾

The Cat from Outer Space An extraterrestrial cat named Jake crashes his spaceship on Earth and leads a group of people on endless escapades. Enjoyable Disney fare.
1978 (G) 103m/C Ken Berry, Sandy Duncan, Harry Morgan, Roddy McDowall, McLean Stevenson; **D:** Norman Tokar. **VHS, Beta** *DIS, OM* 𝄫𝄫

Cat Girl A young bride on her honeymoon finds she has inherited the family curse—she has a psychic link to a ferocious leopard. Numerous murders ensue. Poor production value and a weak script, despite Shelley's fine acting, make this an unworthwhile film.
1957 69m/B Barbara Shelley, Robert Ayres, Kay Callard, Paddy Webster; **D:** Alfred Shaughnessy. **VHS $9.95** *PAR, COL* 𝄫

Cat in the Cage A young man finds many things have changed at home while he was in a mental institution. Dad has remarried, the housekeeper is practicing witchcraft, the chauffeur is after his mistress, and the cat is gone. So where'd that cat go?
1968 96m/C Colleen Camp, Sybil Danning, Mel Novak, Frank De Kova; **D:** Tony Zarin Dast. **VHS, Beta $24.95** *GHV* 𝄫½

The Cat o' Nine Tails A blind detective and a newsman team up to find a sadistic killer. A gory murder mystery.
1971 (PG) 112m/C *GE FR IT* Karl Malden, James Franciscus, Catherine Spaak, Cinzia de Carolis, Carlo Alighiero; **D:** Dario Argento; **W:** Dario Argento; **M:** Ennio Morricone. **VHS, 8mm** *SIM* 𝄫𝄫

Cat on a Hot Tin Roof Tennessee Williams' powerful play about greed and deception in a patriarchal Southern family. Big Daddy (Ives) is dying. Members of the family greedily attempt to capture his inheritance, tearing the family apart. Taylor is a sensual wonder as Maggie the Cat, though the more controversial elements of the play were toned down for the film version. Intense, believable performances from Ives and Newman.
1958 108m/C Paul Newman, Burl Ives, Elizabeth Taylor, Jack Carson, Judith Anderson; **D:** Richard Brooks; **W:** Richard Brooks, James Poe. Academy Awards '56 Nominations: Best Director (Brooks); Academy Awards '58: Best Actor (Newman), Best Actress (Taylor), Best Adapted Screenplay, Best Color Cinematography, Best Picture; National Board of Review Awards '58: 10 Best Films of the Year. **VHS, Beta $19.98** *MGM, FCT, CCB* 𝄫𝄫𝄫½

Cat on a Hot Tin Roof In this adaptation of the Tennessee Williams play, fights over the family inheritance tear a family apart.
1984 122m/C Jessica Lange, Tommy Lee Jones, Rip Torn, David Dukes; **D:** Jack Hofsiss. **VHS, Beta $19.98** *MGM, LIV, VES* 𝄫𝄫

Cat People A young dress designer is the victim of a curse that changes her into a deadly panther who must kill to survive. A classic among the horror genre with unrelenting terror from beginning to end. First horror film from producer Val Lewton.
1942 73m/B Jane Randolph, Elizabeth Russell, Jack Holt, Alan Napier, Simone Simon, Kent Smith, Tom Conway; **D:** Jacques Tourneur. **VHS, Beta $19.95** *MED, BTV, RKO* 𝄫𝄫𝄫

Cat People A beautiful young woman learns that she has inherited a strange family trait—she turns into a vicious panther when sexually aroused. The only person with whom she can safely mate is her brother, a victim of the same genetic heritage. Kinski is mesmerizing as the innocent, sensual woman. Remake of the 1942 film.
1982 (R) 118m/C Nastassia Kinski, Malcolm McDowell, John Heard, Annette O'Toole, Ruby Dee, Ed Begley Jr., John Larroquette; **D:** Paul Schrader; **W:** Alan Ormsby. **VHS, Beta $14.98** *MCA, FCT* 𝄫𝄫½

Cat Women of the Moon Scientists land on the moon and encounter an Amazon-like force of skimpily attired female chauvinists. Remade as "Missile to the Moon." Featuring the Hollywood Cover Girls as various cat women. Available in its original 3-D format. **AKA:** Rocket to the Moon.
1953 65m/B Sonny Tufts, Victor Jory, Marie Windsor, Bill Phipps, Douglas Fowley, Carol Brewster, Suzanne Alexander, Susan Morrow; **D:** Arthur Hilton; **M:** Elmer Bernstein. **VHS, Beta $12.95** *RHI, SNC, MWP* 𝄫𝄫

Cataclysm A swell flick about a sadistic demon who spends his time either finding people willing to join him or killing the people who won't. Also on video as "Satan's Supper."
1981 (R) 94m/C Cameron Mitchell, Marc Lawrence, Faith Clift, Charles Moll; **D:** Tom McGowan, Greg Tallas, Philip Marshak. **VHS, Beta $49.95** *FOX, ACA* 𝄫𝄫½

Catacombs An investigative monk and a beautiful photographer stumble across a mysterious, centuries-old evil power.
1989 (R) 112m/C Timothy Van Patten, Laura Schaefer, Ian Abercrombie, Jeremy West; **D:** David Schmoeller; **W:** C. Courtney Joyner; **M:** Pino Donaggio. **VHS, Beta $89.95** *TWE* 𝄫

The Catamount Killing The story of a small town bank manager and his lover. They decide to rob the bank and run for greener pastures only to find their escape befuddled at every turn.
1974 82m/C *GE* Horst Buchholz, Ann Wedgeworth; **D:** Krzysztof Zanussi. **VHS, Beta** *NO* 𝄫½

Catch as Catch Can An Italian male model is comically besieged by animals of every type, making a mess of his life and career. Dubbed. **AKA:** Lo Scatenato.
1968 95m/C *IT* Vittorio Gassman, Martha Hyer, Gila Golan; **D:** Franco Indovina. **VHS, Beta $59.98** *NLC* 𝄫

Catch Me a Spy A foreign agent attempts to lure an innocent man into becoming part of a swap for an imprisoned Russian spy. **AKA:** To Catch a Spy.
1971 94m/C *GB FR* Kirk Douglas, Tom Courtenay, Trevor Howard, Marlene Jobert, Bernard Blier, Patrick Mower, Bernadette LaFont; **D:** Dick Clement; **W:** Dick Clement, Ian LaFrenais; **M:** Claude Bolling. **VHS, Beta $59.95** *PSM* 𝄫½

Catch Me...If You Can High school class president Melissa doesn't want to see the school torn down. To raise fast cash, she teams up with a drag racer and the fun begins.
1989 (PG) 105m/C Matt Lattanzi, Loryn Locklin, M. Emmet Walsh, Geoffrey Lewis; **D:** Stephen Sommers. **VHS, Beta $89.95** *MCG* 𝄫𝄫

Catch the Heat Alexander is an undercover narcotics agent sent to infiltrate Steiger's South American drug operation. **AKA:** Feel the Heat.
1987 (R) 90m/C Tiana Alexandra, David Dukes, Rod Steiger; **D:** Joel Silberg; **W:** Sterling Silliphant; **M:** Tom Chase, Steve Rucker. **VHS, Beta $79.95** *MED, VTR* 𝄫

Catch-22 Buck Henry's adaptation of Joseph Heller's black comedy about a group of fliers in the Mediterranean during WWII. A biting anti-war satire portraying the insanity of the situation in both a humorous and disturbing manner. Perhaps too literal to the book's masterfully chaotic structure, causing occasional problems in the "are you following along department?" Arkin heads a fine and colorful cast.
1970 (R) 121m/C Alan Arkin, Martin Balsam, Art Garfunkel, Jon Voight, Richard Benjamin, Buck Henry, Bob Newhart, Paula Prentiss, Martin Sheen, Charles Grodin, Anthony Perkins, Orson Welles, Jack Gilford; **D:** Mike Nichols; **W:** Buck Henry. **VHS, Beta $14.95** *PAR* 𝄫𝄫𝄫

The Catered Affair Davis, anti-typecast as a Bronx housewife, and Borgnine, as her taxi-driving husband, play the determined parents of soon-to-be-wed Reynolds set on giving her away in a style to which she is not accustomed. Based on Paddy Chayefsky's teleplay, the catered affair turns into a familial trial, sharing the true-to-life poignancy that marked "Marty," the Oscar-winning Chayefsky drama of the previous year. **AKA:** Wedding Breakfast.
1956 92m/B Bette Davis, Ernest Borgnine, Debbie Reynolds, Barry Fitzgerald, Rod Taylor, Robert Simon; **D:** Richard Brooks; **W:** Gore Vidal. **VHS $19.98** *MGM, FCT, CCB* 𝄫𝄫𝄫

Catherine & Co. Lonely, penniless girl arrives in Paris and "opens shop" on the streets of Paris. As business booms, she takes a cue from the big corporations and sells stock in herself.
1976 (R) 91m/C *FR IT* Jane Birkin, Patrick Dewaere, Jean-Pierre Aumont, Jean-Claude Brialy; **D:** Michel Boisrond. **VHS, Beta** *NO* 𝄫½

Catherine the Great Slow but lavish and engrossing British dramatization of the tortured and doomed love affair between Catherine, Empress of Russia, and her irrational, drunken husband Peter. **AKA:** The Rise of Catherine the Great.
1934 88m/B *GB* Douglas Fairbanks Jr., Elisabeth Bergner, Flora Robson; **D:** Paul Czinner. **VHS, Beta $14.98** *SUE, BAR, VYY* 𝄫𝄫½

Catholic Hour A dramatized version of the life story of Thomas Frederick Price who co-founded the Maryknoll Missionaries in the early 1900's.
1960 30m/B Edward Cullen, Arthur Gary. **VHS, Beta $19.95** *VYY* 𝄫

Catholics A sensitive exploration of contemporary mores and changing attitudes within the Roman Catholic church. Sheen is sent by the Pope to Ireland to reform some priests. Based on Brian Moore's short novel and made for television. **AKA:** The Conflict.
1973 86m/C Martin Sheen, Trevor Howard; **D:** Jack Gold; **M:** Carl Davis. **VHS, Beta** *NO* 𝄫𝄫

Cathy's Curse The spirit of her aunt, who died as a child, possesses a young girl in this Canadian-French collaboration. Tries to capitalize on the popularity of "The Exorcist," but falls seriously short. **AKA:** Cauchemares.
1977 90m/C *FR CA* Alan Scarfe, Beverly Murray; **D:** Eddy Matalon. **VHS, Beta** *NO* 𝄫

Catlow A comedic western with Brynner aiming to steal 2 million dollars in gold from under the nose of his friend, lawman Crenna. Based on the novel by Louis L'Amour.
1971 (PG-13) 103m/C Yul Brynner, Richard Crenna, Leonard Nimoy, JoAnn Pflug, Jeff Corey, Michael Delano, David Ladd, Bessie Love; **D:** Sam Wanamaker; **W:** Scot Finch, J.J. Griffith. **VHS $19.98** *MGM* 𝄫𝄫½

Cat's Eye An anthology of three Stephen King short stories connected by a stray cat who wanders through each tale.
1985 (PG-13) 94m/C Drew Barrymore, James Woods, Alan King, Robert Hays, Candy Clark, Kenneth McMillan, James Naughton, Charles S. Dutton; **D:** Lewis Teague; **W:** Stephen King. **VHS, Beta $19.99** *FOX, FCT* 𝄫𝄫

C

Cat's Play A widowed music teacher makes a ceremonial occassion of a weekly dinner with an old flame. Then an old friend from her youth suddenly reappears and begins an affair with the gentleman, causing self-destructive passions to explode. In Hungarian with English subtitles.
1974 115m/C *HU* Margit Dayka, Margit Makay, Elma Bulla; *D:* Karoly Makk. **VHS** $59.95 *CVC, ING* ♫♫

Cattle Queen of Montana Reagan stars as an undercover federal agent investigating livestock rustlings and Indian uprisings.
1954 88m/C Ronald Reagan, Barbara Stanwyck, Jack Elam, Gene Evans, Lance Fuller, Anthony Caruso; *D:* Allan Dwan. **VHS, Beta NO** ♫♫½

Caught A woman marries for wealth and security and is desperately unhappy. She runs away and takes a job with a struggling physician, and falls in love with him. Her husband finds her, forcing her to decide between a life of security or love.
1949 90m/B James Mason, Barbara Bel Geddes, Robert Ryan, Curt Bois, Natalie Schafer, Art Smith; *D:* Max Ophuls. **VHS** $14.98 *REP* ♫♫♫

Caught in the Act Scott McNally (Harrison) is an out-of-work actor who teaches acting classes to make a buck. Into one of his classes walks the sultry Rachel (Hope) and they start a hot affair. Then Rachel calls Scott, claiming to be kidnapped, he suddenly finds 10 million dollars in his bank account, and his landlord is murdered. Scott finds himself the pawn in an embezzlement scheme and framed for murder. But this is one script Scott doesn't want and he intends to work with a new script of his own devise. Made for cable television.
1993 (PG-13) 93m/C Gregory Harrison, Leslie Hope, Patricia Clarkson, Kevin Tighe; *D:* Deborah Reinisch; *W:* Ken Hixon. **VHS** $89.98 *MCA* ♫♫½

Caught in the Draft Hope's funniest role has him as a Hollywood star trying to evade the draft in WW II, but he ends up accidentally enlisting himself. Lamour plays the daughter of a colonel in the Army whom Hope plans to marry, thinking it will get him out of the service. Very funny military comedy and one of Hope's best. Based on a story by Harry Tugend.
1941 82m/B Bob Hope, Dorothy Lamour, Lynne Overman, Eddie Bracken, Clarence Kolb, Paul Hurst, Ferike Boros, Irving Bacon; *D:* David Butler; *W:* Harry Tugend. **VHS** $14.98 *MCA, BTV* ♫♫♫

Cauldron of Blood Blind sculptor Karloff unwittingly uses human skeletons supplied by his crazed wife Lindfors as the framework of his art pieces. *AKA:* Blind Man's Bluff; El Coleccionista de Cadaveres.
1967 (PG) 95m/C *SP* Boris Karloff, Viveca Lindfors, Jean-Pierre Aumont, Rosenda Monteros, Rueben Rojo, Dianik Zurakowska; *D:* Edward Mann; *W:* Edward Mann. **VHS** $14.98 *REP, VDC, FCT* ♫½

Cause for Alarm A jealous husband recovering from a heart attack begins to lose his mind. He wrongly accuses his wife of having an affair and attempts to frame her for his own murder. A fast-paced thriller with a nifty surprise ending.
1951 74m/C Loretta Young, Barry Sullivan, Bruce Cowling, Margalo Gillmore, Irving Bacon, Carl "Alfalfa" Switzer; *D:* Tay Garnett. **VHS** $16.95 *NOS, SNC, MGM* ♫♫½

Cavalcade Traces the lives of the British Marryot family from the death of Queen Victoria, through WWI, the Jazz Age, and the Depression. A wistful adaptation of the hit play by Noel Coward with its touching portrayal of one family trying to weather good times and bad together.
1933 110m/B Diana Wynyard, Clive Brook, Herbert Mundin, Una O'Connor, Ursula Jeans, Beryl Mercer, Merle Tottenham, Frank Lawton, John Warburton, Margaret Lindsay, Billy Bevan; *D:* Frank Lloyd. Academy Awards '33: Best Director (Lloyd), Best Interior Decoration, Best Picture; Nominations: Best Actress (Wynyard). **VHS** $19.98 *FXV, BTV* ♫♫♫

Cavalcade of the West Typical western with two brothers, separated by a kidnapping, growing up on opposite sides of the law. Much later they meet, and the question is: will the outlaw be reformed and reunited with his happy family?
1936 70m/B Hoot Gibson, Rex Lease, Marion Shilling, Earl Dwire; *D:* Harry Fraser. **VHS, Beta** $19.95 *GPV, DVT, VCN* ♫

The Cavalier Chinese cavalier faces love, danger and intrigue while deploying martial arts skills.
198? 90m/C Tang Wei, Lung Fei, Yeh Yuen, Tseng Tsao. **VHS, Beta** $29.95 *UNI* ♫

Cavalier of the West An Army captain is the only negotiating force between the white man and a primitive Indian tribe.
1931 66m/B Harry Carey Sr., Kane Richmond, George "Gabby" Hayes; *D:* John P. McCarthy. **VHS, Beta** $19.95 *NOS* ♫

Cavalry A Union Army Lieutenant is reunited with his family after the Civil War, bringing them happiness and joy.
1936 60m/B Bob Steele, Frances Grant, Karl Hackett, Hal Price; *D:* Robert North Bradbury. **VHS, Beta** $19.90 *NOS, DVT* ♫½

Cavalry Charge Vance Britton (Reagan) is the captain of a brigade of Confederate troops wreaking havoc on Union outposts. His brother Jeb (Bennett) is a Union soldier sent to the western frontier to take care of the Confederate problem. Vance's former fiance Julie (Fleming) is also living in the territories with her new husband. All three converge when the Union fort, where Julie is living and Jeb is defending, is attacked by Apaches. Brother Vance rides to the rescue. Lots of action.
1951 72m/C **VHS** $29.95 *IVY* ♫♫½

Cavalry Command Good will and integrity characterize the U.S. soldiers called into a small village to quiet a guerrilla rebellion. *AKA:* Cavalleria Commandos.
1963 77m/C John Agar, Richard Arlen, Myron Healey, Alicia Vergel, William Phipps, Eddie Infante; *D:* Eddie Romero; *W:* Eddie Romero. **VHS, Beta** *RHI* ♫

Cave Girl After falling through a time-warp during a high-school field trip, a social pariah makes a hit with a pre-historic honey. Sexist teen exploitation film, with few original ideas and a not-so-hot cast. *AKA:* Cavegirl.
1985 (R) 85m/C Daniel Roebuck, Cindy Ann Thompson, Saba Moor, Jeff Chayette; *D:* David Oliver; *W:* David Oliver. **VHS, Beta** $79.95 *COL* Woof!

Cave Girls A critically acclaimed experimental short by a group of female filmmakers depicting how a society of stone-age women prior to the evolution of thought processes would interact with each other and relate to their surroundings.
1982 28m/C *D:* Cara Brownell, Kiki Smith, Ellen Cooper; *M:* Bush Tetras, Y Pants. **VHS** $29.95 *FCT, MWF* Woof!

Cave of the Living Dead Mad professor with a past is up to something in a cave under castle. Villagers summon Inspector Doren of Interpol to solve a rash of nasty murders that they've blamed on green-eyed, cave-dwelling vampires. A challenge to watch till the end. Filmed in Sepiatone. *AKA:* Der Fluch Der Gruenen Augen.
1965 87m/B *GE YU* Adrian Hoven, Erika Remberg, Carl Mohner, Wolfgang Preiss, Karin Field, John Kitzmiller, Akos Von Rathony; *D:* Akos Von Rathony. **VHS, Beta** $39.95 *MSP* Woof!

Caveman Starr stars in this prehistoric spoof about a group of cavemen banished from different tribes who band together to form a tribe called "The Misfits."
1981 (PG) 92m/C Ringo Starr, Barbara Bach, John Matuszak, Dennis Quaid, Jack Gilford, Shelley Long, Cork Hubbert; *D:* Carl Gottlieb; *W:* Carl Gottlieb, Rudy DeLuca. **VHS, Beta** $14.95 *MGM, FOX* ♫

CB4: The Movie Falling somewhere between a serious attempt and parody, CB4 tries to do both and succeeds at neither. Written in the key of "Wayne's World" by "Saturday Night Live's" Rock, it starts out as a "rockumentary" (please refer to "This is Spinal Tap"), but quickly turns into a sitcom after two gangsta rap members assume the identity of a local club owner when he is in jail. Hartman, also of SNL, appears as a right-wing city councilman. Chock full of violence, sexism, and profanity tucked into a wandering plot.
1993 (R) 83m/C Chris Rock, Allen Payne, Deezer D, Phil Hartman, Charlie Murphy, Khandi Alexander, Art Evans, Chris Elliott, Willard Pugh, Theresa Randle; *D:* Tamra Davis; *W:* Chris Rock, Nelson George, Robert Locash. **VHS** $19.98 *MCA* ♫½

Cease Fire The story of a troubled Vietnam vet who finds solace in a veterans' therapy group. Adapted from the play by George Fernandez.
1985 (R) 97m/C Don Johnson, Robert F. Lyons, Lisa Blount; *D:* David Nutter; *M:* Gary Fry. **VHS, Beta** $14.95 *CNG* ♫♫

Ceiling Zero Cagney is an irrepressible pilot who does as he pleases and loves to aggravate his soft-hearted boss O'Brien. He falls for aviatrix Travis and neglects his duties to woo her, which leads to tragedy. Naturally, this sobers Cagney up and he volunteers for a dangerous test flight. Lots of fast-paced action and Cagney is at his swaggering best. Based on a play by Frank Wead, who also wrote the screenplay. Remade in 1941 as "International Squadron."
1935 95m/B James Cagney, Pat O'Brien, June Travis, Stuart Erwin, Henry Wadsworth, Isabel Jewell, Barton MacLane; *D:* Howard Hawks; *W:* Frank Wead. **VHS** $19.98 *MGM, FCT* ♫♫♫

Celebrity In this television film, a tragic childhood secret must be confronted by three friends when one is charged with murder. Based on the Thomas Thompson novel.
1985 313m/C Michael Beck, Ben Masters, Joseph Bottoms; *D:* Paul Wendkos. **VHS, Beta** *NO* ♫½

Celeste Adlon (who later made the offbeat comedy "Sugarbaby") directed this longish but finely detailed and beautifully photographed biographical look at French writer Marcel (Remembrance of Things Past) Proust. Based on the memoirs of Proust's housekeeper, Celeste Albaret, an uneducated farmgirl, portraying the woman's devoted relationship ('til death did them part) with the middle-aged, homosexual author. It does so with wit, poignancy, and insight, but is not entirely successful in its attempt to render Proust's verbal literary style into a visual medium. In German with English subtitles.
1981 107m/C *GE* Eva Mattes, Jurgen Arndt, Norbert Wartha, Wolf Euba; *D:* Percy Adlon; *W:* Percy Adlon. **VHS** $79.95 *NYF, FCT, APD* ♫♫♫

Celia: Child Of Terror Set in the 1950s, this film deals with the awful results of a young girl's inability to handle disappointment.
1989 110m/C Rebecca Smart, Nicholas Eadie, Victoria Longley, Mary-Anne Fahey; **D:** Ann Turner. **VHS, Beta** *NO* 🎬🎬

The Cellar A young boy finds an ancient Comanche monster spirit in the basement of his home. His parents, as usual, don't believe him, so he must battle the monster alone.
1990 (PG-13) 90m/C Patrick Kilpatrick, Suzanne Savoy, Chris Miller, Ford Rainey; **D:** Kevin S. Tenney. **VHS $14.95** *HMD* 🎬🎬½

Cellar Dweller A cartoonist moves into an old house and soon discovers it's haunted by a demonic cartoonist who killed himself thirty years earlier. What a coincidence. Low-budget scare-'em-upper filmed on one set and lit by a floodlamp.
1987 78m/C Pamela Bellwood, Deborah Muldowney, Brian Robbins, Vince Edwards, Jeffrey Combs, Yvonne De Carlo; **D:** John Carl Buechler. **VHS, Beta $19.95** *STE, NWV* Woof!

The Cemetery Club Story of three Jewish widows who make weekly visits to their husband's graves while attempting to cope with the loss of their lives. Doris (Dukakis) is loyal to the memory of her husband and acts as the moral conscience of the trio. Lucille (Ladd) is a merry widow who wears clothes more suitable for younger women, but she also harbors a painful secret. Esther (Burstyn) struggles with her loneliness until a widowed cab driver begins to woo her. Commendably, the characters are given more dimension than Hollywood usually grants women of a certain age. Based on the play "The Cemetary Club" by Menchell, who also wrote the screenplay.
1993 (PG-13) 114m/C Ellen Burstyn, Olympia Dukakis, Diane Ladd, Danny Aiello, Lainie Kazan, Christina Ricci, Bernie Casey, Alan Mason, Sam Schwartz, Jeff Howell, Robert Costanzo, Wallace Shawn, Louis Guss; **D:** Bill Duke; **W:** Ivan Menchell; **M:** Elmer Bernstein. **VHS, Beta $19.99** *TOU, BTV* 🎬🎬½

Cemetery High Beautiful high school girls decide to lure the local boys into a trap and kill them.
1989 80m/C Debi Thibeault, Karen Nielsen, Lisa Schmidt, Ruth Collins, Simone, Tony Kruk, David Coughlin, Frank Stewart; **D:** Gorman Bechard. **VHS, Beta $79.95** *UNI, HHE* 🎬

Center of the Web John Phillips is a victim of mistaken identity—someone thinks he's a professional hit man. After surviving an apparent mob attempt on his life, Phillips is persuaded by a CIA operative to go along with the deception in order to capture a potential political assassin. At least that's what Phillips is told, but he soon realizes that the deeper he gets into his new role, the deadlier the plot becomes. Davi is one of the best bad guys around and the fast-paced stunts and plot twists make this watchable.
1992 (R) 88m/C Ted Prior, Robert Davi, Tony Curtis, Charlene Tilton, Bo Hopkins, Charles Napier; **D:** David A. Prior. **VHS $89.95** *AIP* 🎬🎬

The Centerfold Girls Microscopic storyline involves a deranged man who is determined to kill all the voluptuous young women who have posed nude for a centerfold.
1974 (R) 93m/C Andrew Prine, Tiffany Bolling, Aldo Ray, Jeremy Slate, Ray Danton, Francine York; **D:** John Peyser. **VHS, Beta $54.95** *MED* Woof!

Certain Fury Two timid women go on the lam when they are mistaken for escaped prostitutes who shot up a courthouse. The sooner they get caught, the better.
1985 (R) 88m/C Tatum O'Neal, Irene Cara, Peter Fonda, Nicholas Campbell, Moses Gunn; **D:** Stephen Gyllenhaal. **VHS, Beta $14.95** *NWV, STE* 🎬

Certain Sacrifice Nineteen-year-old Madonna expresses herself in her film debut. Seeking revenge on the man who raped her, she murders him in a strange ritualistic manner underneath the Brooklyn Bridge. Poor is the man whose pleasures depend on the permission of another?
1980 60m/C Madonna, Jeremy Pattnosh, Charles Kurtz; **D:** Stephen Lewicki. **VHS, Beta** *WOV, MVD* 🎬

Cesar This is the third and most bittersweet part of Pagnol's famed trilogy based on his play depicting the lives and loves of the people of Provence, France. Marius returns after a 20-year absence to his beloved Fanny and his now-grown son, Cesariot. The first two parts of the trilogy were "Marius" and "Fanny" and were directed by Alexander Korda and Marc Allegret respectively. In French with English subtitles.
1936 117m/B *FR* Raimu, Pierre Fresnay, Orane Demazis, Charpin, Andre Fouche, Alida Rauffe; **D:** Marcel Pagnol; **W:** Marcel Pagnol; **M:** Vincent Scotto. **VHS, Beta $24.95** *NOS, MRV, INT* 🎬🎬🎬🎬

Cesar & Rosalie Acclaimed French comedy depicts the love triangle between a beautiful divorcee, her aging live-in companion and a younger man. Engaging portrait of how their relationship evolves over time. In French with English subtitles.
1972 (PG) 110m/C *FR* Romy Schneider, Yves Montand, Sami Frey, Umberto Orsini; **D:** Claude Sautet. **VHS, Beta $29.95** *TPV, ING, AUD* 🎬🎬🎬

Chain Gang Killings Pair of shackled prisoners, one black, the other white, escape from a truck transporting them to prison.
1985 99m/C Ian Yule, Ken Gampu. **VHS, Beta** *NO* 🎬

Chain Gang Women Sordid violence. Two escaped convicts plunder, rob, and rape until a victim's husband comes looking for revenge.
1972 (R) 85m/C Robert Lott, Barbara Mills, Michael Stearns, Linda York; **D:** Lee Frost. **VHS** *NO* Woof!

Chain Lightning Bogart stars as a bomber pilot who falls in love with a Red Cross worker (Parker) while fighting in Europe in 1943. They lose touch after the war until Bogie goes to work as a test pilot for the same shady airplane manufacturer (Massey) where Parker works. He is given the chance to test a new plane, which has already cost the life of one of his friends. Bogart has more success, along with rekindling the flames of romance. Average script but the flying sequences are well-done.
1950 94m/B Humphrey Bogart, Eleanor Parker, Raymond Massey, Richard Whorf; **D:** Stuart Heisler. **VHS $19.98** *MGM* 🎬🎬

Chain of Desire Lots of sexual encounters, including telephone sex, exhibitionism, and voyeurism, so who needs a plot.
1993 107m/C Linda Fiorentino, Elias Koteas, Malcolm McDowell, Grace Zabriskie, Tim Guinee, Assumpta Serna, Patrick Bauchau, Seymour Cassel; **D:** Temistocles Lopez; **W:** Temistocles Lopez. **VHS, Beta $92.95** *PSM* 🎬🎬

Chain Reaction When a nuclear scientist is exposed to radiation after an accident at an atomic power plant, he must escape to warn the public of the danger. *AKA:* Nuclear Run.
1980 87m/C Steve Bisley, Ross Thompson; **D:** Ian Barry. **VHS, Beta** *NO* 🎬½

Chained Crawford and Gable star in this love triangle that somehow never sizzles. Crawford, in love with married businessman Kruger, takes a South American cruise to get away from it all, meets Gable, and of course falls in love. Seems simple enough, but wait! Crawford goes back to New York City and marries Kruger (his wife grants him a divorce) and is miserable. But then Gable shows up, further complicating matters. Choices, choices. Predictable script was not helped by half-hearted performances.
1934 73m/B Joan Crawford, Clark Gable, Otto Kruger, Stuart Erwin, Una O'Connor; **D:** Clarence Brown. **VHS, Beta $19.98** *MGM, CCB* 🎬🎬½

Chained for Life Daisy and Violet Hilton, real life Siamese twins, star in this old-fashioned "freak" show. When a gigolo deserts one twin on their wedding night, the other twin shoots him dead. The twins go on trial and the judge asks the viewer to hand down the verdict. Exploitative and embarrassing to watch.
1951 81m/B Daisy Hilton, Violet Hilton; **D:** Harry Fraser. **VHS, Beta $16.95** *SNC, NOS, RHI* Woof!

Chained Heat Seamy tale of the vicious reality of life for women behind bars. Naive Blair is imprisoned again (after another bad jailhouse gig in "Born Innocent") and has usual assortment of negative experiences with domineering prisoners, degenerate guards, and the creepy warden who maintains a prison bachelor pad equipped with hot tub. Needless to say, she grows up in a hurry. Trashifying, archetypal women-in-prison effort that aims to satisfy full range of low-quality audience demands. Sequel to 1982 "Concrete Jungle."
1983 (R) 97m/C Linda Blair, Stella Stevens, Sybil Danning, Tamara Dobson, Henry Silva, John Vernon, Nita Talbot, Louisa Moritz; **D:** Paul Nicholas. **VHS, Beta $29.98** *VES* 🎬🎬

Chained Heat 2 Another sordid tale of women behind bars. Nielsen stars as the psychotic stiletto-heeled warden of an infamous prison, complete with sadistic heroin-smuggling guards. This drug ring also deals in prostitution, which results in two imprisoned sisters (innocent, naturally) being separated from one another. One sister is determined to find true justice.
1992 (R) 98m/C Brigitte Nielsen, Paul Koslo, Kari Whitman, Kimberley Kates; **D:** Lloyd A. Simandl; **W:** Chris Hyde. **VHS $89.95** *NLC* 🎬½

Chains A Chicago gangland feud entraps two couples in its web, and the innocents must take care of themselves when the situation goes from bad to worse.
1989 (R) ?m/C Jim Jordan, Michael Dixon, John L. Eves; **D:** Roger J. Barski. **VHS $89.95** *IMP* 🎬🎬

Chains of Gold Kind social worker (Travolta) befriends teen who wants to get out of the crack-dealing gang in which he's involved. He infiltrates the gang and risks his life helping the boy get out. Originally aired on cable television.
1992 (R) 95m/C John Travolta, Marilu Henner, Bernie Casey, Hector Elizondo, Joey Lawrence; **D:** Rod Holcomb; **M:** Trevor Jones. **VHS $89.95** *ACA* 🎬🎬

The Chair The penitentiary where an evil superintendent was fried in his own electric chair during an inmate uprising is reopened after two decades. The new warden (Benedict), who used to be a subordinate to the dead man, believes in rigid control of the inmates and locks horns with the big-house shrink (Coco), who on the surface is an intelligent humanitarian, but may have a darker side. This acrimonious dispute takes a back seat, when it appears that the spirit of the late warden has come back to make the inmates pay for his untimely death. *AKA:* Hot Seat.

1987 (R) ?m/C James Coco, Paul Benedict, Stephen Geoffreys, Trini Alvarado, John Bentley; *D:* Waldemar Korzeniowsky. VHS **$89.95** IMP *ℤℤ*

The Chalk Garden A woman with a mysterious past takes on the job of governess for an unruly 14-year-old girl, with unforeseen consequences. An excellent adaptation of the Enid Bagnold play although not as suspenseful as the stage production.

1964 106m/C *GB* Deborah Kerr, Hayley Mills, Edith Evans, John Mills, Elizabeth Sellars, Felix Aylmer; *D:* Ronald Neame; *W:* John Michael Hayes; *M:* Malcolm Arnold. Academy Awards '64 Nominations: Best Supporting Actress (Evans); National Board of Review Awards '64: 10 Best Films of the Year, Best Supporting Actress (Evans). VHS, Beta **$14.98** MCA *ℤℤℤ*

The Challenge Story of the courageous party of explorers who conquered the Matterhorn. Incredible avalanche scenes.

1938 77m/B Luis Trenker, Robert Douglas. VHS, Beta **$19.98** DVT, VYY, HEG *ℤℤℤ*

Challenge When his entire family is killed, dad decides to seek revenge with his shotgun. Very bloody and violent and very nearly plotless.

1974 (PG) 90m/C Earl Owensby, William T. Hicks, Katheryn Thompson, Johnny Popwell; *D:* Martin Beck. VHS **$59.98** FOX Woof!

The Challenge A contemporary action spectacle which combines modern swordplay with the mysticism and fantasy of ancient Samurai legends.

1982 (R) 108m/C Scott Glenn, Toshiro Mifune; *D:* John Frankenheimer; *W:* John Sayles, Richard Maxwell; *M:* Jerry Goldsmith. VHS, Beta **$59.95** FOX *ℤℤ½*

Challenge of a Lifetime Marshall stars as a divorcee whose dream is to compete in the Hawaiian Ironman Triathlon. Cult favorite; Woronov has a substantial supporting role.

1985 100m/C Penny Marshall, Richard Gilliland, Jonathan Silverman, Mary Woronov, Paul Gleason, Mark Spitz, Cathy Rigby; *D:* Russ Mayberry. VHS **$59.98** TTC, MOV *ℤℤ½*

Challenge of McKenna Run-of-the-prairie horse opera has drifter Ireland stumble upon danger and intrigue when he enters a mysterious town.

1983 90m/C John Ireland, Robert Woods. VHS PMH *ℤℤ*

Challenge of the Masters A young Kung-Fu artist wins a new tutor in a contest. Soon he's fighting for a friend to protect his family's honor.

1989 97m/C Liu Chia Hui, Liu Chia-Yung, Chen Kuan-Tai, Chiang Yang; *D:* Lu Chia-Liang. VHS **$14.95** HMD *ℤ*

Challenge the Ninja One talented fighter defends a town from high-kicking hordes. Lots of kung fu action for martial arts fans.

198? 92m/C Bruce Baron, Pierre Tremblay, Richard Berman, Eric Redner. VHS, Beta **$59.95** TWE *ℤ*

Challenge To Be Free Action adventure geared toward a young audience depicting the struggles of a man being pursued by 12 men and 100 dogs across a thousand miles of frozen wilderness. The last film directed by Garnett, who has a cameo as Marshal McGee. Produced in 1972, the release wasn't until 1976. *AKA:* Mad Trapper of the Yukon.

1976 (G) 90m/C Mike Mazurki, Jimmy Kane; *Cameos:* Tay Garnett; *D:* Tay Garnett. VHS, Beta **$9.98** MED, VTR *ℤℤ*

Challenge to Lassie When Lassie's Scottish master dies, the faithful pup remains at his grave. An unsympathetic policeman orders Lassie to leave the premises, inspiring a debate among the townsfolk as to the dog's fate. Based on a true story (although the original hero was in Skye Terrier); remade as "Greyfriar's Bobby."

1949 (G) 76m/C Edmund Gwenn, Donald Crisp, Geraldine Brooks, Reginald Owen, Alan Webb, Henry Stephenson, Alan Napier, Sara Allgood; *D:* Richard Thorpe; *M:* Andre Previn. VHS, Beta **$14.95** MGM, FCT *ℤℤ½*

Challenge to White Fang A courageous dog prevents a scheming businessman from taking over an old man's gold mine.

1986 (PG) 89m/C Harry Carey Jr., Franco Nero; *D:* Lucio Fulci. VHS, Beta **$69.95** TWE *ℤ½*

The Challengers Young Mackie wants to join local rock band The Challengers, only to discover their main rule is no girls. So Mackie disguises herself as her male cousin Mac—getting ever more confused as she tries to juggle her dual identities. Then she gets found out.

1993 97m/C Gema Zamprogna, Gwynyth Walsh, Eric Christmas, Eric Till; *W:* Clive Endersby. VHS **$89.95** TRI *ℤℤ½*

Chamber of Horrors A family is brought together at an English castle to claim a fortune left by an aristocrat. However, there's a catch—seven keys may open the vault with the fortune, or leave the key turner dead. Based on the work by Edgar Wallace. *AKA:* The Door With Seven Locks.

1940 80m/B *GB* Leslie Banks, Lilli Palmer; *D:* Norman Lee. VHS, Beta **$16.95** NOS, MRV, SNC *ℤℤ½*

Chameleon A freeform dramatic examination of a day in the life of a Los Angeles pusher.

1981 90m/C Bob Glaudini; *D:* Jon Jost. VHS, Beta FCT *ℤℤ½*

Chameleon Street Entertaining fact-based account of William Douglas Street, a Detroit man who successfully impersonated, among others, a Time magazine reporter and a surgeon until he was caught and sent to prison. He escaped and went to Yale, faked his identity as a student, and then returned to Michigan to impersonate a lawyer for the Detroit Human Rights Commission. Harris wrote and directed this insightful look into the man who fooled many people, including the mayor of Detroit, Coleman A. Young, who appears briefly as himself.

1989 (R) 95m/C Wendell B. Harris Jr., Angela Leslie, Amina Fakir, Paula McGee, Mano Breckenridge, Richard Kiley, Anthony Ennis; *D:* Wendell B. Harris Jr.; *W:* Wendell B. Harris Jr. VHS **$89.95** ACA, FCT *ℤℤℤ*

The Champ A washed up boxer dreams of making a comeback and receives support from no one but his devoted son. Minor classic most notorious for jerking the tears and soiling the hankies, this was the first of three Beery/Cooper screen teamings.

1931 87m/B Wallace Beery, Jackie Cooper, Irene Rich, Roscoe Ates, Edward Brophy, Hale Hamilton, Jesse Scott, Marcia Mae Jones; *D:* King Vidor; *W:* Francis Marion. Academy Awards '32: Best Actor (Beery), Best Original Screenplay; Nominations: Best Director (Vidor), Best Picture. VHS, Beta **$19.98** MGM, FCT, BTV *ℤℤℤ*

The Champ An ex-fighter with a weakness for gambling and drinking is forced to return to the ring in an attempt to keep custody of his son. Excessive sentiment may cause cringing. Remake of the 1931 classic.

1979 (PG) 121m/C Jon Voight, Faye Dunaway, Rick Schroder, Jack Warden, Arthur Hill, Strother Martin, Joan Blondell, Elisha Cook Jr.; *D:* Franco Zeffirelli; *M:* Dave Grusin. VHS, Beta **$59.95** MGM *ℤ½*

Champagne A socialite's father fakes bankruptcy to teach his irresponsible daughter a lesson. Early, silent endeavor from Hitchcock is brilliantly photographed.

1928 93m/B *GB* Betty Balfour, Gordon Harker, Ferdinand von Alten, Clifford Heatherly, Jack Trevor; *D:* Alfred Hitchcock; *W:* Alfred Hitchcock. VHS **$19.99** GPV, MLB, VEC *ℤℤ*

Champagne for Breakfast Sex comedy follows the fun-filled adventures of "Champagne," a free-spirited beauty living life to the fullest.

1935 (R) 69m/B Mary Carlisle, Hardie Albright, Joan Marsh, Lila Lee, Sidney Toler, Bradley Page, Emerson Tracy; *D:* Melville Brown. VHS NO *ℤ*

Champagne for Caesar The laughs keep coming in this comedy about a self-proclaimed genius-on-every-subject who goes on a television quiz show and proceeds to win everything in sight. The program's sponsor, in desperation, hires a femme fatale to distract the contestant before the final program. Wonderful spoof of the game-show industry.

1950 90m/B Ronald Colman, Celeste Holm, Vincent Price, Art Linkletter, Barbara Britton; *D:* Richard Whorf. VHS, Beta **$39.95** VCI *ℤℤℤ*

Champion An ambitious prizefighter alienates the people around him as he desperately fights his way to the top. When he finally reaches his goal, he is forced to question the cost of his success. From a story by Ring Lardner. Certainly one of the best films ever made about boxing, with less sentiment than "Rocky" but concerned with sociological correctness.

1949 99m/B Kirk Douglas, Arthur Kennedy, Marilyn Maxwell, Ruth Roman, Lola Albright; *D:* Mark Robson. Academy Awards '49: Best Film Editing; Nominations: Best Actor (Douglas), Best Black and White Cinematography, Best Screenplay, Best Supporting Actor (Kennedy), Best Original Score. VHS **$19.98** REP *ℤℤℤ½*

The Champion/His New Job Two classic silent shorts by Chaplin, with music; the first is alternately entitled "Champion Charlie." *AKA:* Champion Charlie.

1915 53m/B Charlie Chaplin, Edna Purviance, Ben Turpin, Gloria Swanson, Mack Swain, Billy Anderson; *D:* Charlie Chaplin. VHS, Beta, 8mm **$19.95** VYY *ℤℤℤ*

Champion Operation Hong Kong heavies pose as police officers. The action follows them from the slums to the red-light district. Lots of martial arts action.

1987 100m/C Tong Chun Chung, Yu Ka Hei, Tang Ho Kwong. VHS **$49.95** OCE *ℤ*

Champions Moving but cliched story of Bob Champion, a leading jockey who overcame cancer to win England's Grand National Steeplechase. A true story, no less.

1984 113m/C *GB* John Hurt, Gregory Jones, Mick Dillon, Ann Bell, Jan Francis, Peter Barkworth, Edward Woodward, Ben Johnson, Kirstie Alley, Alison Steadman; *D:* John Irvin; *W:* Evan Jones; *M:* Carl Davis. VHS, Beta **$9.98** SUE, NLC *ℤℤ*

Chan is Missing Two cab drivers try to find the man who stole their life savings. Wry, low-budget comedy filmed in San Francisco's Chinatown was an art-house smash.

The first full-length American film produced exclusively by an Asian-American cast and crew.
1982 80m/B Wood Moy, Marc Hayashi, Laureen Chew, Judy Mihei, Peter Wang, Presco Tabios; **D:** Wayne Wang; **W:** Terrel Seltzer. **VHS $79.95** NYF, ING ✍✍✍

Chance With over a million dollars in diamonds missing, Haggerty and Jacobs throw out all the stops to recover them in this action thriller.
1989 90m/C Dan Haggerty, Lawrence Hilton-Jacobs, Addison Randall, Roger Rudd, Charles Gries, Pamela Dixon; **D:** Addison Randall, Charles Kanganis. **VHS** PMH ✍½

Chances Are After her loving husband dies in a chance accident, a pregnant woman remains unmarried, keeping her husband's best friend as her only close male companion. Years later, her now teenage daughter brings a friend home for dinner, but due to an error in heaven, the young man begins to realize that this may not be the first time he and this family have met. A wonderful love-story hampered only minimally by the unbelievable plot.
1989 (PG) 108m/C Cybill Shepherd, Robert Downey Jr., Ryan O'Neal, Mary Stuart Masterson, Josef Sommer, Christopher McDonald, Joe Grifasi, James Noble, Susan Ruttan, Fran Ryan; **D:** Emile Ardolino; **W:** Perry Howze, Randy Howze; **M:** Maurice Jarre. VHS, Beta, 8mm **$19.95** COL, FCT ✍✍✍

Chandu on the Magic Island Chandu the Magician takes his powers of the occult to the mysterious lost island of Lemuri to battle the evil cult of Ubasti. Sequel to "Chandu the Magician" and just as campy.
1934 67m/B Bela Lugosi, Maria Alba, Clara Kimball Young. **VHS, Beta $19.95** NOS, SNC, VYY ✍✍

Chandu the Magician Bad guy searches desperately for the secret of a powerful death ray so he can (surprise!) destroy civilization. Not well received in its day, but makes for great high-camp fun now. One of Lugosi's most melodramatic performances.
1932 70m/B Edmund Lowe, Bela Lugosi, Irene Ware, Henry B. Walthall; **D:** William Cameron Menzies, Marcel Varnel. **VHS, Beta** MLB, RXM ✍✍

Chanel Solitaire Uninspiring biography follows the fabulous (simply fabulous) career of dress designer Gabrielle "Coco" Chanel. Ah, go sew something.
1981 (R) 124m/C Marie-France Pisier, Rutger Hauer, Timothy Dalton, Karen Black, Brigitte Fossey; **D:** George Kaczender. **VHS, Beta $19.95** MED, FCT ✍✍

Chang: A Drama of the Wilderness A farmer and his family has settled a small patch of ground on the edge of the jungle and must struggle for survival against numerous wild animals. The climatic elephant stampede is still thrilling. Shot on location in Siam.
1927 67m/B D: Ernest B. Schoedsack; **W:** Merian C. Cooper, Ernest B. Schoedsack. **VHS $39.95** MIL ✍✍✍½

Change of Habit Three novitiates undertake to learn about the world before becoming full-fledged nuns. While working at a ghetto clinic a young doctor forms a strong, affectionate relationship with one of them. Presley's last feature film. ♫Change of Habit; Let Us Pray; Rubberneckin'.
1969 (G) 93m/C Elvis Presley, Mary Tyler Moore, Barbara McNair, Ed Asner, Ruth McDevitt, Regis Toomey; **D:** William A. Graham; **M:** Billy Goldenberg. **VHS, Beta $14.95** MCA, GKK ✍✍

A Change of Seasons One of them so-called sophisticated comedies that look at the contemporary relationships and values of middle-class, middle-aged people who should know better. The wife of a college professor learns of her husband's affair with a seductive student and decides to have a fling with a younger man. The situation reaches absurdity when the couples decide to vacation together.
1980 (R) 102m/C Shirley MacLaine, Bo Derek, Anthony Hopkins, Michael Brandon, Mary Beth Hurt; **D:** Richard Lang; **W:** Erich Segal. **VHS, Beta $59.98** FOX ✍✍

The Changeling A music teacher moves into an old house and discovers that a young boy's ghostly spirit is his housemate. The ghost wants revenge against the being that replaced him upon his death. Scary ghost story with some less than logical leaps of script.
1980 (R) 114m/C CA George C. Scott, Trish Van Devere, John Russell, Melvyn Douglas, Jean Marsh; **D:** Peter Medak. **VHS, Beta $19.98** VES ✍✍½

Changes A young man leaves home and thumbs across the California coast in order to find himself. On the road again.
1969 (PG) 103m/C Kent Lane, Michele Carey, Jack Albertson, Marcia Strassman; **D:** Hall Bartlett. **VHS, Beta $79.95** PSM ✍

The Channeler The traditional dopey students probe an old Colorado mine and encounter black-robed, demon whazzits. A spunky cast and nice scenery didn't stop the Hound from switching channels on this one.
1989 90m/C Dan Haggerty, Richard Harrison, Jay Richardson, David Homb, Oliver Darrow, Robin Sims, Charles Solomon; **D:** Grant Austin Waldman. **VHS, Beta** NO ✍

Chantilly Lace Ensemble cast tries hard in this story of modern American women and friendship in the nineties. Val (Eilenberry) gathers a group of seven close friends at her new house in Sundance. Turns out trying to "have it all" is causing some emotional crises to surface, which are explored over the course of a year. Actresses improvised their dialogue from basic character information. Lots of weeping and bonding. Made for cable television.
1993 (R) 102m/C Jill Eikenberry, Ally Sheedy, Helen Slater, Lindsay Crouse, JoBeth Williams, Martha Plimpton, Talia Shire; **D:** Linda Yellen; **W:** Linda Yellen, Rosanne Ehrlich; **M:** Patrick Seymour. **VHS** COL ✍✍½

Chapayev Striking propagandist drama dealing with the exploits of a legendary Red Army commander during the 1919 battle with the White Russians. Stunning, and carefully choreographed, battle scenes. Adapted from a biographical novel by Dmitri Furmanov. In Russian with English subtitles.
1934 101m/B RU Boris Babochkin, Leonid Kmit; **D:** Sergei Vasiliev, Gregory Vasiliev. **VHS, Beta $14.95** VYY, AUD, IHF ✍✍✍

Chaplin The life and career of "The Little Tramp" is chronicled by director Attenborough and brilliantly portrayed by Downey, Jr, as Chaplin. A flashback format traces his life from its poverty-stricken Dickensian origins in the London slums through his directing and acting career, to his honorary Oscar in 1972. Slow-moving at parts, but captures Chaplin's devotion to his art and also his penchant towards jailbait. In a clever casting choice, Chaplin's own daughter from his fourth marriage to Oona O'Neill, Geraldine Chaplin, plays her own grandmother who goes mad.
1992 (PG-13) 135m/C Robert Downey Jr., Dan Aykroyd, Geraldine Chaplin, Kevin Dunn, Anthony Hopkins, Milla Jovovich, Moira Kelly, Kevin Kline, Diane Lane, Penelope Ann Miller, Paul Rhys, John Thaw, Marisa Tomei, Nancy Travis, James Woods, David Duchovny, Deborah Maria Moore, Bill Paterson, John Standing, Robert Stephens; **D:** Richard Attenborough; **W:** Bryan Forbes, William Boyd, William Goldman; **M:** John Barry. Academy Awards '92 Nominations: Best Actor (Downey), Best Art Direction/Set Decoration, Best Original Score; British Academy Awards '93: Best Actor (Downey). **VHS $19.98** LIV, MOV, FCT ✍✍✍

Chaplin: A Character Is Born The evolution of Chaplin's "Little Tramp" is shown in scenes from his early classics, "The Pawnshop," "The Rink," and "The Immigrant."
1979 40m/B Charlie Chaplin. **VHS, Beta** NO ✍✍✍

Chaplin: A Character Is Born/ Keaton: The Great Stone Face Wynn narrates "A Character Is Born," with scenes from "Little Champ," "The Pawnshop," "The Rink" and "The Immigrant." Buttons presents "The Great Stone Face" featuring scenes from "Cops," "The Playhouse," "The Boat" and "The General."
19?? 90m/C Charlie Chaplin. **VHS, Beta** NO ✍✍½

Chaplin Essanay Book 1 Two of Chaplin's early shorts: "The Tramp" and "The Champion."
1915 51m/B Charlie Chaplin, Edna Purviance, Ben Turpin. **VHS, Beta $19.98** CCB ✍✍½

The Chaplin Revue The "Revue," put together by Chaplin in 1958, consists of three of his best shorts: "A Dog's Life" (1918), the WWII comedy "Shoulder Arms" (1918), and "The Pilgrim," in which a convict hides out in a clerical guise (1922). Chaplin added self-composed score, narration, and some documentary on-the-set material.
1958 121m/B Charlie Chaplin, Edna Purviance, Sydney Chaplin, Mack Swain; **D:** Charlie Chaplin. **VHS, Beta $19.98** FOX ✍✍½

Chapter in Her Life An early silent film by Lois Weber which examines the relationships between an orphaned child and the adults in her life.
1923 87m/B D: Lois Weber. **VHS, Beta $19.95** GVV ✍✍½

Chapter Two Loosely based on Neil Simon's marriage to Mason and his Broadway hit of the same name. A writer, grief-stricken over the death of his first wife, meets the woman who will become his second. Witty dialogue in first half deteriorates when guilt strikes.
1979 (PG) 124m/C James Caan, Marsha Mason, Valerie Harper, Joseph Bologna; **D:** Robert Moore; **W:** Neil Simon. **VHS, Beta $69.95** COL ✍✍

Charade Mason and wife Pamela star in this trilogy of love and violence. "Portrait of a Murderer" has a young artist sketching the picture of the man who—unknown to her—has just murdered his girlfriend. "Duel at Dawn" concerns an 1880s Austrian officer who steals a woman from another officer and is then challenged to a duel. "The Midas Touch" revolves around a successful but dissatisfied man who abandons his riches to find the meaning of life. Mason himself had said he hoped "this curiosity" would disappear.
1953 83m/B James Mason, Pamela Mason, Scott Forbes, Paul Cavanagh, Bruce Lester, Sean McClory, Vince Barnett; **D:** Roy Kellino. **VHS $19.95** NOS ✍✍

Charade After her husband is murdered, a young woman finds herself on the run from crooks and double agents who want the $250,000 her husband stole during WWII. Hepburn and Grant are charming and sophisticated as usual in this stylish intrigue filmed in Paris. Based on the story "The Unsuspecting Wife" by Marc Behm and Peter Stone. 1963 113m/C Cary Grant, Audrey Hepburn, Walter Matthau, James Coburn, George Kennedy; *D:* Stanley Donen; *W:* Peter Stone; *M:* Henry Mancini. Academy Awards '63 Nominations: Best Song ("Charade"); British Academy Awards '64: Best Actress (Hepburn); Edgar Allan Poe Awards '63: Best Screenplay. VHS, Beta $8.95 CNG, MRV, MCA 🎞🎞🎞½

The Charge of the Light Brigade A British army officer stationed in India deliberately starts the Balaclava charge to even an old score with Surat Khan, who's on the other side. Still an exciting film, though it's hardly historically accurate. De Havilland is along to provide the requisite romance with Flynn. Also available colorized. 1936 (PG-13) 115m/B Olivia de Havilland, Errol Flynn, David Niven, Nigel Bruce, Patric Knowles, Donald Crisp, Sir C. Aubrey Smith, J. Carroll Naish, Henry Stephenson, E.E. Clive, Scotty Beckett; *D:* Michael Curtiz, Jack Sullivan. VHS, Beta $19.98 MGM, FCT, FOX 🎞🎞🎞

The Charge of the Light Brigade Political indictment of imperialistic England in this revisionist retelling of the notorious British defeat by the Russians at Balaclava. Battle scenes are secondary to this look at the stupidity of war. Fine cast; notable animation sequences by Richard Williams. 1968 (PG-13) 130m/C *GB* Trevor Howard, John Gielgud, David Hemmings, Vanessa Redgrave, Harry Andrews, Jill Bennett, Peter Bowles, Mark Burns, Alan Dobie, T.P. McKenna, Corin Redgrave, Norman Rossington, Rachel Kempson, Donald Wolfit; *D:* Tony Richardson; *W:* Charles Wood; *M:* John Addison. VHS $19.98 MGM 🎞🎞½

The Charge of the Model T's Comedy about a WWI German spy who tries to infiltrate the U.S. army. 1976 (G) 90m/C Louis Nye, John David Carson, Herb Edelman, Carol Bagdasarian, Arte Johnson; *D:* Jim McCullough. VHS, Beta $9.99 SUE 🎞½

Chariots of Fire A lush telling of the parallel stories of Harold Abraham and Eric Liddell, English runners who competed in the 1924 Paris Olympics. One was compelled by a hatred of anti-Semitism, the other by the love of God. Outstanding performances by the entire cast. 1981 (PG) 123m/C *GB* Ben Cross, Ian Charleson, Nigel Havers, Ian Holm, Alice Krige, Brad Davis, Dennis Christopher, Patrick Magee, Cheryl Campbell, John Gielgud, Lindsay Anderson, Nigel Davenport; *D:* Hugh Hudson; *W:* Colin Welland; *M:* Vangelis. Academy Awards '81: Best Costume Design, Best Original Screenplay, Best Picture, Best Score; Nominations: Best Director (Hudson), Best Supporting Actor (Holm); British Academy Awards '81: Best Film, Best Supporting Actor (Holm). VHS, Beta $19.98 WAR, FCT, BTV 🎞🎞🎞½

Charles & Diana: A Palace Divided Trashy scandalous tale of the disintegration of the fairytale romance and marriage of Prince Charles and Princess Diana. Oxenberg stars as Princess Di, a role she played a decade ago in "The Royal Romance of Charles and Diana," and Rees does a fine job playing the conservative Prince Charles. Although the film covers all of the couple's highly-publicized troubles, it's such a quick superficial treatment that it's often hard to follow. Nonetheless, it's a flashingly inviting look into the privileged House of Windsor. 1993 92m/C Roger Rees, Catherine Oxenberg, Benedict Taylor, Tracy Brabin, Amanda Walker, David Quilter, Jane How; *D:* John Power. VHS $89.98 TTC 🎞🎞½

Charles et Lucie A has-been couple are ripped off, pursued, persecuted, and saddled with very bad luck in the South of France. Essentially a character study; semi-acclaimed. In French with subtitles. 1979 96m/C *FR* Daniel Ceccaldi, Ginette Garcin, Jean-Marie Proslier, Samson Fainsilber; *D:* Nelly Kaplan. VHS, Beta FCT 🎞🎞🎞

Charleston Renoir's third film, a simple erotic dance fantasy that caused much controversy in its day. Silent, with jazz score and historical introduction. 1926 30m/B Catherine Hessling; *D:* Jean Renoir. VHS, Beta FCT 🎞🎞🎞

Charley and the Angel Touching story of a man who changes his cold ways with his family when informed by an angel that he hasn't much time to live. Amusing Disney movie set in the Great Depression. 1973 (G) 93m/C Fred MacMurray, Cloris Leachman, Harry Morgan, Kurt Russell, Vincent Van Patten, Kathleen Cody; *D:* Vincent McEveety. VHS DIS, OM 🎞🎞½

Charley Chase Festival, Vol. 1 Six classic Charley Chase comedies: "At First Sight" (1923), "Fighting Fluid" (1924), "Young Oldfield" (1924), "Ten Minute Egg" (1924), "Stolen Goods" (1924), and "Long Fliv the King" (1926). 1923 70m/B Charley Chase. VHS, Beta $19.95 VDM 🎞🎞

Charley Varrick Matthau, a small-town hood, robs a bank only to find out that one of its depositors is the Mob. Baker's the vicious hit-man assigned the job of getting the loot back. A well-paced, on-the-mark thriller. 1973 (PG) 111m/C Walter Matthau, Joe Don Baker, Felicia Farr, John Vernon, Sheree North, Norman Fell, Andrew (Andy) Robinson; *D:* Don Siegel. VHS, Beta $14.98 MCA 🎞🎞🎞

Charley's Aunt Amusing Victorian farce in which two young male students convince an older fellow student to dress up as their female chaperon so they can pitch woo to two local lovelies. Fun performances and well-paced direction by Sidney. Based on the Brandon Thomas farce, the movie was remade in 1930, starring Charles Ruggles, and again in 1941, with Jack Benny. 1925 75m/B Sydney Chaplin, Ethel Shannon, Lucien Littlefield, Alec B. Francis; *D:* Scott Sidney. VHS, Beta $24.95 GPV, FCT 🎞🎞½

Charlie and the Great Balloon Chase When a grandfather takes his grandson on a cross-country balloon trip, they are hotly pursued by the boy's mother, her stuffy fiance (who wants the boy in military school), the FBI, a reporter, and the Mafia. Made for television. 1982 98m/C Jack Albertson, Adrienne Barbeau, Slim Pickens, Moosie Drier; *D:* Larry Elikann. VHS, Beta $59.95 TLF 🎞🎞

Charlie Boy The new owner of an ancient African idol enters the world of the supernatural when he casts a death spell on six people. 1981 60m/C Leigh Lawson, Angela Bruce, Marius Goring; *D:* Robert M. Young. VHS, Beta $29.95 LIV 🎞½

Charlie Bravo A commando group is commanded to rescue a captured nurse in Vietnam. Dubbed. 198? (R) 94m/C *FR* Bruno Pradal, Karen Verlier, Jean-Francois Poron; *D:* Rene Demoulin. VHS, Beta $59.95 GEM 🎞

A Charlie Brown Celebration The Peanuts gang in an extended adventure in which Lucy courts Schroeder, Patty goes to obedience school, and Charlie Brown finally kicks the football. 1984 49m/C *D:* Bill Melendez. VHS, Beta $14.95 BAR, WTA 🎞

A Charlie Brown Christmas Disillusioned by the commercialization of the holiday season, Charlie Brown sets out to find the true meaning of Christmas. 1965 30m/C *D:* Bill Melendez. VHS, Beta $9.95 MED, SHV, VTR 🎞

A Charlie Brown Thanksgiving The Peanuts gang learns that Thanksgiving is more than just turkey and stuffing in this family favorite. 1981 25m/C *D:* Bill Melendez, Phil Roman. VHS, Beta $14.95 BAR, KAR, WTA 🎞

Charlie Brown's All-Stars Charlie Brown and the whole Peanuts gang is here to delight young and old alike. 1966 26m/C *D:* Bill Melendez. VHS $9.98 MED, VTR, WTA 🎞

Charlie Chan and the Curse of the Dragon Queen The famed Oriental sleuth confronts his old enemy the Dragon Queen, and reveals the true identity of a killer. 1981 (PG) 97m/C Peter Ustinov, Lee Grant, Angie Dickinson, Richard Hatch, Brian Keith, Roddy McDowall, Michelle Pfeiffer, Rachel Roberts; *D:* Clive Donner. VHS, Beta $9.95 MED 🎞½

Charlie Chan at the Opera The great detective investigates an amnesiac opera star (Karloff) who may have committed murder. Considered one of the best of the series. Interesting even to those not familiar with Charlie Chan. 1936 66m/B Warner Oland, Boris Karloff, Keye Luke, Charlotte Henry, Thomas Beck, Nedda Harrigan, William Demarest; *D:* H. Bruce Humberstone. VHS $19.98 FOX 🎞🎞🎞

Charlie Chan at the Wax Museum Charlie and number one son must find a criminal hiding out in a wax museum. Chills abound when the fugitive heads for the chamber of horrors. 1940 63m/B Sidney Toler, Sen Yung, C. Henry Gordon, Marc Lawrence, Joan Valerie, Marguerite Chapman, Ted Osborn, Michael Visaroff; *D:* Lynn Shores. VHS $19.98 FOX 🎞½

The Charlie Chan Collection "The Secret Service," "Meeting at Midnight," "The Chinese Cat," "The Jade Mask," "The Scarlet Clue," and "The Shanghai Cobra" are included on a four-disc boxed set. 194? 391m/C $99.98 MGM 🎞½

Charlie Chan in Paris Chan scours the city of lights to track down a trio of counterfeiters. Top-notch plot and plenty of suspense will please all. 1935 72m/B Warner Oland, Mary Brian, Thomas Beck, Erik Rhodes, John Miljan, Minor Watson, John Qualen, Keye Luke, Henry Kolker; *D:* Lewis Seiler. VHS $19.98 FOX 🎞🎞½

Charlie Chan in Rio Local police call on Chan to help solve a double murder. One of the series' weaker entries but with fine setting and music. 1941 60m/B Sidney Toler, Mary Beth Hughes, Cobina Wright Jr., Ted North, Victor Jory, Harold Huber, Sen Yung; *D:* Harry Lachman. VHS $19.98 FOX 🎞🎞

Charlie Chan in the Secret Service Toler's Chan is now a government agent who is assigned to find the killer of an inventor. Moreland joins up as Chan's taxi-driving, constantly terrified sidekick. The series moved from 20th-century Fox to low-budget Monogram Pictures with this entry, with an ensuing drop in production quality. **1944** 64m/B Sidney Toler, Mantan Moreland, Gwen Kenyon, Arthur Loft, Marianne Quon, Lela Tyler, Benson Fong; *D:* Phil Rosen. **VHS** $19.98 MGM *&&* ½

Charlie Chan's Secret Chan must solve the murder of the heir to a huge fortune. A good, logical script with plenty of suspects to keep you guessing. **1935** 72m/B Warner Oland, Rosina Lawrence, Charles Quigley, Henrietta Crosman, Edward Trevor, Astrid Allwyn; *D:* Gordon Wiles. **VHS** $19.98 FOX *&&*

Charlie Chaplin Carnival, Four Early Shorts This tape features: "The Vagabond," "The Fireman," "The Count," and "Behind the Screen." Sound effects and music added. Silent. **1916** 80m/B Charlie Chaplin. **VHS, Beta** $44.95 HHT, HEG *&&*

Charlie Chaplin Cavalcade, Mutual Studios Shorts A compilation tape which features Chaplin's: "One A.M.," "Pawnshop," "Floorwalker," and "The Rink." **1916** 81m/B Charlie Chaplin, Edna Purviance; *D:* Charlie Chaplin. **VHS, Beta** $19.95 VDM, HHT, KIV *&&*

Charlie Chaplin Centennial Collection Chaplin is up to his stunts again in an anthology of comedy shorts. **191?** 87m/B Charlie Chaplin; *D:* Charlie Chaplin. **VHS** $19.98 FOX *&&*

Charlie Chaplin Festival This video features four classic Chaplin shorts: "The Immigrant," "The Adventurer," "The Cure," and "Easy Street." **1917** 80m/B Charlie Chaplin, Edna Purviance, Henry Bergman, Eric Campbell; *D:* Charlie Chaplin. **VHS, Beta** PSM *&&*

Charlie Chaplin Festival Four Chaplin shorts: "The Immigrant," "The Fireman," "Behind the Screen" and "The Adventurer." **1917** 60m/B Charlie Chaplin. **VHS, Beta** $24.95 DVT *&&*

Charlie Chaplin: Night at the Show Chaplin plays two different mugs, both out for a night on the town. Mr. Pest, a sharp-dressed upper-cruster, clings to his disgusting habits, and Mr. Rowdy is his working-class doppelganger. Both obnoxious Chaplins-in-disguise collaborate to wreak havoc on a local theater. Contains original organ score. **1915** ?m/B Charlie Chaplin, Edna Purviance; *D:* Charlie Chaplin; *W:* Charlie Chaplin. **VHS, Beta** VYY *&&&*

Charlie Chaplin: Rare Chaplin A collection of three Chaplin shorts: "The Bank," "Shanghaied," and "A Night in the Snow." **1915** 60m/B Charlie Chaplin, Edna Purviance, Bud Jamison, Billy Armstrong; *D:* Charlie Chaplin. **VHS, Beta** $29.95 KIV *&&* ½

Charlie Chaplin: The Early Years, Vol. 1 This video package includes Chaplin's "The Immigrant," "The Count," and "Easy Street." Silent. **1917** 62m/B Charlie Chaplin, Edna Purviance, John Rand, Eric Campbell. **VHS** $19.98 REP, FCT, KIV *&&* ½

Charlie Chaplin: The Early Years, Vol. 2 This video package includes Chaplin's "The Pawnshop" (1916), "The Adventurer" (1917) and "One A.M." (1916).

1917 61m/B Charlie Chaplin, Edna Purviance, Eric Campbell, Albert Austin, Henry Bergman, John Rand. **VHS** $19.98 REP, FCT, KIV *&&* ½

Charlie Chaplin: The Early Years, Vol. 3 This video package includes Chaplin's "The Cure" (1916), "The Floorwalker" (1916), and "The Vagabond." **1916** 64m/B Charlie Chaplin, Edna Purviance, Eric Campbell, Albert Austin. **VHS** $19.98 REP, FCT, KIV *&&* ½

Charlie Chaplin: The Early Years, Vol. 4 This video package includes Chaplin's "Behind the Screen," "The Fireman" (1916), and "The Rink" (1916). **1916** 63m/B Charlie Chaplin, Edna Purviance, Eric Campbell, Lloyd Bacon, Albert Austin. **VHS, Beta** $19.98 REP, FCT, KIV *&&* ½

Charlie Chaplin...Our Hero! Two shorts from 1915 written and directed by Chaplin, "Night at the Show" and "In the Park," as well as a 1914 film, "Hot Finish," in which Charlie plays the villain. **1915** 58m/B Charlie Chaplin, Edna Purviance, Lloyd Bacon, Mabel Normand, Chester Conklin, Mack Sennett; *D:* Charlie Chaplin. **VHS, Beta, 8mm** $24.95 VYY *&&* ½

Charlie Chaplin's Keystone Comedies #1 Six one-reelers which Chaplin filmed in 1914, his first movie-making year: "Making a Living," Chaplin's first, in which he plays a villain; "Kid Auto Races," in which Charlie now sports baggy pants, bowler hat and cane; "A Busy Day," featuring Charlie in drag; "Mabel's Married Life;" "Laughing Gas;" and "The New Janitor." Silent with musical score. **1914** 59m/B Charlie Chaplin, Mabel Normand, Mack Swain. **VHS, Beta** $24.95 VYY, KIV *&&* ½

Charlie Chaplin's Keystone Comedies #2 Three hilarious early Chaplin shorts, "His Trysting Place," "Getting Acquainted" and "The Fatal Mallet." Silent with musical score. **1914** 60m/B Charlie Chaplin, Mabel Normand, Mack Swain, Mack Sennett. **VHS, Beta** $19.95 VYY, KIV *&&* ½

Charlie Chaplin's Keystone Comedies #3 Three more vintage early Chaplin shorts: "Caught in a Cabaret," "The Masquerader," and "Between Showers." Silent, includes a musical score. **1914** 59m/B Charlie Chaplin, Mack Swain, Mabel Normand, Chester Conklin; *D:* Charlie Chaplin. **VHS, Beta** $19.95 VYY, KIV *&&* ½

Charlie Chaplin's Keystone Comedies #4 Four classic silent shorts featuring Chaplin in 1914, Including "Caught in the Rain (in the Park)," "His Million Dollar Job," "Mabel's Busy Day," and "The Face on the Bar Room Floor." With musical score. **1914** 54m/B Charlie Chaplin, Mack Swain, Alice Davenport, Fatty Arbuckle, Mabel Normand, Chester Conklin, Slim Summerville, Cecile Arnold, Alice Howell. **VHS, Beta, 8mm** $19.95 VYY, KIV *&&* ½

Charlie Chaplin's Keystone Comedies #5 Four classic silent features: "Mabel's Strange Predicament," "The Rounders," "Tango Tangles," and "The Star Border." **1914** 57m/B Charlie Chaplin; *D:* Charlie Chaplin. **VHS** $19.95 VYY, KIV *&&* ½

Charlie Chase and Ben Turpin Three silent comedy classics, "All Wet," "Publicity Pays," and "A Clever Dummy." **1921** 67m/B Ben Turpin, Charley Chase, Wallace Beery, Juanita Hansen. **VHS, Beta** $29.95 VYY *&&* ½

Charlie Grant's War The true story of a Canadian businessman who hears of Nazi brutality and determines to save European Jews from persecution during the Holocaust. Not among the more distinguished works of its kind. **1980** 130m/C GB Jan Rubes, R.H. Thomson. **VHS, Beta** $59.99 MOV *&&*

Charlie, the Lonesome Cougar Life for a rugged logger will never be the same after he adopts an orphaned cougar. From the Disney factory. **1967** (G) 75m/C Linda Wallace, Jim Wilson, Ron Brown, Brian Russell, Clifford Peterson; *D:* Winston Hibler. **VHS, Beta** $69.95 DIS *&&*

Charlotte Forten's Mission: Experiment in Freedom Fact-based story, set during the Civil War. A wealthy, educated black woman, determined to prove to President Lincoln that blacks are equal to whites, journeys to a remote island off the coast of Georgia. There she teaches freed slaves to read and write. Part of the "American Playhouse" series on PBS. Preceded by "Solomon Northrup's Odyssey." *AKA:* Half Slave, Half Free 2. **1985** 120m/C Melba Moore, Mary Alice, Ned Beatty, Carla Borelli, Micki Grant, Moses Gunn, Anna Maria Horsford, Bruce McGill, Glynn Turman, Roderick Wimberly; *D:* Barry Crane; *W:* Samm-Art Williams. **VHS** $59.95 FCT, PTB, XVC *&&&*

Charlotte's Web E.B. White's classic story of a friendship between a spider and a pig is handled only adequately by Hanna-Barbera studios. Some okay songs. **1979** (G) 94m/C *V:* Charles A. Nichols; *V:* Debbie Reynolds, Agnes Moorehead, Paul Lynde, Henry Gibson. **VHS, Beta** $14.95 KUI, PAR, FCT *&&*

Charly A retarded man becomes intelligent after brain surgery, then romances a kindly caseworker before slipping back into retardation. Moving account is well served by leads Roberston and Bloom. Adapted by Sterling Silliphant from the Daniel Keyes novel "Flowers for Algernon." **1968** 103m/C Cliff Robertson, Claire Bloom, Lilia Skala, Leon Janney, Dick Van Patten, William Dwyer; *D:* Ralph Nelson; *W:* Sterling Silliphant. **VHS, Beta** $19.98 FOX, BTV *&&*

Charm of La Boheme A vintage German musical based on the Puccini opera. With English subtitles. **1936** 90m/B GE Jan Keipura, Martha Eggerth, Paul Kemp; *D:* Geza von Bolvary. **VHS, Beta** $29.95 NOS, DVT, APD *&&* ½

The Charmer Havers stars as Ralph Gorse, a charming but amoral con man who uses any means to get what he wants. This includes using the affection (and money) of an older woman, blackmail, and even murder. Set in the late 30s. Made for British television miniseries on 6 cassettes. **1989** 312m/C GB Nigel Havers, Rosemary Leach, Bernard Hepton, Fiona Fullerton, Abigail McKern, George Baker, Judy Parfitt; *D:* Alan Gibson; *W:* Allan Prior. **VHS** $129.95 SIG *&&* ½

Charro! Presley in a straight role as a reformed bandit hounded by former gang members. Western fails on nearly all accounts, with Presley hopelessly acting outside the bounds of his talent. Furthermore, he sings only one song. **1969** (G) 98m/C Elvis Presley, Ina Balin, Victor French, Lynn Kellogg, Barbara Werle, Paul Brinegar, James B. Sikking; *D:* Charles Marquis Warren; *W:* Hugo Montenego. **VHS** $19.98 WAR *&*

The Chase Not realizing that his boss-to-be is a mobster, Cummings takes a job as a chauffeur. Naturally, he falls in love with the gangster's wife (Morgan), and the two plan to elope. Somewhat miffed, the cuckolded mafioso and his bodyguard (Lorre) pursue the elusive couple as they head for Havana. The performances are up to snuff, but the story's as unimaginative as the title, with intermittent bouts of suspense.
1946 86m/B Robert Cummings, Michele Morgan, Peter Lorre, Steve Cochran, Lloyd Corrigan, Jack Holt, Don "The Dragon" Wilson; **D:** Arthur Ripley; **W:** Philip Yordan. **VHS, Beta $16.95** NOS, MRV, SNC ½½½

The Chase Southern community is undone when rumors circulate of a former member's prison escape and return home. Excellent cast only partially shines. Brando is outstanding as the beleaguered, honorable sheriff, and Duvall makes a splash in the more showy role of a cuckold who fears the escapee is returning home to avenge a childhood incident. Reliable Dickinson also makes the most of her role as Brando's loving wife. Fonda, however, was not yet capable of fashioning complex characterizations, and Redford is under-utilized as the escapee. Adapted from the play by Horton Foote. Notorious conflicts among producer, director, and writer kept it from being a winner.
1966 135m/C Marlon Brando, Robert Redford, Angie Dickinson, E.G. Marshall, Jane Fonda, James Fox, Janice Rule, Robert Duvall, Miriam Hopkins, Martha Hyer; **D:** Arthur Penn; **W:** Lillian Hellman, Horton Foote; **M:** John Barry. **VHS, Beta $14.95** COL ½½½

Chase A big-city lawyer returns to her small hometown to defend a killer and ends up at odds with the town, including an ex-lover. Routine made for television drama.
1985 104m/C Jennifer O'Neill, Robert Woods, Richard Farnsworth, Michael Parks; **D:** Rod Holcomb; **M:** Charles Bernstein. **VHS, Beta $59.98** FOX ½½

The Chase Routine made for television actioner. An ex-con killer leads a ruthless cop and a TV news team on a wild chase. Loosely based on a true story.
1991 (PG-13) 93m/C Casey Siemaszko, Ben Johnson, Gerry Bamman, Robert Beltran, Barry Corbin, Ricki Lake, Megan Follows; **VMK** ½½

The Chase Heiress Natalie Voss (Swanson) is in the wrong place at the wrong time when she's carjacked by escaped con Jack Hammond (Sheen) who uses a Butterfinger for his weapon. Frantic chases ensues as it turns out that Daddy Voss is a media hungry millionaire and he's followed by not only the cops but the media as well. One-dimensional characters aren't helped by a one-dimensional script, but slick filmmaking and a little charm helps. Skewers the media hype that surrounds crime, taking on news programs that offer immediate coverage and reality based shows with glee.
1993 (PG-13) 87m/C Kristy Swanson, Charlie Sheen, Josh Mostel, Ray Wise, Henry Rollins, Flea; **D:** Adam Rifkin; **W:** Adam Rifkin; **M:** Richard Gibbs. **VHS** FXV ½½½

Chasers Gruff Navy petty officer Rock Reilly (Berenger) and his conniving partner Eddie Devane (McNamara) are stuck escorting maximum security prisoner Toni Johnson (Eleniak) to a Charleston naval base. Imagine their surprise when Toni turns out to be a beautiful blonde whose one purpose is to escape her jail-sentence for going AWOL. Considering how dumb her jailers are this

shouldn't be too difficult. Lots of sneering, leering, and macho posturing.
1994 (R) 100m/C Tom Berenger, William McNamara, Erika Eleniak; *Cameos:* Gary Busey, Crispin Glover, Dean Stockwell, Seymour Cassel, Frederic Forrest, Marilu Henner, Dennis Hopper; **D:** Dennis Hopper; **W:** Joe Batteer, John Rice, Dan Gilroy; **M:** Dwight Yoakam, Pete Anderson. **VHS** WAR ½½

Chasing Dreams Sickly melodrama about a farmboy who finds fulfillment as a baseball player. Lame film promoted as Costner baseball vehicle, but the star of "Bull Durham" and "Field of Dreams" appears only briefly in a secondary role.
1981 (PG) 96m/C David G. Brown, John Fife, Jim Shane, Lisa Kingston, Matt Clark, Kevin Costner; **D:** Sean Roche, Therese Conte. **VHS, Beta $79.95** PSM ½½

Chasing Those Depression Blues Four '30s comedy shorts: "Money on Your Life," "Dental Follies," "Any Day in Hollywood" and "Art in the Raw."
1935 58m/B Danny Kaye, Pinky Lee, Edgar Kennedy, Ben Turpin. **VHS, Beta $19.95** VYY ½½

Chato's Land An Indian is tracked by a posse eager to resolve a lawman's death. Conventional violent Bronson vehicle is bolstered by presence of masterful Palance.
1971 (PG) 100m/C Charles Bronson, Jack Palance, Richard Basehart, James Whitmore, Simon Oakland, Richard Jordan, Ralph Waite, Victor French, Lee Patterson; **D:** Michael Winner. **VHS, Beta $14.95** MGM, VTR ½½½

Chattahoochee A man suffering from post-combat syndrome lands in a horrifying institution. Strong cast, with Oldman fine in the lead, and Hopper memorable in extended cameo. Fact-based film is, unfortunately, rather conventionally rendered.
1989 97m/C Gary Oldman, Dennis Hopper, Frances McDormand, Pamela Reed, Ned Beatty, M. Emmet Walsh, William De Acutis, Lee Wilkof, Matt Craven, Gary Klar; **D:** Mick Jackson. **VHS $89.99** HBO, IME, FCT ½½½

Chattanooga Choo Choo A football team owner must restore the Chattanooga Choo Choo and make a 24-hour run from Chattanooga to New York in order to collect one-million dollars left to him in a will. The train never leaves the station.
1984 (PG) 102m/C Barbara Eden, George Kennedy, Melissa Sue Anderson, Joe Namath, Bridget Hanley, Christopher McDonald, Clu Gulager, Tony Azito; **D:** Bruce Bilson. **VHS, Beta $59.99** HBO ½½

Chatterbox A starlet's life and career are severely altered when her sex organs begin speaking. So why didn't they warn her about movies like this? Plenty of B-queen Rialson on view. Good double bill with "Me and Him."
1976 73m/C Candice Rialson, Larry Gelman, Jean Kean, Perry Bullington; **D:** Tom De Simone. **VHS, Beta $59.98** LIV, VES ½½

The Cheap Detective Neil Simon's parody of the "Maltese Falcon" gloriously exploits the resourceful Falk in a Bogart-like role. Vast supporting cast—notable Brennan, DeLuise, and Kahn—equally game for fun in this consistently amusing venture.
1978 (PG) 92m/C Peter Falk, Ann-Margret, Eileen Brennan, Sid Caesar, Stockard Channing, James Coco, Dom DeLuise, Louise Fletcher, John Houseman, Madeline Kahn, Fernando Lamas, Marsha Mason, Phil Silvers, Vic Tayback, Abe Vigoda, Paul Williams, Nicol Williamson; **D:** Robert Moore; **W:** Neil Simon. **VHS $19.95** CSM, COL ½½½

Cheap Shots Cheap best describes this. Two guys running a sleazy New York State resort motel plot to videotape patrons having sex, but capture an apparent mob murder instead. More of a character study than sexploitation, but who needs these characters? Not a stellar writing/directing debut for Ureles and Stoeffhaas.
1991 (PG-13) 90m/C Louis Zorich, David Patrick Kelly, Mary Louise Wilson, Michael Twaine, Patience Moore; **D:** Jeff Ureles; **W:** Jeff Ureles, Jerry Stoeffhaas; **M:** Jeff Beal. **VHS $9.95** HMD ½½

Cheaper to Keep Her Alleged comedy about a private detective hired to track likely alimony dodgers. Loathsome, repellent fare, with Davis hopeless in the lead.
1980 (R) 92m/C Mac Davis, Tovah Feldshuh, Jack Gilford, Rose Marie; **D:** Ken Annakin; **W:** Herschel Weingrod, Timothy Harris. **VHS, Beta $54.95** MED Woof!

The Cheat Ward plays a frivolous socialite heavily indebted to Hayakawa as the Japanese money lender. Hayakawa makes Ward pay with her honor and her flesh by branding her. A dark and captivating drama. Silent with piano score.
1915 55m/B Fannie Ward, Sessue Hayakawa; **D:** Cecil B. DeMille. **VHS, Beta $14.95** GPV ½½½

The Cheaters A young gambler runs away with his boss's son's girlfriend, and is pursued therein.
1976 (R) 91m/C IT Dayle Haddon, Luc Merenda, Lino Troisi, Enrico Maria Salerno; **D:** Sergio Martino. **VHS, Beta $59.95** PSM ½

Cheaters Two middle class couples are having affairs with each other's spouses. Complications arise when their respective children decide to marry each other.
1984 103m/C Peggy Cass, Jack Kruschen. **VHS, Beta $39.95** RKO ½½

Cheatin' Hearts Kirkland is a woman beset by woe: she's about to lose her house, her philandering husband (Brolin) wanders back to town with his latest bimbo in tow, and her daughter's getting married. This should be a good thing, except hubby makes a fool of himself at the wedding and nearly ruins everything. Well, at least local rancher Kristofferson is around to lift a woman's spirits. And yes, there's a (predictably) happy ending.
1993 (R) 88m/C Sally Kirkland, James Brolin, Kris Kristofferson. **VHS $92.95** VMK ½½½

Check & Double Check Radio's original Amos 'n' Andy (a couple of black-faced white guys) help solve a lover's triangle in this film version of the popular radio series. Interesting only as a novelty. Duke Ellington's band plays "Old Man Blues" and "Three Little Words."
1930 85m/B Freeman Gosden, Charles Correll, Duke Ellington; **D:** Melville Brown. **VHS, Beta $19.95** NOS, MRV, VYY ½

Check Is in the Mail Lame comedy about a financier determined to make his home entirely independent from the rat-race of capitalist society. Dependables Dennehy and Archer are wasted.
1985 (R) 83m/C Brian Dennehy, Anne Archer, Dick Shawn; **D:** Joan Darling. **VHS, Beta $79.95** MED, VTR ½½

Check Your Guns A crooked judge and a gang of outlaws team up to prey on law-abiding folk and cause headaches for the new sheriff, who's pushing an unsuccessful Old West version of gun control. Nothing really noteworthy here.

1985 (R) 83m/C Brian Dennehy, Anne Archer, Dick Shawn; **D:** Joan Darling. **VHS, Beta $79.95** MED, VTR ½½

1948 55m/B Eddie Dean, Roscoe Ates, Nancy Gates, George Cheseboro, I. Stanford Jolley, Mikel Conrad, Bill Fawcett; D: Ray Taylor. VHS $19.95 NOS 🎬🎬

The Checkered Flag Lame auto-racing drama about an aging, millionaire race car driver with an alcoholic wife who would like nothing more than to see him dead. She talks a young rookie into helping her dispose of hubby. Plans go awry—with horrifying results. Racing scenes overshadow incredibly weak script and performances.
1963 110m/C Joe Morrison, Evelyn King, Charles G. Martin, Peggy Vendig; D: William Grefe; W: William Grefe. VHS $16.95 SNC 🎬

Checking Out Black comedy about a manic hypochondriac who is convinced that his demise will soon occur. You'll pray that he's right. Daniels can't make it work, and supporters Mayron and Magnuson also have little chance in poorly conceived roles.
1989 (R) 95m/C Jeff Daniels, Melanie Mayron, Michael Tucker, Kathleen York, Ann Magnuson, Allen Havey, Jo Harvey Allen, Felton Perry, Alan Wolfe; D: David Leland; W: Joe Eszterhas; M: Carter Burwell. VHS, Beta NO 🎬½

Cheech and Chong: Still Smokin' Not really. More like still trying to make a buck. Veteran marijuana-dazed comedy duo travel to Amsterdam to raise funds for a bankrupt film festival group by hosting a dope-a-thon. Lots of concert footage used in an attempt to hold the slim plot together. Only for serious fans of the dopin' duo. AKA: Still Smokin'.
1983 (R) 91m/C Richard "Cheech" Marin, Thomas Chong; D: Thomas Chong; M: George S. Clinton. VHS, Beta $14.95 PAR 🎬½

Cheech and Chong: Things Are Tough All Over Stoner comedy team are hired by two rich Arab brothers (also played by Cheech and Chong in acting stretch) and unwittingly drive a car loaded with money from Chicago to Las Vegas. Tired fourth in the series.
1982 (R) 87m/C Richard "Cheech" Marin, Thomas Chong, Shelby Fiddis, Rikki Marin, Evelyn Guerrero, Rip Taylor; D: Tom Avildsen. VHS, Beta $9.95 COL 🎬🎬

Cheech and Chong's Next Movie A pair of messed-up bumblers adventure into a welfare office, massage parlor, nightclub, and flying saucer, while always living in fear of the cops. Kinda funny, like. Sequel to "Up in Smoke."
1980 (R) 95m/C Richard "Cheech" Marin, Thomas Chong, Evelyn Guerrero, Edie McClurg, Paul (Pee Wee Herman) Reubens, Phil Hartman; D: Thomas Chong. VHS, Beta $14.95 MCA 🎬🎬

Cheech and Chong's Nice Dreams The spaced-out duo are selling their own "specially mixed" ice cream to make cash and realize their dreams. Third in the series.
1981 (R) 97m/C Richard "Cheech" Marin, Thomas Chong, Evelyn Guerrero, Stacy Keach, Paul (Pee Wee Herman) Reubens; D: Thomas Chong, Timothy Leary. VHS, Beta $14.95 COL 🎬🎬

Cheech and Chong's, The Corsican Brothers Wretched swashbuckler features the minimally talented duo in a variety of worthless roles. Dumas would vomit in his casket if he knew about this. Fifth in the series.
1984 (PG) 91m/C Richard "Cheech" Marin, Thomas Chong, Roy Dotrice, Rae Dawn Chong, Shelby Fiddis, Rikki Marin, Edie McClurg; D: Thomas Chong. VHS $79.98 LIV Woof!

Cheech and Chong's Up in Smoke A pair of free-spirited burn-outs team up for a tongue-in-cheek spoof of sex, drugs, and rock and roll. First and probably the best of the dopey duo's cinematic adventures. A box-office bonanza when released and still a cult favorite.
1979 (R) 87m/C Richard "Cheech" Marin, Thomas Chong, Stacy Keach, Tom Skerritt, Edie Adams, Strother Martin, Cheryl "Rainbeaux" Smith; D: Lou Adler. VHS, Beta $14.95 PAR 🎬🎬½

The Cheerful Fraud Denny, who appeared in some two hundred-odd films in his career, masquerades as a butler to be near the girl he loves. A fool for love is a cheerful fraud. A zanily romantic silent comedy.
1927 64m/B Reginald Denny, Gertrude Olmsted, Emily Fitzroy, Gertrude Astor; D: William A. Seiter. VHS, Beta $24.95 GPV 🎬🎬½

Cheering Section High school football teams compete for the grand prize—the privilege of ravishing the losing school's cheerleaders. Rah, rah, rah.
1973 (R) 84m/C Rhonda Foxx, Tom Leindecker, Gregg D'Jah, Patricia Michelle, Jeff Laine; D: Harry Kerwin. VHS NO Woof!

Cheerleader Camp Nubile gals are stalked by a psychopath while they cavort semi-clad at summer camp. AKA: Bloody Pom Poms.
1988 (R) 89m/C Betsy Russell, Leif Garrett, Lucinda Dickey, Lorie Griffin, George Flower, Teri Weigel, Rebecca Ferratti; D: John Quinn. VHS, Beta $14.95 PSM, PAR Woof!

The Cheerleaders Dimwitted exploitation effort has the usual suspects—moronic jocks and lamebrained gals—cavorting exuberantly. Followed by "Revenge of the Cheerleaders."
1972 (R) 84m/C Stephanie Fondue, Denise Dillaway, Jovita Bush, Debbie Lowe, Sandy Evans; D: Paul Glickler. VHS, Beta $9.99 STE, PSM, IME Woof!

Cheerleaders' Wild Weekend Group of cheerleaders are held captive by a disgruntled former football star. Pom poms wave.
1985 (R) 87m/C Jason Williams, Kristine DeBell; D: Jeff Werner. VHS, Beta $69.98 LIV, VES Woof!

Cheers for Miss Bishop The story of a woman who graduates from college then teaches at the same institution for the next 50 years. Somewhat moving. Based on Bess Streeter Aldrich's novel.
1941 95m/C Martha Scott, William Gargan, Edmund Gwenn, Sterling Holloway, Rosemary DeCamp; D: Tay Garnett; M: Edward Ward. VHS, Beta $19.95 NOS, MRV, VYY 🎬🎬½

Cheetah Two California kids visiting their parents in Kenya embark on the adventure of their lives when, with the help of a young Masai, they adopt and care for an orphaned cheetah. Usual Disney kids and animals story.
1989 (G) 80m/C Keith Coogan, Lucy Deakins, Collin Mothupi; D: Jeff Blyth. VHS $89.98 DIS 🎬🎬

Cherry Hill High Five teen girls compete for former-virgin status. Pass on this one.
1976 (R) 92m/C Linda McInnerney, Carrie Olsen, Nina Carson, Lynn Hastings, Gloria Upson, Stephanie Lawlor; D: Alex E. Goiten. VHS, Beta $59.95 MCA Woof!

Cherry 2000 Futuristic flick concerns a man who short-circuits his sex-toy robots and embarks on a search for replacement parts across treacherous territory, only to meet a real female—Griffith. Offbeat, occasionally funny.
1988 (PG-13) 94m/C Melanie Griffith, David Andrews, Ben Johnson, Tim Thomerson, Michael C. Gwynne; D: Steve DeJarnatt. VHS, Beta $9.98 ORI 🎬🎬

Chesty Anderson USN Ultra-lame sexploitation about female naval recruits. Minimal nudity. AKA: Anderson's Angels.
1976 90m/C Shari Eubank, Dorri Thompson, Rosanne Katon, Marcie Barkin, Scatman Crothers, Frank Campanella, Fred Willard; D: Ed Forsyth. VHS, Beta NO 🎬

Cheyenne Autumn The newly restored version of the ambitious, ultimately hit-and-miss western epic about three hundred Cheyenne Indians who migrate from Oklahoma to their Wyoming homeland in 1878. The cavalry, for once, are not the good guys. Widmark is strong in the lead. Stewart is memorable in his comic cameo as Wyatt Earp. Last film from genre master Ford, capturing the usual rugged panoramas. Based on a true story as told in the Mari Sandoz novel.
1964 156m/C Richard Widmark, Carroll Baker, Karl Malden, Dolores Del Rio, Sal Mineo, Edward G. Robinson, Ricardo Montalban, Gilbert Roland, Arthur Kennedy, John Carradine, Victor Jory, Mike Mazurki, George O'Brien, John Qualen; Cameos: James Stewart; D: John Ford. VHS, Beta $19.98 WAR, FCT 🎬🎬½

Cheyenne Kid Determined bronco buster is up against a gang of bad guys.
1933 40m/B Tom Keene, Mary Mason, Roscoe Ates. VHS, Beta $19.95 NOS, DVT 🎬½

Cheyenne Rides Again Cheyenne poses as an outlaw to hunt a gang of rustlers.
1938 60m/B Tom Tyler, Lucille Browne, Lon Chaney Jr., Roger Williams, Charles "Slim" Whitaker; D: Robert F. Hill. VHS, Beta $19.95 NOS, VYY, VCN 🎬½

The Cheyenne Social Club Stewart inherits a brothel and Fonda helps him operate it. Kelly directs, sort of. Some laughs, but this effort is beneath this trio.
1970 (PG) 103m/C Henry Fonda, James Stewart, Shirley Jones, Sue Ane Langdon, Elaine Devry; D: Gene Kelly. VHS $14.95 WAR 🎬🎬

Cheyenne Takes Over Lash sniffs out the bad guy in the case of a murdered ranch heir.
1947 56m/B Lash LaRue, Al "Fuzzy" St. John, George Cheseboro; D: Ray Taylor. VHS, Beta $12.95 COL 🎬

Chicago Joe & the Showgirl A London-based GI befriends a loopy showgirl and helps her in various crimes during WWII. Appealing Lloyd overwhelms Sutherland, who shows only limited acting ability here. Kensit and Pigg are fine in smaller roles.
1990 (R) 105m/C GB Emily Lloyd, Kiefer Sutherland, Patsy Kensit, Keith Allen, Liz Fraser, Alexandra Pigg, Ralph Nossek, Colin Bruce; D: Bernard Rose. VHS $89.95 LIV, IME 🎬½

The Chicken Chronicles An affluent high school dude longs to get horizontal with his dream girl. Set in the 1960s. First feature film appearance for Guttenberg.
1977 (PG) 94m/C Phil Silvers, Ed Lauter, Steve Guttenberg, Lisa Reeves, Meredith Baer; D: Francis Simon. VHS, Beta $14.95 COL, SUE 🎬

Chiefs A police chief in a Southern town discovers a series of murders concealed by town big wigs. Made for TV film boasts a surprisingly strong cast, but provides otherwise conventional entertainment.

1983 200m/C Charlton Heston, Paul Sorvino, Keith Carradine, Brad Davis, Billy Dee Williams, Wayne Rogers, Stephen Collins, Tess Harper, Victoria Tennant; *D:* Jerry London. **VHS, Beta** $29.95 STE, NWV ⅋⅋

Child Bride of Short Creek A young Korean war veteran returns to his community where polygamy is allowed, to find that his father intends to marry again, this time to a 15-year-old. Conflict ensues. Made for television. Based on an actual event that occurred in the 1950s.
1981 100m/C Diane Lane, Conrad Bain, Christopher Atkins, Kiel Martin, Helen Hunt; *D:* Robert Lewis. **VHS, Beta** $59.95 PSM ⅋⅋½

Child in the Night A shaken eight-year old boy is a witness to murder in his family, and a psychologist with plenty of her own problems must get him to testify. First film for Wood. Middling TV-movie suspense.
1990 (R) 93m/C Tom Skerritt, JoBeth Williams, Darren McGavin, Season Hubley, Elijah Wood; *D:* Mike Robe. **VHS, Beta** $79.95 TRI ⅋⅋

A Child is Waiting Poignant and provocative story of teachers in an institution for the mentally retarded. Fine performances include Lancaster as the institution's administrator and Garland as a teacher who cares too much for everyone's good. Cassavetes incorporates footage using handicapped children as extras—not entirely seamlessly—providing a sensitive and candid edge.
1963 105m/B Burt Lancaster, Judy Garland, Gena Rowlands, Steven Hill, Bruce Ritchey; *D:* John Cassavetes; *W:* Abby Mann; *M:* Ernest Gold. **VHS, Beta** $19.98 MGM ⅋⅋⅋

Child of Darkness, Child of Light A priest is sent to investigate two virgin pregnancies and discovers that one child will be a savior and the other the Anti-Christ. Totally mindless brain candy resembling the "Omen" movies and "Rosemary's Baby." Made for cable television. Adapted from James Patterson's book "Virgin."
1991 (PG-13) 85m/C Anthony John Denison, Brad Davis, Paxton Whitehead, Claudette Nevins, Sydney Penny, Kristin Datillo, Viveca Lindfors, Sela Ward, Alan Oppenheimer, Eric Christmas; *D:* Marina Sargenti; *W:* Brian Taggert. **VHS, Beta** PAR ⅋½

Child of Glass A young boy's family moves into a huge New Orleans mansion, and soon after encounters a young girl's ghost and lost treasure from the Civil War. A Disney made for TV movie.
1978 93m/C Barbara Barrie, Biff McGuire, Anthony Zerbe, Nina Foch, Steve Shaw, Katy Kurtzman, Olivia Barash; *D:* John Erman. **VHS, Beta** $69.95 DIS ⅋⅋

Child of the Prairie An early Mix film about a young cowboy and his city-loving wife down on their luck in a western town. Silent with music score.
1918 63m/B Tom Mix. **VHS, Beta, 8mm** $24.95 VYY ⅋

The Children Familiar nuclear leak leads to monster mutants done to a novel (though extremely low-budget) turn: after a school bus passes through radioactive fog, the kiddies inside assume the ability to incinerate whoever they hug. They also assume a certain zombie-like demeanor and sport black fingernails. None of this is noted by their uncaring and less-than-observant parents, many of whom are enticed into a very warm hug. This may be intended as social satire. Not only are the little microwaves extremely dangerous, the only way to kill them is to chop off their hands, leading to a wild limbless finale.

1980 (R) 89m/C Martin Shaker, Gale Garnett, Gil Rogers; *D:* Max Kalmanowicz. **VHS, Beta** $14.95 VES, FCT, RHI Woof!

The Children Kingsley stars as a middle-aged engineer who finds himself caring for seven children in this touching love story from novelist Edith Wharton. Shot on location in Venice, the cinematography is excellent and the cast is superb, but the film lags in places. A remake of "The Marriage Playground."
1990 90m/C GB GE Ben Kingsley, Kim Novak, Siri Neal, Geraldine Chaplin, Joe Don Baker, Britt Ekland, Donald Sinden, Karen Black, Robert Stephens, Rupert Graves, Rosemary Leach; *D:* Tony Palmer. **VHS** $89.95 HMD ⅋⅋½

The Children Are Watching Us Sobering drama of a family dissolution as seen by a child. Worthy example of Italian neo-realism marks the first collaboration between Zavattini and De Sica. In Italian with subtitles. *AKA:* The Little Martyr; I Bambini Ci Guardano.
1944 92m/B IT Luciano de Ambrosis, Isa Pola, Emilio Cigoli; *D:* Vittorio De Sica; *W:* Cesare Zavattini, Vittorio De Sica. **VHS, Beta** $79.95 FCT ⅋⅋⅋

Children in the Crossfire When youngsters from war-torn Northern Ireland spend a summer in America with children from the Republic of Ireland, both sides find their nationalistic prejudices falling away. But a great challenge awaits them when they return home from their summer of fun. Nicely done drama made for television.
1984 96m/C Charles Haid, Karen Valentine, Julia Duffy, David Hoffman; *D:* George Schaefer; *M:* Brad Fiedel. **VHS** $79.98 LIV, VES ⅋⅋½

Children of a Lesser God Based upon the play by Mark Medoff, this sensitive, intelligent film deals with an unorthodox speech teacher at a school for the deaf, who falls in love with a beautiful and rebellious ex-student. Inarguably romantic; the original stage production won the Best Play Tony in 1980. Hurt and Matlin reportedly continued their romance off-screen as well.
1986 (R) 119m/C William Hurt, Marlee Matlin, Piper Laurie, Philip Bosco, E. Katherine Kerr; *D:* Randa Haines; *W:* Hesper Anderson, Mark Medoff; *M:* Michael Convertino. Academy Awards '86: Best Actress (Matlin); Nominations: Best Actor (Hurt), Best Adapted Screenplay, Best Picture, Best Supporting Actress (Laurie); Golden Globe Awards '87: Best Actress—Drama (Matlin). **VHS, Beta, 8mm** $19.95 PAR, BTV, JCF ⅋⅋⅋½

The Children of An Lac Three women attempt to rescue hundreds of Vietnamese orphans before Saigon falls to the communists. The film derives actress Balin's actual wartime experience. Made for television.
1980 100m/C Shirley Jones, Ina Balin, Beulah Quo, Alan Fudge, Ben Piazza, Lee Paul, Kieu Chinh, Vic Diaz. **VHS, Beta** $14.95 FRH ⅋⅋½

Children of Divorce Made-for-television drama shows divorce from the children's point of view. Standard fare.
1980 96m/C Barbara Feldon, Lance Kerwin, Stacey Nelkin, Billy Dee Williams; *D:* Joanna Lee. **VHS, Beta** $39.95 LIV ⅋½

Children of Nature A 78-year-old man unwillingly enters a nursing home where he meets a long-ago sweetheart. The two fall in love again and decide to escape from the home and return to their childhood village. Sweet love story about late-blooming passions laced with fantasy and humor. Iceland's first Academy Award nomination. In Icelandic with English subtitles. *AKA:* Born Natturunnar.

1992 85m/C Gisli Halldorsson, Sigridur Hagalin, Bruno Ganz; *D:* Fridrik Thor Fridriksson; *W:* Fridrik Thor Fridriksson, Einar Mar Gudmundsson; *M:* Hilmar Orn Hilmarsson. **VHS** $89.98 FXL, ING ⅋⅋½

Children of Paradise Considered by many to be the greatest film ever made, certainly one of the most beautiful. In the Parisian theatre district of the 1800s an actor falls in love with a seemingly unattainable woman. Although circumstances keep them apart, their love never dies. Produced in France during WWII right under the noses of Nazi occupiers; many of the talent (including the writer, poet Jacques Prevert) were active resistance fighters. Laserdisc version features: interview with director Marcel Carne, production photos, analysis of influences of French painting on the film, and audio essay by film authority Brian Stonehill. In French with English subtitles. *AKA:* Les Enfants du Paradise.
1944 188m/B FR Jean-Louis Barrault, Arletty, Pierre Brasseur, Maria Casares, Albert Remy, Leon Larive, Marcel Herrand, Pierre Renoir; *D:* Marcel Carne; *W:* Jacques Prevert; *M:* Maurice Thiriet, Joseph Kosma, George Mouque. **VHS** $79.95 HMV, VYG, CRC ⅋⅋⅋⅋

Children of Rage High-minded and long-winded drama dealing with the Israeli/Palestinian war and terrorism from the viewpoint of an Israeli doctor yearning for peace.
1975 (PG) 106m/C GB IS Simon Ward, Cyril Cusack, Helmut Griem, Olga Georges-Picot; *D:* Arthur Seidelman; *W:* Richard Alferi. **VHS, Beta** $69.95 ACA ⅋⅋½

Children of Sanchez Mexican man attempts to provide for his family with very little except faith and love. U.S./Mexican production based on Oscar Lewis' novel.
1979 (PG) 103m/C MX Anthony Quinn, Dolores Del Rio, Katy Jurado, Lupita Ferrer; *D:* Hall Bartlett; *W:* Hall Bartlett; *M:* Chuck Mangione. **VHS, Beta** $39.95 MON ⅋⅋

Children of the Corn Young couple lands in a small Iowa town where children appease a demon by murderously sacrificing adults. Time to move or dispense with some major spankings. Infrequently scary. Another feeble attempt to translate the horror of a Stephen King book to film.
1984 (R) 93m/C Peter Horton, Linda Hamilton, R.G. Armstrong, John Franklin, Courtney Gains, Robbie Kiger; *D:* Fritz Kiersch; *M:* Jonathan Elias. **VHS, Beta** $9.98 SUE, STE ⅋½

Children of the Corn 2: The Final Sacrifice Reporter working for a tabloid paper gets more than he bargained for when he decides to do a story on the adults murdered in the town of Gatlin, Nebraska. Gatlin's surviving children, who killed their parents in the first film, are now living in a neighboring town and free to kill again. This youthful satanic cult does in authority figures in a number of sacrifical ways, working ever more smartly to create the prime attraction—blood flow. Not based on anything written by Stephen King.
1992 (R) 93m/C Terence Knox, Paul Scherrer, Rosalind Allen, Christie Clark, Ned Romero, Ryan Bollman, Ted Travelstead; *D:* David F. Price; *W:* Gilbert Adler, A.L. Katz. **VHS** PAR ⅋½

Children of the Damned Six children, who are a sample of what man will evolve to in a million years, are born all around the world with genius IQs, ray-gun eyes, and murderous dispositions. Two investigators bring the children together, and while they are being examined by scientists they escape. The children hide out in a church, but they are doomed because their destiny is to be destroyed to teach a lesson

to modern man. A sequel to "Village of the Damned" based loosely on the novel "The Midwich Cuckoos" by John Wyndham.
1963 90m/B *GB* Ian Hendry, Alan Badel, Barbara Ferris, Alfred Burke, Sheila Allen, Clive Powell, Frank Summerscales, Mahdu Mathen, Gerald Delsol, Roberta Rex, Franchesca Lee, Harold Goldblatt; *D:* Anton Leader; *W:* John Briley. **VHS** *$19.98 MGM* 🎦🎦

Children of the Full Moon A young couple find themselves lost in a forest that is the home of a family of werewolves. Earns praise only for brevity. Even bad movie aficionados will want to skip this howler.
1984 60m/C *GB* Christopher Cazenove, Celia Gregory, Diana Dors, Jacof Witken, Robert Urquhart; *D:* Tom Clegg. **VHS, Beta** *$29.95 LIV* 🎦

Children of the Night Allburg seems like a typically quiet small town far removed from any danger—until a vampire is released from an underground crypt and decides to make the town his bloodthirsty target. When a teacher, whose girlfriend is visiting Allburg, learns of the supernatural goings on he decides to investigate, which may be a deadly mistake.
1992 (R) 92m/C Peter DeLuise, Karen Black, Ami Dolenz; *D:* Tony Randel. **VHS** *$89.95 COL* 🎦½

Children of the Wild Adventure story about a pack of dogs surviving in the Rocky Mountain wilderness. Splendid scenery and some interesting sequences. *AKA:* Killers of the Wild.
1937 65m/B Patsy Moran. **VHS** *$24.95 VYY* 🎦🎦½

The Children of Theatre Street Absorbing documentary follows three children attending the renowned Kirov Ballet School. A show for all ages that may be especially enjoyed by kids who are interested in ballet. Kelly's last film appearance.
1977 90m/C *D:* Robert Dornhelm, Earle Mack; *Performed by:* Kirov Ballet. **VHS, Beta** *$39.95 MVD, PBC, KUL* 🎦🎦🎦½

The Children of Times Square A mother pursues her son who has fled home and joined a gang of drug dealers in New York City's seedy Times Square. Ordinary television film despite strong casting of Cassidy and Rollins.
1986 95m/C Joanna Cassidy, Howard E. Rollins Jr., Brandon Douglas, David Ackroyd, Griffin O'Neal, Danny Nucci, Larry B. Scott; *D:* Curtis Hanson; *M:* Patrick Gleeson. **VHS, Beta** *$14.95 FRH* 🎦🎦

Children Shouldn't Play with Dead Things A band of foolhardy hippie filmmakers on an island cemetary skimp on special effects by using witchcraft to revive the dead. The plan works. Soon the crew has an island full of hungry ghouls to contend with. Film strives for yucks, frequently succeeds. A late night fave, sporting some excellent dead rising from their grave scenes as well as a selection of groovy fashions. Screenwriter/star Ormsby went on to write the remake of "Cat People," while director Clark would eventually helm "Porky's." *AKA:* Revenge of the Living Dead.
1972 85m/C Alan Ormsby, Valerie Mamches, Jeff Gillen, Anya Ormsby, Paul Cronin, Jane Daly, Roy Engelman, Robert Philip, Bruce Solomon, Alecs Baird, Seth Sklarey; *D:* Bob (Benjamin) Clark; *W:* Alan Ormsby, Bob (Benjamin) Clark. **VHS, Beta** *$19.95 VCI, MPI* 🎦🎦½

Children's Carol The winter solstice brings no special joy to Walton's mountain; WWII has taken many men, with short wave reports indicating the Nazi terror spreading

across Europe. But huddled in the glow of Walton's barn, the children rediscover the true meaning of Christmas. *AKA:* The Waltons: The Children's Carol.
1980 94m/C Judy Norton-Taylor, Jon Walmsley, Mary McDonough, Eric Scott, Kami Cotler, Joe Conley, Ronnie Clare, Leslie Winston, Peggy Rea; *D:* Lawrence Dobkin. **VHS, Beta** *$14.98 LHV*

The Children's Hour The teaching careers of two women are ruined when girls begin circulating vicious rumors. Only an occasionally taut drama despite forceful handling of a lesbian theme. Updated version of Lillian Hellman's play (adapted by Hellman) is more explicit, but less suspenseful in spite of excellent performances from the talented cast. Remake of Wyler's own "These Three." *AKA:* The Loudest Whisper.
1961 107m/C Shirley MacLaine, Audrey Hepburn, James Garner, Miriam Hopkins, Veronica Cartwright, Fay Bainter; *D:* William Wyler. **VHS** *$19.98 MGM, BTV, FCT* 🎦🎦

Children's Island A two-volume saga, sold in one package, about children who, after being shipwrecked on an island during WWII, begin a democratic mini-society.
1984 100m/C **VHS, Beta** *NO* 🎦🎦

Child's Christmas in Wales A film of Dylan Thomas's Christmas story about an old, traditional Christmas in Wales circa 1910.
1988 55m/C Mathonwy Reeves; *D:* Don McBrearty. **VHS, Beta** *$9.98 LIV, VES, HMV* 🎦🎦

Child's Play A boy discovers that his new doll named Chucky is actually the embodiment of a deranged killer. His initially skeptical mom and a police officer come around after various killings. Exciting, if somewhat moronic, fare, with fine special effects. Followed by "Child's Play 2."
1988 (R) 95m/C Catherine Hicks, Alex Vincent, Chris Sarandon, Dinah Manoff, Brad Dourif, Tommy Swerdlow, Jack Colvin; *D:* Tom Holland; *W:* Don Mancini, John Lafia, Tom Holland; *M:* Joe Renzetti. **VHS, Beta** *$14.95 MGM* 🎦🎦½

Child's Play 2 Chuckie lives. Basic doll-on-a-rampage story, a metaphor for the Reagan years, lives on in the sequel (you remember: somehow guy-doll Chuckie made it past the quality control people with a highly inflammable temper). A little dotty from playing with dolls, young Vincent finds himself fostered by two new parents, and plagued by an obnoxious and very animated doll that fosters ill will toward all. What's worse is the doll is transmigratory, craving the boy's body as his next address. Chef d'effects Kevin Yagher's new toy is bad, real bad, and so are the other part two FX. Little Chuckie's saga, however grows a tad tiresome. A bad example for small children.
1990 (R) 84m/C Alex Vincent, Jenny Agutter, Gerrit Graham, Christine Elise, Grace Zabriskie; *D:* John Lafia; *W:* Don Mancini; *M:* Graeme Revell; *V:* Brad Dourif. **VHS, Beta** *$19.98 MCA Woof!*

Child's Play 3 Possessed doll Chucky returns to life again in search of a new child to control, and luckily finds his old pal (Whalin) at a military school filled with the usual stereotypes. Gory sequel in a mostly awful series. "Don't F— With the Chuck" was its catch phrase; that should indicate the level of this junk.
1991 (R) 89m/C Justin Whalin, Perrey Reeves, Jeremy Sylvers, Peter Haskell, Dakin Matthews, Travis Fine, Dean Jacobson, Matthew Walker, Andrew (Andy) Robinson; *D:* Jack Bender; *W:* Don Mancini, Cory Lerios; *M:* John D'Andrea; *V:* Brad Dourif. **VHS, Beta** *$19.98 MCA* 🎦

Chill Factor A television reporter for an investigative news show uncovers evidence of an international conspiracy. Plot twists abound.
1990 (R) ?m/C Paul Williams, Patrick Macnee, Andrew Prine, Carrie Snodgress, Patrick Wayne, Gary Crosby; *D:* David L. Stanton. **VHS** *NO* 🎦🎦

Chillers Travellers waiting for a bus are besieged by carnivorous zombies and voracious vampires. How this is different from the standard bus trip is unclear.
1988 90m/C Jesse Emery, Marjorie Fitzsimmons, Laurie Pennington, Jim Wolfe, David Wohl; *D:* Daniel Boyd; *W:* Daniel Boyd. **VHS, Beta** *$9.95 SIM, PSM* 🎦

The Chilling Corpses preserved in a deep freeze come alive and plague Kansas City as flesh-chomping zombies. Utterly worthless film doesn't even provide convincing effects. *AKA:* Gamma 693.
1989 (R) 91m/C Linda Blair, Dan Haggerty, Troy Donahue, Jack A. De Rieux, Ron Vincent; *D:* Deland Nuse, Jack A. Sunseri. **VHS** *$9.95 HMD Woof!*

Chilly Scenes of Winter Quirky comedy with a cult following about a man obsessed with regaining the love of a former girlfriend who is now married. He must also deal with an insane mom and various other problems. Strong, subtle performances from Heard and Riegert. Hurt is somewhat less satisfying as the supposedly fascinating woman. Released with a different, inferior ending as "Head Over Heels." Adapted by Joan Micklin Silver from Ann Beattie's first novel. Watch for Beattie's cameo as a waitress. *AKA:* Head Over Heels.
1979 (PG) 96m/C John Heard, Mary Beth Hurt, Peter Riegert, Kenneth McMillan, Gloria Grahame, Nora Heflin, Griffin Dunne; *Cameos:* Ann Beattie; *D:* Joan Micklin Silver; *W:* Joan Micklin Silver. **VHS, Beta** *$19.98 MGM* 🎦🎦½

Chimes at Midnight Classic tragedy—derived by Welles from five Shakespeare plays—about a corpulent blowhard and his friendship with a prince. Crammed with classic sequences, including a battle that is both realistic and funny. The love scene between massive Welles and a nonetheless willing Moreau also manages to be both sad and amusing. Great performances all around, but Welles understandably dominates. The film's few flaws (due to budget problems) are inconsequential before considerable strengths. This one ranks among Welles', and thus the entire cinema's, very best. *AKA:* Falstaff; Campanadas a Medianoche.
1967 115m/B *SP SI* Orson Welles, Jeanne Moreau, Margaret Rutherford, John Gielgud, Marina Vlady, Keith Baxter, Fernando Rey, Norman Rodway; *D:* Orson Welles; *W:* Orson Welles; *M:* Angelo Francesco Lavagnino. **VHS, Beta** *FCT* 🎦🎦🎦🎦

China Beach TV movie/pilot launched the acclaimed series about American military women behind the lines during the chaos of the Vietnam War. Nurse McMurphy has only seven days left on her first tour of duty, and in spite of her hate of the brutality of the war, she has mixed feelings about leaving her friends and her work. A USO singer on a one week tour finds her search for men brings the war too close for comfort. Cherry, a new Red Cross volunteer, shows up at the Beach. Skillfully introduces the viewer to all the characters, their problems and joys, without melodrama or redundancy.
1988 95m/C Dana Delany, Chloe Webb, Robert Picardo, Nan Woods, Michael Boatman, Marg Helgenberger, Tim Ryan, Concetta Tomei, Jeff Kober, Brian Wimmer; *D:* Rod Holcomb; *W:* John Sacret Young. **VHS, Beta** *$79.95 WAR* 🎦🎦🎦

China Cry Based on the true story of Sung Negn Yee who escaped from Communist China to the freedom of Hong Kong in the early '60s. Fine portrayal of the young woman from a privileged background who witnessed some of the atrocities of Mao's government policies.
1991 (PG-13) 103m/C Julia Nickson-Soul, Russell Wong, James Shigeta, France Nuyen; **D:** James F. Collier. VHS $24.95 ING, IGP *ℤℤ* ½

China Gate A band of multi-national troops follows a French officer against a communist stronghold in Indochina. Conventional fare bolstered considerably by director Fuller's flair for action. Weak male leads, but Dickinson shines.
1957 97m/B Gene Barry, Angie Dickinson, Nat King Cole, Paul Dubov, Lee Van Cleef, George Givot, Marcel Dalio; **D:** Samuel Fuller; **W:** Samuel Fuller. VHS $19.98 REP *ℤℤℤ*

China Girl An Italian-American boy and a Chinese-American girl romance despite a war between gangs in their respective NYC communities. This often violent drama is enriched by director Ferrara's slick, high-energy approach.
1987 (R) 90m/C Richard Panebianco, James Russo, Sari Chang, Russell Wong, David Caruso, Joey Chin; **D:** Abel Ferrara; **W:** Nicholas St. John; **M:** Joe Delia. VHS, Beta $79.98 VES *ℤℤ* ½

The China Lake Murders A made for cable crazy cop on the loose fable in which a serial killer disguised as a highway patrolman practices population control on the inhabitants of a small town in the Mojave desert. Meanwhile the local sheriff (Skerritt), unwittingly befriends the killer-patrolman.
1990 (PG-13) 100m/C Tom Skerritt, Michael Parks, Nancy Everhard, Lauren Tewes, Bill McKinney, Loni Chapman; **D:** Alan Metzger; **W:** N.D. Schreiner. VHS, Beta $79.95 MCA *ℤℤ* ½

China Moon Convoluted police thriller, set in Florida, about beautiful Rachel (Stowe), who's married to rich-but-abusive Rupert (Dance). Kyle (Harris) is the lonely homicide detective who's besotted by Rachel and conveniently helps her dispose of her murdered husband's body. Kyle's problems increase when his rookie partner (Del Toro) turns out to be smarter than anyone thinks. Good performances but the suspense is only average.
1991 (R) 99m/C Ed Harris, Madeleine Stowe, Benicio Del Toro, Charles Dance; **D:** John Bailey; **W:** Roy Carlson; **M:** George Fenton. VHS NYR *ℤℤ* ½

China, My Sorrow Thirteen-year-old "Little Four Eyes" is sent to a Chinese re-education camp for the crime of playing a love song to a girl. There he befriends another enemy of the revolution and a Buddhist monk who help him maintain his familial traditions and identity. Tragi-comic look at how freedom's spirit survived the Cultural Revolution. In Mandarin and Shanghaiese with English subtitles.
1989 86m/C CH Guo Yiang Yi, Tieu Quan Nghieu, Vong Han Lai, Chi-Vy Sam, Chang Cheung Siang; **D:** Dai Sijie; **W:** Dai Sijie, Shan Yuan Zhu; **M:** Chen Qi Gang. VHS $79.95 CVC, FCT *ℤℤ* ½

China O'Brien Gorgeous police officer with martial arts expertise returns home for a little R & R, but finds she has to kick some major butt instead. Violent, dimwitted action drama proves only that cleavage can be macho too.

1988 (R) 90m/C Cynthia Rothrock, Richard Norton, Patrick Adamson, David Blackwell, Steven Kerby, Robert Tiller, Lainie Watts, Keith Cooke; **D:** Robert Clouse. VHS $19.95 IMP, BTV *ℤ* ½

China O'Brien 2 The unbreakable China, now a sheriff, battles the standard-issue Vietnam-vet druglord who invades her little town. Made back-to-back with the first film (note that both pics' bad guys have the same gang of henchman!), and in both films Rothrock is basically invincible, so there's no suspense.
1989 (R) 85m/C Cynthia Rothrock, Richard Norton, Keith Cooke; **D:** Robert Clouse. VHS $89.95 IMP *ℤ* ½

China Seas The captain of a commercial steamship on the China route has to fight off murderous Malay pirates, a spurned woman, and a raging typhoon to reach port safely. Fast-moving romantic action taken from Crosbie Garstin's novel.
1935 89m/B Clark Gable, Jean Harlow, Wallace Beery, Rosalind Russell, Lewis Stone, Sir C. Aubrey Smith, Dudley Digges, Robert Benchley; **D:** Tay Garnett. VHS, Beta $19.98 MGM *ℤℤℤ*

China Sky An American doctor fights alongside Chinese guerillas against the Japanese during WWII. Drama, to its credit, often opts for character conflict instead of warfare, but this makes it merely dull instead of cliched. Adapted from a Pearl S. Buck novel.
1944 78m/B Randolph Scott, Ellen Drew, Ruth Warrick, Anthony Quinn, Carol Thurston, Richard Loo, Philip Ahn; **D:** Ray Enright. VHS, Beta $19.98 TTC *ℤℤ*

The China Syndrome A somewhat unstable executive at a nuclear plant uncovers evidence of a concealed accident, takes drastic steps to publicize the incident. Lemmon is excellent as the anxious exec, while Fonda and Douglas are scarcely less distinguished as a sympathetic TV journalist and camera operator, respectively. Tense, prophetic thriller that ironically preceded the Three Mile Island accident by just a few months. Produced by Douglas.
1979 (PG) 123m/C Jane Fonda, Jack Lemmon, Michael Douglas, Scott Brady, James Hampton, Peter Donat, Wilford Brimley, James Karen; **D:** James Bridges; **W:** Mike Gray, T.S. Cook, James Bridges. Academy Awards '78 Nominations: Best Actress (Fonda), Best Original Screenplay; Academy Awards '79: Best Actor (Lemmon), Best Art Direction/Set Decoration; Cannes Film Festival '79: Best Film; British Academy Awards '79: Best Actor (Lemmon), Best Actress (Fonda); National Board of Review Awards '79: 10 Best Films of the Year. VHS, Beta $12.98 COL *ℤℤℤ* ½

China White Violence erupts in the streets of Paris, Amsterdam and Bangkok, when international drug cartels battle over the ownership of China White - premium heroin, its sources and its outlets. Rousing, realistic action.
1991 (R) ?m/C Billy Drago, Russell Wong, Lisa Schrage, Steven Leigh; **D:** Ronny Yu. VHS $89.98 IMP *ℤℤℤ* ½

Chinatown Private detective finds himself overwhelmed in a scandalous case involving the rich and powerful of Los Angeles. Gripping, atmospheric mystery excels in virtually every aspect, with strong narrative drive and outstanding performances from Nicholson, Dunaway, and Huston. Director Polanski also appears in a suitable unsettling cameo. Fabulous. A sneaky, snaking delight filled with seedy characters and plots-within-plots. Followed more than 15 years later by "The Two Jakes."

1974 (R) 131m/C Jack Nicholson, Faye Dunaway, John Huston, Diane Ladd, John Hillerman, Burt Young, Perry Lopez, Darrell Zwerling; **Cameos:** Roman Polanski; **D:** Roman Polanski; **W:** Robert Towne; **M:** Jerry Goldsmith. Academy Awards '74: Best Original Screenplay; Nominations: Best Actor (Nicholson), Best Actress (Dunaway), Best Art Direction/Set Decoration, Best Cinematography, Best Costume Design, Best Director (Polanski), Best Film Editing, Best Picture, Best Original Score; British Academy Awards '74: Best Actor (Nicholson), Best Director (Polanski); Golden Globe Awards '75: Best Actor—Drama (Nicholson), Best Director (Polanski), Best Film—Drama, Best Screenplay; National Board of Review Awards '74: 10 Best Films of the Year; New York Film Critics Awards '74: Best Actor (Nicholson); National Society of Film Critics Awards '74: Best Actor (Nicholson). VHS, Beta, 8mm $19.95 PAR *ℤℤℤℤ*

Chinatown After Dark Ludicrous, inane melodrama about a white girl raised by the Chinese.
1931 50m/B Rex Lease, Barbara Kent, Carmel Myers; **D:** Ralph M. Like. VHS $12.95 SNC, NOS, DVT *ℤ*

Chinatown Connection For some inexplicable reason, local drug dealers start selling poisoned cocaine. Two renegade cops discover the super-secret organization doing the poisoning, arm themselves heavily, and kill lots of people while putting an end to the poisonings. Violent, foolish film with dull performances.
1990 (R) 94m/C Bruce Ly, Lee Majors, Pat McCormick, Art Camacho, Susan Frailey, Scott Richards; **D:** Jean-Paul Ouellette. VHS NO *ℤ*

The Chinatown Kid Tan Tung escapes from Red China on a ship bound for San Francisco. There he becomes involved in a local extortion racket and he'll need all his martial arts skills to overcome the two gangs fighting for power.
1978 115m/C Alexander Fu Sheng, Sun Chein, Shirley Yu, Shaw Yin-Yin; **D:** Chen Chen. VHS $14.95 HMD, FXL *ℤ*

The Chinatown Murders: Man Against the Mob A tough cop is up against the Chinese mafia and his own corrupt police force as he tries to stay alive and find some justice.
1992 (R) 96m/C George Peppard, Charles Haid, Richard Bradford, Ursula Andress. VHS $89.95 VMK *ℤℤ*

Chinese Boxes An American man in Berlin is framed in a murder and becomes caught in an international web of crime and intrigue. Low budget but interesting thriller.
1984 87m/C GE GB Will Patton, Adelheid Arndt, Robbie Coltrane; **D:** Christopher Petit. VHS, Beta $69.98 LIV, VES *ℤℤ* ½

The Chinese Cat Poorly scripted formula mystery has the younger Chan smitten with a girl who needs the elder Chan's detective skills in finding her father's killer.
1944 65m/B Sidney Toler, Benson Fong, Mantan Moreland, Weldon Heyburn, Joan Woodbury, Ian Keith, Sam Flint; **D:** Phil Rosen. VHS $19.98 MGM *ℤ*

Chinese Connection A martial arts expert tracks sadistic brutes who slew his instructor. Wild action sequences provide a breathtaking view of Lee's skill. Dubbed. **AKA:** Fist of Fury; The Iron Hand.
1973 (R) 90m/C CH Bruce Lee, James Tien, Robert Baker; **D:** Lo Wei. VHS, Beta $19.98 FOX, MRV, REP *ℤℤℤ*

Chinese Connection 2 A martial-arts expert learns that the school where he trained is now run by an unappealing master. Conflict ensues. Bruce Li is not Bruce Lee,

but he is fairly good in action portions of this otherwise dull, sloppy venture.
1984 96m/C Bruce Li. **VHS, Beta** $39.95 *TWE &&*

Chinese Roulette A host of unappealing characters convene at a country house for sexual shenanigans and a cruel game masterminded by a sadistic crippled girl. Cold effort from German master Fassbinder. In German with English subtitles.
1986 96m/C *GE* Anna Karina, Margit Carstensen, Ulli Lommel, Brigitte Mira, Macha Meril, Andrea Schober, Volker Spengler; *D:* Rainer Werner Fassbinder; *W:* Rainer Werner Fassbinder. **VHS, Beta** $79.95 *CVC, ING &&* 1/2

Chinese Web Spiderman adventure in which Spidey becomes entwined in international intrigue and corrupt officials.
1978 95m/C Nicholas Hammond, Robert F. Simon, Rosalind Chao, Ted Danson; *D:* Donald McDougall. **VHS, Beta** $24.98 *FOX &*

Chino A half-Indian horse rancher struggles to maintain his livelihood in this spaghetti western. Not among Bronson's stronger—that is, more viscerally effective—films. Adapted from Lee Hoffman's novel. *AKA:* Valdez the Half Breed; The Valdez Horses.
1975 (PG) 97m/C *IT* Charles Bronson, Jill Ireland, Vincent Van Patten; *D:* John Sturges. **VHS, Beta** $59.95 *MPI, MRV, VTR &&*

The Chipmunk Adventure The three animated chipmunks, Simon, Theodore and Alvin, get involved with a diamond smuggling ring. Original songs. In HiFi Stereo.
1987 76m/C *D:* Janice Karman; *M:* Randy Edelman. **VHS, Beta** $79.95 *LHV, WAR, WTA &&*

Chips, the War Dog A WWII Army recruit, who's scared of dogs, is assigned to train a German shepherd for duty. Made for cable television.
1990 90m/C Brandon Douglas, Ned Vaughn, Paxton Whitehead, Ellie Cornell, Robert Miranda, William Devane; *D:* Ed Kaplan. **VHS** *DIS &&* 1/2

The Chisholms If you're into oaters, here's a high fiber six-hour serial: Chisolm (Preston) leads the family as they head west and find trouble with a capital "T" en route from Virginia to Californ-i-a. Originally a network miniseries, it's now a two-cassette rentable; adapted by Evan Hunter from his novel.
1979 300m/C Robert Preston, Rosemary Harris, Brian Keith, Ben Murphy, Charles Frank; *D:* Mel Stuart; *M:* Elmer Bernstein. **VHS, Beta** $69.95 *LIV &&* 1/2

Chisum Cattle baron faces various conflicts, including a confrontation with Billy the Kid. Lame Wayne vehicle contributes nothing to exhausted western genre. Laserdisc available in widescreen letterbox edition.
1970 (G) 111m/C John Wayne, Forrest Tucker, Geoffrey Deuel, Christopher George, Ben Johnson, Bruce Cabot, Patric Knowles, Richard Jaeckel, Glenn Corbett; *D:* Andrew V. McLaglen; *W:* Andrew J. Fenady. **VHS, Beta** $19.98 *WAR, TLF &* 1/2

Chitty Chitty Bang Bang An eccentric inventor spruces up an old car and, in fantasy, takes his children to a land where the evil rulers have forbidden children. Poor special effects and forgettable score stall effort. Loosely adapted by Roald Dahl and Hughes from an Ian Fleming story. ♫Chitty Chitty Bang Bang; Hushabye Mountain; Truly Scrumptious; You Two; Toot Sweet; Me Ol' Bam-Boo; Lovely Lonely Man; Posh; The Roses of Success; Chu-Chi Face; Doll on a Music Box.

1968 (G) 142m/C *GB* Dick Van Dyke, Sally Ann Howes, Lionel Jeffries, Gert Frobe, Anna Quayle, Benny Hill; *D:* Ken Hughes; *W:* Ken Hughes, Roald Dahl. **VHS, Beta** $19.98 *FOX, MGM, TLF &*

Chloe in the Afternoon A married man finds himself inexplicably drawn to an ungainly young woman. Sixth of the "Moral Tales" series is typical of director Rohmer's talky approach. Not for all tastes, but rewarding for those who are drawn to this sort of thing. In French with English subtitles.
1972 (R) 97m/C *FR* Bernard Verley, Zouzou, Francoise Verley, Daniel Ceccaldi, Malvina Penne, Babette Ferrier, Suze Randall, Marie-Christine Barrault; *D:* Eric Rohmer; *W:* Eric Rohmer. **VHS, Beta** $59.95 *ING, FCT &&&*

Chocolat A woman recalls her childhood spent in French West Africa and the unfulfilled sexual tension between her mother and black servant. Vivid film provides a host of intriguing characters and offers splendid panoramas of rugged desert landscapes. Profound, if somewhat personal filmmaking from novice director Denis. In French with English subtitles.
1988 (PG-13) 105m/C Mireille Perrier, Emmet Judson Williamson, Cecile Ducasse, Giulia Boschi, Francois Cluzet, Isaach de Bankole, Kenneth Cranham; *D:* Claire Denis; *W:* Claire Denis, Jean-Pol Fargeau. **VHS, Beta** $79.98 *ORI, ING &&&* 1/2

The Chocolate Soldier Dull musical in which an opera star tests his wife's fidelity. Lovers of the musical genre will find that his one has too much talking, not enough singing. Lovers of fine films will realize that more singing would hardly improve things. Based loosely on Molnar's play "The Guardsman."
1941 102m/B Nelson Eddy, Rise Stevens, Nigel Bruce, Florence Bates, Dorothy Gilmore, Nydia Westman; *D:* Roy Del Ruth. **VHS** $19.98 *MGM &*

The Chocolate War An idealistic student and a hardline headmaster butt heads at a Catholic boys' school over an unofficial candy business in this tense, unsettling drama. Glover is notable in his familiar villain role, and Gordon is effective in his first effort as director. Based on the Robert Cormier novel.
1988 (R) 95m/C John Glover, Jenny Wright, Wally Ward, Bud Cort, Ilan Mitchell-Smith, Adam Baldwin; *D:* Keith Gordon; *W:* Keith Gordon. **VHS, Beta** $89.98 *MCG &&&*

The Choice A young woman must make the choice between aborting or keeping her baby in this fairly insipid television drama.
1981 96m/C Susan Clark, Jennifer Warren, Mitchell Ryan, Largo Woodruff; *D:* David Greene. **VHS, Beta** $39.95 *LIV &&*

Choice of Arms A gangster's rural retirement is undone by a dimwitted criminal in this sometimes gripping drama. Montand and Deneuve are serviceable in undemanding roles of the gangster and his glamorous wife; Depardieu is more impressive as the troublemaking punk. In French with English subtitles.
1983 114m/C *FR* Gerard Depardieu, Catherine Deneuve, Yves Montand; *D:* Alain Corneau. **VHS, Beta** $59.95 *ING, MED &&* 1/2

Choice of Weapons Ex-cop trying to solve murders focuses on a curious group of 20th-century men who live within a 12th-century fantasy—jousting for sport and chivalrous honor. Offbeat lance thruster notable for incongruity and all-star cast. *AKA:* A Dirty Knight's Work; Trial by Combat.
1976 88m/C *GB* David Birney, Peter Cushing, Donald Pleasence, Barbara Hershey, John Mills, Margaret Leighton; *D:* Kevin Connor; *W:* Julian Bond. **VHS, Beta** *NO &&*

Choices A hearing-impaired athlete suffers alienation when banned from the football squad. What? Controversial covergirl Moore is a supporting player in this, her first film.
1981 90m/C Paul Carafotes, Victor French, Lelia Goldoni, Val Avery, Dennis Patrick, Demi Moore; *D:* Rami Alon. **VHS, Beta** $49.95 *VHE, HHE, VTR &* 1/2

Choices Scott is a 62-year-old man with a lovely second wife (Bisset) and a rebellious grown daughter (Gilbert), who announces she's pregnant and is getting an abortion. Meanwhile, his wife also discovers she's pregnant and wants the child, although Scott is adamantly opposed to raising a second family at his age. Family strife carried by fine performances. Made for television.
1986 95m/C George C. Scott, Jacqueline Bisset, Melissa Gilbert; *D:* David Lowell Rich. **VHS** *CAF &&* 1/2

The Choirboys Thoroughly mediocre production about overbearing L.A. cops and their off-hours handling of job stress. Few of the strong cast emerge unscathed. Based on the Joseph Wambaugh novel.
1977 (R) 120m/C Charles Durning, Louis Gossett Jr., Perry King, Clyde Kusatsu, Stephen Macht, Tim McIntire, Randy Quaid, Chuck Sacci, Don Stroud, James Woods, Burt Young, Robert Webber, Barbara Rhoades, Vic Tayback, Blair Brown, Charles Haid, Jim Davis; *D:* Robert Aldrich. **VHS, Beta** $14.98 *MCA &*

Choke Canyon An environmentalist thwarts the henchmen of an industrialist eager to coverup a nuclear dump in a picturesque canyon. Good intentions do not necessarily make for a good movie.
1986 (PG) 95m/C Stephen Collins, Bo Svenson, Lance Henriksen; *D:* Chuck Bail. **VHS, Beta** $79.95 *MED &&*

C.H.O.M.P.S. Comedy in which a youthful inventor and a popular robot guard dog become the target of a business takeover. Harmless but unfunny and unfun.
1979 (PG) 90m/C Jim Backus, Valerie Bertinelli, Wesley Eure, Conrad Bain, Chuck McCann, Red Buttons; *D:* Don Chaffey. **VHS, Beta** *NO &* 1/2

Choose Me Comedy-drama about sad, lonely, and often quirky characters linked to an unlikely L.A. radio sex therapist. Moody, memorable fare features especially strong playing from Bujold as a sexually inexperienced sex therapist and Warren as one of her regular listeners. Typically eccentric fare from director Rudolph.
1984 (R) 106m/C Keith Carradine, Genevieve Bujold, Lesley Ann Warren, Rae Dawn Chong, John Larroquette, John Considine; *D:* Alan Rudolph; *W:* Alan Rudolph. **VHS, Beta** $9.98 *MED &&&* 1/2

Chopper Chicks in Zombietown Tough but sexy Chopper Chicks show up in that American vacation mecca, Zombietown, for a little rest and relaxation. Little do they know that a mad mortician has designs on turning our hot heroines into mindless zombie slaves. Can the buxom biker babes thwart the evil embalmer before it's too late, or will they abandon their Harleys to shuffle about in search of human flesh? From the Troma Team.
1991 (R) 86m/C Jamie Rose, Catherine Carlen, Lycia Naff, Vicki Frederick, Kristina Loggia, Martha Quinn, Don Calfa; *D:* Dan Hoskins; *W:* Dan Hoskins. **VHS** $19.95 *COL, NLC &&*

The Choppers Naw, not a fable about false teeth. Teen punk Hall operates a car theft ring made up of fellow punksters. Rock'n'roll tunes by the Hall-meister include the much-overlooked "Monkey in my Hatband."

1961 66m/B Arch Hall Jr., Marianne Gaba, Robert Paget, Tom Brown, Rex Holman, Bruno Ve Sota; *D:* Leigh Jason. **VHS, Beta $16.95** *SNC* ⅔

Chopping Mall A freak electric storm unleashes killer security robots on a band of teens trapped inside the mall. Nobody shops. Premise undone by obscure humor, lack of flairful action, or horror. Updated imitation of the 1973 TV movie "Trapped." *AKA:* Kill-bots.
1986 (R) 77m/C Paul Bartel, Mary Woronov, Barbara Crampton, John Terlesky, Dick Miller; *D:* Jim Wynorski; *W:* Jim Wynorski. **VHS, Beta $19.98** *LIV* ⅔½

A Chorus Line A range of performers reveal their insecurities and aspirations while auditioning before a hardnosed director in this adaptation of the popular, overblown Broadway musical. Singing and dancing is rarely rousing. Director Attenborough probably wasn't the right choice for this one. ♫ Dance 10, Looks 3; What I Did for Love; At the Ballet; I Can Do That; Let Me Dance For You; I Hope I Get It; Nothing; The Music and the Mirror; And...; Hello Twelve, Hello Thirteen, Hello Love; Surprise, Surprise; One.
1985 (PG-13) 118m/C Michael Douglas, Audrey Landers, Gregg Burge, Alyson Reed, Janet Jones, Michael Blevins, Terrence Mann, Cameron English, Vicki Frederick, Nicole Fosse, Michelle Johnson; *D:* Richard Attenborough; *M:* Arnold Schulman; *M:* Marvin Hamlisch, Ralph Burns. **VHS, Beta, 8mm $14.98** *SUE, SUP, NLC* ⅔⅔

A Chorus of Disapproval Adaptation of prolific Alan Ayckbourn's play about a withdrawn, somewhat dimwitted British widower who attempts social interaction by joining community theater, then finds himself embroiled in romantic shenanigans and theatrical intrigue. Irons is fine in the lead, but Hopkins sparkles in the more spectacular role of the musical production's demanding but beleaguered director. Seagrove is impressive as an amoral sexpot. Sharper focus from director Winner would have improved this one, but the film is fun even when it isn't particularly funny.
1989 (PG) 105m/C *GB* Jeremy Irons, Anthony Hopkins, Jenny Seagrove, Lionel Jeffries, Patsy Kensit, Gareth Hunt, Prunella Scales, Sylvia Syms, Richard Briers, Barbara Ferris; *D:* Michael Winner; *W:* Michael Winner; *M:* John Du Prez. **VHS, Beta** *NO* ⅔½

The Chosen Executive of a nuclear power facility located in the Sahara Desert realizes that his son is the Anti-Christ born on the world's destruction. This truly horrible film provides nothing in terms of entertainment. It's rarely even laughably bad. *AKA:* Holocaust 2000.
1977 (R) 102m/C Kirk Douglas, Simon Ward, Agostina Belli, Anthony Quayle, Virginia McKenna, Alexander Knox; *D:* Alberto De Martino; *M:* Ennio Morricone. **VHS, Beta $59.98** *FOX, LIV, VES* Woof!

Christ Stopped at Eboli Subdued work about an anti-Fascist writer exiled to rural Italy in the 1930s. Excellent performances from the lead Volante and supporting players Papas and Cuny. Slow, contemplative film is probably director Rosi's masterpiece. Adapted from Carlo Levi's book. In Italian with English subtitles. *AKA:* Eboli.
1979 118m/C *IT FR* Gian Marie Volonte, Irene Papas, Paolo Bonacelli, Francois Simon, Alain Cuny, Lea Massari; *D:* Francesco Rosi; *W:* Francesco Rosi. **VHS, Beta $59.95** *COL, APD, ING* ⅔⅔⅔⅔

Christabel Condensed version of the BBC mini-series based on the true-life WWII exploits of Christabel Bielenberg, a British woman who battled to save her German husband from the horrors of the Ravensbruck concentration camp.
1989 148m/C *GB* Elizabeth Hurley, Stephen Dillon, Nigel le Vaillant, Geoffrey Palmer; *W:* Dennis Potter. **VHS, Beta $19.98** *FOX, ING* ⅔⅔

Christian the Lion The true story of Christian, a lion cub raised in a London zoo, who is transported to Africa to learn to live with other lions. With the principals from "Born Free."
1976 (G) 87m/C *GB* Virginia McKenna, Bill Travers, George Adamson, James Hill; *D:* Bill Travers. **VHS, Beta $29.95** *UNI* ⅔⅔½

Christiane F. Gripping, visually impressive story of a bored German girl's decline into drug use and prostitution. Based on a West German magazine article. Sobering and dismal look at a milieu in which innocence and youth have run amok. The film's impact is only somewhat undermined by poor dubbing. Bowie appears in a concert sequence.
1982 (R) 120m/C *GE* Natja Brunkhorst, Thomas Haustein, David Bowie; *D:* Uli Edel; *M:* David Bowie. **VHS, Beta $69.95** *MED, GLV* ⅔⅔

Christina Gloomy suspense fare in which a beautiful woman pays a forlorn fellow $25,000 to marry her, then disappears as he begins to actually fall in love with her. His search takes him to various gothic settings. Intriguing, but not really fulfilling. Parkins, however, is appropriately mysterious in the lead.
1974 (PG) 95m/C *CA* Barbara Parkins, Peter Haskell; *D:* Paul Krasny. **VHS, Beta $59.95** *MPI* ⅔⅔½

Christine Unassuming teen gains possession of a classic auto equipped with a murderous will. The car more than returns the care and consideration its owner provides it. Are you listening GMC? Based on a novel by Stephen King.
1984 (R) 110m/C Keith Gordon, John Stockwell, Alexandra Paul, Robert Prosky, Harry Dean Stanton, Kelly Preston; *D:* John Carpenter; *W:* Bill Phillips; *M:* John Carpenter, Alan Howarth. **VHS, Beta, 8mm $14.95** *COL* ⅔⅔½

A Christmas Carol An early version of Dickens' classic tale about miser Scrooge, who is instilled with the Christmas spirit after a grim evening with some ghosts. Good playing from Owen as Scrooge and Lockhart as the hapless Bob Cratchett. Scary graveyard sequence too.
1938 70m/B Reginald Owen, Gene Lockhart, Terence Kilburn, Leo G. Carroll, Lynne Carver, Ann Rutherford; *D:* Edwin L. Marin. **VHS, Beta $19.95** *MGM* ⅔⅔⅔

A Christmas Carol A fine retelling of the classic tale about a penny-pinching holiday hater who learns appreciation of Christmas following a frightful, revealing evening with supernatural visitors. Perhaps the best rendering of the Dickens classic. "And God bless Tiny Tim!" *AKA:* Scrooge.
1951 86m/B *GB* Alastair Sim, Kathleen Harrison, Jack Warner, Michael Hordern, Patrick Macnee, Mervyn Johns, Hermione Baddeley, Clifford Mollison, George Cole, Carol Marsh, Miles Malleson, Ernest Thesiger, Hattie Jacques, Peter Bull, Hugh Dempster; *W:* Noel Langley; *M:* Richard Addinsell. **VHS, Beta $19.95** *MLB, HMV* ⅔⅔⅔⅔

A Christmas Carol Musical version of the Dickens' classic about a stingy old man who is visited by three ghosts on Christmas Eve.
1954 54m/B Fredric March, Basil Rathbone, Ray Middleton, Bob Sweeney, Christopher Cook. **VHS, Beta** *CFV* ⅔⅔

The Christmas Coal Mine Miracle Syrupy made-for-television story about miners struggling for survival in a collapsed mine on Christmas Eve. Also titled "Christmas Miracle in Caulfield, U.S.A."
1977 98m/C Mitchell Ryan, Kurt Russell, Andrew Prine, John Carradine, Barbara Babcock, Melissa Gilbert, Don Porter, Shelby Leverington; *D:* Judd Taylor. **VHS, Beta $59.98** *FOX* ⅔½

Christmas Comes to Willow Creek Mutually antagonistic brothers are enlisted to deliver Christmas gifts to an isolated Alaskan community. Can brotherly love be far off? Two leads played together in the rowdy TV series "Dukes of Hazzard." This is hardly an improvement.
1987 96m/C John Schneider, Tom Wopat, Hoyt Axton, Zachary Ansley, Kim Delaney; *D:* Richard Lang; *M:* Charles Fox. **VHS, Beta $14.98** *LIV, FHE* ⅔⅔

Christmas in Connecticut Lightweight comedy about a housekeeping magazine's successful columnist who isn't quite the expert homemaker she presents herself to be. When a war veteran is invited to her home as part of a publicity gimmick, she must master the ways of housekeeping or reveal her incompetence. Stanwyck is winning in the lead role. Also available in a colorized version. *AKA:* Indiscretion.
1945 101m/B Barbara Stanwyck, Reginald Gardiner, Sydney Greenstreet, Dennis (Stanley Morner) Morgan, S.Z. Sakall, Una O'Connor, Robert Shayne, Joyce Compton; *D:* Peter Godfrey. **VHS, Beta $19.98** *MGM* ⅔⅔⅔

Christmas in Connecticut Cannon hosts a weekly television show as America's favorite homemaker/hostess. A local forest ranger (Kristofferson) becomes a hero by saving a little boy's life and her network stages a media event by inviting him to her home for a traditional Christmas dinner. There's only one problem: she can't cook. Schwarzenegger's directorial debut lacks challenge in this fluffy remake. See the original instead. Made for cable television.
1992 93m/C Dyan Cannon, Kris Kristofferson, Tony Curtis, Richard Roundtree, Kelly Cinnante, Gene Lithgow, Vivian Bonnell; *D:* Arnold Schwarzenegger. **VHS $14.95** *TTC* ⅔⅔

Christmas in July A young man goes on a spending spree when he thinks he's won a sweepstakes. Things take a turn for the worse when he finds out that it was all a practical joke. Powell provides a winning performance in this second film from comic master Sturges.
1940 67m/B Dick Powell, Ellen Drew, Raymond Walburn, William Demarest, Franklin Pangborn; *D:* Preston Sturges. **VHS, Beta $14.98** *MCA, FCT* ⅔⅔⅔½

The Christmas Kid A desperado struggles to determine his true identity while stopping in a frontier town. Gunplay ensues. Don't bother with this one.
1968 87m/C *SP* Jeffrey Hunter, Louis Hayward, Gustavo Rojo, Perla Cristal, Luis Prendes; *D:* Sidney Pink. **VHS** *NO* ⅔½

Christmas Lilies of the Field This made-for-television sequel to "Lilies of the Field" follows an ex-soldier who returns to the church he helped build. This time he sets out to build an orphanage.
1984 98m/C Billy Dee Williams, Maria Schell, Fay Hauser, Judith Piquet; *D:* Ralph Nelson. **VHS, Beta $29.95** *MPI* ⅔½

A Christmas Story Unlikely but winning comedy of a boy's single-minded obsession to acquire a Red Ryder BB-gun for Christmas. Particularly great sequence involving an impatient department-store Santa.

Fun for everyone. Based on "In God We Trust, All Others Pay Cash," an autobiographical story by Jean Shepard.
1983 (PG) 95m/C Peter Billingsley, Darren McGavin, Melinda Dillon, Ian Petrella; *D:* Bob (Benjamin) Clark; *W:* Bob (Benjamin) Clark, Leigh Brown, Jean Shepherd. **VHS, Beta $19.98** *MGM &&&*

The Christmas That Almost Wasn't Loathsome humbug decides to destroy Christmas forever by removing Santa Claus from the North Pole. Crude Italian-made children's film nonetheless remembered fondly by a generation of kids. ♫The Christmas That Almost Wasn't; Christmas is Coming; Hustle Bustle; I'm Bad; Kids Get All the Breaks; The Name of the Song is Prune; Nothing to do But Wait; Santa Claus; Time For Christmas; What Are Children Like When They're Fast Asleep?; Why Can't Every Day Be Christmas?. *AKA:* Il Natale Che Quasi Non Fu.
1966 (G) 95m/C *IT* Rossano Brazzi, Paul Tripp, Lidia Brazzi, Sonny Fox, Mischa Auer; *D:* Rossano Brazzi. **VHS, Beta $9.99** *HBO &½*

A Christmas to Remember Depression-era Minnesota farmer who has lost his son in WWI brings his city-bred grandson to the farm for a holiday visit. Somber, occasionally poignant film buoyed by Robards presence, and Saint's as well. Made for television.
1978 (G) 96m/C Jason Robards Jr., Eva Marie Saint, Joanne Woodward; *D:* George Englund. **VHS, Beta $69.95** *NO &&½*

The Christmas Wife A lonely man pays a woman to be his holiday companion at a mountain retreat. Sturdy performances by Robards and Harris manage to keep this one from going to the dogs. Based on a story by Helen Norris. Made for cable television.
1988 73m/C Jason Robards Jr., Julie Harris, Don Francks, Patricia Hamilton, Deborah Grover, James Eckhouse; *D:* David Jones. **VHS, Beta $79.99** *HBO &&½*

A Christmas Without Snow Made-for-television film about a lonely divorced woman finding communal happiness within a local church choir led by a crusty choir master.
1980 96m/C Michael Learned, John Houseman, Ramon Bieri, James Cromwell, Valerie Curtin, Ruth Nelson, Beah Richards, Calvin Levels; *D:* John Korty. **VHS, Beta $59.98** *FOX &&½*

Christopher Columbus Step-by-step biography of the fifteenth-century explorer, his discovery of America, the fame that first greeted him, and his last days.
1949 103m/C *GB* Fredric March, Florence Eldridge, Francis L. Sullivan; *D:* David MacDonald. **VHS, Beta $19.95** *LCA, IGP &&½*

Christopher Columbus The man who explored the New World is shown in all his flawed complexity in this film that takes a contemporary approach to the discoveries and character of Christopher Columbus. Shot on location in Spain, Malta, and the Dominican Republic, the film features an exact replica of Columbus' flagship, the Santa Maria. Originally aired as a six-hour television miniseries.
1985 128m/C Gabriel Byrne, Faye Dunaway, Oliver Reed, Max von Sydow, Eli Wallach, Nicol Williamson, Jose Ferrer, Virna Lisi, Raf Vallone; *D:* Alberto Lattuada. **VHS $89.95** *WAR &&½*

Christopher Columbus: The Discovery The 500th anniversary of Columbus' voyage brought this lame excursion in historical biography to the screen briefly. Columbus is portrayed as a swashbuckling adventurer who finally gets the Queen of Spain to agree to finance his voyage of discovery (which primarily consists of discovering a lot of bare-breasted native women). Story is secondary to the banality of the entire production, including the acting. Brando is briefly seen as Torquemada—another film in which he took his substantial paycheck and ran.
1992 (PG-13) 120m/C Georges Corraface, Rachel Ward, Tom Selleck, Marlon Brando, Robert Davi, Oliver Cotton, Benicio Del Toro, Catherine Zeta Jones, Matthieu Carriere, Nigel Terry, Branscombe Richmond; *D:* John Glen; *M:* Cliff Eidelman. **VHS, Beta $94.99** *WAR &*

Christopher Strong Interesting Hepburn turn as a daredevil aviatrix who falls in love with a married British statesman.
1933 77m/B Katharine Hepburn, Billie Burke, Colin Clive, Helen Chandler; *D:* Dorothy Arzner. **VHS, Beta $19.98** *RKO, TTC &&½*

Chrome and Hot Leather A Green Beret is out for revenge after vicious bikers kill his fiance. Conventional, tasteless genre fare notable only as Gaye's first film.
1971 (PG) 91m/C William Smith, Tony Young, Michael Haynes, Peter Brown, Marvin Gaye, Michael Stearns, Katherine Baumann, Wes Bishop, Herbert Jeffries; *D:* Lee Frost. **VHS** *NO &½*

Chrome Hearts Rebel biker rescues a buxom gal from a fate worse than death, than vies for control of the gang. Laughable, with Namath hopeless in his film debut. Redeemed only by Ann-Margret in continual disarray. *AKA:* C.C. & Company.
1970 (R) 91m/C Joe Namath, Ann-Margret, William Smith, Jennifer Billingsley, Teda Bracci, Greg Mullavey, Sid Haig, Bruce Glover; *D:* Seymour Robbie. **VHS, Beta $14.95** *COL, SUE, SIM &*

Chrome Soldiers Five Vietnam veterans come together to avenge a friend's murder in a town controlled by drug dealers. Busey, as the murdered man's brother, leads the "Chrome Soldiers" in their battle to expose the killers and end local corruption.
1992 92m/C Gary Busey, Ray Sharkey, William Atherton, Yaphet Kotto, Nicholas Guest, Kim Robillard, Norman Skaggs, D. David Morin; *D:* Thomas J. Wright; *W:* Nick Randall. **VHS, Beta $14.95** *PAR &&*

The Chronicles of Narnia Exceptional BBC production of the C.S. Lewis fantasy about four brave children who battle evil in a mythical land where the animals talk and strange creatures roam the countryside. In three volumes; aired on PBS as part of the "Wonderworks" family movie series.
1989 180m/C *GB* Barbara Kellerman, Jeffery Perry, Richard Dempsey, Sophie Cook, Jonathan Scott, Sophie Wilcox, David Thwaites, Tom Baker; *D:* Alex Kirby. **VHS $29.95** *FCT, PME, TVC &&*

Chu Chu & the Philly Flash A has-been baseball player and a lame dance teacher meet while hustling the same corner; he sells hot watches, she's a one-woman band. A briefcase full of government secrets soon involves them with the feds, the mob, and a motley collection of back-alley bums. Insipid comedy is actually worse than its title, with Burnett and Arkin both trying too hard. Supporters Warden, Aiello, and Glover don't help either.
1981 (PG) 102m/C Alan Arkin, Carol Burnett, Jack Warden, Danny Aiello, Ruth Buzzi, Danny Glover, Lou Jacobi; *D:* David Lowell Rich. **VHS, Beta $59.98** *FOX Woof!*

Chuck Amuck: The Movie An in-depth look at legendary animator/director Chuck Jones.

1991 51m/C Chuck Jones. **VHS $14.95** *WAR, FCT, WTA Woof!*

Chuck Berry: Hail! Hail! Rock 'n' Roll Engaging, energetic portrait of one of rock's founding fathers, via interviews, behind-the-scenes footage and performance clips of Berry at 60. Songs featured: "Johnny B. Goode," "Roll Over Beethoven," "Maybelline," and more. Appearances by Eric Clapton, Etta James, John and Julian Lennon, Roy Orbison, Linda Ronstadt, Bo Diddley and Bruce Springsteen among others.
1987 (PG) 121m/C Chuck Berry, Eric Clapton, Etta James, Robert Cray, Julian Lennon, Keith Richards, Linda Ronstadt, John Lennon, Roy Orbison, Bo Diddley, Jerry Lee Lewis, Bruce Springsteen, Kareem Abdul-Jabbar; *D:* Taylor Hackford. **VHS, Beta $19.95** *MCA, MVD, FCT &&&½*

C.H.U.D. Cannibalistic Humanoid Underground Dwellers are what it's about. Exposed to toxic wastes, a race of flesh-craving, sewer-dwelling monstrosities goes food shopping on the streets of New York. Don't be fooled by the presence of real actors, this one is inexcusable. Followed by a sequel.
1984 (R) 90m/C John Heard, Daniel Stern, Christopher Curry, Kim Greist, John Goodman; *D:* Douglas Cheek. **VHS, Beta $9.99** *STE, MRV Woof!*

C.H.U.D. 2: Bud the Chud Asinine teens steal a corpse that is actually a zombie cannibal capable of passing the trait to anyone it bites (but doesn't eat entirely). Graham excels as the kidnapped corpse, but this horror-comedy is consistently repellent. Contains one of Jagger's few film appearances, a situation of no despair.
1989 (R) 84m/C Brian Robbins, Bill Calvert, Gerrit Graham, Tricia Leigh Fisher, Bianca Jagger, Robert Vaughn, Larry Cedar; *D:* David Irving. **VHS, Beta $14.98** *LIV, VES, IME Woof!*

Chuka A gunfighter tries to resolve a conflict between Indians and unlikeable troops while simultaneously romancing the fort's beautiful occupant. Pedestrian western features convincing playing from the always reliable Taylor.
1967 105m/C Rod Taylor, Ernest Borgnine, John Mills, Lucianna Paluzzi, James Whitmore, Angela Dorian, Louis Hayward, Michael Cole, Hugh Reilly; *D:* Gordon Douglas. **VHS $14.95** *PAR, FCT &&½*

A Chump at Oxford Two street cleaners foil a bank robbery and receive an all-expenses-paid education at Oxford as their reward. This loopy Laurel and Hardy vehicle provides regular amusement in detailing the duo's exploits in Britain.
1940 63m/B Stan Laurel, Oliver Hardy, James Finlayson, Wilfrid Lucas, Peter Cushing, Charlie Hall; *D:* Alfred Goulding. **VHS, Beta $14.98** *MED, CCB, FCT &&½*

The Church Italian thrill-meister Argento scripted and produced this ecclesiastical gorefest. A gargoyle-glutted gothic cathedral which happens to stand on the site of a gruesome mass murder is renovated, and the kirk-cleaning turns into a special-effects loaded demonic epiphany. It'll have you muttering your pater noster. Unrated, it's also available in an R-rated version. *AKA:* La Chiesa.
1990 110m/C *IT* Tomas Arana, Hugh Quarshine, Feodor Chaliapin; *D:* Michele (Michael) Soavi; *W:* Dario Argento; *M:* Keith Emerson. **VHS** *NO &&½*

Churchill and the Generals The true story of how Winston Churchill led England away from the bleak Dunkirk battle and rallied the Allied generals to a D-Day victory. Based upon Churchill's memoirs.

1981 180m/C Timothy West, Joseph Cotten, Arthur Hill, Eric Porter, Richard Dysart. **VHS, Beta** $14.99 *PSM ♂♂*

C.I.A.: Code Name Alexa Alexa is the beautiful and deadly protege of Victor, who heads an international crime ring. A CIA agent decides the best way to stop Victor is to turn Alexa against her boss. Lots of action and violence.
1992 (R) 93m/C Kathleen Kinmont, Lorenzo Lamas, Alex Cord, O.J. Simpson, Stephen Quadros, Pamela Dixon, Michael Smith; *D:* Joseph Merhi. **VHS** $89.95 *PMH ♂½*

C.I.A. 2: Target Alexa When a nuclear guidance system is stolen from a government facility CIA agent Mark Graver (Lamas) reteams with former terrorist Alexa (Kinmont) to retrieve the system from international terrorist Franz Klug (Savage). Complicating things are ex-CIA agent Straker (Ryan), who now heads his own commando army and wants to sell the device to the highest bidder.
1994 90m/C Lorenzo Lamas, Kathleen Kinmont, John Savage, John P. Ryan, Pamela Dixon, Larry Manetti; *D:* Lorenzo Lamas; *W:* Michael January. **VHS** *PMH ♂♂*

Ciao Federico! Fellini Directs Satyricon A documentary of Frederico Fellini's filming of Petronius' "Satyricon." Portrays the Italian filmmaker's larger-than-life directorial approach and relationship with his actors. In English and Italian, with English subtitles.
1969 60m/C Federico Fellini, Martin Potter, Hiram Keller, Roman Polanski, Sharon Tate; *D:* Gideon Bachmann. **VHS, Beta** $29.95 *MFV, ING, TPV ♂♂*

The Cigarette Girl of Mosselprom A lowly cigarette girl is thrust into the world of moviemaking in this sharp Russian satire. Silent with orchestral score.
1924 78m/B *RU D:* Yuri Zhelyabuzhsky. **VHS** $29.95 *KIV, FCT, ING ♂♂½*

Cimarron Hopelessly overblown saga of an American frontier family from 1890 to 1915. Hokey, cliched, with only sporadic liveliness. How did this one win an Oscar? An adaptation of Edna Ferber's novel, featuring Dunne in an early major role. Remade in 1960.
1930 130m/B Richard Dix, Irene Dunne, Estelle Taylor, Nance O'Neill, William Collier Jr., Roscoe Ates, George E. Stone, Stanley Fields, Edna May Oliver, Dennis O'Keefe; *D:* Wesley Ruggles. Academy Awards '31: Best Adapted Screenplay, Best Interior Decoration, Best Picture; Nominations: Best Actor (Dix), Best Actress (Dunne), Best Cinematography, Best Director (Ruggles); National Board of Review Awards '31: 10 Best Films of the Year. **VHS, Beta** $19.98 *MGM, BTV ♂♂*

Cimarron Director Mann's remake of the 1931 Academy Award-winning film about frontier life in Oklahoma. This version features Ford as a carefree survivor of the Old West with an extreme case of wanderlust. Schell plays his civilizing wife. Based on Edna Ferber's novel.
1960 140m/C Glenn Ford, Maria Schell, Anne Baxter, Arthur O'Connell, Russ Tamblyn, Mercedes McCambridge, Vic Morrow, Robert Keith, Charles McGraw; *D:* Anthony Mann; *W:* Arnold Schulman; *M:* Franz Waxman. **VHS** $19.98 *MGM ♂♂½*

The Cincinnati Kid Cardsharks gather for a major stakes poker game, with some romance on the side. Conventional fare helped along by serviceable performances and some stunning cinematography. Sam Peckinpah was dismissed as director from this one. Guess he took the script with him.

1965 104m/C Steve McQueen, Edward G. Robinson, Ann-Margret, Tuesday Weld, Karl Malden, Joan Blondell, Rip Torn, Jack Weston, Cab Calloway; *D:* Norman Jewison; *W:* Ring Lardner Jr., Terry Southern. **VHS, Beta** $19.98 *MGM ♂♂½*

Cinderella Classic Disney animated fairytale about the slighted beauty who outshines her evil stepsisters at a royal ball, then returns to her grim existence before the handsome prince finds her again. Engaging film, with a wicked stepmother, kindly fairy godmother, and singing mice. ♫ Cinderella; Bibbidy-Bobbidi-Boo; So This Is Love; A Dream Is a Wish Your Heart Makes; The Work Song; Oh Sing, Sweet Nightingale.
1950 76m/C *D:* Wilfred Jackson; *V:* Ilene Woods, William Phipps, Verna Felton, James MacDonald. Academy Awards '50 Nominations: Best Song ("Bibbidy-Bobbidi-Boo"), Best Sound, Best Original Score; Venice Film Festival '50: Special Jury Prize. **VHS, Beta** $26.99 *DIS, KUI ♂♂♂½*

Cinderella A made-for-television rendition of the fairy tale as scored by Rodgers and Hammerstein. Songs include "The Loveliness of Evening," "Ten Minutes Ago" and "Do I Love You (Because You're Beautiful?)."
1964 83m/C Lesley Ann Warren, Ginger Rogers, Walter Pidgeon, Stuart Damon, Celeste Holm; *D:* Charles S. Dubin; *M:* Richard Rodgers, Oscar Hammerstein. **VHS, Beta** $19.98 *FOX, FCT ♂♂*

Cinderella From the "Faerie Tale Theatre" comes the classic tale of a poor girl who goes to a ball to meet the man of her dreams, despite her nasty stepmother and stepsisters.
1984 60m/C Jennifer Beals, Jean Stapleton, Matthew Broderick, Eve Arden; *D:* Mark Cullingham. **VHS, Beta** $14.98 *KUI, FOX, FCT ♂♂*

Cinderella Liberty Bittersweet romance in which a kindly sailor falls for a brash hooker with a son. Sometimes funny, sometimes moving, with sometimes crude direction overcome by truly compelling performances from Caan and Mason. Story written by Darryl Ponicsan from his novel.
1973 (R) 117m/C James Caan, Marsha Mason, Eli Wallach, Kirk Calloway, Burt Young, Bruce Kirby, Dabney Coleman, Sally Kirkland; *D:* Mark Rydell; *W:* Darryl Ponicsan; *M:* John Williams. Academy Awards '73 Nominations: Best Actress (Mason), Best Song ("You're So Nice to Be Around"), Best Original Score; Golden Globe Awards '74: Best Actress—Drama (Mason). **VHS, Beta** $59.98 *FOX ♂♂♂*

Cinderella 2000 Soft-core musical version of the classic fairy tale. It's the year 2047 and sex is outlawed, except by computer. Strains of Sugarman's score, including "Doin' Without" and "We All Need Love," set the stage for Erhardt's Cinderella to meet her Prince Charming at that conventional single prince romance venue, a sex orgy. Trouble is, it wasn't a shoe Cinderella lost before she fled, and the charming one must interface, as it were, with the local pretenders to the throne in order to find his lost princess. Touching.
1978 (R) 86m/C Catharine Erhardt, Jay B. Larson, Vaughn Armstrong; *D:* Al Adamson; *M:* Sparky Sugarman. **VHS** *NO ♂♂*

Cinderfella This twist on the classic children's fairy tale features Lewis as the hapless buffoon guided by his fairy godfather. Somewhat overdone, with extended talking sequences and gratuitous musical interludes. Lewis, though, mugs effectively.
1960 88m/C Jerry Lewis, Ed Wynn, Judith Anderson, Anna Maria Alberghetti, Henry Silva, Count Basie, Robert Hutton; *D:* Frank Tashlin; *W:* Frank Tashlin. **VHS, Beta** $59.95 *LIV ♂♂½*

Cinema Paradiso Memoir of a boy's life working at a movie theatre in small-town Italy after WWII. Film aspires to both majestic sweep and stirring poignancy, but only occasionally hits its target. Still manages to move the viewer, and it features a suitably low-key performance by the masterful Noiret. Autobiographically inspired script written by Tornatore. The version shown in America is approximately a half-hour shorter than the original Italian form. *AKA:* Nuovo Cinema Paradiso.
1988 123m/C *IT* Philippe Noiret, Jacques Perrin, Salvatore Cascio, Mario Leonardi, Agnes Nano, Leopoldo Trieste; *D:* Giuseppe Tornatore; *W:* Giuseppe Tornatore; *M:* Ennio Morricone. **VHS, 8mm** $89.99 *HBO, APD, ING ♂♂♂½*

Cinema Shrapnel A tour through the wonderful world of screen hype and bad movies, with scenes from terrible trailers, maudlin fundraising shorts, and glitzy movie premieres.
1987 60m/C **VHS, Beta** *NO ♂♂♂*

Cinemagic A compilation of four short horror and science fiction films including "Nightfright," "Dr. Dobermind," "Illegal Alien" and "The Thing in the Basement."
1985 60m/C **VHS, Beta** $39.95 *MPI ♂♂♂*

Circle Canyon In a remote canyon two opposing outlaw gangs battle to the death.
1933 48m/B Buddy Roosevelt. **VHS, Beta** *NO ♂*

Circle Man A made-for-video action drama about the underground sporting phenomenon, bare-knuckle fighting.
1987 90m/C William Sanderson. **VHS, Beta** $79.95 *ACA ♂*

Circle of Death Average formula western about a white boy who is raised as an Indian. Later he falls in love with a white girl and leaves the tribe.
1936 55m/B Monte Montana, Yakima Canutt. **VHS, Beta** $19.95 *NOS, VDM ♂½*

Circle of Fear An ex-hitman who worked for the Mob upends the black market for sex and drugs in the Philippines while looking for his daughter who was sold into a sex slave ring. El cheapo exploiter.
1989 (R) 90m/C *PH* Patrick Dollaghan, Welsey Pfenning, Joey Aresco, Vernon Wells; *D:* Clark Henderson. **VHS, Beta** $44.98 *MGM ♂½*

Circle of Iron Plenty of action and martial arts combat abound in this story of one man's eternal quest for truth. Originally co-written by and intended for Bruce Lee as a rib-crunching vehicle, until he died before production began and was replaced by Kung-Fu Carradine. A cut above most chopsocky actioners. Filmed in Israel. *AKA:* The Silent Flute.
1978 (R) 102m/C *GB* Jeff Cooper, David Carradine, Roddy McDowall, Eli Wallach, Christopher Lee; *D:* Richard Moore; *W:* Bruce Lee, James Coburn, Sterling Silliphant. **VHS, Beta** $24.98 *SUE ♂♂½*

Circle of Love Episodic melodrama drifts from romance to romance in contemporary Paris. A somewhat pretentious remake of Ophuls classic "La Ronde," which was in turn adapted from Arthur Schnitzler's play. Credible performers are undone by Vadim's strained direction.
1964 110m/C *FR* Jane Fonda, Francine Berge, Marie DuBois, Jean-Claude Brialy, Catherine Spaak, Claude Giraud; *D:* Roger Vadim; *W:* Jean Anouilh. **VHS, Beta** *JEF ♂♂*

Circle of Power Mimieux must cure various business men of their problems (homosexuality, alcoholism and the like) to help them become better executives. Intriguing and somewhat disturbing, supposedly

based on a true story. *AKA:* Brainwash; The Naked Weekend; Mystique.
1983 (R) 103m/C *GB* Yvette Mimieux, John Considine, Terence Knox, Cindy Pickett, Christopher Allport; **D:** Bobby Roth. **VHS $59.95** *MED* &woove;&woove;½

Circle of Two A platonic friendship between an aging artist and a young girl is misunderstood by others. Well, of course they do meet in a porno theater. Pedestrian fare adapted from a story by Marie Therese Baird.
1980 (PG) 90m/C *CA* Richard Burton, Tatum O'Neal, Kate Reid; **D:** Jules Dassin. **VHS, Beta $69.95** *VES, VTR* &woove;&woove;

Circonstances Attenuantes French classic about a retired judge who moves to the outskirts of Paris with his wife and attempts to convert the locals from disreputable to law-abiding citizens. Also available dubbed. *AKA:* Extenuating Circumstances.
1936 90m/B *FR* Michel Simon, Arletty; **D:** Jean Boyer. **VHS $59.95** *FRA, FCT* &woove;&woove;½

Circuitry Man Post-apocalyptic saga of future American life as a woman tries to deliver a briefcase full of computer chips to the underground Big Apple. Along the way she runs into Plughead, a humanoid with electrical outlets that allow him to "plug in" to other people's fantasies. Intelligent retelling of a standard tale with an inspired soundtrack by Deborah Holland. Witty and original.
1990 (R) 85m/C Jim Metzler, Dana Wheeler-Nicholson, Lu Leonard, Vernon Wells, Barbara Alyn Woods, Dennis Christopher; **D:** Steven Lovy; **W:** Steven Lovy; **M:** Deborah Holland. **VHS $19.95** *COL* &woove;&woove;½

The Circus Classic comedy silent details the tramp's exploits as a member of a traveling circus, including a romance with the bareback rider. Hilarious, less sentimental than most of Chaplin's feature films. Chaplin won a special Academy Award for "versatility and genius in writing, acting, directing and producing" for this one. Outrageous final scenes.
1919 105m/B Charlie Chaplin, Merna Kennedy; **D:** Charlie Chaplin. **VHS $19.98** *FOX* &woove;&woove;&woove;½

Circus Angel The renowned director of "The Red Balloon" creates a fantasy about a klutzy burglar transformed by a found nightgown into an angel. He begins to serve the dreams and actions of an odd lot of characters. Subtitled in English.
1965 80m/B *FR* Philippe Avron, Mirielle Negre; **D:** Albert Lamorisse. **VHS, Beta $14.98** *SUE, NLC* &woove;&woove;&woove;

Circus of Fear A travelling troupe is stalked by a murderer. The unedited version is occasionally scary. *AKA:* Psycho-Circus.
1967 92m/C *GB GE* Christopher Lee, Leo Genn, Anthony Newlands, Heinz Drache, Eddi Arent, Klaus Kinski, Margaret Lee, Suzy Kendall; **D:** John Llewellyn Moxey. **VHS, Beta $19.95** *INC, SNC, NOS* &woove;½

Circus of Horrors Nip 'n tuck horror about a plastic surgeon who takes over a circus to escape a disfigured patient bent on revenge. The circus is staffed by former patients with new faces who, one by one, fall victim in fine circus style. A bloody one-ring extravaganza.
1960 87m/C *GB* Donald Pleasence, Anton Diffring, Erika Remberg, Yvonne Monlaur, Jane Hylton, Kenneth Griffith; **D:** Sidney Hayers. **VHS, Beta $9.98** *REP* &woove;

Circus World A circus boss tries to navigate a reckless, romancing crew through a European tour while searching for aerialist he loved 15 years before and whose daugh-

---

ter he has reared. Too long and too familiar, but nonetheless well done with an excellent finale. *AKA:* The Magnificent Showman.
1964 132m/C John Wayne, Rita Hayworth, Claudia Cardinale, Lloyd Nolan, Richard Conte; **D:** Henry Hathaway; **W:** Ben Hecht, James Edward Grant, Julian Halevy. **VHS, Beta $29.98** *VCI* &woove;&woove;½

The Cisco Kid Renaldo is the heroic Cisco, a do-gooder who, with his sidekick Pancho, championed the poor and downtrodden. The first TV series shown in color. Features two episodes: "Quarterhorse" and "The Postmaster." Additional episodes are available.
1950 60m/C Duncan Renaldo, Leo Carrillo. **VHS** *HEG, MOV* &woove;&woove;½

The Cisco Kid The Cisco Kid and his sidekick Pancho went from O. Henry's short story, to silent movies, talkies, a '50s TV series, and now this made for TV movie. Benito Juarez is leading an uprising to overthrow the French-backed Emperor Maximilian in 1867 Mexico. Cisco's (Smits) supplying the rebels with guns while carrying on romantic escapades (watch for the tango). Meanwhile, true-believer Pancho tries to convince his friend to become a revolutionary. Lighthearted with pedestrian action shots. Filmed on location in Mexico.
1994 96m/C Jimmy Smits, Richard "Cheech" Marin, Sadie Frost, Tim Thomerson, Bruce Payne; **D:** Luis Valdez; **W:** Michael Kane, Luis Valdez. **VHS** *TTC* &woove;&woove;½

The Citadel From the A.J. Cronin novel, the intelligent and honest Hollywood drama about a young British doctor who is morally corrupted by his move from a poor mining village to a well-off practice treating wealthy hypochondriacs. Somewhat hokey but still consistently entertaining, with Donat fine in the lead.
1938 114m/C *GB* Robert Donat, Rosalind Russell, Rex Harrison, Ralph Richardson, Emlyn Williams, Penelope Dudley Ward; **D:** King Vidor. Academy Awards '38 Nominations: Best Actor (Donat), Best Director (Vidor), Best Picture, Best Screenplay; National Board of Review Awards '38: 10 Best Films of the Year; New York Film Critics Awards '38: Best Film. **VHS, Beta $24.95** *MGM, HMV* &woove;&woove;&woove;

Citizen Cohn An appallingly fascinating look at a human monster. Told in hallucinatory flashbacks, as he lays dying from AIDS, Roy Cohn is a lawyer and power broker, probably best-remembered as the malevolent sidekick to Communist-hunting Senator Joseph McCarthy. But his contempt also extended to antisemitism and gay-bashing (though Cohn was both homosexual and Jewish), and his past comes, literally, back to haunt him. Woods does an exceptional job in bringing this sociopathic heel to wretched life. Adapted from the biography by Nicholas von Hoffman. Made for cable television.
1992 (R) 112m/C James Woods, Joe Don Baker, Joseph Bologna, Ed Flanders, Frederic Forrest, Lee Grant, Pat Hingle; **D:** Frank Pierson; **W:** David Franzoni. **VHS $89.99** *HBO, BTV* &woove;&woove;

Citizen Kane Extraordinary film is an American tragedy of a newspaper tycoon (based loosely on William Randolph Hearst) from his humble beginnings to the solitude of his final years. One of the greatest films ever made—a stunning tour-de-force in virtually every aspect, from the fragmented narration to breathtaking, deep-focus cinematography; from a vivid soundtrack to fabulous ensemble acting. Welles was only 25 when he co-wrote, directed, and starred in this masterpiece. Three disc laser edition was reproduced from a superior negative and features liner notes and running commentary from film

---

historian Robert J. Carringer. Watch for Ladd and O'Connell as reporters.
1941 119m/B Orson Welles, Joseph Cotten, Everett Sloane, Dorothy Comingore, Ruth Warrick, George Coulouris, Ray Collins, William Alland, Paul Stewart, Erskine Sanford, Agnes Moorehead, Alan Ladd, Gus Schilling, Philip Van Zandt, Harry Shannon, Sonny Bupp, Arthur O'Connell; **D:** Orson Welles; **W:** Orson Welles, Herman J. Mankiewicz; **M:** Bernard Herrmann. Academy Awards '41: Best Original Screenplay; Nominations: Best Actor (Welles), Best Black and White Cinematography, Best Director (Welles), Best Film Editing, Best Interior Decoration, Best Picture, Best Sound, Best Original Score; National Board of Review Awards '41: 10 Best Films of the Year; New York Film Critics Awards '41: Best Film. **VHS, Beta, 8mm $19.98** *RKO, VYG, CRC* &woove;&woove;&woove;&woove;

Citizens Band Episodic, low-key comedy about people united by their CB use in a midwestern community. Notable performance from Clark as a soft-voiced guide for truckers passing through. Demme's first comedy is characteristically idiosyncratic. *AKA:* Handle With Care.
1977 (PG) 98m/C Paul LeMat, Candy Clark, Ann Wedgeworth, Roberts Blossom, Charles Napier, Marcia Rodd, Bruce McGill, Ed Begley Jr., Alix Elias; **D:** Jonathan Demme; **W:** Paul Brickman; **M:** Bill Conti. **VHS, Beta $59.95** *PAR* &woove;&woove;&woove;

The City Police desperately search for a psychotic determined to kill a country singer. He shouldn't be too hard to find. Made for television.
1976 78m/C Don Johnson, Robert Forster, Ward Costello, Jimmy Dean, Mark Hamill; **D:** Harvey Hart. **VHS, Beta $49.95** *WOV* &woove;

The City and the Dogs A brutal, cynical adaptation of Mario Vargas Llosa's novel. A young military recruit rebels against the authority establishments around him. In Spanish with English subtitles. *AKA:* La Ciudad y los Perros.
1985 135m/C *SP* **D:** Francisco J. Lombardi Pery. **VHS, Beta $34.95** *FCT, ING* &woove;&woove;&woove;

City Boy At the turn of the century the orphaned Nick makes his way from Chicago to the Pacific Northwest in search of his natural father. He takes a job guarding Limberlost, a valuable old-growth forest, from thieves and is torn between the ideals of two new friends. His mentor Tom sees the forest as timber that will build homes and provide jobs, while Angelica sees the forest as an irreplaceable sanctuary. Filmed on location in Vancouver, British Columbia. Adaptation of "Freckles" by Gene Stratton Porter.
1993 120m/C *GB CA* Christian Campbell, James Brolin, Sarah Chalke, Wendel Meldrum, Christopher Bolton; **D:** John Kent Harrison; **W:** John Kent Harrison. **VHS $29.95** *PME, BTV, HMV* &woove;&woove;&woove;

City for Conquest Two lovers go their separate ways to pursue individual careers. He attempts to become a boxing champ, but is blinded in the ring and ends up selling newspapers. She takes a shot at a dancing career but hooks up with an unscrupulous partner. Will the ill-fated pair find happiness again?
1940 101m/B James Cagney, Ann Sheridan, Frank Craven, Donald Crisp, Arthur Kennedy, Frank McHugh, George Tobias, Anthony Quinn, Blanche Yurka, Elia Kazan, Bob Steele; **D:** Anatole Litvak. **VHS, Beta $19.98** *MGM, CCB* &woove;&woove;

City Girl Friedrich Murnau, who directed the silent vampire classic "Nosferatu," was removed from the director's chair before "City Girl" was completed and it shows. But so do the marks of his inimitable camera direction. The story concerns a Minnesota grain grower who visits the Windy City and returns with a waitress as his wife. Frustratingly inconsistent, leading you to wonder what could have been had Murnau remained behind the camera (he died the following year). Silent. *AKA:* Our Daily Bread.

1930 90m/B Charles Farrell, Mary Duncan; *D:* F.W. Murnau. **VHS, Beta $39.95** GPV, FCT *♬♬* ½

City Heat A hardnosed cop and a plucky private eye berate each other while opposing the mob in this overdone comedy. Both Eastwood and Reynolds spoof their screen personas, but the results are only slightly satisfactory. Good back-up, though, from Alexander and Kahn as the dames. Screenplay written by Blake Edwards under the pseudonym Sam O. Brown.

1984 (PG) 98m/C Clint Eastwood, Burt Reynolds, Jane Alexander, Irene Cara, Madeline Kahn, Richard Roundtree, Rip Torn, Tony LoBianco, William Sanderson; *D:* Richard Benjamin; *W:* Blake Edwards. **VHS, Beta $19.98** WAR *♬♬* ½

City in Fear Stellar cast lights up a made-for-television drama about a tired newspaper columnist (Janssen) who communicates directly with a murdering psychotic (Rourke), as publisher Vaughn applauds and hypes. Rourke's first role, Janssen's last, and Smithee is actually Jud Taylor.

1980 135m/C David Janssen, Robert Vaughn, Mickey Rourke, William Daniels, Perry King, Susan Sullivan, William Prince; *D:* Alan Smithee. **VHS, Beta $69.98** LIV, HHE *♬♬♬*

City in Panic A detective and radio talk show host try to catch a psychotic mass murderer busy offing homosexuals throughout the city. Violent with no redeeming social qualities.

1986 85m/C Dave Adamson, Ed Chester, Leeann Westegard; *D:* Robert Bouvier. **VHS, Beta $19.98** TWE *♬*

City Killer A lunatic tries to blackmail the girl he loves into going out on a few dates by committing huge destructive acts of inner-city terrorism (flowers won't do). Made for television.

1987 120m/C Heather Locklear, Gerald McRaney, Terence Knox, Peter Mark Richman, John Harkins; *D:* Robert Lewis. **VHS, Beta $9.99** PSM *♬*

City Lights Masterpiece that was Chaplin's last silent film. The "Little Tramp" falls in love with a blind flower seller. A series of lucky accidents permits him to get the money she needs for a sight-restoring surgery. One of the most eloquent movies ever filmed, due to Chaplin's keen balance between comedy and tragedy.

1931 86m/B Charlie Chaplin, Virginia Cherrill, Florence Lee, Hank Mann, Harry Myers, Henry Bergman, Jean Harlow; *D:* Charlie Chaplin. **VHS, Beta $19.98** FOX *♬♬♬♬*

City Limits In a post-apocalyptic city, gangs of young people on choppers clash.

1985 (PG-13) 85m/C John Stockwell, Kim Cattrall, Darrell Larson, Rae Dawn Chong, Robby Benson, James Earl Jones, Jennifer Balgobin; *D:* Aaron Lipstadt. **VHS, Beta $79.98** VES, LIV, HHE *♬*

City of Blood A South African doctor is embroiled in mystery with racial overtones when prostitutes are being killed with a spiked club. Packaged as a horror film, this movie actually deals with the questions of South African racial tensions in a sophisticated, ultimately tragic manner.

1988 (R) 96m/C SA Joe Stewardson, Ian Yule, Susan Coetzer; *D:* Darrell Roodt. **VHS, Beta** NO *♬♬* ½

City of Hope The picture that "Bonfire of the Vanities" wanted to be, an eventful few days in the fictional metropolis of Hudson: an ugly racial incident threatens to snowball, the corrupt mayor pushes a shady real-estate deal, and a botched robbery has profound implications. Some of the subplots resolve too easily, but this cynical, crazy-quilt of urban life is worthy of comparison with "American Graffiti" and "Nashville" as pure Americana.

1991 (R) 132m/C Vincent Spano, Tony LoBianco, Joe Morton, Todd Graff, David Strathairn, Anthony John Denison, Barbara Williams, Angela Bassett, Gloria Foster, Lawrence Tierney, John Sayles, Maggie Renzi, Kevin Tighe, Chris Cooper, Jace Alexander, Frankie Faison, Tom Wright, Michael Mantell, Josh Mostel, Joe Grifasi, Louis Zorich, Gina Gershon, Rose Gregorio, Bill Raymond, Maeve Kinkead, Ray Aranha; *D:* John Sayles; *W:* John Sayles; *M:* Mason Daring. **VHS, 8mm** COL *♬♬♬*

City of Joy Disillusioned American heart surgeon Swayze flees to India after losing a patient. In Calcutta he is beaten by a street gang and loses his money and passport, but finds help from a farmer (Puri) who takes him to a nearby clinic in the City of Joy, one of Calcutta's poorest areas. Collins runs the clinic and recruits the reluctant doctor, who undergoes a life-changing transformation. The squalor of Calcutta is shown, but the city's portrayal as a magical place where problems miraculously disappear is unrealistic. Swayze lacks the emotional range for his part, but Collins and Puri are excellent in their roles. Adapted from the book by Dominique Lapierre.

1992 (PG-13) 134m/C GB FR Patrick Swayze, Pauline Collins, Om Puri, Shabana Azmi, Art Malik, Ayesha Dharker, Santu Chowdhury, Imran Badsah Khan, Shyamanand Jalan; *Cameos:* Sam Wanamaker; *D:* Roland Joffe; *W:* Mark Medoff; *M:* Ennio Morricone. **VHS $19.95** COL *♬♬*

City of Shadows Twins separated at birth are reunited by a criminal mind with evil intentions. Double trouble?

1986 (R) 97m/C John P. Ryan, Paul Coufos, Tony Rosato; *D:* David Mitchell; *M:* Tangerine Dream. **VHS, Beta $19.95** STE, NWV *♬♬*

City of the Walking Dead Eco-misery as a community must contend with prowling, radiation-zapped zombies who enjoy chewing through human flesh. *AKA:* Nightmare City; Nightmare.

1983 92m/C IT SP Mel Ferrer, Hugo Stiglitz, Laura Trotter, Francesco Rabal; *D:* Umberto Lenzi. **VHS** NO *♬*

City of Women Visually stunning, but otherwise thin fantasy/drama about a man smothered with women. A journalist wanders through a feminist theme park replete with a roller rink and screening room. Some worthwhile adventures are mixed in with rather dull stretches. Not among the best from either Mastroianni, who is under utilized, or Fellini, who here seems incapable of separating good ideas from bad. Plenty of buxom babes, but otherwise undistinguished. In Italian with English subtitles.

1981 (R) 140m/C IT Marcello Mastroianni, Ettore Manni, Anna Prucnal, Bernice Stegers; *D:* Federico Fellini; *W:* Federico Fellini. **VHS, Beta $79.95** NYF, FCT, ING *♬♬*

City on Fire An arsonist starts a fire that could engulf an entire city. Flaming bore.

1978 (R) 101m/C CA Barry Newman, Susan Clark, Shelley Winters, Leslie Nielsen, Henry Fonda, Ava Gardner; *D:* Alvin Rakoff. **VHS, Beta $9.98** SUE Woof!

City Slickers Three men with mid-life crises leave New York City for a cattle-ranch vacation that turns into an arduous, character-building stint. Many funny moments supplied by leads Crystal, Stern, and Kirby, but Palance steals the film as a salty, wise cowpoke. Slater is fetching as the lone gal vacationer on the cattle drive. Box office winner notable for a realistic calf birthing scene, one of few in cinema history. From an idea by Crystal, who also produced. Palance stole the show from Oscar ceremonies host Crystal a second time when he accepted his award and suddenly started doing one-arm pushups, startling the audience into laughter.

1991 (PG-13) 114m/C Billy Crystal, Daniel Stern, Bruno Kirby, Patricia Wettig, Helen Slater, Jack Palance, Noble Willingham, Tracy Walter, Josh Mostel, David Paymer, Bill Henderson, Jeffrey Tambor, Phill Lewis, Kyle Secor, Yeardley Smith, Jayne Meadows; *D:* Ron Underwood; *W:* Lowell Ganz, Babaloo Mandel; *M:* Marc Shaiman. **VHS, Beta, 8mm $19.95** COL, NLC *♬♬♬*

City Slickers 2: The Legend of Curly's Gold Mid-life crisis meets the wild west, part deux. Crystal and his fellow urban dudes discover a treasure map in the hat of departed trail boss Curly and decide to go a-huntin'. Palance is back as Curly's evil twin. Lovitz occupies the screen as Crystal's ne'er-do-well brother, replacing sidekick Bruno Kirby. A bit of a rehash, formulaic and occasionally straining for a punchline, it's still pretty darn funny, especially when the boys start to improvise.

1994 (PG-13) 116m/C Billy Crystal, Daniel Stern, Jon Lovitz, Jack Palance, Patricia Wettig, Pruitt Taylor Vince, Bill McKinney, Lindsay Crystal, Noble Willingham, David Paymer, Josh Mostel; *D:* Paul Weiland; *W:* Billy Crystal, Lowell Ganz, Babaloo Mandel; *M:* Marc Shaiman. **VHS** NYR *♬♬* ½

City That Never Sleeps A Chicago cop must decide whether or not to run off with an entertainer, or continue his life with his family. Decisions, decisions. Moody but dated melodrama that's finely acted and indecisively directed, with good use of dim city lights. Nothing new here.

1953 90m/B Gig Young, Mala Powers, Edward Arnold, Paula Raymond, Chill Wills, Marie Windsor; *D:* John H. Auer. **VHS $19.98** REP *♬♬* ½

City Without Men Melodramatic story about a boarding house near a prison where the women tenants await the release of their imprisoned men. Little plot, no suspense.

1943 75m/B Linda Darnell, Sara Allgood, Michael Duane, Edgar Buchanan, Leslie Brooks, Glenda Farrell, Margaret Hamilton, Sheldon Leonard; *D:* Sidney Salkow. **VHS** RXM *♬* ½

The City's Edge A young man becomes involved with the mysterious residents of a boarding house on the edge of the ocean.

1983 86m/C AU **VHS, Beta $59.95** MGM *♬* ½

Civil War Diary Too young to go to war, a young man struggles for the survival of his family amidst harsh winters, the devastation of the Civil War and his own personal nightmares. Winner of the International Heritage Award in 1990. Based on the Newberry Award winning young people's novel "Across Five Aprils."

1990 82m/C **VHS $79.98** RHI *♬* ½

The Civil War, Episode 1: The Cause—1861 The blowout PBS hit miniseries, five years in the making by author and filmmaker Ken Burns, is a staggering historical achievement. Episode 1 focuses on the causes of the Civil War from the schism created by Lincoln's election, John Brown's

assault on Harper's Ferry, and the firing on Fort Sumpter. Also available as a set for $179.95.
1990 99m/C D: Ken Burns; **W:** Ken Burns. **VHS $79.95** *PBS, SIG, KUI* 🎬🎬🎬🎬

The Civil War, Episode 2: A Very Bloody Affair—1862 Second in the enormously popular PBS series looks at the unexpectedly extreme costs in human life of the War Between the States.
1990 69m/C D: Ken Burns; **W:** Ken Burns. **VHS $59.95** *PBS, SIG, KUI* 🎬🎬🎬🎬

The Civil War, Episode 3: Forever Free—1862 Third volume in the PBS Emmy-nominated mini-series covers Antietam, Robert E. Lee and Stonewall Jackson planning Confederate strategy, and Lincoln's decision to free the slaves.
1990 76m/C D: Ken Burns; **W:** Ken Burns. **VHS $19.95** *PBS, SIG, KUI* 🎬🎬🎬🎬

The Civil War, Episode 4: Simply Murder—1863 Union forces meet disaster at Fredericksburg, and Gen. Lee wins a victory but loses Stonewall Jackson in the fourth episode of the Emmy-nominated PBS mini-series.
1990 62m/C D: Ken Burns; **W:** Ken Burns. **VHS $59.95** *PBS, SIG, KUI* 🎬🎬🎬🎬

The Civil War, Episode 5: The Universe of Battle—1863 Gettysburg, the battleground which claimed 150,000 American lives, is examined in the 5th episode of the Emmy-nominated PBS mini-series.
1990 95m/C D: Ken Burns; **W:** Ken Burns. **VHS $79.95** *PBS, SIG, KUI* 🎬🎬🎬🎬

The Civil War, Episode 6: Valley of the Shadow of Death—1864 Profiles of Grant and Lee are offered, plus Sherman's assault on Atlanta, in this volume from the Emmy-nominated PBS mini-series.
1990 70m/C D: Ken Burns; **W:** Ken Burns. **VHS $59.95** *PBS, SIG, KUI* 🎬🎬🎬🎬

The Civil War, Episode 7: Most Hallowed Ground—1864 The nation re-elects Abraham Lincoln, and the North turns General Lee's mansion into Arlington National Cemetery in this episode of the Emmy-nominated PBS mini-series.
1990 72m/C D: Ken Burns; **W:** Ken Burns. **VHS $59.95** *PBS, SIG, KUI* 🎬🎬🎬🎬

The Civil War, Episode 8: War is All Hell—1865 Sherman marches to the sea and Lee surrenders to Grant in this episode from the Emmy-nominated PBS mini-series.
1990 69m/C D: Ken Burns; **W:** Ken Burns. **VHS $59.95** *PBS, SIG, KUI* 🎬🎬🎬🎬

The Civil War, Episode 9: The Better Angels of Our Nature—1865 In this final episode of the Emmy-nominated PBS mini-series, Lincoln's assassination is examined, and the central characters of the war are summarized.
1990 68m/C D: Ken Burns; **W:** Ken Burns. **VHS $59.95** *PBS, SIG, KUI* 🎬🎬🎬🎬

Civilization A silent epic about the horrors and immorality of war as envisioned by the ground-breaking film pioneer Ince, who was later murdered. Famous scene involves Christ walking through body-ridden battlefields.
1916 80m/B Howard Hickman, Enid Markey, Lola May; **D:** Thomas Ince. **VHS, Beta $19.95** *GPV, VYY, GVV* 🎬🎬🎬

Claire of the Moon Famous satirist Claire goes to a women writers retreat in the Pacific Northwest where she's assigned a room with Noel, a solemn sex therapist. Noel's recovering from a disasterous love affair while Claire is promiscuous and unwilling to commit. Inspite of their differences, the two women find themselves drawn together. Too many philosophical debates slow the story down but the gentle romance works well.
1992 102m/C Trisha Todd, Karen Trumbo, Faith McDevitt, Damon Craig; **D:** Nicole Conn; **W:** Nicole Conn; **M:** Michael Allen Harrison. **VHS $89.95** *FXL, FCT, BTV* 🎬🎬

Claire's Knee A grown man about to be married goes on a holiday and develops a fixation on a young girl's knee. Another of Rohmer's Moral Tales exploring sexual and erotic obsessions. Lots of talk, little else. You'll either find it fascinating or fail to watch more than 10 minutes. Most, however, consider it a classic. Sophisticated dialogue, lovely visions of summer on Lake Geneva. In French with English subtitles.
1971 105m/C *FR* Jean-Claude Brialy, Aurora Cornu, Beatrice Romand; **D:** Eric Rohmer; **W:** Eric Rohmer. **VHS, Beta $59.95** *ING, MED, FCT* 🎬🎬🎬½

Clambake Noxious Elvis vehicle about a rich man's son who wants success on his own terms, so he trades places with a water-skiing teacher. Inane, even in comparison to other Elvis ventures. 🎵Clambake; The Girl I Never Loved; Hey, Hey, Hey; Confidence; Who Needs Money?; A House That Has Everything.
1967 98m/C Elvis Presley, Shelley Fabares, Bill Bixby, James Gregory, Gary Merrill, Will Hutchins, Harold Peary; **D:** Arthur Nadel. **VHS, Beta $14.95** *MGM* 🎬

The Clan of the Cave Bear A scrawny cavegirl is taken in by Neanderthals after her own parents are killed. Hannah is lifeless as a primitive gamine, and the film is similarly DOA. Ponderous and only unintentionally funny. Based on the popular novel by Jean M. Auel.
1986 (R) 100m/C Daryl Hannah, James Remar, Pamela Reed, John Doolittle, Thomas G. Waites; **D:** Michael Chapman; **W:** John Sayles. **VHS, Beta $14.98** *FXV, FOX* 🎬½

Clara's Heart A Jamaican maid enriches the lives of her insufferable, bourgeois employers and their particularly repellent son. A kinder, gentler waste of film and Goldberg; sentimental clap-trap which occasionally lapses into comedy.
1988 (PG-13) 108m/C Whoopi Goldberg, Michael Ontkean, Kathleen Quinlan, Neil Patrick Harris, Spalding Gray, Beverly Todd, Hattie Winston; **D:** Robert Mulligan; **W:** Mark Medoff; **M:** Dave Grusin. **VHS, Beta $19.98** *WAR, FCT* 🎬

Clarence Clarence, the benevolent angel from the classic "It's a Wonderful Life" is back, risking his wings for a beautiful young woman. Made for cable.
1991 (G) 92m/C Robert Carradine, Kate Trotter; **D:** Eric Till. **VHS $79.98** *REP* 🎬🎬½

Clarence Darrow Riveting one-man stage performance shot for television and based on Darrow's writings, adapted from the play by Irving Stone.
1978 81m/C Henry Fonda; **D:** John Rich. **VHS, Beta $39.95** *ALL, KAR, IME* 🎬🎬🎬

Clarence, the Cross-eyed Lion Follows the many adventures of a cross-eyed lion and his human compatriots. Great family viewing from the creator of "Flipper."

1965 98m/C Marshall Thompson, Betsy Drake, Richard Haydn, Cheryl Miller, Rockne Tarkington, Maurice Marsac; **D:** Andrew Marton. **VHS $19.98** *MGM, FCT* 🎬🎬🎬

Clark & McCullough The zany duo, a hit in burlesque and night clubs, transferred some of their crazy antics onto film. Their comedy shorts include "Fits in a Fiddle" (1933), "Love and Kisses" (1934), "Alibi Bye Bye" (1935), and a rehearsal of "Mademoiselle from New Rochelle" from "Strike Up the Band" (with George Gershwin on piano).
1933 53m/B Bobby Clark, Paul McCullough, George Gershwin, James Finlayson. **VHS, Beta $57.95** *GVV, DVT, VYY* 🎬🎬½

Clash by Night A wayward woman marries a fisherman, then beds his best friend. Seamy storyline is exploited to the hilt by master filmmaker Lang. An utterly unflinching melodrama. Early Monroe shines in a supporting role too. Based on the Clifford Odets play.
1952 105m/B Barbara Stanwyck, Paul Douglas, Marilyn Monroe, Robert Ryan, J. Carroll Naish; **D:** Fritz Lang. **VHS, Beta $15.95** *VCI* 🎬🎬🎬½

Clash of the Ninja Evil Occidental ninja runs medical smuggling operation. Interpol ninja sets out to stop him. Wild ninja nonsense includes ninja with rotating head and exploding ninja. Dubbed poorly.
1986 90m/C *HK* Paul Torcha, Louis Roth, Eric Neff, Bernie Junker, Joe Redner, Klaus Mutter, Eddie Chan, Max Kwan, Tom Allen, Stanley Tong; **D:** Wallace Chan; **W:** Kurt Spielberg. **VHS, Beta $59.95** *TWE* 🎬½

Clash of the Titans Mind-numbing fantasy derived from Greek legends about heroic Perseus, who slays the snake-haired Medusa and rescues a semi-clad maiden from the monstrous Kraken. Wooden Hamlin plays Perseus and fares better than more accomplished Olivier and Smith, who seem in need of enemas as they lurch about Mt. Olympus. Only Bloom seems truly godlike in a supporting role. Some good, some wretched special effects from pioneer Harryhausen.
1981 (PG) 118m/C *GB* Laurence Olivier, Dame Maggie Smith, Claire Bloom, Ursula Andress, Burgess Meredith, Harry Hamlin, Sian Phillips, Judi Bowker; **D:** Desmond Davis; **W:** Beverly Cross. **VHS, Beta $69.95** *MGM, MLB* Woof!

Class A prep school student discovers that his mother is the lover whom his roommate has bragged about. Lowe is serviceable as the stunned son of sexy Bisset, who woos McCarthy, even in an elevator. Too ludicrous to be enjoyed, but you may watch just to see what happens next.
1983 (R) 98m/C Jacqueline Bisset, Rob Lowe, Andrew McCarthy, Cliff Robertson, John Cusack, Stuart Margolin, Casey Siemaszko; **D:** Lewis John Carlino; **M:** Elmer Bernstein. **VHS, Beta $29.98** *VES* 🎬🎬

Class Act Rappers Kid 'N' Play team up once again in this role reversal comedy. A straight-laced brain and a partying, macho bully find their school records and identifications switched when they enroll in a new high school. This turns out to be good for the character of both young men, as the egghead learns to loosen up and the bully learns what it feels like to be respected for his ideas rather than a fierce reputation. Comedy is very uneven but the duo are energetic and likable.
1991 (PG-13) 98m/C Christopher Reid, Christopher Martin, Meshach Taylor, Karyn Parsons, Doug E. Doug, Rick Ducommun, Lamont Jackson, Rhea Perlman; **D:** Randall Miller; **M:** Vassal Benford. **VHS $19.98** *WAR* 🎬🎬½

Class Action 1960s versus 1990s ethics clash when a father and daughter, both lawyers, wind up on opposing sides of a litigation against an auto manufacturer. Hackman and Mastrantonio give intense, exciting performances, almost surmounting the melodramatic script.
1991 (R) 110m/C Mary Elizabeth Mastrantonio, Gene Hackman, Joanna Merlin, Colin Friels, Laurence "Larry" Fishburne, Donald Moffatt, Jan Rubes, Matt Clark, Fred Dalton Thompson, Jonathan Silverman, Dan Hicks; *D:* Michael Apted; *W:* Samantha Shad; *M:* James Horner. VHS, Beta $19.98 FXV ↗↗↗

Class of Fear The new kid in school is having a particularly rough time. He's been framed for murdering a teacher and must prove his innocence before he winds up in prison.
1991 (R) 105m/C Julianne McNamara, Noah Blake. VHS $79.99 MNC, MOV ↗↗½

Class of '44 The sequel to "Summer of '42" finds insufferable boys becoming insufferable men at military school. Worse than its predecessor, and notable only in that it is Candy's film debut.
1973 (PG) 95m/C Gary Grimes, Jerry Houser, Oliver Conant, Deborah Winters, William Atherton, Sam Bottoms, John Candy; *D:* Paul Bogart. VHS, Beta $14.95 WAR ↗↗½

The Class of Miss MacMichael A dedicated instructor inherits and ultimately inspires a class of high school misfits and malcontents. Derivative venture is beneath considerable talents of Jackson. Based on a novel by Sandy Hutson.
1978 (R) 95m/C *GB* Glenda Jackson, Oliver Reed, Michael Murphy, Rosalind Cash; *D:* Silvio Narizzano. VHS, Beta $9.95 FOX, MED ↗↗

Class of 1984 Teacher King must face a motley crew of teenagers in the classroom. Ring leader and student psychopath Van Patten leads his groupies on a reign of terror through the high school halls, stopping to gang rape King's wife. Teacher attempts revenge. Bloody and thoughtless update of "Blackboard Jungle." Early Fox appearance. Followed by "Class of 1999."
1982 (R) 93m/C *CA* Perry King, Roddy McDowall, Timothy Van Patten, Michael J. Fox, Merrie Lynn Ross, Stefan Arngrim, Al Waxman; *D:* Mark L. Lester; *W:* Mark L. Lester, Tom Holland. VHS, Beta $29.98 VES Woof!

Class of 1999 Freewheeling sci-fi set in the near future where teen gangs terrorize seemingly the entire country. A high school principal determines to enforce law and order by installing human-like robots with rocket launchers for arms. Violent, crude entertainment. Class dismissed. Sequel to "Class of 1984" and available in an unrated version.
1990 (R) 98m/C Bradley Gregg, Traci Lin, Malcolm McDowell, Stacy Keach, Patrick Kilpatrick, Pam Grier, John P. Ryan, Darren E. Burrows, Joshua Miller; *D:* Mark L. Lester; *W:* C. Courtney Joyner. VHS, Beta VES, LIV ↗

Class of 1999 2: The Substitute High school in 1999 is filled with violent gangs who murder at random. Enter substitute teacher John Bolen, who has his own ideas of discipline—leading to an even higher body count. John just doesn't seem human and when a CIA agent starts investigating, school may never be the same.
1993 (R) 90m/C Sasha Mitchell, Nick Cassavetes, Caitlin Dulany, Jack Knight, Gregory West, Rick Hill; *D:* Spiro Razatos; *W:* Mark Sevi. VHS $92.95 VMK ↗½

Class of Nuke 'Em High Team Troma once again experiments with the chemicals, with violent results. Jersey high school becomes a hotbed of mutants and

maniacs after a nuclear spill occurs. Good teens Chrissy and Warren succumb, the school blows, life goes on. High camp, low budget, heavy gore. Followed by "Class of Nuke 'Em High Part 2."
1986 (R) 84m/C Janelle Brady, Gilbert Brenton; *D:* Richard W. Haines. VHS, Beta $9.98 MED ↗↗½

Class of Nuke 'Em High, Part 2: Subhumanoid Meltdown The Troma team brings us back into the world of the strange. In this adventure, the evil Nukamama Corporation holds secret experiments at their "college" and create sub-humanoids as slave labor, swelling unemployment and wrecking the economy. This does not fare too well with the rest of society, including our heroes Roger the reporter, Professor Holt, and the scantily clad sub-humanoid Victoria.
1991 m/C Lisa Gaye, Brick Bronsky, Leesa Rowland; *D:* Eric Louzil. VHS, Beta $19.98 VTR, MED, FXV ↗

Class of '63 An unfulfilled woman finally discovers the lover she lost nearly ten years ago at her college reunion. Nearly average made for television drama.
1973 74m/C James Brolin, Joan Hackett, Cliff Gorman, Ed Lauter; *D:* John Korty. VHS, Beta $59.95 LHV ↗↗

Class Reunion Sexual highjinks are the order of the day at a 10-year high school reunion. Insipid softcore effort. It's cheaper just to cut out heads from yearbooks and paste 'em to skin mags torsos. Not to be confused with "National Lampoon's Class Reunion," equally bad but nonetheless distinct.
1987 (X) 90m/C Marsha Jordan, Renee Bond, Terry Johnson. VHS, Beta $29.95 MED Woof!

Class Reunion Massacre Typically lame-brained horror about the mysterious deaths of former school jerks who've reconvened for the 10-year reunion. Worthless flick stars someone named Finkbinder. Contains graphic violence that is not for the squeamish. Also titled "The Redeemer."
1977 (R) 87m/C T.K. Finkbinder, Damien Knight, Nick Carter. VHS, Beta $39.98 VCI Woof!

Classic Comedy Video Sampler A collection of classic comedy shorts featuring Amos and Andy, The Three Stooges, and Abbott and Costello.
1949 78m/B Bud Abbott, Lou Costello, Moe Howard, Larry Fine, Curly Howard. VHS, Beta $29.95 VCI Woof!

Claudia A wealthy woman who's part of London's high society falls for a lowly musician while trying to escape her dominating husband. Melodramatic meanderings not likely to move you.
1985 (R) 88m/C Deborah Raffin, Nicholas Ball; *D:* Anwar Kawadri. VHS $19.95 TTC ↗↗

The Claw A young British profligate goes to Africa to prove his manhood to the woman who rejected him. Silent.
1927 ?m/B Claire Windsor, Norman Kerry; *D:* Sidney Olcott. VHS, Beta, 8mm $55.95 GVV ↗↗

Claws A woodsman, a game commissioner and an Indian band together to stop a grizzly bear who is killing residents of a small Alaskan town.
1977 (PG) 100m/C Leon Ames, Jason Evers, Anthony Caruso, Glenn Sipes, Carla Layton, Myron Healey; *D:* Richard Bansbach, R.E. Pierson. VHS, Beta $59.95 GEM ↗

Claws A lone farmboy is subjected to repeated attacks by feline mutants. Meow, baby.

1985 84m/C Jason Roberts, Brian O'Shaughnessy, Sandra Prinsloo. VHS, Beta NO *Woof!*

The Clay Pigeon Seaman comes to in the hospital after a long coma and discovers he's about to be court-martialed for treason and murder. Effective suspense as he goes after the man who incriminated him.
1949 63m/B Bill Williams, Barbara Hale, Richard Loo; *D:* Richard Fleischer. VHS, Beta $34.95 RKO ↗↗½

Clayton County Line Plucky buddies decide to end a cruel sheriff's reign of terror. Derivative and unredeeming.
1987 80m/C Kelly Bradish, Vince Csapos, Michael Heinz, Donald Kenney, Kathy Kenney, Gregg Schultz, Dan Quine, Steve Szilagyi, Dean Wilson; *D:* Dean Wilson. VHS NO ↗

Clean and Sober A drug addict hides out at a rehabilitation clinic and actually undergoes treatment. A serious, subtle, and realistic look at the physical/emotional detoxification of an obnoxious, substance-abusing real estate broker; unpredictable and powerful without moralizing. Keaton is fine in unsympathetic lead, with both Baker and Freeman excelling in lesser roles. Not for all tastes, but its certainly a worthwhile work. Caron, creator of TV's "Moonlighting," debuts here as director.
1988 (R) 124m/C Michael Keaton, Kathy Baker, Morgan Freeman, M. Emmet Walsh, Claudia Christian, Pat Quinn, Ben Piazza, Brian Benben, Luca Bercovici, Tate Donovan, Henry Judd Baker, Mary Catherine Martin; *D:* Glenn Gordon Caron. VHS, Beta, 8mm $19.98 WAR, FCT ↗↗↗½

Clean Slate Private-eye Maurice Pogue (Carvey) sustains injuries that cause a rare type of amnesia making every day seem like the first day of his life. As the only witness to a crime, he bumbles through mix-ups with the mob and his job as a bodyguard. Lightweight comedy fare is good for a few yuks but doesn't work as well as the similar "Groundhog Day." Barkley the sight-impaired dog steals nearly every scene he's in.
1994 (PG-13) 107m/C Dana Carvey, Valeria Golino, James Earl Jones, Kevin Pollak, Michael Murphy, Michael Gambon, Jayne Brook, Vyto Ruginis, Olivia D'Abo; *D:* Mick Jackson; *W:* Robert King; *M:* Alan Silvestri. VHS NYR ↗↗

Clear and Present Danger Ford returns for a second go at CIA agent Jack Ryan in the third installment of Tom Clancy's bestselling adventures. With the Cold War over, the U.S. government is the bad guy as Ryan discovers a link between a South American drug cartel and a Presidential advisor. Viewers will also finally get an answer to that nagging question at the end of "Patriot Games:" is it a boy or a girl? Archer's back as Ryan's annoying wife, and Birch and Jones also return. Keep alert for complex plot twists in lieu of tons of action, though there's enough to keep action fans happy. Better than "Patriot Games" but not quite up to "The Hunt for Red October."
1994 ?m/C Harrison Ford, Anne Archer, James Earl Jones, Willem Dafoe, Thora Birch, Henry Czerny, Harris Yulin, Raymond Cruz, Joaquim de Almeida, Miguel Sandoval, Donald Moffatt, Theodore Raimi; *D:* Phillip Noyce; *W:* Steven Zaillian, Donald Stewart, John Milius. VHS NYR ↗↗↗

Clearcut Progressive lawyer finds his liberalism and his survival skills tested among modern Canadian Indians, when a militant native resorts to kidnapping the businessman who threatens their land. Well-acted, brutal drama that asks tough questions; it includes what purports to be the first authentic sweat-lodge ceremony ever filmed.

1992 (R) 98m/C *CA* Graham Greene, Ron Lea, Michael Hogan, Floyd "Red Crow" Westerman, Rebecca Jenkins; *D:* Richard Bugajski. **VHS** $89.95 *ACA* 🐾🐾½

Clearing the Range Hoot wants the bad guy who knocked off his brother so he poses as a cringing coward in the hopes of uncovering the villain. Eilers is the love interest as well as his real-life wife.
1931 64m/B Hoot Gibson, Sally Eilers, Hooper Atchley; *D:* Otto Brower. **VHS, Beta** $19.95 *NOS, VCN, DVT* 🐾½

Cleo from 5 to 7 A singer strolls through Paris for 90 minutes, and reconsiders her life while awaiting the results of medical tests for cancer. Typical documentary-like effort from innovative filmmaker Varda, who constructed the film in real time. Look for a brief appearance of master director Jean-Luc Godard. In French with English subtitles. *AKA:* Cleo de 5 a 7.
1961 90m/B *FR* Corinne Marchand, Antoine Bourseiller, Dorothee Blanck, Michel Legrand, Jean-Claude Brialy, Jean-Luc Godard, Anna Karina, Eddie Constantine, Sami Frey; *D:* Agnes Varda; *W:* Agnes Varda. **VHS, Beta** $79.95 *FCT* 🐾🐾🐾½

Cleo/Leo Crude and sexist jerk Leo gets chased into the East River by a gun-toting feminist. Reincarnated, Leo returns as Cleo and endures the same Neanderthal remarks and attitudes that "he" used to dish out. Tasteless, exploitive comedy only cynically explores the sex reversal theme.
1989 (R) 94m/C Jane Hamilton, Scott Thompson Baker, Kevin Thomas, Alan Naggar, Ginger Lynn Allen; *D:* Chuck Vincent. **VHS** $19.95 *STE, MED* 🐾

Cleopatra Early Hollywood DeMille version of the Egyptian temptress's lust for Marc Antony after Julius Caesar's death. Intermittently interesting extravaganza. Colbert seems to be enjoying herself in the lead role in this hokey, overdone epic. Includes the original theatrical trailer on laser-track 2. Remade in 1963.
1934 100m/B Claudette Colbert, Henry Wilcoxon, Warren William, Gertrude Michael, Joseph Schildkraut, Sir C. Aubrey Smith; *D:* Cecil B. DeMille. Academy Awards '34: Best Cinematography; Nominations: Best Film Editing, Best Picture, Best Sound. **VHS, Beta** $14.95 *MCA* 🐾🐾

Cleopatra And we thought DeMille's version was extravagant. After the death of Julius Caesar, Cleopatra, Queen of Egypt, becomes infatuated with Mark Antony. Costly four-hour epic functions like a blimp-sized, multi-colored sleeping tablet. Historical characters are utterly dwarfed by the film's massive scope, and audiences are benumbed by a spectacle of crowd scenes and opulent, grotesque interiors. Taylor looks and often acts like a sex bomb ruler, while Harrison has some notion of Caesar's majesty. Burton, however, is hopelessly wooden. Hard to believe this came from director Mankiewicz.
1963 246m/C Elizabeth Taylor, Richard Burton, Rex Harrison, Roddy McDowall, Martin Landau, Pamela Brown, Michael Hordern, Kenneth Haigh, Andrew Keir, Hume Cronyn, Carroll O'Connor; *D:* Joseph L. Mankiewicz; *W:* Joseph L. Mankiewicz. Academy Awards '63: Best Art Direction/Set Decoration (Color), Best Color Cinematography, Best Costume Design (Color), Best Visual Effects; Nominations: Best Actor (Harrison), Best Film Editing, Best Picture, Best Sound, Best Original Score; National Board of Review Awards '63: Best Actor (Harrison). **VHS, Beta** $29.98 *FOX* 🐾

Cleopatra Jones Lean and lethal government agent with considerable martial arts prowess takes on loathsome drug lords. Dobson is fetching as the lead performer in this fast-paced, violent flick. Followed by "Cleopatra Jones and the Casino of Gold."
1973 (PG) 89m/C Tamara Dobson, Shelley Winters, Bernie Casey, Brenda Sykes; *D:* Jack Starrett. **VHS, Beta** $14.95 *WAR* 🐾🐾

Cleopatra Jones & the Casino of Gold Dobson returns as the lethal, physically imposing federal agent to Hong Kong to take on a powerful druglord in this sequel to "Cleopatra Jones." Watch for sexy Stevens as the Dragon Lady.
1975 (R) 96m/C Tamara Dobson, Stella Stevens, Norman Fell; *D:* Chuck Bail. **VHS, Beta** $14.95 *WAR* 🐾🐾

The Clergyman's Daughter A clergyman's daughter calls upon detectives Tommy and Tuppence to investigate some murders at the family's country house. Made for British television and based on the Agatha Christie story.
1984 60m/C *GB* James Warwick, Francesca Annis. **VHS, Beta** $14.95 *TPV* 🐾½

The Client Another legal thriller from the Grisham factory. Sarandon is the troubled attorney hired by an 11-year-old boy who witnessed the suicide of a Mafia attorney and now knows more than he should. Jones is the ambitious federal prosecutor who's willing to risk the boy's life in exchange for career advancement. Lacks the mega-big Hollywood names of "The Firm" and "The Pelican Brief" but gains solid acting in return. No frills, near-faithful adaptation by Schumacher basically travels down the path of least resistance. Filmed on location in Memphis.
1994 (PG-13) 120m/C Susan Sarandon, Tommy Lee Jones, Brad Renfro, Mary-Louise Parker, Anthony LaPaglia, Bradley Whitford, Anthony Edwards, Ossie Davis, Walter Olkewicz, J.T. Walsh, Will Patton, Anthony Heald; *D:* Joel Schumacher; *W:* Robert Getchell, Akiva Goldsman. **VHS**

Cliffhanger Action-packed thriller. Expert climber Gabe Walker (Stallone) faces his greatest challenge when criminal mastermind Lithgow and his henchman appear on the scene. Turner plays fellow climber and love interest. Lithgow makes a particularly convincing, if not downright chilling, murderous thief. Filmed in the Italian Alps with a budget of $70 million-plus; boasts stunning cinematography and breathtaking footage of the Dolomite mountain range. Harlin's expert pacing and direction combine to produce maximum thrills and suspense. The hit Stallone's been waiting for, placing eighth on the list of top 1993 box office grossers.
1993 (R) 113m/C Sylvester Stallone, John Lithgow, Michael Rooker, Janine Turner, Rex Linn, Caroline Goodall, Leon, Paul Winfield, Ralph Waite, Craig Fairbrass, Michelle Joyner, Max Perlich; *D:* Renny Harlin; *W:* Sylvester Stallone, Michael France; *M:* Trevor Jones. **VHS, Beta, 8mm** $99.95 *COL, BTV, FCT* 🐾🐾🐾

Clifford Short plays a 10-year-old in an effort delayed by Orion's financial crisis. Creepy little Clifford's uncle Martin (Grodin) rues the day he volunteered to babysit his nephew to prove to his girlfriend (Steenburgen) how much he likes kids. Clifford terrorizes Grodin in surprisingly nasty ways when their plans for visiting Dinosaurworld fall through, the uncle loses the girl, and takes his revenge on the "child." Not just bad in the conventional sense, but bad in a bizarre sort of alien fashion that raises questions about who was controlling the bodies of the

producers. To create the effect of Short really being short, other actors stood on boxes and sets were built slightly larger.
1992 (PG) 90m/C Martin Short, Charles Grodin, Mary Steenburgen, Dabney Coleman, Sonia Jackson; *D:* Paul Flaherty; *W:* Bobby Von Hayes, Jay Dee Rock, Steven Kampmann; *M:* Richard Gibbs. **VHS** *NYR* Woof!

A Climate for Killing Arizona police are baffled when a woman murdered 16 years earlier is again found dead. Case open? Hunks Bauer and Beck are earnest in leads, and Ross and Sara are foxy. Passable entertainment.
1991 (R) 104m/C Steven Bauer, John Beck, Katharine Ross, Mia Sara, John Diehl, Phil Brock, Dedee Pfeiffer, Lu Leonard, Jack Dodson, Eloy Casados; *D:* J.S. Cardone; *W:* J.S. Cardone; *M:* Robert Folk. **VHS, Beta** $89.98 *MED* 🐾🐾½

The Climb German mountain climbers attempt to conquer the Himalayan Nanga Parbat, the world's fifth highest peak. Sometimes compelling film based on 1953 expedition in which only one member succeeded in reaching the summit.
1987 (PG) 90m/C Bruce Greenwood, James Hurdle, Kenneth Welsh; *D:* Donald Shebib; *W:* Donald Shebib; *M:* Peter Jermyn. **VHS, Beta** $19.95 *IME* 🐾🐾½

Clipped Wings The Bowery Boys are at their best as they inadvertantly join the army while visiting a friend and in the process of their usual bumblings, uncover a Nazi plot.
1953 62m/B Leo Gorcey, Huntz Hall, Bernard Gorcey, David Condon, Bennie Bartlett, June Vincent, Mary Treen, Philip Van Zandt, Elaine Riley, Jeanne Dean, Lyle Talbot; *D:* Edward L. Bernds. **VHS** $14.98 *WAR* 🐾🐾½

Cloak and Dagger An American physicist joins the secret service during WWII and infiltrates Nazi territory to release a kidnapped scientist who is being forced to build a nuclear bomb. Disappointing spy show with muted anti-nuclear tone.
1946 106m/B Gary Cooper, Lilli Palmer, Robert Alda, James Flavin, Vladimir Sokoloff, J. Edward Bromberg, Marc Lawrence, Ludwig Stossel; *D:* Fritz Lang; *W:* Ring Lardner Jr., Albert Maltz. **VHS** $19.95 *REP, FCT* 🐾🐾

Cloak & Dagger A young boy, last seen befriending E.T., depends upon his imaginary super-friend to help him out when some real-life agents are after his video game. Coleman is particularly fun as both dad and fantasy hero in an interesting family adventure.
1984 (PG) 101m/C Dabney Coleman, Henry Thomas, Michael Murphy, John McIntire, Jeanette Nolan; *D:* Richard Franklin; *W:* Tom Holland. **VHS, Beta** $19.95 *MCA* 🐾🐾½

The Clock Appealing romance about an office worker who meets and falls in love with a soldier on two-day leave in New York City. Charismatic Walker and likeable Garland make a fine screen couple, and Wynn is memorable as the drunk. The original theatrical trailer is included on the laserdisc format. *AKA:* Under the Clock.
1945 91m/B Judy Garland, Robert Walker, James Gleason, Marshall Thompson, Keenan Wynn; *D:* Vincente Minnelli. **VHS** $19.98 *BTV, MGM, FCT* 🐾🐾🐾

The Clockmaker Contemplative drama about a clockmaker whose life is shattered when his son is arrested as a political assassin. Tavernier regular Noiret excels in the lead. In French with English subtitles.
1976 105m/C *FR* Philippe Noiret, Jean Rochefort, Jacques Denis, William Sabatier, Christine Pascal; *D:* Bertrand Tavernier. **VHS, Beta** $34.95 *FCT, LUM* 🐾🐾🐾½

Clockwise Monty Python regular Cleese is a teacher preoccupied by punctuality. His neurosis proves his undoing when he falls victim to misadventure while traveling to deliver a speech. Cleese is acceptable, dialogue and story is less so, though sprinkled with a fair amount of humor.
1986 (PG) 96m/C GB John Cleese, Penelope Wilton, Alison Steadman, Stephen Moore, Sharon Maiden; D: Christopher Morahan; W: Michael Frayn; M: George Fenton. VHS $14.98 REP ⅛⅛½

A Clockwork Orange In the Britain of the near future, a sadistic punk leads a gang on nightly rape and murder sprees, then is captured and becomes the subject of a grim experiment to eradicate his violent tendencies in this extraordinary adaptation of Anthony Burgess's controversial novel. The film is an exhilarating experience, with an outstanding performance by McDowell as the funny, fierce psychopath. Many memorable, disturbing sequences, including a rape conducted while assailant McDowell belts "Singing in the Rain." Truly outstanding, provocative work from master filmmaker Kubrick.
1971 (R) 137m/C GB Malcolm McDowell, Patrick Magee, Adrienne Corri, Michael Bates, Warren Clarke, Aubrey Morris, James Marcus, Steven Berkoff, David Prowse; D: Stanley Kubrick; W: Stanley Kubrick. Academy Awards '71 Nominations: Best Adapted Screenplay, Best Director (Kubrick), Best Film Editing, Best Picture; New York Film Critics Awards '71: Best Director (Kubrick), Best Film. VHS, Beta $19.98 WAR, FCT, FUS ⅛⅛⅛⅛

Clodhopper A farmboy decides to head out for New York where he achieves fame on Broadway for his dance number, the "Clophooper Glide." He stays true to his hometown girl, however, and returns to save his father's farm from financial ruin.
1917 47m/B Charles Ray, Margery Wilson; D: Victor Schertzinger. VHS, Beta $16.95 GPV, CCB, DVT ⅛⅛

The Clones A doctor discovers a government experiment engineered to murder him with a perfect clone.
1973 (PG) 90m/C Michael Greene, Gregory Sierra; D: Paul Hunt, Lamar Card. VHS, Beta $69.98 LIV, HHE ⅛⅛

Clones of Bruce Lee It's a martial arts free-for-all as bold masters from throughout the world duel for supremacy in the realm of self defense. If you like martial arts movies, you'll probably like this one. If you don't know if you like martial arts movies, find out with one of the actual Bruce Lee's flicks.
1980 (R) 87m/C Dragon Lee, Bruce Le, Bruce Lai, Bruce Thai; D: Joseph Kong. VHS, Beta $49.95 MED ⅛⅛

The Clonus Horror A scientist discovers a government plot to clone the population by freezing bodies alive and using their parts in surgery. AKA: Parts: The Clonus Horror.
1979 90m/C Tim Donnelly, Keenan Wynn, Peter Graves, Dick Sargent, Paulette Breen; D: Robert S. Fiveson. VHS, Beta $69.98 LIV ⅛½

Close Encounters of the Third Kind Middle-American strangers become involved in the attempts of benevolent aliens to contact earthlings. Despite the sometimes mundane nature of the characters, this Spielberg epic is a stirring achievement. Studded with classic sequences; the ending is an exhilarating experience of special effects and peace-on-earth feelings. Dreyfuss and Dillon excel as friends who are at once bewildered and obsessed by the alien presence, and French filmmaker Truffaut is also strong as the stern, ultimately kind scientist. Laserdisc includes formerly edited scenes, live interviews with Spielberg, special effects man Douglas Trumbull, and composer Williams, publicity materials, and over 1,000 production photos.
1977 (PG) 152m/C Richard Dreyfuss, Teri Garr, Melinda Dillon, Francois Truffaut, Bob Balaban, Cary Guffey; D: Steven Spielberg; W: Steven Spielberg; M: John Williams. Academy Awards '77: Best Cinematography, Best Sound Effects Editing; Nominations: Best Art Direction/Set Decoration, Best Director (Spielberg), Best Film Editing, Best Sound, Best Supporting Actress (Dillon), Best Original Score; National Board of Review Awards '77: 10 Best Films of the Year. VHS, Beta $14.95 COL, CRC, FUS ⅛⅛⅛⅛

Close My Eyes A hot, steamy summer arouses vibrant passions in a brother and sister, and neither marriage nor blood relation can halt the inevitable.
1991 (R) 105m/C Alan Rickman, Clive Owen, Saskia Reeves; D: Stephen Poliakoff. VHS $89.95 ACA ⅛⅛

Close to Eden A peasant couple living in inner Mongolia with their three children are prevented by strict Chinese law from having a fourth. The husband sets out from his village to obtain birth control from the nearby town. While on his way, the farmer (Bayaertu) saves a Russian truck driver (Gostukhin) after he drives into a lake. Sergei is introduced to another way of life when he's taken home by his rescuer to meet the family and becomes accustomed to the tranquility of farm life in the rural Mongolian steppe. Essentially a story about the changes modern civilization can bring to a rural way of life. Filmed in Mongolia. In Russian with English subtitles. AKA: Urga.
1990 (PG) 109m/C RU Baoyinhexige, Badema, Nikita Mikhalkov; D: Nikita Mikhalkov; W: Rustam Ibragimbekov; M: Eduard Artemyev. Academy Awards '92 Nominations: Best Foreign Language Film; Venice Film Festival '91: Best Film. VHS, Beta $94.95 PAR, FCT ⅛⅛

Close to Home A runaway fleeing a home life of abuse and neglect befriends a TV journalist doing a story on similar girls. She turns to him for support after she is arrested and returned home. Merely mediocre.
1986 93m/C CA Daniel Allman, Jillian Fargey, Anne Petrie; D: Rick Beairsto. VHS, Beta $79.95 TWE ⅛⅛

Closely Watched Trains A novice train dispatcher attempts to gain sexual experience in German-occupied Czechoslovakia during WWII. Many funny scenes in this film regarded by some as a classic. Based upon the Czech novel by Bohumil Hrabal. In Czech with English subtitles.
1966 89m/B CZ Vaclav Neckar, Jitka Bendova, Vladimir Valenta, Josef Somr; D: Jiri Menzel. VHS, Beta $79.95 FXL, ING, COL ⅛⅛⅛½

The Closer Aiello is "The Closer," a high-powered salesman whose world is falling apart. Somewhere between the money and the power, he's lost touch with his family and the truly important things in life. Is it too late to get them back?
1991 (R) 87m/C Danny Aiello, Michael Pare, Joe Cortese, Justine Bateman, Diane Baker, James Karen, Rick Aiello, Michael Lerner; D: Dimitri Logothetis; W: Robert Keats, Louis LaRusso II; M: Al Kasha. VHS $19.95 ACA ⅛⅛½

Closet Cases of the Nerd Kind In this comical takeoff on "Close Encounters of the Third Kind," a zany assortment of mortals meet up with extraterrestrials. All of the memorable scenes of the Spielberg film are recreated and spoofed.
1980 12m/C VHS, Beta PYR ⅛⅛½

Closet Land Severe, stylized political allegory aims high but fails to convincingly distill totalitarian repression into just two characters—a government inquisitor and his captive, a woman subjected to hideous mental and physical torture. Child-molesting emerges as an ill-advised subtheme. A better video on the same subject: "Interrogation," from Poland.
1990 (R) 95m/C Madeleine Stowe, Alan Rickman; D: Radha Bharadwaj; W: Radha Bharadwaj; M: Richard Einhorn. VHS, Beta $92.98 FXV, VTR ⅛⅛

Cloud Dancer A self-absorbed acrobat uses and abuses those around him, including his girlfriend. Carradine and O'Neill fail to distinguish themselves in this mediocre film.
1980 (PG) 107m/C David Carradine, Jennifer O'Neill, Joseph Bottoms, Colleen Camp; D: Barry Brown; W: William Goodhart. VHS, Beta $9.99 PSM ⅛⅛

Cloud Waltzing The screen version of a Harlequin romance about a journalist who arrives in France to interview a vinter and finds romance and danger. Melodrama bolstered by the presence of photogenic Beller.
1987 103m/C Kathleen Beller, Francois-Eric Gendron, Paul Maxwell, Therese Liotard, Claude Gensac, David Baxt; D: Gordon Flemyng. VHS, Beta $19.95 PAR ⅛⅛½

Clouds Over Europe A test pilot and a man from Scotland Yard team up to find out why new bomber planes are disappearing. AKA: Q Planes.
1939 82m/B Laurence Olivier, Valerie Hobson, Ralph Richardson; D: Tim Whelan. VHS, Beta $49.95 SUE ⅛⅛⅛

Clown A broken-down funny man with a worshipful son obtains one last career opportunity. This "Champ"-derived tearjerker features credible playing from Skelton and Considine as father and son, respectively.
1953 91m/B Red Skelton, Jane Greer, Tim Considine, Steve Forrest; D: Robert Z. Leonard. VHS, Beta $49.95 MGM ⅛⅛½

Clown House Young brothers are stalked in their home by three demonic clowns.
1988 (R) 95m/C Nathan Forrest Winters, Brian McHugh, Sam Rockwell, Viletta Skillman, Timothy Enos, Tree; D: Victor Salva. VHS, Beta $89.95 COL ⅛

Clown Murders Posh Halloween party is undone when a cruel group fakes a kidnapping to ruin a too-prosperous pal's business deal. Awkward thriller boasts little suspense. Candy plays it straight, mostly, in this one.
1983 94m/C John Candy, Al Waxman, Susan Keller, Lawrence Dane; D: Martyn Burke. VHS, Beta $59.95 TWE ⅛½

Clowning Around Simon, who has lived in foster homes all his life, dreams of becoming a famous circus clown. When he's sent to a new home, his new foster parents think his idea is silly, so he runs away and joins the circus. There he meets Anatole, a European clown has-been who can no longer perform because of injuries. Simon believes Anatole can teach him about clowning, so he follows Anatole to Paris to help make his dream come true. Part of the "Wonderworks" series.
1992 165m/C AU Clayton Williamson, Jean-Michel Dagory, Ernie Dingo. VHS $29.95 PME, HMV, BTV ⅛⅛½

Clowning Around 2 The continuing story of Sim, whose dream is to become a world-famous clown. Now a member of the Winter Circus in Paris, he is still training with his mentor Anatole. But Sim is dissatisfied and when he befriends Eve, another young

clown, he learns an experimental style of clowning which gets them both fired. He first follows Eve to her home in Montreal but then returns to his own home in Australia where he has been left the co-owner of a less-than-successful circus by a former employer. Filmed on location in Paris, France and Perth, Australia.
1993 120m/C *AU* Clayton Williamson, Jean-Michel Dagory, Ernie Dingo, Frederique Fouche; *D:* George Whaley. VHS $29.95 *PME, BTV* ♫♫♫½

The Clowns An idiosyncratic documentary about circus clowns. Director Fellini has fashioned an homage that is sincere, entertaining, and personal. Contains some truly poignant sequences. Made for Italian television with English subtitles.
1971 (G) 90m/C *IT D:* Federico Fellini; *W:* Federico Fellini; *M:* Nino Rota. VHS, Beta $39.95 *HTV, NOS, MRV* ♫♫♫½

The Club A soccer coach tries to train and motivate a mediocre squad into on worthy of playing for—and perhaps even winning—the league cup. Conventional sports story is significantly improved by Thompson's rendering of the coach. *AKA:* Players.
1981 (PG) 99m/C *AU* Jack Thompson, Graham Kennedy, Frank Wilson, John Howard, Alan Cassell; *D:* Bruce Beresford; *W:* David Williamson. VHS, Beta $19.95 *ACA* ♫♫♫

The Club Typical teens-in-peril flick finds the high school prom held in a mysterious old castle with ghouls out to get the unfortunate seniors. Visuals are decent but frights are tepid.
1994 (R) 88m/C Kim Coates, Joel Wyner, Andrea Roth, Rino Romano, Zack Ward, Kelli Taylor, Matthew Ferguson; *D:* Benton Spencer; *W:* Robert Cooper; *M:* Paul Zaza. VHS $92.95 *IMP* ♫

Club Extinction A near-future thriller in which Berlin is plagued by a wave of suicides. An investigator suspects a spa representative and a media tycoon of being involved. Features a fine international cast, but the film is a lesser venture from prolific master Chabrol. *AKA:* Docteur M.
1989 (R) 105m/C *GE* Alan Bates, Andrew McCarthy, Jennifer Beals, Jan Niklas, Hanns Zischler, Benoit Regent, Peter Fitz, Wolfgang Preiss, Isolde Barth; *D:* Claude Chabrol. VHS, Beta $89.95 *PSM, FCT* ♫♫½

Club Fed A rigid prison warden's plot to impose greater discipline is undone by inmate highjinks. Crude laughs and one-dimensional play from a cast of recognizable names and faces.
1990 (PG-13) 93m/C Judy Landers, Sherman Hemsley, Karen Black, Burt Young, Rick Schmidt, Allen (Gooritz) Garfield, Joseph Campanella, Lyle Alzado, Mary Woronov, Debbie Lee Carrington; *D:* Nathaniel Christian. VHS, Beta $19.95 *PSM* ♫½

Club Havana A benevolent nightclub owner tries to save one of his singers from the depths of despair by reuniting her with her boyfriend. Minor musical with minor musical numbers. ♫Besame Mucho; Tico Tico.
1946 62m/B Tom Neal, Margaret Lindsay, Don Douglas, Isabelita, Dorothy Morris, Ernest Truex; *D:* Edgar G. Ulmer. VHS, Beta $16.95 *SNC* ♫½

Club Life A hardened biker finds sex, drugs, and violence on the Hollywood streets. What did he expect? Peace, love, and understanding?
1986 (R) 93m/C Tony Curtis, Dee Wallace Stone, Tom Parsekian, Michael Parks, Jamie Barrett; *D:* Norman Thaddeus Vane. VHS, Beta $9.99 *PSM* ♫

Club Med An insecure comedian and his goofy friend try to make the most of a ski vacation. Perhaps your only chance to see Thicke, Killy, and Coolidge together.
1983 (PG) 60m/C Alan Thicke, Jim Carrey, Jean-Claude Killy, Rita Coolidge, Ronnie Hawkins; *D:* David Mitchell, Bob Giraldi; *M:* Peter Bernstein. VHS, Beta $39.95 *AHV* ♫♫

Club Paradise A Chicago fireman flees the big city for a faltering tropical resort and tries to develop some night life. Somewhat disappointing with Williams largely playing the straight man. Most laughs provided by Martin, particularly when she is assaulted by a shower, and Moranis, who gets lost while windsurfing.
1986 (PG-13) 96m/C Robin Williams, Peter O'Toole, Rick Moranis, Andrea Martin, Jimmy Cliff, Brian Doyle-Murray, Twiggy, Eugene Levy, Adolph Caesar, Joanna Cassidy, Mary Gross, Carey Lowell, Robin Duke, Simon Jones; *D:* Harold Ramis; *W:* Harold Ramis, Brian Doyle-Murray; *M:* David Mansfield, Van Dyke Parks. VHS, Beta $19.98 *WAR* ♫♫½

Clue The popular boardgame's characters must unravel a night of murder at a spooky Victorian mansion. The entire cast seems to be subsisting on sugar, with wild eyes and frantic movements the order of the day. Butler Curry best survives the uneven script and direction. Warren is appealing too. The theatrical version played with three alternative endings, and the video version shows all three successively.
1985 (PG) 96m/C Lesley Ann Warren, Tim Curry, Martin Mull, Madeline Kahn, Michael McKean, Christopher Lloyd, Eileen Brennan, Howard Hesseman, Lee Ving, Jane Wiedlin, Colleen Camp, Bill Henderson; *D:* Jonathan Lynn; *W:* Jonathan Lynn, John Landis; *M:* John Morris. VHS, Beta $19.95 *PAR* ♫♫½

The Clutching Hand The Clutching Hand seeks a formula that will turn metal into gold and detective Craig Kennedy is out to prevent him from doing so. A serial in 15 chapters on three cassettes.
1936 268m/B Jack Mulhall, Rex Lease. VHS, Beta $26.95 *SNC, NOS, VDM* ♫♫

Coach Sexy woman is unintentionally hired to coach a high school basketball team and mold rookies into lusty young champions. Low-grade roundball fever.
1978 (PG) 100m/C Cathy Lee Crosby, Michael Biehn, Keenan Wynn, Sidney Wicks; *D:* Bud Townsend. VHS, Beta $9.95 *MED* ♫½

Coal Miner's Daughter A strong bio of country singer Loretta Lynn, who rose from Appalachian poverty to Nashville riches. Spacek is perfect in the lead, and she even provides acceptable rendering of Lynn's tunes. Band drummer Helm shines as Lynn's father, and Jones is strong as Lynn's down-home husband. Uneven melodrama toward the end, but the film is still a good one. ♫Coal Miner's Daughter; Sweet Dreams of You; I'm a Honky-Tonk Girl; You're Lookin' at Country; One's On the Way; You Ain't Woman Enough to Take My Man; Back in My Baby's Arms.
1980 (PG) 125m/C Sissy Spacek, Tommy Lee Jones, Levon Helm, Beverly D'Angelo; *D:* Michael Apted. Academy Awards '80: Best Actress (Spacek); Nominations: Best Adapted Screenplay, Best Art Direction/Set Decoration, Best Cinematography, Best Film Editing, Best Picture; Golden Globe Awards '81: Best Actress—Musical/Comedy (Spacek), Best Film—Musical/Comedy; Los Angeles Film Critics Association Awards '80: Best Actress (Spacek); National Board of Review Awards '80: 10 Best Films of the Year, Best Actress (Spacek); National Society of Film Critics Awards '80: Best Actress (Spacek). VHS, Beta $14.95 *MCA, BTV* ♫♫♫

The Coast Patrol B. Reeves Eason, responsible for the chariot scene in the silent "Ben Hur" and the action scenes in "The Charge of the Light Brigade," directed Fay in one of her earliest parts, eight years before the role that prompted her to say "I didn't realize that King Kong and I were going to be together for the rest of our lives, and longer..." Much Eason-style high action when smugglers meet the coast patrol.
1925 63m/B Kenneth McDonald, Claire De Lorez, Fay Wray; *D:* B. Reeves Eason. VHS, Beta $19.95 *NOS, GPV, FCT* ♫♫½

Coast to Coast A wacky woman escapes from a mental institution and teams with a pugnacious trucker for a cross-country spree. Ostensibly freewheeling comedy is only occasionally worthwhile despite appropriate playing from leads Cannon and Blake, who deserve better.
1980 (PG) 95m/C Dyan Cannon, Robert (Bobby) Blake, Quinn Redeker, Michael Lerner, Maxine Stuart, William Lucking; *D:* Joseph Sargent; *M:* Charles Bernstein. VHS, Beta $14.95 *PAR* ♫♫

Cobra To pay off the debts incurred by his profligate playbuoyance, Valentino takes a job with an antique dealer, falls for the dealer's secretary and arranges an assignation with the dealer's wife, who is inconveniently killed at the designated rendezvous. Complications abound as Valentino finds himself Shiek out of luck. Lesser Valentino effort was released a year before the famous heartthrob's untimely death and enjoyed a rather acrid critical reception. Which isn't to say the public didn't flock to see the Italian stallion flare his nostrils.
1925 70m/B Rudolph Valentino, Nita Naldi, Casson Ferguson, Gertrude Olmsted; *D:* Joseph Henabery. VHS, Beta $24.95 *VYY, FCT, GPV* ♫

The Cobra A tightlipped U.S. agent ogles a voluptuous siren when not fighting opium smugglers from the Middle East. A must for all admirers of Ekberg. *AKA:* Il Cobra; El Cobra.
1968 93m/C Dana Andrews, Anita Ekberg; *D:* Mario Sequi. VHS *NO* ♫

Cobra A hired killer destroys most of a mob family and becomes the target of revenge for the lone survivor. Moody thriller boasts an international cast. *AKA:* le Sant de l'Ange.
1971 93m/C *FR IT* Sterling Hayden, Senta Berger, Jean Yanne; *D:* Yves Boisset. VHS, Beta $59.95 *UNI* ♫♫½

Cobra A cold-blooded cop protects a model from a gang of deranged killers. Low-brow, manipulative action fare void of feeling. Truly exploitive, with little expression from the leads. Highlight is the extended chase sequence.
1986 (R) 87m/C Sylvester Stallone, Reni Santoni, Brigitte Nielsen, Andrew (Andy) Robinson; *D:* George P. Cosmatos; *W:* Sylvester Stallone. VHS, Beta $14.95 *WAR* ♫

Cobra Against Ninja Once again, two martial arts experts try to kill each other. Can't be many of these fellas left.
1987 88m/C Jimmy Bosco, Paul Branney, Gary Carter, Alan Friss, Alfred Pears; *D:* Joseph Lai. VHS $59.95 *IMP* ♫

The Cobra Strikes Nosey thief gets more than he bargained for when he works his way through an inventor's studio. Low-budget and unexceptional.
1948 62m/B Sheila Ryan, Richard Fraser, Leslie Brooks, Herbert Heyes; *D:* Charles F. Reisner. VHS $19.95 *NOS, MOV, RXM* ♫½

Cobra Woman Technicolor adventure fantasy about the jungle queen (Montez) of a cobra-worshiping cult and her evil twin sister who wants the throne for herself.

1944 70m/C Maria Montez, Jon Hall, Sabu, Edgar Barrier, Lois Collier, Lon Chaney Jr.; *D:* Robert Siodmak; *W:* Richard Brooks. **VHS** $12.95 *GPV* 🐾🐾½

The Cobweb Shady goings on are uncovered at a psychiatric ward run by a bunch of neurotic administrators. A strong cast, director and producer do not add much to this dull outing.
1955 125m/C **Lauren Bacall, Richard Widmark, Gloria Grahame, Charles Boyer, Lillian Gish, John Kerr, Susan Strasberg, Oscar Levant, Tommy Rettig, Paul Stewart, Adele Jergens, Bert Freed, Sandy Descher, Fay Wray, Virginia Christine;** *D:* Vincente Minnelli. $39.98 *MGM* 🐾🐾

The Coca-Cola Kid A smug sales executive treks to Australia to improve regional sales and becomes embroiled in sexual and professional shenanigans. Roberts is strong in the difficult lead role, and Scacchi is compelling in an awkwardly constructed part. Ambitious satire is somewhat scattershot, with more storylines than it needs. Still, filmmaker Makavejev is usually capable of juggling the entire enterprise.
1984 (R) 94m/C *AU* Eric Roberts, Greta Scacchi, Bill Kerr; *D:* Dusan Makavejev. **VHS, Beta** $19.95 *LIV, VES, FCT* 🐾🐾🐾½

Cocaine Cowboys Lame rockers support themselves between gigs by peddling drugs then find out they've run afoul of the mob. Palance is the one worthwhile aspect of this rambling venture produced at Andy Warhol's home.
1979 (R) 90m/C Jack Palance, Andy Warhol, Tom Sullivan, Suzanna Love; *D:* Ulli Lommel. **VHS, Beta** *MED, OM* 🐾½

Cocaine Fiends Drug use leads siblings into a squalid life of addiction, crime, prostitution, and eventually suicide. Ostensibly straight morality tale functions better as loopy camp. Features memorable slang. *AKA:* The Pace That Kills.
1936 74m/B Lois January, Noel Madison; *D:* W.A. Conner. **VHS, Beta** $16.95 *SNC, NOS, MED* 🐾🐾

Cocaine: One Man's Seduction Made-for-television film documents one man's degeneration into drug addiction. Weaver snorts convincingly in lead.
1983 97m/C Dennis Weaver, Karen Grassle, Pamela Bellwood, David Ackroyd; *D:* Paul Wendkos; *M:* Brad Fiedel. **VHS, Beta** $14.95 *FRH* 🐾🐾½

Cocaine Wars An undercover U.S. agent kills dozens while trying to rescue his kidnapped girlfriend from an evil South American drug tycoon. Violent, but otherwise unaffecting.
1986 82m/C John Schneider, Kathryn Witt, Royal Dano; *D:* Hector Olivera. **VHS, Beta** $19.95 *MED, VTR* 🐾

Cockeyed Cavaliers Wheeler and Woolsey are stockaded for stealing the Duke's horses and carriage. To escape jail they swap clothes with some drunken royalty.
1934 70m/B Bert Wheeler, Robert Woolsey, Dorothy Lee, Thelma Todd; *D:* Mark Sandrich. **VHS, Beta** $34.98 *CCB* 🐾🐾

Cockfighter A unique, grim portrait of a cockfighting trainer. Oates, in the lead, provides voiceover narrations, but the film otherwise remains silent until the end. Strong support from Stanton. Interesting, violent fare. *AKA:* Gamblin' Man; Born to Kill; Wild Drifters.
1974 (R) 84m/C Warren Oates, Harry Dean Stanton, Richard B. Shull, Troy Donahue, Millie Perkins; *D:* Monte Hellman; *M:* Michael Franks. **VHS, Beta** $59.98 *SUE* 🐾🐾🐾

Cocktail A smug young man finds fame and fortune as a proficient, flashy bartender, charming the ladies with his bottle and glass juggling act. Slick, superficial film boasts a busy soundtrack and serviceable exchanges between male leads Cruise and Brown. There's less chemistry between Cruise and love interest Shue. Filmed in a high-tech rock video style.
1988 (R) 103m/C Tom Cruise, Bryan Brown, Elisabeth Shue, Lisa Banes, Laurence Luckinbill, Kelly Lynch, Gina Gershon, Ron Dean, Paul Benedict; *D:* Roger Donaldson; *W:* Heywood Gould; *M:* J. Peter Robinson. **VHS, Beta, 8mm** $19.99 *TOU* 🐾🐾½

The Cocoanuts In their film debut, the Marx Brothers create their trademark, indescribable mayhem. Stagey, technically crude comedy nonetheless delights with zany, free-for-all exchanges, antics. Includes famous "viaduct" exchange.
1929 96m/B Groucho Marx, Chico Marx, Harpo Marx, Zeppo Marx, Margaret Dumont, Kay Francis, Oscar Shaw, Mary Eaton; *D:* Robert Florey, Joseph Santley; *W:* George S. Kaufman, Morrie Ryskind; *M:* Irving Berlin. **VHS, Beta** $14.98 *MCA* 🐾🐾½

Cocoon Humanist fantasy in which senior citizens discover their fountain of youth is actually a breeding ground for aliens. Heart-warming, one-of-a kind drama showcases elderly greats Ameche, Brimley, Gilford, Cronyn, and Tandy. A commendable, recommendable venture. Based on David Saperstein's novel and followed by "Cocoon: The Return."
1985 (PG-13) 117m/C Wilford Brimley, Brian Dennehy, Steve Guttenberg, Don Ameche, Tahnee Welch, Jack Gilford, Hume Cronyn, Jessica Tandy, Gwen Verdon, Maureen Stapleton, Tyrone Power Jr., Barret Oliver, Linda Harrison, Herta Ware, Clint Howard; *D:* Ron Howard; *W:* Tom Benedek; *M:* James Horner. **VHS, Beta** $19.98 *FOX, FCT, BTV* 🐾🐾🐾

Cocoon: The Return Old timers who left with aliens in "Cocoon" return to earth and face grave problems. Less compelling sequel misses guiding hand of earlier film's director, Ron Howard. Still, most of cast from the original is on board here, and the film has its moments.
1988 (PG) 116m/C Don Ameche, Wilford Brimley, Steve Guttenberg, Maureen Stapleton, Hume Cronyn, Jessica Tandy, Gwen Verdon, Jack Gilford, Tahnee Welch, Courteney Cox, Brian Dennehy, Barret Oliver; *D:* Daniel Petrie; *M:* James Horner. **VHS, Beta** $19.98 *FOX* 🐾🐾

C.O.D. Bosom buddies must develop advertising campaign for brassiere producer or find their careers are bust. Premise milked for all its worth, so you may want to keep abreast of this one. On the other hand, you may not give a hoot. Oh well, tit for tat.
1983 (PG) 96m/C Chris Lemmon, Olivia Pascal, Jennifer Richards, Corinne Alphen, Teresa Ganzel, Carole Davis; *D:* Chuck Vincent; *W:* R.J. Marx. **VHS, Beta** $69.95 *VES, LIV* 🐾

Code Name Alpha You don't have to have a federal case of intelligence to figure out where this FBI story's going and how it's going to get there. Someone's smuggling sophisticated electrical components to the communists, and a team of intelligence agents, including Granger and Schiaffino, hike over to Hong Kong to break up the party. Based on the story "Le Riviere des Trois Jonques" by Georges Godefroy. *AKA:* Red Dragon; A-009 Missione Hong Kong.
1967 89m/C *IT GE* Stewart Granger, Rosanna Schiaffino, Harald Juhnke, Paul Klinger, Helga Sommerfeld, Horst Frank; *D:* Ernest Hofbauer. **VHS** $14.99 *VTR, SNC* 🐾🐾

Code Name: Chaos A political spoof featuring a group of renegade spies trying to come up with a get-rich-quick scheme. It involves inventing a global crisis in a small Asian country but the plan comes under the scrutiny of a CIA agent who's not in on the scheme. *AKA:* Spies, Lies, and Alibis.
1990 (R) 96m/C Robert Loggia, Diane Ladd, David Warner, Alice Krige, Brian Kerwin; *D:* Antony Thomas. **VHS** $89.98 *LIV, MOV, LIV* 🐾🐾

Code Name: Dancer A retired spy leaves her peaceful life, husband and family to take care of business in Cuba. Made for television.
1987 93m/C Kate Capshaw, Jeroen Krabbe, Gregory Sierra, Cliff DeYoung. **VHS** $89.95 *VMK* 🐾🐾

Code Name: Diamond Head In Hawaii, a secret agent is assigned to retrieve a deadly chemical that has been hidden by a master of disguises. Made for television.
1977 78m/C Roy Thinnes, France Nuyen, Zulu, Ian McShane; *D:* Jeannot Szwarc. **VHS, Beta** $49.95 *WOV* 🐾

Code Name: Emerald WWII drama in which an American agent must stop an enemy spy with knowledge of impending D-Day invasion. Conventional TV fare boasts a fine performance by von Sydow, but Stolz is hopelessly miscast as an adult. Perhaps the only film featuring both Bucholz and Berger. First feature film by NBC-TV network.
1985 (PG) 95m/C Ed Harris, Max von Sydow, Eric Stoltz, Horst Buchholz, Helmut Berger, Cyrielle Claire, Patrick Stewart, Graham Crowden; *D:* Jonathan Sanger; *M:* John Addison. **VHS, Beta** $79.98 *FOX* 🐾🐾

Code Name: Zebra The Zebra Force helps the cops put bad guys away. When the bad guys get out, they want revenge. The result: lots of violence and action. Wasn't released theatrically.
1984 96m/C Jim Mitchum, Mike Lane, Tim Brown, Joe Dante, Deana Jurgens, Frank Sinatra Jr.; *D:* Joe Tornatore. **VHS, Beta** $79.95 *TWE* 🐾½

Code of Honor A young woman vows revenge on the military commanders who caused her brother's demise. Neatly made psychological thriller is surprisingly good for a TV movie. *AKA:* Sweet Revenge.
1984 105m/C Kevin Dobson, Wings Hauser, Alec Baldwin, Merritt Butrick, Kelly McGillis, Alfre Woodard, Savannah Smith, Helen Hunt, Dana Elcar; *D:* David Green. **VHS** $59.95 *XVC, VTR* 🐾🐾½

Code of Honor Prominent businessman embarks on mission of revenge when police fail to apprehend his wife's rapist. No surprise here. You either enjoy this sort of thing or you lead a reasonably fulfilling life.
1988 90m/C Cameron Mitchell, Mark Sabin. **VHS** *NO* 🐾

Code of Silence A police loner must contend with both a gang war and police department corruption. Hectic, violent action-drama with some wild stunts.
1985 (R) 100m/C Chuck Norris, Henry Silva, Bert Remsen, Molly Hagan, Nathan Davis, Dennis Farina; *D:* Andrew Davis; *W:* Michael Butler, Mike Gray. **VHS, Beta** *NO* 🐾🐾

Code of the Fearless A cowboy wins the heart of a beautiful maiden while bringing evildoers to justice.
1939 56m/B Fred Scott, Claire Rochelle, John Merton, Harry Harvey, Walter McGrail, Roger Williams; *D:* Raymond K. Johnson. **VHS** $19.95 *NOS, DVT* 🐾

C

Codename: Foxfire An attractive secret agent is framed for wrongdoing and must clear her name by tracking the enemy spy lurking within the intelligence network. Always interesting Cassidy is an asset, but this by-the-numbers TV film is otherwise a misappropriation of the term "intelligence" in relation to espionage. *AKA:* Slay It Again, Sam.
1985 99m/C Joanna Cassidy, John McCook, Sheryl Lee Ralph, Henry Jones, Luke Andreas; *D:* Corey Allen. **VHS, Beta** $39.95 *MCA 🎬🎬*

Codename: Icarus A young mathematical genius, enrolled at a special school for accelerated study uncovers evil government plots to use the students for espionage. Made for British television.
1985 106m/C *GB* Barry Angel, Jack Galloway; *D:* Marilyn Fox. **VHS, Beta** $19.95 *FOX, TVC 🎬🎬*

Codename Kyril Woodward plays a British spy pitted against Soviet assassin Kyril (Charleson) who's been sent to England by the KGB to rout out a double agent. Turns out there's more to it than Kyril knows, and nobody loves an assassin. Based on John Trenhaile's "A Man Called Kyril," the script is slow from the gun, but eventually builds something akin to momentum. Made for cable TV.
1991 115m/C Edward Woodward, Ian Charleson, Denholm Elliott, Joss Ackland, Richard E. Grant, Sven-Bertil Taube, Catherine Nielson, John McEnery, Peter Vaughan, James Laurenson; *D:* Ian Sharp; *W:* John Hopkins. **VHS** $79.98 *TTC 🎬🎬½*

Codename: Terminate Title says it all in this tender exploration of the human condition. Jungle-trained mercenaries grab their guns and go after an American pilot shot down behind enemy lines.
1990 84m/C Robert Mason, Jim Gaines. **VHS** *NO 🎬½*

Codename: Vengeance A macho fellow tries to stop a killer holding the shah's wife and son hostage. Dated.
1987 97m/C Robert Ginty, Cameron Mitchell, Shannon Tweed; *D:* David Winters. **VHS** $79.98 *VTR, MCG 🎬*

Codename: Wildgeese The big-name cast of this meandering mercenary macho-rama probably wish they'd been credited under code names; solid histrionics cannot a silly script save. A troop of commandos-for-hire are engaged by the Drug Enforcement Administration to obliterate an opium operation in Asia's infamous Golden Triangle, and much mindless agitation ensues. *AKA:* Geheimecode Wildganse.
1984 (R) 101m/C *IT GE* Lewis Collins, Lee Van Cleef, Ernest Borgnine, Klaus Kinski, Mimsy Farmer; *D:* Anthony M. (Antonio Margheretí) Dawson. **VHS** $19.95 *STE, NWV 🎬½*

Cody A former bronco buster wants his son "take it like a man" when the boy's dog dies. Then a mystical goose arrives to mellow the old man. That's really the plot.
1967 82m/C Tony Becker, Terry Evans. **VHS, Beta** *NO 🎬*

A Coeur Joie Sixties set piece about a gorgeous woman who must choose between her much older lover or her newfound stud. Bardot and U.K. scenery keep this one from sinking entirely. In French with English subtitles. *AKA:* Two Weeks in September.
1967 100m/C *FR* Brigitte Bardot, Laurent Terzieff; *D:* Serge Bourguignon. **VHS, Beta** $19.95 *BAR 🎬🎬*

Coffy A beautiful woman feigns drug addiction to discover and destroy the evil dealers responsible for her sister's death. Grier is everything in this exploitative flick full of violence and nudity.
1973 (R) 91m/C Pam Grier, Booker Bradshaw, Robert DoQui, Allan Arbus; *D:* Jack Hill. **VHS, Beta** $9.98 *ORI, FCT 🎬🎬*

Cohen and Tate Two antagonistic mob hitmen kidnap a 9-year-old who witnessed his parent's recent murder by the mob. In order to survive, the boy begins to play one psycho off the other.
1988 (R) 113m/C Roy Scheider, Adam Baldwin, Harley Cross, Cooper Huckabee; *D:* Eric Red; *W:* Eric Red; *M:* Bill Conti. **VHS, Beta** $19.98 *SUE, NLC 🎬🎬*

Cold Blood A small dubbed Dutch film about a pair of kidnap victims who turn the tables on their captors.
197? (R) 90m/C *NL* Rutger Hauer. **VHS, Beta** $9.95 *SIM 🎬½*

Cold Blooded Murder A martial arts master assists the cops in a hunt for a Jack-the-Ripper-style killer. Among Lee's more obscure appearances.
197? 96m/C Lau Dan, Stephen Leung, Chan Wai, Carter Wong; *D:* Albert Law. **VHS** *NO 🎬*

Cold Comfort A father arranges his teen daughter's romance, but finds his plans going awry in this Canadian thriller. Nominated for several Canadian television awards, including Best Actress, Best Actor, Best Picture and Best Musical Score.
1990 (R) 90m/C *CA* Margaret Langrick, Maury Chaykin; *D:* Vic Sarin. **VHS** $89.98 *REP 🎬🎬½*

Cold Days Four men await execution for their part in the WWII massacre of Jews and Serbs. Their reminiscences and justifications, if any, are examined. Stunning cinematography and unusual theme for 1960s Hungarian political climate.
1966 102m/C *HU D:* Andras Kovacs. **VHS** $59.95 *FCT 🎬🎬½*

Cold Eyes of Fear A man and his girlfriend are besieged by a raving convict whom his uncle, a judge, had put away years before. Shades of "Cape Fear" on a low budget.
197? 88m/C Fernando Rey, Frank Wolfe, Karin Schubert; *D:* Enzo G. Castellari; *M:* Ennio Morricone. **VHS, Beta** $59.95 *TWE 🎬*

Cold Feet Light romantic comedy about a television director just recovering from a failed marriage and his fall for a lab researcher who just went through a break-up herself.
1984 (PG) 96m/C Griffin Dunne, Marissa Chibas, Blanche Baker, Mark Cronogue; *D:* Bruce Van Dusen. **VHS, Beta** $29.95 *FOX 🎬🎬*

Cold Feet Modern-day western in which a trio of loopy desperados smuggle jewels inside a racehorse's stomach. Quirky comedy offers wild performances from Waits and sex-bomb Kirkland, but could use a few more laughs. Filmed largely on McGuane's ranch.
1989 (R) 94m/C Keith Carradine, Tom Waits, Sally Kirkland, Rip Torn, Kathleen York, Bill Pullman, Vincent Schiavelli; *D:* Robert Dornhelm; *W:* Thomas McGuane, Jim Harrison; *M:* Tom Bahler. **VHS, Beta** $89.95 *LIV 🎬🎬½*

Cold Front A hired assassin turned serial killer is hunted by two dedicated cops.
1989 (R) 94m/C Martin Sheen, Michael Ontkean, Beverly D'Angelo, Kim Coates; *D:* Paul Bnarbic. **VHS, Beta** $89.99 *HBO 🎬½*

Cold Heat When a custody battle rocks a crime boss' world, he pulls out all the stops in the war against his wife.

1990 85m/C John Phillip Law, Britt Ekland, Robert Sacchi, Roy Summerset, Joanne Watkins, Chance Michael Corbitt; *D:* Ulli Lommel. **VHS, Beta** $14.95 *AIP 🎬🎬*

Cold Heaven Alex and Marie Davenport are on vacation when an accident occurs and Alex dies—or does he? The next day his body disappears and his unfaithful wife begins to have paranoid delusions that he is returning to exact retribution for her affair. But these aren't her only visions, for during the past year Marie has also had religious visions she believes are part of a personal battle with God. Harmon does what he can with his role as the alleged corpse but Russell is uncharacteristically whiny and bland. Convoluted story of marriage, death, and spirituality; doesn't pan out on any accounts. Based on a novel by Brian Moore.
1992 (R) 103m/C Theresa Russell, Mark Harmon, James Russo, Talia Shire, Will Patton, Richard Bradford; *D:* Nicolas Roeg; *W:* Allan Scott. **VHS** $9.95 *HMD, FCT 🎬½*

Cold Justice An ex-prizefighter (Daltrey) and his friends welcome an English priest into their tough southside Chicago neighborhood. The good father seems too good to be true as he befriends the locals—even raising funds for the children's hospital. When the funds never make it to the hospital and the neighborhood begins to experience a number of violent tragedies, the residents decide to take their own revenge.
1989 (R) 106m/C Dennis Waterman, Roger Daltrey, Penelope Milford, Ron Dean, Bert Rosario; *D:* Terry Green; *W:* Terry Green. **VHS** $89.95 *COL 🎬🎬*

Cold River An experienced guide takes his two children on an extended trip through the Adirondacks. For the children, it's a fantasy vacation until their father succumbs to a heart attack in the chilly mountains. "Cold River" is a journey of survival, and an exploration of human relationships.
1981 (PG) 94m/C Pat Petersen, Richard Jaeckel, Suzanne Weber; *D:* Fred G. Sullivan. **VHS, Beta** $59.98 *FOX 🎬🎬½*

Cold Room College student on vacation with her father in East Berlin discovers the horrors hidden in an antiquated hotel room next to hers. Made for cable television. From the novel by Jeffrey Caine. *AKA:* The Prisoner.
1984 95m/C George Segal, Renee Soutendijk, Amanda Pays, Warren Clarke, Anthony Higgins; *D:* James Dearden. **VHS, Beta** $59.95 *FOX 🎬½*

Cold Sassy Tree Endearing romance of a scandalous May-December marriage as perceived by the younger woman's teenage son. Dunaway and Widmark shine, and small town pettiness is vividly rendered. Adapted from the books by Olive Ann Burns. A superior made-for-cable production.
1989 95m/C Faye Dunaway, Richard Widmark, Neil Patrick Harris, Frances Fisher, Lee Garlington, John M. Jackson; *D:* Joan Tewkesbury; *W:* Joan Tewkesbury; *M:* Brad Fiedel. **VHS** $14.98 *TTC 🎬🎬🎬½*

Cold Steel Standard revenge drama about a hardnosed Los Angeles cop tracking his father's disfigured psycho-killer. Cast includes the always intense Davis, ex-pop star Ant, and screen scorchstress Stone. Still it's predictable, low-grade fare.
1987 91m/C Brad Davis, Jonathan Banks, Adam Ant, Sharon Stone; *D:* Dorothy Ann Puzo. **VHS, Beta** $79.95 *COL 🎬½*

Cold Steel for Tortuga An Italian epic about a mercenary rescuing his woman and his gold from an evil governor. Dubbed.

1965 95m/C *IT* Guy Madison, Rick Battaglia, Ingeborg Schoener; *D:* Luigi Capuano. **VHS, Beta** *NO ♂*

Cold Sweat A brutal drug trader takes his ultra-violent revenge after his wife is captured by a drug boss' moronic henchmen. Typical Bronson flick boasts superior supporting cast of Ullman and Mason. Writing and direction, however, are mediocre. *AKA:* L'Uomo Dalle Due Ombre; De la Part des Copains.
1974 (PG) 94m/C *IT FR* Charles Bronson, Jill Ireland, Liv Ullmann, James Mason; *D:* Terence Young. **VHS, Beta** $59.95 *GEM, MRV ♂♂*

Cold Sweat A professional hit man (Cross) is literally haunted by the ghost of his last victim (who happens to be female and usually appears naked), so he decides his next assignment will be his last. A ruthless businessman suspects his very sexy wife (Tweed) has been unfaithful but she has lots of other secrets to hide.
1993 (R) 93m/C Ben Cross, Shannon Tweed, Adam Baldwin, Dave Thomas; *D:* Gail Harvey; *W:* Richard Beattie. **VHS, Beta** *PAR, VTR ♂♂*

Cold Turkey Often witty satire about what happens when an entire town tries to stop smoking for a contest. Van Dyke is fine as the anti-smoking minister; newscasters Bob and Ray are riotous; oldtimer Horton's swansong. Wholesome, somewhat tame fare.
1971 (PG) 99m/C Dick Van Dyke, Pippa Scott, Tom Poston, Bob Newhart, Vincent Gardenia, Barnard Hughes, Jean Stapleton, Graham Jarvis, Edward Everett Horton; *D:* Norman Lear; *W:* Norman Lear. **VHS, Beta** $19.95 *MGM ♂♂♂*

Cold War Killers Soviet and British agents vie for control of prized cargo plane recently retrieved from the sea floor.
1986 (PG) 85m/C *GB* Terence Stamp; *D:* William Brayne. **VHS, Beta** *NO ♂ 1/2*

Coldfire Two rookie cops work to undo the havoc unleashed on the streets of LA because of a deadly new drug sought for its powerful high. Not many surprises here.
1990 90m/C Wings Hauser, Kamar Reyes, Robert Viharo, Gary Swanson; *D:* Wings Hauser. **VHS** $19.95 *PMH ♂♂*

The Colditz Story Prisoners of war from the Allied countries join together in an attempt to escape from Colditz, an allegedly escape-proof castle-prison deep within the Third Reich.
1955 93m/B John Mills, Eric Portman, Lionel Jeffries, Bryan Forbes, Ian Carmichael, Anton Diffring; *D:* Guy Hamilton. **VHS, Beta** $14.95 *CNG ♂♂1/2*

Cole Justice An older man, haunted by the memory of his girlfriend's rape and murder thirty-five years earlier, takes to the streets to protect innocent citizens from lowlife criminals. Somewhat unusual revenge pic filmed in and around Tulsa, Oklahoma.
1989 90m/C Carl Bartholomew, Keith Andrews, Mike Wiles, Nick Zickefoose; *D:* Carl Bartholomew. **VHS, Beta** *NO ♂♂*

The Collector Compelling adaptation of the John Fowles novel about a withdrawn butterfly collector who decides to add to his collection by kidnapping a beautiful girl he admires. He locks her in his cellar hoping she will fall in love with him. Chilling, unsettling drama with Stamp unnerving, yet sympathetic in lead.
1965 119m/C *GB* Terence Stamp, Samantha Eggar, Maurice Dallimore, Mona Washbourne; *D:* William Wyler; *M:* Maurice Jarre. Academy Awards '65 Nominations: Best Actress (Eggar), Best Adapted Screenplay, Best Director (Wyler); Cannes Film Festival '65: Best Actor (Stamp),

Best Actress (Eggar). **VHS, Beta** $59.95 *COL ♂♂♂ 1/2*

Collector's Item Two lovers reunite after 16 years and a flurry of memories temporarily rekindles their passion, which comes dangerously close to obsession. Casting of the physically bountiful Antonelli helps this effective erotic drama.
1989 99m/C *IT* Tony Musante, Laura Antonelli, Florinda Bolkan; *D:* Giuseppe Patroni Griffi. **VHS, Beta** *NO ♂♂*

College A high school valedictorian tries out for every sport in college, hoping to win the girl. Vintage Keaton antics, including disaster as a soda jerk, an attempt to be a track star, and the pole vault through a window to rescue the damsel in distress.
1927 60m/B Buster Keaton, A. Cornwall, Harold Goodwin; *D:* James W. Horne; *M:* John Muri. **VHS, Beta** $19.95 *DVT, MRV, CCB ♂♂♂ 1/2*

College Swing Lightweight, lackluster musical about Allen inheriting a small town college which she turns into a hangout for her vaudeville pals. Top cast is basically wasted performing many forgettable songs and familiar routines. Based on an adaptation by Frederick Hazlitt Brennan from a story by Ted Lesser. ♫College Swing; What Did Romeo Say to Juliet?; I Fall In Love With You Every Day; You're a Natural; The Old School Bell; Moments Like This; How D'ja Like to Love Me?; What a Rumba Does to Romance. *AKA:* Swing, Teacher, Swing.
1938 86m/B George Burns, Gracie Allen, Martha Raye, Bob Hope, Edward Everett Horton, Ben Blue, Betty Grable, Jackie Coogan, John Payne; *D:* Raoul Walsh. **VHS** $14.98 *MCA, BTV ♂ 1/2*

Collision Course A wise-cracking cop from Detroit teams up with Japan's best detective to nail a ruthless gang leader. Release was delayed until 1992 due to a lawsuit, but it was resolved in time to coordinate the release with Leno's debut as the host of "The Tonight Show." Pretty marginal, but diehard fans of Leno may appreciate it. Filmed on location in Detroit.
1989 (PG) 90m/C Noriyuki "Pat" Morita, Jay Leno, Chris Sarandon, Al Waxman. **VHS, Beta** $89.99 *HBO ♂*

The Colombian Connection America's best undercover agent battles a powerful cocaine empire deep in the jungles of the Amazon, where slave labor and political corruption abound.
1991 90m/C Miles O'Keeffe, Henry Silva. **VHS, Beta** *NO ♂ 1/2*

Colonel Effingham's Raid A retired army colonel uses military tactics to keep an old historical courthouse open, while defeating some crooked politicians in the process. *AKA:* Man of the Hour.
1945 70m/B Joan Bennett, Charles Coburn, William Eythe, Donald Meek; *D:* Irving Pichel. **VHS, Beta** $19.95 *NOS, HEG ♂♂ 1/2*

Colonel Redl Absorbing, intricately rendered psychological study of an ambitious officer's rise and fall in pre-WWI Austria. Brandauer is excellent as the vain, insecure homosexual ultimately undone by his own ambition and his superior officer's smug loathing. Muller-Stahl and Landgrebe are particularly distinguished among the supporting players. The second in the Szabo/Brandauer trilogy, after "Mephisto" and before "Hanussen." In German with English subtitles.
1984 (R) 114m/C *GE HU* Klaus Maria Brandauer, Armin Mueller-Stahl, Gudrun Landgrebe, Jan Niklas, Hans-Christian Blech, Laszlo Mensaros, Andras Balint; *D:* Laszlo Szabo. **VHS, Beta** $29.95 *FCT, GLV, ING ♂♂♂♂*

Colonel Wolodyjowski An adaptation of the monumental novels by Henryk Sinkiewicz chronicling the attack on Poland's eastern border by the Turks in 1668. In Polish with English subtitles.
1969 160m/C *PL* Tadeusz Loniski, Magdalena Zawadzka, Daniel Olbrychski; *D:* Jerzy Hoffman. **VHS** $49.95 *FCT ♂♂ 1/2*

Color Me Blood Red Artist decides that the red in his paintings is best rendered with human blood. He even manages to continue his art career—when not busy stabbing and mutilating the unsuspecting citizenry. Short and shoddy. Also known as "Model Massacre." *AKA:* Model Massacre.
1964 74m/C Don Joseph, Sandi Conder; *D:* Herschell Gordon Lewis. **VHS, Beta** $29.95 *NO Woof!*

Color Me Dead A victim of an extremely slow-acting poison frantically spends his final days trying to uncover his killer. Another inferior remake of B-thriller "D.O.A." Rent that one instead.
1969 (R) 97m/C *AU* Tom Tryon, Carolyn Jones, Rick Jason, Patricia Connolly, Tony Ward; *D:* Eddie Davis. **VHS** *REP ♂ 1/2*

The Color of Money Flashy, gripping drama about former pool hustler Fast Eddie Felsen (Newman) who, after years off the circuit, takes a brilliant but immature pool shark (Cruise) under his wing. Strong performances by Newman as the grizzled veteran, Cruise as the showboating youth, and Mastrantonio and Shaver as the men's worldly girlfriends. Worthy sequel to '50s classic "The Hustler."
1986 (R) 119m/C Paul Newman, Tom Cruise, Mary Elizabeth Mastrantonio, Helen Shaver, John Turturro, Forest Whitaker; *D:* Martin Scorsese; *W:* Richard Price. Academy Awards '86: Best Actor (Newman); Nominations: Best Adapted Screenplay, Best Art Direction/Set Decoration, Best Supporting Actress (Mastrantonio). **VHS, Beta** $19.95 *TOU, BTV ♂♂♂ 1/2*

Color of Night Psychologist Dr. Bill Capa (Willis) takes over a murdered colleague's therapy group hoping to find out the killer's identity. Then he meets temptress Rose (March) and gets involved in a hot affair but she's not what she seems—nor is anyone else in the group. Sex scenes between Willis and March were toned down to avoid the dreaded NC-17 rating but push the limits nonetheless.
1994 (R) ?m/C Bruce Willis, Jane March, Scott Bakula, Ruben Blades, Lesley Ann Warren, Lance Henriksen, Kevin J. O'Connor, Andrew Lowery, Brad Dourif; *D:* Richard Rush; *W:* Matthew Chapman, Billy Ray, Richard Rush. **VHS** *NYR ♂♂*

The Color of Pomegranates Paradjanov's depiction of the life of Armenian poet Arutiun Sayadin, known as Sayat Nova, who rises from carpet weaver to court minstrel to archbishop. Eloquent imagery and symbols are derived from Armenian paintings, poetry and history. In Armenian with English subtitles. Also includes "Hagop Hovnatanian," a 12-minute short on the artist. *AKA:* Sayat Nova; Tsvet Granata.
1969 80m/C *RU* Sofiko Chiaureli, M. Aleksanian, V. Galstian; *D:* Sergei Paradjanov; *W:* Sergei Paradjanov. **VHS** $79.95 *CVC, FCT ♂♂♂*

The Color Purple Celie is a poor black girl who fights for her self-esteem when she is separated from her sister and forced into a brutal marriage. Spanning 1909 to 1947 in a small Georgia town, the movie chronicles the joys, pains, and people in her life. Adaptation of Alice Walker's acclaimed book features strong lead from Goldberg (her screen debut), Glover, Avery, and talk-show host Win-

frey (also her film debut). It's hard to see director Spielberg as the most suited for this one, but he acquits himself nicely, avoiding the facileness that sometimes flaws his pics. Brilliant photography by Allen Davian and musical score by Jones (who co-produced) compliment this strong film.
1985 (PG-13) 154m/C Whoopi Goldberg, Danny Glover, Oprah Winfrey, Margaret Avery, Adolph Caesar, Rae Dawn Chong, Willard Pugh, Akosua Busia; *D:* Steven Spielberg; *M:* Quincy Jones. Academy Awards '85 Nominations: Best Actress (Goldberg), Best Adapted Screenplay, Best Art Direction/Set Decoration, Best Cinematography, Best Costume Design, Best Makeup, Best Picture, Best Song ("Miss Celie's Blues (Sister)"), Best Supporting Actress (Avery, Winfrey), Best Original Score; Directors Guild of America Awards '85: Best Director (Spielberg); Golden Globe Awards '86: Best Actress—Drama (Goldberg); National Board of Review Awards '85: 10 Best Films of the Year, Best Actress (Goldberg). **VHS, Beta $19.98** WAR, FCT �411½

Colorado Roy tries to find his brother, a Union deserter, during the Civil War.
1940 54m/B Roy Rogers, George "Gabby" Hayes, Milburn Stone; *D:* Joseph Kane. **VHS, Beta $9.99** NOS, MED, DVT �4½

Colorado Serenade Standard oater has Dean, Sharpe and Ates trying to prevent a young outlaw from bullying the local citizenry. Sharpe shows off his athletic prowess, and King provides some laughs. Other than that, it's pretty routine stuff.
1946 68m/C Eddie Dean, David Sharpe, Roscoe Ates, Forrest Taylor, Dennis Moore, Warner Richmond, Bob Duncan, Charles "Blackie" King; *D:* Robert Emmett. **VHS $19.95** NOS, RXM, HEG ✄✄

Colorado Sundown A conniving brother and sister attempt to cheat a man out of his inheritance.
1952 67m/B Rex Allen, Mary Ellen Kay, Slim Pickens, June Vincent, Koko; *D:* William Witney. **VHS $19.95** NOS, DVT ✄

Colors Vivid, realistic cop drama pairs sympathetic veteran Duvall and trigger-tempered rookie Penn on the gang-infested streets of East Los Angeles. Fine play from leads is one of the many assets in this controversial, unsettling depiction of deadly streetlife. Colorful, freewheeling direction from the underrated Hopper. Rattling rap soundtrack too. Additional footage has been added for video release.
1988 (R) 120m/C Sean Penn, Robert Duvall, Maria Conchita Alonso, Trinidad Silva, Randi Brooks, Grand Bush, Don Cheadle, Rudy Ramos; *D:* Dennis Hopper; *W:* Michael Schiffer; *M:* Herbie Hancock. **VHS, Beta $9.98** ORI, FCT ✄✄✄½

Colossus and the Amazon Queen Idle gladiators are unwillingly recruited for service to Amazons. Doesn't seem like the worst way to make a living. But lead actor Taylor—so notable in comedies, thrillers, and action flicks—is too good for this sort of thing. Dubbed.
1964 94m/C *IT* Rod Taylor, Dorian Gray, Ed Fury. **VHS, Beta, 8mm $24.95** VYY ✄½

Colossus of the Arena In 4th century Rome, Forest plays a mighty gladiator who uncovers a plot to imprison a beautiful princess. Through an incredible series of feats and combats, he exposes an evil duke as a traitor.
1960 ?m/C Mark Forest, Scilla Gabel. **VHS $16.95** SNC ✄✄

Colossus: The Forbin Project A computer designed to manage U.S. defense systems teams instead with its Soviet equal and they attempt world domination. Wiretight, suspenseful film seems at once dated

yet timely. Based on the novel by D.F. Jones. *AKA:* The Forbin Project.
1970 100m/C Eric (Hans Gudegast) Braeden, Susan Clark, Gordon Pinsent; *D:* Joseph Sargent; *W:* James Bridges; *M:* Michel Colombier. **VHS, Beta $14.98** MCA ✄✄✄

Colt Comrades A bad guy's monopoly on water rights is jeopardized when Boyd and Clyde strike water while drilling for oil. Nothing really notable here, except for Bob (Robert) Mitchum and George ("Superman") Reeves in minor roles.
1943 67m/B William Boyd, Andy Clyde, Jay Kirby, George Reeves, Gayle Lord, Earle Hodgins, Victor Jory, Douglas Fowley, Herbert Rawlinson, Robert Mitchum; *D:* Lesley Selander. **VHS $19.95** NOS ✄✄

Colt is My Law Bandits steal a railroad-funding gold shipment, and are pursued relentlessly by mysterious masked men. *AKA:* Mi Revolver es la Ley.
19?? 95m/C Anthony Clark, Lucy Gilly, Michael Martin. **VHS, Beta** NO ✄½

Columbo: Murder By the Book The rumpled, cigar-smoking television detective investigates the killing of a mystery writer. Scripted by Bochco of "Hill Street Blues" and "L.A. Law" fame.
1971 79m/C Peter Falk, Jack Cassidy, Rosemary Forsyth, Martin Milner; *D:* Steven Spielberg; *W:* Steven Bochco. **VHS, Beta $39.95** MCA ✄✄½

Columbo: Prescription Murder Peter Falk's debut as the raincoat-clad lieutenant investigating the death of a psychiatrist's wife. Rich with subplots. Good mystery fare.
1967 99m/C Peter Falk, Gene Barry, Katherine Justice, William Windom, Nina Foch, Anthony James, Virginia Gregg; *D:* Richard Irving. **VHS, Beta** MCA ✄✄✄

Coma A doctor discovers murder and corpse-nabbing at her Boston hospital, defies her male bosses, and determines to find out what's going on before more patients die. Exciting, suspenseful fare, with Bujold impressive in lead. Based on the novel by Robin Cook.
1978 (PG) 113m/C Genevieve Bujold, Michael Douglas, Elizabeth Ashley, Rip Torn, Richard Widmark, Lois Chiles, Hari Rhodes, Tom Selleck, Ed Harris; *D:* Michael Crichton; *W:* Michael Crichton; *M:* Jerry Goldsmith. **VHS, Beta $14.95** MGM ✄✄✄

The Comancheros Texas Ranger Wayne and his prisoner fight with the Comancheros, an outlaw gang who is supplying guns and liquor to the dreaded Comanche Indians. Musical score adds flavor. Last film by Curtiz.
1961 108m/C John Wayne, Ina Balin, Stuart Whitman, Nehemiah Persoff, Lee Marvin, Bruce Cabot; *D:* Michael Curtiz; *M:* Elmer Bernstein. **VHS, Beta $19.98** FOX ✄✄✄

Combat! Morrow and Jason starred in this gritty series about an Army platoon in Europe during the final years of WWII. In "The Bridge at Chalons" Marvin guest stars as a demolitions expert. Additional episodes available.
1962 50m/B Vic Morrow, Rick Jason, Lee Marvin. **VHS, Beta $19.95** GKK, MOV ✄✄✄

Combat Academy Weak comedy about two goofballs sent to a military academy to straighten out, but instead turn the academy on its ear with their antics. Unremarkable.
1986 96m/C Keith Gordon, Jamie Farr, Sherman Hemsley, John Ratzenberger, Bernie Kopell, Charles Moll; *D:* Neal Israel. **VHS $19.95** STE, NWV ✄

Combat Killers A WWII Army captain grabs for individual glory on the battlefield, and jeopardizes the lives of his platoon.

1980 96m/C Paul Edwards, Marlene Dauden, Claude Wilson; *D:* Ken Loring. **VHS, Beta $59.95** MED ✄✄

Combat Shock A Vietnam veteran returns home and can't cope with the stresses of modern life, including the lowlifes who have been taking over the streets. So he goes after some scum who have been trying to kill him, succeeds, but things don't end well. Familiar plot handled in a conventional manner. *AKA:* American Nightmares.
1984 (R) 85m/C Ricky Giovinazzo, Nick Nasta, Veronica Stork; *D:* Buddy Giovinazzo. **VHS, Beta $9.99** PSM ✄✄

Combination Platter Anxious young immigrant Robert (Lau), newly arrived from Hong Kong, becomes a waiter at the Szechuan Inn in Queens, New York, where he gets a crash course in American culture and romance (as well as tipping). Gentle comedy works best with little details that ring true: overheard customer conversations, staff banter, the kitchen scenes. Lau's earnest, but effort feels like a series of small vignettes rather than a complete story. Still, a worthy first effort for the then 24-year-old Chan, who directed on a $250,000 budget, using his parents restaurant after hours on a set.
1993 84m/C Jeff Lau, Colleen O'Brien, Lester Chan, Thomas S. Hsiung, David Chung; *D:* Tony Chan; *W:* Tony Chan, Edwin Baker. **VHS** NYR ✄✄½

Come Along with Me A made-for-television adaptation of Shirley Jackson's unfinished novel about a woman who sells all and leaves her hometown when her husband dies, determined to start a new career as a seer.
1984 60m/C Estelle Parsons, Barbara Baxley, Sylvia Sidney; *D:* Joanne Woodward. **VHS, Beta $24.95** MON, KAR ✄✄½

Come and Get It A classic adaptation of the Edna Ferber novel about a lumber king battling against his son for the love of a woman. Farmer's most important Hollywood role. *AKA:* Roaring Timber.
1936 99m/B Frances Farmer, Edward Arnold, Joel McCrea, Walter Brennan, Andrea Leeds, Charles Halton; *D:* William Wyler, Howard Hawks. Academy Awards '36: Best Supporting Actor (Brennan); Nominations: Best Film Editing. **VHS, Beta $19.98** HBO, SUE, BTV ✄✄✄

Come and See Harrowing, unnerving epic which depicts the horrors of war as a boy soldier roams the Russian countryside during the Nazi invasion. Some overwhelming sequences, including tracer-bullets flashing across an open field. War has rarely been rendered in such a vivid, utterly grim manner. Outstanding achievement from Soviet director Klimov. In Russian with English subtitles. *AKA:* Idi i Smotri; Go and See.
1985 142m/C *RU* Alexei Kravchenko, Olga Mironova, Lubomiras Lauciavicus; *D:* Elem Klimov. **VHS $59.95** KIV, FCT, TPV ✄✄✄✄

Come Back, Africa A classic documentary about a Zulu family surviving under apartheid in South Africa.
1960 83m/B VHS, Beta $29.95 MFV, FCT, TPV ✄✄✄

Come Back Little Reba A semi-educational film about a young black boy and his lovable aging dog.
1986 60m/C VHS, Beta PAR ✄

Come Back, Little Sheba Unsettling drama about a worn-out housewife, her abusive, alcoholic husband and a comely boarder who causes further marital tension. The title refers to the housewife's despairing search for her lost dog. Booth, Lancaster, and Moore are all excellent. Based on the

play by William Inge, this film still packs an emotional wallop.
1952 99m/B Burt Lancaster, Shirley Booth, Terry Moore, Richard Jaeckel, Philip Ober, Liza Golm, Walter Kelley; **D:** Daniel Mann. Academy Awards '52: Best Actress (Booth); Nominations: Best Film Editing, Best Supporting Actress (Moore); Cannes Film Festival '53: Best Actress (Booth); Golden Globe Awards '53: Best Actress—Drama (Booth). **VHS, Beta $19.95** *PAR, FCT, BTV* ♦♦♦½

Come Back to the Five & Dime Jimmy Dean, Jimmy Dean Five women convene at a run-down Texas drug-store for a 20-year reunion of a local James Dean fan club. The women recall earlier times and make some stunning revelations. Altman's filming of Ed Graczyk's sometimes funny, sometimes wrenching play proves fine vehicle for the actresses. Cher is probably the most impressive, but Dennis and Black are also memorable.
1982 (PG) 109m/C Sandy Dennis, Cher, Karen Black, Kathy Bates, Sudie Bond, Marta Heflin; **D:** Robert Altman. **VHS, Beta $19.98** *SUE* ♦♦♦

Come Blow Your Horn Neil Simon's first major Broadway success is a little less successful in its celluloid wrapper, suffering a bit from a familiar script. Sinatra's a playboy who blows his horn all over town, causing his close-knit New York Jewish family to warp a bit. Dad's not keen on his son's pledge of allegiance to the good life, and kid brother Bill would like to be his sibling's understudy in playboyhood.
1963 115m/C Frank Sinatra, Lee J. Cobb, Tony Bill, Molly Picon, Barbara Rush, Jill St. John; **D:** Bud Yorkin; **W:** Norman Lear. **VHS, Beta $14.95** *PAR* ♦♦♦

Come On, Cowboys The Three Mesquiteers rescue an old circus friend from certain death. Part of "The Three Mesquiteers" series.
1937 54m/B Bob Livingston, Ray Corrigan. **VHS, Beta $25.00** *MED, DVT* ♦½

Come On Danger! Keene makes his "B" Western debut, out to avenge the death of his brother and battle an outlaw gang. Haydon is forced into a life of crime in order to save her ranch from villain Ellis and only Texas Ranger Keene can set her free.
1932 60m/B Tom Keene, Julie Haydon, Roscoe Ates, Robert Ellis, Wade Boteler; **D:** Robert F. Hill; **W:** Bennett Cohen. **VHS $19.99** *MOV* ♦♦½

Come On Rangers Also called "Come On Ranger." Rogers and his friends go to Texas to avenge the death of a comrade.
1938 54m/B Roy Rogers, George "Gabby" Hayes. **VHS, Beta $19.95** *NOS, DVT, RXM* ♦

Come On Tarzan Maynard and his trusty horse Tarzan save wild horses from the bad guys who want to turn them into dog food.
1932 60m/B Ken Maynard. **VHS, Beta $19.95** *NOS, VDM, DVT* ♦½

Come See the Paradise Jack McGurn (Quaid) takes a job at a movie theatre in Los Angeles' Little Tokyo and falls for owner's daughter Lily (Tomita). They marry, but after the bombing of Pearl Harbor all Japanese-Americans are interned. Told in flashback, the story offers a candid look at the racism implicit in the relocations and the hypocrisy that often lurks beneath the surface of the pursuit of liberty and justice for all. Sometimes melodramatic script indulges a bit too much in the obvious, but the subject is worthwhile, one that has not yet been cast into the vast bin of Hollywood cliches. The cast, apart from Quaid's misguided attempt at seriousness, is excellent.

1990 (R) 135m/C Dennis Quaid, Tamlyn Tomita, Sab Shimono, Shizuko Hoshi, Stan Egi, Ronald Yamamoto, Akemi Nishino, Naomi Nakano, Brady Tsurutani, Pruitt Taylor Vince, Joe Lisi; **D:** Alan Parker; **W:** Alan Parker; **M:** Randy Edelman. **VHS, Beta $19.98** *FOX, FCT, CCB* ♦♦♦

The Comeback A singer attempting a comeback in England finds his wife murdered. **AKA:** The Day the Screaming Stopped.
1977 100m/C *GB* Jack Jones, Pamela Stephenson, David Doyle, Bill Owen, Sheila Keith, Richard Johnson; **D:** Pete Walker. **VHS, Beta $19.98** *LHV* ♦

Comeback The story of a disillusioned rock star, played by Eric Burdon (the lead singer of the Animals), who gives up his life in the fast lane and tries to go back to his roots.
1983 105m/C Eric Burdon; **D:** Christel Bushmann. **VHS, Beta $24.95** *MGM* ♦♦½

Comeback Kid An ex-big league baseball player is conned into coaching an urban team of smarmy street youths, and falls for their playground supervisor. Made for television.
1980 97m/C John Ritter, Susan Dey; **D:** Peter Levin. **VHS, Beta $9.98** *SUE, NLC* ♦

The Comedians Disturbing and powerful drama of political intrigue set against the murderous dictatorship of "Papa Doc" Duvalier. Burton plays the cynical owner of a resort hotel with Taylor as his German mistress. Ustinov is great as he does his usual scene-stealing in his role as a South American ambassador married to Taylor. Excellent cast was somewhat held back by sluggish direction and an uninspired script. Based on the novel of the same name by Graham Greene.
1967 148m/C Elizabeth Taylor, Richard Burton, Alec Guinness, Peter Ustinov, Paul Ford, Lillian Gish, Raymond St. Jacques, Zakes Mokae; **D:** Peter Glenville; **W:** Graham Greene. **VHS $19.98** *MGM* ♦♦½

Comedy Classics Three early comedy shorts: "Double Trouble," with Pollard; "So and Sew," with Ball; and "Technocrazy," directed by Al Christie.
1935 60m/B Snub Pollard, Oliver Hardy, Lucille Ball, Billy Bevan, Monty Collins. **VHS, Beta $59.95** *JEF* ♦♦½

Comedy Classics of Mack Sennett and Hal Roach Three comedy silent films: "Love, Loot and Crash;" "Looking for Trouble;" and "A Desperate Scoundrel."
1915 51m/B **VHS, Beta $24.95** *VYY* ♦♦½

Comedy Festival #1 Collection of three comic films: "Speed in the Gay Nineties," with Clyde; "Disorder in the Court," with the Three Stooges; "Hail Brother," with Gilbert.
193? 53m/B Andy Clyde, Billy Gilbert, Curly Howard, Moe Howard, Larry Fine. **VHS, Beta $34.95** *HHT* ♦♦½

Comedy Festival #2 Collection of comedy films: "Bashful Romeo," with Lamb; "Super Snooper," with Clyde; "Super Stupid," with Gilbert.
193? 53m/B Gil Lamb, Andy Clyde, Billy Gilbert. **VHS, Beta $34.95** *HHT* ♦♦½

Comedy Festival #3 Collection of comic films: "Big Flash," with Langdon; "Half A Hero," and "Pardon My Papa," with Temple.
193? 53m/B Harry Langdon, Shirley Temple. **VHS, Beta $34.95** *HHT* ♦♦½

Comedy Festival #4 A collection of comic films: "His Weak Moment," "Fainting Lover," and "Shopping with the Wife."

193? 53m/B Andy Clyde. **VHS, Beta $34.95** *HHT* ♦♦½

The Comedy of Terrors Comedy in which some deranged undertakers take a hands-on approach to insuring their continued employment. Much fun is supplied by the quartet of Price, Lorre, Karloff, and Rathbone, all veterans of the horror genre.
1964 84m/C Vincent Price, Peter Lorre, Boris Karloff, Basil Rathbone, Joe E. Brown, Joyce Jameson; **D:** Jacques Tourneur; **W:** Richard Matheson; **M:** Les Baxter. **VHS $79.98** *MOV* ♦♦♦

Comedy Reel, Vol. 1 Contains three W.C. Fields shorts: "Golf Specialist," "Fatal Glass of Beer," and "The Dentist."
197? 60m/B W.C. Fields. **VHS, Beta $23.95** *CAB* ♦♦½

Comedy Reel, Vol. 2 These comedy shorts feature the Three Stooges in "Disorder in the Court," Edgar Kennedy and Franklin Pangborn in "Next Door Neighbors," and W.C. Fields in "The Barbershop."
197? 60m/B Moe Howard, Edgar Kennedy, Franklin Pangborn, W.C. Fields. **VHS, Beta $23.95** *CAB* ♦♦½

Comes a Horseman Robards is a cattle baron, attempting to gobble up all the oil-rich land his neighbor owns. Neighbor Fonda has the courage to stand up to him, with the help of a WWII veteran and the local old timer Farnsworth, in this slow-moving but intriguing western drama.
1978 (PG) 119m/C James Caan, Jane Fonda, Jason Robards Jr., George Grizzard, Richard Farnsworth, Jim Davis, Mark Harmon; **D:** Alan J. Pakula. Academy Awards '78 Nominations: Best Supporting Actor (Farnsworth); National Board of Review Awards '78: 10 Best Films of the Year, Best Supporting Actor (Farnsworth). **VHS, Beta** *FOX* ♦♦½

Comfort and Joy After his kleptomaniac girlfriend deserts him, a Scottish disc jockey is forced to reevaluate his life. He becomes involved in an underworld battle between two mob-owned local ice cream companies. Another odd comedy gem from Forsyth, who did "Gregory's Girl" and "Local Hero". Music by Dire Straits guitarist Knopfler.
1984 (PG) 93m/C *GB* Bill Paterson, Eleanor David, C.P. Grogan, Alex Norton, Patrick Malahide, Rikki Fulton, Roberto Berrardi; **D:** Bill Forsyth; **M:** Mark Knopfler. **VHS, Beta $69.95** *MCA* ♦♦♦½

The Comfort of Strangers Atmospheric psychological thriller. Mary and Colin (Richardson and Everett), a handsome young British couple, take a Venetian holiday to rediscover the passion in their relationship. Lost in the city, they chance, it seems, upon Robert (Walken), a sort of Virgil in an Italian suit. He later reappears, and, abetted by his wife Caroline (Mirren), gradually leads the couple on an eerie tour of urbane decadence that hints at danger. Psychologically tantalizing and horrifyingly erotic, the movie's based on Ian McEwan's novel.
1991 (R) 102m/C Christopher Walken, Natasha Richardson, Rupert Everett, Helen Mirren; **D:** Paul Schrader; **W:** Harold Pinter; **M:** Angelo Badalamenti. **VHS, Beta $79.95** *PAR, FCT* ♦♦♦

The Comic Van Dyke is terrific as a silent screen comedian (a composite of several real-life screen comics) whose ego destroys his career. Recreations of silent films, and the blend of comedy and pathos, are especially effective.
1969 (PG) 96m/C Dick Van Dyke, Mickey Rooney, Michele Lee, Cornel Wilde, Nina Wayne, Pert Kelton, Jeannine Riley; **D:** Carl Reiner; **W:** Carl Reiner. **VHS, Beta $59.95** *COL* ♦♦♦

The Comic In a future police state, a young comedian kills the star and takes his place in the show. His future rises, but who cares?
1985 90m/C Steve Munroe, Bernard Plant, Jeff Pirie; *D:* Richard Driscoll. **VHS, Beta** NO *⌐*

Comic Book Kids Two youngsters enjoy visiting their friend's comic strip studio, since they have the power to project themselves into the cartoon stories. Viewers will be less impressed.
1982 (G) 90m/C Joseph Campanella, Mike Darnell, Robyn Finn, Jim Engelhardt, Fay De Witt. **VHS, Beta** GEM *⌐⌐½*

Comic Cabby A day in the life of an introvert cabby seems to last forever. From "New York City Cab Driver's Joke Book" by Jim Pietsch.
1987 59m/C Bill McLaughlin, Al Lewis. **VHS, Beta** $59.95 VES, LIV Woof!

Comin' Round the Mountain The duo are caught in a Kentucky family feud while seeking a fortune in gold. Funniest bit has backwoods witch Hamilton squaring off with Costello when he refuses to pay for the love potion she's made him.
1951 77m/B Bud Abbott, Lou Costello, Dorothy Shay, Kirby Grant, Joseph Sawyer, Margaret Hamilton, Glenn Strange, Guy Wilkerson; *D:* Charles Lamont; *W:* John Grant, Robert Lees, Fred Rinaldo. **VHS** $14.98 MCA *⌐⌐½*

Coming Home Looks at the effect of the Vietnam War on home front. The wife of a gung-ho Marine officer volunteers as an aide in a Veteran's Hospital, befriends and eventually falls in love with a Vietnam vet, paralyzed from war injuries. His attitudes, pain, and first-hand knowledge of the war force her to re-examine her previously automatic responses. Honest look at the everyday life of disabled veterans, unusual vision of the possibilities of simple friendship between men and women. Fonda and Voight are great; Dern's character suffers from weak scriptwriting late in the film. Critically acclaimed. Compelling score from late '60s music.
1978 (R) 130m/C Jane Fonda, Jon Voight, Bruce Dern, Penelope Milford, Robert Carradine, Robert Ginty; *D:* Hal Ashby; *W:* Robert C. Jones. Academy Awards '78: Best Actor (Voight), Best Actress (Fonda), Best Screenplay; Nominations: Best Director (Ashby), Best Film Editing, Best Picture, Best Supporting Actor (Dern), Best Supporting Actress (Milford); Cannes Film Festival '78: Best Actor (Voight); Golden Globe Awards '79: Best Actor—Drama (Voight), Best Actress—Drama (Fonda). **VHS, Beta** $14.95 MGM, FOX, FCT *⌐⌐⌐½*

The Coming of Amos A wonderful send-up of all those Fairbanks-style melodramas, with La Rocque as an Aussie on vacation on the French Riviera falling for and eventually rescuing Goudal, as the Russian princess held captive by the lustful Beery.
1925 60m/B Rod La Rocque, Jetta Goudal, Noah Beery Sr., Florence Vidor; *D:* Paul Sloane. **VHS, Beta** GVV *⌐⌐⌐*

Coming Out Alive Tense thriller about a woman and her hired mercenary who try to rescue her kidnapped son from his estranged father—a radical is involved in an assassination plot. Hylands is especially compelling.
1984 73m/C Helen Shaver, Scott Hylands, Michael Ironside, Monica Parker. **VHS, Beta** $59.95 TWE *⌐⌐½*

Coming Out of the Ice Engrossing true story of Victor Herman, an outstanding American athlete who worked in Russia (for 38 years!) for refusing to renounce his American citizenship. Made for television.

1982 (PG) 100m/C John Savage, Willie Nelson, Ben Cross, Francesca Annis, Peter Vaughan; *D:* Waris Hussein; *M:* Maurice Jarre. **VHS, Beta** $59.98 FOX *⌐⌐⌐*

Coming Through Writer D.H. Lawrence meets the married Frieda von Richthofen and begins a scandalous affair which intertwines with his own writings, and the life of a young man in the present day. Made for British television production lacks passion.
1990 78m/C GB Kenneth Branagh, Helen Mirren, Alison Steadman, Philip Martin Brown, Norman Rodway; *D:* Peter Barber-Fleming; *W:* Alan Plater. **VHS** $29.95 TVC, BFS *⌐⌐½*

Coming to America An African prince (Murphy) decides to come to America in search of a suitable bride. He lands in Queens, and quickly finds American women to be more confusing than he imagined. Sometimes overly-cute entertainment relieved by clever costume cameos by Murphy and Hall. Later lawsuit resulted in columnist Art Buchwald being given credit for story.
1988 (R) 116m/C Eddie Murphy, Arsenio Hall, James Earl Jones, John Amos, Madge Sinclair, Shari Headley, Don Ameche, Louie Anderson, Paul Bates, Allison Dean, Eriq LaSalle, Calvin Lockhart, Samuel L. Jackson, Cuba Gooding Jr., Vanessa Bell, Frankie Faison, Vondie Curtis-Hall; *D:* John Landis; *W:* David Sheffield, Barry W. Blaustein; *M:* Nile Rodgers. **VHS, Beta, 8mm** $14.95 PAR, FCT *⌐⌐*

Coming Up Roses Pleasant comedy about the residents of a small mining village in the South of Wales who fight to keep their local movie house from being shut down. In Welsh with English subtitles. *AKA:* Rhosyn A Rhith.
1987 (PG) 95m/C GB Dafydd Hywel, Iola Gregory, Olive Michael, Mari Emlyn, Bill Paterson; *D:* Stephen Bayly; *W:* Ruth Carter; *M:* Michael Storey. **VHS, Beta** $29.95 FCT, ING *⌐⌐½*

Command Decision Upon realizing he must send his men on missions-of-no-return to destroy German jet production, Gable's WWII flight commander becomes tactically at odds with his political superior, Pidgeon (who's not keen to have his precision bombing plans placed in an unflattering light). Based on the stage hit by William Wister Haines, it's a late war pic by Wood, who earlier directed such diverse efforts as "A Night at the Opera," "The Devil and Miss Jones," and "Our Town." Vintage war-is-hell actioner.
1948 112m/B Clark Gable, Walter Pidgeon, Van Johnson, Brian Donlevy, Charles Bickford, John Hodiak; *D:* Sam Wood; *M:* Miklos Rozsa. **VHS** $19.98 MGM, FCT *⌐⌐½*

Commando An ex-commando leader's daughter is kidnapped in a blackmail scheme to make him depose a South American president. He fights instead, and proceeds to rescue his daughter amid a torrential flow of falling bodies. Violent action spiced with throwaway comic lines.
1985 (R) 90m/C Arnold Schwarzenegger, Rae Dawn Chong, Dan Hedaya, Vernon Wells, James Olson, David Patrick Kelly, Alyssa Milano, Bill Duke; *D:* Mark L. Lester; *W:* Steven E. de Souza; *M:* James Horner. **VHS, Beta** $14.98 FXV, TLF *⌐⌐⌐*

Commando Attack A tough sergeant leads a group of misfit soldiers to blow up a German radio transmitter the day before D-Day.
1967 90m/C Michael Rennie, Monica Randall, Bob Sullivan. **VHS, Beta** $59.95 UNI *⌐½*

Commando Invasion When an army captain is accused of murder, he hunts down the man he knows is responsible for the crime. Jungle revenge mayhem is confusing. Set in Viet Nam.
1987 90m/C Jim Gaines, Michael James, Gordon Mitchell, Carol Roberts, Pat Vance, Ken Watanabe; *D:* John Gale. **VHS** NO *⌐*

Commando Squad During WWII, soldiers go to battle to prevent the development of a device that re-animates flesh. The script stays dead.
1976 (R) 82m/C Chuck Alford, Peter Owen, April Adams; *D:* Charles Nizet. **VHS, Beta** $24.95 GHV *⌐*

Commando Squad Story of drug agents undercover in Mexico, and a female agent who rescues her kidnapped lover. Firepower is wasted, but Shower is a former "Playboy" Playmate of the Year.
1987 (R) 90m/C Brian Thompson, William Smith, Kathy Shower, Sid Haig, Robert Quarry, Ross Hagen, Mel Welles, Marie Windsor, Russ Tamblyn; *D:* Fred Olen Ray. **VHS, Beta** $79.95 TWE *⌐*

Commandos Commando operation against Rommel's forces in North Africa during WWII. Too much said, not enough action. Also know as "Sullivan's Marauders."
1973 (PG) 100m/C GE IT Lee Van Cleef, Jack Kelly; *D:* Armando Crispino. **VHS, Beta** $49.95 GEM, MRV, PSM *⌐½*

Commandos Strike at Dawn Norwegian villagers, including Muni, fight the invading Nazis, and eventually help the British Navy battle them over an Arctic supply line. Okay script helped along by veteran actors Muni and Gish. Based on a C.S. Forester story.
1943 100m/B Paul Muni, Lillian Gish, Cedric Hardwicke, Anna Lee, Ray Collins, Robert Coote, Alexander Knox, Rosemary DeCamp; *D:* John Farrow; *W:* Irwin Shaw. **VHS, Beta** $69.95 COL *⌐⌐½*

Comment Ca Va? The boss and workers in a Communist publishing house decide to make a simple film about how information is manufactured. But Odette, one of the workers, has some strange ideas about filmmaking. In French with English subtitles. *AKA:* How Is It Going?.
1976 76m/C FR Anne-Marie Mieville; *D:* Jean-Luc Godard. **VHS** $59.95 FCT *⌐⌐*

The Commies are Coming, the Commies are Coming Cult classic will leave viewers red from laughing in disbelief. Webb narrates this anti-communist movie about the Russians taking over the United States. Filmed in a documentary style, it captures the paranoia of the times. Re-released in 1984, just before the Evil Empire collapsed.
1957 60m/B Jack Webb, Andrew Duggan, Robert Conrad, Jack Kelly, Peter Brown; *D:* George Waggner. **VHS, Beta** $39.95 RHI *⌐⌐*

Commissar Before the Soviet Union ended up in the ashcan of history, this film was labeled as "treason" and shelved in Red Russia. Now, even Americans can view the story of a female Soviet soldier who becomes pregnant during the civil war of 1922. The Soviet military has no policy regarding pregnancy, so the woman is dumped on a family of outcast Jews to complete her pregnancy. This film makes the strong statement that women were just as discriminated against in the U.S.S.R. as were many races or creeds, especially Jews. In Russian with English subtitles. Released in the U.S. in 1988. *AKA:* Komissar.

1968 105m/B *RU* Nonna Mordyukova, Rolan Bykov; *D:* Alexander Askoldov. **VHS** $59.95 KIV ✗✗✗✗

The Commitments Convinced that they can bring soul music to Dublin, a group of working-class youth form a band. High-energy production paints an interesting, un-romanticized picture of modern Ireland and refuses to follow standard showbiz cliches, even though its lack of resolution hurts. Honest, whimsical dialog laced with poetic obscenities, delivered by a cast of mostly unknowns. Very successful soundtrack features the music of Wilson Pickett, James Brown, Otis Redding, Aretha Franklin, Percy Sledge, and others, and received a Grammy nomination. Based on the book "The Commitments" by Roddy Doyle, part of a trilogy which includes "The Snapper" and "The Van."
1991 (R) 116m/C *IR* Andrew Strong, Bronagh Gallagher, Glen Hansard, Michael Aberne, Dick Massey, Ken McCluskey, Robert Arkins, Dave Finnegan, Johnny Murphy, Angeline Ball, Felim Gormley, Maria Doyle, Colm Meaney; *D:* Alan Parker; *W:* Dick Clement, Roddy Doyle, Ian LaFrenais. Academy Awards '91 Nominations: Best Film Editing; British Academy Awards '92: Best Director (Parker), Best Film. **VHS, Beta** $19.98 FXV, CCB, IME ✗✗✗

Committed Schlock-meister Levey's latest directorial effort is a step above his earlier "Slumber Party" and "Happy Hooker Goes to Washington," a statement ringing with the faintest of praise. Thinking she's applying for a job at an asylum, a nurse discovers she has committed herself. Try as she may, not even a committed nurse can snake her way out of the pit of madness they call "The Institute."
1991 (R) 93m/C Jennifer O'Neill, William Windom, Robert Forster, Ron Palillo, Sydney Lassick; *D:* William A. Levey. **VHS** $89.98 MED, VTR ✗ ½

The Committee Comedy film of the seminal comedy troupe "The Committee," specialists in short, punchy satire. Dated, but of interest to comedy buffs.
1968 (PG) 88m/C Wolfman Jack, Howard Hesseman, Barbara Bosson, Peter Bonerz, Garry Goodrow, Carl Gottlieb; *D:* Jack Del. **VHS, Beta** NO ✗

Common Bonds After being put together in an experimental outreach program, two mismatched partners struggle to break free from a system that threatens to destroy them both.
1991 (PG) 109m/C Rae Dawn Chong, Michael Ironside, Brad Dourif; *D:* Allan Goldstein; *M:* Graeme Coleman. **VHS, Beta** $89.95 ACA ✗✗½

Common Law Wife Made-for-the-drive-in flick about a man whose common law marriage is threatened by his niece, who wants his money. Murder and mayhem abound when the man's moonshine is poisoned. Cheap and exploitative.
1963 (R) 81m/B Lacy Kelly, Shugfoot Rainey, Annabelle Lee, Jody Works, Anne MacAdams, George Edgely; *D:* Eric Sayers. **VHS** $16.95 SNC ✗

Common Threads: Stories from the Quilt The heavily awarded, made-for-cable-TV documentary about the Quilt: an immense 14-acre blanket created by the survivors of AIDS victims as a monument to their loved ones' premature deaths. All proceeds from the sale of this tape go to the NAMES Project Foundation in support of the Quilt and AIDS service providers.
1989 79m/C *D:* Robert Epstein, Jeffrey Friedman. **VHS, Beta** $19.98 WAR, HBO, IME ✗

Communion A serious adaptation of the purportedly nonfictional bestseller by Whitley Strieber about his family's abduction by extraterrestrials. Spacey new age story is overlong and hard to swallow.
1989 (R) 103m/C Christopher Walken, Lindsay Crouse, Frances Sternhagen, Joel Carlson, Andreas Katsulas, Basil Hoffman; *D:* Philippe Mora; *M:* Eric Clapton. **VHS, Beta** NO ✗✗

Como Dos Gotas de Agua Twin sisters trade places with each other in this limp musical comedy in Spanish. *AKA:* Like Two Drops of Water.
197? 104m/C *SP* Pili & Mili, Isabel Garces, Luis Davila, Manolo Moran. **VHS, Beta** $49.95 MAD ✗

Company Business Sam Boyd is a retired CIA agent who's brought back to swap Pyiotr Grushenko (Baryshnikov), a Russian mole in the State Department, for a U-2 pilot being held in Moscow. The swap is to be made in Berlin and also involves two million dollars of what turns out be to Colombian drug money. When things inevitably go wrong (both intelligence agencies would like them out of the way permanently) the two men find they must depend on each other if they want to stay alive. An unimaginative plot wastes a stalwart cast in this old-fashioned spy drama.
1991 (PG-13) 104m/C Gene Hackman, Mikhail Baryshnikov, Kurtwood Smith, Terry O'Quinn; *D:* Nicholas Meyer; *W:* Nicholas Meyer. **VHS** $14.95 MGM ✗ ½

Company Limited The story of a young Indian sales executive working for a British owned firm, set in contemporary Calcutta. English subtitles.
197? 112m/B *IN* **VHS, Beta** CIG ✗✗

The Company of Wolves A young girl on the threshold of womanhood listens to her grandmother tell fairy tales and dreams of a medieval fantasy world inhabited by wolves and werewolves. An adult "Little Red Riding Hood" type comedy heavy on Freudian symbolism. Not really for kids.
1985 (R) 95m/C Angela Lansbury, David Warner, Stephen Rea, Tusse Silberg, Sarah Patterson, Brian Glover, Danielle Dax, Graham Crowden, Micha Bergese; *D:* Neil Jordan; *W:* Neil Jordan, Angela Carter; *M:* George Fenton. **VHS, Beta** $19.98 VES, LIV ✗✗✗

The Competition Two virtuoso pianists meet at an international competition and fall in love. Will they stay together if one of them wins? Can they have a performance career and love too? Is he trying to distract her with sex, so he can win? Dreyfuss and Irving are fine (they practiced for four months to look like they were actually playing the pianos), and Remick's character has some interesting insights into the world of art.
1980 (PG) 125m/C Richard Dreyfuss, Amy Irving, Lee Remick, Sam Wanamaker, Joseph Cali, Ty Henderson, Priscilla Pointer, James B. Sikking; *D:* Joel Oliansky. **VHS, Beta** $14.95 COL, TVC ✗✗✗

The Compleat Beatles Music, interviews, film clips, animation and live performances make up this "rockumentary" on the Beatles. New interviews are featured, as well as vintage film clips and studio footage with narration by Malcolm McDowell. The first U.S. press conference, legendary Hamburg footage, and an in-depth interview with George Martin are highlights.
1982 120m/C John Lennon, Paul McCartney, Ringo Starr, George Harrison, George Martin, Brian Epstein, Billy Preston, Milt Oken, Bruce Johnston, Roger McGuinn, Mike McCartney, Mick Jagger; *D:* Patrick Montgomery. **VHS, Beta** $19.95 MVD, MGM ✗✗✗

The Complete Showboat Deluxe collector's edition contains footage from three versions of the classic Jerome Kern-Oscar Hammerstein musical, showcasing the talents of Ava Gardner, Robert Sterling, Irene Dunne, Agnes Moorehead, Paul Robeson, and more. Four-disc set features such tunes as "Old Man River," "Bill," and "Can't Help Loving That Man."
19?? 360m/C $124.98 MGM ✗✗✗

Complex Cute tale of a clever dog (aren't they all?) who annoys his swinish, beer-guzzling master by learning how to play chess, speak French, and read Dostoevsky.
1985 12m/C **VHS, Beta** $160.00 BFA ✗✗✗

Complex World The Heartbreak Hotel is a notorious rock club which may not be around much longer. It seems the young owner's father is an ex-CIA redneck who is running for President and his son's profession is a political liability. Meanwhile, the town's mayor wants to replace the club with a shopping mall. A bomb is planted in the club's basement, terrorists lurk, and a gang of bikers is spoiling for a fight but the crowd at the Heartbreak just rocks on.
1992 (R) 81m/C Dan Welch, Bob Owczarek, Jay Charbonneau, Tilman Gandy Jr., David P.B. Stephens; *D:* James Wolpaw; *W:* James Wolpaw. **VHS** NO ✗ ½

Compromising Positions A philandering dentist is killed on Long Island, and a bored housewife begins to investigate, uncovering scandal after scandal. Black comedy mixed unevenly with mystery makes for unsatisfying brew. However, Ivey is a standout as Sarandon's best friend. Screenplay was written by Susan Isaacs, based on her novel of the same title.
1985 (R) 99m/C Susan Sarandon, Raul Julia, Edward Herrmann, Judith Ivey, Mary Beth Hurt, Joe Mantegna, Josh Mostel, Anne DeSalvo; *D:* Frank Perry; *M:* Brad Fiedel. **VHS, Beta** $19.95 PAR ✗✗

Computer Beach Party A couple of surf-head college computer hackers foil their mayor's plans to develop their favorite beach. The title, at least, is original.
1988 97m/C Hank Amigo, Stacey Nemour, Andre Chimene; *D:* Gary A. Troy. **VHS, Beta** $69.98 VES, LIV ✗

Computer Wizard Boy genius builds a powerful electronic device. His intentions are good, but the invention disrupts the town and lands him in big trouble. Not the "Thomas Edison Story."
1977 (G) 91m/C Henry Darrow, Kate Woodville, Guy Madison, Marc Gilpin; *D:* John Florea. **VHS, Beta** NO ✗

The Computer Wore Tennis Shoes Disney comedy (strictly for the kids) about a slow-witted college student who turns into a genius after a "shocking" encounter with the campus computer. His new brains give the local gangster headaches. Sequel: "Now You See Him, Now You Don't."
1969 (G) 87m/C Kurt Russell, Cesar Romero, Joe Flynn, William Schallert, Alan Hewitt, Richard Bakalayan; *D:* Robert Butler. **VHS, Beta** DIS, OM ✗ ½

Comrade X Gable is an American correspondent in Moscow who is blackmailed into marrying die-hard Communist Lamarr in this comedic spinoff of "Ninotchka." The two stars failed to create any sparks as a love duo, although their previous film "Boom Town" was a hit. Based on a story by Walter Reisch.

1940 87m/B Clark Gable, Hedy Lamarr, Oscar Homolka, Felix Bressart, Eve Arden, Sig Rumann, Natash Lytess, Vladimir Sokoloff; **D:** King Vidor; **W:** Ben Hecht, Charles Lederer. VHS $19.98 MGM ✍✍½

Comrades in Arms When an international drug cartel threatens to take over the world, the United States and Russia must set their differences aside and team up to stop them.
1991 (R) 91m/C Lyle Alzado, Rick Washburne, John Christian, Lance Henriksen; **D:** J. Christian Ingvordsen; **W:** J. Christian Ingvordsen. VHS $89.98 REP ✍½

The Comrades of Summer Mantegna plays big-league baseball coach Sparky Smith, whose fiery temper gets him into big trouble. Out of a job, he discovers the only team willing to take a chance on him happens to be Russian. Sparky finds the players of the Russian National team need a lot of help—and not just with their English. Made for cable television.
1992 (R) 90m/C Joe Mantegna, Natalia Negoda, Mark Rolston, John Fleck, Eric Allen Kramer, Michael Lerner, Ian Tracey; **D:** Tommy Lee Wallace; **W:** Robert Rodat; **M:** William Olvis. VHS $89.99 HBO ✍✍½

The Con Artists After con man Quinn is sprung from prison, he and his protege set up a sting operation against the beautiful Capucine. Not clever or witty enough for the caper to capture interest. **AKA:** The Con Man.
1980 86m/C IT Anthony Quinn, Adriano Celentano, Capucine, Corinne Clery; **D:** Sergio Corbucci. VHS, Beta $19.98 HHE ✍½

Con Man Robin Mitchell is a small-time con man on the fringes of London's underworld. He witnesses a brutal mob hit, which means they want him dead, and his girlfriend has decided it's just too dangerous being a part of his life. But Mitchell is convinced his luck will change for the better as he puts together a million-dollar long-shot that could secure him for life—if he survives.
1992 91m/C Ian McShane, Gayle Hunnicutt, Keith Barron, Alan Lake, Luan Peters; **D:** Francis Megahy. VHS NO ✍✍

Conagher A lyrical, if poorly plotted Western about a veteran cowboy who takes the whole movie to decide to end up in the arms of the pretty widow lady. Cable-TV adaptation of Louis L'Amour's novel doesn't have much intensity, though Elliott captures his character well. **AKA:** Louis L'Amour's Conagher.
1991 94m/C Sam Elliott, Katharine Ross, Barry Corbin, Buck Taylor, Dub Taylor, Daniel Quinn, Anndi McAfee, Billy Green Bush, Ken Curtis; **D:** Reynaldo Villalobos. VHS, Beta $9.98 TTC ✍✍½

Conan the Barbarian A fine sword and sorcery tale featuring brutality, excellent production values, and a rousing score. Conan's parents are killed and he's enslaved. But hardship makes him strong, so when he is set free he can avenge their murder and retrieve the sword bequeathed him by his father. Sandahl Bergman is great as The Queen of Thieves, and Schwarzenegger maintains an admirable sense of humor throughout. Jones is dandy as always. Based on the character created by Robert E. Howard. Sequel: "Conan the Destroyer."
1982 (R) 115m/C Arnold Schwarzenegger, James Earl Jones, Max von Sydow, Sandahl Bergman, Mako, Ben Davidson, Valerie Quennessen, Cassandra Gaviola, William Smith; **D:** John Milius; **W:** John Milius, Oliver Stone. VHS, Beta $14.95 MCA ✍✍✍

Conan the Destroyer Conan is manipulated by Queen Tamaris into searching for a treasure. In return she'll bring Conan's love Valeria back to life. On his trip he meets Jones and Chamberlain, who later give him a hand. Excellent special effects, good humor, camp fun, somewhat silly finale. Sequel to the better "Conan the Barbarian."
1984 (PG) 101m/C Arnold Schwarzenegger, Grace Jones, Wilt Chamberlain, Sarah Douglas, Mako, Olivia D'Abo, Jeff Corey; **D:** Richard Fleischer. VHS, Beta $14.95 MCA ✍✍½

The Concentratin' Kid An unusual horse opera sans shootouts and fisticuffs. Hoot's fiancee is kidnapped and taken to the range so that the renegade cowpokes can, uh, benefit from a female perspective on home decorating. Despite being outnumbered, Hoot concentrates and sets the rescue in motion, taking on the gang of rustlers without firing a shot.
1930 54m/B Hoot Gibson, Kathryn Crawford, Duke Lee, Robert E. Homans, James Mason; **D:** Arthur Rosson. VHS, Beta $9.95 GPV ✍

The Concorde: Airport '79 A supersonic film in the "Airport" tradition has the Concorde chased by missiles and fighter aircraft before it crashes in the Alps. Incredibly far-fetched nonsense with an all-star cast doesn't fly. **AKA:** Airport '79.
1979 (PG) 103m/C Alain Delon, Susan Blakely, Robert Wagner, Sylvia Kristel, John Davidson, Charo, Sybil Danning, Jimmie Walker, Eddie Albert, Bibi Andersson, Monica Lewis, Andrea Marcovicci, Martha Raye, Cicely Tyson, Mercedes McCambridge, George Kennedy, David Warner; **D:** David Lowell Rich; **W:** Eric Roth. VHS, Beta $14.98 MCA ✍

Concrete Angels A poignant glimpse at the influence of rock music in its infancy. A group of deprived teens in Toronto form a band and audition to open for the Beatles. Lack of nostalgia is refreshing, but too much of this is amateurish.
1987 (R) 97m/C CA Joseph Dimambro, Luke McKeehan, Omie Craden, Dean Bosacki. VHS, Beta $29.95 ACA ✍

Concrete Beat A newspaper reporter simultaneously searches for a murderer, tries to win his ex-wife back, and writes front page stories for his editor/ex-father-in-law. Tough assignment. Made for television.
1984 74m/C Kenneth McMillan, John Getz, Darlanne Fluegel, Rhoda Gemignani; **D:** Robert Butler. VHS, Beta $59.95 PSM ✍½

The Concrete Cowboys Two bumbling cowboys from Montana come to the metropolis of Nashville and promptly turn detective to foil a blackmail scheme and locate a missing singer. Barbara Mandrell and Roy Acuff play themselves. Silly made-for-TV pilot of short-lived series. **AKA:** Ramblin' Man.
1979 100m/C Jerry Reed, Tom Selleck, Morgan Fairchild, Claude Akins, Gene Evans, Roy Acuff, Barbara Mandrell; **D:** Burt Kennedy. VHS FOX, EDV, HHE ✍½

The Concrete Jungle After being set up by her no-good boyfriend, Bregman is sent to a correctional facility for drug smuggling. There she must learn to fend for herself (or else). Typical prison for gals fare with cute babes in revealing outfits, a topless riot, the bad warden, and a concerned social worker. Followed by "Chained Heat." **AKA:** The Criminal.
1982 106m/C Tracy Bregman, Jill St. John, Barbara Luna, Peter Brown, Aimee Eccles, Nita Talbot, Sondra Currie; **D:** Tom De Simone. VHS, Beta $59.95 COL ✍½

Condemned to Hell A tough-as-iron street punk gets thrown into a women's prison, where she must fight for her existence. Low-brow violence galore.
198? 97m/C IT Leonor Benedetto. VHS, Beta $59.95 TWE Woof!

Condemned to Live Mild-mannered doctor Ralph Morgan and his fiancee Maxine Doyle seem like your average early 20th Century Middle-European couple...but the doctor's hunchbacked servant Mischa Auer is a tipoff that this is a horror movie of some sort. Like many men, the doctor has suffered from a vampire curse all his life. And, like many men, he is unaware of his blood-sucking habit, thanks to the concealment efforts of his loyal (hunchback) servant. Doyle discovers her fiance's sanguine secret, but not before she finds out she really loves Gleason, anyway. Answers the question: just how do you jilt a vampire?
1935 68m/B Ralph Morgan, Maxine Doyle, Russell Gleason, Pedro de Cordoba, Mischa Auer, Lucy Beaumont, Carl Stockade; **D:** Frank Strayer. VHS $19.98 SNC, LSV ✍✍

Condorman Woody Wilkins, an inventive comic book writer, adopts the identity of his own character, Condorman, in order to help a beautiful Russian spy defect. A Disney film, strictly for the small fry.
1981 (PG) 90m/C Michael Crawford, Oliver Reed, Barbara Carrera, James Hampton, Jean-Pierre Kalfon, Dana Elcar; **D:** Charles Jarrott. VHS, Beta $69.95 DIS ✍✍

Conduct Unbecoming Late nineteenth century India is the setting for a trial involving the possible assault of a British officer's wife. Ambitious production based on a British stage play suffers from claustrophobic atmosphere but is greatly redeemed by the first rate cast.
1975 (PG) 107m/C GB Michael York, Richard Attenborough, Trevor Howard, Stacy Keach, Christopher Plummer, Susannah York, James Faulkner, Michael Culver, Persis Khambatta; **D:** Michael Anderson Sr. VHS CRV ✍✍½

The Conductor A famous Polish-born conductor (Gielgud) returns to his birthplace after 50 years of living in the U.S. A dying man, he decides to work with a struggling provincial orchestra, much to the dismay of their own conductor. But the conductor finds himself being used in government schemes to take advantage of his return. In English and Polish with subtitles. **AKA:** Dyrygent.
1980 101m/C PL John Gielgud, Krystyna Janda, Andrzej Seweryn, Jan Ciercierski, Tadeusz Czechowski; **D:** Andrzej Wajda; **W:** Andrzej Kijowski. VHS $79.95 NYF, ING ✍✍

Coneheads Comedy inspired by once popular characters from "Saturday Night Live" coasts in on the coattails of "Wayne's World." Aykroyd and Curtin reprise their roles as Beldar and Prymaat, the couple from the planet Remulak who are just trying to fit in on Earth. Newman, who created the role of teenage daughter Connie, appears as Beldar's sister, while Burke takes over as Connie (toddler Connie is Aykroyd's daughter, in her film debut). One-joke premise is a decade late and a dime short, though cast of comedy all-stars provides a lift.
1993 (PG) 86m/C Dan Aykroyd, Jane Curtin, Laraine Newman, Jason Alexander, Michelle Burke, Chris Farley, Michael Richards, Lisa Jane Persky, Sinbad, Shishir Kurup, Michael McKean, Phil Hartman, David Spade, Dave Thomas, Jan Hooks, Chris Rock, Adam Sandler, Julia Sweeney, Danielle Aykroyd; **D:** Steven Barron; **W:** Dan Aykroyd, Tom Davis, Bonnie Turner, Terry Turner. VHS, Beta PAR, BTV ✍✍½

Conexion Mexico Not-bad actioner about the Mexican police fighting against drug traffickers who are aided by a group of vicious women.
1987 85m/C *MX* Sergio Goyri, Victor Junco, Silvia Manriquez, Sergio Bustamante. **VHS, Beta** $75.00 *MAD* 𝄞𝄞½

Conexion Oriental A journalist investigates an Oriental crime syndicate. Not much mystery to the mystery. Dubbed into Spanish. *AKA:* East Connection.
1970 90m/C Dale Robertson, Lucianna Paluzzi, Calisto Calisti. **VHS, Beta** *NO* 𝄞½

The Confession A priest hears a killer's confession and must protect the oath of confidentiality, even as his own brother is being convicted of the murder.
1920 78m/B Henry B. Walthall, Francis McDonald, William H. Clifford, Margaret McWade, Margaret Landis; *D:* Bertram Bracken. **VHS** $14.95 *GPV* 𝄞𝄞½

The Confessional A mad priest unleashes a monster from his confessional to wreak havoc upon the world. Pray for your VCR. *AKA:* House of Mortal Sin.
1975 (R) 108m/C *GB* Anthony Sharp, Susan Penhaligon, Stephanie Beacham, Norman Eshley, Sheila Keith; *D:* Pete Walker. **VHS, Beta** $59.95 *PSM* 𝄞

Confessions of a Hit Man Nephew who stole millions from his mobster uncle must amend his sordid past.
1994 (R) 93m/C James Remar, Michael Wright, Emily Longstreth; *D:* Larry Leahy; *W:* Tony Cinciripini, Larry Leahy; *M:* Billy Talbot. **VHS** $92.95 *HMD* 𝄞𝄞

Confessions of a Police Captain A dedicated police captain tries to wipe out the bureaucratic corruption that is infecting his city. Balsam gives a fine performance in a heavy-going tale.
1972 (PG) 104m/C *IT* Martin Balsam, Franco Nero, Marilu Tolo; *D:* Damiano Damiani. **VHS, Beta** $59.98 *SUE* 𝄞𝄞

Confessions of a Serial Killer True story based on the life of Henry Lee Lucas, one of the nation's most vicious killers. Burns plays Lucas in this grisly account of his most violent murders. Shocking realistic look inside the mind of a serial killer.
1987 85m/C Robert Burns, Dennis Hill; *D:* Mark Blair. **VHS** $89.98 *NHO* 𝄞𝄞

Confessions of a Vice Baron Vice Baron Lombardo makes it big as a drug dealer and flesh peddler, then loses it all when he falls in love. Sleazy exploitation.
1942 70m/B Willy Castello; *D:* Harvey Thew. **VHS, Beta** $16.95 *SNC* 𝄞

Confessions of Tom Harris Somewhere between all the prize-fighting, leg-breaking for the mob, and jail terms for rape, Tom Harris finds time for a life-changing encounter with love. Based on true story. *AKA:* Tale of the Cock; Childish Things.
1972 (PG) 90m/C Don Murray, Linda Evans, David Brian, Gary Clarke, Logan Ramsey, Angelique Pettyjohn; *D:* John Derek, David Nelson; *W:* Don Murray. **VHS, Beta** *NO* 𝄞

Confidential A G-man goes under cover to infiltrate a crime ring. Well made and full of action, fun array of character actors. Naish particularly good as nasty killer.
1935 67m/B Donald Cook, Evelyn Knapp, Warren Hymer, J. Carroll Naish, Herbert Rawlinson, Morgan Wallace, Kane Richmond, Theodore von Eltz, Reed Howes; *D:* Edward L. Cahn. **VHS** $24.95 *VYY* 𝄞𝄞½

Confidential A '40s detective tries to solve a decades-old axe murder, only to disappear himself. Horrible fare from our friends north of the border.

1986 (R) 95m/C *CA* Neil Munro, August Schellenberg, Chapelle Jaffe, Tom Butler; *D:* Bruce Pittman. **VHS, Beta** *NO Woof!*

Confidentially Yours Truffaut's homage to Hitchcock, based on Charles Williams' "The Long Saturday Night." A hapless small-town real estate agent is framed for a rash of murders and his secretary, who is secretly in love with him, tries to clear his name. Truffaut's last film is stylish and entertaining. In French with English subtitles. *AKA:* Vivement Dimanche!; Finally, Sunday.
1983 (PG) 110m/B *FR* Fanny Ardant, Jean-Louis Trintignant, Philippe Morier-Genoud, Philippe Laudenbach, Caroline Sihol; *D:* Francois Truffaut; *W:* Suzanne Schiffman; *M:* Georges Delerue. **VHS, Beta** $59.98 *FOX, ING, HMV* 𝄞𝄞𝄞

Conflict Bogart falls for his sister-in-law and asks his wife for a divorce. She refuses, he plots her murder, and thinks up the alibi. When the police fail to notify him of her death, Bogart is forced to report his wife missing. But is she dead? Her guilty husband smells her perfume, sees her walking down the street, and discovers the body is missing from the scene of the crime. Suspenseful thriller also features Greenstreet as a psychologist/family friend who suspects Bogart knows more than he's telling.
1945 86m/B Humphrey Bogart, Alexis Smith, Sydney Greenstreet, Rose Hobart, Charles Drake, Grant Mitchell; *D:* Curtis Bernhardt. **VHS** $19.98 *MGM* 𝄞𝄞𝄞

Conflict of Interest Gideon (Nelson) is a thug who runs stolen cars, drugs, and women from his heavy-metal club on the wrong side of town. Mickey Flannery (McDonald) is the new cop determined to get Gideon behind bars, especially after Gideon kills Mickey's wife, sets up his son on a phony murder rap, and kidnaps his son's girlfriend. Now it's personal and Mickey will stop at nothing to get his revenge. Over-the-top performance by Nelson will have the viewer hoping he gets it soon and puts the film out of its misery.
1992 (R) 88m/C Judd Nelson, Christopher McDonald, Alyssa Milano, Dey Young, Gregory Alan Harris; *D:* Gary Davis; *W:* Gregory Miller, Michael Angeli. **VHS** $89.99 *HBO* 𝄞½

The Conformist Character study of young Italian fascist, plagued by homosexual feelings, who must prove his loyalty by killing his old professor. Decadent and engrossing story is brilliantly acted. Based on the novel by Alberto Moravia. *AKA:* Il Conformist.
1971 (R) 108m/C *IT FR GE* Jean-Louis Trintignant, Stefania Sandrelli, Dominique Sanda, Pierre Clementi, Gastone Moschin, Pasquale Fortunato; *D:* Bernardo Bertolucci; *W:* Bernardo Bertolucci; *M:* Georges Delerue. Academy Awards '71 Nominations: Best Adapted Screenplay; National Board of Review Awards '71: 5 Best Foreign Films of the Year; National Society of Film Critics Awards '71: Best Director (Bertolucci). **VHS, Beta** $44.95 *ING, PAR, APD* 𝄞𝄞𝄞𝄞

Congress Dances A rare German musical about a romance in old Vienna. Popular in its day, it was subsequently banned by the Nazis in 1937. In German with English subtitles. *AKA:* Der Kongress Tanzt.
1931 92m/B *GE* Lilian Harvey, Conrad Veidt, Willy Fritsch; *D:* Erik Charell. **VHS, Beta** $44.95 *ING, NOS, HHT* 𝄞𝄞

A Connecticut Yankee A charming, if somewhat dated, version of the popular Mark Twain story, "A Connecticut Yankee in King Arthur's Court." Rogers is a radio shop owner who dreams his way back to the Knights of the Round Table. Story rewritten to fit Rogers' amiable style and to make

then-current wisecracks. Great cast overcomes weak points in the script.
1931 96m/B Will Rogers, Myrna Loy, Maureen O'Sullivan, William Farnum; *D:* David Butler. **VHS** $19.98 *FOX, FCT* 𝄞𝄞𝄞

A Connecticut Yankee in King Arthur's Court A pleasant version of the famous Mark Twain story about a 20th century man transported to Camelot and mistaken for a dangerous wizard. This was the third film version of the classic, which was later remade as "Unidentified Flying Oddball," a made for television movie and an animated feature. ♫Once and For Always; Busy Doin' Nothin'; If You Stub Your Toe on the Moon; When Is Sometime?; Twixt Myself and Me. *AKA:* A Yankee in King Arthur's Court.
1949 108m/C Bing Crosby, Rhonda Fleming, William Bendix, Cedric Hardwicke, Henry Wilcoxon, Murvyn Vye, Virginia Field; *D:* Tay Garnett. **VHS, Beta** $14.98 *MCA* 𝄞𝄞½

The Connection The Living Theatre's ground-breaking performance of Jack Gelber's play about heroin addicts waiting for their connection to arrive, while a documentary filmmaker hovers nearby with his camera.
1961 105m/B Warren Finnerty, Carl Lee, William Redfield, Freddie Redd Quartet, Roscoe Lee Browne, Garry Goodrow, James Anderson, Jackie McLean; *D:* Shirley Clarke. **VHS, Beta** $29.95 *MFV, FCT* 𝄞𝄞𝄞½

The Connection During steps in to work a deal between hotel jewel thieves and the insurance company. Complex plot handled deftly by all concerned. Made for television.
1973 74m/C Charles Durning, Ronny Cox, Dennis Cole, Zohra Lampert, Heather MacRae, Dana Wynter; *D:* Tom Gries. **VHS, Beta** $59.95 *VMK* 𝄞𝄞½

The Conqueror Wayne in pointed helmet and goatee is comically miscast as Genghis Khan in this woeful tale of the warlord's early life and involvement with the kidnapped daughter of a powerful enemy. Rife with stilted, unintentionally funny dialogue, Oriental western was very expensive to make (with backing by Howard Hughes), and is now listed in the "Fifty Worst Films of All Time." No matter; it's surreal enough to enable viewer to approximate an out-of-body experience. Even those on the set suffered; filming took place near a nuclear test site in Utah and many members of the cast and crew eventually developed cancer.
1956 111m/C John Wayne, Susan Hayward, William Conrad, Agnes Moorehead, Lee Van Cleef, Pedro Armendariz Sr., Thomas Gomez, John Hoyt; *D:* Dick Powell; *W:* Oscar Millard. **VHS, Beta** $19.95 *MCA Woof!*

Conqueror & the Empress Low-budget tale of English explorers who roust an island prince from his throne, motivating him to engage in inspired blood-letting.
1964 89m/C Guy Madison, Ray Danton, Mario Petri, Alberto Farnese. **VHS, Beta** *NO Woof!*

Conqueror of the World The adventures of a caveman named Bog. Really. Based on the novel by Albert Cavallone. Available in Spanish.
1985 90m/C **VHS, Beta** *NO Woof!*

The Conqueror Worm Price turns in a fine performance portraying the sinister Matthew Hopkins, a real-life 17th century witch-hunter. No "ham" in this low-budget, underrated thriller. The last of three films from director Reeves, who died from an accidental overdose in 1969. Also available with "Tomb of Ligeia" on Laser Disc. *AKA:* Witchfinder

General; Edgar Allan Poe's Conqueror Worm.
1968 95m/C *GB* Vincent Price, Ian Ogilvy, Hilary Dwyer, Rupert Davies, Robert Russell, Patrick Wymark, Wilfrid Brambell; *D:* Michael Reeves. **VHS $59.99** *HBO, FCT* ✂✂✂

Conquest Garbo, as the Polish countess Marie Walewska, tries to persuade Napoleon (Boyer) to free her native Poland from the Russian Tsar. Garbo, Boyer, and Ouspenskaya are outstanding, while the beautiful costumes and lavish production help, but the script is occasionally weak. "Conquest" was a box office flop in the United States and ended up costing MGM more than any movie it had made up until that time. *AKA:* Marie Walewska.
1937 115m/B Greta Garbo, Charles Boyer, Reginald Owen, Alan Marshal, Henry Stephenson, Leif Erickson, May Whitty, Maria Ouspenskaya, Vladimir Sokoloff, Scotty Beckett; *D:* Clarence Brown. **VHS, Beta $19.98** *MGM, FCT* ✂✂✂

Conquest Sword and sorcery tale of two mighty warriors against an evil sorceress who seeks world domination. Excellent score.
1983 (R) 92m/C *IT SP MX* Jorge Rivero, Andrea Occhipinti, Violeta Cela, Sabrina Siani; *D:* Lucio Fulci; *M:* Claudio Simonetti. **VHS, Beta $59.95** *MED* ✂½

Conquest of Cochise Mediocre oater about a cavalry officer who must stop the war between the Apache and Comanche tribes and a group of Mexicans in the Southwest of the 1850s.
1953 70m/C John Hodiak, Robert Stack, Joy Page; *D:* William Castle. **VHS, Beta $14.99** *GKK* ✂✂

Conquest of Mycene Hercules battles an evil queen and this time he may actually lose! Muscleman mayhem will entertain the kids. *AKA:* Ercole Contro Molock.
1963 102m/C *IT* Gordon Scott, Rosalba (Sara Bay) Neri, Jany Clair; *D:* Giorgio Ferroni. **VHS $16.95** *SNC* ✂½

Conquest of Space A spaceship sets off to explore Mars in spite of the commander's attempts to sabotage the voyage. He believes the flight is an heretical attempt to reach God. An uneasy mixture of religion and space exploration detracts from the nifty special effects which are the only reason to watch.
1955 81m/C Walter Brooke, Eric Fleming, Mickey Shaughnessy, Phil Foster, William Redfield, William Hopper, Benson Fong, Ross Martin; *D:* Byron Haskin. **VHS** *PAR* ✂½

Conquest of the Normans During the Norman invasion of England, Oliver is accused of kidnapping the King. To save his life, Oliver must find the true identity of the abductors. With so much plot, there should have been some suspense.
1962 83m/C Cameron Mitchell. **Beta $39.95** *AIP* ✂

Conquest of the Planet of the Apes The apes turn the tables on the human Earth population when they lead a revolt against their cruel masters in the distant year of 1990. Sure, there's plenty of cliches—but the story drags you along. The 4th film in the series. Followed by "Battle for the Planet of the Apes."
1972 (PG) 87m/C Roddy McDowall, Don Murray, Ricardo Montalban, Natalie Trundy, Severn Darden, Hari Rhodes; *D:* J. Lee Thompson. **VHS, Beta $19.98** *FOX* ✂✂½

Conrack The true story of Pat Conroy, who tried to teach a group of illiterate Black children in South Carolina by using commonsense teaching techniques to inspire their interest. Voight is convincing as the earnest teacher. Based on Conroy's novel "The Water Is Wide."
1974 (PG) 111m/C Jon Voight, Paul Winfield, Madge Sinclair, Hume Cronyn, Martin Ritt; *D:* Martin Ritt; *W:* Harriet Frank Jr., Irving Ravetch; *M:* John Williams. **VHS, Beta $59.98** *FOX* ✂✂✂

Consenting Adult Made for television movie about a distressed family coming to terms with a favorite son's homosexuality. Restrained exploration of the controversial subject. Based on Laura Z. Hobson's novel.
1985 100m/C Marlo Thomas, Martin Sheen, Barry Tubb, Talia Balsam, Ben Piazza, Corinne Michaels; *D:* Gilbert Cates; *W:* John McGreevey. **VHS** *NO* ✂✂½

Consenting Adults Cookie-cutter thriller capitalizes on popular "psycho-destroys-your-normal-life" theme. Average yuppie couple (Kline and Mastrantonio) are startled and then seduced by the couple moving in next door (Spacey and Miller), who conduct a considerably less-restrained lifestyle. Wife-swapping leads to murder and an innocent man is framed. Plot and characters are underdeveloped yet manage to hold interest through decent performances.
1992 (R) 100m/C Kevin Kline, Mary Elizabeth Mastrantonio, Kevin Spacey, Rebecca Miller, Forest Whitaker, E.G. Marshall, Billie Neal; *D:* Alan J. Pakula; *W:* Matthew Chapman. **VHS, Beta $94.95** *HPH, IME* ✂✂

Consolation Marriage A couple meet and marry after being jilted by others, then must make a choice when their old flames return. Dunne and O'Brien make a charming couple in this early talkie. One of Dunne's early starring roles. *AKA:* Married in Haste.
1931 82m/B Irene Dunne, Pat O'Brien, John Halliday, Matt Moore, Myrna Loy, Lester Vail; *D:* Paul Sloane. **VHS, Beta $19.98** *TTC* ✂✂½

Conspiracy Defense Secretary William Baine is haunted by a past sexual encounter, and a top secret team moves in to avert any hint of what could become a "sex scandal." Based on a true story.
1989 (R) 87m/C James Wilby, Kate Hardie, Glyn Houston; *D:* Christopher Barnard. **VHS, Beta $29.95** *ACA* ✂✂

Conspiracy of Hearts A convent of nuns hide Jewish children in 1943 Italy despite threats to their personal safety. Suspenseful tale despite the familiar plot.
1960 113m/B *GB* Lilli Palmer, Yvonne Mitchell, Sylvia Syms, Ronald Lewis; *D:* Ralph Thomas. **VHS, Beta** *LCA* ✂✂✂

A Conspiracy of Love A made-for-television movie about three generations of a divorce-torn family trying to pull itself back together. Sugary domestic tale tries to be uplifting, succeeds in being cliche-ridden.
1987 93m/C Robert Young, Drew Barrymore, Glynnis O'Connor, Elizabeth Wilson, Michael Laurence, John Fujioka, Alan Fawcett; *D:* Noel Black. **VHS $19.95** *STE, NWV* ✂

Conspiracy of Terror Married detectives investigate a series of murders and unearth a grisly cult in a quiet suburb. Standard fare with a few too cute lines concerning the leads' mixed-faith marriage. Made for television pilot.
1975 78m/C Michael Constantine, Barbara Rhoades, Mariclare Costello, Roger Perry, David Opatoshu, Logan Ramsey; *D:* John Llewellyn Moxey. **VHS** *LIV* ✂✂

Conspiracy: The Trial of the Chicago Eight Courtroom drama focuses on the rambunctious trial of the Chicago Eight radicals, charged with inciting a riot at the Democratic National Convention of 1968. Dramatized footage mixed with interviews with the defendants. Imaginative reconstruction of history.
1987 118m/C Peter Boyle, Elliott Gould, Robert Carradine, Martin Sheen, David Clennon, David Kagen, Michael Lembeck, Robert Loggia; *D:* Jeremy Paul Kagan. **VHS, Beta $79.95** *HBO* ✂✂✂

Conspirator Somewhat engrossing drama about a beautiful young girl who discovers that her new husband, a British army officer, is working with the Communists. Elizabeth Taylor stars as the naive American wife and Robert Taylor plays her Russkie agent husband. Although madly in love with his wife, he is given orders to kill her. Picture falls apart at end due to weak script. Based on the novel by Humphrey Slater.
1949 85m/B *GB* Robert Taylor, Elizabeth Taylor, Robert Flemyng, Harold Warrender, Honor Blackman, Marjorie Fielding, Thora Hird; *D:* Victor Saville; *W:* Sally Benson, Gerard Fairlie. **VHS $19.98** *MGM* ✂✂½

Consuming Passions A ribald, food-obsessed English comedy about a young idiot who rises within the hierarchy of a chocolate company via murder. You'll never guess what the secret ingredient in his wonderful chocolate is. Based on a play by Michael Palin and Terry Jones (better known as part of the Monty Python troupe), the film is sometimes funny, more often gross, and takes a single joke far beyond its limit.
1988 (R) 95m/C *GB* Vanessa Redgrave, Jonathan Pryce, Tyler Butterworth, Freddie Jones, Prunella Scales, Sammi Davis-Voss, Thora Hird; *D:* Giles Foster; *W:* Michael Palin. **VHS, Beta** *NO* ✂½

Contagion Innocent real estate agent meets a reclusive, eccentric millionaire who offers him unlimited wealth and beautiful women, but only if he kills someone. Interesting ethical premise loses its philosophical purity.
1987 90m/C *AU* John Doyle, Nicola Bartlett, Roy Barrett, Nathy Gaffney, Pamela Hawksford; *D:* Karl Zwicky. **VHS, Beta** *NO* ✂½

Contempt A film about the filming of a new version of "The Odyssey," and the rival visions of how to tell the story. Amusing look at the film business features Fritz Lang playing himself, Godard as his assistant. Bardot is pleasant scenery. Adapted from Moravia's "A Ghost at Noon." *AKA:* Le Mepris; Il Disprezzo.
1964 102m/C *IT FR* Brigitte Bardot, Jack Palance, Fritz Lang, Georgia Moll, Michel Piccoli; *D:* Jean-Luc Godard; *W:* Jean-Luc Godard; *M:* Georges Delerue. **VHS, Beta $19.95** *COL, ING, SUE* ✂✂✂½

Continental Divide A hard-nosed political columnist takes off for the Colorado Rockies on an "easy assignment"—interviewing a reclusive ornithologist, with whom he instantly falls in love. A city slicker, he first alienates her, but she eventually falls for him, too. But it's not exactly a match made in heaven. Story meanders to a conclusion of sorts. Probably the most normal Belushi ever was on screen.
1981 (PG) 103m/C John Belushi, Blair Brown, Allen (Gooritz) Garfield, Carlin Glynn, Val Avery, Tony Ganios, Tim Kazurinsky; *D:* Michael Apted; *W:* Lawrence Kasdan. **VHS, Beta $14.95** *MCA* ✂✂

Contra Company A teenage girl and an embittered ex-terrorist narrowly escape from a terrorist-infested region in this confusing film about politics, drugs, and sinister dealings.
1988 (R) 110m/C VHS, Beta NO *I*

Contraband The leader of a smuggling gang escapes from an ambush in which his brother was murdered. He searches for a haven of safety while his cronies seek brutal revenge. Average crime yarn lacks much excitement. Dubbed into English.
1986 95m/C *IT* Fabio Testi, Ivana Monti; *D:* Lucio Fulci. **VHS, Beta** NO *I ½*

Control Tedious tale of fifteen volunteers for a 20-day fallout shelter habitation experiment who become trapped when a real nuclear emergency occurs. Filmed in Rome. Made for cable TV.
1987 83m/C *IT* Burt Lancaster, Kate Nelligan, Ben Gazzara, Andrea Ferreol, Lavinia Segurini, Andrea Occhipinti, Cyrielle Claire, Jean Benguigui, Kate Reid, Erland Josephson, Ingrid Thulin; *D:* Giuliano Montaldo. **VHS, Beta $14.95** CNG, HBO *I ½*

The Conversation Hackman plays a surveillance expert increasingly uneasy about his job as he begins to suspect he is an accomplice to murder. Powerful statement about privacy, responsibility and guilt. One of the best movies of the '70s.
1974 (PG) 113m/C Gene Hackman, John Cazale, Frederic Forrest, Allen (Gooritz) Garfield, Cindy Williams, Robert Duvall, Teri Garr, Michael Higgins, Elizabeth McRae, Harrison Ford; *D:* Francis Ford Coppola; *W:* Francis Ford Coppola. Academy Awards '74 Nominations: Best Original Screenplay, Best Picture, Best Sound; Cannes Film Festival '74: Best Film; National Board of Review Awards '74: 10 Best Films of the Year, Best Actor (Hackman), Best Director (Coppola). **VHS, Beta $14.95** PAR *III ½*

Conversation Piece An aging art historian's life is turned upside down when a Countess and her daughters rent out the penthouse in his estate. Sometimes-talky examination of scholarly pretensions. *AKA:* Violence et Passion; Gruppo di Famiglia in un Interno.
1975 (R) 112m/C *IT FR* Burt Lancaster, Silvana Mangano, Helmut Berger, Claudia Cardinale; *D:* Luchino Visconti. **VHS, Beta** NO *III*

Convicted Lean thriller about a woman cleared of a murder charge, but only when a second, identical murder occurs while she is jailed.
1932 57m/B Aileen Pringle, Jameson Thomas, Harry Myers, Dorothy Christy, Richard Tucker; *D:* Christy Cabanne. **VHS, Beta $19.95** NOS *II ½*

Convicted Solid story of innocent man imprisoned for rape, and his wife's determined efforts to free him. Larroquette does well in unexpected role. Based on a true story. Made for television.
1986 94m/C John Larroquette, Carroll O'Connor, Lindsay Wagner; *D:* David Lowell Rich; *M:* Stephen Dorff. **VHS, Beta $69.98** TTC *II ½*

Convicted: A Mother's Story Jillian embezzles cash from her employer, all for the sake of a bum of a boyfriend, and goes to jail. Odd casting hinders a ho-hum plot. Made for television.
1987 95m/C Ann Jillian, Kiel Martin, Fred Savage, Gloria Loring, Christa Denton; *D:* Richard T. Heffron. **VHS, Beta $79.95** JTC *I*

Convicts at Large An escaped convict steals the clothes of an inept architect. Left with only prison duds, the architect stumbles into the bad side of town and gets involved with the mob. Inane.
1938 58m/B Ralph Forbes, Paula Stone. **VHS, Beta** NO *I*

Convoy Life aboard a convoy ship in the North Sea during WWII. The small cruiser is picked on by a German U-Boat. Will a rescuer appear? Noted for technical production values.
1940 95m/B Clive Brook, John Clements, Edward Chapman, Judy Campbell, Edward Rigby, Stewart Granger, Michael Wilding, George Benson; *D:* Pen Tennyson. **VHS $19.95** NOS *II ½*

Convoy A defiant trucker leads an indestructible truck convoy to Mexico to protect high gasoline prices. Lightweight stuff was inspired by the song "Convoy" by C.W. McCall.
1978 (R) 106m/C Kris Kristofferson, Ali MacGraw, Ernest Borgnine, Burt Young, Madge Sinclair, Franklin Ajaye, Cassie Yates; *D:* Sam Peckinpah. **VHS, Beta** NO *II*

Coogan's Bluff An Arizona deputy sheriff (Eastwood) travels to New York in order to track down a killer on the loose. First Eastwood/Siegel teaming is tense actioner. The television series "McCloud" was based on this film.
1968 (PG) 100m/C Clint Eastwood, Lee J. Cobb, Tisha Sterling, Don Stroud, Betty Field, Susan Clark, Tom Tully; *D:* Don Siegel. **VHS, Beta $19.95** MCA *III*

The Cook, the Thief, His Wife & Her Lover An exclusive restaurant houses four disturbing characters. Greenaway's powerful vision of greed, love, and violence may be too strong for some tastes. Available in several different versions: the standard unrated theatrical release, the unrated version in a letterboxed format, an R-rated cut which runs half an hour shorter, and a Spanish-subtitled version.
1990 (R) 123m/C *GB* Richard Boringer, Michael Gambon, Helen Mirren, Alan Howard, Tim Roth; *D:* Peter Greenaway; *W:* Peter Greenaway. **VHS $19.95** VMK *III ½*

Cookie Light comedy about a Mafia don's daughter trying to smart mouth her way into the mob's good graces. A character-driven vehicle, this plot takes a backseat to casting. Wiest is superb as Falk's moll.
1989 (R) 93m/C Emily Lloyd, Peter Falk, Dianne Wiest, Jerry Lewis, Brenda Vaccaro, Ricki Lake, Lionel Stander, Michael Gazzo, Adrian Pasdar, Bob Gunton, Rockets Redglare, G. Anthony Sirico; *D:* Susan Seidelman; *W:* Alice Arlen, Nora Ephron; *M:* Thomas Newman. **VHS, Beta, 8mm $19.95** WAR *II ½*

Cooking Up Trouble The crazy trio become foster dads in this "Stooge" type comedy.
1944 ?m/C Shemp Howard, Billy Gilbert, Maxie "Slapsie" Rosenbloom. **VHS $1944** LOO *II*

Cool As Ice "Rapper" Vanilla Ice makes his feature film debut as a rebel with an eye for the ladies, who motors into a small, conservative town. Several so-so musical segments. For teenage girls only.
1991 (PG) 92m/C Vanilla Ice, Kristin Minter, Michael Gross, Sydney Lassick, Dody Goodman, Naomi Campbell, Candy Clark; *D:* David Kellogg; *M:* Stanley Clarke. **VHS, Beta $79.95** MCA *I*

Cool Blue An unsuccessful painter meets the woman of his dreams, has a brief affair, then tries to locate her in the greater Los Angeles metro area. Good luck. Watch for Penn's cameo.
1988 (R) 93m/C Woody Harrelson, Hank Azaria, Ely Pouget, John Diehl; *Cameos:* Sean Penn; *D:* Mark Mullin, Richard Shepard. **VHS, Beta $19.95** COL *I ½*

Cool Change Man and woman from feuding families ally to expose a corrupt conservation movement that threatens cattle herders.

1986 (PG) 79m/C VHS $39.98 FHE, BTV *II ½*

Cool Hand Luke One of the last great men-in-chains films. A man (Newman) sentenced to sweat out a term on a prison farm refuses to compromise with authority. Martin shines in his supporting role as the oily warden, uttering that now-famous phrase, "What we have here is a failure to communicate." Kennedy's performance as leader of the chain gang won him an Oscar. Based on the novel by Donn Pearce.
1967 126m/C Paul Newman, George Kennedy, J.D. Cannon, Strother Martin, Dennis Hopper, Anthony Zerbe, Lou Antonio, Wayne Rogers, Harry Dean Stanton, Ralph Waite, Joe Don Baker, Richard Davalos, Jo Van Fleet; *D:* Stuart Rosenberg; *W:* Frank Pierson. Academy Awards '67: Best Supporting Actor (Kennedy); Nominations: Best Adapted Screenplay, Best Original Score; Academy Awards '67: Best Actor (Newman). **VHS, Beta $19.98** WAR, BTV *III ½*

Cool It, Baby A woman's life is ripped apart when she unknowingly appears in a raunchy stag film while under the influence of drugs.
1967 ?m/B VHS $24.95 SMW, TPV *III ½*

Cool Mikado A jazzy modernization of the Gilbert-Sullivan operetta, in which an American soldier is kidnapped by the gangster fiance of the Japanese girl he loves.
1963 81m/C *GB* Stubby Kaye, Frankie Howerd, Dennis Price; *D:* Michael Winner. **VHS, Beta $79.95** JEF *II*

Cool Runnings Bright, slapstick comedy based on the true story of the Jamaican bobsled team's quest to enter the 1988 Winter Olympics in Calgary. Candy is recruited to coach four unlikely athletes who don't quite exemplify the spirit of the Games. He accepts the challenge not only because of its inherent difficulty but because he needs to reconcile himself to past failures as a former sledder. When our heroes leave their sunny training ground for Calgary, their mettle is tested by serious sledders from more frigid climes who pursue the competition with a stern sense of mission. An upbeat story which will appeal to children, its target audience.
1993 (PG) 98m/C Leon, Doug E. Doug, John Candy, Marco Brambilla, Malik Yoba, Rawle Lewis, Raymond J. Barry, Peter Outerbridge, Larry Gilman, Paul Coeur; *D:* Jon Turteltaub; *W:* Tommy Swerdlow, Lynn Siefert, Michael Goldberg; *M:* Hans Zimmer. **VHS** DIS *II ½*

The Cool Surface Sex and ambition, Hollywood style. Dani, a wannbe actress, and Jarvis, an aspiring screenwriter become lovers. Jarvis turns their hot affair into a sizzling novel and then a script. Dani may have inspired the lead role but that doesn't mean she'll get the part. But it won't be for lack of trying (anything).
1992 (R) 88m/C Robert Patrick, Teri Hatcher, Matt McCoy, Cyril O'Reilly, Ian Buchanan; *D:* Erik Anjou; *W:* Erik Anjou; *M:* Dave Kopplin. **VHS** COL *II*

Cool World Underground cartoonist Jack Deebs enters his own adult cartoon "Cool World," lured by his sex-kitten character "Holli Would," who needs him to leave her animated world and become human. Holli's plan is opposed by the only other human to occupy Cool World, a slick detective whose main job is to prevent noids (humans) and doodles (cartoons) from having sex and destroying the balance between the two existences. A mixture of live-action and wild animation. Director Bakshi's creations are not intended for children but this is less explicit than usual, which may be one of the

problems. Little humor and a flat script leave this film too uninvolving.
1992 (PG-13) 101m/C Gabriel Byrne, Kim Basinger, Brad Pitt, Michele Abrams, Deidre O'Connell, Carrie Hamilton, Frank Sinatra Jr.; **D:** Ralph Bakshi. **VHS, Beta** $14.95 PAR, PMS, WTA *🎧🎧*

Cooley High Black high school students in Chicago go through the rites of passage in their senior year during the '60s. Film is funny, smart and much acclaimed. Great soundtrack featuring Motown hits of the era is a highlight. Sequel to the TV series "What's Happening."
1975 (PG) 107m/C Glynn Turman, Lawrence Hilton-Jacobs, Garrett Morris, Cynthia Davis; **D:** Michael A. Schultz; **W:** Eric Monte. **VHS** $79.98 ORI, FCT, PTB *🎧🎧🎧*

Cooperstown Harry (Arkin) is a former major-league pitcher who now works as a baseball scout in Florida. He's been angry for 30 years over giving up a home-run pitch that kept his team (the ficitional Chicago Barons) out of the World Series. Harry's feels this error cost him his chance at induction into the Baseball Hall of Fame in Cooperstown, New York, and he's always blamed ex-friend and former catcher Raymond (Greene), who's just had the gall to get elected. Only Raymond's just died—but his ghostly figure visits Harry and urges him to take a road trip not only to the baseball shrine but into his past. Made for cable television.
1993 100m/C Alan Arkin, Graham Greene, Hope Lange, Josh Charles, Ed Begley Jr., Maria Pitillo, Ann Wedgeworth, Paul Dooley, Joanna Miles, Charles Haid; **D:** Charles Haid; **W:** Lee Blessing. **VHS** NO *🎧🎧½*

Cop Left by his wife and child, a ruthless and work-obsessed detective goes after a twisted serial killer. Woods' exceptional ability to play sympathetic weirdos is diluted by a script—based on James Ellroy's novel "Blood on the Moon"—that warps the feminist theme, is violent, and depends too heavily on coincidence.
1988 (R) 110m/C James Woods, Lesley Ann Warren, Charles Durning, Charles Haid, Raymond J. Barry, Randi Brooks, Annie McEnroe, Victoria Wauchope; **D:** James B. Harris; **W:** James B. Harris; **M:** Michel Colombier. **VHS, Beta** $19.95 PAR *🎧🎧½*

Cop and a Half Streetwise 8-year-old (Golden) accidentally witnesses a murder and then bullys police into letting him join the force (for a day) when he withholds key information. Enter his partner for the day— hard-edged detective Reynolds, who claims to hate kids, but who we know will learn to love them. Meanwhile, the outlaw (Sharkey) knows Devon saw him and is trying to silence him permanently. Predictable fantasy may appeal to kids, but will make most adults yawn. One of Sharkey's last roles.
1993 (PG) 87m/C Norman D. Golden II, Burt Reynolds, Ruby Dee, Ray Sharkey, Holland Taylor, Frank Sivero, Marc Macaulay, Rocky Giordani, Sammy Hernandez; **D:** Henry Winkler; **W:** Arne Olsen; **M:** Alan Silvestri. **VHS** $19.95 MCA *🎧½*

The Cop & the Girl A cop falls for a teenage runaway, ends up on the lam. Confused story overpowered by camera work. Lots of violence and strong language. Dubbed.
1986 94m/C GE Juergen Prochnow, Annette Von Klier; **D:** Peter Keglevic. **VHS, Beta** NO *🎧*

Cop in Blue Jeans Undercover cop goes after a mob kingpin in this violent, badly dubbed crime yarn.
1978 92m/C Tomas Milian, Jack Palance, Maria Rosaria Omaggio, Guido Mannari; **D:** Bruno Corbucci. **VHS, Beta** $24.95 VMK *🎧*

Cop-Out A cop is framed. His brother is mad. Teamed up with a sexy lawyer, he exposes the filth that is corrupting the city. Okay melodrama.
1991 102m/C David Buff, Kathryn Luster, Dan Ranger, Reggie DeMorton, Lawrence L. Simeone; **D:** Lawrence L. Simeone; **W:** Lawrence L. Simeone. **VHS, Beta** $14.95 AIP *🎧🎧*

Copacabana A shady theatrical agent (Groucho) books a nightclub singer into two shows at the same time at New York's ritzy nightclub. Lots of energy spent trying to enliven a routine script. Also available colorized. ♫Tico Tico; Stranger Things Have Happened; Je Vous Amie; My Heart Was Doing a Bolero; Let's Do the Copacabana; I Haven't Got a Thing to Sell; We've Come to Copa.
1947 91m/B Groucho Marx, Carmen Miranda, Steve Cochran, Gloria Jean, Andy Russell, Earl Wilson; **D:** Alfred E. Green. **VHS** $19.98 REP, FCT, MLB *🎧🎧*

Copkillers Two men desperate for an easy way to make money embark on a murderous shooting spree. Mostly blanks.
1977 93m/C Jason Williams, Bill Osco. **VHS, Beta** $59.95 TWE Woof!

Copper Canyon Milland plays a Confederate Army officer who heads West after the Civil War, meets up with Lamarr, and sparks a romance. Good chemistry between the leads in this otherwise standard western.
1950 84m/B Ray Milland, Hedy Lamarr, MacDonald Carey, Mona Freeman, Harry Carey Jr., Frank Faylen, Taylor Holmes, Peggy Knudsen; **D:** John Farrow. **VHS** $14.95 PAR, FCT *🎧🎧½*

Copperhead A group of copperhead snakes attack a family who possess a stolen Incan gold necklace. This one bites.
1984 (R) 90m/C Jack Renner, Gretta Ratliff, David Fritts, Cheryl Nickerson. **VHS, Beta** $59.95 VCI *🎧*

Cops and Robbers Two cops use a Wall Street parade for returning astronauts as a cover for a multi-million dollar heist. Exceptional caper film thanks to the likable leads and genuine suspense.
1973 (PG) 89m/C Joseph Bologna, Dick Ward, Sheppard Strudwick, John P. Ryan, Ellen Holly, Dolph Sweet, Joe Spinell, Cliff Gorman; **D:** Aram Avakian; **W:** Donald E. Westlake. **VHS** $14.95 MGM, WKV *🎧🎧½*

Cops and Robbersons Bored, dimwitted dad Chase, a TV cop-show junkie, wishes his life had a little more danger and excitement. How lucky for him when hardnosed cop Palance sets up a command post in his house to stake out the mobster living next door (Davi). Predictable plot isn't funny and drags Chase's bumbling idiot persona on for too long; Wiest and Davi are two bright spots, but their talents are wasted, while Palance does little more than reincarnate his "City Slickers" character. Poor effort for otherwise notable director Ritchie.
1994 (PG) 93m/C Chevy Chase, Jack Palance, Dianne Wiest, Robert Davi, Jason James Richter, Fay Masterson, Miko Hughes, Richard Romanus, David Barry Gray; **D:** Michael Ritchie; **W:** Bernie Somers; **M:** William Ross. **VHS** NYR *🎧*

Cops/One Week Two vintage Keaton shorts, with original organ score.
1922 51m/B Buster Keaton; **D:** Buster Keaton, Eddie Cline. **VHS, Beta, 8mm** $19.95 VYY *🎧*

Coquette Pickford's first talkie portrays her as a flirtatious flapper from a well-to-do family who falls in love with a poor man her father despises. So much in fact that daddy kills the young man and then commits suicide, leaving his daughter to face the world

alone. Pickford and Brown get to share a melodramatic death scene and audiences flocked to hear "America's Sweetheart" speak onscreen. Based on a play by George Abbott and Anne Preston.
1929 75m/B Mary Pickford, Johnny Mack Brown, Matt Moore, John St. Polis, Henry Kolker, George Irving, Louise Beavers, William Janney; **D:** Sam Taylor. **VHS** $19.98 MGM *🎧🎧½*

Cord & Dischords/Naughty Nurse Two vintage silent shorts featuring some lesser known slapstick clowns cavorting in blackface.
1928 50m/B Fred Parker, Jack Cooper, Ella MacKenzie, Spencer Williams Jr. **VHS, Beta** $14.95 VYY *🎧*

Cordelia A dramatization of an actual court case in turn-of-the century Quebec, in which an "overly" vivacious woman is accused of murdering her husband.
1987 115m/C CA **VHS, Beta** NFB *🎧*

Coriolanus, Man without a Country When the Romans begin to abuse their rights, the Plebians call upon the brave and mighty Coriolanus to lead them into battle against their oppressors. Predictable muscle man outing.
1964 ?m/C IT Gordon Scott, Alberto Lupo, Lilla Brignone. **VHS, Beta** $16.95 SNC *🎧*

Corleone Limp tale about two boyhood friends who grow up to fight the evil landowners who dominate Italy. To accomplish this, one becomes a mobster, the other a politician.
1979 (R) 115m/C IT Claudia Cardinale, Giuliano Gemma; **D:** Pasquale Squitieri. **VHS, Beta** $79.95 MGM *🎧*

The Corn is Green Touching story of a school teacher in a poor Welsh village who eventually sends her pet student to Oxford. Davis makes a fine teacher, though a little young, while the on-site photography provides atmosphere. Based on the play by Emlyn Williams. Remade in 1979.
1945 115m/B Bette Davis, John Dall, Nigel Bruce, Joan Lorring, Arthur Shields, Mildred Dunnock, Rhys Williams, Rosalind Iven; **D:** Irving Rapper; **M:** Max Steiner. **VHS, Beta** $19.95 MGM, FCT *🎧🎧🎧*

Cornbread, Earl & Me A high school basketball star from the ghetto is mistaken for a murderer by cops and shot, causing a subsequent furor of protest and racial hatred. Superficial melodrama.
1975 (R) 95m/C Moses Gunn, Rosalind Cash, Bernie Casey, Tierre Turner, Madge Sinclair, Keith Wilkes, Antonio Fargas; **D:** Joseph Manduke. **VHS, Beta** $59.95 HBO *🎧🎧*

Cornered Tough Powell plays an airman released from a German prison camp who pursues a Nazi war criminal to avenge the death of his wife and child.
1945 102m/B Dick Powell, Walter Slezak, Micheline Cheirel, Luther Adler; **D:** Edward Dmytryk. **VHS, Beta** $19.98 RKO, TTC *🎧🎧🎧*

Coroner Creek Scott's fiancee commits suicide during an Indian attack on her stagecoach, and the couple's dowry is stolen. Scott sets out to trace the loot and exact his revenge. A superior production, notable for being one of the first westerns with an adult theme.
1948 89m/B Randolph Scott, Marguerite Chapman, George Macready, Sally Eilers, Edgar Buchanan, Wallace Ford, Forrest Tucker; **D:** Ray Enright. **VHS** NO *🎧🎧½*

Corporate Affairs A ruthless business woman climbing her way to the top literally seduces her boss to death.

1990 (R) 92m/C Peter Scolari, Mary Crosby, Chris Lemmon, Ken Kercheval; **D:** Terence H. Winkless; **W:** Terence H. Winkless. VHS $79.98 MGM ♂♂

The Corpse Grinders Low-budget bad movie classic in which a cardboard corpse-grinding machine makes nasty cat food that makes cats nasty. Sets are cheap, gore effects silly, and cat attacks ridiculous. 1971 (R) 73m/C Sean Kenney, Monika Kelly, Sandford Mitchell; **D:** Ted V. Mikels; **W:** Ted V. Mikels. VHS, Beta NO Woof!

The Corpse Vanishes Lugosi at his chilling best as a diabolical scientist who snatches young brides and drains their blood in an effort to keep his 70-year-old wife eternally youthful. Not for newlyweds! 1942 64m/B Bela Lugosi, Luana Walters, Tristram Coffin, Elizabeth Russell, Vince Barnett, Joan Barclay, Angelo Rossitto; **D:** Wallace Fox. VHS, Beta $19.95 NOS, MRV, SNC ♂♂½

Corregidor A love triangle develops between doctors treating the wounded during the WWII battle. A poor propaganda piece which contains only shaky stock footage for its "action" sequences. 1943 73m/B Otto Kruger, Elissa Landi, Donald Woods, Rick Vallin, Frank Jenks, Wanda McKay, Ian Keith; **D:** William Nigh. VHS $19.95 NOS, MOV, HEG ♂♂

Corrida Interdite Slow-motion sequences reveal the beauty of the bullfighting ritual without neglecting the deadly nature of the sport. 1958 10m/C VHS, Beta FLI ♂♂

The Corridor: Death Two Americans are involved in a car accident in Israel which triggers a debate on the Jewish perspective of death and the afterlife. Filmed on location at Hadassah Hospital on St. Scopus, Jerusalem. The final part of the trilogy preceded by "The Eighth Day: Circumcision" and "The Journey: Bar Mitzvah." 19?? 25m/C VHS, Beta $39.95 ERG ♂♂

Corridors of Blood Karloff is a doctor, in search of a viable anesthetic, who accidently becomes addicted to drugs, then turns to grave robbers to support his habit. Karloff plays usual threatening doctor to perfection. **AKA:** The Doctor from Seven Dials. 1958 86m/C GB Boris Karloff, Betta St. John, Finlay Currie, Christopher Lee, Francis Matthews, Adrienne Corri, Nigel Green; **D:** Robert Day. VHS, Beta $39.95 MPI ♂♂½

Corrina, Corrina Newly-widowed jingle-writer Liotta needs someone to care for his withdrawn eight year-old daughter. Enter Whoopi, as housekeeper and eventual love interest. Sweet, nostalgic romance set in the 1950's. Goldberg also found off-screen romance (again), this time with the film's union organizer Lyle Trachtenberg. Last role for Ameche. 1994 (PG) ?m/C Whoopi Goldberg, Ray Liotta, Don Ameche, Tina Majorino, Wendy Crewson, Jenifer Lewis, Larry Miller, Erica Yohn; **Cameos:** Anita Baker; **D:** Jessie Nelson; **W:** Jessie Nelson. VHS NYR ♂♂½

Corrupt Bad narcotics cop goes after murderer, but mysterious Lydon gets in the way. An acquired taste, best if you appreciate Lydon, better known as Johnny Rotten of the Sex Pistols. **AKA:** Order of Death; Cop Killers. 1984 (PG) 99m/C IT Harvey Keitel, John (Johnny Rotten) Lydon, Sylvia Sidney, Nicole Garcia, Leonard Mann; **D:** Roberto Faenza; **M:** Ennio Morricone. VHS, Beta $69.95 VTR ♂♂♂

The Corrupt Ones Everyone's after a photographer who has a medallion that will lead to buried treasure in China. Great characters hampered by pedestrian script. **AKA:** Il Sigillo de Pechino; Die Holle von Macao; Les Corrompus; The Peking Medallion; Hell to Macao. 1967 87m/C Robert Stack, Elke Sommer, Nancy Kwan, Christian Marquand, Werner Peters; **D:** James Hill; **W:** Brian Clemens. VHS, Beta $49.95 SUE, NLC ♂♂½

Corruption Mostly soft-porn. Alleged plot: The Mob is interested in having Shea work for them, and makes it worth his while. 1989 (R) 80m/C Mary McGee, Patrick Shea. VHS NO Woof!

Corsair Actioner about a gorgeous debutante and a handsome gangster who find themselves caught up with a gang of bootlegging pirates. Todd is always worth watching. 1931 73m/B Chester Morris, Thelma Todd, Frank McHugh, Ned Sparks, Mayo Methot; **D:** Roland West. VHS, Beta $12.95 GPV, RXM, HEG ♂♂

The Corsican Brothers Alexander Dumas' classic about twins who, although separated, remain spiritually tied throughout their various adventures. Fairbanks takes on dual roles in this entertaining swashbuckler. Remade for television in 1984. 1942 111m/B Douglas Fairbanks Jr., Akim Tamiroff, Ruth Warrick, J. Carroll Naish, H.B. Warner, Henry Wilcoxon, Veda Ann Borg; **D:** Gregory Ratoff. VHS, Beta VTR, LIV ♂♂½

Corvette Summer After spending a semester restoring a Corvette in his high school shop class, an L.A. student must journey to Las Vegas to recover the car when it is stolen. There he meets a prostitute, falls in love, and steps into the "real world" for the first time. Potts intriguing as the low-life love interest, but she can't save this one. **AKA:** The Hot One. 1978 (PG) 104m/C Mark Hamill, Annie Potts, Eugene Roche, Kim Milford, Richard McKenzie, William Bryant; **D:** Matthew Robbins; **W:** Matthew Robbins. VHS, Beta $59.95 MGM ♂

Cosh Boy Vicious male youths stalk women on the streets of London in this low-budget Jack the Ripper rip-off. **AKA:** The Slasher. 1961 90m/B Joan Collins, James Kennedy. VHS, Beta NO Woof!

The Cosmic Eye Animated tale of three musicians from outer space who come to earth to spread the message of worldwide peace and harmony. A variety of cultural perspectives about the origins and destiny of the Earth are offered. Rather moralizing but the animation is impressive. 1971 71m/C **D:** Faith Hubley; **V:** Dizzy Gillespie, Maureen Stapleton, Benny Carter. VHS, Beta $59.98 LTY, WTA, DIS ♂♂♂

The Cosmic Man An alien arrives on Earth with a message of peace and restraint. He is regarded with suspicion by us nasty Earthlings. Essentially "The Day the Earth Stood Still" without the budget, but interesting nonetheless. 1959 72m/B Bruce (Herman Brix) Bennett, John Carradine, Angela Greene, Paul Langton, Scotty Morrow; **D:** Herbert Greene. VHS, Beta $14.95 RHI, SNC ♂½

The Cosmic Monsters Scientist accidentally pops a hole in the ionosphere during a magnetism experiment. Then huge, mean insects arrive to plague mankind. Coincidence? You figure it out. **AKA:** The Strange World of Planet X.

1958 75m/B Forrest Tucker, Gaby Andre, Alec Mango, Hugh Latimer, Martin Benson; **D:** Gilbert Gunn. VHS, Beta $14.95 RHI, MRV, SNC ♂½

Cosmo Jones, Crime Smasher Murder mystery based on a forties radio program. 1943 ?m/C Mantan Moreland, Frank Graham. VHS $16.95 SNC ♂♂

Cosmos: War of the Planets The ultimate battle for survival is fought in outer space, though not very well and on a small budget. Special effects especially laughable. **AKA:** Cosmo 2000: Planet Without a Name; War of the Planets. 1980 (PG) 90m/C IT Katia Christine, West Buchanan, John Richardson, Yanti Somer; **D:** Al Bradley. VHS, Beta NO Woof!

Cottage to Let Propaganda thriller about a Nazi plot to kidnap the inventor of a new bombsight. Focused cast struggles with lackluster script. **AKA:** Bombsight Stolen. 1941 90m/B GB Leslie Banks, Alastair Sim, John Mills, Jeanne de Casalis, Carla Lehmann, George Cole, Michael Wilding, Frank Cellier, Wally Patch, Catherine Lacey; **D:** Anthony Asquith. VHS, Beta $16.95 SNC ♂½

Cotter A Native American rodeo clown feels responsible for a cowboy's death, returns home to reflect on his life. Fair story, best at the small town feeling. 1972 94m/C Don Murray, Carol Lynley, Rip Torn, Sherry Jackson; **D:** Paul Stanley. VHS, Beta $39.95 XVC, VCI ♂

Cotton Candy Follows the faintly interesting trials and tribulations of a high school senior who tries to form a rock band. At first he meets failure, but is ultimately successful with the band and romance. Made for television. Joint script-writing venture by brothers Clint and Ron Howard. 1982 97m/C Charles Martin Smith, Clint Howard, Leslie King; **D:** Ron Howard; **W:** Clint Howard, Ron Howard. VHS, Beta TLF ♂♂

The Cotton Club With $50 million in his pocket, Francis reaches for an epic and delivers: handsome production, lots of dance, bit of singing, confused plot, uneven performances, tad too long. A musician playing at The Cotton Club falls in love with gangster Dutch Schultz's girlfriend. A black tap dancer falls in love with a member of the chorus line who can pass for white. These two love stories are told against a background of mob violence and music. Excellent performances by Hoskins and Gwynne. ♫Minnie the Moocher; Ill Wind; The Mooch; Ring Dem Bells; Drop Me Off in Harlem; Cotton Club Stomp; Truckin; Mood Indigo; Copper Colored Gal; Crazy Rhythm; The Jitter Bug. 1984 (R) 121m/C Diane Lane, Richard Gere, Gregory Hines, Lonette McKee, Bob Hoskins, Fred Gwynne, James Remar, Nicolas Cage, Lisa Jane Persky, Allen (Gooritz) Garfield, Gwen Verdon, Joe Dallesandro, Jennifer Grey, Tom Waits, Diane Venora; **D:** Francis Ford Coppola; **W:** Francis Ford Coppola, William Kennedy, Mario Puzo; **M:** John Barry. VHS, Beta, 8mm $14.98 SUE, NLC ♂♂♂

Cotton Comes to Harlem Cambridge and St. Jacques star as Harlem plainclothes detectives Grave Digger Jones and Coffin Ed Johnson in this successful mix of crime and comedy. They're investigating a suspicious preacher's back-to-Africa scheme which they suspect is a swindle. Directorial debut of Davis. Filmed on location in Harlem, New York. Based on the novel by Chester Himes. Followed by a weak sequel, "Come Back, Charleston Blue."

1970 (R) 97m/C Godfrey Cambridge, Raymond St. Jacques, Calvin Lockhart, Judy Pace, Redd Foxx, John Anderson, Emily Yancy, J.D. Cannon, Teddy Wilson, Eugene Roche, Cleavon Little, Lou Jacobi; **D:** Ossie Davis. VHS $14.95 MGM *🎬🎬🎬*

Cotton Queen Romance and light intrigue plague the children of two rival textile mill owners. **AKA:** Crying Out Loud.
1937 80m/B Will Fyffe, Stanley Holloway; **D:** Joe Rock. VHS, Beta, 8mm $24.95 VYY, FCT *🎬½*

The Couch Trip Aykroyd is an escapee from a mental institution who passes himself off as a radio psychologist and becomes a media sensation. There are a few laughs and some funny characters but for the most part this one falls flat.
1987 (R) 98m/C Dan Aykroyd, Walter Matthau, Charles Grodin, Donna Dixon, Richard Romanus, Arye Gross, David Clennon, Mary Gross; **D:** Michael Ritchie; **M:** Michel Colombier. VHS, Beta $9.98 ORI *🎬½*

Could It Happen Here? A lurid Italian spectacle about a metropolis thrown into a state of chaotic martial law by terrorism. Dubbed.
198? 90m/C *IT* Luc Merenda, Marcella Michelangeli; **D:** Massimo Pirri. VHS, Beta NO *🎬*

The Count Chaplin pretends to be the secretary of his boss, who in turn is posing as a count. Silent with musical soundtrack added.
1916 20m/B Charlie Chaplin; **D:** Charlie Chaplin. VHS, Beta CAB *🎬🎬½*

Count/Adventurer Two Chaplin two-reelers: "The Count (The Phoney Nobleman)" (1916), in which Charlie impersonates a count at the home of Miss Moneybags, and "The Adventurer" (1917), Chaplin's final film for Mutual, in which he plays an escaped convict with the law relentlessly on his trail. Silent with musical score.
1917 52m/B Charlie Chaplin, Eric Campbell, Edna Purviance, Frank Coleman; **D:** Charlie Chaplin. VHS, Beta $19.95 VYY *🎬🎬½*

Count Dracula Passable version of the Dracula legend (based on the novel by Bram Stoker) has Lee as the thirsty count on the prowl for fresh blood.
1971 (R) 90m/C *SP GE IT* Christopher Lee, Herbert Lom, Klaus Kinski, Frederick Williams, Maria Rohm, Soledad Miranda; **D:** Jess (Jesus) Franco. VHS $14.98 REP, FCT *🎬🎬½*

Count Dracula's Great Love European horror superstar Naschy plays Dracula; stylishly done in the Hammer tradition. Considered by many to be Naschy's best horror film.
1972 ?m/C Paul Naschy. VHS $16.95 SNC, SMW *🎬🎬*

The Count of Monte Cristo One of the first full-length features starring popular stage stars of the day. The first truly American feature, it was based on the classic tale of revenge by Alexander Dumas. Silent. Remade many times. Lead actor O'Neill was the father of famed American playwright, Eugene O'Neill, who covered his father's success in this role in his own family drama "Long Day's Journey Into Night."
1912 90m/B James O'Neill; **D:** Edwin S. Porter. VHS, Beta $19.95 NOS, VYY, DVT *🎬🎬½*

The Count of Monte Cristo A true swashbuckling revenge tale about Edmond Dantes, who unjustly spends years prison. After escaping, he gains ever so sweet and served quite cold revenge. Adaptation of the Alexandre Dumas classic.

1934 114m/B Robert Donat, Elissa Landi, Louis Calhern, Sidney Blackmer, Irene Hervey, Raymond Walburn, O.P. Heggie; **D:** Rowland V. Lee. VHS, Beta $9.99 CCB, MED, MOV *🎬🎬🎬*

The Count of Monte Cristo The Alexander Dumas classic about an innocent man (Chamberlain) who is imprisoned, escapes, and finds the treasure of Monte Cristo, which he uses to bring down those who wronged him. Good version of the historical costumer. Originally shown in theaters in Europe, but broadcast on television in the U.S.
1974 104m/C *GB* Richard Chamberlain, Kate Nelligan, Donald Pleasence, Alessio Orano, Tony Curtis, Louis Jourdan, Trevor Howard, Taryn Power; **D:** David Greene. VHS, Beta $19.98 LIV, FUS *🎬🎬½*

The Count of the Old Town Feisty townsfolk settle the score after a gang of booze smugglers trick them out of their money. Bergman's film debut as a maid swept off her feet by a mysterious young stranger. Adapted from the play "Greven fran Gamla Sta'n" by Arthur and Sigfried Fischer. In Swedish with English subtitles. **AKA:** Munkbrogreven.
1934 90m/B *SW* Edvin Adolphson, Ingrid Bergman, Sigurd Wallen, Valdemar Dahlquist; **D:** Edvin Adolphson, Sigurd Wallen; **W:** Gosta Stevens. VHS, Beta $29.95 WAC, ING *🎬🎬*

Count Yorga, Vampire The vampire Count Yorga is practicing his trade in Los Angeles, setting up a coven and conducting seances. Good update of the traditional character, with Quarry suitably solemn and menacing. Followed by "The Return of Count Yorga." Also available with "Cry of the Banshee" on laserdisc.
1970 (PG) 90m/C Robert Quarry, Roger Perry, Michael Murphy, Michael Macready, Donna Anders, Judith Lang; **D:** Bob Kelljan. VHS, Beta NO *🎬🎬½*

Countdown Documentary-type fictional look at the first moon mission and its toll on the astronauts and their families. Timely because the U.S. was trying to send a man to the moon in 1968. Interesting as a look at the developing Altman style.
1968 102m/C James Caan, Robert Duvall, Michael Murphy, Ted Knight, Joanna Moore, Barbara Baxley, Charles Aidman, Steve Ihnat, Robert Altman; **D:** Robert Altman. VHS, Beta $19.98 WAR *🎬🎬½*

Counter Attack Story of murder and insurance fraud takes place on the back lots of the Hong Kong film industry. As good as these get.
1984 105m/C Bruce Li, Dan Inosanto, John Ladalski, Young Kong; **D:** Bruce Li. VHS, Beta WVE *🎬½*

Counter Measures A helicopter pilot stumbles on to a bizarre chain of crimes and disasters.
198? 98m/C Monte Markham; **D:** Gerban Ceth. VHS, Beta NO *🎬*

Counter Punch Blake is a boxer framed for the murder of his manager who sets out to clear his name by finding the killers. Fair rendition of a familiar plot. **AKA:** Ripped Off; The Boxer; Uomo Dalla Pelle Dura.
1971 (R) 72m/C *IT* Robert (Bobby) Blake, Ernest Borgnine, Gabriel Ferzetti, Catherine Spaak, Tomas Milian; **D:** Franco Prosperi. VHS, Beta $9.95 SIM, LIV *🎬🎬*

Counterblast A Nazi spy assumes the role of a British scientist in order to gain classified information for the Fatherland. The trouble begins when he refuses to carry out an order to execute a pretty young assistant. Appealing performances distract from the

somewhat confusing plot. **AKA:** The Devil's Plot.
1948 99m/B *GB* Robert Beatty, Mervyn Johns, Nova Pilbeam, Margaretta Scott, Sybilla Binder, Marie Lohr, Karel Stepanek, Alan Wheatley; **D:** Paul Stein. VHS, Beta $16.95 SNC, RXM *🎬🎬*

The Counterfeit Traitor Suspense thriller with Holden playing a double agent in Europe during WWII. Based on the true adventures of Eric Erickson, the top Allied spy of WW II, who was captured by the Gestapo but escaped.
1962 140m/C William Holden, Lilli Palmer, Hugh Griffith, Werner Peters, Eva Dahlbeck; **D:** George Seaton; **W:** George Seaton. VHS, Beta $29.95 PAR *🎬🎬🎬½*

Counterforce A rough group of mercenaries is hired to guard a Mideastern leader being chased by his country's ruling despot. Mild action with predictable story.
1987 (R) 98m/C George Rivero, George Kennedy, Andrew Stevens, Isaac Hayes, Louis Jourdan, Kevin Bernhardt, Hugo Stiglitz, Robert Foster, Susana Dosamantes; **D:** J. Anthony Loma. VHS, Beta $89.95 LIV *🎬*

Country Strong story of a farm family in crisis when the government attempts to foreclose on their land. Good performances all around and an excellent portrayal of the wife by Lange. "The River" and "Places In the Heart," both released in 1984, also dramatized the plight of many American farm families in the early 1980s.
1984 (PG) 109m/C Jessica Lange, Sam Shepard, Wilford Brimley, Matt Clark, Therese Graham, Levi L. Knebel; **D:** Richard Pearce; **W:** Bill Wittliff. VHS, Beta $79.95 TOU *🎬🎬🎬*

The Country Diary of an Edwardian Lady Biographical dramatization of the life of English writer Edith Holden. Chronicles her life from 1877 until her mysterious death.
1988 90m/C VHS $26.98 BFS, BTV *🎬🎬½*

Country Gentlemen Vaudeville team, Olsen and Johnson, play fast-talking conmen who sell shares in a worthless oil field to a bunch of WWI veterans. What a surprise when oil is actually found there. Not one of the duo's better performances.
1936 54m/B Ole Olsen, Chic Johnson, Joyce Compton, Lila Lee, Ray Corrigan, Donald Kirke, Pierre Watkin; **D:** Ralph Staub. VHS, Beta $24.95 NOS, MRV, VYY *🎬*

Country Girl In the role that completely de-glamorized her (and won her an Oscar) Kelly plays the wife of alcoholic singer Crosby who tries to make a comeback with the help of director Holden. One of Crosby's four dramatic parts, undoubtedly one of his best. Seaton won an Oscar for his adaptation of the Clifford Odets play. Remade in 1982. 🎵The Search is Through; Dissertation on the State of Bliss; It's Mine, It's Yours; The Land Around Us.
1954 104m/B Bing Crosby, Grace Kelly, William Holden, Gene Reynolds, Anthony Ross; **D:** George Seaton; **W:** George Seaton. Academy Awards '54: Best Actress (Kelly), Best Screenplay; Nominations: Best Actor (Crosby), Best Black and White Cinematography, Best Director (Seaton), Best Picture; Academy Awards '56: Best Art Direction/Set Decoration (B & W); Golden Globe Awards '55: Best Actress—Drama (Kelly); National Board of Review Awards '54: 10 Best Films of the Year, Best Actress (Kelly). VHS, Beta $14.95 PAR, BTV *🎬🎬🎬½*

Country Girl Aging, alcoholic actor is desperate for a comeback. His director blames his fiercely loving wife for the downfall. Poor cable TV remake of 1954 version with Bing Crosby.

1982 137m/C Dick Van Dyke, Faye Dunaway, Ken Howard. **VHS, Beta** NO ✂️

The Country Kid A freckle-faced teen-ager and his two brothers are beset by a wicked uncle out to steal their inheritance. One of Barry's best-remembered films.
1923 60m/B Wesley Barry, "Spec" O'Donnell, Bruce Guerin, Kate Toncray, Helen Jerome Eddy, George Nichols; **D:** William Beaudine. **VHS, Beta** NO ✂️✂️✂️

Country Lovers, City Lovers Two adaptations of short stories by South African novelist Nadine Gordimer about interracial love.
1972 121m/C **VHS, Beta** $69.95 MGM ✂️✂️½

Countryman A dope-smuggling woman crashes her plane in Jamaica and is rescued by Countryman, a rasta super hero. Not very good, but at least there's great music by Bob Marley and others.
1983 (R) 103m/C Hiram Keller, Kristine Sinclair; **D:** Dickie Jobson. **VHS, Beta** $59.95 MVD, MED ✂️✂️

County Fair This early silent film is an adaptation of Neil Burgess' play about life in New England.
1920 60m/B Helen Jerome Eddy, David Butler. **VHS, Beta** $24.95 NOS, DVT, HEG ✂️✂️

Coup de Grace Engaging political satire about a wealthy aristocratic woman in Latvia during the 1919-1920 Civil War, and how she attempts to maintain her lifestyle as German soldiers are housed on her estate. Her unrequited love for a German officer adds to her troubles. In German with English subtitles. Co-written by von Trotta and based on the novel by Marguerite Yourcenar.
1978 96m/B GE FR Margarethe von Trotta, Matthias Habich, Rudiger Kirschstein, Matthieu Carriere; **D:** Volker Schlondorff; **W:** Margarethe von Trotta. **Beta** $59.95 COL, APD, GLV ✂️✂️½

Coup de Torchon Set in 1938 French West Africa, Noiret plays corrupt police chief Lucien Cordier who is consistently harrassed by his community, particularly by the town pimp. He usually overlooks the pimp's crimes, but when Cordier catches him and a friend shooting at plague victims' bodies floating down the river he decides to murder them in cold blood. Based on the novel "POP 1280" by Jim Thompson. In French with English subtitles. **AKA:** Clean Slate.
1981 128m/C FR Philippe Noiret, Isabelle Huppert, Guy Marchand, Stephane Audran, Eddy Mitchell, Jean-Pierre Marielle; **D:** Bertrand Tavernier; **W:** Bertrand Tavernier. **VHS** NO ✂️✂️✂️

Coupe de Ville Three brothers are forced by their father to drive mom's birthday present from Detroit to Florida in the summer of '63. Period concerns and music keep it interesting.
1990 (PG-13) 98m/C Patrick Dempsey, Daniel Stern, Arye Gross, Joseph Bologna, Alan Arkin, Annabeth Gish, Rita Taggart, James Gammon; **D:** Joe Roth; **W:** Mike Binder; **M:** James Newton Howard. **VHS, Beta** $19.95 MCA ✂️✂️½

Couples and Robbers Rich couple and a poor couple are unexpectedly brought together.
1984 29m/C **VHS, Beta** DCL ✂️

Courage Based on fact, a television movie about a Hispanic mother in New York City who, motivated by her drug-troubled children, goes undercover and exposes a multi-million-dollar drug ring. Loren is great in a decidedly non-glamorous role.
1986 141m/C Sophia Loren, Billy Dee Williams, Hector Elizondo, Val Avery, Dan Hedaya, Ron Rifkin, Jose Perez; **D:** Jeremy Paul Kagan. **VHS, Beta** $29.95 STE, NWV ✂️✂️✂️

Courage Mountain If you're looking for a good sequel to Johanna Spyri's classic "Heidi" this isn't it. Europe is on the brink of WWI when teenage Heidi leaves her beloved mountain for an exclusive boarding school in Italy. Not surprisingly in a war zone, the military takes over and the kids are sent to an orphanage run by nasties (see also "Oliver!"). The girls escape to the mountains and are saved by none other than Sheen as Heidi's pal Peter (who cast the twentysomething Sheen as a teenager? Bad mistake.) Ridiculous sequel to the classic tale will appeal to kids despite what the critics say.
1989 (PG) 92m/C Juliette Caton, Joanna Clarke, Nicola Stapleton, Charlie Sheen, Jan Rubes, Leslie Caron, Jade Magri, Kathryn Ludlow, Yorgo Voyagis; **D:** Christopher Leitch; **W:** Weaver Webb; **M:** Sylvester Levay. **VHS, Beta** $14.95 COL, FCT ✂️

Courage of Black Beauty Another version of the perennial heart warmer about a boy and his horse.
1957 80m/C Johnny Crawford, Mimi Gibson, John Bryant, Diane Brewster, J. Pat O'Malley; **D:** Harold Schuster. **VHS, Beta** $12.95 LIV ✂️½

Courage of Lassie Fourteen-year-old Taylor is the heroine in this girl loves dog tale. In this case, the dog is actually called Bill, not Lassie, in spite of the film's title. Bill is found wounded by Taylor and she nurses him back to health. He proves to be loving, loyal, and useful, so much so that, through a complicated plotline, he winds up in the Army's K-9 division and returns home with the doggie version of shell-shock. Taylor's still there to nurse him back to his old kind self again. **AKA:** Blue Sierra.
1946 (G) 93m/C Elizabeth Taylor, Frank Morgan, Tom Drake, Selena Royle, Harry Davenport; **D:** Fred M. Wilcox. **VHS** $14.95 MGM ✂️✂️½

Courage of Rin Tin Tin Rusty and his faithful dog Rin Tin Tin help the cavalry soldiers of Fort Apache keep law and order in a small Arizona town. The perennial kid-pleasing German Shepherd comes through again.
1983 90m/C James Brown, Lee Aaker. **VHS, Beta** $24.95 MON ✂️

Courage of the North The Mounties break up a fur-stealing ring with the help of Captain Dog and Dynamite Horse. Bound to set your hair on end.
1935 55m/B John Preston, June Love, William Desmond, Tom London, Jimmy Aubrey, Dynamite Horse, Captain Dog. **VHS, Beta** NO ✂️½

Courageous Avenger A sheriff brings a treacherous ore mine foreman to justice.
1935 59m/B Johnny Mack Brown. **VHS, Beta** MLB ✂️

Courageous Dr. Christian Dr. Christian is faced with an epidemic of meningitis among the inhabitants of a shanty town. Typical entry in the "Dr. Christian" series.
1940 66m/B Jean Hersholt, Dorothy Lovett, Tom Neal, Robert Baldwin, Maude Eburne; **D:** Bernard Vorhaus. **VHS, Beta** $19.95 NOS, VYY, DVT ✂️

The Courageous Mr. Penn Slow-moving British film, outlining the achievements of William Penn, the Quaker founder of Pennsylvania. **AKA:** Penn of Pennsylvania.
1941 79m/B GB Clifford Evans, Deborah Kerr, Dennis Arundell, Aubrey Mallalieu, D.J. Williams, O.B. Clarence, Charles Carson, Henry Oscar, J.H. Roberts; **D:** Lance Comfort. **VHS, Beta** $19.95 NOS, VYY, VEC ✂️✂️

The Courier A former drug addict seeks revenge on the dealers who killed his friend. Only thing that saves it are the songs by U2, The Pogues, and Hothouse Flowers. Musical score by Elvis Costello.

1988 (R) 85m/C IR Gabriel Byrne, Ian Bannen, Padraig O'Loingsigh, Cait O'Riordan, Patrick Bergin; **D:** Frank Deasy, Joe Lee; **M:** Elvis Costello. **VHS, Beta** $79.98 VES, LIV ✂️✂️

Courier of Death A courier is embroiled in a mob war/struggle over a locked briefcase with mysterious contents.
1984 77m/C Joey Johnson, Barbara Garrison; **D:** Tom Shaw. **VHS, Beta** $69.95 VES, LIV ✂️

Court Jester Swashbuckling comedy stars Danny Kaye as a former circus clown who teams up with a band of outlaws trying to dethrone a tyrant king. Kaye poses as the court jester so he can learn of the evil king's intentions. Filled with more color, more song, and more truly funny lines than any three comedies put together, this is Kaye's best performance. ♫They'll Never Outfox the Fox; Baby, Let Me Take You Dreaming; My Heart Knows a Lovely Song; The Maladjusted Jester.
1956 101m/C Danny Kaye, Glynis Johns, Basil Rathbone, Angela Lansbury, Cecil Parker, John Carradine, Mildred Natwick, Robert Middleton; **D:** Norman Panama, Melvin Frank; **W:** Norman Panama. **VHS, Beta** $14.95 PAR ✂️✂️✂️½

The Court Martial of Billy Mitchell Terrific courtroom drama depicts the secret trial of Billy Mitchell, head of the Army Air Service in the 1920s, who predicted the role of airpower in subsequent warfare and the danger of war with Japan. Mitchell incurred the wrath of the military by publicly faulting the lack of U.S. preparedness for invasion. Steiger is outstanding as the attorney; Cooper is great as Mitchell. Debut for Montgomery. **AKA:** One-Man Mutiny.
1955 100m/C Gary Cooper, Charles Bickford, Ralph Bellamy, Rod Steiger, Elizabeth Montgomery, Fred Clark, James Daly, Jack Lord, Peter Graves, Darren McGavin, Robert Simon, Jack Perrin, Charles Dingle; **D:** Otto Preminger. **VHS** $19.98 REP ✂️✂️✂️

The Court Martial of Jackie Robinson True story of a little known chapter in the life of the famous athlete. During his stint in the Army, Robinson refused to take a back seat on a bus and subsequently faced the possibility of court martial. Originally made for cable television.
1990 (R) 94m/C Andre Braugher, Daniel Stern, Ruby Dee, Stan Shaw, Paul Dooley, Bruce Dern; **D:** Larry Peerce. **VHS, Beta** $79.98 TTC, FCT ✂️✂️✂️½

The Courtesans of Bombay Gritty docudrama, set in Pavanpul, the poverty-stricken brothel section of Bombay, looks at how the impoverished women support themselves through a combination of prostitution and performing. Made for British television.
1985 74m/C GB Kareem Samar, Zohra Segal, Saeed Jaffrey; **D:** Ismail Merchant, James Ivory, Ruth Prawer Jhabvala. **VHS, Beta** $19.95 SUE, ING, NLC ✂️✂️✂️

Courtin' Wildcats Early Gibson programmer in which he plays a frail eastern college boy who was sent west by his father to toughen up. Once there, he meets Gilbert and ends up marrying her.
1929 56m/B Hoot Gibson, Eugenia Gilbert, Monte Montague; **D:** Jerome Storm. **VHS** $9.95 GPV ✂️½

The Courtney Affair An aristocratic young Britisher causes a stir when he marries an Irish maid. As a result, the couple must face terrific social ostracism. Classy soap opera family saga was a big money maker in England. **AKA:** The Courtneys of Curzon Street.

1947 112m/B *GB* Anna Neagle, Michael Wilding, Gladys Young, Michael Medwin, Coral Browne, Jack Watling, Bernard Lee; *D:* Herbert Wilcox. VHS $24.95 *VYY* 🎬🎬½

Courtship From renowned playwright Horton Foote comes this touching story about a sheltered, upper-crust young girl who shocks her family and friends by eloping with a traveling salesman. Made for television.
1987 84m/C Hallie Foote, William Converse-Roberts, Amanda Plummer, Rochelle Oliver, Michael Higgins; *D:* Howard Cummings. VHS, Beta $19.98 *LHV, WAR* 🎬🎬🎬

The Courtship of Eddie's Father A clever nine-year-old boy plays matchmaker for his widowed dad in this rewarding family comedy-drama (the inspiration for the TV series). Some plot elements are outdated, but young Howard's performance is terrific; he would later excel at direction. Based on the novel by Mark Toby.
1962 117m/C Glenn Ford, Shirley Jones, Stella Stevens, Dina Merrill, Ron Howard, Jerry Van Dyke; *D:* Vincente Minnelli; *W:* John Gay. VHS $19.98 *MGM, FCT* 🎬🎬🎬

Cousin, Cousine Pleasant French comedy about distant cousins who meet at a round of family parties, funerals, and weddings and become friends, but their relationship soon becomes more than platonic. Remade in the U.S. in 1989 as "Cousins." In French with English subtitles.
1976 (R) 95m/C *FR* Marie-Christine Barrault, Marie-France Pisier, Victor Lanoux, Guy Marchand, Ginette Garcin, Sybil Maas; *D:* Jean-Charles Tacchella. Academy Awards '76 Nominations: Best Actress (Barrault), Best Foreign Language Film, Best Original Screenplay; Cesar Awards '76: Best Supporting Actress (Pisier); National Board of Review Awards '76: 5 Best Foreign Films of the Year. VHS, Beta $29.95 *TPV, IME, FOX* 🎬🎬🎬½

The Cousins Set against the backdrop of Parisian student life, two very different cousins (one twisted, the other saintly) vie for the hand of Maynier. This country mouse, city mouse adult fable ultimately depicts the survival of the fittest. Chabrol's lovely but sad second directorial effort. *AKA:* Les Cousins.
1959 112m/B *FR* Jean-Claude Brialy, Gerard Blain, Juliette Maynier, Claude Cerval, Genevieve Cluny; *D:* Claude Chabrol; *W:* Claude Chabrol. VHS *PAR* 🎬🎬🎬

Cousins An American remake of "Cousin, Cousine," in which two distant cousins-by-marriage meet at a wedding and, due to their respective spouses' infidelities, fall into each other's arms. A gentle love story with a humorous and biting look at the foibles of extended families.
1989 (PG-13) 110m/C Isabella Rossellini, Sean Young, Ted Danson, William L. Petersen, Norma Aleandro, Lloyd Bridges, Keith Coogan; *D:* Joel Schumacher; *W:* Stephen Metcalfe; *M:* Angelo Badalamenti. VHS, Beta $19.95 *PAR, FCT, HMV* 🎬🎬🎬½

Cover Girl A vintage wartime musical about a girl who must decide between a nightclub career and a future as a cover model. Hayworth is beautiful, Kelly dances like a dream, and Silvers and Arden are hilarious. Cinematography by Rudolph Mate. ♫ Cover Girl; Sure Thing; Make Way For Tomorrow; Put Me to the Test; Long Ago and Far Away; That's the Best of All; The Show Must Go On; Who's Complaining?; Poor John.
1944 107m/C Rita Hayworth, Gene Kelly, Phil Silvers, Otto Kruger, Lee Bowman, Jinx Falkenberg, Eve Arden, Edward Brophy, Anita Colby; *D:* Charles Vidor; *M:* Ira Gershwin, Jerome Kern. Academy Awards '44: Best Score;

Nominations: Best Color Cinematography, Best Interior Decoration, Best Song ("Long Ago and Far Away"), Best Sound. VHS, Beta $19.95 *COL* 🎬🎬🎬

Cover Girl Models An action-packed seventies adventure in which beautiful models are forced to fight for survival.
1975 82m/C Lindsay Bloom, Pat Anderson, John Kramer, Rhonda Leigh Hopkins, Mary Woronov; *D:* Cirio H. Santiago. VHS, Beta *SUE* 🎬

The Cover Girl Murders Six beautiful models have been brought together on a remote island to shoot a magazine's popular swimsuit issue. Each one wants to be the cover model—but someone is willing to kill to get the job.
1993 (PG-13) 87m/C Lee Majors, Jennifer O'Neill, Adrian Paul, Beverly Johnson, Vanessa Angel; *D:* James A. Contner; *W:* Douglas Barr, Bernard Maybeck; *M:* Rick Marotta. VHS, Beta *PAR* 🎬🎬½

Cover-Up Terrorist attacks on U.S. military bases in Israel are just a smokescreen for a greater threat. The below-par actioner stands out only for the hokey religious symbolism in its Good Friday climax.
1991 (R) 89m/C Dolph Lundgren, Louis Gossett Jr., John Finn; *D:* Manny Coto. VHS $39.95 *LIV, IME* 🎬½

The Covered Wagon Prototypical silent Western began the genre. Wagon train moves cross-country, battling weather and wild Indians. By today's standards, somewhat bucolic and uneventful, but the location photography holds up quite well. Big budget film in its day, and enormously popular.
1923 98m/B Warren Kerigan, Lois Wilson, Alan Hale, Ernest Torrence; *D:* James Cruze. VHS $14.95 *PAR* 🎬🎬½

Covered Wagon Days The Three Mesquiteers set out after silver smugglers who have framed Rico's brother for murder.
1940 54m/B Bob Livingston, Raymond Hatton, Duncan Renaldo, John Merton, Reed Howes; *D:* George Sherman. VHS $9.95 *REP* 🎬🎬

Covered Wagon Trails Substandard Western has good guy Randall dealing with the shifty cattleman's association and making the West safe for the hardworking locals. Future Frankenstein monster Strange plays the hired muscle.
1940 52m/B Jack Randall, Sally Cairns, David Sharpe, Lafe McKee, Budd Buster, Glenn Strange; *D:* Raymond K. Johnson; *W:* Tom Gibson. VHS $19.99 *MOV* 🎬

Covergirl Wealthy man decides to relieve his boredom by molding a young woman into a supermodel. She finds the glamorous life isn't always what it's cracked up to be. TV-type melodrama. *AKA:* Dreamworld.
1983 (R) 98m/C *CA* Jeff Conaway, Irena Ferris, Cathie Shirriff, Roberta Leighton, Deborah Wakeham; *D:* Jean-Claude Lord. VHS, Beta $19.99 *STE* 🎬½

Covert Action A drug kingpin who desires to protect his business tries to frame a captain for a crime he did not commit.
1988 85m/C Rick Washburne, John Christian, Stuart Garrison Day, Amanda Zinsser, Johnny Stumper; *D:* J. Christian Ingvordsen. VHS, Beta $79.98 *MCG* 🎬🎬

Cow Town A range war results when ranchers begin fencing in their land to prevent cattle rustling. Autry's 72nd film has some good songs and a dependable cast.
1950 70m/B Gene Autry, Gail Davis, Jock Mahoney, Harry Shannon; *D:* John English. VHS, Beta $29.98 *CCB* 🎬🎬

Coward of the County A devout pacifist is put to the test when his girlfriend is raped. Good performances by all concerned. Based on the lyrics of Kenny Rogers' hit song of the same name. Made for television.
1981 115m/C Kenny Rogers, Frederic Lehne, Largo Woodruff, Mariclare Costello, Ana Alicia, Noble Willingham; *D:* Dick Lowry. VHS, Beta $19.98 *LHV, WAR* 🎬🎬½

Cowboy Film chronicling the determination of cattle-herders in the West.
1954 69m/C VHS, Beta *RXM* 🎬½

The Cowboy & the Ballerina A television movie about an aging rodeo star who falls in love with a petite ballerina defecting from a Russian Dance Company. Good cast makes it watchable.
1984 96m/C Lee Majors, Leslie Wing, Christopher Lloyd, Anjelica Huston, George de la Pena; *D:* Jerry Jameson; *M:* Bruce Broughton. VHS, Beta $79.95 *PSM* 🎬🎬

Cowboy & the Bandit A cowboy comes to the aid of a widow being victimized by outlaws.
1935 58m/B Rex Lease, Bobby Nelson, William Desmond; *D:* Albert Herman. VHS, Beta $19.95 *NOS* 🎬

The Cowboy and the Lady Oberon plays a madcap heiress who is deposited by her politician father on their Florida estate to keep her out of trouble while he seeks the Presidential nomination. She is bored and decides to go to a local rodeo where she meets cowboy Cooper. Both are instantly smitten and marry on impulse. Cooper doesn't know about her wealth and when her father finds out about the marriage he's appalled that his daughter has married beneath her. Since this is a comedy all comes out right in the end. Good cast, weak story.
1938 91m/B Gary Cooper, Merle Oberon, Patsy Kelly, Walter Brennan, Fuzzy Knight, Mabel Todd, Henry Kolker, Harry Davenport; *D:* H.C. Potter. Academy Awards '38: Best Sound; Nominations: Best Song ("The Cowboy and the Lady"), Best Original Score. VHS $19.98 *FCT, HBO* 🎬🎬½

Cowboy & the Senorita A cowboy solves the mystery of a missing girl and wins her lovely cousin. The first film that paired Rogers and Evans, who went on to become a winning team, on and offscreen.
1944 56m/B Roy Rogers, John Hubbard, Dale Evans. VHS, Beta $9.95 *NOS, MRV, DVT* 🎬🎬

Cowboy Commandos Improbable plot has cowboys riding out after Nazi spies, who want to steal valuable ore.
1943 53m/B Ray Corrigan, Dennis Moore, Max Terhune, Budd Buster, John Merton; *D:* S. Roy Luby. VHS $19.95 *DVT, RXM, HEG* 🎬½

Cowboy Counselor Cowboy Hoot Gibson helps an enchanting girl clear her innocent brother's name.
1933 60m/B Hoot Gibson. VHS, Beta *VCI* 🎬

Cowboy Millionaire An Englishwoman comes to an American dude ranch and falls in love with one of the ranch hands. Entertaining Western comedy.
1935 65m/B George O'Brien, Evalyn Bostock, Edgar Kennedy, Alden Chase; *D:* Eddie Cline. VHS $19.95 *NOS, DVT, RXM* 🎬

The Cowboy Way A mess from start to finish made somewhat watchable by cowpoke charm of the leads and one good horse chase. Two rodeo stars (Harrelson and Sutherland) from New Mexico ride into New York City to avenge a pal's death, with Hudson as a mounted NYC cop who always yearned to be a cowboy. Great premise is overcome by tasteless humor and a patched-up plot shot full of holes. Good for a gander is the

90-foot Times Square billboard of Harrelson's character as a Calvin Klein underwear model, which stopped traffic even in jaded New York. **1994 (PG-13) 106m/C** Woody Harrelson, Kiefer Sutherland, Dylan McDermott, Ernie Hudson, Cara Buono, Marg Helgenberger, Tomas Milian, Joaquin Martinez; *Cameos:* Travis Tritt; *D:* Gregg Champion; *W:* Bill Wittliff, Rob Thompson; *M:* David Newman. **VHS** *NYR ♂♂½*

The Cowboys Wayne stars as a cattle rancher who is forced to hire eleven schoolboys to help him drive his cattle 400 miles to market. Clever script makes this one of Wayne's better Westerns. Carradine's film debut. Inspired the television series. Laserdisc available in widescreen letterbox edition. **1972 (PG) 128m/C** John Wayne, Roscoe Lee Browne, A. Martinez, Bruce Dern, Colleen Dewhurst, Slim Pickens, Robert Carradine; *D:* Mark Rydell; *W:* Harriet Frank Jr., Irving Ravetch; *M:* John Williams. **VHS, Beta $19.98** *WAR, TLF ♂♂♂*

Cowboys Don't Cry When a modern cowboy's wife is killed in an automobile accident, he must change his immature ways and build a solid future with his teenage son or perish in loneliness. **1988 96m/C** Rebecca Jenkins, Ron White, Janet-Laine Green. **VHS, Beta** *MCA ♂♂*

Cowboys from Texas The Three Mesquiteers bring about a peaceful settlement to a fight between cattlemen and homesteaders. Part of "The Three Mesquiteers" series. **1939 54m/B** Bob Livingston, Raymond Hatton, Duncan Renaldo, Carole Landis. **VHS, Beta** *MED ♂½*

Cowboys of the Saturday Matinee The history of B-movie westerns is traced from the beginning of the sound era. **1984 75m/B** Gene Autry, Tex Ritter, Roy Rogers. **VHS, Beta $19.98** *LHV, FCT, WAR ♂½*

Coyote Trails Standard western adventure has cowboy Tyler helping a damsel in distress. **1935 68m/B** Tom Tyler. **VHS, Beta $19.95** *NOS, VCN, RXM ♂½*

Crack House A man seeks revenge for the murder of a relative by drug dealers. Average exploitation flick. **1989 (R) 91m/C** Jim Brown, Richard Roundtree, Anthony Geary, Angel Tompkins, Greg Gomez Thomsen, Clyde Jones, Cheryl Kay; *D:* Michael Fischa. **VHS, Beta $14.95** *MGM, WAR ♂♂*

Crack Shadow Boxers Through a series of misadventures, Wu Lung and Chu San battle to protect the inhabitants of a small village from the onslaught of relentless bandits. **197? 91m/C** *HK* Ku Feng, Chou Li Lung, Han Guo Gai; *D:* Weng Yao Hai. **VHS, Beta $54.95** *OCE ♂*

Crack-Up Largely ignored at the time of its release, this tense tale is now regarded as a minor classic of film noir. An art expert suffers a blackout while investigating a possible forgery and must piece together the missing hours to uncover a criminal conspiracy. **1946 70m/B** Pat O'Brien, Claire Trevor, Herbert Marshall, Ray Collins, Wallace Ford, Damian O'Flynn, Erskine Sanford; *D:* Irving Reis. **VHS, Beta $19.98** *TTC ♂♂½*

The Cracker Factory Wood is impressive as a woman committed to a mental institution who attempts to charm her way out of treatment. Made for television. **1979 90m/C** Natalie Wood, Perry King, Shelley Long, Vivian Blaine, Juliet Mills, Peter Haskell; *D:* Burt Brinckerhoff; *M:* Billy Goldenberg. **VHS, Beta** *NO ♂♂½*

Crackers The offbeat story of two bumbling thieves who round up a gang of equally inept neighbors and go on the wildest crime spree you have ever seen. A would-be comic remake of "Big Deal on Madonna Street." **1984 (PG) 92m/C** Donald Sutherland, Jack Warden, Sean Penn, Wallace Shawn, Larry Riley, Trinidad Silva, Christine Baranski, Charlaine Woodard, Tasia Valenza; *D:* Louis Malle. **VHS, Beta $59.95** *MCA ♂♂*

Cracking Up Accident-prone misfit's mishaps on the road to recovery create chaos for everyone he meets. Lewis plays a dozen characters in this overboard comedy with few laughs. *AKA:* Smorgasbord. **1983 (PG) 91m/C** Jerry Lewis, Herb Edelman, Foster Brooks, Milton Berle, Sammy Davis Jr., Zane Buzby, Dick Butkus, Buddy Lester; *D:* Jerry Lewis. **VHS, Beta $19.98** *WAR ♂½*

The Crackler During the '20s, a husband-and-wife private investigation team (Tommy and Tuppence) set out to find a gang of forgers operating in high society circles. Based on a story by Agatha Christie. Made for British television. **1984 60m/C** *GB* James Warwick, Francesca Annis. **VHS, Beta $14.95** *TPV ♂♂*

The Cradle Will Fall A made-for-television adaptation of the pulpy bestselling mystery by Mary Higgins Clark about a woman who cannot convince anyone she witnessed a murder. The cast of "The Guiding Light" appear. Poor script and poor direction do not a thriller make. **1983 103m/C** Lauren Hutton, Ben Murphy, James Farentino, Charita Bauer, Peter Simon; *D:* John Llewellyn Moxey. **VHS, Beta $19.98** *LHV, WAR Woof!*

Craig's Wife A classic soap opera about a pitiful woman driven to total ruin by her desire for social acceptance and material wealth. Russell makes her surprisingly sympathetic. Based on a Pulitzer Prize-winning George Kelly play. Remake of a silent film, was also remade as "Harriet Craig." **1936 75m/B** Rosalind Russell, John Boles, Alma Kruger, Jane Darwell, Billie Burke; *D:* Dorothy Arzner. **VHS, Beta** *NO ♂♂♂*

Crainquebille The classic satire based on the Anatole France story about a street merchant in Paris unfairly imprisoned and eventually surviving peacefully as a tramp. Silent. **1923 50m/B** *FR* Maurice Feraudy; *D:* Jacques Feyder. **VHS, Beta $34.95** *FCT, GPV ♂♂♂*

The Cranes are Flying When her lover goes off to fight during WWII, a girl is seduced by her cousin. Touching love story is free of politics. Filmed in Russia; English subtitles. *AKA:* Letyat Zhuravit. **1957 91m/B** *RU* Tatyana Samoilova, Alexei Batalov, Vasily Merkuryev, A. Shvorin; *D:* Mikhail Kalatozov. **VHS, Beta $35.95** *IHF, CVC ♂♂♂½*

Crash and Burn Rebels in a repressive future police state reactivate a huge, long-dormant robot to battle the establishment's army of powerful androids. Special effects by David Allen make the mayhem interesting. **1990 (R) 85m/C** Ralph Waite, Paul Ganus, Eva LaRue, Bill Moseley; *D:* Charles Band; *M:* Richard Band. **VHS, Beta $19.95** *PAR ♂½*

Crash Dive WWII glory film provides comic relief in the form of romance. Second-in-command Power falls hopelessly in love with school teacher Baxter, only to find out later that she is Lt. Commander Andrews' fiance. Once this little tidbit of information is disclosed, the two officers embark on a mission to destroy a Nazi U-Boat responsible for laying mines in the North Atlantic. Fantastic special effects and sound. Based on the story by W.R. Burnett. **1943 105m/B** Tyrone Power, Anne Baxter, Dana Andrews, James Gleason, May Whitty, Henry Morgan, Ben Carter, Frank Conroy, Florence Lake, John Archer, Minor Watson, Kathleen Howard, Stanley Andrews, Thurston Hall, Trudy Marshall; *D:* Archie Mayo; *M:* David Buttolph. **VHS $19.99** *FXV ♂♂½*

The Crash of Flight 401 A plane, full of recognizable TV stars, crashes in the Florida Everglades. "Airport" for a smaller screen. Based on a real event. Made for televisiion. **1978 97m/C** William Shatner, Adrienne Barbeau, Eddie Albert, Brooke Bundy, Christopher Connelly, Lorraine Gary, Ron Glass, Sharon Gless, Brett Halsey, George Maharis, Gerald S. O'Loughlin; *D:* Barry Shear. **VHS, Beta $14.95** *FRH ♂½*

Crashout Six men break out of prison in this entertaining melodrama. Bendix plays the gang's leader to nasty perfection. **1955 82m/B** William Bendix, Gene Evans, Arthur Kennedy, Luther Adler, William Talman, Marshall Thompson, Beverly Michaels; *D:* Lewis R. Foster. **VHS $19.98** *REP ♂♂½*

The Crater Lake Monster The dormant egg of a prehistoric creature hatches after a meteor rudely awakens the dozing dino. He's understandably miffed and begins a revenge campaign. Prehistoric yawner. **1977 (PG) 85m/C** Richard Cardella, Glenn Roberts, Mark Siegel, Bob Hyman, Kacey Cobb; *D:* William R. Stromberg. **VHS, Beta $19.95** *VCI, MRV Woof!*

The Craving Naschy returns as El Hombre Lobo for the umpteenth time and once again battles a female vampire (see "Werewolf vs. the Vampire Woman"). Although continental Europe's biggest horror star, this film was such a box office disaster that Naschy went bankrupt. He was then forced to turn to Japan for financing (see "The Human Beasts"). Naschy also directed under a pseudonym. **1980 (R) 93m/C** *MX* Paul Naschy, Julie Saly; *D:* Jack Molina. **VHS, Beta $69.95** *VES, LIV ♂*

The Crawlers Illegal radioactive dumping has caused a living, lethal organism to invade in a small western town. Seems the local sheriff and the nuclear plant manager were partners in a toxic dumping scheme that went awry and two teenagers are the only ones willing to expose the truth. More to the point—scary monster attacks woman with artistically enhanced cleavage. **1993 (R) 94m/C** Jason Saucier, Mary Sellers; *D:* Martin Newlin; *W:* Dan Price, Martin Newlin. **VHS $79.95** *COL ♂*

The Crawling Eye Hidden in a radioactive fog on a mountaintop, the crawling eye decapitates its victims and returns these humans to Earth to threaten mankind. Average acting, but particularly awful special effects. Based on a British TV series. *AKA:* The Trollenberg Terror. **1958 87m/B** *GB* Forrest Tucker, Laurence Payne, Janet Munro, Jennifer Jayne, Warren Mitchell; *D:* Quentin Lawrence; *W:* Jimmy Sangster. **VHS, Beta $19.95** *SNC, MRV, MED ♂♂*

The Crawling Hand An astronaut's hand takes off without him on an unearthly spree of stranglings. Silly stuff is a hands-down loser. **1963 98m/B** Alan Hale Jr., Rod Lauren, Richard Arlen, Peter Breck, Kent Taylor, Arline Judge, Allison Hayes; *D:* Herbert L. Strock. **VHS, Beta $9.95** *NOS, RHI, GEM Woof!*

Crawlspace Beautiful girls lease rooms from a murdering, perverted doctor who spies on them, then kills. You may find Kinski amusing but not terrifying.
1986 (R) 86m/C Klaus Kinski, Talia Balsam, Joyce Van Patten, Sally Brown, Barbara Whinnery; *D:* David Schmoeller; *W:* David Schmoeller; *M:* Pino Donaggio. **VHS, Beta** $19.98 *VES, LIV* 🎬

Craze Tongue-in-cheek tale of a crazed antique dealer who slays a number of women as sacrifices to an African idol named Chuku. *AKA:* The Infernal Idol; Demon Master.
1974 (R) 96m/C Jack Palance, Diana Dors, Julie Ege, Suzy Kendall, Michael Jayston, Edith Evans, Hugh Griffith, Trevor Howard; *D:* Freddie Francis. **VHS, Beta** *MRV* 🎬

Crazed Dull plodder about a psychopath who keeps a dead girl's body in his boarding house and kills all intruders to keep his secret.
1982 88m/C Laslo Papas, Belle Mitchell, Beverly Ross; *D:* Richard Cassidy. **VHS, Beta** $49.95 *TWE* **Woof!**

Crazed Cop A man's mind snaps when his wife is found raped and murdered, and nothing will stop him on his quest for revenge. Low budget and violent.
1988 85m/C Ivan Rogers, Sandy Brooke, Rich Sutherlin, Doug Irk, Abdulah the Great; *D:* Paul Kyriazi. **VHS, Beta** $69.95 *UNI* 🎬

The Crazies A poisoned water supply makes the residents of a small town go on a chaotic, murderous rampage. When the army is called into to quell the anarchy, a small war breaks out. Message film about the military is muddled and derivative. *AKA:* Code Name: Trixie.
1973 (R) 103m/C Lane Carroll, W.G. McMillan, Harold W. Jones, Lloyd Hollar, Lynn Lowry; *D:* George A. Romero; *W:* George A. Romero. **Beta** *NO* 🎬🎬

Crazy Fat Ethel II A fat, hungry, homicidal female psychopath gets released from the asylum and goes on a cannibalistic rampage. Offensive junk. Sequel to "Criminally Insane."
1985 90m/C Priscilla Alden, Michael Flood, Jane Lambert, Robert Copple; *D:* Nick Phillips. **VHS, Beta** *NO* **Woof!**

Crazy for Love A village idiot stands to inherit the town inn if he can get a diploma within a year. With English subtitles.
1952 80m/B *FR* Brigitte Bardot, Bourvil, Jane Marken, Nadine Basile. **VHS, Beta** $24.95 *DVT, ING, GVV* 🎬🎬½

Crazy from the Heart Sweet made-for-cable TV tale of a high school principal in a small south Texas town who discovers the romance of her life one weekend with a Mexican janitor. Strong, nuanced performances from Lahti and Blades make this chestnut of a story work beautifully, with able help from supporting actors.
1991 104m/C Christine Lahti, Ruben Blades, Mary Kay Place, Brent Spiner, William Russ, Louise Latham, Tommy Muntz, Robin Lively, Bibi Besch, Kamala Lopez; *D:* Thomas Schlamme. **VHS, Beta** $89.98 *TTC* 🎬🎬🎬

Crazy Horse and Custer: "The Untold Story" Long before Little Big Horn, two legendary enemies find themselves trapped together in deadly Blackfoot territory. George Armstrong Custer and Crazy Horse are forced to form a volatile alliance in their life-or- death struggle against the murderous Blackfoot Tribe. History takes a back seat to Hollywood scriptwriting.
1990 (R) 120m/C Slim Pickens, Wayne Maunder, Mary Ann Mobley, Michael Dante. **VHS** *NO* 🎬

Crazy in Love Three generations of women live on an island in the home that has been in their family for years. Hunter is wildly in love with her husband, but misses (and doesn't quite trust) him when he is away on business. Enter Sands, who showers her with affection and fills the void in her life. The supporting cast fleshes out the story nicely and illustrates the reasons behind Hunter's insecurity. Enjoyable romantic comedy doesn't throw out anything heavy. Adapted from the novel by Luanne Rice; made for television.
1992 93m/C Holly Hunter, Gena Rowlands, Bill Pullman, Julian Sands, Frances McDormand, Herta Ware, Joannne Baron; *D:* Martha Coolidge. **VHS** $89.98 *TTC* 🎬🎬½

Crazy Mama Three women go on a crime spree from California to Arkansas, picking up men and having a hoot. Crime and comedy in a campy romp. Set in the 1950s and loaded with period kitsch.
1975 (PG) 81m/C Cloris Leachman, Stuart Whitman, Ann Sothern, Jim Backus, Linda Purl; *D:* Jonathan Demme. **VHS, Beta** $69.98 *SUE* 🎬🎬½

Crazy Moon A rich high school nerd falls in love with a deaf girl, and must struggle against his domineering father's and older brother's prejudices. The viewer must struggle against the romantic cliches and heavy-handed message to enjoy a basically tender tale of romance. *AKA:* Huggers.
1987 (PG-13) 89m/C Kiefer Sutherland, Vanessa Vaughan, Peter Spence, Ken Pogue, Eve Napier; *D:* Allan Eastman; *W:* Tom Berry, Stefan Wodoslowsky; *M:* Lou Forestieri. **VHS, Beta** $14.95 *SUE, NLC* 🎬🎬½

Crazy People Advertising exec Emory Leeston (Moore) writes commercials that describe products with complete honesty, and is committed to a mental hospital as a result. He meets a variety of characters at the hospital, including Hannah, with whom he falls in love. Tepid box-office blunder sounds funnier than it is. We give half a bone for the ad slogans, the funniest part of the movie. Our favorite: "Most of our passengers arrive alive" for an airline.
1990 (R) 91m/C Dudley Moore, Daryl Hannah, Paul Reiser, Mercedes Ruehl, J.T. Walsh, Ben Hammer, Dick Cusack, Alan North, David Paymer, Danton Stone, Doug Yasuda, Bill Smitrovich, Paul Bates, Floyd Vivino; *D:* Tony Bill; *W:* Mitch Markowitz; *M:* Cliff Eidelman. **VHS, Beta** $14.95 *PAR* 🎬½

The Crazy Ray The classic silent fantasy about a mad scientist who endeavors to put the whole population of Paris in a trance. Vintage Clair nonsense. *AKA:* Paris Qui Dort.
1922 60m/B *FR* Henri Rollan, Albert Prejean, Marcel Vallee, Madeleine Rodrigue; *D:* Rene Clair. **VHS, Beta** $16.95 *SNC, FCT, MRV* 🎬🎬🎬

Crazy Streets Cop Baldwin becomes involved in a deadly game of intrigue when a drug deal goes sour.
198? 85m/C Alec Baldwin, Deborah Harry; *D:* Amos Kollek; *W:* Amos Kollek. **VHS** *MTX* 🎬🎬🎬

The Creation of the Humanoids Set in the familiar post-holocaust future, this is a tale of humans outnumbered by androids and the resulting struggle for survival. Slow and silly low-budget sets. For some reason, Andy Warhol was reported to love this film.
1962 84m/C Don Megowan, Frances McCann, Erica Elliot, Don Doolittle, Dudley Manlove; *D:* Wesley E. Barry. **VHS, Beta** $39.95 *MON, MRV, SNC* **Woof!**

Creator A Frankenstein-like scientist plans to clone a being based on his wife, who died thirty years ago. As his experiments begin to show positive results, his romantic attention turns towards his beautiful lab assistant. O'Toole as the deranged scientist almost saves this one. Based on a novel by Jeremy Leven.
1985 (R) 108m/C Peter O'Toole, Mariel Hemingway, Vincent Spano, Virginia Madsen, David Ogden Stiers, John Dehner, Karen Kopins, Jeff Corey; *D:* Ivan Passer. **VHS, Beta** *NO* 🎬🎬

Creature A two thousand-year-old alien life form is killing off astronauts exploring the planet Titan. "Alien" rip-off has its moments, but not enough of them. Kinski provides some laughs. *AKA:* Titan Find.
1985 (R) 97m/C Klaus Kinski, Stan Ivar, Wendy Schaal, Lyman Ward, Annette McCarthy, Diane Salinger; *D:* William Malone; *M:* Tom Chase, Steve Rucker. **VHS, Beta** $9.98 *MED* 🎬

Creature from Black Lake Two anthropology students from Chicago travel to the Louisiana swamps searching for the creature from Black Lake. Predictably, they find him. McClenny, incidentally, is Morgan Fairchild's sister.
1976 (PG) 95m/C Jack Elam, Dub Taylor, Dennis Fimple, John David Carson, Bill Thurman, Catherine McClenny; *D:* Joy Houck Jr. **VHS, Beta** $59.95 *MRV, VES, LIV* 🎬

Creature from the Black Lagoon An anthropological expedition in the Amazon stumbles upon the Gill-Man, a prehistoric humanoid fish monster who takes a fancy to fetching Adams, a coed majoring in "science," but the humans will have none of it. Originally filmed in 3-D, this was one of the first movies to sport top-of-the-line underwater photography and remains one of the most enjoyable monster movies ever made. Gershenson's score became a "Creature Features" standard. Based on a story by Maurice Zimm. Sequels: "Revenge of the Creature" and "The Creature Walks Among Us."
1954 79m/C Richard Carlson, Julie Adams, Richard Denning, Antonio Moreno, Whit Bissell, Nestor Paiva, Ricou Browning; *D:* Jack Arnold; *W:* Arthur Ross; *M:* Joseph Gershenson, Henry Mancini. **VHS, Beta** $14.95 *MCA, GKK* 🎬🎬🎬

Creature from the Haunted Sea Monster movie satire set in Cuba shortly after the revolution and centering around an elaborate plan to loot the Treasury and put the blame on a strange sea monster. Corman comedy is predictably low budget but entertaining. "Wain" is really Robert Towne, winner of an Oscar for screenwriting. Remake of "Naked Paradise."
1960 76m/C Antony Carbone, Betsy Jones-Moreland, Beach Dickerson, Edward Wain, Edmundo Rivera Alvarez, Robert Bean; *D:* Roger Corman, Monte Hellman; *W:* Charles B. Griffith. **VHS, Beta** $19.95 *NOS, MRV, SNC* 🎬

Creature of Destruction A beautiful young woman is hypnotized and inadvertantly reverted to her past life as a hideous sea monster. Buchanan's remake of his own 1956 production, "The She Creature."
1967 ?m/B Les Tremayne, Aron Kincaid, Pat Delaney, Neil Fletcher, Ann McAdams; *D:* Larry Buchanan. **VHS** *NO* 🎬

Creature of the Walking Dead Scientist brings his grandfather back to life with horrifying results for the cast and the audience. Made cheaply and quickly in Mexico in Mexico in 1960, then released with added footage directed by Warren. *AKA:* La Marca del Muerto.
1960 74m/B *MX* Rock Madison, Ann Wells, George Todd, Willard Gross, Bruno Ve Sota; *D:* Frederic Corte, Jerry Warren. **VHS** $16.95 *NOS, MRV, SNC* 🎬½

The Creature Walks Among Us Sequel to "Revenge of the Creature" has the Gill-Man once again being captured by scientists for studying purposes. Through an accidental lab fire, the creature's gills are burned off and he undergoes surgery in an attempt to live out of water. Final entry in the Creature series has little magic of the original. Also shot in 3-D. Available on laserdisc as part of a special Encore Edition Double Feature with "Revenge of the Creature."
1956 79m/B Jeff Morrow, Rex Reason, Leigh Snowden, Gregg Palmer; **D:** John Sherwood; **W:** Arthur Ross; **M:** Henry Mancini. **VHS $14.98** MCA, FCT ♫♫½

Creature with the Blue Hand A German horror film based on a passable Edgar Wallace story about a man unjustly convicted of murders actually committed by a lunatic. Dubbed.
1970 92m/C *GE* Klaus Kinski, Harald Leopold, Hermann Leschau, Diana Kerner, Carl Lange, Ilse Page; **D:** Alfred Vohrer. **VHS, Beta** NO ♫♫

Creatures the World Forgot A British-made bomb about two tribes of cavemen warring over power and a cavewoman. No special effects, dinosaurs, or dialogue.
1970 96m/C *GE* Julie Ege, Robert John, Tony Bonner, Rosalie Crutchley, Sue Wilson; **D:** Don Chaffey. **VHS, Beta $69.95** COL, MLB Woof!

The Creeper After experimenting with a variety of serums, a doctor turns into a murderous monster with feline paws.
1948 65m/B Eduardo Ciannelli, Onslow Stevens, June Vincent, Ralph Morgan; **D:** Jean Yarborough. **VHS, Beta $14.95** MLB ♫♫

Creepers A young girl talks to bugs and gets them to follow her instructions, which comes in handy when she battles the lunatic who is killing her school chums. Argento weirdness—and graphic gore—may not be for all tastes. **AKA:** Phenomena.
1985 (R) 82m/C *IT* Jennifer Connelly, Donald Pleasence, Daria Nicolodi, Elenora Giorgi, Dalia di Lazzaro, Patrick Bauchau, Fiore Argento; **D:** Dario Argento; **W:** Dario Argento, Franco Ferrini. **VHS, Beta $79.95** MED ♫♫½

The Creeping Flesh A scientist decides he can cure evil by injecting his patients with a serum derived from the blood of an ancient corpse. Some truly chilling moments will get your flesh creeping.
1972 (PG) 89m/C *GB* Peter Cushing, Christopher Lee, Lorna Heilbron, George Benson; **D:** Freddie Francis. **VHS, Beta $49.95** COL, IME, MLB ♫♫½

Creeping Terror Gigantic alien carpet monster (look for the tennis shoes sticking out underneath) devours slow-moving teenagers. Partially narrated because some of the original soundtrack was lost, with lots of bad acting, a worse script, laughable sets, and a ridiculous monster. Beware of the thermometer scene. **AKA:** The Crawling Monster; Dangerous Charter.
1964 81m/B Vic Savage, Shannon O'Neal, William Thourlby, Louise Lawson, Robin James; **D:** Art J. Nelson. **VHS, Beta $54.95** VCI Woof!

Creepozoids In the near future, a monster at an abandoned science complex stalks army deserters hiding out there. Violent nonsense done better by others.
1987 72m/C Linnea Quigley, Ken Abraham, Michael Aranda; **D:** David DeCoteau. **Beta** NO ♫

Creepshow Stephen King's tribute to E.C. Comics, those pulp horror comic books of the 1950s that delighted in grizzly, grotesque, and morbid humor, the film tells five horror tales. Features King himself in one segment, as a none-too-bright farmer who unknowingly cultivates a strange, alien-origin

moss. With despicable heroes and gory monsters, this is sure to delight all fans of the horror vein. Those easily repulsed by cockroaches beware!
1982 (R) 120m/C Hal Holbrook, Adrienne Barbeau, Viveca Lindfors, E.G. Marshall, Stephen King, Leslie Nielsen, Carrie Nye, Fritz Weaver, Ted Danson, Ed Harris; **D:** George A. Romero; **W:** Stephen King. **VHS, Beta $19.98** WAR ♫♫½

Creepshow 2 Romero adapted three Stephen King stories for this horror anthology which presents gruesome looks at a hit-and-run driver, a wooden Indian, and a vacation gone wrong. Gory and childish stuff from two masters of the genre. Look for King as a truck driver.
1987 (R) 92m/C Lois Chiles, George Kennedy, Dorothy Lamour, Tom Savini, Domenick John, Frank S. Salsedo, Holt McCallany, David Holbrook, Page Hannah, Daniel Beer, Stephen King; **D:** Michael Gornick; **W:** George A. Romero. **VHS, Beta $19.95** STE, NWV ♫½

The Cremators A meteorite carrying an alien lands at a seaside resort and everyone begins bursting into flames. Low budget effort from the scripter of "It Came from Outer Space."
1972 90m/C Marvin Howard, Maria de Aragon; **D:** Harry Essex. **VHS, Beta** NO Woof!

Cria The award-winning story of a 9-year-old girl's struggle for maturity in a hostile adult world. In Spanish with English subtitles. **AKA:** Cria Cuervos; Raise Ravens.
1976 (PG) 115m/C *SP* Geraldine Chaplin, Ana Torrent, Conchita Perez; **D:** Carlos Saura. Cannes Film Festival Nominations: cs '76: Best Film; National Board of Review Awards '77: 5 Best Foreign Films of the Year. **VHS, Beta $59.95** INT, TPV, APD ♫♫♫

Cricket on the Hearth An adaptation of Charles Dickens' short story about a mail carrier and his bride, who find the symbol of good luck, a cricket on the hearth, when they enter their new home. Silent with organ score.
1923 68m/B Paul Gerson, Virginia Brown Faire, Paul Moore, Joan Standing. **VHS, Beta $24.98** CCB ♫♫

Cries and Whispers As a woman dies slowly of tuberculosis, three women care for her: her two sisters, one sexually repressed, the other promiscuous, and her servant. The sisters remember family love and closeness, but are too afraid to look death in the face to aid their sister. Only the servant can touch her in her dying and only the servant believes in God and his will. Beautiful imagery, focused through a nervous camera, which lingers on the meaningless and whisks away from the meaningful. Absolute mastery of cinematic art by Bergman. **AKA:** Viskingar Och Rop.
1972 (R) 91m/C *SW* Harriet Andersson, Ingrid Thulin, Liv Ullmann, Kary Sylway, Erland Josephson, Henning Moritzen; **D:** Ingmar Bergman; **W:** Ingmar Bergman. Academy Awards '73: Best Cinematography; Nominations: Best Costume Design, Best Director (Bergman), Best Picture, Best Story & Screenplay; National Board of Review Awards '73: 5 Best Foreign Films of the Year, Best Director (Bergman). **VHS, Beta $39.95** HMV, ING, WAR ♫♫♫

Crime & Passion Two scheming lovers plan to get rich by having the woman marry a multimillionaire and sue for a quick divorce. The multimillionaire is no patsy, however, and seeks a deadly revenge. Three scripts by six writers were combined to create this story. That explains the many problems.
1975 (R) 92m/C Omar Sharif, Karen Black, Joseph Bottoms, Bernhard Wicki; **D:** Ivan Passer. **VHS, Beta $69.95** VES, LIV ♫½

Crime and Punishment Original French production (preceding the American version by just one week) of Dostoyevski's novel, the tale of a young murderer, his crime, and ultimately, his confession. Generally considered better than the American version, the French throw out all that is not dramatic, keeping the psychology and suspense. Remade in 1958. **AKA:** Crime et Chatiment.
1935 110m/B Harry Baur, Pierre Blanchar, Madeleine Ozeray, Marcelle Geniat, Lucienne Lemarchand; **D:** Pierre Chenal; **W:** Marcel Ayme, Chenal, Christian Stengel, Wladimir Strijewski; **M:** Arthur Honegger. **VHS $59.95** FCT ♫♫♫♫

Crime and Punishment Pared down but well-executed adaptation of the Dostoyevski novel. Lorre is superb as Raskolnikov, who robs and murders an elderly pawnbroker. Believing he has committed the perfect murder, he accepts the invitation of police inspector Porfiry (Arnold) to observe the investigation. Gradually Raskolnikov's conscience begins to overwhelm him as Porfiry slowly works to wring a confession from the killer. Von Sternberg's subdued directorial approach worked well to explore the psychological aspects of guilt, although the melodramatic French film version (released at the same time) scored better with the critics.
1935 88m/B Peter Lorre, Edward Arnold, Marian Marsh, Tala Birell, Elisabeth Risdon, Robert Allen, Douglass Dumbrille, Gene Lockhart; **D:** Josef von Sternberg; **W:** S.K. Lauren, Joseph Anthony. **VHS $19.95** COL ♫♫♫

Crime and Punishment Ponderous, excruciatingly long adaptation of the Dostoyevski classic involving a haunted murderer and the relentless policeman who seeks to prove him guilty. In Russian with English subtitles.
1970 200m/B *RU* Georgi Taratorkin, Victoria Fyodorova; **D:** Lev Kulijanov; **W:** Lev Kulijanov. **VHS $59.95** ING, DVT, HEG ♫♫

Crime Busters Two guys attempt to pull off a bank heist but accidentally join the Miami police force instead. Hill and Spencer are enjoyable as usual but the film suffers from poor dubbing. Remake of "Two Supercops."
1978 (PG) 114m/C *IT* Terence Hill, Bud Spencer, Laura Gemser, Luciana Catenacci, David Huddleston; **D:** E.B. Clucher. **VHS, Beta $19.98** WAR ♫½

Crime Killer Confusing shenanigans about an explosive ex-CIA agent enlisted by the FBI to battle a brutal crime syndicate shipping guns to nasty Arabs.
1985 90m/C George Pan-Andreas, Leo Morrell, Althan Karras; **D:** George Pan-Andreas. **VHS, Beta $19.95** STE, NWV ♫

Crime Lords When a pair of cops are suspended from the force for committing a blunder, they travel to Hong Kong to continue their investigation. Little do they know their sleuthing has drawn then into a confrontation with one of largest crime syndicates in the world. Lots of action, beautiful women, and exotic locations keep this basic buddy plot moving well.
1991 (R) 96m/C Wayne Crawford, Martin Hewitt, Susan Byun, Mel Castelo, James Hong; **D:** Wayne Crawford. **VHS $19.95** ACA ♫♫

The Crime of Dr. Crespi A doctor takes his revenge on a man who is after his girlfriend by injecting him with suspended animation serum. Extremely campy performance from von Stroheim; Frye's biggest role in terms of screen time.

1935 64m/B Erich von Stroheim, Dwight Frye, Paul Guilfoyle, Harriett Russell, John Bohn; **D:** John H. Auer. **VHS, Beta** $16.95 *NOS, SNC, MLB* ♦♦

Crime of Honor A European executive goes public with his company's corruption, and his family suffers predictable ruin as a result. Based on a true story.
1985 95m/C Maria Schneider, David Suchet; **D:** John Goldschmidt. **VHS, Beta** $29.95 *ACA* ♦

The Crime of Monsieur Lange Charming French socialist fantasy wherein the workers of a publishing company turn the business into a thriving cooperative while their evil boss is gone. When he returns, they plot to kill him. Rather talky, but humorous. In French with subtitles. French script booklet also available. *AKA:* Le Crime de Monsieur Lange.
1936 90m/B *FR* Rene Lefevre, Jules Berry, Florelle, Sylvia Bataille, Jean Daste, Nadia Sibirskaia; **D:** Jean Renoir; **W:** Jacques Prevert. **VHS, Beta** $29.95 *FCT, INT, APD* ♦♦♦

Crime of Passion Stanwyck plays a femme fatale whose ambitions for detective hubby lead to murder. Good performances from Stanwyck, Hayden, and Burr make this an above-average, although outlandish, crime-drama.
1957 85m/B Barbara Stanwyck, Sterling Hayden, Raymond Burr, Fay Wray, Royal Dano, Virginia Grey, Dennis Cross, Robert Griffin, Jay Adler, Malcolm Atterbury, S. John Launer; **D:** Gerd Oswald; **W:** Joe Eisinger. **VHS** $19.98 *MGM, FCT* ♦♦½

Crime Story: The Complete Saga All 42 episodes of the 1986-1988 NBC cops-versus-mobsters series set first in Chicago in 1963, and later in Las Vegas. The series was created by Michael Mann, the executive producer of "Miami Vice." Del Shannon updated the lyrics to his hit "Runaway" for the series theme. Available as a boxed set of ten tapes or individually.
1986 ?m/C Dennis Farina, Anthony John Denison, Bill Smitrovich, Steve Ryan, Bill Campbell, Paul Butler, Stephen Lang, Darlanne Fluegel. **VHS** $14.98 *STE, MOV* ♦♦½

Crime Zone In a totalitarian, repressive, future society, two young lovers try to beat the system and make it on their own. A well-made, if occasionally muddled, low-budget film shot in Peru, of all places.
1988 (R) 96m/C David Carradine, Peter Nelson, Sherilyn Fenn, Orlando Sacha, Don Manor, Michael Shaner; **D:** Luis Llosa; **M:** Rick Conrad. **VHS** $79.95 *MGM* ♦♦½

Crimebusters A man exacts revenge against a government conspiracy that kidnapped his loved ones.
1979 (PG) 90m/C Henry Silva, Antonio Sabato; **D:** Michael Tarantini. **VHS, Beta** *NO* ♦♦½

Crimes & Misdemeanors One of Allen's most mature films, exploring a whole range of moral ambiguities through the parallel and eventually interlocking stories of a nebbish filmmaker—who agrees to make a profile of a smug Hollywood television comic and then sabotages it—and an esteemed ophthalmologist who is being threatened with exposure by his neurotic mistress. Intriguing mix of drama and comedy few directors could pull off. Look for Daryl Hannah in an unbilled cameo.
1989 (PG-13) 104m/C Martin Landau, Woody Allen, Alan Alda, Mia Farrow, Joanna Gleason, Anjelica Huston, Jerry Orbach, Sam Waterston, Claire Bloom, Jenny Nichols, Caroline Aaron; *Cameos:* Daryl Hannah, Nora Ephron, Jerry Zaks; **D:** Woody Allen; **W:** Woody Allen. **VHS, Beta** $14.98 *ORI* ♦♦♦

Crimes at the Dark House In this campy, melodramatic adaptation of Wilkie Collins's novel "The Woman in White," a man kills his rich wife and puts a disguised mental patient in her place. Later remade using the book's title.
1939 69m/B *GB* Tod Slaughter, Hilary Eaves, Sylvia Marriott, Hay Petrie, Geoffrey Wardwell; **D:** George King. **VHS** $19.95 *NOS, MRV, SNC* ♦♦♦

Crimes of Dr. Mabuse Supernatural horror classic about the evil Dr. Mabuse controlling an underworld empire while confined to an insane asylum. One of the best "mad doctor" movies ever made. Also known as "The Testament of Dr. Mabuse" or "The Last Will of Dr. Mabuse."
1932 120m/B *GE* Rudolf Klein-Rogge, Otto Wernicke, Gustav Diesl, Karl Meixner; **D:** Fritz Lang. **VHS** $16.95 *SNC* ♦♦♦½

Crimes of Passion Vintage whacked-out Russell, not intended for the kiddies. A business-like fashion designer becomes a kinky prostitute at night. A disturbed street preacher makes her the heroine of his erotic fantasies. A dark terrifying vision of the underground sex world and moral hypocrisy. Sexually explicit and violent, with an extremely black comedic center. Turner's portrayal is honest and believable, Perkins overacts until he nearly gets a nosebleed, but it's all for good effect. Cut for "R" rating to get it in the theatres; this version restores some excised footage. Also available in rated version.
1984 101m/C Kathleen Turner, Anthony Perkins, Annie Potts, John Laughlin, Bruce Davison, Norman Burton; **D:** Ken Russell; **W:** Barry Sandler; **M:** Rick Wakeman. **VHS, Beta** $14.95 *NWV, STE* ♦♦♦

The Crimes of Stephen Hawke The world knows Stephen Hawke as a big-hearted money lender. What they don't know is his favorite hobby is breaking peoples' spines. An entertaining thriller set in the 1800s. *AKA:* Strangler's Morgue.
1936 65m/B *GB* Tod Slaughter, Marjorie Taylor, D.J. Williams, Eric Portman, Ben Soutten; **D:** George King. **VHS, Beta** $16.95 *SNC, MRV, HEG* ♦♦

Crimes of the Heart Based on Beth Henley's acclaimed play. A few days in the lives of three very strange Southern sisters, one of whom has just been arrested for calmly shooting her husband after he chased her black lover out of town. Spacek as the suicidal sister is a lark. A tart, black comedy that works better as a play than a film.
1986 (PG-13) 105m/C Sissy Spacek, Diane Keaton, Jessica Lange, Sam Shepard, Tess Harper, Hurd Hatfield; **D:** Bruce Beresford; **W:** Beth Henley; **M:** Georges Delerue. Academy Awards '86 Nominations: Best Actress (Spacek), Best Adapted Screenplay, Best Supporting Actress (Harper); Golden Globe Awards '87: Best Actress—Musical/Comedy (Spacek). **VHS, Beta** $19.98 *LHV, WAR* ♦♦½

Crimewave Zany spoof about serial killers set in Detroit (director Raimi's hometown). A rhapsody to comic book style, short on plot and long on style. With such credentials you expect more. *AKA:* The XYZ Murders; Broken Hearts and Noses.
1985 (PG-13) 83m/C Louise Lasser, Paul Smith, Brion James, Bruce Campbell, Reed Birney, Sheree J. Wilson, Edward R. Pressman, Julius W. Harris; **D:** Sam Raimi; **W:** Ethan Coen, Joel Coen, Sam Raimi. **VHS, Beta** $19.98 *NLC* ♦

Criminal Act A newspaper editor hits the street to prove she's still a tough reporter, but uncovers a dangerous scandal in the process.

1988 94m/C Catherine Bach, Charlene Dallas, Nicholas Guest, John Saxon, Vic Tayback; **D:** Mark Byers. **VHS, Beta** $79.95 *PSM* ♦♦½

Criminal Code Aging melodrama about a young man who's jailed for killing in self-defense. His life worsens at the hands of a prison warden when the head guy's daughter falls for him. Remade as "Penitentiary" and "Convicted."
1931 98m/B Walter Huston, Phillips Holmes, Boris Karloff, Constance Cummings, Mary Doran, DeWitt Jennings, John Sheehan; **D:** Howard Hawks. **VHS, Beta** $59.95 *COL, MLB* ♦♦½

Criminal Court A man accused of murdering his blackmailer hires the real killer as his attorney. Hard to follow, with an interesting premise that turns flat.
1946 63m/B Tom Conway, Martha O'Driscoll, Robert Armstrong, Addison Richards, June Clayworth, Pat Gleason, Steve Brodie; **D:** Robert Wise. **VHS, Beta** *RKO* ♦♦

Criminal Justice A black man is accused of a crime by a woman with whom he was involved. Is it justice or revenge? Strong cast in important story. Made for cable TV.
1990 (R) 92m/C Forest Whitaker, Jennifer Grey, Rosie Perez, Anthony LaPaglia, Tony Todd; **D:** Andy Wolk; **W:** Andy Wolk. **VHS** $89.95 *HBO* ♦♦♦

Criminal Law An ambitious young Boston lawyer gets a man acquitted for murder, only to find out after the trial that the man is guilty and renewing his killing spree. Realizing he's the only one privy to the killer's trust, the lawyer decides to stop him himself. A white-knuckled thriller burdened by a weak script.
1989 (R) 113m/C Kevin Bacon, Gary Oldman, Karen Young, Joe Don Baker, Tess Harper; **D:** Martin Campbell; **M:** Jerry Goldsmith. **VHS, Beta** $14.95 *HBO, WAR* ♦♦

The Criminal Life of Archibaldo de la Cruz Seeing the death of his governess has a lasting effect on a boy. He grows up to be a demented cretin whose failure with women leads him to conspire to kill every one he meets, a task at which he also fails. Hilarious, bitter Bunuelian diatribe. In Spanish with English subtitles. *AKA:* Ensayo de un Crimen; Rehearsal for a Crime.
1955 95m/B *MX SP* Ernesto Alonso, Ariadne Welter, Rita Macedo, Rodolfo Landa, Andrea Palma, Miroslava Stern; **D:** Luis Bunuel. **VHS, Beta** $39.95 *FCT, WBF* ♦♦♦

Criminally Insane Authorities release 250 pounds of cleaver-wielding maniacal fury from the loony bin. She seeks food and human blood. They should have known better. Followed by "Crazy Fat Ethel II."
1975 61m/C Priscilla Alden, Michael Flood; **D:** Nick Phillips. **VHS, Beta** *NO* ♦

Criminals Within A scientist working on a top secret formula is murdered and a detective tries to nail the spy ring responsible. Very confusing, poor usage of some fine female cast members. *AKA:* Army Mystery.
1941 67m/B Eric Linden, Ann Doran, Constance Worth, Donald Curtis, Weldon Heyburn, Ben Alexander; **D:** Joseph H. Lewis. **VHS, Beta** $16.95 *SNC* ♦

The Crimson Cult Eden and his girlfriend are invited to a mysterious mansion. They discover that Lee is out to enact revenge as his ancestor was burned for witchcraft by Eden's. An all-star horror disaster. Karloff was eighty and confined to a wheelchair. Despite ads claiming this as his last film, he made four more in Mexico. Highlights include the scantily clad Steele in sado-masochistic sequences and a psychedelic party with strippers and body painters.

AKA: The Crimson Altar; Curse of the Crimson Altar. **1968** (PG) 87m/C *GB* Boris Karloff, Christopher Lee, Mark Eden, Barbara Steele, Virginia Wetherell, Michael Gough, Rupert Davies; **D:** Vernon Sewell. VHS $79.98 MOV 🎬

Crimson Pirate An 18th-century buccaneer pits his wits and brawn against the might of a ruthless Spanish nobleman. Considered by many to be one of the best swashbucklers, laced with humor and enthusiastically paced. Showcase for Lancaster and Cravat's acrobatic talents. **1952** 104m/C *GB* Burt Lancaster, Eva Bartok, Torin Thatcher, Christopher Lee, Nick Cravat; **D:** Robert Siodmak. VHS, Beta $19.98 WAR 🎬🎬🎬½

Crimson Romance Two unemployed American pilots in Europe decide to join the German airforce for want of anything better to do. Conflicts revolve around a warmongering Commandant and his pilot. **1934** 70m/B Ben Lyon, Sari Maritza, James Bush, Erich von Stroheim, Jason Robards Sr., Herman Bing, Vince Barnett; **D:** David Howard. VHS, Beta, 8mm $19.95 NOS, VYY, RXM 🎬🎬

The Crimson Trail Buck believes his uncle may be involved in cattle rustling. Lots of action, minimal plot. **1935** 56m/B Buck Jones, Polly Ann Young, Carl Stockdale, Charles French, Ward Bond, Robert F. (Bob) Kortman, Bud Osborne, Charles Brinley, Robert Walker; **D:** Al Raboch; **W:** Jack Natteford. VHS $11.95 GPV 🎬🎬½

Crisis at Central High A dramatic television recreation of the events leading up to the 1957 integration of Central High in Little Rock, Arkansas. Based on teacher Elizabeth Huckaby's journal. Emmy-nominated performance by Woodward as Huckaby. **1980** 120m/C Joanne Woodward, Charles Durning, William Ross, Henderson Forsythe; **D:** Lamont Johnson; **M:** Billy Goldenberg. VHS, Beta NO 🎬🎬🎬

Criss Cross A classic grade-B film noir, in which an armored car driver is suckered into a burglary by his ex-wife and her hoodlum husband. Multiple back-stabbings and double-crossings ensue. **1948** 98m/B Burt Lancaster, Yvonne De Carlo, Dan Duryea, Stephen McNally, Richard Long, Tony Curtis; **D:** Robert Siodmak; **W:** Daniel Fuchs; **M:** Miklos Rozsa. VHS, Beta $59.95 MCA 🎬🎬🎬

Crisscross It's 1969 and Tracy Cross is a divorced mom whose ex-husband is a traumatized Vietnam vet who has left her alone to raise their 12 year-old son Chris during some hard times. She works two jobs, as a waitress and, unbeknownst to her son, as a stripper in a local club. When Chris sneaks into the club and sees her act he takes drastic measures to help out—by selling drugs. Film is sluggish and relies too much on voice-overs to explain thoughts but Hawn gives a convincing and restrained performance as the mother. **AKA:** Alone Together. **1992** (R) 107m/C Goldie Hawn, David Arnott, Arliss Howard, James Gammon, Keith Carradine, J.C. Quinn, Steve Buscemi, Paul Calderone; **D:** Chris Menges; **M:** Trevor Jones. VHS $14.95 MGM 🎬🎬½

Critical Condition During a blackout, a criminal masquerades as a doctor in a city hospital. Limp comedy embarrassing for Pryor. **1986** (R) 99m/C Richard Pryor, Rachel Ticotin, Ruben Blades, Joe Mantegna; **D:** Michael Apted. VHS, Beta $19.95 PAR 🎬🎬

Critters A gang of furry, razor-toothed aliens escapes from its prison ship to Earth with their bounty hunters right behind them. They make it to a small town in Kansas

where they begin to attack anything that moves. Not just a thrill-kill epic, but a sarcastic other-worldly thrill-kill epic. **1986** (PG-13) 86m/C Dee Wallace Stone, M. Emmet Walsh, Billy Green Bush, Scott Grimes, Nadine Van Der Velde, Terrence Mann, Billy Zane; **D:** Stephen Herek; **W:** Stephen Herek; **M:** David Newman. VHS, Beta $14.95 COL 🎬🎬½

Critters 2: The Main Course Sequel to the hit horror-comedy, wherein the voracious alien furballs return in full force to Grovers Bend, Kansas, from eggs planted two years before. Occasionally inspired "Gremlins" rip. **1988** (PG-13) 93m/C Scott Grimes, Liane Curtis, Don Opper, Barry Corbin, Terrence Mann; **D:** Mick Garris; **W:** Mick Garris, David N. Twohy. VHS, Beta $14.95 COL 🎬🎬

Critters 3 The not-so-loveable critters are back, terrorizing the occupants of a tenement building. **1991** (PG-13) 86m/C Francis Bay, Aimee Brooks, Leonardo DiCaprio, Don Opper; **D:** Kristine Peterson; **W:** David J. Schow. VHS $14.95 COL, NLC 🎬🎬

Critters 4 The ghoulish critters are back, and this time a strain of genetically engineered mutant critters (what's the difference?) wants to take over the universe. **1991** (PG-13) 94m/C Don Opper, Paul Whitthorne, Angela Bassett, Brad Dourif, Terrence Mann; **D:** Rupert Harvey; **W:** David J. Schow. VHS $19.95 NLC, COL 🎬🎬

Crocodile Giant crocodile attacks a beach town, killing and devouring dozens of people. The locals sit around trying to figure a way to stop the critter. Special effects include rear-projected croc. Lots of blood but lacking humor of "Alligator." Filmed in Thailand and Korea. **1981** (R) 95m/C Nat Puvanai, Tiny Tim; **D:** Herman Cohen. VHS, Beta NO Woof!

Crocodile Dundee New York reporter Sue Charlton is assigned to the Outback to interview living legend Mike Dundee. When she finally locates the man, she is so taken with him that she brings him back to New York with her. There, the naive Aussie wanders about, amazed at the wonders of the city and unwittingly charming everyone he comes in contact with, from high-society transvestites to street hookers. One of the surprise hits of 1986. **1986** (PG-13) 98m/C *AU* Paul Hogan, Linda Kozlowski, John Meillon, David Gulpilil, Mark Blum; **D:** Peter Faiman. Academy Awards '86 Nominations: Best Original Screenplay; Golden Globe Awards '87: Best Actor—Musical/Comedy (Hogan). VHS, Beta, 8mm $14.95 PAR 🎬🎬🎬½

Crocodile Dundee 2 In this sequel Mike Dundee, the loveable rube, returns to his native Australia looking for new adventure, having "conquered" New York City. He inadvertently gets involved in stopping a gang of crooks active in Australia and New York. Lacks the charm and freshness of the first film. **1988** (PG) 110m/C Paul Hogan, Linda Kozlowski, Kenneth Welsh, John Meillon, Ernie Dingo, Juan Fernandez, Charles S. Dutton; **D:** John Cornell; **W:** Paul Hogan. VHS, Beta $14.95 PAR 🎬🎬½

Cromwell A lavish British-made spectacle about the conflict between Oliver Cromwell and Charles I, and the British Civil War. History is twisted as Cromwell becomes the liberator of the oppressed. Harris gives a commanding performance and the battle scenes are stunners.

1970 (G) 139m/C *GB* Richard Harris, Alec Guinness, Robert Morley, Frank Finlay, Patrick Magee, Timothy Dalton; **D:** Ken Hughes; **W:** Ken Hughes. Academy Awards '70: Best Costume Design; Nominations: Best Original Score. VHS, Beta $19.95 COL, TVC 🎬🎬½

The Crooked Circle More comedy than mystery as slapstick policeman Gleason goes under cover as a swami. Not helped at all by a weak script and poor photography. **1932** 68m/B Ben Lyon, ZaSu Pitts, James Gleason, C. Henry Gordon, Raymond Hatton, Roscoe Karns; **D:** H. Bruce Humberstone. VHS $12.95 SNC, NOS 🎬🎬

Crooked Hearts Dysfunctional family drama means well but lays it on too thick, as a father/son rivalry threatens to sunder the tight-knit Warrens. Based on a novel by Robert Boswell. **1991** (R) 113m/C Peter Coyote, Jennifer Jason Leigh, Peter Berg, Cindy Pickett, Vincent D'Onofrio; **D:** Michael Bortman. VHS, Beta $14.95 MGM 🎬🎬

Crooked Trail A lawman and bad guy become friends. **1936** 58m/B Johnny Mack Brown. VHS, Beta NO 🎬

Crooklyn Director Lee turns from the life of Malcolm X to the early lives of Generation X in this profile of an African-American middle class family growing up in 1970's Brooklyn. Lee's least politically charged film to date is a joint effort between him and sibs Joie and Cinque, and profiles the only girl in a family of five children coming of age. Tender and real performances from all, especially newcomer Harris, propel the sometimes messy, music-laden trip to nostalgia land. **1994** (PG-13) 112m/C Alfre Woodard, Delroy Lindo, Zelda Harris, David Patrick Kelly, Carlton Williams, Sharif Rashed, Tse-March Washington, Christopher Knowings, Jose Zuniga, Isaiah Washington, Ivelka Reyes, N. Jeremi Duru, Frances Foster, Norman Matlock, Patriece Nelson, Joie Lee, Vondie Curtis-Hall, Tiasha Reyes, Spike Lee; **D:** Spike Lee; **W:** Joie Lee, Cinque Lee; **M:** Terence Blanchard. VHS NYR 🎬🎬🎬

Crooks & Coronets Two-bit crooks plot to rob the country estate of an eccentric British dowager. **AKA:** Sophie's Place. **1969** (PG) 106m/C *GB* Cesar Romero, Telly Savalas, Warren Oates, Edith Evans; **D:** James O'Connolly. VHS, Beta $19.98 WAR 🎬½

The Cross & the Switchblade An idealistic priest tries to bring the message of religion to the members of a vicious street gang. They don't wanna listen. Spanish language version available. **1972** (PG) 105m/C Pat Boone, Erik Estrada, Jackie Giroux, Jo-Ann Robinson; **D:** Don Murray. VHS, Beta $19.95 VGD, VBL 🎬½

Cross Country Action revolves around the brutal murder of a call girl, with initial suspicion falling on a television advertising director involved with the woman. The story twists and turns from the suspect to investigating detective Ironside without becoming particularly interesting. **1983** (R) 95m/C *CA* Richard Beymer, Nina Axelrod, Michael Ironside; **D:** Paul Lynch. VHS, Beta $9.98 SUE, STE, NLC 🎬½

Cross Creek Based on the life of Marjorie Kinnan Rawlings, author of "The Yearling," who, after 10 years as a frustrated reporter/writer, moves to the remote and untamed Everglades. There she meets colorful local characters and receives the inspiration to write numerous bestsellers. Well acted though overtly sentimental at times.

1983 (PG) 115m/C Mary Steenburgen, Rip Torn, Peter Coyote, Dana Hill, Alfre Woodard, Malcolm McDowell; *D:* Martin Ritt. VHS, Beta $14.98 REP ♂♂½

Cross Examination A boy is charged with his father's murder, and a defense attorney struggles to acquit him.
1932 61m/B H.B. Warner, Sally Blane, Sarah Padden. VHS, Beta NO ♂½

Cross Mission Predictable actioner about a photographer and a soldier who are captured by the enemy. Packed with a bit of ninja, ammo, and occult.
1989 (R) 90m/C Richard Randall; *D:* Al Bradley. VHS $59.95 CAN ♂

Cross My Heart Light comedy about two single people with complicated, post-divorce lives who go on a date and suffer accordingly. Will true love prevail?
1988 (R) 91m/C Martin Short, Annette O'Toole, Paul Reiser, Joanna Kerns; *D:* Armyan Bernstein; *M:* Bruce Broughton. VHS, Beta $79.95 MCA ♂♂

Cross My Heart A group of school children conspire to hide the death of one of the group's mothers. This will prevent his placement in the state orphanage. Interesting premise is blandly treated by Fansten. Child actors don't seem realistic, photography is without flair. In French with English subtitles.
1991 ?m/C FR Sylvain Copans; *D:* Jacques Fansten. VHS, Beta $89.95 FXL ♂♂

Cross of Iron During WWII, two antagonistic German officers clash over personal ideals as well as strategy in combatting the relentless Russian attack. Followed by "Breakthrough."
1976 (R) 120m/C James Coburn, Maximilian Schell, James Mason, David Warner, Senta Berger; *D:* Sam Peckinpah; *W:* Julius J. Epstein; *M:* Ernest Gold. VHS, Beta $19.95 MED ♂♂½

Crossbar Aaron Kornylo is determined to reach Olympic qualifications in the high jump despite having only one leg. Inspired by a true story, this program dramatically shows how far determination and work can take a person.
1979 77m/C John Ireland, Brent Carver, Kate Reid; *D:* John Trent. VHS, Beta $49.95 TWE, LCA ♂♂

Crossfire A Jewish hotel guest is murdered and three soldiers just back from Europe are suspected of the crime. The first Hollywood film that explored racial bigotry. Due to the radical nature of its plot, the director and the producer were eventually black-listed for promoting "un-American" themes. Loosely based on Richard Brooks' "The Brick Foxhole."
1947 86m/B Robert Young, Robert Mitchum, Robert Ryan, Gloria Grahame, Paul Kelly; *D:* Edward Dmytryk. Academy Awards '46 Nominations: Best Picture; Academy Awards '47: Best Director (Dmytryk), Best Screenplay, Best Supporting Actor (Ryan), Best Supporting Actress (Grahame); Edgar Allan Poe Awards '47: Best Screenplay; National Board of Review Awards '47: 10 Best Films of the Year. VHS, Beta $19.95 MED ♂♂♂½

Crossfire Two bandits are almost hung in the midst of the Mexican revolution. Released in the U.S. in 1979. *AKA:* The Bandit.
1967 (PG) 82m/C MX Robert Conrad, Jan-Michael Vincent, Manuel Lopez Ochoa, Roy Jenson; *D:* Robert Conrad, Alfredo Zacharias. VHS, Beta $59.95 ACA ♂

Crossfire A rescue team heads to Vietnam to pick up their MIA comrades. With no help from the government and the enemy at every turn, can they possibly succeed?

1989 (R) 99m/C Richard Norton, Michael Meyer, Daniel Dietrich, Don Pemrick, Eric Hahn, Wren Brown, Steve Young; *D:* Anthony Maharaj. VHS $19.98 SUE ♂

The Crossing Powerful coming-of-age story in which Meg, a sheltered young woman, falls in love with an ambitious artist named Sam. When he decides to leave their small town to pursue his career, she turns to his best friend for comfort and companionship. However, when Sam unexpectedly returns, Meg is forced to make a choice that could drastically change all of their lives.
1992 (R) 92m/C AU Russell Crowe, Danielle Spencer, Robert Mammone; *W:* Ranald Allan; *M:* Martin Armiger. VHS $89.98 REP ♂♂

Crossing Delancey Jewish woman (Bozyk), in old world style, plays matchmaker to her independent thirtysomething granddaughter. Charming modern-day New York City fairy tale deftly manipulates cliches and stereotypes. Lovely performance from Irving as the woman whose heart surprises her. Riegert is swell playing the gentle but never wimpy suitor. Perfectly cast Bozyk was a star on the Yiddish vaudeville stage, this is her film debut. Appealing music by the Roches, with Suzzy Roche giving a credible performance as Irving's friend. Adapted for the big screen by Sandler from her play of the same name.
1988 (PG) 97m/C Amy Irving, Reizl Bozyk, Peter Riegert, Jeroen Krabbe, Sylvia Miles, Suzzy Roche, George Martin, John Bedford Lloyd, Rosemary Harris, Amy Wright, Claudia Silver; *D:* Joan Micklin Silver; *W:* Suzzy Roche, Susan Sandler. VHS, Beta, 8mm $19.98 WAR, FCT, JCF ♂♂♂

Crossing the Bridge An after high-school tale of three buddies and their restless lives as they take their uncertain steps towards adulthood. It's 1975 in Detroit and Mort, Danny, and Tim cling to high-school memories as they pass time on petty jobs, drinking, and cruising across the Ambassador Bridge to check out the Canadian strip joints. Their big moment—for better or worse—comes when they are offered the chance to make a lot of quick cash if they'll smuggle hash from Toronto to Detroit. Directorial debut of Binder.
1992 (R) 105m/C Josh Charles, Jason Gedrick, Stephen Baldwin, Cheryl Pollak, Jeffrey Tambor; *D:* Mike Binder; *W:* Mike Binder. VHS, Beta $94.95 TOU ♂♂

Crossing the Line Two motocross racers battle it out for the championship.
1990 (R) 90m/C Jon Stafford, Rick Hearst, Paul Smith, Cameron Mitchell, Vernon Wells, Colleen Morris, John Saxon; *D:* Gary Graver. VHS, Beta $79.95 COL ♂

Crossover A devoted male nurse works the graveyard shift in the psychiatric ward and neglects his personal life.
1982 (R) 96m/C James Coburn, Kate Nelligan; *D:* John Guillermin. VHS, Beta $69.95 VES, LIV ♂½

Crossover Dreams Actor and musician Blades moves this old story along. Sure that he has at last made the international Big Time, a salsa artist becomes a self-important back-stabber after cutting an album. Great music. Blades's first film. ♫Good For Baby; Liz's Theme; Sin Fe; Todos Vuelven; Libra Timbero; Elegua; Merecumbe; Judy, Part 2; Yiri Yiri Bon.
1985 86m/C Ruben Blades, Shawn Elliott, Elizabeth Pena, Virgilio Marti, Tom Signorelli, Frank Robles, Joel Diamond, Amanda Barber, John Hammil; *D:* Leon Ichaso; *W:* Leon Ichaso, Manuel Arce; *M:* Mauricio Smith. VHS, Beta $14.95 CNG ♂♂½

Crossroads A blues-loving young white man, classically trained at Juilliard, befriends an aging black blues-master. After helping the old man escape from the nursing home, the two hop trains to the South where it's literally a duel with the devil. Fine performances by Macchio, Gertz, and Morton, and a wonderful score.
1986 (R) 100m/C Ralph Macchio, Joe Seneca, Jami Gertz, Joe Morton, Robert Judd, Harry Carey Jr.; *D:* Walter Hill; *W:* John Fusco; *M:* Ry Cooder. VHS, Beta $19.95 COL ♂♂½

The Crow Revenge-fantasy finds Eric Draven (Lee) resurrected on Devil's Night, a year after his death, in order to avenge his own murder and that of his girlfriend. 90% of the scenes are at night, in the rain, or both, and it's not easy to tell what's going on (a blessing considering the violence level). Very dark, but with good performances, particularly from Lee, in his last role before an unfortunate on set accident caused his death. That footage has been destroyed, but use of a stunt double and camera trickery allowed for the movie's completion. Film was dedicated to Lee and his fiance Eliza. Based on the comic strip by James O'Barr.
1993 (R) 100m/C Brandon Lee, Ernie Hudson, Michael Wincott, David Patrick Kelly, Rochelle Davis, Angel David, Michael Massee, Bai Ling, Lawrence Mason, Bill Raymond, Marco Rodriguez, Anna Thomson, Sofia Shinas, Jon Polito, Tony Todd; *D:* Alex Proyas; *W:* David J. Schow, John Shirley; *M:* Graeme Revell. VHS NYR ♂♂½

Crow Hollow A Victorian mansion inhabited by three whacko sisters is the site of a murder committed in an attempt to cash in on an inheritance. When a young woman investigates, eyebrows are raised.
1952 69m/B GB Donald Houston, Nastasha Parry, Nora Nicholson, Esma Cannon, Melissa Stribling; *D:* Michael McCarthy. VHS, Beta $16.95 SNC, RXM ♂♂

The Crowd A look at the day-to-day trials of a working-class family set against the backdrop of wealthy society. True-to-life, it's peppered with some happy moments, too. One of the best silent films. Available on laserdisc as a double feature with another '20s classic, "The Wind."
1928 104m/B Eleanor Boardman, James Murray, Bert Roach, Daniel G. Tomlinson, Dell Henderson, Lucy Beaumont; *D:* King Vidor. VHS, Beta $29.95 MGM ♂♂♂♂

Crucible of Horror Chilling story of a terrorized wife, who, along with her daughter, plots to murder her sadistic husband to end his abusive treatment of them. However, he isn't yet ready to die and comes back to drive them mad. *AKA:* Velvet House; The Corpse.
1969 91m/C GB Michael Gough, Yvonne Mitchell, Sharon Gurney; *D:* Viktors Ritelis. VHS, Beta $14.95 MGM, FCT ♂♂

Crucible of Terror Mad sculptor covers beautiful models with hot wax, then imprisons them in a mold of bronze.
1972 95m/C Mike Raven, Mary Maude, James Bolam. VHS, Beta $49.95 PSM, MRV, GEM Woof!

The Crucifer of Blood A disappointing Sherlock Holmes yarn, made for cable TV. Heston is adequate as the Baker Street sleuth, but the mystery—about two retired British soldiers who share an accursed secret and a vengeful comrade—unreels clumsily in the form of flashbacks that give away most of the puzzle from the start. Interesting only in that Dr. Watson has a love affair, more or less. Adapted from a play (and looking like it) by Paul Giovanni, inspired by Arthur Conan Doyle's "The Sign of Four."

1991 105m/C Charlton Heston, Richard Johnson, Susannah Harker, John Castle, Clive Wood, Simon Callow, Edward Fox; *D:* Fraser Heston. VHS, Beta $89.98 *TTC* ♫♫ ½

The Crucified Lovers A shy scroll-maker falls in love with his master's wife. Excellent Japanese tragedy with fine performances all around. *AKA:* Chikamatsu Monogatari.
1954 100m/B *JP* Kazuo Hasegawa, Kyoko Kagawa, Yoko Minamida, Eitaro Shindo, Sakae Ozawa; *D:* Kenji Mizoguchi. VHS *FCT* ♫♫♫½

Cruel Sea Well-made documentary-like account of a Royal Navy corvette on convoy duty in the Atlantic during WWII.
1953 121m/B *GB* Jack Hawkins, Stanley Baker, Denholm Elliott, Virginia McKenna; *D:* Charles Frend. VHS, Beta $9.98 *REP, BMV, HMV* ♫♫♫

The Cruel Story of Youth A teenage girl and her criminal boyfriend use sex to get money out of rich, middle-aged men in this controversial look at the disillusionment of youth and the breaking of old values and traditions in Japan after WWII. In Japanese with English subtitles. *AKA:* Seishun Zanoku Monogatari; Naked Youth; A Story of the Cruelties of Youth.
1960 96m/C *JP* Yusuke Kawazu, Miyuki Kuwano, Yoshiko Kuga; *D:* Nagisa Oshima; *W:* Nagisa Oshima. VHS $79.95 *NYF* ♫♫♫

Cruise into Terror A sarcophagus brought aboard a pleasure cruise ship unleashes an evil force that slowly starts to kill off the ship's passengers, most of whom likely thought they were on the Love Boat. Made for television.
1978 100m/C Ray Milland, Hugh O'Brian, John Forsythe, Christopher George, Dirk Benedict, Frank Converse, Lynda Day George, Stella Stevens; *D:* Bruce Kessler. VHS, Beta $49.95 *PSM* Woof!

Cruise Missile Unique task force is on a mission to keep the world from nuclear holocaust.
1978 100m/C Peter Graves, Curt Jurgens, Michael Dante; *D:* Ted V. Mikels. VHS, Beta *NO* ♫

Cruisin' High Two city street gangs battle it out.
1975 (R) 109m/C David Kyle, Kelly Yaegermann, Rhodes Reason. VHS, Beta $69.95 *VES, LIV* ♫

Cruising Rookie cop Pacino is deep undercover investigating the bizarre murders of homosexuals in New York's West Village. Sexually explicit but less than suspenseful mystery. Release was sensationalized, with many gay rights groups voicing loud disapproval of the sordid gay characterization, while others feared copy-cat crimes. Excellent NYC cinematography.
1980 (R) 102m/C Al Pacino, Paul Sorvino, Karen Allen, Powers Boothe; *D:* William Friedkin; *W:* William Friedkin; *M:* Jack Nitzsche. VHS, Beta $19.98 *WAR* ♫♫

Crush Christina is a local New Zealand literary critic on her way to interview Colin, a reclusive novelist. Along for the ride is her seductive American friend Lane who manages to crash the car but walk away with hardly a scratch. Christina appears to be dead and Lane abandons her, finding her way to the home Colin shares with his teenage daughter Angela. Lane promptly sets out to seduce Colin, making Angela jealous, (oh, and Christina's not dead after all). Poor script finds the characters actions baffling and why Lane is so wildly attractive is never apparent.

1993 97m/C *NZ* Marcia Gay Harden, Donough Rees, William Zappa, Caitlin Bossley; *D:* Alison Maclean; *W:* Alison Maclean, Anne Kennedy. VHS $89.98 *ORI* ♫♫

The Crush Wealthy 14-year-old temptress Silverstone (in her debut) develops an obsessive crush on handsome 28-year-old Elwes, who rents her family's guest house. In an attempt to win his heart, she rewrites his poorly composed magazine articles. This doesn't convince him they should mate for life, so she sabotages his apartment to vent her rage. Sound familiar? The plot's lifted right out of "Fatal Attraction" and Shapiro doesn't offer viewers anything inventively different. He does manage to substitute new methods for the spurned lover to snare her prey. Limp plot would have been exciting if we hadn't seen it so many times before.
1993 (R) 89m/C Cary Elwes, Alicia Silverstone, Jennifer Rubin, Kurtwood Smith, Gwynyth Walsh, Amber Benson; *D:* Alan Shapiro; *W:* Alan Shapiro; *M:* Graeme Revell. VHS, Beta *WAR* ♫½

Crusoe A lushly photographed version of the Daniel Defoe classic. Crusoe is an arrogant slave trader stranded on a desert island populated by unfriendly natives. Themes of prejudice, fear, and choice appear in this never-padded, thoughtful film. Quinn gives an excellent performance as the stranded slave-trader.
1989 (PG-13) 94m/C Aidan Quinn, Ade Sapara, Jimmy Nail, Timothy Spall, Colin Bruce, Michael Higgins, Shane Rimmer, Hepburn Grahame; *D:* Caleb Deschanel; *W:* Walon Green, Christopher Logue; *M:* Michael Kamen. VHS, Beta *NO* ♫♫½

Cry-Baby An homage and spoof of '50s teen-rock melodramas by the doyen of cinematic Bad Taste, involving a terminal bad-boy high schooler who goes with a square blond and starts an inter-class rumble. Musical numbers, throwaway gags and plenty of knee-bending to Elvis, with a weak story supported by offbeat celeb appearances.
1990 (PG-13) 85m/C Johnny Depp, Amy Locane, Polly Bergen, Traci Lords, Ricki Lake, Iggy Pop, Susan Tyrrell, Patty Hearst, Kim McGuire, Darren E. Burrows, Troy Donahue, Willem Dafoe, David Nelson, Mink Stole, Joe Dallesandro, Joey Heatherton, Robert Walsh; *D:* John Waters; *W:* John Waters; *M:* Patrick Williams. VHS, Beta $19.95 *MCA* ♫♫♫

Cry Danger A falsely imprisoned man is released from jail, and he searches for those who framed him.
1951 80m/B Dick Powell, Rhonda Fleming, William Conrad, Richard Erdman; *D:* Robert Parrish. VHS $19.98 *REP* ♫♫♫

A Cry for Love An amphetamine addict and an alcoholic meet, fall in love, and help each other recover. Based on the best seller by Jill Schary Robinson, "Bedtime Story."
1980 96m/C Susan Blakely, Powers Boothe, Gene Barry, Charles Siebert, Herb Edelman, Fern Fitzgerald, Lainie Kazan; *D:* Paul Wendkos. VHS, Beta $14.95 *FRH* ♫♫

Cry Freedom A romantic look at the short life of South African activist Steven Biko, and his friendship with the white news editor, Donald Woods. The film focuses on Woods' escape from Africa while struggling to bring Biko's message to the world. Based on a true story.
1987 (PG) 157m/C Kevin Kline, Denzel Washington, Penelope Wilton, Kevin McNally, John Thaw, Timothy West, John Hargreaves, Alec McCowen, Zakes Mokae, Ian Richardson, Juanita Waterman; *D:* Richard Attenborough; *W:* John Briley; *M:* George Fenton, Jonas Gwangwa. VHS, Beta $14.98 *MCA, KUI, FCT* ♫♫½

Cry from the Mountain Heavily religious film about a father and son who go on a kayak trip through Alaska's wilderness so the father can break the news of his impending divorce. A series of events occurs that change their lives, and they meet a mysterious mountain man who relies on his faith in God to get by in the wilderness. Features an appearance by Rev. Billy Graham.
1985 (PG) 78m/C James Cavan, Wes Parker, Rita Walter, Chris Kidd, Coleen Gray, Jerry Ballew, Allison Argo, Glen Alsworth, Myrna Kidd; *D:* James F. Collier. VHS, Beta $59.95 *LIV* ♫

A Cry from the Streets Drama about the plight of orphan children and dedicated social workers in England.
1957 100m/C *GB* Max Bygraves, Barbara Murray, Kathleen Harrison, Colin Petersen; *D:* Lewis Gilbert; *M:* Larry Adler. VHS $29.95 *FCT* ♫♫

A Cry in the Dark Tight film story of the infamous Australian murder trial of Lindy Chamberlain, who was accused of killing her own baby, mostly because of the intensely adverse public opinion, aroused by vicious press, that surrounded the case. Chamberlain blamed the death on a wild dingo dog. Near-documentary style, with Streep excellent as the religious, unknowable mother. Based on the book "Evil Angels" by John Bryson and released in Australia under that title. This case was also detailed in the film "Who Killed Baby Azaria?"
1988 (PG-13) 120m/C *AU* Meryl Streep, Sam Neill, Bruce Myles, Charles Tingwell, Nick Tate, Neil Fitzpatrick, Maurice Fields, Lewis Fitzgerald; *D:* Fred Schepisi; *W:* Fred Schepisi, Robert Caswell. Academy Awards '88 Nominations: Best Actress (Streep); Australian Film Institute '88: Best Actor (Neill), Best Actress (Streep); New York Film Critics Awards '88: Best Actress (Streep). VHS, Beta, 8mm $19.98 *WAR, FCT* ♫♫♫½

A Cry in the Night After Jenny (Higgins Clark) marries an internationally-acclaimed artist, she thinks her life is complete. However, once she and her two daughters move into his country estate, her life takes a tragic turn as she's haunted by the mysterious deaths of her ex-husband and newborn child. King plays the new husband who turns out to have a few psychological quirks of his own. Based on the bestselling novel by Mary Higgins Clark. Actress Higgins Clark is the novelist's daughter. Made for television.
1993 (PG-13) 99m/C Perry King, Carol Higgins Clark; *D:* Robin Spry; *W:* Robin Spry. VHS $89.98 *REP* ♫♫½

A Cry in the Wild A 14 year old boy must find his way back to civilization when he's the lone survivor of an airplane crash. Strong acting from Rushton, excellent nature photography make this well-used story work again.
1990 (PG) 93m/C Jared Rushton, Ned Beatty, Pamela Sue Martin, Stephen Meadows; *D:* Mark Griffiths. VHS $14.95 *MGM* ♫♫♫

Cry of a Prostitute: Love Kills Former prostitute joins with a professional assassin in an effort to pacify rival gangsters in Italy.
1972 (R) 86m/C Henry Silva, Barbara Bouchet; *D:* Andrew Bianchi. VHS, Beta $59.95 *PSM* ♫

Cry of Battle Anxious for the challenges of manhood, a well-heeled young man joins a guerrilla militia in the Philippines. *AKA:* To Be a Man.
1963 99m/B Van Heflin, Rita Moreno, James MacArthur; *D:* Irving Lerner. VHS, Beta $49.95 *PSM, MRV, FGF* ♫♫½

Cry of the Banshee Witch-hunter Price and family are tormented by Satanic powers seeking revenge. Superior horror period piece. Also available with "Count Yorga, Vampire" on Laserdisc.
1970 (PG) 87m/C *GB* Vincent Price, Elisabeth Bergner, Essy Persson, Hugh Griffith, Hilary Dwyer, Sally Geeson, Patrick Mower; *D:* Gordon Hessler; *M:* Les Baxter. **VHS, Beta $79.99** *HBO* 🎬🎬½

Cry of the Black Wolves A trapper wrongly accused of murder saves the life of a bounty hunter hired to capture him.
197? 90m/C Ron Ely, Catherine Conti. **VHS, Beta** *VTR* 🎬

Cry of the Innocent An action-packed thriller about a Vietnam veteran who is out to find a group of Irish terrorists that killed his family.
1980 93m/C Cyril Cusack, Alexander Knox, Rod Taylor, Joanna Pettet, Nigel Davenport; *D:* Michael O'Herlihy. **VHS, Beta** *NO* 🎬🎬🎬

The Cry of the Owl Robert (Malavoy) has divorced the dreadful Veronique (Thevenet) and struck up a friendship with Juliette (May). He admires the way her life seems so satisfied and orderly but Juliette decides she doesn't like this idea of herself and impulsively drops her swinish fiance Patrick (Penot) and pursues Robert instead. But Robert is only interested in friendship, leading to some very twisted revenge plots. Suspenseful look at what obsessions can drive people to do. Adapted from the novel by Patricia Highsmith. In French with English subtitles. *AKA:* Le Cri du Hibou.
1992 102m/C *FR IT* Christophe MaLavoy, Mathilda May, Virginie Thevenet, Jacques Penot, Jean-Pierre Kalfon, Patrice Kerbrat; *D:* Claude Chabrol; *W:* Claude Chabrol, Odile Barski; *M:* Matthieu Chabrol. **VHS $89.95** *CVC* 🎬🎬

Cry of the Werewolf A beautiful New Orleans gypsy protects her mother's mummified remains by periodically turning into a werewolf and killing people.
1944 63m/B Nina Foch, Stephen Crane, Osa Massen, Blanche Yurka, Barton MacLane, Ivan Triesault, John Abbott, Fritz Leiber; *D:* Henry Levin. **VHS $14.99** *MOV* 🎬🎬

Cry Panic A man is thrown into a strange series of events after accidentally running down a man on a highway. Made for television.
1974 74m/C John Forsythe, Anne Francis, Earl Holliman, Claudia McNeil, Ralph Meeker; *D:* James Goldstone. **VHS, Beta $49.95** *PSM* 🎬🎬

Cry Terror Two escaped convicts take two beautiful women hostage hoping to gain their own freedom. Only a quick-thinking undercover police officer can save the girls. Made for television.
1974 71m/C *GB* Bob Hoskins, Susan Hampshire, Gabrielle Drake. **VHS, Beta** *NO* 🎬🎬

Cry, the Beloved Country A black country minister travels to Johannesberg to be with his son after the youth is accused of killing a white man. Through the events of the trial, the horror, oppression, and destruction of South Africa's apartheid system are exposed. Startling and moving, the first entertainment feature set against the backdrop of apartheid. Still trenchant; based on the novel by Alan Paton. *AKA:* African Fury.
1951 111m/B *GB* Canada Lee, Charles Carson, Sidney Poitier, Joyce Carey, Geoffrey Keen; *D:* Zoltan Korda. **VHS $69.95** *MON, FCT* 🎬🎬🎬½

Cry Uncle Comic account of a private eye who investigates a blackmailing case involving a film of orgies in which, much to his chagrin, he participated.

1971 85m/C Allen (Gooritz) Garfield, Paul Sorvino; *D:* John G. Avildsen. **VHS, Beta $79.95** *PSM* 🎬🎬½

Cry Vengeance A falsely-imprisoned detective gets out of jail and searches for the people who framed him and killed his family.
1954 83m/B Mark Stevens, Joan Vohs, Martha Hyer, Skip Homeier; *D:* Mark Stevens. **VHS, Beta $19.98** *REP* 🎬🎬½

The Crying Game PR lesson in how to launch a small movie into the hypersphere and ensure critical silence on salient characterization. Jordan's gritty drama is on par with his best, a complex blend of violence, love, betrayal, guilt, and redemption and is not about what it seems to be about much of the time. Wonderful performances by all, including Rea as the appealing, conscience-stricken Fergus; Richardson as the cold, violent IRA moll Jude; and Davidson, in a film debut, as the needy, charismatic Dil. Whitaker is terrific in his 15 minutes of intense screen time. Filled with definite surprises and unexpected pleasures. Title is taken from a top-5 British hit of 1964, three versions of which are heard.
1992 (R) 112m/C *IR* Stephen Rea, Jaye Davidson, Miranda Richardson, Forest Whitaker, Adrian Dunbar, Jim Broadbent, Ralph Brown, Breffini McKenna, Joe Savino, Birdie Sweeney, Andre Bernard; *D:* Neil Jordan; *W:* Neil Jordan; *M:* Anne Dudley. Academy Awards '92: Best Original Screenplay; Nominations: Best Actor (Rea), Best Director (Jordan), Best Film Editing, Best Picture, Best Supporting Actor (Davidson); Australian Film Institute '93: Best Foreign Film; Chicago Film Critics Awards '92: Best Foreign Film; Independent Spirit Awards '93: Best Foreign Film; Los Angeles Film Critics Association Awards '92: Best Foreign Film; New York Film Critics Awards '92: Best Supporting Actress (Richardson); National Society of Film Critics Awards '92: Best Actor (Rea). **VHS $19.98** *LIV, MOV, BTV* 🎬🎬🎬½

Crypt of Dark Secrets Vietnam veteran recovering from wounds in the Louisiana swamps encounters a friendly Indian spirit who saves him from death.
1976 (R) 100m/C Maureen Chan, Ronald Tanet, Wayne Mack, Herbert G. Jahncke; *D:* Jack Weis. **VHS, Beta** *NO* 🎬

Crypt of the Living Dead An undead woman from the 13th century makes life miserable for visitors on Vampire Island.
1973 (PG) 75m/C Andrew Prine, Mark Damon, Teresa Gimpera, Patty Shepard, Francisco (Frank) Brana; *D:* Ray Danton. **VHS, Beta** *NO* Woof!

Crystal Heart A medically isolated songwriter with an incurable disease falls in love with a lovely rock singer.
1987 (R) 103m/C Lee Curreri, Tawny Kitaen, Lloyd Bochner; *D:* Gil Bettman; *M:* Joel Goldsmith. **VHS, Beta $19.95** *STE, NWV* 🎬

Crystalstone A wooden cross leads a pair of orphans on a dangerous search for the legendary Crystalstone.
1988 (PG) 103m/C Frank Grimes, Kamlesh Gupta, Laura Jane Goodwin, Sydney Bromley; *D:* Antonio Pelaez. **VHS, Beta $79.98** *MCG* 🎬🎬

Cthulhu Mansion The oldest-looking juvenile delinquents you've ever seen release evil spirits when they take over a magician's estate. Not very special effects and abominable dialogue; it claims to be based on H.P. Lovecraft stories, but that's a load of dung.
1991 (R) 95m/C Frank Finlay, Marcia Layton, Brad Fisher, Melanie Shatner, Luis Fernando Alves, Kaethe Cherney, Paul Birchard, Francisco (Frank) Brana; *D:* J.P. Simon; *W:* J.P. Simon. **VHS $9.98** *REP* Woof!

Cuba Cynical, satirical adventure/love story. Mercenary soldier rekindles an old affair during the Castro revolution. Charismatic cast and good direction make for an entertaining, if overlooked, Connery vehicle.
1979 (R) 121m/C Sean Connery, Brooke Adams, Jack Weston, Hector Elizondo, Denholm Elliott, Chris Sarandon, Lonette McKee; *D:* Richard Lester; *W:* Charles Wood. **VHS, Beta $14.95** *MGM, FOX* 🎬🎬🎬

Cujo A rabid dog goes berserk and attacks a mother and her child who are trapped inside a broken-down Pinto. Frighteningly realistic film is based on Stephen King's bestseller.
1983 (R) 94m/C Dee Wallace Stone, Daniel Hugh-Kelly, Danny Pintauro, Ed Lauter, Christopher Stone; *D:* Lewis Teague; *M:* Charles Bernstein. **VHS, Beta $19.98** *WAR* 🎬🎬

Cul de Sac A macabre, psychological thriller set in a dreary castle on a small island off the British coast. Pleasance is an eccentric, middle-aged hermit living acrimoniously with his young, nymphy wife (Dorleac) when their home is invaded by two wounded gangsters (Stander and MacGowran), who proceed to hold the couple hostage. MacGowran soon dies of his wounds, leaving Stander and Pleasance to fight it out, encouraged by the luscious Dorleac, who finds her fun where she can. A bleak, sinister film considered one of Polanski's best.
1966 111m/C *GB* Donald Pleasence, Francoise Dorleac, Lionel Stander, Jack MacGowran, Jacqueline Bisset; *D:* Roman Polanski; *W:* Roman Polanski, Gerard Brach. **VHS $29.95** *FCT* 🎬🎬🎬

Culpepper Cattle Co. A young, starry-eyed yokel wants to be a cowboy and gets himself enlisted in a cattle drive, where he learns the harsh reality of the West.
1972 (PG) 92m/C Gary Grimes, Billy Green Bush, Bo Hopkins, Charles Martin Smith, Geoffrey Lewis; *D:* Dick Richards; *M:* Jerry Goldsmith. **VHS, Beta $19.98** *FOX* 🎬🎬½

Cult of the Cobra Mysterious horror film that became minor camp classic. It seems ex-servicemen are being killed by exotic snake-lady Domergue. Cheesy film that can be fun. Based on a story by Jerry Davis.
1955 75m/B Faith Domergue, Richard Long, Marshall Thompson, William Reynolds, Jack Kelly, Kathleen Hughes; *D:* Francis D. Lyon; *W:* Jerry Davis. **VHS $14.98** *MCA* 🎬🎬

Cult People Interviews and film clips featuring a host of filmmaking's favorite cult personalities.
1989 60m/C Patrick Macnee, Cameron Mitchell, James Karen, Russ Meyer, Curtis Harrington, Waris Hussein, Michael Sarne. **VHS $19.95** *FCT* 🎬½

Cup Final The similarities and contradictions in war and sports, where passions and competition run high, are depicted in this emotional drama. Set in 1982 during Israel's invasion of Lebanon. Cohen is an Israeli soldier passionately interested in the World Cup soccer tournament. When he is taken prisoner by the PLO he discovers his captor Ziad shares his interest in the Italian national team. This common interest brings the two antagonists reluctantly together. In Hebrew and Arabic with English subtitles. *AKA:* G'mar Giviya.
1992 107m/C *IS* Moshe Ivgi, Muhamad Bacri, Suheil Haddad; *D:* Eran Riklis; *W:* Eyal Halfon; *M:* Raviv Gazit. **VHS $59.95** *ICA, BTV* 🎬🎬

The Cure Chaplin arrives at a spa to take a rest cure, accompanied by a trunk full of liquor that somehow gets dumped into the water at the resort. Silent with music track.

1917 20m/B Charlie Chaplin, Edna Purviance, Eric Campbell, Albert Austin; D: Charlie Chaplin. VHS, Beta VYY, GVV, CAB ♦♦

Curfew A young woman rushes home so she doesn't break her curfew, only to find two killers with time on their hands waiting for her. Violent.
1988 (R) 86m/C John Putch, Kyle Richards, William Wellman Jr., Bert Remsen; D: Gary Winick. VHS, Beta $19.95 STE, NWV ♦♦

Curiosity Kills Young people find more than they bargained for when they begin to investigate the death of a fellow tenant. Tense made-for-cable thriller.
1990 (R) 86m/C Rae Dawn Chong, C. Thomas Howell, Courteney Cox, Paul Guilfoyle, Jeff Fahey; D: Colin Bucksey; W: Joe Batteer, John Rice. VHS, Beta $79.95 MCA ♦♦

The Curious Dr. Humpp A mad scientist (Barbero) kidnaps exotic dancers and extracts their libidos to preserve his youth. Under the guise of research, he encourages his victims to engage in trysts so that their carnal energies will increase. Everything is hunky dory until a reporter (Bauleo) starts snooping around the laboratory, discovering Dr. Humpp observing multiple couplings via closed-circuit television. Boldly exploitative, the American distributor added about 10 minutes of raunchy hard-core footage of exotic dance routines.
1970 87m/B AR Ricardo Bauleo, Aldo Barbero; D: Emilio Vieyra. VHS $23.00 SMW, TPV ♦

Curley High-spirited youngsters play pranks on their schoolteacher. A part of the Hal Roach Comedy Carnival.
1947 53m/C Larry Olsen, Frances Rafferty, Eilene Janssen, Walter Abel; D: Bernard Carr. VHS, Beta $19.95 DVT, NOS, HHT ♦♦

Curly Sue Adorable, homeless waif Porter and her scheming, adoptive father Belushi plot to rip off single, career-minded female attorney Lynch in order to take in some extra cash. Trouble is, all three heartstrings are tugged, and the trio develop a warm, caring relationship. A throwback to the Depression era's Shirley Temple formula films met with mixed reviews. Undiscriminating younger audiences should have a good time, though. Available in widescreen format on laserdisc.
1991 (PG) 102m/C James Belushi, Kelly Lynch, Alison Porter, John Getz, Fred Dalton Thompson; D: John Hughes; W: John Hughes; M: Georges Delerue. VHS, Beta, 8mm $19.98 WAR, CCB ♦♦

Curly Top Orphan Temple helps land a husband for her beautiful sister. Along the way, she sings ''Animal Crackers in My Soup.'' Remake of the silent ''Daddy Long Legs,'' which was remade again in 1955.
1935 74m/B Shirley Temple, John Boles, Rochelle Hudson, Jane Darwell, Esther Dale, Arthur Treacher, Rafaela Ottiano; D: Irving Cummings. VHS, Beta $19.98 FOX, MLT ♦♦½

The Curse After a meteorite lands near a small farming community and contaminates the area, a young boy tries to prevent residents from turning into slime-oozing mutants. Remake of ''Die, Monster, Die.'' AKA: The Farm.
1987 (R) 92m/C Wil Wheaton, Claude Akins, Malcolm Danare, Cooper Huckabee, John Schneider, David Keith, Amy Wheaton, David Chaskin; D: David Keith; W: David Chaskin. VHS, Beta $14.95 MED, VTR, IME ♦

Curse 2: The Bite Radiation affected snakes are transformed into deadly vipers whose bites change their unsuspecting victims into horrible creatures.
1988 (R) 97m/C Jill Schoelen, J. Eddie Peck, Jamie Farr, Savina Gersak, Bo Svenson; D: Fred Goodwin. VHS, Beta $89.95 TWE ♦

Curse 3: Blood Sacrifice An African sugar cane plantation becomes host to a horrible nightmare when a voodoo curse is placed on the owners. The monstrous God of the Sea is summoned to avenge the accidental death of a baby, and the hellish journey into insanity begins. AKA: Panga.
1990 (R) 91m/C Christopher Lee, Jenilee Harrison, Henry Cele; D: Sean Barton. VHS $79.95 COL ♦

Curse 4: The Ultimate Sacrifice Beneath the monastery at San Pietro lies buried the beast of the Apocalypse. For 400 years the secret has been kept and then an American priest and a lovely school teacher unwittingly break the seal and unleash the cursed beast upon an unsuspecting world.
1992 (R) 84m/C Timothy Van Patten, Laura Schaefer, Jeremy West, Ian Abercrombie; D: David Schmoeller. VHS $79.95 COL ♦½

The Curse of Frankenstein Young Victor Frankenstein reenacts his father's experiments with creating life from the dead resulting in a terrifying, hideous creature. The first in Hammer's Frankenstein series and followed by ''Revenge of Frankenstein.'' From the Shelley story. Make-up by Jack Pierce, who also created the famous make-up for Universal's Frankenstein monster.
1957 83m/C GB Peter Cushing, Christopher Lee, Hazel Court, Robert Urquhart, Valerie Gaunt; D: Terence Fisher; W: Jimmy Sangster. VHS, Beta $14.95 WAR, MLB ♦♦½

The Curse of King Tut's Tomb Made-for-television movie is set in 1922 where archaeologists have just opened Tutankhamen's tomb. The curse of the boy king is unleashed as tragic events bring the adventurers uncommon gloom. Oh boy.
1980 98m/C Robin Ellis, Harry Andrews, Eva Marie Saint, Raymond Burr, Wendy Hiller; D: Philip Leacock. VHS, Beta $9.95 GKK ♦♦

Curse of the Alpha Stone A professor experiments with an ancient formula on a student, creating a babbling maniac who slaughters freshman girls.
1985 90m/C VHS, Beta $49.95 VCI Woof!

The Curse of the Aztec Mummy A mad scientist schemes to rob a Mayan pyramid of its treasure but the resident mummy will have none of it. Sequel to ''Robot vs. the Aztec Mummy'' and followed by ''Wrestling Women vs. the Aztec Mummy.'' AKA: La Maldicion de la Momia Azteca.
1959 65m/B MX Ramon Gay, Rosita Arenas, Crox Alvarado; D: Rafael Portillo. VHS $16.95 SNC Woof!

Curse of the Aztec Mummy/ Robot vs. the Aztec Mummy Vengeful mummy of an Aztec warrior stalks those who attempt to steal a fabulous treasure. A mad criminal scientist wants the treasure and uses gangsters and a human robot to get what he wants.
1959 130m/B Ramon Gay, Rosita Arenas, Crox Alvarado, Luis Aceves Cantaneda; D: Rafael Portillo. VHS, Beta HHT Woof!

Curse of the Black Widow An investigator follows a trail of brutal murders to the lair of a supernatural gigantic spider in the middle of Los Angeles. Made for television. AKA: Love Trap.
1977 100m/C Patty Duke, Anthony (Tony) Franciosa, Donna Mills, June Lockhart, Sid Caesar, Vic Morrow, June Allyson, Roz Kelly, Jeff Corey; D: Dan Curtis. VHS, Beta NO ♦

Curse of the Blue Lights Mysterious lights begin appearing at the local romantic spot. Little do the young lovers know, it hails the arrival of a ghoul, intent on raising the dead. Also available in an unedited

version. Unfortunately, nothing can resurrect this film.
1988 (R) 93m/C Brent Ritter; D: John H. Johnson. VHS, Beta NO Woof!

Curse of the Cat People A young sensitive girl is guided by the vision of her dead mother. Sequel to ''Cat People.'' Available in a colorized version.
1944 70m/B Simone Simon, Kent Smith, Jane Randolph, Elizabeth Russell, Ann Carter; D: Robert Wise, Gunther Von Fritsch. VHS, Beta $19.95 MED, TTC ♦♦♦

The Curse of the Crying Woman Unknowing descendant of a witch is lured to her aunt's home to perform the act that will revive the monstrous crying woman and renew a reign of evil. AKA: La Maldicion de a Llorona; La Casa Embrujada.
1961 74m/B MX Rosita Arenas, Abel Salazar, Rita Macedo, Carlos Lopez Moctezuma. VHS, Beta $59.95 SNC, HHT ♦♦½

Curse of the Crystal Eye A gunrunner tries to get the treasure of Ali Baba aided by the requisite lovely lady and opposed by your usual bad guys.
1993 (PG-13) 90m/C Jameson Parker, Cynthia Rhodes, Mike Lane, David Sherwood, Andre Jacobs. VHS $92.98 NHO ♦

Curse of the Demon A famous psychologist investigates a colleague's mysterious death and enters a world of demonology and the occult, climaxing in a confrontation with a cult's patron demon. Superb thriller based upon the story ''Casting the Runes'' by M.R. James. AKA: Night of the Demon.
1957 81m/B GB Dana Andrews, Peggy Cummins, Niall MacGinnis, Maurice Denham; D: Jacques Tourneur; W: Charles Bennett. VHS, Beta $9.95 GKK, MLB ♦♦♦½

Curse of the Devil This time Naschy is turned into a werewolf by annoyed gypsies whose ancestors were slain by his. AKA: El Retorno de la Walpurgis.
1973 (R) 73m/C MX SP Paul Naschy, Maria Silva, Patty Shepard, Fay Falcon; D: Carlos Aured; W: Paul Naschy. VHS $19.98 SNC, VCI ♦½

Curse of the Headless Horseman The headless horseman rides again, bringing terror to all who cross his path!
1972 80m/C Don Carrara, Claudia Dean, B.G. Fisher, Margo Dean, Lee Byers, Joe Cody; D: John Kirkland. VHS NO ♦½

Curse of the Living Corpse A millionaire comes back to rotting life to kill his negligent relatives. Scheider's first film.
1964 84m/C Candace Hilligoss, Roy Scheider, Helen Warren, Margot Hartman; D: Del Tenney. VHS, Beta $39.95 PSM ♦

Curse of the Living Dead Two siblings are forced to eat flesh for eternity after their witch-doctor mother puts a curse on them.
1989 90m/C D: Lawrence Foldes. VHS, Beta ELV, HHE ♦

Curse of the Pink Panther Clifton Sleigh, an inept New York City detective played by Wass, is assigned to find the missing Inspector Clouseau. His efforts are complicated by an assortment of gangsters and aristocrats who cross paths with the detective. So-so attempt to keep popular series going after Seller's death. Niven's last film.
1983 (PG) 110m/C Ted Wass, David Niven, Robert Wagner, Herbert Lom, Joanna Lumley, Capucine, Robert Loggia, Harvey Korman, Leslie Ash, Denise Crosby; D: Blake Edwards; W: Blake Edwards. VHS, Beta $14.95 MGM ♦♦

Curse of the Queerwolf A man is bitten on the butt by gay werewolf and transforms into the title character. Filmed in Santa Barbara in 8mm; some funny moments. From the director of "A Polish Vampire in Burbank."
1987 90m/C Michael Palazzolo, Kent Butler, Taylor Whitney; *D:* Mark Pirro. VHS $9.95 *HHE 🎞🎞*

Curse of the Screaming Dead An unpredictable zombie yarn.
1984 90m/C VHS, Beta *NO Woof!*

Curse of the Stone Hand A pair of stone hands causes folks to do suicidal things. A mutation of a Mexican and a Chilean horror film, each purchased and monster-mashed into one by Warren.
1964 72m/B MX John Carradine, Ernest Walch, Sheila Bon, Katherine Victor, Lloyd Nelson; *D:* Jerry Warren. VHS $15.95 *NOS, LOO Woof!*

Curse of the Swamp Creature A mad scientist in the Everglades attempts to create human/half alligator monsters. In turn, a geologic expeditional force attempts to stop his experimentation. Low budget thrills courtesy of Larry Buchanan.
1966 80m/C John Agar, Francine York, Shirley McLine, Bill Thurman, Jeff Alexander; *D:* Larry Buchanan. VHS $19.98 *MOV, VDM 🎞*

The Curse of the Werewolf Horror film about a 19th-century European werewolf that is renowned for its ferocious departure from the stereotypical portrait of the beast.
1961 91m/C GB Oliver Reed, Clifford Evans, Yvonne Romain, Catherine Feller, Anthony M. (Antonio Margheretti) Dawson, Michael Ripper; *D:* Terence Fisher. VHS, Beta $14.98 *MCA, TLF, MLB 🎞🎞½*

Curse of the Yellow Snake Voluminous yarn features a running battle over an ancient Chinese artifact, with crazed Chinese cultists running through foggy London streets.
1963 98m/C GE Joachim Berger, Werner Peters; *D:* Franz Gottlieb. VHS, Beta $24.95 *VYY 🎞🎞*

The Cursed Mountain Mystery Two petty thieves steal a legendary precious gem rumored to cursed. The immortal warrior supposed to guard the gem lures the crooks to Sher Mountain, where he intends to eliminate them and return the stone to its keeper.
1993 (R) 87m/C Phillip Avalon, Tom Richards, Joe Bugner; *D:* Vince Martin; *W:* Denis Whitburn. VHS $89.95 *COL 🎞½*

Curtain Up "Little theatre" dramatics and the exasperating temperaments of amateur theatricals are exposed in this adaptation of the play "On Monday Next," by Philip King.
1953 82m/C GB Robert Morley, Margaret Rutherford, Olive Sloane; *D:* Ralph Smart; *M:* Malcolm Arnold. VHS, Beta *LCA 🎞🎞*

Curtains Director has a clash of wills with a film star that spells "Curtains" for a group of aspiring actresses gathered together at a haunted house for an audition. Hamfest with no thrills, chills, gore, or gratuitous skin. No wonder why director Richard Ciupka hides behind pseudonym Stryker.
1983 (R) 90m/C CA John Vernon, Samantha Eggar; *D:* Jonathan Stryker; *W:* Robert Guza Jr. VHS, Beta $69.95 *VES Woof!*

Custer's Last Fight Re-enactment of the American West period when the Sioux and Cheyenne Indian tribes bitterly opposed the white man. Silent.
1912 50m/B *D:* Francis Ford. VHS, Beta $19.95 *NOS, DVT, CAM 🎞½*

Custer's Last Stand Feature-length version of the Mascot serial recounting the last days of the famous General.
1936 70m/B Frank McGlynn, Rex Lease, Nancy Caseell, Lona Andre, William Farnum, Reed Howes, Jack Mulhall, Josef Swickard, Ruth Mix; *D:* Elmer Clifton. VHS, Beta $69.95 *VCN, GPV 🎞½*

Cut and Run Two journalists follow a lead to the former South American home of Jim Jones, and are instantly captured by local guerrillas.
1985 (R) 87m/C Michael Berryman, Willie Aames, Lisa Blount, Karen Black. VHS, Beta $19.95 *STE, NWV 🎞*

The Cut Throats Americans stumble upon an isolated Nazi outpost stocked with gold and beautiful women. Exploitation at its worst.
1989 (R) 80m/C Jay Scott, Joanne Douglas, Jeff Letham, Pat Michaels, Barbara Lane; *D:* John Hayes; *W:* John Hayes. VHS $24.95 *TPV 🎞*

Cutter's Way An embittered and alcoholic disabled Vietnam vet and his small-time crook/gigolo friend wrestle with justice and morality when the drifter uncovers a murder but declines to get involved. An unusually cynical mystery from the novel by Newton Thorburg. *AKA:* Cutter and Bone.
1981 (R) 105m/C Jeff Bridges, John Heard, Lisa Eichhorn, Ann Dusenberry, Stephen Elliott, Nina Van Pallandt, George Dickerson; *D:* Ivan Passer; *M:* Jack Nitzche. VHS, Beta $69.95 *MGM 🎞🎞*

Cutting Class Murders proliferate in a high school, where a student with a history of mental illness is number one on the suspect list. Tongue-in-cheek mayhem.
1989 (R) 91m/C Jill Schoelen, Roddy McDowall, Donovan Leitch, Martin Mull, Brad Pitt; *D:* Rospo Pallenberg. VHS $9.98 *REP 🎞*

The Cutting Edge Take one spoiled figure skater who can't keep a partner, team her with a cocky ex-hockey player who thinks the only sport on ice IS hockey and you've got a winning combo. Rather thin plot revolves around their quest for Olympic gold and can't be taken too seriously, but the sparks fly between Kelly and Sweeney—the reason this movie works.
1992 (PG) 101m/C D.B. Sweeney, Moira Kelly, Roy Dotrice, Terry O'Quinn, Dwier Brown, Rachelle Ottley, Jo Jo Starbuck; *D:* Paul Michael Glaser; *W:* Tony Gilroy; *M:* Patrick Williams. VHS $19.98 *MGM 🎞🎞½*

Cyborg In a deathly, dirty, post-holocaust urban world, an able cyborg battles a horde of evil mutant thugs. Poorly-made action flick.
1989 (R) 85m/C Jean-Claude Van Damme, Deborah Richter, Vincent Klyn, Dayle Haddon; *D:* Albert Pyun; *W:* Kitty Chalmers. VHS, Beta $14.95 *MGM 🎞*

Cyborg 2 In the year 2074 cyborgs have replaced humans at all levels. A devious company which manufactures cyborgs decides to get rid of its chief competition by literally killing them off. They plan to inject cyborg Cash Reese (Jolie) with a liquid explosive that will detonate her and everything else in sight. Tech-master Mercy (Palance) clues Cash in and she escapes with the help of the human Colton (Koteas) but they've become prey to a group of ruthless hunters.
1993 (R) 99m/C Angelina Jolie, Elias Koteas, Jack Palance, Billy Drago. VHS *VMK 🎞🎞*

Cyborg Cop DEA agent Phillip (Jenson) is captured during a foreign drug raid and is turned into a half-man, half-machine by mad scientist Kessel (Rhys-Davies), who wants to sell his cyborgs as unstoppable hitmen.

Phillip's brother Jack (Bradley) tries to come to his rescue. Lots of stunts and car chases and even a minor romantic subplot with Jack and a tough reporter (Shaw).
1993 (R) 97m/C David Bradley, John Rhys-Davies, Todd Jensen, Alonna Shaw. VHS $92.95 *VMK 🎞½*

Cycle Psycho Two girls are abused by a crazed motorcycle gang. *AKA:* Numbered Days.
19?? (R) 80m/C Joe Turkel, Tom Drake, Stephen Oliver. VHS, Beta $59.95 *ACA Woof!*

Cycle Vixens Three girls jump on their hogs and head from Colorado to California. Much leather, motor revving and other obligatory motorcycle-trash trimmings. *AKA:* The Young Cycle Girls.
1979 (R) 90m/C Loraine Ferris, Daphne Lawrence, Deborah Marcus, Lonnie Pense, Kevin O'Neill, Bee Lechat, Billy Bullet; *D:* Peter Perry. VHS $9.95 *SIM Woof!*

Cyclone The girlfriend of a murdered scientist must deliver a secretly devised motorcycle into righteous government hands, much to the dismay of evil agents and corrupt officials. Good fun, sparked by a stellar "B" cast.
1987 (R) 89m/C Heather Thomas, Jeffrey Combs, Ashley Ferrare, Dar Robinson, Martine Beswick, Robert Quarry, Martin Landau, Huntz Hall, Troy Donahue, Michael Reagan, Dawn Wildsmith, Bruce Fairbairn, Russ Tamblyn; *D:* Fred Olen Ray. VHS, Beta $79.95 *COL 🎞🎞*

Cyclone Cavalier A dauntless hero travels through Central America on an adventurous spree.
1925 58m/B Reed Howes; *D:* Albert Rogell. VHS, Beta $16.95 *GPV, GVV 🎞🎞*

Cyclone of the Saddle Typical Western about a range war.
1935 53m/B Rex Lease, Bobby Nelson, William Desmond, Yakima Canutt; *D:* Elmer Clifton. VHS, Beta *NO 🎞*

Cyclops When an expedition party searches throughout Mexico for a woman's long lost fiance, they are shocked when they find out that radiation has turned him into a one-eyed monster.
1956 72m/B Tom Drake, Gloria Talbott, Lon Chaney Jr., James Craig; *D:* Bert I. Gordon. VHS, Beta $29.95 *LIV, MLB 🎞🎞*

Cyclotrode "X" The Crimson Ghost attempts to kidnap the inventor of the title machine, which would enable him to rule the world. Moore (The Lone Ranger) plays a bad guy. Serial in 12 episodes. Also available in a 93-minute colorized edition. *AKA:* The Crimson Ghost.
1946 100m/B Charles Quigley, Linda Stirling, I. Stanford Jolley, Clayton Moore, Kenne Duncan; *D:* William Witney, Fred Brannon. VHS, Beta $29.98 *VCN, REP, MLB 🎞🎞*

Cyrano de Bergerac Edmund Rostand's famous story of a large nosed yet poetic cavalier, who finds himself too ugly to be loved. He bears the pain of his devotion to Roxanne from afar, and helps the handsome but tongue-tied Christian to romance her. Ferrer became famous for this role, which won him an Oscar. Based on Brian Hooke's translation of the play. Also available colorized.
1950 112m/B Jose Ferrer, Mala Powers, William Prince, Elena Verdugo, Morris Carnovsky; *D:* Michael Gordon; *W:* Carl Foreman; *M:* Dimitri Tiomkin. VHS $9.95 *CNG, MRV, NOS 🎞🎞🎞🎞*

Cyrano de Bergerac Edmund Rostand's gallant poet and swordsman, with the extraordinary nose, is well-portrayed by Jacobi in this Royal Shakespeare Company

production. Translated and adapted by Anthony Burgess.
1985 177m/C *GB* Derek Jacobi, Sinead Cusack. **VHS $29.95** *TVC, TTC* 🎬🎬🎬🎬

Cyrano de Bergerac Depardieu brings to exhilarating life Rostand's well-loved play about the brilliant but grotesque-looking swordsman/poet, afraid of nothing—except declaring his love to the beautiful Roxanne. One of France's costliest modern productions, a multi-award winner for its cast, costumes, music and sets. English subtitles (by Anthony Burgess) are designed to capture the intricate rhymes of the original French dialogue.
1990 (PG) 135m/C *FR* Gerard Depardieu, Jacques Weber, Anne Brochet, Vincent Perez, Roland Bertin, Josiane Stoleru, Phillipe Volter, Philippe Morier-Genoud, Pierre Maguelon; *D:* Jean-Paul Rappeneau; *W:* Jean-Claude Carriere, Jean-Paul Rappeneau. Academy Awards '90: Best Costume Design; Nominations: Best Actor (Depardieu), Best Art Direction/Set Decoration, Best Foreign Language Film, Best Makeup; Cannes Film Festival '90: Best Actor (Depardieu); Cesar Awards '91: Best Actor (Depardieu), Best Director (Rappeneau), Best Film, Best Supporting Actor (Weber). **VHS $19.98** *ORI, FCT, BTV* 🎬🎬🎬🎬

D-Day on Mars Alien invader the Purple Monster is bent on taking over Earth. Originally a 15-part Republic serial titled "The Purple Monster Strikes."
1945 100m/B Dennis Moore, Linda Stirling, Roy Barcroft, James Craven, Bud Geary, Mary Moore; *D:* Spencer Gordon Bennet, Fred Brannon. **VHS $29.98** *REP* 🎬🎬

D-Day, the Sixth of June An American soldier has an affair with a Englishwoman weeks before D-Day, where he unhappily finds himself fighting side by side with her husband. Based on the novel by Lionel Shapiro. *AKA:* The Sixth of June.
1956 106m/C Richard Todd, Dana Wynter, Robert Taylor, Edmond O'Brien, John Williams, Jerry Paris, Richard Stapley; *D:* Henry Koster. **VHS, Beta $14.98** *FXV* 🎬🎬🎬

Da A middle-aged man returns to Ireland for his father's funeral. As he sorts out his father's belongings, his father returns as a ghostly presence to chat with him about life, death, and their own relationship. Based on the Hugh Leonard play with Hughes recreating his Tony-award winning role.
1988 (PG) 102m/C Barnard Hughes, Martin Sheen, William Hickey, Hugh O'Conor; *D:* Matt Clark; *W:* Hugh Leonard; *M:* Elmer Bernstein. **VHS, Beta** *NO* 🎬🎬½

Dad Hoping to make up for lost time, a busy executive rushes home to take care of his father who has just had a heart attack. What could have easily become sappy is made bittersweet by the convincing performances of Lemmon and Danson. Based on the novel by William Wharton.
1989 (PG) 117m/C Jack Lemmon, Ted Danson, Ethan Hawke, Olympia Dukakis, Kathy Baker, Zakes Mokae, J.T. Walsh, Kevin Spacey, Chris Lemmon; *D:* Gary David Goldberg; *W:* Gary David Goldberg; *M:* James Horner. Academy Awards '89 Nominations: Best Makeup; National Media Owl Awards '90: First Prize. **VHS, Beta $19.95** *MCA* 🎬🎬½

Daddy Long Legs Far from the great musicals, but enjoyable. An eccentric millionaire glimpses a French orphan and becomes her anonymous benefactor. Her musing over his identity spawns some surreal (often inexplicable) dance numbers, but love conquers all, even lesser Johnny Mercer songs. From a story by Jean Webster, also done in 1919 with Mary Pickford, 1931 with Janet Gaynor and 1935 with Shirley Temple as "Curly Top." 🎵Daddy Long Legs; Something's Got

To Give; Sluefoot; Dream; History of the Beat; C-A-T Spells Cat; Welcome Egghead.
1955 126m/C Fred Astaire, Leslie Caron, Terry Moore, Thelma Ritter, Fred Clark, Charlotte Austin, Larry Keating; *D:* Jean Negulesco. **VHS $19.98** *FXV, FCT* 🎬🎬🎬

Daddy Nostalgia Birkin plays the estranged daughter of Bogarde, who rushes from her home in England to France to be with her seriously ill father. She must come to terms with her feelings for him just as Bogarde must deal with his own mortality. Wonderful performances, with Bogarde a charming and dominating presence. In French with English subtitles. *AKA:* These Foolish Things.
1990 105m/C *FR* Dirk Bogarde, Jane Birkin, Odette Laure; *D:* Bertrand Tavernier; *W:* Colo Taverniev O'Hagan; *M:* Antoine Duhamel. **VHS $29.98** *FCT* 🎬🎬🎬

Daddy-O Drag racer Daddy-O traps the killers of his best friend and lands the blonde bombshell Jana. It might seem bad since it's dated, but, hey, it may have been bad in 1959, too! *AKA:* Out on Probation.
1959 74m/B Dick Contino, Sandra Giles; *D:* Lou Place; *W:* David Moessinger. **VHS $9.95** *COL* 🎬

Daddy's Boys Since farming during the Depression is a rather low-paying endeavor, this family turns to thieving instead. But all-for-one and one-for-all is not the credo for one of the sons who decides to branch out on his own. Produced by Roger Corman.
1987 (R) 90m/C Daryl Haney, Laura Burkett, Raymond J. Barry, Dan Shor; *D:* Joe Minion; *W:* Daryl Haney. **VHS, Beta $69.95** *COL* 🎬½

Daddy's Dyin'...Who's Got the Will? Based on the critically acclaimed play, this bittersweet comedy stars Bridges and D'Angelo as two members of the spiteful Turnover clan. When Daddy is on his deathbed, the entire family uses the opportunity to stab each other in the back. Non-stop humor and deep-hearted honesty carries this delightful adaptation quickly from beginning to end.
1990 (PG-13) 95m/C Beau Bridges, Beverly D'Angelo, Tess Harper, Judge Reinhold, Amy Wright, Keith Carradine, Patrika Darbo, Molly McClure, Bert Remsen; *D:* Jack Fisk; *W:* Del Shores; *M:* David McHugh. **VHS, Beta $14.95** *MGM* 🎬🎬½

Daddy's Gone A-Hunting It's an eye for an eye, a baby for a baby in this well-done psychological thriller. A happily married woman is stalked by her deranged ex-boyfriend, whose baby she aborted years before. Now he wants the life of her child as just compensation for the loss of his.
1969 (PG) 108m/C Carol White, Paul Burke, Scott Hylands, Rachel Ames, Mala Powers, James B. Sikking; *D:* Mark Robson; *W:* Larry Cohen; *M:* John Williams. **VHS $19.98** *WAR* 🎬🎬🎬

Daffy Duck's Movie: Fantastic Island A compilation of classic Warner Brothers cartoons, starring Daffy Duck, Speedy Gonzales, Bugs Bunny, Porky Pig, Sylvester, Tweety, Pepe Le Pew, Pirate Sam, Granny, Foghorn Leghorn and the Tasmanian Devil.
1983 (G) 78m/C *D:* Friz Freleng. **VHS, Beta $14.95** *WAR, FCT, WTA* 🎬🎬🎬

Daffy Duck's Quackbusters Daffy, with help from pals Bugs and Porky, sets up his own "ghostbusting" service. Good compilation of old classics such as "Night of the Living Duck," plus a new feature, "The Duxorcist." Video is also available in Spanish.
1989 (G) 79m/C *D:* Greg Ford, Terry Lennon; *V:* Mel Blanc. **VHS, Beta $14.95** *WAR, FCT, APD* 🎬🎬🎬

Dagger Eyes A political assassin at work is inadvertently captured on film by a photographer. The assassin's mob employers will go to any lengths to destroy the film. Say cheeeeeese!
1987 84m/C Carol Bouquet, Philip Coccioletti, John Steiner; *D:* Carlo Vanzina. **VHS, Beta** *NO* 🎬½

The Dagger of Kamui Jiro is pursued by minions of the evil Tenkai as he races from Japan to the American Old West and back again. He's trying to avenge the murder of his father and Jiro's only weapon is the mysterious Dagger of Kamui, which holds the secret to a treasure and the future of Japan. In Japanese with English subtitles.
1985 132m/C *JP* **VHS $39.95** *ANI, WTA* 🎬🎬½

Dagora, the Space Monster Giant, slimy, pulsating mass from space lands on Earth and begins eating everything in sight. Scientists join together in a massive effort to destroy the creature. Believe it or not, it's sillier than most of the Japanese sci-fi genre. *AKA:* Dagora; Space Monster Dagora; Uchudai Dogora; Uchu Daikaiju Dogora.
1965 80m/C *JP* Yosuke Natsuki, Yoko Fujiyama; *W:* Shinichi Sekizawa. **VHS, Beta $24.95** *VYY* Woof!

The Dain Curse In 1928, private eye Hamilton Nash must recover stolen diamonds, solve a millionaire's suicide, avoid being murdered, and end a family curse. Based on the novel by Dashiell Hammett. Made-for-television as a 312-minute miniseries. *AKA:* Dashiell Hammett's The Dain Curse.
1978 138m/C James Coburn, Jason Miller, Jean Simmons, Beatrice Straight, Hector Elizondo, Nancy Addison; *D:* E.W. Swackhamer. **VHS, Beta $92.95** *EHV, MTX, SUE* 🎬🎬

Daisy Miller Shepherd portrays the title character in this adaptation of the Henry James novella about a naive young American woman travelling through Europe and getting a taste of the Continent during the late 19th century. Though it is intelligently written and has a good supporting cast, the film seems strangely flat, due in large part to Shepherd's hollow performance.
1974 (G) 93m/C Cybill Shepherd, Eileen Brennan, Cloris Leachman, Mildred Natwick; *D:* Peter Bogdanovich; *W:* Frederic Raphael. Academy Awards '74 Nominations: Best Costume Design; National Board of Review Awards '74: 10 Best Films of the Year. **VHS, Beta $14.95** *PAR* 🎬🎬½

Dakota Fine cast becomes embroiled in railroad land dispute. In the meantime, love strikes The Duke. Standard Wayne western saga never quite gets on track.
1945 82m/B John Wayne, Vera Ralston, Walter Brennan, Ward Bond, Ona Munson; *D:* Joseph Kane. **VHS $14.98** *REP* 🎬🎬

Dakota A troubled half-breed teenager works for a rancher, romances his daughter, and befriends his crippled 12-year-old son. A well-meaning, but predictable drama.
1988 (PG) 96m/C Lou Diamond Phillips, Dee Dee Norton, Eli Cummins, Herta Ware; *D:* Fred Holmes. **VHS, Beta $89.99** *HBO* 🎬🎬

Dakota Incident Decent western about stagecoach passengers travelling through Dakota Territory who must defend themselves against an Indian attack.
1956 88m/C Dale Robertson, Ward Bond, Linda Darnell, John Lund; *D:* Lewis R. Foster. **VHS $19.98** *REP* 🎬🎬

Daleks—Invasion Earth 2150 A.D. A sequel to "Dr. Who and the Daleks," wherein the popular British character endeavors to save the Earth from a robotic threat. *AKA:* Invasion Earth 2150 A.D.
1966 81m/C *GB* Peter Cushing, Andrew Keir, Jill Curzon, Ray Brooks; *D:* Gordon Flemyng. **VHS, Beta** NO *♪♪½*

Dam Busters Well-done and exciting film details the efforts of British scientists trying to devise a method of destroying a strategic dam in Nazi Germany during WWII. Definitely one of the better in the war movie genre.
1955 119m/B *GB* Michael Redgrave, Richard Todd, Ursula Jeans, Basil Sydney; *D:* Michael Anderson Sr. **VHS, Beta** $59.99 HMV, CNG *♪♪♪½*

Damage The elegant Irons portrays Stephen, a middle-aged, married British politican who has always been completely in control of his life, especially where his feelings are concerned. Then he meets Anna (Binoche), his son's less-than-innocent fiance, and immediately begins an obsessive, wildly sexual affair with her. Stephen should have listened to Anna's warning about herself "Damaged people are dangerous, they know they can survive," because their passion leads to betrayal and tragedy. Binoche is more icon than human being but the film still hypnotizes as an exploration of passion. Based on the novel by Josephine Hart. An unrated version is also available.
1992 (R) 111m/C *FR GB* Jeremy Irons, Juliette Binoche, Rupert Graves, Miranda Richardson, Ian Bannen, Leslie Caron, Peter Stormare, Gemma Clark, Julian Fellowes; *D:* Louis Malle; *W:* David Hare; *M:* Zbigniew Preisner. Academy Awards '92 Nominations: Best Supporting Actress (Richardson); British Academy Awards '93: Best Supporting Actress (Richardson). **VHS** $19.95 COL, IME, MOV *♪♪♪*

Dames A millionaire with fanatically religious beliefs tries to stop the opening of a Broadway show. In the last of the grand budget-breaking spectacles before the "production code" came into being, distinguished choreographer Busby Berkeley took his imagination to the limit: watch for the dancing clothes on an ironing board and dancing girls with puzzle pieces on their backs which form the real Keeler. ♫Dames; I Only Have Eyes For You; When You Were a Smile on Your Mother's Lips and a Twinkle in Your Father's Eye; Try To See It My Way; The Girl at the Ironing Board.
1934 95m/B Dick Powell, Joan Blondell, Ruby Keeler, ZaSu Pitts, Guy Kibbee, Busby Berkeley; *D:* Ray Enright; *W:* Delmer Daves. **VHS, Beta** $19.98 MGM, FOX *♪♪♪*

Damien: Omen 2 Sequel to "The Omen" about Damien, a young boy possessed with mysterious demonic powers, who kills those people who anger him. Followed by "The Final Conflict."
1978 (R) 110m/C William Holden, Lee Grant, Lew Ayres, Robert Foxworth, Sylvia Sidney, Lance Henriksen; *D:* Don Taylor; *M:* Mike Hodges; *M:* Jerry Goldsmith. **VHS, Beta** $19.98 FOX *♪♪*

Damien: The Leper Priest True story of a Roman Catholic priest who doomed himself by voluntarily serving on a leper colony one hundred years ago. Somewhat disappointing considering the dramatic material. Originally a vehicle for David Janssen, who died prior to filming. Made for television. *AKA:* Father Damien: The Leper Priest.
1980 100m/C Ken Howard, Mike Farrell, Wilfrid Hyde-White, William Daniels, David Ogden Stiers; *D:* Steven Gethers. **VHS, Beta** $59.95 LIV *♪♪*

Damn the Defiant Adventure abounds when Guinness, as captain of the HMS Defiant during the Napoleonic wars, finds himself up against not only the French but his cruel second-in-command (Bogarde) and a mutinous crew as well. In the end, both a fleet-wide mutiny and a French invasion of England are avoided. Much attention is paid to period detail in this well-crafted film. *AKA:* HMS Defiant.
1962 101m/C *GB* Alec Guinness, Dirk Bogarde, Maurice Denham, Anthony Quayle; *D:* Lewis Gilbert. **VHS, Beta** $14.95 COL, FCT *♪♪♪*

Damn Yankees Musical feature adapted from the Broadway hit. A baseball fan frustrated by his team's lack of success makes a pact with the devil to become the team's new star. Verdon is dynamite as the devil's accomplice. Great Bob Fosse choreography. ♫Whatever Lola Wants; (You Gotta Have) Heart; Shoeless Joe From Hannibal Mo; Goodbye, Old Girl; A Little Brains, a Little Talent; Who's Got the Pain; Two Lost Souls; There's Something About an Empty Chair; Those Were the Good Old Days; Six Months Out of Every Year; Heart. *AKA:* What Lola Wants.
1958 110m/C Gwen Verdon, Ray Walston, Tab Hunter, Jean Stapleton, Russ Brown; *D:* George Abbott, Stanley Donen. **VHS, Beta** $19.98 WAR, FCT, HMV *♪♪♪*

Damnation Alley A warrior, an artist, and a biker jump in tank and set off in search of civilization after Armageddon. They go to Albany instead. So-so attempt to revive the post-nuclear holocaust genre which was more successfully accomplished by the "Mad Max" series. Adapted from Roger Zelazny's novel.
1977 (PG) 87m/C George Peppard, Jan-Michael Vincent, Paul Winfield, Dominique Sanda, Jackie Earle Haley; *D:* Jack Smight; *W:* Alan Sharp, Lukas Heller; *M:* Jerry Goldsmith. **VHS, Beta** $59.98 FOX *♪½*

The Damned Depicts the Nazi takeover of a German industrialist family and their descent into greed, lust, and madness. Comes in dubbed or subtitled formats.
1969 (R) 146m/C *IT GE* Dirk Bogarde, Ingrid Thulin, Helmut Griem, Charlotte Rampling, Helmut Berger; *D:* Luchino Visconti; *M:* Maurice Jarre. Academy Awards '69 Nominations: Best Story & Screenplay; National Board of Review Awards '69: 5 Best Foreign Films of the Year. **VHS, Beta** $59.95 WAR, APD, ING *♪♪½*

Damned River Four friends take a guided tour down Zimbabwe's Zambezi River, only to find midway down that their guide is a murderous psycho. Survival becomes a priority.
1989 (R) 93m/C Stephen Shellan, Lisa Aliff, John Terlesky, Marc Poppel, Bradford Bancroft; *D:* Michael Schroeder. **VHS, Beta** $89.98 FOX *♪½*

A Damsel in Distress Astaire falls for an upper-class British girl, whose family wants her to have nothing to do with him. Features memorable songs from the Gershwins. ♫A Foggy Day in Londontown; Nice Work If You Can Get It; Stiff Upper Lip; Put Me to the Test; I Can't Be Bothered Now; The Jolly Tar and the Milkmaid; Things Are Looking Up; Sing of Spring; Ah Che a Voi Perdoni Iddio.
1937 101m/B Fred Astaire, Joan Fontaine, George Burns, Gracie Allen, Ray Noble, Montagu Love, Reginald Gardiner; *D:* George Stevens; *M:* George Gershwin, Ira Gershwin. **VHS, Beta** $14.98 CCB, MED, TTC *♪♪♪*

Dan Candy's Law A Canadian mountie becomes a driven hunter, and then desperate prey, when he tries to track down the Indian who killed his partner. *AKA:* Alien Thunder.
1973 90m/C *CA* Donald Sutherland, Gordon Tootoosis, Chief Dan George, Kevin McCarthy; *D:* Claude Fournier; *M:* Georges Delerue. **VHS, Beta** $79.95 PSM, SIM *♪½*

Dance Two ballet dancers struggle to find love amidst the backstage treacheries and demanding schedules of their profession.
1990 90m/C John Revall, Ellen Troy, Carlton Wilborn, Charlene Campbell; *D:* Robin Murray. **VHS, Beta** AIP *♪½*

Dance Fools Dance Fast-paced drama has Crawford and Bakewell as a pair of spoiled rich kids who are forced to face poverty when the stock market crashes. He meets up with Gable, who's producing liquor illegally, while she gets a job at a newspaper. When Gable arranges something akin to the St. Valentine's Day Massacre, Bakewell's investigative reporting of the situation produces fatal results. The Hays Office had a problem with Crawford and friends appearing in their underwear. Cast notes: Gable was just starting out at MGM, which is why he was billed sixth; the William Holden here is not THE William Holden, and Edwards went on to provide the voice of Jiminy Cricket in "Pinocchio."
1931 82m/B Joan Crawford, Lester Vail, Cliff Edwards, William "Billy" Bakewell, William Holden, Clark Gable; *D:* Harry Beaumont. **VHS, Beta** $19.98 MGM, FCT *♪♪♪*

Dance, Girl, Dance The private lives and romances of a wartime nightclub dance troupe. Standard Hollywood potpourri of dance, drama, comedy. ♫Mother, What Do I Do Now?; Jitterbug Bite; Morning Star.
1940 88m/B Maureen O'Hara, Louis Hayward, Lucille Ball, Virginia Field, Ralph Bellamy, Maria Ouspenskaya, Mary Carlisle, Katherine Alexander, Edward Brophy; *D:* Dorothy Arzner. **VHS, Beta** $19.98 RKO, TTC *♪♪*

The Dance Goes On After the death of an uncle, Keach and his estranged son Almond reunite at the old Quebec family farm left to them. The father is country-bred and appreciates the property but his Los Angeles-reared son wants to sell for a quick profit. Director Almond cast his own son in the starring role as well as his ex-wife Bujold, who plays the ambitious showbiz mother.
1992 104m/C James Keach, Matt Almond, Genevieve Bujold, Cary Lawrence; *D:* Paul Almond; *W:* Paul Almond. **VHS** $89.95 MNC *♪♪*

Dance Hall A Pennsylvania dance hall owner is propelled into romantic confusion with the introduction of a sultry blond dancer into his club.
1941 73m/C Cesar Romero, Carole Landis, William Henry, June Storey, Charles Halton; *D:* Irving Pichel. **VHS, Beta** $19.95 NOS, BAR, HEG *♪½*

Dance Hall Racket A sleazy, stilted expose of dance hall vice featuring a brief appearance by Bruce and his wife, Harlow.
1958 60m/B Lenny Bruce, Honey Harlow; *D:* Phil Tucker. **VHS, Beta** $19.98 DVT, HEG *♪♪*

Dance Macabre Englund takes on a dual role as a man with a split personality—one of whom is deadly. Jessica, an American ballerina, enrolls in a Russian dance academy and meets mesmerizing choreographer, Anthony. Unfortunately for Jessica she happens to look exactly like Anthony's long-dead lover and he becomes obsessed with her. Also, her fellow dancers are being brutally murdered. Are the events connected?

1991 (R) 97m/C Robert Englund, Michelle Zeitlin, Marianna Moen, Julene Renee, Alexander Sergeyev; *D:* Greydon Clark; *W:* Greydon Clark. **VHS** $89.95 *COL* 🎞

Dance of Death Just before his death, Karloff agreed to appear in footage for four Mexican cheapies that were practically thrown together (Karloff actually filmed his scenes in Los Angeles). If they had mixed the footage instead of matched it, the flicks couldn't be any worse. This one concerns a lunatic toy-maker whose toys kill and maim his heirs. *AKA:* House of Evil; Macabre Serenade.
1968 89m/C MX Boris Karloff, Julissa, Andres Garcia, Jack Hill; *D:* Juan Ibanez. **VHS, Beta** $59.95 *SNC, MPI* Woof!

Dance of Death A girl learns kung fu and kills many warriors by kicking them in the ribs and head.
1984 81m/C Mao Ying, Shih Tien, Shiao Bou-Lo, Chien Pay, Chia Kai, Noh Tikki. **VHS, Beta** $39.95 *UNI* 🎞

Dance of Life A look at the backstage goings-on at a burlesque theater. A successful entertainer's life goes down the tubes when he hits the bottle. His wife leaves him because of his philandering, but returns when she sees how much he really needs her. One scene of the Ziegfeld Follies uses two-tone Technicolor technology. This was re-made twice: as "Swing High, Swing Low" in 1937 and as "When My Baby Smiles at Me" in 1948. Carroll replaced the stage lead, who was said to have no "name recognition"—Barbara Stanwyck. 🎵True Blue Lou; King of Jazzmania; Cuddlesome Baby; Flippity Flop; Ladies of the Dance; The Mightiest Matador; Sweet Rosie O'Grady; In the Gloaming; Sam, the Accordion Man.
1929 115m/B Nancy Carroll, Hal Skelly, Ralph Theadore, Charles D. Brown, Dorothy Revier, Al "Fuzzy" St. John, Oscar Levant; *D:* John Cromwell. **VHS** $19.95 *NOS, MLB* 🎞🎞½

Dance of the Damned A case where low-budget isn't synonymous with bomb. Fascinating noir-ish plot concerning a vampire who wants to learn more about the life of his next victim, a deep-thinking stripper, who has lost the will to live it. Surprisingly well-done and acted; above-par for this genre.
1988 (R) 83m/C Cyril O'Reilly, Starr Andreeff; *D:* Katt Shea Ruben; *W:* Katt Shea Ruben, Andy Ruben. **VHS, Beta** *NO* 🎞🎞

Dance or Die Just goes to show that in Las Vegas you can't have your dance and drugs too, because if the Mob doesn't get you, the Feds will. Made for video (though maybe it shouldn't have been made at all). In HiFi Stereo.
1987 90m/C Ray Kieffer, Rebecca Barrington; *D:* Richard W. Munchkin. **VHS, Beta** *NO* 🎞

Dance with a Stranger The engrossing and factual story of Ruth Ellis who gained notoriety as the last woman hanged in Great Britain. This emotional and sometimes violent film mirrors the sensationalism produced in the 1950s. The film follows Ellis's pre-trial life and her perpetual struggle to maintain her independence. Newcomer Richardson portrays the Marilyn Monroe look-alike barmaid.
1985 (R) 101m/C GB Miranda Richardson, Rupert Everett, Ian Holm, Joanne Whalley-Kilmer; *D:* Mike Newell; *W:* Shelagh Delaney. **VHS, Beta** $19.98 *VES, LIV* 🎞🎞🎞½

Dance with Death When strippers turn up brutally murdered, a young journalist goes undercover to solve the case.
1991 (R) 90m/C Maxwell Caulfield, Barbara Alyn Jones, Martin Mull, Drew Snyder, Catya Sassoon; *D:* Charles Philip Moore. **VHS** $89.98 *HBO* 🎞

Dance with Me, Henry When Lou becomes involved with Bud's gambling debts and the local district attorney turns up dead, Lou's not only wanted by the law, but by the mafia as well. This was the great comedy duo's last picture together and it's clear the pair are not happy about working with each other, even on this mediocre effort.
1956 90m/B Bud Abbott, Lou Costello, Gigi Perreau, Rusty Hamer, Mary Wickes, Ted de Corsia; *D:* Charles T. Barton. **VHS** $19.98 *MGM* 🎞🎞

Dancers During the filming of the ballet "Giselle" in Italy, a famous, almost-over-the-hill dancer (Baryshnikov, ten years after his role in "The Turning Point") coaches a young, inexperienced starlet. He hopes to revitalize his life and his dancing. Features dancers from the Baryshnikov-led American Ballet Theatre.
1987 (PG) 99m/C Mikhail Baryshnikov, Leslie Browne, Julie Kent, Mariangela Melato, Alessandra Ferri, Lynn Seymour, Victor Barbee, Tommy Rall; *D:* Herbert Ross; *M:* Pino Donaggio. **VHS, Beta** $19.98 *CTH, WAR, FCT* 🎞½

Dances with Wolves The story of a U.S. Army soldier, circa 1870, whose heroism in battle allows him his pick of posts. His choice, to see the West before it disappears, changes his life. He meets, understands and eventually becomes a member of a Lakota Sioux tribe in the Dakotas. Costner's first directorial attempt proves him a talent of vision and intelligence. This sometimes too objective movie lacks a sense of definitive character, undermining its gorgeous scenery and interesting perspective on the plight of Native Americans. Lovely music and epic proportions. Adapted by Blake from his novel.
1990 (PG-13) 181m/C Kevin Costner, Mary McDonnell, Graham Greene, Rodney Grant, Floyd "Red Crow" Westerman, Tantoo Cardinal, Robert Pastorelli, Charles Rocket, Maury Chaykin, Jimmy Herman, Nathan Lee Chasing His Horse, Wes Studi; *D:* Kevin Costner; *W:* Michael Blake; *M:* John Barry. Academy Awards '90: Best Adapted Screenplay, Best Cinematography, Best Director (Costner), Best Film Editing, Best Picture, Best Sound, Best Score; Nominations: Best Actor (Costner), Best Art Direction/Set Decoration, Best Costume Design, Best Supporting Actor (Greene), Best Supporting Actress (McDonnell), Best Original Score; Directors Guild of America Awards '90: Best Director (Costner); Golden Globe Awards '91: Best Director (Costner), Best Film—Drama, Best Screenplay; National Board of Review Awards '90: 10 Best Films of the Year, Best Director (Costner). **VHS, Beta** $14.98 *ORI, FCT, IME* 🎞🎞🎞½

Dancing in the Dark An interesting but slow-moving Canadian film about the perfect housewife who learns that after 20 years of devotion to him, her spouse has been unfaithful. Realizing how her life has been wasted she murders her husband and, in the end, suffers a mental breakdown.
1986 (PG-13) 93m/C CA Martha Henry, Neil Munro, Rosemary Dunsmore, Richard Monette; *D:* Leon Marr; *W:* Leon Marr; *M:* Erik Satie. **VHS, Beta** $19.95 *STE, NWV* 🎞🎞½

Dancing Lady Rarely seen film is MGM's answer to "42nd Street," with Crawford as a small-time hoofer trying to break into Broadway. The screen debuts of Astaire and Eddy. 🎵Everything I Have Is Yours; Heigh-Ho! The Gang's All Here; Hold Your Man; That's the Rhythm of the Day; My Dancing Lady; Let's Go Bavarian; Hey Young Fella.

1933 93m/B Clark Gable, Joan Crawford, Fred Astaire, Franchot Tone, Nelson Eddy, Ted Healy, Moe Howard, Shemp Howard, Larry Fine; *D:* Robert Z. Leonard. **VHS, Beta** $19.98 *MGM, TTC, FCT* 🎞🎞½

Dancing Man A gigolo romances both mother and daughter and winds up implicated in murder as a result. Dismissable.
1933 65m/B Judith Allen, Reginald Denny, Natalie Moorhead; *D:* Albert Ray. **VHS, Beta, 8mm** $24.95 *VYY* 🎞½

Dancing Mothers A fast-living woman becomes involved with her mother's roguish boyfriend in this silent film with accompanying musical score.
1926 85m/B Clara Bow, Alice Joyce, Conway Tearle, Donald Keith; *D:* Herbert Brenon. **VHS, Beta** $19.95 *NOS, MRV, DVT* 🎞🎞½

Dancing Pirate A Boston dance instructor is kidnapped by pirates and jumps ship in Mexico, where he romances a mayor's daughter. The silly story boasts some Rodgers and Hart tunes, plus the early use of Technicolor, exploited here for all it was worth and then some. 🎵Are You My Love?; When You're Dancing the Waltz.
1936 83m/C Charles Collins, Frank Morgan, Steffi Duna, Luis Alberni, Victor Varconi, Jack LaRue; *D:* Lloyd Corrigan. **VHS** $19.95 *NOS, LOO* 🎞🎞

The Dancing Princesses When five naughty princesses wear the soles of their slippers out every night, their father the King must foot the bill. He soon tires of this expense and offers a reward to the person who can discover how this happens. A handsome prince becomes invisible to follow the lovely ladies and discover their secret. From the "Faerie Tale Theatre" series. Made for television.
1984 60m/C Lesley Ann Warren, Peter Weller, Sachi Parker, Roy Dotrice; *D:* Peter Medak. **VHS, Beta** $14.98 *KUI, FOX, FCT* 🎞

Dandelions German soft-core flick starring Hauer in an early role as a man jilted by his wife. To make himself feel better he decides to explore the sleazier side of life. Meaningless film evokes no sympathy but some may appreciate the titillation. Dubbed.
1974 92m/C GE Rutger Hauer, Dagmar Lassander; *D:* Adrian Hoven. **VHS, Beta** *NO* 🎞

Dandy in Aspic A double-agent is assigned to kill himself in this hard to follow British spy drama. The film is based on Derek Marlowe's novel. Mann died midway through shooting and Harvey finished direction.
1968 (R) 107m/C GB Laurence Harvey, Tom Courtenay, Lionel Stander, Mia Farrow, Harry Andrews, Peter Cook, Per Oscarsson; *D:* Anthony Mann; *M:* Quincy Jones. **VHS, Beta** $69.95 *COL* 🎞½

Danger Ahead! Comedy short featuring an exciting train chase.
1926 15m/B **VHS, Beta** $49.95 *IUF* 🎞½

Danger Ahead Newill stars again as Renfrew of the Mounties—this time he tries to rid the north woods of the baddies who are trying to take over.
1940 57m/B James Newill, Dorothea Kent, Guy Usher, Dave O'Brien, Bob Terry; *D:* Ralph Staub. **VHS** $19.95 *DVT, HEG* 🎞

Danger: Diabolik A superthief called Diabolik (Law) continuously evades the law while performing his criminal antics. *AKA:* Diabolik.
1968 (PG-13) 99m/C IT John Phillip Law, Marisa Mell, Michel Piccoli, Terry-Thomas; *D:* Mario Bava; *M:* Ennio Morricone. **VHS** *PAR* 🎞

D

Danger in the Skies An alcoholic airline pilot tries to straighten out his life when he nearly loses everything while drinking on the job. Made for cable television. *AKA:* The Pilot.
1979 (PG) 99m/C Cliff Robertson, Diane Baker, Dana Andrews, Gordon MacRae, Milo O'Shea, Frank Converse, Edward Binns; *D:* Cliff Robertson. VHS, Beta $79.95 VCI, HHE ♪½

Danger Lights Depicts the railroads and the railroad men's dedication to each other and their trains.
1930 73m/B Jean Arthur, Louis Wolheim, Robert Armstrong; *D:* George B. Seitz. VHS, Beta $19.95 PEN, MRV, NOS ♪½

Danger Man British tv series starring McGoohan as NATO agent John Drake. Half-hour episodes were known as "Danger Man" in England, when the series went to 60 minutes the title was changed to "Secret Agent" with the premise remaining the same. Additional episodes available.
1961 30m/B *GB* Patrick McGoohan. VHS $14.95 MPI, MOV ♪½

Danger on the Air A radio program sponsor—a much-despised misogynist—is murdered, and the sound engineer attempts to solve the mystery. Features Cobb in one of his earliest roles; Garrett also directed "Lady in the Morgue" that year.
1938 70m/B Donald Woods, Nan Grey, Berton Churchill, Jed Prouty, William Lundigan, Richard "Skeets" Gallagher, Edward Van Sloan, George Meeker, Lee J. Cobb, Johnny Arthur, Linda Hayes, Louise Stanley; *D:* Otis Garrett. VHS, Beta $16.95 SNC ♪♪

Danger Trails Rehashed western programmer. Features the hero who must save the rancher's honor as well as the ranch, while fighting detestable hombres with the traditional fare as an arsenal.
1935 55m/B Guinn Williams, Marjorie Gordon, Wally Wales, John Elliott, Ace Cain, Edmund Cobb; *D:* Bob Hill. VHS $19.95 NOS, DVT, GPV ♪½

Danger UXB During the 1940 London blitz "Danger UXB" was scrawled wherever there was, or thought to be, an unexploded German bomb. This miniseries covers the exploits of the Royal Engineers whose job it was, with little training and lots of nerve, to defuse the bombs. Based on the memoirs of Major A.B. Hartley of the Royal Engineers. On five cassettes. Made for television.
1981 660m/C *GB* Anthony Andrews, Judy Geeson, Maurice Roeves, Kenneth Cranham, Jeremy Sinden, Iain Cuthbertson, George Innes, Norman Chappell, Kenneth Farrington, Gordon Kane, Ken Kitson, Robert Longden, Robert Pugh, Deborah Watling. VHS $149.95 SIG, TVC, FUS ♪♪½

Danger Zone A man is hired to bid for a saxophone at an auction and then has the instrument stolen from him. He discovers it contained stolen jewelry and tries to recover it.
1951 56m/B Hugh Beaumont, Tom Neal, Richard Travis, Virginia Dale. VHS, Beta NO ♪♪

Danger Zone A low-budget, low-brow flick about an all-female rock band whose bus breaks down in the middle of the desert, leaving the girls to defend themselves against a merciless motorcycle gang. You'll wish this one was a mirage.
1987 (R) 90m/C Robert Canada, Jason Williams, Kriss Braxton, Dana Dowell, Jamie Ferreira; *D:* Henry Vernon. VHS, Beta $19.98 NLC Woof!

Danger Zone 2 A pernicious biker is released from prison on a technicality and decides to pay a social call to the undercover cop who set him up.

1989 (R) 95m/C Jason Williams, Robert Random; *D:* Geoffrey G. Bowers. VHS $79.98 MCG ♪

Danger Zone 3: Steel Horse War The "Danger Zone" dude is back and this time he's taken on a bevy of biker-types in a most gruesome battle to make our deserts safe.
1990 (R) 91m/C Jason Williams, Robert Random, Barne Suboski, Juanita Ranney, Rusty Cooper, Giles Ashford; *D:* Douglas Bronco. VHS, Beta $79.98 PMR ♪

Dangerous Davis won her first Oscar for her rather overdone portrayal of a has-been alcoholic actress reformed by a smitten architect who recognizes her from her days as a star.
1935 72m/B Bette Davis, Franchot Tone, Margaret Lindsay, Alison Skipworth, John Eldridge, Dick Foran; *D:* Alfred E. Green. VHS, Beta $19.98 MGM, BTV ♪♪½

A Dangerous Age A young girl, hoping to marry her lover, runs away from boarding school.
1957 ?m/C Ben Piazza, Ann Pearson. VHS $16.95 SNC ♪½

Dangerous Appointment Story of an innocent store clerk accused of theft and attempted murder.
1934 ?m/C Charles Starrett, Dorothy Wilson. VHS $16.95 SNC ♪♪

Dangerous Charter A group of fishermen discover a deserted yacht and man its helm. But their good fortune takes a decided turn for the worst as they become caught in mob-propelled danger.
1962 76m/C Chris Warfield, Sally Fraser, Richard Foote, Peter Foster, Wright King; *D:* Robert Gottschalk. VHS, Beta $19.95 NOS, ACA ♪½

Dangerous Curves Two friends are assigned to deliver a new Porsche to a billionaire's daughter - one of them talks the other into taking a little detour, and the trouble begins. This one went straight to video.
1988 (PG) 93m/C Robert Stack, Tate Donovan, Danielle von Zernaeck, Robert Klein, Elizabeth Ashley, Leslie Nielsen; *D:* David Lewis. VHS, Beta $79.98 VES, LIV ♪½

Dangerous Game A computer hacker leads his friends through a department store's security system, only to find they can't get out until morning. They soon discover they are not alone when one of the group turns up dead.
1990 (R) 102m/C Miles Buchanan, Sandy Lillingston, Kathryn Walker, John Polson; *D:* Stephen Hopkins. VHS, Beta $29.95 ACD ♪½

Dangerous Game Abrasive filmmaker Eddie Israel's (Keitel) new movie is about a couple's disintegrating marriage turning violent. Stars Sarah (Madonna) and Francis (Russo) find the on-camera violence spilling over into their tangled private lives while Eddie finds his personal traumas intruding more and more into the fictional material. Very raw movie within a movie features volatile Keitel (who also worked with Ferrera on "Bad Lieutenant") and suitably histrionic Russo; Madonna manages to hold her own in the least showy role, a cinematic first. Eddie's betrayed and bewildered wife is sympathetically portrayed by Ferrara, director Abel's wife. Also available in an unrated version. *AKA:* Snake Eyes.
1993 (R) 107m/C Harvey Keitel, James Russo, Madonna, Nancy Ferrara; *D:* Abel Ferrara; *W:* Nicholas St. John. VHS MGM ♪♪

Dangerous Heart A crooked undercover cop steals a bundle from a drug dealer and gets himself killed for his troubles. Only the dealer doesn't know where the money is. So he decides to befriend the cop's widow, get romantically involved, and see what she knows.
1993 (R) 93m/C Timothy Daly, Lauren Holly, Jeffrey Nordling, Alice Carter, Joe Pantoliano; *D:* Michael Scott; *W:* Patrick Cirillo. VHS $89.98 MCA ♪♪

Dangerous Holiday A young violin prodigy would rather be just "one of the boys" than be forced to practice all the time. He decides to run away but has everyone in an uproar thinking he's been kidnapped.
1937 54m/B Hedda Hopper, Guinn Williams, Jack La Rue, Franklin Pangborn, Grady Sutton. VHS, Beta $19.95 VYY ♪♪

Dangerous Hours An anti-communist propaganda film with Hughes as the innocent young college boy who gets duped by the evil Marxists until he realizes the truth of his all-American upbringing. Silent with original organ score.
1919 88m/B Lloyd Hughes; *D:* Fred Niblo. VHS, Beta, 8mm $24.95 VYY, FCT, GPV ♪♪

Dangerous Liaisons A couple take each other to the brink of destruction via their insatiable desire for extra-marital affairs. Vadim attempted to repeat his success with Brigitte Bardot by featuring wife Annette as a new sex goddess, but lightning didn't strike twice. *AKA:* Les Liaisons Dangereuses; Dangerous Love Affairs.
1960 111m/B *FR IT* Gerard Philippe, Jeanne Moreau, Jeanne Valeri, Annette Vadim, Simone Renant, Jean-Louis Trintignant, Nikolas Vogel; *D:* Roger Vadim; *W:* Roger Vadim. VHS $59.95 INT, APD, ING ♪♪

Dangerous Liaisons Stylish and absorbing, this adaptation of the Laclos novel and the Christopher Hampton play centers around the relationship of two decadent members of 18th-century French nobility. The two, Close and Malkovich, spend their time testing and manipulating the loves of others. They find love often has a will of its own. Possibly the best of the several versions available. Interesting to comparison-view with director Milos Forman's version of this story, 1989's "Valmont."
1988 (R) 120m/C John Malkovich, Glenn Close, Michelle Pfeiffer, Uma Thurman, Keanu Reeves, Swoosie Kurtz, Mildred Natwick, Peter Capaldi; *D:* Stephen Frears; *W:* Christopher Hampton; *M:* George Fenton. Academy Awards '88: Best Adapted Screenplay, Best Art Direction/Set Decoration, Best Costume Design; Nominations: Best Actress (Close), Best Picture, Best Supporting Actress (Pfeiffer), Best Original Score; British Academy Awards '89: Best Supporting Actress (Pfeiffer); Cesar Awards '90: Best Foreign Film. VHS, Beta, 8mm $19.98 WAR, FCT ♪♪♪

Dangerous Life Explosive drama brings to the screen the story of the Philippine uprising. It shows the horrible events that lead to the fall of Marcos and permitted the rise of Corazon Aquino.
1989 163m/C Gary Busey; *W:* David Williamson. VHS, Beta NO ♪♪

Dangerous Love Advice to the lovelorn: Avoid this one. Female members of a video dating service are being filmed in a death scene—their own.
1987 87m/C Lawrence Monoson, Brenda Bakke, Peter Marc, Elliott Gould, Anthony Geary; *D:* Marty Ollstein. VHS, Beta $79.95 MED Woof!

A Dangerous Man: Lawrence after Arabia At the 1919 Paris Peace Conference, T.E. Lawrence serves as the liaison to the Hashemite delegation in an effort to have the Allies agree to Arab independence. He finds the diplomatic fields more treacherous than anything he encountered during WWI. Fiennes does well in the difficult role of the reluctant, ambivalent hero. Made for television.
1991 104m/C *GB* Ralph Fiennes, Denis Quilley, Siddig el Fadil, Nicholas Jones, Roger Hammond, Peter Copley, Paul Freeman, Polly Walker; *D:* Christopher Menaul; *W:* Tim Rose Price. VHS $29.95 PBS *♂♂♂*

Dangerous Mission A young woman witnesses a mob murder in New York and flees to the Midwest, pursued by killers and the police. Good cast couldn't do much with this one.
1954 75m/B Victor Mature, Piper Laurie, Vincent Price, William Bendix; *D:* Louis King; *W:* W.R. Burnett, Charles Bennett. VHS, Beta $19.95 MED *♂½*

Dangerous Moonlight Polish concert pianist becomes a bomber pilot for the British in WWII, though his wife wants him to stay at the piano. Great battle and music sequences; the piece "Warsaw Concerto" became a soundtrack hit. *AKA:* Suicide Squadron.
1941 97m/B *GB* Anton Walbrook, Sally Gray, Derrick De Marney, Cecil Parker, Percy Parsons, Kenneth Kent, Guy Middleton, John Laurie, Frederick Valk; *D:* Brian Desmond Hurst. VHS, Beta $19.98 TTC *♂♂♂*

Dangerous Moves A drama built around the World Chess championship competition between a renowned Russian master and a young, rebellious dissident. The chess game serves as both metaphor and background for the social and political tensions it produces. With English subtitles. *AKA:* La Diagonale du Fou.
1984 (PG) 96m/C *SI* Liv Ullmann, Michel Piccoli, Leslie Caron, Alexandre Arbatt; *D:* Richard Dembo. VHS, Beta $59.95 LHV, IME *♂♂*

Dangerous Obsession A woman kidnaps the doctor she blames for her boyfriend's death and instead of exacting revenge, she makes him her personal sex slave. In the case of this flick, it's really a fate worse than death. *AKA:* Divine Obsession; Mortal Sins.
1988 (R) 81m/C *IT* Corinne Clery, Brett Halsey; *D:* Lucio Fulci; *M:* Simon Boswell. VHS $79.95 AIP *♂*

Dangerous Orphans Not completely awful tale of three brothers, orphaned as boys when their father is murdered before their very eyes, and the vendetta they have against the killer.
1986 (R) 90m/C *NZ* Peter Stevens, Peter Bland, Ian Mune, Ross Girven, Jennifer Ward-Lealand; *D:* John Laing. VHS, Beta $29.95 ACA *♂½*

Dangerous Passage A ne'er-do-well inherits 200 grand but gets in trouble before he can collect it. He ends up falling in with assorted misfits aboard a tramp steamer.
1944 60m/B Robert Lowery, Phyllis Brooks, Jack La Rue, Victor Kilian; *D:* William Berke. VHS, Beta, 8mm $19.95 VYY *♂♂*

Dangerous Pursuit A woman discovers that a man she slept with years ago is an assassin. Knowing too much, she finds herself next on his hit list. Decent psycho-thriller that was never released theatrically.
1989 95m/C Gregory Harrison, Alexandra Powers, Scott Valentine, Brian Wimmer, Elena Stiteler; *D:* Sandor Stern. VHS, Beta $89.99 PAR *♂♂*

Dangerous Relations Made for TV drama with Gossett as a tough convict at the end of 15-year prison sentence whose authority is challenged by young punk prisoner Underwood. Imagine his surprise when the old con realizes the punk is the son he hasn't seen since he started his time behind bars. Things don't improve (well, not at first) when they are paroled into each other's custody. *AKA:* Father & Son: Dangerous Relations.
1993 (PG-13) 93m/C *D:* Louis Gossett Jr., Blair Underwood, Rae Dawn Chong, Clarence Williams III. VHS $89.95 ACA *♂♂½*

Dangerous Summer In Australia, an American businessman building a resort is the victim of elaborate arson/murder insurance schemes. *AKA:* The Burning Man.
1982 100m/C *AU* Tom Skerritt, James Mason, Ian Gilmour, Wendy Hughes; *D:* Quentin Masters; *W:* David Ambrose. VHS, Beta NO *♂♂*

Dangerous When Wet A typical Williams water-musical. A farm girl dreams of fame by swimming the English Channel. One famous number pairs Williams with cartoon characters Tom & Jerry in an underwater frolic. ♫I Got Out of Bed on the Right Side; Ain't Nature Grand; I Like Men; Fifi; In My Wildest Dreams.
1953 96m/C Esther Williams, Fernando Lamas, Charlotte Greenwood, William Demarest, Jack Carson; *D:* Charles Walters; *M:* Arthur Schwartz, Johnny Mercer. VHS, Beta $19.98 MGM *♂♂*

A Dangerous Woman No, this isn't the femme fatale romance the word "dangerous" suggests. Instead, the eponymous character is a mildly retarded woman, Martha (Winger), whose simplistic view on life places her in ethically compromising positions. When a hunky Irish handyman (Byrne) comes on the scene and seduces both her and the aunt with whom she lives (Hershey), Martha awakens to feelings she has never experienced. Winger's performance is both sensitive and provocative, but is wasted in a film filled with two-dimensional characters, and really, not too much of a point. Adapted from a novel by Mary McGarry Morris. Screenplay by Foner, wife of director Gyllenhaal.
1993 (R) 101m/C Debra Winger, Barbara Hershey, Gabriel Byrne, David Strathairn, Chloe Webb, John Terry, Jan Hooks, Paul Dooley, Viveka Davis, Richard Riehle, Laurie Metcalf; *D:* Stephen Gyllenhaal; *W:* Naomi Foner; *M:* Carter Burwell. VHS MCA *♂♂*

Dangerously Close A group of anti-crime high school students organize a hall monitoring gang that becomes a group of neo-fascist disciplinarian elite.
1986 (R) 96m/C John Stockwell, Carey Lowell, J. Eddie Peck; *D:* Albert Pyun. VHS, Beta $9.98 MED, VTR *♂½*

Daniel The children of a couple who were executed for espionage (patterned after the Rosenbergs) struggle with their past in the dissident 1960s. So-so adaptation of E.L. Doctorow's "The Book of Daniel."
1983 (R) 130m/C Timothy Hutton, Amanda Plummer, Mandy Patinkin, Lindsay Crouse, Ed Asner, Ellen Barkin; *D:* Sidney Lumet. VHS, Beta $59.95 PAR *♂♂½*

Daniel and the Towers Daniel and his friends enjoy making fun of Sam, the man who is building glass towers in Watts, California. But when Daniel must pay for the repairs of a shopkeeper's window, he turns to Sam for help. Sam agrees to fix the windows if Daniel helps him collect glass for the towers. In the process, Sam and Daniel become friends and Sam teaches Daniel valuable lessons about beauty and determination. Although this story is fictional, the glass towers, built by Sam Rodia, really

stand in Watts. A viewers' guide is included. Part of the "Wonderworks" series.
199? 58m/C Allan Arbus, Michael McKean, Carmen Zapata, Miguel Alamo. VHS $29.95 PME, BTV *♂♂½*

Daniel Boone Daniel Boone guides a party of settlers from North Carolina to the fertile valleys of Kentucky, facing Indians, food shortages and bad weather along the way. O'Brien turns in a fine performance as the early American frontier hero.
1934 75m/B George O'Brien, Heather Angel, John Carradine; *D:* David Howard. VHS, Beta $19.95 NOS, MRV, VCN *♂♂½*

Daniel Boone: Trail Blazer Low-budget, though surprisingly well-acted rendition of the frontiersman's heroics, filmed in Mexico.
1956 75m/B Bruce (Herman Brix) Bennett, Lon Chaney Jr., Faron Young, Damian O'Flynn, Fred Kohler Jr., Claudio Brook, Kem Dibbs; *D:* Ismael Rodriguez, Albert C. Gannaway; *W:* John Patrick, John Hubbard. VHS $19.95 NOS, MRV, REP *♂♂½*

Danielle Steel's Changes Ladd is a successful, divorced New York television anchorwoman who turns her life upside-down when she marries an equally successful, widowed Los Angeles surgeon (Nouri). Can they overcome their bicoastal careers to make things work? What do you think. Made for television. *AKA:* Changes.
1991 96m/C Cheryl Ladd, Michael Nouri, Christopher Gartin, Randee Heller, Charles Frank, James Sloyan, Cynthia Bain; *D:* Charles Jarrott. VHS $89.95 WOV *♂♂½*

Danielle Steel's "Daddy" Ad exec Oliver Watson (Duffy) is happily married to Sarah (Mulgrew) and living the good life with their three kids—or so he thinks. Then Sarah announces she's leaving and Oliver's left to cope with family crisis as a single parent. A move to a new job in LA finds Oliver falling for an actress (Carter) and wondering if his family can ever be put back together again. Made for television. *AKA:* Daddy.
1992 95m/C Patrick Duffy, Lynda Carter, Kate Mulgrew; *D:* Michael Miller. VHS $89.95 WOV *♂♂½*

Danielle Steel's Kaleidoscope Three sisters are separated in childhood, after the mysterious deaths of their parents. Then a detective is hired to reunite the adult siblings. But Hilary, the eldest, has secrets she doesn't want her sisters to share. Made for television. *AKA:* Kaleidoscope.
1992 96m/C Jaclyn Smith, Perry King, Colleen Dewhurst, Donald Moffatt; *D:* Judd Taylor. VHS $89.95 WOV *♂♂½*

Danny Charming story of a lonely young girl who receives an injured horse that was no longer fit for the spoiled daughter of the rich owners.
1979 (G) 90m/C Rebecca Page, Janet Zarish, Barbara Jean Earhardt, Gloria Maddox, George Luce; *D:* Gene Feldman. VHS, Beta $59.95 MON, WOM, HHE *♂♂½*

Danny Boy Veteran dog, returning from the war, has difficulty adjusting to life back home. Things get worse for him and his young master when Danny Boy is assumed to be shell-shocked and dangerous. One of the few shell-shocked dog stories ever filmed.
1946 67m/B VHS, Beta $24.95 VYY *♂½*

Danny Boy Takes place in Ireland where a young saxophonist witnesses a murder and, in an effort to understand it, sets out to find the killer. Thought-provoking film is meant to highlight the continuing struggles in Ireland.

1984 (R) 92m/C *IR* Stephen Rea, Veronica Quilligan, Honor Heffernan, Marie Kean, Donal McCann, Ray McAnally; **D:** Neil Jordan; **W:** Neil Jordan. **VHS, Beta $59.95** COL &&&

Dante's Inferno Abandon all hope you who watch this film. A one-time friend sends his ruthless capitalist nemesis a copy of Dante's "Inferno," and the man reads the book and dreams he's gone to hell (would that be the dress circle?) A silent film that was controversial in its day: the body-stockinged actors were believed to be nude (which would have made it the first nudie Comedy).
1924 54m/B Lawson Butt, Howard Gaye, Ralph Lewis, Pauline Starke, Josef Swickard; **D:** Henry Otto. **VHS $10.95** CNM &&&

Dante's Inferno: Life of Dante Gabriel Rossetti The flamboyant life of mid-19th century English Pre-Raphaelite artist/poet Dante Gabriel Rossetti is depicted with the usual Russell flair. The drunken, drug-taking, womanizing Rossetti was part of the leading intellectual group of his age, which included Swinburne, Morris, Ruskin, and Rossetti's sister, the poet Christina Rossetti.
1969 90m/B *GB* Oliver Reed; **D:** Ken Russell. **VHS $39.95** ING, TPV &&

Danton A sweeping account of the reign of terror following the French Revolution. Focuses on the title character (wonderfully portrayed by Depardieu) and is directed with searching parallels to modern-day Poland by that country's premier filmmaker, Andrzej Wajda. Well-done period sets round out a memorable film. In French with English subtitles.
1982 (PG) 136m/C *PL FR* Gerard Depardieu, Wojciech Pszoniak, Patrice Chereau, Angela Winkler, Boguslaw Linda; **D:** Andrzej Wajda; **W:** Jean-Claude Carriere, Agnieszka Holland, Boleslaw Michalek, Jacek Gasiorowski, Andrzej Wajda. **VHS, Beta $59.95** COL, ING &&&&

Danzon Julia (Rojo), a single, working-class mom escapes the drudgery of her simple existence by going to a Mexico City dance hall every Wednesday. There she loses herself to the movement of the danzon, a dance with Haitian roots, popular in Mexico for over 100 years. When her partner of six years, Carmelo (Rergis), doesn't show up one night, her life is turned upside down. So begins a search for Carmelo—and herself. Quiet and restrained, like the ballroom-style danzon at the center of the plot. Applauded at Cannes. In Spanish with English subtitles.
1991 (PG) 103m/C *SP* Maria Rojo, Carmen Salinas, Blanca Guerra, Tito Vasconcelos, Victor Carpinteiro, Victor Vasconcelos; **D:** Maria Novaro; **W:** Maria Novaro, Betriz Novaro. **VHS $94.95** COL, ACY &&&½

Darby O'Gill & the Little People Set in Ireland, a roguish old story teller tumbles into a well and visits the land of leprechauns who give him three wishes in order to rearrange his life. When he tries to tell his friends what happened, they think that it is only another one of his stories. A wonderful Disney production (despite its disappointing box-office performance) with wit, charm and an ounce or two of terror.
1959 (G) 93m/C Albert Sharpe, Janet Munro, Sean Connery, Estelle Winwood; **D:** Robert Stevenson. **VHS, Beta $19.99** DIS &&&½

Darby's Rangers WWII pot-boiler with Garner as the leader of a commando team put together for covert operations in North Africa and Italy. Successful battle sequences combine with slow-paced romantic scenes as the soldiers chase women when not chasing the enemy. **AKA:** Young Invaders.

1958 122m/B James Garner, Jack Warden, Edd Byrnes, Peter Brown, Stuart Whitman, David Janssen, Etchika Choreau, Venetia Stevenson, Torin Thatcher, Joan Elan, Corey Allen, Murray Hamilton; **D:** William A. Wellman; **W:** Guy Trosper; **M:** Max Steiner **VHS $19.98** WAR &&½

Daredevils of the Red Circle Three young men set out to free a man held prisoner by an escaped convict. A serial in twelve chapters.
1938 195m/B Charles Quigley, Bruce (Herman Brix) Bennett, Carole Landis; **D:** John English, William Witney. **VHS $59.95** REP, VCN, MLB &&½

Daring Danger McCoy is nearly killed in a fight with the villainous Alexander. When he recovers he finds Alexander has joined forces with a rustler (Ellis), so McCoy battles both of them—while his horse goes for help.
1932 58m/B Tim McCoy, Richard Alexander, Robert Ellis, Alberta Vaughn, Wallace MacDonald, Murdock McQuarrie, Max Davidson; **D:** David Ross Lederman. **VHS $11.95** GPV &½

Daring Dobermans In this sequel to "The Doberman Gang," the barking bank-robbers have a new set of crime-planning masters. A young Indian boy who loves the dogs enters the picture and may thwart their perfect crime.
1973 (PG) 88m/C Charles Robinson, Tim Considine, David Moses, Claudio Martinez, Joan Caulfield; **D:** Byron Ross Chudnow. **VHS, Beta $59.98** FOX &&

Daring Game A group of scuba divers nicknamed the Flying Fish attempt to rescue a woman's husband and daughter from an island dictatorship. Failed series pilot by producer Ivan Tors, better known for "Sea Hunt" and "Flipper."
1968 100m/C Lloyd Bridges, Brock Peters, Michael Ansara, Joan Blackman; **D:** Laslo Benedek. **VHS, Beta $39.98** NO &&

Dario Argento's Trauma When a teenage girl's parents are decapitated, she and an artist friend start following the clues to a psychotic killer known as "The Headhunter." Trademark horror work for Italian cult director Argento with high suspense quotient and equally high gore. An unrated version is also available. **AKA:** Trauma.
1993 (R) 106m/C Christopher Rydell, Asia Argento, Laura Johnson, James Russo, Brad Dourif, Frederic Forrest, Piper Laurie; **D:** Dario Argento; **W:** Ted Klein, Dario Argento. **VHS $89.95** WOV &&

The Dark A supernatural beast commits a string of gruesome murders. **AKA:** The Mutilator.
1979 (R) 92m/C William Devane, Cathy Lee Crosby, Richard Jaeckel, Keenan Wynn, Vivian Blaine; **D:** John Cardos. **VHS, Beta $9.95** MED &½

The Dark Cop and scientist seek a mysterious graveyard creature who holds both the power to heal and destroy. One man wants to kill it, one man wants to save it, and they race to be the first to find it.
1994 (R) 90m/C Brion James, Jaimz Woolvett, Cynthia Belliveau, Stephen McHattie; **D:** Craig Pryce. **VHS $92.95** IMP &½

Dark Age An Australian conservationist must track down a rampaging, giant, semi-mythical alligator before it is killed by bounty hunters. Based on the novel (and Aboriginal legend) "Numunwari."
1988 (R) 90m/C *AU* John Jarratt, David Gulpilil, Max Phipps, Ray Meagher, Nikki Coghill, Burnam Burnam; **D:** Arch Nicholson. **VHS, Beta $19.98** NLC &&½

The Dark Angel Maud is the young and innocent heiress to a fortune in this gothic mystery of creeping unease. She is intrigued by the romantic portrait of her youthful and unknown Uncle Silas. But her mysterious uncle is no longer the Byronic hero. What secret wickedness does his ravaged face hide? And what about Maud's drug-addicted governess and the brutish young man in the cemetary? Does Uncle Silas just want Maud's fortune or Maud herself? Watch and see. Excellent performances by O'Toole as the decadent uncle and Edney as the innocent-but-not-stupid Maud. Based on the novel "Uncle Silas" by J.S. Le Fanu. Made for British television.
1991 150m/C *GB* Peter O'Toole, Beatie Edney, Jane Lapotaire, Tim Woodward, Alan MacNaughton, Barbara Shelley, Guy Rolfe; **D:** Peter Hammond. **VHS $19.98** FOX &&&

Dark August A New Yorker drops out and transplants to rural Vermont, where he accidentally kills a young girl and then suffers numerous horrors as a result of a curse put on him by the girl's grandfather.
1976 (PG) 87m/C J.J. Barry, Carole Shelyne, Kim Hunter, William Robertson; **D:** Martin Goldman. **VHS, Beta $59.95** VES, LIV &½

The Dark Backward A dark, subversive comedy about a garbage man who dreams of making it big in show biz as a stand-up comedian. He's terrible until a third arm starts growing out of his back and the sheer grotesqueness of his situation makes him a temporary star. Caan and Newton are interestingly cast, but young, first-time director Rifkin's foray into David Lynch territory was not well received by critics.
1991 (R) 97m/C Judd Nelson, Bill Paxton, Wayne Newton, Lara Flynn Boyle, James Caan, Rob Lowe, Claudia Christian; **D:** Adam Rifkin; **W:** Adam Rifkin. **VHS $89.95** COL &½

Dark Before Dawn American farmers and Vietnam veterans team up against corrupt government officials and ruthless businessmen in this violent film about the plight of the underdog.
1989 (R) 95m/C Doug McClure, Sonny Gibson, Ben Johnson, Billy Drago, Rance Howard, Morgan Woodward, Buck Henry, Jeffery Osterhage, Red Steagall, John Martin, Gary Cooper; **D:** Robert Totten. **VHS, Beta $79.98** VES, LIV &½

Dark Command The story of Quantrell's Raiders who terrorized the Kansas territory during the Civil War until one man came along to put a stop to it. Colorful and talented cast add depth to the script. Also available colorized.
1940 95m/B John Wayne, Walter Pidgeon, Claire Trevor, Roy Rogers, Marjorie Main, George "Gabby" Hayes; **D:** Raoul Walsh. **VHS, Beta $9.98** REP, FCT &&&

Dark Corner Gripping, intricate film noir about a detective, already framed once, who may go up the river yet again—this time for the murder of his ex-partner, the guy who framed him the first time. Loyal secretary Ball helps to extricate him from this tangled web.
1946 99m/B Lucille Ball, Mark Stevens, Clifton Webb, William Bendix, Cathy Downs, Reed Hadley, Constance Collier, Kurt Kreuger; **D:** Henry Hathaway. **VHS, Beta $59.98** FOX &&&

The Dark Crystal Jen and Kira, two of the last surviving Gelflings, attempt to return a crystal shard (discovered with the help of a sorceress) to the castle where the Dark Crystal lies, guarded by the cruel and evil Skeksis. Designed by Brian Froud. From the creators of the Muppets.
1982 (PG) 93m/C **D:** Jim Henson; **M:** Trevor Jones. **VHS, Beta** NO &&&

Dark Eyes An acclaimed Italian film based on a several short stories by Anton Chekov. Mastroianni is a weak-willed Italian, trapped in a marriage of convenience, who falls in love with a mysterious, also married, Russian beauty he meets in a health spa. He embarks on a journey to find her and, perhaps, his lost ideals. Hailed as Mastroianni's consummate performance. In Italian with English subtitles. *AKA:* Les Yeux Noirs; Oci Ciornie.
1987 118m/C *IT* Marcello Mastroianni, Silvana Mangano, Elena Sofonova, Marthe Keller; *D:* Nikita Mikhalkov. Academy Awards '87 Nominations: Best Actor (Mastroianni); Cannes Film Festival '87: Best Actor (Mastroianni). **VHS, Beta** $79.98 *GHV, FOX* 𝄞𝄞𝄞½

Dark Forces A faith-healer promises to help a senator's dying son and finds the politician's wife also desires his assistance. This Australian film is uneven and predictable. Though rated "PG," beware of two rather brief, but explicit, nudity scenes. *AKA:* Harlequin.
1983 (PG) 96m/C *AU* Robert Powell, David Hemmings, Broderick Crawford, Carmen Duncan; *D:* Simon Wincer. **VHS, Beta** $9.95 *MED* 𝄞𝄞

Dark Habits An early Almodovar farce about already-demented nuns in a failing convent trying to raise funds with the help of a nightclub singer who is on the run. Although certainly irreverant, it doesn't quite have the zing of his later work. In Spanish with subtitles. *AKA:* Entre Tinieblas.
1984 116m/C *SP* Carmen Maura, Christina Pascual, Julieta Serrano, Marisa Paredes; *D:* Pedro Almodovar; *W:* Pedro Almodovar. **VHS, Beta** $79.95 *ING, CCN, TPV* 𝄞𝄞½

The Dark Half Flawed chiller based on a Stephen King novel. Thad Beaumont's serious novels have been failures, but writing as George Stark, he's had phenomenal success with grisly horror stories. In a publicity stunt Thad kills off and publicly buries George (who doesn't want to stay dead). Soon everyone who's crossed Thad is brutally murdered. Hutton acquits himself well in a change of pace dual role. Otherwise, the psychological thrills are few and the gore is plentiful. Pittsburgh serves as location double for King's usual New England territory. Film's release was delayed due to Orion's bankruptcy problems.
1991 (R) 122m/C Timothy Hutton, Amy Madigan, Michael Rooker, Julie Harris, Robert Joy, Kent Broadhurst, Beth Grant, Rutanya Alda, Tom Mardirosian, Chelsea Field, Royal Dano; *D:* George A. Romero; *W:* George A. Romero; *M:* Christopher Young. **VHS** *NYR* 𝄞

Dark Horse Meyers is a young woman distraught over the death of her mother. She gets into trouble and is assigned to do community service work at a horse farm where she finds herself caring for a prize-winning horse.
1992 (PG) 98m/C Ari Meyers, Mimi Rogers, Ed Begley Jr., Donovan Leitch, Samantha Eggar; *D:* David Hemmings. **VHS** $19.98 *LIV, MOV, FCT* 𝄞𝄞½

The Dark Hour Two detectives team up to solve a murder in which multiple suspects are involved. Based on Sinclair Gluck's "The Last Trap."
1936 72m/B Ray Walker, Irene Ware, Berton Churchill, Hedda Hopper, Hobart Bosworth, E.E. Clive; *D:* Charles Lamont. **VHS, Beta** $16.95 *NOS, LOO, SNC* 𝄞½

Dark Journey WWI Stockholm is the setting for a love story between a double agent and the head of German Intelligence. Clever, sophisticated production; Leigh is stunning. *AKA:* The Anxious Years.

1937 82m/B *GB* Vivien Leigh, Conrad Veidt, Joan Gardner, Anthony Bushell, Ursula Jeans; *D:* Victor Saville. **VHS, Beta** $19.95 *NOS, MRV, CAB* 𝄞𝄞𝄞

Dark Justice Judge by day, avenger by night in this actioner created from three episodes of the late-night television series. Judge Nicholas Marshall is disgusted by the criminals sprung on legal loopholes and backroom deals. So he decides to take justice into his own hands.
1991 99m/C Ramy Zada, Dick O'Neill, Clayton Prince, Begona Plaza. **VHS** *WAR* 𝄞𝄞½

Dark Mirror A psychologist and a detective struggle to determine which twin sister murdered a prominent physician. Good and evil siblings finely-acted by de Havilland.
1946 85m/B Olivia de Havilland, Lew Ayres, Thomas Mitchell, Garry Owen; *D:* Robert Siodmak. **VHS** $14.98 *REP* 𝄞𝄞𝄞

Dark Mountain A forest ranger rescues his gal from the clutches of a hardened criminal.
1944 56m/B Robert Lowery, Ellen Drew, Regis Toomey, Eddie Quillan, Elisha Cook Jr.; *D:* William H. Pine, William C. Thomas. **VHS** $24.95 *NOS, DVT* 𝄞½

Dark Night of the Scarecrow Thriller with a moral. Prejudiced townspeople execute a retarded man who was innocently befriended by a young girl. After his death unusual things begin to happen. Slow to start but effective. Made for television.
1981 100m/C Charles Durning, Tanya Crowe, Larry Drake; *D:* Frank de Felitta. **VHS, Beta** $59.98 *FOX, HHE* 𝄞𝄞½

Dark Obsession Byrne portrays a husband who lives out his dark erotic fantasies with his wife (Donohoe), and is involved in a hit-and-run accident. Driven by guilt, madness slowly begins to take him. Ugly and depressing. Based on a true scandal. Available in an "NC-17" rated version. *AKA:* Diamond Skulls.
1990 (R) 97m/C Gabriel Byrne, Amanda Donohoe, Michael Hordern, Judy Parfitt, Douglas Hodge, Sadie Frost, Ian Carmichael; *D:* Nick Broomfield; *W:* Tim Rose Price. **VHS, Beta** $29.95 *PSM* 𝄞𝄞

Dark of the Night A young woman, new to the city, purchases a used Jaguar and finds she must share it with the car's former owner—a woman murdered inside the Jag. Decent psycho-thriller with some suspenseful and amusing moments. *AKA:* Mr. Wrong.
1985 88m/C *NZ* Heather Bolton, David Letch, Gary Stalker, Michael Haigh, Danny Mulheron, Kate Harcourt; *D:* Gaylene Preston; *W:* Gaylene Preston, Geoff Murphy, Graham Tetley; *M:* Jonathan Crayford. **VHS, Beta** $79.98 *LIV* 𝄞𝄞½

Dark of the Sun Lots of action; routine plot. Taylor is a tough mercenary hired to retrieve a supply of uncut diamonds from a beseiged town in the Congo during the 1950's rebellion. Oh, and if he can help out the town's inhabitants that's okay too. Based on the novel by Wilbur A. Smith. *AKA:* The Mercenaries.
1968 (PG) 101m/C *GB* Rod Taylor, Jim Brown, Yvette Mimieux, Kenneth More, Peter Carsten, Calvin Lockhart, Andre Morell; *D:* Jack Cardiff; *W:* Quentin Werty, Adrian Spies; *M:* Jacques Loussier. **VHS** $19.98 *MGM* 𝄞𝄞½

Dark Passage Bogart plays a convict who escapes from San Quentin to prove he was framed for the murder of his wife. He undergoes plastic surgery and is hidden and aided by Bacall as he tries to find the real killer. Stars can't quite compensate for a far-fetched script and so-so direction.

1947 107m/B Humphrey Bogart, Lauren Bacall, Agnes Moorehead, Bruce (Herman Brix) Bennett, Tom D'Andrea; *D:* Delmer Daves. **VHS, Beta** $19.95 *FOX* 𝄞𝄞½

The Dark Past A crazy, escaped convict holds a psychologist and his family hostage, and the two men engage in psychological cat-and-mouse combat. An underrated thriller with off-beat casting.
1949 75m/B William Holden, Lee J. Cobb, Nina Foch, Adele Jergens; *D:* Rudolph Mate; *M:* George Duning. **VHS, Beta** $69.95 *COL* 𝄞𝄞

Dark Places Masquerading as a hospital administrator, a former mental patient inherits the ruined mansion of a man who had killed his wife and children and died insane. As he lives in the house, the spirit of its former owner seems to overcome him with a need to repeat the crime. Meanwhile, Lee, Collins, and Lom think the nut is hiding money they would like to get their collective hands on. Low-budget but fairly effective.
1973 (PG) 91m/C *GB* Joan Collins, Christopher Lee, Robert Hardy; *D:* Don Sharp. **VHS, Beta** $24.98 *SUE* 𝄞𝄞

The Dark Power Ex-cowboy LaRue and his trusty whip provide this flick with its only excitement. As sheriff, he must deal with the dead Mexican warriors who rise to wreak havoc when a house is built on their burial ground.
1985 87m/C Lash LaRue, Anna Lane Tatum; *D:* Phil Smoot. **VHS, Beta** *NO* 𝄞

The Dark Ride Lunatic picks up women with the intention of raping and killing them. Ugly thriller based on the evil deeds of serial murderer Ted Bundy.
1984 83m/C James Luisi, Susan Sullivan, Martin Speer; *D:* Jeremy Hoenack. **VHS, Beta** $69.95 *MED* 𝄞½

Dark Rider Dark Rider is a mysterious, motorcycle riding hero who comes to the rescue of a small town. Besieged by a gangster who buys up all their land, the townspeople must abandon their homes and indeed, their very dreams. That is until Dark Rider rolls into to town to enact his own unique brand of vengeance.
1991 94m/C Joe Estevez, Doug Shanklin, Alicia Kowalski, David Shark, Chuck Williams; *W:* Chuck Williams, Bob Ivy. **VHS** $79.95 *AIP* 𝄞½

Dark River: A Father's Revenge When his daughter is killed in a toxic waste dump accident, a man begins revenge on the company and its managers. Tense, with important message.
1990 95m/C Helen Hunt, Mike Farrell, Tess Harper. **VHS** $79.98 *TTC* 𝄞𝄞

Dark Sanity Uninvolving attempt at horror has a recently de-institutionalized woman envisioning death and destruction (something you'll wish the film would do) while everyone else just thinks she's losing her marbles. Problem is we don't really care. *AKA:* Straight Jacket.
1982 89m/C Aldo Ray, Kory Clark, Andy Gwyn, Bobby Holt; *D:* Martin Greene. **VHS, Beta** $59.95 *PSM* Woof!

The Dark Secret of Harvest Home An urban couple confront a pagan cult in the New England town into which they've moved. Based upon the Thomas Tryon novel. Made for television.
1978 118m/C Bette Davis, Rosanna Arquette, David Ackroyd, Rene Auberjonois, Michael O'Keefe; *D:* Leonard Penn. **VHS, Beta** $59.95 *MCA* 𝄞𝄞½

Dark Shadows "Dark Shadows" had already been on television for about eight months when the character of Barnabas Collins was introduced. This volume serves to familiarize the viewer with characters and situations that were running on the series at that time. These are the first five episodes that feature Barnabas. Original air dates are April 17 to May 1, 1967. Contains both B&W and color episodes. Additional episodes available.

1967 120m/B Joan Bennett, Kathryn Leigh Scott, John Karlen, Alexandra Moltke, Jonathan Frid, David Selby, Kate Jackson; *D:* John Sedwick. **VHS $29.95** *MPI, MOV* ♫♫½

The Dark Side of Love A young girl gets involved with the rougher side of New Orleans society, gets pregnant, and realizes how she's been degraded.

1979 94m/C James Stacy, Glynnis O'Connor, Jan Sterling, Mickey Rooney. **VHS, Beta $59.95** *GEM* ♫½

Dark Side of Midnight A super-detective tracks down a psychopathic killer. *AKA:* The Creeper.

1986 (R) 108m/C James Moore, Wes Olsen, Sandy Schemmel, Dave Bowling. **VHS, Beta $79.95** *PSM* ♫½

Dark Side of the Moon Members of a space ship sent on a routine mission to the far side of the moon, discover an unknown force that feeds on human emotion and consumes the soul. Lukewarm science fiction/horror.

1990 (R) 96m/C William Bledsoe, Alan Blumenfeld, John Diehl, Robert Sampson, Wendy MacDonald, Camilla More, Joe Turkel; *D:* D.J. Webster. **VHS $89.95** *VMK* ♫

Dark Star John Carpenter's directorial debut is a low-budget, sci-fi satire which focuses on a group of scientists whose mission is to destroy unstable planets. During their journey, they battle their alien mascot (who closely resembles a walking beach ball), as well as a "sensitive" and intelligent bombing device which starts to question the meaning of its existence. Enjoyable early feature from John "Halloween" Carpenter and Dan "Aliens" O'Bannon. Fun, weird, and unpredictable.

1974 (G) 95m/C Dan O'Bannon, Brian Narelle; *D:* John Carpenter; *W:* Dan O'Bannon, John Carpenter; *M:* John Carpenter. **VHS, Beta $19.95** *HHT, IME, VCI* ♫♫♫

Dark Tide Erotic action thriller about a pair of deep sea divers whose love life is disturbed when their boat captain becomes sexually fixated on the woman. Also available in an uncut, unrated version.

1993 (R) 92m/C Brigitte Bako, Richard Tyson, Chris Sarandon. **VHS $92.95** *VMK* ♫♫

Dark Tower Decent cast is wasted in yet another inept attempt at horror. An architect is dismayed to learn that an evil force is inhabiting her building and it might just be the ghost of her dearly departed husband.

1987 (R) 91m/C Michael Moriarty, Jenny Agutter, Theodore Bikel, Carol Lynley, Anne Lockhart, Kevin McCarthy; *D:* Ken Barnett. **VHS, Beta $79.98** *VTR, IME* ♫

Dark Universe An alien terror wants to conquer the Earth and make its inhabitants their new food source.

1993 (R) 83m/C Blake Pickett, Cherie Scott, Bently Tittle, John Maynard, Paul Austin Saunders, Tom Ferguson, Steve Barkett, Joe Estevez, Patrick Moran; *D:* Steve Latshaw; *W:* Patrick Moran. **VHS, Beta $79.95** *PSM* ♫½

Dark Victory A spoiled young heiress discovers she is dying from a brain tumor. She attempts to pack a lifetime of parties into a few months, but is rescued by her doctor, with whom she falls in love. Classic final scene with Davis at the top of her form. Bogart plays an Irish stable hand, but not

especially well. Also available in a colorized version.

1939 106m/B Bette Davis, George Brent, Geraldine Fitzgerald, Humphrey Bogart, Ronald Reagan, Henry Travers; *D:* Edmund Goulding. **VHS, Beta $19.95** *MGM* ♫♫♫½

Dark Waters The drowning death of her parents has left a young woman mentally unstable. She returns to her family home in the backwaters of Louisiana with her peculiar aunt and uncle to serve as guardians. It eventually becomes apparent that someone is trying to drive her insane. This one tends to be rather murky and it's not simply due to the plentiful scenes of misty swampland.

1944 93m/B Merle Oberon, Franchot Tone, Thomas Mitchell, Fay Bainter, Elisha Cook Jr., John Qualen, Rex Ingram; *D:* Andre de Toth; *M:* Miklos Rozsa. **VHS, Beta $19.95** *STE* ♫♫

The Dark Wind The first of Tony Hillerman's popular Native American mysteries comes to the screen in a lame adaptation. Phillips stars as the Navaho cop investigating a murder on a New Mexico Indian reservation. Since the Navaho believe a "dark wind" enters a man's soul when he does evil, expect some "spirited" goings-on as well.

1991 (R) 111m/C Lou Diamond Phillips; *D:* Errol Morris. **VHS $92.98** *LIV* ♫½

Darker than Amber John D. MacDonald's houseboat-dwelling detective Travis McGee (Taylor) rescues a girl (Kendall) he's fallen for, and soon discovers that the mugs who thugged her were part of a collection racket. A violent action melodrama upgraded from its original "R" rating.

1970 (R) 96m/C Rod Taylor, Suzy Kendall, Theodore Bikel, Jane Russell, James Booth, Janet MacLachlan, William Smith, Anna Capri, Chris Robinson; *D:* Robert Clouse. **VHS** *NO* ♫♫

Darkest Africa Legendary animal trainer Beatty is the hero of this 15 episode cliffhanger serial as he vies with beasts—both animal and human. *AKA:* Batmen of Africa; King of the Jungleland.

1936 270m/B Clyde Beatty, Manuel King, Elaine Shepard. **$49.98** *REP, MOV* ♫♫

Darkman Raimi's disfigured-man-seeks-revenge suspenser is comicbook kitsch cross-pollinated with a strain of gothic horror. Neeson plays a scientist who's on the verge of discovering the key to cloning body parts; brutally attacked by the henchmen of a crooked politico, his lab is destroyed and he's left for dead. Turns out he's not dead—just horribly disfigured and a wee bit chafed—and he stalks his deserving victims from the shadows, using his lab know-how to disguise his rugged bad looks. Exquisitely violent. Montage by Pablo Ferro.

1990 (R) 96m/C Liam Neeson, Frances McDormand, Larry Drake, Colin Friels, Nelson Mashita, Jenny Agutter, Rafael H. Robledo; *D:* Sam Raimi; *W:* Sam Raimi, Ivan Raimi; *M:* Danny Elfman. **VHS, Beta $19.95** *MCA, CCB* ♫♫♫

Darkroom An unstable young man devises a scheme to photograph his father in bed with his mistress, and then use the pics to blackmail dear ol' dad.

1990 90m/C Jill Pierce, Jeffrey Allen Arbaugh, Sara Lee Wade, Aaron Teich; *D:* Terrence O'Hara. **VHS** *NO* ♫½

The Darkside In this frightening drama, a young prostitute and an innocent cabbie attempt to escape the clutches of a maniacal film producer with a secret he won't let them reveal.

1987 (R) 95m/C Tony Galati, Cyndy Preston; *D:* Constantino Magnatta. **VHS $79.95** *VMK* ♫½

Darktown Strutters Effort to satirize racial stereotypes is humorless and ineffective. Black female motorcycle gang searches for the kidnapped mother of one of the members. *AKA:* Get Down and Boogie.

1974 (PG) 85m/C Trina Parks, Roger E. Mosley, Shirley Washington; *D:* William Witney. **VHS, Beta $59.98** *NLC* ♫

Darling Young amoral model tries to hold boredom at bay by having a number of love affairs. She joins the international jet set and manages to reach the top of European society by marrying a prince. She then learns what an empty life she has. Christie won an Oscar for her portrayal of the disillusioned, cynical young woman.

1965 122m/B *GB* Julie Christie, Dirk Bogarde, Laurence Harvey; *D:* John Schlesinger; *W:* Frederic Raphael. Academy Awards '65: Best Actress (Christie), Best Costume Design (B & W), Best Story; Nominations: Best Director (Schlesinger), Best Picture; British Academy Awards '65: Best Actor (Bogarde), Best Actress (Christie); National Board of Review Awards '65: 10 Best Films of the Year, Best Actress (Christie), Best Director (Schlesinger). **VHS, Beta $19.95** *COL, VYG, BTV* ♫♫♫½

Darling Lili Big-budget WWI spy comedy/musical with Andrews as a German spy posing as an English music hall performer who falls in love with squadron leader Hudson and finds she can't betray him. A critical flop when first released, film has its charm though director Edwards did much better for Andrews in "Victor/Victoria." ♫Whistling Away the Dark; The Girl In No Man's Land; Smile Away Each Rainy Day; I'll Give You Three Guesses; Your Good Will Ambassador; Darling Lili; The Little Birds.

1970 136m/C Julie Andrews, Rock Hudson, Jeremy Kemp, Jacques Marin, Michael Witney, Vernon Dobtcheff; *D:* Blake Edwards; *W:* Blake Edwards, William Peter Blatty; *M:* Henry Mancini, Johnny Mercer. **VHS $19.98** *PAR* ♫♫½

D.A.R.Y.L. The little boy found by the side of the road is too polite, too honest and too smart. His friend explains to him the necessity of imperfection (If you don't want the grown-ups to bother you too much) and he begins to become more like a real little boy. But the American military has a top-secret interest in this child, since he is in fact the combination of a cloned body and a computer brain. More interesting when it's involved with the human beings and less so when it focuses on science.

1985 (PG) 100m/C Mary Beth Hurt, Michael McKean, Barret Oliver, Colleen Camp; *D:* Simon Wincer; *W:* David Ambrose, Allan Scott; *M:* Marvin Hamlisch. **VHS, Beta $14.95** *PAR* ♫♫

Das Boot Superb detailing of life in a German U-boat during WWII. Intense, claustrophobic atmosphere complemented by nail-biting action provides a realistic portrait of the stressful conditions that were endured on these submarines. Excellent performances, especially from Prochnow. With English subtitles. Originally a 6-hour special made for German television. Also available in a dubbed version. From the novel by Lothar-Guenther Buccheim. *AKA:* The Boat.

1981 (R) 150m/C *GE* Juergen Prochnow, Herbert Gronemeyer, Klaus Wennemann, Hubertus Bengsch, Martin Semmelrogge, Bernd Tauber, Erwin Leder, Martin May; *D:* Wolfgang Petersen; *W:* Wolfgang Petersen; *M:* Klaus Doldinger. **VHS, Beta $19.95** *COL, APD, ING* ♫♫♫♫

Das Testament des Dr. Mabuse The third, and only sound, Mabuse film by Lang. The infamous crime lord/megalomaniac plots the world's destruction from the confines of an asylum cell. In German, with

English subtitles. Released as "The Last Will of Dr. Mabuse" in the U.S. in 1943.
1933 122m/B *GE* Rudolf Klein-Rogge, Otto Wernicke, Gustav Diesl, Karl Meixner; *D:* Fritz Lang. VHS, Beta $29.98 *SNC, SUE, GLV* 𝄞𝄞𝄞½

Date Bait When a teen couple decides—much to their parents' chagrin—to elope, they find themselves on a date with danger when their post-nuptials are plagued by pushers and assorted other bad guys.
1960 71m/B Gary Clarke, Marlo Ryan, Richard Gering, Danny Logan; *D:* O'Dale Ireland. VHS, Beta $16.95 *SNC* 𝄞

Date with an Angel When aspiring musician Knight fishes a beautiful angel out of the swimming pool, he is just trying to rescue her. But the beauty of the angel overwhelms him and he finds himself questioning his upcoming wedding to Cates, a cosmetic mogul's daughter. Sickeningly cute and way too sentimental, though Beart's beauty is other-wordly.
1987 (PG) 114m/C Emmanuelle Beart, Michael E. Knight, Phoebe Cates, David Dukes, Bibi Besch, Albert Macklin, David Hunt, Michael Goodwin; *D:* Tom McLoughlin. VHS, Beta $19.99 *HBO* 𝄞½

A Date with Judy Standard post-war musical dealing with teenage mix-ups in and around a big high school dance. Choreography by Stanley Donen. ♫Cuanto La Gusto; Strictly on the Corny Side; It's a Most Unusual Day; Judaline; I've Got a Date with Judy; I'm Gonna Meet My Mary; Temptation; Mulligatawny.
1948 114m/C Jane Powell, Elizabeth Taylor, Carmen Miranda, Wallace Beery, Robert Stack, Xavier Cugat, Selena Royle, Leon Ames, The Scorpions; *D:* Richard Thorpe. VHS, Beta $19.98 *MGM, MLB* 𝄞𝄞

Daughter of Death A little mentally off-center since she witnessed the gruesome rape and murder of her mother, a teenage girl doesn't bond well with her new mom when dad remarries. *AKA:* Julie Darling.
1982 (R) 100m/C *CA GE* Anthony (Tony) Franciosa, Isabelle Mejias, Sybil Danning, Cindy Gurling, Paul Hubbard, Benjamin Schmoll; *D:* Paul Nicholas. VHS $59.99 *FCT* 𝄞

The Daughter of Dr. Jekyll The doc's daughter believes she may have inherited her father's evil curse when several of the locals are found dead.
1957 71m/B John Agar, Arthur Shields, John Dierkes, Gloria Talbott; *D:* Edgar G. Ulmer. VHS, Beta $39.98 *FOX* 𝄞½

Daughter of Don Q Delores' father is very rich with a huge real estate empire and she is his only heir. Greedy cousin Carlos would like to change that—by killing Delores. Delores must dodge speeding cars, hurling harpoons, and more to escape Carlos' evil plot. Part of "The Cliffhanger Serials" series.
1946 166m/B Adrian Booth, Kirk Alyn, Leroy Mason. VHS $29.98 *REP, MOV* 𝄞𝄞

Daughter of Horror A young woman finds herself involved with a porcine mobster who resembles her abusive father. Trouble is, Dad's dead, and daughter dearest abetted his departure. Obscure venture into expressionism that was initially banned by the New York State Board of Censors. Shot on a low budget (how low was it? So low that McMahon narrated because shooting with sound was too expensive). The 55 minutes tend to lag, although the film should be intriguing to genre enthusiasts and to fans of things pseudo-Freudian. *AKA:* Dementia.
1955 60m/B Adrienne Barrett, Bruno Ve Sota, Ben Roseman; *D:* John Parker; *W:* John Parker. VHS $19.98 *NOS, SNC, MRV* 𝄞𝄞

Daughter of the Dragon Fu Manchu is again on the prowl, this time sending his daughter to murder Fletcher to avenge the death of his wife and son during China's Boxer Rebellion. Based on a Sax Rohmer story.
1931 70m/B Anna May Wong, Warner Oland, Sessue Hayakawa, Bramwell Fletcher, Holmes Herbert; *D:* Lloyd Corrigan. VHS $19.95 *NOS* 𝄞𝄞

Daughter of the Tong FBI agent gets tong twisted when he tries to put a lid on a smuggling ring headed by a woman (who's beautiful, of course). Something that resembles acting is wasted in a mess of a movie.
1939 56m/B Evelyn Brent, Grant Withers, Dorothy Short, Dave O'Brien; *D:* Raymond K. Johnson. VHS, Beta $16.95 *NOS, SNC* 𝄞

Daughters of Darkness Newlyweds on their way to England stop at a posh French hotel. There they meet a beautiful woman whom the hotel owner swears had been there forty years ago, even though she hasn't aged a bit. When she introduces herself as Countess of Bathory (the woman who bathed in the blood of virgins to stay young) folks begin to wonder. A really superb erotic vampire film charged with sensuality and a sense of dread. *AKA:* Le Rouge aux Levres.
1971 (R) 87m/C *BE GE IT FR* Delphine Seyrig, John Karlen, Daniele Ouimet, Andrea Rau, Paul Esser, Georges Jamin, Joris Collet, Fons Rademakers; *D:* Harry Kumel. VHS, Beta *NO* 𝄞𝄞𝄞

Daughters of Satan Selleck, in an early role as a virile museum buyer, antagonizes a coven of witches when he purchases a painting. His wife, played by Grant, becomes a target of the witches' revenge and salacious shenanigans ensue.
1972 (R) 96m/C Tom Selleck, Barra Grant, Paraluman, Tani Phelps Guthrie; *D:* Hollingsworth Morse. VHS, Beta *NO* 𝄞𝄞

Daughters of the Dust Five women of a Gullah family living on the Sea Islands off the Georgia coast in 1902 contemplate moving to the mainland in this emotional tale of change. The Gullah are descendants of West African slaves and their isolation has kept their superstitions and native dialect (a mixture of Western African, Creole, and English) intact. Family bonds and memories are celebrated with a quiet narrative and beautiful cinematography in Dash's feature-film directorial debut.
1992 113m/C Cora Lee Day, Barbara O, Alva Rogers, Kaycee Moore, Cheryl Lynn Bruce, Adisa Anderson; *D:* Julie Dash; *W:* Julie Dash; *M:* John Barnes. VHS $79.95 *KIV, FCT, PMS* 𝄞𝄞𝄞½

Dave Regular guy Dave Kovic (Kline) is a dead ringer for the President, launching him into the White House after the prez suffers a stroke in embarrassing circumstances. Seamless comedy prompts lots of hearty laughs and the feel-good faith that despite the overwhelming odds, everything will turn out just fine. Political cameos abound: look for real-life Senators Alan Simpson, Paul Simon, Howard Metzenbaum, Tom Harkin, and Christopher Dodd as well as the commentators from TV's "The McLaughlin Group," and Stone, poking fun at himself on "Larry King Live," as he tries to convince the public there's a conspiracy going on.
1993 (PG-13) 110m/C Kevin Kline, Sigourney Weaver, Frank Langella, Kevin Dunn, Ving Rhames, Ben Kingsley, Charles Grodin, Faith Prince, Laura Linney, Bonnie Hunt, Parley Baer, Stefan Gierasch, Anna Deavere Smith, Bonnie Bartlett; *Cameos:* Oliver Stone, Arnold Schwarzenegger, Jay Leno, Larry King; *D:* Ivan

Reitman; *W:* Gary Ross; *M:* James Newton Howard. VHS, Beta $95.99 *WAR, BTV, FCT* 𝄞𝄞𝄞

David A haunting portrait of the survival of a Jewish teenager in Berlin during the Nazi reign of terror, based on the novel by Joel Koenig. Universally acclaimed, this was the first film about the Holocaust made in Germany by a German Jew. In German with English subtitles.
1979 106m/C *GE* Mario Fischel, Walter Taub, Irene Vrkjan, Torsten Hentes, Eva Mattes; *D:* Peter Lilienthal. VHS, Beta $79.95 *KIV, GLV, ING* 𝄞𝄞𝄞½

David and Bathsheba The Bible story comes alive in this lush and colorful Fox production. Peck and Hayward are great together and Peck is properly concerned about the wrath of God over his transgressions. Terrific costumes and special effects, lovely music and a fine supporting cast keep this a notch above other Biblical epics.
1951 116m/C Gregory Peck, Susan Hayward, Raymond Massey, Kieron Moore, James Robertson Justice, Jayne Meadows, John Sutton, Dennis Hoey, Francis X. Bushman, George Zucco; *D:* Henry King; *W:* Philip Dunne. VHS $19.98 *FXV, FOX* 𝄞𝄞½

David and Lisa Director Perry was given an Oscar for this sensitive independently-produced film. Adapted from Theodore Isaac Rubin's true case history novel concerning a young man and woman who fall in love while institutionalized for mental illness. Dullea and Margolin are excellent in the title roles of this sleeper.
1962 94m/B Keir Dullea, Janet Margolin, Howard da Silva, Neva Patterson, Clifton James; *D:* Frank Perry. VHS, Beta $69.95 *COL, MRV* 𝄞𝄞𝄞

David Copperfield Superior adaptation of Charles Dickens' great novel. An orphan grows to manhood in Victorian England with a wide variety of help and harm. Terrific acting by Bartholomew, Fields, Rathbone, and all the rest. Lavish production, lovingly filmed.
1935 132m/B Lionel Barrymore, W.C. Fields, Freddie Bartholomew, Maureen O'Sullivan, Basil Rathbone, Lewis Stone, Frank Lawton, Madge Evans, Roland Young, Edna May Oliver, Lennox Pawle, Elsa Lanchester, Una O'Connor, Arthur Treacher; *D:* George Cukor; *W:* Howard Estabrook, Hugh Walpole; *M:* Herbert Stothart. Academy Awards '35 Nominations: Best Film Editing; Academy Awards '36: Best Picture; National Board of Review Awards '35: 10 Best Films of the Year. VHS, Beta $19.98 *MGM* 𝄞𝄞𝄞𝄞

David Copperfield This British made-for-television production is more faithful to the Dickens classic than any of its predecessors. The added material, however, fails to highlight any one character as had the successful 1935 MGM version. Still, the exceptional (and largely stage-trained) cast do much to redeem the production.
1970 118m/C Richard Attenborough, Cyril Cusack, Edith Evans, Pamela Franklin, Susan Hampshire, Wendy Hiller, Ron Moody, Laurence Olivier; *D:* Delbert Mann; *M:* Malcolm Arnold. VHS *FOX* 𝄞𝄞½

David Holzman's Diary Director McBride helmed this fake underground movie, a legendary put-on focusing on film student pretensions. Holzman is a sincere geek who seeks the meaning of life by filming his own existence in oh-so-chic grainy black and white verite. He learns reality is more important than film. Drolly captures the state of the art in late '60's America.
1967 71m/B L.M. Kit Carson; *D:* Jim McBride; *W:* L.M. Kit Carson, Jim McBride. VHS $79.95 *FXL* 𝄞𝄞𝄞

DaVinci's War Frank DaVinci's sister is murdered and he wants revenge. So he hooks up with a professional killer and a bunch of Vietnam vets and gets the firepower he needs to blow the bad guys away.
1992 (R) 94m/C Joey Travolta, Michael Nouri, Vanity, Richard Foronjy, Branscombe Richmond, Sam Jones, Jack Bannon; *Cameos:* Brian Robbins, James Russo; *D:* Raymond Martino; *W:* Raymond Martino; *M:* Jeff Lass. **VHS $89.95** TRI ⅒

Davy Crockett and the River Pirates Another Disney splice and dice of two episodes from the television series, chronicling the further adventures of our frontier hero. Davy meets up with Mike Fink, the King of the Ohio River, and the two engage in a furious keelboat race, and then unite to track down a group of thieves masquerading as Indians and threatening the peace.
1956 (G) 81m/C Fess Parker, Buddy Ebsen, Jeff York; *D:* Norman Foster. **VHS, Beta** DIS, OM ⅒½

Davy Crockett, King of the Wild Frontier Three episodes of the popular Disney television series are blended together here to present the life and some of the adventures of Davy Crockett. These include his days as an Indian fighter and his gallant stand in defense of the Alamo. Well-done by a splendid cast, the film helped to spread Davy-mania among the children of the 1950s.
1955 (PG) 93m/C Fess Parker, Buddy Ebsen, Hans Conried, Ray Whiteside, Pat Hogan, William "Billy" Bakewell, Basil Ruysdael, Kenneth Tobey; *D:* Norman Foster. **VHS, Beta $19.99** DIS, BTV ⅒½

Dawn! True story of Dawn Fraser, an Olympic champion swimmer and an unfulfilled woman willing to fight for her happiness.
1983 114m/C Bronwyn MacKay-Payne, Tom Richards. **VHS, Beta** NO ⅒

Dawn Express Nazi spies infiltrate the U.S. in search of a secret formula designed to enhance the power of gasoline. Another film made to contribute to the war effort that doesn't make much sense.
1942 63m/B Michael Whalen, Anne Nagel, William "Billy" Bakewell, Constance Worth, Hans von Twardowski, Jack Mulhall, George Pembroke, Kenneth Harlan, Robert Frazer; *D:* Albert Herman. **VHS, Beta $16.95** SNC ⅒

Dawn of the Dead Romero's gruesome sequel to his "Night of the Living Dead." A mysterious plague causes the recently dead to rise from their graves and scour the countryside for living flesh. Very violent, gory, graphic, and shocking, yet not without humor. Gives interesting consideration to the violence created by the living humans in their efforts to save themselves.
1978 126m/C David Emge, Ken Foree, Gaylen Ross; *D:* George A. Romero; *W:* George A. Romero. **VHS, Beta $14.98** REP, FCT ⅒⅒½

Dawn of the Mummy Lousy plot and bad acting—not to mention gore galore—do this one in. A photographer and a bevy of young fashion models travel to Egypt for a special shoot. They unwittingly stumble upon an ancient tomb, teeming with vengeance-minded mummies.
1982 93m/C Brenda King, Barry Sattels, George Peck, Joan Levy; *D:* Frank Agrama. **VHS, Beta** NO Woof!

Dawn of the Pirates An adventurer stumbles upon a murderous tribe of Tughs and the beautiful white woman they captured. *AKA:* La Secta de los Tughs.
19?? 95m/C SP **VHS, Beta** NO ⅒½

Dawn on the Great Divide Jones' last film before his tragic and untimely death trying to save people from a fire at the Coconut Grove in Boston. Wagon train has to battle not only Indians, but bad guys as well. Plot provides more depth than the usual western fare.
1942 57m/B Buck Jones, Tim McCoy, Raymond Hatton, Mona Barrie, Robert Lowery, Betty Blythe, Jan Wiley, Harry Woods, Roy Barcroft; *D:* Howard Bretherton. **VHS, Beta $19.95** NOS, MRV, VCN ⅒½

Dawn Patrol Flynn plays a flight commander whose nerves are shot in this story of the British Royal Flying Corps during WWI. The focus is on the effects that the pressures and deaths have on all those concerned. Fine performances from all in this well-done remake of the 1930 film.
1938 103m/B Errol Flynn, David Niven, Basil Rathbone, Donald Crisp, Barry Fitzgerald, Melville Cooper; *D:* Edmund Goulding. **VHS, Beta $19.98** FOX, MGM ⅒⅒

Dawn Rider Formula western has all the right ingredients: Wayne as a cowboy out to get revenge on the gang that murdered his father. Features stuntman Canutt in rare acting role.
1935 60m/B John Wayne, Marion Burns, Yakima Canutt; *D:* Robert North Bradbury. **VHS $8.95** CNG, REP, MRV ⅒

Dawn Rider/Frontier Horizon A double feature of two of Wayne's earliest western films.
1939 114m/B John Wayne, Jennifer Jones, Marion Burns; *D:* Robert North Bradbury, George Sherman. **VHS, Beta $34.95** REP ⅒

The Dawning An Irish revolutionary in the 1920's draws a young woman into his dangerous world of romance, intrigue and death. Howard's last film. Based on the novel "Old Jest" by Jennifer Johnston.
1988 97m/C Anthony Hopkins, Jean Simmons, Trevor Howard, Rebecca Pidgeon, Hugh Grant, Tara MacGowan; *D:* Robert Knights. **VHS $89.98** LIV, PMS ⅒½

The Dawson Patrol Royal Canadian Mountie dog-sled race turns into a dramatic battle for survival.
1978 75m/C George R. Robinson, Tim Henry, Neil Dainaro, James B. Douglas; *D:* Peter Kelly. **VHS, Beta $49.95** TWE ⅒½

The Day After Powerful drama graphically depicts the nuclear bombing of a midwestern city and its after-effects on the survivors. Made for television, and very controversial when first shown, gathering huge ratings and vast media coverage.
1983 126m/C Jason Robards Jr., JoBeth Williams, John Lithgow, Steve Guttenberg; *D:* Nicholas Meyer. **VHS, Beta $9.98** SUE ⅒⅒

The Day and the Hour A woman becomes accidentally involved in the resistance movement during the Nazi occupation of France in WWII. *AKA:* Today We Live; Le Jour et L'Heure; Il Giorno e L'Ora; Viviamo Oggi.
1963 110m/C FR JP Simone Signoret, Stuart Whitman, Genevieve Page, Michel Piccoli, Reggie Nalder, Pierre Dux, Billy Kearns; *D:* Rene Clement; *M:* Claude Bolling. **VHS, Beta $24.95** ING, MON ⅒½

A Day at the Races Though it seems labored at times, the brilliance of the brothers Marx still comes through in this rather weak tale of a patient in a sanitorium who convinces horse doctor Groucho to take on running the place. ♫A Message from the Man in the Moon; On Blue Venetian Waters;

Tomorrow is Another Day; All God's Chillun Got Rhythm.
1937 111m/B Groucho Marx, Harpo Marx, Chico Marx, Sig Rumann, Douglass Dumbrille, Margaret Dumont, Allan Jones, Maureen O'Sullivan; *D:* Sam Wood. **VHS, Beta $19.95** MGM, CCB ⅒⅒½

Day for Night A wryly affectionate look at the profession of moviemaking—its craft, character, and the personalities that interact against the performances commanded by the camera. In French with English subtitles. *AKA:* La Nuit Americaine.
1973 (PG) 116m/C FR Jean-Pierre Leaud, Jacqueline Bisset, Jean-Pierre Aumont, Valentina Cortese, Alexandra Stewart, Dani, Nathalie Baye, Francois Truffaut; *D:* Francois Truffaut; *W:* Suzanne Schiffman, Jean-Louis Richard, Francois Truffaut; *M:* Georges Delerue. Academy Awards '73: Best Foreign Language Film; Nominations: Best Director (Truffaut), Best Original Screenplay, Best Supporting Actress (Cortese); British Academy Awards '73: Best Director (Truffaut), Best Film, Best Supporting Actress (Cortese); National Society of Film Critics Awards '73: Best Director (Truffaut), Best Film, Best Supporting Actress (Cortese). **VHS, Beta $19.95** ING, WAR, APD ⅒⅒⅒

A Day for Thanks on Walton's Mountain Many of the original television-show cast members returned for this sentimental Thanksgiving reunion on Walton's Mountain. Made for television.
1982 97m/C Ralph Waite, Ellen Corby, Judy Norton-Taylor, Eric Scott, Jon Walmsley, Robert Wightman, Mary McDonough, David W. Harper, Kami Cotler, Joe Conley, Ronnie Clair Edwards, Richard Gilliland, Melinda Naud; *D:* Harry Harris. **VHS $19.98** WAR ⅒

A Day in October Niels Jensen (Sweeney) is a Danish resistance fighter fighting in Copenhagen as the Nazis prepare to invade Denmark in 1943. During a sabotage attempt he's injured and rescued by Sara, a young Jewish woman. Her family reluctantly hides the young man as they finally face up to the Nazi reality. Based on historical fact. Good performances help what is otherwise an average script. Filmed on location in Denmark.
1992 (PG-13) 96m/C D.B. Sweeney, Kelly Wolf, Tovah Feldshuh, Daniel Benzali, Ole Lemmeke, Kim Romer, Anders Peter Bro, Lars Oluf Larsen; *D:* Kenneth Madsen; *W:* Damian F. Slattery; *M:* Jens Lysdal. **VHS $89.95** ACA, FOX ⅒½

A Day in the Country The son of the famed painter gives us the moving tale of a young woman's sudden and intense love for a man she meets while on a picnic with her family. Beautifully adapted from a story by Guy de Maupassant. Renowned photographer Henri Cartier-Bresson contributed to the wonderful cinematography. In French with English subtitles. *AKA:* Une Partie de Campagne.
1946 40m/B FR Sylvia Bataille, Georges Darnoux, Jane Marken, Paul Temps; *D:* Jean Renoir. **VHS, Beta $24.95** NOS, MRV, DVT ⅒⅒⅒½

A Day in the Death of Joe Egg Based on the Peter Nichols play, an unlikely black comedy about a British couple trying to care for their retarded/autistic child, nearly destroying their marriage in the process. They begin to contemplate euthanasia as a solution. Well-acted, but potentially offensive to some.
1971 (R) 106m/C GB Alan Bates, Janet Suzman, Elizabeth Robillard, Peter Bowles, Joan Hickson, Sheila Gish; *D:* Peter Medak; *W:* David Deutsch. **VHS, Beta $69.95** COL ⅒⅒⅒

The Day It Came to Earth Completely silly and unbelievable sci-fi flick has meteor crashing into the watery grave of a mobster. The decomposed corpse is revived

by the radiation and plots to take revenge on those who fitted him with cement shoes.
1977 (PG) 89m/C Roger Manning, Wink Roberts, Bob Ginnaven, Rita Wilson, Delight de Bruine; **D:** Harry Z. Thomason. **VHS, Beta** *NO Woof!*

Day of Atonement It's a war for power between rival druglords when Hanin is released from prison and finds out his son and cousin are battling over turf. Then Walken is dragged into the fracas. Beals is the government agent trying to regain some control of the dangerous situation.
1993 (R) 127m/C Christopher Walken, Jennifer Beals, Jill Clayburgh, Roger Hanin, Richard Berry. **VHS** $92.95 *VMK* ♂♂½

Day of Judgment A mysterious stranger arrives in a town to slaughter those people who violate the Ten Commandments.
1981 101m/C William T. Hicks, Harris Bloodworth, Brownlee Davis; **D:** C.D.H. Reynolds. **VHS, Beta** *NO* ♂½

Day of the Animals Nature gone wild. It seems a depleted ozone layer has exposed the animals to the sun's radiation, turning Bambi and Bugs into brutal killers. A group of backpackers trek in the Sierras, unaware of the transformation. Far-fetched and silly (we hope). **AKA:** Something is Out There.
1977 (PG) 95m/C Christopher George, Leslie Nielsen, Lynda Day George, Richard Jaeckel, Michael Ansara, Ruth Roman, Jon Cedar, Susan Backlinie, Andrew Stevens, Gil Lamb; **D:** William Girdler; **W:** William W. Norton Sr. **VHS** $59.95 *MED* ♂

Day of the Assassin A Mideast shah's yacht explodes, sending a huge fortune to the bottom of a murky bay. This sets off a rampage of treasure hunting by a variety of ruthless mercenaries.
1981 94m/C Glenn Ford, Chuck Connors, Richard Roundtree, Henry Silva, Jorge Rivero; **D:** Brian Trenchard-Smith. **VHS, Beta** $79.95 *PSM* ♂

Day of the Cobra A corrupt narcotics bureau official hires an ex-cop to find a heroin kingpin on the back streets of Genoa, Italy.
1984 95m/C *IT* Franco Nero, Sybil Danning, Mario Maranzana, Licinia Lentini, William Berger; **D:** Enzo G. Castellari. **VHS, Beta** $49.95 *MED* ♂½

Day of the Dead The third in Romero's trilogy of films about flesh-eating zombies taking over the world. Romero hasn't thought up anything new for the ghouls to do, and the humans are too nasty to care about this time around. For adult audiences.
1985 91m/C Lori Cardillo, Terry Alexander, Joseph Pilato, Jarleth Conroy; **D:** George A. Romero; **W:** George A. Romero. **VHS, Beta** $19.95 *MED, IME, VTR* ♂½

The Day of the Dolphin Research scientist, after successfully working out a means of teaching dolphins to talk, finds his animals kidnapped; espionage and assassination are involved. Dolphin voices by Henry, who also wrote the screenplay.
1973 (PG) 104m/C George C. Scott, Trish Van Devere, Paul Sorvino, Fritz Weaver, Jon Korkes, John Dehner, Edward Herrmann, Severn Darden; **D:** Mike Nichols; **W:** Buck Henry; **M:** Georges Delerue; **V:** Buck Henry. Academy Awards '73 Nominations: Best Sound; National Board of Review Awards '73: 10 Best Films of the Year. **VHS, Beta** $14.98 *SUE, NLC* ♂♂

The Day of the Jackal Frederick Forsyth's best-selling novel of political intrigue is splendidly brought to the screen by Zinnemann. A brilliant and ruthless assassin hired to kill Charles de Gaulle skirts the international intelligence pool, while intuitive police work to stop him. Tense, suspenseful,

beautiful location photography. Excellent acting by Fox, Cusack and Britton.
1973 (PG) 142m/C Edward Fox, Alan Badel, Tony Britton, Derek Jacobi, Cyril Cusack, Olga Georges-Picot; **D:** Fred Zinneman; **M:** Georges Delerue. **VHS, Beta** $59.95 *MCA* ♂♂♂½

The Day of the Locust Compelling adaptation of Nathaniel West's novel concerning the dark side of 1930s' Hollywood. A no-talent amoral actress's affair with a meek accountant leads to tragedy and destruction. Told from the view of a cynical art director wise to the ways of Hollywood.
1975 (R) 140m/C Donald Sutherland, Karen Black, Burgess Meredith, William Atherton, Billy Barty, Bo Hopkins, Richard Dysart, Geraldine Page; **D:** John Schlesinger; **M:** John Barry. Academy Awards '75 Nominations: Best Cinematography, Best Supporting Actor (Meredith); National Board of Review Awards '75: 10 Best Films of the Year. **VHS, Beta** $14.95 *PAR* ♂♂♂½

Day of the Maniac Psychotic drug addict will stop at nothing to support his growing habit.
1977 (R) 89m/C George Hilton, Susan Scott; **D:** Sergio Martino. **VHS, Beta** $69.95 *REP* ♂½

Day of the Panther The Panthers—the world's most formidable martial artists—are mighty torqued when panther-Linda is pithed, and they're not known to turn the other cheek. Much chop-socky kicking and shrilling.
1988 86m/C John Stanton, Eddie Stazak; **D:** Brian Trenchard-Smith. **VHS, Beta** $79.95 *CEL* ♂½

Day of the Triffids The majority of Earth's population is blinded by a meteor shower which also causes plant spores to mutate into giant carnivores. Well-done adaptation of John Wyndham's science fiction classic.
1963 94m/C Howard Keel, Janet Scott, Nicole Maurey, Kieron Moore, Mervyn Johns; **D:** Steve Sekely; **W:** Philip Yordan. **VHS, Beta** $29.95 *MED, MRV, PSM* ♂♂♂

Day of Triumph A dynamic version of the life of Christ as seen through the eyes of the apostles Andrew and Zadok, the leaders of the Zealot underground.
1954 110m/C Lee J. Cobb, Robert Wilson, Ralph Freud; **D:** Irving Pichel. **VHS** $39.95 *REP* ♂♂♂

Day of Wrath An involving psychological thriller based on records of witch trials from the early 1600s. An old woman, burned at the stake as a witch, puts a curse on the local parson and his family. Grim and unrelentingly pessimistic, moving from one horrific scene to another, director Dreyer creates a masterpiece of terror. Based on a play by Hans Wiers Jenssen. In Danish with English subtitles. **AKA:** Vredens Dag.
1943 110m/B DK Thorkild Roose, Sigrid Neiiendam, Lisbeth Movin, Preben Lerdorff, Anna Svierker; **D:** Carl Theodor Dreyer; **W:** Carl Theodor Dreyer; **M:** Poul Schierbeck. **VHS, Beta** $49.95 *ING, NOS, SNC* ♂♂♂♂

Day One Vivid recreation of one of the most turbulent periods of American history—the WWII race to build the atomic bomb. Chronicles the two year top-secret efforts of the Manhattan Project, with General Leslie Groves (Dennehy) having to supervise the project and contain the scientific rivalries. Outstanding cast, with Strathairn notable as physicist J. Robert Oppenheimer. Adapted from "Day One: Before Hiroshima and After" by Peter Wyden. Made for television.

1989 141m/C Brian Dennehy, David Strathairn, Michael Tucker, Hume Cronyn, Richard Dysart, Barnard Hughes, Hal Holbrook, David Ogden Stiers, John McMartin; **D:** Joseph Sargent; **W:** David Rintel; **M:** Mason Daring. **VHS** *WOV* ♂♂♂

The Day that Shook the World Slow-moving but intriguing account of events surrounding the assassination of Archduke Ferdinand of Austria that triggered WWI. Garnered an R-rating due to some disturbingly graphic scenes.
1978 (R) 111m/C Christopher Plummer, Florinda Bolkan, Maximilian Schell; **D:** Veljko Bulajic. **VHS** *NO* ♂♂

Day the Bookies Wept Decent yarn about cabbies tricked into buying a "racehorse." Turns out she's old as the hills and hooked on alcohol to boot, but they enter her in the big race anyway.
1939 50m/B Betty Grable, Joe Penner, Tom Kennedy, Richard Lane; **D:** Leslie Goodwins. **VHS, Beta** $34.98 *CCB* ♂♂

The Day the Earth Caught Fire The earth is knocked out of orbit and sent hurtling toward the sun when nuclear testing is done simultaneously at both the North and South Poles. Realistic and suspenseful, this is one of the best of the sci-fi genre.
1962 95m/B Janet Munro, Edward Judd, Leo McKern; **D:** Val Guest. **VHS, Beta** $9.98 *REP, KAR, CNG* ♂♂♂½

The Day the Earth Froze Witch steals the sun because she couldn't have a magical mill that produced grain, salt, and gold. Everything on Earth freezes. Based on a Finnish epic poem.
1959 67m/B FI RU Nina Anderson, Jon Powers, Ingrid Elhardt, Paul Sorenson; **D:** Gregg Sebelious. **VHS** $16.95 *SNC* ♂♂

The Day the Earth Stood Still A gentle alien lands on Earth to deliver a message of peace and a warning against experimenting with nuclear power. He finds his views echoed by a majority of the population, but not the ones who are in control. In this account based loosely on the story of Christ, Rennie is the visitor backed by the mighty robot Gort. One of the greatest science fiction films of all time.
1951 92m/B Michael Rennie, Patricia Neal, Hugh Marlowe, Sam Jaffe, Francis Bavier, Lock Martin, Bobby Gray; **D:** Robert Wise; **M:** Bernard Herrmann. **VHS, Beta** $14.98 *FOX, FCT, MLB* ♂♂♂½

The Day the Sky Exploded Sci-fi disaster drama doesn't live up to the grandiose title, as a runaway rocket ship hits the sun, unleashing an asteroid shower that threatens Earth with tidal waves, earthquakes, heat waves and terrible dialogue. The highlight of this Franco-Italian effort is the cinematography by horror director Mario Bava. **AKA:** Death From Outer Space; La Morte Viene Dalla Spazio; Le Danger Vient de l'Escape.
1957 80m/B FR IT Paul Hubschmid, Madeleine Fischer, Fiorella Mari, Ivo Garrani, Dario Michaelis; **D:** Richard Benson. **VHS** $29.95 *NOS, FCT* ♂½

The Day the Women Got Even Four suburban homemakers take up the life of vigilantes to save unsuspecting actresses from a talent agent's blackmail scheme. Made for television.
1980 98m/C JoAnn Pflug, Tina Louise, Georgia Engel, Barbara Rhoades, Julie Hagerty, Ed O'Neill; **D:** Burt Brinckerhoff; **M:** Brad Fiedel. **VHS, Beta** *TLF* ♂½

D

Day the World Ended The first science fiction film of exploitation director Roger Corman. Five survivors of nuclear holocaust discover a desert ranch house fortress owned by a survivalist (Birch) and his daughter (Nelson). With relatively abundant supplies, they fatuously wallow in false misery until a disfigured visitor, wasting away from radiation, stumbles into their paradise. His mutation into an alien being confronts them with the horror that lurks outside.
1955 79m/B Paul Birch, Lori Nelson, Adele Jergens, Raymond Hatton, Paul Dubov, Richard Denning, Touch Connors; **D:** Roger Corman. VHS $9.98 COL &

Day Time Ended A pair of glowing UFO's streaking across the sky and an alien mechanical device with long menacing appendages are only two of the bizarre phenomena witnessed from a lone house in the desert. Good special effects. Also released as "Time Warp" (1978). **AKA:** Vortex.
1980 80m/C Chris Mitchum, Jim Davis, Dorothy Malone; **D:** John Cardos; **W:** David Schmoeller; **M:** Richard Band. VHS, Beta MED, MRV &&

The Day Will Dawn Suspenseful British-made WWII thriller about a reporter and a young Norwegian girl who plot to sabotage a secret Nazi U-boat base near the girl's town. **AKA:** The Avengers.
1942 100m/B GB Deborah Kerr, Hugh Williams, Griffith Jones, Ralph Richardson, Francis L. Sullivan, Roland Culver, Niall MacGinnis, Finlay Currie, Patricia Medina; **D:** Harold French; **W:** Terence Rattigan. VHS, Beta, 8mm $24.95 VYY &&&

Day with Conrad Green Set in 1927, this program presents a somewhat farcical look at a successful Broadway producer as he attempts to cope with a full schedule of personal and business problems on the day of the funeral of his longtime assistant.
1980 60m/C Fred Gwynne. VHS, Beta MTP &&&

Daybreak In the near future America has been decimated by a nameless, sexually transmitted disease (read AIDS parable) and public policy is to quarantine the infected in concentration camp-like prisons. This leads to a quasi-official group of green-shirted thugs roaming the streets and imprisoning or killing anyone they suspect has the disease. A small resistance movement is lead by Torch (Gooding, Jr.), who happens to fall in love with Blue (Kelly), the sister of one of the fascist leaders. Based on Alan Bowne's play "Beirut, Daybreak." Made for cable television.
1993 (R) 91m/C Cuba Gooding Jr., Moira Kelly, Omar Epps, Martha Plimpton, Alice Drummond, David Eigenberg, John Savage; **Cameos:** Phil Hartman; **D:** Stephen Tolkin; **W:** Stephen Tolkin. VHS HBO && 1/2

The Daydreamer Actor/director/writer Richard stars as a bumbling fool let loose in the French corporate world with comical results. In French with subtitles. **AKA:** Absent-Minded; Le Distrait.
1975 90m/C FR Pierre Richard, Bernard Blier, Maria Pacome, Marie-Christine Barrault; **D:** Pierre Richard; **W:** Pierre Richard; **M:** Vladimir Cosma. VHS, Beta $19.95 FCT && 1/2

Days and Nights in the Forest Four men living in Calcutta decide to leave the city for a brief vacation. Each has a different emotional experience which will change him forever, including a brief love affair and finding true romance. In Bengali with English subtitles.
1970 120m/C IN **D:** Satyajit Ray. VHS $39.95 FCT && 1/2

Days of Glory Peck's screen debut finds him as a Russian peasant bravely fighting the Nazi blitzkrieg almost single-handedly.
1943 86m/B Tamara Toumanova, Gregory Peck, Alan Reed, Maria Palmer, Lowell Gilmore, Hugo Haas; **D:** Jacques Tourneur. VHS, Beta $19.98 TTC && 1/2

Days of Heaven Drifter Gere, his younger sister, and a woman he claims is his sister become involved with a Texas sharecropper. Told through the eyes of the younger girl, this is a sweeping vision of the U.S. before WWI. Loss and loneliness, deception, frustration, and anger haunt these people as they struggle to make the land their own. Deservedly awarded an Oscar for breathtaking cinematography.
1978 (PG) 95m/C Richard Gere, Brooke Adams, Sam Shepard, Linda Manz, Stuart Margolin; **D:** Terence Malick; **W:** Terence Malick; **M:** Ennio Morricone. Academy Awards '78: Best Cinematography; Nominations: Best Costume Design, Best Sound, Best Original Score; Cannes Film Festival '79: Best Film; Cannes Film Festival '79: Best Director (Malick); National Board of Review Awards '78: 10 Best Films of the Year; New York Film Critics Awards '78: Best Director (Malick); National Society of Film Critics Awards '78: Best Director (Malick). VHS, Beta $14.95 PAR &&& 1/2

Days of Hell Forgettable tale of four mercenaries who are hired to rescue a doctor and his daughter held captive by guerrillas somewhere in Afghanistan only to find out they're pawns in an even bigger scheme. **AKA:** I Giorni Dell'Inferno.
1984 90m/C Conrad Nichols, Richard Raymond, Stephen Elliott, Kinako Harada; **D:** Anthony Richmond. VHS, Beta NO &

Days of Thrills and Laughter Delightful compilation of clips from the era of silent films, showcasing the talents of the great comics as well as daring stuntman.
1961 93m/B Buster Keaton, Charlie Chaplin, Harold Lloyd, Stan Laurel, Oliver Hardy, Douglas Fairbanks Sr.; **D:** Robert Youngson. VHS, Beta $29.95 MPI &&&

Days of Thunder "Top Gun" in race cars! Cruise follows the same formula he has followed for several years now (with the notable exception of "Born on the Fourth of July.") Cruise and Towne co-wrote the screenplay concerning a young kid bursting with talent and raw energy who must learn to deal with his mentor, his girlfriend, and eventually the bad guy. First film that featured cameras that were actually on the race cars. If you like Cruise or race cars then this is the movie for you.
1990 (PG-13) 108m/C Tom Cruise, Robert Duvall, Randy Quaid, Nicole Kidman, Cary Elwes, Michael Rooker, Fred Dalton Thompson; **D:** Tony Scott; **W:** Tom Cruise, Robert Towne; **M:** Hans Zimmer. VHS, Beta $14.95 PAR, SUP &&

Days of Wine and Roses The original "Playhouse 90" television version of J.P. Miller's story which was adapted for the big screen in 1962. An executive on the fast track and his young wife, initially only social drinkers, find themselves degenerating into alcoholism. A well-acted, stirring drama.
1958 89m/B Cliff Robertson, Piper Laurie; **D:** John Frankenheimer. VHS, Beta $14.95 RHI, MGM, BTV &&&

Days of Wine and Roses A harrowing tale of an alcoholic advertising man who gradually drags his wife down with him into a life of booze. Part of the "A Night at the Movies" series, this tape simulates a 1962 movie evening with a Bugs Bunny cartoon, "Martian Through Georgia," a newsreel, and coming attractions for "Gypsy" and "Rome

Adventure." Big screen adaptation of the play originally shown on television.
1962 138m/B Jack Lemmon, Lee Remick, Charles Bickford, Jack Klugman, Jack Albertson; **D:** Blake Edwards; **M:** Henry Mancini, Johnny Mercer. Academy Awards '62: Best Song ("Days of Wine and Roses"); Nominations: Best Actor (Lemmon), Best Actress (Remick), Best Art Direction/Set Decoration (B & W), Best Costume Design (B & W). VHS, Beta $19.98 WAR &&& 1/2

Dayton's Devils Nielsen is the leader of a motley crew of losers who plan to rob a military base bank in this action-packed heist flick.
1968 107m/C Rory Calhoun, Leslie Nielsen, Lainie Kazan, Eric (Hans Gudegast) Braeden, Georg Stanford Brown; **D:** Jack Shea. VHS, Beta NO &&

Dazed and Confused A day in the life of a bunch of high school seniors should prove to be a trip back in time for those coming of age in the 70's. Eight students faced with life after high school have one last hurrah, as they search for Aerosmith tickets and haze the incoming freshmen. Keen characterization by writer/director Linklater captures the spirit of a generation shaped by Watergate, the Vietnam War, feminism, and marijuana. Groovy soundtrack features Alice Cooper, Deep Purple, KISS, and Foghat.
1993 (R) 97m/C Jason London, Rory Cochrane, Sasha Jensen, Wiley Wiggins, Michelle Burke, Adam Goldberg, Anthony Rapp, Marissa Ribisi; **D:** Richard Linklater; **W:** Richard Linklater. VHS MCA &&&

D.C. Cab A rag-tag group of Washington, D.C. cabbies learn a lesson in self-respect in this endearing comedy. Though not without flaws, it's charming all the same.
1984 (R) 100m/C Mr. T, Leif Erickson, Adam Baldwin, Charlie Barnett, Irene Cara, Anne DeSalvo, Max Gail, Gloria Gifford, Gary Busey, Jill Schoelen, Marsha Warfield; **D:** Joel Schumacher; **W:** Joel Schumacher, Topper Carew. VHS, Beta $19.95 MCA && 1/2

The Dead The poignant final film by Huston, based on James Joyce's short story. At a Christmas dinner party in turn-of-the-century Dublin, a man discovers how little he knows about his wife when a song reminds her of a cherished lost love. Beautifully captures the spirit of the story while providing Huston an opportunity to create a last lament on the fickle nature of time and life.
1987 (PG) 82m/C GB Anjelica Huston, Donal McCann, Marie Kean, Donal Donnelly, Dan O'Herlihy, Helen Carroll, Frank Patterson; **D:** John Huston. Academy Awards '87 Nominations: Best Adapted Screenplay, Best Costume Design; Independent Spirit Awards '88: Best Director (Huston), Best Supporting Actress (Huston); National Society of Film Critics Awards '87: Best Film. VHS, Beta $89.98 LIV, VES, TVC &&& 1/2

Dead Again Branagh's first film since his brilliant debut as the director/star of "Henry V" again proves him a visionary force on and off camera. As the smart L.A. detective hired to discover the identity of a beautiful, but mute woman, he's realistic, clever, tender and cynical. He finds that he's apparently trapped in a nightmarish cycle of murder begun years before. Literate, lovely to look at, suspenseful, with a sense of humor to match its high style.
1991 (R) 107m/C Kenneth Branagh, Emma Thompson, Andy Garcia, Lois Hall, Richard Easton, Derek Jacobi, Hanna Schygulla, Campbell Scott, Wayne Knight, Christine Ebersole; **Cameos:** Robin Williams; **D:** Kenneth Branagh; **W:** Scott Frank; **M:** Patrick Doyle. VHS $19.95 PAR, CCB &&& 1/2

Dead Ahead: The Exxon Valdez Disaster
Focuses on the first crucial days after the March 24, 1989 oil spill when the Exxon Valdez ran aground off Alaska in Prince William Sound. Portrays the inadequate precautions, incompetence, greed, and petty bureaucracy that made an appalling situation even worse. Lloyd stars as Exxon official Frank Iarossi, in charge of the official cleanup, caught between onsite confusion and corporate bungling while Heard is outraged environmentalist Dan Lawn. News and home videotapes of the actual spill are used to enhance the dramatization. Filmed in Vancouver, British Columbia. Made for cable television. **AKA:** Disaster at Valdez.
1992 (PG-13) 90m/C Christopher Lloyd, John Heard, Rip Torn, Michael Murphy, Don S. Davies, Ken Walsh, Bob Gunton, Mark Metcalf, Paul Guilfoyle, David Morse, Jackson Davies; **D:** Paul Seed; **W:** Michael Baker; **M:** David Ferguson. **VHS $89.95** IMP ✗✗✗

Dead Aim
A dud about Soviet spies who introduce even more drugs into New York City, ostensibly to bring about the downfall of the U.S. Obviously a completely far-fetched plot.
1987 (R) 91m/C Ed Marinaro, Isaac Hayes, Corbin Bernsen; **D:** William Vanderkloot. **VHS $89.98** LIV, HHE Woof!

Dead Alive
This outrageously over-the-top horror flick from New Zealand is a gore aficionado's delight (think "Evil Dead" movies for comparison). Set in 1957 and satirizing the bland times, the "plot" has the mom of a nerdy son getting bitten by an exotic monkey, which promptly turns her into a particularly nasty ghoul. This condition is apparently contagious (except for her son who tries to hide the fact mom is literally a monster) and calls for lots of spurting blood and body parts which take on lives of their own. For those with strong stomachs and senses of humor.
1993 (R) 97m/C NZ Timothy Balme, Elizabeth Moody, Diana Penalver, Ian Watkin; **D:** Peter Jackson; **W:** Peter Jackson. **VHS $94.95** VMK, FCT ✗✗✗½

Dead and Buried
Farentino is the sheriff who can't understand why the victims of some pretty grisly murders seem to be coming back to life. Eerily suspenseful.
1981 (R) 95m/C James Farentino, Jack Albertson, Melody Anderson, Lisa Blount, Bill Quinn, Michael Pataki; **D:** Gary Sherman; **W:** Dan O'Bannon. **VHS, Beta $19.98** VES ✗✗½

Dead as a Doorman
A young writer takes a part-time post as a doorman and becomes the target of a murderous lunatic.
1985 83m/C Bradley Whitford, Sharon Schlarth, Bruce Taylor; **D:** Gary Youngman. **VHS, Beta $69.98** LIV, VES ✗✗½

Dead Bang
A frustrated cop uncovers a murderous white supremacist conspiracy in L.A. Frankenheimer's deft directorial hand shapes a somewhat conventional cop plot into an effective vehicle for Johnson.
1989 (R) 102m/C Don Johnson, Bob Balaban, William Forsythe, Penelope Ann Miller, Tim Reid, Frank Military, Michael Higgins, Michael Jeter, Evans Evans, Tate Donovan; **D:** John Frankenheimer; **W:** Robert Foster; **M:** Gary Chang, Michael Kamen. **VHS, Beta, 8mm $19.98** WAR ✗✗½

Dead Boyz Can't Fly
Disturbing look at urban violence. Dysfunctional punk leads his equally amoral cohorts on a looting spree in a near-empty highrise in revenge against a patronizing businessman. The unrated version contains 10 more minutes of violence.

1993 (R) 92m/C Delia Sheppard, Sheila Kennedy, Ruth Collins, Mark McCulley, Brad Friedman; **D:** Howard Winters. **VHS $59.95** VCI ✗✗

Dead Calm
A taut Australian thriller based on a novel by Charles Williams. A young married couple is yachting on the open seas when they happen upon the lone survivor of a sinking ship. They take him on board only to discover he's a homicidal maniac. Makes for some pretty suspenseful moments that somewhat make up for the weak ending.
1989 (R) 97m/C AU Sam Neill, Billy Zane, Nicole Kidman, Rod Mullinar; **D:** Phillip Noyce; **W:** Terry Hayes; **M:** Graeme Revell. **VHS, Beta, 8mm $19.98** WAR, FCT ✗✗✗

Dead Certain
A "Silence of the Lambs" rip-off. Dourif (again specializing in weirdos) is the jailed serial killer providing tantalizing clues to the identity of a new killer on the loose.
1992 (R) 93m/C Brad Dourif, Francesco Quinn, Karen Russell, Joel Kaiser; **D:** Anders Palm; **W:** Anders Palm. **VHS $9.95** HMD ✗

Dead Connection
Beautiful reporter Bonet is in cahoots with cop Madsen to see justice brought the "phone sex killer" who is terrorizing Los Angeles.
1994 (R) 93m/C Michael Madsen, Lisa Bonet, Gary Stretch; **D:** Nigel Dick; **W:** Larry Grolin; **M:** Rolfe Kent. **VHS $94.99** PGV ✗✗

The Dead Don't Die
Unbelievable plot set in the 1930s has Hamilton as a detective trying to prove his brother was wrongly executed for murder. He ultimately clashes with the madman who wants to rule the world with an army of zombies. Perhaps if they had cast Hamilton as Master of the Zombies. Made for television.
1975 74m/C George Hamilton, Ray Milland, Linda Cristal, Ralph Meeker, Joan Blondell, James McEachin; **D:** Curtis Harrington. **VHS, Beta $49.95** WOV, GKK ✗

Dead Easy
Livin' ain't easy for a Sydney sleaze-club owner, his working-girl girlfriend, and a slandered cop when they're caught between machete-wielding enemy gangs (it seems somebody made the crime boss REALLY mad). The three flee in that quintessential escape vehicle—a two-ton truck—to qualify the effort as an Australian contender for greatest chase scene ever (heavy chassis category).
1982 92m/C AU Scott Burgess, Rosemary Paul; **D:** Bert Deling. **VHS, Beta $59.95** MCG ✗✗

Dead End
Sidney Kingsley play, adapted for the big screen by Lillian Hellman, traces the lives of various inhabitants of the slums on New York's Lower East Side as they try to overcome their surroundings. Gritty drama saved from melodrama status by some genuinely funny moments. Film launched the Dead End Kids. **AKA:** Cradle of Crime.
1937 92m/B Sylvia Sidney, Joel McCrea, Humphrey Bogart, Wendy Barrie, Claire Trevor, Allen Jenkins, Marjorie Main, Leo Gorcey, Charles Halton; **D:** William Wyler. **VHS, Beta $19.98** MGM, SUE, MLB ✗✗✗½

Dead End City
Street-wise resident of L.A. organizes fellow citizens into a vigilante force to fight the gangs for control of the city.
1988 88m/C Dennis Cole, Greg Cummins, Christine Lunde, Robert Z'Dar, Darrell Nelson, Alena Downs; **D:** Peter Yuval. **VHS, Beta $9.95** AIP ✗½

Dead End Drive-In
In a surreal, grim future a man is trapped at a drive-in theater-cum-government-run concentration camp, where those considered to be less than

desirable members of society are incarcerated.
1986 (R) 92m/C AU Ned Manning, Natalie McCurray, Peter Whitford; **D:** Brian Trenchard-Smith. **VHS, Beta $19.95** STE, NWV ✗✗

Dead End Street
Young prostitute attempts to change her self-destructive lifestyle. It's not easy.
1983 86m/C IS Anat Atzman, Yehoram Gaon. **VHS, Beta $59.95** TWE ✗½

Dead Eyes of London
Blind old German men are dying to lower their premiums in this geriatric thriller: someone (perhaps the director of the home for the blind?) is killing off the clientele for their insurance money, and a Scotland Yard inspector aims to expose the scam. Relatively early vintage Kinski, it's a remake of the eerie 1939 Lugosi vehicle, "The Human Monster" (originally titled "Dark Eyes of London"), adapted from Edgar Wallace's "The Testament of Gordon Stuart." **AKA:** Dark Eyes of London; Die Toten Augen von London.
1961 95m/B GE Joachim Fuchsberger, Karin Baal, Dieter Borsche, Ady Berber, Klaus Kinski, Eddi Arent, Wolfgang Lukschy; **D:** Alfred Vohrer. **VHS $19.98** SNC ✗✗½

Dead for a Dollar
A Colonel, a con man, and a mysterious woman team up in the Old West to search for the two hundred thousand dollars they stole from a local bank.
1977 92m/C John Ireland, George Hilton, Piero Vida, Sandra Milo. **VHS, Beta $49.95** UNI, MOV ✗½

Dead Girls
A rock group whose lyrics focus on suicide goes on vacation. The members find themselves stalked by a serial killer who decides to take matters out of the musicians' hands and into his own. Graphic violence.
1990 40m/C Diana Karanikas, Angela Eads; **D:** Dennis Devine. **VHS** HHE ✗

Dead Heat
Some acting talent and a few funny moments unfortunately don't add up to a fine film, though they do save it from being a complete woofer. In this one even the cops are zombies when one of them is resurrected from the dead to help his partner solve his murder and rid the city of the rest of the undead.
1988 (R) 86m/C Joe Piscopo, Treat Williams, Lindsay Frost, Darren McGavin, Vincent Price, Keye Luke, Clare Kirkconnell; **D:** Mark Goldblatt. **VHS, Beta $19.95** STE, NWV ✗½

Dead Heat on a Merry-Go-Round
Coburn turns in a great performance as the ex-con who masterminds the heist of an airport safe. Intricately woven plot provides suspense and surprises. The film is also notable for the debut of Ford in a bit part (he has one line as a hotel messenger).
1966 (R) 108m/C James Coburn, Camilla Sparv, Aldo Ray, Nina Wayne, Robert Webber, Rose Marie, Todd Armstrong, Marian Moses, Severn Darden, Harrison Ford; **D:** Bernard Girard. **VHS, Beta $69.95** COL ✗✗✗

Dead in the Water
Brown is Charlie Deegan, a big-time lawyer with a rich wife that he'd rather see dead. Charlie and his mistress plot the perfect murder to dispose of his spouse and collect her money. When plans go awry, he ends up as a suspect for the wrong murder in this story of infidelity and greed.
1991 (PG-13) 90m/C Bryan Brown, Teri Hatcher, Anne DeSalvo, Veronica Cartwright; **D:** Bill Condon; **W:** Eleanor Gaver, Robert Seidenberg, Walter Klenhard. **VHS, Beta $79.95** MCA ✗½

Dead Lucky A novice tries gambling and wins a fortune, but his luck leads him into an entanglement with an assassin, a scam artist, and a beautiful woman. Based on the novel "Lake of Darkness."
1960 91m/B *GB* Vincent Ball, Betty McDowall, John Le Mesurier, Alfred Burke, Michael Ripper; **D:** Montgomery Tully. **VHS, Beta $19.98** *FCT* ✗½

Dead Man Out Both Glover and Blades turn in exceptional performances in this thought-provoking drama. A convict on Death Row (Blades) goes insane and therefore cannot be executed. The state calls in a psychiatrist (Glover) to review the case and determine whether he can be cured so that the sentence can be carried out. Powerful and riveting morality check.
1989 87m/C Danny Glover, Ruben Blades, Tom Atkins, Larry Block, Sam Jackson, Maria Ricossa; **D:** Richard Pearce; **M:** Cliff Eidelman. **VHS, Beta $89.99** *HBO* ✗✗✗

Dead Man Walking In a post-holocaust future, half the population has been stricken with a deadly plague. Hauser is a mercenary, dying from the disease, who is hired to rescue a young woman who was kidnapped and is being held in the plague zone.
1988 (R) 90m/C Wings Hauser, Brion James, Pamela Ludwig, Sy Richardson, Leland Crooke, Jeffrey Combs; **D:** Gregory Brown; **W:** R.J. Marx. **VHS $9.98** *REP* ✗✗

Dead Man's Revenge Ruthless railroad mogul Payton McCay (Dern) doesn't let anyone stand in his way—even if it means framing innocent homesteader Hatcher (Ironside) in order to get his land. Hatcher escapes from jail and goes after McCay, trailed by bounty hunter Bodeen (Couloris). But Bodeen's not what he seems and has his own plans on getting even with the villainous McCay.
1993 (PG-13) 92m/C Bruce Dern, Michael Ironside, Keith Couloris, Randy Travis; **D:** Alan J. Levi; **W:** Jim Byrnes, David Chisholm. **VHS** *MCA* ✗✗½

Dead Mate A woman marries a mortician after a whirlwind romance only to discover that, to her husband, being an undertaker is not just a job, it's a way of life.
1988 93m/C Elizabeth Mannino, David Gregory, Lawrence Bockus, Adam Wahl; **D:** Straw Weisman. **VHS, Beta $79.95** *PSM* ✗

Dead Men Don't Die An anchorman is slain by criminals but resurrected as a shambling voodoo zombie. Few viewers notice the difference in this inoffensive but repetitious farce. The living-dead Gould appears to be having a lot of fun.
1991 (PG-13) 94m/C Elliott Gould, Melissa Anderson, Mark Moses, Philip Bruns, Jack Betts, Mabel King; **D:** Malcolm Marmorstein; **W:** Malcolm Marmorstein. **VHS $19.95** *ACA* ✗½

Dead Men Don't Wear Plaid Martin is hilarious as a private detective who encounters a bizarre assortment of suspects while trying to find out the truth about a scientist's death. Ingeniously interspliced with clips from old Warner Brothers films. Features Humphrey Bogart, Bette Davis, Alan Ladd, Burt Lancaster, Ava Gardner, Barbara Stanwyck, Ray Milland and others. Its only flaw is that the joke loses momentum by the end of the film.
1982 (PG) 89m/B Steve Martin, Rachel Ward, Reni Santoni, George Gaynes, Frank McCarthy, Carl Reiner; **D:** Carl Reiner; **W:** Steve Martin, Carl Reiner. **VHS, Beta $14.95** *MCA, FCT, HMV* ✗✗½

Dead Men Walk A decent, albeit low budget, chiller about twin brothers (Zucco in a dual role); one a nice, well-adjusted member of society, the other a vampire who wants to suck his bro's blood. Sibling rivalry with a bite.
1943 65m/B George Zucco, Mary Carlisle, Dwight Frye, Nedrick Young, Al "Fuzzy" St. John; **D:** Sam Newfield. **VHS, Beta $14.95** *NOS, MRV, SNC* ✗✗

The Dead Next Door Eerily reminiscent of "Night of the Living Dead." A scientist manufactures a virus which inhabits corpses and multiplies while replacing the former cells with its own. But the newly living corpses need human flesh to survive. In response, the government creates "The Zombie Squad" who do heroic battle with the stiffs. When a bizarre cult whose goal is the eradication of the human race befriend the dead, the battle gets ugly.
1989 84m/C Scott Spiegel, Peter Terry. **VHS $20.00** *TEM, MOV* ✗

Dead of Night The template for episodic horror films, this suspense classic, set in a remote country house, follows the individual nightmares of five houseguests. Redgrave turns in a chillingly convincing performance as a ventriloquist terrorized by a demonic dummy. Not recommended for light-sleepers. Truly spine-tingling.
1945 102m/B *GB* Michael Redgrave, Sally Ann Howes, Basil Radford, Naunton Wayne, Mervyn Johns, Roland Culver, Googie Withers, Frederick Valk, Antony Baird, Judy Kelly, Miles Malleson, Ralph Michael; **D:** Alberto Cavalcanti, Charles Crichton, Basil Dearden, Charles Hamer; **W:** T.E.B. Clarke, John Baines, Angus MacPhail; **M:** Georges Auric. **VHS, Beta $9.98** *REP, RXM, CNG* ✗✗✗✗

Dead of Night This trilogy features Richard Matheson's tales of the Supernatural: "Second Chance," "Bobby," and "No Such Thing As a Vampire," all served up by your hostess, Elvira.
1977 76m/C Joan Hackett, Ed Begley Jr., Patrick Macnee, Anjanette Comer; **D:** Dan Curtis. **VHS, Beta $39.95** *LIV* ✗½

Dead of Winter A young actress is suckered into a private screen test for a crippled old director, only to find she is actually being remodeled in the guise of a murdered woman. Edge-of-your-seat suspense as the plot twists.
1987 (R) 100m/C Mary Steenburgen, Roddy McDowall, Jan Rubes, Ken Pogue, William Russ; **D:** Arthur Penn; **W:** Mark Shmuger, Mark malone; **M:** Richard Einhorn. **VHS, Beta $14.95** *MGM, FOX* ✗✗✗

Dead On Illicit lovers want to get rid of their inconvenient spouses so they can be together always. But their perfect plan doesn't work out as expected. Also available in an unrated version.
1993 (R) 87m/C Matt McCoy, Shari Shattuck, David Ackroyd, Tracy Scoggins, Thomas Wagner; **D:** Ralph Hemecker; **W:** April Wayne. **VHS** *ORI* ✗½

Dead on the Money Adequate made for TV suspenser about a woman who believes her lover plots a dire fate for her cousin. But nothing is what it seems here. Confusing, droopy in spots, but fun.
1991 92m/C Corbin Bernsen, Amanda Pays, John Glover, Eleanor Parker, Kevin McCarthy; **D:** Mark Cullingham; **W:** Gavin Lambert. **VHS, Beta $89.98** *TTC* ✗✗½

Dead or Alive Tex and the Texas Rangers pretend to be outlaws in order to join a gang terrorizing a town.

1941 54m/B Tex Ritter, Dave O'Brien, Guy Wilkerson, Charles "Blackie" King, Bud Osborne, Reed Howes; **D:** Elmer Clifton. **VHS, Beta $11.95** *GPV, RXM, VCN* ✗½

Dead Pit Leave this one in the pit it crawled out of. Twenty years ago a mad scientist was killed as a result of horrible experiments he was conducting on mentally ill patients at an asylum. A young woman stumbles across his experiments, awakening him from the dead.
1989 (R) 90m/C Jeremy Slate, Steffen Gregory Foster; **D:** Brett Leonard. **VHS, Beta $89.95** *IMP* Woof!

Dead Poets Society An idealistic English teacher inspires a group of boys in a 1950s' prep school to pursue individuality and creative endeavor, resulting in clashes with school and parental authorities. Williams shows he can master the serious roles as well as the comic with his portrayal of the unorthodox educator. Big box office hit occasionally scripted with a heavy hand in order to elevate the message. The ensemble cast is excellent.
1989 (PG) 128m/C Robin Williams, Ethan Hawke, Robert Sean Leonard, Josh Charles, Gale Hansen, Kurtwood Smith, James Waterston, Dylan Kussman, Lara Flynn Boyle, Melora Hardin; **D:** Peter Weir; **W:** Tom Schulman; **M:** Maurice Jarre. Academy Awards '89: Best Original Screenplay; Nominations: Best Actor (Williams), Best Director (Weir), Best Picture; British Academy Awards '89: Best Film; Cesar Awards '91: Best Foreign Film. **VHS, Beta, 8mm $19.99** *TOU* ✗✗✗½

The Dead Pool Dirty Harry Number Five features a new twist on the sports pool: a list of celebrities is distributed and bets are placed on who will be first to cross the finish line, literally. Unfortunately someone seems to be hedging their bet by offing the celebs themselves. When Harry's name appears on the list, he decides to throw the game.
1988 (R) 92m/C Clint Eastwood, Liam Neeson, Patricia Clarkson, Evan C. Kim, David Hunt, Michael Currie, Michael Goodwin; **D:** Buddy Van Horn. **VHS, Beta, 8mm $19.98** *WAR, TLF* ✗½

Dead Reckoning Bogart and Prince are two WWII veterans en route to Washington when Prince disappears. Bogart trails Prince to his Southern hometown and discovers he's been murdered. Blackmail and more murders follow as Bogie tries to uncover the truth. Suspenseful with good performances from all, especially Bogart.
1947 100m/B Humphrey Bogart, Lizabeth Scott, Morris Carnovsky, Charles Cane, Wallace Ford, William Prince, Marvin Miller; **D:** John Cromwell. **VHS, Beta $19.98** *CCB, COL* ✗✗✗

Dead Reckoning A plastic surgeon and his lovely wife embark on a cruise aboard his new luxury yacht. The intrigue begins with a storm, an isolated island, and the discovery that the captain is the wife's former lover.
1989 (R) 95m/C Cliff Robertson, Susan Blakely, Rick Springfield; **D:** Robert Lewis. **VHS $79.95** *MCA* ✗½

Dead Right A black man is unjustly put into prison in the Deep South. He manages to escape in order to try and prove his innocence. *AKA:* If He Hollers, Let Him Go.
1968 111m/C Raymond St. Jacques, Dana Wynter, Kevin McCarthy, Barbara McNair. **VHS, Beta $79.95** *PSM* ✗½

Dead Ringers A stunning, unsettling chiller, based loosely on a real case and the bestseller by Bari Wood and Jack Geasland. Irons, in an excellent dual role, is effectively disturbing as the twin gynecologists who descend into madness when they can no longer handle the fame, fortune, drugs, and

women in their lives. Acutely upsetting film made all the more so due to its graphic images and basis in fact.
1988 (R) 117m/C *CA* Jeremy Irons, Genevieve Bujold, Heidi von Palleske, Shirley Douglas, Stephen Lack; *D:* David Cronenberg; *W:* Norman Snider, David Cronenberg; *M:* Howard Shore. VHS, Beta $9.99 *CCB, MED, VTR* 🎞🎞🎞

Dead Silence Screenwriter Cliff Morgan has written a classic film noir screenplay... with the money, it seems all Cliff's problems are solved... or are they?
1990 (R) 92m/C Clete Keith, Doris Anne Soyka, Joseph Scott, Craig Fleming; *D:* Harrison Ellenshaw. VHS *NO* 🎞

Dead Sleep A nurse discovers that co-matose patients at a private clinic have been used as guinea pigs by an overzealous doctor. This minor-league chiller from Down Under is said to have been inspired by an actual medical scandal.
1991 (R) 95m/C Linda Blair, Tony Bonner; *D:* Alec Mills. VHS $89.98 *VES* 🎞🎞

Dead Solid Perfect Quaid stars as a golf pro whose life on the PGA tour is handicapped by his taste for scotch and his eye for the ladies. Based on the book by Dan Jenkins.
1988 97m/C Randy Quaid, Kathryn Harrold, Jack Warden, Larry Riley, Brett Cullen, Corinne Bohrer; *D:* Bobby Roth; *W:* Dan Jenkins, Bobby Roth. VHS, Beta $79.99 *WAR, BTV* 🎞🎞

Dead Space Dead space lay between the ears of whoever thought we needed this remake of 1982's "Forbidden World." At a lab on a hostile planet an experimental vaccine mutates into a prickly puppet monster who menaces the medicos. Needed: a vaccine against cheapo "Alien" ripoffs.
1990 (R) 72m/C Marc Singer, Laura Tate, Bryan Cranston, Judith Chapman; *D:* Fred Gallo. VHS $79.95 *COL* 🎞

Dead Women in Lingerie When beautiful models are turning up dead, a detective is called in to solve the mystery. Perhaps they committed suicide to avoid being in this picture any longer than necessary. Title sounds like the next episode of "Geraldo."
1990 (R) 87m/C June Lockhart, Lyle Waggoner, John Romo, Jerry Orbach, Maura Tierney; *D:* Erika Fox. VHS $79.98 *MNC* Woof!

Dead Wrong Undercover agent falls in love with the drug smuggler she's supposed to bring to justice.
1983 93m/C Britt Ekland, Winston Rekert, Jackson Davies. VHS, Beta $49.95 *MED* 🎞½

Dead Wrong: The John Evans Story The true story of Evans' life of crime and eventual execution in the electric chair, using footage of an interview taped before his death.
1984 45m/C VHS *AFC* 🎞½

Dead Zone A man gains extraordinary psychic powers following a near-fatal accident. He is forced to decide between seeking absolute seclusion in order to escape his frightening visions, or using his "gift" to save mankind from impending evil. A good adaptation of the Stephen King thriller.
1983 (R) 104m/C Christopher Walken, Brooke Adams, Tom Skerritt, Martin Sheen, Herbert Lom, Anthony Zerbe, Colleen Dewhurst; *D:* David Cronenberg; *W:* Jeffrey Boam; *M:* Michael Kamen. VHS, Beta $14.95 *PAR* 🎞🎞🎞

Deadbolt Divorced med student Marty Hiller (Bateman) desperately needs a room-mate and Alec Danz (Baldwin) seems per-fect. Soon they're sharing more than the rent, until Danz kills her friends and imprisons her in the apartment (equipped of course

with soundproof walls and bulletproof glass—one wonders why she doesn't bang on the floor to gain attention.) Predictable and silly would-be thriller attempts to capital-ize on the roommate from hell theme that started with "Single White Female," but isn't nearly as effective. Went straight to video and showed up on network TV several months later.
1992 (R) 95m/C Justine Bateman, Adam Baldwin, Michelle Scarabelli, Chris Mulkey, Cyndi Pass, Isabelle Truchon, Douglas Jackson. VHS $89.95 *NLC* 🎞🎞

Deadfall Father/son grifters plan an elabo-rate scam that goes wrong when son Joe (Biehn) inadvertently kills dear old dad (Co-burn). When Joe is going through his father's effects he finds out about an unknown twin uncle, who also turns out to be a racketeer. Along with Uncle Lou's mistrustful henchman Eddie (Cage), they plan another con but swindles and vendettas abound.
1993 (R) 99m/C Michael Biehn, Sarah Trigger, Nicolas Cage, James Coburn, Charlie Sheen, Peter Fonda; *D:* Christopher Coppola; *W:* David Peoples. VHS $94.95 *VMK* 🎞🎞½

The Deadliest Art: The Best of the Martial Arts Films The masters of bare-handed combat team up in this look at the best of the martial arts movies. Action packed.
1990 ?m/C Yuen Biao, Jackie Chan, Samo Hung, Kareem Abdul-Jabbar, Sho Kosugi, Bruce Lee, Angela Mao, Cynthia Rothrock; *D:* Sandra Weintraub; *W:* Sandra Weintraub. VHS $89.98 *FXV* 🎞🎞½

Deadline Journalist must find out the truth behind a minor earthquake in Australia.
1981 94m/C Barry Newman, Trisha Noble, Bill Kerr. VHS, Beta $7.50 *WOV* 🎞½

Deadline Eerie tale of horror writer's life as it begins to reflect his latest story in this play on the "truth is stranger than fiction" adage.
1982 85m/C Stephen Young, Sharon Masters, Cindy Hinds, Phillip Leonard; *D:* Mario Azzopardi. VHS, Beta *NO* 🎞

Deadline Walken is a cynical American journalist assigned to cover the warring factions in Beirut. He finds himself becoming more and more involved in the events he's supposed to report when he falls in love with a German nurse who is aiding the rebel forces. Tense, though sometimes murky drama.
1987 (R) 110m/C *GE* Christopher Walken, Hywel Bennett, Marita Marschall; *D:* Nathaniel Gutman. VHS, Beta *VTR* 🎞🎞

Deadline Assault Kate McSweeny is a beautiful young reporter who is brutally at-tacked and raped by a gang of savage youths. Kate must now face the unsettling facts; they're still on the streets and they may be stalking her again. *AKA:* Act of Violence.
1990 (R) 90m/C Elizabeth Montgomery, James Sloyan, Sean Frye, Biff McGuire, Michael Goodwin, Linden Chiles; *D:* Paul Wendkos. VHS *ELV, HHE* 🎞½

Deadline at Dawn Hayward is an aspiring actress who tries to help a sailor (Williams) prove that he is innocent of murd-er. Based on a novel by Cornell Woolrich.
1946 82m/B Bill Williams, Susan Hayward, Lola Lane, Paul Lukas, Joseph Calleia; *D:* Harold Clurman; *W:* Clifford Odets. VHS, Beta $19.98 *RKO, MLB, TTC* 🎞🎞

Deadline Auto Theft A fun lovin' guy drives fast cars and meets beautiful women. Nudge, nudge, wink, wink.

1983 90m/C H.B. Halicki, Hoyt Axton, Marion Busia, George Cole, Judi Gibbs, Lang Jeffries Jr.; *D:* H.B. Halicki. VHS, Beta $79.95 *IMP* 🎞

Deadlock Hauer and Rogers star as in-mates in a prison of the future. This prison has no walls, no fences and no guards - and no one EVER escapes. Each prisoner wears an explosive collar that is tuned to the same frequency as one of the other prisoner's. Should the two separate by more than 100 yards, the collars explode. When Rogers convinces Hauer that they are on the same frequency, the two escape. Trouble is, they are being pursued not only by the police, but by Hauer's former partners in crime as well. Can the two find the freedom they are looking for - without losing their heads? Originally made for cable television.
1991 (R) 103m/C Rutger Hauer, Mimi Rogers, Joan Chen, James Remar, Stephen Tobolowsky, Basil Wallace; *D:* Lewis Teague. VHS, Beta $19.98 *VTR, FXV, MED* 🎞🎞½

Deadly Alliance Two impecunious film-makers (who happen to be hunks) and a babe (for good measure) poke their noses in where they're not wanted (in the shady business of an international oil cartel). "Deadly Dull" would be a more appropriate moniker.
1978 90m/C Kathleen Arc, Tony de Fonte, Michele Marsh, Walter Prince; *D:* Paul S. Parco. VHS, Beta *NO* 🎞

The Deadly and the Beautiful Dr. Tsu sends her "deadly but beautiful" task force to kidnap the world's prime male athletes for use in her private business enterprise. *AKA:* Wonder Women.
1973 (PG) 82m/C *PH* Nancy Kwan, Ross Hagen, Maria de Aragon, Roberta Collins, Tony Lorea, Sid Haig, Vic Diaz, Shirley Washington, Gale Hansen; *D:* Robert Vincent O'Neil. VHS, Beta $29.95 *MED* 🎞

Deadly Bet A made-for-video saga of a kickboxer who loses his money and his girl when he loses the big match. Lots of fight sequences as he works to regain his career.
1991 (R) 93m/C Jeff Wincott, Charlene Tilton, Steven Leigh; *D:* Richard W. Munchkin. VHS $29.95 *PMH* 🎞½

Deadly Blessing A young, recently wi-dowed woman is visited in her rural Pennsyl-vania home by some friends from the city. Something's not quite right about this coun-try life and they become especially suspi-cious after meeting their friend's very reli-gious in-laws.
1981 (R) 104m/C Maren Jensen, Susan Buckner, Sharon Stone, Ernest Borgnine, Karen Jensen, Jeff East, Lisa Hartman, Lois Nettleton; *D:* Wes Craven; *W:* Wes Craven, Glenn Benest; *M:* James Horner. VHS, Beta $24.98 *SUE* 🎞🎞

Deadly Breed Beware your friendly neighborhood cop. A band of white suprema-cists has infiltrated the local police force, intent on causing violence, not keeping the peace.
1989 90m/C William Smith, Addison Randall, Blake Bahner, Joe Vance; *D:* Charles Kanganis. VHS $29.95 *PMH* 🎞½

Deadly Business The true story of a man who turned from crime to become a government informant. As a garbage man, he works to stop the illegal dumping of chemi-cals in New Jersey. An interesting made-for-televison drama.
1986 100m/C Alan Arkin, Armand Assante, Michael Learned, Jon Polito, George Morfogen, James Rebhorn; *D:* John Korty. VHS *WOV* 🎞🎞🎞

Deadly Business Hard-nosed collection man for a lethal loan shark finds he is the one with the debt to pay as he's stalked through the city street by hit men.
197? 95m/C David Peterson, John Lazarus, Leo Gabrowski. **VHS, Beta** NO 🎬🎬½

Deadly Commando When terrorists begin kidnapping diplomats, only the Deadly Commandos have a chance of saving them.
197? 88m/C **VHS, Beta** MOV 🎬

Deadly Companions Keith is an ex-gunslinger who agrees to escort O'Hara through Apache territory in order to make up for inadvertely killing her son. Director Peckinpah's first feature film.
1961 90m/C Maureen O'Hara, Brian Keith, Chill Wills, Steve Cochran; **D:** Sam Peckinpah. **VHS, Beta** $19.95 STE, NWV 🎬🎬½

Deadly Conspiracy Saxon plays a corrupt businessman who kills an employee about to blow the whistle on his shady dealings. Hauser is the good cop, with the bad personal life, who makes it his mission to bring Saxon to justice. The prolific Hauser brings some fast-paced action to this routine story.
1991 (R) 92m/C Wings Hauser, John Saxon, Frances Fisher, Patti D'Arbanville, Margaux Hemingway, Greg Mullavey; **D:** Paul Leder. **VHS** $89.95 MNC 🎬

Deadly Currents Scott plays a former sea captain who owns a bar on the island of Curacao and enjoys regaling his patrons with his sea-going tales. Petersen is the exiled CIA agent stuck as the security officer of the American consulate. The dangerous pasts of both men catch them up and find them caught in a web of international intrigue. Based on the novel "The Prince of Malta" by James David Buchanan.
1993 (R) 93m/C George C. Scott, William L. Petersen, Julie Carmen, Alexei Sayle, Trish Van Devere, Philip Anglim, Maria Ellingsen; **D:** Carl Schultz; **W:** James David Buchanan. **VHS** COL 🎬🎬

Deadly Dancer It's up to a lone cop to find out who's been offing the hoofers in L.A.
1990 88m/C Adolfo "Shabba Doo" Quinones, Smith Wordes, Walter W. Cox, Steve Jonson; **D:** Kimberly Casey; **W:** David A. Prior. **VHS** $79.95 AIP 🎬½

Deadly Daphne's Revenge Gory story of rape and revenge from the Troma Team. Hitchhiker Cindy is beaten and raped by Charlie Johnson. When she seeks justice via the local police, Johnson makes plans to have her snuffed out. Meantime, another of his victims escapes from the asylum she's been in and comes looking for him with murder on her mind.
1993 98m/C **VHS** $89.95 AIP 🎬½

Deadly Darling Muddled, completely awful tale centering on two different rapes with no discernible attempt made to link the two or establish a plot.
1985 91m/C Fonda Lynn, Warren Chan, Bernard Tsui, Cherry Kwok; **D:** Karen Young. **VHS, Beta** $49.95 UNI Woof!

Deadly Desire Seduced by the beautiful Harrold, security guard Scalia finds himself putting his life on the line when Harrold asks him to help cheat her husband out of millions in an insurance scam. Trouble ensues when they try to outsmart Harrold's powerful entrepreneurial husband.
1991 (R) 93m/C Jack Scalia, Kathryn Harrold, Will Patton, Joe Santos; **D:** Charles Correll. **VHS** PAR, HHE 🎬🎬

Deadly Diamonds Cop is on the trail of diamond smugglers who leave a trail of death in their wake.
1991 90m/C Dan Haggerty, Troy Donahue, Eli Rich, Kathleen Kane, Kenna Grob, Nicholas Mercer; **D:** Thomas Atcheson; **W:** Ron Herbst. **VHS, Beta** GNS, PHX, HHT 🎬🎬

Deadly Dreams A young boy's parents are killed by a maniac who then commits suicide. Years later, he dreams that he is being stalked anew by the same killer. Nightmares turn into reality in this decent horror/suspense flick.
1988 (R) 79m/C Mitchell Anderson, Xander Berkeley, Thom Babbes, Juliette Cummins; **D:** Kristine Peterson. **VHS, Beta** NO 🎬🎬

Deadly Embrace Sordid tale of wealthy man (Vincent) who wants to get rid of his wife—permanantly. He enlists the aid of a beautiful young coed. Soft-core sleaze with nary a redeemable quality.
1988 82m/C Jan-Michael Vincent, Jack Carter, Ty Randolph, Linnea Quigley, Michelle (McClellan) Bauer, Ken Abraham; **D:** Ellen Cabot. **VHS, Beta** $79.95 PSM Woof!

Deadly Encounter Thrilling actioner in which Hagman portrays a helicopter pilot—a former war ace—who allows an old flame to talk him into helping her escape from the mobsters on her trail. Terrific edge-of-your-seat aerial action.
1972 90m/C Larry Hagman, Susan Anspach, Michael C. Goetz, James Gammon; **D:** William A. Graham. **VHS, Beta** NO 🎬🎬🎬

Deadly Encounter Lacking any redeemable qualities, this film shows just how low some people go. Merrill hosts a dinner to garner financial support for a budding playwright, but what we get is a look at the lifestyles of the rich and perverse.
1978 (R) 90m/C Dina Merrill, Carl Betz, Leon Ames, Vicki Powers, Mark Rasmussen, Susan Logan; **D:** R. John Hugh. **VHS, Beta** $19.95 CNG Woof!

Deadly Exposure Benson stars as a burned-out journalist doing his own investigation of the right-wing extremist group that killed his father. Aspiring reporter Johnson helps out and turns up a conspiracy between the extremists, the government, and a plot to assassinate a U.S. senator. Also available in an unrated version.
1993 (R) 100m/C Robby Benson, Laura Johnson, Paul Hampton, Andrew Prine, Bentley Mitchum, Isaac Hayes; **D:** Lawrence Mortorff; **W:** Asher Brauner. **VHS** $89.95 AVE 🎬🎬

Deadly Eyes After eating grain laced with steroids a group of rats grows to mammoth proportions (dachshunds in rat drag were used). Their appetites grow accordingly—now they crave humans. Amid the nibbling by the giant rat-dogs, romance blooms. Silly adaptation by Charles Eglee of Frank Herbert's "The Rats." **AKA:** The Rats.
1982 (R) 93m/C Sam Groom, Sara Botsford, Scatman Crothers, Lisa Langlois, Cec Linder; **D:** Robert Clouse. **VHS, Beta** $19.98 WAR 🎬½

Deadly Fieldtrip Four female students and their teacher are abducted by a biker gang and held hostage on a deserted farm.
1974 91m/C Zalman King, Brenda Fogarty, Robert Porter; **D:** Earl Barton. **VHS, Beta** $79.95 MNC 🎬½

Deadly Force Ex-cop turned private detective stalks a killer in Los Angeles who has left an "X" carved in the forehead of each of his 17 victims. If he had just signed his name, things could have been tidied up much earlier.

1983 (R) 95m/C Wings Hauser, Joyce Ingalls, Paul Shenar, Al Ruscio, Arlen Dean Snyder, Lincoln Kilpatrick; **D:** Paul Aaron; **W:** Robert Vincent O'Neil, Barry Schneider. **VHS, Beta** $14.98 SUE, NLC 🎬½

Deadly Friend A well-meaning horror flick? That's what Wes Craven has tried to provide for us. When the girlfriend of a lonely teenage genius is accidentally killed, he decides to insert his robot's "brain" in her body, though the results aren't entirely successful. The same can be said for the film which was based on Diana Henstell's more effective novel "Friend."
1986 (R) 91m/C Matthew Laborteaux, Kristy Swanson, Michael Sharrett, Anne Twomey, Richard Marcus, Anne Ramsey; **D:** Wes Craven; **W:** Bruce Joel Rubin; **M:** Charles Bernstein. **VHS, Beta** $14.95 WAR 🎬🎬

Deadly Game A reunion at a remote hotel leads to an ordeal of psychological terror and murderous intrigue.
1982 (R) 108m/C George Segal, Robert Morley, Trevor Howard, Emlyn Williams, Alan Webb; **D:** George Schaefer. **VHS, Beta** $59.98 SUE 🎬🎬

Deadly Game Much-maligned and preyed-upon witness is protected by a weary cop, who speaks with the use of English subtitles.
1983 90m/C GE Mel Ferrer, Helmut Berger, Barbara Sukowa; **D:** Karoly Makk, Dieter Geissler. **VHS, Beta** $39.95 VCD, GLV 🎬½

The Deadly Game East-West intrigue prior to the fall of the Berlin Wall finds a Western operative returning from a dangerous mission, only to walk into a trap set by his own side.
198? 104m/C GB David Hemmings. **VHS** $59.99 HBO, FCT, ING 🎬🎬

Deadly Game Horribly burned, a vengeful millionaire invites seven people he believes have wronged him to spend the weekend on his isolated island. He has promised them each a reward for their good deeds, but instead plans to have a big-game hunt with his "guests" as the prey.
1991 (R) 93m/C Roddy McDowall, Jenny Seagrove, Marc Singer, Michael Beck; **D:** Tom Wright. **VHS, Beta** PAR 🎬½

Deadly Games Ineffective plot involving a series of murders in a small town is seemingly played out by the principal characters in a horror board game. Film is saved from being a complete waste by Groom's good performance as the local cop.
1980 94m/C Sam Groom, Jo Ann Harris, Steve Railsback, Dick Butkus, June Lockhart, Colleen Camp; **D:** Scott Mansfield. **VHS, Beta** $39.95 MON 🎬½

Deadly Harvest Scientists' worst fears have been realized—due to ecological abuse and over-development of the land, food has become extremely scarce. This in turn has caused people to become a bit savage. They are particularly nasty to a farmer and his family. Not a bad plot, but a poorly acted film.
1972 (PG) 86m/C Clint Walker, Nehemiah Persoff, Kim Cattrall, David G. Brown, Gary Davies; **D:** Timothy Bond. **VHS, Beta** $19.95 STE, NWV 🎬

Deadly Hero Gripping tale of a young woman who becomes the prey of a New York City cop after questioning the brutal methods he employed while saving her from being assaulted, ultimately killing her attacker. Williams makes film debut in this chilling suspenser.
1975 (R) 102m/C Don Murray, James Earl Jones, Diahn Williams, Lilia Skala, Conchata Ferrell, George S. Irving, Treat Williams, Josh Mostel; **D:** Ivan Nagy; **M:** Brad Fiedel. **VHS, Beta** $39.98 SUE 🎬🎬🎬

Deadly Illusion Williams is a private detective who manages to get himself tangled in a complex web of intrigue and winds up framed for murder. Decent outing for all. *AKA:* Love You to Death.
1987 (R) 95m/C Billy Dee Williams, Morgan Fairchild, Vanity, John Beck, Joe Cortese; *D:* William Tannen, Larry Cohen; *W:* Larry Cohen; *M:* Patrick Gleeson. VHS, Beta $79.95 COL �她

Deadly Impact Las Vegas casinos are targeted for rip-off by means of a computer. Svenson and Williamson give good performances, but that's not enough to save this one.
1984 90m/C *IT* Bo Svenson, Fred Williamson, Marcia Clingan, John Morghen, Vincent Conti; *D:* Larry Ludman. VHS, Beta $29.98 LIV, VES �她½

Deadly Innocence A shy, lonely girl works at an isolated gas station. After her father's death, she takes in a boarder—a mysterious woman being chased by her past.
1988 (R) 90m/C Mary Crosby, Andrew Stevens, Amanda Wyss; *D:* John D. Patterson, Hugh Parks. VHS NO 🌂½

Deadly Intent The widow of a murdered archeologist becomes the target of fortune hunters when they try to get their hands on the priceless jewel her husband brought back from a dig.
1988 83m/C Lisa Eilbacher, Steve Railsback, Maud Adams, Lance Henriksen, Fred Williamson, Persis Khambatta; *D:* Nigel Dick. VHS $29.95 FRH 🌂🌂

Deadly Intruder Quiet vacation spot is being terrorized by an escapee from a mental institution. So much for a little R and R.
1984 86m/C Chris Holder, Molly Creek. VHS, Beta NO 🌂½

The Deadly Mantis A gigantic praying mantis lies in a million-year-old sleep in the frozen reaches of the Arctic. Then a volcanic eruption releases the critter and it's flying beastie does its destructive best on Washington, DC and New York City until the military can gas it into oblivion. Typically silly fifties sci-fi with decent special effects. *AKA:* The Incredible Praying Mantis.
1957 79m/B Craig Stevens, William Hopper, Alix Talton, Pat Conway, Donald Randolph; *D:* Nathan Juran; *W:* Martin Berkeley. VHS $14.98 MCA 🌂½

Deadly Matrimony A womanizing mob lawyer (Williams) murders the wife who wants to leave him and dumps her body in a canal to make it seem she's disappeared. When the body is accidentally recovered, tough-but-honest Chicago cop John Reed (Dennehy) works to put the lawyer away. Only the lawyer and his mob connections have a significant number of the police force on the payroll and Jack's investigation may cost him more than his pension. Okay crime-drama with Dennehy and Williams always worth watching. Based on a true story. Made for television.
1992 ?m/C Brian Dennehy, Treat Williams, Embeth Davidtz, Susan Ruttan, John M. Jackson, Lisa Eilbacher, Terry Kinney, George Morfogen. 🌂🌂½

Deadly Mission Five soldiers in WWII France are convicted of crimes against the Army, only to escape from lock-up and become focal points in a decisive battle.
1978 (R) 99m/C Bo Svenson, Peter Hooten, Fred Williamson. VHS, Beta $69.98 LIV 🌂½

Deadly Neighbor New neighbor moves in, dead neighborhood housewives move out. Another neighbor becomes suspicious and investigates.
1991 90m/C Don Leifert, George Stover, Lydia Laurans; *D:* Donald M. Dohler. VHS $59.95 VCI 🌂🌂

Deadly Obsession A disfigured lunatic stalks a young co-ed hoping to extort $1 million from the wealthy dean of the school.
1988 (R) 93m/C Jeffrey R. Iorio; *D:* Jeno Hodl. VHS $14.98 REP, FCT 🌂½

Deadly Passion A James Cain-like thriller about a private eye getting carnally involved with a beautiful and treacherous woman who is manipulating her late husband's estate through murder and double-crossing.
1985 (R) 100m/C *SA* Brent Huff, Ingrid Boulting, Harrison Coburn, Lynn Maree; *D:* Larry Larson. VHS, Beta $79.98 LIV 🌂½

Deadly Possession A college student plays amateur detective when she tries to clear her ex-husband's name after he is accused of the horrible murder of a fellow student.
1988 99m/C *AU* Penny Cook, Anna-Maria Winchester, Liddy Clark, Olivia Hamnett; *D:* Craig Lahiff. VHS, Beta $79.98 LIV, VES 🌂🌂

Deadly Prey Prior is up against a fully outfitted army of bloodthirsty mercenaries who are using innocent people as "live targets" at their secret bootcamp. Plot lifted from "The Most Dangerous Game" has more than its share of gruesome violence.
1987 (R) 87m/C Cameron Mitchell, Troy Donahue, Ted Prior, Fritz Matthews; *D:* David A. Prior; *W:* David A. Prior. VHS, Beta NO Woof!

Deadly Reactor In a post-nuclear future a lone preacher turns into an armed vigilante to protect the people of a town being terrorized by a vicious motorcycle gang.
1989 88m/C David Heavener, Stuart Whitman, Darwyn Swalve, Allyson Davis; *D:* David Heavener. VHS, Beta $9.95 AIP 🌂🌂

Deadly Recruits The Russians did it! The Russians did it! Stamp is convinced that the downfall of several top students at Oxford, amid scandal and rumor, is due to a KGB conspiracy.
1986 92m/C *GB* Terence Stamp, Michael Culver, Carmen Du Sautoy, Robin Sachs; *D:* Roger Tucker. VHS, Beta NO 🌂½

Deadly Revenge Action-adventure pic with not much adventure and even less action. Small-town reporter finds himself up against a mob boss when he takes over the nightclub business of a friend killed by the mobsters. Dubbed.
1983 (R) 90m/C *IT* Rodolfo Ranni, Julio de Grazia, Silvia Montanari, Fred Commoner; *D:* Juan Carlos Sesanzo. VHS, Beta $59.95 UNI 🌂

Deadly Rivals Stevens plays a laser specialist in Miami for a top-secret weapons conference. A beauty takes a interest in him but then she's first accused of being a spy and then mistaken for a courier in the pay of a ruthless crime boss. Can Stevens find the truth?
1992 (R) 93m/C Andrew Stevens, Cela Wise, Joseph Bologna, Margaux Hemingway, Richard Roundtree, Francesco Quinn, Randi Ingerman; *D:* James Dodson; *W:* Redge Mahaffey; *M:* Ashley Irwin. VHS MCA 🌂🌂

Deadly Sanctuary Censors stopped production of this film several times. The Marquis de Sade's writings provided the inspiration (though there's nothing inspired about it) for this tale of two recently orphaned young women who get caught up in prostitution, an S&M club, and murder.
1968 92m/C Jack Palance, Mercedes McCambridge, Sylva Koscina, Klaus Kinski, Akim Tamiroff, Romina Power; *D:* Jess (Jesus) Franco. VHS, Beta $39.95 MON Woof!

The Deadly Secret Randall Parks is a successful real estate agent with a past he has managed to hide for twenty years. When he is blackmailed, he decides to take matters into his own hands and track down his accusers.
1994 98m/C Joe Estevez, Tracy Spaulding, Reggie Cale, Douglas Stalgren; *D:* Jason Hammond; *W:* Douglas Stalgren; *M:* Erik Hansen. VHS $89.95 AIP 🌂🌂

Deadly Spygames A special agent for the United States Special Operations Bureau finds himself in deep trouble.
1989 ?m/C Troy Donahue, Tippi Hedren; *D:* Jack M. Sell; *W:* Jack M. Sell. VHS $59.95 UNI 🌂🌂

Deadly Sting Silva devises an intricate scheme to gain revenge on the men who cheated him out of his share of a gold bullion heist.
1982 90m/C *FR* Henry Silva, Philip Clay, Andre Pousse; *D:* Jean-Claude Roy. VHS, Beta NO 🌂½

Deadly Stranger Fluegel's talents could have been put to much better use than as the selfish mistress of a plantation owner who is taking advantage of the migrant workers toiling on his land. Moore is a drifter and hired hand who rallies the workers to stand up to the owner. *AKA:* Border Heat.
1988 93m/C Darlanne Fluegel, Michael J. Moore, John Vernon, Ted White; *D:* Max Kleven. VHS $79.98 MCG 🌂

Deadly Strangers Two people meet up on the road and decide to share a ride. We discover that one of them is an insane killer who's escaped from a mental institltution. Suspense builds nicely, but the ending is flawed.
1982 89m/C *GB* Hayley Mills, Simon Ward, Sterling Hayden, Ken Hutchison; *D:* Sidney Hayers. VHS, Beta NO 🌂🌂

Deadly Sunday A family's weekly Sunday drive turns terrifying when desperate jewel thieves detour them and hold them hostage.
1982 85m/C Dennis Ely, Henry Sanders, Gylian Roland, Douglas Alexander; *D:* Donald M. Jones. VHS, Beta $59.98 LIV 🌂½

Deadly Surveillance Two tough policemen investigate a series of drug-related murders and stake out a possible suspect—a beautiful woman who's the lover of one of the lawmen. Tension in this Canadian-made cop opera evaporates in the third act for a standard buddy-buddy action finale. Made for television.
1991 (R) 92m/C Michael Ironside, Christopher Bondy, Susan Almgren, Vlasta Vrana, David Carradine; *D:* Paul Ziller. VHS $89.98 REP 🌂🌂

Deadly Thief A former jewel thief comes out of retirement to challenge those who are now tops in the profession to try and steal the world's most precious ruby from him. Of course all they have to lose is their lives. What could have been an exciting adventure is made curiously boring. *AKA:* Shalimar.
1978 90m/C *IN* Rex Harrison, John Saxon, Sylvia Miles, Dharmendra, Zenat Aman, Shammi Kapoor; *D:* Krishna Shah. VHS, Beta $49.95 PSM 🌂🌂

The Deadly Trackers If gorey oaters are your thing, this one's definitely for you; if not, make tracks. Harris plays a spiteful sheriff who heads south of the border to get his pound of flesh from the outlaws who slew his family in a bank robbery. Overlong revenge-o-rama based on Samuel Fuller's short story, "Riata"; might have been bearable if Fuller hadn't been bumped from the director's chair (as it is, he and other contributors refused to be listed in the credits).

1973 (PG) 104m/C Richard Harris, Rod Taylor, Al Lettieri, Neville Brand, William Smith, Paul Benjamin, Pedro Armendariz Jr.; *D:* Barry Shear. **VHS $59.95** WAR, FCT *Ⅱ*

The Deadly Trap Confusing thriller that couldn't. Dunaway is the mentally unstable wife of an ex-spy. His former employers have targeted him with plans to use her and her fragile state-of-mind to their advantage. *AKA:* Death Scream.
1971 (PG) 96m/C *FR IT* Faye Dunaway, Frank Langella, Barbara Parkins, Maurice Ronet; *D:* Rene Clement. **VHS** FCT *Ⅱ*

Deadly Twins After being beaten and gang-raped, twin sister singers are out to get revenge. Nothing new here; don't waste your time.
1985 87m/C Audrey Landers, Judy Landers, Ellie Russell, Wayne Allison; *D:* Joe Oaks. **VHS, Beta $79.95** PSM *Woof!*

Deadly Vengeance It's strictly low budget as the mob kills Jones's boyfriend, forcing her to mount a vengeful but inexpensive offensive against the crime syndicate's bigwigs.
1981 84m/C Grace Jones, Alan Marlowe, Arthur Roberts. **VHS, Beta** NO *Ⅱ*

Deadly Weapon It's a bit of nerdish wish fulfillment when 15-year-old geek Eastman finds a secret anti-matter weapon conveniently lost by the military in an Arizona stream. You won't like the kid any more than you'll like the story of this low rent boy-gets-back-at-bullies sci fi fiasco.
1988 (PG-13) 89m/C Rodney Eastman, Gary Frank, Michael Horse, Ed Nelson, Kim Walker; *D:* Michael Miner; *W:* Michael Miner. **VHS $79.95** TWE, HHE *Ⅱ*

Deadly Weapons Chesty Morgan, she of the 73-inch bustline, takes on the mob using only her God-given abilities. One of Joe Bob Brigg's "Sleaziest Movies in the History of the World" series, and he is welcome to it.
1970 (R) 90m/C Chesty Morgan, Harry Reems; *D:* Doris Wishman. **VHS** NO *Ⅱ*

Deadman's Curve Decent bio pic detailing the lives of Jan Berry and Dean Torrence who, as Jan and Dean, started the surf music wave only to wipe out after an almost-fatal car wreck. Shows how they deal with and recover from the tragedy. Made for television.
1978 100m/C Richard Hatch, Bruce Davison, Pamela Bellwood, Susan Sullivan, Dick Clark, Wolfman Jack; *D:* Richard Compton. **VHS $59.95** GEM *ⅡⅡ*

Deadtime Stories Mother Goose it's not. Fairy tales "Little Red Riding Hood" and "Goldilocks and the Three Bears," among others, are presented like you've never before seen them—as low-budget horror tales.
1986 93m/C Michael Mesmer, Brian DePersia, Scott Valentine, Phyllis Craig, Melissa Leo, Nicole Picard; *D:* Jeffrey Delman. **VHS, Beta** NO *Ⅱ½*

Deadwood In the untamed West, a young cowboy is mistaken for the notorious Billy the Kid. Cinematography by Vilmos Zsigmond.
1965 100m/C Arch Hall Jr., Jack Lester, Melissa Morgan, Robert Dix; *D:* James Landis. **VHS, Beta $29.95** RHI, FCT *Ⅱ½*

Deadwood Pass Below-standard fare has Tyler rescuing Monti more times than seems reasonable. Monti was once an all-around helper to W.C. Fields.
1933 62m/B Tom Tyler, Alice Dahl, Wally Wales, Buffalo Bill Jr., Lafe McKee, Bud Osborne, Charles "Slim" Whitaker, Charlotte (Carlotta) Monti; *D:* J.P. McGowan. **VHS $19.95** DVT, HEG, GPV *Ⅱ*

Deal of the Century A first-rate hustler and his cohorts sell second-rate weapons to third-world nations; unfortunately, their latest deal threatens to blow up in their faces—literally.
1983 (PG) 99m/C Chevy Chase, Sigourney Weaver, Gregory Hines, Richard Libertini, Wallace Shawn; *D:* William Friedkin; *W:* Paul Brickman. **VHS, Beta $19.98** WAR *ⅡⅡ*

Dealers Two money-hungry stock traders mix business and pleasure, then set their sights on one final all or nothing score.
1989 (R) 92m/C *GB* Rebecca DeMornay, Paul McGann, Derrick O'Connor; *D:* Colin Bucksey. **VHS, Beta $29.95** ACA, IME *Ⅱ½*

Dear America: Letters Home from Vietnam Acclaimed documentary featuring pictures and film of the war with voice-overs by dozens of Hollywood stars reading the words of American GIs. Initially made for cable television.
1988 (PG) 84m/C *D:* Bill Couturie; *M:* Todd Boekelheide. **VHS, Beta $89.98** HBO, AMB *ⅡⅡⅡ½*

Dear Boys A stylized film of sexual fantasies and romance between a moody writer and a carefree young man who relentlessly pursues excitement. Based on the novel by Gerald Reve.
1980 90m/C *NL* Hugo Netsers, Hans Dagelet, Bill Van Dijk, Albert Mol; *D:* Paul de Lussanet. **VHS $69.95** FCT *Ⅱ*

Dear Brigitte A young American kid ("Lost in Space" tyke Mumy) writes a love letter to Brigitte Bardot and travels to Paris to meet her in person. Based on the novel "Erasmus with Freckles" by John Haase.
1965 100m/C James Stewart, Billy Mumy, Glynis Johns, Fabian, Cindy Carol, John Williams, Jack Kruschen, Brigitte Bardot, Ed Wynn, Alice Pearce; *D:* Henry Koster; *W:* Hal Kanter. **VHS, Beta $19.98** FOX *ⅡⅡ*

Dear Dead Delilah Moorehead is Delilah, the matriarch of a southern family, who is on her deathbed. Her heirs are fighting to the bitter—and bloody—end to be the first to find Delilah's money, buried somewhere on her land.
1972 90m/C Agnes Moorehead, Will Geer, Michael Ansara, Patricia Carmichael, Dennis Patrick; *D:* John Farris. **VHS, Beta $59.98** SUE *Ⅱ½*

Dear Detective Vaccaro is the head of the police homicide unit who is trying to track down the killer of several politicians. In the midst of her investigation, she falls for an old friend, a professor of Greek language. Made for television and based on a French television series. *AKA:* Dear Inspector; Tendre Poulet.
1978 90m/C Brenda Vaccaro, Arlen Dean Snyder, Michael MacRae, John Dennis Johnston, Jack Ging, Stephen McNally, M. Emmet Walsh, Constance Forslund, R.G. Armstrong; *D:* Dean Hargrove; *M:* Georges Delerue. **VHS** NO *ⅡⅡ*

Dear Murderer A husband suspects his wife of having an affair, and devises an ingenious, if complicated, trap for her. Inspired performances from the leads, but the plot is grim and confusing.
1947 94m/B *GB* Eric Portman, Greta Gynt, Dennis Price, Jack Warner, Maxwell Reed, Hazel Court, Andrew Crawford, Jane Hylton; *D:* Arthur Crabtree. **VHS, Beta $16.95** SNC *Ⅱ*

Dear Wife Comedy about those ties that bind. Even though her father is runnning for reelection to the State Senate, Freeman wants her brother-in-law (Holden) to run against him. Sequel to "Dear Ruth."
1949 88m/B William Holden, Joan Caulfield, Edward Arnold, Billy DeWolfe, Mona Freeman; *D:* Richard Haydn. **VHS, Beta $19.95** BAR *ⅡⅡ½*

Death at Love House A screen writer becomes obsessed when he is hired to write the life story of a long dead silent movie queen. Filmed at the Harold Lloyd estate. Made for television.
1975 74m/C Robert Wagner, Kate Jackson, Sylvia Sidney, Joan Blondell, John Carradine; *D:* E.W. Swackhamer. **VHS, Beta $59.95** PSM *Ⅱ½*

Death Be Not Proud Based on the book by John Gunther detailing the valiant battle fought by his son against the brain tumor that took his life at the age of 17. Wonderfully acted by the three principals, especially Alexander, this film leaves us feeling hopeful despite its subject. Made for television.
1975 74m/C Arthur Hill, Robby Benson, Jane Alexander, Linden Chiles, Wendy Phillips; *D:* Donald Wrye. **VHS, Beta** LCA *ⅡⅡⅡ*

Death Becomes Her Aging actress Streep will do anything to stay young and beautiful, especially when childhood rival Hawn shows up, 200 pounds lighter and out to revenge the loss of her fiance, Streep's henpecked hubby. Doing anything arrives in the form of a potion that stops the aging process (and keeps her alive forever). Watch for the hilarious party filled with dead celebrities who all look as good as the day they died. Great special effects and fun performances by Streep and Hawn playing their glamour-girl roles to the hilt add merit to this biting commentary on Hollywood's obsession with beauty and youth.
1992 (PG-13) 105m/C Meryl Streep, Bruce Willis, Goldie Hawn, Isabella Rossellini, Sydney Pollack, Michael Caine, Ian Ogilvy, Adam Storke, Nancy Fish, Alaina Reed Hall, Michelle Johnson, Mimi Kennedy, Jonathan Silverman; *Cameos:* Fabio Lanzoni; *D:* Robert Zemeckis; *W:* Martin Donovan, David Koepp; *M:* Alan Silvestri. **VHS, Beta $95.00** MGM, PMS *ⅡⅡⅡ*

Death Before Dishonor Formula actioner stars Dryer as a tough Marine sergeant who battles ruthless Middle Eastern terrorists after they slaughter his men and kidnap his commanding officer (Keith).
1987 (R) 95m/C Fred Dryer, Brian Keith, Joanna Pacula, Paul Winfield; *D:* Terry J. Leonard. **VHS, Beta $19.95** NWV, STE *Ⅱ½*

Death Blow The victims of a violent rapist team together to stop the criminal after he repeatedly skirts conviction.
1987 90m/C Martin Landau, Frank Stallone, Jerry Van Dyke, Terry Moore, Henry Darrow, Jack Carter, Peter Lapis, Don Swayze, Donna Denton; *D:* Raphael Nussbaum. **VHS, Beta** NO *Ⅱ½*

Death by Dialogue Muddled story of some teenagers who discover an old film script from a project never produced because it was haunted by tragic accidents.
1988 (R) 90m/C Laura Albert, Ken Sagoes; *D:* Tom Dewier. **VHS, Beta** NO *Ⅱ*

Death by Prescription After adjusting his patients' wills to benefit himself, an evil physician sees to their mysterious deaths.
198? 75m/C Vincent Van Patten, Nigel Davenport. **VHS, Beta $29.95** ACA, MOV *Ⅱ½*

Death Challenge Gangs battle without weapons, motive or discretion in this kung fu extravaganza.
1980 94m/C Steve Leving, Susan Wong. **VHS, Beta $39.95** UNI *Ⅱ½*

Death Chase An average Joe, just jogging down the street, is thrown into a desperate game of cat-and-mouse when a body lands at his feet.
1987 86m/C William Zipp, Paul Smith, Jack Starrett, Bainbridge Scott; *D:* David A. Prior. **VHS, Beta** NO *Ⅱ½*

D

▲ 313 • VIDEOHOUND'S GOLDEN MOVIE RETRIEVER

Death Collector In the future when insurance companies run the world, if you don't pay your premium, you die.
1989 (R) 90m/C Daniel Chapman, Ruth Collins; *D:* Tom Gniazdowski. VHS, Beta *VTR &½*

Death Cruise The six winners of a free cruise find that there is a fatal catch to the prize in this made-for-TV movie.
1974 74m/C Kate Jackson, Celeste Holm, Tom Bosley, Edward Albert, Polly Bergen, Michael Constantine, Richard Long; *D:* Ralph Senesky. VHS, Beta $39.95 *AHV &½*

The Death Curse of Tartu Another aspiring cult classic. (Read: A low-budget flick so bad it's funny). Students accidentally disturb the burial ground of an Indian medicine man who comes to zombie-like life with a deadly prescription.
1966 84m/C Fred Pinero, Doug Hobart, William Grefe. VHS, Beta *NO Woof!*

Death Dreams Crista thinks she has a perfect life with her wealth, beautiful daughter Jennie, and handsome new husband George. Then Jennie tragically drowns. It appears to be an accident until Jennie contacts her mother from beyond the grave to tell what really happened. Is the tragedy turning Crista's mind or is there truly something sinister going on—something that involves George? Based on the novel by William Katz. Routine suspenser originally appeared on cable television.
1992 94m/C Marg Helgenberger, Christopher Reeve, Fionnula Flanagan; *D:* Martin Donovan; *W:* Robert Glass. VHS $89.95 *NLC &&*

Death Driver In order to make a comeback, a stuntman attempts to do a stunt that was responsible for ending his career ten years earlier. Obviously brave but none too smart.
1978 93m/C Earl Owensby, Mike Allen, Patty Shaw, Mary Ann Hearn; *D:* Jimmy Huston. VHS, Beta *NO &½*

Death Drug Cliched alarmist film about a talented musician ruining his career by becoming addicted to the drug angel dust.
1983 73m/C Philip Michael Thomas, Vernee Watson, Rosalind Cash; *D:* Oscar Williams. VHS, Beta $29.95 *ACA &½*

Death Feud A man tries to save the woman he loves from the man who would destroy her and her former pimp.
1989 94m/C Karen Mayo Chandler, Chris Mitchum, Frank Stallone. VHS, Beta $14.95 *HMD &½*

Death Force When a Vietnam veteran comes to New York City, he becomes a hitman for the Mafia.
1978 (R) 90m/C Jayne Kennedy, Leon Isaac Kennedy, James Inglehart, Carmen Argenziano; *D:* Cirio H. Santiago. VHS, Beta *NO &½*

Death from a Distance A reporter and a detective put the moves on a group of astronomers who may be responsible for a murder.
1936 73m/B Russell Hopton, Lola Lane, George F. Marion Sr., John St. Polis, Lee Kohlmar, Lew Kelly, Wheeler Oakman, Robert Frazer, Cornelius Keefe; *D:* Frank Strayer. VHS, Beta $16.95 *SNC &½*

Death Games Two young men shooting a documentary about an influential music promoter ask too many wrong questions, causing the powers-that-be to want them out of the picture for good.
1982 78m/C Lou Brown, David Clendenning, Jennifer Cluff. VHS, Beta *NO &½*

Death Goes to School A strangler is loose in a girl's school, and the music teacher has a hunch as to who it is.

1953 65m/B *GB* Barbara Murray, Gordon Jackson, Pamela Allan, Jane Aird, Beatrice Varley; *D:* Stephen Clarkson. VHS, Beta $16.95 *SNC &&*

Death House Kerek Keillor is on Death Row at Townsend State Prison when he discovers a plot to use inmates for scientific experiments in biological warfare. He decides the best way to get out is to volunteer, which means convincing the man who put him in prison that they're now on the same side.
19?? 92m/C Dennis Cole, Anthony (Tony) Franciosa, John Saxon. VHS $89.95 *AIP &½*

Death Hunt A man unjustly accused of murder pits his knowledge of the wilderness against the superior numbers of his pursuers.
1981 (R) 98m/C Charles Bronson, Lee Marvin, Ed Lauter, Andrew Stevens, Carl Weathers, Angie Dickinson; *D:* Peter Hunt; *W:* Mark Victor, Michael Grais. VHS, Beta $14.98 *FXV, FOX &&*

Death in Deep Water A sensuous woman lures a man into a plot to kill her incredibly rich husband.
1974 71m/C Bradford Dillman, Suzan Farmer. VHS, Beta $29.95 *LIV &&*

Death in the Shadows A young woman searches for her mother while trying to avoid a killer. Filmed entirely in Holland.
19?? 96m/C *D:* Vivian Pieters. VHS *NO &½*

Death in Venice A lush, decadent adaptation of the Thomas Mann novella about an aging and jaded composer, here suggested to be Gustav Mahler, tragically obsessed with ideal beauty as personified in a young boy. *AKA:* Morte a Venezia.
1971 (PG) 124m/C *IT* Dirk Bogarde, Mark Burns, Bjorn Andresen, Marisa Berenson, Silvana Mangano; *D:* Luchino Visconti; *M:* Gustav Mahler. VHS, Beta $59.95 *WAR, ING, PME &&&½*

Death is Called Engelchen An influential, important work of the Czech new wave. A survivor of WWII remembers his experiences with the SS leader Engelchen in a series of flashbacks. In Czech with subtitles. *AKA:* For We Too Do Not Forgive.
1963 111m/B *CZ* Jan Kadar, Elmar Klos. VHS, Beta $59.95 *FCT &&&½*

Death Journey Producer and director Williamson portrays private eye Jesse Crowder, hired by the New York D.A. to escort a key witness cross-country. A regular Williamsonfest.
1976 (R) 90m/C Fred Williamson, D'Urville Martin, Bernie Kuby, Heidi Dobbs, Stephanie Faulkner; *D:* Fred Williamson. VHS, Beta $49.95 *UNI &½*

The Death Kiss Creepy thriller about eerie doings at a major Hollywood film studio where a sinister killer does away with his victims while a cast-of-thousands movie spectacular is in production.
1933 72m/B Bela Lugosi, David Manners, Adrienne Ames, Edward Van Sloan, Vince Barnett; *D:* Edwin L. Marin. VHS, Beta, 8mm $14.95 *NOS, SNC, CAB &&½*

Death Kiss When a man hires a psychopath to murder his wife, his plan doesn't proceed exactly as expected.
1977 (R) 90m/C Larry Daniels, Dorothy Moore. VHS, Beta $49.95 *PSM, LSV &½*

Death Machines Young karate student must face the "Death Machines," a team of deadly assassins who are trained to kill on command.
1976 (R) 93m/C Ron Marchini, Michael Chong, Joshua Johnson; *D:* Paul Kyriazi. VHS, Beta *NO &½*

Death Magic A group of five ceremonial magicians performs a spell to bring someone back from the dead, but the man they bring back, a soldier from the Civil War, decides to go on a vicious murdering spree to kill the descendants of the people who convicted him of murder in 1875. A suspenseful first entry from director Clinco.
1992 93m/C Anne Coffrey, Keith DeGreen, Jack Dunlap, Danielle Frons, Norman Stone; *D:* Paul E. Clinco; *W:* Paul E. Clinco. VHS *NO &½*

Death Mask of the Ninja Two princes, separated at birth, reunite and kick everyone in the head. Dubbed.
198? 95m/C Joey Lee, Tiger Tung, Jon Chen. VHS, Beta $54.95 *MOV &½*

The Death Merchant Foundering attempt at a nuclear thriller. A modern mad man hopes to sell a computer chip to third world countries but is thwarted by a secret agent. Confusing, illogical plot highlighted by mediocre performances.
1991 90m/C Lawrence Tierney, Martina Castle, Melody Munyan, Monika Schnarre; *D:* Jim Winburn; *W:* Kari Holman. VHS $14.95 *AIP &*

Death Nurse Fresh from "Crazy Fat Ethel II," aspiring Queen of Camp Alden takes takes up residence in a health care establishment, much to the dismay of the patients who give up their lives in exchange for their money.
1987 80m/C Priscilla Alden, Michael Flood; *D:* Nick Phillips. VHS $29.98 *VCD &&*

Death of a Bureaucrat A Cuban hero dies, and in tribute, the Communist government buries him with his union card. His widow, however, needs the card in order to collect a pension, and she enlists her nephew's help to retrieve it. The nephew soon finds himself buried in red tape, and digs himself in ever-deeper as he seeks to disinter his late uncle. A wry satire of the communist bureaucracy in Cuba, brimming with comedic tributes to Harold Lloyd, Buster Keaton and Laurel & Hardy. Alea's film was only briefly released in 1966 and was promptly banned, eventually finding its way to the U.S. in 1979. In Spanish with English subtitles.
1966 87m/B Salvador Wood, Silvia Planas, Manuel Estanillo, Gaspar de Santelices, Carlos Ruiz de la Tejera, Omar Alfonso, Ricardo Suarez, Luis Romay, Elsa Montero; *D:* Thomas Gutierrez Alea. VHS, Beta $69.95 *NYF, FCT, ING &&&*

Death of a Centerfold Drama based on the life and tragic death of Playboy model and actress Dorothy Stratten. More effectively handled in Bob Fosse's "Star 80."
1981 96m/C Jamie Lee Curtis, Bruce Weitz, Robert Reed, Mitchell Ryan, Bibi Besch; *D:* Gabrielle Beaumont. VHS, Beta $59.95 *MGM &&*

Death of a Gunfighter A western town courting eastern investors and bankers seeks a way to kill their ex-gunslinger sheriff.
1969 (PG) 94m/C Richard Widmark, Lena Horne, Carroll O'Connor, John Saxon, Larry Gates; *D:* Don Siegel; *W:* Robert Totten. VHS, Beta $9.95 *MCA &&*

Death of a Salesman A powerful made-for-television adaptation of the famous Arthur Miller play. Hoffman won an Emmy (as did Malkovich) for his stirring portrayal of Willy Loman, the aging salesman who realizes he's past his prime and tries to come to grips with the life he's wasted and the family he's neglected. Reid also turns in a fine performance as his long-suffering wife.
1986 135m/C Dustin Hoffman, John Malkovich, Charles Durning, Stephen Lang, Kate Reid, Louis Zorich; *D:* Volker Schlondorff. VHS, Beta $19.98 *LHV, FCT, WAR &&&½*

Death of a Scoundrel A womanizing entrepreneur is murdered and the culprit could be any one of his many jealous romantic conquests. *AKA:* Loves of a Scoundrel.
1956 119m/B George Sanders, Zsa Zsa Gabor, Yvonne De Carlo, Victor Jory; *D:* Charles Martin. VHS, Beta $15.95 VCI ♂♂½

Death of a Soldier During WWII, the uneasy U.S.-Australian alliance explodes when a psychotic American soldier murders three Melbourne women. The lawyer hired to defend him has to fight political as well as legal influences. Based on a true story.
1985 (R) 93m/C *AU* James Coburn, Reb Brown, Maurie Field, Belinda Darey; *D:* Philippe Mora. VHS, Beta $79.98 FOX ♂♂

The Death of Adolf Hitler British made-for-television film depicting Hitler's last ten days in an underground bunker. Drug-addled, suicidal, and Eva Braun-haunted, he receives the news of the fall of the Third Reich. While the film avoids cliche, it lacks emotional depth.
1984 107m/C *GB* Frank Finlay, Caroline Mortimer; *D:* Rex Firlin. VHS, Beta $59.95 LHV, TLF, WAR ♂♂½

Death of an Angel When her crippled daughter runs away to join a cult in Mexico, a recently ordained priest (Bedelia) follows her, only to become caught up herself with the leader of the group.
1986 95m/C Bonnie Bedelia, Nick Mancuso, Pamela Ludwig, Alex Colon; *D:* Petru Popescu; *M:* Jay Michael Ferguson. VHS, Beta NO ♂♂½

The Death of Richie Gazzara does a fine job as a father driven to kill his drug-addicted teenage son, portrayed by Benson. Occasionally lapses into melodrama, but all-in-all a decent adaptation of Thomas Thompson's book "Richie" which was based on a true story. Made for television. *AKA:* Richie.
1976 97m/C Ben Gazzara, Robby Benson, Eileen Brennan, Clint Howard; *D:* Paul Wendkos. VHS, Beta $59.95 PSM, LCA ♂♂

Death of the Incredible Hulk Scientist David Banner's new job just may provide the clues for stopping his transformation into the monstrous Incredible Hulk. But first there are terrorists after the Hulk who need to be defeated and Banner's new romance to contend with. Made for television.
1990 96m/C Bill Bixby, Lou Ferrigno, Elizabeth Gracen, Philip Sterling; *D:* Bill Bixby. VHS $79.95 RHI ♂½

Death of the Rat A serious/comic meditation on the tragedy of modern technological life.
1975 6m/C *D:* Pascal Aubier. VHS, Beta FFM ♂♂½

Death on the Nile Agatha Christie's fictional detective, Hercule Poirot, is called upon to interrupt his vacation to uncover who killed an heiress aboard a steamer cruising down the Nile. Ustinov's first stint as the Belgian sleuth. Anthony Powell's costume design won an Oscar.
1978 (PG) 135m/C *GB* Peter Ustinov, Jane Birkin, Lois Chiles, Bette Davis, Mia Farrow, David Niven, Olivia Hussey, Angela Lansbury, Jack Warden, Dame Maggie Smith, George Kennedy, Simon MacCorkindale, Harry Andrews, Jon Finch; *D:* John Guillermin; *W:* Anthony Shaffer. VHS, Beta $14.98 REP ♂♂½

Death Promise Ho-hum excuse for a horror flick has murderous landlord trying to evict his tenants using whatever means are necessary.
1978 (R) 90m/C Charles Bonet. VHS, Beta NO ♂

Death Race 2000 In the 21st century, five racing car contenders challenge the national champion of a cross country race in which drivers score points by killing pedestrians. Gory fun. Based on the 1956 story by Ib Melchior, and followed by "Deathsport." Made for television.
1975 (R) 80m/C David Carradine, Simone Griffeth, Sylvester Stallone, Mary Woronov; *D:* Paul Bartel; *W:* Charles B. Griffith, Robert Thom. VHS, Beta $19.95 VDM, MRV ♂♂½

Death Rage A hitman comes out of retirement to handle the toughest assignment he has ever faced: search for and kill the man who murdered his brother. He finds out he's the victim of a Mafia doublecross.
1977 (R) 92m/C *IT* Yul Brynner, Martin Balsam; *D:* Anthony M. (Antonio Margheretti) Dawson. VHS, Beta NO ♂½

Death Ray It's a race to the finish as terrorists threaten to unleash the world's most powerful weapon.
19?? 93m/C Gordon Scott. VHS, Beta $19.99 BFV, MRV ♂½

Death Ray 2000 Bondian superspy T.R. Sloane must search out the whereabouts of a stolen military device that could kill all life on Earth. TV pilot for the series "A Man Called Sloane." *AKA:* T.R. Sloane.
1981 100m/C Robert F. Logan, Ann Turkel, Maggie Cooper, Dan O'Herlihy; *D:* Lee H. Katzin. VHS, Beta $49.95 WOV, MOV ♂½

Death Rides the Plains Western with a twist. A man lures prospective buyers to his ranch, kills them, and steals their money. It's up to our heroes to ride to the rescue.
1944 53m/B Bob Livingston, Al "Fuzzy" St. John, Nica Doret, Ray Bennett; *D:* Sam Newfield. VHS, Beta $19.95 VYY, VDM ♂♂

Death Rides the Range Russian spies start a range war as a cover for an operation to pipe helium off a ranch and over the border. Maynard, an undercover FBI agent posing as a cowboy, is out to stop them.
1940 58m/B Ken Maynard, Fay McKenzie, Ralph Peters, Julian Rivero, Charles "Blackie" King, John Elliott, Bud Osborne; *D:* Sam Newfield. VHS $11.95 GPV, NOS, DVT ♂½

Death Ring Basic action/martial arts tale about three men who must battle the bad guys to ensure their own survival.
1993 (R) 91m/C Mike Norris, Chad McQueen, Don Swayze, Billy Drago, Isabel Glasser; *D:* Robert J. Kizer; *W:* George T. LeBrun. VHS COL, NLC ♂

Death Row Diner A movie mogul, executed for a crime he didn't commit, is brought back to life by a freak electrical storm. Nothing will stop him from exacting revenge.
1988 90m/C Jay Richardson, Michelle (McClellan) Bauer, John Content, Tom Schell, Dennis Mooney, Frank Sarcinello Sr., Dana Mason. VHS, Beta NO ♂½

Death Scream Drama based on the New York murder of Kitty Genovese, whose cries for help while being assaulted went ignored by her neighbors. Good casting but the pacing deteriorates. Made for television.
1975 100m/C Raul Julia, John P. Ryan, Lucie Arnaz, Ed Asner, Art Carney, Diahann Carroll, Kate Jackson, Cloris Leachman, Tina Louise, Nancy Walker, Eric (Hans Gudegast) Braeden, Allyn Ann McLerie, Tony Dow, Sally Kirkland; *D:* Richard T. Heffron; *W:* Sterling Silliphant. VHS ACE ♂♂

Death Screams Attractive college coeds have a party and get hacked to pieces for their troubles by a machete-wielding maniac.
1983 (R) 88m/C Susan Kiger, Jennifer Chase, Jody Kay, William T. Hicks, Martin Tucker. VHS, Beta GEM ♂

Death Sentence When a woman juror on a murder case finds out that the wrong man is on trial, she is stalked by the real killer. Made for television. *AKA:* Murder One.
1974 74m/C Cloris Leachman, Laurence Luckinbill, Nick Nolte, William Schallert; *D:* E.W. Swackhamer. VHS, Beta $49.95 PSM ♂♂½

Death Ship A luxury liner is destroyed by an ancient, mysterious freighter on open seas, leaving the survivors to confront the ghost ship's inherent evil in this slow-going horror flick.
1980 (R) 91m/C *GB CA* George Kennedy, Richard Crenna, Nick Mancuso, Sally Ann Howes, Saul Rubinek, Kate Reid; *D:* Alvin Rakoff. VHS, Beta $19.98 SUE, NLC ♂

Death Shot Two plainclothes detectives (who seem just as sleazy as the criminals they're trying to bust) try to break up a drug ring and find that, with a little coercion, their best sources of information are the pimps and junkies they want to stop. Senseless attempt to make an action pic.
1973 90m/C Richard C. Watt, Frank Himes; *D:* Mitch Brown. VHS NO ♂

Death Spa A health club is possessed by the spirit of a vengeful woman. The fitness craze takes on a campy new twist.
1987 (R) 87m/C William Bumiller, Brenda Bakke, Merritt Butrick; *D:* Michael Fischa. VHS $79.98 MPI Woof!

Death Sport In this sequel to the cult hit "Death Race 2000," a group of humans play a game of death in the year 3000. The object is to race cars and kill as many competitors as possible. Not as good as the original, but still watchable.
1978 (R) 83m/C David Carradine, Claudia Jennings, Richard Lynch, William Smithers, Will Walker, David McLean, Jesse Vint; *D:* Henry Suso, Allan Arkush. VHS, Beta WAR, OM ♂♂

The Death Squad A police commissioner hires an ex-cop to find a group of vigilante cops who are behind a series of gangland-style executions. Good cast, though that's about all this flick has got going for it. Made for television.
1973 74m/C Robert Forster, Melvyn Douglas, Michelle Phillips, Mark Goddard, Bert Remsen, Claude Akins; *D:* Harry Falk. VHS, Beta $59.95 PSM ♂♂½

Death Stalk Dream vacation turns nightmarish for two couples when the wives are taken hostage by several escaped convicts. Made for television.
1974 90m/C Vince Edwards, Vic Morrow, Anjanette Comer, Robert Webber, Carol Lynley, Neville Brand, Norman Fell; *D:* Robert Day. VHS, Beta $14.95 CNG, GEM, HHE ♂½

Death Target Three former mercenaries team up for one last mission that gets sidetracked when one of the soldiers-of-fortune falls for a worker with a habit.
1983 72m/C Jorge Montesi, Elaine Lakeman; *D:* Peter Hyams. VHS, Beta $49.95 PSM ♂½

Death Tide Hoodlums pirate a ship full of diamonds in this story of death and crime on the high seas.
1958 ?m/C Frank Silvera. VHS $16.95 SNC ♂♂

Death Train Dead man seems to have been struck by a train, but clueless investigator can't figure out where the train came from.

1979 96m/C Hugh Keays-Byrne, Ingrid Mason, Max Meldrum; *D:* Igor Auzins. **VHS, Beta** *NO 𝄢½*

Death Valley Greed turns gold prospectors in Death Valley against each other.
1946 70m/C Robert Lowery, Helen Gilbert, Sterling Holloway; *D:* Lew Landers. **VHS, Beta** *NO 𝄢½*

Death Valley Good cast, lousy plot. Youngster (Billingsley) gets caught up with a psycho cowpoke while visiting mom in Arizona.
1981 (R) 90m/C Paul LeMat, Catherine Hicks, Peter Billingsley, Wilford Brimley, Edward Herrmann, Stephen McHattie; *D:* Dick Richards. **VHS, Beta** $79.95 *MCA 𝄢½*

Death Valley Days: No Gun Behind His Badge Western anthology series which ran on television from 1952-1970 and was noted for its longtime sponsor, 20 Mule Team Borax, as well as its hosts, including Stanley Andrews, Ronald Reagan, Robert Taylor, and Dale Robertson. On this tape: the premiere episode plus "Halo for a Bad Man." Each additional tape contains two episodes.
1965 55m/C Robert Taylor, Ronald Reagan. **VHS** $9.95 *RHI, MOV 𝄢½*

Death Valley Manhunt A marshal hired to protect a man's oil wells discovers that the company manager is keeping the profits for himself.
1943 55m/B Wild Bill Elliott, George "Gabby" Hayes, Anne Jeffreys; *D:* John English. **VHS, Beta** $29.95 *DVT 𝄢*

Death Valley Rangers The hero pretends to be an outlaw to expose a gang robbing gold-laden stagecoaches.
1944 59m/B Ken Maynard, Hoot Gibson, Bob Steele, Linda Brent, Kenneth Harlan; *D:* Robert Tansey. **VHS** $19.95 *NOS, DVT 𝄢½*

Death Warmed Up A crazed brain surgeon turns ordinary people into blood-thirsty mutants, and a small group of young people travel to his secluded island to stop him.
1985 83m/C Michael Hurst, Margaret Umbers, David Letch; *D:* David Blyth. **VHS, Beta** $69.98 *LIV, VES 𝄢½*

Death Warrant Van Damme whams and bams a little less than usual in this cop-undercover-in-prison testosterone fest. As a Royal Canadian Mountie undercover in prison—where inmates are perishing under mysterious circumstances—the pectoral-perfect Muscles from Brussels is on the brink of adding two plus two when an inmate transferee threatens his cover. Contains the requisite gratuitous violence, prison bromide, and miscellaneous other Van Dammages.
1990 (R) 111m/C Jean-Claude Van Damme, Robert Guillaume, Cynthia Gibb, George Dickerson, Patrick Kilpatrick; *D:* Deran Sarafian. **VHS** $14.95 *MGM 𝄢𝄢*

Death Watch In the future, media abuse is taken to an all time high as a terminally ill woman's last days are secretly filmed by a man with a camera in his head. Intelligent, adult science fiction with an excellent cast.
1980 (R) 128m/C *FR GE* Romy Schneider, Harvey Keitel, Harry Dean Stanton, Max von Sydow; *D:* Bertrand Tavernier; *W:* Bertrand Tavernier, David Rayfiel. **VHS** $29.98 *SUE 𝄢𝄢𝄢*

Death Weekend A woman is stalked by a trio of murderous, drunken hoodlums who seek to spoil her weekend. *AKA:* House by the Lake.
1976 89m/C *CA* Brenda Vaccaro, Don Stroud, Chuck Shamata, Richard Ayres, Kyle Edwards; *D:* William Fruet. **VHS, Beta** $69.98 *LIV, VES 𝄢½*

Death Wish A middle-aged businessman turns vigilante after his wife and daughter are violently attacked and raped by a gang of hoodlums (one is Goldblum in his film debut). He stalks the streets of New York seeking revenge on other muggers, pimps, and crooks, making the neighborhood safer for those less macho.
1974 (R) 93m/C Charles Bronson, Vincent Gardenia, William Redfield, Hope Lange, Jeff Goldblum, Stuart Margolin, Olympia Dukakis; *D:* Michael Winner; *W:* Wendell Mayes; *M:* Herbie Hancock. **VHS, Beta** $14.95 *MGM, PAR 𝄢𝄢½*

Death Wish 2 Bronson recreates the role of Paul Kersey, an architect who takes the law into his own hands when his family is victimized once again. Extremely violent sequel to the successful 1974 movie. Followed by "Death Wish 3" (1985) and 4 (1987) in which Bronson continues to torture the street scum and the viewers as well.
1982 (R) 89m/C J.D. Cannon, Charles Bronson, Jill Ireland, Vincent Gardenia, Anthony (Tony) Franciosa; *D:* Michael Winner. **VHS, Beta** $19.98 *WAR, OM Woof!*

Death Wish 3 Once again, Charles Bronson blows away the low lifes who have killed those who were dear to him and were spared in the first two films.
1985 (R) 100m/C Charles Bronson, Martin Balsam, Deborah Raffin, Ed Lauter, Alex Winter, Marina Sirtis; *D:* Michael Winner. **VHS, Beta** $14.98 *MGM 𝄢½*

Death Wish 4: The Crackdown The four-times-weary urban vigilante hits crack dealers this time, hard.
1987 (R) 100m/C Charles Bronson, John P. Ryan, Kay Lenz; *D:* J. Lee Thompson. **VHS, Beta** $19.95 *MED, VTR 𝄢*

Death Wish 5: The Face of Death Paul Kersey (Bronson) returns to vigilantism when his clothing manufacturer fiancee Olivia (Downs) has her business threatened by mobsters, one of whom turns out to be her sadistic ex (Parks). Bronson looks bored with the rehashed material. Lots of explicit and grisly violence.
1994 (R) 95m/C Charles Bronson, Lesley-Anne Down, Michael Parks, Kenneth Welsh; *D:* Allan Goldstein; *W:* Allan Goldstein; *M:* Terry Plumer. **VHS** $94.99 *VMK Woof!*

Death Wish Club Young woman gets involved in a club with an unusual mission—suicide. *AKA:* Carnival of Fools.
1983 93m/C Meridith Haze, Rick Barns, J. Martin Sellers, Ann Fairchild; *D:* John Carr. **VHS, Beta** *NO 𝄢½*

Deathcheaters Australian Secret Service offers two stuntmen a top secret mission in the Philippines.
1976 (G) 96m/C John Hargreaves, Grant Page, Noel Ferrer; *D:* Brian Trenchard-Smith; *W:* Michael Cove. **VHS, Beta** $69.98 *VES 𝄢½*

Deathdream In this reworking of the "Monkey's Paw" tale, a mother wishes her dead son would return from Vietnam. He does, but he's not quite the person he used to be. Gripping plot gives new meaning to the saying, "Be careful what you wish for—it might come true." *AKA:* Dead of Night; Night Walk; The Veteran.
1972 98m/C John Marley, Richard Backus, Lynn Carlin; *D:* Bob (Benjamin) Clark; *W:* Alan Ormsby. **VHS, Beta** $59.95 *MPI 𝄢𝄢½*

Deathfight Let's face it, no one watches these movies because they have a plot. This is a fast-paced B-grade martial arts flick with numerous butts getting kicked. Oh, all right, if you insist on a plot—Norton's evil half-brother (Guerrero) is trying to turn their legitimate family business into a criminal front by framing Norton for murder.
1993 (R) 92m/C Richard Norton, Franco Guerrero, Karen Moncrieff, Chuck Jeffrys, Ron Vreeken, Tetchie Agbayani, Jose Mari Avellano; *D:* Anthony Maharaj; *W:* Tom Huckabee. **VHS** $92.95 *ACA 𝄢½*

Deathhead Virgin An evil virgin spirit is waiting to possess one of two men eager to find a sunken fortune. The fate of the fortunate one is only death!
1974 (R) 94m/C Jock Gaynor, Larry Ward, Diane McBain, Vic Diaz. **VHS, Beta** *NO 𝄢½*

Deathmask A four-year-old boy's corpse is found buried in a cardboard box, and a medical examiner—whose daughter met a similar fate—investigates the murder. Could've been done more tastefully.
1969 102m/C Farley Granger, Ruth Warrick, Danny Aiello; *D:* Richard S. Friedman. **VHS, Beta** $69.95 *PSM, PRD 𝄢𝄢*

Deathmoon A businessman plagued by recurring werewolf nightmares goes on a Hawaiian vacation to try to forget his troubles. Made for television.
1978 90m/C Robert Foxworth, Joe Penny, Debralee Scott, Dolph Sweet, Charles Haid; *D:* Bruce Kessler. **VHS, Beta** *NO 𝄢½*

Deathrow Gameshow Condemned criminals can either win their freedom or die in front of millions on a new television show that doesn't win the host many friends.
1988 78m/C John McCafferty, Robin Bluthe, Beano, Mark Lasky; *D:* Mark Pirro; *W:* Mark Pirro. **VHS, Beta** *MED 𝄢½*

Deathstalker Deathstalker sets his sights on seizing the evil wizard Munkar's magic amulet so he can take over Munkar's castle. The only excuse for making such an idiotic film seems to have been to fill it with half-naked women. Filmed in Argentina and followed by two sequels that were an improvement. *AKA:* El Cazador de la Muerte.
1983 (R) 80m/C Richard Hill, Barbi Benton, Richard Brooker, Victor Bo, Lana Clarkson; *D:* John Watson. **VHS, Beta** $29.98 *LIV, VES Woof!*

Deathstalker 2: Duel of the Titans Campy fantasy comically pits the lead character against an evil wizard. Sword-and-sorcery spoof doesn't take itself too seriously.
1987 85m/C John Terlesky, Monique Gabrielle, John Lazar, Toni Naples, Maria Socas, Queen Kong; *D:* Jim Wynorski; *W:* Jim Wynorski. **VHS, Beta** $29.98 *LIV, VES 𝄢𝄢*

Deathstalker 3 Another humorous entry in the Deathstalker saga. This time there's action, romance, magic and the Warriors From Hell. *AKA:* Deathstalker 3: The Warriors From Hell.
1989 (R) 85m/C John Allen Nelson, Carla Herd, Terri Treas, Thom Christopher; *D:* Alfonso Corona. **VHS, Beta** $79.98 *LIV, VES, HHE 𝄢½*

Deathstalker 4: Clash of the Titans The sword and sorcery epic continues, with our hero revealing yet more musculature in his efforts to defeat an evil queen and her legion of stone warriors.
1992 (R) 85m/C Richard Hill, Maria Ford, Michelle Moffett, Brent Baxter Clark; *D:* Howard R. Cohen. **VHS** $89.98 *NHO 𝄢*

Deathtrap A creatively-blocked playwright, his ailing rich wife, and a former student who has written a surefire hit worth killing for, are the principals in this compelling comedy-mystery. Cross and double-cross are explored in this film based on the Broadway hit by Ira Levin.

1982 (PG) 118m/C Henry Jones, Michael Caine, Christopher Reeve, Dyan Cannon, Irene Worth; *D:* Sidney Lumet; *W:* Jay Presson Allen. **VHS, Beta** $19.98 *WAR ♪♪*

The Decameron Pasolini's first epic pageant in his "Trilogy of Life" series. An acclaimed, sexually explicit adaptation of a handful of the Boccaccio tales. In Italian with English subtitles.
1970 (R) 111m/C *FR IT GE* Franco Citti, Ninetto Davoli, Angela Luce, Patrizia Capparelli, Jovan Jovanovich, Silvana Mangano, Pier Paolo Pasolini; *D:* Pier Paolo Pasolini; *M:* Ennio Morricone. **VHS, Beta** $79.95 *WBF, ING, APD ♪♪♪ ½*

Decameron Nights Story of Boccaccio's pursuit of a recently-widowed young women is interwoven amongst the three of the fourteenth-century Italian writer's bawdy tales.
1953 87m/C *GB* Louis Jourdan, Joan Fontaine, Binnie Barnes, Joan Collins, Marjorie Rhodes; *D:* Hugo Fregonese. **VHS, Beta** $19.95 *NOS, MRV, GEM ♪♪ ½*

Deceit A sci-fi sex comedy with an environmental premise. Bailey and Brick are two aliens working for their planet's Environmental Protection Agency, whose idea of protection is to vaporize polluter planets. Guess which planet is next on their hit list. But before they get down to business, our two alien studs want to do the horizontal bop with two of the local lovelies, who decide that isn't how they want to spend their last moments on earth. It has a happy ending.
1993 (R) 92m/C Scott Paulin, Norbert Weisser, Samantha Phillips; *D:* Albert Pyun; *W:* Kitty Chalmers. **VHS** $89.95 *COL ♪♪*

Deceived A successful career woman with a passionate husband and a young daughter feels she has it all until her husband is apparently killed in a bizarre tragedy. But just how well did she know the man she married? Who was he really and what secrets are hidden in his past? As she struggles to solve these mysteries, her own life becomes endangered in this psychological thriller.
1991 (PG-13) 115m/C Goldie Hawn, John Heard, Ashley Peldon, Jan Rubes, Amy Wright, Maia Filar, Robin Bartlett, Tom Irwin, Beatrice Straight, Kate Reid; *D:* Damien Harris; *W:* Mary Agnes Donoghue, Derek Saunders; *M:* Thomas Newman. **VHS, Beta** $92.95 *TOU ♪♪ ½*

The Deceivers Brosnan stars as a British officer sent on a dangerous undercover mission in 1820s India. He's to infiltrate the notorious Thuggee cult, known for robbing and murdering unwary travelers. Interesting premise falters due to slow pacing and Brosnan's lack of believability.
1988 (PG-13) 112m/C *IN GB* Pierce Brosnan, Saeed Jaffrey, Shashi Kapoor, Keith Michell; *D:* Nicholas Meyer. **VHS, Beta** $19.98 *WAR ♪♪*

December Four prep-school students in New Hampshire must confront the reality of war when the Japanese bomb Pearl Harbor. A touching story of courage and friendship that takes place in one night during the suprise-attack.
1991 (PG) 92m/C Wil Wheaton, Chris Young, Brian Krause, Balthazar Getty, Jason London; *D:* Gabe Torres; *W:* Gabe Torres. **VHS** *NO ♪♪*

December Flower A young woman arrives at her aunt's estate so she can nurse her back to health, but she finds her aunt a bit down in the mouth: seems someone is trying to kill her, and she could be next in line.
19?? 65m/C Jean Simmons, Mona Washbourne, Bryan Forbes. **VHS** $19.99 *FCT, MOV ♪♪ ½*

December 7th: The Movie Banned for 50 years by the U.S. Government, this planned Hollywood explanation to wartime audiences of the Pearl Harbor debacle offers such "offensive" images as blacks fighting heroically alongside whites, loyal Japanese-Americans, and Uncle Sam asleep on the morning of the attack. The Chief of Naval Operations confiscated the original film, claiming it demeaned the Navy. The battle scenes were so realistic they fooled even documentarians. This isn't the most incisive video on the event—just an unforgettable snapshot.
1991 82m/B Walter Huston, Harry Davenport; *D:* John Ford. **VHS** $19.95 *KIT, CPM, FUS ♪♪ ½*

Deception Davis is a pianist torn between two loves: her intensely jealous sponsor (Rains) and her cellist boyfriend (Henreid). Plot in danger of going over the melodramatic edge is saved by the very effective performances of the stars.
1946 112m/B Bette Davis, Paul Henreid, Claude Rains, John Abbott, Benson Fong; *D:* Irving Rapper. **VHS, Beta** $19.95 *MGM ♪♪♪*

Deception Talented cast is wasted in an old-fashioned mystery that lacks a coherent script. MacDowell is married to Mortensen, the owner of an aircraft salvage company. He's supposedly killed in a plane crash but she thinks he's just pulled a fast one and sets off to find him. Tracking her hubby's secret bank accounts takes her all over the world, and finally to Cairo, Egypt where she meets Neeson. Together they discover Mortensen's scam involves smuggling poison gas and the duo then try to outwit the hoods on their trail. Film was originally released at 110 minutes. *AKA:* Ruby Cairo.
1992 (PG-13) 90m/C Andie MacDowell, Liam Neeson, Viggo Mortensen, Jack Thompson, Jeff Corey, Miriam Reed, Luis Cortes, Paco Mauri; *D:* Graeme Clifford; *W:* Robert Dillon, Michael Thomas; *M:* John Barry. **VHS** *LIV ♪ ½*

Deceptions A risque, semi-erotic thriller about a wealthy society woman (Sheridan) who kills her husband. Sheridan claims that she acted in self-defense, but macho cop Hamlin has a different view. He interrogates her, grows increasingly attracted, and is drawn into her web of seduction.
1990 (R) 105m/C Harry Hamlin, Nicollette Sheridan. **VHS** $89.98 *REP ♪♪*

The Decline of the American Empire The critically acclaimed French-Canadian film about eight academic intellectuals who spend a weekend shedding their sophistication and engaging in intertwining sexual affairs. Examines the differing attitudes of men and women in regards to sex and sexuality. In French with English subtitles. *AKA:* Le Declin De L'Empire Americain.
1986 (R) 102m/C *CA* Dominique Michel, Dorothee Berryman, Louise Portal, Genevieve Rioux; *D:* Denys Arcand; *W:* Denys Arcand. Academy Awards '86 Nominations: Best Foreign Language Film; Genie Awards '87: Best Director (Arcand), Best Film, Best Supporting Actor (Arcand), Best Supporting Actress (Portal). **VHS, Beta** $79.95 *MCA, ING ♪♪♪ ½*

Decline of Western Civilization 1 The L.A. hard core punk scene. Music by X, Circle Jerks, Black Flag, Fear and more.
1981 100m/C *D:* Penelope Spheeris. **VHS, Beta** $49.95 *MVD, MED ♪♪♪*

Decline of Western Civilization 2: The Metal Years Following Spheeris's first documentary about hardcore punk, she in turn delves into the world of heavy metal rock. We are given a look at some of the early rockers, as well as some of the smaller bands still playing L.A. clubs. Features appearances by Alice Cooper, Ozzy Osbourne, Poison, Gene Simmons and Megadeth.
1988 (R) 90m/C Alice Cooper, Ozzy Osbourne, Gene Simmons, Lizzie Borden; *D:* Penelope Spheeris. **VHS, Beta** $14.95 *COL, MVD, FCT ♪♪♪*

Decoration Day Garner plays a retired Southern judge who aids an angry childhood friend who has refused to accept his long-overdue Medal of Honor. Investigating the past leads to a decades-old mystery and a tragic secret that has repercussions for everyone involved. Based on the novel by John William Corrington. A Hallmark Hall of Fame presentation.
1990 (PG) 99m/C James Garner, Bill Cobbs, Judith Ivey, Ruby Dee, Laurence "Larry" Fishburne, Jo Anderson; *D:* Robert Markowitz. **VHS** $14.98 *REP ♪♪♪*

Dedee d'Anvers A gritty dockside melodrama about a drunken prostitute abused by her pimp. A sailor and a local barkeep don't like it. In French with subtitles. *AKA:* Dedee; Woman of Antwerp.
1949 95m/B Simone Signoret, Marcel Dalio, Bernard Blier, Marcel Pagliero, Jane Marken; *D:* Yves Allegret. **VHS, Beta** $24.95 *NOS, FCT, ING ♪♪ ½*

A Dedicated Man A lonely woman agrees to act as a wife for a businessman to lend him credibility. A British "Romance Theater" presentation.
1986 60m/C *GB* Alec McCowen, Joan Plowright; *D:* Robert Knights. **VHS** $11.95 *PSM ♪♪ ½*

The Deep An innocent couple get involved in an underwater search for a shipwreck, and they quickly find themselves in over their heads. Gorgeous photography manages to keep this slow mover afloat. Famous for Bisset's wet T-shirt scene. Based on the novel by Peter Benchley. The laserdisc edition offers widescreen format.
1977 (PG) 123m/C Nick Nolte, Jacqueline Bisset, Robert Shaw, Louis Gossett Jr., Eli Wallach; *D:* Peter Yates; *W:* Peter Benchley, Tracy Keenan Wynn; *M:* John Barry. **VHS, Beta** $14.95 *GKK ♪♪*

Deep Cover A man dares to go beyond the walls of a mysterious English manor in order to expose the secrets that lie within the manor.
1988 (R) 81m/C Tom Conti, Donald Pleasence, Denholm Elliott, Kika Markham, Phoebe Nicholls; *D:* Richard Loncraine. **VHS, Beta** $79.95 *PSM, PAR ♪ ½*

Deep Cover Fishburne plays Russell Stevens Jr., a straight-arrow cop who goes undercover to infiltrate a Latin American cocaine cartel. While undercover, he becomes partners with drug dealer David Jason (Goldblum), and undergoes an inner transformation until he realizes he is betraying his cause. Confusing and commercial, yet marked with a moral rage.
1992 (R) 107m/C Laurence "Larry" Fishburne, Jeff Goldblum, Victoria Dillard, Charles Martin Smith, Sydney Lassick, Clarence Williams III, Gregory Sierra, Robert Guenveur Smith, Cory Curtis, Glynn Turman, Def Jef; *D:* Bill Duke; *W:* Michael Tolkin, Henry Bean; *M:* Michel Colombier. **VHS** $19.95 *COL, NLC ♪♪ ½*

Deep End A 15-year-old boy working as an attendant in a bath house falls in love with a 20-year-old woman in this tragic tale of a young man obsessed. Good British cast and music by Cat Stevens.
1970 88m/C *GB GE* Jane Asher, John Moulder-Brown, Diana Dors; *D:* Jerzy Skolimowski; *M:* Cat Stevens. **VHS** *FCT ♪♪♪*

Deep in My Heart A musical biography of the life and times of composer Sigmund Romberg, with guest appearances by many MGM stars. ♫ Leg of Mutton; You Will Remember Vienna; Softly, as in a Morning Sunrise; Mr. & Mrs.; I Love to Go Swimmin' with Wimmin; The Road to Paradise; Will You Remember; It; Serenade; One Alone; Your Land and My Land; Lover, Come Back to Me; Stouthearted Men; When I Grow Too Old to Dream; The Desert Song; Goodbye Girls; Fat, Fat Fatima; Jazza, Jazza Doo Do; Miss U.S.A.; Auf Wiedersehn.
1954 132m/C Jose Ferrer, Merle Oberon, Paul Henreid, Walter Pidgeon, Helen Traubel, Rosemary Clooney, Jane Powell, Howard Keel, Cyd Charisse, Gene Kelly, Ann Miller; **D:** Stanley Donen. **VHS, Beta $19.98** *MGM ♫♫ ½*

Deep in the Heart When a young teacher is raped at gunpoint on a second date, she takes the law into her own hands. Just-off-the-target film tries to take a stand against the proliferation of guns in the U.S. Thought-provoking all the same. **AKA:** Handgun.
1983 (R) 99m/C *GB* Karen Young, Clayton Day, Ben Jones, Suzie Humphreys; **D:** Tony Garnett; **W:** Tony Garnett. **VHS, Beta $69.99** *HBO ♫♫*

Deep Red When a young girl has an encounter with an extra-terrestrial spacecraft her blood chemistry is mysteriously altered. Now the proteins her body manufactures can lead to immortality and ruthless scientist Newmar wants to take advantage of the fact—any way he can.
1994 (R) 85m/C Michael Biehn, Joanna Pacula, John de Lancie; **D:** Craig R. Baxley; **W:** D. Brent Mote. **VHS $89.98** *MCA ♫♫*

Deep Red: Hatchet Murders A stylish but gruesome rock music-driven tale of a composer who reads a book on the occult which happens to relate to the sadistic, sangfroid murder of his neighbor. When he visits the book's author, he discovers that she has been horribly murdered as well. **AKA:** The Hatchet Murders; Profundo Rosso; Dripping Deep Red.
1975 100m/C David Hemmings, Daria Nicolodi; **D:** Dario Argento. **VHS, Beta $19.99** *HBO, QVD ♫♫ ½*

Deep Six A WWII drama that examines the conflict between pacifism and loyalty. A staunch Quaker is called to active duty as a lieutenant in the U.S. Navy, where his beliefs put him into disfavor with shipmates.
1958 110m/C Alan Ladd, William Bendix, James Whitmore, Keenan Wynn, Efrem Zimbalist Jr., Joey Bishop; **D:** Rudolph Mate. **VHS, Beta $54.95** *VCI ♫♫ ½*

Deep Space A flesh-eating alien lands on earth and, after devouring a cop, is stalked by his partner. An "Alien" rip-off. Some humorous moments keep us from thinking too hard about how much the monster resembles our friend from "Alien."
1987 90m/C Charles Napier, Ann Turkel, Ron Glass, Bo Svenson, Julie Newmar; **D:** Fred Olen Ray. **VHS, Beta $79.95** *TWE ♫♫ ½*

Deepstar Six When futuristic scientists try to set up an undersea research and missile site, a group of subterranean monsters get in the way.
1989 (R) 97m/C Taurean Blacque, Nancy Everhard, Greg Evigan, Miguel Ferrer, Matt McCoy, Nia Peeples, Cindy Pickett, Marius Weyers; **D:** Sean S. Cunningham. **VHS, Beta NO ♫ ½**

The Deer Hunter A powerful and vivid portrait of Middle America with three steel-working friends who leave home to face the Vietnam War. Controversial, brutal sequences in Vietnam are among the most wrenching ever filmed; the rhythms and rituals of home are just as purely captured. Neither pro- nor anti-war, but rather the perfect evocation of how totally and forever altered these people are by the war. Emotionally shattering; not to be missed.
1978 (R) 183m/C Robert De Niro, Christopher Walken, Meryl Streep, John Savage, George Dzundza, John Cazale, Chuck Aspegren, Rutanya Alda, Shirley Stoler, Amy Wright; **D:** Michael Cimino; **W:** Deric Washburn, Michael Cimino; **M:** John Williams. Academy Awards '78: Best Director (Cimino), Best Film Editing, Best Picture, Best Sound, Best Supporting Actor (Walken); Nominations: Best Actor (De Niro), Best Cinematography, Best Original Screenplay, Best Supporting Actress (Streep); Golden Globe Awards '79: Best Director (Cimino); Los Angeles Film Critics Association Awards '78: Best Director (Cimino); New York Film Critics Awards '78: Best Film, Best Supporting Actor (Walken). **VHS, Beta $14.95** *MCA, FCT, BTV ♫♫♫♫*

The Deerslayer Low-budget snoozer based on the classic novel by James Fenimore Cooper. Frontiersman Hawkeye and his Indian companion Chingachgook set out to rescue a beautiful Indian maiden and must fight bands of hostile Indians and Frenchmen along the way.
1978 98m/C Steve Forrest, Ned Romero, John Anderson, Joan Prather; **D:** Richard Friedenberg. **VHS, Beta $19.95** *STE, VCI ♫ ½*

Def by Temptation A potent horror fantasy about a young black theology student who travels to New York in search of an old friend. There he meets an evil woman who is determined to seduce him and force him to give in to temptation. Great soundtrack.
1990 (R) 95m/C James Bond III, Kadeem Hardison, Bill Nunn, Samuel L. Jackson, Minnie Gentry, Rony Clanton; **D:** James Bond III. **VHS, Beta $89.98** *SGE, IME ♫♫*

Def-Con 4 Three marooned space travelers return to a holocaust-shaken Earth to try to start again, but some heavy-duty slimeballs are in charge and they don't want to give it up. Good special effects bolster a weak script.
1985 (R) 85m/C Maury Chaykin, Kate Lynch, Tim Choate; **D:** Paul Donovan. **VHS, Beta $14.95** *NWV, STE ♫ ½*

The Defender CBS "Studio One" presentation of a live courtroom drama. First shown in 1957. Made for television.
1957 112m/B Steve McQueen, William Shatner, Ralph Bellamy, Martin Balsam. **VHS, Beta $29.95** *FCT, RHI ♫♫ ½*

Defenders of the Law Early action talkie concerned with gang warfare and law enforcement.
1931 64m/B John Holland, Mae Busch, Alan Cooke, Joseph Girard, Edmund Breese, Catherine Dale Owen, Robert Gleckler; **D:** Joseph Levering. **VHS $9.95** *GPV ♫♫*

Defending Your Life Brooks' cock-eyed way of looking at the world travels to the afterlife in this uneven comedy/romance. In Judgement City, where everyone goes after death, past lives are examined and judged. If you were a good enough person you get to stay in heaven (where you wear funny robes and eat all you want without getting fat). If not, it's back to earth for another go-round. Brooks plays an L.A. advertising executive who crashes his new BMW and finds himself defending his life. When he meets and falls in love with Streep, his interest in staying in heaven multiplies. Occasionally charming, seldom out-right hilarious.
1991 (PG) 112m/C Albert Brooks, Meryl Streep, Rip Torn, Lee Grant, Buck Henry, George Wallace, Lillian Lehman, Peter Schuck; **D:** Albert Brooks; **W:** Albert Brooks; **M:** Michael Gore. **VHS, 8mm $19.98** *WAR ♫♫♫*

The Defense Never Rests Perry Mason, the lawyer who never loses a case, aids his friend and secretary, Della Street, in this made-for-television movie.
1990 95m/C Raymond Burr, Barbara Hale, Al Freeman Jr., William Katt, Patrick O'Neal. **VHS, Beta $29.98** *MCG ♫♫*

Defense of the Realm A British politician is accused of selling secrets to the KGB through his mistress and only a pair of dedicated newspapermen believe he is innocent. In the course of finding the answers they discover a national cover-up conspiracy. An acclaimed, taut thriller.
1985 (PG) 96m/C *GB* Gabriel Byrne, Greta Scacchi, Denholm Elliott, Ian Bannen, Bill Paterson, Fulton Mackay, Robbie Coltrane; **D:** David Drury. **VHS, Beta $14.95** *COL, SUE ♫♫♫ ½*

Defense Play Two teenagers are unwittingly stuck in the middle of a Soviet plot to steal the plans that created a technologically advanced helicopter.
1988 (PG) 95m/C David Oliver, Susan Ursitti, Monte Markham, William Frankfather, Patch MacKenzie; **D:** Monte Markham. **VHS, Beta $19.98** *TWE ♫ ½*

Defenseless Hershey tries hard in an unplayable part as a giddy attorney who finds herself trapped in a love-affair/legal case that turns murderous. Good cast and interesting twists contend with a sexist subtext, which proves a woman can't "have it all."
1991 (R) 106m/C Barbara Hershey, Sam Shepard, Mary Beth Hurt, J.T. Walsh, Sheree North; **D:** Martin Campbell; **M:** Trevor Jones. **VHS $19.98** *LIV ♫♫*

Defiance A former merchant seaman moves into a tenement in a run-down area of New York City. When a local street gang begins terrorizing the neighborhood, he decides to take a stand. Familiar plotline handled well in this thoughtful film.
1979 (PG) 101m/C Jan-Michael Vincent, Art Carney, Theresa Saldana, Danny Aiello; **D:** John Flynn; **W:** Tom Donnelly. **VHS, Beta $9.98** *ORI, LIV, VES ♫♫*

Defiant Two rival street gangs clash when one admits a young orphan girl. **AKA:** The Wild Pack; The Sandpit Generals.
1970 93m/C Kent Lane, John Rubinstein, Tisha Sterling; **D:** Hall Bartlett. **VHS, Beta $69.98** *LIV ♫ ½*

The Defiant Ones Thought-provoking story about racism revolves around two escaped prisoners (one black, one white) from a chain gang in the rural South. Their societal conditioning to hate each other dissolves as they face constant peril together. Critically acclaimed.
1958 97m/B Tony Curtis, Sidney Poitier, Theodore Bikel, Lon Chaney Jr., Charles McGraw, Cara Williams; **D:** Stanley Kramer; **W:** Nathan E. Douglas, Harold Jacob Smith; **M:** Stephen Dorff. Academy Awards '58: Best Black and White Cinematography, Best Original Screenplay; Nominations: Best Actor (Curtis), Best Actor (Poitier), Best Director (Kramer), Best Film Editing, Best Picture, Best Supporting Actor (Bikel), Best Supporting Actress (Williams); British Academy Awards '58: Best Actor (Poitier); Edgar Allan Poe Awards '58: Best Screenplay; Golden Globe Awards '59: Best Film—Drama. **VHS, Beta $19.95** *MGM, FOX ♫♫♫♫*

The Defilers Disturbing, low-budget J.D. movie in which two thugs imprison a young girl in a basement and force her to be their love slave.

1965 (R) ?m/B Byron Mabe, Jerome Eden, Mae Johnson; **D:** David Friedman. VHS $16.95 SNC, TPV ✠

Deja Vu A lame romantic thriller about the tragic deaths of two lovers and their supposed reincarnation 50 years later. **1984 (R) 95m/C** *GB* Jaclyn Smith, Nigel Terry, Claire Bloom, Shelley Winters; **D:** Anthony Richmond; **W:** Ezra D. Rappaport; **M:** Pino Donaggio. VHS, Beta $79.95 MGM ✠

Deja Vu Thriller set in 1925 and moving between Chicago and Odessa. A Chicago hitman is hired by the mob to kill a traitor who has fled to Odessa. Niczypur, the traitor, has been using the newly opened Chicago-Constantinople-Odessa shipping line for his own smuggling operation. Filled with shoot-outs, brawls, and chases. In English, Russian, and Polish with English subtitles. **1989 108m/C** *PL* Jerzy Stuhr, Galina Pietrowa, Nikolai Karaczencow, Wladimir Golowin; **D:** Juliusz Machulski. VHS $59.95 FCT ✠✠

The Deliberate Stranger Harmon is engrossing as charismatic serial killer Ted Bundy, sentenced to death for several Florida murders and suspected in the killings of a least 25 women in several states. After eluding police for five years Bundy was finally arrested in Florida in 1979. His case became a cause celebre on capital punishment as it dragged on for nine years. Bundy was finally executed in 1989. Based on the book "Bundy: The Deliberate Stranger" by Richard W. Larsen. Made for television. **1986 188m/C** Mark Harmon, M. Emmet Walsh, Frederic Forrest, John Ashton, George Grizzard, Ben Masters, Glynnis O'Connor, Bonnie Bartlett, Billy Green Bush, Lawrence Pressman; **D:** Marvin J. Chomsky. VHS, Beta $69.99 WAR, PMS ✠✠✠

The Delicate Delinquent Lewis's first movie without Dean Martin finds him in the role of delinquent who manages to become a policeman with just the right amount of slapstick. **1956 101m/B** Jerry Lewis, Darren McGavin, Martha Hyer, Robert Ivers, Horace McMahon; **D:** Don McGuire; **W:** Don McGuire. VHS, Beta $24.95 PAR ✠✠½

Delicatessen Set in 21st-century Paris, this hilarious debut from directors Jeunot and Caro focuses on the lives of the oddball tenants of an apartment building over a butcher shop. Although there is a famine, the butcher shop is always stocked with fresh meat—made from the building's tenants. Part comedy, part horror, part romance, this film merges a cacophony of sights and sounds with intriguing results. Watch for the scene involving a symphony of creaking bed springs, a squeaky bicycle pump, a cello, and clicking knitting needles. In French with English subtitles. **1992 95m/C** *FR* Marie-Laure Dougnac, Dominique Pinon, Karin Viard, Jean Claude Dreyfus, Ticky Holgado, Anne Marie Pisani, Edith Ker, Patrick Paroux, Jean-Luc Caron; **D:** Jean-Marie Jeunet, Marc Caro; **W:** Adrien Gilles; **M:** Carlos D'Alessi. VHS, Beta $89.95 PAR, ING, BTV ✠✠✠

Delightfully Dangerous Often Deadly Dull. A farfetched musical rooted in yesteryear about mismatched sisters, one a 15-year-old farm girl, the other a New York burlesque dancer, in competition on Broadway. ♫I'm Only Teasin'; In a Shower of Stars; Mynah Bird; Through Your Eyes to Your Heart; Delightfully Dangerous; Once Upon a Song. **1945 92m/B** Jane Powell, Ralph Bellamy, Constance Moore, Arthur Treacher, Louise Beavers; **D:** Arthur Lubin. VHS $19.95 DVT, NOS, VDM ✠✠

Delinquent Daughters Slow-paced drama about a high school girl who commits suicide and the cop and reporter who try to find out why so darn many kids are getting into trouble. **1944 71m/B** June Carlson, Fifi d'Orsay, Teala Loring; **D:** Albert Herman. VHS, Beta $16.95 SNC, VYY ✠½

Delinquent Parents A wayward girl gives up her baby for adoption. She turns her life around and becomes a juvenile court judge. Years later, who should come up before her for misdeeds but her long-lost daughter. The Hound cannot improve on a contemporary critic who renamed this "Delinquent Producers." **1938 62m/B** Doris Weston, Maurice Murphy, Helen MacKellar, Terry Walker, Richard Tucker, Morgan Wallace; **D:** Nick Grinde. VHS $15.95 NOS, LOO ✠½

Delinquent School Girls Three escapees from an asylum get more than they bargained for when they visit a Female Correctional Institute to fulfill their sexual fantasies. Buys into just about every conceivable stereotype. **AKA:** Bad Girls. **1984 (R) 89m/C** Michael Pataki, Bob Minos, Stephen Stucker; **D:** Gregory Corarito. VHS, Beta $69.98 LIV, VES *Woof!*

Delirious A writer for a television soap opera wakes from a bash on the head to find himself inside the story where murder and mayhem are brewing. Can he write himself back to safety, and find romance along the way? Somehow Candy just isn't believeable as a romantic lead and the film set laughs. **1991 (PG) 96m/C** John Candy, Mariel Hemingway, Emma Samms, Raymond Burr, David Rasche, Dylan Baker, Charles Rocket, Jerry Orbach, Renee Taylor, Robert Wagner; **D:** Tom Mankiewicz; **M:** Cliff Eidelman. VHS, Beta, 8mm $14.95 MGM ✠½

Delirium Homicidal maniac goes on a killing spree and has just one thing in mind—women. Angry group of citizens inadvertently includes the demonic villain in their vigilante club. Nothing redeeming here. **AKA:** Psycho Puppet. **1977 94m/C** Turk Cekovsky, Debi Shanley, Terry Ten Brock; **D:** Peter Maris. VHS, Beta NO *Woof!*

Deliverance Terrifying exploration of the primal nature of man and his alienation from nature, based on the novel by James Dickey, which he adapted for the film (he also makes an appearance as a sheriff). Four urban professionals, hoping to get away from it all for the weekend, canoe down a southern river, encounter crazed backwoodsmen, and end up battling for survival. Excellent performances all around, especially by Voight. Debuts for Beatty and Cox. Watch for O'Neill as a sheriff, and director Boorman's son Charley as Voight's son. "Dueling Banjos" scene and tune are memorable as is scene where the backwoods boys promise to make the fellows squeal like pigs. **1972 (R) 109m/C** Jon Voight, Burt Reynolds, Ronny Cox, Ned Beatty, James Dickey, Bill McKinney, Ed O'Neill, Charley Boorman; **D:** John Boorman; **W:** James Dickey; **M:** Eric Weissburg. Academy Awards '72 Nominations: Best Director (Boorman), Best Film Editing, Best Picture; National Board of Review Awards '72: 10 Best Films of the Year. VHS, Beta $19.98 WAR, FCT ✠✠✠✠

Delivery Boys The "Delivery Boys," three breakdancers aiming to win the $10,000 New York City Break-Off, find unusual perils that may keep them from competing.

1984 (R) 94m/C Joss Marcano, Tom Sierchio, Jim Soriero, Mario Van Peebles, Samantha Fox; **D:** Ken Handley. VHS, Beta $19.95 STE, NWV ✠½

Delos Adventure A geological expedition in South America stumbles upon covert Russian activities and must battle to survive in this overly-violent actioner. **1986 (R) 98m/C** Roger Kern, Jenny Neumann, Kevin Brophy; **D:** Joseph Purcell. VHS, Beta $79.95 TWE ✠

Delta Force Based on the true hijacking of a TWA plane in June 1985. Arab terrorists take over an airliner; the Delta Force, led by Lee Marvin and featuring Norris as its best fighter, rescue the passengers in ways that cater directly to our nationalistic revenge fantasies. Average thriller, exciting and tense at times, with fine work from Marvin, Norris, and Forster. **1986 (R) 125m/C** Lee Marvin, Chuck Norris, Shelley Winters, Martin Balsam, George Kennedy, Hanna Schygulla, Susan Strasberg, Bo Svenson, Joey Bishop, Lainie Kazan, Robert Forster, Robert Vaughn, Kim Delaney; **D:** Menahem Golan. VHS, Beta $9.99 MED, VTR ✠✠

Delta Force 2: Operation Stranglehold Delta Force is back with martial artist and military technician Norris at the helm. Action-packed and tense. **1990 (R) 110m/C** John P. Ryan, Chuck Norris, Billy Drago, Richard Jaeckel, Paul Perri; **D:** Aaron Norris; **W:** Lee Reynolds. VHS, Beta $89.98 MED, BTV, VTR ✠½

Delta Force 3: The Killing Game A terrorist mastermind plants an atomic bomb in an American city, and the President has only one choice...call in the Delta Force. The leading men in this lackluster thriller are the sons of some of Hollywood's biggest stars. **AKA:** Young Commandos. **1991 (R) 97m/C** Nick Cassavetes, Eric Douglas, Mike Norris, Matthew Penn, John P. Ryan, Sandy Ward; **D:** Sam Firstenberg. VHS $89.99 CAN ✠½

Delta Force Commando Two U.S. Fighter pilots fight against terrorism in the deadly Nicaraguan jungle. **1987 (R) 90m/C** Fred Williamson, Bo Svenson. VHS $19.95 VES, RHI ✠½

Delta Force Commando 2 The celluloid was hardly dry on the first "Delta Force Commando" before the resourceful Italians began grinding out this follow-up, with the lead commando getting the Force entangled in a deadly international conspiracy. **AKA:** Priority Red One. **1990 (R) 100m/C** *IT* Richard Hatch, Fred Williamson, Giannina Facio, Van Johnson; **D:** Frank Valenti. VHS $89.95 LIV ✠

Delta Fox Delta Fox is carrying a million dollars for the mob, but the mob is carrying a grudge and the chase is on. **1977 90m/C** Priscilla Barnes, Richard Lynch, Stuart Whitman, John Ireland; **D:** Beverly Sebastian, Ferd Sebastian. VHS, Beta NO ✠✠

Delta Heat A new designer drug hits L.A. and detective Mike Bishop (Edwards) follows his partner to the drug's source in Louisiana. When Bishop arrives he has his partner has been tortured and murdered in order to keep the drug lord's foes in line. Bishop must then save himself and find justice in the steamy streets of New Orleans. Routine lone guy vs. bad guys actioner. **1992 (R) 91m/C** Anthony Edwards, Lance Henriksen, Betsy Russell, Linda Dona, Rod Masterson, John McConnell, Clyde Jones; **D:** Michael Rischa. VHS $89.95 ACA ✠½

Deluge Tidal waves causd by earthquakes have destroyed most of New York (though some may think this is no great loss) in this early sci-fi pic.
1933 72m/B Edward Van Sloan, Peggy Shannon, Sidney Blackmer, Fred Kohler Jr., Matt Moore, Samuel S. Hinds, Lane Chandler; *D:* Felix Feist. **VHS, Beta** *MWP ♂♂*

Delusion Gothic thriller in which invalid Cotten and family are harassed by a possibly supernatural killer as told by Cotten's nurse. Filmed in 1980. Ending is a let-down. *AKA:* The House Where Death Lives.
1984 (R) 93m/C Patricia Pearcy, David Hayward, John Dukakis, Joseph Cotten, Simone Griffeth; *D:* Alan Beattie. **VHS, Beta $24.98** *SUE ♂*

Delusion A yuppie with an embezzled fortune is held up in the Nevada desert by a psycho hood with a showgirl lover. But who's really in charge here? The snappy, hip, film-noir thriller takes a few unlikely twists and has an open Lady-or-the-Tiger finale that may infuriate. Available in a widescreen edition on laserdisc.
1991 (R) 100m/C Jim Metzler, Jennifer Rubin, Kyle Secor, Robert Costanzo, Tracy Walter, Jerry Orbach; *D:* Carl Colpaert; *W:* Carl Colpaert, Kurt Voss; *M:* Barry Adamson. **VHS $89.98** *COL ♂♂½*

Delusions of Grandeur A French comedy of court intrigue set in 17th-century Spain. In French with English subtitles. Based loosely on Victor Hugo's "Ruy Blas." *AKA:* La Folie des Grandeurs.
1976 85m/C *FR* Yves Montand, Louis de Funes, Alice Sapritch, Karin Schubert, Gabriele Tinti; *D:* Gerard Oury. **VHS, Beta $24.95** *FCT ♂♂½*

Demented Beautiful and talented woman is brutally gang-raped by four men, but her revenge is sweet and deadly as she entices each to bed and gives them a big dose of their own medicine. All-too-familiar plot offers nothing new.
1980 (R) 92m/C Sallee Elyse, Bruce Gilchrist. **VHS, Beta $54.95** *MED ♂*

Dementia 13 This eerie thriller, set in a creepy castle, is an early Coppola film about the members of an Irish family who are being offed by an axe murderer one-by-one. *AKA:* The Haunted and the Hunted.
1963 75m/B William Campbell, Luana Anders, Bart Patton, Patrick Magee; *D:* Francis Ford Coppola; *W:* Francis Ford Coppola. **VHS, Beta $19.95** *NOS, MRV, SNC ♂♂½*

Demetrius and the Gladiators A sequel to "The Robe," wherein the holy-robe-carrying slave is enlisted as one of Caligula's gladiators and mixes with the trampy empress Messalina.
1954 101m/C Victor Mature, Susan Hayward, Michael Rennie, Debra Paget, Anne Bancroft, Jay Robinson, Barry Jones, Richard Egan, William Marshall, Ernest Borgnine; *D:* Delmer Daves; *W:* Philip Dunne. **VHS, Beta $19.98** *FOX ♂♂½*

The Demi-Paradise Tongue-in-cheek look at people's perceptions of foreigners has Olivier as a Russian inventor (?!) who comes to England with some trepidation. Though the Brits are plenty quirky, he manages to find romance with Ward in this charming look at British life. *AKA:* Adventure for Two.
1943 110m/B *GB* Laurence Olivier, Penelope Dudley Ward, Margaret Rutherford, Wilfrid Hyde-White; *D:* Anthony Asquith. **VHS, Beta $19.95** *NOS, VDM, DVT ♂♂♂*

Demolition Ex-international courier finds that the "simple" task he has consented to do for his old employers is deceptively hazardous.

1977 90m/C John Waters, Belinda Giblin, Fred Steele, Vincent Ball; *D:* Kevin Dobson. **VHS, Beta** *NO ♂½*

Demolition Man No-brain sci-fier rests on the action skills of Stallone and Snipes. Psychovillain Snipes (a shocking blond!) is pursued by equally violent cop Stallone in the late 1990s. Then they're cryogenically frozen, defrosted in 2032, and back to their old tricks. One problem. This is not a fun future: virtual reality sex is the only kind allowed and puritan ethics and political correctness are enforced to the max. So cop and bad guy get to show this highly orderly society some really violent times. Implausible plot and minimal acting, but lots of action and violence for fans.
1993 (R) 115m/C Sylvester Stallone, Wesley Snipes, Sandra Bullock, Nigel Hawthorne; *D:* Marco Brambilla; *W:* Daniel Waters, Robert Reneau, Peter M. Lenkov; *M:* Elliot Goldenthal. **VHS, Beta, 8mm** *WAR ♂♂*

The Demon A small town may be doomed to extinction, courtesy of a monster's thirst for the blood of its inhabitants.
1981 (R) 94m/C Cameron Mitchell, Jennifer Holmes. **VHS, Beta $14.98** *VCI ♂½*

Demon Barber of Fleet Street Loosely based on an actual event, this film inspired the 1978 smash play "Sweeney Todd." Slaughter stars as a mad barber who doesn't just cut his client's hair. He happens to have a deal cooked up with the baker to provide him with some nice 'juicy' filling for his meat pies. Manages to be creepy and funny at the same time. *AKA:* Sweeney Todd: The Demon Barber of Fleet Street.
1936 68m/B *GB* Tod Slaughter, Eve Lister, Bruce Seton; *D:* George King. **VHS, Beta $14.95** *VYY, MRV, SNC ♂♂½*

Demon City Shinjuku In the near future the evil Levih Rah has created a Demon City in Shinjuku, located in the heart of Tokyo, where he commands his army of thugs and monsters. Sayama and the streetwise Kyoya venture into Shinjuku in search of Sayama's kidnapped father. They encounter the mystical Mephisto, who may be able to help them, but time is running out—Levih Rah is set to destroy the entire planet in three days! In Japanese with English subtitles.
1993 82m/C *JP* **VHS $29.95** *CPM ♂♂½*

Demon for Trouble Outlaws are murdering land buyers in this routine western.
1934 58m/B Bob Steele. **VHS, Beta $19.95** *NOS, HEG, RXM ♂*

Demon Hunter Terror reigns while a deranged killer stalks his next victim.
1988 90m/C George Ellis, Erin Fleming, Marrianne Gordon; *D:* Massey Cramer. **VHS, Beta** *NO ♂*

A Demon in My View In a role similar to his infamous Norman Bates in "Psycho," Perkins stars as a man who hides a terrible secret—he is a former serial killer. When a fellow tenant in his apartment house accidentally destroys his doll, Perkins' tenuous sanity is shaken and he begins killing again. A smart thriller. Perkins last big-screen role.
1992 (R) 98m/C Anthony Perkins, Sophie Ward, Stratford Johns; *D:* Petra Hafter. **VHS $89.95** *VMK, MOV ♂♂½*

The Demon Lover Leader of a satanic cult calls forth the devil when he doesn't get his way. Poorly acted and badly produced. Features comic book artists Val "Howard the Duck" Mayerick and Gunnar "Leatherface" Hansen. Also on video as "Devil Master" and "Master of Evil."

1977 (R) 87m/C Christmas Robbins, Val Mayerick, Gunnar Hansen, Tom Hutton, David Howard; *D:* Donald G. Jackson, Jerry Younkins; *W:* Donald G. Jackson, Jerry Younkins. **VHS, Beta $9.95** *UNI, PMR* Woof!

Demon Lust A couple's lovely country vacation is turned into a nightmare when two drifters terrorize them.
19?? 76m/C *D:* Bernard Buys. **VHS, Beta $59.95** *GHV ♂*

Demon of Paradise Dynamite fishing off the coast of Hawaii unearths an ancient, man-eating lizard-man. Uneven, unexciting horror attempt.
1987 (R) 84m/C Kathryn Witt, William Steis, Leslie Huntly, Laura Banks; *D:* Cirio H. Santiago. **VHS, Beta $14.95** *WAR* Woof!

Demon Possessed When Tom is critically injured in a snowmobile race in a remote woods, he and his friends find shelter in a deserted children's camp. It turns out the camp was run by a secret religious cult that practiced occult murder and the demon that haunted the place has never left. When Tom dies this satanic spirit finds the perfect host to return to human form and continue its bloody work.
1993 (R) 97m/C Dawn Laurrie, Aaron Kjenass, David Fields, Eve Montgomery; *D:* Christopher Webster; *W:* Julian Weaver; *M:* John Tatgenhorst. **VHS $89.95** *AIP ♂½*

Demon Queen A vampirish woman seduces, then murders, many men.
1987? 70m/C Mary Fanaro, Dennis Stewart, Cliff Dance; *D:* Donald Farmer. **VHS, Beta** *NO ♂*

Demon Rage Neglected housewife drifts under the spell of a phantom lover. *AKA:* Satan's Mistress; Fury of the Succubus; Dark Eyes.
1982 (R) 98m/C Britt Ekland, Lana Wood, Kabir Bedi, Don Galloway, John Carradine, Sherry Scott; *D:* James Polakof. **VHS, Beta $59.95** *HHE ♂½*

Demon Seed When a scientist and his wife separate so he can work on his computer, the computer takes over the house and impregnates the wife. Bizarre and taut.
1977 (R) 97m/C Julie Christie, Fritz Weaver, Gerrit Graham, Berry Kroeger, Ron Hays; *D:* Donald Cammell; *V:* Robert Vaughn. **VHS, Beta $19.98** *MGM ♂♂♂*

Demon Warrior An Indian shaman curses a land-stealing white man and revenge comes in the form of the Demon Warrior, who can appear but once every ten years.
19?? 82m/C **VHS $79.98** *MNC, MOV ♂♂*

Demon Wind A gateway to Hell opens up on a secluded farm and various heroic types try to close it. Meanwhile, demons attempt to possess those humans in their midst. Zombies abound in this near-woof.
1990 (R) 97m/C Eric Larson, Francine Lapensee, Rufus Norris; *D:* Charles Philip Moore. **VHS, Beta $19.95** *PAR ♂½*

Demon Witch Child A wrongly accused old woman commits suicide and possesses a young girl who takes revenge on everyone.
1975 90m/C **VHS, Beta** *NO* Woof!

Demon with a Glass Hand In the vein of "The Terminator," a man goes back two hundred years in time to escape the evil race that rules the planet.
1964 63m/B Robert Culp, Arlene Martel, Abraham Sofaer. **VHS, Beta $14.95** *MGM ♂½*

Demonic Toys The possessed playthings attack a bunch of unfortunates in a warehouse, and pumped-up lady cop Scoggins deserves an award for keeping a

straight face. Skimpily scripted gore from the horror assembly-line at Full Moon Productions. Far more entertaining are the multiple behind-the-scenes featurettes on the tape.
1991 (R) 86m/C Tracy Scoggins, Bentley Mitchum, Michael Russo, Jeff Weston, Daniel Cerney, Pete Schrum; *D:* Peter Manoogian. **VHS, Beta** PAR ♫½

Demonoid, Messenger of Death Discovery of an ancient temple of Satan worship drastically changes the lives of a young couple when the husband becomes possessed by the Demonoid, which initially takes on the form of a severed hand. Poor script needs hand, producing a number of unintentionally laughable moments. *AKA:* Macabra.
1981 (R) 85m/C Samantha Eggar, Stuart Whitman, Roy Cameron Jenson; *D:* Alfredo Zacharias. **VHS, Beta $9.95** MED ♫

The Demons As she slips into death, a tortured woman curses her torturers.
1974 (R) 90m/C Anne Libert, Britt Nichols, Doris Thomas. **VHS, Beta $49.95** UNI ♫

Demons A horror film in a Berlin theater is so involving that its viewers become the demons they are seeing. The new monsters turn on the other audience members. Virtually plotless, very explicit. Rock soundtrack by Accept, Go West, Motley Crue, and others. Revered in some circles, blasted in others. Followed by "Demons 2." *AKA:* Demoni.
1986 (R) 89m/C *IT* Urbano Barberini, Natasha Hovey, Paolo Cozza, Karl Zinny, Fiore Argento, Fabiola Toledo, Nicoletta Elni; *D:* Lamberto Bava. **VHS, Beta $19.95** STE, NWV ♫½

Demons 2 Inferior sequel to "Demons." The son of horror-meister Mario Bava, Lamberto collaborated with Italian auteur Argento (who co-wrote and produced) to create an improbable sequel (storywise) which seems to have been edited by some kind of crazed cutting room slasher with equally hackneyed dubbing. Residents of a chi-chi high rise watching a documentary about the events of "Demons"—a sort of high-tech play-within-a-play ploy—when a demon emerges from the TV, spreads his creepy cooties, and causes the tenants to sprout fangs and claws and nasty tempers. Lots of blood drips from ceilings, plumbing fixtures, and various body parts.
1987 88m/C *IT* David Knight, Nancy Brill, Coralina Cataldi Tassoni, Bobby Rhodes, Asia Argento, Virginia Bryant; *D:* Lamberto Bava; *W:* Lamberto Bava, Dario Argento. **VHS $29.99** IMP ♫½

Demons in the Garden Centers on the disintegration of a family after the end of the Spanish Civil War, due to sibling rivalries and a variety of indiscretions. Problems mount as two brothers become involved with their stepsister. Story takes on poignancy in its narration by a young boy. Beautiful cinematography. In Spanish with English subtitles. *AKA:* Demonios En El Jardin.
1982 (R) 100m/C *SP* Angela Molina, Ana Belen, Encarna Paso, Imanol Arias; *D:* Manuel Gutierrez Aragon. **VHS $29.95** CVC, TPV, ING ♫½

Demons of Ludlow Demons attend a small town's bicentennial celebration intent on raising a little hell of their own.
1975 83m/C Paul von Hauser, Stephanie Cushna, James Robinson, Carol Perry; *D:* Steven Kuether. **VHS, Beta $59.95** TWE ♫

Demons of the Mind A sordid psychological horror film about a baron in 19th century Austria who imprisons his children, fearing that mental illness is a family trait. Also on video as "Blood Evil."

1972 (R) 85m/C *GB* Michael Hordern, Patrick Magee, Yvonne Mitchell, Robert Hardy, Gillian Hills, Virginia Wetherell, Shane Briant, Paul Jones; *D:* Peter Sykes. **VHS, Beta $59.99** ACA, MLB ♫♫

Demonstone A television reporter becomes possessed by a Filipino demon and carries out an ancient curse against the family of a corrupt government official. *AKA:* Heartstone.
1989 (R) 90m/C R. Lee Ermey, Jan-Michael Vincent, Nancy Everhard; *D:* Andrew Prowse. **VHS, Beta $29.95** FRH ♫

Demonstrator A father and son are at odds when dad heads an Asian military coalition and junior protests. Notable for being one of the first major Australian films to use an entirely native cast.
1971 82m/C *AU* Joe James, Irene Inescort, Gerard Maguire, Wendy Lingham, Harold Hopkins; *D:* Warwick Freeman **VHS $19.95** ACA ♫♫½

Demonwarp A vengeance-minded hunter journeys into an evil, primeval forest to kill the monsters that abducted his daughter.
1987 91m/C George Kennedy, Emmett Alston. **VHS, Beta $79.95** VMK Woof!

Dempsey In this made for television film based on Jack Dempsey's autobiography, Williams plays the role of the famed world heavyweight champ. His rise through the boxing ranks as well as his personal life are chronicled. A bit slow-moving considering the pounding fists and other action.
1983 110m/C Treat Williams, Sam Waterston, Sally Kellerman, Victoria Tennant, Peter Mark Richman, Jesse Vint, Bonnie Bartlett, James Noble; *D:* Gus Trikonis; *M:* Billy Goldenberg. **VHS, Beta** MED ♫♫

Denial: The Dark Side of Passion A strong-willed woman tries to put a destructive love affair behind her—but if she succeeded there'd be no movie. Torrid stuff with a watchable cast.
1991 (R) 103m/C Robin Wright, Jason Patric, Barry Primus, Christina Harnos, Rae Dawn Chong; *D:* Eric Dignam; *W:* Eric Dignam. **VHS $89.98** REP ♫♫

Dennis the Menace Straight from the Hughes kiddie farm comes Kevin McAllister—oops!—Dennis Mitchell (newcomer Gamble), curious, crafty, and blond 5-year-old. He dreams and schemes but everything he does manages to be a threat to the physical and mental well-being of hot-head neighbor Mr. Wilson (Matthau, perfectly cast as the grump). Lloyd is very nasty as protagonist Switchblade Sam; Plowright, Thompson, and Stanton round out the cast as Mrs. Wilson and the Mitchell parents, respectively. Sure to please young kids, but parents may be less enthralled with this adaptation of the popular '50s comic strip and subsequent TV series.
1993 (PG) 96m/C Walter Matthau, Mason Gamble, Joan Plowright, Christopher Lloyd, Lea Thompson, Robert Stanton, Billie Bird, Paul Winfield, Amy Sakasitz, Kellen Hathaway, Arnold Stang; *D:* Nick Castle; *W:* John Hughes; *M:* Jerry Goldsmith. **VHS, Beta, 8mm $24.96** WAR ♫♫½

Dennis the Menace: Dinosaur Hunter Another version of Hank Ketchum's mischievous cartoon character brought to life to have adventures and disturb his neighbor Mr. Wilson. This time Dennis discovers a huge, primitive bone in his backyard and when an archaeologist declares it's a dinosaur bone, news crews, tourists, and scientists are suddenly everywhere. This badly disturbs Mr. Wilson's retirement and Dennis

and his friends must save the day (and their neighborhood).
1993 (G) 118m/C Victor Dimattia, William Windom, Pat Estrin, Jim Jansen, Patsy Garrett. **VHS $89.95** VMK ♫♫½

The Dentist Fields treats several oddball patients in his office. After watching the infamous tooth-pulling scene, viewers will be sure to brush regularly.
1932 22m/B W.C. Fields, Elise Cavanna, Babe Kane, Bud Jamison, Zedna Farley. **VHS, Beta $19.98** CCB, GVV ♫♫♫½

The Denver & Rio Grande Action-packed western about two rival railroads competing to be the first to complete a line through the Royal Gorge. Plot is predictable, but the scene featuring two trains crashing into each other is worth it (Haskin used actual trains for this stunt).
1951 89m/C Edmond O'Brien, Sterling Hayden, Dean Jagger, ZaSu Pitts, J. Carroll Naish; *D:* Byron Haskin. **VHS** PAR ♫♫½

Departamento Compartido A notorious ladies' man and his shy friend become unlikely roommates after their wives kick them out of their homes.
1985 100m/C *SP* Alberto Olmedo, Tato Bores, Graciela Alfano, Camila Perisse; *D:* Hugo Sofovich. **VHS, Beta $29.95** MED ♫

Department Store Confusing crime-drama involving a store manager who mistakes an ex-convict for his employer's heir. Based on a story by H. F. Maltby. *AKA:* Bargain Basement.
1935 65m/B *GB* Garry Marsh, Eve Gray, Sebastian Shaw, Geraldine Fitzgerald, Jack Melford; *D:* Leslie Hiscott. **VHS $19.95** DVT ♫

The Deputy Drummer Second-rate early British musical, notable as a later vehicle for silent-era star Lane. He plays a penniless composer who impersonates an aristocrat to attend a party, and catches jewel robbers in the act.
1935 71m/B *GB* Lupino Lane, Jean Denis, Kathleen Kelly, Wallace Lupino, Margaret Yarde, Syd Crossley. **VHS $19.95** NOS ♫½

Deputy Marshall Hall trails a pair of bankrobbers, fights off landgrabbers, and finds romance as well.
1950 75m/B Jon Hall, Frances Langford, Dick Foran. **VHS, Beta** RXM ♫½

Der Purimshpiler A drifter embarks on a quest for happiness, which takes him to various small towns. In one, he meets and falls in love with a shoemaker's daughter. In Yiddish with English subtitles. *AKA:* The Purim Player; The Jester; The Jewish Jester.
1937 90m/B *PL* Miriam Kressyn, Zygmund Turkow, Hymie Jacobsen; *D:* Joseph Green. **VHS, Beta $79.95** ERG ♫♫½

Deranged Of the numerous movies based on the cannibalistic exploits of Ed Gein ("Psycho," "Texas Chainsaw Massacre," etc.), this is the most accurate. A dead-on performance by Blossom and a twisted sense of humor help move things along nicely. The two directors, Gillen and Ormsby, previously worked together on the classic "Children Shouldn't Play with Dead Things." An added attraction is the early special effect work of gore wizard Tom Savini.
1974 (R) 82m/C *CA* Roberts Blossom, Cosette Lee, Robert Warner, Marcia Diamond, Brian Sneagle; *D:* Jeff Gillen, Alan Ormsby. **VHS $18.00** FRG, MRV ♫♫♫

Deranged A mentally unstable, pregnant woman is attacked in her apartment after her husband leaves town. She spends the rest of the movie engaged in psychotic encounters, real and imagined. Technically not bad, but

extremely violent and grim. Not to be confused with 1974 movie of the same name.
1987 (R) 85m/C Jane Hamilton, Paul Siederman, Jennifer Delora, James Gillis, Jill Cumer, Gary Goldman; *D:* Chuck Vincent. **VHS $14.95** REP *♂♂*

Derby The documentary story of the rise to fame of roller-derby stars on the big rink.
1971 (R) 91m/C Charlie O'Connell, Lydia Gray, Janet Earp, Ann Colvello, Mike Snell; *D:* Robert Kaylor. **VHS, Beta $49.95** PSM, FFF *♂♂♂*

Dersu Uzala An acclaimed, photographically breathtaking film about a Russian surveyor in Siberia who befriends a crusty, resourceful Mongolian. They begin to teach each other about their respective worlds. Produced in Russia; one of Kurosawa's stranger films.
1975 124m/C JP RU Yuri Solomin, Maxim Munzuk; *D:* Akira Kurosawa. **VHS, Beta $29.98** SUE, KIV *♂♂♂½*

Descending Angel The premise is familiar: a swastika-friendly collaborator is forced out of the closet. But the cast and scripting makes this made-for-cable there's-a-Nazi-in-the-woodwork suspenser better than average, despite its flawed finale. Scott plays a well-respected Romanian refugee—active in the community, in the church, and in Romanian-American activities—whose daughter's fiance (Roberts) suspects him of Nazi collusion.
1990 (R) 96m/C George C. Scott, Diane Lane, Eric Roberts, Mark Margolis, Vyto Ruginis, Amy Aquino, Richard Jenkins, Jan Rubes; *D:* George C. Scott, Jeremy Paul Kagan; *W:* George C. Scott. **VHS $89.99** HBO *♂♂♂*

Desde el Abismo After the birth of her son, a young mother takes to drink while in the throes of post-partum depression. In Spanish.
19?? 115m/C SP Thelma Biral, Alberto Argibay, Olga Zubarry. **VHS, Beta $29.95** MED *♂½*

Desert Bloom On the eve of a nearby nuclear bomb test, a beleaguered alcoholic veteran and his family struggle through tensions brought on by a promiscuous visiting aunt and the chaotic, rapidly changing world. Gish shines as the teenage daughter through whose eyes the story unfolds. From a story by Corr and Linda Ramy.
1986 (PG) 103m/C Jon Voight, JoBeth Williams, Ellen Barkin, Annabeth Gish, Allen (Gooritz) Garfield, Jay Underwood; *D:* Eugene Corr; *W:* Eugene Corr; *M:* Brad Fiedel. **VHS, Beta** NO *♂♂♂*

Desert Commandos When the Allies appear to be winning WWII, the Nazis devise a plan to eliminate all of the opposing forces' leaders at once.
196? ?m/C Kenneth Clark, Horst Frank, Jeanne Valeri, Carlo Hinterman, Gianni Rizzo. **VHS** NO *♂♂*

The Desert Fox Big-budgeted portrait of German Army Field Marshal Rommel, played by Mason, focuses on the soldier's defeat in Africa during WWII and his subsequent, disillusioned return to Hitler's Germany. Mason played Rommel again in 1953's "Desert Rats." *AKA:* Rommel—Desert Fox.
1951 87m/B James Mason, Cedric Hardwicke, Jessica Tandy, Luther Adler; *D:* Henry Hathaway. **VHS, Beta $19.98** FOX, TLF *♂♂♂*

Desert Gold A fierce Indian chief battles a horde of greedy white men over his tribe's gold mine. Based on a novel by Zane Grey.
1936 58m/B Buster Crabbe, Robert Cummings, Marsha Hunt, Tom Keene, Raymond Hatton, Monte Blue, Leif Erickson; *D:* Charles T. Barton. **VHS, Beta $19.95** NOS, DVT *♂½*

Desert Guns/Six-Shootin' Sheriff Double feature includes a rare Tearle "B" film and a Maynard oater from 1938.
1936 ?m/C Conway Tearle, Ken Maynard. **VHS $18** RXM *♂♂*

Desert Hearts An upstanding professional woman travels to Reno, Nevada in 1959 to obtain a quick divorce, and slowly becomes involved in a lesbian relationship with a free-spirited casino waitress.
1986 (R) 93m/C Helen Shaver, Audra Lindley, Patricia Charbonneau, Andra Akers, Dean Butler, Jeffrey Tambor, Denise Crosby, Gwen Welles; *D:* Donna Deitch; *W:* Natalie Cooper. **VHS, Beta $29.98** LIV, VES *♂♂♂*

Desert Kickboxer A border guard takes on a cocaine dealer and his henchmen, fighting for gold and, of course, a beautiful woman. Lots of kickboxing action.
1992 (R) 86m/C John Haymes Newton, Judie Aronson, Sam DeFrancisco, Paul Smith; *D:* Isaac Florentine. **VHS $89.99** HBO *♂♂*

Desert of the Lost Wales flees to Mexico after shooting a man in self-defense. He's aided by Montgomery and, in turn, helps save her from a forced marriage.
1927 58m/B Wally Wales, Peggy Montgomery, William J. Dyer, Edward Cecil, Richard Neill, Kelly Cafford, Ray Murro, George Magrill, Charles "Slim" Whitaker; *D:* Richard Thorpe. **VHS $16.95** GPV *♂♂½*

The Desert of the Tartars Story of a young soldier who dreams of war and discovers that the real battle for him is with time. *AKA:* Le Desert des Tartares.
1976 (PG) 140m/C Jacques Perrin; *M:* Ennio Morricone. **VHS, Beta $59.95** SUE *♂*

Desert Phantom Villains threaten to rob a woman of her ranch until a stranger rescues her.
1936 66m/B Johnny Mack Brown, Sheila Manners, Charles "Blackie" King, Ted Adams, Hal Price, Nelson McDowell; *D:* S. Roy Luby. **VHS, Beta $9.95** GPV *♂½*

The Desert Rats A crusty British captain (Burton) takes charge of an Australian division during WWII. Thinking they are inferior to his own British troops, he is stiff and uncaring to the Aussies until a kind-hearted drunk and the courage of the division win him over. Crack direction from Wise and Newton's performance (as the wag) simply steal the movie. Mason reprises his role as Germany Army Field Marshal Rommel from "The Desert Fox."
1953 88m/B Richard Burton, Robert Newton, Robert Douglas, Torin Thatcher, Chips Rafferty, Charles Tingwell, James Mason; *D:* Robert Wise. **VHS, Beta $19.98** FXV, FCT *♂♂♂*

Desert Snow Here's a non-formulaic dope opera oater: cowboys 'n' drug runners battle it out for an out-of-the-way, underpopulated western town. About as clever as the title.
1989 (R) 90m/C Frank Capizzi, Flint Carney, Shelley Hinkle, Sam Incorvia, Carolyn Jacobs; *D:* Paul de Cruccio. **VHS, Beta** VTR *♂♂*

The Desert Song MacRae secretly leads a band of do-gooders against the evil forces of a dastardly sheik. Grayson is the general's daughter who falls in love with our disguised hero. Third filmed version of the Sigmund Romberg operetta creaks along with the talents of MacRae and Grayson rising about the hackneyed plot. ♫The Desert Song; Gay Parisienne; Long Live the Night; One Alone; One Flower; The Riff Song; Romance.

1953 96m/C Gordon MacRae, Kathryn Grayson, Raymond Massey, Steve Cochran, Dick Wesson, Allyn Ann McLerie, Ray Collins, William Conrad; *D:* Robert Florey; *W:* Paul Buckner; *M:* Max Steiner. **VHS $29.99** FCT *♂♂½*

The Desert Tigers Allied soldiers escape from a German POW camp and battle for survival across the African deserts. *AKA:* Los Tigres del Desierto.
19?? 95m/C Richard Harrison, Lea Lander. **VHS, Beta $39.98** MOV *♂½*

Desert Trail Wayne is a championship rodeo rider accused of bank robbery.
1935 57m/B John Wayne, Paul Fix, Mary Kornman; *D:* Robert North Bradbury. **VHS, Beta $9.98** REP, COL, MRV *♂½*

Desert Warrior Earth becomes a waste site after a nuclear war. Ferrigno stars as a post-nuke hero in this low-budget action film. Very bad acting.
1988 (PG-13) 89m/C Lou Ferrigno, Shari Shattuck, Kenneth Peer, Anthony East; *D:* Jim Goldman. **VHS, Beta $79.95** PSM *♂*

The Deserters Sergeant Hawley, a Vietnam-era hawk, hunts deserters and draft-dodgers in Canada. There, he confronts issues of war and peace head-on.
198? 110m/C Alan Scarfe, Dermot Hennelly, Jon Bryden, Barbara March; *M:* Michael Conway Baker. **VHS, Beta** MOV *♂½*

Designing Woman Bacall and Peck star in this mismatched tale of romance. She's a chic high-fashion designer, he's a rumpled sports writer. The fun begins when they try to adjust to married life together. Neither likes the other's friends or lifestyle. Things get even crazier when Bacall has to work with her ex-lover Helmore on a fashion show and Peck's former love Gray shows up as well. And as if that weren't enough, Peck is being hunted by the mob because of a boxing story he's written. It's a fun, quick, witty tale that is all entertainment and no message. Bacall's performance is of note because Bogart was dying of cancer at the time.
1957 118m/C Gregory Peck, Lauren Bacall, Dolores Gray, Sam Levene, Tom Helmore, Mickey Shaughnessy, Jesse White, Chuck Connors, Edward Platt, Alvy Moore, Jack Cole; *D:* Vincente Minnelli; *W:* George Wells. **VHS, Beta $19.98** MGM *♂♂♂*

Desire A free-spirited woman finds herself attracted to a local fisherman. Hardly her intellectual equal but then want she really wants is his body.
1993 (R) 108m/C Greta Scacchi, Vincent D'Onofrio; *D:* Andrew Birkin. **VHS $89.95** ACA *♂♂*

Desire and Hell at Sunset Motel Low-budget thriller takes place at the Sunset Motel in 1950s Anaheim. Fenn is the bombshell wife of a toy salesman who's in town for a sales meeting, while she just wants to visit Disneyland. She's soon fooling around with another guy and her husband hires a psychotic criminal to spy on her as her new lover plots to kill hubby. Very confusing plot isn't worth figuring out. Film's only redeeming quality is the imaginative and creative work used in the visuals. Castle's directorial debut.
1992 (PG-13) 90m/C Sherilyn Fenn, Whip Hubley, David Hewlett, David Johansen, Paul Bartel; *D:* Alien Castle; *W:* Alien Castle. **VHS, Beta $89.98** FXV, VTR *♂½*

Desire Under the Elms Ives, the patriarch of an 1840s New England farming family, takes a young wife (Loren) who promptly has an affair with her stepson.

D

Loren's American film debut. Based on the play by Eugene O'Neill.
1958 114m/B Sophia Loren, Anthony Perkins, Burl Ives, Frank Overton; **D:** Delbert Mann; **M:** Elmer Bernstein. **VHS, Beta $19.95** BAR, FCT, PAR ♫♫½

Desiree A romanticized historical epic about Napoleon and his 17-year-old mistress, Desiree. Based on the novel by Annemarie Selinko. Slightly better than average historical fiction piece.
1954 110m/C Marlon Brando, Jean Simmons, Merle Oberon, Michael Rennie, Cameron Mitchell, Elizabeth Sellars, Cathleen Nesbitt; **D:** Henry Koster; **W:** Daniel Taradash. **Beta $19.98** FOX, IME ♫♫½

Desk Set One of the later and less dynamic Tracy/Hepburn comedies, about an efficiency expert who installs a giant computer in an effort to update a television network's female-run reference department. Still, the duo sparkle as they bicker, battle, and give in to love. Based on William Marchant's play. **AKA:** His Other Woman.
1957 103m/C Spencer Tracy, Katharine Hepburn, Joan Blondell, Gig Young, Dina Merrill, Neva Patterson; **D:** Walter Lang. **VHS, Beta $19.98** FOX, FCT ♫♫♫

Despair A chilling and comic study of a victimized chocolate factory owner's descent into madness, set against the backdrop of the Nazi rise to power in the 1930s. Adapted from the Nabokov novel by Tom Stoppard.
1978 120m/C GE Dirk Bogarde, Andrea Ferreol, Volker Spengler, Klaus Lowitsch; **D:** Rainer Werner Fassbinder; **W:** Tom Stoppard; **M:** Peer Raben. **VHS, Beta** GLV ♫♫♫

Despedida de Casada After their divorce, a man and a woman concentrate on making the other's life miserable.
1987 101m/C MX Ana Louisa Peluffo, Mauricio Garces, Hector Suarez. **VHS, Beta $55.95** MAD ♫♫

Desperados After the Civil War, a murderous renegade and two of his sons go on a looting rampage, eventually kidnapping the child of the third son who just wants to live in peace. Made in Spain.
1969 (PG) 90m/C SP Jack Palance, Vince Edwards, Christian Roberts, George Maharis, Neville Brand, Sylvia Syms; **D:** Henry Levin. **VHS, Beta $14.95** COL ♫♫½

The Desperados When a young woman is raped by outlaws robbing her stagecoach, a bevy of western heroes band together to avenge her.
198? 86m/C Keenan Wynn, Henry Silva, Michele Carey, John Anderson, Joe Turkel; **D:** Ron Joy. **VHS $14.95** SIM, COL ♫♫½

Desperate An honest truck driver witnesses a mob crime and must escape with his wife in this minor film noir. Eventually, the law is on his tail, too.
1947 73m/B Steve Brodie, Audrey Long, Raymond Burr, Jason Robards Sr., Douglas Fowley, William Challee, Ilka Gruning, Nan Leslie; **D:** Anthony Mann. **VHS, Beta $19.98** TTC ♫♫½

Desperate Cargo Two showgirls stranded in a Latin American town manage to get aboard a clipper ship with hoodlums who are trying to steal the vessel's cargo.
1941 69m/B Ralph Byrd, Carol Hughes, Jack Mulhall. **VHS, Beta $24.95** NOS, DVT, HEG ♫♫½

Desperate Characters A slice-of-city-life story about a middle-class couple living in a once-fashionable section of Brooklyn, New York, who watch their neighborhood disintegrate around them. Their marriage on remote control, the two find their lives a series of small disappointments, routine work, uncertain friendships, and pervasive violence. Ex-

cellent performances, especially by MacLaine as the harried wife, but the film's depressing nature made it a complete box office flop.
1971 (R) 87m/C Shirley MacLaine, Kenneth Mars, Gerald S. O'Loughlin, Sada Thompson, Michael Higgins, Rose Gregorio, Jack Somack, Chris Gampel, Mary Ellen Hokanson, Patrick McVey, Carol Kane; **D:** Frank D. Gilroy; **W:** Frank D. Gilroy. **VHS** PAR ♫♫♫

Desperate Crimes Two rival mobs battle over the prostitution and drug trade. When an innocent woman is murdered her brother looks for revenge with the help of a beautiful prostitute.
1993 92m/C Traci Lords, Denise Crosby, Franco Columbu, Van Quattro, Rena Niehaus, Nicoletta Boris, Elizabeth Kaitan, Randi Ingerman; **D:** Andreas Marfori. **VHS $89.95** AIP ♫♫

Desperate Hours A tough, gritty thriller about three escaped convicts taking over a suburban home and holding the family hostage. Plenty of suspense and fine acting. Based on the novel and play by Joseph Hayes.
1955 112m/B Humphrey Bogart, Fredric March, Martha Scott, Arthur Kennedy, Gig Young, Dewey Martin, Mary Murphy, Robert Middleton, Richard Eyer; **D:** William Wyler. **VHS, Beta $14.95** PAR ♫♫♫

Desperate Hours An escaped prisoner holes up in a suburban couple's home, waiting for his lawyer/accomplice to take him to Mexico. Tensions heighten between the separated couple and the increasingly nerve-wracked criminals. Terrific, if not downright horrifying, performance by Rourke in an overall tepid remake of the 1955 thriller.
1990 (R) 105m/C Mickey Rourke, Anthony Hopkins, Mimi Rogers, Kelly Lynch, Lindsay Crouse, Elias Koteas, David Morse, Shawnee Smith, Danny Gerard, Matt McGrath; **D:** Michael Cimino; **W:** Mark Rosenthal. **VHS, Beta $14.95** MGM, FHE ♫♫

Desperate Journey Flynn and Reagan are two of five Allied fighters shot down over Nazi occupied Poland. They go through various tight squeezes such as stealing Goering's car in Berlin, and eliminating a few Nazis at a chemical factory to get back to the safety of England. All the while they are hunted by Massey as Nazi Major Otto Baumester, who of course bumbles and fumbles the whole affair. Strictly propaganda intended to keep up morale on the homefront. Flynn was not pleased about having Reagan as his co-star, seeing as he was usually paired with female leads.
1942 108m/B Errol Flynn, Ronald Reagan, Raymond Massey, Nancy Coleman, Alan Hale, Arthur Kennedy, Helmut Dantine; **D:** Raoul Walsh. **VHS, Beta $19.98** MGM ♫♫½

Desperate Lives High school siblings come into contact with drugs and join their guidance counselor in the war against dope. Average made for TV fare.
1982 100m/C Diana Scarwid, Doug McKeon, Helen Hunt, William Windom, Art Hindle, Tom Atkins, Sam Bottoms, Diane Ladd, Dr. Joyce Brothers; **D:** Robert Lewis; **M:** Bruce Broughton. **VHS, Beta $49.95** LIV ♫♫

Desperate Living Typical John Waters trash. A mental patient (Stole) is released and becomes paranoid that her family may be out to kill her. After aiding in the murder of her husband (the hefty maid, Hill, suffocates him by sitting on him), Stole and Hill escape to Mortville, a town populated by outcasts such as transsexuals, murderers, and the woefully disfigured.
1977 90m/C Jean Hill, Mink Stole, Edith Massey, Mary Vivian Pearce, Liz Renay, Susan Lowe; **D:** John Waters; **W:** John Waters. **VHS, Beta $19.95** COL, NLC ♫♫½

Desperate Motives Keith and his fiancee Helgenberger are a charming couple who arrive to stay with Keith's distant cousin (Katt) and his family. Only what the family doesn't realize is that the duo have escaped from an asylum for the criminally insane and want to take over their lives. **AKA:** Distant Cousins.
1992 (R) 92m/C David Keith, Marg Helgenberger, William Katt, Mel Harris, Mary Crosby, Brian Bonsall, Cyndi Pass; **D:** Andrew Lane; **W:** C. Courtney Joyner. **VHS $89.98** NLC ♫♫

Desperate Moves An Oregon-transplanted geek in San Francisco sets out to make himself over in order to win his dream girl. Sometimes effective, often sappy treatment of his coming to terms with the big city.
1986 90m/C Isabel Sanford, Steve Tracy, Paul Benedict, Christopher Lee, Eddie Deezen; **D:** Oliver Hellman. **VHS, Beta $19.98** TWE ♫♫

Desperate Scoundrel/The Pride of Pikeville Two classic comedy films back to back featuring the best of the early silent comics.
1922 44m/B Ford Sterling, Ben Turpin, The Keystone Cops. **VHS, Beta $19.98** CCB ♫♫

Desperate Target Courageous people fight against all odds to survive.
1980 90m/C Chris Mitchum. **VHS, Beta** NO ♫½

Desperate Teenage Lovedolls A trashy view of the formation of a tacky all-girl punk group.
1984 60m/C Jennifer Schwartz, Hilary Rubens, Steve McDonald, Tracy Lea; **D:** David Markey. **VHS, Beta $28.95** HHT ♫

Desperate Women Made for television western about three unjustly accused female convicts rescued en route to prison by an ex-hired gun.
1978 98m/C Susan St. James, Dan Haggerty, Ronee Blakley, Ann Dusenberry, Susan Myers; **D:** Earl Bellamy. **VHS $59.95** LIV ♫½

Desperately Seeking Susan A bored New Jersey housewife gets her kicks reading the personals. When she becomes obsessed with a relationship between two lovers who arrange their meetings through the columns, she decides to find out for herself who they are. But when she is involved in an accident the housewife loses her memory and thinks she is Susan, the free-spirited woman in the personals. Unfortunately, Susan is in a lot of trouble with all sorts of unsavory folk and our innocent housewife finds herself caught in the middle. Terrific characters, with special appeal generated by Arquette and Madonna. Quinn winningly plays the romantic interest.
1985 (PG-13) 104m/C Rosanna Arquette, Madonna, Aidan Quinn, Mark Blum, Robert Joy, Laurie Metcalf, Steven Wright, John Turturro, Richard Hell, Annie Golden, Ann Magnuson; **D:** Susan Seidelman. **VHS, Beta $14.98** FCT ♫♫

Destination Moon Story of man's first lunar voyage contains Chesley Bonstell's astronomical artwork and a famous Woody Woodpecker cartoon. Includes previews of coming attractions from classic science fiction films.
1950 91m/C Warner Anderson, Tom Powers, Dick Wesson, Erin O'Brien Moore; **D:** Irving Pichel. Academy Awards '50: Best Special Effects; Nominations: Best Art Direction/Set Decoration (Color). **VHS, Beta $19.95** SNC, MED ♫♫½

Destination Moonbase Alpha In the 21st century, an explosion has destroyed half the moon, causing it to break away from the Earth's orbit. The moon is cast far away, but the 311 people manning Alpha, a re-

search station on the moon, must continue their search for other life forms in outer space. A thankless task. Pilot for the television series "Space: 1999."
1975 93m/C Martin Landau, Barbara Bain, Barry Morse. **VHS, Beta** FOX II

Destination Saturn Buck Rogers awakens from suspended animation in the twenty-fifth century. *AKA:* Buck Rogers.
1939 90m/B Buster Crabbe, Constance Moore; *D:* Ford Beebe. **VHS, Beta** $19.95 NOS, CAB, VYY II

Destination Tokyo A weathered WWII submarine actioner, dealing with the search-and-destroy mission of a U.S. sub sent into Tokyo harbor. Available in a colorized version.
1943 135m/B Cary Grant, John Garfield, Alan Hale, Dane Clark, John Ridgely, Warner Anderson, William Prince, Robert Hutton, Tom Tully, Peter Whitney, Faye Emerson, John Forsythe; *D:* Delmer Daves. **VHS, Beta** $19.98 MGM II

Destroy All Monsters When alien babes take control of Godzilla and his monstrous colleagues, it looks like all is lost for Earth. Adding insult to injury, Ghidra is sent in to take care of the loose ends. Can the planet possibly survive this madness? Classic Toho monster slugfest also features Mothra, Rodan, Son of Godzilla, Angila, Varan, Baragon, Spigas and others. *AKA:* Kaiju Soshingeki.
1968 (G) 88m/C JP Akira Kubo, Jun Tazaki, Yoshio Tsuchiya, Kyoko Ai, Yukiko Kobayashi, Kenji Sahara, Andrew Hughes; *D:* Inoshiro Honda. **VHS** $18.00 FRG II ½

Destroy All Planets Aliens whose spaceships turn into giant flying squids are attacking Earth. It's up to Gammera, the flying, fire-breathing turtle to save the day.
1968 ?m/C JP Peter Williams, Kojiro Hongo, Toru Takatsuka. **VHS** $16.95 SNC II

Destroyer Trials and tribulations aboard a WWII destroyer result in tensions, but when the time comes for action, the men get the job done.
1943 99m/B Edward G. Robinson, Glenn Ford, Marguerite Chapman, Edgar Buchanan, Leo Gorcey, Regis Toomey, Edward Brophy, Larry Parks; *D:* William A. Seiter. **VHS, Beta** NO III

Destroyer Small-budget film crew goes to an empty location to shoot, and are stalked by the ghost/zombie remains of a huge serial killer given the electric chair 18 months before.
1988 (R) 94m/C Anthony Perkins, Deborah Foreman, Lyle Alzado; *D:* Robert Kirk. **VHS, Beta** IV

The Destructors An American narcotics enforcement officer in Paris seeks the help of a hitman in order to catch a druglord. *AKA:* The Marseille Contract.
1974 (PG) 89m/C GB Anthony Quinn, Michael Caine, James Mason, Maureen Kerwin, Alexandra Stewart; *D:* Robert Parrish. **VHS, Beta** $69.98 LIV, VES, HHE II

Destry Rides Again An uncontrollably lawless western town is whipped into shape by a peaceful, unarmed sheriff. A vintage Hollywood potpourri with Dietrich's finest post-Sternberg moment; standing on the bar singing "See What the Boys in the Back Room Will Have." The second of three versions of this Max Brand story. First was released in 1932; the third in 1954. *AKA:* Justice Rides Again.
1939 94m/B James Stewart, Marlene Dietrich, Brian Donlevy, Charles Winninger, Mischa Auer, Irene Hervey, Una Merkel, Billy Gilbert, Jack Carson, Samuel S. Hinds, Allen Jenkins; *D:* George Marshall; *W:* Gertrude Purcell, Felix

Jackson, Henry Meyers; *M:* Frank Skinner. **VHS, Beta** $14.98 MCA, FCT IIII

Details of a Duel: A Question of Honor A butcher and a teacher collide in this comedy, and prodded by the church, militia and town officals, must duel before the entire town. In Spanish with English subtitles.
1989 97m/C SP D: Sergio Cabrera. **VHS** $59.95 ING, FCT II ½

The Detective Based on G.K. Chesterton's "Father Brown" detective stories, a slick, funny English mystery in which the famous priest tracks down a notorious, endlessly crafty antique thief. *AKA:* Father Brown.
1954 91m/B GB Alec Guinness, Peter Finch, Joan Greenwood, Cecil Parker, Bernard Lee; *D:* Robert Hamer; *M:* Jerry Goldsmith. **VHS, Beta** $19.95 COL III

The Detective A New York detective investigating the mutilation murder of a homosexual finds political and police department corruption. Fine, gritty performances prevail in this suspense thriller. Based on the novel by Roderick Thorpe.
1968 114m/C Frank Sinatra, Lee Remick, Ralph Meeker, Jacqueline Bisset, William Windom, Robert Duvall, Tony Musante, Jack Klugman, Al Freeman Jr.; *D:* Gordon Douglas; *W:* Abby Mann. **VHS, Beta** $59.98 FOX III

Detective Sadie & Son A television movie about an elderly detective and her young son cracking a case.
1984 96m/C Debbie Reynolds, Sam Wanamaker, Brian McNamara. **VHS, Beta** NO II

Detective School Dropouts Since they couldn't pass detective school, are they smart enough to outwit a kidnapper? Find out and get a few laughs at the same time. *AKA:* Dumb Dicks.
1985 (PG) 92m/C Lorin Dreyfuss, David Landsberg, Christian de Sica, George Eastman; *D:* Filippo Ottoni. **VHS, Beta** $79.95 MGM II

Detective Story Intense drama about a New York City police precinct with a wide array of characters led by a disillusioned and bitter detective (Douglas). Excellent casting is the strong point, as the film can be a bit dated. Based on Sydney Kingsley's Broadway play.
1951 103m/B Kirk Douglas, Eleanor Parker, Lee Grant, Horace McMahon, William Bendix, Craig Hill, Cathy O'Donnell, Bert Freed, George Macready, Joseph Wiseman, Gladys George, Frank Faylen, Warner Anderson, Gerald Mohr; *D:* William Wyler; *W:* William Wyler, Philip Yordan. Academy Awards '51 Nominations: Best Actress (Parker), Best Director (Wyler), Best Screenplay, Best Supporting Actress (Grant); Cannes Film Festival '52: Best Actress (Grant); Edgar Allan Poe Awards '51: Best Screenplay. **VHS** PAR III ½

Detonator A renegade Russian general has stolen a nuclear bomb and is transporting it from Germany to Iraq via a hijacked train commandeered by his hired band of mercenaries. Stewart is the U.N. troubleshooter delegated to stop the plot, aided by a commando team featuring Brosnan and Paul. Based on the novel "Death Train" by Alistair MacLean. Made for cable television. *AKA:* Alistair MacLean's Death Train; Death Train.
1993 (R) 98m/C Pierce Brosnan, Patrick Stewart, Ted Levine, Alexandra Paul, Christopher Lee; *D:* David S. Jackson; *W:* David S. Jackson. **VHS** $89.95 NLC, COL III

Detour Considered to be the creme de la creme of "B" movies, a largely unacknowledged but cult-followed noir downer. Well-designed, stylish, and compelling, if a bit contrived and sometimes annoyingly shrill. Shot in only six days with six indoor sets.

Down-on-his-luck pianist Neal hitches cross-country to rejoin his fiancee. His first wrong turn involves the accidental death of the man who picked him up, then he's en route to Destiny with a capital "D" when he picks up fatal femme Savage, as vicious a vixen as ever ruined a good man. Told in flashback, it's also been called the most despairing of all "B"-pictures. As noir as they get.
1946 67m/B Tom Neal, Ann Savage, Claudia Drake, Edmund MacDonald; *D:* Edgar G. Ulmer. **VHS, Beta** $19.95 BAR, MRV, SNC III

Detour to Danger Two young men set out on a fishing expedition and run into crooks and damsels in distress. Unintentionally hilarious "acting" by the no-name cast make this a grade-Z "B" movie. Of interest only because it was filmed in the three-color Kodachrome process used primarily in documentaries.
1945 56m/C Britt Wood, John Day, Nancy Brinckman; *D:* Richard Talmadge. **VHS, Beta, 8mm** $19.95 VYY Woof!

Detroit 9000 A pair of Detroit policemen investigate a robbery that occurred at a black congressman's fundraising banquet. Also on video as "Detroit Heat."
1973 (R) 106m/C Alex Rocco, Scatman Crothers, Hari Rhodes, Lonette McKee, Herbert Jefferson Jr.; *D:* Arthur Marks. **VHS, Beta** NO II ½

Deutschland im Jahre Null The acclaimed, unsettling vision of post-war Germany as seen through the eyes of a disturbed boy who eventually kills himself. Lyrical and grim, in German with subtitles.
1947 75m/B GE Franz Gruber; *D:* Roberto Rossellini. **VHS, Beta** $29.95 FCT, GLV III ½

Devastator A Vietnam vet exacts violent revenge on the murderer of an old army buddy. *AKA:* Kings Ransom; The Destroyers.
1985 (R) 79m/C Richard Hill, Katt Shea Ruben, Crofton Hardester; *D:* Cirio H. Santiago. **VHS, Beta** $79.95 MGM I

Devi A minor film in the Ray canon, it is, nonetheless, a strange and compelling tale of religious superstition. An Indian farmer becomes convinced that his beautiful daughter-in-law is the reincarnation of the goddess Kali. The girl is then pressured into accepting a worship that eventually drives her mad. In Bengali with English subtitles.
1960 96m/B IN Chhabi Biswas, Sharmila Tagore, Soumitra Chatterjee; *D:* Satyajit Ray. **VHS, Beta** $49.95 ING, WFV, DVT III ½

The Devil The last remaining humans try to fight off demonic lifeforms that need to feed on their flesh.
1984 90m/C **VHS, Beta** $39.95 VCD I

The Devil & Daniel Webster In 1840s New Hampshire, a young farmer, who sells his soul to the devil, is saved from a trip to Hell when Daniel Webster steps in to defend him. This classic fantasy is visually striking and contains wonderful performances. Adapted from the story by Stephen Vincent Benet who based it on Goethe's Faust. *AKA:* All That Money Can Buy; Here Is a Man; A Certain Mr. Scratch.
1941 106m/B James Craig, Edward Arnold, Walter Huston, Simone Simon, Gene Lockhart, Jane Darwell, Anne Shirley, John Qualen, H.B. Warner; *D:* William Dieterle. **VHS, Beta** $24.95 HMV, SUE, VYG III ½

Devil & Leroy Basset Keema Gregwolf kills a deputy, breaks from jail with the Basset brothers, hijacks a church bus, kidnaps a family, and gets into other troublesome situations while on a posse-eluding cross-country adventure.

1973 (PG) 85m/C Cody Bearpaw, John Goff, George Flower; **D:** Robert E. Pearso; **M:** Les Baxter. **VHS, Beta** $59.95 *PSM ℐ*

The Devil & Max Devlin Good cast wanders aimlessly in Disney family fantasy. The recently deceased Max Devlin strikes a bargain with the devil. He will be restored to life if he can convince three mortals to sell their souls.
1981 (PG) 95m/C Elliott Gould, Bill Cosby, Susan Anspach, Adam Rich, Julie Budd; **D:** Steven Hilliard Stern; **W:** Jimmy Sangster; **M:** Marvin Hamlisch, Buddy Baker. **VHS, Beta** *DIS, OM ℐℐ½*

The Devil & Miss Jones Engaging romantic comedy finds a big business boss posing as an ordinary salesclerk to weed out union organizers. He doesn't expect to encounter the wicked management or his beautiful co-worker, however.
1941 90m/B Jean Arthur, Robert Cummings, Charles Coburn, Edmund Gwenn, Spring Byington, William Demarest, S.Z. Sakall; **D:** Sam Wood. **VHS** $19.98 *REP ℐℐℐ½*

The Devil at 4 O'Clock An alcoholic missionary and three convicts work to save a colony of leper children from a South Seas volcano. Quality cast barely compensates for mediocre script.
1961 126m/B Spencer Tracy, Frank Sinatra, Kerwin Mathews, Jean-Pierre Aumont; **D:** Mervyn LeRoy; **M:** George Duning. **VHS, Beta** $39.95 *GKK, IME ℐℐ½*

The Devil Bat Madman Lugosi trains a swarm of monstrous blood-sucking bats to attack whenever they smell perfume. Followed by the sequel "Devil Bat's Daughter." **AKA:** Killer Bats.
1941 67m/B Bela Lugosi, Dave O'Brien, Suzanne Kaaren, Yolande Donlan; **D:** Jean Yarborough. **VHS, Beta** $19.95 *NOS, SNC, PSM ℐℐ*

The Devil Bat's Daughter A young woman, hoping to avoid becoming insane like her batty father, consults a psychiatrist when she starts to have violent nightmares. Unsuccessful sequel to "Devil Bats."
1946 66m/B Rosemary La Planche, Michael Hale, John James, Molly Lamont; **D:** Frank Wisbar. **VHS, Beta** $14.95 *COL, MRV ℐℐ*

Devil Diamond Mystery-suspense yarn about two amateur detectives who find themselves facing danger after tracking down a gang of evil jewel thieves.
1937 ?m/C Kane Richmond, Frankie Darro. **VHS** $16.95 *SNC, VYY ℐℐ*

Devil Dog: The Hound of Hell A family has trouble with man's best friend when they adopt a dog that is the son of the "Hound of Hell" in this made for television movie.
1978 95m/C Richard Crenna, Yvette Mimieux, Kim Richards, Victor Jory; **D:** Curtis Harrington. **VHS, Beta** *NO ℐ*

Devil Dogs of the Air Cagney and O'Brien team up in another air drama with Cagney once again the cocky pilot who, this time, joins the Marine Air Corp. O'Brien plays his flying idol (and later rival). Cagney finds all his wisecracking and luck are no match for knowledge and experience but he learns. Good stunt flying; shot on location at the San Diego naval air base.
1935 85m/B James Cagney, Pat O'Brien, Margaret Lindsay, Frank McHugh, Robert Barratt, Russell Hicks, Ward Bond; **D:** Lloyd Bacon. **VHS** $19.98 *MGM, FCT ℐℐ½*

Devil Doll An escaped convict uses a mad scientist's human-shrinking formula to evil ends—he sends out miniature assassins in the guise of store-bought dolls. Rarely seen horror oldie.
1936 80m/B Lionel Barrymore, Maureen O'Sullivan, Frank Lawton; **D:** Tod Browning; **W:** Tod Browning, Erich von Stroheim. **VHS, Beta** $19.95 *MGM, MLB ℐℐ*

Devil Doll Ventriloquist's dummy, which contains the soul of a former performer, eyes a beautiful victim in the crowd. Newspaper guy senses trouble. Cut above the usual talking, stalking dummy story.
1964 80m/B GB Bryant Holiday, William Sylvester; **D:** Lindsay Shonteff. **VHS, Beta** $59.95 *MPI ℐℐ*

Devil Girl from Mars Sexy female from Mars and her very large robot arrive at a small Scottish inn to announce that a Martian feminist revolution has occurred. The distaff aliens then undertake a search of healthy Earth males for breeding purposes. Believe it or not, the humans don't want to go and therein lies the rub. A somewhat enjoyable space show.
1954 76m/B GB Hugh McDermott, Hazel Court, Patricia Laffan, Peter Reynolds, Adrienne Corri, Joseph Tomelty, Sophie Stewart, John Laurie, Anthony Richmond; **D:** David MacDonald. **VHS, Beta** $16.95 *NOS, MRV, SNC ℐℐ½*

Devil Horse A boy's devotion to a wild horse marked for destruction as a killer leads him into trouble. A serial in twelve, thirteen-minute chapters.
1932 156m/B Frankie Darro, Harry Carey Sr., Noah Beery Sr.; **D:** Otto Brower, Richard Talmadge. **VHS, Beta** $14.95 *GPV, VCN, DVT ℐℐ*

The Devil in Silk A composer marries a woman, not knowing that she is psychotically jealous. After she commits suicide, he must prove to the police that he did not kill her. Original dialogue in German.
1956 102m/B GE Lilli Palmer, Curt Jurgens, Winnie Markus; **D:** Rolf Hansen. **VHS, Beta** $16.95 *NOS, SNC ℐℐ½*

Devil in the Flesh Acclaimed drama about a French soldier's wife having a passionate affair with a high school student while her husband is away fighting in WWI. From the novel by Raymond Radiguet. Dubbed. Updated and remade in 1987. **AKA:** Le Diable au Corps.
1946 112m/B FR Gerard Philippe, Micheline Presle, Denise Grey; **D:** Claude Autant-Lara. **VHS, Beta** $14.98 *NOS, FCT, APD ℐℐℐ*

Devil in the Flesh A angst-ridden, semi-pretentious Italian drama about an obsessive older woman carrying on an affair with a schoolboy, despite her terrorist boyfriend and the objections of the lad's psychiatrist father, who had treated her. In Italian with subtitles. Famous for a graphic sex scene, available in the unrated version. Updated remake of the 1946 French film. **AKA:** Il Diavolo in Corpo.
1987 (R) 110m/C IT Maruschka Detmers, Federico Pitzalis; **D:** Marco Bellochio; **W:** Marco Bellochio. **VHS, Beta** $14.98 *ORI, ING ℐℐ*

Devil Kiss Gothic horror including zombies, virgins, sorcery, and the inevitable living dead.
1977 93m/C Oliver Mathews, Evelyn Scott. **VHS, Beta** $59.95 *HMV ℐ*

Devil Monster A world-weary traveler searches for a girl's fiance in the South Pacific, and is attacked by a large manta.
1946 65m/B Barry Norton, Blanche Mehaffey; **D:** S. Edward Graham. **VHS, Beta** $16.95 *SNC ℐ*

Devil of the Desert Against the Son of Hercules The grandson of Zeus ventures into the wasteland to take on a feisty foe.
1962 ?m/C IT Kirk Morris, Michele Girardon; **D:** Riccardo (Robert Hampton) Freda. **VHS, Beta** $16.95 *SNC ℐℐ½*

Devil on Horseback A miner's son journeys to London to become a jockey in this comedy/drama. As he tries to bully his way into the racing circuit, he succeeds, but not in the way he anticipated.
1954 88m/B GB Googie Withers, John McCallum, Jeremy Spenser, Liam Redmond; **D:** Cyril Frankel; **M:** Malcolm Arnold. **VHS, Beta, 8mm** $24.95 *VYY ℐℐ*

The Devil on Wheels Inspired by his dad's reckless driving, a teenager becomes a hot rodder and causes a family tragedy. A rusty melodrama that can't be described as high-performance.
1947 67m/B James B. Cardwell, Noreen Nash, Darryl Hickman, Jan Ford, Damian O'Flynn, Lenita Love. **VHS** $15.95 *NOS, LOO ℐℐ*

Devil Rider A monster from Hell, the Devil Rider, once rode the plains in search of human fodder. In the present day, a pleasure ranch is built on his old territory, and people begin dying in the most horrific manners. Could this mean the return of the Devil Rider?
1991 90m/C VHS *NO ℐ½*

Devil Riders Unspectacular horse opera has a crooked lawyer trying to get his grubby hands on some choice land. Enter Crabbe to set things straight.
1944 56m/B Buster Crabbe, Al "Fuzzy" St. John, Patti McCarty, Charles "Blackie" King, John Merton, Kermit Maynard, Frank LaRue, Jack Ingram, George Cheseboro, Edward Cassidy; **D:** Sam Newfield. **VHS** $19.95 *NOS, MRV ℐ½*

The Devil Thumbs a Ride A naive traveller picks up a hitchhiker, not knowing he's wanted for murder. Will history repeat itself in this interesting noir?
1947 63m/B Ted North, Lawrence Tierney, Nan Leslie; **D:** Felix Feist. **VHS, Beta** $34.95 *RKO ℐℐ*

The Devil Thumbs a Ride/ Having Wonderful Crime A mystery double feature. In "Devil Thumbs a Ride," a ruthless killer-bank robber hitches a ride from an inebriated travelling salesman. In "Having Wonderful Crime," a criminal lawyer investigates the disappearance of a magician.
1947 132m/B Lawrence Tierney, Pat O'Brien, George Murphy, Carole Landis, Nan Leslie, George Zucco; **D:** Felix Feist, Edward Sutherland. **VHS, Beta** $39.95 *RKO ℐℐℐ*

Devil Times Five To take revenge for being incarcerated in a mental hospital, five children methodically murder the adults who befriend them. **AKA:** People Toys; The Horrible House on the Hill.
1974 (R) 87m/C Gene Evans, Sorrell Booke, Shelly Morrison; **D:** Sean McGregor. **VHS, Beta** $54.95 *MED ℐ½*

Devil Wears White A student's vacation is disrupted when he becomes involved in a war with an insane arms dealer who wants to take over a Latin American Republic.
1986 (R) 92m/C Robert Livesy, Jane Higginson, Guy Ecker, Anthony Cordova; **D:** Steven A. Hull. **VHS, Beta** $79.95 *TWE ℐ*

Devil Woman A Filipino Gorgon-woman seeks reptilian revenge on the farmers who killed her family. Bad news.
1976 (R) 79m/C PH Rosemarie Gil; **D:** Albert Yu, Felix Vilars. **VHS** $19.98 *SNC Woof!*

D

VIDEOHOUND'S GOLDEN MOVIE RETRIEVER • ▲ 325

Devilfish A small seaside community is ravaged by berserk manta rays in this soggy saga.
1984 92m/C *IT* **D:** Lamberto Bava. **VHS, Beta $59.95** *VMK* ⊘

The Devils In 1631 France, a priest is accused of commerce with the devil and sexual misconduct with nuns. Since he is also a political threat, the accusation is used to denounce and eventually execute him. Based on Aldous Huxley's "The Devils of Loudun," the movie features masturbating nuns and other excesses—shocking scenes typical of film director Russell. Supposedly this was Russell's attempt to wake the public to their desensitization of modern horrors of war. Controversial and flamboyant.
1971 (R) 109m/C *GB* Vanessa Redgrave, Oliver Reed, Dudley Sutton, Max Adrian, Gemma Jones, Murray Melvin; **D:** Ken Russell; **W:** Ken Russell. **VHS, Beta $19.98** *WAR, ING* ⊘⊘⊘

Devil's Angels A motorcycle gang clashes with a small-town sheriff. Cheap 'n' sleazy fare.
1967 84m/C John Cassavetes, Beverly Adams, Mimsy Farmer, Salli Sachse, Nai Bonet, Leo Gordon; **D:** Daniel Haller; **W:** Charles B. Griffith. **VHS** *NO* ⊘

The Devil's Brigade "Dirty Dozen" style film with Holden as the leader of special commando brigade consisting of the usual misfits and oddballs. The team is trained to take on the Nazis in Scandanavia but has their assignment cancelled. Instead, they take them on in the Italian Alps, making for some perilous adventures. Non-acting notables include former football great Hornung and former boxing champ Gene Fullmer.
1968 130m/C William Holden, Cliff Robertson, Vince Edwards, Michael Rennie, Dana Andrews, Gretchen Wyler, Andrew Prine, Claude Akins, Carroll O'Connor, Richard Jaeckel, Jack Watson, Paul Hornung, Jeremy Slate, Don Megowan, Patric Knowles, James Craig, Richard Dawson, Tom Stern, Luke Askew; **D:** Andrew V. McLaglen; **W:** William Roberts. **VHS, Beta $19.98** *MGM* ⊘⊘

The Devil's Brother In one of their lesser efforts, Laurel and Hardy star as bumbling bandits in this comic operetta based on the 1830 opera by Daniel F. Auber. Also available with "Laurel & Hardy's Laughing 20's" on laserdisc. **AKA:** Fra Diavolo; Bogus Bandits; The Virtuous Tramps.
1933 88m/B Stan Laurel, Oliver Hardy, Dennis King, Thelma Todd, James Finlayson, Lucille Browne; **D:** Charles "Buddy" Rogers, Hal Roach. **VHS $19.98** *MGM, MLB, CCB* ⊘⊘

Devil's Canyon An ex-lawman, serving time in an Arizona prison, is beset by a jailed killer seeking vengeance for his own incarceration. Filmed in 3-D.
1953 92m/B Dale Robertson, Virginia Mayo, Stephen McNally, Arthur Hunnicutt, Robert Keith, Jay C. Flippen, Whit Bissell; **D:** Alfred Werker. **VHS, Beta $19.98** *TTC* ⊘⊘

The Devil's Cargo When a man is accused of killing a racetrack operator, he calls in the Falcon to clear his name. The master detective finds this to be a most difficult task however, especially when the accused is found poisoned in his cell. One of the final three "Falcon" films, in which Calvert replaced Tom Conway.
1948 61m/B John Calvert, Rochelle Hudson, Roscoe Karns, Lyle Talbot, Tom Kennedy; **D:** John F. Link. **VHS, Beta $16.95** *SNC* ⊘½

The Devil's Commandment A lurid melodrama about a Parisian newspaperman's journey into a network of crime and perversion. Cinematography by Mario Bava. **AKA:** I, Vampiri; Lust of the Vampires.

1956 90m/B *FR* Giana Maria Canale, Dario Michaelis, Carlo D'Angelo, Wandisa Guida, Paul Muller, Renato Tontini; **D:** Riccardo (Robert Hampton) Freda. **VHS, Beta $16.95** *SNC* ⊘⊘

Devil's Crude Adventurous sailor and a young oil heir uncover a conspiracy within a giant corporation.
1971 85m/C *IT* Franco Nero. **VHS, Beta $59.95** *TWE* ⊘

The Devil's Daughter A sister's hatred and voodoo ceremonies play an important part in this all-black drama. **AKA:** Pocomania; Poncomania.
1939 60m/B Nina Mae McKinney, Jack Carter, Ida James, Hamtree Harrington. **VHS, Beta $16.95** *SNC, VYY, DVT* ⊘½

The Devil's Daughter Satan, in a desperate bid to take over the planet, orders his minions to flood the earth with horrific evil. Only one woman can prevent the Hell-Master from succeeding, and she may be too late!
1991 (R) 112m/C *IT* Kelly Curtis, Herbert Lom, Maria Angela Giordano, Michel Hans Adatte, Carla Cassola, Angelika Maria Boeck, Tomas Arana; **D:** Michele (Michael) Soavi; **W:** Dario Argento; **M:** Pino Donaggio. **VHS $89.98** *REP* ⊘½

The Devil's Disciple Entertaining adaptation of George Bernard Shaw play set during the American Revolution. Standout performances by Douglas as a romantic rogue, Lancaster as a New England pastor, and Olivier as British General Burgoyne. Film suffers from choppy direction, but the excellent cast more than makes up for it.
1959 82m/B *GB* Burt Lancaster, Kirk Douglas, Laurence Olivier, Janet Scott, Eva LeGallienne, Harry Andrews, Basil Sydney, George Rose; **D:** Guy Hamilton; **M:** Richard Rodney Bennett. **VHS $19.98** *MGM* ⊘⊘⊘

The Devil's Eye The devil dispatches Don Juan to tempt and seduce a young virgin bride-to-be, a reverend's daughter, no less. Based on the Danish radio play "Don Juan Returns." **AKA:** Djavulens Oga.
1960 90m/B *SW* Bibi Andersson, Jarl Kulle; **D:** Ingmar Bergman; **W:** Ingmar Bergman. **VHS, Beta $29.98** *SUE, ING, NLC* ⊘⊘

Devil's Gift A young boy's toy is possessed by a demon and havoc ensues.
1984 112m/C Bob Mendlesolin, Vicki Saputo, Steven Robertson; **D:** Kenneth Berton. **VHS, Beta $69.98** *LIV, VES* Woof!

The Devil's Hand When Alda finds a doll that represents his ideal woman in a curio shop, the shop's owner (Hamilton, aka Commissioner Gordon), tells him the dream girl who modeled for the doll lives nearby. Trouble is, she's part of a voodoo cult, and guess who's head voodoo-man. Big trouble for Alda; big snooze for you. **AKA:** Devil's Doll; The Naked Goddess; Live to Love.
1961 71m/B Linda Christian, Robert Alda, Neil Hamilton, Ariadne Welter; **D:** William Hole Jr. **VHS $19.98** *NOS, SNC, LOO* ⊘

The Devil's Harvest A vintage "Reefer Madness"-style cautionary film about pot, the "smoke of Hell."
193? 52m/B **VHS, Beta** *NO* Woof!

The Devil's Mistress A gang of criminals on a pillaging spree murder a man and rape his Indian wife, only to find out she's a she-demon who won't let bygones be bygones. Lame.
1968 66m/C Joan Stapleton, Robert Gregory, Forrest Westmoreland, Douglas Warren, Oren Williams, Arthur Resley; **D:** Orville Wanzer; **W:** Orville Wanzer. **VHS $19.98** *SNC* ⊘½

The Devil's Nightmare A woman leads seven tourists (representing the seven deadly sins) on a tour of a medieval European castle. There they experience demonic tortures. Lots of creepy moments. Euro-horror/sex star Blanc is fantastic in this otherwise mediocre production. **AKA:** Succubus; The Devil Walks at Midnight.
1971 (R) 88m/C *BE IT* Erika Blanc, Jean Servais, Daniel Emilfork, Lucien Raimbourg, Jacques Monseau, Colette Emmanuelle, Ivana Novak, Shirley Corrigan, Frederique Hender; **D:** Jean Brismee. **VHS, Beta $59.95** *MON, APP* ⊘½

The Devil's Partner Yet another uninspired devil yarn in which an old-timer trades in his senior citizenship by dying and coming back in the form of his younger self. Young again, he takes a new wife and indulges in multiple ritual sacrifices. Noteworthy only by virtue of the cast's later TV notoriety—Buchanan and Foulger would later appear on "Petticoat Junction," Nelson played Dr. Rossi on "Peyton Place," and Crane beached a role on "Hawaiian Eye."
1958 75m/B Ed Nelson, Jean Allison, Edgar Buchanan, Richard Crane, Spencer Carlisle, Byron Foulger, Claire Carleton; **D:** Charles R. Rondeau. **VHS $19.98** *SNC, MRV, CNM* ⊘½

Devil's Party A tenement boy's reunion party turns into a night of horror when one of the guests is killed. As a result, the childhood friends band together to uncover the murderer's identity.
1938 65m/B Victor McLaglen, Paul Kelly, William Gargan, Samuel S. Hinds, Scotty Beckett; **D:** Ray McCarey. **VHS, Beta $24.95** *NOS, MRV, DVT* ⊘½

The Devil's Playground Sexual tension rises in a Catholic seminary, distracting the boys from their theological studies. The attentions of the priests only further their sexual confusion. Winner of many Australian film awards.
1976 107m/C *AU* Arthur Dignam, Nick Tate, Simon Burke, Charles Frawley, Jonathon Hardy, Gerry Dugan, Thomas Keneally; **D:** Fred Schepisi; **W:** Fred Schepisi. **Beta $79.95** *ALL* ⊘⊘⊘

The Devil's Possessed A Middle Ages despot tortures and maims the peasants in his region until they rise up and enact an unspeakable revenge.
1974 90m/C *AR SP* Paul Naschy; **D:** Leon Klimovsky. **VHS, Beta** *NO* ⊘½

Devil's Rain The rituals and practices of devil worship, possession, and satanism are gruesomely related. Interesting cast.
1975 (PG) 85m/C Ernest Borgnine, Ida Lupino, William Shatner, Eddie Albert, Keenan Wynn, John Travolta, Tom Skerritt; **D:** Robert Fuest. **VHS, Beta $19.95** *VCI* ⊘½

The Devil's Sleep When a crusading woman sets out to break up a teen narcotics ring, the threatened thugs attempt to draw her daughter into their sleazy affairs, thus assuring the mother's silence.
1951 81m/B Lita Grey Chaplin, Timothy Farrell, John Mitchum, William Thomason, Tracy Lynn; **D:** W. Merle Connell. **VHS, Beta $16.95** *SNC* ⊘

Devil's Son-in-Law A black stand-up comic makes a deal with a devil.
1977 (R) 95m/C Rudy Ray Moore; **D:** Cliff Roguemore. **VHS, Beta** *NO* Woof!

The Devil's Undead When a Scottish orphanage is besieged by a rash of cold-blooded murders, the detectives Lee and Cushing are summoned to investigate. Interesting spin on that old possessed by demons theme.

1975 (PG) 90m/C *GB* Christopher Lee, Peter Cushing; *D:* Peter Sasdy. VHS, Beta $59.95 MON, MLB 🎬🎬½

Devil's Wanton A young girl tries to forget an unhappy relationship by beginning a new romance with an equally frustrated beau. Gloomy, but hopeful. *AKA:* Fangelse; Prison.
1949 80m/B *SW* Doris Svedlund, Eva Henning, Hasse Ekman; *D:* Ingmar Bergman; *W:* Ingmar Bergman. VHS, Beta $24.95 VYY, MRV, DVT 🎬🎬½

The Devil's Web A demonic nurse infiltrates, manipulates, and corrupts three beautiful sisters.
1974 (PG) 73m/C Diana Dors, Andrea Marcovicci, Ed Bishop, Cec Linder, Michael Culver. VHS, Beta $29.95 LIV 🎬½

Devil's Wedding Night An archaeologist and his twin brother fight over a ring that lures virgins into Count Dracula's Transylvanian castle. Vampire queen Bay seduces the dimwit twins and strips at every chance she gets.
1973 (R) 85m/C Mark Damon, Rosalba (Sara Bay) Neri, Frances Davis; *D:* Paul Solvay. VHS, Beta $49.95 VCI Woof!

Devlin Devlin is a tough cop with an alcohol problem and a bad marriage. His father-in-law, Brennan, is a powerful local political boss. When Brennan's son is murdered, Devlin is the fall guy. Seeking to clear himself, he discovers a conspiracy going back thirty years. Made for cable television.
1992 (R) 110m/C Bryan Brown, Roma Downey, Lloyd Bridges; *D:* Rick Rosenthal. VHS, Beta $89.98 FXV, VTR 🎬🎬

Devlin Connection Retired private investigator helps his son learn the ropes as he embarks on a Los Angeles crime fighting career. Hudson's last starring television series, excluding his "Dynasty" role. All thirteen episodes are available separately.
1982 50m/C Rock Hudson, Jack Scalia, Louis Giambalvo, Leigh Taylor-Young, Jack Kruschen; *D:* Christian Nyby. VHS, Beta $39.95 TWE 🎬🎬

Devonsville Terror Strange things begin to happen when a new school teacher arrives in Devonsville, a town that has a history of torture, murder, and witchcraft. The hysterical townspeople react by beginning a 20th-century witchhunt.
1983 (R) 97m/C Suzanna Love, Donald Pleasence, Deanna Haas, Mary Walden, Robert Walker Jr., Paul Wilson; *D:* Ulli Lommel; *W:* Ulli Lommel. VHS, Beta $9.98 SUE 🎬🎬

Devotion A lovesick British miss disguises herself as a governess so she can be near the object of her affection, a London barrister.
1931 80m/B Ann Harding, Leslie Howard, Robert Williams, O.P. Heggie, Louise Closser Hale, Dudley Digges; *D:* Robert Milton. VHS $19.98 TTC 🎬🎬½

D.I. A tough drill sergeant is faced with an unbreakable rebellious recruit, threatening his record and his platoon's status. Webb's film features performances by actual soldiers.
1957 106m/B Jack Webb, Don Dubbins, Jackie Loughery, Lin McCarthy, Virginia Gregg; *D:* Jack Webb. VHS, Beta $59.95 WAR 🎬🎬

The Diabolical Dr. Z When dad dies of cardiac arrest after the medical council won't let him make the world a kinder gentler place with his personality-altering technique, his dutiful daughter—convinced the council brought on dad's demise—is out to change some personalities in a big way. *AKA:* Miss Muette; Dans les Griffes du Maniaque.
1965 86m/B *SP FR* Mabel Karr, Fernando Montes, Estella Blain, Antonio J. Escribano, Howard Vernon; *D:* Jess (Jesus) Franco. VHS $19.98 SNC 🎬🎬

Diabolically Yours A French thriller about an amnesiac who struggles to discover his lost identity. Tensions mount when his pretty spouse and friends begin to wonder if it's all a game. Dubbed. *AKA:* Diaboliquement Votre.
1967 94m/C *FR* Alain Delon, Senta Berger; *D:* Julien Duvivier. VHS, Beta $59.95 UNI 🎬🎬½

Diabolique The mistress and the wife of a sadistic schoolmaster conspire to murder the man, carry it out, and then begin to wonder if they have covered their tracks effectively. Plot twists and double-crosses abound. In French with English subtitles. Remade for television as "Reflections of Murder." *AKA:* Les Diabolique.
1955 107m/B *FR* Simone Signoret, Vera Clouzot, Paul Meurisse, Charles Vanel, Michel Serrault; *D:* Henri-Georges Clouzot. VHS, Beta, 8mm $24.95 VYY, NOS, SNC 🎬🎬🎬½

Dial Help A lame Italian-made suspenser about a model plagued by ghostly phone calls.
1988 (R) 94m/C *IT* Charlotte Lewis, Marcello Modugno, Mattia Sbragia, Victor Cavallo; *D:* Ruggero Deodato. VHS, Beta $79.95 PSM 🎬½

Dial "M" for Murder An unfaithful husband devises an elaborate plan to murder his wife for her money, but when she accidentally stabs the killer-to-be, with scissors no less, he alters his methods. Part of the "A Night at the Movies" series, this tape simulates a 1954 movie evening with a Daffy Duck cartoon, "My Little Duckaroo," a newsreel, and coming attractions for "Them" and "A Star is Born." Filmed in 3-D. Based on the play by Frederick Knotts.
1954 123m/C Ray Milland, Grace Kelly, Robert Cummings, John Williams, Anthony M. (Antonio Marghereti) Dawson; *D:* Alfred Hitchcock; *M:* Dimitri Tiomkin. VHS, Beta $19.98 WAR, TLF 🎬🎬🎬

Diamante, Oro y Amor A pair of amateur gangsters find themselves in some crazy situations.
1987 93m/C *MX* Julio Aleman, Hilda Aguirre, Hector Suarez, Adriana Roel, Chucho Salinas. VHS, Beta $59.95 MAD 🎬🎬

Diamond Fleece Rick (Cross) is a convicted diamond thief who's given a parole just so he can guard the world's largest uncut gemstone. But Inspector Outlaw (Dennehy) figures Rick will never be able to resist stealing the gem himself and the law can finally lock Rick away for good. Oh, and Holly, she thinks a maybe-ex-diamond thief will bring a little romance to her life.
1992 93m/C Ben Cross, Brian Dennehy, Kate Nelligan; *D:* Al Waxman; *W:* Michael Norell. VHS $79.95 PSM 🎬🎬½

Diamond Head A Hawaiian landowner brings destruction and misery to his family via his stubbornness. Based on the Peter Gilman novel.
1962 107m/C Charlton Heston, Yvette Mimieux, George Chakiris, France Nuyen, James Darren; *D:* Guy Green; *M:* John Williams. VHS, Beta $69.95 COL 🎬🎬½

Diamond Ninja Force Non-adventure minimally hosted by Sho Kosugi pitting reluctant ninjas against innocent mortal enemies with the usual half-hearted revenge motif. Shabby ninja imitator.
198? 90m/C VHS, Beta $59.95 TWE Woof!

Diamond Run A streetwise American expatriate frantically searches for his girlfriend after unwittingly involving her in an assassination plot.
1990 (R) 89m/C William Bell Sullivan, Ava Lazar, Ayu Azhari, David Thornton, Peter Fox; *D:* Robert Chappell. VHS, Beta NO 🎬½

Diamond Trail East Coast jewel thieves bring their operation to the West, trailed by a New York reporter.
1933 58m/B Rex Bell, Frances Rich, Bud Osborne, Lloyd Whitlock, Norman Feusier; *D:* Harry Fraser. VHS, Beta $19.95 NOS, DVT 🎬½

The Diamond Trap A Manhatten detective finds himself in the middle of a diamond heist and involved with a con artist. Made for television.
1991 (PG) 93m/C Howard Hesseman, Brooke Shields, Ed Marinaro, Antonio J. Escribano; *D:* Don Taylor; *W:* David Peckinpah. VHS $89.95 VMK 🎬

Diamonds A tense film in which the Israel Diamond Exchange is looted by a motley array of criminal heisters. Shaw plays a dual role as twin brothers.
1972 (PG) 108m/C *IS* Robert Shaw, Richard Roundtree, Barbara Hershey, Shelley Winters; *D:* Menahem Golan. VHS, Beta $59.98 NLC 🎬🎬

Diamonds are Forever 007 once again battles his nemesis Blofeld, this time in Las Vegas. Bond must prevent the implementation of a plot to destroy Washington through the use of a space-orbiting laser. Fabulous stunts include Bond's wild drive through the streets of Vegas in a '71 Mach 1. Connery returned to play Bond in this film after being offered the then record-setting salary of one million dollars.
1971 (PG) 120m/C *GB* Sean Connery, Jill St. John, Charles Gray, Bruce Cabot, Jimmy Dean, Lana Wood, Bruce Glover, Putter Smith, Norman Burton, Joseph Furst, Bernard Lee, Desmond Llewelyn, Laurence Naismith, Leonard Barr, Lois Maxwell, Margaret Lacey, Joe Robinson, Donna Garrat, Trina Parks; *D:* Guy Hamilton; *W:* Tom Mankiewicz; *M:* John Barry. VHS, Beta $19.98 MGM, TLF 🎬🎬🎬½

Diamond's Edge An adolescent private eye and his juvenescent brother snoop into the affairs of the Fat Man, and find out that the opera ain't over until they find out what's in the Fat Man's mysterious box of bonbons. A genre-parodying kid mystery, written by Horowitz, based on his novel, "The Falcon's Malteser." *AKA:* Just Ask for Diamond.
1988 (PG) 83m/C Susannah York, Peter Eyre, Patricia Hodge, Nickolas Grace; *D:* Stephen Bayly; *W:* Anthony Horowitz; *M:* Trevor Jones. VHS, Beta $79.99 HBO 🎬🎬

Diamonds of the Night A breakthrough masterpiece of the Czech new wave, about two young men escaping from a transport train to Auschwitz and scrambling for survival in the countryside. Surreal, powerfully expressionistic film, one of the most important of its time. In Czech with English subtitles. Accompanied by Nemec's short "A Loaf of Bread." *AKA:* Demanty Noci.
1964 71m/B *CZ* Ladislav Jansky, Antonin Kumbera, Ilse Bischofova; *D:* Jan Nemec; *W:* Arnost Lustig, Jan Nemec. VHS, Beta $59.95 FCT 🎬🎬🎬🎬

Diamonds on Wheels A Disney film about three British teenagers, amid a big road rally, discovering stolen diamonds and getting pursued by gangsters.
1973 84m/C VHS, Beta $69.95 DIS 🎬

Diana: Her True Story Britain's royals are held up to scandalous review in this made for tv adaptaion of Andrew Morton's sympathetic bio of the Princess of Wales.

Taking Diana from her lonely childhood to her "fairytale" nuptials and subsequent disillusionment with being a royal, including her bulimia and half-hearted suicide attempts. Charles is portrayed as an arrogant, emotional cold fish, only interested in farming and continuing his liaison with Camilla Parker-Bowles. Handsome production with appropriate impersonations by the cast.

1993 180m/C Serena Scott Thomas, David Threlfall, Elizabeth Garvie, Jemma Redgrave, Tracy Hardwick, Anne Stallybrass, Jeffrey Harmer, Donald Douglas; *D:* Kevin Connor; *W:* Stephen Zito. **VHS** $95.25 EHV ♦♦½

Diane Overstuffed medieval drama featuring Turner as Diane de Poitier, the mistress of a sixteenth century French King. Moore plays the king in his Hollywood debut. Gorgeous sets and costumes couldn't boost this film at the box office, which had disappointing figures in spite of the expense bestowed upon it. Based on the novel "Diane de Poitier" by John Erskine.

1955 110m/C Lana Turner, Pedro Armendariz Sr., Roger Moore, Marisa Pavan, Cedric Hardwicke, Torin Thatcher, Taina Elg, John Lupton, Henry Daniell, Sean McClory, Michael Ansara; *D:* David Miller; *W:* Christopher Isherwood. **VHS** $19.98 MGM ♦♦

Diary of a Chambermaid A chambermaid wants to marry a rich man and finds herself the object of desire of a poor servant willing to commit murder for her. Excellent comic drama, but very stylized in direction and set design. Produced during Renoir's years in Hollywood. Adapted from a story by Octave Mirbeau, later turned into a play. Remade in 1964 by Luis Bumel.

1946 86m/B Paulette Goddard, Burgess Meredith, Hurd Hatfield, Francis Lederer, Judith Anderson, Florence Bates, Almira Sessions, Reginald Owen; *D:* Jean Renoir. **VHS** $19.98 REP, FCT ♦♦♦

Diary of a Chambermaid Vintage Bunuelian social satire about a young girl taking a servant's job in a provincial French family, and easing into an atmosphere of sexual hypocrisy and decadence. In French with English subtitles. Remake of the 1946 Jean Renoir film. *AKA:* Le Journal d'une Femme de Chambre; Il Diario di una Cameriera.

1964 97m/C *FR* Jeanne Moreau, Michel Piccoli, Georges Geret, Francoise Lugagne, Daniel Ivernel; *D:* Luis Bunuel; *W:* Luis Bunuel, Jean-Claude Carriere. **VHS, Beta** $19.98 ING, APD, IME ♦♦♦½

Diary of a Country Priest With "Balthazar" and "Mouchette," this is one of Bresson's greatest, subtlest films, treating the story of an alienated, unrewarded young priest with his characteristic austerity and Catholic humanism. In French and English subtitles. *AKA:* Le Journal d'un Cure de Campagne.

1950 120m/B *FR* Claude Layou, Jean Riveyre, Nicole Ladmiral; *D:* Robert Bresson; *W:* Robert Bresson. **VHS, Beta** $59.95 DVT, APD, ING ♦♦♦½

Diary of a Hitman A hitman is hired to knock off the wife and child of a commodities broker who claims his wife is a drug addict and the infant is a crack baby and not his. The hired killer wants out of the business, but needs to pull off one more job for a down payment on his apartment. Beset by doubts, he breaks conduct by conversing with the victim and discovers the broker lied. Based on the play "Insider's Price" by Pressman.

1991 (R) 90m/C Forest Whitaker, James Belushi, Sherilyn Fenn, Sharon Stone, Seymour Cassel, Lewis Smith, Lois Chiles, John Bedford-Lloyd; *D:* Roy London; *W:* Kenneth Pressman; *M:* Michel Colombier. **VHS** $19.95 COL ♦♦½

Diary of a Lost Girl The second Louise Brooks/G.W. Pabst collaboration (after "Pandora's Box") in which a frail but mesmerizing German girl plummets into a life of hopeless degradation. Dark and gloomy, the film chronicles the difficulties she faces, from rape to an unwanted pregnancy and prostitution. Based on the popular book by Margarete Boehme. Silent. Made after flapper Brooks left Hollywood to pursue greater opportunities and more challenging roles under Pabst's guidance.

1929 99m/B *GE* Louise Brooks, Fritz Rasp, Josef Rovensky, Sybille Schmitz; *D:* G.W. Pabst. **VHS, Beta** $19.95 GPV, MRV, VDM ♦♦♦

Diary of a Mad Housewife Despairing of her miserable family life, a housewife has an affair with a writer only to find him to be even more selfish and egotistical than her no-good husband. Snodgrass plays her character perfectly, hearing the insensitive absurdity of her husband and her lover over and over again, enjoying her martyrdom even as it drives her crazy.

1970 (R) 94m/C Carrie Snodgrass, Richard Benjamin, Frank Langella; *D:* Frank Perry. Academy Awards '70 Nominations: Best Actress (Snodgrass); Golden Globe Awards '71: Best Actress—Musical/Comedy (Snodgrass); National Board of Review Awards '70: 10 Best Films of the Year, Best Supporting Actor (Langella). **VHS, Beta** $14.95 GKK ♦♦♦

Diary of a Mad Old Man A wistful drama about an old man who's lost everything except his desire for his daughter-in-law, which sends him into fits of nostalgia. *AKA:* Dagboek Van Een Oude Dwaas.

1988 (PG-13) 93m/C Derek De Lint, Ralph Michael, Beatie Edney. **VHS, Beta** $79.95 MED ♦♦

Diary of a Madman Price is once again possessed by an evil force in this gothic thriller. Fairly average Price vehicle, based on Guy de Maupassant's story.

1963 96m/C Vincent Price, Nancy Kovack, Chris Warfield, Ian Wolfe, Nelson Olmstead; *D:* Reginald LeBorg. **VHS, Beta** $14.95 MGM, FCT ♦♦

Diary of a Rebel A fictional account of the rise of Cuban rebel leader Che Guevara.

1984 89m/C John Ireland, Francesco Rabal. **VHS, Beta** NO ♦

Diary of a Teenage Hitchhiker Teen girl ignores family restrictions and police warnings about a homicidal rapist stalking the area and continues to thumb rides to her job at a beach resort. One night she's picked up for ride she'll never forget.

1982 96m/C Charlene Tilton, Dick Van Patten; *D:* Ted Post. **VHS, Beta** NO ♦

Diary of a Young Comic New York comedian searches for the meaning of lunacy. He finds it after Improvisation in Los Angeles.

1979 74m/C Stacy Keach, Dom DeLuise, Richard Lewis, Bill Macy, George Jessel, Gary Muledeer, Nina Van Pallandt; *D:* Gary Weis. **VHS, Beta** NO ♦

The Diary of Anne Frank In June 1945, a liberated Jewish refugee returns to the hidden third floor of an Amsterdam factory where he finds the diary kept by his youngest daughter, Anne. The document recounts their years in hiding from the Nazis. Based on the actual diary of 13-year-old Anne Frank, killed in a death camp during WWII.

1959 150m/B Millie Perkins, Joseph Schildkraut, Shelley Winters, Richard Beymer, Gusti Huber, Ed Wynn, Lou Jacobi, Diane Baker; *D:* George Stevens. Academy Awards '59: Best Art Direction/Set Decoration (B & W), Best Black and White Cinematography, Best Supporting Actress (Winters); Nominations: Best Costume Design (B & W), Best Director (Stevens), Best Picture, Best Supporting Actor (Wynn), Best Original Score. **VHS, Beta** $79.98 KUI, FOX, BTV ♦♦♦½

Diary of Forbidden Dreams A beautiful young girl finds herself drawn into bizarre incidents at an eccentric millionaire's mansion that cause her to go insane. Set on the Italian Riviera, it's the most offbeat rendition of "Alice in Wonderland" you're apt to find. Unfortunately, the convoluted plot lessens its appeal. Unedited version, under the original title "What!," released at 113 minutes, is also available. *AKA:* What?; Che?.

1973 (R) 94m/C *IT* Marcello Mastroianni, Hugh Griffith, Sydne Rome, Roman Polanski; *D:* Roman Polanski; *W:* Roman Polanski, Gerard Brach. **VHS, Beta** $19.95 VDM, TWE, FCT ♦♦♦

Diary of the Dead A newlywed kills his aggravating mother-in-law, only to have her repeatedly return from the grave.

1987 (PG) 93m/C Hector Elizondo, Geraldine Fitzgerald, Salome Jens; *D:* Arvin Brown. **Beta** NO ♦

Dias de Ilusion The fantasy world in which Lucia and her sister live was created for only one reason, and only Lucia's diary has the secret. In Spanish.

1980 94m/C *SP* Andrea Del Boca, Luisina Brando. **VHS, Beta** $29.95 MED ♦½

Dick Barton, Special Agent Dick Barton is called in when a mad scientist threatens to attack London with germ-carrying bombs. The first film production for Hammer Studios, later to be known for its horror classics.

1948 70m/B *GB* Don Stannard, Geoffrey Ford, Jack Shaw; *D:* Alfred Goulding. **VHS, Beta** $16.95 SNC, VYY ♦

Dick Barton Strikes Back "Mr. French" Cabot has a nuclear weapon and is willing to use it; that is, until Dick Barton arrives to put the Frenchman out of commission. Generally considered the best of the Dick Barton film series.

1948 73m/B *GB* Don Stannard, Sebastian Cabot, Jean Lodge; *D:* Godfrey Grayson. **VHS, Beta** $16.95 SNC, VYY ♦♦½

Dick Tracy Serial, based on the comic-strip character, in fifteen chapters. Tracy tries to find his kidnapped brother as he faces the fiend "Spider." The first chapter is thirty minutes and each additional chapter is twenty minutes.

1937 310m/B Ralph Byrd, Smiley Burnette, Irving Pichel, Jennifer Jones; *D:* John English. **VHS, Beta** $29.95 SNC, VYY, VCI ♦♦½

Dick Tracy Beatty wears the caps of producer, director, and star, performing admirably on all fronts. One minor complaint: his Tracy is somewhat flat in comparison to the outstanding performances and makeup of the unique villains, especially Pacino. Stylistically superior, shot in only 7 colors, the timeless sets capture the essence rather than the reality of the city, successfully bringing the comic strip to life. Madonna is fine as the seductive Breathless Mahoney, belting out Stephen Sondheim like she was born to do it. People expecting the gothic technology of "Batman" may be disappointed, but moviegoers searching for a memory made real will be thrilled.

D

1990 (PG) 105m/C Warren Beatty, Madonna, Charlie Korsmo, Glenne Headly, Al Pacino, Dustin Hoffman, James Caan, Mandy Patinkin, Paul Sorvino, Charles Durning, Dick Van Dyke, R.G. Armstrong, Catherine O'Hara, Estelle Parsons, Seymour Cassel, Michael J. Pollard, William Forsythe, Kathy Bates, James Tolkan; *D:* Warren Beatty; *W:* Jim Cash, Jack Epps Jr.; *M:* Danny Elfman, Stephen Sondheim. Academy Awards '90: Best Art Direction/Set Decoration, Best Makeup, Best Song ("Sooner or Later"); Nominations: Best Cinematography, Best Costume Design, Best Sound, Best Supporting Actor (Pacino). VHS, Beta $19.99 *TOU, FCT, IME* 🎬🎬🎬½

Dick Tracy, Detective The first Dick Tracy feature film, in which Splitface is on the loose, a schoolteacher is murdered, the Mayor is threatened, and a nutty professor uses a crystal ball to give Tracy the clues needed to connect the crimes.
1945 62m/B Morgan Conway, Anne Jeffreys, Mike Mazurki, Jane Greer, Lyle Latelle; *D:* William Burke. VHS, Beta $16.95 *SNC, MED, VYY* 🎬🎬🎬

Dick Tracy, Detective/The Corpse Vanishes On one tape, the first Dick Tracy feature film and Lugosi's minor epic about a mad scientist using virgin's blood to restore youth to an aging countess.
1942 126m/B Bela Lugosi, Morgan Conway, Luana Walters, Tristram Coffin, Mike Mazurki, Jane Greer, Lyle Latelle; *D:* William Berke. VHS, Beta *AOV* 🎬½

Dick Tracy Double Feature #1 Mystery-adventure double feature presents Chester Gould's popular comic strip hero in live action. Includes "Dick Tracy, Detective" and "Dick Tracy's Dilemma."
1945 122m/B Ralph Byrd, Lyle Latelle, Morgan Conway, Anne Jeffreys. VHS, Beta $54.95 *VCI* 🎬½

Dick Tracy Double Feature #2 Chester Gould's famous comic strip character is personified in "Dick Tracy Meets Gruesome" and "Dick Tracy vs. Cueball," a double-feature videocassette featuring Dick Tracy battling two of his arch-enemies.
1947 127m/B Boris Karloff, Ralph Byrd, Morgan Conway, Anne Jeffreys. VHS, Beta $54.95 *VCI* 🎬🎬

Dick Tracy Meets Gruesome Gruesome and his partner in crime, Melody, stage a bank robbery using the secret formula of Dr. A. Tomic. Tracy has to solve the case before word gets out and people rush to withdraw their savings, destroying civilization as we know it. *AKA:* Dick Tracy's Amazing Adventure; Dick Tracy Meets Karloff.
1947 66m/B Boris Karloff, Ralph Byrd, Lyle Latelle; *D:* John Rawlins. VHS, Beta $14.95 *NOS, MRV, SNC* 🎬🎬

Dick Tracy Returns 15-chapter serial. Public Enemy Paw Stark and his gang set out on a wave of crime that brings them face to face with dapper Dick.
1938 100m/B Ralph Byrd, Charles Middleton; *D:* William Witney. VHS, Beta $79.95 *VCI, IME, MLB* 🎬🎬

Dick Tracy: The Original Serial, Vol. 1 The first seven parts of the original popular serial. The comic strip character comes to life and tries to stop the spider, a dangerous criminal.
1937 150m/B Ralph Byrd, Smiley Burnette, Kay Hughes, Francis X. Bushman, Lee Van Atta; *D:* Ray Taylor; *W:* Alan James. VHS, Beta $24.95 *GKK* 🎬🎬🎬

Dick Tracy: The Original Serial, Vol. 2 The last eight chapters of the highly acclaimed serial. Tracy is still tracking down the Spider in this action-packed adventure.
1937 160m/B Ralph Byrd, Smiley Burnette, Kay Hughes, Francis X. Bushman, Lee Van Atta; *D:* Ray Taylor; *W:* Alan James. VHS, Beta $24.95 *GKK* 🎬🎬🎬

Dick Tracy: The Spider Strikes Dick Tracy, his bumbling sidekick, and his beautiful, brainy assistant go up against the master criminal, The Spider.
1937 60m/B Ralph Byrd, Francis X. Bushman. VHS, Beta $9.95 *KAR* 🎬🎬🎬

Dick Tracy vs. Crime Inc. Dick Tracy encounters many difficulties when he tries to track down a criminal who can make himself invisible. A serial in 15 chapters.
1941 100m/B Ralph Byrd, Ralph Morgan, Michael Owen; *D:* William Witney; *W:* John English. VHS, Beta $79.95 *VCI, IME, MLB* 🎬🎬

Dick Tracy vs. Cueball Dick Tracy has his work cut out for him when the evil gangster Cueball appears on the scene. Based on Chester Gould's comic strip.
1946 62m/B Morgan Conway, Anne Jeffreys; *D:* Gordon Douglas. VHS, Beta $14.95 *NOS, VCI, VYY* 🎬🎬🎬

Dick Tracy's Dilemma The renowned police detective Dick Tracy tries to solve a case involving the Claw. Based on the Chester Gould comic strip. *AKA:* Mark of the Claw.
1947 60m/B Ralph Byrd, Lyle Latelle, Kay Christopher, Jack Lambert, Ian Keith, Jimmy Conlin; *D:* John Rawlins. VHS, Beta *MRV, VCI, VYY* 🎬🎬

Dick Turpin In this rare film, Mix plays the famed English highwayman who seeks adventure in historical Britain.
1925 60m/B Tom Mix, Alan Hale; *D:* John Blystone. VHS, Beta $47.50 *GVV* 🎬🎬½

Didn't You Hear? An alienated college student discovers that dreams have a life of their own when he becomes immersed in his own fantasy world.
1983 (PG) 94m/C Dennis Christopher, Gary Busey, Cheryl Waters, John Kauffman. VHS, Beta $49.95 *PSM* 🎬

Die! Die! My Darling! A young widow visits her mad ex-mother-in-law in a remote English village, and is imprisoned by the mourning woman as revenge for her son's death. Bankhead's last role. *AKA:* Fanatic.
1965 97m/C *GB* Tallulah Bankhead, Stefanie Powers, Peter Vaughan, Maurice Kaufman, Donald Sutherland, Gwendolyn Watts, Yootha Joyce, Winifred Dennis; *D:* Silvio Narizzano; *W:* Richard Matheson. Beta $9.95 *COL, MLB* 🎬½

Die Grosse Freiheit Nr. 7 A man tries to stop his niece's love affair with a sailor. Nazi propaganda minister Goebbels banned this film in Germany, since it showed German soldiers getting drunk and also had Hildebrand cast as a prostitute. After the war, however, it enjoyed great popularity throughout Germany. Albers sings the classic "Auf der Reeperbahn." In German with no English translation.
1945 100m/C *GE* Hans Albers, Hilde Hildebrand. VHS, Beta $35.95 *IHF* 🎬½

Die Hard High-voltage action thriller pits a lone New York cop against a band of ruthless high-stakes terrorists who attack and and hold hostage the employees of a large corporation as they celebrate Christmas in a new L.A. high rise. It's just as unbelievable as it sounds, but you'll love it anyway. Rickman, who later charmed audiences as the villain in "Robin Hood: Prince of Thieves," turns in a marvelous performance as the chief bad guy. Based on the novel "Nothing Lasts Forever" by Roderick Thorp.
1988 (R) 114m/C Bruce Willis, Bonnie Bedelia, Alan Rickman, Alexander Godunov, Paul Gleason, William Atherton, Reginald Vel Johnson, Hart Bochner, James Shigeta, Mary Ellen Trainor, De'voreaux White, Robert Davi, Rick Ducommun; *D:* John McTiernan; *W:* Jeb Stuart, Steven E. de Souza; *M:* Michael Kamen. VHS, Beta $19.98 *FOX* 🎬🎬🎬

Die Hard 2: Die Harder Fast, well-done sequel brings another impossible situation before the wise-cracking, tough-cookie cop. Our hero tangles with a group of terrorists at an airport under siege, while his wife remains in a plane circling above as its fuel dwindles. Obviously a repeat of the plot and action of the first "Die Hard," with references to the former in the script. While the bad guys lack the fiendishness of their predecessors, this installment features energetic and finely acted performances. Fairly gory, especially the icicle-in-the-eyeball scene. Adapted from the novel "58 Minutes" by Walter Wager and characters created by Roderick Thorp.
1990 (R) 124m/C Bruce Willis, William Atherton, Franco Nero, Bonnie Bedelia, John Amos, Reginald Vel Johnson, Dennis Franz, Art Evans, Fred Dalton Thompson, William Sadler, Sheila McCarthy, Robert Patrick, John Leguizamo, Robert Costanzo, Tom Verica; *D:* Renny Harlin; *W:* Doug Richardson, Steven E. de Souza; *M:* Michael Kamen. VHS $19.98 *FOX* 🎬🎬🎬

Die Laughing A cab driver unwittingly becomes involved in murder, intrigue, and the kidnapping of a monkey that has memorized a scientific formula that can destroy the world. Writer/actor/composer Benson might consider renaming it "Die from Embarassment."
1980 (PG) 108m/C Robby Benson, Charles Durning, Bud Cort, Elsa Lanchester, Peter Coyote; *D:* Jeff Werner; *W:* Robby Benson, Scott Parker; *M:* Robby Benson. VHS, Beta $19.98 *WAR* Woof!

Die, Monster, Die! A reclusive scientist experiments with a radioactive meteorite and gains bizarre powers. Karloff is great in this adaptation of H.P. Lovecraft's "The Color Out of Space." *AKA:* Monster of Terror.
1965 80m/C *GB* Boris Karloff, Nick Adams, Suzan Farmer, Patrick Magee; *D:* Daniel Haller. VHS $19.99 *HBO* 🎬🎬

Die Screaming, Marianne A girl is on the run from her father, a crooked judge, who wants to kill her before her 21st birthday, when she will inherit evidence that will put him away for life. *AKA:* Die, Beautiful Marianne.
1973 81m/C *GB* Michael Rennie, Susan George, Karin Dor; *D:* Pete Walker. VHS, Beta $49.95 *UNI* 🎬

Die Sister, Die! Thriller about a gothic mansion with an eerie secret in the basement features a battle between a senile, reclusive sister and her disturbed, tormenting brother.
1974 88m/C Jack Ging, Edith Atwater, Antoinette Bower, Kent Smith, Robert Emhardt; *D:* Randall Hood. VHS, Beta $59.95 *MPI* 🎬

Die Watching Sleazy erotic thriller about a video director (Atkins) who not only likes to film some hot Hollywood babes but may also like to kill them as well. His latest discovery just could be the next victim.
1993 (R) 92m/C Christopher Atkins, Vali Ashton, Tim Thomerson, Carlos Palomino, Mike Jacobs Jr.; *D:* Charles Davis; *W:* Kenneth J. Hall. VHS $89.95 *TRI* 🎬½

A Different Kind of Love A romantic novel on tape, in modern settings. Love, frustration, tragedy.
1985 60m/C Joyce Redman. Beta $11.95 *PSM* ✍️

Different Story Romance develops when a lesbian real estate agent offers a homosexual chauffeur a job with her firm. Resorts to stereotypes when the characters decide to marry.
1978 107m/C Perry King, Meg Foster, Valerie Curtin, Peter Donat, Richard Bull; *D:* Paul Aaron. VHS, Beta $19.95 *SUE, NLC* ✍️✍️½

Digby, the Biggest Dog in the World Poor comedy-fantasy about Digby, a sheepdog, who wanders around a scientific laboratory, drinks an experimental fluid, and grows and grows and grows.
1973 (G) 88m/C *GB* Jim Dale, Angela Douglas, Spike Milligan, Dinsdale Landen; *D:* Joseph McGrath. VHS, Beta $59.95 *PSM* ✍️

Digging Up Business Johnson tries to save the family funeral home business from financial ruin with some unique interment services. This film needs a decent burial.
1991 (PG) 89m/C Lynn-Holly Johnson, Billy Barty, Ruth Buzzi, Murray Langston, Yvonne Craig, Gary Owens; *D:* Mark Byers. VHS $79.95 *MNC* Woof!

Diggstown Lightweight, good-natured sports comedy about a boxing scam. Con man Gabriel Caine (Woods), fresh out of prison, heads for Diggstown and the unregulated boxing matches arranged by town boss, John Gillon (Dern). The bet is that Caine's one boxer can beat any 10 boxers, chosen by Gillon, in a 24-hour period. So Caine decides to hook up with an old friend, former prizefighter "Honey" Roy Palmer (Gosset Jr.), to run the scam of his life. Dern is sufficiently nasty and Woods his usual nervy self but it's Gossett Jr. who manages to hold everything together as the aging boxer. Based on the novel "The Diggstown Ringers" by Leonard Wise.
1992 (R) 97m/C James Woods, Louis Gossett Jr., Bruce Dern, Oliver Platt, Heather Graham, Randall "Tex" Cobb, Thomas Wilson Brown, Duane Davis, Willie Green, George Wallace; *D:* Michael Ritchie; *W:* Steven McKay; *M:* James Newton Howard. VHS, Beta $19.98 *MGM* ✍️✍️½

Dillinger John Dillinger's notorious career, from street punk to public enemy number one, receives a thrilling fast-paced treatment. Tierney turns in a fine performance in this interesting account of the criminal life.
1945 70m/C Lawrence Tierney, Edmund Lowe, Anne Jeffreys, Elisha Cook Jr.; *D:* Max Nosseck; *W:* Philip Yordan. VHS, Beta $14.98 *FOX, FCT* ✍️✍️

Dillinger The most colorful period of criminality in America is brought to life in this story of bank-robber John Dillinger, "Baby Face" Nelson, and the notorious "Lady in Red."
1973 (R) 106m/C Warren Oates, Michelle Phillips, Richard Dreyfuss, Cloris Leachman, Ben Johnson, Harry Dean Stanton; *D:* John Milius; *W:* John Milius. VHS, Beta $69.98 *LIV, VES* ✍️✍️

Dim Sum: A Little Bit of Heart The second independent film from the director of "Chan Is Missing." A Chinese-American mother and daughter living in San Francisco's Chinatown confront the conflict between traditional Eastern ways and modern American life. Gentle, fragile picture made with humor and care. In English and Chinese with subtitles.
1985 (PG) 88m/C Laureen Chew, Kim Chew, Victor Wong, Ida F.O. Chong, Cora Miao, John Nishio, Joan Chen; *D:* Wayne Wang; *W:* Terrel Seltzer; *M:* Todd Boekelheide. VHS, Beta $29.95 *FCT, IME, ING* ✍️✍️✍️

Dimples When Shirley's pickpocket grandfather is caught red-handed, she steps in, takes the blame, and somehow ends up in show business. Re-issued version is rated. Also available colorized. ♫Hey, What Did the Bluebird Say?; He Was a Dandy; Picture Me Without You; Oh Mister Man Up in the Moon; Dixie-Anna; Get On Board; Swing Low Sweet Chariot.
1936 (PG) 78m/B Shirley Temple, John Carradine, Frank Morgan, Helen Westley, Berton Churchill, Robert Kent, Delma Byron; *D:* William A. Seiter. VHS, Beta $14.98 *FOX* ✍️✍️

Diner A group of old high school friends meet at "their" Baltimore diner to find that more has changed than the menu. A bittersweet look at the experiences of a group of Baltimore post-teenagers growing up, circa 1959. Particularly notable was Levinson's casting of "unknowns" who have since become household names. Features many humorous moments and fine performances.
1982 (R) 110m/C Steve Guttenberg, Daniel Stern, Mickey Rourke, Kevin Bacon, Ellen Barkin, Timothy Daly, Paul Reiser, Michael Tucker; *D:* Barry Levinson. VHS, Beta $19.95 *MGM* ✍️✍️✍️

Dingaka A controversial drama from the writer and director of "The Gods Must Be Crazy" about a South African tribesman who avenges his daughter's murder by tribal laws, and is then tried by white man's laws. A crusading white attorney struggles to acquit him.
1965 96m/C Stanley Baker, Juliet Prowse, Ken Gampu; *D:* Jamie Uys. VHS, Beta $14.95 *COL, NLC, FCT* ✍️✍️½

The Dining Room Six performers play more than 50 roles in this adaptation of A.R. Gurney Jr.'s play set in a dining room, where people live out dramatic and comic moments in their lives. From the "American Playhouse" series.
1986 90m/C Remak Ramsay, Pippa Perthree, John Shea, Frances Sternhagen; *D:* Allan Goldstein. VHS, Beta $59.95 *PBS, ACA* ✍️✍️½

Dinner at Eight A social-climbing woman and her husband throw a dinner party for various members of the New York elite. During the course of the evening, all of the guests reveal something about themselves. Special performances all around, especially Barrymore, Dressler, and Harlow. Superb comedic direction by Cukor. Adapted from the play by Edna Ferber and George Kaufman.
1933 110m/C John Barrymore, Lionel Barrymore, Wallace Beery, Madge Evans, Jean Harlow, Billie Burke, Marie Dressler, Phillips Holmes, Jean Hersholt, Lee Tracy, Edmund Lowe, Karen Morley, May Robson; *D:* George Cukor; *W:* Herman J. Mankiewicz, Francis Marion, Donald Ogden Stewart. VHS, Beta, 8mm $24.95 *MGM* ✍️✍️✍️

Dinner at Eight A social-climbing romance novelist throws an elegant dinner party. Made for television remake of the 1933 film does not compare well.
1989 100m/C Lauren Bacall, Charles Durning, Ellen Greene, Harry Hamlin, John Mahoney, Marsha Mason, Tim Kazurinsky; *D:* Ron Lagomarsino. VHS, Beta $139.98 *TTC* ✍️✍️

Dinner at the Ritz Daughter of a murdered Parisian banker vows to find his killer with help from her fiance.
1937 78m/B *GB* David Niven, Annabella, Paul Lukas, Patricia Medina; *D:* Harold Schuster. VHS, Beta $19.95 *NOS, MRV, VYY* ✍️✍️½

Dino Social worker joins a young woman in helping a seventeen-year-old delinquent re-enter society.

1957 96m/B Sal Mineo, Brian Keith, Susan Kohner; *D:* Thomas Carr. VHS, Beta $39.95 *REP* ✍️½

Dinosaur Island Five military men survive a plane crash and discover an island where scantily-clad (leather bikinis being the fashion choice) lascivious ladies live. Will the awesome power of testosterone overcome the fierce dinosaurs which stand between the men and their objects of desire?
1993 (R) 85m/C Ross Hagen, Richard Gabai, Antonia Dorian, Peter Spellos, Tom Shell, Griffin Drew, Steve Barkett, Toni Naples; *D:* Jim Wynorski, Fred Olen Ray; *W:* Bob Sheridan, Christopher Wooden. VHS *NHO, HVL* ✍️

Dinosaurus! Large sadistic dinosaurs appear in the modern world. They eat, burn, and pillage their way through this film. Also includes a romance between a Neanderthal and a modern-age woman.
1960 85m/C Ward Ramsey, Kristina Hanson, Paul Lukather; *D:* Irvin S. Yeawarth Jr. VHS, Beta $9.95 *NWV, SNC* ✍️

Diplomaniacs Wheeler and Woolsey, official barbers on an Indian reservation, are sent to the Geneva peace conference to represent the interests of their tribe. Slim plot nevertheless provides quite a few laughs. Fun musical numbers.
1933 62m/B Bert Wheeler, Robert Woolsey, Marjorie White, Hugh Herbert; *D:* William A. Seiter; *W:* Joseph L. Mankiewicz, Henry Meyers. VHS, Beta $19.98 *CCB, IME, TTC* ✍️✍️

Diplomatic Courier Cold-war espionage saga has secret agent Power attempting to re-steal sensitive documents from the hands of Soviet agents. Involved and exciting thriller. Michael Ansara, Charles Bronson and Lee Marvin made brief appearances.
1952 97m/B Tyrone Power, Patricia Neal, Stephen McNally, Hildegarde Neff, Karl Malden; *D:* Henry Hathaway. VHS *TCF* ✍️✍️✍️

Diplomatic Immunity Vicious killer gets off scot-free due to his diplomatic immunity. That is, until the victim's ex-soldier father follows this low-life to the jungles of Paraguay to exact revenge. A heap o' action.
1991 (R) 95m/C Bruce Boxleitner, Billy Drago, Meg Foster, Robert Forster; *D:* Peter Maris. VHS, Beta $89.95 *FRH, IME* ✍️½

Dirkham Detective Agency Three children team up to form the Dirkham Detective Agency and are hired by a veterinarian to recover two dognapped poodles.
1983 60m/C Sally Kellerman, Stan Shaw, John Quade, Gordon Jump, Randy Morton. VHS, Beta *NO* ✍️½

Dirt Bike Kid A precocious brat is stuck with a used motorbike that has a mind of its own. Shenanigans follow in utterly predictable fashion as he battles bankers and bikers with his bad bike.
1986 (PG) 91m/C Peter Billingsley, Anne Bloom, Stuart Pankin, Patrick Collins, Sage Parker, Chad Sheets; *D:* Hoite C. Caston; *W:* Lewis Colick, David Brandes. VHS, Beta, 8mm $14.95 *COL, NLC* ✍️½

Dirt Gang A motorcycle gang terrorizes the members of a film crew on location in the desert.
1971 (R) 89m/C Paul Carr, Michael Pataki, Michael Forest; *D:* Jerry Jameson. VHS, Beta $59.95 *MPI* ✍️

Dirty Dancing An innocent 17-year-old (Grey) is vacationing with her parents in the Catskills in 1963. Bored with the program at the hotel, she finds the real fun at the staff dances. Falling for the sexy dance instructor (Swayze), she finds love, sex, and rock and roll dancing. An old story, with little to save it, but Grey and Swayze are appealing, the dance sequences fun, and the music great. Swayze, classically trained in ballet, also performs one of the sound-track songs. **1987 (PG-13) 97m/C** Patrick Swayze, Jennifer Grey, Cynthia Rhodes, Jerry Orbach, Jack Weston, Jane Brucker, Kelly Bishop, Lonny Price, Charles "Honi" Coles, Bruce Morrow; *D:* Emile Ardolino; *W:* Eleanor Bergstein; *M:* John Morris. **VHS, Beta $19.98** *LIV, VES* 🎬🎬🎬

Dirty Dishes A French film sardonically examining the fruitless life of the average housewife as she confronts a series of bizarre but pointless experiences during the day. Dubbed and subtitled versions available. The director is the American daughter-in-law of the late Luis Bunuel. **1982 (R) 99m/C** *FR* Carol Laurie, Pierre Santini; *D:* Joyce Bunuel. **VHS, Beta $29.98** *SUE* 🎬🎬🎬

The Dirty Dozen A tough Army major is assigned to train and command twelve hardened convicts offered absolution if they participate in a suicidal mission into Nazi Germany in 1944. Well-made movie is a standout in its genre. Rough and gruff Marvin is good as the group leader. Three made-for-television sequels followed in the '80s. **1967 (PG) 149m/C** Lee Marvin, Ernest Borgnine, Charles Bronson, Jim Brown, George Kennedy, John Cassavetes, Clint Walker, Donald Sutherland, Telly Savalas, Robert Ryan, Ralph Meeker, Richard Jaeckel, Trini Lopez; *D:* Robert Aldrich. Academy Awards '67: Best Sound Effects Editing; Nominations: Best Film Editing, Best Sound, Best Supporting Actor (Cassavetes). **VHS, Beta $19.98** *MGM, TLF* 🎬🎬🎬

The Dirty Dozen: The Deadly Mission A second made-for-TV sequel to the '67 movie finds Borgnine ordering another suicide mission. Savalas (killed in the original, he's playing a new character) must pick 12 convicted army prisoners for an assault on a Nazi-held French monastery. Their mission is to rescue six scientists who are working on a deadly new nerve gas. Followed by "The Dirty Dozen: The Fatal Mission." **1987 96m/C** Ernest Borgnine, Telly Savalas, Vince Edwards, Gary Graham, James Van Patten, Vincent Van Patten, Bo Svenson; *D:* Lee H. Katzin. **VHS $19.98** *MGM* 🎬🎬½

The Dirty Dozen: The Fatal Mission This third TV sequel has Borgnine learning of a plan to bring a group of high-ranking Nazis to Instanbul via the Orient Express. Naturally, he assigns Savalas the task of getting his motley gang together to thwart the Nazi schemes. To add intrigue, a female has joined the ranks of the Dirty Dozen and a spy may also have infiltrated the group. **1988 91m/C** Ernest Borgnine, Telly Savalas, Hunt Block, Jeff Conaway, Erik Estrada, Ray "Boom Boom" Mancini, Heather Thomas, Alex Cord; *D:* Lee H. Katzin. **VHS $19.98** *MGM* 🎬🎬½

The Dirty Dozen: The Next Mission Disappointing made for television sequel to the 1967 hit, with Marvin reprising his role as the leader of the motley pack. In this installment, the rag-tag toughs are sent on yet another suicide mission inside Nazi Germany, this time to thwart an assassination attempt of Hitler. Followed by two more sequels. **1985 97m/C** Lee Marvin, Ernest Borgnine, Richard Jaeckel, Ken Wahl, Larry Wilcox, Sonny Landham, Ricco Ross; *D:* Andrew V. McLaglen. **VHS, Beta $79.95** *MGM* 🎬½

Dirty Games Nicola Kendra is part of a team sent to Africa to inspect a nuclear waste site. Once there, the scientists discover terrorists are plotting to blow up the

nuclear complex unless Nicola and her new allies can prevent it. **1993 97m/C** Jan-Michael Vincent, Valentina Vargas, Ronald France, Michael McGovern; *D:* Grey Hofmeyr. **VHS $89.95** *AIP* 🎬½

Dirty Gertie from Harlem U.S.A. All-black cast performs a variation of W. Somerset Maugham's "Rain." Gertie goes to Trinidad to hide out from her jilted boyfriend. **1946 60m/B** Gertie LaRue, Spencer Williams Jr., Francine Everett, Don "The Dragon" Wilson. **VHS, Beta $19.95** *VYY, DVT, VYY* 🎬🎬

Dirty Hands A woman and her lover conspire to murder her husband. A must for fans of the sexy Schneider. Cinematography provides moments that are both interesting and eerie. *AKA:* Les Innocents aux Mains Sales. **1976 102m/C** *FR* Rod Steiger, Romy Schneider, Paul Giusti, Jean Rochefort, Hans-Christian Blech; *D:* Claude Chabrol. **VHS** *FCT* 🎬🎬

Dirty Harry Rock-hard cop Harry Callahan attempts to track down a psychopathic rooftop killer before a kidnapped girl dies. Harry abuses the murderer's civil rights, however, forcing the police to return the criminal to the streets, where he hijacks a school bus and Harry is called on once again. The only answer to stop this vicious killer seems to be death in cold blood, and Harry is just the man to do it. Taut, suspenseful direction by Siegel, who thoroughly understands Eastwood's on-screen character. Features Callahan's famous "Do you feel lucky?" line, the precursor to his "Go ahead, make my day." **1971 (R) 103m/C** Clint Eastwood, Harry Guardino, John Larch, Andrew (Andy) Robinson, Reni Santoni, John Vernon; *D:* Don Siegel. **VHS, Beta, 8mm $14.95** *WAR, TLF* 🎬🎬🎬½

Dirty Heroes A band of escaped WWII POWs battle the Nazis for a precious treasure in the war's final days. *AKA:* Dalle Ardenne All'Inferno. **1971 (R) 117m/C** John Ireland, Curt Jurgens, Adolfo Celi, Daniela Bianchi, Michael Constantine; *D:* Alberto De Martino; *M:* Ennio Morricone. **VHS, Beta $59.95** *VTR* 🎬🎬

Dirty Laundry Insipid wreck of a comedy about a klutz who accidentally gets his laundry mixed up with $1 million dollars in drug money. Features Olympians Lewis and Louganis. Never released theatrically. **1987 (PG-13) 81m/C** Leigh McCloskey, Jeanne O'Brien, Frankie Valli, Sonny Bono, Carl Lewis, Greg Louganis, Nicholas Worth; *D:* William Webb. **VHS, Beta** *NO Woof!*

Dirty Mary Crazy Larry A racecar driver, his mechanic, and a sexy girl hightail it from the law after pulling off a heist. Great action, great fun, and an infamous surprise ending. **1974 (PG) 93m/C** Peter Fonda, Susan George, Adam Roarke, Vic Morrow, Roddy McDowall; *D:* John Hough. **VHS, Beta** *FOX* 🎬🎬🎬

Dirty Mind of Young Sally Sally's erotic radio program broadcasts from a mobile studio, which must stay one step ahead of the police. **1972 (R) 84m/C** Sharon Kelly. **VHS, Beta $24.95** *TPV Woof!*

Dirty Rotten Scoundrels A remake of the 1964 "Bedtime Story," in which two confidence tricksters on the Riviera endeavor to rip off a suddenly rich American woman, and each other. Caine and Martin are terrific, Martin has some of his best physical comedy ever, and Headly is charming as the prey who's always one step ahead of them. Fine direction from Oz, the man who brought us

the voice of Yoda in "The Empire Strikes Back." **1988 (PG) 112m/C** Steve Martin, Michael Caine, Glenne Headly, Anton Rodgers, Barbara Harris, Dana Ivey; *D:* Frank Oz; *W:* Dale Launer; *M:* Miles Goodman. **VHS, Beta $9.98** *ORI* 🎬🎬🎬

Dirty Tricks History professor Gould fights with bad guys for a letter written by George Washington. Thoroughly forgettable comedy lacking in laughs. **1981 (PG) 91m/C** *CA* Elliott Gould, Kate Jackson, Arthur Hill, Rich Little; *D:* Alvin Rakoff; *W:* William W. Norton Sr.; *M:* Hagood Hardy. **VHS, Beta $14.95** *COL, SUE* 🎬½

Dirty Work A drug-dealing bail bondsman (Ashton) steals counterfeit money from the mob and then sets up his partner (Dobson) as the fall guy. Can Dobson survive long enough to set things straight? **1992 (R) 88m/C** John Ashton, Kevin Dobson, Roxann Biggs, Donnelly Rhodes, Jim Byrnes, Mitchell Ryan; *D:* John McPherson; *W:* Aaron Julien. **VHS, Beta** *PAR* 🎬🎬

Disappearance A hired assassin discovers an ironic link between his new target and his missing wife. **1981 (R) 80m/C** *CA* Donald Sutherland, David Hemmings, John Hurt, Christopher Plummer, David Warner, Virginia McKenna; *D:* Stuart Cooper. **VHS, Beta $19.95** *VES, RHI* 🎬🎬

The Disappearance of Aimee Dramatic recreation of events surrounding the 1926 disappearance of evangelist Aimee Semple McPherson. She claimed she was abducted, but her mother insisted she ran away to have an affair. Excellent made for television movie with an exceptional cast. Originally to star Ann-Margret. **1976 110m/C** Faye Dunaway, Bette Davis, James Sloyan, James Woods, John Lehne, Lelia Goldoni, Barry Brown, Severn Darden; *W:* Anthony Harvey. **VHS, Beta $59.95** *LIV* 🎬🎬🎬

The Disappearance of Christina Successful entrepreneur Joe Seldon (Stamos) is married to heiress Christina (Yarlett) and they seem to be the perfect couple. But when Christina mysteriously vanishes during a sailing trip, was it really an accident? Detective Nora Davis (Pounder) doesn't think so and naturally, Joe is suspect numero uno. **1993 (PG-13) 93m/C** John Stamos, Kim Delaney, Robert Carradine, Claire Yarlett, CCH Pounder; *D:* Karen Arthur; *W:* Camille Thomasson. **VHS $89.98** *MCA* 🎬🎬½

Disaster at Silo 7 When the engine of a Titan missile goes on the fritz, the Air Force tries to prevent a nuclear disaster. Based on an actual Titan II missile incident near Little Rock, Arkansas. Made for television. **1988 92m/C** Peter Boyle, Patricia Charbonneau, Perry King, Michael O'Keefe, Joe Spano, Dennis Weaver; *D:* Larry Elikann; *W:* Douglas Lloyd McIntosh. **VHS $89.95** *TRI* 🎬🎬

Disciple Vintage silent western wherein Hart's unsmiling good-bad guy tries to clean up a lawless town and win back his wife, who has shamefully fallen in with a corrupt saloon-keeper. **1915 80m/B** William S. Hart, Dorothy Dalton, Robert McKim, Jean Hersholt; *D:* William S. Hart; *W:* Thomas Ince. **VHS, Beta, 8mm $24.95** *VYY* 🎬½

Disciple of Death Raven plays "The Stranger," a ghoul who sacrifices virgins to the Devil. **1972 (R) 82m/C** *GB* Mike Raven, Ronald Lacey, Stephen Bradley, Virginia Wetherell; *D:* Tom Parkinson. **VHS, Beta $49.95** *UNI* 🎬

Disconnected "Sorry, Wrong Number" is updated, with more than ample doses of sex and violence.
1987 81m/C Mark Walker. **VHS, Beta $7.00** VTR ♬½

Discontent An early silent film by Lois Weber in which a cantankerous old vet goes to live with his wealthy nephew. The harmonious family life is disrupted by his meddling ways.
1916 30m/B *D:* Lois Weber. **VHS, Beta $42.50** GVV ♬½

The Discovery Program Four award-winning short films on one video: "Ray's Male Heterosexual Dance Hall," "Greasy Lake," "The Open Window," and "Hearts of Stone." The subjects range from humorous and offbeat to tragic and deadly serious.
1989 106m/C VHS, Beta $79.95 FCT ♬♬½

The Discreet Charm of the Bourgeoisie Bunuel in top form, satirizing modern society. These six characters are forever sitting down to dinner, yet they never eat. Dreams and reality, actual or contrived, prevent their feast. *AKA:* Le Charme Discret de la Bourgeoisie.
1972 (R) 100m/C *FR* Fernando Rey, Delphine Seyrig, Jean-Pierre Cassel, Bulle Ogier, Michel Piccoli, Stephane Audran, Luis Bunuel; *D:* Luis Bunuel; *W:* Luis Bunuel, Jean-Claude Carriere. Academy Awards '72: Best Foreign Language Film; Nominations: Best Story & Screenplay; British Academy Awards '73: Best Actress (Seyrig); National Board of Review Awards '72: 5 Best Foreign Films of the Year; National Society of Film Critics Awards '72: Best Director (Bunuel), Best Film. **VHS, Beta $59.95** ING, MED, APD ♬♬♬♬

Discretion Assured Successful businessman Trevor McCabe (York) finds himself in a romantic quandry with three women, leading to his involvement in embezzlement and murder.
1993 97m/C Michael York, Jennifer O'Neill, Dee Wallace Stone, Elizabeth Gracen; *D:* Odorico Mendes. **VHS $92.95** MNC ♬♬½

Dishonored Dated spy drama has Dietrich playing secret agent X-27 in WWI and masquerading on the side as a peasant girl. Although not one of the more famous Dietrich-Sternberg productions, its camp plot and Dietrich's lavish performance make it worth watching. Based on the infamous spy Mata Hari, who was shot by the French in 1917 for espionage.
1931 91m/B Marlene Dietrich, Victor McLaglen, Lew Cody, Gustav von Seyffertitz, Warner Oland, Barry Norton, Davison Clark, Wilfrid Lucas; *D:* Josef von Sternberg; *W:* Josef von Sternberg, Daniel N. Rubin. **VHS $14.98** MCA, FCT ♬♬½

Dishonored Lady After her ex-boyfriend is murdered, a female art director finds that she's the number one suspect. When put on trial for the dastardly deed, she takes the fifth in this mediocre melodrama.
1947 85m/B Hedy Lamarr, Dennis O'Keefe, William Lundigan, John Loder; *D:* Robert Stevenson. **VHS, Beta $16.95** SNC, NOS, CAB ♬½

Disney's Storybook Classics A collection of classic children's fables, featuring "Little Toot" (1948, excerpted from "Melody Time"), the story of a little harbor tugboat; "Chicken Little" (1943); "The Grasshopper and the Ant" (1934, a "Silly Symphony"); and "Peter and the Wolf" (1946, excerpted from "Make Mine Music"), a Disneyized version of Prokofiev's famous concert piece.
1982 121m/C Sterling Holloway, The Andrews Sisters. **VHS, Beta** DIS ♬½

Disorderlies Members of the popular rap group cavort as incompetent hospital orderlies assigned to care for a cranky millionaire. Fat jokes abound with performances by the Fat Boys.
1987 (PG) 86m/C The Fat Boys, Ralph Bellamy; *D:* Michael A. Schultz; *M:* Anne Dudley. **VHS, Beta $19.98** WAR ♬

Disorderly Orderly When Jerry Lewis gets hired as a hospital orderly, nothing stands upright long with him around. Vintage slapstick Lewis running amuck in a nursing home.
1964 90m/C Jerry Lewis, Glenda Farrell, Everett Sloane, Kathleen Freeman, Susan Oliver; *D:* Frank Tashlin. **VHS, Beta $14.95** PAR ♬½

Disorganized Crime On the lam from the law, Bernsen attempts to organize a group of his ex-con buddies to pull off the perfect heist. Before the boys can organize, however, the cops are hot on Bernsen's trail, and he must vacate the meeting place. Good cast attempts to lift this movie beyond script.
1989 (R) 101m/C Lou Diamond Phillips, Fred Gwynne, Corbin Bernsen, Ruben Blades, Hoyt Axton, Ed O'Neill, Daniel Roebuck, William Russ; *D:* Jim Kouf. **VHS, Beta $89.95** TOU ♬♬

The Displaced Person In this television adaptation of Flannery O'Connor's story, the inhabitants of a 1940s Georgia farm find their lives disrupted by a Polish refugee family. The strong work ethic practiced by the foreigners makes their less-productive, if not lazy, neighbors regard them with caution and contempt. Well-crafted depiction of the prejudice faced by many immigrants aspiring to realize the American dream.
1976 58m/C Irene Worth, John Houseman, Henry Fonda, Shirley Stoler, Lane Smith, Earl Jones; *D:* Glenn Jordan. **VHS, Beta $24.95** MON, KAR ♬♬♬½

Disraeli Arliss deservedly won the Best Actor Oscar for his title role as the famed British prime minister to Queen Victoria. This particular slice of the cunning statesman's life depicts his efforts to secure the Suez Canal for England against the Russians. Arliss' wife also played his screen spouse. One of Warner's earliest and best biographical pictures. Based on a play by Louis Napoleon Parker.
1929 87m/B George Arliss, Joan Bennett, Florence Arliss, Anthony Bushell, David Torrence, Doris Lloyd, Ivan Simpson, Gwendolyn Logan; *D:* Alfred E. Green. Academy Awards '30: Best Actor (Arliss); Nominations: Best Picture, Best Writing. **VHS $19.98** MGM ♬♬♬

Distant Drums A small band of adventurers tries to stop the Seminole War in the Florida Everglades.
1951 101m/C Gary Cooper, Mari Aldon, Robert Barratt, Richard Webb, Ray Teal, Arthur Hunnicutt; *D:* Raoul Walsh. **VHS $19.98** REP, FCT ♬♬

Distant Thunder A bitter, unrelenting portrait of a small Bengali neighborhood as the severe famines of 1942, brought about by the "distant thunder" of WWII, take their toll. A mature achievement from Ray; in Bengali with English subtitles.
1973 92m/C *IN* Soumitra Chatterjee, Sandhya Roy, Babita, Gobinda Chakravarty, Romesh Mukerji; *D:* Satyajit Ray. **VHS, Beta $44.95** FCT ♬♬♬½

Distant Thunder A scarred Vietnam vet, who has become a recluse, and his estranged son reunite in the Washington State wilderness, causing him to reflect on his isolation. Strong premise and cast watered down by weak script.

1988 (R) 114m/C *CA* John Lithgow, Ralph Macchio, Kerrie Keane, Janet Margolin, Rick Rosenthal; *D:* Rick Rosenberg; *M:* Maurice Jarre. **VHS, Beta $14.95** PAR ♬♬

Distant Voices, Still Lives A profoundly executed, disturbing film chronicling a British middle-class family through the maturation of the three children, under the dark shadow of their abusive, malevolent father. An evocative, heartbreaking portrait of British life from WWII on, and of the rhythms of dysfunctional families. A film festival favorite.
1988 87m/C *GB* Freda Dowie, Peter Postlethwaite, Angela Walsh, Dean Williams, Lorraine Ashbourne; *D:* Terence Davies; *W:* Terence Davies. **VHS, Beta $89.95** LIV ♬♬♬

The Distinguished Gentleman A small-time con man (Murphy) manages to scam his way into a political career and winds up in Congress. The other characters serve mostly as foils for Murphy's comedic talent. Viewers will laugh despite the story's predictablity.
1992 (R) 122m/C Eddie Murphy, Lane Smith, Sheryl Lee Ralph, Joe Don Baker, Victoria Rowell, Grant Shaud, Kevin McCarthy, Charles S. Dutton, James Garner; *D:* Jonathan Lynn; *W:* Marty Kaplan; *M:* Randy Edelman. **VHS $94.95** BVV ♬♬

Distortions Hussey is a widow whose evil aunt (Laurie) is holding her hostage. What the film lacks in suspense throughout most of the movie is made up for in the end.
1987 (PG) 90m/C Piper Laurie, Steve Railsback, Olivia Hussey, Edward Albert, Rita Gam, Terence Knox; *D:* Armand Mastroianni. **VHS, Beta $29.95** ACA ♬♬

Disturbance The two personas of a young schizophrenic get him entangled in a mysterious string of murders.
1989 81m/C Timothy Greeson, Lisa Geoffreion; *D:* Cliff Guest. **VHS, Beta** NO ♬½

Disturbed Lusty mental hospital director McDowell meets sex starved and suicidal Gidley in this less-than-stellar erotic creeper. Redeemed only by McDowell's performance and more evidence that the droog's career hasn't been just peachy since "Clockwork Orange."
1990 (R) 96m/C Malcolm McDowell, Geoffrey Lewis, Priscilla Pointer, Pamela Gidley, Clint Howard; *D:* Charles Winkler; *W:* Emerson Bixby, Charles Winkler. **VHS $89.95** LIV ♬

Diva While at a concert given by his favorite star, a young French courier secretly tapes a soprano who has refused to record. The film follows the young man through Paris as he flees from two Japanese recording pirates, and a couple of crooked undercover police who are trying to cover-up for the chief who not only has a mistress, but runs a prostitution ring. Brilliant and dazzling photography compliment the eclectic soundtrack.
1982 (R) 123m/C *FR* Frederic Andrei, Roland Bertin, Richard Bohringer, Gerard Darmon, Jacques Fabbri, Wilhelmenia Wiggins Fernandez, Dominique Pinon; *D:* Jean-Jacques Beineix; *W:* Jean-Jacques Beineix; *M:* Vladimir Cosma. **VHS, Beta $29.95** MGM, APD ♬♬♬½

The Dive Two North Sea oil-rig workers are trapped far below the waves when the lifeline to their diving bell snaps in rough seas.
1989 (PG-13) 90m/C Bjorn Sundquist, Frank Grimes, Einride Eidsvold, Michael Kitchen; *D:* Tristan De Vere Cole. **VHS, Beta** NO ♬♬

Dive Bomber Exciting aviation film that focuses on medical problems related to flying. Flynn stars as an aviator-doctor who conducts experiments to eliminate pilot-blackout. MacMurray, Toomey, and Heydt

D

perform well as three flyboys stationed in Hawaii. Great flying sequences filmed at San Diego's naval base with extra scenes shot at Pensacola. Warner Bros. released this film just months before the Japanese attacked Pearl Harbor. Based on the story "Beyond the Blue Sky" by Frank Wead.
1941 130m/B Errol Flynn, Fred MacMurray, Ralph Bellamy, Alexis Smith, Regis Toomey, Robert Armstrong, Allen Jenkins, Craig Stevens; *D:* Michael Curtiz; *W:* Frank Wead, Robert Buckner. VHS $19.98 *MGM* ⚜⚜⚜

Divine Two Divine flicks from Waters. First, Divine plays a naughty girl who, not surprisingly, since this one is titled "The Diane Linkletter Story," ends up a successful suicide. "The Neon Woman" is a rare live performance, with Divine a woman who owns a strip joint and has a slew of problems you won't read about in Dear Abbey.
1990 110m/C Divine; *D:* John Waters. VHS $29.99 *FCT* ⚜⚜½

The Divine Enforcer A monsignor in a crime-ridden L.A. neighborhood reaches his wit's end in trying to stave off perpetrators of injustice. Fortunately, help arrives in the form of a mysterious priest who is equally handy with his fists, nunchakus, and guns. From then on it's no more mister nice guy, and the criminals haven't a prayer.
1991 90m/C Jan-Michael Vincent, Erik Estrada, Jim Brown, Judy Landers, Don Stroud, Robert Z'Dar, Michael Foley, Carrie Chambers, Hiroko; *D:* Robert Rundle. VHS, Beta $79.95 *PSM* ⚜½

Divine Madness Bette Midler is captured at her best in a live concert at Pasadena Civic Auditorium.
1980 (R) 87m/C Bette Midler; *D:* Michael Ritchie. VHS, Beta $14.95 *WAR* ⚜½

Divine Nymph Charts the erotic adventures of the beautiful and young Manuela, who is dangerously pursued by two cousins.
1971 (R) 100m/C *IT* Laura Antonelli, Marcello Mastroianni, Terence Stamp; *D:* Giuseppe Patroni Griffi; *M:* Ennio Morricone. VHS, Beta $59.95 *MPI* ⚜½

Diving In Have you heard the one about the acrophobic diver? It seems a paralyzing fear of heights is the only thing between a young diver and Olympic gold. Much splashing about and heartstring-tugging.
1990 (PG-13) 92m/C Burt Young, Matt Adler, Kristy Swanson, Matt Lattanzi, Richard Johnson, Carey Scott, Yolanda Jilot; *D:* Strathford Hamilton. VHS, Beta $89.95 *PAR, FCT* ⚜⚜

Divorce His, Divorce Hers The first half of this drama shows the crumbling of a marriage through the husband's eyes. The second half offers the wife's perspective. Made for television.
1972 144m/C Richard Burton, Elizabeth Taylor; *D:* Waris Hussein. VHS, Beta *NO* ⚜⚜

Divorce—Italian Style A middle-aged baron bored with his wife begins directing his amorous attentions to a teenage cousin. Since divorce in Italy is impossible, the only way out of his marriage is murder—and the baron finds a little-known law that excuses a man from murdering his wife if she is having an affair (since he would merely be defending his honor). A hilarious comedy with a twist ending. Available in Italian with English subtitles or dubbed in English. *AKA:* Divorzio All'Italiana.
1962 104m/B *IT* Marcello Mastroianni, Daniela Rocca, Leopoldo Trieste; *D:* Pietro Germi; *W:* Pietro Germi, Ennio de Concini, Alfredo Giannetti. Academy Awards '62: Best Screenplay; Nominations: Best Actor (Mastroianni), Best Director (Germi); British Academy Awards '63: Best Actor (Mastroianni); Golden Globe Awards

'63: Best Actor—Musical/Comedy (Mastroianni), Best Foreign Film. VHS $39.95 *HTV, ING* ⚜⚜⚜½

The Divorce of Lady X A spoiled British debutante, in the guise of "Lady X," makes a woman-hating divorce lawyer eat his words through romance and marriage. Based on the play by Gilbert Wakefield.
1938 92m/C *GB* Merle Oberon, Laurence Olivier, Ralph Richardson, Binnie Barnes; *D:* Tim Whelan; *M:* Miklos Rozsa. VHS, Beta $19.95 *NOS, MRV, UNI* ⚜⚜½

The Divorcee Early Leonard film (he'd later direct "The Great Ziegfield" and "Pride and Prejudice") casts Shearer as a woman out to beat her husband at philandering. Married to a journalist, she cavorts with her husband's best friend and a discarded old flame as only a pre-production code gal could. Shearer—who Lillian Hellman described as having "a face unclouded by thought"—grabbed an Oscar. Based on the novel "Ex-Wife" by Ursula Parrott.
1930 83m/B Norma Shearer, Chester Morris, Conrad Nagel, Robert Montgomery, Mary Doran, Tyler Brooke, George Irving, Helen Johnson; *D:* Robert Z. Leonard. Academy Awards '30: Best Actress (Shearer); Nominations: Best Director (Leonard), Best Picture, Best Writing. VHS $19.98 *MGM, FCT, BTV* ⚜⚜½

Dixiana A Southern millionaire falls for a circus performer shortly before the start of the Civil War. Part color. ♫Dixiana; Here's to the Old Days; A Tear, a Kiss, a Smile; My One Ambition is You; A Lady Loved a Soldier; Mr. & Mrs. Sippi; Guiding Star.
1930 99m/B Bebe Daniels, Bert Wheeler, Robert Woolsey, Dorothy Lamour, Bill Robinson; *D:* Luther Reed. VHS, Beta $24.95 *NOS, DVT* ⚜½

Dixie: Changing Habits A New Orleans madam and a Mother Superior go head to head in this amusing made-for-television movie. In the end all benefit as the nuns discover business sense and pay off a debt, while the former bordello owner cleans up her act. Above-average scripting and directing for the medium.
1985 100m/C Suzanne Pleshette, Cloris Leachman, Kenneth McMillan, John Considine, Geraldine Fitzgerald, Judith Ivey; *D:* George Englund. VHS $59.95 *LIV* ⚜⚜⚜

Dixie Dynamite The two daughters of a Georgia moonshiner set out to avenge the murder of their father. The music is performed by Duane Eddy and Dorsey Burnette.
1976 (PG) 88m/C Warren Oates, Christopher George, Jane Anne Johnstone, Kathy McHaley, R.G. Armstrong, Wes Bishop; *D:* Lee Frost. VHS, Beta $49.95 *VCI* ⚜

Dixie Jamboree Low-budget musical has gangster on the lam using an unusual method to escape from St. Louis—the last Mississippi Showboat. ♫Dixie Showboat; No, No, No; If It's a Dream; You Ain't Right with the Lord; Big Stuff.
1944 69m/B Guy Kibbee, Frances Langford, Louise Beavers, Charles Butterworth; *D:* Christy Cabanne. VHS, Beta $19.95 *NOS, VYY, DVT* ⚜

Dixie Lanes A relentlessly nostalgic comedy set in a small town at the end of WWII. A woman, troubled by her nephew's restless antics, puts him to work. Unfortunately she adds to his plight, as her business involves the Black Market.
1988 92m/C Hoyt Axton, Karen Black, Art Hindle, John Vernon, Ruth Buzzi, Tina Louise, Pamela Springsteen, Nina Foch; *D:* Don Cato. VHS, Beta $79.95 *CEL* ⚜

Django Django is a stranger who arrives in a Mexican-border town to settle a dispute between a small band of Americans and Mexicans.

1968 (PG) 90m/C Franco Nero, Loredana Nusciak, Angel Alvarez; *D:* Sergio Corbucci. VHS, Beta *NO* ⚜½

Django Shoots First Spaghetti western with usual amount of action and plot twists.
1974 96m/C Glen Saxson, Evelyn Stewart, Alberto Lupo. VHS, Beta $24.95 *VYY* ⚜½

Do or Die Former "Playboy" centerfolds Speir and Vasquez team up as a couple of federal agent babes who take on international crime boss Morita. But the crimelord is ready for our scantily clad heroines with a sick game of revenge—and the stakes are their very lives!
1991 (R) 97m/C Erik Estrada, Dona Speir, Roberta Vasquez, Noriyuki "Pat" Morita, Bruce Penhall, Carolyn Liu, Stephanie Schick; *D:* Andy Sidaris; *W:* Andy Sidaris. VHS $79.95 *COL* ⚜½

Do the Right Thing An uncompromising, brutal comedy about the racial tensions surrounding a white-owned pizzeria in the Bed-Stuy section of Brooklyn on the hottest day of the summer, and the violence that eventually erupts. Ambivalent and, for the most part, hilarious; Lee's coming-of-age.
1989 (R) 120m/C Spike Lee, Danny Aiello, Richard Edson, Ruby Dee, Ossie Davis, Giancarlo Esposito, Bill Nunn, John Turturro, John Savage, Rosie Perez, Frankie Faison; *D:* Spike Lee; *W:* Spike Lee. VHS, Beta $19.95 *MCA, FCT* ⚜⚜⚜½

D.O.A. A man is given a lethal, slow-acting poison. As his time runs out, he frantically seeks to learn who is responsible and why he was targeted for death. Dark film noir remade in 1969 as "Color Me Dead" and in 1988 with Dennis Quaid and Meg Ryan. Also available colorized.
1949 83m/B Edmond O'Brien, Pamela Britton, Luther Adler, Neville Brand, Beverly Garland; *D:* Rudolph Mate; *M:* Dimitri Tiomkin. VHS, Beta $16.95 *SNC, NOS, VYY* ⚜⚜⚜½

D.O.A. Well-done remake of the 1949 thriller with Quaid portraying a college professor who is poisoned and has only 24 hours to identify his killer. His search for the suspect is further complicated by the fact that he is being sought by the police on phony charges of murder. Directed by the same people who brought "Max Headroom" to television screens.
1988 (R) 98m/C Dennis Quaid, Meg Ryan, Charlotte Rampling, Daniel Stern, Jane Kaczmarek, Christopher Neame, Jay Patterson; *D:* Rocky Morton, Annabel Jankel; *W:* Charles Edward Pogue; *M:* Chaz Jankel. VHS, Beta $89.95 *TOU* ⚜⚜½

D.O.A.: A Right of Passage Often-depressing documentary about the British punk rock movement of the late '70s. The performance scenes are exciting. Also contains footage of the late Sid Vicious with his girlfriend Nancy Spungen, whom he was later accused of murdering.
1981 (R) 93m/C The Sex Pistols, X-Ray Specs. VHS, Beta $54.95 *VES, LIV, MVD* ⚜½

The Doberman Gang Clever thieves train a gang of Dobermans in the fine art of bank robbery. Sequelled by "The Daring Dobermans."
1972 (PG) 85m/C Byron Mabe, Hal Reed, Julie Parrish, Simmy Bow, JoJo D'Amore; *D:* Byron Ross Chudnow; *W:* Frank Ray Perilli. VHS, Beta $59.98 *FOX* ⚜⚜

Doc Hollywood A hotshot young physician on his way to a lucrative California practice gets stranded in a small Southern town. Will the wacky woodsy inhabitants persuade the city doctor to stay? There aren't many surprises in this fish-out-of-water comedy, but the cast injects it with

considerable charm. Adapted from Neil B. Shulman's book "What?...Dead Again?"
1991 (PG-13) 104m/C Michael J. Fox, Julie Warner, Woody Harrelson, Barnard Hughes, David Ogden Stiers, Frances Sternhagen, Bridget Fonda, George Hamilton, Roberts Blossom, Helen Martin, Macon McCalman, Barry Sobel; *D:* Michael Caton-Jones; *W:* Daniel Pyne, Jeffrey Price, Peter S. Seaman; *M:* Carter Burwell. **VHS, Beta, 8mm $19.98** *WAR* 🎬🎬½

Doc Savage Doc and "The Amazing Five" fight a murderous villain who plans to take over the world. Based on the novels of Kenneth Robeson.
1975 (PG) 100m/C Ron Ely, Pamela Hensley; *D:* Michael Anderson Sr. **VHS, Beta $19.98** *WAR* 🎬🎬½

Docks of New York Von Sternberg made his mark in Hollywood with this silent drama about two dockside losers finding love amid the squalor. A rarely seen, early masterpiece.
1928 60m/B George Bancroft, Betty Compson, Olga Baclanova; *D:* Josef von Sternberg; *M:* Gaylord Carter. **VHS, Beta $29.95** *PAR* 🎬🎬🎬

The Doctor A hotshot doctor develops throat cancer and gets treated at his own hospital, an ordeal that teaches him a respect and compassion for patients that he formerly lacked. Potential melodrama is saved by fine acting and strong direction. Based on the autobiographical book "A Taste of My Own Medicine" by Dr. Edward Rosenbaum.
1991 (PG-13) 125m/C William Hurt, Elizabeth Perkins, Christine Lahti, Mandy Patinkin, Wendy Crewson, Charlie Korsmo, Adam Arkin, Bill Macy; *D:* Randa Haines; *W:* Robert Caswell; *M:* Michael Convertino. **VHS, Beta $92.95** *TOU* 🎬🎬½

Dr. Alien Alien poses as beautiful scientist and turns a college freshman into a sex-addicted satyr. Likewise, the cast turns this flick into a dog.
1988 (R) 90m/C Billy Jacoby, Olivia Barash, Stuart Fratkin, Troy Donahue, Arlene Golonka, Judy Landers; *D:* David DeCoteau. **VHS, Beta $19.95** *PAR* 🎬

The Doctor and the Devils Based on an old screenplay by Dylan Thomas, this is a semi-Gothic tale about two criminals who supply a physician with corpses to study, either digging them up or killing them fresh.
1985 (R) 93m/C *GB* Timothy Dalton, Julian Sands, Jonathan Pryce, Twiggy, Stephen Rea, Beryl Reid, Sian Phillips, Patrick Stewart, Phyllis Logan, T.P. McKenna; *D:* Freddie Francis; *W:* Ronald Harwood; *M:* John Morris. **VHS, Beta $79.98** *FOX* 🎬🎬½

Doctor at Large A fledgling doctor seeks to become a surgeon at a hospital for the rich. Humorous antics follow. The third of the "Doctor" series.
1957 98m/C *GB* Dirk Bogarde, Muriel Pavlow, James Robertson Justice, Shirley Eaton, Donald Sinden, Anne Heywood; *D:* Ralph Thomas. **VHS, Beta** *NO* 🎬🎬½

Doctor at Sea To escape a troublesome romantic entanglement and the stresses of his career, a London physician signs on a cargo boat as a ship's doctor and becomes involved with French bombshell Bardot. The second of the "Doctor" series.
1956 93m/C *GB* James Robertson Justice, Dirk Bogarde, Brigitte Bardot; *D:* Ralph Thomas. **VHS, Beta $19.98** *FCT* 🎬🎬½

Dr. Bethune Canadian surgeon Norman Bethune was a larger-than-life hero with equally great flaws. A crusader for socialized medicine and an outspoken opponent of Fascism (as well as an alcoholic womanizer), he worked for the Loyalist forces in the Spanish Civil War and was instrumental in

developing mobile medical units for treating battlefield wounded. He's also credited with bringing modern medical care to China, where he attended to Mao's revolutionary forces. Sutherland's strong performance shows the intensity and vision of a complicated man; he previously played the doctor in 1977's "Bethune." Awkward jumps in time and place rob the story of narrative drive. *AKA:* Bethune, The Making of a Hero.
1990 115m/C *CA FR* Donald Sutherland, Helen Mirren, Helen Shaver, Colm Feore, Anouk Aimee, Ronald Pickup, Harrison Liu; *D:* Phillip Borsos; *W:* Ted Allan; *M:* Alan Reeves. **VHS $92.98** *FXL, ING* 🎬🎬🎬

Dr. Black, Mr. Hyde Not-so-horrifying tale of a black Jekyll who metamorphoses into a white monster with the help of the special potion. Unintended laughs lessen suspense. *AKA:* Dr. Black and Mr. White; The Watts Monster.
1976 (R) 88m/C Rosalind Cash, Stu Gilliam, Bernie Casey, Marie O'Henry; *D:* William Crain. **VHS, Beta $29.95** *VCI* 🎬

Doctor Blood's Coffin The aptly named doctor performs hideous experiments on the unsuspecting denizens of a lonely village. Good cast in this effective chiller.
1962 92m/C *GB* Kieron Moore, Hazel Court, Ian Hunter; *D:* Sidney J. Furie. **VHS $16.95** *SNC* 🎬🎬½

Doctor Butcher M.D. Mad doctor's deranged dream of creating "perfect people" by taking parts of one person and interchanging them with another backfires as his monstrosities develop strange side effects. The M.D., by the way, stands for "Medical Deviate." Dubbed. *AKA:* Queen of the Cannibals.
1980 (R) 81m/C *IT* Ian McCulloch, Alexandra Cole, Peter O'Neal, Donald O'Brien; *D:* Frank Martin. **VHS, Beta** *NO* Woof!

Dr. Caligari The granddaughter of the original Dr. Caligari promotes "better living through chemistry" in her insane asylum while using her patients as guinea pigs in her bizarre sexual experiments. Nothing outstanding here in terms of story or performance, but "Dick Tracy" has nothing on the visually compelling set designs and make-up.
1989 (R) 80m/C Madeleine Reynal, Fox Harris, Laura Albert, Jennifer Balgobin, John Durbin, Gene Zerna, David Parry, Barry Phillips; *D:* Stephen Sayadian. **VHS** *FCT* 🎬

Dr. Christian Meets the Women This entry in the "Dr. Christian" series of films has the small-town physician once again exposing a con man trying to filch the townspeople.
1940 63m/B Jean Hersholt, Edgar Kennedy, Rod La Rocque, Dorothy Lovett, Veda Ann Borg; *D:* William McGann. **VHS, Beta, 8mm $24.95** *VYY* 🎬½

Dr. Cyclops The famous early Technicolor fantasia about a mad scientist miniaturizing a group of explorers who happen upon his jungle lab. Landmark F/X and a slow-moving story.
1940 76m/C Albert Dekker, Janice Logan, Victor Kilian, Thomas Coley, Charles Halton; *D:* Ernest B. Schoedsack. **VHS, Beta $14.98** *MCA, FCT, MLB* 🎬🎬½

Dr. Death, Seeker of Souls Evil doctor discovers a process for transmigrating his soul into the bodies of people he murdered 1000 years ago. Now he seeks to revive his wife. Final role for 77-year-old "Stooge" Moe Howard.

1973 (R) 93m/C John Considine, Barry Coe, Cheryl Miller, Stewart Moss, Leon Askin, Jo Morrow, Florence Marly, Sivi Aberg, Athena Lorde, Moe Howard; *D:* Eddie Saeta. **VHS, Beta $59.95** *PSM* 🎬

Doctor Detroit Aykroyd is funny in thin film, portraying a meek college professor who gets involved with prostitutes and the mob, under the alias "Dr. Detroit." Aykroyd later married actress Donna Dixon, whom he worked with on this film. Features music by Devo, James Brown, and Pattie Brooks.
1983 (R) 91m/C Dan Aykroyd, Howard Hesseman, Donna Dixon, T.K. Carter, Lynn Whitfield, Lydia Lei, Fran Drescher, Kate Murtagh, George Furth, Andrew Duggan, James Brown, Glenne Headly; *D:* Michael Pressman; *W:* Carl Gottlieb. **VHS, Beta $14.95** *MCA* 🎬🎬

Doctor Dolittle An adventure about a 19th century English doctor who dreams of teaching animals to speak to him. Realistic premise suffers from poor script. Based on Hugh Lofting's acclaimed stories. 🎵 Doctor Dolittle; My Friend the Doctor; Talk to the Animals; I've Never Seen Anything Like It; Beautiful Things; When I Look in Your Eyes; After Today; Fabulous Places; Where Are the Words?; I Think I Like You; Something in Your Smile; The Vegetarian; At the Crossroads; Like Animals.
1967 144m/C Rex Harrison, Samantha Eggar, Anthony Newley, Richard Attenborough, Geoffrey Holder, Peter Bull; *D:* Richard Fleischer; *W:* Leslie Bricusse. Academy Awards '67: Best Song ("Talk to the Animals"), Best Visual Effects; Nominations: Best Cinematography, Best Sound, Best Original Score; Academy Awards '67: Best Film Editing, Best Picture; Golden Globe Awards '68: Best Supporting Actor (Attenborough); National Board of Review Awards '67: 10 Best Films of the Year. **VHS, Beta $14.98** *FOX, FCT, MLT* 🎬🎬

Doctor Duck's Super Secret All-Purpose Sauce Conglomeration of video, music, and comedy clips directed by the former Monkee done in the style of his popular "Elephant Parts."
1985 90m/C Michael Nesmith, Whoopi Goldberg, Jimmy Buffett, Rosanne Cash, Jay Leno; *D:* Michael Nesmith. **VHS, Beta $9.95** *MVD* 🎬🎬

Doctor Faustus A stilted, stagy, but well-meaning adaptation of the Christopher Marlowe classic about Faust, who sold his soul to the devil for youth and the love of Helen of Troy.
1968 93m/C Richard Burton, Andreas Teuber, Elizabeth Taylor, Ian Marter; *D:* Richard Burton, Nevill Coghill. **VHS, Beta $69.95** *COL* 🎬½

Dr. Frankenstein's Castle of Freaks Dr. Frankenstein and his dwarf assistant reanimate a few Neanderthals that are terrorizing a nearby Rumanian village.
1974 (PG) 87m/C *IT* Rossano Brazzi, Michael Dunn, Edmund Purdom, Christiane Royce; *D:* Robert Oliver. **VHS, Beta** *SNC* 🎬

Dr. Giggles Drake plays the psycho-genius Dr. Giggles, an escaped mental patient who sets out to avenge the death of his psycho-genius father (dementia runs in the family). He returns to his family home to procure the necessary medical instruments, most notably a hypodermic needle, and starts killing people—on screen with the tools and in the audience with remarkably stupid one-liners. Opening scenes are especially mired in gore.
1992 (R) 96m/C Larry Drake, Holly Marie Combs, Glenn Quinn, Keith Diamond, Cliff DeYoung; *D:* Manny Coto; *W:* Graeme Whifler, Manny Coto. **VHS, Beta $19.98** *MCA* 🎬

Dr. Goldfoot and the Bikini Machine A mad scientist employs gorgeous female robots to seduce the wealthy and powerful, thereby allowing him to take over the world. Title song by the Supremes.
1966 90m/C Vincent Price, Frankie Avalon, Dwayne Hickman, Annette Funicello, Susan Hart, Kay Elkhardt, Fred Clark, Deanna Lund, Deborah Walley; **D:** Norman Taurog; **M:** Les Baxter. VHS AIP *½

Dr. Hackenstein A doctor tries to revive his wife by "borrowing" parts from unexpected (and unsuspecting) guests.
1988 (R) 88m/C David Muir, Stacy Travis, Catherine Davis Cox, Dyanne DiRosario, Anne Ramsey, Logan Ramsey; **D:** Richard Clark. VHS, Beta $79.98 MCG *½

Dr. Heckyl and Mr. Hype A naughty, comical version of the Jekyll and Hyde story. Exuberantly wicked performances from Reed and Coogan; stellar cast of "B" veterans.
1980 100m/C Oliver Reed, Sunny Johnson, Maia Danzinger, Mel Welles, Virgil Frye, Kedrick Wolfe, Jackie Coogan, Corinne Calvet, Dick Miller, Lucretia Love; **D:** Charles B. Griffith; **W:** Charles B. Griffith; **M:** Richard Band. VHS, Beta NO *½

Doctor in Distress Aging chief surgeon falls in love for the first time. His assistant tries to further the romance as well as his own love life. Comedic fourth in the six-film "Doctor" series.
1963 102m/C GB Dirk Bogarde, James Robertson Justice, Leo McKern, Samantha Eggar; **D:** Ralph Thomas. VHS, Beta NO *½½

Doctor in the House Four medical student/roommates seek only to examine lovely women and make lots of cash. In the process, they are also tempted by the evils of drink, but rally to make their grades. A riotous British comedy with marvelous performances all around. Led to six sequels and a television series.
1953 92m/C GB Dirk Bogarde, Muriel Pavlow, Kenneth More, Donald Sinden, Kay Kendall, James Robertson Justice, Donald Houston, Geoffrey Keen, George Coulouris, Shirley Eaton, Joan Hickson, Richard Wattis; **D:** Ralph Thomas. VHS $19.95 PAR, HMV *½½½

Dr. Jack/For Heaven's Sake In "Dr. Jack" (1922) and "For Heaven's Sake" (1926) Lloyd acts respectively as an unorthodox doctor and as a debonair millionaire who falls in love with a poor girl. Silent comedy shorts from Lloyd.
1926 88m/B Harold Lloyd, Jobyna Ralston; **D:** Sam Taylor. VHS, Beta TLF *½½½½

Dr. Jekyll and Mr. Hyde The first American film version of Robert Louis Stevenson's horror tale about a doctor's experiments that lead to his developing good and evil sides to his personality. Silent. Kino Video's edition also contains the rarely seen 1911 version of the film, as well as scenes from a different 1920 version.
1920 96m/B John Barrymore, Martha Mansfield, Brandon Hurst, Charles Lane, J. Malcolm Dunn, Nita Naldi; **D:** John S. Robertson. VHS $16.95 SNC, REP, MRV *½½½

Dr. Jekyll and Mr. Hyde The hallucinatory, feverish classic version of the Robert Louis Stevenson story, in which the good doctor becomes addicted to the formula that turns him into a sadistic beast. Possibly Mamoulian's and March's best work, and a masterpiece of subversive, pseudo-Freudian creepiness. Eighteen minutes from the original version, lost until recently, have been restored, including the infamous whipping scene.
1931 96m/B Fredric March, Miriam Hopkins, Halliwell Hobbes, Rose Hobart, Holmes Herbert, Edgar Norton; **D:** Rouben Mamoulian. Academy Awards '32: Best Actor (March); Nominations: Best Adapted Screenplay, Best Cinematography; Venice Film Festival '31: Best Actor (March). VHS, Beta $19.98 MGM, BTV *½½½

Dr. Jekyll and Mr. Hyde Strangely cast adaptation of the Robert Louis Stevenson story about a doctor's experiment on himself to separate good and evil.
1941 113m/B Spencer Tracy, Ingrid Bergman, Lana Turner, Donald Crisp; **D:** Victor Fleming. VHS, Beta $19.98 MGM *½½½

Dr. Jekyll and Mr. Hyde Yet another production of Robert Louis Stevenson's classic story of a split-personality.
1968 90m/C Jack Palance. VHS, Beta $49.95 LIV *½½½

Dr. Jekyll and Mr. Hyde Dr. Jekyll discovers a potion that turns him into the sinister Mr. Hyde. Based on the classic story by Robert Louis Stevenson.
1973 90m/C Kirk Douglas, Michael Redgrave, Susan George, Donald Pleasence; **D:** David Winters. VHS, Beta $59.95 IME *½½

Dr. Jekyll and Sister Hyde A tongue-in-cheek variation on the split-personality theme, which has the good doctor transforming himself into a sultry, knife-wielding woman who kills prostitutes.
1971 (R) 94m/C GB Ralph Bates, Martine Beswick, Gerald Sim; **D:** Roy Ward Baker; **W:** Brian Clemens. VHS, Beta $59.99 MLB *½½½

Dr. Jekyll and the Wolfman Naschy's sixth stint as El Hombre Lobo. This time he visits a mysterious doctor in search of a cure but ends up turning into Mr. Hyde, a man who likes to torture women. *AKA:* Dr. Jekyll y el Hombre Lobo.
1971 (R) 85m/C SP Paul Naschy, Shirley Corrigan, Jack Taylor; **D:** Leon Klimovsky. VHS $19.98 SNC *½

Dr. Jekyll vs. the Werewolf A man afflicted with the characteristics of a wolf seeks a cure from Dr. Jekyll's grandson.
1971 ?m/C Paul Naschy, Jack Taylor. VHS $16.95 SNC *½½

Dr. Jekyll's Dungeon of Death Dr. Jekyll and his lobotomized sister, Hilda, scour the streets of San Francisco looking for human blood to recreate his great-grandfather's secret serum. Also on video as "Dr. Jekyll's Dungeon of Darkness."
1982 (R) 90m/C James Mathers, Dawn Carver Kelly, John Kearney, Jake Pearson; **D:** James Wood. VHS, Beta GHV *

Dr. Judym The screen adaptation of writer Stefan Zeromski's story of an impoverished youth who grows up to become an idealistic physician. In Polish with English subtitles.
19?? 94m/C PL **D:** Wlodzimierz Haupe. VHS $49.95 FCT, MOV *½½

Dr. Kildare's Strange Case Dr. Kildare administers a daring treatment to a man suffering from a mental disorder of a dangerous nature. One in the film series.
1940 76m/B Lew Ayres, Lionel Barrymore, Laraine Day; **D:** Harold Bucquet. VHS, Beta $19.95 NOS, HHT, DVT *½½

Dr. Mabuse the Gambler The massive, two-part crime melodrama, introducing the raving mastermind/extortionist/villain to the world. The film follows Dr. Mabuse through his life of crime until he finally goes mad. Highly influential and inventive. Lang meant this to be a criticism of morally bankrupt post-WWI Germany. Followed some time later by "Testament of Doctor Mabuse" and "The Thousand Eyes of Dr. Mabuse." Silent. *AKA:* Doktor Mabuse der Spieler.
1922 242m/B GE Rudolf Klein-Rogge, Aud Egede Nissen, Alfred Abel, Gertrude Welcker, Lil Dagover, Paul Richter; **D:** Fritz Lang. VHS, Beta $16.95 SNC, MRV, NOS *½½½

Dr. Mabuse vs. Scotland Yard A sequel to the Fritz Lang classics, this film features the arch-criminal attempting to take over the world with a mind-controlling camera.
1964 90m/B GE Sabine Bethmann, Peter Van Eyck; **D:** Paul May. VHS, Beta $24.95 VYY, SNC, GLV *½½

Doctor Mordrid: Master of the Unknown Two immensely powerful sorcerers from the 4th dimension cross over into present time with two very different missions—one wants to destroy the Earth, one wants to save it.
1992 (R) 102m/C Jeffrey Combs, Yvette Nipar, Jay Acovone, Brian Thompson; **D:** Albert Band, Charles Band; **M:** Richard Band. VHS, Beta PAR *½

Dr. No The world is introduced to British secret agent 007, James Bond, when it is discovered that a mad scientist is sabotaging rocket launchings from his hideout in Jamaica. The first 007 film is far less glitzy than any of its successors but boasts the sexiest "Bond girl" of them all in Andress, and promptly made stars of her and Connery. On laserdisc, the film is in wide-screen transfer and includes movie bills, publicity photos, location pictures, and the British and American trailers. The sound effects and musical score can be separated from the dialogue. Audio interviews with the director, writer, and editor are included as part of the disc.
1962 (PG) 111m/C GB Sean Connery, Ursula Andress, Joseph Wiseman, Jack Lord, Zena Marshall, Eunice Gayson, Margaret LeWars, John Kitzmiller, Lois Maxwell, Bernard Lee, Anthony M. (Antonio Margheriti) Dawson; **D:** Terence Young; **M:** John Barry. VHS, Beta $19.98 MGM, VYG, CRC *½½½

Dr. Orloff's Invisible Horror In this horror film, Dr. Orloff creates an invisible ape-monster that escapes and goes on a rampage.
1972 ?m/C Howard Vernon. VHS $16.95 SNC *½½

Dr. Orloff's Monster As if "The Awful Dr. Orloff" wasn't awful enough, the doctor is back, this time eliminating his enemies with his trusty killer robot. Awful awful.
1964 88m/B SP Jose Rubio, Agnes Spaak; **D:** Jess (Jesus) Franco. VHS $19.98 SNC, VYY Woof!

Dr. Otto & the Riddle of the Gloom Beam Ernest is in your face again. Fresh from the TV commercials featuring "Ernest" comes Varney playing a villain out to wreck the global economy. He also plays all the other characters, too. Way bizarre, "Know whut I mean?"
1986 (PG) 92m/C Jim Varney; **D:** John R. Cherry III. VHS, Beta $59.95 GKK *½

Doctor Phibes Rises Again The despicable doctor contines his quest to revive his beloved wife. Fun, superior sequel to "The Abominable Dr. Phibes."
1972 (PG) 89m/C GB Vincent Price, Robert Quarry, Peter Cushing, Beryl Reid, Hugh Griffith, Terry-Thomas; **D:** Robert Fuest. VHS, Beta $19.98 LIV, VES, ORI *½½

Doctor Quinn, Medicine Woman The small western town of Colorado Springs has advertised for a doctor and is pleased to hire Dr. "Mike" Quinn from Boston. Only to

VIDEOHOUND'S GOLDEN MOVIE RETRIEVER

the town's surprise, and dismay, who should arrive but Dr. Michaela Quinn. This eastern lady has her work cut out for her just trying to convince the townsfolk that a woman can practice medicine. But she's determined and with the aid of the brooding, handsome Sully she opens her practice. Made for television.
1992 ?m/C Jane Seymour, Diane Ladd, Joe Lando. VHS **$89.98** FXV 🐾🐾½

Doctor Satan's Robot Indestructible robot is battled by insane Dr. Satan in reedited serial, "Mysterious Dr. Satan."
1940 100m/B Eduardo Ciannelli, Robert Wilcox, William Newell, Ella Neal; D: William Whitney, John English. VHS **$29.95** VCN 🐾🐾½

Dr. Strange A made-for-television pilot based upon the Marvel Comics character who, with the help of a sorcerer, practices witchcraft in order to fight evil.
1978 94m/C Peter Hooten, Clyde Kusatsu, Jessica Walter, Eddie Benton, John Mills; D: Philip DeGuere. VHS, Beta **$39.95** MCA 🐾🐾½

Dr. Strangelove, or: How I Learned to Stop Worrying and Love the Bomb Sellers plays a tour-de-force triple role in Kubrick's classic black anti-war comedy. While a U.S. President (Sellers) deals with the Russian situation, a crazed general (Hayden) implements a plan to drop the A-bomb on the Soviets. Famous for Pickens' wild ride on the bomb, Hayden's character's "purity of essence" philosophy, Scott's gumchewing militarist, a soft-drink vending machine dispute, and countless other scenes. Based on the novel "Red Alert" by Peter George.
1964 93m/B GB Peter Sellers, George C. Scott, Sterling Hayden, Keenan Wynn, Slim Pickens, James Earl Jones, Peter Bull; D: Stanley Kubrick; W: Terry Southern, Peter George, Stanley Kubrick; M: Laurie Johnson. Academy Awards '64 Nominations: Best Actor (Sellers), Best Adapted Screenplay, Best Director (Kubrick), Best Picture; British Academy Awards '64: Best Film; New York Film Critics Awards '64: Best Director (Kubrick). VHS, Beta, 8mm **$19.95** COL, HMV 🐾🐾🐾🐾

Dr. Syn The story of a seemingly respectable vicar of Dymchurch who is really a former pirate. The last film of George Arliss.
1937 90m/B GB George Arliss, Margaret Lockwood, John Loder; D: Roy William Neill. VHS, Beta **$19.95** NOS, MRV, CAB 🐾🐾🐾

Dr. Syn, Alias the Scarecrow A mild-mannered minister is, in reality, a smuggler and pirate avenging King George III's injustices upon the English people. Originally broadcast in three parts on the Disney television show.
1964 (G) 129m/C Patrick McGoohan, George Cole, Tony Britton, Michael Hordern, Geoffrey Keen, Kay Cole; D: James Neilson. VHS, Beta **$69.95** DIS 🐾🐾½

Doctor Takes a Wife A fast, fun screwball comedy wherein two ill-matched career people are forced via a publicity mix-up to fake being married.
1940 89m/B Ray Milland, Loretta Young, Reginald Gardiner, Gail Patrick, Edmund Gwenn, George Metaxa, Charles Halton; D: Alexander Hall; W: George Seaton. VHS, Beta **$69.95** COL 🐾🐾🐾

Dr. Tarr's Torture Dungeon A mysterious man is sent to the forest to investigate the bizarre behavior of Dr. Tarr who runs a torture asylum.
1975 (R) 90m/C Claudio Brook, Ellen Sherman, Robert Dumont. VHS, Beta NO Woof!

Dr. Terror's House of Horrors On a train, six traveling companions have their fortunes told by a mysterious doctor. Little do they realize that their final destination has

changed. Creepy and suspenseful, especially the severed-hand chase sequence. **AKA:** The Blood Suckers.
1965 92m/C GB Christopher Lee, Peter Cushing, Donald Sutherland; D: Freddie Francis. VHS **$14.95** REP, MLB 🐾🐾½

Doctor Who: An Unearthly Child In the British series' first episode, Doctor Who and his granddaughter travel to prehistoric times to witness the discovery of fire.
1963 98m/B GB William Hartnell, William Russell; D: Waris Hussein. VHS **$19.98** FXV, MOV 🐾🐾½

Doctor Who and the Daleks The Time Lord and his two grandchildren accidentally transport themselves to a futuristic planet inhabited by the Daleks, who capture the travelers and hold them captive. A feature film version of the long-running British television show.
1965 78m/C GB Peter Cushing, Roy Castle; D: Gordon Flemyng. VHS, Beta **$9.98** REP 🐾🐾

Doctor Who: Cybermen—The Early Years Baker, the 6th Doctor, hosts this look at the Time Lord's favorite enemies, the robotic and ruthless Cybermen from their first appearance in "The Tenth Planet" to "Tomb of the Cyberman" and "The Invasion."
1992 120m/C GB VHS **$19.99** FXV, MOV 🐾🐾½

Doctor Who: Daleks Invasion of Earth 2150 A.D. The Tardis lands in an empty and decayed city—it's London in the next century! What's happened? Why the Daleks of course! The evil aliens have conquered Earth! Can the Doctor destroy the creatures once and for all?
196? 80m/B GB William Hartnell. VHS **$9.98** REP 🐾🐾½

Doctor Who: Day of the Daleks From the long-running British television show. The Doctor must stop the evil Daleks from gaining control of Earth. Hailed as one of the best episodes by fans.
1972 90m/C GB Jon Pertwee; D: Paul Bernard. VHS, Beta **$19.98** FOX, MOV 🐾🐾½

Doctor Who: Death to the Daleks The Doctor and Sarah must battle the Daleks in order to find an antidote to a deadly virus threatening all life in the universe.
1974 90m/C GB Jon Pertwee, Elisabeth Sladen; D: Michael E. Briant. VHS, Beta **$19.98** FOX, MOV 🐾🐾½

Doctor Who: Earthshock The Doctor finds himself in the middle of a 26th-century murder mystery on an abandoned planet—and it seems his old enemies the Cybermen are involved!
1982 99m/C GB Peter Davison. VHS **$19.99** FXV, MOV 🐾🐾½

Doctor Who: Mawdryn Undead The evil Black Guardian influences a school boy in a plot to assassinate the Doctor. Meanwhile, the Tardis is in orbit inside a huge space ship, the resting place of Mawdryn and his fellow scientists who are trapped in a state of perpetual regeneration. Only the Doctor's own life force can free them but the price is high!
198? ?m/C GB Peter Davison. VHS **$19.98** FOX 🐾🐾½

Doctor Who: Pyramids of Mars Join the Doctor and Sarah Jane as they battle a professor possessed by the God of Darkness who must be stopped before he destroys humankind. From the British television series.
1975 91m/C GB Tom Baker, Elisabeth Sladen; D: Paddy Russell. VHS, Beta **$19.98** FOX, MOV 🐾🐾½

Doctor Who: Revenge of the Cybermen The Doctor, Sarah Jane, and Harry must free a space station from the deadly grip of the half-robot, half-human Cybermen.
1975 92m/C GB Tom Baker, Elisabeth Sladen; D: Michael E. Briant. VHS, Beta **$19.98** FOX, MOV 🐾🐾½

Doctor Who: Robots of Death The Doctor and new-on-the-scene Leela must solve a series of murders on a planet inhabited by robots.
1977 91m/C GB Tom Baker, Louise Jameson; D: Michael E. Briant. VHS, Beta **$19.98** FOX, MOV 🐾🐾½

Doctor Who: Shada The Doctor, Romana, and K-9 seek the help of a Time Lord living incognito on Earth. A six-part Time Lord cycle never aired on television. The story was not completed due to a BBC strike but the available scenes have been linked with narration by Baker.
1980 110m/C GB Tom Baker. VHS **$19.98** FOX, TVC, MOV 🐾🐾½

Doctor Who: Spearhead from Space Earth is in peril at the hands of murderous mannequins and only Doctor Who can stop them. From the British television series.
1970 92m/C GB Jon Pertwee. VHS, Beta **$19.98** FOX, MOV 🐾🐾½

Doctor Who: Terror of the Zygons Still more hideous aliens threaten the Earth. Their instrument of destruction? The Loch Ness Monster. Unless of course the Doctor can stop them. From the British television series.
1975 92m/C GB Tom Baker, Elisabeth Sladen. VHS, Beta **$19.98** FOX, MOV 🐾🐾½

Doctor Who: The Ark in Space The Doctor, Sarah Jane, and Harry find the last survivors of Earth living in a giant space ark. They're threatened by insect-like aliens who want to use the humans as host bodies.
1974 90m/C GB Tom Baker, Elisabeth Sladen. VHS, Beta **$19.98** FOX, MOV 🐾🐾½

Doctor Who: The Brain of Morbius The Doctor and Sarah find a space scientist has kept alive the brain of the evil renegade Time Lord, Morbius, and plans to transplant the brain into a new body. The original version aired at 90 minutes.
1976 91m/C GB Tom Baker, Elisabeth Sladen; D: Christopher Barry. VHS, Beta **$19.98** FOX, MOV 🐾🐾½

Doctor Who: The Caves of Androzani A four-part story, the last featuring Davison as Doctor No. 5, has our hero battling wits with android creator Sharaz Jek for control of a mysterious and addictive substance.
1984 101m/C GB Peter Davison. VHS **$19.98** FOX, TVC, MOV 🐾🐾½

Doctor Who: The Curse of Fenric In this adventure, the Doctor's battle with the wolves of Fenric take him back to WWII Britain.
1989 104m/C GB Sylvester McCoy. VHS **$19.98** FOX, MOV 🐾🐾½

Doctor Who: The Deadly Assassin On his home planet of Gallifrey the Doctor stands accused of murder before the council of the Time Lords. Can he prove his innocence and battle that arch-fiend "The Master?"
1976 90m/C GB Tom Baker; D: David Maloney. VHS, Beta **$19.98** FOX, MOV 🐾🐾½

Doctor Who: The Five Doctors
Literally the best of the best. The Doctor's five regenerations, numerous companions, lots of bad guys, even the Master, reunite for a spectacular showdown. An exceptional treat for fans.
1983 90m/C GB Peter Davison, Jon Pertwee, Patrick Troughton, Tom Baker, Richard Hurndall; **D:** Peter Moffatt. VHS, Beta $19.98 FOX, MOV ♂♂♂½

Doctor Who: The Hartnell Years
Seventh Doctor McCoy hosts this look at the first three seasons of the long-running program and the first of the Doctors, Hartnell.
1991 88m/B GB William Hartnell. VHS $19.98 FOX, MOV ♂♂½

Doctor Who: The Keeper of Traken The empire of Traken faces disaster at the hands of the evil Melkur. So the sacred Keeper calls on the Doctor, and his latest assistant Nyssa, for help.
197? ?m/C GB Tom Baker. VHS $19.98 FOX ♂♂½

Doctor Who: The Masque of Mandragora The Tardis travels back to 15th century Earth where the Doctor is entangled in a power struggle for the Dukedom of San Martino against the mysterious cult of Demnos.
197? ?m/C GB Tom Baker. VHS $19.98 FOX ♂♂½

Doctor Who: The Mind Robber An emergency forces the Tardis out of the time space dimension and it lands outside of reality. The Doctor enters a fantasy world of white robots, fictional monsters come to life, and great danger.
196? ?m/C GB Patrick Troughton. VHS $19.98 FOX ♂♂½

Doctor Who: The Pertwee Years
A compilation of highlights from the 1970s featuring Pertwee's adventures as the Time Lord in the long-running British television series.
1992 88m/C GB Jon Pertwee. VHS $19.98 FOX, TVC, MOV ♂♂½

Doctor Who: The Seeds of Death Martian Ice Warriors plan to infect 21st-century Earth with a deadly fungus carried by seed pods. Can the Doctor and his companions prevent the catastrophe?
1969 137m/B GB Patrick Troughton; **D:** Michael Ferguson. VHS, Beta $19.98 FOX, MOV ♂♂½

Doctor Who: The Sontaran Experiment/The Genesis of the Daleks Two Tom Baker adventures from the British sci-fi series. "The Sontaran Experiment" finds the Doctor visiting Piccadilly Circus 10,000 years in the future. The land is ruled by a mysterious alien and the Doctor is the subject of a lethal experiment. "The Genesis of the Daleks" finds the Doctor back on Skaro where the Timelords themselves have ordered him to destroy the Daleks before they can evolve and face their evil creator.
197? ?m/C GB Tom Baker. VHS $29.98 FOX ♂♂½

Doctor Who: The Talons of Weng-Chiang The Doctor and Leela face off against a murderous time-traveling magician in Victorian London.
1977 140m/C GB Tom Baker, Louise Jameson; **D:** Michael E. Briant. VHS, Beta $19.98 FOX, MOV ♂♂½

Doctor Who: The Three Doctors
This 10th-anniversary special highlights three incarnations of the Doctor as they join forces to battle a renegade Time Lord known as Omega.
1973 99m/C GB Jon Pertwee, Patrick Troughton, William Hartnell. VHS $19.98 FOX, MOV ♂♂½

Doctor Who: The Time Warrior
When scientists begin disappearing, the Doctor pursues them into the Middle Ages, where he finds an unscrupulous Sontaran fleet commander is prepared to exploit his superior technology to no good end. From the British television series.
1974 90m/C GB Jon Pertwee, Elisabeth Sladen. VHS, Beta $19.98 FOX, MOV ♂♂½

Doctor Who: The Tom Baker Years Baker starred the longest as the Doctor, for seven seasons, and here he looks at his favorite epissdes and other highlights from the series.
1992 170m/C GB VHS $19.99 FXV, MOV ♂♂½

Doctor Who: The Troughton Years The third Doctor serves as host to highlight the accomplishments of his predecessor in all his adventures. Collection of rare episodes and photos from 1966 to 1969.
1991 84m/B GB Patrick Troughton. VHS $19.98 FOX, MOV ♂♂½

Doctor Who: The Twin Dilemma
Twins Romulus and Remus are a kidnapped pair of mathematical geniuses about to be used in a scheme for galactic domination. The Doctor must save the day but in his newly-regenerated state his behavior is even more erratic than usual. Baker's first episode as the sixth Doctor.
1984 99m/C GB Colin Baker. VHS $19.99 FXV, MOV ♂♂½

Doctor Who: The War Games The Doctor, Zoe, and Jamie find themselves involved in an alien-staged, life-sized war simulation using soldiers plucked from different centuries. Can the Time Lord save the day? On two cassettes.
1969 243m/B GB Patrick Troughton; **D:** David Maloney. VHS $19.98 FOX, MOV ♂♂½

Doctor Who: Tomb of the Cyberman The Doctor, Jamie, and Victoria visit an archeological dig which unfortunately uncovers the deadly robotic Cybermen.
1967 100m/B GB Patrick Troughton. VHS $19.98 FOX, TVC, MOV ♂♂½

Doctor X An armless mad scientist uses a formula for "synthetic flesh" to grow temporary limbs and commit murder. A classic, rarely seen horror oldie, famous for its very early use of two-color Technicolor.
1932 77m/C Lionel Atwill, Fay Wray, Lee Tracy, Preston Foster; **D:** Michael Curtiz. VHS, Beta $19.95 MGM, MLB ♂♂½

Doctor Zhivago Sweeping adaptation of the Nobel Prize-winning Boris Pasternak novel. An innocent Russian poet-intellectual is caught in the furor and chaos of the Bolshevik Revolution. Essentially a poignant love story filmed as a historical epic. Panoramic film popularized the song "Lara's Theme." Overlong, with often disappointing performances, but gorgeous scenery. Lean was more successful in "Lawrence of Arabia," where there was less need for ensemble acting.
1965 197m/C Omar Sharif, Julie Christie, Geraldine Chaplin, Rod Steiger, Alec Guinness, Klaus Kinski, Ralph Richardson, Rita Tushingham, Siobhan McKenna, Tom Courtenay; **D:** David Lean; **W:** Robert Bolt; **M:** Maurice Jarre. Academy Awards '65: Best Adapted Screenplay, Best Art Direction/Set Decoration (Color), Best Color Cinematography, Best Costume Design (Color), Best Original Score; Nominations: Best Director (Lean), Best Film Editing, Best Picture, Best Sound, Best Supporting Actor (Courtenay); Golden Globe Awards '66: Best Actor—Drama (Sharif), Best Director (Lean), Best Film—Drama, Best Screenplay, Best Score; National Board of Review Awards '65: 10 Best Films of the Year, Best Actress (Christie). VHS, Beta $29.98 MGM, RDG, HMV ♂♂♂

Doctors and Nurses A children's satire of soap operas wherein the adults play the children and vice-versa.
1982 90m/C Rebecca Rigg, Drew Forsythe, Graeme Blundell; **D:** Maurice Murphy. VHS, Beta NO ♂♂

Doctors' Wives An adaptation of the Frank Slaughter potboiler about a large city hospital's doctors, nurses, and their respective spouses, with plenty of affairs, medical traumas, and betrayals.
1970 (R) 102m/C Dyan Cannon, Richard Crenna, Gene Hackman, Carroll O'Connor, Rachel Roberts, Janice Rule, Diana Sands, Ralph Bellamy, John Colicos; **D:** George Schaefer; **W:** Daniel Taradash; **M:** Elmer Bernstein. VHS, Beta $69.95 COL ♂♂

Dodes 'ka-den In this departure from his samurai-genre films, Kurosawa depicts a throng of fringe-dwelling Tokyo slum inhabitants in a semi-surreal manner. Fascinating presentation and content. **AKA:** Clickety Clack.
1970 140m/C JP Yoshitaka Zushi, Junzaburo Ban, Kiyoko Tange; **D:** Akira Kurosawa. VHS, Beta $19.98 ING, SUE ♂♂♂½

Dodge City Flynn stars as Wade Hutton, a roving cattleman who becomes the sheriff of Dodge City. His job: to run a ruthless outlaw and his gang out of town. De Havilland serves as Flynn's love interest, as she did in many previous films. A broad and colorful shoot-em-up!
1939 104m/C Errol Flynn, Olivia de Havilland, Bruce Cabot, Ann Sheridan, Alan Hale, Frank McHugh, Victor Jory, Henry Travers, Charles Halton; **D:** Michael Curtiz. VHS, Beta $19.98 MGM, FOX, FCT ♂♂♂

Dodsworth The lives of a self-made American tycoon and his wife are drastically changed when they take a tour of Europe. The success of their marriage seems questionable as they re-evaluate their lives. Huston excels as does the rest of the cast in this film, based upon the Sinclair Lewis novel.
1936 101m/B Walter Huston, David Niven, Paul Lukas, John Payne, Mary Astor, Ruth Chatterton, Maria Ouspenskaya, Charles Halton; **D:** William Wyler. Academy Awards '36: Best Interior Decoration; Nominations: Best Actor (Huston), Best Adapted Screenplay, Best Director (Wyler), Best Picture, Best Sound, Best Supporting Actress (Ouspenskaya). VHS, Beta $19.98 HBO, SUE ♂♂♂½

Does This Mean We're Married? A stand-up comedian is trying to find success in the comedy clubs of Paris but without her green card she may soon be deported. She finds a sleazy marriage broker who fixes her up with a womanizing songwriter who needs money. As usual, immigration officials suspect that the marriage is a fake and the mismatched couple must live together to prove them wrong.
1990 (PG-13) 93m/C Patsy Kensit, Stephane Freiss; **D:** Carol Wiseman. VHS $19.95 COL, NLC ♂♂

Dog Day An American traitor, who is on the lam from the government, and his cronies, takes refuge on a small farm. A surprise awaits him when the farmers come up with an unusual plan to bargain for his life. *AKA:* Canicule.
1983 101m/C *FR* Lee Marvin, Miou-Miou, Victor Lanoux; *D:* Yves Boisset. **VHS, Beta $79.98** *LIV* 🎬🎬½

Dog Day Afternoon Based on a true story, this taut, yet fantastic thriller centers on a bi-sexual and his slow-witted buddy who rob a bank to obtain money to fund a sex change operation for the ringleader's lover. Pacino is breathtaking in his role as the frustrated robber, caught in a trap of his own devising. Very controversial for its language and subject matter when released, it nevertheless became a huge success. Director Lumet keeps up the pace, fills the screen with pathos without gross sentiment.
1975 (R) 124m/C Al Pacino, John Cazale, Charles Durning, James Broderick, Chris Sarandon, Carol Kane, Lance Henriksen, Dick Williams; *D:* Sidney Lumet; *W:* Frank Pierson. Academy Awards '75: Best Original Screenplay; Nominations: Best Actor (Pacino), Best Director (Lumet), Best Film Editing, Best Picture, Best Supporting Actor (Sarandon); British Academy Awards '75: Best Actor (Pacino); National Board of Review Awards '75: 10 Best Films of the Year, Best Supporting Actor (Durning). **VHS, Beta $19.98** *WAR* 🎬🎬🎬½

Dog Eat Dog Centering on a heist scheme by Mitchell, this one has nothing to offer except Mansfield's attributes. *AKA:* Einer Frisst den Anderen; La Morte Vestita di Dollar.
1964 86m/B Cameron Mitchell, Jayne Mansfield, Isa Miranda; *D:* Ray Nazarro. **VHS, Beta, 8mm $24.95** *VYY, HEG* 🎬

A Dog of Flanders A young Dutch boy and his grandfather find a severely beaten dog and restore it to health.
1959 96m/C David Ladd, Donald Crisp, Theodore Bikel, Max Croiset, Monique Ahrens; *D:* James B. Clark. **VHS, Beta $14.95** *PAR* 🎬🎬½

Dog Pound Shuffle Two drifters form a new song-and-dance act in order to raise the funds necessary to win their dog's freedom from the pound. Charming Canadian production. *AKA:* Spot.
1975 (PG) 98m/C *CA* Ron Moody, David Soul; *D:* Jeffrey Bloom; *W:* Jeffrey Bloom. **VHS, Beta $59.98** *FOX* 🎬🎬

The Dog Soldier This "video novel" dramatically depicts a state of future events whereby a lone human in flight struggles to preserve his right to be free.
1972 40m/B **VHS, Beta** *PCV* 🎬½

Dog Star Man The silent epic by the dean of experimental American film depicts man's spiritual and physical conflicts through Brakhage's characteristics freeform collage techniques.
1964 78m/C *D:* Stan Brakhage. **VHS, Beta $29.95** *MFV, FCT, TPV* 🎬🎬🎬

The Dog Who Stopped the War A Canadian children's film about a dog who puts a halt to an escalating snowball fight between rival gangs.
1984 (G) 90m/C *CA D:* Andre Melancon. **VHS, Beta** *NO* 🎬🎬

Dogfight It's 1963 and a baby-faced Marine and his buddies are spending their last night in San Francisco before leaving the U.S. for a tour of duty in Vietnam. They agree to throw a "dogfight," a competition to see who can bring the ugliest date to a party. Birdlace (Phoenix) chooses Taylor, a shy, average-looking waitress who dreams of

becoming a folk singer and realizes too late that she doesn't deserve the treatment he's about to subject her to. This quiet film didn't see a wide release, but is worth renting due to an above average script which is held up by the splendid performances of Phoenix and Taylor.
1991 (R) 94m/C River Phoenix, Lili Taylor, Richard Panebianco, Anthony Clark, Mitchell Whitfield, E.G. Daily, Holly Near, Brendan Fraser, Peg Phillips; *D:* Nancy Savoca; *W:* Bob Comfort. **VHS, Beta, 8mm $19.98** *WAR* 🎬🎬🎬

Dogs in Space A low-budget Australian film about a clique of aimless Melbourne rock kids in 1978, caught somewhere between post-hippiedom and punk, free love and heroin addiction. Acclaimed. Includes music by Hutchence, Brian Eno, Iggy Pop, and others.
1987 109m/C *AU* Michael Hutchence, Saskia Post, Nique Needles, Tony Helou, Deanna Bond; *D:* Richard Lowenstein; *W:* Richard Lowenstein. **VHS, Beta $79.98** *FOX* 🎬🎬

Dogs of Hell The sheriff of an idyllic resort community must stop a pack of killer dogs from terrorizing the residents.
1983 (R) 90m/C Earl Owensby, Bill Gribble, Jerry Rushing; *D:* Worth Keeter. **VHS, Beta $59.95** *MED* 🎬½

The Dogs of War A graphic depiction of a group of professional mercenaries, driven by nothing but their quest for wealth and power, hired to overthrow the dictator of a new West African nation. Has some weak moments which break up the continuity of the movie. Based on the novel by Frederick Forsyth.
1981 (R) 102m/C *GB* Christopher Walken, Tom Berenger, Colin Blakely, Paul Freeman, Hugh Millais, Victoria Tennant, JoBeth Williams; *D:* John Irvin; *W:* Gary De Vore. **VHS, Beta $14.95** *MGM* 🎬🎬

Doin' Time At the John Dillinger Memorial Penitentiary, the inmates take over the prison under the supervision of warden "Mongo." Silliness prevails.
1985 (R) 80m/C Jeff Altman, Dey Young, Richard Mulligan, John Vernon, Colleen Camp, Melanie Chartoff, Graham Jarvis, Pat McCormick, Eddie Velez, Jimmie Walker, Judy Landers, Nicholas Worth, Mike Mazurki, Muhammad Ali, Melinda Fee, Francesca "Kitten" Natavidad, Ron Palillo; *D:* George Mendeluk; *M:* Charles Fox. **VHS, Beta $19.98** *WAR* 🎬

Doin' Time on Planet Earth A young boy feels out of place with his family and is convinced by two strange people (aliens themselves?) that he is really an extraterrestrial. Amusing, aimless fun directed by the son of Walter Matthau.
1988 (PG-13) 83m/C Adam West, Candice Azzara, Hugh O'Brian, Matt Adler, Timothy Patrick Murphy, Roddy McDowall, Maureen Stapleton, Andrea Thompson; *D:* Charles Matthau. **VHS, Beta $19.98** *WAR* 🎬🎬½

Dolemite An ex-con attempts to settle the score with some of his former inmates. He forms a band of kung-fu savvy ladies. Strange combination of action and comedy.
1975 (R) 88m/C Rudy Ray Moore, Jerry Jones; *D:* D'Urville Martin. **VHS** *XVC* 🎬½

Dolemite 2: Human Tornado Nobody ever said Moore was for everybody's taste. But, hey, when blaxploitation movies were the rage, Rudy the standup comic was out there rapping through a series of trashy movies that, when viewed today, have survived the test of time. This one's just as vile, violent, and sexist as the day it was released. When Rudy is surprised in bed with a white sheriff's wife, he flees and meets up with a madam and a house of kung-fu-skilled girls

who are embroiled in a fight with a local mobster. *AKA:* The Human Tornado.
1976 (R) 98m/C Rudy Ray Moore, Lady Reed. **VHS** *XVC* 🎬½

The Doll A lonely night watchman happens upon two burglars and, in the chase, the thieves knock over a mannequin. The watchman reports the mannequin stolen, brings it home and begins to have conversations with it. Soon, the doll's needs cause him to steal jewelry and clothes, until his brutish neighbor discovers his secrets. In Swedish with English subtitles. *AKA:* La Poupee; He, She or It.
1962 96m/B *SW* Per Oscarsson, Gio Petre, Tor Isedal, Elsa Prawitz; *D:* Arne Mattson. **VHS $29.95** *FCT, DVT, AUD* 🎬🎬

Doll Face Story of a stripper who wants to go legit and make it on Broadway. Film was adapted from the play "The Naked Genius" by tease queen Gypsy Rose Lee. ♫Dig You Later; Here Comes Heaven Again; Chico-Chico; Somebody's Walkin' In My Dreams; Red Hot and Beautiful. *AKA:* Come Back to Me.
1946 80m/B Vivian Blaine, Dennis O'Keefe, Perry Como, Carmen Miranda, Martha Stewart, Reed Hadley; *D:* Lewis Seiler. **VHS, Beta $19.99** *NOS, HHT, DVT* 🎬🎬½

The Doll Squad Three voluptuous special agents fight an ex-CIA agent out to rule the world. *AKA:* Hustler Squad.
1973 (PG) 93m/C Michael Ansara, Francine York, Anthony Eisley, Tura Satana; *D:* Ted V. Mikels. **VHS, Beta $39.95** *GHV, MRV* 🎬

Dollar The actress wife of an industrialist, convinced that he is having an affair, follows him to a ski lodge in attempt to catch him in the act. In Swedish with English subtitles.
1938 74m/B *SW* Georg Rydeberg, Ingrid Bergman, Kotti Chave, Tutta Rolf, Hakan Westergren, Elsa Burnett, Edvin Adolphson, Gosta Cederlund, Eric Rosen; *D:* Gustaf Molander. **VHS, Beta $29.95** *WAC, ING* 🎬🎬

Dollars A bank employee and his dizzy call-girl assistant plan to steal the German facility's assets while installing its new security system. Lighthearted fun. *AKA:* The Heist.
1971 (R) 119m/C Warren Beatty, Goldie Hawn, Gert Frobe, Scott Brady, Robert Webber; *D:* Richard Brooks; *W:* Richard Brooks; *M:* Quincy Jones. **VHS, Beta $9.95** *GKK* 🎬🎬🎬

The Dollmaker Excellent made for television adaptation of Harriette Arnow's novel. A strong-willed Kentucky mother of five helps move her family to Detroit in the 1940s. Petrie's direction moves the story along and creates a lovely period vision.
1984 140m/C Jane Fonda, Levon Helm, Geraldine Page, Amanda Plummer, Susan Kingsley; *D:* Daniel Petrie. **VHS, Beta $79.98** *FOX* 🎬🎬½

Dollman An ultra-tough cop from an Earth-like planet (even swear words are the same) crashes in the South Bronx—and on this world he's only 13 inches tall. The filmmakers squander a great premise and cast with bloody shootouts and a sequel-ready nonending.
1991 (R) 86m/C Tim Thomerson, Jackie Earle Haley, Kamala Lopez, Humberto Ortiz, Nicholas Guest, Michael Halsey, Eugene Glazer, Judd Omen, Frank Collison, Vincent Klyn; *D:* Albert Pyun. **VHS, Beta $19.95** *PAR* 🎬½

Dollman vs Demonic Toys Let's combine elements from three separate films and make one disgusting sequel: "Dollman," the 13-inch cop from the planet Arturus; his new girlfriend, Dollchick, who was shrunk to a diminutive 10 inches in "Bad Channels;"

and tough cop Judith Grey, who's once again battling those loathsome playthings from "Demonic Toys." If you feel the need for a plot—Dollchick is kidnapped by Baby Doll and needs to be rescued.
1993 (R) 84m/C Tim Thomerson, Tracy Scoggins, Melissa Behr, Phil Brock, Phil Fondacaro; *D:* Charles Band; *W:* Craig Hamann; *M:* Richard Band. VHS, Beta PAR *ℐ*

The Dolls A tropically located photographer recruits an area beauty into the fashion world with his winning smile and macho charm, only to learn native traditions forbid her to follow him.
1983 96m/C Tetchie Agbayani, Max Thayer, Carina Schally, Richard Seward; *D:* Hubert Frank. VHS, Beta $69.98 LIV, VES Woof!

Dolls A group of people is stranded during a storm in an old, creepy mansion. As the night wears on, they are attacked by hundreds of antique dolls. Tongue-in-cheek.
1987 (R) 77m/C Ian Patrick Williams, Carolyn Purdy-Gordon, Carrie Lorraine, Stephen Lee, Guy Rolfe, Bunty Bailey, Cassie Stuart, Hilary Mason; *D:* Stuart Gordon; *W:* Ed Naha; *M:* Richard Band. VHS, Beta $14.98 LIV, VES *ℐℐ½*

A Doll's House An all-star cast is featured in this original television production of Henrik Ibsen's classic play about an independent woman's quest for freedom in nineteenth-century Norway.
1959 89m/B Julie Harris, Christopher Plummer, Jason Robards Jr., Hume Cronyn, Eileen Heckart, Richard Thomas. VHS, Beta $39.95 MGM, FCT *ℐℐ½*

A Doll's House Fonda plays Nora, a subjugated 19th-century housewife who breaks free to establish herself as an individual. Based on Henrik Ibsen's classic play; some controversy regarding Fonda's interpretation of her role.
1973 (G) 98m/C Jane Fonda, Edward Fox, Trevor Howard, David Warner, Delphine Seyrig; *D:* Joseph Losey; *W:* Christopher Hampton; *M:* John Barry. Beta $9.99 STE, PSM *ℐℐℐ½*

A Doll's House A Canadian production of the Henrik Ibsen play about a Norwegian woman's search for independence.
1989 (G) 96m/C CA Claire Bloom, Anthony Hopkins, Ralph Richardson, Denholm Elliott, Anna Massey, Edith Evans; *D:* Patrick Garland. VHS, Beta $9.99 HMD *ℐℐℐ*

Dolly Dearest Strange things start happening after an American family takes over a run-down Mexican doll factory. They create a new doll called "Dolly Dearest" with deadly results. In the same tradition as the "Chucky" series.
1992 (R) 94m/C Rip Torn, Sam Bottoms, Denise Crosby; *D:* Maria Lease. VHS $92.95 VMK *ℐ½*

The Dolphin A dolphin visits a Brazilian fishing village each full moon, turns himself into a man, and casts a spell of seduction over the women. Villagers are both enchanted and angered by the dolphin-man, since his presence creates desire in local women but scares fish from the waters. In Portuguese with English subtitles.
1987 95m/C BR Carlos Alberto Riccelli, Cassia Kiss, Ney Latorraca; *D:* Walter Lima Jr.; *W:* Walter Lima Jr. VHS $79.95 FXL, ING *ℐℐ½*

Dominick & Eugene Dominick is a little slow, but he makes a fair living as a garbageman—good enough to put his brother through medical school. Both men struggle with the other's faults and weaknesses, as they learn the meaning of family and friendship. Well-acted, especially by Hulce, never melodramatic or weak.

1988 (PG-13) 96m/C Ray Liotta, Tom Hulce, Jamie Lee Curtis, Todd Graff, Bill Cobbs, David Strathairn; *D:* Robert M. Young; *W:* Alvin Sargent, Corey Blechman; *M:* Trevor Jones. VHS, Beta $19.98 ORI, FCT *ℐℐℐ*

Dominique is Dead A woman is driven to suicide by her greedy husband; now someone is trying to drive him mad. A.K.A. "Dominique" and "Avenging Spirit."
1979 (PG) 95m/C Cliff Robertson, Jean Simmons, Jenny Agutter, Simon Ward, Ron Moody; *D:* Michael Anderson Sr. VHS, Beta $9.95 PSM *ℐℐ*

Domino A beautiful woman and a mysterious guy link up for sex, murder and double-crosses. Dubbed. Tries to be arty and avant-garde, but only succeeds in being a piece of soft-core fluff.
1988 (R) 95m/C IT Brigitte Nielsen, Tomas Arana, Daniela Alzone; *D:* Ivana Massetti. VHS, Beta $89.95 LIV *ℐ*

The Domino Principle It's got nothing to do with pizza. Viet vet Hackman is a doltish convict sprung from the joint by a government organization to do some dirty work: working as a political assassin. Heavy-handed direction and lack of suspense make it less than it should be. *AKA:* The Domino Killings.
1977 (R) 97m/C Gene Hackman, Candice Bergen, Richard Widmark, Mickey Rooney, Edward Albert, Eli Wallach; *D:* Stanley Kramer; *M:* Billy Goldenberg. VHS, Beta $9.99 CCB, FOX *ℐℐ½*

Don Amigo/Stage to Chino A western double feature: The Cisco Kid and Pancho ride together again in "Don Amigo," and in "Stage to Chino," a postal inspector investigates a gang who robs rival stage lines.
194? 122m/B Duncan Renaldo, Leo Carrillo, George O'Brien, Roy Barcroft; *D:* Edward Killy. VHS, Beta $34.95 RKO, TTC *ℐℐ*

Don Daredevil Rides Again A greedy political boss tries to take over homesteaders' claims for their mineral rights. One settler adopts the identity of an ancestor (Don Daredevil), and a black mask, and becomes a frontier avenger. A 12-episode serial.
1951 180m/B Ken Curtis, Aline Towne, Roy Barcroft. VHS, Beta $29.98 REP, MLB, MED *ℐ*

The Don is Dead A violent Mafia saga wherein a love triangle interferes with Family business, resulting in gang wars. *AKA:* Beautiful But Deadly.
1973 (R) 96m/C Anthony Quinn, Frederic Forrest, Robert Forster, Al Lettieri, Ina Balin, Angel Tompkins, Charles Cioffi; *D:* Richard Fleischer; *M:* Jerry Goldsmith. VHS, Beta $59.95 MCA *ℐℐ*

Don Juan Barrymore stars as the swashbuckling Italian duke with Spanish blood who seduces a castleful of women in the 1500s. Many exciting action sequences, including classic sword fights in which Barrymore eschewed a stunt double. Great attention is also paid to the detail of the costumes and settings of the Spanish-Moor period. Noted for employing fledgling movie sound effects and music-dubbing technology, which, ironically, were responsible for eclipsing the movie's reputation. Watch for Loy as an Asian vamp and Oland as a pre-Charlie Chan Cesare Borgia.
1926 90m/B John Barrymore, Mary Astor, Willard Louis, Estelle Taylor, Helene Costello, Myrna Loy, June Marlowe, Warner Oland, Montagu Love, Hedda Hopper, Gustav von Seyffertitz; *D:* Alan Crosland. VHS $29.95 MGM, FCT *ℐℐℐ½*

Don Juan, My Love Sexy comedy finds the ghost of Don Juan given a chance, after 450 years in Purgatory, to perform a good deed and free his soul. In Spanish with English subtitles. *AKA:* Don Juan, Mi Querido Fantasma.
1990 96m/C SP Juan Luis Galiardo, Rossy de Palma, Maria Barranco, Loles Leon; *D:* Antonio Mercero; *M:* Bernardo Bonazzi. VHS $79.95 FXL, FCT *ℐℐℐ*

Don Q., Son of Zorro Zorro's son takes up his father's fight against evil and injustice. Silent sequel to the 1920 classic.
1925 111m/B Douglas Fairbanks Sr., Mary Astor. VHS, Beta $19.95 NOS, WFV, CCB *ℐℐ*

Don Quixote Miguel de Cervantes' tale of the romantic who would rather be a knight in shining armor than shining armor at night. Chaliapin stars as the knight-errant on his nightly errands, tilting at windmills and charging flocks of sheep. Certain scenes were adapted to fit the pre-WWII atmosphere, as it was filmed during the same time that the Nazis were burning books.
1935 73m/B Feodor Chaliapin, George Robey, Sidney Fox, Miles Mander, Oscar Asche, Emily Fitzroy, Wally Patch; *D:* G.W. Pabst; *W:* Paul Morand, Alexandre Arnoux; *M:* Jacques Ibert. VHS $19.95 NOS, MLB, VEC *ℐℐℐℐ*

Don Quixote The lauded, visually ravishing adaptation of the Cervantes classic, with a formal integrity inherited from Eisenstein and Dovshenko. In Russian with English subtitles.
1957 110m/B SP RU Nikolai Cherkassov, Yuri Tobubeyev; *D:* Grigori Kosintsev. VHS, Beta $34.95 FCT, AUD *ℐℐℐ½*

Don Segundo Sombra An interesting film seen through the eyes of an old gaucho, who is the mentor of a young boy growing to manhood. Based on the novel by Ricardo Guiraldes. In Spanish with English subtitles.
1969 110m/C SP Juan Carballido, Juan Carlos Gene, Soledad Silveyra, Alejandra Boero; *D:* Manuel Antin. VHS, Beta $54.95 MED, ING *ℐℐ½*

Don Winslow of the Coast Guard Serial in 13 episodes features comic-strip character Winslow as he strives to keep the waters of America safe for democracy.
1943 234m/B Don Terry, Elyse Knox; *D:* Ford Beebe, Ray Taylor. VHS, Beta $49.95 NOS, MED, VDM *ℐℐ½*

Don Winslow of the Navy Thirteen episodes centered around the evil Scorpion, who plots to attack the Pacific Coast, but is thwarted by comic-strip hero Winslow.
1943 234m/B Don Terry, Walter Sande, Anne Nagel; *D:* Ford Beebe, Ray Taylor. VHS, Beta $39.95 VYY, MED, MLB *ℐℐ½*

Dona Flor and Her Two Husbands A woman becomes a widow when her philandering husband finally expires from drink, gambling, and ladies. She remarries, but her new husband is so boring and proper that she begins fantasizing spouse number one's return. But is he only in her imagination? Based on the novel by Jorge Amado. In Portuguese with English subtitles. Remade as "Kiss Me Goodbye." *AKA:* Dona Flor e Seus Dois Maridos.
1978 106m/C BR Sonia Braga, Jose Wilker, Mauro Mendonca; *D:* Bruno Barreto. VHS, Beta $79.95 FXL, IME, ING *ℐℐℐ*

Dona Herlinda & Her Son A Mexican sex comedy about a mother who manipulates her bisexual son's two lovers (one male, one female), until all four fit together into a seamless unit. In Spanish with English subtitles. Slow, but amusing. *AKA:* Dona Herlinda y Su Hijo.

D

VIDEOHOUND'S GOLDEN MOVIE RETRIEVER • 339 ▲

1986 90m/C MX Guadalupe Del Toro, Arturo Meza, Marco Antonio Trevino, Leticia Lupersio; D: Jaime Humberto Hermosillo. **VHS, Beta** $79.95 TPV, ING, CCN 🎞️🎞️

Donde Duermen Dos...Duermen Tres
A Spanish "Mr. Mom"-flavored domestic comedy.
198? 94m/C SP Susana Gimenez, Juan Carlos Calabro. **VHS, Beta** $57.95 UNI 🎞️

Donkey Skin
A charming, all-star version of the medieval French fairy tale about a king searching for a suitable wife in a magical realm after his queen dies. In his quest for the most beautiful spouse, he learns that his daughter is that woman. She prefers Prince Charming, however. In French with English subtitles. AKA: Peau d'Ane.
1970 89m/C FR Catherine Deneuve, Jean Marais, Delphine Seyrig, Jacques Perrin; D: Jacques Demy. **VHS, Beta** $19.95 ING, SUE 🎞️🎞️🎞️

Donner Pass: The Road to Survival
Tame retelling of the western wagon-train pioneers who were forced to resort to cannibalism during a brutal snowstorm in the Rockies. The tragedy is lightly implied, keeping the film suitable for family viewing.
1984 98m/C Robert Fuller, Diane McBain, Andrew Prine, John Anderson, Michael Callan; D: James L. Conway. **VHS, Beta** $19.95 STE, VCI, HHE 🎞️🎞️

Donovan's Brain
A scientist maintains the still-living brain of a dead millionaire and begins to be controlled by its powerful force. Based on Curt Siodmak's novel.
1953 85m/B Lew Ayres, Gene Evans, Nancy Davis, Steve Brodie; D: Felix Feist. **VHS, Beta** $14.95 MGM, IME, MLB 🎞️🎞️🎞️

Donovan's Reef
Two WWII buddies meet every year on a Pacific atoll to engage in a perpetual bar-brawl, until a stuck-up Bostonian maiden appears to find her dad, a man who has fathered a brood of lovable half-casts. A rollicking, good-natured film from Ford.
1963 109m/C John Wayne, Lee Marvin, Jack Warden, Elizabeth Allan, Dorothy Lamour, Mike Mazurki, Cesar Romero; D: John Ford. **VHS, Beta** $19.95 PAR, TLF 🎞️🎞️🎞️

Don's Party
A rather dark comedy focusing on Australian Yuppie-types who decide to watch the election results on television as a group. A lot more goes on at this party, however, than talk of the returns. Sexual themes surface. Cast members turn fine performances, aided by top-notch script and direction.
1976 90m/C AU Pat Bishop, Graham Kennedy, Candy Raymond, Veronica Lang, John Hargreaves; D: Bruce Beresford; W: David Williamson. **VHS, Beta** $14.98 FCT 🎞️🎞️🎞️

Don't Answer the Phone
Deeply troubled photographer stalks and attacks the patients of a beautiful psychologist talk-show hostess. AKA: The Hollywood Strangler.
1980 (R) 94m/C James Westmoreland, Flo Gerrish, Ben Frank; D: Robert Hammer. **VHS, Beta** $19.95 MED 🎞️

Don't Be Afraid of the Dark
A young couple move into their dream house only to find that demonic little critters are residing in their basement and they want more than shelter. Made for TV with creepy scenes and eerie makeup for the monsters.
1973 74m/C Kim Darby, Jim Hutton, Barbara Anderson, William Demarest, Pedro Armendariz Jr.; D: John Newland. **VHS, Beta** $49.95 LIV 🎞️🎞️½

Don't Bother to Knock
As a mentally unstable hotel babysitter, Monroe meets a pilot (Widmark) and has a brief rendezvous with him. When the little girl she is babysitting interrupts, Monroe is furious, and later tries to murder the girl. This is one of Monroe's best dramatic roles. Bancroft's film debut as the Widmark's girlfriend.
1952 76m/B Richard Widmark, Marilyn Monroe, Anne Bancroft, Elisha Cook Jr., Jim Backus, Lurene Tuttle, Jeanne Cagney, Donna Corcoran; D: Roy Ward Baker; W: Daniel Taradash. **VHS** $14.98 FXV 🎞️🎞️½

Don't Change My World
To preserve the natural beauty of the north woods, a wildlife photographer must fight a villainous land developer and a reckless poacher. Eco-correct.
1983 (G) 89m/C Roy Tatum, Ben Jones. **VHS, Beta** $59.98 LIV 🎞️½

Don't Cry, It's Only Thunder
A young army medic who works in a mortuary in Saigon becomes involved with a group of Vietnamese orphans and a dedicated army doctor. Based on a true story.
1982 (PG) 108m/C Dennis Christopher, Susan St. James, Roger Brown, Li Lu, Thu Thuy, James Whitmore; D: Peter Werner; M: Maurice Jarre. **VHS, Beta** $59.95 COL 🎞️🎞️½

Don't Drink the Water
Based on Woody Allen's hit play, this film places an average Newark, New Jersey, family behind the Iron Curtain, where their vacation phototaking gets them accused of spying.
1969 (G) 100m/C Jackie Gleason, Estelle Parsons, Joan Delaney, Ted Bessell, Michael Constantine; D: Howard Morris. **VHS, Beta** $9.95 COL, SUE 🎞️🎞️½

Don't Go in the House
Long-dormant psychosis is brought to life by the death of a young man's mother.
1980 (R) 90m/C Dan Grimaldi, Robert Osth, Ruth Dardick; D: Joseph Ellison; M: Richard Einhorn. **VHS, Beta** $54.95 MED 🎞️

Don't Go in the Woods
Routine exercise in "don't do that" terror genre (includes warnings about going into houses, answering phones, looking into basements, opening windows, etc.). This time, four young campers are stalked by a crazed killer armed with prerequisite ax.
1981 (R) 88m/C **VHS, Beta** $59.98 VES Woof!

Don't Go Near the Water
Somewhat amusing comedy about the happenings at a Naval installation on a South Pacific tropical paradise. Clark outshines the others in his role as a frustrated officer. Based on the novel by William Brinkley.
1957 107m/C Glenn Ford, Gia Scala, Earl Holliman, Anne Francis, Keenan Wynn, Fred Clark, Eva Gabor, Russ Tamblyn; D: Charles Walters; W: Dorothy Kingsley, George Wells. **VHS** $19.98 MGM 🎞️🎞️

Don't Go to Sleep
After a fatal car crash, a young girl misses mom and dad so much she returns from the grave to take them where they can be one big happy family again. Better than most made-for-TV junk-food fright-fests, written by Keenan Wynn's son, Ned.
1982 93m/C Dennis Weaver, Valerie Harper, Robin Ignico, Kristin Cummings, Ruth Gordon, Robert Webber; D: Richard Lang; W: Ned Wynn. **VHS** $29.95 UNI 🎞️🎞️

Don't Hang Up
Handicapped New York actress Sarah (Arquette) wants to do a production of agoraphobic London writer Joe's (Suchet) play. So she calls him up to get his permission and the two begin a phone relationship that develops from business to romance.

1990 84m/C GB Rosanna Arquette, David Suchet. **VHS** $59.95 WBF 🎞️🎞️½

Don't Look Back
A famous documentary about Bob Dylan at the beginning of his career: on the road, in performance and during private moments. From the director of "Monterey Pop."
1967 95m/B Bob Dylan, Joan Baez, Donovan; D: D.A. Pennebaker. **VHS, Beta** $19.98 WRV, MVD, PAR 🎞️🎞️🎞️

Don't Look Back: The Story of Leroy "Satchel" Paige
Drama of the legendary baseball pitcher who helped break down racial barriers, based on his autobiography. Made-for-TV fare. Gossett hits a home run in the lead, but the overall effort is a ground-rule double.
1981 98m/C Louis Gossett Jr., Beverly Todd, Cleavon Little, Clifton Davis, John Beradino, Jim Davis, Ossie Davis, Hal Williams; D: George C. Scott, Richard A. Colla. **VHS** ABC 🎞️🎞️½

Don't Look in the Attic
A couple finds a haunted house with cows in the attic.
1981 90m/C Beba Loncar, Jean-Pierre Aumont; D: Carl Ausino. **VHS, Beta** NO Woof!

Don't Look in the Basement
Things get out of hand at an isolated asylum and a pretty young nurse is caught in the middle. Straight-jacketed by a low budget.
1973 (R) 90m/C Rosie Holotik, Anne MacAdams, William Bill McGhee, Rhea MacAdams, Gene Ross, Betty Chandler, Camilla Carr, Robert Dracup, Jessie Kirby, Hugh Feagin, Harryete Warren, Jessie Lee Fulton, Michael Harvey; D: S.F. Brownrigg. **VHS, Beta** $14.98 MPI 🎞️½

Don't Look Now
A psychological thriller about a couple's trip to Venice after their child drowns. Notable for a steamy love scene and a chilling climax. Based on the novel by Daphne Du Maurier.
1973 (R) 110m/C Donald Sutherland, Julie Christie, Hilary Mason; D: Nicolas Roeg; W: Chris Bryant, Allan Scott; M: Pino Donaggio. **VHS, Beta** $49.95 PAR 🎞️🎞️🎞️

Don't Mess with My Sister!
A married, New York junkyard worker falls in love with a belly dancer he meets at a party. The affair leads to murder and subsequently, revenge. An interesting, offbeat film from the director of "I Spit on Your Grave."
1985 90m/C Joe Perce, Jeannine Lemay, Jack Gurci, Peter Sapienza, Laura Lanfranchi; D: Mier Zarchi. **VHS, Beta** NO 🎞️½

Don't Open the Door!
A young woman is terrorized by a killer located inside her house.
1974 (PG) 90m/C Susan Bracken, Gene Ross, Jim Harrell; D: S.F. Brownrigg. **VHS, Beta** $24.95 GEM Woof!

Don't Open Till Christmas
A weirdo murders various Santa Clauses in assorted gory ways. Best to take this one back to the department store.
1984 86m/C GB Edmund Purdom, Caroline Munro, Alan Lake, Belinda Mayne, Gerry Sundquist, Mark Jones; D: Edmund Purdom. **VHS, Beta** $69.98 LIV, VES Woof!

Don't Raise the Bridge, Lower the River
After his wife leaves him, an American with crazy, get-rich-quick schemes turns his wife's ancestral English home into a Chinese discotheque. Domestic farce that comes and goes; if mad for Lewis, rent "The Nutty Professor."
1968 (G) 99m/C Jerry Lewis, Terry-Thomas, Jacqueline Pearce; D: Jerry Paris. **VHS, Beta** $59.95 COL 🎞️🎞️

Don't Shove/Two Gun Gussie
Two early Harold Lloyd shorts feature the comedian's embryonic comic style as a young fellow impressing his date at a skating rink ("Don't

Shove") and a city slicker out West ("Two Gun Gussie"). Silent with piano scores.
1919 27m/B Harold Lloyd, Bebe Daniels, Noah Young, Snub Pollard. VHS, Beta $19.95 CCB *Woof!*

Don't Tell Her It's Me Guttenberg is determined to win the heart of an attractive writer. With the assistance of his sister, he works to become a dream man. Clever premise, promising cast, lame comedy. From the novel by Sarah Bird. *AKA:* The Boyfriend School.
1990 (PG-13) 101m/C Steve Guttenberg, Jami Gertz, Shelley Long, Kyle MacLachlan, Madchen Amick; *D:* Malcolm Mowbray; *W:* Sarah Bird; *M:* Michael Gore. VHS, Beta $92.99 HBO *Woof!*

Don't Tell Mom the Babysitter's Dead Their mother traveling abroad, the title situation leaves a houseful of teenagers with the whole summer to themselves. Eldest daughter Applegate cons her way into the high-powered business world while the metalhead son parties hardy. Many tepid comic situations, not adding up to very much.
1991 (PG-13) 105m/C Christina Applegate, Keith Coogan, Joanna Cassidy, John Getz, Josh Charles, Concetta Tomei, Eda Reiss Merin; *D:* Stephen Herek. VHS, Beta, 8mm $19.98 HBO *Woof! 1/2*

The Doolins of Oklahoma Scott is the leader of the last of the southwestern outlaw gangs, pursued by lawmen and changing times with the onset of the modern age. Fast-paced and intelligent. *AKA:* The Great Manhunt.
1949 90m/B Randolph Scott, George Macready, Louise Allbritton, John Ireland, Virginia Huston, Charles Kemper, Noah Beery Jr.; *D:* Gordon Douglas; *M:* George Duning. VHS, Beta $14.99 GKK *Woof! Woof! 1/2*

Doom Asylum Several sex kittens wander into a deserted sanatorium and meet up with the grisly beast wielding autopsy instruments. The people involved with this spoof should have been (more) committed.
1988 (R) 77m/C Patty Mullen, Ruth Collins, Kristen Davis, William Hay, Kenny L. Price, Harrison White, Dawn Alvan, Michael Rogan; *D:* Richard S. Friedman. VHS, Beta $29.95 ACA *Woof!*

Doomed at Sundown Decent Steele vehicle has the tough cowpoke as a sheriff's son known for playing practical jokes. When his father gets knifed, it's no laughing matter and he takes off after the killers. Based on a story by Fred Myton.
1937 55m/B Bob Steele, Laraine Day, Warner Richmond, Harold Daniels, David Sharpe; *D:* Sam Newfield; *W:* George Plympton. VHS $9.95 GPV, DVT *Woof! 1/2*

Doomed Caravan Hoppy and his pals lend a hand when some villains try to monopolize the wagon train business. Location shooting was done in the valleys of central California.
1941 60m/B William Boyd, Russell Hayden, Andy Clyde, Minna Gombell, Morris Ankrum, Georgia Hawkins, Trevor Bardette, Pat O'Brien; *D:* Lesley Selander. VHS $19.95 NOS *Woof! Woof! Woof!*

Doomed Love Love is hell, especially when the object of your affection happens to be deceased. A professor of literature in the throes of unrequited love decides to reunite himself with his lost love. Won awards when released in Berlin.
1983 75m/C Bill Rice; *D:* Andrew Horn. VHS $59.95 MWF, FCT *Woof! 1/2*

Doomed to Die Cargo of stolen bonds leads to a tong war and the murder of a shipping millionaire. Part of Mr. Wong series. Worth a look if only for Karloff's performance.

1940 67m/B Boris Karloff, Marjorie Reynolds, Grant Withers; *D:* William Nigh. VHS, Beta $19.95 NOS, MRV, SNC *Woof! Woof!*

Doomsday Vidor marries for wealth instead of love and, in classic fashion, finds that money doesn't buy happiness.
1928 73m/B Florence Vidor, Gary Cooper, Lawrence Grant; *D:* Rowland V. Lee. VHS $19.95 GPV *Woof! Woof! 1/2*

The Doomsday Flight Uneven made-for-television thriller. O'Brien plants an altitude-triggered bomb on a jet in an effort to blackmail the airline. Search for the bomb provides some suspenseful and well-acted moments.
1966 100m/C Jack Lord, Edmond O'Brien, Van Johnson, Jim Saxon, Katherine Crawford, Michael Sarrazin, Ed Asner, Greg Morris, Richard Carlson, Don Stewart; *D:* William A. Graham; *W:* Rod Serling. VHS, Beta $39.95 MCA *Woof! Woof!*

Doomwatch A scientist discovers a chemical company is dumping poison into local waters, deforming the inhabitants of an isolated island when they eat the catch of the day. Unsurprising.
1972 89m/C GB Ian Bannen, Judy Geeson, John Paul, Simon Oates, George Sanders; *D:* Peter Sasdy. VHS, Beta MON, SUE *Woof! Woof! 1/2*

Door to Door A made-for-cable comedy about two door-to-door salesmen who race to stay one step ahead of the law and their own company. Fairly lightweight, but it has its moments.
1984 93m/C Ron Leibman, Jane Kaczmarek, Arliss Howard, Alan Austin; *D:* Patrick Bailey. VHS, Beta $9.95 MED *Woof! Woof!*

Door to Door Maniac Criminals hold a bank president's wife hostage, unaware that the husband was looking to get rid of her in favor of another woman. Cash's screen debut. Aside from the strange cast ensemble, not particularly worth seeing. *AKA:* Five Minutes to Live.
1961 80m/B Johnny Cash, Ron Howard, Vic Tayback, Donald Woods, Cay Forrester, Pamela Mason; *D:* Bill Karn. VHS, Beta $19.95 VDM, AOV *Woof! 1/2*

Door with the Seven Locks Bizarre Edgar Wallace story of man who leaves seven keys to a treasure vault in his will. Remake of "Chamber of Horrors."
1962 96m/C GE Eddi Arent, Heinz Drache, Klaus Kinski, Ady Berber; *D:* Alfred Vohrer. VHS $16.95 SNC *Woof! Woof!*

The Doors Stone approached Jim Morrison with an early incarnation of this docudrama, but it's hard to believe even the Lizard King could play himself with any more convincing abandon than Kilmer, in a great performance. Trouble is, the story—one of drugs, abuse, and abject self-indulgence—grows tiresome, and the audience, with the exception of die-hard fans, may lose sight of any sympathy they might have had. Ryan is forgettable as Morrison's hippie-chick wife, MacLachlan sports a funny wig and dabbles on the keyboards as Ray Manszarek, and Quinlan is atypically cast as a sado-masochistic journalist paramour. Based on "Riders on the Storm" by John Densmore.
1991 (R) 138m/C Val Kilmer, Meg Ryan, Kevin Dillon, Kyle MacLachlan, Frank Whaley, Michael Madsen, Kathleen Quinlan, Crispin Glover, Josh Evans, John Densmore, William Jordan, Mimi Rogers, Paul Williams, Bill Graham, Billy Vera, William Kunstler, Wes Studi, Costas Mandylor, Billy Idol, Michael Wincott, Dennis Burkley; *D:* Oliver Stone; *W:* Oliver Stone, Ralph Thomas, Randy Johnson, J. Randall Johnson. VHS, 8mm $14.98 COL, FCT, VES *Woof! Woof! 1/2*

The Doors: Soft Parade, a Retrospective The Doors' final TV appearance in 1969 forms the centerpiece of this concert-video tie-in to the Oliver Stone film. Fans should a-Door previously unreleased backstage interviews and a notable version of "The Unknown Soldier."
1969 50m/C *D:* Ray Manzarek. VHS $19.95 MCA *Woof! Woof! 1/2*

Dope Mania A potpourri of anti-drug propaganda spanning from the '30's to the '60's, campily detailing the degradation thought to result instantly from pot and cocaine.
1986 60m/C VHS, Beta $29.95 RHI *Woof! Woof!*

Doppelganger: The Evil Within Holly Gooding (Barrymore) seems like such a nice girl—until the police suspect her of the brutal murder of her mother. Her new friend Patrick (Newbern) begins to see another side to the vulnerable Holly—a seductress capable of doing anything to get what she wants.
1990 (R) 105m/C Drew Barrymore, George Newbern, Dennis Christopher, Sally Kellerman, Leslie Hope; *D:* Avi Nesher; *W:* Avi Nesher. VHS $89.98 FXV *Woof! Woof!*

Dorf and the First Games of Mount Olympus The video comedy character bungles his way through a parody of the ancient Greek Olympics.
1987 30m/C Tim Conway; *D:* Lang Elliott. VHS, Beta $29.95 JTC *Woof! Woof!*

Dorf Goes Auto Racing Wacky "Doozle Dorf" shows us mortals how to race cars through Europe.
1989 30m/C Tim Conway. VHS, Beta $29.95 PMR *Woof! Woof!*

Dorian Gray Modern-day version of the famous tale by Oscar Wilde about an ageless young man whose portrait reflects the ravages of time and a life of debauchery. More sex, less acting with Berger in lead. Not nearly as good as the original version, "The Picture of Dorian Gray." *AKA:* The Secret of Dorian Gray; Il Dio Chiamato a Dorian; Das Bildness des Dorian Gray.
1970 (R) 92m/C GE IT Richard Todd, Helmut Berger, Herbert Lom; *D:* Massimo Dallamano. VHS $14.98 REP, FCT *Woof! 1/2*

Dorm That Dripped Blood Five college students volunteer to close the dorm during their Christmas vacation. A series of grisly and barbaric incidents eliminates the youngsters one by one. As the terror mounts, the remaining students slowly realize that they are up against a terrifyingly real psychopathic killer. Merry Christmas.
1982 (R) 84m/C Laura Lopinski, Stephen Sachs, Pamela Holland; *D:* Stephen Carpenter, Jeffrey Obrow. VHS, Beta $59.95 MED *Woof!*

Dos Chicas de Revista A former film actor now recovering from a mental breakdown and drug addiction comes across a book written about him when he was bigtime. He meets the girl who wrote the book and they enjoy a happy relationship. In Spanish.
19?? 90m/C SP Lina Morgan, Manolo Gomez Bur. VHS, Beta $19.95 MED *Woof! 1/2*

Dos Cruces en Danger Pass Charming fairy tale about a widowed king in search of a beautiful wife. Gorgeous color production. Also known as "Peau D'Ane." In French with English subtitles.
1971 0090m/C FR Catherine Deneuve, Jacques Perrin, Jean Marais, Delphine Seyrig; *D:* Jacques Demy. VHS, Beta $29.98 SUE *Woof! Woof! Woof!*

Dos Esposas en Mi Cama A man finds himself in trouble when he must choose between his present wife and the wife he thought was dead. In Spanish.
1987 90m/C *MX* Joaquin Cordero, Teresa Velasquez, Hector Lechuga, Roxana Bellini. **VHS, Beta** $57.95 *MAD* ✗✗

Dos Postolas Gemelas Two teenage girls sing in the old West. In Spanish.
1965 84m/C *MX* Pili & Mili, Sean Flynn, Jorge Rigaud, Beni Deus. **VHS, Beta** $49.95 *MAD* ✗✗

Double Agents Two double agents are sent on a rendezvous to exchange vital government secrets. Dubbed in English. *AKA:* La Nuit Des Espions; Night Encounter.
1959 81m/B *FR* Marina Vlady, Robert Hossein. **VHS, Beta** $24.95 *VYY* ✗

Double Cross Tank Polling (Connery), a British journalist, uses the secrets of an ex-hooker (Donohoe) to get back at a corrupt politician who ruined Polling's life five years earlier. Lots of action and a few graphic murders in this thriller.
1992 (R) 96m/C Amanda Donohoe, Peter Wyngarde, Jason Connery; *D:* James Marcus. **VHS** $79.95 *MNC, VTR* ✗

Double-Crossed In 1984 Barry Seal agrees to inform on Colombia's Medellin Cartel and its links to the Sandanista government of Nicaragua in exchange for leniency on drug-smuggling charges. Little does he know that the personal consequences will turn deadly when his cover is blown and the government double-crosses him. Hopper's hyped-up performance as drug smuggler turned DEA informant Seal showcases this true-crime tale.
1991 111m/C Dennis Hopper, Robert Carradine, G.W. Bailey, Adrienne Barbeau. **VHS** $79.99 *WAR* ✗✗½

Double Deal An honest man and a gangster are rivals in love. The gangster robs a jewelry store and tries to pin the crime on the good guy. This is a movie with a moral so don't expect him to get away with it.
1939 60m/C Monte Hawley, Jeni Le Gon, Edward Thompson, Florence O'Brien; *D:* Arthur Dreifuss. **VHS** $34.95 *FCT* ✗✗

Double Deal Murder, mayhem, and industrial espionage come into play as parties fight over an oil field.
1950 65m/B Marie Windsor, Richard Denning, Taylor Holmes; *D:* Abby Berlin. **VHS, Beta** $24.95 *DVT* ✗½

Double Deal Unfaithful woman and her lover plot to steal priceless opal from hubby. Lifeless and silly.
1984 90m/C Louis Jourdan, Angela Punch McGregor; *D:* Brian Kavanagh. **VHS, Beta** NO ✗½

Double Dynamite A bank teller is at a loss when his racetrack winnings are confused with the cash lifted from his bank during a robbery. Forgettable, forgotten shambles. Originally filmed in 1948. *AKA:* It's Only Money.
1951 80m/B Frank Sinatra, Jane Russell, Groucho Marx, Don McGuire, Howard Freeman, Harry Hayden, Nestor Paiva, Lou Nova, Joe Devlin; *D:* Irving Cummings; *W:* Melville Shavelson. **VHS, Beta** $19.98 *RKO, TTC* ✗½

Double Edge The Palestinian-Israeli conflict is the focus of this drama about an ambitious reporter (Dunaway). On her first foreign assignment, New Yorker Faye Milano finds herself way out of her depth when she covers a colleague's beat in Jerusalem. Unable to remain a detached observer, Faye instead becomes an active participant, alternating between her affair with an Israeli reserves officer and her friendship with a

family of Palestinian intifada leaders. Dunaway and Kollek are unfortunately stiff in their performances but the location (Israel and the West Bank) is interesting and the story surprisingly balanced.
1992 (PG-13) 85m/C *IS* Faye Dunaway, Amos Kollek, Muhamad Bakri, Shmuel Shilo, Makram Khouri, Michael Schneider, Anat Atzman, Ann Belkin; *D:* Amos Kollek; *W:* Amos Kollek. **VHS, Beta** $89.99 *WAR* ✗✗

Double Exposure A young photographer's violent nightmares become the next day's headlines. Unsurprising vision.
1982 (R) 95m/C Michael Callan, James Stacy, Joanna Pettet, Cleavon Little, Pamela Hensley, Seymour Cassel; *D:* William B. Hillman. **VHS, Beta** $59.98 *VES* ✗✗

Double Exposure A possessive husband discovers his wife's infidelity and decides to get revenge, only his plan doesn't work out as he intends.
1993 (R) 93m/C Ron Perlman, Ian Buchanan, Jennifer Gatti, William R. Moses, James McEachin, Dedee Pfeiffer; *D:* Claudia Hoover; *W:* Christine Colfer, Bridget Hoffman, Claudia Hoover. **VHS** $92.95 *PSM* ✗½

Double Exposure: The Story of Margaret Bourke-White Beautifully shot but slow biography of a woman who became a well-known professional photographer for "Life" magazine during the 1930s and 1940s, as well as the first official female photojournalist of WWII. Made for cable television. *AKA:* Margaret Bourke-White.
1989 105m/C Farrah Fawcett, Frederic Forrest, Mitchell Ryan, David Huddleston, Jay Patterson, Ken Marshall; *D:* Lawrence Schiller. **VHS** $9.98 *TTC* ✗✗½

Double Face A wealthy industrialist kills his lesbian wife with a car bomb, but she seems to haunt him through pornographic films.
1970 84m/C Klaus Kinski, Annabella Incontrera. **VHS, Beta** $49.95 *UNI* ✗½

Double Identity Former college professor turned criminal Mancuso moves to a corn patch called New Hope in hopes of returning to the straight and narrow. He finds a good woman to stand by him, but, alas, crime, like smoking, is easier to start than to quit. Much intrigue and deceit.
1989 (PG-13) 95m/C *CA FR* Nick Mancuso, Leah K. Pinsent, Patrick Bauchau, Anne LeTourneau, Jacques Godin; *D:* Yves Boisset. **VHS** $29.95 *MNC* ✗✗½

Double Impact Van Damme plays twins re-united in Hong Kong to avenge their parents' murder by local bad guys, but this lunkhead kick-em-up doesn't even take advantage of that gimmick; the basic story would have been exactly the same with just one Jean-Claude. Lots of profane dialogue and some gratuitous nudity for the kiddies.
1991 (R) 107m/C Jean-Claude Van Damme, Cory Everson, Geoffrey Lewis; *D:* Sheldon Lettich; *W:* Jean-Claude Van Damme, Sheldon Lettich. **VHS, Beta, 8mm** $19.95 *COL, CCB* ✗½

Double Indemnity The classic seedy story of an insurance agent seduced by a deadly woman into killing her husband so they can collect together from his company. Terrific, influential film noir, the best of its kind. Based on the James M. Cain novel.
1944 107m/B Fred MacMurray, Barbara Stanwyck, Edward G. Robinson, Tom Powers, Porter Hall, Jean Heather, Byron Barr, Fortuna Bonavona; *D:* Billy Wilder; *W:* Raymond Chandler, Billy Wilder; *M:* Miklos Rozsa. **VHS, Beta** $19.95 *MCA, FCT* ✗✗✗✗

Double Jeopardy Boxleitner stars as a married man who risks his family and life when his sexy ex-lover returns to town. She easily involves him in deception—and murder. A cake-walk for Ward as the femme fatale. Made for cable television.
1992 (R) 101m/C Bruce Boxleitner, Rachel Ward, Sela Ward, Sally Kirkland; *D:* Lawrence Schiller. **VHS, Beta** $89.98 *FXV, PMS* ✗✗

A Double Life Colman plays a Shakespearean actor in trouble when the characters he plays begin to seep into his personal life and take over. Things begin to look really bad when he is cast in the role of the cursed Othello. Colman won an Oscar for this difficult role, and the moody musical score garnered another for Rozsa.
1947 103m/B Ronald Colman, Shelley Winters, Signe Hasso, Edmond O'Brien, Ray Collins, Millard Mitchell; *D:* George Cukor; *W:* Ruth Gordon, Garson Kanin; *M:* Miklos Rozsa. Academy Awards '47: Best Actor (Colman), Best Score; Nominations: Best Director (Cukor), Best Original Screenplay; Golden Globe Awards '48: Best Actor—Drama (Colman). **VHS** $14.98 *REP, FCT, BTV* ✗✗✗

The Double Life of Veronique They say everyone has a twin, but this is ridiculous. Two women—Polish Veronika and French Veronique—are born on the same day in different countries, share a singing talent, a cardiac ailment, and, although the two never meet, a strange awareness of each other. Jacob is unforgettable as the two women, and director Krzysztof creates some spellbinding scenes but the viewer has to be willing to forgo plot for atmosphere. *AKA:* La Double Vie de Veronique.
1991 (R) 96m/C *FR PL* Irene Jacob, Phillipe Volter, Sandrine Dumas, Aleksander Bardini, Louis Ducreux, Claude Duneton, Halina Gryglaszewska, Kalina Jedrusik; *D:* Krzysztof Kieslowski; *W:* Krzysztof Kieslowski, Krzysztof Piesiewicz. **VHS, Beta** *PAR* ✗✗

The Double McGuffin A plot of international intrigue is uncovered by teenagers—a la the Hardy Boys—when a prime minister and her security guard pay a visit to a small Virginia community. They're not believed, though. Action-packed from the makers of Benji. Dogs do not figure prominently here.
1979 (PG) 100m/C Ernest Borgnine, George Kennedy, Elke Sommer, Ed "Too Tall" Jones, Lisa Whelchel, Vincent Spano; *D:* Joe Camp; *V:* Orson Welles. **VHS, Beta** $69.95 *VES* ✗✗

The Double Negative A photojournalist pursues his wife's killer in a confusing story. Based on Ross MacDonald's "The Three Roads." *AKA:* Deadly Companion.
1980 96m/C *CA* Michael Sarrazin, Susan Clark, Anthony Perkins, Howard Duff, Kate Reid, Al Waxman, Elizabeth Shepherd, John Candy; *D:* George Bloomfield. **VHS, Beta** *BFV, VTR* ✗½

The Double O Kid Lance is a 17-year-old video game master who's interning at the Agency, a covert spy organization. Ordered to rush a package to Los Angeles, Lance discovers that a madman computer virus designer and his henchwoman desperately want what he's carrying. Aided by the prerequisite pretty girl, Lance must avoid all the hazards sent his way.
1992 (PG-13) 95m/C Corey Haim, Wallace Shawn, Brigitte Nielsen, Nicole Eggert, John Rhys-Davies, Basil Hoffman, Karen Black; *Cameos:* Anne Francis; *D:* Duncan McLachlan; *W:* Andrea Buck, Duncan McLachlan. **VHS, Beta** $89.95 *PSM* ✗✗½

Double Obsession College roommates Heather (Hemingway) and Claire (d'Abo) are inseparable friends—until Claire falls in love. Heather becomes possessive and, though the years pass, her obsession with Claire only grows. When Heather's affections turn deadly, can Claire stop her?
1993 (R) 88m/C Margaux Hemingway, Maryam D'Abo, Frederic Forrest, Scott Valentine; **D:** Eduardo Montes; **W:** Jeffrey Delman, R.J. Marx, Eduardo Montes. **VHS** COL ⨌½

Double Revenge Two men feel they have a score to settle after a bank heist gone sour leaves two people dead.
1989 90m/C Joe Dallesandro, Nancy Everhard, Leigh McCloskey, Richard Rust, Theresa Saldana; **D:** Armand Mastroianni. **VHS $9.98** REP ⨌½

Double Standard You'll be less concerned with the plot—a community discovers that a prominent judge has maintained two marriages for nearly twenty years—than with the possibility that such dim-witted myopes might actually have existed in the real world. This made-for-TV slice of bigamy is for fans of the oops-I-forgot-I'm-married genre only.
1988 95m/C Robert Foxworth, Michelle Greene, Pamela Bellwood, James Kee; **D:** Louis Rudolph. **VHS $14.95** FRH ⨌½

Double Suicide From a play by Monzarmon Chikamatsu, a tragic drama about a poor salesman in 18th century Japan who falls in love with a geisha and ruins his family and himself trying to requite the hopeless passion. Stylish with Iwashita turning in a wonderful dual performance. In Japanese with subtitles. **AKA:** Shinju Ten No Amijima.
1969 105m/B JP Kichiemon Nakamura, Shima Iwashita, Yusuke Takita, Hosei Komatsu; **D:** Masahiro Shinoda. **VHS, Beta $59.95** ING ⨌⨌⨌

Double Threat An aging sex star makes her return to the screen opposite a younger actor with whom she is having an affair. When the director wants to include nude sex scenes in the film she agrees to use a younger body-double. Then the actress discovers her lover is involved in off-screen action with the double as well. This does not please her and she decides to take a deadly revenge. An unrated version is also available.
1992 (R) 94m/C Sally Kirkland, Andrew Stevens, Lisa Shane, Richard Lynch, Anthony (Tony) Franciosa, Sherrie Rose, Chick Vennera; **D:** David A. Prior. **VHS $89.95** AIP ⨌½

Double Trouble When rock star Presley falls in love with an English heiress, he winds up involved in an attempted murder. The king belts out "Long Legged Girl" while evading cops, criminals, and crying women. A B-side. Based on a story by Marc Brandell.
1967 92m/C Elvis Presley, Annette Day, John Williams, Yvonne Romain, The Wiere Brothers, Michael Murphy, Chips Rafferty; **D:** Norman Taurog; **W:** Jo Heims. **VHS, Beta $14.95** MGM ⨌⨌

Double Trouble Twin brothers—one a cop, one a jewel thief—team up to crack the case of an international jewel smuggling ring headed by a wealthy and politically well-connected businessman and his righthand man.
1991 (R) 87m/C David Paul, Peter Paul, James Doohan, Roddy McDowall, Steve Kanaly, A.J. Johnson, David Carradine; **D:** John Paragon. **VHS $89.95** COL ⨌

Double Vision Suspense thriller starring Cattrall as Caroline, a medical student who goes to London to check out the strange disappearance of her twin sister, Lisa. Assuming her identity, Caroline gets deeply involved in a kinky lifestyle that may result in

murder. Based on a short story by Mary Higgins Clark.
1992 (PG-13) 92m/C Kim Cattrall, Gale Hansen, Christopher Lee; **D:** Robert Knights. **VHS $89.98** REP ⨌⨌

Double Wedding Madcap comedy starring Powell as a wacky painter who doesn't believe in working and Loy as a workaholic dress designer. Loy has chosen a fiance for her younger sister, Irene, to marry, but Irene has plans of her own. When Irene and her beau meet bohemian Powell, the fun really begins. Script suffers slightly from too much slapstick and not enough wit, although the stars (in their seventh outing as a duo) play it well. Based on the play "Great Love" by Ferenc Molnar.
1937 86m/B William Powell, Myrna Loy, Florence Rice, John Beal, Jessie Ralph, Edgar Kennedy, Sidney Toler, Mary Gordon; **D:** Richard Thorpe; **W:** Jo Swerling. **VHS $19.98** MGM ⨌⨌⨌

Doubting Thomas Rogers' last film, which was in theatres when he was killed in a plane crash. Silly story of a husband and his doubts about his wife and her amateur-acting career. The show goes on in spite of his doubts, her forgotten lines, and wardrobe goofs. Remake of 1922's silent film "The Torch Bearers."
1935 78m/B Will Rogers, Billie Burke, Alison Skipworth, Sterling Holloway; **D:** David Butler. **VHS $19.98** FOX, FCT ⨌⨌½

Doughboys Keaton's second talkie is a so-so comedy about a rich man who mistakenly enlists in the Army during WWI. He manages to bumble his way through basic training and win the heart of a pretty girl. There are a few bright moments, particularly a musical number between Keaton and "Ukulele Ike" Edwards. **AKA:** Forward March.
1930 80m/B Buster Keaton, Cliff Edwards, Edward Brophy, Sally Eilers, Victor Potel, Arnold Korff, Frank Mayo; **D:** Edward Sedgwick. **VHS $19.98** MGM ⨌⨌½

Doughnuts & Society Two elderly ladies who run a coffee shop suddenly strike it rich and find that life among the bluebloods is not all it's cracked up to be. No sprinkles.
1936 70m/B Louise Fazenda, Maude Eburne, Eddie Nugent, Ann Rutherford, Hedda Hopper, Franklin Pangborn. **VHS, Beta $24.95** VYY ⨌½

The Dove A hilarious short spoof of the Ingmar Bergman films "Wild Strawberries," "The Seventh Seal," and "The Silence." English sub-titles.
1968 15m/B Madeline Kahn; **M:** John Barry. **VHS, Beta** PYR ⨌⨌⨌

The Dove The true story of a 16-year-old's adventures as he sails around the world in a 23-foot sloop. The trip took him five years and along the way he falls in love with a girl who follows him to exotic locales. Photography and scenery are magnificent.
1974 (PG-13) 105m/C Joseph Bottoms, Deborah Raffin, Dabney Coleman, Peter Gwynne; **D:** Charles Jarrott. **VHS, Beta $14.95** PAR, BMV ⨌⨌½

Down Among the Z Men Enlisted man helps a girl save an atomic formula from spies. Funny in spots but weighed down by musical numbers from a female entourage. From the pre-Monty Python comedy troupe "The Goons."
1952 71m/B GB Peter Sellers, Spike Milligan, Harry Secombe, Michael Bentine, Carole Carr; **D:** Maclean Rogers. **VHS, Beta** NO ⨌⨌

Down & Dirty A scathing Italian satire about a modern Roman family steeped in petty crime, incest, murder, adultery, drugs, and arson. In Italian with English subtitles. **AKA:** Brutti, Sporchi, e Cattivi.
1976 115m/C IT Nino Manfredi, Francesco Anniballi, Maria Bosco; **D:** Ettore Scola; **W:** Ettore Scola. **VHS, Beta $59.94** MED, ING ⨌⨌⨌

Down and Out in Beverly Hills A modern retelling of Jean Renoir's classic "Boudu Sauve des Eaux" with some nice star turns. A spoiled wealthy couple rescue a suicidal bum from their swimming pool. He, in turn, beds the wife, the maid and the daughter, solves the dog's identity crisis, rescues the man and his son from frustration and finds he doesn't like being a bum. A box-office hit.
1986 (R) 103m/C Nick Nolte, Bette Midler, Richard Dreyfuss, Little Richard, Tracy Nelson, Elizabeth Pena, Evan Richards, Valerie Curtin, Barry Primus, Dorothy Tristan, Alexis Arquette, Mike the Dog; **D:** Paul Mazursky; **W:** Paul Mazursky, Leon Capetanos; **M:** Andy Summers. **VHS, Beta $19.95** TOU ⨌⨌½

Down Argentine Way A lovely young woman falls in love with a suave Argentinian horse breeder. First-rate Fox musical made a star of Grable and was Miranda's first American film. ♫South American Way; Down Argentina Way; Two Dreams Met; Mama Yo Quiero; Sing to Your Senorita.
1940 90m/C Don Ameche, Betty Grable, Carmen Miranda, Charlotte Greenwood, J. Carroll Naish, Henry Stephenson, Leonid Kinskey; **D:** Irving Cummings. **VHS, Beta $19.98** FOX, MLB ⨌⨌⨌

Down by Law In Jarmusch's follow-up to his successful "Stranger than Paradise," he introduces us to three men: a pimp, an out-of-work disc jockey, and an Italian tourist. When the three break out of prison, they wander through the Louisiana swampland with some regrets about their new-found freedom. Slow-moving at times, beautifully shot throughout. Poignant and hilarious, the film is true to Jarmusch form: some will love the film's offbeat flair, and others will find it bothersome.
1986 (R) 107m/C John Lurie, Tom Waits, Roberto Benigni, Ellen Barkin, Billie Neal, Rockets Redglare, Vernel Bagneris, Nicoletta Braschi; **D:** Jim Jarmusch; **W:** Jim Jarmusch; **M:** John Lurie, Tom Waits. **VHS, Beta $79.98** FOX ⨌⨌⨌

Down Dakota Way Strange coincidence between a recent murder and a fatal cow epidemic. Rogers helps some locals bring the link to light.
1949 67m/C Roy Rogers, Dale Evans, Pat Brady, Monte Montana, Elisabeth Risdon, Byron Barr, James B. Cardwell, Roy Barcroft, Emmett Vogan; **D:** William Witney. **VHS $12.98** REP ⨌½

Down Mexico Way Two cowboys come to the aid of a Mexican town whose residents have been hoodwinked by a phony movie company. Very exciting chase on horseback, motorcycle, and in automobiles.
1941 78m/B Gene Autry, Smiley Burnette, Fay McKenzie, Duncan Renaldo, Champion; **D:** Joseph Santley. **VHS, Beta $19.95** CCB ⨌⨌

Down Texas Way One of the "Rough Riders" series. When one of the boys is accused of murdering his best friend, his two companions search for the real killer.
1942 57m/B Buck Jones, Tim McCoy, Raymond Hatton; **D:** Howard Bretherton. **VHS, Beta $9.99** NOS, VCN, TIM ⨌⨌

Down the Drain A broad-as-a-city-block farce about an unscrupulous criminal lawyer and his assortment of crazy clients. A fine first half but someone pulls the plug in the middle of the bath.

1989 (R) 90m/C Andrew Stevens, John Matuszak, Teri Copley, Joseph Campanella, Don Stroud, Stella Stevens, Jerry Mathers, Benny "The Jet" Urquidez; *D:* Robert C. Hughes. **VHS, Beta** $89.95 *COL* 🐶🐶

Down the Wyoming Trail Western hero Ritter battles some rustlers who are terrorizing farmers during the winter, while still managing to find time to warble some tunes.
1939 52m/B Tex Ritter, Horace Murphy, Mary Brodel, Bobby Lawson, Charles "Blackie" King, Bob Terry; *D:* Al Herman; *W:* Peter Dixon, Roger Merton. **VHS** $19.99 *MOV* 🐶

Down to Earth Ever-gallant lover Fairbanks overruns a mental hospital to save his sweetheart. Once inside, he's determined to show the patients that their illness is illusion, and reality's the cure. A quixotic gem from Fairbanks' pre-swashbuckling social comic days. Director Emerson's wife was the scenarist, and Victor Fleming, who went on to direct "The Wizard of Oz" and "Gone with the Wind" (to name a few), was the man behind the camera.
1917 68m/B Douglas Fairbanks Sr., Eileen Percy, Gustav von Seyffertitz, Charles P. McHugh, Charles Gerrard, William H. Keith, Ruth Allen, Fred Goodwine; *D:* John Emerson. **VHS, Beta** $24.95 *GPV, FCT* 🐶🐶🐶

Down to Earth A lackluster musical and box office flop with an impressive cast. Hayworth is the Greek goddess of dance sent to Earth on a mission to straighten out Broadway producer Parks and his play that ridicules the Greek gods. Anita Ellis dubs the singing of Hayworth. A parody of "Here Comes Mr. Jordan," remade in 1980 as "Xanadu."
1947 101m/C Rita Hayworth, Larry Parks, Marc Platt, Roland Culver, James Gleason, Edward Everett Horton, Adele Jergens, George Macready, William Frawley, James Burke, Fred F. Sears, Lynn Merrick, Myron Healey; *D:* Alexander Hall; *M:* George Duning. **VHS** $19.95 *COL, CCB* 🐶🐶

Down to the Sea in Ships Bow made her movie debut in this drama about the whalers of 19th-century Massachusetts. Highlighted by exciting action scenes of an actual whale hunt. Silent with music score and original tinted footage. *AKA:* The Last Adventurers.
1922 83m/B Marguerite Courtot, Raymond McKee, Clara Bow; *D:* Elmer Clifton. **VHS, Beta** $19.95 *NOS, CCB, GPV* 🐶🐶½

Down Twisted A young woman gets involved with a thief on the run in Mexico in this "Romancing the Stone" derivative. The muddled plot deserves such a confusing title.
1989 (R) 89m/C Carey Lowell, Charles Rocket, Trudi Dochtermann, Thom Mathews, Linda Kerridge, Courteney Cox; *D:* Albert Pyun; *W:* Albert Pyun. **VHS, Beta** $89.95 *MED* 🐶

Down Under Two gold-hungry beach boys go to Australia looking for riches, and document their adventures on film. Essentially a crudely shot, tongue-in-cheek travelogue narrated by Patrick Macnee.
1986 90m/C Don Atkinson, Donn Dunlop, Patrick Macnee. **VHS, Beta** $79.95 *VCI* 🐶

Downhill Racer An undisciplined American skier locks ski-tips with his coach and his new-found love while on his way to becoming an Olympic superstar. Character study on film. Beautiful ski and mountain photography keep it from sliding downhill.
1969 (PG) 102m/C Robert Redford, Camilla Sparv, Gene Hackman, Dabney Coleman; *D:* Michael Ritchie. **VHS, Beta** $14.95 *PAR* 🐶🐶½

Downtown Urban comedy about a naive white suburban cop who gets demoted to the roughest precinct in Philadelphia, and gains a streetwise black partner. Runs a routine beat.
1989 (R) 96m/C Anthony Edwards, Forest Whitaker, Joe Pantoliano, Penelope Ann Miller; *D:* Richard Benjamin. **VHS, Beta** $89.98 *FOX* 🐶½

D.P. A black orphan attaches to the only other black in post-WWII Germany. From a story by Kurt Vonnegut, Jr. Made for television.
1985 60m/C Stan Shaw, Rosemary Leach, Julius Gordon. **VHS** $24.95 *MON, KAR* 🐶½

Drachenfutter Powerful story dealing with a Pakistani immigrant's attempts to enter the Western world. Themes of alienation and helplessness are emphasized. Dialogues occur in 12 languages, predominantly German and Mandarin Chinese; subtitled in English. *AKA:* Dragon's Food; Dragon Chow.
1987 75m/B *GE SI* Bhasker, Ric Young, Buddy Uzzaman; *D:* Jan Schutte; *W:* Thomas Strittmatter; *M:* Claus Bantzer. **VHS, Beta** $69.95 *NYF, ING* 🐶🐶

Dracula Lugosi, in his most famous role, plays a vampire who terrorizes the countryside in his search for human blood. From Bram Stoker's novel. Although short of a masterpiece due to slow second half, deservedly rated a film classic. What would Halloween be like without this movie? Sequelled by "Dracula's Daughter."
1931 75m/B Bela Lugosi, David Manners, Dwight Frye, Helen Chandler, Edward Van Sloan; *D:* Tod Browning. **VHS, Beta** $14.95 *MCA, TLF, HMV* 🐶🐶🐶

Dracula Count on squinty-eyed Palance to shine as the Transylvanian vampire who must quench his thirst for human blood. A made-for-television adaptation of the Bram Stoker novel that really flies.
1973 105m/C Jack Palance, Simon Ward, Fiona Lewis, Nigel Davenport; *D:* Dan Curtis. **VHS, Beta** $29.95 *LIV* 🐶🐶½

Dracula Langella recreates his Broadway role as the count who needs human blood for nourishment. Notable for its portrayal of Dracula as a romantic and tragic figure in history. Overlooked since the vampire spoof "Love at First Bite" came out at the same time.
1979 (R) 109m/C Frank Langella, Laurence Olivier, Kate Nelligan, Donald Pleasence; *D:* John Badham; *W:* W.D. Richter; *M:* John Williams. **VHS, Beta** $19.95 *MCA* 🐶🐶½

Dracula: A Cinematic Scrapbook A look at the blood-sucking monster in both film and legend, featuring rare film trailers and interviews with actors such as Bela Lugosi, Christopher Lee, and Lon Chaney, Jr. In color and B&W.
1991 60m/C *D:* Ted Newsom; *W:* Ted Newsom. **VHS, Beta** $9.95 *RHI, FCT* 🐶🐶½

Dracula & Son Dracula spoof in which the count fathers a son who prefers girls and football to blood. Poor English dubbing and choppy ending drive a stake through the heart. *AKA:* Dracula Pere et Fils.
1976 (PG) 88m/C *FR* Christopher Lee, Bernard Menez, Marie Breillat; *D:* Edouard Molinaro; *M:* Vladimir Cosma. **VHS, Beta** $9.95 *GKK* 🐶

Dracula Blows His Cool Three voluptuous models and their photographer restore an ancient castle and open a disco in it. The vampire lurking about the castle welcomes the party with his fangs.
1982 (R) 91m/C John Garco, Betty Verges; *D:* Carlo Ombra; *W:* Carlo Ombra. **VHS, Beta** *MED* 🐶

Dracula/Garden of Eden The abridged version of the chilling vampire film "Nosferatu" is coupled with "The Garden of Eden," in which Tini Le Brun meets her Prince Charming while vacationing with her Baroness friend. Silent.
1928 52m/B Max Schreck, Alexander Granach, Corrine Griffith, Charles Ray, Louise Dresser. **VHS, Beta** $19.95 *CCB* 🐶🐶

Dracula Has Risen from the Grave Lee's Dracula is foiled by the local priest before he can drain the blood from innocent villagers. Effectively gory. One of the Hammer series of Dracula films followed by "Taste the Blood of Dracula."
1968 (G) 92m/C *GB* Christopher Lee, Rupert Davies, Veronica Carlson, Barbara Ewing, Barry Andrews, Michael Ripper; *D:* Freddie Francis. **VHS** $19.98 *WAR* 🐶🐶½

Dracula Rising A modern-day art historian (Travis) turns out to have been a witch, burned at the stake, in a past life. She was also the blood-drinking Count's lost love. Now Dracula's a monk and when he sees this reincarnated beauty is he going to be able to keep his hands—er, fangs—off her?
1993 (R) ?m/C Christopher Atkins, Stacy Travis; *D:* Fred Gallo. **VHS** $89.98 *NHO* 🐶🐶½

Dracula (Spanish Version) Filmed at the same time as the Bela Lugosi version of "Dracula," using the same sets and the same scripts, only in Spanish. Thought to be more visually appealing and more terrifying than the English-language counterpart. The only thing it's missing is a presence like Lugosi. Based on the novel by Bram Stoker.
1931 104m/B Carlos Villarias, Lupita Tova, Eduardo Arozamena, Pablo Alvarez Rubio, Barry Norton, Carmen Guerrero; *D:* George Melford; *W:* Garrett Fort. **VHS** $14.98 *MCA* 🐶🐶½

Dracula Sucks A soft-core edit of a hardcore sex parody about Dracula snacking on the usual bevy of screaming quasi-virgins.
1979 (R) 90m/C James Gillis, Reggie Nalder, Annette Haven, Kay Parker, Serena, Seka, John Leslie; *D:* Philip Marshak. **VHS, Beta** *UNI, OM* 🐶

Dracula: Up in Harlem When the Prince of Darkness gets together with the people of the night, the Pentagon rolls out the heavy metal. This may suck your brain out.
1983 90m/C **VHS, Beta** *NO Woof!*

Dracula vs. Frankenstein An alien reanimates Earth's most infamous monsters in a bid to take over the planet. Rennie's last role. Also on video as, "Assignment: Terror."
1969 91m/C *IT GE SP* Michael Rennie, Paul Naschy, Karin Dor, Patty Shepard; *D:* Hugo Fregonese, Tulio Demicheli; *W:* Paul Naschy. **VHS** $29.95 *UAV* 🐶

Dracula vs. Frankenstein The Count makes a deal with a shady doctor to keep him in blood. Vampire spoof that's very bad but fun. Last film for both Chaney and Naish. Features a cameo by genre maven Forrest J. Ackerman. *AKA:* Blood of Frankenstein; They're Coming to Get You; Dracula Contra Frankenstein; The Revenge of Dracula.
1971 (R) 90m/C *SP* J. Carroll Naish, Lon Chaney Jr., Regina Carrol, Russ Tamblyn, Jim Davis, Anthony Eisley, Zandor Vorkov, John Bloom, Angelo Rossitto; *Cameos:* Forrest J. Ackerman; *D:* Al Adamson. **VHS** *NO Woof!*

Dracula's Daughter Count Dracula's daughter, Countess Marya Zaleska, heads to London supposedly to find the cure to a mysterious illness. Instead she finds she has a taste for human blood, especially female blood. She also finds a man, falls in love, and tries to keep him by casting a spell on him. A

D

good script and cast keep this sequel to Bela Lugosi's "Dracula" entertaining.
1936 71m/B Gloria Holden, Otto Kruger, Marguerite Churchill, Irving Pichel, Edward Van Sloan, Nan Grey, Hedda Hopper; **D:** Lambert Hillyer. VHS **$14.98** MCA ♂♂♂

Dracula's Great Love Four travellers end up in Dracula's castle for the night, where the horny Count takes a liking to one of the women. Left out in the sun too long. **AKA:** Gran Amore del Conde Dracula; Count Dracula's Great Love; Dracula's Virgin Lovers.
1972 (R) 96m/C SP Paul Naschy, Charo Soriano; **D:** Javier Aguirre. VHS, Beta **$59.95** SNC, MPI Woof!

Dracula's Last Rites Blood-curdling tale of a sheriff and a mortician in a small town who are up to no good. Technically inept: film equipment can be spotted throughout. Don't stick your neck out for this one. **AKA:** Last Rites.
1979 (R) 86m/C Patricia Lee Hammond, Gerald Fielding, Victor Jorge; **D:** Domonic Paris. VHS, Beta **$14.95** MGM, CAN, FCT Woof!

Dracula's Widow Countess Dracula, missing her hubby and desperately in need of a substitute, picks innocent Raymond as her victim. His girlfriend and a cynical cop fight to save his soul from the Countess' damnation. Directed by the nephew of Frances Ford Coppola.
1988 (R) 85m/C Sylvia Kristel, Josef Sommer, Lenny Von Dohlen; **D:** Christopher Coppola. VHS, Beta **$14.99** HBO ♂♂

Dragnet Sgt. Joe Friday and Officer Frank Smith try to solve a mob slaying but have a rough time. Alexander plays the sidekick in "Dragnet" pre-Morgan days. Just the facts: feature version of the TV show that's suspenseful and well-acted.
1954 88m/C Jack Webb, Ben Alexander, Richard Boone, Ann Robinson; **D:** Jack Webb. VHS, Beta **$14.95** MCA ♂♂½

Dragnet Detectives Joe Friday and Frank Smith make the streets of Los Angeles safe in this police series which ran from 1951-1959. Two episodes per tape.
1952 55m/C Jack Webb, Ben Alexander. VHS **$19.99** MOV, MRV ♂♂½

Dragnet Semi-parody of the vintage '60s television cop show. Sgt. Joe Friday's straight-laced nephew and his sloppy partner take on the seamy crime life of Los Angeles. Neither Aykroyd nor Hanks can save this big-budget but lackluster spoof that's full of holes.
1987 (PG-13) 106m/C Dan Aykroyd, Tom Hanks, Christopher Plummer, Harry Morgan, Elizabeth Ashley, Dabney Coleman; **D:** Tom Mankiewicz; **W:** Dan Aykroyd, Tom Mankiewicz, Alan Zweibel. VHS, Beta **$14.95** MCA ♂♂

Dragon Force Korean martial artists fend off Japanese invaders in the 1930s.
1982 101m/C Kangjo Lee; **D:** Key-Nam Nam. VHS, Beta CNG ♂½

Dragon Princess When the king of karate and his dragon princess confront the blind master of the bloody blades, sparks fly.
197? 90m/C Sonny Chiba, Sue Shiomi. VHS, Beta NO ♂

The Dragon Returns A young man desperately kicks and chops to save the woman he loves from slave traders.
19?? 90m/C Bruce Le, Meng Fei, Lo Lieh. VHS, Beta OCE ♂

Dragon Seed The lives of the residents of a small Chinese village are turned upside down when the Japanese invade it. Based on the Pearl S. Buck novel. Lengthy and occa-

sionally tedious, though generally well-made with heart-felt attempts to create Oriental characters, without having Asians in the cast.
1944 145m/B Katharine Hepburn, Walter Huston, Agnes Moorehead, Akim Tamiroff, Hurd Hatfield, J. Carroll Naish, Henry Travers, Turhan Bey, Aline MacMahon; **D:** Jack Conway. VHS, Beta **$19.98** MGM, FCT ♂♂½

Dragon: The Bruce Lee Story Entertaining, inspiring account of the life of Chinese-American martial-arts legend Bruce Lee. Jason Scott Lee (no relation) is great as the talented artist, exuding his joy of life and gentle spirit, before his mysterious brain disorder death at the age of 32. Ironically, this release coincided with son Brandon's accidental death on a movie set. The martial arts sequences in "Dragon" are extraordinary, but there's also romance as Lee meets and marries his wife (Holly, who acquits herself well). Based on the book "Bruce Lee: The Man Only I Knew" by his widow, Linda Lee Caldwell.
1993 (PG-13) 121m/C Jason Scott Lee, Lauren Holly, Robert Wagner, Michael Learned, Nancy Kwan, Kay Tong Lim, Sterling Macer, Ric Young, Sven Ole-Thorsen; **D:** Rob Cohen; **W:** Edward Khmara, John Raffo, Rob Cohen; **M:** Randy Edelman. VHS **$19.98** MCA, BTV, FCT ♂♂♂

Dragon the Odds A man named Mo masters Kung Fu "maniac style" in order to repossess the gymnasium that was willed to him.
198? 90m/C VHS, Beta **$39.95** TWE ♂

Dragon vs. Needles of Death It's a battle to the finish against the unstoppable deadly needles in this Kung-Fu adventure.
1982 86m/C Don Chien, Wong Ting. VHS, Beta FOX ♂

Dragonard Slaves on a West Indies island rebel against their cruel masters.
1988 (R) 93m/C Eartha Kitt, Oliver Reed, Annabel Schofield, Patrick Warburton; **D:** Gerard Kikione; **W:** R.J. Marx. VHS, Beta **$79.95** WAR ♂½

Dragonfight Corporations rule the world and vie for supremacy through gladiator combat in this action-adventure saga set in the near future. Fights are to the death and when the current champ refuses a new challenger the corporate honchos decide to provoke him into battle by having the challenger mow down innocent bystanders. Several execs also decide the slaughter has to stop but they may be the next targets.
1992 (R) 84m/C Robert Z'Dar, Michael Pare, Paul Coufos, Charles Napier, James Hong, Alexa Hamilton, Fawna MacLaren. VHS, Beta **$89.99** WAR ♂½

Dragonfly Squadron Korean war drama about pilots and their romantic problems. Never gets off the ground.
1954 82m/C John Hodiak, Barbara Britton, Bruce (Herman Brix) Bennett, Jess Barker; **D:** Lesley Selander. VHS NO ♂♂

Dragon's Claw A young man's parents are murdered, and he trains in shaolin skills in order to exact revenge.
198? 90m/C Jimmy Liu, Hwang Cheng Li; **D:** Joseph Kuo. VHS, Beta **$59.95** GEM ♂

The Dragon's Showdown After witnessing the brutal decapitations of his parents, a young man learns Kung-Fu to avenge their deaths.
1983 90m/C Dragon Lee; **D:** Godfrey Ho. VHS, Beta **$59.95** GEM ♂

Dragonslayer A sorcerer's apprentice suddenly finds himself the only person who can save the kingdom from a horrible, fire-breathing dragon. Extreme violence but won-

derful special effects, smart writing, and a funny performance by Richardson.
1981 (PG) 110m/C Peter MacNicol, Caitlin Clarke, Ralph Richardson, John Hallam, Albert Salmi, Chloe Salaman; **D:** Matthew Robbins; **W:** Matthew Robbins. VHS, Beta **$19.95** PAR, COL ♂♂

Dragonworld Five-year-old Johnny McGowan is sent to Scotland to live with grandfather. A wish for a friend has Johnny mysteriously awakening a baby dragon he names Yowler. Years later, the financially strapped adult Johnny agrees to loan Yowler to an amusement park only to find out the park's owner never intends to give Yowler back. Both baby dragon and young Johnny are unbearably cute.
1994 (PG) 86m/C Sam Mackenzie, Courtland Mead, Brittney Powell, John Calvin, Andrew Keir, Lila Kaye, John Woodvine; **D:** Ted Nicolaou; **W:** Ted Nicolaou, Suzanne Glazener Naha; **M:** Richard Band. VHS, Beta PAR ♂♂½

Dragstrip Girl An 18-year-old girl comes of age while burning rubber at the dragstrip—the world of boys, hot rods, and horsepower. A definite "B" movie that may seem dated.
1957 70m/B Fay Spain, Steven Terrell, John Ashley, Frank Gorshin; **D:** Edward L. Cahn. VHS **$9.95** COL ♂♂

The Drake Case A slight courtroom drama made during the waning days of the silent era. You'll probably recognize Brit Lloyd from her later career.
1929 56m/B Robert Frazer, Doris Lloyd, Gladys Brockwell. VHS, Beta **$19.95** GPV, FCT ♂♂

The Draughtsman's Contract A beguiling mystery begins when a wealthy woman hires an artist to make drawings of her home. Their contract is quite unusual, as is their relationship. Everything is going along at an even pace until murder is suspected, and things spiral down to darker levels. A simple story turned into a bizarre puzzle. Intense enough for any thriller fan.
1982 (R) 103m/C GB Anthony Higgins, Janet Suzman, Anne Louise Lambert, Hugh Fraser; **D:** Peter Greenaway; **W:** Peter Greenaway. VHS **$19.99** MGM, FCT ♂♂♂

Draw! Two has-been outlaws warm up their pistols again in this old-fashioned Western. Star power and some smart moments make it worthwhile. Made for TV.
1981 98m/C Kirk Douglas, James Coburn, Alexandra Bastedo, Graham Jarvis; **D:** Steven Hilliard Stern. VHS, Beta **$69.95** MED ♂♂

Dreadnaught Rivals A student is taught by his drunken servant how to avenge himself on the culprits who kidnapped his girlfriend. Dubbed.
198? 90m/C Sinon Lin, Kent Ko, Louisa Monk. VHS, Beta **$54.95** MOV ♂

Dream a Little Dream Strange teen transformation drama about an old man and his wife trying mystically to regain their youth. When they collide bikes with the teenagers down the street, their minds are exchanged and the older couple with the now young minds are transported to a permanent dream-like state. Same old switcheroo made bearable by cast.
1989 (PG-13) 114m/C Corey Feldman, Corey Haim, Meredith Salenger, Jason Robards Jr., Piper Laurie, Harry Dean Stanton, Victoria Jackson, Alex Rocco, Billy McNamara; **D:** Marc Rocco; **W:** Marc Rocco. VHS, Beta **$89.98** LIV, VES, HHE ♂♂

Dream Chasers A bankrupt old codger and an 11-year-old boy stricken with cancer run away together during the Great Depression.

1984 (PG) 97m/C Harold Gould, Justin Dana. VHS, Beta $79.98 FOX ℐℐ

Dream Date Lovely teenager is wooed by hip, playful suitor until trouble ensues when goofball sidekick enters the picture. Family entertainment.
1993 (PG-13) 96m/C Tempestt Bledsoe, Clifton Davis, Kadeem Hardison, Anne-Marie Johnson, Pauly Shore, Richard Moll; D: Anson Williams. VHS $89.95 TRI, PMS ℐℐ½

A Dream for Christmas Earl Hamner, Jr. (best known for writing the "The Waltons") wrote this moving story of a black minister whose church in Los Angeles is scheduled to be demolished. Made for television.
1973 100m/C Hari Rhodes, Beah Richards, George Spell, Juanita Moore, Joel Fluellen, Robert DoQui, Clarence Muse; D: Ralph Senesky. VHS $19.98 LIV, HBO, WAR ℐℐℐ

Dream Lover Terrifying nightmares after an assault lead McNichol to dream therapy. Treatment causes her tortured unconscious desires to take over her waking behavior, and she becomes a violent schizophrenic. Slow, heavy, and not very thrilling.
1985 (R) 105m/C Kristy McNichol, Ben Masters, Paul Shenar, Justin Deas, Joseph Culp, Gayle Hunnicutt, John McMartin; D: Alan J. Pakula. VHS, Beta $14.95 MGM ℐℐ

Dream Lover Divorced architect Ray (Spader) meets and marries Lena (Amick), beautiful and seemingly perfect, who nonetheless warns him that she's just your average mixed-up gal. Suspense is supposed to come into play as Ray suspects Lena's been lying to him about her past. Visually appealing (considerably helped by the attractive leads) but good looks don't make up for the lack of substance and the minimal number of surprises expected in a thriller. Directorial debut of Kazan.
1993 (R) 103m/C James Spader, Madchen Amick, Frederic Lehne, Bess Armstrong, Larry Miller, Kathleen York, Blair Tefkin, Scott Coffey, William Shockley, Clyde Kusatsu; D: Nicholas Kazan; W: Nicholas Kazan; M: Christopher Young. VHS NYR ℐℐ

Dream Machine A childish teen comedy, based on that old urban legend of the lucky kid given a free Porshe by the vengeful wife of a wealthy philanderer. The gimmick is that the husband's body is in the trunk; the murderer is in pursuit. The tape includes an anti-drug commerical—but nothing against reckless driving, which the picture glorifies.
1991 (PG) 88m/C Corey Haim, Evan Richards, Jeremy Slate, Randall England, Tracy Fraim, Brittney Lewis, Susan Seaforth Hayes; D: Lyman Dayton. VHS $89.95 LIV ℐℐ½

Dream No Evil A mentally disturbed woman is forced to commit bizarre murders to protect her warped fantasy world.
1975 93m/C Edmond O'Brien, Brooke Mills, Marc Lawrence, Arthur Franz; D: John Hayes. VHS, Beta $19.95 AHV ℐ½

A Dream of Kings Quinn is exceptional in this Petrakis story of an immigrant working to get his dying son home to Greece. Last film appearance for Stevens before committing suicide at age 36.
1969 (R) 107m/C Anthony Quinn, Irene Papas, Inger Stevens, Sam Levene, Val Avery; D: Daniel Mann. VHS $59.95 WAR ℐℐℐ

A Dream of Passion A woman imprisoned in Greece for murdering her children becomes the object of a publicity stunt for a production of "Medea," and the lead actress begin to exchange personalities. Artificial gobbledygook.

1978 (R) 105m/C GR SI Ellen Burstyn, Melina Mercouri, Andreas Voutsinas; W: Jules Dassin. VHS, Beta $9.98 NLC ℐℐ½

Dream Street A weak morality tale of London's lower classes. Two brothers, both in love with the same dancing girl, woo her in their own way, while a Chinese gambler plans to take her by force. Silent with music score. Based on Thomas Burke's "Limehouse Nights."
1921 138m/B Tyrone Power Sr., Carol Dempster, Ralph Graves, Charles Mack; D: D.W. Griffith. VHS, Beta $39.95 VYY ℐℐ

The Dream Team On their way to a ball game, four patients from a mental hospital find themselves lost in New York City after their doctor is knocked out by murderers. Some fine moments from a cast of dependable comics. Watch for numerous nods to "One Flew Over the Cuckoo's Nest," another Lloyd feature. Keaton fans won't want to miss this one.
1989 (PG-13) 113m/C Michael Keaton, Christopher Lloyd, Peter Boyle, Stephen Furst, Lorraine Bracco, Milo O'Shea, Dennis Boutsikaris, Philip Bosco, James Remar, Cynthia Belliveau; D: Howard Zieff; W: Jon Connolly, David Loucka; M: David McHugh. VHS, Beta $19.95 MCA ℐℐ½

Dream to Believe Slice of the life of your typical high school coed—mom's dying, stepdad's from hell, sports injury hurts, and, oh yeah, championship gymnastic competitions loom. Designed to make you feel oh-so-good in that MTV kind of way. Reeves is most excellent as the girl's blushing beau.
1985 96m/C Rita Tushingham, Keanu Reeves, Olivia D'Abo; D: Paul Lynde. VHS, Beta $79.98 HHE ℐℐ

Dream Trap A young man is obsessed with a girl in his dreams. When he meets a girl who really exists, fantasy louses up every opportunity for the real thing.
1990 90m/C Kristy Swanson, Sasha Jensen, Jeanie Moore, Hugh Parks; D: Tom Logan; W: Tom Logan. VHS NO ℐℐ½

Dreamchild A poignant story of the autumn years of Alice Hargreaves, the model for Lewis Carroll's "Alice in Wonderland." Film follows her on a visit to New York in the 1930s, with fantasy sequences including Wonderland characters created by Jim Henson's Creature Shop invoking the obsessive Reverend Dodgson (a.k.a. Carroll).
1985 (PG) 94m/C GB Coral Browne, Ian Holm, Peter Gallagher, Jane Asher, Nicola Cowper, Amelia Shankley, Caris Corfman, Shane Rimmer, James Wilby; D: Gavin Millar; W: Dennis Potter; M: Max Harris, Stanley Myers. VHS, Beta $14.95 MGM ℐℐℐ

Dreamer The excitement of bowling is exploited for all it's worth in this "strike or die" extravaganza. One of a kind.
1979 (PG) 86m/C Tim Matheson, Susan Blakely, Jack Warden, Richard B. Shull; D: Noel Nosseck; M: Bill Conti. VHS $59.98 FOX ℐℐ

The Dreaming A young doctor stumbles upon a dimension where reality and fantasy are blurred, and where the supernatural reigns supreme.
1989 87m/C AU VHS, Beta NO ℐ

Dreaming Lips An orchestra conductor's wife falls in love with her husband's violinist friend. Tragedy befalls the couple. Bergner outstanding in a familiar script.
1937 70m/B GB Raymond Massey, Elisabeth Bergner, Romney Brent, Joyce Bland, Charles Carson, Felix Aylmer; D: Paul Czinner, Lee Garmes. VHS, Beta $24.95 VYY, CCB ℐℐ½

Dreaming Out Loud Screen debut of popular radio team Lum 'n Abner. The boys get involved in several capers to bring progress to their small Arkansas town. Rural wisecracks make for pleasant outing. First in film series for the duo.
1940 65m/B Frances Langford, Phil Harris, Clara Blandick, Robert Wilcox, Chester Lauck, Norris Goff, Frank Craven, Bobs Watson, Irving Bacon; D: Harold Young. VHS, Beta $24.95 NOS, DVT, VYY ℐℐ

Dreams Unfocused film about the lives and loves of two successful women. Subtitled. AKA: Kvinn odrom; Journey into Autumn.
1955 86m/B SW Harriet Andersson, Gunnar Bjornstrand, Eva Dahlbeck, Ulf Palme; D: Ingmar Bergman; W: Ingmar Bergman. VHS, Beta $14.95 VDM, ING, SUE ℐℐ

Dreams Come True Silly young comedy-romance about two young lovers who discover the trick of out-of-body travel, and have various forms of spiritual contact while their bodies are sleeping.
1984 (R) 95m/C Michael Sanville, Stephanie Shuford; D: Max Kalmanowicz. VHS, Beta $59.95 MED ℐ

Dreams Lost, Dreams Found A young widow journeys from the U.S. to Scotland in search of her heritage. The third "Harlequin Romance Movie," made for cable television.
1987 102m/C Kathleen Quinlan, Betsy Brantley, Charles Gray; D: Willi Patterson. VHS $19.95 PAR ℐ½

Dreams of Desire Engaged couple goes to Hong Kong to enjoy that city's sensual pleasures.
1982 80m/C VHS, Beta NO ℐ

Dreamscape When a doctor teaches a young psychic how to enter into other people's dreams in order to end their nightmares, somebody else wants to use this psychic for evil purposes. The special effects are far more convincing than the one man-saves-the-country-with-his-psychic-powers plot.
1984 (PG-13) 99m/C Dennis Quaid, Max von Sydow, Christopher Plummer, Eddie Albert, Kate Capshaw, David Patrick Kelly, George Wendt, Jana Taylor; D: Joseph Ruben; M: Maurice Jarre. VHS, Beta $19.99 IME ℐℐ½

Dreamwood A myth-packed experimental film by James Broughton with muse-figures, angels, flower-children, and the like.
1972 45m/C D: James Broughton. VHS, Beta $29.95 MFV, TPV ℐℐℐ

Dress Gray Fine, exciting adaptation of the Lucian K. Truscott IV novel about a coverup at an Eastern military academy. Baldwin is cadet Slaight, an upperclassman who finds more secrets than he can handle when a younger cadet (Cassidy), with whom he had an adversarial relationship, is murdered. He's torn between investigating the death or keeping quiet—for the sake of his career if not his life. Originally a television miniseries.
1986 192m/C Alec Baldwin, Hal Holbrook, Eddie Albert, Lloyd Bridges, Susan Hess, Timothy Van Patten, Patrick Cassidy, Alexis Smith, James B. Sikking, Lane Smith; D: Glenn Jordan; W: Gore Vidal; M: Billy Goldenberg. VHS, Beta $79.99 WAR ℐℐ

Dressed for Death A tale of true love gone bad as a woman is chased and murdered in her castle by the psychopath she loves. AKA: Straight on Till Morning; Til Dawn Do Us Part.

1974 (R) 121m/C *GB* Rita Tushingham, Shane Briant, Tom Bell, Annie Ross, Katya Wyeth, James Bolam, Claire Kelly; **D:** Peter Collinson. **VHS, Beta** $19.95 *ACA* 🎬½

Dressed to Kill Sherlock Holmes finds that a series of music boxes holds the key to plates stolen from the Bank of England. The plot's a bit thin, but Rathbone/Bruce, in their final Holmes adventure, are always a delight. **1946** 72m/B Basil Rathbone, Nigel Bruce, Patricia Morison, Edmund Breon, Tom Dillon; **D:** Roy William Neill. **VHS** $14.98 *CNG, MRV, REP* 🎬🎬½

Dressed to Kill Contemporary thriller merges bombastic DePalma with a tense Hitchcockian flare. Sexually unsatisfied Dickinson ends up in bed with a man who catches her eye in a museum. Then she's found brutally murdered. Her son teams up with a prostitute to track and lure the killer into their trap. Suspenseful and fast paced. Dickinson's museum scene is wonderfully photographed and edited. DePalma was repeatedly criticized for using a stand-in during the Dickinson shower scene; he titled his next film "Body Double" as a rebuttal. **1980 (R)** 105m/C Angie Dickinson, Michael Caine, Nancy Allen, Keith Gordon, Dennis Franz, David Margulies, Brandon Maggart; **D:** Brian DePalma; **W:** Brian DePalma; **M:** Pino Donaggio. **VHS, Beta** $19.98 *WAR, OM* 🎬🎬½

The Dresser The film adaptation of Ronald Harwood's Broadway play about an aging English actor/manager, his dresser, and their theater company touring England during WWII. Marvelous showbiz tale is lovingly told, superbly acted. **1983 (PG)** 119m/C Albert Finney, Tom Courtenay, Edward Fox, Michael Gough, Zena Walker, Eileen Atkins, Cathryn Harrison; **D:** Peter Yates; **W:** John Michael Hayes; **M:** James Horner. Academy Awards '83 Nominations: Best Actor (Courtenay), Best Actor (Finney), Best Adapted Screenplay, Best Director (Yates), Best Picture; Golden Globe Awards '84: Best Actor—Drama (Courtenay). **VHS, Beta** $12.95 *COL* 🎬🎬🎬½

Dressmaker French comedian Fernandel stars as a man's tailor who designs dresses in secret so as not to compete with his dressmaker wife. Lightweight but entertaining. English subtitled. **1956** 95m/B *FR* Fernandel, Francoise Fabian; **D:** Jean Boyer. **VHS, Beta** $29.95 *NOS, GVV, DVT* 🎬🎬½

The Dressmaker Two sisters in WWII Liverpool must deal with their young niece's romantic involvement with an American soldier. Plowright and Whitelaw turn in fine performances as the two siblings with very different outlooks on life. **1989** 90m/C *GB* Joan Plowright, Billie Whitelaw, Peter Postlethwaite, Jane Horrocks, Tim Ransom; **D:** Jim O'Brien; **M:** George Fenton. **VHS** $79.95 *CAP, ING* 🎬🎬½

Drift Fence Good early oater about a Texas ranger who goes in search of the man responsible for the murder of his buddy. Routine story saved by high quality production. Based on the story "Nevada" by Zane Grey. **AKA:** Texas Desperadoes. **1936** 57m/B Buster Crabbe, Katherine DeMille, Tom Keene, Benny Baker; **D:** Otto Lovering; **W:** Stuart Anthony, Robert Yost. **VHS** $19.95 *DVT, GPV* 🎬🎬½

The Drifter A lumberjack makes sacrifices for the love between his brother and the lumbermill owner's daughter. **1932** 56m/B William Farnum, Noah Beery Sr., Phyliss Barrington. **VHS, Beta** $19.95 *NOS, VYY, HEG* 🎬🎬

The Drifter It's psychos, psychos everywhere as a beautiful young woman learns to regret a one-night stand. A good, low-budget version of "Fatal Attraction." Director Brand plays the cop. **1988 (R)** 90m/C Kim Delaney, Timothy Bottoms, Miles O'Keeffe, Al Shannon, Thomas Wagner, Larry Brand; **D:** Larry Brand; **M:** Rick Conrad. **VHS** $79.95 *MGM* 🎬🎬

The Driftin' Kid Poorly produced western has Keene posing as a rancher in order to nab a bunch of cattle rusters. So bad that even the sound of the punches are seconds off from the blows. **1941** 57m/B Tom Keene, Betty Miles, Frank Yaconelli, Slim Andrews, Stanley Price, Glenn Strange; **D:** Robert Tansey; **W:** Robert Tansey, Frances Kavanaugh. **VHS** $19.99 *MOV* 🎬

Driftin' River A shipment of horses bound for the Army is hijacked and the soldiers sent to investigate the theft are murdered. Investigators Deans and Ates are sent to take care of the culprits. Routine oater. **1946** 57m/B Eddie Dean, Roscoe Ates, Shirley Patterson, William Fawcett, Dennis Moore, Bob Callahan, Lottie Harrison, Forrest Taylor; **D:** Robert Tansey; **W:** Frances Kavanaugh. **VHS** $11.95 *GPV* 🎬🎬½

Drifting A controversial Israeli film about a homosexual filmmaker surviving in modern-day Jerusalem. First such movie to be made in Israel. In Hebrew with English titles. **AKA:** Nagooa. **1982** 103m/C *IS* Jonathan Sagalle, Ami Traub, Ben Levine, Dita Arel; **D:** Amos Guttman. **VHS, Beta** $69.95 *FCT* 🎬🎬½

Drifting Souls In order to save her father's life, a beautiful young woman marries for money instead of love. **1932** 65m/C Lois Wilson, Theodore von Eltz, Shirley Grey, Raymond Hatton, Gene Gowing, Bryant Washburn; **D:** Louis King. **VHS, Beta** $12.95 *GPV* 🎬🎬

Drifting Weeds A remake by Ozu of his 1934 silent film about a troupe of traveling actors whose leader visits his illegitimate son and his lover after years of separation. Classic Ozu in his first color film. In Japanese with English subtitles. **AKA:** Floating Weeds; The Duckweed Story; Ukigusa. **1959** 128m/B *JP* Ganjiro Nakamura, Machiko Kyo, Haruko Sugimura, Ayako Wakao; **D:** Yasujiro Ozu. **VHS, Beta** $29.95 *HMV, MRV, HEG* 🎬🎬🎬½

Driller Killer Frustrated artist goes insane and begins to kill off Manhattan residents with a carpenter's drill. Likewise, the plot is full of holes. **1974 (R)** 78m/C Jimmy Laine, Carolyn Marz, Bob DeFrank; **D:** Abel Ferrara; **M:** Joe Delia. **VHS, Beta** *NO* Woof!

Drive-In A low-budget bomb showing a night in the life of teenage yahoos at a Texas drive-in. **1976 (PG)** 96m/C Lisa Lemole, Glen Morshower, Gary Cavagnaro; **D:** Rod Amateau. **VHS, Beta** $69.95 *COL* Woof!

Drive-In Massacre Two police detectives investigate a bizarre series of slasher murders at the local drive-in. Honk the horn at this one. **1974 (R)** 78m/C Jake Barnes, Adam Lawrence. **VHS, Beta** *NO* Woof!

Driven to Kill No-name cast assemble in low-rent suspenser portraying the ugly side of love: bent on revenge, a man is out to obliterate the thugs who made his life a horrible experience highlighted by misery and boredom.

1990 ?m/C Jake Jacobs, Chip Campbell, Michele McNeil. **VHS** $79.95 *PMH* 🎬🎬

The Driver A police detective will stop at nothing to catch "The Driver," a man who has the reputation of driving the fastest getaway car around. Chase scenes win out over plot. **1978 (PG)** 131m/C Ryan O'Neal, Bruce Dern, Isabelle Adjani, Ronee Blakley, Matt Clark; **D:** Walter Hill; **W:** Walter Hill. **VHS, Beta** $59.98 *FOX* 🎬🎬½

Driver's Seat Extremely bizarre film with a cult following that was adapted from the novel by Muriel Spark. Liz stars as a deranged woman trying to keep a rendezvous with her strange lover in Rome. In the meantime she wears tacky clothes and delivers stupid lines. **AKA:** Psychotic; Identikit. **1973 (R)** 101m/C *IT* Elizabeth Taylor, Ian Bannen, Mona Washbourne, Andy Warhol; **D:** Giuseppe Patroni Griffi. **VHS, Beta** $24.98 *SUE* Woof!

Driving Force In an effort to capitalize on the popularity of the "Road Warrior" movies, features a lone trucker battling a gang of roadhogs in another post-holocaust desert. Ultimately, runs off the road. **1988** 90m/C Sam Jones, Catherine Bach, Don Swayze; **D:** A.J. Prowse; **W:** Patrick Edgeworth. **VHS, Beta** $29.95 *ACA* 🎬

Driving Me Crazy When an East German car inventor comes to America, it's laughs in the fast lane in this all-star comedy. **1991 (PG-13)** 88m/C Billy Dee Williams, Thomas Gottschalk, Dom DeLuise, Milton Berle, Steve Kanaly, Michelle Johnson, Richard Moll, Morton Downey Jr., George Kennedy; **D:** Jon Turteltaub. **VHS** *NO* 🎬½

Driving Miss Daisy Tender and sincere portrayal of a 25-year friendship between an aging Jewish woman and the black chauffeur forced upon her by her son. Humorous and thought-provoking, skillfully acted and directed, it subtly explores the effects of prejudice in the South. The development of Aykroyd as a top-notch character actor is further evidenced here. Part of the fun is watching the changes in fashion and auto design. Adapted from the play by Alfred Uhry. **1989 (PG)** 99m/C Jessica Tandy, Morgan Freeman, Dan Aykroyd, Esther Rolle, Patti LuPone; **D:** Bruce Beresford; **W:** Alfred Uhry. Academy Awards '89: Best Actress (Tandy), Best Adapted Screenplay, Best Makeup, Best Picture; Nominations: Best Actor (Freeman), Best Costume Design, Best Film Editing, Best Supporting Actor (Aykroyd); British Academy Awards '90: Best Actress (Tandy); Golden Globe Awards '90: Best Actor—Musical/Comedy (Freeman), Best Actress—Musical/Comedy (Tandy), Best Film—Musical/Comedy; National Board of Review Awards '89: 10 Best Films of the Year, Best Actor (Freeman). **VHS, Beta, 8mm** $19.98 *WAR, FCT, BTV* 🎬🎬🎬½

Drop Dead Fred As a little girl, Lizzie Cronin had a manic, imaginary friend named Fred, who protected her from her domineering mother. When her husband dumps her twenty years later, Fred returns to "help" as only he can. Although the cast is fine, incompetent writing and direction make this a truly dismal affair. Plus, gutter humor and mean-spirited pranks throw the whole "heart-warming" premise out the window. Filmed in Minneapolis. **1991 (PG-13)** 103m/C Phoebe Cates, Rik Mayall, Tim Matheson, Marsha Mason, Carrie Fisher, Daniel Gerroll, Ron Eldard; **D:** Ate De Jong; **M:** Randy Edelman. **VHS** $92.95 *LIV* Woof!

Drop-Out Mother A woman gives up her executive position to become a house-wife and full-time mom; expected domestic turmoil follows. Standard made for television fare and sort of a sequel to "Drop-Out Father," shown in 1982.
1988 100m/C Valerie Harper, Wayne Rogers, Carol Kane, Kim Hunter, Danny Gerard; **D:** Charles S. Dubin. **VHS $39.95** *FRH* ✍️

The Dropkick Erstwhile D.W. Griffith leading man Barthelmess stars in this pigskin whodunnit: a coach's suicide looks like murder, and the prime suspect is the team's most valuable player. Cast includes ten bona fide university football players and Hedda "nobody's interested in sweetness and light" Hopper, while The Duke makes cameo. Webb later went on to direct a musical with Eddie Cantor and Rudy Vallee ("Glorifying the American Girl"). Silent. Based on the story "Glitter" by Katherine Brush.
1927 62m/B Richard Barthelmess, Barbara Kent, Dorothy Revier, Eugene Strong, Alberta Vaughn, Brooks Benedict, Hedda Hopper; **Cameos:** John Wayne; **D:** Millard Webb; **W:** Winifred Dunn. **VHS, Beta $24.95** *GPV, FCT* ✍️

Drowning by Numbers Three generations of women, each named Cissie Colpitts, solve their marital problems by drowning their husbands and making deals with a bizarre coroner. Further strange visions from director Greenaway, complemented by stunning cinematography courtesy of Sacha Vierny. A treat for those who appreciate Greenaway's uniquely curious cinematic statements.
1987 (R) 121m/C *GB* Bernard Hill, Joan Plowright, Juliet Stevenson, Joely Richardson; **D:** Peter Greenaway; **W:** Peter Greenaway. **VHS $19.98** *LIV* ✍️✍️✍️½

The Drowning Pool Newman returns as detective Lew Harper (of "Harper" by Ross MacDonald) to solve a blackmail case. Uneventful script and stodgy direction, but excellent character work from all the cast members keep this watchable. Title is taken from a trap set for Newman, from which he must escape using most of his female companion's clothing. Adapted from a character created by Ross MacDonald.
1975 (PG) 109m/C Paul Newman, Joanne Woodward, Anthony (Tony) Franciosa, Murray Hamilton, Melanie Griffith, Richard Jaeckel; **D:** Stuart Rosenberg; **W:** Tracy Keenan Wynn, Walter Hill; **M:** Charles Fox. **VHS, Beta $19.98** *WAR* ✍️✍️

Drug Wars 2: The Cocaine Cartel Muddled drama featuring crazy unpredictable DEA agents executing the downfall of Colombia's Medellin drug kingpins. Average sequel to the award-winning miniseries "Drug Wars."
1992 200m/C Alex McArthur, Dennis Farina, Julie Carmen, John Glover, Karen Young, Michele Placido, Gustav Vintas, Geno Silva; **D:** Paul Krasny. **VHS** *MCA* ✍️✍️

Drugstore Cowboy A gritty, uncompromising depiction of a pack of early 1970s drugstore-robbing junkies as they travel around looking to score. Brushes with the law and tragedy encourage them to examine other life-styles, but the trap seems impossible to leave. A perfectly crafted piece that reflects the "me generation" era, though it tends to glamorize addiction. Dillon's best work to date. Based on a novel by prison inmate James Fogle.
1989 (R) 100m/C Matt Dillon, Kelly Lynch, James Remar, James LeGros, Heather Graham, William S. Burroughs, Beah Richards, Grace Zabriskie, Max Perlich; **D:** Gus Van Sant; **W:** Gus Van Sant; **M:** Elliot Goldenthal. **VHS, Beta $19.95** *LIV, FCT* ✍️✍️✍️½

Drum This steamy sequel to "Mandingo" deals with the sordid interracial sexual shenanigans at a Southern plantation. Bad taste at its best.
1976 (R) 101m/C Ken Norton, Warren Oates, Pam Grier, Yaphet Kotto, Fiona Lewis, Isela Vega, Cheryl "Rainbeaux" Smith; **D:** Steve Carver. **VHS, Beta $19.98** *LIV, VES, WAR Woof!*

Drum Beat An unarmed Indian fighter sets out to negotiate a peace treaty with a renegade Indian leader. Bronson is especially believable as chief. Based on historical incident.
1954 111m/C Alan Ladd, Charles Bronson, Marisa Pavan, Robert Keith, Rodolfa Acosta, Warner Anderson, Elisha Cook Jr., Anthony Caruso; **D:** Delmer Daves. **VHS, Beta $54.95** *VCI* ✍️✍️

Drum Taps Maynard saves the day for a young girl who is being pushed off her land by a group of speculators.
1933 55m/B Ken Maynard, Dorothy Dix, Frank "Junior" Coghlan, Kermit Maynard; **D:** J.P. McGowan. **VHS, Beta $19.95** *NOS, VDM, VYY* ✍️✍️

Drums A native prince helps to save the British army in India from being annihilated by a tyrant. Rich melodrama with interesting characterizations and locale. **AKA:** The Drum.
1938 96m/B *GB* Sabu, Raymond Massey, Valerie Hobson, Roger Livesey, David Tree; **D:** Zoltan Korda. **VHS, Beta $14.98** *SUE* ✍️✍️½

Drums Along the Mohawk Grand, action-filled saga about pre-Revolutionary America, detailing the trials of a colonial newlywed couple as their village in Mohawk Valley is besieged by Indians. Based on the Walter Edmonds novel, and vintage Ford.
1939 104m/C Henry Fonda, Claudette Colbert, Edna May Oliver, Eddie Collins, John Carradine, Dorris Bowdon, Arthur Shields, Ward Bond, Jessie Ralph, Robert Lowery; **D:** John Ford. **VHS, Beta $19.98** *FOX* ✍️✍️✍️½

Drums in the Deep South A rivalry turns ugly as two former West Point roommates wind up on opposite sides when the Civil War breaks out. Historical drama hampered by familiar premise.
1951 87m/C James Craig, Guy Madison, Craig Stevens, Barbara Payton, Barton MacLane; **D:** William Cameron Menzies; **W:** Philip Yordan. **VHS, Beta $19.95** *NOS, MRV, VGR* ✍️✍️

Drums of Fu Manchu Fu Manchu searches for the scepter of Genghis Khan, an artifact that would give him domination over the East. Brandon smoothly evil as the Devil Doctor. Originally a serial in 15 chapters.
1940 150m/B Henry Brandon, Robert Kellard, George Cleveland, Dwight Frye, Gloria Franklin, Tom Chatterton; **D:** William Witney, John English. **VHS, Beta $69.95** *VCN, MLB* ✍️✍️✍️

Drums of Jeopardy A father wanders through czarist Russia and the U.S. to seek revenge on his daughter's killer. Cheap copy of "Dr. Fu Manchu." **AKA:** Mark of Terror.
1931 65m/B Warner Oland, June Collyer, Lloyd Hughes, George Fawcett, Mischa Auer; **D:** George B. Seitz. **VHS $24.95** *NOS, SNC, DVT* ✍️

Drums O'Voodoo A voodoo princess fights to eliminate the town bad guy in this all-black feature that is greatly hampered by shoddy production values. **AKA:** She Devil.
1934 70m/B Laura Bowman, J. Augustus Smith, Edna Barr; **D:** Arthur Hoerl. **VHS, Beta $16.95** *SNC Woof!*

Drunken Angel Alcoholic doctor gets mixed up with local gangster. Kurosawa's first major film aided by strong performances. With English subtitles.
1948 108m/B *JP* Toshiro Mifune, Takashi Shimura, Choko Iida; **D:** Akira Kurosawa. **VHS, Beta $39.95** *DVT, MRV, ING* ✍️✍️✍️

A Dry White Season A white Afrikaner living resignedly with apartheid confronts the system when his black gardener, an old friend, is persecuted and murdered. A well-meaning expose that, like many others, focuses on white people.
1989 (R) 105m/C Donald Sutherland, Marlon Brando, Susan Sarandon, Zakes Mokae, Janet Suzman, Juergen Prochnow, Winston Ntshona, Susannah Harker, Thoko Ntshinga, Rowan Elmes; **D:** Euzhan Palcy; **W:** Colin Welland, Euzhan Palcy; **M:** Dave Grusin. **VHS, Beta $19.98** *FOX, FCT* ✍️✍️✍️

Drying Up the Streets Tepid message tale of a police drug squad out to terminate the pattern that has young women turning to a life of prostitution and drugs.
1976 90m/C *CA* Len Cariou, Don Francks, Sarah Torgov, Calvin Butler; **D:** Robin Spry. **VHS, Beta $69.98** *LIV, VES* ✍️

D2: The Mighty Ducks When an injury forces Gordon (Estevez) out of the minor leagues, he is tapped by promotor Tibbles (Tucker) to coach Team U.S.A. in the Junior Goodwill Games. Upon arriving in LA, the coach's head is turned by the money to be made in endorsements, and he soon gets a lesson in character-building (hey, it's Disney). The duck redux premise is lame, but kids will want ice time to see more of the hockey action that made the first a hit. **AKA:** The Mighty Ducks 2.
1994 (PG) 107m/C Emilio Estevez, Michael Tucker, Jan Rubes, Kathryn Erbe, Shaun Weiss, Kenan Thompson, Ty O'Neal; **Cameos:** Kristi Yamaguchi, Kareem Abdul-Jabbar, Wayne Gretzky; **D:** Sam Weisman; **W:** Steven Brill; **M:** J.A.C. Redford. **VHS $19.99** *DIS* ✍️✍️

Dual Alibi Identical twin trapeze artists murder a colleague for a winning lottery ticket. Lom plays the brothers in a dual role.
1947 87m/B *GB* Herbert Lom, Terence de Marney, Phyllis Dixey, Ronald Frankau, Abraham Sofaer, Harold Berens, Sebastian Cabot; **D:** Alfred Travers. **VHS, Beta $16.95** *NOS, SNC* ✍️✍️

Dual Flying Kicks Chinese provincial mayor allies himself with a group of bandits amid much high kicking.
1982 90m/C Chen Hsing, Tan Tao Liang. **VHS, Beta** *WVE* ✍️

Dubarry Early sound version of the romantic experiences of Madame Dubarry, the alluring French heroine of David Belasco's "DuBarry." Talmadge's last film.
1930 81m/B Norma Talmadge, Conrad Nagel, William Farnum, Hobart Bosworth, Alison Skipworth; **D:** Sam Taylor. **VHS, Beta $24.95** *NOS, DVT, HEG* ✍️✍️½

DuBarry Was a Lady Skelton is a washroom attendant who daydreams that he is King Louis XV of France. Dorsey's band gets to dress in period wigs and costumes. ♫DuBarry Was a Lady; Do I Love You, Do I?; Friendship; Well, Did You Evah; Taliostro's Dance; Katie Went to Haiti; Madame, I Love Your Crepes Suzettes; Thinking of You; A Cigarette, Sweet Music and You; Sleepy Lagoon; You Are My Sunshine; I'm Getting Sentimental Over You; Salome; Ladies of the Bath; Get Me a Taxi; On to Combat; No Matter How You Slice It, It's Still Salome.
1943 112m/C Lucille Ball, Gene Kelly, Red Skelton, Virginia O'Brien, Zero Mostel, Dick Haymes, Rags Ragland, Donald Meek, George Givot, Louise Beavers; **D:** Roy Del Ruth. **VHS, Beta $19.98** *MGM, CCB* ✍️✍️½

Dubeat-E-O A filmmaker races against time to finish making a documentary about the Los Angeles underground hardcore punk scene, and becomes immersed in the subculture. Somewhat of a haphazard exercise in filmmaking that is best appreciated by rock fans.
1984 84m/C Ray Sharkey, Joan Jett, Derf Scratch, Len Lesser, Nora Gaye; **D:** Alan Sacks. **VHS, Beta** $59.95 MVD, MED ♂️½

The Duchess and the Dirtwater Fox Period western strung together with many failed attempts at humor, all about a music-hall hooker who meets a bumbling card shark on the make.
1976 (PG) 105m/C George Segal, Goldie Hawn, Conrad Janis, Thayer David; **D:** Melvin Frank; **W:** Barry Sandler; **M:** Charles Fox. **VHS, Beta** $19.98 FOX ♂️½

Duchess of Idaho Williams tries to help her roommate patch up a romance gone bad, but ends up falling in love herself. MGM guest stars liven up an otherwise routine production. ♫Baby Come Out of the Clouds; You Can't Do Wrong Doin' Right; Let's Choo Choo to Idaho; Of All Things; Or Was It Spring; Warm Hands, Cold Heart; Singlefoot Serenade; You Won't Forget Me.
1950 98m/C Esther Williams, Van Johnson, John Lund, Paula Raymond, Amanda Blake, Eleanor Powell, Lena Horne; **D:** Robert Z. Leonard. **VHS** $19.98 MGM ♂️♂️½

Duck Soup The Marx Brothers satiric masterpiece (which failed at the box office). Groucho becomes the dictator of Freedonia, and hires Chico and Harpo as spies. Jampacked with the classic anarchic and irreverent Marx shtick; watch for the mirror scene. Zeppo plays a love-sick tenor, in this, his last film with the brothers.
1933 70m/B Groucho Marx, Chico Marx, Harpo Marx, Zeppo Marx, Louis Calhern, Margaret Dumont, Edgar Kennedy, Raquel Torres, Leonid Kinskey, Charles Middleton; **D:** Leo McCarey; **W:** Harry Ruby, Nat Perrin, Bert Kalmar, Arthur Sheekman; **M:** Harry Ruby, Bert Kalmar. **VHS, Beta** $14.98 MCA, FCT ♂️♂️♂️♂️

DuckTales the Movie: Treasure of the Lost Lamp Uncle Scrooge and company embark on a lost-ark quest, ala Harrison Ford, for misplaced treasure (a lamp that can make the sky rain ice cream). Based on the daily Disney cartoon of the same name, it's more like an extended-version Saturday morning sugar smacks'n'milk 'toon. See it with someone young.
1990 (G) 74m/C D: Bob Hathcock; **W:** Alan Burnett; **M:** David Newman; **V:** Alan Young, Christopher Lloyd, Rip Taylor, June Foray, Chuck McCann, Richard Libertini, Russi Taylor, Joan Gerber, Terence McGovern. **VHS, Beta** $22.99 DIS, WTA ♂️½

Dude Bandit An unscrupulous moneylender tries to gain control of a ranch but Gibson comes to the rescue. Gibson actually plays three roles: the rancher's best friend, an aw-shucks cowpoke disguise in order to find out what's going on, and the title character used to bedevil the crooks.
1932 68m/B Hoot Gibson, Gloria Shea. **VHS, Beta** $24.95 VYY, VCI, VCN ♂️♂️

Dude Ranger Well-acted Zane Grey story about an easterner who gets caught up in a range war and cattle rustling when he takes possession of some property out west.
1934 58m/B Smiley Burnette, George O'Brien, Irene Hervey; **D:** Eddie Cline. **VHS, Beta** $19.95 VDM ♂️♂️½

Dudes Three city kids head for the desert and run afoul of some rednecks. Tired grade-6 revenge story.
1987 (R) 90m/C Jon Cryer, Catherine Mary Stewart, Daniel Roebuck, Flea, Lee Ving, Calvin Bartlett, Pete Willcox, Glenn Withrow; **D:** Penelope Spheeris; **M:** Charles Bernstein. **VHS, Beta** NO ♂️

Duel Spielberg's first notable film, a made-for-television exercise in paranoia. A docile traveling salesman is repeatedly attacked and threatened by a huge, malevolent tractor-trailer on an open desert highway. Released theatrically in Europe.
1971 90m/C Dennis Weaver, Lucille Benson, Eddie Firestone, Cary Loftin; **D:** Steven Spielberg; **W:** Richard Matheson; **M:** Billy Goldenberg. **VHS, Beta** $39.95 MCA ♂️♂️♂️

Duel at Diablo An exceptionally violent film that deals with racism in the Old West. Good casting; western fans will enjoy the action.
1966 103m/C James Garner, Sidney Poitier, Bibi Andersson, Dennis Weaver, Bill Travers; **D:** Ralph Nelson. **VHS** $19.98 MGM ♂️♂️♂️

Duel in the Eclipse A strategically timed eclipse permits a gringo to avenge his brother's murder.
19?? 100m/C Fernando Sancho. **VHS, Beta** $39.95 TWE ♂️

Duel in the Sun A lavish, lusty David O. Selznick production of a minor western novel about a vivacious half-breed Indian girl, living on a powerful dynastic ranch, who incites two brothers to conflict. Selznick's last effort at outdoing his epic success with "Gone With the Wind."
1946 130m/C Gregory Peck, Jennifer Jones, Joseph Cotten, Lionel Barrymore, Lillian Gish, Butterfly McQueen, Harry Carey Sr., Walter Huston, Charles Bickford, Herbert Marshall; **D:** King Vidor. **VHS, Beta** $19.98 FOX ♂️♂️♂️

Duel of Champions It's ancient Rome, and the prodigal gladiator has come home. Now the family must have a duel to decide who will rule. **AKA:** Orazi e Curiazi.
1961 90m/C IT SP Alan Ladd, Francesca Bett; **D:** Ferdinando Baldi. **VHS, Beta** NO ♂️

Duel of Fists When the owner of a boxing institute dies, he instructs his son in his will to go searching for his long-lost brother in Thailand. All he can go on is an old photograph and the knowledge that his brother is a Thai boxer.
1989 111m/C David Chiang, Chen Hsing, Ti Lung, Tang Ti. **VHS, Beta** $14.95 HMD, MOV ♂️

Duel of Hearts Beautiful Caroline falls in love with wealthy Lord Vane Brecon, who unfortunately is accused of murder. When Caroline tries to help him clear his name she discovers he's hiding a number of secrets. Based on the romance novel "Duel of Love" by Barbara Cartland. Nothing too inspiring here, although regency romance fans will appreciate the attention to detail. Originally made for cable television.
1992 (PG-13) 95m/C GB Alison Doody, Michael York, Geraldine Chaplin, Benedict Taylor, Billie Whitelaw, Virginia McKenna, Richard Johnson, Jeremy Kemp, Beryl Reid, Suzanna Hamilton, Jolyon Baker, Julie Kate; **D:** John Hough. **VHS, Beta** $89.98 TTC ♂️♂️

Duel of the Iron Fist Master of the martial arts must do battle with a brutal gang to save his own group from extinction.
1972 (R) 98m/C David Chiang, Ti Lung, Wang Ping, Yu Hui. **VHS, Beta** $59.95 HHT, VCI ♂️

Duel of the Seven Tigers Nine of the world's greatest Kung Fu and Karate exponents team up in this martial arts spectacular.
1980 80m/C Cliff Lok, Ka Sa Fa, Chio Chi Ling, Lam Men Wei, Yang Pan Pan, Charlie Chan. **VHS, Beta** $39.95 TWE ♂️♂️

The Duellists A beautifully photographed picture about the long-running feud between two French officers during the Napoleonic wars. Based on "The Duel" by Joseph Conrad.
1977 (PG) 101m/C GB Keith Carradine, Harvey Keitel, Albert Finney, Edward Fox, Tom Conti, Christina Raines, Diana Quick; **D:** Ridley Scott. **VHS, Beta** $49.95 PAR ♂️♂️♂️

Duelo en el Dorado A white man and Indian fight over the custody of an orphan.
19?? 90m/C SP Luis Aguilar, Lola Beltran, Emilio Fernandez, German Valdes. **VHS, Beta** $78.95 MAD ♂️½

Duet for One A famous concert violinist learns she is suffering from multiple sclerosis and is slowly losing her ability to play. Convinced that her life is meaningless without music, she self-destructively drifts into bitter isolation. From the play by Tom Kempinski.
1986 (R) 108m/C Julie Andrews, Max von Sydow, Alan Bates, Liam Neeson; **D:** Andrei Konchalovsky. **VHS, Beta** $14.95 MGM ♂️♂️

The Duke is the Tops In Horne's earliest existing film appearance, she's off to attempt the "big-time," while her boyfriend joins a traveling medicine show. ♫I Know You Remember.
1938 80m/C Ralph Cooper, Lena Horne, The Basin Street Boys, Rubber Neck Boys, Marie Bryant. **VHS, Beta** $39.95 NOS, MRV, VCN ♂️½

Duke of the Derby A scheming racehorse handicapper bets over his head and ruins his higher-than-means lifestyle. In French with English subtitles. **AKA:** Le Gentleman D'epsom.
1962 83m/C FR Jean Gabin; **D:** Gilles Grangier. **VHS, Beta** $19.95 FCT, DVT, HEG ♂️♂️

Duke: The Films of John Wayne A gift-pack collection of three of Wayne's finest: "Flying Leathernecks," "Fort Apache," and "She Wore a Yellow Ribbon."
1989 332m/C John Wayne. **VHS** $59.95 TTC ♂️♂️

Dumb Waiter A mini-play by Harold Pinter about two hitmen awaiting instructions for a job in an empty boardinghouse, and getting comically mixed messages. Made for television.
1987 60m/C John Travolta, Tom Conti; **D:** Robert Altman; **W:** Harold Pinter. **VHS, Beta** $79.95 PSM ♂️♂️

Dumbo Animated Disney classic about a baby elephant growing up in the circus who is ridiculed for his large ears, until he discovers he can fly. The little elephant who could fly then becomes a circus star. Expressively and imaginatively animated, highlighted by the hallucinatory dancing pink elephants sequence. Endearing songs by Frank Churchill, Oliver Wallace, and Ned Washington, including "Baby Mine," "Pink Elephants on Parade," and "I See an Elephant Fly."
1941 63m/C D: Ben Sharpsteen; **W:** Joe Grant, Dick Huemer; **M:** Frank Churchill, Oliver Wallace; **V:** Sterling Holloway, Edward Brophy, Verna Felton, Herman Bing, Cliff Edwards. Academy Awards '41: Best Score; Nominations: Best Song ("Baby Mine"); National Board of Review Awards '41: 10 Best Films of the Year. **VHS, Beta** $24.99 DIS, KUI, APD ♂️♂️♂️♂️

The Dummy Talks When a ventriloquist is murdered, a midget goes undercover as a dummy to find the killer. Watch closely and you might see his lips move.
1943 85m/B GB Jack Warner, Claude Hulbert, Beryl Orde, Derna-Hazell, Ivy Benson, Manning Whiley; **D:** Oswald Mitchell. **VHS, Beta** $16.95 SNC ♂️♂️

Dune Lynch sci-fi opus based on the Frank Herbert novel boasting great set design, muddled scripting, and a good cast. The story: controlling the spice drug of Arrakis permits control of the universe in the year 10991. Paul, the heir of the Atreides family, leads the Freemen in a revolt against the evil Harkhonens who have violently seized control of Arrakis, also known as Dune, the desert planet. That's as clear as it ever gets.
1984 (PG-13) 137m/C Kyle MacLachlan, Francesca Annis, Jose Ferrer, Sting, Max von Sydow, Juergen Prochnow, Linda Hunt, Freddie Jones, Dean Stockwell, Virginia Madsen, Brad Dourif, Kenneth McMillan, Silvana Mangano, Jack Nance, Sian Phillips, Paul Smith, Richard Jordan, Everett McGill, Sean Young; **D:** David Lynch; **W:** David Lynch; **M:** Brian Eno, Toto. VHS, Beta $24.95 MCA, FCT *夏夏*

Dune Warriors Earth is a parched planet in the year 2040. Renegade bands cruise the desert, making short shrift of civilized people who band together in remote villages. When peaceful farmer Carradine's family falls prey to the pillagers, surely he and the most evil warlord of all must clash. Good action and stunts, if the dummy plot doesn't get you first.
1991 (R) 77m/C David Carradine, Richard Hill, Luke Askew, Jillian McWhirter, Blake Boyd; **D:** Cirio H. Santiago. VHS $89.95 COL *夏 1/2*

The Dunera Boys Hoskins shines in this story about Viennese Jews who, at the onset of WWII, escape to England where they are suspected as German spies. Subsequently, the British shipped them all to an Australian prison camp, where they recreated in peace their Viennese lifestyle.
1985 (R) 150m/C AU Bob Hoskins, Joe Spano, Warren Mitchell, Joseph Furst, Moshe Kedem, Dita Cobb, John Meillon, Mary-Anne Fahey, Simon Chilvers, Steven Vidler; **D:** Sam Lewin. VHS, Beta $9.99 STE, PSM *夏夏夏*

Dungeon of Harrow Unbelievably cheap tale of shipwrecked comrades who encounter a maniacal family on an otherwise deserted island. Not your stranded-on-a-desert-island fantasy come true. Filmed in San Antonio, a harrowing bore.
1964 74m/B Russ Harvey, Helen Hogan, Bill McNulty, Pat Boyette; **D:** Pat Boyette. VHS $19.98 SNC *夏*

Dungeonmaster A warlord forces a computer wiz to participate in a bizarre "Dungeons and Dragons" styled game in order to save a girl held captive. Consists of seven segments, each by a different director. Save yourself the trouble.
1985 (PG-13) 80m/C Jeffrey Byron, Richard Moll, Leslie Wing, Danny Dick; **D:** John Carl Buechler, Charles Band, David Allen, Stephen Ford, Peter Manoogian, Ted Nicolaou, Rosemarie Turko; **M:** Richard Band. VHS, Beta $29.98 LIV *夏 1/2*

The Dunwich Horror Young warlock acquires a banned book of evil spells, starts trouble on the astral plane. Stockwell hammy. Loosely based on H. P. Lovecraft story.
1970 90m/C Sandra Dee, Dean Stockwell, Lloyd Bochner, Ed Begley Sr., Sam Jaffe, Joanna Moore; **D:** Daniel Haller; **W:** Curtis Hanson; **M:** Les Baxter. VHS, Beta $9.98 SUE *夏夏*

Duplicates Harrison and Greist are a married couple whose young son has disappeared. When the boy is found he has no memory of his former life or parents. The couple discover he's the victim of secret experiments which transfer human memories into computer banks. Will they become the next targets?
1992 (PG-13) 92m/C Gregory Harrison, Kim Greist, Cicely Tyson, Lane Smith, William Lucking, Kevin McCarthy; **D:** Sandor Stern. VHS, Beta PAR, PMS *夏夏*

Durango Valley Raiders Sheriff is the leader of the outlaws, and a young cowboy finds out.
1938 55m/B Bob Steele; **D:** Sam Newfield. VHS, Beta $19.95 VCN, DVT *夏 1/2*

Dust A white woman in South Africa murders her father when he shows affection for a young black servant. Controversial and intense.
1985 87m/C FR BE Jane Birkin, Trevor Howard, John Matshikiza, Nadine Uwampa, Lourdes Christina Sayo, Rene Diaz; **D:** Marion Hansel; **W:** Marion Hansel; **M:** Martin St. Pierre. VHS, Beta $79.95 TPV *夏夏夏*

Dust Devil Three travelers find themselves in Namibia's vast desert: a policeman, a woman on the run, and her abusive husband. They all have the misfortune of meeting up with a supernatural being known as the "Dust Devil," who kills humans in order to steal their souls and increase his other worldly powers.
1993 (R) 87m/C Robert Burke, Chelsea Field, Zakes Mokae, Rufus Swart, John Matshikiza, William Hootkins, Marianne Sagebrecht; **D:** Richard Stanley; **W:** Richard Stanley; **M:** Simon Boswell. VHS, Beta PAR *夏夏*

Dust to Dust A short mystery made for British television about an aging gentleman who answers a request for correspondence and discovers ulterior, and evil, motives.
1985 60m/C GB Patricia Hodge, Michael Jayston, Judy Campbell. VHS, Beta $59.95 PSM *夏夏*

Dusty Touching story of a wild dingo dog raised by an Australian rancher and trained to herd sheep. Filmed in the Australian bush and based on the children's book by Frank Dalby Davison.
1985 89m/C AU Bill Kerr, Noel Trevarthen, Carol Burns, Nicholas Holland, John Stanton; **D:** John Richardson. VHS, Beta $19.95 MED, FCT, FHE *夏夏*

Dutch Working class boob attempts to pick up his girlfriend's son from boarding school. Their trip together gives them an unexpected chance to connect, if they don't kill each other first. Silly premise from the Hughes factory has little innovation and uses typecasting instead of acting.
1991 (PG-13) 107m/C Ed O'Neill, Ethan Randall, JoBeth Williams; **D:** Peter Faiman; **W:** John Hughes. VHS $19.98 FXV, IME *夏 1/2*

Dutch Girls Muddled mayhem as a horny high school field hockey team travels through Holland, cavorts about, and discovers the meaning of life.
1987 83m/C GB Bill Paterson, Colin Firth, Timothy Spall; **D:** Giles Foster. VHS, Beta $29.95 ACA Woof!

Dutch Treat Two nerds con a sultry, all-girl rock band into thinking they're powerful record company execs. Nobody's buying.
1986 (R) 95m/C Lorin Dreyfuss, David Landsberg; **D:** Boaz Davidson. VHS, Beta $79.95 MGM *夏*

Dutchman Film presentation of Amiri Baraka's one act play depicting the claustrophobic reality of the black man's situation in America. Black man shares subway conversation with a white woman who questions his race and middle class aspirations. Enraged, one takes the other's life.
1967 55m/C GB Al Freeman Jr., Shirley Knight; **D:** Anthony Harvey; **M:** John Barry. VHS $195.00 CAL *夏夏夏*

D.W. Griffith Triple Feature A collection of three short D.W. Griffith films including "The Battle of Elderbush Gulch," "Iola's Promise," and "The Goddess of Sagebrush Gulch."
1913 50m/B Mae Marsh, Lillian Gish, Mary Pickford, Blanche Sweet, Charles West; **D:** D.W. Griffith. VHS, Beta $19.95 BAR, FCT *夏夏 1/2*

The Dybbuk A man's bride is possessed by a restless spirit. Set in the Polish-Jewish community before WWI and based on the play by Sholom Anski. Considered a classic for its portrayal of Jewish religious and cultural mores. In Yiddish with English subtitles.
1937 123m/B PL Abraham Morewski, Isaac Samberg, Moshe Lipman, Lili Liliana, Dina Halpern; **D:** Michal Waszynski. VHS, Beta $39.95 IHF, FCT, NCJ *夏夏夏 1/2*

Dying Room Only Travelling through the desert, a woman's husband suddenly disappears after they stop at a secluded roadside diner. Made for television flick is a real spooker.
1973 74m/C Cloris Leachman, Ross Martin, Ned Beatty, Louise Latham, Dana Elcar, Dabney Coleman; **D:** Philip Leacock; **W:** Richard Matheson; **M:** Charles Fox. VHS $49.95 LIV *夏夏 1/2*

Dying to Remember A fashion designer (Gilbert) regresses to a past life during hypnotherapy and discovers she was murdered in 1963. She flies to San Francisco to discover more about her past but finds that someone wants to keep things secret—and is willing to kill again. Tedious and predictable.
1993 (PG-13) 87m/C Melissa Gilbert, Ted Shackleford, Scott Plank, Christopher Stone, Jay Robinson; **D:** Arthur Seidelman; **W:** George Schenck, Frank Cardea, Brian L. Ross. VHS, Beta PAR *夏 1/2*

The Dying Truth A wrongfully accused prisoner lies dying in his cell. Trouble is, he can't die in peace until he solves the murder they say he committed. Interesting mix of the supernatural and mystery, although perhaps not one of Carradine's more memorable roles.
1991 80m/C David Carradine, Stephanie Beacham, Stephen Greif, Stephan Chase, Larry Carby, Lesley Dunlop; **D:** John Hough. VHS NO *夏夏*

Dying Young Muted romance has a wealthy leukemia victim hire a spirited, unschooled beauty as his nurse. They fall in love, but the film is either too timid or too unimaginative to mine emotions denoted by the title. Nobody dies, in fact, a grim ending (faithful to the Marti Leimbach novel on which this was based) got scrapped after testing poorly with audiences. The actors try their best, photography is lovely, and Kenny G's mellow music fills the soundtrack. Scott is the late Dewhurst's son.
1991 (R) 111m/C Julia Roberts, Campbell Scott, Vincent D'Onofrio, Colleen Dewhurst, Ellen Burstyn, David Selby; **D:** Joel Schumacher; **W:** Richard Friedenberg. VHS $19.98 FXV *夏 1/2*

Dynamite Romance explodes as two young demolitions experts vie for the same girl. Stand back.
1949 68m/B William Gargan, Virginia Welles, Richard Crane, Irving Bacon; **D:** William H. Pine. VHS, Beta $24.95 NOS, DVT, HEG *夏*

Dynamite and Gold Nelson and crew embark on a search for lost gold, battling hostile Indians, the Mexican army and assorted bandits along the way. A mediocre television movie. **AKA:** Where the Hell's the Gold?.

1988 (PG) 91m/C Willie Nelson, Delta Burke, Jack Elam, Alfonso Arau, Gregory Sierra, Michael Wren, Gerald McRaney; *D:* Burt Kennedy; *W:* Burt Kennedy. VHS $19.95 *ACA, VTR* ��

The Dynamite Brothers Two tough guys, one a Hong Kong immigrant with martial arts skills, the other a brother from the streets of the ghetto, team up to rid Los Angeles of a Chinese crimelord.
19?? (R) 90m/C James Hong, Aldo Ray, Alan Tang, Timothy Brown, Carolyn Ann Speed, Don Oliver; *D:* Al Adamson; *M:* Charles Earland. VHS $19.95 *RHI* ��

Dynamite Canyon Average oater has villain Price committing murder in order to keep secret the location of a lode of copper. Standard western fare.
1941 58m/B Tom Keene, Evelyn Finley, Sugar Dawn, Stanley Price, Kenne Duncan; *D:* Robert Tansey; *W:* Robert Tansey, Frances Kavanaugh. VHS $19.95 *DVT* ��

Dynamite Chicken Melange of skits, songs, and hippie satire is dated. Includes performances by Joan Baez, Lenny Bruce, B.B. King, and others.
1970 (R) 75m/C Joan Baez, Richard Pryor, Lenny Bruce, Jimi Hendrix, Sha-Na-Na; *D:* Ernie Pintoff. VHS, Beta *NO* ����

Dynamite Dan A man knocks out the heavyweight boxing champion after he flirts with his girlfriend and decides to give up his day job to become a championship boxer. He is a success, and in the end he has to face the champion again. Will he win?
1924 62m/B Kenneth McDonald, Frank Rice, Boris Karloff, Eddie Harris, Diana Alden, Harry Woods, Jack Richardson; *D:* Bruce Mitchell. VHS, Beta $16.95 *GPV, LSV* ����

Dynamite Pass Offbeat oater about disgruntled ranchers attempting to stop the construction of a new road.
1950 61m/B Tim Holt, Richard Martin, Regis Toomey, Lynn (Mary Hart) Roberts, Denver Pyle; *D:* Lew Landers. VHS, Beta *MED* ����

Dynamite Ranch Ranchers fight tooth and nail to keep their rights and property in this Maynard oater.
1932 60m/B Ken Maynard. VHS, Beta $19.95 *NOS, VCI, DVT* ��

Dynamo A glamorous advertising executive pursues a kung fu expert to sign a contract with her agency for a kick boxing contest.
1980 (R) 81m/C VHS, Beta $9.98 *SUE, ORI* ��

Dynasty A leader of the Ming Dynasty is killed by evil Imperial Court eunuch and his son the monk sets out to avenge him. In 3-D. Run-of-the-mill kung-fu stunts.
1977 94m/C Bobby Ming, Lin Tashing, Pai Ying, Tang Wei, Jin Gang; *D:* Zhang Meijun. VHS, Beta $29.95 *BFV* ��

Dynasty Pulitzer Prize-winning author James Michener creates the usual sweeping saga of a family torn by jealousy, deception, and rivalry in love and business as husband, wife, and brother-in-law seek their fortune in the Ohio frontier of the 1820s.
1982 90m/C Sarah Miles, Harris Yulin, Stacy Keach. VHS, Beta *TLF* ����

Dynasty of Fear Matters get rather sticky at a British boys' school when the headmaster's wife seduces her husband's assistant. Together they conspire to murder her husband and share his fortune. *AKA:* Fear in the Night; Honeymoon of Fear.
1972 (PG) 93m/C *GB* Peter Cushing, Joan Collins, Ralph Bates, Judy Geeson, James Cossins; *D:* Jimmy Sangster; *W:* Jimmy Sangster. VHS, Beta $9.98 *REP, ACA, CNG* ����

E. Nick: A Legend in His Own Mind Satire of videos and magazines designed for adults.
1984 75m/C Don Calfa, Cleavon Little, Andra Akers, Pat McCormick; *D:* Robert Hegyes. VHS, Beta $39.95 *LIV* ����

Each Dawn I Die Cagney stars as a reporter who is a fervent critic of the political system. Framed for murder and imprisoned, he is subsequently befriended by fellow inmate, Raft, a gangster. Once hardened by prison life, Cagney shuns his friend and becomes wary of the system. Despite its farfetched second half and mediocre script, the film makes interesting viewing thanks to a stellar performance from Cagney.
1939 92m/B James Cagney, George Raft, George Bancroft, Jane Bryan, Maxie "Slapsie" Rosenbloom, Alan Baxter, Thurston Hall, Stanley Ridges, Victor Jory; *D:* William Keighley. VHS, Beta $19.95 *MGM* ����½

The Eagle In this tale of a young Cossack "Robin Hood," Valentino assumes the persona of the Eagle to avenge his father's murder. The romantic rogue encounters trouble when he falls for the beautiful Banky much to the chagrin of the scorned Czarina Dresser. Fine performances from Valentino and Dresser. Silent, based on a Alexander Pushkin story. Released on video with a new score by Davis.
1925 77m/B Rudolph Valentino, Vilma Banky, Louise Dresser, George Nichols, James Marcus; *D:* Clarence Brown; *M:* Carl Davis. VHS, Beta $19.95 *NOS, HBO, VYY* �“✓✓

Eagle Claws Champion A ninja master accidentally kills a friend, goes to prison, gets released and returns to fight again.
198? 90m/C Sho Kosugi. VHS, Beta $29.98 *TWE* ✓

The Eagle Has Landed Duvall, portraying a Nazi colonel in this WWII spy film, commissions Sutherland's Irish, English-hating character to aid him in his mission to kill Prime Minister Winston Churchill. Adapted from the bestselling novel by Jack Higgins. A restored version is available at 134 minutes.
1977 (PG) 123m/C Michael Caine, Donald Sutherland, Robert Duvall, Larry Hagman, Jenny Agutter, Donald Pleasence, Treat Williams, Anthony Quayle; *D:* John Sturges; *W:* Tom Mankiewicz. VHS, Beta $19.98 *FOX, FCT* ✓✓✓

Eagles Attack at Dawn After escaping from an Arab prison, an Israeli soldier vows to return with a small commando force to kill the sadistic warden.
1974 (PG) 96m/C *IS* Rick Jason, Peter Brown, Joseph Shiloal. VHS, Beta *NO* ✓½

Eagle's Shadow After a poor orphan boy rescues an aged beggar, the grateful old man tutors the lad in Snake-Fist techniques.
1984 101m/C Jackie Chan, Juan Jan Lee, Simon Yuen, Roy Horan; *D:* Yuen Woo Ping. VHS, Beta *WVE* ✓

Eagle's Wing John Briley, screenwriter of the award-winning epic "Gandhi," attempts to weave the threads of allegory smoothly in this white man vs. red man Western from England. The mediocre story finds Native American Waterston dueling white trapper Sheen in a quest to capture an elusive, exotic white stallion.
1979 111m/C *GB* Martin Sheen, Sam Waterston, Harvey Keitel, Stephane Audran, Caroline Langrishe; *D:* Anthony Harvey; *W:* John Briley. VHS, Beta $19.95 *MED* ✓½

Early Cinema Vol. 1 A compendium of early silent shorts, mostly predating 1920, which includes: Melies' "Conquest of the North Pole"; Linder's "Man and the Statue" and "Max's Mother In Law"; Drew's "Aun-

tie's Portrait"; Normand's "Mabel's Dramatic Career"; Mix's "An Angelic Attitude" Sennett and Swain's "Cowboy Ambrose"; Lloyd's "Just Neighbors" and Parrott's "Take the Air."
1919 118m/B Mabel Normand, Harold Lloyd, Sidney Drew, Max Linder, Paul Parrott, Tom Mix, Mack Swain; *D:* Mabel Normand, Harold Lloyd, Max Linder, Georges Melies, Mack Sennett. VHS, Beta *FCT* ✓½

Early Days A cantankerous, salty, once-powerful politician awaits death.
1981 67m/C Ralph Richardson. VHS, Beta $49.98 *FOX* ✓✓

Early Frost Near suspenseful whodunit centering around a simple divorce investigation that leads to the discovery of a corpse.
1984 95m/C Diana McLean, Jon Blake, Janet Kingsbury, David Franklin; *D:* Terry O'Connor. VHS, Beta *NO* ✓½

An Early Frost Highly praised, surprisingly intelligent made-for-television drama following the anguish of a successful lawyer who tells his closed-minded family that he is gay and dying of AIDS. Sensitive performance by Quinn in one of the first TV films to focus on the devastating effects of HIV. Rowlands adeptly displays her acting talents as the despairing mother.
1985 97m/C Aidan Quinn, Gena Rowlands, Ben Gazzara, John Glover, D.W. Moffett, Sylvia Sidney; *D:* John Erman. VHS, Beta $69.95 *COL* ✓✓✓½

Early Russian Cinema, Vol. 1: Beginnings Four films from 1908-1911, including a documentary and the first film adaptation of a Chekhov play. English subtitles.
1911 45m/B *RU* VHS $29.95 *MIL* ✓✓✓½

Early Russian Cinema, Vol. 2: Folklore & Legend Four films from 1909-1912: two depicting typical Russian folktales and two, directed by Goncharov, featuring national and cultural themes of the day. English subtitles.
1912 55m/B *RU* *D:* Vasilii Goncharov. VHS $29.95 *MIL* ✓✓✓½

Early Russian Cinema, Vol. 3: Starewicz's Fantasies Three films by director Starewicz, known for his use of puppet animation. This selection also includes a live-action fantasy from a Gogol story and an anti-German war allegory. English subtitles.
1915 58m/B *RU* *D:* Wladislaw Starewicz. VHS $29.95 *MIL* ✓✓✓½

Early Russian Cinema, Vol. 4: Provincial Variations The provincial Latvian film "Wedding Day" highlights Jewish life while the melodrama "Merchant Bashkirov's Daughter" follows a scandal based on an actual murder. English subtitles.
1913 55m/B *RU* VHS $29.95 *MIL* ✓✓✓½

Early Russian Cinema, Vol. 5: Chardynin's Pushkin Actor-director Chardynin's adaptations of two Pushkin stories. English subtitles.
1913 45m/B *RU* Ivan Mosjoukine; *D:* Petr Chardynin. VHS $29.95 *MIL* ✓✓✓½

Early Russian Cinema, Vol. 6: Class Distinctions The hardship of rural life and a view of servants and masters are depicted in two films. English subtitles.
1914 94m/B *RU* *D:* Vasilii Goncharov, Evgenii Bauer. VHS $29.95 *MIL* ✓✓✓½

Early Russian Cinema, Vol. 7: Evgenii Bauer Three films from the prolific director of some 80 films, covering both melodrama and erotic comedy. English subtitles.
1915 95m/B *RU* D: Evgenii Bauer. **VHS $29.95** MIL ✂✂✂½

Early Russian Cinema, Vol. 8: Iakov Protazanov Two films from director Protazanov, including his controversial film on the last days of Tolstoy which provoked legal action from the writer's family due to its scandalous depiction. English subtitles.
1916 104m/B *RU* D: Iakov Protazanov. **VHS $29.95** MIL ✂✂✂½

Early Russian Cinema, Vol. 9: High Society Three films covering social and urban topics, including a newsreel on the death of Russia's greatest star of the day. English subtitles.
1919 72m/B *RU* D: Evgenii Bauer. **VHS $29.95** MIL ✂✂✂½

Early Russian Cinema, Vol. 10: The End of an Era Three films, including Bauer's last film "For Luck" and a fragment with the husband-wife acting team of Lisenko and Mosjoukine before their departure into exile. English subtitles.
1917 72m/B *RU* Ivan Mosjoukine, Natalia Lisenko; D: Evgenii Bauer. **VHS $29.95** MIL ✂✂✂½

Early Sound Films This series of experimental shorts from throughout the silent era depicts the various methods of devising sound film, prior to "The Jazz Singer" in 1927.
1928 90m/B **VHS, Beta $59.50** GVV ✂✂✂½

Early Summer A classic from renowned Japanese director Ozu, this film chronicles family tensions in post-WWII Japan caused by newly-independent women rebelling against the social conventions they are expected to fulfill. Perhaps the best example of this director's work. Winner of Japan's Film of the Year Award. In Japanese with English subtitles. *AKA:* Bakushu.
1951 150m/B *JP* Ichiro Sugai, Chishu Ryu, Setsuko Hara, Chikage Awashima, Chieko Higashiyama, Haruko Sugimura, Kuniko Miyake, Kan Nihon-yanagi, Shuji Sano, Toyoko Takahashi, Seiji Miyaguchi; D: Yasujiro Ozu. **VHS, Beta $59.95** FCT, ING ✂✂✂

The Earrings of Madame De... A simple story about a society woman who sells a pair of diamond earrings that her husband gave her, then lies about it. Transformed by Ophuls into his most opulent, overwrought masterpiece, the film displays a triumph of form over content. In French with English subtitles. *AKA:* Diamond Earrings; Madame De.
1954 105m/C *FR* Charles Boyer, Danielle Darrieux, Vittorio De Sica, Lea di Lea, Jean Debucourt; D: Max Ophuls. **VHS, Beta $69.95** FCT, MRV, ING ✂✂✂

Earth Classic Russian silent film with English subtitles. Problems begin in a Ukrainian village when a collective farm landowner resists handing over his land. Outstanding camera work. Kino release runs 70 minutes. *AKA:* Zemlya; Soul.
1930 57m/B *RU* Semyon Svashenko, Mikola Nademsy, Stephan Shkurat, Yelena Maximova; D: Alexander Dovzhenko. **VHS, Beta $24.95** VYY, CCB, IHF ✂✂✂✂

Earth Entranced A complex political lamentation from Rocha, the premiere director of Brazil's own new wave cinema. Here a writer switches his allegiance from one politician to another, only to find that he (and the masses) lose either way. In Portuguese with English subtitles. *AKA:* Terra in Transe.
1966 105m/C *BR* Jose Lewgoy, Paulo Gracindo, Jardel Filho, Glauce Rocha; D: Glauce Rocha; W: Glauce Rocha. **VHS** NO ✂✂

Earth Girls are Easy Valley girl Valerie is having a bad week: first she catches her fiancee with another woman, then she breaks a nail, then furry aliens land in her swimming pool. What more could go wrong? When the aliens are temporarily stranded, she decides to make amends by giving them a head-to-toe makeover. Devoid of their excessive hairiness, the handsome trio of fun-loving extraterrestrials set out to experience the Southern California lifestyle. Sometimes hilarious sci-fi/musical, featuring bouncy shtick and a gleeful dismantling of modern culture.
1989 (PG) 100m/C Geena Davis, Jeff Goldblum, Charles Rocket, Julie Brown, Jim Carrey, Damon Wayans, Michael McKean, Angelyne, Larry Linville, Rick Overton; D: Julien Temple; W: Julie Brown, Charlie Coffey, Terrance McNally; M: Nile Rodgers. **VHS, Beta $14.98** LIV, VES ✂✂½

Earth vs. the Flying Saucers Extraterrestrials land on Earth and issue an ultimatum to humans concerning their constant use of bombs and missiles. Peace is threatened when the military disregards the extraterrestrials' simple warning. Superb special effects by Ray Harryhausen. *AKA:* Invasion of the Flying Saucers.
1956 83m/B Hugh Marlowe, Joan Taylor, Donald Curtis, Morris Ankrum; D: Fred F. Sears; W: Curtis Siodmak. **VHS, Beta $9.95** COL, MLB ✂✂½

Earth vs. the Spider Man-eating giant mutant (teenage ninja?) tarantula makes life miserable for a small town in general and high school partyers in particular. Silly old drive-in fare is agony for many, camp treasure for a precious few. *AKA:* The Spider.
1958 72m/B Edward Kemmer, June Kennedy, Gene Persson, Gene Roth, Hal Torey, Mickey Finn; D: Bert I. Gordon. **VHS $9.95** COL, MLB ✂

Earthling A terminally ill Holden helps a young Schroder survive in the Australian wilderness after the boy's parents are killed in a tragic accident. Lessons of life and the power of the human heart are passed on in this panoramic, yet mildly sentimental film.
1980 (PG) 102m/C *AU* William Holden, Rick Schroder, Jack Thompson, Olivia Hamnett, Alwyn Kurts; D: Peter Collinson. **VHS, Beta $69.98** LIV, VES ✂✂½

Earthquake Less-than mediocre drama centers on a major earthquake in Los Angeles and its effect on the lives of an engineer, his spoiled wife, his mistress, his father-in-law, and a suspended policeman. Filmed in much-hyped Sensurround—a technique intended to shake up the theater a bit, but which will have no effect on your television set. Good special effects, but not enough to compensate for lackluster script.
1974 (PG) 123m/C Charlton Heston, Ava Gardner, George Kennedy, Lorne Greene, Genevieve Bujold, Richard Roundtree, Marjoe Gortner, Barry Sullivan, Victoria Principal, Lloyd Nolan, Walter Matthau; D: Mark Robson; W: Mario Puzo; M: John Williams. Academy Awards '74: Best Sound, Best Visual Effects; Nominations: Best Art Direction/Set Decoration, Best Cinematography, Best Film Editing. **VHS, Beta $14.98** MCA ✂✂

Earthworm Tractors Ambitious tractor salesman Alexander Botts will do anything to make a sale. Brown excels as the fast-talking lead. Comedy is strengthened by its supporting cast. Based on characters first appearing in the "Saturday Evening Post."
1936 63m/B Joe E. Brown, June Travis, Guy Kibbee, Dick Foran, Carol Hughes, Gene Lockhart, Olin Howland; D: Ray Enright. **VHS $19.95** NOS, RXM, HEG ✂✂½

East and West Morris Brown, a worldly New York Jew, returns home to Galicia with his daughter Mollie for a traditional family wedding. She teaches the young villagers to dance and box but meets her romantic match in a young yeshiva scholar who forsakes tradition to win her heart. Picon shines as the exuberant flapper. With English and Yiddish intertitles.
1923 85m/B Molly Picon, Jacob Kalish, Sidney Goldin; D: Sidney Goldin. **VHS $72.00** NCJ ✂✂✂

East End Hustle High-priced call girl rebels against her pimp and sets out to free other prostitutes as well. Also available in an 88-minute unrated version.
1976 (R) 86m/C **VHS, Beta $69.98** LIV, VES ✂

East L.A. Warriors A mobster, Hilton-Jacobs, manipulates Los Angeles gangs in this non-stop action adventure.
1989 90m/C Tony Bravo, Lawrence Hilton-Jacobs, Kamar Reyes, William Smith; D: Addison Randall. **VHS, Beta $69.95** PAR ✂

East of Borneo Tropical adventure involving a "lost" physician whose worried wife sets out to find him in the jungle. She locates her love only to discover he has a prestigious new job tending to royalty and didn't want to be found.
1931 76m/B Charles Bickford, Rose Hobart, Georges Renavent; D: George Melford. **VHS, Beta $16.95** SNC, DVT, CAB ✂½

East of Eden Steinbeck's contemporary retelling of the biblical Cain and Abel story receives superior treatment from Kazan and his excellent cast. Dean, in his first starring role, gives a reading of a young man's search for love and acceptance that defines adolescent pain. Though filmed in the 1950s, this story still rivets today's viewers with its emotional message.
1954 115m/C James Dean, Julie Harris, Richard Davalos, Raymond Massey, Jo Van Fleet, Burl Ives, Albert Dekker; D: Elia Kazan; W: Paul Osborn; M: Leonard Rosenman. Academy Awards '55: Best Supporting Actress (Van Fleet); Nominations: Best Actor (Dean), Best Director (Kazan), Best Screenplay; Golden Globe Awards '56: Best Film—Drama; National Board of Review Awards '55: 10 Best Films of the Year. **VHS, Beta $19.98** WAR, BTV, HMV ✂✂✂✂

East of Eden Remade into a television mini series, this Steinbeck classic tells the tale of two brothers who vie for their father's affection and the woman who comes between them. Seymour is notable as the self-serving mother who abandons her babies to lead a disreputable life. Rife with biblical symbolism and allusions.
1980 375m/C Jane Seymour, Bruce Boxleitner, Warren Oates, Lloyd Bridges, Anne Baxter, Timothy Bottoms, Soon-Teck Oh, Karen Allen, Hart Bochner, Sam Bottoms, Howard Duff, Richard Masur, Wendell Burton, Nicholas Pryor, Grace Zabriskie, M. Emmet Walsh, Matthew "Stymie" Beard; D: Harvey Hart. **VHS, Beta $29.95** STE, LIV ✂✂½

East of Elephant Rock In 1948, a young first secretary of the British Embassy returns from leave in England to a tense atmosphere in a colony in southeast Asia. Beautiful scenery can't make up for weak plot.
1976 93m/C *GB* John Hurt, Jeremy Kemp, Judi Bowker, Christopher Cazenove; D: Don Boyd; W: Don Boyd. **VHS, Beta $59.98** SUE ✂½

East of Kilimanjaro A freelance photographer and a doctor search frantically to find the carrier of a fatal disease near the slopes of the majestic Mt. Kilimanjaro. Routine killer virus flick filmed in Africa. Also know as "The Big Search."
1959 75m/C Marshall Thompson, Gaby Andre, Fausto Tozzi; *D:* Arnold Belgard. **VHS** SUE 🐾🐾

East Side Kids Early East Side kids. A hoodlum wants to prevent his brother from beginning a similar life of crime.
1940 60m/B Leon Ames, Harris Berger, Dennis Moore, Joyce Bryant; *D:* Robert F. Hill. **VHS, Beta** $19.95 NOS, MRV, DVT 🐾🐾

East Side Kids/The Lost City The first East Side Kids film introduces some soon-familiar faces. "The Lost City" is a composite of all twelve episodes of the serial; edited for brevity.
1935 135m/B Dennis Moore, Vince Barnett, William Boyd, Kane Richmond. **VHS, Beta** AOV 🐾🐾

East Side, West Side Stanwyck and Mason try hard to make this simple-minded soaper work, with mixed results. A wealthy couple experiences marital woes, aggravated by a ambitious young woman and a soft-hearted man suffering from unrequited love. Based on the popular novel by Marcia Davenport.
1949 110m/B Barbara Stanwyck, James Mason, Ava Gardner, Van Heflin, Gale Sondergaard, William Frawley, Nancy Davis; *D:* Mervyn LeRoy; *M:* Miklos Rozsa. **VHS** $19.98 MGM 🐾🐾

Easter Parade A big musical star (Astaire) splits with his partner (Miller) claiming that he could mold any girl to replace her in the act. He tries and finally succeeds after much difficulty. Astaire and Garland in peak form, aided by a classic Irving Berlin score. ♫Happy Easter; Drum Crazy; It Only Happens When I Dance With You; Everybody's Doin' It; I Want to Go Back to Michigan; Beautiful Faces Need Beautiful Clothes; A Fella With an Umbrella; I Love a Piano; Snookey Ookums; Ragtime Violin; When the Midnight Choo-Choo Leaves for Alabam; Shaking the Blues Away; Steppin' Out With My Baby; A Couple of Swells; The Girl on the Magazine Cover; Better Luck Next Time; Easter Parade.
1948 103m/C Fred Astaire, Judy Garland, Peter Lawford, Ann Miller, Jules Munshin, Joi Lansing; *D:* Charles Walters; *W:* Sidney Sheldon; *M:* Irving Berlin. **VHS, Beta** $19.98 MGM, HMV 🐾🐾🐾½

Easy Come, Easy Go Elvis, as a Navy frogman, gets excited when he accidentally discovers what he believes is a vast sunken treasure. Music is his only solace when he finds his treasure to be worthless copper coins. ♫Easy Come, Easy Go; The Love Machine; Yoga is as Yoga Goes; Sing, You Children; You Gotta Stop; I'll Take Love.
1967 96m/C Elvis Presley, Dodie Marshall, Pat Priest, Elsa Lanchester, Frank McHugh, Pat Harrington; *D:* John Rich. **VHS, Beta** $14.95 PAR 🐾🐾

Easy Kill A man takes the law into his own hands to exact revenge on drug lords.
1989 100m/C Jane Badler, Cameron Mitchell, Frank Stallone; *D:* Josh Spencer. **VHS, Beta** NO 🐾½

The Easy Life Haunting film about a hedonistic man from a small Italian village who takes a mild-mannered student pleasure-seeking. The ride turns sour and the playboy is ultimately destroyed by his own brutality.
1963 105m/B *IT* Vittorio Gassman, Catherine Spaak, Jean-Louis Trintignant, Luciana Angiolillo; *D:* Dino Risi. **VHS** FST 🐾🐾🐾

Easy Living Compromised melodrama about an over-the-hill football player who must cope with his failing marriage and looming retirement. Based on an Irwin Shaw story.
1949 77m/B Victor Mature, Lucille Ball, Jack Paar, Lizabeth Scott, Sonny Tufts, Lloyd Nolan, Paul Stewart; *D:* Jacques Tourneur. **VHS, Beta** $19.95 MED, TTC 🐾🐾

Easy Money A basic slob has the chance to inherit $10 million if he can give up his loves: smoking, drinking, and gambling among others. Dangerfield is surprisingly restrained in this harmless, though not altogether unpleasing comedy.
1983 (R) 95m/C Rodney Dangerfield, Joe Pesci, Geraldine Fitzgerald, Jennifer Jason Leigh, Tom Ewell, Candice Azzara, Taylor Negron; *D:* James Signorelli. **VHS, Beta** $19.98 VES 🐾🐾

Easy Rider Slim-budget, generation-defining movie. Two young men in late 1960s undertake a motorcycle trek throughout the Southwest in search of the real essence of America. Along the way they encounter hippies, rednecks, prostitutes, drugs, Nicholson, and tragedy. One of the highest-grossing pictures of the decade, undoubtedly an influence on two generations of "youth-oriented dramas," which all tried unsuccessfully to duplicate the original accomplishment. Psychedelic scenes and a great role for Nicholson are added bonuses. Look for the graveyard dancing scene in New Orleans. Features one of the best '60s rock scores around, including "Mean Streets" and "The Wanderers."
1969 (R) 94m/C Peter Fonda, Dennis Hopper, Jack Nicholson, Karen Black, Toni Basil, Robert Walker Jr.; *D:* Dennis Hopper; *W:* Terry Southern. **VHS, Beta, 8mm** $19.95 COL, CCB 🐾🐾🐾½

Easy Street Chaplin portrays a derelict who, using some hilarious methods, reforms the residents of Easy Street. Chaplin's row with the town bully is particularly amusing. Silent with musical soundtrack added.
1916 20m/B Charlie Chaplin; *D:* Charlie Chaplin. **VHS, Beta** CAB 🐾🐾🐾

Easy to Love Williams is in love with her boss, but he pays her no attention until a handsome singer vies for her affections. Set at Florida's Cypress Gardens, this aquatic musical features spectacular water ballet productions choreographed by Busby Berkeley, and the title song penned by Cole Porter. ♫Easy to Love; Coquette; Beautiful Spring; That's What Rainy Day is For; Look Out! I'm Romantic; Didja Ever.
1953 96m/C Esther Williams, Van Johnson, Tony Martin, John Bromfield, King Donovan, Carroll Baker; *D:* Charles Walters; *W:* William Roberts. **VHS** $19.98 MGM 🐾🐾½

Easy Virtue Hitchcock directs this adaptation of a Noel Coward play as a social melodrama. Larita is an unhappily married socialite with a lover. When her husband discovers her infidelity they divorce and she is marked as a woman of loose morals. Her reputation is not enhanced by her marriage to a younger man whose family diapproves.
1927 79m/B *GB* Isabel Jeans, Ian Hunter, Frank Dyall, Eric Bransby Williams, Robin Irvine, Violet Farebrother; *D:* Alfred Hitchcock. **VHS, Beta** $16.95 GPV, MRV, NOS 🐾🐾½

Easy Wheels Like most decent biker movies, "Wheels" is propelled by bad taste and a healthy dose of existentialist nihilism. But there's an unusual plot twist in this parody. A biker named She-Wolf and her gang kidnap female babies and let wolves rear the children. Their elaborate plan is to create a race of super women who will

subdue the troublesome male population. But can this "noble" plan succeed?
1989 94m/C Paul LeMat, Eileen Davidson, Marjorie Bransfield, Jon Menick, Mark Holton, Karen Russell, Jami Richards, Roberta Vasquez, Barry Livingston, George Plimpton; *D:* David O'Malley; *W:* Ivan Raimi, Celia Abrams, David O'Malley; *M:* John Ross. **VHS, Beta** $29.95 FRH 🐾🐾½

Easyriders Video Magazine A series based on the popular magazine, ripe with a variety of features from the biker world, including coverage of Daytona Bike Week 89, Rodeo Action, the Wall of Death, Grateful Dead Roadies, the Black Hills Rally, Midwest Ice Racing, Malcom Forbes' Last Ride, David Mann's original Daytona collection, plus wild biker chicks and plenty of good times.
1991 (NC-17) 60m/C VHS $29.95 EAS 🐾🐾½

Eat a Bowl of Tea Endearing light drama-comedy concerning a multi-generational Chinese family. They must learn to deal with the problems of life in America and in particular, marriage, when Chinese women are finally allowed to immigrate with their husbands to the United States following WWII. Adaptation of Louis Chu's story, directed by the man who brought us "Dim Sum." A PBS "American Playhouse" presentation.
1989 (PG-13) 102m/C Cora Miao, Russell Wong, Lau Siu Ming, Eric Tsiang Chi Wai, Victor Wong, Jessica Harper, Lee Sau Kee; *D:* Wayne Wang; *W:* Judith Rascoe. **VHS, Beta** $19.98 COL 🐾🐾🐾

Eat and Run A bloody comedy about a 400-pound alien with a taste for Italian (people, that is).
1986 (R) 85m/C Ron Silver, R.L. Ryan, Sharon Schlarth; *D:* Christopher Hart. **VHS, Beta** $19.95 STE, NWV 🐾

Eat My Dust Teenage son of a California sheriff steals the best stock cars from a race track to take the town's heartthrob for a joy ride. Subsequently he leads the town on a wild car chase. Brainless but fast-paced.
1976 (PG) 89m/C Ron Howard, Christopher Norris, Dave Kemmerling, Rance Howard, Clint Howard, Corbin Bernsen; *D:* Charles B. Griffith. **VHS, Beta** $9.98 SUE 🐾½

Eat the Peach An idiosyncratic Irish comedy about two young unemployed rebels who attempt to break free from their tiny coast town by becoming motorcycle champs after seeing the Elvis Presley film "Roustabout." Together they create the "wall of death,"—a large wooden barrel in which they can perform various biker feats.
1986 90m/C *IR* Stephen Brennan, Eamon Morrissey, Catherine Byrne, Niall Toibin, Tony Doyle, Joe Lynch; *D:* Peter Ormrod; *W:* Peter Ormrod, Leslie McKibbin; *M:* Donal Lunny. **VHS, Beta** $79.98 FOX 🐾🐾½

Eat the Rich A British farce about a group of terrorists who take over the popular London restaurant, Bastard's. Led by a former, disgruntled transvestite employee, they turn diners into menu offerings. Music by Motorhead.
1987 (R) 89m/C *GB* Nosher Powell, Lanah Pellay, Fiona Richmond, Ronald Allen, Sandra Dorne; *Cameos:* Paul McCartney, Bill Wyman, Koo Stark, Miranda Richardson; *D:* Peter Richardson. **VHS, Beta** $89.95 COL 🐾

Eaten Alive A Southerner takes an unsuspecting group of tourists into a crocodile death trap. Director Tobe Hooper's follow-up to "The Texas Chainsaw Massacre." Englund is more recognizable with razor fingernails as Freddy Krueger of the "Nightmare on Elm Street" films. *AKA:* Death Trap; Starlight Slaughter; Legend of the Bayou; Horror Hotel Massacre.

1976 (R) 96m/C Neville Brand, Mel Ferrer, Carolyn Jones, Marilyn Burns, Stuart Whitman, Robert Englund; *D:* Tobe Hooper. VHS, Beta $59.95 PSM 🎞🎞

Eating Set in Southern California, women gather to celebrate birthdays for three of their friends who are turning 30, 40 and 50. As the party commences, women from two generations discuss their attitudes towards food and men...and discover hilarious parallels.
1990 (R) 110m/C Nelly Alard, Frances Bergen, Mary Crosby, Lisa Richards, Gwen Welles, Daphna Kastner, Elizabeth Kemp, Marlena Giovi, Marina Gregory, Toni Basil; *D:* Henry Jaglom; *W:* Henry Jaglom. VHS, Beta PAR 🎞🎞½

Eating Raoul The Blands are a happily married couple who share many interests: good food and wine, entrepreneurial dreams, and an aversion to sex. The problem is, they're flat broke. So, when the tasty swinger from upstairs makes a pass at Mary and Paul accidentally kills him, they discover he's got loads of money; Raoul takes a cut in the deal by disposing of—or rather recycling—the body. This may just be the way to finance that restaurant they've been wanting to open. Wonderful, offbeat, hilariously dark comedy.
1982 (R) 83m/C Mary Woronov, Paul Bartel, Buck Henry, Ed Begley Jr., Edie McClurg, Robert Beltran, John Paragon; *D:* Mary Woronov, Paul Bartel. VHS, Beta $19.98 FOX 🎞🎞🎞½

Ebony Dreams WWII documentary focuses on the experience of female factory workers during and after the war. Five contemporary women relate their personal endeavors and struggles to retain their jobs once the war ended. Excellent use of newsreel footage and interesting interviews with the women.
1980 85m/C Philomena Nowlin; *D:* Bill Brame. VHS $19.95 LPC 🎞🎞🎞½

Ebony Tower Based on the John Fowles novel about a crusty old artist who lives in a French chateau with two young female companions. They are visited by a handsome young man, thereby initiating sexual tension and recognizably Fowlesian plot puzzles. Made for British television. Features some partial nudity.
1986 80m/C GB Laurence Olivier, Roger Rees, Greta Scacchi, Toyah Wilcox; *D:* Robert Knights; *M:* Richard Rodney Bennett. Beta NO 🎞🎞½

Echo Murders A Sexton Blake mystery wherein he investigates a mine owner's mysterious death, opening up a veritable can of murdering, power-hungry worms.
1945 75m/B David Farrar, Dennis Price. VHS, Beta $19.95 NOS, VYY 🎞½

Echo Park An unsung sleeper comedy about three roommates living in Los Angeles' Echo Park: a body builder, a single-mother waitress, and an itinerant songwriter. Charts their struggles as they aim for careers in showbiz. Offbeat ensemble effort.
1986 (R) 93m/C AU Tom Hulce, Susan Dey, Michael Bowen, Richard "Cheech" Marin, Christopher Walker, Shirley Jo Finney, Cassandra Peterson, Yana Nirvana, Timothy Carey; *D:* Robert Dornhelm; *W:* Michael Ventura; *M:* David Ricketts. VHS, Beta $19.98 BAR 🎞🎞½

Echoes A young painter's life slowly comes apart as he is tormented by nightmares that his stillborn twin brother is attempting to murder him.
1983 (R) 90m/C Gale Sondergaard, Mercedes McCambridge, Richard Alfieri, Ruth Roman, John Spencer, Nathalie Nell; *D:* Arthur Seidelman; *W:* Richard Alfieri. VHS, Beta NO 🎞🎞

Echoes in the Darkness Television mini series based on the true-life Joseph Wambaugh bestseller about the "Main Line" murder investigation in Pennsylvania in 1979. Police are baffled when a teacher is murdered and her children vanish. Suspicion falls on a charismatic coworker and the school's principal. On two tapes.
1987 234m/C Peter Coyote, Robert Loggia, Stockard Channing, Peter Boyle, Cindy Pickett, Gary Cole, Zeljko Ivanek, Alex Hyde-White, Treat Williams; *D:* Glenn Jordan. VHS $29.95 NWV 🎞🎞½

Echoes of Conflict The turbulent Middle East and Arab-Israeli tensions are spotlighted in three new wave films from Israel. Includes "The Cage," "The Movie," and "Don't Get Involved." In Hebrew with English subtitles. In color and black and white.
1989 91m/C IS VHS $79.95 FCT, ING, KIV 🎞🎞

Echoes of Paradise After a series of earth-shattering events, a depressed woman journeys to an island where she falls for a Balinese dancer. Soon she must choose between returning home or beginning life anew in paradise. *AKA:* Shadows of the Peacock.
1986 (R) 90m/C AU Wendy Hughes, John Lone, Rod Mullinar, Peta Toppano, Steve Jacobs, Gillian Jones; *D:* Phillip Noyce. VHS, Beta $14.95 ACA 🎞🎞½

The Eclipse The last of Antonioni's trilogy (after "L'Avventura" and "La Notte"), wherein another fashionable and alienated Italian woman passes from one lover to another searching unsuccessfully for truth and love. Highly acclaimed. In Italian with subtitles. *AKA:* L'eclisse.
1966 123m/B IT Monica Vitti, Alain Delon, Francesco Rabal, Louis Seigner; *D:* Michelangelo Antonioni; *W:* Michelangelo Antonioni. VHS, Beta $29.95 TPV, MRV, FCT 🎞🎞🎞½

Ecstasy A romantic, erotic story about a young woman married to an older man, who takes a lover. Features Lamarr, then Hedy Kiesler, before her discovery in Hollywood. Film subsequently gained notoriety for Lamarr's nude scenes. In Czech with English subtitles. *AKA:* Extase; Ekstase; Symphony of Love.
1933 90m/B CZ Hedy Lamarr, Jaromir Rogoz; *D:* Gustav Machaty. VHS, Beta, 8mm $24.95 VYY, NOS, MRV 🎞🎞½

Ecstasy Soft core fluff about a film director's wife's erotic adventures.
1984 (R) 82m/C Tiffany Bolling, Franc Luz, Jack Carter, Britt Ekland, Julie Newmar. VHS, Beta $19.95 MGM Woof!

Ed and His Dead Mother Ed's just an average guy who happens to really love his mother. So much so that when she dies Ed tries to bring her back from the dead—and succeeds. Only death has made a few changes in Mom's personality. Now she's a bug-eating, chainsaw-wielding fiend. Just what's a good son supposed to do?
1993 (PG-13) 93m/C Ned Beatty, Steve Buscemi, John Glover, Miriam Margolyes; *D:* Jonathan Wacks; *W:* Chuck Hughes. VHS FXV 🎞🎞

Ed Wood Leave it to Burton to bring to the screen the story of the least talented movie director of all time. Depp is convincing as Ed Wood, Jr., the cross-dressing, angora-sweater-wearing, low-budget auteur of such notoriously "bad" cult films as "Glen or Glenda" and "Plan 9 From Outer Space." Landau has a choice role as drug-addicted horror movie star Bela Lugosi. Worth seeing for Depp's performance alone.
1994 ?m/B Johnny Depp, Sarah Jessica Parker, Martin Landau, Bill Murray, Jim Myers, Patricia Arquette, Jeffrey Jones, Lisa Marie, Vincent D'Onofrio; *D:* Tim Burton; *W:* Scott Alexander, Larry Karaszewski. VHS 🎞🎞🎞

Eddie and the Cruisers In the early 1960s, rockers Eddie and the Cruisers score with one hit album. Amid their success, lead singer Pare dies mysteriously in a car accident. Years later, a reporter decides to write a feature on the defunct group, prompting a former band member to begin a search for missing tapes of the Cruisers' unreleased second album. Questions posed at the end of the movie are answered in the sequel. Enjoyable soundtrack by John Cafferty and the Beaver Brown Band.
1983 (PG) 90m/C Tom Berenger, Michael Pare, Ellen Barkin, Joe Pantoliano, Matthew Laurance; *D:* Martin Davidson. VHS, Beta, 8mm $14.95 MVD, SUE, NLC 🎞🎞

Eddie and the Cruisers 2: Eddie Lives! A sequel to the minor cult favorite, in which a rock star believed to be dead emerges under a new name in Montreal to lead a new band. The Beaver Brown Band again provides the music.
1989 (PG-13) 106m/C CA Michael Pare, Marina Orsini, Matthew Laurance, Bernie Coulson; *D:* Jean-Claude Lord. VHS, Beta $9.99 CCB, IME 🎞½

Eddie Macon's Run Based on a true story; Eddie Macon has been unjustly jailed in Texas and plans an escape to run to Mexico. He is followed by a tough cop who is determined to catch the fugitive. Film debut of Goodman.
1983 (PG) 95m/C Kirk Douglas, John Schneider, Lee Purcell, John Goodman, Leah Ayres; *D:* Jeff Kanew. VHS, Beta $69.95 MCA 🎞🎞

Eddie Murphy "Delirious" Murphy raps about life, sex, childhood etc. in this scathing, scatalogical, stand-up performance. Strong language.
1983 (R) 69m/C Eddie Murphy, Richard Tienken, Robert Wachs; *D:* Bruce Gowers. VHS, Beta $14.95 PAR 🎞½

Eddie Murphy: Raw Murphy's second stand-up performance film, featuring many of his woman-bashing observations on life.
1987 (R) 90m/C Eddie Murphy; *D:* Robert Townsend. VHS, Beta, 8mm $14.95 PAR 🎞🎞

The Eddy Duchin Story Glossy tearjerker that profiles the tragic life of Eddy Duchin, the famous pianist/bandleader of the 30s and 40s. Features almost 30 songs, including classics by Cole Porter, George and Ira Gershwin, Hammerstein, Chopin, and several others.
1956 123m/C Tyrone Power, Kim Novak, Victoria Shaw, James Whitmore, Rex Thompson; *D:* George Sidney; *M:* George Duning. VHS $19.95 COL, MVD, TVC 🎞🎞

Eden Eden is a luxury resort designed to cater to personal fantasies and filled with numerous intrigues. Part-owner Eve Sinclair faces a number of professional and personal complications, including the tragic death of her husband, a brother-in-law who's interested in more than business, and an old friend with uncertain motives. Lots of sex in beautiful settings. Made for cable television.
1992 ?m/C Barbara Alyn Woods, Jack Armstrong, Steve Chase, Darcy Demoss, Jeff Griggs; *D:* Victor Lobl; *W:* Stephen Black, Henry Stern. VHS $79.95 UND 🎞🎞

Eden 2 The continuing saga of the luxury resort Eden. Owner Eve is still having erotic dreams of late husband Grant while fending off the very real advances of his brother Josh and becoming attracted to Paul, her late

husband's best friend. The guests are equally caught up in erotic dilemmas involving sexual blackmail. Made for cable television.
1993 (R) 102m/C Barbara Alyn Woods, Jack Armstrong, Steve Chase, Darcy Demoss, Jeff Griggs; **D:** Kristine Peterson; **W:** Stephen Black, Henry Stern. VHS **$79.95** UND *♫♫*

Eden 3 Yet another chapter in this sexy made for cable saga. Eve Sinclair risks losing her share of the tropical resort unless she remarries, which she doesn't want to do, although fitness trainer Randi would be delighted to pick up the option. Meanwhile, an heiress discovers her new bridegroom has murderous intentions.
1993 (R) ?m/C Barbara Alyn Woods, Jack Armstrong, Steve Chase, Darcy Demoss, Jeff Griggs, Dean Scofield; **D:** Victor Lobl. VHS **$79.95** UND *♫♫*

Eden 4 Further adventures in the cable series. Eve, Eden's co-owner, must cope with both Josh's jealous rage and Randi's continuing scheming as she tries to keep her guests happy at the posh resort. One of the guests, a beautiful author, gets too caught up in her sexual fantasies and may find herself in danger.
1993 (R) ?m/C Barbara Alyn Woods, Jack Armstrong, Steve Chase, Darcy Demoss, Jeff Griggs, Dean Scofield; **D:** Kristine Peterson. VHS **$79.95** UND *♫♫*

Edge of Darkness Compelling war-drama about the underground movement in Norway during Nazi takeover of WWII. Flynn plays a Norwegian fisherman who leads the local underground movement and Sheridan is his loyal fiancee. Although several problems occurred throughout filming, this picture earned high marks for its superb performances and excellent camerawork. Based on the novel by William Woods.
1943 120m/B Errol Flynn, Ann Sheridan, Walter Huston, Nancy Coleman, Helmut Dantine, Judith Anderson, Ruth Gordon, John Beal; **D:** Lewis Milestone; **W:** Robert Rossen. VHS **$19.98** MGM *♫♫♫½*

Edge of Darkness Originally produced as a mini series for British television, this mystery involves a police detective who investigates his daughter's murder and uncovers a web of espionage and intrigue.
1986 307m/C GB Joe Don Baker, Bob Peck, Jack Woodson, John Woodvine, Joanne Whalley-Kilmer; **D:** Martin Campbell; **M:** Eric Clapton, Michael Kamen. VHS, Beta **$29.95** FOX, TVC *♫♫*

Edge of Honor Young Eagle Scouts camping in the Pacific Northwest discover a woodland weapons cache and wage guerilla war against killer lumberjacks out to silence them. A boneheaded, politically correct action bloodbath; you don't have to like the logging industry to disapprove of the broad slurs against its men shown here.
1991 (R) 92m/C Corey Feldman, Meredith Salenger, Scott Reeves, Ken Jenkins, Christopher Neame, Don Swayze; **D:** Michael Spence; **W:** David O'Malley. VHS **$19.95** ACA *♫½*

Edge of Sanity An overdone Jekyll-Hyde reprise, with cocaine serving as the villainous substance. The coke-created Hyde is posited as a prototype for Jack the Ripper. Not for the easily queasy. Available in a 90 minute, unrated version.
1989 (R) 85m/C GB Anthony Perkins, Glynis Barber, David Lodge, Sarah Maur-Thorp; **D:** Gerard Kikione. VHS, Beta NO *♫½*

Edge of the Axe A small town is held in the grip of terror by a demented slasher.
1989 91m/C Barton Faulks, Christina Marie Lane, Page Moseley, Fred Hollyday; **D:** Joseph Braunstein. VHS, Beta **$79.98** MCG *♫½*

Edge of the World Moody, stark British drama of a mini-society in its death throes, expertly photographed on a six-square-mile island in the Shetlands. A dwindling fishing community of fewer than 100 souls agonize over whether to migrate to the mainland; meanwhile the romance of a local girl with an off-islander takes a tragic course. Choral effects were provided by the Glasgow Orpheus Choir.
1937 80m/B GB Finlay Currie, Niall MacGinnis, Grant Sutherland, John Laurie, Michael Powell; **D:** Michael Powell; **W:** Michael Powell. VHS **$19.95** NOS *♫♫*

Edie in Ciao! Manhattan Real-life story of Edie Sedgwick, Warhol superstar and international fashion model, whose life in the fast lane led to ruin. AKA: Ciao! Manhattan.
1972 (R) 84m/C Edie Sedgwick, Baby Jane Holzer, Roger Vadim, Paul America, Viva. VHS, Beta **$14.95** FCT, PBS *♫½*

Edison the Man Story of Tommy Edison's early years of experimentation in the basement. The young genious eventually invents light bulbs, motion pictures, and a sound recording device. Well played by Tracy.
1940 108m/C Spencer Tracy, Rita Johnson, Lynne Overman, Charles Coburn, Gene Lockhart, Henry Travers, Felix Bressart; **D:** Clarence Brown. VHS, Beta **$19.98** MGM *♫♫½*

Edith & Marcel A fictionalization of the love affair between chanteuse Edith Piaf and boxer Marcel Cerdan (played by his son, Marcel Cerdan, Jr.). In French, with English subtitles.
1983 104m/C FR Evelyne Bouix, Marcel Cerdan Jr., Charles Aznavour, Jacques Villeret; **D:** Claude Lelouch. VHS, Beta **$59.95** MED *♫½*

Educating Rita Walters and Caine team beautifully in this adaptation of the successful Willy Russell play which finds an uneducated hairdresser determined to improve her knowledge of literature. In so doing, she enlists the aid of a tutor: a disillusioned alcoholic, adeptly played by Caine. Together, the two find inspiration in one another's differences and experiences. Ultimately, the teacher receives a lesson in how to again appreciate his work and the classics as he observes his pupil's unique approach to her studies. Some deem this a "Pygmalion" for the '80s.
1983 (PG) 110m/C GB Michael Caine, Julie Walters, Michael Williams, Maureen Lipman; **D:** Lewis Gilbert; **W:** Willy Russell. Academy Awards '83 Nominations: Best Actor (Caine), Best Actress (Walters), Best Adapted Screenplay; British Academy Awards '83: Best Actor (Caine), Best Actress (Walters), Best Film; Golden Globe Awards '84: Best Actor—Musical/Comedy (Caine), Best Actress—Musical/Comedy (Walters). VHS, Beta, 8mm **$14.95** COL *♫♫♫½*

The Education of Sonny Carson Chilling look at the tribulations of a black youth living in a Brooklyn ghetto amid drugs, prostitution, crime, and other forms of vice. Based on Sonny Carson's autobiography. Still pertinent some twenty years after its theatrical release.
1974 (R) 104m/C Rony Clanton, Don Gordon, Paul Benjamin; **D:** Michael Campus. VHS, Beta **$59.95** MED *♫♫½*

Edvard Munch Biographical portrait of the Norwegian Expressionist painter and his tormented life in the stuffy society of 19th-century Oslo. Concentrates mainly on his early years, including the deaths of his mother and younger sister, his brother's suicide, Munch's affair with a married woman, and his struggle to maintain his sanity.

Based on Munch's memoirs. In German and Norwegian with English subtitles.
1974 167m/C NO Geir Westby, Gro Fraas, Eli Ryg; **D:** Peter Watkins; **W:** Peter Watkins. VHS **$79.95** FCT, NYF *♫♫*

Edward and Mrs. Simpson Made-for-television dramatic reconstruction of the years leading to the abdication of King Edward VIII, who forfeited the British throne in 1936 so that he could marry American divorcee Wallis Simpson. Originally aired on PBS.
1980 270m/C Edward Fox, Cynthia Harris; **D:** Waris Hussein. VHS, Beta **$79.95** HBO, TVC *♫♫*

Edward Scissorhands Depp's a young man created by loony scientist Price, who dies before he can attach hands to his boy-creature. Then the boy is rescued from his lonely existence outside of suburbia by an ingratiating Avon lady. With scissors in place of hands, he has more trouble fitting into suburbia than would most new kids on the block, and he struggles with being different and lonely in a cardboard-cutout world. Visually captivating fairy tale full of splash and color, however predictable the Hollywood-prefab denouement.
1990 (PG-13) 100m/C Johnny Depp, Winona Ryder, Dianne Wiest, Vincent Price, Anthony Michael Hall, Alan Arkin, Kathy Baker, Conchata Ferrell, Caroline Aaron, Dick Anthony Williams, Robert Oliveri, John Davidson; **D:** Tim Burton; **W:** Caroline Thompson, Tim Burton; **M:** Danny Elfman. VHS, Beta **$19.98** FOX, FCT *♫♫♫*

Edward II Jarman's controversial adaptation of Christopher Marlowe's play "The Troublesome Reign of Edward II" portrays the weak-willed monarch as neglecting his kingdom for love. Unfortunately, it's not for his queen but for his commoner male lover. His neglect of both queen and country lead to a swift and brutal downfall. Jarman's use of contemporary anachronisms, stream of conscienceness approach, and heavy symbolism may leave more than one viewer wondering what's going on.
1992 (R) 91m/C GB Steven Waddington, Kevin Collins, Andrew Tiernan, John Lynch, Dudley Sutton, Tilda Swinton, Jerome Flynn, Jody Graber, Nigel Terry, Annie Lennox; **D:** Derek Jarman; **W:** Derek Jarman; **M:** Simon Fisher Turner. VHS **$19.95** COL, ING *♫♫½*

Eegah! Another Arch Hall (Merriwether) epic in which an anachronistic Neanderthal falls in love in '60s California. Reputed to be one of the worst films of all time.
1962 93m/C Marilyn Manning, Richard Kiel, Arch Hall Jr., William Waters; **D:** Ray Dennis Steckler. VHS, Beta **$9.95** RHI, FCT Woof!

The Effect of Gamma Rays on Man-in-the-Moon Marigolds A wonderful drama based on the Pulitzer Prize winning play by Paul Zindel. The story centers around eccentric young Beatrice and her depressed family. Beatrice is preparing her experiment for the school science fair, determined to beat her competition. Her exhibit shows how radiation sometimes kills the helpless marigolds, but sometimes causes them to grow into even more beautiful mutations. This mirrors Beatrice, who flowers even amidst the drunkenness of her mother and the dullness of her sister.
1973 (PG) 100m/C Joanne Woodward, Nell Potts, Roberta Wallach, Judith Lowry, Richard Venture; **D:** Paul Newman. Cannes Film Festival Nominations: cs 73: Best Film; Cannes Film Festival '73: Best Actress (Woodward). VHS NO *♫♫♫*

Effi Briest A 19th-century tragedy well-played by Schygulla and empowered with Fassbinder's directorial skills. Effi (Schygulla) is a 17 year-old beauty, unhappily married to a much older man. She drifts into a brief affair, which is not discovered for several years. When her husband does discover her past infidelity, the Prussian legal code permits him a chilling revenge. Based on a popular 19th-century novel by Theodor Fontane. In German with English subtitles. *AKA:* Fontane Effi Briest.
1974 135m/B *GE* Hanna Schygulla, Wolfgang Schenck, Lilo Pempeit, Ulli Lommel; *D:* Rainer Werner Fassbinder; *W:* Rainer Werner Fassbinder. **VHS $79.95** *NYF, ING, PMS* ♫♫♫½

The Efficiency Expert Lighthearted Australian comedy about a dingy moccasin factory where a rigid efficiency consultant is invited to save the eccentric family-run company from bankruptcy. Predictable ending contains a nevertheless timely message about the importance of the bottom line.
1992 (PG) 97m/C *AU* Anthony Hopkins, Ben Mendelsohn, Alwyn Kurts, Bruno Lawrence, Angela Punch McGregor, Russell Crowe, Rebecca Rigg, Toni Collette; *D:* Mark Joffe; *W:* Andrew Knight; *M:* Rikki Fataar. **VHS, Beta $14.95** *PAR, BTV* ♫♫½

Egg Striking film from Holland chronicles the life of a quiet, middle-aged baker who answers a personal ad from a schoolteacher. After much correspondence, the teacher visits the baker in his village, and the townspeople take great interest in what happens next. In Dutch with English subtitles.
1988 58m/C *NL* Johan Leysen, Marijke Vengelers; *D:* Danniel Danniel. **VHS $29.95** *KIV, LUM, ING* ♫♫½

Egg and I Based on the true-life adventures of best-selling humorist Betty MacDonald. A young urban bride agrees to help her new husband realize his life-long dream of owning a chicken farm. A dilapidated house, temperamental stove, and suicidal chickens test the bride's perseverance, as do the zany antics of her country-bumpkin neighbors, Ma and Pa Kettle, who make their screen debut. Plenty of old-fashioned laughs.
1947 104m/B Claudette Colbert, Fred MacMurray, Marjorie Main, Percy Kilbride, Louise Allbritton, Richard Long, Billy House, Donald MacBride; *D:* Chester Erskine. **VHS, Beta $14.95** *MCA* ♫♫♫

The Egyptian Based on the sword-and-sandal novel by Mika Waltari, this is a ponderous big-budget epic about a young Egyptian in Akhnaton's epoch who becomes physician to the Pharaoh.
1954 140m/C Edmund Purdom, Victor Mature, Peter Ustinov, Bella Darvi, Gene Tierney, Henry Daniell, Jean Simmons, Michael Wilding, Judith Evelyn, John Carradine, Carl Benton Reid; *D:* Michael Curtiz; *W:* Philip Dunne, Casey Robinson. **VHS, Beta $19.98** *FOX, IME* ♫♫½

The Eiger Sanction An art teacher returns to the CII (a fictionalized version of the CIA) as an exterminator hired to assassinate the killers of an American agent. In the process, he finds himself climbing the Eiger. Beautiful Swiss Alps scenery fails to totally compensate for several dreary lapses. Based on the novel by Trevanian.
1975 (R) 125m/C Clint Eastwood, George Kennedy, Vonetta McGee, Jack Cassidy, Thayer David; *D:* Clint Eastwood; *W:* John Williams. **VHS, Beta $19.95** *MCA, TLF* ♫♫

8 1/2 The acclaimed Fellini self-portrait of a revered Italian film director struggling with a fated film project wanders through his intermixed life, childhood memories, and halluci-

natory fantasies. Subtitled in English. *AKA:* Otto E Mezzo; Federico Fellini's 8 1/2.
1963 135m/B *IT* Marcello Mastroianni, Claudia Cardinale, Anouk Aimee, Sandra Milo, Barbara Steele, Rossella Falk, Eddra Gale, Mark Herron, Madeleine LeBeau, Caterina Boratto; *D:* Federico Fellini; *W:* Tullio Pinelli, Ennio Flaino, Brunello Rondi, Federico Fellini; *M:* Nino Rota. Academy Awards '63: Best Costume Design (B & W), Best Foreign Language Film; Nominations: Best Art Direction/Set Decoration (B & W), Best Director (Fellini), Best Story & Screenplay; National Board of Review Awards '63: 5 Best Foreign Films of the Year; New York Film Critics Awards '63: Best Foreign Film. **VHS, Beta $69.95** *VES, MRV, MPI* ♫♫♫♫

800 Leagues Down the Amazon A journey through the Amazonian jungle. Also available in Spanish.
199? (PG-13) 100m/C Daphne Zuniga, Barry Bostwick, Adam Baldwin, Tom Verica, E.E. Bell; *D:* Luis Llosa; *W:* Laura Schiff, Jackson Barr. **VHS $89.98** *NHO* ♫♫♫½

Eight Men Out Taken from Eliot Asinof's book, a moving, full-blooded account of the infamous 1919 "Black Sox" scandal, in which members of the Chicago White Sox teamed to throw the World Series for $80,000. A dirge of lost innocence, this is among Sayles' best films. Provides an interesting look at the "conspiracy" that ended "shoeless" Joe Jackson's major-league career. The actual baseball scenes are first-rate, and Straithairn, Sweeney, and Cusack give exceptional performances. Sayles makes an appearance as Ring Lardner. Enjoyable viewing for even the non-sports fan.
1988 (PG) 121m/C John Cusack, D.B. Sweeney, Perry Lang, Jane Alexander, Bill Irwin, Clifton James, Michael Rooker, Michael Lerner, Christopher Lloyd, Studs Terkel, David Strathairn, Charlie Sheen, Kevin Tighe, John Mahoney, John Sayles, Gordon Clapp, Richard Edson, James Reed, Don Harvey, John Anderson, Maggie Renzi; *D:* John Sayles; *W:* John Sayles; *M:* Mason Daring. **VHS, Beta $9.98** *ORI, FCT* ♫♫♫

8 Million Ways to Die An ex-cop hires himself out to rescue a pimp-bound hooker, and gets knee-deep in a mess of million-dollar drug deals, murder, and prostitution. Slow-moving but satisfying. Based on the book by Lawrence Block.
1985 (R) 115m/C Jeff Bridges, Rosanna Arquette, Andy Garcia, Alexandra Paul; *D:* Hal Ashby; *W:* Oliver Stone; *M:* James Newton Howard. **VHS, Beta $19.98** *FOX* ♫♫

8 Seconds Love, not sports, dominates the true-life story of rodeo star Lane Frost (Perry), a world champion bull rider killed in the ring at the age of 25 in 1990. A decent guy, he finds quick success on the rodeo circuit, marries (to Geary), and finds his career getting in the way of their happiness. Bull-riding sequences are genuinely stomach churning, the performances low-key. Title refers to the amount of time a rider must stay aboard his animal. *AKA:* The Lane Frost Story.
1994 (PG-13) 104m/C Luke Perry, Cynthia Geary, Stephen Baldwin, James Rebhorn, Carrie Snodgress, Red Mitchell, Ronnie Clair Edwards; *D:* John G. Avildsen; *W:* Monte Merrick; *M:* Bill Conti. **VHS** *NYR* ♫♫½

Eight Witnesses Suspense thriller about a man being murdered in front of eight blind witnesses.
1954 ?m/C Peggy Ann Garner. **VHS $15.95** *LOO* ♫♫

18 Again! After a bump on the head, an 81-year-old man and his 18-year-old grandson mentally switch places, giving each a new look at his life. Lightweight romp with

Burns in especially good form, but not good enough to justify redoing this tired theme.
1988 (PG) 100m/C George Burns, Charlie Schlatter, Anita Morris, Jennifer Runyon, Tony Roberts, Red Buttons, Miriam Flynn, George DiCenzo; *D:* Paul Flaherty; *W:* Jonathan Prince, Josh Goldstein; *M:* Billy Goldenberg. **VHS, Beta $19.95** *STE, NWV* ♫♫½

Eighteen Jade Arhats A kung fu epic with a blind heroine who nevertheless kicks other people in the eyes.
1984 95m/C Chia Ling, Ou-Yang Ksiek, Sun Chia-Lin, Otae Mofo. **VHS, Beta $57.95** *UNI* ♫

1860 During the Battle of Calatafimi in May of 1860, Sicilian peasants revolted against the King of Naples' army. The story focuses on four people caught up in the fighting: the spouse of a revolutionary, a foppish intellectual, a rebel priest, and the young shepherd who is sent with a message to Genoa asking for assistance. Blasetti made great use of location filming and natural light. In Italian with English subtitles.
1933 72m/C *IT* *D:* Alexandro Blasetti. **VHS $29.95** *FCT, ING, WBF* ♫♫

The Eighties A comic, pseudo-documentary romp through the making of a musical. Not just another dime-a-dozen song-and-dance flick, but plays with the genre with humor and intelligence, treating us to an insider's view of a performance arranged at a shopping plaza, from the rigorous auditions to the tedium of the production of songs and routines. Treated in a light-hearted, sensitive, just on the verge of laughable manner, it concludes with 30 minutes of song and dance. In French with English subtitles.
1983 86m/C *FR* Aurore Clement, Lio, Magali Noel, Pascale Salkin; *D:* Chantal Akerman; *W:* Chantal Akerman, Jean Gruault. **VHS $79.95** *WAC, FCT, ING* ♫♫½

84 Charing Cross Road A lonely woman in New York and a book-seller in London begin corresponding for business reasons. Over a twenty-year period, their relationship grows into a friendship, and then a romance, though they communicate only by mail. Based on a true story.
1986 (PG) 100m/C Anne Bancroft, Anthony Hopkins, Judi Dench, Jean De Baer, Maurice Denham, Eleanor David, Mercedes Ruehl, Daniel Gerroll, Hugh Whitemore; *D:* David Jones; *M:* George Fenton. **VHS, Beta $19.95** *COL, TVC, HMV* ♫♫♫

84 Charlie Mopic A widely acclaimed drama about the horrors of Vietnam seen through the eyes of a cameraman assigned to a special front-line unit. Filled with a cast of unknowns, this is an unsettling film that sheds new light on the subject of the Vietnam war. Powerful and energetic; music by Donovan.
1989 (R) 89m/C Richard Brooks, Christopher Burgard, Nicholas Cascone, Jonathon Emerson, Glen Morshower, Jason Tomlins, Byron Thames; *D:* Patrick Duncan; *W:* Patrick Duncan; *M:* Donovan. **VHS, Beta $89.95** *COL* ♫♫♫

Eijanaika A gripping story of a poor Japanese man who returns to his country after a visit to America in the 1860s. Memorable performances make this an above-average film. In Japanese with English subtitles. *AKA:* Why Not?.
1981 151m/C *JP* Ken Ogata, Shigeru Izumiya; *D:* Shohei Imamura. **VHS $79.95** *KIV, FCT, ING* ♫♫♫½

El Ametralladora A retired general tussles with a man known as "The Machine Gun."
1965 90m/C *MX* Pedro Infante, Margarita Mora, Alfredo Varela. **VHS, Beta $44.95** *MAD* ♫♫

E

El Amor Brujo An adaptation of the work of Miguel de Falla, in which flamenco dancers enact the story of a tragic romance.
1986 100m/C Antonio Gades, Christina Hoyos, Laura Del Sol; **D:** Carlos Saura. **VHS, Beta** $29.95 CTH, FCT, APD *ƒƒ*

El Aviador Fenomeno A private eye goes undercover to investigate several murders.
1947 90m/B MX Adalberto "Resortes" Martinez, Maria Eugenia San Martin, David Silva, Pedro de Aguillon. **VHS, Beta** $39.95 MAD, PMS *ƒƒ*

El Aviso Inoportuno Two men journey to Mexico City to become actors, but are unable to find jobs in their chosen field.
1987 121m/C MX Enrique Cuenca, Eduardo Manzano, Carlos Lopez Moctezuma. **VHS, Beta** $57.95 MAD *ƒƒ*

El Barbaro In the beginning of civilization, when evil powers rule, a barbarian has two ambitions in life: to seek revenge for his friend's death and to rescue the world from a sorcerer's power.
1984 88m/C SP Andrea Occhipinti, Maria Scola, Violeta Cela, Sabrina Sellers. **VHS, Beta** MED *ƒ*

El Bruto A mid-Mexican-period Bunuel drama, about a brainless thug who is used as a bullying pawn in a struggle between a brutal landlord and discontented tenants. In Spanish with English titles. **AKA:** The Brute.
1952 83m/B MX Pedro Armendariz Sr., Katy Jurado, Andres Soler, Rosita Arenas; **D:** Luis Bunuel. **VHS, Beta** $59.95 ING, FCT, APD *ƒƒ ½*

El Callao A Puerto Rican gang in New York City searches for their former leader. When they mistakenly kill a priest who looks like him, trouble begins. **AKA:** The Silent One.
197? 90m/C Jose Albar, Olga Agostini. **VHS, Beta** NO *ƒ ½*

El Ceniciento An innocent man gets into trouble because he can't stop thinking about a beautiful princess.
1947 90m/B MX Tin Tan, Alicia Caro, Andres Soler. **VHS, Beta** $48.95 MAD *ƒƒ*

El Ciclon An invincible lawman comes to town to clean things up.
1947 120m/B MX Miguel Aceves Mejia, Flor Silvestre, Sonia Furio, Raul Ramirez. **VHS, Beta** $45.95 MAD *ƒƒ*

El Cid Charts the life of Rodrigo Diaz de Bivar, known as El Cid, who was the legendary eleventh-century Christian hero who freed Spain from Moorish invaders. Noted for its insanely lavish budget, this epic tale is true to its setting and features elaborate battle scenes.
1961 184m/C Charlton Heston, Sophia Loren, Raf Vallone, Hurd Hatfield, Genevieve Page; **D:** Anthony Mann; **W:** Philip Yordan; **M:** Miklos Rozsa. **VHS, Beta** $29.95 BFV, VCI, FCT *ƒƒƒ*

El Cochecito The great Spanish actor, Jose Isbert, stars as the head of a large family whose closest friends are all joined together in a kind of fraternity defined by the fact that they each use a wheelchair. He feels excluded because he does not have or need one, so he goes to great lengths to gain acceptance in this "brotherhood." In Spanish with English subtitles. **AKA:** The Wheelchair.
1960 90m/B SP Jose Isbert; **D:** Marco Ferreri. **VHS, Beta** $69.95 KIV *ƒƒƒ*

El Condor Two drifters search for gold buried in a Mexican fort.
1970 (R) 102m/C SP Jim Brown, Lee Van Cleef, Patrick O'Neal, Marianna Hill, Iron Eyes Cody, Elisha Cook Jr.; **D:** John Guillermin; **W:** Larry Cohen; **M:** Maurice Jarre. **VHS** $59.95 WAR, SIM *ƒ ½*

El Cristo de los Milagros After a ruthless thief has a vision of Christ, he changes his criminal ways. In Spanish.
1987? 90m/C SP Juan Gallardo, Norma Lazarendo, Claudio Lanuza, Julio Cesar. **VHS, Beta** $74.95 MAD *ƒ*

El Cuarto Chino A madman terrorizes the ports of Acapulco, Mexico. **AKA:** The Chinese Room.
1971 97m/C MX Cathy Crosby, Guillermo Murray, Carlos Rivas, Regina Torne. **VHS, Beta** $69.95 MAD *ƒ*

El Derecho de Comer A good natured vagrant finds a purse filled with money and a love letter. **AKA:** The Right to Eat.
1987 86m/C MX Arturo Correa, Findingo, Lissette, Luis Cosme. **VHS, Beta** $54.95 MAD *ƒƒ ½*

El Diablo A young man finds the West more wild than he expected. He finds "help" in the shape of Gossett as he tries to free a young girl who's being held by the notorious El Diablo. Made for television. Better than average.
1990 (PG-13) 107m/C Louis Gossett Jr., Anthony Edwards, John Glover, Robert Beltran, M.C. Gainey, Miguel Sandoval, Sarah Trigger, Joe Pantoliano; **D:** Peter Markle; **W:** John Carpenter, Bill Phillips. **VHS** $19.98 WAR, HBO *ƒƒ*

El Diablo Rides A fierce feud between cattlemen and sheepmen develops, with touches of comedy in between.
1939 57m/B Bob Steele, Carleton Young, Kit Guard. **VHS, Beta** $19.95 VDM, VCN, VYY *ƒ ½*

El Diputado A famous politician jeopardizes his career when he has an affair with a young man. In Spanish. Also available with English subtitles. **AKA:** The Deputy.
1978 111m/C SP Jose Sacristan, Maria Luisa San Jose, Jose Alonso; **D:** Eloy De La Iglesia. **VHS, Beta** $79.95 FCT *ƒƒƒ*

El Dorado A gunfighter rides into the frontier town of El Dorado to aid a reckless cattle baron in his war with farmers over land rights. Once in town, the hired gun meets up with an old friend—the sheriff—who also happens to be the town drunkard. Switching allegiances, the gunslinger helps the lawman sober up and defend the farmers. This Hawks western displays a number of similarities to the director's earlier "Rio Bravo" (1959), staring Wayne, Dean Martin, and Ricky Nelson—who charms viewers as the young sidekick "Colorado" much like Caan does as "Mississippi" in El Dorado.
1967 126m/C John Wayne, Robert Mitchum, James Caan, Charlene Holt, Ed Asner, Arthur Hunnicutt, Christopher George, R.G. Armstrong, Jim Davis, Paul Fix, Johnny Crawford, Michele Carey; **D:** Howard Hawks. **VHS, Beta** $14.95 PAR, TLF *ƒƒƒ*

El Fego Baca: Six-Gun Law An Arizona DA tackles a seemingly clear-cut murder case. Compiled from Walt Disney television episodes.
1962 77m/C Robert Loggia, James Dunn, Lynn Bari, Annette Funicello. **VHS, Beta** $69.95 DIS *ƒ ½*

El Forastero Vengador A man arrives in town and challenges an evil woman dictator.
1965 95m/C MX Jaime Fernandez, Eleazar Garcia Chelelo, Ofelia Guillman. **VHS, Beta** $39.95 MAD *ƒƒ*

El Fugitivo A man convicted of a crime he didn't commit waits for the right moment to exact his revenge.
1965 95m/C MX Luis Aguilar, Lucha Villa, Amparo Rivelles, Rita Macedo. **VHS, Beta** $58.95 MAD *ƒƒ*

El Gallo de Oro Two rival gamblers bet everything on a big cockfight in Mexico. This film examines the story behind the cockfights and what they mean in Mexican tradition. **AKA:** The Golden Rooster.
1965 94m/C MX Ignacio Lopez Tarso, Lucha Villa, Narciso Busquets. **VHS, Beta** $68.00 MAD, APD *ƒ*

El Gavilan Pollero A singing man in the West enthralls many a beautiful lady in this western. Packed full with gambling, horse racing, music, and women.
1947 90m/B MX Pedro Infante, Antonio Badu, Lilia Prado. **VHS, Beta** $44.95 MAD *ƒƒ*

El Gendarme Desconocido Cantinflas bungles his way into becoming a police officer after accidentally apprehending a gang of criminals in this bumble-filled comedy.
1941 110m/B MX Cantinflas, Mapita Cortes, Gloria Marin, Daniel "Chino" Herrera, Carlos Lopez Moctezuma; **D:** Miguel M. Delgado. **VHS, Beta** NO *ƒ*

El Hombre Contra el Mundo A Mexican comic-book hero comes to life so he can battle a variety of evils.
1987 100m/C MX Jorge Rivero, Nadia Milton, Narciso Busquets, Tito Junco. **VHS, Beta** $75.95 MAD *ƒƒ ½*

El Hombre de la Furia The son of a rancher seeks to avenge his father's death. **AKA:** Man of Fury.
1965 90m/B MX Javier Solis, Dacia Gonzales, Fernando Soto. **VHS, Beta** $49.95 MAD *ƒƒ ½*

El Libro de Piedra An isolated ranch harbors dark, horrible secrets. There's no telling what could be causing such strange occurrences.
1968 100m/C MX Margo Lopez, Joaquin Cordero; **D:** Carlos Enrique Taboada. **VHS, Beta** $59.95 UNI *ƒ*

El Mariachi Extremely low-budget but clever mixture of humor and violence in a tale of mistaken identity set in a small Mexican border town. 24-year-old director Rodriguez makes his feature film debut with this $7000 feature, originally intended only for the Spanish-language market. Film festival awards and critical attention brought the work to wider release. In Spanish with English subtitles or dubbed. The laserdisc version includes director's commentary and Rodriguez's 8 minute film "Bedhead."
1993 (R) 81m/C Carlos Gallardo, Consuelo Gomez, Peter Marquardt, Jaime de Hoyos, Reinol Martinez, Ramiro Gomez; **D:** Robert Rodriguez; **W:** Carlos Gallardo, Robert Rodriguez. Independent Spirit Aw Nominations: rds '94: Best Director (Rodriguez); Independent Spirit Awards '94: Best First Feature. **VHS, Beta, 8mm** $19.95 COL, FCT, BTV *ƒƒƒ*

El Monte de las Brujas A mad widow burns her daughter alive in a satanistic ritual. In Spanish.
197? 90m/C Patty Shepard. **VHS, Beta** $57.95 UNI *ƒ*

El Muerto In 19th-century Buenos Aires, a young man flees his home after killing an enemy. Arriving in Montevideo, he becomes a member of a smuggling ring. In Spanish with English subtitles.
1975 103m/C SP Thelma Biral, Juan Jose Camero, Francesco Rabal; **D:** Hector Olivera. **VHS, Beta** $24.98 ING, MED *ƒ ½*

El Norte Gripping account of a Guatemalan brother and sister, persecuted in their homeland, who make an arduous journey north ("El Norte") to America. Their difficult saga continues as they struggle against overwhelming odds in an attempt to realize their dreams. Passionate, sobering, and

powerful. In English and Spanish with English subtitles. Produced in association with the "American Playhouse" series for PBS. Produced by Anna Thomas who also co-wrote the story with Nava.
1983 (R) 139m/C *SP* David Villalpando, Zaide Silvia Gutierrez, Ernesto Cruz, Eracio Zepeda, Stella Quan, Alicia del Lugo, Lupe Ontiveros; *D:* Gregory Nava; *W:* Anna Thomas, Gregory Nava. **VHS, Beta $68.00** *FOX, APD* 🐾🐾🐾

El Paso Stampede Cowboy investigates raids on cattle herds used to feed Americans fighting in the Spanish-American War.
1953 50m/B Allan "Rocky" Lane, Eddy Waller, Phyllis Coates; *D:* Harry Keller. **VHS, Beta $29.95** *VCN* 🐾🐾

El Penon de las Animas Spanish film features a classic premise—two long-feuding families find complications in their bitter relationship as their children fall in love with one another.
1947 90m/B *MX* Maria Felix, George Negrete. **VHS, Beta $44.95** *MAD* 🐾🐾

El Profesor Hippie A freewheeling college history professor befriends a group of students, taking them to a far-off part of the country where adventures befall them. In Spanish.
1969 95m/C *MX* Luis Sandrini, Soledad Silveyra; *D:* Fernando Ayala. **VHS, Beta $29.95** *MED* 🐾🐾

El Rey The story of "The King," a rebel during the Mexican Revolution.
1987 93m/C *MX* Antonio Aguilar, Carmen Montejo, Pancho Cordova, Gerardo Reyes. **VHS, Beta $58.95** *MAD* 🐾🐾

El Robo al Tren Correo A young man must confront a ruthless band of outlaws to prove that he didn't steal a gold shipment.
1947 90m/B *MX* Carlos Cortez, Noe Murayama, Julissa. **VHS, Beta $39.95** *MAD* 🐾🐾

El Sabor de la Venganza A man's wife and son vow to avenge his murder.
1965 92m/C *MX* Isela Vega, Jorge Luke, Cameron Mitchell, Mario Almada. **VHS, Beta $59.95** *MAD* 🐾🐾

El Super A Cuban refugee, still homesick after many years, struggles to make a life for himself in Manhattan as an apartment superintendent. In Spanish with English subtitles; an American production shot on location in New York City.
1979 90m/C *SP* Raymundo Hidalgo-Gato, Orlando Jiminez-Leal, Zully Montero, Raynaldo Medina, Juan Granda, Hilda Lee, Elizabeth Pena; *D:* Leon Ichaso; *W:* Leon Ichaso, Manuel Arce. **VHS** *APD, ING, NYF* 🐾🐾🐾

El Tesoro de Chucho el Roto A widow with half of a treasure map must fend off thieves while she searches for the other half.
1947 90m/B *MX* Joaquin Cordero, Ana Berta Lepe, Manuel Lopez Ochoa. **VHS, Beta $44.95** *MAD* 🐾🐾

El: This Strange Passion Disturbing drama in which a man, convinced he is cuckolded, slowly descends into madness. Bunuel's surreal, almost Freudian look at the Spanish male's obsession with female fidelity. In Spanish with English subtitles.
1952 82m/B *SP* Arturo de Cordova, Delia Garces, Luis Beristain, Aurora Walker; *D:* Luis Bunuel. **VHS $59.95** *HTV, FCT* 🐾🐾🐾

El Zorro Blanco A man in a white mask rescues a kidnapped heiress.
1987 90m/C *MX* Juan Miranda, Hilda Aguirre, Carlos Agosti. **VHS, Beta $59.95** *MAD* 🐾🐾

El Zorro Vengador Zorro's best friend is killed and his bride abducted. And, you better believe he's going to make those baddies pay.
1947 90m/B *MX* Luis Aguilar, Maria Eugenia San Martin. **VHS, Beta $39.95** *MAD* 🐾🐾

Ele, My Friend The British Raj still rules India in the 1920s, when 10-year-old Charles comes across a herd of wild elephants living in the jungle. Charles befriends a baby elephant he names Ele but what can he do when hunters also discover the animals? Filmed on location in south India.
1993 104m/C Jacob Paul Guzman, Gazan Khan, R.S. Shivaji, Amjad Khan, Prabhu; *D:* Dharan Mandrayar; *W:* Dharan Mandrayar; *M:* Barry Phillips. **VHS $89.95** *VCI, BTV* 🐾🐾½

Eleanor & Franklin An exceptional television dramatization of the personal lives of President Franklin D. Roosevelt and his wife Eleanor. Based on Joseph Lash's book, this Emmy award-winning film features stunning performances by Alexander and Herrmann in the title roles.
1976 208m/C Jane Alexander, Edward Herrmann, Ed Flanders, Rosemary Murphy, MacKenzie Phillips, Pamela Franklin, Anna Lee, Linda Purl, Linda Kelsey, Lindsay Crouse; *D:* Daniel Petrie; *M:* John Barry. **VHS, Beta $59.95** *SIG, TLF* 🐾🐾🐾½

Eleanor: First Lady of the World Stapleton plays the former first lady after her husband's death as she goes on to work at the United Nations and emerges as even more of an influential public figure. Made for television.
1982 104m/C Jean Stapleton, E.G. Marshall, Coral Browne, Joyce Van Patten, Gail Strickland, Kenneth Kimmins; *D:* John Erman; *M:* John Addison. **VHS $59.95** *COL* 🐾🐾½

Electra Glide in Blue An Arizona motorcycle cop uses his head in a world that's coming apart at the seams. Good action scenes; lots of violence.
1973 (R) 113m/C Robert (Bobby) Blake, Billy Green Bush, Mitchell Ryan, Jeannine Riley, Elisha Cook Jr., Royal Dano; *D:* James W. Guercio. **VHS $14.95** *MGM* 🐾🐾🐾

Electric Dreams A young man buys a computer that yearns to do more than sit on a desk. First it takes over his apartment, then it sets its sights on the man's cello-playing neighbor—the same woman his owner is courting. To win her affections, the over-eager computer tries to dazzle her with a variety of musical compositions from his unique keyboard. Cort supplies the voice of Edgar the computer in this film that integrates a rock-music video format.
1984 (PG) 95m/C Lenny Von Dohlen, Virginia Madsen, Maxwell Caulfield, Bud Cort, Koo Stark; *D:* Steven Barron. **VHS, Beta $79.95** *MGM* 🐾🐾½

The Electric Horseman Journalist Fonda sets out to discover the reason behind the kidnapping of a prized horse by an ex-rodeo star. The alcoholic cowboy has taken the horse to return it to its native environment, away from the clutches of corporate greed. As Fonda investigates the story she falls in love with rebel Redford. Excellent Las Vegas and remote western settings.
1979 (PG) 120m/C Robert Redford, Jane Fonda, John Saxon, Willie Nelson, Valerie Perrine, Wilford Brimley, Nicholas Coster, James B. Sikking; *D:* Sydney Pollack; *M:* Dave Grusin. **VHS, Beta $14.98** *MCA* 🐾🐾½

The Electronic Monster Insurance claims investigator Cameron looks into the death of a Hollywood starlet and discovers an exclusive therapy center dedicated to hypnotism. At the facility, people vacation for weeks in morgue-like body drawers, while

evil Dr. Illing uses an electronic device to control the sleeper's dreams and actions. Eerie. Intriguingly, it is one of the first films to explore the possibilities of brainwashing and mind control. *AKA:* Escapement; The Electric Monster.
1957 72m/B *GB* Rod Cameron, Mary Murphy, Meredith Edwards, Peter Illing; *D:* Montgomery Tully. **VHS $16.95** *SNC* 🐾🐾

The Elegant Criminal Based on the true story of France's most infamous killer, Pierre Lacenaire. The film begins with Lacenaire in prison, writing his memoirs, receiving his admirers, and awaiting his execution (in 1836). A series of flashbacks detail his life and the supposed social clime which hindered his better instincts and turned him to the criminal life. However, Auteuil has such a wonderful time playing the charming bad guy that any blame to society fails to convince. In French with English subtitles.
1992 120m/C *FR* Daniel Auteuil, Jean Poiret, Jacques Weber, Marie-Armelle DeGuy, Maiwenn Le Besco, Patrick Pineau; *D:* Francis Girod; *W:* George Conchon, Francis Girod. **VHS $89.95** *FXL, BTV, FCT* 🐾🐾½

The Element of Crime In a monochromatic, post-holocaust future, a detective tracks down a serial killer of young girls. Made in Denmark, this minor festival favorite features an impressive directional debut and awaits cult status. Filmed in Sepiatone. *AKA:* Forbrydelsens Element.
1984 104m/C *DK* Michael Elphick, Esmond Knight, Jerold Wells, Meme Lei, Astrid Henning-Jensen, Preben Leerdorff-Rye, Gotha Andersen; *D:* Lars von Trier. **VHS, Beta $79.95** *UNI, ING, TPV* 🐾🐾½

Elena and Her Men The romantic entanglements and intrigues of a poor Polish princess are explored in this enjoyable French film. Beautiful cinematography by Claude Renoir. In French with subtitles. *AKA:* Paris Does Strange Things; Elena et les Hommes.
1956 98m/C *FR* Ingrid Bergman, Jean Marais, Mel Ferrer, Jean Richard, Magali Noel, Pierre Bertin, Juliette Greco; *D:* Jean Renoir. **VHS, Beta $59.95** *INT, FCT, ING* 🐾🐾

Eleni The true story of "New York Times" reporter Nicholas Gage and his journey to Athens to discover the truth about his mother's execution by Communists during the Greek rebellion after WWII. Adapted by Steve Tesich from Gage's bestselling book.
1985 (PG) 117m/C John Malkovich, Kate Nelligan, Linda Hunt, Oliver Cotton, Ronald Pickup, Dimitra Arliss, Rosalie Crutchley; *D:* Peter Yates; *W:* Steve Tesich. **VHS, Beta, 8mm $14.98** *COL, IGP, ING* 🐾🐾

Elephant Boy An Indian boy helps government conservationists locate a herd of elephants in the jungle. Sabu's first film. Available in digitally remastered stereo.
1937 80m/B *GB* Sabu, Walter Hudd, W.E. Holloway; *D:* Robert Flaherty, Zoltan Korda. **VHS, Beta $19.98** *HBO, SUE, WAR* 🐾🐾🐾

The Elephant Man A biography of John Merrick, a severely deformed man who, with the help of a sympathetic doctor, moved from freak shows into posh London society. Lynch's first mainstream film, shot in black and white, it presents a startlingly vivid picture of the hypocrisies evident in the social mores of the Victorian era. Moving performance from Hurt in title role.
1980 (PG) 125m/B Anthony Hopkins, John Hurt, Anne Bancroft, John Gielgud, Wendy Hiller, Freddie Jones, Kenny Baker; *D:* David Lynch; *W:* Eric Bergren, Christopher DeVore, David Lynch; *M:* John Morris, Samuel Barber. Acad. Awards '80 Nominations: Best Actor (Hurt), Best Art Direction/Set Decoration, Best Costume

Design, Best Director (Lynch), Best Film Editing, Best Picture, Best Original Score; British Academy Awards '80: Best Actor (Hurt), Best Film; Cesar Awards '82: Best Foreign Film; National Board of Review Awards '80: 10 Best Films of the Year. **VHS, Beta $14.95** PAR 𝄞𝄞𝄞𝄞

Elephant Walk Sri Lanka's balmy jungles provide the backdrop for a torrid love triangle in this post-prime Dieterle effort. Taylor, ignored by her wealthy drunkard hubby, finds solace in the arms of her spouse's sexy right-hand man. As if keeping the affair secret weren't a big enough task, she also braves a cholera epidemic and a pack of vengeful elephants who take an unscheduled tour of her humble home. Lethargic lead performances make this more of a sleep walk, but Sofaer and Biberman's supporting roles are worth the price of rental. Taylor replaced Vivian Leigh early in the filming after she fell ill, but footage of Leigh in faraway shots is included.
1954 103m/C Elizabeth Taylor, Dana Andrews, Peter Finch, Abraham Sofaer, Abner Biberman; **D:** William Dieterle. **VHS $14.95** PAR, FCT 𝄞𝄞½

11 Harrowhouse The Consolidated Selling System at 11 Harrowhouse, London, controls much of the world's diamond trade. Four adventurous thieves plot a daring heist relying on a very clever cockroach. A rather successful stab at spoofing detailed "heist" films. **AKA:** Anything for Love; Fast Fortune.
1974 (PG) 95m/C GB Charles Grodin, Candice Bergen, James Mason, Trevor Howard, John Gielgud; **D:** Aram Avakian; **W:** Jeffrey Bloom. **VHS, Beta $59.98** FOX 𝄞𝄞𝄞

Eli Eli An American Yiddish film about a family forced to live apart because of their farm's failure. Lighthearted and fun. In Yiddish with English titles.
1940 85m/B Esther Feild, Lazar Fried, Muni Serebroff; **D:** Joseph Seiden; **M:** Sholom Secunda. **VHS, Beta $14.95** VYY, AUD, FCT 𝄞𝄞½

The Eliminators A cyborgian creature endeavors to avenge himself on his evil scientist creator with help from a kung fu expert and a Mexican. The group uses time travel and other devices to achieve their mission.
1986 (PG) 95m/C Roy Dotrice, Patrick Reynolds, Denise Crosby, Andrew Prine, Conan Lee; **D:** Peter Manoogian; **W:** Danny Bilson, Paul DeMeo; **M:** Richard Band. **VHS, Beta $79.98** FOX 𝄞

Elizabeth of Ladymead Four generations of a British family live through their experiences in the Crimean War, Boer War, WWI, and WWII. Neagle, playing the wives in all four generations, aptly explores the woman's side of war. Enjoyable performances from husband and wife team Neagle and Wilcox.
1948 97m/C Anna Neagle, Hugh Williams, Bernard Lee, Michael Lawrence, Nicholas Phipps, Isabel Jeans; **D:** Herbert Wilcox. **VHS, Beta $24.95** DVT, VEC 𝄞𝄞½

Elizabeth, the Queen Historical drama recreates the struggle for power by Robert Devereaux, Earl of Essex, whom the aging Queen Elizabeth I both loved and feared, and whose downfall she finally invoked. Part of "George Schaefer's Showcase Theatre." **AKA:** The Private Lives of Elizabeth and Essex.
1968 76m/C Judith Anderson, Charlton Heston; **D:** George Schaefer. **VHS, Beta** FHS 𝄞𝄞

Eliza's Horoscope A frail Canadian woman uses astrology in her search for love in Montreal, and experiences bizarre and surreal events. An acclaimed Canadian film.
1970 120m/C CA Tommy Lee Jones, Elizabeth Moorman; **D:** Gordon Sheppard. **VHS, Beta $24.95** AHV 𝄞𝄞½

Ella Cinders The American mania for breaking into the movies is satirized in this look at a girl who wins a trip to Hollywood in a small-town beauty contest. Silent with original organ score.
1926 60m/B Colleen Moore, Harry Langdon, Lloyd Hughes, Jed Prouty, Vera Lewis; **D:** Alfred E. Green. **VHS, Beta $19.95** NOS, GPV, VYY 𝄞𝄞𝄞

Elle Voit des Nains Partout A film of France's "Cafe Theatre Show," wherein various fairy tale characters' stories are revised per modern situations. In French with subtitles.
1983 83m/C FR **D:** Jean-Claude Sussfeld. **VHS, Beta $59.95** FCT 𝄞𝄞½

Ellie A murderous widow's stepdaughter tries to save her father from being added to the woman's extensive list of dearly departed husbands.
1984 (R) 90m/C Shelley Winters, Sheila Kennedy, Pat Paulsen, George Gobel, Edward Albert; **D:** Peter Wittman. **VHS, Beta $79.98** LIV, VES 𝄞½

Elmer Follows the adventures of a temporarily blinded youth and a lovable hound dog who meet in the wilderness and together set off in search of civilization.
1976 (G) 82m/C Elmer Swanson, Phillip Swanson; **D:** Christopher Cain. **VHS, Beta $59.98** LIV, WTA 𝄞

Elmer Gantry The classic multi-Oscar-winning adaptation of the Sinclair Lewis novel written to expose and denounce the flamboyant, small-town evangelists spreading through America at the time. In the film, Lancaster is the amoral Southern preacher who exacts wealth and power from his congregation, and takes a nun as a mistress. Jones stars as his ex-girlfriend who resorts to a life of prostitution.
1960 146m/C Burt Lancaster, Shirley Jones, Jean Simmons, Dean Jagger, Arthur Kennedy, Patti Page, Edward Andrews, John McIntire, Hugh Marlowe, Rex Ingram; **D:** Richard Brooks; **W:** Richard Brooks. Academy Awards '60: Best Actor (Lancaster), Best Adapted Screenplay, Best Supporting Actress (Jones); Nominations: Best Picture, Best Original Score; National Board of Review Awards '60: 10 Best Films of the Year, Best Supporting Actress (Jones). **VHS, Beta $19.95** FOX, MGM, FCT 𝄞𝄞𝄞½

Elsa, Elsa Satire of moviemaking life finds a scriptwriter-director distracted by the loss of his girlfriend and unable to concentrate on writing a memoir of his career as a child actor. He creates a subplot dealing with his romantic problems, and puts the film in jeopardy. Fine acting and witty dialogue. In French with English subtitles.
1985 85m/C FR **D:** Didier Haudepin. **VHS $49.95** FCT 𝄞𝄞𝄞½

The Elusive Corporal Set in a P.O.W. camp on the day France surrendered to Germany, this is the story of the French and Germans, complete with memories of a France that is no more. **AKA:** Le Caporal Epingle.
1962 108m/B Jean-Pierre Cassel, Claude Brasseur, O.E. Hasse, Claude Rich; **D:** Jean Renoir. **VHS, Beta $24.95** VYY, INT, APD 𝄞𝄞𝄞½

The Elusive Pimpernel Niven sparkles in this otherwise undistinguished adaptation of Baroness Orczy's "The Scarlet Pimpernel." **AKA:** The Fighting Pimpernel.
1950 109m/C GB David Niven, Margaret Leighton, Jack Hawkins, Cyril Cusack, Robert Coote, Edmund Audran, Danielle Godet, Patrick Macnee; **D:** Michael Powell; **W:** Michael Powell, Emeric Pressburger. **VHS, Beta $59.95** HMV, FCT 𝄞𝄞½

Elves A group of possessed, neo-Nazi elves performs serious human harm at Christmas time in this tongue-in-check thriller.
1989 (PG-13) 95m/C Dan Haggerty, Deanna Lund, Julie Austin, Borah Silver; **D:** Jeffrey Mandel. **VHS, Beta $79.95** AIP 𝄞

Elvira Madigan Chronicles the 19th-century Swedish romance between a young officer and a beautiful circus tight-rope walker. Based on a true incident. Exceptional direction and photography. In Swedish with English subtitles.
1967 (PG) 90m/C SW Pia Degermark, Thommy Berggren, Lennart Malmer, Nina Widerberg, Cleo Jensen; **D:** Bo Widerberg; **W:** Bo Widerberg. **VHS, Beta $24.98** WAC, FCT, TPV 𝄞𝄞𝄞

Elvira, Mistress of the Dark A manic comedy based on Peterson's infamous B-movie horror-hostess character. The mega-busted terror-queen inherits a house in a conservative Massachusetts town and causes double-entendre chaos when she attempts to sell it.
1988 (PG-13) 96m/C Cassandra Peterson, Jeff Conaway, Susan Kellerman, Edie McClurg, Daniel Greene, W. Morgan Shepherd; **D:** James Signorelli. **VHS, Beta $9.99** STE, NWV 𝄞𝄞

Elvis and Me A TV mini series based on Priscilla Beaulieu Presley's autobiography about her life with the Pelvis. Features many of Presley's biggest hits, sung by country star Ronnie McDowell. Film may aggravate Elvis fans, however, as the King is often depicted negatively from his ex-wife's point of view.
1988 187m/C Dale Midkiff, Susan Walters, Billy Green Bush, Linda Miller, Jon Cypher; **D:** Larry Peerce. **VHS, Beta $29.95** STE, NWV 𝄞½

The Elvis Files Documentary examining the strange details surrounding Elvis's death. Contains some rare footage and interviews in support of Brewer's theory that Elvis's death was faked.
1990 55m/C VHS $19.98 MED, TTC, VTR 𝄞½

Elvis in Hollywood A tribute highlighting Presley's first four films, "Love Me Tender," "Loving You," "Jailhouse Rock," and "King Creole," completed prior to his reporting for active duty in the army. Features his 1956 screen test at Paramount Studios; photos from the movie sets; interviews with co-stars, directors, writers, business associates, songwriters, and friends; and home movies as well as out-take footage from "Jailhouse Rock."
1993 65m/C D: Frank Martin. **VHS $19.98** BMG, BTV 𝄞𝄞𝄞

Elvis in the Movies All of the King's movies are covered, complete with scenes and highlights from each. A must for Elvis fans. A must for Elvis impersonators. A must for average Elvis look-alikes. Essentially, a must for fans of all types and ages.
1990 ?m/C Elvis Presley. **VHS** COL 𝄞𝄞𝄞

Elvis Memories A video scrapbook of Elvis' career, including concert appearances, home movies, and contemporary interviews.
1985 48m/C Elvis Presley, Priscilla Presley, Cybill Shepherd, Dick Clark. **VHS, Beta $29.95** MVD, LIV, VES 𝄞𝄞𝄞

Elvis on Tour A revealing glimpse of Elvis Presley, onstage and off, during a whirlwind concert tour.
1972 (G) 93m/C Elvis Presley; **D:** Pierre Adidge, Robert Abel. **VHS, Beta $14.95** MGM 𝄞𝄞𝄞

Elvis: One Night with You The celebrated crooner performs such memorables as "Heartbreak Hotel," "Blue Suede Shoes," and "Are You Lonesome Tonight"

in this unedited performance from his 1968 Christmas Special.
1968 53m/C Elvis Presley. **VHS, Beta $19.95** *MVD, MED, LTY* 𝄞𝄞𝄞

Elvis Presley's Graceland Elvis' ex-wife (Priscilla Beaulieu Presley) takes the viewer on a tour of Graceland, the famous Memphis, Tennessee, mansion, which was home to the rock star from 1957 until his death in 1977.
1984 60m/C VHS, Beta $19.95 *CNG, KAR* 𝄞𝄞𝄞

Elvis: Rare Moments with the King Footage of Elvis from news conferences, his wedding and media newsreels.
1990 60m/B Elvis Presley. **VHS, Beta $12.95** *MVD, GKK* 𝄞𝄞𝄞

Elvis Stories Collection of humorous shorts dealing with the King, from Mojo Nixon's song "Elvis Is Everywhere" to Cusack as a burger maker who claims to receive messages from Elvis through his patties.
1989 30m/C John Cusack, Ben Stiller, Joel Murray, Mojo Nixon, Rick Saucedo. **VHS, Beta $14.95** *MVD, RHI* 𝄞𝄞

Elvis: The Echo Will Never Die Celebrities chat about the King and how much they miss him, recounting anecdotes about his rise to fame.
1986 50m/C Tom Jones, B.B. King, Sammy Davis Jr., Casey Kasem, Ursula Andress. **VHS, Beta $29.95** *IHF, MVD, MPI* 𝄞𝄞𝄞

Elvis: The Lost Performances A video collection of live performances and rehearsal footage that was discovered in MGM's underground vaults in 1986. Includes outtakes from "Elvis: That's the Way It Is" and "Elvis on Tour." A must for fans and collectors of Elvis memorabilia.
1992 60m/C Elvis Presley. **VHS $19.98** *WAR, MGM* 𝄞𝄞𝄞

Elvis: The Movie A made-for-television biography of the legendary singer, from his high school days to his Las Vegas comeback. Russell gives a convincing performance and lip syncs effectively to the voice of the King (provided by country singer Ronnie McDowell). Also available in 150-minute version.
1979 117m/C Kurt Russell, Season Hubley, Shelley Winters, Ed Begley Jr., Dennis Christopher, Pat Hingle, Bing Russell, Joe Mantegna; *D:* John Carpenter. **VHS, Beta $14.98** *LIV, VES* 𝄞𝄞½

Emanon A coming-of-age tale about a young kid and the Christ-like vagabond, named Emanon (or "no name" if spelled in reverse), he befriends.
1986 (PG-13) 101m/C Stuart Paul, Cheryl Lynn, Jeremy Miller; *D:* Stuart Paul. **VHS, Beta $19.98** *NLC* 𝄞½

Embassy In this mediocre espionage thriller, von Sydow is a Soviet defector under asylum at the U.S. embassy in Beirut. Colonel Connors, a Russian spy, penetrates embassy security and wounds von Sydow. He is caught, escapes, is captured, escapes, and is caught again. Great cast, but script is often too wordy and contrived. *AKA:* Target: Embassy.
1972 90m/C *GB* Richard Roundtree, Chuck Connors, Max von Sydow, Ray Milland, Broderick Crawford, Marie-Jose Nat; *D:* Gordon Hessler. **VHS $79.95** *WVE* 𝄞𝄞

Embassy A made-for-television movie about an American family in Rome that unknowingly possesses a secret computer chip, and thus is pursued by ruthless agents.

1985 104m/C Nick Mancuso, Blanche Baker, Eli Wallach, Sam Wanamaker, Richard Gilliland, Mimi Rogers, George Grizzard, Richard Masur, Kim Darby; *D:* Robert Lewis. **VHS, Beta** *NO* 𝄞𝄞

Embryo An average sci-fi drama about a scientist who uses raw genetic material to artificially produce a beautiful woman, with ghastly results. *AKA:* Created to Kill.
1976 (PG) 108m/C Rock Hudson, Barbara Carrera, Diane Ladd, Roddy McDowall, Ann Schedeen, John Elerick, Dr. Joyce Brothers; *D:* Ralph Nelson. **VHS, Beta $19.95** *STE, LIV* 𝄞𝄞

The Emerald Forest Captivating adventure about a young boy who is kidnapped by a primitive tribe of Amazons while his family is traveling through the Brazilian jungle. Boothe is the father who searches 10 years for him. An engrossing look at tribal life in the vanishing jungle. Beautifully photographed and based upon a true story. Features the director's son as the kidnapped youth.
1985 (R) 113m/C Powers Boothe, Meg Foster, Charley Boorman, Dira Pass, Rui Polonah; *D:* John Boorman; *W:* Rospo Pallenberg. **VHS, Beta, 8mm $14.98** *SUE, SUP, NLC* 𝄞𝄞𝄞

Emerald Jungle While searching for her missing sister in the jungle, Agren encounters cannibal tribes and a colony of brainwashed cult followers. Originally titled "Eaten Alive by Cannibals," this Italian feature was cut for its U.S. release. *AKA:* Eaten Alive by Cannibals.
1980 92m/C *IT* Robert Kerman, Janet Agren, Mel Ferrer, Luciano Martino, Mino Loy; *D:* Umberto Lenzi. **VHS, Beta** *NO* 𝄞½

Emerald of Artama Anyone viewing the most precious and sought after stone in the history of man does not live to tell about it.
1967 93m/C Rory Calhoun. **VHS** *NO* 𝄞

Emergency Scenes from the Living Theatre's works after their return to America from four years of self-imposed exile, including "Frankenstein," "Mysteries," and "Paradise Now."
1968 29m/C Julian Beck, Judith Malina; *D:* Gwen Brown. **VHS, Beta $29.95** *MFV* 𝄞𝄞𝄞

The Emigrants Farmer von Sydow decides to gather his wife (Ullmann) and family together and leave 19th-century Sweden for the promise of a new life in America. Film is divided into their leaving, the voyage over, and the journey to a settlement in Minnesota. Pacing is somewhat slow; notable cinematography (by director Troell). Adapted from the novels by Vilhelm Moberg. Dubbed into English. Followed by "The New Land." Also edited with the sequel for TV as "The Emigrant Saga." *AKA:* Utvandrarna.
1972 (PG) 151m/C *SW* Max von Sydow, Liv Ullmann, Allan Edwall, Eddie Axberg, Svenolof Bern, Aina Alfredsson, Monica Zetterlund, Pierre Lindstedt; *D:* Jan Troell; *W:* Jan Troell, Bengt Forslund; *M:* Erik Nordgren. Academy Awards '72 Nominations: Best Actress (Ullmann), Best Adapted Screenplay, Best Director (Troell), Best Picture; New York Film Critics Awards '72: Best Actress (Ullmann). **VHS $29.99** *WAR, MOV* 𝄞𝄞𝄞

Emil and the Detective A German ten-year-old is robbed of his grandmother's money by gangsters, and subsequently enlists the help of pre-adolescent detectives to retrieve it. Good Disney dramatization of the Erich Kastner children's novel. Remake of the 1931 German film starring Rolf Wenkhaus. *AKA:* Emil Und Die Detektive.
1964 99m/C Walter Slezak, Roger Mobley; *D:* Peter Tewkesbury. **VHS, Beta $69.95** *DIS* 𝄞𝄞½

Emiliano Zapata Zapata was a hero of the Mexican Revolution who sacrificed everything because of the high hopes he had for his country.
1987 139m/C *MX* Antonio Aguilar, Jaime Fernandez, Mario Almada, Patricia Aspillaga. **VHS, Beta $59.95** *MAD* 𝄞𝄞

Emilio Varela vs. Camelia La Texana A pair of criminals encounter trouble when one tries to reform while the other insists on a life of crime.
1987 110m/C *MX* Maria Almada, Jorge Russek, Silvia Manriquez. **VHS, Beta $59.95** *MAD* 𝄞𝄞

Emily Returning from her exclusive Swiss finishing school, licentious young Emily discovers mama is a prostitute and deals with the scalding news by delving into a series of erotic encounters at the hands of her willing "instructors." Stark's first venture into the realm of soft porn.
1977 87m/C Koo Stark; *D:* Henry Herbert. **VHS, Beta $59.95** *MGM* Woof!

Eminent Domain A communist party member wakes up to find himself stripped of power in a Kafkaesque purge, not knowing what he is accused of—or why. A potent premise, indifferently handled despite filming on location in Poland. Based on actual events that befell the family of scriptwriter Androej Krakowski.
1991 (PG-13) 102m/C Donald Sutherland, Anne Archer, Paul Freeman, Bernard Hepton, Francoise Michaud, Jodhi May; *D:* John Irvin; *W:* Andrzej Krakowski, Richard Greggson; *M:* Zbigniew Preisner. **VHS $39.95** *IME* 𝄞𝄞½

Emissary An American politician and his wife are blackmailed in Africa by the Russians into revealing state secrets that could spark WWIII.
1989 (R) 98m/C *SA* Robert Vaughn, Ted Leplat, Terry Norton, Andre Jacobs; *D:* Jan Scholtz. **VHS, Beta** *NO* 𝄞𝄞

Emmanuelle Filmed in Bangkok, a young, beautiful woman is introduced by her husband to an uninhibited world of sensuality. Above-average soft-core skin film, made with sophistication and style. Kristel maintains a vulnerability and awareness, never becoming a mannequin.
1974 92m/C *FR* Sylvia Kristel, Alain Cuny, Marika Green; *D:* Just Jaeckin. **VHS, Beta $84.95** *COL* 𝄞𝄞½

Emmanuelle 4 Emmanuelle flees a bad relationship and undergoes plastic surgery to mask her identity. Ultimately, she becomes a beautiful young model in the form of a different actress, of course.
1984 (R) 95m/C *FR* Sylvia Kristel, Mia Nygren, Patrick Bauchau; *D:* Francis Giacobetti. **VHS, Beta $14.95** *MGM* 𝄞

Emmanuelle 5 This time around sexy Emmanuelle flees aboard a convenient yacht when she's chased by adoring fans at the Cannes Film Festival. But she winds up being forced to join an Arab sheik's harem of slaves. A good example of a series that should have quit while it was ahead.
1987 (R) 78m/C *FR* Monique Gabrielle, Charles Foster; *D:* Steve Barnett, Walerian Borowczyk. **VHS $89.98** *NHO* 𝄞½

Emmanuelle 6 The saga of the sexy beauty continues. This time Emmanuelle and a group of models head for the paradise of an Amazon jungle where they promptly become the prized captives of a drug lord.
1992 (R) 80m/C VHS $89.98 *NHO* 𝄞

Emmanuelle & Joanna A mistreated newlywed bride goes to her sister's whorehouse and stumbles across lots of soft-core antics.

1986 90m/C *FR* Sherry Buchanan, Danielle Dublino. VHS, Beta $29.95 *MED ⅟*

Emmanuelle in Bangkok Emanuelle's exotic, erotic experiences in the Far East include a royal masseuse, suspense, and the Asian art of love.
1978 (R) 94m/C *FR* VHS, Beta *NO ⅟*

Emmanuelle in Soho Yet another episode of the sleaze-queen's sexual exploits, this time in London's porn-saturated Soho district.
198? 90m/C *FR* VHS, Beta $59.95 *PSM ⅟*

Emmanuelle in the Country Emmanuelle becomes a nurse in an attempt to bring comfort and other pleasures to those in need.
1978 90m/C *FR* Laura Gemser. VHS, Beta *IME ⅟*

Emmanuelle on Taboo Island Marooned young man discovers a beautiful woman on his island. This delights him.
1976 (R) 95m/C *FR* Laura Gemser, Paul Giusti, Arthur Kennedy. VHS, Beta *NO ⅟½*

Emmanuelle, the Joys of a Woman The amorous exploits of a sensuous, liberated couple take them and their erotic companions to exotic Hong Kong, Bangkok, and Bali.
1976 94m/C *FR* Sylvia Kristel, Umberto Orsini, Catherine Rivet, Frederic Lagache; *D:* Francis Giacobetti. VHS, Beta, 8mm $69.95 *PAR ⅟*

Emmanuelle, the Queen Seeking revenge, Emmanuelle plots the murder of her sadistic husband. The lecherous assassin she hires tries to blackmail her, and she challenges him at his own game of deadly seduction.
1975 90m/C Laura Gemser. VHS, Beta *NO ⅟*

Emmanuelle's Daughter A Greek-made thriller in which a vapidly sensuous heroine cavorts amid episodes of murder, blackmail, and rape.
1979 91m/C *GR* Laura Gemser, Gabriele Tinti, Livia Russa, Vagelis Varton, Nadia Neri. Beta *NO ⅟*

Emma's Shadow In the 1930s, a young girl fakes her own kidnapping to get away from her inattentive family and comes to befriend an ex-convict sewer worker. In Danish with English subtitles. Winner of the Prix de la Jeunesse at Cannes, it was voted 1988's Best Danish Film. *AKA:* Skyggen Af Emma.
1988 93m/C *DK* Bjorje Ahistedt, Line Kruse; *D:* Soeren Kragh-Jacobsen. VHS $79.95 *FXL, FCT, ING ⅟⅟⅟*

Emperor Jones Loosely based on Eugene O'Neill's play, film portrays the rise and fall of a railroad porter whose exploits take him from a life sentence on a chain gang to emperor of Haiti. Robeson recreates his stage role in his first screen appearance.
1933 72m/B Paul Robeson, Dudley Digges, Frank Wilson, Fredi Washington, Ruby Elzy; *D:* Dudley Murphy. VHS, Beta $12.95 *SNC, NOS, HHT ⅟⅟½*

Emperor Jones/Paul Robeson: Tribute to an Artist A classic, rarely viewed version of the Eugene O'Neill play about a criminal who schemes his way into becoming the king of a Caribbean island. Robeson's only true dramatic film appearance. The film is accompanied by a documentary profile of Robeson, made in 1979.
1933 102m/B Paul Robeson, Dudley Digges, Frank Wilson; *D:* Dudley Murphy. VHS, Beta $14.95 *COL, SUE, HMV ⅟⅟½*

Emperor of the Bronx A look at crime, sleaze, violence, and the actions of bad guys in the inner-city.
1989 90m/C William Smith. VHS, Beta $29.95 *HHE ⅟*

The Emperor's New Clothes The story of an emperor and the unusual outfit he gets from his tailor. A "Faerie Tale Theatre" presentation.
1984 60m/C Art Carney, Alan Arkin, Dick Shawn; *D:* Peter Medak. VHS, Beta $14.98 *KUI, FOX, FCT ⅟*

The Empire of Passion A peasant woman and her low-life lover kill the woman's husband, but find the future they planned with each other is not to be. The husband's ghost returns to haunt them, and destroy the passionate bond which led to the murder. Oshima's follow-up to "In the Realm of the Senses." In Japanese with English subtitles.
1976 110m/C *JP* Nagisa Oshima, Kazuko Yoshiyuki, Tatsuya Fuji, Takahiro Tamura, Takuzo Kawatani; *D:* Nagisa Oshima. Cannes Film Festival Nominations: cs 78: Best Film; Cannes Film Festival '78: Best Director (Oshima). VHS $89.95 *FCT ⅟⅟⅟*

Empire of Spiritual Ninja Ninja student gone bad encounters his former teacher. Tedious pseudo ninja adventure with more talking than action and more gunplay than chop socky action. Dubbed.
197? 90m/C *HK* Tom Berlin, Hubert Hays; *D:* Bruce Lambert; *W:* Jerry Sawyer. VHS $59.95 *TWE Woof!*

Empire of the Air: The Men Who Made Radio Documentary traces the history of radio from 1906-1955 and profiles its three rival creators: Lee de Forest, Edwin Howard Armstrong and David Sarnoff.
1991 120m/C VHS $19.95 *PBS Woof!*

Empire of the Ants A group of enormous, nuclear, unfriendly ants stalk a real estate dealer and prospective buyers of undeveloped oceanfront property. Story originated by master science-fiction storyteller H. G. Wells.
1977 (PG) 90m/C Joan Collins, Robert Lansing, John David Carson, Albert Salmi, Jacqueline Scott, Robert Pine; *D:* Bert I. Gordon. VHS, Beta $9.98 *SUE ⅟½*

Empire of the Dragon Rip-roaring martial arts adventure featuring standard number of wide-ranging kicks.
198? 90m/C Chen Tien Tse, Chia Kai, Chang Shan. VHS, Beta *NO ⅟*

Empire of the Sun Spielberg's mature, extraordinarily vivid return to real story-telling, from the best-selling J.G. Ballard novel. Yearns to be a great film, but occasional flat spots keep it slightly out of contention. Young, wealthy British Bale lives in Shanghai, but is thrust into a life of poverty and discomfort when China is invaded by Japan at the onset of WWII and he's separated from his family and interred in a prison camp. A mysterious, breathtaking work, in which Spielberg's heightened juvenile romanticism has a real, heartbreaking context. Two other 1987 releases explore the WWII memories of young boys: "Au Revoir Les Enfants" and "Hope and Glory."
1987 (PG) 153m/C Christian Bale, John Malkovich, Miranda Richardson, Nigel Havers, Joe Pantoliano, Leslie Phillips, Rupert Frazer, Ben Stiller, Robert Stephens, Burt Kwouk, Masato Ibu, Emily Richard; *Cameos:* J.G. Ballard; *D:* Steven Spielberg; *W:* Tom Stoppard; *M:* John Williams. Academy Awards '87 Nominations: Best Art Direction/Set Decoration, Best Cinematography, Best Costume Design, Best Film Editing, Best Sound, Best Original Score; National Board of Review Awards '87: 10

Best Films of the Year, Best Director (Spielberg). VHS, Beta, 8mm $19.98 *WAR, ING ⅟⅟⅟*

Empire State When his friend disappears from a posh London nightclub, a young man searches for him and finds more action and intrigue than he can handle. Even so, this movie's still pretty bland.
1987 (R) 102m/C *GB* Cathryn Harrison, Martin Landau, Ray McAnally; *D:* Ron Peck. VHS, Beta $79.95 *VMK ⅟*

The Empire Strikes Back Second film in the epic "Star Wars" trilogy finds young Luke Skywalker and the Rebel Alliance plotting new strategies as they prepare to battle the evil Darth Vader and the forces of the Dark Side. Luke learns the ways of a Jedi knight from master Yoda, while Han and Leia find time for romance and a few adventures of their own. Introduces the charismatic Lando Calrissian, vulgar and drooling Jabba the Hut, and a mind-numbing secret from Vadar. Offers the same superb special effects and hearty plot as set by 1977's excellent "Star Wars." Followed by "Return of the Jedi" in 1983. Also available on Laserdisc with "The Making of 'Star Wars'."
1980 (PG) 124m/C Mark Hamill, Carrie Fisher, Harrison Ford, Billy Dee Williams, Alec Guinness, David Prowse, Kenny Baker, Frank Oz, Anthony Daniels, Peter Mayhew, Clive Revill, Julian Glover, John Ratzenberger; *D:* Irvin Kershner; *W:* Leigh Brackett, Lawrence Kasdan; *M:* John Williams; *V:* James Earl Jones. Academy Awards '80: Best Sound, Best Visual Effects; Nominations: Best Art Direction/Set Decoration, Best Original Score; People's Choice Awards '81: Best Film. VHS, Beta $19.98 *FOX, FCT, RDG ⅟⅟⅟⅟*

Employees' Entrance William stars as a ruthless department store manager in this story about commerce and compromise during the Depression. Young gives an excellent performance as the wife of one of his employees. Outrageous, and racy, this pre-Code film was expertly-directed by veteran craftsman Del Ruth. Based on a play by David Boehm.
1933 74m/B Warren William, Loretta Young, Wallace Ford, Alice White, Allen Jenkins; *D:* Roy Del Ruth; *W:* Robert Presnell. VHS $19.98 *MGM ⅟⅟⅟*

The Empty Beach A tough private detective investigates the disappearance of a wealthy business tycoon.
1985 87m/C *AU* Bryan Brown, Anna Maria Monticelli; *D:* Chris Thomson. VHS, Beta $69.98 *LIV ⅟½*

An Empty Bed Award-winning independent production depicting Bill Frayne, an older homosexual, and the challenges of his everyday life. Told mostly in flashbacks as Bill encounters people and places during the course of one day, this is a delicate drama with important statements about homosexuality, aging and honesty.
1990 60m/C John Wylie, Mark Clifford Smith, Conan McCarty, Dorothy Stinnette, Kevin Kelly, Thomas Hill, Harriet Bass; *D:* Mark Gasper; *W:* Mark Gasper. VHS $59.99 *YOC, FCT, ING ⅟⅟⅟*

Empty Canvas A spiritually-bankrupt artist becomes obsessively jealous of his mistress who refuses to marry him in the hope that someone better will come along. Based on the Alberto Moravia novel. *AKA:* La Noia: L'Ennui Et Sa Diversion, L'Erotisme.
1964 118m/B *FR IT* Horst Buchholz, Catherine Spaak, Bette Davis; *D:* Damiano Damiani. VHS, Beta $59.98 *SUE, MLB ⅟½*

Empty Suitcases A woman becomes alienated from society when she commutes between a lover in New York City and a job in Chicago.

1984 55m/C VHS, Beta *NO* 🎬🎬

Enchanted April Two women, tired of their overbearing husbands, rent a villa in Portofino, Italy for a month with two other very different women—a beautiful but bored socialite, and a crusty old woman with an impeccable literary pedigree. The effects of the charming villa, with plenty of wisteria and sunshine, do wonders for the women. A charming and romantic period piece. Based on the 1922 novel by Elizabeth von Arnim. 1992 (PG) 93m/C *GB* Miranda Richardson, Joan Plowright, Josie Lawrence, Polly Walker, Alfred Molina, Jim Broadbent, Michael Kitchen, Adriana Fachetti; *D:* Mike Newell; *W:* Peter Barnes; *M:* Richard Rodney Bennett. Academy Awards '92 Nominations: Best Adapted Screenplay, Best Costume Design, Best Supporting Actress (Plowright); Golden Globe Awards '93: Best Actress—Musical/Comedy (Richardson), Best Supporting Actress (Plowright). VHS, Beta $19.95 *PAR, MOV, WAR* 🎬🎬½

The Enchanted Cottage Represents Hollywood's "love conquers all" fantasy hokum, as a disfigured war vet and a homely girl retreat from the horrors of the world into a secluded cottage, where they both regain youth and beauty. A four-tissue heart-tugger. Adopted from the Arthur Pinero play. 1945 91m/B Dorothy McGuire, Robert Young, Herbert Marshall, Mildred Natwick, Spring Byington, Hillary Brooke, Richard Gaines, Robert Clarke; *D:* John Cromwell. VHS, Beta $19.98 *NOS, RKO, TTC* 🎬🎬½

The Enchanted Forest An elderly man teaches a boy about life and the beauty of nature when the boy gets lost in a forest. 1945 78m/C *AR* Harry Davenport, Edmund Lowe, Brenda Joyce; *D:* Lew Landers. VHS, Beta $19.95 *NOS, NWV, HEG* 🎬🎬½

Enchanted Island Sailor stops on an island to find provisions and ends up falling in love with a cannibal princess. Thinly based upon Herman Melville's "Typee." 1958 94m/C Jane Powell, Dana Andrews, Arthur Shields; *D:* Allan Dwan. VHS, Beta $15.95 *VCI* 🎬½

The Enchantress A daring boy experiences his first true loves and passions when he journeys through a mystical land in order to find a beautiful fairy. In Greek with subtitles. *AKA:* I Skiachtra. 1985 93m/C *GR* Alkis Kourkoulos, Sofia Aliberti, Lily Kokodi, Antogone Amanitou, Vicky Koulianou, Nicols Papaconstantinou, Stratos Pachis; *D:* Manoussos Manoussakis. VHS, Beta $59.95 *FCT* 🎬½

Encino Man Two, like, totally uncool Valley dudes dig up a 10,000-year old caveman in the backyard. After giving him a makeover and teaching him the necessities like the four basic food groups (Milk Duds in the dairy group, Sweet Tarts in the fruit group), they use the gnarly caveman as their ticket to popularity and dates to the prom. Juvenile humor appealing to teens; strictly brain candy. *AKA:* California Man. 1992 (PG) 88m/C Sean Astin, Brendan Fraser, Pauly Shore, Megan Ward, Robin Tunney, Rick Ducommun, Mariette Hartley, Richard Masur, Michael DeLuise; *D:* Les Mayfield; *W:* Shawn Schepps. VHS, Beta $19.99 *HPH* 🎬🎬

Encore The third W. Somerset Maugham omnibus (following "Quartet" and "Trio") which includes: "Winter Cruise," "The Ant and the Grasshopper," and "Gigolo and Gigolette." 1952 85m/B *GB* Nigel Patrick, Kay Walsh, Roland Culver, John Laurie, Glynis Johns, Ronald Squire, Noel Purcell, Peter Graves; *D:* Pat Jackson, Anthony Pelissier, Harold French. VHS, Beta *NO* 🎬🎬🎬

Encounter at Raven's Gate Punk rockers and extraterrestrials meet amid hard rock and gallons of gore. 1988 (R) 85m/C Eddie Cleary, Steven Vidler; *D:* Rolf de Heer. VHS, Beta $29.95 *IME* 🎬½

Encounter with the Unknown Relates three fully documented supernatural events including a death prophesy and a ghost. 1975 90m/C Rosie Holotik, Gene Ross; *D:* Harry Z. Thomason. VHS, Beta $29.95 *VCI* 🎬🎬½

The End Reynolds plays a young man who discovers he is terminally ill. He decides not to prolonging his suffering and attempts various tried-and-true methods for committing suicide, receiving riotous help from the crazed DeLuise. 1978 (R) 100m/C Burt Reynolds, Sally Field, Dom DeLuise, Carl Reiner, Joanne Woodward, Robby Benson, Kristy McNichol, Norman Fell, Pat O'Brien, Myrna Loy, David Steinberg; *D:* Burt Reynolds; *W:* Jerry Belson. VHS, Beta $14.95 *MGM, FOX* 🎬🎬🎬

End of August A spinster of New Orleans Creole aristocracy, circa 1900, breaks out of her sheltered life and experiences new sexual and romantic awareness. Adapted from "The Awakening" by Kate Chopin. 1982 (PG) 104m/C Sally Sharp, David Marshall Grant, Paul Roebling; *D:* Bob Graham; *W:* Anna Thomas, Gregory Nava. VHS, Beta $59.98 *NLC* 🎬🎬

End of Desire Schell discovers that her husband, Marquand, has married her for her money and is having an affair with the maid in this melodrama based on De Maupassant's story, "Une Vie." A period piece that is a little on the slow side. In French with English subtitles. 1962 86m/C *FR* Maria Schell, Christian Marquand, Pascale Petit, Ivan Desny; *D:* Alexandre Astruc. VHS *NO* 🎬🎬

The End of Innocence In her attempts to please everyone in her life, a woman experiences a nervous breakdown. Released two years after Schaeffer's murder. 1990 (R) 102m/C Dyan Cannon, John Heard, George Coe, Lola Mason, Rebecca Schaeffer, Stephen Meadows, Billie Bird, Michael Madsen, Madge Sinclair, Renee Taylor, Viveka Davis; *D:* Dyan Cannon; *W:* Dyan Cannon; *M:* Michael Convertino. VHS, Beta $89.95 *PAR, FCT* 🎬🎬

The End of St. Petersburg A Russian peasant becomes a scab during a workers' strike in 1914. He is then forced to enlist in the army prior to the 1917 October Revolution. Fascinating, although propagandistic film commissioned by the then-new Soviet government. Silent. 1927 75m/B Ivan Chuvelov; *D:* Vsevolod Pudovkin. VHS, Beta $24.95 *NOS, MRV, WFV* 🎬🎬🎬

End of the Line Two old-time railroad workers steal a locomotive for a cross-country jaunt to protest the closing of the local railroad company. Produced by Steenburgen. 1988 (PG) 103m/C Wilford Brimley, Levon Helm, Mary Steenburgen, Kevin Bacon, Holly Hunter, Barbara Barrie, Bob Balaban, Howard Morris, Bruce McGill, Clint Howard, Trey Wilson, Rita Jenrette; *D:* Jay Russell; *W:* John Wohlbruck; *M:* Andy Summers. VHS, Beta $79.95 *BAR, LHV, WAR* 🎬🎬½

End of the Road Keach is a troubled college professor whose bizarre treatment by his physician (Jones) produces tragic results. He eventually enters into an affair with the wife of a co-worker. Fascinating, if uneven script adapted from John Barth's

story. Rated X upon release for adult story and nudity. 1970 (X) 110m/C Stacy Keach, James Earl Jones, James Coco, Harris Yulin, Dorothy Tristan; *D:* Aram Avakian; *W:* Terry Southern. VHS, Beta $59.98 *FOX* 🎬🎬½

End of the World A coffee machine explodes, sending a man through a window and into a neon sign, where he is electrocuted. A priest witnesses this and retreats to a convent where he meets his alien double and heads for more trouble with outer space invaders. Interesting premise. 1977 (PG) 88m/C Christopher Lee, Sue Lyon, Lew Ayres, MacDonald Carey, Dean Jagger, Kirk Scott; *D:* John Hayes. VHS, Beta $29.95 *MED* Woof!

Endangered Species Offbeat thriller with sci-fi leanings about a retired New York cop on vacation in America's West who is drawn into a female sheriff's investigation of a mysterious series of cattle killings. Could it be UFOs? Based on a true story. 1982 (R) 97m/C Robert Urich, JoBeth Williams, Paul Dooley, Hoyt Axton, Peter Coyote, Harry Carey Jr., Dan Hedaya, John Considine; *D:* Alan Rudolph; *W:* Alan Rudolph. VHS, Beta $69.95 *MGM* 🎬🎬½

Endgame Grotesquely deformed survivors of WWIII fight their way out of radioactive New York City to seek a better life. 1985 98m/C Al Oliver, Moira Chen, Jack Davis, Bobby Rhodes, Jill Elliot; *D:* Steve Benson. VHS, Beta $59.95 *MED* 🎬

Endless Descent At least it seems endless. A group of scientist-types set out in search of a sunken sub, but somehow take a wrong turn into the rift, the deepest chasm at the bottom of the sea. There, they discover unimaginable horrors—that is, if you've never seen "Alien," or just about any other icky-monster flick. A Spanish film, shot in English, by director Simon, whose other works of art include "Pieces" and "Slugs." *AKA:* La Grieta. 1990 (R) 79m/C *SP* Jack Scalia, R. Lee Ermey, Ray Wise, Deborah Adair, Ely Pouget; *D:* J.P. Simon. VHS, Beta $89.95 *LIV* Woof!

The Endless Game Cold War suspenser has British secret-agent-man Finney attempting to solve the murder of his erstwhile fellow agent-lover, much to the dismay of the government. Written by director Forbes, this made-for-cable would-be thriller is a decidedly mediocre waste of a talented cast. Also of note, it was actor-director Sir Anthony Quayle's final appearance. 1989 (PG-13) 123m/C *GB* Albert Finney, George Segal, Derek De Lint, Monica Guerritore, Ian Holm, John Standing, Anthony Quayle, Kristin Scott Thomas; *M:* Ennio Morricone. VHS $89.95 *PSM, FCT* 🎬🎬

Endless Love Although only 17, David and Jade are in love. Her parents think they are too serious and demand that the two spend time apart. David attempts to win her parents' affection and approval, goes mad in the process, and commits a foolish act (he burns the house down) that threatens their love forever. Based on the novel by Scott Spencer. Of interest only to those with time on their hands or smitten by a love so bad that this movie will seem grand in comparison. Features Cruise's first film appearance. 1981 (R) 115m/C Brooke Shields, Martin Hewitt, Don Murray, Shirley Knight, Beatrice Straight, Richard Kiley, Tom Cruise, James Spader, Robert Moore, Jami Gertz; *D:* Franco Zeffirelli; *W:* Judith Rascoe. VHS, Beta $14.98 *LIV, VES* 🎬🎬

Endless Night An adaptation of an Agatha Christie tale. Focuses on a young chauffeur who wants to build a dream house, and his chance meeting with an American heiress. *AKA:* Agatha Christie's Endless Night.

1971 95m/C *GB* Hayley Mills, Hywel Bennett, Britt Ekland, George Sanders, Per Oscarsson, Peter Bowles; *D:* Sidney Gilliat. **VHS, Beta** $9.98 *REP &&&*

The Endless Summer Classic surfing documentary about the freedom and sense of adventure that surfing symbolizes. Director Brown follows two young surfers around the world in search of the perfect wave. (They finally find it at a then-unknown break off Cape Saint Francis in South America.) Besides the excellent surfing photography, Big Kahuna Brown provides the amusing tongue-in-cheek narrative. Considered by many to be the best surf movie ever.

1966 90m/C Mike Hynson, Robert August; *D:* Bruce Brown; *W:* Bruce Brown. **VHS, Beta** $24.95 *FCT, HMV, PBS &&&*

The Endless Summer 2 You don't have to personally hang ten to get stoked about this long-awaited sequel that once again follows two surfer dudes in their quest for the perfect wave. This time out pro surfers O'Connell and Weaver circle the globe seeking adventure and the world's best waves. Traces the evolution of surfing, from the lazy, golden days of the '60s to the worldwide phenomenon it is today, complete with its own pro tour circuit. Breathtaking scenery and spectacular surfing sequences highlight this look at a unique subculture. Thirty years later and it's still a great ride, though the travelogue wears thin and the sub-culture's now fairly well exploited. *AKA:* Bruce Brown's The Endless Summer 2.

1994 (PG) 107m/C Robert "Wingnut" Weaver, Pat O'Connell, Robert August; *D:* Bruce Brown; *W:* Bruce Brown, Dana Brown. **VHS** *&&&*

Endplay An Australian-made crime/horror drama in which two brothers cover for each other in a series of murders involving blonde hitchhikers. Based on a novel by Russell Braddon.

1975 110m/C *AU* George Mallaby, John Waters, Ken Goodlet, Delvene Delaney, Charles Tingwell, Robert Hewett, Kevin Miles; *D:* Tim Burstall. **VHS** $14.95 *ACA &&½*

Enemies, a Love Story A wonderfully resonant, subtle tragedy based on the novel by Isaac Bashevis Singer. A post-Holocaust Jew, living in Coney Island, can't choose between three women—his current wife (who hid him during the war), his tempestuous lover, and his reappearing prewar wife he presumed dead. A hilarious, confident tale told with grace and patience.

1989 (R) 119m/C Ron Silver, Lena Olin, Anjelica Huston, Margaret Sophie Stein, Paul Mazursky, Alan King, Judith Malina, Rita Karin, Phil Leeds, Elya Baskin, Marie-Adele Lemieux; *D:* Paul Mazursky; *W:* Paul Mazursky; *M:* Maurice Jarre. Academy Awards '89 Nominations: Best Adapted Screenplay, Best Supporting Actress (Huston, Olin); New York Film Critics Awards '89: Best Director (Mazursky), Best Supporting Actress (Olin). **VHS, Beta** $89.98 *MED, VTR &&&½*

Enemy Below Suspenseful WWII sea epic, in which an American destroyer and a German U-Boat chase one another and square off in the South Atlantic.

1957 98m/C Robert Mitchum, Curt Jurgens, David Hedison, Theodore Bikel, Doug McClure, Russell Collins; *D:* Dick Powell. **VHS, Beta** $19.98 *FOX, FCT &&&*

Enemy Gold A crime czar and a beautiful killer without a conscience go after federal agents who have stumbled across a cache of Confederate gold. Basically, a babes-with-guns blowout.

1993 (R) 92m/C Bruce Penhall, Rodrigo Obregon, Mark Barriere, Suzi Simpson, Tai Collins, Julie Strain; *D:* Drew Sidaris; *W:* Wess Rahn, Christian Sidaris. **VHS, Beta** $89.95 *PSM &&½*

Enemy Mine A space fantasy in which two pilots from warring planets, one an Earthling, the other an asexual reptilian Drac, crash land on a barren planet and are forced to work together to survive.

1985 (PG-13) 108m/C Dennis Quaid, Louis Gossett Jr., Brion James, Richard Marcus, Lance Kerwin; *D:* Wolfgang Petersen; *M:* Maurice Jarre. **VHS, Beta** $19.98 *FOX &&*

Enemy of the Law Texas rangers battle evil in an old frontier town.

1945 59m/B Tex Ritter, Dave O'Brien; *D:* Harry Fraser. **VHS, Beta** $19.95 *NOS, VCN, DVT &&½*

Enemy of Women Chronicles the life and loves of Nazi propagandist Dr. Joseph Goebbels. *AKA:* The Private Life of Paul Joseph Goebbels.

1944 90m/B Claudia Drake, Paul Andor, Donald Woods, H.B. Warner, Sigrid Gurie, Ralph Morgan, Gloria Stuart, Charles Halton; *D:* Alfred Zeisler; *W:* Alfred Zeisler. **VHS, Beta** $24.95 *NOS, DVT, GLV &&½*

Enemy Territory A handful of citizens trapped in a New York City housing project after dark are stalked by a violent, murderous street gang.

1987 (R) 89m/C Ray Parker Jr., Jan-Michael Vincent, Gary Frank, Frances Foster; *D:* Peter Manoogian. **VHS, Beta** $79.98 *FOX &&*

Enemy Unseen A bickering squad of mercenaries slog through the African jungle to find a girl abducted by crocodile-worshipping natives. Dull Jungle-Jim-style adventure, notable for the hilariously phony crocs that occasionally clamp onto the characters.

1991 (R) 90m/C Vernon Wells, Stack Pierce, Ken Gampu, Michael McCabe, Angela O'Neill; *D:* Elmo De Witt. **VHS** $14.95 *AIP &*

The Enforcer A district attorney goes after an organized gang of killers in this film noir treatment of the real-life "Murder, Inc." case. *AKA:* Murder, Inc.

1951 87m/B Humphrey Bogart, Zero Mostel, Ted de Corsia, Everett Sloane, Roy Roberts, Lawrence Tolan, King Donovan, Bob Steele, Adelaide Klein, Don Beddoe, Tito Vuolo, John Kellogg; *D:* Bretaigne Windust, Raoul Walsh; *W:* Martin Rackin. **VHS** $19.95 *REP &&½*

The Enforcer Dirty Harry takes on a female partner and a vicious terrorist group that is threatening the city of San Francisco. See how many "punks" feel lucky enough to test the hand of the tough cop.

1976 (R) 96m/C Clint Eastwood, Tyne Daly, Harry Guardino, Bradford Dillman, John Mitchum; *D:* James Fargo; *W:* Sterling Silliphant. **VHS, Beta** $19.98 *WAR &&*

Enforcer from Death Row An ex-con is recruited by a secret international peacekeeping organization to track down and eliminate a band of murderous spies.

1978 87m/C Cameron Mitchell, Leo Fong, Darnell Garcia, Booker T. Anderson, John Hammond, Mariwin Roberts. **VHS, Beta** $69.98 *LIV, GHV &*

An Englishman Abroad During the Cold War, a British actress visits Moscow and chances to meet a notorious English defector. Behind their gossip and small talk is a tragicomic portrait of the exiled traitor/spy. He was the infamous Guy Burgess; the actress was Coral Browne, here playing herself in a pointed recreation. Made for British TV; nuances may be lost on yank viewers. Winner of several British awards.

1983 63m/C *GB* Alan Bates, Coral Browne, Charles Gray; *D:* John Schlesinger; *W:* Alan Bennett; *M:* George Fenton. **VHS** *FOX, FCT, PRV &&&*

Enid is Sleeping Well-done comedy noir in the now-popular there's-a-corpse-in-the-closet subgenre. A woman in a mythical New Mexican town tries to hide the body of her sister Enid, who she's accidentally killed. Enid, it turns out, wasn't thrilled to discover her sister sleeping with her police-officer husband. Phillips and Perkins restored the film to its original state after it was ruthlessly gutted by the studio. *AKA:* Over Her Dead Body.

1990 (R) 105m/C Elizabeth Perkins, Judge Reinhold, Rhea Perlman; *D:* Maurice Phillips; *W:* Maurice Phillips. **VHS** $89.98 *VES, LIV &&*

Enigma Trapped behind the Iron Curtain, a double agent tries to find the key to five pending murders by locating a Russian coded microprocessor holding information that would unravel the assassination scheme.

1982 (PG) 101m/C *FR* Martin Sheen, Brigitte Fossey, Sam Neill, Derek Jacobi, Frank Finlay, Michael Lonsdale, Warren Clarke; *D:* Jeannot Szwarc; *W:* John Briley. **VHS, Beta** $69.98 *SUE &&*

Enigma Secret Three Polish mathematicians use their noggins to break the Nazi secret code machine during WWII. Based on a true story; in Polish with English subtitles.

1979 158m/C *PL* Tadeusz Borowski, Piotr Fronczewski, Piotr Garlicki. **VHS** $49.95 *FCT &&*

Enola Gay: The Men, the Mission, the Atomic Bomb Based on the bestselling book by Gordon Thomas and Max Gordon Witts, this made for television drama tells the story of the airmen aboard the B-29 that dropped the first atomic bomb. Details the events during WWII leading up to the decision to bomb Hiroshima and the concerns of the crew assigned the task.

1980 150m/C Patrick Duffy, Billy Crystal, Kim Darby, Gary Frank, Gregory Harrison, Ed Nelson, Robert Walden, Stephen Macht, Robert Pine, James Shigeta, Henry Wilcoxon; *D:* David Lowell Rich; *M:* Maurice Jarre. **VHS, Beta** $69.95 *PSM &&*

Enormous Changes Three stories about New York City women and their personal relationships. Based on the stories of Grace Paley. *AKA:* Enormous Changes at the Last Minute.

1983 115m/C Ellen Barkin, David Strathairn, Ron McLarty, Maria Tucci, Lynn Milgrim, Kevin Bacon; *D:* Mirra Bank; *W:* John Sayles. **VHS, Beta** $79.95 *VMK &&&*

Enrapture A chauffeur is the prime suspect when a promiscuous passenger is murdered in his limousine. The driver did it?

1990 (R) 87m/C Ona Simms, Harvey Siegel, Richard Parnes; *D:* Chuck Vincent. **VHS** $79.95 *ATL &½*

Ensign Pulver A continuation of the further adventures of the crew of the U.S.S. Reluctant from "Mister Roberts," which was adapted from the Broadway play.

1964 104m/C Walter Matthau, Robert Walker Jr., Larry Hagman, Jack Nicholson, Millie Perkins, James Coco, James Farentino, Burl Ives, Gerald S. O'Loughlin, Al Freeman Jr.; *D:* Joshua Logan. **VHS, Beta** $19.98 *WAR &&*

Entangled David Mirkin (Nelson) is a struggling writer living in Paris with his beautiful girlfriend Annabelle (Treil). As she becomes ever more successful as a fashion model, David becomes ever more jealous

and mistrustful. So he hires a detective (Brosnan) to spy on her. And then there's the small matter of a murder. Adapted from the novel "Les Veufs" by Boileau Narcejac.
1993 (R) 98m/C Judd Nelson, Pierce Brosnan, Laurence Treil, Roy Dupuis; D: Max Fischer. VHS $92.00 COL ⅉⅉ

Enter Laughing Based on Reiner's semi-autobiographical novel and play, depicts the botched efforts of a Bronx-born schlump to become an actor. Worthwhile, but doesn't live up to the original.
1967 112m/C Reni Santoni, Jose Ferrer, Elaine May, Shelley Winters, Jack Gilford, Don Rickles, Michael J. Pollard, Janet Margolin, Rob Reiner; D: Carl Reiner; W: Carl Reiner; M: Quincy Jones. VHS, Beta NO ⅉⅉ

Enter the Dragon The American film that broke Bruce Lee worldwide combines Oriental conventions with 007 thrills. Spectacular fighting sequences including Karate, Judo, Tae Kwon Do, and Tai Chi Chuan are featured as Lee is recruited by the British to search for opium smugglers in Hong Kong. AKA: The Deadly Three.
1973 (R) 98m/C Bruce Lee, John Saxon, Jim Kelly; D: Robert Clouse. VHS, Beta $19.98 WAR ⅉⅉⅉ

Enter the Ninja First and most serious of the Cannon canon of relatively well-done ninja epics (faint praise) that created original box-office stir for genre (mostly among adolescents needing outlet). Ninja Nero visits old friend in Philippines who's being pressured by ruthless evil guy George to give up the farm. Nero dispatches numerous thugs before indulging in ninja slugfest with Kosugi.
1981 (R) 99m/C Franco Nero, Susan George, Sho Kosugi, Christopher George, Alex Courtney; D: Menahem Golan. VHS, Beta $14.95 MGM ⅉⅉ

Enter the Panther Amidst, and regardless of, a double-crossing plot featuring a treacherous family and a sought-after gold mine, a young man kicks heads and punches his way to fame.
1979 91m/C Bruce Li, Tsai Chin, Tse Lan. VHS, Beta $24.95 GEM ⅉ

Enter Three Dragons Kung Fu artistry abounds in this head-kicking action-adventure film.
1981 (R) 90m/C Dragon Lee, Bruce Lea, Yang Tsze, Samuel Walls, Chang Li, Bruce Li, Jackie Chin. VHS SUN ⅉ

The Entertainer Splendid drama of a down and out vaudevillian who tries vainly to gain the fame his dying father once possessed. His blatant disregard for his alcoholic wife and his superficial sons brings his world crashing down around them, and he discovers how self-destructive his life has been. Remade in 1975 for television. Adapted from the play by John Osborne.
1960 97m/B GB Laurence Olivier, Brenda de Banzie, Roger Livesey, Joan Plowright, Daniel Massey, Alan Bates, Shirley Anne Field, Albert Finney, Thora Hird; D: Tony Richardson; W: John Osborne; M: John Addison. VHS $39.95 FCT, TPV ⅉⅉⅉ½

Entertaining Mr. Sloane Playwright Joe Orton's masterpiece of black comedy concerning a handsome criminal who becomes the guest and love interest of a widow and her brother.
1970 90m/C Beryl Reid, Harry Andrews, Peter McEnery, Alan Webb; D: Douglas Hickox. VHS, Beta NO ⅉⅉ½

The Entity Supposedly based on a true story about an unseen entity that repeatedly rapes a woman. Hershey's the victim whom nobody believes. She eventually ends up at a university for talks with parapsychologist

Silver. Pseudo-science to the rescue as the over-sexed creature is frozen dead in its tracks. Exploitative violence, gore, and nudity aplenty, balanced to a degree by Hershey's strong performance.
1983 (R) 115m/C Barbara Hershey, Ron Silver, Alex Rocco; D: Sidney J. Furie; W: Frank DeFelitta; M: Charles Bernstein. VHS, Beta $14.98 FOX ⅉⅉ

Entr'acte Clair's famous dada-surrealist classic short, reflecting his sense of humor, as various eccentric characters become involved in a crazy chase. Silent.
1924 21m/B FR D: Rene Clair. VHS, Beta MRV, ING, GVV ⅉⅉ

Entre-Nous Two attractive, young French mothers find in each other the fulfillment their husbands cannot provide. One of the women was confined in a concentration camp during WWII; the other is a disaffected artist. In French with English subtitles. AKA: Between Us; Coup de Foudre.
1983 (PG) 112m/C FR Isabelle Huppert, Miou-Miou, Guy Marchand; D: Diane Kurys; W: Diane Kurys. VHS, Beta $19.98 MGM, ING ⅉⅉⅉ½

Epic That Never Was A fascinating documentary of the circumstances under which a big-budgeted 1937 adaptation of Graves' "I, Claudius," filmed by Von Sternberg, was shelved after Oberon's auto accident and director/star disagreements. Features both interviews made 30 years later and much of the existing footage, a testament to its unfulfilled potential as a masterpiece.
1965 74m/C Charles Laughton, Flora Robson, Merle Oberon, Emlyn Williams, Robert Newton, Josef von Sternberg, Robert Graves. VHS, Beta, 8mm $24.95 NOS, VYY, VRS ⅉⅉⅉ½

Epitaph An average American family's life is disrupted by the mother's habitual axe-murdering.
1987 90m/C D: Joseph Merhi. VHS, Beta NO ⅉ

The Equalizer: Memories of Manon Feature-length episode of the popular television crime thriller about an ex-agent who uses guns and espionage tactics to help people who are being persecuted by ruthless villians on the streets of New York City. In this installment, McCall, the Equalizer, learns that he has a daughter and that her life is in peril.
1988 96m/C Edward Woodward, Melissa Sue Anderson, Anthony Zerbe, George DiCenzo, Jon Polito, Robert Lansing, Keith Szarabajka; D: Tony Wharmby. VHS, Beta $39.95 MCA ⅉⅉ½

Equalizer 2000 A warrior in a post-holocaust future plots to overthrow a dictatorship by using a high-powered gun.
1986 (R) 85m/C Richard Norton, Corinne Wahl, William Steis; D: Cirio H. Santiago. VHS, Beta $79.95 MGM ⅉ

Equinox Young archaeologists uncover horror in a state forest. The ranger, questing for a book of spells that the scientists have found, threatens them with wonderful special effects, including winged beasts, huge apes, and Satan. Though originally an amateur film, it is deemed a minor classic in its genre.
1971 (PG) 80m/C Edward Connell, Barbara Hewitt, Frank Bonner, Robin Christopher, Jack Woods, Fritz Leiber; D: Jack Woods. VHS NO ⅉⅉⅉ

Equinox Modine gets to try his hand (and does well) at a dual role, with his portrayal of identical twins, separated at birth and raised in completely different environs. Garage worker Henry lives in a tenement while slick brother Freddie is a gangster's chauffeur married to the materialistic Sharon (Singer). Fate brings the brothers together when a

janitor discovers a letter that reveals their parentage and the fact that a fortune has been left to them. Set in the near future, in the surreal and decaying city of Empire, this is typical Rudolph with its moody stylized appearance and convoluted plot.
1993 (R) 110m/C Matthew Modine, Lara Flynn Boyle, Lori Singer, Marisa Tomei, Fred Ward, M. Emmet Walsh, Tyra Ferrell, Tate Donovan, Kevin J. O'Connor, Gailard Sartain; D: Alan Rudolph; W: Alan Rudolph. VHS $94.95 COL, FCT ⅉⅉ

Equinox Flower Ozu's first color film tells the sensitive story of two teenage girls who make a pact to protect each other from the traditional prearranged marriages their parents have set up. Lovely film that focuses on the generation gap between young and old in the Japanese family. In Japanese with English subtitles.
1958 118m/C JP Shin Saburi, Kinuyo Tanaka, Ineko Arima, Miyuki Kuwano, Chishu Ryu; D: Yasujiro Ozu. VHS $69.95 NYF, ART, FCT ⅉⅉ

Equus A psychiatrist undertakes the most challenging case of his career when he tries to figure out why a stable-boy blinded horses. Based upon the successful play by Peter Shaffer, but not well transferred to film.
1977 (R) 138m/C Richard Burton, Peter Firth, Jenny Agutter, Joan Plowright, Colin Blakely, Harry Andrews; D: Sidney Lumet; W: Peter Shaffer; M: Richard Rodney Bennett. Academy Awards '77 Nominations: Best Actor (Burton), Best Adapted Screenplay, Best Supporting Actor (Firth); British Academy Awards '77: Best Supporting Actress (Agutter); Golden Globe Awards '78: Best Actor—Drama (Burton), Best Supporting Actor (Firth). VHS, Beta $14.95 MGM ⅉⅉⅉ

Era Notte a Roma An American, Russian, and British soldier each escape from a concentration camp in the waning days of WWII and find refuge in the home of a young woman.
1960 145m/B IT D: Roberto Rossellini; W: Roberto Rossellini. VHS NO ⅉⅉⅉ

Eraserhead The infamous cult classic about a numb-brained everyman wandering through what amounts to a sick, ironic parody of the modern urban landscape, innocently impregnating his girlfriend and fathering a pestilent embryonic mutant. Surreal and bizarre, the film has an inner, completely unpredictable logic all its own. Lynch's first feature-length film stars Nance, who later achieved fame in Lynch's "Twin Peaks" as Pete the Logger.
1978 90m/B Jack Nance, Charlotte Stewart, Jack Fisk, Jeanne Bates; D: David Lynch; W: David Lynch. VHS, Beta COL, OM ⅉⅉⅉ

Erendira Based on Gabriel Garcia-Marquez's story about a teenage girl prostituting herself to support her witch-like grandmother after accidentally torching the elder's house. The film follows the two as they travel across the desert trying out new and inventive ways to survive. Unusual ending tops off a creative, if not eclectic, movie. In Spanish with English subtitles.
1983 103m/C FR MX GE Irene Papas, Claudia Ohana, Michael Lonsdale, Rufus, Jorge Fegan; D: Ruy Guerra. VHS, Beta $24.95 XVC, MED, APD ⅉⅉ½

Eric Made-for-television tear-jerker about a young athlete who fights for his life after he's diagnosed with leukemia. Based on the true-life account written by Eric's mother Doris Lund.
1975 100m/C Patricia Neal, John Savage, Claude Akins, Sian Barbara Allen, Mark Hamill, Nehemiah Persoff, Tom Clancy; D: James Goldstone; M: Dave Grusin. VHS, Beta $39.95 LIV ⅉⅉⅉ

Erik An ex-government agent working in Central America finds his loyalties divided when he is approached by a female activist and his old CIA friends. They want him to help expose his current boss as a drug smuggler.
1990 90m/C Stephen McHattie, Deborah Van Valkenburgh. **VHS, Beta** NO &&

Erik, the Viking The Norse Warrior discovers not only the New World but traitorous subordinates among his crew, calling for drastic measures.
1972 95m/C Giuliano Gemma, Gordon Mitchell. **VHS, Beta** $59.95 UNI &

Erik the Viking A mediocre Monty Pythonesque farce about a Viking who grows dissatisfied with his barbaric way of life and decides to set out to find the mythical Asgaard, where Norse gods dwell. Great cast of character actors is wasted.
1989 (PG-13) 104m/C GB Tim Robbins, Terry Jones, Mickey Rooney, John Cleese, Imogen Stubbs, Anthony Sher, Gordon John Sinclair, Freddie Jones, Eartha Kitt; **D:** Terry Jones; **W:** Terry Jones. **VHS, Beta** $89.98 ORI &&½

Ernest Goes to Camp A screwball, slapstick summer camp farce starring the character Ernest P. Worrell as an inept camp counselor. When progress threatens the camp, Ernest leads the boys on a turtle-bombing, slop-shooting attack on the construction company. Followed by "Ernest Saves Christmas" and "Ernest Goes to Jail."
1987 (PG) 92m/C Jim Varney, Victoria Racimo, John Vernon, Iron Eyes Cody, Lyle Alzado, Gailard Sartain, Daniel Butler, Hakeem Abdul-Samad; **D:** John R. Cherry III. **VHS, Beta** $19.99 TOU &½

Ernest Goes to Jail The infamous loon Ernest P. Worrell winds up in the jury box and the courtroom will never be the same again. Jury duty suddenly becomes hard-time in the slammer for poor Ernest when he is mistaken for a big-wig organized crime boss. Sequel to "Ernest Goes to Camp" and "Ernest Saves Christmas."
1990 (PG) 81m/C Jim Varney, Gailard Sartain, Randall "Tex" Cobb, Bill Byrge, Barry Scott, Charles Napier; **D:** John R. Cherry III. **VHS** $89.95 BVV, TOU &&

The Ernest Green Story Made-for-cable drama based on the integration of Central High in Little Rock, Arkansas by nine black students in 1957. Green was the only senior in the group and the movie follows a year of verbal and physical abuse, vandalism, and unfair academic treatment, as he struggles to withstand every difficulty in order to graduate.
1993 92m/C Morris Chestnut, CCH Pounder, Gary Grubbs, Tina Lifford, Avery Brooks, Ruby Dee, Ossie Davis; **D:** Eric Laneuville. **VHS** DIS &&½

Ernest Rides Again Ernest P. "Know-whutImean?" Worrell (Varney) is back, aiding a college professor friend who has a cockamamie theory that the British crown jewels were hidden in a Revolutionary War cannon. Naturally he's right and Ernest must battle British spies and a greedy antiquities collector to get the gems back. Goofy slapstick sticks to the formula of the other films.
1993 (PG) 93m/C Jim Varney, Ron James, Duke Ernsberger, Jeffrey Pillars, Linda Kash, Tom Butler; **D:** John Cherry; **W:** John Cherry, William M. Akers; **M:** Bruce Arnston, Kirby Shelstad. **VHS** $94.95 MNC &&½

Ernest Saves Christmas Ernest P. Worrell is back. When Santa decides that it's time to retire, Ernest must help him recruit a has-been children's show host who is a bit

reluctant. For Ernest fans only, and only the most dedicated of those. Second in the series featuring the nimble-faced Varney, the first of which was "Ernest Goes to Camp," followed by "Ernest Goes to Jail."
1988 (PG) 91m/C Jim Varney, Douglas Seale, Oliver Clark, Noelle Parker, Billie Bird; **D:** John R. Cherry III. **VHS, Beta** $14.99 TOU &½

Ernest Scared Stupid Pea-brained Ernest P. Worrell returns yet again in this silly comedy. When he accidentally releases a demon from a sacred tomb a 200-year-old curse threatens to destroy his hometown, unless Ernest can come to the rescue. Would you want your town depending on Ernest's heroics? Who would have thought that the annoying Ernest P. Worrell could appear in one movie, let alone four?
1991 (PG) 93m/C Jim Varney, Eartha Kitt, Austin Nagler, Jonas Moscartolo, Shay Astar; **D:** John R. Cherry III; **M:** Bruce Arnston. **VHS, Beta** $14.99 TOU &½

Ernesto A lushly erotic Italian film depicting the troubled relationship between a young, devil-may-care gay youth and his older, coolly seducing lover. In Italian with subtitles.
1979 98m/C IT Martin Halm, Michele Placido; **D:** Salvatore Samperi. **VHS, Beta** $79.50 FCT &&½

Ernie Kovacs: Between the Laughter A made for television version of the television comic's life and career, ending with his tragic death in a car accident in 1962. Shows the brand of humor that made Kovacs famous as well as the devastation that he suffered after the tragic kidnapping of his children by his first wife during divorce proceedings. Kovac's second wife, Edie Adams, makes a brief appearance.
1984 95m/C Jeff Goldblum, Cloris Leachman, Melody Anderson, Madolyn Smith, John Glover; **Cameos:** Edie Adams; **D:** Lamont Johnson; **M:** Ralph Burns. **VHS, Beta** NO &&

Erotic Dreams The Devil tries to persuade a young guy to come to Hell by showing him a tableau of lusty soft-core vignettes.
1987 70m/C VHS, Beta $59.95 CEL Woof!

Erotic Escape Soft-core fun about party girls taking over a small French town. Originally in French, but dubbed in English. Check your brain at the door.
1986 86m/C FR Marie-Claire Davy, Pauline Larrieu. **VHS, Beta** $29.95 MED &

Erotic Images A beautiful psychology teacher publishes her doctoral thesis on sex and becomes a best-selling author, which threatens her marriage.
1985 (R) 93m/C Britt Ekland, Edd Byrnes, John McCann; **D:** Declan Langan. **VHS, Beta** $69.98 LIV, VES Woof!

Erotic Touch of Hot Skin Sex, murder, false identities, car crashes, and striptease in the Riviera.
1965 78m/B Fabienne Dali, Sophie Hardy, Jean Valmont, Francois Dryek; **D:** Max Pecas. **VHS, Beta** $19.95 VDM &

The Errand Boy Jerry Lewis' patented babbling schnook hits Hollywood in search of a job. When he lands a position as an errand boy, Hollywood may never be the same again in this prototypical comedy; a must for Lewis fans only.
1961 92m/B Jerry Lewis, Brian Donlevy, Dick Wesson, Howard McNear, Felicia Atkins, Fritz Feld, Sig Rumann, Renee Taylor, Doodles Weaver, Mike Mazurki, Lorne Greene, Michael Landon, Dan Blocker, Pernell Roberts, Snub Pollard, Kathleen Freeman; **D:** Jerry Lewis; **W:** Jerry Lewis. **VHS, Beta** $59.95 LIV &&½

Escapade Sons thinking their parents are en route to divorce court create a scheme to achieve peace worldwide. The pacifist father's reaction juxtaposes idealistic youth with the cynicism of adulthood. Adapted from a play by Roger MacDougall.
1955 87m/B GB John Mills, Yvonne Mitchell, Alastair Sim, Jeremy Spenser, Andrew Ray, Marie Lohr, Peter Asher; **D:** Philip Leacock. **VHS** $24.95 VYY, MOV &&&

Escapade in Florence As two students in Florence paint their way to immortality, an elaborate art-forging ring preys upon their talents.
1962 81m/C Tommy Kirk, Ivan Desny; **D:** Steve Previn. **VHS, Beta** $69.95 DIS &

Escapade in Japan A Japanese youth helps an American boy frantically search the city of Tokyo for his parents. Shot in Japan.
1957 93m/C Cameron Mitchell, Teresa Wright, Jon Provost, Roger Nakagawa, Philip Ober, Clint Eastwood; **D:** Arthur Lubin. **VHS, Beta** $15.95 VCI &&

Escape A fun-loving, care-free Irish officer is sent to oversee the toughest POW prison in Scotland. There, he becomes consumed with keeping the facility secure despite the intricate escape plans laid out by a group of rioters.
1990 (PG) 90m/C Brian Keith, Helmut Griem; **D:** Lamont Johnson. **VHS** NO &&

Escape A woman attempts to track down her brother's killer and finds an entire town mysteriously controlled by a sadistic and powerful man. Features General Hospital's bad-boy Shriner.
1990 (R) 100m/C Elizabeth Jeager, Kim Richards, Kin Shriner; **D:** Richard Styles. **VHS** HHE &½

The Escape Artist Award-winning cinematographer Deschanel's first directorial effort is this quirky film about a teenage escape artist who sets out to uncover the identity of his father's killers.
1982 96m/C Griffin O'Neal, Raul Julia, Teri Garr, Joan Hackett, Desi Arnaz Sr., Gabriel Dell, Huntz Hall, Jackie Coogan; **D:** Caleb Deschanel; **W:** Melissa Mathison; **M:** Georges Delerue. **VHS, Beta** $79.98 LIV, VES &&&

Escape from Alcatraz A fascinating account of the one and only successful escape from the maximum security prison at Alcatraz in 1962. The three men were never heard from again.
1979 (PG) 112m/C Clint Eastwood, Patrick McGoohan, Roberts Blossom, Fred Ward, Danny Glover; **D:** Don Siegel. **VHS, Beta** $14.95 PAR &&&

Escape from Cell Block 3 Five escaped female convicts take it on the lam for Mexico and freedom.
1978 82m/C Carolyn Judd, Teri Guzman, Bonita Kalem. **VHS, Beta** $9.99 PSM &

Escape from Death Row Convicted criminal mastermind, sentenced to die, devises a brilliant and daring plan of escape on the eve of his execution.
1976 (R) 85m/C Lee Van Cleef, James Lane, Barbara Moore, Alice Belios. **VHS, Beta** NO &

Escape from DS-3 Bostwick and "Police Academy" alumnus Smith team up in a familiar story: framed for a serious crime, a man attempts to escape from a maximum security satellite prison. About as good as you'd expect.
198? 88m/C Jackson Bostwick, Bubba Smith. **VHS** $79.99 MNC, MOV &

Escape from El Diablo Two juvenile delinquents harass guards at a Mexican prison. Being from California, they use frisbees and skateboards to help their escape.
1983 (PG) 92m/C *SP GB* Jimmy McNichol, Timothy Van Patten, John Ethan Wayne; *D:* Gordon Hessler. **VHS, Beta** $9.95 *MED* 🎬

Escape from Fort Bravo A Civil War era western set in an Arizona stockade. Holden is the hard-bitten Union cavalry officer who ruthlessly guards his Confederate prisoners, who are led by Forsythe. Parker is a southern spy whose job is to break the rebels out of jail by seducing Holden from his duty, which she does. When Holden discovers what's happened, he recaptures his prisoners only to be beset by hostile Mescalero Indians while trying to get everyone back to the fort. It's an old story but well-executed with lots of action.
1953 98m/C William Holden, Eleanor Parker, John Forsythe, William Demarest, William Campbell, Polly Bergen, Richard Anderson, Carl Benton Reid, John Lupton, Howard McNear, Alex Montoya, Forrest Lewis, Fred Graham, William Newell; *D:* John Sturges; *W:* Frank Fenton. **VHS, Beta** $19.98 *MGM, FCT* 🎬🎬½

Escape from Galaxy Three A pair of space travelers fight off a bevy of evil aliens.
1976 (G) 90m/C James Milton, Cheryl Buchanan. **VHS, Beta** $79.95 *PSM* 🎬

Escape from Hell Two scantily clad women escape from a jungle prison and are pursued by their sadistic warden. *AKA:* Hellfire on Ice, Part 2: Escape from Hell.
1989 ?m/C Anthony Steffen, Ajita Wilson; *D:* Edward Muller. **VHS** $59.95 *HHE* Woof!

Escape from New York The ultimate urban nightmare: a ruined, future Manhattan is an anarchic prison for America's worst felons. When convicts hold the President hostage, a disgraced war hero unwillingly attempts an impossible rescue mission. Cynical but largely unexceptional sci-fi action, putting a good cast through tight-lipped peril.
1981 (R) 99m/C Kurt Russell, Lee Van Cleef, Ernest Borgnine, Donald Pleasence, Isaac Hayes, Adrienne Barbeau, Harry Dean Stanton, Season Hubley; *D:* John Carpenter; *W:* John Carpenter, Nick Castle; *M:* John Carpenter. **VHS, Beta** $14.98 *SUE, NLC, FUS* 🎬🎬½

Escape from Planet Earth A spaceship is damaged deep in space and only a few of the crew can make it back to Earth. But who will decide who lives or dies? (Unfortunately, the Earth has been totally destroyed so who cares anyway.) Lousy special effects. *AKA:* The Doomsday Machine.
1967 91m/B Grant Williams, Bobby Van, Ruta Lee, Henry Wilcoxon, Mala Powers, Casey Kasem, Mike Farrell, Harry Hope; *D:* Lee Sholem. **VHS** $59.95 *ACA* 🎬

Escape from Safehaven Brutal slimeballs rule a mad, sadistic world in the post-apocalyptic future, and a family tries to escape them. In very poor taste.
1988 (R) 87m/C Rick Gianasi, Mollie O'Mara, John Wittenbauer, Roy MacArthur, William Beckwith; *D:* Brian Thomas Jones, James McCalmont. **VHS, Beta** *NO* Woof!

Escape from Sobibor Nail-biting, true account of the largest successful escape from a Nazi prison camp, adapted from Richard Rashke's book. Made for TV.
1987 (PG-13) 120m/C Alan Arkin, Joanna Pacula, Rutger Hauer, Hartmut Becker, Jack Shepherd; *D:* Jack Gold; *M:* Georges Delerue. **VHS** $89.98 *LIV* 🎬🎬🎬

Escape from the Bronx Invading death squads seek to level the Bronx. Local street gangs cry foul and ally to defeat the uncultured barbarians. Sequel to "1990: The Bronx Warriors."
1985 (R) 82m/C Mark Gregory, Henry Silva, Valeria D'Obici, Timothy Brent, Andrea Coppola; *D:* Enzo G. Castellari. **VHS, Beta** $69.95 *MED* 🎬

Escape from the KGB A CIA agent escapes from a Soviet prison, taking plans for a new space installation with him.
1987 99m/C Thomas Hunter, Ivan Desny, Marie Versini, Walter Barns; *D:* Harald Phillipe. **VHS, Beta** *NO* Woof!

Escape from the Planet of the Apes Reprising their roles as intelligent, English-speaking apes, McDowall and Hunter flee their world before it's destroyed, and travel back in time to present-day America. In L.A. they become the subjects of a relentless search by the fearful population, much like humans Charlton Heston and James Franciscus were targeted for experimentation and destruction in simian society in the earlier "Planet of the Apes" and "Beneath the Planet of the Apes." Sequelled by "Conquest of the Planet of the Apes" and a television series.
1971 (G) 98m/C Roddy McDowall, Kim Hunter, Sal Mineo, Ricardo Montalban, William Windom, Bradford Dillman, Natalie Trundy, Eric (Hans Gudegast) Braeden; *D:* Don Taylor; *M:* Jerry Goldsmith. **VHS, Beta** $19.98 *FOX, FUS* 🎬🎬🎬

Escape Me Never Flynn plays a struggling composer in this sappy period piece about poverty-stricken artists in Italy at the turn of the century. Flynn falls for his brother's wealthy fiancee (Parker), although he is married to the faithful Lupino. Atypical role for Flynn and definitely not one of his best. Based on the novel "The Fool of the Family," by Margaret Kennedy and the play "Escape Me Never" by Kennedy.
1947 101m/B Errol Flynn, Ida Lupino, Eleanor Parker, Gig Young, Reginald Denny, Isobel Elsom; *D:* Peter Godfrey; *W:* Thomas Williamson. **VHS** $19.98 *MGM* 🎬½

Escape to Athena A motley group is stuck in a German P.O.W. camp on a Greek island during WWII.
1979 (PG) 102m/C *GB* Roger Moore, Telly Savalas, David Niven, Claudia Cardinale, Richard Roundtree, Stefanie Powers, Sonny Bono, Elliott Gould, William Holden; *D:* George P. Cosmatos; *W:* Edward Anhalt. **VHS, Beta** $19.98 *FOX* 🎬🎬½

Escape to Burma A man on the run for a murder he did not commit finds refuge and romance in an isolated jungle home.
1955 86m/C Barbara Stanwyck, Robert Ryan, Reginald Denny; *D:* Allan Dwan. **VHS, Beta** $39.95 *DIS, BVV* 🎬½

Escape to Love Beautiful student helps a famous dissident escape from Poland, only to lose him to another heroic venture.
1982 105m/C Clara Perryman, Louis Jourdan; *D:* Herbert Stein. **Beta** $14.95 *PSM* 🎬½

Escape to Paradise The last of Breen's films for RKO has him as a South American motorcycle-taxi driver acting as a guide for tourist Taylor. When Breen sets Taylor up with Shelton, trouble ensues. 🎵Tra-La-La; Rhythm of the Rio; Ay, Ay, Ay.
1939 60m/B Bobby Breen, Kent Taylor, Maria Shelton, Joyce Compton, Rosina Galli, Frank Yaconelli; *D:* Erle C. Kenton. **VHS** $19.95 *NOS, RXM* 🎬½

Escape to the Sun Pair of Russian university students plan to flee their homeland so they can be allowed to live and love free from oppression. *AKA:* Habricha el Hashemesh.

1972 (PG) 94m/C *IS* Laurence Harvey, Josephine Chaplin, John Ireland, Jack Hawkins, Lila Kedrova, Clive Revill; *D:* Menahem Golan. **VHS, Beta** *NO* 🎬½

Escape to Witch Mountain Two young orphans with supernatural powers find themselves on the run from a greedy millionaire who wants to exploit their amazing gift. Adapted from a novel by Alexander Key.
1975 (G) 97m/C Kim Richards, Ike Eisenmann, Eddie Albert, Ray Milland, Donald Pleasence; *D:* John Hough. **VHS, Beta** $19.99 *DIS, BTV* 🎬🎬🎬

Escape 2000 In a future society where individuality is considered a crime, those who refuse to conform are punished by being hunted down in a jungle. Gross, twisted takeoff of Richard Connell's "The Most Dangerous Game." *AKA:* Turkey Shoot.
1981 (R) 80m/C *AU* Steve Railsback, Olivia Hussey, Michael Craig; *D:* Brian Trenchard-Smith; *W:* George Schenck. **VHS, Beta** $9.98 *SUE, STE* Woof!

Escapes In the tradition of "The Twilight Zone," Vincent Price introduces five short thrillers featuring time travel, aliens, and telepathy. Produced with computer assistance for sharper, more contrasted images.
1986 72m/C Vincent Price, Jerry Grisham, Lee Canfield, John Mitchum, Gil Reade; *D:* David Steensland. **VHS, Beta** $9.99 *STE, PSM* 🎬🎬

Escapist A professional escape artist becomes involved in a perverted corporate plot and must escape to save his life and livelihood.
1983 87m/C Bill Shirk, Peter Lupus; *D:* Eddie Beverly Jr. **VHS, Beta** $69.98 *LIV, VES* Woof!

E.S.P. A young man is given the amazing power of extra-sensory perception.
1983 96m/C Jim Stafford, George Deaton. **VHS, Beta** *BFV* Woof!

Esposa y Amante While her daughter contemplates suicide, a mother remembers the happy early years of her marriage, followed by the wrong-doings of her husband which caused her to seek comfort in the arms of an old lawyer friend. Her daughter is now suffering for the problems of her own marriage. In Spanish.
1977 102m/C *SP* Ramiro Oliveros, Ricardo Merino, Victoria Abril, Frika Wallner. **VHS, Beta** $29.95 *MED* 🎬

Esta Noche Cena Pancho A Spanish comedy about the antics of men at a bachelor party.
1987 90m/C *SP* Alfonso Zayas, Carmen Salinas, Armando Silvestre, Alberto Rojas; *D:* Victor Manuel Castro. **VHS, Beta** *MED* 🎬

Estate of Insanity An English lord and his second wife become involved in a web of death when a maniac stalks their ancient estate.
1970 90m/C John Turner, Heather Sears, Ann Lynn; *D:* Robert Hartford-Davis. **VHS, Beta** *NO* 🎬

Et La Tenoresse?...Bordel! A French comedy about a color-blind painter and his kinky fashion photographer roommate living in Paris. In French with subtitles.
1984 100m/C *FR D:* Patrick Schulmann. **VHS, Beta** $59.95 *FCT* 🎬

E.T.: The Extra-Terrestrial Spielberg's famous fantasy, one of the most popular films in history, portrays a limpid-eyed alien stranded on earth and his special bonding relationship with a young boy. A modern fairy tale providing warmth, humor and sheer wonder. Held the first place spot as the highest grossing movie of all time for years until a new Spielberg hit replaced it— "Jurassic Park." Debra Winger contributed to the voice of E.T.

1982 (PG) 115m/C Henry Thomas, Dee Wallace Stone, Drew Barrymore, Robert MacNaughton, Peter Coyote, C. Thomas Howell, Sean Frye, K.C. Martel; *D:* Steven Spielberg; *M:* John Williams. Academy Awards '82: Best Sound, Best Visual Effects, Best Original Score; Nominations: Best Film Editing; Academy Awards '82: Best Cinematography, Best Director (Spielberg), Best Picture, Best Sound; Golden Globe Awards '83: Best Film— Drama, Best Score; People's Choice Awards '83: Best Film. **VHS, Beta $24.95** *MCA, APD, RDG* 𝘐𝘐𝘐𝘐

Eternal Evil A bored television director is taught how to have out-of-body experiences by his devil-worshipping girlfriend. He eventually realizes that when he leaves his body, it runs around killing people.
1987 (R) 85m/C Karen Black, Winston Rekert, Lois Maxwell; *D:* George Mihalka. **VHS, Beta $79.98** *LIV* 𝘐

Eternal Return A lush modern retelling of the Tristan/Isolde legend. A young man falls passionately in love with his aunt, only to die of unrequited love. In French with English subtitles. *AKA:* L'Eternel Retour; Love Eternal.
1943 100m/B *FR* Jean Marais, Madeleine Sologne; *D:* Jean Delannoy; *W:* Jean Cocteau. **VHS, Beta $29.98** *SUE, ING, NLC* 𝘐𝘐½

The Eternal Waltz Overly sentimental chronicle of the life of composer Johann Strauss. Only director Verhoeven's touch holds the viewer's interest, though the production values are excellent. *AKA:* Ewiger Walzer.
1954 97m/C Bernhard Wicki, Hilde Krahl, Annemarie Duerringer, Friedl Loor, Eduard Strauss Jr., Jeffrey V. Thompson; *D:* Paul Verhoeven. **VHS $24.95** *NOS* 𝘐𝘐

Eternally Yours A witty magician's career threatens to break up his marriage.
1939 95m/B David Niven, Loretta Young, Hugh Herbert, Broderick Crawford, Sir C. Aubrey Smith, Billie Burke, Eve Arden, ZaSu Pitts; *D:* Tay Garnett. **VHS, Beta $19.95** *NOS, MRV, HHT* 𝘐𝘐½

Eternity While trying to uncover corrupt corporate America a television reporter falls in love with a model who works for a media king and puts his credibility on the line. He believes he and the woman shared romance in a past life.
1990 (R) 122m/C Jon Voight, Armand Assante, Wilford Brimley, Eileen Davidson, Kaye Ballard, Lainie Kazan, Joey Villa, Steven Keats, Eugene Roche, Frankie Valli, John P. Ryan; *D:* Steven Paul. **VHS $14.95** *ACA* 𝘐

Ethan A missionary in the Philippines falls in love with a woman and exiles himself for his fall from grace.
1971 91m/C Robert Sampson, Rosa Rosal, Eddie Infante; *D:* Michael DuPont. **VHS, Beta $24.95** *GHV* 𝘐½

Ethan Frome Neeson stars as the lonely, poverty-stricken 19th-century New England farmer who has long and faithfully cared for his bitter, invalid wife. When his wife's distant young cousin comes to take over as housekeeper they both succumb to their forbidden passion with tragic results. The performers carry the burden of the film's sluggish pacing, where the bleak setting of Massachusetts in winter tends to overwhelm the events. Based on the novel by Edith Wharton.
1992 (PG) 107m/C Liam Neeson, Patricia Arquette, Joan Allen, Tate Donovan, Katherine Houghton, Stephen Mendillo; *D:* John Madden; *W:* Richard Nelson. **VHS, Beta $94.95** *TOU, FCT* 𝘐𝘐½

Eubie! The popular Broadway musical revue based on the life and songs of Eubie Blake is presented in a video transfer. Some of Eubie's best known songs, performed here by members of the original cast, include "I'm Just Wild About Harry," "Memories of You," "In Honeysuckle Time" and "The Charleston Rag."
1982 100m/C Gregory Hines, Maurice Hines, Leslie Dockery, Alaina Reed, Lynnie Godfrey, Mel Johnson Jr., Jeffrey V. Thompson; *D:* Julianne Boyd. **VHS, Beta $19.98** *WAR, OM* 𝘐𝘐½

Eureka! A bizarre, wildly symbolic slab of Roegian artifice that deals with the dream-spliced life of a rich, bored gold tycoon who becomes tortured over his daughter's marriage and his own useless wealth. Eventually he is bothered by the Mafia and led to the courtroom by business competitors. From the book by Paul Mayersberg.
1981 (R) 130m/C *GB* Gene Hackman, Theresa Russell, Joe Pesci, Rutger Hauer, Mickey Rourke, Ed Lauter, Jane Lapotaire; *D:* Nicolas Roeg. **VHS, Beta $14.95** *MGM* 𝘐𝘐½

Eureka Stockade Four early Australian gold prospectors join forces to fight their governor and the police for the rights to dig on the continent. *AKA:* Massacre Hill.
1949 103m/B *AU* Chips Rafferty, Peter Finch, Jane Barrett, Peter Illing; *D:* Harry Watt. **VHS, Beta $24.95** *NOS, DVT, HEG* 𝘐𝘐

Europa, Europa The incredible, harrowing and borderline-absurdist true story of Solomon Perel, a young Jew who escaped the Holocaust by passing for German at an elite, Nazi-run academy. Such a sharp evocation of the era that the modern German establishment wouldn't submit it for the Academy Awards. In German and Russian with English subtitles.
1991 (R) 115m/C *GE* Marco Hofschneider, Klaus Abramowsky, Michele Gleizer, Rene Hofschneider, Nathalie Schmidt, Delphine Forest; *D:* Agnieszka Holland; *W:* Agnieszka Holland. Academy Awards '91 Nominations: Best Adapted Screenplay; Golden Globe Awards '92: Best Foreign Film; National Board of Review Awards '91: 5 Best Foreign Films of the Year; New York Film Critics Awards '91: Best Foreign Film. **VHS $19.98** *ORI, ING, BTV* 𝘐𝘐𝘐½

Europa '51 The despairing portrait of post-war malaise, as an American woman, whose son committed suicide, lives in Rome searching for some semblance of meaning, and ends up in an asylum. One of Bergman & Rossellini's least-loved films. In Italian with subtitles. *AKA:* The Greatest Love.
1952 110m/B Ingrid Bergman, Alexander Knox, Ettore Giannini, Giulietta Masina; *D:* Roberto Rossellini. **VHS, Beta $59.95** *FCT* 𝘐𝘐½

The Europeans Fine adaptation of Henry James's satiric novel. British brother and sister visit their staid American cousins in 19th-century New England in an effort to improve their prospects through fortuitous marriages.
1979 90m/C Lee Remick, Lisa Eichhorn, Robin Ellis, Wesley Addy, Tim Woodward; *D:* James Ivory; *W:* Ruth Prawer Jhabvala. Academy Awards '79 Nominations: Best Costume Design; Cannes Film Festival '79: Best Film; National Board of Review Awards '79: 10 Best Films of the Year. **VHS, Beta $59.95** *CVC, ING, LUM* 𝘐𝘐𝘐

Eve of Destruction Hell knows no fury like a cutting-edge android-girl on the warpath. Modeled after her creator, Dr. Eve Simmons, Eve VII has android-babe good looks and a raging nuclear capability. Wouldn't you know, something goes haywire during her trial run, and debutante Eve turns into a PMS nightmare machine, blasting all the good Doctor's previous beaux. That's where military agent Hines comes in, though

you wonder why. Dutch actress Soutendijk plays dual Eves in her first American film.
1990 (R) 101m/C Gregory Hines, Renee Soutendijk, Kevin McCarthy, Ross Malinger; *D:* Duncan Gibbins; *W:* Duncan Gibbins. **VHS, Beta $19.95** *COL, NLC, SUE* Woof!

Evel Knievel The life of motorcycle stuntman Evel Knievel is depicted in this movie, as portrayed by George Hamilton. Stunts will be appreciated by Evel Knievel fans.
1972 (PG) 90m/C George Hamilton, Bert Freed, Rod Cameron, Sue Lyon; *D:* Marvin J. Chomsky; *W:* John Milius. **VHS, Beta $59.95** *MPI* 𝘐𝘐

Evelyn Prentice Powell and Loy again team up as a married couple (after their "The Thin Man" success) but this time things aren't so rosy. He is an attorney with a wandering eye who has an affair with Russell (in her film debut). Loy finds out and turns for sympathy to Stephens but then she decides to stay with her husband after all. Only she's written some steamy letters to Stephens and he tries blackmailing her—and winds up dead. Dramatic courtroom scene straightens things up. Adapted from the novel by W.E. Woodward. Film was remade as "Stronger Than Desire" in 1939.
1934 78m/B Myrna Loy, William Powell, Harvey Stephens, Isabel Jewell, Una Merkel, Rosalind Russell, Henry Wadsworth, Edward Brophy, Cora Sue Collins, Jessie Ralph, Sam Flint, Pat O'Malley; *D:* William K. Howard; *W:* Lenore Coffee. **VHS $29.98** *MGM* 𝘐𝘐½

Even Angels Fall One of heartthrob singer Humperdinck's scattered dramatic projects, a mystery thriller about a romance novelist moving into a New York brownstone whose previous inhabitant committed suicide—or was it murder?
1990 ?m/C Morgan Fairchild, Engelbert Humperdinck; *D:* Thomas Calabrese. **VHS** *NO* 𝘐𝘐

Even Cowgirls Get the Blues '70s counterculture loses its ill-defined charm in a meandering adaptation of cult author Tom Robbins 1976 novel. An interesting failure, but likely to alienate both Van Sant and Robbins fans. Sissy Hackshaw (Thurman) possesses enormous thumbs which she hopes will make her the greatest hitchhiker in the world. But first they take her to a NYC modeling career for The Countess (Hurt in a high camp performance), who sends her to the Rubber Rose ranch, recently liberated by female cowhands, who are happy to welcome her. Theatrical release was delayed numerous times as Van Sant recut but it doesn't matter—the only successful feature is the soundtrack.
1994 (R) 106m/C Uma Thurman, John Hurt, Rain Phoenix, Lorraine Bracco, Noriyuki "Pat" Morita, Angie Dickinson, Keanu Reeves; *Cameos:* Sean Young, Crispin Glover, Roseanne (Barr) Arnold, Ed Begley Jr.; *D:* Gus Van Sant; *W:* Gus Van Sant; *M:* k.d. lang, Ben Mink. **VHS** *NYR* 𝘐½

An Evening with Robin Williams Robin Williams explodes all over the screen in this live nightclub performance taped at the Great American Music Hall in San Francisco.
1983 92m/C Robin Williams. **VHS, Beta $14.95** *PAR* 𝘐½

Evergreen The daughter of a retired British music hall star is mistaken for her mother and it is thought that she has discovered the secret of eternal youth. ♫Daddy Wouldn't Buy Me a Bow-Wow; When You've Got a Little Springtime in Your Heart; If I Give in to You; Tinkle, Tinkle, Tinkle; Dear, Dear; Dancing on the Ceiling; Just by Your Example; Over My Shoulder;

1934 91m/B *GB* Jessie Matthews, Sonnie Hale, Betty Balfour, Barry Mackay; *D:* Victor Saville; *M:* Richard Rodgers, Harry Woods, Lorenz Hart, Harry Woods. **VHS, Beta $24.95** *VYY, HMV, VMK* ✂✂½

The Everlasting Secret Family
Politics and family life make strange bedfellows. A top political figure joins a secret homosexual organization in his search for power.
1988 93m/C *AU* Arthur Dignam, Mark Lee, Dennis Miller, Heather Mitchell; *D:* Michael Thornhill. **VHS $79.95** *FCT, CCN, TPV* ✂✂

Eversmile New Jersey
A dentist travels through Patagonia, offering dental care and advice to anyone in need, and a young woman, taken with the dental knight, dumps her boyfriend and stows away with him. When he discovers his admirer, he is less than ecstatic, but a chance tooth extraction on the road reveals the young woman's natural dental talents, and the two bond. From the director of "The Official Story."
1989 (PG) 88m/C *AR* Daniel Day-Lewis, Mirjana Jokovic; *D:* Carlos Sorin; *W:* Jorge Goldenberg, Roberto Scheuer, Carlos Sorin. **VHS, Beta $89.98** *FXV, MED* ✂½

Every Breath
A kinky couple's games can be deadly and now they have someone new to play with. Jimmy couldn't resist the wife's seductive allure and if he wants to survive, he'll have to beat them at their own game.
1993 (R) 88m/C Judd Nelson, Joanna Pacula, Patrick Bauchau; *D:* Steve Bing; *W:* Judd Nelson, Andrew Fleming, Steve Bing; *M:* Nils Lofgren. **VHS** *COL* ✂✂

Every Day's a Holiday
In the 1890s, West stars as confidence woman Peaches O'Day, who sells the Brooklyn Bridge and is run out of New York City. But she comes back, in disguise as a French singer, to expose some crooked cops. The Hays office again came down heavily on Mae's suggestive behavior, which left her with little to rely on. West's last film for Paramount.
1938 79m/B Mae West, Edmund Lowe, Charles Butterworth, Charles Winninger, Walter Catlett, Lloyd Nolan, Herman Bing; *D:* Edward Sutherland; *W:* Mae West. **VHS $14.98** *MCA, BTV* ✂✂½

Every Girl Should Be Married
A shopgirl sets her sights on an eligible bachelor doctor.
1948 84m/B Cary Grant, Betsy Drake, Diana Lynn, Franchot Tone; *D:* Don Hartman. **VHS, Beta $19.98** *RKO, TTC* ✂✂½

Every Girl Should Have One
A rambunctious comedy about a chase following a million-dollar diamond theft.
1978 90m/C Zsa Zsa Gabor, Robert Alda, Alice Faye, Sandra Vacey, John Lazar. **VHS, Beta $59.95** *GEM* ✂½

Every Man for Himself & God Against All
Kaspar Hauser is a young man who mysteriously appears in the town square of Nuremberg, early in the 19th century. He cannot speak or stand upright and is found to have been kept in a dungeon for the first 18 years of his life. He becomes an attraction in society with his alternate vision of the world and attempts to reconcile with reality. A lovely, though demanding film which is based on a true story. In German with English subtitles. *AKA:* The Mystery of Kaspar Hauser; Jeder Fur Sich Und Gott Gegen Alle; The Enigma of Kaspar Hauser.
1975 110m/C *GE* Bruno S, Brigitte Mira, Walter Ladengast, Hans Musaus, Willy Semmelrogge, Michael Kroecher, Henry van Lyck; *D:* Werner Herzog; *W:* Werner Herzog; *M:* Albinoni.

Pachelbel, Orlando Di Lasso. **VHS, Beta $79.95** *NYF, APD, GLV* ✂✂✂✂

Every Man's Law
A cowboy who poses as a hired gunman is almost lynched by ranchers who think he is a murderer.
1935 60m/B Johnny Mack Brown. **VHS, Beta $19.95** *VCN* ✂½

Every Time We Say Goodbye
In 1942, Jerusalem, an American flyboy falls in love with a young Sephardic Jewish girl, whose family resists the match.
1986 (PG-13) 97m/C Tom Hanks, Christina Marsillach, Benedict Taylor, Anat Atzman, Gila Almagor; *D:* Moshe Mizrahi; *W:* Moshe Mizrahi; *M:* Philippe Sarde. **VHS, Beta $79.98** *LIV* ✂✂½

Every Which Way But Loose
Fairly pointless Eastwood foray featuring Clint as a beer-guzzling, country-music loving truck driver earning a living as a barroom brawler. He and his orangutan travel to Colorado in pursuit of the woman he loves. Behind him are a motorcycle gang and an L.A. cop. All have been victims of his fists. Sequel is "Any Which Way You Can."
1978 (R) 119m/C Clint Eastwood, Sondra Locke, Geoffrey Lewis, Beverly D'Angelo, Ruth Gordon; *D:* James Fargo; *M:* Stephen Dorff. **VHS, Beta $19.98** *WAR* ✂✂

Everybody Sing
A down-on-their-luck theatrical family, including Garland (who is kicked out of boarding school for singing Mendelssohn with a swing beat) decides to put on a show in hopes of making a comeback. Dumb plot and boring songs make this one for die-hard Garland fans only. ♫Swing, Mr. Mendelssohn, Swing; The One I Love; Down on Melody Farms; The Show Must Go On; I Wanna Swing; Never Was There Such a Perfect Day; Quainty Dainty Me; Why? Because; Snooks; Cosi, Cosa; Swing Low, Sweet Chariot.
1938 80m/B Allan Jones, Fanny Brice, Judy Garland, Reginald Owen, Billie Burke, Reginald Gardiner, Lynne Carver, Monty Woolley; *D:* Edwin L. Marin. **VHS $19.98** *MGM, MVD* ✂✂

Everybody Wins
A mystery-romance about a befuddled private eye trying to solve a murder and getting caught up with the bizarre prostitute who hired him. Arthur Miller based this screenplay on his stage drama "Some Kind of Love Story." Confused and, given its pedigree, disappointing mystery.
1990 (R) 110m/C Nick Nolte, Debra Winger, Will Patton, Jack Warden, Kathleen Wilhoite, Frank Converse, Frank Military, Judith Ivey; *D:* Karel Reisz; *W:* Arthur Miller. **VHS, Beta $89.98** *ORI* ✂

Everybody's All American
Shallow, sentimental melodrama about a college football star and his cheerleader wife whose lives, subsequent to their youthful glories, is a string of disappointments and tragedies. Decently acted and based on Frank Deford's novel.
1988 (R) 127m/C Jessica Lange, Dennis Quaid, Timothy Hutton, John Goodman, Carl Lumbly, Ray Baker, Savannah Smith; *D:* Taylor Hackford; *M:* James Newton Howard. **VHS, Beta, 8mm $14.95** *WAR* ✂✂

Everybody's Dancin'
A ballroom proprietor's business is marred by random killings in her establishment as the bands play on. ♫Foolish Tears; Oblivious; Deep Freeze Dinah; I Shook; Rhumba Boogie.
1950 66m/B Spade Cooley, Dick Lane, Hal Derwin, The Pioneers, Roddy McDowall; *D:* Will Jason. **VHS, Beta** *NO* ✂✂½

Everybody's Fine
Mastroianni stars in this bittersweet story of a father on a mission to reunite his five grown children. His journey takes him all over Italy as he tries to bring them together in this touching film about

enduring family love. In Italian with English subtitles. *AKA:* Stanno Tutti Bene.
1990 (PG-13) 115m/C *IT* Marcello Mastroianni, Salvatore Cascio, Valeria Cavalli, Norma Martelli, Marino Cenna, Roberto Nobile, Michele Morgan, Fabio Iellini; *D:* Giuseppe Tornatore, Giuseppe Tornatore; *W:* Giuseppe Tornatore, Tonino Guerra; *M:* Ennio Morricone. **VHS $19.95** *COL, ING* ✂✂½

Everything Happens at Night
Rival reporters Milland and Cummings are torn between the woman they love and the story of a lifetime. One of Henie's best romantic skating vehicles due to the strong performances by the leading men. Henie does take to the ice for a couple of numbers, but this film was largely designed to expand her image as a serious actress. Although it failed to do that, it's good entertainment nonetheless.
1939 76m/B Sonja Henie, Ray Milland, Robert Cummings, Maurice Moscovich, Leonid Kinskey, Alan Dinehart, Fritz Feld; *D:* Irving Cummings; *W:* Art Arthur, Robert Herari. **VHS $19.98** *FXV* ✂✂✂

Everything You Always Wanted to Know About Sex (But Were Afraid to Ask)
Satiric comical sketches about sex includes a timid sperm cell, an oversexed court jester, a sheep folly, and a giant disembodied breast. Quite entertaining in its own jolly way. Based on the book by Dr. David Reuben.
1972 (R) 88m/C Woody Allen, John Carradine, Lou Jacobi, Louise Lasser, Anthony Quayle, Geoffrey Holder, Lynn Redgrave, Tony Randall, Burt Reynolds, Gene Wilder, Robert Walden, Jay Robinson; *D:* Woody Allen; *W:* Woody Allen. **VHS, Beta $14.95** *MGM, FOX, FCT* ✂✂✂

The Evictors
Young couple moves into an abandoned, haunted farmhouse in a small Louisiana town. Unfortunately, they don't know anything about its horrible bloody history. And the real estate agent acts kinda funny. AIP Amityville scare-a-thon.
1979 (PG) 92m/C Vic Morrow, Michael Parks, Jessica Harper, Sue Ane Langdon, Dennis Fimple; *D:* Charles B. Pierce; *W:* Charles B. Pierce. **VHS, Beta $59.98** *LIV, VES* Woof!

The Evil
A psychologist must destroy an evil force that is killing off the members of his research team residing at an old mansion.
1978 (R) 80m/C Richard Crenna, Joanna Pettet, Andrew Prine, Victor Buono, Cassie Yates; *D:* Gus Trikonis. **VHS, Beta $19.98** *SUE* ✂✂

Evil Altar
A man controls a small town, but only so long as he offers sacrifices to the devil!
1989 (R) 90m/C William Smith, Robert Z'Dar, Pepper Martin, Theresa Cooney, Ryan Rao; *D:* Jim Winburn. **VHS $14.95** *HMD* ✂

The Evil Below
A couple hits the high seas in search of the lost treasure ship "El Diablo," resting on the ocean floor. In the process they trigger an evil curse and then must attempt to thwart it.
1987 90m/C *SA* June Chadwick, Wayne Crawford; *D:* Jean-Claude Dubois. **VHS, Beta** *NO* ✂

Evil Clutch
A young couple vacationing in the Alps encounter several creepy locals when they find themselves in the midst of a haunted forest. The cinematography is extremely amateurish in this Italian gorefest and the English dubbing is atrocious. However, the special makeup effects are outstanding and the musical score adds a touch of class to this otherwise inept horror film.
1989 (R) 88m/C *IT* Coralina Cataldi Tassoni, Diego Riba, Elena Cantarone, Luciano Crovato, Stefano Molinari; *D:* Andreas Marfori; *W:* Andreas Marfori. **VHS $79.95** *UND, RHI* ✂½

Evil Dead Five vacationing college students unwittingly resurrect demons which transform the students into evil monsters. Exuberantly gory low-budgeter followed by two sequels.
1983 126m/C Bruce Campbell, Ellen Sandweiss, Betsy Baker, Hal Delrich; *D:* Sam Raimi; *W:* Sam Raimi. VHS, Beta $14.99 IME ♫♫½

Evil Dead 2: Dead by Dawn A gory, tongue-in-cheek sequel/remake of the original festival of gag and gore, in which an ancient book of magic invokes a crowd of flesh-snacking, joke-tossing ghouls. Followed by yet a third bloodfest.
1987 (R) 84m/C Bruce Campbell, Sarah Berry, Dan Hicks, Kassie Wesley, Theodore Raimi, Denise Bixler, Richard Domeier; *D:* Sam Raimi; *W:* Sam Raimi, Scott Spiegel; *M:* Joseph Lo Duca. VHS, Beta $14.98 LIV, VES ♫♫½

Evil Judgement A young girl investigates a series of murders and finds the culprit is a psychopathic judge.
1985 93m/C Pamela Collyer, Jack Langedijk, Nanette Workman; *D:* Claude Castravelli. VHS, Beta $69.95 MED ♫½

Evil Laugh Medical students and their girlfriends party at an abandoned orphanage, until a serial killer decides to join them.
1986 (R) 90m/C Tony Griffin, Kim McKamy, Jody Gibson, Dominick Brascia; *D:* Dominick Brascia. VHS $79.95 CEL *Woof!*

The Evil Mind A fraudulent mind reader predicts many disasters that start coming true. *AKA:* The Clairvoyant.
1934 80m/B Claude Rains, Fay Wray, Jane Baxter, Felix Aylmer; *D:* Maurice Elvey; *W:* Charles Bennett. VHS, Beta $16.95 SNC, NOS, BAR ♫♫½

The Evil of Frankenstein The third of the Hammer Frankenstein films, with the mad doctor once again finding his creature preserved in ice and thawing him out. Preceded by "The Revenge of Frankenstein" and followed by "Frankenstein Created Woman."
1964 84m/C *GB* Peter Cushing, Duncan Lamont, Peter Woodthorpe, Sandor Eles, Kiwi Kingston, Katy Wild; *D:* Freddie Francis. VHS, Beta $14.98 MCA, MLB ♫♫

Evil Spawn A fading movie queen takes an experimental drug to restore her youthful beauty, but it only turns her into a giant silverfish. Releases under several alternate titles, and with varying running times. *AKA:* Deadly Sting; Alive by Night; Alien Within.
1987 80m/C Bobbie Bresee, John Carradine, Drew Godderis, John Terrance, Dawn Wildsmith; *D:* Kenneth J. Hall. VHS, Beta NO ♫

Evil Spirits Boardinghouse tenants are murdered while the crazy landlady cashes their social security checks. This seedy horror cheapie doesn't take itself seriously, and like-minded genre buffs may enjoy the cult-film cast.
1991 (R) 95m/C Karen Black, Arte Johnson, Virginia Mayo, Michael Berryman, Martine Beswick, Bert Remsen, Yvette Vickers, Robert Quarry, Mikel Angel, Debra Lamb; *D:* Gary Graver. VHS, Beta $79.95 PSM ♫½

The Evil That Men Do A hitman comes out of retirement to break up a Central American government's political torture ring and, in the process, brings a friend's killer to justice. Based on the novel by R. Lance Hill.
1984 (R) 90m/C Charles Bronson, Theresa Saldana, Joseph Maher, Jose Ferrer, Rene Enriquez, John Glover, Raymond St. Jacques, Antoinette Bower, Enrique Lucero, Jorge Luke; *D:* J. Lee Thompson. VHS, Beta, 8mm $14.95 COL ♫♫

Evil Toons A quartet of lovely coeds on a cleaning job venture into a deserted mansion. There they accidentally release a vulgar, lustful, animated demon who proceeds to cause their clothes to fall off. Can the girls escape the haunted mansion with their sanity, virtue and wardrobes intact?
1990 (R) 86m/C David Carradine, Dick Miller, Monique Gabrielle, Suzanne Ager, Stacy Nix, Madison Stone, Don Dowe, Arte Johnson, Michelle (McClellan) Bauer; *D:* Fred Olen Ray. VHS, Beta $79.95 PSM ♫½

Evil Town In this poorly made film, a wandering guy discovers a town overrun with zombies created by a mad doctor.
1987 (R) 88m/C Dean Jagger, James Keach, Robert Walker Jr., Doria Cook, Michele Marsh; *D:* Edward Collins. VHS, Beta $79.95 TWE, HHE ♫

Evil Under the Sun An opulent beach resort is the setting as Hercule Poirot attempts to unravel a murder mystery. Based on the Agatha Christie novel.
1982 (PG) 112m/C *GB* Peter Ustinov, Jane Birkin, Dame Maggie Smith, Colin Blakely, Roddy McDowall, Diana Rigg, Sylvia Miles, James Mason, Nicholas Clay; *D:* Guy Hamilton; *W:* Anthony Shaffer. VHS, Beta $14.98 REP ♫♫

Evil's Commandment Original vampire film which started the classic Italian horror cycle. A gorgeous Countess needs blood to stay young, otherwise she reverts to a 200-year-old vampire.
1956 ?m/B *IT* Giana Maria Canale; *D:* Riccardo (Robert Hampton) Freda. VHS $20 SMW ♫♫½

Evils of the Night Teenage campers are abducted by sex-crazed alien vampires. Bloody naked mayhem follows.
1985 85m/C John Carradine, Julie Newmar, Tina Louise, Neville Brand, Aldo Ray, Karrie Emerson, Bridget Hollman; *D:* Mardi Rustam. VHS, Beta $69.98 LIV ♫

Evilspeak Bumbling misfit enrolled at a military school is mistreated by the other cadets. With the help of his computer, he retaliates with satanic power. Bits, bytes, and gore.
1982 (R) 89m/C Clint Howard, Don Stark, Lou Gravance, Lauren Lester, R.G. Armstrong, Joe Cortese, Claude Earl Jones, Haywood Nelson; *D:* Eric Weston. VHS, Beta $59.98 FOX *Woof!*

The Ewok Adventure Those adorable, friendly and funny characters from "Return of the Jedi" make the jump from film to television in a new adventure from George Lucas. In this installment, the Ewoks save a miraculous child from harm with the help of a young human. This fun-filled adventure has Lucas's thumbprint all over it and great special effects. Followed by "Ewoks: The Battle for Endor."
1984 (G) 96m/C Warwick Davis, Eric Walker, Aubree Miller, Fionnula Flanagan; *D:* John Korty; *M:* Elmer Bernstein. VHS, Beta $14.95 MGM, FCT ♫♫½

The Ewoks: Battle for Endor A television movie based on the furry creatures from "Return of the Jedi," detailing their battle against an evil queen to retain their forest home. Preceded by "The Ewok Adventure."
1985 98m/C Wilford Brimley, Warwick Davis, Aubree Miller, Sian Phillips, Paul Gleason, Eric Walker, Carel Struycken, Niki Botelho; *D:* Jim Wheat, Ken Wheat. VHS, Beta $14.95 MGM, FCT ♫♫½

Ex-Cop Pete Danberg is a cop with a drinking problem. He's fired from the force but not before he puts away the "Las Vegas Slasher." Unfortunately for Pete the Slasher makes parole and is out for revenge—using Pete's kidnapped daughter as bait.

1993 97m/C Rick Savage, Sandy Hackett, Joan Chamberlain, Douglas Terry, Angi Davidson, Richard Cornell, Jim Williams; *D:* Patrick Kerby; *W:* Daniel S. Sample. VHS $89.95 AIP ♫♫

Ex-Lady Davis stars as a liberated woman who loves advertising writer Raymond, but doesn't want to marry him. However, she believes living together is the most suitable arrangement. The two open up an ad agency and complications ensue. Remake of "Illicit," which was filmed only two years earlier with Barbara Stanwyck in the lead role.
1933 65m/B Bette Davis, Gene Raymond, Frank McHugh, Claire Dodd, Monroe Owsley, Ferdinand Gottschalk; *D:* Robert Florey. VHS $19.98 MGM ♫

Ex-Mrs. Bradford Amateur sleuth Dr. Bradford teams up with his ex-wife to solve a series of murders at the race track. Sophisticated comedy-mystery; witty dialogue.
1936 80m/B William Powell, Jean Arthur, James Gleason, Eric Blore, Robert Armstrong; *D:* Stephen Roberts. VHS, Beta $19.95 NOS, MED ♫♫♫

Excalibur A sweeping, visionary retelling of the life of King Arthur, from his conception, to the sword in the stone, to the search for the Holy Grail and the final battle with Mordred. An imperfect, sensationalized version, but still the best yet filmed.
1981 (R) 140m/C Nigel Terry, Nicol Williamson, Nicholas Clay, Helen Mirren, Cherie Lunghi, Paul Geoffrey, Gabriel Byrne, Liam Neeson, Patrick Stewart, Charley Boorman, Corin Redgrave; *D:* John Boorman; *W:* Rospo Pallenberg; *M:* Trevor Jones. VHS, Beta $19.98 WAR, TVC ♫♫♫½

Excessive Force Routine actioner lives up to its title by offering lots of violence, but little else. Gang leader Young seeks revenge on the cops who he believes ruined a $3 million drug deal. Loner cop Griffith is the only one to survive the grudge killings and goes after Young himself. Talented cast underachieves. Limited theatrical release sent this one almost straight to video.
1993 (R) 87m/C Thomas Ian Griffith, Lance Henriksen, James Earl Jones, Charlotte Lewis, Tony Todd, Burt Young, W. Earl Brown; *D:* Jon Hess; *W:* Thomas Ian Griffith; *M:* Charles Bernstein. VHS $19.95 COL, IME ♫½

The Execution A made-for-television film about five female friends who discover that the Nazi doctor who brutalized them in a concentration camp during WWII is now living a normal life in California. Together they plot his undoing.
1985 92m/C Loretta Swit, Valerie Harper, Sandy Dennis, Jessica Walter, Rip Torn, Barbara Barrie, Robert Hooks, Michael Lerner; *D:* Paul Wendkos; *M:* Georges Delerue. VHS $9.99 STE, PSM ♫½

The Execution of Private Slovik This quiet powerhouse of a TV movie recounts in straightforward terms the case of Eddie Slovik, a WWII misfit who became the only American soldier executed for desertion since the Civil War. The Levinson/Link screenplay (based on the book by William Bradford Huie) ends up defying Slovik, which some might find hard to take. But there's no arguing the impact of the drama, or of Sheen's unaffected lead performance.
1974 122m/C Martin Sheen, Mariclare Costello, Ned Beatty, Gary Busey, Matt Clark, Ben Hammer, Warren Kemmerling; *D:* Lamont Johnson; *W:* Richard Levinson, William Link. VHS $14.98 MCA ♫♫♫½

Execution of Raymond Graham The lawyers and family of Raymond Graham struggle to keep him from being executed for murder. Based on a true story; made for television.

1985 104m/C Morgan Freeman, Jeff Fahey, Kate Reid, Laurie Metcalf, Josef Sommer; *D:* Daniel Petrie. VHS, Beta *NO* 🎬🎬½

The Executioner A thriller wherein a British spy must prove that his former colleague is a double agent. Elements of backstabbing, betrayal, and espionage abound.
1970 (PG) 107m/C *GB* Judy Geeson, Oscar Homolka, Charles Gray, Nigel Patrick, George Peppard, Joan Collins, Keith Mitchell; *D:* Sam Wanamaker. VHS, Beta $9.95 *COL, GKK* 🎬🎬

The Executioner A very cheap, very "Godfather"-like story of a mafia family gone awry. Also known as "Like Father, Like Son" and "Massacre Mafia Style." *AKA:* Like Father, Like Son; Massacre Mafia Style.
1978 (R) 84m/C Duke Mitchell, Vic Caesar, Dominic Micelli, John Strong, Jim Williams, Lorenzo Dodo; *D:* Duke Mitchell; *W:* Duke Mitchell. VHS, Beta *GEM, MRV* 🎬

Executioner of Venice Marauding pirates with time on hands swarm in from the Adriatic Sea and attempt to rob the Venetians blind. The Doge and his godson come to the rescue.
1963 90m/C Guy Madison, Lex Barker, Alessandra Panaro; *D:* Louis Capauno. VHS, Beta *NO* 🎬

The Executioner, Part 2: Frozen Scream Brutal feud rocks the Mafia, and a crime kingpin's passionate son seeks revenge on his father's slayers. Not a sequel to any other films bearing similar titles. Strange thing is, no "Executioner, Part I" was ever made. Pretty laughable.
1984 (R) 150m/C Chris Mitchum, Aldo Ray, Antoine John Mottet, Renee Harmon; *D:* James Bryant. VHS, Beta $49.98 *GEM* 🎬

The Executioner's Song European version of the television movie based on Norman Mailer's Pulitzer Prize-winner, recounting the life and death of convicted murderer Gary Gilmore. Features adult-minded footage not seen in the U.S. version.
1982 157m/C Tommy Lee Jones, Rosanna Arquette, Eli Wallach, Christine Lahti, Jenny Wright, Jordan Clark, Steven Keats; *D:* Lawrence Schiller. VHS, Beta $29.95 *STE, LIV* 🎬🎬½

Executive Action Political thriller providing a different look at the events leading to the assassination of JFK. In this speculation, a millionaire pays a professional spy to organize a secret conspiracy to kill President Kennedy. Ryan's final film. Adapted by Dalton Trumbo from Mark Lane's "Rush to Judgement."
1973 (PG) 91m/C Burt Lancaster, Robert Ryan, Will Geer, Gilbert Green, John Anderson; *D:* David Miller; *M:* Randy Edelman. VHS, Beta $19.98 *WAR* 🎬🎬½

Executive Suite One of the first dog-eat-dog dramas about high finance and big business. The plot centers on the question of a replacement for the freshly buried owner of a gigantic furniture company.
1954 104m/B William Holden, June Allyson, Barbara Stanwyck, Fredric March, Walter Pidgeon, Louis Calhern, Shelley Winters, Paul Douglas, Nina Foch, Dean Jagger; *D:* Robert Wise; *W:* Ernest Lehman. VHS, Beta $19.98 *MGM* 🎬🎬🎬

Exiled in America A Central American freedom fighter (Albert) flees his country for the United States, settling in a small town with his wife. She gets a waitressing job at a local diner, telling the owner her husband died in an accident, and the owner's son winds up falling in love with her. Things get complicated when the death squad, led by a corrupt CIA agent, follows Albert to his hiding

place, and the local sheriff threatens to blow his cover.
1990 84m/C Maxwell Caulfield, Edward Albert, Viveca Lindfors, Kamala Lopez, Stella Stevens, Wings Hauser; *D:* Paul Leder; *W:* Paul Leder. VHS $79.95 *PSM* 🎬🎬

Exiled to Shanghai A couple of newsreel men invent a television device that revolutionizes the business.
1937 65m/B Wallace Ford, June Travis, Dean Jagger, William "Billy" Bakewell, Arthur Lake, Jonathan Hale, William Harrigan, Sarah Padden; *D:* Armand Schaefer. VHS $24.95 *NOS, DVT, HEG* 🎬🎬½

Exit the Dragon, Enter the Tiger Story about the death of karate master Bruce Lee.
1976 84m/C VHS, Beta $24.95 *VCI, TWE* 🎬½

Exodus Chronicles the post-WWII partition of Palestine into a homeland for Jews; the anguish of refugees from Nazi concentration camps held on ships in the Mediterranean; the struggle of the tiny nation with forces dividing it from within and destroying it from the outside; and the heroic men and women who saw a job to be done and did it. Based on the novel by Leon Uris; filmed in Cyprus and Israel. Preminger battled the Israeli government, the studio, and the novel's author to complete this epic. Cost more than $4 million, a phenomenal amount at the time.
1960 208m/C Paul Newman, Eva Marie Saint, Lee J. Cobb, Sal Mineo, Ralph Richardson, Hugh Griffith, Gregory Ratoff, Felix Aylmer, Peter Lawford, Jill Haworth, John Derek, David Opatoshu, Marius Goring, Alexandra Stewart, Michael Wager, Martin Benson, Paul Stevens, George Maharis; *D:* Otto Preminger; *W:* Dalton Trumbo; *M:* Ernest Gold. Academy Awards '60: Best Original Score; Nominations: Best Color Cinematography, Best Supporting Actor (Mineo); Golden Globe Awards '61: Best Supporting Actor (Mineo). VHS, Beta $29.98 *FOX, SWC* 🎬🎬🎬

Exorcism A satanic cult in a small English village commits a series of gruesome crimes that have the authorities baffled.
1974 90m/C Paul Naschy, Maria Perschy; *D:* Juan Bosch. VHS, Beta $19.95 *HHE* 🎬½

Exorcism's Daughter While running an insane asylum, a man discovers that a woman has lost her mind because as a child, she witnessed her mother's death during an exorcism. Pretty grim but interesting for genre fans. A natural double feature with "House of Psychotic Women." *AKA:* House of Insane Women.
1974 (R) 93m/C *SP* Amelia Gade, Francesco Rabal, Espartaco Santoni; *D:* Rafael Morena Alba. VHS $16.95 *SNC* 🎬

The Exorcist Truly terrifying story of a young girl who is possessed by a malevolent spirit. Brilliantly directed by Friedkin, with underlying themes of the workings and nature of fate. Impeccable casting and unforgettable, thought-provoking performances. A rare film that remains startling and engrossing with every viewing, it spawned countless imitations and changed the way horror films were made. Based on the bestseller by Blatty, who also wrote the screenplay. Not for the squeamish. When first released, the film created mass hysteria in theaters, with people fainting and paramedics on the scene.
1973 (R) 120m/C Ellen Burstyn, Linda Blair, Jason Miller, Max von Sydow, Jack MacGowran, Lee J. Cobb, Kitty Winn; *D:* William Friedkin; *W:* William Peter Blatty; *M:* Jack Nitzsche. Academy Awards '73: Best Adapted Screenplay, Best Sound; Nominations: Best Actress (Burstyn), Best Art Direction/Set Decoration, Best Cinematography, Best Director (Friedkin), Best Film Editing, Best Picture, Best Supporting Actor (Miller), Best Supporting Actress (Blair); Golden

Globe Awards '74: Best Director (Friedkin), Best Film—Drama, Best Screenplay, Best Supporting Actress (Blair). VHS, Beta $19.98 *WAR* 🎬🎬🎬½

The Exorcist 2: The Heretic Unnecessary sequel to the 1973 hit "The Exorcist" which featured extensive recutting by Boorman. After four years, Blair is still under psychiatric care, suffering from the effects of being possessed by the devil. Meanwhile, a priest investigates the first exorcist's work as he tries to help the head-spinning lass. Decent special effects.
1977 (R) 118m/C Richard Burton, Linda Blair, Louise Fletcher, Kitty Winn, James Earl Jones, Ned Beatty, Max von Sydow; *D:* John Boorman; *M:* Ennio Morricone. VHS, Beta $14.95 *WAR* 🎬🎬

The Exorcist 3 Apparently subscribing to the two wrongs make a right school of sequels, this time novelist Blatty is the director. The result is slightly better than the first sequel, but still a far cry from the original. Fifteen years after later, Detective Kinderman (Scott) is faced with a series of really gross murders bearing the mark of a serial killer who was flambeed in the electric chair on the same night as the exorcism of the pea-soup expectorating devil of the original. With the aid of priests Flanders and Douriff the detective stalks the transmigratory terror—without the help of Linda Blair, who was at the time spoofing "The Exorcist" in "Repossessed."
1990 (R) 105m/C George C. Scott, Ed Flanders, Jason Miller, Nicol Williamson, Scott Wilson, Brad Dourif, Nancy Fish, George DiCenzo, Viveca Lindfors; *D:* William Peter Blatty; *W:* William Peter Blatty. VHS, Beta $19.98 *FOX, CCB* 🎬🎬

The Expendables A rugged captain turns a platoon of criminals and misfits into a tough fighting unit for a particularly dangerous mission from which they might not return. See the "Dirty Dozen" instead.
1989 (R) 89m/C Anthony Finetti, Peter Nelson, Loren Haynes, Kevin Duffis; *D:* Cirio H. Santiago. VHS, Beta $79.95 *MED* 🎬

Experience Preferred... But Not Essential An English schoolgirl gets her first job at a resort where she learns about life. Made for British television.
1983 (PG) 77m/C *GB* Elizabeth Edmonds, Sue Wallace, Geraldine Griffith, Karen Meagher, Ron Bain, Alun Lewis, Robert Blythe; *D:* Peter Duffell; *W:* June Roberts. VHS, Beta $59.95 *MGM* 🎬🎬½

Experiment in Terror A psychopath kidnaps a girl in order to blackmail her sister, a bank teller, into embezzling $100,000.
1962 123m/B Lee Remick, Glenn Ford, Stefanie Powers, Ross Martin; *D:* Blake Edwards; *M:* Henry Mancini. VHS, Beta $59.95 *COL, IME* 🎬🎬🎬

Experiment Perilous A psychologist and a recently widowed woman band together to find her husband's murderer. An atmospheric vintage mystery.
1945 91m/B Hedy Lamarr, Paul Lukas, George Brent, Albert Dekker; *D:* Jacques Tourneur. VHS, Beta $19.95 *MED* 🎬🎬🎬

Expertos en Pinchazos In this comedy from Spain, Albert and George, experts at giving injections to women, inject a patient with venom by mistake. Now they must find her within 48 hours. In Spanish.
1979 100m/C *SP* Alberto Olmedo, Jorge Porcel. VHS, Beta $29.95 *MED* 🎬½

The Experts When the KGB needs real Americans for their spies to study, they kidnap two out-of-work New Yorkers who mistakenly believe that they have been hired to open a nightclub in Nebraska. Shot on location in Canada. Sometimes funny and

directed by former Second City TV MacKenzie Brother, Dave Thomas.
1989 (PG-13) 94m/C John Travolta, Arye Gross, Charles Martin Smith, Kelly Preston, James Keach, Deborah Foreman, Brian Doyle-Murray; **D:** Dave Thomas; **W:** Nick Thiel; **M:** Marvin Hamlisch. **VHS, Beta, 8mm** $14.95 PAR ♂♂

Explorers Intelligent family fare involving three young boys who use a contraption from their makeshift laboratory to travel to outer space. From the director of "Gremlins," displaying Dante's characteristic surreal wit and sense of irony.
1985 (PG) 107m/C Ethan Hawke, River Phoenix, Jason Presson, Amanda Peterson, Mary Kay Place, Dick Miller, Robert Picardo, Dana Ivey, Meshach Taylor, Brooke Bundy; **D:** Joe Dante; **W:** Eric Luke; **M:** Jerry Goldsmith. **VHS, Beta** $14.95 PAR ♂♂½

Explosion Distraught and disturbed young man evades the draft after losing a brother in Vietnam. Arriving in Canada, he meets another draft-dodger with whom he embarks on a murderous rampage.
1969 (R) 96m/C Don Stroud, Gordon Thomson, Michele Chicoine, Richard Conte; **D:** Jules Bricken. **VHS, Beta** $59.95 TWE ♂♂½

Exposed High fashion model Kinski falls in with a terrorist gang through a connection with violinist Nureyev. Weak plotting undermines the end of this political thriller. However, Kinski is brilliant, stripping the barrier between performance and audience.
1983 (R) 100m/C Nastassia Kinski, Rudolf Nureyev, Harvey Keitel, Ian McShane, Bibi Andersson; **D:** James Toback; **W:** James Toback; **M:** Georges Delerue. **VHS, Beta** $79.95 MGM ♂♂

Exposure A rugged American photographer (Coyote) on assignment in Rio turns vigilante to locate the vicious killer of a young prostitute. Coyote and his girlfriend (Pays) get caught up in the deadly underworld of international arms trading and drug running as they search for the murderer.
1991 99m/C Peter Coyote, Amanda Pays, Tcheky Karyo; **M:** Todd Boekelheide. **VHS** $92.99 HBO ♂

Express to Terror Passengers aboard an atomic-powered train en route to Los Angeles attempt to kill a sleazy theatrical agent. Pilot for the "Supertrain" series.
1979 120m/C Steve Lawrence, George Hamilton, Vic Morrow, Broderick Crawford, Robert Alda, Don Stroud, Fred Williamson, Stella Stevens, Don Meredith; **D:** Dan Curtis. **VHS, Beta** $49.95 PSM ♂♂½

Exquisite Corpses An Oklahoma hayseed charges to New York with a new, slick image. He meets the wife of a wealthy man, and together they organize a murderous operation.
1988 95m/C Zoe Tamerlaine Lund, Gary Knox, Daniel Chapman, Ruth Collins; **D:** Temistocles Lopez. **VHS** $79.95 MNC ♂♂½

The Exterminating Angel A fierce, funny surreal nightmare, wherein dinner guests find they cannot, for any definable reason, leave the dining room; full of dream imagery and characteristically scatological satire. One of Bunuel's best, in Spanish with English subtitles.
1962 95m/B MX SP Silvia Pinal, Enrique Rambal, Jacqueline Andere, Jose Baviera, Augusto Benedico, Luis Beristain; **D:** Luis Bunuel. **VHS, Beta** $59.95 ING, HTV, FCT ♂♂♂½

Exterminator Vietnam veteran hunts down the gang that assaulted his friend and becomes the target of the police, the CIA and the underworld in this bloody banal tale of murder and intrigue. Followed by creatively titled "Exterminator II."
1980 (R) 101m/C Christopher George, Samantha Eggar, Robert Ginty; **D:** James Glickenhaus. **VHS, Beta** $14.98 SUE, NLC ♂

Exterminator 2 The Exterminator battles the denizens of New York's underworld after his girlfriend is crippled, then murdered by the ruthless Mr. X. Violence galore.
1984 (R) 88m/C Robert Ginty, Mario Van Peebles, Deborah Geffner, Frankie Faison; **D:** Mark Buntzman. **VHS, Beta** $14.95 MGM ♂

Exterminators of the Year 3000 The Exterminator and his mercenary girlfriend battle with nuclear mutants over the last remaining tanks of purified water on Earth. Low-budget Road Warrior rip-off.
1983 (R) 101m/C IT Robert Jannucci, Alicia Moro, Alan Collins, Fred Harris; **D:** Jules Harrison. **VHS, Beta** NO Woof!

Extra Girl A silent melodrama/farce about a farm girl, brilliantly played by Normand, who travels to Hollywood to be a star. Once in the glamour capital, she gets used and abused for her trouble.
1923 87m/B Mabel Normand, Ralph Graves, Vernon Dent; **D:** F. Richard Jones; **W:** Mack Sennett. **VHS, Beta, 8mm** $29.95 VYY, GPV ♂♂

The Extraordinary Adventures of Mr. West in the Land of the Bolsheviks The first achievement from the Kuleshov workshop, a wacky satire on American insularity depicting a naive and prejudiced American visiting Russia and being taken advantage of. Silent.
1924 55m/B Vsevolod Pudovkin, Boris Barnett; **D:** Lev Kuleshov. **VHS, Beta** $29.95 FCT, ING, KIV ♂♂

Extreme Justice A violent expose of the Special Investigations Section of the Los Angeles Police Department, an elite, undercover squad which specialized in catching violent repeat offenders. But their tactics left something to be desired. They were accused of stalking their prey until they committed a crime and then dealing with the criminal by shooting them in the act. Lots of gunplay. Originally a theatrical film that was pulled for release in the wake of the Rodney King verdict.
1993 (R) 96m/C Lou Diamond Phillips, Scott Glenn, Yaphet Kotto, Ed Lauter, Chelsea Field. **VHS** $92.95 VMK ♂♂½

Extreme Prejudice A redneck Texas Ranger fights a powerful drug kingpin along the U.S.-Mexican border. Once best friends, they now fight for justice and the heart of the woman they both love.
1987 (R) 104m/C Nick Nolte, Powers Boothe, Maria Conchita Alonso, Michael Ironside, Rip Torn; **D:** Walter Hill; **W:** Deric Washburn; **M:** Jerry Goldsmith. **VHS, Beta** $14.95 LIV ♂♂

Extreme Vengeance Police officer David puts mafia crime boss Mario Blanco away for ten years, then exposes police corruption and goes into hiding. When Blanco gets out, he seeks revenge on David's family, forcing David out of hiding to protect what is his. Available in Spanish subtitles.
1993 97m/C **VHS** $89.95 NHO ♂♂

Extremities An adaptation of the topical William Mastrosimone play about an intended rape victim who turns on her attacker, captures him, and plots to kill him. Violent and exploitive.
1986 (R) 83m/C Farrah Fawcett, Diana Scarwid, James Russo, Alfre Woodard; **D:** Robert M. Young; **W:** William Mastrosimone. **VHS, Beta, 8mm** $19.95 PAR ♂♂

The Eye Creatures Alien creatures in the form of eyeballs are fought off by a teenager and his girlfriend. A low-budget, gory, science fiction feature.
1965 80m/B John Ashley, Cynthia Hull, Warren Hammack, Chet Davis, Bill Peck; **D:** Larry Buchanan. **VHS** $16.98 NOS, SNC ♂

An Eye for an Eye A story of pursuit and revenge with Norris as an undercover cop pitted against San Francisco's underworld and high society.
1981 (R) 106m/C Chuck Norris, Christopher Lee, Richard Roundtree, Matt Clark, Mako, Maggie Cooper; **D:** Steve Carver; **M:** William Goldstein. **VHS, Beta** $19.98 SUE, NLC ♂♂

Eye of the Demon A couple moves to a small town in Massachusetts and discovers that the area had once been a haven for witchcraft. To their horror, they soon find that old habits die hard, and the spellcasting continues in a nearby graveyard. Made for cable television.
1987 92m/C Tim Matheson, Pamela Sue Martin, Woody Harrelson, Barbara Billingsley, Susan Ruttan; **D:** Carl Schenkel. **VHS** $89.95 VMK ♂

Eye of the Eagle A special task force is given a dangerous assignment during the Vietnam war.
1987 (R) 84m/C Brett Clark, Ed Crick, Robert Patrick, William Steis, Cec Verrell; **D:** Cirio H. Santiago. **VHS, Beta** $14.95 MGM ♂½

Eye of the Eagle 2 When his platoon is betrayed and killed in Vietnam, a surviving soldier joins with a beautiful girl and seeks revenge.
1989 (R) 79m/C Todd Field, Andy Wood, Ken Jacobson, Ronald Lawrence; **D:** Carl Franklin. **VHS, Beta** $14.95 MGM ♂

Eye of the Eagle 3 Filipino-made Vietnam-War shoot-em-up, rack-em-up, shoot-em-up again, with U.S. forces pinned down against seemingly overwhelming odds. Violent.
1991 (R) 90m/C Steve Kanaly, Ken Wright, Peter Nelson, Carl Franklin; **D:** Cirio H. Santiago; **W:** Carl Franklin. **VHS** $89.98 NHO ♂½

Eye of the Needle Based on Ken Follett's novel about a German spy posing as a shipwrecked sailor on a deserted English island during WWII. Lonely, sad, yet capable of terrible violence, he is stranded on an isolated island while en route to report to his Nazi commander. He becomes involved with an English woman living on the island, and begins to contemplate his role in the war.
1981 (R) 112m/C Donald Sutherland, Kate Nelligan, Ian Bannen, Christopher Cazenove, Philip Brown; **D:** Richard Marquand. **VHS, Beta** $14.95 MGM, FOX ♂♂½

Eye of the Octopus Based on a true story of a boy who traveled to a Pacific Island to learn the ways of the people there.
1982 23m/C **VHS, Beta** JOU ♂

Eye of the Storm At the highway gas station/motel/diner where they live, two young brothers witness their parent's murder. Their younger brother is blinded in the same incident. Ten years later both brothers are still there and the tragedy may have turned one of them psychotic. When the abusive Gladstone and his young and sexy wife are stranded at the gas station it brings out the worst in everyone, with a violent climax during an equally violent thunderstorm.
1991 (R) 98m/C Craig Sheffer, Bradley Gregg, Lara Flynn Boyle, Dennis Hopper, Leon Rippy; **D:** Yuri Zeltser. **VHS** $89.95 NLC ♂♂½

Eye of the Stranger Suspenser about a nameless stranger who sets out to solve the mystery of a small western town and its corrupt mayor.
1993 (R) 96m/C David Heavener, Sally Kirkland, Martin Landau, Don Swayze, Stella Stevens, John Pleshette, Joe Estevez, Thomas F. Duffy; *D:* David Heavener; *W:* David Heavener; *M:* Robert Garrett. VHS **$89.95** *MNC ₰₰½*

Eye of the Tiger A righteous ex-con battles a crazed, crack-dealing motorcycle gang that terrorized and murdered his wife, and is moving on to infest his town.
1986 (R) 90m/C Gary Busey, Yaphet Kotto, Seymour Cassel, Bert Remsen, William Smith; *D:* Richard Sarafian. VHS, Beta **$14.95** *LIV ₰₰*

Eye on the Sparrow A couple (Winningham and Carradine) desperately want to raise a child of their own, but the system classifies them as unfit parents since they are both blind. Together they successfully fight the system in this inspiring made for television movie that was based on a true story.
1991 (PG) 94m/C Mare Winningham, Keith Carradine, Conchata Ferrell, Sandy McPeak, Karen Lee, Bianca Rose; *D:* John Korty. VHS **$89.98** *REP ₰₰½*

Eye Witness An American attorney goes abroad to free a friend from the British legal system. A book of poems becomes the necessary device in deducing the whereabouts of the witness testifying to his friend's alibi. *AKA:* Your Witness.
1949 104m/B *GB* Robert Montgomery, Felix Aylmer, Leslie Banks, Michael Ripper, Patricia Wayne; *D:* Robert Montgomery. VHS **$16.95** *NOS, SNC, RXM ₰₰½*

Eyeball An intrepid policeman is stumped by a madman who is removing eyeballs from his victims. At least they won't have to watch this movie. *AKA:* Gatto Rossi In Un Labirinto Do Vetro.
1978 (R) 87m/C *IT* John Richardson, Martine Brochard; *D:* Umberto Lenzi. VHS, Beta **$59.95** *PSM Woof!*

Eyes Behind the Stars A news photographer accidentally gets a few pictures of invading aliens, but nobody takes him seriously, particularly the government.
1972 95m/C *IT* Martin Balsam, Robert Hoffman, Nathalie Delon, Sherry Buchanan; *D:* Roy Garrett. VHS, Beta **$49.95** *CNG ₰*

Eyes of a Stranger Terrifying maniac stalks his female prey by watching their every move. Tewes is cast as a journalist, the stronger of the two sisters in this exploitative slasher.
1981 85m/C Lauren Tewes, John Disanti, Jennifer Jason Leigh; *D:* Ken Wiederhorn; *M:* Richard Einhorn. VHS, Beta **$14.95** *WAR Woof!*

Eyes of Fire In early rural America, a group of pioneers set up camp in the wilderness and are besieged during the night by Indian witchcraft.
1984 (R) 86m/C Dennis Lipscomb, Rebecca Stanley, Fran Ryan, Rob Paulsen, Guy Boyd, Karlene Crockett; *D:* Avery Crounse; *M:* Brad Fiedel. VHS, Beta **$79.95** *VES ₰*

Eyes of Julia Deep Rare silent film featuring the ill-fated Minter as Julia, a woman who prevents Terry (Forrest) from killing himself. Piano scored.
1918 54m/B Mary Miles Minter, Alan Forrest, Alice Wilson, George Periolat; *D:* Lloyd Ingraham. VHS **$16.95** *GPV ₰₰*

Eyes of Laura Mars A photographer exhibits strange powers—she can foresee a murder before it happens through her snapshots. In time she realizes that the person responsible for a series of killings is tracking

her. Title song performed by Barbra Streisand.
1978 (R) 104m/C Faye Dunaway, Tommy Lee Jones, Brad Dourif, Rene Auberjonois, Raul Julia, Darlanne Fluegel, Michael Tucker; *D:* Irvin Kershner; *W:* John Carpenter, David Zelag Goodman. VHS, Beta **$14.95** *GKK ₰₰½*

Eyes of Texas Bryant, a lawyer who uses a pack of killer dogs to get the land she wants, is pursued by a U.S Marshal played decently by Rogers.
1948 54m/B Roy Rogers, Lynn (Mary Hart) Roberts, Andy Devine, Nana Bryant, Roy Barcroft; *D:* William Witney. VHS, Beta **$9.99** *NOS, VCN, TIM ₰½*

The Eyes of the Amaryllis A young girl becomes involved in a mysterious game when she arrives in Nantucket to care for her insane, invalid grandmother. Based on the story by Natalie Babbitt and filmed on location on Nantucket Island.
1982 (R) 94m/C Martha Byrne, Ruth Ford, Guy Boyd, Jonathan Bolt, Katherine Houghton; *D:* Frederick King Keller. VHS, Beta **$69.98** *LIV, VES ₰½*

Eyes of the Beholder Janice is a psychopathic serial killer who suffered brain damage from a botched surgical attempt to reverse his insanity. Now he's escaped from the state mental institution, heading straight for the secluded home of the doctor who made him crazier than ever. During a raging storm, Janice stalks the doctor, his wife, and their two hapless dinner guests in a sadistic game of cat-and-mouse.
1992 (R) 89m/C Lenny Von Dohlen, Joanna Pacula, Matt McCoy, George Lazenby, Kylie Travis, Charles Napier; *D:* Lawrence L. Simeone; *W:* Lawrence L. Simeone; *M:* Greg Turner. VHS **$92.87** *COL ₰₰*

Eyes of the Panther One of Shelley Duvall's "Nightmare Classics" series, this adaptation of an Ambrose Bierce story concerns a pioneer girl haunted for years by the animal urges of a wild cat.
1990 60m/C Daphne Zuniga, C. Thomas Howell, John Stockwell; *D:* Noel Black. VHS, Beta **$59.95** *NO ₰*

Eyes of Turpin Are Upon You! Two early Turpin silent comedies: "Idle Eyes" and "A Small Town Idol."
1921 56m/B Ben Turpin, Ramon Novarro, Marie Prevost, James Finlayson. VHS, Beta **$19.95** *VYY ₰₰*

The Eyes of Youth A young woman searches her soul for answers: to marry or not to marry is the question. A little foresight, in the form of a glimpse into the hypothetical future, helps her make the right choice. Very early Valentino fare in which the sheik plays a cad.
1919 78m/B Clara Kimball Young, Edmund Lowe, Rudolph Valentino. VHS, Beta **$24.95** *VYY, FCT, VYY ₰₰*

Eyes Right! Based on a story by Ernest Grayman, this portrayal of life in a military prep school has its main character experience struggle, recognition, love, jealousy, and triumph. Silent.
1926 46m/B Francis X. Bushman. VHS, Beta **$24.95** *VYY, GPV ₰₰*

The Eyes, the Mouth A young man has an affair with his dead twin brother's fiancee. Happiness eludes them as they are haunted by the deceased's memory and the family's grief. Available with English subtitles.
1983 (R) 100m/C *FR IT* Lou Castel, Angela Molina; *D:* Marco Bellochio; *W:* Marco Bellochio. VHS, Beta **$59.95** *COL, ING ₰₰*

Eyewitness When a murder occurs in the office building of a star-struck janitor, he fabricates a tale in order to initiate a relationship with the television reporter covering the story. Unfortunately the killers think he's telling the truth, which plunges the janitor and reporter into a dangerous and complicated position, pursued by both police and foreign agents. Somewhat contrived, but Hurt and Weaver are always interesting. Woods turns in a wonderful performance as Hurt's somewhat-psychotic best friend. *AKA:* The Janitor.
1981 (R) 102m/C William Hurt, Sigourney Weaver, Christopher Plummer, James Woods, Kenneth McMillan, Pamela Reed, Irene Worth, Steven Hill, Morgan Freeman; *D:* Peter Yates; *W:* Steve Tesich. VHS, Beta **$14.98** *FXV, FOX ₰₰½*

Eyewitness to Murder Stevens plays a cop who is assigned to protect beautiful artist Wolter. They both have their tragic flaws: he is a grieving widower, she has been blinded by an unknown attacker. Their flaws may draw them together. Somewhat more engaging than a television police action drama.
1993 75m/C Andrew Stevens, Adrian Zmed, Sherilyn Wolter, Carl Strano, Robie Drue; *D:* Jag Mundhra. VHS *NHO ₰½*

F. Scott Fitzgerald in Hollywood Dramatization begins in the late 1930s when Fitzgerald was lured to Hollywood to work in the burgeoning film industry. It covers the period when, with his wife in a mental institution, he lived with Sheila Graham and struggled against alcoholism. Interesting story made dull and depressing by Miller's uninspired performance, but it's almost saved by Weld's portrayal of Zelda. Made for television.
1976 98m/C Jason Miller, Tuesday Weld, Julia Foster, Dolores Sutton, Michael Lerner, James Woods; *D:* Anthony Page. VHS, Beta *NO ₰₰*

F/X A Hollywood special effects expert is contracted by the government to fake an assassination to protect a mob informer. After completing the assignment, he learns that he's become involved in a real crime and is forced to reach into his bag of F/X tricks to survive. Twists and turns abound in this fast-paced story that was the sleeper hit of the year. Followed by a sequel.
1986 (R) 109m/C Bryan Brown, Cliff DeYoung, Diane Venora, Brian Dennehy, Jerry Orbach, Mason Adams, Joe Grifasi, Martha Gehman; *D:* Robert Mandel; *W:* Robert T. Megginson, Gregory Fleeman; *M:* Bill Conti. VHS, Beta **$14.98** *HBO, FCT ₰₰₰*

F/X 2: The Deadly Art of Illusion Weak follow-up finds the special-effects specialist set to pull off just one more illusion for the police. Once again, corrupt cops use him as a chump for their scheme, an over-complicated business involving a stolen Vatican treasure.
1991 (PG-13) 107m/C Bryan Brown, Brian Dennehy, Rachel Ticotin, Philip Bosco, Joanna Gleason; *D:* Richard Franklin. VHS **$14.98** *ORI, IME ₰₰*

Fabiola The first of the big Italian spectacle movies, this one opened the door for a flood of low-budget imitators. Fabiola, the daughter of a Roman senator, becomes a Christian when her father's Christian servants are accused of murdering him. In the meantime, the Emperor Constantine speeds toward Rome to convert it to Christian status. You can bet plenty of Christians will lose their heads, be thrown to the lions and generally burn at the stake before he does.

1948 96m/C *IT* Michel Simon, Henri Vidal, Gino Cervi; *D:* Alexandro Blasetti. VHS $16.95 SNC, FCT ♂♂♂

The Fable of the Beautiful Pigeon Fancier
A powerful man who has always gotten what he wanted spies a beautiful young married woman and sets out to make her his own. Based on the Gabriel Gracia Marquez novel "Love in the Time of Cholera." In Spanish with English subtitles. *AKA:* Fabula de la Bella Palomera.
1988 73m/C *SP* Ney Latorraca, Claudia Ohana, Tonia Carrero, Dina Stat, Chico Diaz; *D:* Ruy Guerra. VHS $79.95 FXL, FCT, ING ♂♂½

Fabulous Adventures of Baron Munchausen
The legendary Baron Munchausen, known for his tall tales, relates the story of his trek to the strange and beautiful land of Trukesban in a mixture of live action and animation. Wonderful special effects but a boring storyline. In German with English subtitles.
1961 84m/C *GE* Milos Kopecky, Jana Brejchova, Rudolph Jelinek, Jan Werich; *D:* Karel Zeman. VHS, Beta $19.98 LIV, VES, TPV ♂♂

The Fabulous Baker Boys
Two brothers have been performing a tired act as nightclub pianists for fifteen years. When they hire a sultry vocalist to revitalize the routine, she inadvertently triggers long-suppressed hostility between the "boys." The story may be a bit uneven, but fine performances by the three leading actors, the steamy 1940s atmosphere, and Pfeiffer's classic rendition of "Makin' Whoopee," are worth the price of the rental.
1989 (R) 116m/C Michelle Pfeiffer, Jeff Bridges, Beau Bridges, Elie Raab, Jennifer Tilly; *D:* Steven Kloves; *W:* Steven Kloves; *M:* Dave Grusin. Academy Awards '89 Nominations: Best Actress (Pfeiffer), Best Cinematography, Best Film Editing, Best Original Score; Golden Globe Awards '90: Best Actress—Drama (Pfeiffer); Los Angeles Film Critics Association Awards '89: Best Actress (Pfeiffer); National Board of Review Awards '89: Best Actress (Pfeiffer); New York Film Critics Awards '89: Best Actress (Pfeiffer). VHS, Beta, 8mm $19.95 LIV, FCT ♂♂♂

The Fabulous Dorseys
The musical lives of big band leaders Tommy and Jimmy Dorsey are portrayed in this less than fabulous biography that's strong on song but weak on plot. Guest stars include Art Tatum, Charlie Barnet, Ziggy Elman, Bob Eberly and Helen O'Connell. Highlights are the tunes. ♫At Sundown; I'll Never Say Never Again; To Me; Green Eyes; Dorsey Concerto; Art's Blues; Everybody's Doin' It; The Object of My Affection; Runnin' Wild; When You and I Were Young, Maggie; Waitin' at the Gate for Katy; Marie.
1947 91m/B Tommy Dorsey, Jimmy Dorsey, Janet Blair, Paul Whiteman, Sara Allgood, Arthur Shields; *D:* Alfred E. Green. VHS $19.95 NOS, MRV, HHT ♂♂

Fabulous Joe
A talking dog named Joe gets involved in the life of a hen-pecked husband.
1947 54m/C Walter Abel, Donald Meek, Margot Grahame, Marie Wilson; *D:* Bernard Carr. VHS, Beta $19.95 NOS ♂♂

The Face at the Window
Melodramatic crime story of a pair of ne'er-do-well brothers who terrorize Paris to conceal their bank robberies.
1939 65m/B Tod Slaughter, Marjorie Taylor, John Warwick, Robert Adair, Harry Terry; *D:* George King. VHS $14.99 NOS, MRV, HEG ♂♂

A Face in the Crowd
Journalist (Neal) discovers a down-home philosopher (Griffith) and puts him on her television show. His aw-shucks personality soon wins him a

---

large following and increasing influence—even political clout. Off the air he reveals his true nature to be insulting, vengeful, and power-hungry—all of which Neal decides to expose. Marks Griffith's spectacular film debut as a thoroughly despicable character and debut of Remick as the pretty cheerleader in whom he takes an interest. Schulburg wrote the screenplay from his short story "The Arkansas Traveler." He and director Kazan collaborated equally well in "On the Waterfront."
1957 126m/B Andy Griffith, Patricia Neal, Lee Remick, Walter Matthau, Anthony (Tony) Franciosa; *D:* Elia Kazan; *W:* Budd Schulberg. VHS, Beta $19.98 WAR, FCT ♂♂♂½

A Face in the Fog
Two newspaper reporters set out to solve a number of murders that have plagued the cast of a play. Also interested is the playwright. Good low-budget thriller.
1936 66m/B June Collyer, Lloyd Hughes, Lawrence Gray, Al "Fuzzy" St. John, Jack Mulhall, Jack Cowell, John Elliott, Sam Flint, Forrest Taylor, Edward Cassidy; *D:* Bob Hill. VHS, Beta $16.95 NOS, SNC ♂♂

Face of Another
A severely burned man gets a second chance when a plastic surgeon makes a mask to hide the disfigurement. Unfortunately this face leads him to alienation, rape, infidelity, and murder. In Japanese with English subtitles.
1966 124m/B *JP* Tatsuya Nakadai, Machiko Kyo; *D:* Hiroshi Teshigahara. VHS, Beta $59.95 ING ♂♂

Face of the Screaming Werewolf
Originally a Mexican horror/comedy that was bought for U.S. distribution by Jerry Warren, who earned his spot in the horror hall of fame with "The Incredible Petrified World" and "Teenage Zombies." A scientist brings a mummy back to life, but when he removes the bandages (gasp), the subject turns out to be of the canine persuasion. Suffers from comic evisceration; not much to scream about. *AKA:* La Casa Del Terror; House of Terror.
1959 60m/B *MX* Lon Chaney Jr., Landa Varle, Raymond Gaylord; *D:* Gilberto Martinez Solares, Jerry Warren. VHS $16.95 SNC, MRV ♂½

Face the Music
Ringwald and Dempsey were once stormily married and pursuing successful, collaborative careers as singer/songwriters for the movies. But they've abandoned the work, along with the marriage, until a movie producer makes them a very lucrative offer for a new song. Only Dempsey's new girlfriend has some voracious objections.
1992 (PG-13) 93m/C Patrick Dempsey, Molly Ringwald, Lysette Anthony. VHS $89.98 LIV ♂½

Face to Face
Dramatic adaptation of two short stories, "The Secret Sharer," by Joseph Conrad, and Stephen Crane's "The Bride Comes to Yellow Sky." The Conrad story features Mason as a sea captain who discovers a fugitive stowaway aboard his ships. The Crane story features Preston as a sheriff threatened by an old-time gunfighter.
1952 92m/B Bretaigne Windust, James Mason, Michael Pate, Robert Preston, Marjorie Steele, Gene Lockhart, Minor Watson; *D:* John Brahm. VHS RKO ♂♂½

Face to Face
Bergman's harrowing tale of a mental breakdown. Ullmann has a bravura role as a psychiatrist deciding to vacation at her grandparent's house in the country. Once there she begins to experience depression and hallucinations tied to her past with both her mother and grandmother. Her deeply repressed feelings eventually lead to a suicide attempt, which brings

---

some much needed help. Originally a four-hour series made for Swedish television. In Swedish with English subtitles.
1976 136m/C *SW* Liv Ullmann, Erland Josephson, Gunnar Bjornstrand, Aino Taube-Henrikson, Sven Lindberg; *D:* Ingmar Bergman; *W:* Ingmar Bergman. Academy Awards '76 Nominations: Best Actress (Ullmann), Best Director (Bergman); Golden Globe Awards '77: Best Foreign Film. VHS PAR ♂♂♂

Faces of Death, Part 1
Morbid, gruesome, "shockumentary" looks at death experiences around the world; uncensored film footage offers graphic coverage of autopsies, suicides, executions, and animal slaughter.
1974 88m/C VHS, Beta $19.98 MPI ♂♂♂

Faces of Death, Part 2
Mindless sequel to "Faces of Death" further explores violent termination of man by man and by nature in a graphic and grisly gala. Not for the squeamish.
1985 84m/C VHS, Beta $79.95 MPI Woof!

Fade to Black
Young man obsessed with movies loses his grip on reality and adopts the personalities of cinematic characters (Hopalong Cassidy and Dracula among them) to seek revenge on people who have wronged him. Thoroughly unpleasant, highlighted by clips from old flicks.
1980 (R) 100m/C Dennis Christopher, Tim Thomerson, Linda Kerridge, Mickey Rourke, Melinda Fee; *D:* Vernon Zimmerman. VHS, Beta $9.95 MED, MLB Woof!

Fade to Black
Busfield stars as a college professor with voyeuristic tendencies and a handy camcorder. After viewing his latest tape, he realizes he's filmed his neighbor's murder and that he can recognize the killer. Before he can warn the killer's girlfriend, she disappears and our nosy prof is framed for the death.
1993 (R) 84m/C Timothy Busfield, Heather Locklear, Michael Beck, Louis Giambalvo, Cloris Leachman, David Byron; *D:* John McPherson; *W:* Douglas Barr. VHS, Beta PAR ♂♂

Fahrenheit 451
Chilling adaptation of the Ray Bradbury novel about a futuristic society that has banned all reading material and the firemen whose job it is to keep the fires at 451 degrees: the temperature at which paper burns. Werner is a fireman who begins to question the rightness of his actions when he meets the book-loving Christie—who also plays the dual role of Werner's TV-absorbed wife. Truffaut's first color and English-language film.
1966 112m/C *FR* Oskar Werner, Julie Christie, Cyril Cusack, Anton Diffring; *D:* Francois Truffaut. VHS, Beta $19.98 MCA, MLB, ING ♂♂♂

Fail-Safe
A nail-biting nuclear age nightmare, in which American planes have been erroneously sent to bomb the USSR, with no way to recall them. An all-star cast impels this bitterly serious thriller, the straight-faced flipside of "Dr. Strangelove."
1964 111m/B Henry Fonda, Dan O'Herlihy, Walter Matthau, Larry Hagman, Fritz Weaver, Dom DeLuise; *D:* Sidney Lumet. VHS, Beta $14.95 COL ♂♂♂½

Fair Game
Hedonistic maniacs roam rural areas killing, looting and raping, until a beautiful woman they capture fights back.
1985 (R) 90m/C Kim Trengove, Kerry Mack, Marie O'Loughlina, Karen West; *D:* Christopher Fitchett. VHS, Beta $79.95 IMP Woof!

Fair Game
A psychotic but imaginative ex-boyfriend locks his former girlfriend in her apartment with a lethal giant Mamba snake. Understandably uninterested in its serpentine attention, the young woman must trespass

against the Hollywood code and keep her wits in the face of danger. Guaranteed not to charm you.
1989 (R) 81m/C Greg Henry, Trudie Styler, Bill Moseley; **D:** Mario Orfini. **VHS $89.95** *VMK Woof!*

Fairytales A ribald musical fantasy for adults. In order to save the kingdom, the prince must produce an heir. The problem is that only the girl in the painting of "Princess Beauty" can "interest" the prince and she must be found. Good-natured smut.
1979 (R) 83m/C Don Sparks, Prof. Irwin Corey, Brenda Fogarty, Sy Richardson, Nai Bonet, Martha Reeves; **D:** Harry Tampa. **VHS, Beta $39.95** *MED ⅓⅓*

Faith When young dancer Faith's parents are killed in an accident she winds up in a frightening foster home. Running away, she meets a gentlemanly mobster who helps her attain her dance dreams. Laughably implausible.
1992 (R) 104m/C Sylvia Seidel, Ami Dolenz, Richard Maldone. **VHS $92.95** *VMK ⅓*

Fake Out Nightclub singer is caught between the mob and the police who want her to testify against her gangland lover. Typical vanity outing for Zadora. *AKA:* Nevada Heat.
1982 89m/C Pia Zadora, Telly Savalas, Desi Arnaz Jr.; **D:** Matt Cimber. **VHS, Beta $14.95** *CNG, VTR ⅓*

Falcon Brave knight battles for the honor of a beautiful maiden; with or without the Falcon's help.
1974 105m/C Franco Nero. **VHS, Beta $59.95** *TWE ⅓*

The Falcon and the Snowman True story of Daulton Lee and Christopher Boyce, two childhood friends who, almost accidentally, sell American intelligence secrets to the KGB in 1977. Hutton and Penn are excellent, creating a relationship we care about and strong characterizations.
1985 (R) 110m/C Sean Penn, Timothy Hutton, Lori Singer, Pat Hingle, Dorian Harewood, Richard Dysart, David Suchet, Jennifer Runyon, Priscilla Pointer, Nicholas Pryor, Joyce Van Patten, Mady Kaplan, Michael Ironside; **D:** John Schlesinger; **W:** Steven Zaillian; **M:** Lyle Mays, Pat Metheny. **VHS, Beta $29.98** *LIV, VES ⅓⅓⅓*

The Falcon in Hollywood The falcon gets caught up with the murder of an actor who was part of a Tinseltown love triangle. The film takes place on RKO's back lot for a behind-the-scenes view of Hollywood. Part of the popular "Falcon" series from the 1940s.
1944 67m/B Tom Conway, Barbara Hale, Veda Ann Borg, Sheldon Leonard, Frank Jenks, Rita Corday, John Abbott; **D:** Gordon Douglas. **VHS $59.98** *MED ⅓⅓½*

The Falcon in Mexico When paintings from a supposedly dead artist turn up for sale in New York City, the Falcon and the artist's daughter wind up journeying to Mexico to solve the mystery. Part of "The Falcon" series.
1944 70m/B Tom Conway, Mona Maris, Nestor Paiva; **D:** William Berke. **VHS, Beta** *MED ⅓½*

Falcon Takes Over/Strange Bargain A mystery double feature. In "The Falcon Takes Over," The Falcon becomes involved in a series of murder and an ex-con's last love, and in "Strange Bargain," an underpaid bookkeeper gets in on an insurance swindle.
1949 131m/B George Sanders, Ward Bond, Allen Jenkins, Martha Scott, Harry Morgan, James Gleason, Anne Revere, Hans Conried, Turhan Bey; **D:** Irving Reis. **VHS, Beta $34.95** *TTC, RKO ⅓⅓*

Falcon's Adventure/Armored Car Robbery A mystery double feature: The Falcon uncovers a vicious plot to steal a formula for synthetic diamonds in "The Falcon's Adventure," and four participants in an armored car robbery flee after slaying a policeman in "Armored Car Robbery."
1950 122m/B Tom Conway, Madge Meredith, William Talman, Charles McGraw, Adele Jergens; **D:** William Berke. **VHS, Beta $34.95** *TTC, RKO ⅓½*

The Falcon's Brother Enemy agents intent on killing a South American diplomat are foiled by the Falcon's brothers at a steep personal cost. The plot enabled Sanders' real-life brother Conway to take over the title role in "The Falcon" mystery series, a role which he played nine more times.
1942 64m/B Tom Conway, George Sanders, Keye Luke, Jane Randolph; **D:** Stanley Logan. **VHS, Beta** *MED ⅓⅓*

Fall and Rise of Reginald Perrin 1 Starring Leonard Rossiter, this BBC show has Reginald getting out of the rat race.
1978 107m/C *GB* Leonard Rossiter. **VHS $29.95** *BFS, HMV, FUS ⅓⅓⅓*

Fall and Rise of Reginald Perrin 2 After part one's escape from the rat race, this time Reginald is back in suburbia.
1978 120m/C *GB* Leonard Rossiter. **VHS $29.95** *BFS, HMV, FUS ⅓⅓⅓*

Fall from Innocence A girl is driven to a life of prostitution and drugs by the sexual abuse inflicted upon her by her father.
1988 81m/C Isabelle Mejias, Thom Haverstock, Amanda Smith, Rob McEwan; **D:** Carey Connor. **VHS $79.95** *MNC ⅓½*

The Fall of the House of Usher Lord Roderick Usher is haunted by his sister's ghost in this poor adaptation of the Poe classic.
1952 70m/B *GB* Kay Tendeter, Gwen Watford, Irving Steen, Lucy Pavey; **D:** Ivan Barnett. **VHS $16.95** *SNC, FCT ⅓*

The Fall of the House of Usher The moody Roger Corman/Vincent Price interpretation, the first of their eight Poe adaptations, depicting the collapse of the famous estate due to madness and revenge. Terrific sets and solid direction as well as Price's inimitable presence. *AKA:* House of Usher.
1960 85m/C Vincent Price, Myrna Fahey, Mark Damon; **D:** Roger Corman; **W:** Richard Matheson; **M:** Les Baxter. **VHS, Beta** *NO ⅓⅓⅓*

The Fall of the House of Usher Another version of Edgar Allan Poe's classic tale of a family doomed to destruction. Stray to the Roger Corman/Vincent Price version to see how it should have been done.
1980 (PG) 101m/C Martin Landau, Robert Hays, Charlene Tilton, Ray Walston; **D:** James L. Conway. **VHS, Beta $19.98** *VCI ⅓½*

The Fall of the Roman Empire An all-star, big budget extravaganza set in ancient Rome praised for its action sequences. The licentious son of Marcus Aurelius arranges for his father's murder and takes over as emperor while Barbarians gather at the gate. Great sets, fine acting, and thundering battle scenes.
1964 187m/C Sophia Loren, Alec Guinness, James Mason, Stephen Boyd, Christopher Plummer, John Ireland, Anthony Quayle, Eric Porter, Mel Ferrer, Omar Sharif; **D:** Anthony Mann; **W:** Philip Yordan. Academy Awards '64 Nominations: Best Original Score; Golden Globe Awards '65: Best Score. **VHS, Beta $29.95** *BFV, VCI, KAR ⅓⅓*

Fallen Angel Television movie about a child pornographer and a particular young girl he finds easily exploitable because of her unbalanced home situation. Fine cast, solid direction.
1981 100m/C Dana Hill, Richard Masur, Melinda Dillon, Ronny Cox; **D:** Robert Lewis. **Beta $59.95** *COL ⅓⅓½*

Fallen Angels 1 Trilogy of hard-boiled, film noirish tales set in Los Angeles. "The Frightening Frammis" concerns a grifter (Gallagher) who meets his match in a mystery woman (Rossellini) in this adaptation of a Jim Thompson story. Cruise's directorial debut. "Murder, Obliquely" finds a plain Jane (Dern) falling for a heel (Rickman) who may have murdered his previous girl in a Cornell Woolrich tale. "Since I Don't Have You" has Buzz Meeks (Busey) hired to find a dame sought by both Howard Hughes (Matheson) and gangster Mickey Cohen (Woods). From a story by James Elroy. Made for cable television.
1993 90m/C Peter Gallagher, Isabella Rossellini, Nancy Travis, John Reilly, Bill Erwin, Laura Dern, Alan Rickman, Diane Lane, Robin Bartlett, Gary Busey, Tim Matheson, James Woods, Aimee Graham, Dick Miller, Ken Lerner; **D:** Tom Cruise, Alfonso Cuaron, Jonathan Kaplan; **W:** Jon Robin Baitz, Howard A. Rodman, Amanda Silver, Steven Katz; **M:** Elmer Bernstein. **VHS $89.99** *PGV ⅓⅓⅓*

Fallen Angels 2 Three more film noir stories set in L.A. "Dead End for Delia" finds a police detective (Oldman) arriving at a murder scene to find his estranged wife (Anwar) the victim. Based on a short story by William Campbell Gault. "I'll Be Waiting" has Kirby as a hapless hotel detective who falls for a beautiful guest (Helgenberger) and winds up a mob pawn. Adaptation of a Raymond Chandler tale. "The Quiet Room" has Bedelia and Mantegna as a pair of corrupt cops who find their shakedown schemes going very wrong. From a story by Jonathan Craig. Made for cable television.
1993 90m/C Gary Oldman, Gabrielle Anwar, Meg Tilly, Patrick Masset, Vondie Curtis-Hall, Paul Guilfoyle, Dan Hedaya, John Putch, Wayne Knight, Bruno Kirby, Marg Helgenberger, Jon Polito, Peter Scolari, Dick Miller, Joe Mantegna, Bonnie Bedelia, Vinessa Shaw, J.E. Freeman, Peter Gallagher, Patrick Breen, Genia Michaela, Wayne Grace; *Cameos:* Tom Hanks; **D:** Phil Joanou, Tom Hanks, Steven Soderberg; **W:** Scott Frank, C. Gaby Mitchell, Howard A. Rodman. **VHS $89.99** *PGV ⅓⅓⅓*

Fallen Champ: The Untold Story of Mike Tyson Director Kopple's provocative documentary on the boxing champ, from his roots in a Brooklyn ghetto to his conviction for rape in 1991. Tyson is shown as pathetic, vulnerable, and violent—psychologically unprepared for both acclaim and responsibility, as well as easily manipulated by promoters and opportunists. A mixture of ring footage and interviews with sportswriters, promoters, trainers, and others as well as media coverage of Tyson. Made for television.
1993 93m/C D: Barbara Kopple. **VHS $59.95** *COL, BTV ⅓⅓⅓*

The Fallen Idol A young boy wrongly believes that a servant he admires is guilty of murdering his wife. Unwittingly, the child influences the police investigation of the crime so that the servant becomes the prime suspect. Richardson as the accused and Henrey as the boy are notable. Screenplay adapted by Greene from his short story, "The Basement Room." *AKA:* The Lost Illusion.

1949 92m/B *GB* Ralph Richardson, Bobby Henrey, Michele Morgan, Sonia Dresdel, Jack Hawkins, Bernard Lee; *D:* Carol Reed; *W:* Graham Greene. Academy Awards '49 Nominations: Best Director (Reed), Best Screenplay; British Academy Awards '48: Best Film; National Board of Review Awards '49: 10 Best Films of the Year, Best Actor (Richardson). **VHS, Beta** $19.95 *NOS, MRV, PSM* 𝆑𝆑𝆑

The Fallen Sparrow Garfield is superb as a half-mad veteran of the Spanish Civil War. Captured and brutalized, he never revealed the whereabouts of a valuable possession. His return to the U.S. continues his torture as Nazi agent Slezak uses the woman Garfield loves to set a trap and finish the job. Solid performances and good plot are highlights.
1943 94m/B John Garfield, Maureen O'Hara, Walter Slezak, Patricia Morison, Martha O'Driscoll, Bruce Edwards, John Miljan, John Banner, Hugh Beaumont; *D:* Richard Wallace. **VHS, Beta** $29.95 *MED, IME* 𝆑𝆑𝆑

Falling Down Douglas is "D-FENS" (taken from his license plate), a normally law-abiding white-collar geek who snaps while stuck in a traffic jam on a hot day in LA. Like Charles Bronson in "Death Wish," he decides to take matters into his own hands. Unlike Bronson, he is not avenging an attack by a specific criminal, but raging against whomever gets in his way. Duvall is a detective on his last day before retirement, Hershey has the thankless role of Douglas' ex. Essentially a revenge fantasy that was vilified by some for catering to the baser emotions.
1993 (R) 112m/C Michael Douglas, Robert Duvall, Barbara Hershey, Rachel Ticotin, Tuesday Weld, Frederic Forrest, Lois Smith, D.W. Moffett, Dedee Pfeiffer, Vondie Curtis-Hall, Michael Paul Chan, Raymond J. Barry, Jack Kehoe, John Diehl; *D:* Joel Schumacher; *W:* Ebbe Roe Smith; *M:* James Newton Howard. **VHS** $19.98 *WAR, FCT* 𝆑𝆑

Falling from Grace Bud Parks (Mellencamp) is a successful country singer who, accompanied by his wife and daughter, returns to his small Indiana hometown to celebrate his grandfather's 80th birthday. He's tired of both his career and his marriage and finds himself taking up once again with an old girlfriend (Lenz), who is not only married to Bud's brother but is also having an affair with his father. Bud believes he's better off staying in his old hometown but the problems caused by his return may change his mind. Surprisingly sedate, although literate, family drama with good ensemble performances. Actor-director debut for Mellencamp.
1992 (PG-13) 100m/C John Cougar Mellencamp, Mariel Hemingway, Kay Lenz, Claude Akins, Dub Taylor, Brent Huff, Deidre O'Connell, Larry Crane; *D:* John Cougar Mellencamp; *W:* Larry McMurtry. **VHS** $19.95 *COL, FCT* 𝆑𝆑½

Falling in Love Two married New Yorkers unexpectedly fall in love after a coincidental meeting at the Rizzoli Book Store. Weak but gracefully performed reworking of "Brief Encounter," where no one seems to ever complete a sentence. An unfortunate reteaming for Streep and De Niro after their wonderful work in "The Deer Hunter."
1984 (PG-13) 106m/C Robert De Niro, Meryl Streep, Harvey Keitel, Dianne Wiest, George Martin, Jane Kaczmarek, David Clennon; *D:* Ulu Grosbard; *W:* Michael Cristofer; *M:* Dave Grusin. **VHS, Beta** $19.95 *PAR* 𝆑𝆑½

Falling in Love Again Romantic comedy about middle-aged dreamer Gould and realistic wife York. They travel from Los Angeles to their hometown of New York for

his high school reunion, where Gould is suddenly attacked by nostalgia vibes for his youth, seen in countless flashbacks, and prominently featuring Pfeiffer, notable in her film debut. Like watching a home movie about people you don't care about. *AKA:* In Love.
1980 (PG) 103m/C Elliott Gould, Susannah York, Michelle Pfeiffer; *D:* Steven Paul; *W:* Ted Allan. **VHS, Beta** $24.98 *SUE* 𝆑½

False Arrest A woman is falsely accused of killing her husband's business partner and winds up in prison where she continues to fight to prove her innocence. Mills does well in this less-than-glamorous role. Based on a true story. Made for television.
1992 102m/C Donna Mills, Steven Bauer, James Handy, Lane Smith, Lewis Van Bergen, Dennis Christopher, Robert Wagner; *D:* Bill L. Norton. **VHS, Beta** $89.98 *TTC, PMS* 𝆑𝆑½

False Colors Hopalong Cassidy unmasks a crook posing as a ranch heir. This was the 49th Hopalong Cassidy feature.
1943 54m/B William Boyd, Robert Mitchum, Andy Clyde, Jimmy Rogers; *D:* George Archainbaud. **VHS, Beta** $9.99 *NOS, MRV, VYY* 𝆑

False Faces A ruthless, money-hungry quack is hounded by the law and the victims of his unscrupulous plastic surgery.
1932 80m/B Lowell Sherman, Peggy Shannon, Lila Lee, Joyce Compton, Berton Churchill, David Landau, Eddie Anderson, Ken Maynard, Veda Ann Borg; *D:* Lowell Sherman. **VHS, Beta** $24.95 *VYY* 𝆑½

False Identity A radio psychologist buys a Purple Heart medal at a garage sale and then tries to find out about the original recipient. But her questions are making a number of folks uneasy, including a potentially dangerous stranger.
1990 (PG-13) 97m/C Genevieve Bujold, Stacy Keach, Veronica Cartwright, Tobin Bell, Mimi Maynard; *D:* James Keach. **VHS, Beta** $89.99 *PAR* 𝆑½

False Note Against a background of vibrant colors and collages, a little, crippled beggar-musician roams through a modern city, playing his small barrel organ which inevitably emits a sour note. He discovers a kindred spirit in an abandoned carousel horse.
1972 10m/C **VHS, Beta** *IFB* 𝆑½

False Witness A New Orleans district attorney and her lover, a private investigator, find themselves working the same rape-murder case. When their methods disagree both find themselves in danger. Adapted from a novel by Dorothy Uhnak. Made for television.
1989 96m/C Phylicia Rashad, Philip Michael Thomas, Terri Austin, George Grizzard; *D:* Arthur Seidelman; *M:* Charles Fox. **VHS** *STE* 𝆑𝆑½

Fame Follows eight talented teenagers from their freshmen year through graduation from New York's High School of Performing Arts. Insightful and absorbing, director Parker allows the kids to mature on screen, revealing the pressures of constantly trying to prove themselves. A faultless parallel is drawn between these "special" kids and the pressures felt by high schoolers everywhere. Great dance and music sequences. The basis for the television series. ♫Fame; Red Light; I Sing the Body Electric; Dogs in the Yard; Hot Lunch Jam; Out Here On My Own; Is It OK If I Call You Mine?.
1980 (R) 133m/C Irene Cara, Barry Miller, Paul McCrane, Anne Meara, Joanna Merlin, Richard Belzer, Maureen Teefy; *D:* Alan Parker; *M:* Michael Gore. Academy Awards '80: Best Song ("Fame"), Best Original Score; Nominations: Best Film Editing, Best Film Editing, Best Original

Screenplay, Best Song ("Out Here on My Own"), Best Sound; Golden Globe Awards '81: Best Song ("Fame"). **VHS, Beta** $19.99 *MGM, FCT* 𝆑𝆑𝆑

Fame is the Spur A lengthy but interesting look at the way power corrupts, plus an insight into the Conservative versus Labor dynamics of British government. Redgrave is a poor, idealistic worker who decides to help his fellow workers by running for Parliament. There, he falls prey to the trappings of office with surprising consequences. Look hard for Tomlinson, who went on to star in "Mary Poppins" and "Bedknobs and Broomsticks" for Disney.
1947 116m/B *GB* Michael Redgrave, Rosamund John, Bernard Miles, Hugh Burden, Guy Verney, Carla Lehmann, Seymour Hicks, David Tomlinson; *D:* Roy Boulting. **VHS** $19.95 *NOS, VEC* 𝆑𝆑½

The Family As a New Orleans hit-man who resists joining the mob, Bronson initiates an all-out war on the syndicate and its boss, played by Savalas. A poorly dubbed Italian action film.
1973 94m/C *IT* Charles Bronson, Jill Ireland, Telly Savalas; *D:* Sergio Sollima. **VHS, Beta** $59.95 *MPI* 𝆑½

The Family An 80-year-old patriarch prepares for his birthday celebration reminiscing about his family's past triumphs, tragedies and enduring love. The charming flashbacks, convincingly played, all take place in the family's grand old Roman apartment. In Italian with English subtitles or dubbed. *AKA:* La Famiglia.
1987 128m/C *IT* Vittorio Gassman, Fanny Ardant, Philippe Noiret, Stefania Sandrelli, Andrea Occhipinti, Jo Ciampa; *D:* Ettore Scola; *W:* Ettore Scola, Ruggero Maccari, Furio Scarpelli; *M:* Armando Trovajoli. **VHS, Beta** $19.98 *LIV, VES, ING* 𝆑𝆑𝆑

Family Business A bright Ivy Leaguer, impressed by the exploits and vitality of his criminal grandfather, recruits him and his ex-con dad to pull off a high-tech robbery, which goes awry. Caper film, with its interest in family relationships and being true to one's nature. Casting Connery, Hoffman, and Broderick as the three leaves a big believability problem in the family department.
1989 (R) 114m/C Sean Connery, Dustin Hoffman, Matthew Broderick, Rosana De Soto, Janet Carroll, Victoria Jackson, Bill McCutcheon, Deborah Rush, Marilyn Cooper, Salem Ludwig, Rex Everhart, James Tolkan; *D:* Sidney Lumet; *W:* Vincent Patrick; *M:* Cy Coleman. **VHS, Beta, 8mm** $19.95 *COL, FCT* 𝆑𝆑½

Family Dog: Complete Series Ten episodes from the animated television series executive produced by Tim Burton and Steven Spielberg. This put-upon pup is property of the Binfords family and succeeds in getting himself involved in all sorts of unhappy situations.
1992 235m/C *D:* Chris Buck; *W:* Dennis Klein; *V:* Daniel Mann, Martin Mull, Molly Cheek, Zak Huxtable Epstein, Cassie Cole. **VHS** *MCA* 𝆑𝆑½

Family Enforcer A small-time hoodlum is bent on becoming the best enforcer in an underworld society. *AKA:* Death Collector.
1976 (R) 82m/C Joe Cortese, Lou Criscuola, Joe Pesci, Anne Johns, Keith Davis; *D:* Ralph De Vito. **VHS, Beta** $19.95 *VCI, VTR* 𝆑

The Family Game An obsessive satire about a poor, belligerent college student hired by a wealthy contemporary Japanese family to tutor their spoiled teenage son. Provides an all-out cultural assault on the Japanese bourgeoisie. From an original story by Yohei Honma. In Japanese with English subtitles.

1983 107m/C JP Junichi Tsujita, Yusaku Matsuda, Juzo Itami, Saori Yuki, Ichirota Miyagawa; **D:** Yoshimitsu Morita; **W:** Yoshimitsu Morita. **VHS, Beta** $59.95 FCT, ING ✂✂✂

Family Jewels A spoiled child-heiress has to choose among her six uncles to decide which should be her new father. If you like Jerry Lewis, you can't miss this! In addition to playing all six uncles, Lewis plays the chauffeur, as well as serving as producer, director, and coauthor of the script. **1965 100m/C** Jerry Lewis, Donna Butterworth, Sebastian Cabot, Robert Strauss; **D:** Jerry Lewis; **W:** Jerry Lewis. **VHS, Beta** $19.95 PAR ✂✂

Family Life A portrait of a 19-year-old girl battling her parents to establish her own identity. She is subjected to increasingly vigorous psychological interventions in this documentary-style effort originally made for British television. **AKA:** Wednesday's Child. **1971 108m/C** GB Sandy Ratcliff, Bill Dean, Grace Cave; **D:** Ken Loach. **VHS, Beta** $59.95 COL ✂✂½

The Family Man A brief encounter-between a married Manhattanite (Asner) and a much younger single woman (Baxter Birney) is sensitively handled in this film which explores their passionate affair. Made-for-television. **1979 98m/C** Ed Asner, Meredith Baxter Birney, Paul Clemens, Mary Joan Negro, Anne Jackson, Martin Short, Michael Ironside; **D:** Glenn Jordan; **M:** Billy Goldenberg. **VHS, Beta** TLF ✂✂

A Family Matter A Mafia chieftain adopts a child whose father was killed by hit men. She grows into a beautiful woman bent on revenge. Melodramatic Italian-American co-production, made for TV. **AKA:** Vendetta: Secrets of a Mafia Bride. **1991 (R) 100m/C** Eric Roberts, Carol Alt, Eli Wallach, Burt Young. **VHS** $89.95 VMK ✂✂

Family Pictures A photographer remembers growing up in the 50's with her autistic brother, the mother who lavished her attention on him almost to the exclusion of her five other children, and the father who blamed his wife for their son's deficiencies. Interesting portrait of a typical American family, which eventually cracks under pressure and splits up. Adapted from the novel by Sue Miller (no relation to screenwriter Jennifer). **1993 240m/C** Anjelica Huston, Sam Neill, Kyra Sedgwick, Dermot Mulroney, Gemma Barry, Tara Charendoff, Torri Higginson, Jamie Harold; **D:** Philip Saville; **W:** Jennifer Miller. **VHS** NYR ✂✂✂

Family Plot Alfred Hitchcock's last film focuses on the search for a missing heir which is undertaken by a phony psychic and her private-eye boyfriend, with all becoming involved in a diamond theft. Campy, lightweight mystery that stales with time and doesn't fit well into Hitchcock's genre. **1976 (PG) 120m/C** Karen Black, Bruce Dern, Barbara Harris, William Devane, Ed Lauter, Katherine Helmond; **D:** Alfred Hitchcock; **W:** Ernest Lehman; **M:** John Williams. **VHS, Beta** $19.95 MCA ✂✂½

Family Prayers Coming-of-age drama, set in 1969 Los Angeles, about 13-year-old Andrew and his family troubles. His father Martin (Mantegna) is a compulsive gambler which causes wife Rita (Archer) untold anxiety and constant friction between the two. Tension is heightened by Nan (LuPone), Rita's opinionated older sister who has bailed the family out of their money problems more than once. Meanwhile, Andrew tries to look out for his younger sister and prepare for his bar-mitzvah. A little too much of a nostalgic

golden glow surrounds what is essentially a family tragedy. **1991 (PG) 109m/C** Tzvi Ratner-Stauber, Joe Mantegna, Anne Archer, Patti LuPone, Paul Reiser, Allen (Gooritz) Garfield, Conchata Ferrell, David Margulies; **D:** Scott Rosenfelt; **W:** Steven Ginsburg. **VHS** $89.95 COL ✂✂½

Family Reunion A young man brings a pretty hitchhiker to his family reunion where they mistake her for his fiancee (who recently dumped him). **1988 97m/C** David Eisner, Rebecca Jenkins, Henry Beckman, Linda Sorensen; **D:** Dick Sarin. **VHS, Beta** $19.95 MNC ✂½

Family Secrets A made-for-television drama about a daughter, mother, and grandmother overprotecting and manipulating each other during a weekend together. **1984 96m/C** Maureen Stapleton, Stefanie Powers, Melissa Gilbert, James Spader; **D:** Jack Hofsiss. **Beta** NO ✂✂½

Family Sins A television movie about a domineering father who dotes on his sports-oriented son while willfully neglecting the other. Eventually this leads to calamity. **1987 93m/C** James Farentino, Jill Eikenberry, Andrew Bendarski, Mimi Kuzyk, Brent Spiner, Michael Durrell, Tom Bower; **D:** Jerrold Freedman. **VHS** $79.98 REP ✂✂

Family Upside Down An aging couple fight their separation after the husband has a heart attack and is put into a nursing home. The fine cast received several Emmy nominations, with Astaire the winner. Made-for-television. **1978 100m/C** Helen Hayes, Fred Astaire, Efrem Zimbalist Jr., Patty Duke; **D:** David Lowell Rich; **M:** Henry Mancini. **VHS, Beta** $59.95 COL ✂✂

Family Viewing Surrealistic depiction of a family—obsessed with television and video—whose existence is a textbook model of home sweet dysfunctional home. An early, experimental film from Canada's Egoyan, it won considerable praise for its social commentary. **1988 92m/C** CA David Hemblen, Adian Tierney, Gabrielle Rose, Arsinee Khanjian; **D:** Atom Egoyan; **W:** Atom Egoyan; **M:** Mychael Danna. **VHS** $79.95 FXL, FCT, ING ✂✂✂

Famous Five Get Into Trouble Four precocious youngsters and a dog get involved with a criminal plot and cutely wile their way out of it. Scandinavian; dubbed in English. **1987 90m/C** Astrid Villaume, Ove Sprogoe, Lily Broberg; **D:** Trine Hedman. **VHS, Beta** $69.95 TWE ✂

The Fan A Broadway star is threatened and her immediate circle cut down when a lovestruck fan feels he has been rejected by his idol. The stellar cast makes this bloody and familiar tale seem better than it is. **1981 (R) 95m/C** Lauren Bacall, Maureen Stapleton, James Garner, Hector Elizondo, Michael Biehn, Griffin Dunne; **D:** Edward Bianchi; **M:** Pino Donaggio. **VHS, Beta** $14.95 PAR ✂✂

Fancy Pants Remake of "Ruggles of Red Gap" features Hope, a British actor posing as a butler. Also featuring Ball, an amusing contrast. Fine performances all around. ♫Fancy Pants; Home Cookin'. **1950 92m/C** Bob Hope, Lucille Ball, Bruce Cabot, Jack Kirkwood, Lea Penman, Eric Blore, John Alexander, Norma Varden; **D:** George Marshall. **VHS, Beta** $14.95 PAR ✂✂½

Fandango Five college friends take a wild weekend drive across the Texas Badlands for one last fling before graduation and the prospect of military service. Expanded by Reynolds with assistance from Steven Spielberg, from his student film. Provides a look at

college and life during the '60s Vietnam crisis. **1985 (PG) 91m/C** Judd Nelson, Kevin Costner, Sam Robards, Chuck Bush, Brian Cesak, Elizabeth Daily, Suzy Amis, Glenne Headly, Pepe Serna, Marvin J. McIntyre; **D:** Kevin Reynolds; **W:** Kevin Reynolds; **M:** Alan Silvestri. **VHS, Beta** $19.98 WAR ✂✂½

Fangoria's Weekend of Horrors A documentary about the making of horror films, featuring interviews with the industry's most scream-invoking artists. Copious film clips. **1986 60m/C** Rick Baker, Wes Craven, Tobe Hooper, Robert Englund. **VHS, Beta** $9.98 MED ✂✂½

Fangs Unfriendly reptile-stomping villagers take the life of Mr. Snakey's favorite serpent. He sends his slithering pets on a vengeful and poisonous spree. **1975 (R) 90m/C** Les Tremayne, Janet Wood, Bebe Kelly, Marvin Kaplan, Alice Nunn; **D:** Vittorio Schiraldi. **VHS, Beta** $24.95 GEM, MRV ✂½

Fangs of Fate A gang of bad guys battles the town's new marshal. **1925 67m/B** Bill Patton, Dorothy Donald. **VHS, Beta, 8mm** $24.95 GPV, VYY ✂½

Fangs of the Living Dead When a young woman inherits a castle, her uncle, who happens to be a vampire, tries to persuade her to remain among the undead. **AKA:** Malenka, the Vampire; La Nipote del Vampiro. **1968 80m/C** SP IT Anita Ekberg, Rossana Yanni, Diana Lorys, Fernando Bilbao, Paul Muller, John Hamilton, Julian Ugarte, Andriana Ambesi; **D:** Armando de Ossorio; **W:** Armando de Ossorio. **VHS** $19.98 SNC ✂½

Fangs of the Wild When a young boy witnesses a murder at his father's hunting lodge, no one but the killer believes him. When the killer decides to get rid of the boy, Buck the Wonder Dog gets involved. **AKA:** Follow the Hunter. **1954 72m/B** Charles Chaplin Jr., Onslow Stevens, Margia Dean, Freddy Ridgeway, Phil Tead, Robert Stevenson, Buck the Wonder Dog; **D:** William Claxton. **VHS** $19.95 NOS, DVT, HEG ✂✂

Fanny Second part of Marcel Pagnol's trilogy depicting the lives of the people of Provence, France. The poignant tale of Fanny, a young woman who marries an older man when Marius, her young lover, leaves her pregnant when he goes to sea. Remade several times but the original holds its own very well. "Marius" was first in the trilogy; "Cesar" was third. **1932 128m/B** FR Raimu, Charpin, Orane Demazis, Pierre Fresnay, Alida Rauffe; **D:** Marc Allegret; **W:** Marcel Pagnol; **M:** Vincent Scotto. **VHS, Beta** $64.95 INT, MRV, HHT ✂✂✂

Fanny Young girl falls in love with an adventurous sailor, and finds herself pregnant after he returns to the sea. With the help of the sailor's parents, she finds, marries, and eventually grows to love a much older man, who in turn cares for her and adores her son as if he were his own. When the sailor returns, all involved must confront their pasts and define their futures. Beautifully made, with fine performances and a plot which defies age or nationality. Part of the "A Night at the Movies" series, this tape simulates a 1961 movie evening, with a Tweety Pie cartoon, a newsreel and coming attractions for "Splendor in the Grass" and "The Roman Spring of Mrs. Stone."

1961 148m/C *FR* Leslie Caron, Maurice Chevalier, Charles Boyer, Horst Buchholz, Lionel Jeffries; *D:* Joshua Logan; *W:* Julius J. Epstein, Philip C. Epstein. Academy Awards '60 Nominations: Best Color Cinematography; Academy Awards '61: Best Actor (Boyer), Best Film Editing, Best Picture, Best Original Score; National Board of Review Awards '61: 10 Best Films of the Year. **VHS, Beta** $19.98 *NOS, WAR 𝄞𝄞𝄞*

Fanny and Alexander The culmination of Bergman's career, this autobiographical film is set in a rural Swedish town in 1907. It tells the story of one year in the lives of the Ekdahl family, as seen by the young children, Fanny and Alexander. Magic and religion, love and death, reconciliation and estrangement are skillfully captured in this carefully detailed, lovingly photographed film. In Swedish with English subtitles or dubbed. *AKA: Fanny Och Alexander.*
1983 (R) 197m/C *SW* Pernilla Allwin, Bertil Guve, Gunn Walgren, Allan Edwall, Ewa Froling, Erland Josephson, Harriet Andersson, Jarl Kulle, Jan Malmsjo; *D:* Ingmar Bergman; *W:* Ingmar Bergman. Academy Awards '83: Best Art Direction/Set Decoration, Best Cinematography, Best Costume Design, Best Foreign Language Film; Nominations: Best Director (Bergman), Best Original Screenplay; Cesar Awards '84: Best Foreign Film; Golden Globe Awards '84: Best Foreign Film. **VHS, Beta** $29.95 *COL, ING, NLC 𝄞𝄞𝄞𝄞*

Fanny Hill A softcore adaptation of the racy Victorian classic.
1983 (R) 80m/C *GB* Lisa Raines, Shelley Winters, Wilfrid Hyde-White, Oliver Reed. **VHS, Beta** $79.95 *MGM 𝄞*

Fanny Hill: Memoirs of a Woman of Pleasure Sexual exploits of an innocent in bawdy 18th-century London, as directed by notorious "Super Vixen" Meyer (though by Meyer standards, proceedings are fairly innocuous, if inept). Based on the novel.
1964 105m/B Miriam Hopkins, Walter Giller, Alexander D'Arcy, Leticia Roman; *D:* Russ Meyer. **VHS, Beta** *NO Woof!*

Fantasia Disney's most personal animation feature first bombed at the box office and irked purists who couldn't take the plotless, experimental mix of classical music and cartoons. It became a cult movie, embraced by more liberal generations of moviegoers. Reissue of the original version, painstakingly restored, ceased because of a planned remake. ♫Toccata & Fugue in D; The Nutcracker Suite; The Sorcerer's Apprentice; The Rite of Spring; Pastoral Symphony; Dance of the Hours; Night on Bald Mountain; Ave Maria; The Cossack Dance.
1940 116m/C Mickey Mouse; *Performed by:* Philadelphia Symphony Orchestra. **VHS** $24.99 *DIS, FCT, RDG 𝄞𝄞𝄞𝄞*

Fantasies Teenage lovers Derek and Hooten return to their Greek island home and decide to improve their village by turning it into a tourist haven. First collaboration of the Dereks is a loser, lacking plot, direction, and decent acting. Bo shows no talent but the obvious one and is actually credited as Kathleen Collins. *AKA: And Once Upon a Love.*
1973 (R) 81m/C Bo Derek, Peter Hooten, Anna Alexiades; *D:* John Derek. **VHS, Beta** $59.98 *FOX Woof!*

The Fantasist Sex crime thriller features a deranged killer who makes obscene, yet seductive phone calls to young ladies before murdering them.
1989 (R) 98m/C Timothy Bottoms, Christopher Cazenove; *D:* Robin Hardy. **VHS** $79.98 *REP 𝄞*

Fantastic Balloon Voyage Three men embark on a journey across the equator in a balloon, experiencing myriad adventures along the way. Much hot air.
198? (G) 100m/C Hugo Stiglitz, Jeff Cooper. **VHS, Beta** $29.95 *GEM 𝄞*

Fantastic Planet A critically acclaimed French, animated, sci-fi epic based on the drawings of Roland Topor. A race of small humanoids are enslaved and exploited by a race of giants on a savage planet, until one of the small creatures manages to unite his people and fight for equality. *AKA: La Planete Sauvage.*
1973 (PG) 68m/C *FR D:* Rene Laloux; *V:* Barry Bostwick. **VHS, Beta** $24.95 *VYY, MRV, SNC 𝄞𝄞𝄞*

Fantastic Seven The Fantastic Seven is a daredevil team sent to rescue a Hollywood sex symbol who has been kidnapped and held for ransom while shooting on location off the coast of Miami.
1982 96m/C Elke Sommer, Christopher Connelly. **VHS, Beta** *TLF 𝄞½*

Fantastic Voyage An important scientist, rescued from behind the Iron Curtain, is so severely wounded by enemy agents that traditional surgery is impossible. After being shrunk to microscopic size, a medical team journeys inside his body where they find themselves threatened by the patient's natural defenses. Great action, award-winning special effects. *AKA: Microscopia; Strange Journey.*
1966 100m/C Stephen Boyd, Edmond O'Brien, Raquel Welch, Arthur Kennedy, Donald Pleasence, Arthur O'Connell, William Redfield, James Brolin; *D:* Richard Fleischer. Academy Awards '66: Best Art Direction/Set Decoration (Color), Best Visual Effects; Nominations: Best Color Cinematography, Best Film Editing. **VHS, Beta** $19.98 *FOX, CCB 𝄞𝄞*

The Fantastic World of D.C. Collins Gary Coleman plays a daydreaming teenager who thinks he is being pursued by mysterious strangers seeking a videotape that was unknowingly slipped to him. Made for television.
1984 100m/C Gary Coleman, Bernie Casey, Shelley Smith, Fred Dryer, Marilyn McCoo, Phillip Abbott, George Gobel, Michael Ansara; *D:* Leslie Martinson. **VHS** $19.95 *STE, NWV 𝄞*

Fantasy Island Three people fly ("De plane, boss!") to an island paradise and get to live out their fantasies for a price. Made for television; the basis for the TV series.
1976 100m/C Ricardo Montalban, Bill Bixby, Sandra Dee, Peter Lawford, Carol Lynley, Hugh O'Brian, Eleanor Parker, Dick Sargent, Victoria Principal; *D:* Richard Lang. **VHS, Beta** $49.95 *PSM 𝄞*

Fantasy Man A restless middle-aged man tries to relieve his mid-life crisis with the help of three women.
1984 100m/C *AU* Harold Hopkins, Jeanie Drynan, Kerry Mack, Kate Fitzpatrick; *D:* John Meagher; *W:* John Meagher. **VHS, Beta** $59.95 *VCD 𝄞½*

Far and Away Meandering old-fashioned epic about immigrants, romance, and settling the American West. In the 1890s, Joseph Donelly (Cruise) is forced to flee his Irish homeland after threatening the life of his landlord, and emigrates to America in the company of the landlord's daughter, feisty Shannon Christie (Kidman). Particularly brutal scenes of Cruise earning his living as a bare-knuckled boxer contrast with the expansiveness of the land rush ending. Slow, spotty, and a little too slick for its own good, though real-life couple Cruise and Kidman are an attractive pair. Filmed in 70-mm Panavision on location in Ireland and Montana. Also available in a letter boxed version.
1992 (PG-13) 140m/C Tom Cruise, Nicole Kidman, Thomas Gibson, Robert Prosky, Barbara Babcock, Colm Meaney, Eileen Pollock, Michelle Johnson, Cyril Cusack, Clint Howard, Rance Howard; *D:* Ron Howard; *W:* Bob Dolman; *M:* John Williams. **VHS, Beta** $19.98 *MCA 𝄞𝄞½*

Far Away and Long Ago Based on the autobiographical novel by Guillermo Hudson which details the memories which haunted his childhood—the Argentinian pampas, its gauchos, witchcraft, and women. In Spanish with English subtitles.
1974 91m/C *AR* Juan Jose Camero, Leonor Manso; *D:* Manuel Antin. **VHS** $24.98 *ING 𝄞𝄞½*

Far Country Cattlemen must battle the elements and frontier lawlessness in this classic. Stewart leads his herd to the Yukon in hopes of large profits, but ends up having to kidnap it back from the crooked sheriff and avenging the deaths of his friends. Entertaining and the Yukon setting takes it out of the usual Western arena.
1955 97m/C James Stewart, Ruth Roman, Walter Brennan, Harry Morgan, Corinne Calvet, Jay C. Flippen, John McIntire; *D:* Anthony Mann; *M:* Henry Mancini. **VHS, Beta** $14.95 *BAR 𝄞𝄞𝄞*

Far Cry from Home A battered wife attempts to escape from her domineering husband before it's too late.
197? 87m/C Mary Ann McDonald, Richard Monette. **VHS, Beta** $49.95 *TWE 𝄞*

Far East Two ex-lovers meet in Southeast Asia and join forces to find the woman's missing husband, a reporter.
1985 105m/C Bryan Brown, Helen Morse; *D:* John Duigan. **VHS, Beta** $59.95 *LHV, VTR 𝄞½*

Far from Home Drew Barrymore is the seductive teen being scoped by a psychotic killer while on vacation with her father. Lots of over-the-top performances by the familiar cast.
1989 (R) 86m/C Matt Frewer, Drew Barrymore, Richard Masur, Karen Austin, Susan Tyrrell, Anthony Rapp, Jennifer Tilly, Andras Jones, Dick Miller; *D:* Meiert Avis; *M:* Jonathan Elias. **VHS** $89.98 *LIV, VES 𝄞𝄞*

Far from the Madding Crowd A lavish, long adaptation of Thomas Hardy's nineteenth century classic about the beautiful Bathsheba and the three very different men who love her. Her first love is a handsome and wayward soldier (Stamp), her second the local noble lord (Finch) and her third the everloving and long-patient farmer (Bates). Christie is well cast as the much-desired beauty. Gorgeous cinematography by Nicolas Roeg.
1967 (PG) 165m/C *GB* Julie Christie, Terence Stamp, Peter Finch, Alan Bates, Prunella Ransome; *D:* John Schlesinger; *W:* Frederic Raphael; *M:* Richard Rodney Bennett. Academy Awards '67 Nominations: Best Original Score; National Board of Review Awards '67: 10 Best Films of the Year, Best Actor (Finch). **VHS, Beta** $29.98 *MGM 𝄞𝄞𝄞*

Far Frontier Roy Rogers saves the day by thwarting a band of outlaws who are being smuggled across the border in soybean oil cans. Includes musical numbers and horse tricks.
1948 60m/B Roy Rogers, Andy Devine, Clayton Moore. **VHS** $9.95 *NOS, TIM, REP 𝄞𝄞*

Far North Quirky comedy about a woman who returns to her rural family homestead after her father is seriously injured by a horse, and tries to deal with her eccentric family's travails. Fine cast never reaches its potential. Shepard's directing debut.

1988 (PG-13) 96m/C Jessica Lange, Charles Durning, Tess Harper, Donald Moffatt, Ann Wedgeworth, Patricia Arquette, Nina Draxton; *D:* Sam Shepard; *W:* Sam Shepard; *M:* Red Clay Ramblers. VHS, Beta, 8mm $19.95 NLC 🎞️🎞️½

A Far Off Place Adolescent boy, adolescent girl, adolescent bushperson, and mature dog set out across the African desert to escape elephant poachers who want to kill them. The boy and girl find romance in the sand, bushperson finds water by listening, and dog gets very nice walk. Strong performances by the youthful leads lend charm to this Disney/Amblin flick, particularly Bok as the bushperson. Unusually violent film for studios involved (animals and people bite sand), though care is taken to add actual blood shed on screen. Filmed in Zimbabwe and Namibia and based on the books "A Story Like the Wind" and "A Far Off Place" by Laurens van der Post. **1993** (PG-13) 107m/C Reese Witherspoon, Ethan Randall, Sarel Bok, Jack Thompson, Maximilian Schell, Robert Burke, Patricia Kalember, Daniel Gerroll, Miles Anderson; *D:* Mikael Salomon; *W:* Robert Caswell, Jonathan Hensleigh, Sally Robinson; *M:* James Horner. VHS, Beta $94.95 DIS 🎞️🎞️

Far Out Man An unalterable middle-aged hippie is sent by his worried family and his psychiatrist on a cross-country journey to rediscover himself. The script makes no sense and has very few laughs. **1989** (R) 105m/C Thomas Chong, Rae Dawn Chong, C. Thomas Howell, Shelby Chong, Martin Mull, Paris Chong, Paul Bartel, Judd Nelson, Michael Winslow, Richard "Cheech" Marin; *D:* Thomas Chong. VHS, Beta $89.95 COL Woof!

The Far Pavilions A British officer falls in love with an Indian princess during the second Afghan War. Cross is appropriately noble and stiff-upper-lipped but Irving is miscast as his ethnic love. Based on the romantic bestseller by M.M. Kaye, this lavish production was made for cable television. *AKA:* Blade of Steel. **1984** 108m/C Ben Cross, Amy Irving, Omar Sharif, Benedict Taylor, Rossano Brazzi, Christopher Lee; *D:* Peter Duffell; *M:* Carl Davis. VHS, Beta $14.95 CNG, KAR 🎞️🎞️½

Faraway, So Close! Wenders' erratic follow-up to his magnificent "Wings of Desire." Cassiel (Sander), the angel left behind when Damiel (Ganz) chose to become human, once again surveys Berlin, noticing the changes (not necessarily for the better). Angelic companion Raphaela (Kinski) watches events passively, including an old man's (Ruhamnn) reflections on life and the philosophical musings of Emit Flesti (Dafoe, Time Itself, get it?), even as Cassiel impulsively views humanity over his heavenly world. Falk makes a return appearance to little effect. Overlong and under-developed. *AKA:* In Weiter Ferne, So Nah!. **1993** (PG-13) 146m/C GE Otto Sander, Peter Falk, Horst Buchholz, Nastassia Kinski, Heinz Ruhmann, Bruno Ganz, Solveig Dommartin, Ruediger Vogler, Willem Dafoe, Lou Reed; *D:* Wim Wenders; *W:* Ulrich Zieger, Richard Reitinger, Wim Wenders; *M:* Laurent Petitgand. Cannes Film Festival Nominations: cs 93: Best Film; Golden Globe Awards '94: Best Song ("Stay"); Cannes Film Festival '93: Jury Prize. VHS COL 🎞️🎞️

Farewell My Concubine Exotic film covers 50 years of sexual, social, and political Chinese history wrapped around the story of two male Peking Opera stars. Deposited as boys at the Opera's training school Douzi and Shitou become fast friends in their hermetically sealed world, but their friendship is tested during the chaos of Communism and the cultural revolution. Sumptuous and well-acted, but the sheer length and emotional detachment prove to be drawbacks. Adapted from a novel by Lee, who based the work on a 2000-year-old Chinese opera about an imperial concubine. Filmed on location in Beijing. In Mandarin Chinese with subtitles. *AKA:* Bawang Bie Ji. **1993** (R) 157m/C HK Leslie Cheung, Zhang Fengyi, Gong Li, Lu Qi, Ying Da, Ge You; *D:* Chen Kaige; *W:* Lilian Lee, Lu Wei; *M:* Zhao Jiping. Academy Awards '93 Nominations: Best Cinematography, Best Foreign Language Film; British Academy Awards '93: Best Foreign Language Film; Golden Globe Awards '94: Best Foreign Language Film; Cannes Film Festival '93: Best Film; Los Angeles Film Critics Association Awards '93: Best Foreign Language Film; National Board of Review Awards '93: Best Foreign Language Film; New York Film Critics Awards '93: Best Foreign Language Film, Best Supporting Actress (Li). VHS TOU, KIV 🎞️🎞️

Farewell, My Lovely A remake of the 1944 Raymond Chandler mystery, "Murder, My Sweet," featuring private eye Phillip Marlowe hunting for an ex-convict's lost sweetheart in 1941 Los Angeles. Perhaps the most accurate of Chandler adaptations, but far from the best, this film offers a nicely detailed production. Mitchum is a bit too world-weary as the see-it-all detective. **1975** (R) 95m/C GB Robert Mitchum, Charlotte Rampling, Sylvia Miles, John Ireland, Anthony Zerbe, Jack O'Halloran, Harry Dean Stanton, Sylvester Stallone, Cheryl "Rainbeaux" Smith; *D:* Dick Richards; *W:* David Zelag Goodman. Academy Awards '75 Nominations: Best Supporting Actress (Miles); National Board of Review Awards '75: 10 Best Films of the Year. VHS, Beta $24.98 SUE 🎞️🎞️🎞️

A Farewell to Arms The original film version of Ernest Hemingway's novel about the tragic love affair between an American ambulance driver and an English nurse during the Italian campaign of WWI. The novelist disavowed the ambiguous ending, but the public loved the film. Fine performances and cinematography. **1932** 85m/B Helen Hayes, Gary Cooper, Adolphe Menjou, Mary Philips, Jack LaRue, Blanche Frederici; *D:* Frank Borzage. Academy Awards '33: Best Cinematography, Best Sound; Nominations: Best Interior Decoration, Best Picture; National Board of Review Awards '32: 10 Best Films of the Year. VHS, Beta $9.95 CNG, MRV, NOS 🎞️🎞️🎞️

Farewell to the King During WWII, a ship-wrecked American deserter becomes the chief of a tribe of Borneo headhunters until his jungle kingdom is caught between the forces of the U.S. and Japanese. With the help of a British officer he helps them defend themselves when the Japanese invade. An old-fashioned war epic with a beautiful location and solid if uninspired-performances by the leads. Based on Pierre Schoendoerffer's novel "L'Adieu Au Roi." **1989** (PG-13) 114m/C Nick Nolte, Nigel Havers, Marius Weyers, Frank McRae, Marilyn Tokuda, Elan Oberon, William Wise, James Fox, Aki Aleong; *D:* John Milius; *W:* John Milius; *M:* Basil Poledouris. VHS, Beta $19.98 ORI 🎞️🎞️½

Fargo Express When the kid brother of Maynard's true love is falsely accused of robbing a stagecoach, Maynard works to clear his name. Routine stuff. **1932** 60m/B Ken Maynard, Helen Mack, Paul Fix; *D:* Alan James. VHS, Beta $19.95 NOS, VCN, DVT 🎞️½

The Farmer Takes a Wife Henry Fonda's first film, recreating his stage role, as a mid-nineteenth century farmer at odds with the Erie canal builders and struggling to court the woman he loves. Remade as a musical in 1953. **1935** 91m/B Janet Gaynor, Henry Fonda, Charles Bickford, Slim Summerville, Jane Withers; *D:* Victor Fleming. VHS TCF 🎞️🎞️½

The Farmer Takes a Wife Poor musical remake of the 1935 drama, about the trials of a struggling 1850s farmer and the Erie canal boat cook he loves. Contains no memorable music and Robertson can't compete with Henry Fonda's original role as the farmer. ♫We're in Business; On the Erie Canal; We're Doing it for the Natives in Jamaica; When I Close My Door; Today I Love Everybody; Somethin' Real Special; With The Sun Warm Upon Me; Can You Spell Schenectady?. **1953** 81m/C Betty Grable, Dale Robertson, Thelma Ritter, John Carroll, Eddie Foy Jr.; *D:* Henry Levin. VHS, Beta $19.98 FOX 🎞️🎞️

The Farmer's Daughter Young portrays Katrin Holmstrom, a Swedish farm girl who becomes a maid to Congressman Cotten and winds up running for office herself (not neglecting to find romance as well). The outspoken and multi-talented character charmed audiences and was the basis of a television series in the 1960s. **1947** 97m/B Loretta Young, Joseph Cotten, Ethel Barrymore, Charles Bickford, Harry Davenport, Lex Barker, James Arness, Rose Hobart; *D:* H.C. Potter. Academy Awards '47: Best Actress (Young); Nominations: Best Supporting Actor (Bickford). VHS, Beta $59.98 FOX, BTV 🎞️🎞️🎞️

The Farmer's Other Daughter A rural comedy about Farmer Brown whose lovely daughter is eyed by all the farmhands. He also has to contend with dastardly Mr. Barksnapper who wants to take his farm away from him until one of his daughter's beaus comes to the rescue. *AKA:* Farm Girl. **1965** 84m/C Ernest Ashworth, Judy Pennebaker, Bill Michael; *D:* John Patrick Hayes. VHS $19.95 COL 🎞️🎞️

The Farmer's Wife Silent British comedy about a recently widowed farmer searching for a new wife. Meanwhile, his lovely housekeeper would be the perfect candidate. Based on Eden Philpott's play. **1928** 97m/B GB Jameson Thomas, Lillian Hall-Davies, Gordon Harker; *D:* Alfred Hitchcock; *W:* Alfred Hitchcock. VHS $9.98 REP, SNC, MLB 🎞️🎞️½

Fashions of 1934 A typical, lightweight thirties musical with impressive choreography by Busby Berkeley. Powell plays a disreputable clothing designer who goes to Paris to steal the latest fashion designs and winds up costuming a musical and falls in love. ♫Spin a Little Web of Dreams; Broken Melody. *AKA:* Fashions. **1934** 78m/B Bette Davis, William Powell, Frank McHugh, Hugh Herbert, Reginald Owen, Busby Berkeley; *D:* William Dieterle. VHS, Beta $19.95 VDM 🎞️🎞️

Fass Black Yet another man against the mob flick straight out of Bartlett's familiar plot lines. Amidst gratuitous music and violence, a disco owner locks horns with the syndicate after they try to take over his place. There's a good reason disco is dead. **1977** (R) 105m/C John Poole, Jeanne Bell, Cal Wilson, Harold Nicholas, Nicholas Lewis; *D:* D'Urville Martin. VHS $39.95 XVC 🎞️🎞️

The Fast and the Furious On the lam after being falsely charged with murder, Ireland picks up a fast car and a loose woman (or is it a loose car and a fast woman?) and makes a run for the border by entering the Pebble Beach race.

1954 73m/B John Ireland, Dorothy Malone, Bruce Carlisle, Iris Adrian; **D:** John Ireland, Edwards Sampson. VHS $19.95 NOS &&

Fast Break New York deli clerk who is a compulsive basketball fan talks his way into a college coaching job. He takes a team of street players with him, with predictable results on and off the court. Kaplan's screen debut.
1979 (PG) 107m/C Gabe Kaplan, Harold Sylvester, Randee Heller; **D:** Jack Smight. VHS, Beta $19.95 GKK &1/2

Fast Bullets Texas Rangers fight a gang of smugglers and rescue a kidnap victim in this typical western.
1944 52m/B Tom Tyler, Rex Lease. VHS, Beta $19.95 NOS, VCN, DVT &1/2

Fast Company The life story of champion race car driver Lonnie Johnson including women, money, and the drag racing sponsors.
1978 90m/C William Smith, John Saxon, Claudia Jennings, Nicholas Campbell, Don Francks; **D:** David Cronenberg; **W:** David Cronenberg. VHS, Beta AOV &&

Fast Fists During the reign of the Min Kou Government, the Red Light Net gang of bandits terrorizes the countryside. One fateful evening, the gang's leader attempts to kidnap and kill a famous actress. This is the incredible story of what happened.
19?? 90m/C Jimmy Wang Yu. VHS, Beta $57.95 OCE &

Fast Food A super-cheap, strangulated attempt at low comedy, wherein an entrepreneurial hamburger peddler invents a secret aphrodisiac sauce. Look for former porn-star Traci Lords.
1989 90m/C Clark Brandon, Tracy Griffith, Randal Patrick, Traci Lords, Kevin McCarthy, Michael J. Pollard, Jim Varney; **D:** Michael A. Simpson. VHS, Beta $29.95 FRH &

Fast Forward A group of eight teenagers from Ohio learn how to deal with success and failure when they enter a national dance contest in New York City. A break-dancing variation on the old show business chestnut. ♫Fast Forward; How Do You Do; As Long As We Believe; Pretty Girl; Mystery; Curves; Showdown; Do You Want It Right Now?; Hardrock; Taste.
1984 (PG) 110m/C John Scott Clough, Don Franklin, Tracy Silver, Cindy McGee; **D:** Sidney Poitier; **W:** Richard Wesley; **M:** Tom Bahler. VHS, Beta $79.95 COL &1/2

Fast Getaway Chases scenes proliferate when a teen criminal mastermind plots bank heists for his outlaw father. Relatively painless adolescent action-comedy, cleverly acted, quickly forgotten.
1991 (PG) 91m/C Corey Haim, Cynthia Rothrock, Leo Rossi, Ken Lerner, Marcia Strassman; **D:** Spiro Razatos. VHS, Beta, 8mm $89.95 COL &&

Fast Kill A terrorist plot begins to fall apart when the conspirators fight among themselves.
1973 94m/C Tom Adams, Susie Hampton, Michael Culver, Peter Halliday; **D:** Lindsay Shonteff. VHS, Beta $19.95 GEM &

Fast Lane Fever A drag racer challenges a factory worker to a no-holds-barred race.
1982 (R) 94m/C VHS, Beta $69.95 MGM &

Fast Money Three pals can't resist the temptation of big bucks from flying drugs in from Mexico, but they find danger along the way.
1983 92m/C Sammy Allred, Sonny Carl Davis; **D:** Doug Holloway. VHS, Beta $39.95 LIV &1/2

Fast Talking The story of a quick-talking, incorrigible, fifteen-year-old Australian boy's humorous though tragic criminal schemes. The young protagonist slides his way through a life marked by a degenerate home life, a brother who forces him to sell drugs, and a future that holds no promise.
1986 93m/C AU Steve Bisley, Tracey Mann, Peter Hehir, Dennis Moore, Rod Zuanic, Toni Allaylis, Chris Truswell; **D:** Ken Cameron; **W:** Ken Cameron. VHS, Beta $19.98 SUE, NLC &&

Fast Times at Ridgemont High Teens at a Southern California high school revel in sex, drugs, and rock 'n' roll. A full complement of student types meet at the Mall—that great suburban microcosm percolating with angst-ridden teen trials—to contemplate losing their virginity, plot skipping homeroom, and move inexorably closer to the end of their adolescence. The talented young cast became household names: Sean Penn is most excellent as the California surfer dude who antagonizes teacher, Walston, aka "Aloha Mr. Hand." Based on the best-selling book by Cameron Crowe, it's one of the best of this genre.
1982 (R) 91m/C Sean Penn, Jennifer Jason Leigh, Judge Reinhold, Robert Romanus, Brian Backer, Phoebe Cates, Ray Walston, Scott Thomson, Vincent Schiavelli, Amanda Wyss, Forest Whitaker, Kelli Maroney, Eric Stoltz, Pamela Springsteen, James Russo, Martin Brest, Anthony Edwards; **D:** Amy Heckerling; **W:** Cameron Crowe. VHS, Beta $14.95 MCA &&&

Fast Walking A prison guard is offered fifty-thousand dollars to help a militant black leader escape from jail, the same man his cousin has contracted to kill.
1982 (R) 116m/C James Woods, Kay Lenz, M. Emmet Walsh, Robert Hooks, Tim McIntire, Timothy Carey, Susan Tyrrell; **D:** James B. Harris. VHS, Beta $19.98 FOX, HHE &&

Faster Pussycat! Kill! Kill! It doesn't get any better than this! Three sexy go-go dancers get their after-work kicks by hot-rodding in the California desert. They soon find themselves enveloped in murder, kidnapping, lust and robbery after a particular race gets out of hand. Easily the most watchable, fun and funny production to spring from the mind of Russ Meyer. Those who haven't seen this cannot truly be called "cool."
1966 83m/B Tura Satana, Haji, Lori Williams, Susan Bernard, Stuart Lancaster, Paul Trinka, Dennis Busch, Ray Barlow, Mickey Foxx; **D:** Russ Meyer; **W:** Jack Moran. VHS $79.95 RMF, FCT, TPV &&

Fastest Guitar Alive Debut of the legendary Orbison is strictly for inveterate fans only. Rebel operative/crooner during the Civil War, whose rhythm is good but timing is bad, steals a Union gold supply, but the war ends before he makes it back to the land of Dixie. Seems that makes him a common thief.
1968 88m/C Roy Orbison, Sammy Jackson, Margaret Pierce, Joan Freeman; **D:** Michael Moore; **W:** Roy Orbison. VHS, Beta $14.95 MGM, MVD &1/2

Fastest Gun Alive Suspenseful western with ex-gunfighter Ford challenged to a showdown by Crawford.
1956 89m/C Glenn Ford, Jeanne Crain, Broderick Crawford, Russ Tamblyn, Allyn Joslyn, Leif Erickson, John Dehner, Noah Beery Jr., J.M. Kerrigan, Rhys Williams; **D:** Russel Rouse; **W:** Russel Rouse, Frank D. Gilroy. VHS $19.98 MGM &&

Fat and the Lean An early short film from Roman Polanski that satirizes government tyranny and absurdity.

1961 16m/C **D:** Roman Polanski. VHS, Beta IHF, FLI, GVV &&&

Fat City One of Huston's later triumphs, a seedy, street-level drama based on the Leonard Gardner novel about an aging alcoholic boxer trying to make a comeback and his young worshipful protege. Highly acclaimed. Tyrrell earned an Oscar nomination as the boxer's world-weary lover.
1972 (PG) 93m/C Stacy Keach, Jeff Bridges, Susan Tyrrell, Candy Clark, Nicholas Colasanto; **D:** John Huston; **M:** Marvin Hamlisch. VHS, Beta $19.95 COL &&&1/2

Fat Guy Goes Nutzoid A crude farce about an obese mental patient who escapes from the mental hospital and joins two teenagers on a wild trip to New York City. **AKA:** Zeisters.
1986 85m/C Tibor Feldman, Peter Linari, John MacKay, Joan Allen; **D:** John Golden. VHS, Beta $79.95 PSM Woof!

Fat Man and Little Boy A lavish, semi-fictional account of the creation of the first atomic bomb, and the tensions between J. Robert Oppenheimer and his military employer, Gen. Leslie Groves. Overlong but interesting. Cusack, whose character never existed, is especially worthwhile as an idealistic scientist.
1989 (PG-13) 127m/C Paul Newman, Dwight Schultz, Bonnie Bedelia, John Cusack, Laura Dern, John C. McGinley, Natasha Richardson, Ron Frazier; **D:** Roland Joffe; **W:** Bruce Robinson, Tony Garnett, Roland Joffe; **M:** Ennio Morricone. VHS, Beta, 8mm $14.95 PAR, FCT, HMV &&1/2

Fatal Attraction Couple meet after an auto accident. They begin an affair which turns dark and bizarre. Fine cast doesn't get far with this peculiar premise, although every one tries hard. **AKA:** Head On.
1980 (R) 90m/C CA Sally Kellerman, Stephen Lack, John Huston, Lawrence Dane; **D:** Michael Grant. VHS, Beta $29.98 VES &&

Fatal Attraction When a very married New York lawyer is seduced by a beautiful blonde associate, the one-night stand leads to terror as she continues to pursue the relationship. She begins to threaten his family and home with possessive, violent acts. An expertly made, manipulative thriller; one of the most hotly discussed films of the 1980s. A successful change of role for Close as the sexy, scorned, and deadly other woman. Also available in a special "director's series" edition, featuring Lyne's original, controversial ending.
1987 (R) 120m/C Michael Douglas, Glenn Close, Anne Archer, Stuart Pankin, Ellen Hamilton-Latzen, Ellen Foley, Fred Gwynne, Meg Mundy, J.J. Johnston; **D:** Adrian Lyne; **W:** James Dearden; **M:** Maurice Jarre. Academy Awards '87 Nominations: Best Actress (Close), Best Adapted Screenplay, Best Director (Lyne), Best Film Editing, Best Picture, Best Supporting Actress (Archer); People's Choice Awards '88: Best Film—Drama. VHS, Beta, 8mm, CDV $14.95 PAR, FCT, CCB &&&

Fatal Beauty A female undercover cop in Los Angeles tracks down a drug dealer selling cocaine (from which the title is taken). Elliott is the mob bodyguard who helps her out. Violent and sensational, the film tries to capitalize on the success of "Beverly Hills Cop" and fails miserably. Goldberg is wasted in this effort and the picture tiptoes around the interracial romance aspects that are implied.
1987 (R) 104m/C Whoopi Goldberg, Sam Elliott, Ruben Blades, Harris Yulin, Richard "Cheech" Marin, Brad Dourif; **D:** Tom Holland; **M:** Harold Faltermeyer. VHS, Beta $14.95 MGM &1/2

Fatal Bond Blair plays a small-town hairdresser caught in an obsessive love affair with a drifter. When she suspects her boyfriend is committing a string of rape-murders, will she turn him in or protect him? Or is she next?
1991 (R) 89m/C Linda Blair, Jerome Elhers, Stephen Leeder, Donal Gibson, Caz Lederman, Tao Gerbert, Penny Pederson, Joe Bugner; D: Vincent Monton; W: Phillip Avalon. VHS COL *½

Fatal Charm There's a serial killer at work in a small town. So far six women have been raped and murdered. But cute-teen Valerie can't believe it when the townspeople accuse that sweet guy Adam, especially since he's the one boy Valerie is so very attracted to.
1992 (R) 90m/C Christopher Atkins, Amanda Peterson, Mary Frann, James Remar, Andrew (Andy) Robinson, Peggy Lipton; D: Alan Smithee; W: Nicholas Niciphor. VHS $89.95 ACA **

Fatal Chase Van Cleef is a U.S. Marshal assigned to protect ex-hitman Musante from his vengeful former employers. And you thought you didn't get along with your boss. Typical made-for-TV fodder written by Anhalt, who usually manages to be a trifle more entertaining. AKA: Nowhere to Hide.
1977 78m/C Lee Van Cleef, Tony Musante, Charles Robinson, Lelia Goldoni, Noel Fournier, Russell Johnson, Edward Anhalt; D: Jack Starrett; W: Edward Anhalt. VHS $9.95 SIM **

Fatal Confinement Wrenching drama finds Crawford, having lived 15 years in seclusion with her young daughter, forced to sell her land to a giant corporation bent on expansion. Interesting also for the similarities to Crawford's real-life "Mommie Dearest" lifestyle.
1964 70m/C GB Joan Crawford, Paul Burke, Charles Bickford; D: Robert Guest. VHS $39.95 FCT, MOV, TPV **½

Fatal Error Dutch police thriller about the investigation of a cop killing. Dubbed. AKA: Outsider in Amsterdam; The Outsider; Grijpstra and de Gier.
1983 85m/C NL Rutger Hauer, Rijk de Gooyer, Willeke Van Ammelrooy, Donald M. Jones; D: Wim Verstappen; M: Ennio Morricone. VHS, Beta NO *½

Fatal Exposure The insatiably sanguinary Jack the Ripper lives on in the form of his great grandson, who avails himself of modern technology to capture those magic moments on videotape. Just goes to show home movies don't have to be bland.
1990 ?m/C Blake Bahner, Ena Henderson, Julie Austin, Dan Schmale, Renee Cline, Gary Wise, Joy Ovington. VHS HHE *

Fatal Exposure A divorcee on vacation with her young sons accidentally picks up the wrong snapshots at the developers'. It turns out she has her hands on some incriminating photos, and the subject will resort to anything, even murder, to keep her quiet. Originally made for television.
1991 (PG-13) 89m/C Mare Winningham, Nick Mancuso, Christopher McDonald, Geoffrey Blake; D: Alan Metzger. VHS, Beta PAR **

Fatal Fix A French film expose of urban heroin addiction. Music by the Pretenders.
198? 90m/C FR Helmut Berger, Corinne Clery; D: Massimo Pirri; M: The Pretenders. VHS, Beta NO *½

Fatal Games Young female athletes are mysteriously disappearing at the Falcon Academy of Athletics and a crazed killer is responsible.
1984 88m/C Sally Kirkland, Lynn Banashek, Sean Masterson. VHS, Beta $59.95 MED *½

The Fatal Glass of Beer Fields' son returns to his home in the north woods after serving a jail term in this slapstick comedy short.
1933 18m/B W.C. Fields, Rosemary Theby, George Chandler, Richard Cramer. VHS, Beta $19.98 CCB, GVV *½

The Fatal Hour Karloff is enlisted to aid police in solving the murder of a detective. As Karloff is rounding up suspects, three more murders take place. Feeble.
1940 68m/B Boris Karloff, Marjorie Reynolds, Grant Withers, Charles Trowbridge, John Hamilton, Frank Puglia, Jason Robards Sr.; D: William Nigh. VHS, Beta, 8mm $14.95 VYY, SNC *½

The Fatal Image A mother and daughter on vacation in Paris inadvertently videotape an international mob hit, making them the target of ruthless assassins. Filmed on location in Paris. Made for television.
1990 96m/C Michele Lee, Justine Bateman, Francois Dunoyer, Jean-Pierre Cassel, Sonia Petrovna; D: Thomas J. Wright. VHS $89.95 WOV **½

Fatal Images A camera mysteriously causes all the models who pose for it to die, prompting the photographer to investigate.
1982 90m/C Lane Coyle. VHS, Beta $49.95 AHV *

Fatal Instinct A tough-guy cop trying to solve a murder instead finds himself a victim of sexual obsession in this erotic thriller. Also available in an unrated version. Not to be confused with (but doesn't everything sound familiar) "Basic Instinct."
1992 (R) 93m/C Michael Madsen, Laura Johnson, Tony Hamilton; D: John Dirlam. VHS $89.95 NLC, COL *½

Fatal Instinct Spoof on erotic thrillers such as "Fatal Attraction" and "Basic Instinct." Suave Assante plays a guy with dual careers—he's both cop and attorney, defending the criminals he's arrested. Young plays a lovelorn psycho who's lost her panties. Plot is worth mentioning only in passing, since the point is to mercilessly skewer the entire film noir tradition. The gags occasionally hit deep-chuckle level, though for every good joke there's at least three that misfire. Clemmons of "E Street Band" fame wanders around with sax for background music purposes, typical of the acute self-consciousness of the film.
1993 (PG-13) 90m/C Armand Assante, Sean Young, Sherilyn Fenn, Kate Nelligan, Christopher McDonald, James Remar, Tony Randall; Cameos: Clarence Clemmons, Doc Severinsen; D: Carl Reiner; W: David O'Malley; M: Richard Gibbs. VHS MGM **

Fatal Justice Mars is a topnotch assassin who's been in the business too long and knows too much so the agency he works for decides to kill him off. They send young and beautiful professional Diana to do the job but will she be able to when she discovers Mars is actually her father?
199? 90m/C Joe Estevez. VHS $89.95 AIP *

Fatal Mission A Vietnam soldier captures a female Chinese guerilla and uses her as his hostage and guide through the jungle.
1989 (R) 84m/C Peter Fonda, Mako, Tia Carrere. VHS, Beta $79.98 MED, VTR *

Fatal Pulse Sorority girls are being killed off in grisly ways. Basic slasher/gore.
1988 90m/C Michelle McCormick, Ken Roberts, Joe Phelan, Alex Courtney. VHS, Beta $19.95 CEL Woof!

Fatal Skies An evil schemer plots to dump toxic waste in a small town's water supply until a group of teens comes to the rescue.
1990 88m/C Timothy Leary. VHS, Beta $14.95 AIP *

Fatal Vision The television film version of Joe McGinniss' controversial book about the murder trial of Dr. Jeffrey MacDonald, the Marine corps physician accused of murdering his whole family and blaming the killings on crazed hippies. McGinniss first believed MacDonald may have been innocent but his subsequent investigation, and his book, proved otherwise. The starring debut for Cole. MacDonald still protests his innocence.
1984 192m/C Gary Cole, Karl Malden, Eva Marie Saint, Andy Griffith, Barry Newman; D: David Greene. VHS, Beta $69.95 COL **½

Fate Sweet comedy. A young man plans his love-affair carefully, but his biggest problem is meeting the girl of his dreams. Cheerful acting from Lynn and Paul. Stylish and charming.
1990 (PG-13) 115m/C Cheryl Lynn, Stuart Paul, Kaye Ballard, Susannah York; D: Stuart Paul. VHS $19.95 ACA **½

The Fate of Lee Khan Much blood is shed as a rebellion is led against the Mongols during the Yuan dynasty.
1973 107m/C Roy Chaid, Angela Mao; D: Kinghu. VHS, Beta FCT *

Father After WWII, a Hungarian youth makes up stories about his dead father's heroism that enhance his own position. Eventually he becomes obsessed with the facts surrounding his father's death at the hands of the enemy and, learning the truth, lays the past to rest. In Hungarian with English subtitles.
1967 89m/B HU Andras Balint, Miklos Gabor; D: Istvan Szabo; W: Istvan Szabo. VHS, Beta $24.95 VYY, DVT, ING ***

Father A woman receives an anonymous telephone call telling her to watch a television news program and learn the truth about her beloved father. What she sees is her father's face superimposed over that of a young Nazi soldier and an aging, unstable woman accusing her father of war crimes. The daughter fiercely believes her father to be a victim of mistaken identity but questions keep nagging at her. Very similiar in plot to "Music Box" and just as pedestrian in spite of some good performances.
1990 (PG-13) 106m/C AU Max von Sydow, Carol Drinkwater, Julia Blake, Steve Jacobs; D: John Power. VHS $79.95 MNC **

The Father Clements Story The true story of a black priest in Chicago who battled the Roman Catholic hierarchy in order to adopt a troubled teenager. Made for television.
1987 100m/C Louis Gossett Jr., Malcolm Jamal Warner, Carroll O'Connor, Leon Robinson, Rosetta LeNoire, Ron McClarty; D: Edwin Sherin. VHS $19.98 LIV **½

Father Figure When a divorced man attends his ex-wife's funeral, he discovers that he must take care of his estranged sons. Based on young adult writer Richard Peck's novel; a well-done made-for-television movie.
1980 94m/C Hal Linden, Timothy Hutton, Cassie Yates, Martha Scott, Jeremy Licht; D: Jerry London; M: Billy Goldenberg. VHS, Beta NO *½

Father Goose During WWII, a liquor-loving plane-spotter stationed on a remote Pacific isle finds himself stuck with a group of French refugee schoolgirls and their teacher. Some predictable gags, romance, and heroism fill out the running time pleasantly.

Scriptwriters Stone and Tarloff, who were competitors, not collaborators on the project, shared an Oscar.
1964 116m/C Cary Grant, Leslie Caron, Trevor Howard; **D:** Ralph Nelson; **W:** Peter Stone, Frank Tarloff; **M:** Cy Coleman. Academy Awards '64: Best Story & Screenplay; Nominations: Best Film Editing, Best Sound. **VHS $14.98** REP ♫♫½

Father Hood Family drama has Swayze playing a small-time criminal whose daughter tracks him down after leaving the foster-care shelter where she and her brother are being abused. The family takes to the road, running from both the police and a journalist (Berry) who wants to expose the corrupt foster-care system. The children are obnoxious, Swayze is miscast, and the entire film is a misfire.
1993 (PG-13) 94m/C Patrick Swayze, Halle Berry, Sabrina Lloyd, Brian Bonsall, Diane Ladd, Michael Ironside, Bob Gunton; **D:** Darrell Roodt; **W:** Scott Spencer. **VHS** BVV ♫

Father of the Bride A classic, quietly hilarious comedy about the tribulations of a father preparing for his only daughter's wedding. Tracy is suitably overwhelmed as the loving father and Taylor radiant as the bride. A warm vision of American family life, accompanied by the 1940 MGM short "Wedding Bills." Also available in a colorized version. Followed by "Father's Little Dividend" and later a television series. Remade in 1991.
1950 94m/C Spencer Tracy, Elizabeth Taylor, Joan Bennett, Billie Burke, Leo G. Carroll, Russ Tamblyn, Don Taylor, Moroni Olsen; **D:** Vincente Minnelli; **W:** Francis Goodrich, Albert Hacket. **VHS, Beta $19.98** MGM ♫♫♫½

Father of the Bride Remake of the 1950 comedy classic portrays one of the most overextravagant weddings in recent film history, but falls short of the original. Predictable plot and characters don't hide any surprises, but nothing detracts from the purpose of the film: to be a nice, charming movie. Martin is fine as the reluctant dad but Keaton is little more than window dressing as the bride's mom; Short is annoying as the pretentious wedding coordinator. Williams pulls off a nice film debut—and was almost immediately cast in a TV ad as a young-bride-to-be calling her dad long distance to tell him she's engaged. Adapted from a novel by Edward Streeter.
1991 (PG) 105m/C Steve Martin, Diane Keaton, Kimberly Williams, Kieran Culkin, George Newbern, Martin Short, B.D. Wong, Peter Michael Goetz, Kate McGregor Stewart, Martha Gehman; **Cameos:** Eugene Levy; **D:** Charles Shyer; **W:** Charles Shyer, Nancy Meyer; **M:** Alan Silvestri. **VHS, Beta $94.95** TOU ♫♫½

Fathers and Sons Max is a brooding, former bad-boy movie director living on the Jersey Shore. His wife's death causes him to rethink his life and deal with his drinking problem. He also tries to get to know his equally brooding teenage son, Ed. Turns out addiction may run in the family as Ed experiments with drugs. Ill-fitting subplot deals a serial killer stalking the community. Goldblum brings an uneasy gentleness to the father's role in an otherwise slow, talky, and obviously symbolic flick.
1992 (R) 100m/C Jeff Goldblum, Rory Cochrane, Mitchell Marchand, Famke Janssen, Natasha Gregson Wagner, Ellen Greene, Samuel L. Jackson, Joie Lee, Rosanna Arquette, Michael Disend; **D:** Paul Mones; **W:** Paul Mones; **M:** Mason Daring. **VHS** COL ♫½

Father's Little Dividend Tracy expects a little peace and quiet now that he's successfully married off Taylor in this charming sequel to "Father of the Bride." However, he's quickly disillusioned by the news he'll soon be a grandfather - a prospect that

causes nothing but dismay. Reunited the stars, director, writers, and producer from the successful first film.
1951 82m/B Spencer Tracy, Joan Bennett, Elizabeth Taylor, Don Taylor, Billie Burke, Russ Tamblyn, Moroni Olsen; **D:** Vincente Minnelli; **W:** Francis Goodrich, Albert Hacket. **VHS, Beta $9.95** CNG, MRV, NOS ♫♫♫

A Father's Revenge Dennehy is the only reason to bother with this average hostage drama. He's the father of a stewardess who's one of a group being held by terrorists. They're scheduled to die in 72 hours unless Dennehy can find a way to rescue them. Made for television.
1988 (R) 93m/C Brian Dennehy, Joanna Cassidy, Ron Silver; **D:** John Herzfeld; **M:** Klaus Doldinger. **VHS $89.95** VMK ♫♫½

Fatso After the shocking death of his obese cousin, an obsessive overeater struggles to overcome his neurosis with the aid of his sister and a self-help group called "Chubby Checkers." Bancroft's first work as both writer and director.
1980 (PG) 93m/C Dom DeLuise, Anne Bancroft, Ron Carey, Candice Azzara; **D:** Anne Bancroft; **W:** Anne Bancroft. **VHS, Beta $14.98** FOX ♫½

Fatty and Mabel Adrift/Mabel, Fatty and the Law Fatty and Mabel have problems enjoying their wedded bliss in these two silent shorts, which have a newly recorded orchestral score on the soundtrack.
1916 40m/B Fatty Arbuckle, Mabel Normand, Al "Fuzzy" St. John, Minta Durfee, Teddy the Dog. **VHS, Beta $19.98** CCB, GVV ♫½

Fatty Finn A children's gagfest about young kids and bullies during the Depression, based on Syd Nicholls' comic strip.
1984 91m/C AU Ben Oxenbould, Bart Newton; **D:** Maurice Murphy. **VHS, Beta** NO ♫½

Faust The classic German silent based upon the legend of Faust, who sells his soul to the devil in exchange for youth. Based on Goethe's poem, and directed by Murnau as a classic example of Germanic expressionism. Remade as "All That Money Can Buy" in 1941.
1926 117m/B GE Emil Jannings, Warner Fuetterer, Gosta Ekman, Camilla Horn; **D:** F.W. Murnau. **VHS, Beta $19.95** GPV, MRV, NOS ♫♫♫½

Faust Joan Sutherland introduces the opera based on Goethe's dramatic poem telling of a man who makes a pact with the devil. Some of the most beautiful moments in French opera are presented. Puppet characters help explain the story and make it accessible to youngsters.
1973 30m/C Joan Sutherland. **VHS, Beta** BFA ♫♫♫½

The Favor Lighthearted romance rife with comic confusion, vivid fantasies, secrets, and the all-important favor. Kathy (Kozak) seeks to relieve the boredom of her marriage through best friend Emily's (McGovern) tryst with Kathy's old beau, Tom. Or so she thinks, until Em spills all the juicy details. In a change of pace, the males take a back seat to the women. Good comic performances from Kozak and McGovern and witty dialogue help overcome the plot's sheer silliness. Damian Elwes (actor Cary's brother) provided Pitt's paintings. Theatrical release was delayed three years due to financial crisis at Orion Pictures.
1994 (R) 97m/C Harley Jane Kozak, Elizabeth McGovern, Bill Pullman, Brad Pitt, Ken Wahl, Larry Miller, Holland Taylor; **D:** Donald Petrie; **W:** Josann McGibbon, Sara Parriott; **M:** Thomas Newman. **VHS** NYR ♫♫½

The Favor, the Watch, & the Very Big Fish Set in a fairytale version of Paris. Hoskins is a photographer of religious subjects searching for a man to pose as Jesus. He discovers his subject in the hirsute Goldblum, a mad bar pianist who actually thinks he's the savior. Richardson plays the object of Hoskin's shy affections, an actress who does dubbing work by providing the moaning and groaning for porno flicks. Messy attempt at screwball-comedy with some brief humorous moments.
1992 (R) 89m/C GB FR Bob Hoskins, Jeff Goldblum, Natasha Richardson, Michel Blanc, Jacques Villeret, Angela Pleasence, Jean-Pierre Cassel, Bruce Altman; **D:** Ben Lewin; **W:** Ben Lewin; **M:** Vladimir Cosma. **VHS $92.95** VMK, FCT ♫

Fawlty Towers Cleese stars as the most obnoxious and inept hotel proprietor on earth in these three comedy episodes from the BBC series: "A Touch of Class," "Hotel Inspectors," and "The Germans," (which features Cleese's extraordinary goose-stepping). Additional episodes available.
1977 90m/C GB John Cleese, Prunella Scales, Connie Booth, Andrew Sachs; **W:** John Cleese, Connie Booth. **VHS $19.98** FOX, MOV, SIG ♫♫

FBI Girl An FBI clerk is used as bait to trap a murderer and break up a gang. Burr, pre-Perry Mason, plays a bad guy.
1952 74m/C Cesar Romero, George Brent, Audrey Totter, Raymond Burr, Tom Drake; **D:** William Berke. **VHS, Beta** RXM ♫♫

The FBI Murders A fact-based chiller about the bloody 1986 shootout between Miami FBI agents and a pair of violent killers (Soul and Gross playing against type). This made for television drama was shown on TV as "In the Line of Duty: The FBI Murders."
1988 95m/C David Soul, Michael Gross, Ronny Cox, Bruce Greenwood, Doug Sheehan, Teri Copley; **D:** Dick Lowry; **W:** Tracy Keenan Wynn. **VHS $79.95** CAF ♫♫♫

The FBI Story Mr. Stewart goes to Washington in this anatomy of the Federal Bureau of Investigation. If you're a fan of the gangster genre (LeRoy earlier directed "Little Caesar"), and not especially persnickety about fidelity to the facts, this actioner offers a pseudo-factual (read fictional) glimpse—based on actual cases from the 1920s through the 1950s—into the life of a fictitious agent-family man.
1959 149m/C James Stewart, Vera Miles, Nick Adams, Murray Hamilton, Larry Pennell; **D:** Mervyn LeRoy. **VHS $19.98** WAR, FCT, CCB ♫♫♫

Fear An impoverished medical student murders the professor he believes is tormenting him and his life suddenly gets better. He falls in love and gets a scholarship but the police are closing in on his crime. Except...did any of it really happen? Or is he suffering from hallucinations. Low-budget psycho-drama with some good paranoid moments.
1946 68m/B Peter Cookson, Warren William, Anne Gwynne, James B. Cardwell, Nestor Paiva; **D:** Alfred Zeisler. **VHS** VES ♫♫

Fear A vacationing family is plagued by a murderous Vietnam vet and other psychotic cons.
1988 (R) 96m/C Frank Stallone, Cliff DeYoung, Kay Lenz, Robert Factor; **D:** Robert A. Ferretti. **VHS, Beta** NO ♫

Fear A young psychic (Sheedy) delves into the minds of serial killers and writes novels about her experiences. But what happens when the next killer is also a psychic and decides to play mind-games with her? Above average suspense sustains this made-for-cable thriller.

1990 (R) 98m/C Ally Sheedy, Lauren Hutton, Michael O'Keefe, Stan Shaw, Dina Merrill, John Agar, Marta DuBois; **D:** Rockne S. O'Bannon; **M:** Henry Mancini. **VHS $89.98** VES ⅟₂⅟₂

Fear, Anxiety and Depression A neurotic aspiring playwright in New York has various problems with his love life. Sub-Woody Allen comedy attempt, with a few bright spots. The dregs of New York, with all the violence and degradation, are brought to the screen here.
1989 (R) 84m/C Todd Solondz, Stanley Tucci; **D:** Todd Solondz; **W:** Todd Solondz. **VHS, Beta** NO ⅟₂⅟₂

The Fear Chamber Hardly a Karloff vehicle. Boris shot the footage for this and three other Mexican "horror" films in LA, an unfortunate swan song to his career, though he was fortunate to be quickly written out of this story. The near plot concerns a mutant rock that thrives on human fear. Doctor Karloff and his assistants make sure the rock is rolling in sacrificial victims (women, of course). A prodigious devaluation of the "B"-grade horror flick, it's so bad it's just bad. **AKA:** Torture Zone; Chamber of Fear; La Camara Del Terror.
1968 88m/C MX Boris Karloff, Yerye Beirut, Julissa, Carlos East; **D:** Juan Ibanez, Jack Hill. **VHS $19.99** SNC, MPI Woof!

Fear City Two partners who own a talent agency are after the psychopath who is killing off their prized strippers with the aid of a local cop. Sleazy look at Manhattan low life.
1985 (R) 93m/C Billy Dee Williams, Tom Berenger, Jack Scalia, Melanie Griffith, Rae Dawn Chong, Joe Santos, Maria Conchita Alonso, Rossano Brazzi; **D:** Abel Ferrara; **W:** Nicholas St. John. **VHS, Beta** NO ⅟₂⅟₂

Fear in the City The Sicilian Mafia and a black crime gang battle for control of the streets.
1981 90m/C IT Michael Constantine, Fred Williamson, Gianni Manera; **D:** Gianni Manera. **VHS, Beta** NO ⅟₂

Fear in the Night Suspenseful tale of a murder committed by a man under hypnosis. Fearing his nightmares are real Kelley talks his detective friend into investigating his "crime", which leads them to a mansion, a mirrored room, and a plot that takes some clever and unexpected twists. Remade in 1956 as "Nightmare."
1947 72m/B Paul Kelly, DeForest Kelley, Ann Doran, Kay Scott, Robert Emmett Keane; **D:** Maxwell Shane. **VHS $59.99** SNC ⅟₂⅟₂⅟₂

The Fear Inside Lahti plays a woman suffering from agoraphobia who, because of her fear, has not left her home in more than a year. To help out, Lahti invites a seemingly charming college student to live with her. When the young woman's equally charming "brother" comes to visit, Lahti discovers the two aren't so charming after all. A standard woman-in-terror film with a better-than-average cast. Made for cable television.
1992 (R) 100m/C Christine Lahti, Jennifer Rubin, Dylan McDermott, David Ackroyd, Thomas Ian Nicholas, Paul Linke, Leon Ichaso. **VHS, Beta $89.98** FXV, VTR ⅟₂⅟₂⅟₂

Fear No Evil A teenager who is the human embodiment of the demon Lucifer commits acts of demonic murder and destruction. His powers are challenged by an 18-year-old girl, who is the embodiment of the archangel Gabriel. First feature from La Loggia is better than it sounds.
1980 (R) 90m/C Stefan Arngrim, Kathleen Rowe McAllen, Elizabeth Hoffman; **D:** Frank Laloggia; **W:** Frank Laloggia. **VHS, Beta $9.95** COL, SUE ⅟₂⅟₂

Fear Strikes Out Perkins plays Jimmy Piersall, star outfielder for the Boston Red Sox, and Malden, his demanding father, in the true story of the baseball star's battle for sanity. One of Perkins' best screen performances.
1957 100m/B Anthony Perkins, Karl Malden, Norma Moore, Adam Williams, Perry Wilson; **D:** Robert Mulligan; **M:** Elmer Bernstein. **VHS, Beta $14.95** PAR ⅟₂⅟₂⅟₂

Fearless An Italian detective has found a Viennese banker's daughter, but continues to pursue the unanswered questions of the case, embroiling himself in a web of intrigue and plotting.
1978 89m/C Joan Collins, Maurizio Merli, Franz Antel. **VHS, Beta $19.95** NWV ⅟₂

Fearless Two plane crash survivors reach out to each other as they try and cope with everday life. Bridges is riveting as the transformed Max, and Perez compelling as the sorrowful Carla. Hulce provides dead-on amusement as a casualty lawyer who knows he's slime but can't help himself. Opening sequences of smoke in the corn fields are haunting as are flashbacks of the crash itself. Weir provides an engrossing look at facing death, both psychological and spiritual, but the ending is something of a letdown in its sappiness. Based on the novel by Yglesias.
1993 (R) 122m/C Jeff Bridges, Isabella Rossellini, Rosie Perez, Tom Hulce, John Turturro, Benicio Del Toro, Deidre O'Connell, John de Lancie; **D:** Peter Weir; **W:** Rafael Yglesias; **M:** Maurice Jarre. Academy Awards '94 Nominations: Best Supporting Actress (Perez); Golden Globe Awards '94: Best Supporting Actress (Perez); Los Angeles Film Critics Association Awards '93: Best Supporting Actress (Perez). **VHS, Beta** WAR ⅟₂⅟₂⅟₂

Fearless Tiger Martial arts action flick includes the usual combination of fierce swordplay, hand-to-hand showdowns, and the intrigue of exotic locations.
1994 (R) ?m/C Bolo Yeung, Monika Schnarre, Jamie Farr, Jalal Merhi; **D:** Ron Hulme; **W:** Ron Hulme; **M:** Varouje. **VHS $92.95** IMP ⅟₂⅟₂

The Fearless Vampire Killers Underrated, off-off-beat, and deliberately campy spoof of vampire films in which Tate is kidnapped by some fangy villains. Vampire trackers MacGowran and Polanski pursue the villains to the haunted castle and attempt the rescue. Only vampire movie with a Jewish bloodsucker ("Boy, have you got the wrong vampire," he proclaims to a maiden thrusting a crucifix at him). Inside the castle, Polanski is chased by the count's gay vampire son. Highlight is the vampire ball with a wonderful mirror scene. Many other amusing moments. **AKA:** Pardon Me, Your Teeth are in My Neck; Dance of the Vampires.
1967 98m/C GB Jack MacGowran, Roman Polanski, Alfie Bass, Jessie Robbins, Sharon Tate, Ferdinand "Ferdy" Mayne, Iain Quarrier; **D:** Roman Polanski; **W:** Roman Polanski, Gerard Brach. **VHS, Beta $19.98** MGM ⅟₂⅟₂⅟₂

Fearmaker After the mysterious death of her father, the heiress to his fortune is tangled in a web of treachery created by other potential inheritors. **AKA:** House of Fear; Violent Rage.
1989 (PG) 90m/C MX Katy Jurado, Paul Picerni, Sonia Amelio, Carlos East; **D:** Anthony Carras. **VHS, Beta $59.95** PSM ⅟₂⅟₂⅟₂

Feast for the Devil A woman searches for her missing sister in a mysterious coastal village, only to fall under the occult spell of a mad doctor.
197? 90m/C Krista Nell, Teresa Gimpera. **VHS, Beta** NO ⅟₂⅟₂

Federal Agent Lots of cliches fill this crime film about a federal agent chasing foreign spys who are looking for a new explosive.
1936 53m/B William Boyd, Charles A. Browne, Irene Ware, George Cooper, Lentia Lace, Dan Alvarado; **D:** Sam Newfield. **VHS, Beta $8.95** GPV ⅟₂⅟₂

Federal Agents vs. Underworld, Inc. Super G-Man Dave Worth goes up against Nila, a greedy villainess bent on finding the golden hands of Kurigal so she may rule the world. A 12-episode serial edited onto two cassettes. **AKA:** Golden Hands of Kurigal.
1949 167m/B Kirk Alyn, Rosemary La Planche, Roy Barcroft, Carol Forman, James Dale, Bruce Edwards; **D:** Fred Brannon. **VHS $29.98** REP, MLB ⅟₂⅟₂

Federal Operator 99 A fortune in stolen jewels, a chemical plant, and a priceless violin all figure in this 12 chapter serial. And it's up to Jerry Blake, Federal Operator 99, to save the day. Part of "The Cliffhanger Serials" series.
1945 169m/B Marten Lamont, Helen Talbot, George Lewis. **VHS $29.98** REP, MOV ⅟₂⅟₂⅟₂

Feds Two women enter the FBI Academy and take on the system's inherent sexism with feebly comic results.
1988 (PG-13) 82m/C Rebecca DeMornay, Mary Gross, Ken Marshall, Fred Dalton Thompson, Larry Cedar, James Luisi, Raymond Singer; **D:** Dan Goldberg; **W:** Dan Goldberg, Len Blum; **M:** Randy Edelman. **VHS, Beta** WAR ⅟₂⅟₂

Feel My Pulse Silent comedy about a rich fanatic who leaves everything in his will to his young niece on the stipulation that she lead a germ-free life; when she reaches 21, she moves into the sanitarium she's inherited, not knowing it has become a base for prohibition-era rum runners.
1928 86m/B Bebe Daniels, Richard Arlen, William Powell; **D:** Gregory La Cava. **VHS, Beta $24.95** VYY ⅟₂⅟₂

Feel the Motion A female auto-mechanic wants to make it big in the music biz. She sees her chance when she slips her demo tape onto a hit TV-music show.
1986 98m/C Sissy Kelling, Frank Meyer-Brockman, Ingold Locke, Falco, Meatloaf. **VHS, Beta $69.95** VMK ⅟₂

Feelin' Screwy A couple of misfit dweebs attempt to rid their town of the local drug dealer in order to impress a couple of babes in this limp coming-of-ager.
1990 90m/C Quincy Reynolds, Larry Gamal, Darin McBride, Hassan Jamal, Marsha Carter, Brooks Morales, Anna Fuentes; **D:** Riffat A. Khan; **W:** Riffat A. Khan. **VHS** NO ⅟₂

Feelin' Up A young man sells all his possessions to come to New York in search of erotic adventures.
1976 (R) 84m/C Malcolm Groome, Kathleen Seward, Rhonda Hansome, Tony Collado, Charles Douglass; **D:** David Secter. **VHS, Beta $69.95** LIV, VES Woof!

Feet First A shoe salesman puts on "upper crust" airs as he begins a shipboard romance with a girl who thinks he's wealthy. Lloyd's second sound film shows him grappling with technique and has scenes that recall highlights of his silent hits.
1930 85m/B Harold Lloyd, Barbara Kent, Robert McWade; **D:** Clyde Bruckman. **VHS, Beta** TLF ⅟₂⅟₂

Feet Foremost A made-for-British-television horror story about an industrialist haunted by the spirit of a teenage girl.
1985 60m/C GB Jeremy Kemp. **VHS, Beta $59.95** PSM ⅟₂⅟₂

Felix the Cat: The Movie Classic cartoon creation Felix returns in a trite feature. The feline and his bag of tricks enter a dimension filled with He-Man/Mutant Ninja Turtles leftovers; new-age princess, comic reptiles, robots and a Darth Vader clone who's defeated with ridiculous ease. Strictly for undemanding kids.
1991 83m/C VHS, Beta $19.99 BVV, FCT, WTA ♢♢½

Fellini Satyricon Fellini's famous, garish, indulgent pastiche vision of ancient Rome, based on the novel "Satyricon" by Petronius, follows the adventures of two young men through the decadences of Nero's reign. Actually an exposition on the excesses of the 1960s, with the actors having little to do other than look good and react to any number of sexual situations. Crammed with excesses of every variety. In Italian with English subtitles. Also available on laserdisc with additional footage and letterboxing. AKA: Satyricon.
1969 (R) 129m/C IT Martin Potter, Capucine, Hiram Keller, Salvo Randone, Max Born; D: Federico Fellini; W: Federico Fellini. VHS, Beta $19.98 MGM, VYG, FCT ♢♢♢

Fellini's Roma Fellini reviews his youth in this stream-of-consciousness homage to Rome and Italy. Best left for fervent Fellini fans. AKA: Roma.
1972 (R) 128m/C FR IT Peter Gonzales, Britta Barnes, Pia de Doses, Fiona Florence, Marne Maitland, Renato Giovannoli; D: Federico Fellini; W: Federico Fellini; V: Federico Fellini. VHS, Beta $19.98 MGM, FCT, APD ♢♢½

Fellow Traveler Two old friends, an actor and a screenwriter, both successful, get blacklisted for reputed Communist leanings in 1950s Hollywood. Good performances and a literate script. Made for cable television.
1989 97m/C Ron Silver, Hart Bochner, Daniel J. Travanti, Imogen Stubbs, Katherine Borowitz, Jonathan Hyde; D: Philip Saville. VHS, Beta $89.95 PAR ♢♢♢

Female Feminist look at life in the 30's stars Chatterton as the wealthy president of an auto factory who wines and dines the office men and then gives them the strictly business line the next day. However, she finally meets her match when Brent walks through the door. (The two stars were a real-life married couple at the time.) Funny, role-reversal story directed by Curtiz of "Casablanca" fame. Based on a story by Donald Henderson Clark.
1933 60m/B Ruth Chatterton, George Brent, Philip Reed, Ruth Donnelly, Johnny Mack Brown, Lois Wilson, Gavin Gordon, Ferdinand Gottschalk; D: Michael Curtiz, William Dieterle; W: Gene Markey, Kathryn Scola. VHS $19.98 MGM ♢♢½

The Female Bunch The man-free world of an all-woman settlement is shattered by the arrival of a handsome stranger. Some of this garbage was filmed on location at the notorious Charles Manson ranch, and that's the least of its flaws.
1969 (R) 86m/C Jennifer Bishop, Russ Tamblyn, Lon Chaney Jr., Nesa Renet, Geoffrey Land, Regina Carrol; D: Al Adamson, John Cardos. VHS $16.95 SNC Woof!

The Female Jungle Below-average whocares whodunnit directed by Roger Corman stock-company actor Ve Sota. Police sergeant Tierney is caught between a rock and a hard place. The prime suspect in a murder case, Tierney discovers a series of clues that implicate his friend Carradine. Interesting only for the screen debut of the nympho-typecast Miss Jayne—of whom

Bette Davis said "Dramatic art in her opinion is knowing how to fill a sweater." AKA: The Hangover.
1956 56m/B Lawrence Tierney, John Carradine, Jayne Mansfield, Burt Kaiser, Kathleen Crowley, James Kodl, Rex Thorson, Jack Hill; D: Bruno Ve Sota. VHS $9.95 COL, FCT ♢

Female Trouble Divine leads a troublesome existence in this $25,000 picture. She turns to a life of crime and decadence, seeking to live out her philosophy: "Crime is beauty." Look closely at the Divine rape scene where she plays both rapist and victim. Climax of her deviant ways comes with her unusual night club act, for which the law shows no mercy. Trashy, campy; for die-hard Waters fans.
1974 (R) 95m/C Divine, David Lochary, Mary Vivian Pearce, Mink Stole, Edith Massey, Danny Mills, Cookie Mueller, Susan Walsh; D: John Waters; W: John Waters. VHS, Beta NO ♢♢½

Femme Fatale When a man's new bride disappears he teams up with an artist pal to track her down. Their search reveals her secret double life and takes them to L.A.'s avant-garde art scene—and deeper into deception and mystery. Billy Zane (Elijah) and Lisa Zane are brother and sister. AKA: Fatal Woman.
1990 (R) 96m/C Colin Firth, Lisa Zane, Billy Zane, Scott Wilson, Lisa Blount; D: Andre Guttfreund. VHS $89.98 REP ♢♢½

Femmes de Paris A funny and risque French musical comedy about the comings and goings of the cast of a naughty nightclub shows. In French with English subtitles.
1953 79m/C FR Robert Dhery, Collette Brosset, Louis de Funes, Bluebell Girls. VHS, Beta $29.95 VDM, TPV ♢♢

Fer-De-Lance A stricken submarine is trapped at the bottom of the sea, with a nest of deadly snakes crawling through the ship. Made for television. AKA: Operation Serpent.
1974 120m/C David Janssen, Hope Lange, Ivan Dixon, Jason Evers; D: Russ Mayberry. VHS, Beta $49.95 WOV ♢½

Fergie & Andrew: Behind Palace Doors More soap-opera from the British royals in this tale of feisty redhead, Sarah Ferguson, and the neglectful Prince Andrew. He's away a lot, she's bored by all the palace propriety and causes too many scandals, and their marriage falls apart. Made for television.
1993 92m/C Pippa Hinchley, Sam Miller, Peter Cellier, Harold Innocent, Edita Brychta; D: Michael Switzer. VHS, Beta $89.98 TTC ♢♢

Fernandel the Dressmaker Fernandel dreams of designing exquisite dresses, but when the opportunity arises, he finds his cheating partners get in the way. In French with English subtitles.
1957 95m/B FR Fernandel, Suzy Delair, Francoise Fabian, Georges Chamarat; D: Jean Boyer. VHS, Beta, 8mm $24.95 VYY, FCT ♢♢½

Ferngully: The Last Rain Forest Animated eco-musical follows the adventures of independent-minded flying sprite Crysta, who lives in a rain forest beset by pollution. She discovers the outside world and becomes smitten with the human Zak, who is helping to cut down the forest. Crysta decides to reduce him to her size and show him the error of his ways. She's aided by fellow sprite, Pips, and a crazy bat (Batty Koda with a voice provided by the lively Williams). So-so script with politically pristine environmental message may grow tiresome for both adults and children, though decent animation and brilliant coloring enlivens the tale.

1992 (G) 72m/C D: Bill Kroyer; M: Alan Silvestri; V: Samantha Mathis, Christian Slater, Robin Williams, Tim Curry, Jonathan Ward, Grace Zabriskie, Richard "Cheech" Marin, Thomas Chong, Tone Loc, Jim Cox. VHS $24.98 FXV, MLT ♢♢½

Ferocious Female Freedom Fighters A typical foreign-made action flick with female wrestlers is spoofed by the L.A. Connection comedy troupe which did the totally ridiculous dubbed dialog.
1988 90m/C Eva Arnaz, Barry Prima. VHS, Beta MED, IME ♢

Ferris Bueller's Day Off It's almost graduation and if Ferris can get away with just one more sick day—it had better be a good one. He sweet talks his best friend into borrowing his dad's antique Ferrari and sneaks his girlfriend out of school to spend a day in Chicago. Their escapades lead to fun, adventure, and almost getting caught. Broderick is charismatic as the notorious Bueller with Grey amusing as his tattle-tale sister doing everything she can to see him get caught. Early Sheen appearance as a juvenile delinquent who pesters Grey. Led to TV series. One of Hughes' more solid efforts.
1986 (PG-13) 103m/C Matthew Broderick, Mia Sara, Alan Ruck, Jeffrey Jones, Jennifer Grey, Cindy Pickett, Edie McClurg, Charlie Sheen, Del Close, Virginia Capers, Max Perlich, Louis Anderson; D: John Hughes; W: John Hughes; M: Ira Newborn. VHS, Beta, 8mm $14.95 PAR, TLF ♢♢♢

Ferry to Hong Kong World-weary, heavy drinking traveler comes aboard the "Fat Annie," a ship skippered by the pompous Captain Hart. The two men clash, until an act of heroism brings them together. Embarrassingly hammy performance by Welles as the ferry skipper.
1959 103m/C Curt Jurgens, Orson Welles, Sylvia Syms; D: Lewis Gilbert. VHS $9.95 SUE ♢½

The Feud A wacky comedy about the ultimate "family feud." The Bullards of Millville and the Bealers of Hornbeck engage in a battle of the witless, and no one in either town is safe. A silly, irreverent comedy of the slapstick variety. Based on a novel by Thomas Berger.
1990 (R) 87m/C Rene Auberjonois, Ron McLarty, Joe Grifasi, David Strathairn, Gale Mayron; D: Bill D'Elia. VHS $89.95 VMK ♢♢

Feud Maker Steele rides to the rescue in this range war between the bad guys and the cowmen. Hackett plays a schemer who falsely befriends both sides, plotting to buy up cheap land when the participants have killed each other off. Based on a story by Harry F. Olmsted.
1938 55m/B Bob Steele, Marion Weldon, Karl Hackett, Frank Ball, Budd Buster, Lew Meehan, Roger Williams; D: Sam Newfield; W: George Plympton. VHS $19.99 MOV ♢½

Feud of the Trail A cowboy saves a range family's gold and falls in love with their daughter in the process. Tyler plays both the hero and the villain here.
1937 56m/B Tom Tyler, Harlin Wood, Guinn Williams; D: Robert F. Hill. VHS, Beta $19.95 NOS, DVT ♢

Feud of the West Old West disagreements settled with guns in this outing for cowboy star Gibson, here portraying a rodeo performer.
1935 60m/B Hoot Gibson, Buzz Barton, Robert F. (Bob) Kortman, Edward Cassidy, Joan Barclay, Nelson McDowell, Reed Howes, Lew Meehan; D: Harry Fraser. VHS, Beta $19.95 NOS, VCI, VCN ♢½

Fever Controversial Polish film based on Andrzej Strug's novel "The Story of One Bomb." Focusing on a period in Polish history marked by anarchy, violence, resistance, and revolution, it was banned before it won eventual acclaim at the Gdansk Film Festival. In Polish with English subtitles. **1981** 115m/C **PL D:** Agnieszka Holland. **VHS** $49.95 FCT 𝄢𝄢𝄢

Fever A once-honest cop trades his good life in for a shot at dealing drugs. Meanwhile, his wife's lover wants to murder him. **1988 (R)** 83m/C Bill Hunter, Gary Sweet, Mary Regan, Jim Holt; **D:** Craig Lahiff. **VHS, Beta** $14.95 ACA 𝄢

Fever An ex-con and a high-powered lawyer join forces to rescue the woman both of them love from a vicious killer. Made for cable television. Available in Spanish. **1991 (R)** 99m/C Armand Assante, Sam Neill, Marcia Gay Harden, Joe Spano; **D:** Larry Elikann. **VHS** $89.98 HBO 𝄢𝄢

Fever Mounts at El Pao A minor effort from director Bunuel about the regime of a dictator in an imaginary South American country. In Spanish with English subtitles. **AKA:** Los Ambiciosos. **1959** 97m/B **MX** Gerard Philippe, Jean Servais; **D:** Luis Bunuel. **VHS, Beta** $24.95 NOS, FCT, FST 𝄢𝄢½

Fever Pitch Sordid story of a sports writer (O'Neal) who becomes addicted to gambling. Very poor script. **1985 (R)** 95m/C Ryan O'Neal, Catherine Hicks, Giancarlo Giannini, Bridgette Anderson, Chad Everett, John Saxon, William Smith, Patrick Cassidy, Chad McQueen; **D:** Richard Brooks; **W:** Richard Brooks; **M:** Thomas Dolby. **VHS, Beta** $79.98 FOX Woof!

A Few Good Men Strong performances by Cruise and Nicholson carry this story of a peacetime military coverup. Cruise is a smart aleck Navy lawyer sleepwalking through his comfortable career in DC. He's ready to write off two soldiers pinned for the murder of their cohort until he interviews their commanding officer, Nicholson. Cruise smells a rat, but Nicholson practically dares him to prove it. Moore is another military lawyer assigned to the case, though her function seems to be holding Kaffee's hand (there's no actual romance between the two). Incredible fireworks between Cruise and Nicholson in the courtroom. Based on the play by Sorkin, who also wrote the screenplay. **1992 (R)** 138m/C Tom Cruise, Jack Nicholson, Demi Moore, Kevin Bacon, Kevin Pollak, Kiefer Sutherland, James Marshall, J.T. Walsh, Christopher Guest, J.A. Preston, Matt Craven, Wolfgang Bodison, Xander Berkeley, Cuba Gooding Jr.; **D:** Rob Reiner; **W:** Aaron Sorkin; **M:** Marc Shaiman. Academy Awards '92 Nominations: Best Film Editing, Best Picture, Best Sound, Best Supporting Actor (Nicholson); Chicago Film Critics Awards '93: Best Supporting Actor (Nicholson); MTV Movie Awards '93: Best Film; People's Choice Awards '93: Best Film, Best Film—Drama. **VHS, Beta, 8mm** $19.95 COL, CRC, MOV 𝄢𝄢𝄢½

A Few Moments with Buster Keaton and Laurel and Hardy Three short appearances: "The Tree in a Test Tube," a government film with Stan & Ollie about wood's role in the war effort; an episode of "The Ed Sullivan Show," with the duo, and a commercial for Simon Pure Beer featuring Keaton. **1963** 17m/B Stan Laurel, Oliver Hardy, Buster Keaton, Ed Sullivan, Pete Smith. **VHS, Beta, 8mm** $9.95 VYY 𝄢𝄢𝄢

ffolkes Rufus Excalibur Ffolkes is an eccentric underwater expert who is called upon to stop a madman (Perkins, indulging himself) from blowing up an oil rig in the North Sea. Entertaining farce with Moore playing the opposite of his usual suave James Bond character. **AKA:** Assault Force; North Sea Hijack. **1980 (PG)** 99m/C Roger Moore, James Mason, Anthony Perkins, David Hedison, Michael Parks; **D:** Andrew V. McLaglen. **VHS, Beta** $59.95 MCA 𝄢𝄢

Fiction Makers Roger Moore stars as Simon Templar, also known as "The Saint," a sophisticated detective who is hired to help Amos Klein. Klein turns out to be an alias for a beautiful novelist who is being threatened by the underworld crime ring. Based on the Leslie Chateris' character. **1967** 102m/C Roger Moore, Sylvia Syms. **VHS, Beta** FOX 𝄢𝄢

Fictitious Marriage Eldad Ilan, a high school teacher experiencing a mid-life crisis, travels to Israel to get away from his family in order to consider his life's direction. In Hebrew with English subtitles. **1988** 90m/C Shlomo Bar-Aba, Irit Sheleg, Ofra Veingarten; **D:** Haim Bouzaglo. **VHS** $79.95 ERG 𝄢𝄢

Fiddler on the Roof Based on the long-running Broadway musical. The poignant story of Tevye, a poor Jewish milkman at the turn of the century in a small Ukrainian village, and his five dowry-less daughters, his lame horse, his wife, and his companionable relationship with God. Topol, an Israeli who played the role in London, is charming, if not quite as wonderful as Zero Mostel, the Broadway star. Finely detailed set decoration and choreography, strong performances from the entire cast create a sense of intimacy in spite of near epic proportions of the production. Play was based on the Yiddish stories of Tevye the Dairyman, written by Sholem Aleichem. ♫ Tradition; Matchmaker, Matchmaker; If I Were a Rich Man; Sabbath Prayer; To Life; Miracle of Miracles; Tevye's Dream; Sunrise, Sunset; Wedding Celebration; Do You Love Me?; Far from the Home I Love; Chava Ballet; Anatevka. **1971 (G)** 184m/C Chaim Topol, Norma Crane, Leonard Frey, Molly Picon; **D:** Norman Jewison; **M:** John Williams. Academy Awards '71: Best Cinematography, Best Sound, Best Score; Nominations: Best Actor (Topol), Best Art Direction/Set Decoration, Best Director (Jewison), Best Picture, Best Supporting Actor (Frey); Golden Globe Awards '72: Best Actor—Musical/Comedy (Topol), Best Film—Musical/Comedy. **VHS, Beta** $29.97 FOX, MGM, TLF 𝄢𝄢𝄢½

The Fiddlin' Buckaroo Maynard plays a government agent who disguises himself as a musical ventriloquist to capture Kohler and his band of outlaws. Everybody sings a lot. **1933** 63m/B Ken Maynard, Gloria Shea, Fred Kohler Sr., Frank Rice, Jack Mower, Charles "Slim" Whitaker, Robert F. (Bob) Kortman, Hank Bell, Jack Rockwell; **D:** Ken Maynard; **W:** Nate Gatzert. **VHS** $11.95 GPV 𝄢½

The Field After an absence from the big screen, intense and nearly over the top Harris won acclaim as an iron-willed peasant fighting to retain a patch of Irish land he's tended all his life, now offered for sale to a wealthy American. His uncompromising stand divides the community in this glowing adaptation of John B. Keane's classic play, an allegory of Ireland's internal conflicts. **1990 (PG-13)** 113m/C **GB** Richard Harris, Tom Berenger, John Hurt, Sean Bean, Brenda Fricker, Frances Tomelty, Sean McGinley, Jenny Conroy; **D:** Jim Sheridan; **W:** Jim Sheridan. **VHS** $19.98 LIV, TVC 𝄢𝄢𝄢½

Field of Dreams Uplifting mythic fantasy based on W.P. Kinsella's novel "Shoeless Joe." Iowa corn farmer heeds a mysterious voice that instructs "If you build it, he will come" and cuts a baseball diamond in his corn field. Soon the ball field is inhabited by the spirit of Joe Jackson and others who were disgraced in the notorious 1919 "Black Sox" baseball scandal. Jones, as a character based on reclusive author J.D. Salinger, is reluctantly pulled into the mystery. It's all about chasing a dream, maintaining innocence, finding redemption, reconciling the child with the adult, and celebrating the mythic lure of baseball. Costner and Madigan are strong, believable characters. **1989 (PG)** 106m/C Kevin Costner, Amy Madigan, James Earl Jones, Burt Lancaster, Ray Liotta, Timothy Busfield, Frank Whaley, Gaby Hoffman; **D:** Phil Alden Robinson; **W:** Phil Alden Robinson; **M:** James Horner. **VHS, Beta** $19.95 MCA, FCT, HMV 𝄢𝄢𝄢½

Field of Fire One of America's top military experts has been taken hostage and it's up to a top general to rescue him. But the rescue doesn't come off as planned and all must fight their way through the Cambodian jungle to safety. **1992 (R)** 96m/C David Carradine; **D:** Cirio H. Santiago; **W:** Thomas McKelvey Cleaver. **VHS** $89.99 HBO 𝄢𝄢

Field of Honor A look at the harrowing experience of jungle combat through the eyes of a Dutch infantryman in Korea. **1986 (R)** 93m/C Everett McGill, Ron Bradsteder, Hey Young Lee; **D:** Hans Scheepmaker. **VHS, Beta** $19.98 MGM 𝄢𝄢½

Field of Honor A quiet French anti-war drama set during the Franco-Prussian war in 1869 in which a peasant boy volunteers to fight in place of a rich man's son. He is befriended behind enemy lines by a young boy and both try to avoid capture. In French with English subtitles. **AKA:** Champ d'Honneur. **1987 (PG)** 87m/C **FR** Cris Campion, Eric Wapler, Pascale Rocard, Frederic Mayer; **D:** Jean-Pierre Denis. **VHS, Beta** $19.98 ORI, ING 𝄢𝄢½

The Fiend A religious cultist, already unbalanced, grabs a knife and starts hacking away Jack-the-Ripper style. **1971 (R)** 87m/C **GB** Ann Todd, Patrick Magee, Tony Beckley, Madeline Hinde, Suzanna Leigh, Percy Herbert; **D:** Robert Hartford-Davis. **VHS, Beta** $39.95 MON 𝄢

Fiend Glowing supernatural thing flits around graveyard before animating dead guy who needs to kill in order to go on living. Murderous dead guy becomes a small-town music teacher feeding parasitically on his students to satisfy his supernatural hunger. His neighbor suspects some discord. Low-budget time waster. **1983** 93m/C Don Leifert, Richard Nelson, Elaine White, George Stover; **D:** Donald M. Dohler. **VHS, Beta** $49.95 PSM Woof!

Fiend Without a Face An isolated air base in Canada is the site for a scientist using atomic power in an experiment to make a person's thoughts materialize. Only his thoughts are evil and reveal themselves as flying brains with spinal cords that suck human brains right out of the skull. Tons of fun for fifties SF fans and anyone who appreciates the sheer silliness of it all.

1958 77m/B Marshall Thompson, Kim Parker, Terence Kilburn, Michael Balfour, Gil Winfield, Shane Cordell; *D:* Arthur Crabtree. VHS $19.98 *CCB, REP, MLB* ♂♂

The Fiendish Plot of Dr. Fu Manchu
A sad farewell from Sellers, who in his last film portrays Dr. Fu in his desperate quest for the necessary ingredients for his secret life-preserving formula. Sellers portrays both Dr. Fu and the Scotland Yard detective on his trail, but it's not enough to save this picture, flawed by poor script and lack of direction.
1980 (PG) 100m/C *GB* Peter Sellers, David Tomlinson, Sid Caesar, Helen Mirren; *D:* Piers Haggard. VHS, Beta $19.98 *WAR, FCT Woof!*

Fiesta
A girl comes from Mexico City to her father's hacienda where her old boyfriend awaits her return with a proposal of marriage. Full of authentic Mexican dances and music. ♫Fantasia Mexican; La Bamba; La Luna Enamorada; Miriano; Romeria Vasca.
1947 44m/C Anne Ayars, George Negrete, Armida; *D:* Richard Thorpe. VHS, Beta $19.95 *VYY, DVT* ♂♂

Fifth Avenue Girl
An unhappy millionaire brings home a poor young woman to pose as his mistress to make his family realize how they've neglected him. As this below-par social comedy drones toward its romantic conclusion, the rich folks see the error of their ways and love conquers all.
1939 83m/B Ginger Rogers, Walter Connolly, Tim Holt, James Ellison, Franklin Pangborn; *D:* Gregory La Cava. VHS, Beta $29.95 *RKO, IME, TTC* ♂½

Fifth Day of Peace
In the aftermath of the WWI armistice, two German soldiers are tried and executed for desertion by their commander, even though the Allies forbade German military trials. An interesting plot that is marred by too obvious plot twists. Based on a true story.
1972 (PG) 95m/C *IT* Richard Johnson, Franco Nero, Larry Aubrey, Helmut Schneider; *D:* Guiliano Montaldo. VHS, Beta $19.95 *PSM* ♂♂

The Fifth Floor
College disco dancer overdoses on drugs and winds up in an insane asylum, complete with menacing attendant Hopkins and apathetic doctor Ferrer. Pathetic, exploitative trash.
1980 (R) 90m/C Bo Hopkins, Dianne Hull, Patti D'Arbanville, Mel Ferrer; *D:* Howard (Hikmet) Avedis; *W:* Howard (Hikmet) Avedis. VHS, Beta $59.95 *MED Woof!*

The Fifth Monkey
A man embarks on a journey to sell four monkeys in order to fill a dowry for his bride, but along the way he encounters all sorts of obstacles and adventures. Filmed on location in Brazil
1990 (PG-13) 93m/C Ben Kingsley; *D:* Eric Rochant; *W:* Eric Rochant. VHS $89.98 *COL, FCT* ♂½

The Fifth Musketeer
A campy adaptation of Dumas's "The Man in the Iron Mask," wherein a monarch's evil twin impersonates him while imprisoning the true king. A good cast and rich production shot in Austria make for a fairly entertaining swashbuckler. *AKA:* Behind the Iron Mask.
1979 (PG) 90m/C *GB* Beau Bridges, Sylvia Kristel, Ursula Andress, Cornel Wilde, Ian McShane, Alan Hale Jr., Helmut Dantine, Olivia de Havilland, Jose Ferrer, Rex Harrison, Helmut Dantine; *D:* Ken Annakin; *W:* David Ambrose. Beta $19.95 *COL* ♂♂

The Fifth Seal
A group of friends are arrested when one makes a casual remark that offends a commandant. This leads to a series of tasks that test their commitment to their moral ideals. Set at the close of WWII in Hungary. In Hungarian with English subtitles.
1976 116m/C *HU D:* Zoltan Fabri. VHS $59.95 *FCT* ♂♂

Fifty/Fifty
Jake and Frenchie are a couple of mercenaries forced by the CIA not only to work together but with a bunch of incompetent guerillas to overthrow a Southeast Asian dictator. Weller handles the violence, Hays handles the comedy, and both get chased a lot.
1993 (R) 101m/C Robert Hays, Peter Weller, Ramona Rahman, Charles Martin Smith; *D:* Charles Martin Smith; *W:* Dennis Shryack, Michael Butler; *M:* Peter Bernstein. VHS $19.98 *WAR, CAN* ♂♂

$50,000 Reward
Maynard's first western finds him being victimized by an unscrupulous banker who wants Maynard's land deeds for property on which a new dam is being built.
1925 49m/B Ken Maynard, Esther Ralston. VHS, Beta $14.95 *GPV, CCB, HEG* ♂½

52 Pick-Up
After a fling, a wealthy industrialist is blackmailed by a trio of repulsive criminals and determines to save himself. First he becomes deeply caught in their web of murder. Based on an Elmore Leonard novel with lots of gruesome violence and good performances.
1986 (R) 111m/C Roy Scheider, Ann-Margret, Vanity, John Glover, Doug McClure, Clarence Williams III, Kelly Preston, Robert Trebor, Loni Chapman; *D:* John Frankenheimer; *W:* John Steppling, Elmore Leonard; *M:* Gary Chang. VHS, Beta $19.95 *MED, VTR* ♂♂½

55 Days at Peking
A costume epic depicting the Chinese Boxer Rebellion and the fate of military Britishers caught in the midst of the chaos. Standard fare superbly handled by director Ray and an all-star cast.
1963 150m/C Charlton Heston, Ava Gardner, David Niven, John Ireland, Flora Robson, Paul Lukas, Jacques Sernas; *D:* Nicholas Ray; *W:* Philip Yordan. VHS, Beta $29.95 *BFV, VCI, KAR* ♂♂♂

The Fig Tree
After her mother passes away, Miranda becomes tormented by the fear of death. Now her aunt must help her cope with this difficult part of life. Adapted from the short story by Katherine Anne Porter. Aired on PBS as part of the "Wonderworks" family movie series.
1987 58m/C Olivia Cole, William Converse-Roberts, Doris Roberts, Teresa Wright, Karron Graves; *D:* Calvin Skaggs. VHS $14.95 *PME, FCT, BTV* ♂♂♂

Fight for Gold
In the frozen wastes of the North, a man becomes embroiled in a violent quest for gold.
1986 107m/C *GE* Doug McClure, Harald Leipnitz, Heinz Reinl, Roberto Bianco, Angelica Ott, Kristina Nel; *D:* Harald Reinl. VHS $14.95 *ACA* ♂

A Fight for Jenny
Miami Viceroy Thomas and Warren play an interracial couple who fight for custody of the wife's child from a previous marriage. Standard madefor-TV meaningful drama (bite-sized issues served with a modicum of melodrama).
1990 (PG) 95m/C Philip Michael Thomas, Lesley Ann Warren, Jean Smart, Lynne Moody, William Atherton; *D:* Gilbert Moses. VHS $79.95 *PSM* ♂♂

Fight for Survival
Young female aspirant of kung fu must recover sacred books that were stolen by disguised kung fu masters.
1977 (R) 101m/C Shangkuan Ling-Feng. VHS, Beta *FOX* ♂½

Fight for the Title
Benny Leonard's reign as the lightweight boxing champ has just begun when WWII is declared. Against his manager's wishes, Benny decides to enlist.
1957 30m/C Michael Landon, George Brenlin; *D:* Eric Kenton. VHS $14.95 *FCT, RHI* ♂♂

Fight for Us
A social activist, recently released from prison, takes on the death squads terrorizing the countryside in post-Marcos Philippines. In Spanish with English subtitles. *AKA:* L'Insoumis.
1989 92m/C Phillip Salvador, Dina Bonnevie, Gina Alajar, Benbol Roco. VHS, Beta $59.95 *NO* ♂♂½

Fight for Your Life
Three escaped convicts—a white bigot, an Asian, and a Chicano—take a black minister's family hostage. After suffering all manner of vicious torture, the family exacts an equally brutal revenge. Shades of "The Desperate Hours" and "Extremities," but with much more graphic violence and a racial twist.
1979 89m/C *CA* William Sanderson, Robert Judd, Lela Small. VHS, Beta $59.95 *MON* ♂

Fight to the Death
An evil businessman hires a group of deadly assassins to assist with the Japanese invasion of China at the start of WWII. Includes self-defense tips segment.
1983 100m/C Chang Li, Ron Van Cliff. VHS *NO* ♂

The Fighter
A Mexican patriot, involved in a struggle to overthrow a dictator, falls for a co-revolutionist. Flashbacks show the destruction of his family and village, and his pugilistic expertise, which he uses to fight for a huge purse to help the cause. Adapted from Jack London's "The Mexican." *AKA:* The First Time.
1952 78m/B Richard Conte, Vanessa Brown, Lee J. Cobb, Frank Silvera, Roberta Haynes, Hugh Sanders, Claire Carleton, Martin Garralaga; *D:* Herbert Kline. VHS *DVT, HEG* ♂♂♂

Fighter Attack
Story of a WWII pilot, based in Corsica, who is shot down during a mission to destroy a Nazi supply station. He meets with a woman of the Italian underground, and succeeds in destroying his target with her help.
1953 80m/C Sterling Hayden, J. Carroll Naish, Joy Page; *D:* Lesley Selander. VHS $19.98 *REP* ♂♂

Fightin' Ranch
A famous lawman saves his reputation, previously tainted. A Maynard classic.
1930 60m/B Ken Maynard. VHS, Beta *VCI* ♂♂

The Fighting American
A frat boy proposes to a girl on a brotherly dare, and, unflattered by the fraternal proposal, the girl flees to the Far East to return to the bosom of her family. But it turns out the boy really does love the girl, by golly, and he's got just enough of that fighting American spirit to prove it. Predates Oland's Charlie Chan career by seven years.
1924 65m/B Pat O'Malley, Mary Astor, Raymond Hatton, Warner Oland; *D:* Tom Forman. VHS, Beta $16.95 *GPV, FCT* ♂♂

Fighting Back
Reactionary tale of an angry resident in a crime-ridden Philadelphia neighborhood who organizes a patrol of armed civilian vigilantes. The police attempt to head off a racial confrontation in this effective drama graced with some fine performances. *AKA:* Death Vengeance.
1982 (R) 96m/C Tom Skerritt, Patti LuPone, Michael Sarrazin, Yaphet Kotto; *D:* Lewis Teague; *W:* David Zelag Goodman. VHS, Beta $14.95 *PAR* ♂♂

Fighting Black Kings Martial arts and karate masters appear in this tale of action.
1976 (PG) 90m/C William Oliver, Charles Martin, Willie Williams, Mas Oyama. **VHS, Beta $19.98** WAR, OM *♫*

Fighting Caballero Lease and his pals effectively handle a gang of mine-harassing outlaws.
1935 60m/B Rex Lease; **D:** Elmer Clifton. **VHS, Beta** NO *♫*

Fighting Caravans In this early big-budget western, based on a story by Zane Grey, a wagon train sets out west from Missouri. Cooper emerges as the hero after warding off an Indian attack that takes the lives of the original leaders. AKA: Blazing Arrows.
1931 80m/B Gary Cooper, Ernest Torrence, Tully Marshall, Fred Kohler Jr., Lili Damita; **D:** Otto Brower, David Burton. **VHS, Beta $19.95** NOS, MRV, VYY *♫♫*

Fighting Champ Cowpunching gives way to boxing as Steele steps into the ring and takes on all comers. Poor combination of riding and boxing makes for a disappointing Western.
1933 57m/B Bob Steele, Arletta Duncan, George "Gabby" Hayes, Charles "Blackie" King, Lafe McKee, Kit Guard, George Cheseboro; **W:** John P. McCarthy. **VHS $19.99** MOV *♫*

Fighting Cowboy Bill settles a tungsten mine dispute with a greedy miner and some outlaws.
1933 50m/B Buffalo Bill Jr.; **D:** Denver Dixon. **VHS, Beta** NO *♫*

Fighting Devil Dogs Two Marine lieutenants are assigned the task of obtaining a deadly secret weapon controlled by crooks. A serial in twelve chapters.
1938 195m/B Lee Powell, Herman Brix; **D:** John English, William Witney. **VHS $29.98** REP, VCN, MLB *♫*

Fighting Duel of Death Subculture evildoers threaten a convict and his lady friend. The two fight back with astounding expertise and effective results.
19?? 88m/C Mah Sah, Richard Chui. **VHS $14.99** CNG *♫ 1/2*

Fighting Father Dunne Mega-hokey Hollywood steamroller about a tough priest caring for St. Louis newsboys in the early 1900s. Based on a true story.
1948 92m/B Pat O'Brien, Darryl Hickman, Charles Kemper, Una O'Connor, Arthur Shields, Harry Shannon, Joseph Sawyer, Anna Q. Nilsson, Donn Gift, Myrna Dell; **D:** Ted Tetzlaff. **VHS, Beta** RKO, TTC *♫♫*

Fighting Fists of Shanghai Joe Fearsome fighting man from the Far East engages a vile American land baron in a battle of honor.
1965 94m/C Klaus Kinski, Gordon Mitchell, Carla Romanelli, Robert Hundar, Chen Lee; **D:** Mario Ciano. **VHS, Beta $59.95** TWE *♫*

Fighting Fool Average oater has McCoy as a sheriff constantly in pursuit of an outlaw named "The Shadow." Of course, romance blossoms between McCoy and Day, too. The real identity of "The Shadow" turns out to be quite a surprise for McCoy.
1932 57m/B Tim McCoy, Marceline Day, Robert Ellis, Arthur Rankin, Dorothy Granger; **D:** Lambert Hillyer. **VHS $19.99** MOV *♫*

Fighting Jack After he saves a girl from a watery death, a man is accused of horse stealing and trespassing.
1926 52m/B Bill Bailey, Hazel Deane, Frona Hale, John Byron, Sailor Sharkey, Herma Cordova; **D:** Louis Chaudet. **VHS, Beta $14.95** GPV *♫♫*

The Fighting Kentuckian Homeward bound from the Battle of New Orleans in 1814, a Kentucky rifleman lingers in a French settlement in Alabama. His romance with the daughter of a French general is blocked by the father until the American saves the community from an assault by land grabbers. Hardy as a frontiersman is well worth the view. An action-packed, well-photographed hit.
1949 100m/B John Wayne, Oliver Hardy, Vera Ralston, Marie Windsor, Philip Dorn, John Howard, Hugo Haas, Grant Withers; **D:** George Waggner. **VHS $9.98** REP *♫♫ 1/2*

The Fighting Legion Maynard shows his foresight here, making this one of the first westerns to fully exploit sound by adding music and singing. Standard plot has Maynard going after the villain who murdered his brother.
1930 69m/B Ken Maynard, Dorothy Dwan, Ernie Adams, Stanley Blystone, Frank Rice; **D:** Harry Joe Brown. **VHS $16.95** GPV, DVT, HEG *♫♫*

Fighting Life The tale of two brothers who overcome immense physical and emotional handicaps and become vital members of society. The two stars of the film are both physically handicapped.
1980 90m/C **VHS, Beta** NO *♫♫*

Fighting Mad A singing Mountie tangles with border-crossing robbers and saves the reputation of a woman they exploit. One of the "Renfrew of the Mounties" series.
1939 57m/B James Newill, Milburn Stone, Sally Blane; **D:** Sam Newfield. **VHS, Beta $39.98** VDM *♫ 1/2*

Fighting Mad A peaceful land owner is driven to violence when he discovers that the business men who want his property are planning to murder two of his family members in order to get it. The local sheriff's apathy forces the man to take the law into his own hands. Unlike other Fonda films of the time which consist of chaotic violence and car crashes, this story is a well performed character study.
1976 (R) 90m/C Peter Fonda, Lynn Lowry, John Doucette, Phil Carey, Scott Glenn, Kathleen Miller; **D:** Jonathan Demme; **W:** Jonathan Demme. **VHS** NO *♫♫ 1/2*

Fighting Mad Soldiers leave their buddy for dead in wartime Vietnam. He is alive, but captured by Japanese soldiers who believe they are still fighting in WWII. AKA: Fierce.
1977 (R) 96m/C James Inglehart, Jayne Kennedy, Leon Isaac Kennedy; **D:** Cirio H. Santiago. **VHS** NO *♫ 1/2*

Fighting Marines U.S. Marines are trying to establish an air base on Halfway Island in the Pacific, but are thwarted by the "Tiger Shark," a modern-day pirate. First appeared as a serial.
1936 69m/B Jason Robards Sr., Grant Withers, Ann Rutherford, Pat O'Malley; **D:** Joseph Kane, B. Reeves Eason. **VHS, Beta $24.95** VYY, VCN, VDM *♫ 1/2*

The Fighting Marshal After serving time for a crime he didn't commit, McCoy assumes the identity of a dead sheriff and tries to find the felons who done him wrong.
1932 58m/B Tim McCoy, Dorothy Gulliver, Mary Carr, Matthew Betz, Pat O'Malley; **D:** David Ross Lederman. **VHS $19.99** MOV *♫♫*

Fighting Parson In order to infiltrate a lawless town Gibson, a gunsling cowboy, dresses as a revivalist preacher.
1935 65m/B Hoot Gibson, Marceline Day, Robert Frazer, Stanley Blystone, Skeeter Bill Robbins, Charles "Blackie" King; **D:** Harry Fraser. **VHS, Beta** VCI, GPV *♫*

Fighting Pilot Talmadge is a real fighter in this classic talkie. His assignment is to rescue the plans for a secret aircraft from ill fate.
1935 62m/B Richard Talmadge, Victor Mace, Gertrude Messinger, Eddie Davis, Robert Frazer; **D:** Noel Mason. **VHS, Beta $24.95** NOS, DVT, GPV *♫*

The Fighting Prince of Donegal An Irish prince battles the invading British in 16th Century Ireland. Escaping their clutches, he leads his clan in rescuing his mother and his beloved in this Disney swashbuckler. Based on the novel "Red Hugh, Prince of Donegal" by Robert T. Reilly.
1966 110m/C Peter McEnery, Susan Hampshire, Tom Adams, Gordon Jackson, Andrew Keir; **D:** Michael O'Herlihy. **VHS, Beta $69.95** DIS *♫♫ 1/2*

The Fighting Redhead Final entry in the "Red Ryder" series has Hart as a cattle rustling murderer and Bannon as the hero, Red Ryder. Based on the comic strip, "Red Ryder."
1950 55m/C Jim Bannon, Don Reynolds, Emmett Lynn, Marin Sais, Peggy Stewart, John Hart, Lane Bradford; **D:** Lewis D. Collins; **W:** Paul Franklin, Jerry Thomas. **VHS $19.99** MOV *♫♫*

Fighting Renegade The search for an Indian burial ground in Mexico prompts two murders and McCoy, disguised as a notorious bandit part of the time, is wrongly accused. Justice triumphs in the end.
1939 60m/B Tim McCoy; **D:** Sam Newfield. **VHS, Beta $19.95** NOS, VCN, DVT *♫ 1/2*

The Fighting Rookie LaRue, better known for playing hoods, is a rookie cop set up and disgraced by the mob. But he fights back to regain his honor and bring the gang to justice.
1934 65m/B Jack LaRue; **D:** Spencer Gordon Bennet. **VHS, Beta, 8mm $24.95** VYY *♫ 1/2*

Fighting Seabees As a hot-tempered construction foreman who battles Navy regulations as well as the Japanese, Wayne emerges as a larger-than-life hero in this action-packed saga of the Pacific theater of WWII. Extremely popular patriotic drama depicts the founding of the Seabees, the naval construction corps, amidst the action and the would-be romance with a woman reporter. Also available colorized.
1944 100m/B John Wayne, Susan Hayward, Dennis O'Keefe, William Frawley; **D:** Edward Ludwig. **VHS $9.98** REP *♫♫ 1/2*

Fighting Shadows McCoy plays a tough lawman who rids his town of an unscrupulous bandit gang guilty of harassing the locals. Highlighted by some excellent trick riding—for which Western star McCoy was known.
1935 58m/B Tim McCoy, Robert Allen, Geneva Mitchell, Ward Bond, Si Jenks; **D:** David Selman; **W:** Ford Beebe. **VHS $19.99** MOV *♫ 1/2*

The Fighting Sheriff Routine oater mixes action and romance when a sheriff is thrown together with a society debutante.
1931 65m/B Buck Jones, Loretta Sayers, Robert Ellis, Harlan E. Knight, Paul Fix, Lilian Worth; **D:** Louis King; **W:** Stuart Anthony. **VHS $19.99** MOV *♫*

The Fighting 69th Cornball but entertaining WWI drama with lots of action. Cagney is a Brooklyn street tough who joins the all-Irish 69th New York regiment but could care less about its famed military history. He promptly defies his superiors and barely scrapes through his training. Sent to France the swaggering Cagney turns coward when confronted by the horrors of war but eventually redeems himself. O'Brien is the famed

regimental chaplain Father Duffy, while Brent is commander "Wild Bill" Donovan, who would later found the OSS in WWII. Lots of heart-tugging emotion backed with a fine supporting cast.
1940 90m/B James Cagney, Pat O'Brien, George Brent, Jeffrey Lynn, Alan Hale, Frank McHugh, Dennis (Stanley Morner) Morgan, William Lundigan, Dick Foran, Guinn Williams, Henry O'Neill, John Litel, George Reeves; **D:** William Keighley; **W:** Fred Niblo, Norman Reilly Raine, Dean Franklin. **VHS $19.98** MGM, FCT ⅛⅛⅛

The Fighting Stallion Canutt stars as a drifter hired by a rancher who's determined to capture a beautiful wild stallion (played by Boy the Wonder Horse). Silent with original organ score.
1926 76m/B Yakima Canutt, Neva Gerber, Bud Osborne. **VHS, Beta, 8mm $16.95** GPV, VYY ⅛⅛⅛

The Fighting Sullivans The true story of five brothers killed on the Battleship Juneau at Guadalcanal during WWII. The tale tells of the fury felt by the siblings after Pearl Harbor, their enlistment to fight for their country, and their tragic fate in the heat of battle. Truly a stirring tribute to all lives lost in combat. **AKA:** The Sullivans.
1942 110m/B Anne Baxter, Thomas Mitchell, Selena Royle, Eddie Ryan, Trudy Marshall, James B. Cardwell, Roy Roberts, Ward Bond, Mary McCarty, Bobby Driscoll, Addison Richards, Selmer Jackson, Mae Marsh, Harry Strang, Barbara Brown; **D:** Lloyd Bacon. **VHS** IVY, MLB ⅛⅛⅛ ½

Fighting Texans An entire town invests in an oil well, on the advice of young salesman Bell, that the bankers are sure is a dud. Imagine their surprise when it turns out to be a gusher.
1933 60m/B Rex Bell, Luana Walters, Betty Mack, Gordon DeMain; **D:** Armand Schaefer. **VHS $19.95** NOS, DVT ⅛

Fighting Thru Maynard fights off the bad guys and wins the girl after some nifty riding in his first all-talkie western. **AKA:** California in 1878.
1930 60m/B Ken Maynard, Jeanette Loff; **D:** William Nigh. **VHS, Beta $19.95** NOS, DVT ⅛

The Fighting Trooper Based on the James Oliver Curwood story, "Footprints," this frontier tale presents a Mountie who goes undercover as a trapper in the Northwest. He is out to catch a murderer.
1934 57m/B Kermit Maynard. **VHS, Beta $9.95** NOS, VDM, DVT ⅛ ½

Fighting Valley Texas Rangers O'Brien, Newill, and Wilkerson ride off to break up an outlaw gang that is trying to monopolize the ore smelting business. O'Brien later went on to directing for TV and also wrote for Red Skelton.
1943 60m/B Dave O'Brien, James Newill, Guy Wilkerson, Patti McCarty, John Merton, Curly Dresden; **D:** Oliver Drake; **W:** Oliver Drake. **VHS $19.95** DVT, HEG ⅛

Fighting Vigilantes A villainous food distributor is terrorizing his rivals until LaRue whips him. Holt and her father put together a committee called "The Vigilantes" to help out. Holt is the daughter of movie good guy Jack Holt.
1947 61m/B Lash LaRue, Al "Fuzzy" St. John, Jennifer Holt, George Cheseboro, Lee Morgan, Russell Arms, Steve Clark; **D:** Ray Taylor. **VHS $19.95** NOS ⅛⅛

The Fighting Westerner Scott stars as a mining engineer who becomes entangled in mysterious murders. Mrs. Leslie Carter stars in a rare screen role. **AKA:** Rocky Mountain Mystery.
1935 54m/B Randolph Scott, Chic Sale, Ann Sheridan, Charles T. Barton. **VHS, Beta, 8mm $19.95** VYY, MRV ⅛ ½

Fighting with Kit Carson Famous guide and Indian fighter lead bands of settlers westward. Action-packed. Twelve chapters.
1933 230m/B Johnny Mack Brown, Noah Beery Sr., Noah Beery Jr., Betsy King Ross; **D:** Armand Schaefer, Colbert Clark. **VHS, Beta $24.95** VYY, VCN, VDM ⅛⅛

Film House Fever A compilation of clips from sleazy, cult-type movies, including "Blood Feast" and "Hot Night at the Go Go Lounge."
1986 58m/C Jamie Lee Curtis, James Keach, Lon Chaney Jr., Harvey Korman. **VHS, Beta $59.98** LIV, VES ⅛

Films by Peter Thompson Three semi-experimental documentary shorts by Thompson, each using film form to comment on matters of both personal and public history: "Two Portraits," a memoir about Thompson's parents; "Universal Hotel," a meditation on photographs of a Polish POW forced into deep-cold medical experiments in Dachau, and "Universal Citizen," about a Guatemalan smuggler who was once an inmate at Dachau.
1987 74m/C D: Peter Thompson. **VHS, Beta** FCT ⅛

Filthy Harry Eastwood and Bronson look-alikes send up the vigilante film.
19?? 90m/C VHS $59.95 TPV, HHE ⅛ ½

Fin de Fiesta When a corpse is found in the swimming pool, the party takes a dive. Spanish pool party fans will lap this one up. In Spanish.
1971 91m/C SP Isela Vega, Hector Suarez, Ana Martin; **D:** Mauricio Walerstein. **VHS, Beta $49.95** MED ⅛

The Final Alliance A tough loner takes on a vicious motorcycle gang that's terrorizing a small town, and realizes that they're also responsible for his family's death.
1989 (R) 90m/C David Hasselhoff, John Saxon, Bo Hopkins, Jeanie Moore; **D:** Mario Di Leo. **VHS, Beta $79.95** COL ⅛

Final Analysis Glossy thriller starring Gere as a San Francisco psychiatrist who falls for the glamorous sister of one of his patients. Basinger plays the femme fatale and Thurman is Gere's sexually neurotic patient. Although heavily influenced by "Vertigo," this film never comes close to attaining the depth of Hitchcock's cinematic masterpiece. Roberts gives the most gripping performance in this slick suspense movie as Basinger's sleazy gangster husband.
1992 (R) 125m/C Richard Gere, Kim Basinger, Uma Thurman, Eric Roberts, Paul Guilfoyle, Keith David, Robert Harper, Jolyon Baker, Harris Yulin, Agustin Rodriguez; **D:** Phil Joanou; **W:** Wesley Strick; **M:** George Fenton. **VHS $19.98** WAR ⅛⅛ ½

Final Approach Test pilot Jason Halsey (Sikking) crashes in the desert and awakens in the office of psychiatrist Dio Gottlieb (Elizondo). Halsey can't remember anything about his past, or his own name for that matter, but through word association games and psychological tests, he begins to remember as Gottlieb tries to pry information from his brain. Showy computer effects are excellent, but they only serve to fill holes in a story that has an unsatisfying ending. Notable as first film mde with digital sound. Also available in a letterboxed version.

1991 (R) 100m/C James B. Sikking, Hector Elizondo, Madolyn Smith, Kevin McCarthy, Cameo Kneuer, Wayne Duvall; **D:** Eric Steven Stahl. **VHS $92.95** VMK ⅛⅛

Final Assignment A Canadian television reporter agrees to smuggle a dissident Soviet scientist's ill granddaughter out of Russia for treatment along with a videotape documenting tragic experiments on children with steroids. She manages to evade the KGB while carrying on with a Russian press officer, and enlists the support of a Jewish fur trader. Location shooting in Canada instead of Russia is just one pitfall of this production. Also on video as, "The Moscow Chronicle."
1980 101m/C CA Genevieve Bujold, Michael York, Burgess Meredith, Colleen Dewhurst; **D:** Paul Almond. **VHS, Beta $69.98** LIV, VES ⅛

Final Comedown A black revolutionary attempts to get white radicals behind his war against racism. He fails and starts a racial bloodbath.
1972 (R) 84m/C Billy Dee Williams, D'Urville Martin, Celia Kaye, Raymond St. Jacques, Pamela Jones, R.G. Armstrong; **D:** Oscar Williams. **VHS, Beta $59.98** NLC, SIM ⅛

The Final Conflict Unwelcomed third installment in the "Omen" series, concerning Satan's son Damien. Now 32, and the head of an international conglomerate, he is poised for world domination but fears another savior is born. Several monks and many babies meet gruesome deaths before he gets his comeuppance. The last theatrical release was then followed by a made-for-television movie called "Omen 4: The Awakening" (1991). **AKA:** The Omen 3.
1981 (R) 108m/C Sam Neill, Lisa Harrow, Barnaby Holm, Rossano Brazzi; **D:** Graham Baker; **W:** Andrew Birkin; **M:** Jerry Goldsmith. **VHS, Beta $19.98** FOX ⅛ ½

The Final Countdown A U.S. nuclear-powered aircraft carrier, caught in a time warp, is transported back to 1941, just hours before the bombing of Pearl Harbor. The commanders face the ultimate decision—leave history intact or stop the incident and thus avoid WWII. Excellent photography and a surprise ending.
1980 (PG) 92m/C Kirk Douglas, Martin Sheen, Katharine Ross, James Farentino, Charles Durning; **D:** Don Taylor; **W:** Thomas Hunter, David Ambrose. **VHS, Beta $19.98** VES ⅛⅛⅛

Final Cut While filming in a secluded swampland, a crew stumbles on a local sheriff's crooked scheme and one by one, the crew members disappear.
1988 92m/C Carla De Lane, T.J. Kennedy, Joe Rainer, Brett Rice, Jordan Williams; **D:** Larry G. Brown. **VHS, Beta $79.95** VMK ⅛ ½

Final Embrace When Laurel's famous sister is murdered she decides to do a little investigating on her own. She's aided by a young cop who just happened to be obsessed with the murdered woman.
1992 (R) ?m/C Robert Rusler, Nancy Valen, Dick Van Patten, Linda Dona; **D:** Oley Sassone; **W:** R.J. Robertson, Jim Wynorski; **M:** Daniel Licht. **VHS $89.98** NHO ⅛ ½

Final Exam Psychotic killer stalks college students during exam week. This one's too boring to be scary. You root for the psycho to off everyone just to have the movie over.
1981 (R) 90m/C Cecile Bagdadi, Joel Rice; **D:** Jimmy Huston. **VHS, Beta $14.95** COL, SUE Woof!

The Final Executioner A valiant man finds a way to stop the slaughter of innocent people in a post-nuclear world. **AKA:** The Last Warrior.

1983 95m/C William Mang, Marina Costa, Harrison Muller, Woody Strode; **D:** Romolo Guerrieri. **VHS, Beta** $59.95 MGM �...

Final Extra Ambitious reporter's career gets a boost when he's assigned to investigate the murder of a rival. Silent with music score.
1927 60m/B Grant Withers, Marguerite de la Motte. **VHS, Beta, 8mm** $19.95 NOS, VYY, DVT ⅛⅛

Final Impact Nick Taylor seeks vengeance on reigning kickboxing champ Jake Gerard through his prodigy, Danny Davis. Will sweet revenge for the wicked beating, suffered at the hands of Gerard years earlier, be his?
1991 (R) 90m/C Lorenzo Lamas, Kathleen Kinmont, Mimi Lesseos, Kathrin Lautner, Jeff Langton, Mike Worth; **D:** Joseph Merhi, Stephen Smoke; **M:** John Gonzalez. **VHS** $29.95 PMH ⅛½

Final Judgement Daniel Tyrone (Dourif) is a former gang member, now a troubled priest, who's the prime suspect in the Los Angeles murder of a beautiful stripper. Determined to find the killer Father Tyrone heads into L.A.'s underground sex industry to search for clues, which brings him face to face with evil and his own desires.
1992 (R) 90m/C Brad Dourif, Isaac Hayes, Maria Ford, Karen Black, Orson Bean, David Ledingham; **D:** Louis Morneau; **W:** Kirk Honeycutt, Louis Morneau. **VHS** $89.95 COL ⅛⅛

Final Justice A small-town Texan sheriff wages a war against crime and corruption that carries him to Italy and the haunts of Mafia hitmen.
1984 (R) 90m/C Joe Don Baker, Rossano Brazzi, Patrizia Pellegrino; **D:** Greydon Clark. **VHS, Beta** $79.95 VES ⅛

Final Mission Vengeful one-man army follows the professional hit man who slaughtered his family from L.A. to Laos. His pursuit leads to a jungle showdown. Gee, sounds like "Rambo, First Blood," though obviously less grand and glorious.
1984 97m/C Richard Young, John Dresden, Kaz Garas, Christine Tudor; **D:** Cirio H. Santiago. **VHS, Beta** $14.98 REP ⅛

Final Notice A detective tracking a serial killer has as his only evidence a trail of shredded photos of nude women. Not released theatrically.
1989 91m/C Gil Gerard, Steve Landesburg, Jackie Burroughs, Melody Anderson, Louise Fletcher, David Ogden Stiers, Kevin Hicks; **D:** Steven Hilliard Stern; **W:** John Gay; **M:** Tom Scott. **VHS, Beta** $59.99 PAR ⅛

The Final Option An agent of England's Special Air Services team goes undercover as one of a band of anti-nuclear terrorists that take over the U.S. Embassy in London. Violent, but unconvincing. **AKA:** Who Dares Wins.
1982 (R) 125m/C GB Lewis Collins, Judy Davis, Richard Widmark, Robert Webber, Edward Woodward, Ingrid Pitt, Kenneth Griffith, Tony Doyle, John Duttine; **D:** Ian Sharp; **W:** Reginald Rose. **VHS, Beta** $79.95 MGM ⅛

The Final Programme In this futuristic story, a man must rescue his sister—and the world—from their brother, who holds a microfilmed plan for global domination. Meanwhile, he must shield himself from the advances of a bisexual computer programmer who wants to make him father to a new, all-purpose human being. Based on the Michael Moorcock "Jerry Cornelius" stories, the film has gained a cult following. **AKA:** The Last Days of Man on Earth.

1973 85m/C GB Hugh Griffith, Harry Andrews, Jon Finch, Jenny Runacre, Sterling Hayden, Patrick Magee, Sarah Douglas; **D:** Robert Fuest. **VHS, Beta** $59.95 SUE ⅛⅛½

Final Round A kickboxer and his girlfriend are kidnapped by a millionaire who stages hunt the humans games for the pleasure of his gambling syndicate. Stiff but with a few good action sequences.
1993 (R) 90m/C Lorenzo Lamas, Anthony de Longis, Kathleen Kinmont, Clark Johnson, Isabelle Jamieson; **D:** George Erschbamer; **W:** Arne Olsen; **M:** Graeme Coleman. **VHS** $89.95 WOV ⅛½

Final Sanction After a nuclear holocaust exhausts their military resources, the U.S. and the Soviets each send one-man armies to battle each other for final control of the world.
1989 90m/C Robert Z'Dar, Ted Prior; **D:** David A. Prior; **W:** David A. Prior. **VHS, Beta** AIP, HHE ⅛⅛½

Final Shot: The Hank Gathers Story Inspirational story of Gathers, who rose from the ghetto to become one of America's top college basketball stars at Loyola Marymount, until tragedy strikes during a game.
1992 92m/C Victor Love, Duane Davis, Nell Carter, George Kennedy. **VHS, Beta** $79.95 PSM ⅛⅛

The Final Terror Group of young campers is stalked by a mad killer in a desolate, backwoods area. Better-than-average stalked-teens entry is notable for the presence of some soon-to-be stars. **AKA:** Campsite Massacre; Bump in the Night; The Forest Primeval.
1983 (R) 90m/C John Friedrich, Rachel Ward, Adrian Zmed, Daryl Hannah, Joe Pantoliano, Ernest Harden, Mark Metcalf, Lewis Smith, Cindy Harrel, Akosua Busia; **D:** Andrew Davis. **VHS, Beta** $29.98 LIV, VES ⅛⅛

Final Verdict A trial lawyer defends a man he knows is guilty, throwing his life and his family into turmoil. Made for cable television.
1991 93m/C Treat Williams, Glenn Ford, Amy Wright, Olivia Burnette; **D:** Jack Fisk. **VHS, Beta** $89.98 TTC ⅛⅛½

Final Warning A dramatization of actual events surrounding the 1986 melt-down of the nuclear power plant at Chernobyl. Made for television. **AKA:** Chernobyl: The Final Warning.
1990 94m/C Jon Voight, Jason Robards Jr., Sammi Davis-Voss; **D:** Anthony Page. **VHS** $79.98 TTC ⅛⅛½

Find the Lady Candy assumes a supporting role as a bumbling cop who is part of an incompetent police team trying to rescue a kidnapped socialite. **AKA:** Call the Cops; Kopek and Broom.
1975 (R) 100m/C CA John Candy, Peter Cook, Mickey Rooney, Lawrence Dane, Alexandra Bastedo; **D:** John Trent. **VHS, Beta** VTR ⅛

Finders Keepers A wild assortment of characters on board a train en route from California to Nebraska search for five million dollars hidden in the baggage car.
1984 (R) 96m/C Michael O'Keefe, Beverly D'Angelo, Ed Lauter, Louis Gossett Jr., Pamela Stephenson, Jim Carrey, David Wayne, Brian Dennehy, John Schuck; **D:** Richard Lester; **W:** Ronny Graham. **VHS, Beta** $59.98 FOX ⅛⅛

Fine Gold A false charge of embezzlement leaves a man without home and family, so he decides to turn the tables on those who betrayed him.

19?? 91m/C Andrew Stevens, Ray Walston, Ted Wass, Stewart Granger, Lloyd Bochner, Jane Badler. **VHS, Beta** $79.99 MCG ⅛

A Fine Madness A near-classic comedy about a lusty, rebellious poet thrashing against the pressures of the modern world, and fending off a bevy of lobotomy-happy psychiatrists. Shot on location in New York City, based on Elliot Baker's novel.
1966 104m/C Sean Connery, Joanne Woodward, Jean Seberg, Patrick O'Neal, Colleen Dewhurst, Clive Revill, John Fiedler; **D:** Irvin Kershner; **M:** John Addison. **VHS, Beta** $19.98 WAR ⅛⅛⅛

A Fine Mess Two buffoons cash in when one overhears a plan to dope a racehorse, but they are soon fleeing the plotters' slapstick pursuit. The plot is further complicated by the romantic interest of a gangster's wife. The television popularity of the two stars did not translate to the big screen; perhaps it's Edwards' fault.
1986 (PG) 100m/C Ted Danson, Howie Mandel, Richard Mulligan, Stuart Margolin, Maria Conchita Alonso, Paul Sorvino; **D:** Blake Edwards; **W:** Blake Edwards. **VHS, Beta** $19.95 COL ⅛½

A Fine Romance An improbable romance set in Paris features Andrews and Mastroianni as abandoned spouses falling in love. Andrews is the prim English Pamela who has been abandoned by her docter husband. Mastroianni is the irrepresible Cesareo, whose wife has just happened to run off with the aforementioned doctor. They meet to plan how to get their spouses back and wind up with opposites attracting. Not much story and the charm is spread thin. Based on the play "Tchin, Tchin" by Francois Billetdoux.
1992 (PG-13) 83m/C Julie Andrews, Marcello Mastroianni, Ian Fitzgibbon, Jean-Pierre Castaldi, Jean-Jacques Dulon, Maria Machado, Jean-Michel Cannone, Catherine Jarrett, Gene Saks; **W:** Ronald Harwood; **M:** Pino Donaggio. **VHS** $89.95 ACA ⅛⅛

Fine Things Bernie Fine thinks everything will be dandy now that he has a beautiful new bride and a cute stepdaughter. Then his wife dies and his stepdaughter's unreliable father wants sole custody. What's a nice guy to do? Based on the novel by Danielle Steel. Made for television. **AKA:** Danielle Steel's Fine Things.
1990 145m/C D.W. Moffett, Tracy Pollan, Judith Hoag, Cloris Leachman, Noley Thornton; **D:** Tom Moore; **W:** Peter Lefcourt. **VHS** $89.95 WOV ⅛⅛½

Finessing the King Private eyes Tommy and Tuppence follow a mysterious newspaper notice to a masked ball where a murder is about to occur. Based on the Agatha Christie story. Made for British television.
1984 60m/C GB James Warwick, Francesca Annis. **VHS, Beta** $14.95 TPV ⅛⅛½

The Finest Hour Two Navy buddies have a falling out when they both fall for the same woman. But they must put aside their differences when their next mission sends them to Iraq to deal with the deadly threat of biological warfare.
1991 (R) 105m/C Rob Lowe, Gale Hansen, Tracy Griffith, Eb Lottimer; **D:** Shimon Dotan; **W:** Shimon Dotan. **VHS** $19.95 COL ⅛½

The Finger Man An ex-con cooperates with the feds rather than return to jail. The deal is that he gets the dirt on an underworld crime boss. Solid performances.
1955 82m/B Frank Lovejoy, Forrest Tucker, Peggy Castle, Timothy Carey, Glenn Gordon; **D:** Harold Schuster. **VHS** $19.98 REP ⅛⅛½

Finger on the Trigger Veterans from both sides of the Civil War are after a hidden supply of gold, but find that they must band together to fend off an Indian attack. Routine. *AKA:* El Dedo En El Gatillo.
1965 89m/C Rory Calhoun, James Philbrook, Todd Martin, Silvia Solar, Brad Talbot; *D:* Sidney Pink. VHS, Beta $7.00 *VTR* 🎬🎬

Fingerprints Don't Lie A fingerprint expert pins the murder of the town mayor on an innocent guy, then suspects a frame-up.
1951 56m/B Richard Travis, Sheila Ryan, Tom Neal; *D:* Sam Newfield. VHS, Beta *NO* 🎬

Fingers Keitel is Johnny Fingers, a mobster's son, reluctantly working as a mob debt-collector, all the while dreaming of his ambitions to be a concert pianist. The divisions between his dreams and reality cause him to crack. Toback's first film generates psychological tension and excellent performances.
1978 (R) 89m/C Harvey Keitel, Tisa Farrow, Jim Brown, Danny Aiello, Tanya Roberts, Marian Seldes, Michael Gazzo, James Toback; *D:* James Toback; *W:* James Toback. VHS, Beta $29.98 *TTC* 🎬🎬🎬

Finian's Rainbow A leprechaun comes to America to steal back a pot of gold taken by an Irishman and his daughter in this fanciful musical comedy based on a 1947 Broadway hit. Both the sprite and the girl find romance; the share-cropping locals are saved by the cash; a bigot learns the error of his ways; and Finian (Astaire) dances off to new adventures. The fine production and talented cast are not used to their best advantage by the director who proved much better suited for "The Godfather." Entertaining, nonetheless. 🎵How Are Things in Glocca Morra?; Look To the Rainbow; That Old Devil Moon; If This Isn't Love; Something Sort of Grandish; The Be-Gat; This Time of Year; The Great Come and Get It Day; When I'm Not Near the Girl I Love; When the Idle Poor Become the Idle Rich; Rain Dance Ballet.
1968 (G) 141m/C Fred Astaire, Petula Clark, Tommy Steele, Keenan Wynn, Al Freeman Jr., Don Francks, Susan Hancock, Dolph Sweet; *D:* Francis Ford Coppola. VHS, Beta $19.98 *WAR, MVD* 🎬🎬🎬

Finish Line A high school track star turns to steroids to enhance his performance after being pushed by an overzealous father. The father-and-son Brolins play the pair. Made for cable.
1989 100m/C James Brolin, Josh Brolin, Mariska Hargitay, Kristoff St. John, John Finnegan, Billy Vera, Stephen Lang; *D:* John Nicolella. VHS $139.96 *TTC* 🎬🎬½

Finishing School Girls' school roommates Rogers and Dee experience heartaches and loves lost while enduring disinterested parents and snobbish peers. Box office bomb when released, despite a strong cast.
1933 73m/B Ginger Rogers, Frances Dee, George Nichols, Beulah Bondi, Bruce Cabot, Billie Burke, John Halliday, Sara Haden, Jack Norton, Joan Barclay, Jane Darwell; *D:* George Nichols. VHS, Beta $19.98 *TTC* 🎬½

The Finishing Touch Someone is stalking L.A.'s most gorgeous women and Detective Sam Stone (Nader) is assigned to the case. Stone discovers his prime suspect is a video artist with a taste for pornography. When Stone's investigation is cut short, his ex-wife, Detective Hannah Stone (Hack) is brought in to take over the case. Unfortunately, she finds herself falling for the suspect in this erotic thriller.

1992 (R) 82m/C Michael Nader, Shelley Hack, Arnold Vosloo, Art Evans, Clark Johnson, Theodore Raimi; *D:* Fred Gallo. VHS $89.95 *COL* 🎬🎬

Finnegan Begin Again A middle-aged schoolteacher and a grouchy, 65-year-old newspaper editor find romance despite their other obligations. Winning performances add charm to this cable TV movie.
1984 112m/C Mary Tyler Moore, Robert Preston, Sam Waterston, Sylvia Sidney, David Huddleston; *D:* Joan Micklin Silver. VHS, Beta $14.95 *CNG, HBO, KAR* 🎬🎬

Finnegan's Wake Portions of the filmed adaptation of James Joyce's novel are shown in this program along with an interview with producer/director Mary Ellen Bute. *AKA:* Passages from "Finnegans Wake"; Passages from James Joyce's "Finnegans Wake".
1963 92m/B VHS, Beta *CMR, NYS* 🎬🎬

Fiorile Covers several generations of a Tuscan clan living under a family curse which dates back to Napoleon's invasion of Italy. At that time Jean, a handsome French lieutenant, falls in love with Tuscan peasant girl Elisabetta, nicknamed Fiorile. When Jean is executed for a theft committed by her brother, the pregnant Fiorile vows revenge. Throughout sucessive generations, haunted by the past, the family's personal bad luck persists. Several of the actors play their character's ancestors, lending continuity. Attractive cast does well with the Taviani brothers' visual style and romantic narrative. In Italian with English subtitles. *AKA:* Wild Flower.
1993 (PG-13) 118m/C *IT* Michael Vartan, Galatea Ranzi, Claudio Bigagli, Lino Capolicchio, Constanze Engelbrecht, Athina Cenci, Giovanni Guidelli, Chiara Caselli; *D:* Paolo Taviani, Vittorio Taviani; *W:* Paolo Taviani, Vittorio Taviani, Sandro Petraglia; *M:* Nicola Piovani. VHS *NLC* 🎬🎬🎬

Fire A fire started by an escaped convict rages through Oregon timberland in this suspenseful made-for-television Irwin Allen disaster drama.
1977 98m/C Ernest Borgnine, Vera Miles, Patty Duke, Alex Cord, Donna Mills; *D:* Earl Bellamy. VHS, Beta $59.95 *WAR* 🎬½

Fire Alarm A change of scene for Western star Brown as he portrays a fireman who, in-between his work, romances a career girl.
1938 67m/B Johnny Mack Brown, Noel Francis; *D:* Karl Brown. VHS, Beta $19.95 *NOS, VYY, HEG* 🎬

Fire and Ice An animated adventure film that culminates in a tense battle between good and evil, surrounded by the mystical elements of the ancient past. Designed by Frank Frazetta.
1983 (PG) 81m/C Randy Norton, Cynthia Leake; *D:* Ralph Bakshi; *V:* Susan Tyrrell, William Ostrander. VHS, Beta $12.98 *COL, WTA* 🎬🎬½

Fire and Ice A tale of love on the slopes. Two skiers realize that their feelings for each other are perhaps even stronger than their feelings about skiing. You won't care though, except for some fine ski footage.
1987 (PG) 83m/C Suzy Chaffee, John Eaves; *D:* Willy Bogner; *W:* George Schlatter; *M:* Harold Faltermeyer. VHS, Beta $14.95 *SUE* 🎬

Fire and Rain Based on the real-life crash of a Delta Airlines plane in Dallas and the rescue efforts made following the disaster. Familiar cast-members turn in decent performance. Made for television.
1989 89m/C Angie Dickinson, Charles Haid, Tom Bosley, David Hasselhoff, Robert Guillaume, Susan Ruttan, John Beck, Patti LaBelle, Dean Jones, Lawrence Pressman, Penny Fuller; *D:*

Jerry Jameson; *W:* Gary Sherman. VHS, Beta $59.99 *PAR* 🎬🎬

Fire and Sword A Cornish knight must choose between loyalty for king and country and the love of an Irish woman in this medieval drama. A not very inspired retelling of the Tristan and Isolde legend.
1982 84m/C *GB* Peter Firth, Leigh Lawson, Antonia Preser, Christopher Waitz; *D:* Veith von Furstenberg. VHS, Beta $69.98 *LIV* 🎬

Fire Birds Army attack helicopters and the people who fly them are used in the war on drugs in South America. Failed to match either the exciting flight sequences, the romantic interest or the box office of "Top Gun." *AKA:* Wings of the Apache.
1990 (PG-13) 85m/C Nicolas Cage, Tommy Lee Jones, Sean Young, Bryan Kestner, Dale Dye, Mary Ellen Trainor, J.A. Preston, Peter Onorati; *D:* David Green; *W:* Nick Thiel, Paul F. Edwards; *M:* David Newman. VHS, Beta $19.99 *TOU* 🎬

Fire Down Below Hayworth is the been-around-the-block beauty who persuades Mitchum and Lemmon, two small-time smugglers, to take her to a safe haven, no questions asked. Both men fall for her obvious charms, causing them to have a falling out until a life or death situation puts their friendship to the test. An unoriginal melodrama indifferently acted by everyone but Lemmon. Good location work in Trinidad and Tobago.
1957 116m/C *GB* Robert Mitchum, Jack Lemmon, Rita Hayworth, Herbert Lom, Anthony Newley; *D:* Robert Parrish. VHS, Beta $19.95 *COL, COL, CCB* 🎬½

Fire, Ice and Dynamite Moore is onscreen only briefly as an eccentric tycoon who fakes suicide to watch several teams of challengers scramble in a madcap winter-sports contest for his millions. A German-made avalanche of crazy stunts, bad jokes, and product plugs for countless European companies, commencing with a literal parade of guests, from astronaut Buzz Aldrin to soul man Isaac Hayes. Numbing; must be seen to be believed.
1991 (PG) 105m/C Roger Moore, Shari Belafonte-Harper, Simon Shepherd, Uwe Ochsenknecht, Marjoe Gortner; *D:* Willy Bogner. VHS $89.98 *VES, LIV* 🎬½

Fire in the Night In a small Southern town, a beautiful and sure-footed woman battles the limitless resources of the town's predominant dynastic family.
1985 89m/C Graciela Casillas, John Martin. VHS, Beta $19.95 *STE, NWV* 🎬½

Fire in the Sky Mysterious disappearance of Sweeney sparks a criminal investigation, until he returns, claiming he was abducted by aliens. Though everybody doubts his story, viewers won't, since the alleged aliens have already made an appearance, shifting the focus to Sweeney as he tries to convince skeptics that his trauma is genuine. Perhaps this mirrors what director Lieberman went through while trying to convince backers the film should be made. He could have benefitted by understanding the difference between what he was telling viewers and what he was showing them. Captivating special effects are one of the few bright spots. Based on a story that might be true.
1993 (PG-13) 98m/C D.B. Sweeney, Robert Patrick, Craig Sheffer, Peter Berg, James Garner, Henry Thomas; *D:* Robert Lieberman; *W:* Tracy Torme; *M:* Mark Isham. VHS, Beta *PAR* 🎬🎬

The Fire in the Stone A young boy discovers an opal mine and dreams of using the treasure to reunite his family. However, when the jewels are stolen from him, he enlists his friends to help get them back. Based on the novel by Colin Thiele.

1985 97m/C *AU* Paul Smith, Linda Hartley, Theo Pertsinidis. **VHS, Beta $39.95** *WAR ℐℐ*

Fire Maidens from Outer Space
Fire maidens prove to be true to the space opera code that dictates that all alien women be in desperate need of male company. Astronauts on an expedition to Jupiter's thirteenth moon discover the lost civilization of Atlantis, which, as luck would have it, is inhabited by women only. Possibly an idea before its time, it might've been better had it been made in the sixties, when space-exploitation came into its own.

1956 80m/B *GB* Anthony Dexter, Susan Shaw, Paul Carpenter, Harry Fowler, Jacqueline Curtiss, Sydney Tafler, Maya Koumani, Jan Holden, Kim Parker; *D:* Cy Roth; *W:* Cy Roth. **VHS $16.95** *CNM, MLB ℐ*

Fire Monsters Against the Son of Hercules
The son of the muscular one does battle with a hydra-headed monster in this average war and sandal adventure.

1962 ?m/C Reg Lewis. **VHS $16.95** *SNC ℐℐ*

The Fire Next Time
In the year 2017, the United States is being ravaged by an ecological holocaust caused by a deadly combination of pollution and global warming. Nelson, Bedelia and their children are forced from their Louisiana home by a natural disaster and decide to head for better times in Canada. Their travels aren't easy. Made for television.

1993 195m/C Craig T. Nelson, Bonnie Bedelia, Juergen Prochnow, Richard Farnsworth, Justin Whalin, Charles Haid, Sal Lopez, Shawn Toovey, Ashley Jones; *Cameos:* Odetta; *D:* Tom McLoughlin; *W:* James Henerson. **VHS $14.95** *CAF ℐℐ½*

Fire Over England
Young naval officer volunteers to spy at the Spanish court to learn the plans for the invasion of his native England and to identify the traitors among the English nobility. He arouses the romantic interest of his queen, Elizabeth I, one of her ladies, and a Spanish noblewoman who helps with his missions, and later leads the fleet to victory over the huge Spanish Armada. The first on-screen pairing of Olivier and Leigh is just one of the many virtues of this entertaining drama.

1937 81m/B *GB* Flora Robson, Raymond Massey, Laurence Olivier, Vivien Leigh, Leslie Banks, James Mason; *D:* William K. Howard. **VHS, Beta $19.95** *NOS, MRV, VYY ℐℐℐ*

Fire with Fire
A boy at a juvenile detention center and a Catholic school girl fall in love. However, they find themselves on the run from the law when he escapes to be with her. Sheffer and Madsen are appealing in this otherwise unspectacular film.

1986 (PG-13) 103m/C Craig Sheffer, Virginia Madsen, Jon Polito, Kate Reid, Jean Smart, D.B. Sweeney; *D:* Duncan Gibbins; *W:* Bill Phillips. **VHS $79.95** *PAR ℐℐ*

The Fire Within
Ronet plays an alcoholic writer recently released from a sanitorium after a breakdown. Believing his life will only continue its downward spiral, he pays a final visit to friends and calmly plots his suicide. Malle clearly and pitilessly describes a man beyond despair. Based on a novel by Pierre Drieu La Rochelle, which itself fictionalized the suicide of writer Jacques Rigaut. In French with English subtitles. *AKA:* Le Feu Follet; Fuoco Fatuo.

1964 104m/B *FR* Maurice Ronet, Lena Skerla, Yvonne Clech, Hubert Deschamps, Jean-Paul Moulinot; *D:* Louis Malle; *W:* Louis Malle. **VHS $69.95** *NYF, ING, PMS ℐℐℐ*

Fireback
A Vietnam vet's wife is kidnapped by the mob, causing him to take up arms and spill blood yet again.

1978 90m/C Bruce Baron, Richard Harrison. **VHS, Beta $39.95** *LIV ℐ½*

Fireball Forward
A battalion fighting in France during WWII is having a bad time until Gazzara takes over and turns them into a crack fighting team. Uses some battle footage from the movie "Patton." Made for television.

1972 (PG) 100m/C Ben Gazzara, Eddie Albert, Ricardo Montalban, Dana Elcar, L.Q. Jones, Anne Francis; *D:* Marvin J. Chomsky. **VHS $9.99** *QVD ℐℐ½*

Fireballs
Sexploitaton pic set at a firehouse, where a batch of female recruits turn up the heat for three stud hose-bearers. The title should give you some idea of the intellectual level.

1990 89m/C Mike Shapiro, Goren Kalezik; *D:* Mike Shapiro. **VHS $79.95** *ATL ℐ½*

Firebird 2015 A.D.
Dreary action adventure set in a 21st century society where automobile use is banned because of an extreme oil shortage. Private cars are hunted down for destruction by the Department of Vehicular Control. One over-zealous enforcer decides to make it a package deal and throws in the owners as well. Everyone connected with effort should have been cited for running stop sign.

1981 (PG) 97m/C Darren McGavin, George Touliatos, Doug McClure; *D:* David Robertson. **VHS, Beta $69.98** *SUE ℐ*

Firecracker
Female martial arts expert retaliates against the crooks who murdered her sister.

1971 83m/C Jillian Kesner, Darby Hinton; *D:* Cirio H. Santiago. **VHS, Beta** *NO ℐ*

Firecreek
Fonda and his thugs terrorize a small town protected by part-time sheriff Stewart. Beautiful photography and competent cast, but meandering and long.

1968 104m/C Henry Fonda, James Stewart, Inger Stevens, Gary Lockwood, Dean Jagger, Ed Begley Sr., Jay C. Flippen, Jack Elam, Barbara Luna; *D:* Vincent McEveety. **VHS $29.99** *WAR, VTR, MTX ℐℐ½*

Firefall
Wildlife photog Katy Mazur (Gidley) has a brief affair with sportsman Grant Orion (Roberts) while on assignment in Africa. When they meet again, Orion tells Katy he's actually an Interpol agent who's assigned to protect her—although she has no idea why. Katy's fiance (Fahey) thinks this is strange.

1994 95m/C Pamela Gidley, Eric Roberts, Jeff Fahey; *D:* John Irvin. **VHS $94.95** *VMK ℐℐ*

Firefight
After a nuclear holocaust, convicted criminals endeavor to rule the wasteland.

1987 100m/C James Pfeiffer, Janice Carraher, Jack Tucker; *D:* Scott Pfeiffer. **VHS, Beta $69.95** *TWE ℐ*

The Firefly
Although slow-paced and long, this adaptation of the 1912 Rudolf Friml operetta was one of MacDonald's most popular films. Co-star Jones gets to sing the best song in the film, "Donkey Serenade," while MacDonald sings most of the others. ♫Love Is Like a Firefly; English March; A Woman's Kiss; He Who Loves and Runs Away; When a Maid Comes Knocking at Your Heart; When the Wine Is Full of Fire; The Donkey Serenade; Giannina Mia; Sympathy.

1937 140m/B Jeanette MacDonald, Allan Jones, Warren William, Billy Gilbert, Henry Daniell, Douglass Dumbrille, George Zucco; *D:* Robert Z. Leonard. **VHS $19.98** *MGM ℐℐ½*

Firefox
A retired pilot sneaks into the Soviet Union for the Pentagon to steal a top-secret, ultra-sophisticated warplane and fly it out of the country. Best for the low-altitude flight and aerial battle sequences, but too slow on character and much too slow getting started.

1982 (PG) 136m/C Clint Eastwood, Freddie Jones, David Huffman, Warren Clarke, Ronald Lacey, Kenneth Colley, Nigel Hawthorne, Kai Wulff; *D:* Clint Eastwood; *M:* Maurice Jarre. **VHS, Beta $19.98** *WAR ℐℐ½*

Firehawk
Several American soldiers survive the crash of their helicopter into the jungles of Vietnam. They think their only enemy is the Vietcong but when they discover the copter has been sabotaged the hunt is on for the traitor among them.

1992 (R) 92m/C Martin Kove, Matt Salinger, Vic Trevino; *D:* Cirio H. Santiago; *W:* Jeff Yonis. **VHS $89.95** *LIV ℐℐ*

Firehead
A pyrokinetic Soviet defector begins using his powers to destroy American munitions in the name of peace. When a clandestine pro-war organization hears of this, they attempt to capture the man and use him for their own evil purposes.

1990 (R) 88m/C Christopher Plummer, Chris Lemmon, Martin Landau, Gretchen Becker, Brett Porter; *D:* Peter Yuval. **VHS, Beta $89.98** *AIP ℐℐ½*

Firehouse
Tempers ignite in a lily-white firehouse when a black rookie replaces an expired veteran. March—of "Paper Lion" renown—directed this made-for-TV emergency clone, which ran ever-so-briefly as an adventure series on TV in 1974 (with a largely different cast).

1972 73m/C Richard Roundtree, Vince Edwards, Andrew Duggan, Richard Jaeckel, Sheila Frazier, Val Avery, Paul LeMat, Michael Lerner; *D:* Alex March. **VHS $59.95** *XVC ℐℐ*

Firehouse
In the style of "Police Academy," three beautiful and sex-starved firefighting recruits klutz up an urban firehouse. A softcore frolic.

1987 (R) 91m/C Barrett Hopkins, Shannon Murphy, Violet Brown, John Anderson; *D:* J. Christian Ingvordsen. **VHS, Beta $14.95** *ACA ℐ*

The Fireman
Chaplin portrays a fireman who becomes a hero. Silent with musical soundtrack added.

1916 20m/B Eric Campbell, Edna Purviance, Charlie Chaplin; *D:* Charlie Chaplin. **VHS, Beta $39.95** *CAB, GVV, VYY ℐℐ½*

The Firemen's Ball
A critically acclaimed comedy about a small-town ball held for a retiring fire chief. Plans go amusingly awry as beauty contestants refuse to show themselves, raffle prizes and other items—including the gift for the guest of honor—are stolen, and the firemen are unable to prevent an old man's house from burning down. Forman's second film is sometimes interpreted as political allegory; in Czechoslovacian, with English subtitles.

1968 73m/C *CZ* Vaclav Stockel, Josef Svet; *D:* Milos Forman. **VHS, Beta $39.95** *HMV, ING, COL ℐℐℐ*

Firepower
Loren blames her chemist husband's death on a rich industrialist and hires hitman Coburn to take care of the matter. Less than compelling.

1979 (R) 104m/C Sophia Loren, James Coburn, O.J. Simpson, Christopher F. Bean; *D:* Michael Winner; *W:* Michael Winner. **VHS, Beta $59.98** *FOX ℐ½*

Firepower Two cops chase "The Swordsman" into a federally sanctioned area of legalized gambling, prostitution and crime (Las Vegas?), risking life and limb in the treacherous "Caged Ring of Death."
1993 (R) ?m/C Chad McQueen, Gary Daniels, Jim Hellwig, Joseph Ruskin, George Murdock. **VHS $89.95** PMH *️⃣½

Fires on the Plain A grueling Japanese anti-war film about an unhinged private in the Philippines during WWII who roams the war-torn countryside encountering all manner of horror and devastation. In Japanese with English subtitles. *AKA:* Nobi.
1959 105m/B JP Eiji Funakoshi, Osamu Takizawa, Mickey Custis, Asao Suno; *D:* Kon Ichikawa. **VHS, Beta $29.98** SUE, MRV, HHT *️⃣*️⃣*️⃣

Fires Within A curiously flat romance with political overtones. After eight years as a political prisoner in Cuba, Nestor (Smits) is released and goes to Miami to be reunited with his wife and daughter. Once there he finds his wife has fallen in love with another man. Now Nestor must choose between his politics and the chance to win back his family. Secondary plot lines fizzle out and a talented cast is largely wasted. Scacchi is beautiful but hardly believable as the Cuban wife.
1991 (R) 90m/C Jimmy Smits, Greta Scacchi, Vincent D'Onofrio; *D:* Gillian Armstrong; *W:* Cynthia Cidre. **VHS, Beta $14.95** MGM *️⃣*️⃣

Firesign Theatre Presents Nick Danger in the Case of the Missing Yolks Firesign characters Nick Danger and Rocky Rococo are featured in this story of a truly interactive family who live through their television set.
1983 60m/C Phil Proctor, Phil Austin, Peter Bergman. **VHS, Beta** NO *️⃣*️⃣½

Firestarter A C.I.A.-like organization is after a little girl who has the ability to set anything on fire in this filmed adaptation of Stephen King's bestseller. Good special effects help a silly plot.
1984 (R) 115m/C David Keith, Drew Barrymore, Freddie Jones, Martin Sheen, George C. Scott, Heather Locklear, Louise Fletcher, Moses Gunn, Art Carney, Antonio Fargas, Drew Snyder; *D:* Mark L. Lester. **VHS, Beta $19.95** MCA *️⃣*️⃣

Firewalker An "Indiana Jones" clone about three mercenaries endeavoring to capture a fortune in hidden gold. Paper-mache sets and a villain with an eye patch that consistently changes eyes are just some of the gaffes that make this one of the worst edited movies in history.
1986 (PG) 106m/C Chuck Norris, Louis Gossett Jr., Melody Anderson; *D:* J. Lee Thompson; *M:* Gary Chang. **VHS, Beta $19.95** MED, VTR *️⃣

The Firing Line The Central American government hires a mercenary rebel-buster to squash insurgents. Everything's great until he finds out he agrees with the rebel cause, and he trains them to fight the government. Below average renegade-with-a-hidden-heart warpic.
1991 93m/C Reb Brown, Shannon Tweed; *D:* John Gale. **VHS $79.95** AIP *️⃣*️⃣

The Firm Top-flight cast promises a good time—the script based on the top-selling 1991 novel by John Grisham nearly guarantees it. Ambitious, idealistic Ivy League law school grad Cruise accepts a great offer from a small but wealthy Memphis law firm. As with anything that seems too good to be true, he finds out too late that nothing in life is free. Good performances by nearly everyone involved makes up for predictability. Sorvino has an uncredited cameo as a mob boss. Book fans beware: the script is fairly

faithful until the end. The movie rights were snapped up before the book was published. Placed third in the 1993 race for top box office grosses.
1993 (R) 154m/C Tom Cruise, Jeanne Tripplehorn, Gene Hackman, Hal Holbrook, Terry Kinney, Wilford Brimley, Ed Harris, Holly Hunter, David Strathairn, Gary Busey, Steven Hill, Tobin Bell, Barbara Garrick, Jerry Hardin, Karina Lombard, John Beal; *Cameos:* Paul Sorvino; *D:* Sydney Pollack; *W:* Robert Towne, David Rayfiel; *M:* Dave Grusin. **VHS, Beta, CDV $99.95** PAR, BTV, FCT *️⃣*️⃣*️⃣

First Affair A made-for-television film about a young innocent girl undergoing the pressures of freshman life at college, including her first love affair, which is with the husband of a female professor.
1983 95m/C Loretta Swit, Melissa Sue Anderson, Joel Higgins; *D:* Gus Trikonis. **VHS, Beta $59.98** FOX *️⃣*️⃣*️⃣

First & Ten A failing football team emphasizes sexual, rather than athletic conquests, under the guidance of their female owner. Made for cable TV and followed by "First & Ten: The Team Scores Again."
1985 88m/C Delta Burke, Geoffrey Scott, Reid Shelton, Ruta Lee, Fran Tarkenton; *D:* Donald Kushner. **VHS, Beta $69.98** LIV, VES *️⃣*️⃣

First & Ten: The Team Scores Again A sequel to the made-for-cable-television comedy "First and Ten" about a football team's relationship with their female owner.
1985 101m/C Delta Burke, Geoffrey Scott, Ruta Lee, Reid Shelton, Clayton Landey, Fran Tarkenton. **VHS, Beta $69.98** LIV, VES *️⃣*️⃣

First Blood Stallone is a former Green Beret survivor of Vietnam whose nightmares of wartime horrors are triggered by a wrongful arrest in a small town. He escapes into the mountains of the Northwest and leads his pursuers to all manner of bloody ends. Finally, the Army is summoned to crush him. Extremely violent and frequently confused, fueled on the revenge fantasy and not much concerned with the rules of plot realism. Screen debut of Caruso. Based on David Morrell's novel. A box-office hit that launched the "Rambo" series. Followed by "Rambo: First Blood, Part 2."
1982 (R) 96m/C Sylvester Stallone, Richard Crenna, Brian Dennehy, Jack Starrett, David Caruso; *D:* Ted Kotcheff; *W:* Sylvester Stallone; *M:* Jerry Goldsmith. **VHS, Beta $14.95** LIV, TLF *️⃣*️⃣

First Born In search of romance, divorced mother Garr finds an intriguing man, Weller. Trouble erupts when her son learns Weller is a cocaine dealer. Talented cast makes most of story.
1984 (PG-13) 100m/C Teri Garr, Peter Weller, Christopher Collet, Corey Haim, Sarah Jessica Parker, Robert Downey Jr.; *D:* Michael Apted. **VHS, Beta $14.95** PAR *️⃣*️⃣½

The First Deadly Sin Police lieutenant Sinatra tracks down a homicidal killer in spite of wife Dunaway's illness and his impending retirement. Read Lawrence Sanders' best-selling novel; it's a lot more exciting than this.
1980 (R) 112m/C Frank Sinatra, Faye Dunaway, David Dukes, Brenda Vaccaro, James Whitmore; *D:* Brian G. Hutton. **VHS, Beta $59.95** WAR *️⃣½

First Family Flat satire of life in the White House. The humor is weak and silly at best, despite the excellent comedy cast. Henry's first directorial effort.
1980 (R) 100m/C Bob Newhart, Madeline Kahn, Gilda Radner, Richard Benjamin; *D:* Buck Henry; *W:* Buck Henry; *M:* Ralph Burns. **VHS, Beta $19.98** WAR *️⃣½

First Legion Boyer and Addy are seminarians struggling with their faith when they are confronted with a supposed miracle. Low-key examination of religion and conflict within a religious community.
1951 77m/B Charles Boyer, Barbara Rush, William Demarest, Leo G. Carroll; *D:* Douglas Sirk. **VHS, Beta $59.98** LIV *️⃣*️⃣½

First Love A sixteen year old lad falls in love with a slightly older woman only to have his feelings rejected and to discover that she's his father's mistress. Actor Schell's directorial debut.
1970 (R) 90m/C GE SI John Moulder-Brown, Dominique Sanda, Maximilian Schell, Valentina Cortese; *D:* Maximilian Schell. **VHS, Beta $49.95** CNG *️⃣*️⃣

First Love A story of an idealistic college student who takes love (and especially making love) more seriously than the rest of his peers, including his girlfriend. Based on Harold Brodkey's story "Sentimental Education." Darling's directorial debut.
1977 (R) 92m/C William Katt, Susan Dey, John Heard, Beverly D'Angelo, Robert Loggia; *D:* Joan Darling; *M:* John Barry. **VHS, Beta $49.95** PAR *️⃣*️⃣½

First Man into Space An astronaut returns to Earth covered with strange space dust and with an organism feeding inside him (shades of "Alien"). The alien needs human blood to survive and starts killing in order to get it. *AKA:* Satellite of Blood.
1959 78m/B Marshall Thompson, Marla Landi, Bill Edwards; *D:* Robert Day. **VHS, Beta $19.98** DVT, RHI, HEG *️⃣*️⃣

First Men in the Moon A fun, special effects-laden adaptation of the H. G. Wells novel about an Edwardian civilian spacecraft visiting the moon and the creature found there. Visual effects by Ray Harryhausen. Finch makes a brief appearance.
1964 103m/C GB Martha Hyer, Edward Judd, Lionel Jeffries, Erik Chitty, Peter Finch; *D:* Nathan Juran; *W:* Nigel Kneale, Jan Read. **VHS, Beta $14.95** COL, MLB *️⃣*️⃣

First Monday in October A comedy concerning the first woman appointed to the Supreme Court, a conservative, and her colleague, a crusty but benign liberal judge. Though based on a Broadway hit, it ended up seeming to foreshadow the real-life appointment of Sandra Day O'Connor, which occurred at about the time the film was released. The title refers to the date the court begins its sessions.
1981 (R) 99m/C Walter Matthau, Jill Clayburgh, Barnard Hughes, James Stephens, Jan Sterling; *D:* Ronald Neame. **VHS, Beta $84.95** PAR *️⃣*️⃣½

The First Movie Cowboy Three shorts featuring the very first movie cowboy, Bronco Billy.
1913 47m/B G.M. Anderson; *D:* G.M. Anderson. **VHS, Beta, 8mm $19.95** VYY *️⃣*️⃣½

First Name: Carmen Carmen, although posing as an aspiring filmmaker, really is a bank robber and terrorist. She is also such a femme fatale that during a bank robbery one of the guards decides to run away with her. Godard cast himself as Carmen's uncle. Amusing late Godard. *AKA:* Prenom: Carmen.
1983 95m/C FR Maruschka Detmers, Jacques Bonaffe, Jean-Luc Godard, Myriem Roussel, Christophe Odent; *D:* Jean-Luc Godard. **VHS, Beta $29.95** CVC, ING, TPV *️⃣*️⃣

The First Nudie Musical A producer tries to save his studio by staging a 1930s style musical, but with a naked cast and risque lyrics. Has attained semi-cult/trash status. ♫The First Nudie Musical; The Lights

F

and the Smiles; Orgasm; Lesbian Butch Dyke; Dancing Dildos; Perversion; Honey, What Ya Doin' Tonight; Let 'Em Eat Cake; I Don't Have to Hide Anymore; Where Is a Man.

1975 (R) 93m/C Cindy Williams, Stephen Nathan, Diana Canova, Bruce Kimmel; **D:** Mark Haggard. **VHS, Beta $59.95** *MED, HHT* 🎞🎞

The First Olympics: Athens 1896 Recounts the organization and drama surrounding the first modern-day Olympic games when the inexperienced American team shocked the games with their success. Made for television.

1984 260m/C Louis Jourdan, Angela Lansbury, David Ogden Stiers, Virginia McKenna, Jason Connery, Alex Hyde-White, Honor Blackman, Bill Travers; **D:** Alvin Rakoff; **M:** Bruce Broughton. **VHS, Beta $29.95** *COL* 🎞🎞

The First Power A detective and psychic join forces to track down a serial killer who, after being executed, uses his satanic powers to kill again.

1989 90m/C Lou Diamond Phillips, Tracy Griffith, Jeff Kober, Mykel T. Williamson, Elizabeth Arlen; **D:** Robert Resnikoff; **W:** Robert Resnikoff; **M:** Stewart Copeland. **VHS, Beta, 8mm $14.95** *COL, SUE, NLC* 🎞🎞½

First Spaceship on Venus Eight scientists from various countries set out for Venus and find the remains of a civilization far in advance of Earth's that perished because of nuclear weapons. A sometimes compelling anti-nuclear sci-fi effort made with German and Polish backing. Originally released at 130 minutes. *AKA:* Der Schweigende Stern; Milczaca Gwiazda.

1960 78m/C *GE PL* Yoko Tani, Oldrich Lukes, Ignacy Machowski, Julius Ongewe, Michal Postnikov, Kurt Rackelmann, Gunther Simon, Tang-Hua-Ta, Lucyna Winnicka; **D:** Kurt Maetzig. **VHS, Beta $19.95** *NOS, MRV, SNC* 🎞🎞🎞

First Strike The United States and the USSR engage in nuclear submarine warfare when the Soviets hijack a U.S. sub and aims its weapons at Arab oil fields.

1985 90m/C Stuart Whitman, Persis Khambatta. **VHS, Beta $69.95** *VCD* 🎞

The First Time It's pre-Porky's zaniness as a vacationing youth understandably wants to spend his "first time" with Bisset. Other than her presence, this film has little to offer. *AKA:* You Don't Need Pajamas at Rosie's; The Beginners Three; The Beginners; They Don't Wear Pajamas at Rosie's; Doin' It.

1969 (R) 90m/C Jacqueline Bisset, Wes Stern, Rick Kelman, Wink Roberts; **D:** James Neilson. **VHS** *NO* 🎞½

First Time A comedy about a college student who can't quite succeed with women, despite coaching from his roommate and counseling from a psychology professor whose assistance is part of a research project. *AKA:* Doin' It.

1982 90m/C Tim Choate, Krista Errickson, Marshall Efron, Wallace Shawn, Wendie Jo Sperber, Cathryn Damon; **D:** Charles Loventhal. **VHS, Beta** *NO* 🎞🎞½

First Turn On Not to be confused with "The Thomas Edison Story," this sex-comedy follows the adventures of several young campers who decide to die happy when an avalanche leaves them trapped in a cave. A longer unrated version is available.

1983 (R) 84m/C Georgia Harrell, Michael Sanville, Googy Gress, Jenny Johnson, Heide Basset, Vincent D'Onofrio, Sheila Kennedy; **D:** Michael Herz, Lloyd Samuel Weil Kaufman. **VHS, Beta $69.98** *LIV* 🎞

First Yank into Tokyo An American army pilot who grew up in Japan undergoes plastic surgery in order to infiltrate Japanese lines and get information from an American scientist. Some last minute editing to capitalize on current events made this the first American film to deal with the atomic bomb. *AKA:* Mask of Fury.

1945 83m/B Tom Neal, Richard Loo, Barbara Hale, Marc Cramer; **D:** Gordon Douglas. **VHS, Beta $19.98** *RKO, TTC* 🎞🎞

A Fish Called Wanda Absurd, high-speed farce about four criminals trying to retrieve $20 million they've stolen from a safety deposit box—and each other. Meanwhile, barrister Cleese falls in love with the female thief (Curtis). Some sick, but tastelessly funny, humor involves Palin's problem with stuttering and some very dead doggies. Written by Monty Python alum Cleese and director Crichton, who understand that silence is sometimes funnier than speech, and that timing is everything. Wickedly funny.

1988 (R) 98m/C John Cleese, Kevin Kline, Jamie Lee Curtis, Michael Palin, Tom Georgeson, Maria Aitken, Patricia Hayes, Geoffrey Palmer; **D:** Charles Crichton; **W:** John Cleese, Charles Crichton; **M:** John Du Prez. Academy Awards '88: Best Supporting Actor (Kline); Nominations: Best Director (Crichton), Best Original Screenplay; British Academy Awards '88: Best Actor (Cleese), Best Supporting Actor (Palin). **VHS, Beta $14.95** *MGM, BTV, FOX* 🎞🎞🎞

Fish Hawk When an alcoholic Indian, Fish Hawk, meets a young boy in the forest, they strike up a friendship and he attempts to clean up his act. Attempts to be heartwarming.

1979 (G) 95m/C *CA* Will Sampson, Charlie Fields; **D:** Donald Shebib. **VHS, Beta $19.95** *MED, VTR* 🎞½

The Fish that Saved Pittsburgh A floundering basketball team hires an astrologer to try and change their luck. She makes sure all the team members' signs are compatible with their star's Pisces sign (the fish). Produced a disco soundtrack with several Motown groups who also performed in the movie.

1979 (PG) 104m/C Jonathan Winters, Stockard Channing, Flip Wilson, Julius Erving, Margaret Avery, Meadowlark Lemon, Nicholas Pryor, James Bond III, Kareem Abdul-Jabbar, Jack Kehoe, Debbie Allen; **D:** Gilbert Moses. **VHS, Beta $59.95** *LHV, WAR* 🎞🎞

The Fisher King In derelict-infested Manhattan a down-and-out radio deejay meets a crazed vagabond (Williams) obsessed with medieval history and in search of the Holy Grail. At first the whimsical mix of Arthurian myth and modern urban hell seems amazingly wrongheaded. In retrospect it still does. But while this picture runs it weaves a spell that pulls you in, especially in its quiet moments. Your reaction to the silly ending depends entirely on how well you're bamboozled by a script that equates madness with enlightment and the homeless with holy fools. Filmed on the streets of New York, with many street people playing themselves.

1991 (R) 138m/C Robin Williams, Jeff Bridges, Amanda Plummer, Mercedes Ruehl, Michael Jeter, Harry Shearer, John de Lancie; **D:** Terry Gilliam; **W:** Richard LaGravenese. Academy Awards '91: Best Supporting Actress (Ruehl); Nominations: Best Actor (Williams), Best Art Direction/Set Decoration, Best Original Screenplay, Best Original Score; Chicago Film Critics Awards '91: Best Supporting Actress (Ruehl); Golden Globe Awards '92: Best Actor—Musical/Comedy (Williams), Best Supporting Actress (Ruehl). **VHS, Beta, 8mm $19.95** *COL, CCB* 🎞🎞🎞

Fisherman's Wharf Breen stars as an orphan adopted by a San Francisco fisherman who runs away when his aunt and bratty cousin come to live with them.

1939 72m/B Bobby Breen, Leo Carrillo, Henry Armetta, Lee Patrick, Rosina Galli, Leon Belasco; **D:** Bernard Vorhaus. **VHS $19.95** *NOS* 🎞½

F.I.S.T. A young truck driver turns union organizer for idealistic reasons, but finds himself teaming with gangsters to boost his cause. His rise to the top of the union comes at the cost of his integrity, as Stallone does a character resembling Jimmy Hoffa.

1978 (R) 145m/C Sylvester Stallone, Rod Steiger, Peter Boyle, David Huffman, Melinda Dillon, Tony LoBianco, Kevin Conway, Peter Donat, Cassie Yates, Brian Dennehy; **D:** Norman Jewison; **W:** Sylvester Stallone; **M:** Bill Conti. **VHS, Beta $14.95** *MGM, FOX* 🎞🎞½

Fist Street fighter battles his way through the urban jungle seeking personal freedom and revenge.

1979 (R) 84m/C Richard Lawson, Annazette Chase, Dabney Coleman. **VHS, Beta** *NO* 🎞

Fist Fighter The ups and downs of a professional bare-knuckle fighter as he avenges a friend's murder.

1988 (R) 99m/C George Rivero, Edward Albert, Brenda Bakke, Mike Connors, Simon Andrew, Matthias Hues; **D:** Frank Zuniga. **VHS, Beta** *NO* 🎞½

A Fist Full of Talons A sexy maiden, a young warrior, and a goofy thief team up to fight evil in the early Chinese republic.

19?? 100m/C **VHS, Beta $34.95** *OCE* 🎞

Fist of Fear, Touch of Death Madison Square Garden is the scene for a high stakes martial arts face-off. Standard kung-fu film highlighted by short clips of the late Bruce Lee.

1977 90m/C Fred Williamson, Ron Van Cliff, Adolph Caesar, Aaron Banks, Bill Louie; **D:** Matthew Mallinson. **VHS, Beta $39.95** *LIV* 🎞

Fist of Honor A young boxer seeks to avenge his fiance's death, a beautiful girl squares off against a bad-cop, and two mobster leaders try to take control of the same city. When a member of one family breaks a truce and begins killing rival family members, the violence escalates and old scores will be settled.

1992 (R) 90m/C Sam Jones, Joey House, Harry Guardino, Nicholas Worth, Frank Sivero, Abe Vigoda, Bubba Smith; **D:** Richard Pepin; **W:** Charles Kanganis. **VHS $89.95** *PMH* 🎞

Fist of Steel In this futuristic martial arts film, modern day gladiators fight to the death in tournaments run by a vicious syndicate. When top gladiator Amp makes an escape bid he's hunted by henchman Mainframe, who plans to meet Amp in a fixed fight in order to become the new champion.

1993 97m/C Dale "Apollo" Cook, Greg Douglass, Cynthia Khan, Don Nakaya Nielsen, Jim Gaines, Ned Hourani, Nick Nicholson, Kris Aguilar; **D:** Irvin Johnson; **W:** Anthony Jesu. **VHS $89.95** *AIP* 🎞½

The Fist, the Kicks, and the Evils A young man who's father is murdered learns kung fu and sets out for revenge.

1980 90m/C Kao Fei, Bruce Liang. **VHS, Beta $29.95** *OCE* 🎞½

Fistful of Death Kinski portrays a vengefully violent and desperate cowpoke in the days of the old West.

1967 84m/C Klaus Kinski. **VHS, Beta $59.95** *TWE* 🎞

A Fistful of Dollars The epitome of the "spaghetti western" pits Eastwood as "the man with no name" against two families who are feuding over land. A remake of Kurosawa's "Yojimbo," and followed by Leone's "For a Few Dollars More", and "The Good, The Bad, and The Ugly."
1964 (R) 101m/C *IT* Clint Eastwood, Gian Marie Volonte, Marianne Koch; *D:* Sergio Leone; *M:* Ennio Morricone. VHS, Beta $19.98 *MGM, FCT, TLF* ✍✍✍

A Fistful of Dynamite A spaghetti western, with Leone's trademark humor and a striking score by Morricone. An Irish demolitions expert and a Mexican peasant team up to rob a bank during a revolution in Mexico. *AKA:* Duck, You Sucker; Giu la Testa.
1972 (PG) 138m/C *IT* James Coburn, Rod Steiger, Romolo Valli; *D:* Sergio Leone; *M:* Ennio Morricone. VHS, Beta $59.95 *MGM* ✍✍

Fists of Blood A martial arts expert seeks revenge on the drug baron who murdered his friend and kidnapped his girl.
1987 90m/C *AU* Eddie Stazak; *D:* Brian Trenchard-Smith. VHS, Beta $39.95 *CEL* ✍½

Fists of Dragons Vengeful, sacrificial bloodshed abounds in this Chinese boxing extravaganza.
1969 92m/C Huang I Lung, Ou Ti; *D:* Yeh Yung Chu. VHS, Beta $29.95 *TWE* ✍

Fists of Fury Bruce Lee stars in this violent but charming Kung Fu action adventure in which he must break a solemn vow to avoid fighting in order to avenge the murder of his teacher by drug smugglers. *AKA:* The Big Boss.
1973 (R) 102m/C Bruce Lee, Maria Yi; *D:* Lo Wei. VHS, Beta $19.98 *FOX* ✍✍✍

Fists of Fury 2 Chen Shan must survive the Organizations' onslaughts to kill him. He escapes their perilous plots only to return to battle against them after they kill his mother for her inability to disclose Chen's hiding place. Finally Chen defeats the Evil Organization himself.
1980 (R) 90m/C Bruce Li, Ho Chung Do, Shum Shim Po. VHS, Beta $19.98 *GEM* ✍½

Fit for a King A reporter becomes a princess' knight in shining armor when he foils an assassination plot in this screwball romance.
1937 73m/B Joe E. Brown, Leo Carrillo, Helen Mack, Paul Kelly, Harry Davenport; *D:* Edward Sedgwick. VHS, Beta $24.95 *NOS, DVT, HEG* ✍✍

Fit to Kill Once again special agents Donna Hamilton and Nicole Justine (former Playboy centerfolds Speir and Vasquez) re-team for an adventure that matches them with an old enemy, double agents, diamonds, and revenge. Filmed on location in Hawaii.
1993 90m/C Dona Speir, Roberta Vasquez, R.J. Moore, Bruce Penhall, Julie Strain, Rodrigo Obregon, Cynthia Brimhall, Tony Peck; *D:* Andy Sidaris; *W:* Andy Sidaris. VHS $89.95 *COL* ✍½

Fitzcarraldo Although he failed to build a railroad across South America, Fitzcarraldo is determined to build an opera house in the middle of the Amazon jungles and have Enrico Caruso sing there. Based on a true story of a charismatic Irishman's impossible quest at the turn of the century. Of note: No special effects were used in this movie—everything you see actually occurred during filming, including hauling a large boat over a mountain.
1982 (PG) 157m/C *GE* Klaus Kinski, Claudia Cardinale, Jose Lewgoy, Miguel Angel Fuentes, Paul Hittscher; *D:* Werner Herzog; *M:* Popul Vuh. Cannes Film Festival Nominations: cs 82: Best Film; Cannes Film

Festival '82: Best Director (Herzog). VHS, Beta $69.95 *WAR, APD, ING* ✍✍✍

Five Came Back When a plane with twelve passengers crashes in the South American jungle, only five can ride in the patched-up wreck. Since the remainder will be left to face head hunters, intense arguments ensue. Same director remade this as "Back from Eternity" in 1956.
1939 93m/B Lucille Ball, Chester Morris, John Carradine, Wendy Barrie, Kent Taylor, Joseph Calleia, Sir C. Aubrey Smith, Patric Knowles; *D:* John Farrow. VHS, Beta $29.95 *RKO, TTC* ✍✍

Five Card Stud Five members of a lynching party are being killed one by one, and a professional gambler, who tried to prevent the lynching, attempts to ensnare the killer with the aid of a preacher with a gun. The poor script was based on a novel by Ray Gaulden.
1968 (PG) 103m/C Robert Mitchum, Dean Martin, Inger Stevens, Roddy McDowall, Yaphet Kotto, John Anderson, Katherine Justice; *D:* Henry Hathaway; *M:* Maurice Jarre. VHS, Beta $14.95 *PAR* ✍½

Five Corners A quixotic, dramatic comedy about the inhabitants of the 5 Corners section of the Bronx in 1964, centering around a girl being wooed by a psychotic rapist, her crippled boyfriend, and the hero-turned-racial-pacifist who cannot rescue her out of principle.
1988 (R) 92m/C Jodie Foster, John Turturro, Todd Graff, Tim Robbins, Elizabeth Berridge, Rose Gregorio, Gregory Rozakis, Rodney Harvey, John Seitz; *D:* Tony Bill; *W:* John Patrick Shanley; *M:* James Newton Howard. VHS, Beta $14.95 *MGM* ✍✍✍

Five Days One Summer Set in 1932, the story of a haunting and obsessive love affair between a married Scottish doctor and a young woman who happens to be his niece. While on vacation in the Swiss Alps, the doctor must vie for her love with their handsome young mountain climbing guide. Based on a story by Kay Boyle.
1982 (PG) 108m/C Sean Connery, Betsy Brantley, Lambert Wilson; *D:* Fred Zinneman; *M:* Elmer Bernstein. VHS, Beta $19.98 *WAR* ✍✍

Five Easy Pieces Nicholson's superb acting brings to life this character study of a talented musician who has given up a promising career and now works on the oil rigs. After twenty years he returns home to attempt one last communication with his dying father and perhaps, reconcile himself with his fear of failure and desire for greatness. Black, Anspach, and Bush create especially memorable characters. Nicholson ordering toast via a chicken salad sandwich is a classic.
1970 (R) 98m/C Jack Nicholson, Karen Black, Susan Anspach, Lois Smith, Billy Green Bush, Fannie Flagg, Ralph Waite, Sally Struthers, Helena Kallianiotes; *D:* Bob Rafelson; *W:* Adrien (Carole Eastman) Joyce, Bob Rafelson. Academy Awards '70 Nominations: Best Actor (Nicholson), Best Picture, Best Story & Screenplay, Best Supporting Actress (Black); Golden Globe Awards '71: Best Supporting Actress (Black). VHS, Beta, 8mm $14.95 *COL, VYG, WME* ✍✍✍✍

Five Fighters from Shaolin Five high-kicking fighters endeavor to recapture their temple from an evil duke.
197? 88m/C Chang Shen, Lung Kwan, Dhiu Min Shien; *D:* Ko Shu-How. VHS, Beta $39.95 *MPI, MOV* ✍

Five Fingers Under the alias "Cicero," Albanian valet Mason joins the espionage ring, selling highly confidential British war papers to the Germans during WWII. True story with odd real-life ending—unconvinced

of document authenticity, the Nazis never acted on the information, even when they had the time and date of the European invasion! Fast-paced and absorbing. Adapted from the book "Operation Cicero" by L.C. Moyzisch. *AKA:* Operation Cicero.
1952 108m/B James Mason, Danielle Darrieux, Michael Rennie, Walter Hampden, Oscar Karlweis, Herbert Berghof, John Wengraf, Michael Pate, Ivan Triesault, Hanne Axman, David Wolfe, Nestor Paiva, Richard Loo, Keith McConnell; *D:* Joseph L. Mankiewicz; *W:* Michael Wilson; *M:* Bernard Herrmann. VHS $19.99 *FXV* ✍✍✍½

Five for Hell The army picks five of its meanest men for a suicide mission during WWII. They must go behind German lines and find the plans for the enemy offensive.
1967 88m/C *IT* Klaus Kinski, John Garko, Nick Jordan, Margaret Lee; *D:* Frank Kramer. VHS, Beta $59.95 *TWE* ✍

Five Giants from Texas El cheapo spaghetti western features Madison, television's former Wild Bill Hickock, as a rancher fighting off displaced Mexican peasants and outlaws. *AKA:* I Cinque Della Vendetta.
1966 103m/C Guy Madison, Monica Randall; *D:* Aldo Florio. VHS, Beta $59.95 *TWE* ✍

Five Golden Dragons A typical action film about an American running afoul of ruthless gold trafficking in Hong Kong. Even this stellar cast can't help the script.
1967 92m/C *GB* Robert Cummings, Christopher Lee, Brian Donlevy, Klaus Kinski, George Raft, Dan Duryea, Margaret Lee; *D:* Jeremy Summers. VHS, Beta $59.98 *NO* ✍

The Five Heartbeats Well told story of five black singers in the 1960s, their successes and failures as a group and as individuals. Although every horror story of the music business is included, the story remains fresh and the acting excellent. Music is fine, but secondary to the people. Well written characters with few cliches. Skillfully directed by Townsend (of "Hollywood Shuffle") who did research by talking to the Dells. Less than memorable showing at the box office but fun and entertaining.
1991 (R) 122m/C Robert Townsend, Tressa Thomas, Michael Wright, Harry J. Lennix, Diahann Carroll, Leon, Hawthorne James, Chuck Patterson, Roy Fegan, Tico Wells, John Canada Terrell, Harold Nicholas, Paul Benjamin; *D:* Robert Townsend; *W:* Robert Townsend, Keenan Ivory Wayans; *M:* Stanley Clarke. VHS, Beta $19.95 *FXV* ✍✍✍

Five Miles to Midnight Brett and Danny have to depend on a photographer (Collins) for help to smuggle a gangster out of Italy. From the British "Persuaders" adventure series. Made for television.
1980 52m/C *GB* Roger Moore, Tony Curtis, Joan Collins. VHS *NO* ✍✍✍

Five Minutes to Love McClanahan (one of TV's "Golden Girls") plays a young, sleazy hussy named "Poochie, the girl from the shack." This exploitation schlocker appears to be McClanahan's first film. *AKA:* The Rotten Apple; It Only Take Five Minutes.
1963 85m/B Rue McClanahan, Paul Leder, King Moody; *D:* John Hayes. VHS $16.95 *SNC, TPV* ✍

The Five of Me A man with five personalities finds that livin' ain't easy and seeks professional help. Made for television, based on the autobiography of Henry Hawksworth.
1981 100m/C David Birney, Dee Wallace Stone, Mitchell Ryan, John McLiam, James Whitmore Jr., Ben Piazza; *D:* Paul Wendkos. VHS $39.95 *LIV* ✍✍½

The Five Pennies Sentimental biography starring Kaye as famed jazzman Red Nichols features performances by legendary musicians Bob Crosby, Bobby Troup, Ray Anthony and Louis Armstrong. This movie marked Weld's film debut. ♫Good Night Sleep Tight; The Five Pennies; Battle Hymn of the Republic; When the Saints Go Marching In; The Music Goes 'Round and Around; Jingle Bells; Carnival of Venice; Paradise.
1959 117m/C Danny Kaye, Louis Armstrong, Barbara Bel Geddes, Tuesday Weld, Harry Guardino; *D:* Melville Shavelson; *W:* Melville Shavelson, Jack Rose. **VHS, Beta $14.95** *PAR* ♫♫½

The 5000 Fingers of Dr. T In Dr. Seuss' only non-animated movie, a boy tries to evade piano lessons and runs right into the castle of the evil Dr. Terwilliger, where hundreds of boys are held captive for piano lessons. Worse yet, they're forced to wear silly beanies with "happy fingers" waving on top. Luckily, the trusted family plumber is on hand to save the day through means of an atomic bomb. Wonderful satire, horrible music, mesmerizing Seussian sets. The skating brothers (who are joined at their beards) are a treat.
1953 88m/C Peter Lind Hayes, Mary Healy, Tommy Rettig, Hans Conried; *D:* Roy Rowland; *W:* Dr. Seuss, Allan Scott. **VHS, Beta $59.95** *COL, XVC, FCT* ♫♫♫

Five Weeks in a Balloon This adaptation of the Jules Verne novel follows the often-comic exploits of a 19th-century British expedition that encounters many adventures on a balloon trek across Africa. Pleasant fluff with a good cast.
1962 101m/C Fabian, Peter Lorre, Red Buttons, Cedric Hardwicke, Barbara Eden; *D:* Irwin Allen; *W:* Charles Bennett, Irwin Allen. **VHS, Beta $19.98** *FOX, FCT* ♫♫

The $5.20 an Hour Dream Lavin is a divorced mother and factory worker burdened with debt and determined to get and keep a job on the higher-paying, traditionally all-male assembly line. Lesser feminist drama on the heels of "Norma Rae." Made for television.
1980 96m/C Linda Lavin, Richard Jaeckel, Nicholas Pryor, Pamela McMyler, Mayf Nutter, Taurean Blacque, Robert Davi, Dennis Fimple, Dana Hill, Ernie Hudson; *D:* Russ Mayberry. **VHS, Beta** *TLF* ♫♫

The Fix A group of cocaine smugglers get their just desserts as the federal government catches them in a sting operation. *AKA:* The Agitators.
1984 95m/C Vince Edwards, Richard Jaeckel, Julie Hill, Charles Dierkop, Byron Cherry, Robert Tessier; *D:* Will Zens. **VHS, Beta** *NO* ♫

The Fixer Based on the true story of a Jewish handyman (Bates) in 1911 Tsarist Russia who's accused of murdering a gentile boy. Wrongly imprisoned he's tortured to confess to the crime, which he refuses to do. Bogarde is the lawyer who tries to help him. Strong direction and acting in an unrelenting drama. Adapted from Bernard Malamud's Pulitzer Prize-winning novel.
1968 (PG-13) 132m/C Alan Bates, Dirk Bogarde, Georgia Brown, Hugh Griffith, Elizabeth Hartman, Ian Holm, David Opatoshu, David Warner, Carol White, Murray Melvin, Peter Jeffrey, William Hutt; *D:* John Frankenheimer; *W:* Dalton Trumbo; *M:* Maurice Jarre. **VHS $19.98** *MGM* ♫♫♫

Flambards In the early 1900's teenaged orphan Christine is sent to live with her tyrannical Uncle Russell and his two sons on their crumbling English estate, Flambards. Bitter rivalries and jealousies abound between arrogant, tradition bound Mark and

younger brother William, who's obsessed with the new-fangled airplane. Quarrels intensify as both young men fall in love with Christine and WWI begins, leading to sacrifice and tragedy. Based on the trilogy by K.M. Peyton. Made for British television; 12 episodes on 6 cassettes.
19?? 676m/C *GB* Christine McKenna, Stephen Grives, Alan Parnaby, Edward Judd, Sebastian Abineri, Peter Settelen, Carol Leader, Frank Mills. **VHS $139.95** *TVC* ♫♫½

The Flame & the Arrow Dardo the Arrow, a Robin Hood-like outlaw in medieval Italy, leads his band of mountain fighters against a mercenary warlord who has seduced his wife and kidnapped his son. Spectacular acrobatics, with Lancaster performing his own stunts, add interest to the usual swashbuckling.
1950 88m/C Burt Lancaster, Virginia Mayo, Aline MacMahon, Nick Cravat, Robert Douglas, Frank Allenby; *D:* Jacques Tourneur; *M:* Max Steiner. **VHS, Beta $19.98** *WAR* ♫♫♫

The Flame is Love A made-for-television adaptation of one of Barbara Cartland's romantic novels. An American heiress falls tragically in love with a Parisian journalist despite her engagement to an Englishman. Takes place at the turn of the century.
1979 98m/C Linda Purl, Timothy Dalton, Shane Briant; *D:* Michael O'Herlihy. **VHS, Beta $69.98** *LIV* ♫♫

Flame of the Barbary Coast A rancher from Montana vies with a gambling czar for a beautiful dance hall queen and control of the Barbary Coast district of San Francisco. The great earthquake of 1906 provides the plot with a climax. Also available colorized.
1945 91m/B John Wayne, Ann Dvorak, Joseph Schildkraut, William Frawley; *D:* Joseph Kane. **VHS $14.98** *MED, REP* ♫♫½

Flame of the Islands De Carlo plays a smoldering, passionate chanteuse who struggles with love and gangsters for possession of a Bahamian casino in this tropical heat wave.
1955 92m/C Yvonne De Carlo, Howard Duff, Zachary Scott, James Arness, Kurt Kasznar, Barbara O'Neil; *D:* Edward Ludwig. **VHS, Beta $39.98** *NO* ♫♫

Flame Over India When Moslems lay siege to a British fortress in India, Governess Wyatt (Bacall) and Captain Scott (More) save the Maharaja's son and escape by commandeering a train. Along the way they find treason, adventure and love. *AKA:* Northwest Frontier.
1960 130m/C *GB* Kenneth More, Lauren Bacall, Herbert Lom, Wilfrid Hyde-White, I.S. Johar, Ursula Jeans, Ian Hunter, Eugene Deckers, Jack Gwillim, Govind Raja Ross, Frank Olegario; *D:* J. Lee Thompson. **VHS** *HEG, SUE, DVT* ♫♫♫

Flame to the Phoenix A WWII drama about the Polish cavalry forces' decimation to German Panzer tanks.
1985 80m/C *GB* Paul Geoffrey, Ann Firbank, Frederick Treves; *D:* William Brayne. **VHS, Beta** *NO* ♫½

The Flame Trees of Thika In 1913, a British family travels to East Africa to start a coffee plantation. Seen through the eyes of the young daughter, her childhood consists of the local Masai and Kikuyu tribes, the eccentric and sometimes unhappy English neighbors, and the wild animals that roam the plains. Based on the memoirs of writer Elspeth Huxley. On four cassettes. Shown on PBS "Masterpiece Theatre."
198? 366m/C *GB* Hayley Mills, Holly Aird, David Robb, Ben Cross. **VHS $129.95** *SIG, TVC* ♫♫♫

Flaming Bullets Last of the Texas Rangers series has solid action scenes, but little else. Ritter leads the Texas Rangers in breaking up a gang with a devious scheme: breaking men out of jail, then killing them for the cash reward.
1945 55m/B **VHS $19.99** *MOV* ♫♫

Flaming Frontiers A frontier scout matches wits against gold mine thieves. In fifteen episodes.
1938 300m/B Johnny Mack Brown, Eleanor Hanson, Ralph Bowman; *D:* Ray Taylor. **VHS, Beta $39.95** *VYY, VCN, NOS* ♫½

Flaming Lead A hard-drinkin' ranch owner hires a nightclub cowboy to help him get an Army horse contract.
1939 57m/B Ken Maynard, Eleanor Stewart, Walter Long, Tom London; *D:* Max Alexander. **VHS $19.95** *NOS, DVT, HEG* ♫½

Flaming Signal Featuring Flash the Wonder Labrador, this action-packed film deals with a pilot who crash-lands near a Pacific island, just as the natives, provoked by an exploitative German trader, are rising up against the whites. Both Flash and his master manage to rescue the missionary's pretty daughter.
1933 64m/B Noah Beery Sr., Marceline Day, Carmelita Geraghty, Mischa Auer, Henry B. Walthall. **VHS, Beta $16.95** *SNC, LSV, RXM* ♫½

Flaming Star In 1870s Texas, a family with a white father and an Indian mother is caught in the midst of an Indian uprising. The mixed-blood youth, excellently played by Presley, must choose a side with tragic results for all. A stirring, well-written drama of frontier prejudice and one of Presley's best films.
1960 101m/C Elvis Presley, Dolores Del Rio, Barbara Eden, Steve Forrest, John McIntire, Richard Jaeckel, L.Q. Jones; *D:* Don Siegel. **VHS, Beta $14.98** *FOX, MVD* ♫♫♫

The Flaming Teen-Age Schlocky pseudo-documentary demonstrating the evils of drugs and alcohol. Exploitative, and the teenagers look really old. Cheaply made, and it shows.
1956 67m/B Noel Reyburn, Ethel Barrett, Jerry Frank, Shirley Holmes; *D:* Irvin S. Yeaworth Jr., Charles Edwards. **VHS $16.95** *SNC* ♫

The Flaming Urge A small town is plagued by mysterious fires. Could a pyromaniac be on the loose?
1953 67m/B Harold Lloyd Jr., Cathy Downs. **VHS, Beta $16.95** *SNC* ♫

The Flamingo Kid Brooklyn teen Dillon gets a summer job at a fancy beach club on Long Island. His father, a plumber, remembers how to dream but is also aware of how rough the world is on dreamers. Suddenly making lots of money at a mostly easy job, the kid's attracted to the high style of the local sports car dealer, and finds his father's solid life a bore. By the end of the summer, he's learned the true value of both men, and the kind of man he wants to be. Excellent performances all around, nice ensemble acting among the young men who play Dillon's buddies. Great sound track. Film debut of Jones, who seems a little old for her part as a California college sophomore.
1984 (PG-13) 100m/C Matt Dillon, Hector Elizondo, Molly McCarthy, Martha Gehman, Richard Crenna, Jessica Walter, Carole Davis, Janet Jones, Fisher Stevens, Bronson Pinchot; *D:* Garry Marshall. **VHS, Beta $29.98** *LIV, VES* ♫♫♫

Flamingo Road A scandalously entertaining melodrama in which Crawford portrays a carnival dancer who intrigues Scott and Brian in a small Southern town where the

carnival stops. Crawford shines in a role that demands her to be both tough and sensitive in a corrupt world full of political backstabbing and sleazy characters. Remade as a TV movie and television soap-opera series in 1980.
1949 94m/B Joan Crawford, Zachary Scott, David Brian, Sydney Greenstreet, Gertrude Michael, Gladys George, Virginia Huston, Fred Clark, Alice White; **D:** Michael Curtiz; **W:** Edmund H. North, Robert Wilder. **VHS** $19.98 *MGM ぽぽ*

The Flash When police scientist Barry Allen is accidentally doused by chemicals and then struck by lightening the combination makes him into a new superhero. His super quickness help his quest in fighting crime in Central City where he's aided by fellow scientist Tina McGee (the only other person to know his secret). In this adventure, the Flash seeks out the violent and mesmerizing leader of a biker gang who caused the death of Barry's brother. Based on the DC comic book character, this is the pilot episode for the short-lived television series. The look is dark and stylized and not played for camp.
1990 94m/C John Wesley Shipp, Amanda Pays, Michael Nader; **M:** Danny Elfman. **VHS, Beta** $19.98 *WAR ぽぽ*

The Flash 2: Revenge of the Trickster Every good superhero needs his nemesis—and this time around the Flash (Shipp) has that murderous mischiefmaker the Trickster (Hamill) who, along with his femme fatale sidekick Prank, is determined to outwit our hero. Can super speed and strength be enough to keep Central City safe? Based on the DC comic book character and taken from two episodes of the television series.
1991 92m/C John Wesley Shipp, Amanda Pays, Mark Hamill, Richard Belzer. **VHS, Beta** *WAR ぽぽ½*

Flash & Firecat A beautiful blonde and a crazy thief steal and race their way across the country in a dune buggy with the police hot on their trail.
1975 (PG) 90m/C Roger Davis, Tricia Sembera, Dub Taylor, Richard Kiel; **D:** Ferd Sebastian. **VHS, Beta** *NO ぽ*

Flash Gordon Camp version of the adventures of Flash Gordon in outer space. This time, Flash and Dale Arden are forced by Dr. Zarkov to accompany him on a mission to far-off Mongo, where Ming the Merciless is threatening the destruction of Earth. Music by Queen.
1980 (PG) 111m/C Sam Jones, Melody Anderson, Chaim Topol, Max von Sydow, Ornella Muti, Timothy Dalton, Brian Blessed; **D:** Mike Hodges; **M:** Queen, Howard Blake. **VHS, Beta** $14.98 *MCA ぽぽ*

Flash Gordon Conquers the Universe Ravaging plague strikes the earth and Flash Gordon undertakes to stop it. A serial in twelve chapters. *AKA:* Purple Death from Outer Space.
1940 240m/B Buster Crabbe, Carol Hughes, Charles Middleton, Frank Shannon. **VHS, Beta** $39.95 *VYY, MRV, SNC ぽぽ*

Flash Gordon: Mars Attacks the World The earth is plagued by the evil Ming, but Flash Gordon steps in. From the serial. *AKA:* The Deadly Rays From Mars; Flash Gordon's Trip to Mars.
1938 87m/B Buster Crabbe, Jean Rogers, Charles Middleton. **VHS, Beta** $39.95 *CAB ぽぽ*

Flash Gordon: Rocketship Re-edited from the original Flash Gordon serial in which Flash and company must prevent the planet Mongo from colliding with Earth. Good

character acting and good clean fun. *AKA:* Spaceship to the Unknown; Perils from Planet Mongo; Space Soldiers; Atomic Rocketship.
1936 97m/B Buster Crabbe, Jean Rogers, Frank Shannon, Charles Middleton, Priscilla Lawson, Jack Lipson; **D:** Frederick Stephani. **VHS, Beta** $29.95 *VYY, PSM, CAB ぽぽ½*

Flash Gordon: Vol. 1 Join Flash Gordon and Dale Arden as they struggle to maintain peace in the galaxy in this pair of episodes from the series.
1953 60m/B Steve Holland, Irene Champlin. **VHS, Beta** $29.95 *DVT ぽぽ½*

Flash Gordon: Vol. 2 Flash and Dale continue their quest for intergalactic tranquility in this pair of episodes from the series.
1953 60m/B Steve Holland, Irene Champlin. **VHS, Beta** $29.95 *DVT ぽぽ½*

Flash Gordon: Vol. 3 The struggle for intergalactic peace continues as Flash Gordon battles Ming the Merciless in this pair of episodes from the series.
1953 60m/B VHS, Beta $29.95 *DVT ぽぽ½*

A Flash of Green A crooked politician is helping a construction firm exploit valuable waterfront property. He enlists the influence of a hesitant local journalist, who then falls for the woman leading the homeowner's conservation drive against the development plan. Made for American Playhouse and produced by costar Jordon. Based on the work of John D. MacDonald.
1985 122m/C Ed Harris, Blair Brown, Richard Jordan, George Coe; **D:** Victor Nunez; **W:** Victor Nunez; **M:** Charles Engstrom. **VHS, Beta** $59.95 *MED ぽぽ*

Flashback FBI agent Sutherland's assignment sounds easy: escort aging 1960s radical Hopper to prison. But Hopper is cunning and decides not to go without a fight. He uses his brain to outwit the young Sutherland and to turn him against himself. Good moments between the two leads and with Kane, as a woman who never left the sixties behind.
1989 (R) 108m/C Dennis Hopper, Kiefer Sutherland, Carol Kane, Cliff DeYoung, Paul Dooley, Michael McKean, Richard Masur; **D:** Franco Amurri; **M:** Barry Goldberg. **VHS, Beta** $89.99 *PAR ぽぽぽ*

Flashdance 18-year-old Alex wants to dance. She works all day as a welder (and has a hot affair going with her boss), dances at a local bar at night, and hopes someday to get enough courage to audition for a spot at the School of Ballet. Glossy music video redeemed somewhat by exciting choreography with Marine Jahan doing the dancing for Beals. Oscar-winning title song sung by Irene Cara. Inspired the torn-sweatshirt trend in fashion of the period. ♫Flashdance...What a Feeling; I Love Rock 'n Roll; Manhunt; Gloria; Lady, Lady, Lady; Seduce Me Tonight.
1983 (R) 95m/C Jennifer Beals, Michael Nouri, Belinda Bauer, Lilia Skala, Cynthia Rhodes, Sunny Johnson, Lee Ving, Kyle T. Heffner, Ron Karabatsos, Robert Wuhl, Elizabeth Sagal; **D:** Franca Pasut. Academy Awards '83: Best Song ("Flashdance...What a Feeling"); Nominations: Best Cinematography, Best Film Editing, Best Song ("Maniac"); Golden Globe Awards '84: Best Song ("Flashdance...What a Feeling"), Best Score. **VHS, Beta, 8mm** $14.95 *PAR ぽぽ*

Flashpoint A pair of Texas border patrolmen discover an abandoned jeep that contains a fortune in cash, apparently from the 1960s. As they try to figure out how it got there, they become prey to those who want to keep the secret. With this cast, flick ought to be better.

1984 (R) 95m/C Treat Williams, Kris Kristofferson, Tess Harper, Rip Torn, Miguel Ferrer, Roberts Blossom; **D:** William Tannen; **W:** Michael Butler. **VHS, Beta** *NO ぽぽ*

Flashpoint Africa When a news team follows a terrorist group's activities it winds up in a power struggle with terrifying consequences.
1984 99m/C Trevor Howard, Gayle Hunnicutt, James Faulkner. **VHS, Beta** *NO ぽ½*

Flat Top The training of Navy fighter pilots aboard "flat top" aircraft carriers during WWII provides the drama here. A strict commander is appreciated only after the war when the pilots realize his role in their survival. The film makes good use of actual combat footage; fast-paced and effective.
1952 85m/C Sterling Hayden, Richard Carlson, Keith Larsen, John Bromfield; **D:** Lesley Selander. **VHS, Beta** $9.98 *REP, FCT ぽぽ½*

Flatbed Annie and Sweetiepie: Lady Truckers A couple of good ol' gals hit the road and encounter a variety of bad guys out to steal their truck. Made for television. *AKA:* Flatbed Annie.
1979 100m/C Annie Potts, Kim Darby, Harry Dean Stanton, Arthur Godfrey, Rory Calhoun, Bill Carter; **D:** Robert Greenwald. **VHS, Beta** $79.99 *HBO, CNG ぽぽ½*

Flatfoot Tough police officer will let nothing stop him from finding and arresting drug smugglers. Good for laughs as well as lots of action. *AKA:* The Knock-Out Cop.
1978 (PG) 113m/C *IT* Bud Bodo, Werner Pochat, Bud Spencer, Enzo Cannavale, Dagmar Lassander, Joe Stewardson; **D:** Steno. **VHS, Beta** *NO ぽぽ*

Flatliners A group of medical students begin after-hours experimentation with death and out-of-body experiences. Some standard horror film images but Roberts and Sutherland create an energy that makes it worth watching.
1990 (R) 111m/C Kiefer Sutherland, Julia Roberts, William Baldwin, Oliver Platt, Kevin Bacon, Kimberly Scott, Joshua Rudoy; **D:** Joel Schumacher; **M:** James Newton Howard. **VHS, Beta, 8mm** $19.95 *COL ぽぽ*

Flesh An Andy Warhol-produced seedy urban farce about a bisexual street hustler who meets a variety of drug-addicted, deformed, and sexually deviant people. Dallesandro fans will enjoy his extensive exposure (literally).
1968 90m/C Joe Dallesandro, Geraldine Smith, Patti D'Arbanville; **D:** Paul Morrissey. **VHS, Beta** $29.95 *TPV, PAR, FCT ぽぽぽ*

Flesh and Blood An unjustly convicted lawyer is released from prison to find out his wife has died. He vows revenge on those who falsely imprisoned him and assumes the disguise of a crippled beggar to begin his plot. Silent with musical score.
1922 75m/B Lon Chaney Sr.; **D:** Irving Cummings. **VHS, Beta, 8mm** $16.95 *SNC, VYY, GVV ぽぽ*

Flesh and Blood A rowdy group of 16th Century hellions makes off with a princess who is already spoken for and pillage and plunder their way to revenge. Hauer leads the motley group through sword fights, raids, and the like. Dutch director Verhoeven's first English language film. Not for children; with rape scenes, nudity, and graphic sex. *AKA:* The Rose and The Sword.
1985 (R) 126m/C Rutger Hauer, Jennifer Jason Leigh, Tom Burlinson, Susan Tyrrell, Jack Thompson, Ronald Lacey, Brion James, Bruno Kirby; **D:** Paul Verhoeven; **W:** Paul Verhoeven, Gerard Soeteman; **M:** Basil Poledouris. **VHS, Beta** $19.99 *LIV, VES ぽぽ½*

Flesh and Blood Show Rehearsal turns into an execution ritual for a group of actors at a mysterious seaside theatre. Truth in titling: features blood, gore, and some sex. Shot in part in 3-D. *AKA:* Asylum of the Insane.
1973 (R) 93m/C *GB* Robin Askwith, Candace Glendenning, Tristan Rogers, Ray Brooks, Jenny Hanley, Luan Peters, Patrick Barr; *D:* Pete Walker. **VHS, Beta $59.95** *MON* 𝄞

Flesh and Bone Quaid is exact as a vending machine distributor with a desolate rural Texas circuit, haunted by the memory of a decades-old murder committed by his father (Caan) during a botched farm-house robbery. Alcoholic Ryan (Quaid's real-life wife) emerges from a bad marriage and helps Quaid rebuild his life, never suspecting that they may have met before. Challenging but successful role for Ryan, better known for her girlish, romantic-comedy appeal. Paltrow's unforgettable as a heartless casket robber and Caan's partner/girlfriend. Director Kloves extracts moments of earthy beauty from the bleak, humble West Texas setting.
1993 (R) 127m/C Dennis Quaid, Meg Ryan, James Caan, Gwyneth Paltrow, Scott Wilson, Christopher Rydell; *D:* Steven Kloves; *W:* Steven Kloves; *M:* Thomas Newman. **VHS, Beta** *PAR* 𝄞𝄞𝄞

The Flesh and the Devil Classic Garbo at her seductive best as a woman who causes a feud between two friends. Gilbert is an Austrian officer, falls for the married Garbo and winds up killing her husband in a duel. Banished to the African Corps he asks his best friend (Hanson) to look after his lady love. But Hanson takes his job too seriously, falling for the lady himself. Great silent movie with surprise ending to match. The first Gilbert and Garbo pairing.
1927 112m/B John Gilbert, Greta Garbo, Lars Hanson, Barbara Kent, George Fawcett, Eugenie Besserer; *D:* Clarence Brown. **VHS $29.95** *MGM* 𝄞𝄞𝄞½

Flesh and the Spur A cowboy tracks the killer of his brother. Future Mannix Mike Connors (nicknamed 'Touch' at the time) joins the search. Unedifying western with oddball touches, notably a theme song by Chipmunks creator Ross Bagdasarian.
1957 78m/C John Agar, Marla English, Mike Connors, Raymond Hatton, Maria Monay, Joyce Meadows, Kenne Duncan; *D:* Edward L. Cahn. **VHS $15.95** *NOS, LOO* 𝄞½

The Flesh Eaters A claustrophobic low-budget thriller about a film queen and her secretary who crash-land on an island inhabited by your basic mad scientist. His latest experiment is with tiny flesh-eating sea creatures. Shock ending.
1964 87m/C Martin Kosleck, Rita Morley, Byron Sanders, Barbara Wilkin, Ray Tudor; *D:* Jack Curtis. **VHS, Beta $39.95** *SNC* 𝄞½

Flesh Eating Mothers Housewives are transformed into cannibals after a mystery virus hits their town. Their kids must stop the moms from eating any more people.
1989 90m/C Robert Lee Oliver, Donatella Hecht, Valorie Hubbard, Neal Rosen, Terry Hayes; *D:* James Aviles Martin. **VHS, Beta $14.95** *ACA* 𝄞

Flesh Feast Classically horrendous anti-Nazi bosh, in which a mad female plastic surgeon (Lake) rejuvenates Hitler and then tortures him to death with maggots to avenge her mother's suffering. Lake's last film, and the sorriest sign-off any actress ever had.
1969 (R) 72m/C Veronica Lake, Phil Philbin, Heather Hughes, Martha Mischon, Yanka Mann, Dian Wilhite, Chris Martell; *D:* Brad F. Ginter. **VHS, Beta** *NO* Woof!

Flesh Gordon Soft-core spoof of the "Flash Gordon" series. Flesh takes it upon himself to save Earth from the evil Wang's sex ray; Wang, of course, being the leader of the planet Porno. Lackluster special effects and below par story dull an already ridiculous movie. Look for cameo by real-life porn starlet Candy Samples.
1972 70m/C Jason Williams, Suzanne Fields, Joseph Hudgins, John Hoyt, Howard Zieff, Michael Benveniste; *Cameos:* Candy Samples; *D:* Mike Light. **VHS, Beta $19.98** *MED, IME* 𝄞

Fleshburn An Indian Vietnam War veteran escapes from a mental institution to get revenge on the four psychiatrists who committed him.
1984 (R) 91m/C Steve Kanaly, Karen Carlson, Sonny Landham, Macon McCalman; *D:* George Gage. **VHS, Beta $59.95** *MED* 𝄞𝄞

Fleshpot on 42nd Street Stark, realistic look at the streetwalking profession. Dusty leaves her blue collar boyfriend to move in with a transvestite and then she meets a dashing young Staten Island native (like the director). Their romance blooms until he is run over by a car, sending Dusty into a tailspin which lands her back on 42nd Street. Along the way, various rustic hookers and venerable old floozies liven up director Mulligan's version of New York. Less emphasis on the sleaze than the grittiness.
1971 78m/C Diana Lewis, Lynn Flanagan, Bob Walters; *D:* Andy Milligan. **VHS $23.00** *SMW, TPV* 𝄞

Fleshtone Artist Matthew Greco's (Kmep) work is not for the faint-hearted since he paints grisly suicides and murders. No wonder he's lonely—so lonely that he answers a phone-sex ad and is hooked up with Edna (Cutter), who becomes an obsession. Matthew even depicts her murder in one of his paintings and then she's found dead—only in turns out not to be Edna, who doesn't exist. Just what has Matthew gotten himself into? Provocative but ending is a letdown. An unrated version is also available.
1994 (R) 89m/C Martin Kemp, Lise Cutter, Tim Thomerson; *D:* Harry Hurwitz; *W:* Harry Hurwitz. **VHS $92.95** *PSM* 𝄞𝄞

Fletch Somewhat charming comedy. When newspaper journalist Fletch goes undercover to get the scoop on the local drug scene, a wealthy young businessman enlists his help in dying. Something's rotten in Denmark when the man's doctor knows nothing of the illness and Fletch comes closer to the drug scene than he realizes. Throughout the entire film, Chevy Chase assumes a multitude of flippant comic characters to discover the truth. Based on Gregory McDonald's novel.
1985 (PG) 98m/C Chevy Chase, Tim Matheson, Joe Don Baker, Dana Wheeler-Nicholson, M. Emmet Walsh, Kenneth Mars, Geena Davis, Richard Libertini, George Wendt, Kareem Abdul-Jabbar, Alison La Placa; *D:* Michael Ritchie; *W:* Andrew Bergman; *M:* Harold Faltermeyer. **VHS, Beta $14.95** *MCA* 𝄞𝄞

Fletch Lives In this sequel to "Fletch," Chase is back again as the super-reporter. When Fletch learns of his inheritance of a Southern estate he is eager to claim it. During his down-home trip he becomes involved in a murder and must use his disguise skills to solve it before he becomes the next victim. Based on the novels of Gregory MacDonald.
1989 (PG) 95m/C Chevy Chase, Hal Holbrook, Julianne Phillips, Richard Libertini, R. Lee Ermey, Cleavon Little; *D:* Michael Ritchie; *W:* Leon Capetanos; *M:* Harold Faltermeyer. **VHS, Beta $14.95** *MCA* 𝄞𝄞

Flicks A compilation of skits parodying the tradition of Saturday afternoon matinees, including coming attractions and a cartoon. Never released theatrically. *AKA:* Hollyweird; Loose Joints.
1985 (R) 79m/C Martin Mull, Joan Hackett, Pamela Sue Martin, Betty Kennedy, Richard Belzer; *D:* Peter Winograd. **VHS, Beta $69.95** *MED* 𝄞𝄞

The Flight A non-narrative view of glider planes as they soar over the countryside and rivers of the Laurentians and Canadian Rockies. Useful in language arts classes.
1989 96m/C Eli Danker, Sandy McPeak, Lindsay Wagner; *D:* Paul Wendkos. **VHS, Beta $79.95** *VES, IME* 𝄞𝄞

Flight from Glory A group of pilots fly supplies over the Andes from their isolated base camp to even more isolated mines. Morris is their leader who watches as, one by one, the men are killed on their dangerous flights. To make a bad situation worse, Heflin arrives as a new recruit—along with his pretty wife.
1937 66m/B Chester Morris, Onslow Stevens, Whitney Bourne, Van Heflin; *D:* Lew Landers. **VHS, Beta** *RKO* 𝄞𝄞½

Flight from Singapore Transporting desperately needed blood to Malaysia, a flight crew is forced to crash land in the jungle. Nicely done if trite.
1962 74m/B *GB* Patrick Allen, Patrick Holt, William Abney, Harry Fowler; *D:* Dudley Birch; *W:* Dudley Birch. **VHS, Beta $16.95** *SNC* 𝄞½

Flight from Vienna A high-ranking Hungarian security officer, disenchanted with communism, stages a daring escape from his country. In Vienna, he asks the British for political asylum, but is sent back to Hungary to help a scientist escape in order to prove his loyalty. Cold war drama hangs together on strength of Bikel's performance.
1958 54m/B Theodore Bikel, John Bentley, Donald Gray. **VHS, Beta $19.95** *VYY* 𝄞𝄞

Flight of Black Angel Wacked-out F-16 pilot fancies himself an angel of death, and, after annihilating a number of trainees, sets out to make Las Vegas a nuked-out ghost town. Squadron commander Strauss, however, is not pleased with his pilot's initiative. Made for cable TV script runs out of gas and heads into a nosedive.
1991 (R) 102m/C Peter Strauss, William O'Leary, James O'Sullivan, Michael Keys Hall; *D:* Jon Mostow; *W:* Henry Dominick. **VHS $89.95** *VMK* 𝄞𝄞½

Flight of Dragons Animated tale takes place between the Age of Magic and the Age of Science, in a century when dragons ruled the skies.
1982 98m/C *D:* Arthur Rankin Jr., Jules Bass; *V:* John Ritter, Victor Buono, James Earl Jones. **VHS, Beta $19.98** *WAR, WTA* 𝄞𝄞½

A Flight of Rainbirds In a dual role, Krabbe plays a biologist who dreams he must lose his virginity within a week or die and his alter ego who joins him in the search for the perfect woman. In Dutch with English subtitles.
1981 94m/C *NL* Jeroen Krabbe; *D:* Ate de Jong. **VHS $79.95** *ING* 𝄞𝄞

Flight of the Eagle Based on the actual ill-fated expedition of Salomon Andree who, with two friends, attempted to fly from Sweden to the North Pole in a hydrogen balloon in 1897. The last half of the film drags somewhat as the three struggle to survive in the frozen north after their balloon crashes. Beautifully photographed adventure. In Swedish with English subtitles.

1982 115m/C *SW* Max von Sydow, Goran Stangertz, Clement Harari, Sverre Anker; *D:* Jan Troell. **VHS, Beta** $24.95 *AHV* ♫♫♫

Flight of the Grey Wolf A tame, innocent wolf is mistaken for a killer and must run for his life with the help of his boy-owner.
1976 82m/C Bill Williams, Barbara Hale, Jeff East. **VHS, Beta** $69.95 *DIS* ♫♫½

Flight of the Innocent The innocent 10-year-old Vito comes from a family who make their living as kidnappers. He is the only witness (and the only survivor) when his family is massacred by a rival gang. Vito flees the carnage and sets off to find his cousin who lives in Rome. But his journey truly ends when he is taken in by a wealthy industrialist family whose own son has been kidnapped. Directorial debut of Carlei who tends to rely on striking visuals rather than his characters. In Italian with English subtitles.
1993 (R) 105m/C *IT* Manuel Colao, Francesca Neri, Jacques Perrin, Frederico Pacifici, Sal Borgese; *D:* Carlo Carlei; *W:* Carlo Carlei, Gualtiero Rosella. **VHS** *MGM* ♫♫½

Flight of the Intruder Vietnam naval pilots aboard an aircraft carrier don't like the way the war is being handled, so they go rogue and decide to go on a mission to bomb an enemy air base in Hanoi. Loads of male bonding.
1990 (PG-13) 115m/C Danny Glover, Willem Dafoe, Brad Johnson, Rosanna Arquette, Tom Sizemore; *D:* John Milius; *W:* Robert Dillon. **VHS, Beta** $14.95 *PAR* ♫½

Flight of the Navigator A boy boards an alien spacecraft and embarks on a series of time-travel adventures with a crew of wisecracking extraterrestrial creatures. When he returns home eight years later, a NASA investigation ensues. Paul Reubens, better known as Pee Wee Herman, provides the voice of the robot.
1986 (PG) 90m/C Joey Cramer, Veronica Cartwright, Cliff DeYoung, Sarah Jessica Parker, Matt Adler, Howard Hesseman; *D:* Randal Kleiser; *M:* Michael Burton, Matt MacManus; *V:* Alan Silvestri; *V:* Paul (Pee Wee Herman) Reubens. **VHS, Beta** $19.99 *DIS* ♫♫½

The Flight of the Phoenix A group of men stranded in the Arabian desert after a plane crash attempt to rebuild their plane in order to escape before succumbing to the elements. Big budget, all-star survival drama based on the novel by Elleston Trevor.
1965 147m/C James Stewart, Richard Attenborough, Peter Finch, Hardy Kruger, Dan Duryea, George Kennedy, Ernest Borgnine, Ian Bannen; *D:* Robert Aldrich. **VHS, Beta** $19.98 *FOX* ♫♫♫

Flight to Fury A cheap independent adventure film, featuring the novice Hellman-Nicholson team, about a few assorted mercenaries searching for a horde of diamonds when their plane crashes in the wilderness of the Philippines. Based on a story by director/producer Hellman.
1966 73m/B Jack Nicholson, Dewey Martin, Fay Spain, Vic Diaz, Jacqueline Hellman; *D:* Monte Hellman; *W:* Jack Nicholson. **VHS, Beta** $59.95 *WAR* ♫½

Flight to Mars An expedition crash lands on the red planet and discovers an advanced underground society that wants to invade earth using the U.S. spacecraft. Includes previews of coming attractions from classic science fiction films. First movie of this genre to be shot in color.
1952 72m/C Cameron Mitchell, Marguerite Chapman, Arthur Franz; *D:* Lesley Selander. **VHS, Beta** $19.95 *MED, IME* ♫♫

Flight to Nowhere An FBI agent tracks down a stolen map of atomic bomb source material with the help of a charter pilot and a dizzy blonde. Muddled plot and no discernable acting.
1946 74m/B Alan Curtis, Evelyn Ankers, Jack Holt; *D:* William Rowland. **VHS, Beta** $16.95 *SNC, VYY* Woof!

Flim-Flam Man A con man teams up with an army deserter to teach him the fine art of flim-flamming as they travel through small southern towns. Love may lead the young man back to the straight and narrow, but not his reprobate mentor. Scott is wonderful; and the slapstick episodes move at a good pace. *AKA:* One Born Every Minute.
1967 104m/C George C. Scott, Michael Sarrazin, Slim Pickens, Sue Lyon, Jack Albertson, Harry Morgan; *D:* Irvin Kershner; *M:* Jerry Goldsmith. **VHS, Beta** $59.98 *FOX* ♫♫

The Flintstones The foibles of the two Stone Age families, the Flintstones and the Rubbles, are chronicled in these two animated episodes of the classic series.
1960 50m/C *V:* Alan Reed, Mel Blanc, Jean Vander Pyl, Bea Benadaret. **VHS, Beta** $29.95 *TTC* ♫♫

The Flintstones Preceded by massive hype, popular '60s cartoon comes to life thanks to a huge budget and creative sets and props. Seems that Fred's being set up by evil corporate types MacLachlan and Barry to take the fall for their embezzling scheme. Soon he gives up dining at RocDonald's for Cavern on the Green and cans best buddy Barney (Moranis). Forget the lame plot (32 writers took a shot at it) and sit back and enjoy the spectacle. Goodman's an amazingly true-to-type Fred, O'Donnell has Betty's giggle down pat, and Perkins looks a lot like Wilma. Wilma's original voice, VanderPyl, has a cameo; listen for Korman's voice as the Dictabird. Add half a bone if you're under 12.
1994 (PG) 92m/C John Goodman, Rick Moranis, Elizabeth Perkins, Rosie O'Donnell, Elizabeth Taylor, Kyle MacLachlan, Halle Berry, Jonathan Winters, Richard Moll, Irwin Keyes, Dann Florek; *Cameos:* Laraine Newman, Jean VanDerPyl, Jay Leno; *D:* Brian Levant; *W:* Tom S. Parker, Jim Jennewein, Steven E. de Souza; *M:* David Newman; *V:* Harvey Korman. **VHS** *NYR* ♫♫½

Flipper A fisherman's son befriends an injured dolphin, is persuaded to return him to the wild, and earns the animal's gratitude. Prime kids' fare, as its sequels and television series attest.
1963 87m/C Chuck Connors, Luke Halpin, Kathleen Maguire, Connie Scott; *D:* James B. Clark. **VHS, Beta** $19.98 *MVD, MGM* ♫♫♫

Flipper's New Adventure Believing they are to be separated, Flipper and Sandy travel to a remote island. Little do they know, a British family is being held for ransom on the island they have chosen. It's up to the duo to save the day. An enjoyable, nicely done family adventure. *AKA:* Flipper and the Pirates.
1964 103m/C Luke Halpin, Pamela Franklin, Tom Helmore, Francesca Annis, Brian Kelly, Joe Higgins, Ricou Browning; *D:* Leon Benson. **VHS, Beta** $19.98 *MGM, FCT* ♫♫

Flipper's Odyssey Flipper has disappeared and his adopted family goes looking for him, but when one of the boys gets trapped in a cave, Flipper is his only hope.
1966 77m/C Flipper, Luke Halpin, Brian Kelly, Tommy Norden; *D:* Paul Landres. **VHS, Beta** $14.95 *CNG, PSM* ♫½

Flirtation Walk West point musical that has cadet Powell falling in love with the general's daughter (Keeler), who is already engaged to lieutenant Eldredge. Some fairly good numbers, including "Mr. and Mrs. Is The Name," and "Flirtation Walk." In an attempt to change her image, Keeler hardly dances at all, which is too bad for the viewer. Based on a story by Lou Edelman and Delmer Daves.
1934 98m/B Dick Powell, Ruby Keeler, Pat O'Brien, Ross Alexander; *D:* Frank Borzage; *W:* Delmer Daves. **VHS** $19.98 *MGM* ♫♫½

Flirting Set in an Australian boarding school in 1965, a charming story following the misadventures of the adolescent Danny Embling, who has the misfortune to be both bright and sensitive, putting him seriously at odds with his masculine peers. He finds love with an outcast at the neighboring girls boarding school, the daughter of a diplomat from Uganda. Kidman has a supporting role as a snobbish older boarding school girl, not quite as bad as she seems. Tender and amusing. The second of director Duigan's coming-of-age trilogy, preceded by "The Year My Voice Broke" (the third film isn't yet completed).
1989 (R) 100m/C *AU* Noah Taylor, Thandie Newton, Nicole Kidman, Bartholomew Rose, Felix Nobis, Josh Picker, Kiri Paramore, Marc Gray, Joshua Marshall, David Wieland, Craig Black, Leslie Hill; *D:* John Duigan; *W:* John Duigan. **VHS** $94.95 *VMK, BTV* ♫♫♫

Flirting with Fate Early Fairbanks-cum-acrobat vehicle. Having hired a hitman to rub himself out, a young man decides he doesn't want to die, after all. Seems there's a girl involved...
1916 51m/B Douglas Fairbanks Sr., Jewel Carmen, Howard Gaye, William E. Lawrence, George Beranger, Dorothy Hadel, Lillian Langdon; *D:* Christy Cabanne. **VHS, Beta** $24.95 *NOS, GPV, FCT* ♫♫♫

Flood! Irwin Allen's first made-for-television disaster film. A dam bursts and devastates a small town, so a helicopter pilot must save the day. Good cast is swept along in a current of disaster-genre cliches.
1976 98m/C Robert Culp, Martin Milner, Barbara Hershey, Richard Basehart, Carol Lynley, Roddy McDowall, Cameron Mitchell, Teresa Wright, Francine York; *D:* Earl Bellamy. **VHS, Beta** $59.95 *WAR* ♫♫

The Floorwalker Chaplin becomes involved with a dishonest floorwalker in a department store. Silent.
1917 20m/B Charlie Chaplin; *D:* Charlie Chaplin. **VHS, Beta** *CAB, GVV* ♫♫♫

The Floorwalker/By the Sea Two early Chaplin short comedies, featuring a hilarious scene on an escalator in the first film. Silent.
1915 51m/B Charlie Chaplin, Edna Purviance, Eric Campbell; *D:* Charlie Chaplin. **VHS, Beta, 8mm** $19.95 *VYY* ♫♫♫

Flor Silvestre The son of a rich rancher romances a young woman against the background of the Mexican Revolution. *AKA:* Wild Flower.
1958 90m/B *MX* Dolores Del Rio, Pedro Armendariz Sr.; *D:* Emilio Fernandez. **VHS, Beta** $64.95 *MAD* ♫

The Florida Connection An action thriller set in the Florida Swamps with a collection of villains and a vague plot about smuggling.
1974 90m/C Dan Pastorini, June Wilkinson. **VHS, Beta** $9.95 *UNI* ♫

Florida Straits A recently released Cuban prisoner hires a few losers and their boat to return to the island, supposedly to find the girl he loves. The real quest is for gold buried during the Bay-of-Pigs invasion in this none-

too-original made-for-cable movie that at least offers a good cast.
1987 (PG-13) 98m/C Raul Julia, Fred Ward, Daniel H. Jenkins, Antonio Fargas; **D:** Mike Hodges; **W:** Stephen Metcalfe; **M:** Michel Colombier. VHS, Beta $9.98 ORI ♫♫

Flower Drum Song The Rodgers and Hammerstein musical played better on Broadway than in this overblown adaptation of life in San Francisco's Chinatown. Umeki plays the young girl who arrives from Hong Kong for an arranged marriage. Her intended (Soo) is a fast-living nightclub owner already enjoying the love of singer Kwan. Meanwhile Umeki falls for the handsome Shigeta. Naturally, everything comes together in a happy ending. ♫I Enjoy Being A Girl; Don't Marry Me; Grant Avenue; You Are Beautiful; A Hundred Million Miracles; Fan Tan Fanny; Chop Suey; The Other Generation; I Am Going to Like It Here; Love Look Away; Sunday.
1961 133m/C Nancy Kwan, Jack Soo, James Shigeta, Miyoshi Umeki, Juanita Hall; **D:** Henry Koster; **M:** Richard Rodgers, Oscar Hammerstein. VHS, Beta $39.98 MCA, FCT ♫♫

Flowers in the Attic Based on the V.C. Andrews bestseller, a would-be thriller about four young siblings locked for years in their family's old mansion by their grandmother with their mother's selfish acquiescence. A chicken-hearted, clumsy flop that skimps on the novel's trashier themes.
1987 (PG-13) 93m/C Victoria Tennant, Kristy Swanson, Louise Fletcher, Jeb Stuart Adams; **D:** Jeffrey Bloom; **W:** Jeffrey Bloom. VHS, Beta $19.95 NWV, STE ♫♫

Flowers of Reverie A former soldier is imprisoned for his work in the resistance during the Hungarian Revolution (1848-9), leading to tragedy. In Hungarian with English subtitles.
1984 106m/C HU **D:** Laszlo Lugossy. VHS $59.95 FCT ♫♫

The Flowers of St. Francis Rossellini's presentation of St. Francis and his friars' attainment of spiritual harmony. In Italian with English subtitles. This is the British release version, 10-15 minutes longer than the U.S. version.
1950 75m/B IT Federico Fellini; **D:** Roberto Rossellini. VHS, Beta $34.95 FCT ♫♫♫

Flush Unorthodox comedy involving funny noises.
1981 90m/C William Calloway, William Bronder, Jeannie Linero; **D:** Andrew J. Kuehn. VHS NO ♫♫

Flush It While working in the honey factory, Harvey finds a clue that leads him on a wild escapade in search of a buried treasure. Surprises abound along the way.
1976 (R) 90m/C VHS, Beta NO ♫♫

The Flustered Comedy of Leon Errol The popular Depression-era comedian Errol is showcased in three shorts: "Crime Rave," "Man-I-Cured," and "A Panic in the Parlor."
1939 56m/B Leon Errol, Vivian Tobin, Dorothy Granger, Frank Faylen, Virginia Vale. VHS, Beta, 8mm $19.95 VYY ♫♫

The Fly The historic, chillingly original '50s sci-fi tale about a hapless scientist experimenting with teleportation who accidentally gets anatomically confused with a housefly. Campy required viewing; two sequels followed, and a 1986 remake which itself has spawned one sequel.
1958 94m/C Vincent Price, David Hedison, Herbert Marshall, Patricia Owens; **D:** Kurt Neumann; **W:** James Clavell. VHS, Beta $14.98 FOX ♫♫♫

The Fly A sensitive, humanistic remake of the 1958 horror film about a scientist whose flesh is genetically intermixed with a housefly via his experimental transportation device. A thoughtful, shocking horror film, with fine performances from Goldblum and Davis and a brutally emotional conclusion. Followed by "The Fly II" in 1989.
1986 (R) 96m/C Jeff Goldblum, Geena Davis, John Getz, Joy Boushel; **D:** David Cronenberg; **W:** David Cronenberg, Charles Edward Pogue; **M:** Howard Shore. VHS, Beta $19.98 FOX ♫♫♫

The Fly 2 Inferior sequel to Cronenberg's opus, in which the offspring of Seth Brundle achieves full genius maturity in three years, falls in love, and discovers the evil truth behind his father's teleportation device and the corporate auspices that backed it.
1989 (R) 105m/C Eric Stoltz, Daphne Zuniga, Lee Richardson, John Getz, Harley Cross; **D:** Chris Walas; **W:** Mick Garris, Jim Wheat, Ken Wheat, Frank Darabont. VHS, Beta $19.98 FOX, CCB ♫♫

Fly with the Hawk A troubled teenager gets lost in the wilderness for a year, and learns some important things from nature to take back to civilization.
19?? 90m/C Peter Ferri, Peter Snook, Shelley Lynne Speigel; **D:** Robert Tanos. VHS NO ♫♫

Flying Blind Foreign agents are thwarted in their attempt to steal a vital air defense secret. Unconvincing espionage plot cobbled into a story about a Los Angeles-Las Vegas puddle jumper.
1941 69m/B Richard Arlen, Jean Parker, Marie Wilson. VHS, Beta $24.95 NOS, DVT, HEG ♫♫

The Flying Deuces Ollie's broken heart lands Laurel and Hardy in the Foreign Legion. The comic pair escape a firing squad only to suffer a plane crash that results in Hardy's reincarnation as a horse. A musical interlude with a Laurel soft shoe while Hardy sings "Shine On, Harvest Moon" is one of the film's highlights. **AKA:** Flying Aces.
1939 65m/B Stan Laurel, Oliver Hardy, Jean Parker, Reginald Gardiner, James Finlayson; **D:** Edward Sutherland. VHS, Beta $9.95 CNG, MRV, NOS ♫♫♫

Flying Discman from Mars A Martian warlord battles a brave pilot and his secretary in this exciting serial not seen in 30 years. The original 12 episodes are edited together on two cassettes.
1951 167m/B VHS $29.95 REP, MLB ♫♫♫

Flying Down to Rio The first Astaire-Rogers musical, although they are relegated to supporting status behind Del Rio and Raymond. Still, it was enough to make them stars and a team that epitomizes the height of American musical films. The slim story revolves around singer Del Rio's two suitors and receives a splendid, art deco production. Showgirls dancing on plane wings in flight provide another memorable moment. ♫Music Makes Me; The Carioca; Orchids in the Moonlight; Flying Down to Rio.
1933 89m/B Fred Astaire, Ginger Rogers, Dolores Del Rio, Eric Blore, Gene Raymond, Franklin Pangborn; **D:** Thornton Freeland; **M:** Vincent Youman. VHS, Beta $14.98 TTC, MED ♫♫½

The Flying Fool Ace pilot Bill returns from the war to find his younger brother has fallen for a singer. When Bill meets the lady, he also notices her charms and the two brothers have a duel in the skies to see who'll get the girl.
1929 75m/B William Boyd, Marie Prevost, Russell Gleason; **D:** Tay Garnett; **W:** Russell Gleason. VHS, Beta $14.95 VYY, RXM, GPV ♫♫

Flying from the Hawk A 12-year-old boy sees something he shouldn't and soon finds that his friends and relatives are mysteriously vanishing.
1986 110m/C John Ireland, Diane McBain. VHS, Beta $19.95 CNG ♫½

Flying Karamazov Brothers Comedy Hour The wild and crazy Karamazov brothers show what they can do in this fun-filled video of comedy, acrobatics, and juggling.
1983 59m/C The Flying Karamazov Brothers. VHS, Beta $19.98 MCG ♫½

Flying Leathernecks Tough squadron leader Wayne fights with his fellow officer Ryan in Guadalcanal when their leadership styles clash. But when the real fighting begins all is forgotten as Wayne leads his men into victorious battle, winning the admiration and devotion of his fliers. Memorable WWII film deals with war in human terms.
1951 102m/C John Wayne, Robert Ryan, Janis Carter; **D:** Nicholas Ray. VHS, Beta $14.98 RKO, TLF, TTC ♫♫♫

The Flying Saucer U.S. and Russian scientists clash over their search for a huge flying saucer that is hidden under a glacier. The first movie to deal with flying saucers. The cassette includes animated opening and closing sequences plus previews of coming attractions.
1950 120m/B Mikel Conrad, Pat Garrison, Hanz von Teuffen; **D:** Mikel Conrad. VHS, Beta $14.95 RHI, MWP, VCI ♫½

Flying Saucers Over Hollywood: The Plan 9 Companion This documentary looks at what many consider to be the worst film of all time, "Plan 9 from Outer Space," released in 1959. The cult classic, directed by the equally bizarre Edward D. Wood, Jr., is revealed in all its absurdity, including interviews with cast, crew, and fans.
1993 111m/C VHS $24.95 ATM ♫½

The Flying Scotsman A fired railroad worker tries to wreck an express train on the engineer's last journey. The daughter of the intended victim saves the day. Silent, with sound added.
1929 60m/B Ray Milland, Pauline Johnson, Moore Marriot; **D:** Castleton Knight. VHS, Beta $24.95 NOS, DVT, HEG ♫½

Flying Tigers Salutes the All-American Volunteer Group which flew for China under General Claire Chennault against the Japanese before the U.S. entered WWII. A squadron leader and a brash new recruit both vie for the affections of a pretty nurse in-between their flying missions. Romance and a few comic touches take a back seat to graphic scenes of aerial battles and dramatization of heroic sacrifice in this rousing war film.
1942 101m/B John Wayne, Paul Kelly, John Carroll, Anna Lee, Mae Clarke, Gordon Jones; **D:** David Miller. VHS $9.98 REP ♫♫½

Flying Wild A gang of saboteurs is out to steal top-secret airplane blueprints. Who else but the Bowery Boys could conceivably stop them? No Satch in this one.
1941 62m/B Leo Gorcey, Bobby Jordan, Donald Haines, Joan Barclay, David Gorcey, Bobby Stone, Sammy Morrison; **D:** William West. VHS $19.95 NOS, LOO ♫½

FM The disc jockeys at an L.A. radio station rebel in the name of rock'n'roll. Despite the promising cast and setting (Mull makes his movie debut as a memorable space case), this is just disjointed and surprisingly unhip; one producer took his name off it due to

creative difficulties. The decent soundtrack includes concert footage of Jimmy Buffet and Linda Ronstadt. ♫FM; Do It Again; FM Reprise; Livingston Saturday Night; The Key To My Kingdom; Green Grass and High Tides; Life In The Fast Lane; Bad Man; Poor, Poor, Pitiful Me; Love Me Tender; Life's Been Good To Me; Cold As Ice; Feels Like the First Time; Slow Ride; Night Moves; Sentimental Lady; Fly Like An Eagle; Just The Way You Are; Lido Shuffle; Hollywood; Your Smiling Face; We Will Rock You; More Than A Feeling. *AKA:* Citizen's Band.
1978 (PG-13) 104m/C Eileen Brennan, Alex Karras, Cleavon Little, Martin Mull, Cassie Yates, Linda Ronstadt, Jimmy Buffett; *D:* Lamont Johnson. **VHS $14.98** *MCA* ⅋⅋

The Fog John Carpenter's blustery follow-up to his success with "Halloween." An evil fog containing murderous, vengeful ghosts envelops a sleepy seaside town and subjects the residents to terror and mayhem.
1978 (R) 91m/C Hal Holbrook, Adrienne Barbeau, Jamie Lee Curtis, Janet Leigh, John Houseman; *D:* John Carpenter; *W:* John Carpenter; *M:* John Carpenter. **VHS, Beta, 8mm $14.95** *COL, SUE* ⅋⅋

Fog Island Murder and terror lurk after a greedy inventor, who was framed for fraud by his business partner, is released from prison. He plots revenge by inviting his foes to his island home.
1945 72m/B George Zucco, Lionel Atwill, Terry Morse, Jerome Cowan, Veda Ann Borg; *D:* Terry Morse. **VHS, Beta $19.95** *NOS, SNC, VCN* ⅋½

Folks! Selleck is a Chicago stockbroker whose wife and kids have left him, the FBI is after him, and, worst of all, his parents have moved in with him. His parents don't want to be a burden, so Selleck decides that the best way to solve his financial woes is to help his parents commit suicide so he can collect on their insurance policies. Tasteless comedy that makes fun of aging and Alzheimer's Disease. Selleck is too sweet and cuddly for his role, but Ameche is good as the senile father, and Ebersole is great as Selleck's unpleasant sister.
1992 (PG-13) 109m/C Tom Selleck, Don Ameche, Anne Jackson, Christine Ebersole, Wendy Crewson, Robert Pastorelli, Michael Murphy, Kevin Timothy Chevalia, Margaret Murphy; *D:* Ted Kotcheff; *M:* Michel Colombier. **VHS** *FXV* ⅋

Follies Girl There's folly in expecting that this wartime tuner would hold up today. An army private romances a dress designer and a musical show somehow results. ♫Keep the Flag A-Flying; No Man In The House; Someone to Love; I Told A Lie; Shall We Gather at the Rhythm?; Fascination; I Knew Your Father's Son; Thoity Poiple Boids.
1943 74m/B Wendy Barrie, Doris Nolan, Gordon Oliver, Anne Barrett, Arthur Pierson; *D:* William Rowland. **VHS $15.95** *NOS, LOO* ⅋⅋

Follies in Concert A filmed record of the famed Stephen Sondheim musical play, performed at Lincoln Center in New York with an all-star cast. Songs include "I'm Still Here," "Losing My Mind," "Broadway Baby" and "The Ladies Who Lunch."
1985 90m/C Carol Burnett, Lee Remick, Betty Comden, Andre Gregory, Adolph Green, Mandy Patinkin, Phyllis Newman, Elaine Stritch, Jim Walton, Licia Albanese. **VHS, Beta $19.95** *MVD, FRH* ⅋⅋

Follow Me Round-the-world odyssey of three moon doggies searching for adventure—and the perfect wave. Spectacular surfing scenes are complemented by songs performed by Dino, Desi, and Billy.

1969 (G) 90m/C Claude Codgen, Mary Lou McGinnis, Bob Purvey; *D:* Gene McCabe. **VHS** *BEI* ⅋⅋

Follow Me, Boys! A Disney film about a simple man who decides to put down roots and enjoy the quiet life, after one year too many on the road with a ramshackle jazz band. That life is soon interrupted when he volunteers to lead a high-spirited boy scout troop.
1966 120m/C Fred MacMurray, Vera Miles, Lillian Gish, Charlie Ruggles, Elliott Reid, Kurt Russell, Luanna Patten, Ken Murray; *D:* Norman Tokar. **VHS, Beta $69.95** *DIS* ⅋⅋⅋

Follow Me Quietly Serial strangler who only kills in the rain is stalked by Lundigan. Very good little thriller which packs a punch in less than an hour.
1949 59m/B William Lundigan, Dorothy Patrick, Jeff Corey, Nestor Paiva, Charles D. Brown, Paul Guilfoyle; *D:* Richard Fleischer. **VHS, Beta $19.95** *TTC, MLB, RXM* ⅋⅋⅋

Follow That Camel Foreign Legion sergeant who invents acts of heroism finally gets a chance to really help out a friend in need. Part of the "Carry On" series.
1967 95m/C *GB* Phil Silvers, Kenneth Williams, Anita Harris, Jim Dale; *D:* Gerald Thomas. **VHS, Beta** *NO* ⅋½

Follow That Car Three southern kids become FBI agents and begin a thigh-slappin', rip-snortin' down-home escapade.
1980 (PG) 96m/C Dirk Benedict, Tanya Tucker, Teri Nunn; *D:* Daniel Haller. **VHS, Beta $59.98** *NLC* ⅋

Follow That Dream Elvis plays a musical hillbilly whose family is trying to homestead on government land along the sunny Florida coast. Based on Richard C. Powell's novel "Pioneer Go Home." The songs-the only reason to see this movie—include "Angel", and "What a Wonderful Life", and the title track.
1961 (G) 111m/C Elvis Presley, Arthur O'Connell, Anne Helm, Simon Oakland, Jack Kruschen, Joanna Moore, Howard McNear; *D:* Gordon Douglas. **VHS, Beta $14.95** *MGM* ⅋⅋

Follow That Rainbow Believing that her long-lost father is a popular touring singer, a young lass pursues him from Switzerland to South Africa.
1966 90m/C Joe Stewardson, Memory Jane, Joan Bickhill. **VHS, Beta** *NO* ⅋

Follow the Fleet A song-and-dance man joins the Navy and meets two sisters in need of help in this Rogers/Astaire bon-bon featuring a classic Berlin score. Look for Betty Grable, Lucille Ball, and Tony Martin in minor roles. Hilliard went on to be best known as the wife of Ozzie Nelson in TV's "The Adventures of Ozzie and Harriet." ♫Let's Face the Music and Dance; We Saw the Sea; I'm Putting All My Eggs In One Basket; Get Thee Behind Me, Satan; But Where Are You?; I'd Rather Lead a Band; Let Yourself Go.
1936 110m/B Fred Astaire, Ginger Rogers, Randolph Scott, Harriet Hilliard Nelson, Betty Grable, Lucille Ball; *D:* Mark Sandrich; *M:* Irving Berlin. **VHS, Beta $14.98** *RKO, MED, TTC* ⅋⅋⅋

Follow the Leader On leave from the Army, Hall and Gorcey discover that one of the gang has been jailed on a trumped-up charge and set about finding the real culprit. ♫Now and Then; All I Want to Do Play the Drums. *AKA:* East of the Bowery.
1944 65m/B Leo Gorcey, Huntz Hall, Gabriel Dell, Jack LaRue, Joan Marsh, Billy Benedict, Mary Gordon, Sammy Morrison; *D:* William Beaudine; *M:* Gene Austin, Sherrill Sisters. **VHS $19.95** *NOS* ⅋⅋

Food of the Gods On a secluded island giant rats, chickens, and other creatures crave human flesh, blood, bones, etc. This cheap, updated version of the H. G. Wells novel suffers from lousy performances and a lack of imagination.
1976 (PG) 88m/C Marjoe Gortner, Pamela Franklin, Ralph Meeker, Ida Lupino, Jon Cypher; *D:* Bert I. Gordon. **VHS, Beta $19.98** *LIV, VES* Woof!

Food of the Gods: Part 2 The killer beasts and animals of the first film (and of H.G. Wells' classic novel) strike again; gigantic rats maim young girls. Easily as bad as the original. *AKA:* Gnaw: Food of the Gods 2.
1988 (R) 93m/C Paul Coufos, Lisa Schrage; *D:* Damian Lee. **VHS, Beta** *NO* Woof!

Fool for Love Explores the mysterious relationship between a modern-day drifter and his long-time lover, who may or may not be his half-sister, as they confront each other in a seedy New Mexico motel. Adapted by Shepard from his play.
1986 (R) 108m/C Sam Shepard, Kim Basinger, Randy Quaid, Harry Dean Stanton; *D:* Robert Altman; *W:* Sam Shepard; *M:* George Burt. **VHS, Beta $14.95** *MGM* ⅋⅋

The Fool Killer In the post-Civil War south, a 12 year-old boy learns that a terrifying legend about an axe-murderer may be all too real. Offbeat film with striking visuals and photography. Debut film for Albert and another choice psycho role for Perkins. *AKA:* Violent Journey.
1965 100m/B Anthony Perkins, Edward Albert, Dana Elcar, Henry Hull, Salome Jens, Arnold Moss; *D:* Servando Gonzalez. **VHS $19.98** *REP* ⅋⅋½

A Fool There Was The rocket that blasted Theda Bara to stardom and launched the vamp film genre. One of the few extant Bara films, it tells the now familiar story of a good man whom crumbles from the heights of moral rectitude thanks to the inescapable influence of an unredeemable vamp. Bette Davis described Bara as "divinely, hysterically, insanely malevolent." Much heavy emoting; subtitled (notoriously) "Kiss Me, My Fool!" Based on Rudyard Kipling's "The Vampire."
1914 70m/B Theda Bara, Edward Jose, Runa Hodges, Clifford Bruce; *D:* Frank Powell. **VHS, Beta $24.95** *VYY, FCT, GVV* ⅋⅋

Foolin' Around An innocent Oklahoma farm boy arrives at college and falls in love with a beautiful heiress. He will stop at nothing to win her over, including crashing her lavish wedding ceremony.
1980 (PG) 101m/C Gary Busey, Annette O'Toole, Eddie Albert, Tony Randall, Cloris Leachman; *D:* Richard T. Heffron; *W:* Michael Kane; *M:* Charles Bernstein. **VHS, Beta $24.98** *SUE* ⅋⅋½

Foolish Wives A remake of Von Stroheim's classic depicting the confused milieu of post-war Europe as reflected through the actions of a bogus count and his seductive, corrupt ways. Comes as close as possible to the original film.
1922 107m/B Erich von Stroheim, Mae Busch, Maude George, Cesare Gravina, Harrison Ford; *D:* Erich von Stroheim. **VHS, Beta $29.95** *KIV, CCB, HHT* ⅋⅋⅋½

Fools Two lonely people—he an aging horror film actor and she a young woman estranged from her husband—start a warm romance when they meet in San Francisco. The husband reacts violently. Good cast seems lost.
1970 (PG) 93m/C Jason Robards Jr., Katharine Ross, Scott Hylands; *D:* Tom Gries. **VHS, Beta $59.95** *PSM* ⅋

Fools of Fortune Adaptation of William Trevor's novel depicting Willie Clinton's childhood and adult experiences of family dramatics played against the backdrop of post-WWI Ireland. During the Irish war for independence, a family is attacked by British soldiers, creating emotional havoc for the survivors. Though well-acted and poignant, it's a rather disjointed and straying shamrock opera.
1990 (PG-13) 104m/C *GB* Mary Elizabeth Mastrantonio, Iain Glen, Julie Christie, Michael Kitchen, Sean McClory, Frankie McCafferty; **D:** Pat O'Connor; **W:** Michael Hirst; **M:** Hans Zimmer. **VHS $89.95** *COL, FCT* 🎬🎬 ½

Footlight Frenzy The Law Moan Spectacular comedy troupe are at it again as they perform a benefit play where everything goes wrong.
1984 110m/C *GB* Alan Shearman, Diz White, Ron House, Frances Tomelty, Michael Aldridge, Ron Pember. **VHS, Beta $39.95** *RKO* 🎬🎬

Footlight Parade Broadway producer Cagney is out of work. Sound films have scared off his backers until his idea for staging live musical numbers before the cinema features lures them back. Lots of authentic backstage action precedes three spectacular Busby Berkeley-choreographed numbers that climax the film, including the giant water ballet featuring more than 100 performers. 🎵Ah, the Moon is Here; Sittin' on a Backyard Fence; Honeymoon Hotel; By A Waterfall; Shanghai Lil.
1933 104m/B James Cagney, Joan Blondell, Dick Powell, Ruby Keeler, Guy Kibbee, Ruth Donnelly; **D:** Lloyd Bacon. **Beta $19.98** *MGM, FOX* 🎬🎬🎬

Footlight Serenade A boxer falls for a beautiful dancer with whom he's costarring in a Broadway play. Unfortunately, she's secretly married to another of the actors and her husband is becoming jealous of the boxer's intentions. Light, fun musical. One of a series of Grable movies made to boost morale during WWII. 🎵Are You Kidding?; I'm Still Crazy About You; I Hear the Birdies Sing; Living High; I'll Be Marching to a Love Song; Land On Your Feet; I'm Stepping Out With a Memory Tonight.
1942 80m/B Betty Grable, Victor Mature, John Payne, Jane Wyman, Phil Silvers, James Gleason, Mantan Moreland; **D:** Gregory Ratoff. **VHS, Beta $19.98** *FOX* 🎬🎬 ½

Footloose When a city boy moves to a small Midwestern town, he discovers some disappointing news: rock music and dancing have been forbidden by the local government. Determined to bring some '80s-style life into the town, he sets about changing the rules and eventually enlists the help of the daughter of the man responsible for the law. Rousing music, talented young cast, and plenty of trouble make this an entertaining musical-drama. 🎵Footloose; Let's Hear it for the Boy; The Girl Gets Around; Dancing in the Sheets; Somebody's Eyes; Almost Paradise; I'm Free; Never; Holding Out for a Hero.
1984 (PG) 107m/C Kevin Bacon, Lori Singer, Christopher Penn, John Lithgow, Dianne Wiest, John Laughlin, Sarah Jessica Parker; **D:** Herbert Ross; **M:** Miles Goodman. **VHS, Beta, 8mm $14.95** *PAR* 🎬🎬 ½

For a Few Dollars More The Man With No Name returns as a bounty hunter who teams up with a gunslinger/rival to track down the sadistic leader of a gang of bandits. Violent. Sequel to "A Fistful of Dollars" (1964) and followed by "The Good, The Bad, and The Ugly". Letterboxed laserdisc edition features the original movie trailer.

1965 (PG) 127m/C *IT* Clint Eastwood, Lee Van Cleef, Klaus Kinski, Gian Marie Volonte; **D:** Sergio Leone; **M:** Ennio Morricone. **VHS, Beta $19.95** *FOX, MGM, FCT* 🎬🎬 ½

For Auld Lang Syne: The Marx Brothers Four classic comedy shorts: "Monkey Business Special," "Gai Dimanche," "Hooks and Jabs," and "For Auld Lang Syne."
1932 46m/B Chico Marx, Groucho Marx, Alan Marx, Harpo Marx. **VHS, Beta $19.95** *VYY* 🎬🎬 ½

For Better and For Worse A nice young couple is planning to have your average nice wedding when one of their friends gets hold of an invitation and decides to jokingly invite the Pope to attend. But the joke is on them when the Pope accepts. Talk about upstaging the bride!
1992 (PG) 94m/C Patrick Dempsey, Kelly Lynch. **VHS $89.98** *LIV* 🎬🎬 ½

For Heaven's Sake Lloyd's first film for Paramount has him making an accidental donation to a skid row mission, then marrying the preacher's daughter and converting all the neighborhood tough guys.
1926 60m/B Harold Lloyd, Jobyna Ralston, Noah Young, James Mason, Paul Weigel; **D:** Sam Taylor. **VHS** *NO* 🎬🎬🎬

For Heaven's Sake A bumbling basketball team is lent some heavenly assistance in the form of a meddling angel. But can he hit the jumper? Made for television.
1979 90m/C Ray Bolger, Kent McCord. **VHS $49.99** *LIV* 🎬 ½

For Keeps Two high school sweethearts on the verge of graduating get married after the girl becomes pregnant, and suffer all the trials of teenage parenthood. Tends toward the unrealistic and trite.
1988 (PG-13) 98m/C Molly Ringwald, Randall Batinkoff, Kenneth Mars; **D:** John G. Avildsen; **W:** Tim Kazurinsky, Denise DeClue; **M:** Bill Conti. **VHS, Beta $14.95** *COL* 🎬 ½

For Ladies Only A struggling actor takes a job as a male stripper to pay the rent. Among the leering ladies is Davis, daughter of former President Reagan. Made for television.
1981 100m/C Gregory Harrison, Patricia Davis, Dinah Manoff, Louise Lasser, Lee Grant, Marc Singer, Viveca Lindfors, Steven Keats; **D:** Mel Damski. **VHS, Beta** *NO* 🎬🎬

For Love Alone A young Australian college co-ed in the 1930s falls in love with a handsome, controversial teacher and follows him to London, only to discover he's not her Mr. Right after all.
1986 102m/C *AU* Helen Buday, Sam Neill, Hugo Weaving; **D:** Stephen Wallace. **VHS, Beta $69.95** *LIV* 🎬🎬

For Love of Ivy Poitier is a trucking executive who has a gambling operation on the side. Ivy is the Black maid of a rich white family who is about to leave her job to look for romance. The two are brought together but the road to true love doesn't run smooth. Based on a story by Poitier.
1968 (PG) 102m/C Sidney Poitier, Abbey Lincoln, Beau Bridges, Carroll O'Connor, Nan Martin; **D:** Daniel Mann; **M:** Quincy Jones. **VHS, Beta $19.98** *FOX* 🎬🎬

For Love or Money A super-rich hotel owner wants her lawyer to find her three beautiful daughters. However, she doesn't trust him enough not to meddle in the search. Lavish production and a good cast can't overcome the mediocrity of the script and direction.

1963 108m/C Kirk Douglas, Mitzi Gaynor, Thelma Ritter, William Bendix, Julie Newmar, Gig Young, Leslie Parrish, William Windom, Richard Sargent; **D:** Michael Gordon. **VHS** *NO* 🎬🎬

For Love or Money Made-for-television fare about game-show contestants finding money and romance.
1984 91m/C Jamie Farr, Suzanne Pleshette, Gil Gerard, Ray Walston, Lawrence Pressman, Mary Kay Place; **D:** Terry Hughes; **M:** Billy Goldenberg. **VHS, Beta $39.95** *IME* 🎬 ½

For Love or Money A real estate man with Career on the mind has to choose between the woman in his life and the condo development that stands firmly between them and happily-ever-afterdom.
1988 (PG) ?m/C Timothy Daly, Haviland Morris, Kevin McCarthy. **VHS** *NO* 🎬🎬

For Love or Money Struggling hotel concierge with a heart of gold finds himself doing little "favors" for a slimy entrepreneur who holds the key to his dreams—the cash to open an elegant hotel of his own. Romantic comedy is reminiscent of the classic screwball comedies of the '30s and '40s, but lacks the trademark tight writing and impeccable timing. Fox is appealing and likable as the wheeling and dealing concierge, a role undermined by a mediocre script offering too few laughs.
1993 (PG) 89m/C Michael J. Fox, Gabrielle Anwar, Isaac Mizrahi, Anthony Higgins, Michael Tucker, Bobby Short, Dan Hedaya, Bob Balaban, Udo Kier, Patrick Breen, Paula Laurence; **D:** Barry Sonnenfeld; **W:** Mark Rosenthal, Larry Konner; **M:** Bruce Broughton. **VHS** *MCA* 🎬🎬 ½

For Me and My Gal In his film debut, Kelly plays an opportunistic song-and-dance man who lures a young vaudevillian (Garland) away from her current partners. WWI interrupts both their career and romance, but you can count on them being reunited. Loaded with vintage tunes. 🎵For Me and My Gal; They Go Wild, Simply Wild Over Me; The Doll Shop; Oh, Johnny, Oh; Oh, You Beautiful Doll; When You Wore A Tulip; Don't Leave Me Daddy; Do I Love You; By The Beautiful Sea; After You've Gone; Till We Meet Again; Tell Me; We Don't Want The Bacon; Ballin' the Jack; Mademoiselle From Armentieres; What Are You Going to Do to Help the Boys?; How Ya Gonna Keep 'Em Down on the Farm?; Where Do We Go From Here?; Goodbye Broadway, Hello France; Smiles; It's A Long Way to Tipperary; Oh Frenchy; Pack Up Your Troubles; When Johnny Comes Marching Home.
1942 104m/B Gene Kelly, Judy Garland, George Murphy, Martha Eggerth, Ben Blue, Richard Quine, Keenan Wynn, Stephen McNally; **D:** Busby Berkeley. **VHS, Beta $19.98** *MGM* 🎬🎬 ½

For Pete's Sake Topsy-turvy comedy about a woman whose efforts to get together enough money to put her husband through school involve her with loan sharks, a madame, and even cattle rustling in New York City. Not one of Streisand's best. **AKA:** July Pork Bellies.
1974 (PG) 90m/C Barbra Streisand, Michael Sarrazin, Estelle Parsons, William Redfield, Molly Picon; **D:** Peter Yates. **VHS, Beta $9.95** *COL* 🎬🎬

For Richer, For Poorer A very rich, successful businessman notices his son is happy just to sit back and let dad earn all the dough while he waits for his share. In order to teach his son a lesson, Dad decides to give all his money away. But the plan backfires when both realize that earning a second fortune may not be as easy as they assumed. Below average made for cable fare. **AKA:** Father, Son and the Mistress.

1992 (PG) 90m/C Jack Lemmon, Talia Shire, Joanna Gleason, Jonathan Silverman, Madeline Kahn, George Wyner; *D:* Jay Sandrich. VHS $89.99 *HBO* 🎬🎬½

For the Boys Midler stars as Dixie Leonard, a gutsy singer-comedian who hooks up with Eddie Sparks (Caan) to become one of America's favorite USO singing, dancing, and comedy teams. The movie spans 50 years and three wars—including Korea and Vietnam—and raises such issues as the blacklist and the role of politics in showbiz. Glitzy Hollywood entertainment falters despite Midler's strong performance. ♫Billy-A-Dick; Come Rain or Come Shine; In My Life; Stuff Like That There.
1991 (R) 120m/C Bette Midler, James Caan, George Segal, Patrick O'Neal, Christopher Rydell, Arye Gross, Norman Fell, Rosemary Murphy, Dori Brenner, Bud Yorkin, Jack Sheldon, Melissa Manchester, Brandon Call; *Cameos:* Arliss Howard; *D:* Mark Rydell; *W:* Marshall Brickman, Neal Jimenez, Lindy Laub; *M:* Dave Grusin. Academy Awards '91 Nominations: Best Actress (Midler); Golden Globe Awards '92: Best Actress—Musical/Comedy (Midler). VHS $19.98 *FXV* 🎬🎬

For the First Time In his last film, Lanza plays an opera singer who tours European cities to raise money for his deaf girlfriend's medical treatment. ♫Oh Mon Amour; Bavarian Drinking Song; Ave Maria; Vesti La Giubba; La Donna e Mobile; Niun Mi Tema; Grand March; O Solo Mio; Ich Liebe Dich; Come Prima; Capri, Capri; Pineapple Picker.
1959 97m/C Mario Lanza, Zsa Zsa Gabor, Johanna von Koczian, Kurt Kasznar, Hans Sohnker, Peter Capell, Renzo Cesana, Sandro Giglio; *D:* Rudolph Mate; *W:* Andrew Solt. VHS $19.98 *MGM* 🎬🎬½

For the Love of Angela Pretty and young shop clerk involves herself with both the shopkeeper and his son.
1986 90m/C Louis Jourdan. Beta $14.95 *PSM* 🎬½

For the Love of Benji In this second "Benji" film, the adorable little dog accompanies his human family on a Greek vacation. He is kidnapped to be used as a messenger for a secret code, but escapes, to have a series of comic adventures in this entertaining family fare.
1977 (G) 85m/C Benji, Patsy Garrett, Cynthia Smith, Allen Finzat, Ed Nelson; *D:* Joe Camp. VHS, Beta $19.99 *FCT, APD, BFV* 🎬🎬

For the Love of It Television stars galore try to hold together this farce about car chases in California, stolen secret documents, and (of course) true love. Outstandingly mediocre. Made for television.
1980 100m/C Deborah Raffin, Jeff Conaway, Tom Bosley, Norman Fell, Don Rickles, Henry Gibson, Noriyuki "Pat" Morita, William Christopher, Lawrence Hilton-Jacobs, Adrian Zmed, Barbi Benton, Adam West; *D:* Hal Kanter. VHS, Beta $14.95 *FRH* 🎬½

For Those About to Rock: Monsters in Moscow A tribute to the young people who defended Russia's new freedom during 1991's attempted coup. The first open-air festival-style concert ever to take place in Russia features the music of AC/DC, Metallica, The Black Crowes, Pantera, and Russia's Electro Shock Therapy.
1991 (R) 84m/C *D:* Wayne Isham. VHS, Beta $14.95 *WAR, MVD, PMS* 🎬🎬½

For Us, the Living The life and assassination of civil rights activist Medgar Evers are dramatically presented in this production of "American Playhouse" for PBS. Provides insight into Evers' character, not just a

recording of the events surrounding his life. Adapted from the biography written by Evers' widow.
1988 84m/C Howard E. Rollins Jr., Rocky Aoki, Paul Winfield, Irene Cara, Margaret Avery, Roscoe Lee Browne, Laurence "Larry" Fishburne, Janet MacLachlan, Dick Anthony Williams; *D:* Michael A. Schultz. VHS, Beta $79.95 *MED, FCT* 🎬🎬

For Your Eyes Only In this James Bond adventure, 007 must keep the Soviets from getting hold of a valuable instrument aboard a sunken British spy ship. Sheds the gadgetry of its more recent predecessors in the series in favor of some spectacular stunt work and the usual beautiful girl and exotic locale. Glen's first outing as director, though he handled second units on previous Bond films. Sheena Easton sang the hit title tune.
1981 (PG) 136m/C *GB* Roger Moore, Carol Bouquet, Chaim Topol, Lynn-Holly Johnson, Julian Glover, Cassandra Harris, Jill Bennett, Michael Gothard, John Wyman, Jack Hedley, Lois Maxwell, Desmond Llewelyn, Geoffrey Keen, Walter Gotell, Charles Dance; *D:* John Glen; *W:* Michael G. Wilson; *M:* Bill Conti. VHS, Beta $19.98 *MGM, FOX, TLF* 🎬🎬🎬

For Your Love Only A beautiful young student falls in love with her teacher and is blackmailed, leading her to murder her tormentor. Soap opera made for German television. Dubbed in English.
1979 90m/C *GE* Nastassia Kinski, Christian Quadflieg, Judy Winter, Klaus Schwarzkopf; *D:* Wolfgang Petersen. VHS, Beta *GLV* 🎬🎬

Forbidden In Nazi Germany, a German countess has an affair with a Jewish intellectual, and she winds up hiding him from the S.S. Based on the novel "The Last Jews of Berlin" by Leonard Gross. Slow made-for-cable movie.
1985 116m/C Jacqueline Bisset, Juergen Prochnow, Irene Worth, Peter Vaughan, Amanda Cannings, Avis Bunnage; *D:* Anthony Page; *W:* Leonard Gross. VHS, Beta $79.95 *SWC* 🎬🎬½

The Forbidden City San San is a young Chinese maiden who has the misfortune to fall in love with a Western diplomat. After he is sent away on business San San keeps secret the fact she has born her lover a child but her actions are unforgiven by her father, a deposed mandarin.
1918 72m/B Norma Talmadge, Thomas Meighan; *D:* Sidney Franklin. VHS, Beta $24.95 *VYY, GVV, GPV* 🎬🎬

The Forbidden Dance The first of several quickies released in 1990 applying hackneyed plots to the short-lived Lambada dance craze. The nonsensible plot has a Brazilian princess coming to the U.S. in order to stop further destruction of the rain forest. Instead, she winds up falling for a guy, teaching him to Lambada, and going on TV for a dance contest. Features an appearance by Kid Creole and the Coconuts.
1990 (PG-13) 90m/C Laura Herring, Jeff James, Sid Haig, Richard Lynch, Kid Creole & the Coconuts; *D:* Greydon Clark. VHS, Beta $19.95 *COL* Woof!

Forbidden Games Famous anti-war drama about two French children play-acting the dramas of war amid the carnage of WWII. Young refugee Fossey sees her parents and dog killed. She meets a slightly older boy whose family takes the girl in. The children decide to bury the animals they have seen killed in the same way that people are buried—even stealing crosses from the cemetery to use over the animal graves. Eventually they are discovered and Fossey is again separated from her newfound home. Acclaimed; available in both dubbed and En-

glish-subtitled versions. *AKA:* Les Jeux Interdits.
1952 90m/B *FR* Brigitte Fossey, Georges Poujouly, Amedee, Louis Herbert; *D:* Rene Clement. Academy Awards '52: Best Foreign Language Film; Nominations: Best Story, Best Story; British Academy Awards '53: Best Film; National Board of Review Awards '52: 5 Best Foreign Films of the Year; New York Film Critics Awards '52: Best Foreign Film; Venice Film Festival '52: Best Film. VHS, Beta $29.98 *NOS, SUE, APD* 🎬🎬🎬🎬

Forbidden Love A man in his early 20's falls in love with a woman twice his age, much to the chagrin of her daughters. Made for television.
1982 96m/C Andrew Stevens, Yvette Mimieux, Dana Elcar, Lisa Lucas, Jerry Hauser, Randi Brooks, Lynn Carlin, Hildy Brooks, John Considine; *D:* Steven Hilliard Stern; *M:* Hagood Hardy. VHS, Beta *CNG* 🎬

Forbidden Passion: The Oscar Wilde Movie A British-made look at Wilde's later years, emphasizing his homosexuality and the Victorian repression that accompanied it.
1987 120m/C *GB* Michael Gambon, Robin Lermitte. VHS, Beta $79.95 *VMK* 🎬🎬½ *D*

Forbidden Planet In 2200 A.D., a space cruiser visits the planet Altair-4 to uncover the fate of a previous mission of space colonists. They are greeted by Robby the Robot and discover the only survivors of the Earth colony which has been preyed upon by a terrible space monster. A classic science fiction version of the Shakespearean classic "The Tempest." Laserdisc features formerly "cut" scenes, production and publicity photos, the original screen treatment, and special effects outtakes.
1956 98m/C Walter Pidgeon, Anne Francis, Leslie Nielsen, Warren Stevens, Jack Kelly, Richard Anderson, Earl Holliman, George Wallace; *D:* Fred M. Wilcox. VHS, Beta $19.98 *MGM, VYG, CRC* 🎬🎬½

Forbidden Sun An Olympic gymnastics coach and her dozen beautiful students go to Crete to train. When one of them is brutally raped, vengeance is meted out by the girls.
1989 (R) 88m/C Lauren Hutton, Cliff DeYoung, Renee Estevez; *D:* Zelda Barron. VHS, Beta $14.95 *ACA* 🎬

Forbidden Trails Rough Riders adventure has Silver the horse saving his owner from the vengeance of two outlaws. Two more heroes go under cover to bring the bad guys to justice.
1941 60m/B Buck Jones, Tim McCoy, Raymond Hatton; *D:* Robert North Bradbury. VHS, Beta $9.95 *NOS, VCN, DVT* 🎬½

Forbidden World Lives of a genetic research team become threatened by the very life form they helped to create: a man-eating organism capable of changing its genetic structure as it grows and matures. Corman-produced quickie follow-up to "Galaxy of Terror" is a graphically violent rip-off of "Alien." *AKA:* Mutant.
1982 (R) 82m/C Jesse Vint, Dawn Dunlap, June Chadwick, Linden Chiles; *D:* Allan Holzman; *W:* Jim Wynorski, R.J. Robertson. VHS, Beta $69.98 *SUE* Woof!

Forbidden Zone A sixth dimension kingdom is ruled by the midget, King Fausto, and inhabited by dancing frogs, bikini-clad tootsies, robot boxers, and degraded beings of all kinds. Original music by Oingo Boingo, and directed by founding member Elfman.
1980 (R) 75m/B Herve Villechaize, Susan Tyrrell, Kipper Kids, Viva; *D:* Richard Elfman; *W:* Matthew Bright, Richard Elfman; *M:* Danny Elfman. VHS, Beta $39.95 *MED* 🎬½

Force Five A group of ex-cons form an anti-crime undercover force turning their skills toward justice. Nothing new in this made for television pilot.
1975 78m/C Gerald Gordon, Nicholas Pryor, James Hampton, David Spielberg, Leif Erickson, Bradford Dillman; *D:* Walter Grauman. VHS, Beta $54.95 *MED* ℤℤ

Force: Five Mercenary gathers a group of like-minded action groupies together to rescue the daughter of a powerful man from a religious cult. All action and no brains.
1981 (R) 95m/C Joe Lewis, Pam Huntington, Master Bong Soo Han; *D:* Robert Clouse; *M:* William Goldstein. VHS, Beta $54.95 *MED* ℤ

Force of Evil A cynical attorney who works for a mob boss and for Wall Street tries to save his brother from the gangster's takeover of the numbers operation. The honorable, though criminal, brother refuses the help of the amoral lawyer, and he is finally forced to confront his conscience. Garfield's sizzling performance and the atmospheric photography have made this a film noir classic.
1949 80m/B John Garfield, Thomas Gomez, Marie Windsor, Sheldon Leonard, Ray Roberts; *D:* Abraham Polonsky; *W:* Abraham Polonsky. VHS $19.98 *REP* ℤℤℤ

Force of Evil A paroled murderer returns to his hometown to brutalize the family that refused to fabricate an alibi for him. Made for television.
1977 100m/C Lloyd Bridges, Eve Plumb, William Watson, Pat Crowley; *D:* Richard Lang. VHS, Beta $49.95 *WOV, GKK* ℤ

Force of Impulse J.D. schlocker featuring an impressive cast involved with everything from hot rods to robbery to parental problems.
1960 ?m/C J. Carroll Naish, Robert Alda, Tony Anthony, Christina Crawford, Jody McCrea, Lionel Hampton. VHS $16.95 *SNC* ℤ

Force of One A team of undercover narcotics agents is being eliminated mysteriously, and karate expert Norris saves the day in this sequel to "Good Guys Wear Black."
1979 (PG) 91m/C Chuck Norris, Bill Wallace, Jennifer O'Neill, Clu Gulager; *D:* Paul Aaron. VHS, Beta $54.95 *MED* ℤℤ

Force on Thunder Mountain A father and son go camping and encounter ancient Indian lore and flying saucers.
1977 93m/C Christopher Cain, Todd Dutson. VHS, Beta $19.95 *VCI* ℤ

Force 10 from Navarone So-so sequel to Alistair MacLean's "The Guns of Navarone," follows a group of saboteurs whose aim is to blow up a bridge vital to the Nazi's in Yugoslavia. Keep an eye out for Ford, Nero, and Bach. Lots of double-crosses and action sequences, but doesn't quite hang together.
1978 (PG) 118m/C Robert Shaw, Harrison Ford, Barbara Bach, Edward Fox, Carl Weathers, Richard Kiel, Franco Nero; *D:* Guy Hamilton. VHS, Beta $19.98 *WAR, OM* ℤℤ

Forced Entry Psychopathic killer-rapist hesitates over one of his victims, and she murders him instead. *AKA:* The Last Victim.
1975 (R) 92m/C Tanya Roberts, Ron Max, Nancy Allen; *D:* Jim Sotos. VHS, Beta *NO* ℤ

Forced March On location in Hungary, an actor portrays a poet who fought in WWII and became a victim of the Holocaust. However, the deeper he gets into his role, the thinner the line between illusion and reality becomes. Flat drama.
1990 104m/C Chris Sarandon, Renee Soutendijk, Josef Sommer, John Seitz; *D:* Rick King. VHS, Beta $89.99 *SGE, MOV, IME* ℤℤ½

Forced to Kill A repo man is on his way to deliver a Jaguar when he's captured by a bizarre family and forced to fight in an illegal bare-fist tournament run by the local lunatic sheriff. Professional stuntman Eubanks has his work cut out for him in this actioner.
1993 (R) 91m/C Corey Michael Eubanks, Michael Ironside, Rance Howard, Don Swayze, Clint Howard, Brian Avery, Kari Whitman, Mickey Jones, Carl Ciarfalio, Cynthia J. Blessington, Alan Gelfant; *D:* Russell Solberg; *W:* Corey Michael Eubanks. VHS $89.95 *PMH* ℤ½

Forced Vengeance Vietnam vet pits himself against the underworld in Hong Kong. With Norris in the lead, you can take it for granted there will be plenty of martial arts action.
1982 (R) 103m/C Chuck Norris, Mary Louise Weller; *D:* James Fargo; *M:* William Goldstein. VHS, Beta $19.95 *MGM* ℤℤ

Ford: The Man & the Machine Episodic biography of ruthless auto magnate Henry Ford I from the building of his empire to his personal tragedies. The cast lacks spark and Robertson (Ford) is positively gloomy. The only one appearing to have any fun is Thomas (Ford's mistress). Based on the biography by Robert Lacey.
1987 200m/C Cliff Robertson, Hope Lange, Heather Thomas, Michael Ironside, Chris Wiggins, R.H. Thomson; *D:* Allan Eastman. VHS $79.95 *CAF* ℤℤ

Foreign Affairs Vinnie Miller (Woodward) is a prim New England college teacher off to London on a research sabbatical. On the flight Vinnie's seatmate is boisterous good-ole-boy Chuck Mumpson (Dennehy), with whom she appears to have nothing in common. Naturally the two middle-aged romantics find a funny, though bittersweet, love together. A rather distracting subplot find's Vinnie's young colleague Fred (Stolz) involved in an affair with an older, eccentric British actress (Beacham). Based on the novel by Alison Lurie. Made for cable television.
1993 100m/C Joanne Woodward, Brian Dennehy, Eric Stoltz, Stephanie Beacham, Ian Richardson, Robert Hands; *D:* Jim O'Brien; *W:* Chris Bryant. VHS $89.98 *TTC* ℤℤℤ

Foreign Body An Indian (played by "Passage to India" star, Banerjee) visiting London pretends to be a doctor and finds women flocking to him. Excellent overlooked British comedy. Based on the novel by Roderick Mann.
1986 (PG-13) 108m/C GB Victor Banerjee, Warren Mitchell, Trevor Howard, Geraldine McEwan, Amanda Donohoe, Denis Quilley, Eve Ferret, Anna Massey; *D:* Ronald Neame; *W:* Celine La Freniere; *M:* Ken Howard. VHS $19.99 *HBO* ℤℤ½

Foreign Correspondent A classic Hitchcock tale of espionage and derring-do. A reporter is sent to Europe during WWII to cover a pacifist conference in London, where he becomes romantically involved with the daughter of the group's founder and befriends an elderly diplomat. When the diplomat is kidnapped, the reporter uncovers a Nazi spy-ring headed by his future father-in-law.
1940 120m/B Joel McCrea, Laraine Day, Herbert Marshall, George Sanders, Robert Benchley, Albert Basserman, Edmund Gwenn, Eduardo Ciannelli, Harry Davenport, Martin Kosleck, Charles Halton; *D:* Alfred Hitchcock; *W:* Robert Benchley, Charles Bennett, Joan Harrison, James Hilton; *M:* Alfred Newman. Academy Awards '40 Nominations: Best Black and White Cinematography, Best Interior Decoration, Best Original Screenplay, Best Picture, Best Supporting Actor (Basserman); National Board of Review Awards '40: 10 Best Films of the Year. VHS, Beta $59.95 *WAR* ℤℤℤℤ

The Foreigner Secret agent who comes to New York City to meet his contact becomes entrapped in a series of mysterious events revolving around the underground club scene.
1978 90m/B Eric Mitchell, Patti Astor, Deborah Harry; *D:* Amos Poe; *W:* Amos Poe. VHS, Beta $59.95 *FCT* ℤ

The Foreman Went to France Industrial engineer travels to France during WWII to help prevent secret machinery from falling into the hands of the Nazis and their allies. *AKA:* Somewhere in France.
1942 88m/B GB Clifford Evans, Constance Cummings, Robert Morley; *D:* Charles Frend. VHS, Beta $24.95 *NOS, MRV, DVT* ℤ½

Foreplay Inane trilogy of comedy segments involving characters with White House connections. Stories are introduced by former President Mostel discussing his downfall in a television interview. Lame rather than risque, wasting talents of all involved. Each segment was scripted and directed by a different team. *AKA:* The President's Women.
1975 100m/C Pat Paulsen, Jerry Orbach, Estelle Parsons, Zero Mostel; *D:* Bruce Malmuth, John G. Avildsen. VHS, Beta $59.98 *LIV, VES* Woof!

The Forest Spooks and a cannibalistic killer terrorize a group of campers. Nothing that hasn't been done countless times before.
1983 90m/C *D:* Donald M. Jones. VHS, Beta $59.95 *PSM* ℤ

Forest of Little Bear A man returns to his impoverished family in 1928 and decides to seek the reward put on the head of a one-eared man-eating bear. He kills the bear but faces a dilemma when he sees the bear left a helpless cub behind. In Japanese with English subtitles.
1979 124m/C JP *D:* Toshio Goto. VHS $59.95 *FCT* ℤℤ

Forever A teenage girl experiences true love for the first time and struggles with its meaning. Made for television adaptation of Judy Blume's novel.
1978 100m/C Stephanie Zimbalist, Dean Butler, John Friedrich, Beth Raines, Diana Scarwid; *D:* John Korty. VHS $59.95 *GEM* ℤℤ½

Forever: A Ghost of a Love Story Coogan is a hot-shot music video director who moves into a haunted house and soon meets the resident ghost, who just happens to be a beautiful woman. He falls for the ghostly presence but his all-too-real female agent is also making her moves.
1992 (R) 93m/C Keith Coogan, Sean Young, Diane Ladd, Sally Kirkland, Terence Knox, Nicholas Guest, Renee Taylor, Steve Railsback; *D:* Thomas Palmer Jr.; *W:* Thomas Palmer Jr. VHS, Beta $89.95 *PSM* ℤℤ½

Forever Amber Seventeenth century rags to riches story features Darnell as the poverty stricken girl who uses sex to gain wealth and status. She makes it to the bed of King Charles II, only to lose the one man she ever really loved (Wilde). The censorship of the 1940s hindered the film's erotic potential. Adapted from the best-selling novel by Kathleen Winsor.
1947 140m/C Linda Darnell, Cornel Wilde, Richard Greene, George Sanders, Richard Haydn, Jessica Tandy, Anne Revere, John Russell, Leo G. Carroll, Robert Coote, Margaret Wycherly, Alma Kruger, Edmund Breon, Alan Napier, Bill Ward, Richard Bailey, Skelton Knaggs, Norma Varden, Edith Evanson, Ellen Corby; *D:* Otto Preminger; *W:* Philip Dunne, Ring

Lardner Jr.; *M:* David Raskin. VHS $19.99 FXV 🎬🎬½

Forever and a Day Tremendous salute to British history centers around a London manor originally built by an English admiral during the Napoleonic era and the exploits of succeeding generations. The house even manages to survive the blitz of WWII showing English courage during wartime. Once-in-a-lifetime casting and directing. 1943 104m/B Brian Aherne, Robert Cummings, Ida Lupino, Charles Laughton, Herbert Marshall, Ray Milland, Anna Neagle, Merle Oberon, Claude Rains, Victor McLaglen, Buster Keaton, Jessie Matthews, Roland Young, Sir C. Aubrey Smith, Edward Everett Horton, Elsa Lanchester, Edmund Gwenn; *D:* Rene Clair, Edmund Goulding, Cedric Hardwicke, Frank Lloyd, Victor Saville, Robert Stevenson, Herbert Wilcox, Kent Smith; *W:* Charles Bennett, Michael Hogan, Peter Godfrey, Christopher Isherwood, Gene Lockhart, Donald Ogden Stewart. VHS $19.95 HTV, MLB, TPV 🎬🎬🎬🎬

Forever Darling Mixed effort from the reliable comedy duo sees Desi playing a dedicated chemist who neglects his wife while pursuing the next great pesticide. Lucy calls on her guardian angel (Mason) to help her rekindle her marriage. He advises her to go with Desi when he tests his new bug killer, and a series of hilarious, woodsy calamities occur. Lucy and Desi are always fun to watch, but '60s TV sitcom fans will enjoy the fact that Mrs. Howell (Schaefer) and Jane Hathaway (Kulp) appear in the same picture. 1956 91m/C Lucille Ball, Desi Arnaz Sr., James Mason, Louis Calhern, John Emery, John Hoyt, Natalie Schafer, Nancy Kulp; *D:* Alexander Hall. VHS, Beta $19.98 MGM, CCB 🎬🎬

Forever Emmanuelle Sensual young woman finds love and the ultimate erotic experience in the wilds of the South Pacific in this sequel to the porn-with-production-values "Emmanuelle." 1982 (R) 89m/C Annie-Belle, Emmanuelle Arsan, Al Cliver. VHS, Beta $29.98 LIV, VES 🎬

Forever Evil The vacationing denizens of a secluded cabin are almost killed off by the cult followers of a mythic god. 1987 107m/C Red Mitchell, Tracey Huffman, Charles Trotter, Howard Jacobsen, Kent Johnson. VHS, Beta $79.95 VCI 🎬

Forever Female Bright comedy about show business, egos, and love. Holden is a young playwright whose first play is accepted by stage producer Douglas on the condition that the lead role, featuring a 19-year-old heroine, be rewritten for his ex-wife Rogers. She's an aging leading lady smitten by Holden's charms—as is the ingenue Crowley, who would be perfect for the role as written. Complications and manipulations abound as the play makes its way to production. Adaptation of the Sir James Barrie play "Rosalind." 1953 93m/B Ginger Rogers, William Holden, Paul Douglas, Pat Crowley, James Gleason, Jesse White, George Reeves, Marjorie Rambeau, King Donovan, Vic Perrin, Marion Ross; *D:* Irving Rapper; *W:* Julius J. Epstein, Philip G. Epstein. VHS PAR 🎬🎬🎬

Forever James Dean A profile of the legendary actor/cult hero, examining his life, short career and remaining legacy. Also includes the original previews of his three feature films. A must for serious Dean fans. 1988 69m/C James Dean, Julie Harris, William Bast, Kenneth Kendall; *D:* Ara Chekmayan. VHS, Beta $29.98 WAR, FCT 🎬🎬🎬

Forever, Lulu A down-on-her-luck novelist winds up involved with the mob and a gangster's girlfriend. Completely laughless comedy with amateurish direction. *AKA:* Crazy Streets. 1987 86m/C Hanna Schygulla, Deborah Harry, Alec Baldwin, Annie Golden, Paul Gleason, Dr. Ruth Westheimer; *D:* Amos Kollek. VHS, Beta $79.95 COL 🎬

Forever Mary A teacher tries to better the lives of the boys sentenced to a reformatory in Palermo, Sicily, when a teenage transvestite prostitute (the title character) is admitted to the school. In Italian with English subtitles. *AKA:* Mery per Sempre. 1989 100m/C *IT* Michele Placido, Alesandro DiSanzo, Francesco Benigno; *D:* Marco Risi; *W:* Sandro Petraglia. VHS $79.95 CCN, ING 🎬🎬🎬

Forever Young A young boy immerses himself in Catholicism. Admiring a priest, he is unaware that the priest's friend is involved with his mother. Tangled, but delicate handling of the coming-of-age story. Made originally for British television. 1985 85m/C *GB* James Aubrey, Nicholas Gecks, Alec McCowen; *D:* David Drury. VHS, Beta $59.95 MGM 🎬🎬

Forever Young When test pilot Gibson's girlfriend is hit by a car and goes into a coma, he volunteers to be cryogenically frozen for one year. Oops!—he's left frozen for fifty years, until he is accidentally thawed out by a couple of kids. Predictable, designed to be a tear jerker, though it serves mostly as a star vehicle for Gibson who bumbles with 90s technology, finds his true love, and escapes from government heavies, adorable as ever. Through all the schmaltz, the relationship Gibson develops with the young Wood turns out to be the most authentic and endearing love in the film. 1992 (PG) 102m/C Mel Gibson, Jamie Lee Curtis, Elijah Wood, Isabel Glasser, George Wendt, Joe Morton, Nicolas Surovy, David Marshall Grant, Art LaFleur; *D:* Steve Miner; *W:* Jeffrey Abrams; *M:* Jerry Goldsmith. VHS, 8mm $19.98 WAR, BTV 🎬🎬½

Forger of London Edgar Wallace tale in which Scotland Yard investigates a counterfeit ring connected to a prime suspect, an amnesiac playboy. 1961 91m/C *GE* Eddi Arent, Karin Dor, Viktor de Kowa, Hellmut Lange, Robert Graf; *D:* Harald Reinl. VHS $16.95 SNC 🎬🎬

Forget Mozart On the day of Mozart's death, the head of the secret police gathers a group together for questioning. They include the composer's wife, his lyricist, the head of a Masonic lodge, and Salieri, Mozart's rival. Each has a different story to tell to the investigator about the composer's life and death. The film makes use of a number of sets and costumes from "Amadeus" and was also filmed on location in Prague. In German with English subtitles. *AKA:* Zabudnite na Mozarta. 1985 93m/C *GE* Armin Mueller-Stahl, Catarina Raacke; *D:* Salvo Luther. VHS $79.95 WBF 🎬🎬

The Forgotten After 17 years as POWs, six Green Berets are freed, only to face a treacherous government conspiracy aimed at eliminating them. Made for television. 1989 96m/C Keith Carradine, Steve Railsback, Stacy Keach, Pepe Serna, Don Opper, Richard Lawson; *D:* James Keach; *W:* Keith Carradine, Steve Railsback, James Keach. VHS, Beta $59.95 PAR 🎬🎬

The Forgotten One An uninspired author and a female reporter become mixed up in a century-old murder and the restless ghost it spawned.

1989 (R) 89m/C Kristy McNichol, Terry O'Quinn, Blair Parker, Elisabeth Brooks; *D:* Phillip Badger. VHS, Beta $14.95 ACA 🎬½

Forgotten Prisoners Celluloid proof that conviction and true grit do not always entertainment make. Greenwald—whose credits range from "Xanadu" to "The Burning Bed"—directed this righteous but stationary drama about an Amnesty International official (Silver) who's assigned to look into the incarceration and egregious mistreatment of Turkish citizens. Made for cable TV. *AKA:* Forgotten Prisoners: The Amnesty Files. 1990 (R) 92m/C Ron Silver, Roger Daltrey, Hector Elizondo; *D:* Robert Greenwald; *M:* Brad Fiedel. VHS, Beta $79.98 TTC, FCT 🎬🎬

A Forgotten Tune for the Flute A delightful, Glasnost-era romantic comedy. A bureaucrat caught up in a dull, stuffy existence has a heart attack and winds up falling in love with his nurse. He then must decide between his comfortable, cared-for life or the love which beckons him. In Russian with English subtitles. 1988 131m/C *RU* Leonid Filatov, Tatiana Dogileva, Irina Kupchenko; *D:* Edgar Ryazanov. VHS, Beta $29.95 FRH, ING 🎬🎬🎬

Forgotten Warrior Vengeance is the name of the game as a Vietnam vet tracks down the fellow officer who tried to kill him and shot his commander. 1986 (R) 76m/C Quincy Frazer, Sam T. Lapuzz, Ron Marchini, Joe Meyer; *D:* Nick Cacas, Charlie Ordonez. VHS, Beta $79.95 MNC 🎬½

Forlorn River Nevada and Weary, two law-abiding men, seek to return their hometown to peace by eliminating a gang of outlaws. Based on a novel by Zane Grey. 1937 62m/B Buster Crabbe, June Martel, John D. Patterson, Harvey Stephens, Chester Conklin, Lew Kelly, Syd Saylor; *D:* Charles T. Barton. VHS $19.95 NOS, DVT, RXM 🎬½

The Formula Convoluted story about a secret formula for synthetic fuel that meanders it's way from the end of WWII to the present. A U.S. soldier waylays, and then joins forces with, a German general entrusted with the formula. Years later, after the American is murdered, his friend, a hardnosed L.A. cop, starts investigating, meeting up with spies and a reclusive oil billionaire. Scott and Brando have one good confrontation scene but the rest of the movie is just hot air. From the novel by Steve Shagan. 1980 (R) 117m/C Marlon Brando, George C. Scott, Marthe Keller, G.D. Spradlin, Beatrice Straight, John Gielgud, Richard Lynch; *D:* John G. Avildsen; *M:* Bill Conti. VHS, Beta $19.98 MGM 🎬½

Formula for a Murder A very rich but paralyzed woman marries a scheming con artist who plots to kill her and inherit everything. 1985 89m/C Christina Nagy, David Warbeck, Rossano Brazzi. VHS, Beta $69.98 LIV 🎬

Forrest Gump Grandly ambitious and slightly flawed, amounting to a wonderful bit of movie magic. As the intelligence-impaired Gump with a heart of gold and more than enough character and dignity, Hanks supplies another career highlight. Field contributes a nice turn as his dedicated mama (they were last together in "Punchline"), while Sinise is particularly effective as a handicap Vietnam veteran with a bad attitude. Incredible special effects put Gump in the middle of historic events over a four-decade period, but the real story is the life-affirming, nonjudgmental power of Gump to transform the

lives of those around him. From the novel by Winston Groom.
1994 142m/C Tom Hanks, Robin Wright, Sally Field, Gary Sinise, Mykelti Williamson; **D:** Robert Zemeckis; **W:** Eric Roth. VHS *NYR ↙↙↙↙*

Forsaking All Others Screwball comedy featuring several MGM superstars. Friends since childhood, Gable has been in love with Crawford for 20 years, but she never realizes it and plans to marry Montgomery. Crawford is very funny in this delightful story of a wacky romantic triangle.
1935 84m/B Joan Crawford, Clark Gable, Robert Montgomery, Charles Butterworth, Billie Burke, Rosalind Russell, Frances Drake; **D:** Woodbridge S. Van Dyke; **W:** Joseph L. Mankiewicz. VHS $19.98 *MGM ↙↙½*

Fort Apache The first of director Ford's celebrated cavalry trilogy, in which a fanatical colonel (Fonda) leads his reluctant men to an eventual slaughter, recalling George Custer at Little Big Horn. In residence: Ford hallmarks of spectacular landscapes and stirring action, as well as many vignettes of life at a remote outpost. Don't forget to catch "She Wore a Yellow Ribbon" and "Rio Grande," the next films in the series. Also available in a colorized version.
1948 125m/B John Wayne, Henry Fonda, Shirley Temple, John Agar, Pedro Armendariz Sr., Victor McLaglen, Ward Bond, Anna Lee; **D:** John Ford. VHS, Beta $19.95 *TTC, RKO, TLF ↙↙↙½*

Fort Apache, the Bronx A police drama set in the beleaguered South Bronx of New York City, based on the real-life experiences of two former New York cops who served there. Newman is a decent cop who goes against every kind of criminal and crazy and against his superiors in trying to bring law and justice to a downtrodden community.
1981 (R) 123m/C Paul Newman, Ed Asner, Ken Wahl, Danny Aiello, Rachel Ticotin, Pam Grier, Kathleen Beller; **D:** Daniel Petrie; **W:** Heywood Gould. VHS, Beta $14.95 *WAR, VES, CCB ↙↙↙*

Fortress A teacher and her class are kidnapped from their one-room schoolhouse in the Australian outback. They must use their ingenuity and wits to save their lives in this violent made-for-cable-television suspense drama.
1985 (R) 90m/C *AU* Rachel Ward, Sean Garlick, Rebecca Rigg; **D:** Arch Nicholson. VHS, Beta $14.95 *CNG, HBO ↙*

Fortress How come the future is never a place you'd want to be? Thanks to overpopulation a woman is only allowed one pregnancy. When John and Karen Bennick are caught trying to have a second child they are shipped to the Fortress, an underground prison in the middle of the desert. Discipline is enforced with numerous sadistic toys, including the intestinator, so-called because it's implanted in the stomach of each prisoner and infractions result in excruciating laser-activated pain. Lambert does well with his action hero but it's character actor Smith as the warden, a techno-human with some sick fantasies, who has the real fun in this horrific depiction of the future.
1993 (R) 91m/C Christopher Lambert, Kurtwood Smith, Loryn Locklin, Lincoln Kilpatrick; **D:** Stuart Gordon; **W:** Steve Feinberg, Troy Nabors, Terry Curtis Fox. VHS $92.98 *LIV ↙↙*

Fortress of Amerikka In the not-too-distant future, mercenaries get their hands on a secret weapon that could allow them to take over the USA.
1989 ?m/C Gene Le Brock, Kellee Bradley. VHS $79.99 *IMP ↙½*

Fortune and Men's Eyes Exploitative and depressing film about life in a Canadian prison. A naive young man is sent to prison for marijuana possession and has to make a difficult choice—be regularly sodomized by a man who will protect him or be raped by everyone else. Based on the play by John Herbert.
1971 (R) 102m/C Wendell Burton, Michael Greer, Zooey Hall, Danny Freedman; **D:** Harvey Hart; **W:** John Herbert. VHS $19.98 *MGM ↙↙*

The Fortune Cookie After receiving a minor injury during a football game, a TV cameraman is convinced by his seedy lawyer brother-in-law to exaggerate his injury and start an expensive lawsuit. A classic, biting comedy by Wilder. First of several Lemmon-Matthau comedies. The letterbox laserdisc version contains the original theatrical trailer. **AKA:** Meet Whiplash Willie.
1966 125m/B Jack Lemmon, Walter Matthau, Ron Rich, Cliff Osmond, Judi West, Lurene Tuttle; **D:** Billy Wilder; **W:** Billy Wilder, I.A.L. Diamond. Academy Awards '66: Best Supporting Actor (Matthau); Nominations: Best Art Direction/Set Decoration (B & W), Best Black and White Cinematography, Best Story & Screenplay. VHS, Beta $19.95 *FOX, MGM, FCT ↙↙↙*

Fortune Dane Police detective Fortune Dane goes undercover to clear his name after he is framed for murder.
1986 (PG) 83m/C Carl Weathers, Adolph Caesar; **D:** Nicholas Sgarro; **W:** Charles Correll. VHS, Beta $29.95 *VMK ↙½*

Fortune's Fool A beef king and profiteer marries a younger woman and soon discovers the problems that ambition can cause. Silent.
1921 60m/B *GE* Emil Jannings, Daguey Servaes, Reinhold Schunzel; **D:** Reinhold Schunzel. VHS, Beta $24.95 *NOS, MRV, VYY ↙↙*

Fortunes of War British professor Guy Pringle arrives with his bride, Harriet, to take up a teaching post in the Balkans in 1939. The idealistic Guy soon becomes enmeshed in anti-fascist politics and involved with the local members of the British embassy. When threatened by war they travel to Athens and then Cairo, where Guy's increasing involvement in the political situation, and his neglect of Harriet, causes a crisis in their marriage. Slow-moving drama with some self-centered characters is redeemed by the acting skills of those involved. Based on the autobiographial novels of Olivia Manning. Originally shown on "Masterpiece Theater" on PBS.
1987 160m/C *GB* Kenneth Branagh, Emma Thompson, Rupert Graves, Ronald Pickup, Robert Stephens, Charles Kay, James Villers, Harry Burton, Ciaran Madden, Diana Hardcastle, Greg Hicks, Alan Bennett, Jeremy Brundell, Jeremy Sinden; **D:** James Cellan Jones; **W:** Alan Plater. VHS $29.98 *FOX, FCT, TVC ↙↙↙*

Forty Carats Ullmann plays the just-turned forty divorcee who has a brief fling with the half-her-age Albert while on vacation in Greece. She figures she'll never see him again but, back in New York, he turns up on the arm of her beautiful daughter (Raffin). Except he's still interested in mom. The rest of the movie is spent trying to convince Ullmann that love can conquer all. Ullmann's very attractive but not well-suited for the part; Raffins's screen debut. Based on the Broadway hit.
1973 (PG) 110m/C Liv Ullmann, Edward Albert, Gene Kelly, Binnie Barnes, Deborah Raffin, Nancy Walker; **D:** Milton Katselas; **W:** Jay Presson Allen. VHS, Beta $59.95 *COL ↙↙½*

Forty Days of Musa Dagh Based on the true story of Armenia's fight for freedom against Turkey in the 1914 uprising and the dreadful cost. From the novel by Franz Werfel.
1985 120m/C Michael Constantine, David Opatoshu. VHS, Beta $69.95 *VCD ↙↙*

The Forty-Niners A forgettable oater about the hysteria surrounding the finding of gold in California.
1932 59m/B Tom Tyler, Betty Mack, Alan Bridge, Fern Emmett, Gordon Wood, Frank Ball; **D:** John P. McCarthy. VHS $19.95 *DVT, HEG, GPV ↙*

The Forty-Ninth Parallel Six Nazi servicemen, seeking to reach neutral American soil, are trapped and their U-boat sunk by Royal Canadian Air Force bombers, forcing them into Canada on foot, where they run into an array of stalwart patriots. Dated wartime propaganda made prior to the U.S. entering the war; riddled with entertaining star turns. **AKA:** The Invaders.
1941 90m/B *GB* Laurence Olivier, Leslie Howard, Eric Portman, Raymond Massey, Glynis Johns, Finlay Currie, Anton Walbrook; **D:** Michael Powell; **W:** Emeric Pressburger, Rodney Ackland. VHS, Beta $29.95 *VYG ↙↙↙*

Forty Thousand Horsemen The story of the ANZACS of Australia, created to fight Germany in the Middle East during WWII. This Australian war drama is full of cavalry charges, brave young lads, and "Waltzing Matilda."
1941 86m/B *AU* Chips Rafferty, Grant Taylor, Betty Bryant, Pat Twohill. VHS, Beta $24.95 *VYY, FCT ↙↙½*

42nd Street A Broadway musical producer faces numerous problems in his efforts to reach a successful opening night. Choreography by Busby Berkeley. A colorized version of the film is also available. ♫You're Getting to Be a Habit With Me; Shuffle Off to Buffalo; Young and Healthy; Forty-Second Street; It Must Be June.
1933 89m/B Warner Baxter, Ruby Keeler, Bebe Daniels, George Brent, Dick Powell, Guy Kibbee, Ginger Rogers, Una Merkel, Busby Berkeley, Ned Sparks, George E. Stone; **D:** Lloyd Bacon; **W:** Rian James, James Seymour; **M:** Harry Warren, Al Dubin. VHS, Beta $19.98 *MGM, FOX, HMV ↙↙↙↙*

47 Ronin, Part 1 Turn of the 18th-century epic chronicling the samurai legend. The warriors of Lord Asano set out to avenge their leader, tricked into committing a forced seppuku, or hara-kiri. The photography is generously laden with views of 18th century gardens as well as panoramic vistas. This is the largest and most popular film of the Kabuki version of the story by Seika Mayama. In Japanese with English subtitles. **AKA:** The Loyal 47 Ronin; 47 Samurai.
1942 111m/C *JP* **D:** Kenji Mizoguchi. VHS *ING ↙↙*

47 Ronin, Part 2 Second half of the film in which the famous Japanese folktale of Lord Asano and his warriors is told. The film follows Asano's samurai as they commit themselves to avenging their leader in 1703. In Japanese with English subtitles.
1942 108m/C *JP* **D:** Kenji Mizoguchi. VHS *ING ↙↙*

48 Hrs. An experienced San Francisco cop (Nolte) springs a convict (Murphy) from jail for 48 hours to find a vicious murdering drug lord. Murphy's film debut is great and Nolte is perfect as his gruff foil.
1982 (R) 97m/C Nick Nolte, Eddie Murphy, James Remar, Annette O'Toole, David Patrick Kelly, Sonny Landham, Brion James, Denise Crosby; **D:** Walter Hill; **W:** Walter Hill, Larry

Gross, Steven E. de Souza, Roger Spottiswoode; *M:* James Horner. VHS, Beta $14.95 *PAR* 🐾🐾

48 Hours to Live A reporter travels to a nuclear scientist's secluded island only to find the scientist held hostage by nuclear weapon-seeking terrorists. *AKA:* Man in the Middle.
1960 86m/B Anthony Steel, Ingemar Johannson, Marlies Behrens. VHS, Beta *NO* 🐾

Fotografo de Senoras A novice photographer finds himself being mistaken for a rapist when naked women keep popping up in front of his camera.
1985 110m/C *SP* Jorge Porcel, Graciela Alfano, Tristan. VHS, Beta *MED* 🐾

Foul Play Bearing no similarity to the Goldie Hawn vehicle of the same name, this Polish crimer is based on a true story, and stars two of Poland's Olympic boxers. A young man, accused of theft, is coerced by the Warsaw police to go undercover in return for having the charges against him dropped. With English subtitles.
1976 98m/C *PL* Marek Powowski, Jan Szcepanski, Jerzy Kulej. VHS $14.95 *FCT* 🐾🐾

Foul Play Hawn is a librarian who picks up a hitchhiker which leads to nothing but trouble. She becomes involved with San Francisco detective Chase in an effort to expose a plot to kill the Pope during his visit to the city. Also involved is Moore as an English orchestra conductor with some kinky sexual leanings. Chase is charming (no mugging here) and Hawn both bubbly and brave. A big winner at the box office; features Barry Manilow's hit tune "Ready to Take a Chance Again."
1978 (PG) 116m/C Goldie Hawn, Chevy Chase, Dudley Moore, Burgess Meredith, Billy Barty, Rachel Roberts, Eugene Roche, Brian Dennehy, Chuck McCann, Bruce Solomon; *D:* Colin Higgins; *M:* Charles Fox. VHS, Beta, 8mm $19.95 *PAR* 🐾🐾🐾

Found Alive After a painful divorce, a woman kidnaps her son and steals away into the Mexican jungle, with only the help of her faithful butler.
1934 65m/B Barbara Bedford, Maurice Murphy, Robert Frazer, Edwin Cross; *D:* Charles Hutchinson. VHS, Beta $16.95 *SNC* 🐾

The Fountainhead Cooper is an idealistic, uncompromising architect who refuses to change his designs. When he finds out his plans for a public housing project have been radically altered he blows up the building and winds up in court defending his actions. Neal is the sub-plot love interest. Based on the novel by Ayn Rand.
1949 113m/C Gary Cooper, Patricia Neal, Raymond Massey, Ray Collins, Henry Hull; *D:* King Vidor. VHS, Beta $19.98 *MGM, FOX* 🐾🐾🐾

Four Adventures of Reinette and Mirabelle Small but touching Rohmer tale of the friendship between two women—one a naive country girl (Miquel, as Reinette), the other a sophisticated Parisian (Forde, as Mirabelle)—who share an apartment and a number of experiences, but who have a very different manner of inhabiting those experiences. A thoroughly French human comedy, one of Rohmer's better studies. In French with English subtitles.
1989 95m/C *FR* Joelle Miquel, Jessica Forde, Philippe Laudenbach, Marie Riviere, Beatrice Romand, Yasmine Haury; *D:* Eric Rohmer; *W:* Eric Rohmer. VHS $69.95 *NYF, FCT, ING* 🐾🐾🐾

Four Bags Full A bitter comedy about two smugglers during WWII who try to get a slaughtered pig to the black market under the Nazis' noses. In French with English subtitles.
1956 82m/C *FR* Jean Gabin, Louis de Funes, Bourvil, Jeanette Batti; *D:* Claude Autant-Lara. VHS, Beta $14.95 *VDM, FCT* 🐾🐾 ½

Four Daughters Classic, three-hankie outing in which four talented daughters of music professor Rains fall in love and marry. Garfield shines, in a role tailor-made for him, as the world-weary suitor driven to extremes in the name of love. Great performances from all. Based on the novel "Sister Act" by Fannie Hurst.
1938 90m/B Claude Rains, John Garfield, May Robson, Priscilla Lane, Lola Lane, Rosemary Lane, Gale Page, Dick Foran, Jeffrey Lynn; *D:* Michael Curtiz. VHS $19.98 *MGM, CCB* 🐾🐾🐾

Four Days in July Two couples from Belfast, one Catholic and one Protestant, find they have something in common when they meet in the maternity ward as both couples become first-time parents. Script and dialog were mainly improvised, which provides both dull stretches and the film's charm.
1984 99m/C *GB* Des McAleer, Brid Brennan, Charles Lawson, Paula Hamilton, Shane Connaughton, Eileen Pollock, Stephen Rea; *D:* Mike Leigh. VHS $79.95 *WBF, BTV* 🐾🐾

Four Deuces Gang war is underway between the Chico Hamilton mob and Vic Morano and the Four Deuces during the Depression. Comedy and action combine with elements of strong language, strong sex, and strong violence.
1975 87m/C Jack Palance, Carol Lynley, Warren Berlinger, Adam Roarke; *D:* William H. Bushnell Jr. VHS, Beta $59.99 *HBO, VTR* 🐾 ½

Four Eyes and Six Guns In 1882 a New York optometrist, who's a fan of the popular dime-store western novels, moves to Tombstone, Arizona in search of adventure. He's just in time too because Sheriff Wyatt Earp is trying to rid the town of those pesky Doom Brothers but is having a problem with his eyesight (causing his gunshots to go astray). Now if the greenhorn can just get Earp to wear his new glasses. Silly but harmless fluff. Made for cable television.
1993 92m/C Judge Reinhold, Patricia Clarkson, Dan Hedaya, M. Emmet Walsh, Austin Pendleton, Fred Ward; *D:* Piers Haggard; *W:* Leon Prochnik. VHS, Beta $9.98 *TTC* 🐾🐾 ½

Four Faces West McCrea is an honest rancher who nevertheless robs the local bank in order to save his father's ranch from foreclosure. His humanity in helping a diphtheria-ridden family leads to his capture, but the sheriff promises a light sentence, since he is not a typical bad guy. Fine performances strengthen this low-key western. *AKA:* They Passed This Way.
1948 90m/B Joel McCrea, Frances Dee, Charles Bickford; *D:* Alfred E. Green. VHS $14.95 *REP* 🐾🐾 ½

The Four Feathers A grand adventure from a story by A.E.W. Mason. After resigning from the British Army a young man is branded a coward and given four white feathers as symbols by three of his friends and his lady love. Determined to prove them wrong he joins the Sudan campaign of 1898 and rescues each of the men from certain death. They then take back their feathers as does his girl upon learning of his true courage. Excellent performances by Smith and Richardson.

1939 99m/C *GB* John Clements, Ralph Richardson, Sir C. Aubrey Smith, June Duprez, Donald Gray, Jack Allen, Clive Barker, Allan Jeayes; *D:* Zoltan Korda; *W:* R.C. Sheriff; *M:* Miklos Rozsa. VHS, Beta $14.98 *SUE, FCT, HMV* 🐾🐾🐾🐾

The Four Feathers Determined to return the symbols of cowardice, four feathers, to his friends and fiancee, a man courageously saves his friends' lives during the British Sudan campaign and regains the love of his lady. Made-for-television movie is the fifth remake.
1978 95m/C Beau Bridges, Jane Seymour, Simon Ward, Harry Andrews, Richard Johnson, Robert Powell; *D:* Don Sharp. VHS, Beta $14.98 *REP* 🐾🐾

Four for Texas Perhaps Aldrich's later success with "The Dirty Dozen" can be attributed, in part, to this exercise in how not to make a comic western; poorly made, over long, and far too dependant on the feminine charisma of Ekberg and Andress. Slow-moving Sinatra-Martin vehicle tells the tale of con men in the Old West who battle bandits and bad bankers for a stash of loot.
1963 124m/C Frank Sinatra, Dean Martin, Anita Ekberg, Ursula Andress, Charles Bronson, Victor Buono, Jack Elam; *D:* Robert Aldrich. VHS, Beta $14.95 *WAR, FCT* 🐾

Four Friends The magical good and bad dream of the 1960s is remembered in this story of four friends. A young woman and the three men in love with her first come together in high school and then separate, learning from college, war and drug abuse, and each other in this ambitious movie from Steve Tesich, the writer of "Breaking Away." Good performances by all. *AKA:* Georgia's Friends.
1981 (R) 114m/C James Leo Herlihy, Craig Wasson, Jodi Thelen, Michael Huddleston, Jim Metzler, Reed Birney; *D:* Arthur Penn; *W:* Steve Tesich. VHS, Beta $19.98 *WAR, OM* 🐾🐾🐾

The Four Hands of Death: Wily Match Two martial artists are the best of friends, in and out of the ring—until they both fall for the same woman!
19?? 90m/C Cheung Fu Hung, Jimmy Lee, Mo Man Sau. VHS, Beta $49.95 *OCE* 🐾 ½

The Four Horsemen of the Apocalypse Silent classic and star maker for Valentino concerning an Argentine family torn apart by the outbreak of WWI. Valentino is a painter who moves from his native Argentina to France and is persuaded to enlist by a recruiter who invokes the image of the Biblical riders. His excellence as a soldier, however, proves to be his undoing. The 1962 remake can't hold a candle to original, adapted from a novel by Vicente Blasco-Ibanez.
1921 110m/B Rudolph Valentino, Alice Terry, Pomeroy Cannon, Josef Swickard, Alan Hale, Mabel van Buren, Nigel de Brulier, Bowditch Turner, Wallace Beery; *D:* Rex Ingram. VHS *NO* 🐾🐾🐾 ½

The Four Horsemen of the Apocalypse The members of a German family find themselves fighting on opposite sides during WWII. This remake of the vintage Valentino silent failed at the box office, with complaints about its length, disjointed script, and uninspired performances. The title refers to the horrors of conquest, pestilence, war, and death. Adapted from the book by Vincente Blasco-Ibanez.
1962 153m/C Glenn Ford, Charles Boyer, Lee J. Cobb, Paul Henreid, Yvette Mimieux; *D:* Vincente Minnelli; *W:* John Gay. VHS, Beta $19.98 *MGM* 🐾🐾 ½

The 400 Blows The classic, groundbreaking semi-autobiography that initiated Truffaut's career and catapulted him to international acclaim, about the trials and rebellions of a 12-year-old French schoolboy. One of the greatest and most influential of films, and the first of Truffaut's career-long Antoine Doinel series. With English subtitles. *AKA:* Les Quatre Cents Coups.
1959 97m/B FR Jean-Pierre Leaud, Claire Maurier, Albert Remy, Guy Decomble, Georges Flament, Patrick Auffay, Jeanne Moreau, Jean-Claude Brialy, Jacques Demy, Francois Truffaut; *D:* Francois Truffaut; *W:* Marcel Moussey, Francois Truffaut; *M:* Jean Constantin. Academy Awards '59 Nominations: Best Story & Screenplay; Cannes Film Festival '59: Best Director (Truffaut); New York Film Critics Awards '59: Best Foreign Film. **VHS, Beta $39.95** *HMV, MRV, APD 🎬🎬🎬🎬*

Four in a Jeep In Vienna in 1945, soldiers from different countries are serving as an international military police force. They clash as a result of political demands and their love for the same woman. Shot on location in Austria.
1951 83m/B Ralph Meeker, Viveca Lindfors, Joseph Yadin, Michael Medwin; *D:* Leopold Lindtberg. **VHS, Beta $19.95** *NOS 🎬🎬½*

Four Jacks and a Jill Four musicians are left in the lurch when their band singer leaves them for her gangster boyfriend and they must frantically search for a replacement. Not completely uninteresting, but rather bland and old now. Earlier versions of the story were released as "Street Girl" and "That Girl from Paris." 🎵I'm in Good Shape For the Shape I'm In; You Go Your Way and I'll Go Crazy; I Haven't A Thing to Wear; Wherever You Are; Boogie Woogie Conga.
1941 68m/B Anne Shirley, Ray Bolger, Desi Arnaz Sr., Jack Durant, June Havoc, Eddie Foy Jr., Fritz Feld; *D:* Jack Hively. **VHS, Beta $19.98** *TTC 🎬🎬*

The Four Musketeers A fun-loving continuation of "The Three Musketeers," reportedly filmed simultaneously. Lavish swashbuckler jaunts between France, England, and Italy, in following the adventures of D'Artagnan and his cohorts. Pictures give an amusing depiction of Lester-interpreted seventeenth-century Europe, with fine performances especially by Dunaway as an evil countess seeking revenge on our heroes and Welch as the scatterbrained object of York's affections. Followed, in 1989, by "The Return of the Musketeers." *AKA:* The Revenge of Milady.
1975 (PG) 108m/C Michael York, Oliver Reed, Richard Chamberlain, Frank Finlay, Raquel Welch, Christopher Lee, Faye Dunaway, Jean-Pierre Cassel, Geraldine Chaplin, Simon Ward, Charlton Heston, Roy Kinnear, Nicole Calfan; *D:* Richard Lester. **VHS, Beta** *LIV, OM 🎬🎬🎬*

Four Robbers The ruthless Ma initiates his series of crimes throughout the Far East, somehow staying ahead of the cops. When the final showdown occurs, it's an all out kung fu massacre.
197? 90m/C Lau Chun, Shek Hon, Kong Seng, Lee Wing Shan. **VHS, Beta $49.95** *OCE 🎬*

Four Rode Out A Mexican outlaw is pursued by his girlfriend, one-time partner, and the law. Brutal, inferior western.
1969 99m/C Pernell Roberts, Sue Lyon, Leslie Nielsen, Julian Mateos; *D:* John Peyser. **VHS** *NO 🎬*

The Four Seasons Three upper-middle-class New York couples share their vacations together, as well as their friendship, their frustrations and their jealousies. Alda's first outing as a film director is pleasant and easy on the eyes.
1981 (PG) 108m/C Alan Alda, Carol Burnett, Sandy Dennis, Len Cariou, Jack Weston, Rita Moreno, Bess Armstrong; *D:* Alan Alda; *W:* Alan Alda. **VHS, Beta $19.95** *MCA 🎬🎬½*

Four Sided Triangle Two mad scientists find their friendship threatened when they discover that they are both in love with the same woman. So they do what anyone would do in this situation—they invent a machine and duplicate her.
1953 81m/B GB James Hayter, Barbara Payton, Stephen Murray, John Van Eyssen, Percy Marmont; *D:* Terence Fisher; *M:* Malcolm Arnold. **VHS $19.98** *NOS, SNC, MLB 🎬*

Four Ways Out Four average guys are fed up by their lot in life and stage a box-office robbery of their local soccer stadium. They don't get to enjoy their ill-gotten gains. In Italian with subtitles or dubbed.
1957 77m/B IT Gina Lollobrigida, Renalto Baldini, Paul Muller; *D:* Pietro Germi. **VHS $16.95** *SNC, VYY 🎬🎬½*

Four Weddings and a Funeral Refreshing, intelligent adult comedy filled with upper-class sophistication and wit. Thirtyish Brit bachelor Charles (Grant) attends the weddings of his friends, but won't take the plunge himself—even as he falls in love with Carrie (MacDowell). Great beginning offers loads of laughs as the first two weddings unfold, then becomes decidedly bittersweet. Grant is terrific as the romantic bumbler, but MacDowell seems slightly out of place. Supporting characters are superb, especially Coleman as the "flirty" Scarlett and Atkinson as a new minister. Surprising box office hit found a broad audience.
1993 (R) 118m/C GB Hugh Grant, Andie MacDowell, Simon Callow, Kristin Scott Thomas, James Fleet, John Hannah, Charlotte Coleman, David Bower, Corin Redgrave, Rowan Atkinson; *D:* Mike Newell; *W:* Richard Curtis; *M:* Richard Rodney Bennett. **VHS** *PGV 🎬🎬🎬½*

The 4D Man A physicist makes two fateful discoveries while working on a special project that gets out of control, leaving him able to pass through matter and see around corners. He also finds that his touch brings instant death. Cheap but effective sci-fier. Young Duke has a small part.
1959 85m/C Robert Lansing, Lee Meriwether, James Congdon, Guy Raymond, Robert Strauss, Patty Duke; *D:* Irvin S. Yeaworth Jr. **VHS, Beta $19.95** *NWV, MLB 🎬🎬½*

1492: Conquest of Paradise Large-scale Hollywood production striving for political correctness is a drawn-out account of Columbus's (Depardieu) discovery and subsequent exploitation of the "New World." Skillful directing and impressive scenery add interest, yet don't make up for a script which chronicles events but tends towards trite dialogue and characterization. Available in both pan-and-scan and letterbox formats.
1992 (PG-13) 142m/C Gerard Depardieu, Sigourney Weaver, Armand Assante, Frank Langella, Loren Dean, Angela Molina, Fernando Rey, Michael Wincott, Steven Waddington, Tcheky Karyo, Kario Salem; *D:* Ridley Scott; *W:* Roselyne Bosch; *M:* Vangelis. **VHS, Beta $95.95** *PAR, BTV 🎬🎬½*

The 4th Man Steeped in saturated colors and jet black comedy, with an atmospheric score, Verhoeven's nouveau noir mystery enjoyed considerable art-house success but was not released in the US until 1984. The story is decidedly non-linear, the look stylish and symbolic. Krabbe is an alcoholic bisexual Catholic writer who inadvertently becomes the hypotenuse of a love triangle involving Herman, a young man he encounters at a railway station, and his lover Christine, who owns the Sphinx beauty parlor and whose three husbands died, shall we say, mysteriously. In Dutch with English subtitles. *AKA:* Blunt.
1979 104m/C NL Jeroen Krabbe, Renee Soutendijk, Thom Hoffman, Jon DeVries, Geert De Jong; *D:* Paul Verhoeven; *M:* Loek Dikker. **VHS, Beta $24.95** *XVC, MED, ING 🎬🎬🎬½*

The Fourth Protocol Well-made thriller based on the Frederick Forsyth bestseller about a British secret agent trying to stop a young KGB agent from destroying NATO and putting the world in nuclear jeopardy. Brosnan, as the totally dedicated Russkie, gives his best performance to date while Caine, as usual, is totally believable as he goes about the business of tracking down the bad guys.
1987 (R) 119m/C GB Michael Caine, Pierce Brosnan, Ned Beatty, Joanna Cassidy, Julian Glover, Ray McAnally, Michael Gough, Ian Richardson, Betsy Brantley, Matt Frewer, Peter Cartwright, David Conville; *D:* John MacKenzie; *W:* Frederick Forsyth, Richard Burridge, George Axelrod; *M:* Lalo Schifrin, Francis Shaw. **VHS, Beta $19.98** *LHV, WAR 🎬🎬🎬*

Fourth Story A misfit detective is hired by a beautiful woman to find her missing husband. The investigation reveals some unseemly facts about the gentleman. Characterizations and plot twists keep this made-for-cable mystery interesting.
1990 (PG-13) 91m/C Mark Harmon, Mimi Rogers, Cliff DeYoung, Paul Gleason, M. Emmet Walsh; *D:* Ivan Passer; *W:* Andrew Guerdat. **VHS, Beta $89.98** *MED, IME, VTR 🎬🎬🎬*

The Fourth War Scheider and Prochnow are American and Russian colonels, respectively, assigned to guard the West German-Czechoslovakian border against each other. With the end of the cold war looming, these two frustrated warriors begin to taunt each other with sallies into the other's territory, threatening to touch off a major superpower conflict.
1990 (R) 109m/C Roy Scheider, Juergen Prochnow, Tim Reid, Lara Harris, Harry Dean Stanton; *D:* John Frankenheimer; *M:* Bill Conti. **VHS, Beta $89.99** *HBO 🎬🎬*

Fourth Wise Man A Biblical Easter story about a rich physician searching for Christ in Persia.
1985 72m/C Martin Sheen, Lance Kerwin, Alan Arkin, Harold Gould, Eileen Brennan, Ralph Bellamy, Adam Arkin, Richard Libertini. **VHS, Beta $19.98** *LIV, VES, IGP 🎬🎬*

Fourth Wish When a single father learns that his son is dying, he vows to make his son's last months as fulfilling as possible. Bring lots of hankies.
1975 107m/C John Meillon, Robert Bettles, Robyn Nevin; *D:* Don Chaffey. **VHS, Beta $49.95** *SUE 🎬🎬*

Fowl Play An unlikely threesome encounter various hardships and mishaps on their way to the first cock-fighting Olympics. Let's hope it's the last cock-fighting Olympics.
1983 90m/C Nancy Kwan. **VHS, Beta** *NO Woof!*

Fox and His Friends Fassbinder's breakthrough tragi-drama, about a lowly gay carnival barker who wins the lottery, thus attracting a devious, exploiting lover, who takes him for everything he has. In German with English subtitles. *AKA:* Faustrecht der Freiheit; Fist Right of Freedom.

1975 123m/C *GE* Rainer Werner Fassbinder, Peter Chatel, Karl-Heinz Boehm, Adrian Hoven, Harry Baer, Ulla Jacobsson, Kurt Raab; *D:* Rainer Werner Fassbinder. **VHS, Beta $79.95** FCT, NYF, ING 🎬🎬🎬 ½

The Fox and the Hound Sweet story of the friendship shared by a fox and hound. Young and naive, the animals become friends and swear their allegiance to one another when they are separated for a season. Upon return, the hound has become his master's best hunting dog and warns his friend the fox to stay clear of their hunting grounds, for the master is determined to catch the docile fox. Saddened, the fox retreats but soon finds himself boldly standing his ground against a bear that attacks the hound, and the hound inevitably protects the fox from the mean-spirited hunter. Very good animation, but not in the same class as other Disney favorites like "Beauty and the Beast."
1981 (G) 83m/C *D:* Art Stevens, Ted Berman, Richard Rich; *W:* Art Stevens, Peter Young, Steve Hulett, Earl Kress, Vance Gerry, Laury Clemmons, Dave Michener, Burny Mattinson; *M:* Buddy Baker; *V:* Mickey Rooney, Kurt Russell, Pearl Bailey, Jack Albertson, Sandy Duncan, Jeanette Nolán, Pat Buttram, John Fiedler, John McIntire, Richard Bakalayan, Paul Winchell, Keith Mitchell, Corey Feldman. **VHS, Beta $24.99** DIS, WTA, BTV 🎬🎬🎬

Foxes Four young California girls grow up with little supervision from parents still trying to grow up themselves. They rely on each other in a world where they have to make adult choices, yet are not considered grown-up. They look for no more than a good time and no tragic mistakes.
1980 (R) 106m/C Jodie Foster, Cherie Currie, Marilyn Kagan, Scott Baio, Sally Kellerman, Randy Quaid, Laura Dern; *D:* Adrian Lyne. **VHS, Beta $14.95** MGM, FOX 🎬🎬

Foxfire In the role that won her Tony and Emmy awards, Tandy stars as Annie Nations, a woman who has lived her entire life in the Blue Ridge Mountains. Widowed, all she has left are the memories of her beloved husband, with whom she regularly communes. Her son tries to convince her to move, and it becomes a clash of the wills as Annie tries to decide to stay in her past or change her future. Made for television.
1987 (PG) 118m/C Jessica Tandy, Hume Cronyn, John Denver, Gary Grubbs, Harriet Hall; *D:* Judd Taylor. **VHS $14.98** REP 🎬🎬🎬

Foxfire Light A young woman vacationing in the Ozarks is drawn into a romance with a cowboy. But her mother's social ambitions and her own indecesion may tear them apart.
1984 (PG) 102m/C Tippi Hedren, Lara Parker, Leslie Nielsen, Barry Van Dyke; *D:* Allen Baron. **VHS, Beta $79.95** PSM 🎬

Foxstyle A wealthy nightclub owner struggles with his country roots and his city sophistication.
1973 84m/C Juanita Moore, Richard Lawson, John Taylor, Jovita Bush; *D:* Clyde Houston. **VHS, Beta** MOV 🎬½

Foxtrap An L.A. courier is hired to find a runaway girl and, upon finding her in Europe, discovers he's been led into a trap. A low budget Italian co-production.
1985 89m/C *IT* Fred Williamson, Christopher Connelly, Arlene Golonka; *D:* Fred Williamson. **VHS, Beta $69.95** VES 🎬

Foxtrot A wealthy count isolates himself, his wife, and their two servants, on an island but cannot escape his past or the horrors of WWII. Even the good cast can't save the pretentious script and inadequate production. *AKA:* The Other Side of Paradise.
1976 (R) 91m/C *SI MX* Peter O'Toole, Charlotte Rampling, Max von Sydow, Jorge Luke; *D:* Arturo Ripstein. **VHS, Beta $59.98** NLC 🎬🎬

Foxy Brown A bitter woman poses as a prostitute to avenge the mob-backed deaths of her drug dealer brother and undercover cop boyfriend. Extremely violent black exploitation flick.
1974 (R) 92m/C Pam Grier, Terry Carter, Antonio Fargas, Kathryn Loder; *D:* Jack Hill. **VHS, Beta $9.98** ORI, FCT 🎬

F.P. 1 An artifical island (Floating Platform 1) in the Atlantic is threatened by treason. This slow-moving 1930s technothriller is the English-language version of the German "F.P. 1 Antwortet Nicht" ("F.P. 1 Doesn't Answer"). Both were directed at the same time by Hartl, using different casts.
1933 74m/B Leslie Fenton, Conrad Veidt, Jill Esmond. **VHS $19.95** NOS 🎬🎬

F.P. 1 Doesn't Answer A mid-Atlantic refueling station (Floating Platform 1) is threatened by treason and a pilot sets out to put things right. Features pre-Hollywood vintage Lorre; Albers was Germany's number one box office draw at the time. In German. *AKA:* F.P. 1 Antwortet Nicht.
1933 74m/B *GE* Hans Albers, Sybille Schmitz, Paul Hartmann, Peter Lorre, Hermann Speelmanns; *D:* Karl Hartl. **VHS $16.95** SNC, LSV 🎬🎬

Frame Up A small town sheriff is trying to investigate a murder tied to a fraternity's initiation. However, he runs into opposition from the most powerful man in town.
1991 (R) 90m/C Wings Hauser, Bobby DiCicco, Frances Fisher, Dick Sargent, Robert Picardo; *D:* Paul Leder. **VHS $9.98** REP 🎬🎬

Framed A nightclub owner is framed for murder, which understandably irks him. He's determined to get paroled and then seek revenge on the crooked cops responsible for his incarceration. This action melodrama features the writer, director and star of "Walking Tall."
1975 (R) 106m/C Joe Don Baker, Gabriel Dell, Brock Peters, Conny Van Dyke, John Marley; *D:* Phil Karlson. **VHS, Beta $24.95** PAR 🎬🎬

Framed An art forger gets tripped up by a beautiful con artist. However, when they meet again he is willingly drawn into her latest swindle.
1990 87m/C Jeff Goldblum, Kristin Scott Thomas, Todd Graff. **VHS $89.99** HBO 🎬🎬

Fran A young woman is torn between her desperate need for a male companion and the care of her children. Well made, albeit depressing, Australian production.
1985 92m/C *AU* Noni Hazlehurst, Annie Byron, Alan Fletcher; *D:* Glenda Hambly. **VHS, Beta** NO 🎬

France/Tour/Detour/Deux/ Enfants A twelve-part television series made for French television in which Godard and Mieville chronicle, in their characteristically reflexive fashion, the lives of two French schoolchildren and how their everyday growth is informed by television and the media. In French with English subtitles.
1978 26m/C *FR D:* Jean-Luc Godard, Anne-Marie Mieville. **VHS, Beta** EAI 🎬🎬

Frances The tragic story of Frances Farmer, the beautiful and talented screen actress of the 30's and early 40's, who was driven to a mental breakdown by bad luck, drug and alcohol abuse, a neurotic, domineering mother, despicable mental health care, and her own stubbornness. After being in and out of mental hospitals, she is finally reduced to a shadow by a lobotomy. Not nearly as bleak as it sounds, this film works because Lange understands this character from the inside out, and never lets her become melodramatic or weak.
1982 134m/C Jessica Lange, Kim Stanley, Sam Shepard; *D:* Graeme Clifford; *W:* Christopher DeVore, Nicholas Kazan, Eric Bergren; *M:* John Barry. **VHS, Beta $14.98** REP 🎬🎬🎬

Francesco Set in 13th-century Italy and depicting the life of St. Francis of Assisi. Follows the pleasure-loving son of a wealthy merchant through his religious awakening, and the founding of the Franciscan order of monks. Rourke, in a definite change-of-pace role, is actually believable, while Bonham Carter offers fine support as a devoted disciple.
1993 (R) 119m/C Mickey Rourke, Helena Bonham Carter; *D:* Liliana Cavani. **VHS $89.95** HMD 🎬🎬

The Franchise Affair A teenage girl in need of an alibi accuses two reclusive women of kidnapping and abusing her. It's up to a lawyer to sort out the truth. Based on the novel by Josephine Tey.
1952 149m/C *GB* Michael Denison, Dulcie Gray, Anthony Nicholls, Marjorie Fielding, Athene Seyler, Ann Stephens, Patrick Troughton; *D:* Lawrence Huntington. **VHS $49.95** FCT 🎬🎬

The Franchise Affair A scandal is about to overtake the sleepy village of Milford in 1947. An elderly lady and her daughter, the owners of a forbidding country house, are accused by of kidnapping and beating a teenaged girl until she agreed to work as their servant. A British TV production based on the novel by Josephine Tey and previously filmed for the big screen in 1952.
19?? 155m/C *GB* Patrick Malahide, Rosalie Crutchley, Joanna McCallum. **VHS $26.98** BFS 🎬🎬½

Francis Gary Powers: The True Story of the U-2 Spy A television dramatization of the true experiences of Gary Powers, a CIA spy pilot whose plane was shot down over the Soviet Union in 1960. His capture, trial, and conviction are all portrayed in detail, taken from Power's own reminiscences.
1976 120m/C Lee Majors, Noah Beery Jr., Nehemiah Persoff, Lew Ayres, Brooke Bundy; *D:* Delbert Mann. **VHS, Beta** WOV 🎬🎬½

Francis Goes to the Races The second in the talking-mule series finds O'Connor and Francis taking up residence on Kellaway's failing horse ranch. When mobsters seize control of the property to pay off a debt, Francis decides to check with the horses at the Santa Anita race track and find a sure winner to bet on.
1951 88m/B Donald O'Connor, Piper Laurie, Cecil Kellaway, Jesse White, Barry Kelley, Hayden Rorke, Vaughn Taylor, Larry Keating; *D:* Arthur Lubin; *W:* Oscar Brodney; *M:* Frank Skinner; *V:* Chill Wills. **VHS** MCA 🎬🎬½

Francis in the Navy The precocious talking mule, Francis, is drafted, and his buddy, played by O'Connor, comes to the rescue. The loquacious beast proves he has the superior grey matter however, and ends up doing all the thinking. Look for Clint Eastwood in his second minor role.
1955 80m/B Donald O'Connor, Martha Hyer, Jim Backus, Paul Burke, David Janssen, Clint Eastwood, Martin Milner; *D:* Arthur Lubin. **VHS $9.95** MCA 🎬🎬

Francis Joins the WACs The fifth entry in the series finds O'Connor working as a bank clerk when he is mistakenly drafted back into the military—and sent to a WAC base. Francis tries to keep him out of trouble with the ladies. Wills, the voice of Francis, also turns up as a general.
1954 94m/B Donald O'Connor, Julie Adams, Chill Wills, Mamie Van Doren, Lynn Bari, ZaSu Pitts, Joan Shawlee, Mara Corday, Allison Hayes; *D:* Arthur Lubin; *V:* Chill Wills. VHS MCA 🐾🐾½

Francis the Talking Mule The first of the silly but funny series about, what else, a talking mule. Peter Stirling (O'Connor) is the dim-bulb G.I. who hooks up with Francis while fighting in Burma. Francis helps Peter become a war hero but of course everyone thinks he's crazy when Peter insists the mule can talk. The joke is that Francis is smarter than any of the humans. O'Connor starred in six of the films, with Mickey Rooney taking over the final adventure. Director Lubin went on to create the television series "Mr. Ed," about a talking horse. *AKA:* Francis.
1949 91m/B Donald O'Connor, Patricia Medina, ZaSu Pitts, Ray Collins, John McIntire, Eduard Franz, Howland Chamberlin, Frank Faylen, Tony Curtis; *D:* Arthur Lubin; *M:* Frank Skinner; *V:* Chill Wills. VHS $14.98 MCA 🐾🐾🐾

Frankenhooker Jeffrey Franken is a nice guy; he didn't mean to mow his fiancee down in the front lawn. But sometimes bad things just happen to good people. Luckily Jeff thought to save her head and decides to pair it up with the body of some sexy streetwalkers. Voila! You have Frankenhooker: the girlfriend with more than a heart. The posters say it best, "A Terrifying Tale of Sluts and Bolts." Also available in an "R" rated version.
1990 (R) 90m/C James Lorinz, Patty Mullen, Charlotte J. Helmkamp, Louise Lasser; *D:* Frank Henenlotter. VHS SGE, FCT 🐾½

Frankenstein The definitive expressionistic Gothic horror classic that set the mold. Adapted from the Mary Shelley novel about Dr. Henry Frankenstein, the scientist who creates a terrifying, yet strangely sympathetic monster. Great performance by Karloff as the creation, which made him a monster star. Several powerful scenes, excised from the original version, have been restored. Side two of the laser disc version contains the original theatrical trailer, plus a collection of photos and scenes replayed for study purposes.
1931 71m/B Boris Karloff, Colin Clive, Mae Clarke, John Boles, Dwight Frye, Edward Van Sloan, Frederick Kerr, Lionel Belman; *D:* James Whale; *W:* Francis Edwards Faragoh, Garrett Fort, John Balderston, Robert Florey; *M:* David Brockman. VHS, Beta $14.95 MCA, TLF, HMV 🐾🐾🐾🐾

Frankenstein A brilliant scientist plays God, unleashing a living monster from the remains of the dead. A TV movie version of the legendary horror story. Good atmosphere provided by producer Dan "Dark Shadows" Curtis.
1973 130m/C Robert Foxworth, Bo Svenson, Willie Aames, Susan Strasberg; *D:* Glenn Jordan. VHS, Beta MPI 🐾🐾½

Frankenstein A remake of the horror classic, closely following the original story, wherein the creature speaks (and waxes philosophical), the doctor sees him as his dark subconscious, and the two die in an arctic confrontation.
1982 81m/C Robert Powell, Carrie Fisher, David Warner, John Gielgud; *D:* James Ormerod. VHS, Beta $59.98 LIV 🐾🐾½

Frankenstein Yet another remake of Mary Shelley's 1818 novel. Bergin stars as Dr. Victor Frankenstein, fanatically believing in the power of science to solve all mankind's ills. This leads him to prove his theories on the "secret of life" with his creation of the monster (Quaid), which Frankenstein finds he cannot ultimately control. Slow-moving story but while the monster isn't really terrifying, he's vengeful and intelligent enough to be a good enemy. Made for cable television.
1993 117m/C Patrick Bergin, Randy Quaid, John Mills, Lambert Wilson, Fiona Gilles, Jacinta Mulcahy, Timothy Stark; *D:* David Wickes; *W:* David Wickes. VHS $92.98 TTC, BTV 🐾🐾½

Frankenstein: A Cinematic Scrapbook A behind the scenes look at the world's most infamous monster, featuring interviews with Boris Karloff, Bela Lugosi and Lon Chaney, Jr. Also included are original movie trailers. In color and B&W.
1991 60m/C *D:* Ted Newsom; *W:* Ted Newsom. VHS, Beta $9.95 RHI, FCT 🐾🐾½

Frankenstein and the Monster from Hell A young doctor is discovered conducting experiments with human bodies and thrown into a mental asylum run by none other than Dr. Frankenstein himself. They continue their gruesome work together, creating a monster who develops a taste for human flesh. This really lame film was the last of the Hammer Frankenstein series.
1974 (R) 93m/C Peter Cushing, Shane Briant, Madeleine Smith, David Prowse, John Stratton; *D:* Terence Fisher. VHS PAR 🐾🐾

Frankenstein '80 Guy named Frankenstein pieces together a monster who goes on a killing spree. Bottom of the barrel Italian production with funky music and lots of gore.
1979 88m/C IT GE John Richardson, Gordon Mitchell, Leila Parker, Dada Galloti, Marisa Travers; *D:* Mario Mancini. VHS, Beta $59.95 NO Woof!

Frankenstein General Hospital A completely laughless horror spoof wherein the twelfth grandson of the infamous scientist duplicates his experiments in the basement of a modern hospital. A must see for Frankenstein fans; considered by some the worst Frankenstein movie ever made.
1988 90m/C Mark Blankfield, Kathy Shower, Leslie Jordan, Irwin Keyes; *D:* Deborah Roberts. VHS, Beta NO Woof!

Frankenstein Island Four balloonists get pulled down in a storm and end up on a mysterious island. They are greeted by one Sheila Frankenstein and encounter monsters, amazons, and other obstacles. Completely inept; Carradine "appears" in a visionary sequence wearing his pajamas.
1981 (PG) 97m/C Cameron Mitchell, Andrew Duggan, John Carradine; *D:* Jerry Warren. VHS, Beta NO Woof!

Frankenstein Meets the Space Monster A classic grade-Z epic about a space robot gone berserk among Puerto Rican disco dancers. *AKA:* Mars Invades Puerto Rico; Frankenstein Meets the Spacemen.
1965 80m/B James Karen, Nancy Marshall, Marilyn Hanold; *D:* Robert Gaffney. VHS, Beta $39.95 PSM Woof!

Frankenstein Meets the Wolfman The two famous Universal monsters meet and battle it out in this typical grade-B entry, the fifth from the series. The Werewolf wants Dr. Frankenstein to cure him, but only his monster (played by Lugosi) remains.

1942 73m/C Lon Chaney Jr., Bela Lugosi, Patric Knowles, Lionel Atwill, Maria Ouspenskaya; *D:* Roy William Neill. VHS, Beta $14.98 MCA, MLB 🐾🐾🐾

Frankenstein Unbound Corman returns after nearly 20 years with a better than ever B movie. Hurt plays a nuclear physicist time traveler who goes back to the 1800s and runs into Lord Byron, Percy and Mary Shelley and their neighbor Dr. Frankenstein and his monster. Great acting, fun special effects, intelligent and subtle message, with a little sex to keep things going. *AKA:* Roger Corman's Frankenstein Unbound.
1990 (R) 86m/C John Hurt, Raul Julia, Bridget Fonda, Jason Patric, Michael Hutchence, Catherine Rabett, Nick Brimble, Catherine Corman, Mickey Knox; *D:* Roger Corman; *W:* Roger Corman, F.X. Feeney; *M:* Carl Davis; *V:* Terri Treas. VHS, Beta $14.98 FOX 🐾🐾🐾

Frankenstein's Daughter Demented descendant of Dr. Frankenstein sets a den of gruesome monsters loose, including the corpse of a teenaged girl he revitalizes, as he continues the mad experiments of his forefathers. *AKA:* She Monster of the Night.
1958 85m/B John Ashley, Sandra Knight; *D:* Richard Cunha. VHS, Beta $9.95 NOS, MRV, RHI 🐾

Frankenstein's Great Aunt Tillie An excruciatingly bad send up of the Frankenstein saga with the good doctor about to be evicted from his estate because of back taxes. Gabor appears for a few seconds in a flashback.
1983 99m/C Donald Pleasence, Yvonne Furneaux, Aldo Ray, June Wilkinson, Zsa Zsa Gabor; *D:* Myron G. Gold; *W:* Myron G. Gold. VHS, Beta $59.95 VCD Woof!

Frankenweenie "Frankenweenie" is the tale of a lovable spunky dog named Sparky and his owner, Victor Frankenstein. When Sparky is hit by a car, Victor brings him back to life through the use of electric shock. This affectionate parody of "Frankenstein" launched renowned director Burton's career.
1984 (PG) 27m/B Shelley Duvall, Daniel Stern, Barret Oliver, Paul Bartel; *D:* Tim Burton; *W:* Tim Burton. VHS, Beta $14.99 BVV Woof!

Frankie and Johnny Based on the song of the same name, famed torch singer Morgan portrays a singer in a bordello who shoots her unfaithful lover. Release was delayed two years by the Hays Office's intervention in how a house of prostitution could be portrayed on screen. Too bad they reached an agreement. Not even Morgan's rendition of the title song redeems this.
1936 68m/B Helen Morgan, Chester Morris; *D:* Chester Erskine. VHS, Beta $24.98 CCB 🐾

Frankie and Johnny Elvis is a riverboat gambler/singer with lousy luck until Kovack changes the odds. This upsets his girlfriend Douglas who shoots him (but not fatally). Elvis wears period costumes, but this is otherwise similar to his contemporary films. 🎵When the Saints Go Marching In; Look Out Broadway; Shout It Out; Frankie and Johnny; Chesay; Come Along; Petunia; The Gardner's Daughter; Beginner's Luck; What Every Woman Lives For; Everybody Come Aboard; Hard Luck; Please Don't Stop Loving Me.
1965 88m/C Elvis Presley, Donna Douglas, Harry Morgan, Audrey Christie, Anthony Eisley, Sue Ane Langdon, Robert Strauss, Nancy Kovack; *D:* Fred de Cordova. VHS, Beta $14.95 MGM 🐾🐾½

Frankie and Johnny Ex-con gets a job as a short-order cook and falls for a world-weary waitress. She doesn't believe in romance, but finally gives into his pleas for a chance and finds out he may not be such a

bad guy after all. Nothing can make Pfeiffer dowdy enough for this role, but she and Pacino are charming together. In a change of pace role, Nelligan has fun as a fellow waitress who loves men. Based on the play "Frankie and Johnny in the Clair de Lune" by McNally who also wrote the screenplay.
1991 (R) 117m/C Al Pacino, Michelle Pfeiffer, Hector Elizondo, Nathan Lane, Kate Nelligan, Jane Morris, Greg Lewis, Al Fann, K. Callan, Phil Leeds, Tracy Reiner, Dey Young; *D:* Garry Marshall; *W:* Terrance McNally; *M:* Marvin Hamlisch. VHS **$14.95** *PAR, CCB* 🎬🎬🎬

Frantic From Louis Malle comes one of the first French New Wave film noir dramas. A man kills his boss with the connivance of the employer's wife, his lover, and makes it look like suicide. Meanwhile, teenagers have used his car and gun in the murder of a tourist couple and he is indicted for that crime. Their perfectly planned murder begins to unravel into a panic-stricken nightmare. A suspenseful and captivating drama. Director Malle's first feature film. Musical score by jazz legend Miles Davis. *AKA:* Elevator to the Gallows; Ascenseur Pour L'Echafaud.
1958 92m/B *FR* Maurice Ronet, Jeanne Moreau, Georges Poujouly; *D:* Louis Malle; *M:* Miles Davis. VHS, Beta, 8mm **$16.95** *SNC, NOS, VYY* 🎬🎬🎬

Frantic While in Paris, an American surgeon's wife is kidnapped when she inadvertantly picks up the wrong suitcase. Her kidnappers want their hidden tresure returned, which forces the husband into the criminal underground and into unexpected heroism when he seeks to rescue her. Contrived ending weakens on the whole, but Polanski is still master of the dark film thriller.
1988 (R) 120m/C Harrison Ford, Betty Buckley, John Mahoney, Emmanuelle Seigner, Jimmie Ray Weeks, Yorgo Voyagis, David Huddleston, Gerard Klein; *D:* Roman Polanski; *W:* Gerard Brach, Roman Polanski; *M:* Ennio Morricone. VHS, Beta **$14.95** *WAR, FCT* 🎬🎬🎬

Franz A French mercenary and an insecure woman struggle with a doomed love affair. In French with English subtitles.
1972 90m/C *FR* Jacques Brel; *D:* Jacques Brel. VHS, Beta **$19.95** *BAR, ING* 🎬

Frasier the Sensuous Lion A zoology professor is able to converse with Frasier, a lion known for his sexual stamina and whose potency is coveted by a billionaire (shadow of monkey glands rejuvenation therapy). A fairly typical, if slightly risque, talking critter film. *AKA:* Frasier the Lovable Lion.
1973 (PG) 97m/C Michael Callan, Katherine Justice, Frank De Kova, Malachi Throne, Victor Jory, Peter Lorre Jr., Marc Lawrence; *D:* Pat Shields. VHS, Beta **$9.99** *PSM* 🎬🎬

Fraternity Vacation Two college fraternity men show a nerd the greatest time of his life while he's on vacation in Palm Springs.
1985 (R) 95m/C Stephen Geoffreys, Sheree J. Wilson, Cameron Dye, Leigh McCloskey, Tim Robbins, Matt McCoy, Amanda Bearse, John Vernon, Nita Talbot, Barbara Crampton, Kathleen Kinmont, Max Wright, Julie Payne, Franklin Ajaye, Charles Rocket, Britt Ekland; *D:* James Frawley; *M:* Brad Fiedel. VHS, Beta **$9.95** *NWV, STE* 🎬

Frauds Collins is an immoral insurance investigator who takes his victims for everything he can. Then he meets a couple who are out to beat him at his own game.
1993 (R) 94m/C Phil Collins, Hugo Weaving, Josephine Byrnes. VHS **$49.98** *LIV* 🎬🎬½

Freaked Bizarre little black comedy throws everything at the screen, hoping some of the gross-out humor will prove amusing (and some does). Greedy TV star Ricky Coogin (Winter) agrees to be the spokesman for E.E.S. Corporation, which markets a toxic green slime fertilizer to the third world. He's sent to South America to promote the product and is captured by the mad scientist proprietor (Quaid) of a mysterious sideshow, who douses him with the fertilizer. Before you know it he's an oozing half-man, half-beast, perfect to join other freaks as the latest attraction. Lots of yucky makeup. Reeves has an uncredited cameo as the Dog Boy.
1993 (PG-13) 80m/C Alex Winter, Randy Quaid, Megan Ward, Michael Stoyanov, Brooke Shields, William Sadler, Derek McGrath, Mr. T, Alex Zuckerman, Karyn Malchus; *Cameos:* Keanu Reeves; *D:* Alex Winter, Tom Stern; *W:* Alex Winter, Tim Burns, Tom Stern; *M:* Kevin Kiner; *V:* Bob(cat) Goldthwait. VHS *FXV* 🎬🎬

The Freakmaker Mad professor attempts to breed plants with humans in his lab and has the usual bizarre results. Experiments that fail go to Dunn, a dwarf who runs a freak show. Shamelessly includes real freaks as if plot was not strange enough. *AKA:* Mutations; The Mutation.
1973 (R) 90m/C *GB* Donald Pleasence, Tom Baker, Brad Harris, Julie Ege, Michael Dunn, Jill Haworth; *D:* Jack Cardiff. VHS, Beta **$19.98** *VDC* 🎬🎬

Freaks The infamous, controversial, cult-horror classic about a band of circus freaks that exact revenge upon a beautiful aerialist and her strongman lover after enduring humiliation and exploitation. Based on Ted Robbins story "Spurs." It was meant to out-horror "Frankenstein" but was so successful that it was repeatedly banned. Browning's film may be a shocker but it is never intended to be exploitative since the "Freaks" are the only compassionate, loyal, and loving people around. *AKA:* Nature's Mistakes; Forbidden Love; The Monster Show.
1932 66m/B Wallace Ford, Olga Baclanova, Leila Hyams, Roscoe Ates, Harry Earles; *D:* Tod Browning. VHS, Beta **$19.98** *MGM* 🎬🎬🎬½

Freaky Friday A housewife and her teenage daughter inadvertently switch bodies and each then tries to carry on the other's normal routine. Mary Rodgers' popular book is brought to the screen with great charm in this above average Disney film.
1976 (G) 95m/C Barbara Harris, Jodie Foster, Patsy Kelly, Dick Van Patten, Ruth Buzzi; *D:* Gary Nelson. VHS, Beta **$19.99** *DIS* 🎬🎬½

Freddie as F.R.O.7 Britain's most ambitious animated film features a French frog ("frog" incidentally being the derisive British term for the French) hired to recover stolen British national treasures. The frog is, of course, a former prince suffering under a curse from his evil murderous aunt. His new amphibious form, however, doesn't hinder him from jumping all over Europe in his quest for justice. Beautiful animation and voices, but assumes a rather high awareness of French/English relations for the children at which the tale is aimed.
1992 (PG) 90m/C *GB D:* Jon Acevski; *W:* Jon Acevski; *M:* David Dundas; *V:* Ben Kingsley, Phyllis Logan, John Sessions, Billie Whitelaw, Brian Blessed, Jonathan Pryce, Jenny Agutter. VHS *NYR* 🎬

Freddy's Dead: The Final Nightmare Freddy's daughter journeys to Springwood, Ohio to put a stop to her father's evil ways. Will she be able to destroy this maniac, or is a new reign of terror just

beginning? The sixth, and supposedly last, film in the "Nightmare" series. *AKA:* Nightmare on Elm Street 6: Freddy's Dead.
1991 (R) 96m/C Robert Englund, Lisa Zane, Shon Greenblatt, Leslie Deane, Ricky Dean Logan, Breckin Majer, Yaphet Kotto, Elinor Donahue, Roseanne (Barr) Arnold, Johnny Depp, Alice Cooper; *D:* Rachel Talalay. VHS **$19.95** *COL, NLC* 🎬🎬

Free Amerika Broadcasting A drama about an alternate reality in which Richard Nixon was assassinated, leaving Spiro Agnew president. As a result, the country turns to violent revolution.
1989 80m/C Brian Kincaid; *D:* Dean Wilson. VHS *NO* 🎬🎬

Free and Easy Keaton plays the incompetent manager of a beauty contest winner (Page) from Gopher City, Kansas. Page and her overbearing mother, accompanied by Keaton, go to Hollywood to make the girl a star. They gate-crash the MGM studio where all cause havoc and it turns out Keaton is the one who lands in front of the cameras (Page has to settle for romancing Montgomery). Provides a behind-the-scenes look at the MGM studio, with a number of MGM stars making cameo appearances. *AKA:* Easy Go.
1930 92m/B Buster Keaton, Anita Page, Robert Montgomery, Trixie Friganza, Fred Niblo; *Cameos:* Cecil B. DeMille, Jackie Coogan, Lionel Barrymore, William Haines; *D:* Edward Sedgwick. VHS **$19.98** *MGM* 🎬🎬½

Free Grass A gang of thoughtless hippie drug smugglers and abusers escape from the police, drink acid-spiked wine, shoot each other, and have love-ins. *AKA:* Scream Free!.
1969 82m/C Russ Tamblyn, Richard Beymer, Casey Kasem, Lana Wood, Warren Finnerty. VHS, Beta *NO* 🎬

Free Ride A kooky kid steals a sportscar to impress a girl, and gets involved with local hoods. They chase each other around.
1986 (R) 92m/C Gary Hershberger, Reed Rudy, Dawn Schneider, Peter DeLuise, Brian MacGregor. VHS, Beta **$19.95** *LIV* 🎬

A Free Soul Tippling litigator Barrymore helps low-life mobster Gable beat a murder rap, only to discover the hood has stolen his daughter's heart. Bargaining with his ditzy daughter, he vows to eschew the bottle if she'll stay away from good-for-nothing Gable. Directed by Brown, best known for his work with Garbo, and based on the memoirs of Adela Rogers St. John. The final courtroom scene—a cloak-and-gavel classic—cinched Barrymore's Oscar. Remade with Liz Taylor as "The Girl Who Had Everything" (although, ironically, the earlier version is the racier of the two).
1931 94m/B Norma Shearer, Leslie Howard, Lionel Barrymore, Clark Gable, James Gleason, Lucy Beaumont; *D:* Clarence Brown. Academy Awards '31: Best Actor (Barrymore); Nominations: Best Actress (Shearer), Best Director (Brown). VHS **$19.98** *MGM, FCT, BTV* 🎬🎬½

Free to Love Screen idol Bow plays a young woman, fresh out of prison, who is taken in by a kindly, affluent patron. But, as the silent drama axiom would have it, there's no escaping the past, and she's forced to defend her former life when her guardian is murdered.
1925 61m/B Clara Bow, Donald Keith, Raymond McKee; *D:* Frank O'Connor. VHS, Beta **$16.95** *GPV, FCT* 🎬

Free, White, and 21 A black motel owner is accused of raping a white civil rights worker. Produced in a "pseudo-documentary" form which sometimes drags.

1962 104m/B Frederick O'Neal, Annalena Lund, George Edgely, John Hicks, Hugh Crenshaw, George Russell; **D:** Larry Buchanan. **VHS** *NO* ♂♂

Free Willy Sentimental story about a 12-year-old runaway (Richter) who befriends a whale. Should appeal to children for its heartwarming story and delightful sea acrobatics. An electronically operated stand-in whale was used for far-off shots; a domesticated performing whale named Keiko for the close-ups. Director Wincer was known to grumble about the temperamental Keiko during shooting. Suggested viewing for students of animal behavior. Proof that family films can make money, "Free Willy" placed tenth for total box office receipts in 1993. **1993** (PG) 112m/C Jason James Richter, Lori Petty, Jayne Atkinson, August Schellenberg, Michael Madsen; **D:** Simon Wincer; **W:** Keith A. Walker, Corey Blechman; **M:** Basil Poledouris. MTV Movie Awards ' Nominations: 4: Breakthrough Performance (Richter), Best Kiss (Jason James Richter/Willy); MTV Movie Awards '94: Best Song ("Will You Be There"). **VHS, 8mm** $24.95 *WAR, BTV* ♂♂½

Freebie & the Bean Two San Francisco cops nearly ruin the city in their pursuit of a numbers-running mobster. Top-flight car chases and low-level, bigoted humor combine. Watch for Valerie Harper's appearance as Arkin's wife. Followed by a flash-in-the-pan television series. **1974** (R) 113m/C Alan Arkin, James Caan, Loretta Swit, Valerie Harper, Jack Kruschen, Mike Kellin; **D:** Richard Rush. **VHS, Beta** $19.98 *WAR* ♂½

Freedom A young man finds the price of freedom to be very high when he tries to escape from Australian society in a silver Porsche. **1981** 102m/C Jon Blake, Candy Raymond, Jad Capelja, Reg Lye, John Clayton. **VHS, Beta** *NO* ♂½

Freedom is Paradise With his mother dead and his father missing, thirteen-year-old Sasha is growing up in a bleak reform school. Every time he runs away he is caught and severely beaten upon his return. When Sasha learns of his father's whereabouts he sets out on a 1,000 mile journey to the gulag-style prison where is father is being held. Bodrov's directorial debut. In Russian with English subtitles. **1989** 75m/C *RU* **D:** Sergei Bodrov. **VHS** $69.95 *FCT* ♂♂♂

Freedom Road A made for television drama about a Reconstruction Era ex-slave, portrayed by heavyweight champion Ali, who is elected to the U.S. Senate and subsequently killed while trying to obtain total freedom for his race. Based on a novel by Howard Fast. **1979** 186m/C Ron O'Neal, Edward Herrmann, John McLiam, Ernest Dixon, Alfre Woodard, Kris Kristofferson, Muhammad Ali; **D:** Jan Kadar. **VHS, Beta** $69.95 *WOV, FCT* ♂♂

Freejack Futuristic thriller set in the year 2009, where pollution, the hole in the ozone layer, and the financial gap between the social classes have grown to such horrific proportions that the rich must pillage the past to find young bodies to replace their own. Estevez is a young race car driver whose sudden death makes him an ideal candidate for this bizarre type of surgery. Once transported to the future, he becomes a "Freejack" who must run for his life. Good cast including Jagger and Hopkins brings this one up slightly. Adapted from the novel "Immortality Inc." by Robert Sheckley. **1992** (R) 110m/C Emilio Estevez, Mick Jagger, Rene Russo, Anthony Hopkins, Jonathan Banks, David Johansen, Amanda Plummer, Grand Bush, Frankie Faison, Esai Morales, John Shea; **D:** Geoff Murphy; **W:** Dan Gilroy, Ronald Shusett, Steven Pressfield; **M:** Trevor Jones. **VHS, Beta** $19.98 *WAR* ♂♂½

Freeway A nurse attempts to find the obsessive killer who shot her husband. The murderer phones a radio psychiatrist from his car, using Biblical quotes, while cruising for new victims. Okay thriller, based on the L.A. freeway shootings. **1988** (R) 91m/C Darlanne Fluegel, James Russo, Billy Drago, Richard Belzer, Michael Callan, Steve Franken, Kenneth Tobey, Clint Howard; **D:** Francis Delia; **W:** Larry Ketron, Darrell Fetty, Francis Delia; **M:** Joe Delia. **VHS, Beta** $14.98 *NWV, STE* ♂♂½

The Freeway Maniac A low budget thriller about an escaped convict who ends up on a movie set where he continues his former career: murder. Music by former "Doors" guitarist Robby Krieger. **1988** (R) 94m/C Loren Winters, James Courtney, Shepard Sanders, Donald Hotton; **D:** Paul Winters; **M:** Robby Krieger. **VHS, Beta** $79.95 *MED* ♂

Freeze-Die-Come to Life First feature film from Kanevski, who spent 8 years in a labor camp before glasnost. The story of two children who overcome the crushing poverty and bleakness of life in a remote mining community with friendship and humor. Beautifully filmed images, fine acting, touching but never overly sentimental story. The title comes from a children's game of tag. In Russian with English subtitles. *AKA:* Zamri Oumi Voskresni. **1990** 105m/B *RU* Pavel Nazarov, Dinara Drukarova; **D:** Vitaly Kanevski. **VHS** $89.95 *FXL, ART, BST* ♂♂♂

Freeze Frame Doherty is a high school TV reporter who's determined to capture a biotech conspiracy on video in this funny, fast-paced action flick. Nothing objectionable here. **1992** 78m/C Shannen Doherty, Charles Haid, Robyn Douglass, Seth Michaels; **D:** William Bindley; **W:** William Bindley. **VHS** $89.95 *COL, NLC* ♂♂½

French Can-Can Dramatically sparse but visually stunning depiction of the can-can's revival in Parisian nightclubs. Gabin plays the theater impressario who discovers laundress Arnoul and decides to turn her into the dancing star of his new revue at the Moulin Rouge. In French with English subtitles. *AKA:* Only the French Can!. **1955** 93m/C *FR* Jean Gabin, Francoise Arnoul, Maria Felix, Jean-Roger Caussimon, Edith Piaf, Patachou; **D:** Jean Renoir. **VHS, Beta** $39.95 *INT, APD, ING* ♂♂♂

The French Connection Two NY hard-nosed narcotics detectives stumble onto what turns out to be one of the biggest narcotics rings of all time. Cat-and-mouse thriller will keep you on the edge of your seat; contains one of the most exciting chase scenes ever filmed. Hackman's portrayal of Popeye Doyle is exact and the teamwork with Scheider special. Won multiple awards. Based on a true story from the book by Robin Moore. Followed in 1975 by "French Connection 2." **1971** (R) 102m/C Gene Hackman, Roy Scheider, Fernando Rey, Tony LoBianco, Eddie Egan, Sonny Grosso, Marcel Bozzuffi; **D:** William Friedkin. Academy Awards '71: Best Actor (Hackman), Best Adapted Screenplay, Best Director (Friedkin), Best Film Editing, Best Picture; Nominations: Best Cinematography, Best Sound, Best Supporting Actor (Scheider); British Academy Awards '72: Best Actor (Hackman); Directors Guild of America Awards '71: Best Director (Friedkin); Edgar Allan Poe Awards '71: Best Screenplay; Golden Globe Awards '72: Best Actor—Drama (Hackman), Best Director (Friedkin), Best Film—Drama; National Board of Review Awards '71: 10 Best Films of the Year, Best Actor (Hackman). **VHS, Beta** $19.98 *FOX* ♂♂♂½

French Connection 2 New York policeman "Popeye" Doyle goes to Marseilles to crack a heroin ring headed by his arch nemesis, Frog One, who he failed to stop in the United States. Dour, super-gritty sequel to the 1971 blockbuster, and featuring one of Hackman's most uncompromising performances. **1975** (R) 118m/C Gene Hackman, Fernando Rey, Bernard Fresson; **D:** John Frankenheimer; **W:** Robert Dillon. **VHS, Beta** $19.98 *FOX* ♂♂♂

The French Detective Two detectives, one an old-time tough guy and the other a young cynic, are after a ruthless politician and his pet hood. Grim but entertaining. **1975** 90m/C *FR* Lino Ventura, Patrick Dewaere, Victor Lanoux; **D:** Pierre Granier-Deferre. **VHS, Beta** $59.95 *COL* ♂♂♂

French Intrigue International agents track drug lords from the U.S. to France in a so-so spy thriller. **19??** 90m/C Jane Birkin, Curt Jurgens. **VHS, Beta** $19.99 *BFV* ♂♂

The French Lesson A romantic British farce from a screenplay by cartoonist Simmonds, dealing with an English girl who goes to school in Paris and finds love. *AKA:* The Frog Prince. **1986** (PG) 90m/C *GB* Alexandre Sterling, Jane Snowdon; **D:** Brian Gilbert; **W:** Posy S. Simmonds. **VHS, Beta** $69.95 *WAR* ♂♂½

The French Lieutenant's Woman Romantic love and tragedy in the form of two parallel stories, that of an 19th-century woman who keeps her mysterious past from the scientist who loves her, and the lead actor and actress in the film of the same story managing an illicit affair on the set. Extraordinary performances and beautifully shot. Based on the John Fowles novel. **1981** (R) 124m/C Meryl Streep, Jeremy Irons, Leo McKern, Lynsey Baxter; **D:** Karel Reisz; **W:** Harold Pinter; **M:** Carl Davis. Academy Awards '81 Nominations: Best Actress (Streep), Best Adapted Screenplay, Best Art Direction/Set Decoration, Best Costume Design, Best Film Editing; British Academy Awards '81: Best Actress (Streep); Golden Globe Awards '82: Best Actress—Drama (Streep). **VHS, Beta** $19.95 *MGM, FOX* ♂♂♂

The French Line A millionairess beauty travels incognito while trying to sort out which men are after her money, and which ones aren't. The 3-D presentation of Russell's physique in skimpy costumes earned this the condemnation of the Catholic Legion of Decency, which pumped the box office even higher. Lacks the charm of "Gentlemen Prefer Blonds," which it imitates. ♫Comment Allez-Vous; Well, I'll Be Switched; Any Gal From Texas; What Is This That I Feel?; With A Kiss; By Madame Fuelle; Wait Till You See Paris; Poor Andre; The French Line. **1954** 102m/C Jane Russell, Gilbert Roland, Craig Stevens, Kim Novak, Arthur Hunnicutt, Joi Lansing; **D:** Lloyd Bacon. **VHS, Beta** $19.98 *CCB, TTC* ♂♂

French Postcards Three American students study all aspects of French culture when they spend their junior year of college at the Institute of French Studies in Paris. By the same writers who penned "American Graffiti" a few years earlier.

1979 (PG) 95m/C Miles Chapin, Blanche Baker, Valerie Quennessen, Debra Winger, Mandy Patinkin, Marie-France Pisier; **D:** Willard Huyck; **W:** Gloria Katz, Willard Huyck. **VHS, Beta** $59.95 PAR ⅋⅋

French Quarter A dual story about a young girl in the modern-day French Quarter of New Orleans who is also the reincarnation of a turn-of-the-century prostitute. Everyone gets to play two roles but this film is more curiosity than anything else.
1978 (R) 101m/C Bruce Davison, Virginia Mayo, Lindsay Bloom, Alisha Fontaine, Lance LeGault, Anne Michelle; **D:** Dennis Kane. **VHS, Beta** $19.95 VCI ⅋⅋½

French Quarter Undercover Two undercover cops in New Orleans thwart a terrorist plot aimed at the World's Fair.
1985 (R) 84m/C Michael Parks, Bill Holiday; **D:** Joe Catalanotto. **VHS, Beta** $69.95 LIV ⅋

French Silk Homicide detective (Horsley) falls for a lingerie designer (Lucci) who's a murder suspect. Filmed on location in New Orleans. Made for TV production with additional footage. "R" rating is for nudity (not Lucci's).
1994 (PG-13) 90m/C Susan Lucci, Lee Horsley, Shari Belafonte-Harper, R. Lee Ermey, Sarah Marshall, Bobby Hosea, Jim Metzler, Joe Warfield, Paul Rosenberg. **VHS** APX ⅋⅋½

The French Touch Fernandel stars in this French farce about a shepherd who decides to open his own clip joint as a hairdresser and finds himself at home with the Parisiennes. Fair to middling comedy.
1954 84m/C FR Fernandel, Renee Devillers, Georges Chamarat; **D:** Jean Boyer. **VHS** $24.95 NOS ⅋⅋½

The French Way One of the legendary Baker's few films, in which she portrays a Parisian nightclub owner playing matchmaker for a young couple. In French with English subtitles.
1940 72m/B FR Josephine Baker, Micheline Presle, Georges Marchal; **D:** Jacques de Baroncelli. **VHS, Beta** $29.95 VDM, FCT ⅋⅋½

The French Woman Soft-core story of blackmail, murder, and sex involving French cabinet ministers mixing passion and politics. From the director of "Emmanuelle."
1979 (R) 97m/C Francoise Fabian, Klaus Kinski; **D:** Just Jaeckin; **M:** Serge Gainsbourg. **VHS, Beta** NO ⅋

Frenchman's Farm A young woman witnesses a killing at a deserted farmhouse. When she tells the police, they tell her that the murder happened forty years before. Average thriller that probably won't keep you on the edge of your seat.
1987 (R) 90m/C AU Tracey Tainsh, David Reyne, John Meillon, Norman Kaye, Tui Bow; **D:** Ron Way. **VHS, Beta** NO ⅋½

Frenzy A sculptor, pushed over the brink of sanity when he discovers that his wife is having an affair, turns to his art for solace...and seals his wife's corpse in a statue. Creepy. **AKA:** Latin Quarter.
1946 75m/B GB Derrick DeMarney, Frederick Valk, Joan Greenwood, Joan Seton, Valentine Dyall, Martin Miller; **D:** Vernon Sewell; **W:** Vernon Sewell. **VHS** $19.98 SNC ⅋⅋

Frenzy The only film in which Hitchcock was allowed to totally vent the violence and perverse sexuality of his distinctive vision, in a story about a strangler stalking London women in the late '60s. Finch plays the convicted killer-only he's innocent and must escape prison to find the real killer. McGowen is wonderful as the put-upon police inspector. A bit dated, but still ferociously hostile and cunningly executed.

1972 (R) 116m/C GB Jon Finch, Barry Foster, Barbara Leigh-Hunt, Anna Massey, Alec McCowen, Vivien Merchant, Billie Whitelaw, Jean Marsh; **D:** Alfred Hitchcock; **W:** Anthony Shaffer. **VHS, Beta** $19.95 MCA ⅋⅋⅋

Fresh Horses A wrong-side-of-the-tracks Depression-era romance. McCarthy is the engaged college boy who falls for backwoods girl Ringwald, who turns out to have a destructive secret.
1988 (PG-13) 92m/C Molly Ringwald, Andrew McCarthy, Patti D'Arbanville, Ben Stiller; **D:** David Anspaugh; **M:** David Foster. **VHS, Beta** $89.95 COL ⅋⅋

Fresh Kill A young guy from Chicago goes to Hollywood, and gets mixed up in drugs and murder. Made for video.
1987 90m/C Flint Keller, Patricia Parks; **D:** Joseph Merhi. **VHS, Beta** NO ⅋

The Freshman Country boy Lloyd goes to college and, after many comic tribulations, saves the day with the winning touchdown at the big game and wins the girl of his dreams. This was one of the comedian's most popular films.
1925 75m/B Harold Lloyd, Jobyna Ralston, Brooks Benedict, James Anderson, Hazel Keener; **D:** Fred Newmeyer, Sam Taylor; **W:** Fred Newmeyer. **VHS, Beta** TLF ⅋⅋⅋

The Freshman Brando, in an incredible parody of his Don Corleone character, makes this work. Broderick is a college student in need of fast cash, and innocent enough to believe that any work is honest. A good supporting cast and a twisty plot keep things interesting. Sometimes heavy handed with its sight gags, but Broderick and Brando push the movie to hilarious conclusion. Don't miss Burt Parks' musical extravaganza.
1990 (PG) 102m/C Marlon Brando, Matthew Broderick, Penelope Ann Miller, Maximilian Schell, Bruno Kirby, Frank Whaley, Jon Polito, Paul Benedict, Richard Gant, B.D. Wong, Bert Parks; **D:** Andrew Bergman; **W:** Andrew Bergman; **M:** David Newman. **VHS, Beta, 8mm** $19.95 COL, FCT ⅋⅋½

Frida The life of controversial Mexican painter Frido Kahlo is told via deathbed flashbacks using the artist's paintings to set the scenes. In Spanish with English subtitles.
1984 108m/C SP Ofelia Medina, Juan Jose Gurrola, Max Kerlow; **D:** Paul Leduc. **VHS, Beta** $29.95 CVC, IME, APD ⅋⅋

Friday Foster A beautiful, young photographer investigates an assassination attempt and uncovers a conspiracy against black politicians. Based on the Chicago Tribune comic strip.
1975 (R) 90m/C Pam Grier, Yaphet Kotto, Thalmus Rasulala, Carl Weathers, Godfrey Cambridge; **D:** Arthur Marks. **VHS, Beta** $59.98 ORI, FCT ⅋½

Friday the 13th Notable as among the first in a very long series of slasher flicks, with effects by Tom Savini. A New Jersey camp reopens after it's been closed for 20 years after a history of "accidental" deaths. And the horror begins again. Six would-be counselors arrive to get the place ready. Each is progressively murdered: knifed, speared, and axed. Followed by numerous, equally gory sequels.
1980 (R) 95m/C Betsy Palmer, Adrienne King, Harry Crosby, Laurie Bartram, Mark Nelsor, Kevin Bacon; **D:** Sean S. Cunningham. **VHS, Beta** $14.95 PAR ⅋⅋

Friday the 13th, Part 2 New group of teen camp counselors are gruesomely executed by the still undead Jason. Equally as graphic as the first installment; followed by several more gorefests.

1981 (R) 87m/C Amy Steel, John Furey, Adrienne King, Betsy Palmer; **D:** Steve Miner. **VHS, Beta** $14.95 PAR Woof!

Friday the 13th, Part 3 Yet another group of naive counselors at Camp Crystal Lake fall victim to the maniacal Jason. The 3-D effects actually helped lessen the gory effects, but this is still awful. Followed by more disgusting sequels.
1982 (R) 96m/C Dana Kimmell, Paul Krata, Richard Brooker; **D:** Steve Miner. **VHS, Beta** $14.95 PAR Woof!

Friday the 13th, Part 4: The Final Chapter Jason escapes from the morgue to once again slaughter and annihilate teenagers at a lakeside cottage. Preceded by three earlier "Friday the 13th" films, equally as graphic. The title's also a lie since there's several more sequels to look forward to.
1984 (R) 90m/C Erich Anderson, Judie Aronson, Kimberly Beck, Peter Barton, Tom Everett, Corey Feldman, Crispin Glover; **D:** Joseph Zito. **VHS, Beta** $14.95 PAR Woof!

Friday the 13th, Part 5: A New Beginning Jason rises from the dead to slice up the residents of a secluded halfway house. The sequels, and the sameness, never stop. See Part 6...
1985 (R) 92m/C John Shepherd, Melanie Kinnaman, Shavar Ross, Richard Young, Juliette Cummins, Corey Feldman; **D:** Danny Steinmann. **VHS, Beta** $14.95 PAR Woof!

Friday the 13th, Part 6: Jason Lives One of the few youths not butchered by Jason digs him up and discovers he's not (and never will be) dead. Carnage ensues...and the sequels continue.
1986 (R) 87m/C Thom Mathews, Jennifer Cooke, David Kagen; **D:** Tom McLoughlin. **VHS, Beta** $14.95 PAR Woof!

Friday the 13th, Part 7: The New Blood A young camper with telekinetic powers accidentally unchains Jason from his underwater lair with the now-familiar results. There's still another bloody sequel to go.
1988 (R) 90m/C Lar Park Lincoln, Kevin Blair, Susan Blu; **D:** John Carl Buechler; **W:** Daryl Haney. **VHS, Beta** $14.95 PAR Woof!

Friday the 13th, Part 8: Jason Takes Manhattan Yet another sequel, with the ski-masked walking slaughterhouse transported to New York. Most of the previous action in the movie takes place on a cruise ship. This one is less gruesome than others in the series. Followed by "Jason Goes to Hell: The Final Friday."
1989 (R) 96m/C Jensen Daggett, Scott Reeves, Peter Mark Richman, Barbara Bingham; **D:** Rob Hedden; **W:** Rob Hedden. **VHS, Beta** $14.95 PAR ⅋

Fridays of Eternity A romantic comedy about loyalty, fidelity, love, and lovers all with a tinge of the supernatural. In Spanish with English subtitles.
1981 89m/C AR Thelma Biral, Hector Alterio; **D:** Hector Olivera. **VHS** $24.98 ING ⅋⅋

Fried Green Tomatoes Two stories about four women, love, friendship, Southern charm, and eccentricity are untidily held together by wonderful performances. Unhappy, middle-aged Evelyn (Bates), meets the talkative 83-year-old Ninny Threadgoode (Tandy). Ninny reminisces about her Depression-era life in the town of Whistle Stop, Alabama and the two women, Idgie (Masterson) and Ruth (Parker), who ran the local cafe. Back-and-forth narrative as it tracks multiple storylines is occasionally confusing, though strong character development holds

interest. Surprising box office hit adapted by Fannie Flagg from her novel "Fried Green Tomatoes at the Whistle Stop Cafe."
1991 (PG-13) 130m/C Kathy Bates, Jessica Tandy, Mary Stuart Masterson, Mary-Louise Parker, Cicely Tyson, Chris O'Donnell, Stan Shaw, Gailard Sartain, Timothy Scott, Gary Basaraba, Lois Smith, Grace Zabriskie; **D:** Jon Avnet; **W:** Fannie Flagg, Carol Sobieski; **M:** Thomas Newman. Academy Awards '91 Nominations: Best Adapted Screenplay, Best Supporting Actress (Tandy); National Media Owl Awards '92: First Prize. **VHS, Beta $19.98** *MCA* ⅃⅃⅃

Frieda An RAF officer brings his German wife home after the war and she is naturally distrusted by his family and neighbors. An interesting look at post-war bigotry.
1947 97m/B *GB* David Farrar, Glynis Johns, Mai Zetterling, Flora Robson, Albert Lieven; **D:** Basil Dearden. **VHS $19.95** *NOS, VYY, VEC* ⅃⅃½

Friendly Fire Based on a true story of an American family in 1970 whose soldier son is killed by "friendly fire" in Vietnam, and their efforts to uncover the circumstances of the tragedy. Touching and powerful, with an excellent dramatic performance by Burnett. Made for television.
1979 146m/C Carol Burnett, Ned Beatty, Sam Waterston, Timothy Hutton; **D:** David Greene. **VHS, Beta $59.98** *FOX* ⅃⅃⅃

Friendly Persuasion Earnest, solidly acted tale about a peaceful Quaker family struggling to remain true to its ideals in spite of the Civil War which touches their farm life in southern Indiana. Cooper and McGuire are excellent as the parents with Perkins fine as the son worried he's using his religion to hide his cowardice. Based on a novel by Jessamyn West. **AKA:** Except For Me and Thee.
1956 140m/C Gary Cooper, Dorothy McGuire, Anthony Perkins, Marjorie Main, Charles Halton; **D:** William Wyler; **M:** Dimitri Tiomkin. Academy Awards '56 Nominations: Best Adapted Screenplay, Best Director (Wyler), Best Picture, Best Song ("Friendly Persuasion (Thee I Love)"), Best Sound, Best Supporting Actor (Perkins); Cannes Film Festival '57: Best Film. **VHS, Beta $59.98** *FOX* ⅃⅃⅃

Friends Ho-hum drama about an orphaned French girl and an unloved English boy who meet, become friends, and decide to run away together, setting up house in a deserted beach cottage. They even have a baby before they're discovered. Provides no insight into the teenagers dilemmas. Followed by "Paul and Michelle."
1971 (R) 101m/C *GB* Sean Bury, Anicee Alvina, Pascale Roberts, Sady Rebbot, Ronald Lewis; **D:** Lewis Gilbert; **M:** Elton John. **VHS $14.95** *PAR* ⅃

Friends Forever Conformity, sexuality, and friendship are explored in this coming-of-age drama. Kristian is a shy, conformist sixteen-year-old, starting off at a new school. He finds himself drawn to two different young men who equally dominate his class. Henrik's androgynous sexual charm is equaled by his independence while the moody Patrick is the leader of a band of troublemakers. Kristian gains in self-confidence by their friendship but is tested when he learns Patrick is gay.
1986 95m/C *DK* **D:** Stefan Christian Henszelman. **VHS $69.95** *FCT* ⅃⅃⅃

Friends, Lovers & Lunatics A weekend turns into a romantic nightmare/laugh-fest when a man visits his ex-girlfriend and her new "friend", and winds up in a new romance himself. **AKA:** Crazy Horse; She Drives Me Crazy.

1989 87m/C *CA* Daniel Stern, Deborah Foreman, Sheila McCarthy, Page Fletcher, Elias Koteas; **D:** Stephen Withrow. **VHS, Beta $29.95** *FRH, IME* ⅃½

A Friendship in Vienna The friendship of two young teenage girls, one Jewish, and the other the daughter of a Nazi collaborator, is tested as WWII looms over Europe and the Nazis begin their persecution of Austrian Jews. Adapted from the book "Devil in Vienna" by Doris Orgel. Made for cable television.
1988 100m/C Jenny Lewis, Ed Asner, Jane Alexander, Stephen Macht, Rosemary Forsyth, Ferdinand "Ferdy" Mayne, Kamie Harper; **D:** Arthur Seidelman; **W:** Richard Alfieri. **VHS** *DIS* ⅃⅃½

Fright A woman—convinced that she died in 1889 as part of a suicide pact with Prince Rudolph of Austria—seeks help from a psychiatrist who promptly falls in love with her (didn't Freud say it was supposed to be the other way around?). **AKA:** Spell of the Hypnotist.
1956 ?m/B Nancy Malone, Eric Fleming, Frank Marth, Humphrey Davis, Ned Glass, Norman Burton; **D:** W. Lee Wilder. **VHS $19.98** *SNC* ⅃

Fright A baby-sitter is menaced by a mental hospital escapee. He turns out to be the father of the boy she is watching. Tense but violent thriller. **AKA:** Night Legs.
1971 (PG) 84m/C *GB* Susan George, Honor Blackman, Ian Bannen, John Gregson, George Cole, Dennis Waterman; **D:** Peter Collinson. **VHS $9.98** *REP, MOV* ⅃⅃

Fright House Two stories of terror. "Fright House" features witches preparing an old mansion for a visit from the Devil. "Abandon" explains the prolonged youth of a teacher to her young student.
1989 (R) 110m/C Al Lewis, Duane Jones; **D:** Len Anthony. **VHS, Beta** *NO* ⅃

Fright Night It's Dracula-versus-the-teens time when Charley suspects that his new neighbor descends from Count Vlad's line. He calls in the host of "Fright Night," the local, late-night, horror-flick series, to help de-ghoul the neighborhood. But they have a problem when the vampire discovers their plans (and nobody belives them anyway). Sarandon is properly seductive as the bloodsucker. Followed by sequel.
1985 (R) 106m/C William Ragsdale, Chris Sarandon, Amanda Bearse, Roddy McDowall, Stephen Geoffreys, Jonathan Stark, Dorothy Fielding; **D:** Tom Holland; **W:** Tom Holland; **M:** Brad Fiedel. **VHS, Beta $19.95** *COL* ⅃⅃½

Fright Night 2 The sequel to the 1985 release "Fright Night," in which the harassed guy from the original film learns slowly that the vampire's sister and her entourage have come to roost around his college. Not quite as good as the original but the special effects are worth a look.
1988 (R) 108m/C Roddy McDowall, William Ragsdale, Traci Lin, Julie Carmen; **D:** Tommy Lee Wallace; **W:** Tommy Lee Wallace, Tim Metcalfe; **M:** Brad Fiedel. **VHS, Beta $14.95** *LIV* ⅃⅃

Frightmare A seemingly quiet British couple do indulge in one strange habit—they're cannibals. Released on video as "Frightmare 2" to avoid confusion with the 1981 film. **AKA:** Frightmare 2.
1974 (R) 86m/C *GB* Deborah Fairfax, Kim Butcher, Rupert Davies, Sheila Keith; **D:** Pete Walker. **VHS, Beta $59.98** *PSM* ⅃⅃½

Frightmare Great horror star dies, but he refuses to give up his need for adoration and revenge.

1981 (R) 84m/C Ferdinand "Ferdy" Mayne, Luca Bercovici, Nita Talbot, Peter Kastner; **D:** Norman Thaddeus Vane. **VHS, Beta $59.95** *VES* ⅃

Frightshow Four independent short horror films; "Nightfright," "Thing in the Basement," "Dr. Dobermind," and "Illegal Alien."
1984 60m/C **VHS $29.98** *MPI* ⅃

The Fringe Dwellers An Aborigine family leave their shantytown and move to the white, middle-class suburbs of Australia, encountering prejudice and other difficulties. Well acted and interesting but the ending's a letdown.
1986 (PG) 98m/C *AU* Kristina Nehm, Justine Saunders, Bob Maza, Kylie Belling, Denis Walker, Ernie Dingo; **D:** Bruce Beresford; **W:** Bruce Beresford, Rhoisin Beresford; **M:** George Dreyfus. **VHS, Beta** *NO* ⅃⅃½

The Frisco Kid An innocent orthodox rabbi (Wilder) from Poland is sent to the wilds of San Francisco during the 1850s gold rush to lead a new congregation. He lands in Philadelphia, joins a wagon train and is promptly robbed and abandoned. He eventually meets up with a not-too-bright robber (Ford) who finds himself unexpectedly befriending the man and undergoing numerous tribulations in order to get them both safely to their destination. This isn't a laugh riot and some scenes fall distinctly flat but Wilder is sweetness personified and lends the movie its charm. **AKA:** No Knife.
1979 (R) 119m/C Gene Wilder, Harrison Ford, Ramon Bieri, George DiCenzo, Penny Peyser, William Smith; **D:** Robert Aldrich. **VHS, Beta $19.98** *WAR* ⅃⅃

Fritz the Cat Ralph Bakshi's animated tale for adults about a cat's adventures as he gets into group sex, college radicalism, and other hazards of life in the '60s. Loosely based on the underground comics character by Robert Crumb. Originally X-rated.
1972 77m/C **D:** Ralph Bakshi. **VHS, Beta** *WAR, OM* ⅃⅃⅃

Frog A boy adds a frog to his reptile collection but gets the surprise of his life when he finds it's really an enchanted Prince! Followed by "Frogs!" Part of the "Wonderworks" series.
1989 55m/C Paul Williams, Scott Grimes, Shelley Duvall, Elliott Gould, David Grossman. **VHS, Beta $9.98** *ORI, IME* ⅃⅃⅃

Frogs An environmental photographer working on a small island in Florida interrupts the birthday celebration of a patriarch. He and the folks at the party soon realize that various amphibians animals in the surrounding area are going berserk and attacking humans. One of the first environmentally-motivated animal-vengeance films, and one of the best to come out of the '70s.
1972 (PG) 91m/C Ray Milland, Sam Elliott, Joan VanArk, Adam Roarke, Judy Pace, Lynn Borden, Mae Mercer, David Gilliam, George Skaff; **D:** George McCowan; **M:** Les Baxter. **VHS, Beta** *WAR, OM* ⅃⅃½

Frogs! Arlo is almost the most popular boy in school and is hoping to be crowned the king of his school's Spring Fling dance—until he and his friend Gus are turned into frogs by a witch. When Arlo and Gus discover their frog pond is being poisoned, they turn to the geeky Hannah for help. A sequel to "Frog." A viewers' guide is included. Part of the "Wonderworks" series.
199? 55m/C Shelley Duvall, Elliott Gould, Paul Williams, Scott Grimes, Judith Ivey. **VHS $29.95** *PME, HMV, BTV* ⅃⅃½

F

Frolics on Ice Pleasant comedy-musical about a family man saving to buy the barber shop he works at. Irene Dare is featured in several ice skating production numbers.
1940 65m/B Roscoe Karns, Lynn (Mary Hart) Roberts, Irene Dare, Edgar Kennedy. **VHS, Beta** $24.95 *VYY* ✲✲

From Beyond A gruesome, tongue-in-cheek adaptation of the ghoulish H.P. Lovecraft story. Scientists discover another dimension through experiments with the pineal gland. From the makers of "Re-Animator," and just as funny.
1986 (R) 90m/C Jeffrey Combs, Barbara Crampton, Ted Sorel, Ken Foree, Carolyn Purdy-Gordon, Bunny Summers, Bruce McGuire; **D:** Stuart Gordon; **W:** Dennis Paoli, Brian Yuzna; **M:** Richard Band. **VHS, Beta** $19.98 *LIV, VES* ✲✲✲

From Beyond the Grave This horror compendium revolves around a mysterious antique shop whose customers experience various supernatural phenomena, especially when they try to cheat the shop's equally mysterious owner. **AKA:** Creatures.
1973 (PG) 98m/C *GB* Peter Cushing, David Warner, Ian Bannen, Donald Pleasence, Margaret Leighton, Lesley-Anne Down, Diana Dors, Ian Ogilvy; **D:** Kevin Connor. **VHS, Beta** $59.95 *WAR* ✲✲

From Hell to Borneo A mercenary must defend his secluded island from pirates and gangsters.
1964 (PG) 90m/C George Montgomery, Torin Thatcher, Julie Gregg, Lisa Moreno; **D:** George Montgomery. **VHS, Beta** *NO* ✲½

From Hell to Victory Group of friends of different nationalities vow to meet each year in Paris on the same date but WWII interrupts their lives and friendships. Director Lenzi used the alias Hank Milestone. Good battle scenes but nothing special.
1979 (PG) 100m/C *SP FR* George Peppard, George Hamilton, Horst Buchholz, Jean-Pierre Cassel, Capucine, Sam Wanamaker, Anny Duperey, Ray Lovelock; **D:** Umberto Lenzi. **VHS, Beta** $9.95 *SIM, MED, HHE* ✲✲

From Here to Eternity Complex, hard-hitting look at the on and off-duty life of soldiers at the Army base in Honolulu in the days before the Pearl Harbor attack. There's sensitive Pvt. Pruitt (Clift), who's always in trouble best friend Maggio (Sinatra), and their good-guy top sergeant (Lancaster) who just happens to be having a torrid affair with the commander's wife (Kerr). Pruitt, meanwhile, is introduced to a club "hostess" (Reed) who is a lot more vulnerable than she's willing to admit. A movie filled with great performances. Still has the best waves-on-the-beach love scene in filmdom. Based on the novel by James Jones, which was toned down by the censors.
1953 118m/B Burt Lancaster, Montgomery Clift, Frank Sinatra, Deborah Kerr, Donna Reed, Ernest Borgnine, Philip Ober, Jack Warden, Mickey Shaughnessy, George Reeves, Claude Akins; **D:** Fred Zinneman; **W:** Daniel Taradash; **M:** George Duning. Academy Awards '53: Best Black and White Cinematography, Best Director (Zinneman), Best Film Editing, Best Picture, Best Screenplay, Best Sound, Best Supporting Actor (Sinatra), Best Supporting Actress (Reed); Nominations: Best Actor (Clift), Best Actor (Lancaster), Best Actress (Kerr), Best Costume Design (B & W); Golden Globe Awards '54: Best Director (Zinneman); Golden Globe Awards '54: Best Supporting Actor (Sinatra); National Board of Review Awards '53: 10 Best Films of the Year; New York Film Critics Awards '53: Best Actor (Lancaster), Best Director (Zinneman), Best Film. **VHS, Beta, 8mm** $19.95 *COL, BTV* ✲✲✲✲

From Here to Eternity From here to eternity...and back on the silver screen. Remake of the 1953 classic is based on James Jones' novel about life on a Hawaiian military base just before WWII. Decent actioner, but no Oscar-winner this time around. Made for television.
1979 (PG-13) 110m/C Natalie Wood, Kim Basinger, William Devane, Steve Railsback, Peter Boyle, Will Sampson, Andy Griffith, Roy Thinnes; **D:** Buzz Kulik. **VHS, Beta** $89.95 *VMK, FCT* ✲✲½

From Here to Maternity A made-for-television soap opera-based spoof about modern maternity. Three women want to be pregnant but their significant others aren't interested in paternity.
1985 40m/C Carrie Fisher, Arleen Sorkin, Lauren Hutton, Griffin Dunne, Paul Reiser. **VHS, Beta** $59.95 *LIV, VES* ✲✲½

From Hollywood to Deadwood A beautiful starlet is kidnapped and the private eye searching for her discovers blackmail and danger.
1989 (R) 90m/C Scott Paulin, Jim Haynie, Barbara Schock; **D:** Rex Pickett. **VHS, Beta** $19.98 *MED, FCT, IME* ✲✲

From Noon Till Three A change of pace role for Bronson as a two-bit gunfighter in a spoof of western legends. Bronson has a brief romance with Ireland who, believing him dead, fictionalizes their relationship in a series of books and builds the mediocre Dorsey into a western hero. When he turns up alive no one, including Ireland, believes that he is the real Dorsey and he's gradually driven crazy. Good script, weak direction but Bronson is likeable.
1976 (PG) 99m/C Charles Bronson, Jill Ireland, Douglas Fowley, Stan Haze, Damon Douglas; **D:** Frank D. Gilroy; **W:** Frank D. Gilroy; **M:** Elmer Bernstein. **VHS** $14.95 *MGM* ✲✲½

From Russia with Love Bond is back and on the loose in exotic Istanbul looking for a super-secret coding machine. He's involved with a beautiful Russian spy and has the SPECTRE organization after him, including villainess Rosa Klebb (she of the killer shoe). Lots of exciting escapes but not an over-reliance on the gadgetry of the later films. The second Bond feature, thought by many to be the best. The laserdisc edition includes interviews with director Terence Young and others on the creative staff. The musical score and special effects can be separated from the actors' dialogue. Also features publicity shots, American and British trailers, on-location photos, and movie posters.
1963 (PG) 125m/C *GB* Sean Connery, Daniela Bianchi, Pedro Armendariz Sr., Lotte Lenya, Robert Shaw, Eunice Gayson, Walter Gotell, Lois Maxwell, Bernard Lee, Desmond Llewelyn, Nadja Regin, Alizia Gur, Martine Beswick, Leila; **D:** Terence Young; **M:** John Barry. **VHS, Beta** $19.98 *MGM, VYG, CRC* ✲✲✲

From "Star Wars" to "Jedi": The Making of a Saga Using copious amounts of actual footage from the films, this movie follows the production of all three "Star Wars" sagas, concentrating on the special effects involved.
1983 65m/C David Prowse, Harrison Ford, Carrie Fisher, Billy Dee Williams, Alec Guinness; **D:** George Lucas. **VHS, Beta** $19.98 *FOX, FLI* ✲✲✲½

From the Dead of Night A spooky chiller about a near-death experience. Fashion designer Wagner narrowly escapes death but gets close enough to the other side that six of the dead feel cheated that she didn't join them. They decide to rectify the mistake

and Wagner is pursued by the shadowy figures. Based on the novel "Walkers" by Gary Bradner. Made for television.
1989 192m/C Lindsay Wagner, Bruce Boxleitner, Diahann Carroll, Robert Prosky, Robin Thomas, Merritt Butrick, Joanne Linville; **D:** Paul Wendkos. **VHS, Beta** $89.95 *AIP* ✲✲✲

From the Earth to the Moon A mad scientist invents a new energy source and builds a rocket which takes him, his daughter, and two other men for some adventures on the moon. Based on the novel by Jules Verne.
1958 100m/C George Sanders, Joseph Cotten, Debra Paget, Don Dubbins; **D:** Byron Haskin. **VHS, Beta** $15.95 *VCI* ✲✲

From the Hip A young lawyer (Nelson) gets the chance of a lifetime when his office assigns a murder case to him. The only problem is that he suspects his client is very guilty indeed and must discover the truth without breaking his code of ethics. Nelson's courtroom theatrics are a bit out of hand, as he flares his nostrils at every opportunity. The movie is encumbered by a weak script and plot as well as a mid-story switch from comedy to drama.
1986 (PG) 112m/C Judd Nelson, Elizabeth Perkins, John Hurt, Ray Walston; **D:** Bob (Benjamin) Clark; **W:** Bob (Benjamin) Clark, David Kelly. **VHS, Beta** $19.98 *LHV, WAR* ✲✲

From the Life of the Marionettes A repressed man in a crumbling marriage rapes and kills a young prostitute. Another look at the powers behind individual motivations from Bergman, who uses black and white and color to relate details of the incident.
1980 (R) 104m/C *SW* Robert Atzorn, Christine Buchegger, Martin Benrath, Rita Russek, Lola Muethel, Walter Schmidinger, Heinz Bennent; **D:** Ingmar Bergman; **W:** Ingmar Bergman. **VHS, Beta** $39.95 *LIV* ✲✲✲

From the Terrace Newman is a wealthy Pennsylvania boy who goes to New York and marries into even more money and social position when he weds Woodward. He gets a job with her family's investment company and neglects his wife for business. She turns to another man and when he goes home for a visit he also finds a new romance which leads to some emotional soul searching. The explicitness of O'Hara's very long novel was diluted by the censors and Newman's performance is a stilted disappointment. Loy, as Newman's alcoholic mother, earned the best reviews.
1960 144m/C Paul Newman, Joanne Woodward, Myrna Loy, Ina Balin, Felix Aylmer, Leon Ames, George Grizzard, Patrick O'Neal, Barbara Eden, Mae Marsh; **D:** Mark Robson; **W:** Ernest Lehman; **M:** Elmer Bernstein. **VHS, Beta** $19.98 *FOX* ✲✲½

The Front Woody is the bookmaker who becomes a "front" for blacklisted writers during the communist witch hunts of the 1950s in this satire comedy. The scriptwriter and several of the performers suffered blacklisting themselves during the Cold War. Based more or less on a true story.
1976 (PG) 95m/C Woody Allen, Zero Mostel, Herschel Bernardi, Michael Murphy, Danny Aiello, Andrea Marcovicci; **D:** Martin Ritt; **M:** Dave Grusin. Academy Awards '76 Nominations: Best Original Screenplay; National Board of Review Awards '76: 10 Best Films of the Year. **VHS, Beta** $12.95 *COL* ✲✲✲

The Front Page The original screen version of the Hecht-MacArthur play about the shenanigans of a battling newspaper reporter and his editor in Chicago. O'Brien's film debut here is one of several hilarious

performances in this breathless pursuit of an exclusive with an escaped death row inmate.
1931 101m/B Adolphe Menjou, Pat O'Brien, Edward Everett Horton, Mae Clarke, Walter Catlett; *D:* Lewis Milestone. Academy Awards '31 Nominations: Best Actor (Menjou), Best Director (Milestone), Best Picture; National Board of Review Awards '31: 10 Best Films of the Year. **VHS, Beta $19.95** *NOS, MRV, HHT 𝄞𝄞𝄞 ½*

The Front Page A remake of the Hecht-MacArthur play about the managing editor of a 1920s Chicago newspaper who finds out his ace reporter wants to quit the business and get married. But first an escaped convicted killer offers the reporter an exclusive interview.
1974 (PG) 105m/C Jack Lemmon, Walter Matthau, Carol Burnett, Austin Pendleton, Vincent Gardenia, Charles Durning, Susan Sarandon; *D:* Billy Wilder; *W:* Billy Wilder, I.A.L. Diamond. **VHS $89.95** *MCA 𝄞𝄞½*

Frontera If you're looking for action, go to the Border! Anything goes on the dangerous, exciting "Frontera." *AKA:* The Border.
19?? ?m/C *SP* Fernando Allende, Daniela Romo. **VHS, Beta** *VVC 𝄞 ½*

Frontera Sin Ley The son of Santo fights against local gangsters' crime and abuse in Pueblo Viejo.
19?? ?m/C *MX* Mil Mascaras, Eleazar Garcia Chelelo, Carmen Del Valle, Hijo Del Santo. **VHS, Beta** *NO 𝄞𝄞*

Frontier Days Cody goes undercover to capture the leader of a gang of stagecoach robbers. He also manages to capture a killer along the way.
1934 60m/B Bill Cody, Ada Ince, Wheeler Oakman; *D:* Sam Newfield. **VHS, Beta $19.95** *NOS, DVT 𝄞 ½*

Frontier Fugitives When a trapper is murdered—allegedly by Indians—the Texas Rangers ride in to investigate.
1945 58m/B Tex Ritter, Dave O'Brien, Guy Wilkerson, Lorraine Miller, I. Stanford Jolley, Jack Ingram; *D:* Harry Fraser. **VHS $19.95** *NOS 𝄞 ½*

Frontier Horizon Wayne and the Three Mesquiteers help out ranchers whose land is being bought up by crooked speculators.
1939 55m/B John Wayne, Jennifer Jones, Ray Corrigan, Raymond Hatton; *D:* George Sherman. **VHS, Beta $19.95** *REP, CAB 𝄞𝄞*

Frontier Justice Gibson is the foolish son of a cattle owner who has been forced into an insane asylum because of a battle over water rights. Naturally, he must take on responsibility and rescue his father.
1935 56m/B Hoot Gibson, Richard Cramer; *D:* Robert McGowan. **VHS, Beta $19.95** *NOS, VCN, DVT 𝄞𝄞*

Frontier Law Hayden and the boys ride into town to clean out the bad guys and clear a friend wrongly accused of murder.
1943 55m/B Russell Hayden, Jennifer Holt, Dennis Moore, Fuzzy Knight, Jack Ingram, Hal Taliaferro; *D:* Elmer Clifton; *W:* Elmer Clifton. **VHS $19.99** *MOV 𝄞 ½*

Frontier Outlaws A gang of villains is selling stolen cattle, and Crabbe poses as an interested buyer to catch them in the act. Laughs are provided by Lynn as a judge, and "Fuzzy" St. John as Crabbe's sidekick.
1944 58m/B Buster Crabbe, Al "Fuzzy" St. John, Frances Gladwin, Marin Sais, Charles "Blackie" King, Jack Ingram, Kermit Maynard, Edward Cassidy, Emmett Lynn, Budd Buster; *D:* Sam Newfield. **VHS $9.95** *GPV, MRV, NOS 𝄞𝄞*

Frontier Pony Express Roy and Trigger do their best to help the Pony Express riders who are being attacked by marauding gangs in California during the time of the Civil War. Plenty of action here.
1939 54m/B Roy Rogers; *D:* Joseph Kane. **VHS, Beta $19.95** *NOS, MED, DVT 𝄞𝄞*

Frontier Scout Action-packed western has Wild Bill Hickock, portrayed by former opera singer Houston, forcing Lee's surrender in the Civil War before pursuing cattle rustlers out West.
1938 m/B George Houston, Mantan Moreland; *D:* Sam Newfield. **VHS, Beta $19.95** *NOS, DVT, RXM 𝄞𝄞*

Frontier Uprising Stunning cinematography makes up for weak narrative in this otherwise routine oater. Davis stars as a frontier scout battling hordes of Mexicans and Indians while trying to gain control of California for the U.S. Based on the short story "Kit Carson" by George Bruce.
1961 68m/B Jim Davis, Nancy Hadley, Ken Mayer, Nestor Paiva, Don O'Kelly; *D:* Edward L. Cahn; *W:* Owen Harris. **VHS $19.95** *DVT 𝄞 ½*

Frontier Vengeance Barry is falsely accused of murder and works to clear his name while at the same time romancing a stagecoach driver who's trying to win a race with a rival stagecoach line.
1940 54m/B Donald (Don "Red") Barry, Nate Watt. **VHS, Beta** *MED, RXM 𝄞 ½*

The Frontiersman Things plod along at the little red schoolhouse until Hoppy and the guys have to take off after some rustlers. Features the members of the St. Brendan Boys Choir as the schoolboys. Unusual for its lack of gunplay until near the end.
1938 71m/B William Boyd, George "Gabby" Hayes, Russell Hayden, Evelyn Venable, Clara Kimball Young, Charles Hughes, Dick Jones, Roy Barcroft, Emily Fitzroy; *D:* Lesley Selander. **VHS $19.95** *NOS 𝄞𝄞*

Frozen Alive A scientist experiments with suspended animation but, wouldn't you know, someone murders his wife while he's on ice. Apparently being frozen stiff does not an alibi make, and he becomes the prime suspect. Much unanimated suspense.
1964 80m/B *GB GE* Mark Stevens, Marianne Koch, Delphi Lawrence, Joachim Hansen, Walter Rilla, Wolfgang Lukschy; *D:* Bernard Knowles. **VHS $19.98** *MOV 𝄞*

Frozen Assets Pathetic attempt at comedy from Long and Bernsen. He's an ambitious executive who finds the "bank" of his corporation's latest acquisition deals in sperm and not cash. Still, he expects this acquisition to be a success and comes up with a number of tacky ways, much to the horror of the facility's administrator, to make that profit margin grow.
1992 (PG-13) 93m/C Corbin Bernsen, Shelley Long, Larry Miller, Dody Goodman, Gerrit Graham, Paul Sand, Teri Copley, Matt Clark; *D:* George Miller; *W:* Don Klein, Tom Kartozian. **VHS $94.98** *FXV 𝄞*

Frozen Terror A madman resembling both Jack Frost and Jack the Ripper claims victims at random.
1980 (R) 93m/C Bernice Stegers; *D:* Lamberto Bava. **VHS, Beta $69.95** *LIV, VES 𝄞*

Fu Manchu Villainous arch-criminal Fu Manchu plots to enslave the world in "The Golden God" and "The Master Plan," two episodes from the television series.
1956 60m/B Glenn Gordon, Laurette Luez, Clark Howat, Lee Matthews. **VHS, Beta $24.95** *DVT 𝄞*

Fuerte Perdido Settlers battle for their lives against hostile Indians led by Geronimo. In Spanish. *AKA:* Fort Lost.

1978 90m/C *SP* Esther Rojo, German Cobos, Mario Vidal. **VHS, Beta $59.95** *HHT 𝄞*

The Fugitive Fonda is a priest devoted to God and the peasants under his care when he finds himself on the run after religion is outlawed in this nameless South-of-the-border dictatorship. Despite the danger of capture, he continues to minister to his flock. His eventual martyrdom unites the villagers in prayer. Considered Fonda's best performance; Ford's favorite film. Shot on location in Mexico. Excellent supporting performances. Based on the Graham Greene novel "The Power and the Glory" although considerably cleaned up for the big screen—Greene's priest had lost virtually all of his faith and moral code. Here the priest is a genuine Ford hero. A gem.
1948 99m/B Henry Fonda, Dolores Del Rio, Pedro Armendariz Sr., J. Carroll Naish, Leo Carrillo, Ward Bond, Robert Armstrong, John Qualen; *D:* John Ford; *W:* Dudley Nichols. **VHS, Beta $19.98** *TTC 𝄞𝄞𝄞𝄞*

The Fugitive Exciting big-screen version of the '60s TV series with the same basic storyline: Dr. Richard Kimble's wife is murdered and he's implicated, so he goes on the lam to find the real killer, the mysterious one-armed man. Lots of mystery and action, particularly a spectacular train/bus crash sequence, keeps the tension high. Due to illness, Richard Jordan was replaced by Krabbe after production had begun. Alec Baldwin was originally slated to star as Kimble, but backed out and Ford was cast. Sound familiar? Ford also replaced Baldwin as Jack Ryan in "Patriot Games." The second highest grossing movie of 1993.
1993 (PG-13) 127m/C Harrison Ford, Tommy Lee Jones, Jeroen Krabbe, Julianne Moore, Sela Ward, Joe Pantoliano, Andreas Katsulas, Daniel Roebuck; *D:* Andrew Davis; *W:* David N. Twohy, Jeb Stuart; *M:* James Newton Howard. Academy Awards '93: Best Supporting Actor (Jones); Nominations: Best Cinematography, Best Film Editing, Best Original Screenplay, Best Picture, Best Sound, Best Sound Effects Editing; British Academy Awards '93: Best Supporting Actor (Jones); Directors Guild of America Awards '93: Best Director (Davis); Golden Globe Awards '94: Best Actor—Drama (Ford), Best Director (Davis); Golden Globe Awards '94: Best Supporting Actor (Jones); Los Angeles Film Critics Association Awards '93: Best Supporting Actor (Jones); MTV Movie Awards '94: Best On-Screen Duo (Harrison Ford/Tommy Lee Jones), Best Action Sequence. **VHS $24.96** *WAR 𝄞𝄞𝄞½*

Fugitive Alien Alien and Earth forces battle it out. Dubbed for Japanese.
1986 103m/C *JP* **VHS, Beta $39.95** *CEL Woof!*

The Fugitive Kind A young drifter walks into a sleepy Mississippi town and attracts the attention of three of its women with tragic results. Based upon the Tennessee Williams' play "Orpheus Descending." good performances but the writing never hangs well-enough together for coherence.
1960 122m/B Marlon Brando, Anna Magnani, Joanne Woodward, Victor Jory, R.G. Armstrong, Maureen Stapleton; *D:* Sidney Lumet. **VHS, Beta $19.98** *MGM, FOX 𝄞𝄞 ½*

The Fugitive: Premiere Episode In this introductory episode to the television series, Janssen plays Dr. Richard Kimble, who's wrongly convicted of murdering his wife. After a train taking him to prison derails, he makes his escape and begins his search for the real culprit, the mysterious one-armed man. But Kimble's pursued by the relentless Lt. Gerard. Additional episodes available.
1963 45m/B David Janssen, Barry Morse, Vera Miles, Brian Keith. **VHS $12.99** *MOV, GKK*

Fugitive Road The great von Stroheim stars as a crusty but soft-hearted border guard who arbitrarily detains people at the crossing.
1934 69m/B Erich von Stroheim, Wera Engels, Leslie Fenton, Harry Holman; *D:* Frank Strayer. **VHS** $19.95 *NOS* ✂✂

The Fugitive: Taking of Luke McVane An early silent western in which Hart upholds the cowboy code of honor.
1915 28m/B William S. Hart, Enid Markey. **VHS, Beta** $24.95 *VYY* ✂✂

The Fugitive: The Final Episode The final episode of the acclaimed series, aired on August 29, 1967, in which Dr. Richard Kimble meets up with the one-armed man who murdered his wife and tries to bring him to justice before Lt. Gerard can bring Kimble in. Episode was the most watched television program up to that time.
1967 78m/C David Janssen, Barry Morse, Bill Raisch, Diane Baker, Joseph Campanella, Michael Constantine. **VHS** $14.99 *MOV* ✂✂

Fugitive Valley Muddled plot has villains-turned-heroes on the trail of some outlaws and stolen money. Terhune shows off some of his vaudeville skills, and King sings some songs.
1941 61m/B Ray Corrigan, John "Dusty" King, Max Terhune, Julie Duncan, Glenn Strange, Robert F. (Bob) Kortman, Tom London, Reed Howes; *D:* S. Roy Luby. **VHS** $19.95 *NOS, HEG* ✂½

Fulfillment Ladd stars as Mary Gray, a turn-of-the-century woman comfortably married to good but unexciting farmer, Jonathan (Levine). He's unable to give his wife the child they both desperately want and when his younger brother, Aaron (Smith), visits, the hope is Aaron can be persuaded to help out. The naturally volatile situation is heightened by the fact Mary is very drawn to the handsome Aaron anyway, and the feeling is mutual. Based on the novel "The Fulfillment" by LaVyrle Spencer. Made for television. *AKA:* The Fulfillment of Mary Gray.
1989 (PG-13) 96m/C Cheryl Ladd, Ted Levine, Lewis Smith; *D:* Piers Haggard. **VHS** $89.98 *REP* ✂½

Full Circle Peter Straub wrote this eerie tale about a grief-stricken young woman whose child has recently died. To overcome her loss, she moves into a new house—which is haunted by the ghost of a long-dead child. *AKA:* The Haunting of Julia.
1977 (R) 96m/C *CA GB* Mia Farrow, Keir Dullea, Tom Conti, Jill Bennett, Robin Gammell; *D:* Richard Loncraine. **VHS, Beta** *MED* ✂✂

Full Contact Farmhand Luke Powers heads for the decadence of Los Angeles to find his older brother. When three thugs make the mistake of trying to rob him, Luke shows off his martial arts skills. When Luke finds out his brother has been murdered by gamblers involved in an illegal back alley kickboxing circuit, he vows to get revenge.
1993 97m/C Jerry Trimble, Howard Jackson, Alvin Prouder, Gerry Blanck, Denise Buick; *D:* Rick Jacobson; *W:* Beverly Gray. **VHS** $89.95 *COL* ✂✂

Full Eclipse Max Dire (Van Peebles) is seduced by the fetching Casey (Kensit) into joining a fierce elite group of underground cops whose mission is to wipe out crime. However, Max soon learns that the secret of their power is a serum which turns them into werewolves. Max is now faced with a decision: join forces with them, or expose them. Either way, blood will flow. Interesting special effects. Unrated version also available.

1993 (R) 97m/C Mario Van Peebles, Patsy Kensit, Bruce Payne, Anthony John Denison; *D:* Anthony Hickox. **VHS** $92.99 *HBO* ✂✂

Full Exposure: The Sex Tape Scandals Sleazy drama about a murdered call girl who was blackmailing her clients with sex videos. A cop and his inexperienced female partner are assigned to catch the killer. Made for television.
1989 (R) 95m/C Jennifer O'Neill, Lisa Hartman, Vanessa Williams, Anthony John Denison, Peter Jurasik; *D:* Noel Nosseck; *M:* Dana Kaproff. **VHS** $89.95 *WOV* ✂½

Full Fathom Five Central American militants, angered by America's invasion of Panama, hijack a submarine and threaten a nuclear assault on Houston. Boring and dumb.
1990 (PG) 81m/C Michael Moriarty, Maria Rangel, Michael Cavanaugh, John Lafayette, Todd Field, Daniel Faraldo; *D:* Carl Franklin. **VHS, Beta** $14.95 *MGM* ✂½

Full Hearts & Empty Pockets Follows the happy-go-lucky adventures of a young, handsome, impoverished gentleman on the loose in Rome. Dubbed in English.
1963 88m/B *IT GE* Linda Christian, Gino Cervi, Senta Berger; *D:* Camillo Mastrocinque. **VHS, Beta** $24.95 *VYY* ✂½

Full Metal Jacket A three-act Vietnam War epic, about a single Everyman impetuously passing through basic training then working in the field as an Army photojournalist and fighting at the onset of the Tet offensive. First half of the film is the most realistic bootcamp sequence ever done. Unfocused but powerful. Based on the novel by Hasford, who also co-scripted.
1987 (R) 116m/C Matthew Modine, R. Lee Ermey, Vincent D'Onofrio, Adam Baldwin, Dorian Harewood, Arliss Howard, Kevyn Major Howard; *D:* Stanley Kubrick; *W:* Michael Herr, Gustav Hasford, Stanley Kubrick. **VHS, Beta, 8mm** $19.98 *WAR, FCT* ✂✂✂½

Full Metal Ninja When his family is kidnapped, a trained martial artist trails their abductors and swears revenge.
1989 90m/C Patrick Allen, Pierre Kirby, Sean Odell, Jean Paul, Renato Sala; *D:* Charles Lee. **VHS, Beta** $59.95 *IMP* ✂

Full Moon in Blue Water His wife's been dead a year, he owes back taxes on his bar, his father has Alzheimer's, and his only form of entertainment is watching old home movies of his wife. Floyd has problems. Enter Louise, a lonely spinster who feels that it is her personal duty to change his life. If she doesn't do it, the bizarre things that happen after her arrival will.
1988 (R) 96m/C Gene Hackman, Teri Garr, Burgess Meredith, Elias Koteas, Kevin Cooney, David Doty; *D:* Peter Masterson; *W:* Bill Bozzone; *M:* Phil Marshall. **VHS, Beta** $19.98 *MED, VTR* ✂✂½

Full Moon in Paris A young woman in Paris moves out on her architect lover in order to experience freedom. Through a couple of random relationships, she soon finds that what she hoped for is not what she really wanted. *AKA:* Les Nuits De La Pleine.
1984 (R) 101m/C *FR* Pascale Ogier, Tcheky Karyo, Fabrice Luchini; *D:* Eric Rohmer; *W:* Eric Rohmer. **VHS, Beta** $24.95 *XVC, MED, ING* ✂✂½

Full of Life Holliday stars in this domestic comedy about a non-religious young woman who had married, in a civil ceremony, into a strict, Italian-Catholic family. Although she is now eight months pregnant the family still wants the couple to have a church wedding. Holliday is a winning personality and the humor is lightly handled.

1956 91m/C Judy Holliday, Richard Conte, Salvatore Baccaloni, Ester Minciotti; *D:* Richard Quine. **VHS** $19.95 *FCT* ✂✂½

The Fuller Brush Girl Lots of slapstick with Ball as a door-to-door saleswoman unexpectedly involved in a murder. She and dim-bulb boyfriend Albert are chased by cops, murderers, and smugglers in this frantic farce. Sequel to Red Skelton's (who has a cameo) 1948 film "The Fuller Brush Man."
1950 84m/B Lucille Ball, Eddie Albert, Carl Benton Reid, Gale Robbins, Jeff Donnell, John Litel, Fred Graham, Lee Patrick; *Cameos:* Red Skelton; *D:* Lloyd Bacon; *W:* Frank Tashlin. **VHS** $19.95 *COL* ✂✂½

Fuller Brush Man A newly hired Fuller Brush man becomes involved in murder and romance as he tries to win the heart of his girlfriend. A slapstick delight for Skelton fans. *AKA:* That Man Mr. Jones.
1948 93m/B Red Skelton, Janet Blair, Don McGuire, Adele Jergens; *D:* Frank Tashlin. **VHS, Beta** $19.95 *COL* ✂✂½

Fun & Fancy Free Part-animated, part-live-action feature is split into two segments: "Bongo" with Dinah Shore narrating the story of a happy-go-lucky circus bear; and "Mickey and the Beanstalk"—a "new" version of an old fairy tale.
1947 96m/C Edgar Bergen, Charlie McCarthy, Jiminy Cricket, Mickey Mouse, Donald Duck, Goofy, Dinah Shore. **VHS, Beta** *DIS* ✂✂½

Fun Down There This smalltown boy-comes-to-the-big city is so bad, it's...bad. A naive—and unsympathetic—gay man from upstate New York moves to Greenwich Village and has fun down there (and they don't mean Australia).
1988 110m/C Michael Waite, Nickolas Nagurney, Gretschen Somerville, Martin Goldin, Kevin Och; *D:* Roger Stigliano; *W:* Michael Waite, Roger Stigliano. **VHS** $29.95 *WBF, FCT, ING* Woof!

Fun in Acapulco Former trapeze artist Elvis romances two beauties and acts as a part-time lifeguard and night club entertainer. He must conquer his fear of heights for a climactic dive from the Acapulco cliffs. Features ten musical numbers. ♫ Fun in Acapulco; Vino, Dinero y Amor; Mexico; The Bullfighter Was A Lady; El Toro; Marguerita; (There's) No Room To Rhumba (In A Sports Car); I Think I'm Going To Like It Here; You Can't Say No In Acapulco; Guadalajara.
1963 97m/C Elvis Presley, Ursula Andress, Elsa Cardenas, Paul Lukas, Alejandro Rey, Larry Domasin, Howard McNear; *D:* Richard Thorpe. **VHS, Beta** $14.98 *FOX, MVD* ✂✂

Fun with Dick and Jane An upper-middle class couple turn to armed robbery to support themselves when the husband is fired from his job. Though it has good performances, the film never develops its intended bite.
1977 (PG) 104m/C George Segal, Jane Fonda, Ed McMahon; *D:* Ted Kotcheff; *W:* Jerry Belson, David Giler, Mordecai Richler; *M:* Ernest Gold. **VHS, Beta** $9.95 *COL* ✂✂

The Funeral A sharp satire of the clash of modern Japanese culture with the old. The hypocrisies, rivalries and corruption in an average family are displayed at the funeral of its patriarch who also happened to own a house of ill repute. Itami's breakthrough film, in Japanese with English subtitles.
1984 112m/C *JP* Tsutomu Yamazaki, Nobuko Miyamoto, Kin Sugai, Ichiro Zaitsu, Nekohachi Edoya, Shoji Otake; *D:* Juzo Itami. **VHS** $19.98 *REP, FCT, ING* ✂✂✂½

Funeral for an Assassin A professional assassin seeks revenge for his imprisonment by the government of South Africa, a former client. Planning to kill all of the country's leading politicians, he masquerades as a black man, a cover which is designed to fool the apartheid establishment. **1977 (PG) 92m/C** Vic Morrow, Peter Van Dissel; *D:* Ivan Hall. **VHS, Beta $59.95** *GEM, MRV, VTR* ✰✰½

Funeral Home Terrified teen spends her summer vacation at her grandmother's tourist home, a former funeral parlor. Rip-off of "Psycho." *AKA:* 2 Cries in the Night. **1982 90m/C** *CA* Lesleh Donaldson, Kay Hawtry; *D:* William Fruet. **VHS, Beta** *NO* ✰✰½

Funeral in Berlin Second of the Caine-Harry Palmer espionage films (following on "Ipcress File"), in which the deadpan British secret serviceman arranges the questionable defection of a Russian colonel. Good look at he spy biz and postwar Berlin. "Billion Dollar Brain" continues the series. **1966 102m/C** Michael Caine, Eva Renzi, Oscar Homolka; *D:* Guy Hamilton; *W:* Evan Jones. **VHS, Beta $14.95** *PAR* ✰✰✰

The Funhouse Four teenagers spend the night at a carnival funhouse, witness a murder, and become next on the list of victims. From the director of cult favorite "Texas Chainsaw Massacre," but nothing that hasn't been seen before. **1981 (R) 96m/C** Elizabeth Berridge, Shawn Carson, Cooper Huckabee, Largo Woodruff, Sylvia Miles; *D:* Tobe Hooper. **VHS, Beta $14.98** *MCA* ✰✰½

Funland In the world's weirdest amusement park a clown goes nuts over the new corporate owners' plans for the place and decides to seek revenge. **1989 (PG-13) 86m/C** David Lander, William Windom, Bruce Mahler, Michael McManus; *D:* Michael A. Simpson. **VHS $79.98** *LIV, IME, VES* ✰

Funny About Love Fairly absurd tale with dashes of inappropriate black humor about a fellow with a ticking biological clock. Nimoy sheds his Spock ears to direct a star-studded cast in this lame tale of middle-aged cartoonist Wilder who strays from wife Lahti after having problems on the conception end into the welcoming arms of fertile college co-ed Masterson in his quest to contribute to the population count. **1990 (PG-13) 107m/C** Gene Wilder, Christine Lahti, Mary Stuart Masterson, Robert Prosky, Stephen Tobolowsky, Anne Jackson, Susan Ruttan, David Margulies; *D:* Leonard Nimoy; *W:* Norman Steinberg, David Frankel. **VHS, Beta, 8mm $14.95** *PAR* ✰½

Funny, Dirty Little War An Argentinian farce about the petty rivalries in a small village erupting into a violent, mini-civil war. In Spanish with English subtitles. **1983 80m/C** *AR* Federico Luppi, Julio de Grazia, Miguel Angel Sola; *D:* Hector Olivera. **VHS, Beta $24.95** *XVC, ING* ✰✰½

Funny Face A musical satire on beatniks and the fashion scene also features the May-December romance between Astaire and the ever-lovely Hepburn. He is a high-fashion photographer (based on Richard Avedon); she is a Greenwich Village bookseller fond of shapeless, drab clothing. He decides to take her to Paris and show her what modeling's all about. The elegant musical score features classic Gershwin. The laserdisc includes the original theatrical trailer and is available in widescreen. ♫Let's Kiss and Make Up; He Loves and She Loves; Funny Face; How Long Has This Been Going On?; Clap Yo'

Hands; S'Wonderful; Bonjour Paris; On How To Be Lovely; Marche Funebre; Think Pink. **1957 103m/C** Fred Astaire, Audrey Hepburn, Kay Thompson, Suzy Parker; *D:* Stanley Donen; *M:* George Gershwin, Ira Gershwin. **VHS, Beta, 8mm $14.95** *PAR, FCT* ✰✰✰

The Funny Farm Comedy about a group of ambitious young comics striving to make it in the crazy world of comedy at Los Angeles' famous comedy club, The Funny Farm. **1982 90m/C** *CA* Miles Chapin, Eileen Brennan, Peter Aykroyd; *D:* Ron Clark. **VHS, Beta $19.95** *STE* ✰✰

Funny Farm Chevy Chase as a New York sportswriter finds that life in the country is not quite what he envisioned. The comedy is uneven throughout, with the best scenes coming at the end. **1988 (PG) 101m/C** Chevy Chase, Madolyn Smith, Joseph Maher, Jack Gilpin, Brad Sullivan, MacIntyre Dixon; *D:* George Roy Hill; *W:* Jeffrey Boam; *M:* Elmer Bernstein. **VHS $19.98** *WAR, STE* ✰✰

Funny Girl Follows the early career of comedian Fanny Brice, her rise to stardom with the Ziegfeld Follies and her stormy romance with gambler Nick Arnstein in a fun and funny look at back stage music hall life in the early 1900s. Streisand's film debut followed her auspicious performance of the role on Broadway. Score was augmented by several tunes sung by Brice during her performances. Excellent performances from everyone, captured beautifully by Wyler in his musical film debut. Followed by "Funny Lady." ♫My Man; Second Hand Rose; I'd Rather Be Blue Over You; People; Don't Rain On My Parade; I'm The Greatest Star; Sadie, Sadie; His Love Makes Me Beautiful; You Are Woman, I Am Man; If A Girl Isn't Pretty; The Swan; Roller Skate Rag; Funny Girl. **1968 (G) 151m/C** Barbra Streisand, Omar Sharif, Walter Pidgeon, Kay Medford, Anne Francis; *D:* William Wyler. Academy Awards '68: Best Actress (Streisand); Nominations: Best Cinematography, Best Film Editing, Best Picture, Best Song ("Funny Girl"), Best Sound, Best Supporting Actress (Medford), Best Original Score; Golden Globe Awards '69: Best Actress—Musical/Comedy (Streisand). **VHS, Beta $19.95** *COL, BTV* ✰✰✰

Funny Lady A continuation of "Funny Girl," recounting Fanny Brice's tumultuous marriage to showman Billy Rose in the 1930s and her lingering affection for first husband Nick Arnstein. One of the rare sequels which are just as good, or at least almost, as the original. ♫How Lucky Can You Get?; Great Day; More Than You Know; Blind Date; So Long, Honey Lamb; Isn't This Better; Let's Hear It For Me; I Like Him/I Like Her; It's Only a Paper Moon; I Found a Million Dollar Baby In a Five and Ten Cent Store; Beautiful Face, Have a Heart; If You Want the Rainbow, You Must Have the Rain; I Caught a Code In My Dose; Am I Blue?; Clap Hands, Here Comes Charley; Me and My Shadow; If I Love Again; Isn't It Better. **1975 (PG) 137m/C** Barbra Streisand, Omar Sharif, James Caan, Roddy McDowall, Ben Vereen, Carole Wells, Larry Gates, Heidi O'Rourke; *D:* Herbert Ross; *W:* Jay Presson Allen, Arnold Schulman. **VHS, Beta $19.95** *COL, FCT* ✰✰½

Funny Money Pointed, satirical look at the British habit of financing life with the almighty credit card. Sometimes uneven comedy. **1982 92m/C** *GB* Greg Henry, Elizabeth Daily, Gareth Hunt, Derren Nesbitt, Annie Ross; *D:* James Kenelm Clarke. **VHS, Beta $69.95** *LIV* ✰

A Funny Thing Happened on the Way to the Forum A bawdy Broadway farce set in ancient Rome where a conniving, slave plots his way to freedom by aiding in the romantic escapades of his master's inept son. Terrific performances by Mostel and Gilford. Keaton's second-to-last film role. The Oscar-winning score includes such highlights as "Comedy Tonight," "Lovely," and "Everybody Ought to Have a Maid." **1966 100m/C** Zero Mostel, Phil Silvers, Jack Gilford, Buster Keaton, Michael Hordern, Michael Crawford, Annette Andre; *D:* Richard Lester; *M:* Ken Thorne. **VHS, Beta $19.99** *FOX, FCT* ✰✰✰

Furia Pasional A hot, passionate film about a lusty couple in romantic trouble. **19?? ?m/C** *SP* Alfonso Muguia, Hilda Cibar, Manuel Cepeda. **VHS, Beta** *MAD* ✰½

Furious The sister of a young martial arts apprentice is killed by the master, with a great deal of action and special effects. **1983 (PG) 85m/C** Simon Rhee, Howard Jackson, Arlene Montano. **VHS, Beta $49.95** *VHE* ✰

The Furious Avenger A released convict, on his way to avenging his family's murder, stops a rape and takes on one opponent after another in this rousing kick-fest. Dubbed. **1976 84m/C** Hsiung Fei, Fan Ling, Chen Pei Ling, Tien Yeh, Wang Mo Chou. **VHS, Beta $39.95** *UNI* ✰

The Further Adventures of Tennessee Buck Mercenary adventurer travels through tropical jungles acting as a guide to a dizzy couple. Along the way, they encounter cannibals, headhunters, and other bizarre jungle things in this lame take on "Indiana Jones." Shot on location in Sri Lanka. **1988 (R) 90m/C** David Keith, Kathy Shower, Brant Van Hoffman; *D:* David Keith; *M:* John Debney. **VHS, Beta $19.98** *MED, VTR* ✰

Further Adventures of the Wilderness Family, Part 2 Also known as the "Further Adventures of the Wilderness Family." Depicts the Robinson family who left civilization for the freedom of the Colorado wild. Predictable retread, but more good family adventure drama from the makers of "Adventures of the Wilderness Family." *AKA:* Wilderness Family, Part 2. **1977 (G) 104m/C** Heather Rattray, Ham Larsen, George Flower, Robert F. Logan, Susan Damante Shaw; *D:* Frank Zuniga. **VHS, Beta $9.98** *MED, VTR* ✰✰½

Fury Tracy gives an excellent performance as an innocent young man framed for kidnapping and then nearly murdered by a lynch mob. His plans for revenge are thwarted by his girlfriend, who fears that he will turn into the murderer he has been accused of being. Powerful anti-violence message is well-made, with strong ensemble acting. Lang's favorite of his American-made films. **1936 96m/B** Spencer Tracy, Sylvia Sidney, Walter Abel, Bruce Cabot, Edward Ellis, Walter Brennan, Frank Albertson; *D:* Fritz Lang. **VHS, Beta $19.98** *MGM* ✰✰✰½

The Fury The head of a government institute for psychic research finds that his own son is snatched by supposed terrorists who wish to use his lethal powers. The father tries to use another a young woman with psychic power to locate him, with bloody results. A real chiller. **1978 (R) 117m/C** Kirk Douglas, John Cassavetes, Carrie Snodgress, Andrew Stevens, Amy Irving, Charles Durning, Daryl Hannah; *D:* Brian DePalma; *M:* John Williams. **VHS, Beta $19.98** *FOX* ✰✰

Fury A man and woman meet in the Amazonian jungle and the sparks begin to fly. 1987 75m/C Stuart Whitman, Laura Gemser. VHS, Beta *NO* 🐾

Fury is a Woman A Polish version of Shakespeare's Macbeth which ranks with the greatest film translations of his work. In Czarist Russia the passionate wife of a plantation owner begins an affair with a farm hand, and poisons her father-in-law when he finds them out. As her madness grows, she plots the murder of the husband. Letterbox format. In Serbian with English subtitles. 1961 93m/C *RU* Olivera Markovic, Ljuba Tadic, Kapitalina Eric; *D:* Andrzej Wajda. VHS $59.95 *HTV, ING* 🐾🐾🐾½

The Fury of Hercules It's up to the mighty son of Zeus to free an enslaved group of people from an oppressive, evil ruler. Surely all who stand in his way will be destroyed. Another Italian muscleman film. *AKA:* La Furia Di Ercole; Fury of Samson. 1961 95m/C *IT* Brad Harris, Brigitte Corey, Mara Berni, Carlo Tamberlani, Serge Gainsbourg, Elke Arendt, Alan Steel; *D:* Gianfranco Parolini. VHS $9.95 *GKK, SNC* 🐾🐾

The Fury of the Wolfman A murdering werewolf is captured by a female scientist who tries to cure his lycanthropy with drugs and brain implants. Pretty slow going, but hang in there for the wolfman versus werewoman climax. 1970 80m/C *SP* Paul Naschy, Perla Cristal; *D:* Jose Maria Zabalza; *W:* Paul Naschy. VHS, Beta $49.95 *UNI, NLC, LOO* 🐾

Fury on Wheels Tale of men who race cars and wreak havoc and vice versa. 1971 (PG) 89m/C Judd Hirsch, Tom Ligon, Paul Sorvino, Logan Ramsey, Collin Wilcox-Horne. VHS, Beta *NO* 🐾

Fury to Freedom: The Life Story of Raul Ries A young man raised in the volatile world of abusive and alcoholic parents grows into an abusive and violent adult. One night, however, he meets something he can't beat up, and it changes his life. 1985 78m/C Gil Gerard, John Quade, Tom Silardi. VHS $29.95 *VCI* 🐾🐾

Future Cop A hard-nosed, old-fashioned cop is forced to team with the ultimate partner—a robot. Silly made-for-TV movie, but likable leads. *AKA:* Trancers. 1976 78m/C Ernest Borgnine, Michael J. Shannon, John Amos, John Larch, Herbert Nelson, Ronnie Clair Edwards; *D:* Judd Taylor; *W:* Danny Bilson, Paul DeMeo. VHS *PAR* 🐾🐾

Future Force In the crime-filled future cops can't maintain order. They rely on a group of civilian mercenaries to clean up the streets. 1989 (R) 90m/C David Carradine, Robert Tessier, Anna Rapagna, William Zipp. VHS, Beta $79.95 *AIP* 🐾

Future Hunters In the holocaust-blitzed future, a young couple searches for a religious artifact that may decide the future of the planet. 1988 96m/C Robert Patrick, Linda Carol, Ed Crick, Bob Schott; *D:* Cirio H. Santiago. VHS, Beta $19.98 *LIV, VES* 🐾

Future Kill Anti-nuclear activists battle fraternity brothers in this grim futuristic world. Shaky political alliances form between revenge-seeking factions on both sides. 1985 (R) 83m/C Edwin Neal, Marilyn Burns, Doug Davis; *D:* Ronald W. Moore; *W:* Ronald W. Moore. VHS, Beta $19.98 *LIV, VES* 🐾

Future Shock Dr. Russell Langdon is a psychiatrist who has been experimenting with virtual reality technology. Unbeknownst to three of his patients he decides to use them as guinea pigs in his work. But confronting their deepest fears only leads to new terrors. Also available in an unrated version. 1993 (PG-13) 93m/C Bill Paxton, Vivian Schilling, Brion James, Martin Kove; *D:* Eric Parkinson. VHS $89.95 *HMD* 🐾🐾

Future Zone In an attempt to save his father from being murdered, a young man travels backwards in time. 1990 (R) 88m/C David Carradine, Charles Napier, Ted Prior; *D:* David A. Prior. VHS $79.95 *AIP* 🐾🐾

Futurekick In the not so distant future, a kickboxer with an attitude and cyborg capabilities must use every ounce of strength in a battle against evil. 1991 (R) 80m/C Don "The Dragon" Wilson, Meg Foster, Christopher Penn, Eb Lottimer; *D:* Damian Klaus; *W:* Damian Klaus. VHS *NHO* 🐾½

Futureworld In the sequel to "Westworld," two reporters junket to the new "Futureworld" theme park, where they first support a scheme to clone and control world leaders. Includes footage shot at NASA locations. 1976 (PG) 107m/C Peter Fonda, Blythe Danner, Arthur Hill, Yul Brynner, Stuart Margolin; *D:* Richard T. Heffron; *W:* George Schenck. VHS, Beta $19.98 *WAR, OM* 🐾🐾

Futz Story from off-Broadway is of a man who loves his pig and the world that can't understand the attraction. Better in original stage production. 1969 90m/C John Pakos, Victor Lipari, Sally Kirkland; *D:* Tom O'Horgan. VHS, Beta *NO* 🐾½

Fuzz Reynolds in the Boston cop on the track of a bomber killing policemen, punks setting winos on fire, and some amorous fellow officers. Combines fast action and some sharp-edged humor. 1972 (PG) 92m/C Burt Reynolds, Tom Skerritt, Yul Brynner, Raquel Welch, Jack Weston, Charles Martin Smith; *D:* Richard A. Colla; *M:* Dave Grusin. VHS, Beta $14.95 *MGM, FOX* 🐾🐾½

Fyre Young beautiful girl moves from the Midwest to Los Angeles and becomes a prostitute. 1978 (R) 90m/C Allen (Gooritz) Garfield, Lynn Theel, Tom Baker, Cal Haynes, Donna Wilkes, Bruce Kirby; *D:* Richard Grand. VHS, Beta *MED* 🐾½

"G" Men Powerful story based loosely on actual events that occurred during FBI operations in the early 1930s, with Cagney on the right side of the law, though still given to unreasonable fits of anger. Raised and educated by a well-known crime kingpin, a young man becomes an attorney. When his friend the FBI agent is killed in the line of duty, he joins the FBI to seek vengeance on the mob. But his mob history haunts him, forcing him to constantly prove to his superiors that he is not under its influence. Tense and thrilling classic. 1935 86m/B James Cagney, Barton MacLane, Ann Dvorak, Margaret Lindsay, Robert Armstrong, Lloyd Nolan, William Harrigan, Regis Toomey; *D:* William Keighley. VHS, Beta $19.98 *MGM, CCB* 🐾🐾🐾½

G-Men Never Forget Moore, former stunt-man and future Lone Ranger, stars in this 12-part serial about FBI agents battling the bad guys. Lots of action. On two cassettes. *AKA:* Code 645.

1948 167m/B Clayton Moore, Roy Barcroft, Ramsay Ames, Drew Allen, Tommy Steele, Eddie Acuff; *D:* Fred Brannon, Yakima Canutt. VHS $29.98 *REP, MLB* 🐾🐾½

G-Men vs. the Black Dragon Reedited serial of "Black Dragon of Manzanar" stars Cameron as Fed who battles Asian Axis agents during WWII. Action-packed. 1943 244m/B Rod Cameron, Roland Got, Constance Worth, Nino Pipitone, Noel Cravat; *D:* William Witney. VHS $29.98 *REP, MED, MLB* 🐾🐾½

Gabriel Over the White House Part political satire, part fantasy, and completely fascinating. Huston is a venal politician, completely in thrall to his crooked cohorts, who manages to get elected President. While recuperating from an auto accident Huston thinks he's sees a vision of the Archangel Gabriel, who essentially tells him to change his crooked ways. From bought man Huston changes to righteous do-gooder, much to the dismay of his criminal companions, who'll stop at nothing to get rid of the man they think has simply gone insane. Huston gives a powerful performance in this decidedly oddball film. 1933 86m/B Walter Huston, Karen Morley, Arthur Byron, Franchot Tone, Dickie Moore, C. Henry Gordon, David Landau, Samuel S. Hinds, Jean Parker; *D:* Gregory La Cava. VHS $19.98 *MGM, MOV, BTV* 🐾🐾🐾

Gabriela A sultry romance develops between a Brazilian tavern keeper and the new cook he's just hired. Derived from Jorge Amado's novel. In Portuguese with English subtitles. 1984 (R) 102m/C *BR* Sonia Braga, Marcello Mastroianni, Nelson Xavier, Antonio Cantafora; *D:* Bruno Barreto; *M:* Antonio Carlos. VHS, Beta $19.98 *MGM, ING* 🐾🐾🐾

Gaby: A True Story The story of a woman with congenital cerebral palsy who triumphs over her condition with the help of family and loved ones, and ends up a college graduate and acclaimed author. Based on a true story. 1987 (R) 115m/C Rachel Levin, Liv Ullmann, Norma Aleandro, Robert Loggia, Lawrence Monoson, Robert Beltran, Tony Goldwyn; *D:* Luis Mandoki; *W:* Martin Salinas, Michael James Love; *M:* Maurice Jarre. VHS, Beta $79.95 *COL* 🐾🐾🐾

Gaiety Explores the lighter side of lion hunting. 1943 40m/B Antonio Moreno, Armida, Anne Ayars. VHS, Beta *NO* 🐾½

Gal Young 'Un Set during the Prohibition era, a rich, middle-aged woman living on her property in the Florida backwoods finds herself courted by a much younger man. She discovers she is being used to help him set up a moonshining business. Unsentimental story of a strong woman. Based on a Marjorie Kinnan Rawlings story. 1979 105m/C Dana Preu, David Peck, J. Smith; *D:* Victor Nunez. VHS, Beta $29.95 *ACA, ICA* 🐾🐾🐾

Galactic Gigolo An alien broccoli (yes, the vegetable) descends to earth on vacation, and discovers he's irresistible to Connecticut women. Must be something in the water. Amateurish effort intended as science-fiction satire, but there's more sleaze than humor. 1987 80m/C Carmine Capobianco, Debi Thibeault, Ruth Collins, Angela Nicholas, Frank Stewart; *D:* Gorman Bechard. Beta *NO Woof!*

Galaxina In the 31st century, a beautiful robot woman capable of human feelings is created. Stumbling parody of superspace fantasies features murdered Playmate Stratten in one of few film appearances.
1980 (R) 95m/C Dorothy Stratten, Avery Schreiber, Stephen Macht; **D:** William Sachs. **VHS, Beta** $59.95 *MCA ♂♂½*

Galaxy Invader Chaos erupts when an alien explorer crash lands his spacecraft in a backwoods area of the United States.
1985 (PG) 90m/C Richard Ruxton, Faye Tilles, Don Leifert. **VHS, Beta** $24.95 *CNG ♂*

Galaxy of Terror Astronauts sent to rescue a stranded spaceship get killed by vicious aliens. Big first: Moran (Joanie on "Happy Days") explodes. Inferior Corman-produced "Alien" imitation still manages to shock and displays generous gore. Followed by "Forbidden World." **AKA:** Mindwarp: An Infinity of Terror; Planet of Horrors.
1981 (R) 85m/C Erin Moran, Edward Albert, Ray Walston, Grace Zabriskie, Zalman King; **D:** B.D. Clark; **W:** Mark Siegler, B.D. Clark. **VHS, Beta** $9.98 *SUE ♂♂½*

Gallagher's Travels A screwball male/female reporting team chase an animal smuggling ring through the wilds of Australia.
1987 94m/C *AU* Ivar Kants, Joanne Samuel, Stuart Campbell, Jennifer Hagan; **D:** Michael Caulfield. **VHS, Beta** $79.95 *TWE ♂*

The Gallant Fool A man is wrongly accused of murder and tries to clear his name while eluding the law.
1933 57m/B Bob Steele, Arletta Duncan, George "Gabby" Hayes, John Elliott; **D:** Robert North Bradbury; **W:** Robert North Bradbury. **VHS** $11.95 *GPV ♂♂½*

The Gallant Hours Biography of Admiral "Bull" Halsey (Cagney) covers five weeks, October 18 through December 1, 1942, in the WWII battle of Guadalcanal in the South Pacific. Director Montgomery forgoes battle scenes to focus on the human elements in a war and what makes a great leader. Fine performance by Cagney.
1960 115m/B James Cagney, Dennis Weaver, Ward Costello, Richard Jaeckel, Les Tremayne, Robert Burton, Raymond Bailey, Karl Swenson, Harry Landers, James T. Goto; **D:** Robert Montgomery; **W:** Frank D. Gilroy. **VHS** $19.98 *MGM ♂♂♂*

Gallipoli History blends with the destiny of two friends as they become part of the legendary WWI confrontation between Australia and the German-allied Turks. A superbly filmed, gripping commentary on the wastes of war. Haunting score; excellent performances by Lee and a then-unknown Gibson. Remake of a lesser 1931 effort "Battle of Gallipoli."
1981 (PG) 111m/C *AU* Mel Gibson, Mark Lee, Bill Kerr, David Argue, Tim McKenzie, Robert Grubb; **D:** Peter Weir; **W:** David Williamson, Peter Weir. **VHS, Beta** $19.95 *PAR ♂♂♂♂*

Galloping Dynamite Early western based on a James Oliver Curwood story. A ranger avenges the death of his brother killed for gold.
1937 58m/B Kermit Maynard; **D:** Harry Fraser. **VHS, Beta** $19.95 *VDM ♂♂½*

The Galloping Ghost A 12-chapter serial starring football great "Red" Grange about big games, gambling, and underworld gangs. Grange is ousted from football when he's accused of throwing a game and he sets out to prove his innocence.
1931 226m/B Harold "Red" Grange, Dorothy Gulliver, Walter Miller, Tom Dugan; **D:** B. Reeves Eason. **VHS, Beta** $29.95 *VYY, VDM, NOS ♂♂½*

Galloping Romeo Steele stars as a heartthrob on horseback in this romantic Western. Steele had a hard time pulling off the light comedy he was asked to do, so clips from his previous films were used to pad the movie.
1933 59m/B Bob Steele, Doris Hill, George "Gabby" Hayes, Frank Ball, Ernie Adams; **D:** Robert North Bradbury; **W:** Harry Fraser. **VHS** $9.95 *GPV, MOV ♂½*

Galyon Soldier of fortune is recruited by an oil tycoon to find his daughter and son-in-law who have been kidnapped by terrorists in South America.
1977 (PG) 92m/C Stan Brock, Lloyd Nolan, Ina Balin. **VHS, Beta** *NO ♂*

Gambit Caine's first Hollywood film casts him as a burglar who develops a "Topkapi"-style scheme to steal a valuable statue with MacLaine as the lure and Lom as the equally devious owner. Once Caine's careful plan is put into operation, however, everything begins to unravel.
1966 109m/C Shirley MacLaine, Michael Caine, Herbert Lom, Roger C. Carmel; **D:** Ronald Neame; **W:** Alvin Sargent; **M:** Maurice Jarre. **VHS, Beta** $19.98 *MCA ♂♂½*

The Gamble A young man (Modine) seeks to rescue his father from gambling debts by wagering himself against a lustful countess (Dunaway). When he loses the bet, however, he flees and joins up with a runaway (Beals) with the countess and her henchmen in close pursuit.
1988 (R) 108m/C Matthew Modine, Jennifer Beals, Faye Dunaway; **D:** Carlo Vanzina. **VHS, Beta** $89.98 *PSM ♂♂*

Gamble on Love Woman returns to her father's Las Vegas casino and falls for the man who manages the gaming room.
1986 90m/C Beverly Garland; **D:** Jim Balden. **Beta** $14.95 *PSM ♂*

The Gambler College professor Axel Freed has a gambling problem so vast that it nearly gets him killed by his bookies. He goes to Las Vegas to recoup his losses and wins big, only to blow the money on stupid sports bets that get him deeper into trouble. Excellent character study of a compulsive loser on a downward spiral.
1974 (R) 111m/C James Caan, Lauren Hutton, Paul Sorvino, Burt Young, James Woods; **D:** Karel Reisz; **W:** James Toback. **VHS, Beta** $69.95 *PAR ♂♂♂*

The Gambler & the Lady A successful London-based gambler and casino owner endeavors to climb the social ladder by having an affair with a member of the British aristocracy. He not only has to contend with his jilted nightclub singer girlfriend but also with the gangsters who would like to take over his clubs. Dull direction and a mediocre script.
1952 72m/B *GB* Dane Clark, Naomi Chance, Kathleen Byron; **D:** Patrick Jenkins. **VHS, Beta** *NO ♂½*

The Gambler Returns: The Luck of the Draw You'll see lots of familiar western television stars as Rogers returns yet again as debonair gambler Brady Hawkes. This time he's on a cross country trip to San Francisco and the biggest card game around—only some varmints are out to stop him playing that first hand.
1993 180m/C Kenny Rogers, Reba McEntire, Rick Rossovich, Chuck Connors, Patrick Macnee, Linda Evans, James Drury, Mickey Rooney, Jere Burns, Clint Walker, Claude Akins, Gene Barry, Doug McClure, Hugh O'Brian, Brian Keith, Park Overall, Jack Kelly, David Carradine, Johnny Crawford, Marianne Rogers; **D:** Dick Lowry. **VHS** $89.95 *CAF ♂♂½*

Gambler's Choice A police lieutenant and his boyhood friend find themselves on opposite sides of the law in this crime drama. Even though both men are romantically involved with the same woman, their friendship remains intact.
1944 66m/B Chester Morris, Nancy Kelly, Russell Hayden, Sheldon Leonard, Lee Patrick, Lloyd Corrigan, Tom Dugan, Lyle Talbot, Charles Arnt; **D:** Frank McDonald. **VHS** $19.95 *NOS ♂♂*

The Gambling Samurai A samurai returns to his village to find it besieged by a ruthless government. Instead of attacking, he bides his time and works to undermine the government—finally achieving his revenge. In Japanese with English subtitles. **AKA:** Kunisada Chuji.
1960 101m/C *JP* Toshiro Mifune, Michiyo Aratama; **D:** Senkichi Taniguhi. **VHS, Beta** $59.95 *VDA ♂♂*

The Gambling Terror A cowboy goes after a mobster selling protection to hapless ranchers.
1937 53m/B Johnny Mack Brown, Charles "Blackie" King; **D:** Sam Newfield. **VHS, Beta** $19.95 *NOS, VCN, HEG ♂♂*

The Game Three friends arrange a puzzle-murder-mystery for a selected group of guilty people, with $1 million as the prize—and death for the losers.
1989 91m/C Tom Blair, Debbie Martin. **VHS, Beta** $69.95 *TWE ♂*

Game for Vultures Racial unrest in Rhodesia is the backdrop for this tale of a black revolutionary who fights racist sanctions. The noble topic suffers from stereotypes and oversimplification.
1986 (R) 113m/C *GB* Richard Harris, Richard Roundtree, Joan Collins, Ray Milland; **D:** James Fargo. **VHS, Beta** $19.98 *TWE ♂½*

The Game is Over A wealthy neglected wife falls in love with her grown stepson, causing her to divorce her husband and shatter her life. A good performance by Fonda, then Vadim's wife. Modern version of Zola's "La Curee."
1966 (R) 96m/C *FR* Jane Fonda, Peter McEnery, Michel Piccoli; **D:** Roger Vadim. **VHS, Beta** $69.95 *MED ♂♂½*

A Game of Crime Intriguing murder story with strong horror overtones.
1960 ?m/C John Blythe Barrymore Jr., Luisa Rivelli. **VHS** $15.95 *LOO ♂♂*

Game of Death Bruce Lee's final kung fu thriller about a young martial arts movie star who gets involved with the syndicate. Lee died halfway through the filming of this movie and it was finished with out-takes and a double. **AKA:** Goodbye Bruce Lee: His Last Game of Death; Bruce Lee's Game of Death.
1979 (R) 100m/C Bruce Lee, Dean Jagger, Kareem Abdul-Jabbar, Colleen Camp, Chuck Norris; **D:** Robert Clouse; **M:** John Barry. **VHS, Beta** $19.98 *FOX ♂♂*

The Game of Love Olin presides over Henry's bar, the lost and found of lonely hearts and lust, where people go to quench that deep thirst for love.
1990 (PG) 94m/C Ed Marinaro, Belinda Bauer, Ken Olin, Robert Rusler, Tracy Nelson, Max Gail, Janet Margolin, Brynn Thayer; **D:** Bobby Roth. **VHS** $19.95 *ACA ♂½*

Game of Seduction A murdering, womanizing playboy pursues a married woman and gets caught up in a treacherous cat-and-mouse game. Dubbed.
1986 81m/C Sylvia Kristel, Jon Finch, Nathalie Delon; **D:** Roger Vadim. **VHS, Beta** *NO ♂*

Game of Survival A young rebel warrior from another planet is sent to earth to battle six of the galaxy's most brutal warriors.
1989 85m/C Nikki Hill, Cindy Coatman, Roosevelt Miller Jr.; *D:* Armand Gazarian. VHS, Beta *NO* &

Gamera, the Invincible This Japanese monster flick features the ultimate nuclear super-turtle who flies around destroying cities and causing panic. First in the series of notoriously bad films, this one is cool in black and white and has some impressive special effects. Dubbed in English. *AKA:* Gamera; Gammera; Daikaiju Gamera.
1966 86m/B *JP* Brian Donlevy, Albert Dekker, Diane Findlay, John Baragrey, Dick O'Neill, Eiji Funakoshi; *D:* Noriaki Yuasa. VHS $9.99 *JFK*, SNC &&½

Gamera vs. Barugon The monstrous turtle returns to Earth from his outer space prison, now equipped with his famous leg-jets. He soon wishes he had stayed airborne, however, when he is forced to do battle with 130-foot lizard Barugon and his rainbow-melting ray. Tokyo and Osaka get melted in the process. *AKA:* Gamera Tai Barugon; Gambara vs. Barugon; The War of the Monsters.
1966 101m/C *JP* Kojiro Hongo, Kyoko Enami; *D:* Shigeo Tanaka. VHS, Beta $9.99 *JFK* &½

Gamera vs. Gaos Now fully the good guy, Gamera slugs it out with a bat-like critter named Gaos. Suspense rules the day when Gaos tries to put out the super turtle's jets with his built-in fire extinguisher but luckily for Earth, Gamera has a few tricks of his own up his shell. *AKA:* The Return of the Giant Monsters; Gamera vs. Gyaos; Boyichi and the Supermonster; Gamera Tai Gaos.
1967 87m/C *JP* Kojiro Hongo, Kichijiro Ueda, Naoyuki Abe; *D:* Noriaki Yuasa. VHS, Beta $9.99 *JFK* &½

Gamera vs. Guiron Gamera risks it all to take on an evil, spear-headed monster on a distant planet. Highlight is the sexy, leotard clad aliens who want to eat the little Earth kids' brains. *AKA:* Attack of the Monsters; Gamera Tai Guiron.
1969 88m/C *JP* Nobuhiro Kashima, Christopher Murphy, Miyuki Akiyama, Yuko Hamada, Eiji Funakoshi; *D:* Noriaki Yuasa. VHS, Beta $9.99 *JFK* &

Gamera vs. Zigra Gamera the flying turtle chose an ecological theme for this, his final movie. It seems that the alien Zigrans have come to Earth to wrest the planet from the hands of the pollutive humans who have nearly destroyed it. The aliens kill the staunch turtle, but the love and prayers of children revive him that he may defend Earth once more. *AKA:* Gamera Tai Shinkai Kaiju Jigara; Gamera vs. the Deep Sea Monster Zigra.
1971 91m/C *JP* Reiko Kasahara, Mikiko Tsubouchi, Koji Fujiyama, Arlene Zoellner, Gloria Zoellner; *D:* Noriaki Yuasa. VHS, Beta $9.99 *JFK* &

Games Girls Play The daughter of an American diplomat organizes a contest at a British boarding school to see which of her classmates can seduce important dignitaries. *AKA:* The Bunny Caper; Sex Play.
1975 90m/C Christina Hart, Jane Anthony, Jill Damas, Drina Pavlovic; *D:* Jack Arnold. VHS, Beta *NO* &½

The Gamma People A journalist discovers a Balkan doctor shooting children with gamma rays, creating an army of brainless zombies. Cult-renowned grade-Z tripe.
1956 83m/B *GB* Walter Rilla, Paul Douglas, Eva Bartok; *D:* John Gilling. VHS, Beta *NO* Woof!

Gandhi The biography of Mahatma Gandhi from the prejudice he encounters as a young attorney in South Africa, to his role as spiritual leader to the people of India and his use of passive resistance against the country's British rulers, and his eventual assassination. Kingsley is a marvel in his Academy Award-winning role and the picture is a generally riveting epic worthy of its eight Oscars.
1982 (PG) 188m/C *GB* Ben Kingsley, Candice Bergen, Edward Fox, John Gielgud, John Mills, Saeed Jaffrey, Trevor Howard, Ian Charleson, Roshan Seth, Athol Fugard, Martin Sheen, Daniel Day-Lewis, Rohini Hattangady; *D:* Richard Attenborough; *W:* John Briley; *M:* George Fenton. Academy Awards '82: Best Actor (Kingsley), Best Art Direction/Set Decoration, Best Cinematography, Best Costume Design, Best Director (Attenborough), Best Film Editing, Best Original Screenplay, Best Picture; Nominations: Best Makeup, Best Original Score; British Academy Awards '82: Best Actor (Kingsley), Best Director (Attenborough), Best Film, Best Supporting Actress (Hattangady); Golden Globe Awards '83: Best Actor—Drama (Kingsley), Best Director (Attenborough), Best Foreign Film, Best Screenplay; New York Film Critics Awards '82: Best Film. VHS, Beta $29.95 COL, BTV, HMV &&&&

Gang Bullets Mobster tries to continue his dirty systems in a new town, but finds the legal force incorruptible.
1938 62m/B Anne Nagel, Robert Kent, Charles Trowbridge, Morgan Wallace, J. Farrell MacDonald, Arthur Loft, John Merton; *D:* Lambert Hillyer. VHS, Beta $16.95 SNC &

Gang Busters Prisoners plan a breakout. Slow and uninteresting adaptation of the successful radio series. Filmed in Oregon.
1955 78m/B Myron Healey, Don Harvey, Sam Edwards, Frank Gerstle; *D:* Bill Karn. VHS $19.95 NOS, SNC &½

Gang Justice Low-budget melodrama finds sensitive Asian student Paul (Kim) battling racists at school and his crippled alcoholic father at home. Some martial arts fight scenes but this is amateur time.
1994 92m/C Joon Kim, Jonathan Gorman, Erik Estrada, Angel Dashek; *D:* Richard W. Park. VHS $89.95 AIP &

Gang War Low-budget gangster film with an all-back cast about two gangs fighting for control of the city's jukebox business.
1940 60m/B Ralph Cooper, Gladys Snyder, Reggie Fenderson, Lawrence Criner, Monte Hawley, Jesse C. Brooks, Maceo B. Sheffield; *D:* Leo Popkin. VHS $24.95 NOS, RXM &

Gang Wars There's a riot going on as Puerto Rican, Black, and Chinese gangs fight it out for control of the city. *AKA:* Devil's Express.
1975 (R) 82m/C Warhawk Tanzania, Larry Fleishman, Sam DeFazio, Wilfred Roldan, Elsie Roman, Sarah Nyrick; *D:* Barry Rosen. VHS $9.95 SUN &

Gangbusters Men battle crime in the city in this serial in thirteen episodes based on the popular radio series of the same name.
1938 253m/B Kent Taylor, Irene Hervey, Robert Armstrong. VHS, Beta $49.95 NOS, CAB, VCN &

The Gang's All Here Darro joins a trucking firm whose rigs are being run off the road and hijacked by a competitor. Features "Charlie Chan" regulars Luke and Moreland.
1941 63m/B Frankie Darro, Marcia Mae Jones, Jackie Moran, Mantan Moreland, Keye Luke; *D:* Jean Yarborough. VHS $19.95 NOS, RXM, MOV &½

Gangs, Inc. A woman is sent to prison for a hit-and-run accident, actually the fault of a wealthy playboy. When she learns his identity she vows revenge and turns to crime to achieve her evil ends. Okay thriller suffers from plot problems. Ladd has a minor role filmed before he became a star. *AKA:* Crimes, Inc.; Paper Bullets.
1941 72m/B Joan Woodbury, Lash LaRue, Linda Ware, John Archer, Vince Barnett, Alan Ladd; *D:* Phil Rosen. VHS, Beta $19.95 NOS, MRV, DVT &&

The Gangster Sullivan plays a small-time slum-bred hood who climbs to the top of the underworld, only to lose his gang because he allows his fears to get the better of him. (There's nothing to fear except when someone knows you're afeared.) Noir crimer with an interesting psychological perspective, though a bit sluggish at times.
1947 84m/B Barry Sullivan, Joan Lorring, Akim Tamiroff, Harry Morgan, John Ireland, Fifi d'Orsay, Shelley Winters; *D:* Gordon Wiles. VHS $14.98 FOX, FCT &&½

Gangster Wars A specially edited-for-video version of the television mini-series "The Gangster Chronicles." Based on fact, it deals with the growth of organized crime in America from the early days of this century, through the eyes of three ghetto kids who grow up to become powerful mobsters.
1981 121m/C Michael Nouri, Joe Penny, Brian Benben, Kathleen Lloyd, Madeleine Stowe, Robert Davi; *D:* Richard Sarafian. VHS, Beta $59.95 MCA &&

Gangsters City is ruled by the mob and nothing can stop their bloody grip except "The Special Squad."
1979 90m/C *IT* Michael Gazzo, Tony Page, Vicki Sue Robinson, Nai Bonet; *D:* Mac Ahlberg. VHS, Beta $39.95 VCD, HHE, MTX &

Gangster's Den A gang of renegades scare a woman out of buying a gold-laden piece of land and Billy the Kid comes to her rescue.
1945 56m/B Buster Crabbe, Kermit Maynard, Al "Fuzzy" St. John, Charles "Blackie" King; *D:* Sam Newfield. VHS, Beta $ VDM &

Gangster's Law A look at a seedy gangster's downfall. Filmed on location in Italy. Dubbed.
1986 89m/C Klaus Kinski, Maurice Poli, Susy Anderson, Max Delys; *D:* Siro Marcellini. VHS, Beta $69.95 TWE Woof!

Gangsters of the Frontier The people of Red Rock are forced to work in the town mines by two prison escapees until Ritter and his friends ride to the rescue. Part of the "Texas Ranger" series.
1944 56m/B Tex Ritter, Dave O'Brien; *D:* Elmer Clifton; *W:* Elmer Clifton. VHS, Beta $19.95 NOS, DVT, RXM &

Gangway Pat Wayne (Matthews), a London newspaper reporter, is mistaken for a jewel thief and kidnapped by gangsters aboard a New York-bound ocean liner. In the meantime, the real thief is aboard posing as a Hollywood actress (Blakeney), and it's up to Scotland Yard inspector Bob Deering (Mackay) to solve the crime. Matthews was considered by many to be the English equivalent of America's Eleanor Powell. Based on an original story by Dwight Taylor.
1937 90m/B *GB* Jessie Matthews, Barry Mackay, Olive Blakeney, Liane Ordeyne, Patrick Ludlow, Nat Pendleton, Noel Madison, Alastair Sim, Doris Rogers, Laurence Anderson, Bennie

Dorn; **D:** Sonnie Hale; **W:** Sonnie Hale, Lesser Samuels. **VHS** HEG ♪♪½

Ganjasaurus Rex Monster spoof about a giant green dinosaur emerging from the pot-laden hills of California. Maybe it's all in your head, man.
1987 (R) 100m/C Paul Bassis, Dave Fresh, Rosie Jones; **D:** Ursi Reynolds. **VHS, Beta $59.95** RHI ♪

Gappa the Trifibian Monster Researchers visiting a tropical island find a giant egg and take it back to Tokyo with them, dismaying the egg's giant monster parents. Dubbed. **AKA:** Daikyoju Gappa; Monster from a Prehistoric Planet.
1967 (PG) 90m/C JP **VHS, Beta $19.98** ORI ♪½

The Garbage Pail Kids Movie The disgusting youngsters, stars of bubblegum cards, make their first and last film appearance in this live action dud. The garbage is where it should be thrown.
1987 (PG) 100m/C Anthony Newley, MacKenzie Astin, Katie Barberi; **D:** Rod Amateau. **VHS, Beta $14.95** PAR, BAR, IME Woof!

Garbo Talks A dying eccentric's last request is to meet the reclusive screen legend Greta Garbo. Bancroft amusingly plays the dying woman whose son goes to extreme lengths in order to fulfill his mother's last wish.
1984 (PG-13) 104m/C Anne Bancroft, Ron Silver, Carrie Fisher, Catherine Hicks, Steven Hill, Howard da Silva, Dorothy Loudon, Harvey Fierstein, Hermione Gingold; **D:** Sidney Lumet; **M:** Cy Coleman. **VHS, Beta $19.98** MGM, FOX ♪♪

The Garden of Allah Dietrich finds hyper-romantic encounters in the Algerian desert with Boyer, but his terrible secret may doom them both. This early Technicolor production, though flawed, is an absolute must for Dietrich fans. Yuma, Ariz. substituted for the exotic locale.
1936 85m/C Marlene Dietrich, Charles Boyer, Basil Rathbone, Sir C. Aubrey Smith, Tilly Losch, Joseph Schildkraut, Henry Kleinbach (Brandon), John Carradine; **D:** Richard Boleslawski. **VHS $59.98** FOX ♪♪♪

The Garden of Delights A wicked black comedy about a millionaire, paralyzed and suffering from amnesia after a car accident. His horrendously greedy family tries to get him to remember and reveal his Swiss bank account number. Acclaimed; in Spanish with English subtitles.
1970 95m/C SP Jose Luis Lopez Vasquez, Lina Canelajas, Luchy Soto, Francisco Pierra, Charo Soriano; **D:** Carlos Saura. **VHS, Beta $29.95** HMV, CVC, FCT ♪♪♪

The Garden of Eden Milestone—whose "Two Arabian Nights" had won an Academy Award the previous year, and who went on to direct "All Quiet on the Western Front" and "Of Mice and Men"—directed this sophisticated ersatz Lubitsch sex comedy. Griffith, the so-called "Orchid Lady," is a young girl who dreams of diva-dom but falls deep into the underbelly of the seedy side of Budapest. With the aid of a fallen baroness, however, she finds her way to Monte Carlo and has her turn in the limelight. A handsome production designed by William Cameron Menzies, art director for "Gone With the Wind."
1928 115m/B Corrine Griffith, Louise Dresser, Charles Ray, Lowell Sherman; **D:** Lewis Milestone. **VHS, Beta, 8mm $19.95** NOS, VYY ♪♪♪

The Garden of the Finzi-Continis Acclaimed film by De Sica about an aristocratic Jewish family living in Italy under increasing Fascist oppression on the eve of WWII. The garden wall symbolizes the distance between the Finzi-Continis and the Nazi reality about to engulf them. Flawless acting and well-defined direction. Based on the novel by Giorgio Bassani, who collaborated on the script but later repudiated the film. Music by De Sica's son, Manuel. In Italian with English subtitles or dubbed. **AKA:** Il Giardino Del Finzi-Contini.
1971 (R) 90m/C IT Dominique Sanda, Helmut Berger, Lino Capolicchio, Fabio Testi, Romolo Valli; **D:** Vittorio De Sica; **W:** Cesare Zavattini; **M:** Manuel De Sica. Academy Awards '71: Best Foreign Language Film; Nominations: Best Adapted Screenplay; Berlin International Film Festival '71: Golden Berlin Bear; National Board of Review Awards '71: 5 Best Foreign Films of the Year. **VHS, Beta $39.98** LHV, IME, APD ♪♪♪♪

Gardens of Stone A zealous young cadet during the Vietnam War is assigned to the Old Guard patrol at Arlington Cemetery, and clashes with the patrol's older officers and various pacifist civilians. Falls short of the mark, although Jones turns in an excellent performance.
1987 (R) 112m/C James Caan, James Earl Jones, D.B. Sweeney, Anjelica Huston, Dean Stockwell, Lonette McKee, Mary Stuart Masterson, Bill Graham, Sam Bottoms, Casey Siemaszko, Laurence "Larry" Fishburne; **D:** Francis Ford Coppola; **M:** Carmine Coppola. **VHS, Beta $89.98** FOX ♪♪♪

Garringo Lawmen attempt to bring to justice a man who is intent on killing the soldiers responsible for his father's death.
1969 95m/C IT SP Anthony Steffen, Peter Lee Lawrence, Jose Bodalo; **D:** Rafael Romero Marchent. **VHS, Beta $44.95** MAD ♪♪

Gas This dog has tycoon Hayden buying up all the gas stations in town to create a crisis that will make him richer. Everyone in the cast wastes their time, especially Sutherland as a hip DJ reporting on the gas shortage.
1981 (R) 94m/C CA Donald Sutherland, Susan Anspach, Sterling Hayden, Peter Aykroyd, Howie Mandel, Helen Shaver; **D:** Les Rose; **W:** Dick Wolf. **VHS, Beta $79.95** PAR Woof!

Gas Food Lodging Saga casts Adams as Nora, a weary waitress in Laramie, New Mexico, trying her best to raise two teenaged daughters on her own. The daughters, Skye and Balk, are disillusioned about love and family. Balk's special friend is Darius, an eccentric window dresser, played by Leitch, Skye's brother. Nothing works out quite as intended but multi-dimensional characters, poignant situtations, and enormous emotional appeal highlight the directorial debut of Anders. Based on the Richard Peck novel "Don't Look and It Won't Hurt."
1992 (R) 100m/C Brooke Adams, Ione Skye, Fairuza Balk, James Brolin, Rob Knepper, Donovan Leitch, David Lansbury, Jacob Vargas, Chris Mulkey, Tiffany Anders; **D:** Allison Anders; **W:** Allison Anders; **M:** J. Mascis. **VHS $19.95** COL ♪♪♪

Gas Pump Girls Comedy about five lovely ladies who manage a gas station and use their feminine wiles to win the battle against a shady oil sheik.
1979 (R) 102m/C Kirsten Baker, Dennis Bowen, Huntz Hall, Steve Bond, Leslie King, Linda Lawrence; **D:** Joel Bender. **VHS, Beta** VES ♪½

Gas-s-s-s! A gas main leak in an Alaskan defense plant kills everyone beyond thirty-something and the post-apocalyptic pre-boomer survivors are left to muddle their way through the brume. Trouble is, AIP edited the

heck out of the movie, much to Corman's chagrin, and the result is a truncated comedy; Corman was so displeased, in fact, he left to create New World studios. **AKA:** Gas-s-s-s... or, It May Become Necessary to Destroy the World in Order to Save It.
1970 (PG) 79m/C Robert Corff, Elaine Giftos, Pat Patterson, George Armitage, Alex Wilson, Ben Vereen, Cindy Williams, Bud Cort, Talia Shire, Country Joe & the Fish; **D:** Roger Corman. **VHS, Beta** NO ♪♪½

Gaslight A forgotten British classic that fell victim to the American production of the same title and theme that was filmed only five years later. Set in late Victorian London, Wynyard is the rich innocent married to the calculating Walbrook, who slowly tries driving his bride insane in order to discover some hidden family jewels. She comes under the protection of a Scotland Yard detective (Pettingell) who suspects Walbrook has already murdered once. An outstandingly eerie psychological thriller. Based on the play "Angel Street" by Patrick Hamilton. **AKA:** Angel Street.
1939 84m/C GB Anton Walbrook, Diana Wynyard, Frank Pettingell, Cathleen Cordell; **D:** Thorold Dickinson. **VHS $29.95** FCT ♪♪♪½

Gaslight Lavish remake of the 1939 film, based on the Patrick Hamilton play "Angel Street." A man tries to drive his beautiful wife insane while searching for priceless jewels. Her only clue to his evil acts is the frequent dimming of their gaslights. A suspenseful Victorian era mystery. Lansbury's film debut, as the tarty maid. **AKA:** The Murder in Thorton Square.
1944 114m/B Charles Boyer, Ingrid Bergman, Joseph Cotten, Angela Lansbury, Terry Moore, May Whitty, Barbara Everest, Emil Rameau, Edmund Breon, Halliwell Hobbes, Tom Stevenson; **D:** George Cukor. Academy Awards '44: Best Actress (Bergman), Best Interior Decoration; Nominations: Best Actor (Boyer), Best Black and White Cinematography, Best Picture, Best Screenplay, Best Supporting Actress (Lansbury); Golden Globe Awards '45: Best Actress—Drama (Bergman). **VHS, Beta $19.98** MGM, BTV, VEC ♪♪♪½

The Gate Kids generally like to explore and Dorff and Tripp are no exception. When a large hole is exposed in their backyard, it would be a childhood sin not to see what's in it, right? What they don't know is that this hole is actually a gateway to and from Hell. The terror they unleash includes more than just run-of-the-mill demons. Good special effects. Followed by "Gate 2."
1987 (PG-13) 85m/C Christa Denton, Stephen Dorff, Louis Tripp; **D:** Tibor Takacs. **VHS, Beta $14.98** LIV, VES ♪♪

Gate 2 Tripp returns in his role as Terry, a young student of demonology in this lame sequel to "The Gate." Terry and a few of his teen buddies call up a group of demons that have been confined behind a gate for billions of years. The demons are used to grant modest wishes, but the wishes end up having very evil effects. Incredibly weak plot saved only by the special monster effects, which include live action and puppetry.
1992 (R) 90m/C Louis Tripp, Simon Reynolds, Pamela Segall, James Villemaire, Neil Munro, James Kidnie, Andrea Ladanyi; **D:** Tibor Takacs; **W:** Michael Nankin. **VHS** COL ♪½

Gate of Hell Set in 12th-century Japan. A warlord desires a beautiful married woman and seeks to kill her husband to have her. However, he accidentally kills her instead. Filled with shame and remorse, the warlord abandons his life to seek solace as a monk. Heavily awarded and critically acclaimed; the first Japanese film to use color photography.

In Japanese with English subtitles. *AKA:* Jigokumen.
1954 89m/C *JP* Kazuo Hasegawa, Machiko Kyo; *D:* Teinosuke Kinugasa. **VHS, Beta, 8mm $24.95** *VYY, SUE, DVT* 🎬🎬🎬½

Gates of Hell Salem, Massachusetts, must battle the risen dead in this gorefest that tried to disguise itself under many other titles. *AKA:* Paura Nella Citta Dei Morti Viventi; City of the Living Dead; The Fear; Twilight of the Dead; Fear in the City of the Living Dead.
1983 90m/C Christopher George, Janet Agren, Katherine MacColl, Robert Sampson; *D:* Lucio Fulci. **VHS, Beta** *IGP Woof!*

The Gathering A dying man seeks out the wife and family he has alienated for a final Christmas gathering. James Poe authored this well-acted holiday tearjerker that won the 1977-78 Emmy for outstanding TV drama special.
1977 94m/C Ed Asner, Maureen Stapleton, Lawrence Pressman, Stephanie Zimbalist, Bruce Davison, Gregory Harrison, Veronica Hamel, Gail Strickland; *D:* Randal Kleiser; *M:* John Barry. **VHS, Beta $49.95** *WOV* 🎬🎬½

A Gathering of Eagles Hudson portrays a hard-nosed Air Force colonel during peacetime whose British wife must adjust to being a military spouse.
1963 115m/C Rock Hudson, Rod Taylor, Mary Peach, Barry Sullivan, Kevin McCarthy, Henry Silva, Leif Erickson; *D:* Delbert Mann; *M:* Jerry Goldsmith. **VHS** *MGM* 🎬🎬½

The Gathering: Part 2 Sequel in which a widow has a Christmas reunion with her family, but conflict arises when she introduces a new man in her life. Not as effective as the original, also made for TV.
1979 98m/C Maureen Stapleton, Efrem Zimbalist Jr., Jameson Parker, Bruce Davison, Lawrence Pressman, Gail Strickland, Veronica Hamel; *D:* Charles S. Dubin. **VHS** *TTC* 🎬🎬

The Gathering Storm Based on the first book of memoirs from Sir Winston Churchill, this drama examines the pre-WWII years.
1974 72m/C Richard Burton, Virginia McKenna, Ian Bannen; *D:* Herbert Wise. **Beta $14.95** *PSM* 🎬🎬

The Gatling Gun Poor tale of the Cavalry, Apache Indians, and renegades all after the title weapon. *AKA:* King Gun.
1972 (PG) 93m/C Guy Stockwell, Woody Strode, Patrick Wayne, Robert Fuller, Barbara Luna, John Carradine, Pat Buttram, Phil Harris; *D:* Robert Gordon. **VHS** *HHE* 🎬½

Gator Sequel to "White Lightning" (1973) follows the adventures of Gator (Reynolds), who is recruited to gather evidence to convict a corrupt political boss who also happens to be his friend. Reynolds in his good ole' boy role with lots of chase scenes. Talk show host Michael Douglas made his film debut in the role of the governor. First film Reynolds directed.
1976 (PG) 116m/C Burt Reynolds, Jerry Reed, Lauren Hutton, Jack Weston, Alice Ghostley, Dub Taylor; *D:* Burt Reynolds; *W:* William W. Norton Sr.; *M:* Charles Bernstein. **VHS, Beta $14.95** *MGM, FOX* 🎬🎬

Gator Bait The Louisiana swamp is home to the beautiful Desiree, and woe be unto any man who threatens her family. Aims to please fans of the raunchy and violent. Followed by an equally vile sequel.
1973 (R) 91m/C Claudia Jennings, Clyde Ventura, Bill Thurman, Janet Baldwin; *D:* Ferd Sebastian, Beverly Sebastian; *W:* Ferd Sebastian, Beverly Sebastian. **VHS, Beta $19.95** *PAR* 🎬½

Gator Bait 2: Cajun Justice A city girl comes to the Louisiana swamp and turns violent in an effort to exact revenge on the men who have been tormenting her.
1988 (R) 94m/C Jan MacKenzie, Tray Loren, Paul Muzzcat, Brad Kepnick, Jerry Armstrong, Ben Sebastian; *D:* Ferd Sebastian, Beverly Sebastian; *W:* Ferd Sebastian, Beverly Sebastian. **VHS, Beta $19.95** *PAR* 🎬

The Gauntlet A cop is ordered to Las Vegas to bring back a key witness for an important trial—but the witness turns out to be a beautiful prostitute being hunted by killers. Violence-packed action.
1977 (R) 111m/C Clint Eastwood, Sondra Locke, Pat Hingle, Bill McKinney; *D:* Clint Eastwood; *W:* Michael Butler. **VHS, Beta $19.98** *WAR, TLF* 🎬🎬

The Gay Divorcee Astaire pursues Rogers to an English seaside resort, where she mistakes him for the hired correspondent in her divorce case. Based on the musical play "The Gay Divorce" by Dwight Taylor and Cole Porter. The title was slightly changed for the movie because of protests from the Hays Office. 🎵Don't Let It Bother You; A Needle in a Haystack; Let's K-nock K-nees; Night and Day; The Continental. *AKA:* The Gay Divorce.
1934 107m/B Fred Astaire, Ginger Rogers, Edward Everett Horton, Eric Blore, Alice Brady, Erik Rhodes, Betty Grable; *D:* Mark Sandrich. Academy Awards '34: Best Song ("The Continental"); Nominations: Best Interior Decoration, Best Picture, Best Sound, Best Score. **VHS, Beta $14.98** *MED, TTC* 🎬🎬🎬

The Gay Lady Light romantic comedy set in the 1890s about an actress who climbs to stardom in London theater and winds up marrying into the aristocracy. Look for Christopher Lee and Roger Moore in early bit parts. *AKA:* Trottie True.
1949 95m/C *GB* Jean Kent, James Donald, Hugh Sinclair, Lana Morris, Bill Owen, Michael Medwin, Andrew Crawford; *D:* Brian Desmond Hurst. **VHS** *MOV, UNI* 🎬🎬½

Gay Purr-ee Delightful tale of feline romance in the City of Lights. For all ages.
1962 85m/C *D:* Abe Levitow; *W:* Chuck Jones; *M:* Harold Arlen; *V:* Judy Garland, Robert Goulet, Red Buttons, Hermione Gingold, Mel Blanc. **VHS $14.95** *WAR, FCT, WTA* 🎬🎬

The Gay Ranchero Rogers, without Dale Evans, in an average tale of old west meets new crooks. Rogers is the sheriff who foils gangsters trying to take over an airport. The action doesn't stop him from singing a duet with leading lady Frazee on "Wait'll I Get My Sunshine in the Moonlight."
1942 55m/B Roy Rogers, Andy Devine, Tito Guizar, Jane Frazee, Estelita Rodriguez; *D:* William Witney. **VHS, Beta $9.99** *NOS, VCN, CAB* 🎬🎬

The Gazebo Wacky comedy about a TV writer who is being blackmailed by someone who has nude photos of his Broadway star wife. He decides murder is the only solution to this problem. Reynolds sings "Something Called Love." Based on a play by Alec Coppel from a story by Myra and Alec Coppel.
1959 102m/B Glenn Ford, Debbie Reynolds, Carl Reiner, John McGiver, Doro Merande, Bert Freed, Martin Landau; *D:* George Marshall; *W:* George Wells. **VHS $19.98** *MGM* 🎬🎬🎬

Geek Maggot Bingo It's too bad director Zed waited until mid-"Bingo" to post a sign warning "Leave Now, It Isn't Going Get Any Better!" Conceived by the New York underground's don of the "Cinema of Transgression" to be an off-the-rack cult classic, this horror spoof is too long on in-jokes and short on substance to earn its

number in the cult hall of fame. It does, however, boast Death as Scumbalina the vampire queen and Hell as a punk cowboy crooner (before alternative country hit the airwaves). TV horror-meister Zacherle narrates. *AKA:* The Freak From Suckweasel Mountain.
1983 70m/C Richard Hell, Donna Death, John Zacherle; *D:* Nick Zedd. **VHS $39.99** *MWF, MOV* 🎬

Geheimakte WB1 Historical drama centering on the invention of the U-boat by Sergeant Wilhelm Bauer during Denmark's WWII blockade of the ports of Schleswig-Holstein. In German with no subtitles. *AKA:* Secret Paper WB1.
1942 91m/B *GE* Alexander Golling; *D:* Herbert Selpin. **VHS, Beta $35.95** *IHF* 🎬🎬

A Geisha Miyoharu (Kogure) is a passive elderly geisha who agrees to train the naive young Eiko (Wakao) in her new role. But Eiko discovers her romantic notions of the geisha life are far from it's modern reality. Poignant look at the changing status of the geisha in Japan after WWII and the country's social upheavals. In Japanese with English subtitles. *AKA:* Gion Bayashi; Gion Festival Music.
1953 86m/B *JP* Michiyo Kogure, Ayako Wakao, Seizaburo Kawazu, Chieko Naniwa, Eitaro Shindo; *D:* Kenji Mizoguchi; *W:* Yoshikata Yoda; *M:* Ichiro Saito. **VHS $79.95** *NYF, FCT, BTV* 🎬🎬🎬

The Geisha Boy Jerry is a floundering magician who joins the USO and tours the Far East. His slapstick confrontations with the troupe leader and an officer who dreams of attending his own funeral provide hearty laughs, plus Lewis finds romance with a Japanese widow after her son claims him as a father. Pleshette's film debut, with an appearance by the Los Angeles Dodgers.
1958 98m/C Jerry Lewis, Marie McDonald, Sessue Hayakawa, Barton MacLane, Suzanne Pleshette, Nobu McCarthy; *D:* Frank Tashlin. **VHS $14.95** *PAR* 🎬🎬

Gemini Affair Two women go to Hollywood to become rich and famous but end up being very disappointed.
198? 88m/C Marta Kristen, Kathy Kersh, Anne Seymour. **VHS, Beta $49.95** *UNI* 🎬

Gene Autry Matinee Double Feature #1 Includes "Blue Canadian Rockies" (1952), where Autry must investigate a series of murders, and "Last of the Pony Riders" (1953), in which the final days of the pony express yield a sinister conspiracy.
1953 117m/C Gene Autry; *D:* George Archainbaud. **VHS $39.98** *NO* 🎬

Gene Autry Matinee Double Feature #2 An exciting western double feature: A cowboy goes after the man who stole his rodeo winnings in "Melody Trail" and a territorial ranger investigates a series of Indian raids in "Winning of the West."
1953 117m/B Gene Autry, Champion, Smiley Burnette, Alan Bridge; *D:* George Archainbaud, Joseph Kane. **VHS, Beta $39.98** *NO* 🎬

Gene Autry Matinee Double Feature #3 Gene stars in "Prairie Moon," in which he teaches some tough kids a lesson about life, and "On Top of Old Smokey," which sees a young woman trying to save her small town.
1953 113m/B Gene Autry, Smiley Burnette; *D:* George Archainbaud, Ralph Staub. **VHS, Beta $39.98** *NO* 🎬

The Gene Krupa Story The story of the famous jazz drummer and his career plunge after a drug conviction. Krupa recorded the soundtrack, mimed by Mineo, who was too young for a convincing portrayal. Gavin McLeod (of "Love Boat" fame) has a small part as Mineo's dad.

1959 101m/B Sal Mineo, James Darren, Susan Kohner, Susan Oliver, Anita O'Day, Red Nichols; **D:** Don Weis. VHS, Beta $19.95 COL, FCT ♂♂½

The General Keaton's masterpiece and arguably the most formally perfect and funniest of silent comedies. Concerns a plucky Confederate soldier who single-handedly retrieves a pivotal train from Northern territory. Full of eloquent man-vs-machinery images and outrageous sight gags. Remade as "The Great Locomotive Chase" in 1956 with Fess Parker.

1927 78m/B Buster Keaton, Marion Mack, Glen Cavender, Jim Farley, Joe Keaton; **D:** Buster Keaton, Clyde Bruckman. VHS, Beta, 8mm $24.95 VYY, HHT, NOS ♂♂♂♂

The General Died at Dawn A clever, atmospheric suspense film about an American mercenary in Shanghai falling in love with a beautiful spy as he battles a fierce Chinese warlord who wants to take over the country. Playwright-to-be Odets' first screenplay; he, O'Hara and '30s gossip hound Skolsky have cameos as reporters.

1936 93m/B Gary Cooper, Madeleine Carroll, Akim Tamiroff, Dudley Digges, Porter Hall, William Frawley, Philip Ahn; **Cameos:** John O'Hara, Clifford Odets, Sidney Skolsky; **D:** Lewis Milestone; **W:** Clifford Odets. VHS, Beta $14.98 MCA ♂♂♂

The General Line Eisenstein's classic pro-Soviet semi-documentary about a poor farm woman who persuades her village to form a cooperative. Transgresses its party-line instructional purpose by vivid filmmaking. The director's last silent film. **AKA:** The Old and the New.

1929 90m/B RU Marfa Lapkina; **D:** Sergei Eisenstein. VHS, Beta $24.95 NOS, MRV, DVT ♂♂♂♂

General Spanky The only feature "Our Gang" comedy goofed by transplanting them to a Civil War milieu popular at the time. Confederate kids Spanky and Alfalfa play soldier, ultimately outsmarting Union troops. The rascals are still funny sometimes, but Buckwheat's role as an eager slave is disturbing today.

1936 73m/B George "Spanky" McFarland, Phillips Holmes, Ralph Morgan, Irving Pichel, Rosina Lawrence, Billie "Buckwheat" Thomas, Carl "Alfalfa" Switzer, Louise Beavers; **D:** Fred Newmeyer. VHS $19.98 MGM, FCT ♂♂

Generale Della Rovere A WWII black marketeer is forced by the Nazis to go undercover in a local prison. To find out who the resistance leaders are, he poses as a general. But when prisoners begin to look to him for guidance, he finds the line between his assumed role and real identity diminished, leading to a tragic conclusion. Acclaimed film featuring a bravura lead performance by veteran director De Sica. In Italian with English subtitles. **AKA:** Il Generale Della-Rovere.

1960 139m/B IT Vittorio De Sica, Otto Messmer, Sandra Milo; **D:** Roberto Rossellini. VHS, Beta $29.95 NOS, CVC, HHT ♂♂♂½

A Generation During WWII, a young man escapes from the Warsaw Ghetto and finds his way to the Polish Resistance. He falls in love with the leader of the local group and finds the courage to fight for his freedom. Strong directorial debut from Wajda. Par 1 of his "War Trilogy," followed by "Kanal" and "Ashes and Diamonds." Scripted by Czeszko from his novel "Pokolenie." In Polish with English subtitles.

1954 90m/B PL Tadeusz Lomnicki, Ursula Modrzynska, Zbigniew Cybulski, Roman Polanski; **D:** Andrzej Wajda; **W:** Bohdan Czeszko. VHS $24.95 FCT, HMV, PME ♂♂♂

Generation A very pregnant bride informs everyone she'll give birth at home without doctors, and creates a panic. Based on the Broadway play by William Goodhart. **AKA:** A Time For Caring.

1969 109m/C David Janssen, Kim Darby, Carl Reiner, Peter Duel, Andrew Prine, James Coco, Sam Waterston; **D:** George Schaefer; **W:** William Goodhart; **M:** Dave Grusin. VHS, Beta $69.98 SUE ♂♂

Generations: Mind Control-From the Future Max Lang has lost all self-control and is being driven by evil forces beyond time, forced to kill while fleeing total extinction.

1980 54m/C VHS, Beta BEI ♂

Genevieve A 1904 Darracq roadster is the title star of this picture which spoofs "classic car" owners and their annual rally from London to Brighton. Two married couples challenge each other to a friendly race which becomes increasingly intense as they near the finish line.

1953 86m/C GB John Gregson, Dinah Sheridan, Kenneth More, Kay Kendall; **D:** Henry Cornelius; **M:** Larry Adler. Academy Awards '54 Nominations: Best Story & Screenplay, Best Original Score; British Academy Awards '53: Best Film; Golden Globe Awards '55: Best Foreign Film. VHS, Beta LCA ♂♂♂

Genie of Darkness The ashes of Nostradamus himself are retrieved in a bid to destroy his vampiric descendent. Edited from a Mexican serial; if you were able to sit through this one, look for "Curse of Nostradamus" and "The Monster Demolisher."

1960 ?m/B MX German Robles; **D:** Frederick Curiel. VHS $16.95 SNC, NOS, LOO ♂

Gente Violenta A crook who steals a million dollars worth of diamonds has to flee from both the police and his old gang.

1987 90m/C MX Armando Silvestre, Antonio De Hudd, Rebeca Silva, Victor Junco. VHS, Beta $58.95 MAD ♂♂

Gentle Giant An orphaned bear is taken in by a boy and his family and grows to be a 750 pound giant who must be returned to the wild. "Gentle Ben" TV series was derived from this feature.

1967 93m/C Dennis Weaver, Vera Miles, Ralph Meeker, Clint Howard, Huntz Hall; **D:** James Neilson. VHS $14.98 REP ♂♂

Gentle Savage When an Indian is wrongly accused of raping and beating a white woman, the white community seeks revenge. The vengeful mob, led by the victim's step-father, is unaware that it's really their ringleader who is responsible for the crime. When the accused's brother is slain, the Indian community retaliates. Violent but well-crafted. **AKA:** Camper John.

1973 (R) 85m/C William Smith, Gene Evans, Barbara Luna, Joe Flynn; **D:** Sean McGregor. VHS $29.95 LIV ♂♂½

Gentleman Bandit So-so drama about Father Bernard Pagano, a Boston priest mistakenly arrested as a stickup artist. Based on a true story. Made for television.

1981 96m/C Ralph Waite, Julie Bovasso, Jerry Zaks, Joe Grifasi, Estelle Parsons, Tom Aldredge; **D:** Jonathan Kaplan. VHS, Beta $59.95 MTI ♂♂

The Gentleman from California The dashing son of a Mexican landowner returns home and finds his people's land stolen from them by greedy tax collectors. **AKA:** The Californian.

1937 56m/B Ricardo Cortez, Marjorie Weaver, Katherine DeMille; **D:** Gus Meins. VHS, Beta, 8mm $19.95 VYY ♂

Gentleman from Dixie After LaRue is released from prison, he looks to change his life by joining his brother on a farm and seeking revenge on the man who put him in the pokey.

1941 61m/B Jack LaRue, Marian Marsh, Clarence Muse, Mary Ruth, Robert Kellard, John Holland, Herbert Rawlinson; **D:** Al Herman. VHS $19.99 MOV ♂♂

Gentleman from Texas Ropin', ridin', and romance figure in this less than dramatic oater.

1946 55m/B Johnny Mack Brown, Raymond Hatton, Claudia Drake, Reno Blair, Christine McIntyre; **D:** Lambert Hillyer. VHS $19.95 NOS, DVT ♂

Gentleman Jim A colorful version of the life of oldtime heavyweight boxing great Jim Corbett, transformed from a typical Warner Bros. bio-pic by director Walsh into a fun-loving, anything-for-laughs donnybrook. Climaxes with Corbett's fight for the championship against the great John L. Sullivan. One of Flynn's most riotous performances.

1942 104m/B Errol Flynn, Alan Hale, Alexis Smith, Jack Carson, Ward Bond, Arthur Shields, William Frawley; **D:** Raoul Walsh. VHS, Beta $19.98 MGM, FOX ♂♂♂½

The Gentleman Killer A man-with-no-name clears a ravaged border town of murdering bandits.

1978 95m/C Anthony Steffen, Silvia Solar. VHS, Beta $49.95 UNI ♂

Gentleman's Agreement A magazine writer (Peck) looks for a new angle for an article on anti-Semitism by pretending to be Jewish. His new identity pervades his life in unexpected ways, almost destroys his relationships, but contributes to the success of his magazine series. This movie was Hollywood's first major attack on anti-Semitism. Controversial in its day, yet still timely.

1947 118m/B Gregory Peck, Dorothy McGuire, John Garfield, Celeste Holm, Anne Revere, June Havoc, Albert Dekker, Jane Wyatt, Dean Stockwell, Nicholas Joy; **D:** Elia Kazan; **W:** Moss Hart. Academy Awards '47: Best Director (Kazan), Best Picture, Best Supporting Actress (Holm); Nominations: Best Actress (McGuire); Academy Awards '47: Best Actor (Peck), Best Film Editing, Best Screenplay, Best Supporting Actress (Revere). VHS $19.98 FXV, BTV, JCF ♂♂♂

Gentlemen Prefer Blondes Amusing satire involving two show-business girls from Little Rock trying to make it big in Paris. Seeking rich husbands or diamonds, their capers land them in police court. Monroe plays Lorelei Lee, Russell is her sidekick. Despite an occasionally slow plot, the music, comedy, and performances are great fun. Film version of a Broadway adaption of a story by Anita Loos. Followed by (but without Monroe) "Gentlemen Marry Brunettes." ♪♫ (Two) Little Girl(s) From Little Rock; Bye, Bye Baby; Ain't There Anyone Here For Love?; When Love Goes Wrong; Diamonds Are A Girl's Best Friend.

1953 91m/C Marilyn Monroe, Jane Russell, Charles Coburn, Elliott Reid, Tommy Noonan, George Winslow; **D:** Howard Hawks. VHS, Beta $14.98 FOX ♂♂♂

Genuine Risk Gorgeous young woman turns off her crime boss boyfriend bigtime when she seduces his bodyguard. Genuine tripe.

1989 (R) 89m/C Terence Stamp, Michelle Johnson, Peter Berg, M.K. Harris; **D:** Kurt Voss; **W:** Kurt Voss. VHS $89.95 COL ♂½

George! A carefree bachelor takes his girlfriend and his 250-pound St. Bernard on a trip to the Swiss Alps where he proves that a dog is not always man's best friend.
1970 (G) 87m/C Marshall Thompson, Jack Mullaney, Inge Schoner; *D:* Wallace C. Bennett; *W:* Wallace C. Bennett. VHS, Beta $39.95 *VCI* ♪♪ ½

George Balanchine's The Nutcracker Pas de deux redeux. Tchaikovsky's classic ballet about the magic of Christmas and a little girl (Cohen) who dreams on Christmas Eve that she is in an enchanted kingdom. Culkin lamely grins through his wooden performance as the Nutcracker Prince, but the talent of the Sugarplum Fairy (Kistler) and the other dancers is such that conventional camera techniques sometimes fail to keep up with their exacting moves. Adapted from the 1816 book by E.T.A. Hoffmann. *AKA:* The Nutcracker.
1993 (G) 93m/C Macaulay Culkin, Jessica Lynn Cohen, Bart Robinson Cook, Darci Kistler, Damian Woetzel, Kyra Nichols, Wendy Whelan, Gen Horiuchi, Margaret Tracey, New York City Ballet; *D:* Emile Ardolino; *W:* Susan Cooper; *M:* Piotr Ilich Tchaikovsky. VHS *NYR* ♪♪ ½

George Carlin: Doin' It Again When this unassuming comic opens his mouth, expect to hear some of the filthiest routines on the stand-up circuit. Should appeal to the true Carlin fanatic and the shock-hungry. Includes the sketches "Rape Can Be Funny," "Feminist Blowjob," and "I Love My Dog."
1994 60m/C *D:* Rocco Urbisci; *W:* George Carlin; *Performed by:* George Carlin. VHS $39.95 *COL* ♪♪ ½

George Carlin: Jammin' in New York Carlin as social critic in this stand-up performance which takes devastating aim at the government, male sexuality, the military, golfers, yellow ribbons, the upper class, eating disorders, the news media, environmentalists, and average Americans.
1993 59m/C VHS $39.95 *COL* ♪♪ ½

The George McKenna Story Washington stars as the newly appointed principal of George Washington High in Los Angeles. The school is located in South Central, a gang and drug-infested war zone where the students are armed for their own protection. The situation appears hopeless but McKenna refuses to give up. Based on a true story. Made for television.
1986 95m/C Denzel Washington, Lynn Whitfield, Akosua Busia, Richard Masur; *D:* Eric Laneuville; *W:* Charles Eric Johnson; *M:* Herbie Hancock. VHS $79.95 *PSM* ♪♪ ½

George Washington Bostwick stars as the father of our country in this made for television adaptation of James Thomas Flexner's biography. The destitute young Washington develops a close friendship with the wealthy Will Fairfax (Dukes), who provides him with the support to pursue his dreams, even though Washington has secretly fallen in love with Sally (Smith), Will's flirtatious wife. George himself has married the widowed Martha (Duke) and begins his military career, leading the American colonies against the Brits in the Revolutionary War. On three cassettes.
1984 398m/C Barry Bostwick, David Dukes, Jaclyn Smith, Patty Duke, Hal Holbrook, Lloyd Bridges, Jose Ferrer, Trevor Howard, Richard Kiley, James Mason, Clive Revill, Robert Stack; *W:* Richard Fielder. VHS, Beta *WAR* ♪♪ ½

George Washington Slept Here Hilarious side-splitter about a couple who moves from their Manhattan apartment to an old, broken-down country home in Connecticut. It's one catastrophe after another as the couple tries to renovate their home and deal with a greedy neighbor. Based on the play by George S. Kaufman and Moss Hart.
1942 93m/B Jack Benny, Ann Sheridan, Charles Coburn, Percy Kilbride, Hattie McDaniel, William Tracy; *D:* William Keighley. VHS $19.98 *MGM* ♪♪♪

George Washington: The Forging of a Nation Sequel to the "George Washington" miniseries finds Bostwick and Duke reprising their roles as George and Martha. Unfortunately, the later part of Washington's life isn't nearly as exciting.
1986 208m/C Barry Bostwick, Patty Duke, Penny Fuller, Jeffrey Jones, Richard Bekins; *D:* William A. Graham; *M:* Bruce Broughton. VHS $29.98 *MGM* ♪♪ ½

George White's Scandals A lightweight musical comedy look at the show biz world and why the show must go on. Based on White's Broadway extravaganzas. Jazz numbers by Gene Krupa and his band. Preceded by "George White's Scandals" of 1934 and 1935. ♪Bolero in the Jungle; E.H.S.; Leave Us Leap; I Want to be a Drummer in the Band; How Did You Get Out of My Dreams?; I Wake Up in the Morning; Who Killed Vaudeville?; Scandals; Liza; Os Pintinhos No Perreiro; Wishing; Life is Just a Bowl of Cherries; Bouquet and Lace.
1945 95m/B Joan Davis, Jack Haley, Jane Greer, Phillip Terry, Margaret Hamilton, Martha Holliday; *D:* Felix Feist. VHS, Beta $39.98 *CCB* ♪♪

George's Island When young George is placed with the worst foster parents in the world, his eccentric grandfather helps him escape. They wind up on Oak's Island, where legend has it, Captain Kidd's ghost and buried treasure reside. They soon find out the legends are true!
1991 (PG) 89m/C Ian Bannen, Sheila McCarthy, Maury Chaykin, Nathaniel Moreau, Vicki Ridler, Brian Downey, Gary Reineke; *D:* Paul Donovan; *W:* J. William Ritchie; *M:* Marty Simon. VHS $19.95 *COL, NLC* ♪♪♪

Georgia Tough lawyer Nina Bailey (Davis) explores her past when she begins a search for information on her biological mother, Georgia White, a photographer who drowned herself years before. Only Nina has no idea about the Pandora's box of secrets she's about to unleash. Frequent flashbacks to Georgia's mysterious life and death (Davis well plays both roles).
1987 90m/C *AU* Judy Davis, Julia Blake, John Bach; *D:* Ben Lewin. VHS $89.98 *ORI, FXL* ♪♪

Georgia, Georgia Sands is a black entertainer on tour in Sweden who falls for a white photographer. Her traveling companion, who hates whites, takes drastic action to separate the lovers. Poor acting, script, and direction. Based on a book by Maya Angelou.
1972 (R) 91m/C Diana Sands, Dirk Benedict, Minnie Gentry; *D:* Stig Bjorkman; *W:* Maya Angelou. VHS, Beta $59.95 *PSM* ♪ ½

Georgy Girl Redgrave finely plays the overweight ugly-duckling Georgy who shares a flat with the beautiful and promiscuous Meredith (Rampling). Georgy is, however, desired by the wealthy and aging Mason and soon by Meredith's lover (Bates) who recognizes her good heart. When Meredith becomes pregnant, Georgy persuades her to let her raise the baby, leaving Georgy with the dilemma of marrying the irresponsible Bates (the baby's father) or the settled Mason. The film and title song (sung by the Seekers) were both huge hits. Based on the novel by Margaret Foster who also co-wrote the screenplay.
1966 100m/B *GB* Lynn Redgrave, James Mason, Charlotte Rampling, Alan Bates, Bill Owen, Claire Kelly, Rachel Kempson; *D:* Silvio Narizzano. Academy Awards '66 Nominations: Best Actress (Redgrave), Best Black and White Cinematography, Best Song ("Georgy Girl"), Best Supporting Actor (Mason); Golden Globe Awards '67: Best Actress—Musical/Comedy (Redgrave); National Board of Review Awards '66: 10 Best Films of the Year; New York Film Critics Awards '66: Best Actress (Redgrave). VHS, Beta $19.95 *FCT, COL* ♪♪♪

Germany in Autumn Twelve West German filmmakers offer political statements and artistic commentary on the political situation in their country after the kidnapping and murder of industrialist Hans Martin Schleyer. In German with English subtitles. *AKA:* Deutschland im Herbst.
1978 124m/C *GE D:* Volker Schlondorff, Rainer Werner Fassbinder, Alf Brustellin, Alexander Kluge, Maximiliane Mainka, Edgar Reitz, Katja Rupe, Hans Peter Cloos, Bernhard Sinkel, Beate Mainka-Jellinghaus, Peter Schubert, Heinrich Boll; *W:* Heinrich Boll. VHS $79.95 *WAC, FCT* ♪♪

Germicide Scientist tries to warn the world of the threat posed by a horrifying bacterial weapon. Terrorists and his mistress hatch plots against him.
1974 90m/C Rod Taylor, Bibi Andersson. Beta $59.95 *PSM* ♪

Geronimo In typical Hollywood casting Connors stars as the Indian leader on the warpath against the cavalry over broken treaties. Lots of action and the Indians are actually the good guys.
1962 101m/C Chuck Connors, Ross Martin, Pat Conway, Kamala Devi, Adam West, Lawrence Dobkin, Denver Pyle, Enid Jaynes, Armando Silvestre, John Anderson; *D:* Arnold Laven. VHS $14.95 *MGM* ♪♪ ½

Geronimo Not to be confused with the big screen version, this made for cable television drama uses three actors to portray the legendary Apache warrior (1829-1909) at various stages of his life. The intrepid teenager who leads attacks on Mexican troops, the adult fighting the duplicitous bluecoats, and the aged man witnessing the destruction of his way of life. The true story is told from the point of view of Native American culture and historical records. Somewhat overly earnest.
1993 120m/C Joseph Runningfox, Jimmy Herman, Ryan Black, Nick Ramus, Michelle St. John, Michael Greyeyes, Tailinh Forest Flower, Kimberly Norris, August Schellenberg, Geno Silva, Harrison Lowe; *D:* Roger Young; *W:* J.T. Allen; *M:* Patrick Williams. VHS *TTC* ♪♪♪

Geronimo: An American Legend Well-intentioned bio-actioner about the legendary Apache leader who fought the U.S. Army over forcing Native Americans onto reservations. Narrator is young Army officer Gatewood (Patric), whose division is to round up the renegades led by Geronimo (Studi), whom he naturally comes to admire. Hackman and Duvall (as a General and a scout respectively) steal any scene they're in although the leads manage to hold their own. Too noble for its own good and somewhat plodding. Great location filming around Moab, Utah.
1993 (PG-13) 115m/C Wes Studi, Jason Patric, Robert Duvall, Gene Hackman, Matt Damon, Rodney Grant, Kevin Tighe, Carlos Palomino, Stephen McHattie; *D:* Walter Hill; *W:* John Milius, Larry Gross; *M:* Ry Cooder. VHS, 8mm *COL* ♪♪ ½

Geronimo's Revenge When Geronimo starts a battle with the settlers, a rancher he has befriended finds himself caught in the middle. The fourth soggy Disney TV oater from the "Tales of Texas John Slaughter" series.
1960 77m/C Tom Tryon, Darryl Hickman; *D:* Harry Keller. **VHS, Beta** *NO ⅞ ½*

Gertrud The simple story of an independent Danish woman rejecting her husband and lovers in favor of isolation. Cold, dry, minimalistic techniques make up Dreyer's final film. In Danish with subtitles.
1964 116m/B *DK* Nina Pens Rode, Bendt Rothe, Ebbe Rode; *D:* Carl Theodor Dreyer; *W:* Carl Theodor Dreyer. **VHS, Beta $34.95** *FCT, DVT, HEG ⅞⅞⅞*

Gervaise The best of several films of Emile Zola's "L'Assommoir." A 19th-century middle-class family is destroyed by the father's plunge into alcoholism despite a mother's attempts to save them. Well acted but overwhelmingly depressing. In French with English subtitles.
1956 89m/B *FR* Maria Schell, Francois Perier, Suzy Delair, Armand Mestral; *D:* Rene Clement; *M:* Georges Auric. Academy Awards '56 Nominations: Best Foreign Language Film; British Academy Awards '56: Best Actor (Perier), Best Film; National Board of Review Awards '57: 5 Best Foreign Films of the Year; New York Film Critics Awards '57: Best Foreign Film; Venice Film Festival '56: Best Actress (Schell). **VHS, Beta $29.95** *DVT, FST, WFV ⅞⅞⅞*

Get Christie Love! Vintage blaxploitation from the genre's halcyon days, when going undercover meant a carte blanche for skimpy outfits. Based on Dorothy Uhnak's detective novel, the eponymous policewoman goes undercover to bring a thriving drug empire to it knees. The outcome: a TV series. Graves previously appeared on television as one of the "Laugh-In" party girls.
1974 95m/C Teresa Graves, Harry Guardino, Louise Sorel, Paul Stevens, Andy Romano, Debbie Dozier; *D:* William A. Graham. **VHS $59.95** *XVC ⅞⅞*

Get Crazy The owner of the Saturn Theatre is attempting to stage the biggest rock-and-roll concert of all time on New Year's Eve 1983, and everything is going wrong in this hilarious, off-beat film.
1983 90m/C Malcolm McDowell, Allen (Goorita) Garfield, Daniel Stern, Gail Edwards, Ed Begley Jr., Lou Reed, Bill Henderson; *D:* Allan Arkush; *M:* Michael Boddicker. **VHS, Beta $9.98** *SUE, NLC ⅞⅞½*

Get Out Your Handkerchiefs Unconventional comedy about a husband desperately attempting to make his sexually frustrated wife happy. Determined to go to any lengths, he asks a Mozart-loving teacher to become her lover. She is now, however, bored by both men. Only when she meets a 13-year-old genius at the summer camp where the three adults are counselors does she come out of her funk and find her sexual happiness. Laure is a beautiful character, but Depardieu and Dewaere are wonderful as the bewildered would-be lovers. Academy Award winner for best foreign film. In French with English subtitles. *AKA:* Preparez Vous Mouchoirs.
1978 (R) 109m/C *FR* Gerard Depardieu, Patrick Dewaere, Carole Laure; *D:* Bertrand Blier; *M:* Georges Delerue. **VHS, Beta $19.98** *WAR, INT, ING ⅞⅞⅞½*

Get Rita Italian prostitute sets up her gangster boyfriend for a murder she committed, and she winds up as mob boss.
19?? 90m/C Sophia Loren, Marcello Mastroianni; *D:* Tom Rowe. **VHS, Beta $19.95** *CTC ⅞⅞*

Get Smart, Again! Would you believe Maxwell Smart is back again as CONTROL's most incompetent agent? How about Agent 99 as his sidekick? Hymie the robot and those no-good-niks at KAOS? Well, it's all true. This second reunion movie (following "The Nude Bomb") from the '60s TV show highlights all the wacky gadgetry, including the shoe phone, but fails to find the show's original outlandishness. Made for television.
1989 93m/C Don Adams, Barbara Feldon, Dick Gautier, Bernie Kopell, Kenneth Mars, Harold Gould, Roger Price, Fritz Feld, Robert Karvelas, King Moody; *D:* Gary Nelson. **VHS $89.95** *WOV ⅞⅞½*

Get That Girl Minor western action pic marred by former silent-screen player Talmadge's heavy German accent which soon lead to him giving up acting for a directing career.
1932 54m/B Richard Talmadge, Shirley Grey, Carl Stockdale; *D:* George Crone. **VHS $14.95** *GPV ⅞*

Get That Man When a cabby is mistaken for the murdered heir to a vast fortune, his life suddenly becomes complex.
1935 57m/B Wallace Ford, Leon Ames, Lillian Miles, E. Allen Warren; *D:* Spencer Gordon Bennet. **VHS, Beta $19.95** *NOS ⅞⅞*

The Getaway McQueen plays a thief released on a parole arranged by his wife (McGraw) only to find out a corrupt politician wants him to rob a bank. After the successful holdup, McQueen finds out his cohorts are in the politician's pocket and trying to doublecross him. McQueen and McGraw are forced into a feverish chase across Texas to the Mexican border, pursued by the politician's henchmen and the state police. Completely amoral depiction of crime and violence with McQueen taciturn as always and McGraw again showing a complete lack of acting skills. Based on a novel by Jim Thompson. McQueen and McGraw had a romance during filming and later married. Remade in 1993.
1972 (PG) 123m/C Steve McQueen, Ali MacGraw, Ben Johnson, Sally Struthers, Al Lettieri, Slim Pickens, Jack Dodson, Dub Taylor, Bo Hopkins; *D:* Sam Peckinpah; *W:* Walter Hill; *M:* Quincy Jones. **VHS, Beta** *FCT ⅞⅞*

The Getaway It was a bad movie in 1972 and the remake hasn't improved the situation. Doc and Carol are husband and wife crooks (played by marrieds Basinger and Baldwin). Doc gets double-crossed and winds up in a Mexican jail; Carol gets a well-connected crook (Woods) to spring her hubby—by sleeping with him and promising Doc will pull off another heist. The robbery's botched, there are double-crosses galore, and the couple go on the run. The stars are pretty but everything's predictable. An unrated version is also available.
1993 (R) 110m/C Alec Baldwin, Kim Basinger, James Woods, Michael Madsen, Jennifer Tilly, David Morse; *D:* Roger Donaldson; *W:* Walter Hill, Amy Jones; *M:* Mark Isham. **VHS** *MCA ⅞½*

Getting Even A maniac threatens to poison the entire population of Texas with a deadly gas unless he gets $50 million. An adventurous businessman sets out to stop him. *AKA:* Hostage: Dallas.
1986 (R) 90m/C Edward Albert, Joe Don Baker, Audrey Landers; *D:* Dwight Little. **VHS, Beta $79.95** *LIV, VES ⅞½*

Getting Even Dundee and Evans served together in Vietnam. Fifteen years later they're reunited by the FBI to track a former Marine, who once betrayed Evans to the enemy. Seems he's now a drug trafficker and arms dealer who also gets his sadistic plea-

sures by killing women. The two ex-Marines find they have one last battle to fight.
1992 (R) 93m/C Richard Roundtree, Michael J. Aronin; *D:* Leandro Lucchetti. **VHS $89.95** *COL ⅞⅞*

Getting Even with Dad Crook Danson can't find the money he stole in his last heist. Why? because his precocious son has hidden it with the intention of blackmailing dear old dad into going straight and acting like a real father. Title is unintentionally funny in light of Mac's domineering dad Kit, who makes everybody in Hollywood want to go hide when he appears. Fairly bland family film squanders charm of Danson and Culkin, running formulaic plot into ground. Headly is likewise wasted as district attorney who prosecutes and then falls for Pops. And hey, Macaulay's precocious days are down to a precious few.
1994 (PG) 108m/C Macaulay Culkin, Ted Danson, Glenne Headly, Hector Elizondo, Saul Rubinek, Gailard Sartain, Kathleen Wilhoite, Sam McMurray; *D:* Howard Deutch; *W:* Tom S. Parker, Jim Jennewein. **VHS** *NYR ⅞½*

Getting It On High school student uses his new-found video equipment for voyeuristic activity.
1983 (R) 100m/C Martin Yost, Heather Kennedy, Jeff Edmond, Kathy Rockmeier, Mark Alan Ferri; *D:* William Olsen. **VHS, Beta $69.95** *LIV, VES ⅞*

Getting It Right A sweet-natured British comedy about an inexperienced, shy adult male who is quite suddenly pursued by a middle-aged socialite, a pregnant, unstable rich girl, and a modest single mother. Novel and screenplay by Elizabeth Jane Howard.
1989 (R) 101m/C *GB* Jesse Birdsall, Helena Bonham Carter, Lynn Redgrave, Peter Cook, John Gielgud, Jane Horrocks, Richard Huw, Shirley Anne Field, Pat Haywood, Judy Parfitt, Bryan Pringle; *D:* Randal Kleiser; *W:* Elizabeth Jane Howard; *M:* Colin Towns, Steve Tyrell. **VHS, Beta** *VTR ⅞⅞*

The Getting of Wisdom A 13-year-old girl from the Australian outback tries to establish her identity, and her individuality, within the restricting confines of a Victorian girl's boarding school. Based on the novel by Henry Handel Richardson.
1977 100m/C *AU* Susannah Fowle, Hilary Ryan, Alix Longman, Sheila Helpmann, Patricia Kennedy, Barry Humphries, John Waters; *D:* Bruce Beresford. **VHS, Beta** *FOX ⅞⅞½*

Getting Over A black promoter is hired as a figurehead by a bigoted record company president and proceeds to try to run the company his own way. He develops an all-girl group called "The Love Machine" and gets involved in a singer's kidnapping and a record company run by gangsters. Filled with cliches and stereotypes.
1981 108m/C John Daniels, Gwen Brisco, Mary Hopkins, John Goff, Andrew "Buzz" Cooper; *D:* Bernie Rollins; *W:* Bernie Rollins. **VHS, Beta $59.95** *UNI ⅞*

Getting Physical After being mugged, a secretary decides to get in shape and enters the world of female body building. Crammed with workout scenes and disco music. Made for television.
1984 95m/C Alexandra Paul, Sandahl Bergman, David Naughton; *D:* Steven Hilliard Stern; *M:* William Goldstein. **VHS, Beta $59.98** *FOX ⅞½*

Getting Straight A returning Vietnam soldier (Gould) goes back to his alma mater to secure a teaching degree and gets involved in the lives of his fellow students and the turbulence of the end of the '60s, including campus riots. A now-dated "youth" picture somewhat watchable for Gould's performance.

1970 (R) 124m/C Elliott Gould, Candice Bergen, Jeff Corey, Cecil Kellaway, Jeannie Berlin, Harrison Ford, John Rubinstein, Robert F. Lyons, Max Julien; *D:* Richard Rush. VHS, Beta $59.95 COL *ℤℤ*

Getting Up and Going Home Jack (Skerritt) is a married man with a midlife crisis. So what does he do? Get involved with not one, but two, other women. Is he asking for trouble or what? Adapted from the book by Robert Anderson.
1992 93m/C Tom Skerritt, Blythe Danner, Roma Downey, Julianne Phillips, Bruce Kirby, Gary Frank, Dorian Harewood, Paul Sand; *D:* Steven Schachter; *W:* Peter Nelson. VHS, Beta $79.95 PSM *ℤℤ* ½

Getting Wasted Set in 1969 at a military academy for troublesome young men, chaos ensues when the cadets meet hippies.
1980 (PG) 98m/C Brian Kerwin, Stephen Furst, Cooper Huckabee. VHS, Beta $19.95 VCI *ℤ* ½

Gettysburg Civil War buff Ted Turner (who has a cameo as a Confederate soldier) originally intended Michael Shaara's Pulitzer Prize-winning novel "The Killer Angels" to be adapted as a three-part miniseries for his "TNT" network, but the lure of the big screen prevailed, marking the first time the battle has been committed to film and the first time a film crew has been allowed to film battle scenes on the Gettysburg National Military Park battlefield. The greatest battle of the war and the bloodiest in U.S. history is realistically staged by more than 5,000 Civil War re-enactors. The all-male cast concentrates on presenting the human cost of the war, with Daniels particularly noteworthy as the scholarly Colonel Chamberlain, determined to hold Little Big Top for the Union. Last film role for Jordan, to whom the movie is co-dedicated. The full scale recreation of Pickett's Charge is believed to be the largest period scale motion-picture sequence filmed in North America since D.W. Griffith's "Birth of a Nation."
1993 (PG) 254m/C Jeff Daniels, Martin Sheen, Tom Berenger, Sam Elliott, Richard Jordan, Stephen Lang, Kevin Conway, C. Thomas Howell, Maxwell Caulfield, Andrew Prine, James Lancaster, Royce D. Applegate, Brian Mallon; *Cameos:* Ken Burns, Ted Turner; *D:* Ronald Maxwell; *W:* Ronald Maxwell; *M:* Randy Edelman. VHS TTC *ℤℤℤ* ½

The Ghastly Ones Three couples must stay in a haunted mansion to inherit an estate, but they're soon being violently killed off. No budget and no talent. Remade as "Legacy of Blood."
1968 81m/C Don Williams, Maggie Rogers, Hal Belsoe, Veronica Redburn; *D:* Andy Milligan. VHS, Beta NO Woof!

Ghetto Blaster A Vietnam vet takes on out-of-control street gangs to make his neighborhood safe.
1989 (R) 86m/C R.G. Armstrong, Richard Hatch, Richard Jaeckel, Harry Caesar, Rose Marie; *D:* Alan L. Stewart. VHS, Beta $79.95 PSM *ℤ*

Ghetto Revenge An embittered Vietnam vet gets caught between white supremacists and black radical activists in this coming home story. He returns and tries to build a life but succumbs to the desire for vengeance and things are never the same.
19?? ?m/C Mike Sims. VHS NO *ℤ*

Ghidrah the Three Headed Monster When a three-headed monster from outer-space threatens the world, humans, having nowhere else to turn, appeal to the friendly Mothra, Rodan, and Godzilla. Rock'em, sock 'em giant thrashing about as Tokyo once again gets trampled. Dependable afternoon monster fare complete with

usual dubious dubbing. *AKA:* Ghidorah Sandai Kaiju Chikyu Saidai No Kessan; Ghidora, The Three-Headed Monster; Ghidrah; The Greatest Battle on Earth; The Biggest Right on Earth; Monster of Monsters.
1965 85m/C JP Yosuke Natsuki, Yuriko Hoshi; *D:* Inoshiro Honda. VHS, Beta $19.95 HHT, VCN, VHE *ℤℤ* ½

The Ghost A woman is driven mad by her supposedly dead husband and their evil housekeeper. Sequel to "The Horrible Dr. Hichcock." *AKA:* Lo Spettro.
1963 96m/C IT Barbara Steele, Peter Baldwin, Leonard Eliott, Harriet White; *D:* Riccardo (Robert Hampton) Freda. VHS, Beta $14.95 SNC, LPC *ℤ* ½

Ghost Zucker, known for overboard comedies like "Airplane!" and "Ruthless People," changed tack and directed this undemanding romantic thriller, which was the surprising top grosser of 1990. Swayze is a murdered investment consultant attempting (from somewhere near the hereafter) to protect his lover, Moore, from imminent danger when he learns he was the victim of a hit gone afoul. Goldberg is the medium who suddenly discovers that the powers she's been faking are real. A winning blend of action, special effects (from Industrial Light and Magic) and romance.
1990 (PG-13) 127m/C Patrick Swayze, Demi Moore, Whoopi Goldberg, Tony Goldwyn, Rick Aviles, Vincent Schiavelli, Gail Boggs, Armelia McQueen, Phil Leeds; *D:* Jerry Zucker; *W:* Bruce Joel Rubin; *M:* Maurice Jarre. Academy Awards '90: Best Original Screenplay, Best Supporting Actress (Goldberg); Nominations: Best Film Editing, Best Picture, Best Original Score; Golden Globe Awards '91: Best Supporting Actress (Goldberg); People's Choice Awards '91: Best Film—Drama. VHS, Beta, 8mm $14.95 PAR, SUP, FCT *ℤℤℤ*

The Ghost and Mrs. Muir A charming, beautifully orchestrated fantasy about a feisty widow who, with her young daughter, buys a seaside house and refuses to be intimidated by the crabby ghost of its former sea captain owner. When the widow falls into debt, the captain dictates his sea adventures, which she adapts into a successful novel. The ghost also falls in love with the beautiful lady. Tierney is exquisite and Harrison is sharp-tongued and manly. Based on R. A. Dick's novel.
1947 104m/B Gene Tierney, Rex Harrison, George Sanders, Edna Best, Anna Lee, Vanessa Brown, Robert Coote, Natalie Wood, Isobel Elsom; *D:* Joseph L. Mankiewicz; *W:* Philip Dunne; *M:* Bernard Herrmann. VHS, Beta $19.98 FOX, HMV *ℤℤℤ*

The Ghost and the Guest Newlyweds spend their honeymoon in a house in the country only to find that gangsters are using the place as a hideout. Chases involving secret passages ensue.
1943 59m/B James Dunn, Florence Rice, Mabel Todd; *D:* William Nigh; *W:* Morey Amsterdam. VHS, Beta $16.95 SNC, VYY *ℤℤ* ½

The Ghost Breakers As a follow-up to the Hope/Goddard 1939 comedy thriller "The Cat and the Canary," this spooky comedy was even better. Lots of laughs and real chills as Hope and Goddard investigate a haunted mansion that she's inherited in Cuba. Effective horror scenes are expertly handled by director Marshall. Remade in 1953 as "Scared Stiff" with Dean Martin and Jerry Lewis. Based on the play by Paul Dickey and Charles Goddard.
1940 83m/B Bob Hope, Paulette Goddard, Richard Carlson, Paul Lukas, Willie Best, Pedro de Cordoba, Noble Johnson, Anthony Quinn; *D:* George Marshall. VHS $14.98 MCA, BTV *ℤℤℤ*

The Ghost Camera Slight story of a man falsely accused of murder. A photograph taken at the murder scene can prove his innocence if only the missing camera can be discovered.
1933 68m/B GB Henry Kendall, Ida Lupino, John Mills; *D:* Bernard Vorhaus. VHS HCV *ℤℤ* ½

Ghost Chase A young filmmaker desperate for funds inherits his dead relative's clock, from which issues the ghost of the deceased's butler. The ghostly retainer aids in a search for the departed's secret fortune. Neither scary nor funny.
1988 (PG-13) 89m/C Jason Lively, Jill Whitlow, Tim McDaniel, Paul Gleason, Chuck "Porky" Mitchell; *D:* Roland Emmerich. VHS, Beta NO *ℤ* ½

Ghost Chasers The Bowery Boys become mixed up in supernatural hijinks when a seance leads to the appearance of a ghost that only Sach can see.
1951 70m/B Leo Gorcey, Huntz Hall, Billy Benedict, David Gorcey, Buddy Gorman, Bernard Gorcey, Jan Kayne, Philip Van Zandt, Lloyd Corrigan; *D:* William Beaudine. VHS $14.98 WAR *ℤℤ* ½

Ghost City Our hero must deal with a masked gang that is "haunting" a town.
1932 60m/B Bill Cody, Helen Foster, Ann Rutherford, John Shelton, Reginald Owen; *D:* Harry Fraser. VHS $19.95 NOS, DVT, HEG *ℤ*

Ghost Crazy Three wild comedians and a gorilla create mayhem in a haunted house.
1944 ?m/C Shemp Howard, Billy Gilbert, Maxie "Slapsie" Rosenbloom. VHS $15.95 LOO *ℤℤ*

Ghost Dad A widowed workaholic dad is prematurely killed and returns from the dead to help his children prepare for the future. Cosby walks through doors, walls, and other solid objects for the sake of comedy—only none of it is funny.
1990 (PG) 84m/C Bill Cosby, Denise Nicholas, Ian Bannen, Christine Ebersole, Dana Ashbrook, Arnold Stang; *D:* Sidney Poitier; *W:* S.S. Wilson; *M:* Henry Mancini. VHS, Beta $19.95 MCA *ℤ*

Ghost Dance Sacred Indian burial ground is violated, with grim results.
1983 93m/C Sherman Hemsley, Henry Ball, Julie Amato; *D:* Peter Bufa. VHS, Beta $49.95 TWE *ℤ*

Ghost Fever Two bumbling cops try to evict the inhabitants of a haunted house and get nowhere. A bad rip-off of "Ghostbusters." Alan Smithee is a pseudonym used when a director does not want his or her name on a film—no wonder.
1987 (PG) 86m/C Sherman Hemsley, Luis Avalos; *D:* Alan Smithee; *W:* Oscar Brodney. VHS, Beta $19.98 NLC Woof!

The Ghost Goes West A brash American family buys a Scottish castle and transports the pieces to the United States along with the Scottish family ghost (Donat). Also along is the ghost's modern-day descendant (also played by Donat) who is the new castle caretaker and in love with the new owner's daughter. It turns out to be up to the ghost to get the two lovers together and find his own eternal rest. A rather lovable fantasy. Rene Clair's first English film. Available in digitally remastered stereo with original movie trailer.
1936 85m/B GB Robert Donat, Jean Parker, Eugene Pallette, Elsa Lanchester; *D:* Rene Clair; *W:* Robert Sherwood. VHS, Beta $19.98 HBO, SUE *ℤℤℤ*

Ghost in the Machine Serial killer dies while undergoing an X-ray scan and somehow, because of a lightning storm and a power outage, his soul manages to infiltrate the hospital's computer and go on to

terrorize more victims via their home computers and appliances. (You expect this to make sense?) Outlandish, predictable flick hovers between high-tech horror and satiric comedy and wastes some pretty decent talent. Horror buffs may get a kick out of it but be forewarned: You may never view your microwave, dishwasher, or electrical outlets in quite the same way again.
1993 (R) 104m/C Karen Allen, Chris Mulkey, Ted Marcoux, Jessica Walter, Rick Ducommun, Wil Horneff, Nancy Fish, Brandon Adams; *D:* Rachel Talalay; *W:* William Davies, William Osborne; *M:* Graeme Revell. VHS FXV *‡‡*½

Ghost in the Noonday Sun Crew of a treasure-seeking pirate ship sets sail for high sea silliness in this slapstick adventure film. Not a theatrical release for one obvious reason—it's terrible.
1974 90m/C *GB* Peter Sellers, Spike Milligan, Anthony (Tony) Franciosa, Clive Revill, Rosemary Leach, Peter Boyle; *D:* Peter Medak. VHS, Beta NO Woof!

Ghost Keeper Three girls are trapped in a mansion with an old hag and various supernatural apparitions.
1980 87m/C Riva Spier, Murray Ord, Georgie Collins; *D:* Vernon Sewell. VHS, Beta $59.95 NWV *‡*

The Ghost of Fletcher Ridge Two friends on a hunting trip run into some backwoodsmen and uncover their moonshining operation. When one of the men is killed, the other flees to the forest in a desperate bid for survival.
198? 90m/C Campbell Scott, Bernie White, Virginia Lantry, Len Lesser; *D:* Michael Bordon. VHS NO *‡*

The Ghost of Frankenstein Fourth Frankenstein film in the Universal Studios series with Chaney filling in for Karloff as the monster. Not as good as its predecessors, but the cast is enjoyable, especially Lugosi as the monster's deformed sidekick, Ygor. Based on a story by Eric Taylor.
1942 68m/B Cedric Hardwicke, Lon Chaney Jr., Lionel Atwill, Ralph Bellamy, Bela Lugosi, Evelyn Ankers, Dwight Frye; *D:* Erle C. Kenton; *W:* W. Scott Darling. VHS $14.98 MCA, FCT *‡‡‡*

Ghost of Hanley House Obscure, low-budget ghost story, shot in Texas.
1968 ?m/B VHS $20 SMW *‡‡*

The Ghost of Rashmon Hall Doctor tries to rid his home of the ghosts of a sailor, his wife and her lover. *AKA:* Night Comes Too Soon.
1947 52m/B Valentine Dyall, Anne Howard, Alex Flavorsham, Howard Douglas, Beatrice Marsden, Arthur Brander. VHS, Beta $16.95 SNC, MWP *‡*

The Ghost of Yotsuya Based on the Japanese legend of a man who must betray his wife to get the power he seeks. When he does, however, what follows is a horrifying revenge. In Japanese with English subtitles.
1958 100m/C *JP* Shigeru Amachi. VHS, Beta $59.95 VDA, TPV *‡*½

Ghost Patrol A cowboy duo kidnaps the inventor of a ray gun in order to hijack mail planes, but they're stopped by G-Man McCoy and friends. An odd hybrid of science fiction and western, to say the least.
1936 57m/B Tim McCoy, Walter Miller, Wheeler Oakman; *D:* Sam Newfield. VHS, Beta $9.95 GPV, VCI, VCN *‡*½

Ghost Rider A lawman is aided in his outlaw-nabbing efforts by the ghost of a gunfighter.
1935 56m/B Rex Lease; *D:* Jack Levine. VHS, Beta $19.95 NOS *‡*

Ghost Rider Former footballer Brown rides the range once again, this time with an element of the supernatural nipping at his heels.
1943 58m/B Johnny Mack Brown, Raymond Hatton, Tim Seidel, Beverly Boyd, Milburn Morante; *D:* Wallace Fox. VHS $11.95 GPV *‡‡*

Ghost Ship Young couple is tortured by ghostly apparitions when they move into an old yacht with a dubious past. Grade "b" haunting featuring the murdered wife of the ship's former owner as the poltergeist.
1953 69m/B *GB* Dermot Walsh, Hazel Court, Hugh Burden, John Robinson; *D:* Vernon Sewell. VHS, Beta $14.95 NOS, SNC *‡*½

Ghost Stories: Graveyard Thriller A compilation of stories with ghosts, vampires and other creatures of the night.
1986 56m/C *D:* Lynn Silver. VHS, Beta $59.98 LIV, VES *‡*½

Ghost Story Four elderly men, members of an informal social club called the Chowder Society, share a terrible secret buried deep in their pasts—a secret that comes back to haunt them to death. Has moments where it's chilling, but unfortunately they're few. Based on the best-selling novel by Peter Straub.
1981 (R) 110m/C Fred Astaire, Melvyn Douglas, Douglas Fairbanks Jr., John Houseman, Craig Wasson, Alice Krige, Patricia Neal; *D:* John Irvin. VHS, Beta $19.95 MCA *‡‡*

Ghost Town Good guy Carey saves a mine from claim jumpers, but not before he is mistakenly incarcerated as his friend's murderer, and then proved innocent.
1937 65m/B Harry Carey Sr.; *D:* Harry Fraser. VHS, Beta $19.95 VDM *‡*

Ghost Town Fine sleeper about a modern sheriff who must rid a ghost town of its age-old curse.
1988 (R) 85m/C Franc Luz, Catherine Hickland, Jimmie F. Skaggs, Penelope Windust, Bruce Glover, Blake Conway, Laura Schaefer; *D:* Richard Governor; *W:* Duke Sandefur; *M:* Harvey R. Cohen. VHS $19.95 STE, NWV *‡‡*½

Ghost Town Gold The Three Mesquiteers series continues as the trio outwits bank robbers who have hidden their loot in a ghost town.
1936 53m/B Bob Livingston, Ray Corrigan, Max Terhune; *D:* Joseph Kane. VHS, Beta $19.95 NOS, DVT *‡*

Ghost Town Law The Rough Riders step in to save the day when a group of outlaws defend their hideout by murdering anyone who approaches.
1942 62m/B Buck Jones, Tim McCoy, Raymond Hatton; *D:* Howard Bretherton. VHS, Beta $9.99 NOS, VCN, CAB *‡*½

Ghost Town Renegades A pair of government agents prevent a crook from gaining control of a mining town.
1947 57m/B Lash LaRue, Al "Fuzzy" St. John, Jennifer Holt; *D:* Ray Taylor. VHS, Beta $12.95 COL *‡*

Ghost Town Riders An outlaw gang is holed up in an abandoned town, threatening to steal Shannon's gold mine, until Baker comes to the rescue.
1938 55m/B Bob Baker, Fay Shannon, George Cleveland, Glenn Strange, Forrest Taylor, Hank Worden, Murdock McQuarrie; *D:* George Waggner. VHS $11.95 GPV *‡*½

The Ghost Train Passengers stranded at a train station are told tales of a haunted train. Forced to stay at the station overnight, they encounter a number of comically spooky situations.

1941 85m/B *GB* Arthur Askey, Richard Murdock, Kathleen Harrison; *D:* Walter Forde. VHS, Beta $16.95 NOS, SNC *‡‡*

Ghost Valley When Keene and Kennedy inherit land rich in unmined ore, the administrator (Harris) attempts to scare them off. To foil his plan, Keene conceals his identity and takes a job as the administrator's assistant. Based on a story by Adele Buffington.
1932 54m/B Tom Keene, Merna Kennedy, Mitchell Harris, Billy Franey, Harry Bowen, Kate Campbell, Ted Adams, Buck Moulton, Harry Semels, Al Taylor, Charles "Slim" Whitaker; *D:* Fred Allen. VHS HEG *‡‡*½

The Ghost Walks A playwright has his new masterpiece acted out in front of an unsuspecting producer, who thinks that a real murder has taken place. But when the cast really does start disappearing, who's to blame?
1934 69m/B John Miljan, June Collyer, Richard Carle, Spencer Charters, Johnny Arthur, Henry Kolker; *D:* Frank Strayer. VHS $12.95 SNC, NOS, DVT *‡‡*

Ghost Writer A writer discovers the ghost of a movie star haunting her beach house, and together they solve the dead vamp's murder.
1989 (PG) 94m/C Audrey Landers, Judy Landers, Jeff Conaway, David Doyle, Anthony (Tony) Franciosa, Joey Travolta, John Matuszak, David Paul, Peter Paul; *D:* Kenneth J. Hall. VHS, Beta $79.95 PSM *‡*

Ghostbusters After losing their scholastic funding, a group of "para-normal" investigators decide to go into business for themselves, aiding New York citizens in the removal of ghosts, goblins and other annoying spirits. This comedy-thriller about Manhattan being overrun by ghosts, contains great special effects, zany characters, and some of the best laughs of the decade. Also available in a laserdisc version with letterboxing, analysis of all special effects, complete screenplay, and original trailer. Followed by a sequel.
1984 (PG) 103m/C Bill Murray, Dan Aykroyd, Harold Ramis, Rick Moranis, Sigourney Weaver, Annie Potts, Ernie Hudson, William Atherton; *D:* Ivan Reitman; *W:* Dan Aykroyd, Harold Ramis, Harold Ramis; *M:* Elmer Bernstein. VHS, Beta, 8mm $19.95 COL, VYG, APD *‡‡‡*

Ghostbusters 2 After being sued by the city for the damages they did in the original "Ghostbusters," the boys in khaki are doing kiddie shows at birthday parties. When a river of slime is actually the physical version of evil is discovered running beneath the city, the Ghostbusters are back in action. They must do battle with a wicked spirit in a painting or the entire world will fall prey to its ravaging whims.
1989 (PG) 102m/C Bill Murray, Dan Aykroyd, Sigourney Weaver, Harold Ramis, Rick Moranis, Ernie Hudson, Peter MacNicol, David Margulies, Wilhelm von Homburg, Harris Yulin, Annie Potts; *D:* Ivan Reitman; *W:* Harold Ramis; *M:* Randy Edelman. VHS, Beta, 8mm $19.95 COL *‡‡*½

Ghosthouse It looks like an average suburban house, but it's haunted by the ghost of a little girl—and when she comes, evil is sure to follow.
1988 91m/C Lara Wendell, Gregg Scott; *D:* Humphrey Humbert. VHS, Beta $79.95 IMP *‡*

Ghostriders One hundred years after their hanging, a band of ghostly outlaws take revenge on the townfolk's descendents.
1987 85m/C Bill Shaw, Jim Peters, Ricky Long, Cari Powell, Mike Ammons, Arland Bishop; *D:* Alan L. Stewart. VHS, Beta $9.99 PSM *‡*

Ghosts Can Do It The Hound doesn't like jumping to conclusions, but is it possible this obscurity was titled to be reminiscent of the more publicized Bo Derek vehicle "Ghosts Can't Do it?" comedy about a man who returns to his sexy wife despite her efforts at killing him.
1990 88m/C Garry McDonald, Pamela Stephenson. **VHS $59.95** *ATL, HHE* ⅞½

Ghosts Can't Do It Another wet-shirted, Bo-dacious softcore epic, involving a young woman who would like to have the spirit of her virile, but unfortunately dead, husband return to inhabit a living body.
1990 (R) 91m/C Bo Derek, Anthony Quinn, Don Murray, Leo Damian; *D:* John Derek. **VHS, Beta $59.95** *COL, TTC* ⅞

Ghosts of Berkeley Square The ghosts of two retired soldiers of the early 18th century are doomed to haunt their former home, and only a visit from a reigning monarch can free them.
1947 85m/B Wilfrid Hyde-White, Robert Morley, Felix Aylmer; *D:* Vernon Sewell. **VHS, Beta $19.95** *VYY* ⅞⅞½

The Ghosts of Hanley House No-budget spooker with no-brain plot. Several unlucky guests spend an evening in a creepy mansion...sound familiar? Shot in Texas.
1968 80m/C Barbara Chase, Wilkie De Martel, Elsie Baker, Cliff Scott. **VHS, Beta $16.95** *SNC* ⅞½

Ghosts That Still Walk Spooky phenomena occur. The demons possessing a young lad's soul may be responsible.
1977 92m/C Ann Nelson, Matt Boston, Jerry Jenson, Caroline Howe, Rita Crafts; *D:* James T. Flocker. **VHS, Beta $29.95** *VCI, MRV* ⅞

Ghostwarrior A 16th century samurai warrior's ice-packed body is revived and runs amuck in the streets of modern-day Los Angeles.
1986 91m/C Hiroshi Fujioka, Janet Julian, Andy Wood, John Calvin; *D:* Larry Carroll. **VHS, Beta $79.98** *VES* ⅞

Ghostwriter Based on Philip Roth's best-selling novel, the story is of a writer coming to terms with his past. Roth co-wrote the screenplay. First seen on PBS.
1984 90m/C Sam Wanamaker, Claire Bloom, Rose Arrick, MacIntyre Dixon, Cecile Mann, Joseph Wiseman, Mark Linn-Baker, Paulette Smit; *D:* Tristam Powell; *W:* Phillip J. Roth. **VHS, Beta $69.95** *PBS* ⅞

The Ghoul An eccentric English Egyptologist desires a sacred jewel to be buried with him and vows to come back from the grave if the gem is stolen. When that happens, he makes good on his ghostly promise. A minor horror piece with Karloff only appearing at the beginning and end of the film. This leaves the middle very dull.
1934 73m/B *GB* Boris Karloff, Cedric Hardwicke, Ernest Thesiger, Dorothy Hyson, Ralph Richardson, Anthony Bushell; *D:* T. Hayes Hunter. **VHS $14.95** *VYY, SNC, DVT* ⅞⅞½

The Ghoul A defrocked clergyman has a cannibal son to contend with—especially after the drivers in a local auto race begin to disappear. Hurt is the lunatic family gardener.
1975 (R) 88m/C *GB* Peter Cushing, John Hurt, Alexandra Bastedo, Don Henderson, Stewart Bevan; *D:* Freddie Francis. **VHS, Beta $19.95** *MED* ⅞⅞

Ghoul School A spoof of horror films and college flicks, with lots of scantily clad women and bloody creatures in dark hallways.
1990 (R) 90m/C Joe Franklin, Nancy Siriani, William Friedman. **VHS $79.95** *HHE* ⅞

Ghoulies A young man gets more than he bargained for when he conjures up a batch of evil creatures when dabbling in the occult. Ridiculous but successful. Followed by two sequels.
1985 (PG-13) 81m/C Lisa Pelikan, Jack Nance, Scott Thomson, Tamara DeTreaux, Mariska Hargitay, Bobbie Bresee; *D:* Luca Bercovici; *M:* Richard Band. **VHS, Beta $29.98** *LIV, VES, HHE* ⅞

Ghoulies 2 Inept sequel to "Ghoulies" (1985), wherein the little demons haunt a failing carnival horror house, whose revenues begin to soar. Followed by a second sequel.
1988 (R) 89m/C Damon Martin, Royal Dano, Phil Fondacaro, J. Downing, Kerry Remsen; *D:* Albert Band. **VHS, Beta $14.98** *LIV, VES* ⅞

Ghoulies 3: Ghoulies Go to College Third in the series has the best special effects and the worst storyline. Not satisfied with ripping off "Gremlins," this one imposes Three Stooges personae upon a trio of demons at large on a beer- and babe-soaked campus.
1991 (R) 94m/C Kevin McCarthy, Griffin O'Neal, Evan Mackenzie; *D:* John Carl Buechler. **VHS $14.98** *VES, LIV* Woof!

G.I. Blues Three G.I.'s form a musical combo while stationed in Germany. Prowse is the nightclub singer Presley falls for. Presley's first film after his military service. ♫Shopping Around; Tonight Is So Right For Love; What's She Really Like?; Frankfurt Special; Didya Ever; Big Boots; Pocketful of Rainbows; Doin' the Best I Can; Blue Suede Shoes; G.I. Blues; Wooden Heart.
1960 104m/C Elvis Presley, Juliet Prowse, Robert Ivers, Leticia Roman, Ludwig Stossel, James Douglas, Jeremy Slate; *D:* Norman Taurog. **VHS, Beta $14.98** *FOX, MVD* ⅞

G.I. Executioner An adventure set in Singapore featuring a Vietnam veteran turned executioner. *AKA:* Wit's End; Dragon Lady.
1971 (R) 86m/C Tom Kenna, Victoria Racimo, Angelique Pettyjohn, Janet Wood, Walter Hill; *D:* Joel M. Reed. **VHS, Beta $69.95** *VES* ⅞

G.I. Jane A television producer faints when he gets his draft notice and dreams his company is stranded at a desert post with a company of WACs.
1951 62m/B Jean Porter, Tom Neal, Iris Adrian, Jimmy Lloyd, Mara Lynn, Michael Whalen; *D:* Reginald LeBorg. **VHS, Beta** *NO* ⅞

Giant Based on the Edna Ferber novel, this epic saga covers two generations of a wealthy Texas cattle baron (Hudson) who marries a strong-willed Virginia woman (Taylor) and takes her to live on his vast ranch. It explores the problems they have adjusting to life together, as well as the politics and prejudice of the time. Dean plays the resentful ranch hand (who secretly loves Taylor) who winds up striking oil and beginning a fortune to rival that of his former boss. Dean's last movie—he died in a car crash shortly before filming was completed.
1956 201m/C Elizabeth Taylor, Rock Hudson, James Dean, Carroll Baker, Chill Wills, Dennis Hopper, Rod Taylor, Earl Holliman, Jane Withers, Sal Mineo, Mercedes McCambridge; *D:* George Stevens. Academy Awards '56: Best Director (Stevens); Nominations: Best Actor (Dean), Best Actor (Hudson), Best Adapted Screenplay, Best Art Direction/Set Decoration (Color), Best Costume Design (Color), Best Film Editing, Best Picture, Best Supporting Actress (McCambridge), Best Original Score; Directors Guild of America Awards '56: Best Director (Stevens). **VHS, Beta $29.98** *WAR, BTV* ⅞⅞⅞½

The Giant Claw Giant, winged (and stringed) bird attacks from outer space and scientists Morrow, Corday and Ankrum attempt to pluck it. Good bad movie; Corday was Playboy's Miss October, 1958.
1957 76m/B Jeff Morrow, Mara Corday, Morris Ankrum, Louis D. Merrill, Edgar Barrier, Robert Shayne, Morgan Jones, Clark Howat; *D:* Fred F. Sears. **VHS $14.98** *MOV* ⅞½

Giant from the Unknown Giant conquistador is revived after being struck by lightning and goes on a murderous rampage. Unbelievably bad.
1958 80m/B Edward Kemmer, Buddy Baer, Bob Steele, Sally Fraser; *D:* Richard Cunha. **VHS, Beta $16.95** *NOS, SNC, MWP* Woof!

The Giant Gila Monster A giant lizard has the nerve to disrupt a local record hop, foolishly bringing upon it the wrath of the local teens. Rear-projection monster isn't particularly effective, but the film provides many unintentional laughs.
1959 74m/B Don Sullivan, Lisa Simone, Shug Fisher, Jerry Cortwright, Beverly Thurman, Don Flourney, Pat Simmons; *D:* Ray Kellogg. **VHS $9.95** *NOS, RHI, SNC* ⅞½

The Giant of Marathon Reeves shrugs off the role of Hercules to play Philippides, a marathoner (who uses a horse) trying to save Greece from invading Persian hordes. Lots of muscle on display, but not much talent. Cinematography by Mario Bava.
1960 90m/C Steve Reeves, Mylene Demongeot, Daniela Rocca, Ivo Garrani, Alberto Lupo, Sergio Fantoni; *D:* Jacques Tourneur. **VHS $16.95** *SNC, MLB* ⅞

The Giant of Metropolis Muscle-bound hero goes shirtless to take on the evil, sadistic ruler of Atlantis (still above water) in 10,000 B.C. Ordinary Italian adventure, but includes interesting sets and bizarre torture scenes. *AKA:* Il Gigante Di Metropolis.
1961 92m/C *IT* Gordon Mitchell, Roldano Lupi, Bella Cortez, Liana Orfei; *D:* Umberto Scarpelli. **VHS $19.98** *SNC* ⅞⅞

The Giant Spider Invasion A meteorite carrying spider eggs crashes to Earth and soon the alien arachnids are growing to humongous proportions. Notoriously bad special effects, but the veteran "B" cast has a good time.
1975 (PG) 76m/C Steve Brodie, Barbara Hale, Leslie Parrish, Robert Easton, Alan Hale Jr., Dianne Lee Hart, Bill Williams, Christianne Schmidtmer; *D:* Bill Rebane. **VHS** *MOV* ⅞

Giant Steps Williams plays Slate Hopson, a moody jazz legend idolized by a talented young trumpet player. When the two meet Hopson clues the boy into some of life's lessons and rediscovers his own joy at making music.
19?? 94m/C Billy Dee Williams, Michael Mahonen; *M:* Eric Leeds. **VHS $89.95** *MNC* ⅞⅞

Giants of Rome Rome is in peril at the hands of a mysterious secret weapon that turns out to be a giant catapult. Ludicrous all around.
1963 87m/C *IT* Richard Harrison, Ettore Manni. **VHS, Beta $16.95** *SNC* Woof!

The Giants of Thessaly Jason and Orpheus search for the Golden Fleece, encountering and defeating monsters, wizards, and a scheming witch.
1960 86m/C *IT* Roland Carey, Ziva Rodann, Massimo Girotti, Alberto Farnese; *D:* Riccardo (Robert Hampton) Freda. **VHS $16.95** *SNC* ⅞⅞

Gideon's Trumpet True story of Clarence Earl Gideon, a Florida convict whose case was decided by the Supreme Court and set the precedent that everyone is entitled to defense by a lawyer, whether or not they can

pay for it. Based on the book by Anthony Lewis. Made for television.
1980 104m/C Henry Fonda, Jose Ferrer, John Houseman, Dean Jagger, Sam Jaffe, Fay Wray; **D:** Robert Collins. **VHS, Beta $14.95** WOV *ℐℐ* ½

Gidget A plucky, boy-crazy teenage girl (whose nickname means girl midget) discovers romance and wisdom on the beaches of Malibu when she becomes involved with a group of college-aged surfers. First in a series of Gidget/surfer films. Based on a novel by Frederick Kohner about his daughter.
1959 95m/C Sandra Dee, James Darren, Cliff Robertson, Mary Laroche, Arthur O'Connell, Joby Baker; **D:** Paul Wendkos. **VHS, Beta $9.95** COL *ℐℐ*

Gidget Goes Hawaiian Gidget is off to Hawaii with her parents and is enjoying the beach (and the boys) when she is surprised by a visit from boyfriend "Moondoggie." Sequel to "Gidget" and followed by "Gidget Goes to Rome."
1961 102m/C Deborah Walley, James Darren, Carl Reiner, Peggy Cass, Michael Callan, Eddie Foy Jr.; **D:** Paul Wendkos. **VHS, Beta $14.95** COL *ℐℐ*

Gidget Goes to Rome Darren returns in his third outing as boyfriend "Moondoggie" to yet another actress playing "Gidget" as the two vacation in Rome and find themselves tempted by other romances. Second sequel to "Gidget."
1963 104m/C Cindy Carol, James Darren, Jeff Donnell, Cesare Danova, Peter Brooks, Jessie Royce Landis; **D:** Paul Wendkos; **W:** John Williams. **VHS, Beta $19.95** COL *ℐ* ½

The Gift Story of a 55-year-old man who chooses early retirement in the hopes of changing his dull and boring life. Unbeknownst to him, his co-workers arrange the ultimate retirement gift - a woman. Silly French sexual farce. Dubbed.
1982 (R) 105m/C FR Pierre Mondy, Claudia Cardinale, Clio Goldsmith, Jacques Francois, Cecile Magnet, Remy Laurent; **D:** Michael Lang. **VHS, Beta $19.95** FCT *ℐℐ* ½

The Gift Real life husband and wife Farrell and Niccoli play fictitious characters of the same names in this darkly comic look into the world of the junkie. They revolve between the streets, drug treatment centers, and the shooting gallery they call home as the film moves toward its inevitable conclusion. Farrell is a former member of the band "Jane's Addiction."
19?? 83m/C VHS $19.98 WEA *ℐℐ*

The Gift Horse A WWII British naval officer dispatches his duties with an iron hand in an attempt to overturn the legacy of a court-martial eight years earlier. Angry rumblings from his crew threaten to upset the ship's stability. Against this foreboding backdrop, the Nazis give battle. Not historically accurate, but exciting. Based on a story by Ivan Goff and Ben Roberts. **AKA:** Glory at Sea.
1952 99m/B GB Trevor Howard, Richard Attenborough, Sonny Tufts, Bernard Lee; **D:** Compton Bennett. **VHS, Beta $39.95** MON, DVT, HEG *ℐℐ*

The Gift of Love Saccharine, made-for-television adaption of O. Henry's Christmas romance "The Gift of the Magi."
1990 96m/C James Woods, Marie Osmond, Timothy Bottoms, June Lockhart, David Wayne; **D:** Don Chaffey. **VHS, Beta $24.95** MON, KAR *ℐℐ* ½

The Gig In this small, independently-made film, a band of middle-aged amateur jazz musicians give up their stable occupations for a once-in-a-lifetime shot at a two-week

gig in the Catskills. Film succeeds on the strength of it's well fleshed-out characters.
1985 95m/C Wayne Rogers, Cleavon Little, Warren Vache, Joe Silver, Daniel Nalbach, Andrew Duncan, Jay Thomas, Jerry Matz; **D:** Frank D. Gilroy; **W:** Frank D. Gilroy. **VHS, Beta $79.95** LHV, WAR *ℐℐ* ½

Gigi Based on Colette's story of a young Parisian girl (Caron) trained to become a courtesan to the wealthy Gaston (Jourdan). But he finds out he prefers her to be his wife rather than his mistress. Chevalier is Gaston's roguish father who casts an always admiring eye on the ladies, Gingold is Gigi's grandmother and former Chevalier flame, and Gabor amuses as Gaston's current, and vapid, mistress. One of the first MGM movies to be shot on location, this extravaganza features some of the best tributes to the French lifestyle ever filmed. Score includes memorable classics. ♫Gigi; Ah Yes, I Remember It Well; Thank Heaven For Little Girls; The Night They Invented Champagne; She's Not Thinking of Me; It's a Bore; Gossip; I'm Glad I'm Not Young Anymore; The Parisians; Gaston's Soliloquy; Say A Prayer For Me Tonight; A Toujours.
1958 119m/C Leslie Caron, Louis Jourdan, Maurice Chevalier, Hermione Gingold, Eva Gabor, Isabel Jeans, Jacques Bergerac; **D:** Vincente Minnelli; **W:** Alan Jay Lerner; **M:** Frederick Loewe. **VHS, Beta, 8mm $19.98** MGM, BTV *ℐℐℐℐ*

Gilda An evil South American gambling casino owner hires young American Ford as his trusted aide, unaware that Ford and his sultry wife Hayworth have engaged in a steamy affair. Hayworth does a striptease to "Put the Blame on Mame" in this prominently sexual film. This is the film that made Hayworth into a Hollywood sex goddess.
1946 110m/B Rita Hayworth, Glenn Ford, George Macready, Joseph Calleia; **D:** Charles Vidor. **VHS, Beta $19.95** COL *ℐℐℐ* ½

The Gilded Cage Two brothers are falsely accused of art theft and must find the real crooks in order to clear their names.
1954 77m/B GB Alex Nicol, Veronica Hurst, Clifford Evans, Ursula Howells, Elwyn Brook-Jones, John Stuart; **D:** John Gilling. **VHS, Beta $16.95** SNC *ℐℐ*

Gilligan's Island: Meet the Crew Join Gilligan and the Skipper of the S.S. Minnow and their unfortunate passengers—Ginger, Mary Ann, the Professor, and Mr. and Mrs. Thurston Howell III—as they try to survive life (and each other) on an uncharted desert isle. Three episodes per cassette from the slapstick television series. Additional episodes available.
1964 ?m/C Bob Denver, Alan Hale Jr., Jim Backus, Natalie Schafer, Tina Louise, Russell Johnson, Dawn Wells. VHS CMB *ℐℐ*

Gimme an F The handsome cheerleading instructor at Camp Beaver View ruffles a few pom-poms when he discovers that the camp's owner is about to enter into a shady deal with some foreigners. The film certainly deserves an "F" for foolishness if nothing else. **AKA:** T & A Academy 2.
1985 (R) 100m/C Stephen Shellan, Mark Keyloun, John Karlen, Jennifer Cooke; **D:** Paul Justman. **VHS, Beta $79.98** FOX Woof!

Gimme Shelter The sixties ended as violence occurred at a December 1969 free Rolling Stones concert attended by 300,000 people in Altamont, California. This "Woodstock West" became a bitter remembrance in rock history, as Hell's Angels (hired for security) do some ultimate damage to the spectators. A provocative look at an out-of-control situation.

1970 91m/C Mick Jagger, Keith Richards, Charlie Watts, Bill Wyman, Mick Taylor; **D:** David Maysles. **VHS, Beta $29.95** COL, MVD Woof!

Gin Game Taped London performance of the Broadway play about an aging couple who find romance in an old age home. Two-character performance won awards; touching and insightful.
1984 82m/C Jessica Tandy, Hume Cronyn; **D:** Mike Nichols. **VHS, Beta $39.95** RKO, STS, TTC *ℐℐℐ*

Ginger Fabulous super-sleuth Ginger faces the sordid world of prostitution, blackmail and drugs. Prequel to "The Abductors" and followed eventually by "Girls Are for Loving."
1972 90m/C Cheri Caffaro, William Grannell; **D:** Don Schain. **VHS, Beta $39.95** MON *ℐ*

Ginger Ale Afternoon A smutty comedy revolving around a triangle formed by a married couple and their sexy next-door neighbor. The film tries for fizz but only comes up flat.
1989 88m/C Dana Anderson, John M. Jackson, Yeardley Smith; **D:** Rafal Zeilinski; **W:** Gina Wendkos; **M:** Willie Dixon. **VHS, Beta $29.95** ACA, IME *ℐ*

Ginger & Fred An acclaimed story of Fellini-esque poignancy about an aging dance team. Years before they had gained success by reverently impersonating the famous dancing duo of Astaire and Rogers. Now, after thirty years, they reunite under the gaudy lights of a high-tech television special. Wonderful performances by the aging Mastroianni and the still sweet Masina. In Italian with English subtitles.
1986 (PG-13) 126m/C IT Marcello Mastroianni, Giulietta Masina, Franco Fabrizi, Frederick Von Ledenberg, Martin Blau, Toto Mignone; **D:** Federico Fellini; **W:** Federico Fellini, Tonino Guerra, Tullio Pinelli; **M:** Nicola Piovani. **VHS, Beta $19.98** MGM, FCT, APD *ℐℐℐ*

Ginger in the Morning A salesman is enamored of a young hitchhiker whom he picks up on the road. This is the same year Spacek played the innocent-gone-twisted in "Badlands."
1973 90m/C Sissy Spacek, Slim Pickens, Monte Markham, Susan Oliver, Mark Miller; **D:** Gordon Wiles. **VHS, Beta** NO *ℐℐ*

The Girl The first of Meszaros' trilogy, dealing with a young girl who leaves an orphanage to be reunited with her mother, a traditional country peasant. In Hungarian with English subtitles. Meszaros' first film. Followed by "Riddance" (1973) and "Adoption" (1975).
1968 86m/B HU **D:** Marta Meszaros. **VHS, Beta $69.95** KIV, ING *ℐℐℐ*

The Girl Nero is a wealthy attorney who agrees to pay Powney 300 crowns to have his way with her. Although somewhat ambivalent because of her scandalous age, he takes her anyway. Soon he informs his wife he needs to go on a long business trip, which fits in with her own adulterous plans. A snooping reporter (Brennan) out for some dirt upsets the apple cart, eventually leading to murder.
1986 (R) 104m/C Franco Nero, Christopher Lee, Bernice Stegers, Clare Powney, Frank Brennan; **D:** Arne Mattson. **VHS, Beta $19.95** STE, NWV *ℐ* ½

A Girl, a Guy and a Gob A shy rich boy falls in love with a girl who has her sights on another. Silly but enjoyable cast. **AKA:** The Navy Steps Out.
1941 91m/B Lucille Ball, Edmond O'Brien, George Murphy, Franklin Pangborn, Henry Travers, Lloyd Corrigan; **D:** Richard Wallace. **VHS, Beta $19.98** RKO, TTC *ℐℐ*

The Girl Can't Help It Satiric rock and roll musical comedy about a retired mobster who hires a hungry talent agent to promote his girlfriend, a wannabe no-talent singer. Mansfield's first starring role. Classic performances by some of the early greats including Eddie Cochran, Gene Vincent, The Platters, Little Richard and Fats Domino.
1956 99m/B Jayne Mansfield, Tom Ewell, Edmond O'Brien, Julie London, Ray Anthony; *D:* Frank Tashlin. VHS, Beta $59.98 FOX 🎜🎜 ½

Girl Crazy A wealthy young playboy is sent to an all-boy school in Arizona to get his mind off girls. Once there, he still manages to fall for a local girl who can't stand the sight of him. The eighth film pairing for Rooney and Garland. 🎜Sam and Delilah; Embraceable You; I Got Rhythm; Fascinating Rhythm; Treat Me Rough; Bronco Busters; Bidin' My Time; But Not For Me; Do; When It's Cactus Time in Arizona; Boy, What Love Has Done to Me; Barbary Coast; Could You Use Me?. *AKA:* When the Girls Meet the Boys.
1943 99m/B Mickey Rooney, Judy Garland, Nancy Walker, June Allyson; *D:* Norman Taurog; *M:* George Gershwin, Ira Gershwin. VHS, Beta $19.98 MGM, TTC, FCT 🎜🎜

Girl from Calgary A female rodeo champ ropes her boyfriends much like she ropes her cows, but not without a knockdown, drag-out fight between the two which forces our cowgirl to make the choice she seems to know is fated. Stock rodeo footage is intercut with the heroine riding an obviously mechanical bucking bronc.
1932 66m/B Fifi d'Orsay, Paul Kelly; *D:* Philip H. Whitman. VHS, Beta $19.95 VYY 🎜

Girl from Chicago In this crime melodrama a secret service agent falls in love while on assignment in Mississippi. When he's back in New York he finds a good friend of his girl's in serious trouble with the numbers racket.
1932 69m/C Starr Calloway, Grace Smith, Eugene Brooks, Frank Wilson; *D:* Oscar Micheaux. VHS $34.95 FCT, BTV 🎜

Girl from Hunan Turn-of-the-century China, a 12-year-old girl is married to a 2-year-old boy in a typical arranged marriage. She grows into womanhood treating her toddler husband with sibling affection, but conducts a secret love affair with a farmer. Intolerant village laws against adultry place her life in jeopardy. In Mandarin with English subtitles.
1986 99m/C Na Renhua, Deng Xiaotuang, Yu Zhang; *D:* Xie Fei. VHS $79.95 NYF, ING 🎜🎜🎜

The Girl from Missouri Cute comedy in which Harlow tries to snag a millionaire without sacrificing her virtues. Lots of laughs and hilarious action, especially the scene where Harlow arrives at the yacht in Florida. Kelly is great as Harlow's wise-cracking girlfriend. Witty dialogue by Emerson and Loos, who also wrote "Gentleman Prefer Blondes." *AKA:* One Hundred Percent Pure.
1934 75m/B Jean Harlow, Lionel Barrymore, Franchot Tone, Lewis Stone, Patsy Kelly, Alan Mowbray, Clara Blandick, Russell Hopton; *D:* Jack Conway; *W:* Anita Loos, John Emerson. VHS $19.98 MGM 🎜🎜

The Girl from Petrovka A high-spirited Russian ballerina falls in love with an American newspaper correspondent. Their romance is complicated by the suspicious KGB. Bittersweet with a bleak ending.
1974 (PG) 103m/C Goldie Hawn, Hal Holbrook, Anthony Hopkins; *D:* Robert Ellis Miller; *W:* Chris Bryant, Allan Scott; *M:* Henry Mancini. VHS, Beta $59.95 MCA 🎜 ½

The Girl from Tobacco Row A Southern slut involved with a cache of stolen cash fools with both a convict and the sheriff.
1966 90m/C Tex Ritter, Rachel Romen, Earl Richards, Tim Ormond, Rita Faye, Ralph Emery; *D:* Ron Ormond. VHS, Beta NO 🎜

Girl Happy The King's fans will find him in Fort Lauderdale, Florida this time as the leader of a rock 'n' roll group. His mission: to chaperon the daughter of a Chicago mobster who naturally falls for him. Why not? 🎜Girl Happy; Cross My Heart and Hope to Die; Do Not Disturb; Spring Fever; Wolf Call; Do the Clam; Fort Lauderdale Chamber of Commerce; Puppet On a String; I've Got to Find About My Baby; The Meanest Girl in Town; Startin' Tonight.
1965 96m/C Elvis Presley, Harold J. Stone, Shelley Fabares, Gary Crosby, Nita Talbot, Mary Ann Mobley, Jackie Coogan; *D:* Boris Sagal. VHS, Beta $19.95 MGM 🎜🎜

Girl Hunters That intrepid private eye, Mike Hammer (played by his creator, Spillane), is caught up with communist spies, wicked women, and a missing secretary. Hammer is his usual judge-and-jury character but the action is fast-paced.
1963 103m/B Mickey Spillane, Lloyd Nolan, Shirley Eaton, Hy Gardner, Scott Peters; *D:* Roy Rowland. VHS, Beta $16.95 SNC, NOS, DVT 🎜🎜 ½

A Girl in a Million Williams dumps his verbose wife and seeks peace and quiet in a men-only War Department office. All is well until the arrival of a colonel and his daughter, mute from trauma. Finding her silence appealing, he marries her, but another trauma restores her speech. Sexist comedy may have played better in its day.
1946 90m/B GB Hugh Williams, Joan Greenwood, Naunton Wayne, Wylie Watson, Garry Marsh; *D:* Francis Searle. VHS $19.95 NOS 🎜🎜

The Girl in a Swing An Englishman impulsively marries a beautiful German girl and both are subsequently haunted by phantoms from her past - are they caused by her psychic powers? Cliche-ridden silliness. Based on the Richard Adams novel.
1989 (R) 119m/C Meg Tilly, Rupert Frazer, Elspet Gray, Lynsey Baxter, Nicholas Le Prevost, Jean Both; *D:* Gordon Hessler. VHS, Beta $89.99 HBO 🎜 ½

Girl in Black The shy daughter of a once wealthy household gets the chance to escape her genteel poverty when she falls in love with the young man boarding with her family. He is attracted to her but a shocking tragedy changes everything. In Greek with English subtitles.
1956 100m/C GR Ellie Lambetti; *D:* Michael Cacoyannis. VHS, Beta $59.95 FCT 🎜🎜

Girl in Black Stockings Beautiful women are mysteriously murdered at a remote, Utah hotel. Interesting, little known thriller similar to Hitchcock's "Psycho," but pre-dating it by three years.
1957 75m/B Lex Barker, Anne Bancroft, Mamie Van Doren, Ron Randell, Marie Windsor, John Dehner, John Holland, Diana Van Der Vlis; *D:* Howard W. Koch; *M:* Les Baxter. VHS $18.00 FRG 🎜🎜

The Girl in Blue A lawyer, ill at ease with his current romance, suddenly decides to search for a beautiful woman he saw once, and instantly fell in love with, years before.
1974 (R) 103m/C CA Maud Adams, David Selby, Gay Rowan, William Osler, Diane Dewey, Michael Kirby; *D:* George Kaczender. VHS, Beta $79.95 PSM 🎜🎜

A Girl in Every Port Navy buddies acquire an ailing racehorse and try to conceal it aboard ship along with a healthy horse they plan to switch it with in an upcoming race. Groucho flies without his brothers in this zany film.
1952 86m/B Groucho Marx, William Bendix, Marie Wilson, Don DeFore, Gene Lockhart; *D:* Chester Erskine. VHS, Beta $19.98 CCB 🎜🎜 ½

Girl in Gold Boots Aspiring starlet meets up with a draft evader and a biker on her way to Hollywood where she gets a job as a go-go dancer in a sleazy club. But things don't go smoothly when a murder and a drug theft are revealed. 🎜Do You Want to Laugh or Cry?; For You; Hello, Michelle; One Good Time, One Good Place; Lonesome Man; You Gotta Come Down; Everything I Touch Turns to Gold; Cowboy Santa; Wheels of Love; Sin; Minnie Shimmy; Jimmy's Girl; Strange Things.
1969 94m/C Jody Daniels, Leslie McRae, Tom Pace, Mark Herron; *D:* Ted V. Mikels. VHS, Beta NO 🎜

Girl in His Pocket Mad scientist creates a potion that turns things into three-inch statues. He uses it mostly to have trysts with his lab assistant so his fiancee won't find out. Based on "The Diminishing Draft" by Waldemar Kaempfert. *AKA:* Amour de Poche; Nude in His Pocket.
1962 82m/C FR Jean Marais, Genevieve Page, Agnes Laurent; *D:* Pierre Kast. VHS $16.95 SNC 🎜🎜

The Girl in Lover's Lane A drifter falls in love with a small town girl but becomes a murder suspect when she turns up dead. Interesting mainly for Elam's uncharacteristic portrayal of a village idiot.
1960 78m/B Brett Halsey, Joyce Meadows, Lowell Brown, Jack Elam; *D:* Charles R. Rondeau. VHS, Beta $16.95 SNC 🎜🎜

The Girl in Room 2A A young woman is trapped in a mansion with the elderly owner and her demented son. Routine horrorfest.
1976 (R) 90m/C Raf Vallone, Daniela Giordano. VHS, Beta $59.95 PSM Woof!

The Girl in the Picture Sinclair stars in this light comedy as an unlucky photo clerk who discovers only too late that his ex-girlfriend may be the woman of his dreams. Typical understated but entertaining effort from the U.K.'s Forsyth.
1986 (PG-13) 89m/C GB John Gordon-Sinclair, Irina Brook, David McKay, Catherine Guthrie, Paul Young, Gregory Fisher; *D:* Cary Parker. VHS, Beta $79.95 VES 🎜🎜 ½

The Girl Most Likely Light musical comedy about a romance-minded girl who dreams of marrying a wealthy, handsome man. She runs into a problem when she finds three prospects. Remake of 1941's "Tom, Dick and Harry" with Ginger Rogers. Choreography by great Gower Champion. 🎜The Girl Most Likely; All the Colors of the Rainbow; I Don't Know What I Want; Balboa; We Gotta Keep Up With the Joneses; Crazy Horse.
1957 98m/C Jane Powell, Cliff Robertson, Tommy Noonan, Kaye Ballard, Una Merkel; *D:* Mitchell Leisen. VHS, Beta $15.95 VCI 🎜🎜 ½

Girl of the Golden West A musical version of the David Belasco chestnut about a Canadian frontier girl loving a rogue. One of Eddy and MacDonald's lesser efforts but features Ebsen's song and dance talents. 🎜Camptown Races; Shadows on the Moon; Soldiers of Fortune; Soldiers of Fortune Reprise; Shadows on the Moon Reprise; The Wind in the Trees; Liebestraum; Ave Maria;

Senorita; Who Are We to Say; Who Are We to Say Reprise.
1938 120m/B Jeanette MacDonald, Nelson Eddy, Walter Pidgeon, Leo Carrillo, Buddy Ebsen, Leonard Penn, Priscilla Lawson, Bob Murphy, Olin Howland, Cliff Edwards, Billy Bevan; **D:** Robert Z. Leonard. **VHS, Beta $19.98** MGM 🎬🎬

A Girl of the Limberlost A young Indiana farmgirl fights to bring her estranged parents back together, in spite of a meddling aunt and the unexplained phenomena that haunt her. Fine acting and beautiful scenery. Originally broadcast on public television as part of the "Wonderworks" family movie series, it's best appreciated by young teens. Adapted from Gene Stratton Porter's much-filmed novel.
1990 120m/C Annette O'Toole, Joanna Cassidy, Heather Fairfield. **VHS $29.95** PME, HMV, FCT 🎬🎬

Girl on a Chain Gang A girl on the run gets caught by police and does her time on a chain gang—an otherwise all-male chain gang. Predictable.
1965 96m/C William Watson, Julie Ange, R.K. Charles; **D:** Jerry Gross; **W:** Jerry Gross. **VHS, Beta $16.95** SNC Woof!

The Girl on a Motorcycle Singer Faithfull is a bored housewife who dons black leather and hops on her motorcycle to meet up with her lover (Delon), all the while remembering their other erotic encounters. **AKA:** Naked Under Leather; La Motocyclette.
1968 (R) 92m/C GB Alain Delon, Marianne Faithfull, Roger Mutton; **D:** Jack Cardiff. **VHS, Beta $59.95** MLB 🎬🎬

A Girl on Her Own A young actress embarking on her first big role in Paris must also deal with her family and political considerations in this drama set during the political upheaval of 1935.
1976 112m/C FR Sophie Chemineau, Bruno La Brasca; **D:** Philippe Nahoun. **VHS $49.95** FCT 🎬🎬

Girl Rush Two bad vaudeville comics are stuck in California during the gold rush and are promised sacks of gold if they can persuade some women to come to a rowdy mining town. ♫ Annabella's Bustle; Rainbow Valley; If Mother Could Only See Us Now; Walking Arm in Arm With Jim.
1944 65m/B Wally Brown, Alan Carney, Frances Langford, Vera Vague, Robert Mitchum, Paul Hurst, Patti Brill, Sarah Padden, Cy Kendall; **D:** Gordon Douglas. **VHS, Beta** RKO, TTC 🎬

The Girl Said No A sleazy bookie poses as a theatrical producer in order to get even with a dance hall floozy who once stiffed him. **AKA:** With Words and Music.
1937 72m/B Robert Armstrong, Irene Hervey, William Haines; **D:** Andrew L. Stone; **W:** Andrew L. Stone. **VHS, Beta $19.95** NOS, DVT, VYY 🎬½

Girl Shy Harold is a shy tailor's apprentice who is trying to get a collection of his romantic fantasies published. Finale features Lloyd chasing wildly after girl of his dreams.
1924 65m/B Harold Lloyd, Jobyna Ralston, Richard Daniels; **D:** Fred Newmeyer; **W:** Sam Taylor. **VHS, Beta** TLF 🎬🎬🎬

The Girl, the Body and the Pill Sexploitation pic from director Lewis has a high school instructor getting fired for her sex education lectures—so she continues them in the privacy of her own home. Meanwhile, her students take up playing musical beds and learn about "the pill."
1967 ?m/C Bill Rogers, Nancy Lee Noble; **D:** Herschell Gordon Lewis. **VHS $19.99** MOV 🎬

A Girl to Kill for A temptress lures a randy college guy into a plot of murder and betrayal.

1990 (R) 85m/C Sasha Jensen, Karen Austin, Alex Cord, Rod McCary, Karen Medak; **D:** Richard Oliver. **VHS, Beta $79.95** COL 🎬½

Girl Under the Sheet A con-man/archaeologist moves into an ancient castle and begins romancing a beautiful resident ghost.
196? 89m/C Chelo Alonso, Walter Chiari. **VHS, Beta** NO 🎬

The Girl Who Had Everything Good melodrama with top cast, intelligent script and smooth direction. Taylor plays the spoiled daughter of a criminal lawyer (Powell) who falls for her father's client (Lamas), a suave, underground syndicate boss. Remake of the 1931 film "A Free Soul," which starred Norma Shearer, Clark Gable, and Lionel Barrymore. Based on the novel of the same name by Adela Rogers St. John.
1953 69m/B Elizabeth Taylor, Fernando Lamas, William Powell, Gig Young, James Whitmore, Robert Burton; **D:** Richard Thorpe. **VHS $19.98** MGM 🎬🎬½

The Girl Who Spelled Freedom A young Cambodian girl, speaking little English, strives to adjust to life in Chattanooga, Tennessee. She faces her challenges by becoming a champion at the national spelling bee. Based on a true story. Made-for-television.
1986 90m/C Wayne Rogers, Mary Kay Place, Jade Chinn, Kieu Chinh, Kathleen Sisk; **D:** Simon Wincer. **VHS, Beta $59.95** DIS 🎬🎬🎬

The Girl with the Hat Box Early Russian production about a poor working girl who's paid with a lottery ticket rather than rubles (an ironic pre-communist theme?). When she strikes it rich in the lottery, her boss gives chase and silent antics ensue. Silent with orchestral score.
1927 67m/B RU Anna Sten, Vladimar Fogel, Serafina Birman, Ivan Koval-Samborsky; **D:** Boris Barnett. **VHS $29.95** KIV, FCT, ING 🎬🎬

Girlfriend from Hell The Devil inhabits the body of a teenage wallflower and turns her into an uncontrollable vamp.
1989 (R) 95m/C Liane Curtis, Dana Ashbrook, Leslie Deane, James Daughton, Anthony Barrie, James Karen; **D:** Daniel M. Peterson; **W:** Daniel M. Peterson. **VHS, Beta $14.95** LIV 🎬

Girlfriends Bittersweet story of a young Jewish photographer learning to make it on her own. Directorial debut of Weill reflects her background in documentaries as the true-to-life episodes unfold.
1978 (PG) 87m/C Melanie Mayron, Anita Skinner, Eli Wallach, Christopher Guest, Amy Wright, Viveca Lindfors, Bob Balaban; **D:** Claudia Weill; **W:** Vicki Polon. **VHS, Beta $19.98** WAR 🎬🎬🎬

Girls Are for Loving Undercover agent Ginger faces real adventure when she battles it out with her counterpart, a seductive enemy agent. Her third adventure following "Ginger" (1970) and "The Abductors" (1971).
1973 90m/C Cheri Caffaro, Timothy Brown; **D:** Don Schain. **VHS, Beta $39.95** MON 🎬

A Girl's Folly A country girl falls in love with the leading man of a film shooting on location. She wants to become a rich actress, but fails miserably. The actor offers her all the luxuries she wants if she'll become his mistress. When she finally agrees, her mother shows up. What will our country maid do now?
1917 66m/B Robert Warwick, Doris Kenyon, June Elvidge, Johnny Hines; **D:** Maurice Tourneur. **VHS, Beta, 8mm $19.95** VYY, GPV 🎬🎬½

Girls! Girls! Girls! Poor tuna boat fisherman Elvis moonlights as a nightclub singer to get his father's boat out of hock. He falls for a rich girl pretending to be poor; and after some romantic trials, there's the usual happy ending. ♫ The Nearness of You; Never Let Me Go; Girls, Girls, Girls; Return to Sender; We're Coming in Loaded; A Boy Like Me, A Girl Like You; Song of the Shrimp; Earth Boy; The Walls Have Ears; Thanks to the Rolling Sea; Because of You; Where Do We Come From?; We'll Be Together, Mama; I Don't Wanna Be Tied; I Don't Want To.
1962 106m/C Elvis Presley, Stella Stevens, Laurel Goodwin, Jeremy Slate, Benson Fong, Robert Strauss, Ginny Tiu, Guy Lee, Beulah Quo; **D:** Norman Taurog. **VHS, Beta $14.98** FOX, MVD 🎬🎬

Girls in Chains Girls in a reformatory, a teacher, a corrupt school official, and the detective trying to nail him. There's also a murder with the killer revealed at the beginning of the film.
1943 72m/B Arline Judge, Roger Clark, Robin Raymond, Barbara Pepper, Dorothy Burgess, Clancy Cooper; **D:** Edgar G. Ulmer. **VHS, Beta $16.95** NOS, SNC 🎬½

Girls in Prison Anne Carson is sent to prison for a bank robbery she didn't commit, and although the prison chaplain believes her story, the other prisoners think she knows where the money is hidden. They plan a prison break, forcing Carson to go with them and get the money, but they soon run across the real robber, also searching for the loot. A below-average "B" prison movie, lacking the camp aspects of so many of these films.
1956 87m/B Richard Denning, Joan Taylor, Adele Jergens, Helen Gilbert, Lance Fuller, Jane Darwell, Raymond Hatton; **D:** Edward L. Cahn. **VHS $9.95** COL 🎬½

Girls Just Want to Have Fun An army brat and her friends pull out all the stops and defy their parents for a chance to dance on a national television program. Based loosely upon Cyndi Lauper's song of the same name.
1985 (PG) 90m/C Sarah Jessica Parker, Helen Hunt, Ed Lauter, Holly Gagnier, Morgan Woodward, Lee Montgomery, Shannen Doherty, Biff Yeager; **D:** Alan Metter. **VHS, Beta $9.95** NWV, STE 🎬½

Girls Next Door A bevy of boisterous beauties cavort and cause havoc in buffoon-cluttered suburbia.
1979 (R) 85m/C Kirsten Baker, Perry Lang, Leslie Cederquist, Richard Singer; **D:** James Hong. **VHS, Beta** NO 🎬

Girls Night Out Ex-cop must stop a killer who is murdering participants in a sorority house scavenger hunt and leaving cryptic clues on the local radio station. **AKA:** The Scaremaker.
1983 (R) 96m/C Hal Holbrook, Rutanya Alda, Julia Montgomery, James Carroll; **D:** Robert Deubel. **VHS, Beta $69.95** HBO 🎬

The Girls of Huntington House A teacher in a school for unwed mothers finds herself becoming increasingly absorbed in her students' lives. Made for television.
1973 73m/C Shirley Jones, Mercedes McCambridge, Sissy Spacek, William Windom, Pamela Sue Martin, Darrell Larson; **D:** Alf Kjellin. **VHS $59.95** LIV 🎬🎬

Girls of the White Orchid A naive American girl thinks she's getting a job singing in a Japanese nightclub, but it turns out to be a front for a prostitution ring run by the Japanese Yakuza. A made-for-television movie based on real stories, though the producers concentrate on the seamy side. **AKA:** Death Ride to Osaka.

1985 96m/C Ann Jillian, Jennifer Jason Leigh; *D:* Jonathan Kaplan; *M:* Brad Fiedel. VHS, Beta $59.95 *LHV* ⅟

Girls on the Road Two girls are just out for fun cruising the California coast. But that handsome hitchhiker turns out to be a deadly mistake.
1973 91m/C *CA* Kathleen Cody, Michael Ontkean, Dianne Hull, Ralph Waite; *D:* Thomas J. Schmidt. VHS, Beta $59.95 *UNI* ⅟⅟

Girls Riot Young, female juvenile delinquents have had enough! They decide to give their warden-like headmistress a taste of her own violence.
1988 100m/C Jocelyne Boisseau, Cornelia Calwer, Angelica Domrose, Ute Freight; *D:* Manfred Purzer. VHS, Beta $39.95 *ACN* ⅟

Girls School Screamers Six young women and a nun are assigned to spend the weekend checking the contents for sale in a scary mansion bequeathed to their school. Unfortunately, the psychotic killer inhabiting the place doesn't think that's a good idea.
1986 (R) 85m/C Mollie O'Mara, Sharon Christopher, Vera Gallagher; *D:* John P. Finegan. VHS, Beta $69.98 *LIV* ⅟

Girls' Town Typical bad girls and drag racing fifties flick has Van Doren sent to a correctional institute, run by nuns. This tough girl sees the error of her wicked ways and turns into a goody-two-shoes. *AKA:* The Innocent and the Damned.
1959 90m/B Mamie Van Doren, Mel Torme, Paul Anka, Ray Anthony, Maggie Hayes, Cathy Crosby, Elinor Donahue, Gigi Perreau, Jim Mitchum, Gloria Talbott, Harold Lloyd Jr., Charles Chaplin Jr.; *D:* Charles Haas; *W:* Robert Smith. VHS $9.98 *REP* ⅟

Girly An English gothic about an excessively weird family that lives in a crumbling mansion and indulges in murder, mental aberration, and sexual compulsion. *AKA:* Mumsy, Nanny, Sonny, and Girly.
1970 (R) 101m/C *GB* Michael Bryant, Ursula Howells, Pat Heywood, Howard Trevor, Vanessa Howard, Michael Ripper; *D:* Freddie Francis. VHS, Beta $79.95 *PSM* ⅟

Git! A young runaway and his faithful dog are taken in by a wealthy dog-breeder and trained by him into a crack hunting team.
1965 90m/C Jack Chaplain, Richard Webb, Heather North; *D:* Ellis Kadison. VHS, Beta $14.95 *COL, NLC* ⅟⅟

Git Along Little Dogies It's cattle ranchers versus oil men with Autry caught in the middle of the petro/cow war. But Gene still finds a little time to romance the town banker's pretty daughter.
1937 60m/B William Farnum, Gene Autry, Judith Allen, Champion, Smiley Burnette; *D:* Joseph Kane. VHS, Beta $19.95 *NOS, VYY, DVT* ⅟⅟

Give a Girl a Break Three talented but unknown babes vie for the lead in a stage production headed for Broadway after the incumbent prima donna quits. After befriending one of the various men associated with the production, each starlet thinks she's a shoe-in for the part. Entertaining but undistinguished musical with appealing dance routines of Fosse and the Champions. Ira Gershwin, collaborating for the first and only time with Burton Lane, wrote the lyrics to two of the songs. ♫Give the Girl a Break; In Our United State; It Happens Every Time; Nothing is Impossible; Applause, Applause; Challenge Dance.
1953 84m/C Marge Champion, Gower Champion, Debbie Reynolds, Helen Wood, Bob Fosse, Kurt Kasznar, Richard Anderson, William Ching, Larry Keating, Donna Martell; *D:* Stanley Donen. VHS $19.98 *MGM, TTC, FCT* ⅟⅟½

Give 'Em Hell, Harry! James Whitmore's one-man show as Harry S. Truman filmed in performance on stage; Whitmore was nominated for a Tony.
1975 103m/C James Whitmore; *D:* Steve Binder. VHS, Beta $19.95 *WOV* ⅟⅟½

Give My Regards to Broad Street McCartney film made for McCartney fans. Film features many fine versions of the ex-Beatle's songs that accompany his otherwise lackluster portrayal of a rock star in search of his stolen master recordings. ♫Eleanor Rigby; Ballroom Dancing; Good Day, Sunshine; Silly Love Songs; No Values; No More Lonely Nights; Yesterday; Not Such a Bad Boy; The Long and Winding Road.
1984 (PG) 109m/C *GB* Paul McCartney, Bryan Brown, Ringo Starr, Barbara Bach, Tracey Ullman, Ralph Richardson, Linda McCartney; *D:* Peter Webb. VHS, Beta $19.95 *MVD, FOX* ⅟⅟

The Gladiator Brown stars as a mild-mannered collegiate who accidently ingests a serum which turns him into a real he-man. Things take a turn for the funniest when the effects wear off, just as he is to wrestle Man Mountain Dean. Chock-full of Brown's trademark physical humor.
1938 70m/B Joe E. Brown, Man Mountain Dean, June Travis, Dickie Moore, Lucien Littlefield, Robert Kent, Ethel Wales; *D:* Edward Sedgwick. VHS $19.95 *NOS* ⅟⅟⅟½

The Gladiator An angry Los Angeles citizen turns vigilante against drunk drivers after his brother is one of their victims. Made for television.
1986 94m/C Ken Wahl, Nancy Allen, Robert Culp, Stan Shaw, Rosemary Forsyth; *D:* Abel Ferrara. VHS, Beta $19.95 *STE, NWV, HHE* ⅟½

Gladiator When suburban Golden Gloves boxing champion Tommy Riley (Marshall) is forced to move to the inner city because of his father's gambling debts, he becomes involved with an evil boxing promotor who thrives on pitting different ethnic races against each other in illegal boxing matches. Eventually Riley is forced to fight his black friend Lincoln (Gooding), even though Lincoln has been warned that another blow to the head could mean his life. Although this film tries to serve some moral purpose, it falls flat on the mat.
1992 (R) 98m/C Cuba Gooding Jr., James Marshall, Robert Loggia, Ossie Davis, Brian Dennehy, Cara Buono, John Heard, John Seda, Lance Slaughter; *D:* Rowdy Herrington. VHS *COL* ⅟⅟

Gladiator of Rome A gladiator flexes his pecs to save a young girl from death at the hands of evil rulers. *AKA:* Il Gladiatore Di Roma.
1963 105m/C *IT* Gordon Scott, Wandisa Guida, Roberto Risso, Ombretta Colli, Alberto Farnese; *D:* Mario Costa. VHS $16.95 *SNC* ⅟

The Gladiators Televised gladiatorial bouts are designed to subdue man's violent tendencies in a futuristic society until a computer makes a fatal error. *AKA:* The Peace Game; Gladiatorerna.
1970 90m/C Arthur Pentelow, Frederick Danner; *D:* Peter Watkins. VHS, Beta *VCI* ⅟

Gladiators 7 Sparta must be freed from the tyrannical rule of the Romans. In lieu of samurai or cowboys, who better than the Gladiators 7 to do the deed? Plenty of sword-to-sword action and scantily clad Italian babes.
1962 92m/C *SP IT* Richard Harrison, Loredana Nusciak, Livio Lorenzon, Gerard Tichy, Edoardo Toniolo, Joseph Marco, Barta Barry; *D:* Pedro Lazaga. VHS, Beta $16.95 *SNC* ⅟½

Glass A normally complacent man is driven to the brink of savagery when a killer begins stalking his employees.
1990 92m/C Alan Lovell, Lisa Peers, Adam Stone, Natalie McCurray. VHS $59.95 *ATL* ⅟½

The Glass Bottom Boat A bubbly but transparent Doris Day comedy, in which she falls in love with her boss at an aerospace lab. Their scheme to spend time together get her mistaken for a spy. Made about the time they stopped making them like this anymore, it's innocuous slapstick romance with a remarkable 1960's cast, including a Robert Vaughn cameo as the Man From U.N.C.L.E. Doris sings "Que Sera, Sera" and a few other numbers.
1966 110m/C Doris Day, Rod Taylor, Arthur Godfrey, Paul Lynde, Eric Fleming, Alice Pearce, Ellen Corby, John McGiver, Dom DeLuise, Dick Martin, Edward Andrews; *Cameos:* Robert Vaughn; *D:* Frank Tashlin; *W:* Everett Freeman. VHS, Beta $19.98 *MGM* ⅟⅟½

The Glass House Alda stars as a middle-aged college professor, convicted on a manslaugter charge, who is sent to a maximum security prison and must learn to deal with life inside. Filmed at Utah State Prison, real-life prisoners add supporting cast add to the drama. Still has the power to chill, with Morrow particularly effective as one of the inmate leaders. Adapted from a Truman Capote story. Made for television. *AKA:* Truman Capote's The Glass House.
1972 92m/C Alan Alda, Vic Morrow, Clu Gulager, Billy Dee Williams, Dean Jagger, Kristopher Tabori; *D:* Tom Gries; *M:* Billy Goldenberg. VHS, Beta $49.95 *MOV, HHT* ⅟⅟⅟

The Glass Jungle Will a cab driver save Los Angeles? When armed terrorists and the FBI battle it out in the sunny California city an innocent cabby seems to hold the solution to survival.
1988 94m/C Lee Canalito, Joe Filbeck, Diana Frank, Mark High, Frank Scala; *D:* Joseph Merhi. VHS, Beta $69.95 *HHE* ⅟⅟⅟

The Glass Key The second version of Dashiell Hammet's novel, a vintage mystery movie concerning a nominally corrupt politician (Donlevy) being framed for murder, and his assistant sleuthing out the real culprit. One of Ladd's first starring vehicles; Lake is the mystery woman who loves him, and Bendix a particularly vicious thug.
1942 85m/B Alan Ladd, Veronica Lake, Brian Donlevy, William Bendix, Bonita Granville, Richard Denning, Joseph Calleia, Moroni Olsen, Dane Clark; *D:* Stuart Heisler. VHS, Beta $14.98 *MCA* ⅟⅟⅟

The Glass Menagerie An aging Southern belle deals with her crippled daughter Laura, whose one great love is her collection of glass animals. The third film adaptation of the Tennessee Williams classic, which preserves the performances of the Broadway revival cast, is a solid-but-not-stellar adaptation of the play. All-star acting ensemble.
1987 (PG) 134m/C Joanne Woodward, Karen Allen, John Malkovich, James Naughton; *D:* Paul Newman; *W:* Tennessee Williams; *M:* Henry Mancini. VHS, Beta $19.98 *MCA, KUI* ⅟⅟⅟

The Glass Slipper In this version of the "Cinderella" saga, Caron plays an unglamourous girl gradually transformed into the expected beauty. Winwood is the fairy godmother who inspires the girl to find happiness, rather then simply providing it for her magically. The film is highlighted by the stunning dance numbers, choreographed by Roland Petit and featuring the Paris ballet.

1955 93m/C Leslie Caron, Michael Wilding, Keenan Wynn, Estelle Winwood, Elsa Lanchester, Barry Jones, Amanda Blake, Lurene Tuttle; **D:** Charles Walters. **VHS, Beta** $19.98 MGM, FCT ✐✐

Glass Tomb At a circus, a man performs the world's longest fast inside a glass cage, and becomes the raison d'etre for murder. **AKA:** The Glass Cage.
1955 59m/B John Ireland, Honor Blackman, Eric Pohlmann, Tonia Bern, Sidney James; **D:** Montgomery Tully. **VHS, Beta** NO ✐✐

Gleaming the Cube A skateboarding teen investigates his brother's murder. Film impresses with its stunt footage only. For those with adolescent interests.
1989 (PG-13) 102m/C Christian Slater, Steven Bauer, Min Luong, Art Chudabala, Le Tuan; **D:** Graeme Clifford; **W:** Michael Tolkin; **M:** Jay Michael Ferguson. **VHS, Beta** $14.98 LIV, VES ✐✐½

Glen and Randa Two young people experience the world after it has been destroyed by nuclear war. Early McBride, before the hired-gun success of "The Big Easy."
1971 (R) 94m/C Steven Curry, Shelley Plimpton; **D:** Jim McBride; **W:** Rudy Wurlitzer, Jim McBride. **VHS, Beta** $59.95 VCI, IME ✐✐½

Glen or Glenda An appalling, quasi-docudrama about transvestism, interspersed with meaningless stock footage, inept dream sequences and Lugosi sitting in a chair spouting incoherent prattle at the camera. Directorial debut of Wood, who, using a pseudonym, played the lead; one of the phenomenally bad films of this century. An integral part of the famous anti-auteur's canon. **AKA:** He or She; I Changed My Sex; I Led Two Lives; The Transvestite.
1953 70m/B Bela Lugosi, Edward D. Wood Jr., Lyle Talbot, Donald Woods; **D:** Edward D. Wood Jr. **VHS, Beta** $19.95 NOS, MRV, SNC Woof!

Glengarry Glen Ross A seven-character study chronicling 48-hours in the lives of some sleazy real estate men in danger of getting the ax from their hard-driving bosses. A standout cast includes Pacino as the glad-handing sales leader, Lemmon as the hustler fallen on dim prospects, and Baldwin, briefly venomous, as the company hatchet-man. Brutal and hard-edged with very strong language. Mamet scripted from his Tony-award winning Broadway play.
1992 (R) 100m/C Al Pacino, Jack Lemmon, Ed Harris, Alec Baldwin, Alan Arkin, Kevin Spacey, Jonathan Pryce, Bruce Altman, Jude Ciccolella; **D:** James Foley; **W:** David Mamet; **M:** James Newton Howard. Academy Awards '92 Nominations: Best Supporting Actor (Pacino); National Board of Review Awards '93: Best Actor (Lemmon); Venice Film Festival '93: Best Actor (Lemmon). **VHS** $94.98 LIV, MOV, BTV ✐✐✐

The Glenn Miller Story The music of the Big Band Era lives again in this warm biography of the legendary Glenn Miller, following his life from the late '20s to his untimely death in a WWII plane crash. Stewart's likably convincing and even fakes the trombone playing well. ♫Moonlight Serenade; In the Mood; Tuxedo Junction; Little Brown Jug; Adios; String of Pearls; Pennsylvania 6-5000; Stairway to the Stars; American Patrol; I Know Why; Chattanooga Choo Choo; Bidin' My Time; I Dreamed I Dwelt in Marble Halls; St. Louis Blues March; Basin Street Blues; Over the Rainbow.
1954 (G) 113m/C James Stewart, June Allyson, Harry Morgan, Gene Krupa, Louis Armstrong, Ben Pollack; **D:** Anthony Mann; **W:** Oscar Brodney; **M:** Henry Mancini. Academy Awards '54: Best Sound; Nominations: Best Story &

Screenplay, Best Original Score. **VHS, Beta** $19.95 MCA, RDG ✐✐✐

Glitch! A throng of beautiful Hollywood hopefuls draw two youngsters unconnected with the film into posing as the film's director and producer in the hopes of conducting personal interviews on the casting couch. Straight to video.
1988 (R) 88m/C Julia Nickson-Soul, Will Egan, Steve Donmyer, Dan Speaker, Dallas Cole, Ji Tu Cambuka, Dick Gautier, Ted Lange, Teri Weigel, Fernando Carzon, John Kreng, Lindsay Carr; **D:** Nico Mastorakis; **W:** Nico Mastorakis. **VHS, Beta** $29.95 ACA ✐½

The Glitter Dome Two policemen discover the sleazier side of Hollywood when they investigate the murder of a pornographer. Based upon the novel by Joseph Wambaugh. Made for television.
1984 90m/C Stuart Margolin, John Marley, James Garner, John Lithgow, Margot Kidder, Colleen Dewhurst; **D:** Stuart Margolin. **VHS, Beta** NO ✐½

Glitz A Miami cop and an Atlantic City lounge singer team up to investigate a call-girl's death and wind up too close to a drug ring. Based on the novel by Elmore Leonard. Made for television.
1988 96m/C Jimmy Smits, John Diehl, Markie Post, Ken Foree, Madison Mason, Robin Strasser; **D:** Sandor Stern. **VHS, Beta** $79.95 WAR ✐✐½

A Global Affair Hope is a department head in the United Nations who finds an abandoned baby in the building. The inept bachelor is wooed by a number of international beauties seeking to adopt the child for their various countries but he becomes increasingly attached to the little tyke.
1963 84m/B Bob Hope, Lilo (Liselotte) Pulver, Michele Mercier, Yvonne De Carlo, Miiko Taka, Robert Sterling, Nehemiah Persoff, John McGiver, Mickey Shaughnessy; **D:** Jack Arnold; **W:** Charles Lederer, Arthur Marx, Bob Fisher. **VHS, Beta** $19.98 MGM, FCT ✐½

Gloria She used to be a Mafia moll, now she's outrunning the Mob after taking in the son of a slain neighbor. He's got a book that they want, and they're willing to kill to get it. Trademark Cassavetes effort in which he has actors plumb their souls to discomfiting levels.
1980 (PG) 123m/C Gena Rowlands, John Adams, Buck Henry, Julie Carmen; **D:** John Cassavetes; **M:** Bill Conti. Academy Awards '80 Nominations: Best Actress (Rowlands); Venice Film Festival '80: Best Film. **VHS, Beta** $69.95 COL ✐✐½

Glorifying the American Girl Eaton's a chorus girl performing in the Ziegfeld Follies, which lends itself to numerous production numbers. The only film Ziegfeld ever produced. ♫What I Wouldn't Do For That Man; Blue Skies; I'm Just a Vagabond Lover; Baby Face; At Sundown; Beautiful Changes; Sam the Old Accordian Man; There Must Be Someone Waiting For Me.
1930 96m/B Mary Eaton, Dan Healey, Eddie Cantor, Rudy Vallee; **D:** Millard Webb. **VHS, Beta** $19.95 NOS, HHT, DVT ✐✐

Glory O'Brien is a racehorse owner who tussles with her grandmother over how to keep the family farm open on a shoestring budget. Brennan enters the picture as the financial guru who lands them back on track, with enough left over to enter their prize filly in the Kentucky Derby. Lupton plays O'Brien's love interest. No surprises here.
1956 100m/C Margaret O'Brien, Walter Brennan, Charlotte Greenwood; **D:** Dick Butler. **VHS, Beta** $15.95 VCI ✐✐

Glory A rich, historical spectacle chronicling the 54th Massachusetts, the first black volunteer infantry unit in the Civil War. The film manages to artfully focus on both the 54th and their white commander, Robert Gould Shaw. Based on Shaw's letters, the film uses thousands of accurately costumed "living historians" (re-enactors) as extras in this panoramic production. A haunting, bittersweet musical score pervades what finally becomes an anti-war statement. Stunning performances throughout, with exceptional work from Freeman and Washington.
1989 (R) 122m/C Matthew Broderick, Morgan Freeman, Denzel Washington, Cary Elwes, Jihmi Kennedy, Andre Braugher, John Finn, Donovan Leitch, John Cullum, Bob Gunton, Jane Alexander, Raymond St. Jacques; **D:** Edward Zwick; **W:** Kevin Jarre; **M:** James Horner. Academy Awards '89: Best Cinematography, Best Sound, Best Supporting Actor (Washington); Nominations: Best Film Editing. **VHS, Beta, 8mm** $19.95 COL, FCT, BTV ✐✐½

Glory Boys A secret agent is hired to protect an Israeli scientist who is marked for assassination by the PLO and IRA.
1984 110m/C Rod Steiger, Anthony Perkins, Gary Brown, Aaron Harris; **D:** Michael Ferguson. **VHS, Beta** $59.95 PSM, VTR ✐½

Glory Enough for All: The Discovery of Insulin The drama behind the discovery of insulin in the 1920s focuses on the research of four men, sometimes not-so-friendly rivals, searching for a treatment for diabetes mellitus. Dr. Frederick Banting and science student Charles Best are granted permission by James Macleod, a Professor of Physiology at the University of Toronto, to conduct experiments on the pancreas. Macleod then assigns biochemist James Collip to assist them on developing a viable serum, an extract named insulin. Banting and Macleod were awarded the Nobel prize in 1923 for their discovery (though Banting felt Macleod was undeserving). Adapted from "The Discovery of Insulin" by Michael Bliss. Made for Canadian television.
1992 196m/C CA R.H. Thomson, Robert Wisden, John Woodvine, Michael Zelniker, Martha Henry, Heather Hess; **D:** Eric Till; **W:** Grahame Woods. **VHS** $150.00 CCC ✐✐½

Glory! Glory! Slashing satire about TV evangelism. Thomas as the meek son of founder of Church of the Champions of Christ brings in lewd female rock singer to save the money-machine ministry from financial ruin. Rock music, sex, and MTV-like camera work make it worth seeing. Whitmore is a treat.
1990 (R) 152m/C Ellen Greene, Richard Thomas, Barry Morse, James Whitmore, Winston Reckert; **D:** Lindsay Anderson. **VHS, Beta** $59.98 ORI, IME ✐✐✐

The Glory Stompers Hopper prepares for his Easy Rider role as the leader of a motorcycle gang who battles with a rival leader over a woman. Very bad, atrocious dialogue, and a "love-in" scene that will be best appreciated by insomniacs.
1967 85m/C Dennis Hopper, Jody McCrea, Chris Noel, Jock Mahoney, Lindsay Crosby, Robert Tessier, Casey Kasem; **D:** Anthony M. Lanza. **VHS** NO Woof!

The Glory Trail A group of railroad workers and soldiers are constantly harassed by Indian attacks. **AKA:** Glorious Sacrifice.
1936 63m/B Tom Keene, Joan Barclay, James Bush, Frank Melton, Walter Long; **D:** Lynn Shores. **VHS** $12.95 GPV ✐½

Glory Years Three old friends find themselves in charge of the scholarship fund at their 20th high school reunion. Unfortunately, they decide to increase the fund by gambling in Las Vegas and lose it all on a fixed fight!
1987 150m/C George Dzundza, Archie Hahn, Tim Thomerson, Tawny Kitaen, Donna Pescow, Donna Denton; *D:* Arthur Seidelman. VHS, Beta **$79.95** HBO *✒*

The Glove Ex-cop turned bounty hunter has his toughest assignment ever. It's his job to bring in a six-and-a-half foot, 250-pound ex-con who's been wreaking havoc with an unusual glove—it's made of leather and steel. *AKA:* The Glove: Lethal Terminator; Blood Mad.
1978 (R) 93m/C John Saxon, Roosevelt Grier, Joanna Cassidy, Joan Blondell, Jack Carter, Aldo Ray; *D:* Ross Hagen. VHS, Beta **$19.95** MED *✒½*

The Gnome-Mobile A lumber baron and his two grandchildren attempt to reunite a pair of forest gnomes with a lost gnome colony. Brennan has a dual role as both a human and a gnome grandfather. Wynn's last film. Based on a children's novel by Upton Sinclair.
1967 84m/C Walter Brennan, Richard Deacon, Ed Wynn, Karen Dotrice, Matthew Garber; *D:* Robert Stevenson; *M:* Buddy Baker. VHS, Beta DIS, OM *✒✒*

The Go-Between Wonderful tale of hidden love. Young boy Guard acts as a messenger between the aristocratic Christie and her former lover Bates. But tragedy befalls them all when the lovers are discovered. The story is told as the elderly messenger (now played by Redgrave) recalls his younger days as the go-between and builds to a climax when he is once again asked to be a messenger for the lady he loved long ago. Based on a story by L.P. Hartley.
1971 (PG) 116m/C *GB* Julie Christie, Alan Bates, Dominic Guard, Margaret Leighton, Michael Redgrave, Michael Gough, Edward Fox; *D:* Joseph Losey; *W:* Harold Pinter. Academy Awards '71 Nominations: Best Supporting Actress (Leighton); British Academy Awards '71: Best Supporting Actor (Fox), Best Supporting Actress (Leighton). VHS CSM, MGM *✒✒✒½*

Go Down Death In this early all-black film, a minister is caught in a moral dilemma literally between Heaven and Hell. Scenes of the afterlife are taken from early silent films.
1941 63m/B Myra D. Hemmings, Samuel H. James, Eddy L. Houston, Spencer Williams Jr., Amos Droughan; *D:* Spencer Williams Jr. VHS, Beta **$19.95** VYY, DVT, TIM *✒½*

Go for Broke! Inexperienced officer Johnson heads a special WWII attack force which is made up of Japanese Americans. Sent to fight in Europe, they prove their bravery and loyalty to all. Good, offbeat story.
1951 92m/B Van Johnson, Giana Maria Canale, Warner Anderson, Lane Nakano, George Miki; *D:* Robert Pirosh. VHS, Beta **$19.95** NOS, MRV, VYY *✒✒½*

Go for Broke Motorcycle stunts, fights, and car chases highlight this action film.
1990 ?m/C VHS VYY *✒✒½*

Go for It Oddball supercops go after a mad scientist—who has created a deadly "K"-bomb—and they encounter killer whales, karate busboys and malevolent Shirley Temple clones along the way.
1983 (PG) 109m/C *IT* Bud Spencer, Terence Hill, David Huddleston; *D:* E.B. Clucher. VHS, Beta **$79.95** WAR *✒½*

Go for the Gold A young marathon runner risks his girlfriend's love when he decides to pursue fame and fortune.

1984 98m/C James Ryan, Cameron Mitchell, Sandra Horne. VHS, Beta **$69.98** LIV *✒*

The Go-Getter Wild slapstick fun in the world of business.
1954 ?m/C Hank McCune, Beverly Garland. VHS **$15.95** LOO *✒✒*

Go, Johnny Go! Rock promoter Alan Freed molds a young orphan into rock sensation "Johnny Melody." Musical performances include Ritchie Valens (his only film appearance), Eddie Cochran, Jackie Wilson.
1959 75m/B Alan Freed, Sandy Stewart, Chuck Berry, The Cadillacs, Jimmy Clanton, Eddie Cochran, Jackie Wilson, Ritchie Valens; *D:* Paul Landres. VHS, Beta **$14.95** MED, AOV, VTR *✒✒*

Go Kill and Come Back A bounty hunter tracks down a notoriously dangerous train robber.
1968 (PG) 95m/C Gilbert Roland, George Helton, Edd Byrnes; *D:* Enzo G. Castellari. VHS, Beta **$24.95** MON *✒*

The Go-Masters Historic co-production between Japan and China, centering on the ancient strategy board game "Go." A young competitor becomes obsessed with winning at any price. Episodic tale of the relationships between a Japanese and Chinese family spans 30 years and was critically acclaimed in both China and Japan. In Japanese and Chinese with English subtitles. *AKA:* Mikan No Taikyoku.
1982 134m/C *JP CH* Huang Zong-Ying, Du Peng, Yu Shao-Kang, Lui Xin, Yoshiko Mita, Keiko Matsuzaka, Mayumi Ogawa, Rentaro Mikuni, Sun Dao-Lin, Shen Guan-Chu, Misako Honno; *D:* Junya Sato, Duan Jishun. VHS, Beta **$59.95** ING, FCT *✒✒✒*

Go Tell the Spartans In Vietnam, 1964, a hard-boiled major is ordered to establish a garrison at Muc Wa with a platoon of burned out Americans and Vietnamese mercenaries. Blundering but politically interesting war epic pre-dating the flood of 1980s American-Vietnam apologetics. Based on Daniel Ford's novel.
1978 (R) 114m/C Burt Lancaster, Craig Wasson, David Clennon, Marc Singer; *D:* Ted Post; *W:* Wendell Mayes. VHS, Beta **$19.98** VES *✒✒✒*

Go West The brothers Marx help in the making and un-making of the Old West. Weak, late Marx Bros., but always good for a few yucks.
1940 80m/B Groucho Marx, Chico Marx, Harpo Marx, John Carroll, Diana Lewis; *D:* Edward Buzzell. VHS, Beta **$19.95** MGM, CCB *✒✒½*

Go West, Young Man West is a movie star whose latest film is premiering in a small town, where she's naturally a sensation. Scott is the muscular farm boy who catches her eye and she decides to hang around in order to catch the rest of him as well. The censors again cut West's most overt sexual and satiric barbs.
1936 80m/B Mae West, Randolph Scott, Warren William, Alice Brady, Elizabeth Patterson, Lyle Talbot, Isabel Jewell; *D:* Henry Hathaway; *W:* Mae West. VHS **$14.98** MCA, BTV *✒✒½*

The Goalie's Anxiety at the Penalty Kick A chilling landmark film that established Wenders as one of the chief film voices to emerge from post-war Germany. The story deals with a soccer player who wanders around Vienna after being suspended, commits a random murder, and slowly passes over the brink of sanity and morality. A suspenseful, existential adaptation of the Peter Handke novel. In German with English subtitles.
1971 101m/C *GE* Arthur Brauss, Erika Pluhar, Kai Fischer; *D:* Wim Wenders. VHS, Beta **$29.95** FCT, GLV, ING *✒✒✒½*

Goblin Newlywed couple regret the purchase of their new home when the devilish creature once brought to life by the previous homeowner, a witchcraft performing farmer, is raised from the depths of hell to rip to pieces anyone in its view. Any movie whose promo says "You won't believe your eyes...until he rips them from their sockets" is sure to be a crowd pleaser. Enjoy.
1993 75m/C Bobby Westrick, Jenny Admire. VHS TEM Woof!

God Bless the Child A young single mother loses her home and she and her seven-year-old daughter are forced to live on the streets. Harrowing made for television drama providing no easy answers to the plight of the homeless.
1988 93m/C Mare Winningham, Dorian Harewood, Grace Johnston, Charlaine Woodard, Obba Babatunde, L. Scott Caldwell; *D:* Larry Elikann; *W:* Dennis Nemec. VHS **$89.95** WOV *✒✒✒*

God, Man and Devil A wager between God and Satan begins this allegory of money versus the spirit. A poor Torah scribe, Hershele Dubrovner, has a life that glorifies God until Satan, disguised as a business partner, turns him greedy and dishonest. Dubrovner's success destroys both his religion and his community leaving only betrayal and abandonment. In Yiddish with English subtitles.
1949 100m/B Mikhal Mikhalesko, Gustav Berger; *D:* Joseph Seiden. VHS **$54.00** NCJ *✒✒½*

God Told Me To A religious New York cop is embroiled in occult mysteries while investigating a series of grisly murders. He investigates a religious cult that turns out to be composed of half-human, half-alien beings. A cult-fave Larry Cohen epic. *AKA:* Demon.
1976 (R) 89m/C Tony LoBianco, Deborah Raffin, Sylvia Sidney, Sandy Dennis, Richard Lynch; *D:* Larry Cohen; *W:* Larry Cohen. VHS, Beta **$19.98** NLC *✒✒½*

Godard/Truffaut Shorts A pair of early shorts directed by two French "new wave" masters: Jean-Luc Godard's "All the Boys Are Called Patrick" from 1957 and Francois Truffaut's "Les Mistons" from 1958.
1958 39m/B *FR D:* Francois Truffaut, Jean-Luc Godard. VHS, Beta **$29.95** DVT, MRV, ING *✒✒✒*

The Goddess Sordid story of a girl who rises to fame as a celluloid star by making her body available to anyone who can help her career. When the spotlight dims, she keeps going with drugs and alcohol to a bitter end.
1958 105m/B Kim Stanley, Lloyd Bridges, Patty Duke; *D:* John Cromwell; *W:* Paddy Chayefsky. VHS, Beta NO *✒✒✒*

The Godfather Coppola's award-winning adaptation of Mario Puzo's novel about a fictional Mafia family in the late 1940s. Revenge, envy, and parent-child conflict mix with the rituals of Italian mob life in America. Minutely detailed, with excellent performances by Pacino, Brando, and Caan as the violence-prone Sonny. Film debut of Coppola's daughter Sophia, the infant in the baptism scene, who returns in "Godfather III." The horrific horse scene is an instant chiller. Indisputably an instant piece of American culture. Followed by two sequels.
1972 (R) 171m/C Marlon Brando, Al Pacino, Robert Duvall, James Caan, Diane Keaton, John Cazale, Talia Shire, Richard Conte, Richard Castellano, Abe Vigoda, Alex Rocco, Sterling Hayden, John Marley, Al Lettieri, Sofia Coppola, Al Martino, Morgana King; *D:* Francis Ford Coppola; *W:* Mario Puzo, Francis Ford Coppola;

M: Nino Rota. Academy Awards '72: Best Actor (Brando), Best Adapted Screenplay, Best Picture; Nominations: Best Costume Design, Best Director (Coppola), Best Film Editing, Best Sound, Best Supporting Actor (Caan, Duvall, Pacino); Directors Guild of America Awards '72: Best Director (Coppola); Golden Globe Awards '73: Best Actor—Drama (Brando), Best Director (Coppola), Best Film—Drama, Best Screenplay, Best Score; National Board of Review Awards '72: 10 Best Films of the Year, Best Supporting Actor (Pacino); National Society of Film Critics Awards '72: Best Actor (Pacino). **VHS, Beta, 8mm** $29.95 *PAR, BTV* 🐾🐾🐾🐾

The Godfather 1902-1959: The Complete Epic Coppola's epic work concerning the lives of a New York crime family. Comprises the first two "Godfather" films, reedited into a chronological framework of the Corleone family history, with much previously discarded footage restored. **1981 386m/C** Marlon Brando, Al Pacino, Robert Duvall, James Caan, Richard Castellano, Diane Keaton, Robert De Niro, John Cazale, Lee Strasberg, Talia Shire, Michael Gazzo, Troy Donahue, Joe Spinell, Abe Vigoda, Alex Rocco, Sterling Hayden, John Marley, Richard Conte, G.D. Spradlin, Bruno Kirby, Harry Dean Stanton, Roger Corman, Al Lettieri; *D:* Francis Ford Coppola; *W:* Mario Puzo, Francis Ford Coppola; *M:* Nino Rota. **VHS, Beta** $99.95 *PAR, FCT* 🐾🐾🐾🐾

The Godfather, Part 2 A continuation and retracing of the first film, interpolating the maintenance of the Corleone family by the aging Michael, and its founding by the young Vito (De Niro, in a terrific performance) 60 years before in New York City's Little Italy. Often considered the second half of one film, the two films stand as one of American film's greatest efforts, and as a 1970s high-water mark. Combined into one work for television presentation. Followed by a sequel. **1974 (R) 200m/C** Al Pacino, Robert De Niro, Diane Keaton, Robert Duvall, James Caan, Danny Aiello, John Cazale, Lee Strasberg, Talia Shire, Michael Gazzo, Troy Donahue, Joe Spinell, Abe Vigoda, Marianna Hill, Fay Spain, G.D. Spradlin, Bruno Kirby, Harry Dean Stanton, Roger Corman, Kathleen Beller, John Aprea, Morgana King; *D:* Francis Ford Coppola; *W:* Mario Puzo, Francis Ford Coppola; *M:* Nino Rota, Carmine Coppola. Academy Awards '74: Best Adapted Screenplay, Best Art Direction/Set Decoration, Best Director (Coppola), Best Picture, Best Supporting Actor (De Niro), Best Original Score; Nominations: Best Actor (Pacino), Best Costume Design, Best Supporting Actor (Gazzo, Strasberg), Best Supporting Actress (Shire); Directors Guild of America Awards '74: Best Director (Coppola); National Society of Film Critics Awards '74: Best Director (Coppola). **VHS, Beta, 8mm** $29.95 *PAR, BTV* 🐾🐾🐾🐾

The Godfather, Part 3 Don Corleone (Pacino), now aging and guilt-ridden, determines to buy his salvation by investing in the Catholic Church, which he finds to be a more corrupt brotherhood than his own. Meanwhile, back on the homefront, his young daughter discovers her sexuality as she falls in love with her first cousin. Weakest entry of the trilogy is still a stunning and inevitable conclusion to the story; Pacino adds exquisite finishing touches to his time-worn character. Beautifully photographed in Italy by Gordon Willis. Video release contains the final director's cut featuring nine minutes of footage not included in the theatrical release. **1990 (R) 170m/C** Al Pacino, Diane Keaton, Andy Garcia, Joe Mantegna, George Hamilton, Talia Shire, Sofia Coppola, Eli Wallach, Don Novello, Bridget Fonda, John Savage, Al Martino, Raf Vallone, Franc D'Ambrosio, Donal Donnelly, Richard Bright, Helmut Berger; *D:* Francis Ford Coppola; *W:* Mario Puzo, Francis Ford Coppola;

M: Nino Rota, Carmine Coppola. **VHS, Beta, 8mm** $79.98 *PAR, SUP, FCT* 🐾🐾🐾

God's Bloody Acre Three backwoods mountain-dwelling brothers kill construction workers in order to defend their land, and then begin preying on vacationers. **1975 (R) 90m/C** Scott Lawrence, Jennifer Gregory, Sam Moree, Shiang Hwa Chyang; *D:* Harry Kerwin. **VHS, Beta** $69.95 *TWE Woof!*

God's Country A loner kills a man in self-defense and escapes the pursuing law by disappearing into California Redwood country with his dog. **1946 62m/C** Robert Lowery, Helen Gilbert, William Farnum, Buster Keaton; *D:* Robert Tansey. **VHS, Beta** *NO* 🐾🐾

God's Country and the Man Typical western adventurer about a cowboy out to nab a gunman who's been threatening the life of a dance hall girl. Plenty of two-fisted action when law-abiding Keene shows up. **1937 56m/B** Tom Keene, Betty Compson, Charlotte Henry, Charles "Blackie" King, Billy Bletcher, Ed Parker; *D:* Robert North Bradbury; *W:* Robert Emmett. **VHS** $19.99 *MOV* 🐾🐾

God's Gun Preacher who was once a gunfighter seeks revenge on the men who tried to kill him. *AKA:* A Bullet from God. **1975 (R) 93m/C** Richard Boone, Lee Van Cleef, Jack Palance, Sybil Danning; *D:* Frank Kramer. **VHS, Beta** $9.99 *CCB, VTR* 🐾

God's Little Acre Delves into the unexpectedly passionate lives of Georgia farmers. One man, convinced there's buried teasure on his land, nearly brings himself and his family to ruin trying to find it. Based on the novel by Erskine Caldwell. **1958 110m/B** Robert Ryan, Tina Louise, Michael Landon, Buddy Hackett, Vic Morrow, Jack Lord, Aldo Ray; *D:* Anthony Mann; *W:* Philip Yordan; *M:* Elmer Bernstein. **VHS, Beta** $19.95 *PSM, VEC* 🐾🐾

The Gods Must Be Crazy An innocent and charming film. A peaceful Bushman travels into the civilized world to return a Coke bottle "to the gods." Along the way he meets a transplanted schoolteacher, an oafishly clumsy microbiologist and a gang of fanatical terrorists. A very popular film, disarmingly crammed with slapstick and broad humor of every sort. Followed by a weak sequel. **1984 (PG) 109m/C** N!xau, Marius Weyers, Sandra Prinsloo, Louw Verwey, Jamie Uys, Michael Thys, Nic de Jager; *D:* Jamie Uys. **VHS, Beta** $19.39 *FOX, FCT, TVC* 🐾🐾🐾½

The Gods Must Be Crazy 2 A slapdash sequel to the original 1981 African chortler, featuring more ridiculous shenanigans in the bush. This time the bushman's children find themselves in civilization and N!xau must use his unique ingenuity to secure their safe return. **1989 (PG) 90m/C** N!xau, Lena Farugia, Hans Strydom, Eiros Nadies, Eric Bowen; *D:* Jamie Uys; *M:* Charles Fox. **VHS, Beta** $19.95 *COL, TTC, FCT* 🐾🐾½

Gods of the Plague Fassbinder goes noir—or grey with lots of sharp lighting—in this gangster-auteur tale of robbery gone awry. The requisite trappings of the crime genre (guys and dolls and cops and robbers) provide a vague backdrop (and a vague plot) for a moody story full of teutonic angst and alienation, and that certain Fassbinder feeling (which, need we say, isn't to everyone's taste). An early effort by the director, who remade the story later the same year as "The American Soldier" (Fassbinder acts in both). In German with (difficult-to-read) English subtitles. *AKA:* Gotter der Pest.

1969 92m/C *GE* Hanna Schygulla, Harry Bear; *D:* Rainer Werner Fassbinder. **VHS** $39.99 *TPV, ING* 🐾🐾🐾

The Godsend "Omen" rip-off about a little girl who is thrust upon a couple. After adopting her, they lose their natural family to her evil ways. **1979 (R) 93m/C** *CA* Cyd Hayman, Malcolm Stoddard, Angela Pleasence, Patrick Barr; *D:* Gabrielle Beaumont. **VHS, Beta** $59.98 *VES* 🐾

Godson Emotionless assassin lives a barren life under the surveillance of Paris police who suspect him in a recent killing. He suddenly discovers that his boss has a contract out on his life. Delon's performance raises this to an above-average crime drama. **1972 103m/C** *FR* Alain Delon, Nathalie Delon, Francois Perier; *D:* Jean-Pierre Melville. **VHS** *PSV* 🐾🐾🐾

Godzilla, King of the Monsters An underwater prehistoric reptile emerges from the depths to terrorize Tokyo after he has been awakened by atomic testing. Burr's scenes are intercut in the American version, where he serves as a narrator telling the monster's tale in flashbacks. Ridiculously primitive special effects even in its own day. One of the first post-WWII Japanese films to break through commercially in the U.S. *AKA:* Gojira. **1956 80m/B** *JP* Raymond Burr, Takashi Shimura; *D:* Terry Morse. **VHS, Beta** *PAR, VES* 🐾🐾½

Godzilla 1985 Godzilla is awakened from underwater slumber by trolling nuclear submarines belonging to the superpowers near Japan. The giant monster's newly acquired appetite for nuclear energy inadvertently precipitates an international incident. Burr is called in (as the only living American witness to Godzilla's destructive 1955 outburst) to help mediate the conflict. Film released to coincide with the 30th anniversary of the original. **1985 (PG) 91m/C** *JP* Raymond Burr, Keiju Kobayashi, Ken Tanaka, Yasuka Sawaguchi; *D:* Kohji Hashimoto, Robert J. Kizer. **VHS, Beta** $9.95 *NWV, STE* 🐾½

Godzilla on Monster Island Even Godzilla himself cannot hope to take on both Ghidra and Gigan alone and hope to succeed. Therefore he summons his pal Angillus for help. Together, they offer Earth its only hope of survival. Though the terror may repel you, the movie is a must for Godzilla fans; it's his first speaking part. *AKA:* Godzilla vs. Gigan. **1972 89m/C** *JP* Hiroshi Ishikawa, Tomoko Umeda, Yuriko Hishimi, Minoru Takashima, Zan Fujita; *D:* Jun Fukuda. **VHS** $9.95 *SNC, MRV, NWV* 🐾

Godzilla Raids Again Warner Bros. had a problem securing rights to Godzilla's name. Yearning for a change of pace, the King of Monsters opts to destroy Osaka instead of Tokyo, but the spiny Angorous is out to dethrone our hero. Citizens flee in terror when the battle royale begins. The first Godzilla sequel. *AKA:* Gigantis, the Fire Monster; Godzilla's Counter Attack. **1959 78m/B** *JP* Hugo Grimaldi, Makayama, Minoru Chiaki. **VHS** $14.99 *VTR* 🐾

Godzilla vs. Biollante Doctor Surigama's secret plant formula could free the industrialized world from oil dependency. He also runs his pet Godzilla experiment from the same laboratory. When terrorist thieves attempt to steal the plant formula, a petri dish mixup unleashes the abominable fury of Biollante. The return of the real Godzilla is the world's only hope, but not before another

Japanese city is crushed in the reptilian rumble.

1989 (PG) 104m/C *JP* **D:** Kazuki Ohmori; **W:** Kazuki Ohmori. **VHS $69.99** *HBO* 🎬🎬

Godzilla vs. Megalon Godzilla's creators show their gratitude to misguided but faithful American audiences by transforming the giant monster into a good guy. This time, the world is threatened by Megalon, the giant cockroach, and Gigan, a flying metal creature, simultaneously. Fortunately, the slippery hero's robot pal Jet Jaguar is on hand to slug it out side by side with Tokyo's ultimate defender. **AKA:** Gojira Tai Megaro.

1976 (G) 80m/C *JP* Katsuhiko Sasakai, Hiroyuki Kawase, Yutaka Hayashi, Robert Dunham; **D:** Jun Fukuda. **VHS $19.95** *NOS, MRV, NWV* 🎬½

Godzilla vs. Monster Zero Novel Godzilla adventure with the big guy and Rodan in outer space. Suspicious denizens of Planet X require the help of Godzilla and Rodan to rid themselves of the menacing Ghidra, whom they refer to as Monster Zero. Will they, in return, help Earth as promised, or is this just one big, fat double cross? **AKA:** Monster Zero; Battle of the Astros; Invasion of the Astro-Monsters; Invasion of the Astros; Invasion of Planet X; Kaiju Daisenso.

1968 (G) 93m/C *JP* Nick Adams; **D:** Inoshiro Honda. **VHS, Beta $19.95** *PAR, FUS* 🎬🎬

Godzilla vs. Mothra Mighty Mothra is called in to save the populace from Godzilla, who is on a rampage; and he's aided by two junior Mothras who hatch in the nick of time. The hesitant moth avoids the fire-breathing behemoth until succumbing to the pleadings of the Peanut Sisters to save humanity. Hilarious special effects inspire more laughter from derision than anything else. **AKA:** Godzilla vs. the Thing; Godzilla vs. the Giant Moth; Godzilla Fights the Giant Moth; Mothra vs. Godzilla; Mosura Tai Goira.

1964 88m/C *JP* Akira Takarada, Yuriko Hoshi, Hiroshi Koizumi; **D:** Inoshiro Honda. **VHS, Beta $19.95** *PAR, FUS* 🎬🎬

Godzilla vs. the Cosmic Monster Godzilla's worst nightmares become a reality as he is forced to take on the one foe he cannot defeat - a metal clone of himself! To make matters worse, Earth is in dire peril at the hands of cosmic apes. We all need friends, and Godzilla is never more happy to see his buddy King Seeser, who gladly lends a claw. **AKA:** Godzilla Versus the Bionic Monster; Godzilla vs. Mechagodzilla; Gojira Tai Meka-Gojira.

1974 (G) 80m/C *JP* Masaaki Daimon, Kazuya Aoyama, Reiko Tajima, Barbara Lynn, Akihiko Hirata; **D:** Jun Fukuda. **VHS $9.95** *NWV, MRV, VYY* 🎬🎬

Godzilla vs. the Sea Monster Godzilla makes friends with former rival Mothra (a giant moth) and together they bash on Ebirah, an enormous lobster backed by an evil cadre of (human) totalitarians. The unrepentant crusteacean turns the tables on our heroes, however, by growing a new tentacle everytime one is ripped off. Meanwhile, a frenzied batch of helpless humans are trapped on an island about to explode, if they aren't drowned first in a shower of reptilian backwash. **AKA:** Nankai No Kai Ketto; Ebirah, Terror of the Deep; Big Duel in the North.

1966 80m/C *JP* **D:** Jun Fukuda. **VHS, Beta $44.95** *DVT, MRV, HHT* Woof!

Godzilla vs. the Smog Monster Godzilla battles a creature borne of pollution, a 400-pound sludge blob named Hedora. Early 1970's period piece conveys interesting attitude towards pollution; it's treated as a

sinister force that people are powerless to stop. Japanese teenagers marshal their dancing talents to combat the threat amid the hypnotic swirl of disco lighting. Great opening song: "Save the Earth." Dubbed in English. **AKA:** Gojira Tai Hedora; Godzilla vs. Hedora.

1972 (G) 87m/C *JP* Akira Yamauchi, Hiroyuki Kawase, Toshio Shibaki; **D:** Yoshimitu Banno. **VHS, Beta $19.98** *ORI* 🎬

Godzilla's Revenge A young boy who is having problems dreams of going to Monster Island to learn from Minya, Godzilla's son. Using the lessons in real life, the boy captures some bandits and outwits a bully. Uses footage from "Godzilla vs. the Sea Monster" and "Son of Godzilla" for battle scenes. One of the silliest Godzilla movies around. **AKA:** Oru Kaiju Daishingeki.

1969 70m/C *JP* Kenji Sahara, Tomonori Yazaki, Machiko Naka, Sachio Sakai, Chotaro Togin, Yoshibumi Tujima; **D:** Inoshiro Honda. **VHS** *NO* 🎬

Goetz von Berlichingen During the reign of Emperor Maximilian, a brave knight fights injustice in the service of the Emperor and becomes a hunted man. In German with English subtitles. **AKA:** Iron Hand.

1980 100m/C *GE* **VHS, Beta $39.95** *VCD, GLV* 🎬🎬

Goin' Coconuts Donny and Marie are miscast as Donny and Marie in this smarmy story of crooks and jewels. Seems someone covets the chanteuse's necklace, and only gratuitous crooning can spare the twosome from certain swindling. Big bore on the big island.

1978 (PG) 93m/C Donny Osmond, Marie Osmond, Herb Edelman, Kenneth Mars, Ted Cassidy, Marc Lawrence, Harold Sakata; **D:** Howard Morris. **VHS** *NO* 🎬

Goin' South An outlaw is saved from being hanged by a young woman who agrees to marry him in exchange for his help working a secret gold mine. They try to get the loot before his old gang gets wind of it. A tongue-in-cheek western that served as Nicholson's second directorial effort. Movie debuts of Steenburgen and Belushi.

1978 (PG) 109m/C Jack Nicholson, Mary Steenburgen, John Belushi, Christopher Lloyd, Veronica Cartwright, Richard Bradford, Danny DeVito, Luana Anders, Ed Begley Jr., Anne Ramsey; **D:** Jack Nicholson; **W:** Charles Shyer. **VHS, Beta $19.95** *PAR* 🎬🎬🎬

Goin' to Town Complicated yarn with West as a woman who inherits an oil field and becomes the wealthiest woman in the state. She falls for British engineer Cavanagh and decides to become a "lady" in order to get his attention. There's a subplot about Buenos Aires and a crooked horse race, an in-name-only marriage to a high society type, and a murder before Mae finally gets her man.

1935 71m/B Mae West, Paul Cavanagh, Gilbert Emery, Ivan Lebedeff, Marjorie Gateson, Tito Coral, Monroe Owsley; **D:** Alexander Hall; **W:** Mae West. **VHS $14.98** *MCA, BTV* 🎬🎬

Going Ape! Danza inherits a bunch of orangutans. If the apes are treated well, a legacy of $5 million will follow. This is all you need to know.

1981 (PG) 87m/C Tony Danza, Jessica Walter, Danny DeVito, Art Metrano, Rick Hurst; **D:** Jeremy Joe Kronsberg; **M:** Elmer Bernstein. **VHS, Beta $49.95** *PAR* 🎬½

Going Back Four friends reunite after college to relive a memorable summer they spent together after graduating from high school.

1983 85m/C Bruce Campbell, Christopher Howe, Perry Mallette, Susan W. Yamasaki; **D:** Ron Teachworth. **VHS, Beta $69.98** *LIV, VES* 🎬½

Going Bananas Wacky adventure about a chimp who is being chased by a sinister circus owner. The monkey runs through Africa dragging along a boy, his caretaker, and a guide. The cast says it all.

1988 (PG) 95m/C Dom DeLuise, Jimmie Walker, David Mendenhall, Herbert Lom; **D:** Boaz Davidson. **VHS, Beta $19.95** *MED, VTR* 🎬🎬

Going Berserk The members of SCTV's television comedy troupe are featured in this comedy which lampoons everything from religious cults to kung fu movies to "Father Knows Best." Should have been more fun.

1983 (R) 85m/C *CA* John Candy, Joe Flaherty, Eugene Levy, Paul Dooley, Pat Hingle, Richard Libertini, Ernie Hudson; **D:** David Steinberg. **VHS, Beta $69.95** *MCA* 🎬½

Going for the Gold: The Bill Johnson Story Biographical tale of the American downhill skier who went from hard-luck punk to Olympic champion in the 1984 games at Sarajevo, Yugoslavia.

1985 100m/C Anthony Edwards, Dennis Weaver, Sarah Jessica Parker, Deborah Van Valkenburgh, Wayne Northrop; **D:** Don Taylor. **VHS $14.95** *COL* 🎬🎬

Going Hollywood Amusing musical/romantic fluff about a French teacher (Davies) who falls in love with a radio crooner (Crosby in his first MGM film). He's got the movie bug and heads for Hollywood, where he becomes an overnight sensation with a sultry costar (D'Orsay). Davies follows and proceeds to get Crosby out of D'Orsay's clutches and winds up replacing her rival in the film, promptly becoming a star herself. The underrated Davies was a fine light comedienne and supplied glamour to the production as well. Kelly, in her film debut, supplied the slapstick. The last Hearst-Cosmopolitan production made with MGM. ♫Temptation; We'll Make Hay While the Sun Shines; Going Hollywood; Our Big Love Scene; After Sundown; Cinderella's Fella; Beautiful Girl; Just an Echo in the Valley.

1933 78m/B Marion Davies, Bing Crosby, Fifi d'Orsay, Stuart Erwin, Patsy Kelly, Ned Sparks; **D:** Walter Walsh; **W:** Donald Ogden Stewart. **VHS $19.98** *MGM* 🎬🎬🎬

Going Home During WWI, Canadian soldiers held in British camps awaiting transport back home stage a riot over the endless delays and intolerable conditions. A fact-based story of the events leading up to this tragedy.

1986 100m/C Nicholas Campbell, Paul Maxwell, Eugene Lipinski. **VHS** *NO* 🎬🎬½

Going in Style Three elderly gentlemen, tired of doing nothing, decide to liven up their lives by pulling a daylight bank stick-up. They don't care about the consequences because anything is better than sitting on a park bench all day long. The real fun begins when they get away with the robbery. Great cast makes this a winner.

1979 (PG) 91m/C George Burns, Art Carney, Lee Strasberg; **D:** Martin Brest. **VHS, Beta $19.98** *WAR* 🎬🎬🎬½

Going My Way A musical-comedy about a progressive young priest assigned to a downtrodden parish who works to get the parish out of debt, but clashes with his elderly curate, who's set in his ways. Followed by "The Bells of St. Mary's." Fitzgerald's Oscar-winning Supporting Actor performance was also nominated in the Best Actor category. ♫The Day After Forever; Swingin'

On a Star; Too-ra-loo-ra-loo-ra; Going My Way; Silent Night; Habanera; Ave Maria. **1944 126m/B** Bing Crosby, Barry Fitzgerald, Rise Stevens, Frank McHugh, Gene Lockhart, Porter Hall; *D:* Leo McCarey; *W:* Frank Butler, Frank Cavett, Leo McCarey. Academy Awards '44: Best Actor (Crosby), Best Director (McCarey), Best Picture, Best Song ("Swinging on a Star"), Best Story & Screenplay, Best Supporting Actor (Fitzgerald); Nominations: Best Actor (Fitzgerald), Best Black and White Cinematography, Best Film Editing; National Board of Review Awards '44: 10 Best Films of the Year; New York Film Critics Awards '44: Best Actor (Fitzgerald), Best Director (McCarey), Best Film. **VHS, Beta $14.98** *MCA, IGP, BTV* 🐾🐾🐾½

Going Places A cynical, brutal satire about two young thugs traversing the French countryside raping, looting and cavorting as they please. Moreau has a brief role as an ex-con trying to go straight. An amoral, controversial comedy that established both its director and two stars. In French with English subtitles or dubbed. *AKA:* Les Valseuses; Making It. **1974 (R) 122m/C** *FR* Gerard Depardieu, Patrick Dewaere, Miou-Miou, Isabelle Huppert, Jeanne Moreau, Brigitte Fossey; *D:* Bertrand Blier. **VHS, Beta $59.95** *COL, INT, ING* 🐾🐾🐾

Going to Congress/Don't Park There Two typical silent Rogers shorts. With original organ score. **1924 57m/B** Will Rogers. **VHS, Beta, 8mm $19.95** *VYY* 🐾🐾🐾

Going to Town Radio team Lum and Abner in one of their last films, as two conmen who scheme to make money from a phony oil well. **1944 77m/B** Barbara Hale, Grady Sutton, Florence Lake. **VHS, Beta** *GVV* 🐾

Going Under Subsurface military satire about the U.S.S. Sub Standard, the worst nuclear vessel in the Navy. It's so poorly constructed that the brass would rather sink than inspect it - if only they could. Interesting cast sinks with script headed for dry dock. **1991 (PG) 81m/C** Bill Pullman, Wendy Schaal, Ned Beatty, Robert Vaughn, Bud Cort, Michael Winslow. **VHS, Beta $19.98** *WAR* 🐾

Going Undercover A bumbling private investigator is hired to protect a rich, beautiful, and spoiled young woman on her European vacation. Poor excuse for a comedy. **1988 (PG-13) 90m/C** Lea Thompson, Jean Simmons, Chris Lemmon; *D:* James Kenelm Clarke. **VHS, Beta $29.95** *VMK* 🐾

The Gold & Glory Two brothers, one a musician, the other an athlete, vie for the affections of the same girl by competing in a footrace for a golden purse. **1988 (PG-13) 102m/C** Colin Friels, Josephine Smulders, Grant Kenny. **VHS, Beta $39.95** *LIV* 🐾

Gold Diggers of 1933 In this famous period musical, showgirls help a songwriter save his Busby Berkeley-choreographed show. Followed by two sequels. 🎵We're in the Money; Shadow Waltz; I've Got to Sing a Torch Song; Pettin' in the Park; Remember My Forgotten Man. **1933 96m/B** Joan Blondell, Ruby Keeler, Aline MacMahon, Dick Powell, Guy Kibbee, Warren William, Ned Sparks, Ginger Rogers; *D:* Mervyn LeRoy. **VHS, Beta $19.98** *MGM, FOX* 🐾🐾🐾½

Gold Diggers of 1935 The second Gold Diggers film, having something to do with a New England resort, romance, and a charity show put on at the hotel. Plenty of Berkeleian large-scale drama, especially the bizarre, mock-tragic "Lullaby on Broadway" number, which details the last days of a Broadway baby. 🎵I'm Going Shopping With

You; The Words Are in My Heart; Lullaby of Broadway. **1935 95m/B** Dick Powell, Adolphe Menjou, Gloria Stuart, Alice Brady, Frank McHugh, Glenda Farrell, Grant Mitchell, Hugh Herbert, Wini Shaw; *D:* Busby Berkeley. **VHS, Beta $29.95** *MGM, MLB* 🐾🐾🐾

The Gold of Naples A four-part omnibus film about life in Naples, filled with romance and family tragedies, by turns poignant, funny and pensive. Originally six tales; two were trimmed for U.S. release. In Italian with subtitles. *AKA:* L'Oro Di Napoli. **1954 107m/B** *IT* Vittorio De Sica, Eduardo de Filippo, Toto, Sophia Loren, Paolo Stoppa, Silvana Mangano; *D:* Vittorio De Sica. **VHS, Beta $19.95** *NOS, FCT, APD* 🐾🐾🐾

Gold of the Amazon Women When two explorers set out to find gold, they stumble onto a society of man-hungry women who follow them into the urban jungle of Manhattan. Made for television. There is also a European "R" rated version. *AKA:* Amazon Women. **1979 94m/C** Bo Svenson, Anita Ekberg, Bond Gideon, Donald Pleasence; *D:* Mark L. Lester. **VHS, Beta $59.98** *SUE, VTR* 🐾

Gold Raiders Larry, Moe, and Shemp team up with an insurance agent to take on the bad guys in the wild west. The Stooges are long past their prime. **1951 56m/B** George O'Brien, Moe Howard, Moe Howard, Shemp Howard, Larry Fine, Sheila Ryan, Clem Bevans, Lyle Talbot; *D:* Edward L. Bernds. **VHS** *MED* 🐾

Gold Raiders Team of secret agents are sent to the Jungles of Laos to find a plane carrying $200 million worth of gold, and nothing will get in their way. **1984 106m/C** Robert Ginty, Sarah Langenfeld, William Steven. **VHS, Beta $69.95** *MED* 🐾½

The Gold Rush Chaplin's most critically acclaimed film. The best definition of his simple approach to film form; adept maneuvering of visual pathos. The "Little Tramp" searches for gold and romance in the Klondike in the mid-1800s. Includes the dance of the rolls, pantomime sequence of eating the shoe, and Chaplin's lovely music. **1925 85m/B** Charlie Chaplin, Mack Swain, Tom Murray, Georgina Hale; *D:* Charlie Chaplin. **VHS, Beta, 8mm $9.95** *CNG, NOS, CAB* 🐾🐾🐾🐾

Gold Rush/Payday Chaplin drifts along the Arctic tundra, searching for gold and love in "The Gold Rush." In "Payday," he goes out drinking with his buddies. **1925 92m/B** Charlie Chaplin, Georgina Hale, Mack Swain. **VHS, Beta $19.98** *FOX* 🐾🐾🐾🐾

Golden Age of Comedy The great comedians of silent cinema are seen in clips from some of their funniest films. **1958 78m/B** Ben Turpin, Harry Langdon, Will Rogers, Jean Harlow, Carole Lombard, Stan Laurel, Oliver Hardy, The Keystone Cops. **VHS, Beta $14.98** *MLB* 🐾🐾🐾🐾

Golden Age of Hollywood This episode of "Life Goes to the Movies" examines Hollywood as it quickly became the ultimate dream factory, providing escape from the grimness of the depression. **1977 34m/C** Henry Fonda, Shirley MacLaine. **VHS, Beta** *TLF* 🐾🐾🐾🐾

Golden Boy Holden plays a young and gifted violinist who earns money for his musical education by working as a part-time prizefighter. Fight promoter Menjou has Stanwyck cozy up to the impressionable young man to convince him to make the fight game his prime concern. She's successful but it leads to tragedy. Holden's screen debut, with Cobb as his immigrant father and

Stanwyck successfully slinky as the corrupting love interest. Classic pugilistic drama with well-staged fight scenes. Based on Clifford Odet's play with toned down finale. **1939 99m/B** William Holden, Adolphe Menjou, Barbara Stanwyck, Lee J. Cobb, Joseph Calleia, Sam Levene, Don Beddoe, Charles Halton; *D:* Rouben Mamoulian; *W:* Daniel Taradash, Victor Heerman, Sarah Y. Mason. **VHS, Beta $9.95** *GKK* 🐾🐾🐾

The Golden Child When a Tibetan child with magic powers is kidnapped and transported to Los Angeles, Chandler, a professional "finder of lost children" must come to the rescue. The search takes him through Chinatown in a hunt that cliches every Oriental swashbuckler ever made. Good fun. **1986 (PG-13) 94m/C** Eddie Murphy, Charlotte Lewis, Charles Dance, Victor Wong, Randall "Tex" Cobb, James Hong; *D:* Michael Ritchie; *M:* Michel Colombier. **VHS, Beta, 8mm $19.95** *PAR* 🐾🐾

The Golden Coach Based on a play by Prosper Merimee, the tale of an 18th century actress in Spanish South America who takes on all comers, including the local viceroy who creates a scandal by presenting her with his official coach. Rare cinematography by Claude Renoir. *AKA:* Le Carrosse D'Or. **1952 101m/C** *FR* Anna Magnani, Odoardo Spadaro, Nada Fiorelli, Dante Rino, Duncan Lamont; *D:* Jean Renoir. **VHS, Beta $29.95** *FCT, CRC, INT* 🐾🐾🐾

Golden Demon An acclaimed Japanese epic, from the novel by Koyo Ozaki, about the destructive powers of wealth on the lives of two star-crossed lovers in medieval Japan. In Japanese with English subtitles. *AKA:* Konjiki Yasha. **1953 95m/C** *JP* Jun Negami, Fujiko Yamamoto; *D:* Koji Shima. **VHS, Beta $29.95** *SUE, NLC, ING* 🐾🐾½

Golden Earrings Enjoyable, yet incredulous story about British agent Milland joining up with gypsy Dietrich for espionage work. Absurd film was so bad it became a camp classic overnight. Although Dietrich and Milland couldn't stand each other and battled constantly during production, the movie did quite well at the box office. Based on a novel by Yolanda Foldes. **1947 95m/B** Ray Milland, Marlene Dietrich, Bruce Lester, Dennis Hoey, Quentin Reynolds, Reinhold Schunzel, Ivan Triesault, Mitchell Leisen; *W:* Abraham Polonsky, Frank Butler, Helen Deutsch. **VHS $14.98** *MCA, FCT* 🐾🐾½

Golden Exterminators Two brothers battle the forces of evil who have killed their martial arts master with the heels of their formidable feet. **197? 86m/C** Raymond Chan. **VHS, Beta $39.95** *UNI* 🐾

Golden Gate Young Fed Dillon is thrown into the hysteria of the communist witch hunt in 1952 San Francisco. He snares Song, a Chinese labor activist, on some very dubious charges. Ten years later he finds himself getting involved with Song's daughter Marilyn (Chen), who knows nothing about her lover's involvement with her family. Then she finds out. Everchanging moods, sometimes film noir, sometimes a love story, sometimes a nostalgic look back, are confusing. Promising storyline meanders and fades as Director Madden tries to do too much in a short time. Beware of broad stereotypes in every character. **1993 (R) 95m/C** Matt Dillon, Joan Chen, Bruno Kirby, Teri Polo, Tzi Ma, Stan Egi, Peter Murnik; *D:* John Madden; *W:* David Henry Hwang; *M:* Elliot Goldenthal. **VHS** *NYR* 🐾🐾

The Golden Honeymoon Ring Lardner's story about an elderly couple who journey to St. Petersburg to celebrate their 50th anniversary. There they encounter the wife's suitor of 50 years past, who is also vacationing with his spouse. Curiosity draws the couples together, and jealousy, doubt and a simmering competitive spirit momentarily jar the marriage. Part of the American Short Story Collection. Made for television.
1980 52m/C James Whitmore, Teresa Wright; *D:* Noel Black. VHS, Beta MON, MTI ✐✐

Golden Lady Beautiful woman leads her female gang in a deadly game of international intrigue.
1979 90m/C Christina World, Suzanne Danielle, June Chadwick; *D:* Joseph Larraz. VHS, Beta NO ✐½

Golden Ninja Warrior Lady ninjas endeavor to capture a golden statue and gain superiority over chauvinists everywhere.
198? 92m/C VHS, Beta $59.95 TWE ✐

Golden Rendezvous A tale of treachery aboard a "gambler's paradise" luxury liner which is hijacked and held for ransom. Based on Alistair MacLean's novel. *AKA:* Nuclear Terror.
1977 103m/C Richard Harris, David Janssen, John Carradine, Burgess Meredith, Ann Turkel, John Vernon; *D:* Ashley Lazarus. VHS, Beta $69.95 VES ✐✐

The Golden Salamander Howard shines in otherwise lackluster adventure about archaeologist searching for ancient ruins in Tunisia who must deal with gun runners and their evil leader, while torridly romancing a beautiful Tunisian girl. Filmed on location in Tunis. Based on the novel by Victor Canning.
1951 96m/B GB Trevor Howard, Anouk Aimee, Herbert Lom, Miles Malleson, Walter Rilla, Jacques Sernas, Wilfrid Hyde-White, Peter Copely, Eugene Deckers, Henry Edwards, Marcel Poncin, Percy Walsh, Sybilla Binder, Kathleen Boutall, Valentine Dyall; *D:* Ronald Neame. VHS $29.95 FCT ✐✐

The Golden Seal Tale of a small boy's innocence put in direct conflict, because of his love of a rare wild golden seal and her pup, with the failed dreams, pride and ordinary greed of adults.
1983 (PG) 94m/C Steve Railsback, Michael Beck, Penelope Milford, Torquil Campbell; *D:* Frank Zuniga; *M:* John Barry. VHS, Beta, 8mm $19.98 SUE ✐✐½

The Golden Stallion Trigger falls in love with a stunning mare. He sees her villainous owners abusing her and kills them. Roy takes the blame for his equine pal, but true love triumphs to save the day.
1949 67m/B Roy Rogers, Dale Evans, Estelita Rodriguez, Pat Brady, Douglas Evans, Frank Fenton; *D:* William Witney. VHS $12.98 REP ✐½

Golden Sun Young Kung Fu student decides to investigate the death of his hero, Bruce Lee, and comes up against a sinister conspiracy.
198? 90m/C Lei Hsiao Lung, Chen Pei Ling, Ou-Yang Chung. VHS, Beta $29.95 UNI ✐

The Golden Triangle Big battle of the drug pushers set in the mountainous region surrounded by Laos, Thailand, and Burma. Rival gangs fight for control of the world's opium crop.
1980 (PG) 90m/C Lo Lieh, Sambat Metanen, Tien Ner. VHS, Beta $59.98 OCE ✐½

Golden Voyage of Sinbad In the mysterious ancient land of Lemuria, Sinbad and his crew encounter magical and mystical creatures. A statue of Nirvana comes to life and engages in a sword fight with Sinbad. He later meets up with a one-eyed centaur and a griffin. Ray Harryhausen can once again claim credit for the unusual and wonderful mythical creatures springing to life.
1973 (G) 105m/C John Phillip Law, Caroline Munro, Tom Baker, Douglas Wilmer, Martin Shaw, John David Garfield, Gregoire Aslan; *D:* Gordon Hessler; *W:* Brian Clemens. VHS, Beta $14.95 COL, MLB ✐✐½

Goldengirl A neo-Nazi doctor tries to make a superwoman of his daughter who has been specially fed, exercised, and emotionally conditioned since childhood to run in the Olympics. Anton's starring debut.
1979 (PG) 107m/C Susan Anton, James Coburn, Curt Jurgens, Robert Culp, Leslie Caron, Harry Guardino, Jessica Walter; *D:* Joseph Sargent; *M:* Bill Conti. VHS, Beta $14.95 COL, SUE ✐✐

Goldenrod A successful rodeo champion is forced to reevaluate his life when he sustains a crippling accident in the ring. Made for television.
1977 100m/C CA Tony LoBianco, Gloria Carlin, Donald Pleasence, Donnelly Rhodes; *D:* Harvey Hart. VHS, Beta $59.95 PSM ✐½

Goldfinger Ian Fleming's James Bond, Agent 007, attempts to prevent international gold smuggler Goldfinger and his pilot Pussy Galore from robbing Fort Knox. Features villainous assistant Oddjob and his deadly bowler hat. The third in the series is perhaps the most popular. Shirley Bassey sings the theme song. The laserdisc edition includes audio interviews with the director, the writer, the editor, and the production designer; publicity stills, movie posters, trailers, and on-location photos. A treat for Bond fans.
1964 (PG) 117m/C GB Sean Connery, Honor Blackman, Gert Frobe, Shirley Eaton, Tania Mallet, Harold Sakata, Cec Linder, Bernard Lee, Lois Maxwell, Desmond Llewelyn, Nadja Regin; *D:* Guy Hamilton; *M:* John Barry. VHS, Beta $19.98 MGM, VYG, CRC ✐✐✐

Goldilocks & the Three Bears Entry from "Faerie Tale Theatre" tells the story of Goldilocks, who wanders through the woods and finds the home of three bears—only in this version Goldilocks is a nasty child, and it's the bears who'll get your sympathy.
1983 60m/C Tatum O'Neal, Alex Karras, Brandis Kemp, Donovan Scott, Hoyt Axton, John Lithgow, Carole King; *D:* Gilbert Cates. VHS, Beta $14.98 KUI, FOX, FCT ✐✐✐

The Goldwyn Follies Lavish disjointed musical comedy about Hollywood. A movie producer chooses a naive girl to give him advice on his movies. George Gershwin died during the filming. ♫Romeo and Juliet; Water Nymph; Here, Pussy, Pussy; Serenade To a Fish; Love Walked In; Love is Here to Stay; Spring Again; I Was Doing Alright; La Serenata; I Love to Rhyme.
1938 115m/C Adolphe Menjou, Vera Zorina, The Ritz Brothers, Helen Jepson, Phil Baker, Bobby Clark, Ella Logan, Andrea Leeds, Edgar Bergen; *D:* George Marshall; *M:* George Gershwin, Ira Gershwin. VHS, Beta $19.98 SUE, HBO ✐✐

Goldy: The Last of the Golden Bears Orphaned child and a lonely prospector risk their lives to save a Golden Bear from a circus owner. Followed by "Goldy 2: The Saga of the Golden Bear."
1984 91m/C VHS, Beta $14.98 LIV, VES ✐½

Goldy 2: The Saga of the Golden Bear Continues the adventures in the High Sierras of an orphan girl and her friend, the Golden Bear.
1985 96m/C VHS, Beta $14.98 LIV, VES ✐

The Golem A huge clay figure is given life by a rabbi in hopes of saving the Jews in the ghetto of medieval Prague. Rarely seen Wegener expressionist myth-opus that heavily influenced the "Frankenstein" films of the sound era.
1920 80m/B GE Paul Wegener, Albert Steinruck, Ernst Deutsch, Syda Salmonova; *D:* Paul Wegener. VHS, Beta $16.95 SNC, NOS, MRV ✐✐✐

Goliath Against the Giants Goliath takes on Bokan, who has stolen his throne. Goliath must fight Amazons, storms, and sea monsters to save the lovely Elea. Goliath conquers all. *AKA:* Goliath Contro I Giganti; Goliat Contra Los Gigantes; Goliath and the Giants.
1963 95m/C IT SP Brad Harris, Gloria Milland, Fernando Rey, Barbara Carroll; *D:* Guido Malatesta. VHS, Beta $19.98 SNC ✐½

Goliath and the Barbarians Goliath and his men go after the barbarians who are terrorizing and ravaging the Northern Italian countryside during the fall of the Roman Empire. A basic Reeves muscleman epic. *AKA:* Il Terror Dei Baraberi.
1960 86m/C IT Steve Reeves, Bruce Cabot; *D:* Carlo Campogalliani. VHS, Beta $59.95 MGM ✐✐

Goliath and the Dragon Even Goliath must have doubts as he is challenged by the evil and powerful King Eurystheus. A must for fans of ridiculous movies with ridiculous monsters. *AKA:* La Vendetta De Ercole.
1961 90m/C IT FR Bruce Cabot, Mark Forest, Broderick Crawford, Gaby Andre, Leonora Ruffo; *D:* Vittorio Cottafavi. VHS, Beta $19.98 SNC Woof!

Goliath and the Sins of Babylon Well-sculpted Forest plays yet another mesomorph to the rescue in this poorly dubbed spaghetti legend. Goliath must spare twenty-four virgins whom the evil Crisa would submit as human sacrifice. Forest—who played the mythic Maciste in a number of films—was randomly assigned the identity of Goliath, Hercules or Samson for US viewing; go figure. *AKA:* Maciste, L'Eroe Piu Grande Del Mondo.
1964 80m/C IT Mark Forest, Eleanora Bianchi, Jose Greco, Giuliano Gemma, Paul Muller; *D:* Michele Lupo. VHS $19.98 SNC ✐✐

Goliath Awaits Harmon plays an oceanographer who discovers a ship that was sunk by German U-boats during WWI. Nothing much new there, except that the survivors still reside on board the vessel, some 40 years after the oceanliner was torpedoed. And get this: they're living a quasi-Utopian existence. Kind of hard to swallow. Made for TV, it originally aired in two parts.
1981 110m/C Mark Harmon, Robert Forster, Christopher Lee, Eddie Albert, John Carradine, Alex Cord, Emma Samms, Jean Marsh; *D:* Kevin Connor; *M:* George Duning. VHS VMK ✐✐

Goliathon A ten-story-tall gorilla resides in the jungle and is sought by a group of Hong Kong businessmen who want to display the creature. Johnny, the hunter hired to find the beast, discovers both the gorilla and a beautiful jungle goddess. Incredibly campy, with badly dubbed and hilariously awful dialogue. *AKA:* The Mighty Peking Man.
1979 81m/C HK Lee Hassen, Evelyn Kraft. VHS $24.95 VYY Woof!

Gone are the Days Shaky adaptation of the play, "Purlie Victorious." A black preacher wants to cause the ruin of a white plantation owner. Alda's screen debut. *AKA:* The Man From C.O.T.T.O.N., Purlie Victorious.

1963 97m/B Ossie Davis, Ruby Dee, Sorrell Booke, Godfrey Cambridge, Alan Alda, Beah Richards; *D:* Nicholas Webster. **VHS, Beta** $69.95 *DIS* 🎞🎞½

Gone are the Days Government agent (Korman) is assigned to protect a family who witnessed an underworld shooting, but the family would like to get away from both the mob and the police. Made-for-cable Disney comedy is well-acted but done in by cliches.
1984 90m/C Harvey Korman, Susan Anspach, Robert Hogan; *D:* Gabrielle Beaumont. **VHS, Beta** $69.95 *DIS* 🎞🎞

Gone in 60 Seconds Car thief working for an insurance adjustment firm gets double-crossed by his boss and chased by the police. Forty minutes are consumed by a chase scene which destroyed more than 90 vehicles.
1974 105m/C H.B. Halicki, Marion Busia, George Cole, James McIntyre, Jerry Daugirda; *D:* H.B. Halicki. **VHS, Beta** $9.95 *MED* 🎞½

Gone to Ground Mad killer terrorizes a group of vacationers who are trapped in an isolated beach house.
1976 74m/C Charles Tingwell, Elaine Lee, Eric Oldfield, Marion Johns, Robyn Gibbes, Judy Lynne, Dennis Grosvenor, Alan Penney, Marcus Hale. **VHS, Beta** *NO* 🎞

Gone with the West Little Moon and Jud McGraw seek revenge upon the man who stole their cattle.
1972 92m/C James Caan, Stefanie Powers, Sammy Davis Jr., Aldo Ray, Michael Conrad, Michael Walker Jr.; *D:* Bernard Giraudeau. **VHS, Beta** $49.95 *UNI* 🎞½

Gone with the Wind Epic Civil War drama focuses on the life of petulant southern belle Scarlett O'Hara. Starting with her idyllic lifestyle on a sprawling plantation, the film traces her survival through the tragic history of the South during the Civil War and Reconstruction, and her tangled love affairs with Ashley Wilkes and Rhett Butler. Classic Hollywood doesn't get any better than this; one great scene after another, equally effective in intimate drama and sweeping spectacle. The train depot scene, one of the more technically adroit shots in movie history, involved hundreds of extras and dummies, and much of the MGM lot was razed to simulate the burning of Atlanta. Based on Margaret Mitchell's novel, screenwriter Howard was assisted by producer Selnick and novelist F. Scott Fitzgerald. For its 50th anniversary, a 231-minute restored version was released that included the trailer for "The Making of a Legend: GWTW." The laserdisc is available in a limited, numbered edition, fully restored to Technicolor from the original negative, with an enhanced soundtrack and seven minutes of rare footage, including the original trailer.
1939 231m/C Clark Gable, Vivien Leigh, Olivia de Havilland, Leslie Howard, Thomas Mitchell, Hattie McDaniel, Butterfly McQueen, Evelyn Keyes, Harry Davenport, Jane Darwell, Ona Munson, Barbara O'Neil, William "Billy" Bakewell, Rand Brooks, Ward Bond, Laura Hope Crews, Yakima Canutt, George Reeves, Marjorie Reynolds, Ann Rutherford, Victor Jory, Carroll Nye, Paul Hurst, Isabel Jewell, Cliff Edwards, Eddie Anderson, Oscar Polk, Eric Linden, Violet Kemble-Cooper; *D:* Victor Fleming; *W:* Sidney Howard; *M:* Max Steiner. Academy Awards '39: Best Actress (Leigh), Best Color Cinematography, Best Director (Fleming), Best Film Editing, Best Interior Decoration, Best Picture, Best Screenplay, Best Supporting Actress (McDaniel); Nominations: Best Actor (Gable), Best Sound, Best Special Effects, Best Supporting Actress (de Havilland), Best Original Score; New York Film Critics Awards '39: Best

Actress (Leigh). **VHS, Beta** $19.98 *MGM, FUS, BTV* 🎞🎞🎞🎞

Gonza the Spearman A gifted samurai lancer is accused of having an affair with the wife of the lord of his province. The lancer must leave to save the woman's honor, because to stay would mean death to them both. In Japanese with English subtitles.
1986 126m/C *JP* Hiromi Goh, Shima Iwashita; *D:* Masahiro Shinoda. **VHS** $79.95 *KIV, ING* 🎞🎞½

The Good Earth Pearl S. Buck's classic recreation of the story of a simple Chinese farm couple beset by greed and poverty. Outstanding special effects. MGM's last film produced by master Irving Thalberg and dedicated to his memory. Rainer won the second of her back-to-back Best Actress Oscars for her portrayal of the self-sacrificing O-Lan.
1937 138m/B Paul Muni, Luise Rainer, Charley Grapewin, Keye Luke, Walter Connolly; *D:* Sidney Franklin. Academy Awards '37: Best Actress (Rainer), Best Cinematography; Nominations: Best Director (Franklin), Best Film Editing, Best Picture. **VHS, Beta** $19.98 *MGM, KUI, BTV* 🎞🎞🎞½

Good Evening, Mr. Wallenberg Raoul Wallenberg was an upper-class Swede who imported luxury goods from Hungary. He was also responsible for saving thousands of Hungarian Jews from extermination by the Nazis. Using phony documents he first had small groups of Jews smuggled to safety but when he learns that the 65,0000 Jews of the Budapest ghetto are to be killed he uses a bluff to prevent the deaths. Later taken prisoner by the Soviet Army, Wallenberg's fate has never been determined. Characters are dwarfed by the immensity of the events and Wallenberg remains an enigma. In Swedish, German, and Hungarian with English subtitles.
1993 115m/C *SW* Stellan Skarsgard, Erland Josephson, Katharina Thalbach; *D:* Kjell Grede; *W:* Kjell Grede. **VHS** $89.98 *FXL, ORI, FCT* 🎞🎞½

The Good Father An acclaimed British TV movie about a bitter divorced man trying to come to terms with his son, his ex-wife, and his own fury by supporting the courtroom divorce battle of a friend.
1987 (R) 90m/C *GB* Anthony Hopkins, Jim Broadbent, Harriet Walter, Frances Viner, Joanne Whalley-Kilmer, Simon Callow, Michael Byrne; *D:* Mike Newell; *W:* Christopher Hampton; *M:* Richard Hartley. **VHS, Beta** $79.95 *MED, FOX* 🎞🎞🎞

The Good Fight Grace Cragin (Lahti) is a lawyer at a small firm who's asked by her son's best friend to represent him in a tough case against a powerful corporation. The young man is dying of mouth cancer and he wants to sue the tobacco company that makes the chewing tobacco he blames for his illness. Grace is wary of the high-powered litigation necessary but with the increasingly personal aid of her prominent lawyer ex-husband (O'Quinn), she is ready to battle the odds. Another fine performance by Lahti in this made for cable television drama.
1992 91m/C Christine Lahti, Terry O'Quinn, Kenneth Welsh, Lawrence Dane, Adam Trese, Tony Rosato, Andrea Roth, Jonathan Crombie; *D:* John David Coles; *W:* Beth Gutcheon; *M:* W.G. Snuffy Walden. **VHS, Beta** $79.95 *PSM* 🎞🎞

Good Grief, Charlie Brown That lovably misunderstood Charlie Brown is featured again in this Peanuts production.
1983 30m/C *D:* Bill Melendez, Sam Jaimes, Phil Roman. **VHS** $14.95 *BAR* 🎞🎞½

The Good Guys and the Bad Guys When Kennedy is abandoned by his gang of outlaws for being too old to keep up, he finds himself being hunted by lifelong marshall nemesis Mitchum.
1969 (PG) 91m/C Robert Mitchum, George Kennedy, David Carradine, Tina Louise, Douglas Fowley, Lois Nettleton, Martin Balsam, John Carradine; *D:* Burt Kennedy. **VHS** $29.99 *WAR* 🎞🎞½

Good Guys Wear Black A mild-mannered professor keeps his former life as leader of a Vietnam commando unit under wraps until he discovers that he's number one on the CIA hit list. Sequel is "A Force of One."
1978 (PG) 96m/C Chuck Norris, Anne Archer, James Franciscus; *D:* Ted Post; *W:* Mark Medoff. **VHS, Beta** $14.95 *WAR, HBO, VES* 🎞🎞

Good Morning, Babylon The Taviani brothers' first American film. Two young Italian brothers skilled in cathedral restoration come to America and find success building the sets to D.W. Griffith's "Intolerance." Eventually, their fortune is shattered by the onslaught of WWI. *AKA:* Good Morning Babilonia.
1987 (PG-13) 113m/C Vincent Spano, Joaquim de Almeida, Greta Scacchi, Charles Dance, Desiree Becker, Omero Antonutti, David Brandon; *D:* Paolo Taviani, Vittorio Taviani; *W:* Paolo Taviani, Vittorio Taviani, Tonino Guerra; *M:* Nicola Piovani. **VHS, Beta** $79.98 *LIV, VES* 🎞🎞🎞

Good Morning, Vietnam Based on the story of Saigon DJ Adrian Cronauer, although Williams' portrayal is reportedly a bit more extroverted than the personality of Cronauer. Williams spins great comic moments that may have been scripted but likely were not as a man with no history and for whom everything is manic radio material. The character adlibs, swoops and swerves, finally accepting adult responsibility. Engaging all the way with an outstanding period soundtrack.
1987 (R) 121m/C Robin Williams, Forest Whitaker, Bruno Kirby, Richard Edson, Robert Wuhl, J.T. Walsh, Noble Willingham, Floyd Vivino, Tung Thanh Tran, Chintara Sukapatana; *D:* Barry Levinson; *W:* Mitch Markowitz; *M:* Alex North. Academy Awards '87 Nominations: Best Actor (Williams); Golden Globe Awards '88: Best Actor—Musical/Comedy (Williams). **VHS, Beta, 8mm** $29.95 *TOU, BVV* 🎞🎞🎞

The Good Mother A divorced mother works at creating a fulfilling life for herself and her daughter, with an honest education for her daughter about every subject, including sex. But her ex-husband, unsure of how far this education is being taken, fights for custody of their 8-year old daughter after allegations of sexual misconduct against the mother's new lover. Based on Sue Miller's bestselling novel. Well acted, weakly edited and scripted.
1988 (R) 104m/C Diane Keaton, Liam Neeson, Jason Robards Jr., Ralph Bellamy, James Naughton, Teresa Wright, Asia Vieira, Joe Morton, Katey Sagal, Tracy Griffith, Charles Kimbrough; *D:* Leonard Nimoy; *W:* Michael Bortman; *M:* Elmer Bernstein. **VHS, Beta** $89.95 *TOU* 🎞🎞½

Good Neighbor Sam A married advertising executive (Lemmon) agrees to pose as a friend's husband in order for her to collect a multi-million dollar inheritance. Complications ensue when his biggest client mistakes the friend for his actual wife and decides they're the perfect couple to promote his wholesome product—milk.

1964 130m/C Jack Lemmon, Romy Schneider, Dorothy Provine, Mike Connors, Edward G. Robinson, Joyce Jameson; **D:** David Swift. VHS, Beta $9.95 GKK ♫♫♫

Good News A vintage Comden-Green musical about the love problems of a college football star, who will flunk out if he doesn't pass his French exams. Revamping of the 1927 Broadway smash features the unlikely sight of Lawford in a song-and-dance role. ♫Varsity Drag; He's a Lady's Man; Good News; Tait Song; Students Are We; Just Imagine; If You're Not Kissing Me; Football; I Feel Pessimistic; I'd Like to Make You Happy; My Blue Heaven; Pass That Peace Pipe; The French Lesson; Lucky in Love; The Best Things in Life Are Free.
1947 92m/C June Allyson, Peter Lawford, Joan McCracken, Mel Torme; **D:** Charles Walters. VHS, Beta $19.98 MGM, FCT ♫♫½

Good Sam An incurable "Good Samaritan" finds himself in one jam after another as he tries too hard to help people. Lots of missed opportunities for laughs with McCrarey's mediocre direction.
1948 116m/B Gary Cooper, Ann Sheridan, Ray Collins, Edmund Lowe, Joan Lorring, Ruth Roman; **D:** Leo McCarey. VHS $19.98 REP ♫♫

The Good Son In a grand departure from cute, Culkin tackles evil as a 13-year-old obsessed with death and other unseemly hobbies. During a stay with his uncle, Mark (Wood) watches as his cousin (Culkin) gets creepier and creepier, and tries to alert the family. But will they listen? Nooo—they choose to ignore the little warning signs like the doll hanging by a noose in Culkin's room. And then there's the untimely death of a sibling. Hmmm. Culkin isn't as bad as expected, but doesn't quite get all the way down to bone-chilling terror either. Original star Jesse Bradford was dropped when Papa Culkin threatened to pull Mac off "Home Alone 2" if he wasn't cast in the lead.
1993 (R) 87m/C Macaulay Culkin, Elijah Wood, Wendy Crewson, David Morse, Daniel Hugh-Kelly, Quinn Culkin; **D:** Joseph Ruben; **W:** Ian McEwan; **M:** Elmer Bernstein. VHS FXV ♫♫

The Good, the Bad, and Huckleberry Hound Journeying out West to begin a ranch, Huckleberry Hound winds up becoming a sheriff in the small town of Two-Bit. Huckleberry stands up against a group of bully brothers who have been terrorizing the town.
1988 94m/C **D:** Ray Patterson; **V:** Daws Butler. VHS, Beta $29.95 TTC, IME, WTA ♫♫

The Good, the Bad and the Ugly Leone's grandiloquent, shambling tribute to the American Western. Set during the Civil War, it follows the seemingly endless adventures of three dirtbags in search of a cache of Confederate gold buried in a nameless grave. Violent, exaggerated, beautifully crafted, it is the final and finest installment of the "Dollars" trilogy: a spaghetti Western chef d'oeuvre.
1967 161m/C IT Clint Eastwood, Eli Wallach, Lee Van Cleef, Chelo Alonso, Luigi Pistilli; **D:** Sergio Leone; **W:** Sergio Leone; **M:** Ennio Morricone. VHS, Beta $19.98 FOX, MGM, FCT ♫♫♫½

Good Time with a Bad Girl A married millionaire visiting Las Vegas experiments with exotic sexual pleasures when he meets up with Sue, a teenage nymphomaniac. **AKA:** A Good Time, A Bad Girl.
1967 61m/B VHS, Beta $19.95 VDM, TPV ♫

The Good Wife A bored and sexually frustrated wife scandalizes her small Australian town by taking up with the new hotel barman. There's no denying Ward's sexuality, but overall the movie is too predictable. **AKA:** The Umbrella Woman.
1986 (R) 97m/C AU Rachel Ward, Bryan Brown, Sam Neill, Steven Vidler, Bruce Barry, Jennifer Claire; **D:** Ken Cameron; **M:** Cameron Allan. VHS, Beta BAR, IME ♫♫½

Goodbye Again A romantic drama based on the novel by Francoise Sagan. Bergman is a middle-aged interior decorator whose lover, Montand, has a roaming eye. She finds herself drawn to the son (Perkins) of a client and begins an affair—flattered by the young man's attentions. Montand is outraged and vows to change his ways and marry Bergman if she will give up the young man. A bit soapy, but a must for Bergman fans. **AKA:** Aimez-Vous Brahms.
1961 120m/B Jessie Royce Landis, Ingrid Bergman, Anthony Perkins, Yves Montand, Diahann Carroll; **D:** Anatole Litvak. VHS $19.98 MGM, FCT ♫♫½

The Goodbye Bird Frank is accused by his school principal of stealing her prized talking parrot. With the aid of a kindly veterinarian Frank tries to discover who the thief really is.
1993 (G) 91m/C Cindy Pickett, Concetta Tomei, Wayne Rogers, Christopher Pettiet; **D:** William Clark. VHS $89.95 WOV ♫♫½

Goodbye Columbus Philip Roth's novel about a young Jewish librarian who has an affair with the spoiled daughter of a nouveau riche family is brought to late-'60s life, and vindicated by superb performances all around. Benjamin and McGraw's first starring roles.
1969 (PG) 105m/C Richard Benjamin, Ali MacGraw, Jack Klugman, Nan Martin, Jaclyn Smith; **D:** Larry Peerce; **M:** Charles Fox. VHS, Beta $14.95 PAR ♫♫♫

Goodbye Cruel World Black comedy about a suicidal television anchorman who decides to spend his last day filming the relatives who drove him to the brink.
1982 (R) 90m/C Dick Shawn, Cynthia Sikes, Chuck "Porky" Mitchell; **D:** David Irving. VHS, Beta $69.98 LIV ♫½

Goodbye Emmanuelle Follows the further adventures of Emmanuelle in her quest for sexual freedom and the excitement of forbidden pleasures. The second sequel to "Emmanuelle."
1979 (R) 92m/C Sylvia Kristel. VHS, Beta NO ♫½

The Goodbye Girl Neil Simon's story of a former actress, her precocious nine-year-old daughter and the aspiring actor who moves in with them. The daughter serves as catalyst for the other two to fall in love. While Mason's character is fairly unsympathetic, Dreyfuss is great and Simon's dialogue witty.
1977 (PG) 110m/C Richard Dreyfuss, Marsha Mason, Quinn Cummings, Barbara Rhoades, Marilyn Sokol; **D:** Herbert Ross; **W:** Neil Simon; **M:** Dave Grusin. Academy Awards '77: Best Actor (Dreyfuss); Nominations: Best Picture; Academy Awards '77: Best Actress (Mason), Best Original Screenplay, Best Supporting Actress (Cummings); British Academy Awards '78: Best Actor (Dreyfuss); Golden Globe Awards '78: Best Actor—Musical/Comedy (Dreyfuss), Best Actress—Musical/Comedy (Mason), Best Film—Musical/Comedy, Best Screenplay; Los Angeles Film Critics Association Awards '77: Best Actor (Dreyfuss). VHS, Beta $19.98 MGM, BTV ♫♫♫

Goodbye Love Dull comedy about a group of ex-husbands who refuse to pay alimony and end up in jail.
1934 65m/B Charlie Ruggles, Verree Teasdale, Sidney Blackmer, Mayo Methot, Phyllis Barry, Ray Walker, John Kelly, Hale Grace, Luis Alberni; **D:** Herbert Ross. VHS $29.95 FCT ♫½

Goodbye, Miss 4th of July Inspired by the true story of the teenage daughter of Greek immigrants living in pre-WWI West Virginia, the prejudice they encounter, the relationship that begins between the family and an aging African-American ex-boxer, and the girl's efforts in the influenza epidemic. Based on the 1985 book by her brother.
1988 89m/C Roxana Zal, Louis Gossett Jr., Chris Sarandon, Chantal Contouri, Chynna Phillips, Mitchell Anderson, Conchata Ferrell, Ed Lauter; **D:** George Miller. VHS $39.99 DIS ♫♫½

Goodbye, Mr. Chips An MGM classic, the sentimental rendering of the James Hilton novel about a shy Latin professor in an English school who marries the vivacious Garson only to tragically lose her. He spends the rest of his life devoting himself to his students and becoming a school legend. Multi award-winning soaper featuring Garson's first screen appearance, which was Oscar nominated. Special two-tape letter-boxed laserdisc edition includes the original trailer and an extra-special production featurette. Remade in 1969 as a fairly awful musical starring Peter O'Toole.
1939 115m/B Robert Donat, Greer Garson, Paul Henreid, John Mills; **D:** Sam Wood. Academy Awards '39: Best Actor (Donat); Nominations: Best Actress (Garson), Best Director (Wood), Best Film Editing, Best Picture, Best Screenplay, Best Sound; National Board of Review Awards '39: 10 Best Films of the Year. VHS, Beta $24.98 MGM, BTV, HMV ♫♫♫½

Goodbye, Mr. Chips Ross debuted as director with this big-budget (but inferior) musical re-make of the classic James Hilton novel about a gentle teacher in an English all-boys private school and the woman who helps him demonstrate his compassion and overcome his shyness. O'Toole, although excellent, is categorically a non-singer, while Clark, a popular singer at the time ("Downtown"), musters very little talent in front of the camera. The plot is altered unnecessarily and updated to the WWII era for little reason; the music is thoroughly forgettable. ♫Fill The World With Love; Where Did My Childhood Go; London is London; And the Sky Smiled; When I Am Older; Walk Through the World; What Shall I Do with Today?; What a Lot of Flowers; Schooldays; When I Was Younger; You and I.
1969 151m/C Peter O'Toole, Petula Clark, Michael Redgrave, George Baker, Sian Phillips, Michael Bryant, Jack Hedley, Herbert Ross; **D:** Herbert Ross; **M:** Leslie Bricusse, John Williams. Academy Awards '69 Nominations: Best Actor (O'Toole), Best Original Score; Golden Globe Awards '70: Best Actor—Musical/Comedy (O'Toole). VHS, Beta $19.98 MGM ♫♫

Goodbye, My Lady Based on the novel by James Street, this is a tear-jerking film about a young Mississippi farmboy who finds and cares for a special dog that he comes to love but eventually must give up.
1956 95m/B Brandon de Wilde, Walter Brennan, Sidney Poitier, Phil Harris, Louise Beavers; **D:** William A. Wellman. VHS, Beta $14.95 WAR, FCT ♫♫

Goodbye, New York A New York yuppie on a vacation finds herself penniless and stranded in Israel. She makes the best of the situation by joining a kibbutz and falling for a part-time soldier. Well, of course.

1985 (R) 90m/C *IS* Julie Hagerty, Amos Kollek, Shmuel Shilo; *D:* Amos Kollek. **VHS, Beta** $79.95 *VES ♫♫*

Goodbye, Norma Jean Detailed and sleazy recreation of Marilyn Monroe's early years in Hollywood. Followed by "Goodnight, Sweet Marilyn."
1975 (R) 95m/C Misty Rowe, Terrence Locke, Patch MacKenzie; *D:* Larry Buchanan. **VHS, Beta** *NO ♫*

The Goodbye People Balsam is an elderly man who decides to reopen his Coney Island hot dog stand that folded 22 years earlier. Hirsch and Reed help him realize his impossible dream in this sweetly sentimental film.
1983 104m/C Judd Hirsch, Martin Balsam, Pamela Reed, Ron Silver; *D:* Herb Gardner; *W:* Herb Gardner. **VHS, Beta** $14.95 *COL, SUE ♫♫½*

Goodbye Pork Pie With the police on their trail, two young men speed on a 1000-mile journey in a small, brand-new, yellow stolen car. Remember: journey of thousand miles always begin in stolen car.
1981 (R) 105m/C *NZ* Tony Barry, Kelly Johnson; *D:* Geoff Murphy. **VHS, Beta** $69.98 *SUE ♫½*

Goodfellas Quintessential picture about "wise guys," at turns both violent and funny. A young man grows up in the mob, works hard to advance himself through the ranks, and enjoys the life of the rich and violent, oblivious to the horror of which he is a part. Cocaine addiction and many wise-guy missteps ultimately unravel his climb to the top. Excellent performances (particularly Liotta and Pesci, with De Niro pitching in around the corners), with visionary cinematography and careful pacing. Watch for Scorsese's mom as Pesci's mom. Based on the life of Henry Hill, ex-mobster now in the Witness Protection Program. Adapted from the book by Nicholas Pileggi.
1990 (R) 146m/C Robert De Niro, Ray Liotta, Joe Pesci, Paul Sorvino, Lorraine Bracco, Frank Sivero, Mike Starr, Frank Vincent, Samuel L. Jackson, Henny Youngman, Tony Darrow, Chuck Low, Frank DiLeo, Christopher Serrone, Jerry Vale; *D:* Martin Scorsese; *W:* Nicholas Pileggi, Martin Scorsese. Academy Awards '90: Best Supporting Actor (Pesci); Nominations: Best Adapted Screenplay, Best Director (Scorsese), Best Film Editing, Best Picture, Best Supporting Actress (Bracco); British Academy Awards '90: Best Director (Scorsese), Best Film; Los Angeles Film Critics Association Awards '90: Best Director (Scorsese), Best Film, Best Supporting Actor (Pesci), Best Supporting Actress (Bracco); New York Film Critics Awards '90: Best Director (Scorsese), Best Film; National Society of Film Critics Awards '90: Best Director (Scorsese), Best Film. **VHS, Beta, 8mm** $19.98 *WAR, FCT, BTV ♫♫♫♫*

Goodnight God Bless A depressing movie about a mentally disturbed priest who wanders into an elementary school with murder on his mind. He kills the teacher and all the children—except one. Will he find that one too? It's not worth it to find out.
1987 (R) 90m/C **VHS, Beta** *NO ♫*

Goodnight, Michelangelo Funny, engaging and somewhat confusing story of the life of an Italian immigrant family as seen through the eyes of its youngest member, eight-year-old Michelangelo. Winner of the 1990 Best Comedy Award at the Greater Fort Lauderdale Film Festival.
1989 (R) 91m/C *IT* Lina Sastri, Kim Cattrall, Giancarlo Giannini, Daniel Desanto; *D:* Carlo Liconti; *W:* Carlo Liconti. **VHS** *NO ♫♫½*

Goodnight, Sweet Marilyn Supposed "never-before-told" story of Marilyn Monroe's tragic death. According to this, her death was the result of pre-arranged "mercy-killing." Follow-up to director Buchanan's "Goodbye, Norma Jean" (1977) with Lane as the 1960s Marilyn intercut with scenes of Rowe from the first film as young Marilyn. You'd be better off leaving "Sweet Marilyn" to rest in peace.
1989 (R) 100m/C Paula Lane, Jeremy Slate, Misty Rowe; *D:* Larry Buchanan. **VHS, Beta** *NO ♫*

Goof Balls The tourist denizens of a island golf resort putt and cavort about, and golf isn't all that's on their minds.
1987 (R) 87m/C Ben Gordon, Laura Robinson. **VHS, Beta** $29.95 *ACA Woof!*

Goon Movie The cast of "The Goon Show," Britain's popular radio comedy series, perform some of their best routines in this, their only film appearance. *AKA:* Stand Easy.
1953 75m/B Peter Sellers, Spike Milligan, Harry Secombe. **VHS, Beta** $19.95 *VDM ♫♫*

The Goonies Two brothers who are about to lose their house conveniently find a treasure map. They pick up a couple of friends and head for the "X." If they can recover the treasure without getting caught by the bad guys, then all will be saved. Steven Spielberg produced this high-energy action fantasy for kids of all ages. The laserdisc edition comes in a widescreen format.
1985 (PG) 114m/C Sean Astin, Josh Brolin, Jeff B. Cohen, Corey Feldman, Martha Plimpton, John Matuszak, Anne Ramsey, Mary Ellen Trainor, Jonathan Ke Quan, Kerri Green, Joe Pantoliano; *D:* Richard Donner; *W:* Chris Columbus, Steven Spielberg; *M:* Dave Grusin. **VHS, Beta** $14.95 *WAR ♫♫½*

Gor Sword and sorcery: a magic ring sends a meek college professor to "Gor," a faraway world in which survival goes to the fittest and the most brutal. Followed by "Outlaw of Gor."
1988 (PG) 95m/C Urbano Barberini, Rebecca Ferratti, Jack Palance, Paul Smith, Oliver Reed; *D:* Fritz Kiersch; *W:* R.J. Marx. **VHS, Beta** $19.98 *WAR ♫½*

Gorath The world's top scientists are racing to stop a giant meteor from destroying the Earth. *AKA:* Yosei Gorasu.
1964 77m/C *JP D:* Inoshiro Honda. **VHS, Beta** $19.95 *GEM, PSM ♫♫*

Gordon's War When a Vietnam vet returns to his Harlem home, he finds his wife overdosing on the drugs that have infiltrated his neighborhood. He leads a vigilante group in an attempt to clean up the area, which makes for a lot of action; however, there's also an excessive amount of violence.
1973 (R) 89m/C Paul Winfield, Carl Lee, David Downing, Tony King, Grace Jones; *D:* Ossie Davis; *M:* Angelo Badalamenti. **VHS, Beta** $59.98 *FOX ♫♫*

The Gore-Gore Girls Splatter horror director Lewis' final film follows a detective's search for a madman who's been mutilating and killing beautiful young bar dancers.
1972 84m/C *D:* Herschell Gordon Lewis. **VHS** $19.99 *MOV ♫*

Gore-Met Zombie Chef From Hell A demon/vampire opens up a seafood restaurant and slaughters his customers. Deliberately campy and extremely graphic.
1987 90m/C Theo Depuay, Kelley Kunicki, C.W. Casey, Alan Marx, Michael O'Neill; *D:* Don Swan. **VHS, Beta** *NO Woof!*

Gore Vidal's Billy the Kid An unusual treatment of the William Bonney legend in which the Kid is merely a misunderstood teenager caught up in the midst of the brutal range wars. Made for cable television.
1989 100m/C Val Kilmer, Duncan Regehr, Wilford Brimley, Julie Carmen, Michael Parks, Rene Auberjonois, Albert Salmi; *D:* William A. Graham. **VHS** $9.98 *TTC ♫♫½*

Gore Vidal's Lincoln Waterston is a low-key but sympathetic Lincoln, with Moore as his high-strung wife Mary, in this made for television adaptation of the Vidal best-seller. Follows the couple from their first day in Washington, through the Civil War, family tragedies, up to the day of the President's burial. *AKA:* Lincoln.
1988 190m/C Sam Waterston, Mary Tyler Moore, John Houseman, Richard Mulligan, John McMartin, Ruby Dee, Cleavon Little, Jeffrey DeMunn, James Gammon, Deborah Adair, Robin Gammell; *D:* Lamont Johnson; *W:* Ernest Kinoy; *M:* Ernest Gold. **VHS** $89.95 *AVE ♫♫½*

The Gorgeous Hussy Crawford stars in this fictionalized biography of Peggy Eaton, Andrew Jackson's notorious belle, who disgraces herself and those around her. A star-studded cast complete with beautiful costumes isn't enough to save this overly long and dull picture.
1936 102m/B Joan Crawford, Robert Taylor, Lionel Barrymore, Melvyn Douglas, James Stewart, Franchot Tone, Louis Calhern; *D:* Clarence Brown. **VHS** $19.98 *MGM ♫*

Gorgo An undersea explosion off the coast of Ireland brings to the surface a prehistoric sea monster, which is captured and brought to a London circus. Its irate mother appears looking for her baby, creating havoc in her wake.
1961 76m/C *GB* Bill Travers, William Sylvester, Vincent Winter, Bruce Seton, Christopher Rhodes; *D:* Eugene Lourie. **VHS, Beta** $19.95 *NOS, MRV, VCI ♫♫*

The Gorgon In pre-WWI Germany, the lovely assistant to a mad brain surgeon moonlights as a snake-haired gorgon, turning men to stone. A professor arrives in the village to investigate, only to become another victim.
1964 83m/C *GB* Peter Cushing, Christopher Lee, Richard Pasco, Barbara Shelley, Michael Goodliffe, Patrick Troughton; *D:* Terence Fisher. **VHS, Beta** $9.95 *GKK, MLB ♫♫*

The Gorilla Bumbling Ritzes are hired to protect a country gentleman receiving threats from a killer. Lugosi portrays the menacing butler. Derived from the play by Ralph Spence.
1939 67m/B The Ritz Brothers, Anita Louise, Patsy Kelly, Lionel Atwill, Bela Lugosi; *D:* Allan Dwan. **VHS, Beta** $19.95 *NOS, SNC, MRV ♫♫*

Gorilla A rampaging gorilla is sought by the local game warden and a journalist researching the natives. Filmed on location in the Belgian Congo.
1956 79m/B *SW* Gio Petre, Georges Galley; *D:* Sven Nykvist, Lar Henrik Ottoson. **VHS, Beta** $19.95 *FCT, VYY ♫♫*

Gorillas in the Mist The life of Dian Fossey, animal rights activist and world-renowned expert on the African Gorilla, from her pioneering contact with mountain gorillas to her murder at the hands of poachers. Weaver is totally appropriate as the increasingly obsessed Fossey, but the character moves away from us, just as we need to see and understand more about her. Excellent special effects.
1988 (PG-13) 117m/C Sigourney Weaver, Bryan Brown, Julie Harris, Iain Cuthbertson, John Omirah Miluwi, Constantin Alexandrov, Waigwa Wachira; *D:* Michael Apted; *W:* Anna Hamilton Phelan; *M:* Maurice Jarre. Academy Awards '88 Nominations: Best Actress (Weaver), Best Adapted Screenplay, Best Film Editing, Best Sound, Best Original Score; Golden Globe Awards '88: Best Actress—Drama (Weaver);

Golden Globe Awards '89: Best Score. **VHS, Beta $19.95** MCA, HMV 🎬🎬🎬

Gorky Park Adaptation of Martin Cruz Smith's bestseller. Three strange, faceless corpses are found in Moscow's Gorky Park. There are no clues for the Russian police captain investigating the incident. He makes the solution to this crime his personal crusade, and finds himself caught in a web of political intrigue. Excellent police procedure yarn.
1983 (R) 127m/C William Hurt, Lee Marvin, Brian Dennehy, Joanna Pacula; **D:** Michael Apted; **W:** Dennis Potter; **M:** James Horner. **VHS, Beta $29.98** VES 🎬🎬🎬

Gorp Sex, fun, and lewd, sophomoric humor reign at a summer camp. For the bored and witless or those who aspire.
1980 (R) 90m/C Dennis Quaid, Rosanna Arquette, Michael Lembeck, Philip Casnoff, Frank Drescher; **D:** Joseph Ruben. **VHS, Beta $79.99** HBO Woof!

The Gospel According to St. Matthew Perhaps Pasolini's greatest film, retelling the story of Christ in gritty, neorealistic tones and portraying the man less as a divine presence than as a political revolutionary. The yardstick by which all Jesus-films are to be measured. In Italian with English subtitles or dubbed. **AKA:** Il Vangelo Secondo Matteo; L'Evangile Selon Saint-Matthieu.
1964 142m/B IT Enrique Irazoqui, Susanna Pasolini, Margherita Caruso, Marcello Morante, Mario Socrate; **D:** Pier Paolo Pasolini; **W:** Pier Paolo Pasolini. Academy Awards '66 Nominations: Best Art Direction/Set Decoration (B & W), Best Costume Design (B & W), Best Original Score; National Board of Review Awards '66: 5 Best Foreign Films of the Year. **VHS, Beta, 8mm $24.95** NOS, MRV, WBF 🎬🎬🎬🎬

The Gospel According to Vic A Scottish comedy about a skeptical teacher at a remedial school, who, having survived miraculously from a fall, is taken for proof of the sainthood of the school's patron namesake. **AKA:** Heavenly Pursuits.
1987 (PG-13) 92m/C GB Tom Conti, Helen Mirren; **D:** Charles Gormley. **VHS, Beta $79.98** FOX 🎬🎬

Gotcha! The mock assassination game "Gotcha!" abounds on the college campus and sophomore Edwards is one of the best. What he doesn't know is that his "assassination" skills are about to take on new meaning when he meets up with a female Czech graduate student who is really an international spy.
1985 (PG-13) 97m/C Anthony Edwards, Linda Fiorentino, Alex Rocco, Nick Corri, Marla Adams, Klaus Loewitsch, Christopher Rydell; **D:** Jeff Kanew; **W:** Dan Gordon; **M:** Bill Conti. **VHS, Beta $14.98** MCA 🎬🎬½

Gotham A wealthy financier hires private-eye Jones to track down beautiful wife Madsen. It seems that she keeps dunning her husband for money. Sounds easy enough to Jones until he learns that she has been dead for some time. Mystery ventures into the afterlife and back as it twists its way to its surprise ending. Intriguing throwback to '40s detective flicks. Made for television.
1988 100m/C Tommy Lee Jones, Virginia Madsen, Colin Bruce, Kevin Jarre, Denise Stephenson, Frederic Forrest; **D:** Lloyd Fonvielle; **M:** George S. Clinton. **VHS $19.98** CAN 🎬🎬🎬

Gothic Mary Shelley, Lord Byron, Percy Bysshe Shelley, and John Polidori spend the night in a Swiss villa telling each other ghost stories and experimenting with laudanum and sexual partner combinations. The dreams and realizations of the night will color

their lives ever after. Interesting premise, well-carried out, although burdened by director Russell's typical excesses. Soundtrack by Thomas Dolby.
1987 (R) 87m/C Julian Sands, Gabriel Byrne, Timothy Spall, Natasha Richardson, Miriam Cyr; **D:** Ken Russell; **W:** Stephen Volk; **M:** Thomas Dolby. **VHS, Beta $14.98** LIV, VES 🎬🎬🎬

Gotta Dance, Gotta Sing Compilation of memorable dance routines from great Hollywood films.
1984 53m/C Fred Astaire, Ginger Rogers, Shirley Temple, Carmen Miranda, Betty Grable. **VHS, Beta $39.95** RKO 🎬🎬🎬

Government Agents vs. Phantom Legion Agent Hal Duncan must stop an evil group who is stealing uranium shipments from under the government's nose. Edited from 12 episodes of the original serial on two cassettes.
1951 167m/B Walter Reed, Mary Ellen Kay, Dick Curtis, John Pickard. **VHS, Beta $29.98** REP, MLB 🎬🎬🎬

Grace Quigley An elderly woman, tired of life, hires a hitman to kill her. Instead they go into business together, bumping off other elderly folk who decide they'd rather be dead. Notoriously inept black comedy noted for being the career embarrassment for both of its stars. **AKA:** The Ultimate Solution of Grace Quigley.
1984 (PG) 87m/C Katharine Hepburn, Nick Nolte, Walter Abel, Chip Zien, Elizabeth Wilson, Kit Le Fever, William Duell, Jill Eikenberry; **D:** Anthony Harvey; **M:** John Addison. **VHS, Beta $14.95** MGM 🎬½

Grad Night The anticipation for graduation in a small town high school brings surprises no one could have predicted, unless they've seen all the other typical adolescent films.
1981 (R) 85m/C Joey Johnson, Suzanna Fagan, Barry Stolze, Sam Whipple, Caroline Bates; **D:** John Tenorio. **VHS, Beta $79.95** MNC 🎬

The Graduate Famous, influential slice of comic Americana stars Hoffman as Benjamin Braddock, a shy, aimless college graduate who, without any idea of responsibility or ambition, wanders from a sexual liaison with a married woman (the infamous Mrs. Robinson) to pursuit of her engaged daughter. His pursuit of Elaine right to her wedding has become a film classic. Extremely popular and almost solely responsible for establishing both Hoffman and director Nichols. The career advice given to Benjamin, "plastics," became a catchword for the era. Watch for Dreyfuss in the Berkeley rooming house, Farrell in the hotel lobby, and screenwriter Henry as the desk clerk. Based on the novel by Charles Webb. Laserdisc edition includes screen tests, promotional stills, and a look at the creative process involved in making a novel into a movie. A 25th Anniversary Limited Edition is also available, presented in a wide-screen format and including the original movie trailer and interviews with the cast and crew.
1967 (PG) 106m/C Dustin Hoffman, Anne Bancroft, Katharine Ross, Murray Hamilton, Brian Avery, Marion Lorne, Alice Ghostley, William Daniels, Elizabeth Wilson, Norman Fell, Buck Henry, Richard Dreyfuss, Mike Farrell; **D:** Mike Nichols; **W:** Buck Henry, Calder Willingham; **M:** Paul Simon, Art Garfunkel, Dave Grusin. Academy Awards '67: Best Director (Nichols); Nominations: Best Adapted Screenplay, Best Cinematography, Best Supporting Actress (Ross); British Academy Awards '68: Best Director (Nichols), Best Film; Directors Guild of America Awards '67: Best Director (Nichols); Golden Globe Awards '68: Best Actress—Musical/Comedy (Bancroft), Best Director (Nichols), Best

Film—Musical/Comedy; National Board of Review Awards '67: 10 Best Films of the Year; New York Film Critics Awards '67: Best Director (Nichols). **VHS, Beta, 8mm $19.95** NLC, VYG, CRC 🎬🎬🎬🎬

Graduation Day Another teen slasher about the systematic murder of members of a high school track team. Notable mainly for brief appearance by Vanna White.
1981 (R) 85m/C Christopher George, Patch MacKenzie, E. Danny Murphy, Vanna White; **D:** Herb Freed. **VHS, Beta $69.95** COL 🎬

Graffiti Bridge Prince preaches love instead of sex and the result is boring. The Lavender One is a Minneapolis nightclub owner who battles with Day over the love of a beautiful woman. Chauvinistic attitudes toward women abound, but the females in the film don't seem to mind. Which must mean they were "acting." Visually interesting, although not as experimental as "Purple Rain." Music made Top Ten.
1990 (PG-13) 90m/C Prince, Morris Day, Jerome Benton, The Time, Jill Jones, Mavis Staples, George Clinton, Ingrid Chavez; **D:** Prince; **W:** Prince. **VHS, Beta $14.95** MVD, WAR 🎬1½

Grain of Sand Based on a true story, an understated French drama about a troubled woman searching her past, and her home town in Corsica, for the man of her dreams. Directorial debut of Meffre. In French with English subtitles.
1984 90m/C FR Delphine Seyrig, Genevieve Fontanel, Coralie Seyrig, Michel Aumont; **D:** Pomme Meffre. **VHS, Beta $59.95** FCT 🎬🎬🎬

Grambling's White Tiger The true story of Jim Gregory, the first white man to play on Grambling College's all-black football team. Jenner's a little too old, but Belafonte, in his TV acting debut, is fine as legendary coach Eddie Robinson. Based on book by Bruce Behrenberg. Made for television.
1981 98m/C Bruce Jenner, Harry Belafonte, LeVar Burton, Ray Vitte, Byron Stewart; **D:** Georg Stanford Brown; **M:** John D'Andrea. **VHS, Beta $39.95** MCA 🎬🎬½

Grampa's Monster Movies Grampa (star of "The Munsters" TV show) hosts a tribute to Frankenstein, Dracula, Wolfman and the Mummy, with legends Bela Lugosi, Boris Karloff, Lon Chaney Jr. and Vincent Price.
1990 65m/C VHS, Beta NO 🎬🎬½

Grampa's Sci-Fi Hits Sequel to Grampa's "Monster Movies," this one carries some of the more fantastic sci-fi creatures from beyond.
1990 65m/C VHS, Beta NO 🎬🎬½

Gran Valor en la Facultad de Medicina A Spanish simpleton is mistakenly admitted to medical school.
1987 90m/C SP Juan Carlos Calabro, Adriana Aguirre. **VHS, Beta $57.95** UNI 🎬

Grand Canyon Diverse group of characters is thrown together through chance encounters while coping with urban chaos in L.A. The main focus is the growing friendship between an immigration lawyer (Kline) and a tow-truck driver (Glover) who meet when Kline's car breaks down in a crime-ridden neighborhood. First-rate performances by the cast make up for numerous moral messages thrown at viewers with the subtlety of a brick. Sometimes funny, sometimes preachy became more relevant in light of the violence that exploded in L.A. during the summer of '92.
1991 (R) 134m/C Danny Glover, Kevin Kline, Steve Martin, Mary McDonnell, Mary-Louise Parker, Alfre Woodard, Jeremy Sisto, Tina Lifford, Patrick Malone, Mary Ellen Trainor; **D:**

Lawrence Kasdan; **W:** Lawrence Kasdan, Meg Kasdan; **M:** James Newton Howard. Academy Awards '91 Nominations: Best Original Screenplay; National Board of Review Awards '91: 10 Best Films of the Year. **VHS $19.98** *FXV* 🦴🦴🦴

Grand Canyon Trail Our hero is the owner of a played-out silver mine who is the target of an unscrupulous engineer who thinks there's silver to be found if you know where to look. The first appearance of the Riders of the Purple Sage, who replaced the Sons of the Pioneers.
1948 68m/B Roy Rogers, Andy Devine, Charles Coleman, Jane Frazee, Robert Livingston; **D:** William Witney. **VHS, Beta $9.99** *NOS, MED, DVT* 🦴 ½

The Grand Duchess and the Waiter Menjou is a French millionaire who disguises himself as a waiter in order to enter the service of a grand duchess with whom he has fallen in love.
1926 70m/B Adolphe Menjou, Florence Vidor, Lawrence Grant; **D:** Malcolm St. Clair. **VHS, Beta** *GVV* 🦴🦴🦴

The Grand Duel More spaghetti thrills as Lee plays a mysterious gunman who also acts as protector of a young ruffian falsely accused of murder.
1973 ?m/C *IT* Lee Van Cleef, Peter O'Brien, Jess Hahn, Horst Frank. **VHS $16.95** *SNC, VTR* 🦴🦴

Grand Hotel A star-filled cast is brought together by unusual circumstances at Berlin's Grand Hotel and their lives become hopelessly intertwined over a 24 hour period. Adapted (and given the red-carpet treatment) from a Vicki Baum novel; notable mostly for Garbo's world-weary ballerina. Time has taken its toll on the concept and treatment, but still an interesting star vehicle.
1932 112m/B Greta Garbo, John Barrymore, Joan Crawford, Lewis Stone, Wallace Beery, Jean Hersholt, Lionel Barrymore; **D:** Edmund Goulding. **VHS, Beta $19.98** *MGM, FCT, BTV* 🦴🦴🦴 ½

Grand Illusion Unshakably classic anti-war film by Renoir, in which French prisoners of war attempt to escape from their German captors during WWI. An indictment of the way Old World, aristocratic nobility was brought to modern bloodshed in the Great War. Renoir's optimism remains relentless, but was easier to believe in before WWII. In French, with English subtitles. The laserdisc version includes an audio essay by Peter Crowe.
1937 111m/B *FR* Jean Gabin, Erich von Stroheim, Pierre Fresnay, Marcel Dalio, Julien Carette, Gaston Modot, Jean Daste, Dita Parlo; **D:** Jean Renoir. Academy Awards '38 Nominations: Best Picture; National Board of Review Awards '38: 5 Best Foreign Films of the Year; New York Film Critics Awards '38: Best Foreign Film. **VHS, Beta, 8mm $24.95** *VYY, MRV, FOX* 🦴🦴🦴🦴

Grand Isle At the turn of the century Grand Isle is the place Louisiana gentry leisurely spend their summers. This is where Edna Pontellier (McGillis), the wife of a rich stockbroker, meets sensitive Creole artist Robert LeBrun (Pasdar). Robert gives Edna all the attention sorely lacking in her marriage and they fall in love. However, Edna's attempts to liberate herself from the strictures of society lead her to tragedy. Based on "The Awakening" by Kate Chopin. Made for cable television.
1992 94m/C Kelly McGillis, Adrian Pasdar, Julian Sands, Jon DeVries, Glenne Headly, Anthony De Sando, Ellen Burstyn; **D:** Mary Lambert; **W:** Hesper Anderson. **VHS $89.98** *TTC* 🦴🦴½

Grand Larceny The daughter of a millionaire/thief has to prove that she can take over the family "business." Lots of action and stunts.
19?? 95m/C Marilu Henner, Omar Sharif, Ian McShane, Louis Jourdan. **VHS $49.95** *CAF* 🦴🦴

Grand Prix A big-budget look at the world of Grand Prix auto racing, as four top competitors circle the world's most famous racing circuits. Strictly for those who like cars racing round and round; nothing much happens off the track. Letterboxed screen is featured in the laserdisc format.
1966 161m/C James Garner, Eva Marie Saint, Yves Montand, Toshiro Mifune, Brian Bedford; **D:** John Frankenheimer; **M:** Maurice Jarre. **VHS, Beta $29.99** *MGM, FCT* 🦴🦴

Grand Theft Auto In Howard's initial directorial effort, a young couple elopes to Las Vegas in a Rolls Royce owned by the bride's father. The father, totally against the marriage and angered by the stolen Rolls, offers a reward for their safe return and a cross-country race ensues.
1977 (PG) 84m/C Ron Howard, Nancy Morgan, Marion Ross, Barry Cahill, Clint Howard; **D:** Ron Howard; **W:** Ron Howard. **VHS, Beta $19.98** *WAR* 🦴🦴

Grand Tour: Disaster in Time Greenglen is a quiet, small Midwestern town, until it is visited by a sinister group of time traveling aliens. Daniels plays a widowed innkeeper who must save the town from destruction and save his daughter from being kidnapped by the fiends. Made for cable television.
1992 (PG-13) 98m/C Jeff Daniels, Ariana Richards, Emilia Crow, Jim Haynie, Nicholas Guest, Marilyn Lightstone, George Murdock; **D:** David N. Twohy; **W:** David N. Twohy. **VHS $89.95** *ACA* 🦴🦴

Grandes Amigos A young boy finds out the meaning of having a true friend in this comedy-drama in Spanish. **AKA:** Great Friends.
19?? 105m/C *SP* Nino Del Arco. **VHS, Beta $49.95** *MAD* 🦴

Grandma's House A brother and sister discover that the house in which they live with their grandmother is chock-full of secrets and strange happenings, including madness, incest, and murder.
1988 (R) 90m/C Eric Foster, Kim Valentine, Brinke Stevens, Ida Lee; **D:** Peter Rader. **VHS, Beta $79.95** *ACA* 🦴

Grandview U.S.A. A low-key look at low-rent middle America, centering on a foxy local speedway owner and the derby-obsessed boys she attracts. Pre-"Dirty Dancing" choreography from Patrick Swayze and wife Lisa Niemi.
1984 (R) 97m/C Jamie Lee Curtis, Patrick Swayze, C. Thomas Howell, M. Emmet Walsh, Troy Donahue, William Windom, Jennifer Jason Leigh, Ramon Bieri, John Cusack, Joan Cusack, Jason Court; **D:** Randal Kleiser. **VHS, Beta $19.98** *FOX* 🦴🦴½

The Grapes of Wrath John Steinbeck's classic American novel about the Great Depression. We follow the impoverished Joad family as they migrate from the dust bowl of Oklahoma to find work in the orchards of California and as they struggle to maintain at least a little of their dignity and pride. A sentimental but dignified, uncharacteristic Hollywood epic.
1940 129m/B Henry Fonda, Jane Darwell, John Carradine, Charley Grapewin, Zeffie Tilbury, Dorris Bowdon, Russell Simpson, John Qualen, Eddie Quillan, O.Z. Whitehead, Grant Mitchell; **D:** John Ford; **W:** Nunnally Johnson. Academy Awards '40: Best Director (Ford), Best

Supporting Actress (Darwell); Nominations: Best Actor (Fonda), Best Adapted Screenplay, Best Picture, Best Sound, Best Original Score; New York Film Critics Awards '40: Best Director (Ford), Best Film. **VHS, Beta $19.98** *KUI, FOX, BTV* 🦴🦴🦴½

The Grass is Always Greener Over the Septic Tank Based on Erma Bombeck's best-seller. A city family's flight to the supposed peace of the suburbs turns out to be a comic compilation of complications. Made for television.
1978 98m/C Carol Burnett, Charles Grodin, Linda Gray, Alex Rocco, Robert Sampson, Vicki Belmonte, Craig Richard Nelson, Anrae Walterhouse, Eric Stoltz; **D:** Robert Day. **VHS, Beta** *NO* 🦴

The Grass is Greener An American millionaire invades part of an impoverished Earl's mansion and falls in love with the lady of the house. The Earl, who wants to keep his wife, enlists the aid of an old girlfriend in a feeble attempt to make her jealous. The two couples pair off properly in the end.
1961 105m/C Cary Grant, Deborah Kerr, Jean Simmons, Robert Mitchum; **D:** Stanley Donen. **VHS $19.98** *REP* 🦴🦴½

Grave of the Fireflies In post-war Japan, in the city of Kobe's train station, a young boy lies dying. A janitor finds a metal canister lying next to the boy and when he opens it ashes fall out. As fireflies gather around, ghostly figures of the boy and his little sister appear, as the story flashes back to the orphaned, homeless Seita and his sister. The two youngsters struggle in the Japanese countryside but find they cannot escape the hardships of war and have no chance for survival. Stunning animated testimony to the human spirit. Based on the novel by Akiyuki Nosaka. In Japanese with English subtitles.
1988 88m/C *JP* **D:** Isao Takahata; **W:** Isao Takahata. **VHS $39.95** *CPM, WTA* 🦴🦴🦴

Grave of the Vampire A vampire rapes and impregnates a modern-day girl. Twenty years later, their son, who grows up to be a bitter bloodsucker, sets out to find his father and kill him. **AKA:** Seed of Terror.
1972 (R) 95m/C William Smith, Michael Pataki, Lyn Peters, Diane Holden, Jay Adler, Kitty Vallacher, Jay Scott, Lieux Dressler; **D:** John Hayes. **VHS, Beta $49.95** *UNI* 🦴

Grave Secrets A professor of psychic phenomena teams up with a medium to find out who—or what—is controlling the life of a young woman.
1989 (R) 90m/C Paul LeMat, Renee Soutendijk, David Warner, Olivia Barash, Lee Ving; **D:** Donald P. Borchers. **VHS $89.98** *SGE* 🦴½

Grave Secrets: The Legacy of Hilltop Drive The Williams family finds out their dream house is built on the site of an old graveyard. The spirits are not only restless, they're deadly. Based on a true story.
1992 94m/C Jonelle Allen, Patty Duke, David Selby, David Soul, Blake Clark; **D:** John D. Patterson. **VHS $89.95** *WOV, PMS* 🦴🦴

The Graveyard A mommy spends many years torturing her little boy, David. In one blood-filled day, the fellow seeks his revenge. **AKA:** Persecution; Terror of Sheba; Sheba.
1974 90m/C Lana Turner, Trevor Howard, Ralph Bates, Olga Georges-Picot, Suzan Farmer; **D:** Don Chaffey. **VHS, Beta** *ELV* 🦴🦴

Graveyard of Horror His wife and baby dead, a man seeking revenge discovers a horrible secret: his brother, a doctor, is stealing the heads from corpses. Dubbed.

1971 105m/C SP Bill Curran, Francisco (Frank) Brana, Beatriz Lacy; D: Miguel Madrid. VHS, Beta NO ⅟

Graveyard Shift A New York cabby on the night shift is actually a powerful vampire who uses his fares to build an army of vampires. Not to be confused with the 1990 Stephen King scripted film. Followed by "Understudy: Graveyard Shift II."
1987 (R) 89m/C IT Silvio Oliviero, Helen Papas, Cliff Stoker; D: Gerard Ciccoritti. VHS, Beta VTR ⅟ ½

Graveyard Shift Just because Stephen King wrote the original story doesn't mean its celluloid incarnation is guaranteed to stand your hair on end; unless that's your response to abject boredom. When a man takes over the night shift at a recently reopened textile mill, he starts to find remnants...and they aren't fabric. Seems there's a graveyard in the neighborhood. *AKA:* Stephen King's Graveyard Shift.
1990 (R) 89m/C David Andrews, Kelly Wolf, Stephen Macht, Brad Dourif; D: Ralph S. Singleton; W: Stephen King, John Esposito. VHS, Beta $14.95 PAR, FCT ⅟

Gray Lady Down A nuclear submarine sinks off the coast of Cape Cod and with their oxygen running out, a risky escape in an experimental diving craft seems to be their only hope. Dull, all-semi-star suspenser.
1977 (PG) 111m/C Charlton Heston, David Carradine, Stacy Keach, Ned Beatty, Ronny Cox, Christopher Reeve, Michael O'Keefe, Rosemary Forsyth; D: David Greene. VHS, Beta $59.95 MCA ⅟⅟

Grayeagle When a frontier trapper's daughter is kidnapped by Cheyenne Indians, he launches a search for her recovery. More style than pace in this Western, but worth a look for fans of Johnson.
1977 (PG) 104m/C Ben Johnson, Iron Eyes Cody, Lana Wood, Alex Cord, Jack Elam, Paul Fix, Cindy Butler, Charles B. Pierce; D: Charles B. Pierce; W: Charles B. Pierce. VHS, Beta $19.98 WAR, OM ⅟⅟

Grazuole A nine-year-old girl is mockingly made "Beauty Queen" by her malicious playmates.
1969 71m/B D: Arunas Zhebrunas. VHS, Beta IHF ⅟

Grease Film version of the hit Broadway musical about summer love. Set in the 1950s, this spirited musical follows a group of high-schoolers throughout their senior year. The story offers a responsible moral: act like a tart and you'll get your guy; but, hey, it's all in fun anyway. Followed by a weak sequel. ♫Grease; Summer Nights; Hopelessly Devoted To You; You're the One That I Want; Sandy; Beauty School Dropout; Look at Me, I'm Sandra Dee; Greased Lightnin'; It's Raining on Prom Night; Alone at a Drive-In Movie; Blue Moon; Rock 'n' Roll Is Here To Stay; Those Magic Changes; Hound Dog; Born to Hand-Jive; Tears On My Pillow; Mooning; Freddy My Love; Rock 'n' Roll Party Queen; There Are Worse Things I Could Do; We Go Together; Love is a Many Splendored Thing.
1978 (PG) 110m/C John Travolta, Olivia Newton-John, Jeff Conaway, Stockard Channing, Eve Arden, Sha-Na-Na, Frankie Avalon, Sid Caesar; D: Randal Kleiser. Academy Awards '78 Nominations: Best Song ("Hopelessly Devoted to You"); People's Choice Awards '79: Best Film. VHS, Beta $14.95 PAR, FCT ⅟⅟⅟

Grease 2 Continuing saga of the T-Birds, the Pink Ladies, and young love at Rydell High. Newton-John and Travolta have graduated, leaving Pfeiffer to lead on love-struck book-neb Caulfield. Some okay tunes, though lame story lacks good-humor flair of the original.
1982 (PG) 115m/C Maxwell Caulfield, Michelle Pfeiffer, Adrian Zmed, Lorna Luft, Didi Conn, Eve Arden, Sid Caesar, Tab Hunter; D: Patricia Birch. VHS, Beta $14.95 PAR ⅟⅟

Greased Lightning The story of the first black auto racing champion, Wendell Scott, who had to overcome racial prejudice to achieve his success. Slightly-better-than-average Pryor comedy vehicle.
1977 (PG) 95m/C Richard Pryor, Pam Grier, Beau Bridges, Cleavon Little, Vincent Gardenia; D: Michael A. Schultz; W: Leon Capetanos, Melvin Van Peebles. VHS, Beta $59.95 WAR ⅟⅟ ½

Greaser's Palace Seaweedhead Greaser, owner of the town's saloon, faces his arch-nemesis in this wide-ranging satiric Christ allegory from the director of "Putney Swope."
1972 91m/C Albert Henderson, Allan Arbus; D: Robert Downey; M: Jack Nitzsche. VHS, Beta COL, OM ⅟⅟ ½

The Great Adventure Two farm boys capture and attempt to train a wild otter. Unfortunately, the otter longs to once again join his kind despite the boys' efforts. Arne Sucksdorff won an Oscar for his arresting view of animal life. *AKA:* Det Stora Aventyret.
1953 73m/B SW Anders Norberg, Kjell Sucksdorff, Arne Sucksdorff; D: Arne Sucksdorff; W: Arne Sucksdorff. VHS, Beta MED ⅟⅟⅟ ½

Great Adventure In the severe environment of the gold rush days on the rugged Yukon territory, a touching tale unfolds of a young orphan boy and his eternal bond of friendship with a great northern dog. Based on a Jack London story. Paul Elliots is a pseudonym for Gianfranco Baldanello and Fred Romer is actually Fernando Romero.
1975 (PG) 90m/C IT SP Jack Palance, Joan Collins, Fred Romer, Elisabetta Virgili, Remo de Angelis, Manuel de Blas; D: Paul Elliotts. VHS, Beta $19.95 MED, VTR ⅟⅟

The Great Alligator As if you couldn't guess, this one's about a huge alligator who does what other huge alligators do...terrorizes the people at a resort. *AKA:* Il Fiume Del Grande Caimano.
1981 89m/C Barbara Bach, Mel Ferrer, Richard Johnson; D: Sergio Martino. VHS, Beta MPI ⅟

The Great American Broadcast Two WWI vets want more than anything to strike it rich. After many failed endeavors, the two try that new-fangled thing called radio. The station takes off, as does the plot. The girlfriend of one vet falls for his partner and numerous other misunderstandings and complications ensue. Charming and crazy musical with an energetic cast. ♫I've Got a Bone To Pick With You; It's All In a Lifetime; I Take to You; Long Ago Last Night; Where You Are; The Great American Broadcast; Albany Bound; Give My Regards to Broadway; If I Didn't Care.
1941 92m/B Alice Faye, John Payne, Jack Oakie, Cesar Romero, The Four Ink Spots, James Newill, Mary Beth Hughes; D: Archie Mayo. VHS MLB ⅟⅟⅟

Great American Traffic Jam A made-for-television farce about the humorous variety of characters interacting on the interstate during a massive California traffic jam. *AKA:* Gridlock.
1980 (PG) 97m/C Ed McMahon, Vic Tayback, Howard Hesseman, Abe Vigoda, Noah Beery Jr., Desi Arnaz Jr., John Beck, Shelley Fabares, James Gregory; D: James Frawley. VHS, Beta $59.98 FOX ⅟ ½

The Great Armored Car Swindle An anonymous English businessman becomes involved in international intrigue when he becomes a pawn in a plan to transfer money to a Middle Eastern government under communist rule. But thanks to his wife things don't go off as planned.
1964 58m/B Peter Reynolds, Dermot Walsh, Joanna Dunham, Lisa Gastoni, Brian Cobby; D: Lance Comfort. VHS, Beta $16.95 SNC ⅟⅟

Great Balls of Fire A florid, comic-book film of the glory days of Jerry Lee Lewis, from his first band to stardom. Most of the drama is derived from his marriage to his 13-year-old cousin. Somewhat overacted but full of energy. The soundtrack features many of the "Killer's" greatest hits re-recorded by Jerry Lee Lewis for the film.
1989 (PG-13) 108m/C Dennis Quaid, Winona Ryder, Alec Baldwin, Trey Wilson, John Doe, Lisa Blount, Steve Allen, Stephen Tobolowsky, Lisa Jane Persky, Michael St. Gerard, Peter Cook; D: Jim McBride; W: Jack Baran, Jim McBride; M: Jack Baran, Jim McBride. VHS, Beta $19.98 ORI ⅟⅟ ½

Great Bank Hoax Three bank managers decide to rob their own bank to cover up the fact that all the assets have been embezzled. *AKA:* The Great Georgia Bank Hoax; Shenanigans.
1978 (PG) 89m/C Richard Basehart, Ned Beatty, Burgess Meredith, Michael Murphy, Paul Sand, Arthur Godfrey; D: Joseph Jacoby. VHS, Beta $19.98 WAR ⅟⅟ ½

Great Bikini Off-Road Adventure Duke Abbey is about to lose his jeep tour company because business is so slow that he can't pay the rent. Then Duke's niece Lori decides to get her bikini-clad friends to hire on as drivers, showing lots of sights on their desert tours.
1994 (R) ?m/C Avalon Anders, Lauren Hays, Floyd Irons, Laura Hudspeth, Dan Frank; D: Gary Orona. VHS $89.95 IMP, IME ⅟ ½

The Great Caruso The story of opera legend Enrico Caruso's rise to fame, from his childhood in Naples, Italy, to his collapse on the stage of the Metropolitan Opera House. Lanza is superb as the singer, and there are 27 musical numbers to satisfy the opera lover. ♫The Loveliest Night of the Year; Over the Waves; Vesti la Giubba; M'Appari; Celeste Aida; Numi, Pieta; La Fatal Pietra; Sextet from Lucia di Lammermoor; La Donne a Mobile.
1951 113m/C Mario Lanza, Ann Blyth, Dorothy Kirsten; D: Richard Thorpe. Academy Awards '51: Best Sound; Nominations: Best Costume Design (Color), Best Original Score. VHS, Beta $19.98 MGM ⅟⅟ ½

Great Chase A historical anthology of the funniest and most suspenseful classic movie chases, especially "The General."
1963 79m/B Buster Keaton, Lillian Gish, Pearl White, Noah Beery Jr.; M: Larry Adler. VHS, Beta $24.98 SUE, NLC ⅟⅟

The Great Commandment Young man throws himself into a revolution against the overbearing Roman Empire in 30 A.D. His brother joins him but is killed. The man, who has become influenced by the teachings of Christ, decides to give up his revolution and go off with his brother's widow. (He always loved her anyway.)
1941 78m/B John Beal, Maurice Moscovich, Albert Dekker, Marjorie Cooley, Warren McCollum; D: Irving Pichel. VHS $29.98 REP ⅟

Great Dan Patch The story of the great Dan Patch, the horse that went on to become the highest-earning harness racer in history.

1949 92m/B Dennis O'Keefe, Gail Russell, Ruth Warrick; D: Joseph M. Newman. VHS, Beta $19.95 VEC ♪♪½

Great Day A soap opera set around the wartime visit of first lady Eleanor Roosevelt to a small British town. It focuses mainly on the wife and daughter of a bitter, alcoholic WWI vet.
1946 62m/B Eric Portman, Flora Robson, Sheila Sim, Isabel Jeans, Walter Fitzgerald, Philip Friend, Marjorie Rhodes, Maire O'Neill, Beatrice Varley; D: Lance Comfort. VHS, Beta $19.98 TTC ♪½

Great Day in the Morning A rebel sympathizer and a Northern spy are both after Colorado gold to help finance the Civil War. But our Southern gentlemen soon find themselves equally interested in the local ladies.
1956 92m/C Robert Stack, Ruth Roman, Raymond Burr, Virginia Mayo, Alex Nicol, Regis Toomey; D: Jacques Tourneur. VHS, Beta $15.95 VCI ♪♪½

The Great Dictator Chaplin's first all-dialogue film, a searing satire on Nazism in which he has dual roles as a Jewish barber with amnesia who is mistaken for a Hitlerian dictator, Adenoid Hynkel. A classic scene involves Hynkel playing with a gigantic balloon of the world. Hitler banned the film's release to the German public due to its highly offensive portrait of him. The film also marked Chaplin's last wearing of the Little Tramp's (and Hitler's equally little) mustache.
1940 126m/B Charlie Chaplin, Paulette Goddard, Jack Oakie, Billy Gilbert, Reginald Gardiner, Henry Daniell, Maurice Moscovich; D: Charlie Chaplin; W: Charlie Chaplin. Academy Awards '40 Nominations: Best Actor (Chaplin), Best Original Screenplay, Best Picture, Best Supporting Actor (Oakie), Best Original Score; National Board of Review Awards '40: 10 Best Films of the Year; New York Film Critics Awards '40: Best Actor (Chaplin). VHS, Beta $19.98 FOX, HMV, GLV ♪♪♪

The Great Escape During WWII, troublesome allied POW's are thrown by the Nazis into an escape-proof camp, where they join forces in a single mass break for freedom. One of the great war movies, with a superb ensemble cast and lots of excitement. The story was true, based on the novel by Paul Brickhill. McQueen performed most of the stunts himself, against the wishes of director Sturges. Laserdisc features an analysis of the true story that inspired the movie, actual photos of the camp, prisoners, and guards, commentary by director Sturges, composer Bernstein, and stuntman Bud Ekins, excerpts from the script by novelist/ screenwriter Clavell, over 250 production photos, and the original movie trailer. Followed by a made for TV movie 25 years later.
1963 170m/C Steve McQueen, James Garner, Richard Attenborough, Charles Bronson, James Coburn, Donald Pleasence, David McCallum, James Donald, Gordon Jackson; D: John Sturges; W: James Clavell, W.R. Burnett; M: Elmer Bernstein. VHS, Beta $29.98 MGM, FOX, VYG ♪♪♪½

The Great Escape 2: The Untold Story Bland actioner can't decide whether it's a remake of the original or a sequel; it pretends to be a sequel yet spends a lot of time retelling—poorly—the first great escape. Once it gets around to the sequel part, it dispenses with protocol: Pleasance, an escapee in the original, is a Nazi bad guy in this go-round. Poor casting, especially Reeves, unconvincing as a German-speaking British officer who rallies the surviving escapees in revenge against their WWII captors.

Made for television and originally shown in two parts, but mercifully shortened for video.
1988 93m/C Christopher Reeve, Judd Hirsch, Ian McShane, Donald Pleasence, Anthony John Denison, Judd Taylor, Charles Haid; D: Michael Nader, Paul Wendkos. VHS $89.95 VMK, TLF ♪♪

Great Expectations Lean's magisterial adaptation of the Dickens tome, in which a young English orphan is graced by a mysterious benefactor and becomes a well-heeled gentleman. Hailed and revered over the years; possibly the best Dickens on film. Well-acted by all, but especially notable is Hunt's slightly mad and pathetic Miss Havisham. Remake of the 1934 film.
1946 118m/B John Mills, Valerie Hobson, Anthony Wager, Alec Guinness, Finlay Currie, Jean Simmons, Bernard Miles, Francis L. Sullivan, Martita Hunt, Ivan Barnard, Freda Jackson, Torin Thatcher, Eileen Erskine, Hay Petrie; D: David Lean; W: David Lean. Academy Awards '47: Best Art Direction/Set Decoration (B & W), Best Black and White Cinematography; Nominations: Best Director (Lean), Best Picture, Best Screenplay; National Board of Review Awards '47: 10 Best Films of the Year. VHS, Beta $79.98 PAR, LCA, HMV ♪♪♪♪

Great Expectations A British television mini-series adaptation of the Dickens epic about Pip and his mysterious benefactor in Victorian London. On two tapes.
1981 300m/C Gerry Sundquist, Stratford Johns, Joan Hickson. VHS, Beta $29.98 KUI, FOX, SIG ♪♪

Great Expectations Dickens classic retold on 3 cassettes. A mysterious benefactor turns a poor orphan boy into a gentleman of means.
1989 325m/C Jean Simmons, Anthony Hopkins, John Rhys-Davies; D: Kevin Connor. VHS, Beta $49.95 DIS ♪♪♪

Great Expectations: The Untold Story Magwitch is an escaped convict, hiding out in the Victorian English countryside, who is aided by the young orphan, Pip. Captured and sent to the penal colonies in Australia, Magwitch serves his time and then discovers a fortune in gold, which he decides to use to make Pip into a gentleman. But Magwitch's enemies would like to get Pip's inheritance for themselves. Based on the Dickens classic, this three-tape miniseries is also available in a 102-minute feature length version.
1987 287m/C John Stanton, Sigrid Thornton, Robert Coleby, Todd Boyce, Anne Louise Lambert, Ron Haddrick, Noel Ferrier; D: Tim Burstall. VHS $89.95 FCT ♪♪½

Great Flamarion A woman-hating trickshot artist is nevertheless duped into murdering the husband of his femme fatale assistant after he comes to believe she loves him. He's wrong.
1945 78m/B Dan Duryea, Erich von Stroheim, Mary Beth Hughes; D: Anthony Mann. VHS, Beta $16.95 SNC, NOS, DVT ♪♪½

The Great Gabbo A ventriloquist can express himself only through his dummy, losing his own identity and going mad at the end. Von Stroheim's first talkie. May quite possibly be the first mentally-twisted-ventriloquist story ever put on film. Von Strohein hated the movie, believing it to be analogous to his own life. When he tried to buy the rights to the film, presumably to destroy the prints, he found that the property had been already purchased by real-life ventriloquist, Edgar Bergen. Based on a story by Ben Hecht. ♫The New Step; I'm Laughing Ickey; I'm in Love With You; The Ga-Ga Bird; The Web of Love; Every Now and Then.

1929 82m/B Erich von Stroheim, Betty Compson, Don Douglas, Marjorie Kane; D: James Cruze. VHS, Beta $16.95 SNC, NOS, DVT ♪♪

The Great Gatsby Adaptation of F. Scott Fitzgerald's novel of the idle rich in the 1920s. A mysterious millionaire crashes Long Island society, and finds his heart captured by an impetuous and emotionally impoverished girl. Skillful acting and directing captures the look and feel of this era, but the movie doesn't have the power of the book.
1974 (PG) 144m/C Robert Redford, Mia Farrow, Bruce Dern, Karen Black, Patsy Kensit, Sam Waterston, Howard da Silva, Edward Herrmann; D: Jack Clayton; W: Francis Ford Coppola; M: Nelson Riddle. VHS, Beta $14.95 PAR, FCT ♪♪½

The Great Gildersleeve Throckmorton P. Gildersleeve adds another problem to his list; the sister of a local judge wants to marry him. His niece and nephew won't allow it and his attempts to juggle everyone's desires make for fine fun. Peary was also the voice for the popular radio series of the same name.
1943 62m/B Harold Peary, Jane Darwell, Nancy Gates, Charles Arnt, Thurston Hall; D: Gordon Douglas. VHS MED ♪♪

Great Gold Swindle A dramatization of the 1982 swindling of the Perth Mint in Australia of over $650,000 worth of gold.
1984 101m/C John Hargreaves, Robert C. Hughes, Tony Rickards, Barbara Llewellyn. VHS, Beta $69.98 LIV ♪♪

The Great Gundown A violent tale set in the Old West. The peace of frontier New Mexico erupts when a half-breed Indian leads a brutal assault on an outlaw stronghold.
1975 98m/C Robert Padilla, Richard Rust, Milila St. Duval; D: Paul Hunt. VHS, Beta $29.95 HHT ♪½

Great Guns Stan and Ollie enlist in the army to protect a spoiled millionaire's son but wind up being targets at target practice instead. Not one of their better efforts.
1941 74m/B Stan Laurel, Oliver Hardy, Sheila Ryan, Dick Nelson; D: Montague Banks. VHS, Beta $29.98 FOX, MLB ♪♪

Great Guy One of Cagney's lesser roles as an ex-boxer turned food inspector who wipes out graft in his town. AKA: Pluck of the Irish.
1936 50m/B James Cagney, Mae Clarke, Edward Brophy; D: John Blystone. VHS, Beta $19.95 NOS, MRV, PSM ♪½

The Great Hunter A village militia captain and his girlfriend seek to destroy the men who killed the girl's father.
1975 91m/C Chia Ling, Wang Yu, Hsu Feng. VHS, Beta $29.95 UNI ♪

The Great Impostor The true story of Ferdinand Waldo Demara, Jr., who during the 1950s, hoodwinked people by impersonating a surgeon, a college professor, a monk, a prison warden and a schoolteacher, with the FBI always one step behind him.
1961 112m/C Tony Curtis, Edmond O'Brien, Arthur O'Connell, Gary Merrill, Raymond Massey, Karl Malden, Mike Kellin, Frank Gorshin; D: Robert Mulligan; M: Henry Mancini. VHS, Beta $59.95 MCA ♪♪½

Great Jesse James Raid Jesse James comes out of retirement to carry out a mine theft. Routine.
1949 73m/C Willard Parker, Barbara Payton, Tom Neal, Wallace Ford; D: Reginald LeBorg. VHS, Beta RXM, MRV ♪½

Great K & A Train Robbery A railroad detective is hired to find and stop the bandits who have been preying on the K & A Railroad. Silent.
1926 55m/B Tom Mix, Dorothy Dwan, William Walling, Harry Grippe, Carl Miller; *D:* Lewis Seiler. VHS, Beta $19.95 *GPV, GVV* 🎦🎦½

The Great Land of Small Two children enter a fantasy world and try to save it from Evil. For kids.
1986 (G) 94m/C Karen Elkin, Michael Blouin, Michael Anderson Jr., Ken Roberts; *D:* Vojtech Jasny. VHS, Beta $19.95 *STE, NWV, HHE* 🎦🎦

Great Leaders of the Bibles The inspiring stories of two Old Testament heroes, Gideon and Samson, are dramatized in this beautifully constructed film.
197? 105m/C Ivo Garrani, Fernando Rey, Giorgio Ceridni. VHS, Beta $49.95 *VCI* 🎦🎦

The Great Lie A great soaper with Davis and Astor as rivals for the affections of Brent, an irresponsible flyer. Astor is the concert pianist who marries Brent and then finds out she's pregnant after he's presumed dead in a crash. The wealthy Davis offers to raise the baby so Astor can continue her career. But when Brent does return, who will it be to? Sparkling, catty fun. Astor's very short, mannish haircut became a popular trend.
1941 107m/B Bette Davis, Mary Astor, George Brent, Lucile Watson, Hattie McDaniel, Grant Mitchell, Jerome Cowan; *D:* Edmund Goulding. VHS, Beta $19.95 *MGM, BTV* 🎦🎦🎦

The Great Locomotive Chase During the Civil War, Parker and his fellow soldiers head into Confederate territory to disrupt railroad supply lines. They take over a locomotive, but are pursued by Confederate Hunter, the conductor of another train; and soon a pursuit is underway. Based on the true story of Andrew's Raiders. *AKA:* Andrews' Raiders.
1956 85m/C Fess Parker, Jeffrey Hunter, Kenneth Tobey; *D:* Francis D. Lyon. VHS, Beta *DIS* 🎦🎦½

The Great Los Angeles Earthquake Made-for-TV disaster movie is the same old story; multiple soap-opera plotlines are spun around terrifying special effects, as L.A. is devastated by three major earth tremors and attendant disasters. Condensed from a two-part miniseries, also known as "The Big One: The Great Los Angeles Earthquake."
1991 106m/C Ed Begley Jr., Joanna Kerns; *D:* Larry Elikann. VHS $89.98 *VMK* 🎦½

Great Love Experiment Everyone in a high school learns a valuable lesson about beauty and friendship when four popular students try to change the personality of an awkward classmate.
1984 52m/C Tracy Pollan, Esai Morales, Kelly Wolf, Scott Benderer. VHS, Beta *NO* 🎦

The Great Lover Aboard an ocean liner, a bumbler chaperoning school kids gets involved with a gambler, a duchess and a murder. Vintage Bob Hope.
1949 80m/B Bob Hope, Rhonda Fleming, Roland Young, Roland Culver, George Reeves, Jim Backus; *D:* Alexander Hall. VHS, Beta $14.95 *COL, FCT* 🎦🎦½

The Great Madcap A wealthy man believes in lavishly indulging himself which drives his excessively conservative family crazy. Bunuel satirizes behavioral extremes, Christianity, advertising, sex, and a number of other popular absurdities. In Spanish with English subtitles.
1949 90m/B Fernando Soler, Rosario Granados, Ruben Rogo; *D:* Luis Bunuel. VHS $79.95 *WBF, ING* 🎦🎦

The Great Man Votes Alcoholic college professor Barrymore falls into a deep depression after his wife's death. His children then plan to create a situation wherein his vote will decide the fate of the new town mayor, thus instilling in him a newly found sense of importance for himself and his children. Satiric and funny.
1938 72m/B John Barrymore, Peter Holden, Virginia Weidler, Katherine Alexander, Donald MacBride, Elisabeth Risdon, Granville Bates, Luis Alberni, J.M. Kerrigan, William Demarest, Roy Gordon; *D:* Garson Kanin. VHS, Beta $19.98 *TTC* 🎦🎦🎦

The Great McGinty Sturges' directorial debut, about the rise and fall of a small-time, bribe-happy politician is an acerbic, ultra-cynical indictment of modern politics that stands, like much of his other work, as bracingly courageous as anything that's ever snuck past the Hollywood censors. Political party boss Tamiroff chews the scenery with gusto while Donlevy, in his first starring role, is more than his equal as the not-so-dumb political hack. *AKA:* Down Went McGinty.
1940 82m/B Brian Donlevy, Muriel Angelus, Akim Tamiroff, Louis Jean Heydt, Arthur Hoyt, William Demarest; *D:* Preston Sturges; *W:* Preston Sturges. VHS, Beta $14.98 *MCA* 🎦🎦🎦½

Great McGonagall Tale of an unemployed Scot trying to become Britain's poet laureate. Sellers adds a semi-bright spot with his portrayal of Queen Victoria!
1975 95m/C Peter Sellers, Spike Milligan, Julia Foster; *D:* Joseph McGrath. VHS $49.95 *MOV, VTR* 🎦½

The Great Mike Unlikely but moving story of a young boy who convinces track management that his work horse has a chance against the touted thoroughbred. Sentimental, with little innovation, but generally well-acted.
1944 72m/B Stuart Erwin, Robert "Buzzy" Henry, Pierre Watkin, Gwen Kenyon, Carl "Alfalfa" Switzer, Edythe Elliott, Marion Martin; *D:* Wallace Fox. VHS $19.95 *NOS* 🎦🎦½

Great Missouri Raid Follows the famous adventures of the James/Younger gang and their eventual demise.
1951 81m/C Wendell Corey, MacDonald Carey, Ellen Drew, Ward Bond; *D:* Gordon Douglas. VHS, Beta $19.95 *BAR* 🎦🎦

The Great Moment Story of the Boston dentist who discovered ether's use as an anesthetic in 1845. Confusing at times, changing from comedy to drama and containing flashbacks that add little to the story. Surprisingly bland result from ordinarily solid cast and director.
1944 87m/B Joel McCrea, Betty Field, Harry Carey Sr., William Demarest, Franklin Pangborn, Porter Hall; *D:* Preston Sturges. VHS, Beta $14.98 *MCA* 🎦🎦

The Great Mouse Detective Animated version of the book "Basil of Baker Street" by Eve Titus. Fun adventure about Sherlock-of-the-mouse-world. Not as good as some of the other Disney animated features, but kids will enjoy it nonetheless. In 1992 it was rereleased. *AKA:* The Adventures of the Great Mouse Detective.
1986 (G) 74m/C *D:* John Musker, Ron Clements, Dave Michener, Burny Mattinson; *W:* Dave Michener; *M:* Henry Mancini; *V:* Vincent Price, Barrie Ingham, Val Bettin, Susanne Pollatschek, Candy Candido, Eve Brenner, Alan Young, Melissa Manchester. VHS, Beta $24.99 *DIS, OM* 🎦🎦🎦

Great Movie Stunts & the Making of Raiders of the Lost Ark Two television specials: "Movie Stunts" demonstrates how major action sequences were designed and executed, and "Making of Raiders" captures the cast and crew as they tackle the many problems created in filming the spectacular scenes.
1981 107m/C Harrison Ford. VHS, Beta $12.95 *PAR* 🎦🎦🎦

The Great Muppet Caper A group of hapless reporters (Kermit, Fozzie Bear, and Gonzo) travel to London to follow up on a major jewel robbery.
1981 (G) 95m/C Jim Henson's Muppets, Charles Grodin, Diana Rigg; *Cameos:* John Cleese, Robert Morley, Peter Ustinov, Peter Falk, Jack Warden; *D:* Jim Henson; *W:* Jack Rose; *V:* Frank Oz. VHS, Beta $22.99 *JHV, FOX* 🎦🎦🎦

The Great Northfield Minnesota Raid The Younger/James gang decides to rob the biggest bank west of the Mississippi, but everything goes wrong. Uneven, offbeat western, but Duvall's portrayal of the psychotic Jesse James and Robertson's cunning Cole Younger are notable.
1972 (PG) 91m/C Cliff Robertson, Robert Duvall, Elisha Cook Jr., Luke Askew, R.G. Armstrong, Donald Moffatt, Matt Clark; *D:* Philip Kaufman; *W:* Philip Kaufman; *M:* Dave Grusin. VHS, Beta $14.98 *MCA* 🎦🎦½

The Great Outdoors Good cast is mostly wasted in another John Hughes' tale of vacation gone bad. A family's peaceful summer by the lake is disturbed by their uninvited, trouble-making relatives. Aykroyd and Candy are two funny guys done in by a lame script that awkwardly examines friendship and coming of age and throws in a giant bear when things get unbearably slow. May be fun for small fry.
1988 (PG) 91m/C Dan Aykroyd, John Candy, Stephanie Faracy, Annette Bening, Chris Young, Lucy Deakins; *D:* Howard Deutch; *W:* John Hughes. VHS, Beta $14.95 *MCA* 🎦🎦

Great Race A dastardly villain, a noble hero and a spirited suffragette are among the competitors in an uproarious New York-to-Paris auto race circa 1908, complete with pie fights, saloon brawls, and a confrontation with a feisty polar bear. Overly long and only sporadically funny.
1965 160m/C Jack Lemmon, Tony Curtis, Natalie Wood, Peter Falk, Keenan Wynn, George Macready; *D:* Blake Edwards; *M:* Henry Mancini. Academy Awards '65: Best Sound Effects Editing; Nominations: Best Color Cinematography, Best Film Editing, Best Song ("The Sweetheart Tree"), Best Sound. VHS, Beta $19.98 *WAR, FCT* 🎦🎦½

Great Ride State police are after two dirt bikers who are riding through areas where bike riding is illegal.
1978 90m/C Perry Lang, Michael MacRae, Michael Sullivan; *D:* Don Hulette. VHS, Beta *NO* 🎦

The Great Riviera Bank Robbery A genius executes a bank robbery on the French Riviera netting fifteen million dollars. Based on a true story, the film chronicles the unfolding of the heist.
1979 98m/C Ian McShane, Warren Clarke, Stephen Greif, Christopher Malcolm; *D:* Francis Megahy. VHS, Beta $59.95 *MPI* 🎦🎦½

The Great Rupert Durante and family are befriended by a helpful squirrel (a puppet) in obtaining a huge fortune. Good fun; Durante shines.
1950 86m/B Jimmy Durante, Terry Moore, Tom Drake, Frank Orth, Sara Haden, Queenie Smith; *D:* Irving Pichel. VHS, Beta $19.98 *DVT, HEG, VYY* 🎦🎦🎦

The Great St. Trinian's Train Robbery
Train robbers hide their considerable loot in an empty country mansion only to discover, upon returning years later, it has been converted into a girls' boarding school. When they try to recover the money, the thieves run up against a band of pestiferous adolescent girls, with hilarious results. Based on the cartoon by Ronald Searle. Sequel to "The Pure Hell of St. Trinian's."
1966 90m/C Dora Bryan, Frankie Howerd, Reg Varney, Desmond Walter Ellis; *D:* Sidney Gilliat, Frank Launder; *M:* Malcolm Arnold. **VHS, Beta** *NO 𝄞𝄞*

The Great Santini
Lt. Col. Bull Meechum, the "Great Santini," a Marine pilot stationed stateside, fights a war involving his frustrated career goals, repressed emotions, and family. His family becomes his company of marines, as he abuses them in the name of discipline, because he doesn't allow himself any other way to show his affection. With a standout performance by Duvall, the film successfully blends warm humor and tenderness with the harsh cruelties inherent with dysfunctional families and racism. Based on Pat Conroy's autobiographical novel, the movie was virtually undistributed when first released, but re-released due to critical acclaim. *AKA:* Ace.
1980 (PG) 118m/C Robert Duvall, Blythe Danner, Michael O'Keefe, Julie Ann Haddock, Lisa Jane Persky, David Keith; *D:* Lewis John Carlino; *M:* Elmer Bernstein. Academy Awards '80 Nominations: Best Actor (Duvall), Best Supporting Actor (O'Keefe); Montreal World Film Festival '80: Best Actor (Duvall); National Board of Review Awards '80: 10 Best Films of the Year. **VHS, Beta, 8mm $19.98** *WAR 𝄞𝄞𝄞*

Great Scout & Cathouse Thursday
Marvin and Reed vow to take revenge on their third partner, Culp, who made off with all their profits from a gold mine. The title refers to Marvin's May-December romance with prostitute Lenz. Already forgotten, unfunny, all-star comedy with cutesy title. *AKA:* Wildcat.
1976 (PG) 96m/C Lee Marvin, Oliver Reed, Robert Culp, Elizabeth Ashley, Kay Lenz; *D:* Don Taylor. **VHS, Beta $69.98** *LIV, VES 𝄞 1/2*

The Great Skycopter Rescue
Ruthless businessmen hire a motorcycle gang to terrorize and scare away the inhabitants of an oil-rich town. A local teenage flying enthusiast organizes his friends into an attack force to fight back.
1982 96m/C William Marshall, Aldo Ray, Russell Johnson, Terry Michos, Terry Taylor; *D:* Lawrence Foldes. **VHS, Beta $59.95** *MGM 𝄞*

Great Smokey Roadblock
While in the hospital, a sixty-year-old truck driver's rig is repossessed by the finance company. Deciding that it's time to make one last perfect cross country run, he escapes from the hospital, steals his truck, picks up six prostitutes, heads off into the night with the police on his tail, and becomes a folk hero. *AKA:* Last of the Cowboys.
1976 (PG) 84m/C Henry Fonda, Eileen Brennan, Susan Sarandon, John Byner; *D:* John Leone. **VHS, Beta $59.95** *MED 𝄞𝄞*

The Great Texas Dynamite Chase
Two sexy young women drive across Texas with a carload of dynamite. They leave a trail of empty banks with the cops constantly on their trail. *AKA:* Dynamite Women.
1976 (R) 90m/C Claudia Jennings, Jocelyn Jones, Johnny Crawford, Chris Pennock, Tara Strohmeier, Miles Watkins, Bart Braverman; *D:* Michael Pressman. **VHS, Beta $39.98** *WAR, OM 𝄞 1/2*

The Great Train Robbery
A dapper thief arranges to heist the Folkstone bullion express in 1855, the first moving train robbery. Well-designed, fast-moving costume piece based on Crichton's best-selling novel. *AKA:* The First Great Train Robbery.
1979 (PG) 111m/C Sean Connery, Donald Sutherland, Lesley-Anne Down, Alan Webb; *D:* Michael Crichton; *W:* Michael Crichton; *M:* Jerry Goldsmith. **VHS, Beta $14.95** *MGM, FCT, HMV 𝄞𝄞𝄞*

The Great Train Robbery: Cinema Begins
Three pioneering film shorts: "Billy Whiskers," a collection of Lumiere footage from their most famous films, and the title short.
1903 42m/B Billy Anderson; *D:* Edwin S. Porter, Auguste Lumiere, Hans A. Spanuth. **VHS, Beta, 8mm $19.95** *VYY 𝄞𝄞𝄞*

Great Treasure Hunt
Four Western rogues help a blind man steal a wealthy crook's gold.
197? 90m/C Mark Damon, Stan Cooper, Luis Marin; *D:* Tonino Ricci. **VHS, Beta $69.95** *TWE 𝄞*

The Great Waldo Pepper
Low key and (for Hill) less commercial film about a WWI pilot-turned-barnstormer who gets hired as a stuntman for the movies. Features spectacular vintage aircraft flying sequences.
1975 (PG) 107m/C Robert Redford, Susan Sarandon, Margot Kidder, Bo Svenson, Scott Newman, Geoffrey Lewis, Edward Herrmann; *D:* George Roy Hill; *W:* William Goldman; *M:* Henry Mancini. **VHS, Beta $19.95** *MCA 𝄞𝄞𝄞*

A Great Wall
A Chinese-American family travels to mainland China to discover the country of their ancestry and to visit relatives. They experience radical culture shock. Wang's first independent feature. In English and Chinese with subtitles. *AKA:* The Great Wall is a Great Wall.
1986 (PG) 103m/C Peter Wang, Sharon Iwai, Kelvin Han Yee, Lin Qingin, Hy Xiaoguang; *D:* Peter Wang; *W:* Peter Wang, Shirley Sun; *M:* David Liang, Ge Ganru. **VHS, Beta $29.95** *FCT, IME, APD 𝄞𝄞𝄞*

The Great Wallendas
The true story of the tragedies and triumphs of the Wallendas, a seven-person acrobatic family, who were noted for creating a pyramid on the high wire without nets below them. Made for television.
1978 96m/C Lloyd Bridges, Britt Ekland, Cathy Rigby; *D:* Larry Elikann. **VHS, Beta** *NO 𝄞𝄞*

The Great Waltz
The first of two musical biographies on the life of Johann Strauss sees the musician quit his banking job to pursue his dream of becoming a successful composer. A fine, overlooked production rich with wonderful music and romantic comedy. ♫Tales of Vienna Woods; There'll Come A Time; One Day When We Were Young; Voices of Spring; Du und Du; The Bat; I'm In Love With Vienna; Revolutionary March.
1938 102m/B Luise Rainer, Fernand Gravet, Milza Korjus, Hugh Herbert, Lionel Atwill, Curt Bois, Leonid Kinskey, Al Shear, Minna Gombell, George Houston, Bert Roach, Herman Bing, Alma Kruger, Sig Rumann; *D:* Julien Duvivier. **VHS $19.98** *MGM, FOX, FCT 𝄞𝄞𝄞*

The Great War
Two Italian soldiers find themselves in the midst of WWI, much against their will. They try a number of schemes to get out of fighting and working, but their circumstance dictates otherwise. Slightly muddled, but generally good acting. *AKA:* La Grande Guerre.
1959 118m/B Vittorio Gassman, Alberto Sordi, Silvana Mangano, Folco Lulli; *D:* Mario Monicelli. **VHS $69.95** *FCT 𝄞𝄞*

The Great White Hope
A semi-fictionalized biography of boxer Jack Johnson, played by Jones, who became the first black heavyweight world champion in 1910. Alexander makes her film debut as the boxer's white lover, as both battle the racism of the times. Two Oscar-nominated performances in what is essentially an "opened-out" version of the Broadway play.
1970 (PG) 103m/C James Earl Jones, Jane Alexander, Lou Gilbert, Joel Fluellen, Chester Morris, Robert Webber, Hal Holbrook, R.G. Armstrong, Moses Gunn, Scatman Crothers; *D:* Martin Ritt. **VHS, Beta $39.98** *FOX, FCT 𝄞𝄞 1/2*

The Great Ziegfeld
Big bio-pic of the famous showman; acclaimed in its time as the best musical biography ever done, still considered the textbook for how to make a musical. Look for cameo roles by many famous stars, as well as a walk-on role by future First Lady Pat Nixon. The movie would have stood up as a first-rate biography of Ziegfeld, even without the drop-dead wonderful songs. ♫Won't You Come Play With Me?; It's Delightful to be Married; If You Knew Susie; Shine on Harvest Moon; A Pretty Girl is Like a Melody; You Gotta Pull Strings; She's a Follies Girl; You; You Never Looked So Beautiful.
1936 179m/B William Powell, Luise Rainer, Myrna Loy, Frank Morgan, Reginald Owen, Nat Pendleton, Ray Bolger, Virginia Bruce, Harriet Hocter, Ernest Cossart, Robert Greig, Gilda Gray, Leon Errol, Dennis (Stanley Morner) Morgan, Mickey Daniels, William Demarest; *Cameos:* Fanny Brice; *D:* Robert Z. Leonard; *W:* William Anthony McGuire. Academy Awards '36: Best Actress (Rainer), Best Picture; Nominations: Best Director (Leonard), Best Film Editing, Best Interior Decoration, Best Story; New York Film Critics Awards '36: Best Actress (Rainer). **VHS, Beta $29.98** *MGM, BTV 𝄞𝄞𝄞 1/2*

The Greatest
Autobiography of Cassius Clay, the fighter who could float like a butterfly and sting like a bee. Ali plays himself, and George Benson's hit "The Greatest Love of All" is introduced.
1977 (PG) 100m/C Muhammad Ali, Robert Duvall, Ernest Borgnine, James Earl Jones, John Marley, Roger E. Mosley, Dina Merrill, Paul Winfield; *D:* Tom Gries; *W:* Ring Lardner Jr. **VHS, Beta $14.95** *COL 𝄞 1/2*

The Greatest Question
Gish is a girl menaced by a married couple whom she saw commit a murder years before. A rush job by Griffith to fulfill his studio obligations but Gish's performance is fine.
1919 80m/B Lillian Gish, Robert Harron, Ralph Graves, Eugenie Besserer, George Fawcett, George Nichols, Josephine Crowell, Carl Stockdale; *D:* D.W. Griffith. **VHS $18.95** *GPV 𝄞𝄞 1/2*

The Greatest Show on Earth
DeMille is in all his epic glory here in a tale of a traveling circus wrought with glamour, romance, mysterious clowns, a tough ringmaster, and a train wreck.
1952 149m/C Betty Hutton, Cornel Wilde, James Stewart, Charlton Heston, Dorothy Lamour, Lawrence Tierney; *D:* Cecil B. DeMille. Academy Awards '52: Best Picture, Best Story; Nominations: Best Costume Design (Color), Best Director (DeMille), Best Film Editing; Golden Globe Awards '53: Best Director (DeMille), Best Film—Drama. **VHS, Beta $29.95** *PAR, BTV 𝄞𝄞𝄞*

The Greatest Story Ever Told
Christ's journey from Galilee to Golgotha is portrayed here in true international-all-star-epic treatment by director Stevens. A lackluster version of Christ's life, remarkable only for Heston's out-of-control John the Baptist.

1965 196m/C Max von Sydow, Charlton Heston, Sidney Poitier, Claude Rains, Jose Ferrer, Telly Savalas, Angela Lansbury, Dorothy McGuire, John Wayne, Donald Pleasence, Carroll Baker, Van Heflin, Robert Loggia, Shelley Winters, Ed Wynn, Roddy McDowall; **D:** George Stevens. Academy Awards '65 Nominations: Best Art Direction/Set Decoration (Color), Best Color Cinematography, Best Costume Design (Color); National Board of Review Awards '65: 10 Best Films of the Year. **VHS, Beta $29.98** MGM, RDG, TVC &&

Greed A wife's obsession with money drives her husband to murder. Although the original version's length (eight hours) was trimmed to 140 minutes, it remains one of the greatest and most highly acclaimed silent films ever made. Effective use of Death Valley locations. Adapted from the Frank Norris novel, "McTeague."
1924 140m/B Dale Fuller, Gibson Gowland, ZaSu Pitts, Jean Hersholt, Chester Conklin; **D:** Erich von Stroheim. **VHS $29.95** MGM &&&&

The Greed of William Hart Re-working of the Burke and Hare legend has grave robbers providing Edinburgh medical students with the requisite cadavers. **AKA:** Horror Maniacs.
1948 78m/B Tod Slaughter, Henry Oscar, Jenny Lynn, Winifred Melville; **D:** Oswald Mitchell. **VHS $19.98** SNC &&

Greedy Money-grubbing family suck up to elderly millionaire uncle (Douglas) when they fear he'll leave his money to the sexy, young former pizza delivery girl (d'Abo) he's hired as his nurse. Fox is the long-lost nephew who comes to the rescue. Wicked comedy from veterans Ganz and Mandel should zing, but instead falls flat thanks to a descent into the maudlin. Fox bares his backside and Douglas has fun as the mean old miser, but check out Hartman, a riot as a snarky relative.
1994 (PG-13) 109m/C Kirk Douglas, Michael J. Fox, Olivia D'Abo, Phil Hartman, Nancy Travis, Ed Begley Jr., Bob Balaban, Colleen Camp, Jere Burns, Khandi Alexander; **Cameos:** Jonathan Lynn; **D:** Jonathan Lynn; **W:** Lowell Ganz, Babaloo Mandel; **M:** Randy Edelman. **VHS** MCA &½

Greedy Terror A cross-country motorcycle trip becomes a real nightmare when two young men realize they're being stalked by a maniac with a thirst for blood.
1978 90m/C Michael MacRae, Perry Lang. **VHS, Beta** NO &

Greek Street The owner of small cafe in London discovers a poor girl singing in the street for food. He takes her in and spotlights her songs in his cafe. **AKA:** Latin Love.
1930 51m/B Sari Maritza, Arthur Ahmbling, Martin Lewis; **D:** Sinclair Hill. **VHS, Beta $19.95** VYY, DVT, HEG &&

The Greek Tycoon Old familiar story about widow of an American president who marries a billionaire shipping magnate and finds that money cannot buy happiness. A transparent depiction of the Onassis/Kennedy marriage, done to a turn.
1978 (R) 106m/C Anthony Quinn, Jacqueline Bisset, James Franciscus, Raf Vallone, Edward Albert; **D:** J. Lee Thompson. **VHS, Beta $59.95** MCA &½

Green Archer Fifteen episodes of the famed serial, featuring a spooked castle complete with secret passages and tunnels, trapdoors, and the mysterious masked figure, the Green Archer.
1940 283m/B Victor Jory, Iris Meredith, James Craven, Robert Fiske; **D:** James W. Horne. **VHS, Beta $39.95** VYY, NOS, VCN &&

The Green Berets Cliched wartime heroics co-directed by Wayne and based on Robin Moore's novel. The Duke stars as a Special Forces colonel, leading his troops against the Viet Cong. Painfully insipid pro-war propaganda, notable as the only American film to come out in support of U.S. involvement in Vietnam. Truly embarrassing but did spawn the hit single "Ballad of the Green Beret" by Barry Sadler.
1968 (G) 135m/C John Wayne, David Janssen, Jim Hutton, Aldo Ray, George Takei, Raymond St. Jacques; **D:** John Wayne. **VHS, Beta $19.98** WAR, TLF Woof!

Green Card Some marry for love, some for money, others for an apartment in the Big Apple. Refined, single MacDowell covets a rent-controlled apartment in Manhattan, but the lease stipulates that the apartment be let to a married couple. Enter brusque and burly Depardieu, who covets the elusive green card. The counterpoint between MacDowell, as a stuffy horticulturist, and Depardieu, as a French composer works well, and the two adroitly play a couple whose relationship covers the romantic continuum. Director Weir wrote the screenplay with Depardieu in mind. Depardieu's English-language debut.
1990 (PG-13) 108m/C Gerard Depardieu, Andie MacDowell, Bebe Neuwirth, Gregg Edelman, Robert Prosky, Jessie Keosian, Ann Wedgeworth, Ethan Phillips, Mary Louise Wilson, Lois Smith, Simon Jones; **D:** Peter Weir; **W:** Peter Weir; **M:** Hans Zimmer. Academy Awards '90 Nominations: Best Original Screenplay; Golden Globe Awards '91: Best Actress— Musical/Comedy (MacDowell); Golden Globe Awards '91: Best Actor—Musical/Comedy (Depardieu), Best Film—Musical/Comedy. **VHS, Beta $19.99** TOU &&½

Green Dolphin Street Flimsy romantic epic set in 19th century New Zealand. A young girl marries the beau she and her sister are battling over in this Oscar-winning special effects show which features one big earthquake. Based on the Elizabeth Goudge novel, this was one of MGM's biggest hits in 1947.
1947 161m/B Lana Turner, Van Heflin, Donna Reed, Edmund Gwenn; **D:** Victor Saville. Academy Awards '47: Best Special Effects; Nominations: Best Black and White Cinematography, Best Film Editing, Best Sound. **VHS, Beta $19.98** MGM &&½

Green Dragon Inn When trying to escort an accused murderer to trial, a Ming court emissary finds himself battling against Kung Fu masters.
1982 94m/C Yue Hwa, Lo Lei, Shangkuan Ling-Feng. **VHS, Beta** WVE &

Green Eyes A costume party in a country mansion sets the scene for a routine murder mystery when the guests find their host stabbed to death in a closet. Based on the novel "The Murder of Stephen Kester" by H. Ashbrook.
1934 68m/B Shirley Grey, Charles Starrett, Claude Gillingwater, John Wray, Dorothy Revier; **D:** Richard Thorpe; **W:** Melville Shyer. **VHS $12.95** SNC &½

Green Eyes Winfield, an ex-GI, returns to post-war Vietnam to search for his illegitimate son who he believes will have green eyes. A highly acclaimed, made-for-television drama featuring moving performances by Winfield and Jonathan Lippe.
1976 100m/C Paul Winfield, Rita Tushingham, Jonathon Lippe, Victoria Racimo, Royce Wallace, Claudia Bryar; **D:** John Erman. **VHS $29.95** LIV &&&½

Green Fields A quiet romance based on Peretz Hirschbein's legendary tale of a young scholar of the Talmud who leaves the shelter of the synagogue in order to learn about people in the real world. The search takes him to the countryside where he finds himself in the middle of a battle between two families who both want him as a tutor and a suitor for their daughters. In Yiddish with English subtitles. **AKA:** Grine Felder; Gruner Felder.
1937 95m/B Michael Goldstein, Herschel Bernardi, Helen Beverly; **D:** Jacob Ben-Ami. **VHS, Beta $79.95** ERG, NCJ &&½

Green Fire The screen sizzles when emerald miner Granger meets plantation-owner Kelly in the exotic jungles of South America. Usual plot complications muddle the story, but who cares when the stars are this attractive?
1955 100m/C Stewart Granger, Grace Kelly, Paul Douglas, John Ericson, Murvyn Vye, Jose Torvay, Robert Tafur, Nacho Galindo; **D:** Andrew Marton; **W:** Ivan Goff, Ben Roberts; **M:** Miklos Rozsa. **VHS $19.98** MGM &&½

Green for Danger A detective stages a chilling mock operation to find a mad killer stalking the corridors of a British hospital during WWII. Sim's first great claim to fame (pre-"A Christmas Carol").
1947 91m/B Trevor Howard, Alastair Sim, Leo Genn; **D:** Sidney Gilliat. **VHS, Beta $39.95** HMV, RXM &&&

The Green Glove A jewel thief steals a beautiful relic from a tiny church. WWII makes it impossible for him to fence it and the church finds a relentless ally to track the thief. Excellent action sequences lift this standard plot slightly above the ordinary.
1952 88m/B Glenn Ford, Geraldine Brooks, Cedric Hardwicke, George Macready, Gaby Andre, Roger Treville, Juliette Greco, Jean Bretonniere; **D:** Rudolph Mate; **W:** Charles Bennett. **VHS $19.95** NOS, FCT, TIM &&½

Green Grow the Rushes The English government tries to put a stop to brandy smuggling on the coast, but the townspeople drink up the evidence. A young Burton highlights this watered-down comedy. Based on a novel by co-scripter Harold Clewes. **AKA:** Brandy Ashore.
1951 77m/B Roger Livesey, Honor Blackman, Richard Burton, Frederick Leister; **D:** Derek Twist. **VHS $19.95** NOS, TIM, VYY &½

Green Horizon A bucolic old codger faces a dilemma when he must choose between his granddaughter's future and his disaster-prone natural environment. **AKA:** Afurika Monogatari; A Tale of Africa.
1983 80m/C James Stewart, Philip Sayer, Elenora Vallone. **VHS, Beta $29.95** FHE &½

The Green Hornet The feature version of the original serial, in which the Green Hornet and Kato have a series of crime-fighting adventures.
1939 100m/B Gordon Jones, Keye Luke, Anne Nagel, Wade Boteler, Walter McGrail, Douglas Evans, Cy Kendall. **VHS, Beta $49.95** NOS, GKK, GPV &&&

Green Ice An American electronics expert gets involved with a brutal South American government dealing with emeralds and plans a heist with his girlfriend and other cohorts. A little bit of romance, a little bit of action, a lot of nothing much.
1981 109m/C Ryan O'Neal, Anne Archer, Omar Sharif, John Larroquette; **D:** Ernest Day; **W:** Edward Anhalt. **VHS, Beta** NO &&

Green Inferno A wealthy eccentric who lives deep in the South American jungle incites the natives to rebel. Mercenary agents are then hired to kill him.

198? 90m/C Richard Yesteran, Didi Sherman, Caesar Burner. VHS, Beta NO ⋆

The Green Man Maurice Allington (Finney), the alcoholic and randy owner of the Green Man Inn in rural England, jokes about the spirits that supposedly haunt the inn. It's not too funny, however, when he discovers the spirits are real and he has to figure out who the spirit of a 17th-century murderer is inhabiting before he kills again. A classy ghost story based on the novel by Kingsley Amis.
1991 150m/C Albert Finney, Sarah Berger, Linda Marlowe, Michael Hordern, Nickolas Grace, Michael Culver; **D:** Elijah Moshinsky; **W:** Malcolm Bradbury. VHS $89.95 AAE, ING, ART ⋆⋆⋆

Green Mansions Screen adaptation of W. H. Hudson's novel suffers due to miscasting of Hepburn as Rima the Bird Girl, who is not permitted to leave her sanctuary. Perkins is good as the male lead who fled to the jungle in search of wealth and instead finds a powerful love. Hepburn was married to director Ferrer at the time.
1959 104m/C Audrey Hepburn, Anthony Perkins, Lee J. Cobb, Sessue Hayakawa, Henry Silva, Nehemiah Persoff, Michael Pate; **D:** Mel Ferrer; **W:** Dorothy Kingsley. VHS $19.98 MGM ⋆⋆

Green Pastures An adaptation of Marc Connelly's 1930 Pulitzer Prize-winning play which attempts to retell Biblical stories in Black English Vernacular of the '30s. Southern theater owners boycotted the controversial film which had an all-Black cast.
1936 93m/C Rex Ingram, Oscar Polk, Eddie Anderson, George Reed, Abraham Graves, Myrtle Anderson, Frank Wilson; **D:** William Keighley, Marc Connelly. VHS, Beta $19.98 MGM, MOV, FOX ⋆⋆⋆

The Green Promise A well-meaning but domineering farmer and his four motherless children face disaster as a result of the father's obstinacy. But when he is laid up, the eldest daughter takes over, tries modern methods and equipment, and makes the farm a success. **AKA:** Raging Waters.
1949 90m/B Walter Brennan, Marguerite Chapman, Robert Paige, Natalie Wood; **D:** William D. Russell. VHS, Beta $24.95 NOS, DVT, TIM ⋆⋆

The Green Room Truffaut's haunting tale of a man who, valuing death over life, erects a shrine to all the dead he has known. Offered a chance at love, he cannot overcome his obsessions to take the risk. Based on the Henry James story "Altar of the Dead." In French with subtitles. **AKA:** La Chambre Verte.
1978 (PG) 95m/C Francois Truffaut, Nathalie Baye, Jean Daste; **D:** Francois Truffaut. VHS, Beta $19.98 MGM ⋆⋆

The Green Slime Danger and romance highlight the journey of a space ship assigned to intercept an oncoming asteroid. Little do the astronauts realize, but they have brought aboard the ship the malevolent alien creatures known as green slime (and we ain't talking jello here). Cheap, U.S./Japanese co-production will leave you feeling lousy in the morning. The title song is legendary among genre aficionados. **AKA:** Gamma Sango Uchu Daisakusen; Battle Beyond the Stars; Death and the Green Slime.
1968 (G) 90m/C Robert Horton, Richard Jaeckel, Lucianna Paluzzi, Bud Widom, Ted Gunther, Robert Dunham; **D:** Kinji Fukasaku. VHS, Beta $19.98 MGM Woof!

The Green Wall A city-dwelling young man attempts to homestead with his family in the Amazon. A lovely and tragic film with stunning photography of the Peruvian for-

ests. First Peruvian feature to be shown in the U.S. In Spanish with English subtitles.
1970 110m/C Julio Aleman, Sandra Riva; **D:** Armando Robles; **W:** Armando Robles. VHS $79.95 FCT, DVT, HEG ⋆⋆⋆

Greenstone The green stone is a glowing rock in the forbidden forest that conveys a young boy into an exciting new world.
1985 (G) 48m/C Joseph Corey, John Riley, Kathleen Irvine, Jack Mauck; **D:** Kevin Irvine. VHS, Beta $19.95 AHV ⋆⋆

Greetings De Niro stars in this wild and crazy comedy about a man who tries to help his friend flunk his draft physical. One of DePalma's first films, and a pleasantly anarchic view of the late '60s, wrought with a light, intelligent tone. Followed by the sequel "Hi, Mom."
1968 (R) 88m/C Robert De Niro, Gerrit Graham, Allen (Gooritz) Garfield; **D:** Brian DePalma; **W:** Brian DePalma. VHS, Beta $79.95 VMK ⋆⋆⋆

Gregory's Girl Sweet, disarming comedy established Forsyth. An awkward young Scottish schoolboy falls in love with the female goalie of his soccer team. He turns to his ten-year-old sister for advice, but she's more interested in ice cream than love. His best friend is no help, either, since he has yet to fall in love. Perfect mirror of teen-agers and their instantaneous, raw, and all-consuming loves. Very sweet scene with Gregory and his girl lying on their backs in an open space illustrates the simultaneous simplicity and complexity of young love.
1980 91m/C Gordon John Sinclair, Dee Hepburn, Jake D'Arcy, Chic Murray, Alex Norton, John Bett, Clare Grogan; **D:** Bill Forsyth; **W:** Bill Forsyth. VHS, Beta $69.98 SUE, TVC ⋆⋆⋆ ½

Gremlins Comedy horror with deft satiric edge. Produced by Spielberg. Fumbling gadget salesman Rand Peltzer is looking for something really special to get his son Billy. He finds it in a small store in Chinatown. The wise shopkeeper is reluctant to sell him the adorable "mogwai" but relents after fully warning him "Don't expose him to bright light, don't ever get him wet, and don't ever, ever feed him after midnight." Naturally, this all happens and the result is a gang of nasty gremlins who decide to tear up the town on Christmas Eve. Followed by "Gremlins 2, the New Batch" which is less black comedy, more parody, and perhaps more inventive.
1984 (PG) 106m/C Zach Galligan, Phoebe Cates, Hoyt Axton, Polly Holliday, Frances Lee McCain, Keye Luke, Dick Miller, Corey Feldman, Judge Reinhold; **D:** Joe Dante; **W:** Chris Columbus; **M:** Jerry Goldsmith. VHS, Beta, 8mm $14.95 WAR, TLF ⋆⋆⋆

Gremlins 2: The New Batch The sequel to "Gremlins" is superior to the original, which was quite good. Set in a futuristic skyscraper in the Big Apple, director Dante presents a less violent but far more campy vision, paying myriad surreal tributes to scores of movies, including "The Wizard of Oz" and musical extravaganzas of the past. Also incorporates a Donald Trump parody, takes on television news, and body slams modern urban living. Great fun.
1990 (PG-13) 107m/C Phoebe Cates, Christopher Lee, John Glover, Zach Galligan; **Cameos:** Jerry Goldsmith; **D:** Joe Dante; **M:** Jerry Goldsmith. VHS, Beta, 8mm $14.95 WAR, HHE ⋆⋆⋆ ½

Grendel, Grendel, Grendel An utterly urbane dragon wants to be friends, but for some reason people are just terrified of Grendel. It's true, he bites a head off once in a while, but nobody's perfect! An ingenious, animated retelling of Beowulf.

1982 90m/C **D:** Alexander Stitt; **V:** Peter Ustinov, Arthur Dignam, Julie McKenna, Keith Michell. VHS, Beta $29.95 FHE ⋆⋆

Greta During WWII, a young Polish boy escapes from a detention camp. Now on the run, several bizarre twists of fate place him in the care of Greta, a young girl whose father is an officer in the S.S. In Polish with English subtitles.
1986 60m/C Janusz Grabowski, Agnieszka Kruszewska, Eva Borowik, Tomasz Grochoczki, Andrzej Precig; **D:** Krzysztof Gruber. VHS, Beta $39.50 EVD, ING ⋆⋆

The Grey Fox A gentlemanly old stagecoach robber tries to pick up his life after thirty years in prison. Unable to resist another heist, he tries train robbery, and winds up hiding out in British Columbia where he meets an attractive photographer, come to document the changing West. Farnsworth is perfect as the man who suddenly finds himself in the 20th century trying to work at the only craft he knows. Based on the true story of Canada's most colorful and celebrated outlaw, Bill Miner.
1983 (PG) 92m/C Richard Farnsworth, Jackie Burroughs, Wayne Robson, Timothy Webber, Ken Pogue; **D:** Phillip Borsos; **M:** Michael Conway Baker. VHS, Beta $19.95 MED ⋆⋆⋆ ½

Greyfriars Bobby A true story of a Skye terrier named Bobby who, after his master dies, refuses to leave the grave. Even after being coaxed by the local children into town, he still returns to the cemetery each evening. Word of his loyalty spreads, and Bobby becomes the pet of 19th century Edinburgh. Nicely told, with fine location photography and good acting. Great for children and animal lovers.
1961 91m/C Donald Crisp, Laurence Naismith, Kay Walsh; **D:** Don Chaffey. VHS $69.95 DIS ⋆⋆ ½

Greystoke: The Legend of Tarzan, Lord of the Apes The seventh Earl of Greystoke becomes a shipwrecked orphan and is raised by apes. Ruling the ape-clan in the vine-swinging persona of Tarzan, he is discovered by an anthropologist and returned to his ancestral home in Scotland, where he is immediately recognized by his grandfather. The contrast between the behavior of man and ape is interesting, and Tarzan's introduction to society is fun, but there's no melodrama or cliffhanging action, as we've come to expect of the Tarzan genre. Due to her heavy southern accent, Andie MacDowell (as Jane) had her voice dubbed by Glenn Close.
1984 (PG) 130m/C Christopher Lambert, Ralph Richardson, Ian Holm, James Fox, Andie MacDowell, Ian Charleson, Cheryl Campbell, Nigel Davenport; **D:** Hugh Hudson. VHS, Beta $19.98 WAR ⋆⋆

Grievous Bodily Harm Morris Martin's wife Claudine is missing. When he finds a videotape of Claudine in very compromising positions, he becomes murderously determined to find out where she has gone.
1989 (R) 136m/C John Waters, Colin Friels, Bruno Lawrence; **D:** Mark Joffe. VHS, Beta $29.95 FRH ⋆⋆

Griffin and Phoenix: A Love Story A sentimental film about the mortality of two vital people. Falk deserts his family when he learns he has terminal cancer. Clayburgh, also terminally ill, meets him for a short but meaningful affair. Good performances help overcome the tear-jerker aspects of the story. Made for television.
1976 110m/C Peter Falk, Jill Clayburgh, Dorothy Tristan, John Lehne; **D:** Daryl Duke. VHS $59.98 FOX ⋆⋆ ½

Griffith Biograph Program Some of the best Biograph shorts are featured: "The Lonely Villa," "The Lonedale Operator," "The New York Hat," "Friends," and "The Unseen Enemy," all produced between 1909 and 1912.
1909 50m/B Mary Pickford, Blanche Sweet, Lillian Gish, Dorothy Gish; *D:* D.W. Griffith. **VHS, Beta** *GVV* ♫♫½

The Grifters Evocative rendering of a terrifying sub-culture. Huston, Cusak, and Bening are con artists, struggling to stay on top in a world where violence, money, and lust are the prizes. Bening and Huston fight for Cusak's soul, while he's determined to decide for himself. Seamless performances and dazzling atmosphere, along with superb pacing, make for a provocative film. Based on a novel by Jim Thompson.
1990 114m/C Anjelica Huston, John Cusack, Annette Bening, Pat Hingle, J.T. Walsh, Charles Napier, Henry Jones, Gailard Sartain; *D:* Stephen Frears; *W:* Donald E. Westlake; *M:* Elmer Bernstein. Academy Awards '90 Nominations: Best Actress (Huston), Best Adapted Screenplay, Best Director (Frears), Best Supporting Actress (Bening); Independent Spirit Awards '91: Best Actress (Huston), Best Film; Los Angeles Film Critics Association Awards '90: Best Actress (Huston); National Society of Film Critics Awards '90: Best Actress (Huston), Best Supporting Actress (Bening). **VHS, Beta $19.98** *MCA, HBO, FCT* ♫♫♫½

Grim Prairie Tales A city slicker and a crazed mountain man meet by a campfire in the high plains one night and pass the time sharing four tales of Western horror. Dourif and Jones are fun, the stories scary, making for an interesting twist on both the horror and the Western genres.
1989 (R) 90m/C Brad Dourif, James Earl Jones, Marc McClure, William Atherton, Scott Paulin; *D:* Wayne Coe; *W:* Wayne Coe. **VHS $29.95** *ACA, FCT* ♫♫

The Grim Reaper 22-year-old Bertolucci directed his first feature with this grim and brutal treatment of the investigation of the murder of a prostitute, told via flashbacks and from the disparate perspectives of three people who knew the woman. A commercial bust, the critics were no kinder than the public at the time; not until two years later, with "Before the Revolution," did Bertolucci earn his directorial spurs. The script was written by Pasolini, with whom the erstwhile poet had collaborated on "Accattone" the previous year (as assistant). In Italian with English subtitles. *AKA:* La Commare Secca.
1962 100m/B Francesco Rulu, Giancarlo de Rosa; *D:* Bernardo Bertolucci; *W:* Pier Paolo Pasolini. **VHS $29.95** *CVC, FCT, ING* ♫♫

Grim Reaper Mia Farrow's sister is one of a group of American students vacationing on a Greek island. Farrow learns of the twisted cannibalistic murderer who methodically tries to avenge the tragic deaths of his family.
1981 (R) 81m/C Tisa Farrow, George Eastman; *D:* Joe D'Amato. **VHS, Beta $39.95** *MON* ♫½

The Grissom Gang Remake of the 1948 British film "No Orchids for Miss Blandish." Darby is a wealthy heiress kidnapped by a family of grotesques, led by a sadistic mother. The ransom gets lost in a series of bizarre events, and the heiress appears to be falling for one of her moronic captors. Director Robert Aldrich skillfully blends extreme violence with dark humor. Superb camera work, editing, and 1920s period sets.
1971 (R) 127m/C Kim Darby, Scott Wilson, Tony Musante, Ralph Waite, Connie Stevens, Robert Lansing, Wesley Addy; *D:* Robert Aldrich. **VHS $29.99** *FOX* ♫♫♫

Grit of the Girl Telegrapher/In the Switch Tower A pair of silent railroad dramas, which feature thrilling chase sequences, nefarious schemers and virginal heroines. Silent with piano scores.
1915 47m/B Anna Q. Nilsson, Hal Clements, Walter Edwards, Frank Borzage; *M:* Jon Mirsalis. **VHS, Beta $19.98** *CCB, PEN, GVV* ♫♫♫

Grizzly Giant, killer grizzly terrorizes a state park in this blatant "Jaws" rip-off. From the same folks who produced "Abby," a blatant "Exorcist" rip-off. Filmed in Georgia. *AKA:* Killer Grizzly.
1976 92m/C Christopher George, Richard Jaeckel, Andrew Prine, Victoria (Vicki) Johnson, Charles Kissinger; *D:* William Girdler. **VHS, Beta $9.95** *MED* ♫

Grizzly Adams: The Legend Continues A small town is saved from three desperados by Grizzly and his huge grizzly bear pet, Martha.
1990 90m/C Gene Edwards, Link Wyler, Red West, Tony Caruso, Acquanetta, L.Q. Jones; *D:* Ken Kennedy. **VHS** *NO* ♫½

Grizzly Mountain Man moves to the Sierra Mountains and befriends an Indian.
1980 96m/C VHS, Beta *NO* ♫½

The Groove Tube A television series called "The Groove Tube" is the context for these skits that spoof everything on television from commercials to newscasts. Chevy Chase's movie debut.
1972 (R) 75m/C Lane Sarasohn, Chevy Chase, Richard Belzer, Marcy Mendham, Bill Kemmill; *D:* Ken Shapiro. **VHS, Beta $19.95** *MED* ♫♫½

Gross Anatomy Lightweight comedy/drama centers on the trials and tribulations of medical students. Modine is the very bright, but somewhat lazy, future doctor determined not to buy into the bitter competition among his fellow students. His lack of desire inflames Lahti, a professor dying of a fatal disease who nevertheless believes in modern medicine. She pushes and inspires him to focus on his potential, and his desire to help people. Worth watching, in spite of cheap laughs. Interesting cast of up-and-comers.
1989 (PG-13) 107m/C Matthew Modine, Daphne Zuniga, Christine Lahti, John Scott Clough, Alice Carter, Robert Desiderio, Zakes Mokae, Todd Field; *D:* Thom Eberhardt; *W:* Ron Nyswaner; *M:* David Newman. **VHS, Beta $19.99** *TOU* ♫♫½

Grotesque After slaughtering a young woman's family as they vacationed in a remote mountain cabin, a gang of bloodthirsty punks are attacked by the family secret, the deformed son. The title says it all.
1987 (R) 79m/C Linda Blair, Tab Hunter, Guy Stockwell, Donna Wilkes, Nels Van Patten; *D:* Joe Tornatore. **VHS, Beta $79.95** *MED* Woof!

Ground Zero Political thriller, set in the Australian outback in the fifties, in which a man searches for the reasons for his father's murder in the films of the British nuclear tests.
1988 (R) 109m/C Colin Friels, Jack Thompson, Donald Pleasence, Natalie Bate, Simon Chilvers, Neil Fitzpatrick, Bob Maza, Peter Cummins; *D:* Bruce Myles, Michael Pattinson. **VHS, Beta $14.95** *LIV* ♫♫

Ground Zero Ground Zero is the term used to describe the site of a nuclear explosion. San Francisco is threatened with just such a new name in this story of nuclear blackmail. Someone plants an atomic bomb on the Golden Gate Bridge. It must be defused and the culprit caught.
1988 (R) 90m/C Ron Casteel, Melvin Belli, Yvonne D'Angiers; *D:* James T. Flocker. **VHS, Beta $39.95** *GHV, VTR* ♫½

Groundhog Day Phil, (Murray) an obnoxious weatherman, is in Punxatawney, PA to cover the annual emergence of the famous rodent from its hole. After he's caught in a blizzard that he didn't predict, he finds himself trapped in a time warp, doomed to relive the same day over and over again until he gets it right. Lighthearted romantic comedy takes a funny premise and manages to carry it through to the end. Murray has fun with the role, although he did get bitten by the groundhog during the scene when they're driving. Elliott, who has been missed since his days as the man under the seats on "Late Night with David Letterman" is perfectly cast as a foul-mouthed cameraman.
1993 (PG) 103m/C Bill Murray, Andie MacDowell, Chris Elliott, Stephen Tobolowsky, Brian Doyle-Murray, Marita Geraghty, Angela Paton; *D:* Harold Ramis; *W:* Harold Ramis, Daniel F. Rubin; *M:* George Fenton. **VHS $19.95** *COL, FCT, BTV* ♫♫♫

The Groundstar Conspiracy Spy thriller brings to life L.P. Davies' novel, "The Alien." After an explosion kills all but one space project scientist, Peppard is sent to investigate suspicions of a cover-up. Meanwhile, the surviving scientist (Sarrazin) suffers from disfigurement and amnesia. He pursues his identity while Peppard accuses him of being a spy. Splendid direction by Lamont Johnson. Sarrazin's best role.
1972 (PG) 96m/C George Peppard, Michael Sarrazin, Christine Belford, Cliff Potts, James Olson, Tim O'Connor, James McEachin, Alan Oppenheimer; *D:* Lamont Johnson. **VHS $59.50** *MCA* ♫♫♫

The Group Based upon the novel by Mary McCarthy, the well-acted story deals with a group of graduates from a Vassar-like college as they try to adapt to life during the Great Depression. Has some provocative subject matter, including lesbianism, adultery, and mental breakdowns. Soapy, but a good cast with film debuts of Bergen, Hackett, Pettet, Widdoes, and Holbrook.
1966 150m/C Candice Bergen, Joanna Pettet, Shirley Knight, Joan Hackett, Elizabeth Hartman, Jessica Walter, Larry Hagman, Kathleen Widdoes, Hal Holbrook, Mary-Robin Redd, Richard Mulligan, James Broderick, Carrie Nye; *D:* Sidney Lumet. **VHS, Beta $59.98** *FOX* ♫♫½

Group Marriage Six young professionals fall into a marriage of communal convenience and rapidly discover the many advantages and drawbacks of their thoroughly modern arrangement.
1972 (R) 90m/C Victoria Vetri, Aimee Eccles, Zack Taylor, Jeff Pomerantz, Claudia Jennings, Jayne Kennedy, Milt Kamen; *D:* Stephanie Rothman. **VHS, Beta $39.95** *VCI* ♫♫½

Growing Pains A young couple discover that their newly adopted son possesses extraordinary powers.
1982 60m/C Gary Bond, Barbara Keilermann, Norman Beaton. **VHS, Beta $29.95** *LIV* ♫♫

Grown Ups A newly married couple move into their first home only to discover that the wife's ditzy sister expects to live with them and that their next door neighbor was their former high school teacher.
1980 95m/C Philip Davis, Leslie Manville, Sam Kelly, Lindsay Duncan, Brenda Blethyn, Janine Duvitsky; *D:* Mike Leigh; *W:* Mike Leigh. **VHS $79.95** *WBF, BTV, FCT* ♫♫

Grown Ups A journalist watches his family slowly disintegrating around him in this adaptation of Jules Feiffer's play.
1986 106m/C Jean Stapleton, Martin Balsam, Charles Grodin, Marilu Henner, Kerry Segal; *D:* John Madden. **VHS, Beta $59.95** *LHV, WAR* ♫♫

Gruesome Twosome Another guts/ cannibalism/mutilation fun-fest by Lewis, about someone who's marketing the hair of some very recently deceased college coeds. **1967 75m/C** Elizabeth Davis, Chris Martell; *D:* Herschell Gordon Lewis. **VHS, Beta $39.98** *RHI* *I*

Grumpy Old Men Lemmon and Matthau team for their seventh movie, in parts that seem written just for them. Boyhood friends and retired neighbors, they have been feuding for so long that neither of them can remember why. Doesn't matter much, when it provides a reason for them to spout off at each other every morning and play nasty practical jokes every night. This, and ice-fishing, is life as they know it, until feisty younger woman Ann-Margret moves into the neighborhood and lights some long dormant fires. Eighty-three-year old Meredith is a special treat playing Lemmon's ninety-something father. Filmed in Wabasha, Minnesota, and grumpy, in the most pleasant way. **1993 (PG-13) 104m/C** Jack Lemmon, Walter Matthau, Ann-Margret, Burgess Meredith, Daryl Hannah, Kevin Pollak, Ossie Davis, Buck Henry, Christopher McDonald; *D:* Donald Petrie; *W:* Mark Steven Johnson; *M:* Alan Silvestri. **VHS, 8mm** *WAR* *III*

Grunt! The Wrestling Movie A spoof of documentaries about the behind-the-scenes world of wrestling. For fans only. **1985 (R) 91m/C** Wally Greene, Steven Cepello, Dick Murdoch, John Tolos; *D:* Allan Holzman. **VHS, Beta $19.95** *STE, NWV* Woof!

Gryphon Ricky's new teacher can do all sorts of magical things. Hidden among her tricks are lessons about creativity, beauty, and imagination. Adapted from the short story by Charles Baxter. Aired on PBS as part of the "Wonderworks" family movie series. **1988 58m/C** Amanda Plummer, Sully Diaz, Alexis Cruz; *D:* Mark Cullingham. **VHS $14.95** *PME, FCT, BTV* Woof!

Guadalcanal Diary A vintage wartime flag-waver, with a typical crew of Marines battling the "Yellow Menace" over an important base on the famous Pacific atoll. Based on Richard Tregaskis' first-hand account. **1943 93m/B** Preston Foster, Lloyd Nolan, William Bendix, Richard Conte, Anthony Quinn, Richard Jaeckel, Roy Roberts, Minor Watson, Miles Mander, Ralph Byrd, Lionel Stander, Reed Hadley; *D:* Lewis Seiler. **VHS, Beta $39.98** *FOX, IME* *II½*

The Guardian Residents of a chic New York apartment building hire a security expert/ex-military man to aid them in combatting their crime problem. But one of the liberal tenants thinks their guard's methods may come at too high a cost. Made for cable television. **1984 (R) 102m/C** Martin Sheen, Louis Gossett Jr., Arthur Hill; *D:* David Greene. **VHS, Beta $69.98** *LIV, VES* *I½*

The Guardian A young couple unwittingly hires a human sacrificing druid witch as a babysitter for their child. Based on the book "The Nanny" by Dan Greenburg. **1990 (R) 92m/C** Jenny Seagrove, Dwier Brown, Carey Lowell; *D:* William Friedkin; *W:* William Friedkin. **VHS, Beta $19.98** *MCA* *I*

Guardian of the Abyss A young couple who buy an antique mirror get more than they bargained for when they discover that it is the threshold to Hell and the devil wants to come through. **1982 60m/C** Ray Lonnen, Rosalyn Landor, Paul Darrow, Barbara Ewing; *D:* Don Sharp. **VHS, Beta $29.95** *LIV* *I*

Guarding Tess Long-suffering Secret Service agent Cage is nearing the end of his three year assignment to crotchety widowed First Lady MacLaine when the Prez extends his tour of duty. Feels like a TV movie, not surprising since writers Torokvei and Wilson have several sitcoms to their credit, including "WKRP in Cinncinnati." Nice chemistry between Cage and MacLaine results in a few funny moments, but there are too many formulaic plot twists. End result: a pleasant, if somewhat slow buddy comedy. **1994 (PG-13) 98m/C** Shirley MacLaine, Nicolas Cage, Austin Pendleton, Edward Albert, Richard Griffiths; *D:* Hugh Wilson; *W:* Peter Torokvei, Hugh Wilson; *M:* Michael Convertino. **VHS** *NYR* *II*

The Guardsman Broadway's illustrious couple Lunt and Fontanne shine in this adaptation of the clever marital comedy by French playwright Molnar in which they also starred. This sophisticated comedy was their only starring film, although they were offered large sums of money to appear in other movies—they just couldn't tear themselves away from the stage. Remade as "The Chocolate Soldier" and "Lily in Love." **1931 89m/B** Alfred Lunt, Lynn Fontanne, Roland Young, ZaSu Pitts, Maude Eburne, Herman Bing, Ann Dvorak; *D:* Sidney Franklin. **VHS $19.98** *MGM* *III*

Guerilla Brigade A rarely seen Ukrainian epic about Russian/Ukrainian solidarity during the Civil War. In Russian with English subtitles. *AKA:* Riders. **1939 90m/B** *D:* Igor Savchenko. **VHS, Beta $59.95** *FCT* *II½*

Guess What We Learned in School Today? Parents in a conservative suburban community protest sex education in the schools. Intended as a satire, but it only reinforces stereotypes. **1970 (R) 85m/C** Richard Carballo, Devin Goldenberg; *D:* John G. Avildsen. **VHS, Beta** *NO* Woof!

Guess Who's Coming to Dinner Controversial in its time. A young white woman brings her black fiance home to meet her parents. The situation truly tests their open-mindedness and understanding. Hepburn and Tracy (in his last film appearance) are wonderful and serve as the anchors in what would otherwise have been a rather sugary film. Houghton, who portrays the independent daughter, is the real-life niece of Hepburn. **1967 108m/C** Katharine Hepburn, Spencer Tracy, Sidney Poitier, Katherine Houghton, Cecil Kellaway; *D:* Stanley Kramer; *W:* William Rose. Academy Awards '67: Best Actress (Hepburn), Best Original Screenplay; Nominations: Best Actor (Tracy), Best Picture, Best Supporting Actor (Kellaway); British Academy Awards '68: Best Actor (Tracy), Best Actress (Hepburn). **VHS, Beta $14.95** *COL, FCT, COL* *III*

Guest in the House A seemingly friendly young female patient is invited to stay in the family home of her doctor. She skillfully attempts to dissect the family's harmony in the process. **1945 121m/B** Anne Baxter, Ralph Bellamy, Ruth Warrick, Marie McDonald, Margaret Hamilton; *D:* John Brahm. **VHS, Beta $19.95** *NOS, CAB, VYY* *II½*

Guest Wife Determined to impress his sentimental boss, a quick-thinking bachelor talks his best friend's wife into posing as his own wife, but the hoax gets a bit out of hand and nearly ruins the real couple's marriage. **1945 90m/B** Claudette Colbert, Don Ameche, Dick Foran, Charles Dingle, Wilma Francis; *D:* Sam Wood. **VHS** *REP* *II½*

A Guide for the Married Man One suburban husband instructs another in adultery, with a cast of dozens enacting various slapstick cameos. Based on Frank Tarloff's novel of the same name. Followed by "A Guide for the Married Woman." **1967 91m/C** Walter Matthau, Robert Morse, Inger Stevens, Sue Ane Langdon, Claire Kelly, Elaine Devry; *Cameos:* Lucille Ball, Sid Caesar, Jack Benny, Wally Cox, Jayne Mansfield, Louis Nye, Carl Reiner, Phil Silvers, Terry-Thomas, Sam Jaffe, Jeffrey Hunter, Polly Bergen; *D:* Gene Kelly; *W:* Frank Tarloff; *M:* John Williams. **VHS, Beta $59.98** *FOX* *III*

A Guide for the Married Woman A bored housewife tries to take the romantic advice of a girlfriend to add a little spice to her life. A poor made-for-television follow-up to "A Guide for the Married Man." **1978 96m/C** Cybill Shepherd, Barbara Feldon, Eve Arden, Chuck Woolery, Peter Marshall, Charles Frank; *D:* Hy Averback. **VHS, Beta $59.95** *FOX* *II*

Guilty as Charged A butcher rigs his own private electric chair and captures and executes paroled killers in his personal quest for justice. But when a politician frames an innocent man for murder how far will this vigilante go? **1992 (R) 95m/C** Rod Steiger, Lauren Hutton, Heather Graham, Isaac Hayes; *D:* Sam Irvin; *M:* Steve Bartek. **VHS $89.98** *COL* *I½*

Guilty as Sin Johnson is a ruthless Casanova accused of murdering his very wealthy wife and decides lawyer DeMornay is just the woman to defend him. Question is, who'll defend DeMornay from him? Johnson has fun as the menacing smoothie but De-Mornay's supposedly hotshot criminal attorney is just plain dumb. It sounds like "Jagged Edge" but there's no sexual involvement between client and lawyer and no thrill in this thriller. **1993 (R) 120m/C** Don Johnson, Rebecca DeMornay, Jack Warden, Stephen Lang, Dana Ivey, Ron White, Sean McCann, Luis Guzman; *D:* Sidney Lumet; *W:* Larry Cohen. **VHS, Beta** *HPH, BTV, TOU* *I½*

Guilty by Suspicion Examination of the 1950's McCarthy investigations by the House Un-American Activities Committee comes off like a bland history lesson. De Niro plays a director who attended a Communist party meeting in the '30s but who otherwise doesn't have any red connections. He takes the moral high ground and refuses to incriminate his buddy (Wendt) to get off the hook and finds himself blacklisted. Characterized by average performances (excepting Wettig who goes overboard) and a lightweight script. "The Front" (1976) does a better job on this topic. Directorial debut for producer Winkler. Available in widescreen on laserdisc. **1991 (PG-13) 105m/C** Robert De Niro, Annette Bening, George Wendt, Patricia Wettig, Sam Wanamaker, Chris Cooper, Ben Piazza, Martin Scorsese, Barry Primus, Gailard Sartain, Stuart Margolin, Barry Tubb, Roxann Biggs, Adam Baldwin, Robin Gammell, Brad Sullivan, Luke Edwards; *D:* Irwin Winkler; *W:* Irwin Winkler; *M:* James Newton Howard. **VHS, 8mm $19.98** *WAR* *II½*

Guilty of Innocence A young African-American man finds he's guilty until proven innocent when he runs into the law in Texas. A bold lawyer joins his fight for justice. Based on a true story and made for television. **1987 (PG) 95m/C** Dorian Harewood, Dabney Coleman, Hoyt Axton, Paul Winfield, Dennis Lipscomb, Debbi Morgan, Marshall Colt, Victor Love; *D:* Richard T. Heffron. **VHS $89.98** *VMK* *II*

Guilty of Treason A documentary on the life and times of Joszef Cardinal Mindszenty of Hungary, who was imprisoned by the communists as an enemy of the state for speaking out against the totalitarian regime. At the trial, it was revealed that the Cardinal's confession was obtained only by the use of drugs, hypnosis, and torture. A realistic look at the dark side of Communism.
1950 86m/B Charles Bickford, Paul Kelly, Bonita Granville, Richard Derr, Berry Kroeger, Elisabeth Risdon, Roland Winters, John Banner; **D:** Felix Feist. **VHS $24.95** *NOS, MRV, TIM* 🎞🎞½

Guitarras Lloren Guitarras A popular artist gets frustrated when the girl he loves falls for his brother.
1947 111m/B Cuco Sanchez, Lucha Villa, Fernando Soto Mantequilla. **VHS, Beta $54.95** *MAD* 🎞🎞½

Gulag An American sportscaster is wrongly sentenced to ten years of hard labor in a Soviet prison, and plans his escape from the cruel guards. Good suspense. Made for television.
1985 130m/C David Keith, Malcolm McDowell, David Suchet, Warren Clarke, John McEnery; **D:** Roger Young; **M:** Elmer Bernstein. **VHS, Beta $69.95** *PSM* 🎞🎞½

Gulliver A farce about an escaped convict who hides out with a community of dwarves, manipulates them, and eventually impels them to murder.
197? 100m/C Fernando Gomez, Yolanda Farr. **VHS, Beta** *NO* 🎞½

Gulliver's Travels The Fleischer Studio's animated version of Jonathan Swift's classic about the adventures of Gulliver, an English sailor who is washed ashore in the land of Lilliput, where everyone is about two inches tall.
1939 74m/C **D:** Dave Fleischer; **V:** Lanny Ross, Jessica Dragonette. **VHS $8.95** *CNG, MRV, NOS* 🎞🎞½

Gulliver's Travels In this partially animated adventure the entire land of Lilliput has been constructed in miniature. Cartoon and real life mix in a 3-dimensional story of Dr. Lemuel Gulliver and his discovery of the small people in the East Indies. From the classic by Jonathan Swift.
1977 (G) 80m/C Richard Harris, Catherine Schell; **D:** Peter Hunt. **VHS, Beta $19.95** *VCI, VTR, HHE* 🎞🎞

Gumball Rally An unusual assortment of people converge upon New York for a cross country car race to Long Beach, California where breaking the rules is part of the game.
1976 (PG) 107m/C Michael Sarrazin, Gary Busey, Raul Julia, Nicholas Pryor, Tim McIntire, Susan Flannery; **D:** Chuck Bail; **W:** Leon Capetanos. **VHS, Beta $59.95** *WAR* 🎞🎞

Gumshoe An homage to American hard-boiled detectives. Finney plays a small-time worker in a Liverpool nightclub who decides to become a detective like his movie heroes. He bumbles through a number of interconnecting cases, but finds his way in the end. Good satire of film noir detectives.
1972 (G) 85m/C Albert Finney, Billie Whitelaw, Frank Finlay, Janice Rule, Carolyn Seymour; **D:** Stephen Frears; **M:** Andrew Lloyd Webber. **VHS, Beta** *NO* 🎞🎞½

The Gumshoe Kid A college-bound kid enters the family detective business to prevent his mother from being evicted. He gets in over his head though, trying to track the fiancee of a wealthy mobster. *AKA:* The Detective Kid.

1989 (R) 98m/C Jay Underwood, Tracy Scoggins, Vince Edwards, Arlene Golonka, Pamela Springsteen; **D:** Joseph Manduke. **VHS, Beta $29.95** *ACA* 🎞

Gun Cargo Muddled story about a conniving shipowner who fires his crew for demanding shore leave. He replaces them with assorted low-lifes, resulting in the usual hijinks. A terrible performance by an otherwise great cast.
1949 49m/C Rex Lease, Smith Ballew, William Farnum, Gibson Gowland. **VHS, Beta, 8mm $19.95** *VYY* 🎞

Gun Code The white-hatted cowboy-hero puts a stop to small-town racketeering.
1940 52m/B Tim McCoy, Ina Guest; **D:** Peter Stewart. **VHS, Beta $19.95** *VDM* 🎞½

Gun Crazy Annie Laurie Starr—Annie Oakley in a Wild West show—meets gun-lovin' Bart Tare, who says a gun makes him feel good inside, ''like I'm somebody.'' Sparks fly, and the two get married and live happily ever after—until the money runs out and fatal femme Laurie's craving for excitement and violence starts to flare up. The two become lovebirds-on-the-lam. Now a cult fave, it's based on a MacKinlay Kantor story. Ex-stuntman Russell Harlan's photography is daring; the realism of the impressive robbery scenes is owed in part to the technical consultation of former train robber Al Jennings. And watch for a young Tamblyn as the 14-year-old Bart. *AKA:* Deadly is the Female.
1949 87m/B Peggy Cummins, John Dall, Berry Kroeger, Morris Carnovsky, Anabel Shaw, Nedrick Young, Trevor Bardette, Russ Tamblyn; **D:** Joseph H. Lewis. **VHS $19.98** *FOX, FCT* 🎞🎞🎞

Gun Crazy A gambler becomes enmeshed in an arranged marriage with a cursed Mexican family. Lightweight comedy, good cast. *AKA:* A Talent for Loving.
1969 110m/C Richard Widmark, Chaim Topol, Cesar Romero, Genevieve Page, Judd Hamilton, Caroline Munro; **D:** Richard Quine. **VHS $9.95** *SIM* 🎞🎞½

Gun Fight at Red Sands Landmark western in the history of Italian cinema. Long before Leone's Eastwood trilogy, this film introduced the theme of an avenging stranger to the genre. Harrison stars as the dark, brooding hero who is out for revenge after learning that his family has been attacked by a gang of bandits. *AKA:* Gringo; Duello Nel Texas.
1963 ?m/C Richard Harrison, Giacomo ''Jack'' Rossi-Stuart, Sara Lezana; **M:** Ennio Morricone. **VHS $16.95** *SNC* 🎞🎞

Gun Fury A panoramic western about a Civil War veteran pursuing the bandits who kidnapped his beautiful bride-to-be. First screened as a 3-D movie.
1953 83m/C Rock Hudson, Donna Reed, Phil Carey, Lee Marvin; **D:** Raoul Walsh. **VHS, Beta $14.95** *COL* 🎞🎞½

Gun Girls Campy exploitation flick about a gun-toting gang of girls who rob anything or anyone. The guy who fences their goods ends up getting one of them pregnant.
1956 ?m/C Timothy Farrell, Jean Ferguson, Jacquelyn Park, Jean Ann Lewis; **D:** Robert Deltano. **VHS $16.95** *SNC* 🎞

Gun Glory Granger plays Tom Early, a gunslinger who returns home after three years to find the town would rather not have him. He regains the town's respect when he stops a murderer from invading the town with his cattle herd. Based on the novel ''Man of the West'' by Philip Yordan.

1957 88m/C Stewart Granger, Rhonda Fleming, Chill Wills, Steve Rowland, James Gregory, Jacques Aubuchon, Arch Johnson, William Fawcett, Lane Bradford, Michael Dugan, Bud Osborne, May McAvoy, Charles Herbert, Carl Pitti; **D:** Roy Rowland; **W:** William Ludwig; **M:** Jeff Alexander. **VHS $19.98** *MGM* 🎞🎞½

Gun Grit An FBI agent is sent west to break up a protection racket.
1936 51m/B Jack Perrin, Ethel Beck, David Sharpe, Roger Williams, Budd Buster; **D:** William Berke. **VHS $11.95** *GPV* 🎞½

The Gun in Betty Lou's Handbag Shy, small town librarian with a dull marriage is looking for excitement when she stumbles across a gun used in a murder. She decides excitement will follow her (false) confession to the crime leaving her husband thunderstruck, the police confused, and the gossip line humming. She also intrigues the real bad guy, who comes looking for her. Lame silliness is redeemed somewhat by Miller, but there's some surprisingly nasty violence given the comedy label.
1992 (PG-13) 99m/C Penelope Ann Miller, Eric Thal, Alfre Woodard, Cathy Moriarty, William Forsythe, Julianne Moore, Xander Berkeley, Michael O'Neill, Christopher John Fields; **D:** Allan Moyle; **W:** Grace Cary Bickley; **M:** Richard Gibbs. **VHS, Beta $19.99** *TOU* 🎞🎞

A Gun in the House While being attacked in her own home, a woman shoots one of her assailants. The police find no conclusive evidence of attack and arrest the woman for murder. Exploitive drama on gun control. Made-for-television.
1981 100m/C Sally Struthers, David Ackroyd, Joel Bailey, Jeffrey Tambor; **D:** Ivan Nagy. **VHS, Beta $49.95** *VHE, HHE* 🎞🎞

Gun Law The hero tackles the Sonora Kid, an outlaw terrorizing Arizona folk. One of the few sound westerns with Hoxie, a silent-era star who hung up his spurs when his voice proved non-photogenic.
1933 59m/B Jack Hoxie, Paul Fix, Mary Carr, Edmund Cobb, Robert Burns; **D:** Lewis Collins. **VHS, Beta** *GPV* 🎞½

Gun Lords of Stirrup Basin A cattleman and the daughter of a homesteader are in love in the Old West, but a seedy lawyer wants to douse their flame. Bullets and fists fly as a result.
1937 55m/B Bob Steele, Louise Stanley, Karl Hackett, Ernie Adams, Frank LaRue, Frank Ball, Steve Clark; **D:** Sam Newfield. **VHS $19.95** *NOS, DVT* 🎞

Gun Packer When an outlaw gang robs stagecoaches of their gold and uses the booty to salt barren mine shafts so the unsuspecting can be swindled out of their money on worthless gold mine certificates, hard-riding Randall is called in to save the day.
1938 51m/B Jack Randall, Louise Stanley, Charles ''Blackie'' King, Glenn Strange; **D:** Wallace Fox; **W:** Robert Emmett. **VHS $19.99** *MOV* 🎞🎞

Gun Play Brother and sister venture west to run their father's ranch. Mexican bandits believe the ranch's property houses a revolutionary fortune, and set about recovering it. The brother defends his father's ranch along with a sidekick, who sweeps the sister off her feet. *AKA:* Lucky Boots.
1936 59m/B Guinn Williams, Frank Yaconelli, Marion Shilling, Wally Wales, Charles French; **D:** Albert Herman. **VHS $19.95** *NOS, DVT* 🎞🎞

The Gun Ranger Our hero plays a Texas Ranger who becomes fed up with soft judges and shady prosecutors and decides to take the law into his own hands.

1934 56m/B Bob Steele, Eleanor Stewart, John Merton, Ernie Adams, Budd Buster; **D:** Robert North Bradbury. **VHS, Beta $19.95** NOS, DVT, GPV ♫♫½

Gun Riders Gunman must seek out and stop a murderer of innocent people. **AKA:** Five Bloody Graves; Five Bloody Days to Tombstone; Lonely Man.
1969 98m/C Scott Brady, Jim Davis, John Carradine; **D:** Al Adamson. **VHS, Beta** CCB ♫♫½

Gun Smugglers/Hot Lead A western double feature: Tim Holt and his sidekick Chito must recover a shipment of stolen guns in "Gun Smugglers," and the duo gallop into action against a gang of train robbers in "Hot Lead."
1951 120m/B Tim Holt, Richard Martin, Martha Hyer. **VHS, Beta $34.95** RKO, TTC ♫

Gunblast A convict is released from San Quentin and wastes no time in getting involved with mob-powered drug smuggling.
197? 70m/C Lloyd Allan, Christine Cardan, James Cunningham. **VHS, Beta** NO ♫

Guncrazy Girl from the wrong side of the tracks, abused her entire life, finds her freedom in a gun. She winds up killing the man who raped her, takes up with an equally lost ex-con, and the two armed misfits go on the run from the law. Barrymore's convincing and the movie is another well-made variation on the lovers-on-the-run theme. Film was inspired by, but is not a remake of, the 1949 movie "Gun Crazy."
1992 (R) 97m/C Drew Barrymore, James LeGros, Billy Drago, Rodney Harvey, Ione Skye, Joe Dallesandro, Michael Ironside; **D:** Tamra Davis; **W:** Matthew Bright. **VHS, Beta $89.95** ACA, PMS ♫♫

A Gunfight When Cash is stranded in a small Western town, he meets up with fellow old-time gunfighter Douglas. The two strike up a friendship, but discover the town folk expect a gun battle. Needing money, the two arrange a gunfight for paid admission — winner take all. Cash makes his screen debut.
1971 (PG) 90m/C Kirk Douglas, Johnny Cash, Jane Alexander, Karen Black, Dana Elcar, Keith Carradine, Raf Vallone; **D:** Lamont Johnson. **Beta $59.95** ALL, MTX, VTR ♫♫

Gunfight at Sandoval A Texas Ranger investigates the headquarters of a criminal gang while hunting for the bandits who killed his partner. Adapted from the "Texas John Slaughter" episodes of the Disney television series.
1959 72m/C Tom Tryon, Beverly Garland, Dan Duryea. **VHS, Beta $69.95** DIS ♫½

Gunfight at the O.K. Corral The story of Wyatt Earp and Doc Holliday joining forces in Dodge City to rid the town of the criminal Clanton gang. Filmed in typical Hollywood style, but redeemed by its great stars.
1957 122m/C Burt Lancaster, Kirk Douglas, Rhonda Fleming, Jo Van Fleet, John Ireland, Kenneth Tobey, Lee Van Cleef, Frank Faylen, DeForest Kelley, Earl Holliman; **W:** Leon Uris. **VHS, Beta $14.95** PAR, FCT ♫♫♫

The Gunfighter A mature, serious, Hollywood-western character study about an aging gunfighter searching for peace and quiet but unable to avoid his reputation and the duel-challenges it invites. One of King's best films.
1950 85m/B Gregory Peck, Helen Westcott, Millard Mitchell, Jean Parker, Karl Malden, Skip Homeier, Mae Marsh; **D:** Henry King. **VHS, Beta $19.98** FOX ♫♫♫½

The Gunfighters Lackluster pilot of a proposed Canadian series pits three individualistic relatives against a powerful empire-builder.
1987 100m/C Art Hindle, Reiner Schoene, Tony Addabbo, George Kennedy, Michael Kane, Lori Hallier; **D:** Clay Borris. **VHS $19.99** VMK ♫½

Gunfire A Frank James look-alike cavorts, robs and loots the countryside until the real James decides to set things straight.
1950 59m/B Donald (Don "Red") Barry, Robert Lowery, Pamela Blake, Wally Vernon; **D:** William Berke. **VHS, Beta** HHE ♫½

Gunfire A gunfighter is rescued from the hangman's noose by railroad tycoons who want him to kill a farmer. He doesn't kill the man, but runs off with his wife instead, and the incensed railway honchos send assassins after the double-crossing gunman. Peckinpah's part is pretty puny in this leisurely horse opera. **AKA:** China 9, Liberty 37.
1978 94m/C Fabio Testi, Warren Oates, Jenny Agutter, Sam Peckinpah; **D:** Monte Hellman; **M:** Pino Donaggio. **VHS $9.95** SIM ♫♫

Gung Ho! Carlson's Raiders are a specially trained group of Marine jungle fighters determined to retake the Pacific island of Makin during WWII.
1943 88m/B Robert Mitchum, Randolph Scott, Noah Beery Jr., Alan Curtis, Grace McDonald; **D:** Ray Enright. **VHS, Beta $9.98** REP, MRV, CNG ♫♫

Gung Ho A Japanese firm takes over a small-town U.S. auto factory and causes major cultural collisions. Keaton plays the go-between for employees and management while trying to keep both groups from killing each other. From the director of "Splash" and "Night Shift." Made into a short-lived television series.
1985 (PG-13) 111m/C Michael Keaton, Gedde Watanabe, George Wendt, Mimi Rogers, John Turturro, Clint Howard, Michelle Johnson, So Yamamura, Sab Shimono; **D:** Ron Howard; **W:** Babaloo Mandel, Lowell Ganz. **VHS, Beta, 8mm $14.95** PAR ♫♫½

Gunga Din The prototypical "buddy" film. Three veteran British sergeants in India try to suppress a native uprising, but it's their water boy, the intrepid Gunga Din, who saves the day. Friendship, loyalty, and some of the best action scenes ever filmed. Based loosely on Rudyard Kipling's famous poem, the story is credited to Ben Hecht, Charles MacArthur and William Faulkner (who is uncredited). Also available colorized.
1939 117m/B Cary Grant; Victor McLaglen, Douglas Fairbanks Jr., Sam Jaffe, Eduardo Ciannelli, Montagu Love, Joan Fontaine, Abner Biberman, Robert Coote, Lumsden Hare, Cecil Kellaway; **D:** George Stevens; **W:** Fred Guiol, Joel Sayre; **M:** Alfred Newman. **VHS, Beta $14.98** RKO, TTC, MLB ♫♫♫♫

Gunman from Bodie Second of the Rough Rider series. Jones, McCoy, and Hatton rescue a baby orphaned by rustlers and then go after the bad guys. **AKA:** Gun Man from Bodie.
1941 62m/B Tim McCoy, Buck Jones, Raymond Hatton; **D:** Spencer Gordon Bennet. **VHS, Beta $9.95** NOS, MRV, VCN ♫½

Gunmen A reluctant buddy team face down some bad guys. DEA agent Cole (Van Peebles) teams up with smuggler Dani (Lambert) to find stolen drug money also wanted by wheelchair-bound villain Loomis (Stewart) and his violence-loving henchman (Leary). Adds comedy to the mix as well as shameless action rip-offs from spaghetti westerns.

1993 (R) 90m/C Christopher Lambert, Mario Van Peebles, Denis Leary, Patrick Stewart, Kadeem Hardison, Sally Kirkland; **Cameos:** Big Daddy Kane, Ed Lover, Eric B. Rakim, Dr. Dre; **D:** Deran Sarafian; **W:** Stephen Sommers; **M:** John Debney. **VHS $94.98** LIV ♫♫

Gunners & Guns Vintage western starring King.
1934 51m/B Black King, Edmund Cobb, Edna Asetin, Eddie Davis; **D:** Ray Nazarro. **VHS, Beta $29.95** VCN ♫

Gunplay Two cowboys befriend a boy whose father has been killed and search for the murderer.
1951 61m/B Tim Holt, Joan Dixon, Richard Martin. **VHS, Beta** MED ♫½

Gunpowder Two Interpol agents endeavor to stop a crime lord from causing the collapse of the world economy.
1984 85m/C David Gilliam, Martin Potter, Gordon Jackson, Anthony Schaeffer. **VHS, Beta $69.98** LIV, VES ♫

The Gunrunner Costner plays a Canadian mobster, involved in liquor smuggling, who aids a Chinese rebellion in this 1920s drama. Interesting concept. Received more attention after Costner gained notoriety in later films.
1984 (R) 92m/C Kevin Costner, Sara Botsford, Paul Soles; **D:** Nardo Castillo. **VHS $19.95** STE, HHE ♫½

Guns An international gunrunner puts the moves on buxom women between hair-raising adventures.
1990 (R) 95m/C Erik Estrada, Dona Speir; **D:** Andy Sidaris; **W:** Andy Sidaris. **VHS $79.95** COL ♫♫

The Guns and the Fury Two American oil riggers in the Middle East, circa 1908, are forced to fight off an attack by a vicious Arab sheik and his tribe.
1983 90m/C Peter Graves, Cameron Mitchell, Michael Ansara, Albert Salmi; **D:** Tony Zarindast. **VHS, Beta** NO ♫½

Guns at Batasi Attenborough plays a tough British Sergeant Major stationed in Africa during the anti-colonial 1960s. Ultimately the regiment is threatened by rebel Africans. Fine performances make this rather predictable film watchable.
1964 103m/B Richard Attenborough, Jack Hawkins, Mia Farrow, Flora Robson, John Leyton; **D:** John Guillermin; **M:** John Addison. **VHS** TCF, RXM ♫♫½

Guns Don't Argue Entertaining schlocker about the rise and fall of famous criminal Dillinger. Non-stop action also features Bonnie and Clyde, Pretty Boy Floyd and Baby Face Nelson.
1957 ?m/C Myron Healey, Jim Davis, Richard Crane. **VHS $16.95** SNC ♫♫

Guns for Dollars Mex-Western has four men, including a secret agent and a cossack, tangled up in the Mexican Revolution as they search for a fortune in smuggled jewels. **AKA:** They Call Me Hallelujah.
1973 94m/C George Hilton, Charles Southwood, Agata Flory, Roberto Camardiel, Paolo Gozlino, Rick Boyd; **D:** Anthony Ascot. **VHS $19.95** ACA ♫♫

Guns in the Dark A cowboy vows never to use a gun again when he believes that he accidentally shot his best friend.
1937 60m/C Johnny Mack Brown, Claire Rochelle; **D:** Sam Newfield. **VHS, Beta $19.95** NOS, DVT, RXM ♫

Guns of Diablo Wagon train master Bronson has to fight a gang that controls the supply depot, all the while showing his young helper (beardless boy Russell) the fascinating tricks of the trade.
1964 91m/C Charles Bronson, Kurt Russell, Susan Oliver; **D:** Boris Sagal. **VHS $39.99** ACE, MTX, VTR ♪♪

Guns of Fury Cisco and Pancho solve the troubles of a small boy in this standard oater.
1945 60m/B Duncan Renaldo. **VHS, Beta $19.95** NOS, VCI, VCN ♪♪

Guns of Justice Undercover Colorado rangers stop a swindler from forcing homesteaders off their land. **AKA:** Colorado Ranger.
1950 60m/B James Ellison, Russell Hayden, Tom Tyler, Raymond Hatton; **D:** Thomas Carr. **VHS, Beta** NO ♪

The Guns of Navarone During WWII, British Intelligence in the Middle East sends six men to the Aegean island of Navarone to destroy guns manned by the Germans. Consistently interesting war epic based on the Alistair MacLean novel, with a vivid cast.
1961 159m/C Gregory Peck, David Niven, Anthony Quinn, Richard Harris, Stanley Baker, Anthony Quayle, James Darren, Irene Papas; **D:** J. Lee Thompson. Academy Awards '61: Best Special Effects; Nominations: Best Adapted Screenplay, Best Director (Thompson); Golden Globe Awards '62: Best Film—Drama, Best Score. **VHS, Beta $19.95** COL ♪♪♪½

Guns of the Law The Texas Rangers try to stop a shifty lawyer who attempts to swindle a family out of a potential fortune in property.
1944 56m/B Dave O'Brien, James Newill, Guy Wilkerson, Jack Ingram, Robert F. (Bob) Kortman, Robert Barron; **D:** Elmer Clifton; **W:** Elmer Clifton. **VHS $19.99** MOV ♪½

Guns of the Magnificent Seven The third remake of "The Seven Samurai." Action-packed western in which the seven free political prisoners grant them to kill. The war party then heads out to rescue a Mexican revolutionary being held in an impregnable fortress.
1969 (G) 106m/C George Kennedy, Monte Markham, James Whitmore, Reni Santoni, Bernie Casey, Joe Don Baker, Scott Thomas, Michael Ansara, Fernando Rey; **D:** Paul Wendkos; **M:** Elmer Bernstein. **VHS $19.98** MGM ♪♪½

Guns of War This is the true story of how a group of Yugoslavians formed a partisan army to stop the reign of Nazi terror in their native land.
1975 114m/C **VHS, Beta** NO ♪♪½

The Gunslinger A woman marshall struggles to keep law and order in a town overrun by outlaws. Unique western with a surprise ending.
1956 83m/C John Ireland, Beverly Garland, Allison Hayes, Jonathan Haze, Dick Miller, Bruno Ve Sota; **D:** Roger Corman; **W:** Charles B. Griffith. **VHS $19.95** MLB, TIM, SNC ♪½

Gunslinger Armed to the teeth with weaponry, Sartana shows a mining town's heavies how to sling a gun or two.
197? 90m/C John Garko, Tony Vilar; **D:** Anthony Ascot. **VHS, Beta $19.98** VDC ♪½

Gunsmoke: Return to Dodge The first of the made-for-television movies which reunited most of the cast of the classic television western. Matt Dillon returns to Dodge and Miss Kitty after 12 years only to be trailed by a ruthless adversary.
1987 100m/C James Arness, Amanda Blake, Buck Taylor, Fran Ryan, Earl Holliman, Steve Forrest; **D:** Vincent McEveety. **VHS** FXV ♪♪½

Gunsmoke Trail Cowpoke Randall saves an heiress from losing her estate to a phony uncle in low-budget Western. Also features the prolific "Fuzzy" St. John in his cowboy's sidekick stage (interestingly, St. John, a nephew of Fatty Arbuckle, later co-starred in the "Lone Rider" series with Randall's brother, Robert Livingston).
1938 59m/C Jack Randall, Al "Fuzzy" St. John. **VHS $19.99** NOS, MRV, MOV ♪½

Gus A Disney film about the California Atoms, a football team that has the worst record in the league until they begin winning games with the help of their field goal kicking mule of a mascot, Gus. The competition then plots a donkey-napping. Enjoyable comedy for the whole family.
1976 (G) 96m/C Ed Asner, Tim Conway, Dick Van Patten, Ronnie Schell, Bob Crane, Tom Bosley; **D:** Vincent McEveety. **VHS, Beta** COL, DIS ♪♪½

GUY: Awakening of the Devil Guy and Raina, two despicable intergalactic soldiers of fortune, embark on a continuous sky-raid adventure. Available in general release and uncut versions. Japanese with English subtitles.
1993 ?m/C **VHS $29.95** CPM, WTA ♪♪

The Guy from Harlem He's mad, he's from Harlem, and he's not going to take it any more.
1977 86m/C Loye Hawkins, Cathy Davis, Patricia Fulton, Wanda Starr; **D:** Rene Martinez Jr. **VHS** XVC ♪♪

A Guy Named Joe A sentimental, patriotic Hollywood fantasy about the angel of a dead WWII pilot guiding another young pilot through battle and also helping him to romance his girl, who's still too devoted to his memory. Remade in 1989 as "Always."
1944 121m/B Spencer Tracy, Irene Dunne, Van Johnson, Ward Bond, James Gleason, Lionel Barrymore, Esther Williams; **D:** Victor Fleming; **W:** Dalton Trumbo. **VHS, Beta $19.95** MGM ♪♪½

The Guyana Tragedy: The Story of Jim Jones Dramatization traces the story of the Reverend Jim Jones and the People's Temple from its beginnings in 1953 to the November 1978 mass suicide of more than 900 people. Boothe is appropriately hypnotic as the Reverend. Made for television.
1980 240m/C Powers Boothe, Ned Beatty, Randy Quaid, Brad Dourif, Brenda Vaccaro, LeVar Burton, Colleen Dewhurst, James Earl Jones; **D:** William A. Graham; **M:** Elmer Bernstein. **VHS, Beta $59.95** VHE, HHE ♪♪

Guys and Dolls New York gambler Sky Masterson takes a bet that he can romance a Salvation Army lady. Based on the stories of Damon Runyon with Blaine, Kaye, Pully, and Silver recreating their roles from the Broadway hit. Brando's not-always-convincing musical debut. ♪More I Cannot Wish You; My Time of Day; Guys and Dolls; Fugue for Tinhorns; Follow the Fold; Sue Me; Take Back Your Mink; If I Were a Bell; Luck Be a Lady.
1955 150m/C Marlon Brando, Jean Simmons, Frank Sinatra, Vivian Blaine, Stubby Kaye, Sheldon Leonard, Veda Ann Borg; **D:** Joseph L. Mankiewicz; **W:** Joseph L. Mankiewicz; **M:** Frank Loesser. Academy Awards '55 Nominations: Best Art Direction/Set Decoration (Color), Best Color Cinematography, Best Costume Design (Color), Best Original Score; Golden Globe Awards '56: Best Actress—Musical/Comedy (Simmons), Best Film—Musical/Comedy. **VHS, Beta $19.98** FOX, FCT ♪♪♪

The Guyver A young college student is transformed into a super-human fighting machine thanks to his discovery of an alien device, "The Guyver." A CIA agent (Hamill) must keep the secret device from falling into the hands of human mutants, the Zoanoids. Based on a Japanese comic book.
1991 92m/C Mark Hamill, Vivian Wu, David Gale, Jeffrey Combs, Michael Berryman; **D:** Steve Wang. **VHS $19.95** COL, NLC ♪½

Gymkata A gymnast (Olympian Thomas) must use his martial arts skills to conquer and secure a military state in a hostile European country.
1985 (R) 89m/C Kurt Thomas, Tetchie Agbayani, Richard Norton, Conan Lee; **D:** Robert Clouse. **VHS, Beta $79.95** MGM ♪

Gypsy The life story of America's most famous striptease queen, Gypsy Rose Lee. Russell gives a memorable performance as the infamous Mama Rose, Gypsy's stage mother. Based on both Gypsy Rose Lee's memoirs and the hit Broadway play by Arthur Laurents. ♪Small World; All I Need is the Girl; You'll Never Get Away From Me; Let Me Entertain You; Some People; Everything's Coming Up Roses; You Gotta Have a Gimmick; Baby Jane and the Newsboys; Mr. Goldstone, I Love You.
1962 144m/C Rosalind Russell, Natalie Wood, Karl Malden, Ann Jillian, Parley Baer, Paul Wallace, Betty Bruce; **D:** Mervyn LeRoy. Academy Awards '62 Nominations: Best Color Cinematography, Best Costume Design (Color), Best Original Score; Golden Globe Awards '63: Best Actress—Musical/Comedy (Russell). **VHS, Beta $19.98** WAR ♪♪♪

Gypsy A modern day gypsy-blooded Robin Hood cavorts between heists and romantic trysts. Dubbed.
1975 90m/C Alain Delon, Annie Girardot, Paul Meurisse; **D:** Jose Giovanni. **VHS, Beta $59.95** FCT ♪♪

Gypsy If you like Bette brassy and larger than life, as only she can be, than this is the production for you. This television recreation of the 1959 Broadway musical stars Midler as notorious stage mother Mama Rose, who tries to realize all her frustrated ambitions by pushing her two young daughters, June and Louise, into vaudeville show biz. Her wish eventually comes true, in an unexpected fashion, when an adult Louise (Gibb) transforms herself into stripper Gypsy Rose Lee. ♪Everything's Coming Up Roses; You've Gotta Have a Gimmick; All I Need Is the Girl; Rose's Turn; Some People; Mr. Goldstone, I Love You; You'll Never Get Away From Me; Together, Wherever We Go.
1993 150m/C Bette Midler, Peter Riegert, Cynthia Gibb, Ed Asner, Christine Ebersole, Michael Jeter, Andrea Martin, Jennifer Beck, Linda Hart, Rachel Sweet; **D:** Emile Ardolino; **W:** Arthur Laurents; **M:** Jules Styne, Stephen Sondheim. **VHS $89.95** CAF ♪♪½

Gypsy Angels A daredevil stunt pilot has a terrifying accident and develops amnesia. With the help of a stripper (who is in love with him), he tries to rebuild his life, this time with her in it. White's no actress and unless you like stunt flying (and there's a lot of it), fly by this one. (You'll note the director won't admit to this, since Smithee is a pseudonym.)
1994 (R) 92m/C Vanna White, Richard Roundtree, Gene Bicknell; **D:** Alan Smithee. **VHS $92.95** VMK ♪

Gypsy Blood One of the first screen versions of "Carmen," closer to Prosper Merrimee's story than to the opera, depicting the fated love between a dancing girl and a matador. Lubitsch's first notable film. Silent.

1918 104m/B Pola Negri. *D:* Ernst Lubitsch. VHS, Beta $44.95 *FCT, GPV* 🎬🎬

Gypsy Colt Gypsy is the horse beloved by the young Corcoran. But a drought forces her family to sell the animal to a racing stable 500 miles from their home. Gypsy is having none of this, escapes the stables, and returns home to be with Corcoran. Both horse and child actress are naturally appealing.
1954 (G) 72m/C Donna Corcoran, Ward Bond, Frances Dee, Lee Van Cleef, Larry Keating; *D:* Andrew Marton. VHS $14.98 *MGM, FCT* 🎬🎬½

The Gypsy Warriors Two Army captains during WWII infiltrate Nazi-occupied France in order to prevent the distribution of a deadly toxin and are aided by a band of Gypsies. Made for television.
1978 77m/C Tom Selleck, James Whitmore Jr., Joseph Ruskin, Lina Raymond; *D:* Lou Antonio. VHS, Beta $39.95 *MCA* 🎬½

H-Bomb Mitchum stars as a CIA agent who is sent to Bangkok to retrieve two stolen nuclear warheads from a terrorist. It just so happens that his ex-girlfriend's father is the terrorist he must contend with in this stupid movie.
1971 98m/C Olivia Hussey, Chris Mitchum, Krung Savilai; *D:* P. Chalong. VHS, Beta *NO Woof!*

H-Man A Japanese sci-fi woofer about a radioactive mass of slime festering under Tokyo. Extremely lame special effects get quite a few unintentional laughs. Dubbed. *AKA:* Bijo to Ekitainigen.
1959 79m/C Koreya Senda, Kenji Sahara, Yumi Shirakawa, Akihiko Hirata; *D:* Inoshiro Honda. VHS, Beta $19.95 *COL Woof!*

Hack O'Lantern Granddad worships Satan, and gets his grandson involved: the result is much bloodshed, violence and evil.
1987 90m/C *D:* Jag Mundhra. VHS, Beta *NO* 🎬

Hadley's Rebellion A Georgia farm boy adjusts to relocation at an elitist California boarding school by flaunting his wrestling abilities.
1984 (PG) 96m/C Griffin O'Neal, Charles Durning, William Devane, Adam Baldwin, Dennis Hage, Lisa Lucas; *D:* Fred Walton; *W:* Fred Walton. VHS, Beta $59.98 *FOX* 🎬½

Hail A biting satire of what-might-have-been if certain key cabinet members had their way. *AKA:* Hail to the Chief; Washington, B.C.
1973 (PG) 85m/C Richard B. Shull, Dick O'Neill, Phil Foster, Joseph Sirola, Dan Resin, Willard Waterman, Gary Sandy; *D:* Fred Levinson. VHS, Beta *NO* 🎬🎬

Hail Caesar His job at an eraser factory is the only thing standing between Julius Caesar MacGruder (Hall) and fame and fortune as a rock 'n roll singer.
1994 (PG) 93m/C Anthony Michael Hall, Robert Downey Jr., Frank Gorshin, Samuel L. Jackson, Judd Nelson, Nicholas Pryor, Leslie Danon, Bobbie Philips; *D:* Anthony Michael Hall; *W:* Robert Mittenthal; *M:* Roger Tallman. VHS, Beta $92.95 *PSM* 🎬🎬½

Hail, Hero! A dated Vietnam War era drama about a confused hippie rebelling against his parents and the draft. First film for both Douglas and Strauss. Adapted from the novel by John Weston. Includes music by Gordon Lightfoot.
1969 (PG) 97m/C Michael Douglas, Arthur Kennedy, Teresa Wright, John Larch, Charles Drake, Deborah Winters, Peter Strauss; *D:* David Miller. VHS, Beta $59.98 *FOX* 🎬½

Hail Mary A modern-day virgin named Mary inexplicably becomes pregnant in this controversial film that discards notions of divinity in favor of the celebration of a lively, intellectual humanism. Godard rejects ortho-

dox narrative structure and bourgeois prejudices. Very controversial, but not up to his breathless beginning work. In French with English subtitles. *AKA:* Je Vous Salue Marie.
1985 (R) 107m/C Myriem Roussel, Thierry Rode, Philippe Lacoste, Manon Anderson, Juliette Binoche, Johan Leysen; *D:* Jean-Luc Godard; *W:* Jean-Luc Godard. VHS, Beta $29.98 *LIV, VES, ING* 🎬🎬½

Hail the Conquering Hero A slight young man is rejected by the Army. Upon returning home, he is surprised to find out they think he's a hero. Biting satire with Demarest's performance stealing the show.
1944 101m/B Eddie Bracken, Ella Raines, William Demarest, Franklin Pangborn, Raymond Walburn; *D:* Preston Sturges. VHS $14.98 *MCA* 🎬🎬½

Hair Film version of the explosive 1960s Broadway musical about the carefree life of the flower children and the shadow of the Vietnam War that hangs over them. Great music, as well as wonderful choreography by Twyla Tharp help portray the surprisingly sensitive evocation of the period so long after the fact. Forman has an uncanny knack for understanding the textures of American life. Watch for a thinner Nell Carter.
1979 (PG) 122m/C Treat Williams, John Savage, Beverly D'Angelo, Annie Golden, Nicholas Ray; *D:* Milos Forman; *W:* Michael Weller. VHS, Beta $19.95 *MGM* 🎬🎬½

The Hairdresser's Husband Antoine (Rochefort) has had an odd obsession since boyhood—hairdressers—and in middle age he finds love with Mathilde (Galiena), a hairdresser he meets and proposes to as she cuts his hair. She accepts, and the two live their quiet lives in her barber shop as she cuts hair and he watches, occasionally breaking out in Arabian dances. A dark and odd yet refreshing film with fine performances by Rochefort and Galiena in this story about fetishism, obsession, and hair. In French with English subtitles.
1992 (R) 84m/C Jean Rochefort, Anna Galiena, Roland Bertin, Maurice Chevit, Philippe Clevenot, Jacques Mathou, Claude Aufaure; *D:* Patrice Leconte; *W:* Patrice Leconte. VHS $19.95 *PAR, BTV* 🎬🎬

Hairspray Waters' first truly mainstream film, if that's even possible, and his funniest. Details the struggle among teenagers in 1962 Baltimore for the top spot in a local TV dance show. Deals with racism and stereotypes, as well as typical "teen" problems (hair-do's and don'ts). Filled with refreshingly tasteful, subtle social satire (although not without typical Waters touches that will please die-hard fans). Lake is lovable and appealing as Divine's daughter; Divine, in his last film, is likeable as an iron-toting mom. Look for Waters in a cameo and Divine as a man. Great '60s music, which Waters refers to as "the only known remedy to today's Hit Parade of Hell."
1988 (PG) 94m/C Ricki Lake, Divine, Jerry Stiller, Colleen Fitzpatrick, Sonny Bono, Deborah Harry, Ruth Brown, Pia Zadora, Ric Ocasek, Michael St. Gerard, Leslie Ann Powers, Shawn Thompson; *Cameos:* John Waters; *D:* John Waters; *W:* John Waters. VHS, Beta $14.95 *COL, FCT* 🎬🎬🎬

The Hairy Ape Screen adaptation of the Eugene O'Neill play. A beast-like coal stoker becomes obsessed with a cool and distant passenger aboard an ocean liner.
1944 90m/B William Bendix, Susan Hayward, John Loder, Dorothy Comingore, Roman Bohnen, Alan Napier; *D:* Alfred Santell. VHS $19.95 *NOS, MRV, FCT* 🎬🎬

Half a Lifetime The stakes are too high for four friends playing a game of poker.

1986 85m/C Keith Carradine, Gary Busey, Nick Mancuso, Saul Rubinek. VHS, Beta $79.95 *HBO* 🎬🎬

Half a Loaf of Kung Fu The worthy bodyguards of Sern Chuan are called upon to deliver a valuable jade statue. Thwarted again and again by ruthless robbers, they falter. Only Chan carries on, meeting the enemy alone. Fast action, good story.
1985 98m/C Jackie Chan. VHS, Beta *NO* 🎬

Half a Sixpence Former musician Sidney, who earlier directed "Showboat" and "Kiss Me Kate," shows a bit less verve in this production. Based on H.G. Wells' 1905 novel, "Kipps," it sports much of the original cast from its Broadway incarnation. Edwardian orphan Steele, a cloth-dealer-in-training, comes into a large sum of money and proceeds to lose it with great dispatch. Somewhere along the way he loses his girlfriend, too, but she takes him back because musicals end happily. ♫Half a Sixpence; Flash, Bang, Wallop!; All In The Cause Of Economy; I'm Not Talking To You; Money To Burn; The Race Is On; I Don't Believe A Word Of It; A Proper Gentleman; She's Too Far Above Me.
1967 148m/B Tommy Steele, Julia Foster, Penelope Horner, Cyril Ritchard, Grover Dale; *D:* George Sidney; *W:* Beverly Cross. VHS $19.95 *PAR, FCT* 🎬🎬🎬

Half a Soldier A spoiled girl gets a big surprise when she steals a car and discovers the body of a gangster in the trunk.
1940 59m/B Heather Angel, John "Dusty" King. VHS, Beta $24.95 *NOS, DVT, HEG* 🎬🎬

The Half-Breed Routine oater with settlers and Apaches fighting, and the obligatory half-breed stuck in the middle.
1951 81m/B Robert Young, Jack Buetel, Janis Carter, Barton MacLane, Reed Hadley, Porter Hall, Connie Gilchrist; *D:* Stuart Gilmore. VHS, Beta $19.98 *TTC* 🎬🎬

Half Human Dull Japanese monster movie about an ape-human who terrorizes Northern Japan. When released in the U.S., Carradine and Morris were added. Without subtitles, just Carradine's narration. Director Honda made better movies before and after, with Godzilla and Rodan.
1958 78m/B John Carradine, Akira Takarada, Morris Ankrum; *D:* Inoshiro Honda. VHS $14.95 *RHI, SNC, MLB* 🎬½

Half Moon Street A brilliant woman scientist supplements her paltry fellowship salary by becoming a hired escort and prostitute, which leads her into various incidents of international intrigue. Adapted from a story by Paul Theroux, "Dr. Slaughter." *AKA:* Escort Girl.
1986 (R) 90m/C Sigourney Weaver, Michael Caine, Keith Buckley, Ian MacInnes; *D:* Bob Swaim. VHS, Beta, 8mm $14.98 *SUE, NLC* 🎬🎬

Half of Heaven A critically popular film about a young Spanish woman who begins to share certain telepathic powers with her wizened grandmother. In Spanish with English subtitles. *AKA:* La Mitad del Cielo.
1986 95m/C Angela Molina, Margarita Lozano; *D:* Manuel Gutierrez Aragon. VHS, Beta $29.95 *PBS, FCT, APD* 🎬🎬🎬

Half-Shot at Sunrise Madcap vaudeville comedians play AWOL soldiers loose in 1918 Paris. Continuous one-liners, sight gags, and slapstick nonsense. First film appearance of comedy team Wheeler and Woolsey.
1930 78m/B Bert Wheeler, Robert Woolsey, Dorothy Lee, Robert Rutherford, Edna May Oliver; *D:* Paul Sloane. VHS, Beta $24.95 *VYY, CAB, DVT* 🎬🎬

Half Slave, Half Free The true story of a free black man in the 1840s who is kidnapped and forced into slavery for 12 years. Made for television as part of the "American Playhouse" series on PBS. Followed by "Charlotte Forten's Mission: Experiment in Freedom." AKA: Solomon Northrup's Odyssey.
1985 113m/C Avery Brooks, Mason Adams, Petronia Paley, John Saxon, Joe Seneca, Michael Tolan, Lee Bryant, Rhetta Greene, Janet League; **D:** Gordon Parks. **VHS, Beta $59.95** XVC, KAR, KUI 🎬🎬½

Hallelujah! Haynes plays an innocent young man who turns to religion and becomes a charasmatic preacher after a family tragedy. He retains all his human weaknesses, however, including falling for the lovely but deceitful McKinney. Great music included traditional spirituals and songs by Berlin, such as "At the End of the Road" and "Swanee Shuffle." Shot on location in Tennessee. The first all-black feature film and the first talkie for director Vidor was given the go-ahead by MGM production chief Irving Thalberg, though he knew the film would be both controversial and get minimal release in the deep South.
1929 90m/B Daniel L. Haynes, Nina Mae McKinney, William Fontaine, Harry Gray, Fannie Belle DeKnight, Everett McGarrity; **D:** King Vidor; **M:** Irving Berlin. **VHS $19.98** MGM, MOV, BTV 🎬🎬🎬½

Hallelujah, I'm a Bum A happy-go-lucky hobo reforms and begins a new life for the sake of a woman. Bizarre Depression-era musical with a Rodgers and Hart score and continuously rhyming dialogue. The British version, due to the slang meaning of "bum," was retitled, substituting "tramp." 🎵You Are Too Beautiful; I'll Do It Again; I've Got To Get Back To New York; What Do You Want With Money?; Hallelujah, I'm A Bum; My Pal Bumper; Dear June; Bumper Found a Grand. AKA: Hallelujah, I'm a Tramp; The Heart of New York; Happy Go Lucky; Lazy Bones.
1933 83m/B Al Jolson, Madge Evans, Frank Morgan, Chester Conklin; **D:** Lewis Milestone; **W:** Ben Hecht, S.N. Behrman; **M:** Richard Rodgers, Lorenz Hart. **VHS, Beta** LCA, MLB 🎬🎬½

The Hallelujah Trail Denver mining town in the late 1800s is about to batten down the hatches for a long winter, and there's not a drop of whiskey to be had. The U.S. Cavalry sends a shipment to the miners, but temperance leader Cora Templeton Massingale (Remick) and her bevy of ladies against liquor stand between the shipment and the would-be whistle whetters. Limp Western satire directed by Preston Sturges' brother, who fared much better when he kept a straight face (he also directed "The Great Escape"). Based on Bill Gulick's novel, "The Hallelujah Train." Two-laserdisc set includes additional footage (though it's already overlong), the original trailer, and a letterboxing.
1965 166m/C Burt Lancaster, Lee Remick, Jim Hutton, Pamela Tiffin, Donald Pleasence, Brian Keith, Martin Landau; **D:** John Sturges; **W:** John Gay; **M:** Elmer Bernstein. **VHS $29.99** MGM, FCT 🎬🎬

Halloween John Carpenter's horror classic has been acclaimed "the most successful independent motion picture of all time." A deranged youth returns to his hometown with murderous intent after fifteen years in an asylum. Very, very scary—you feel this movie more than see it.
1978 (R) 90m/C Jamie Lee Curtis, Donald Pleasence, Nancy Loomis, P.J. Soles; **D:** John Carpenter; **W:** John Carpenter; **M:** John Carpenter. **VHS, Beta $19.98** MED, VTR 🎬🎬🎬½

Halloween 2: The Nightmare Isn't Over! Trying to pick up where "Halloween" left off, the sequel begins with the escape of vicious killer Michael, who continues to murder and terrorize the community of Haddonfield, Illinois. Lacking the innovative intentions of its predecessor, it relies on old-fashioned buckets of blood. No chills, just trauma. Co-scripted by Carpenter, director of the original.
1981 (R) 92m/C Jamie Lee Curtis, Donald Pleasence, Jeffrey Kramer, Charles Cyphers, Lance Guest; **D:** Rick Rosenthal; **W:** John Carpenter; **M:** John Carpenter. **VHS, Beta $14.98** MCA 🎬½

Halloween 3: Season of the Witch Modern druid plans to kill 50 million children with his specially made Halloween masks. Produced by John Carpenter, this second sequel to the 1978 horror classic is not based on the events or characters of its predecessors or successors. Followed by "Halloween 4," and "Halloween 5: The Revenge of Michael Myers" (1989).
1982 (R) 98m/C Tom Atkins, Stacey Nelkin, Dan O'Herlihy, Ralph Strait; **D:** Tommy Lee Wallace; **M:** John Carpenter. **VHS, Beta $14.98** MCA 🎬🎬

Halloween 4: The Return of Michael Myers The third sequel, wherein the lunatic that won't die returns home to kill his niece.
1988 (R) 88m/C Donald Pleasence, Ellie Cornell, Danielle Harris, Michael Pataki; **D:** Dwight Little. **VHS, Beta $14.98** FOX 🎬

Halloween 5: The Revenge of Michael Myers Fifth in the series, this Halloween is an improvement over 2, 3, and 4, thanks to a few well-directed scare scenes. Unfortunately, the plot remains the same: a psycho behemoth chases down and kills more teens. An open ending promises yet another installment.
1989 (R) 96m/C Donald Pleasence, Ellie Cornell, Danielle Harris, Don Shanks, Betty Carvalho; **D:** Dominique Othenin-Girard; **W:** Shem Bitterman. **VHS, Beta $14.98** FOX 🎬½

Halloween Night Ancient evil rises up to destroy the perfect small town.
1990 (R) 90m/C Hy Pyke, Katrina Garner; **D:** Emilio P. Miraglio. **VHS $59.95** ATL 🎬🎬

Halloween with the Addams Family A really pathetic production spawned during the "reunion" craze of the late '70s, sparked only by the lively performance of Coogan's Uncle Fester and the always lovable Lurch. Made for television.
1979 87m/C John Astin, Carolyn Jones, Jackie Coogan, Ted Cassidy. **VHS, Beta** GKK Woof!

The Halls of Montezuma Large, bombastic WWII combat epic. Depicts the Marines fighting the Japanese in the Pacific.
1950 113m/C Richard Widmark, Jack Palance, Reginald Gardiner, Robert Wagner, Karl Malden, Richard Boone, Richard Hylton, Skip Homeier, Jack Webb, Neville Brand, Martin Milner, Bert Freed; **D:** Lewis Milestone. **VHS, Beta $14.98** FOX 🎬🎬½

Hallucination Early flower-power exploiter about expatriate acid heads who murder an antique dealer under the influence of LSD and then attempt to hide at a monastery. Depicts LSD as the catalyst in bringing out the group's criminal behavior. In sepia while everyone's cool, breaking into color during the head trips. AKA: Hallucination Generation.
1967 90m/C George Montgomery, Danny Stone; **D:** Edward Mann. **VHS, Beta $19.98** VDC Woof!

Hallucinations of a Deranged Mind A compilation of all the magic moments ever censored by the Brazilian military dictatorship. Includes scenes banned from over 10 different Marins films, including his "Coffin Joe" character. In Spanish with English subtitles.
1970 ?m/C Jose Mojica Marins; **D:** Jose Mojica Marins. **VHS $20.00** SMW, FCT 🎬

Hambone & Hillie An elderly woman makes a 3000-mile trek across the United States to search for the dog she lost in an airport.
1984 (PG) 97m/C Lillian Gish, Timothy Bottoms, Candy Clark, O.J. Simpson, Robert Walker Jr., Jack Carter, Alan Hale Jr., Anne Lockhart; **D:** Roy Watts. **VHS, Beta $19.95** STE 🎬

Hamburger Hill Popular war epic depicting the famous battle between Americans and Viet Cong over a useless hill in Vietnam. Made in the heyday of 1980s Vietnam backlash, and possibly the most realistic and bloodiest of the lot.
1987 (R) 104m/C Michael Dolan, Daniel O'Shea, Dylan McDermott, Tommy Swerdlow, Courtney B. Vance, Anthony Barille, Michael Boatman, Don Cheadle, Tim Quill, Don James, M. A. Nickles; **D:** John Irvin; **W:** Jim Carabatsos; **M:** Philip Glass. **VHS, Beta $14.98** LIV, VES, FCT 🎬🎬½

Hamburger...The Motion Picture The life and times of students at Busterburger U., the only college devoted to hamburger franchise management.
1986 (R) 90m/C Leigh McCloskey, Dick Butkus, Randi Brooks, Sandy Hackett; **D:** Mike Marvin; **M:** Elmer Bernstein. **VHS, Beta $9.95** MED 🎬

Hamlet Splendid adaptation of Shakespeare's dramatic play. Hamlet vows vengeance on the murderer of his father in this tight version of the four hour stage play. Some scenes were cut out, including all of Rosencrantz and Guildenstern. Beautifully photographed in Denmark. An Olivier triumph. Remade several times.
1948 153m/B Laurence Olivier, Basil Sydney, Felix Aylmer, Jean Simmons, Stanley Holloway, Peter Cushing, Christopher Lee, Eileen Herlie, John Laurie, Esmond Knight, Anthony Quayle; **D:** Laurence Olivier; **W:** Alan Dent; **M:** William Walton; **V:** John Gielgud. Academy Awards '48: Best Actor (Olivier), Best Art Direction/Set Decoration (B & W), Best Costume Design (B & W), Best Picture; Nominations: Best Director (Olivier), Best Supporting Actress (Simmons), Best Original Score; British Academy Awards '48: Best Film; Golden Globe Awards '49: Best Actor—Drama (Olivier). **VHS $19.95** PAR, BTV, HMV 🎬🎬🎬🎬

Hamlet Williamson brings to the screen his stage performance as the classic Shakespeare character. Something is lost in the process, although there are some redeeming moments including those with Faithfull as Ophelia.
1969 (G) 114m/C Nicol Williamson, Anthony Hopkins, Marianne Faithfull, Gordon Jackson, Judy Parfitt, Mark Dingham, Anjelica Huston; **D:** Tony Richardson. **VHS, Beta $19.95** COL 🎬🎬½

Hamlet Zeffirelli—in his fourth attempt at Shakespeare—creates a surprisingly energetic and accessible interpretation of the Bard's moody play. Gibson brings charm, humor and a carefully calculated sense of violence, not to mention a good deal of solid flesh, to the eponymous role, and handles the language skillfully (although if you seek a poetic Dane, stick with Olivier). Exceptional work from Scofield and Bates; Close seems a tad hysterical (not to mention too young to play Gibson's mother), but brings insight and nuance to her role. Purists beware: this isn't a completely faithful adaptation. Beautifully

costumed; shot on location in Northern Scotland.
1990 (PG) 135m/C Mel Gibson, Glenn Close, Alan Bates, Paul Scofield, Ian Holm, Helena Bonham Carter; **D:** Franco Zeffirelli; **W:** Franco Zeffirelli, Christopher DeVore. **VHS, Beta, 8mm** $19.98 WAR, BTV, FCT ♫♫♫½

Hammersmith is Out A violent lunatic cons an orderly into letting him escape. Chases, romance and craziness follow.
1972 (R) 108m/C Richard Burton, Elizabeth Taylor, Peter Ustinov, Beau Bridges, John Schuck; **D:** Peter Ustinov. **VHS, Beta** $59.95 PSM ♫½

Hammett After many directors and script rewrites, Wenders was assigned to this arch neo-noir what-if scenario. Depicts Dashiell Hammett solving a complex crime himself, an experience he uses in his novels. Interesting, but ultimately botched studio exercise, like many from executive producer Francis Coppola, who is said to have reshot much of the film.
1982 (PG) 98m/C Frederic Forrest, Peter Boyle, Sylvia Sidney, Elisha Cook Jr., Marilu Henner; **D:** Wim Wenders; **M:** John Barry. **VHS, Beta** $69.95 WAR, ING ♫♫

Hamsin A Jewish landowner and an Arab worker encounter difficulties in their relationship when the government announces plans to confiscate Arab land. In Hebrew with English subtitles.
1983 90m/C Shlomo Tarshish, Yasin Shawap, Hemda Levy, Ruth Geler; **D:** Daniel Wachsmann. **VHS, Beta** $79.95 ERG ♫♫♫

The Hand During WWII, three British POWs are tortured by the Japanese. Refusing to give information, two of them have their right hands cut off. The third opts to talk, thereby keeping his hand. After the war, a series of murders occur in London where the victims have their hands amputated. Could there be a connection?
1960 61m/B Derek Bond, Ronald Lee Hunt, Reed de Rouen, Ray Cooney, Brian Coleman; **D:** Henry Cass. **VHS, Beta** $16.95 SNC ♫½

The Hand A gifted cartoonist's hand is severed in a car accident. Soon, the hand is on the loose with a mind of its own, seeking out victims with an obsessive vengeance. Stone's first film is a unique, surreal psycho-horror pastiche consistently underrated by most critics.
1981 (R) 105m/C Michael Caine, Andrea Marcovicci, Annie McEnroe, Bruce McGill, Viveca Lindfors; **D:** Oliver Stone; **M:** James Horner. **VHS, Beta** $19.98 WAR ♫♫♫

The Hand that Rocks the Cradle DeMornay is Peyton Flanders, the nanny from hell in an otherwise predictable thriller. Sciorra's role is a thankless one as pregnant and unbelievably naive Claire Bartel, who unwittingly starts a horrific chain of events when she levels charges of molestation against her obstetrician. Transparent plot preys on the worst fears of viewers, and doesn't offer anything innovative or new. See this one for DeMornay's Jekyll and Hyde performance.
1992 (R) 110m/C Annabella Sciorra, Rebecca DeMornay, Matt McCoy, Ernie Hudson, Julianne Moore, Madeline Zima, John de Lancie, Mitchell Laurance; **D:** Curtis Hanson; **W:** Amanda Silver; **M:** Graeme Revell. **VHS, Beta** $94.95 HPH ♫♫½

A Handful of Dust A dry, stately adaptation of the bitter Evelyn Waugh novel about a stuffy young aristocrat's wife's careless infidelity and how it sends her innocent husband to a tragic downfall. A well-meaning version that captures Waugh's cynical satire almost in spite of itself. Set in post-WWI England.

1988 (PG) 114m/C James Wilby, Kristin Scott Thomas, Rupert Graves, Alec Guinness, Anjelica Huston, Judi Dench, Cathryn Harrison, Pip Torrens; **D:** Charles Sturridge; **W:** Tim Sullivan, Derek Granger, Charles Sturridge; **M:** George Fenton. Academy Awards '88 Nominations: Best Costume Design; British Academy Awards '88: Best Supporting Actress (Dench). **VHS, Beta** $19.95 COL, TVC ♫♫♫

The Handmaid's Tale A cool, shallow but nonetheless chilling nightmare based on Margaret Atwood's bestselling novel, about a woman caught in the machinations of a near-future society so sterile it enslaves the few fertile women and forces them into being child-bearing "handmaids."
1990 (R) 109m/C Natasha Richardson, Robert Duvall, Faye Dunaway, Aidan Quinn, Elizabeth McGovern, Victoria Tennant, Blanche Baker, Traci Lind; **D:** Volker Schlondorff; **W:** Harold Pinter. **VHS, Beta** $19.98 HBO, FCT, IME ♫♫½

Hands Across the Border A musical western in which Roy helps a woman find the men who killed her father.
1943 72m/B Roy Rogers, Ruth Terry, Guinn Williams, Onslow Stevens, Mary Treen, Joseph Crehan; **D:** Joseph Kane. **VHS** $19.95 NOS, DVT, TIM ♫½

Hands of a Stranger Another undistinguished entry in the long line of remakes of "The Hands of Orlac." A pianist who loses his hands in an accident is given the hands of a murderer, and his new hands want to do more than tickle the ivories. Kellerman has a very small role as does former "Sheena" McCalla.
1962 95m/B Paul Lukather, Joan Harvey, James Stapleton, Sally Kellerman, Irish McCalla; **D:** Newton Arnold. **VHS** $19.98 SNC ♫♫

Hands of a Stranger Policeman's wife is raped during an adulterous tryst. As the painful truth dawns on the cop, he himself dallies with a compassionate lady D.A. while hunting the attacker. About as sordid as a network TV-movie gets without toppling into sleaze; strong acting and a sober script pull it through. But the plot, from Robert Daly's novel, doesn't justify miniseries treatment; the two-cassette package is excessively long.
1987 179m/C Armand Assante, Beverly D'Angelo, Blair Brown, Michael Lerner, Philip Casnoff, Arliss Howard; **D:** Larry Elikann; **W:** Arthur Kopit. **VHS** $89.95 WOV ♫♫½

Hands of Death Thieves use their Ninja skills to stop any one in their path to evil. Action-packed, somewhat contrived.
1988 90m/C Richard Harrison, Mike Abbott; **D:** Godfrey Ho. **VHS, Beta** IMP ♫

The Hands of Orlac Classic silent film about a pianist whose hands are mutilated in an accident. His hands are replaced by those of a murderer, and his urge to kill becomes overwhelming. Contains restored footage.
1925 ?m/B Conrad Veidt, Fritz Kortner, Carmen Cartellieri, Paul Adkonas; **D:** Robert Wiene. **VHS** $19.95 LSV ♫♫

The Hands of Orlac Third remake of Maurice Renard's classic tale. When a concert pianist's hands are mutilated in an accident, he receives a graft of a murderer's hands. Obsession sweeps the musician, as he believes his new hands are incapable of music, only violence. Bland adaptation of the original story. **AKA:** Hands of the Strangler.
1960 95m/B Mel Ferrer, Christopher Lee, Felix Aylmer, Basil Sydney, Donald Wolfit, Donald Pleasence; **D:** Edmond T. Greville; **M:** Claude Bolling. **VHS** $16.95 SNC ♫♫

Hands of Steel A ruthless cyborg carries out a mission to find and kill an important scientist. Terrible acting, and lousy writing: an all-around woofer!
1986 (R) 94m/C Daniel Greene, John Saxon, Janet Agren, Claudio Cassinelli, George Eastman; **D:** Martin Dolman. **VHS, Beta** $79.98 LIV Woof!

Hands of the Ripper Jack the Ripper's daughter returns to London where she works as a medium by day and stalks the streets by night. Classy Hammer horror variation on the perennial theme.
1971 (R) 85m/C Eric Porter, Angharad Rees, Jane Merrow, Keith Bell; **D:** Peter Sasdy; **M:** Christopher Gunning. **VHS, Beta** $19.98 MLB ♫♫½

Hands Up Jaunty Confederate spy (played by much-overlooked American comedian Griffith) attempts, amidst much comic nonsense, to thwart Yankee gold mining during the Civil War. Silent.
1926 50m/B Raymond Griffith, Mack Swain, Marion Nixon, Montagu Love; **D:** Clarence Badger. **VHS, Beta** $19.95 GPV ♫♫½

Hands Up Famed Polish film finished in 1967 but not released until 1981 for political reasons (prologue shot in '81 included). Doctors at a medical school reunion reflect upon the effect of Stalinist rule on their education and lives. In Polish with English subtitles. **AKA:** Rece do Gory.
1981 78m/C **D:** Jerzy Skolimowski. **VHS, Beta** $49.95 FCT ♫♫♫

Hang 'Em High A cowboy is saved from a lynching and vows to hunt down the gang that nearly killed him in this American-made spaghetti western. Eastwood's first major vehicle made outside of Europe.
1967 114m/C Clint Eastwood, Inger Stevens, Ed Begley Sr., Pat Hingle, James MacArthur; **D:** Ted Post. **VHS, Beta** $19.98 MGM, TLF ♫♫½

Hangar 18 Silly sci-fi drama about two astronauts who collide with a UFO during a shuttle flight. Later they learn that the government is hiding it in a hangar and they try to prove its existence. Shown on TV as "Invasion Force" with an entirely new ending. **AKA:** Invasion Force.
1980 (PG) 97m/C Darren McGavin, Robert Vaughn, Gary Collins, James Hampton, Phillip Abbott, Pamela Bellwood, Tom Hallick, Cliff Osmond, Joseph Campanella; **D:** James L. Conway; **W:** David O'Malley. **VHS, Beta** $19.99 WOV ♫½

The Hanged Man Tale of a gunslinger in the Old West who mystically escapes death by hanging. Reborn, he re-evaluates the meaning of justice. Made for television.
1974 78m/C Steve Forrest, Cameron Mitchell, Sharon Acker, Dean Jagger, Will Geer, Barbara Luna, Rafael Campos; **D:** Michael Caffey. **VHS** NO ♫♫

Hangfire When a New Mexican prison is evacuated thanks to a nasty chemical explosion, several prisoners decide it's time for a furlough, and they elect the local sheriff's wife as a traveling companion. Another mediocre actioner from director Maris, it gets an extra bone for stunts kids shouldn't try at home.
1991 91m/C Brad Davis, Yaphet Kotto, Lee De Broux, Jan-Michael Vincent, George Kennedy, Kim Delaney; **D:** Peter Maris; **W:** Brian D. Jeffries. **VHS** $89.98 COL ♫♫

Hangin' with the Homeboys One night in the lives of four young men. Although the Bronx doesn't offer much for any of them, they have little interest in escaping its confines, and they are more than willing to complain. Characters are insightfully written and well portrayed, with strongest work from

Serrano as a Puerto Rican who is trying to pass himself off as Italian. Lack of plot may frustrate some viewers.
1991 (R) 89m/C Mario Joyner, Doug E. Doug, John Leguizamo, Nestor Serrano, Kimberly Russell, Mary B. Ward; **D:** Joseph P. Vasquez; **W:** Joseph P. Vasquez. **VHS $19.95** COL, FCT ✍✍✍

Hanging on a Star A small rock band encounters many comic adventures as it climbs its way up the charts. Raffin stars as the band's persistent and competent road agent.
1978 (PG) 92m/C Deborah Raffin, Lane Caudell, Wolfman Jack, Jason Parker, Danil Torppe; **D:** Mike MacFarland. **VHS, Beta $79.95** MGM ✍

The Hanging Tree Cooper plays a frontier doctor who rescues a thief (Piazza) from a lynch mob and nurses a temporarily blind girl (Schell). Malden is the bad guy who tries to attack Schell and Cooper shoots him. The townspeople take Cooper out to "The Hanging Tree" but this time it's Schell and Piazza who come to his rescue. Slow-paced western with good performances. Scott's screen debut.
1959 108m/B Gary Cooper, Maria Schell, Ben Piazza, Karl Malden, George C. Scott, Karl Swenson, Virginia Gregg, King Donovan; **D:** Delmer Daves; **W:** Wendell Mayes, Halsted Welles; **M:** Max Steiner. **VHS $19.98** WAR ✍✍✍

The Hanging Woman A man is summoned to the reading of a relative's will, and discovers the corpse of a young woman hanging in a cemetery. As he investigates the mystery, he uncovers a local doctor's plans to zombify the entire town. Not bad at all and quite creepy once the zombies are out in force. Euro-horror star Naschy plays the necrophiliac grave digger, Igor. **AKA:** Return of the Zombies; Beyond the Living Dead.
1972 91m/C Stan Cooper, Vickie Nesbitt, Marcella Wright, Catherine Gilbert, Gerard Tichy, Paul Naschy; **D:** John Davidson. **VHS, Beta $59.95** VCI, TIM ✍✍½

Hangman's Knot Members of the Confederate Cavalry rob a Union train, not knowing that the war is over. Now facing criminal charges, they are forced to take refuge in a stagecoach stop. Well-done horse opera with a wry sense of humor.
1952 80m/C Randolph Scott, Donna Reed, Claude Jarman Jr., Frank Faylen, Glenn Langan, Richard Denning, Lee Marvin, Jeanette Nolan; **D:** Roy Huggins. **VHS, Beta** GKK ✍✍½

Hangmen Ex-CIA agents battle it out on the East side of New York. If you're into very violent, very badly-acted films, then this one's for you.
1987 (R) 88m/C Jake La Motta, Rick Washburne, Doug Thomas; **D:** J. Christian Ingvordsen. **VHS, Beta $29.95** ACA Woof!

Hanky Panky Insipid comic thriller in which Wilder and Radner become involved in a search for top-secret plans.
1982 (PG) 107m/C Gene Wilder, Gilda Radner, Richard Widmark, Kathleen Quinlan; **D:** Sidney Poitier. **VHS, Beta $14.95** COL ✍½

Hanna K. Story of divided passions set in the tumultuous state of Israel. American lawyer Clayburgh tries to settle her personal and political affairs with various Middle-Eastern men. Mediocre Disappointing. Release generated controversy over pro-Palestine stance.
1983 (R) 111m/C Jill Clayburgh, Gabriel Byrne, Jean Yanne, Muhamad Bakri, David Clennon, Oded Kotler; **D:** Constantin Costa-Gavras. **VHS, Beta $59.95** MCA ✍✍

Hannah and Her Sisters Allen's grand epic about a New York showbiz family, its three adult sisters and their various complex romantic entanglements. Excellent performances by the entire cast, especially Caine and Hershey. Classic Allen themes of life, love, death, and desire are explored in an assured and sensitive manner. Witty, ironic, and heartwarming.
1986 (PG) 103m/C Mia Farrow, Barbara Hershey, Dianne Wiest, Michael Caine, Woody Allen, Maureen O'Sullivan, Lloyd Nolan, Sam Waterston, Carrie Fisher, Max von Sydow, Julie Kavner, Daniel Stern, Tony Roberts, John Turturro; **D:** Woody Allen; **W:** Woody Allen. Academy Awards '86: Best Original Screenplay, Best Supporting Actor (Caine), Best Supporting Actress (Wiest); Nominations: Best Art Direction/Set Decoration; Academy Awards '86: Best Director (Allen), Best Film Editing, Best Picture; Golden Globe Awards '87: Best Film—Musical/Comedy; New York Film Critics Awards '86: Best Film. **VHS, Beta $19.99** HBO, BTV ✍✍✍½

Hanna's War A moving film about Hanna Senesh, a young Hungarian Jew living in Palestine, who volunteered for a suicide mission behind Nazi lines during WWII. After her capture by the Germans, she was killed, and is now considered by many to have been a martyr. Detmers is very believable as Hanna and Burstyn puts in a good performance as her mother.
1988 (PG-13) 148m/C Ellen Burstyn, Maruschka Detmers, Anthony Andrews, Donald Pleasence, David Warner, Denholm Elliott, Vincenzo Ricotta, Ingrid Pitt; **D:** Menahem Golan; **W:** Menahem Golan; **M:** Dov Seltzer. **VHS, Beta $9.99** CCB, MED, SWC ✍✍½

Hannie Caulder A woman hires a bounty hunter to avenge her husband's murder and her own rape at the hands of three bandits. Excellent casting but uneven direction. Boyd is uncredited as the preacher.
1972 (R) 87m/C Raquel Welch, Robert Culp, Ernest Borgnine, Strother Martin, Jack Elam, Christopher Lee, Diana Dors, Stephen Boyd; **D:** Burt Kennedy; **W:** Burt Kennedy. **VHS $14.95** PAR, FCT, VTR ✍✍

Hanoi Hilton A brutal drama about the sufferings of American POWs in Vietnamese prison camps. Non-stop torture, filth, and degradation.
1987 (R) 126m/C Michael Moriarty, Paul LeMat, Jeffrey Jones, Lawrence Pressman, Stephen Davies, David Soul, Rick Fitts, Aki Aleong, Gloria Carlin; **D:** Lionel Chetwynd; **W:** Lionel Chetwynd. **VHS, Beta** WAR ✍½

Hanover Street An American bomber pilot and a married British nurse fall in love in war-torn Europe. Eventually the pilot must work with the husband of the woman he loves on a secret mission. A sappy, romantic tearjerker.
1979 (PG) 109m/C Harrison Ford, Lesley-Anne Down, Christopher Plummer, Alec McCowen; **D:** Peter Hyams; **W:** Peter Hyams; **M:** John Barry. **VHS, Beta $14.95** COL ✍✍

Hans Brinker Young Hans Brinker and his sister participate in an ice skating race, hoping to win a pair of silver skates. A musical version of the classic tale.
1969 103m/C Robin Askwith, Eleanor Parker, Richard Basehart, Cyril Ritchard, John Gregson; **D:** Robert Scheerer. **VHS, Beta $19.98** WAR, OM ✍✍½

Hans Christian Andersen Sentimental musical story of Hans Christian Andersen, a young cobbler who has a great gift for storytelling. Digitally remastered editions available with stereo sound and original trailer. ♫The King's New Clothes; I'm Hans Christian Andersen; Wonderful Copenhagen; Thumbelina; The Ugly Duckling; Anywhere I Wander; The Inch Worm; No Two People.
1952 112m/C Danny Kaye, Farley Granger, Zizi Jeanmarie, Joey Walsh; **D:** Charles Vidor; **W:** Moss Hart; **M:** Frank Loesser. **VHS, Beta $14.98** HBO, SUE, FCT ✍✍✍

Hansel and Gretel From Shelly Duvall's "Faerie Tale Theatre" comes the story of two young children who get more than they bargained for when they eat a gingerbread house.
1982 51m/C Rick Schroder, Joan Collins, Paul Dooley, Bridgette Anderson; **D:** James Frawley. **VHS, Beta $14.98** KUI, FOX, FCT ✍✍

Hanussen The third of Szabo and Brandauer's price-of-fame trilogy (after "Mephisto" and "Colonel Redl"), in which a talented German magician and clairvoyant (based on a true life figure) collaborates with the Nazis during their rise to power in the 1930s, although he can foresee the outcome of their reign. In German with English subtitles.
1988 (R) 110m/C Klaus Maria Brandauer, Erland Josephson, Walter Schmidinger; **D:** Istvan Szabo. **VHS, Beta $79.95** COL, ING ✍✍✍½

The Happiest Days of Your Life During the London Blitz, a girls academy is evacuated to the country and mistakeningly billeted with a boys school. The headmaster and headmistress clash and the bewildered students all try to get along. Good cast, lots of laughs. Adapted from a play by John Dighton.
1950 81m/B Alastair Sim, Margaret Rutherford, Joyce Grenfell, Edward Rigby, Guy Middleton, John Bentley, Bernadette O'Farrell, Richard Wattis, Muriel Aked, Patricia Owens, John Turnbull, Arthur Howard; **D:** Frank Launder; **W:** Frank Launder, John Dighton; **M:** Mischa Spoliansky. **VHS $39.95** HMV, ING ✍✍✍

The Happiest Millionaire A Disney film about a newly immigrated lad who finds a job as butler in the home of an eccentric millionaire. Based on the book "My Philadelphia Father," by Kyle Chrichton. ♫What's Wrong With That?; Watch Your Footwork; Valentine Candy; Strengthen the Dwelling; I'll Always be Irish; Bye-Yum Pum Pum; I Believe in This Country; Detroit; There Are Those.
1967 118m/C Fred MacMurray, Tommy Steele, Greer Garson, Geraldine Page, Lesley Ann Warren, John Davidson; **D:** Norman Tokar. **VHS, Beta** DIS, OM ✍✍

Happily Ever After Las Vegas starmaker recruits and manipulates two green performers. Show business life in Vegas is given a truthful treatment in made-for-television drama.
1982 95m/C Suzanne Somers, John Rubinstein, Eric (Hans Gudegast) Braeden; **D:** Robert Scheerer. **VHS, Beta $69.95** TLF ✍✍

Happily Ever After A Brazilian housewife meets a bisexual transvestite and has a passionate affair, bringing her into the depths of the criminal underworld. In Portuguese with English subtitles. Contains nudity. **AKA:** Alem Da Paixao.
1986 106m/C Regina Duarte, Paul Castelli; **D:** Bruno Barreto. **VHS, Beta $69.95** FCT, ING, TPV ✍✍

Happily Ever After Sequel to "Snow White" begins where the original ends, but isn't connected to the Walt Disney classic. Snow White and her Prince prepare for their wedding when the Wicked Queen is found dead by her brother, who vows revenge. So it's up to Snow and the Dwarfelles (Disney said no to using the Dwarfs), female cousins of the original Dwarfs, to rescue him. Interesting choices from the casting department:

H

Diller is Mother Nature and Asner provides the voice of a rapping owl. Poorly animated drivel designed to ride in on Disney's coattails. While the kids might enjoy it, save your money for the original, finally slated for a video release.
1993 (G) 80m/C D: John Howley; **W:** Martha Moran, Robby London; **V:** Dom DeLuise, Phyllis Diller, Zsa Zsa Gabor, Ed Asner, Sally Kellerman, Irene Cara, Carol Channing, Tracey Ullman. **VHS $24.95** *WOV, WTA ✍️½*

Happiness Another zany comedy from the land of the hammer and sickle. Banned in Russia for 40 years, it was deemed to be risque and a bit too biting with the social satire. Silent with orchestral score.
1934 69m/B D: Alexander Medvedkin. **VHS $29.95** *KIV, FCT, ING ✍️✍️*

Happy Anniversary 007: 25 Years of James Bond Film clip retrospective of the dashing British spy created by Ian Fleming. Hosted by Roger Moore.
1987 59m/C Sean Connery, Roger Moore, George Lazenby, Timothy Dalton; **D:** Mel Stuart. **VHS, Beta $14.98** *FOX ✍️½*

Happy Birthday, Gemini A coming-of-age comedy about a young man on his 21st birthday worrying about his sexual identity. Based on the play "Gemini" by Albert Innaurato. The closeness of the characters on stage did not translate to the screen.
1980 (R) 107m/C Robert Viharo, Madeline Kahn, Rita Moreno, Alan Rosenberg, Sarah Holcomb, David Marshall Grant, David McIlwraith; **D:** Richard Benner; **W:** Richard Benner. **VHS $14.95** *MGM ✍️½*

Happy Birthday to Me Several elite seniors at an exclusive private school are mysteriously killed by a deranged killer who has a fetish for cutlery.
1981 (R) 108m/C Melissa Sue Anderson, Glenn Ford, Tracy Bregman, Jack Blum, Matt Craven; **D:** J. Lee Thompson. **VHS, Beta $69.95** *COL ✍️½*

The Happy Ending Woman struggles with a modern definition of herself and her marriage, causing pain and confusion for her family. Simmons is solid as the wife and mother seeking herself. Michel LeGrand's theme song "What Are You Doing With the Rest of Your Life?" was a big hit.
1969 (PG) 112m/C Jean Simmons, John Forsythe, Lloyd Bridges, Shirley Jones, Teresa Wright, Dick Shawn, Nanette Fabray, Bobby Darin, Tina Louise; **D:** Richard Brooks; **W:** Richard Brooks. **VHS** *NO ✍️✍️½*

Happy Go Lovely An unscrupulous theatrical producer casts a chorus girl in a leading role in order to get closer to her boyfriend's fortune. Tired plot, but good performances in this lightweight musical. ♫One-Two-Three; Would You, Could You; London Town.
1951 95m/C Vera-Ellen, David Niven, Cesar Romero, Bobby Howes; **D:** H. Bruce Humberstone. **VHS, Beta $24.95** *NOS, MRV, DVT ✍️✍️*

The Happy Hooker Xaviera Hollander's cheeky (and bestselling) memoir of her transition from office girl to "working girl" has been brought to the screen with a sprightly (though sanitary) air of naughtiness, with Redgrave enjoyable in title role. Followed by "The Happy Hooker Goes to Washington" and "The Happy Hooker Goes Hollywood."
1975 (R) 96m/C Lynn Redgrave, Jean-Pierre Aumont, Nicholas Pryor; **D:** Nicholas Sgarro. **VHS, Beta $29.95** *CAN, VES ✍️✍️½*

The Happy Hooker Goes Hollywood Third film inspired by the title of Xaviera Hollander's memoirs, in which the fun-loving Xaviera comes to Hollywood with the intention of making a movie based on her book, but soon meets up with a series of scheming, would-be producers.
1980 (R) 86m/C Martine Beswick, Chris Lemmon, Adam West, Phil Silvers; **D:** Alan Roberts. **VHS, Beta $39.98** *CAN, MCA ✍️*

The Happy Hooker Goes to Washington Further adventures of the world's most famous madam. Heatherton (not Redgrave) is Xaviera Hollander this time, testifying before the U.S. Senate in defense of sex. Fairly stupid attempt to milk box office of original. Second in the holy trilogy of Happy Hooker pictures, which also include "The Happy Hooker" and "The Happy Hooker Goes Hollywood."
1977 (R) 89m/C Joey Heatherton, George Hamilton, Ray Walston, Jack Carter; **D:** William A. Levey. **VHS, Beta $69.95** *CAN, VES ✍️½*

Happy Hour A young brewing scientist discovers a secret formula for beer, and everyone tries to take it from him. Little turns in a good performance as a superspy.
1987 (R) 88m/C Richard Gilliland, Jamie Farr, Tawny Kitaen, Ty Henderson, Rich Little; **D:** John DeBello. **VHS, Beta $19.95** *LIV ✍️½*

Happy Landing Predictable, yet entertaining Henie vehicle about a plane that makes a forced landing in Norway near Henie's home. Romance follows with bandleader Romero and manager Ameche. ♫Hot and Happy; Yonny and his Oompah; You Are The Music to the Words in my Heart; A Gypsy Told Me; You Appeal to Me.
1938 102m/B Sonja Henie, Don Ameche, Jean Hersholt, Ethel Merman, Cesar Romero, Billy Gilbert, Wally Vernon, El Brendel; **D:** Roy Del Ruth; **W:** Milton Sperling, Boris Ingster. **VHS $19.98** *FXV ✍️½*

Happy New Year Charming romantic comedy in which two thieves plan a robbery but get sidetracked by the distracting woman who works next door to the jewelry store. Available in both subtitled and dubbed versions. Remade in 1987. **AKA:** The Happy New Year Caper.
1974 114m/C Francoise Fabian, Lino Ventura, Andre Falcon; **D:** Claude Lelouch; **W:** Claude Lelouch. **VHS, Beta $29.98** *SUE ✍️✍️*

A Happy New Year! Two men and a woman, all engineers in a chemical plant, try to fight off a hangover as they deal with the comings and goings of friends throughout the day and night. In Hungarian with English subtitles.
1979 84m/C Istvan Bujtor, Erika Bodnar, Cecilia Esztergalyos, Andras Balint; **D:** Reszo Szoreny; **W:** Peter Modos, Reszo Szoreny. **VHS $59.95** *FCT ✍️✍️*

Happy New Year Two sophisticated thieves plan and execute an elaborate jewel heist that goes completely awry. Remake of the 1974 French film of the same name.
1987 (PG) 86m/C Peter Falk, Wendy Hughes, Tom Courtenay, Charles Durning, Joan Copeland; **D:** John G. Avildsen; **W:** Warren Lane; **M:** Bill Conti. **VHS, Beta $79.95** *COL ✍️✍️*

Happy New Year, Charlie Brown Strife upsets the Peanuts gang as the New Year's Eve gala becomes a source of tension.
1982 25m/C D: Bill Melendez, Sam Jaimes. **VHS, Beta $9.95** *BAR, KAR, WTA ✍️✍️½*

Happy Since I Met You Comedy-drama about a scatterbrained drama teacher and a struggling young actor who become romantically involved.

1989 55m/C Julie Walters, Duncan Preston; **Cameos:** Tracey Ullman, Jim Bowen; **D:** Baz Taylor; **W:** Victoria Wood. **VHS, Beta $150.00** *BIJ, WOM ✍️✍️*

Happy Together An eager freshman accidentally gets a beautiful, impulsive girl as his roommate. Together they meet the challenges of secondary education.
1989 (PG-13) 102m/C Helen Slater, Patrick Dempsey, Dan Schneider, Marius Weyers, Barbara Babcock; **D:** Mel Damski; **M:** Robert Folk. **VHS, Beta $89.95** *LIV ✍️*

Hard-Boiled Police Inspector Yuen (Woo regular Yun-fat) is investigating, with his usual excessive force, the Triads organized crime syndicate and a group of gun smugglers who killed his partner. He joins forces with Tony, an undercover cop who's working as a gangster hitman. There's lots of gunplay and betrayals among all the participants. Usual Woo way with violence and action sequences although the plot is more contrived. In Mandarin and Chinese with English subtitles. **AKA:** Lashou Shentan.
1992 126m/C Chow Yun-fat, Tony Leung, Philip Chan, Anthony Wong, Teresa Mo; **D:** John Woo; **W:** Barry Wong; **M:** Michael Gibbs. **VHS $39.95** *FCT ✍️✍️*

Hard-Boiled Mahoney Slip, Sach, and the rest of the Bowery Boys try to solve a mystery involving mysterious women and missing men. The last film in the series for Bobby Jordan, whose career was ended when he was injured in an accident involving a falling elevator.
1947 64m/B Leo Gorcey, Huntz Hall, Bobby Jordan, Billy Benedict, David Gorcey, Gabriel Dell, Teala Loring, Dan Seymour, Bernard Gorcey, Patti Brill, Betty Compson; **D:** William Beaudine. **VHS $14.98** *WAR ✍️✍️½*

Hard Choices A 15-year-old Tennessee boy is unjustly charged as an accessory to murder, until a female social worker decides to help him. From then on, nothing is predictable. Excellent work by Klenck, McCleery, and Seitz. Don't miss Sayles as an unusual drug dealer. Intelligent, surprising, and powerful. Based on a true story, this is a low profile film that deserves to be discovered.
1984 90m/C Margaret Klenck, Gary McCleery, John Seitz, John Sayles, Liane Curtis, J.T. Walsh, Spalding Gray; **D:** Rick King; **W:** Rick King. **VHS, Beta $79.95** *BAR, LHV, WAR ✍️✍️✍️*

Hard Country Caught between her best friend's success as a country singer and the old values of a woman's place, a small town girl questions her love and her life style. A warm and intelligent rural drama. Basinger's debut.
1981 (PG) 104m/C Jan-Michael Vincent, Kim Basinger, Michael Parks, Gailard Sartain, Tanya Tucker, Ted Neeley, Daryl Hannah, Richard Moll; **D:** David Greene; **W:** Michael Kane; **M:** Michael Martin Murphy. **VHS** *NO ✍️✍️½*

A Hard Day's Night The Beatles' first film is a joyous romp through an average "day in the life" of the Fab Four, shot in a pseudo-documentary style with great flair by Lester and noted as the first music video. Laser version includes original trailer and an interview with Lester. ♫A Hard Day's Night; Tell Me Why; I Should Have Known Better; She Loves You; I'm Happy Just To Dance With You; If I Fell; And I Love Her; This Boy; Can't Buy Me Love.
1964 90m/B John Lennon, Paul McCartney, George Harrison, Ringo Starr; **D:** Richard Lester. **VHS, Beta, CDV $19.98** *MVD, MPI, VYG ✍️✍️✍️½*

Hard Drivin' Rowdy action featuring Southern stock car drivers with well shot race scenes from the Southern 500.

VIDEOHOUND'S GOLDEN MOVIE RETRIEVER • 458 ▲

1960 92m/C Rory Calhoun, John Gentry, Alan Hale Jr.; *D:* Paul Helmick. **VHS, Beta** *NO* ⨂

Hard Frame An ex-con returns home hoping all will turn to sweetness and light when he attempts to make nice-nice with his stepdad, who wouldn't stick by him during his trial. Reynolds' debut into TV moviedom; could be the hirsute actor was thinking of this one when he said his movies were the kind they show in prisons and airplanes because nobody can leave. *AKA:* Hunters Are For Killing.
1970 100m/C Burt Reynolds, Melvyn Douglas, Suzanne Pleshette, Larry Storch, Martin Balsam, Peter Brown, Jill Banner, Donald (Don "Red") Barry, Angus Duncan, Ivor Francis; *D:* Bernard Girard. **VHS** $9.95 *SIM* ⨂½

Hard Hombre Gibson rides and shoots across the screen in one of his best western adventures.
1931 60m/B Hoot Gibson, Lena Basquette, Skeeter Bill Robbins, Jack Byron, Glenn Strange; *D:* Otto Brower. **VHS, Beta** $29.95 *GPV, VCN, VCI* ⨂⨂

Hard Hunted Three macho undercover agents try to avoid death at the hands of high-tech guerillas trying to steal nuclear weapons. No-brain actioner, heavy on the display of feminine charms.
1992 (R) 97m/C Dona Speir, Roberta Vasquez, Cynthia Brimhall, Bruce Penhall, R.J. Moore, Tony Peck, Rodrigo Obregon, Al Leong, Michael J. Shane; *D:* Andy Sidaris; *W:* Andy Sidaris. **VHS** $89.95 *COL* ⨂½

Hard Knocks An ex-con goes from one tragic situation to another, and is eventually stalked by shotgun-wielding rednecks in this grim, powerful drama. Excellent performance by Mann holds this picture together.
1980 85m/C Tracey Mann, Jim Arnold, Bill Hunter, Max Cullen, Tony Barry; *D:* Don McLennan. **Beta** *NO* ⨂⨂½

Hard Knocks A young man on the run is tormented by an aging actress and her husband. His attempt to leave a past of violence and pain creates even more havoc.
19?? 90m/C Michael Christian, John Crawford, Donna Wilkes, Keenan Wynn. **VHS, Beta** *NO* ⨂

Hard Knox A hard-nosed Marine pilot is dumped from the service and takes up command at a military school filled with undisciplined punks. A made-for-television movie.
1983 96m/C Robert Conrad, Frank Howard, Alan Ruck, Red West, Bill Erwin, Dean Hill, Joan Sweeney; *D:* Peter Werner. **VHS, Beta** $59.95 *BAR, LHV* ⨂

Hard Part Begins A naive country singer gets sucked into the pratfalls of show business.
1987 87m/C Donnelly Rhodes, Nancy Belle Fuller, Paul Bradley. **VHS, Beta** $49.95 *TWE* ⨂

Hard Promises Absence doesn't necessarily make the heart fonder, as Joey finds out when he's accidentally invited to his wife's wedding. He's been away from home for so long he doesn't even realize he's been divorced and hightails it home to win his sweetheart back. Average performances and script round out this innocuous domestic comedy-drama. Originally made for cable televison.
1992 (PG) 95m/C Sissy Spacek, William L. Petersen, Brian Kerwin, Mare Winningham, Peter MacNicol, Ann Wedgeworth, Amy Wright, Lois Smith, Rip Torn; *D:* Martin Davidson; *M:* George S. Clinton. **VHS, 8mm** *COL* ⨂⨂

Hard Rain-The Tet 1968 An American platoon stationed in Saigon must mobilize in the wake of the North Vietnamese Army's Tet offensive. An episode of televi-

sion's "Tour of Duty." Other episodes are also available on tape.
1989 89m/C Terence Knox, Stephen Caffrey; *D:* Bill L. Norton. **VHS** $59.95 *NWV* ⨂⨂

Hard Rock Zombies Four heavy metal band members die horribly on the road and are brought back from the dead as zombies. This horror/heavy metal spoof is somewhat amusing in a goofy way.
1985 (R) 90m/C E.J. Curcio, Sam Mann; *D:* Krishna Shah. **VHS, Beta** $69.98 *LIV, VES* ⨂½

Hard Target Van Damme continues his action-hero ways as Chance Boudreaux, a Cajun (which explains the accent) merchant seaman, who comes to the rescue of Natasha (Butler), albeit with lots of violence. Brimley provides the humor as Chance's bayou uncle. It's another variation of "The Most Dangerous Game" story but it moves. American directorial debut of over-the-top Hong Kong action director Woo who had to tone down his usual stylistic effects and repeatedly cut some of the more violent scenes to earn an "R" rating.
1993 (R) 97m/C Jean-Claude Van Damme, Lance Henriksen, Yancy Butler, Arnold Vosloo, Wilford Brimley, Kasi Lemmons; *D:* John Woo; *W:* Chuck Pfarrer; *M:* Graeme Revell. **VHS** $19.98 *MCA, BTV* ⨂⨂½

Hard Ticket to Hawaii A shot-on-video spy thriller about an agent trying to rescue a comrade in Hawaii from a smuggling syndicate. Supporting cast includes many Playboy Playmates.
1987 (R) 96m/C Ron Moss, Dona Speir, Hope Marie Carlton, Cynthia Brimhall; *D:* Andy Sidaris. **VHS, Beta** $79.95 *BAR, LHV, WAR* ⨂

Hard Times A Depression-era drifter becomes a bare knuckle street fighter, and a gambler decides to promote him for big stakes. One of grade-B meister Hill's first genre films. A quiet, evocative drama.
1975 (PG) 92m/C Charles Bronson, James Coburn, Jill Ireland, Strother Martin; *D:* Walter Hill; *W:* Walter Hill. **VHS, Beta** $12.95 *GKK* ⨂⨂⨂

Hard to Die Director Wynorski's comic homage to Carol Frank's "Sorority House Massacre." Five beauties (former Playboy Playmates Harris, Taylor, Dare, Moore, and Carney) find employment moving boxes in a deserted lingerie factory. The film takes off from there as they uncover a mysterious spirit called the Sorority House Killer in an ancient "Soul Box." Desperate to extinguish the evil threat, they focus their efforts in an armed struggle involving high-powered weaponry against the building maintenance man, whom they fear is possessed by the spirit. Accompanied by a lovely, touching group shower scene. *AKA:* Tower of Terror.
1990 77m/C Robin Harris, Melissa Moore, Debra Dare, Lindsay Taylor, Bridget Carney, Forrest J. Ackerman; *D:* Jim Wynorski. **VHS** $89.98 *NHO* ⨂

Hard to Hold Rockin' Rick's lukewarm film debut where he falls in love with a children's counselor after an automobile accident. Springfield sings "Love Somebody" with music by Peter Gabriel.
1984 (PG) 93m/C Rick Springfield, Janet Eilber, Patti Hansen, Albert Salmi, Monique Gabrielle; *D:* Larry Peerce. **VHS, Beta** $69.95 *MCA* ⨂½

Hard to Kill Policeman Seagal is shot and left for dead in his bedroom, but survives against the odds, though his wife does not. After seven years, he is well enough to consider evening the score with his assailants. He hides while training in martial arts for the final battle. Strong outing from Seagal, with good supporting cast.

1989 (R) 96m/C Steven Seagal, Kelly Le Brock, William Sadler, Frederick Coffin, Bonnie Burroughs, Zachary Rosencrantz, Dean Norris; *D:* Bruce Malmuth; *M:* Charles Fox. **VHS, Beta, 8mm** $19.98 *WAR* ⨂⨂

Hard Traveling An unemployed Depression-era farmworker is accused of murder. He must fight a hostile court system to maintain his dignity and salvage the love and respect of his wife. Based on a novel by Alvah Bessie.
1985 (PG) 99m/C J.E. Freeman, Ellen Geer, Barry Corbin, James Gammon, Jim Haynie; *D:* Dan Bessie. **VHS, Beta** $19.95 *STE, NWV* ⨂⨂

Hard Vice Vice cops Joe Owens (Jones) and Andrea Thompson (Tweed) have their work cut out for them on their Las Vegas beat. When the bodies start piling up, the prime suspects turn out to be a group of high-priced hookers.
1994 (R) 86m/C Shannon Tweed, Sam Jones, James Gammon, Rebecca Ferratti. **VHS** $92.95 *APX* ⨂½

Hard Way A world-weary assassin is pressured by his boss to perform one last assignment. A surprise awaits him if he accepts.
1980 88m/C Patrick McGoohan, Lee Van Cleef, Donal McCann, Edna O'Brien; *D:* Mihael Dryhurst. **VHS, Beta** $59.95 *TWE* ⨂⨂

The Hard Way Hollywood superstar Fox is assigned to hardened NYC cop Woods to learn the ropes as he trains for a role. Nothing special in the way of script or direction, but Woods and Fox bring such intensity and good humor to their roles that the package works. Fox pokes fun at the LA lifestyle as the annoying, self-absorbed actor, and Marshall has an entertaining appearance as his agent. Woods is on familiar over-the-edge turf as the brittle but dedicated detective. Silly finale almost destroys the film, but other small vignettes are terrific.
1991 (R) 91m/C James Woods, Michael J. Fox, Annabella Sciorra, Stephen Lang, LL Cool J., John Capodice, Christina Ricci, Karen Gorney, Luis Guzman; *Cameos:* Penny Marshall; *D:* John Badham; *W:* Daniel Pyne, Lem Dobbs; *M:* Arthur B. Rubinstein. **VHS, Beta** $19.98 *MCA* ⨂⨂⨂

Hardbodies Three middle-aged men hit the beaches of Southern California in search of luscious young girls. They find them. Mid-life crisis done stupidly. Followed by a sequel.
1984 (R) 88m/C Grant Cramer, Teal Roberts, Gary Wood, Michael Rapport, Sorrels Pickard, Roberta Collins, Cindy Silver, Courtney Gains, Kristi Somers, Crystal Shaw, Kathleen Kinmont, Joyce Jameson; *D:* Mark Griffiths. **VHS, Beta** $79.95 *COL* ⨂

Hardbodies 2 A sequel to the original comedy hit, dealing with film crew in Greece that is distracted by hordes of nude natives. Sophomoric humor dependent on nudity and profanity for laughs.
1986 (R) 89m/C Brad Zutaut, Brenda Bakke, Fabiana Udenio, James Karen; *D:* Mark Griffiths. **VHS, Beta** $9.95 *COL Woof!*

Hardcase and Fist A framed cop leaves prison with his mind on revenge. The godfather who used him is just his first target.
1989 (R) 92m/C Maureen Lavette, Ted Prior; *D:* Tony Zarindast. **VHS, Beta** $79.98 *MCG* ⨂⨂

Hardcore A Midwestern businessman who is raising a strict Christian family learns of his daughter's disappearance while she is on a church trip. After hiring a streetwise investigator, he learns that his daughter has become an actress in pornographic films out in California. Strong performance by Scott and glimpse into the hardcore pornography

industry prove to be convincing points of this film, though it exploits what it condemns. *AKA:* The Hardcore Life.
1979 (R) 106m/C George C. Scott, Season Hubley, Peter Boyle, Dick Sargent; *D:* Paul Schrader; *W:* Paul Schrader; *M:* Jack Nitzsche. VHS, Beta $9.95 COL &&½

The Harder They Come A poor Jamaican youth becomes a success with a hit reggae record after he has turned to a life of crime out of desperation. Songs, which are blended nicely into the framework of the film, include "You Can Get It If You Really Want it" and "Sitting In Limbo."
1972 (R) 93m/C Jimmy Cliff, Janet Barkley, Carl Bradshaw; *D:* Perry Henzell. VHS, Beta $19.95 CRC, FCT &&½

The Harder They Fall A cold-eyed appraisal of the scum-infested boxing world. An unemployed reporter (Bogart in his last role) promotes a fighter for the syndicate, while doing an expose on the fight racket. Bogart became increasingly debilitated during filming and died soon afterward. Based on Budd Schulberg's novel.
1956 109m/B Humphrey Bogart, Rod Steiger, Jan Sterling, Mike Lane, Max Baer Sr.; *D:* Mark Robson; *W:* Philip Yordan. VHS, Beta $19.98 CCB, COL &&&

Hardhat & Legs Comic complications arise when a New York construction worker falls in love with the woman who's teaching the modern sexuality course in which he's enrolled. Made for television.
1980 96m/C Sharon Gless, Kevin Dobson, Ray Serra, Elva Josephson, Bobby Short, Jacqueline Brookes, W.T. Martin; *D:* Lee Philips; *W:* Ruth Gordon; *M:* Brad Fiedel. VHS, Beta NO &&

Hardly Working A circus clown finds it difficult to adjust to real life as he fumbles about from one job to another. Lewis's last attempt at resuscitating his directorial career. His fans will love it, but others need not bother.
1981 (PG) 90m/C Jerry Lewis, Susan Oliver, Roger C. Carmel, Gary Lewis, Deanna Lund; *D:* Jerry Lewis; *W:* Jerry Lewis. VHS, Beta $59.98 FOX &

Hardware Rag-tag ripoff in which McDermott is a post-apocalyptic garbage picker who gives girlfriend Travis some robot remains he collected (ours is not to ask why), oblivious to the fact that the tidy android was a government-spawned population controller programmed to destroy warm bodies. Seems old habits die hard, and that spells danger, danger, Will Robinson. Much violence excised to avoid x-rating.
1990 (R) 94m/C Dylan McDermott, Stacy Travis, John Lynch, Iggy Pop; *D:* Richard Stanley; *M:* Simon Boswell. VHS, Beta $14.95 HBO, WAR &½

Hardware Wars & Other Film Farces A collection of four award-winning spoofs of big-budget film epics, featuring "Hardware Wars," "Porklips Now," "Bambi Meets Godzilla," and "Closet Cases of the Nerd Kind." Some black-and-white segments.
1981 (G) 48m/C VHS, Beta WAR, OM &½

Harem A beautiful stockbroker gets kidnapped by a wealthy OPEC oil minister and becomes part of his harem. Kingsley stars as the lonely sheik who longs for the love of a modern woman.
1985 107m/C Ben Kingsley, Nastassia Kinski; *D:* Alfred Joffe. VHS, Beta $79.98 LIV, VES &

Harem In the early 1900s, a dastardly Turkish sultan kidnaps an American beauty to add to his harem—mightily displeasingly his jealous first wife. Lots of overwrought

romance and drama until she is finally rescued. Made for television.
1986 200m/C Omar Sharif, Nancy Travis, Ava Gardner, Julian Sands, Art Malik, Sarah Miles, Yaphet Kotto, Cherie Lunghi; *D:* Billy Hale. VHS STE &&

Harlan County, U.S.A. The emotions of 180 coal mining families are seen up close in this classic documentary about their struggle to win a United Mine Workers contract in Kentucky. Award-winning documentary.
1976 (PG) 103m/C *D:* Barbara Kopple. VHS, Beta $19.98 COL &&

Harlem Nights Two Harlem nightclub owners in the 1930s battle comically against efforts by the Mob and crooked cops to take over their territory. High-grossing, although somewhat disappointing effort from Murphy, who directed, wrote, produced, and starred in this film.
1989 (R) 118m/C Eddie Murphy, Richard Pryor, Redd Foxx, Danny Aiello, Jasmine Guy, Michael Lerner, Arsenio Hall, Della Reese; *D:* Eddie Murphy; *M:* Herbie Hancock. VHS, Beta $14.95 PAR &½

Harlem on the Prairie This first-ever western with an all-black cast has Jeffries helping a young lady find hidden gold and foiling a villain. Even though the technical standards and acting are below par, this is worth watching for the singing and a comedy routine done by a well-known contemporary black team. ♫Harlem On The Prairie; Romance In The Rain. *AKA:* Bad Man of Harlem.
1938 54m/B Herbert Jeffries, Mantan Moreland, F.E. Miller, Connie Harris, Maceo B. Sheffield, William Spencer Jr.; *D:* Sam Newfield; *M:* The Four Tunes. VHS $24.95 NOS &

Harlem Rides the Range Jeffries must outsmart villainous Brooks, who means to swindle a radium mine away from its rightful owner. Early oater of interest only because of its atypical all-black cast and crew.
1939 58m/B Herbert Jeffries, Lucius Brooks, Artie Young, F.E. Miller, Spencer Williams Jr., Clarence Brooks, Tom Southern, Wade Dumas, The Four Tunes, Leonard Christmas; *D:* Richard C. Kahn; *W:* F.E. Miller, Spencer Williams Jr. VHS $24.95 NOS, MRV, TPV &½

Harley Diamond is Harley, an L.A. thug-on-a-hog, who's on his way to an extended stay at one of the state's luxury institutions when he's sent to a Texas rehabilitation community. There, he bonds with an ex-biker, and may just find his way back down the straight and narrow. And the local longhorn rednecks applaud his efforts...not.
1990 (PG) 80m/C Lou Diamond Phillips, Eli Cummins, DeWitt Jan, Valentine Kim; *D:* Fred Holmes; *W:* Frank Kuntz, Sandy Kuntz. VHS $89.95 VMK &&

Harley Davidson and the Marlboro Man An awful rehash of "Butch Cassidy and the Sundance Kid" with blatant vulgarity and pointless sci-fi touches. The title duo are near-future outlaws who rob a bank to save their favorite bar, then find they've stolen mob money. Some action, but it's mostly talk: lewd, meant-to-be-whimsical soul-probing chats between H.D. and M.M. that would bore even the biker crowd—and did.
1991 (R) 98m/C Mickey Rourke, Don Johnson, Chelsea Field, Tom Sizemore, Vanessa Williams, Robert Ginty, Daniel Baldwin; *D:* Simon Wincer. VHS, Beta, 8mm $19.98 MGM &

Harlow The more lavish of the two Harlow biographies made in 1965, both with the same title. A sensationalized "scandal sheet" version of Jean Harlow's rise to fame

that bears little resemblance to the facts of her life.
1965 125m/C Carroll Baker, Martin Balsam, Red Buttons, Mike Connors, Angela Lansbury, Peter Lawford, Raf Vallone, Leslie Nielsen; *D:* Gordon Douglas; *W:* John Michael Hayes. VHS, Beta $14.95 PAR &&½

Harmagedon When Princess Luna's jetliner explodes she is thrown into a psychic plane where she must battle Genma, an eternal being who has destroyed half the universe. Luna gathers together the heroic Psyonic Warriors and the cyborg Vega to aid in her battle. Animated; in Japanese with English subtitles.
1983 131m/C VHS $39.95 CPM, WTA &&

Harmon of Michigan College football hero Harmon starred in this loosely adapted story of his life in and out of the pros and his career at Michigan.
1941 65m/B Tom Harmon, Anita Louise, Forest Evashevski, Oscar O'Shea, Warren Ashe, Stanley Crown, Ken Christy, Tim Ryan, Lloyd Bridges, William Hall, Chester Conklin, Larry Parks; *D:* Charles T. Barton; *W:* Howard J. Green. VHS $12.95 GPV &&½

Harmony Lane Highly romanticised rendition of the life of American composer, Stephen Collins Foster (1826-1864). Montgomery, as Foster, manages to lend a hint of credibility to the syrupy, melodramatic script. Very little attention is given to historical fact and almost every scene is orchestrated to showcase the composer's songs. The music steals the show. ♫Beautiful Dreamer; Old Folks at Home; Swanee River; Oh! Susanna; De Camptown Races.
1935 84m/B Douglass Montgomery, Evelyn Venable, Adrienne Ames, Joseph Cawthorn, William Frawley, Florence Roberts, Smiley Burnette, Hattie McDaniel; *D:* Joseph Santley. VHS $24.95 DVT, NOS, VYY &&

Harmony Trail Maynard stars in another rip-roaring western adventure.
1944 60m/B Ken Maynard. VHS, Beta $19.95 NOS, VCN, DVT &½

Harold and Maude Cult classic pairs Cort as a dead-pan disillusioned 20-year-old obsessed with suicide (his staged attempts are a highlight) and a loveable Gordon as a fun-loving 80-year-old eccentric. They meet at a funeral (a mutual hobby), and develop a taboo romantic relationship, in which they explore the tired theme of the meaning of life with a fresh perspective. The script was originally the 20-minute long graduate thesis of UCLA student Higgins, who showed it to his landlady, wife of film producer Lewis. Features music by the pre-Islamic Cat Stevens.
1971 (PG) 92m/C Ruth Gordon, Bud Cort, Cyril Cusack, Vivian Pickles, Charles Tyner, Ellen Geer; *D:* Hal Ashby; *W:* Colin Higgins; *M:* Cat Stevens. VHS, Beta, 8mm $14.95 PAR &&&&

Harper A tight, fast-moving genre piece about cynical LA private eye Newman investigating the disappearence of Bacall's wealthy husband. From a Ross McDonald novel, adapted by William Golding. Later sequelled in "The Drowning Pool." *AKA:* The Moving Target.
1966 121m/C Paul Newman, Shelley Winters, Lauren Bacall, Julie Harris, Robert Wagner, Janet Leigh, Arthur Hill; *D:* Jack Smight. VHS, Beta $19.98 WAR &&&

Harper Valley P.T.A. Eden raises hell in Harper Valley after the PTA questions her parental capabilities. Brain candy was adapted from a hit song; TV series followed.

1978 (PG) 93m/C Barbara Eden, Nanette Fabray, Louis Nye, Pat Paulsen, Ronny Cox, Ron Masak, Audrey Christie, John Fiedler, Bob Hastings; **D:** Richard Bennett; **W:** Barry Schneider. **VHS, Beta $19.98** *VES ♂♂*

Harrad Experiment Adaptation of Robert Rimmer's love-power bestseller in which an experiment-minded college establishes a campus policy of sexual freedom. Famous for the Hedren/Johnson relationship, shortly before Johnson married Hedren's real-life daughter Melanie Griffith. Followed by "The Harrad Summer."
1973 (R) 98m/C James Whitmore, Tippi Hedren, Don Johnson, Bruno Kirby, Laurie Walters, Victoria Thompson, Elliot Street, Sharon Taggart, Robert Middleton, Billy Sands, Melanie Griffith; **D:** Ted Post. **VHS, Beta** *VCI, VES ♂½*

Harrad Summer Sequel to "The Harrad Experiment." College coeds take their sex-education to the bedroom where they can apply their knowledge by more intensive means.
1974 (R) 103m/C Richard Doran, Victoria Thompson, Laurie Walters, Robert Reiser, Bill Dana, Marty Allen; **D:** Steven Hilliard Stern. **VHS** *VCI ♂♂*

Harry & Son A widowed construction worker faces the problems of raising his son. Newman is miscast as the old man and we've all seen Benson play the young role too many times.
1984 (PG) 117m/C Paul Newman, Robby Benson, Ellen Barkin, Wilford Brimley, Judith Ivey, Ossie Davis, Morgan Freeman, Joanne Woodward; **D:** Paul Newman. **VHS, Beta $79.98** *VES ♂♂*

Harry and the Hendersons Ordinary American family vacationing in the Northwest has a collision with Bigfoot. Thinking that the big guy is dead, they throw him on top of the car and head home. Lo and behold, he revives and starts wrecking the furniture and in the process, endears himself to the at-first frightened family. Nice little tale efficiently told, with Lithgow fine as the frustrated dad trying to hold his Bigfoot-invaded home together. Basis for the television series.
1987 (PG) 111m/C John Lithgow, Melinda Dillon, Don Ameche, David Suchet, Margaret Langrick, Joshua Rudoy, Kevin Peter Hall, Lainie Kazan, M. Emmet Walsh; **D:** William Dear; **W:** William Dear, William E. Martin, Ezra D. Rappaport; **M:** Bruce Broughton. **VHS, Beta $14.98** *MCA, APD ♂♂½*

Harry and Tonto A gentle comedy about an energetic septuagenarian who takes a cross-country trip with his cat, Tonto. Never in a hurry, still capable of feeling surprise and joy, he makes new friends and visits old lovers. Carney deserved his Oscar. Mazursky has seldom been better.
1974 115m/C Art Carney, Ellen Burstyn, Larry Hagman, Geraldine Fitzgerald, Chief Dan George, Arthur Hunnicutt, Josh Mostel; **D:** Paul Mazursky; **W:** Paul Mazursky; **M:** Bill Conti. Academy Awards '74: Best Actor (Carney); Nominations: Best Original Screenplay; Golden Globe Awards '75: Best Actor—Musical/Comedy (Carney); National Board of Review Awards '74: 10 Best Films of the Year. **VHS, Beta $19.98** *FOX, FCT, BTV ♂♂♂*

Harry & Walter Go to New York At the turn of the century, two vaudeville performers are hired by a crooked British entrepreneur for a wild crime scheme. The cast and crew try their hardest, but it's not enough to save this boring comedy. The vaudeville team of Caan and Gould perhaps served as a model for Beatty and Hoffman in "Ishtar."
1976 (PG) 111m/C James Caan, Elliott Gould, Michael Caine, Diane Keaton, Burt Young, Jack Gilford, Charles Durning, Lesley Ann Warren, Carol Kane; **D:** Mark Rydell. **VHS, Beta $9.95** *COL ♂♂*

Harry Black and the Tiger Jungle adventure involving a one-legged hunter and a man-eating tiger. The hunter initally teams up with the old war buddy who cost him his leg. The motivation grows with each failure to catch the beast and to make matters worse, the friend's wife and son are lost somewhere in the perilous jungle. Filmed in India. *AKA:* Harry Black.
1958 107m/C Stewart Granger, Barbara Rush, Anthony Steel; **D:** Hugo Fregonese. **VHS** *TCF ♂♂*

Harry Tracy Whimsical tale of the legendary outlaw whose escapades made him both a wanted criminal and an exalted folk hero. *AKA:* Harry Tracy—Desperado.
1983 (PG) 111m/C Bruce Dern, Gordon Lightfoot, Helen Shaver, Michael C. Gwynne; **D:** William A. Graham. **VHS, Beta $69.95** *VES ♂♂½*

Harry's War A middle-class, middle-aged American declares military war on the IRS in this overdone comedy.
1984 (PG) 98m/C Edward Herrmann, Geraldine Page, Karen Grassle, David Ogden Stiers; **D:** Keith Merrill. **VHS, Beta $59.95** *TPI ♂♂*

Harum Scarum Elvis tune-fest time! When a movie star (Presley) travels through the Middle East, he becomes involved in an attempted assassination of the king and falls in love with his daughter. He also sings at the drop of a veil: "Shake That Tambourine," "Harem Holiday," and seven others. *AKA:* Harem Holiday.
1965 95m/C Elvis Presley, Mary Ann Mobley, Fran Jeffries, Michael Ansara, Billy Barty, Theo Marcuse, Jay Novello; **D:** Gene Nelson. **VHS, Beta $14.95** *MGM ♂♂*

Harvest A classically Pagnolian rural pageant-of-life melodrama, wherein a pair of loners link up together in an abandoned French town and completely revitalize it and the land around it. From the novel by Jean Giono. In French with English subtitles.
1937 128m/B Fernandel, Gabriel Gabrio, Orane Demazis, Edouard Delmont, Henri Poupon; **D:** Marcel Pagnol; **W:** Marcel Pagnol; **M:** Arthur Honegger. **VHS, Beta $69.95** *INT, MRV, FCT ♂♂♂♂*

The Harvest Sultry temptress Leilani sends Miguel's internal thermometer into convulsions with her preference for ice during lovemaking. However, their tryst turns sour (for him) when she takes Miguel to the beach where mystery thugs beat him unconscious and swipe his kidney. Bizarre story sure to ignite a small cult following.
1992 (R) 97m/C Miguel Ferrer, Leilani Sarelle Ferrer, Harvey Fierstein, Anthony John Denison, Tim Thomerson, Matt Clark, Henry Silva; **D:** David Marconi; **W:** David Marconi; **M:** Dave Allen, Rick Boston. **VHS, Beta $89.95** *COL ♂♂½*

Harvest Melody Singing star Gilda Parker travels to farm country for a mere publicity stunt but decides to stay. Corny in more ways than one. ♫You Could Have Knocked Me Over With A Feather; Put It In Reverse; Let's Drive Out To The Drive-In; Tenderly.
1943 70m/B Rosemary Lane, Johnny Downs, Sheldon Leonard, Charlotte Wynters, Luis Alberni, Claire Rochelle, Syd Saylor; **D:** Sam Newfield. **VHS $19.95** *NOS, LOO ♂♂*

Harvey Straightforward version of the Mary Chase play about a friendly drunk with an imaginary 6-foot rabbit friend named Harvey, and a sister who tries to have him committed. A fondly remembered, charming comedy. Hull is a standout, well deserving her Oscar.
1950 104m/B James Stewart, Josephine Hull, Victoria Horne, Peggy Dow, Cecil Kellaway, Charles Drake, Jesse White, Wallace Ford, Nana Bryant; **D:** Henry Koster. Academy Awards '50: Best Supporting Actress (Hull); Nominations: Best Actor (Stewart); Golden Globe Awards '51: Best Supporting Actress (Hull). **VHS, Beta $14.95** *MCA, BTV, RDG ♂♂♂½*

The Harvey Girls Lightweight musical about a restaurant chain that sends its waitresses to work in the Old West. ♫In the Valley Where the Evening Sun Goes Down; Wait and See; On the Atchison, Topeka and the Santa Fe; It's a Great Big World; The Wild Wild West.
1946 102m/C Judy Garland, Ray Bolger, John Hodiak, Preston Foster, Angela Lansbury, Virginia O'Brien, Marjorie Main, Chill Wills, Kenny L. Baker, Selena Royle, Cyd Charisse; **D:** George Sidney; **M:** Harry Warren, Johnny Mercer. Academy Awards '46: Best Song ("On the Atchison, Topeka and Santa Fe"); Nominations: Best Song ("On the Atchison, Topeka and Santa Fe"), Best Original Score. **VHS, Beta $19.98** *MGM, FCT ♂♂♂*

A Hash House Fraud/The Sultan's Wife "A Hash House Fraud" (1915) features a frenetic Keystone chase. "The Sultan's Wife" (1917) concerns a woman who attracts the unwanted attention of a sultan.
1915 33m/B Louise Fazenda, Hugh Fay, Chester Conklin, Gloria Swanson, Bobby Vernon. **VHS, Beta $19.98** *CCB ♂♂♂*

The Hasty Heart A rowdy, terminally ill Scotsman brings problems and friendships to a makeshift war-time hospital built in the jungles of Burma. Remake of 1949 flick with Richard Todd and Ronald Reagan in leading roles.
1986 100m/C Gregory Harrison, Cheryl Ladd, Perry King; **D:** Martin Speer. **VHS, Beta $59.95** *BAR, LHV, WAR ♂♂*

Hat Box Mystery A detective's secretary is tricked into shooting a woman and private eye Neal is determined to save her from prison. Although not outstanding, it's worth seeing as perhaps the shortest detective film (a mere 44 min.) to ever make it as a feature.
1947 44m/B Tom Neal, Pamela Blake, Allen Jenkins; **D:** Lambert Hillyer. **VHS, Beta $16.95** *SNC, VYY ♂♂*

Hatari An adventure-loving team of professional big game hunters ventures to East Africa to round up animals for zoos around the world. Led by Wayne, they get into a couple of scuffs along the way, including one with lady photographer Martinelli who is doing a story on the expedition. Extraordinary footage of Africa and the animals brought to life by a fantastic musical score.
1962 158m/C John Wayne, Elsa Martinelli, Red Buttons, Hardy Kruger, Gerard Blain, Bruce Cabot; **D:** Howard Hawks; **M:** Henry Mancini. **VHS, Beta $49.95** *PAR ♂♂♂*

Hatchet for the Honeymoon A rather disturbed young man goes around hacking young brides to death as he tries to find out who murdered his wife. Typical sick Bava horror flick; confusing plot, but strong on vivid imagery. *AKA:* Blood Brides; Una Hacka Para la Luna de Miel; Il Roso Segmo Della Pollias.
1970 90m/C Stephen Forsythe, Dagmar Lassander, Laura Betti, Gerard Tichy; **D:** Mario Bava. **VHS, Beta $12.95** *MED, TIM, HEG ♂*

The Hatfields & the McCoys A made-for-television re-telling of the most famous feud in American history—the legendary mountain war between the Hatfields and the McCoys.
1975 90m/C Jack Palance, Steve Forrest, Richard Hatch, Karen Lamm; *D:* Clyde Ware. VHS, Beta $14.98 *WOV* 🎞🎞

Hats Off Clarke and Payne star as opposing press agents in this tedious musical. The only bright spot is the finale, which features white-robed girls on a cloud-covered carousel. 🎵Where Have You Been All My Life?; Little Old Rhythm; Twinkle, Twinkle, Little Star; Let's Have Another; Zilch's Hats; Hats Off.
1937 65m/B Mae Clarke, John Payne, Helen Lynd, Luis Alberni, Richard "Skeets" Gallagher, Franklin Pangborn; *D:* Boris L. Petroff. VHS $19.95 *NOS, MLB* 🎞

The Haunted The ancient curse of an Indian woman haunts a present day family by possessing the body of a beautiful girl. Through the girl, a horrible vengeance is carried out.
1979 81m/C Aldo Ray, Virginia Mayo, Anne Michelle, Jim Negele; *D:* Michael de Gaetano. VHS, Beta $9.95 *SIM, VHE, HHE* 🎞

The Haunted Castle One of Murnau's first films, and a vintage, if crusty, example of German expressionism. A nobleman entertains guests at his country mansion when strange things start to occur. Silent, with English titles. *AKA:* Schloss Vogelod.
1921 56m/B Arnold Korff, Lulu Keyser-Korff; *D:* F.W. Murnau. VHS, Beta $16.95 *SNC, NOS, VYY* 🎞🎞🎞

Haunted Gold A young Wayne, in his first Western for Warners, battles gold-hungry desperadoes and a mysterious cloaked phantom. Remake of "The Phantom City."
1932 57m/B John Wayne, Sheila Terry, Harry Woods; *D:* Mack V. Wright; *W:* Adele Buffington. VHS $19.98 *MGM, GPV* 🎞🎞

Haunted Harbor A high-seas financier has been murdered by a crooked crony and Captain Jim Marsden's alibi is all wet. He's got to find the gold, the girl, and avoid the goons. Part of "The Cliffhanger Serials" series. *AKA:* Pirate's Harbor.
1944 243m/B Kane Richmond, Kay Aldridge, Roy Barcroft. VHS $29.98 *REP, MOV* 🎞🎞½

Haunted Honeymoon Arthritic comedy about a haunted house and a couple trapped there. Sad times for the Mel Brooks alumni participating in this lame horror spoof.
1986 (PG) 82m/C Gene Wilder, Gilda Radner, Dom DeLuise, Jonathan Pryce, Paul Smith, Peter Vaughan, Bryan Pringle, Roger Ashton-Griffiths, Jim Carter; *D:* Gene Wilder; *W:* Gene Wilder. VHS $34.95 *HBO* 🎞

The Haunted Palace Price plays both a 17th-century warlock burned at the stake and a descendant who returns to the family dungeon and gets possessed by the mutant-breeding forebearer. The movie has its own identity crisis, with title and ambience from Poe but story from H.P. Lovecraft's "The Case of Charles Dexter Ward." Respectable but rootless chills, also available with the quasi-Lovecraft "Curse of the Crimson Altar" on laser disc.
1963 87m/C Vincent Price, Debra Paget, Lon Chaney Jr., Frank Maxwell, Leo Gordon, Elisha Cook Jr., John Dierkes; *D:* Roger Corman. VHS, Beta $59.98 *HBO, MLB* 🎞🎞½

Haunted Ranch Reno Red has been murdered and a shipment of gold bullion is missing. A gang on the lookout for the gold tries to convince people that Red's ranch is haunted by his ghost.

1943 56m/B John "Dusty" King, David Sharpe, Max Terhune, Rex Lease, Julie Duncan; *D:* Robert Tansey. VHS, Beta $19.95 *NOS, DVT, VYY* 🎞½

The Haunted Strangler Boris Karloff is a writer investigating a 20-year old murder who begins copying some of the killer's acts. *AKA:* The Grip of the Strangler.
1958 78m/B Boris Karloff, Anthony M. (Antonio Margheriti) Dawson, Elizabeth Allan; *D:* Robert Day. VHS, Beta $49.95 *MED, MPI* 🎞🎞½

Haunted Summer Soft-focus, sex-and-drugs period piece of the bacchanalian summer of 1816 spent by free spirits Lord Byron, Percy Shelley, Mary Shelley, and John Polidori and others that led Mary Shelley to write "Frankenstein." Based on the novel of the same name by Anne Edwards.
1988 (R) 106m/C Alice Krige, Eric Stoltz, Philip Anglim, Laura Dern, Alex Winter; *D:* Ivan Passer. VHS, Beta $79.95 *MED* 🎞🎞

Haunted: The Ferryman Adapted by Julian Bond from a Kingsley Amis story, the film deals with a novelist who is mysteriously confronted with various events and macabre set-pieces from his own novel, including a dead ferryman rising from the grave.
1974 50m/C Jeremy Brett, Nastasha Parry, Lesley Dunlop; *D:* John Irvin. VHS, Beta $59.95 *PSM* 🎞🎞

HauntedWeen All trick, no treat, as a guy nailed by a frat house prank twenty years ago comes-back-for-revenge.
1991 ?m/C Brien Blakely, Blake Pickett, Brad Hanks, Bart White, Leslee Lacey, Ethan Adler; *D:* Doug Robertson. VHS $29.50 *CVD* 🎞½

The Haunting A subtle, bloodless horror film about a weekend spent in a monstrously haunted mansion by a parapsychologist, the mansion's skeptic heir, and two mediums. A chilling adaptation of Shirley Jackson's "The Haunting of Hill House," in which the psychology of the heroine is forever in question.
1963 113m/B Julie Harris, Claire Bloom, Russ Tamblyn, Richard Johnson; *D:* Robert Wise. VHS, Beta $19.98 *MGM, FCT* 🎞🎞🎞½

Haunting Fear Poe's "The Premature Burial" inspired this pale cheapie about a wife with a fear of early interment. After lengthy nightmares and graphic sex, her greedy husband uses her phobia in a murder plot.
1991 88m/C Jan-Michael Vincent, Karen Black, Brinke Stevens, Michael Berryman; *D:* Fred Olen Ray; *W:* Sherman Scott. VHS $79.95 *RHI* 🎞

The Haunting of Barney Palmer Barney Palmer is sure he has inherited the family magic powers because he is haunted by the ghost of his great uncle. To destroy the curse, he must conquer his fears. Based on the book "The Haunting" by Margaret Mahy. Includes a viewers' guide. Part of the "Wonderworks" series.
199? 58m/C Ned Beatty, Alexis Banas, Eleanor Gibson. VHS $29.95 *PME, FCT, BTV* 🎞

Haunting of Harrington House A tame teenage haunted house film originally produced for television.
1982 50m/C Dominique Dunne, Roscoe Lee Browne, Edie Adams, Phil Leeds; *D:* Murray Golden. VHS, Beta $29.95 *GEM* 🎞

The Haunting of Morella Poe-inspired cheapjack exploitation about a an executed witch living again in the nubile body of her teen daughter. Ritual murders result, in between lesbian baths and nude swims. Producer Roger Corman did the same story with more class and less skin in his earlier anthology "Tales of Terror."

1991 (R) 82m/C David McCallum, Nicole Eggert, Maria Ford, Lana Clarkson; *D:* Jim Wynorski; *W:* Jim Wynorski, R.J. Robertson. VHS $89.98 *NHO* 🎞

Haunting of Sarah Hardy Ward, as a recently wed heiress, returns to the scene of her unhappy childhood home. In a standard plot, Ward is torn between an apparent haunting and the question of her own sanity. Made for TV film is redeemed by the creditable acting.
1989 92m/C Sela Ward, Michael Woods, Roscoe Born, Polly Bergen, Morgan Fairchild; *D:* Jerry London. VHS, Beta $59.95 *PAR* 🎞🎞

The Haunting Passion Newlywed Seymour moves into a haunted house only to be seduced by the ghost of the former occupant's dead lover. Effective and erotic presentation. Made for Television.
1983 100m/C Jane Seymour, Gerald McRaney, Millie Perkins, Ruth Nelson, Paul Rossilli, Ivan Bonar; *D:* John Korty. VHS, Beta $39.95 *LIV* 🎞🎞½

Haunts Tormented woman has difficulty distinguishing between fantasy and reality after a series of brutal slayings lead police to the stunning conclusion that dead people have been committing the crimes. *AKA:* The Veil.
1977 (PG) 97m/C Cameron Mitchell, Aldo Ray, May Britt, William Gray Espy, Susan Nohr; *D:* Herb Freed; *M:* Pino Donaggio. VHS, Beta $59.95 *MED* 🎞½

Haunts of the Very Rich A loose remake of "Outward Bound" in which a group of spoiled people on a vacation find themselves spiritually dead. Made for TV.
1972 72m/C Lloyd Bridges, Anne Francis, Donna Mills, Tony Bill, Robert Reed, Moses Gunn, Cloris Leachman, Ed Asner; *D:* Paul Wendkos. VHS, Beta $59.95 *VMK* 🎞🎞½

Havana During the waning days of the Batista regime, a gambler travels to Havana in search of big winnings. Instead, he meets the beautiful wife of a communist revolutionary. Unable to resist their mutual physical attraction, the lovers become drawn into a destiny which is far greater than themselves. Reminiscent of "Casablanca."
1990 (R) 145m/C Robert Redford, Lena Olin, Alan Arkin, Raul Julia, Tomas Milian, Tony Plana, Betsy Brantley, Lise Cutter, Richard Farnsworth, Mark Rydell, Daniel Davis; *D:* Sydney Pollack; *W:* Judith Rascoe, David Rayfiel; *M:* Dave Grusin. VHS, Beta $19.98 *MCA, FCT, MOV* 🎞🎞½

Having It All A wry television comedy about a love triangle. Dyan Cannon stars as a successful business woman with a husband on each coast, who finds dividing her time is more than she bargained for.
1982 100m/C Dyan Cannon, Barry Newman, Hart Bochner, Melanie Chartoff, Sylvia Sidney; *D:* Edward Zwick; *M:* Miles Goodman. VHS, Beta $39.95 *LIV* 🎞🎞

Having Wonderful Crime Madcap comedy-thriller about a newly married couple who combine sleuthing with a honeymoon. With their criminal lawyer friend along, the trio winds up searching for a magician who has vanished. Fast-paced action and quick dialogue.
1945 70m/B Pat O'Brien, George Murphy, Carole Landis, Lenore Aubert, George Zucco; *D:* Edward Sutherland. VHS $19.98 *TTC, FCT, IME* 🎞🎞½

Having Wonderful Time A young girl tries to find culture and romance on her summer vacation at a resort in the Catskills. Film debut of comic Red Skelton, who wasn't always as old as the hills. Based on a Broadway hit by Arthur Kober.

1938 71m/B Ginger Rogers, Lucille Ball, Eve Arden, Red Skelton, Douglas Fairbanks Jr.; **D:** Alfred Santell. VHS, Beta $34.95 RKO ♂♂½

Having Wonderful Time/Carnival Boat
A Ginger Rogers double feature: "Having Wonderful Time" (1938)-fun and frolic at an adult summer camp in the Catskills; and "Carnival Boat" (1932)-the lives and loves of rugged loggers in the Pacific Northwest.
1938 134m/B Ginger Rogers, Douglas Fairbanks Jr., Lucille Ball, Ann Miller, Red Skelton, William Boyd. VHS, Beta $39.95 RKO, TTC ♂♂½

Hawaii
James Michener's novel about a New England farm boy who decides in 1820 that the Lord has commanded him to the island of Hawaii for the purpose of "Christianizing" the natives. Filmed on location. Also available in a 181 minute version with restored footage. Available in director's cut version with an additional 20 minutes.
1966 161m/C Max von Sydow, Julie Andrews, Richard Harris, Carroll O'Connor, Bette Midler, Gene Hackman, Jocelyn Lagarde; **D:** George Roy Hill; **W:** Daniel Taradash, Dalton Trumbo; **M:** Elmer Bernstein. Academy Awards '66 Nominations: Best Color Cinematography, Best Costume Design (Color), Best Song ("My Wishing Doll"), Best Sound, Best Supporting Actress (Lagarde), Best Original Score; Golden Globe Awards '67: Best Supporting Actress (Lagarde), Best Score. VHS, Beta $19.95 FOX ♂♂♂

Hawaii Calls
Two young stowaways on a cruise ship are allowed to stay on after one of them (Breen) struts his stuff as a singer. The two then turn sleuth to catch a gang of spies. More ham than a can of Spam, but still enjoyable. ♫That's The Hawaiian In Me; Hawaii Calls; Down Where The Trade Winds Blow; Macushia; Aloha Oe.
1938 72m/B Bobby Breen, Ned Sparks, Irvin S. Cobb, Warren Hull, Gloria Holden, Pua Lani, Raymond Paige, Philip Ahn, Ward Bond; **D:** Eddie Cline. VHS $19.95 DVT, NOS, HEG ♂♂

Hawaiian Buckaroo
A couple of cowboys fight to save their pineapple plantation from a sneaky foreman.
1938 62m/B Smith Ballew, Evelyn Knapp, Benny Burt, Harry Woods, Pat O'Brien; **D:** Ray Taylor. VHS $19.95 NOS, DVT, GPV ♂

The Hawk
Okay thriller about suburban housewife Annie (Mirren) who suspects that her husband Stephen (Costigan) is a serial killer known as the Hawk. Since Annie has a history of depression and her husband is a known louse, her suspicions are dismissed as delusional. Some surprise twists help the weak story along. Contains some graphic views of corpses. Based on the novel by Ransley.
1993 (R) 84m/C Helen Mirren, George Costigan, Owen Teale, Rosemary Leach; **D:** David Hayman; **W:** Peter Ransley; **M:** Nick Bicat. VHS $92.95 ACA ♂♂½

Hawk and Castile
Bandits murder, pillage, and terrorize the nobility in Medieval Europe until the Hawk comes onto the scene.
19?? 95m/C Tom Griffith, Jerry Cobb, Nurla Forway, Mari Real. VHS, Beta NO ♂♂½

The Hawk of Powder River
Cheapie western has Dean getting involved with a beautiful outlaw gang leader with a murderous streak. A large part of this film was lifted from earlier Dean oaters, as are all the tunes.
1948 54m/B Eddie Dean, Roscoe Ates, Jennifer Holt, June Carlson, Terry Frost, Lane Bradford; **D:** Ray Taylor. VHS $19.99 MOV ♂

Hawk of the Wilderness
A man, shipwrecked as an infant and reared on a remote island by native Indians, battles modern day pirates. Serial in 12 episodes. Also called "Lost Island of Kioga."
1938 195m/B Herman Brix, Mala, William Boyle; **D:** William Witney. VHS, Beta $29.95 VCN, MLB ♂♂

Hawk the Slayer
A comic book fantasy. A good warrior struggles against his villainous brother to possess a magical sword that bestows upon its holder great powers of destruction. Violent battle scenes; Palance makes a great villain.
1981 93m/C Jack Palance, John Terry, Harry Andrews, Roy Kinnear, Ferdinand "Ferdy" Mayne; **D:** Terry Marcel. VHS, Beta $39.95 LIV ♂½

Hawken's Breed
Drifter meets American Indian beauty and hears her tale of woe; the two fall for each other and set out together to avenge the murder of the woman's husband and son. Nothing much to crow about.
1987 (R) 93m/C Peter Fonda, Serene Hedin, Jack Elam; **D:** Charles B. Pierce. VHS, Beta $19.95 STE, VMK, IME ♂♂

Hawkeye
After his best friend is murdered by gangsters in a seedy drug deal, Hawkeye, a rough and tumble Texas cop, and his slick new partner hit the streets of Las Vegas with a vengeance.
1988 90m/C Troy Donahue, Chuck Jeffreys, George Chung, Stan Wertlieb; **D:** Leo Fong. VHS, Beta NO ♂½

Hawks
Somewhere on the road to blackcomedy this film gets waylaid by triviality. Two terminally ill men break out of the hospital, determined to make their way to Amsterdam for some last-minute fun. Mediocre at best.
1989 (R) 105m/C Anthony Edwards, Timothy Dalton, Janet McTeer, Jill Bennett, Sheila Hancock, Connie Booth, Camille Coduri; **D:** Robert Ellis Miller. VHS, Beta, 8mm $34.95 PAR ♂½

The Hawks & the Sparrows
Shortly after "Mr. Ed" came Pasolini's garrulous crow, which follows a father and son's travels through Italy spouting pithy bits of politics. A comic Pasolinian allegory-fest full of then-topical political allusions, the story comes off a bit wooden. Worth watching to see Toto, the Italian comic, in his element. **AKA:** Uccellacci e Uccellini.
1967 91m/B Toto, Ninetto Davoli, Femi Benussi; **D:** Pier Paolo Pasolini; **W:** Pier Paolo Pasolini; **M:** Ennio Morricone. VHS $29.95 WBF, ING ♂♂

Hawmps!
Idiotic comedy about a Civil War lieutenant who trains his men to use camels. When the soldiers and animals begin to grow fond of each other, Congress orders the camels to be set free. Hard to believe this was based on a real life incident.
1976 (G) 98m/C James Hampton, Christopher Connelly, Slim Pickens, Denver Pyle; **D:** Joe Camp. VHS, Beta $79.95 VES Woof!

Hawthorne of the USA
Reid stars as Anthony Hamilton Hawthorne, American extraordinaire. After gambling a fortune away in Monte Carlo, Hawthorne heads to mainland Europe for rest and revelry. Instead, he finds the love of a princess and a Communist coup in the making. Silent with orchestral score.
1919 55m/B Wallace Reid, Harrison Ford, Lila Lee, Tully Marshall; **D:** James Cruze. VHS, Beta $19.95 GPV ♂♂½

Hazel's People
Bitter and hostile college student attends his friend's funeral in Mennonite country. He discovers not only a way of life he never knew existed, but a

personal faith in a living Christ. From the Merle Good novel, "Happy as the Grass Was Green."
1975 (G) 105m/C Geraldine Page, Pat Hingle, Graham Beckel. VHS, Beta $29.95 VCI, VGD ♂½

He is My Brother
Two boys survive a shipwreck, landing on an island that houses a leper colony.
1975 (G) 90m/C Keenan Wynn, Bobby Sherman, Robbie Rist; **D:** Edward Dmytryk. VHS, Beta NO ♂½

He Kills Night After Night After Night
British police are baffled as they seek the man who has been killing women in the style of Jack the Ripper. And he keeps doing it.
1970 88m/C Jack May, Linda Marlowe, Justine Lord. VHS, Beta NO ♂½

He Knows You're Alone
Lame horror flick that focuses on a psychotic killer terrorizing a bride-to-be and her bridal party in his search for a suitable bride of his own.
1980 (R) 94m/C Don Scardino, Elizabeth Kemp, Tom Rolfing, Paul Gleason, Caitlin O'Heaney, Tom Hanks, Patsy Pease; **D:** Armand Mastroianni; **W:** Scott Parker. VHS, Beta $59.95 MGM ♂

He Lives: The Search for the Evil One
A man who was imprisoned by Nazis as a child attempts to keep Hitler, now living in Buenos Aires, from starting a 4th Reich.
1988 90m/C Lee Patterson. VHS, Beta NO ♂

He Said, She Said
Romance is the topic, but this isn't a typical dating film, instead a couple's relationship unfolds from differing points of view: first, the guy's (by Kwapis) and then the girl's (by Silver). Bacon and Perkins, Baltimore journalists and professional rivals, tell how their romance wound up on the rocks, and why (or so they say). The end result is overlong and lacks the zing of other war between the sexes movies, but real-life couple Silver and Kwapis do humorously highlight the fact that men and women often view the same incidents very differently. Bacon overacts, Perkins overreacts, and Stone shines as Bacon's ex-girl.
1991 (R) 115m/C Elizabeth Perkins, Kevin Bacon, Sharon Stone, Nathan Lane, Anthony LaPaglia, Stanley Anderson, Charlaine Woodard, Danton Stone, Phil Leeds, Rita Karin; **D:** Marisa Silver, Ken Kwapis; **W:** Brian Hohlfield; **M:** Miles Goodman. VHS $14.95 PAR, CCB ♂♂½

He Walked by Night
Los Angeles homicide investigators track down a cop killer in this excellent drama. Based on a true story from the files of the Los Angeles police, this first rate production reportedly inspired Webb to create "Dragnet."
1948 80m/B Richard Basehart, Scott Brady, Roy Roberts, Jack Webb, Whit Bissell; **D:** Alfred Werker, Anthony Mann. VHS, Beta $16.95 SNC, NOS, BAR ♂♂♂½

He Who Gets Slapped
Chaney portrays a brilliant scientist whose personal and professional humiliations cause him to join a travelling French circus as a masochistic clown (hence the title). There he falls in love with a beautiful circus performer and plans a spectacular revenge. Brilliant use of lighting and Expressionist devices by director Sjostrom (who used the Americanized version of his name-Seastrom-in the credits). Adapted from the Russian play "He, The One Who Gets Slapped" by Leonid Andreyev.
1924 85m/B Lon Chaney Sr., Norma Shearer, John Gilbert, Tully Marshall, Ford Sterling, Marc McDermott; **D:** Victor Sjostrom; **W:** Carey Wilson, Victor Sjostrom. VHS $29.95 FCT ♂♂♂

He Who Walks Alone Made-for-television film documents the life of Thomas E. Gilmore, who became the South's first elected black sheriff in the 1960s.
1978 74m/C Louis Gossett Jr., Clu Gulager, Mary Alice, James McEachin, Barton Heyman, Barry Brown, Loni Chapman; **D:** Jerrold Freedman. **VHS, Beta** NO &&&

The Head A scientist comes up with a serum that can keep the severed head of a dog alive. Before too long, he tries the stuff out on a woman, transferring the head from her own hunchbacked body to that of a beautiful stripper. Weird German epic sports poor special effects and unintentional laughs, but is interesting nonetheless.
1959 92m/B Horst Frank, Michel Simon, Paul Dahlke, Karin Kernke, Helmut Schmidt; **D:** Victor Trivas; **W:** Victor Trivas. **VHS** $19.98 SNC &&

Head Infamously plotless musical comedy starring the television fab four of the '60s, the Monkees, in their only film appearance. A number of guest stars appear and a collection of old movie clips are also included. ♫Circle Sky; Can You Dig It; Long Title: Do I Have To Do This All Over Again; Daddy's Song; As We Go Along; The Porpoise Song.
1968 (G) 86m/C Peter Tork, Mickey Dolenz, Davy Jones, Michael Nesmith, Frank Zappa, Annette Funicello, Teri Garr; **D:** Bob Rafelson; **W:** Jack Nicholson, Bob Rafelson. **VHS, Beta** $19.95 MVD, COL &&&

Head of the Family After a woman sacrifices her political ideals and career goals for her role as a family matriarch, she eventually falls apart.
1971 (PG) 105m/C Nino Manfredi, Leslie Caron, Ugo Tognazzi, Claudine Auger; **D:** Nanni Loy; **W:** Nanni Loy. **VHS, Beta** $59.95 GEM &&½

Head Office A light comedy revolving around the competition between corporate management and the lower echelon for the available position of chairman.
1986 (PG-13) 90m/C Danny DeVito, Eddie Albert, Judge Reinhold, Rick Moranis, Jane Seymour; **D:** Ken Finkleman; **M:** James Newton Howard. **VHS, Beta** $79.99 HBO &&

Head Over Heels A model married to an older man has an affair with a younger one and cannot decide between them. In French with subtitles.
1967 89m/C Brigitte Bardot, Laurent Terzieff, Michael Same; **D:** Serge Bourguignon. **VHS, Beta** $19.95 FCT &&

Headhunter Voodoo-esque killers are leaving headless bodies all around Miami. Plenty of prosthetic make-up.
1989 92m/C Kay Lenz, Wayne Crawford, John Fatooh, Steve Kanaly, June Chadwick, Sam Williams; **D:** Francis Schaeffer. **VHS, Beta** $29.95 ACA, IME &½

Headin' for the Rio Grande A cowboy and his sheriff brother drive off cattle-rustlers in this Western saga. Ritter's film debut. Songs include "Campfire Love Song," "Jailhouse Lament," and "Night Herding Song."
1936 60m/B Tex Ritter, Eleanor Stewart, Syd Saylor, Warner Richmond, Charles "Blackie" King; **D:** Robert North Bradbury. **VHS, Beta** $19.95 NOS, DVT &

Heading for Heaven A mistaken medical report leaves a frazzled realtor believing he has only three months to live, and when he disappears the family suspects the worst. A minor comedy based on a play by Charles Webb.
1947 65m/B Stuart Erwin, Glenda Farrell, Russ Vincent, Irene Ryan, Milburn Stone, George O'Hanlon; **D:** Lewis D. Collins. **VHS** $19.95 NOS, TIM &&

Heading Home A very early version of the Babe Ruth story—starring none other than the Babe himself. A fair print, this film is orchestra scored.
1924 56m/B Babe Ruth. **VHS, Beta** $14.95 GPV &&½

Headless Eyes Gory entry into the psycho-artist category. An artist is miffed when mistaken by a woman as a burglar he loses an eye. Not one to forgive and forget, he becomes quite the eyeball fetishist, culling donations from unsuspecting women. An eye for an eye ad finitum.
1983 78m/C Bo Brundin, Gordon Raman, Mary Jane Early; **D:** Kent Bateman. **VHS** VCI &½

Headline Woman An ongoing feud between a police commissioner and a newspaper's city editor causes a reporter to make a deal with a policeman in exchange for news. A good cast makes this otherwise tired story tolerable.
1935 75m/B Heather Angel, Roger Pryor, Jack LaRue, Ford Sterling, Conway Tearle; **D:** William Nigh. **VHS, Beta** $24.95 NOS, DVT, HEG &&

Heads Unassuming copyreader Guy Franklin (Cryer) gets promoted to reporter and his first assignment is a doozy. He's to cover a series of decapitation murders in a small town. Can he do the job without become the next victim—or being accused of the crimes?
1993 (R) 102m/C Jon Cryer, Jennifer Tilly, Ed Asner, Roddy McDowall; **D:** Paul Shapiro. **VHS** REP &&½

Headwinds Silent romance in which Mr. Right spares helpless girl against her will from marrying Mr. Wrong.
1928 52m/B House Peters, Patsy Ruth Miller. **VHS, Beta** $16.95 GPV &&

Healer A doctor forgets his pledge to help the lame and becomes a fashionable physician. A young crippled lad helps him eventually remember his original purpose was to serve others. **AKA:** Little Pal.
1936 80m/B Mickey Rooney, Ralph Bellamy, Karen Morley, Judith Allen, Robert McWade; **D:** Reginald Barker. **VHS, Beta** $19.95 DVT &½

Hear My Song Mickey O'Neill (Dunbar) is an unscrupulous club promoter, who books singers with names like Franc Cinatra, while trying to revive his failing nightclub in this charming, hilarious comedy. He hires the mysterious Mr. X, who claims he is really the legendary exiled singer Josef Locke, only to find out he is an imposter. To redeem himself with his fiancee and her mother, he goes to Ireland to find the real Locke (Beatty) and bring him to Liverpool to sing. Dunbar is appealing in his role, and Beatty is magnificent as the legendary Locke—so much so that he was nominated for a Golden Globe for Best Supporting Actor.
1991 (R) 104m/C Ned Beatty, Adrian Dunbar, Shirley Anne Field, Tara Fitzgerald, William Hootkins, David McCallum; **D:** Peter Chelsom; **W:** Peter Chelsom. **VHS, Beta** $19.95 PAR &&&½

Hear No Evil Below average thriller with a deaf victim (Matlin) involved in a game of cat-and-mouse with a corrupt cop (Sheen) who's looking for a valuable coin. Weak script plays up the woman in jeopardy theme but lacks the crucial element of suspense. A waste of an otherwise talented cast.
1993 (R) 98m/C Marlee Matlin, D.B. Sweeney, Martin Sheen, John C. McGinley, Christina Carlisi, Greg Elam, Charley Lang; **D:** Robert Greenwald; **W:** R.M. Badat, Kathleen Rowell; **M:** Graeme Revell. **VHS** $19.98 FXV &½

Hearing Voices Joyless Erica is a commercial model who suffers from a form of scoliosis. If she capitalized on her infirmity by advertising medical aids, she could make a lot of money but she firmly refuses her lover's pleas to do this. When her doctor suggests reconstructive surgery, she storms out of his office but not before attracting the attention of Lee, his gay lover. Erica and Lee begin a complex emotional relationship, upsetting to everyone around them. Uninvolving characters, inert direction, and amateurish acting work against Greytak's feature film debut.
1990 87m/C Erika Nagy, Stephen Gatta, Tim Ahearn, Michael Davenport; **D:** Sharon Greytak; **W:** Sharon Greytak. **VHS** $79.95 WAC, FCT &½

The Hearse Incredibly boring horror film in which a young school teacher moves into a mansion left to her by her late aunt and finds her life threatened by a sinister black hearse.
1980 (PG) 97m/C Trish Van Devere, Joseph Cotten; **D:** George Bowers. **VHS, Beta** $54.95 MED Woof!

The Hearst and Davies Affair Married, middle-aged newspaper tycoon William Randolph Hearst falls for teenage Ziegfeld girl Marion Davies and tries to turn her into a Hollywood star. Davies was generally thought to be talented as a comedienne but Hearst insisted on choosing ill-suited dramatic roles for the blonde and her career was problematic. Their lavish lifestyle was enhanced when Hearst built San Simeon for Davies and their scandalous affair lasted 35 years. Made for television.
1985 97m/C Robert Mitchum, Virginia Madsen, Fritz Weaver; **D:** David Lowell Rich. **VHS** $79.95 ABC, PSM &&½

Heart A down-and-out small-time boxer is given a chance to make a comeback, and makes the Rocky-like most of it.
1987 (R) 93m/C Brad Davis, Jesse Doran, Sam Gray, Steve Buscemi, Frances Fisher; **D:** James Lemmo. **VHS, Beta** STE, NWV &½

Heart and Souls Reincarnation comedy casts Downey, Jr. as a mortal whose body is inhabited by four lost souls who died on the night he was born. Now an adult, he must finish what they could not, no matter how outrageous it may be. Talented cast wears plot that's old hat. Downey Jr. must be looking to do a trilogy of tired reincarnated soul roles—this is his second, "Chances Are" was his first.
1993 (PG-13) 104m/C Robert Downey Jr., Charles Grodin, Tom Sizemore, Alfre Woodard, Kyra Sedgwick, Elisabeth Shue, David Paymer; **D:** Ron Underwood; **W:** Brent Maddock, S.S. Wilson, Gregory Hansen, Erik Hansen; **M:** Marc Shaiman. **VHS** $19.98 MCA, BTV &&½

Heart Beat The fictionalized story of Jack Kerouac (author of "On the Road"), his friend and inspiration Neal Cassady, and the woman they shared, Carolyn Cassady. Based on Carolyn Cassady's memoirs. Strong performances, with Nolte as Cassady and Spacek as his wife, overcome the sometimes shaky narrative.
1980 (R) 105m/C Nick Nolte, John Heard, Sissy Spacek, Ann Dusenberry, Ray Sharkey, Tony Bill, Steve Allen, John Larroquette; **D:** John Byrum; **M:** Jack Nitzsche. **VHS, Beta** $59.95 WAR &&½

Heart Condition A deceased black lawyer's heart is donated to a bigoted Los Angeles cop who was stalking the lawyer when he was alive. Soon afterwards the lawyer's ghost returns to haunt the police officer, hoping the officer will help to avenge his murder. Both Hoskins and Washington

display fine performances given the unlikely script.
1990 (R) 95m/C Bob Hoskins, Denzel Washington, Chloe Webb, Ray Baker, Ja'net DuBois, Alan Rachins, Roger E. Mosley, Jeffrey Meek; *D:* James D. Parriott. **VHS, Beta $14.95** *COL* ✓✓ ½

The Heart is a Lonely Hunter Set in the South, Carson McCuller's tale of angst and ignorance, loneliness and beauty comes to the screen with the film debuts of Keach and Locke. Arkin gives an instinctive, gentle performance as the deaf mute; Locke's screen debut.
1968 (G) 124m/C Alan Arkin, Cicely Tyson, Sondra Locke, Stacy Keach, Chuck McCann, Laurinda Barrett; *M:* Dave Grusin. Academy Awards '68 Nominations: Best Actor (Arkin), Best Supporting Actress (Locke); New York Film Critics Awards '68: Best Actor (Arkin). **VHS, Beta $19.98** *KUI, WAR* ✓✓✓

Heart Like a Wheel The story of Shirley Muldowney, who rose from the daughter of a country-western singer to the leading lady in drag racing. The film follows her battles of sexism and choosing whether to have a career or a family. Bedelia's perfomance is outstanding. Fine showings from Bridges and Axton in supporting roles.
1983 (PG) 113m/C Bonnie Bedelia, Beau Bridges, Bill McKinney, Leo Rossi, Hoyt Axton, Dick Miller, Anthony Edwards; *D:* Jonathan Kaplan; *W:* Ken Friedman. **VHS, Beta $59.98** *FOX* ✓✓ ½

Heart of a Champion: The Ray Mancini Story Made-for-TV movie based on the life of Ray "Boom Boom" Mancini, former lightweight boxing champion. Inspired by the career his father never had due to WWII, Mancini fought his way to the top. Sylvester Stallone staged the fight sequences.
1985 94m/C Robert (Bobby) Blake, Doug McKeon, Mariclare Costello; *D:* Richard Michaels. **VHS, Beta $59.98** *FOX* ✓✓

Heart of a Nation Saga of the Montmarte family and their life during three wars, beginning with the Franco-Prussian War and ending with the Nazi occupation in France. Although ordered to be destroyed by the Nazis, this film was saved, along with many others, by the French "Cinema Resistance." In French with English subtitles. *AKA:* Untel Pere et Fils.
1943 111m/B Louis Jouvet, Raimu, Suzy Prim, Michael Morgan, Renee Devillers; *D:* Paul Graetz. **VHS $24.95** *NOS, DVT, HEG* ✓✓✓

Heart of Darkness Joseph Conrad's 1902 menacing novella set in the Belgian Congo is told through flashbacks by Marlow (Roth), whose employers, a Belgian trading company, hire him to find Kurtz (Malkovich), head of a remote trading station, who is rumored to be hoarding a huge cache of ivory. Marlow's journey up the river is beset by obstacles and Kurtz is rumored to be either insane or a prophet in his jungle kingdom. Filmed in Belize; made for television. Francis Ford Coppola's updated adaptation became "Apocalyse Now."
1993 120m/C Tim Roth, John Malkovich, James Fox, Isaach de Bankole, Patrick Ryecart, Geoffrey Hutchings, Peter Vaughan, Phoebe Nicholls, Allan Cordurner, Alan Scarfe, Iman, Timothy Bateson; *D:* Nicolas Roeg; *W:* Benedict Fitzgerald; *M:* Stanley Myers. **VHS** *TTC* ✓✓

The Heart of Dixie Three college co-eds at a southern university in the 1950s see their lives and values change with the influence of the civil rights movement. College newspaper reporter Sheedy takes up the

cause of a black man victimized by racial violence. Lightweight social-conscience fare.
1989 (PG) 96m/C Virginia Madsen, Ally Sheedy, Phoebe Cates, Treat Williams, Kyle Secor, Francesca Roberts, Barbara Babcock, Don Michael Paul, Kurtwood Smith, Richard Bradford; *D:* Martin Davidson. **VHS, Beta $19.98** *ORI* ✓✓

Heart of Glass A pre-industrial Bavarian village becomes deeply troubled when their glassblower dies without imparting the secret of making his unique Ruby glass. The townspeople go to extremes, from madness to murder to magic, to discover the ingredients. From German director Herzog (who hypnotized his cast daily), this somewhat apocalyptic tale is based on legend. The colors are incredible in their intensity. In German with English subtitles.
1974 93m/C Josef Bierbichler, Stefan Autter, Scheitz Clemens, Volker Prechtel, Sonia Skiba; *D:* Werner Herzog. **VHS $79.95** *NYF, ING, FCT* ✓✓✓

Heart of Humanity An intense drama of love, patriotism, and sacrifice just before the war in a small Canadian village. A traveler who is really a Prussian army lieutenant finds his way to the house of a young man who is about to wed. He ends up falling in love with his fiancee and war is declared just before the wedding. A silent film with music score.
1918 133m/B Dorothy Phillips, Erich von Stroheim; *D:* Allen Holubar. **VHS, Beta, 8mm $19.95** *GPV, VYY, GVV* ✓✓✓

Heart of Midnight An emotionally unstable young woman inherits a seedy massage parlor. She works hard to turn it, and herself, into something better. Nice performance by Leigh.
1989 (R) 93m/C Jennifer Jason Leigh, Brenda Vaccaro, Frank Stallone, Peter Coyote, Gale Mayron, Sam Schacht, Denise Dumont; *D:* Matthew Chapman; *W:* Matthew Chapman; *M:* Yanni. **VHS, Beta** *NO* ✓✓ ½

Heart of Texas Ryan Flamboyant cowboy star fights with kidnappers and wins in this silent film.
1916 50m/B Tom Mix. **VHS, Beta $16.95** *GPV, NOS, DVT* ✓ ½

Heart of the Golden West Roy protects ranchers of Cherokee City from unjust shipping charges.
1942 65m/B Roy Rogers, Smiley Burnette, George "Gabby" Hayes, Bob Nolan, Ruth Terry; *D:* Joseph Kane. **VHS, Beta $19.95** *NOS, VYY, VCN* ✓

Heart of the Rio Grande Spoiled young rich girl tries to trick her father into coming to her "rescue" at a western dude ranch.
1942 70m/B Gene Autry, Smiley Burnette, Fay McKenzie, Edith Fellows, Joseph Stauch Jr.; *D:* William M. Morgan. **VHS, Beta $29.98** *CCB, VCN* ✓ ½

Heart of the Rockies The Three Mesquiteers stop a mountain family's rustling and illegal game trappers.
1937 54m/B Bob Livingston, Ray Corrigan, Max Terhune, Lynn (Mary Hart) Roberts, Yakima Canutt, J.P. McGowan; *D:* Joseph Kane. **VHS, Beta $9.95** *NOS, VCN, MED* ✓ ½

Heart of the Rockies Roy, along with his trusty horse and dog, takes care of a highway construction project.
1951 67m/B Roy Rogers, Penny Edwards, Gordon Jones, Ralph Morgan, Fred Graham, Mira McKinney; *D:* William Witney. **VHS $19.95** *NOS, DVT, TIM* ✓ ½

Heart of the Stag On an isolated sheep ranch in the New Zealand outback, a father and daughter suffer the repercussions of an incestuous relationship when she becomes enamored with a hired hand.
1984 (R) 94m/C Bruno Lawrence, Mary Regan, Terence Cooper; *D:* Michael Firth. **VHS, Beta $19.95** *STE, NWV* ✓✓ ½

Heartaches A reporter tries to track down a murderer who has killed twice.
1947 71m/B Chill Wills, Sheila Ryan, Edward Norris, James Seay. **VHS, Beta $19.95** *NOS, DVT, TIM* ✓✓

Heartaches A young pregnant woman (Potts) meets up with a crazy girlfriend (Kidder) in this touching film about love and friendship. Although a study in contrasts, the two end up sharing an apartment together in Toronto. Fine performances from Potts and Kidder give life to this romantic comedy.
1982 90m/C Margot Kidder, Annie Potts, Robert Carradine, Winston Rekert; *D:* Donald Shebib. **VHS, Beta $69.98** *LIV, VES* ✓✓✓

Heartbeat If you thought pointless Hollywood remakes of French films were a new phenomenon (see "Pure Luck," for example), then note this lighthearted remake of a 1940 Gallic farce. Rogers becomes the best student in a Parisian school for pickpockets, but when she tries out her skills on a dashing diplomat they fall in love instead.
1946 100m/B Ginger Rogers, Jean-Pierre Aumont, Adolphe Menjou, Basil Rathbone, Melville Cooper, Mona Maris, Henry Stephenson, Eduardo Ciannelli; *D:* Sam Wood. **VHS $19.95** *NOS, TIM, HEG* ✓✓ ½

Heartbeeps In 1995, two domestic robot servants fall in love and run off together. On a beach they encounter the Energizer Bunny. No, that's not right. Young kids may enjoy the romantic robotic duo of Kaufman and Peters.
1981 (PG) 79m/C Andy Kaufman, Bernadette Peters, Randy Quaid, Kenneth McMillan, Christopher Guest, Melanie Mayron, Jack Carter; *D:* Allan Arkush; *M:* John Williams. **VHS, Beta $39.95** *MCA* ✓✓

Heartbreak Hotel Johnny Wolfe kidnaps Elvis Presley from his show in Cleveland and drives him home to his mother, a die-hard Elvis fan. Completely unbelievable, utterly ridiculous, and still a lot of fun.
1988 (PG-13) 101m/C David Keith, Tuesday Weld, Charlie Schlatter, Angela Goethals, Jacque Lynn Colton, Chris Mulkey, Karen Landry, Tudor Sherrard, Paul Harkins; *D:* Chris Columbus; *W:* Chris Columbus; *M:* Georges Delerue. **VHS, Beta $89.95** *TOU* ✓✓ ½

Heartbreak House A production of George Bernard Shaw's classic play about a captain and his daughter who invite an odd assortment of people into their home for a few days. In the course of their visit, each person shares his ambitions, hopes, and fears. From the "American Playhouse" television series.
1986 118m/C Rex Harrison, Rosemary Harris, Amy Irving; *D:* Anthony Page. **VHS, Beta $59.95** *ACA, PBS* ✓✓

The Heartbreak Kid Director May's comic examination of love and hypocrisy. Grodin embroils himself in a triangle with his new bride and a woman he can't have, an absolutely gorgeous and totally unloving woman he shouldn't want. Walks the fence between tragedy and comedy, with an exceptional performance from Berlin. Based on Bruce Jay Friedman's story.
1972 (PG) 106m/C Charles Grodin, Cybill Shepherd, Eddie Albert, Jeannie Berlin, Audra Lindley, Art Metrano; *D:* Elaine May; *W:* Neil Simon. **VHS, Beta $19.95** *MED, VTR* ✓✓✓

Heartbreak Ridge An aging Marine recon sergeant is put in command of a young platoon to whip them into shape to prepare for combat in the invasion of Grenada. Eastwood whips this old story into shape too, with a fine performance of a man who's given everything to the Marines. The invasion of Grenada, though, is not epic material. (Also available in English with Spanish subtitles.)
1986 (R) 130m/C Clint Eastwood, Marsha Mason, Everett McGill, Arlen Dean Snyder, Bo Svenson, Moses Gunn, Eileen Heckart, Boyd Gaines, Mario Van Peebles; **D:** Clint Eastwood; **W:** Jim Carabatsos; **M:** Lennie Niehaus. **VHS, Beta, 8mm $19.98** *WAR, TLF* 🎞️🎞️🎞️

Heartbreaker Eastern Los Angeles explodes with vicious turf wars when Beto and Hector battle for the affection of Kim, the neighborhood's newest heartbreaker.
1983 (R) 90m/C Fernando Allende, Dawn Dunlap, Michael D. Roberts, Robert Dryer, Apollonia; **D:** Frank Zuniga. **VHS, Beta $49.95** *MED* 🎞️½

Heartbreakers Two male best friends find themselves in the throes of drastic changes in their careers and romantic encounters. On target acting makes this old story new, with a fine performance by Wayne, in her last film before her death.
1984 (R) 98m/C Peter Coyote, Nick Mancuso, Carole Laure, Max Gail, James Laurenson, Carol Wayne, Jamie Rose, Kathryn Harrold; **D:** Bobby Roth; **W:** Bobby Roth; **M:** Tangerine Dream. **VHS, Beta $79.95** *VES* 🎞️🎞️🎞️

Heartburn Based on Nora Ephron's own semi-autobiographical novel about her marital travails with writer Carl Bernstein, this is a tepid, bitter modern romance between writers already shell-shocked from previous marriages.
1986 (R) 109m/C Meryl Streep, Jack Nicholson, Steven Hill, Richard Masur, Stockard Channing, Jeff Daniels, Milos Forman, Catherine O'Hara, Maureen Stapleton, Karen Akers, Joanna Gleason, Mercedes Ruehl, Caroline Aaron, Yakov Smirnoff, Anna Maria Horsford, Wilfrid Hyde-White; **D:** Mike Nichols; **W:** Nora Ephron; **M:** Carly Simon. **VHS, Beta, 8mm $19.95** *PAR* 🎞️🎞️🎞️

Heartland Set in 1910, this film chronicles the story of one woman's life on the Wyoming Frontier, the hazards she faces, and her courage and spirit. Stunningly realistic and without cliche. Based on the diaries of Elinore Randall Stewart.
1981 (PG) 95m/C Conchata Ferrell, Rip Torn, Barry Primus, Lilia Skala, Megan Folson; **D:** Richard Pearce. **VHS, Beta $79.99** *HBO* 🎞️🎞️🎞️½

Hearts & Armour A holy war between Christians and Moors erupts when a Moorish princess is kidnapped. Based on Ludovico Ariosto's "Orlando Furioso."
1983 101m/C Tanya Roberts, Leigh McCloskey, Ron Moss, Rick Edwards, Giovanni Visentin; **D:** Giacomo Battiato. **VHS, Beta $19.98** *WAR, HBO* 🎞️🎞️

Heart's Desire Opera great Tauber stars in this musical of an unknown Viennese singer who falls in love with an English girl.
1937 79m/B Richard Tauber, Lenora Corbett, Kathleen Kelly, Paul Graetz; **D:** Paul Stein. **VHS, Beta $24.95** *NO* 🎞️🎞️

Heart's Haven An insensitive wife (Adams), who doesn't appreciate how wonderful her husband is, winds up running away with another man.
1922 61m/B Claire Adams, Robert McKim, Carl Gantvoort, Jean Hersholt; **D:** Benjamin B. Hampton. **VHS, Beta $16.95** *GPV, FCT* 🎞️🎞️½

Hearts of Darkness: A Filmmaker's Apocalypse This riveting, critically acclaimed documentary about the making of Francis Ford Coppola's masterpiece "Apocalypse Now" is based largely on original footage shot and directed by his wife Eleanor. Also included are recent interviews with cast and crew members including Coppola, Martin Sheen, Robert Duvall, Frederic Forrest and Dennis Hopper.
1991 (R) 96m/C Sam Bottoms, Eleanor Coppola, Francis Ford Coppola, Robert Duvall, Laurence "Larry" Fishburne, Frederic Forrest, Albert Hall, Dennis Hopper, George Lucas, John Milius, Martin Sheen; **D:** Fax Bahr, George Hickenlooper; **W:** Fax Bahr, George Hickenlooper. **VHS, Beta $14.95** *PAR* 🎞️🎞️🎞️🎞️

Hearts of Fire A trio of successful rock 'n roll stars work out their confused romantic entanglements. Barely released and then, not even in the U.S. Sad outing for the cast, especially legendary Dylan.
1987 90m/C Bob Dylan, Fionna, Rupert Everett, Julian Glover; **D:** Richard Marquand; **W:** Joe Eszterhas; **M:** John Barry. **VHS, Beta $14.95** *LHV, WAR* 🎞️

Hearts of Humanity Mawkish melodrama concerning a Jewish antique dealer and his relationship with the son of an Irish cop. An early "Chico and the Man" variant.
1932 56m/B Jean Hersholt, Jackie Searl, J. Farrell MacDonald, Claudia Dell, Charles Delaney, Lucille LaVerne, George Humbert; **D:** Christy Cabanne. **VHS $19.95** *NOS, HEG* 🎞️🎞️

Hearts of the West A fantasy-filled farm boy travels to Hollywood in the 1930s and seeks a writing career. Instead, he finds himself an ill-suited western movie star in this small offbeat comedy-drama that's sure to charm. *AKA:* Hollywood Cowboy.
1975 (PG) 103m/C Jeff Bridges, Andy Griffith, Donald Pleasence, Alan Arkin, Blythe Danner; **D:** Howard Zieff; **W:** Rob Thompson. **VHS, Beta $19.98** *MGM* 🎞️🎞️🎞️½

Hearts of the World A vintage Griffith epic about a young boy who goes off to WWI and the tribulations endured by both him and his family on the homefront. Overly sentimental but powerfully made melodrama, from Griffith's waning years. Silent with music score.
1918 152m/B Lillian Gish, Robert Harron, Dorothy Gish, Erich von Stroheim, Ben Alexander, Josephine Crowell, Noel Coward, Mary Gish; **D:** D.W. Griffith. **VHS, Beta, 8mm $19.95** *GPV, REP, GVV* 🎞️🎞️🎞️

Heartstopper Benjamin Latham, an innocent physician in Pittsburgh, was accused of being a vampire in colonial times and hung. 200 years later, he emerges from the grave, unscathed. While trying to figure out what has happened, he falls in love with a photojournalist, who helps him find his own descendent, Matthew Latham. Unfortunately, his deep freeze has left him with the compulsion to kill, but only evil members of society.
1992 96m/B Moon Zappa, Tom Savini, Kevin Kindlan. **VHS $30.00** *TEM, MOV* 🎞️

Heat Another Andy Warhol-produced journey into drug-addled urban seediness. Features a former child actor/junkie and a has-been movie star barely surviving in a rundown motel. This is one of Warhol's better film productions; even non-fans may enjoy it.
1972 102m/C Joe Dallesandro, Sylvia Miles, Pat Ast; **D:** Paul Morrissey. **VHS, Beta $29.95** *TPV, PAR, FCT* 🎞️🎞️🎞️

Heat A Las Vegas bodyguard avenges the beating of an old flame by a mobster's son, and incites mob retaliation. Based on the William Goldman novel.
1987 (R) 103m/C Burt Reynolds, Karen Young, Peter MacNicol, Howard Hesseman; **D:** R.M. Richards; **W:** William Goldman; **M:** Michael Gibbs. **VHS, Beta $14.95** *PAR* 🎞️½

Heat and Dust A young bride joins her husband at his post in India and is inexorably drawn to the country and its prince of state. Years later her great niece journeys to modern day India in search of the truth about her scandalous and mysterious relative. More than the story of two romances, this is the tale of women rebelling against an unseen caste system which keeps them second-class citizens. Ruth Jhabvala wrote the novel and screenplay.
1982 (R) 130m/C Julie Christie, Greta Scacchi, Shashi Kapoor, Christopher Cazenove, Nickolas Grace; **D:** James Ivory; **W:** Ruth Prawer Jhabvala. **VHS, Beta $59.95** *MCA* 🎞️🎞️🎞️

Heat and Sunlight A photographer becomes obsessively jealous of his lover as their relationship comes to an end. Director Nilsson again used a unique improvisational, video-to-film technique, as he did with his previous film, "Signal 7."
1987 98m/B Rob Nilsson, Consuelo Faust, Bill Bailey, Don Bajema, Ernie Fosselius; **D:** Rob Nilsson; **W:** Rob Nilsson. **VHS, Beta $29.95** *CVC* 🎞️½

Heat of Desire A philosophy professor abandons everything (including his wife) for a woman he barely knows and is conned by her "relatives." With English subtitles. *AKA:* Plein Sud.
1984 (R) 90m/C Clio Goldsmith, Patrick Dewaere, Jeanne Moreau, Guy Marchand; **D:** Luc Beraud. **VHS, Beta $59.95** *COL* 🎞️🎞️

The Heat of the Day A British officer is accused of treason. As he attempts to find those who framed him, he meets a lovely woman all too willing to help. But whose side is she really on? Set in WWII. Tense and well-acted. Originally made for Masterpiece Theatre.
1991 120m/C Michael York, Patricia Hodge, Peggy Ashcroft, Anna Carteret, Michael Gambon; **W:** Harold Pinter. **VHS $19.95** *PBS* 🎞️🎞️

Heat of the Flame A vicious woodsman captures and rapes a beautiful girl. Psychological games, eroticism and exploitive nudity ensue.
1982 88m/C Tony Ferrandis, Ellie MacLure, Raymond Young, Anthony Mayans. **VHS, Beta $39.95** *VCD* 🎞️

Heat Street Two thugs exact revenge on street gangs for the murders of loved ones. Made for video.
1987 90m/C Quincy Adams, Deborah Gibson, Wendy MacDonald, Del Zamora; **D:** Joseph Merhi. **VHS, Beta $39.95** *HHE* 🎞️

Heat Wave A writer gets involved with a "femme fatale" who kills her wealthy husband for the love of a young pianist.
1954 60m/B Alex Nicol, Hillary Brooke, Sidney James, Susan Stephen, Paul Carpenter; **D:** Ken Hughes; **W:** Ken Hughes. **VHS, Beta** *NO* 🎞️½

Heat Wave The Watts ghetto uprising of 1965 is a proving ground for a young black journalist. Excellent cast and fine script portrays the anger and frustration of blacks in Los Angeles and the U.S. in the 1960s and the fear of change felt by blacks and whites when civil rights reform began. Strong drama with minimal emotionalism. Made for cable TV.
1990 (R) 92m/C Blair Underwood, Cicely Tyson, James Earl Jones, Sally Kirkland, Margaret Avery, David Strathairn, Robert Hooks, Adam Arkin, Paris Vaughan, Charlie Korsmo. **VHS, Beta $79.88** *TTC* 🎞️🎞️🎞️

Heated Vengeance A Vietnam vet returns to the jungle to find the woman he left behind, and runs into some old enemies. **1987 (R) 91m/C** Richard Hatch, Michael J. Pollard, Mills Watson, Cameron Dye; **D:** Edward Murphy. **VHS, Beta $79.95** MED ℐ

Heathers Clique of stuck-up girls named Heather rule the high school social scene until the newest member (not a Heather) decides that enough is enough. She and her outlaw boyfriend embark (accidentally on her part, intentionally on his) on a murder spree disguised as a rash of teen suicides. Dense, take-no-prisoners black comedy with buckets of potent slang, satire and unforgiving hostility. Humor this dark is rare; sharply observed and acted, though the end is out of place. Slater does his best Nicholson impression. **1989 (R) 102m/C** Winona Ryder, Christian Slater, Kim Walker, Shannen Doherty, Lisanne Falk, Penelope Milford, Glenn Shadix, Lance Fenton, Patrick Laborteaux; **D:** Michael Lehmann. **VHS, Beta $19.95** STE, NWV, FCT ℐℐ½

The Heat's On Gaxton is a broadway producer with a failing musical and an unhappy star in West. He cranks up the publicity machine and gets the show declared immoral by the Legion of Purity which results in its closing (not what he expected). Gaxton then runs a scam to become the producer of West's new show, which just happens to be financed by some Legion members. Very uneven plot and performances with thrown-in musical numbers. West wrote her own dialogue but unlike her early films she had little control over the production and it showed. West didn't make another movie for 27 years (the appalling "Myra Breckenridge"). ♫Just a Stranger in Town; Hello, Mi Amigo; The White Keys and the Black Keys; There Goes That Guitar; Antonio; The Caissons Go Rolling Along; There Goes My Heart. **AKA:** Tropicana. **1943 79m/B** Mae West, William Gaxton, Victor Moore, Almira Sessions, Lester Allen, Mary Roche, Alan Dinehart, Lloyd Bridges; **D:** Gregory Ratoff; **W:** Fitzroy Davis, George S. George, Fred Schiller. **VHS $19.95** FCT ℐ

Heatwave Local residents oppose a multi-million dollar residential complex in Australia. Davis portrays a liberal activist, who wages war with the developers, and, in return, becomes involved with a possible murder case. **1983 (R) 92m/C** Judy Davis, Richard Moir, Chris Haywood, Bill Hunter, John Gregg, Anna Jemison; **D:** Phillip Noyce. **VHS, Beta** NO ℐℐℐ

Heaven An exploration of "heaven" including the idea, the place, and people's views about it. Questions such as "How do you get there?" and "What goes on up there?" are discussed. Offbeat interviews mixed with a collage of celestial images. **1987 (PG-13) 80m/C D:** Diane Keaton. **VHS, Beta $14.95** FCT ℐℐ½

Heaven & Earth A samurai epic covering the battle for the future of Japan between two feuding warlords. The overwhelming battle scenes were actually filmed on location in Canada. In Japanese with English subtitles. **1990 (PG-13) 104m/C** Masahiko Tsugawa, Takaai Enoki, Atsuko Asano, Tsunehiko Watase, Naomi Zaizen, Binpachi Ito. **VHS $79.98** LIV, ING ℐℐℐ

Heaven and Earth Conclusion of Stone's Vietnam trilogy (after "Platoon" and "Born on the Fourth of July") focuses on Vietnamese woman (film debut of Le) and her life under the French and American occupations. Jones is the American soldier who marries her and eventually brings her to the U.S. Not one for subtleties, Stone chases melodramatic excess with finesse of lumberjack, sawing away at guilt and remorse from a "woman's point of view." Cranky Tommy Lee shows up too late to save flick and is saddled with a perplexing I.D. to boot. Flawed, ambitious, and interesting if a student of Stone. Based on the two autobiographies of Le Ly Haslip, "When Heaven and Earth Changed Places" and "Child of War, Woman of Peace." Filmed on location in Thailand. **1993 (R) 142m/C** Hiep Thi Le, Tommy Lee Jones, Joan Chen, Haing S. Ngor, Debbie Reynolds, Conchata Ferrell, Dustin Nguyen, Liem Whatley, Dale Dye; **D:** Oliver Stone; **W:** Oliver Stone; **M:** Kitaro. **VHS** WAR ℐℐ

Heaven Can Wait Social satire in which a rogue tries to convince the Devil to admit him into Hell by relating the story of his philandering life and discovers that he was a more valuable human being than he thought. A witty Lubitsch treat based on the play "Birthdays." **1943 112m/C** Don Ameche, Gene Tierney, Laird Cregar, Charles Coburn, Marjorie Main, Eugene Pallette, Allyn Joslyn, Spring Byington, Signe Hasso, Louis Calhern, Dickie Moore, Florence Bates, Scotty Beckett, Charles Halton; **D:** Ernst Lubitsch. **VHS, Beta $19.98** FOX, FCT ℐℐℐ

Heaven Can Wait A remake of 1941's "Here Comes Mr. Jordan," about a football player who is mistakenly summoned to heaven before his time. When the mistake is realized, he is returned to Earth in the body of a corrupt executive about to be murdered by his wife. Not to be confused with the 1943 film of the same name. **1978 (PG) 101m/C** Warren Beatty, Julie Christie, Charles Grodin, Dyan Cannon, James Mason, Jack Warden; **D:** Buck Henry; **W:** Warren Beatty, Elaine May; **M:** Dave Grusin. Academy Awards '78: Best Art Direction/Set Decoration; Nominations: Best Actor (Beatty), Best Adapted Screenplay, Best Director (Beatty, Henry), Best Picture, Best Supporting Actor (Warden), Best Supporting Actress (Cannon), Best Original Score; Golden Globe Awards '79: Best Actor—Musical/Comedy (Beatty), Best Film—Musical/Comedy, Best Supporting Actress (Cannon). **VHS, Beta $14.95** PAR, FOX, HMV ℐℐℐ

Heaven Help Us Three mischievous boys find themselves continually in trouble with the priests running their Brooklyn Catholic high school during the mid-1960s. Realistic and humorous look at adolescent life. **AKA:** Catholic Boys. **1985 (R) 102m/C** Andrew McCarthy, Mary Stuart Masterson, Kevin Dillon, Malcolm Danare, Jennie Dundas, Kate Reid, Wallace Shawn, Jay Patterson, John Heard, Donald Sutherland, Yeardley Smith, Sherry Steiner, Calvert Deforest, Philip Bosco, Patrick Dempsey, Christopher Durang; **D:** Michael Dinner; **W:** Charles Purpura; **M:** James Horner. **VHS, Beta** NO ℐℐ½

Heaven is a Playground On Chicago's South Side an inner city basketball coach and an idealistic young lawyer are determined to change the fate of a group of high school boys. The men use the incentive of athletic scholarships to keep their team in school and away from drugs and gangs. **1991 (R) 104m/C** D.B. Sweeney, Michael Warren, Richard Jordan, Victor Love; **D:** Randall Fried; **W:** Randall Fried. **VHS $19.95** COL ℐℐ½

Heaven on Earth The story of two orphaned British children who, along with thousands of orphans shipped from England to Canada between 1867 and 1914, try to make new lives in the Canadian wilderness. **1989 101m/C** R.H. Thomson, Sian Leisa Davies, Torquil Campbell, Fiona Reid; **D:** Allen Kroeker; **W:** Margaret Atwood. **VHS, Beta** NO ℐℐ½

Heaven Tonight Ex-rock star dad copes with midlife crisis by trying for his big comeback, this time with his son. **1993 (R) 97m/C** John Waters, Rebecca Gilling, Guy Pearce, Kim Gyngell; **D:** Pina Amenta. **VHS $89.95** ACA ℐℐ½

Heavenly Bodies A young woman who dreams of owning a health club will stop at nothing to accomplish her goals. When a rival tries to put her out of business, a "dancedown" takes place in this lame low-budget aerobics musical. **1984 (R) 99m/C** Cynthia Dale, Richard Rebrere, Laura Henry, Stuart Stone, Walter George Alton, Cec Linder; **D:** Lawrence Dane. **VHS, Beta $19.98** FOX Woof!

The Heavenly Kid Leather-jacketed "cool" guy who died in a sixties hot rod crash finally receives an offer to exit limbo and enter heaven. The deal requires that he educate his dull earthly son on more hip and worldly ways. A big problem is that the soundtrack and wardrobe are 1955, whereas the cocky cool greaser supposedly died seventeen years ago in 1968. Mildly entertaining. **1985 (PG-13) 92m/C** Lewis Smith, Jane Kaczmarek, Jason Gedrick, Richard Mulligan; **D:** Cary Medoway. **VHS, Beta** NO ℐℐ

Heavens Above A sharp, biting satire on cleric life in England. Sellers stars as the quiet, down-to-earth reverend who is appointed to a new post in space. **1963 113m/B** Peter Sellers, Cecil Parker, Isabel Jeans, Eric Sykes, Ian Carmichael; **D:** John Boulting, Roy Boulting; **M:** Richard Rodney Bennett. **VHS, Beta $19.98** FCT ℐℐℐ

Heaven's Gate The uncut version of Cimino's notorious folly. A fascinating, plotless, and exaggerated account of the Johnson County cattle war of the 1880s. Ravishingly photographed, the film's production almost single-handedly put United Artists out of business. **1981 (R) 220m/C** Kris Kristofferson, Christopher Walken, Isabelle Huppert, John Hurt, Richard Masur, Mickey Rourke, Brad Dourif, Joseph Cotten, Jeff Bridges, Sam Waterston, Terry O'Quinn, Geoffrey Lewis; **D:** Michael Cimino; **W:** Michael Cimino. **VHS, Beta $29.99** MGM, FCT ℐℐ

Heaven's Heroes Dennis Hill, a dedicated policeman, was killed in the line of duty on August 27, 1977. This film recalls his life and deep faith in Jesus. **1988 72m/C** David Ralphe, Heidi Vaughn, James O'Hagen; **D:** Donald W. Thompson. **VHS, Beta $29.95** MIV, BPG ℐ

Heavy Petting A hilarious compilation of "love scene" footage from feature films of the silent era to the sixties, newsreels, news reports, educational films, old TV shows, and home movies. **1989 75m/C** David Byrne, Josh Mostel, Sandra Bernhard, Allen Ginsberg, Ann Magnuson, Spalding Gray, Laurie Anderson, John Oates, Abbie Hoffman, Jacki Ochs; **D:** Obie Benz. **VHS, Beta $29.95** SUE, ACA ℐℐ½

Heavy Traffic Ralph Bakshi's animated fantasy portrait of the hard-edged underside of city life. A young cartoonist draws the people, places, and paranoia of his environment. **1973 76m/C D:** Ralph Bakshi. **VHS, Beta** WAR, OM ℐℐℐ

Hector's Bunyip What's a bunyip? People think it's just Hector's scaly imaginary friend. It therefore comes as quite a surprise when Hector gets kidnapped—by his supposed imaginary friend! Aired on PBS as part of the "Wonderworks" series.

1986 58m/C Scott Bartle, Robert Coleby, Barbara Stephens, Tushka Hose; **D:** Mark Callan. **VHS** $14.95 *PME, FCT, BTV* ❚❚❚

Hedda A dramatization of the Henrik Ibsen play, "Hedda Gabler," about a middle-class pregnant woman. The story finds her frustrated with her life and manipulating those around her with tragic results.
1975 102m/C Glenda Jackson, Peter Eyre, Timothy West, Jennie Linden, Patrick Stewart; **D:** Trevor Nunn. **VHS, Beta** $59.95 *MED* ❚❚½

Hedda Hopper's Hollywood Newsreel version of the gossip-hound's column, featuring scoops on Ball, Cooper, Minelli and many more.
1942 58m/B Hedda Hopper, Gary Cooper, Lucille Ball, Gloria Swanson, Liza Minnelli. **VHS** $19.95 *REP* ❚❚½

Heidi Johanna Spyri's classic tale puts Shirley Temple in the hands of a mean governess and the loving arms of her Swiss grandfather. Also available colorized. Remade in 1967. Also available with "Poor Little Rich Girl" on Laser Disc.
1937 88m/B Shirley Temple, Jean Hersholt, Helen Westley, Arthur Treacher; **D:** Allan Dwan. **VHS, Beta** $14.98 *FXV, HMV, MLT* ❚❚❚

Heidi The Swiss do their own version of the children's classic by Johanna Spyri. A precocious little girl enjoys life in the Swiss Alps with her grandfather, until her stern aunt takes her away to live in the village in the valley.
1952 98m/B Elsbeth Sigmund, Heinrich Gretler, Thomas Klameth, Elsie Attenoff; **D:** Luigi Comencini. **VHS** $8.95 *CNG, MRV, KAR* ❚❚½

Heidi The classic story from Johanna Spyri's novel is filmed beautifully in the Swiss Alps in Eastmancolor. Heidi is kidnapped by her mean aunt and forced to work as a slave for a rich family. Her kindly old grandfather comes to her rescue. Family entertainment for all, dubbed in English.
1965 95m/C Eva Maria Singhammer, Gustav Knuth, Lotte Ledl; **D:** Werner Jacobs. **VHS** *NO* ❚❚❚

Heidi The second American adaptation of the classic Johanna Spyri novel tells the story of an orphaned girl who goes to the Swiss Alps to live with her grandfather. Made for television.
1967 100m/C Maximilian Schell, Jennifer Edwards, Michael Redgrave, Jean Simmons; **D:** Delbert Mann; **M:** John Williams. **VHS, Beta** $19.98 *LIV, VES, GLV* ❚❚

Heidi Yet another version of the children's classic, from German writer Johanna Spyri's 1881 novel. Thornton is charming as the orphan shuttled from relative to relative until she happily ends up with her crotchety grandfather (Robards) in his mountain cabin. Then her cousin comes along and whisks her off to the city to be a companion to the invalid Klara (Randall). Seymour is the snobbish, scowling governess. This "Heidi" is spunky enough to keep the sugar level tolerable. Filmed on location in Austria. Made for television.
1993 (G) 167m/C Noley Thornton, Jason Robards Jr., Jane Seymour, Lexi Randall, Sian Phillips, Patricia Neal, Benjamin Brazier, Michael Simkins, Andrew Bicknell, Jane Hazlegrove; **D:** Michael Rhodes; **W:** Jeanne Rosenberg; **M:** Lee Holdridge. **VHS** $19.99 *DIS* ❚❚❚

The Heiress Based on the Henry James novel "Washington Square," about a wealthy plain Jane, her tyrannical father, and the handsome fortune-seeking scoundrel who seeks to marry her.

1949 115m/B Olivia de Havilland, Montgomery Clift, Ralph Richardson, Miriam Hopkins; **D:** William Wyler; **M:** Aaron Copland. Academy Awards '49: Best Actress (de Havilland), Best Art Direction/Set Decoration (B & W), Best Costume Design (B & W), Best Original Score; Nominations: Best Black and White Cinematography, Best Director (Wyler), Best Picture, Best Supporting Actor (Richardson); Golden Globe Awards '50: Best Actress—Drama (de Havilland); National Board of Review Awards '49: 10 Best Films of the Year, Best Actor (Richardson). **VHS, Beta** $14.95 *MCA, MLB, BTV* ❚❚❚½

The Heist An explosive crime thriller...
1988 (R) 93m/C Lee Van Cleef, Karen Black, Edward Albert, Lionel Stander, Robert Alda. **VHS** *NO* ❚❚

The Heist A made-for-cable-television film about an ex-con who, upon regaining his freedom, sets out to rip off the crook who framed him. Entertaining enough story with a first-rate cast.
1989 97m/C Pierce Brosnan, Tom Skerritt, Wendy Hughes; **D:** Stuart Orme. **VHS, Beta** $89.99 *HBO, HHE* ❚❚

Held for Murder When a vacationing daughter is accused of murder, her mom lovingly takes the blame. Will the daughter come back to clear her mom, or will she let her fry in the electric chair? *AKA:* Her Mad Night.
1932 67m/B Irene Rich, Conway Tearle, Mary Carlisle, Kenneth Thomson, William B. Davidson; **D:** E. Mason Hopper. **VHS, Beta** $16.95 *SNC* ❚

Held Hostage The true story of Jerry Levin, a reporter kidnapped by terrorists while on assignment in Beirut, and his wife, Sis, who struggled with the State Department for his release. Made for television.
1991 95m/C Marlo Thomas, David Dukes, G.W. Bailey, Ed Winter, Robert Harper, William Schallert; **D:** Roger Young. **VHS** *NO* ❚❚

Hell Comes to Frogtown In a post-nuclear holocaust land run by giant frogs, a renegade who is one of the few non-sterile men left on earth must rescue some fertile women and impregnate them. Sci-fi spoof is extremely low-budget, but fun. Stars "Rowdy" Roddy Piper of wrestling fame.
1988 (R) 88m/C Roddy Piper, Sandahl Bergman, Rory Calhoun, Donald G. Jackson; **D:** Robert J. Kizer. **VHS, Beta** $19.95 *STE, NWV* ❚

Hell Commandos Soldiers in WWII struggle to prevent the Nazis from releasing a deadly bacteria that will kill millions. Dubbed.
1969 92m/C Guy Madison, Stan Cooper; **D:** J.L. Merino. **VHS, Beta** *NO* ❚½

Hell Fire Austin Maynard finds himself mixed up with outlaws in the Old West.
1932 60m/B Ken Maynard, Nat Pendleton, Jack Perrin; **D:** Forrest Sheldon. **VHS, Beta** $19.95 *NOS, VCN, DVT* ❚½

Hell Harbor Caribbean love, murder and greed combine to make this early talkie. Exterior shots were filmed on the west coast of Florida and the beauty of the Tampa area in the 1930s is definitely something to see.
1930 65m/B Lupe Velez, Gibson Gowland, Jean Hersholt, John Holland; **D:** Henry King. **VHS, Beta** $47.50 *GVV* ❚❚

Hell High Four high schoolers plan a night of torture and humiliation for an annoying teacher, only to find she has some deadly secrets of her own. Dumber than it sounds.
1986 (R) 84m/C Christopher Stryker, Christopher Cousins, Millie Prezioso, Jason Brill; **D:** Douglas Grossman. **VHS, Beta** $79.95 *PSM* ❚

Hell Hounds of Alaska A man goes searching for a kidnapped boy in the gold rush days of Alaska.
197? (G) 90m/C Doug McClure. **VHS, Beta** *NO* ❚

Hell Hunters Nazi-hunters foil the plot of an old German doctor to poison the population of L.A. Meanwhile, a daughter avenges the death of her mother by blowing up the doctor's jungle compound.
1987 98m/C Stewart Granger, Maud Adams, George Lazenby, Candice Daly, Romulo Arantes, William Berger. **VHS, Beta** *NO* ❚

Hell in the Pacific A marvelously photographed (by Conrad Hall) psycho/macho allegory, about an American and a Japanese soldier stranded together on a tiny island and the mini-war they fight all by themselves. Overly obvious anti-war statement done with style.
1969 (PG) 101m/C Lee Marvin, Toshiro Mifune; **D:** John Boorman. **VHS, Beta** $14.98 *FOX* ❚❚❚

Hell is for Heroes McQueen stars as the bitter leader of a small infantry squad outmanned by the Germans in this tight WWII drama. A strong cast and riveting climax make this a must for action fans.
1962 90m/B Steve McQueen, Bobby Darin, Fess Parker, Harry Guardino, James Coburn, Mike Kellin, Nick Adams, Bob Newhart; **D:** Don Siegel; **W:** Robert Pirosh, Richard Carr. **VHS, Beta** $14.95 *PAR* ❚❚❚½

Hell Night Several young people must spend the night in a mysterious mansion as part of their initiation into Alpha Sigma Rho fraternity in this extremely dull low-budget horror flick.
1981 (R) 100m/C Linda Blair, Vincent Van Patten, Kevin Brophy, Peter Barton, Jenny Neumann; **D:** Tom De Simone; **W:** Randy Feldman. **VHS, Beta** $19.95 *MED* Woof!

Hell on Frisco Bay An ex-waterfront cop, falsely imprisoned for manslaughter, sets out to clear his name. His quest finds him taking on the Mob, in this thirties-style gangster film. Good performances all around, especially Robinson, who steals every scene he's in.
1955 93m/C Alan Ladd, Edward G. Robinson, Joanne Dru, Fay Wray, William Demarest, Jayne Mansfield; **D:** Frank Tuttle. **VHS, Beta** $54.95 *VCI* ❚❚½

Hell on the Battleground Group of inexperienced recruits are led into combat by two battle-hardened veterans. Their only hope for survival is a counterattack by U.S. tanks.
1988 (R) 91m/C William Smith, Ted Prior, Fritz Matthews; **D:** David A. Prior; **W:** David A. Prior. **VHS, Beta** $9.95 *AIP* ❚½

Hell on Wheels Two successful brothers in the racing industry are torn apart by the same girl. Brotherly love diminishes into a hatred so deep that murder becomes the sole purpose of both.
1967 96m/C Marty Robbins, Jennifer Ashley, John Ashley, Gigi Perreau, Robert Dornan, Connie Smith, Frank Gerstle; **D:** Will Zens. **VHS, Beta** $39.95 *ACA* ❚❚

Hell Raiders A force invades a supposedly defenseless Pacific island, and finds itself fiercely attacked.
1968 90m/C John Agar, Richard Webb, Joan Huntington; **D:** Larry Buchanan. **VHS, Beta** $79.95 *JEF* ❚½

Hell River In 1941 Yugoslavia, Yugoslav partisans and Nazis battle it out at a place called Hell River.
1975 (PG) 100m/C Rod Taylor, Adam West; **D:** Stole Jankovic. **VHS, Beta** $69.95 *VCD* ❚❚

Hell-Ship Morgan Bancroft is a womanizing tuna boat captain who falls for and marries Sothern. When they set up married life on the boat, she starts eyeing first mate Jory. And Bancroft finds out.
1936 65m/B George Bancroft, Ann Sothern, Victor Jory, George Regas, Howard Hickman, Ralph Byrd; **D:** David Ross Lederman. **VHS** $9.95 *GPV* ♫♫½

Hell Ship Mutiny Man comes to the aid of a lovely island princess, whose people have been forced to hand over their pearls to a pair of ruthless smugglers. Excellent cast in an unfortunately tepid production.
1957 66m/B Jon Hall, John Carradine, Peter Lorre, Roberta Haynes, Mike Mazurki, Stanley Adams; **D:** Lee Sholem, Elmo Williams. **VHS, Beta** $16.95 *SNC, HEG* ♫½

Hell Squad Lost in North Africa during WWII, five American GIs wander through the desert. They find numerous pitfalls and unexpected help. Overall, dismal and disappointing.
1958 64m/B Wally Campo, Brandon Carroll; **D:** Burt Topper. **VHS** $19.95 *NOS* ♫½

Hell Squad Unable to release his son from the Middle Eastern terrorists who kidnapped him, a U.S. ambassador turns to the services of nine Las Vegas showgirls. These gals moonlight as vicious commandos in this low-budget action film with skin.
1985 (R) 88m/C Bainbridge Scott, Glen Hartford, Tina Lederman; **D:** Kenneth Hartford; **W:** Kenneth Hartford. **VHS, Beta** $59.95 *MGM, GHV* ♫

Hell to Eternity The true story of how WWII hero Guy Gabaldon persuaded 2,000 Japanese soldiers to surrender. Features several spectacular scenes.
1960 132m/B Jeffrey Hunter, Sessue Hayakawa, David Janssen, Vic Damone, Patricia Owens; **D:** Phil Karlson. **VHS, Beta** $14.98 *FOX* ♫♫½

Hell Up in Harlem A black crime lord recuperates from an assassination attempt and tries to regain his power. Poor sequel to the decent film "Black Caesar."
1973 (R) 98m/C Fred Williamson, Julius W. Harris, Margaret Avery, Gerald Gordon, Gloria Hendry; **D:** Larry Cohen; **W:** Larry Cohen. **VHS, Beta** $9.98 *ORI* Woof!

Hellbenders A confederate veteran robs a Union train and must fight through acres of Civil War adversity. Dubbed. Poorly directed and acted. **AKA:** Il Crudeli; Los Despiadados.
1967 (PG) 92m/C Joseph Cotten, Norman Bengell, Julian Mateos; **D:** Sergio Corbucci; **M:** Ennio Morricone. **VHS, Beta** $14.95 *COL, SUE* ♫½

Hellbent A crazed musician and a revenge-obsessed housewife embark on an unusual adventure that challenges their very sanity.
1990 90m/C Phil Ward, Lynn Levand, Cheryl Slean, David Marciano; **D:** Richard Casey; **W:** Richard Casey. **VHS, Beta** *NO* ♫½

Hellbound: Hellraiser 2 In this, the first sequel to Clive Barker's inter-dimensional nightmare, the traumatized daughter from the first film is pulled into the Cenobites' universe. Gore and weird imagery abound. An uncut, unrated version is also available. **AKA:** Hellraiser 2.
1988 (R) 96m/C Ashley Laurence, Clare Higgins, Kenneth Cranham, Imogen Boorman, William Hope, Oliver Smith, Sean Chapman, Doug Bradley; **D:** Tony Randel; **W:** Peter Atkins. **VHS, Beta** $9.99 *STE, NWV* ♫♫

Hellcats A mob of sleazy, leather-clad female bikers terrorize small Midwestern towns in this violent girl-gang thriller. Even biker movie fans might find this one unworthy.
1968 (R) 90m/C Ross Hagen, Dee Duffy, Sharyn Kinzie, Sonny West, Bob Slatzer; **D:** Bob Slatzer. **VHS, Beta** $19.95 *ACA* Woof!

Hellcats of the Navy Soggy true saga of the WWII mission to sever the vital link between mainland Asia and Japan. The only film that Ronald and Nancy Davis Reagan starred in together and the beginning of their grand romance.
1957 82m/B Ronald Reagan, Nancy Davis, Arthur Franz, Robert Arthur; **D:** Nathan Juran. **VHS, Beta** $9.95 *GKK* ♫½

Helldorado A lively western starring the singing cowboy, Roy Rogers. **AKA:** Heldorado.
1946 54m/B Roy Rogers, George "Gabby" Hayes, Dale Evans, Paul Harvey; **D:** William Witney. **VHS, Beta** $19.95 *NOS, VCN, CAB* ♫♫

Heller in Pink Tights The Louis L'Amour story follows the adventures of a colorful theatrical troupe that visits the 1880s West. Performing amid Indians, bill collectors, and thieves, they are often just one step ahead of the law themselves in this offbeat western.
1960 100m/C Sophia Loren, Anthony Quinn, Margaret O'Brien, Steve Forrest, Edmund Lowe, Ramon Novarro; **D:** George Cukor; **W:** Walter Bernstein. **VHS, Beta** $14.95 *BAR, PAR, FCT* ♫♫

Hellfighters Texas oil well fire fighters experience trouble between themselves and the women they love.
1968 (G) 121m/C John Wayne, Katharine Ross, Jim Hutton, Vera Miles, Bruce Cabot, Jay C. Flippen; **D:** Andrew V. McLaglen. **VHS, Beta** $14.95 *MCA* ♫♫

Hellfire A gambler promises to build a church and follow the precepts of the Bible after a minister sacrifices his life for him.
1948 90m/B William Elliott, Marie Windsor, Forrest Tucker, Jim Davis; **D:** R.G. Springsteen. **VHS** $39.98 *REP* ♫♫

The Hellfire Club In 18th century Britain, a young man reaches adulthood and attempts to claim the estate of his father. No ordinary dad, his led the infamous Hellfire Club, an organization specializing in debauchery and depravity. His cousin challenges his claim and kidnaps his fiancee. Historical hokum, complete with swordplay.
1961 88m/C Keith Michell, Kai Fischer, Adrienne Corri, Peter Arne, David Lodge, Bill Owen, Peter Cushing, Francis Matthews, Desmond Walter Ellis; **D:** Robert S. Baker, Monty Berman; **W:** Jimmy Sangster. **VHS, Beta** $16.95 *SNC* ♫♫

Hellgate A woman hitchhiking turns out to be one of the living dead. Her benefactor lives to regret picking her up.
1989 (R) 96m/C Abigail Wolcott, Ron Palillo; **D:** William A. Levey. **VHS** $89.95 *VMK* Woof!

Hellhole A young woman who witnesses her mother's murder is sent to a sanitarium where the doctors are perfecting chemical lobotomies. Extremely weak script and poor acting make this a suspenseless thriller.
1985 (R) 93m/C Judy Landers, Ray Sharkey, Mary Woronov, Marjoe Gortner, Edy Williams, Terry Moore, Dyanne Thorne; **D:** Pierre De Moro. **VHS, Beta** $14.95 *COL* ♫

Hellmaster Your basic sicko mad scientist experiments on some unsuspecting college students by injecting them with an addictive drug. The drug also causes some horrifying mutations and makes its victims superhuman (but also super-ugly). Lots of gore. Creative special effects and make-up will appeal to fans of horror.
1992 92m/C John Saxon, David Emge, Amy Raasch; **D:** Douglas Schulze; **W:** Douglas Schulze. **VHS** $89.95 *AIP* ♫

Hello Again The wife of a successful plastic surgeon chokes to death on a piece of chicken. A year later she returns to life, with comical consequences, but soon discovers that life won't be the same.
1987 (PG) 96m/C Shelley Long, Corbin Bernsen, Judith Ivey, Gabriel Byrne, Sela Ward, Austin Pendleton, Carrie Nye, Robert Lewis, Madeleine Potter; **D:** Frank Perry; **M:** William Goldstein. **VHS, Beta** $19.99 *TOU* ♫

Hello, Dolly! Widow Dolly Levi, while matchmaking for her friends, finds a match for herself. Based on the hugely successful Broadway musical adapted from Thornton Wilder's play "Matchmaker." Lightweight story needs better actors with stronger characterizations. Original Broadway score helps. ♫Hello Dolly; Just Leave Everything to Me; Love is Only Love; Dancing; Walter's Gavotte; It Only Takes a Moment; Ribbons Down My Back; Elegance; It Takes a Woman.
1969 (G) 146m/C Barbra Streisand, Walter Matthau, Michael Crawford, Louis Armstrong, E.J. Peaker, Marianne McAndrew, Tommy Tune; **D:** Gene Kelly; **W:** Ernest Lehman; **M:** Jerry Herman. Academy Awards '69: Best Art Direction/Set Decoration, Best Sound, Best Score; Nominations: Best Cinematography, Best Costume Design, Best Film Editing, Best Picture. **VHS, Beta** $19.98 *FOX, FCT* ♫♫

Hello, Frisco, Hello San Francisco's wild Barbary Coast is the setting for this romantic musical. Smoothie Payne opens up a saloon that features Faye, who's in love with him, as the star singing attraction. Unfortunately, Payne is involved with a society snob and Faye heads off to European success. When she returns, it's to a sadder and wiser man. ♫Hello, Frisco, Hello; You'll Never Know; San Francisco; Ragtime Cowboy Joe; Sweet Cider Time; Has Anybody Here Seen Kelly; King Chanticleer; When You Wore a Tulip; Strike Up the Band, Here Comes a Sailor.
1943 98m/C Alice Faye, John Payne, Jack Oakie, Lynn Bari, Laird Cregar, June Havoc, Ward Bond, Aubrey Mather, John Archer; **D:** H. Bruce Humberstone; **W:** Robert Ellis, Helen Logan. Academy Awards '43: Best Song ("You'll Never Know"); Nominations: Best Color Cinematography. **VHS** $19.98 *FXV* ♫♫½

Hello Mary Lou: Prom Night 2 A sequel to the successful slasher flick, wherein a dead-for-30-years prom queen relegates the current queen to purgatory and comes back to life in order to avenge herself. Wild special effects. **AKA:** The Haunting of Hamilton High; Prom Night 2.
1987 (R) 97m/C Michael Ironside, Wendy Lyon, Justin Louis, Lisa Schrage, Richard Monette; **D:** Bruce Pittman; **W:** Ron Oliver. **VHS, Beta** *NO* ♫½

Hellraiser A graphic, horror fantasy about a woman who is manipulated by the monstrous spirit of her husband's dead brother. In order for the man who was also her lover to be brought back to life, she must lure and kill human prey for his sustenance. Grisly and inventive scenes keep the action fast-paced; not for the faint-hearted.
1987 (R) 94m/C Andrew (Andy) Robinson, Clare Higgins, Ashley Laurence, Sean Chapman, Oliver Smith, Robert Hines; **D:** Clive Barker; **W:** Clive Barker; **M:** Christopher Young. **Beta** $9.99 *STE, NWV* ♫♫½

Hellraiser 3: Hell on Earth Pinhead is back in this film based on characters created by horrormeister Clive Barker. A strange black box holds the key to sending Pinhead back to Hell and is sought by the heroine, a TV newswoman (Farrell). But Pinhead's human henchman, a nasty nightclub owner, isn't going to make things easy. Imaginative special effects and Bradley's commanding presence as Pinhead aid this shocker, which becomes unfortunately mired in excessive gore. An unrated version at 97 minutes is also available.
1992 (R) 91m/C Doug Bradley, Terry Farrell, Kevin Bernhardt, Paula Marshall, Ken Carpenter, Peter Boynton, Ashley Laurence; **D:** Anthony Hickox; **W:** Peter Atkins. VHS *PAR ⅃⅃*

Hellriders A motorcycle gang rides into a small town and subjects its residents to a reign of terror.
1984 (R) 90m/C Adam West, Tina Louise. VHS, Beta $59.95 *TWE* Woof!

Hell's Angels Classic WWI aviation movie is sappy and a bit lumbering, but still an extravagant spectacle with awesome air scenes. Studio owner Hughes fired directors Howard Hawks and Luther Reed, spent an unprecedented $3.8 million, and was ultimately credited as director (although Whale also spent some time in the director's chair). Three years in the making, the venture cost three pilots their lives and lost a bundle. Harlow replaced Swedish Greta Nissen when sound was added and was catapulted into blond bombshelldom as a two-timing dame. And the tinted and two-color scenes—restored in 1989—came well before Ted Turner ever wielded a crayola.
1930 135m/B Jean Harlow, Ben Lyon, James Hall, John Darrow, Lucien Prival; **D:** Howard Hughes; **W:** James Whale. VHS $19.98 *MCA, MRV ⅃⅃⅃*

Hell's Angels Forever A revealing ride into the world of honor, violence, and undying passion for motorcycles on the road. Documentary was filmed with cooperation of the Angels. Features appearances by Willie Nelson, Jerry Garcia, Bo Diddley, Kevin Keating and Johnny Paycheck.
1983 (R) 93m/C Willie Nelson, Jerry Garcia, Johnny Paycheck, Bo Diddley; **D:** Richard Chase. VHS, Beta $59.95 *MED ⅃⅃*

Hell's Angels on Wheels Low-budget, two-wheeled Nicholson vehicle that casts him as a gas station attendant who joins up with the Angels for a cross country trip. Laszlo Kovacs is responsible for the photography. One of the better 1960s biker films.
1967 95m/C Jack Nicholson, Adam Roarke, Sabrina Scharf, Jana Taylor, John Garwood; **D:** Richard Rush. VHS, Beta $39.95 *VMK ⅃⅃½*

Hell's Angels '69 Figuring on robbing Caesar's Palace for the thrill, two wealthy brothers plot a deadly game by infiltrating the ranks of the Hell's Angels. Upon figuring out that they've been duped, the Angels seek revenge. Average biker epic filmed in Nevada features Hell's Angels Oakland chapter.
1969 (PG) 97m/C Tom Stern, Jeremy Slate, Conny Van Dyke; **D:** Lee Madden; **W:** Tom Stern, Jeremy Slate. VHS, Beta $49.95 *MED ⅃⅃*

Hell's Brigade: The Final Assault Low-budget, poorly acted film in which a small band of American commandos is ordered on the most dangerous and important mission of WWII.
1980 (PG) 99m/C Jack Palance, John Douglas, Carlos Estrada; **D:** Henry Mankiewirk. VHS, Beta $59.95 *MPI* Woof!

Hell's Headquarters A startling tale of murder and greed involving a hunt for a fortune in African ivory.
1932 59m/B Jack Mulhall, Barbara Weeks, Frank Mayo; **D:** Andrew L. Stone. VHS $16.95 *SNC, NOS, DVT ⅃*

Hell's Hinges The next to last Hart western, typifying his good/bad cowboy character. Perhaps Hart's best film.
1916 65m/B William S. Hart, Clara Williams, Jack Standing, Robert McKim; **D:** William S. Hart. VHS, Beta $18.95 *GPV, VYY, GVV ⅃⅃*

Hell's House After his mother dies, young lad Durkin goes to the city to live with relatives, gets mixed up with moll Davis and her bootlegger boyfriend O'Brien, and is sent to a brutal reform school. Interesting primarily for early appearances by Davis and O'Brien (before he was typecast as the indefatigable good-guy).
1932 80m/B Junior Durkin, Pat O'Brien, Bette Davis, Frank "Junior" Coghlan, Charley Grapewin, Emma Dunn; **D:** Howard Higgin. VHS, Beta $19.95 *NOS, MRV, CNG ⅃⅃*

Hell's Wind Staff Two boys uncover a plot to sell their townsmen as slaves to other South East Asian countries.
1982 95m/C Hwang Jang Lee, Mang Yuen Man, Mang Hai. VHS, Beta *WVE ⅃*

The Hellstrom Chronicle A powerful quasi-documentary about insects, their formidable capacity for survival, and the conjectured battle man will have with them in the future.
1971 (G) 90m/C Lawrence Pressman; **D:** Walon Green; **W:** David Seltzer. VHS, Beta *COL, OM ⅃⅃⅃*

Helltown A western programmer based on Zane Grey's novel in which Wayne tracks down a cattle rustler.
1938 60m/B John Wayne; **D:** Charles T. Barton. VHS, Beta $19.95 *NOS, DVT, VCN ⅃½*

Helltrain Passengers take the ride of their lives on the "Helltrain."
1980 (R) 90m/C **D:** Alain Payet. VHS $59.95 *VCI* Woof!

Help! Ringo's ruby ring is the object of a search by an Arab cult who chase the Fab Four all over the globe in order to acquire the bauble. The laserdisc version includes a wealth of Beatles memorabilia, rare footage behind the scenes and at the film's premiere, and extensive publicity material. ♫Help!; You're Gonna Lose That Girl; You've Got To Hide Your Love Away; The Night Before; Another Girl; Ticket To Ride; I Need You.
1965 (G) 90m/C John Lennon, Paul McCartney, Ringo Starr, George Harrison, Leo McKern, Eleanor Bron; **D:** Richard Lester; **W:** Charles Wood. VHS, Beta $19.98 *MPI, MVD, CRC ⅃⅃⅃*

Help Wanted Female Jo Jo, a prostitute with kung fu skills who likes to rob traveling salesmen, is in a quandary over her lesbian roommate's acid dropping friends, including Mr. Gregory, who has a penchant for murder. After recounting a previous trip in which he murdered an acquaintance, he succeeds in alienating his current companions, who must fight for their life to escape him.
1968 71m/B Sebastian Gregory, Inga Olsen; **D:** Harold Perkins. VHS $23.00 *SMW, TPV ⅃*

Help Wanted: Male When a magazine publisher discovers that her fiance cannot have children, she looks for someone else who can do the job right. Made for television.
1982 97m/C Suzanne Pleshette, Gil Gerard, Bert Convy, Dana Elcar, Harold Gould, Caren Kaye; **D:** William Wiard. VHS, Beta $39.95 *WOV ⅃½*

Helter Skelter The harrowing story of the murder of actress Sharon Tate and four others at the hands of Charles Manson and his psychotic "family." Based on the book by prosecutor Vincent Bugliosi, adapted by J.P. Miller. Features an outstanding performance by Railsback as Manson. A TV mini-series.
1976 194m/C Steve Railsback, Nancy Wolfe, George DiCenzo, Marilyn Burns; **D:** Tom Gries; **M:** Billy Goldenberg. VHS, Beta $59.98 *FOX ⅃⅃½*

The Henderson Monster Experiments of a genetic scientist are questioned by a community and its mayor. A potentially controversial television drama turns into typical romantic fluff.
1980 105m/C Jason Miller, Christine Lahti, Stephen Collins, David Spielberg, Nehemiah Persoff, Larry Gates; **D:** Waris Hussein. VHS, Beta $39.95 *LIV ⅃⅃½*

Hennessy An IRA man plots revenge on the Royal family and Parliament after his family is violently killed. Tense political drama, but slightly far-fetched.
1975 (PG) 103m/C Rod Steiger, Lee Remick, Richard Johnson, Trevor Howard, Peter Egan, Eric Porter; **D:** Don Sharp; **W:** John Gay. VHS $19.99 *HBO ⅃⅃½*

Henry IV The adaptation of the Luigi Pirandello farce about a modern-day recluse who shields himself from the horrors of the real world by pretending to be mad and acting out the fantasy of being the medieval German emperor Henry IV. In Italian with English subtitles.
1985 94m/C Marcello Mastroianni, Claudia Cardinale, Leopoldo Trieste, Paolo Bonacelli, Luciano Bartoli, Latou Chardons; **D:** Marco Bellochio; **W:** Tonino Guerra, Astor Piazzolla, Marco Bellochio; **M:** Tonino Guerra. VHS, Beta $59.95 *MED, APD, ING ⅃⅃½*

Henry V Classic, epic adaptation of the Shakespeare play, and Olivier's first and most successful directorial effort, dealing with the medieval British monarch that defeated the French at Agincourt. Distinguished by Olivier's brilliant formal experiment of beginning the drama as a 16th Century performance of the play in the Globe Theatre, and having the stage eventually transform into realistic historical settings of storybook color. Filmed at the height of WWII suffering in Britain (and meant as a parallel to the British fighting the Nazis), the film was not released in the U.S. until 1946.
1944 136m/C Laurence Olivier, Robert Newton, Leslie Banks, Esmond Knight, Renee Asherson, Leo Genn, George Robey, Ernest Thesiger, Felix Aylmer, Ralph Truman; **D:** Laurence Olivier, Reginald Beck; **W:** Laurence Olivier, Alan Dent; **M:** William Walton. Academy Awards '46 Nominations: Best Actor (Olivier), Best Interior Decoration, Best Picture, Best Original Score; National Board of Review Awards '46: 10 Best Films of the Year, Best Actor (Olivier). VHS, Beta $19.95 *PAR, HMV ⅃⅃⅃⅃*

Henry V Stirring, expansive retelling of Shakespeare's drama about the warrior-king of England. Branagh stars as Henry, leading his troops and uniting his kingdom against France. Very impressive production rivals Olivier's 1945 rendering but differs by stressing the high cost of war—showing the egomania, doubts, and subterfuge that underlie conflicts. Marvelous film-directorial debut for Branagh (who also adapted the screenplay). Wonderful supporting cast includes some of Britain's finest actors.
1989 138m/C Kenneth Branagh, Derek Jacobi, Brian Blessed, Alec McCowen, Ian Holm, Richard Briers, Robert Stephens, Robbie Coltrane, Christian Bale, Judi Dench, Paul Scofield, Michael Maloney, Emma Thompson; **D:** Kenneth

Branagh; **W:** Kenneth Branagh; **M:** Patrick Doyle. Academy Awards '89: Best Costume Design; Nominations: Best Actor (Branagh), Best Director (Branagh), British Academy Awards '89: Best Director (Branagh). **VHS $19.98** *FOX, SIG, TVC* 𝔍𝔍𝔍𝔍

Henry & June Based on the diaries of writer Anais Nin which chronicled her triangular relationship with author Henry Miller and his wife June, a relationship that provided the erotic backdrop to Miller's "Tropic of Capricorn." Set in Paris in the early '30s, the setting moves between the impecunious expatriate's cheap room on the Left bank—filled with artists, circus performers, prostitutes, and gypsies—to the conservative, well-appointed home of Nin and her husband. Captures the heady atmosphere of Miller's gay Paris; no one plays an American better than Ward (who replaced Alec Baldwin). Notable for having prompted the creation of an NC-17 rating because of its adult theme. **1990 (NC-17) 136m/C** Fred Ward, Uma Thurman, Maria De Medeiros, Richard E. Grant, Kevin Spacey; **D:** Philip Kaufman; **W:** Philip Kaufman. **VHS $19.98** *MCA, FCT* 𝔍𝔍𝔍½

Henry: Portrait of a Serial Killer Based on the horrific life and times of serial killer Henry Lee Lucas, this film has received wide praise for its straight-forward and uncompromising look into the minds of madmen. The film follows Henry and his roommate Otis as they set out on mindless murder sprees (one of which they videotape). Extremely disturbing and graphic film. Unwary viewers should be aware of the grisly scenes and use their own discretion when viewing this otherwise genuinely moving film. **1990 (X) 90m/C** Michael Rooker, Tom Towles, Tracy Arnold; **D:** John McNaughton; **W:** Richard Fire, John McNaughton. **VHS $79.98** *MPI* 𝔍𝔍𝔍𝔍

Hepburn & Tracy The finest moments from the legendary film careers of Hepburn and Tracy, as a team and on their own. Some sequences in black and white. A must for fans. **1984 45m/C** Katharine Hepburn, Spencer Tracy. **VHS, Beta $29.95** *RKO* 𝔍𝔍𝔍𝔍

Her Alibi When successful murder-mystery novelist Phil Blackwood runs out of ideas for good books, he seeks inspiration in the criminal courtroom. There he discovers a beautiful Romanian immigrant named Nina who is accused of murder. He goes to see her in jail and offers to provide her with an alibi. Narrated by Blackwood in the tone of one of his thriller novels. Uneven comedy, with appealing cast and arbitrary plot. **1988 (PG) 95m/C** Tom Selleck, Paulina Porizkova, William Daniels, James Farentino, Hurd Hatfield, Patrick Wayne, Tess Harper, Joan Copeland; **D:** Bruce Beresford; **W:** Charlie Peters; **M:** Georges Delerue. **VHS, Beta, 8mm $14.95** *WAR* 𝔍𝔍

Her Husband's Affairs Tone is an advertising wonder and Ball is his loving wife who always gets credit for his work. Tone does the advertising for an inventor who is searching for the perfect embalming fluid in this rather lifeless comedy. **1947 83m/B** Lucille Ball, Franchot Tone, Edward Everett Horton, Gene Lockhart, Larry Parks; **D:** Sylvan Simon; **M:** George Duning. **VHS $9.95** *GKK* 𝔍

Her Life as a Man A female reporter is refused a job as a sportswriter because of her gender. She makes herself up as a man, gets the job, and creates havoc when she has to deal with lustful women on the man. A made-for-television movie.

1983 93m/C Robyn Douglass, Joan Collins, Robert Culp, Marc Singer, Laraine Newman; **D:** Robert Ellis Miller. **VHS, Beta $59.95** *LHV* 𝔍½

Her Silent Sacrifice A silent melodrama about a French girl torn between material wealth and true love. **1918 42m/B** Alice Brady, Henry Clive. **VHS, Beta $19.95** *VYY* 𝔍½

Herbie Goes Bananas While Herbie the VW is racing in Rio de Janeiro, he is bothered by the syndicate, a pickpocket, and a raging bull. The fourth and final entry in the Disney "Love Bug" movies, but Herbie later made his way to a television series. **1980 (G) 93m/C** Cloris Leachman, Charles Martin Smith, Harvey Korman, John Vernon, Alex Rocco, Richard Jaeckel, Fritz Feld; **D:** Vincent McEveety. **VHS, Beta $69.95** *DIS* 𝔍½

Herbie Goes to Monte Carlo While participating in a Paris-to-Monte-Carlo race, Herbie the VW takes a detour and falls in love with a Lancia. Third in the Disney "Love Bug" series. **1977 (G) 104m/C** Dean Jones, Don Knotts, Julie Sommars, Roy Kinnear; **D:** Vincent McEveety. **VHS, Beta $69.95** *DIS* 𝔍𝔍

Herbie Rides Again In this "Love Bug" sequel, Herbie comes to the aid of an elderly woman who is trying to stop a ruthless tycoon from raising a skyscraper on her property. Humorous Disney fare. Two other sequels followed. **1974 (G) 88m/C** Helen Hayes, Ken Berry, Stefanie Powers, John McIntire, Keenan Wynn; **D:** Robert Stevenson. **VHS, Beta $19.99** *DIS* 𝔍𝔍

Hercules The one that started it all. Reeves is perfect as the mythical hero Hercules who encounters many dangerous situations while trying to win over his true love. Dubbed in English. Cinematography by Mario Bava. **AKA:** La Tatiche de Ercole. **1958 107m/C** Steve Reeves, Sylva Koscina, Fabrizio Mioni, Giana Maria Canale, Arturo Dominici; **D:** Pietro Francisci. **VHS, Beta $14.98** *MRV, IME, VDM* 𝔍𝔍½

Hercules Lackluster remake of 1957 original finds legendary muscle guy Hercules in the person of Ferrigno's Hulkster fighting against the evil King Minos for his own survival and the love of Cassiopeia, a rival king's daughter. **1983 (PG) 100m/C** Lou Ferrigno, Sybil Danning, William Berger, Brad Harris, Ingrid Anderson; **D:** Lewis (Luigi Cozzi) Coates; **W:** Lewis (Luigi Cozzi) Coates; **M:** Pino Donaggio. **VHS, Beta $79.95** *MGM, IME* 𝔍

Hercules 2 The muscle-bound demi-god returns to do battle with more evil foes amidst the same stunningly cheap special effects. **AKA:** The Adventures of Hercules. **1985 (PG) 90m/C** Lou Ferrigno, Claudio Cassinelli, Milly Carlucci, Sonia Viviani, William Berger, Carlotta Green; **D:** Lewis (Luigi Cozzi) Coates; **M:** Pino Donaggio. **VHS $79.95** *MGM* 𝔍

Hercules Against the Moon Men It's no holds barred for the mighty son of Zeus when evil moon men start killing off humans in a desperate bid to revive their dead queen. **AKA:** Maciste la Regina di Samar. **1964 88m/C** Alan Steel, Jany Clair, Anna Maria Polani; **D:** Giacomo Gentilomo. **VHS, Beta $16.95** *SNC, MRV* 𝔍

Hercules and the Captive Women Hercules' son is kidnapped by the Queen of Atlantis, and the bare-chested warrior goes on an all-out rampage to save the boy. Directed by sometimes-lauded Cottafavi. **AKA:** Hercules and the Haunted Wom-

en; Hercules and the Conquest of Atlantis; Ercole Alla Conquista di Atlantide. **1963 93m/C** Reg Park, Fay Spain, Ettore Manni; **D:** Vittorio Cottafavi. **VHS, Beta $9.95** *RHI, MRV, TIM* 𝔍𝔍

Hercules and the Princess of Troy Hercules is up to his pecs in trouble as he battles a hungry sea monster in order to save a beautiful maiden. Originally a pilot for a prospective television series, and shot in English, not Italian, with Hercules played by erstwhile Tarzan Scott. Highlights are special effects and color cinematography. **1965 ?m/C** Gordon Scott, Diana Hyland, Paul Stevens, Everett Sloane. **VHS, Beta $16.95** *SNC, MLB* 𝔍𝔍½

Hercules in New York Motion picture debut of Schwarzenegger (his voice is dubbed) as a Herculean mass of muscle sent by dad Zeus to Manhattan, where he behaves likes a geek out of water and eventually becomes a professional wrestling superstar. 250 pounds of stupid, lighthearted fun. **AKA:** Hercules: The Movie; Hercules Goes Bananas. **1970 (G) 93m/C** Arnold Schwarzenegger, Arnold Stang, Deborah Loomis, James Karen, Ernest Graves; **D:** Arthur Seidelman. **VHS, Beta $59.98** *MPI* 𝔍½

Hercules in the Haunted World Long before the days of 24-hour pharmacies, Hercules—played yet again by Reeves-clone Park—must journey to the depths of Hell in order to find a plant that will cure a poisoned princess. Better than most muscle operas, thanks to Bava. **AKA:** Ercole al Centro Della Terra. **1964 91m/C** Reg Park, Leonora Ruffo, Christopher Lee, George Ardisson; **D:** Mario Bava. **VHS, Beta $9.99** *CCB, RHI, MRV* 𝔍𝔍½

Hercules, Prisoner of Evil Spaghetti myth-opera in which Hercules battles a witch who is turning men into werewolves. Made for Italian television by director Dawson (the nom-de-cinema of Antonio Margheriti). **1964 ?m/C** Reg Park; **D:** Anthony M. (Antonio Margheriti) Dawson. **VHS $19.98** *SNC* 𝔍

Hercules Unchained Sequel to "Hercules" finds superhero Reeves must use all his strength to save the city of Thebes and the woman he loves from the giant Antaeus. **AKA:** Ercole e la Regina di Lidia. **1959 101m/C** Steve Reeves, Sylva Koscina, Silvia Lopel, Primo Carnera; **D:** Pietro Francisci. **VHS, Beta $14.95** *VDM, SUE, MRV* 𝔍𝔍

Here and Elsewhere Godard, Gorin, and Mieville contrast the story of a French family with a look at the Palestine revolution as seen through the media of television, books, and pictures. The film was originally titled "Until Victory" and commissioned by the Palestinians to examine life in the Palestinian camps. After the defeat of the Palestinian army in the Six Day War, Godard and his cohorts transformed the film with their French family ("Here") and their impressions of Palestine ("Elsewhere"). In French with English subtitles. **AKA:** Ici et Ailleurs. **197? ?m/C** Anne-Marie Mieville; **D:** Jean-Pierre Gorin, Jean-Luc Godard. **VHS $59.95** *FCT* 𝔍𝔍

Here Come the Co-Eds Bud & Lou are the caretakers of an all-girl college which is about to go bankrupt unless the boys can find a way to pay off the mortgage. And come to the rescue they do, including Bud getting into the wrestling ring with the "Masked Marvel" (Chaney, Jr. as the villain). There's also a classic silent scene with Lou served a bowl of oyster stew containing a live oyster, which promptly grabs his tie, bites his fingers, and squirts in his face. **1945 90m/B** Bud Abbott, Lou Costello, Lon Chaney Jr., Peggy Ryan, Martha O'Driscoll, June Vincent, Donald Cook, Charles Dingle; **D:** Jean Yarborough; **W:** Arthur T. Horman, John Grant. **VHS $14.98** MCA, FCT ⅟₂

Here Come the Girls An unfunny musical-comedy about a chorus boy (Hope) fired for incompetence and then rehired to set a trap when the new singer (Martin) is stalked by a killer. Weak script, weak songs. ♫Girls Are Here To Stay; Never So Beautiful; You Got Class; Desire; When You Love Someone; Ali Baba Be My Baby; Heavenly Days; See the Circus; Peace. **1953 100m/C** Bob Hope, Tony Martin, Arlene Dahl, Rosemary Clooney, Millard Mitchell, William Demarest, Fred Clark, Robert Strauss; **D:** Claude Binyon; **W:** Hal Kanter. **VHS $14.95** PAR ⅟₂

Here Come the Littles: The Movie A twelve-year-old boy finds many new adventures when he meets The Littles—tiny folks who reside within the walls of people's houses. Adapted from the books and TV series. **1985 76m/C D:** Bernard Deyries. **VHS, Beta $14.98** WTA, FOX ⅟₂

Here Come the Marines The Bowery Boys accidentally join the marines and wind up breaking up a gambling ring. *AKA:* Tell It To the Marines. **1952 66m/B** Leo Gorcey, Huntz Hall, Tim Ryan; **D:** William Beaudine. **VHS $19.95** NOS ⅟⅟

Here Comes Kelly Controlling his temper and hanging on to his job is more than our hero can handle. **1943 63m/C** Eddie Quillan, Joan Woodbury, Maxie "Slapsie" Rosenbloom; **D:** William Beaudine. **VHS, Beta** GPV ⅟⅟₂

Here Comes Mr. Jordan Montgomery is the young prizefighter killed in a plane crash because of a mix-up in heaven. He returns to life in the body of a soon-to-be murdered millionaire. Rains is the indulgent and advising guardian angel. A lovely fantasy/romance remade in 1978 as "Heaven Can Wait." Laserdisc edition includes actress Elizabeth Montgomery talking about her father Robert Montgomery as well as her television show "Bewitched." **1941 94m/B** Robert Montgomery, Claude Rains, James Gleason, Evelyn Keyes, Edward Everett Horton, Rita Johnson, John Emery; **D:** Alexander Hall; **W:** Sidney Buchman, Seton I. Miller; **M:** Morris Stoloff. **VHS, Beta $19.95** COL, VYG, CRC ⅟⅟⅟⅟

Here Comes Santa Claus A young boy and girl travel to the North Pole to deliver a very special wish to Santa Claus. **1984 78m/C** Karen Cheryl, Armand Meffre; **D:** Christian Gion. **VHS, Beta $14.95** NWV, STE ⅟⅟₂

Here Comes the Groom Late, stale Capra-corn, involving a rogue journalist who tries to keep his girlfriend from marrying a millionaire by becoming a charity worker. Includes a number of cameos. **1951 114m/B** Bing Crosby, Jane Wyman, Franchot Tone, Alexis Smith, James Barton, Connie Gilchrist, Robert Keith, Anna Maria Alberghetti, Charles Halton; **Cameos:** Dorothy Lamour, Phil Harris, Louis Armstrong; **D:** Frank Capra. Academy Awards '51: Best Song ("In the Cool, Cool, Cool of the Evening"); Nominations: Best Story. **VHS, Beta $14.95** PAR ⅟⅟

Here We Go Again! Fibber McGee and Molly are planning a cross-country celebration for their 20th anniversary celebration, but complications abound. Based on the popular NBC radio series.

1942 76m/B Marion Jordan, Jim Jordan, Harold Peary, Gale Gordon, Edgar Bergen, Ray Noble; **D:** Allan Dwan. **VHS, Beta $9.95** CCB ⅟⅟

The Hereafter An old church is suddenly overrun by zombies. **1987 92m/C VHS, Beta** NO ⅟

Here's Looking at You, Warner Bros. The 90-year history of Warner Bros. studios is profiled from the silent-era to its current success. Highlights cover the creation of Warners' gangster films, Busby Berkeley musicals, and "Looney Tunes" as well as bloopers and early screen tests by Marlo Brando, Paul Newman, Lana Turner, and Orson Welles. Includes interviews with stars, directors, and producers and numerous film clips. **1993 108m/C D:** Robert Guenette; **W:** Robert Guenette. **VHS $19.95** WAR ⅟⅟⅟

Heritage of the Desert One of the earlier westerns made by the rugged Scott. **1933 62m/B** Randolph Scott, Sally Blane, Guinn Williams; **D:** Henry Hathaway. **VHS, Beta $24.95** DVT, TIM ⅟⅟

The Hero A popular soccer player agrees to throw a game for big cash, and then worries about losing the respect of a young boy who idolizes him. Nothing new in this overly sentimental sports drama. *AKA:* Bloomfield. **1971 (PG) 97m/C** Richard Harris, Romy Schneider, Kim Burfield, Maurice Kaufman; **D:** Richard Harris. **VHS, Beta $59.98** SUE ⅟⅟₂

Hero Interesting twist on Cinderella fable and modern media satire has television reporter Davis looking for the man who saved her life, expecting a genuine hero, and accepting without question the one who fits her vision. Critically considered disappointing, but wait—Garcia and Hoffman make a great team, and Davis is fetching as the vulnerable media person. Strong language and dark edges may keep away some of the kids, but otherwise this is a fine fable. **1992 (PG-13) 116m/C** Geena Davis, Dustin Hoffman, Andy Garcia, Joan Cusack, Kevin J. O'Connor, Chevy Chase, Maury Chaykin, Stephen Tobolowsky, Christian Clemenson, Tom Arnold, Janis Paige, Warren Berlinger, Susie Cusack, James Madio, Richard Riehle, Don Yesso, Darrell Larson; **D:** Stephen Frears; **W:** David Peoples; **M:** George Fenton. **VHS, 8mm $19.95** COL ⅟⅟⅟

A Hero Ain't Nothin' But a Sandwich A young urban black teenager gets involved in drugs and is eventually saved from ruin. Slow-moving, over-directed and talky. However, Scott turns in a fine performance. Based on Alice Childress' novel. **1978 (PG) 107m/C** Cicely Tyson, Paul Winfield, Larry B. Scott, Helen Martin, Glynn Turman, David Groh; **D:** Ralph Nelson. **VHS, Beta $14.95** PAR, FCT ⅟⅟

Hero and the Terror Perennial karate guy Norris plays a sensitive policeman who conquers his fear of a not-so-sensitive maniac who's trying to kill him. Plenty of action and a cheesy subplot to boot. **1988 (R) 96m/C** Chuck Norris, Brynn Thayer, Steve James, Jack O'Halloran, Ron O'Neal, Billy Drago; **D:** William Tannen. **VHS, Beta $89.95** MED, VTR ⅟⅟

Hero at Large An unemployed actor foils a robbery while dressed in a promotional "Captain Avenger" suit, and instant celebrity follows. Lightweight, yet enjoyable. **1980 (PG) 98m/C** John Ritter, Anne Archer, Bert Convy, Kevin McCarthy, Kevin Bacon; **D:** Martin Davidson. **VHS, Beta $59.95** MGM ⅟⅟₂

Hero Bunker Hero bunk about a platoon of heroic Greek soldiers who attempt, at the expense of their personal longevity, to defend an important bunker from enemy invasion. **1971 93m/C** John Miller, Maria Xenia; **D:** George Andrews. **VHS, Beta $39.95** LIV ⅟⅟

Hero of Rome Rome has many who could be called "hero," but one stands biceps and pecs above the rest. **1963 ?m/C** Gordon Scott, Gabriella Pallotti. **VHS, Beta $16.95** SNC ⅟⅟

Hero of the Year The characters from Falk's "Top Dog" return in this story of a Polish television personality who loses his job and is forced to face unemployment and jobseeking. **1985 115m/C D:** Feliks Falk. **VHS $49.99** FCT ⅟⅟

Herod the Great Biblical epic of the downfall of Herod, the ruler of ancient Judea. Scantily clad women abound. Dubbed. **1960 93m/C** Edmund Purdom, Sandra Milo, Alberto Lupo; **D:** Arnaldo Genoino. **VHS $16.95** SNC ⅟

Heroes An institutionalized Vietnam vet (Winkler) escapes, hoping to establish a worm farm which will support all his crazy buddies. On the way to the home of a friend he hopes will help him, he encounters Field. Funny situations don't always mix with serious underlying themes of mental illness and post-war adjustment. **1977 (PG) 97m/C** Henry Winkler, Sally Field, Harrison Ford; **D:** Jeremy Paul Kagan; **W:** Jim Carabatsos; **M:** Jack Nitzsche. **VHS, Beta $59.95** MCA ⅟⅟

Heroes Die Young A cheap independent feature depicting an American command mission with orders to sabotage German oil fields during WWII. **1960 76m/B** Krika Peters, Scott Borland, Robert Getz, James Strother. **VHS, Beta $19.98** FOX, FCT ⅟⅟₂

Heroes for Sale Fascinating melodrama about a WWI veteran who returns home and manages to survive one disaster after another. Barthelmess is great in his performance as an American Everyman who must deal with everything from morphine addiction to finding work during the Depression. Fast-paced, patriotic film is helped by ambitious script and the expert direction of Wellman. **1933 72m/B** Richard Barthelmess, Loretta Young, Aline MacMahon, Robert Barratt, Grant Mitchell, Douglass Dumbrille, Charley Grapewin, Ward Bond; **D:** William A. Wellman; **W:** Robert Lord, Wilson Mizner. **VHS** MGM ⅟⅟⅟

Heroes in Blue Two brothers join the police force, but one goes astray and hooks up with gangsters. Plenty of action distracts from the cliched story. **1939 60m/B** Dick Purcell, Charles Quigley, Bernadene Hayes, Edward Keane; **D:** William Watson. **VHS, Beta $16.95** SNC ⅟⅟

Heroes in Hell Two escaped WWII POWs join the Allied underground in an espionage conspiracy against the Third Reich. **1967 90m/C** Klaus Kinski, Ettore Manni. **VHS, Beta** NO ⅟⅟₂

The Heroes of Desert Storm The human spirit of the people who fought in the high-tech Persian Gulf War is captured in this film that also features real war footage from ABC News. **1991 93m/C** Daniel Baldwin, Angela Bassett, Marshall Bell, Michael Alan Brooks, William Bumiller, Michael Champion, Maria Diaz; **D:** Don Ohlmeyer; **W:** Lionel Chetwynd. **VHS, Beta $79.95** PSM ⅟⅟

Heroes of the Alamo Remember the Alamo...but forget this movie. Dull, threadbare dramatization of the battle that was scorned even back in '37.
1937 75m/B Rex Lease, Lane Chandler, Roger Williams, Earle Hodgins, Julian Rivero; *D*: Harry Fraser. **VHS, Beta** *GPV* ⅃½

Heroes of the Hills The Three Mesquiteers back up a plan that would allow trusted prisoners to work for neighboring ranchers. Part of "The Three Mesquiteers" series.
1938 54m/B Bob Livingston, Ray Corrigan, Max Terhune. **VHS, Beta** *MED* ⅃½

Heroes of the West Early sound action western serial.
1932 70m/B Noah Beery Jr. **VHS, Beta $29.95** *VCN, MLB* ⅃½

Heroes Stand Alone When a U.S. spy plane is downed in Central America, a special force is sent in to rescue the crew. Another "Rambo" rip-off.
1989 (R) 84m/C Bradford Dillman, Chad Everett, Wayne Grace, Rick Dean; *D*: Mark Griffiths; *W*: Thomas McKelvey Cleaver. **VHS, Beta $14.95** *MGM* ⅃

Heroes Three When his crewmate is murdered while on leave in the Far East, a Navy officer enlists the aid of a Chinese detective to track down the killer.
1984 90m/C Rowena Cortes, Mike Kelly, Laurens C. Postma, Lawrence Tan; *D*: S.H. Lau. **VHS, Beta $99.95** *IMP* ⅃

He's My Girl When a rock singer wins a trip for two to Hollywood, he convinces his agent to dress up as a woman so they can use the free tickets.
1987 (PG-13) 104m/C David Hallyday, T.K. Carter, Misha McK, Jennifer Tilly; *D*: Gabrielle Beaumont; *W*: Terence H. Winkless. **VHS, Beta $14.95** *LIV* ⅃½

He's Your Dog, Charlie Brown! An animated Peanuts adventure wherein Charlie Brown decides to send Snoopy back to the Daisy Hill Puppy Farm for obedience lessons.
1968 30m/C **VHS, Beta $9.98** *MED, VTR, WTA* ⅃½

Hester Street Set at the turn of the century, the film tells the story of a young Jewish immigrant who ventures to New York City to be with her husband. As she reacquaints herself with her husband, she finds that he has abandoned her Old World ideals. The film speaks not only to preserving the heritage of the Jews, but to cherishing all heritages and cultures. Highly regarded upon release, unfortunately forgotten today.
1975 89m/C Carol Kane, Doris Roberts, Steven Keats, Mel Howard; *D*: Joan Micklin Silver. **VHS, Beta $39.95** *VES, FRV, ING* ⅃⅃½

Hexed Walter Mitty lives in the person of bellboy Matthew Welsh, who enjoys masquerading as a debonair bon vivant. He finagles his way into the life of Hexina, a beautiful psychotic model who has checked into the hotel where Matthew works in order to murder her blackmailer. She tries to kill Matthew, apparently getting in a little practice, but he'll still follow her anywhere. Inane, charmless comedy that intends to satirize "Fatal Attraction" and similar films.
1993 (R) 93m/C Arye Gross, Claudia Christian, Adrienne Shelly, R. Lee Ermey, Norman Fell, Michael E. Knight; *D*: Alan Spencer; *W*: Alan Spencer. **VHS** *COL* ⅃½

Hey Abbott! A compilation of Abbott and Costello routines from their classic television series. Sketches include "Who's On First," "Oyster Stew," "Floogle Street" and "The Birthday Party."
1978 76m/B Bud Abbott, Lou Costello, Phil Silvers, Steve Allen, Joe Besser. **VHS, Beta** *NO* ⅃½

Hey, Babu Riba A popular Yugoslavian fit of nostalgia about four men convening at the funeral of a young girl they all loved years before, and their happy, Americana-bathed memories therein. In Serbo-Croatian with English subtitles.
1988 (R) 109m/C Gala Videnovic, Nebojsa Bakocevic, Dragan Bjelogrlic, Marko Todorovic, Goran Radakovic, Relja Basic, Milos Zutic; *D*: Jovan Acin. **VHS, Beta $19.98** *ORI, ING* ⅃⅃½

Hey Good Lookin' Ralph Bakshi's irreverent look at growing up in the 1950s bears the trademark qualities that distinguish his other adult animated features, "Fritz the Cat" and "Heavy Traffic."
1982 87m/C *D*: Ralph Bakshi. **VHS, Beta $19.98** *WAR, WTA* ⅃⅃½

Hey There, It's Yogi Bear When Yogi Bear comes out of winter hibernation to search for food, he travels to the Chizzling Brothers Circus. The first feature-length cartoon to come from the H-B Studios.
1964 98m/C *D*: William Hanna; *V*: Daws Butler, James Darren, Mel Blanc, J. Pat O'Malley, Julie Bennett. **VHS, Beta $19.95** *WOV, IME, WTA* ⅃⅃

Hi-De-Ho The great Cab Calloway and his red hot jazz are featured in this film, which has the band caught between rival gangsters. The plot is incidental to the music, anyway. ♫Hi-De-Ho; I Got A Gal Named Nettie; Little Old Lady From Baltimore; A Rainy Sunday.
1935 60m/B Cab Calloway, Ida James, The Peters Sisters; *D*: Josh Binney. **VHS, Beta $19.95** *MVD, NOS, VCN* ⅃⅃½

Hi-Di-Hi A British television comedy about the shenanigans that inevitably follow when a stuffy Cambridge professor becomes the entertainment manager for a holiday camp.
1988 91m/C Simon Cadell, Ruth Madoc, Paul Shane, Jeffrey Holland, Leslie Dwyer. **VHS, Beta $39.98** *FOX* ⅃⅃½

Hi Diddle Diddle Topsy-turvy comedy features young lovers who long for conventional happiness. Instead they are cursed with con-artist parents who delight in crossing that law-abiding line. *AKA*: Diamonds and Crime; Try and Find It.
1943 72m/B Adolphe Menjou, Martha Scott, Dennis O'Keefe, Pola Negri; *D*: Andrew L. Stone. **VHS, Beta $24.95** *NOS, DVT, HEG* ⅃⅃½

Hi-Jacked When a parolee trucker's cargo is stolen, he inevitably becomes a suspect and must set out to find the true culprits.
1950 66m/B Jim Davis, Paul Cavanagh, Marsha Jones. **VHS, Beta** *RXM* ⅃

Hi, Mom! DePalma's follow-up to "Greetings" finds amateur pornographer/movie maker De Niro being advised by a professional in the field (Garfield) of sleazy filmmaking. De Niro films the residents of his apartment building and eventually marries one of his starlets. One of De Palma's earlier and better efforts with De Niro playing a crazy as only he can. *AKA*: Confessions of A Peeping John; Blue Manhattan.
1970 (R) 87m/C Robert De Niro, Charles Durnham, Allen (Gooritz) Garfield, Lara Parker, Jennifer Salt, Gerrit Graham; *D*: Brian DePalma; *W*: Brian DePalma. **VHS** *FCT, HHE* ⅃⅃

Hi-Riders A revenge-based tale about large, mag-wheeled trucks and their drivers.
1977 (R) 90m/C Mel Ferrer, Stephen McNally, Neville Brand, Ralph Meeker; *D*: Greydon Clark. **VHS, Beta $49.95** *VCI* ⅃

The Hidden A seasoned cop (Nouri) and a benign alien posing as an FBI agent (MacLachlan) team up to track down and destroy a hyper-violent alien who survives by invading the bodies of humans, causing them to go on murderous rampages. Much acclaimed, high velocity action film with state-of-the-art special effects.
1987 (R) 98m/C Kyle MacLachlan, Michael Nouri, Clu Gulager, Ed O'Ross, Claudia Christian, Clarence Felder, Richard Brooks, William Boyett; *D*: Jack Sholder; *W*: Bob Hunt; *M*: Michael Convertino. **VHS, Beta $19.95** *MED, CVS, VTR* ⅃⅃⅃

The Hidden 2 The hyper-violent alien of the 1987 movie returns. With its love of fast cars, high-caliber weapons, and heavy metal music, this body-possessing creature appears to be unstoppable.
1994 91m/C Raphael Sbarge, Kate Hodge, Michael Nouri; *D*: Seth Pinsker; *W*: Seth Pinsker; *M*: David McHugh. **VHS** *NLC, COL, IME* ⅃⅃½

Hidden Agenda A human rights activist and an American lawyer uncover brutality and corruption among the British forces in Northern Ireland. Slow-paced but strong performances. The Northern Irish dialect is sometimes difficult to understand as are the machinations on the British police system. Generally worthwhile.
1990 (R) 108m/C Frances McDormand, Brian Cox, Brad Dourif, Mai Zetterling, John Benfield, Des McAleer, Jim Norton, Maurice Roeves; *D*: Ken Loach; *W*: Jim Allen; *M*: Stewart Copeland. **VHS $19.98** *HBO, FCT* ⅃⅃½

Hidden City A film archivist and a statistician become drawn into a conspiracy when a piece of revealing film is spliced onto the end of an innocuous government tape.
1987 112m/C Charles Dance, Cassie Stuart, Alex Norton, Tusse Silberg, Bill Paterson; *D*: Stephen Poliakoff. **VHS, Beta** *NO* ⅃⅃

Hidden Enemy During WWII, a scientist develops a new metal alloy that is stronger than steel yet lighter than aluminum. His nephew must protect his scientist/uncle from spies who would steal the formula to use against the Allies.
1940 63m/B Warren Hull, Kay Linaker, William von Brinken, George Cleveland; *D*: Howard Bretherton. **VHS, Beta $16.95** *SNC, RXM* ⅃½

Hidden Fears Maureen Dietz (Foster) carries the gruesome memories of her husband's murder with her. Years later she goes to the police with new evidence to reopen her husband's case. Only the killers find out and return to finish off the eyewitnesses, and she's next! Based on the novel "Exercise in Terror" by Kaminsky, who also wrote the screenplay.
1993 90m/C Meg Foster, Frederic Forrest, Wally Taylor, Bever-Leigh Banfield, Marc Macaulay, Patrick Cherry, Scott Hayes; *D*: Jean Bodon; *W*: Stuart Kaminsky. **VHS, Beta $89.95** *PSM* ⅃⅃½

The Hidden Fortress Kurosawa's tale of a warrior who protects a princess from warring feudal lords. An inspiration for George Lucas' "Star Wars" series and deserving of its excellent reputation. In Japanese with English subtitles. The laserdisc edition is letter boxed to retain the film's original integrity. *AKA*: Kakushi Toride No San Akunin; Three Rascals in the Hidden Fortress; Three Bad Men in the Hidden Fortress.
1958 139m/B Toshiro Mifune, Misa Vehara, Minoru Chiaki; *D*: Akira Kurosawa. **VHS, Beta $39.95** *HMV, VYG, FCT* ⅃⅃⅃½

Hidden Gold Routine western for Mix, which has him going undercover to win the confidence of three outlaws and discover where they have hidden their loot.

1933 57m/B Tom Mix, Judith Barrie, Raymond Hatton; *D:* Arthur Rosson. **VHS, Beta $11.95** *GPV, VCN, DVT* 🎬½

Hidden Guns Above-average tale of father-and-son lawmen out to reform a town and put the bad guys away. When dad is killed, son goes up against the villain alone. A Greek chorus adds an interesting twist to the action. Erich von Stroheim, Jr. is listed as assistant director.
1956 66m/B Bruce (Herman Brix) Bennett, Richard Arlen, John Carradine, Faron Young, Angie Dickinson, Guinn Williams; *D:* Albert C. Gannaway. **VHS $19.95** *NOS* 🎬🎬🎬

Hidden Obsession Newscaster Ellen is taking a much needed vacation at an isolated cabin when she learns that a serial killer has escaped from a nearby prison. Luckily, she has a hunky police officer neighbor for protection. But though the escaped killer is captured, the killings go on—with Ellen as the next target.
1992 (R) 92m/C Heather Thomas, Jan-Michael Vincent, Nicholas Celozzi; *D:* John Stewart; *W:* David Reskin. **VHS** *MCA* 🎬½

The Hidden Room A doctor finds out about his wife's affair and decides to get revenge on her lover. He kidnaps him, imprisons him in a cellar, and decides to kill him—slowly. Tense melodrama. *AKA:* Obsession.
1949 98m/B Robert Newton, Sally Gray, Naunton Wayne, Phil Brown, Olga Lindo; *D:* Edward Dmytryk. **VHS, Beta $16.95** *NOS, SNC, RXM* 🎬🎬🎬

Hidden Valley Early Steele western in which everyone is fighting over a map that leads to hidden treasure in the valley.
1932 60m/B Bob Steele, Gertrude Messinger, Francis McDonald; *D:* Robert North Bradbury. **VHS $9.95** *GPV* 🎬🎬

Hide and Go Shriek Several high school seniors are murdered one by one during a graduation party. Also available in an unrated, gorier version.
1987 (R) 90m/C Annette Sinclair, Brittain Frye, Rebunkah Jones; *D:* Skip Schoolnik. **VHS, Beta** *NO* 🎬

Hide and Seek When a high school hacker converts his computer into a nuclear weapon, he finds that it has developed a mind of its own.
1977 60m/C Bob Martin, Ingrid Veninger, David Patrick. **VHS, Beta $59.95** *LHV* 🎬

Hide and Seek A study of children living in the land that would soon become Israel. Although they play as normal children, life is particularly difficult. This adversity will lay the foundation for their Israeli citizenry. In Hebrew with English subtitles.
1980 90m/C Gila Almagor, Doron Tavori, Chaim Hadaya; *D:* Dan Wolman. **VHS, Beta $79.95** *ERG, ING, TPV* 🎬

Hide in Plain Sight A distraught blue-collar worker searches for his children who disappeared when his ex-wife and her mobster husband are given new identities by federal agents. Caan's fine directorial debut is based on a true story.
1980 (PG) 96m/C James Caan, Jill Eikenberry, Robert Viharo, Kenneth McMillan, Josef Sommer, Danny Aiello; *D:* James Caan. **VHS, Beta $59.95** *MGM* 🎬🎬🎬

Hide-Out A man running from the law winds up at a small farm, falls in love, and becomes reformed by the good family that takes him in. Good supporting cast includes a very young Rooney.
1934 83m/B Robert Montgomery, Maureen O'Sullivan, Edward Arnold, Elizabeth Patterson, Mickey Rooney, Edward Brophy; *D:* Woodbridge S. Van Dyke. **VHS** *MGM* 🎬🎬½

The Hideaways A 12-year-old girl and her younger brother run away and hide in the Metropolitan Museum of Art. The girl becomes enamored of a piece of sculpture and sets out to discover its creator. Based on the children's novel by E.L. Konigsburg. *AKA:* From the Mixed-Up Files of Mrs. Basil E. Frankweiler.
1973 (G) 105m/C Richard Mulligan, George Rose, Ingrid Bergman, Sally Prager, Johnny Doran, Madeline Kahn; *D:* Fielder Cook. **VHS, Beta $14.95** *WAR, VHE, FCT* 🎬🎬½

Hideous Sun Demon A physicist exposed to radiation must stay out of sunlight or he will turn into a scaly, lizard-like creature. Includes previews of coming attractions from classic sci-fi films. *AKA:* Blood On His Lips; Terror From the Sun; The Sun Demon.
1959 75m/B Robert Clarke, Patricia Manning, Nan Peterson; *D:* Robert Clarke. **VHS, Beta $9.95** *NOS, MRV, RHI* 🎬½

Hider in the House In a peaceful neighborhood a family is about to spend an evening of terror when they discover a psychopath is hiding in the attic of their home.
1990 (R) 109m/C Michael McKean, Gary Busey, Mimi Rogers, Kurt Christopher Kinder, Candy Hutson, Elizabeth Ruscio, Bruce Glover; *D:* Michael Patrick. **VHS, Beta $89.98** *VES, LIV* 🎬🎬½

Hiding Out A young stockbroker testifies against the Mafia and must find a place to hide in order to avoid being killed. He winds up at his cousin's high school in Delaware, but can he really go through all these teenage troubles once again?
1987 (PG-13) 99m/C Jon Cryer, Keith Coogan, Gretchen Cryer, Annabeth Gish, Tim Quill; *D:* Bob Giraldi; *M:* Anne Dudley. **VHS, Beta $19.99** *HBO* 🎬🎬

The Hiding Place True story of two Dutch Christian sisters sent to a concentration camp for hiding Jews during WWII. Film is uneven but good cast pulls it through. Based on the Corrie Ten Boom book and produced by Billy Graham's Evangelistic Association.
1975 145m/C Julie Harris, Eileen Heckart, Arthur O'Connell, Jeanette Clift; *D:* James F. Collier. **VHS $49.95** *VBL, REP, COV* 🎬🎬

High & Low Fine Japanese film noir about a wealthy businessman who is being blackmailed by kidnappers who claim to have his son. When he discovers that they have mistakenly taken his chauffeur's son he must decide whether to face financial ruin or risk the life of a young boy. Based on an Ed McBain novel. In Japanese with English subtitles. *AKA:* Tengoku To Jigoku.
1962 (R) 143m/B Toshiro Mifune, Tatsuya Mihashi, Tatsuya Nakadai; *D:* Akira Kurosawa. **VHS, Beta $29.95** *IME, ING, TPV* 🎬🎬🎬½

High Anxiety Brooks tries hard to please in this low-brow parody of Hitchcock films employing dozens of references to films like "Psycho," "Spellbound," "The Birds," and "Vertigo." Tells the tale of a height-fearing psychiatrist caught up in a murder mystery. The title song performed a la Sinatra by Brooks is one of the film's high moments. Brooks also has a lot of fun with Hitchcockian camera movements. Uneven (What? Brooks?) but amusing tribute.
1977 (PG) 92m/C Mel Brooks, Madeline Kahn, Cloris Leachman, Harvey Korman, Ron Carey, Howard Morris, Dick Van Patten; *D:* Mel Brooks; *W:* Mel Brooks, Ron Clark, Barry Levinson, Rudy DeLuca. **VHS, Beta $14.98** *FOX* 🎬🎬

High Ballin' Truckers Fonda and Reed team up with lady trucker Shaver to take on the gang trying to crush the independent drivers.
1978 (PG) 100m/C Peter Fonda, Jerry Reed, Helen Shaver; *D:* Peter Carter; *W:* Paul F. Edwards. **VHS, Beta $29.98** *LIV, VES* 🎬🎬

High Command To save his daughter from an ugly scandal, the British general of an isolated Colonial African outpost traps a blackmailer's killer.
1937 84m/B Lionel Atwill, Lucie Mannheim, James Mason; *D:* Thorold Dickinson. **VHS, Beta $19.95** *NOS, MRV, VYY* 🎬🎬½

High Country Two misfits, one handicapped, the other an ex-con, on the run from society learn mutual trust as they travel through the Canadian Rockies. *AKA:* The First Hello.
1981 (PG) 101m/C Timothy Bottoms, Linda Purl, George Sims, Jim Lawrence, Bill Berry; *D:* Harvey Hart. **VHS, Beta $79.95** *VES* 🎬🎬

High Country Calling Wolf pups escape their man-made home and set off a cross-country chase.
1975 (G) 84m/C **VHS, Beta $29.95** *GEM, CNG* 🎬½

High Crime A "French Connection"-style suspense story about the heroin trade. Features high-speed chases and a police commissioner obsessed with capturing the criminals.
1973 91m/C James Whitmore, Franco Nero, Fernando Rey; *D:* Enzo G. Castellari. **VHS, Beta $49.95** *MED* 🎬🎬

High Desert Kill A science-fiction tale will keep you guessing. Aliens landing in the New Mexican desert want something totally unexpected, and a trio of friends will be the first to find out what it is. Written for cable by Cook ("The China Syndrome").
1990 (PG) 93m/C Chuck Connors, Marc Singer, Anthony Geary, Micah Grant; *D:* Harry Falk; *W:* T.S. Cook. **VHS, Beta $79.95** *MCA* 🎬🎬

High Frequency Two young men monitoring a satellite relay station witness the murder of a woman. Believing they know who the killer's next victim will be, they set out to warn her. Lack of development mars what could have been a tidy little thriller.
1988 105m/C Oliver Benny, Vincent Spano, Isabelle Pasco, Anne Canovos; *D:* Faliero Rosati. **VHS $79.98** *MCG* 🎬

High Gear Heartstring-tugger about a race car driver, his girlfriend and the orphan son of a driver killed in a crash. Try to guess the outcome.
1933 65m/B James Murray, Joan Marsh, Jackie Searl, Theodore von Eltz, Lee Moran, Gordon DeMain; *D:* Leigh Jason. **VHS $19.95** *NOS, RXM* 🎬

High Heels A black comedy about a doctor who believes beauty is only skin deep and marries a plain woman. However, when he meets her beautiful sister, he begins to wonder. In French with English subtitles. *AKA:* Docteur Popaul; Scoundrel in White.
1972 100m/C Laura Antonelli, Jean-Paul Belmondo, Mia Farrow, Daniel Ivernel; *D:* Claude Chabrol. **VHS, Beta $39.95** *MON* 🎬🎬

High Heels An outrageous combination murder-melodrama-comedy from Almodovar. Rebecca is a TV anchorwoman in Madrid whose flamboyant singer/actress mother has returned to the city for a concert. Rebecca happens to be married to one of her mother's not-so-ex-flames. When her husband winds up dead, Rebecca confesses to his murder during her newscast—but is she telling the truth or just covering up for mom? Mix in a drag queen/judge, a dancing chorus of wom-

en prison inmates, and a peculiar police detective, and see if the plot convolutions make sense. In Spanish with English subtitles. *AKA:* Tacones Lejanos.
1991 (R) 113m/C Victoria Abril, Marisa Paredes, Miguel Bose, Feodor Atkine, Bibi Andersen, Rocio Munoz; *D:* Pedro Almodovar; *W:* Pedro Almodovar; *M:* Ryuichi Sakamoto. **VHS, Beta** PAR *🎬🎬🎬*

High Hopes A moving yet nasty satiric comedy about a pair of ex-hippies maintaining their counter-culture lifestyle in Margaret Thatcher's England, as they watch the signs of conservative "progress" overtake them and their geriatric, embittered Mum. Hilarious and mature.
1989 110m/C Philip Davis, Ruth Sheen, Edna Dore, Philip Jackson, Heather Tobias, Leslie Manville, David Bamber; *D:* Mike Leigh; *W:* Mike Leigh; *M:* Andrew Dixon. **VHS, Beta $29.95** ACA *🎬🎬🎬*

High Ice Forest ranger and a lieutenant colonel are involved in a clash of wills over a rescue mission high in the snow-capped Washington state peaks.
1980 97m/C David Janssen, Tony Musante; *D:* Eugene S. Jones. **VHS, Beta $69.95** VES *🎬1/2*

High Lonesome Barrymore is a drifter in Big Bend country, suspected in a series of mysterious murders. While he is being held captive, the real killers - thought dead - return to exact revenge on those they hold responsible for the range war in which they were wounded. This was LeMay's only stint as a director.
1950 80m/C John Blythe Barrymore Jr., Chill Wills, John Archer, Lois Butler, Kristine Miller, Basil Ruysdael, Jack Elam; *D:* Alan LeMay; *W:* Alan LeMay. **VHS $19.95** NOS *🎬🎬1/2*

High Noon Landmark Western about Hadeyville town marshal Will Kane (Cooper) who faces four professional killers alone, after being abandoned to his fate by the gutless townspeople who profess to admire him. Cooper is the ultimate hero figure, his sheer presence overwhelming. Note the continuing use of the ballad written by Dimitri Tamkin, "Do Not Forsake Me, Oh My Darlin'" (sung by Tex Ritter) to heighten the tension and action. Laserdisc includes the original trailer, an essay by Howard Suber on audio 2, a photo essay of production stills, Carl Foreman's original notes of the film and the complete text of "The Tin Star," the story on which the film is based.
1952 85m/B Gary Cooper, Grace Kelly, Lloyd Bridges, Lon Chaney Jr., Thomas Mitchell, Otto Kruger, Katy Jurado, Lee Van Cleef, Henry Morgan, Robert J. Wilke, Sheb Wooley; *D:* Fred Zinneman; *W:* Carl Foreman; *M:* Dimitri Tiomkin. Academy Awards '52: Best Actor (Cooper), Best Film Editing, Best Song ("High Noon (Do Not Forsake Me, Oh My Darlin')"), Best Score; Nominations: Best Director (Zinneman), Best Picture, Best Screenplay; Golden Globe Awards '53: Best Actor--Drama (Cooper), Best Supporting Actress (Jurado), Best Score; National Board of Review Awards '52: 10 Best Films of the Year; New York Film Critics Awards '52: Best Director (Zinneman), Best Film. **VHS $19.98** REP, VYG, TLF *🎬🎬🎬🎬*

High Noon: Part 2 Majors attempts to fill Gary Cooper's shoes, as Marshal Kane returns a year after the events of the original "High Noon" to remove the corrupt marshal who replaced him. Subtitled "The Return of Will Kane." Made for television.
1980 96m/C Lee Majors, David Carradine, Pernell Roberts, Kathy Cannon; *D:* Jerry Jameson. **VHS, Beta $14.95** FRH, VTR *🎬1/2*

High Plains Drifter A surreal, violent western focusing on a drifter who defends a town from gunmen intent on meting out death. One of Eastwood's most stylistic directorial efforts, indebted to his "Man with No Name" days with Sergio Leone. Laser format is letterboxed and includes chapter stops and the original theatrical trailer.
1973 (R) 105m/C Clint Eastwood, Verna Bloom, Mitchell Ryan, Marianna Hill; *D:* Clint Eastwood. **VHS, Beta $19.95** MCA, TLF *🎬🎬1/2*

High Risk Improbable action-adventure of four unemployed Americans who battle foreign armies, unscrupulous gunrunners, and jungle bandits in a harrowing attempt to steal five million dollars from an expatriate American drug dealer living in the peaceful splendor of his Columbian villa. Interesting in its own run-on way.
1976 (R) 94m/C James Brolin, Anthony Quinn, Lindsay Wagner, James Coburn, Ernest Borgnine, Bruce Davison, Cleavon Little; *D:* Stewart Raffill. **VHS, Beta $9.98** SUE, VTR *🎬1/2*

High Road to China A hard-drinking former WWI air ace is recruited by a young heiress who must find her father before his ex-partner takes over his business. Post-"Raiders of the Lost Ark" thrills and romance, but without that tale's panache.
1983 (PG) 105m/C Bess Armstrong, Tom Selleck, Jack Weston, Robert Morley, Wilford Brimley, Brian Blessed; *D:* Brian G. Hutton; *M:* John Barry. **VHS, Beta $19.98** WAR *🎬🎬*

High Rolling in a Hot Corvette Two carnival workers leave their jobs and hit the road in search of adventure and excitement, eventually turning to crime. *AKA:* High Rolling.
1977 (PG) 82m/C Joseph Bottoms, Greg Taylor, Judy Davis, Wendy Hughes; *D:* Igor Auzins. **VHS, Beta $69.95** VES *🎬*

High School Caesar A seedy teenage exploitation flick about a rich teenager, with no parental supervision, who starts his own gang to run his high school.
1956 75m/B John Ashley; *D:* O'Dale Ireland. **VHS, Beta $9.95** RHI, SNC *🎬*

High School Confidential Teen punk Tamblyn transfers to Santo Bello high school from Chicago and causes havoc among the locals. He soon involves himself in the school drug scene and looks to be the top dog in dealing, but what no one knows is that he's really a narc. A must for midnight movie fans thanks to high camp values, "hep cat" dialogue and the gorgeous Van Doren as Tamblyn's sex-crazed "aunt." *AKA:* Young Hellions.
1958 85m/B Russ Tamblyn, Jan Sterling, John Blythe Barrymore Jr., Mamie Van Doren, Diane Jergens, Jerry Lee Lewis, Ray Anthony, Jackie Coogan, Charles Chaplin Jr., Burt Douglas, Michael Landon, Jody Fair, Phillipa Fallon, Robin Raymond, James Todd, Lyle Talbot, William Wellman Jr.; *D:* Jack Arnold. **VHS, Beta $14.98** REP *🎬🎬*

High School USA A high school class clown confronts the king of the prep-jock-bullies. Antics ensue in this made-for-television flick which features many stars from fifties and sixties sitcoms.
1984 96m/C Michael J. Fox, Nancy McKeon, Bob Denver, Angela Cartwright, Elinor Donahue, Dwayne Hickman, Lauri Hendler, Dana Plato, Tony Dow, David Nelson; *D:* Rod Amateau; *M:* Miles Goodman. **VHS, Beta $59.95** LHV, WAR *🎬1/2*

High Season A satire about a beautiful English photographer (Bisset) stranded on an idyllic Greek island with neither money nor inspiration, and the motley assembly of char-acters who surround her during the tourist season.
1988 (R) 95m/C Jacqueline Bisset, James Fox, Irene Papas, Sebastian Shaw, Kenneth Branagh, Robert Stephens, Leslie Manville; *D:* Clare Peploe; *W:* Mark Peploe, Clare Peploe; *M:* Jason Osborn. **VHS, Beta, 8mm $19.98** SUE, FCT, NLC *🎬🎬1/2*

High Sierra Bogart is Roy "Mad Dog" Earle, an aging gangster whose last job backfires, so he's hiding out from the police in the High Sierras. Bogart's first starring role. Based on the novel by W.R. Burnett. Remade in 1955 as "I Died A Thousand Times." Also available colorized.
1941 96m/B Humphrey Bogart, Ida Lupino, Arthur Kennedy, Joan Leslie, Cornel Wilde, Henry Travers, Henry Hull; *D:* Raoul Walsh; *W:* John Huston, W.R. Burnett. **VHS, Beta $19.95** FOX *🎬🎬🎬*

High Society A wealthy man attempts to win back his ex-wife who's about to be remarried in this enjoyable remake of "The Philadelphia Story." Letterboxed laserdisc format also includes the original movie trailer. 🎵High Society Calypso; Little One; Who Wants to Be a Millionaire?; True Love; You're Sensational; I Love You, Samantha; Now You Has Jazz; Well, Did You Evah?; Mind if I Make Love to You?.
1956 107m/C Frank Sinatra, Bing Crosby, Grace Kelly, Louis Armstrong, Celeste Holm, Sidney Blackmer, Louis Calhern; *D:* Charles Walters; *M:* Cole Porter. **VHS, Beta, 8mm $19.95** MGM *🎬🎬🎬*

High Spirits An American inherits an Irish castle and a sexy 200-year-old ghost. A painful, clumsy comedy by the fine British director that was apparently butchered by the studio before its release.
1988 (PG-13) 99m/C Daryl Hannah, Peter O'Toole, Steve Guttenberg, Beverly D'Angelo, Liam Neeson, Martin Ferrero, Peter Gallagher, Jennifer Tilly; *D:* Neil Jordan; *W:* Neil Jordan; *M:* George Fenton. **VHS, Beta $19.98** MED, VTR *🎬🎬*

High Stakes Kirkland stars as a prostitute who's battling the Mob and falling in love. Limited release in theaters but another fine performance from Kirkland. Also released as "Melanie Rose."
1989 (R) 102m/C Sally Kirkland, Robert LuPone, Richard Lynch, Sarah Gellar, Kathy Bates, W.T. Martin; *D:* Amos Kollek. **VHS $89.95** VMK *🎬🎬*

High Tide A strong and strange drama once again coupling the star and director of "My Brilliant Career." A small-time rock 'n' roll singer who is stranded in a small, beach town fortuitously meets up with her previously-abandoned teenage daughter. Acclaimed.
1987 (PG-13) 120m/C Judy Davis, Jan Adele, Claudia Karvan, Colin Friels, John Clayton, Mark Hembrow, Frankie J. Holden, Monica Trapaga; *D:* Gillian Armstrong; *W:* Laura Jones; *M:* Rikki Fataar, Mark Moffiatt. **VHS, Beta, 8mm $19.98** SUE, FCT, NLC *🎬🎬🎬*

High Velocity Lame adventure about two mercenaries involved in the challenge of a lifetime—rescuing a kidnapped executive from Asian terrorists. Filmed in Manila.
1976 (PG) 105m/C Ben Gazzara, Paul Winfield, Britt Ekland, Keenan Wynn; *D:* Remi Kramer; *M:* Jerry Goldsmith. **VHS, Beta $29.95** MED *🎬1/2*

High Voltage A fast-moving comedy adventure set in the High Sierras.
1929 62m/B Carole Lombard, William Boyd, Gwen Moore, Billy Bevan; *D:* Howard Higgin. **VHS, Beta $19.95** NOS, MRV, BAR *🎬*

Higher and Higher Bankrupt aristocrat conspires with servants to regain his fortune, and tries to marry his daughter into money. Sinatra's first big-screen role. 🎵You Belong in a Love Song; A Most Important Affair; The Music Stopped; Today I'm A Debutante; A

Lovely Way To Spend An Evening; I Couldn't Sleep a Wink Last Night; You're On Your Own; I Saw You First; Disgustingly Rich. **1944** 90m/B Frank Sinatra, Leon Errol, Michele Morgan, Jack Haley, Mary McGuire; **D:** Tim Whelan. **VHS, Beta $19.98** *CCB, IME, TTC* 🎞️🎞️

Higher Education Andy leaves his small town for a big city college and falls head over heels for a student and a teacher. He didn't know college could be so much fun. **1988 (R)** 83m/C Kevin Hicks, Isabelle Mejias, Lori Hallier, Maury Chaykin, Richard Monette; **D:** John Sheppard. **VHS $9.95** *VTR* 🎞️🎞️

The Highest Honor True story set during WWII of a friendship between an Australian army officer, captured while attempting to infiltrate Singapore, and a Japanese security officer. Too long, but gripping. **1984 (R)** 99m/C John Howard, Atsuo Nakamura, Stuart Wilson, Michael Aitkens, Steve Bisley; **D:** Peter Maxwell. **VHS, Beta $19.98** *SUE, STE* 🎞️🎞️½

Highlander A strange tale about an immortal 16th-century Scottish warrior who has had to battle his evil immortal enemy through the centuries. The feud comes to blows in modern-day Manhattan. Connery makes a memorable appearance as the good warrior's mentor. Spectacular battle and death scenes. A cult favorite which spawned a weak sequel and a television series. Based on a story by Gregory Widen. **1986 (R)** 110m/C Christopher Lambert, Sean Connery, Clancy Brown, Roxanne Hart, Beatie Edney, Alan North, Sheila Gish, Jon Polito; **D:** Russell Mulcahy; **W:** Gregory Widen, Peter Bellwood, Larry Ferguson; **M:** Michael Kamen. **VHS, Beta $14.98** *REP* 🎞️🎞️🎞️

Highlander 2: The Quickening The saga of Connor MacLeod and Juan Villa-Lobos continues in this sequel set in the year 2024. An energy shield designed to block out the sun's harmful ultraviolet rays has left planet Earth in perpetual darkness, but there is evidence that the ozone layer has repaired itself. An environmental terrorist and her group begin a sabotage effort and are joined by MacLeod and Villa-Lobos in their quest to save Earth. Stunning visual effects don't make up for the lack of substance. **1991 (R)** 90m/C Christopher Lambert, Sean Connery, Virginia Madsen, Michael Ironside, John C. McGinley; **D:** Russell Mulcahy; **W:** Peter Bellwood; **M:** Stewart Copeland. **VHS, 8mm $14.95** *COL* 🎞️🎞️½

Highlander 3: The Sorcerer Immortal Conner MacLeod (Lambert) battles master illusionist Kane (Van Peebles), who seeks to rule the world. Aiding MacLeod is Alex Smith (Unger), a research scientist who discovers Kane was once buried beneath a mystical mountain along with three other immortal warriors some 300 years before. MacLeod returns to his old Scottish stomping grounds to prepare for battle. Lots of action and special effects. **1994** ?m/C Christopher Lambert, Mario Van Peebles, Deborah Unger; **D:** Andrew Morahan; **W:** Paul Ohl. **VHS** *NYR* 🎞️🎞️½

Highlander: The Gathering Re-edited episodes from the syndicated television series finds good immortals Connor Ma-cLeod (Lambert) and distant relative Duncan (Paul) battling against an evil immortal (Moll as a particularly nasty villain) and a misguided human (Vanity). Lots of sword-play and a little bit of romance (courtesy of Vandernoot).

1993 (PG-13) 98m/C Christopher Lambert, Adrian Paul, Richard Moll, Vanity, Alexandra Vandernoot, Stan Kirsh; **D:** Thomas J. Wright, Ray Austin; **W:** Lorain Despres, Dan Gordon. **VHS $89.95** *HMD* 🎞️🎞️½

Highpoint When an unemployed man becomes the chauffeur of a wealthy family, he finds himself in the middle of a mysterious murder and part of an international CIA plot. Hard to figure what's happening in this one. **1980 (PG)** 91m/C Richard Harris, Christopher Plummer, Beverly D'Angelo, Kate Reid, Saul Rubinek; **D:** Peter Carter. **VHS, Beta $19.95** *STE, SUE* 🎞️

Highway 61 Shy barber Pokey Jones lives in the small Canadian town of Pickerel Falls and becomes a celebrity when he discovers the frozen corpse of an unknown young man in his backyard. Jackie Bangs, a rock roadie who's stolen her band's stash of drugs, finds herself stranded in the same small town. So begins a wild road trip. Lackluster direction undercuts much of the first-rate acting and amusing story quirks. **1991 (R)** 110m/C Valerie Buhagiar, Don McKellar, Earl Pastko, Peter Breck, Art Bergmann; **D:** Bruce McDonald; **W:** Don McKellar. **VHS $89.95** *PAR, FCT* 🎞️🎞️

Highway 13 When a trucker witnesses an "accidental" death at the loading warehouse, he falls under suspicion. He then sets out to clear his name. **1948** 60m/B Robert Lowery, Pamela Blake, Lyle Talbot, Michael Whalen, Maris Wrixon, Clem Bevans; **D:** William Berke. **VHS, Beta** *NO* 🎞️½

Highway to Hell Bergen plays the devil in a horror-comedy about going to hell—even if you're not dead yet. Lowe and Swanson are newlyweds on their way to Las Vegas when they're stopped by a "hellcop," who kidnaps the bride and takes her to the netherworld to be the devil's new plaything. Her human hubby doesn't take kindly to this and goes to hell to rescue his bride. Campy flick is played for laughs and has some good special effects. **1992** 93m/C Patrick Bergin, Adam Storke, Chad Lowe, Kristy Swanson, Richard Farnsworth, C.J. Graham, Lita Ford, Kevin Peter Hall, Pamela Gidley, Brian Helgeland; **Cameos:** Gilbert Gottfried; **D:** Ate De Jong. **VHS $89.99** *HBO* 🎞️🎞️

Hijazo de Mi Vidaza The history of a family as told by a mother to her son. In Spanish. **AKA:** Son of My Life. **197?** 90m/C Enrique Cuenca, Eduardo Manzano, Maria Fernanda, Fernando Casanova. **VHS, Beta $49.95** *MAD* 🎞️

Hill Number One A dramatization of the story of Easter, featuring Dean in one of his first major roles as John the Baptist. Made for television. **1951** 57m/B James Dean, Michael Ansara, Leif Erickson, Ruth Hussey, Roddy McDowall. **VHS, Beta $19.95** *RHI, FCT, HEG* 🎞️

Hill Street Blues, Vol. 1: Hill Street Station Landmark police drama which effectively combined a large cast of characters with plots filled with humor and tragedy. Set in an urban ghetto of a large (unnamed) American city, the precinct was run by Capt. Frank Furillo (Travanti) and staffed with "let's be careful out there!" Sgt. Phil Esterhaus (Conrad), as well as a host of offbeat detectives and beat cops. The pilot epsiode introduced the characters and the characteristic mayhem. Additional episodes available. **1981** 50m/C Daniel J. Travanti, Veronica Hamel, Michael Conrad, Bruce Weitz, James B. Sikking, Joe Spano, Taurean Blacque, Kiel Martin, Rene Enriquez, Michael Warren, Charles Haid, Betty

Thomas, Ed Marinaro, Barbara Babcock. **VHS $14.99** *MOV, MTM* 🎞️

Hill 24 Doesn't Answer Four Zionist soldiers defend a strategic entrance to Jerusalem. While at their posts, they reflect on their lives and devotion to the cause. Made in Israel, in English. The first Israeli feature film. **1955** 101m/B Edward Mulhare, Haya Harareet, Michael Wager; **D:** Thorold Dickinson. **VHS, Beta $79.95** *ERG, ING* 🎞️🎞️🎞️

Hillbillies in a Haunted House Two country and western singers en route to the Nashville jamboree encounter a group of foreign spies "haunting" a house. Features Rathbone's last film performance. Sequel to "Las Vegas Hillbillies" (1966). Giant step down for everyone involved. **1967** 88m/C Ferlin Husky, Joi Lansing, Don Bowman, John Carradine, Lon Chaney Jr., Basil Rathbone; **D:** Jean Yarborough. **VHS, Beta $29.95** *VCI, AOV Woof!*

Hillbilly Blitzkrieg Two soldiers are sent to the boonies to guard a top-secret missile site from enemy agents. Come-to-life comic strip characters Snuffy Smith, Barney Google and Spark Plug join in the antics. **AKA:** Enemy Round-Up. **1942** 63m/B Bud Duncan, Cliff Nazarro, Edgar Kennedy, Doris Linden, Lucien Littlefield, Alan Baldwin; **D:** Roy Mack. **VHS $19.95** *NOS, RXM* 🎞️

The Hills Have Eyes Desperate family battles for survival and vengeance against a brutal band of inbred hillbilly cannibals. Craven gore-fest followed by Hills II. **1977 (R)** 83m/C Susan Lanier, Robert Houston, Martin Speer, Dee Wallace Stone, Russ Grieve, John Steadman, James Whitworth, Michael Berryman; **D:** Wes Craven; **W:** Wes Craven. **VHS, Beta $19.95** *STE Woof!*

The Hills Have Eyes, Part 2 Craven reprises Hills with Eyes number one to ill effect. Ignorant teens disregard warnings of a "Hills Have Eyes" refugee, and go stomping into the grim reaper's proving grounds. Predictably bad things happen. **1984** 86m/C Michael Berryman, Kevin Blair, John Bloom, Janus Blythe, John Laughlin, Tamara Stafford; **D:** Wes Craven; **W:** Wes Craven. **VHS, Beta $34.98** *REP* 🎞️

The Hills of Home Warm sentimental tale about a Scottish doctor and his beloved pet collie. One of the better films in the "Lassie" series. **AKA:** Master of Lassie. **1948** 97m/C Edmund Gwenn, Donald Crisp, Tom Drake, Janet Leigh; **D:** Fred M. Wilcox; **W:** William Ludwig. **VHS $14.95** *MGM, FCT* 🎞️🎞️🎞️

Hills of Oklahoma Allen stars as the leader of a cattlemen's association who decides not to deal with dishonest meatpacker Keane, so he drives his herd across the desert to a slaughterhouse run by an honest businesswoman. Based on an original story by Cooper. **1950** 67m/B Rex Allen, Elisabeth Fraser, Elisabeth Risdon, Fuzzy Knight, Roscoe Ates, Robert Emmett Keane, Trevor Bardette; **D:** R.G. Springsteen; **W:** Olive Cooper, Victor Arthur. **VHS $19.99** *MOV* 🎞️

Hills of Utah Autry finds himself in the middle of a feud between the local mine operator and a group of cattlemen, while searching for his father's murderer. **1951** 70m/B Gene Autry, Pat Buttram, Denver Pyle; **D:** John English. **VHS, Beta $29.98** *CCB* 🎞️½

The Hillside Strangler Made-for-television, crime-of-the-week drama about the investigation to apprehend the serial killer responsible for 10 deaths in 1977-78. **AKA:** The Case of the Hillside Stranglers.

H

1989 91m/C Richard Crenna, Dennis Farina, Billy Zane, Tony Plana, James Tolkan, Tasia Valenza; **D:** Steven Gethers. **VHS, Beta** $79.95 *FRH* ⚜️½

Himatsuri An acclaimed film detailing the conflicts between man and nature, as a lumberjack in a Japanese forest believes he's the protector of the mountains through his divine relationship with the ancient gods. Outraged by the destruction, pollution, and commercial exploitation of the land he turns to violence. In Japanese with English subtitles. **AKA:** Fire Festival.
1985 120m/C Kinya Kitaoji, Kwako Taichi, Ryota Nakamoto, Norihei Miki; **D:** Mitsuo Yanagimachi; **W:** Kenji Nakagami; **M:** Toru Takemitsu. **VHS, Beta** $29.95 *LHV, WAR, AUD* ⚜️⚜️⚜️

The Hindenburg A dramatization of what might have happened on the fateful night the Hindenburg exploded. Scott plays an investigator who is aware that something is up, and has numerous suspects to interrogate. The laser edition features wide-screen format, digital Stereo Surround, the original trailer and chapter stops.
1975 (PG) 126m/C George C. Scott, Anne Bancroft, William Atherton, Roy Thinnes, Gig Young, Burgess Meredith, Charles Durning, Richard Dysart; **D:** Robert Wise. Academy Awards '75: Best Sound Effects Editing, Best Visual Effects; Nominations: Best Art Direction/Set Decoration, Best Cinematography, Best Sound. **VHS, Beta** $14.98 *MCA* ⚜️⚜️

Hips, Hips, Hooray Two supposed "hot shot" salesmen are hired by a cosmetic company to sell flavored lipstick. This lavish musical comedy is one of Wheeler and Woolsey's best vehicles. ♫Tired of It All; Keep Romance Alive; Keep On Doin' What You're Doin'.
1934 68m/B Robert Woolsey, Bert Wheeler, Ruth Etting, Thelma Todd, Dorothy Lee; **D:** Mark Sandrich. **VHS, Beta** $19.95 *CCB* ⚜️⚜️½

Hired Hand Two drifters settle on a farm belonging to one of their wives, only to leave again seeking to avenge the murder of a friend. TV prints include Larry Hagman in a cameo role.
1971 93m/C Peter Fonda, Warren Oates, Verna Bloom, Severn Darden, Robert Pratt; *Cameos:* Larry Hagman; **D:** Peter Fonda. **VHS, Beta** $14.95 *BAR* ⚜️⚜️½

Hired to Kill A pair of Mafia hoods plot against each other over a $6 million drug shipment. **AKA:** The Italian Connection.
1973 (R) 90m/C Henry Silva, Woody Strode, Adolfo Celi, Mario Adorf. **Beta** *NO* ⚜️⚜️

Hired to Kill The granite-hewn Thompson plays a male-chauvinist commando grudgingly leading a squad of beautiful mercenary-ettes on an international rescue mission. Not as bad as it sounds (mainly because the ladies aren't complete bimbos), but between senseless plotting, gratuitous catfights, and a love scene indistinguishable from rape, the Hound found plenty to dislike.
1991 (R) 91m/C Brian Thompson, George Kennedy, Jose Ferrer, Oliver Reed, Penelope Reed, Michelle Moffett, Barbara Lee Alexander, Jordanca Capra; **D:** Nico Mastorakis, Peter Rader; **W:** Nico Mastorakis. **VHS, Beta** *PAR* ⚜️½

Hiroshima Maiden An American family gains new perspective when they meet a young survivor of the atomic bomb. Based on true stories of Japanese women who stayed with Americans while undergoing surgery to minimize their scars. Originally aired on PBS as part of the "Wonderworks" family movie series.
1988 58m/C Susan Blakely, Richard Masur, Tamlyn Tomita; **D:** Joan Darling. **VHS** $29.95 *PME, WNE, HMV* ⚜️½

Hiroshima, Mon Amour A profoundly moving drama exploring the shadow of history over the personal lives of a lonely French actress living in Tokyo and a Japanese architect with whom she's having an affair. Presented in a complex network of flashbacks. Highly influential; adapted by Marguerite Duras from her book. In Japanese with English subtitles.
1959 88m/B Emmanuelle Riva, Eiji Okada, Bernard Fresson, Stella Dassas, Pierre Barbaud; **D:** Alain Resnais; **W:** Marguerite Duras; **M:** Georges Delerue, Giovanni Fusco. Academy Awards '60 Nominations: Best Story & Screenplay; National Board of Review Awards '60: 5 Best Foreign Films of the Year; New York Film Critics Awards '60: Best Foreign Film. **VHS, Beta, 8mm** $24.95 *VYY, MRV, SUE* ⚜️⚜️⚜️

Hiroshima: Out of the Ashes The terrible aftermath of the bombing of Hiroshima, August, 1945, as seen through the eyes of American and Japanese soldiers, the Japanese people, and a priest. Carefully detailed and realistic, creates an amazing emotional response. Don't miss the scene in which Nelson and his buddy find themselves surrounded by Japanese—the enemy—only to realize that their "captors" have been blinded by the blast. Created as an homage for the 45th anniversary of the bombing.
1990 (PG) 98m/C Max von Sydow, Judd Nelson, Mako, Tamlyn Tomita, Stan Egi, Sab Shimono, Noriyuki "Pat" Morita, Kim Miyori; **D:** Peter Werner. **VHS** *VMK* ⚜️⚜️⚜️

His Brother's Ghost When Fuzzy is rubbed out by bandits, Billy Carson (no longer called Billy the Kid thanks to mothers' protestations) convinces his twin brother to impersonate him in order to make the bandits believe they are the victims of hocus pocus from the otherworld. Crabbe—who dressed noir before it was chic—made this during his post sci-fi western period, when he slugged it through some fifty low-rent oaters (usually under the direction of Newfield at PRC studios).
1945 54m/C Buster Crabbe, Al "Fuzzy" St. John, Charles "Blackie" Kraft, Bud Osborne, Karl Hackett, Archie Hall; **D:** Sam Newfield. **VHS** $19.99 *NOS, MRV, HEG* ⚜️⚜️

His Double Life When a shy gentleman's valet dies, his master assumes the dead man's identity and has a grand time. From the play "Buried Alive" by Arnold Bennett. Remade in 1943 as "Holy Matrimony."
1933 67m/B Roland Young, Lillian Gish, Montagu Love; **D:** Arthur Hopkins. **VHS, Beta** $19.95 *NOS, MRV, BAR* ⚜️⚜️½

His Fighting Blood Northwest Mounties in action. Based on a James Oliver Curwood story.
1935 63m/B Kermit Maynard. **VHS, Beta** $19.95 *VDM* ⚜️½

His First Command An early talkie wherein a playboy falls in love with the daughter of a cavalry officer, and enlists in order to win her affections.
1929 60m/B William Boyd, Dorothy Sebastian, Gavin Gordon; **D:** Gregory La Cava. **VHS, Beta, 8mm** $24.95 *VYY* ⚜️½

His First Flame A classic Langdon silent romantic comedy.
1926 62m/B Harry Langdon, Vernon Dent, Natalie Kingston; **W:** Frank Capra. **VHS, Beta** $19.95 *NOS, VYY, GPV* ⚜️⚜️⚜️

His Girl Friday Classic, unrelentingly hilarious war-between-the-sexes comedy in which a reporter and her ex-husband editor help a condemned man escape the law—while at the same time furthering their own ends as they try to get the big scoop on political corruption in the town. One of Hawks' most furious and inventive screen combats in which women are given uniquely equal (for Hollywood) footing, with staccato dialogue and wonderful performances. Based on the Hecht-MacArthur play "The Front Page," which was originally filmed in 1931. Remade again in 1974 as "The Front Page," and in 1988 as "Switching Channels." Also available colorized.
1940 92m/B Cary Grant, Rosalind Russell, Ralph Bellamy, Gene Lockhart, John Qualen, Porter Hall, Roscoe Karns, Abner Biberman, Cliff Edwards, Billy Gilbert, Helen Mack, Ernest Truex, Clarence Kolb, Frank Jenks; **D:** Howard Hawks; **W:** Charles Lederer; **M:** Morris Stoloff. **VHS, Beta** $9.95 *CNG, MRV, NOS* ⚜️⚜️⚜️

His Kind of Woman A fall guy, being used to bring a racketeer back to the U.S. from Mexico, discovers the plan and tries to halt it.
1951 120m/B Robert Mitchum, Jane Russell, Vincent Price, Tim Holt, Charles McGraw, Raymond Burr, Jim Backus; **D:** John Farrow. **VHS, Beta** *NO* ⚜️⚜️

His Majesty O'Keefe Lancaster stars as a South Seas swashbuckler dealing in the lucrative coconut-oil trade of the mid-1800s. The natives see him as a god and allow him to marry a beautiful maiden. When his reign is threatened by unscrupulous traders, Lancaster springs into action to safeguard his kingdom. Based on a real-life American adventurer, this was the first movie ever filmed in the Fiji Islands.
1953 92m/C Burt Lancaster, Joan Rice, Benson Fong, Philip Ahn, Grant Taylor; **D:** Byron Haskin. **VHS, Beta** $59.99 *WAR* ⚜️½

His Majesty, the American William Brooks (Fairbanks) is a young man whose heritage is unknown to him. It turns out he's an heir to a small European kingdom. When Brooks arrives in Alaine he discovers the war minister is trying to overthrow the present king. With his usual dash, our hero saves the day and also wins the hand of a beautiful princess. First picture released by United Artists studios, formed by Fairbanks, Mary Pickford, Charles Chaplin, and D.W. Griffith.
1919 100m/B Douglas Fairbanks Sr., Marjorie Daw, Lillian Langdon, Frank Campeau; **D:** Joseph Henabery. **VHS** $24.95 *GPV, GVV* ⚜️½

His Majesty, the Scarecrow of Oz/The Magic Cloak of Oz The creator of the Oz stories, L. Frank Baum, wrote, produced and directed these two stories himself, with all the characters from his best-selling children's books.
1914 80m/B *D:* L. Frank Baum. **VHS, Beta** $59.95 *GVV* ⚜️½

His Name was King A man goes after the gang who murdered his brother and raped his young wife in the old West.
1985 90m/C Richard Harrison, Klaus Kinski, Anne Puskin; **D:** Don Reynolds. **VHS, Beta** $14.95 *CNG* Woof!

His Picture in the Papers An early silent comedy wherein the robust, red-meat-eating son of a health food tycoon must get his father's permission to marry by getting his picture favorably in the paper for advertising's sake.
1916 68m/B Douglas Fairbanks Sr.; **D:** John Emerson; **W:** Anita Loos, John Emerson. **VHS, Beta, 8mm** $19.95 *NOS, VYY, GPV* ⚜️½

His Prehistoric Past/The Bank Two of Chaplin's classic early shorts.
1915 54m/B Charlie Chaplin, Mack Swain, Edna Purviance; **D:** Charlie Chaplin. **VHS, Beta** $19.95 *VYY, GVV* ⚜️⚜️

His Private Secretary Wayne plays the jet-setting son of a wealthy businessman who wants his boy to settle down. And he does - after he meets the minister's beautiful daughter.
1933 68m/B John Wayne, Evelyn Knapp, Alec B. Francis, Reginald Barlow, Natalie Kingston, Arthur Hoyt, Al "Fuzzy" St. John; *D:* Philip H. Whitman. **VHS, Beta $19.98** *DVT, HEG* ⅛ ½

His Royal Slyness/Haunted Spooks Two Harold Lloyd shorts. "His Royal Slyness" (1919) offers Harold impersonating the king of a small kingdom, while in "Haunted Spooks" (1920), Harold gets suckered into living in a haunted mansion. Both films include music score.
1920 52m/B Harold Lloyd; *D:* Harold Lloyd. **VHS, Beta $24.95** *VYY, CCB, GVV* ⅛ ½

His Wife's Lover An actor disguised as an old man wins the heart of a lovely young woman. He decides to test her fidelity by reverting to his handsome young self and attempting to seduce her. An enchanting comedy in Yiddish with English subtitles. *AKA:* Zayn Vaybs Lubovnik.
1931 77m/B Ludwig Satz, Michael Rosenberg, Isadore Cashier, Lucy Levine; *D:* Sidney Goldin. **VHS, Beta $59.95** *ERG, FCT, ING* ⅛⅛⅛

Historia de un Gran Amor Two children of rival families fall in love against their parents' wishes. *AKA:* History of a Great Love.
1957 155m/B George Negrete, Sara Garcia, Gloria Marin. **VHS, Beta $64.95** *MAD* ⅛ ½

History is Made at Night A wife seeks a divorce from a jealous husband while on an Atlantic cruise; she ends up finding both true love and heartbreak in this story of a love triangle at sea.
1937 98m/B Charles Boyer, Jean Arthur, Leo Carrillo, Colin Clive; *D:* Frank Borzage. **VHS, Beta $19.98** *WAR, FCT* ⅛⅛⅛

History of the World: Part 1 More misses than hits in this Brooks' parody of historic epics. A bluntly satiric vision of human evolution, from the Dawn of Man to the French Revolution told in an episodic fashion. Good for a few laughs.
1981 (R) 90m/C Mel Brooks, Dom DeLuise, Madeline Kahn, Harvey Korman, Cloris Leachman, Gregory Hines, Pamela Stephenson, Paul Mazursky, Beatrice Arthur, Fritz Feld, John Hurt, Jack Carter, John Hillerman, John Gavin, Barry Levinson, Ron Carey, Howard Morris, Sid Caesar, Jackie Mason; *D:* Mel Brooks; *W:* Mel Brooks. **VHS, Beta $14.98** *FOX* ⅛⅛

The History of White People in America A pseudo-documentary look at the complicated life of a white midwestern family. Succeeds in making hilarious fun of many traditional prejudices. Originally made for cable television.
1985 48m/C Martin Mull, Fred Willard, Mary Kay Place, Teri Garr, Bob Eubanks; *D:* Harry Shearer. **VHS, Beta $24.95** *MCA* ⅛⅛

The History of White People in America: Vol. 2 Mull's television-special comedy satirizing WASP society in America.
1985 40m/C Martin Mull; *D:* Harry Shearer. **VHS, Beta $24.95** *MCA* ⅛⅛

Hit! When the 15-year-old daughter of a government agent dies of a drug overdose, he deals his revenge to top French heroin traffickers.
1973 (R) 135m/C Billy Dee Williams, Richard Pryor, Gwen Welles, Paul Hampton, Warren Kemmerling, Sid Melton; *D:* Sidney J. Furie; *W:* Alan R. Trustman, David M. Wolf; *M:* Lalo Schifrin. **VHS, Beta $14.95** *PAR* ⅛⅛

The Hit A feisty young hooker gets mixed-up with two strong-armed hired killers as they escort an unusual stool-pigeon from his exile in Spain to their angry mob bosses. Minor cult-noir from the director of "My Beautiful Launderette" and "Dangerous Liaisons."
1985 (R) 105m/C Terence Stamp, John Hurt, Laura Del Sol, Tim Roth, Fernando Rey, Bill Hunter; *D:* Stephen Frears; *W:* Peter Prince; *M:* Eric Clapton. **VHS, Beta $19.98** *SUE, NLC* ⅛⅛ ½

Hit & Run David Marks, a Manhattan cab driver, is haunted by recurring flashbacks of a freak hit-and-run accident in which his wife was struck down on a city street. *AKA:* Revenge Squad.
1982 96m/C Paul Perri, Claudia Cron; *D:* Charles Braverman; *M:* Brad Fiedel. **VHS, Beta** *NO* ⅛

Hit Lady An elegant cultured woman becomes a hit lady for the syndicate in this predictable, yet slick gangster movie. Made for television.
1974 74m/C Yvette Mimieux, Dack Rambo, Clu Gulager, Keenan Wynn; *D:* Tracy Keenan Wynn. **VHS, Beta $59.95** *PSM* ⅛⅛

The Hit List A regular guy fights back brutally when his wife and child are mistakenly kidnapped by the Mafia. Fast-paced action makes up for thin plot.
1988 (R) 87m/C Jan-Michael Vincent, Leo Rossi, Lance Henriksen, Charles Napier, Rip Torn; *D:* William Lustig. **VHS, Beta $14.95** *COL* ⅛⅛

The Hit List Charles Pike (Fahey) is a professional hitman working for attorney Peter Mayhew (Coburn) to wipe out drug lords. Then Mayhew gives Pike a new assignment. He introduces him to sexy widow Jordan Henning (Butler), who wants Pike to kill the man who murdered her husband. Pike finds himself mixing business with pleasure in a deadly combination that sees him dodging crooked cops and trained assassins.
1993 (R) 97m/C Jeff Fahey, Yancy Butler, James Coburn; *D:* William Webb; *W:* Reed Steiner. **VHS $19.95** *COL* ⅛⅛ ½

The Hit Man A crime drama that profiles the crisis of a man unfit to commit murder but who does for a price. *AKA:* Il Sicario.
1961 100m/B VHS, Beta *CIG* ⅛⅛

Hit Men Double crosses and gun battles highlight this tale of inner-city crime.
1973 90m/C Henry Silva, Mario Adorf, Woody Strode, Adolfo Celi. **VHS, Beta $19.95** *VDC* ⅛ ½

Hit the Deck Second-rate studio musical about sailors on leave and looking for romance. Based on the 1927 Broadway musical. ♫Sometimes I'm Happy; Hallelujah; Why, Oh Why; Keeping Myself For You; More Than You Know; I Know That You Know; Lucky Bird.
1955 112m/C Jane Powell, Tony Martin, Debbie Reynolds, Walter Pidgeon, Vic Damone, Gene Raymond, Ann Miller, Russ Tamblyn, J. Carroll Naish, Kay Armen, Richard Anderson; *D:* Roy Rowland; *M:* Vincent Youmans. **VHS, Beta $19.98** *MGM* ⅛ ½

Hit the Dutchman Routine gangster flick about Dutch Schultz trying to rise to the top of the New York crime community—with or without the help of underworld pals Legs Diamond and Lucky Luciano. An unrated version is also available.
1992 (R) 116m/C Bruce Nozick, Sally Kirkland, Will Kempe; *D:* Menahem Golan. **VHS $89.95** *VMK* ⅛

Hit the Ice Newspaper photographers Bud and Lou are mistaken as gangsters in Chicago and the usual complications ensue. Includes an appearance by Johnny Long & His Orchestra. ♫I'm Like A Fish Out Of Water; Happiness Bound; I'd Like to Set You to Music; Slap Polka.
1943 89m/C Bud Abbott, Lou Costello, Patric Knowles, Elyse Knox, Ginny Simms, Johnny Long & His Orchestra; *D:* Charles Lamont. **VHS, Beta $14.95** *MCA* ⅛⅛

Hit the Saddle The Three Mesquiteers track down a gang involved in capturing wild horses in protected areas although one of three is more interested in the charms of a dance hall girl (played by starlet Rita Cansino who would soon become Rita Hayworth).
1937 54m/B Bob Livingston, Ray Corrigan, Max Terhune, J.P. McGowan, Yakima Canutt, Rita Hayworth; *D:* Mack V. Wright. **VHS, Beta $9.99** *NOS, VCN, REP* ⅛⅛

Hit Woman: The Double Edge Lucci plays a dual role as an FBI agent and the look-alike killer-for-hire that she's tracking. Originally made for television, the video version contains additional footage that earned the "R" rating.
1993 (R) 92m/C Susan Lucci, Robert Urich, Michael Woods, Robert Prosky. **VHS $89.95** *APX* ⅛⅛ ½

The Hitch-Hiker Two young men off on the vacation of their dreams pick up a psychopathic hitchhiker with a right eye that never closes, even when he sleeps. Taut suspense makes this flick worth seeing.
1953 71m/B Edmond O'Brien, Frank Lovejoy, William Talman, Jose Torvay; *D:* Ida Lupino. **VHS $16.95** *SNC* ⅛⅛⅛

Hitchcock Classics Collection: Trailers on Tape Collection of 20 previews for such Hitchcock favorites as "Shadow of a Doubt," "Rear Window," "Vertigo," "North by Northwest" and "Psycho." Some trailers are in black and white.
1985 55m/C *D:* Alfred Hitchcock. **VHS, Beta $79.95** *SFR* ⅛⅛⅛

Hitchcock Collection A collector's set containing three films from the master of suspense. Includes: "The Lady Vanishes," "The 39 Steps," "Vintage Hitchcock"—see him from a set designer to a director. In B/W and color.
1987 200m/C Alfred Hitchcock, Michael Redgrave, Paul Lukas, Robert Donat, Madeleine Carroll; *D:* Alfred Hitchcock. **VHS, Beta $79.95** *MPI* ⅛⅛⅛

Hitcher A young man picks up a hitchhiker on a deserted stretch of California highway only to be tormented by the man's repeated appearances: is he real or a figment of his imagination? Ferociously funny, sadomasochistic comedy with graphic violence.
1986 (R) 98m/C Rutger Hauer, C. Thomas Howell, Jennifer Jason Leigh, Jeffrey DeMunn, John M. Jackson; *D:* Robert Harmon; *W:* Eric Red; *M:* Mark Isham. **VHS, Beta $14.98** *HBO* ⅛⅛ ½

The Hitchhiker HBO's chilling horror anthology series contains a trio of terrifying tales. Additional episodes are available. In this first collection, Hamlin stars in "The Curse," about Yuppie occult vengeance; "W.G.O.D.," finds Busey and Page caught up in radio religion; and "Hired Help," finds Black with a less than human handyman.
1985 90m/C Harry Hamlin, Gary Busey, Geraldine Page, Karen Black. **VHS, Beta $19.98** *WAR, MOV* ⅛⅛ ½

Hitchhiker 2 Three more episodes from HBO's horror series: "Dead Man's Curve," "Nightshift," and "Last Scene."
1985 90m/C Peter Coyote, Margot Kidder, Darren McGavin, Susan Anspach. **VHS, Beta $19.98** *WAR* ⅛⅛ ½

Hitchhiker 3 Three episodes from the anthology mystery series: "Ghost Writer," "And If We Dream," and "True Believer." Made-for-cable television.
1987 90m/C Ornella Muti, Willem Dafoe, Barry Bostwick, Dayle Haddon, Stephen Collins, Robert Weiss, Tom Skerritt. VHS, Beta $19.98 LHV, WAR ⅍⅍½

Hitchhiker 4 Three episodes of the cable-television suspense series: "Man's Best Friend," about a lonely man whose pet dog tears his enemies to bits. "Face to Face," about the revenge exacted upon a drug-abusing cosmetic surgeon after he mucks up an operation; and "Videodate," about a guy being lured into a sinister video performance piece via his use of video dating services.
1987 90m/C Michael O'Keefe, Sybil Danning, Sonja Smits, Robert Vaughn, Shannon Tweed, Greg Henry. VHS, Beta $19.98 LHV, WAR ⅍⅍½

Hitchhikers Trash film about a bunch of scantily clad female hitchhikers who rob the motorists who stop to pick them up. Keep right on going when you spot this roadkill.
1972 (R) 90m/C Misty Rowe, Norman Klar, Linda Avery; D: Ferd Sebastian. VHS, Beta NO Woof!

The Hitchhiker's Guide to the Galaxy The six episode BBC television adaptation of Douglas Adams' hilarious science-fiction books. Features the intergalatic Ford Prefect, sent to Earth to update its planetary listing in the Hitchhiker's Guide; hapless hero Arthur Dent, a typical Englishman caught up in space mayhem; and an odd assortment of aliens, including Marvin the Paranoid Android. The show's sheer cheesiness is part of the charm. Available in both single-cassette and double-cassette versions, the latter includes a copy of the book and a dedication from Adams.
1981 194m/C Simon Jones, David Dixon, Sandra Dickinson, Mark Wing-Davey; D: Alan J.W. Bell. VHS $19.98 FOX, MOV, FUS Woof!

Hitler The true story of the infamous Nazi dictator's rise to power and his historic downfall. AKA: Women of Nazi Germany.
1962 103m/B Richard Basehart, Maria Emo, Cordula Trantow; D: Stuart Heisler. VHS, Beta $59.98 FOX ⅍⅍½

Hitler: Dead or Alive Three ex-cons devise a scheme to gain a million-dollar reward for capturing Adolf Hitler in this low-budget production.
1943 64m/B Ward Bond, Dorothy Tree, Bruce Edwards, Warren Hymer, Paul Fix, Russell Hicks, Bobby Watson; D: Nick Grinde. VHS, Beta $19.95 NOS, MRV, DVT ⅍

Hitler: The Last Ten Days Based on an eyewitness account, the story of Hitler's last days in an underground bunker gives insight to his madness.
1973 (PG) 106m/C Alec Guinness, Simon Ward, Adolfo Celi; D: Ennio de Concini. VHS, Beta $49.95 PAR, GLV ⅍⅍

Hitler's Children Two young people, a German boy and an American girl, are caught in the horror of Nazi Germany. He's attracted to Hitler's rant, she's repelled. Exploitative yet engrossing.
1943 83m/B Tim Holt, Bonita Granville, Otto Kruger, H.B. Warner, Irving Reis, Hans Conried, Lloyd Corrigan; D: Edward Dmytryk. VHS, Beta $19.95 MED, IHF ⅍⅍

Hitler's Daughter Made for TV movie following the trials and tribulations of the illegitimate daughter of Adolf Hitler. She's all grown up now...and wants to rule the United States. She secures a position of power during an election and now Nazi-hunters

must figure out her identity before she takes over the world!
1990 (R) 88m/C Kay Lenz, Veronica Cartwright, Melody Anderson, Patrick Cassidy, Carolyn Dunn, Lindsay Merrithew, George R. Robertson; D: James A. Contner. VHS, Beta PAR ⅍

The Hitman Norris plays a cop undercover as a syndicate hit man in Seattle, where he cleans up crime by triggering a three-way mob bloodbath between beastly Italian mafiosi, snooty French-Canadian hoods, and fanatical Iranian scum. But he teaches a black kid martial arts, so you know he's politically correct. Action addicts will give this a passing grade; all others need not apply.
1991 (R) 95m/C Chuck Norris, Michael Parks, Al Waxman, Alberta Watson, Salim Grant, Ken Pogue, Marcel Sabourin, Bruno Gerussi, Frank Ferrucci; D: Aaron Norris. VHS, 8mm $14.95 CAN, WAR ⅍⅍

The Hitter A former prizefighter, his girlfriend, and a washed-up promoter are all on the run in this adventure tale.
1979 (R) 94m/C Ron O'Neal, Adolph Caesar, Sheila Frazier; D: Christopher Leitch. VHS NO ⅍⅍

Hittin' the Trail The Good Cowboy is mistaken for a murdering varmint, and must prove his innocence.
1937 57m/B Tex Ritter, Charles "Blackie" King, Ray Whitley, The Range Ramblers; D: Robert North Bradbury. VHS, Beta $19.95 NOS, VDM ⅍

Hitz In a Los Angeles barrio, Musico, a Loco gang member, kills two rival gang members. Arrested and convicted when a young boy named Pepe is coerced into testifying against him, Musico is killed in the courtroom. But the violence doesn't stop. The judge, who wants to reform the juvenile court system, tries to protect Pepe, and both are targeted for death by the Loco gang.
1992 (R) 90m/C Elliott Gould, Emilia Crow, Karen Black, Cuba Gooding Jr. VHS $89.95 VMK ⅍½

The Hobbit An animated interpretation of J.R.R. Tolkien's novel of the same name. The story follows Bilbo Baggins and his journeys in Middle Earth and encounters with the creatures who inhabit it. He joins comrades to battle against evil beings and creatures. Made for television.
1978 76m/C D: Arthur Rankin Jr., Jules Bass; V: Orson Bean, John Huston, Otto Preminger, Richard Boone. VHS, Beta, 8mm $14.95 WAR, CHI, FCT ⅍⅍⅍

Hobgoblins Little creatures escape from a studio vault and wreak havoc.
1987 92m/C Jeffrey Culver, Tom Bartlett; D: Rick Sloane. VHS, Beta $79.95 TWE ⅍

The Hoboken Chicken Emergency Arthur's supposed to pick up a turkey for the family Thanksgiving dinner. Instead he returns with a 266-pound live chicken named Henrietta. Originally aired on PBS as part of the "Wonderworks" series.
1984 55m/C Dick Van Patten, Peter Billingsley, Gabe Kaplan, Arlene Golonka; D: Peter Baldwin. VHS $14.95 PME, FCT, BTV ⅍

Hobo's Christmas A man who left his family to become a hobo comes home for Christmas 25 years later. Hughes turns in a delightful performance as the hobo in this made for television special.
1987 94m/C Barnard Hughes, William Hickey, Gerald McRaney, Wendy Crewson; D: Will MacKenzie. VHS, Beta NO ⅍⅍

Hobson's Choice A prosperous businessman in the 1890s tries to keep his daughter from marrying, but the strong-willed daughter has other ideas. Remade for television in 1983.
1953 107m/B Charles Laughton, John Mills, Brenda de Banzie; D: David Lean; M: Malcolm Arnold. VHS, Beta $29.95 ING, NLC, HMV ⅍⅍⅍

Hobson's Choice Made-for-television remake of the old family comedy about a crusty, penny-pinching businessman whose headstrong daughter proves to him she'll not become an old maid. Instead she marries one of his employees. Not bad, but not as good as the original.
1983 95m/C Jack Warden, Sharon Gless, Richard Thomas, Lillian Gish; D: Gilbert Cates. VHS, Beta $59.98 FOX ⅍⅍

Hockey Night A movie for pre- and early teens in which a girl goalie makes the boys' hockey team.
1984 77m/C Megan Follows, Rick Moranis, Gail Youngs, Martin Harburg, Henry Ramer; D: Paul Shapiro. VHS, Beta FHE ⅍⅍

Hocus Pocus The divine Miss M is back, but this time she's not so sweet. Midler, Najimy, and Parker are 17th century witches accidentally conjured up in the 20th century, appropriately enough on Halloween in Salem, Massachusetts. Seems they were hung 300 years back and they take their revenge in some surprisingly gruesome ways, given the Disney label. They rant, they rave, they sing (only once), they fly. See this one for the three stars who make up for the lack of substance with their comedic talents.
1993 (PG) 95m/C Bette Midler, Kathy Najimy, Sarah Jessica Parker, Thora Birch, Doug Jones, Omri Katz, Vinessa Shaw, Stephanie Faracy, Charles Rocket; Cameos: Penny Marshall, Garry Marshall; D: Kenny Ortega; W: Neil Cuthbert, Mick Garris; M: John Debney. VHS, Beta $96.03 DIS, BVV, BTV ⅍⅍½

Hoffa The story of union organizer James R. Hoffa who oversaw the rise of the Teamsters, a labor union composed mostly of truck drivers, from its fledgling infancy during the Great Depression to a membership of 2 million by the 1970's. Powerful performances by Nicholson in the title role and DeVito, who plays a union aide, a fictitious composite of several men who actually served Hoffa. This almost affectionate biographical treatment stands out in contrast from a career bristling with tension and violence. Proceeds through a series of flashbacks from the day Hoffa disappeared, July 30, 1975.
1992 (R) 140m/C Jack Nicholson, Danny DeVito, Armand Assante, J.T. Walsh, Frank Whaley, Kevin Anderson, John P. Ryan, Robert Prosky, Natalija Nogulich, Nicholas Pryor, John Reilly, Karen Young, Cliff Gorman; D: Danny DeVito; W: David Mamet; M: David Newman. VHS $19.98 FXV ⅍⅍⅍

Hog Wild A clique of high school nerds exact revenge on bullies from the local mean motorcycle gang, and a girl is torn between the two factions.
1980 (PG) 97m/C Patti D'Arbanville, Tony Rosato, Michael Biehn; D: Les Rose. VHS, Beta $59.98 NLC ⅍½

The Holcroft Covenant Based upon the complex Robert Ludlum novel. Details the efforts of a man trying to release a secret fund that his Nazi father humanistically set up to relieve the future sufferings of Holocaust survivors. Confusing, and slow, but interesting, nonetheless.
1985 (R) 112m/C Michael Caine, Victoria Tennant, Anthony Andrews, Lilli Palmer, Mario Adorf, Michael Lonsdale; D: John Frankenheimer; W: Edward Anhalt, John Hopkins, George Axelrod. VHS, Beta $14.95 MGM ⅍⅍

H

479 ▲ VIDEOHOUND'S GOLDEN MOVIE RETRIEVER

Hold 'Em Jail Some good laughs with Wheeler and Woolsey starting a competitive football team at Kennedy's Bidemore Prison.
1932 65m/B Bert Wheeler, Robert Woolsey, Edgar Kennedy, Betty Grable, Edna May Oliver; **D:** Norman Taurog. VHS, Beta $34.98 *CCB ⅛⅛½*

Hold Me, Thrill Me, Kiss Me "Offbeat" barely begins to describe this comedy about a hapless loser who finds true love. Eli (Parrish) has escaped marriage to a rich girl named Twinkle (Young), unfortunately it took a little shooting to do it and now Eli's hiding out in a tacky pink trailer park where Sabra (Naschak), an insatiable stripper with a fondness for sex toys, immediately goes after Eli's bod. But he falls for her naive (and virginal) sister, Dannie (Shelly). Hershman manages to keep all the free-wheeling goings on under control. Film debut of former model Parrish; directorial debut feature of Hershman.
1993 (R) Rm/C Max Parrish, Adrienne Shelly, Andrea Naschak, Sean Young, Diane Ladd, Bela Lehoczky, Ania Suli; **Cameos:** Timothy Leary; **D:** Joel Hershman; **W:** Joel Hershman. VHS $92.92 *LIV ⅛⅛½*

Hold That Ghost Abbott and Costello inherit an abandoned roadhouse where the illicit loot of its former owner, a "rubbed out" mobster, is supposedly hidden. **AKA:** Oh, Charlie.
1941 86m/B Bud Abbott, Lou Costello, Joan Davis, Richard Carlson, Mischa Auer, The Andrews Sisters, Ted Lewis & his Band; **D:** Arthur Lubin. VHS, Beta $14.95 *MCA ⅛⅛⅛*

Hold the Dream A made-for-television mini-series sequel to Barbara Taylor Bradford's "A Woman of Substance."
1985 195m/C Jenny Seagrove, Stephen Collins, Deborah Kerr, James Brolin; **D:** Don Sharp. VHS, Beta *NO ⅛*

Hold Your Man Great star vehicle that turns from comedy to drama with Harlow falling for hustler Gable. Harlow and Gable are at their best in this unlikely story of a crooked couple. Direction drags at times, but snappy dialogue and the stars' personalities more than make up for it.
1933 86m/B Jean Harlow, Clark Gable, Stuart Erwin, Dorothy Burgess, Garry Owen, Paul Hurst, Elizabeth Patterson, Laura La Plante; **D:** Sam Wood; **W:** Anita Loos, Howard Emmett Rogers. VHS $19.98 *MGM ⅛⅛⅛*

A Hole in the Head A comedy-drama about a shiftless but charming lout who tries to raise money to save his hotel from foreclosure and learn to be responsible for his young son. Notable for the introduction of the song "High Hopes."
1959 120m/C Frank Sinatra, Edward G. Robinson, Thelma Ritter, Carolyn Jones, Eleanor Parker, Eddie Hodges, Keenan Wynn, Joi Lansing; **D:** Frank Capra; **W:** Arnold Schulman. VHS, Beta $14.95 *MGM ⅛⅛½*

The Holes A Parisian book shop owner's daughter vanishes along with other local citizens and American tourists, and he decides to investigate when the police won't. In French with subtitles. **AKA:** Les Gaspards.
1972 (PG) 92m/C Philippe Noiret, Charles Denner, Michael Serrault, Gerard Depardieu. VHS, Beta $59.95 *FHE, FCT ⅛⅛½*

Holiday The classically genteel screwball comedy about a rich girl who steals her sister's fiance. A yardstick in years to come for sophisticated, urbane Hollywood romanticism. Based on the play by Philip Barry who later wrote "The Philadelphia Story." **AKA:** Free to Live; Unconventional Linda.
1938 93m/B Cary Grant, Katharine Hepburn, Doris Nolan, Edward Everett Horton, Ruth Donnelly, Lew Ayres, Binnie Barnes; **D:** George Cukor; **W:** Donald Ogden Stewart, Sidney Buchman. VHS, Beta $19.95 *COL ⅛⅛⅛½*

Holiday Affair Hollywood yuletide charmer about a pretty widow being courted by two very different men.
1949 86m/B Robert Mitchum, Janet Leigh, Griff Barnett, Wendell Corey, Esther Dale, Henry O'Neill, Henry Morgan, Larry J. Blake; **D:** Don Hartman. VHS, Beta $14.98 *RKO, TTC ⅛⅛½*

Holiday Hotel A group of wild French vacationers let loose at their favorite little resort hotel along the Brittany coast. Available in French with English subtitles or dubbed into English.
1977 (R) 109m/C Sophie Barjae, Daniel Ceccaldi; **D:** Michael Lang. VHS, Beta $29.95 *SUE ⅛⅛*

Holiday in Havana Desi Arnaz is back in Cuba winning hearts and dance contests. Watch only for Desi's presence. ♫Holiday in Havana; The Arnaz Jam; Straw Hat Song; Rhumba Rumbero; Copacobana; Made For Each Other; I'll Take Romance.
1949 73m/B Desi Arnaz Sr., Lolita Valdez, Mary Hatcher, Ann Doran; **D:** Jean Yarborough. VHS *GKK ⅛⅛*

Holiday in Mexico Pidgeon plays the U.S. ambassador to Mexico whose teenage daughter (Powell) tries to run his life along with his household. He falls for a singer while she develops a crush on an older, respected pianist (Iturbi playing himself). Lots of lively production numbers featuring Xavier Cugat and his orchestra. ♫I Think Of You; Walter Winchell Rhumba; Yo Te Amo Mucho—And That's That; And Dreams Remain; Holiday in Mexico; Ave Maria; Les Filles de Cadiz; Italian Street Song; Polonaise in A Flat Major.
1946 127m/C Walter Pidgeon, Jane Powell, Ilona Massey, Jose Iturbi, Roddy McDowall, Xavier Cugat, Hugo Haas; **D:** George Sidney; **W:** Isobel Lennart; **M:** Georgie Stoll. VHS $19.98 *MGM ⅛⅛½*

Holiday Inn Fred Astaire and Bing Crosby are rival song-and-dance men who decide to work together to turn a Connecticut farm into an inn, open only on holidays. Remade in 1954 as "White Christmas." ♫White Christmas; Be Careful, It's My Heart; Plenty to Be Thankful For; Abraham, Abraham; Let's Say It With Firecrackers; I Gotta Say I Love You Cause I Can't Tell A Lie; Let's Start the New Year Right; Happy Holidays; Song of Freedom.
1942 101m/B Bing Crosby, Fred Astaire, Marjorie Reynolds, Walter Abel, Virginia Dale; **D:** Mark Sandrich. Academy Awards '42: Best Song ("White Christmas"); Nominations: Best Story, Best Original Score. VHS, Beta $14.98 *MCA ⅛⅛⅛*

Holiday Rhythm A television promoter is knocked out and dreams of a world-wide trip full of entertainment, comedy, and insanity.
1950 61m/B Mary Beth Hughes, Tex Ritter, David Street, Donald MacBride. VHS, Beta *NO ⅛½*

Hollow Gate Trick or Treat?? Four kids find out when they run into a guy with hungry dogs.
1988 90m/C Addison Randall. VHS, Beta *NO ⅛½*

Hollywood After Dark McClanahan plays a young starlet trying to make it big in Hollywood. Pure exploitation schlock. Not released theatrically until 1968.
1965 ?m/C Rue McClanahan. VHS $16.95 *SNC, TPV ⅛*

Hollywood Bloopers Hilarious outtakes from some of Hollywood's finest movies, featuring stars such as Bette Davis, James Cagney, Humphrey Bogart, Rosalind Russell, Errol Flynn, Kirk Douglas, and many more.
195? 85m/B Lauren Bacall, Ronald Reagan, James Stewart, Joan Blondell, Rosalind Russell, Errol Flynn, Kirk Douglas, Barbara Stanwyck. VHS, Beta $19.95 *VDM, PPI ⅛⅛½*

Hollywood Boulevard Behind-the-scenes glimpse of shoestring-budget movie making offers comical sex, violence, sight gags, one-liners, comedy bits, and mock-documentary footage. Commander Cody and His Lost Planet Airmen are featured.
1976 93m/C Candice Rialson, Mary Woronov, Rita George, Jonathan Kaplan, Jeffrey Kramer, Dick Miller, Paul Bartel; **D:** Joe Dante, Allan Arkush. VHS, Beta $39.98 *WAR, OM ⅛⅛½*

Hollywood Boulevard 2 A "B" movie studio finds its top actresses being killed off and terror reigns supreme as the mystery grows more intense. Could that psycho-bimbo from outer space have something to do with it?
1989 (R) 82m/C Ginger Lynn Allen, Kelly Monteith, Eddie Deezen, Ken Wright, Steve Vinovich; **D:** Steve Barnett. VHS, Beta $79.95 *MGM ⅛*

Hollywood Canteen Star-studded extravaganza with just about every Warner Bros. lot actor in this tribute to love and nationalism. Lovesick G.I. Hutton falls for Leslie, wins a date with her in a phony raffle set up at the Hollywood Canteen, and the sparks fly right away. But he thinks she tricked him as he boards his train and she's not there to see him off. Lame story is redeemed by the talented cast and wonderful musical numbers which make this picture fly with charm and style. Before production began there were arguments over "unpatriotic" actors—labeled as such due to their lack of participation in this, and other similar movies produced at the time. ♫Don't Fence Me In; Sweet Dreams, Sweetheart; You Can Always Tell A Yank; We're Having a Baby; What Are You Doin' the Rest of Your Life; The General Jumped At Dawn; Gettin' Corns For My Country; Voodoo Moon; Tumblin' Tumbleweeds.
1944 124m/B Robert Hutton, Dane Clark, Janis Paige, Jonathan Hale, Barbara Brown, James Flavin, Eddie Marr, Ray Teal, Bette Davis, Joan Leslie, Jack Benny, Jimmy Dorsey, Joan Crawford, John Garfield, Barbara Stanwyck, Ida Lupino, Eddie Cantor, Jack Carson, Eleanor Parker, Alexis Smith, S.Z. Sakall, Peter Lorre, Sydney Greenstreet, Helmut Dantine; **D:** Delmer Daves; **W:** Delmer Daves. VHS $29.98 *FOX, FCT ⅛⅛⅛⅛*

Hollywood Chainsaw Hookers A campy, sexy, very bloody parody about attractive prostitutes who dismember their unsuspecting customers.
1988 (R) 90m/C Linnea Quigley, Gunnar Hansen, Jay Richardson, Michelle (McClellan) Bauer; **D:** Fred Olen Ray. VHS, Beta *NO ⅛*

Hollywood Chaos Director Ballantine's stars quit his production before it even starts, so he gets the next best thing - star look-alikes. However, his problems are just beginning. One of his new "stars" is kidnapped, and his reclusive stage manager is hunted as the object of desire for a female motorcycle gang.
1989 90m/C Carl Ballantine, Tricia Leigh Fisher, Kathleen Freeman; **D:** Sean McNamara. VHS $79.95 *WLA ⅛½*

Hollywood Clowns Glenn Ford narrates this tribute to the screen's greatest comedians, with clips from many classic scenes.
1985 60m/C Buster Keaton, W.C. Fields, Charlie Chaplin, Harold Lloyd, Bud Abbott, Lou Costello, Stan Laurel, Oliver Hardy, Groucho Marx, Harpo Marx, Chico Marx, Jerry Lewis, Dean Martin, Red Skelton, Danny Kaye, Betty Hutton, Bob Hope. **VHS, Beta $29.95** MGM ♫1/2

Hollywood Come Home Ray Milland hosts this look at the history of the movie industry from WWII to the early 60's. Also on this tape is "Hollywood Historama," a collection of video biographies of such luminaries as Mae West and John Barrymore.
1962 54m/B Ray Milland. **VHS, Beta, 8mm $24.99** VVY ♫1/2

Hollywood Confidential A beautiful Eastern girl goes to Hollywood and suffers irrevocable corruption.
193? 55m/B VHS, Beta NO ♫

Hollywood Cop A tough cop in Hollywood goes up against the mob for the sake of a kidnapped boy.
1987 (R) 101m/C Jim Mitchum, David Goss, Cameron Mitchell, Troy Donahue, Aldo Ray; **D:** Amir Shervan. **VHS, Beta $19.95** CEL ♫1/2

Hollywood Crime Wave An examination of crime and criminals as seen in vintage Hollywood gangster films. Features scenes with Humphrey Bogart, James Cagney and Edward G. Robinson.
196? 60m/B VHS, Beta $14.95 MPI ♫1/2

The Hollywood Detective An average TV movie that spoofs "Kojak." A TV detective tries it out for real, and gets into troubles for which he can't pause "for a message from our sponsor."
1989 (PG) 88m/C Telly Savalas, Helene Udy, George Coe, Joe Dallesandro, Tom Reese; **D:** Kevin Connor. **VHS, Beta $79.95** MCA ♫♫

Hollywood Erotic Film Festival A package of soft-core shorts, animated as well as live action, from around the world.
1987 75m/C VHS, Beta $59.95 PAR ♫

Hollywood Ghost Stories A view of supernatural activity in Hollywood, on the screen and behind the scenes. Includes interviews with William Peter Blatty, Sir Arthur Conan Doyle, Elke Sommer and others.
1986 75m/C VHS, Beta $29.98 WAR ♫

Hollywood Goes to War Five shorts produced for the entertainment of G.I.'s overseas or for home front bond drives: "The All-Star Bond Rally" features Hope, Crosby, Harry James and His Orchestra, Sinatra, Grable, Marx, and the Talking Pin-Ups; "Hollywood Canteen Overseas Special" features Shore, Cantor, Durante, and Skelton; "Mail Call (Strictly G.I.)" is a filmed "Mail Call" radio program; "G.I. Movie Weekly-Sing with the Stars" features Miranda and her fruit-basket hat and a Portuguese follow-the-bouncing-ball sing-along; and "Invaders in Greasepaint," the story of the North African USO tour of the "Four Jills in a Jeep." Also includes the Jill's memorable rendition of the wartime classic "Snafu," banned from the airwaves for its racy lyrics.
1954 41m/B Bob Hope, Bing Crosby, Frank Sinatra, Betty Grable, Harpo Marx, Jimmy Durante, Eddie Cantor, Red Skelton, Bud Abbott, Lou Costello, Dinah Shore, Dorothy Lamour, Carmen Miranda. **VHS, Beta $24.95** NO ♫

Hollywood Harry A private-eye mystery/parody, about an inept detective who searches for a missing porn actress. **AKA:** Harry's Machine.

1986 (PG-13) 99m/C Robert Forster, Kathrine Forster, Joe Spinell, Shannon Wilcox; **D:** Robert Forster. **VHS, Beta $79.95** MED ♫

Hollywood Heartbreak It's heartbreak in tinseltown for a young writer who's trying to pitch his movie script but winds up defending himself from slimy agents and persistent starlets. Another entry for Bartlett's familiar plotlines.
1989 90m/C Mark Moses, Carol Mayo Jenkins, Ron Karabatsos, Richard Romanus, James LeGros; **D:** Lance Dickson. **VHS** VTR ♫♫

Hollywood High Four attractive teen couples converge on the mansion of an eccentric silent-film star for an unusual vacation experience in this teenage skin flick. Followed by a sequel.
1977 (R) 81m/C Marcy Albrecht, Sherry Hardin, Rae Sperling, Susanne Kevin Mead; **D:** Patrick Wright. **VHS, Beta $29.98** LIV, VES ♫

Hollywood High, Part 2 Ignored by their boyfriends for the lure of sun and surf, three comely high school students try their best to regain their interest.
1981 (R) 86m/C April May, Donna Lynn, Camille Warner, Lee Thomburg; **D:** Caruth C. Byrd. **VHS, Beta $29.98** LIV, VES ♫

Hollywood Home Movies The home movies of more than 60 celebrities are compiled in this program. Offers a nostalgic look at how the demi-gods of yesteryear lived, worked, played, and relaxed.
1987 (PG) 58m/B Marilyn Monroe, John Wayne, Gregory Peck, Robert Mitchum, Ann-Margret. **VHS, Beta $19.98** IHF, MPI ♫

Hollywood Hot Tubs Teen sex romp has adolescent picking up some extra cash and a lot of fun repairing the hot tubs of the rich and famous.
1984 (R) 103m/C Donna McDaniel, Michael Andrew, Katt Shea Ruben, Paul Gunning, Edy Williams, Jewel Shepard; **D:** Chuck Vincent. **VHS, Beta $79.98** LIV, VES, VTR ♫

Hollywood Hot Tubs 2: Educating Crystal A softcore comedy about a well-tanned ingenue learning about business in Hollywood during numerous hot tub trysts.
1989 (R) 103m/C Jewel Shepard, Patrick Day, Remy O'Neill, David Tiefen, Bart Braverman; **D:** Ken Raich. **VHS, Beta $9.99** CCB ♫

Hollywood in Trouble A bumbling middle-aged fool decides to break into the wacky movie-making business.
1987 90m/C Vic Vallard, Jean Levine, Jerry Tiffe, Pamela Dixon, Jerry Cleary. **VHS, Beta** NO ♫

Hollywood Man A Hollywood actor wants to make his own film but when his financial support comes from the mob there's trouble ahead.
1976 (R) 90m/C William Smith, Don Stroud, Jennifer Billingsley, Mary Woronov; **D:** Jack Starrett. **VHS, Beta** NO ♫♫

Hollywood My Hometown Hollywood host Ken Murray looks at the stars of the glittering movie world.
19?? 60m/B Ken Murray. **VHS, Beta $19.95** VCN, DVT, HHT ♫♫

Hollywood Mystery A publicity agent stops at nothing to promote his would-be starlet girlfriend. **AKA:** Hollywood Hoodlum.
1934 53m/B June Clyde, Frank Albertson, Joe Crespo; **D:** B. Reeves Eason. **VHS $19.95** NOS, LOO ♫1/2

Hollywood or Bust The zany duo take their act on the road as they head for Tinsel Town in order to meet Lewis' dream girl Ekberg. This was the last film for the Martin

& Lewis team and it's not the swan song their fans would have hoped for.
1956 95m/C Dean Martin, Jerry Lewis, Anita Ekberg, Pat Crowley, Maxie "Slapsie" Rosenbloom, Willard Waterman; **D:** Frank Tashlin. **VHS $14.95** PAR, CCB ♫♫1/2

Hollywood Outtakes & Rare Footage A collection of rare and unusual film clips and excerpts that feature dozens of Hollywood stars in screen tests, promotional shorts, home movies, outtakes, television appearances and WWII propaganda shorts. Some segments in black and white.
1983 85m/C Marilyn Monroe, James Dean, Joan Crawford, Judy Garland, Humphrey Bogart, Ronald Reagan, Bette Davis, Vivien Leigh, Carole Lombard. **VHS, Beta $59.95** COL, RXM ♫♫1/2

Hollywood Party Durante plays a film star who decides to throw a Hollywood bash. Any plot is incidental as it is mainly an excuse to have numerous stars of the day appear in brief comic bits or musical numbers. Mickey Mouse and the Big Bad Wolf of Disney fame also appear in color animated footage combined with live action. Numerous MGM directors worked on parts of the film but Dwan was given the task of trying to pull the various scenes together (he is uncredited onscreen). ♫Hollywood Party; Hello; Reincarnation; I've Had My Moments; Feeling High; Hot Chocolate Soldiers.
1934 72m/B Jimmy Durante, Stan Laurel, Oliver Hardy, Lupe Velez, Ted Healy, Moe Howard, Curly Howard, Larry Fine, Robert Young, Charles Butterworth, Polly Moran, George Givot, Tom Kennedy; **D:** Allan Dwan; **V:** Walt Disney, Billy Bletcher. **VHS $19.98** MGM ♫♫1/2

Hollywood Scandals and Tragedies A look at the skeletons-in-the-closet surrounding the deaths and private turmoils of James Dean, Rock Hudson, Vivien Leigh, Frances Farmer, Sal Mineo, Sharon Tate, Jayne Mansfield, and others.
1988 90m/C VHS, Beta $79.95 MPI ♫♫1/2

Hollywood Shuffle Townsend's autobiographical comedy about a struggling black actor in Hollywood trying to find work and getting nothing but stereotypical roles. Written, directed, financed by Townsend, who created this often clever and appealing film on a $100,000 budget.
1987 (R) 81m/C Robert Townsend, Anne-Marie Johnson, Starletta DuPois, Helen Martin, Keenan Ivory Wayans, Damon Wayans, Craigus R. Johnson; **D:** Robert Townsend; **W:** Robert Townsend, Keenan Ivory Wayans; **M:** Patrice Rushen, Udi Harpaz. **VHS, Beta** NO ♫♫1/2

Hollywood Stadium Mystery A boxer turns up dead before a big match and a D.A. investigates. Performances hold this one up, especially by Hamilton who later played Commissioner Gordon on TV's "Batman."
1938 66m/B Neil Hamilton, Evelyn Venable, Jimmy Wallington, Barbara Pepper, Lucien Littlefield, Lynn (Mary Hart) Roberts, Charles Williams, James Spottswood, Reed Hadley, Smiley Burnette; **D:** David Howard. **VHS, Beta $16.95** SNC ♫♫

The Hollywood Strangler Meets the Skid Row Slasher Voiced-over narration, canned music and an unfathomable plot are but a few of this would-be fright fest's finer points. Uninhibited by any narrative connection, two terrors strike fear in the heart of Tinseltown. While a psycho photographer cruises L.A. taking pictures of models he subsequently strangles, a woman working in a bare-bums magazine store takes a stab (with a knife) at lowering the city's derelict population. There's a word for this sort of

dribble, and it isn't versimilitude. Steckler used an alias (not surprisingly) for this one—Wolfgang Schmidt. *AKA:* The Model Killer.
1979 (R) 72m/C Pierre Agostino, Carolyn Brandt, Forrest Duke, Chuck Alford; *D:* Ray Dennis Steckler. **VHS** *NO Woof!*

Hollywood Uncensored A history of Hollywood censorship, including long-suppressed scenes from ''King Kong,'' ''The Outlaw,'' ''Carnal Knowledge,'' ''Baby Doll,'' ''Easy Rider,'' ''Woodstock,'' and more.
1987 75m/C VHS, Beta $9.99 *LIV, FCT Woof!*

Hollywood Varieties A virtually plotless no-star conglomeration of comedy, music, and burlesque.
1950 60m/B The 3 Rio Brothers, Robert Alda, Glenn Vernon, Eddie Ryan. **VHS, Beta** *NO Woof!*

Hollywood Vice Sqaud Explores the lives of Hollywood police officers and the crimes they investigate. Contains three different story lines involving prostitution, child pornography, and organized crime. The film can't decide to be a comedy send-up of crime stories or a drama and is also crippled by a poor script. Written by the real-life chief of the Hollywood Vice Squad.
1986 (R) 100m/C Trish Van Devere, Ronny Cox, Frank Gorshin, Leon Isaac Kennedy, Carrie Fisher, Ben Frank, Robin Wright; *D:* Penelope Spheeris; *M:* Michael Convertino. **VHS $79.98** *VTR, HHE, MTX*

Hollywood without Makeup Home movie footage taken over the years by Ken Murray includes candid shots of over 100 stars of the film world.
1965 51m/C VHS, Beta, 8mm $24.95 *HHT, MRV, VYY*

Hollywood Zap Two losers, one a Southern orphan, the other a video game nut, hit Hollywood and engage in antics that are meant to be funny, but are actually tasteless.
1986 (R) 85m/C Ben Frank, Ivan E. Roth, De Waldron, Annie Gaybis, Chuck ''Porky'' Mitchell; *D:* David Cohen. **VHS, Beta $14.95** *PSM Woof!*

Hollywood's New Blood Young actors making a movie are haunted by a film crew from hell.
1988 90m/C Bobby Johnson, Francine Lapensee; *D:* James Shyman. **VHS, Beta** *VTR*

Holocaust The war years of 1935 to 1945 are relived in this account of the Nazi atrocities, focusing on the Jewish Weiss family, destroyed by the monstrous crimes, and the Dorf family, Germans who thrived under the Nazi regime. Highly acclaimed riveting made-for-television mini-series with an exceptional cast. Won eight Emmys.
1978 475m/C Michael Moriarty, Fritz Weaver, Meryl Streep, James Woods, Joseph Bottoms, Tovah Feldshuh, David Warner, Ian Holm, Michael Beck, Marius Goring; *D:* Marvin J. Chomsky. **VHS, Beta $69.95** *WOV, SWC*

Holocaust Survivors...Remembrance of Love A concentration camp survivor and his daughter attend the 1981 World Gathering of Holocaust Survivors in Tel-Aviv and both find romance. Made for television. *AKA:* Remembrance of Love.
1983 100m/C Kirk Douglas, Pam Dawber, Chana Eden, Yoram Gal, Robert Clary; *D:* Jack Smight; *M:* William Goldstein. **VHS, Beta $69.95** *VMK*

Holt of the Secret Service Secret service agent runs afoul of saboteurs and fifth-columnists in this 15-episode serial.
1942 290m/B Jack Holt, Evelyn Brent, Montague Shaw, Tristram Coffin, John Ward, George Cheseboro; *D:* James W. Horne. **VHS $39.95** *VYY, MED, DVT*

The Holy Innocents A peasant family is torn asunder by their feudal obligations to their patrons. Set in the 1960s in Franco's Spain. In Spanish with English subtitles. *AKA:* Los Santos Inocentes.
1984 (PG) 108m/C Alfredo Landa, Francesco Rabal; *D:* Mario Camus. Cannes Film Festival Nominations: cs 84: Best Film; Cannes Film Festival '84: Best Actor (Landa), Best Actor (Rabal). **VHS, Beta $68.00** *LHV, APD, ING*

Holy Terror The story of Florence Nightingale, who shocked Victorian society by organizing a nursing staff to aid British soldiers in the Crimean War, is told in this presentation from ''George Schaefer's Showcase Theatre.''
1965 76m/C Julie Harris, Denholm Elliott, Torin Thatcher, Kate Reid; *D:* George Schaefer. **VHS, Beta** *FHS*

Hombre A white man in the 1880s, raised by a band of Arizona Apaches, is forced into a showdown. In helping a stagecoach full of settlers across treacherous country, he not only faces traditional bad guys, but prejudice as well. Based on a story by Elmore Leonard.
1967 111m/C Paul Newman, Fredric March, Richard Boone, Diane Cilento, Cameron Mitchell, Barbara Rush, Martin Balsam; *D:* Martin Ritt; *W:* Harriet Frank Jr., Irving Ravetch. **VHS, Beta $19.98** *FOX*

Home Alone 8-year-old Kevin is accidentally left behind when his entire (and large) family makes a frantic rush for the airport. That's the plausible part. Alone and besieged by burglars, Culkin turns into a pint-sized Rambo defending his suburban castle with the wile and resources of a boy genius with perfect timing and unlimited wherewithal. That's the implausible part. Pesci and Stern, the targets of Macauley's wrath, enact painful slapstick with considerable vigor, while Candy has a small but funny part as the leader of a polka band traveling cross-country with mom O'Hara. The highest-grossing picture of 1990, surpassing ''Ghost'' and ''Jaws.''
1990 (PG) 105m/C Macaulay Culkin, Catherine O'Hara, Joe Pesci, Daniel Stern, John Heard, Roberts Blossom, John Candy, Catherine O'Hara, Billie Bird, Angela Goethals, Devin Ratray, Kieran Culkin; *D:* Chris Columbus; *W:* John Hughes; *M:* John Williams. **VHS, Beta $24.98** *FXV, IME, RDG*

Home Alone 2: Lost in New York In an almost exact duplication of the original blockbuster, the harebrained McCallister family leaves Kevin behind in the shuffle to start their Florida vacation. Boarding the wrong plane, Kevin lands in NYC, where wonder of wonders, he meets crooks Pesci and Stern, prison escapees who somehow survived the torture meted out in the first film. And they want revenge. Loaded with cartoon violence and shameless gag replicas from HA1, mega-hit still produces genuine laughs and manages to incorporate fresh material. Culkin is as adorable as ever, with supporting cast all delivering fine performances. Filmed in New York City.
1992 (PG) 120m/C Macaulay Culkin, Joe Pesci, Daniel Stern, Catherine O'Hara, Tim Curry, Brenda Fricker, Devin Ratray, Hillary Wolf, Eddie Bracken, Dana Ivey, Rob Schneider, Kieran Culkin, Gerry Bamman; *Cameos:* Donald Trump; *D:* Chris Columbus; *W:* John Hughes; *M:* John Williams. **VHS $24.98** *FXV, BTV*

The Home and the World Another masterpiece from India's Ray, this film deals with a sheltered Indian woman who falls in love with her husband's friend and becomes politically committed to the turmoil of 1907-1908. Based on Rabindranath Tagore's nov-

el. In Bengali with English subtitles. *AKA:* Ghare Baire.
1984 130m/C Victor Banerjee, Soumitra Chatterjee; *D:* Satyajit Ray. **VHS, Beta $19.95** *COL, ING, SUE*

Home at Last An orphan in turn of the century New York finds himself shipped to Nebraska on an orphan train. There he works on the farm of his adopted family, whose own son has died. The boy finds that he must adjust to a new lifestyle as well as strive to be accepted as someone other than the couple's son. From the ''Wonderworks'' series.
1988 58m/C Adrien Brody, Frank Converse, Caroline Lagerfelt, Sascha Radetsky. **VHS $29.95** *PME, HMV, FCT*

Home Before Midnight A young songwriter falls in love with a 14-year-old, is discovered, and is subsequently charged with statutory rape.
1984 115m/C James Aubrey, Alison Elliott; *D:* Pete Walker. **VHS, Beta $59.95** *LHV, WAR*

Home Feeling In a black ghetto the residents try to make a viable community.
19?? 60m/C VHS, Beta $49.95 *FCT*

Home for Christmas An elderly homeless man, with the love of a young girl, teaches a wealthy family the spirit of Christmas.
1990 96m/C Mickey Rooney, Joel Kaiser; *D:* Peter McCubbin. **VHS $79.95** *RHI*

Home for the Holidays Four daughters are called home on Christmas by their father who is convinced that his second wife is trying to poison them. Made for television. *AKA:* Deadly Desires.
1972 74m/C Eleanor Parker, Walter Brennan, Sally Field, Jessica Walter, Julie Harris; *D:* John Llewellyn Moxey. **VHS, Beta $24.95** *VMK*

Home Free All A Vietnam vet turned revolutionary, turned writer, tries to reacquaint himself with childhood friends only to find one has joined the mob and another is settled in suburbia and none of them are dealing well with adulthood.
1984 92m/C Allan Nicholls, Roland Caccavo, Maura Ellyn, Shelley Wyant, Lucille Rivim; *D:* Stuart Bird. **VHS, Beta $69.98** *LIV, VES*

Home from the Hill A solemn, brooding drama about a southern landowner and his troubled sons, one of whom is illegitimate. This one triumphs because of casting. Cinematography by Milton Krasner.
1960 150m/C Robert Mitchum, George Peppard, George Hamilton, Eleanor Parker, Everett Sloane, Luana Parker, Constance Ford; *D:* Vincente Minnelli; *W:* Harriet Frank Jr., Irving Ravetch. **VHS, Beta $19.98** *MGM*

Home in Oklahoma A boy will be swindled out of his inheritance and a killer will escape justice until Roy comes to the rescue. Standard series fare.
1947 72m/B Roy Rogers, Dale Evans, George ''Gabby'' Hayes, Carol Hughes; *D:* William Witney. **VHS, Beta $9.95** *NOS, TIM, CAB*

Home is Where the Hart is A rich 103-year-old is kidnapped by a nurse wanting to marry him and become heir to his estate. It's up to his sons, all in their 70s, to rescue him.
1988 (PG-13) 94m/C Martin Mull, Leslie Nielsen, Valri Bromfield, Stephen E. Miller, Eric Christmas, Ted Stidder; *D:* Rex Bromfield. **VHS, Beta $19.95** *PAR, IME*

Home Movies Brian DePalma and his film students at Sarah Lawrence College devised this loose, sloppy comedy which hearkens back to DePalma's early films. Tells the story of a nebbish who seeks therapy to gain control of his absurdly chaotic life. **1979 (PG) 89m/C** Kirk Douglas, Nancy Allen, Keith Gordon, Gerrit Graham, Vincent Gardenia, Harry Davenport; *D:* Brian DePalma; *W:* Brian DePalma; *M:* Pino Donaggio. **VHS, Beta $69.98** *LIV, VES, IME* 🎬🎬 1/2

A Home of Our Own An American priest sets up a home in Mexico for orphan boys and changes their lives for the better. A true story of Father William Wasson. **1975 100m/C** Jason Miller. **VHS, Beta $49.95** *WOV* 🎬🎬 1/2

A Home of Our Own Semi-autobiographical tearjerker based on screenwriter Duncan's childhood. Widowed and poor mother of six (Bates) is fired from her job at a Los Angeles potato chip factory, packs up the tribe and heads for a better life and a home to call their own. They end up in Idaho, in a ramshackle house owned by lonely Mr. Moon (Oh) and what follows is a winter of discontent. Bates provides an intense performance as a poor but proud woman with a tough exterior. Furlong provides the story's narration as the eldest son. A story of spiritual triumph, this one is sure to make your heart weep. **1993 (PG-13) 104m/C** Kathy Bates, Edward Furlong, Soon-Teck Oh, Amy Sakasitz, Tony Campisi; *D:* Tony Bill; *W:* Patrick Duncan. **VHS $94.99** *PGV* 🎬🎬 1/2

Home of the Brave A black soldier is sent on a top secret mission in the South Pacific, but finds that he must battle with his white comrades as he is subjected to subordinate treatment and constant racial slurs. Hollywood's first outstanding statement against racial prejudice. **1949 86m/B** Lloyd Bridges, James Edwards, Frank Lovejoy, Jeff Corey; *D:* Mark Robson. **VHS, Beta $19.98** *REP, FCT* 🎬🎬🎬

Home Remedy An introverted New Jersey bachelor's isolated lifestyle is invaded by a flirtatious housewife and her jealous husband. **1988 92m/C** Seth Barrish, Maxine Albert; *D:* Maggie Greenwald. **VHS, Beta** *MNC, ING* 🎬🎬

Home Sweet Home Suggested by the life of John Howard Payne (actor, poet, dramatist, critic, and world-wanderer) who wrote the title song amid the bitterness of his sad life. Silent with musical score. **1914 62m/B** Lillian Gish, Dorothy Gish, Henry B. Walthall, Mae Marsh, Blanche Sweet, Donald Crisp, Robert Harron; *D:* D.W. Griffith. **VHS, Beta $24.95** *VYY, KIV, GPV* 🎬🎬 1/2

Home Sweet Home A murdering psychopath escapes from the local asylum, and rampages through a family's Thanksgiving dinner. *AKA:* Slasher in the House. **1980 84m/C** Jake Steinfeld, Sallee Elyse, Peter de Paula; *D:* Nettie Pena. **VHS, Beta $59.95** *MED* 🎬 1/2

Home to Stay A farmer who has suffered a stroke is fighting off repeated lapses into senility. His son and daughter have conflicting interests as to whether he should be committed to a nursing home. Made for television. **1979 74m/C** Henry Fonda, Frances Hyland, Michael McGuire; *D:* Delbert Mann; *M:* Hagood Hardy. **VHS, Beta $59.95** *TLF* 🎬🎬

Home Town Story A politician is convinced big business is behind his election loss. Fair drama. Watch for Monroe in a bit part. **1951 61m/B** Jeffrey Lynn, Donald Crisp, Marjorie Reynolds, Alan Hale Jr., Marilyn Monroe, Barbara Brown, Melinda Plowman; *D:* Arthur Pierson. **VHS $19.95** *NOS, TPV* 🎬🎬

Homebodies Six senior citizens, disgusted when they learn that they will be callously tossed out of their home, become violent murderers in their shocking attempt to solve their problem. An odd little film made in Cincinnati. **1974 (PG) 96m/C** Ruth McDevitt, Linda Marsh, William Hansen, Peter Brocco, Frances Fuller; *D:* Larry Yust. **VHS, Beta $59.98** *SUE* 🎬🎬

Homeboy A small-time club boxer who dreams of becoming middleweight champ is offered his big break, but the opportunity is jeopardized by his dishonest manager's dealings. Never released theatrically. **1988 (R) 118m/C** Mickey Rourke, Christopher Walken, Debra Feuer, Kevin Conway, Antony Alda, Ruben Blades; *D:* Michael Seresin; *M:* Eric Clapton, Michael Kamen. **VHS, Beta** *NO* 🎬🎬

Homeboy A Black boxer owes his career to the mob. When he tries to break free is wife is murdered - and he seeks revenge. **198? 93m/C** Dabney Coleman, Philip Michael Thomas. **VHS** *NO* 🎬 1/2

Homeboys Two East L.A. brothers find themselves on opposite sides of the law in this quickie designed to cash in on gang violence and ghetto dramas. **1992 91m/C** Todd Bridges, David Garrison, Ron Odriozola, Ken Michaels; *D:* Lindsay Norgard. **VHS $89.95** *AIP* 🎬

Homecoming Two German prisoners of war escape from a Siberian lead mine. One reaches home first and has an affair with his comrade's wife. Silent. **1928 74m/B** Dita Parlo, Lars Hanson, Gustav Froehlich; *D:* Joe May. **VHS, Beta $29.95** *GLV* 🎬🎬🎬

Homecoming Average soap opera starring Gable and Turner set amidst the trenches of WW II. Gable plays a selfish doctor who leaves behind his wife and colleague to enlist in the Medical Corps as a major. Turner is the battlefield nurse who forever changes his life. Film is hindered by a story which is far below the talents of the excellent cast. Although voted by the New York Critics as one of the ten worst movies of 1948, the public loved it. Based on the story "The Homecoming of Ulysses" by Sidney Kingsley. **1948 113m/B** Clark Gable, Lana Turner, Anne Baxter, John Hodiak, Ray Collins, Gladys Cooper, Cameron Mitchell, Art Baker, Lurene Tuttle; *D:* Mervyn LeRoy; *W:* Paul Osborn, Jan Lustig. **VHS $19.98** *MGM* 🎬🎬

Homecoming: A Christmas Story Made-for-television heart-tugger that inspired the television series "The Waltons." A depression-era Virginia mountain family struggles to celebrate Christmas although the whereabouts and safety of their father are unknown. Adapted from the autobiographical novel by Earl Hamner, Jr. **1971 98m/C** Richard Thomas, Patricia Neal, Edgar Bergen, Cleavon Little, Ellen Corby; *D:* Fielder Cook. **VHS, Beta $14.98** *FOX* 🎬🎬 1/2

Homer and Eddie A witless road comedy with Goldberg as a dying sociopath and a mentally retarded Belushi. They take off cross-country to make a little trouble, learn a little about life, and create a less than entertaining movie. **1989 (R) 100m/C** Whoopi Goldberg, James Belushi, Karen Black; *D:* Andrei Konchalovsky; *W:* Patrick Cirillo; *M:* Eduard Artemyev. **VHS, Beta $89.95** *HBO* 🎬

Homer Comes Home A homely and diligent inventor finds nothing but failure, but sticks it out in hopes of turning his luck around. Silent comedy starring down-home Ray.

1920 55m/B Charles Ray. **VHS, Beta $16.95** *GPV* 🎬🎬

Homesteaders of Paradise Valley The Hume brothers oppose Red Ryder and a group of settlers building a dam in Paradise Valley. **1947 54m/B** Allan "Rocky" Lane, Robert (Bobby) Blake. **VHS, Beta $19.95** *NOS, VCN, CAB* 🎬 1/2

Hometown Boy Makes Good Smalltown boy Boyd Geary moved to the big city to go to medical school. But what he never told his proud mom was that he dropped out and doesn't have the successful psychiatry practice she thinks he has, instead he's a barely surviving waiter. But when Boyd travels back home to confess to mom, the local mayor makes him an offer to set up his own practice and won't take no for an answer. **1993 (R) 88m/C** Anthony Edwards, Grace Zabriskie, Cynthia Bain; *D:* David Burton Morris; *W:* Allen Rucker; *M:* Barry Goldberg. **VHS $89.95** *IMP, IME* 🎬🎬 1/2

Hometown U.S.A. Set in Los Angeles in the late 50s' this teenage cruising movie is the brainchild of director Baer who is better known as Jethro from that madcap television series "The Beverly Hillbillies." **1979 (R) 97m/C** Brian Kerwin, Gary Springer, David Wilson, Cindy Fisher, Sally Kirkland; *D:* Max Baer Jr. **VHS, Beta $69.98** *LIV, VES* Woof!

Homeward Bound A dying teenager tries to reunite his long-estranged father and grandfather. Made for television. **1980 (G) 96m/C** David Soul, Moosie Drier, Barnard Hughes; *D:* Richard Michaels. **VHS, Beta $59.95** *HMV* 🎬

Homeward Bound: The Incredible Journey Successful remake of the 1963 Disney release "The Incredible Journey." Two dogs and a cat once again try to find their way home after their family relocates, armed with greater depth of character than the original. Hard not to shed a tear for the brave animal trio who develop a trusting bond through assorted misadventures. Based on the novel by Sheila Burnford. Superior family fare. **1993 (G) 85m/C** Robert Hays, Kim Greist, Jean Smart, Benj Thall, Veronica Lauren, Kevin Timothy Chevalia; *D:* Duwayne Dunham; *W:* Linda Woolverton, Carolyn Thompson; *M:* Bruce Broughton; *V:* Don Ameche, Michael J. Fox, Sally Field. **VHS $22.99** *DIS, BTV* 🎬🎬🎬

Homework Young man's after-school lessons with a teacher are definitely not part of the curriculum. Yawning sexploitation. **1982 (R) 90m/C** Joan Collins, Michael Morgan, Betty Thomas, Shell Kepler, Wings Hauser, Lee Purcell; *D:* James Beshears. **VHS, Beta $19.95** *MCA* 🎬

Homewrecker Benson stars as a scientist who invents a computer, with a female voice, as the ultimate domestic worker. Only the computer turns possessive and against Benson's estranged wife. **1992 (PG-13) 88m/C** Robby Benson, Sydney Walsh, Sarah Rose Karr; *D:* Fred Walton; *W:* Eric Harlacher; *V:* Kate Jackson. **VHS, Beta** *PAR* 🎬🎬

Homicidal Impulse When Assistant D.A. Tim Casey has an affair with his boss' ambitious niece he doesn't realize the danger he's in. His lover decides to kill her uncle so boyfriend Tim will get his job. Some women will do anything for love. Also available in an unrated version. **1992 (R) 84m/C** Scott Valentine, Vanessa Angel. **VHS $89.98** *LIV* 🎬 1/2

Homicide Terrific police thriller with as much thought as action; a driven detective faces his submerged Jewish identity while probing an anti-Semitic murder and a secret society. Playwright/filmmaker Mamet creates nail-biting suspense and shattering epiphanies without resorting to Hollywood glitz. Rich (often profane) dialogue includes a classic soliloquy mystically comparing a lawman's badge with a Star of David.
1991 (R) 100m/C Joe Mantegna, William H. Macy, Natalija Nogulich, Ving Rhames, Rebecca Pidgeon; **D:** David Mamet. **VHS, 8mm $19.95** *COL, BTV* 🎞🎞🎞½

Homo Eroticus/Man of the Year Handsome servant finds it difficult to satisfy the desires of Bergamo, Italy's socialite.
1971 93m/C Lando Buzzanca, Rossana Podesta. **VHS, Beta** *NO* 🎞

Honey Attractive writer pays an unusual visit to the home of a distinguished publisher. Brandishing a pistol, she demands that he read aloud from her manuscript. As he reads, a unique fantasy unfolds, a dreamlike erotic tale that may be the writer's own sexual awakening. Or maybe not.
1981 89m/C Clio Goldsmith, Fernando Rey, Catherine Spaak; **D:** Gianfranco Angelucci. **VHS, Beta $69.95** *VES* 🎞½

Honey, I Blew Up the Kid Screwball suburban inventor Moranis reverses his shrinking process and this time manages to enlarge his two-year-old into a 112-foot giant who gets bigger every time he comes in contact with electricity. Yikes! Loaded with great special effects, this is a charming and funny film that's fit for the whole family. Sequel to "Honey I Shrunk the Kids."
1992 (PG) 89m/C Rick Moranis, Marcia Strassman, Robert Oliveri, Daniel Shalikar, Joshua Shalikar, Lloyd Bridges, John Shea, Keri Russell, Gregory Sierra, Julia Sweeney, Kenneth Tobey, Peter Eibling; **D:** Randal Kleiser; **W:** Thom Eberhardt, Garry Goodrow; **M:** Bruce Broughton. **VHS, Beta $19.99** *DIS* 🎞🎞½

Honey, I Shrunk the Kids The popular Disney fantasy about a suburban inventor. His shrinking device accidentally reduces his kids to 1/4 inch tall, and he subsequently throws them out with the garbage. Now they must journey back to the house through the jungle that was once the back lawn. Accompanied by "Tummy Trouble," the first of a projected series of Roger Rabbit Maroon Cartoons. Followed by "Honey, I Blew Up the Kids."
1989 (G) 101m/C Rick Moranis, Matt Frewer, Marcia Strassman, Kristine Sutherland, Thomas Wilson Brown, Jared Rushton, Amy O'Neill, Robert Oliveri; **D:** Joe Johnston, Rob Minkoff; **W:** Ed Naha, Tom Schulman, Stuart Gordon; **M:** James Horner; **V:** Charles Fleischer, Kathleen Turner, Lou Hirsch, April Winchell. **VHS, Beta $19.99** *DIS, MOV, RDG* 🎞🎞½

The Honey Pot A millionaire feigns death to see the reaction of three of his former lovers. Amusing black comedy with fine performances from all. Based on Moliere's "Volpone." **AKA:** It Comes Up Murder; Anyone for Venice?; Mr. Fox of Venice.
1967 131m/C Rex Harrison, Susan Hayward, Cliff Robertson, Capucine, Edie Adams, Dame Maggie Smith, Adolfo Celi; **D:** Joseph L. Mankiewicz; **W:** Joseph L. Mankiewicz; **M:** John Addison. **VHS $14.95** *MGM* 🎞🎞½

Honeybaby A smooth international soldier of fortune and a bright, sexy American interpreter are entangled in Middle-Eastern turbulence when they must rescue a politician kidnapped by terrorists.
1974 (PG) 94m/C Calvin Lockhart, Diana Sands; **D:** Michael A. Schultz. **VHS $19.95** *GEM, MRV, CNG* 🎞🎞

Honeyboy Estrada tries to win fame, fortune, and a ticket out of the barrio as an up-and-coming boxer. Outstanding fight scenes, but little else in this made for television drama of the boxing scene.
1982 100m/C Erik Estrada, Morgan Fairchild, James McEachin, Robert Costanzo, Yvonne Wilder; **D:** John Berry. **VHS, Beta** *LIV* 🎞½

Honeymoon A young French woman visiting New York learns she will be deported when her boyfriend is arrested for drug-smuggling. To stay, she is set up in a marriage of convenience and told her new husband will never see or bother her. But hubby has other plans!
1987 96m/C John Shea, Nathalie Baye, Richard Berry, Peter Donat; **D:** Patrick Jamain; **W:** Phillip Setbon. **VHS, Beta $19.98** *LHV, WAR* 🎞🎞

Honeymoon Academy Newly married man has lots to learn in this comic outing. His new wife never told him about her unusual line of business—as an undercover agent! **AKA:** For Better or For Worse.
1990 (PG-13) 94m/C Robert Hays, Kim Cattrall, Leigh Taylor-Young; **D:** Gene Quintano; **W:** Gene Quintano; **M:** Robert Folk. **VHS $89.99** *HBO, IME* 🎞🎞

Honeymoon Horror Stranded on an island, three honeymooning couples soon realize their romantic retreat is a nightmare. A crazy man with an axe is tracking them down. Minimally effective.
197? 90m/C Cheryl Black, William F. Pecchi, Bob Wagner. **VHS, Beta** *NO* 🎞

Honeymoon in Vegas Romantic comedy turns frantic after Cage loses his fiancee to Caan in a high stakes Vegas poker game. Cage displays lots of talent for manic comedy as the distraught young groom-to-be who encounters numerous obstacles on his way to the altar. Lightweight and funny, featuring a bevy of Elvis impersonators in every size, shape, and color and new versions of favorite Elvis tunes. Look for former Las Vegas U basketball coach Jerry Tarkanian as one of Caan's gambling buddies.
1992 (PG-13) 95m/C James Caan, Nicolas Cage, Sarah Jessica Parker, Noriyuki "Pat" Morita, John Capodice, Robert Costanzo, Anne Bancroft, Peter Boyle, Seymour Cassel, Tony Shalhoub; **D:** Andrew Bergman; **W:** Andrew Bergman; **M:** David Newman. **VHS $19.95** *COL, NLC, IME* 🎞🎞½

Honeymoon Killers A grim, creepy filmization of a true multiple-murder case wherein an overweight woman and slimy gigolo living on Long Island seduce and murder one lonely woman after another. Independently made and frankly despairing. **AKA:** The Lonely Hearts Killers.
1970 (R) 103m/C Tony LoBianco, Shirley Stoler, Mary Jane Higby, Dortha Duckworth, Doris Roberts, Marilyn Chris, Kip McArdle, Mary Breen, Barbara Cason, Ann Harris, Guy Sorel; **D:** Leonard Kastle. **VHS, Beta $69.98** *LIV, VES* 🎞🎞🎞

The Honeymoon Machine A lightweight comedy about two American sailors and a computer scam. McQueen and Mullaney hook up with computer expert Hutton to use their ship's computer to beat the gambling odds at an Italian casino. Their commander misinterprets the signals and thinks the ship is being attacked. Fast paced and the computer angle was new territory in '61.
1961 87m/C Steve McQueen, Jack Mullaney, Jim Hutton, Dean Jagger, Paula Prentiss, Brigid Bazlen, Jack Weston; **D:** Richard Thorpe. **VHS $19.98** *MGM, MOV* 🎞🎞½

The Honeymooners "Classic 39": TV or Not TV/ Honeymooners Highlights Captain Video and his video rangers are a Kramden

household name after Ralph and Ed pool their resources to buy a television. Also includes clips from each of the remaining 38 episodes in "The Honeymooners" series. Video cover illustration by C.F. Payne. This 20 volumes series contains two episodes per tape.
1955 60m/C VHS $5.98 *FXV* 🎞🎞½

Honeymooners Hidden Episodes, Vol. 1 Three recently-retrieved episodes of the Honeymooners sketches, which were initially aired live as part of the "Jackie Gleason Show." In "Letter to the Boss," Jackie sends some nasty correspondence to his employer when he mistakenly believes that he has been canned. In "Suspense," Ralph fears that Alice is planning his murder when he eavesdrops on her acting practice. In "Dinner Guest," Ralph's plans to suck up to his supervisor meet with hilarious disaster. This "Honeymooners" series contains 28 volumes, which are available separately for purchase. **AKA:** The Honeymooners: The Lost Episodes.
1953 53m/B Jackie Gleason, Audrey Meadows, Art Carney, Joyce Randolph. **VHS, Beta $29.95** *MPI, FOX, MOV* 🎞🎞

Honeysuckle Rose A road-touring country-Western singer whose life is a series of one night stands, falls in love with an adoring young guitar player who has just joined his band. This nearly costs him his marriage when his wife, who while waiting patiently for him at home, decides she's had enough. Easygoing performance by Nelson, essentially playing himself. **AKA:** On the Road Again.
1980 (PG) 120m/C Willie Nelson, Dyan Cannon, Amy Irving, Slim Pickens, Joey Floyd, Charles Levin, Priscilla Pointer; **D:** Jerry Schatzberg; **W:** Bill Wittliff, John Binder, Carol Sobieski; **M:** Richard Baskin. **VHS, Beta $14.95** *WAR, MVD* 🎞🎞½

Hong Kong Nights Two agents attempt to break up a Chinese smuggling ring run by an unscrupulous madman. Good, action-packed low-budget film.
1935 59m/B Tom Keene, Wera Engels, Warren Hymer, Tetsu Komai, Cornelius Keefe; **D:** E. Mason Hopper. **VHS, Beta $16.95** *SNC* 🎞🎞½

Honky An innocent friendship between a black woman and a white man develops into a passionate romance that has the whole town talking.
1971 (R) 92m/C Brenda Sykes, John Nielson, Maria Donzinger; **D:** William A. Graham; **M:** Quincy Jones. **VHS, Beta $49.95** *UNI* 🎞½

Honky Tonk A western soap opera in which ne'er do well Clark marries Lana and tries to live a respectable life. In this, the first of several MGM teamings between Gable and Turner, the chemistry between the two is evident. So much so in fact that Gable's then wife Carole Lombard let studio head Louis B. Mayer know that she was not at all thrilled. The public was pleased however, and made the film a hit.
1941 106m/B Clark Gable, Lana Turner, Frank Morgan, Claire Trevor, Marjorie Main, Albert Dekker, Chill Wills, Henry O'Neill, John Maxwell, Morgan Wallace, Betty Blythe, Francis X. Bushman, Veda Ann Borg; **D:** Jack Conway. **VHS, Beta $19.98** *MGM, CCB* 🎞🎞🎞

Honky Tonk Freeway An odd assortment of people become involved in a small town Mayor's scheme to turn a dying hamlet into a tourist wonderland. You can find better things to do with your evening than watch this accident.

1981 (PG) 107m/C Teri Garr, Howard Hesseman, Beau Bridges, Hume Cronyn, William Devane, Beverly D'Angelo, Geraldine Page; **D:** John Schlesinger; **M:** Stephen Dorff. **VHS, Beta** NO ♂

Honky Tonk Girl Hilarious exploitation film about a hitch-hiking prostitution ring. Also known as "Highway Hell."
1937 ?m/C Mary Chauning. **VHS $16.95** SNC ♂

Honkytonk Man Unsuccessful change-of-pace Eastwood vehicle set during the Depression. Aging alcoholic country singer tries one last time to make it to Nashville, hoping to perform at the Grand Ole Opry. This time he takes his nephew (played by Eastwoood's real-life son) with him.
1982 (PG) 123m/C Clint Eastwood, Kyle Eastwood, John McIntire, Alexa Kenin, Verna Bloom; **D:** Clint Eastwood; **M:** Stephen Dorff. **VHS, Beta $19.98** WAR ♂♂

Honkytonk Nights A honky-tonkin' romp through an evening in a country/western bar, featuring legendary topless dancer Carol Doda, Georgina ("Devil in Mrs. Jones") Spelvin, and the music of The Hot Licks (minus front man Dan Hicks).
197? (R) 90m/C Carol Doda, Georgina Spelvin, Ramblin' Jack Elliot. **VHS, Beta $59.95** TPV ♂

Honolulu A screwball comedy with Powell providing the musical numbers. Young takes on the dual role of a Hollywood star who meets his exact double, a Hawaii plantation owner. They decide to switch identities to give their lives a little oomph. The star sails to Hawaii, falling for fellow passenger Powell, only to discover he's expected to get married upon his arrival in Honolulu. Anderson and Burns and Allen provide the comic relief. ♫The Leader Doesn't Like Music; This Night Was Made For Dreaming; Honolulu; Hymn To The Sun.
1939 83m/B Robert Young, Eleanor Powell, George Burns, Gracie Allen, Rita Johnson, Eddie Anderson, Clarence Kolb; **D:** Edward Buzzell; **W:** Frank Partos, Herbert Fields; **M:** Franz Waxman. **VHS $19.98** MGM ♂♂½

Honor Among Thieves Two former mercenaries reteam for a robbery that doesn't come off as planned. Not as fast paced as others in Bronson canon. **AKA:** Farewell, Friend.
1968 (R) 115m/C Charles Bronson, Alain Delon, Brigitte Fossey, Olga Georges-Picot, Bernard Fresson; **D:** Jean Herman. **VHS, Beta $9.99** CCB, MPI, MON ♂½

Honor and Glory Tracy Pride, an FBI agent and martial arts expert, teams up with an Interpol agent, who doubles as a TV anchorwoman, to stop an international banker from getting his greedy hands on the key to a nuclear arsenal. These fighting gals are up against a team of assassins but they can more than handle themselves.
1992 (R) 90m/C Cynthia Rothrock, Donna Jason, Chuck Jeffreys, Gerald Klein, Robin Shou, Richard Yuen; **D:** Godfrey Hall; **W:** Herb Borkland. **VHS $89.95** IMP ♂

Honor of the Range The good sheriff's lady is whisked away by her evil twin brother and the sheriff must go undercover to get her back. Odd plot twists for a seemingly normal western.
1934 60m/B Ken Maynard, Cecilia Parker, Fred Kohler Jr.; **D:** Ken Maynard. **VHS $19.95** NOS, DVT, HEG ♂♂

Honor Thy Father The everyday life of a real-life Mafia family as seen through the eyes of Bill Bonanno, the son of mob chieftain Joe Bonanno. Adapted from the book by Gay Talese. Made for television.

1973 97m/C Raf Vallone, Richard Castellano, Brenda Vaccaro, Joseph Bologna; **D:** Paul Wendkos; **M:** George Duning. **Beta $14.95** PSM ♂♂

Honor Thy Father and Mother: The True Story of the Menendez Brothers First Amy Fisher won the true-sleaze-on-TV award and now its the turn of Lyle and Erik Menendez. Accused of the gruesome 1989 shotgun murders of their wealthy parents, the trial provided numerous sordid details, including alledged sexual abuse of the brothers by both parents. (Both Menendez trials ended in hung juries and will be retried). Composite characters and compressed time sequences play fast and loose with the facts of the case. Based on public records and on the book "Blood Brothers," by reporters John Johnson and Ronald L. Soble. Made for television.
1994 90m/C Billy Warlock, David Beron, Jill Clayburgh, James Farentino, Susan Blakely, Erin Gray, Elaine Joyce, John Beck, John David Conti, Stanley Kamel; **D:** Paul Schneider; **W:** Michael J. Murray. **VHS $79.95** AVE ♂♂½

Hooch Comedy about three members of the New York Mafia who get some unexpected southern hospitality when they try to muscle in on a southern family's moonshine operation.
1976 (PG) 96m/C Gil Gerard, Erika Fox, Melody Rogers, Danny Aiello, Mike Allen, Ray Serra; **D:** Edward Mann. **VHS, Beta $49.95** PSM ♂½

The Hooded Terror A merciless group of murderers take on a G-man.
1938 70m/B Tod Slaughter, Greta Gynt. **VHS $14.99** NOS, HEG ♂½

The Hoodlum A criminal does his best to rehabilitate and, with a little help from his brother, is able to hold a steady job. However the crime bug dies hard and when he spots an armored truck, he just can't resist the temptation. Tierney's real brother, Edward, plays his screen brother.
1951 61m/B Lawrence Tierney, Allene Roberts, Marjorie Riordan, Liza Golm, Edward Tierney; **D:** Max Nosseck. **VHS, Beta $16.95** SNC ♂♂

Hoodlum Empire A senator enlists the aid of a former gangster, now a war hero, in his battle against the syndicate. Loosely based on the Kefauver investigations of 1950-51.
1952 98m/B Brian Donlevy, Claire Trevor, Forrest Tucker, Vera Ralston, Luther Adler, John Russell, Gene Lockhart, Grant Withers, Taylor Holmes, Roy Barcroft, Richard Jaeckel; **D:** Joseph Kane. **VHS $19.98** REP ♂♂

The Hoodlum Priest Biography of the Rev. Charles Dismas Clark (Murray), a Jesuit priest who dedicated his life to working with juvenile delinquents and ex-cons in St. Louis. Dullea made his screen debut as Billy Lee Jackson, a thief who finds the straight and narrow is a hard road with more detours than he can handle. Fine performances with Murray co-scripting under the pseudonym Don Deer.
1961 101m/B Don Murray, Keir Dullea, Larry Gates, Logan Ramsey, Cindi Wood; **D:** Irvin Kershner; **W:** Don Murray, Joseph Landon. **VHS, Beta $19.98** MGM, FCT ♂♂♂

Hoodoo Ann The story of Hoodoo Ann, from her days in the orphanage to her happy marriage. Silent.
1916 27m/B Mae Marsh, Robert Harron. **VHS, Beta $29.98** CCB ♂♂

Hook Although he said he was never gonna to do it, Peter Pan has grown up. Uptight Peter Banning places work before family and has forgotten all about Neverland and the evil Captain Hook, until Hook kidnaps the Ban-

ning kids and takes them to Neverland. With the help of Tinkerbell, her magic pixie dust, and happy thoughts, Peter rescues his kids and rediscovers his youth while visiting with the Lost Boys. The sets and special effects are spectacular; the direction less so. Big-budget fantasy lacks the charm it needs to really fly. Still, kids seem to love it. You'll have to look hard to spot pirates Crosby and Close. Futurizes the J.M. Barrie classic.
1991 (PG) 142m/C Dustin Hoffman, Robin Williams, Julia Roberts, Bob Hoskins, Dame Maggie Smith, Charlie Korsmo, Caroline Goodall, Amber Scott, Phil Collins, Arthur Malet, Dante Basco; **Cameos:** Glenn Close, David Crosby; **D:** Steven Spielberg; **W:** Nick Castle; **M:** John Williams. **VHS, Beta, 8mm $19.95** COL ♂♂

Hook, Line and Sinker A couple of insurance investigators try to help a young woman restore a hotel, and they find romance and run-ins with crooks. Directed by Cline, who later directed W.C. Fields in "The Bank Dick," "My Little Chickadee," and "Never Give a Sucker an Even Break."
1930 75m/B Bert Wheeler, Robert Woolsey, Dorothy Lee, Jobyna Howland, Ralf Harolde, Natalie Moorhead, George F. Marion Sr., Hugh Herbert; **D:** Eddie Cline. **VHS $19.98** NOS, TTC, FCT ♂♂

The Hooked Generation A group of drug pushers kidnap defenseless victims, rape innocent girls, and even murder their own Cuban drug contacts (and all without the aid of a cohesive plot). Many gory events precede their untimely deaths; few will be entertained.
1969 (R) 92m/C Jeremy Slate, Steve Alaimo. **VHS** NO ♂

Hooper Lightweight behind-the-scenes satire about the world of movie stuntmen. Reynolds is a top stuntman who becomes involved in a rivalry with an up-and-coming young man out to surpass him. Dated good-ole-boy shenanigans.
1978 (PG) 94m/C Burt Reynolds, Jan-Michael Vincent, Robert Klein, Sally Field, Brian Keith, John Marley, James West; **D:** Hal Needham. **VHS, Beta $59.95** WAR ♂♂½

Hoosiers In Indiana, where basketball is the sport of the gods, a small town high school basketball team gets a new, but surprisingly experienced coach. He makes the team, and each person in it, better than they thought possible. Classic plot rings true because of Hackman's complex and sensitive performance coupled with Hopper's touching portrait of an alcoholic basketball fanatic.
1986 (PG) 115m/C Gene Hackman, Barbara Hershey, Dennis Hopper, David Neidorf, Sheb Wooley, Fern Parsons, Brad Boyle, Steve Hollar, Brad Long; **D:** David Anspaugh; **W:** Angelo Pizzo; **M:** Jerry Goldsmith. **VHS, Beta $14.98** LIV ♂♂♂

Hootch Country Boys A film packed with moonshine, sheriffs, busty country girls, and chases. **AKA:** Redneck County; The Great Lester Boggs.
1975 (PG) 90m/C Alex Karras, Scott MacKenzie, Dean Jagger, Willie Jones, Bob Ridgely, Susan Denbo, Bob Ginnaven, David Haney; **D:** Harry Z. Thomason. **VHS, Beta $19.95** ACA, VTR ♂

Hopalong Cassidy In this first of a long series of "Hopalong Cassidy" films, Hoppy and his pals intervene in a brewing range war. A gang of rustlers is helped by a two-timing foreman who's playing both sides off each other. After a career in silent films, Boyd was pretty much washed up before taking on the role of Cassidy. He was originally asked to play the villain and de-

clined, but agreed to be the good guy if the character was cleaned up. "Gabby" Hayes' stock character was killed off in this episode, but was brought back for later installments. *AKA:* Hopalong Cassidy Enters.
1935 60m/B William Boyd, James Ellison, Paula Stone, Robert Warwick, Charles Middleton, Frank McGlynn, Kenneth Thomson, George "Gabby" Hayes, James Mason, Franklin Farnum; *D:* Howard Bretherton. **VHS $19.95** *NOS, MRV* ♂♂♂

Hopalong Cassidy: Borrowed Trouble Hoppy must save a righteous teacher from the clutches of kidnappers who plan to place a saloon right next to the school.
1948 61m/B William Boyd, Andy Clyde, Rand Brooks, Elaine Riley, John Kellogg, Helen Chapman; *D:* George Archainbaud. **VHS** *NO* ♂ 1/2

Hopalong Cassidy: Dangerous Venture "Dangerous Venture" was one of Hoppy's last ventures, produced the final year of the series' 13-year tenure. Hoppy and the gang hunt for Aztec ruins in the great Southwest, and have to deal with renegade Indians and a band of treacherous looters along the way.
1948 55m/B William Boyd, Andy Clyde, Rand Brooks. **VHS, Beta** *NO* ♂♂

Hopalong Cassidy: False Paradise Another late Hopalong has the noir-clad cowboy rushing to the aid of a girl and her dad when control of their ranch is threatened by swindlers with false mining claims.
1948 59m/B William Boyd, Andy Clyde, Rand Brooks; *D:* George Archainbaud. **VHS, Beta** *NO* ♂♂

Hopalong Cassidy: Hoppy's Holiday Boyd—the only celluloid incarnation of Clarence Mulford's pulp hero—plays the Hopster yet again. This time, the non-drinking, non-smoking (what does he do for kicks?) hero and a passel of Bar-20 cowboys visit Mesa City for some well-earned R and R, but find themselves caught in a web of corruption.
1947 60m/B William Boyd, Andy Clyde, Rand Brooks, Jeff Corey; *D:* George Archainbaud. **VHS, Beta** *NO* ♂♂

Hopalong Cassidy: Renegade Trail Hoppy comes to the aid of both a small town sheriff and a widow.
1939 61m/B William Boyd, George "Gabby" Hayes, Russell Hayden, Charlotte Wynters, Russell Hopton, Sonny Bupp, Jack Rockwell, Roy Barcroft, John Merton, Robert F. (Bob) Kortman; *D:* Lesley Selander. **VHS, Beta** *HEG* ♂♂

Hopalong Cassidy: Riders of the Deadline Hoppy turns into a baddie in this episode in order to infiltrate a treacherous gang and apprehend their leader.
1943 70m/B William Boyd, Andy Clyde, Jimmy Rogers, Robert Mitchum; *D:* Lesley Selander. **VHS, Beta** *NO* ♂♂

Hopalong Cassidy: Silent Conflict Lucky is tricked and hypnotized by a traveling medicine man who commands him to rob and kill Hoppy.
1948 61m/B William Boyd, Andy Clyde, Rand Brooks; *D:* George Archainbaud. **VHS, Beta** *NO* ♂♂

Hopalong Cassidy: Sinister Journey Mysterious accidents are plaguing a railroad where an old friend of Hoppy's works, so Hoppy, California, and Lucky take railroad jobs to find out what gives.
1948 58m/B William Boyd, Andy Clyde, Rand Brooks; *D:* George Archainbaud. **VHS, Beta** *NO* ♂♂

Hopalong Cassidy: The Dead Don't Dream Hoppy's sidekick Lucky decides to get married, but happily-ever-afterdom is threatened when the father of Mrs. Lucky-to-be is murdered. When Hoppy sets out to find the killer, he finds himself suspected of the dastardly deed.
1948 55m/B William Boyd, Andy Clyde, Rand Brooks, John Parrish; *D:* George Archainbaud. **VHS, Beta** *NO* ♂♂

Hopalong Cassidy: The Devil's Playground Strange things are afoot in a peaceful valley adjacent to a desolate, forbidding wasteland. When Hoppy and a young woman set out across the wasteland to make a gold delivery, they encounter a band of desperados and begin to unravel the secrets of a dishonest political ring.
1946 65m/B William Boyd, Andy Clyde, Rand Brooks, Elaine Riley; *D:* George Archainbaud. **VHS, Beta** *NO* ♂♂

Hopalong Cassidy: The Marauders After seeking shelter in an abandoned church one rainy night, Hoppy and the boys must defend the kirk when it is threatened by a marauder and his gang.
1947 64m/B William Boyd, Andy Clyde, Rand Brooks; *D:* George Archainbaud. **VHS, Beta** *NO* ♂♂

Hopalong Cassidy: Unexpected Guest When a small fortune is left to a California family, the head count starts to dwindle, and Hoppy aims to find out why.
1947 59m/B William Boyd, Andy Clyde, Rand Brooks, Una O'Connor; *D:* George Archainbaud. **VHS, Beta** *NO* ♂♂ 1/2

Hope and Glory Boorman turns his memories of WWII London into a complex and sensitive film. Father volunteers, and mother must deal with the awakening sexuality of her teen-age daughter, keep her son in line, balance the ration books, and try to make it to the bomb shelter in the middle of the night. Seen through the boy's eyes, war creates a playground of shrapnel to collect and wild imaginings come true. Nice companion film to "Empire of the Sun" and "Au Revoir Les Enfants," two more 1987 releases that explore WWII from the recollections of young boys.
1987 (PG-13) 97m/C Sebastian Rice Edwards, Geraldine Muir, Sarah Miles, Sammi Davis-Voss, David Hayman, Derrick O'Connor, Susan Wooldridge, Jean-Marc Barr, Ian Bannen, Jill Baker, Charley Boorman, Annie Leon, Katrine Boorman, Gerald James; *D:* John Boorman. Academy Awards '87 Nominations: Best Art Direction/Set Decoration, Best Cinematography, Best Director (Boorman), Best Original Screenplay, Best Picture; British Academy Awards '87: Best Film, Best Supporting Actress (Wooldridge); Los Angeles Film Critics Association Awards '87: Best Director (Boorman), Best Film; National Board of Review Awards '87: 10 Best Films of the Year. **VHS, Beta, 8mm $14.98** *SUE, FCT, HMV* ♂♂♂ 1/2

Hoppity Goes to Town Full-length animated feature from the Max Fleischer studios tells the story of the inhabitants of Bugville, who live in a weed patch in New York City. *AKA:* Mr. Bug Goes to Town.
1941 77m/C *D:* Dave Fleischer; *M:* Frank Loesser, Hoagy Carmichael. **VHS $14.98** *REP, MRV, FCT* ♂♂♂ 1/2

Hoppy Serves a Writ In this last of the series to be based on the writings of the original author, Texas sheriff Cassidy tries to bring a gang of outlaws to justice. Look for a young Robert Mitchum as one of the villains.

1943 67m/B William Boyd, Andy Clyde, Jay Kirby, Victor Jory, George Reeves, Hal Taliaferro, Robert Mitchum, Byron Foulger, Earle Hodgins, Roy Barcroft; *D:* George Archainbaud. **VHS $19.95** *NOS, MRV* ♂♂

Hopscotch A C.I.A. agent drops out when his overly zealous chief demotes him to a desk job. When he writes a book designed to expose the dirty deeds of the CIA, he leads his boss and KGB pal on a merry chase. Amiable comedy well-suited for Matthau's rumpled talents.
1980 (R) 107m/C Walter Matthau, Glenda Jackson, Ned Beatty, Sam Waterston, Herbert Lom; *D:* Ronald Neame. **VHS, Beta $9.95** *COL, SUE* ♂♂♂

Horizons West Two brothers go their separate ways after the Civil War. One leads a peaceful life as a rancher but the other, corrupted by the war, engages in a violent campaign to build his own empire. Ryan's outstanding performance eclipses that of the young Hudson.
1952 81m/C Robert Ryan, Julie Adams, Rock Hudson, Raymond Burr, James Arness, John McIntire, Dennis Weaver, Francis Bavier; *D:* Budd Boetticher; *M:* Henry Mancini. **VHS** *MCA* ♂♂ 1/2

The Horizontal Lieutenant Hutton and Prentiss team up again in this moderately funny romantic-comedy about an officer's escapades during WWII. Based on the novel "The Bottletop Affair" by Gordon Cotler.
1962 90m/C Jim Hutton, Paula Prentiss, Jack Carter, Jim Backus, Charles McGraw, Miyoshi Umeki; *D:* Richard Thorpe; *W:* George Wells. **VHS $19.98** *MGM* ♂♂

The Horn Blows at Midnight A band trumpeter falls asleep and dreams he's a bumbling archangel, on Earth to blow the note bringing the end of the world. But a pretty girl distracts him, and...A wild, high-gloss, well-cast fantasy farce, uniquely subversive in its lighthearted approach to biblical Doomsday. Benny made the film notorious by acting ashamed of it in his later broadcast routines.
1945 78m/B Jack Benny, Alexis Smith, Dolores Moran, Allyn Joslyn, Reginald Gardiner, Guy Kibbee, John Alexander, Margaret Dumont; *D:* Raoul Walsh. **VHS $19.98** *MGM, FCT* ♂♂♂

Hornet's Nest Captain Turner (Hudson) is the lone survivor of an Army commando unit which parachuted into the Italian countryside in an effort to blow up a dam being held by the Nazis. He's rescued by a group of boys, the survivors of a German massacre of their nearby town. Turner wants the boys to help him blow up the dam—and they want his help in getting revenge on the Nazis who have occupied their homes.
1970 110m/C Rock Hudson, Sylva Koscina, Sergio Fantoni, Jacques Sernas, Giacomo "Jack" Rossi-Stuart, Andrea Bosic, Gerard Herter, Tom Felleghi; *D:* Phil Karlson; *W:* S.S. Schweitzer. **VHS $19.98** *MGM* ♂♂ 1/2

The Horrible Dr. Hichcock A sicko doctor, who accidentally killed his first wife while engaged in sexual antics, remarries to bring the first missus back from the dead using his new wife's blood. Genuinely creepy. Sequeled by "The Ghost." *AKA:* L'Orribile Segreto Del Dr. Hichcock.
1962 76m/C Robert Flemyng, Barbara Steele; *D:* Riccardo (Robert Hampton) Freda. **VHS $69.95** *SNC* ♂♂ 1/2

The Horror Chamber of Dr. Faustus A wickedly intelligent, inventive piece of Grand Guignol about a mad doctor who kills young girls so he may graft their skin onto the face of his accidentally mutilated daughter. In French with English subtitles.

AKA: Eyes Without a Face; Les Yeux Sans Visage; Occhi Senza Volto.
1959 84m/B Alida Valli, Pierre Brasseur, Edith Scob, Francois Guerin; *D:* Georges Franju; *M:* Maurice Jarre. **VHS, Beta $29.95** *SNC, TPV* 🎵🎵🎵½

Horror Express A creature from prehistoric times, that was removed from its tomb, is transported on the Trans-Siberian railroad. Passengers suddenly discover strange things happening—such as having their souls sucked out of them. *AKA:* Panic on the Trans-Siberian Express; Panico en el Transiberiano.
1972 (R) 88m/C Christopher Lee, Peter Cushing, Telly Savalas; *D:* Gene Martin. **VHS, Beta $59.95** *SNC, MRV, PSM* 🎵🎵½

Horror Hospital Patients are turned into zombies by a mad doctor in this hospital where no anesthesia is used. Those who try to escape are taken care of by the doctor's guards. *AKA:* Computer Killers.
1973 (R) 91m/C Michael Gough, Robin Askwith, Vanessa Shaw, Ellen Pollock, Skip Martin, Dennis Price; *D:* Antony Balch. **VHS, Beta $29.95** *GRG, VCI, MPI* 🎵🎵

Horror Hotel A young witchcraft student visits a small Massachusetts town which has historic ties to witch burnings and discovers a new, and deadly, coven is now active. Well done and atmospheric. *AKA:* The City of the Dead.
1960 76m/B Christopher Lee, Patricia Jessel, Betta St. John, Dennis Lotis, Venetia Stevenson, Valentine Dyall; *D:* John Llewellyn Moxey. **VHS $19.95** *NOS, MRV, SNC* 🎵🎵½

Horror House on Highway 5 Someone in a Nixon mask kills people in this extremely cheap dud.
1986 90m/C *D:* Richard Casey; *W:* Richard Casey. **VHS, Beta** *NO Woof!*

The Horror of Dracula The first Hammer Dracula film, in which the infamous vampire is given a new, elegant and ruthless persona, as he battles Prof. Van Helsing after coming to England. Possibly the finest, most inspired version of Bram Stoker's macabre chestnut, and one that single-handedly revived the horror genre. *AKA:* Dracula.
1958 82m/C Peter Cushing, Christopher Lee, Michael Gough, Melissa Stribling, Carol Marsh, John Van Eyssen, Valerie Gaunt; *D:* Terence Fisher; *W:* Jimmy Sangster. **VHS, Beta $14.95** *WAR, FCT, MLB* 🎵🎵🎵½

The Horror of Frankenstein Spoof of the standard Frankenstein story features philandering ex-med student Baron Frankenstein, whose interest in a weird and esoteric branch of science provides a shocking and up-to-date rendition of the age-old plot. Preceded by "Frankenstein Must Be Destroyed" and followed by "Frankenstein and the Monster from Hell."
1970 93m/C Ralph Bates, Kate O'Mara, Dennis Price, David Prowse; *D:* Jimmy Sangster; *W:* Jimmy Sangster. **VHS, Beta $59.99** *MLB* 🎵🎵

The Horror of It All A multi-faceted look at popular horror stars, including Karloff, Chaney, Lugosi, Price, and others, plus an examination of the dark side of the imaginative minds that produce horror. Also includes a behind-the-scenes peek at the creation of great horror scenes.
1991 58m/C Boris Karloff, Lon Chaney Sr., Bela Lugosi, John Barrymore, Lionel Atwill, John Carradine, Vincent Price. **VHS $24.98** *MPI, FCT* 🎵🎵

Horror of Party Beach Considered to be one of the all-time worst films. Features a mob of radioactive seaweed creatures who eat a slew of nubile, surf-minded teenagers.

🎵Zombie Stomp. *AKA:* Invasion of the Zombies.
1964 71m/C John Scott, Alice Lyon, Allen Laurel; *D:* Del Tenney. **VHS, Beta $39.95** *PSM Woof!*

Horror of the Blood Monsters John Carradine made a career out of being in bad movies, and this one competes as one of the worst. This is an editor's nightmare, made up of black & white film spliced together and colorized. Vampires from outer space threaten to suck all the blood from the people of Earth. *AKA:* Vampire Men of the Lost Planet; Horror Creatures of the Prehistoric Planet; Creatures of the Prehistoric Planet; Creatures of the Red Planet; Flesh Creatures of the Red Planet; The Flesh Creatures; Space Mission of the Lost Planet.
1970 (PG) 85m/C John Carradine, Robert Dix, Vicki Volante, Jennifer Bishop; *D:* Al Adamson, George Joseph. **VHS, Beta** *REP Woof!*

Horror of the Zombies Bikinied models are pursued by hooded zombies on board a pleasure yacht...the horror. Effete final installment in the "blind dead" trilogy; see also "Tombs of the Blind Dead" and "Return of the Evil Dead." *AKA:* El Buque Maldito.
1974 (R) 90m/C Maria Perschy, Jack Taylor; *D:* Armando de Ossorio; *W:* Armando de Ossorio. **VHS** *NO* 🎵

Horror Planet Alien creature needs a chance to breed before moving on to spread its horror. When a group of explorers disturbs it, the years of waiting are over, and the unlucky mother-to-be will never be the same. Graphic and sensationalistic, capitalizing on the popularity of "Aliens." *AKA:* Inseminoid.
1980 (R) 93m/C Robin Clarke, Jennifer Ashley, Stephanie Beacham, Judy Geeson, Stephen Grives, Victoria Tennant; *D:* Norman J. Warren. **VHS, Beta $9.98** *SUE Woof!*

Horror Rises from the Tomb A 15th century knight and his assistant are beheaded for practicing witchcraft. Five hundred years later, they return to possess a group of vacationers and generally cause havoc.
1972 89m/C Paul Naschy, Vic Winner, Emma Cohen, Helga Line; *D:* Carlos Aured. **VHS, Beta $19.95** *FCT, NLC, LOO* 🎵

The Horror Show Serial killer fries in electric chair, an event that really steams him. So he goes after the cop who brought him in. Standard dead guy who won't die and wants revenge flick. *AKA:* House 3.
1989 (R) 95m/C Brion James, Lance Henriksen, Rita Taggart, Dedee Pfeiffer, Aron Eisenberg, Matt Clark; *D:* James Isaac; *W:* Alan Smithee, Leslie Boehm. **VHS, Beta $14.95** *MGM* 🎵

Horrors of Burke & Hare A gory tale about the exploits of a bunch of 19th-century grave robbers.
1971 94m/C Derren Nesbitt, Harry Andrews, Yootha Joyce; *D:* Vernon Sewell. **VHS, Beta $19.95** *NWV* 🎵

Horrors of Spider Island D'Arcy is a Hollywood talent scout who sniffs a goldmine in a team of young female dancers whom he schedules to perform for him in Singapore. Their transport plane crashes in the Pacific Ocean and he and the girls are forced to take refuge on an uncharted isle. Upon landing there they discover it is infested with giant crab-sized spiders. Lots of potential for both shock and arousal, which was probably why it was originally released in both "horror" and "girlie" versions. D'Arcy later admitted to taking over for director Bottger and adding all the horror sequences himself. Dubbed from the German. *AKA:* It's Hot in Paradise;

Ein Toter Hing im Netz; A Corpse Hangs in the Web.
1959 77m/C Alexander D'Arcy, Ursula Lederstger; *D:* Fritz Bottger. **VHS $23.00** *SMW, TPV* 🎵

Horrors of the Red Planet Cheapo epic sees astronauts crash on Mars, meet its Wizard, and stumble into a few Oz-like creatures. Technically advised by Forrest J. Ackerman. *AKA:* The Wizard of Mars.
1964 81m/C John Carradine, Roger Gentry, Vic McGee; *D:* David L. Hewitt. **VHS, Beta $19.99** *GHV, MRV, REP* 🎵

The Horse A moving, mature Turkish film about a father and son trying to overcome socioeconomic obstacles and their own frailties in order to make enough money to send the boy to school. In Turkish with English subtitles. *AKA:* Horse, My Horse.
1982 116m/C *D:* Ali Ozgenturk. **VHS, Beta $69.95** *KIV, ING* 🎵🎵🎵½

Horse Feathers Huxley College has to beef up its football team to win the championship game, and the corrupt new college president knows just how to do it. Features some of the brothers' classic routines, and the songs "Whatever It Is, I'm Against It" and "Everyone Says I Love You."
1932 67m/B Groucho Marx, Chico Marx, Harpo Marx, Zeppo Marx, Thelma Todd, David Landau, Nat Pendleton; *D:* Norman Z. McLeod. **VHS, Beta $14.98** *MCA* 🎵🎵🎵½

The Horse in the Gray Flannel Suit Disney comedy portrays an advertising executive who links his daughter's devotion to horses with a client's new ad campaign.
1968 (G) 114m/C Dean Jones, Ellen Janov, Fred Clark, Diane Baker, Lloyd Bochner, Kurt Russell; *D:* Norman Tokar. **VHS, Beta** *DIS, OM* 🎵🎵½

The Horse of Pride Chabrol takes a telling look at the everyday life of the peasants of Breton—both their pleasures and their sorrows. In French with English subtitles. French script booklet available. *AKA:* Le Cheval D'Orgeuil.
1980 118m/C Jacques Dufilho, Francois Cluzet; *D:* Claude Chabrol. **VHS, Beta $59.95** *INT, APD, AUD* 🎵🎵½

The Horse Soldiers An 1863 Union cavalry officer is sent 300 miles into Confederate territory to destroy a railroad junction and is accompanied by a fellow officer who is also a pacifist doctor. Based on a true Civil War incident.
1959 114m/C John Wayne, William Holden, Hoot Gibson, Anna Lee, Russell Simpson, Strother Martin; *D:* John Ford. **VHS, Beta $19.98** *MGM, FOX* 🎵🎵½

The Horse Thief Noted as the first movie from the People's Republic of China to be released on video, this epic tells the tale of Norbu, a man who, exiled from his people for horse thievery, is forced to wander the Tibetan countryside with his family in search of work. His son dies while he is in exile, and he, a devout Buddhist, is ultimately forced to accept tribal work in a ritual exorcism, after which he pleads to be accepted back into his clan. Beautiful and image-driven, offering a rare glimpse into the Tibet you won't see in travel brochures. Filmed on location with locals as actors. In Mandarin with English subtitles. *AKA:* Daoma Zei.
1987 88m/C *D:* Tian Zhuangzhuang. **VHS $59.95** *KIV, FCT, ING* 🎵🎵🎵

The Horse Without a Head Stolen loot has been hidden in a discarded toy horse which is now the property of a group of poor children. The thieves, however, have different plans. Good family fare originally shown on the Disney television show.

1963 89m/C Jean-Pierre Aumont, Herbert Lom, Leo McKern, Pamela Franklin, Vincent Winter; **D:** Don Chaffey. **VHS, Beta** $69.95 *DIS* 🎬🎬½

Horsemasters A group of young riders enter a special training program in England to achieve the ultimate equestrian title of horse-master, with Annette having to overcome her fear of jumping. Originally a two-part Disney television show, and released as a feature film in Europe.
1961 85m/C Tommy Kirk, Annette Funicello, Janet Munro, Tony Britton, Donald Pleasence, Jean Marsh, John Fraser, Millicent Martin; **D:** William Fairchild. **VHS, Beta** $69.95 *DIS* 🎬🎬

The Horsemen An Afghani youth enters the brutal buzkashi horse tournament to please his macho-minded father. Beautifully shot in Afghanistan and Spain by Claude Renoir.
1970 (PG) 109m/C Omar Sharif, Leigh Taylor-Young, Jack Palance, David De, Peter Jeffrey; **D:** John Frankenheimer; **W:** Dalton Trumbo; **M:** Georges Delerue. **VHS, Beta** $69.95 *COL* 🎬½

Horseplayer A loner is drawn into a mysterious triangle of decadence and desire in this riveting psychothriller.
1991 (R) ?m/C Brad Dourif, Sammi Davis-Voss, M.K. Harris, Vic Tayback; **D:** Kurt Voss. **VHS** $89.98 *REP* 🎬½

The Horse's Mouth An obsessive painter discovers that he must rely upon his wits to survive in London. A hilarious adaptation of the Joyce Cary novel. The laserdisc version is accompanied by an episode of the British documentary series "The Art of Film" profiling Guinness and his screen career. *AKA:* The Oracle.
1958 93m/C Alec Guinness, Kay Walsh, Robert Coote, Renee Houston, Michael Gough; **D:** Ronald Neame. Academy Awards '58 Nominations: Best Adapted Screenplay; National Board of Review Awards '58: 5 Best Foreign Films of the Year, Best Supporting Actress (Walsh). **VHS, Beta** $24.95 *ING, VYG, HMV* 🎬🎬🎬

The Hospital Cult favorite providing savage, unrelentingly sarcastic look at the workings of a chaotic metropolitan hospital beset by murders, witchdoctors, madness, and plain ineptitude.
1971 (PG) 101m/C George C. Scott, Diana Rigg, Barnard Hughes, Stockard Channing, Nancy Marchand, Richard Dysart; **D:** Arthur Hiller; **W:** Paddy Chayefsky. Academy Awards '71: Best Story & Screenplay; Nominations: Best Actor (Scott); Berlin International Film Festival '72: Silver Prize; Golden Globe Awards '72: Best Screenplay. **VHS, Beta** $19.98 *MGM, FOX* 🎬🎬🎬½

Hospital Massacre Psychopathic killer is loose in a hospital. Seems he holds a grudge against the woman who laughed at his valentine when they were children twenty years earlier, and too bad for her that she just checked in as a patient. Former "Playboy" and Hefner playmate Benton frolics in dangerous health care situation presented by the Cannon organization. *AKA:* X-Ray; Ward 13; Be My Valentine, Or Else.
1981 (R) 89m/C Barbi Benton, Jon Van Ness, Chip Lucio; **D:** Boaz Davidson. **VHS, Beta** $59.95 *MGM* Woof!

Hospital of Terror A transmigratory religious fanatic who died on the operating table manages to possess a nurse (Jacobson) before he kicks the bucket, and once in his candystripe incarnation, vents his spleen on the doctors who botched his operation. It's got a little more plasma than Adamson's "AstroZombies." Recommended by many to be a world-class boner. *AKA:* Nurse Sherri; Terror Hospital; Beyond the Living.

1978 (R) 88m/C Jill Jacobson, Geoffrey Land, Marilyn Joi, Mary Kay Pass, Prentiss Moulden, Clayton Foster; **D:** Al Adamson. **VHS** $19.99 *SSI* 🎬½

The Hostage A young teenager is witness to a gruesome and clandestine burial. The two murderers responsible take it upon themselves to see that their secret is never told.
1967 (PG) 84m/C Don O'Kelly, Harry Dean Stanton, John Carradine, Danny Martins; **D:** Russell S. Doughten Jr. **VHS** *NO* 🎬🎬½

Hostage Arab terrorists hijack a plane and the passengers start to fight back. Filmed in South Africa.
1987 (R) 94m/C Karen Black, Kevin McCarthy, Wings Hauser; **D:** Hanro Mohr; **M:** Brad Fiedel. **VHS, Beta** $79.95 *COL* 🎬½

Hostage British Secret Service agent John Rennie is fed up after a difficult mission in Argentina. He thinks he can walk away clean but his superiors beg to differ. He's marked for murder but Rennie has a dangerous plan that could guarantee his safety—only if he returns to Argentina to set things in motion. Based on the novel "No Place to Hide" by Ted Allbeury.
1992 (R) 100m/C Sam Neill, Talisa Soto, James Fox; **D:** Robert W. Young. **VHS, Beta** *PAR, PMS* 🎬🎬

The Hostage Tower In France, a group of international crime figures capture the visiting U.S. president's mother, hold her hostage in the Eiffel Tower and demand $30 million in ransom. Made for television.
1980 (PG) 97m/C Peter Fonda, Maud Adams, Britt Ekland, Billy Dee Williams, Keir Dullea, Douglas Fairbanks Jr., Rachel Roberts, Celia Johnson; **D:** Claudio Guzman. **VHS, Beta** $69.98 *SUE* 🎬🎬

Hostages A gang of criminals kidnap a family on vacation at a Caribbean island.
1979 93m/C Stuart Whitman, Marisa Mell. **VHS, Beta** *NO* 🎬

Hostages Harrowing docudrama about the Beirut hostage crisis combines acutal news footage with scenes of the prisoners and their families. Under desperate conditions hostages John McCarthy, Brian Keenan, Terry Anderson, Thomas Sutherland, Frank Reed, and Terry Waite try to hold on to their sanity and humanity as their families struggle for their release. Filmed on location in England, Israel, and Lebanon. Made for cable TV.
1993 (R) 90m/C Colin Firth, Ciaran Hinds, Jay O. Sanders, Josef Sommer, Harry Dean Stanton, Kathy Bates, Natasha Richardson, Conrad Asquith; **D:** David Wheatley; **W:** Bernard MacLaverty. **VHS** *IMP* 🎬🎬

Hostile Guns A law man discovers a woman he once loved is now an inmate he is transporting across the Texas badlands. Routine with the exception of cameos by veteran actors. Based on a story by Sloan Nibley and James Edward Grant.
1967 91m/C George Montgomery, Yvonne De Carlo, Tab Hunter, John Russell; *Cameos:* Brian Donlevy, Richard Arlen, Fuzzy Knight, Donald (Don "Red") Barry; **D:** R.G. Springsteen; **W:** Steve Fisher, Sloan Nibley. **VHS** $14.95 *PAR* 🎬🎬½

Hostile Takeover A mild-mannered accountant finally cracks and takes his co-workers hostage. He faces the police in a tense showdown. *AKA:* Office Party.
1988 (R) 93m/C David Warner, Michael Ironside, Kate Vernon, Jayne Eastwood; **D:** George Mihalka. **VHS, Beta** $89.95 *LIV* 🎬½

Hot Blood Two bank robbers take an innocent woman hostage and thrust her in the midst of a huge family battle. Another lukewarm entry from the director of "The Arrogant."
1989 89m/C Sylvia Kristel, Alicia Moro, Aldo Sambrel, Gaspar Cano; **D:** Philippe Blot. **VHS, Beta** $79.95 *CAN* 🎬½

Hot Box A Filipino-shot, low budget woofer. Prison flick about women who break out and foment a revolution.
1972 (R) 85m/C Andrea Cagan, Margaret Markov, Rickey Richardson, Laurie Rose; **D:** Joe Viola; **W:** Joe Viola, Jonathan Demme. **VHS, Beta** $24.98 *SUE* Woof!

Hot Bubblegum Three teenagers discover sex, the beach, rock 'n' roll, sex, drag racing, and sex.
1981 (R) 94m/C Jonathan Segall, Zachi Noy, Yftach Katzur. **VHS, Beta** *NO* 🎬

Hot Child in the City A country girl goes to Los Angeles and searches through the city's fleshpots for her sister's killer. Music by Nick Glider, Lou Reed, Billy Idol, and Fun Boy Three.
1987 85m/C Leah Ayres Hendrix, Shari Shattuck, Geof Pryssir; **D:** John Flores. **VHS, Beta** $14.95 *PSM, PAR* 🎬

Hot Chocolate Derek is a sultry Texas tycoon who wants to buy out the French chocolate factory run by Hays. After getting a look at her, work isn't all that's on his mind.
1992 (PG-13) 93m/C Bo Derek, Robert Hays. **VHS** *LIV* 🎬🎬

Hot Dog...The Movie! There's an intense rivalry going on between an Austrian ski champ and his California challenger during the World Cup Freestyle competition in Squaw Valley. Snow movie strictly for teens or their equivalent.
1983 (R) 96m/C David Naughton, Patrick Houser, Shannon Tweed, Tracy N. Smith; **D:** Peter Markle; **M:** Peter Bernstein. **VHS, Beta** $14.95 *MGM, FOX* 🎬½

Hot Foot/A Happy Married Couple Two silent comedies: "Hot Foot" (1920), is about Dunn's hobo character in the Chaplin mold; "A Happy Married Couple" (1916), is about a young married couple whose puppy, as described in a letter, is mistaken for a baby by their parents.
1920 51m/B Bobbie Dunn, Neal Burns, Betty Compson. **VHS, Beta, 8mm** $19.95 *VYY* 🎬½

Hot Lead Typical Holt oater which has the cowpoke and his sidekick Martin trying to avenge the death of a close friend who was killed by a gang of train robbers.
1951 60m/B Tim Holt, Joan Dixon, Ross Elliott, John Dehner; **D:** Stuart Gilmore. **VHS** $19.99 *MOV* 🎬🎬

Hot Lead & Cold Feet Twin brothers (one a gunfighter, the other meek and mild) compete in a train race where the winner will take ownership of a small western town. Dale not only plays both brothers, but also their tough father. Standard Disney fare.
1978 (G) 89m/C Jim Dale, Don Knotts, Karen Valentine; **D:** Robert Butler; **M:** Buddy Baker. **VHS, Beta** $69.95 *DIS* 🎬🎬

The Hot Line The world's two superpowers become befuddled when the hot line connecting Washington and Moscow breaks down. Taylor's final film. *AKA:* The Day the Hot Line Got Hot; Le Rouble a Deux Faces; El Rublo de las dos Caras.
1969 87m/C Robert Taylor, Charles Boyer, George Chakiris, Dominique Fabre, Gerard Tichy; **D:** Etienne Perier. **VHS** *REP* 🎬½

Hot Millions Hysterical comedy about high-class swindling operation with Ustinov as a refined embezzler. Excellent cast and sharp script. Although it didn't do well at the box office, this amusing romp became one of the biggest sleepers of the year.
1968 106m/C Peter Ustinov, Dame Maggie Smith, Karl Malden, Bob Newhart, Robert Morley, Cesar Romero; *D:* Eric Till; *W:* Peter Ustinov, Ira Wallach. **VHS** $19.98 *MGM* ⅃⅃⅃

Hot Money A small-town drama about an ex-con who poses as an assistant sheriff and plots a million-dollar robbery during the town's 4th of July parade. Made shortly before Welles' death, and kept on the shelf for more than five years.
1979 78m/C Orson Welles, Michael Murphy, Bobby Pickett, Michelle Finney. **VHS, Beta** $79.95 *VMK* ⅃

Hot Moves Four high school boys make a pact to lose their virginity before the end of the summer.
1984 (R) 89m/C Michael Zorek, Adam Silbar, Jill Schoelen, Deborah Richter, Monique Gabrielle, Tami Holbrook, Virgil Frye; *D:* Jim Sotos. **VHS, Beta** $79.98 *VES* ⅃

Hot Potato Black Belt Jones rescues a senator's daughter from a megalomaniacal general by using skull-thwacking footwork.
1976 87m/C Jim Kelly, George Memmoli, Geoffrey Binney; *D:* Oscar Williams. **VHS, Beta** $14.95 *WAR* ⅃

Hot Pursuit A woman who has been framed for murder runs from the law and a relentless hitman.
1984 (PG) 94m/C Mike Preston, Dina Merrill, Kerrie Keane. **VHS, Beta** $79.95 *VMK* ⅃½

Hot Pursuit A prep-school bookworm resorts to Rambo-like tactics in tracking down his girlfriend and her family after being left behind for a trip to the tropics.
1987 (PG-13) 93m/C John Cusack, Robert Loggia, Jerry Stiller, Wendy Gazelle; *D:* Steven Lisberger. **VHS, Beta** $79.95 *PAR* ⅃½

Hot Resort Young American lads mix work and play when they sign on as summer help at an island resort. Typical teen sex fantasy.
1985 (R) 92m/C Bronson Pinchot, Tom Parsekian, Michael Berz, Linda Kenton, Frank Gorshin; *D:* John Robins. **VHS, Beta** $79.95 *MGM* ⅃½

The Hot Rock A motley crew of bumbling thieves conspire to steal a huge, priceless diamond; a witty, gritty comedy that makes no moral excuses for its characters and plays like an early-'70s crime thriller gone awry. Adapted from the novel by Donald E. Westlake. The sequel, 1974's "Bank Shot," stars George C. Scott in the role created by Redford. *AKA:* How To Steal a Diamond in Four Easy Lessons.
1970 (PG) 97m/C Robert Redford, George Segal, Ron Leibman, Zero Mostel, Moses Gunn, William Redfield, Charlotte Rae, Topo Swope; *M:* Quincy Jones. **VHS, Beta** *FOX* ⅃⅃⅃

Hot Rod A young California hotrodder battles the evil sponsor of a drag race championship. *AKA:* Rebel of the Road.
1979 97m/C Greg Henry, Robert Culp, Pernell Roberts, Robin Mattson, Grant Goodeve; *D:* George Armitage. **VHS, Beta** $59.98 *NLC* ⅃

Hot Rod Girl A concerned police officer (Conners) organizes supervised drag racing after illegal drag racing gets out of hand in his community. *AKA:* Hot Car Girl.
1956 75m/B Lori Nelson, Chuck Connors, John W. Smith; *D:* Leslie Martinson; *W:* John McGreevey. **VHS** $16.95 *SNC, NOS, MRV* ⅃

Hot Shot An inspirational tale involving a young soccer player who goes to great lengths to take training from a soccer star, played - of course - by Pele.
1986 (PG) 90m/C Pele, Jim Youngs, Billy Warlock, Weyman Thompson, Mario Van Peebles, David Groh; *D:* Rick King. **VHS, Beta** $14.95 *WAR, MVD* ⅃½

Hot Shots! Another entry from "The Naked Gun" team of master movie parodists, this has lots of clever sight gags but the verbal humor often plummets to the ground. Spoofs "Top Gun" and similar gung-ho air corps adventures but doesn't forget other popular films including "Dances with Wolves" and "The Fabulous Baker Boys." Sheen is very funny as ace fighter pilot Sean "Topper" Harley who's to avenge the family honor. Great when you're in the mood for laughs that don't require thought.
1991 (PG-13) 83m/C Charlie Sheen, Cary Elwes, Valeria Golino, Lloyd Bridges, Kevin Dunn, Jon Cryer, William O'Leary, Kristy Swanson, Efrem Zimbalist Jr., Bill Irwin, Heidi Swedberg, Judith Kahan, Pat Proft; *Cameos:* Charles Barkley, Bill Laimbeer; *D:* Jim Abrahams; *W:* Pat Proft, Jim Abrahams; *M:* Sylvester Levay. **VHS** $19.98 *FXV* ⅃⅃⅃

Hot Shots! Part Deux Second "Hot Shots" outing doesn't live up to the first, but it's not bad either. Admiral Tug Benson (Bridges) is elected President (yes, of the U.S.) and calls on Sheen's newly pumped-up Topper to take on Saddam Hussein Rambostyle. Love interest Ramada (Golino), returns but this time she's competing with Michelle (Bakke), a sexy CIA agent. Crenna spoofs his role in the "Rambo" films as Sheen's mentor; look for real-life dad Martin in a take-off of "Apocalypse Now." Shtick flies as fast and furious as the bodies, with Bridges getting a chance to reprise his glory days of "Sea Hunt." Don't miss the credits.
1993 (PG-13) 89m/C Charlie Sheen, Lloyd Bridges, Valeria Golino, Brenda Bakke, Richard Crenna, Miguel Ferrer, Rowan Atkinson, Jerry Haleva, Mitchell Ryan, Gregory Sierra, Ryan Stiles, Michael Colyar; *Cameos:* Martin Sheen, Bob Vila; *D:* Jim Abrahams; *W:* Pat Proft, Jim Abrahams; *M:* Basil Poledouris. **VHS** $96.98 *FXV, BTV* ⅃⅃½

Hot Spell In an attempt to repair her marriage and unify her family, a mother plans a reunion-birthday party for her husband. Despair reigns in this sultry, Southern melodrama.
1958 86m/B Shirley Booth, Anthony Quinn, Shirley MacLaine, Earl Holliman, Eileen Heckart; *D:* Daniel Mann. **VHS, Beta** $19.95 *BAR* ⅃½

Hot Spot An amoral drifter arrives in a small Texas town and engages in affairs with two women, including his boss's over-sexed wife and a young woman with her own secrets. Things begin to heat up when he decides to plot a bank robbery. Based on Charles Williams' 1952 novel "Hell Hath No Fury."
1990 (R) 120m/C Don Johnson, Virginia Madsen, Jennifer Connelly, Charles Martin Smith, William Sadler, Jerry Hardin, Barry Corbin, Leon Rippy, Jack Nance; *D:* Dennis Hopper; *W:* Charles Williams, Nona Tyson; *M:* Jack Nitzsche. **VHS** $14.98 *ORI, FCT* ⅃⅃½

Hot Stuff Officers on a burglary task force decide the best way to obtain convictions is to go into the fencing business themselves.
1980 (PG) 91m/C Dom DeLuise, Jerry Reed, Suzanne Pleshette, Ossie Davis; *D:* Dom DeLuise; *W:* Donald E. Westlake, Michael Kane. **VHS, Beta** $14.95 *COL* ⅃

Hot Summer in Barefoot County A state law enforcement officer on the search for illegal moonshiners finds more than he bargained for.
1974 (R) 90m/C Sherry Robinson, Tonia Bryan, Dick Smith; *D:* Will Zens. **VHS, Beta** *NO* ⅃⅃

Hot T-Shirts A small town bar owner needs a boost for business, finding the answer in wet T-shirt contests. Softcore trash.
1979 (R) 86m/C Ray Holland, Stephanie Lawlor, Pauline Rose, Corinne Alphen; *D:* Chuck Vincent. **VHS, Beta** $39.95 *MCA Woof!*

Hot Target An ideal mother becomes obsessed with the stranger who seduced her, even after she finds out he's a thief planning to rob her home.
1985 (R) 93m/C Simone Griffeth, Steve Marachuk; *D:* Denis Lewiston. **VHS, Beta** $79.98 *LIV, VES* ⅃

The Hot, the Cool, and the Vicious A quiet town turns into a bloody, martial arts playground when three hombres trade blows in a tavern.
198? ?m/C Wang Tao, Tommy Lee, Sun Chia-Lin. **VHS** $34.95 *OCE* ⅃

Hot Times Low-budget comedy about a high school boy who, after striking out with the high school girls, decides to go to New York and have the time of his life.
1974 (R) 80m/C Gail Lorber, Amy Farber, Henry Cory; *D:* Jim McBride; *W:* Jim McBride. **VHS, Beta** $39.95 *MON* ⅃

Hot to Trot! A babbling idiot links up with a talking horse in an updated version of the "Francis, the Talking Mule" comedies, by way of Mr. Ed. The equine voice is provided by Candy. Some real funny guys are wasted here.
1988 (PG) 90m/C Bob(cat) Goldthwait, Dabney Coleman, Virginia Madsen, Jim Metzler, Cindy Pickett, Tim Kazurinsky, Santos Morales, Barbara Whinnery, Garry Kluger; *D:* Michael Dinner; *W:* Charlie Peters; *V:* John Candy. **VHS, Beta** $19.95 *WAR* ⅃

Hot Touch An art forger with a large heist is besieged by a slashing maniac, and must discover the culprit.
198? 92m/C Wayne Rogers, Samantha Eggar, Marie-France Pisier, Melvyn Douglas. **VHS, Beta** $69.95 *TWE, HHE Woof!*

Hot Under the Collar Jerry is a weasel who tries to seduce the luscious Monica by using hypnosis. But his plans backfire and instead Monica enters a convent and takes a vow of chastity. This isn't going to stop Jerry, he tries posing as a priest and even dressing as a nun in order to get her out. Things get even more complicated when a mobster, looking for a fortune in stolen diamonds, sneaks into the convent.
1991 (R) 87m/C Richard Gabai, Angela Visser, Daniel Friedman, Mindy Clarke, Tane McClure; *D:* Richard Gabai. **VHS** $89.99 *HBO* ⅃

Hot Water/Safety Last Two classic Harold Lloyd silent comedies, "Hot Water" (1924) and "Safety Last" (1923). "Safety Last" features one of Lloyd's most famous stunt scenes, where he is hanging from the hands of a giant clock on the side of a building, high above the city.
1924 81m/B Harold Lloyd. **VHS, Beta** *TLF* ⅃½

Hot Wire Tired comedy about the unscrupulous side of the car repossession racket.
197? 92m/C George Kennedy, Strother Martin. **VHS, Beta** *NO* ⅃½

Hotel A pale rehash of the "Grand Hotel" formula about an array of rich characters interacting in a New Orleans hotel. From the Arthur Hailey potboiler; the basis for the television series.
1967 (PG) 125m/C Rod Taylor, Catherine Spaak, Karl Malden, Melvyn Douglas, Merle Oberon, Michael Rennie, Richard Conte, Kevin McCarthy; **D:** Richard Quine; **W:** Wendell Mayes. **VHS, Beta** $59.95 *WAR* 🦴 ½

Hotel Colonial A young Italian idealist ventures to Columbia to retrieve the body of his brother, who reportedly killed himself. Once there, he finds the dead man is not his brother, and decides to investigate.
1988 (R) 103m/C Robert Duvall, John Savage, Rachel Ward, Massimo Troisi; **D:** Cinzia Torrini; **M:** Pino Donaggio. **VHS, Beta, 8mm** $19.98 *SUE, NLC* 🦴 ½

Hotel du Lac A made-for-British-television adaptation of the Anita Brookner novel about a woman writer languishing at a Swiss lakefront hotel.
1986 75m/C Anna Massey, Denholm Elliott, Googie Withers; **D:** Giles Foster; **M:** Carl Davis. **VHS, Beta** $19.95 *FOX, TVC* 🦴 🦴

Hotel Imperial Set in 1917 Budapest, six Hungarian soldiers ride into a frontier town and find it occupied by Russians. Hall plays Lieutenant Almasy, who takes refuge in the Hotel Imperial. Orchestra scored.
1927 84m/B Pola Negri, James Hall, George Siegmann, Max Davidson; **D:** Mauritz Stiller. **VHS** $19.95 *GPV* 🦴 🦴

The Hotel New Hampshire The witless, amoral adaptation of John Irving's novel about a very strange family's adventures in New Hampshire, Vienna and New York City, which include gang rape, incest, and Kinski in a bear suit.
1984 (R) 110m/C Jodie Foster, Rob Lowe, Beau Bridges, Nastassia Kinski, Wallace Shawn, Wilford Brimley, Amanda Plummer, Anita Morris, Matthew Modine, Lisa Banes, Seth Green; **D:** Tony Richardson; **W:** Tony Richardson. **VHS, Beta** $29.98 *VES* 🦴 🦴

Hotel Paradiso Slightly amusing bedroom farce has timid Guinness trying to carry on affair with Italian sexpot Lollibrigida. Guinness fans won't be disappointed, although it's not a top-rate production. Based on the play "L'Hotel du Libre Echange" by Georges Feydeau and Maurice Desvalliers.
1966 100m/C Alec Guinness, Gina Lollobrigida, Akim Tamiroff, Marie Bell, Derek Fowlds; **D:** Peter Glenville; **W:** Peter Glenville, Jean-Claude Carriere. **VHS** $19.98 *MGM* 🦴 🦴 ½

Hotel Reserve A Nazi spy is reportedly afoot in a French resort during WWII, and tension mounts as the guests attempt to flush him out. Critical response to this film is wildly split; some find it obvious, while others call it well-done and suspenseful. Based on the novel "Epitaph for a Spy" by Eric Ambler.
1944 79m/B James Mason, Lucie Mannheim, Raymond Lovell, Julien Mitchell, Martin Miller, Herbert Lom, Frederick Valk, Valentine Dyall, Patricia Medina; **D:** Victor Hanbury, Lance Comfort, Max Greene. **VHS, Beta** $19.98 *TTC, RXM* 🦴 🦴 🦴

Hotel Room A trilogy of stories set in the same drab New York hotel room in three different time periods. "Getting Rid of Robert," set in 1992, has three girlfriends swilling champagne and discussing Sasha's slick, movie exec boyfriend whom she wants to dump. "Tricks," set in 1969, features Darlene, a bored, druggy prostitute; her client, Moe; and the sudden appearance of Moe's talkative friend, Lou. "Blackout" is set in 1936 and features a young husband trying to cope with the madness of his beautiful wife.

Unfortunately, all three stories are rambling and lacking in energy. Made for cable television. **AKA:** David Lynch's Hotel Room.
1993 100m/C Deborah Unger, Mariska Hargitay, Chelsea Field, Griffin Dunne, Glenne Headly, Harry Dean Stanton, Freddie Jones, Crispin Glover, Alicia Witt, Clark Heathcliffe Brolly, Camilla Overbye Roos; **D:** James Signorelli, David Lynch; **W:** Barry Gifford, Jay McInerney; **M:** Angelo Badalamenti. **VHS** $89.95 *WOV, FCT* 🦴 🦴 ½

Hothead A heedless, impulsive soccer player's behavior gets him cut from the team, fired from his mill job, and booted out of his favorite bar. In French with English subtitles or dubbed. **AKA:** Coup de Tete.
1978 98m/C Patrick Dewaere, Jean Bouise, Michel Aumont, France Dougnac; **D:** Jean-Jacques Annaud; **W:** Francis Veber. **VHS, Beta** $59.95 *COL* 🦴 🦴

Hotline After taking a job answering phones at a crisis center, a woman becomes the next target of a psychotic killer. Made for television.
1982 96m/C Lynda Carter, Steve Forrest, Granville Van Dusen, Monte Markham, James Booth; **D:** Jerry Jameson. **VHS** *NO* 🦴 🦴

H.O.T.S. A sex-filled sorority rivalry film, starring a slew of ex-Playboy Playmates in wet shirts. Screenplay co-written by exploitation star Caffaro. **AKA:** T & A Academy.
1979 (R) 95m/C Susan Kiger, Lisa London, Kimberly Cameron, Danny Bonaduce, Steve Bond; **D:** Gerald Seth Sindell; **W:** Cheri Caffaro. **VHS, Beta** $69.98 *LIV, VES* 🦴

Houdini Historically inaccurate but entertaining biopic of the infamous magician and escapologist. Chronicles his rise to stardom, his efforts to contact his dearly departed mother through mediums (a prequel to "Ghost"?), and his heart-stopping logic-defying escapes. First screen teaming of Leigh and Curtis, who had already been married for two years.
1953 107m/C Tony Curtis, Janet Leigh, Torin Thatcher, Angela Clark, Stefan Schnabel, Ian Wolfe, Sig Rumann, Michael Pate, Connie Gilchrist, Mary Murphy, Tor Johnson; **D:** George Marshall; **W:** Philip Yordan. **VHS** $14.95 *PAR, FCT* 🦴 🦴 ½

The Hound of the Baskervilles The curse of a demonic hound threatens descendants of an English noble family until Holmes and Watson solve the mystery. Also available with "Sherlock Holmes Faces Death" on Laser Disc.
1939 80m/B Basil Rathbone, Nigel Bruce, Richard Greene, John Carradine, Wendy Barrie, Lionel Atwill, E.E. Clive; **D:** Sidney Lanfield. **VHS, Beta** $14.95 *KUI, FOX* 🦴 🦴 🦴

The Hound of the Baskervilles Cushing's not half bad as Sherlock Holmes as he investigates the mystery of a supernatural hound threatening the life of a Dartmoor baronet. Dark and moody.
1959 86m/C Peter Cushing, Christopher Lee, Andre Morell; **D:** Terence Fisher. **VHS, Beta** $19.98 *MGM, MLB, FOX* 🦴 🦴 ½

The Hound of the Baskervilles Awful spoof of the Sherlock Holmes classic with Cook as Holmes and Moore as Watson (and Holmes' mother). Even the cast can't save it.
1977 84m/C Dudley Moore, Peter Cook, Denholm Elliott, Joan Greenwood, Spike Milligan, Jessie Matthews, Roy Kinnear; **D:** Paul Morrissey; **W:** Dudley Moore, Peter Cook, Paul Morrissey. **VHS** *ATV* Woof!

The Hound of the Baskervilles Another remake of the Sherlock Holmes story which finds the great detective investigating the murder of Sir Charles Baskerville and a mysterious haunted moor.
1983 100m/C Ian Richardson, Donald Churchill, Martin Shaw, Nicholas Clay, Denholm Elliott, Brian Blessed, Ronald Lacey; **D:** Douglas Hickox. **VHS, Beta** $59.95 *PAR* 🦴 🦴

Hour of Decision When a newspaper columnist turns up dead, a reporter investigates the murder. Things get hairy when he finds the prime suspect is his own wife.
1957 81m/B Jeff Morrow, Hazel Court, Lionel Jeffries, Anthony M. (Antonio Margheretti) Dawson, Mary Laura Wood; **D:** C. Pennington Richards. **VHS, Beta** $16.95 *SNC* 🦴 ½

Hour of the Assassin A mercenary is hired to assassinate a South American ruler, and a CIA operative is sent to stop him. Shot in Peru.
1986 (R) 96m/C Erik Estrada, Robert Vaughn; **D:** Luis Llosa. **VHS, Beta** $79.95 *MGM* 🦴 ½

Hour of the Gun Western saga chronicles what happens after the gunfight at the OK Corral. Garner plays the grim Wyatt Earp on the trail of vengeance after his brothers are killed. Robards is excellent as the crusty Doc Holliday.
1967 100m/C James Garner, Jason Robards Jr., Robert Ryan, Albert Salmi, Charles Aidman, Steve Ihnat, Jon Voight; **D:** John Sturges; **M:** Jerry Goldsmith. **VHS** $14.95 *MGM* 🦴 🦴

The Hour of the Star The poignant, highly acclaimed feature debut by Amaral, about an innocent young woman moving to the city of Sao Paulo from the impoverished countryside of Brazil, and finding happiness despite her socioeconomic failures. Based on Clarice Lispector's novel. In Portuguese with English subtitles. **AKA:** A Hora Da Estrela.
1985 96m/C Marcelia Cartaxo; **D:** Suzana Amaral. **VHS, Beta** $79.95 *KIV, ING* 🦴 🦴 🦴 ½

Hour of the Wolf An acclaimed, surreal view into the tormented inner life of a painter as he and his wife are isolated on a small northern island. Cinematography by Sven Nykvist. In Swedish with English subtitles.
1968 89m/B Max von Sydow, Liv Ullmann, Ingrid Thulin, Erland Josephson, Gertrud Fridh, Gudrun Brost; **D:** Ingmar Bergman; **W:** Ingmar Bergman. **VHS, Beta** $19.98 *MGM, MRV, FCT* 🦴 🦴 🦴 ½

House A horror novelist moves into his dead aunt's supposedly haunted house only to find that the monsters don't necessarily stay in the closets. His worst nightmares come to life as he writes about his Vietnam experiences and is forced to relive the tragic events, but these aren't the only visions that start springing to life. It sounds depressing, but is actually a funny, intelligent "horror" flick. Followed by several lesser sequels.
1986 (R) 93m/C William Katt, George Wendt, Richard Moll, Kay Lenz, Michael Ensign, Mary Stavin, Susan French; **D:** Steve Miner; **W:** Ethan Wiley; **M:** Harry Manfredini. **VHS, Beta** $19.95 *NWV, STE* 🦴 🦴 🦴

House 2: The Second Story The flaccid sequel to the haunted-house horror flick concerns two innocent guys who move into the family mansion and discover Aztec ghosts. Has none of the humor which helped the first movie along.
1987 (PG-13) 88m/C John Ratzenberger, Arye Gross, Royal Dano, Bill Maher, Jonathan Stark; **D:** Ethan Wiley; **W:** Ethan Wiley. **VHS, Beta** $19.95 *NWV, STE* 🦴

House 4: Home Deadly Home Another bad real estate epic on a par with the other unusually inept "House" efforts. When her husband (Katt) is killed in an auto accident, a young woman and her daughter move into a mysterious old house. Terror begins to confront them at every turn, threatening to destroy them both. We can only hope.
1991 (R) 93m/C Terri Treas, Scott Burkholder, Melissa Clayton, William Katt, Ned Romero; *D:* Lewis Abernathy. **VHS $89.95** *COL, NLC* ✗✗½

House Across the Bay Raft, an imprisoned nightclub owner, finds that he is being duped by his attorney who's eager to get his hooks into the lingerie-clad prisoner's wife. But prison isn't going to stop the bitter husband from getting his revenge.
1940 88m/B George Raft, Walter Pidgeon, Joan Bennett, Lloyd Nolan, Gladys George; *D:* Archie Mayo. **VHS, Beta** *NO* ✗✗½

The House by the Cemetery When a family moves into a house close to a cemetery, strange things start to happen to them. *AKA:* Quella Villa Accanto Al Cimitero.
1983 (R) 84m/C Katherine MacColl, Paolo Malco; *D:* Lucio Fulci. **VHS, Beta $69.98** *LIV, VES* ✗

House Calls A widowed surgeon turns into a swinging bachelor until he meets a witty but staid English divorcee. Wonderful dialogue. Jackson is exceptional. Made into a short-lived TV series.
1978 (PG) 98m/C Walter Matthau, Glenda Jackson, Art Carney, Richard Benjamin, Candice Azzara; *D:* Howard Zieff; *W:* Charles Shyer; *M:* Henry Mancini. **VHS, Beta $14.98** *MCA* ✗✗✗

The House in Marsh Road A faithless husband decides to rid himself of She Who Must Be Obeyed, but his wife's ghost-friend intervenes.
1960 70m/B Tony Wright, Patricia Dainton, Sandra Dorne, Derek Aylward, Sam Kydd; *D:* Montgomery Tully. **VHS $19.98** *SNC* ✗✗

A House In The Hills A struggling actress is housesitting at a luxurious estate and innocently lets in the exterminator. Except he's an ex-con looking for revenge on the home's current occupant (whom the actress is pretending to be) and may just exterminate her instead.
1993 (R) 89m/C Helen Slater, Michael Madsen. **VHS $92.98** *LIV* ✗✗

House of Angels Charming comedy, with some serious overtones, about what happens to the gossipy inhabitants of a small Swedish village when two free-spirited newcomers come to stay. Fanny and her friend Zac, who are cabaret performers, show up at the funeral of eccentric Erik, who turns out to be the grandfather Fanny never knew. With her outrageous clothes and attitude, Fanny has most of the neighbors scandalized but what the generous Fanny wants is some information about her past, including who her father might be. What the neighbors want is for Fanny and Zac to leave as quickly as possible. In Swedish with English subtitles. *AKA:* Anglagard; Colin Nutley's House of Angels.
1992 (R) 119m/C Helena Bergstrom, Rikard Wolff, Sven Wollter, Jakob Eklund, Viveka Seldahl, Ernst Gunter, Reine Brynolfsson, Per Oscarsson; *D:* Colin Nutley; *W:* Susanne Falck. **VHS $95.98** *COL, FCT* ✗✗

House of Cards Precocious 6-year-old Sally (Menina) suddenly stops talking after her father is killed in an accident at an archeological site in Mexico. Mom Ruth (Turner) fights to bring her daughter out of her fantasy world and seeks medical advice

from a psychiatrist (a sympathetic Jones) but ignores it when it clashes with her own theories. The ethereal Menina, in her acting debut, gives the best performance in this weakly plotted and confusing family saga.
1992 (PG-13) 109m/C Kathleen Turner, Asha Menina, Tommy Lee Jones, Shiloh Strong, Esther Rolle, Park Overall, Michael Horse, Anne Pitoniak; *D:* Michael Lessac; *W:* Michael Lessac. **VHS $92.98** *LIV, BTV, FCT* ✗✗½

House of Dark Shadows A 150-year-old vampire, accidentally released by a handyman, wreaks havoc on the inhabitants of the Collinswood mansion. Based on the TV daytime soap.
1970 (PG) 97m/C Jonathan Frid, Joan Bennett, Grayson Hall, Kathryn Leigh Scott, Roger Davis, Nancy Barrett, John Karlen, Thayer David; *D:* Dan Curtis. **VHS, Beta $19.98** *MGM, FUS* ✗✗

House of Death The ex-Playmate of the Year runs in hysterical fear from a knife-wielding lunatic.
1982 (R) 88m/C Susan Kiger, William T. Hicks, Jody Kay, Martin Tucker, Jennifer Chase. **VHS, Beta $59.95** *GEM* ✗

The House of Dies Drear A modern-day African American family moves into an old house that turns out to be haunted by the ghost of a long dead abolitionist. The family is transported back to the days of slavery as they interact with the ghost. Based on the story by Virginia Hamilton. Aired on PBS as part of the "Wonderworks" family movie series.
1988 107m/C Howard E. Rollins Jr., Moses Gunn, Shavar Ross, Gloria Foster, Clarence Williams III; *D:* Allan Goldstein. **VHS $29.95** *HMV, PME, FCT* ✗

House of Dracula Sequel to "House of Frankenstein" features several of the Universal monsters. Overly ambitious story gets a bit hokey, but it's entertaining, nonetheless.
1945 67m/B Lon Chaney Jr., Martha O'Driscoll, John Carradine, Lionel Atwill, Onslow Stevens, Glenn Strange, Jane Adams, Ludwig Stossel; *D:* Erle C. Kenton; *W:* Edward T. Lowe. **VHS $14.98** *MCA, FCT* ✗✗½

House of Dreams Berry is a blocked writer coping with domestic difficulties whose dreams reveal a disturbing future. Contains a bit part for Goodnow, now a CNN talking head.
1964 80m/B Robert Berry, Pauline Elliott, Charlene Bradley, Lance Bird, David Goodnow; *D:* Robert Berry. **VHS** *LSV* ✗

The House of Eliott BBC miniseries set in 1920s London finds the orphaned Beatrice and Evangeline Eliott struggling to begin their fashion business as couturiers to the rich and influential, which eventually leads to their founding of the House of Eliott. Lots of romance and intrigue along the way. Boxed set of six cassettes.
1992 600m/C Stella Gonet, Louise Lombard, Aden Gillett, Richard Lintern. **VHS $129.95** *SIG, AAE* ✗

House of Errors Two deliverymen pose as reporters to safeguard a prototype machine gun from the bad guys. Contrived plot consisting of outdated comic routines. This was Marsh's last film.
1942 63m/B Harry Langdon, Marian Marsh, Ray Walker, Betty Blythe, John Holland; *D:* Bernard B. Ray. **VHS $19.95** *NOS* ✗✗

House of Fear Holmes and Watson investigate the murders of several members of the Good Comrades Club, men who were neither good nor comradely.
1945 69m/B Basil Rathbone, Nigel Bruce, Dennis Hoey, Aubrey Mather, Paul Cavanagh, Gavin Muir; *D:* Roy William Neill. **VHS, Beta $14.98** *FOX* ✗✗½

House of Frankenstein An evil scientist (Karloff) escapes from prison, and, along with his hunchback manservant, revives Dracula, Frankenstein's monster, and the Wolfman to carry out his dastardly deeds. An all-star cast helps this horror fest along.
1944 71m/B Boris Karloff, J. Carroll Naish, Lon Chaney Jr., John Carradine, Elena Verdugo, Anne Gwynne, Lionel Atwill, Peter Coe, George Zucco, Glenn Strange, Sig Rumann; *D:* Erle C. Kenton. **VHS $14.98** *MCA* ✗✗½

House of Games The directorial debut of playwright Mamet is a tale about an uptight female psychiatrist who investigates the secret underworld of con-artistry and becomes increasingly involved in an elaborate con game. She's led along her crooked path by smooth-talking con-master Mantegna. A taut, well plotted psychological suspense film with many twists and turns. Stylishly shot, with dialogue which has that marked Mamet cadence. Most of the leads are from Mamet's theater throng (including his wife, Crouse).
1987 (R) 102m/C Joe Mantegna, Lindsay Crouse, Lilia Skala, J.T. Walsh, Meshach Taylor, Ricky Jay, Mike Nussbaum, Willo Hausman; *D:* David Mamet; *W:* David Mamet; *M:* Alaric Jans. **VHS, Beta $19.99** *HBO, FCT* ✗✗✗

House of Horrors Deformed murderer "The Creeper" (Hatton) is used by a mad sculptor in a twisted revenge plot. Marcel De Lange (Kosleck) believes his work has been vilely abused by art critics so he uses his friend's homicidal urges to get rid of anyone who stands in his way.
1946 76m/B Martin Kosleck, Rondo Hatton, Robert Lowery, Virginia Grey, Bill Goodwin, Alan Napier, Joan Shawlee, Howard Freeman; *D:* Jean Yarborough; *W:* George Bricker. **VHS $14.98** *MCA* ✗✗½

The House of Lurking Death Detectives Tommy and Tuppence find a box of chocolates laced with arsenic at the home of Lois Hargreaves, and the mad old maid is the prime suspect. Based on the Agatha Christie story. Made for British television.
1984 60m/C James Warwick, Francesca Annis. **VHS, Beta $14.95** *TPV* ✗½

House of Mystery For a shot at some priceless jewels stolen by the host from a Hindu princess, several guests gather for a weekend in a spine-tingling mansion. A creepy curse keeps them looking over their shoulders.
1934 62m/C Ed Lowry, Verna Hillie, Brandon Hurst, George "Gabby" Hayes; *D:* William Nigh. **VHS $12.95** *SNC, DVT, MLB* ✗✗

House of Mystery Splendid British remake of 1934 film in which the detective does some true sleuthing to catch the culprits. An old widow is killed for her jewels, but the murderers can't locate the goods. After they try a series of fiendish plans to retrieve them, the detective must work to stop the crooks. *AKA:* At the Villa Rose.
1941 61m/B Kenneth Kent, Judy Kelly, Peter Murray Hill, Walter Rilla, Ruth Maitland; *D:* Walter Summers. **VHS $24.95** *NOS, DVT* ✗✗½

The House of 1000 Dolls Doleful, not dollful, exploitation thriller as magician Price drugs young girls and sells them to slavery rings. An international production set in Tangiers; dialogue is dubbed. *AKA:* Haus Der Tausend Freuden.
1967 79m/C Vincent Price, Martha Hyer, George Nader, Ann Smyrner, Maria Rohm; *D:* Jeremy Summers. **VHS, Beta $59.98** *HBO* ✗

House of Psychotic Women Naschy, Spain's premier horror movie star, plays a studly drifter who winds up in the home of three sisters, one with an artificial

arm, one confined to a wheelchair and the other a nymphomaniac. No problemo thinks the hirsute Spaniard, until a series of bizarre murders—in which the victims eyes are ripped out—spoils his fun. Naschy, who usually sprouts fur and fangs, actually doesn't turn into a werewolf. Catchy but inappropriate score. A must for Naschy/bad movie fans. *AKA:* Los Ojos Azules de la Muneca Rota.
1973 (R) 87m/C Paul Naschy, Maria Perschy, Diana Lorys, Eva Leon, Ines Morales, Tony Pica; *D:* Carlos Aured; *W:* Paul Naschy. **VHS, Beta** *NO Woof!*

The House of Secrets A Yank travels to Britain to collect an inheritance and stays in a dusty old mansion filled with an odd assortment of characters.
1937 70m/B Leslie Fenton, Muriel Evans, Noel Madison, Sidney Blackmer, Morgan Wallace, Holmes Herbert; *D:* Roland D. Reed. **VHS, Beta** $16.95 *SNC �↗⅗*

The House of Seven Corpses A crew attempts to film a horror movie in a Victorian manor where seven people died in a variety of gruesome manners. Things take a turn for the ghoulish when a crew member becomes possesed by the house's evil spirits. Good, low budget fun with a competent "B" cast. Filmed in what was the Utah governor's mansion.
1973 (PG) 90m/C John Ireland, Faith Domergue, John Carradine, Carole Wells; *D:* Paul Harrison. **VHS** $29.95 *GEM, MRV, CNG ⅗⅗*

House of Shadows A 20-year-old murder comes back to haunt the victim's friends in this tale of mystery and terror.
1983 90m/C John Gavin, Yvonne De Carlo, Leonor Manso; *D:* Richard Wulicher. **VHS, Beta** $49.95 *MED ⅗⅛*

House of Strangers Conte, in a superb performance, swears vengeance on his brothers, whom he blames for his father's death. Robinson, in a smaller part than you'd expect from his billing, is nevertheless excellent as the ruthless banker father who sadly reaps a reward he didn't count on. Based on Philip Yordan's "I'll Never Go There Again."
1949 101m/B Edward G. Robinson, Susan Hayward, Richard Conte, Luther Adler, Efrem Zimbalist Jr., Debra Paget; *D:* Joseph L. Mankiewicz; *W:* Philip Yordan. **VHS** $39.98 *FOX, FCT ⅗⅗⅗½*

House of Terror A woman and her boyfriend plot to kill her rich boss, while they too are being stalked by some undefined horror.
1987 91m/C Jennifer Bishop, Arell Blanton, Jacquelyn Hyde. **VHS, Beta** $79.95 *TWE ⅓*

The House of the Arrow Investigating the murder of a French widow, who was killed by a poisoned arrow, a detective must sort through a grab bag of potential suspects. Superior adaptation of the A.E.W. Mason thriller.
1953 73m/B Oscar Homolka, Yvonne Furneaux, Robert Urquhart; *D:* Michael Anderson Sr. **VHS, Beta** $16.95 *NOS, SNC ⅗⅗⅗*

House of the Black Death Horror titans Chaney and Carradine manage to costar in this as warring warlocks, yet they share no scenes together! Chaney is the evil warlock (the horns are a giveaway) holding people hostage in the title edifice. *AKA:* Blood of the Man Devil; Night of the Beast.
1965 89m/B Lon Chaney Jr., John Carradine, Katherine Victor, Tom Drake, Andrea King; *D:* Harold Daniels, Reginald LeBorg. **VHS** $15.95 *NOS, LOO ⅗½*

House of the Damned A young woman, a mental hospital, a murdered father, a priceless gold statue—mix together and you get a mystery horror movie. A woman tries to solve her father's murder.
19?? 89m/C Donald Pleasence, Michael Dunn. **VHS, Beta** *NO ⅗½*

House of the Dead Man is trapped inside a haunted house. Scary.
1980 100m/C John Erikson, Charles Aidman, Bernard Fox, Ivor Francis. **VHS** *NO ⅗*

House of the Living Dead Brattling Manor harbors a murderous and flesh-eating secret ready to lure the unsuspecting. Don't you be one. *AKA:* Doctor Maniac.
1973 (PG) 87m/C Mark Burns, Shirley Anne Field, David Oxley; *D:* Ray Austin. **VHS, Beta** $29.95 *VCI, HHE ⅗*

House of the Long Shadows Comedy mixes with gore, as four of the horror screen's best leading men team up for the first time, although they have only minor roles. Might have been a contender, but Arnaz is miscast as author who stays in spooky house on a bet with Todd. Some wit but not enough. Based on the play "Seven Keys to Baldpate" by George M. Cohan (and novel by Earl Derr Biggers).
1982 (PG) 96m/C Vincent Price, Christopher Lee, Peter Cushing, John Carradine, Desi Arnaz Jr., Sheila Keith, Richard Todd; *D:* Pete Walker. **VHS, Beta** $69.95 *MGM ⅗⅛*

House of the Rising Sun A Los Angeles reporter goes under cover for a story on an exclusive brothel only to discover the owner is a psychopath who has very permanent ways of dealing with troublesome employees.
1987 86m/C John York, Bud Davis, Deborah Wakeham, Frank Annese; *D:* Greg Gold; *M:* Tina Turner, Bryan Ferry. **VHS, Beta** $79.95 *PSM, PAR ⅗½*

The House of the Spirits Star-studded adaptation of the novel by Isabel Allende is a multi-generational saga following the fortunes of the powerful Trueba family. The ambitious Esteban (Irons) marries the clairvoyant Clara (Steep), exploits the peasants on his property, and becomes a conservative senator. Their rebellious daughter Blanca (Ryder) falls for rabble-rousing peasant Pedro (Banderas), and the country undergoes a bloody revolution. Magical realism of the novel is lost in screen melodrama, with the international cast ill-served by tepid direction. The child Clara is played by Streep's daughter, Mary Willa (listed in the credits as Jane Gray).
1993 (R) 109m/C Meryl Streep, Jeremy Irons, Glenn Close, Winona Ryder, Antonio Banderas, Armin Mueller-Stahl, Vanessa Redgrave, Sarita Choudhury, Maria Conchita Alonso, Vincent Gallo; *D:* Bille August; *W:* Bille August; *M:* Hans Zimmer. **VHS** *LIV ⅗⅗*

House of the Yellow Carpet A couple try to sell an ancient Persian carpet heirloom, and in doing so transgress some unwritten mystical law. Havoc ensues.
1984 90m/C Roland Josephson, Beatrice Romand; *D:* Carlo Lizzani. **VHS, Beta** $69.98 *LIV ⅗½*

The House of Usher Some serious overacting by Reed (as Roderick) and Pleasance (as his balmy brother) almost elevate this Poe retread to "so bad it's good" status, and there are a few admirably grisly moments. But, without other camp virtues, it's merely dreary. Adapted by Michael J. Murray and filmed in South Africa.
1988 (R) 92m/C Oliver Reed, Donald Pleasence, Romy Windsor; *D:* Alan Birkinshaw; *W:* Michael J. Murray; *M:* Gary Chang. **VHS** $79.95 *COL ⅓*

House of Wax A deranged sculptor (Price, who else?) builds a sinister wax museum which showcases creations that were once alive. A remake of the early horror flick "Mystery of the Wax Museum," and one of the 50s' most popular 3-D films. This one still has the power to give the viewer the creeps, thanks to another chilling performance by Price. Look for a very young Charles Bronson, as well as Carolyn "Morticia Addams" Jones as a victim.
1953 (PG) 88m/C Vincent Price, Frank Lovejoy, Carolyn Jones, Phyllis Kirk, Paul Cavanagh, Charles Bronson; *D:* Andre de Toth. **VHS, Beta** $19.98 *WAR, MLB ⅗⅗⅗*

House of Whipcord Beautiful young women are kidnapped and tortured in this British gore-o-rama. Awful and degrading.
1975 102m/C Barbara Markham, Patrick Barr, Ray Brooks, Penny Irving, Anne Michelle; *D:* Pete Walker. **VHS, Beta** $39.95 *MON, LIV Woof!*

The House on Carroll Street New York 1951, the middle of the McCarthy era. A young woman overhears a plot to smuggle Nazi war criminals into the U.S. She's already lost her job because of accusations of subversion, and it's not easy persuading FBI agent Daniels that she knows what she's talking about. Contrived plot and melodramatic finale help sink this period piece.
1988 (PG) 111m/C Kelly McGillis, Jeff Daniels, Mandy Patinkin, Jessica Tandy; *D:* Peter Yates; *W:* Walter Bernstein; *M:* Georges Delerue. **VHS, Beta** $89.99 *HBO ⅗½*

The House on Chelouche Street In Tel-Aviv, during the summer of 1946, 15-year-old Sami, an Egyptian immigrant, tries to help support his mother and family during the upheavals of Palestine under the British mandate. A well thought-out story detailing the struggles of a North African Jewish family before the creation of the country of Israel. In Hebrew with English subtitles.
1973 111m/C Gila Almagor, Michal Bat-Adam, Shai K. Ophir; *D:* Moshe Mizrahi. **VHS, Beta** $24.95 *VYY, NCJ, AUD ⅗⅗½*

The House on Garibaldi Street Spy drama about the capture of Nazi war criminal Adolph Eichmann in Argentina and his extradition to Israel for trial. Based on the book by Isser Harel. Made for television.
1979 96m/C Chaim Topol, Nick Mancuso, Martin Balsam, Janet Suzman, Leo McKern, Charles Gray, Alfred Burke; *D:* Peter Collinson; *M:* Charles Bernstein. **VHS, Beta** $14.95 *FRH, SWC ⅗⅗½*

House on Haunted Hill A wealthy man throws a haunted house party and offers ten thousand dollars to anyone who can survive the night there. Vintage cheap horror from the master of the macabre Castle. Remembered for Castle's in-theater gimmick of dangling a skeleton over the audiences' heads in the film's initial release. Also available with "Attack of the 50-Foot Woman" on laserdisc.
1958 75m/B Vincent Price, Carol Ohmart, Richard Long, Alan Marshal; *D:* William Castle. **VHS, Beta** $14.98 *FOX, SNC, FCT ⅗⅗½*

House on Marsh Road Rare British mystery involving poltergeists and murder in a haunted house. *AKA:* The Invisible Creature.
1960 ?m/C **VHS** *NO ⅗⅗*

The House on Skull Mountain The four surviving relatives of a deceased voodoo priestess are in for a bumpy night as they gather at the House on Skull Mountain for the reading of her will.

1974 (PG) 85m/C Victor French, Janee Michelle, Mike Evans, Jean Durand; **D:** Ron Honthaner. **VHS, Beta** $59.98 *FOX* 🐢🐢½

The House on Sorority Row Less-than-harrowing story of what happens when seven sorority sisters have a last fling and get back at their housemother at the same time. *AKA:* House of Evil; Seven Sisters.
1983 90m/C Eileen Davidson, Kathy McNeil, Robin Meloy; **D:** Mark Rosman; **M:** Richard Band. **VHS, Beta** $79.95 *VES* 🐢🐢½

The House on Straw Hill A successful novelist who lives in an isolated farmhouse. Her presence inspires gory hallucinations, lust and violence. *AKA:* Expose.
1976 (R) 84m/C Udo Kier, Linda Hayden, Fiona Richmond; **D:** James Kenelm Clarke. **VHS, Beta** $19.95 *NWV, MED* 🐢½

House on the Edge of the Park A frustrated would-be womanizer takes revenge on a parade of women during an all-night party. *AKA:* La Casa Nel Parco.
1984 91m/C David Hess, Annie Belle, Lorraine De Selle; **D:** Ruggero Deodato. **VHS, Beta** $69.98 *LIV, VES* Woof!

The House on Tombstone Hill An old, abandoned mansion seems like a good investment to a group of friends. Wrong! The original owner is still around and doesn't like strangers coming to visit.
1992 95m/C Doug Gibson, John Cerna, Sarah Newhouse; **D:** J. Riffel; **W:** J. Riffel. **VHS** $89.95 *AIP* 🐢🐢½

House Party Light-hearted, black hip-hop version of a '50s teen comedy with rap duo Kid 'n' Play. After his father grounds him for fighting, a high-schooler attempts all sorts of wacky schemes to get to his friend's party. Sleeper hit features real-life music rappers and some dynamite dance numbers.
1990 (R) 100m/C Christopher Reid, Christopher Martin, Martin Lawrence, Tisha Campbell, Paul Anthony, A.J. Johnson, Full Force, Robin Harris; **D:** Reginald Hudlin; **W:** Reginald Hudlin; **M:** Marcus Miller. **VHS, Beta** $14.95 *COL, FCT, NLC* 🐢🐢🐢

House Party 2: The Pajama Jam Rap stars Kid 'N' Play are back in this hip-hop sequel to the original hit. At Harris University Kid 'N' Play hustle up overdue tuition by holding a campus "jammie jam jam." A stellar cast shines in this rap-powered pajama bash.
1991 (R) 94m/C Christopher Reid, Christopher Martin, Tisha Campbell, Iman, Queen Latifah, Georg Stanford Brown, Martin Lawrence, Eugene Allen, George Anthony Bell, Kamron, Tony Burton, Helen Martin, William Schallert; **D:** Doug McHenry, George Jackson; **W:** Rusty Cundieff, Daryl G. Nickens; **M:** Vassal Benford. **VHS** $19.95 *COL, NLC* 🐢🐢½

House Party 3 Kid is engaged to be married and Play tries to set up a blowout bachelor party. The duo are also working on their record producer careers by trying to sign a feisty female rap group (real life TLC). Strikes out early for easy profanity while never coming within spitting distance of first two flicks.
1994 (R) 93m/C Christopher Reid, Christopher Martin, Angela Means, Tisha Campbell, Bernie Mac, Barbara Edwards, Michael Colyar, David Edwards, Betty Lester, Christopher Tucker; **D:** Eric Meza; **W:** Takashi Bufford; **M:** David Allen Jones. **VHS** *COL, IME* 🐢

The House that Bled to Death Strange things happen to a family when they move into a run-down house where a murder occurred years before.

1981 60m/C Nicholas Ball, Rachel Davies, Brian Croucher, Pat Maynard, Emma Ridley. **VHS, Beta** $29.95 *LIV* 🐢

The House that Dripped Blood A Scotland Yard inspector discovers the history of an English country house while investigating an actor's disappearance. Four horror tales comprise the body of this omnibus creeper, following the successful "Tales from the Crypt" mold. Duffell's debut as director.
1971 (PG) 101m/C Christopher Lee, Peter Cushing, Jon Pertwee, Denholm Elliott, Ingrid Pitt, John Bennett, Tom Adams, Joss Ackland, Chloe Franks; **D:** Peter Duffell; **W:** Robert Bloch. **VHS, Beta** $59.95 *PSM* 🐢🐢½

The House that Vanished Semi-exploitative fare about a beautiful young model who witnesses a murder in a house but later can't find the place. Her boyfriend is skeptical. *AKA:* Scream and Die.
1973 (R) 84m/C Andrea Allan, Karl Lanchbury, Judy Matheson, Maggie Walker; **D:** Joseph Larraz. **VHS, Beta** $14.98 *MED, LIV* 🐢

House Where Evil Dwells An American family is subjected to a reign of terror when they move into an old Japanese house possessed by three deadly samurai ghosts. The setting doesn't upgrade the creepiness of the plot.
1982 (R) 88m/C Edward Albert, Susan George, Doug McClure, Amy Barett; **D:** Kevin Connor. **VHS, Beta** $14.95 *MGM* 🐢½

A House Without a Christmas Tree A frustrated middle-aged man denies his young daughter her one desire—a Christmas tree. Charming made for cable television holiday fare.
1972 90m/C Jason Robards Jr., Lisa Lucas, Mildred Natwick; **D:** Paul Bogart. **VHS, Beta** $14.98 *FXV, FCT* 🐢🐢½

Houseboat Widower Grant with three precocious kids takes up residence on a houseboat with Italian maid Loren who is actually a socialite, incognito. Naturally, they fall in love. Light, fun Hollywood froth.
1958 110m/C Cary Grant, Sophia Loren, Martha Hyer, Eduardo Ciannelli, Murray Hamilton, Harry Guardino; **D:** Melville Shavelson; **W:** Melville Shavelson, Jack Rose; **M:** George Duning. **Beta** $19.95 *PAR* 🐢🐢½

Household Saints Chronicling one family from post-WWII Little Italy through the 1970's, this is a quirky little story about sausage, religion, women, and families (not necessarily in that order). Joseph (D'Onofrio) wins his bride (Ullman) in a pinochle game, much to his superstitious Catholic mother's (Malina) chagrin. The product of that union is a slightly obsessive girl (Taylor), who sees visions and wants to be a saint. Interesting study of Italian-American families, and the roles religion and food play in the culture of Little Italy.
1993 (R) 124m/C Tracey Ullman, Vincent D'Onofrio, Lili Taylor, Judith Malina, Michael Rispoli, Victor Argo, Michael Imperioli, Rachael Bella, Illeana Douglas, Joe Grifasi; **D:** Nancy Savoca; **W:** Richard Guay, Nancy Savoca. **VHS** *COL* 🐢🐢🐢

The Householder An early Merchant-Ivory collaboration featuring a young Indian schoolteacher whose widowed mother arranges his marriage to a woman he doesn't know. The immature couple find their adjustment to marriage fraught with, sometimes amusing, complications. *AKA:* Gharbar.
1963 101m/B Shashi Kapoor, Leela Naidu, Durga Khote; **D:** James Ivory; **W:** Ruth Prawer Jhabvala. **VHS** $79.95 *CVC, ING* 🐢🐢

The Housekeeper Tushingham's portrayal of a deranged housekeeper brings this movie to life even as she kills off her employers. *AKA:* A Judgement in Stone.
1986 (R) 97m/C Rita Tushingham, Ross Petty, Jackie Burroughs, Tom Kneebone, Shelly Peterson, Jessica Stern, Jonathan Crombie; **D:** Ousama Rawi. **VHS, Beta** $39.98 *WAR* 🐢🐢

Housekeeping A quiet but bizarre comedy by Forsyth (his first American film). A pair of orphaned sisters are cared for by their newly arrived eccentric, free-spirited aunt in a small and small-minded community in Oregon in the 1950s. Conventional townspeople attempt to intervene, but the sisters' relationship with their offbeat aunt has become strong enough to withstand the coercion of the townspeople. May move too slowly for some viewers. Based on novel by Marilynne Robinson.
1987 (PG) 117m/C Christine Lahti, Sarah Walker, Andrea Burchill; **D:** Bill Forsyth; **W:** Bill Forsyth; **M:** Michael Gibbs. **VHS, Beta** $89.95 *COL* 🐢🐢🐢

Housemaster In a British boys' school the housemaster is kind and understanding of his sometimes-unruly charges. The stern new headmaster is not, and the students conspire against him. An okay but dated comedy, featuring characters with names like Bimbo and Button. Based on "Bachelor Born" by Ian Hay, a London stage hit at the time.
1938 95m/B Otto Kruger, Diana Churchill, Phillips Holmes, Rene Ray, Walter Hudd, John Wood, Cecil Parker, Michael Shepley, Jimmy Hanley, Rosamund Barnes; **D:** Herbert Brenon. **VHS** $19.95 *NOS, MLB* 🐢🐢½

Housesitter Newton Davis (Martin), an architect/dreamer, builds his high school sweetheart (Delany) a beautiful house and surprises her with a marriage proposal. Delany says no, he has a one-night stand with Gwen (Hawn), and Hawn moves into his empty house and assumes the position of Davis's wife, unbeknownst to him. Gwen spins whoppers of lies and soon has the entire town, including Davis's parents and ex-girlfriend, believing her wacky stories. This romantic screwball comedy is a delight, not only because of Martin and Hawn, but also because of the array of other characters who complicate the stories they spin.
1992 (PG) 102m/C Steve Martin, Goldie Hawn, Dana Delany, Julie Harris, Donald Moffatt, Peter MacNicol, Richard B. Shull, Laurel Cronin, Christopher Durang; **D:** Frank Oz; **W:** Mark Stein, Brian Grazer; **M:** Miles Goodman. **VHS, Beta** $19.98 *MCA, PMS, BTV* 🐢🐢½

Housewife A vengeful black man holds an unhappily married Beverly Hills couple hostage in their home.
1972 (R) 96m/C Yaphet Kotto, Andrew Duggan, Joyce Van Patten, Jeannie Berlin; **D:** Larry Cohen. **VHS, Beta** $19.95 *NWV* 🐢

How Come Nobody's On Our Side? Two out-of-work stuntmen try astrology to find the best time to make some easy money smuggling marijuana out of Mexico.
1973 (PG) 84m/C Adam Roarke, Larry Bishop, Alexandra Hay, Rob Reiner, Penny Marshall. **VHS, Beta** $39.95 *MON* 🐢

How Funny Can Sex Be? Eight risque sketches about love and marriage Italian style.
1976 97m/C Giancarlo Giannini, Laura Antonelli, Dulio Del Prete; **D:** Dino Risi. **VHS, Beta** *FOX* 🐢🐢

How Green was My Valley Compelling story of the trials and tribulations of a Welsh mining family, from the youthful perspective of the youngest child (played by a

13-year-old McDowall). Spans 50 years, from the turn of the century, when coal mining was a difficult but fair-paying way of life, and ends, after unionization, strikes, deaths, and child abuse, with the demise of a town and its culture. Considered by many to be director Ford's finest work. When WWII prevented shooting on location, producer Zanuck built a facsimile Welsh valley in California (although Ford, born Sean Aloysius O'Fearna, was said to have been thinking of his story as taking place in Ireland rather than Wales). Based on the novel by Richard Llewellyn.
1941 118m/B Walter Pidgeon, Maureen O'Hara, Donald Crisp, Anna Lee, Roddy McDowall, John Loder, Sara Allgood, Barry Fitzgerald, Patric Knowles, Rhys Williams, Arthur Shields, Ann Todd, Mae Marsh; *D:* John Ford; *W:* Philip Dunne; *M:* Alfred Newman. Academy Awards '41: Best Black and White Cinematography, Best Director (Ford), Best Interior Decoration, Best Picture, Best Supporting Actor (Crisp); Nominations: Best Film Editing, Best Screenplay, Best Sound, Best Supporting Actress (Allgood), Best Original Score. **VHS, Beta $19.98** *FOX, FUS, BTV* 𝄞𝄞𝄞𝄞

How I Got into College
A slack, uninspired satire about a high school senior who barely manages to get into a local college so he may pursue the girl of his dreams.
1989 (PG-13) 87m/C Corey Parker, Lara Flynn Boyle, Christopher Rydell, Anthony Edwards, Phil Hartman, Brian Doyle-Murray, Nora Dunn, Finn Carter, Charles Rocket; *D:* Steve Holland; *W:* Terrel Seltzer. **VHS, Beta $89.98** *FOX* 𝄞𝄞

How I Learned to Love Women
A British comedy of errors involving a car-loving youth who learns about women and love.
1967 95m/C Anita Ekberg, **VHS, Beta** *NO* 𝄞

How I Won the War
An inept officer must lead his battalion out of England into the Egyptian desert to conquer a cricket field. Indulgent, scarcely amusing Richard Lester comedy; Lennon, in a bit part, provides the brightest moments.
1967 (PG) 111m/C John Lennon, Michael Crawford, Michael Hordern; *D:* Richard Lester; *W:* Charles Wood. **VHS, Beta $59.95** *MGM* 𝄞𝄞

How Many Miles to Babylon?
During WWI, two young men become friends despite their different backgrounds. But one is court-martialed for desertion, and the other is supposed to oversee his execution. Made for British television.
1982 106m/C Daniel Day-Lewis, Christopher Fairbank; *D:* Moira Armstrong. **VHS, Beta $19.98** *FOX, TVC, FUS* 𝄞𝄞

How Sweet It Is!
Typical American family takes a zany European vacation. Looks like a TV sitcom and is about as entertaining. National Lampoon's version is a lot more fun.
1968 99m/C James Garner, Debbie Reynolds, Maurice Ronet, Paul Lynde, Erin Moran, Marcel Dalio, Terry-Thomas; *D:* Jerry Paris; *W:* Jerry Belson. **VHS $59.95** *WAR* 𝄞

How the Grinch Stole Christmas
Classic television Christmas special from the Dr. Seuss book about a Christmas-hating grinch who steals Christmas from the town of Whoville. Fun for the whole family.
1965 26m/C *V:* Boris Karloff. **VHS, Beta $14.95** *MGM, KUI, WTA* 𝄞𝄞𝄞

How the West was Won
A panoramic view of the American West, focusing on the trials, tribulations and travels of three generations of one family, set against the background of wars and historical events. Particularly notable for its impressive cast list and expansive western settings.

1963 (G) 165m/C John Wayne, Carroll Baker, Lee J. Cobb, Spencer Tracy, Gregory Peck, Karl Malden, Robert Preston, Eli Wallach, Henry Fonda, George Peppard, Debbie Reynolds, Carolyn Jones, Richard Widmark, James Stewart, Walter Brennan, Andy Devine, Raymond Massey, Agnes Moorehead, Henry Morgan, Thelma Ritter, Russ Tamblyn; *D:* John Ford, Henry Hathaway, George Marshall; *W:* James R. Webb. Academy Awards '63: Best Film Editing, Best Sound, Best Story & Screenplay; Nominations: Best Art Direction/Set Decoration (Color), Best Color Cinematography, Best Costume Design (Color), Best Picture, Best Original Score; National Board of Review Awards '63: 10 Best Films of the Year. **VHS, Beta $29.98** *MGM* 𝄞𝄞𝄞

How to Be a Perfect Person in Just Three Days
Fun comedy for the whole family shows the efforts of a kid striving for perfection before realizing that individuality is more fun. Based on the book by Stephen Mane. Aired on PBS as part of the "Wonderworks" series.
1984 58m/C Wallace Shawn, Ilan Mitchell-Smith, Hermione Gingold, Joan Micklin Silver. **VHS $29.95** *PME, FCT, HMV* 𝄞𝄞𝄞

How to Beat the High Cost of Living
Three suburban housewives decide to beat inflation by taking up robbery, and they start by planning a heist at the local shopping mall. Comedic talent can't salvage whipped script and direction.
1980 (PG) 105m/C Jessica Lange, Susan St. James, Jane Curtin, Richard Benjamin, Eddie Albert, Dabney Coleman, Fred Willard, Cathryn Damon, Art Metrano; *D:* Robert Scheerer. **VHS, Beta $69.98** *LIV, VES* 𝄞½

How to Break Up a Happy Divorce
A divorced woman starts a vigorous campaign to win her ex-husband back by dating another man to make him jealous. Lightweight made-for-television comedy.
1976 74m/C Barbara Eden, Hal Linden, Peter Bonerz, Marcia Rodd, Harold Gould; *D:* Jerry Paris. **VHS, Beta $34.95** *WOV* 𝄞𝄞

How to Commit Marriage
Hope and Wyman have been married for 20 years when they decide to divorce—just when their daughter (Cameron) decides to marry her college boyfriend (Matheson). His father (Gleason) tries to stop the wedding, fails, but sticks around to cause more trouble. Subplots involve the divorced duo's new loves and the fact that they're about to become grandparents but the comedy is completely uninspired.
1969 (PG) 96m/C Bob Hope, Jane Wyman, Jackie Gleason, Joanna Cameron, Tim Matheson, Beatrice Arthur, Leslie Nielsen, Tina Louise, Paul Stewart, Prof. Irwin Corey; *D:* Norman Panama; *W:* Ben Starr, Michael Kanin; *M:* Joseph J. Lilley. **VHS $14.95** *COL* 𝄞½

How to Get Ahead in Advertising
A cynical, energetic satire about a manic advertising idea man who becomes so disgusted with trying to sell a pimple cream that he quits the business. Ultimately he grows a pimple of his own that talks and begins to take over his life. Acerbic and hilarious.
1989 (R) 95m/C Richard E. Grant, Rachel Ward, Susan Wooldridge, Mick Ford, Richard Wilson, John Shrapnel, Jacqueline Tong; *D:* Bruce Robinson; *W:* Bruce Robinson; *M:* David Dundas, Rick Wentworth. **VHS, Beta** *NO* 𝄞𝄞

How to Kill 400 Duponts
Bumbling Scotland Yard detective is off to France to stop a master criminal from trying to kill off the rich Dupont family. Why? So he'll be the only one left with any claim to the remaining family fortune.
1965 98m/C Terry-Thomas, Johnny Dorelli, Margaret Lee. **VHS, Beta** *VCD* 𝄞

How to Make a Doll
Lewis' sex farce about an extremely shy professor whose ineptness with women inspires him to invent android females to satisfy his sexual needs.
1968 ?m/C Robert Wood, Jim Vance, Pamela Rhea; *D:* Herschell Gordon Lewis. **VHS $24.99** *MOV, TPV* 𝄞

How to Make a Monster
In-joke from the creators of youth-oriented '50s AIP monster flicks; a mad makeup man's homebrew greasepaint brainwashes the actors. Disguised as famous monsters, they kill horror-hating movie execs. Mild fun if—and only if—you treasure the genre. Conway repeats his role as Teenage Frankenstein, but the studio couldn't get Michael Landon for the Teenage Werewolf.
1958 73m/B Robert Harris, Paul Brinegar, Gary Conway, Gary Clarke, Malcolm Atterbury, Dennis Cross, John Ashley, Morris Ankrum, Walter Reed, Heather Ames; *D:* Herbert L. Strock. **VHS $9.95** *COL, MLB* 𝄞𝄞

How to Marry a Millionaire
Three models pool their money and rent a lavish apartment in a campaign to trap millionaire husbands. Clever performances by three lead women salvage a vehicle intended primarily to bolster Monroe's career. The opening street scene, with the accompanying theme music, was a state-of-the-art achievement of screen and sound in the first movie to be filmed in CinemaScope. Remake of "The Greeks Had a Word for Them."
1953 96m/C Lauren Bacall, Marilyn Monroe, Betty Grable, William Powell, David Wayne, Cameron Mitchell; *D:* Jean Negulesco; *W:* Nunnally Johnson; *M:* Alfred Newman. **VHS, Beta $14.98** *FOX* 𝄞𝄞

How to Murder Your Wife
While drunk, a cartoonist marries an unknown woman and then frantically tries to think of ways to get rid of her — even contemplating murder. Frantic comedy is tailored for Lemmon.
1964 118m/C Jack Lemmon, Terry-Thomas, Virna Lisi, Eddie Mayehoff, Sidney Blackmer, Claire Trevor, Mary Wickes, Jack Albertson; *D:* Richard Quine; *W:* George Axelrod. **VHS, Beta $19.95** *MGM* 𝄞𝄞𝄞

How to Pick Up Girls
Comic tale based on Eric Weber's bestseller follows the exploits of a small-town boy who moves to New York City and finds the secret to picking up women. Made for television.
1978 93m/C Desi Arnaz Jr., Bess Armstrong, Fred McCarren, Polly Bergen, Richard Dawson, Alan King, Abe Vigoda, Deborah Raffin; *D:* Bill Persky. **VHS, Beta $19.98** *TWE* 𝄞𝄞

How to Seduce a Woman
A playboy attempts to bed five supposedly unattainable women.
1974 108m/C Angus Duncan, Marty Ingels, Lillian Randolph. **VHS, Beta $39.95** *PSM* Woof!

How to Stuff a Wild Bikini
Tired next to last feature in the overlong tradition of Frankie and Annette doing the beach thing, featuring a pregnant Funicello (though this is hidden and not part of the plot). Avalon actually has only a small role as the jealous boyfriend trying to see if Annette will remain faithful while he's away on military duty. Keaton is the witch doctor who helps Frankie keep Annette true. "Playboy" playmates wander about in small swimsuits, garage band extraordinare "The Kingsmen" play themselves, and Brian Wilson of the "Beach Boys" drops by. Followed by "Ghost in the Invisible Bikini," the only movie in the series that isn't on video. ♫After the Party; Better Be Ready; Follow Your Leader; Give Her Lovin'; How About Us?; How to Stuff a Wild

Bikini; I'm the Boy Next Door; Madison Avenue; The Perfect Boy.

1965 90m/C Annette Funicello, Dwayne Hickman, Frankie Avalon, Beverly Adams, Buster Keaton, Harvey Lembeck, Mickey Rooney, Brian Donlevy, Jody McCrea, John Ashley, Marianne Gaba, Len Lesser, Irene Tsu, Bobbi Shaw, Luree Holmes; *D:* William Asher; *W:* William Asher, Leo Townsend; *M:* Les Baxter. **VHS, Beta** *NO* 🐾🐾

How to Succeed in Business without Really Trying Classic musical comedy about a window-washer who charms his way to the top of a major company. Robert Morse repeats his Tony winning Broadway role. Loosely based on a non-fiction book of the same title by Shepherd Mead, whose book Morse purchases on his first day of work. Excellent transfer of stage to film, with choreography by Moreda expanding Bob Fosse's original plan. Dynamite from start to finish. ♫I Believe In You; The Company Way; Coffee Break; The Brotherhood of Man; A Secretary Is Not A Toy; Grand Old Ivy; Been A Long Day; Rosemary; Finch's Frolic.

1967 121m/C Robert Morse, Michele Lee, Rudy Vallee, Anthony Teague, George Fenneman, Maureen Arthur; *D:* David Swift; *W:* David Swift, Abe Burrows; *M:* Frank Loesser. **VHS $19.95** *MGM* 🐾🐾🐾½

How to Succeed with Girls Marginally funny comedy about pious wax salesman (Leder) with a secret fantasy life who unwittingly enlists the aid of his wife's lover (Schrier) to help him overcome his shyness. Several fantasy sequences (in color; the rest of the film is black and white) include an Arabian harem, an old West saloon, and a science laboratory. Brubaker's secretary (Mathes) was Playboy's Miss June 1962. Pete's girlfriend (McClanahan of television's Golden Girls) is credited as either Patty Leigh or Helen Goodman.

1964 83m/C Marissa Mathes, Rue McClanahan, Paul Leder, Leon Schrier; *D:* Edward A. Biery. **VHS $23.00** *SMW, TPV* 🐾

How U Like Me Now? Comedy set on Chicago's south side focuses on Thomas, an attractive but unmotivated guy with low earning potential, and his girl Valerie, a pretentious overachiever who wants much more than he's able to offer. Robert's second directorial effort offers a fresh look at African Americans on film with plenty of lively supporting characters and witty dialogue. Filmed on a $600,000 budget.

1992 (R) 109m/C Darnell Williams, Salli Richardson, Daniel Gardner, Raymond Whitefield, Debra Crable, Jonelle Kennedy, Byron Stewart, Charnele Brown, Daryll Roberts; *D:* Daryll Roberts; *W:* Daryll Roberts; *M:* Kahil El Zabar, Chuck Webb. **VHS** *MCA* 🐾🐾🐾

Howard the Duck A big-budget Lucasfilm adaptation of the short-lived Marvel comic book about an alien, resembling a cigar-chomping duck, who gets sucked into a vortex, lands on Earth and saves it from the Dark Overlords. While he's at it, he befriends a nice young lady in a punk rock band and starts to fall in love. A notorious box-office bomb and one of the '80s' worst major films, although it seems to work well with children, given the simple story line and good special effects.

1986 (PG) 111m/C Lea Thompson, Jeffrey Jones, Tim Robbins; *D:* Willard Huyck; *W:* Willard Huyck, Gloria Katz; *M:* Sylvester Levay, John Barry. **VHS, Beta $14.98** *MCA* 🐾

Howard's End E.M. Forster's 1910 novel about property, privilege, class differences, and Edwardian society is brought to enchanting life by the Merchant Ivory team. A tragic series of events occurs after two impulsive sisters become involved with a working class couple and a wealthy family. Tragedy aside, this is a visually beautiful effort with subtle performances where a glance or a gesture says as much as any dialog. The winner of numerous awards and wide critical acclaim. Thompson is especially notable as the compassionate Margaret, while Hopkins plays the repressed English gentleman brilliantly.

1992 (PG) 143m/C Anthony Hopkins, Emma Thompson, Helena Bonham Carter, Vanessa Redgrave, James Wilby, Sam West, Jemma Redgrave, Nicola Duffett, Prunella Scales, Joseph Bennett; *Cameos:* Simon Callow; *D:* James Ivory; *W:* Ruth Prawer Jhabvala. Academy Awards '92: Best Actress (Thompson), Best Adapted Screenplay, Best Art Direction/Set Decoration; Nominations: Best Cinematography, Best Costume Design, Best Director (Ivory), Best Picture, Best Supporting Actress (Redgrave), Best Original Score; Cannes Film Festival '92: Best Film; British Academy Awards '93: Best Actress (Thompson); Chicago Film Critics Awards '92: Best Actress (Thompson); Golden Globe Awards '93: Best Actress—Drama (Thompson); Los Angeles Film Critics Association Awards '92: Best Actress (Thompson); National Board of Review Awards '92: 10 Best Films of the Year, Best Actress (Thompson), Best Director (Ivory); National Society of Film Critics Awards '92: Best Actress (Thompson). **VHS, 8mm $19.95** *COL, CRC, MOV* 🐾🐾🐾🐾

The Howards of Virginia A lavish Hollywood historical epic, detailing the adventures of a backwoodsman and the rich Virginia girl he marries as their families become involved in the Revolutionary War. *AKA:* Tree of Liberty.

1940 117m/B Cary Grant, Martha Scott, Cedric Hardwicke, Alan Marshal, Richard Carlson, Paul Kelly, Irving Bacon, Tom Drake, Anne Revere, Ralph Byrd, Alan Ladd; *D:* Frank Lloyd. **VHS, Beta $69.95** *COL* 🐾🐾½

The Howling A pretty television reporter takes a rest at a clinic and discovers slowly that its denizens are actually werewolves. Crammed with inside jokes, this horror comedy pioneered the use of the body-altering prosthetic make-up (by Rob Bottin) now essential for on-screen man-to-wolf transformations. At last count, followed by five sequels.

1981 (R) 91m/C Dee Wallace Stone, Patrick Macnee, Dennis Dugan, Christopher Stone, Belinda Balaski, Kevin McCarthy, John Carradine, Slim Pickens, Elisabeth Brooks, Robert Picardo, Dick Miller; *D:* Joe Dante; *W:* John Sayles, Terence H. Winkless; *M:* Pino Donaggio. **VHS, Beta $14.95** *COL, SUE* 🐾🐾🐾

Howling 2: Your Sister is a Werewolf A policeman (the brother of one of the first film's victims) investigates a Transylvanian werewolf-ridden castle and gets mangled for his trouble. Followed by four more sequels.

1985 (R) 91m/C Sybil Danning, Christopher Lee, Annie McEnroe, Marsha Hunt, Reb Brown, Ferdinand "Ferdy" Mayne; *D:* Philippe Mora. **VHS, Beta $14.98** *REP* 🐾

Howling 3: The Marsupials Australians discover a pouch-laden form of lycanthrope. Third "Howling" (surprise), second from Mora and better than his first.

1987 (PG-13) 94m/C Barry Otto, Imogen Annesley, Dasha Blahova, Max Fairchild, Ralph Cotterill, Leigh Biolos, Frank Thring, Michael Pate; *D:* Philippe Mora. **VHS, Beta $19.95** *LIV* 🐾

Howling 4: The Original Nightmare A woman novelist hears the call of the wild while taking a rest cure in the country. This werewolf tale has nothing to do with the other sequels.

1988 (R) 94m/C Romy Windsor, Michael T. Weiss, Antony Hamilton, Susanne Severeid, Lamya Derval; *D:* John Hough. **VHS, Beta $14.95** *LIV* 🐾

Howling 5: The Rebirth The fifth in the disconnected horror series, in which a varied group of people stranded in a European castle are individually hunted down by evil.

1989 (R) 99m/C Philip Davis, Victoria Catlin, Elizabeth She, Ben Cole, William Shockley; *D:* Neal Sundstrom. **VHS, Beta $14.95** *LIV* 🐾

Howling 6: The Freaks Hideous werewolf suffers from multiple sequels, battles with vampire at freak show, and discovers that series won't die. Next up: "Howling 7: The Nightmare that Won't Go Away."

1990 (R) 102m/C Brendan Hughes, Michelle Matheson, Sean Gregory Sullivan, Antonio Fargas, Carol Lynley, Jered Barclay, Bruce Martyn Payne; *D:* Hope Perello. **VHS $14.98** *LIV, IME* 🐾½

Huck and the King of Hearts When a cardshark and his young friend Huck travel the country searching for Huck's long-lost grandfather, they find adventure everywhere from Hannibal, Missouri to L.A. to Vegas. Loose, contemporary adaptation of Mark Twain's "The Adventures of Huckleberry Finn."

1993 (PG) 103m/C Chauncey Leopardi, Graham Greene, Dee Wallace Stone, Joe Piscopo, John Astin, Gretchen Becker; *D:* Michael Keusch; *W:* Christopher Sturgeon; *M:* Chris Saranec. **VHS, Beta $92.95** *PSM* 🐾🐾½

Huckleberry Finn The musical version of the Mark Twain story about the adventures a young boy and a runaway slave encounter along the Mississippi River.

1974 (G) 114m/C Jeff East, Paul Winfield, Harvey Korman, David Wayne, Arthur O'Connell, Gary Merrill, Natalie Trundy, Lucille Benson; *D:* J. Lee Thompson. **VHS, Beta $14.95** *MGM, FOX, FCT* 🐾🐾

Huckleberry Finn Whitewashed version of the Twain classic features post Opie Howard as the incredible Huck and Dano as the sharp witted short storyist. Stars four members of the Howard clan. Made for TV.

1975 (G) 74m/C Ron Howard, Donny Most, Royal Dano, Antonio Fargas, Jack Elam, Merle Haggard, Rance Howard, Jean Howard, Clint Howard, Shug Fisher, Sarah Selby, Bill Erwin; *D:* Robert Totten. **VHS, Beta $14.98** *KUI, FXV, FCT* 🐾🐾½

Huckleberry Finn A version of the classic Mark Twain novel about the adventures a young boy and a runaway slave encounter as they travel down the Mississippi River.

1981 72m/C VHS, Beta $59.98 *LIV, WTA* 🐾½

The Hucksters Account of a man looking for honesty and integrity in the radio advertising world and finding little to work with. All performances are excellent; but Greenstreet, as the tyrannical head of a soap company, is a stand out. Deborah Kerr's American debut.

1947 115m/B Clark Gable, Deborah Kerr, Sydney Greenstreet, Adolphe Menjou, Ava Gardner, Keenan Wynn, Edward Arnold; *D:* Jack Conway. **VHS, Beta $19.98** *MGM, FCT* 🐾🐾🐾

Hud Newman is a hard-driving, hard-drinking, woman-chasing young man whose life is a revolt against the principles of stern father Douglas. Neal is outstanding as the family housekeeper. Excellent photography.

1963 112m/B Paul Newman, Melvyn Douglas, Patricia Neal, Brandon de Wilde, John Ashley; *D:* Martin Ritt; *W:* Irving Ravetch, Harriet Frank Jr.; *M:* Elmer Bernstein. Academy Awards '63: Best Actress (Neal), Best Black and White

Cinematography, Best Supporting Actor (Douglas); Nominations: Best Actor (Newman), Best Adapted Screenplay, Best Art Direction/Set Decoration (B & W), Best Director (Ritt); National Board of Review Awards '63: 10 Best Films of the Year, Best Actress (Neal), Best Supporting Actor (Douglas). **VHS, Beta** $69.95 *PAR, BTV ♨♨♨♨*

Hudson Hawk A big-budget star vehicle with little else going for it. Willis plays a master burglar released from prison, only to find himself trapped by the CIA into one last theft. Everyone in the cast tries to be extra funny, resulting in a disjointed situation where no one is. Weakly plotted, poorly paced.
1991 (R) 95m/C Bruce Willis, Danny Aiello, Andie MacDowell, James Coburn, Sandra Bernhard, Richard E. Grant, Frank Stallone; **D:** Michael Lehmann; **W:** Steven E. de Souza, Daniel Waters. **VHS, Beta, 8mm** $19.95 *COL ♨*

The Hudsucker Proxy In an effort to scare off would-be investors in a public stock offering dim bulb mailboy Robbins is installed as the Prez of Hudsucker Industries (in 1958) by Board Director Newman after corporate magnate Hudsucker (Durning) takes a swan dive from the 44th floor. First truly mainstream effort from the maverick Coen brothers is peppered with obscure references to numerous points on the historical map of cinematic style, and trots out an equally old but instantly recognizable story. Will delight Coen fans, but may be too dark for others. Destined to keep art history profs busy for decades.
1993 (PG) 115m/C Tim Robbins, Paul Newman, Jennifer Jason Leigh, Charles Durning, John Mahoney, Jim True, Bill Cobbs; **Cameos:** Peter Gallagher; **D:** Joel Coen; **W:** Joel Coen, Sam Raimi, Ethan Coen; **M:** Carter Burwell. **VHS** *NYR ♨♨♨*

Hue and Cry Nobody believes a young boy when he discovers crooks are sending coded messages in a weekly children's magazine. A detective writer finally believes his story and they set off to capture the crooks.
1947 82m/B Alastair Sim, Jack Warner, Frederick Piper, Jack Lambert, Joan Dowling; **D:** Charles Crichton. **VHS** $16.95 *SNC, NOS, FCT ♨♨♨*

Hugh Hefner: Once Upon a Time Fascinating look at the "Bunny" king and Playboy Enterprises. His celebrated life of isolation and excess at the Playboy mansions is portrayed as is the founding of "Playboy" magazine in 1953 and the Playboy clubs (with their notorious Bunnies). Includes interviews, home movies, and photographs. Admiring yet not without a few sharp edges.
1992 (R) 91m/C Hugh Hefner; **D:** Robert Heath. **VHS** $89.95 *UND, BTV ♨♨♨*

Hughes & Harlow: Angels in Hell The story of the romance that occurred between Howard Hughes and Jean Harlow during the filming of "Hell's Angels" in 1930.
1977 94m/C Lindsay Bloom, Victor Holchak, David McLean, Royal Dano, Adam Roarke, Linda Cristal; **D:** Larry Buchanan. **VHS, Beta** *NO ♨*

Hugo the Hippo Animated musical about a forlorn baby hippo who struggles to survive in the human jungle of old Zanzibar.
1976 (G) 90m/C V: Paul Lynde, Burl Ives, Robert Morley, Marie Osmond. **VHS, Beta** $49.98 *FOX ♨♨*

Hula Unflappable flapper Bow and her gang frolic on a Pacific island.
1928 64m/B Clara Bow, Clive Brook, Patricia Dupont, Arnold Kent, Agaslino Borgato; **D:** Victor Fleming. **VHS, Beta** $19.95 *GPV, FCT ♨½*

Hullabaloo Over Georgie & Bonnie's Pictures A young maharajah has inherited a priceless collection of Indian miniature paintings he doesn't appreciate and which his greedy sister is anxious for him to sell. They're beseiged by art dealers and collectors who learn about the treasure trove and will do anything to possess it. Among them are the British Ashcroft, who wants the art for the British Museum, and competing American collector Pine. Made for British television.
1978 85m/C Victor Banerjee, Aparna Sen, Larry Pine, Saeed Jaffrey, Peggy Ashcroft; **D:** James Ivory; **W:** Ruth Prawer Jhabvala. **VHS, Beta** $19.95 *SUE, ING, NLC ♨♨½*

Human Beasts Jewel robbers face a tribe of hungry cannibals.
1980 90m/C Paul Naschy, Eiko Nagashima; **D:** Paul Naschy; **W:** Paul Naschy. **VHS, Beta** *NO ♨*

The Human Comedy A small-town boy experiences love and loss and learns the meaning of true faith during WWII. Straight, unapologetically sentimental version of the William Saroyan novel.
1943 117m/B Mickey Rooney, Frank Morgan, James Craig, Fay Bainter, Ray Collins, Donna Reed, Van Johnson, Barry Nelson, Robert Mitchum, Jackie "Butch" Jenkins; **D:** Clarence Brown; **W:** William Saroyan. Academy Awards '43: Best Story; Nominations: Best Actor (Rooney), Best Black and White Cinematography, Best Director (Brown), Best Picture. **VHS, Beta** $24.98 *MGM ♨♨♨½*

The Human Condition: A Soldier's Prayer A Japanese pacifist escapes from his commanders and allows himself to be captured by Russian troops, hoping for better treatment as a P.O.W. The final part of the trilogy preceded by "The Human Condition: No Greater Love" and "The Human Condition: Road to Eternity." In Japanese with English subtitles.
1961 190m/B Tatsuya Nakadai, Michiyo Aratama, Yusuke Kawazu, Tamao Nakamura, Chishu Ryu, Taketoshi Naito, Reiko Hitomi, Kyoko Kishida, Keijiro Morozumi, Koji Kiyomura, Nobuo Kaneko, Fujio Suga; **D:** Masaki Kobayashi. **VHS, Beta** $59.95 *ING ♨♨♨*

The Human Condition: No Greater Love First of a three-part series of films. A pacifist is called into military service and subsequently sent to a run a military mining camp. A gripping look at one man's attempt to retain his humanity in the face of war. Followed by "The Human Condition: Road to Eternity" and "The Human Condition: A Soldier's Prayer." In Japanese with English subtitles.
1958 200m/B Tatsuya Nakadai, Michiyo Aratama, So Yamamura, Eitaro Ozawa, Akira Ishihama, Chikage Awashima, Ineko Arima, Keiji Sada, Shinji Nambara, Seiji Miyaguchi, Toru Abe, Masao Mishima, Eijiro Tono, Yasushi Nagata, Yoshio Kosugi; **D:** Masaki Kobayashi. **VHS, Beta** $59.95 *ING ♨♨♨*

The Human Condition: Road to Eternity A Japanese pacifist is on punishment duty in Manchuria where he is beaten by sadistic officers who try to destroy his humanity. The second part of the trilogy, preceded by "The Human Condition: No Greater Love" and followed by "The Human Condition: A Soldier's Prayer." In Japanese with English subtitles. *AKA:* No Greater Love; Ningen No Joken.
1959 180m/B Tatsuya Nakadai, Michiyo Aratama, Kokinji Katsura, Jun Tatara, Michio Minami, Keiji Sada, Minoru Chiaki, Ryohei Uchida, Kan Yanagidani, Kenjiro Uemura, Yusuke Kawazu, Susumu Fujita; **D:** Masaki Kobayashi. **VHS, Beta** $59.95 *ING ♨♨♨*

Human Desire Femme fatale Grahame and jealous husband Crawford turn out the lights on Crawford's boss (seems there's some confusion about how Miss Gloria managed to convince the guy to let her hubby have his job back). Ford's wise to them but plays see no evil because he's gone crackers for Grahame, who by now has decided she'd like a little help to rid herself of an unwanted husband. Bleak, melodramatic, full of big heat, its Lang through and through. Based on the Emile Zola novel "La Bete Humaine," which inspired Renoir's 1938 telling as well.
1954 90m/B Glenn Ford, Gloria Grahame, Broderick Crawford, Edgar Buchanan, Kathleen Case; **D:** Fritz Lang. **VHS** *GKK ♨♨½*

The Human Duplicators Kiel is an alien who has come to Earth to make androids out of important folk, thus allowing the "galaxy beings" to take over. Cheap stuff, but earnest performances make this more fun than it should be.
1964 82m/C George Nader, Barbara Nichols, George Macready, Dolores Faith, Hugh Beaumont, Richard Kiel, Richard Arlen; **D:** Hugo Grimaldi. **VHS, Beta** $39.95 *LIV ♨♨½*

Human Experiments Psychiatrist in a women's prison conducts a group of experiments in which he destroys the "criminal instinct" in the inmates through brute fear.
1979 (R) 82m/C Linda Haynes, Jackie Coogan, Aldo Ray; **D:** Gregory Goodell. **VHS, Beta** *NO ♨*

The Human Factor Kennedy stars as a computer expert who tracks down his family's murderers using technology. Bloody and violent.
1975 (R) 96m/C George Kennedy, John Mills, Raf Vallone, Rita Tushingham, Barry Sullivan, Arthur Franz; **D:** Edward Dmytryk; **M:** Ennio Morricone. **VHS, Beta** $39.95 *LIV ♨½*

The Human Factor Unexciting spy caper has a British Secret Service agent (Williamson) betraying his country in order to aid a friend. As a result of his actions an innocent man is killed and Williamson is forced to defect to the Soviet Union. Based on a novel by Graham Greene.
1979 (R) 115m/C Nicol Williamson, Richard Attenborough, John Gielgud, Derek Jacobi, Robert Morley, Ann Todd, Richard Vernon, Iman; **D:** Otto Preminger; **W:** Tom Stoppard. **VHS** $19.98 *MGM ♨♨½*

Human Gorilla A thriller involving a mad scientist, an insane asylum, a reporter, and various other mysterious trappings. *AKA:* Behind Locked Doors.
1948 58m/B Richard Carlson, Lucille Bremer, Tor Johnson. **VHS, Beta** $19.95 *NO ♨*

Human Hearts A creaky old silent starring "Phantom of the Opera" leading lady Philbin. A family is torn apart by a con man and his femme fatale.
1922 99m/B House Peters, Russell Simpson, Mary Philbin. **VHS, Beta, 8mm** $24.95 *YYY ♨♨*

The Human Monster Scotland Yard inspector investigates five drownings of the blind patients a phony Dr. Orloff (Lugosi) is exploiting for insurance money. Superior Lugosi effort that's modestly violent and tasteless. Based on the Edgar Wallace novel. *AKA:* Dark Eyes of London.
1939 73m/B Bela Lugosi, Hugh Williams, Greta Gynt; **D:** Walter Summers; **W:** Walter Summers. **VHS, Beta** $19.95 *NOS, MRV, SNC ♨♨½*

The Human Shield A man risks his life on a mission to save his brother during the Persian Gulf War.
1992 (R) 88m/C Michael Dudikoff, Tommy Hinkley, Steve Inwood; **D:** Ted Post. **VHS** $89.99 *WAR, CAN ♨*

The Human Vapor A normal human being has the ability to vaporize himself at will and use it to terrorize Tokyo. *AKA: Gasu Ningen Daiichigo.*
1968 81m/C VHS, Beta $19.95 *GEM, PSM, CNG* 𝄃

Humanoid Defender A made-for-television film about a scientist and an android rebelling against the government that wants to use the android as a warfare prototype.
1985 94m/C Terence Knox, Gary Kasper, Aimee Eccles, William Lucking; *D:* William Lucking. VHS, Beta $39.95 *MCA* 𝄃𝄃

Humanoids from the Deep Mutated salmon-like monsters rise from the depths of the ocean and decide to chop on some bikinied babes. Violent and bloody. *AKA: Monster.*
1980 (R) 81m/C Doug McClure, Ann Turkel, Vic Morrow, Cindy Weintraub, Anthony Penya, Denise Balik; *D:* Barbara Peeters; *M:* James Horner. VHS, Beta *WAR, OM Woof!*

Humongous Brain-dead bevy of teens shipwreck on an island where they encounter a deranged mutant giant who must kill to survive. You'll be rooting for the monster.
1982 (R) 93m/C Janet Julian, David Wallace, Janet Baldwin; *D:* Paul Lynch. VHS, Beta $14.98 *SUE, NLC Woof!*

Humoresque A talented but struggling young musician finds a patron in the married, wealthy, and older Crawford. His appreciation is not as romantic as she hoped. Stunning performance from Crawford, with excellent supporting cast, including a young Robert Blake. Fine music sequences (Isaac Stern dubbed the violin), and lush production values. Laserdisc version features the original movie trailer.
1946 123m/B Joan Crawford, John Garfield, Oscar Levant, J. Carroll Naish, Joan Chandler, Tom D'Andrea, Peggy Knudsen, Ruth Nelson, Craig Stevens, Paul Cavanagh, Richard Gaines, John Abbott, Robert (Bobby) Blake; *D:* Jean Negulesco. VHS $19.98 *MGM, BTV, FCT* 𝄃𝄃𝄃½

The Hunchback of Notre Dame The first film version of Victor Hugo's novel about the tortured hunchback bellringer of Notre Dame Cathedral, famous for the contortions of Lon Chaney's self-transformations via improvised makeup. Silent.
1923 100m/B Lon Chaney Sr., Patsy Ruth Miller, Norman Kerry, Ernest Torrence; *D:* Wallace Worsley. VHS $19.98 *KIV, MRV, NOS* 𝄃𝄃𝄃

The Hunchback of Notre Dame Best Hollywood version of the Victor Hugo classic, infused with sweep, sadness and an attempt at capturing a degree of spirited, Hugoesque detail. Laughton is Quasimodo, a deformed Parisian bellringer, who provides sanctuary to a young gypsy woman accused by church officials of being a witch. The final scene of the townspeople storming the cathedral remains a Hollywood classic. Great performances all around; the huge facade of the Notre Dame cathedral was constructed on a Hollywood set for this film. Remake of several earlier films, including 1923's Lon Chaney silent. Remade in 1957 and later for television.
1939 117m/B Charles Laughton, Maureen O'Hara, Edmond O'Brien, Cedric Hardwicke, Thomas Mitchell, George Zucco, Alan Marshal, Walter Hampden, Harry Davenport, Curt Bois, George Tobias, Rod La Rocque; *D:* William Dieterle; *W:* Sonya Levien, Bruno Frank; *M:* Alfred Newman. VHS, Beta $19.95 *RKO, MED, CCB* 𝄃𝄃𝄃𝄃

The Hunchback of Notre Dame It's not often that a classic novel is remade into a classic movie that's remade into a made-for-TV reprise, and survives its multiple renderings. But it's not often a cast so rich in stage trained actors is assembled on the small screen. Hopkins gives a textured, pre-Hannibal Lecter interpretation of Quasimodo, the Hunchback in Hugo's eponymous novel. Impressive model of the cathedral by production designer John Stoll. *AKA: Hunchback.*
1982 (PG) 102m/C Anthony Hopkins, Derek Jacobi, Lesley-Anne Down, John Gielgud, Tim Pigott-Smith, Rosalie Crutchley, Robert Powell; *D:* Michael Tuchner. VHS $89.95 *VMK* 𝄃𝄃𝄃

Hundra A warrior queen vows revenge when her all-female tribe is slain by men. Nothing can stop her fierce vendetta—except love.
1985 96m/C Laurene Landon, John Gaffari, Ramiro Oliveros, Marissa Casel; *D:* Matt Cimber; *M:* Ennio Morricone. VHS, Beta $59.95 *MED* 𝄃

A Hungarian Fairy Tale Political satire meets fantasy in a magical tale of a fatherless young boy searching for a surrogate dad. Unusual characters as well as an homage to Mozart's "The Magic Flute." In Hungarian with English subtitles. *AKA: Hol Volt, Hol Nem Volt.*
1987 97m/B Arpad Vermes, Maria Varga, Frantisek Husak, Eszter Csakanyi, Szilvia Toth, Judith Pogany, Geza Balkay; *D:* Gyula Gazdag. VHS $59.95 *EVD, ING* 𝄃𝄃𝄃

Hungarian Rhapsody In 1911, a Hungarian nobleman joins the ranks of the rebelling peasants in order to oppose his brother, who represents aristocratic repression. One of Jancso's clearest political films, and one that continues the filmmaker's experiments with long, uncut sequences and dynamic mise-en-scene. In Hungarian with English subtitles.
1978 101m/C Gyorgy Cserhalmi, Lajos Balaszovits, Gabor Koncz, Bertalan Solti; *D:* Miklos Jancso. VHS, Beta $59.95 *FCT, AUD* 𝄃𝄃𝄃

Hunger In the late 1800's a starving Norwegian writer, unable to sell his work, rejects charity out of pride, and retains his faith in his talent. Based on a novel "Sult" by Knut Hamsun. In Danish with English subtitles.
1966 100m/B Per Oscarsson, Gunnel Lindblom. VHS $49.95 *FCT, ING, CVC* 𝄃𝄃

The Hunger A beautiful 2000-year-old vampire needs new blood when she realizes that her current lover, Bowie, is aging fast. Visually sumptuous but sleepwalking modern vampire tale, complete with soft-focus lesbian love scenes between Deneuve and Sarandon. Features a letterboxed screen and original movie trailer on the laserdisc format.
1983 (R) 100m/C Catherine Deneuve, David Bowie, Susan Sarandon, Cliff DeYoung, Ann Magnuson, Dan Hedaya, Willem Dafoe; *D:* Tony Scott; *W:* Michael Thomas. VHS, Beta $79.95 *MGM* 𝄃𝄃

Hunk A computer nerd sells his soul to the devil for a muscular, beach-blonde physique. Answers the question, "Was it worth it?"
1987 (PG) 102m/C John Allen Nelson, Steve Levitt, Deborah Shelton, Rebecca Bush, James Coco, Avery Schreiber; *D:* Lawrence Bassoff. VHS, Beta $79.95 *COL* 𝄃𝄃

The Hunt A teenage boy accompanies three Spanish Civil War veterans on what is supposed to be a friendly rabbit hunt. Things turn violent, however, when old rivalries and tensions begin to surface. In Spanish with English subtitles. *AKA: La Caza.*
1967 93m/B Alfredo Mayo, Ismael Merlo, Jose Maria Prada, Emilio Gutierrez-Caba, Fernando Sanchez Polack; *D:* Carlos Saura. VHS $39.95 *ING, TPV, CVC* 𝄃𝄃𝄃

The Hunt for Red October Based on Tom Clancy's blockbuster novel, a high-tech Cold War yarn about a Soviet nuclear sub turning rogue and heading straight for U.S. waters, as both the U.S. and the U.S.S.R. try to stop it. Complicated, ill-plotted potboiler that succeeds breathlessly due to the cast and McTiernan's tommy-gun direction. Introduces the character of CIA analyst Jack Ryan who returns in "Patriot Games," though in the guise of Harrison Ford.
1990 (PG) 137m/C Sean Connery, Alec Baldwin, Richard Jordan, Scott Glenn, Joss Ackland, Sam Neill, James Earl Jones, Peter Firth, Tim Curry, Courtney B. Vance, Jeffrey Jones, Fred Dalton Thompson; *D:* John McTiernan; *W:* Larry Ferguson, Donald Stewart; *M:* Basil Poledouris. Academy Awards '90: Best Sound Effects Editing; Nominations: Best Film Editing, Best Sound. VHS, Beta, 8mm, CDV $14.95 *PAR, SUP* 𝄃𝄃𝄃

The Hunt for the Night Stalker Another one of those True-Detective quickies so beloved by network TV, following two hardworking L.A. cops who tracked down satanic serial killer Richard Ramirez in the mid-1980s. It originally aired (under the title "Manhunt: The Search for the Night Stalker") on the date of the killer's death-sentence verdict; the videotape lacks that particular timely sparkle.
1991 (PG-13) 95m/C Richard Jordan, A. Martinez, Lisa Eilbacher, Julie Carmen, Alan Feinstein; *D:* Bruce Seth Green. VHS $19.95 *ACA* 𝄃𝄃

Hunt the Man Down An innocent man is charged with murder, and a public defender must find the real killer before time runs out.
1950 68m/B Gig Young, Lynn (Mary Hart) Roberts, Gerald Mohr; *D:* George Archainbaud. VHS, Beta $34.95 *RKO* 𝄃𝄃½

Hunt the Man Down/Smashing the Rackets A double feature: In "Hunt the Man Down" (1950) a public defender tries to clear a captured fugitive's name, and in "Smashing the Rackets" (1938) a special prosecutor takes on the gangsters who have corrupted a big city.
1950 137m/B Gig Young, Lynn (Mary Hart) Roberts, Chester Morris, Frances Mercer, Willard Parker, Gerald Mohr, Paul Frees; *D:* George Archainbaud. VHS, Beta $34.95 *RKO* 𝄃𝄃½

Hunted! A young Jewish boy teams up with a resistance fighter to find his mother in Nazi Germany during WWII.
1979 90m/C VHS, Beta $29.95 *GEM* 𝄃𝄃

Hunted WWII prisoner attempts to escape from demented officer who seems to enjoy bugging him. Hunted by the MPs, he relies on unorthodox guide to sustain feature length footage.
1988 (PG) 75m/C Andrew Buckland, Richard Carlson, Ron Smerczak, Mercia Van Wyk; *D:* David Lister. VHS $34.95 *ACA* 𝄃𝄃

The Hunted Lady In this television pilot, Mills is an undercover policewoman who is framed by the mob. Tired and predictable.
1977 100m/C Donna Mills, Robert Reed, Lawrence Casey, Andrew Duggan, Will Sampson, Alan Feinstein; *D:* Richard Lang. VHS $39.95 *WOV* 𝄃½

Hunter Pilot for a television series that never emerged. A government agent uncovers an enemy brainwashing scam.
1973 90m/C John Vernon, Steve Ihnat, Fritz Weaver, Edward Binns, Sabrina Scharf, Barbara Rhoades; *D:* Leonard Horn. VHS *LHV* 𝄃½

Hunter An attorney is falsely accused of a crime and imprisoned. Released after eight years, he sets out to even the score with the mysterious millionaire who set him up. Made for television.
1977 120m/C James Franciscus, Linda Evans, Broderick Crawford. **VHS, Beta** $59.95 *LHV, WAR* ��

The Hunter Action drama based on the real life adventures of Ralph (Papa) Thorson, a modern day bounty hunter who makes his living by finding fugitives who have jumped bail. McQueen's last.
1980 (PG) 97m/C Steve McQueen, Eli Wallach, Kathryn Harrold, LeVar Burton; *D:* Buzz Kulik; *W:* Peter Hyams; *M:* Charles Bernstein. **VHS, Beta** $19.95 *PAR* ����½

Hunter in the Dark Set in 18th-century Japan, where power, betrayal, and corruption are the dark side of the samurai world. Tanuma is a powerful shogunate minister who becomes involved with Gomyo, the leader of a secret underworld organization of thieves and murderers with a violent honor code. In Japanese with English subtitles.
1980 138m/C Tatsuya Nakadai, Tetsuro Tamba, Sonny Chiba; *D:* Hideo Gosha. **VHS** $79.95 *ING* ����

The Hunters A motley crew of pilots learn about each other and themselves in this melodrama set during Korean war. Incredible aerial photography sets this apart from other films of the genre.
1958 108m/C Robert Mitchum, Robert Wagner, Richard Egan, May Britt, Lee Phillips; *D:* Dick Powell; *W:* Wendell Mayes. **VHS** *NO* ����½

Hunter's Blood Five urbanites plunge into the Southern wilderness to hunt deer, and are stalked by maniacal hillbillies.
1987 (R) 102m/C Sam Bottoms, Kim Delaney, Clu Gulager, Mayf Nutter; *D:* Robert C. Hughes. **VHS, Beta** $19.98 *SUE, NLC* ��½

Hunters of the Golden Cobra Two American soldiers plot to recover the priceless golden cobra from the Japanese general who stole the prized relic during the last days of WWII.
1982 (R) 95m/C David Warbeck, Almanta Suska, Alan Collins, John Steiner; *D:* Anthony M. (Antonio Margheriti) Dawson. **VHS, Beta** $69.98 *LIV, VES* ��

The Hunting A married woman falls for a ruthless businessman and is drawn into a web of blackmail and murder in this low-budget erotic thriller.
1992 (R) 97m/C John Savage, Kerry Armstrong, Guy Pearce, Rebecca Rigg; *D:* Frank Howson; *W:* Frank Howson. **VHS, Beta** $19.95 *PAR* ����

Hurricane A couple on the run from the law are aided by a hurricane and are able to build a new life for themselves on an idyllic island. Filmed two years before the Academy's "special effects" award came into being, but displaying some of the best effects of the decade. Boringly remade in 1979.
1937 102m/B Jon Hall, Dorothy Lamour, Mary Astor, Sir C. Aubrey Smith, Raymond Massey; *D:* John Ford. Academy Awards '37: Best Sound; Nominations: Best Supporting Actor (Mitchell), Best Original Score. **VHS, Beta** $14.98 *SUE* ������

Hurricane Television's answer to the disaster movie craze of the early 1970s. Realistic hurricane footage and an adequate cast cannot save this catastrophe.
1974 78m/C Larry Hagman, Martin Milner, Jessica Walter, Barry Sullivan, Will Geer, Frank Sutton; *D:* Jerry Jameson. **VHS** *NO* ��

Hurricane And the wind cried, "turkey." Robards is the governor of a tropical island beset with environmental and personal concerns. Virginal daughter Farrow falls for hunky native, standard colonial power/indigenous people complications ensue, vital explanatory footage is cut, and overacting reaches epidemic heights. Then too late the big wind blows in, leveling the place. Expensive (most of the $22 million must have gone to catering) and essentially misdirected remake of the 1937 semi-classic. *AKA:* Forbidden Paradise.
1979 (PG) 120m/C Mia Farrow, Jason Robards Jr., Trevor Howard, Max von Sydow, Timothy Bottoms, James Keach; *D:* Jan Troell. **VHS, Beta** $14.95 *PAR* Woof!

Hurricane Express Twelve episodes of the vintage serial, in which the Duke pits his courage against an unknown, powerful individual out to sabotage a railroad.
1932 223m/B John Wayne, Joseph Girard, Conway Tearle, Shirley Grey; *D:* J.P. McGowan, Armand Schaefer. **VHS, Beta** $16.95 *SNC, NOS, RHI* ����½

Hurricane Smith Weathers stars as a roughneck Texan who travels to Australia's Gold Coast in search of his missing sister. While in the land of Oz, he gets entangled in a Mafia-style drug and prostitution ring around the "Surfer's Paradise" section of the Gold Coast. Packed with mind-blowing stunts and a good performance from Weathers, this fast-paced action thriller won't disappoint fans of this genre.
1992 (R) 86m/C Carl Weathers, Juergen Prochnow, Tony Bonner, Cassandra Delaney; *D:* Colin Budds. **VHS** $14.95 *WAR* ����

Hurricane Sword Thriller sets savage sword play against a background of murder, betrayal, prostitution, and reunion.
197? 86m/C Chen Sau Kei, Li Tai Shing. **VHS, Beta** *NO* ��½

Hurry, Charlie, Hurry Husband gets in trouble when he bows out of a trip with his social-climber wife when he tells her he must travel to Washington to see the Vice President.
1941 65m/B Leon Errol. **VHS, Beta** $34.95 *RKO, MLB* ��

Hurry Up or I'll Be Thirty A Brooklyn bachelor celebrates his thirtieth birthday by becoming morose, depressed, and enraged. His friends try to help; they fail, but he finds love anyway. For those seeking a better life through celluloid.
1973 87m/C Danny DeVito, John Lefkowitz, Steve Inwood, Linda DeCoff, Ronald Anton, Maureen Byrnes, Francis Gallagher; *D:* Joseph Jacoby. **VHS, Beta** $69.98 *LIV, VES* ����

Husband Hunting Working girls hit the beach in search of husbands, and find that love isn't easy to find or hold on to.
196? 90m/C Walter Chiari. **VHS, Beta** *NO* ��

Husbands and Lovers Controversial and confusing film focuses on a couple's untraditional marriage. Stephen (Sands) and Alina (Pacula) have agreed to be totally honest with each other and when Alina decides to take a lover, Stephen agrees on the condition that she report back to him every intimate detail of her affair. In the confusion and excitement of this kinky love triangle, everyone starts losing control as sexual boundaries are pushed to the limit. Also available in an unrated version.
1991 (R) 91m/C Julian Sands, Joanna Pacula, Tcheky Karyo; *D:* Mauro Bolognini; *W:* Sergio Bazzini. **VHS** $19.95 *COL* ����

Husbands and Wives Art imitates life as Allen/Farrow relationship dissolves on-screen (and off) and Woody becomes involved with young student. Mature, penetrating look at modern pair bonding and loneliness offers more painful honesty and sadness than outright laughs, though still retains essential Allen charm. Stylistically burdened by experiment with pseudo-documentary telling of tale and spasmodic hand-held cameras that annoy more than entertain. Excellent, intriguing cast, notably Davis as the overwhelming, overbearing wife/friend. Trailers became unintentionally funny in light of the highly publicized personal problems of Allen and Farrow.
1992 (R) 107m/C Woody Allen, Mia Farrow, Judy Davis, Sydney Pollack, Liam Neeson, Juliette Lewis, Lysette Anthony, Blythe Danner; *D:* Woody Allen; *W:* Woody Allen. Academy Awards '92 Nominations: Best Original Screenplay, Best Supporting Actress (Davis); Chicago Film Critics Awards '93: Best Supporting Actress (Davis); Los Angeles Film Critics Association Awards '92: Best Supporting Actress (Davis); National Board of Review Awards '92: Best Supporting Actress (Davis); National Society of Film Critics Awards '92: Best Supporting Actress (Davis). **VHS** $89.99 *COL, MOV* ������½

Husbands, Wives, Money, and Murder A couple is pushed over the edge by a nosey census taker and then must dispose of the consequences.
1986 92m/C Garrett Morris, Greg Mullavey, Meredith MacRae, Timothy Bottoms; *D:* Bruce Cook Jr. **VHS, Beta** $79.95 *TWE, HHE* ��

Hush, Hush, Sweet Charlotte A fading southern belle finds out the truth about her fiance's murder when the case is reopened thirty-seven years later by her cousin in an elaborate plot to drive her crazy. Grisly, superbly entertaining Southern Gothic horror tale, with vivid performances from the aging leads.
1965 134m/B Bette Davis, Olivia de Havilland, Joseph Cotten, Agnes Moorehead, Mary Astor, Bruce Dern; *D:* Robert Aldrich. Academy Awards '64 Nominations: Best Art Direction/Set Decoration (B & W), Best Black and White Cinematography, Best Costume Design (B & W), Best Film Editing, Best Song ("Hush, Hush, Sweet Charlotte"), Best Supporting Actress (Moorehead), Best Original Score; Edgar Allan Poe Awards '64: Best Screenplay; Golden Globe Awards '65: Best Supporting Actress (Moorehead). **VHS, Beta** $19.98 *FOX* ����✝

Hush Little Baby, Don't You Cry A made-for-television drama about a seemingly normal middle-aged family man who is in actuality a child abuser/murderer.
1986 110m/C Emery L. Kedocia, Gary Giem, Tony Grant, Burt Douglas; *D:* Don Hawks. **VHS, Beta** $79.95 *PSM* ✝

Hussy Hooker and her boyfriend find themselves trapped in a web of gangsters and drugs.
1980 (R) 95m/C Helen Mirren, John Shea, Jenny Runacre; *D:* Matthew Chapman; *W:* Matthew Chapman; *M:* George Fenton. **VHS, Beta** $69.95 *VES* ✝

Hustle Gritty urban adventure with Reynolds as an L.A. detective investigating a young call girl's death. He becomes romantically entangled with high-priced call girl Deneuve.
1975 (R) 120m/C Burt Reynolds, Catherine Deneuve; *D:* Robert Aldrich. **VHS, Beta** $24.95 *PAR* ✝✝

The Hustler The original story of Fast Eddie Felsen and his adventures in the seedy world of professional pool. Newman plays the naive, talented and self-destructive Fel-

sen perfectly, Laurie is oustanding as his lover, and Gleason epitomizes the pool great Minnesota Fats. Rivetingly atmospheric, and exquisitely photographed. Parent to the reprise ''The Color of Money,'' made 25 years later.
1961 134m/B Paul Newman, Jackie Gleason, Piper Laurie, George C. Scott, Myron McCormick, Murray Hamilton, Michael Constantine, Jake La Motta, Vincent Gardenia; *D:* Robert Rossen; *W:* Robert Rossen. Academy Awards '61: Best Art Direction/Set Decoration (B & W), Best Black and White Cinematography; Nominations: Best Actor (Newman), Best Actress (Laurie), Best Adapted Screenplay, Best Director (Rossen), Best Picture, Best Supporting Actor (Gleason, Scott); British Academy Awards '61: Best Actor (Newman), Best Film; National Board of Review Awards '61: 10 Best Films of the Year, Best Supporting Actor (Gleason). **VHS, Beta $19.98** FOX, FCT 𝄌𝄌𝄌𝄌

Hustler Squad U.S. Army major and Philippine guerrilla leader stage a major operation to help rid the Philippines of Japanese Occupation forces: they have four combat-trained prostitutes infiltrate a brothel patronized by top Japanese officers. Verrrrry clever.
1976 (R) 98m/C John Ericson, Karen Ericson, Lynda Sinclaire, Nory Wright; *D:* Ted V. Mikels. **VHS, Beta $19.95** VCI, MRV 𝄌

Hustling A reporter writing a series of articles on prostitution in New York City takes an incisive look at their unusual and sometimes brutal world. Notable performance by Remick as the reporter and Clayburgh as a victimized hooker. Made for TV and based on a novel by Gail Sheehy.
1975 96m/C Jill Clayburgh, Lee Remick, Alex Rocco, Monte Markham; *D:* Joseph Sargent. **VHS, Beta $49.95** WOV 𝄌𝄌𝄌

Hyena of London A doctor steals the hyena of London's corpse and injects the rabid protoplasm into his own brain with deadly results.
1962 ?m/C Diana Martin, Bernard Price. **VHS $15.95** LOO 𝄌

Hyper-Sapien: People from Another Star Two cuddly aliens run away from home, are befriended by a lonely farmboy, and are chased all over the wilds of Wyoming.
1986 (PG) 93m/C Sydney Penny, Keenan Wynn, Gail Strickland, Ricky Paull Goldin, Peter Jason, Talia Shire; *D:* Peter Hunt. **VHS, Beta $14.95** WAR 𝄌½

The Hypothesis of the Stolen Painting An art collector guides an interviewer around six paintings by Frederic Tonnerre, an academic 19th century painter, in an attempt to solve the mysterious disappearance of a seventh painting. The film presents the paintings as tableaux vivants in which the actors hold poses as they are examined. Based on the novel ''Baphomet'' by Pierre Klossowski. In French with English subtitles. *AKA:* L'Hypothese du Tableau Vole.
1978 87m/B *D:* Raul Ruiz; *W:* Raul Ruiz. **VHS $59.95** WAC, ING 𝄌𝄌

Hysteria When an American becomes involved in an accident and has amnesia, a mysterious benefactor pays all his bills and gives the man a house to live in. But a series of murders could mean he's the murderer—or the next victim.
1964 (PG) 85m/B Robert Webber, Sue Lloyd, Maurice Denham; *D:* Freddie Francis; *W:* Jimmy Sangster. **VHS, Beta $59.95** MGM, MLB 𝄌½

Hysterical Odd little attempt at a horror flick parody features the Hudson Brothers and involves a haunted lighthouse occupied by the vengeful spirit of a spurned woman. Late-night fun.
1983 (PG) 86m/C Brett Hudson, William Hudson, Mark Hudson, Cindy Pickett, Richard Kiel, Julie Newmar, Bud Cort; *D:* Chris Bearde. **VHS, Beta $9.98** SUE 𝄌𝄌

I Accuse My Parents Juvenile delinquent tries to blame a murder and his involvement in a gang of thieves on his mom and dad's failure to raise him properly.
1945 70m/B Mary Beth Hughes, Robert Lowell, John Miljan. **VHS, Beta $16.95** SNC, NOS, DVT 𝄌½

I Am a Camera A young English writer develops a relationship with a reckless young English girl in Berlin during the 1930s. Based on the Berlin stories by Christopher Isherwood, later musicalized as ''Cabaret.''
1955 99m/C Julie Harris, Shelley Winters, Laurence Harvey, Patrick McGoohan; *D:* Henry Cornelius. **VHS, Beta $24.95** MON 𝄌𝄌𝄌

I Am a Fugitive from a Chain Gang WWI veteran Muni returns home with dreams of traveling across America. After a brief stint as a clerk, he strikes out on his own. Near penniless, Muni meets up with a tramp who takes him to get a hamburger. He becomes an unwilling accomplice when the bum suddenly robs the place. Convicted and sentenced to a Georgia chain gang, he's brutalized and degraded, though he eventually escapes and lives the life of a criminal on the run. Based on the autobiography by Robert E. Burns. Brutal docu-details combine with powerhouse performances to create a classic. Timeless and thought-provoking. *AKA:* I Am a Fugitive From the Chain Gang.
1932 93m/B Paul Muni, Glenda Farrell, Helen Vinson, Preston Foster, Edward Ellis, Allen Jenkins; *D:* Mervyn LeRoy; *W:* Howard J. Green. Academy Awards '33 Nominations: Best Actor (Muni), Best Picture, Best Sound; National Board of Review Awards '32: 10 Best Films of the Year. **VHS, Beta $19.98** MGM, FOX, CCB 𝄌𝄌𝄌𝄌

I Am Curious (Yellow) A woman sociologist is conducting a sexual survey on Swedish society, which leads her to have numerous sexual encounters in all sorts of places. Very controversial upon its U.S. release because of the nudity and sexual content but tame by today's standards. Followed by ''I Am Curious (Blue)'' which was filmed at the same time. In Swedish with English subtitles.
1967 95m/B Lena Nyman, Peter Lindgren; *D:* Vilgot Sjoman. **VHS $59.95** HTV 𝄌𝄌½

I Am the Cheese An institutionalized boy undergoes psychiatric treatment; with the aid of his therapist (Wagner) he relives his traumatic childhood and finds out the truth about the death of his parents. A bit muddled, but with its moments. Adapted from a Robert Cormier teen novel.
1983 95m/C Robert MacNaughton, Hope Lange, Don Murray, Robert Wagner, Sudie Bond; *D:* Robert Jiras. **VHS, Beta $69.98** LIV, VES 𝄌𝄌

I Am the Law Robinson is given the task of stopping gangster activity in the city. Although regularly a law professor, he is made special prosecutor and starts canvassing for people to testify. His witnesses become murder victims as an enemy on the inside attempts to thwart the game plan. Robinson is dismissed from the case but continues to pursue justice in streetclothes. Fine performances but somewhat predictable.

1938 83m/B Edward G. Robinson, Otto Kruger, John Beal, Barbara O'Neil, Wendy Barrie, Arthur Loft, Marc Lawrence, Charles Halton; *D:* Alexander Hall; *W:* Jo Swerling. **VHS, Beta $69.95** COL 𝄌𝄌𝄌

I Beheld His Glory Story based on the experience of Cornelius, the Roman centurion who guarded Christ's tomb.
1953 53m/C George Macready, Robert Wilson, Virginia Wave. **VHS $19.95** REP, MVC 𝄌𝄌𝄌

I Bury the Living A cemetery manager sticks pins in his map of a graveyard and people mysteriously start to die. Well-done suspense film.
1958 76m/B Richard Boone, Theodore Bikel, Peggy Maurer; *D:* Albert Band. **VHS $16.95** SNC, MRV 𝄌𝄌𝄌

I Can't Escape A man attempts to piece his life back together after serving time for a crime he didn't commit. To prove himself to his girlfriend, he tries to break up an illegal stock scam.
1934 60m/B Onslow Stevens, Lila Lee, Russell Gleason, Otis Harlan, Hooper Atchley, Clara Kimball Young; *D:* Otto Brower. **VHS, Beta $16.95** SNC 𝄌𝄌

I, Claudius, Vol. 1: A Touch of Murder/Family Affairs Award-winning Masterpiece Theatre series tells the true story of the Roman Empire and the people determined to rule it. In these first two episodes, Augustus tries to control his conniving second wife, the beautiful Livia, who is determined that her son Tiberius will be the next Roman ruler. Her manipulations lead to bloody mayhem. Brilliant acting. Based on the books by Robert Graves. Also available as a seven-volume set. Made for television.
1991 120m/C Sian Phillips, Brian Blessed, Derek Jacobi; *D:* Herbert Wise. **VHS $24.95** PBS, FCT, SIG 𝄌𝄌

I, Claudius, Vol. 2: Waiting in the Wings/What Shall We Do With Claudius? Continuation of the Masterpiece Theatre series portraying the true story of the Roman Empire and its rulers. In the third and fourth episodes, Tiberius and his mother Livia attempt to capture the throne with a series of brutal manipulations. Young cousin Claudius, considered an ugly dimwit, watches from afar. Based on the books of Robert Graves. Also available as a seven-volume set. Made for television.
1980 120m/C Derek Jacobi, Sian Phillips, Brian Blessed; *D:* Herbert Wise. **VHS $24.95** PBS, FCT, SIG 𝄌𝄌

I, Claudius, Vol. 3: Poison is Queen/Some Justice Episodes 5 and 6 see Emperor Augustus murdered and Tiberius on the throne he's coveted for so long. But how long can he stay, hiding the treachery that brought him there? Good question. Agrippina, wife of his latest victim, is determined to see him punished, and the Roman masses, not so stupid after all, have begun to see a pattern in the deaths of their best and brightest. Based on the books of Robert Graves. Also available as a seven-volume set. Made for television.
1980 120m/C Derek Jacobi, Sian Phillips, Brian Blessed; *D:* Herbert Wise. **VHS $24.95** PBS, FCT, SIG 𝄌𝄌

I, Claudius, Vol. 4: Queen of Heaven/Reign of Terror In episodes 7 and 8, Caligula begins his evil manipulation of Tiberius, involving him in a wide variety of amoral activities and creating a trail of blood. Based on the books of Robert Graves. Also available as a seven-volume set. Made for television.

1980 120m/C Derek Jacobi, Sian Phillips. **VHS** $24.95 *PBS, FCT, SIG* ⅊⅊

I, Claudius, Vol. 5: Zeus, By Jove!/Hail Who? Caligula's schemes result in his rise to the throne after Tiberius. Debauchery rules and murder is a standard procedure that returns to remove the emperor. At last, patient Claudius, the only remaining heir, thought too foolish to be dangerous, ascends the throne. Award-winning Masterpiece Theatre production created by the BBC. Based on the books of Robert Graves. The first episode on this cassette contains the graphic scene of Caligula's evisceration of his sister, as he enacts the life of Zeus in demented belief that he is the god—be forewarned. Also available as a seven-volume set. Made for television.
1980 120m/C Derek Jacobi, John Hurt; *D:* Herbert Wise. **VHS** $24.95 *PBS, FCT, SIG* ⅊⅊

I, Claudius, Vol. 6: Fool's Luck/A God in Colchester Episodes 11 and 12 see Emperor Claudius wise in the ways of statesmanship, but foolish in the ways of love. His young wife Messalina creates a furor when her sexual practices become known. In spite of his love, the emperor must punish her. Award-winning BBC production, shown in U.S. on Masterpiece Theatre. Based on the books of Robert Graves. Also available as a seven-volume set.
1980 120m/C Derek Jacobi; *D:* Herbert Wise. **VHS** $24.95 *PBS, FCT, SIG* ⅊⅊

I, Claudius, Vol. 7: Old King Log Claudius, aging and sad, resigns himself to his destiny, as his wife makes plans for his death. Claudius wants only the time to complete the journal of his life. Brilliant acting from Jacobi in this BBC production shown in the U.S. on Masterpiece Theatre. Based on the books of Robert Graves. Also available as a seven-volume set.
1980 60m/C Derek Jacobi; *D:* Herbert Wise. **VHS** $24.95 *PBS, FCT, SIG* ⅊⅊

I Come in Peace A tough, maverick Texas cop embarks on a one-way ride to Nosebleed City when he attempts to track down a malevolent alien drug czar who kills his victims by sucking their brains. Mindless thrills. *AKA:* Dark Angel.
1990 (R) 92m/C Dolph Lundgren, Brian Benben, Betsy Brantley, Jesse Vint, Michael J. Pollard; *D:* Craig R. Baxley; *M:* Jan Hammer. **VHS, Beta** $89.95 *MED, VTR* ⅊

I Confess When a priest (Clift) hears a murderer's confession, the circumstances seem to point to him as the prime suspect. Tepid, overly serious and occasionally interesting mid-career Hitchcock. Adapted from Paul Anthelme's 1902 play.
1953 95m/B Montgomery Clift, Anne Baxter, Karl Malden, Brian Aherne; *D:* Alfred Hitchcock. **VHS, Beta** $19.98 *WAR, FCT, MLB* ⅊⅊½

I Conquer the Sea Two brothers, who works as whalers, cast their affection on the same woman. Drowns in its own melodrama.
1936 68m/B Steffi Duna, Dennis (Stanley Morner) Morgan, Douglas Walton, George Cleveland, Johnny Pirrone; *D:* Victor Halperin. **VHS, Beta, 8mm** $24.95 *VYY* ⅊½

I Could Go on Singing An aging American songstress, on a tour in Britain, becomes reacquainted with her illegitimate son and his British father, but eventually goes back to the footlights. Garland's last film. Songs include "By Myself" and "It Never Was You." A must for Garland fans. Letterboxed.

1963 99m/C Judy Garland, Dirk Bogarde, Jack Klugman, Aline MacMahon; *D:* Ronald Neame. **VHS, Beta** $19.98 *MGM* ⅊⅊½

I Cover the Waterfront A reporter is assigned to write about a boatman involved in a fishy scheme to smuggle Chinese immigrants into the country wrapped in shark skins. While trying to get the story, the journalist falls in love with the fisherman's daughter. Torrance passed away before its release.
1933 70m/B Claudette Colbert, Ben Lyon, Ernest Torrence, Hobart Cavanaugh; *D:* James Cruze. **VHS, Beta** $19.95 *NOS, MRV, VYY* ⅊⅊½

I Died a Thousand Times Aging gangster Mad Dog Earle (pushup prince Palance) plans one last death-defying heist while hiding from police in the mountains. Meanwhile, the hard boiled gangster softens a bit thanks to surgery-needing girlfriend, but moll Winters doesn't seem to think that three's company. A low rent "High Sierra." From the novel by W.R. Burnett.
1955 109m/C Jack Palance, Shelley Winters, Lori Nelson, Lee Marvin, Earl Holliman, Lon Chaney Jr., Howard St. John; *D:* Stuart Heisler; *W:* W.R. Burnett. **VHS** $59.99 *WAR, FCT* ⅊⅊

I Dismember Mama Classless story of an asylum inmate who escapes to kill his mother. Although he hates women, he likes little girls as evidenced by his nine-year-old love interest. Notably lacking in bloody scenes. *AKA:* Poor Albert and Little Annie.
1974 (R) 81m/C Zooey Hall, Joanne Moore Jordan, Greg Mullavey, Marlene Tracy; *D:* Paul Leder. **VHS, Beta** $24.95 *GEM* Woof!

I Do! I Do! This Los Angeles production of the Broadway musical covers 50 years of a marriage, beginning just before the turn of the century.
1984 116m/C Lee Remick, Hal Linden. **VHS, Beta** $39.95 *RKO, STS, TTC* Woof!

I Don't Buy Kisses Anymore Heartwarming story starring Alexander and Peeples as two mismatched lovers who end up realizing that they're made for each other. Alexander plays Bernie Fishbine, an overweight Jewish shoe store owner who falls for a psychology graduate student (Peeples). Little does he know, but Peeples is studying him for her term paper, appropriately titled "The Psychological Study of an Obese Male." Alexander gives a great performance, as do Kazan and Jacobi who play Bernie's parents.
1992 (PG) 112m/C Jason Alexander, Nia Peeples, Lainie Kazan, Lou Jacobi, Eileen Brennan, Larry Storch, Arleen Sorkin; *D:* Robert Marcarelli; *W:* Jonnie Lindsell; *M:* Cobb Bussinger. **VHS, Beta** *PAR* ⅊⅊½

I Don't Give a Damn An embittered wounded soldier returns home to his loved ones, rejects them, and becomes more and more uninterested in life itself. Subtitled.
1988 (R) 94m/C Ika Sohar, Anat Waxman; *D:* Shmuel Imberman. **VHS, Beta** $59.95 *TWE* ⅊⅊

I Don't Want to Be Born It's got all the right ingredients for overnight camp: a spurned dwarf, a large, howling baby-thing, slice and dice murder and mayhem, and Collins. It could've been so bad. Instead, this "Rosemary's Baby" rehash is just stupid bad. *AKA:* The Devil Within Her.
1975 (R) 90m/C Joan Collins, Eileen Atkins, Donald Pleasence, Ralph Bates, Caroline Munro; *D:* Peter Sasdy. **VHS** *NO* ⅊

I Dood It Young tailor's assistant Skelton falls hard for young actress Powell working near his shop. She agrees to date, and eventually marry him, but only to spite her boyfriend who has just run off with another

woman. All's well however, when Skelton stumbles across a spy ring, is hailed a hero and helps Powell realize she really loves him. ♫Star Eyes; Taking a Chance on Love; Jericho; One O'Clock Jump; So Long Sarah Jane; Hola E Pae; Swing the Jinx Away. *AKA:* By Hook or By Crook.
1943 102m/B Red Skelton, Eleanor Powell, Richard Ainley, Patricia Dane, Sam Levene, Thurston Hall, Lena Horne, Butterfly McQueen, Jimmy Dorsey & His Orchestra; *D:* Vincente Minnelli. **VHS** $19.98 *MGM, CCB* ⅊⅊

I Dream of Jeannie The third and worst bio of Stephen Foster has Foster as a bookkeeper-cum-songwriter alternating between writing tunes and chasing Lawrence. When she dumps him, he goes into a funk. Will he be able to complete the title song? The suspense will kill you. Lots of singing, but not much else.
1952 90m/C Ray Middleton, Bill Shirley, Muriel Lawrence, Lynn Bari, Rex Allen; *D:* Allan Dwan. **VHS** $19.95 *NOS, VEC* ⅊

I Dream Too Much A musical vehicle for opera star Pons, as a French singer who marries an American composer played by Fonda. Songwriter falls into wife's shadow after pushing her into a singing career; she then raises his spirits a couple of octaves by helping him sell a musical comedy. Went into production after a rival company, Columbia, launched opera singer Grace Moore's acting career. Ball later bought this studio, where she was given her second starring role. ♫The Jockey on the Carousel; I'm the Echo; I Got Love; I Dream Too Much; Bell Song; Caro Nome.
1935 90m/B Lily Pons, Henry Fonda, Eric Blore, Lucille Ball, Mischa Auer, Scotty Beckett; *D:* John Cromwell. **VHS, Beta** $19.98 *HHT, TTC* ⅊⅊

I Drink Your Blood Hippie satanists looking for kicks spike an old man's drink with LSD. To get revenge, the old codger's grandson sells the nasty flower children meat pies injected with the blood of a rabid dog. The hippies then turn into cannibalistic maniacs, infecting anyone they bite. From the man responsible for "I Spit on Your Grave;" originally played on a double bill with "I Eat Your Skin."
1971 (R) 83m/C Bhasker, Jadine Wong, Ronda Fultz, Elizabeth Marner-Brooks, George Patterson, Riley Mills, Iris Brooks, John Damon; *D:* David E. Durston. **VHS** $18.00 *FRG, TPV* ⅊½

I Eat Your Skin Cannibalistic zombies terrorize a novelist and his girlfriend on a Caribbean island. Blood and guts, usually shown on a gourmet double bill with "I Drink Your Blood." *AKA:* Zombies; Voodoo Blood Bath; Zombie.
1964 82m/B William Joyce, Heather Hewitt, Betty H. Lindon; *D:* Del Tenney. **VHS** $9.95 *RHI, SNC, FCT* Woof!

I Hate Blondes A group of criminals use a ghostwriter's burglaring stories as instructional manuals. The writer becomes involved with the gang. Relies heavily on visual humor. Notably among the comedy scenes is the author's search for jewels at a get-together. *AKA:* Odio le Bionde.
1983 90m/C *D:* Giorgio Capitani, Giorgio Capitani. **VHS, Beta** *NO* ⅊⅊½

I Heard the Owl Call My Name Poignant story of an Anglican priest who is relocated to an Indian fishing village on the ouskirts of Vancouver, British Columbia. Made for television and based on a Margaret Craven book.
1973 74m/C Tom Courtenay, Dean Jagger, Paul Stanley; *D:* Daryl Duke. **Beta** $14.95 *PSM* ⅊⅊½

I Killed Rasputin The "Mad Monk" who rose to power before the Russian Revolution lost his life in a bizarre assassination by Felix Youssoupoff. Film deals with the friendship between the men that ended in betrayal. Well-intentioned, but overwrought. Dubbed.
1967 95m/C Geraldine Chaplin, Gert Frobe, Peter McEnery; *D:* Robert Hossein. **VHS, Beta** $59.95 *MPI* ℤ½

I Killed That Man A prisoner scheduled to die in the electric chair is given an early ticket out when he is found poisoned. Evidence points to an unusual group of suspects. Effective low-budget thriller offers a few unexpected surprises.
1942 72m/B Ricardo Cortez, Joan Woodbury, Iris Adrian, George Pembroke, Herbert Rawlinson, Pat Gleason, Ralf Harolde, Jack Mulhall, Vince Barnett, Gavin Gordon, John Hamilton; *D:* Phil Rosen. **VHS, Beta** $16.95 *SNC* ℤℤ½

I Know Where I'm Going A young woman (Hiller), who believes that money brings happiness, is on the verge of marrying a rich old man, until she meets a handsome naval officer (Livesey) and finds a happy, simple life. Early on the female lead appears in a dream sequence filmed in the mode of surrealist painter Salvador Dali and avant garde director Luis Bunuel. Scottish setting and folk songs give a unique flavor. Brown provides a fine performance as a native Scot.
1945 91m/B Roger Livesey, Wendy Hiller, Finlay Currie, Pamela Brown; *D:* Michael Powell. **VHS, Beta** $39.95 *HMV, LCA* ℤℤℤ

I Know Why the Caged Bird Sings A black writer's memories of growing up in the rural South during the 1930s. Strong performances from Rolle and Good. Made-for-television film is based on the book by Maya Angelou.
1979 100m/C Diahann Carroll, Ruby Dee, Esther Rolle, Roger E. Mosley, Paul Benjamin, Constance Good; *D:* Fielder Cook. **VHS, Beta** $59.95 *KUI, LIV* ℤℤℤ

I Like Bats Can a psychiatrist help a vampire become a human? Polish dialogue with English subtitles.
1985 90m/C *D:* Grzegorz Warchol. **VHS** $49.95 *FCT* ℤℤℤ

I Live in Fear Nakajima, an elderly, wealthy owner of a foundry, becomes increasingly fearful of atomic war and the threats to his family's safety. He tries to persuade them to leave Japan and move with him to Brazil but they fear the family will be ruined financially. Nakajima then burns down his foundry to force his children to move but instead they go to court and have him declared mentally incompetent. He is placed in an institution where he finds peace in the delusion that he has escaped to another planet and that the Earth has indeed suffered a nuclear holocaust. Provocative look at the fear of atomic warfare and radiation. In Japanese with English subtitles. *AKA:* Record of a Living Being; Kimono No Kiroku.
1955 105m/C Toshiro Mifune, Takashi Shimura, Eiko Miyoshi, Haruko Togo; *D:* Akira Kurosawa. **VHS** $39.95 *FCT* ℤℤℤ

I Live in Grosvenor Square An American soldier in Great Britain falls in love with a major's fiancee. Entertaining if a bit drawn out. *AKA:* A Yank In London.
1946 106m/B Anna Neagle, Rex Harrison, Dean Jagger, Robert Morley, Jane Darwell; *D:* Herbert Wilcox. **VHS, Beta** $19.95 *NOS, DVT* ℤℤ

I Live My Life Stylish glossy flick with Crawford playing a bored New York debutante who travels to Greece and meets a dedicated archaeologist (Aherne). A love/hate relationship ensues in this typical Crawford vehicle where she is witty and parades around in sophisticated fashions, but there is little substance here.
1935 92m/B Joan Crawford, Brian Aherne, Frank Morgan, Aline MacMahon, Eric Blore, Fred Keating, Jessie Ralph, Arthur Treacher, Frank Conroy, Sterling Holloway, Vince Barnett, Hedda Hopper, Lionel Stander; *D:* Woodbridge S. Van Dyke; *W:* Joseph L. Mankiewicz, Gottfried Reinhardt, Ethel B. Borden. **VHS** $19.98 *MGM* ℤℤ½

I Live with Me Dad A vagrant drunk and his son fight the authorities for the right to be together.
1986 86m/C Peter Hehir, Haydon Samuels; *D:* Paul Maloney. **VHS, Beta** $79.98 *FOX* ℤℤ½

I Love All of You Deneuve relives experiences with three former lovers - a composer, a well-intentioned nobody, and a rock star - as she enters into a relationship with a widower.
1983 103m/C Catherine Deneuve, Jean-Louis Trintignant, Gerard Depardieu, Serge Gainsbourg; *D:* Claude Berri. **VHS, Beta** *NO* ℤℤ½

I Love Lucy Everyone's favorite redhead in scrape after scrape, along with her Cuban bandleader husband, Ricky Ricardo, and their neighbors Fred and Ethel Mertz. Episodes on this tape are "Lucy Does a TV Commercial" and "Lucy's Italian Movie." Other episodes available.
1952 51m/B Lucille Ball, Desi Arnaz Sr., Vivian Vance, William Frawley. **VHS** $14.98 *FOX, MOV* ℤℤ½

I Love Melvin Reynolds wants to be a Tinseltown goddess, and O'Connor just wants Reynolds; so he passes himself off as chief lenseman for a famous magazine and promises her a shot at the cover of "Look." Seems he has a little trouble on the follow through. Choreographed by Robert Alton, it's got a best ever football ballet (with Reynolds as pigskin). ♫A Lady Loves; Saturday Afternoon Before The Game; I Wanna Wander; We Have Never Met As Of Yet; Life Has Its Funny Little Ups And Downs; Where Did You Learn To Dance?; And There You Are.
1953 77m/C Donald O'Connor, Debbie Reynolds, Una Merkel, Richard Anderson, Jim Backus, Allyn Joslyn, Les Tremayne, Noreen Corcoran, Robert Taylor, Howard Keel; *D:* Don Weis. **VHS** $19.98 *MGM, TTC, FCT* ℤℤ½

I Love My...Wife A medical student plays doctor with hospital nurses when he and his wife stop having sex during her pregnancy. The marriage becomes more strained when their son is born and his mother-in-law moves in. A comedy without the proper dosage of laughs.
1970 (R) 98m/C Elliott Gould, Brenda Vaccaro, Angel Tompkins; *D:* Mel Stuart. **VHS, Beta** $59.95 *MCA* ℤℤ

I Love N.Y. A young metropolitan couple struggles to find true love amidst disapproving parents and doubting friends. Choppy direction and poor writing contribute to its failure.
1987 100m/C Scott Baio, Kelley Van Der Velden, Christopher Plummer, Jennifer O'Neill, Jerry Orbach, Virna Lisi; *D:* Alan Smithee; *M:* Bill Conti. **VHS, Beta** *NO* ℤ

I Love Trouble Veteran reporter Peter Brackett (sexy veteran Nolte) and ambitious cub reporter Sabrina Petersen (young and sexy Roberts) are competitors working for rival Chicago newspapers. When they begin to secretly exchange information on a big

story, they find their lives threatened and their rivalry turning to romance. Some action, simplistic retro script, one big star, one sorta big star, and you've got the perfect movie package for the Prozac decade. Written, produced and directed by husband/wife team Meyers and Shyer.
1994 (PG) 123m/C Julia Roberts, Nick Nolte, Saul Rubinek, Robert Loggia, James Rebhorn; *D:* Charles Shyer; *W:* Nancy Myers, Charles Shyer. **VHS** *NYR* ℤℤ½

I Love You Man down on his luck mistakenly assumes that a woman he meets is a hooker. She plays along, only to find that they are becoming emotionally involved. Pretentious cat-and-mouse game.
1981 (R) 104m/C Sonia Braga, Paulo Cesar Pereio, Vera Fischer, Tarcisio Meria; *D:* Arnaldo Jabor. **VHS, Beta** $59.95 *MGM* ℤ½

I Love You Again A classic screwball comedy with Powell and Loy working together (wonderfully) in something other than their "Thin Man" series. Powell is a gloomy businessman who's about to be divorced by Loy. But after an accident it turns out Powell had been suffering from amnesia and has now regained his memory (which he keeps a secret). It seems Mr. Respectable used to be a con man and he decides to revert to his criminal ways. He also doesn't remember Loy but falls instantly in love with her and must decide what kind of life he wants. Witty dialog, amusing situations, fine direction.
1940 97m/B William Powell, Myrna Loy, Frank McHugh, Edmund Lowe; *D:* Woodbridge S. Van Dyke. **VHS** $19.98 *MGM* ℤℤℤ½

I Love You, Alice B. Toklas A straight uptight lawyer decides to join the peace and love generation in this somewhat maniacal satire of the hippie culture. Authored by Paul Mazursky and Larry Tucker. Incidentally, the title's Alice B. Toklas was actually the lifemate of "Lost Generation" author Gertrude Stein. *AKA:* Kiss My Butterfly.
1968 94m/C Peter Sellers, Jo Van Fleet, Leigh Taylor-Young, Joyce Van Patten; *D:* Hy Averback; *W:* Paul Mazursky; *M:* Elmer Bernstein. **VHS, Beta** $19.98 *WAR, FCT* ℤℤ½

I Love You Rosa Rosa, a young Jewish widow, wrestles big time with old world values. Required by custom to marry her dearly departed's eldest brother, she's not enamored with her newly betrothed. Not that he's not a nice guy; he seems to plan to take his marital duties very seriously. It's just that he's a tad youthful (eleven years old, to be exact). Much rabbi consulting and soul searching.
1972 90m/C Michal Bat-Adam, Gabi Oterman, Yoseph Shiloah; *D:* Moshe Mizrahi; *W:* Moshe Mizrahi. **VHS** $39.95 *FCT, NCJ* ℤℤ½

I Love You to Death Dry comedy based on a true story, concerns a woman who tries to kill off her cheating husband. Lots of stars, but they never shine. Hurt and Reeves are somewhat amusing as drugged up hit men who struggle with the lyrics to the National Anthem. Watch for director Kasdan as Devo's lawyer. Cates, Kline's real-life wife, has an unbilled part as one of his one-night stands.
1990 (R) 110m/C Kevin Kline, Tracey Ullman, Joan Plowright, River Phoenix, William Hurt, Keanu Reeves, James Gammon, Victoria Jackson, Miriam Margolyes, Heather Graham; *Cameos:* Phoebe Cates; *D:* Lawrence Kasdan; *W:* John Kostmayer; *M:* James Horner. **VHS, Beta** $19.95 *COL* ℤℤ½

I Love You...Goodbye A frustrated housewife, fed up with the constant role of wife and mother, leaves her family in an effort to find a more challenging and fulfilling life. A good performance by Lange compensates for some of its muddledness.
1973 74m/C Hope Lange, Earl Holliman. VHS, Beta *LCA* 🐾🐾

I, Madman A novel-loving horror actress is stalked by the same mutilating madman that appears in the book she's presently reading. We call that bad luck.
1989 (R) 90m/C Jenny Wright, Clayton Rohner, William Cook; *D:* Tibor Takacs; *W:* David Chaskin. VHS, Beta $89.95 *MED* 🐾🐾

I Married a Centerfold Television movie fluff about a young man's amorous pursuit of a model.
1984 100m/C Teri Copley, Timothy Daly, Diane Ladd, Bert Remsen, Anson Williams; *D:* Peter Werner. VHS, Beta *NO* 🐾🐾

I Married a Monster from Outer Space The vintage thriller about a race of monster-like aliens from another planet who try to conquer earth. Despite its head-shaking title, an effective '50s sci-fi creeper.
1958 78m/B Tom Tryon, Gloria Talbott, Maxie "Slapsie" Rosenbloom, Mary Treen, Ty Hardin; *D:* Gene Fowler. VHS, Beta $49.95 *PAR*, *MLB* 🐾🐾½

I Married a Vampire A country girl in the city is romanced and wed by a dashing vampire. Troma-produced hyper-camp.
1987 85m/C Rachel Gordon, Brendan Hickey; *D:* Jay Raskin. VHS, Beta $9.99 *PSM* 🐾🐾

I Married a Witch A witch burned at the stake during the Salem witch trials comes back to haunt the descendants of her accusers and gets romantic with one of them. Wonderfully played fantasy/comedy.
1942 77m/B Veronica Lake, Fredric March, Susan Hayward, Broderick Crawford; *D:* Rene Clair. VHS, Beta $59.95 *MLB*, *WAR* 🐾🐾🐾

I Married a Woman An advertising executive marries a beautiful blonde woman, but finds it very difficult to balance his career and marriage. Low on laughs. Shot in black and white, but includes a fantasy scene in color that features John Wayne. Pay attention to see young Angie Dickinson.
1956 84m/B George Gobel, Diana Dors, Adolphe Menjou, Nita Talbot; *D:* Hal Kanter. VHS, Beta $15.95 *VCI* 🐾🐾

I Married an Angel The last MacDonald/Eddy film. A playboy is lured away from his usual interests by a beautiful angel. Adapted from Rodgers and Hart Broadway play. Strange and less than compelling. 🎵I Married An Angel; I'll Tell the Man in the Street; Spring is Here; Tira Lira La; A Twinkle in Your Eye; Aloha Oe; Caprice Viennoise; Chanson Boheme; Anges Purs.
1942 84m/C Jeanette MacDonald, Nelson Eddy, Binnie Barnes, Edward Everett Horton, Reginald Owen, Mona Maris, Janis Carter, Inez Cooper, Douglass Dumbrille, Leonid Kinskey, Marion Rosamond, Anne Jeffreys, Marek Windheim, Veda Ann Borg; *D:* Woodbridge S. Van Dyke; *W:* Anita Loos; *M:* Richard Rodgers, Lorenz Hart. VHS, Beta $19.98 *MGM*, *MVD* 🐾½

I Met a Murderer A man kills his nagging wife after a bitter argument and flees from his vengeful brother. Fine fugitive drama with a number of interesting twists.
1939 79m/B James Mason, Pamela Kellino, Sylvia Coleridge; *D:* Roy Kellino. VHS $16.95 *SNC*, *NOS*, *DVT* 🐾🐾½

I, Mobster Cochran tells a Senate Sub-Committee of the Underworld—from his humble beginning as a bet collector for a bookie to his position as kingpin of the crime syndicate.
1958 80m/B Steve Cochran, Lita Milan, Robert Strauss, Celia Lovsky; *D:* Roger Corman. VHS *NO* 🐾🐾½

I Never Promised You a Rose Garden A disturbed 16-year-old girl spirals down into madness and despair while a hospital psychiatrist struggles to bring her back to life. Based on the Joanne Greenberg bestseller. Compelling and unyielding exploration of the clinical treatment of schizophrenia.
1977 (R) 90m/C Kathleen Quinlan, Bibi Andersson, Sylvia Sidney, Diane Varsi; *D:* Anthony Page; *W:* Gavin Lambert. VHS, Beta $59.95 *WAR*, *OM* 🐾🐾🐾

I Never Sang For My Father A devoted son must choose between caring for his cantankerous but well-meaning father, and moving out West to marry the divorced doctor whom he loves. While his mother wants him to stay near home, his sister, who fell out of her father's favor by marrying out of the family faith, argues that he should do what he wants. An introspective, stirring story based on the Robert Anderson play.
1970 (PG) 90m/C Gene Hackman, Melvyn Douglas, Estelle Parsons, Dorothy Stickney; *D:* Gilbert Cates; *W:* Robert Anderson. Academy Awards '70 Nominations: Best Actor (Douglas), Best Adapted Screenplay, Best Supporting Actor (Hackman); National Board of Review Awards '70: 10 Best Films of the Year. VHS, Beta $69.95 *COL* 🐾🐾🐾½

I Ought to Be in Pictures After hitch-hiking from New York to Hollywood to break into the movies, a teen-aged actress finds her father, a screenwriter turned alcoholic-gambler. Late, desperately unfunny Neil Simon outing, adapted from a Simon play.
1982 (PG) 107m/C Walter Matthau, Ann-Margret, Dinah Manoff, Lance Guest, Michael Dudikoff; *D:* Herbert Ross; *W:* Neil Simon; *M:* Marvin Hamlisch. VHS, Beta $59.98 *FOX* 🐾🐾

I Posed for Playboy Three women—one a college co-ed, one a stockbroker, and one a 37-year-old mother—quench their private passions by posing for Playboy Magazine. Made for television with additional footage added to give it an "R" rating.
1991 (R) 98m/C Lynda Carter, Michelle Greene, Amanda Peterson, Brittany York; *D:* Stephen Stafford. VHS $29.98 *REP* 🐾🐾

I Remember Mama A true Hollywood heart tugger chronicling the life of a Norwegian immigrant family living in San Francisco during the early 1900s. Dunne triumphs as the mother, with a perfect Norwegian accent, and provides her family with wisdom and inspiration. A kindly father and four children round out the nuclear family. A host of oddball characters regularly pop in on the household—three high-strung aunts and an eccentric doctor who treats a live-in uncle. Adapted from John Van Druten's stage play, based on Kathryn Forbes memoirs, "Mama's Bank Account;" a TV series came later.
1948 95m/B Irene Dunne, Barbara Bel Geddes, Oscar Homolka, Ellen Corby, Cedric Hardwicke, Edgar Bergen, Rudy Vallee, Barbara O'Neil, Florence Bates; *D:* George Stevens. Academy Awards '48 Nominations: Best Actress (Dunne), Best Black and White Cinematography, Best Supporting Actor (Homolka), Best Supporting Actress (Corby, Bel Geddes); Golden Globe Awards '49: Best Supporting Actress (Corby). VHS, Beta $19.98 *CCB*, *RKO*, *TTC* 🐾🐾🐾½

I See a Dark Stranger Cynical yet whimsical postwar British spy thriller about an angry Irish lass who agrees to steal war plans for the Nazis in order to battle her native enemies, the British—then she falls in love with a British officer. A sharply performed, decidedly jaded view of nationalism and wartime "heroism." *AKA:* The Adventuress.
1946 112m/B Deborah Kerr, Trevor Howard, Raymond Huntley; *D:* Frank Laudner. VHS, Beta *NO* 🐾🐾🐾

I Sent a Letter to My Love An aging spinster, faced with the lonely prospect of the death of her paralyzed brother, places a personal ad for a companion in a local newspaper, using a different name. Unknown to her, the brother is the one who answers it, and they begin a romantic correspondence. Well-acted, touching account of relationships that change lives, but it takes its time in telling the story.
1981 102m/C Simone Signoret, Jean Rochefort, Delphine Seyrig; *D:* Moshe Mizrahi; *W:* Moshe Mizrahi, Gerard Brach. VHS, Beta *NO* 🐾🐾🐾

I Shot Billy the Kid Billy the Kid decides to turn over a new leaf and live a decent life. The cards are stacked against him though: He's killed a man for nearly every year of his life, and old habits are hard to break.
1950 58m/B Donald (Don "Red") Barry, Robert Lowery, Tom Neal, Jack Perrin; *D:* William Berke. VHS, Beta *NO* 🐾½

I Shot Jesse James In his first film, director Fuller breathes characteristically feverish, maddened fire into the story of Bob Ford (Ireland) after he killed the notorious outlaw. An essential moment in Fuller's unique, America-as-tabloid-nightmare canon, and one of the best anti-westerns ever made.
1949 83m/B John Ireland, Barbara Britton, Preston Foster, Reed Hadley; *D:* Samuel Fuller; *W:* Samuel Fuller. VHS, Beta *RXM* 🐾🐾🐾

I Spit on Your Corpse A vicious female hired killer engages in a series of terrorist activities. Stars Spelvin in a non-pornographic role. *AKA:* Girls For Rent.
1974 (R) 90m/C Georgina Spelvin, Susan McIver, Kent Taylor; *D:* Al Adamson. VHS, Beta $59.95 *REP* Woof!

I Spit on Your Grave Woman vacationing at an upstate New York lake house is brutally attacked and raped by four men. Left for dead, she recovers and seeks revenge. Not to be confused with the 1962 film of the same title, this one is worth zero as a film; lots of violent terror and gory death, totally irresponsibly portrayed. Also available in a 102-minute version. *AKA:* Day of the Woman.
1977 (R) 98m/C Camille Keaton, Eron Tabor, Richard Pace, Gunter Kleeman; *D:* Mier Zarchi; *W:* Mier Zarchi. VHS, Beta $39.95 *VES* Woof!

I Stand Condemned A Russian officer is tricked into borrowing money from a spy and is condemned for treason. He's saved when a girl who loves him gives herself to a profiteer. Worth seeing only for young Olivier's performance. *AKA:* Moscow Nights.
1936 90m/B Laurence Olivier, Penelope Dudley Ward, Robert Cochran; *D:* Anthony Asquith. VHS, Beta, 8mm $19.95 *NOS*, *MRV*, *VYY* 🐾🐾½

I Take This Oath A cop is shocked to discover that his uncle is a wanted mobster, responsible for the death of a man. Hackneyed plot.
1940 64m/B Gordon Jones, Joyce Compton, Craig Reynolds, J. Farrell MacDonald, Robert E. Homans, Veda Ann Borg; *D:* Sherman Scott. VHS, Beta $16.95 *SNC* 🐾

I

I, the Jury A remake of the 1953 Mike Hammer mystery in which the famed PI investigates the murder of his best friend. Assante mopes around as Hammer and looks out of place in this slowed-down version.
1982 (R) 111m/C Armand Assante, Barbara Carrera, Laurene Landon, Alan King, Geoffrey Lewis, Paul Sorvino, Jessica James, Leigh Anne Harris, Lynette Harris; **D:** Richard T. Heffron; **W:** Larry Cohen; **M:** Bill Conti. VHS, Beta $19.98 FOX ✓✓

I Vitelloni Fellini's semi-autobiographical drama, argued by some to be his finest work. Five young men grow up in a small Italian town. As they mature, four of them remain in Romini and limit their opportunities by roping themselves off from the rest of the world. The characters are multi-dimensional, including a loafer who is supported by his sister and a young stud who impregnates a local woman. The script has some brilliant insights into youth, adulthood and what's in between. **AKA:** The Young and the Passionate; Vitelloni; Spivs.
1953 104m/B Alberto Sordi, Franco Interlenghi, Franco Fabrizi, Leopoldo Trieste; **D:** Federico Fellini; **W:** Federico Fellini, Ennio Flaino. VHS $68.00 MOV, APD, ING ✓✓✓½

I Wake Up Screaming An actress' promoter is accused of her murder. Entertaining mystery with a surprise ending. Remade as "Vicki." **AKA:** Hot Spot.
1941 82m/B Betty Grable, Victor Mature, Carole Landis, Laird Cregar, William Gargan, Alan Mowbray, Allyn Joslyn; **D:** H. Bruce Humberstone. VHS, Beta $19.98 FOX ✓✓✓

I Walked with a Zombie The definitive and eeriest of the famous Val Lewton/Jacques Tourneur horror films. Dee, a young American nurse, comes to Haiti to care for the catatonic matriarch of a troubled family. Local legends bring themselves to bear when the nurse takes the ill woman to a local voodoo ceremony for "healing." Superb, startling images and atmosphere create a unique context for this serious "Jane Eyre"-like story; its reputation has grown through the years.
1943 69m/B Frances Dee, Tom Conway, James Ellison, Christine Gordon, Edith Barrett, Darby Jones, Sir Lancelot; **D:** Jacques Tourneur. VHS, Beta $19.98 MED, FCT, MLB ✓✓✓½

I Wanna Be a Beauty Queen Divine hosts the "Alternative Miss World" pageant featuring all sorts of bizarre contestants.
1985 81m/C Divine, Little Nell, Andrew Logan. VHS, Beta $19.95 AHV, FCT, HHE ✓✓✓½

I Wanna Hold Your Hand Teenagers try to crash the Beatles' appearance on the Ed Sullivan show.
1978 (PG) 104m/C Nancy Allen, Bobby DiCicco, Wendie Jo Sperber, Marc McClure, Susan Kendall Newman, Theresa Saldana, Eddie Deezen, William Jordan; **D:** Robert Zemeckis; **W:** Robert Zemeckis. VHS, Beta $19.98 WAR, FCT ✓✓½

I Want to Live! Based on a scandalous true story, Hayward gives a riveting, Oscar-winning performance as a prostitute framed for the murder of an elderly woman and sentenced to death in the gas chamber. Producer Walter Wanger's seething indictment of capital punishment.
1958 120m/B Susan Hayward, Simon Oakland, Theodore Bikel; **D:** Robert Wise; **M:** Johnny Mandel. Academy Awards '58: Best Actress (Hayward); Nominations: Best Adapted Screenplay, Best Black and White Cinematography, Best Director (Wise), Best Sound; Golden Globe Awards '59: Best Actress—Drama (Hayward). VHS, Beta $19.98 MGM, BTV, CCB ✓✓✓

I Want What I Want A young Englishman wants a sex-change, lives as a woman, falls in love, complications ensue. Not as shocking to watch as it might seem, but more a melodramatic gender-bender.
1972 (R) 91m/C Anne Heywood, Harry Andrews, Jill Bennett; **D:** John Dexter. VHS, Beta $39.95 PSM ✓✓

I Was a Male War Bride Hilarious WWII comedy. French officer Grant falls in love with and marries WAC lieutenant Sheridan in occupied Europe. Planning to leave the continent and settle down in the U.S., the couple hits a roadblock of red tape and Grant must cross-dress as a war bride. Worth watching for Grant's performance alone. Based on the novel by Henri Rochard.
1949 105m/B Cary Grant, Ann Sheridan, Randy Stuart, Kenneth Tobey, William Neff, Marion Marshall; **D:** Howard Hawks; **W:** Charles Lederer, Leonard Spigelgass, William Neff; **M:** Cyril Mockridge. VHS $19.99 FXV ✓✓✓

I Was a Teenage TV Terrorist Two teenagers pull on-the-air pranks at the local cable television, blaming it all on an imaginary terrorist group. Poorly acted, cheaply made, and pointless. **AKA:** Amateur Hour.
1987 85m/C Adam Nathan, Julie Hanlon; **D:** Stanford Singer; **W:** Kevin McDonough. VHS, Beta $79.98 LIV Woof!

I Was a Teenage Werewolf "Rebel Without a Cause" meets "The Curse of the Werewolf" in this drive-in rock'n'roll horror. A troubled young man (pre-Bonanza Landon, in his first feature film appearance) suffers from teen angst and low production values, and falls victim to shrink Bissel. The good doctor turns out to be a bad hypnotist, and Landon's regression therapy takes him beyond childhood into his, gasp, primal past, where he sprouts a premature beard and knuckle hair. Misconstrued and full of terrible longings, the hairy highschooler is understood only by girlfriend Lime and misunderstood hair-sprouting teen viewers. Directorial debut of Fowler.
1957 70m/B Michael Landon, Yvonne Lime, Whit Bissell, Tony Marshall, Dawn Richard, Barney Phillips, Ken Miller, Cindy Robbins, Michael Rougas, Robert Griffin, Joseph Mell, Malcolm Atterbury, Eddie Marr, Vladimir Sokoloff, Louise Lewis, S. John Launer, Guy Williams, Dorothy Crehan; **D:** Gene Fowler; **W:** Ralph Thornton. VHS $9.95 COL, FCT, MLB ✓✓½

I Was a Teenage Zombie Spoof of high school horror films features a good zombie against a drug-pushing zombie. Forget the story and listen to the music by Los Lobos, the Fleshtones, the Waitresses, Dream Syndicate and Violent Femmes.
1987 92m/C Michael Rubin, Steve McCoy, Cassie Madden, Allen Rickman; **D:** John E. Michalakis. VHS, Beta $19.98 NLC ✓

I Was a Zombie for the FBI Intelligence agency toughens its hiring criteria. Much McCarthyian mirth.
1982 105m/B **D:** Maurice Penczner. VHS, Beta NO ✓½

I Will Fight No More Forever A vivid recounting of the epic true story of the legendary Chief Joseph who led the Nez Perce tribe on a 1,600-mile trek to Canada in 1877. Disturbing and powerful. Made for television.
1975 100m/C James Whitmore, Ned Romero, Sam Elliott; **D:** Richard T. Heffron. VHS, Beta $14.95 CNG, MRV, GEM ✓✓✓

I Will, I Will for Now Tacky sex clinic comedy with Keaton and Gould trying to save their marriage through kinky therapy.
1976 (R) 109m/C Diane Keaton, Elliott Gould, Paul Sorvino, Victoria Principal, Robert Alda, Warren Bellinger; **D:** Norman Panama; **W:** Norman Panama. VHS, Beta $69.95 MED ✓✓

I Wonder Who's Killing Her Now? Husband pays to have his wife murdered, then changes his mind. On-again, off-again comedy.
1976 87m/C Bob Dishy, Joanna Barnes, Bill Dana, Vito Scotti; **D:** Steven Hilliard Stern. VHS $59.95 LIV ✓✓

Ice Charley and Ellen Reed are thieves whose latest heist is $60 million in diamonds from mob boss Vito Malta. There's trouble when they try to fence the goods and Ellen is left with the merchandise and on the run from Malta's henchmen.
1993 (R) 91m/C Traci Lords, Phillip Troy, Zach Galligan, Jorge Rivero, Michael Bailey Smith, Jamie Alba, Jean Pflieger, Floyd Levine; **D:** Brook Yeaton; **W:** Sean Dash. VHS $89.95 PMH ✓✓½

Ice Castles A young figure skater's Olympic dreams are dimmed when she is blinded in an accident, but her boyfriend gives her the strength, encouragement, and love necessary to perform a small miracle. Way too schmaltzy.
1979 (PG) 110m/C Robby Benson, Lynn-Holly Johnson, Tom Skerritt, Colleen Dewhurst, Jennifer Warren, David Huffman; **D:** Donald Wrye; **M:** Marvin Hamlisch. VHS, Beta $64.95 COL ✓✓

The Ice Flood Silent family type comedy of a son who proves to the old man that he wrote the book on life, wagering the successful supervision of dad's lumberjacks.
1926 63m/B Kenneth Harlan, Viola Dana; **D:** George B. Seitz. VHS, Beta $9.95 GPV ✓✓

Ice House A sophisticated young lady flees Texas for Hollywood, searching for a better life. When her ex-lover shows up and wants her to go back, the lackless turmoil begins. Pairs real-life couple Gilbert and Brinkman.
1989 81m/C Melissa Gilbert, Bo Brinkman, Andreas Manolikakis, Buddy Quaid; **D:** Eagle Pennell. VHS, Beta $79.95 MNC ✓✓

Ice Palace Two rugged adventurers maintain a lifelong rivalry in the primitive Alaskan wilderness, their relationship dramatizing the development of the 49th state. Silly but entertaining. Based on Edna Ferber's novel.
1960 143m/C Richard Burton, Robert Ryan, Carolyn Jones, Shirley Knight, Martha Hyer, Jim Backus, George Takei; **D:** Vincent Sherman; **M:** Max Steiner. VHS, Beta $19.98 WAR ✓✓

Ice Pawn Alex Dalton may finally get to realize his dream of becoming a gold medal ice skater if he can beat Misha, his Russian rival. He soon finds out that Misha isn't his only problem, as he unknowingly becomes a pawn in a game of corruption and greed that could totally ruin his career.
1992 102m/C Paul Cross, Dan Haggerty, Robert Budaska, Chris Thomas; **D:** Barry Samson; **W:** Paul Cross. VHS NO ✓✓

Ice Pirates Space pirates in the far future steal blocks of ice to fill the needs of a thirsty galaxy. Cool plot has its moments.
1984 (PG) 91m/C Robert Urich, Mary Crosby, Michael D. Roberts, John Matuszak, Anjelica Huston, Ron Perlman, John Carradine, Robert Symonds; **D:** Stewart Raffill; **W:** Stewart Raffill; **M:** Bruce Broughton. VHS, Beta $14.95 MGM ✓½

The Ice Runner Low-key Cold War thriller, filmed in 1991, about a U.S. spy who escapes from the Soviet gulag. Jeffrey West (Albert) gets caught in a botched payoff to a Soviet minister and when the diplomats wash their hands of him a rigged trial has West sentenced to 12 years hard labor. A convenient train wreck lets him assume a different prisoner's name which gets him to a minimum security camp under the eyes of a suspicious commander. Now West needs to escape and cross 39 miles of icy tundra separating his Russian prison from American freedom.
1993 (R) 116m/C Edward Albert, Eugene Lazarev, Olga Kabo, Victor Wong, Alexander Kuznitsov, Basil Hoffman, Bill Bordy, Sergei Ruban; *D:* Barry Samson; *W:* Joyce Warren, Clifford Coleman, Joshua Stallings. **VHS $89.95** *MNC* 🎬🎬½

Ice Station Zebra A nuclear submarine races Soviet seamen to find a downed Russian satellite under a polar ice cap. Suspenseful Cold War adventure based on the novel by Alistair MacLean.
1968 (G) 148m/C Rock Hudson, Ernest Borgnine, Patrick McGoohan, Jim Brown, Lloyd Nolan, Tony Bill; *D:* John Sturges; *M:* Michel Legrand. **VHS, Beta $19.98** *MGM* 🎬🎬½

Icebox Murders A crazed, motiveless, faceless killer hangs his victims in a walk-in freezer. Store this one.
198? 90m/C Jack Taylor, Mirta Miller. **VHS, Beta** *NO Woof!*

Iced Wild fun turns to horror on a ski trip as a group of college friends are hunted by a maniac on the loose. It's all downhill.
1988 86m/C Debra Deliso, Doug Stevenson, Ron Kologie, Elizabeth Gorcey, Alan Johnson; *D:* Jeff Kwitny. **VHS, Beta $79.95** *PSM* 🎬

Iceland Labored romance of an Iceland girl and a Marine with plenty of skating thrown in for good measure. Skating and singing interludes are the best part of an otherwise average film. ♫You Can't Say No to a Soldier; There Will Never Be Another You; Lover's Knot; Let's Bring New Glory to Old Glory; I Like a Military Tune.
1942 79m/B Sonja Henie, John Payne, Jack Oakie, Felix Bressart, Osa Massen, Fritz Feld; *D:* H. Bruce Humberstone; *W:* Robert Ellis, Helen Logan. **VHS $19.98** *FXV* 🎬🎬

Iceman A frozen prehistoric man is brought back to life, after which severe culture shock takes hold. Underwritten but nicely acted, especially by Lone as the primal man.
1984 (PG) 101m/C Timothy Hutton, Lindsay Crouse, John Lone, David Strathairn, Josef Sommer, Danny Glover; *D:* Fred Schepisi; *W:* Chip Proser. **VHS, Beta $69.95** *MCA* 🎬🎬🎬

The Icicle Thief "The Naked Gun" for the art-house crowd. As a stark, black-and-white neo-realist tragedy airs on TV, bright color commercials disrupt the narrative. Soon ads invade the the movie itself, and the film's director jumps into his picture to fix the damage. Study up on your postwar Italian cinema and this'll seem hilarious; otherwise the real fun doesn't lurk in until the halfway point. In Italian with English subtitles. *AKA:* Ladri di Saponette.
1989 93m/C Maurizio Nichetti, Cateria Sylos Labini, Claudio G. Fava, Renato Scarpa, Heidi Komarek; *D:* Maurizio Nichetti. **VHS $89.95** *FXL, FCT, APD* 🎬🎬🎬

Icy Breasts A French psychiatrist tries to prevent his beautiful but psychotic patient from continuing her murdering spree. Dubbed.
1975 105m/C Alain Delon, Mireille Darc; *D:* Georges Lautner. **VHS, Beta $39.95** *FCT* 🎬🎬🎬

I'd Give My Life A gangster's ex-wife is presently married to the governor. He tries to use their honest but framed son to blackmail her.
1936 73m/B Guy Standing, Frances Drake, Tom Brown, Janet Beecher; *D:* Edwin L. Marin. **VHS, Beta $24.95** *VYY* 🎬🎬½

Idaho On a mission to close down houses of ill repute, Rodgers teams up with Autry's old sidekick Burnette.
1943 70m/B Roy Rogers, Harry Shannon, Virginia Grey, Smiley Burnette, Ona Munson; *D:* Joseph Kane. **VHS, Beta $9.95** *NOS, VDM, VCN* 🎬½

Idaho Transfer Fonda's second directorial effort; Carradine's first screen appearance. An obnoxious group of teens travel through time to Idaho in the year 2044. Environmental wasteland story is dull and confused. *AKA:* Deranged.
1973 (PG) 90m/C Keith Carradine, Kelley Bohanan; *D:* Peter Fonda. **VHS, Beta $19.95** *MPI, FCT* Woof!

Identity Crisis Campy fashion maven and flamboyant rapper switch identities causing much tedious overacting. Lifeless murder comedy from father and son Van Peebles.
1990 (R) 98m/C Mario Van Peebles, Ilan Mitchell-Smith, Nicholas Kepros, Shelly Burch, Richard Clarke; *D:* Melvin Van Peebles. **VHS $19.95** *ACA* 🎬

Identity Unknown Shell-shocked veteran goes AWOL to discover who he is, meeting grieving relatives along the way. Interesting premise is sometimes moving.
1945 70m/B Richard Arlen, Cheryl Walker, Roger Pryor, Bobby Driscoll; *D:* Walter Colmes. **VHS, Beta, 8mm $24.95** *VYY* 🎬🎬½

The Idiot Dostoevski's Russian novel is transported by Kurosawa across two centuries to post-war Japan, where the madness and jealousy continue to rage. In Japanese with English subtitles.
1951 166m/B Toshiro Mifune, Masayuki Mori, Setsuko Hara, Yoshiko Kuga, Takashi Shimura; *D:* Akira Kurosawa. **VHS $79.95** *NYF, ING* 🎬🎬🎬🎬

Idiot's Delight At an Alpine hotel, a song and dance man meets a gorgeous Russian countess who reminds him of a former lover. Incredibly, Gable sings and dances through "Puttin' on the Ritz," the film's big highlight. Based on the Pulitzer Prize-winning play by Robert Sherwood.
1939 107m/B Clark Gable, Norma Shearer, Burgess Meredith, Edward Arnold; *D:* Clarence Brown. **VHS, Beta $19.98** *CCB, MGM* 🎬🎬🎬

The Idol Dancer Romance and adventure in the South Seas with a drunken American beachcomber inspired by love to change his ways. There's also a native uprising for added excitement. Minor Griffith but nice Nassau scenery.
1920 93m/B Richard Barthelmess, Clarine Seymour, Creighton Hale, George MacQuarrie, Kate Bruce, Anders Randolf, Walter James, Thomas Carr; *D:* D.W. Griffith. **VHS $19.95** *GPV, GVV* 🎬🎬

Idolmaker A conniving agent can make a rock star out of anyone. Well-acted fluff with Sharkey taking a strong lead. The first film by hack-meister Hackford and somewhat based on true-life teen fab Fabian.
1980 (PG) 119m/C Ray Sharkey, Tovah Feldshuh, Peter Gallagher, Paul Land, Joe Pantoliano, Maureen McCormick, John Aprea, Richard Bright, Olympia Dukakis, Steven Apostlee Peck; *D:* Taylor Hackford. **VHS, Beta $14.95** *MGM* 🎬🎬

If... Three unruly seniors at a British boarding school refuse to conform. A popular, anarchic indictment of staid British society, using the same milieu as Vigo's "Zero de Conduite," with considerably more violence. The first of Anderson and McDowell's trilogy, culminating in "O Lucky Man!" and "Britannia Hospital." In color and black and white.
1969 (R) 111m/C Malcolm McDowell, David Wood, Christine Noonan, Richard Warwick, Robert Swann, Arthur Lowe, Mona Washbourne, Graham Crowden, Simon Ward; *D:* Lindsay Anderson. **VHS, Beta $49.95** *PAR* 🎬🎬🎬🎬

If Ever I See You Again The creator of "You Light Up My Life" stars in the sentimental melodrama. Two adolescent lovers meet again years later and try to rekindle old passions. Done with as much skill as "Light" minus a hit song.
1978 (PG) 105m/C Joseph Brooks, Shelley Hack, Jerry Keller, Jimmy Breslin; *D:* Joseph Brooks; *W:* Joseph Brooks; *M:* Joseph Brooks. **VHS, Beta $69.95** *COL* 🎬

If I Were Rich Gwenn is arranging a meeting at his home for a group of financiers he hopes will back a scheme to save his ailing business. Meanwhile he has to dodge bill collectors and others determined to ruin his plans. *AKA:* Cash; For Love or Money.
1933 63m/B Edmund Gwenn, Wendy Barrie, Robert Donat, Clifford Heatherly; *D:* Zoltan Korda. **VHS, Beta $24.95** *VYY, FCT, NOS* 🎬🎬

If It's a Man, Hang Up A model is terrified by harrowing telephone calls from a stranger.
1975 71m/C Carol Lynley, Gerald Harper. **VHS, Beta $29.95** *LIV* 🎬½

If It's Tuesday, This Must Be Belgium A fast-paced, frantic, and funny look at a group of Americans on a whirlwind European tour. The group does a nine-country, 18-day bus tour with clashing, comic personalities and lots of romantic possibilities. Remade as a 1987 television movie.
1969 (G) 99m/C Suzanne Pleshette, Ian McShane, Mildred Natwick, Norman Fell, Michael Constantine, Peggy Cass, Murray Hamilton, Marty Ingels, Sandy Baron, Pamela Britton, Luke Halpin; *D:* Mel Stuart. **VHS $19.98** *MGM, MOV* 🎬🎬🎬

If Looks Could Kill Would-be film noir about a man spying on a female embezzler and falling in love.
1986 (R) 90m/C Alan Fisler, Tim Gail, Kim Lambert, Jeanne Marie; *D:* Chuck Vincent. **VHS $79.95** *REP* 🎬🎬

If Looks Could Kill TV stud Grieco makes film debut as a high school class cutup who travels to France with his class to parlez vous for extra credit. Mistaken for a CIA agent, he stumbles into a plot to take over all the money in the whole wide world, and much implausible action and eyelash batting follows. Extra kibbles for supporting characterizations. Oh, and don't be put off by the fact that the Parisian scenes were shot in Montreal.
1991 (PG-13) 89m/C Richard Grieco, Linda Hunt, Roger Rees, Robin Bartlett, Gabrielle Anwar, Roger Daltrey, Geraldine James, Carole Davis; *D:* William Dear; *W:* Fred Dekker; *M:* David Foster. **VHS, Beta, 8mm $19.98** *WAR* 🎬🎬½

If Things Were Different Feisty woman struggles to hold her family together after her husband is hospitalized with a nervous breakdown.
1979 96m/C Suzanne Pleshette, Tony Roberts, Arte Johnson, Chuck McCann, Don Murray; *D:* Robert Lewis. **VHS, Beta $34.98** *WOV* 🎬½

If You Could See What I Hear Irritatingly upbeat true-life story of blind singer-musician, Tom Sullivan. Covers his life from college days to marriage. Sophomoric comedy centers around the hero's irresponsible, and often life-endangering, behavior.
1982 (PG) 103m/C Marc Singer, R.H. Thomson, Sarah Torgov, Shari Belafonte-Harper; *D:* Eric Till. **VHS, Beta $79.95** *VES* ✶✶½

If You Don't Stop It...You'll Go Blind A series of gauche and tasteless vignettes from various little-known comedians.
1977 (R) 80m/C Pat McCormick, George Spencer, Patrick Wright; *D:* Bob Levy, Keefe Brasselle. **VHS, Beta $54.95** *MED* ✶½

If You Knew Susie Two retired vaudeville actors find a letter from George Washington which establishes them as descendants of a colonial patriot and the heirs to a seven billion dollar fortune. ♫If You Knew Susie; My Brooklyn Love Song; What Do I Want With Money?; We're Living the Life We Love; My, How the Time Goes By.
1948 90m/B Eddie Cantor, Joan Davis, Allyn Joslyn, Charles Dingle, Charles Halton; *D:* Gordon Douglas. **VHS, Beta $34.98** *CCB* ✶✶

Igor & the Lunatics Tasteless tale of a cannibal cult leader released from prison who picks up where he left off.
1985 (R) 79m/C Joseph Eero, Joe Niola, T.J. Michaels; *D:* Billy Parolini. **VHS, Beta $69.98** *LIV* ✶

Iguana The videocassette box art makes this look like a horror movie, but it's really a stiff, solemn period drama about a deformed sailor with lizardlike features. After a life of mistreatment he reigns mercilessly over a handful of island castaways. An international coproduction with mostly English dialogue, some Spanish and Portuguese with subtitles.
1989 ?m/C Everett McGill; *D:* Monte Hellman. **VHS $79.99** *IMP* ✶✶

Ike Duvall is top brass in this made-for-television epic biography tracing Eisenhower's career during WWII. Previously a six-hour mini-series; also titled "Ike: The War Years." *AKA:* Ike: The War Years.
1979 291m/C Robert Duvall, Lee Remick, Darren McGavin, Dana Andrews, Laurence Luckinbill; *D:* Melville Shavelson. **VHS, Beta $29.95** *VMK* ✶✶½

Ikiru When a clerk finds out he is dying of cancer, he decides to build a children's playground and give something of himself back to the world. Highly acclaimed, heartbreaking drama from the unusually restrained Kurosawa; possibly his most "eastern" film. In Japanese with English subtitles. *AKA:* To Live.
1952 134m/B Takashi Shimura, Nobuo Kaneko, Kyoko Seki, Miki Odagari, Yunosuke Ito; *D:* Akira Kurosawa. **VHS, Beta $39.95** *HMV, VYG, CRC* ✶✶✶✶

Il Bell'Antonio The boastful Antonio has a reputation as a womanizer but when he finally marries, to a lovely young woman, he faces the loss of his libido. Satire of machismo, marriage, and Catholicism. In Italian with English subtitles.
1960 115m/C Marcello Mastroianni, Claudia Cardinale, Pierre Brasseur; *D:* Mauro Bolognini; *W:* Pier Paolo Pasolini, Gino Vissentini. **VHS $59.95** *KIV, FCT* ✶✶½

Il Grido A jilted husband takes his young daughter from village to village in search of the woman who deserted them for another man. Set in the desolate Po Valley of director Antonioni's childhood. In Italian with English subtitles. *AKA:* The Cry; The Outcry.
1957 116m/B Steve Cochran, Alida Valli, Dorian Gray, Betsy Blair, Gabriella Pallotti; *D:* Michelangelo Antonioni; *W:* Michelangelo Antonioni, Ennio de Concini; *M:* Giovanni Fusco. **VHS $59.95** *KIV, FCT* ✶✶

Il Sorpasso A braggart, who has failed at everything, spends all his time traveling around Italy in his sportscar. He takes a repressed law student under his wing and decides to teach him how to have fun. In Italian with English subtitles.
1963 116m/B Vittorio Gassman, Jean-Louis Trintignant; *D:* Dino Risi. **VHS $59.95** *ING* ✶✶½

I'll Cry Tomorrow Hayward brilliantly portrays actress Lillian Roth as she descends into alcoholism and then tries to overcome her addiction. Based on Roth's memoirs. ♫Sing You Sinners; When The Red Red Robin Comes Bob Bob Bobbin' Along; Happiness Is Just a Thing Called Joe; Vagabond King Waltz.
1955 119m/B Susan Hayward, Richard Conte, Eddie Albert, Jo Van Fleet, Margo, Don Taylor, Ray Danton, Veda Ann Borg; *D:* Daniel Mann. Academy Awards '55: Best Costume Design (B & W); Nominations: Best Actress (Hayward), Best Art Direction/Set Decoration (B & W), Best Black and White Cinematography; Cannes Film Festival '56: Best Actress (Hayward). **VHS, Beta $19.98** *MGM* ✶✶✶

I'll Do Anything Hollywood satire finds unemployed actor Matt (Nolte) suddenly forced to care for his six-year-old daughter Jeannie (Wright), whom he hasn't seen in three years. Matt also finally gets a job—as a chauffeur to an obnoxious producer (well-played by Brooks) whose company winds up making the manipulative demon Jeannie into a hot child star. Great work by Kavner as the owner of a test-screening service who romances Brooks. Originally intended as a musical, the test screenings were so disastrous that the numbers were axed. What's left is less jerky than expected; Brooks reportedly based his character in part on mega-mogul Joel Silver.
1993 (PG-13) 115m/C Nick Nolte, Albert Brooks, Julie Kavner, Whittni Wright, Joely Richardson, Tracey Ullman; *D:* James L. Brooks; *W:* James L. Brooks; *M:* Hans Zimmer. **VHS** *COL* ✶✶½

I'll Get You An FBI agent goes to England on the trail of a kidnapping ring. *AKA:* Escape Route.
1953 79m/B George Raft, Sally Gray, Clifford Evans; *D:* Seymour Friedman. **VHS, Beta** *RXM* ✶✶

I'll Name the Murderer Suspense film in which a gossip columnist starts his own investigation into the murder of a club singer.
1936 ?m/C Ralph Forbes, Marion Shilling; *D:* Raymond K. Johnson. **VHS $16.95** *SNC* ✶✶

I'll See You in My Dreams Hokey but fun musical biography of songwriter Gus Kahn (Thomas) and his wife Grace LeBoy (Day). Kahn gets his start in Ziegfeld shows but loses both his career and wife after the 1929 crash. However, she soon returns and everything ends happily ever after. ♫Ain't We Got Fun; Ukelele Lady; The One I Love Belongs To Somebody Else; I'll See You In My Dreams; It Had To Be You; Swingin' Down the Lane; My Buddy; Makin' Whoopee!; Yes Sir, That's My Baby.
1951 109m/B Danny Thomas, Doris Day, Frank Lovejoy, Patrice Wymore, James Gleason, Mary Wickes, Jim Backus, Minna Gombell, William Forrest; *D:* Michael Curtiz; *W:* Melville Shavelson, Jack Rose. **VHS $19.98** *WAR, MVD* ✶✶½

I'll Take Sweden Overprotective father Hope disapproves of teenaged daughter Weld's guitar-playing boyfriend (Avalon). So to keep her out of harm's way he finagles a company transfer to Sweden. Dad falls for an interior decorator (Merrill) while Weld gets involved with a Swedish playboy (Slate). Deciding Avalon is the lesser of two evils, Hope schemes to get the two back together.
1965 96m/C Bob Hope, Tuesday Weld, Frankie Avalon, Dina Merrill, Jeremy Slate, Walter Sande, John Qualen, Roy Roberts, Maudie Prickett; *D:* Fred de Cordova; *W:* Arthur Marx, Bob Fisher, Nat Perrin. **VHS, Beta $19.98** *MGM, FCT* ✶✶½

Illegal Crime melodrama stars Robinson as an attorney who risks all to acquit his assistant of murder. Early Mansfield appearance. Remake of "The Mouthpiece."
1955 88m/B Edward G. Robinson, Nina Foch, Hugh Marlowe, Jayne Mansfield, Albert Dekker, Ellen Corby, DeForest Kelley, Howard St. John; *D:* Lewis Allen. **VHS** *NO* ✶✶½

Illegal Entry: Formula for Fear Tracie's scientist father has invented a formula that could change the world. When he's murdered the formula falls into her unsuspecting hands. Tracie might not know what she has but that doesn't stop some very ruthless efforts to get the information others want.
1993 88m/C Sabryn Gene't, Barbara Lee Alexander, Gregory Vignolle, Arthur Roberts, Carol Hoyt; *D:* Henri Charr; *W:* John B. Pfeifer. **VHS $89.95** *PMH* ✶½

Illegally Yours Miscast comedy about a college student serving on the jury in trial of old girlfriend. Bring down the gavel on this one.
1987 (PG) 94m/C Rob Lowe, Colleen Camp, Kenneth Mars; *D:* Peter Bogdanovich. **VHS, Beta $14.95** *MGM* ✶

Illicit In love, Stanwyck fears that marrying Rennie will only ruin their wonderful relationship. Two years after their marriage her fears are realized when each searches for happiness with a past lover. A melodramatic performance that doesn't quite hit its mark. Remade two years later as "Ex-Lady" with Bette Davis in the lead. Based on the play by Edith Fitzgerald and Robert Riskin.
1931 76m/B Barbara Stanwyck, Ricardo Cortez, Natalie Moorhead, Charles Butterworth, Joan Blondell, Claude Gillingwater; *D:* Archie Mayo; *W:* Harvey Thew. **VHS $19.98** *MGM* ✶✶

Illicit Behavior A dangerous manipulative woman (Severance) is out to claim a $2 million inheritance in this intricate and seductive police thriller. Included among her victims are her husband; a Hollywood vice cop suspended for use of excessive force; his partner; her husband's internal affairs adversary; and her own psychiatrist. Also available in an uncut, unrated version.
1991 (R) 101m/C Joan Severance, Robert Davi, James Russo, Jack Scalia, Kent McCord; *D:* Worth Keeter. **VHS $29.95** *PSM* ✶✶½

The Illusion Travels by Streetcar Odd but enchanting story of two men who restore a streetcar, only to find that it will not be used by the city. In a gesture of defiance, they steal the streetcar and take it for one last ride, picking up an interesting assortment of characters along the way. In Spanish with English subtitles. Not released in the U.S. until 1977. *AKA:* La Illusion en Travnia.
1953 90m/B Lilia Prado, Carlos Navarro, Domingo Soler, Fernando Soto, Agustin Isunza, Miguel Manzano; *D:* Luis Bunuel. **VHS $59.95** *CVC, FCT* ✶✶✶

Illusions Jan (Locklear) is trying to recover from a nervous breakdown and improve her crumbling marriage when her husband's sexy sister arrives and things start to heat up. Jan thinks her husband and sister-in-law are just a little too close, but when she lets her landlord in on her suspicions, he reacts quite strangely. Will Jan have another nervous breakdown? Mysterious with lots of plot twists. Based on Colley's play "I'll Be Back Before Midnight."
19v1 (R) 95m/C Robert Carradine, Heather Locklear, Emma Samms, Ned Beatty; **D:** Victor Kulle; **W:** Peter Colley. **VHS, Beta** $89.95 PSM ♫♫

The Illustrated Man A young drifter meets a tattooed man. Each tattoo causes a fantastic story to unfold. A strange, interesting, but finally limited attempt at literary sci-fi. Based on the story collection by Ray Bradbury.
1969 (PG) 103m/C Rod Steiger, Claire Bloom, Robert Drivas, Don Dubbins; **D:** Jack Smight; **M:** Jerry Goldsmith. **VHS, Beta** $19.98 WAR, FCT, MLB ♫♫♫

Ilsa, Harem Keeper of the Oil Sheiks The naughty Ilsa works for an Arab sheik in the slave trade. More graphic violence and nudity. Plot makes an appearance.
1976 (R) 45m/C Dyanne Thorne, Michael Thayer. **VHS** $59.98 CIC Woof!

Ilsa, She-Wolf of the SS The torture-loving Ilsa runs a medical camp for the Nazis. Plot is incidental to nudity and violence.
1974 (R) 45m/C Dyanne Thorne, Greg Knoph; **D:** Don Edmunds. **VHS** $59.98 CIC Woof!

Ilsa, the Tigress of Siberia Everyone's favorite torturer has been working her wiles on political prisoners in Russia. After escaping to Canada, her past threatens to catch up with her. As usual, no plot, violence.
1979 85m/C Dyanne Thorne, Michel Morin, Tony Angelo, Terry Coady, Howard Mauer; **D:** Jean LaFleur. **VHS** NO Woof!

Ilsa, the Wicked Warden Ilsa is now a warden of a woman's prison in South America, behaving just as badly as she always has, until the prisoners stage an uprising. Lots of skin, no violence, no acting. Also: no plot. **AKA:** Ilsa, the Absolute Power; Greta the Mad Butcher.
1978 (R) 90m/C Dyanne Thorne, Lina Romay, Jess (Jesus) Franco; **D:** Jess (Jesus) Franco. **VHS** $59.98 CIC Woof!

I'm a Fool A two-character romantic study involving an act of insincerity between two race track aficionados. Based on the Sherwood Anderson story. From the American Short Story Collection. Made for television.
1977 38m/C Ron Howard, Amy Irving; **D:** Noel Black. **VHS, Beta** $24.95 MON, KAR ♫♫½

I'm All Right Jack Sellers plays a pompous communist union leader in this hilarious satire of worker-management relations. Based on Alan Hackney's novel "Private Life."
1959 101m/B Peter Sellers, Ian Carmichael, Terry-Thomas, Victor Maddern; **D:** John Boulting. **VHS, Beta** $19.98 FCT ♫♫♫

I'm Dancing as Fast as I Can A successful television producer hopelessly dependent on tranquilizers tries to stop cold turkey. Good story could be better; based on Barbara Gordon's memoirs.
1982 (R) 107m/C Jill Clayburgh, Nicol Williamson, Dianne West, Joe Pesci, Geraldine Page, John Lithgow, Daniel Stern; **D:** Jack Hofsiss; **W:** David Rabe. **VHS, Beta** $69.95 PAR ♫♫

I'm Dangerous Tonight Wallflower Amick (Shelley the Waitress in Twin Peaks) turns into party monster when she dons red dress made from evil ancient Aztec cloak. Many dead soldiers when this girl parties. Based on a Cornell Woolrich short story, it's another in a series of ever more disappointing entries from Hooper, whose cult fave "Texas Chainsaw Massacre" had low as they come production values, but far better scares. Originally cable fare.
1990 (R) 92m/C Madchen Amick, Corey Parker, R. Lee Ermey, Mary Frann, Dee Wallace Stone, Anthony Perkins; **D:** Tobe Hooper; **W:** Alice Wilson. **VHS** $79.95 MCA ♫½

I'm from Arkansas The little town of Pitchfork, Arkansas, goes nuts when a pig gives birth to ten piglets.
1944 68m/B El Brendel, Slim Summerville, Iris Adrian, Harry Harvey, Bruce (Herman Brix) Bennett; **D:** Lew Landers. **VHS, Beta** $24.95 NOS, MRV, DVT ♫

I'm Gonna Git You Sucka Parody of "blaxploitation" films popular during the '60s and '70s. Funny and laced with out-right bellylaughs. A number of stars who made "blaxploitation" films, including Jim Brown, take part in the gags.
1988 (R) 89m/C Keenan Ivory Wayans, Bernie Casey, Steve James, Isaac Hayes, Jim Brown, Ja'net DuBois, Anne-Marie Johnson, Antonio Fargas, Eve Plumb, John Vernon, Clu Gulager, Kadeem Hardison, Damon Wayans, Gary Owens, Clarence Williams III, David Alan Grier, Kim Wayans, Robin Harris, Chris Rock, Dawnn Lewis, Jester Hairston; **Cameos:** Robert Townsend; **D:** Keenan Ivory Wayans; **W:** Keenan Ivory Wayans; **M:** David Michael Frank. **VHS, Beta** $19.95 MGM ♫♫♫

I'm No Angel "Beulah, peel me a grape." Well, you'd be hungry too if you spent your time eyeing playboy Grant as West does. She's a circus floozy who's prone to extorting money from her men (after hashing over their shortcomings with her seen-it-all-maid, the aforementioned Beulah). However, after wooing Grant, she sues for breach of promise. This leads to a comic courtroom scene with Grant bringing in all West's ex-lovers as witnesses. Grant's second film with West, following "She Done Him Wrong."
1933 88m/B Mae West, Cary Grant, Gregory Ratoff, Edward Arnold, Ralf Harolde, Kent Taylor, Gertrude Michael, Russell Hopton, Dorothy Peterson, William B. Davidson, Gertrude Howard; **D:** Wesley Ruggles; **W:** Mae West. **VHS** $14.98 MCA, BTV ♫♫♫

I'm on My Way/The Non-Stop Kid Two classic shorts: "I'm on My Way" (1919), in which Lloyd's dreams of an idyllic marriage are shattered; and "The Non-Stop Kid" (1918), in which Lloyd must contend with a rival for the affection of his beloved.
1918 30m/B Harold Lloyd, Snub Pollard, Bebe Daniels; **D:** Harold Lloyd. **VHS, Beta** $19.98 CCB, GVV ♫♫♫

I'm the Girl He Wants to Kill A woman sees a murder committed, and the murderer sees her. Now he's after her.
1974 71m/C Julie Sommars, Anthony Steel. **VHS, Beta** NO ♫½

I'm the One You're Looking For A famous model obsessively combs Barcelona for the man who raped her. Suspenseful thriller. In Spanish with English subtitles.
1988 85m/C Patricia Adriani, Chus Lampreave, Ricard Borras, Toni Canto, Angel Alcazar, Marta Fedz, Frank Muro, Miriam DeMaeztu; **D:** Jaime Chavarri. **VHS** $79.95 FXL, FCT, IME ♫♫½

The Image Anchorman Finney, the unscrupulous czar of infotainment, does a little soul delving when a man he wrongly implicated in a savings and loan debacle decides to check into the hereafter ahead of schedule. Seems the newsmonger's cut a few corners en route to the bigtime, and his public is mad as hell and...oops, wrong movie (need we say there are not a few echoes of "Network"?). Finney's great. Made for cable.
1989 91m/C Albert Finney, John Mahoney, Kathy Baker, Swoosie Kurtz, Marsha Mason, Spalding Gray; **D:** Peter Werner; **M:** James Newton Howard. **VHS** $89.95 HBO ♫♫½

Image of Bruce Lee Martial arts fight scenes prevail in this story about a jeweler who is swindled out of $1 million worth of diamonds.
197? (G) 88m/C Bruce Li, Chang Wu Lang, Chang Lei, Dana. **VHS, Beta** $29.95 MED ♫

Image of Death Woman plots to take the life of an old school chum, assume her identity, and then blow up the Capitol.
1977 83m/C Cathy Paine, Cheryl Waters, Tony Banner, Barry Pierce, Sheila Helpmann, Pennie Hackforth-Jones; **D:** Kevin Dobson. **VHS, Beta** NO ♫

Image of Passion Weak account of male stripper/lovely advertising executive romance.
1986 90m/C James Horan, Susan Damante Shaw, Edward Bell; **D:** Susan Orlikoff-Simon. **Beta** $14.95 PSM ♫

Imagemaker Uneven story of a presidential media consultant who bucks the system and exposes corruption.
1986 (R) 93m/C Michael Nouri, Jerry Orbach, Jessica Harper, Farley Granger; **D:** Hal Wiener. **VHS, Beta** $79.98 LIV, VES ♫½

Imitation of Life Remake of the successful 1939 Claudette Colbert outing of the same title, and based on Fanny Hurst's novel, with a few plot changes. Turner is a single mother, more determined to achieve acting fame and fortune than function as a parent. Her black maid, Moore, is devoted to her own daughter (Kohner), but loses her when the girl discovers she can pass for white. When Turner discovers that she and her daughter are in love with the same man, she realizes how little she knows her daughter, and how much the two of them have missed by not having a stronger relationship. Highly successful at the box office.
1959 124m/C Lana Turner, John Gavin, Troy Donahue, Sandra Dee, Juanita Moore, Susan Kohner; **D:** Douglas Sirk. Academy Awards '59 Nominations: Best Supporting Actress (Kohner), Best Supporting Actress (Moore); Golden Globe Awards '60: Best Supporting Actress (Kohner). **VHS, Beta** $14.95 MCA, FCT ♫♫♫

Immediate Family Childless couple contact a pregnant, unmarried girl and her boyfriend in hopes of adoption. As the pregnancy advances, the mother has doubts about giving up her baby. A bit sugar-coated in an effort to woo family trade.
1989 (PG-13) 112m/C Glenn Close, James Woods, Kevin Dillon, Mary Stuart Masterson, Kevin Dillon, Linda Darlow, Jane Greer, Jessica James, Mimi Kennedy; **D:** Jonathan Kaplan; **W:** Barbara Benedek; **M:** Brad Fiedel. **VHS, Beta** $19.95 COL ♫♫½

The Immigrant Chaplin portrays a newly arrived immigrant who falls in love with the first girl he meets. Silent with musical soundtrack added.
1917 20m/B Charlie Chaplin; **D:** Charlie Chaplin. **VHS, Beta** CAB, GVV ♫♫♫½

Immortal Bachelor Good cast can't overcome the silliness of this one. A juror daydreams about the dead husband of a cleaning woman on trial for killing her adulterous spouse. She decides the dead man seems a lot more exciting than her own dull and tiresome husband.
1980 (PG) 94m/C Giancarlo Giannini, Monica Vitti, Claudia Cardinale, Vittorio Gassman; *D:* Marcello Fondato. **VHS, Beta** NO *Ⅱ* 1/2

Immortal Battalion Entertaining wartime psuedo-documentary follows newly recruited soldiers as they are molded from an ordinary group of carping civilians into a hardened battalion of fighting men by Niven. Some prints run to 116 minutes. *AKA:* The Way Ahead.
1944 89m/B David Niven, Stanley Holloway, Reginald Tate, Raymond Huntley, William Hartnell, James Donald, Peter Ustinov; *D:* Carol Reed; *W:* Peter Ustinov, Eric Ambler. **VHS, Beta** $14.95 NOS, MRV, VYY *ⅢⅢ*

Immortal Combat An army of men trained in ninja and guerilla warfare have seemingly immortal powers. Can our two violent heroes find an equally destructive way to stop the killing?
1994 (R) 109m/C Roddy Piper, Sonny Chiba, Tiny Lister, Meg Foster; *D:* Daniel Neira. **VHS** $92.95 APX *Ⅱ* 1/2

Immortal Sergeant After the battle death of the squad leader, an inexperienced corporal takes command of North African troops during WWII. Fonda gives a strong performance. Based on a novel by John Brody.
1943 91m/B Henry Fonda, Thomas Mitchell, Maureen O'Hara, Allyn Joslyn, Reginald Gardiner, Melville Cooper, Morton Lowry; *D:* John M. Stahl; *W:* Lamar Trotti. **VHS, Beta** $19.98 FOX *ⅡⅡ* 1/2

Immortal Sins Michael and Susan inherited an old Spanish Castle, complete with its own curse, which comes in the form of a seductive women that has haunted families for centuries.
1991 (R) 80m/C Cliff DeYoung, Maryam D'Abo. **VHS** NO *Ⅱ*

The Immortalizer A mad doctor transfers people's brains into young bodies for a price, although it's not as simple as it sounds.
1989 (R) 85m/C Ron Kay, Chris Crone, Melody Patterson, Clarke Lindsley, Bekki Armstrong; *D:* Joel Bender. **VHS, Beta** $79.95 COL *Ⅱ*

Impact A woman and her lover plan the murder of her rich industrialist husband, but the plan backfires. More twists and turns than a carnival ride.
1949 83m/B Brian Donlevy, Ella Raines; *D:* Arthur Lubin. **VHS, Beta** $14.95 NOS, MRV, DVT *ⅢⅢ*

The Imperial Japanese Empire Epic of the WWII Pacific seen through Japanese eyes.
1985 130m/C Tetsuro Tamba, Tomokazu Miura, Teruhiko Saigo, Teruhiko Aoi, Saburo Shinoda, Keiko Sekine, Masako Natsume, Akiko Kana. **VHS, Beta** $69.95 VCD *Ⅱ*

Imperial Navy A WWII epic as seen from the Japanese perspective, concentrating on their great navy and its suicide squadrons. Dubbed.
198? 145m/C *D:* Paul Aaron. **VHS, Beta** $59.95 MOV *Ⅱ*

Imperial Venus Biography of Napoleon's sister, Paolina Boneparte—with particular focus on her many loves, lusts and tribulations.
1971 (PG) 121m/C Gina Lollobrigida, Stephen Boyd, Raymond Pellegrin; *D:* Jean Delannoy. **VHS, Beta** $49.95 VCI *ⅡⅡ*

Importance of Being Earnest Fine production of classic Oscar Wilde comedy-of-manners. Cast couldn't be better or the story funnier.
1952 95m/C Michael Redgrave, Edith Evans, Margaret Rutherford, Michael Denison, Joan Greenwood; *D:* Anthony Asquith. **VHS, Beta** $19.95 PAR, HMV *ⅢⅢ*

The Imported Bridegroom A comedy set at the turn of the century about a man who returns to Poland in order to find his daughter a proper husband.
1989 93m/C Eugene Trooback, Avi Hoffman, Greta Cowan, Annette Miller; *D:* Pamela Berger; *W:* Pamela Berger. **VHS** $29.95 ERG, ING *ⅡⅡ*

The Impossible Spy True story of Elie Cohen, an unassuming Israeli who doubled as a top level spy in Syria during the 1960s. Cohen became so close to Syria's president that he was nominated to become the Deputy Minister of Defense before his double life was exposed. Well-acted spy thriller made for cable and is worth a look for espionage fans.
1987 96m/C John Shea, Eli Wallach, Michal Bat-Adam, Rami Danon, Sasson Gabray, Chaim Girafi; *D:* Jim Goddard. **VHS** $79.99 HBO, NCJ, FCT *ⅢⅢ*

The Impossible Years Unattractive, leering sex farce about psychiatrist Nivens who has problems with his own young daughter. Dismal adaptation of the hit Broadway play by Bob Fisher and Arthur Marx.
1968 97m/C David Niven, Lola Albright, Chad Everett, Ozzie Nelson, Christina Ferrare, Jeff Cooper, John Harding; *D:* Michael Gordon; *W:* George Wells. **VHS** $19.98 MGM *Ⅱ*

The Imposter Improbable tale of a con artist/ex-con who impersonates a high school principal in order to regain his estranged girlfriend, who works as a teacher. Complications ensue when he tackles the school's drug problems. Made for television.
1984 95m/C Anthony Geary, Billy Dee Williams, Lorna Patterson; *D:* Michael Pressman. **VHS, Beta** $79.95 PSM *Ⅱ* 1/2

Imposters A comedy centering on the romantic problems between a self-indulgent young man and the woman who cheats on him.
1984 110m/C Ellen McElduff, Charles Ludlum, Lisa Todd, Peter Evans. **VHS, Beta** NO *ⅡⅡ*

Impromptu A smart, sassy, romantic comedy set in 1880s Europe among the era's artistic greats—here depicted as scalawags, parasites and early beatniks. The film's ace is Davis in a lusty, dynamic role as mannish authoress George Sand, obsessively in love with the dismayed composer Chopin. Though he's too pallid a character for her attraction to be credible, a great cast and abundant wit make this a treat. Beautiful score featuring Chopin and Liszt. Film debut of stage director Lapine; screenplay written by his wife, Sarah Kernochan.
1990 (PG-13) 108m/C Judy Davis, Hugh Grant, Mandy Patinkin, Bernadette Peters, Julian Sands, Ralph Brown, Georges Corraface, Anton Rodgers, Emma Thompson, Anna Massey; *D:* James Lapine; *W:* Sarah Kernochan. **VHS** $19.95 TVC, MOV *ⅢⅢ*

Improper Channels Mediocre comedy about a couple trying to recover their daughter after being accused of child abuse.
1982 (PG) 91m/C Monica Parker, Alan Arkin, Mariette Hartley; *D:* Eric Till. **VHS, Beta** $69.95 VES *ⅡⅡ*

Impulse When his wife leaves for a visit with her mother, a young man is thrust into cahoots with gangsters, and wrapped up in an affair with another woman.
1955 81m/B Arthur Kennedy, Constance Smith, Joy Shelton; *D:* Charles De Latour. **VHS** $29.95 FCT *Ⅱ* 1/2

Impulse Shatner, a crazed killer, is released from prison and starts to kill again in this low-budget, predictable, critically debased film about child-molesting. *AKA:* Want a Ride, Little Girl?; I Love to Kill.
1974 (PG) 85m/C William Shatner, Ruth Roman, Harold Sakata, Kim Nicholas, Jennifer Bishop, James Dobbs; *D:* William Grefe. **VHS, Beta** $79.95 LIV, VES Woof!

Impulse Small town residents can't control their impulses, all because of government toxic waste in their milk. A woman worried about her mother's mental health returns to town with her doctor boyfriend to discover most of the inhabitants are quite mad. Starts strong but...
1984 (R) 95m/C Tim Matheson, Meg Tilly, Hume Cronyn, John Karlen, Bill Paxton, Amy Stryker, Claude Earl Jones, Sherri Stoner; *D:* Graham Baker. **VHS, Beta** $29.98 VES *ⅡⅡ*

Impulse A beautiful undercover vice cop poses as a prostitute, and gives in to base desires. Russell gives a fine performance in this underrated sleeper.
1990 (R) 109m/C Theresa Russell, Nicholas Mele, Eli Danker, Charles McCaughan, Jeff Fahey, George Dzundza, Alan Rosenberg, Lynne Thigpen, Shawn Elliott; *D:* Sondra Locke; *M:* Michel Colombier. **VHS, Beta** $92.95 WAR *ⅡⅡ* 1/2

Impure Thoughts Four friends meet in the afterlife and discuss their Catholic school days. Odd premise never catches fire.
1986 (PG) 87m/C Brad Dourif, Lane Davies, John Putch, Terry Beaver; *D:* Michael A. Simpson. **VHS, Beta** $19.98 NLC *Ⅱ*

In a Glass Cage A young boy who was tortured and sexually molested by a Nazi official seeks revenge. Years after the war, he shows up at the Nazi's residence in Spain and is immediately befriended by his tormentor's family. Confined to an iron lung, the official is at the mercy of the young man who tortuously acts out the incidents detailed in the Nazi's journal. Suspenseful and extremely graphic, it's well crafted and meaningful but may be just too horrible to watch. Sexual and violent acts place it in the same league as Pasolini's infamous "Salo, or The 120 Days in Sodom." Definitely not for the faint of heart. In Spanish with English subtitles. *AKA:* Tras el Cristal.
1986 110m/C Gunter Meisner, David Sust, Marisa Paredes, Gisela Echevarria; *D:* Agustin Villaronga. **VHS** $79.95 CCN, FCT, ING *ⅡⅡ* 1/2

In a Lonely Place Bogart is outstanding as a volatile Hollywood screenwriter who has an affair with starlet Grahame while under suspicion of murder. Offbeat, yet superb film noir entry became one of the most memorable of the genre. Expertly directed by Ray. Based on the novel by Dorothy B. Hughes and an adaptation by Edmund H. North.
1950 93m/B Humphrey Bogart, Gloria Grahame, Frank Lovejoy, Carl Benton Reid, Art Smith, Jeff Donnell; *D:* Nicholas Ray; *W:* Andrew Solt. **VHS, Beta** $69.95 COL *ⅢⅢ*

In a Moment of Passion A two-bit actor wants to be a star—in the worst way possible. So he kills off the lead actor of a new film, takes his place, and proceeds to eliminate any obstacle that gets in his way. The problem comes in when an aspiring

actress falls for the actor and then figures out what's going on.
1993 (R) 100m/C Maxwell Caulfield, Chase Masterson, Vivian Schilling, Julie Araskog, Joe Estevez, Robert Z'Dar, Zbigniew Kaminski; *Cameos:* Jeff Conaway; *W:* Charles Haigh. VHS $89.95 HMD *₡*½

In a Shallow Grave Shallow treatment of James Purdy's novel about a WWII veteran, badly disfigured in combat at Guadalcanal, who returns to Virginia in an attempt to return to the life he once had with the woman he still loves. Handsome Biehn plays the disfigured vet, Mueller's his ex-fiancee, and Dempsey the drifter who adds a bisexual hypotenuse to the love triangle. Pokey American Playhouse coproduction.
1988 (R) 92m/C Michael Biehn, Maureen Mueller, Patrick Dempsey, Michael Beach, Thomas Boyd Mason; *D:* Kenneth Bowser. VHS WAR *₡₡*

In a Stranger's Hand Urich stars a respected businessman who happens to find a doll which belongs to a kidnapped young girl. The police have their suspicions but Urich teams up with the child's mother to find the girl and winds up uncovering a child-selling ring. Made for television.
1992 93m/C Robert Urich, Megan Gallagher, Brett Cullen, Vondie Curtis-Hall, Dakin Matthews, Alan Rosenberg, Maria O'Brien; *D:* David Greene. VHS $89.98 TTC *₡₡*½

In an Old Manor House Residents of an old house are tormented by the vindictive ghost of a murdered adultress whose husband didn't approve of the, uh, affection she showed his son from a previous marriage. Based on the play by Stanislaw Witkiewicz. In Polish with English subtitles.
1984 90m/C *D:* Jerzy Kotkowski. VHS $49.99 FCT *₡₡*

In Between When Margo, Jack, and Amy wake up they expect it to be another average day. Instead, these three strangers find themselves together in a peculiar house. An angel informs them that the house is a way station between life and the hereafter. The three must look at their pasts, imagine their futures, and decide whether to return to their old lives or accept death and go on to an afterlife.
1992 (PG-13) 92m/C Wings Hauser, Robin Mattson, Alexandra Paul, Robert Forster. VHS $79.95 MNC *₡*½

In Celebration Three successful brothers return to the old homestead for their parents' 40th wedding celebration. Intense drama but somewhat claustrophobic. Based on a play by David Storey.
1975 (PG) 110m/C Alan Bates, James Bolam, Brian Cox; *D:* Lindsay Anderson. VHS NO *₡₡₡*

In Cold Blood Truman Capote's supposedly factual novel provided the basis for this hard-hitting docu-drama about two ex-cons who ruthlessly murder a Kansas family in 1959 in order to steal their non-existent stash of money. Blake is riveting as one of the killers.
1967 133m/B Robert (Bobby) Blake, Scott Wilson, John Forsythe; *D:* Richard Brooks; *W:* Richard Brooks; *M:* Quincy Jones. Academy Awards '67 Nominations: Best Adapted Screenplay, Best Cinematography, Best Director (Brooks), Best Original Score; National Board of Review Awards '67: 10 Best Films of the Year, Best Director (Brooks). VHS, Beta $19.95 COL *₡₡₡*½

In Country Based on Bobbie Ann Mason's celebrated novel, the story of a young Kentuckian high schooler (perfectly played by Lloyd) and her search for her father, killed in Vietnam. Willis plays her uncle, a veteran still

struggling to accept his own survival, and crippled with memories. Moving scene at the Vietnam Veterans Memorial.
1989 (R) 116m/C Bruce Willis, Emily Lloyd, Joan Allen, Kevin Anderson, Richard Hamilton, Judith Ivey, Peggy Rea, John Terry, Patricia Richardson, Jim Beaver; *D:* Norman Jewison; *W:* Frank Pierson, Cynthia Cidre; *M:* James Horner. VHS, Beta, 8mm $19.98 WAR, MVD *₡₡*½

The In Crowd A bright high school student gets involved with a local television dance show circa 1965, and must choose between uncertain fame and an Ivy League college. A fair nostalgic look at the period. Leitch is the son of psychedelic folk singer Donovan.
1988 (PG) 96m/C Donovan Leitch, Jennifer Runyon, Scott Plank, Joe Pantoliano; *D:* Mark Rosenthal; *W:* Mark Rosenthal. VHS, Beta $19.98 ORI *₡₡*

In Dangerous Company Beautiful babe balances beaux and battles abound. A brow lowering experience.
1988 (R) 92m/C Tracy Scoggins, Cliff DeYoung, Chris Mulkey, Henry Darrow, Steven Keats, Richard Portnow; *D:* Ruben Preuss. VHS NO *₡*

In Deadly Heat Crime, revenge, murder, and urban warfare are done once again.
1987 98m/C William Dame, Catherine Dee, M.R. Murphy; *D:* Don Nardo. VHS, Beta JEF *₡*

In Desert and Wilderness Two kidnapped children escape and are thrust into the wilds of Africa, where they must survive with wits and courage. Based on a novel by Nobel prize-winning author Henyk Sienkiewicz. In Polish with English subtitles.
1973 144m/C *D:* Wladyslaw Slesicki. VHS $49.95 FCT *₡₡*½

In for Treatment A terminally ill cancer patient, lost in the bureaucracy of the hospital, fights to rediscover the joy of life. Strong and disturbing story. In Dutch with English subtitles.
1982 92m/C Helmut Woudenberg, Frank Groothof, Hans Man Int Veld; *D:* Eric Van Zuylen, Marja Kok. VHS, Beta NO *₡₡₡*

In Gold We Trust Vincent leads an elite battalion of fighters against a group of rogue American MIAs (!) laying waste to the Vietnamese countryside.
1991 89m/C Jan-Michael Vincent, Sam Jones; *D:* P. Chalong. VHS $89.98 AIP *₡*½

In Harm's Way Overdone story about two naval officers and their response to the Japanese attack at Pearl Harbor. Even the superb cast members (and there are plenty of them) can't overcome the incredible length and overly intricate plot.
1965 165m/B John Wayne, Kirk Douglas, Tom Tryon, Patricia Neal, Paula Prentiss, Brandon de Wilde, Burgess Meredith, Stanley Holloway, Henry Fonda, Dana Andrews, Franchot Tone, Jill Haworth, George Kennedy, Carroll O'Connor, Patrick O'Neal, Slim Pickens, Bruce Cabot, Larry Hagman, Hugh O'Brian, Jim Mitchum, Barbara Bouchet; *D:* Otto Preminger; *W:* Wendell Mayes; *M:* Jerry Goldsmith. Academy Awards '65 Nominations: Best Black and White Cinematography; British Academy Awards '65: Best Actress (Neal). VHS, Beta $14.95 PAR *₡₡*

In Hot Pursuit Convicted for drug smuggling, two young men stage a daring but not too exciting escape from a southern prison.
1982 90m/C Bob Watson, Don Watson, Debbie Washington. VHS, Beta NO *₡*½

The In-Laws A wild comedy with Falk, who claims to be a CIA agent, and Arkin, a dentist whose daughter is marrying Falk's son. The fathers foil a South American

dictator's counterfeiting scheme in a delightfully convoluted plot.
1979 (PG) 103m/C Peter Falk, Alan Arkin, Richard Libertini, Nancy Dussault, Penny Peyser, Arlene Golonka, Michael Lembeck, Ed Begley Jr., Rosana De Soto, Art Evans; *D:* Arthur Hiller; *W:* Andrew Bergman; *M:* John Morris. VHS, Beta $19.98 WAR *₡₡₡*

In Like Flint Sequel to "Our Man Flint" sees our dapper spy confronting an organization of women endeavoring to take over the world. Spy spoofery at its low-level best.
1967 107m/C James Coburn, Lee J. Cobb, Anna Lee, Andrew Duggan, Jean Hale; *D:* Gordon Douglas; *M:* Jerry Goldsmith. VHS, Beta $19.98 FOX *₡₡*½

In Love and War Woods plays Navy pilot Jim Stockdale, whose plane was grounded over hostile territory and who endured nearly eight years of torture as a POW. Meanwhile, wife Sybil is an organizer of POW wives back in the States. Low octane rendering of the US Navy Commander's true story. Aaron earlier directed "The Miracle Worker," and you may recognize Ngor from "The Killing Fields."
1991 (R) 96m/C James Woods, Jane Alexander, Haing S. Ngor, Concetta Tomei, Richard McKenzie, James Pax; *D:* Paul Aaron; *W:* Carol Schreder. VHS $89.95 VMK *₡₡*½

In Love with an Older Woman Ritter takes fewer pratfalls than usual in this film; after all, it's a romantic comedy. Adapted from "Six Months with an Older Woman," the novel by David Kaufelt. Made for television.
1982 100m/C John Ritter, Karen Carlson, Jamie Rose, Robert Mandan, Jeff Altman, George Murdock; *D:* Jack Bender. VHS, Beta $14.95 FRH *₡₡*

In Memoriam Tragic and gripping drama about one man's ability, albeit too late, to cope with his unforgettable past. In Spanish with English subtitles.
1976 96m/C Geraldine Chaplin, Jose Luis Gomez; *D:* Enrique Braso. VHS $59.95 FCT, ING *₡₡*½

In 'n Out An American loser ventures to Mexico to recover a long-lost inheritance, meeting with mildly comic obstacles along the way.
1986 85m/C Sam Bottoms, Pat Hingle. VHS, Beta $19.95 STE, NWV *₡*½

In Name Only Somber drama about a heartless woman who marries for wealth and prestige and holds her husband to a loveless marriage. Based on "Memory of Love" by Bessie Brewer.
1939 102m/B Carole Lombard, Cary Grant, Kay Francis; *D:* John Cromwell. VHS, Beta $19.95 CCB, RKO, MLB *₡₡*½

In Old Caliente Rogers battles the bad guys in the frontier town of Caliente.
1939 60m/B Roy Rogers, Lynn (Mary Hart) Roberts, George "Gabby" Hayes. VHS, Beta $9.95 NOS, VCN, DVT *₡*½

In Old California Plucky story of a young Boston pharmacist who searches for success in the California gold rush and runs into the local crime boss. Also available colorized.
1942 88m/B John Wayne, Patsy Kelly, Binnie Barnes, Albert Dekker, Charles Halton; *D:* William McGann. VHS $9.98 REP *₡₡*½

In Old Cheyenne Bank holdups, cattle rustling, fist fights, and even car crashes mix with some good ol' guitar plunking in this western.
1941 60m/B Roy Rogers, George "Gabby" Hayes. VHS, Beta $19.95 NOS, CAB, TIM *₡*½

In Old Chicago The O'Leary family travels to Chicago to seek their fortune, with mom working as a washerwoman to support her sons. Brothers Power and Ameche become power-broking rivals and when mom comes to break up a brawl between the two, she neglects to properly restrain the family cow. This leads to the great Chicago fire of 1871, supposedly started when the cow kicks over a latern and sets the barn ablaze. The city burns down in a spectacular 20-minute sequence. Based on the story "We the O'Learys" by Niven Busch.
1938 115m/B Tyrone Power, Alice Faye, Don Ameche, Alice Brady, Andy Devine, Brian Donlevy, Phyllis Brooks, Tom Brown, Sidney Blackmer, Gene Reynolds, Berton Churchill, Bobs Watson; *D:* Henry King; *W:* Lamar Trotti, Sonya Levien. **VHS $19.98** *FXV* 🐾🐾🐾

In Old Colorado Ankrum and his cronies try to stir up trouble over water rights, but Boyd and his pals ride to the rescue.
1941 67m/B William Boyd, Russell Hayden, Andy Clyde, Margaret Hayes, Morris Ankrum, Sarah Padden, Cliff Nazarro, Stanley Andrews, James Seay, Morgan Wallace; *D:* Howard Bretherton. **VHS $19.95** *NOS* 🐾🐾½

In Old Montana A Cavalry lieutenant tries to settle a cattleman vs. sheep-herding war.
1939 60m/B Fred Scott, Jeanne Carmen, Harry Harvey, John Merton; *D:* Raymond K. Johnson. **VHS, Beta $19.95** *VDM, GPV* 🐾

In Old New Mexico The Cisco Kid and Pancho reveal the murderer of an old woman—a mysterious doctor who was after an inheritance.
1945 60m/B Duncan Renaldo, Martin Garralaga, Gwen Kenyon, Pedro de Cordoba. **VHS, Beta $19.95** *NOS, VCI, VYY* 🐾

In Old Santa Fe Cowboy star Maynard's best western, and the first film ever with Autry and Burnette. Maynard is framed for murder and his pals save him.
1934 60m/B Ken Maynard, Gene Autry, Smiley Burnette, Evelyn Knapp, George "Gabby" Hayes, Kenneth Thomson, Wheeler Oakman, George Cheseboro; *D:* David Howard, Joseph Kane. **VHS, Beta $19.95** *NOS, VCN, DVT* 🐾🐾½

In Person Spry comedy about a movie star who disguises herself to take a vacation incognito and falls in love with a country doctor who is unaware of her identity. 🎵 Don't Mention Love To Me; Out of Sight, Out of Mind; Got a New Lease on Life.
1935 87m/B Ginger Rogers, George Brent, Alan Mowbray, Grant Mitchell; *D:* William A. Seiter; *M:* Oscar Levant. **VHS, Beta $19.98** *RKO, TTC* 🐾🐾½

In Praise of Older Women Berenger is just right as a young Hungarian who is corrupted by WWII and a large number of older women. Based on a novel by Stephen Vizinczey.
1978 110m/C Karen Black, Tom Berenger, Susan Strasberg, Helen Shaver, Alexandra Stewart; *D:* George Kaczender. **VHS, Beta** *FOX, SUE* 🐾🐾

In Search of a Golden Sky Following their mother's death, a motley group of children move in with their secluded cabin-dwelling uncle, much to the righteous chagrin of the welfare department.
1984 (PG) 94m/C Charles Napier, George Flower, Cliff Osmond; *D:* Jefferson Richard. **VHS, Beta $79.98** *FOX* 🐾🐾

In Search of Anna When a convict is released from jail, he hits the road with a flighty model in search of the girlfriend who corresponded with him in prison. There auto be a law.
1979 90m/C Judy Morris, Richard Moir, Chris Hayward, Bill Hunter; *D:* Esben Storm. **VHS, Beta $24.95** *AHV* Woof!

In Search of the Castaways Stirring adventure tale of a teenage girl and her younger brother searching for their father, a ship's captain lost at sea years earlier. Powerful special effects and strong cast make this a winning Disney effort. Based on a story by Jules Verne.
1962 98m/C Hayley Mills, Maurice Chevalier, George Sanders, Wilfrid Hyde-White, Michael Anderson Jr.; *D:* Robert Stevenson. **VHS, Beta $19.99** *DIS* 🐾🐾🐾

In Society The duo play dimwitted plumbers who are mistakenly invited to a high society party, where they promptly create catastrophe.
1944 84m/B Bud Abbott, Lou Costello, Marion Hutton, Kirby Grant, Anne Gillis, Arthur Treacher, Thomas Gomez, Steve Geray, Margaret Irving, Thurston Hall; *Cameos:* Sid Fields; *D:* Jean Yarborough; *W:* Sid Fields, Hal Fimberg, Edmund Hartmann, John Grant. **VHS $14.98** *MCA, FCT* 🐾🐾½

In the Aftermath: Angels Never Sleep Mix of animation and live-action in this post-nuclear wasteland tale never quite works.
1987 85m/C Tony Markes, Rainbow Dolan; *D:* Carl Colpaert. **VHS, Beta $19.95** *STE, NWV* 🐾🐾½

In the Army Now Pauly dude gets his head shaved, man. Service comedy about a slacker who joins the Army hoping to cash in on military benefits but who winds up in combat instead. Shore drops the Valley Guy shtick and ventures into the land of action when he gets sent on a mission to the Sahara. Strictly for Shore's fans.
1994 ?m/C Pauly Shore, Esai Morales, Lori Petty, David Alan Grier, Ernie Hudson, Andy Dick; *D:* Dan Petrie Jr.; *W:* Dan Petrie Jr., Ken Kaufman, Fairfax Bahr, Stu Krieger, Adam Small. **VHS** 🐾🐾

In the Cold of the Night Another drowsy entry into the "to sleep perchance to have a nightmare genre." A photographer with a vivid imagination dreams he murders a woman he doesn't know, and when said dream girl rides into his life on the back of a Harley, Mr. Foto's faced with an etiquette quandary: haven't they met before? Cast includes Hedren (Hitchcock's Marnie and Melanie Griffith's mother).
1989 (R) 112m/C Jeff Lester, Adrienne Sachs, Shannon Tweed, David Soul, John Beck, Tippi Hedren, Marc Singer; *D:* Nico Mastorakis. **VHS $9.98** *REP* 🐾

In the Custody of Strangers A teenager's parents refuse to help when he is arrested for being drunk and he ends up spending the night in jail. Realistic handling of a serious subject. Sheen and Estevez play the father and son, mimicking their real-life relationship. Made for television.
1982 100m/C Martin Sheen, Jane Alexander, Emilio Estevez, Kenneth McMillan, Ed Lauter, Matt Clark, John Hancock; *D:* Robert Greenwald. **VHS** *MOV* 🐾🐾🐾

In the Days of the Thundering Herd & the Law & the Outlaw In the first feature, a pony express rider sacrifices his job to accompany his sweetheart on a westward trek to meet her father. In the second show, a fugitive falls in love with a rancher's daughter and risks recognition.
1914 76m/B Tom Mix, Myrtle Stedman; *D:* Tom Mix. **VHS, Beta $24.98** *CCB, GPV* 🐾🐾🐾

In the Good Old Summertime This pleasant musical version of "The Shop Around the Corner" tells the story of two bickering co-workers who are also anonymous lovelorn pen pals. Minnelli made her second screen appearance at 18 months in the final scene. 🎵 I Don't Care; Meet Me Tonight In Dreamland; Play That Barbershop Chord; In the Good Old Summertime; Put Your Arms Around Me Honey; Wait Till the Sun Shines Nellie; Chicago; Merry Christmas.
1949 104m/C Judy Garland, Van Johnson, S.Z. Sakall, Buster Keaton, Spring Byington, Liza Minnelli, Clinton Sundberg; *D:* Robert Z. Leonard. **VHS, Beta $19.98** *MGM* 🐾🐾🐾

In the Heat of Passion A low-budget ripoff of "Body Heat" and "Fatal Attraction" starring Kirkland as a married woman who involves a much younger man in a very steamy affair that leads to murder. This movie wants to be a thriller, but is little more than a soft-core sex flick. Also available in an unrated version that contains explicit footage.
1991 (R) 84m/C Sally Kirkland, Nick Corri, Jack Carter, Michael Greene; *D:* Rodman Flender; *W:* Rodman Flender. **VHS $89.95** *COL* 🐾

In the Heat of the Night A wealthy industrialist in a small Mississippi town is murdered. A black homicide expert is asked to help solve the murder, despite resentment on the part of the town's chief of police. Powerful script with underlying theme of racial prejudice is served well by taut direction and powerhouse performances. Poitier's memorable character Virgil Tibbs appeared in two more pictures, "They Call Me Mister Tibbs" and "The Organization."
1967 109m/C Sidney Poitier, Rod Steiger, Warren Oates, Lee Grant; *D:* Norman Jewison; *W:* Sterling Silliphant; *M:* Quincy Jones. Academy Awards '67: Best Actor (Steiger), Best Film Editing, Best Picture, Best Sound; Nominations: Best Director (Jewison); British Academy Awards '67: Best Actor (Steiger); Edgar Allan Poe Awards '67: Best Screenplay; Golden Globe Awards '68: Best Actor—Drama (Steiger), Best Film—Drama, Best Screenplay. **VHS, Beta $14.95** *MGM, FOX, BTV* 🐾🐾🐾½

In the King of Prussia Recreation of the trial of the "Plowshares Eight" radicals who were jailed for sabotaging two nuclear missiles at an electric plant in Pennsylvania.
1983 92m/C Martin Sheen, Rev. Daniel Berrigan. **VHS, Beta $59.95** *MPI, BUL* 🐾

In the Land of the Owl Turds The story of a decidedly eccentric young man who drives a dada art gallery on wheels while searching for love. Blank's senior thesis film.
1987 30m/C *D:* Harrod Blank. **VHS, Beta $39.95** *FFM* 🐾½

In the Line of Duty: Ambush in Waco Insta-television movie made by NBC even before the fire which engulfed the Texas compound and ended the standoff between self-proclaimed "prophet" David Koresh and the federal government. Daly does well as the manipulative, charasmatic Branch Davidian cult leader whose stockpiling of illegal weapons lead to an investigation by the Bureau of Alcohohol, Tobacco and Firearms and a botched raid which caused the ultimately fatal siege. Filmed on location outside Tulsa, Oklahoma.
1993 93m/C Timothy Daly, Dan Lauria, William O'Leary; *D:* Dick Lowry; *W:* Phil Penningroth. **VHS $89.98** *REP* 🐾🐾½

In the Line of Fire Aging Secret Service agent meets his match in a spooky caller who threatens his honor and the president in an exciting, fast paced cat and

mouse game. Terrific performance by Eastwood includes lots of dry humor and an unscripted emotional moment, but is nearly overshadowed by Malkovich's menacing bad guy. Eerie special effects add to the mood. The Secret Service cooperated and most scenes are believable, with a few Hollywood exceptions; the end result clearly pays homage to the agents who protect our presidents. Intriguing trailer showed the number "6" in "1963" slowly turning to "9" to become "1993." The seventh highest grossing movie of 1993.
1993 (R) 128m/C Clint Eastwood, John Malkovich, Rene Russo, Dylan McDermott, Gary Cole, Fred Dalton Thompson, John Mahoney, Gregory Alan Williams; *D:* Wolfgang Petersen; *W:* Jeff Maguire; *M:* Ennio Morricone. VHS, 8mm **$99.95** COL, BTV 🐾🐾🐾½

In the Money Veteran vaudevillian "Skeets" Gallagher introduces a muddled mass of acts, including a poor imitator of boxing great Gene Tunney, a mad scientist who talks to rabbits and writes rubber checks, and a limp-wristed lisper.
1934 66m/B Lois Wilson, Warren Hymer, Arthur Hoyt, Frank "Junior" Coghlan, Louise Beavers; *D:* Frank Strayer. VHS **$19.95** NOS 🐾

In the Mood Based on fact, this is the story of teenager Sonny Wisecarver, nicknamed "The Woo Woo Kid," who in 1944, seduced two older women and eventually landed in jail after marrying one of them. Look for Wisecarver in a cameo role as a mailman in the film.
1987 (PG-13) 98m/C Patrick Dempsey, Beverly D'Angelo, Talia Balsam, Michael Constantine, Betty Jinnette, Kathleen Freeman, Peter Hobbs, Edith Fellows; *Cameos:* Ellsworth Wisecarver; *D:* Phil Alden Robinson; *W:* Phil Alden Robinson; *M:* Ralph Burns. VHS, Beta **$14.95** WAR, LHV, BAR 🐾🐾½

In the Name of the Father Compelling true story of Gerry Conlon and the Guildford Four, illegally imprisoned in 1974 by British officials after a tragic IRA bombing in London. The British judicial system receives a black eye, but so does the horror and cruelty of IRA terrorism. Politics and family life in a prison cell share the focus, as Sheridan captures superior performances from Day-Lewis and Postlethwaite (beware the thick Belfast brogue). Thompson was accused of pro-IRA sympathies in the British press for her role as the lawyer who believed in Conlon's innocence. Adapted from "Proved Innocent," Conlon's prison memoirs; reunites Sheridan and Day-Lewis after "My Left Foot." Includes original songs by U2's Bono, with a haunting theme sung by Sinead O'Connor.
1993 (R) 133m/C Daniel Day-Lewis, Peter Postlethwaite, Emma Thompson, John Lynch, Corin Redgrave, Beatie Edney, John Benfield, Paterson Joseph, Marie Jones, Gerard McSorley, Frank Harper, Mark Sheppard, Don Baker, Britta Smith, Aidan Grennell, Daniel Massey, Bosco Hogan; *D:* Jim Sheridan; *W:* Jim Sheridan, Terry George; *M:* Trevor Jones, Bono, Sinead O'Connor. Academy Awards '93 Nominations: Best Actor (Day-Lewis), Best Adapted Screenplay, Best Director (Sheridan), Best Film Editing, Best Picture, Best Supporting Actor (Postlethwaite), Best Supporting Actress (Thompson); Golden Globe Awards '94: Best Actor—Drama (Day-Lewis), Best Film—Drama, Best Song ("(You Made Me the) Thief of Your Heart"), Best Supporting Actress (Thompson); Berlin International Film Festival '94: Golden Berlin Bear. VHS MCA 🐾🐾🐾½

In the Name of the Pope-King An acclaimed historical epic about the politics and warfare raging around the 1867 Italian wars that made the Pope the sole ruler in Rome. In Italian with English subtitles.
1985 115m/C Nino Manfredi, Danilo Mattei, Carmen Scarpitta, Giovannella Grifea, Carlo Bagno; *D:* Luigi Magni. VHS, Beta **$29.95** WBF, TPV, FCT 🐾🐾🐾

In the Navy Abbott and Costello join the Navy in one of four military-service comedies they cranked out in 1941 alone. The token narrative involves about a singing star (Powell) in uniform to escape his female fans, but that's just an excuse for classic A & C routines. With the Andrews Sisters. ♫Starlight, Starbright; You're Off To See The World; Hula Ba Lua; Gimme Some Skin; A Sailor's Life For Me; We're In The Navy; Anchors Aweigh (instrumental); You're A Lucky Fellow, Mr. Smith (instrumental). *AKA:* Abbott and Costello in the Navy.
1941 85m/B Lou Costello, Bud Abbott, Dick Powell, The Andrews Sisters; *D:* Arthur Lubin. VHS **$14.95** MCA 🐾🐾½

In the Realm of Passion A wife and her lover murder her husband and dump the body in an abandoned well. Guilt over their actions drive the lovers to return to the scene where they are greeted by the vengeful ghost of the betrayed husband—or is it only their consciences torturing them? In Japanese with English subtitles. *AKA:* Empire of Passion.
1980 (R) 108m/C Kazuko Yoshiyuki, Takahiro Tamura, Tatsuya Fuji; *D:* Nagisa Oshima. VHS **$89.95** FXL, ING 🐾🐾

In the Realm of the Senses Taboo-breaking story of a woman and man who turn their backs on the militaristic rule of Japan in the mid-1930s by plunging into an erotic and sensual world all their own. Striking, graphic work that was seized by U.S. customs when it first entered the country. Violent with explicit sex, and considered by some critics as pretentious, while others call it Oshima's masterpiece. In Japanese with English subtitles.
1976 (NC-17) 105m/C Tatsuya Fuji, Eiko Matsuda, Aio Nakajima, Meika Seri; *D:* Nagisa Oshima. VHS **$89.95** FXL, CVC 🐾🐾🐾

In the Region of Ice Award-winning short reveals the complexities of the relationship between a nun and a disturbed student.
1976 38m/B Fionnula Flanagan, Peter Lempert; *D:* Peter Werner. VHS, Beta BFA 🐾🐾🐾

In the Secret State Inspector Strange finds himself faced with the apparent suicide of a colleague on the day of his own retirement from the force. His private investigation into the case finds him mired in murder and espionage.
19?? 107m/C Frank Finlay, Matthew Marsh, Thorley Walters. VHS **$79.95** MOV 🐾🐾

In the Shadow of Kilimanjaro A pack of hungry baboons attacks innocent people in the wilderness of Kenya. Based on a true story but the characters are contrived and just plain stupid at times. Quite gory as well. Filmed on location in Kenya.
1986 (R) 105m/C John Rhys-Davies, Timothy Bottoms, Michele Carey, Irene Miracle, Calvin Jung, Donald Blakely; *D:* Raju Patel. VHS, Beta **$19.95** LIV Woof!

In the Soup Adolpho is a naive New York filmmaker barely scraping by. He decides to sell his script in a classified ad which is answered by the fast-talking Joe, a would-be film producer who's true profession is as a con artist. The two then try numerous (and humorous) ways to raise the money to begin filming. Also available colorized.
1992 (R) 93m/B Steve Buscemi, Seymour Cassel, Jennifer Beals, Will Patton, Pat Moya, Sully Boyar, Stanley Tucci, Rockets Redglare, Elizabeth Bracco, Ruth Maleczech; *Cameos:* Jim Jarmusch, Carol Kane; *D:* Alexandre Rockwell; *W:* Tim Kissell, Alexandre Rockwell; *M:* Mader. VHS **$89.95** ACA 🐾🐾½

In the Spirit New Age couple move from Beverly Hills to New York, where they meet an air-headed mystic and are forced to hide from a murderer. Falk gives solid performance in sometimes rocky production. Berlin is the real-life daughter of May.
1990 (R) 94m/C Elaine May, Marlo Thomas, Jeannie Berlin, Peter Falk, Melanie Griffith, Olympia Dukakis, Chad Burton, Thurn Hoffman, Michael Emil, Christopher Durang, Laurie Jones; *D:* Sandra Seacat; *W:* Jeannie Berlin, Laurie Jones; *M:* Patrick Williams. VHS, Beta **$29.95** ACA 🐾🐾½

In the Steps of a Dead Man A family grieving for a fallen soldier is earmarked for evil by a young man who bears an uncanny resemblance to the dead man. A friend of the family has her suspicions and must find out the truth before something terrible happens.
1974 71m/C Skye Aubrey, John Nolan. VHS, Beta NO 🐾½

In the White City A sailor jumps ship in Lisbon and uses a movie camera to record himself and his search through the twisted streets and alleys of the city for something or someone to connect to. In French, Portuguese, and German with English subtitles. *AKA:* Dans la Ville Blanche.
1983 108m/C Bruno Ganz, Teresa Madruga; *D:* Alain Tanner. VHS **$79.95** NYF, ING 🐾🐾🐾

In This House of Brede A sophisticated London widow turns her back on her worldly life to become a cloistered Benedictine nun. Rigg is outstanding as the woman struggling to deal with the discipline of faith. Made for television and based on the novel by Rumer Godden.
1975 105m/C Diana Rigg; *D:* George Schaefer. VHS, Beta LCA, OM 🐾🐾🐾

In This Our Life Histrionic melodrama handled effectively by Huston about a nutsy woman who steals her sister's husband, rejects him, manipulates her whole family and eventually leads herself to ruin. Vintage star vehicle for Davis, who chews scenery and fellow actors alike. Adapted by Howard Koch from the Ellen Glasgon novel.
1942 101m/B Bette Davis, Olivia de Havilland, Charles Coburn, Frank Craven, George Brent, Dennis (Stanley Morner) Morgan, Billie Burke, Hattie McDaniel, Lee Patrick, Walter Huston, Ernest Anderson; *D:* John Huston; *M:* Max Steiner. VHS, Beta **$19.95** MGM 🐾🐾½

In Too Deep A rock star and a beautiful woman are physically drawn to one another in spite of the fact that any contact between them could have disasterous results.
1990 (R) 106m/C Hugo Race, Santha Press, Rebekah Elmaloglou, John Flaus, Dominic Sweeney; *D:* Colin South. VHS, Beta **$89.95** PAR 🐾½

In Trouble Hard-to-follow and frequently aimless story of a pregnant girl who invents a fake rape story that her dull-witted brothers take seriously, embarking on a cross-country search for the culprit.
1967 82m/C Julie LaChapelle, Katherine Mousseau, Daniel Pilon; *D:* Gilles Carle. VHS, Beta **$59.95** NWV Woof!

In Which We Serve Much stiff upper-lipping in this classic that captures the spirit of the British Navy during WWII. The sinking of the destroyer HMS Torrin during the Battle of Crete is told via flashbacks, with an emphasis on realism that was unusual in wartime flag-wavers. Features the film debuts of Johnson and Attenborough, and the first Lean directorial effort. Coward received a special Oscar for his ''outstanding production achievement,'' having scripted, scored, codirected and costarred.
1943 114m/B Noel Coward, John Mills, Bernard Miles, Celia Johnson, Kay Walsh, James Donald, Richard Attenborough; **D:** Noel Coward, David Lean; **W:** Noel Coward; **M:** Noel Coward. Academy Awards '43 Nominations: Best Original Screenplay, Best Picture; National Board of Review Awards '42: 10 Best Films of the Year. **VHS, Beta $19.95** NOS, SUE ✍✍✍½

In Your Face Little known blaxploitation film about a black family harrassed in a white suburb. A black motorcycle gang comes to their rescue. **AKA:** Abar, the First Black Superman.
1977 (R) 90m/C J.Walter Smith, Tobar Mayo, Roxie Young, Tina James; **D:** Frank Packard. **VHS $59.95** XVC, HHE ✍½

The Incident A gritty, controversial (at-the-time) drama about two abusive thugs who take over a New York subway car late at night, humiliating and terrorizing each passenger in turn. Film debut for Sheen and Musante as the thugs.
1967 99m/B Martin Sheen, Tony Musante, Beau Bridges, Ruby Dee, Jack Gilford, Thelma Ritter, Brock Peters, Ed McMahon, Gary Merrill, Donna Mills, Jan Sterling, Mike Kellin; **D:** Larry Peerce; **M:** Charles Fox. **VHS, Beta $59.98** FOX ✍✍½

The Incident Political thriller set during WWII in Lincoln Bluff, Colorado. Matthau is excellent in his TV debut as a small-town lawyer who must defend a German prisoner of war accused of murder at nearby Camp Bremen. An all-star cast lends powerful performances to this riveting made for TV drama.
1989 95m/C Walter Matthau, Susan Blakely, Harry Morgan, Robert Carradine, Barnard Hughes, Peter Firth, William Schallert; **D:** Joseph Sargent. **VHS $79.95** CAF ✍✍✍

Incident at Channel Q A heavy-metal rock musical about a suburban neighborhood declaring war on a chain-and-leather deejay.
1986 85m/C Al Corley, Bon Jovi, Deep Purple, Motley Crue, The Scorpions. **VHS, Beta $19.95** MVD, BMG ✍½

Incident at Map-Grid 36-80 A Soviet-made combination of espionage and sea-battle. Gripping and fascinating look at the U.S. from the pre-Glasnost era.
1983 85m/C VHS $59.95 KIV, TPV ✍✍

Incident at Oglala: The Leonard Peltier Story Offers a detailed account of the violent events leading to the murder of two FBI agents in Oglala, South Dakota in 1975. American Indian activist Leonard Peltier was convicted of the murders and is presently serving two consecutive life sentences, but he's cited as a political prisoner by Amnesty International. The documentary examines the highly controversial trial and the tensions between the government and the Oglala Nation stemming back to the Indian occupation of Wounded Knee in 1973. Director Apted is sympathetic to Peltier and offers reasons why he should be allowed a retrial; he examined similar incidents in his film ''Thunderheart.''
1992 (PG) 90m/C D: Michael Apted; **M:** John Trudell, Jackson Browne. **VHS $89.98** LIV, FCT ✍✍✍

An Inconvenient Woman When an older married man has an affair with a young seductress, there's suicide, murder, a nasty gossip columnist, a reporter, a knowing society wife, and a lot of cover-ups among the rich and famous. From the novel by Dominick Dunne and based on the Alfred Bloomingdale scandal. Originally a made for television mini-series.
1991 126m/C Rebecca DeMornay, Jason Robards Jr., Jill Eikenberry, Peter Gallagher, Roddy McDowall, Chad Lowe. **VHS, Beta $79.95** ABC, PSM ✍✍

The Incredible Hulk Bixby is a scientist who achieves superhuman strength after he is exposed to a massive dose of gamma rays. But his personal life suffers, as does his wardrobe. Ferrigno is the Hulkster. The pilot for the television series is based on the Marvel Comics character.
1977 94m/C Bill Bixby, Susan Sullivan, Lou Ferrigno, Jack Colvin; **D:** Kenneth Johnson. **VHS, Beta $19.95** MCA ✍✍½

The Incredible Hulk Returns The beefy green mutant is back and this time he wages war against a Viking named Thor. Very little substance in this made for television flick, so be prepared to park your brain at the door. Followed by ''The Trial of the Incredible Hulk.''
1988 100m/C Bill Bixby, Lou Ferrigno, Jack Colvin, Lee Purcell, Charles Napier, Steve Levitt; **D:** Nick Corea. **VHS $19.95** STE, NWV ✍½

The Incredible Journey A labrador retriever, bull terrier and Siamese cat mistake their caretaker's intentions when he leaves for a hunting trip, believing he will never return. The three set out on a 250 mile adventure-filled trek across Canada's rugged terrain. Entertaining family adventure from Disney taken from Sheila Burnford's book.
1963 80m/C D: Fletcher Markle. **VHS, Beta $69.95** DIS ✍✍½

The Incredible Journey of Dr. Meg Laurel A young doctor returns to her roots to bring modern medicine to the Appalachian mountain people during the 1930's. Made for television featuring Wagner in a strong performance.
1979 143m/C Lindsay Wagner, Jane Wyman, Dorothy McGuire, James Woods, Gary Lockwood; **D:** Guy Green. **VHS, Beta $59.95** COL ✍✍✍

Incredible Master Beggars Against all odds, the Beggars challenge the Great Iron Master, using ''Tam Leg'' tactics versus the ''Iron Cloth'' fighting style.
1982 (R) 88m/C Tan Tao Liang, Ku Feng, Han Kuo Tsai, Li Tang Ming, Li Hai Sheng, Lui I. Fan, Pan Yao Kun. **VHS, Beta $59.95** GEM ✍

Incredible Melting Man Two transformations change an astronaut's life after his return to earth. First, his skin starts to melt, then he displays cannibalistic tendencies. Hard to swallow. Special effects by Rick Baker. Look for director Jonathan Demme in a bit part.
1977 (R) 85m/C Alex Rebar, Burr de Benning, Cheryl ''Rainbeaux'' Smith; **D:** William Sachs. **VHS, Beta $69.98** LIV, VES Woof!

The Incredible Mr. Limpet Limp comedy about a nebbish bookkeeper who's transformed into a fish, fulfilling his aquatic dreams. Eventually he falls in love with another fish, and helps the U.S. Navy find Nazi subs during WWII. Partially animated, beloved by some, particularly those under the age of seven. Based on Theodore Pratt's novel.
1964 99m/C Don Knotts, Jack Weston, Carole Cook, Andrew Duggan, Larry Keating, Elizabeth McRae; **D:** Arthur Lubin. **VHS, Beta $14.95** WAR, WTA ✍✍

The Incredible Petrified World Divers are trapped in an underwater cave when volcanic eruptions begin. Suffocating nonsense.
1958 78m/B John Carradine, Allen Windsor, Phyllis Coates, Lloyd Nelson, George Skaff; **D:** Jerry Warren. **VHS $19.95** NOS, SNC Woof!

The Incredible Rocky Mountain Race The townspeople of St. Joseph, fed up with Mark Twain's destructive feud with a neighbor, devise a shrewd scheme to rid the town of the troublemakers by sending them on a road race through the West. Made for television comedy starring the F-Troop.
1977 97m/C Christopher Connelly, Forrest Tucker, Larry Storch, Mike Mazurki; **D:** James L. Conway. **VHS, Beta $19.95** STE ✍✍

The Incredible Sarah A limp adapted stage biography from ''Reader's Digest'' of the great actress Sarah Bernhardt. Jackson chews scenery to no avail.
1976 (PG) 105m/C Glenda Jackson, Daniel Massey, Yvonne Mitchell, Douglas Wilmer; **D:** Richard Fleischer; **M:** Elmer Bernstein. **VHS, Beta $19.95** IME ✍✍

The Incredible Shrinking Man Adapted by Richard Matheson from his own novel, the sci-fi classic is a philosophical thriller about a man who is doused with radioactive mist and begins to slowly shrink. His new size means that everyday objects take on sinister meaning and he must fight for his life in an increasingly hostile, absurd environment. A surreal, suspenseful allegory with impressive special effects. Endowed with the tension usually reserved for Hitchcock films.
1957 81m/B Grant Williams, Randy Stuart, April Kent, Paul Langton, Raymond Bailey; **D:** Jack Arnold; **W:** Richard Matheson. **VHS, Beta $14.98** MCA, MLB ✍✍✍½

The Incredible Shrinking Woman ''...Shrinking Man'' spoof and inoffensive social satire finds household cleaners producing some strange side effects on model homemaker Tomlin, slowly shrinking her to doll-house size. She then encounters everyday happenings as big tasks and not so menial. Her advertising exec husband has a hand in the down-sizing. Sight gags abound but the cuteness wears thin by the end.
1981 (PG) 89m/C Lily Tomlin, Charles Grodin, Ned Beatty, Henry Gibson; **D:** Joel Schumacher; **W:** Jane Wagner. **VHS, Beta $14.98** MCA ✍✍½

The Incredible Two-Headed Transplant Mad scientist Dern has a criminal head transplanted on to the shoulder of big John Bloom and the critter runs amuck. Low-budget special effects guaranteed to give you a headache or two. Watch for onetime Pat ''Marilyn Munster'' Priest in a bikini.
1971 (PG) 88m/C Bruce Dern, Pat Priest, Casey Kasem, Albert Cole, John Bloom, Berry Kroeger; **D:** Anthony M. Lanza. **VHS** NO Woof!

Incredibly Strange Creatures Who Stopped Living and Became Mixed-Up Zombies The infamous, super-cheap horror spoof that established Sheckler (for whom Cash Flagg is a pseudonym), about a carny side show riddled with ghouls and bad rock bands. Assistant cinematographers include the young Laszlo Kovacs and Vilmos Zsigmond. A must-see for connoisseurs of cult and

camp. *AKA:* The Teenage Psycho Meets Bloody Mary; The Incredibly Strange Creatures.
1963 90m/C Cash Flagg, Carolyn Brandt, Brett O'Hara, Atlas King, Sharon Walsh; **D:** Ray Dennis Steckler. **VHS, Beta** *NO Woof!*

Incubus A doctor and his teenaged daughter settle in a quiet New England community, only to encounter the incubus, a terrifying, supernatural demon who enjoys sex murders. Offensive trash.
1982 (R) 90m/C John Cassavetes, Kerrie Keane, Helen Hughes, Erin Flannery, John Ireland; **D:** John Hough. **VHS, Beta $19.98** *VES Woof!*

Indecency Ellie (Beals) is still recovering from a mental breakdown when she goes to work for Marie (Clarkson) at her ad agency. There Ellie must deal with manipulative associate Nia (Davis) and Marie's charming, estranged husband Mick (Remar), who draws the fragile Ellie into an affair. Then Marie commits suicide—or maybe it was murder.
1992 (PG-13) 88m/C Jennifer Beals, James Remar, Sammi Davis-Voss, Barbara Williams, Christopher John Fields, Ray McKinnon; **D:** Marisa Silver; **W:** Amy Holden Jones, Holly Goldberg Sloan, Alan Ormsby. **VHS $89.98** *MCA ⱫⱫ*

Indecent Behavior Tweed is a sex therapist who's accused of murder when one of her clients overdose's on the latest designer drug. Hudson, who plays the genre's hard-boiled cop figure, gets very personally involved investigating the allegations, which really upsets Tweed's hubby, Vincent. Also available in an unrated version.
1993 (R) 93m/C Shannon Tweed, Gary Hudson, Jan-Michael Vincent; **D:** Lawrence Lanoff. **VHS $89.95** *AVE ⱫⱫ*

An Indecent Obsession Colleen McCullough's bestseller about WWII Australian soldiers recuperating in a field hospital mental ward. Hughes plays the nurse everyone's in love with.
1985 100m/C Wendy Hughes, Gary Sweet, Richard Moir, Jonathan Hyde, Bill Hunter, Bruno Lawrence; **D:** Lex Marinos; **W:** Denise Morgan. **VHS, Beta** *NO ⱫⱫ½*

Indecent Proposal High-gloss movie that had couples everywhere discussing the big question: Would you let your wife sleep with a billionaire in exchange for a million bucks? Probably, if all were as goodlooking as the weathered, yet ever gorgeous Redford. Moore and Harrelson are the financially down on their luck, but happy, couple who venture to Vegas on a last-ditch gambling effort. Surreally slick direction from Lyne, but an ultimately empty film that explores the values of marriage in a terribly angst-ridden fashion. Based on the novel by Jack Engelhard. Proof that average movies can make a killing at the box office, landing in sixth place for 1993.
1993 (R) 119m/C Robert Redford, Demi Moore, Woody Harrelson, Seymour Cassel, Oliver Platt, Billy Bob Thornton, Rip Taylor, Billy Connolly, Joel Brooks; *Cameos:* Sheena Easton, Herbie Hancock; *D:* Adrian Lyne; **W:** Amy Holden Jones; **M:** John Barry. MTV Movie Awards Nominations: 4: Best Actress (Moore), Most Desirable Female (Moore); MTV Movie Awards '94: Best Kiss (Demi Moore/Woody Harrelson). **VHS, Beta, CDV $19.95** *PAR ⱫⱫ½*

Independence Dramatically recreates the debates, concerns, and events that led up to the U.S. Declaration of Independence in 1776.
1976 30m/C Eli Wallach, Anne Jackson, Pat Hingle, Patrick O'Neal; **D:** John Huston. **VHS, Beta $19.98** *MPI, KAR, VEC ⱫⱫ½*

Independence Day Uneven romantic drama about a small-town photographer, yearning for the big city, who falls in love with a racing car enthusiast, whose sister is a battered wife. Strong cast, particularly Wiest as the abused wife, is left occasionally stranded by a script reaching too hard for social significance. *AKA:* Follow Your Dreams.
1983 (R) 110m/C Kathleen Quinlan, David Keith, Frances Sternhagen, Dianne Wiest, Cliff DeYoung, Richard Farnsworth, Josef Sommer, Cheryl "Rainbeaux" Smith; **D:** Robert Mandel; **M:** Charles Bernstein. **VHS, Beta $19.98** *WAR, CCB ⱫⱫ*

The Indestructible Man Chaney, electrocuted for murder and bank robbery, is brought back to life by a scientist. Naturally, he seeks revenge on those who sentenced him to death. Chaney does the best he can with the material.
1956 70m/B Lon Chaney Jr., Marian Carr, Casey Adams; **D:** Jack Pollexfen. **VHS $16.95** *NOS, MRV, SNC Ⱬ*

The Indian Fighter Exciting actioner has Douglas as a scout hired to lead a wagon train to Oregon in 1870. The train must past through dangerous Sioux territory and Douglas tries to make peace with the Sioux leader but a secret Indian gold mine and romance cause friction and keep things lively.
1955 88m/C Kirk Douglas, Elsa Martinelli, Walter Abel, Walter Matthau, Diana Douglas, Lon Chaney Jr., Eduard Franz, Alan Hale Jr., Elisha Cook Jr., Harry Landers; **D:** Andre de Toth; **W:** Ben Hecht. **VHS $14.95** *MGM ⱫⱫⱫ*

Indian Paint A pleasant children's film about an Indian boy's love for his horse and his rite of passage. Silverheels was Tonto on television's "The Lone Ranger," while Crawford was the "Rifleman's" son.
1964 90m/C Jay Silverheels, Johnny Crawford, Pat Hogan, Robert Crawford Jr., George Lewis; **D:** Norman Foster. **VHS, Beta $19.95** *VCI ⱫⱫ*

The Indian Runner In Penn's debut as a writer-director, he brings us the story of two brothers in Nebraska during the late '60s, who are forced to change their lives with the loss of their family farm. Joe is a good cop and family man who can't deal with the rage of his brother Frank, who has just returned from Vietnam and is turning to a life of crime. Penn does a decent job of representing the struggle between the responsible versus the rebellious side of human nature. Based on the song "Highway Patrolman" by Bruce Springsteen.
1991 (R) 127m/C David Morse, Viggo Mortensen, Sandy Dennis, Charles Bronson, Valeria Golino, Patricia Arquette, Dennis Hopper; **D:** Sean Penn; **W:** Sean Penn. **VHS $14.95** *MGM ⱫⱫ*

The Indian Scarf Heirs to a dead man's fortune are being strangled one by one at the benefactor's country estate. An Edgar Wallace suspense tale.
1963 85m/C Heinz Drache, Gisela Uhlen, Klaus Kinski; **D:** Alfred Vohrer. **VHS $16.95** *SNC ⱫⱫ*

Indian Summer Yet another addition to the growing 30-something nostalgia genre. Delete the big house, add a crusty camp director (Arkin), change the characters' names (but not necessarily their lives) and you feel like you're experiencing deja vu. This time seven friends and the requisite outsider reconvene at Camp Tamakwa, the real-life summer camp to writer/director Binder. The former campers talk. They yearn. They save Camp Tamakwa and experience personal growth. A must see for those who appreciate listening to situational jokes that are followed by "I guess you had to be there."

1993 (PG-13) 108m/C Alan Arkin, Matt Craven, Diane Lane, Bill Paxton, Elizabeth Perkins, Kevin Pollak, Sam Raimi, Vincent Spano, Julie Warner, Kimberly Williams, Richard Chevolleau; **D:** Mike Binder; **W:** Mike Binder; **M:** Miles Goodman. **VHS, Beta $19.99** *TOU, FCT ⱫⱫ*

Indian Uprising An army captain tries to keep local settlers from causing trouble with Geronimo and his people when gold is discovered on their territory.
1951 75m/C George Montgomery, Audrey Long, Carl Benton Reid, John Baer, Joseph Sawyer; **D:** Ray Nazarro. **VHS, Beta $14.99** *GKK ⱫⱫ*

Indiana Jones and the Last Crusade In this, the third and last (?) Indiana Jones adventure, the fearless archaeologist is once again up against the Nazis in a race to find the Holy Grail. Connery is perfectly cast as Indy's father; opening sequence features Phoenix as a teenage Indy and explains his fear of snakes and the origins of the infamous fedora. Returns to the look and feel of the original with more adventures, exotic places, dastardly villains, and daring escapes than ever before; a must for Indy fans.
1989 (PG) 126m/C Harrison Ford, Sean Connery, Denholm Elliott, Alison Doody, Julian Glover, John Rhys-Davies, River Phoenix, Michael Byrne, Alex Hyde-White; **D:** Steven Spielberg; **W:** Jeffrey Boam; **M:** John Williams. **VHS, Beta, 8mm $14.95** *PAR, SUP, TLF ⱫⱫⱫ*

Indiana Jones and the Temple of Doom Daredevil archaeologist Indiana Jones is back. This time he's on the trail of the legendary Ankara Stone and a ruthless cult that has enslaved hundreds of children. More gore and violence than the original; Capshaw's whining character is an irritant, lacking the fresh quality that Karen Allen added to the original. Enough action for ten movies, special effects galore, and the usual booming Williams score make it a cinematic roller coaster ride, but with less regard for plot and pacing than the original. Though second in the series, it's actually a prequel to "Raiders of the Lost Ark." Followed by "Indiana Jones and the Last Crusade."
1984 (PG) 118m/C Harrison Ford, Kate Capshaw, Ke Huy Quan, Amrish Puri; **D:** Steven Spielberg; **W:** Willard Huyck, Gloria Katz; **M:** John Williams. Academy Awards '84: Best Visual Effects; Nominations: Best Original Score. **VHS, Beta, 8mm $14.95** *PAR, APD ⱫⱫⱫ*

Indio A Marine-trained half-breed takes it on himself to save the Amazon rain forest. Not a peaceful demonstrator, his tactics are violent ones.
1990 (R) 94m/C Marvin Hagler, Francesco Quinn, Brian Dennehy; **D:** Anthony M. (Antonio Margheriti) Dawson. **VHS, Beta $89.98** *MED, VTR Ⱬ*

Indio 2: The Revolt Greedy developers are cutting a highway into the Amazon jungle, destroying everything in their path. All is not lost though, because U.S. Marine Sgt. Iron is on top of things, continuing his struggle to unite the Amazon tribes and save the rainforest, no matter what it takes.
1992 (R) 104m/C Marvin Hagler, Charles Napier; **M:** Pino Donaggio. **VHS $89.98** *LIV Ⱬ*

Indiscreet Empty-headed romantic comedy about a fashion designer whose past catches up with her when her ex-lover starts romancing her sister. No relation to the classic 1958 film with Cary Grant and Ingrid Bergman. ♫Come To Me; If You Haven't Got Love.
1931 81m/B Gloria Swanson, Ben Lyon, Barbara Kent; **D:** Leo McCarey. **VHS, Beta $19.95** *NOS, MRV, REP Ⱬ½*

Indiscreet A charming American diplomat in London falls in love with a stunning actress, but protects himself by saying he is married. Needless to say, she finds out. Stylish romp with Grant and Bergman at their sophisticated best. Adapted by Norman Krasna from his stage play "Kind Sir."
1958 100m/C Cary Grant, Ingrid Bergman, Phyllis Calvert; *D:* Stanley Donen; *M:* Richard Rodney Bennett. **VHS $19.98** *REP, MLB* ♪♪♪

Indiscreet Indistinctive made for TV re-hash of the charming 1958 Grant/Bergman romantic comedy in which a suave American falls for an English actress. Both versions derive from the play "Kind Sir" by Norman Krasna, but this one suffers by comparison.
1988 (PG) 94m/C Robert Wagner, Lesley-Anne Down, Maggie Henderson, Robert McBain, Jeni Barnett; *D:* Richard Michaels. **VHS $79.98** *REP* ♪♪½

The Indiscreet Mrs. Jarvis Lansbury stars as Brenda Jarvis, a woman who takes drastic steps to ensure that her checkered past won't come back to haunt her.
19?? 30m/B Angela Lansbury; *D:* Alan Smithee. **VHS $7.95** *RHI* ♪♪

Indiscretion of an American Wife Set almost entirely in Rome's famous Terminal Station, where an ill-fated couple say goodbye endlessly while the woman tries to decide whether to join her husband in the States. Trimmed down from 87 minutes upon U.S. release. *AKA:* Indiscretion; Terminus Station; Terminal Station Indiscretion.
1954 63m/C Jennifer Jones, Montgomery Clift, Richard Beymer; *D:* Vittorio De Sica; *W:* Truman Capote. **VHS, Beta $19.95** *NOS, FOX, HEG* ♪♪

Indochine Soapy melodrama follows the fortunes of Eliane (Deneuve), a Frenchwoman born and reared in Indochina, from 1930 to the communist revolution 25 years later. She contends with the changes to her country as well as her adopted daughter as she grows up and becomes independent. Deneuve's controlled performance (and unchanging beauty) is eminently watchable. Filmed on location in Vietnam with breathtaking cinematography by Francois Catonne. In French with English subtitles.
1992 (PG-13) 155m/C Catherine Deneuve, Linh Dan Pham, Vincent Perez, Jean Yanne, Dominique Blanc, Henri Marteau, Carlo Brandt, Gerard Lartigau; *D:* Regis Wargnier; *W:* Erik Orsenna, Louis Gardel, Catherine Cohen, Regis Wargnier; *M:* Patrick Doyle. Academy Awards '92: Best Foreign Language Film; Nominations: Best Actress (Deneuve); British Academy Awards '93: Best Foreign Language Film; Cesar Awards '93: Best Actress (Deneuve), Best Supporting Actress (Blanc); National Board of Review Awards '92: Best Foreign Film. **VHS, 8mm $94.95** *COL, FCT, BTV* ♪♪♪

Indomitable Teddy Roosevelt Entertaining mix of newsreel footage and staged scenes traces the career of the feisty president.
1983 93m/C *D:* Harrison Engle. **VHS, Beta** *PSM, CHF* ♪♪½

Infamous Crimes Philo investigates the murders of a playboy and his girlfriends. One of the last of the series whose character was based on the S.S. Van Dine stories. *AKA:* Philo Vance Returns.
1947 64m/B William Wright, Terry Austin, Leon Belasco, Clara Blandick, Iris Adrian, Frank Wilcox; *D:* William Beaudine. **VHS, Beta, 8mm $24.95** *VYY* ♪

Infernal Trio An attorney comes up with a plan involving two sisters (who are his lovers) which will make them both wealthy; but it will also make them both murderers. Sophisticated black comedy based on a true story. In French with English subtitles or dubbed.
1974 100m/C Romy Schneider, Michel Piccoli, Mascha Gonska; *D:* Francis Girod. **VHS $59.95** *CVC, ING* ♪♪½

Inferno Uneven occult horror tale about a young man who arrives in New York to investigate the mysterious circumstances surrounding his sister's death. Dubbed.
1978 (R) 83m/C Leigh McCloskey, Elenora Giorgi, Irene Miracle, Sacha Pitoeff; *D:* Dario Argento; *M:* Keith Emerson. **VHS, Beta $59.98** *FOX* ♪♪

Inferno in Paradise Mucho macho firefighter and bimbous gal pal photographer get hot while trailing a murderous pyromaniac. More like purgatory in the living room (that is, unless you thought Forsyth's earlier "Chesty Anderson, US Navy" was divine comedy).
1988 115m/C Richard Young, Betty Ann Carr, Jim Davis, Andy Jarrell, Dennis Chun; *D:* Ed Forsyth. **VHS $19.95** *ACA* ♪

The Informer Based on Liam O'Flaherty's novel about the Irish Sinn Fein Rebellion of 1922, it tells the story of a hard-drinking Dublin man (Mclaglen) who informs on a friend (a member of the Irish Republican Army) in order to collect a 20-pound reward. When his "friend" is killed during capture, he goes on a drinking spree instead of using the money, as planned, for passage to America. Director Ford allowed McLaglen to improvise his lines during the trial scene in order to enhance the realism, leading to excruciating suspense. Wonderful score.
1935 91m/B Victor McLaglen, Heather Angel, Wallace Ford, Margot Grahame, Joseph Sawyer, Preston Foster, Una O'Connor, J.M. Kerrigan, Donald Meek; *D:* John Ford; *W:* Dudley Nichols; *M:* Max Steiner. Academy Awards '35: Best Actor (McLaglen), Best Director (Ford), Best Screenplay, Best Original Score; Nominations: Best Film Editing, Best Picture; National Board of Review Awards '35: 10 Best Films of the Year; New York Film Critics Awards '35: Best Director (Ford), Best Film. **VHS, Beta $19.98** *MED, BTV, TTC* ♪♪♪♪

Infra-Man If you're looking for a truly bad, hokey flick, this could be it. Infra-man is a superhero who must rescue the galaxy from the clutches of the evil Princess Dragon Mom and her army of prehistoric monsters. Outlandish dialogue (delivered straight) combines with horrible special effects and costumes to create what may well be one of the best camp classics to date. Poorly dubbed in English. *AKA:* The Super Inframan; The Infra Superman.
1976 (PG) 92m/C Li Hsiu-hsien, Wang Hsieh, Yuan Man-tzu, Terry Liu, Tsen Shu-yi, Huang Chien-lung, Lu Sheng; *D:* Hua-Shan; *W:* Peter Fernandez. **VHS, Beta $49.95** *PSM* Woof!

Inga Story of a teenage girl becoming a woman. Sensitive and well-acted.
1967 86m/B **VHS, Beta $24.95** *VPL* Woof!

Inherit the Wind Powerful courtroom drama, based on the Broadway play, is actually a fictionalized version of the infamous Scopes "Monkey Trial" of 1925. Tracy is the defense attorney for the schoolteacher on trial for teaching Darwin's Theory of Evolution to a group of students in a small town ruled by religion. March is the prosecutor seeking to put the teacher behind bars and restore religion to the schools.
1960 128m/B Spencer Tracy, Fredric March, Florence Eldridge, Gene Kelly, Dick York; *D:* Stanley Kramer; *M:* Ernest Gold. Academy Awards '60 Nominations: Best Actor (Tracy), Best Adapted Screenplay, Best Black and White Cinematography, Best Film Editing; Berlin International Film Festival '60: Best Actor

(March); National Board of Review Awards '60: 10 Best Films of the Year. **VHS, Beta $19.98** *FOX, FCT, ADL* ♪♪♪½

Inheritance Victorian-era melodrama of a young heiress endangered by her guardian, who plots to murder his charge for her inheritance. Chilling and moody story based on a novel by Sheridan Le Fanu. *AKA:* Uncle Silas.
1947 103m/B Jean Simmons, Katina Paxinou, Derrick DeMarney, Derek Bond; *D:* Charles Frank. **VHS, Beta $29.98** *DVT* ♪♪♪

The Inheritance Wealthy partiarch becomes sexually involved with scheming daughter-in-law. Tawdry tale is nonetheless engaging. *AKA:* L'Eredita Ferramonti.
1976 (R) 121m/C Anthony Quinn, Fabio Testi, Dominique Sanda; *D:* Mauro Bolognini; *M:* Ennio Morricone. Cannes Film Festival Nominations: cs 76: Best Film; Cannes Film Festival '76: Best Actress (Sanda). **VHS, Beta** NO ♪♪½

The Inheritor Set in a small New England town, this mystery centers on the death of a young woman and her sister's attempts to uncover the murderer. The local celebrity, a writer, seems to be at the heart of the mystery and the sister finds herself growing interested. Keeps you guessing.
1990 (R) 83m/C Dan Haggerty; *D:* Brian Savegar. **VHS** NO ♪♪

The Inheritors Not-too-subtle tale of a young German boy who becomes involved with a Nazi youth group as his home life deteriorates. Heavy-going anti-fascism creates more message than entertainment. In German with English subtitles or dubbed.
1985 89m/C Nikolas Vogel, Roger Schauer, Klaus Novak, Johanna Tomek; *D:* Walter Bannert. **VHS, Beta $29.98** *SUE, APD, GLV* ♪½

Inhibition A beautiful heiress has lots of sex with different people in exotic locales. Softcore soap.
1986 90m/C Claudine Beccaire, Ilona Staller. **VHS, Beta $29.95** *MED* ♪

The Initiation Trying to rid herself of a troublesome nightmare, a coed finds herself face-to-face with a psycho. Gory campus slaughterfest.
1984 (R) 97m/C Vera Miles, Clu Gulager, James Read, Daphne Zuniga; *D:* Larry Stewart. **VHS, Beta $19.95** *STE* ♪

Initiation of Sarah College freshman joins a sorority, undergoes abusive initiation, and gains a supernatural revenge. Made-for-television "Carrie" rip-off.
1978 100m/C Kay Lenz, Shelley Winters, Kathryn Crosby, Morgan Brittany, Tony Bill, Tisa Farrow, Robert Hays, Morgan Fairchild; *D:* Robert Day. **VHS, Beta $49.95** *WOV* ♪

The Inkwell Quiet teenager Drew Tate finds first love when his family spends their vacation with relatives on Martha's Vineyard. Drew is drawn into the party atmosphere of the Inkwell, the area where affluent black professionals have summered for decades. Meanwhile, political differences between Drew's former Black Panther father and his conservative uncle threaten family harmony. Everything about the film has a sugary aura, with conflicts handled tastefully. Rich directs broadly, leading to some overacting. Film is set in 1976.
1994 (R) 112m/C Larenz Tate, Joe Morton, Phyllis Stickney, Jada Pinkett; *D:* Matty Rich; *W:* Tom Ricostronza, Paris Qualles; *M:* Terence Blanchard. **VHS** ♪♪

Inn of Temptation A bunch of bowling buddies take off for Bangkok on an impulsive weekend, and meet lots of Oriental women.
1986 72m/C Michael Jacot, Claude Martin. **VHS, Beta $29.95** *MED* ♪

Inn of the Damned Detective looks into an inn where no one ever gets charged for an extra day; they simply die. Anderson is watchable.

1974 92m/C Alex Cord, Judith Anderson, Tony Bonner, Michael Craig, John Meillon; *D:* Terry Burke. VHS, Beta NO ♫½

The Inn of the Sixth Happiness Inspiring story of Gladys Aylward, an English missionary in 1930s' China, who leads a group of children through war-torn countryside. Donat's last film.

1958 158m/C Ingrid Bergman, Robert Donat, Curt Jurgens; *D:* Mark Robson; *M:* Malcolm Arnold. Academy Awards '58 Nominations: Best Director (Robson); National Board of Review Awards '58: Best Actress (Bergman). VHS, Beta $19.98 FXV ♫♫♫

Inn on the River Scotland Yard investigates a series of murders taking place on the waterfront by the "Shark's" gang. Remake of "The Return of the Frog."

1962 95m/C Klaus Kinski, Joachim Fuchsberger, Brigitte Grothum, Richard Much; *D:* Alfred Vohrer. VHS $16.95 SNC ♫♫½

The Inner Circle A private detective, framed for murder by his secretary, has a limited amount of time to find the real murderer. Confusing.

1946 57m/B Adele Mara, Warren Douglas, William Frawley, Ricardo Cortez, Virginia Christine; *D:* Philip Ford. VHS, Beta $16.95 SNC ♫½

The Inner Circle Ivan Sanshin is a meek, married man working as a movie projectionist for the KGB in 1935 Russia. Sanshin is taken by the KGB to the Kremlin to show movies, primarily Hollywood features, to leader Joseph Stalin, a job he cannot discuss with anyone, even his wife. Under the spell of Stalin's personality, Sanshin sees only what he's told and overlooks the oppression and persecution of the times. Based on the life of the projectionist who served from 1935 until Stalin's death in 1953. Filmed on location at the Kremlin.

1991 (PG-13) 122m/C Tom Hulce, Lolita Davidovich, Bob Hoskins, Alexandre Zbruev, Maria Baranova, Feodor Chaliapin Jr, Bess Meyer; *D:* Andrei Konchalovsky; *W:* Andrei Konchalovsky, Anatoli Usov; *M:* Eduard Artemyev. VHS, 8mm $19.95 COL ♫♫½

Inner Sanctum Adequate tale of a young girl accosted by a gypsy who claims that tragedy awaits her. Based on a radio show of the same name.

1948 62m/B Chuck Russell, Mary Beth Hughes, Lee Patrick, Nana Bryant; *D:* Lew Landers. VHS $16.95 SNC ♫♫

Inner Sanctum Cheating husband hires sensuous nurse to tend invalid wife. You can guess the rest; in fact, you have to because the plot ultimately makes no sense. Available in R-rated and sex-drenched unrated editions.

1991 (R) 87m/C Tanya Roberts, Margaux Hemingway, Joseph Bottoms, Valerie Wildman, William Butler, Brett Clark; *D:* Fred Olen Ray. VHS $19.95 COL Woof!

Innerspace A space pilot, miniaturized for a journey through a lab rat a la "Fantastic Voyage," is accidentally injected into a nebbish supermarket clerk, and together they nab some bad guys and get the girl. Award-winning special effects support some funny moments between micro Quaid and nerdy Short, with Ryan producing the confused romantic interest.

1987 (PG) 120m/C Dennis Quaid, Martin Short, Meg Ryan, Kevin McCarthy, Fiona Lewis, Henry Gibson, Robert Picardo, John Hora, Wendy Schaal, Orson Bean, Chuck Jones, William

Schallert, Dick Miller, Vernon Wells, Harold Sylvester, Kevin Hooks, Kathleen Freeman, Kenneth Tobey; *D:* Joe Dante; *W:* Jeffrey Boam, Chip Proser; *M:* Jerry Goldsmith. VHS, Beta, 8mm $14.95 WAR ♫♫½

Innocence Unprotected A film collage that contains footage from the 1942 film "Innocence Unprotected," the story of an acrobat trying to save an orphan from her wicked stepmother, newsreels from Nazi-occupied Yugoslavia, and interviews from 1968 with people who were in the film. Confiscated by the Nazis during final production, "Innocence Unprotected" was discovered by director Makavejev, who worked it into the collage. Filmed in color and black and white; in Serbian with English subtitles.

1968 78m/C Dragoljub Aleksic, Ana Milosavljevic, Vera Jovanovic; *D:* Dusan Makavejev; *W:* Dusan Makavejev. VHS $59.95 FCT ♫♫½

The Innocent The setting: turn of the century Rome, ablaze with atheism and free love. The story: Giannini's a Sicilian aristocrat who ignores wife Antonelli and dallies with scheming mistress O'Neill. Discovering his wife's infidelity, he's profoundly disillusioned, and his manly notion of self disintegrates. Visconti's last film, it was an art house fave and is considered by many to be his best. Lavishly photographed, well set and costumed, and true to the Gabrielle D'Annunzio's novel. In Italian with English subtitles. *AKA:* L'Innocente.

1976 (R) 125m/C Laura Antonelli, Jennifer O'Neill, Giancarlo Giannini; *D:* Luchino Visconti. VHS, Beta $79.95 VES, FCT, ING ♫♫♫½

The Innocent Cold War thriller has naive British engineer Leonard Markham (Scott) sent to Berlin in 1955 by Brits who are warily cooperating with the U.S. forces. He's turned over to CIA operator Bob Glass (Hopkins) and asked to intercept communications between East Germany and the Soviet Union. Glass continually warns Markham not to trust anyone, including Maria (Rossellini), the married German woman with whom he begins an affair. Failure to build necessary suspense and performances leads to disappointing one-note display. Based on the novel by McEwan.

1993 107m/C Anthony Hopkins, Campbell Scott, Isabella Rossellini, Hart Bochner, James Grant, Jeremy Sinden, Ronald Nitschke; *D:* John Schlesinger; *W:* Ian McEwan; *M:* Gerald Gouriet. VHS NYR ♫♫½

Innocent Blood A mediocre modern-day vampire/gangster combo with the beautiful (though red-eyed) Parillaud as the woman with a taste for someone "Italian." Unfortunately, she doesn't finish off her latest meal—mobster Loggia—who finds being undead very useful to his vicious work. LaPaglia plays the bewildered, love-struck cop involved with the vamp. Parillaud appears nude in several scenes and the gore and violence are stomach-turning.

1992 (R) 112m/C Anne Parillaud, Anthony LaPaglia, Robert Loggia, David Proval, Don Rickles, Rocco Sisto, Kim Coates; *D:* John Landis. VHS, Beta $19.98 WAR, PMS ♫♫

An Innocent Man Uneven story of Selleck, an ordinary family man and airline mechanic, framed as a drug dealer and sent to prison.

1989 (R) 113m/C Tom Selleck, F. Murray Abraham, Laila Robins, David Rasche, Richard Young, Badja Djola; *D:* Peter Yates; *W:* Larry Brothers; *M:* Howard Shore. VHS, Beta $19.99 TOU ♫♫½

Innocent Prey When a woman finally summons the courage to bid hasta la vista to her abusive husband, it turns out he's not so quick to say ciao. Definitely not a highlight in Balsam's career.

1988 (R) 88m/C P.J. Soles, Martin Balsam, Kit Taylor, Grigor Taylor, John Warnock, Susan Stenmark, Richard Morgan; *D:* Colin Eggleston. VHS NO ♫♫

Innocent Victim Convoluted tale of revenge and madness. Bacall plays a mad grandmother who kidnaps a boy to take the place of her dead grandson. The kidnapped boy's stepfather then is accused of murdering him, and starts murdering others to get the boy back. *AKA:* The Tree of Hands.

1990 (R) 100m/C Lauren Bacall, Helen Shaver, Paul McGann, Peter Firth; *D:* Giles Foster. VHS $29.95 ACA ♫

The Innocents Abroad Entertaining adaptation of Mark Twain's novel about a group of naive Americans cruising the Mediterranean. Ensemble cast offers some surprising performances. Originally produced for PBS.

1984 116m/C Craig Wasson, Brooke Adams, David Ogden Stiers. VHS $19.95 MCA ♫♫½

Innocents in Paris A group of seven Britons visit Paris for the first time. A bit long but enough ooo-la-la to satisfy.

1953 89m/B Alastair Sim, Laurence Harvey, Jimmy Edwards, Claire Bloom, Margaret Rutherford; *D:* Gordon Parry. VHS, Beta NO ♫♫½

The Inquiry A new twist on the resurrection of Christ. Carradine senses a cover-up when he's sent from Rome to investigate the problem of Christ's missing corpse. He retraces Christ's final days to solve the case in this interesting, offbeat film. Dubbed.

1987 107m/C Keith Carradine, Harvey Keitel, Phyllis Logan, Angelo Infanti, Lina Sastri; *D:* Damiano Damiani. VHS $79.99 HBO ♫♫½

Inquisition Naschy is a 16th century witch hunting judge who finds himself accused of witchcraft.

1976 85m/C Paul Naschy, Daniela Giordano, Juan Gallardo; *D:* Paul Naschy; *W:* Paul Naschy. VHS, Beta VCD ♫½

Insanity A film director becomes violently obsessed with a beautiful actress.

1982 101m/C Terence Stamp, Fernando Rey, Corinne Clery. VHS, Beta NO ♫

The Insect Woman Chronicles 45 years in the life of a woman who must work with the diligence of an ant in order to survive. Thoughtfully reflects the exploitation of women and the cruelty of human nature in Japanese society. Beautiful performance from Hidari, who ages from girlhood to middle age. In Japanese with English subtitles. *AKA:* The Insect; Nippon Konchuki.

1963 123m/B Sachiko Hidari, Yitsuko Yoshimura, Hiroyuki Nagaes, Sumie Sasaki; *D:* Shohei Imamura. VHS $29.95 CVC ♫♫♫

Inserts A formerly successful director has been reduced to making porno films in this pretentious, long-winded effort set in a crumbling Hollywood mansion in the 1930s. Affected, windbaggish performances kill it.

1976 (R) 99m/C Richard Dreyfuss, Jessica Harper, Veronica Cartwright, Bob Hoskins; *D:* John Byrum. VHS $59.98 FOX ♫

Inside Daisy Clover Wood is the self-sufficient, junior delinquent waif who becomes a teenage musical star and pays the price for fame in this Hollywood saga set in the 1930s. Discovered by tyrannical studio head Plummer, Daisy is given her big break and taken under his wing for grooming as Swan Studio's newest sensation. She falls

for fellow performer, matinee idol Redford, who has some secrets of his own, and eventually has a breakdown from the career pressure. Glossy melodrama is filled with over-the-top performances but its sheer silliness makes it amusing.
1965 128m/C Natalie Wood, Christopher Plummer, Robert Redford, Ruth Gordon, Roddy McDowall, Katharine Bard; **D:** Robert Mulligan; **W:** Gavin Lambert. Academy Awards '65 Nominations: Best Art Direction/Set Decoration (Color), Best Costume Design (Color), Best Supporting Actress (Gordon); Golden Globe Awards '66: Best Supporting Actress (Gordon). **VHS $19.98** *WAR* 🎬🎬½

Inside Edge Urban crime thriller is a complex yet surprisingly uninteresting story of a police officer who falls for the girlfriend of the drug lord he is chasing. Filled with the standard genre violence.
1992 (R) 84m/C Michael Madsen, Richard Lynch, Rosie Vela, Tony Peck, George Jenesky, Branscombe Richmond; **D:** Warren Clark; **W:** William Tannen. **VHS $89.95** *ATV* 🎬🎬

Inside Information With Tarzan's help, a cop searches out the leader of a ring of jewel thieves.
1934 51m/B Rex Lease, Marion Shilling, Philo McCullough. **VHS, Beta** *NO* 🎬

The Inside Man Double agents struggle to find a submarine-detecting laser device. Based on true incidents in which a soviet sub ran aground in Sweden. Made in Sweden; dubbed.
1984 90m/C Dennis Hopper, Hardy Kruger, Gosta Ekman, David Wilson; **D:** Tom Clegg. **VHS, Beta $9.95** *SIM, CEL, VTR* 🎬🎬½

Inside Monkey Zetterland Monkey Zetterland (Antin) is a screenwriter and former actor with an eccentric family. His actress mother is neurotically insecure and a nag; his father is an aging hippie who only shows up at Thanksgiving; his lesbian sister Grace is trying to get over a failed relationship; and his brother Brent is totally self-absorbed. Add to this menage his equally lunatic friends: Imogene, the compulsive talker and exhibitionist; his vicious girlfriend Daphne; and frightening married couple Sophie and Sasha. Meanwhile, Monkey tries to survive amidst the chaos. Interesting cast but lots of camera tricks do not a successful film make and the effort to be hip is all too apparent.
1993 (R) 92m/C Steve Antin, Patricia Arquette, Sandra Bernhard, Sofia Coppola, Tate Donovan, Katherine Helmond, Bo Hopkins, Debi Mazar, Martha Plimpton, Rupert Everett, Ricki Lake; **D:** Jefery Levy; **W:** Steve Antin. **VHS $92.95** *PSM* 🎬🎬

Inside Moves A look at handicapped citizens trying to make it in everyday life, focusing on the relationship between an insecure, failed suicide and a volatile man who is only a knee operation away from a dreamed-about basketball career.
1980 (PG) 113m/C John Savage, Diana Scarwid, David Morse, Amy Wright; **D:** Richard Donner; **W:** Valerie Curtin, Barry Levinson; **M:** John Barry. **VHS, Beta $19.95** *FOX* 🎬🎬½

Inside Out An ex-GI, a jewel thief and a German POW camp commandant band together to find a stolen shipment of Nazi gold behind the Iron Curtain. To find the gold, they help a Nazi prisoner who knows the secret to break out of prison. Good action caper. *AKA:* The Golden Heist; Hitler's Gold.
1975 (PG) 97m/C Telly Savalas, Robert Culp, James Mason, Aldo Ray, Doris Kunstmann; **D:** Peter Duffell. **VHS, Beta $59.95** *WAR* 🎬🎬½

Inside Out Hiding in his apartment from a world which terrifies him, Jimmy doesn't feel he's missing much—since he has the necessary women and bookies come to him. He soon finds he's not quite as safe as he thought, and the only way out is "out there." Fine performance from Gould, suspenseful pacing.
1991 (R) 87m/C Elliott Gould, Jennifer Tilly, Howard Hesseman, Beah Richards, Timothy Scott, Sandy McPeak, Dana Elcar, Meshach Taylor, Nicole Norman; **D:** Robert Taicher; **W:** Robert Taicher. **VHS** *NO* 🎬🎬½

Inside the Law A gang of crooks takes over a bank and must stay "inside the law" and resist their natural inclinations. Lots of comic situations.
1942 65m/B Wallace Ford, Frank Sully, Harry Holman, Luana Walters, Lafayette McKee, Danny Duncan, Earle Hodgins; **D:** Hamilton MacFadden. **VHS $19.95** *NOS* 🎬🎬

Inside the Lines A WWI tale of espionage and counter-espionage.
1930 73m/B Betty Compson, Montagu Love, Mischa Auer, Ralph Forbes. **VHS, Beta $24.95** *VYY* 🎬🎬

Inside the Third Reich A made-for-television mini-series detailing the rise to power within the Third Reich of Albert Speer, top advisor to Hitler. Based on Speer's rather self-serving memoires.
1982 250m/C Derek Jacobi, Rutger Hauer, John Gielgud, Blythe Danner, Maria Schell, Ian Holm, Trevor Howard, Randy Quaid, Viveca Lindfors, Robert Vaughn, Stephen Collins, Elke Sommer, Renee Soutendijk; **D:** Marvin J. Chomsky. **VHS, Beta $34.95** *SUE, GLV* 🎬🎬½

Insignificance A film about an imaginary night spent in a New York hotel by characters who resemble Marilyn Monroe, Albert Einstein, Joe McCarthy, and Joe DiMaggio. Entertaining and often amusing as it follows the characters as they discuss theory and relativity, the Russians, and baseball among other things.
1985 110m/C Gary Busey, Tony Curtis, Theresa Russell, Michael Emil, Will Sampson; **D:** Nicolas Roeg; **W:** Terry Johnson. **VHS, Beta $19.98** *LHV, WAR* 🎬🎬🎬

The Inspector General Classic Kaye craziness of mistaken identities with the master comic portraying a carnival medicine man who is mistaken by the villagers for their feared Inspector General. If you like Kaye's manic performance, you'll enjoy this one. 🎵The Gypsy Drinking Song; Onward Onward; The Medicine Show; The Inspector General; Lonely Heart; Soliloquy For Three Heads; Happy Times; Brodny. *AKA:* Happy Times.
1949 103m/C Danny Kaye, Walter Slezak, Barbara Bates, Elsa Lanchester, Gene Lockhart, Walter Catlett, Alan Hale; **D:** Henry Koster. **VHS, Beta $19.98** *MGM, MRV, NOS* 🎬🎬½

The Inspector General The filmed performance of Gogol's great play by the Moscow Art Theatre, wherein a provincial town panics when they mistake a wandering moron for the Inspector come to check up on them. In Russian with English subtitles.
1954 128m/B **D:** Vladimir Petrov. **VHS, Beta $44.95** *FCT, AUD, ING* 🎬🎬½

Inspector Hornleigh A pair of bumbling detectives arrive on the scene when a Chancellor's fortune is stolen. Fine comedy, although the Scottish and British accents can be rather thick now and again.
1939 76m/B Gordon Harker, Alastair Sim, Miki Hood, Wally Patch, Steve Geray, Edward Underdown, Hugh Williams, Gibb McLaughlin; **D:** Eugene Forde. **VHS, Beta $16.95** *NOS, SNC* 🎬🎬½

Inspiration of Mr. Budd A clever barber helps police trap a murderer. Based on a short story by Dorothy L. Sayers. Part of EBE's "Orson Welles' Great Mysteries" series.
1975 25m/C Orson Welles. **VHS, Beta** *BRT* 🎬🎬½

Instant Justice A professional Marine jeopardizes his military career by avenging his sister's murder, vigilante style. Exclusive action. *AKA:* Marine Issue.
1986 (R) 101m/C Michael Pare, Tawny Kitaen, Charles Napier; **D:** Craig T. Rumar. **VHS, Beta $79.95** *WAR* 🎬½

Instant Karma Would be comedy depicts young man's far fetched attempts to score babewise. Ask no more what happened to erstwhile teen heart throb Cassidy: he suffers from a major bout of bad karma.
1990 94m/C Craig Sheffer, Chelsea Noble, David Cassidy, Alan Blumenfeld, Glen Hirsch, Marty Ingels, Orson Bean; **D:** Roderick Taylor. **VHS, Beta $89.98** *MGM* 🎬½

Instant Kung-Fu Man Twin brothers get involved in a case of mistaken identity in this martial arts effort.
1984 104m/C John Liu, Hwang Jang Lee, Yeh Fei Yang. **VHS, Beta** *WVE* 🎬

The Instructor The head of a karate school proves the value of his skill when threatened by the owner of a rival school.
1983 91m/C Don Bendell, Bob Chaney, Bob Saal, Lynday Scharnott; **D:** Don Bendell. **VHS, Beta $69.98** *LIV, VES* 🎬

Interceptor Hijackers attempt to steal a Stealth Bomber in this action-adventure saga which features virtual reality computer-generated imagery in its combat sequences.
1992 (R) 92m/C Juergen Prochnow, Andrew Divoff, Elizabeth Morehead; **D:** Michael Cohn. **VHS $92.95** *VMK* 🎬

Interface A computer game gets out of hand at a university, turning the tunnels beneath the campus into a battleground of good and evil.
1984 88m/C John Davies, Laura Lane, Matthew Sacks. **VHS, Beta $69.98** *LIV, VES* 🎬½

Interiors Ultra serious, Bergmanesque drama about three neurotic adult sisters, coping with the dissolution of their family. When Father decides to leave mentally unbalanced mother for a divorcee, the daughters are shocked and bewildered. Depressing and humorless, but fine performances all the way around, supported by the elegant camera work of Gordon Willis. Original theatrical trailer available on the laserdisc format.
1978 (R) 95m/C Diane Keaton, Mary Beth Hurt, E.G. Marshall, Geraldine Page, Richard Jordan, Sam Waterston, Kristin Griffith, Maureen Stapleton; **D:** Woody Allen; **W:** Woody Allen. Academy Awards '78 Nominations: Best Actress (Page), Best Director (Allen), Best Original Screenplay, Best Supporting Actress (Stapleton); British Academy Awards '78: Best Supporting Actress (Page). **VHS, Beta $14.95** *MGM* 🎬🎬🎬½

Intermezzo Married violinist Ekman meets pianist Bergman and they fall in love. He deserts his family to tour with Bergman, but the feelings for his wife and children become too much. When Bergman sees their love won't last, she leaves him. Shakily, he returns home and as his daughter runs to greet him, she is hit by a truck and he realizes that his family is his true love. One of the great grab-your-hanky melodramas. In Swedish with English subtitles. 1939 English re-make features Bergman's American film debut. *AKA:* Interlude.

1936 88m/B Gosta Ekman, Inga Tidblad, Ingrid Bergman, Bullen Berglund; *D:* Gustaf Molander. **VHS** $29.95 *WAC, TPV, LUM* 🎞️🎞️🎞️

Intermezzo Fine, though weepy, love story of a renowned, married violinist who has an affair with his stunningly beautiful protege (Bergman), but while on concert tour realizes that his wife and children hold his heart, and he returns to them. A re-make of the 1936 Swedish film, it's best known as Bergman's American debut. Howard's violin playing was dubbed by Jascha Heifetz. *AKA:* Intermezzo: A Love Story.
1939 70m/B Ingrid Bergman, Leslie Howard, Edna Best, Ann Todd; *D:* Gregory Ratoff. **VHS, Beta** $59.98 *FOX, FCT* 🎞️🎞️🎞️

Internal Affairs Wild, sexually charged action piece about an Internal Affairs officer for the L.A.P.D. (Garcia) who becomes obsessed with exposing a sleazy, corrupt street cop (Gere). Drama becomes illogical, but boasts excellent, strung out performances, especially Gere as the creepy degenerate you'd love to bust.
1990 (R) 114m/C Richard Gere, Andy Garcia, Laurie Metcalf, Ron Vawter, Marco Rodriguez, Nancy Travis, William Baldwin, Richard Bradford, Annabella Sciorra, Michael Beach; *D:* Mike Figgis; *M:* Mike Figgis. **VHS, Beta, 8mm** $14.95 *PAR* 🎞️🎞️½

International Crime Radio hero The Shadow solves a tough crime in this adventure film.
1937 62m/B Rod La Rocque, Astrid Allwyn, William von Brinken; *D:* Charles Lamont. **VHS, Beta** $16.95 *SNC, NOS, AOV* 🎞️🎞️

International House A wacky Dada-esque Hollywood farce about an incredible array of travelers quarantined in a Shanghai hotel where a mad doctor has perfected television. Essentially a burlesque compilation of skits, gags, and routines. Guest stars Rudy Vallee, Baby Rose Marie and Cab Calloway appear on the quaint "television" device, in musical sequences. 🎵Tea Cup; Thank Heaven For You; My Bluebirds are Singing the Blues; Reefer Man.
1933 72m/B W.C. Fields, Peggy Hopkins Joyce, Rudy Vallee, George Burns, Cab Calloway, Sari Maritza, Gracie Allen, Bela Lugosi, Sterling Holloway, Baby Rose Marie; *D:* Edward Sutherland. **VHS, Beta** $14.98 *MCA, MLB* 🎞️🎞️½

International Velvet In this long overdue sequel to "National Velvet," adult Velvet, with live-in companion (Plummer), grooms her orphaned niece (O'Neal) to become an Olympic champanion horsewoman. Good photography and performances by Plummer and Hopkins manage to keep the sentiment at a trot.
1978 (PG) 126m/C Tatum O'Neal, Anthony Hopkins, Christopher Plummer; *D:* Bryan Forbes. **VHS, Beta** $59.95 *MGM* 🎞️🎞️½

Internecine Project Stylistic espionage tale with Coburn's English professor acting as the mastermind behind an unusual series of murders where industrial spies kill each other, so Coburn can garner a top government job in D.C. Unexpected ending is worth the viewing. Based on Mort Elkind's novel.
1973 (PG) 89m/C James Coburn, Lee Grant, Harry Andrews, Keenan Wynn; *D:* Ken Hughes; *W:* Barry Levinson. **VHS, Beta** $59.98 *FOX* 🎞️🎞️½

The Interns Finessed hospital soaper about interns on the staff of a large city hospital, whose personal lives are fraught with trauma, drugs, birth, death, and abortion. Good performances and direction keep this medical melodrama moving in a gurney-like manner. Followed by the "The New

Interns" and the basis for a television series. Adapted from a novel by Richard Frede.
1962 120m/C Cliff Robertson, James MacArthur, Michael Callan, Nick Adams, Stefanie Powers, Suzy Parker, Buddy Ebsen, Telly Savalas, Haya Harareet; *D:* David Swift. **VHS, Beta** $59.95 *COL* 🎞️🎞️½

The Interrogation Grueling depiction of Stalin-era Poland proves that nobody makes anticommunist movies better than those who knew tyranny firsthand. A 1950s cabaret starlet is arrested on false charges and endures years of torment in custody. Banned under Polish martial law in 1982, it circulated illegally in the country until 1989. Janda won an award at Cannes for her transformation from showgirl floozy to defiant heroine. In Polish with English subtitles. *AKA:* Przesluchanie.
1982 118m/C Krystyna Janda, Janusz Gajos, Adam Ferency, Agnieszka Holland, Anna Romantowska; *D:* Richard Bugajski. **VHS** $79.95 *KIV, FCT, ING* 🎞️🎞️🎞️

Interrupted Journey A married man runs away to start a new life with another woman. When she is killed in a train accident, he becomes the prime suspect in her murder. Lots of action and speed, but a disappointing ending.
1949 80m/B Richard Todd, Valerie Hobson; *D:* Daniel Birt. **VHS** $16.95 *NOS, SNC* 🎞️🎞️½

Interrupted Melody True story of opera diva Marjorie Lawrence's courageous battle with polio and her fight to appear once more at the Metropolitan Opera. Parker was nominated for an Oscar in her excellent portrayal of the Australian singer who continues her career despite her handicap. Vocals dubbed by opera star Eileen Farrell. Based on the book by Marjorie Lawrence.
1955 106m/C Glenn Ford, Eleanor Parker, Roger Moore, Cecil Kellaway, Evelyn Ellis, Walter Baldwin; *D:* Curtis Bernhardt; *W:* William Ludwig, Sonya Levien. **VHS** $19.98 *MGM* 🎞️🎞️🎞️

Intersection Successful architect Vincent (Gere) is torn between his aloof wife/partner, Sally (Stone), and a sexy journalist mistress, Olivia (Davidovitch). Who to choose? Since he's a completely self-involved boor, you won't care either way. Another retooling of a French film ("Les Choses de la Vie") as a Hollywood star vehicle that doesn't work. Lousy dialogue doesn't help. Does boast some nice location shots of Vancouver, BC.
1993 (R) 98m/C Richard Gere, Sharon Stone, Lolita Davidovich, Martin Landau, David Selby, Jenny Morrison; *D:* Mark Rydell; *W:* Marshall Brickman, David Rayfiel; *M:* James Newton Howard. **VHS, Beta** *PAR* 🎞️½

Interval A middle-aged, globe-trotting woman becomes involved with a young American painter while running from her past. Oberon, 62 at the time, produced and played in this, her last film. Filmed in Mexico.
1973 (PG) 84m/C Merle Oberon, Robert Wolders; *D:* Daniel Mann. **VHS, Beta** $59.95 *NLC* 🎞️🎞️

Intervista A pseudo-documentary look at director Fellini's love of the movies, "Intervista" is a mixture of recollection, parody, memoir, satire, self-examination and fantasy. Fellini himself is the master of ceremonies in this joyous celebration of the studio community that features actors, actresses, bit players, make-up artists, scene painters, publicity agents, technicians, and gate-crashers. The high point of the film arrives with the stars of "La Dolce Vita" re-screening the Fellini masterpiece at Ekberg's country villa. It's a special moment of fantasy vs. reality in this glorious tribute to cinema history. In Italian

with English subtitles. *AKA:* Federico Fellini's Intervista.
1987 108m/C Marcello Mastroianni, Anita Ekberg, Federico Fellini, Sergio Rubini, Lara Wendell, Antonio Cantafora, Antonella Ponziani, Maurizio Mein, Paola Liguori, Nadia Ottaviani; *D:* Federico Fellini; *W:* Federico Fellini, Gianfranco Angelucci; *M:* Nicola Piovani. **VHS** $89.95 *TRI* 🎞️🎞️🎞️

Interzone Humans battle mutants in a post-holocaust world.
1988 97m/C Bruce Abbott; *D:* Deran Sarafian. **VHS, Beta** $79.95 *MED* 🎞️½

Intimate Contact Top executive discovers he has AIDS after a business trip fling. Powerful drama as he and his wife try to cope. Excellent, understated performances from Massey and Bloom. Originally made for cable television.
1987 (PG) 140m/C Claire Bloom, Daniel Massey, Abigail Cruttenden, Mark Kingston, Sylvia Syms, Sally Jane Jackson; *D:* Waris Hussein; *W:* Alma Cullen. **VHS, Beta** $79.99 *HBO* 🎞️🎞️🎞️

Intimate Power True story of French schoolgirl sold into slavery to an Ottoman sultan who becomes the harem queen. She bears an heir and begins to teach her son about his people's rights, in the hope that he will bring about reform in Turkey where she grows up to be a sultan. Good cast supports the exotic storytelling in this made for cable drama.
1989 (R) 104m/C F. Murray Abraham, Maud Adams, Amber O'Shea; *D:* Jack Smight. **VHS, Beta** $89.99 *HBO* 🎞️🎞️½

Intimate Story Intimate story of a husband and wife trying unsuccessfully to have a baby, amid the lack of privacy in a Kibbutz. Each blames the other for the problem and tries to escape the problems by focusing on personal fantasies. In Hebrew with English subtitles.
1981 95m/C Chava Alberstein, Alex Peleg; *D:* Israeli Nadav Levitan. **VHS, Beta** $79.95 *ERG, ING, TPV* 🎞️🎞️½

Intimate Stranger Sexy, would-be rock star by day, Harry sets out in search of a steadier source of income. Rather than wait on tables all day, she chooses instead to become a phone-sex girl. This turns out to be an unwise career move, as she promptly finds herself the target of a phone-psycho who just can't take "no" for an answer. Will Debbie be able to shake this loser, or will he put a permanent end to her life-long dreams? Made for television.
1991 (R) 96m/C Deborah Harry, James Russo, Tim Thomerson, Paige French, Grace Zabriskie; *D:* Allan Holzman. **VHS, Beta** $89.95 *PAR* 🎞️½

Intimate Strangers Taut made-for-television expose on battering and its effects on the family. Weaver and Struthers outshine the material, but the finest performance is a cameo by Douglas as Weaver's irascible aged father.
1977 96m/C Dennis Weaver, Sally Struthers, Quinn Cummings, Tyne Daly, Larry Hagman, Rhea Perlman; *Cameos:* Melvyn Douglas; *D:* John Llewellyn Moxey. **VHS, Beta** $39.95 *WOV* 🎞️🎞️

Into the Badlands Mild made for cable TV thriller presents three suspense tales in "Twilight Zone" fashion, linked by the appearance of a mysterious Man in Black. No, it's not Johnny Cash, but Dern as a sinister bounty hunter in the old west, who inspires strange events on the trail.
1992 (R) 89m/C Bruce Dern, Mariel Hemingway, Helen Hunt, Dylan McDermott, Lisa Pelikan, Andrew (Andy) Robinson; *D:* Sam Pillsbury. **VHS** $89.95 *MCA* 🎞️🎞️

Into the Darkness In the world of fashion models, a maniacal, demented killer stalks his prey.
1986 90m/C Donald Pleasence, Ronald Lacey. **VHS, Beta** NO *⅟₂*

Into the Fire Thriller about a young drifter who, against the backdrop of a Canadian winter, happens upon a roadside lodge and diner, where he gets involved in sex and murder. Title gives a good idea of what to do with this one.
1988 (R) 88m/C Susan Anspach, Art Hindle, Olivia D'Abo, Lee Montgomery; **D:** Graeme Campbell. **VHS, Beta** $79.98 *LIV, VES* *⅟*

Into the Homeland Seasoned ex-cop (Boothe) infiltrates a white supremacist group which had kidnapped his teenage daughter. Failed "message" about neo-nazi ethics, but good confrontation between Boothe and his son (Howell) make this so-so viewing. Made for cable television.
1987 95m/C Powers Boothe, C. Thomas Howell, Paul LeMat; **D:** Lesli Linka Glatter. **VHS, Beta** $79.95 *BAR, LHV, WAR* *⅟⅟*

Into the Night Campy, off-beat thriller about a middle-aged, jilted deadbeat (Goldblum), who meets a beautiful woman (Pfeiffer) when she suddenly drops onto the hood of his car, with a relentless gang of Arabs pursuing. During their search through L.A. and other parts of California for the one person who can help her out of this mess, a whole crew of Hollywood directors make cameo appearances, making this a delight for film buffs, but occasionally tedious for general audiences. B.B. King sings the title song.
1985 (R) 115m/C Jeff Goldblum, Michelle Pfeiffer, David Bowie, Carl Perkins, Richard Farnsworth, Dan Aykroyd, Paul Mazursky, Roger Vadim, Irene Papas, Bruce McGill, Vera Miles, Clu Gulager, Don Steel, Kathryn Harrold; **Cameos:** Jim Henson, Paul Bartel, David Cronenberg, Jack Arnold, Jonathan Demme, Lawrence Kasdan, Amy Heckerling, Don Siegel, Richard Franklin, Colin Higgins, Andrew Marton; **D:** John Landis; **W:** Ron Koslow. **VHS, Beta** $19.95 *MCA* *⅟⅟*

Into the Sun Hall plays a Hollywood star who encounters real-life danger while hanging out with an Air Force pilot (Pare) to prepare for an upcoming role. Spectacular aerial scenes steal the show, which isn't hard to do in this lackluster movie.
1992 (R) 101m/C Anthony Michael Hall, Michael Pare, Terry Kiser, Deborah Maria Moore; **D:** Fritz Kiersch. **VHS** *VMK* *⅟⅟₂*

Into the West Enchanting horse tale set amid the mystic isle of Eire. Brooding, drunken Riley (Byrne), once the leader of a band of travelers (the Irish version of gypsies), leaves the road after his wife's death and settles in a Dublin slum with his two boys. The boys are enraptured when their grandfather turns up with a beautiful white horse, but their happiness is shattered when the police take it away. Boys and horse eventually escape in a wild ride across Ireland and into the west. Spiritual and mythic, with an awe-inspiring performance by the horse. Fitzgerald and Conroy make a run at best performances by kids, while Byrne is convincingly sodden and sulky. Meany and Barkin shine in small parts as sibling travellers.
1992 (PG) 97m/C Gabriel Byrne, Ellen Barkin, Ciaran Fitzgerald, Ruaidhri Conroy, David Kelly, Colm Meaney; **D:** Mike Newell; **W:** Jim Sheridan; **M:** Patrick Doyle. **VHS** $96.83 *TOU* *⅟⅟⅟*

Into Thin Air A mother searches tirelessly for her college bound son who disappeared on a cross-country drive. Well-done television drama with a good performance from Burstyn.
1985 100m/C Ellen Burstyn, Robert Prosky, Sam Robards, Tate Donovan, Caroline McWilliams, Nicholas Pryor, John Dennis Johnston; **D:** Roger Young; **W:** George Rubio, Larry Cohen; **M:** Brad Fiedel. **VHS, Beta** $79.95 *NBI, VTR* *⅟⅟⅟*

Intolerance Griffith's largest film in every aspect. An interwoven, four-story epic about human intolerance, with segments set in Babylon, ancient Judea, and Paris. One of the cinema's grandest follies, and greatest achievements. Silent with music score. Laserdisc version contains supplemental material including cuts from other Griffith works. Black and white with some restored color footage.
1916 175m/B Lillian Gish, Mae Marsh, Constance Talmadge, Bessie Love, Elmer Clifton, Erich von Stroheim, Eugene Pallette, Seena Owen, Alfred Paget; **D:** D.W. Griffith. **VHS** $24.95 *GPV, MRV, KIV* *⅟⅟⅟⅟*

Intrigue Former CIA agent (Loggia) defects to the KGB, but wants to return to the US when he realizes he has a progressive illness. Underground agent and old buddy (Glenn) is recruited with orders to smuggle his former colleague out. Tension continues throughout as murder comes along with the orders. Loads of suspense and twist ending in this made for television nail-biter.
1990 (PG) 96m/C Scott Glenn, Robert Loggia, William Atherton, Martin Shaw, Cherie Lunghi, Eleanor Bron; **D:** David Drury. **VHS** $89.95 *VMK* *⅟⅟⅟*

Intruder A man and his stepson are terrorized by a stranger in a panel truck as they travel from Rome to Paris.
1977 98m/C Jean-Louis Trintignant, Mireille Darc, Adolfo Celi. **VHS, Beta** NO *⅟⅟*

Intruder A psychotic killer stalks an all-night convenience store shopping for fresh meat (customers beware). Slasher movie fans should get a kick out of the plot twist at the end.
1988 (R) 90m/C Elizabeth Cox, Renee Estevez, Alvy Moore; **D:** Scott Spiegel. **VHS, Beta** $79.95 *PAR* *⅟⅟*

Intruder in the Dust A small southern community develops a lynch mob mentality when a black man is accused of killing a white man. Powerful, but largely ignored portrait of race relations in the South. Solid performances from the whole cast; filmed in Mississippi. Adapted from a novel by William Faulkner.
1949 87m/B David Brian, Claude Jarman Jr., Juano Hernandez, Porter Hall, Elizabeth Patterson; **D:** Clarence Brown. **VHS** $19.98 *MGM, MOV, BTV* *⅟⅟⅟⅟₂*

Intruder Within Half-baked thriller about crew on an isolated oil rig in Antarctica who, while drilling, unearth a nasty creature that goes around terrorizing the frost-bitten men and occasional stray woman. Made for television.
1981 91m/C Chad Everett, Joseph Bottoms, Jennifer Warren; **D:** Peter Carter. **VHS, Beta** $69.95 *TWE* *⅟*

Intruders Follows the story of three people who have unexplained lapses of time in their lives which they eventually believe are connected to visits by aliens. The three are brought together by a skeptical psychiatrist. The aliens are your typical bugged-eyed, white-faced spooks but part of the film is genuinely unsettling.
1992 162m/C Richard Crenna, Mare Winningham, Susan Blakely, Ben Vereen, Steven Berkoff, Daphne Ashbrook; **D:** Dan Curtis. **VHS** $89.98 *FXV* *⅟⅟*

Invader When a news reporter is sent to cover a mysterious massacre, he begins to realize that the culprits are vicious aliens thirsty for blood...and now they're after him!
1991 (R) 95m/C Hans Bachman, A. Thomas Smith, Rich Foucheux, John Cooke, Robert Diedermann, Allison Sheehy, Ralph Bluemke; **D:** Phillip Cook. **VHS** $92.95 *VMK* *⅟⅟*

The Invaders Two Viking brothers battle each other and the Britons. *AKA:* Erik the Conqueror; Gli Invasori; La Ruee Des Vikings; Fury of the Vikings.
1963 88m/C Cameron Mitchell, George Ardisson, Andrea Checchi, Francoise Christophe, Joe Robinson; **D:** Mario Bava; **M:** Les Baxter. **VHS, Beta** NO *⅟⅟*

The Invaders The popular science fiction series created by Larry Cohen stars Thinnes, as David Vincent, who attempts to convince people he has witnessed an alien landing and that they want to take over Earth. "Beach Head" is the pilot episode. Additional episodes available.
1967 53m/C Roy Thinnes, Kent Smith, Diane Baker, J.D. Cannon, James Daly, John Milford, Ellen Corby, Vaughn Taylor; **D:** Joseph Sargent. **VHS** $14.99 *GKK, MOV* *⅟⅟*

Invaders from Mars Young boy cries "martian" in this sci-fi cheapy classic. He can't convince the townspeople of this invasion because they've already been possessed by the alien beings. His parents are zapped by the little green things first, making this perhaps an allegory for the missing Eisenhower/Stepford years. Includes previews of coming attractions from classic science fiction films. Remade in 1986 by Tobe Hooper.
1953 78m/C Helena Carter, Arthur Franz, Jimmy Hunt, Leif Erickson; **D:** William Cameron Menzies. **VHS, Beta** $19.95 *MED, MLB* *⅟⅟⅟₂*

Invaders from Mars A high-tech remake of Menzies' 1953 semi-classic about a Martian invasion perceived only by one young boy and a sympathetic (though hysterical) school nurse, played by mother and son Black and Carson. Instant camp.
1986 (PG) 102m/C Hunter Carson, Karen Black, Louise Fletcher, Laraine Newman, Timothy Bottoms, Bud Cort; **D:** Tobe Hooper; **W:** Dan O'Bannon, Don Jakoby. **VHS, Beta** $39.95 *MED, IME* *⅟⅟*

Invasion A hospital opens its doors to an accident victim, and his attractive female visitors don't seem sympathetic to the idea of a long hospital stay. Turns out he's an escaped alien prisoner, and the alien babes, intent on intergalactic extradition, place a force field around the hospital and demand his return. Early effort of director Bridges, who later did "The Shooting Party." Interesting, creepy, atmospheric, with very cool camera moves.
1965 82m/B Edward Judd, Yoko Tani, Valerie Gearon, Lyndon Brook, Tsai Chin, Barrie Ingham; **D:** Alan Bridges. **VHS** $19.98 *MOV* *⅟⅟⅟₂*

Invasion Earth: The Aliens Are Here! A cheap spoof of monster movies, as an insectoid projectionist takes over the minds of a movie audience. Clips of Godzilla, Mothra and other beasts are interpolated.
1987 84m/C Janice Fabian, Christian Lee; **D:** George Maitland. **VHS, Beta** $19.95 *STE, NWV* *⅟*

Invasion Force A terrorist army parachutes into a remote region where a film crew is preparing to set up for an action movie. The moviemakers must scare away

the terrorists with their smokepots and blanks. Sounds promising, but proves to be as empty as the movie props used to scare the terrorists.
1990 93m/C Richard Lynch, David Shark, Renee Cline, Douglas Hartier, Graham Times, Angie Synodis; **D:** David A. Prior. **VHS $14.95** AIP *II*

The Invasion of Carol Enders A woman, almost killed by a prowler, awakens with an expanded consciousness, and tries to convince her near husband that her death wasn't an accident.
1974 72m/C Meredith Baxter Birney, Christopher Connelly, Charles Aidman. **VHS, Beta $29.95** LIV *II½*

Invasion of Privacy Alex is a psycho prison inmate obsessed with high profile journalist, Hilary. When Hilary interviews Alex for a magazine cover story, his obsession only grows stronger. Then Alex gets paroled and goes to work for Hilary. When he discovers Hilary isn't interested in him, Alex turns his fantasies to her daughter, who has no notion what she's getting into. An unrated version is also available. Made for cable television.
1992 (R) 95m/C Robby Benson, Jennifer O'Neill, Lydie Denier, Ian Ogilvy; **D:** Kevin Meyer; **W:** Kevin Meyer. **VHS $89.95** PSM *II*

Invasion of the Animal People Hairy monster from outer space attacks Lapland. Narrated by Carradine, the only American in the cast. Pretty silly. **AKA:** Terror in the Midnight Sun; Space Invasion of Lapland; Horror in the Midnight Sun; Space Invasion from Lapland.
1962 73m/C Robert Burton, Barbara Wilson, John Carradine; **D:** Virgil W. Vogel, Jerry Warren. **VHS $19.95** VMK, SNC, NOS Woof!

Invasion of the Bee Girls California girls are mysteriously transformed into deadly nymphomaniacs in this delightful campy science fiction romp. Written by Meyer who later directed "Star Trek II: The Wrath of Khan." **AKA:** Graveyard Tramps.
1973 85m/C Victoria Vetri, William Smith, Anitra Ford, Cliff Osmond, Wright King, Ben Hammer; **D:** Denis Sanders; **W:** Nicholas Meyer; **M:** Charles Bernstein. **VHS $69.98** SUE *III*

Invasion of the Blood Farmers In a small New York town, members of an ancient Druidic cult murder young women, taking their blood in the hope of finding the precise, rare blood type to keep their queen alive. A real woofer.
1972 (PG) 86m/C Norman Kelley, Tanna Hunter, Bruce Detrick, Jack Neubeck, Cythia Fleming, Paul Craig Jennings; **D:** Ed Adlum. **VHS, Beta** NO Woof!

Invasion of the Body Snatchers The one and only post-McCarthy paranoid sci-fi epic, where a small California town is infiltrated by pods from outer space that replicate and replace humans. A chilling, genuinely frightening exercise in nightmare dislocation. Based upon a novel by Jack Finney. Remade in 1978. The laserdisc version contains commentary by Maurice Yacowar, the text of an interview with Siegel, and the original theatrical trailer. The film itself is presented in its original wide-screen format.
1956 80m/B Kevin McCarthy, Dana Wynter, Carolyn Jones, King Donovan, Don Siegel; **D:** Don Siegel; **W:** Sam Peckinpah. **VHS $14.98** REP, VYG, CRC *III*

Invasion of the Body Snatchers One of the few instances where a remake is an improvement on the original, which was itself a classic. This time, the "pod people" are infesting San Francisco, with only a small group of people aware of the invasion. A

ceaselessly inventive, creepy version of the alien-takeover paradigm, with an intense and winning performance by Sutherland.
1978 (PG) 115m/C Donald Sutherland, Brooke Adams, Veronica Cartwright, Leonard Nimoy, Jeff Goldblum, Kevin McCarthy, Don Siegel, Art Hindle; **D:** Philip Kaufman; **W:** W.D. Richter. **VHS, Beta $14.95** MGM *III½*

Invasion of the Body Stealers Aliens are thought to be the captors when sky-divers begin vanishing in mid-air. Uneven sci-fi with nothing going for it. **AKA:** Thin Air; The Body Stealers.
1969 (PG) 115m/C George Sanders, Maurice Evans, Patrick Allen; **D:** Gerry Levy. **VHS, Beta $29.95** LIV Woof!

Invasion of the Flesh Hunters Group of tortured Vietnam veterans returns home carrying a cannibalistic curse with them. Smorgasbord of gore and sensationalism is not for discriminating tastes. **AKA:** Cannibals in the Streets; Savage Apocalypse; The Slaughterers; Cannibals in the City; Virus.
1982 90m/C John Saxon, Elizabeth Turner; **D:** Anthony M. (Antonio Margheriti) Dawson; **W:** Anthony M. (Antonio Margheriti) Dawson. **VHS, Beta $69.98** LIV, VES Woof!

Invasion of the Girl Snatchers Aliens from another planet, in cahoots with a cult kingpin, subdue young earth girls and force them to undergo bizarre acts that may just rob them of their dignity. Save a bit of your own dignity by staying away. Cheap look, cheap feel, cheap thrills.
1973 90m/C Elizabeth Rush, Ele Grigsby, David Roster; **D:** Lee Jones. **VHS, Beta $39.95** VCI Woof!

Invasion of the Saucer Men Suburban teenagers (Terrell, Castillo) are detained by a little green man at lovers lane. When they return with police to the scene, only the corpse of the town drunk (Gorshin) remains. Fortunately, the dead man's roommate (Osborn) believes them but the trio must convince authorities before the alien creatures multiply and take over the world.
1957 69m/B Steven Terrell, Gloria Castillo, Frank Gorshin, Lyn Osborn, Ed Nelson, Angelo Rossitto; **D:** Edward L. Cahn; **M:** Ronald Stein. **VHS $9.98** COL *II*

Invasion of the Space Preachers Hideous creatures from outer space arrive on Earth with plans for conquest. Led by the seemingly human Reverend Lash, they prey on the innocent and trusting, fleecing God-fearing folk out of their hard earned cash!
1990 100m/C Jim Wolfe, Guy Nelson, Eliska Hahn, Gary Brown, Jesse Johnson, John Riggs; **D:** Daniel Boyd; **W:** Daniel Boyd. **VHS, Beta $79.95** RHI *II*

Invasion of the Vampires Burrito bat fest has Count Frankenhausen doing his vampire thing in a small, 16th century village. Atmospheric sets are highlight. Not a good substitute for No Doze. **AKA:** La Invasion de Los Vampiros.
1961 78m/B Carlos Agosti, Rafael Etienne, Bertha Moss, Tito Junco, Erna Martha Bauman, Fernando Soto, Enrique Garcia Alvarez, David Reynoso; **D:** Miguel Morayta; **W:** Miguel Morayta. **VHS $19.98** SNC *II*

Invasion of the Zombies Bare-fisted wrestler Santo faces of brace of zombies in order to prove that men with short necks can hug other men and still be mucho macho.
1961 85m/B Santo; **D:** Benito Alazraki. **VHS $19.98** SNC, HHT *II*

Invasion U.S.A. A mercenary defends nothing less than the entire country against Russian terrorists landing in Florida and looking for condos. A record-setting amount of people killed. Count them—it's not like you'll miss anything important. Norris is a bit less animated than a wooden Indian, and the acting is more painful to endure than the violence. Glasnost saved the movie industry from additional paranoia movies of this kind.
1985 (R) 108m/C Chuck Norris, Richard Lynch, Melissa Prophet, Alex Colon, Billy Drago; **D:** Joseph Zito. **VHS, Beta $14.95** MGM *II*

Investigation A Frenchman plans to murder his wife so he can marry his pregnant mistress, guaranteeing an heir. Subtle study of small town people so concerned with their own welfare that the dirty deeds of the lead character might be overlooked. Fine performances and story development make this worth investigating. In French with English subtitles.
1979 116m/C Victor Lanoux, Valerie Mairesse; **D:** Etienne Perier. **VHS, Beta $29.98** SUE *II½*

Invincible Martial arts student must find and correct another student who has turned evil. For Bruce Lee fans, as if they haven't already memorized all the memorable lines—"hiyaah," "ugh," "oof," etc.
1980 (R) 93m/C Chen Sing, Ho Chung Dao. **VHS, Beta** GEM *II½*

Invincible Armor Wrong man is accused of murder when an ambitious minister of justice unleashes a sinister plot.
197? 92m/C VHS, Beta $39.95 TWE *II*

Invincible Barbarian A young man leads a tribe of amazing Amazon warriors in a sneak attack against the tribe that annihilated his native village. One of those movies that presumes "primitivism" can be recreated through bad acting.
1983 92m/C Diana Roy, David Jenkins. **VHS, Beta $59.95** PSM Woof!

The Invincible Gladiator A gladiator who saves the evil man ruling a land for a boy-king is given command of an army. He eventually leads the army in revolt when the evil man tries to take over the throne. Plodding with stock characters. **AKA:** Il Gladiatore Invincible.
1963 96m/C Richard Harrison, Isabel Corey, Livio Lorenzon; **D:** Frank Gregory. **VHS $16.95** SNC *II½*

Invincible Gladiators The sons of Hercules labor to aid a prince whose bride had been kidnapped by an evil queen. Laborious to watch.
1964 87m/C Richard Lloyd, Claudia Lange, Tony Freeman; **D:** Robert Mauri. **VHS, Beta** NO Woof!

Invincible Mr. Disraeli Presentation from "George Schaefer's Showcase Theatre" deals with the life and career of Benjamin Disraeli, novelist, philosopher, first Earl of Beaconsfield, statesman, and Prime Minister. Basically a tribute. Made for television.
1963 76m/C Trevor Howard, Greer Garson, Hurd Hatfield, Kate Reid; **D:** George Schaefer. **VHS, Beta** FHS *II½*

The Invincible Six An unlikely band of thieves running from the law winds up protecting a small village from marauding bandits. Plenty of action, as you would expect when thieves take on bandits, but with no scene-stealers or sympathetic characters the story lacks interest. Unremarkable choreography by ballet great Rudolf Nureyev. Filmed in Iran.
1968 96m/C Stuart Whitman, Elke Sommer, Curt Jurgens, Jim Mitchum, Ian Ogilvy; **D:** Jean Negulesco. **VHS, Beta** NO *II*

Invisible Adversaries A photographer uncovers an extra-terrestrial plot to cause excessive aggression in humans. She and her lover attempt to hold on to their crumbling humanity. Movies like this make you mad enough to tear something up. Enjoyed a meek cult following. In German with English subtitles.
1977 112m/C Susanne Widl, Peter Weibel; *D:* Valie Export. **VHS, Beta $59.95** *FCT 🦴🦴*

Invisible Agent Hall plays an agent using the secret formula to outwit the Nazis in this third sequel to ''The Invisible Man.'' Especially enjoyable for the kids. Based on characters suggested in H.G. Well's ''The Invisible Man.''
1942 83m/B Ilona Massey, Jon Hall, Peter Lorre, Cedric Hardwicke, J. Edward Bromberg, Albert Basserman, John Litel, Holmes Herbert; *D:* Edwin L. Marin; *W:* Curtis Siodmak. **VHS $14.98** *MCA, FCT 🦴🦴*

The Invisible Avenger Based on the vintage radio character ''The Shadow.'' A detective who can make himself invisible investigates the murder of a New Orleans jazz musician. The mysterious element successful on radio is lost on film, and only the Shadow knows why. *AKA:* Bourbon St. Shadows.
1958 60m/B Richard Derr, Marc Daniels, Helen Westcott, Jeanne Neher; *D:* John Sledge, Ben Parker. **VHS, Beta $16.95** *SNC, SMW, RXM 🦴🦴*

The Invisible Boy Science fiction story about a young boy and his robot (Robby the Robot from ''Forbidden Planet''). Kids will enjoy this adventure as told through the viewpoint of the child. Based on a story by Edmund Cooper.
1957 (G) 89m/C Richard Eyer, Diane Brewster, Phillip Abbott, Harold J. Stone; *D:* Hermann Hoffman; *W:* Cyril Hume; *M:* Les Baxter. **VHS $19.98** *MGM, FCT 🦴🦴 ½*

The Invisible Dead So many invisible man movies, so little time. A scientist creates an invisible man, imprisons and tortures him. A bit miffed with his host, he who can't be seen escapes, and vents his invisible spleen.
19?? 90m/C Howard Vernon, Britt Carva; *D:* Jess (Jesus) Franco. **VHS $59.95** *VCI 🦴*

The Invisible Dr. Mabuse Possibly the best of the Dr. Mabuse series sees the mad scientist using an invisibility agent in an attempt to take over the world. Preiss also played the title villian in Fritz Lang's ''The Thousand Eyes of Dr. Mabuse.'' *AKA:* The Invisible Horror; Die Unsichtbaren Krallen des Dr. Mabuse.
1962 89m/B Lex Barker, Karin Dor, Siegfried Lowitz, Wolfgang Preiss, Rudolf Fernau; *D:* Harald Reinl. **VHS, Beta $16.95** *SNC 🦴🦴🦴*

The Invisible Ghost A man carries out a series of grisly stranglings while under hypnosis by his insane wife. Typically bad low-budget exploiter about a fun-lovin' crazy couple bringing down property values in the neighborhood.
1941 70m/B Bela Lugosi, Polly Ann Young; *D:* Joseph H. Lewis. **VHS, Beta $19.95** *VYY, MRV, SNC 🦴 ½*

The Invisible Kid A shy teen manages to make himself invisible, a feat which ironically permits him to get people to notice him. Now he can visit places he's only dreamed of, including the girls' locker room. For those who have dreamed about girls' locker rooms.
1988 95m/C Karen Black, Jay Underwood, Chynna Phillips, Wally Ward, Brother Theodore; *D:* Avery Crounse. **VHS, Beta** *MED, VTR 🦴*

The Invisible Killer Someone is killing folks by sending poison through telephone lines. A detective and a reporter team up to find the scoundrel by setting up an answering machine that automatically plays back messages to the caller. Bad connection of events leads to a static resolution.
1940 61m/B Grace Bradley, Roland Drew, William Newell; *D:* Sam Newfield. **VHS, Beta $16.95** *SNC, MLB 🦴 ½*

The Invisible Man The vintage horror-fest based on H. G. Wells' novella about a scientist whose formula for invisibility slowly drives him insane. His mind definitely wandering, he plans plans to use his recipe to rule the world. Rains' first role; though his body doesn't appear until the final scene, his voice characterization is magnificent. The visual detail is excellent, setting standards that are imitated because they are difficult to surpass; with special effects by John P. Fulton.
1933 71m/B Claude Rains, Gloria Stuart, Dudley Digges, William Harrigan, Una O'Connor, E.E. Clive, Dwight Frye; *D:* James Whale; *W:* R.C. Sheriff. **VHS, Beta $14.95** *MCA, MLB 🦴🦴🦴🦴*

The Invisible Man Returns Price stars as the original invisible man's brother. Using the same invisibility formula, Price tries to clear himself after being charged with murder. He reappears at the worst times, and you gotta love that floating gun. Fun sequel to 1933's classic ''The Invisible Man.''
1940 81m/B Cedric Hardwicke, Vincent Price, John Sutton, Nan Grey; *D:* Joe May. **VHS $14.98** *MCA, MLB 🦴🦴🦴*

The Invisible Maniac A crazy voyeur perfects a serum for invisibility and promptly gets a job as a physics teacher in a high school. There he leers at girls taking showers and slaughters students when he is caught. For voyeurs. Get outta here, you maniac.
1990 (R) 87m/C Noel Peters, Shannon Wilsey, Melissa Moore, Robert Ross, Rod Sweitzer, Eric Champnella, Kalei Shellabarger, Gail Lyon, Debra Lamb; *D:* Rif Coogan; *W:* Rif Coogan. **VHS $89.95** *REP Woof!*

The Invisible Man's Revenge Left for dead on a safari five years before, Hall seeks revenge against Sondergaard and Matthews, aided by scientist Carradine who renders Hall invisible. Only problem is Hall doesn't stay that way. Fifth in Universal's ''Invisible Man'' film series.
1944 78m/B Jon Hall, John Carradine, Gale Sondergaard, Lester Matthews, Evelyn Ankers, Alan Curtis, Leon Errol, Doris Lloyd; *D:* Ford Beebe; *W:* Bertram Millhauser. **VHS $14.98** *MCA 🦴🦴 ½*

The Invisible Monster Special investigators Lane Carlson and Carol Richards battle a mad scientist ready to take over the world with his invisible army. 12 episodes of the original serial edited onto two cassettes. *AKA:* Slaves of the Invisible Monster.
1950 167m/B Richard Webb, Aline Towne, Lane Bradford, Stanley Price, John Crawford, George Meeker; *D:* Fred Brannon. **VHS $29.98** *REP 🦴🦴 ½*

The Invisible Ray For a change, this horror film features Lugosi as the hero, fighting Karloff, a scientist who locates a meteor that contains a powerful substance. Karloff is poisoned and becomes a murdering megalomaniac. Watching Karloff and Lugosi interact, and the great special effects—including a hot scene where a scientist bursts into flames—helps you ignore a generally hokey script.

1936 82m/B Boris Karloff, Bela Lugosi, Frances Drake, Frank Lawton, Beulah Bondi, Walter Kingsford; *D:* Lambert Hillyer. **VHS, Beta $14.98** *MCA, MLB 🦴🦴 ½*

The Invisible Strangler A death-row murderer can make himself invisible and rubs out witnesses who helped put him away; woman risks her life to expose him when the police fail to see the problem. Very violent collection of brutal scenes. Not released theatrically until 1984.
1976 (PG) 85m/C Robert Foxworth, Stefanie Powers, Elke Sommer, Sue Lyon, Leslie Parrish, Marianna Hill; *D:* John Florea. **VHS, Beta $59.95** *TWE 🦴 ½*

The Invisible Terror A maniac steals a mad scientist's invisibility formula and uses it on a number of innocent victims.
1963 ?m/C Herbert Stass, Ellen Scheirs. **VHS $16.95** *SNC 🦴🦴*

Invisible: The Chronicles of Benjamin Knight Scientist Benjamin Knight is rendered invisible during a terrible laboratory accident. His only hope of regaining his visible form is a desperate search by Knight and his fellow scientists for just the right chemical antidote.
1993 (R) 80m/C Brian Cousins, Jennifer Nash, Michael DellaFemina, Curt Lowens, David Kaufman, Alan Oppenheimer, Aharon Ipale; *D:* Jack Ersgard; *W:* Earl Kenton. **VHS, Beta** *PAR 🦴🦴 ½*

The Invisible Woman Above average comedy about zany professor Barrymore discovering the secret of invisibility and making luscious model Bruce transparent. Great cast makes this a very likeable movie. Based on a story by Curt Siodmak and Joe May, the same team that wrote ''The Invisible Man Returns.''
1940 73m/B John Barrymore, Virginia Bruce, John Howard, Charlie Ruggles, Oscar Homolka, Margaret Hamilton, Donald MacBride, Edward Brophy, Shemp Howard, Charles Lane, Thurston Hall; *D:* Edward Sutherland; *W:* Robert Lees, Fred Rinaldo, Gertrude Purcell. **VHS $14.98** *MCA, FCT 🦴🦴🦴*

Invitation au Voyage Follows the journey of a twin who refuses to accept the death of his sister, a rock singer. The obsession is played fairly well, but it's a no-twin situation, even though the guy can't admit it. Perversity is played to the point of overkill. From the novel ''Moi, Ma Soeur Images,'' by Jean Bany. In French with English subtitles.
1982 (R) 90m/C Laurent Malet, Nina Scott, Aurore Clement, Mario Adorf; *D:* Peter Del Monte. **VHS, Beta $59.95** *COL, ING 🦴🦴 ½*

Invitation to a Gunfighter Small town politics change when a paid assassin ambles into town and creates a lot of talk among the neighbors. Like a long joke in which the teller keeps forgetting the important details, the plot grows confusing though it's not complicated. Brynner is interesting as an educated, half-black/half-creole, hired gun.
1964 92m/C Yul Brynner, George Segal, Strother Martin, William Hickey, Janice Rule, Mike Kellin, Pat Hingle; *D:* Richard Wilson. **VHS, Beta $19.98** *MGM, HHE 🦴🦴*

Invitation to Hell Tormented maiden has a devil of a time discovering a secret power that can enable her to gracefully decline a satanic summoning. The cliched evil is tormenting.
1984 100m/C Becky Simpson, Joseph Sheahan, Colin Efford, Stephen Longhurst. **VHS, Beta** *NO Woof!*

I

Invitation to Hell "Faust" meets "All My Children" in celluloid suburbia. Never Emmied Lucci is the devil's dirty worker, persuading upwardly mobile suburbanites to join a really exclusive country club in exchange for a little downward mobility. Urich, a space scientist, and family are new in town, and soul searching Lucci's got her devil vixen sights set on space jock and brood. Bound to disappoint both fans of Craven's early independent work ("Last House on the Left") and his later high gloss ("Nightmare on Elm Street") formulas. Made for the small screen.
1984 100m/C Susan Lucci, Robert Urich, Joanna Cassidy, Kevin McCarthy, Patty McCormack, Joe Regalbuto, Soleil Moon Frye; **D:** Wes Craven. **VHS, Beta** *NO* 🐾½

Invitation to the Dance Three classic dance sequences, "Circus," "Ring Around the Rosy," and "Sinbad the Sailor." For dance lovers, featuring excellent performances by Kelly.
1956 93m/C Gene Kelly, Igor Youskevitch, Tamara Toumanova; **D:** Gene Kelly. **VHS, Beta** **$19.98** *MGM, CCB* 🐾½

Invitation to the Wedding When the best friend of a bridegroom falls in love with the bride, he stops at nothing to halt the wedding. Not exactly the Gielgud movie of the year, but there are some excellent scenes between him and Richardson.
1973 (PG) 89m/C John Gielgud, Ralph Richardson, Paul Nicholas, Elizabeth Shepherd; **D:** Joseph Brooks; **M:** Joseph Brooks. **VHS, Beta** **$69.95** *VES* 🐾🐾

The Ipcress File The first of the Harry Palmer spy mysteries that made Caine a star. Based upon the bestseller by Len Deighton, it features the flabby, nearsighted spy investigating the kidnapping of notable British scientists. Solid scenes, including a scary brainwashing session, and tongue-firmly-in-British-cheek humor. Lots of camera play to emphasize Caine's myopia. Two sequels: "Funeral in Berlin" and "Billion Dollar Brain."
1965 108m/C Michael Caine, Nigel Green, Guy Doleman, Sue Lloyd; **D:** Sidney J. Furie; **M:** John Barry. **VHS, Beta** **$14.98** *MCA* 🐾🐾🐾

Iphigenia Based on the classic Greek tragedy by Euripides, this story concerns the Greek leader Agamemnon, who plans to sacrifice his lovely daughter, Iphigenia, to please the gods. Mere mortals protest and start a save-the-babe movement, but Euripides' moral—you can't please 'em all—is devastatingly realized. Fine adaptation that becomes visually extravagant at times, with an equally fine musical score. In Greek with English subtitles.
1977 130m/C Irene Papas, Costa Kazakos, Tatiana Papamoskou; **D:** Michael Cacoyannis; **M:** Mikis Theodorakis. **VHS, Beta** **$59.95** *COL, FHS, ING* 🐾🐾🐾

Iran: Days of Crisis An insightful made-for-cable-TV miniseries recounts America's humiliation at the hands of Iranian radicals in 1979, told from the vantage of a U.S. embassy official married to a Tehran woman. Former Carter administration aides Hamilton Jordan and Gerald Rafshoon devised the docudrama, which spares neither them nor their president in showing how bungled and shortsighted policies led to 52 Americans held hostage for over a year.
1991 185m/C Arliss Howard, Alice Krige, George Grizzard, Jeff Fahey, Tony Goldwyn, Ronald Guttman, Valerie Kaprisky, Daniel Gelin; **D:** Kevin Connor. **VHS** **$89.98** *TTC* 🐾🐾½

Irezumi A Japanese woman has her body elaborately tattooed to please her lover. Things start off well enough. He's an inept lover, so she has directions tattooed, but

then he discovers a "Dear John" letter on her foot just as she gives him the boot. Actually proves an interesting study in obsession and eroticism, with the tattoos drawing the lovers deeper and deeper until they get under each other's skin. In Japanese with English subtitles. *AKA:* Spirit of Tattoo.
1983 88m/C **VHS, Beta** **$29.95** *ING* 🐾🐾🐾

Iris Drama follows the passionate and tragic life of New Zealand writer Iris Wilkinson, an international novelist, poet, and journalist. Wilkinson achieved a great deal of acclaim as a writer, but suffered many personal tragedies, and eventually took her own life at age 33. Well intentioned but clunky treatment of powerful subject matter.
1989 90m/C Helen Morse. **VHS, Beta** **$160.00** *WOM* 🐾🐾

Irish Cinderella A silent version of the Cinderella legend set in Ireland, with thematic stress on Irish politics and patriotism.
1922 72m/B Pattie MacNamara. **VHS, Beta, 8mm** **$24.95** *YYY* 🐾🐾

Irish Luck A bellhop turns detective to figure out the mysterious happenings in his hotel. Becomes terminally cute by playing on a luck o' the Irish theme.
1939 58m/B Frankie Darro, Dick Purcell, Sheila Darcy; **D:** Grant Withers, Scott R. Dunlap. **VHS** **$24.95** *NOS, DVT, HEG* 🐾🐾

The Irishman Set in 1920s Australia, the tale of a proud North Queensland family and their struggles to stay together. The Irish immigrant father is a teamster whose horse-drawn wagons are threatened by progress. His fight to preserve old ways is impressive, but gives way to sentimentality.
1978 108m/C Lou Brown, Michael Craig, Simon Burke, Robyn Nevin, Bryan Brown; **D:** Donald Crombie. **VHS, Beta** **$69.95** *VES* 🐾🐾½

Irma La Douce A gendarme pulls a one-man raid on a back-street Parisian joint and falls in love with one of the hookers he arrests. Lemmon is great as a well-meaning, incompetent boob, and MacLaine gives her all as the hapless hooker. A plodding pace, however, robs it of the original's zip, though it was a box office smash. Broadway musical is lost without the music.
1963 144m/C Jack Lemmon, Shirley MacLaine, Herschel Bernardi; **D:** Billy Wilder; **W:** Billy Wilder, I.A.L. Diamond; **M:** Andre Previn. Academy Awards '63: Best Original Score; Nominations: Best Actress (MacLaine), Best Color Cinematography; Golden Globe Awards '64: Best Actress—Musical/Comedy (MacLaine). **VHS, Beta** **$19.98** *MGM, IME, FOX* 🐾🐾½

Iron & Silk A young American searches for himself while he teaches English and learns martial arts in mainland China. Based on the true story of Salzman's travels. His studies of martial arts and Chinese culture provide a model for his students in their studies of American language and culture. Beautiful photography. Fine performances.
1991 (PG) 94m/C Mark Salzman, Pan Qingfu, Jeanette Lin Tsui, Vivian Wu; **D:** Shirley Sun; **W:** Shirley Sun, Mark Salzman; **M:** Michael Gibbs. **VHS** **$19.98** *LIV* 🐾🐾½

Iron Angel During the Korean War a squadron sets out to silence North Korean guns. They do. Judging by their eternal bickering they must have put the enemy to sleep.
1964 84m/B Jim Davis, Margo Woode, Donald (Don "Red") Barry, L.Q. Jones; **D:** Ken Kennedy; **W:** Ken Kennedy. **VHS** **$15.95** *NOS, LOO* 🐾½

Iron Cowboy Actor finds romance with film editor while audience stifles yawns. Filmed on the set of "Blue," this pre-"Deliverance" Reynolds comedy never made it to the theaters. (Smithee is actually director Jud Taylor.)
1968 86m/C Burt Reynolds, Barbara Loden, Terence Stamp, Noam Pitlik, Ricardo Montalban, Patricia Casey, Jane Hampton, Joseph Perry; **D:** Alan Smithee. **VHS** **$39.98** *ACE* 🐾🐾

The Iron Crown A 13th-century legend inspired this sometime violent spectacle involving the title totem, a symbol of justice ignored by a powerful king at his peril. There's wonderful pagentry and a notable Tarzan imitator, but the pace is terribly slow. Italian dialogue with English subtitles.
1941 100m/C **D:** Alexandro Blasetti. **VHS** **$59.95** *FST* 🐾🐾

Iron Dragon Strikes Back Man seeks out the men who murdered his martial arts instructor.
1984 90m/C Bruce Li. **VHS, Beta** **$39.95** *TWE* 🐾

The Iron Duke Fair to middlin' historical account of the life of the Duke of Wellington, victor over Napoleon at Waterloo.
1934 88m/B George Arliss, Gladys Cooper, A.E. Matthews, Emlyn Williams, Felix Aylmer; **D:** Victor Saville. **VHS, Beta** **$19.95** *NOS, WFV, BAR* 🐾🐾½

Iron Eagle A teenager teams with a renegade fighter pilot to rescue the youth's father from captivity in the Middle East. Predictable but often exciting. Followed by two sequels.
1986 (PG-13) 117m/C Louis Gossett Jr., Jason Gedrick, Tim Thomerson, David Suchet, Larry B. Scott, Caroline Lagerfelt, Jerry Levine, Michael Bowen, Robbie Rist, Bobby Jacoby, Melora Hardin; **D:** Sidney J. Furie; **W:** Kevin Elders, Sidney J. Furie; **M:** Basil Poledouris. **VHS, Beta** **$14.98** *FOX* 🐾🐾½

Iron Eagle 2 Lower-budget extended adventures of a maverick fighter pilot after he is reinstated in the Air Force. This time he links with an equally rebellious commie fighter and blasts away at nuke-happy Ivan. Yahoo fun for all overt Yankees! Followed by "Aces: Iron Eagle 3." Available in Spanish.
1988 (PG) 102m/C Louis Gossett Jr., Mark Humphrey, Stuart Margolin, Alan Scarfe, Maury Chaykin, Sharon H. Brandon; **D:** Sidney J. Furie; **W:** Sidney J. Furie, Kevin Elders. **VHS, Beta** **$14.95** *LIV* 🐾🐾

Iron Horsemen A motorcycle gang leader has a prophetic vision while tripping on LSD, and returns to his former town to challenge its religious establishment. Also available on video under its original title "J.C." *AKA:* J.C.
1971 (R) 97m/C William F. McGaha, Hannibal Penny, Joanna Moore, Burr de Benning, Slim Pickens, Pati Delaney; **D:** William F. McGaha. **VHS, Beta** **$9.95** *SIM, NLC* 🐾

The Iron Major Frank Cavanaugh, a famous football coach, becomes a hero in WWI. Standard flag-waving biography to increase morale back home, but fairly well-made.
1943 85m/B Pat O'Brien, Ruth Warrick, Robert Ryan, Leon Ames, Russell Wade, Bruce Edwards; **D:** Ray Enright. **VHS, Beta** **$19.98** *TTC* 🐾🐾½

The Iron Mask Early swashbuckling extravaganza with a master swordsman defending the French king from a scheme involving substitution by a lookalike. Still fairly exciting, thanks largely to director Dwan's flair. Based on Alexandre Dumas' "Three Musketeers" and "The Man in the Iron Mask" with talking sequences.

1929 87m/B Douglas Fairbanks Sr., Nigel de Brulier, Marguerite de la Motte; **D:** Allan Dwan. **VHS, Beta** $9.98 NOS, CCB, DVT 𝄢𝄢½

Iron Maze
A fascinating notion forms the center of this dramatic scrapheap; the classic Japanese "Rashomon" plot shifted to a rusting Pennsylvania steel town. When a Tokyo businessman is found bludgeoned, witnesses and suspects (including his American-born wife) tell contradictory stories. It's too convoluted and contrived to work, with a hollow happy ending tacked on. Oliver Stone helped produce.
1991 (R) 102m/C Jeff Fahey, Bridget Fonda, Hiroaki Murakami, J.T. Walsh, Gabriel Damon, John Randolph, Peter Allas; **D:** Hiroaki Yoshida; **W:** Tim Metcalfe. **VHS** $89.95 ACA 𝄢½

Iron Thunder
Liberty is in peril and only much kicking and pec flexing will make the world a kinder gentler place. A thundering bore.
1989 85m/C Iron "Amp" Elmore, George M. Young, Julius Dorsey. **VHS** $79.95 XVC, HHE 𝄢½

The Iron Triangle
A U.S. officer taken prisoner by the Viet Cong forms a bond with one of his captors. Film lends the viewer an opportunity to see things from the other sides perspective.
1989 94m/C Beau Bridges, Haing S. Ngor, Liem Whatley; **D:** Eric Weston. **VHS, Beta** $14.98 LIV 𝄢𝄢

Iron Warrior
A barbarian hacks his way through a fantastical world to get to a beautiful princess.
1987 (R) 82m/C Miles O'Keeffe, Savina Gersak, Tim Lane; **D:** Al Bradley. **VHS, Beta** $19.95 MED, VTR 𝄢

Iron Will
Okay Disney family movie based on a true story. Will Stoneman is a 17-year-old farm kid from South Dakota. It's 1917 and because of his father's death there's no money to send Will to college. So he decides to enter the 500 mile winner-take-all dog sled race, with its $10,000 prize. Lots of obstacles, several villains, but Will perseveres.
1993 (PG) 109m/C MacKenzie Astin, Kevin Spacey, David Ogden Stiers, August Schellenberg, George Gerdes, John Terry; **D:** Charles Haid; **W:** John Michael Hayes, Jeffrey Arch, Djordje Milicevic; **M:** Joel McNeely. **VHS** DIS 𝄢𝄢½

Ironclads
Memorable dramatization of the five-hour naval battle between the Confederate's Merrimac and the Union's Monitor during the Civil War. The special effects are the only thing worth watching in this overlong tale that includes standard subplots of loyalty, lost loves, and death from war.
1990 94m/C Virginia Madsen, Alex Hyde-White, Reed Edward Diamond, E.G. Marshall, Fritz Weaver, Philip Casnoff; **D:** Delbert Mann. **VHS** $79.98 TTC 𝄢𝄢½

Ironheart
Slimy Milverstead and his henchman meet lovely young women at dance clubs, drug them, and sell them into slavery. But the trouble really starts when they kill a cop and his former partner, John Keem (Lee), lashes out with his blazing martial arts skills to still the perpetrators.
1992 ?m/C Britton Lee, Bolo Yeung, Richard Norton, Karman Kruschke; **D:** Robert Clouse; **W:** Lawrence Riggins. **VHS** $89.95 IMP 𝄢½

Ironmaster
When a primitive tribesman is exiled from his tribe, he discovers a mysteriously power-filled iron staff on a mountainside.
1983 98m/C George Eastman, Pamela Field. **VHS, Beta** $59.95 PSM 𝄢

Ironweed
Grim and gritty drama about bums living the hard life in Depression-era Albany. Nicholson excels as a former ballplayer turned drunk bothered by visions of the past, and Streep is his equal in the lesser role of a tubercular boozer. Waits also shines. Another grim view from "Pixote" director Babenco. Kennedy scripted based on his Pulitzer Prize-winning tragedy.
1987 (R) 135m/C Jack Nicholson, Meryl Streep, Tom Waits, Carroll Baker, Michael O'Keefe, Fred Gwynne, Diane Venora, Margaret Whitton, Jake Dengel, Nathan Lane, James Gammon, Joe Grifasi, Bethel Leslie, Ted Levine, Frank Whaley; **D:** Hector Babenco; **W:** William Kennedy; **M:** John Morris. **VHS, Beta** $89.98 LIV, VES 𝄢𝄢𝄢

Irreconcilable Differences
When her Beverly Hills parents spend more time working and fretting than giving hugs and love, a ten-year-old girl sues them for divorce on the grounds of "irreconcilable differences." The media has a field day when they hear that she would rather go live with the maid. Well cast, with well-developed characterizations. The script, by the creators of "Private Benjamin," is humanely comic rather than uproariously funny.
1984 (PG) 112m/C Ryan O'Neal, Shelley Long, Drew Barrymore, Sam Wanamaker, Allen (Gooritz) Garfield, Sharon Stone, Luana Anders; **D:** Charles Shyer; **W:** Charles Shyer, Nancy Meyers. **VHS, Beta** $29.98 LIV, VES 𝄢𝄢½

Irving Berlin's America
A documentary depicting Berlin's legacy of patriotic pop tunes, shown in a variety of film and performance clips, plus interviews with the stars who sang them.
1986 83m/C Ginger Rogers, Mary Martin, Howard Keel, Kate Smith, Fred Astaire. **Beta** CMR 𝄢𝄢½

Is Paris Burning?
A spectacularly star-studded but far too sprawling account of the liberation of Paris from Nazi occupation. The script, in which seven writers had a hand, is based on Larrry Collins and Dominique Lapierre's best seller. **AKA:** Paris Brule-T-Il?.
1968 173m/C Jean-Paul Belmondo, Charles Boyer, Leslie Caron, Jean-Pierre Cassel, George Chakiris, Claude Dauphin, Alain Delon, Kirk Douglas, Glenn Ford, Gert Frobe, Daniel Gelin, E.G. Marshall, Yves Montand, Anthony Perkins, Claude Rich, Simone Signoret, Robert Stack, Jean-Louis Trintignant, Pierre Vaneck, Orson Welles, Bruno Cremer, Suzy Delair, Michael Lonsdale; **D:** Rene Clement; **W:** Gore Vidal, Francis Ford Coppola; **M:** Maurice Jarre. **VHS** $29.95 PAR, FCT 𝄢𝄢𝄢

Is There Sex After Death?
Often funny satire on the sexual revolution is constructed as a behind-the-scenes view of the porn film world. Odd cast includes Henry and Warhol superstar Woodlawn. Originally rated "X."
1971 (R) 97m/C Buck Henry, Alan Abel, Marshall Efron, Holly Woodlawn, Earl Doud; **D:** Alan Abel, Jeanne Abel. **VHS, Beta** NO 𝄢𝄢𝄢

Is This Goodbye, Charlie Brown?
Charlie Brown and the gang struggle to understand their loss when a friend moves away.
1983 25m/C **VHS** $14.95 MED, VTR, WTA 𝄢𝄢𝄢

Isadora
A loose, imaginative biography of Isadora Duncan, the cause celebre dancer in the 1920s who became famous for her scandalous performances, outrageous behavior, public love affairs, and bizarre, early death. Redgrave is exceptional in the lead, and Fox provides fine support. Restored from its original 131-minute print length by the director. **AKA:** The Loves of Isadora.

1968 153m/C Vanessa Redgrave, Jason Robards Jr., James Fox, Ivan Tchenko, John Fraser, Bessie Love; **D:** Karel Reisz; **M:** Maurice Jarre. Academy Awards '68 Nominations: Best Actress (Redgrave); Cannes Film Festival '69: Best Film; Cannes Film Festival '69: Best Actress (Redgrave); National Board of Review Awards '69: 10 Best Films of the Year; National Society of Film Critics Awards '69: Best Actress (Redgrave). **VHS, Beta** $19.98 MCA, HEG 𝄢𝄢𝄢

Ishtar
Two astoundingly untalented performers have a gig in a fictional Middle Eastern country and become involved in foreign intrigue. A big-budget box-office bomb produced by Beatty offering few laughs, though it's not as bad as its reputation. Considering the talent involved, though, it's a disappointment, with Beatty and Hoffman laboring to create Hope and Crosby chemistry. Anyone for a slow night?
1987 (PG-13) 107m/C Dustin Hoffman, Warren Beatty, Isabelle Adjani, Charles Grodin; **D:** Elaine May; **W:** Elaine May; **M:** Dave Grusin. **VHS, Beta** $14.95 COL 𝄢𝄢

The Island
Poetic examination of a peasant family's daily struggle for existence on a small island. No dialogue in this slow but absorbing work by one of Japan's master directors. **AKA:** Hadaka No Shima; Naked Island.
1961 96m/B Nobuko Otowa, Taiji Tonoyama, Shinji Tanaka, Masanori Horimoto; **D:** Kaneto Shindo. **VHS, Beta, 8mm** $24.95 IHF, VYY, HHT 𝄢𝄢𝄢½

Island
Tautly paced, the story creates an increasingly complex situation, until a WWI army officer is revealed to be the victim of a shocking and ingenious trap.
1977 30m/C John Hurt; **D:** Robert Fuest. **VHS, Beta** LCA 𝄢𝄢𝄢½

The Island
New York reporter embarks on a Bermuda triangle investigation, only to meet with the murderous but sterile descendants of seventeenth century pirates on a deserted island. Caine is designated as stud service for the last remaining fertile woman. Almost surreal in its badness. Adapted by Benchley from his novel.
1980 (R) 113m/C Michael Caine, David Warner, Angela Punch McGregor, Frank Middlemass, Don Henderson; **D:** Michael Ritchie; **W:** Peter Benchley; **M:** Ennio Morricone. **VHS, Beta** $19.95 MCA Woof!

The Island at the Top of the World
A rich Englishman, in search of his missing son, travels to the Arctic Circle in 1908. The rescue party includes an American archeologist, a French astronaut, and an Eskimo guide. Astonishingly, they discover an unknown, "lost" Viking kingdom. This Jules Verne-style adventure doesn't quite measure up, but kids will like it.
1974 (G) 93m/C David Hartman, Donald Sinden, Jacques Marin, Mako, David Gwillim; **D:** Robert Stevenson; **M:** Maurice Jarre. **VHS, Beta** $69.95 DIS 𝄢𝄢½

Island Claw
A group of marine biologists experimenting on a tropical island discover the "Island Claw," who evolved as the result of toxic waste seeping into the ocean. A festering, oozing woofer. **AKA:** Night of the Claw.
1980 91m/C Barry Nelson, Robert Lansing; **D:** Hernan Cardenas. **VHS, Beta** $69.98 LIV, VES Woof!

Island in the Sun
Racial tension pulls apart the lives of the residents of a Caribbean island. Good cast, but a very poor adaptation of Alec Waugh's novel. Marvelous location shots.

1957 119m/C James Mason, Joan Fontaine, Dorothy Dandridge, John Williams, Harry Belafonte; **D:** Robert Rossen; **M:** Malcolm Arnold. **VHS** *TCF* ⅓

Island Monster Also called "Monster of the Island," this film deals with ruthless, kidnapping drug-smugglers led by "monster" Karloff, and the efforts to bring them to justice.
1953 87m/B Boris Karloff, Renata Vicario, Franco Marzi; **D:** Robert Montero. **VHS, Beta** $29.95 *SNC, HHT, LSV* ⅓ ½

Island of Adventure Four children explore an island and find a gang of criminals inhabiting it.
1981 85m/C **VHS, Beta** $39.98 *SUE* ⅓ ½

Island of Blood Buckets of blood abound on a remote island when a film crew's beset by berserk butcher.
1986 84m/C Jim Williams, Dean Richards. **VHS** $59.98 *AIP, MOV* ⅓ ½

Island of Desire An Army nurse, a doctor, and a young Navy Adonis are trapped on a deserted island. Not surprisingly, a love triangle develops. **AKA:** Saturday Island.
1952 93m/C Tab Hunter, Linda Darnell, Donald Gray; **D:** Stuart Heisler. **VHS, Beta** $59.95 *MLB* ⅓

Island of Dr. Moreau This remake of the "Island of the Lost Souls" (1933) is a bit disappointing but worth watching for Lancaster's solid performance as the scientist who has isolated himself on a Pacific island in order to continue his chromosome research—he can transform animals into near-humans and humans into animals. Neat-looking critters. Adaptation of the H.G. Wells novel of the same title.
1977 (PG) 99m/C Burt Lancaster, Michael York, Nigel Davenport, Barbara Carrera, Richard Basehart; **D:** Don Taylor. **VHS, Beta** $19.98 *WAR, OM* ⅓ ½

Island of Lost Girls Young women are taken to an unknown location in the Far East to be sold as part of a white slave ring.
1973 (R) 85m/C Brad Harris, Tony Kendall, Monica Pardo. **VHS, Beta** $16.95 *SNC* Woof!

Island of Lost Souls Horrifying adaptation of H.G. Wells' "The Island of Dr. Moreau" was initially banned in parts of the U.S. because of its disturbing contents. Laughton is a mad scientist on a remote island obsessed with making men out of jungle animals. When a shipwreck survivor gets stranded on the island, little does he know that Laughton wants to mate him with Lota, the Panther Woman, to produce the first human-animal child. As unsettling today as it was in the '30s. Burke beat out more than 60,000 young women in a nationwide search to play the Panther Woman, winning the role because of her "feline" look. Remade as "The Island of Dr. Moreau."
1932 71m/B Charles Laughton, Bela Lugosi, Richard Arlen, Leila Hyams, Kathleen Burke, Stanley Fields, Robert F. (Bob) Kortman; *Cameos:* Alan Ladd, Randolph Scott, Buster Crabbe; **D:** Erle C. Kenton; **W:** Philip Wylie, Waldemar Young. **VHS** $14.98 *MCA, FCT, BTV* ⅓⅓⅓

The Island of Nevawuz A beautiful island is in trouble when J.B. Trumphorn decides to make lots of money by building factories and refineries on it. Will the Island of Nevawuz end up a polluted mess?
1980 50m/C **VHS, Beta** $39.98 *SUE* ⅓⅓⅓ ½

Island of Terror First-rate science fiction chiller about an island overrun by shell-like creatures that suck the bones out of their living prey. Good performances and interest-

ing twists make for prickles up the spine. **AKA:** Night of the Silicates; The Creepers.
1966 90m/C Peter Cushing, Edward Judd, Carole Gray, Sam Kydd, Niall MacGinnis; **D:** Terence Fisher. **VHS** $14.98 *MCA, SNC, MLB* ⅓⅓⅓

Island of the Blue Dolphins Based on a popular children's book by Scott O'Dell, this is a true story of a young Native American girl who, with her brother, are stranded on a deserted island when their people accidentally leave them. When the boy is killed, the girl learns to survive by her skills and by befriending the leader of a pack of wild dogs. Good family fare.
1964 99m/C Celia Kaye, Larry Domasin, Ann Daniel, George Kennedy; **D:** James B. Clark. **VHS, Beta** $59.95 *MCA* ⅓⅓ ½

Island of the Burning Doomed A brutal heat wave accompanies invading aliens in this British-made outing. Lee and Cushing carry the picture. **AKA:** Island of the Burning Damned; Night of the Big Heat.
1967 94m/C Christopher Lee, Peter Cushing, Patrick Allen, Sarah Lawson, Jane Merrow; **D:** Terence Fisher. **VHS** *NO* ⅓⅓ ½

Island of the Lost An anthropologist's family must fight for survival when they become shipwrecked on a mysterious island.
1968 92m/C Richard Greene, Luke Halpin; **D:** John Florea. **VHS** $19.98 *REP, GHV* ⅓ ½

Island Trader Young lad battles pirates and a crooked tug captain who seek hidden gold that he knows about.
1971 95m/C John Ewart, Ruth Cracknell, Eric Oldfield; **D:** Harold Rubie. **VHS, Beta** *NO* ⅓

The Islander Sixteen-year-old Inga comes of age among the commercial fishermen of Lake Michigan.
1988 99m/C Kit Wholihan, Jeff Weborg, Celia Klehr, Jacob Mills, Julie Johnson, Mary Ann McHugh, Michael Rock, Sheri Parish; **D:** Phyllis Berg-Pigorsch. **VHS, Beta** *NO* ⅓

Islands A made-for-television drama about a middle-aged ex-hippie and a young rebellious punk who clash during a summer together on a secluded island.
1987 55m/C Louise Fletcher. **VHS, Beta** $19.95 *NWV* ⅓⅓

Islands in the Stream Based on Ernest Hemingway's novel, this film is actually two movies in one. An American painter/sculptor, Thomas Hudson, lives a reclusive life on the island of Bimini shortly before the outbreak of WWII. The first part is a sensitive story of a broken family and the coming of the artist's three sons to live with their father after a four year separation. The second part is a second rate action-adventure.
1977 (PG) 105m/C George C. Scott, David Hemmings, Claire Bloom, Susan Tyrrell, Gilbert Roland; **D:** Franklin J. Schaffner; **M:** Jerry Goldsmith. **VHS, Beta** $29.95 *AIM, PAR* ⅓⅓ ½

Isle of Forgotten Sins Deep sea divers and an evil ship's captain vie for treasure. Good cast and direction but unremarkable material. Also released under the title "Monsoon."
1943 82m/B John Carradine, Gale Sondergaard, Sidney Toler, Frank Fenton, Veda Ann Borg; **D:** Edgar G. Ulmer. **VHS, Beta, 8mm** $16.95 *SNC, VYY* ⅓⅓

Isle of Secret Passion A romance novel comes to video life as two lovers thrash out their problems on a Greek island.
1985 90m/C Patch MacKenzie, Michael MacRae, Zohra Lampert. **VHS, Beta** $14.95 *PSM* ⅓

Isle of the Dead A Greek general is quarantined with seemingly all manner of social vermin on a plague-infested island in the early 1900s. The fear is that vampires

walk among them. Characteristically spooky Val Lewton production with some original twists.
1945 72m/B Boris Karloff, Ellen Drew, Marc Cramer; **D:** Mark Robson. **VHS, Beta** $19.95 *TTC, MED, FCT* ⅓⅓ ½

Isn't Life Wonderful Outstanding Griffith film depicts the unbearable conditions in post-WWI Germany. Filmed on location.
1924 90m/B Carol Dempster, Neil Hamilton, Lupino Lane, Hans von Schlettow; **D:** D.W. Griffith; **W:** D.W. Griffith. **VHS, Beta** $19.95 *GPV, GVV* ⅓⅓⅓⅓

Istanbul An American charms a Belgian student into taking part in a kidnap scheme.
1985 (R) 90m/C Brad Dourif, Dominique Deruddere, Ingrid De Vos, Francois Beukelaers; **D:** Marc Didden. **VHS, Beta** *NO* ⅓

Istanbul Believing he has stumbled upon the best story of his career, a journalist soon discovers that he has been pulled into a world of guns and violence. **AKA:** Istanbul, Keep Your Eyes Open.
1990 (PG-13) 88m/C Robert Morley, Timothy Bottoms, Twiggy; **D:** Mats Arehn. **VHS, Beta** *IME* ⅓

It A department store clerk with plenty of sex appeal desires her rich boss. Established Bow as a prominent screen siren. Otherwise, it's not particularly interesting. Silent. Adapted by Elinor Glyn from her own story; Glyn also makes an appearance.
1927 71m/B Clara Bow, Gary Cooper, Antonio Moreno; **D:** Clarence Badger. **VHS, Beta** $19.95 *GPV, VYG, CRC* ⅓⅓ ½

It Came from Beneath the Sea A giant octopus arises from the depths of the sea to scour San Francisco for human food. Ray Harryhausen effects are special.
1955 80m/B Kenneth Tobey, Faith Domergue, Ian Keith, Donald Curtis; **D:** Robert Gordon. **VHS, Beta** $9.95 *GKK, MLB* ⅓⅓⅓

It Came from Hollywood A compilation of scenes from "B" horror and science fiction films of the 1950s, highlighting the funny side of these classic schlock movies. Some sequences in black and white.
1982 (PG) 87m/C **D:** Malcolm Leo. **VHS, Beta** $59.95 *PAR* ⅓⅓⅓

It Came From Outer Space Aliens take on the form of local humans to repair their spacecraft in a small Arizona town. Good performances and outstanding direction add up to a fine science fiction film. Based on the story "The Meteor" by Ray Bradbury, who also wrote the script. Originally filmed in 3-D.
1953 81m/B Richard Carlson, Barbara Rush, Charles Drake, Russell Johnson; **D:** Jack Arnold; **W:** Ray Bradbury; **M:** Henry Mancini. **VHS** $14.98 *MCA, MLB, GKK* ⅓⅓⅓

It Came Upon a Midnight Clear A heavenly miracle enables a retired (and dead) New York policeman to keep a Christmas promise to his grandson. Made for television.
1984 96m/C Mickey Rooney, Scott Grimes, George Gaynes, Annie Potts, Lloyd Nolan, Barrie Youngfellow; **D:** Peter Hunt. **VHS, Beta** $9.95 *GKK* ⅓ ½

It Conquered the World Vegetable critters from Venus follow a probe satellite back to Earth and drop in on scientist Van Cleef, who'd been their intergalactic pen pal (seems he thought a Venusian invasion would improve the neighborhood). Their travelling companions, little bat creatures, turn earth dwellers into murderous zombies, and it starts to look like the Venusians are trying to make earth their planetary exurbia. Early-vintage zero-budget Corman, for schlock

connoisseurs. Remade for television as "Zontar, the Thing from Venus."
1956 68m/B Peter Graves, Beverly Garland, Lee Van Cleef, Sally Fraser, Charles B. Griffith, Russ Bender, Jonathan Haze, Dick Miller, Karen Kadler, Paul Blaisdell; **D:** Roger Corman. **VHS** $9.95 *COL, FCT, MLB* ⅈⅈ½

It Could Happen to You Stepbrothers raised by a gentle immigrant take different paths in life. When one ends up killing someone during a botched robbery, the other—a lawyer—defends him. Standard '30s morality play.
1937 64m/B Alan Baxter, Andrea Leeds, Owen Davis Jr., Astrid Allwyn, Walter Kingsford, Al Shear; **D:** Phil Rosen. **VHS** $19.95 *NOS, BAR* ⅈ½

It Could Happen to You A drunken advertising executive is charged with murder after a dead nightclub singer is found in his car. His wife sets out to clear him.
1939 64m/C Stuart Erwin, Gloria Stuart, Raymond Walburn, Douglas Fowley, June Gale, Paul Hurst, Richard Lane; **D:** Alfred Werker. **VHS, Beta** *NO* ⅈⅈ

It Could Happen to You NYC cop Charlie Lang (Cage) doesn't have any change to leave coffee shop waitress Yvonne (Fonda) a tip, so he promises to split his lottery ticket with her. When he nets four million dollars, he makes good on the promise, much to the chagrin of his upwardly mobile wife (Perez). Capra-corn for the X-crowd is pleasant dinnertime diversion as Cage and Perez shine as henpecked nice guy and the wife committed to making him miserable. Don't look for the diner on your next trip to NYC; it was specially built in TriBeCa and dismantled after the shoot. *AKA:* Cop Tips Waitress $2 Million.
1994 (PG) ?m/C Bridget Fonda, Nicolas Cage, Rosie Perez, Red Buttons, Isaac Hayes, Seymour Cassel, Stanley Tucci, J.E. Freeman, Richard Jenkins, Ann Dowd, Wendell Pierce; **D:** Andrew Bergman; **W:** Jane Anderson, Andrew Bergman. **VHS** *NYR* ⅈⅈ½

It Couldn't Happen Here Fans of the techno-pop duo The Pet Shop Boys can test their loyalty by enduring this feature music-video that actually played a few theaters. The dour pair journey across a surreal England, encountering a sinister blind priest, a philisophical ventriloquist's dummy, and more. Songs, sometimes presented only as muted incidental music, include the title track, "West End Girls," "It's a Sin" and "Always on My Mind."
1988 (PG-13) 87m/C Neil Tennant, Chris Lowe, Joss Ackland, Neil Dickson, Carmen Du Sautoy, Gareth Hunt; **D:** Jack Bond. **VHS** $59.95 *COL, MVD* ⅈ

It Happened at Nightmare Inn Average thriller in which Geeson travels to Spanish inn and confronts two mad sisters who run the hotel. Also known as "Nightmare Hotel."
1970 95m/C Judy Geeson, Aurora Bautista, Esperanza Roy, Victor Alcocer, Lone Fleming; **D:** Eugenio Martin. **VHS** $16.95 *SNC* ⅈ

It Happened at the World's Fair Fun and light romance comedy has Elvis and a companion (O'Brien) being escorted through the Seattle World's Fair by a fetching Chinese girl. ♫I'm Falling In Love Tonight; They Remind Me Too Much Of You; Take Me To The Fair; Relax; How Would You Like To Be; Beyond the Bend; One Broken Heart For Sale; Cotton Candy Land; A World Of Our Own.
1963 105m/C Elvis Presley, Joan O'Brien, Gary Lockwood, Kurt Russell, Edith Atwater, Yvonne Craig; **D:** Norman Taurog. **VHS, Beta** $14.95 *MGM* ⅈⅈ½

It Happened in Brooklyn Former sailor with blue eyes bunks with janitor with big nose in Brooklyn. Sailor and cronies encounter many musical opportunities. Lots of songs and falling in love, little entertainment.
1947 104m/B Frank Sinatra, Kathryn Grayson, Jimmy Durante, Peter Lawford, Gloria Grahame; **D:** Richard Whorf. **VHS** $19.98 *MGM, FCT* ⅈⅈ

It Happened in New Orleans A young boy is cared for by a former slave in post-Civil War New Orleans until his Yankee grandmother claims him and takes him to New York. The boy is resented by his family but manages to overcome their hostilities. *AKA:* Rainbow on the River.
1936 86m/B Bobby Breen, May Robson, Alan Mowbray, Benita Hume. **VHS, Beta** $24.95 *VYY* ⅈ½

It Happened in the Park A rare film exercise for De Sica, wherein the patrons of the Villa Borghese parks are surveyed for a 24-hour period. In French with English dialogue.
1956 72m/B **D:** Vittorio De Sica. **VHS, Beta** $24.95 *NOS, FCT, ING* ⅈ½

It Happened One Night Classic Capra comedy about an antagonistic couple determined to teach each other about life. Colbert is an unhappy heiress who runs away from her affluent home in search of contentment. On a bus she meets newspaper reporter Gable, who teaches her how "real" people live. She returns the favor in this first of the 1930s screwball comedies. The plot is a framework for an amusing examination of war between the sexes. Colbert and Gable are superb as affectionate foes. Remade as the musicals "Eve Knew Her Apples" and "You Can't Run Away From It."
1934 105m/B Clark Gable, Claudette Colbert, Roscoe Karns, Walter Connolly, Alan Hale, Ward Bond; **D:** Frank Capra; **W:** Robert Riskin. **VHS, Beta** $19.95 *COL, BTV, HMV* ⅈⅈⅈⅈ

It Happens Every Spring A chemistry professor, working on a bug repellant for trees, accidentally invents a potion that repels any kind of wood that it comes in contact with. Since he needs some big bucks to pop the question to his sweetie, the prof, who also loves baseball, gets a tryout as a pitcher with a major league team and uses the solution on the baseballs he pitches. Naturally, it's strikeout time and the prof becomes a pitching phenom. Now, if he can only keep his little secret. Wacky baseball footage is a highlight.
1949 87m/B Ray Milland, Jean Peters, Paul Douglas, Ed Begley Sr., Ted de Corsia, Ray Collins, Jessie Royce Landis, Alan Hale Jr., Gene Evans; **D:** Lloyd Bacon; **W:** Valentine Davies; **M:** Leigh Harline. **VHS** $19.99 *FXV* ⅈⅈⅈ½

It Means That to Me Espionage thriller in which Constantine plays a reporter who's hired by the government to transport top secret micro-film.
1963 ?m/C Eddie Constantine, Jean-Louis Richard. **VHS** $16.95 *SNC* ⅈⅈ

It Rained All Night the Day I Left Two drifters find their fortunes change when they are hired by a wealthy widow. Interesting romance adventure.
1978 (R) 100m/C Louis Gossett Jr., Sally Kellerman, Tony Curtis; **D:** Nicolas Gessner. **VHS, Beta** *NO* ⅈ½

It Runs In the Family Humorist Shepherd and director Clark re-team for another period family comedy in the tradition of their first collaboration, "A Christmas

Story," now a video classic. This time dad (Grodin) takes Ralphie (Kieran Culkin) out fishing, and mom (Steenburgen) goes loopy over gravy boats. Charming family fun. *AKA:* My Summer Story.
1994 (PG) ?m/C Charles Grodin, Mary Steenburgen, Kieran Culkin, Chris Culkin; **D:** Bob (Benjamin) Clark; **W:** Bob (Benjamin) Clark, Jean Shepherd, Leigh Brown. **VHS** *NYR* ⅈⅈⅈ

It Should Happen to You An aspiring model attempts to boost her career by promoting herself on a New York City billboard. The results, however, are continually surprising. Fine comedy teamwork from master thespians Holliday and Lemmon in this, the latter's first film.
1954 87m/B Judy Holliday, Jack Lemmon, Peter Lawford; **D:** George Cukor; **W:** Ruth Gordon, Garson Kanin. **VHS, Beta** $9.95 *GKK* ⅈⅈⅈ

It Started in Naples Good performances by both Gable and Loren in this comedy-drama about an American lawyer in Italy who, upon preparing his late brother's estate, finds that his brother's nephew is living with a stripper. A custody battle ensues, but love wins out in the end. Loren is incredible in nightclub scenes.
1960 100m/C Clark Gable, Sophia Loren, Marietto, Vittorio De Sica, Paolo Carlini, Claudio Ermelli, Giovanni Filidoro; **D:** Melville Shavelson; **W:** Melville Shavelson, Jack Rose. **VHS** $14.95 *PAR* ⅈⅈⅈ

It Started with a Kiss Reynolds plays a showgirl who impulsively marries an Air Force sargeant (Ford). When he's transfered to Spain they try to make a go of their hasty marriage among numerous comic complications. Flimsy farce with likeable leads.
1959 104m/C Debbie Reynolds, Glenn Ford, Eva Gabor, Gustavo Rojo, Fred Clark, Edgar Buchanan, Robert Warwick, Henry Morgan, Francis Bavier; **D:** George Marshall. **VHS** $19.98 *MGM, MOV* ⅈⅈ½

It Takes a Thief Tough cookie Jayne's a buxom gangstress who does the hokey pokey with her criminal minions. A former lover who's been released from the big house seems to think she's been minding the mint for him. Au contraire. *AKA:* The Challenge.
1959 93m/B Jayne Mansfield, Anthony Quayle, Carl Mohner, Peter Reynolds, John Bennett; **D:** John Gilling. **VHS** *BBF* ⅈⅈ

It Takes Two A young man spends his last ten days of bachelorhood cruising down Texas highways with a beautiful car saleswoman. Meanwhile, back at the altar, his bride waits patiently. Upbeat with some genuinely funny moments. From the director of "Pass the Ammo."
1988 (PG-13) 79m/C George Newbern, Leslie Hope, Kimberly Foster, Barry Corbin; **D:** David Beaird; **M:** Carter Burwell. **VHS, Beta** $14.95 *MGM* ⅈⅈ

It! The Terror from Beyond Space The sole survivor of a Martian expedition is believed to have murdered his colleagues. He's arrested and brought back to Earth via space ship. En route, a vicious alien, the actual culprit, is discovered on board and begins killing the crew members. A fun science fiction thriller which, 20 years later, would provide Ridley Scott with the plot for "Alien." *AKA:* It! The Vampire From Beyond Space.
1958 68m/B Marshall Thompson, Shawn Smith, Kim Spalding, Ann Doran, Dabbs Greer, Paul Langton, Ray Corrigan; **D:** Edward L. Cahn. **VHS, Beta** $14.95 *MGM, MLB* ⅈⅈ½

It Was a Short Summer, Charlie Brown The Peanuts gang enjoys the summer until it's time to go back to school.

1969 26m/C **D:** Bill Melendez. VHS **$14.95** *WTA* 🐾🐾½

Italian The story of an Italian immigrant family living in the slums of New York during the turn of the century.
1915 78m/B George Beban, Clara Williams, Leo Wills, J. Frank Burke, Fanny Midgley. VHS, Beta **$19.95** *GPV, GVV* 🐾🐾½

The Italian Job Caine and Coward pair up to steal $4 million in gold by causing a major traffic jam in Turin, Italy. During the jam, the pair steals the gold from an armored car. Silliness and chases through the Swiss mountains ensue, culminating in a hilarious ending.
1969 (G) 99m/C Michael Caine, Noel Coward, Benny Hill, Raf Vallone, Tony Beckley, Rossano Brazzi, Margaret Blye; **D:** Peter Collinson; **M:** Quincy Jones. VHS *PAR* 🐾🐾½

The Italian Stallion Stallone plays a man with only one thing on his mind...sex!
1973 90m/C Sylvester Stallone, Henrietta Holm. VHS, Beta **$79.95** *JEF* 🐾

Italian Straw Hat Classic silent about the chain of errors that ensues when a man's horse eats a woman's hat. His vast, unending struggle to replace the hat is the source of continual comedy. From Eugene Labiche's play. *AKA:* Un Chapeau de Paille d'Italie.
1927 72m/B Albert Prejean; **D:** Rene Clair. VHS, Beta **$24.95** *VYY, MRV, INT* 🐾🐾🐾

Italianamerican/The Big Shave Two shorts by Scorsese. "Italianamerican" (1974) features dinner and conversation with his parents in their own Little Italy (New York) apartment. In "The Big Shave," (1967) a young man nicks himself shaving and suddenly has a frightening religious experience.
19?? 54m/C **D:** Martin Scorsese. VHS **$49.95** *HMV* 🐾🐾🐾

It's a Bundyful Life The outrageous family from television's "Married with Children" does Christmas in their own inimitable fashion. This parody of "It's a Wonderful Life" features Kinison earning his wings as father Al's guardian angel. See what the family would have been like if Al had never been born...and what Al decides to do about it. Those seeking traditional family fare should look elsewhere.
1992 47m/C Ed O'Neill, Katey Sagal, Christina Applegate, David Faustino, Sam Kinison, Amanda Bearse, Ted McGinley; **D:** Gerry Cohen. VHS **$14.95** *COL* 🐾🐾🐾

It's a Date A mother and daughter, both actresses, continually get their professional and romantic lives intertwined. It begins when Durbin (the daughter) is offered Kay's (the mother) Broadway role. It continues in Hawaii where the man that Kay is in love with tries to court Durbin. As it's a comedy, of course, all is put right in the end. ♫Musetta's Waltz; Ave Maria; Loch Lomond; Love Is All; It Happened in Kaloha; Rhythm of the Islands; Hawaiian War Chant.
1940 103m/B Deanna Durbin, Kay Francis, Walter Pidgeon, Samuel S. Hinds, S.Z. Sakall, Henry Stephenson, Charles Lane, Leon Belasco; **D:** William A. Seiter; **W:** Norman Krasna. VHS **$29.98** *FOX, FCT, MLB* 🐾🐾

It's a Dog's Life The hero and narrator of this story is a wily bull terrier called Wildfire. Wildfire is a tough dog on the mean streets of the Bowery in turn-of-the-century New York. His master has him in dog fights in the local saloon but eventually abandons him. Wildfire is then taken in by the kindly employee of the rich and dog-hating Jagger but naturally manages to win the codger over. Based on the short story "The Bar Sinister" by Richard Harding Davis. *AKA:* The Bar Sinister.
1955 87m/C Jeff Richards, Edmund Gwenn, Dean Jagger; **D:** Hermann Hoffman; **W:** John Michael Hayes; **M:** Elmer Bernstein. VHS **$19.98** *FCT* 🐾🐾½

It's A Gift A grocery clerk moves his family west to manage orange groves in this classic Fields comedy. Several inspired sequences. The supporting cast shines too. A real find for the discriminating comedy buff. Remake of the silent "It's the Old Army Game."
1934 71m/B W.C. Fields, Baby LeRoy, Kathleen Howard; **D:** Norman Z. McLeod. VHS, Beta **$14.95** *MCA, BAR* 🐾🐾🐾

It's a Great Feeling Another Carson and Day team-up where Carson plays a camera-hogging show-off whom no one wants to direct. He's such an industry piranha that he ends up directing himself! He cons Day, a waitress and would-be actress, by promising her a part in his new film. Some executives hear her sing before she heads back home to Wisconsin, fed up with Hollywood. They make Carson track her down to star in the new picture, but when he arrives she is at the altar with her high school sweetheart.
1949 85m/C Dennis (Stanley Morner) Morgan, Doris Day, Jack Carson, Bill Goodwin, Errol Flynn, Gary Cooper, Joan Crawford, Ronald Reagan, Sydney Greenstreet, Danny Kaye, Eleanor Parker, Edward G. Robinson, Jane Wyman; **D:** David Butler. VHS **$29.98** *FOX, FCT, MLB* 🐾🐾½

It's a Great Life Blondie wants Dagwood to buy a house but instead he buys a horse. He's scheming to impress a client of Mr. Dither's by participating in a fox hunt. Blondie comes to the rescue. 13th entry in series.
1943 75m/B Penny Singleton, Arthur Lake, Larry Simms, Hugh Herbert, Jonathan Hale, Danny Mummert, Alan Dinehart, Irving Bacon, Douglas Leavitt, Marjorie Ann Mutchie; **D:** Frank Strayer; **W:** Karen De Wolf, Connie Leo. VHS **$19.99** *MOV* 🐾🐾½

It's a Joke, Son! Follows the fictional politician, Senator Claghorn from the Fred Allen radio show, during his first run for the U.S. Senate.
1947 67m/B Kenny Delmar, Una Merkel; **D:** Ben Stoloff. VHS **$19.95** *NOS, MRV, DVT* 🐾🐾

It's a Mad, Mad, Mad, Mad World Overblown epic comedy with a cast of notables desperately seeking the whereabouts of stolen money. Ultimately exhausting film undone by its length and overbearing performances. Laserdisc contains 20 minutes of supplemental footage, including interviews with some of the surviving cast members.
1963 155m/C Spencer Tracy, Sid Caesar, Milton Berle, Ethel Merman, Jonathan Winters, Jimmy Durante, Buddy Hackett, Mickey Rooney, Phil Silvers, Dick Shawn, Edie Adams, Dorothy Provine, Buster Keaton, Terry-Thomas, Moe Howard, Larry Fine, Joe DeRita, Jim Backus, William Demarest, Peter Falk, Leo Gorcey, Edward Everett Horton, Joe E. Brown, Carl Reiner, ZaSu Pitts, Eddie Anderson, Jack Benny, Jerry Lewis; **D:** Stanley Kramer; **M:** Ernest Gold. Academy Awards '63: Best Sound Effects Editing; Nominations: Best Color Cinematography, Best Song ("It's a Mad, Mad, Mad, Mad World"), Best Sound, Best Original Score. VHS, Beta **$29.98** *MGM, FOX, FCT* 🐾🐾½

It's a Mystery, Charlie Brown Peanuts adventure in which Snoopy interrogates everyone on the disappearance of Woodstock's birdhouse.
1987 30m/C **D:** Phil Roman. VHS, Beta **$14.95** *BAR, WTA* 🐾🐾

It's a Wonderful Life American classic about a man saved from suicide by a considerate angel, who then shows the hero how important he's been to the lives of loved ones. Corny but inspirational and heartwarming, with an endearing performance by Travers as angel Clarence. Stewart and Reed are typically wholesome. Perfect film for people who want to feel good, joyfully teetering on the border between Hollywood schmaltz and genuine heartbreak. Also available colorized. The laserdisc version includes production and publicity stills, the theatrical trailer, and commentary by film professor Jeanine Basinger. Also available in a 160-minute Collector's Edition with original preview trailer, "The Making of 'It's a Wonderful Life,'" and a new original transfer from the original negative.
1946 125m/B James Stewart, Donna Reed, Henry Travers, Thomas Mitchell, Lionel Barrymore, Samuel S. Hinds, Frank Faylen, Gloria Grahame, H.B. Warner, Ellen Corby, Sheldon Leonard, Beulah Bondi, Ward Bond, Frank Albertson, Todd Karns, Mary Treen, Charles Halton; **D:** Frank Capra; **W:** Francis Goodrich, Albert Hackett, Jo Swerling; **M:** Dimitri Tiomkin. Academy Awards '46 Nominations: Best Actor (Stewart), Best Director (Capra), Best Film Editing, Best Picture, Best Sound; Golden Globe Awards '47: Best Director (Capra). VHS **$9.95** *IGP, MRV, CNG* 🐾🐾🐾🐾

It's Alive! Slow-moving dud about a farmer feeding passersby to the area's cave-dwelling lizard man. The ping pong ball-eyed monster puts in a belated appearance that's not worth the wait.
1968 80m/C Tommy Kirk, Shirley Bonne, Bill Thurman; **D:** Larry Buchanan; **W:** Larry Buchanan. VHS **$15.95** *NOS, LOO* 🐾

It's Alive Cult film about a mutated baby that is born to a normal Los Angeles couple, who escapes and goes on a bloodthirsty, murderous rampage, is a sight to behold. Fantastic score by Bernard Herrmann makes this chilling film a memorable one.
1974 (PG) 91m/C John P. Ryan, Sharon Farrell, Andrew Duggan, Guy Stockwell, James Dixon, Michael Ansara; **D:** Larry Cohen; **W:** Larry Cohen. VHS, Beta **$14.95** *WAR, FCT* 🐾🐾🐾

It's Alive 2: It Lives Again In this sequel to "It's Alive," the original hellspun baby meets up with two more of the same and all three terrorize the city, murdering everyone they can find. Truly horrendous.
1978 (R) 91m/C Frederic Forrest, Kathleen Lloyd, John P. Ryan, Andrew Duggan, John Marley, Eddie Constantine; **D:** Larry Cohen. VHS, Beta **$19.98** *WAR, FCT* Woof!

It's Alive 3: Island of the Alive The second sequel to the tongue-in-cheek horror film, in which the infant mutant of the previous films has been left with other mutations to spawn on a desert island.
1987 (R) 94m/C Michael Moriarty, Karen Black, Laurene Landon, Gerrit Graham, James Dixon, Neal Israel, MacDonald Carey; **D:** Larry Cohen; **W:** Larry Cohen. VHS, Beta **$19.98** *WAR* 🐾

It's All True A look at auteur Welles' ill-fated WWII filmmaking project. Welles served as a special cultural ambassador to South America and, in 1942, began a documentary covering the area's complex political and social issues. Includes footage from "Four Men on a Raft," Welles' recreation about the peasant fishermen of Brazil; surviving excerpts from "The Story of Samba," a Technicolor musical about Carnaval in Rio de Janeiro; and footage from "My Friend Bonito," set against a backdrop of bullfighting in Mexico.

1993 (G) 85m/C **D:** Richard Wilson, Bill Krohn, Myron Meise, Orson Welles; **W:** Richard Wilson, Bill Krohn, Myron Meise. VHS *PAR* 🎦🎦

It's Always Fair Weather Three WWII buddies meet again at a 10-year reunion and find that they don't like each other very much. A surprisingly cynical film. Director Donen produced "Seven Brides for Seven Brothers" the previous year. ♫Stillman's Gym; March, March; Why Are We Here? (Blue Danube); Music Is Better Than Words; Once Upon A Time; The Time For Parting; I Like Myself; Baby You Knock Me Out; Thanks A Lot But No Thanks.
1955 102m/C Gene Kelly, Cyd Charisse, Dan Dailey, Michael Kidd; **D:** Stanley Donen; **W:** Betty Comden, Adolph Green; **M:** Betty Comden, Adolph Green, Andre Previn. VHS, Beta $19.98 *MGM, FHE* 🎦🎦

It's an Adventure, Charlie Brown! A collection of six vignettes featuring Charlie Brown and the whole Peanuts gang.
1983 50m/C **D:** Bill Melendez. VHS, Beta $9.98 *WTA, SHV, VTR* 🎦

It's Arbor Day, Charlie Brown Tribulations aplenty for Charlie Brown as his baseball team turns his field into an Arbor Day garden.
1983 26m/C VHS, Beta $14.95 *BAR, WTA* 🎦🎦

It's Called Murder, Baby The famed porn star gives the viewer a lesson in English vocabulary in this tale of a blackmailed movie queen.
1982 (R) 94m/C John Leslie, Cameron Mitchell, Lisa Trego; **D:** Sam Weston. VHS, Beta $19.98 *LIV* 🎦

It's Flashbeagle, Charlie Brown/ She's a Good Skate, Charlie Brown A Peanuts double header: In "It's Flashbeagle Charlie Brown," Snoopy infects the Peanuts gang with dance fever, and in "She's a Good Skate Charlie Brown," Snoopy trains Peppermint Patty to become a figure skating champion.
1984 55m/C **D:** Bill Melendez. VHS, Beta $29.95 *SHV* 🎦

It's Good to Be Alive The true story of how Brooklyn Dodgers' catcher Roy Campanella learned to face life after an automobile accident left him a quadriplegic. Good performances in this television drama.
1974 100m/C Paul Winfield, Ruby Dee, Louis Gossett Jr.; **D:** Michael Landon. VHS, Beta $59.95 *PSM* 🎦🎦½

It's in the Bag A shiftless flea circus owner sells chairs he has inherited, not knowing that a fortune is hidden in one of them. **AKA:** The Fifth Chair.
1945 87m/B Fred Allen, Don Ameche, Jack Benny, William Bendix, Binnie Barnes, Robert Benchley; **D:** Richard Wallace. VHS $19.95 *REP, MED* 🎦🎦½

It's Love Again A streetwise chorus girl poses as a fictional socialite in a light music-hall comedy. ♫It's Love Again; Heaven In Your Arms.
1936 83m/B Jessie Matthews, Robert Young, Sonnie Hale; **D:** Victor Saville. VHS, Beta $24.95 *NOS, DVT, HEG* 🎦🎦

It's Magic, Charlie Brown/ Charlie Brown's All Star In the first of these two stories, Snoopy, "The Great Houndini," makes Charlie Brown disappear. Problems begin when Snoopy finds it difficult conjuring his master back to reality. In the second story, Charlie Brown's baseball team has lost 999 games in a row, and prospects are bleak. New hope arrives when he gets an

offer to have the team sponsored in a real league.
1981 55m/C **D:** Phil Roman. VHS, Beta $14.95 *SHV, VTR, WTA* 🎦🎦½

It's My Turn A mathematics professor (Clayburgh) struggles in her relationship with live-in lover (Grodin) who sells real-estate in Chicago. She meets retired baseball player (Douglas) and falls in love. "Ho-hum" just about describes the rest.
1980 (R) 91m/C Jill Clayburgh, Michael Douglas, Charles Grodin, Beverly Garland, Steven Hill, Dianne Wiest, Daniel Stern; **D:** Claudia Weill; **W:** Eleanor Bergstein. VHS, Beta $64.95 *COL* 🎦🎦

It's Not the Size That Counts After the Earth's drinking water is contaminated, Lawson is the only man on Earth not to be struck by impotency. Limp sequel to "Percy," the British comedy about the first man to receive a penis transplant. Promising comedy doesn't deliver. **AKA:** Percy's Progress.
1974 90m/C Leigh Lawson, Elke Sommer, Denholm Elliott, Vincent Price; **D:** Ralph Thomas. VHS $59.98 *SUE Woof!*

It's Pat Yet another sketch character from "Saturday Night Live" makes a big screen appearance. The androgynous Pat (Sweeney) falls for the equally gender-suspect Chris (Foley, from Canada's version of SNL, "Kids in the Hall") and all sorts of embarrassing situations arise. Pat's quest to find Pat's self is sketch material stretched thin. A cameo by Harvey Keitel as a priest didn't make the final cut, one of the few flicks in which Keitel has failed to appear during the 90s.
1994 (PG-13) 77m/C Julia Sweeney, David Foley, Charles Rocket, Kathy Griffin, Julie Haydon, Tim Meadows, Arleen Sorkin; **Cameos:** Sally Jesse Raphael, Kathy Najimy; **D:** Adam Bernstein; **W:** Julia Sweeney, Jim Emerson, Stephen Hibbert. VHS *NYR* 🎦

It's the Great Pumpkin, Charlie Brown It's Halloween, and Charlie Brown and his friends are going trick-or-treating, but Linus faithfully awaits the arrival of the Great Pumpkin.
1988 25m/C VHS, Beta $12.95 *PAR, MED, VTR* 🎦🎦

It's the Old Army Game Classic Fields gags in three of his best Ziegfeld Follies sketches: "The Drug Store," "A Peaceful Morning," and "The Family Flivver." The beautiful Brooks serves as his comic foil.
1926 75m/B W.C. Fields, Louise Brooks, Blanche Ring, William Gaxton; **D:** Edward Sutherland. VHS, Beta $24.95 *GPV* 🎦🎦

It's Three Strikes, Charlie Brown Misfortunes abound in the baseball diamond for the Peanuts gang.
1986 41m/C **D:** Bill Melendez, Phil Roman, Robert E. Balzer, Sam Nicholson. VHS, Beta $14.95 *BAR, WTA* 🎦🎦

It's Your First Kiss, Charlie Brown/Someday You'll Find Her, Charlie Brown In "It's Your First Kiss, Charlie Brown," our hero has to escort the school's homecoming queen to the ball. What's worse, he actually has to kiss her in front of everyone! In "Someday You'll Find Her, Charlie Brown" Charlie Brown sees "the most beautiful girl in the world" on television and, after recruiting Linus, embarks upon a door-to-door search to find her.
1977 55m/C **D:** Phil Roman. VHS, Beta $14.95 *SHV, VTR* 🎦🎦

Ivan the Terrible, Part 1 Contemplative epic of Russia's first czar is a classic, innovative film from cinema genius Eisenstein. Visually stunning, with a fine performance by Cherkassov. Ivan's struggles to preserve his country is the main concern of the first half of Eisenstein's masterwork (which he originally planned as a trilogy). In Russian with English subtitles.
1944 96m/B Nikolai Cherkassov, Ludmila Tselikovskaya, Serafina Birman, Piotr Kadochnikov; **D:** Sergei Eisenstein; **W:** Sergei Eisenstein; **M:** Sergei Prokofiev. VHS, Beta, 8mm $24.95 *NOS, MRV, WST* 🎦🎦🎦🎦

Ivan the Terrible, Part 2 Landed gentry conspire to dethrone the czar in this continuation of the innovative epic. More stunning imagery from master Eisenstein, who makes no false moves in this one. Slow going, but immensely rewarding. Russian dialogue with English subtitles; contains color sequences.
1946 84m/B Nikolai Cherkassov, Ludmila Tselikovskaya, Serafina Birman, Piotr Kadochnikov; **D:** Sergei Eisenstein. VHS, Beta, 8mm $24.95 *NOS, MRV, WST* 🎦🎦🎦½

Ivanhoe Knights fight each other and woo maidens in this chivalrous romance derived from the Sir Walter Scott classic. Taylor is suitably noble, while Sanders is familiarly serpentine. Remade in 1982.
1952 107m/C Robert Taylor, Elizabeth Taylor, Joan Fontaine, George Sanders, Finlay Currie, Felix Aylmer; **D:** Richard Thorpe. VHS, Beta $19.98 *MGM* 🎦🎦🎦

Ivanhoe A version of Sir Walter Scott's classic novel of chivalry and knighthood in 12th century England. Made for television. Remake of the 1953 film classic.
1982 142m/C Anthony Andrews, James Mason, Lysette Anthony, Sam Neill, Olivia Hussey, Michael Hordern, Julian Glover, George Innes, Ronald Pickup, John Rhys-Davies, Chloe Franks; **D:** Douglas Camfield. VHS, Beta $19.95 *TVC, COL* 🎦🎦½

I've Always Loved You The drama of love and jealousy explored in an extravagant production filled with classical music. **AKA:** Concerto.
1946 117m/C Philip Dorn, Catherine McLeod; **D:** Frank Borzage. VHS $19.98 *REP, FCT* 🎦🎦½

I've Heard the Mermaids Singing Independent Canadian semi-satiric romantic comedy details the misadventures of a klutzy woman who suddenly obtains a desirable job in an art gallery run by a lesbian on whom she develops a crush. Good-natured tone helped considerably by McCarthy's winning performance.
1987 81m/C Sheila McCarthy, Paule Baillargeon, Ann-Marie MacDonald, John Evans; **D:** Patricia Rozema; **M:** Mark Korven. VHS, Beta $19.98 *NLC, FCT* 🎦🎦🎦

Ivory Hunters Conservationists team up to thwart a massacre of elephants by poachers. Predictable made-for-cable entertainment co-produced by the National Audubon Society. **AKA:** The Last Elephant.
1990 94m/C John Lithgow, Isabella Rossellini, James Earl Jones, Tony Todd, Olek Krupa; **D:** Joseph Sargent; **W:** Richard Guttman, Bill Bozzone; **M:** Charles Bernstein. VHS, Beta $79.98 *TTC* 🎦🎦½

Izzy & Moe Carney and The Great One are reunited for the last time on screen as former vaudevillians who become federal agents and create havoc amid speak-easies and bathtub gin during Prohibition. A made-for-television movie based on true stories.

1985 92m/C Jackie Gleason, Art Carney, Cynthia Harris, Zohra Lampert, Drew Snyder, Dick Latessa; *D:* Jackie Cooper. **VHS, Beta** $79.95 *VMK* 🐾🐾½

J. Edgar Hoover Made for cable adaptation from "My 30 years in Hoover's FBI" by William G. Sullivan and William S. Brown. Biographical drama deals with Hoover's fifty-five year career with the government. Included are his FBI days.
1987 110m/C Treat Williams, Rip Torn, David Ogden Stiers, Andrew Duggan, Art Hindle, Louise Fletcher; *D:* Robert Collins. **VHS, Beta** $79.98 *MCG* 🐾🐾

J-Men Forever! A spoof on early sci-fi/spy serials in which an alien takeover is attempted via rock-n-roll (your parents warned you). Employs an amusing technique of dubbing footage from dozens of Republic dramas intercut with new film featuring the "Firesign Theater" crew.
1979 (PG) 73m/B Peter Bergman, Phil Proctor; *D:* Richard Patterson. **VHS, Beta** $59.98 *VES* 🐾🐾

Jabberwalk A "Mondo Cane," American-style. A reckless and funny view of the bizarre in U.S. life.
1979 (R) 110m/C **VHS, Beta** $59.95 *VCD* 🐾🐾

Jabberwocky Pythonesque chaos prevails in the medieval cartoon kingdom of King Bruno the Questionable, who rules with cruelty, stupidity, lust and dust. Jabberwocky is the big dragon mowing everything down in its path until hero Palin decides to take it on. Uneven, but real funny at times.
1977 (PG) 104m/C Michael Palin, Eric Idle, Max Wall, Deborah Fallender, Terry Jones, John Le Mesurier; *D:* Terry Gilliam; *W:* Terry Gilliam. **VHS, Beta** $19.95 *COL* 🐾🐾½

Jacare First adventure thriller filmed in the Amazon jungle.
1942 ?m/C Frank Buck; *M:* Miklos Rozsa. **VHS** $16.95 *SNC, VYY* 🐾🐾

J'Accuse A Frenchman creates a device he believes will stop the war but it is confiscated by the government and used as part of the national defense. Subsequently, he goes mad. Gance (known for his 1927 "Napoleon"), remade his 1919 silent film, retelling the powerful anti-war message with great sensitivity. Banned in Nazi Germany. *AKA:* I Accuse; That They May Live.
1937 125m/B Victor Francen, Jean Max, Deltaire, Renee Devillers; *D:* Abel Gance. **VHS** $29.95 *CVC, SNC, FCT* 🐾🐾🐾

Jack and His Friends Comic satire of the tribulations of Jack the shoe salesman (Garfield), who is shown the front door by his unfaithful wife. Beset by grief, he drives the streets aimlessly until he is kidnapped by a young couple (Rockwell and Reyes) on the run from the law, who force Jack to take them to his summer house where they all try to decide what to do with their lives.
1992 (R) 93m/C Allen (Gooritz) Garfield, Sam Rockwell, Judy Reyes; *D:* Bruce Ornstein. **VHS** $79.95 *FCT* 🐾🐾

Jack & the Beanstalk While babysitting, Lou falls asleep and dreams he's Jack in this spoof of the classic fairy tale.
1952 78m/B Bud Abbott, Lou Costello, Buddy Baer; *D:* Jean Yarborough. **VHS, Beta** $19.95 *NOS, VCI, VTR* 🐾🐾

Jack & the Beanstalk An animated musical version of the familiar story of Jack, the young boy who climbs a magic beanstalk up into the clouds, where he meets a fearsome giant.
1976 80m/C *D:* Peter J. Solmo; *W:* Peter J. Solmo. **VHS, Beta** *COL* 🐾🐾

Jack & the Beanstalk From the "Faerie Tale Theatre" comes this classic tale of Jack, who sells his family's cow for 5 magic beans, climbs the huge beanstalk that sprouts from them, and encounters an unfriendly giant.
1983 60m/C Dennis Christopher, Katherine Helmond, Elliott Gould, Jean Stapleton, Mark Blankfield; *D:* Lamont Johnson. **VHS, Beta** $14.98 *KUI, FOX, FCT* 🐾🐾

Jack Frost Moving biographical drama that follows a man from the sweat factories of London to his eventual rise to success.
1943 89m/B Michael O'Shea, Susan Hayward. **VHS, Beta, 8mm** *VYY* 🐾🐾½

The Jack Knife Man Sentimental silent treatment of the relationship between a boy and a man. A new mother close to death hands over her bundle of joy to a kindly old river man, and the two bond in a familial way despite incessant adversity. Made the year following Vidor's debut as a feature film director.
1920 70m/B Fred Turner, Todd Harry, Bobby Kelso, Willis Marks, Lillian Leighton, James Corrigan; *D:* King Vidor; *W:* King Vidor. **VHS, Beta** $24.95 *VYY, GPV, FCT* 🐾🐾🐾

Jack London Dramatizes London's most creative years during his careers as oyster pirate, prospector, war correspondent and author. Based on "The Book of Jack London" by Charmian London. *AKA:* The Adventures of Jack London; The Life of Jack London.
1944 94m/B Michael O'Shea, Susan Hayward, Harry Davenport, Virginia Mayo, Frank Craven; *D:* Alfred Santell. **VHS, Beta** $19.95 *NOS, MRV, DVT* 🐾🐾

Jack the Bear Exercise in misery centers on a father and his two sons, trying to pick up the pieces after the death of wife and mother Marcovicci. Dad DeVito is the host of a late-night horror show who's cuddly as a bear—when he's not drinking. While the talent and circumstances might have been enough to create a sensitive study, the emotion is completely overwrought by contrived plot twists, including a kidnapping by the local Nazi. TV's "thirtysomething" director Herskovitz creates an effect not unlike a cement block being dropped on a card house. Point made, but so much for subtlety. Based on a novel by Dan McCall.
1993 (PG-13) 98m/C Danny DeVito, Robert J. Steinmiller Jr., Miko Hughes, Gary Sinise, Art LaFleur, Andrea Marcovicci, Julia Louis-Dreyfus, Reese Witherspoon; *D:* Marshall Herskovitz; *W:* Steven Zaillian; *M:* James Horner. **VHS** $19.98 *FXV* 🐾½

Jack the Giant Killer A young farmer joins a medieval princess on a journey to a distant convent. Along the way, they combat an evil wizard, dragons, sea monsters and other mystical creatures, and are assisted by leprechauns, a dog and a chimp. Generally considered a blatant rip-off of "The Seventh Voyage of Sinbad," the film nonetheless delivers plenty of fun and excitement. Jim Danforth of "Gumby" fame provided the stop-motion animation.
1962 (G) 95m/C Kerwin Mathews, Judi Meredith, Torin Thatcher, Walter Burke, Roger Mobley, Barry Kelley, Don Beddoe, Anna Lee, Robert Gist; *D:* Nathan Juran. **VHS, Beta** $14.95 *MGM, FCT* 🐾🐾

Jack the Ripper An American detective joins Scotland Yard in tracking down the legendary and elusive Jack the Ripper. More gory than most. The last scene is in color.

1960 88m/B Lee Patterson, Betty McDowall, Barbara Burke, John Le Mesurier, George Rose; *D:* Robert S. Baker, Monty Berman. **VHS** $16.95 *SNC, PAR* 🐾🐾

Jack the Ripper The inimitable Kinski assumes the role of the most heinous criminal of modern history—Jack the Ripper.
1980 (R) 82m/C Klaus Kinski, Josephine Chaplin; *D:* Jess (Jesus) Franco. **VHS, Beta** $59.95 *VES* 🐾🐾

Jack the Ripper Another retelling of the life of the legendary serial killer. Caine is the Scotland Yard inspector who tracks down the murderer. Ending is based on recent evidence found by director/co-writer Wickes. Extremely well done made-for-television film.
1988 200m/C Michael Caine, Armand Assante, Ray McNally, Susan George, Jane Seymour, Lewis Collins, Ken Bones; *D:* David Wickes; *W:* David Wickes. **VHS** *VES, LIV* 🐾🐾🐾

Jackie Chan's Police Force Chopsocker Chan's assigned to protect a witness in a drug case. Faced by unsavory thugs, he flies through the air with the greatest of ease. Very cool stunts. *AKA:* The Police Story; Police Force; Jackie Chan's Police Story.
1985 (PG-13) 89m/C Jackie Chan, Bridget Lin, Maggie Cheung, Cho Yuen, Bill Tung, Kenneth Tong; *D:* Jackie Chan. **VHS** *NO* 🐾🐾½

The Jackie Robinson Story Chronicles Robinson's rise from UCLA to his breakthrough as the first black man to play baseball in the major league. Robinson plays himself; the film deals honestly with the racial issues of the time.
1950 76m/B Jackie Robinson, Ruby Dee, Minor Watson, Louise Beavers, Richard Lane, Harry Shannon, Joel Fluellen, Ben Lessy; *D:* Alfred E. Green. **VHS, Beta** $19.98 *MGM, MRV, MOV* 🐾🐾🐾

Jacknife The well-crafted story of a Vietnam veteran who visits his old war buddy and tries to piece together what's happened to their lives since their homecoming. During his visit he encounters anger and hostility from the other veteran, and tenderness from his friend's sister. A masterfully acted, small-scale drama, adapted by Stephen Metcalfe from his play.
1989 (R) 102m/C Robert De Niro, Kathy Baker, Ed Harris, Loudon Wainwright III, Charles S. Dutton; *D:* David Jones; *W:* Stephen Metcalfe; *M:* Bruce Broughton. **VHS, Beta** $89.98 *HBO, IME* 🐾🐾

Jacko & Lise A French lad falls in love with a young girl, and abandons his previously decadent lifestyle to win her. Available with English subtitles or dubbed.
1982 (R) 92m/C Laurent Malet, Annie Girardot; *D:* Walter Bal. **VHS, Beta** $29.98 *SUE* 🐾🐾

The Jackpot An average Joe wins a bushel of money from a radio quiz show but can't pay the taxes. Maybe that was funny before the age of read-my-lips economics, but the all-star cast doesn't deliver on its promise. Lang, noted for mostly mediocre pictures, went on to direct "The King and I."
1950 87m/C James Stewart, Natalie Wood, Barbara Hale, James Gleason, Fred Clark, Patricia Medina; *D:* Walter Lang. **VHS** *NO* 🐾🐾

Jack's Back When a lunatic is killing Los Angeles prostitutes Jack-the-Ripper style, twin brothers get mistakenly involved (Spader in both roles). One of the brothers is accused of the murders and it is up to the other either to clear his name or to provide the final evidence of guilt. A well thought out story with enough twists and turns for any suspense buff.

1987 (R) 97m/C James Spader, Cynthia Gibb, Rod Loomis, Rex Ryon, Robert Picardo, Jim Haynie, Chris Mulkey, Danitza Kingsley; *D:* Rowdy Herrington. **VHS, Beta $19.95** PAR 🎞🎞🎞

Jackson County Jail While driving cross-country, a young woman is robbed, imprisoned, and raped by a deputy, whom she kills. Faced with a murder charge, she flees, with the law in hot pursuit. Also known by its later remade-for-television name, "Outside Chance," this is a minor cult film. 1976 (R) 84m/C Yvette Mimieux, Tommy Lee Jones, Robert Carradine, Severn Darden, Howard Hesseman, Mary Woronov; *D:* Michael Miller; *W:* Donald Stewart. **VHS, Beta $39.98** WAR 🎞🎞½

The Jacksons: An American Dream Made for television miniseries covering the career of the Jackson 5, the working-class family from Gary, Indiana which became a celebrated show business success. The series begins with the courtship of Joseph and Katherine Jackson and ends with the group's farewell tour in 1984, covering both family and career turmoils. Simplistic, glossy biography. 1992 225m/C Lawrence Hilton-Jacobs, Angela Bassett, Wylie Draper, Angel Vargas, Jacen Wilkerson, Terrence DaShon Howard, Jason Weaver, Jermaine Jackson II, Billy Dee Williams, Vanessa Williams, Holly Robinson, Margaret Avery; *D:* Karen Arthur. **VHS $79.95** PGV 🎞🎞½

Jacob Have I Loved A teenage girl struggles to overcome her jealousy of her twin sister and find her own place in life as she comes of age on a Chesapeake island. Based on the book by Katherine Paterson. Part of the "Wonderworks" family movie series from PBS. 1988 57m/C Bridget Fonda, Jenny Robertson, John Kellogg; *D:* Victoria Hochberg. **VHS $29.95** PME, WNE, RHU 🎞🎞½

Jacob's Ladder A man struggles with events he experienced while serving in Vietnam. Gradually, he becomes unable to separate reality from the strange, psychotic world into which he increasingly lapses. His friends and family try to help him before he's lost forever. Great story potential is flawed by too many flashbacks, leaving the viewer more confused than the characters. 1990 (R) 116m/C Tim Robbins, Elizabeth Pena, Danny Aiello, Matt Craven, Pruitt Taylor Vince, Jason Alexander, Patricia Kalember, Eriq LaSalle, Ving Rhames, Macaulay Culkin; *D:* Adrian Lyne; *W:* Bruce Joel Rubin; *M:* Maurice Jarre. **VHS, Beta $92.95** LIV, FCT 🎞🎞½

Jacqueline Bouvier Kennedy A made-for-television biography of the former First Lady, from her childhood to "Camelot," the glorious years with JFK in the White House. Smith bears a physical resemblance to Jackie, but this drama is far too glossy. 1981 150m/C Jaclyn Smith, James Franciscus, Rod Taylor, Donald Moffatt, Dolph Sweet, Stephen Elliott; *D:* Steven Gethers; *M:* Billy Goldenberg. **VHS, Beta $24.95** VMK 🎞½

Jacquot Director Varda offers a loving tribute to her husband, filmmaker Jacques Demy. Based on the memoirs of her husband's childhood as a boy obsessed with movies, Varda re-stages scenes and also uses clips from various Demy films to illustrate her points. In French with English subtitles. *AKA:* Jacquot de Nantes. 1991 (PG) 118m/C Philippe Maron, Edouard Joubeaud, Laurent Monnier, Brigitte de Villepoix, Daniel Dublet; *D:* Agnes Varda; *W:* Agnes Varda. **VHS** COL 🎞🎞

The Jade Mask Chan discovers a murderer and his wife use puppets and masks to make it appear their victims are still alive. Another in the detective series with nothing noteworthy about it. Luke, the brother of actor Keye Luke, takes on the role of Chan's Number Four son. 1945 66m/B Sidney Toler, Mantan Moreland, Edwin Luke, Janet Warren, Hardie Albright, Edith Evanson; *D:* Phil Rosen. **VHS $19.98** MGM 🎞½

The Jagged Edge The beautiful wife of successful newspaper editor, Jack Forester, is killed and the police want to point the guilty finger at Jack. Attorney Teddy Barnes is brought in to defend him and accidentally falls in love. Taut murder mystery will keep you guessing "whodunit" until the very end. 1985 (R) 108m/C Jeff Bridges, Glenn Close, Robert Loggia, Peter Coyote, John Dehner, Leigh Taylor-Young, Lance Henriksen, James Karen, Karen Austin, Michael Dorn, Guy Boyd, Marshall Colt, Louis Giambalvo; *D:* Richard Marquand; *W:* Joe Eszterhas; *M:* John Barry. **VHS, Beta, 8mm $14.95** COL 🎞🎞½

Jaguar Three men leave their homes in Niger in order to find jobs in the cities. When they return to their village, they bring back with them their experiences. 1956 93m/C *D:* Jean Rouch. **VHS** INT 🎞🎞½

Jaguar Lives A high-kicking secret agent tracks down bad boy drug kings around the world. 1979 (PG) 91m/C Joe Lewis, Barbara Bach, Christopher Lee, Woody Strode, Donald Pleasence, Joseph Wiseman, John Huston, Capucine; *D:* Ernie Pintoff. **VHS, Beta $79.95** TWE 🎞

Jail Bait Early Wood film about a group of small-time crooks who are always in trouble with the law; they blackmail a plastic surgeon into using his talents to help them ditch the cops. Not as "bad" as Wood's "Plan 9 From Outer Space," but still bad enough for camp fans to love (check the cheesy score leftover from an equally cheesy Mexican mad-scientist flick). *AKA:* Hidden Face. 1954 80m/B Timothy Farrell, Clancy Malone, Lyle Talbot, Steve Reeves, Herbert Rawlinson; *D:* Edward D. Wood Jr. **VHS, Beta $16.95** SNC, AOV, LSV 🎞½

Jailbait A cop gets involved with an alleged murder witness, a teenaged runaway named Kyle. What they discover is an international crime syndicate that kidnaps runaways to exploit as sex slaves. Now they know too much. An unrated version is also available. 1993 100m/C C. Thomas Howell, Renee Humphrey; *D:* Rafal Zielinksi; *W:* Robert Vincent O'Neil, Alien Castle. **VHS** PAR 🎞🎞

Jailbait: Betrayed By Innocence A man is on trial for statutory rape. Made-for-television. 1986 (R) 90m/C Barry Bostwick, Lee Purcell, Paul Sorvino, Cristen Kauffman, Isaac Hayes; *D:* Elliot Silverstein. **VHS, Beta $79.95** MNC, HHE 🎞½

Jailbird Rock We'd like to tell you that this isn't really a sweet-young-thing-in-prison musical, but it is. When Antin shoots her stepfather (he told her to turn that damn noise down?) she tries to bring down the Big House with song and dance. No kidding. 1988 90m/C Ronald Lacey, Rhonda Aldrich, Robin Antin; *D:* Phillip Schuman. **VHS $79.95** TWE 🎞½

Jailbird's Vacation Two ex-cons pose as lumberjacks in order to exact revenge on the bum that put them away. In French with English subtitles. *AKA:* Les Grandes Gueules.

1965 125m/C Lino Ventura, Bourvil, Marie DuBois; *D:* Robert Enrico. **VHS, Beta $19.95** FCT, BAR, ING 🎞🎞

Jailbreakin' A faded country singer and a rebellious youth team up to break out of jail. 1972 90m/C Erik Estrada. **VHS, Beta $59.95** GEM 🎞

Jailhouse Rock While in jail for manslaughter, a teenager learns to play the guitar. After his release, he slowly develops into a top recording star. Probably the only film that captured the magnetic power of the young Elvis Presley; an absolute must for fans. Also available in a colorized version. 🎵Jailhouse Rock; Treat Me Nice; Baby, I Don't Care; Young and Beautiful; Don't Leave Me Now; I Wanna Be Free; One More Day. 1957 (G) 96m/B Elvis Presley, Judy Tyler, Vaughn Taylor, Dean Jones, Mickey Shaughnessy, William Forrest, Glenn Strange; *D:* Richard Thorpe. **VHS, Beta $14.95** MGM 🎞🎞🎞

Jakarta A love-hardened CIA operative is whisked away to Jakarta for reasons unknown, only to find his thought-to-be-dead lover still alive and caught in a deadly game of espionage. 1988 (R) 94m/C Christopher Noth, Sue Francis Pai, Ronald Hunter; *D:* Charles Kaufman. **VHS, Beta** NO 🎞½

Jake Speed Comic-book mercenary Jake and his loyal associate Remo rescue a beautiful girl from white slave traders. Supposedly a parody of the action adventure genre. 1986 (PG) 93m/C Wayne Crawford, John Hurt, Karen Kopins, Dennis Christopher; *D:* Andrew Lane. **VHS, Beta $14.95** NWV, STE 🎞½

Jamaica Inn In old Cornwall, an orphan girl becomes involved with smugglers. Remade in 1982; based on the story by Daphne Du Maurier. 1939 98m/B Charles Laughton, Maureen O'Hara, Leslie Banks, Robert Newton; *D:* Alfred Hitchcock. **VHS, Beta $16.95** SNC, NOS, CAB 🎞🎞

Jamaica Inn A made-for-television miniseries based on the old Daphne Du Maurier adventure about highwaymen and moor-lurking thieves in Cornwall. Remake of the 1939 Hitchcock film. 1982 192m/C Patrick McGoohan, Jane Seymour; *D:* Lawrence Gordon Clark. **VHS, Beta $29.95** STE, NWV 🎞½

James Dean Dean's friend Bast wrote this behind-the-scenes look at the short life of the enigmatic movie star. Made for television. *AKA:* The Legend. 1976 99m/C Stephen McHattie, Michael Brandon, Candy Clark, Amy Irving, Brooke Adams, Dane Clark, Jayne Meadows, Meg Foster; *D:* William Bast, Robert Butler; *W:* William Bast; *M:* Billy Goldenberg. **VHS, Beta $19.95** STE, NWV 🎞

James Dean Production reflects an exhaustive search through archival film, videotape and photographs, and includes many exclusive interviews with friends of the late actor. 1985 120m/C James Dean; *D:* Claudio Masenza. **VHS, Beta $69.95** BAR 🎞🎞

James Dean Story An intimate portrait of James Dean presented by Robert Altman. The program includes never-before-seen outtakes from "East of Eden" and rare footage from the Hollywood premiere of "Giant" and the infamous Highway Public Safety message Dean made for television. 1957 80m/B James Dean; *D:* George W. George. **VHS, Beta $14.95** FCT, PMS, VEC 🎞🎞

James Dean: The First American Teenager A look at the life and legend of the charismatic filmstar, with scenes from his films and comments from those who knew him best.
1976 (PG) 83m/C James Dean, Elizabeth Taylor, Sammy Davis Jr., Rock Hudson, Sal Mineo, Natalie Wood, Julie Harris, Jack Larson, Nicholas Ray. **VHS, Beta** *NO ✍✍*

James Joyce: A Portrait of the Artist as a Young Man A moving, lyrical adaptation of the author's autobiography, told through the character of Stephen Dedalus. Joyce's characterizations, words, and scenes are beautifully translated to the medium of film. Excellent casting.
1977 93m/C John Gielgud, T.P. McKenna, Bosco Hogan. **VHS** *$29.95 MFV ✍✍✍*

James Joyce's Women Adapted from her one-woman stage show as well as produced by Flanagan, this acclaimed film features enacted portraits of three real-life Joyce associates, including his wife (Nora Barnacle) and three of his famous characters.
1985 (R) 91m/C Fionnula Flanagan, Timothy E. O'Grady, Chris O'Neill; *D:* Michael Pearce; *W:* Fionnula Flanagan. **VHS, Beta** *$69.95 MCA ✍✍✍*

James Stewart: A Wonderful Life Tribute to the popular, slow-talking actor is highlighted by interviews and visits to the sets of some of Stewart's most popular films.
1987 88m/C **VHS, Beta** *$19.98 MGM, FCT, BTV ✍✍✍*

Jamon, Jamon Comedic melodrama satirizing various aspects of the Spanish character, including machismo, sex, and food. A small Spanish town is dominated by two businesses—an underwear factory and a brothel—both run by strong-minded women. The brothel's Carmen and the factory's Conchita clash when Carmen's daughter, Silvia, becomes pregnant by Conchita's son, Manuel. Conchita's appalled and hires stud Raul to seduce Silvia—only to fall for him herself. Oh yes, Raul attributes his sexual prowess to a steady diet of ham and garlic. In Spanish with English subtitles. *AKA:* Ham Ham.
1993 95m/C Penelope Cruz, Anna Galiena, Javier Bardem, Stefania Sandrelli, Juan Diego, Jordi Molla; *D:* Bigas Luna; *W:* Bigas Luna, Cuca Canals; *M:* Nicola Piovani. **VHS** *ACA ✍✍*

Jane & the Lost City A British farce based on the age-old, barely dressed comic-strip character, Jane, as she stumbles on ancient cities, treasures, villains, and blond/blue-eyed heroes. Low-budget camp fun.
1987 (PG) 94m/C Kristen Hughes, Maud Adams, Sam Jones; *D:* Terry Marcel; *W:* Mervyn Haisman; *M:* Harry Robertson. **VHS, Beta** *$14.95 NWV, STE ✍✍½*

Jane Austen in Manhattan Two acting-teachers vie to stage a long-lost play written by a youthful Jane Austen. Dreary, despite the cast. Hodiak is the real-life daughter of Baxter.
1980 108m/C Anne Baxter, Robert Powell, Michael Wager, Sean Young, Kurt Johnson, Katrina Hodiak; *D:* James Ivory; *W:* Ruth Prawer Jhabvala. **VHS, Beta** *$59.95 NLC ✍½*

Jane Doe Valentine plays a young amnesia victim who is linked to a series of brutal slayings. Quite suspenseful for a television movie.
1983 100m/C Karen Valentine, William Devane, Eva Marie Saint, Stephen E. Miller, Jackson Davies; *D:* Ivan Nagy. **VHS, Beta** *$39.95 LIV ✍✍½*

Jane Eyre Stiff, early version of Charlotte Bronte's classic gothic romance. English orphan grows up to become the governess of a mysterious manor. Notable as the first talkie version. Remade several times.
1934 67m/B Virginia Bruce, Colin Clive, Beryl Mercer, Jameson Thomas, Aileen Pringle, David Torrence; *D:* Christy Cabanne. **VHS** *$16.95 SNC ✍✍*

Jane Eyre Excellent adaptation of the Charlotte Bronte novel about the plain governess with the noble heart and her love for the mysterious and tragic Mr. Rochester. Fontaine has the proper backbone and yearning in the title role but to accommodate Welles' emerging popularity the role of Rochester was enlarged. Excellent bleak romantic-Gothic look. Taylor, in her third film role, is seen briefly in the early orphanage scenes.
1944 97m/B Joan Fontaine, Orson Welles, Margaret O'Brien, Peggy Ann Garner, John Sutton, Sara Allgood, Henry Daniell, Agnes Moorehead, Aubrey Mather, Edith Barrett, Barbara Everest, Hillary Brooke, Elizabeth Taylor; *D:* Robert Stevenson; *W:* John Houseman, Aldous Huxley, Robert Stevenson; *M:* Bernard Herrmann. **VHS** *$19.98 FXV, FCT, BTV ✍✍✍*

Jane Eyre A made-for-British-television mini-series based on the famed Charlotte Bronte novel about the maturation of a homeless English waif, her love for the tormented Rochester, and her quest for permanent peace.
1983 239m/C Timothy Dalton, Zelah Clarke; *D:* Julian Aymes. **VHS, Beta** *$29.98 PBS, FOX, SIG ✍✍✍*

Janis: A Film The famous biographical film about Janis Joplin, from her Texas origins to Woodstock and superstardom, featuring performances with Big Brother and the Holding Company and rare interviews.
1974 (R) 79m/C *D:* Howard Alk. **VHS, Beta** *$19.95 MVD, MCA, FCT ✍✍½*

The January Man An unorthodox cop, previously exiled by a corrupt local government to the fire department, is brought back to the force in New York City to track down a serial killer. Written by the "Moonstruck" guy, Shanley, who apparently peaked with the earlier movie.
1989 (R) 97m/C Kevin Kline, Susan Sarandon, Mary Elizabeth Mastrantonio, Harvey Keitel, Rod Steiger, Alan Rickman, Danny Aiello; *D:* Pat O'Connor; *W:* John Patrick Shanley; *M:* Marvin Hamlisch. **VHS, Beta** *$19.98 MGM, FXV ✍✍*

Japanese Connection Warring crime chiefs fight furiously with deadly kung-fu action until end of movie.
1982 96m/C Li Chao, Yang Wei, Wu Ming-Tsai. **VHS, Beta** *$59.95 GEM ✍*

The Jar A recluse discovers a disgusting creature in a jar. He keeps it, only to discover that it is out to kill him.
1984 90m/C Gary Wallace, Karen Sjoberg; *D:* Bruce Toscano. **VHS, Beta** *NO ✍*

Jason and the Argonauts Jason, son of King of Thessaly, sails on the Argo to the land of Colchis, where the Golden Fleece is guarded by a seven-headed hydra. Superb special effects and multitudes of mythological creatures; fun for the whole family.
1963 (G) 104m/C Todd Armstrong, Nancy Kovack, Gary Raymond, Laurence Naismith, Nigel Green, Michael Gwynn, Honor Blackman; *D:* Don Chaffey; *W:* Jan Read, Beverly Cross. **VHS, Beta, 8mm** *$14.95 COL, MLB, FUS ✍✍✍*

Jason Goes to Hell: The Final Friday The supposed last, at least so far, in the "Friday the 13th" gore series. Only through the bodies—dead or alive—of his

Vorhees kin can supernatural killer Jason be reborn, and only at their hands can he truly die. One can only hope that this is finally true. An unrated, even gorier, version is also available.
1993 (R) 89m/C Kane Hodder, John D. LeMay, Kari Keegan, Steven Williams, Steven Culp, Erin Gray, Richard Gant, Leslie Jordan, Billy Green Bush, Rusty Schwimmer; *D:* Adam Marcus; *W:* Dean Lorey, Jay Huguely-Cass; *M:* Harry Manfredini. **VHS** *NLC, IME Woof!*

Java Head Young Chinese wife commits suicide so her husband can marry an English girl. Set in mid-1800s England. Based on the novel by Joseph Hergesheimer.
1935 70m/B Anna May Wong, Elizabeth Allan, John Loder, Edmund Gwenn, Ralph Richardson, George Curzan; *D:* J. Walter Ruben. **VHS, Beta, 8mm** *$24.95 VYY ✍✍✍*

Jaws Early directorial effort by Spielberg from the Peter Benchley potboiler. A tight, very scary, and sometimes hilarious film about the struggle to kill a giant great white shark that is terrorizing an eastern beach community's waters. The characterizations by Dreyfuss, Scheider, and Shaw are much more endurable than the shock effects. Memorable score. Sequelled by "Jaws 2" in 1978, "Jaws 3" 1983, and "Jaws the Revenge" in 1987. Look for Benchley as a TV reporter.
1975 (PG) 124m/C Roy Scheider, Robert Shaw, Richard Dreyfuss, Lorraine Gary, Murray Hamilton, Carl Gottlieb; *Cameos:* Peter Benchley; *D:* Steven Spielberg; *W:* Carl Gottlieb, Peter Benchley; *M:* John Williams. Academy Awards '75: Best Film Editing, Best Sound, Best Original Score; Nominations: Best Picture; Golden Globe Awards '76: Best Score; People's Choice Awards '76: Best Film. **VHS, Beta** *$19.95 MCA ✍✍✍½*

Jaws 2 Unsatisfactory sequel to "Jaws." It's been four years since the man-eating shark feasted on the resort town of Amity; suddenly a second shark stalks the waters and the terror returns. Scheider—who must by now wonder at his tendancy to attract large aquatic carnivores with lunch on their minds—battles without his compatriots from the original. And we haven't seen the last of the mechanical dorsal fin yet; two more sequels follow.
1978 (PG) 116m/C Roy Scheider, Lorraine Gary, Murray Hamilton; *D:* Jeannot Szwarc; *W:* Carl Gottlieb; *M:* John Williams. **VHS, Beta** *$19.95 MCA ✍✍½*

Jaws 3 Same monster, new setting: in a Sea World-type amusement park, a great white shark escapes from its tank and proceeds to cause terror and chaos. Little connection to the previous "Jaws" sagas. Followed by one more sequel, "Jaws: The Revenge." *AKA:* Jaws 3-D.
1983 (PG) 98m/C Dennis Quaid, Bess Armstrong, Louis Gossett Jr., Simon MacCorkindale, Lea Thompson; *D:* Joe Alves; *W:* Richard Matheson, Carl Gottlieb; *M:* John Williams. **VHS, Beta** *$19.95 MCA ✍✍*

Jaws of Death "Jaws"-like saga of shark terror. Jaeckel illogically strikes out to protect his "friends," the sharks. *AKA:* Mako: The Jaws of Death.
1976 91m/C Richard Jaeckel, Harold Sakata, Jennifer Bishop, John Chandler, Buffy Dee; *D:* William Grefe. **VHS, Beta** *NO ✍✍*

Jaws of Justice A Canadian Mountie and his trusty German shepherd track down outlaws in the Canadian Northwest.
1933 55m/B Kazan the Dog, Richard Terry, Lafe McKee. **VHS, Beta, 8mm** *$19.95 VYY ✍½*

Jaws of Satan Weaver is terrorized by a slimy snake who is, in actuality, the Devil. Not released for 2 years after it was filmed, and generally considered a bomb of the first caliber. Unfortunate work for usually worthwhile Weaver. *AKA:* King Cobra.
1981 (R) 92m/C Fritz Weaver, Gretchen Corbett, Jon Korkes, Norman Lloyd, Christina Applegate; *D:* Bob Claver. **VHS** *NO Woof!*

Jaws: The Revenge The third sequel, in which Mrs. Brody is pursued the world over by a seemingly personally motivated Great White Shark. Includes footage not seen in the theatrical release. Each sequel in this series is progressively inferior to the original.
1987 (PG-13) 87m/C Lorraine Gary, Lance Guest, Karen Young, Mario Van Peebles, Michael Caine, Judith Barsi, Lynn Whitfield; *D:* Joseph Sargent. **VHS, Beta $19.95** *MCA ℤ*

The Jayhawkers Chandler and Parker battle for power and women in pre-Civil War Kansas.
1959 100m/C Jeff Chandler, Fess Parker, Nicole Maurey, Henry Silva, Herbert Rudley, Frank De Kova, Don Megowan, Leo Gordon; *D:* Melvin Frank. **VHS $14.95** *PAR, FCT ℤℤ*

The Jayne Mansfield Story Television movie recounting the blond bombshell's career from her first career exposure, through her marriage to a bodybuilder, to the famous car crash that beheaded her. *AKA:* Jayne Mansfield: A Symbol of the '50s.
1980 97m/C Loni Anderson, Arnold Schwarzenegger, Raymond Buktenica, Kathleen Lloyd, G.D. Spradlin, Dave Shelley; *D:* Dick Lowry. **VHS, Beta $39.95** *LIV ℤ*

Jazz Singer A Jewish cantor's son breaks with his family to become a singer of popular music. Of historical importance as the first successful part-talkie; a very early Loy performance. With the classic line "You ain't heard nothing yet!" Remade several times. ♫Toot, Toot, Tootsie Goodbye; Blue Skies; My Gal Sal; Waiting for the Robert E. Lee; Dirty Hands, Dirty Face; Mother, I Still Have You; Kol Nidre; Yahrzeit; My Mammy.
1927 89m/B Al Jolson, May McAvoy, Warner Oland, William Demarest, Eugenie Besserer, Myrna Loy; *D:* Alan Crosland. **VHS, Beta $29.98** *FOX, FCT, MLB ℤℤ½*

Jazz Singer Flat and uninteresting (if not unintentionally funny) remake of the 1927 classic about a Jewish boy who rebels against his father and family tradition to become a popular entertainer. Stick with the original, this is little more than a vehicle for Diamond to sing. ♫America; You Baby Baby; Jerusalem; Love on the Rocks; Summer Love; On the Robert E. Lee; Louise; Songs of Life; Hello Again.
1980 (PG) 115m/C Neil Diamond, Laurence Olivier, Lucie Arnaz, Catlin Adams, Franklin Ajaye; *D:* Richard Fleischer. **VHS, Beta, 8mm $14.98** *REP, PAR Woof!*

Jazzman A comedy set in the late 1920s with a young musician forming a jazz band with two street musicians and a saxophonist who played in the czar's marching band. Their music is condemned as a product of bourgeois society but that doesn't stop them. In Russian with English subtitles.
1984 80m/C Igor Sklyar, Alexander Chorny; *D:* Karen Chakhnazarov. **VHS $59.95** *KIV, FCT ℤℤℤ*

J.D.'s Revenge Attorney in training Glynn Turman is possessed by the spirit of a gangster who was murdered on Bourbon Street in the early 1940s and grisly blaxploitation results. Ever so slightly better than others of the genre. Shot in New Orleans, with a soundtrack by a then-unknown Prince.
1976 (R) 95m/C Louis Gossett Jr., Glynn Turman; *D:* Arthur Marks; *M:* Prince. **VHS $59.98** *ORI, FCT ℤℤ½*

Je Tu Il Elle A hyperactive young woman desperately seeking the answers to life gradually gains experience and maturity as she travels around France. The directorial debut of Ackerman. In French with English subtitles. *AKA:* I You She He.
1974 90m/B Niels Arestrup, Claire Wauthion, Chantal Akerman; *D:* Chantal Akerman. **VHS $29.95** *WAC, FCT, ING ℤℤ½*

Jealousy Three dramatic episodes dealing with jealousy. Made for TV.
1984 95m/C Angie Dickinson, Paul Michael Glaser, David Carradine, Bo Svenson; *D:* Jeffrey Bloom. **VHS, Beta $79.95** *IMP ℤℤ½*

Jean de Florette The first of two films (with "Manon of the Spring") based on Marcel Pagnol's novel. A single spring in drought-ridden Provence, France is blocked by two scheming countrymen (Montand and Auteuil). They await the imminent failure of the farm nearby, inherited by a city-born hunchback, whose chances for survival fade without water for his crops. A devastating story with a heartrending performance by Depardieu as the hunchback. Lauded and awarded; in French with English subtitles.
1987 (PG) 122m/C Gerard Depardieu, Yves Montand, Daniel Auteuil, Elisabeth Depardieu, Ernestine Mazurowna; *D:* Claude Berri; *W:* Gerard Brach, Claude Berri. **VHS, Beta $19.98** *ORI, IME, FCT ℤℤℤ½*

Jeeves & Wooster: Jeeves' Arrival Based on P.G. Wodehouse's spoofs of upper-crust British life in the 1920s. The bungling Bertie Wooster, a young man who just can't stay out of trouble, is taken in hand by the unflappable "gentleman's gentleman," Jeeves. Wonderful period detail and fine acting add up to a charming and funny hour. Additional episodes available.
1991 60m/C Hugh Laurie, Stephen Fry. **VHS $9.95** *MOV, TVC, PBS ℤℤℤ½*

Jekyll & Hyde...Together Again New Wave comic version of the classic story. This time, a serious young surgeon turns into a drug-crazed punk rocker after sniffing a mysterious powder. Mad scientist Blankfield fires and misfires, occasionally eliciting a snort.
1982 (R) 87m/C Mark Blankfield, Bess Armstrong, Krista Errickson, Tim Thomerson; *D:* Jerry Belson; *W:* Monica Johnson, Michael Leeson, Harvey Miller, Jerry Belson. **VHS, Beta $59.95** *PAR ℤℤ*

Jennifer Elaboration of that old "Carrie" theme: a teen-age girl outcast who likes snakes wreaks havoc on her catty classmates in this supernatural thriller. *AKA:* Jennifer (The Snake Goddess).
1978 (PG) 90m/C Lisa Pelikan, Bert Convy, Nina Foch, John Gavin, Wesley Eure; *D:* Brice Mack. **VHS, Beta $69.98** *LIV, VES ℤ½*

Jennifer 8 Mix of familiar genres results in a film about a burned-out cop moving to the suburbs where he finds the eighth victim of a serial killer and falls in love with the chief witness. Garcia is John Berlin, the cop who discovers the hand of the blind female victim, which leads him to her school and Helena Robertson (Thurman), another blind woman who may have the information he needs. Dark and mysterious atmosphere is dramatic, but plot lacks logic and sense of thrill.
1992 (R) 127m/C Andy Garcia, Uma Thurman, Lance Henriksen, Kathy Baker, Graham Beckel, Kevin Conway, John Malkovich; *D:* Bruce Robinson; *W:* Bruce Robinson. **VHS, Beta $19.95** *PAR, BTV ℤℤ*

Jenny A loveless marriage of convenience between a draft-dodger and a film buff gets turned around as they fall in love despite themselves.
1970 (PG) 90m/C Marlo Thomas, Alan Alda, Marian Hailey, Elizabeth Wilson, Vincent Gardenia, Charlotte Rae; *D:* Edgar J. Scherick. **VHS, Beta $59.98** *FOX ℤ*

Jenny Lamour A dark mystery thriller about a singer accused of murdering a man he thought was stealing his woman. Acclaimed genre piece, dubbed into English. *AKA:* Quai des Orfevres.
1947 95m/B Louis Jouvet, Suzy Delair, Bernard Blier, Simone Renant; *D:* Henri-Georges Clouzot. **VHS, Beta $24.95** *NOS, FCT ℤ*

Jenny's War An unbelievable WWII adventure story of an American teacher (Cannon) who outwits the Gestapo and infiltrates a Nazi POW camp in search of her missing soldier son. Actually based on a true story. From the book by Jack Stoneley. Made for television.
1985 (PG) 192m/C Dyan Cannon, Elke Sommer, Robert Hardy, Nigel Hawthorne, Christopher Cazenove, Patrick Ryecart, Hartmut Becker; *D:* Steven Gethers; *W:* Steven Gethers. **VHS $59.95** *COL ℤℤ½*

Jeremiah Johnson The story of a man who turns his back on civilization, circa 1850, and learns a new code of survival in a brutal land of isolated mountains and hostile Indians. In the process, he becomes part of the mountains and their wildlife. A notable and picturesque film.
1972 (PG) 107m/C Robert Redford, Will Geer; *D:* Sydney Pollack; *W:* Edward Anhalt, John Milius. **VHS, Beta $19.98** *WAR, FCT ℤℤℤ*

Jericho Adventures in Africa occur as a court-martialed captain pursues a murderous deserter. *AKA:* Dark Sands.
1938 77m/B Paul Robeson, Henry Wilcoxon, Wallace Ford; *D:* Thornton Freeland. **VHS, Beta $44.95** *NOS, HHT, DVT ℤ*

Jericho Fever A group of terrorists assassinate Palestinian and Israeli negotiators engaged in peace talks in Mexico. Infected with a deadly disease they also escape to the U.S., tracked by Israeli Mossad agents, a border patrolman, and two investigators from the Centers for Disease Control who want to stop the spread of the plague.
1993 (PG-13) 88m/C Stephanie Zimbalist, Perry King, Branscombe Richmond, Alan Scarfe, Elyssa Davalos, Ari Barak; *D:* Sandor Stern; *W:* I.C. Rapoport; *M:* Cameron Allan. **VHS, Beta** *PAR ℤℤ½*

The Jericho Mile A made-for-television drama about a track-obsessed convicted murderer who is given a chance at the Olympics.
1979 97m/C Peter Strauss, Roger E. Mosley, Brian Dennehy; *D:* Michael Mann. **VHS, Beta $9.98** *NLC, SUE ℤℤ*

The Jerk A jerk tells his rags-to-riches-to-rags story in comedic flashbacks, from "I was born a poor Black child," through his entrepreneurial success in his invention of the "Optigrab," to his inevitable decline. Only film in history with a dog named "Shithead." Martin's first starring role, back in his wild and crazy days; his ridiculous misadventures pay tribute to Jerry Lewis movies of the late sixties. Followed by a TV version released in 1984 as "The Jerk Too," with Mark Blankfield as the Jerk.
1979 (R) 94m/C Steve Martin, Bernadette Peters, Catlin Adams, Bill Macy, Jackie Mason; *D:* Carl Reiner; *W:* Steve Martin, Carl Gottlieb. **VHS, Beta $14.95** *MCA ℤℤ½*

Jersey Girl Toby Mastellone (Gertz) is a bright single gal from the Jersey shore who wants something better in her life. Her hard-working dad (Bologna) has fixed her up with an apprentice plumber but she wants a Manhattan guy. And then Toby meets cute with Sal (McDemott), who seems just the ticket, but can you really take the Jersey out of the girl?
1992 (PG-13) 95m/C Jami Gertz, Dylan McDermott, Joseph Bologna, Aida Turturro, Star Jasper, Sheryl Lee, Joseph Mazzello, Molly Price; **D:** David Burton Morris; **W:** Gina Wendkos. **VHS** COL *⅟₂*

Jesse A heroic nurse ministers to remote Death Valley residents, and state bureaucats hound her for practicing medicine without a license. Although based on a true case and well-acted, this made-for-TV drama just lacks import and impact.
1988 (PG) 94m/C Lee Remick, Scott Wilson, Leon Rippy, Priscilla Lopez, Albert Salmi; **D:** Glenn Jordan. **VHS $79.98** REP *⅟₂*

Jesse James A Hollywood biography of the famed outlaw. One of director King's best efforts.
1939 105m/C Henry Fonda, Tyrone Power, Randolph Scott, Henry Hull, Jane Darwell, Brian Donlevy, Charles Halton; **D:** Henry King. **VHS, Beta $19.98** FOX *⅟₂⅟₂⅟₂*

Jesse James at Bay Rodgers is the do-good Jesse who's warring against some crooked railroad execs. Interesting perspective.
1941 54m/B Roy Rogers, George "Gabby" Hayes, Sally Payne; **D:** Joseph Kane. **VHS, Beta $19.95** NOS, MRV, VCN *⅟₂⅟₂*

Jesse James Meets Frankenstein's Daughter The gunslinger and Frankenstein's granddaughter, Maria, meet up in the Old West in this wacky combination of western and horror genres.
1965 95m/C John Lupton, Cal Bolder, Narda Onyx, Steve Geray, Estelita, Jim Davis, William Fawcett, Nestor Paiva; **D:** William Beaudine. **VHS, Beta $19.98** NOS, SUE *⅟₂*

Jesse James Rides Again Originally a serial, this feature depicts the further adventures of the West's most notorious outlaw.
1947 181m/B Clayton Moore, Linda Stirling, Roy Barcroft, Tristram Coffin; **D:** Fred Brannon, Thomas Carr. **VHS $29.98** REP, MLB *⅟₂*

Jesse James Under the Black Flag An interesting western/pseudo biography/flashback in which Coates and James Jr. (the outlaw's son) play themselves. As Coates attempts to gather information from Jesse's decendants, a stranger appears and falls for Jesse's granddaughter, who shuns him. He proceeds to read the Coates biography and the flashback begins, in the Jesse was really a good guy forced off the straight and narrow vein.
1921 59m/B Jesse James Jr., Franklin Coates, Diana Reed, Marguerite Hungerford; **D:** Franklin Coates. **VHS, Beta $24.95** GPV, FCT *⅟₂⅟₂*

The Jesse Owens Story The moving story of the four-time Olympic Gold medal winner's triumphs and misfortunes. A made-for-television movie.
1984 174m/C Dorian Harewood, Debbi Morgan, Georg Stanford Brown, LeVar Burton, George Kennedy, Tom Bosley, Ben Vereen; **D:** Richard Irving. **VHS, Beta $29.95** PAR, FCT *⅟₂*

Jessie's Girls In retaliation for the murder of her husband, an angry young woman frees three female prisoners, and they embark on a bloody course of revenge. Together, they track down the killers, and one by one, they fight to even the score. **AKA:** Wanted Women.
1975 (R) 86m/C Sondra Currie, Regina Carrol, Jennifer Bishop; **D:** Al Adamson. **VHS, Beta $39.95** MON *⅟₂⅟₂*

Jesus A supposedly authenticated life of Christ, using real artifacts.
1979 (G) 118m/C Brian Deacon; **D:** Peter Sykes, John Kirsh. **VHS** VBL *⅟₂*

Jesus Christ, Superstar A rock opera that portrays, in music, the last seven days in the earthly life of Christ, as reenacted by young tourists in Israel. Outstanding musical score was the key to the success of the film. Based on the stage play by Tim Rice and Andrew Lloyd Weber, film is sometimes stirring while exhibiting the usual heavy-handed Jewison approach. ♫Jesus Christ, Superstar; I Don't Know How To Love Him; What's The Buzz?; Herod's Song; Heaven On Their Minds; Strange Thing, Mystifying; Then We Are Decided; Everything's Alright; This Jesus Must Die.
1973 (G) 108m/C Ted Neeley, Carl Anderson, Yvonne Elliman, Josh Mostel; **D:** Norman Jewison. **VHS, Beta $19.98** MCA *⅟₂⅟₂⅟₂*

Jesus of Montreal A vagrant young actor (stage-trained Canadian star Bluteau) is hired by a Montreal priest to produce a fresh interpretation of an Easter passion play. Taking the good book at its word, he produces a contemporized literal telling that captivates audiences, inflames the men of the cloth, and eventually wins the players' faith. Quebecois director Arcand (keep an eye out for him as the judge) tells a compelling, acerbically satirical and haunting story that never forces its Biblical parallels. In French with English subtitles. **AKA:** Jesus de Montreal.
1989 (R) 119m/C Gilles Pelletier, Lothaire Bluteau, Catherine Wilkening, Robert Lepage, Johanne-Marie Tremblay, Remy Girard, Marie-Christine Barrault; **D:** Denys Arcand; **W:** Denys Arcand. Academy Awards '89 Nominations: Best Foreign Language Film; Genie Awards '90: Best Actor (Arcand), Best Director (Arcand), Best Film, Best Supporting Actor (Girard). **VHS $19.98** ORI, FCT, ING *⅟₂⅟₂⅟₂⅟₂*

Jesus of Nazareth A dramatic recreation of the life of Christ from the Annunciation through the Ascension. The film titles are taken from descriptive biblical passages.
1928 85m/B Philip Van Loan, Anna Lehr, Charles McCaffrey. **VHS, Beta, 8mm $24.95** VYY, FCT *⅟₂⅟₂*

Jesus of Nazareth An all-star cast vividly portrays the life of Christ in this made-for-television mini-series. Wonderfully directed and sensitively acted. On three cassettes.
1977 371m/C Robert Powell, Anne Bancroft, Ernest Borgnine, Claudia Cardinale, James Mason, Laurence Olivier, Anthony Quinn; **D:** Franco Zeffirelli; **M:** Maurice Jarre. **VHS, Beta $69.98** LIV, FOX, ECU *⅟₂⅟₂*

The Jesus Trip Hunted motorcyclists take a young nun hostage in the desert.
1971 86m/C Robert Porter, Tippy Walker; **D:** Russ Mayberry. **VHS, Beta $57.95** UNI *⅟₂*

Jet Attack/Paratroop Command A double feature of "B" war movies. "Jet Attack" is a bad movie about a scientist whose plane gets shot down over Korea. He amazingly survives, only to be taken to a hospital and brainwashed. Enter a squad of soldiers leading a rescue mission who meet up with a beautiful Russian aide and some life-saving guerilas. This movie is so bad it's funny. In "Paratroop Command," a paratrooper accidentally kills a member of his squadron. In order to regain his dignity, the paratrooper sets off land mines in North Africa to prove himself.
1958 139m/B John Agar, Audrey Totter, Gregory Walcott, James Dobson, Richard Bakalayan, Jack Hogan, Jimmy Murphy, Ken Lynch; **D:** Edward L. Cahn, William Witney. **VHS $14.95** COL *⅟₂⅟₂*

Jet Benny Show A Buck Rogers/Star Wars-style spoof of Jack Benny's classic TV show.
1986 76m/C Steve Norman, Kevin Dees, Polly MacIntyre, Ted Luedemann; **D:** Roger Evans. **VHS, Beta $69.95** NLC *⅟₂⅟₂*

Jet Over the Atlantic Dangerous situation arises as a bomb is discovered aboard a plane en route from Spain to New York.
1959 92m/B Guy Madison, George Raft, Virginia Mayo, Brett Halsey; **D:** Byron Haskin. **VHS, Beta** NO *⅟₂*

Jet Pilot An American Air Force colonel (Wayne) in charge of an Alaskan Air Force base falls in love with a defecting Russian jet pilot (Leigh). They marry, but Wayne suspects Leigh is a spy planted to find out top U.S. secrets. He pretends to defect with her back to Russia to see what he can find out, but they again flee. Ludicrous plot is saved only by spectacular flying scenes, some performed by Chuck Yeager. Although this was filmed in 1950, it took seven more years to be released because producer Hughes couldn't keep his hands off it.
1957 112m/B John Wayne, Janet Leigh, Jay C. Flippen, Paul Fix, Richard Rober, Roland Winters, Hans Conried, Ivan Triesault; **D:** Josef von Sternberg. **VHS $19.98** MCA *⅟₂⅟₂*

The Jetsons Meet the Flintstones Trouble arises when young Elroy Jetson's time machine takes him and his family back to the 25th century B.C. There they meet the Flintstones and the Rubbles, who accidentally get transported into the future. Will either family ever get back home?
1988 100m/C V: Mel Blanc, Daws Butler, Jean VanDerPyl, George O'Hanlon, Penny Singleton. **VHS, Beta $19.95** TTC, IME, WTA *⅟₂⅟₂*

Jetsons: The Movie The famous outer space family of '60s TV is given a new silver-screened life. George gets a promotion that puts him in charge of an asteroid populated by furry creatures. Ecological concerns are expressed; while this is rare for a cartoon, the story is overall typical.
1990 (G) 82m/C D: William Hanna, Joseph Barbera; **M:** John Debney; **V:** George O'Hanlon, Mel Blanc, Penny Singleton, Tiffany, Patric Zimmerman, Don Messick, Jean VanDerPyl, Ronnie Schell, Patti Deutsch, Dana Hill, Russi Taylor, Paul Kreppel, Rick Dees. **VHS, Beta $14.98** MCA, APD, WTA *⅟₂*

The Jewel in the Crown Epic saga of the last years of British rule in India from 1942-1947 concentrating on a controversial love affair between the Indian Hari Kumar and the English Daphne Manners, which profoundly affects the lives of many. Based on "The Raj Quartet" by Paul Scott. Originally shown on British television, it aired in the United States on the PBS series "Masterpiece Theatre." An excellent mini-series that was shown in fourteen segments. Available on eight cassettes.
1984 750m/C Charles Dance, Susan Wooldridge, Art Malik, Tim Pigott-Smith, Geraldine James, Peggy Ashcroft, Judy Parfitt; **D:** Christopher Morahan, Jim O'Brien; **M:** George Fenton. **VHS, Beta $149.95** AAE *⅟₂⅟₂*

J

The Jewel of the Nile Sequel to "Romancing the Stone" with the same cast but new director. Romance novelist Joan thought she found her true love in Jack but finds that life doesn't always end happily ever. After they part ways, Jack realizes that she may be in trouble and endeavors to rescue her from the criminal hands of a charming North African president. Of course, he can always check out this "jewel" at the same time. Chemistry is still there, but the rest of the film isn't quite up to the "Stone's" charm.
1985 (PG) 106m/C Michael Douglas, Kathleen Turner, Danny DeVito, Avner Eisenberg, The Flying Karamazov Brothers, Spiros Focas, Holland Taylor; **D:** Lewis Teague; **W:** Mark Rosenthal, Larry Konner; **M:** Jack Nitzsche. **VHS, Beta** $19.98 *FOX* 🎞🎞

The Jeweller's Shop A highly spiritual tale of two married couples in Poland whose children meet and fall in love much later in Canada. Based on a play by Karol Wojtyla—who later became Pope Jean-Paul II. Adapted under strict Vatican supervision.
1990 90m/C Burt Lancaster, Ben Cross, Olivia Hussey. **VHS** $29.95 *IGP*

Jezebel Davis is a willful Southern belle who loses fiance Fonda through her selfish and spiteful ways in this pre-Civil War drama. When he becomes ill, she realizes her cruelty and rushes to nurse him back to health. Davis' role won her an Oscar for Best Actress, and certainly provided Scarlett O'Hara with a rival for most memorable female character of all time.
1938 105m/B Bette Davis, George Brent, Henry Fonda, Margaret Lindsay, Fay Bainter, Donald Crisp, Spring Byington, Eddie Anderson; **D:** William Wyler. Academy Awards '38: Best Actress (Davis), Best Supporting Actress (Bainter); Nominations: Best Cinematography, Best Picture, Best Score. **VHS, Beta** $19.98 *MGM, FCT, BTV* 🎞🎞🎞½

Jezebel's Kiss A sizzling young beauty returns to the town where she grew up and proceeds to destroy any man she pleases.
1990 (R) 96m/C Meg Foster, Malcolm McDowell, Meredith Baxter Birney, Everett McGill, Katherine Barrese; **D:** Harvey Keith; **W:** Harvey Keith. **VHS** $79.95 *COL* 🎞🎞

JFK Highly controversial examination of President John F. Kennedy's 1963 assassination, from the viewpoint of New Orleans district attorney Jim Garrison. Hotly debated because of Stone's conspiracy theory, it sparked new calls to open the sealed government records from the 1977 House Select Committee on Assassinations investigation. Outstanding performances from all-star principal and supporting casts, stunning cinematography, and excellent editing. Even Garrison himself shows up as Chief Justice Earl Warren. Considered by some to be a cinematic masterpiece, others see it as revisionist history that should be taken with a grain of salt. Extended version adds 17 minutes.
1991 (R) 189m/C Kevin Costner, Sissy Spacek, Kevin Bacon, Tommy Lee Jones, Laurie Metcalf, Gary Oldman, Michael Rooker, Jay O. Sanders, Beata Pozniak, Joe Pesci, Donald Sutherland, John Candy, Jack Lemmon, Walter Matthau, Ed Asner, Vincent D'Onofrio, Sally Kirkland, Brian Doyle-Murray, Wayne Knight, Tony Plana, Tomas Milian, Sean Stone; *Cameos:* Lolita Davidovich, Frank Whaley, Jim Garrison; **D:** Oliver Stone; **W:** Oliver Stone, Zachary Sklar; **M:** John Williams. Academy Awards '91: Best Cinematography, Best Film Editing; Nominations: Best Adapted Screenplay, Best Director (Stone), Best Picture, Best Sound, Best Supporting Actor (Jones), Best Original Score; Golden Globe Awards '92: Best Director (Stone). **VHS, Beta** $24.98 *WAR* 🎞🎞🎞½

The JFK Conspiracy Did Lee Harvey Oswald act alone? Opinions of government officials, eyewitnesses, and director Oliver Stone, in addition to testimony, photographs, documents, and other evidence, address the perennial American question. Includes footage from the House Select Committee on Assassination. Made for television.
1991 98m/C **VHS** $24.98 *BMG, VTR* 🎞🎞🎞½

JFK: Reckless Youth Glossy made for TV docudrama detailing the youthful exploits of Kennedy as both ladies man and emerging leader and comes perilously close to being a tacky soap. Follows the president-to-be from his party-hearty years at prep school, through his naval career (and PT-109 heroics), and his first forays into politics. Excellent portrayal by Dempsey details JFK's chronic ill health, his ambitions, and the family ties that provided both friction and support. Based on the controversial biography by Nigel Hamilton.
1993 182m/C Patrick Dempsey, Terry Kinney, Loren Dean, Diana Scarwid, Yolanda Jilot, Robin Tunney, Andrew Lowery, Stan Cahill, Malachy McCourt, James Rebhorn; **D:** Harry Winer; **W:** William Broyles Jr. **VHS** *CAF* 🎞🎞½

JFK Remembered A look at John F. Kennedy's 1000-day Presidential term, released on the 25th anniversary of his assassination, features interviews, rare film clips, and famous news footage.
1988 54m/C **VHS, Beta** $14.98 *LIV, VES* 🎞🎞½

Jigsaw Crime drama with a smattering of cameos by Hollywood favorites. A newspaper reporter is murdered. The dead man's friend, an assistant district attorney, seeks the punks responsible. They send in a seductress to keep the D.A. busy, but she too is murdered. Action and tension in a well-made flick. Based on a story by John Roeburt. *AKA:* Gun Moll.
1949 70m/B Franchot Tone, Jean Wallace, Myron McCormick, Marc Lawrence, Winifred Lenihan, Betty Harper, Robert Gist; *Cameos:* Marlene Dietrich, Henry Fonda, Burgess Meredith, John Garfield; **D:** Fletcher Markle. **VHS** $16.95 *SNC, DVT, HEG* 🎞🎞🎞

Jigsaw Missing persons lawman is lured into a cover-up more complex than he had bargained for. A tense drama originated as the pilot for a series. *AKA:* Man on the Move.
1971 100m/C James Wainwright, Vera Miles, Richard Kiley, Andrew Duggan, Edmond O'Brien; **D:** William A. Graham. **VHS** *LIV* 🎞🎞

Jigsaw A developer is found dead the day after his wedding. His widow and a cop team up to find out who, what, where, and why. Lukewarm Australian mystery export.
1990 85m/C Rebecca Gibney, Dominic Sweeny, Michael Coard. **VHS** $59.95 *ATL* 🎞🎞

The Jigsaw Man A British-Russian double agent is sent back to England to retrieve a list of Soviet agents which he hid there many years before.
1984 (PG) 90m/C Michael Caine, Laurence Olivier, Susan George, Robert Powell, Charles Gray, David Patrick Kelly, Michael Medwin; **D:** Terence Young. **VHS, Beta** $14.98 *REP, HBO* 🎞🎞

Jigsaw Murders A macho detective is out to solve a grisly murder, but the only available leads are a jigsaw puzzle and the victim's severed, tattooed lower limb.
1989 98m/C Chad Everett, Michelle Johnson, Yaphet Kotto; **D:** Jag Mundhra. **VHS, Beta** $79.95 *MGM* 🎞🎞

Jim Thorpe: All American The life story of Thorpe, a Native American athlete who gained international recognition for his excellence in many different sports. A must for sports fans. *AKA:* Man of Bronze.

1951 105m/B Burt Lancaster, Phyllis Thaxter, Charles Bickford, Steve Cochran, Dick Wesson; **D:** Michael Curtiz. **VHS, Beta** *WAR* 🎞🎞½

Jimmy Hollywood Wanna-be Hollywood actor Pesci has never acted in his life but longs for stardom—which he gets after he accidentally becomes a community vigilante. Burned-out sidekick Slater helps create the videotapes that will bring Jimmy his 15 minutes of fame. Although appropriately desperate, Pesci's role comes off as mostly schtick; two dogs in a row for the usually talented Levinson (after "Toys").
1994 (R) 110m/C Joe Pesci, Christian Slater, Victoria Abril; *Cameos:* Barry Levinson, Rob Weiss; **D:** Barry Levinson; **W:** Barry Levinson; **M:** Robbie Robertson. **VHS** *NYR* 🎞½

Jimmy, the Boy Wonder Goremeister Lewis' attempt at a "family" film turns out just as weird as expected. A young boy goes on a magical trip to find out who stopped time and meets an absent-minded astronomer, the evil Mr. Fig, and then discovers what happens at world's end.
1966 ?m/C **D:** Herschell Gordon Lewis. **VHS** $19.99 *MOV, TPV* 🎞½

Jimmy the Kid A young boy becomes the unlikely target for an improbable gang of would-be crooks on a crazy, "fool-proof" crime caper. Kiddie comic caper.
1982 (PG) 95m/C Gary Coleman, Cleavon Little, Fay Hauser, Ruth Gordon, Dee Wallace Stone, Paul LeMat, Don Adams; **D:** Gary Nelson; **W:** Sam Bobrick. **VHS, Beta** *NO* 🎞🎞

Jinxed Las Vegas nightclub singer tries to convince a gullible blackjack dealer to murder her crooked boyfriend, but the plan backfires when the gangster electrocutes himself while taking a shower. Offscreen cast disputes were probably much more interesting than onscreen comedy.
1982 (R) 104m/C Bette Midler, Ken Wahl, Rip Torn; **D:** Don Siegel; **W:** David Newman, Frank D. Gilroy; **M:** Miles Goodman. **VHS, Beta** $14.95 *MGM* 🎞🎞

The Jitters The murdered dead turn into zombies and seek revenge on their killers.
1988 (R) 80m/C Sal Viviano, Marilyn Tokuda, James Hong, Frank Dietz; **D:** John Fasano. **VHS, Beta** $79.95 *PSM* 🎞

Jive Junction A group of patriotic teenagers convert a barn into a canteen for servicemen and name it "Jive Junction."
1943 62m/B Dickie Moore, Tina Thayer, Gerra Young, Johnny Michaels, Jack Wagner, Jan Wiley, Beverly Boyd, William Halligan; **D:** Edgar G. Ulmer. **VHS, Beta** $24.95 *NOS, GVV* 🎞🎞

Jive Turkey Cool dude busts heads.
1976 ?m/C Paul Harris, Frank De Kova, Serena; **D:** Bill Brame. **VHS** *MOV* 🎞½

Jo Jo Dancer, Your Life is Calling Pryor directed and starred in this semi-autobiographical price-of-fame story of a comic, hospitalized for a drug-related accident, who must re-evaluate his life. A serious departure from Pryor's slapstick comedies that doesn't quite make it as a drama; Pryor nevertheless deserves credit for the honesty he demonstrates in dealing with his real-life problems.
1986 (R) 97m/C Richard Pryor, Debbie Allen, Art Evans, Fay Hauser, Barbara Williams, Paula Kelly, Wings Hauser, Carmen McRae, Diahnne Abbott, Scoey Mitchell, Billy Eckstine, Virginia Capers, Dennis Farina; **D:** Richard Pryor; **W:** Richard Pryor, Rocco Urbisci; **M:** Herbie Hancock. **VHS, Beta** $14.95 *COL* 🎞🎞½

Joan of Arc A touching and devout look at the life of Joan of Arc. Perhaps unfortunately, the film is accurately based on the play by Maxwell Anderson, and adds up to too much talk and too little action.
1948 100m/C Ingrid Bergman, Jose Ferrer, John Ireland, Leif Erickson; **D:** Victor Fleming. Academy Awards '48: Best Color Cinematography; Nominations: Best Actress (Bergman), Best Art Direction/Set Decoration (Color), Best Film Editing, Best Supporting Actor (Ferrer), Best Original Score; National Board of Review Awards '48: 10 Best Films of the Year. **VHS, Beta** $14.98 IGP, HMV *㊙㊙½*

Joan of Paris A French resistance leader dies so that Allied pilots can escape from the Nazis. A well done, but obviously dated propaganda feature.
1942 91m/B Michele Morgan, Paul Henreid, Thomas Mitchell, Laird Cregar, May Robson, Alexander Granach, Alan Ladd; **D:** Robert Stevenson. **VHS, Beta** $19.98 TTC *㊙㊙㊙½*

Jock Petersen A light-hearted story about a blonde hunk who enrolls in college, cavorting and seducing his way to questionable fame and fortune. **AKA:** Petersen.
1974 (R) 97m/C Jack Thompson, Wendy Hughes; **D:** Tim Burstall. **VHS, Beta** $59.98 NLC *㊙*

Jocks A whiz-kid tennis team competes in a pro meet in Las Vegas, and paints the town red.
1987 (R) 90m/C Christopher Lee, Perry Lang, Richard Roundtree, Scott Strader; **D:** Steve Carver. **VHS, Beta** $79.95 COL *㊙½*

Joe An odd friendship grows between a businessman and a blue-collar worker as they search together for the executive's runaway daughter. Thrust into the midst of the counter-culture, they react with an orgy of violence.
1970 (R) 107m/C Peter Boyle, Susan Sarandon, Dennis Patrick; **D:** John G. Avildsen. **VHS, Beta** $14.95 VES *㊙㊙½*

Joe Kidd A land war breaks out in New Mexico between Mexican natives and American land barons. Eastwood, once again portraying the "mysterious stranger," must decide with whom he should side, all the while falling in love with Garcia. Lackluster direction results in a surprisingly tedious western, in spite of the cast. One of Eastwood's lowest money grossers. The laserdisc edition is letterboxed and features chapter stops, the original trailer and digital sound.
1972 (PG) 88m/C Clint Eastwood, Robert Duvall, John Saxon, Don Stroud, Stella Garcia, James Wainwright, Paul Koslo, Gregory Walcott, Dick Van Patten, Lynn Marta; **D:** John Sturges; **W:** Elmore Leonard. **VHS, Beta** $14.95 MCA *㊙㊙½*

The Joe Louis Story The story of Joe Louis' rise to fame as boxing's Heavyweight Champion of the world.
1953 88m/B Coley Wallace, Paul Stewart, Hilda Simms. **VHS, Beta** $19.95 NOS, DVT, FCT *㊙㊙*

Joe Panther Family drama about a young Seminole Indian who stakes his claim in the Anglo world by wrestling alligators. Montalban plays a wise old chieftain who helps the youth handle the conflict between Indian and white societies.
1976 (G) 110m/C Brian Keith, Ricardo Montalban, Alan Feinstein, Cliff Osmond, A. Martinez, Robert Hoffman; **D:** Paul Krasny. **VHS** WAR *㊙㊙㊙*

Joe Versus the Volcano Expressionistic goofball comedy about a dopey guy who, after finding out he has only months to live, contracts with a millionaire to leap into a volcano alive. Imaginative farce with great

"Metropolis"-pastiche visuals that eventually fizzle out. Watch for Ryan in not one, but three roles, and mysterious symbolism throughout. Special effects courtesy of Industrial Light and Magic.
1990 (PG) 106m/C Tom Hanks, Meg Ryan, Lloyd Bridges, Robert Stack, Amanda Plummer, Abe Vigoda, Dan Hedaya, Barry McGovern, Ossie Davis; **D:** John Patrick Shanley; **W:** John Patrick Shanley; **M:** Georges Delerue. **VHS, Beta, 8mm** $19.98 WAR *㊙㊙*

Joe's Bed-Stuy Barbershop: We Cut Heads Lee's first film takes place inside a neighborhood landmark, the corner barbershop. Lee displays the social awareness and urban humor that he honed in his later, bigger films.
1983 60m/C Leon Errol, Morris Carnovsky, Elyse Knox, Billy House, Trudy Marshall; **D:** Spike Lee; **W:** Spike Lee. **VHS, Beta** ICA *㊙*

Joey Daddy, a former doo-wopper, looks back on his years of musical success as a waste of time. His son takes to the world of rock guitar with blind fervor. Their argument plays against the backdrop of the "Royal Doo-Wopp Show" at New York City's Radio Music Hall. Features multi-generational rock songs.
1985 (PG) 90m/C Neill Barry, James Quinn. **VHS, Beta** NO *㊙½*

Joey Breaker Joey (cult-fave Edson) is a hot-shot Manhattan talent agent who's consumed by his job. A series of encounters (romantic and otherwise) expands his outlook, first among them with Cyan (Marley), a young Jamaican waitress. On his journey to possible enlightenment Joey also meets AIDS-stricken Fondren, who helps Joey see another side of life. Quirky with a reggae beat, small pic works large message with sense of humor and sincere performances. Dedicated to Fondren, who died of AIDS in 1992. Marley, daughter of late reggae superstar Bob, shares a tune on the soundtrack with brother Ziggy. Filmed in da Big Apple and St. Lucia, West Indies.
1993 (R) 92m/C Richard Edson, Cedella Marley, Erik King, Gina Gershon, Philip S. Hoffman, Fred Fondren; **D:** Steven Starr; **W:** Steven Starr; **M:** Paul Aston. **VHS, Beta** $92.95 PAR, FCT *㊙㊙㊙*

John and the Missus After the discovery of a copper mine threatens to destroy a nearby town, the Canadian government begins a relocation process. However, one man refuses to give up his generations-old home. Canadian Pinsent's directorial debut, adapting his own 1973 novel.
1987 (PG) 98m/C Gordon Pinsent, Jackie Burroughs, Randy Follet, Jessica Steen; **D:** Gordon Pinsent. **VHS, Beta** NO *㊙½*

John & Yoko: A Love Story Appalling television movie version of the rock legend's life and marriage. With original Beatles tunes.
1985 146m/C Mark McGann, Kim Miyori, Kenneth Price, Peter Capaldi, Richard Morant, Philip Walsh; **D:** Sandor Stern. **VHS, Beta** $79.95 IME *㊙*

John Cleese on How to Irritate People Cleese, a master at causing irritation, demonstrates how to take care of all those annoying people who irritate you, including job interviewers, bank clerks, waiters, and salesmen. Monty Python alumni Palin and Chapman also join Cleese in the "Airline Pilots" sketch about bored pilots deliberately trying to terrify their passengers. **AKA:** How to Irritate People.
1968 65m/C John Cleese, Michael Palin, Graham Chapman, Connie Booth. **VHS** $19.95 WST, FUS *㊙*

John F. Kennedy A retrospective of JFK's term in office.
1981 104m/C **VHS, Beta** $29.95 FOX *㊙*

John Paul Jones Big bio of the Revolutionary War naval hero ("I have not yet begun to fight!") who wins a lot of battles but can't convince Congress to maintain a strong navy at war's end. He's sent to win sea battles for the Empress Catherine the Great of Russia and then spends his last years in France. Great action scenes, otherwise tedious.
1959 126m/C Robert Stack, Charles Coburn, MacDonald Carey, Marisa Pavan, Jean-Pierre Aumont, Peter Cushing, Erin O'Brien, Bruce Cabot, David Farrar, Basil Sydney, John Crawford; **Cameos:** Bette Davis; **D:** John Farrow; **W:** John Farrow, Jesse Lasky Jr.; **M:** Max Steiner. **VHS** $29.99 WAR *㊙㊙½*

John Wayne Anthology: Star Packer/Lawless Range In addition to two of Wayne's films, this program captures 40 years of the actor's career.
1934 156m/B John Wayne; **D:** Robert North Bradbury. **VHS** $9.95 SIM *㊙㊙½*

Johnnie Gibson F.B.I. Supposedly based on a true story, the adventures of a beautiful, black FBI agent who falls in love with a man she's investigating. **AKA:** Johnnie Mae Gibson: FBI.
1987 96m/C Howard E. Rollins Jr., Lynn Whitfield, William Allen Young, Richard Lawson; **D:** Bill Duke; **M:** Billy Goldenberg. **VHS, Beta** $29.95 ACA, PTB *㊙*

Johnny Angel Merchant Marine captain unravels mystery of his father's murder aboard a ship. Tense film noir.
1945 79m/B George Raft, Claire Trevor, Signe Hasso, Lowell Gilmore, Hoagy Carmichael; **D:** Edwin L. Marin. **VHS, Beta** $19.98 RKO, CCB, TTC *㊙㊙㊙*

Johnny Apollo Upright college student Power keeps his nose clean until Dad's sent to jail for playing with numbers. Scheming to free his old man (Arnold) from the big house, he decides crime will pay for the stiff price tag of freedom. Predictable and melodramatic, but well directed.
1940 93m/B Tyrone Power, Dorothy Lamour, Lloyd Nolan, Edward Arnold, Charley Grapewin, Lionel Atwill; **D:** Yves Allegret. **VHS, Beta** $14.98 FOX, FCT *㊙㊙½*

Johnny Appleseed True story of the legendary American who spent his life planting apple trees across the country. Comedy the entire family will enjoy from Shelly Duvall's "Tall Tales and Legends" series. Originally broadcast on cable television.
1986 60m/C Martin Short, Rob Reiner, Molly Ringwald. **VHS** $19.98 FOX *㊙㊙*

Johnny Barrows, El Malo An ex-Vietnam vet battles crime on urban streets. In Spanish.
197? 90m/C Fred Williamson. **VHS, Beta** $57.95 UNI *㊙½*

Johnny Be Good A too-talented high school quarterback is torn between loyalty to his best friend and to his girlfriend amid bribery and schemings by colleges eager to sign him up.
1988 (R) 91m/C Anthony Michael Hall, Robert Downey Jr., Paul Gleason, Uma Thurman, John Pankow, Steve James, Seymour Cassel, Michael Greene, Marshall Bell, Deborah May; **D:** Bud Smith; **M:** Jay Michael Ferguson. **VHS, Beta** $19.98 ORI *㊙*

Johnny Belinda A compassionate physician cares for a young deaf mute woman and her illegitimate child. Tension builds as the baby's father returns to claim the boy.

1948 103m/B Jane Wyman, Lew Ayres, Charles Bickford, Agnes Moorehead; *D:* Jean Negulesco. Academy Awards '48: Best Actress (Wyman); Nominations: Best Actor (Ayres), Best Art Direction/Set Decoration (B & W), Best Black and White Cinematography, Best Director (Negulesco), Best Film Editing, Best Picture, Best Screenplay, Best Sound, Best Supporting Actor (Bickford), Best Supporting Actress (Moorehead), Best Original Score; Golden Globe Awards '49: Best Actress—Drama (Wyman), Best Film—Drama. **VHS, Beta $19.98** *MGM, BTV, CCB* 🎞🎞🎞

Johnny Belinda A television movie adaptation of the Elmer Harris weepie about a small town doctor who befriends an abused deaf girl. Remake of the 1948 film.
1982 95m/C Richard Thomas, Rosanna Arquette, Dennis Quaid, Candy Clark, Roberts Blossom, Fran Ryan; *D:* Anthony Page. **VHS, Beta $59.95** *LIV* 🎞🎞

Johnny Come Lately An elderly editor helps out an ex-newspaperman with a police charge. The two then team up to expose political corruption despite threats from a rival newspaperman. *AKA:* Johnny Vagabond.
1943 97m/B James Cagney, Grace George, Marjorie Main, Marjorie Lord, Hattie McDaniel, Ed McNamara; *D:* William K. Howard. **VHS $19.98** *REP* 🎞🎞½

Johnny Dangerously A gangster spoof about Johnny Dangerously, who turned to crime in order to pay his mother's medical bills. Now, Dangerously wants to go straight, but competitive crooks would rather see him dead than law-abiding and his mother requires more and more expensive operations. Crime pays in comic ways.
1984 (PG-13) 90m/C Michael Keaton, Joe Piscopo, Danny DeVito, Maureen Stapleton, Marilu Henner, Peter Boyle, Griffin Dunne, Glynnis O'Connor, Dom DeLuise, Richard Dimitri, Ray Walston, Dick Butkus, Alan Hale Jr., Bob Eubanks; *D:* Amy Heckerling; *W:* Norman Steinberg. **VHS, Beta $79.98** *FOX* 🎞🎞

Johnny Eager Glossy crime melodrama starring Taylor as an unscrupulous racketeer and Turner as the daughter of D.A. Arnold who falls for him and ends up becoming a pawn in his schemes. Heflin won an Oscar for his outstanding performance as Taylor's alcoholic confidant. Excellent direction by LeRoy makes this a top-rate gangster film. Based on a story by James Edward Grant.
1942 107m/B Robert Taylor, Lana Turner, Edward Arnold, Van Heflin, Robert Sterling, Patricia Dane, Glenda Farrell, Barry Nelson, Henry O'Neill, Charles Dingle, Cy Kendall; *D:* Mervyn LeRoy; *W:* James Edward Grant, John Lee Mahin. **VHS $19.98** *MGM* 🎞🎞🎞

Johnny Firecloud A modern Indian goes on the warpath when the persecution of his people reawakens his sense of identity.
1975 94m/C Victor Mohica, Ralph Meeker, Frank De Kova, Sacheen Little Feather, David Canary, Christina Hart; *D:* William Allen Castleman. **VHS, Beta $49.95** *PSM* 🎞

Johnny Frenchman Rival fishing groups battle it out, complicated by a romance across the water. Featured in the cast are real fishermen and villagers from Cornwall, as well as authentic Free French Resistance fighters from WWII.
1946 104m/B Francoise Rosay, Tom Walls, Patricia Roc, Ralph Michael, Frederick Piper, Pierre Richard, Carroll O'Connor; *D:* Charles Frend. **VHS $19.95** *NOS* 🎞🎞

Johnny Got His Gun Dalton Trumbo's story of a young war veteran who realizes that his arms and legs have been amputated.

1971 (R) 111m/C Timothy Bottoms, Jason Robards Jr., Donald Sutherland, Diane Varsi, Kathy Field; *D:* Dalton Trumbo. **VHS, Beta $59.95** *MED* 🎞🎞

Johnny Guitar Women strap on six-guns in Nicholas Ray's unintentionally hilarious, gender-bending western. A guitar-playing loner wanders into a small town feud between lovelorn saloon owner Crawford and McCambridge, the town's resident lynchmob-leading harpy. This fascinating cult-favorite has had film theorists arguing for decades: is it a parody, a political McCarthy-era allegory, or Freudian exercise? The off-screen battles of the two female stars are equally legendary. Stick around for the end credits to hear Peggy Lee sing the title song.
1953 110m/C Joan Crawford, Ernest Borgnine, Sterling Hayden, Mercedes McCambridge, Scott Brady, Ward Bond, Royal Dano, John Carradine; *D:* Nicholas Ray; *W:* Philip Yordan. **VHS, Beta $14.98** *REP* 🎞🎞🎞½

Johnny Handsome An ugly, deformed hood, after he's been double-crossed and sent to prison, volunteers for a reconstructive surgery experiment and is released with a new face, determined to hunt down the scum that set him up. A terrific modern B-picture based on John Godey's "The Three Worlds of Johnny Handsome."
1989 (R) 96m/C Mickey Rourke, Ellen Barkin, Lance Henriksen, Elizabeth McGovern, Morgan Freeman, Forest Whitaker, Scott Wilson, Blake Clark; *D:* Walter Hill; *W:* Ken Friedman; *M:* Ry Cooder. **VHS, Beta $19.95** *LIV* 🎞🎞🎞

Johnny Nobody A mysterious stranger murders a writer who has been taunting the residents of a quaint Irish town. A sleeper of a thriller, especially in the treatment of the town's reaction to this murder.
1961 88m/B William Bendix, Aldo Ray, Nigel Patrick, Yvonne Mitchell, Cyril Cusack; *D:* Nigel Patrick. **VHS, Beta** *NO* 🎞🎞½

Johnny Reno Laughable western that has U.S. Marshal Andrews trying to save an accused killer from lynching. Of interest for star-watching only. Based on a story by Steve Fisher, A.C. Lyles, and Andrew Craddock.
1966 83m/C Dana Andrews, Jane Russell, Lon Chaney Jr., John Agar, Lyle Bettger, Tom Drake, Richard Arlen, Robert Lowery; *D:* R.G. Springsteen; *W:* Steve Fisher. **VHS $14.95** *PAR* 🎞½

Johnny Shiloh An underage youth becomes a heroic drummer during the Civil War. Originally a two-part Disney television show.
1963 90m/C Kevin Corcoran, Brian Keith, Darryl Hickman, Skip Homeier; *D:* James Neilson. **VHS, Beta $69.95** *DIS* 🎞🎞

Johnny Stecchino A breathless, charming comedy about mistaken identity, with Benigni starring as both Dante, a mild-mannered Roman bus driver, and his double, a notorious Mafioso known as "Johnny Toothpick." Dante happens to meet a lovely woman who takes exceptional interest in him, even inviting her to visit her home in Palermo. The reason she's interested is that Dante is the exact double of her husband, who has ratted on his fellow mobsters and needs a patsy to take the fall. Benigni's expressive body language and sweetness of character is well-showcased. In Italian with English subtitles.
1992 (R) 100m/C Roberto Benigni, Nicoletta Braschi, Paolo Bonacelli, Ignazio Pappalardo, Franco Volpi; *D:* Roberto Benigni; *W:* Roberto Benigni, Vincenzo Cerami; *M:* Evan Lurie. **VHS $94.95** *NLC, IME, FCT* 🎞🎞🎞

Johnny Suede Hip kid with big hair wanders the city seeking an identity via retro black suede elevator shoes. Sleepy surreal comedy walks Pitt through two romantic entanglements and a rendezvous with his own rock idol in his quest for musical talent and pop singer nirvana (not necessarily in that order). Candidate for induction into the David Lynch Movie Museum of the Weird.
1992 (R) 97m/C Brad Pitt, Calvin Levels, Nick Cave, Wilfredo Giovanni Clark, Alison Moir, Peter McRobbie, Tina Louise, Michael Mulheren, Catherine Keener, Samuel L. Jackson; *D:* Tom DiCillo; *W:* Tom DiCillo; *M:* Jim Farmer. **VHS** *PAR* 🎞🎞½

Johnny Tiger A teacher has his hands full when he arrives at the Seminole Reservation in Florida to instruct the Indian children.
1966 100m/C Robert Taylor, Geraldine Brooks, Chad Everett, Brenda Scott; *D:* Paul Wendkos. **VHS, Beta** *REP* 🎞🎞½

Johnny Tremain & the Sons of Liberty The story of the gallant American patriots who participated in the Boston Tea Party.
1958 85m/C Sebastian Cabot, Hal Stalmaster, Luanna Patten, Richard Beymer; *D:* Robert Stevenson. **VHS, Beta $69.95** *DIS* 🎞🎞

Johnny We Hardly Knew Ye Well-made biographical drama recounts John F. Kennedy's first political campaign for local office in Boston in 1946. Made for television.
1977 90m/C Paul Rudd, Kevin Conway, William Prince, Burgess Meredith, Tom Berenger, Brian Dennehy, Kenneth McMillan; *D:* Gilbert Gates. **VHS, Beta** *TLF* 🎞🎞½

A Joke of Destiny, Lying in Wait Around the Corner Like a Bandit A irreverent satire about a Minister of the Interior (Tognazzi, of "La Cage aux Folles" fame) who becomes trapped in his high-tech limousine before a vital press conference. An exaggerated vision of Italian bureaucracy. With English subtitles. *AKA:* A Joke of Destiny.
1984 (PG) 105m/C Ugo Tognazzi, Piera Degli Esposti, Gastone Moschin, Renzo Montagnani, Valeria Golino; *D:* Lina Wertmuller; *W:* Lina Wertmuller. **VHS, Beta $59.95** *LHV, APD* 🎞🎞

Jokes My Folks Never Told Me Series of blackouts and sketches featuring a bevy of beautiful women.
1977 82m/C Sandy Johnson, Mariwin Roberts; *D:* Gerry Woolery. **VHS, Beta $59.98** *SUE* 🎞

The Jolly Paupers A pre-war comedy made in Warsaw about two small-town Jews who try to achieve fame and fortune in the face of setbacks, community quarrels, and insanity. In Yiddish with English subtitles. *AKA:* Freylekhe Kabtsonim.
1938 62m/B Shimon Dzigan, Yisroel Shumacher, Max Bozyk, Menasha Oppenheim; *D:* Zygmund Turkow. **VHS $89.95** *ALD* 🎞🎞½

Jolson Sings Again This sequel to "The Jolson Story" brings back Larry Parks as the ebullient entertainer, with Jolson himself dubbing Parks's voice for the songs. Picking up where the other film ended, the movie chronicles Jolson's comeback in the 1940s and his tireless work with the USO overseas during WWII and the Korean War. ♫After You've Gone; Chinatown, My Chinatown; Give My Regards to Broadway; I Only Have Eyes For You; I'm Just Wild About Harry; You Made Me Love You; I'm Looking Over a Four-Leaf Clover; Is It True What They Say About Dixie?; Ma Blushin' Rose.
1949 96m/C Larry Parks, William Demarest, Barbara Hale, Bill Goodwin; *D:* Henry Levin; *M:* George Duning. **VHS, Beta $19.95** *COL* 🎞🎞

J

The Jolson Story A smash Hollywood bio of Jolson, from his childhood to superstardom. Features dozens of vintage songs from Jolson's parade of hits. Jolson himself dubbed the vocals for Parks, rejuvenating his own career in the process. ♫Swanee; You Made Me Love You; By the Light of the Silvery Moon; I'm Sitting On Top of the World; There's a Rainbow Round My Shoulder; My Mammy; Rock-A-Bye Your Baby With a Dixie Melody; Liza; Waiting for the Robert E. Lee.
1946 128m/C Larry Parks, Evelyn Keyes, William Demarest, Bill Goodwin, Tamara Shayne, John Alexander, Jimmy Lloyd, Ludwig Donath, Scotty Beckett; *D:* Alfred E. Green; *M:* Morris Stoloff. Academy Awards '46: Best Sound, Best Score; Nominations: Best Actor (Parks), Best Color Cinematography, Best Film Editing, Best Supporting Actor (Demarest). **VHS, Beta $19.95** COL 🎬🎬🎬

Jonah Who Will Be 25 in the Year 2000 A group of eight friends, former 60s radicals, try to adjust to growing older and coping with life in the 70s. The eccentric octet include a disillusioned journalist turned gambler, an unorthodox teacher, and a grocery store cashier who gives away food to the elderly. Wonderful performances highlight this social comedy. In French with English subtitles. *AKA:* Jonas—Qui Aura 25 Ans en l'an 2000.
1976 110m/C Jean-Luc Bideau, Myriam Meziere, Miou-Miou, Jacques Denis, Rufus, Dominique Labourier, Roger Jendly, Miriam Boyer, Raymond Bussieres, Jonah; *D:* Alain Tanner; *W:* Alain Tanner. **VHS $79.95** NYF 🎬🎬🎬½

Jonathan Livingston Seagull Based on the best-selling novella by Richard Bach, this film quietly envisions a world of love, understanding, achievement, hope and individuality.
1973 (G) 99m/C James Franciscus, Juliet Mills; *D:* Hall Bartlett; *M:* Neil Diamond. Academy Awards '73 Nominations: Best Cinematography, Best Film Editing; Golden Globe Awards '74: Best Score. **VHS, Beta $29.95** PAR, WSH 🎬🎬½

Joni An inspirational story based on the real life of Tada (playing herself) who was seriously injured in a diving accident, and her conquering of the odds. A born-again feature film based on the book by Tada.
1979 (G) 75m/C Joni Eareckson Tada, Bert Remsen, Katherine De Hetre, Cooper Huckabee; *D:* James F. Collier. **VHS, Beta $59.95** LIV 🎬🎬

Jornada de Muerte An ex-cop is hired to bring an important anti-Mob witness to trial via transcontinental train, and must fend off Mob attack squads in the process. In Spanish.
198? 90m/C Fred Williamson, Bernie Kuby, Heidi Dobbs. **VHS, Beta $49.95** UNI 🎬

Jory A young man's father is killed in a saloon fight, and he must grow up quickly to survive.
1972 (PG) 96m/C Robby Benson, B.J. Thomas, John Marley; *D:* Jorge Fons. **VHS, Beta $9.95** COL, SUE 🎬🎬

Joseph & His Brethren A full-length dramatization of the Old Testament story. *AKA:* The Story of Joseph and His Brethren; Joseph Sold by His Brothers.
1960 103m/C Geoffrey Horne, Robert Morley; *D:* Irving Rapper. **VHS, Beta $49.95** VCI, VGD, KEP 🎬

Joseph Andrews This adaptation of a 1742 Henry Fielding novel chronicles the rise of Joseph Andrews from servant to personal footman (and fancy) of Lady Booby.
1977 (R) 99m/C Ann-Margret, Peter Firth, Jim Dale, Michael Hordern, Beryl Reid; *D:* Tony Richardson; *W:* Chris Bryant, Allan Scott; *M:* John Addison. **VHS, Beta $49.95** PAR 🎬🎬

Josepha A husband and wife, both actors, are forced to re-examine their relationship when the wife finds a new love while on a film location. In French with English subtitles.
1982 (R) 114m/C Miou-Miou, Claude Brasseur, Bruno Cremer; *D:* Christopher Frank. **VHS, Beta $59.95** COL, ING 🎬🎬🎬

The Josephine Baker Story Made-for-cable bio of exotic entertainer/activist Josephine Baker, an Afro-American woman from St. Louis who found superstardom in pre-WWII Europe, but repeated racism and rejection in the U.S. At times trite treatment turns her eventful life into a standard rise-and-fall showbiz tale, but a great cast and lavish scope pull it through. Whitfield recreates Baker's (sometimes topless) dance routines; Carol Dennis dubs her singing. Filmed on location in Budapest.
1990 (R) 129m/C Lynn Whitfield, Ruben Blades, David Dukes, Craig T. Nelson, Louis Gossett Jr., Kene Holliday, Vivian Bonnell; *D:* Brian Gibson; *M:* Ralph Burns. **VHS $19.98** HBO, FCT 🎬🎬🎬

Josh and S.A.M. Road movie for youngsters with a twist: the driver can barely see over the dashboard. Josh and Sam are brothers whose parents are splitting. They cope by taking off on their own. Sam, meanwhile has been convinced by Josh that he's not a real boy at all, but rather a S.A.M.: Strategically Altered Mutant. Weber's directorial debut will appeal to young kids, but adults will see over the dashboard and through the transparent plot.
1993 (PG-13) 97m/C Jacob Tierney, Noah Fleiss, Martha Plimpton, Joan Allen, Christopher Penn, Stephen Tobolowsky, Ronald Guttman; *D:* Billy Weber; *W:* Frank Deese; *M:* Thomas Newman. **VHS** NLC 🎬🎬

Joshua Western drama about a vigilante who tracks down the group of outlaws that killed his mother. *AKA:* Black Rider.
1976 (R) 75m/C Fred Williamson, Isela Vega; *D:* Larry Spangler. **VHS** NO 🎬

Joshua Then and Now When a Jewish-Canadian novelist (Woods) is threatened by the breakup of his marriage to his WASPy wife, compounded by a gay scandal, he re-examines his picaresque history, including his life with his gangster father (Arkin). A stirring story that is enhanced by a strong performance by Woods, as well as a picturesque Canadian backdrop. Adapted by Mordecai Richler from his own novel.
1985 (R) 102m/C James Woods, Gabrielle Lazure, Alan Arkin, Michael Sarrazin, Chuck Shamata, Linda Sorensen, Alan Scarfe, Alexander Knox, Robert Joy, Ken Campbell; *D:* Ted Kotcheff; *W:* Mordecai Richler; *M:* Philippe Sarde. **VHS, Beta $79.98** FOX 🎬🎬🎬

Jour de Fete Tati's first film, dealing with a French postman's accelerated efforts at efficiency after viewing a motivational film of the American post service. Wonderful slapstick moments. In French with English subtitles. *AKA:* The Big Day; Holiday.
1948 79m/B Jacques Tati, Guy Decomble, Paul Fankeur; *D:* Jacques Tati. **VHS, Beta $19.95** VDM, SUE, VYG 🎬🎬🎬½

Journey Violent story of a girl who is rescued from the Sagueney River and falls in love with her rescuer. Choosing to remain in the remote pioneer community of this "hero," she brings everyone bad luck and misery.
1977 (PG) 87m/C Genevieve Bujold, John Vernon; *D:* Paul Almond. **VHS, Beta $54.95** VCI 🎬

Journey Back to Oz Animated special features Dorothy and Toto returning to visit their friends in the magical land of Oz.
1971 90m/C *V:* Liza Minnelli, Ethel Merman, Paul Lynde, Milton Berle, Mickey Rooney, Danny Thomas. **VHS, Beta $14.95** FHE, KAR, HHE 🎬

Journey Beneath the Desert Three engineers discover the lost-but-always-found-in-the-movies kingdom of Atlantis when their helicopter's forced down in the sunny Sahara. A poor hostess with a rotten disposition, the mean sub-saharan queen doesn't roll out the welcome mat for her grounded guests, so a beautiful slave babe helps them make a hasty exit. Dawdling Euro production with adequate visuals. *AKA:* Antinea, l'Amante Della Citta Sepolta.
1961 105m/C Haya Harareet, Jean-Louis Trintignant, Brad Fulton, Amadeo Nazzari, George Riviere, Giulia Rubini, Gabriele Tinti, Gian Marie Volonte; *D:* Edgar G. Ulmer; Giuseppe Masini, Frank Borzage. **VHS, Beta $16.95** SNC 🎬🎬

Journey for Margaret Young and Day star as an expectant American couple living in London during WWII so Young can cover the war for a newspaper back home. After she loses her baby during an air raid, Day heads back to the States. Young stays in London where he meets two young orphans and takes them under his wing. He decides to take them back to the United States and adopt them, but problems arise. A real tearjerker and a good story that shows the war through the eyes of children. O'Brien's first film. Based on the book by William L. White.
1942 81m/B Robert Young, Laraine Day, Fay Bainter, Signe Hasso, Margaret O'Brien, Nigel Bruce, G.P. Huntley Jr., William Severn, Doris Lloyd, Halliwell Hobbes, Jill Esmond; *D:* Woodbridge S. Van Dyke. **VHS $19.98** MGM, FCT 🎬🎬🎬

Journey into Fear During WWII, an American armaments expert is smuggled out of Istanbul, but Axis agents are close behind. From the novel by Eric Ambler; remade for television in 1974.
1942 71m/B Joseph Cotten, Dolores Del Rio, Orson Welles, Agnes Moorehead, Norman Foster; *D:* Norman Foster. **VHS, Beta $19.95** RKO, MED, RXM 🎬🎬🎬

Journey into Fear A remake of the 1942 Orson Welles classic about a geologist ensnared in Turkish intrigue and murder. *AKA:* Burn Out.
1974 96m/C Sam Waterston, Vincent Price, Shelley Winters, Donald Pleasence, Zero Mostel, Yvette Mimieux, Ian McShane; *D:* Daniel Mann. **VHS, Beta $59.98** LIV 🎬½

Journey into the Beyond A brain-incinerating look at the inexplicable world of the supernatural. Includes examinations of voodoo, bare-handed surgery and psychic sex that are guaranteed to fry your soul.
1976 (R) 83m/C **VHS, Beta** FHE 🎬½

Journey of Honor During a civil war in 17th century Japan, a nearly defeated Shogun sends his son, Lord Mayeda, to Spain to buy guns from King Phillip III. Along the way he must fight shipboard spies and fierce storms, and once Mayeda arrives in Spain, he is confronted by the evil Duke Don Pedro. In defeating Don Pedro, Mayeda saves King Phillip, gets his guns, and wins the love of Lady Cecilia. To get revenge, Don Pedro plots to capture the Japanese ship and enslave everyone on board. Lots of action and fine acting. Based on a story by martial artist Sho Kosugi.

1991 (PG-13) 107m/C Sho Kosugi, David Essex, Kane Kosugi, Christopher Lee, Norman Lloyd, Ronald Pickup, John Rhys-Davies, Dylan Kussman, Toshiro Mifune; *D:* Gordon Hessler. **VHS, Beta** MCA ♫♫½

Journey of Hope Powerful drama about Kurdish family that sells its material possessions in hopes of emigrating legally to Switzerland, where life will surely be better. During the perilous journey, smugglers take their money and the family must attempt crossing the formidable slopes of the Swiss Mountains on foot. Based on a true story. In Turkish with English subtitles.
1990 (PG) 111m/C Necmettin Cobanoglu, Nur Surer, Emin Sivas, Yaman Okay, Mathias Gnaedinger, Dietmar Schoenherr; *D:* Xavier Koller; *W:* Xavier Koller. **VHS $19.98** WAR, HBO, ING ♫♫♫½

The Journey of Natty Gann With the help of a wolf (brilliantly portrayed by a dog) and a drifter, a 14-year-old girl travels across the country in search of her father in this warm and touching film. Excellent Disney representation of life during the Great Depression.
1985 (PG) 101m/C Meredith Salenger, John Cusack, Ray Wise, Scatman Crothers, Lainie Kazan, Verna Bloom; *D:* Jeremy Paul Kagan; *W:* Jeanne Rosenberg; *M:* James Horner. **VHS, Beta $29.95** DIS ♫♫♫½

Journey Through Rosebud A re-enactment of the 1970s protest at Wounded Knee by Native Americans.
1972 93m/C Robert Forster, Eddie Little Sky; *D:* Tom Giles. **VHS, Beta $59.98** NLC ♫♫♫½

Journey to Spirit Island A young Native American girl dreams of her ancestors who are buried on Spirit Island, an ancient burial ground. However, the island is now scheduled to be developed into a resort. With the help of three friends the girl tries to protect the land. Filmed in the Pacific Northwest.
1992 (PG) 93m/C Brandon Douglas, Gabriel Damon, Tony Acierto, Nick Ramus, Marie Antoinette Rodgers, Tarek McCarthy; *D:* Laszlo Pal. **VHS $89.95** ACA ♫♫½

Journey to the Center of the Earth A scientist and student undergo a hazardous journey to find the center of the earth and along the way they find the lost city of Atlantis. Based upon the Jules Verne novel.
1959 132m/C James Mason, Pat Boone, Arlene Dahl, Diane Baker, Thayer David; *D:* Henry Levin. **VHS, Beta $19.98** FOX, FCT, FUS ♫♫♫

Journey to the Center of the Earth An animated version of the Jules Verne classic adventure about a scientist's quest to reach the earth's core.
1976 50m/C **VHS, Beta $19.95** MGM, WTA ♫♫♫

Journey to the Center of the Earth A young nanny and two teenage boys discover Atlantis while exploring a volcano.
1988 (PG) 83m/C Nicola Cowper, Paul Carafotes, Ilan Mitchell-Smith; *D:* Rusty Lemorande; *W:* Rusty Lemorande, Kitty Chalmers. **VHS, Beta $79.95** CAN ♫♫♫

Journey to the Center of Time A scientist and his crew are hurled into a time trap when a giant reactor explodes.
1967 83m/C Lyle Waggoner, Scott Brady, Gigi Perreau, Anthony Eisley; *D:* David L. Hewitt. **VHS, Beta $19.95** ACA, GHV ♫½

Journey to the Far Side of the Sun Chaos erupts in the Earth's scientific community when it is discovered that a second, identical Earth is on the other side of the Sun. Both planets end up sending out identical exploratory missions. The denouement is worth the journey. *AKA:* Doppelganger.
1969 (G) 92m/C Roy Thinnes, Ian Hendry, Lynn Loring, Patrick Wymark, Loni von Friedl, Herbert Lom, Ed Bishop; *D:* Robert Parrish. **VHS, Beta $29.95** MCA ♫♫♫

Journey to the Lost City Architect living in India happens upon a lost city, the rulership of which is being contested by two brothers. In the midst of fighting snakes and tigers, he falls in love with Paget, a beautiful dancer. This feature is actually a poorly edited hybrid of two Lang German adventures, "Der Tiger von Eschnapur" and "Das Indische Grabmal" merged for U.S. release. *AKA:* Tiger of Bengal.
1958 95m/C Debra Paget, Paul Christian, Walter Reyer, Claus Holm, Sabine Bethmann, Valeri Inkizhinov, Rene Deltgen, Lucianna Paluzzi; *D:* Fritz Lang. **VHS, Beta $16.95** SNC ♫½

Journeys from Berlin/1971 This is the true story about a woman who tries to find a solution to her own problems in life.
1984 125m/C **VHS, Beta** NO ♫♫½

Joy House An American woman befriends a handsome French playboy when her husband sends gangsters to kill him. *AKA:* The Love Cage; Les Felins.
1964 98m/B Jane Fonda, Alain Delon, Lola Albright; *D:* Rene Clement. **VHS, Beta $39.95** MON ♫♫

The Joy Luck Club Universal themes in mother/daughter relationships are explored in a context Hollywood first rejected as too narrow, but which proved to be a modest sleeper hit. Tan skillfully weaves the plot of her 1989 best-seller into a screenplay which centers around young June's going-away party. Slowly the stories of four Chinese women, who meet weekly to play mahjongg, are unraveled. Each vignette reveals life in China for the four women and the tragedies they survived, before reaching into the present to capture the relationships between the mothers and their daughters. Powerful, relevant, and moving.
1993 (R) 136m/C Tsai Chin, Kieu Chinh, France Nuyen, Rosalind Chao, Tamlyn Tomita, Lisa Lu, Lauren Tom, Ming-Na Wen, Michael Paul Chan, Andrew McCarthy, Christopher Rich, Russell Wong, Victor Wong, Vivian Wu, Jack Ford, Diane Baker; *D:* Wayne Wang; *W:* Amy Tan. **VHS** BVV, HPH ♫♫♫

The Joy of Knowledge Godard's experimental use of language and image in a plotless narrative. Berto and Leaud sit together on a bare sound stage and are exposed to popular culture through images, word association, and conversation. In French with English subtitles. Also known as "Le Gai Savoir."
1965 96m/C Juliet Berto, Jean-Pierre Leaud; *D:* Jean-Luc Godard; *W:* Jean-Luc Godard. **VHS $39.95** FCT ♫½

Joy of Living Vintage screwball farce about a randy playboy trying to win over a pragmatic songstress. ♫You Couldn't Be Cuter; A Heavenly Party; What's Good About Goodnight; Just Let Me Look At You.
1938 90m/B Irene Dunne, Douglas Fairbanks Jr., Alice Brady, Guy Kibbee, Jean Dixon, Eric Blore, Lucille Ball, Warren Hymer, Billy Gilbert, Frank Milan; *D:* Tay Garnett; *M:* Jerome Kern, Dorothy Fields. **VHS, Beta $19.98** RKO, TTC ♫♫♫

Joy of Sex An undercover narcotics agent is sent to Southern California's Richard M. Nixon High School to investigate the school's extracurricular activities. Typical teen sex flick; no relation to the book.

1984 (R) 93m/C Cameron Dye, Michelle Meyrink, Colleen Camp, Christopher Lloyd, Ernie Hudson, Lisa Langlois; *D:* Martha Coolidge; *W:* Kathleen Rowell. **VHS, Beta $79.95** PAR ♫

Joy Ride to Nowhere Two young women steal a Cadillac with two million dollars in the trunk and ride away with the owner hot on their tail.
1978 (PG) 86m/C Leslie Ackerman, Sandy Serrano, Len Lesser, Mel Welles, Ron Ross, Speed Stearns. **VHS, Beta $19.95** CNG ♫

Joy Sticks Joy sticks in question are down at the arcade. Businessman wants to shut down local video game palace. Inhabitants just say no.
1983 (R) 88m/C Joe Don Baker, Leif Green, Jim Greenleaf, Scott McGinnis, Jonathan Gries; *D:* Greydon Clark. **VHS, Beta $79.95** VES Woof!

Joyful Laughter The dreary life of an Italian movie bit player draws strength from Magnani's powerful emotions as she repeatedly comes near to success only to find disappointment. Set in Rome. With English subtitles.
1954 106m/C *D:* Mario Monicelli. **VHS $59.95** FST ♫♫

Joyless Street Silent film focuses on the dismal life of the middle class in Austria during an economic crisis. Lovely piano score accompanies the film.
1925 96m/B Greta Garbo, Werner Krauss, Asta Nielson; *D:* G.W. Pabst. **VHS, Beta $24.95** VYY, MRV, FST ♫♫♫½

Joyride Mistreated by a union official, three friends steal a car for a joy ride and plummet into a life of crime.
1977 (R) 91m/C Desi Arnaz Jr., Robert Carradine, Melanie Griffith, Anne Lockhart; *D:* Joseph Ruben. **VHS, Beta $29.98** LIV, VES ♫½

Ju Dou Breath-taking story of an aging factory owner in search of an heir. He takes a third wife, but she finds caring in the arms of another man, when her husband's brutality proves too much. Beautiful color cinematography, excellent acting and epic story. Oscar nominee for Best Foreign Film. In Chinese with English subtitles.
1990 (PG-13) 98m/C Gong Li, Li Bao-Tian, Li Wei, Zhang Yi, Zheng Jian; *D:* Zhang Yimou. **VHS $19.98** LIV, BTV, ING ♫♫♫♫

Juarez A revolutionary leader overthrows the Mexican government and then becomes President of the country. Based on the true story of Benito Pablo Juarez.
1939 132m/B Paul Muni, John Garfield, Bette Davis, Claude Rains, Gale Sondergaard, Charles Halton; *D:* William Dieterle. **VHS, Beta $19.95** MGM, FCT ♫♫

Jubal A rancher (Borgnine) seeks advice from a cowhand (Ford) about pleasing his wife, but another cowhand (Steiger) implies that Ford is "advising" Borgnine's wife, as well. A western take on "Othello."
1956 101m/C Glenn Ford, Rod Steiger, Ernest Borgnine, Felicia Farr, Charles Bronson, Valerie French, Noah Beery Jr.; *D:* Delmer Daves. **VHS, Beta $9.95** IME ♫♫

Jubilee Adam Ant stars as a punk who takes over Buckingham Palace and turns it into a recording studio. Music by Eno, Adam and the Ants, and Siouxsie and the Banshees.
1978 103m/C Jordan, Toyah Wilcox, Jenny Runacre, Little Nell; *M:* Siouxsie & the Banshees, Wayne County. **VHS, Beta $29.95** MVD, MFV, ING ♫♫

Jubilee Trail Wagon trail western follows the lives of a group of pioneers from New Orleans to California. A woman goes through a marriage, a baby, and her husband's death.

Ralston has some good tunes in this lush picture.

1954 103m/C Vera Ralston, Joan Leslie, Forrest Tucker, John Russell, Ray Middleton, Pat O'Brien; **D:** Joseph Kane. **VHS $14.95** REP ♫♫½

Jud Society's refusal to understand a young soldier returning from the Vietnam conflict leads him to violence and tragedy. Jennings' first film; music by Phillips of Creedence Clearwater Revival.

1971 (PG) 80m/C Joseph Kaufmann, Robert Deman, Alix Wyeth, Norman Burton, Claudia Jennings, Maurice Sherbanee, Vic Dunlop, Bonnie Bittner; **D:** Gunther Collins; **M:** Stu Phillips. **VHS, Beta $49.95** PSM ♫½

Jud Suess Classic, scandalous Nazi anti-Semitic tract about a Jew who rises to power under the duchy of Wuerttemberg by stepping on, abusing, and raping Aryans. A film that caused riots at its screenings and tragedy for its cast and crew, and the Third Reich's most notorious fictional expression of policy. In German with English subtitles.

1940 100m/B Ferdinand Marian, Werner Krauss, Heinrich George, Kristina Soderbaum, Eugene Klopfer; **D:** Veit Harlan. **VHS, Beta $24.95** NOS, VCD, IHF ♫♫♫

Jude the Obscure Thomas Hardy's last novel is a tragic, bleak story of mismatched lovers and blighted ambitions. Jude is a poor stonemason whose dream is to get a proper education and marry his beloved cousin. Failing to get into Oxford he is seduced by a farm girl, whom he marries and fathers a child by (a gnome-like creature named "Father Time"). Meanwhile, his cousin marries a schoolteacher who disgusts her. Finally, the two thwarted lovers marry, only to find themselves living in poverty and hopelessness. After this novel (said to be Hardy's favorite), he devoted the rest of his long life to poetry. On three cassettes.

1971 ?m/C Robert Powell, Daphne Heard, Alex Marshall, John Franklyn-Robbins, Fiona Walker; **D:** Hugh David; **W:** Harry Green. **VHS $89.98** FOX, FCT ♫♫½

Judex Judex, a sensitive cloaked hero-avenger, fights master criminal gangs. In French with English subtitles. Remake of the silent French serial.

1964 103m/B Channing Pollock, Francine Berge, Jacques Jouanneau; **D:** Georges Franju; **M:** Maurice Jarre. **VHS, Beta $24.95** NOS, SNC, HHT ♫♫½

The Judge A courtroom crime-drama about the consequences of infidelity. A lawyer sends an acquitted hit man to kill his wife and her lover. Things go amiss and the lawyer winds up dead.

1949 69m/B Milburn Stone, Katherine DeMille, Paul Guilfoyle, Jonathan Hale; **D:** Elmer Clifton. **VHS $16.95** SNC ♫½

The Judge and the Assassin Intriguing courtroom drama. A prejudiced judge has his values challenged when he must decide if a child-killer is insane or not. The relationship that develops between the judge and the killer is the film's focus. Excellent direction by Tavernier. In French with English subtitles. *AKA:* Le Juge et L'assassin.

1975 130m/C Philippe Noiret, Michel Galabru, Isabelle Huppert, Jean-Claude Brialy; **D:** Bertrand Tavernier; **W:** Bertrand Tavernier. **VHS, Beta $79.95** CVC, IME, ING ♫♫♫½

Judge Horton and the Scottsboro Boys A courtroom drama focusing on a famous 1931 trial. A courageous judge must battle the South in the case of nine black men charged with gang-raping two white women. Made for television.

1976 100m/C Arthur Hill, Vera Miles, Ken Kercheval, Suzanne Lederer, Tom Ligon; **D:** Fielder Cook. **VHS $59.95** LIV ♫♫½

Judge Priest Small-town judge in the old South stirs up the place with stinging humor and common-sense observances as he tangles with prejudices and civil injustices. Funny, warm slice-of-life is occasionally defeated by racist characterizations. Ford remade it later as "The Sun Shines Bright." Taken from the Irvin S. Cobb stories.

1934 80m/B Will Rogers, Stepin Fetchit, Anita Louise, Henry B. Walthall; **D:** John Ford. **VHS, Beta $19.95** NOS, MRV, PSM ♫♫♫

Judge Roy Bean This western series set in Langtry, Texas in 1870 starred Buchanan as the self-appointed "Law West of the Pecos," trying to maintain order in a lawless territory. Two episodes per tape.

1955 55m/B Edgar Buchanan, Jack Beutel, Jackie Loughery. **VHS, Beta $19.99** MOV, MVC ♫♫♫

The Judge Steps Out Pleasant, light comedy about a hen-pecked, Bostonian judge who decides he's had enough and heads for balmy California. There he finds a job in a restaurant and, more importantly, a sympathetic friend in its female owner. He soon finds himself falling for the woman, and realizes he faces an important decision.

1949 91m/B Alexander Knox, Ann Sothern, George Tobias, Sharyn Moffett, Florence Bates, Frieda Inescort, Myrna Dell, Ian Wolfe, H.B. Warner; **D:** Boris Ingster. **VHS $19.95** TTC ♫♫½

Judgment A devout Catholic couple are shocked to learn that their young son has been molested by the popular priest of their small Louisiana parish. When they find out their son is not the first victim, and other families have been coerced into silence, they vow to fight back. Tasteful treatment of a real court case. Made for cable.

1990 (PG-13) 89m/C Keith Carradine, Blythe Danner, Jack Warden, David Strathairn, Bob Gunton, Mitchell Ryan, Michael Faustino; **D:** Tom Topor; **W:** Tom Topor. **VHS $89.98** HBO ♫♫♫

Judgment at Nuremberg It's 1948 and a group of high-level Nazis are on trial for war crimes. Chief Justice Tracy must resist political pressures as he presides over the trials. Excellent performances throughout, especially by Dietrich and Garland. Considers to what extent an individual may be held accountable for actions committed under orders of a superior officer. Consuming account of the Holocaust and WWII; deeply moving and powerful. Based on a "Playhouse 90" television program.

1961 178m/B Spencer Tracy, Burt Lancaster, Richard Widmark, Montgomery Clift, Maximilian Schell, Judy Garland, Marlene Dietrich, William Shatner; **D:** Stanley Kramer; **W:** Abby Mann; **M:** Ernest Gold. Academy Awards '61: Best Actor (Schell), Best Adapted Screenplay; Nominations: Best Actor (Tracy), Best Art Direction/Set Decoration (B & W), Best Black and White Cinematography, Best Costume Design (B & W), Best Director (Kramer), Best Film Editing, Best Picture, Best Supporting Actor (Clift), Best Supporting Actress (Garland); Golden Globe Awards '62: Best Actor—Drama (Schell), Best Director (Kramer); New York Film Critics Awards '61: Best Actor (Schell). **VHS, Beta $29.98** MGM, FOX, BTV ♫♫♫♫

Judgment Day Four college buddies pick the wrong New England town for their vacation. It seems that the town made a deal with the Devil in 1689 to save themselves from the plague, and now the Dark Master is here to collect.

1988 (PG-13) 93m/C Kenneth McLeod, David Anthony Smith, Monte Markham, Gloria Hayes, Peter Mark Richman, Cesar Romero; **D:** Ferde Grofe Jr. **VHS, Beta** NO ♫

Judgment in Berlin East German family hijacks a U.S. airliner into West Germany, and then must stand trial in Berlin before a troubled American judge. Based on a true 1978 incident and the book by Herbert J. Stern. *AKA:* Escape to Freedom.

1988 (PG) 92m/C Martin Sheen, Sam Wanamaker, Max Gail, Sean Penn, Heinz Hoenig, Carl Lumbly, Max Volkert Martens, Harris Yulin, Jutta Speidel, Juerger Hemrich; **D:** Leonard Penn; **W:** Joshua Sinclair; **M:** Peter Goldfoot. **VHS, Beta $29.95** COL ♫♫½

Judgment Night Four macho buddies on their way to a boxing match detour a highway traffic jam via surface streets and find themselves witnesses to a murder. The rest of their guys-night-out is spent trying to escape a gloomy ghetto and determined killer (played convincingly by Leary). All of the action takes place after dark on the streets and in the sewers and, subsequently, the scenes are extremely dark with only a burnt orange lighting. Lots of action and a little oomph. Based on a story by Lewis Colick and Jere Cunningham.

1993 (R) 109m/C Emilio Estevez, Cuba Gooding Jr., Stephen Dorff, Denis Leary, Jeremy Piven, Peter Greene; **D:** Stephen Hopkins; **W:** Lewis Colick; **M:** Alan Silvestri. **VHS $19.98** MCA ♫♫

Judith of Bethulia A young widow uses her charm and wits to save her city from attack by the Assyrians. Based on the Apocrypha, this is the last film Griffith directed for Biograph. It was re-released as "Her Condoned Sin" in 1971, including two reels of Griffith's outtakes.

1914 65m/B Blanche Sweet, Henry B. Walthall, Mae Marsh, Robert Harron, Lillian Gish, Dorothy Gish, Kate Bruce, Harry Carey Sr.; **D:** D.W. Griffith; **W:** D.W. Griffith. **VHS $14.95** GPV, NOS, VYY ♫♫♫

Judy Garland: The Golden Years at MGM Special collector's edition featuring the engaging Judy Garland, this four-disc boxed set contains "The Harvey Girls," "Summer Stock," "The Pirate," and much more. Also includes the film's original theatrical trailers, a career overview of her days at MGM, excerpts, outtakes, stills, and additional rare materials.

19?? 414m/C Judy Garland, Gene Kelly, Ray Bolger, Cyd Charisse. **$124.98** MGM ♫♫♫

Juggernaut Not the classic disaster film of the '70s. A young woman hires a sinister doctor (Karloff) to murder her wealthy husband. The doctor, who happens to be insane, does away with the husband and then goes on a poisoning spree. Seems to drag on forever.

1937 64m/B Boris Karloff, Mona Goya, Arthur Margetson. **VHS, Beta $19.95** NOS, SNC, VYY ♫½

Juggernaut Well-done drama about a doomed luxury liner. A madman plants bombs aboard a cruise ship and mocks the crew about his plan over the wireless. The countdown ensues, while the bomb experts struggle to find the explosives. Suspenseful with good direction.

1974 (PG-13) 109m/C Richard Harris, Omar Sharif, David Hemmings, Anthony Hopkins, Shirley Knight, Ian Holm, Roy Kinnear, Freddie Jones; **D:** Richard Lester. **VHS $14.95** MGM, FOX ♫♫♫

The Juggler of Notre Dame A hobo and a street juggler embark on an unusual journey that will change the lives of the people they meet. Based on a medieval

folktale about the special gift given to the Virgin Mary on Christmas morning.
1984 110m/C Carl Carlson, Patrick Collins, Melinda Dillon, Merlin Olsen, Gene Roche. **VHS, Beta** PAU 🎬🎬½

Juice Day-to-day street life of four Harlem youths as they try to earn respect ("juice") in their neighborhood. Q, an aspiring deejay, is talked into a robbery by his friends but everything takes a turn for the worse when one of the others, Bishop, gets hold of a gun. The gritty look and feel of the drama comes naturally to Dickerson in his directorial debut. Prior to his first film, Dickerson served as cinematographer for Spike Lee's "Do the Right Thing" and "Jungle Fever."
1992 (R) 95m/C Omar Epps, Jermaine Hopkins, Tupac Shakur, Khalil Kain, Cindy Herron, Vincent Laresca, Samuel L. Jackson; **D:** Ernest R. Dickerson; **W:** Gerard Brown, Ernest R. Dickerson; **M:** Bomb Squad. **VHS $19.95** PAR 🎬🎬½

Juke Joint "Amos 'n Andy" star Spencer Williams acted in and directed this tale of two men who arrive in Hollywood with only 25 cents between them. Features an all-black cast and musical numbers.
1947 60m/B Spencer Williams Jr., Judy Jones, Mantan Moreland; **D:** Spencer Williams Jr. **VHS, Beta $39.95** NOS, VCN, DVT 🎬½

Jules and Jim Beautiful film with perfect casting, particularly Moreau. Spanning from 1912 to 1932, it is the story of a friendship between two men and their twenty-year love for the same woman. Werner is the shy German Jew and Serre the fun-loving Frenchman, who meet as students. The two men discover and woo the bohemian, destructive Moreau, although it is Werner she marries. After WWI, the friends are reunited but the marriage of Moreau and Werner is in trouble and she has an affair with Serre, which leads to tragedy for all three. Adapted from the novel by Henri-Pierre Roche. In French with English subtitles. **AKA:** Jules et Jim.
1962 104m/B Jeanne Moreau, Oskar Werner, Henri Serre, Marie DuBois, Vanna Urbino; **D:** Francois Truffaut; **W:** Jean Gruault; **M:** Georges Delerue. **VHS, Beta $39.95** HMV, APD, FOX 🎬🎬🎬

Julia The story recounted in Lillian Hellman's fictional memoir "Pentimento." Fonda plays Hellman as she risks her life smuggling money into Germany during WWII for the sake of Julia, her beloved childhood friend (Redgrave), who is working in the Resistance. All cast members shine in their performances; watch for Streep in her screen debut.
1977 (PG) 118m/C Jane Fonda, Jason Robards Jr., Vanessa Redgrave, Maximilian Schell, Hal Holbrook, Rosemary Murphy, Meryl Streep, Lisa Pelikan; **D:** Fred Zinneman; **W:** Alvin Sargent; **M:** Georges Delerue. Academy Awards '77: Best Adapted Screenplay, Best Supporting Actor (Robards), Best Supporting Actress (Redgrave); Nominations: Best Actress (Fonda), Best Cinematography, Best Costume Design, Best Director (Zinneman), Best Film Editing, Best Picture, Best Supporting Actor (Schell), Best Original Score; Golden Globe Awards '78: Best Actress—Drama (Fonda), Best Supporting Actress (Redgrave); New York Film Critics Awards '77: Best Supporting Actor (Schell). **VHS, Beta $19.98** FOX, BTV 🎬🎬🎬½

Julia and Julia A beautiful American woman in Trieste is tossed between two seemingly parallel dimensions, one in which her husband died six years earlier in a car crash, and the other in which he didn't. A purposefully obscure Italian-made psychological thriller, filmed in high-definition video and then transferred to film stock, it has a

very different look and feel from other films of the genre. Intriguing and engaging most of the time, slow moving and confusing some of the time, it ultimately challenges but fails adequately to reward the viewer.
1987 (R) 98m/C Kathleen Turner, Sting, Gabriel Byrne, Gabriel Ferzetti, Angela Goodwin; **D:** Peter Del Monte; **M:** Maurice Jarre. **VHS, Beta $19.98** FOX 🎬🎬½

Julia Has Two Lovers Minimalist comedy-drama about a woman torn between two men—her dull fiance and a mysterious phone caller. Mostly a long phone conversation; don't expect blistering action.
1991 87m/C Daphna Kastner, David Duchovny, David Charles; **D:** Bashar Shbib. **VHS $14.95** HMD 🎬🎬

Julia Misbehaves Charming comedy that has Garson returning to ex-husband Pidgeon and daughter Taylor after an 18-year absence. Taylor is about to be married at a chateau in France and wants Garson to be there. While traveling to France from England, Garson encounters a bunch of colorful circus characters who are taking their act to Paris. Wonderful slapstick scenes give the stars a chance to have some real fun. Based on the novel "The Nutmeg Tree" by Margery Sharp.
1948 99m/B Greer Garson, Walter Pidgeon, Peter Lawford, Cesar Romero, Elizabeth Taylor, Lucile Watson, Nigel Bruce, Mary Boland, Reginald Owen, Veda Ann Borg, Joi Lansing; **D:** Jack Conway. **VHS $19.98** MGM 🎬🎬🎬

Juliet of the Spirits Fellini uses the sparse story of a woman (Fellini's real-life wife) deliberating over her husband's possible infidelity to create a wild, often senseless surrealistic film. With a highly symbolic internal logic and complex imagery, Fellini's fantasy ostensibly elucidates the inner life of a modern woman. In Italian with English subtitles. **AKA:** Giulietta Degli Spiriti.
1965 142m/C Giulietta Masina, Valentina Cortese, Sylva Koscina, Mario Pisu; **D:** Federico Fellini; **W:** Federico Fellini, Tullio Pinelli, Ennio Flaino, Brunello Rondi. Academy Awards '66 Nominations: Best Art Direction/Set Decoration (Color), Best Costume Design (Color); National Board of Review Awards '65: 5 Best Foreign Films of the Year; New York Film Critics Awards '65: Best Foreign Film. **VHS, Beta $14.95** VYY, MRV, VDM 🎬🎬🎬

Julius Caesar All-star version of the Shakespearean tragedy, heavily acclaimed and deservedly so. Working directly from the original Shakespeare, director Mankiewicz produced a lifelike, yet poetic production.
1953 121m/B James Mason, Marlon Brando, John Gielgud, Greer Garson, Deborah Kerr, Louis Calhern, Edmond O'Brien, George Macready, John Hoyt, Michael Pate; **D:** Joseph L. Mankiewicz; **W:** Joseph L. Mankiewicz. Academy Awards '53: Best Art Direction/Set Decoration (B & W); Nominations: Best Actor (Brando), Best Black and White Cinematography, Best Picture, Best Original Score; British Academy Awards '53: Best Actor (Brando), Best Actor (Gielgud). **VHS, Beta $19.98** MGM 🎬🎬🎬½

Julius Caesar Subpar adaptation of the Shakespeare play about political greed and corruption within the Roman Empire.
1970 116m/C Charlton Heston, John Gielgud, Jason Robards Jr., Richard Chamberlain, Robert Vaughn, Diana Rigg; **D:** Stuart Burge. **VHS, Beta $19.98** NOS, REP, APD 🎬🎬

July Group A Quaker family's peaceful existence is threatened when kidnappers invade their home and hold them for ransom.
1977? 75m/C Nicholas Campbell, Calvin Butler, Maury Chaykin. **VHS, Beta $59.95** TWE 🎬½

The Jumper An abstract, theatrical narrative about a cast of tragi-comic characters floundering through their meaningless lives. In German with English subtitles. **AKA:** Der Toderspringer.
1985 90m/C **D:** Benno Trachtmann. **VHS, Beta $39.95** FCT, VCD, GLV 🎬🎬½

Jumpin' at the Boneyard Gritty family drama about the trials of two dispossessed brothers, set on the streets of New York. Deeply depressed, out-of-work, divorced Manny hates his recently deceased father, adores his mother, and is estranged from his younger brother, Danny. Danny is a scared crack addict who's supported by a hooker/girlfriend. The two brothers reunite for a trip into their scarred past when Danny tries to rob his brother's apartment to get dope money. Manny starts to believe that the only way to redeem his own life is to get his brother into a rehab program. Good acting helps to overcome some script weaknesses but this is one depressing movie.
1992 (R) 107m/C Tim Roth, Alexis Arquette, Danitra Vance, Samuel L. Jackson, Kathleen Chalfant, Luis Guzman; **D:** Jeff Stanzler; **W:** Jeff Stanzler. **VHS $94.98** FXV 🎬🎬

Jumpin' Jack Flash A bank worker is humorously embroiled in international espionage when her computer terminal picks up distress signals from a British agent in Russia. Marshall's directing debut. Good performances from a fun cast and a particularly energetic effort by Goldberg are held back by an average and predictable script.
1986 (R) 98m/C Whoopi Goldberg, Stephen Collins, Carol Kane, Annie Potts, Jonathan Pryce, James Belushi, Jon Lovitz, John Wood; **Cameos:** Michael McKean, Tracey Ullman, Roscoe Lee Browne, Sara Botsford, Jeroen Krabbe, Phil Hartman, Tracy Reiner, Paxton Whitehead, Jamey Sheridan, Garry Marshall, Peter Michael Goetz; **D:** Penny Marshall; **W:** David Franzoni; **M:** Thomas Newman. **VHS, Beta $19.98** FOX 🎬🎬½

Jumping Jacks Martin and Lewis are a couple of nightclub performers who wind up in the paratroop corps instead of performing their act for the soldiers. Martin gets to sing and Lewis gets to parachute into enemy territory and capture a general.
1952 96m/B Dean Martin, Jerry Lewis, Mona Freeman, Don DeFore, Robert Strauss, Ray Teal; **D:** Norman Taurog. **VHS $14.95** PAR 🎬🎬

Junction 88 Early all-black musical chock full of great dancing and hot music.
1940 60m/B Noble Sissle, Bob Howard. **VHS, Beta $24.95** NOS, DVT 🎬

June Bride Fast-paced and entertaining comedy in which Davis and Montgomery are teamed up as magazine writers. A hilarious battle of the sexes erupts as they're sent to Indiana to do a feature story on June brides. Look for Debbie Reynolds in her film debut.
1948 97m/B Bette Davis, Robert Montgomery, Fay Bainter, Betty Lynn, Tom Tully, Barbara Bates, Jerome Cowan, Mary Wickes; **D:** Bretaigne Windust; **W:** Ranald MacDougall. **VHS $19.98** MGM 🎬🎬🎬

June Night A woman who was victimized by a shooting incident cannot escape the public eye due to her former promiscuous behavior. In Swedish with English subtitles. **AKA:** Juninatten.
1940 90m/C Ingrid Bergman, Marianne Lofgren, Gunnar Sjoberg, Olaf Widgren; **D:** Per Lindberg. **VHS, Beta $29.95** WAC, TPV, LUM 🎬🎬

Jungle A princess and an American adventurer lead an expedition into the Indian wilds to discover the source of recent elephant attacks.

1952 74m/B Rod Cameron, Cesar Romero, Marie Windsor; **D:** William Berke. **VHS, Beta** NO ✍

Jungle Assault Two Vietnam vets with nothing left to lose are called back into the bloodiest action of their lives. Their assignment is to locate and destroy a terrorist base and bring back an American general's brainwashed daughter.
1989 86m/C William Smith, Ted Prior, William Zipp; **D:** David A. Prior. **VHS, Beta** $9.95 AIP ✍

The Jungle Book A lavish version of Rudyard Kipling's stories about Mowgli, the boy raised by wolves in the jungles of India. **AKA:** Rudyard Kipling's Jungle Book.
1942 109m/C Sabu, Joseph Calleia, Rosemary DeCamp, Ralph Byrd, John Qualen; **D:** Zoltan Korda; **M:** Miklos Rozsa. **VHS** $9.95 CNG, MRV, REP ✍✍

The Jungle Book Based on Kipling's classic, a young boy raised by wolves must choose between his jungle friends and human "civilization." Along the way he meets a variety of jungle characters including zany King Louie, kind-hearted Baloo, wise Bagherra and the evil Shere Khan. Great, classic songs including "Trust in Me," "I Wanna Be Like You," and Oscar-nominated "Bare Necessities." Last Disney feature overseen by Uncle Walt himself and a must for kids of all ages.
1967 78m/C **D:** Wolfgang Reitherman; **V:** Phil Harris, Sebastian Cabot, Louis Prima, George Sanders, Sterling Holloway, J. Pat O'Malley, Verna Felton, Darlene Carr. **VHS, Beta** $24.99 DIS, BVV, FCT ✍✍✍

Jungle Bride Three people are shipwrecked and one of them is a suspected murderer.
1933 66m/B Anita Page, Charles Starrett. **VHS, Beta** $16.95 SNC, NOS, VYY ✍✍½

Jungle Drums of Africa Jungle adventures abound as Moore and Coates encounter lions, wind tunnels, voodoo and enemy agents in deepest Africa. A 12-episode serial re-edited onto two cassettes. **AKA:** U-238 and the Witch Doctor.
1953 167m/B Clayton Moore, Phyllis Coates, Roy Glenn, John Cason; **D:** Fred Brannon. **VHS** REP, MLB ✍½

Jungle Fever Married black architect's affair with his white secretary provides the backdrop for a cold look at interracial love. Focuses more on the discomfort of friends and families than with the intense world created by the lovers for themselves. Provides the quota of humor and fresh insight we expect from Lee, but none of the joyous sexuality experienced by the lovers in "She's Gotta Have It." In fact, Lee tells viewers that interracial love is unnatural, never more than skin deep, never more than a blind obsession with the allure of the opposite race. Very fine cast but if you don't agree with Lee, a real disappointment as well.
1991 (R) 131m/C Wesley Snipes, Annabella Sciorra, John Turturro, Samuel L. Jackson, Ossie Davis, Ruby Dee, Lonette McKee, Anthony Quinn, Spike Lee, Halle Berry, Tyra Ferrell, Veronica Webb, Frank Vincent, Tim Robbins, Brad Dourif; **D:** Spike Lee; **W:** Spike Lee; **M:** Terence Blanchard. **VHS, Beta** $19.98 MCA, CCB, FCT ✍✍✍

Jungle Goddess Two mercenaries set out for the reward offered for finding a wealthy heiress last seen in the jungles of Africa.
1949 61m/B George Reeves, Wanda McKay, Ralph Byrd, Armida; **D:** Lewis D. Collins. **VHS, Beta** NO ✍½

Jungle Heat While searching for a pygmy tribe, an anthropologist and her pilot run into a pack of anthropoid mutants. **AKA:** Dance of the Dwarfs.
1984 (PG) 93m/C Peter Fonda, Deborah Raffin; **D:** Gus Trikonis. **VHS, Beta** $59.95 TWE ✍½

Jungle Hell Sabu comes to the rescue of an Indian tribe being harassed by flying saucers, death rays and radioactive debris.
1955 ?m/B Sabu, David Bruce, George E. Stone, K.T. Stevens; **D:** Norman A. Cerf. **VHS, Beta** $16.95 SNC ✍✍

Jungle Holocaust One member of a scientific team survives an attack by a cannibal tribe and in an effort of self-preservation becomes one of them.
1985 90m/C **VHS, Beta** $59.95 VCD ✍

Jungle Inferno Nature boy, a fugitive from the government, fights lions, tigers and pursuing feds in this story of escape and survival.
197? 90m/C Brad Harris. **VHS, Beta** NO ✍

Jungle Master Noble British types hunt for Karzan, the jungle's number one guy, with the aid of a tribal priestess and a lovely photo-journalist. Must see for trash movie fans.
1956 90m/C John Kitzmiller, Simone Blondell, Edward Mann; **D:** Miles Deem. **VHS, Beta** NO ✍

Jungle Patrol In 1943 New Guinea, a squadron of entrapped fliers are confronted with a beautiful USO entertainer. Romance and show tunes follow.
1948 72m/B Kristine Miller, Arthur Franz, Richard Jaeckel, Ross Ford, Tommy Noonan, Gene Reynolds; **D:** Joseph M. Newman. **VHS, Beta** NO ✍½

Jungle Raiders An Indiana Jones-esque mercenary searches the steamy jungles of Malaysia for a valuable jewel, the Ruby of Gloom. **AKA:** Legenda Del Rudio Malese; Captain Yankee.
1985 (PG-13) 102m/C Lee Van Cleef, Christopher Connelly, Marina Costa; **D:** Anthony M. (Antonio Margheretti) Dawson. **VHS, Beta** $79.95 MGM ✍½

Jungle Siren Nazis in Africa try to foment rebellion amongst the black natives against the white residents. Crabbe and a white woman raised in the jungle set things right.
1942 68m/B Ann Corio, Buster Crabbe, Evelyn Wahl, Milton Kibbee; **D:** Sam Newfield. **VHS, Beta** $16.95 SNC, MLB ✍✍

The Jungle Trap Steve Davis thought he could escape his past living in Africa. However, when the judge who wrongly sentenced his brother to death arrives, he plots revenge.
19?? 30m/B Ronald Reagan. **VHS** $7.95 RHI ✍✍

Jungle Warriors Seven fashion models are abducted by a Peruvian cocaine dealer. To escape him, they must become Jungle Warriors.
1984 (R) 96m/C Sybil Danning, Marjoe Gortner, Nina Van Pallandt, Paul Smith, John Vernon, Alex Cord, Woody Strode, Kai Wulff; **D:** Ernst R. von Theumer. **VHS, Beta** $59.95 MED ✍½

Junior A raving, drooling lunatic cuts up girls with a chainsaw.
1986 80m/C Suzanne DeLaurentis, Linda Singer, Jeremy Ruthford, Michael McKeever. **VHS, Beta** $9.99 STE, PSM Woof!

Junior Bonner A rowdy modern-day western about a young drifting rodeo star who decides to raise money for his father's new ranch by challenging a formidable bull.
1972 (PG) 100m/C Steve McQueen, Robert Preston, Ida Lupino, Ben Johnson, Joe Don Baker, Barbara Leigh; **D:** Sam Peckinpah. **VHS, Beta** $19.98 FOX ✍✍✍

Junior G-Men The Dead End Kids fight Fifth Columnists who are trying to sabotage America's war effort. Twelve episodes.
1940 237m/B Billy Halop, Huntz Hall. **VHS, Beta** $39.95 VYY, VCN, NOS ✍✍✍

Junior G-Men of the Air The Dead End Kids become teen-age flyboys in this twelve-episode serial adventure.
1942 215m/B Billy Halop, Huntz Hall. **VHS, Beta** $26.95 SNC, NOS, MED ✍½

Junior High School A comically, on target film detailing the romantic yearnings, petty cruelties, and claustrophobia of 8th grade existence.
1978 60m/C Paula Abdul. **VHS, Beta** $19.95 PIC, TPV ✍✍½

The Junkman Movie maker whose new film is about to be premiered is being chased by a mysterious killer. Promoted as "the ultimate car chase film" since the production used and destroyed over 150 automobiles. From the makers of "Gone in 60 Seconds."
1982 (R) 97m/C H.B. Halicki, Christopher Stone, Susan Shaw, Hoyt Axton, Lynda Day George, Freddy Cannon & the Belmonts; **D:** H.B. Halicki. **VHS, Beta** $18.95 TWE ✍½

Juno and the Paycock Perhaps if Hitchcock hadn't been so faithful to O'Casey this early effort would have been less stagey and more entertaining. In Dublin during the civil uprising, a poor family is torn apart when they receive news of an imminent fortune. Hitchcock's reported to have said that "drama is life with the dull bits left out," though here too many dull bits remain.
1930 96m/B Sara Allgood, Edward Chapman, John Longden, John Laurie, Maire O'Neill; **D:** Alfred Hitchcock; **W:** Alfred Hitchcock. **VHS** $19.98 NOS, VEC, HHT ✍✍✍

Jupiter's Darling This spoof of Hannibal (Keel) and Amytis (Williams) gravely misses the mark in making funny the world of the Roman Empire. Amytis has the job of distracting Hannibal from attacking the Eternal City, and does so through musical interludes and unfunny jokes. ♫I Have A Dream; If This Be Slav'ry; I Never Trust A Woman; Hannibal's Victory March; Don't Let This Night Get Away; The Life Of An Elephant; Horatio's Narration.
1955 96m/C Esther Williams, Howard Keel, George Sanders, Gower Champion, Marge Champion, Norma Varden, Richard Haydn, William Demarest, Douglass Dumbrille, Michael Ansara, Martha Wentworth, Chris Alcaide, William Tannen; **D:** George Sidney. $19.98 MGM ✍✍

Jupiter's Thigh A madcap married pair of treasure-hunters honeymoon in Greece in search of an ancient statue's lost thigh. Available in French with English subtitles, or dubbed into English.
1981 96m/C Annie Girardot, Philippe Noiret; **D:** Philippe de Broca. **VHS, Beta** $29.98 SUE, FCT ✍✍½

Jurassic Park Crichton's spine-tingling thriller translates well (but not faithfully) due to its main attraction: realistic, rampaging dinosaurs. Genetically cloned from prehistoric DNA, all is well until they escape from their pens—smarter and less predictable than expected. Contrived plot and thin characters (except Goldblum), but who cares? The true stars are the dinos, an incredible combination of models and computer animation. Violent, suspenseful, and realistic with gory attack scenes. Not for small kids, though much of

the marketing is aimed at them. Spielberg knocked his own "E.T." out of first place as "JP" became the highest grossing movie of all time. Also available in a letterbox version.
1993 (PG-13) 127m/C Sam Neill, Laura Dern, Jeff Goldblum, Richard Attenborough, Bob Peck, Martin Ferrero, B.D. Wong, Joseph Mazzello, Ariana Richards, Samuel L. Jackson, Wayne Knight; **D:** Steven Spielberg; **M:** John Williams; **V:** Richard Kiley. Academy Awards '93: Best Sound, Best Sound Effects Editing, Best Visual Effects; Nominations: : Best Film, Best Villain (T-Rex), Best Action Sequence. VHS **$24.98** *MCA* 🎬🎬🎬 ½

Just a Gigolo Bowie stars in this unusual melodrama about a Prussian war vet turned male prostitute. He spends most of his time working for the sexiest of women. Splendid cast, but a bit incoherent.
1979 (R) 105m/C David Bowie, Sydne Rome, Kim Novak, David Hemmings, Maria Schell, Curt Jurgens, Marlene Dietrich; **D:** David Hemmings. VHS **$59.95** *ING, MOV, LUM* 🎬🎬 ½

Just Another Girl on the I.R.T. Double debut from two African American women, writer/director Harris, and actress Johnson, captures the sass and wit of a girl from the projects. Seventeen-year-old Chantal has a plan for her life and challenges authority with assurance, even after an unexpected pregnancy puts a twist into her plan. Strong initial statement tends to become weak and cloudy as Chantal loses her focus. This doesn't dismiss the remarkable realism and raw talent portrayed in a picture filmed in just seventeen days for $130,000. Winner of a special jury prize at the Sundance Film Festival.
1993 (R) 96m/C Ariyan Johnson, Kevin Thigpen, Ebony Jerido, Jerard Washington, Chequita Jackson, William Badget; **D:** Leslie Harris; **W:** Leslie Harris. VHS **$89.98** *LIV, FCT* 🎬🎬 ½

Just Another Pretty Face An aging detective catches a gang of jewel smugglers, and gets involved with their young moll. In French with English subtitles. *AKA:* Be Beautiful but Shut Up.
1958 110m/B Henri Vidal, Mylene Demongeot, Isa Miranda; **D:** Henri Verneuil. VHS, Beta **$19.95** *FCT, ING* 🎬🎬

Just Around the Corner Temple helps her Depression-poor father get a job after she befriends a cantankerous millionaire. 🎵This Is A Happy Little Ditty; I'm Not Myself Today; I'll Be Lucky With You; Just Around the Corner; I Love To Walk in the Rain; Brass Buttons and Epaulets.
1938 70m/B Shirley Temple, Charles Farrell, Bert Lahr, Joan Davis, Bill Robinson, Cora Witherspoon, Franklin Pangborn; **D:** Irving Cummings. VHS, Beta **$19.98** *FOX* 🎬 ½

Just Before Dawn Another murderers stalk campers story; humans resort to their animal instincts in their struggle for survival. Not to be confused with the William Castle film (1946) from the "Crime Doctor" series.
1980 (R) 90m/C Chris Lemmon, Deborah Benson, Greg Henry, George Kennedy; **D:** Jeff Lieberman; **M:** Brad Fiedel. VHS, Beta *NO* 🎬🎬

Just Between Friends Two women become friends, not knowing that one is having an affair with the husband of the other. Allan Burns directorial debut.
1986 (PG-13) 110m/C Mary Tyler Moore, Christine Lahti, Sam Waterston, Ted Danson, Jim MacKrell, Jane Greer; **D:** Allan Burns. VHS, Beta **$79.99** *HBO* 🎬🎬

Just for the Hell of It A quartet of teenage punks ruthlessly terrorize their suburban Miami 'hood while an innocent kid gets blamed. More exploitation from schlock king Lewis, who also wrote the theme song,

"Destruction Inc" (pic's alternate title). Essentially the same cast as the director's "She Devils on Wheels," filmed simultaneously. *AKA:* Destruction, Inc.
1968 85m/C Rodney Bedell, Ray Sager, Nancy Lee Noble, Agi Gyenes, Steve White; **D:** Herschell Gordon Lewis. VHS *NO Woof!*

Just for You Entertaining musical about producer Crosby who doesn't have time for his kids until Wyman steps in and shows him the way. Based on Stephen Vincent Benet's novel "Famous." 🎵Zing A Little Zong; He's Just Crazy For Me; The Live Oak Tree; A Flight of Fancy; I'll Si-Si Ya In Bahia; On the 10:10; Just for You.
1952 95m/C Bing Crosby, Jane Wyman, Ethel Barrymore, Robert Arthur, Natalie Wood, Cora Witherspoon; **D:** Elliott Nugent; **W:** Robert Carson. VHS **$14.95** *PAR* 🎬🎬 ½

Just Like Weather Contemporary Hong Kong and the city's looming return to control by mainland China provide the backdrop for the troubled marriage of a young couple. Couple endure abortion, arrest, and veterinarian episodes before departing for on U.S. trip with high hopes.
1986 98m/C Christine Lee, Lee Chi-Keung, Allen Fong; **D:** Allen Fong. VHS **$39.95** *FCT* 🎬🎬🎬

Just Me & You An "It Happened One Night" made-for-television tale of an unlikely couple who fall in love with each other when chance brings them together on a cross-country drive.
1978 100m/C Louise Lasser, Charles Grodin; **D:** Charles Erman; **W:** Louise Lasser. VHS, Beta *NO* 🎬 ½

Just One of the Girls Teen star Haim transfers to a new high school where he dresses in drag in order to avoid the itinerant leader of the school's toughest gang whom he has unwittingly enraged. Palling around with Eggert becomes one of his costume's unexpected perks. Sort of a cross between "Some Like it Hot" and "90210."
1993 (R) 94m/C Corey Haim, Nicole Eggert, Cameron Bancroft; **D:** Michael Keusch. VHS **$92.95** *VMK* 🎬 ½

Just One of the Guys When the school newspaper refuses to accept the work of an attractive young girl, she goes undercover as a boy to prove that her work is good. She goes on to befriend the school's nerd, and even helps him grow out of his awkward stage, falling for him in the process. Very cute, but predictable.
1985 (PG-13) 100m/C Joyce Hyser, Clayton Rohner, Billy Jacoby, Toni Hudson, Leigh McCloskey, Sherilyn Fenn; **D:** Lisa Gottlieb. VHS, Beta **$79.95** *COL* 🎬🎬

Just Suppose Prince in waiting decides he'd prefer the simple life, travels to the land of the free in search of honest work and is felled by cupid's arrow. All's well 'til duty calls, and his princely presence is expected back in the royal fold. Features beautiful boy Barthelmess, whom Lillian Gish described as having "the most beautiful face of any man who ever went before a camera." Silent.
1926 90m/B Richard Barthelmess, Lois Moran, Geoffrey Kerr, Henry Vibart, George Spelvin; **D:** Kenneth Webb. VHS, Beta **$19.95** *GPV* 🎬🎬 ½

Just Tell Me What You Want A wealthy, self-made married man finally drives his longtime mistress away when he refuses to let her take over the operation of a failing movie studio he has acquired. After she falls for another man, the tycoon does everything he can to win her back. The department store battle between MacGraw and King is priceless.

1980 (R) 112m/C Alan King, Ali MacGraw, Myrna Loy, Keenan Wynn, Tony Roberts; **D:** Sidney Lumet; **W:** Jay Presson Allen. VHS, Beta **$19.98** *WAR* 🎬🎬 ½

Just Tell Me You Love Me Three budding con artists plot to make easy money in this Hawaiian romp.
1980 (PG) 90m/C Robert Hegyes, Debralee Scott, Lisa Hartman, Ricci Martin, June Lockhart; **D:** Tony Mordente. VHS, Beta **$69.98** *LIV, VES* 🎬

Just the Way You Are An attractive musician struggles to overcome a physical handicap and winds up falling in love while on vacation in the French Alps.
1984 (PG) 96m/C Kristy McNichol, Robert Carradine, Kaki Hunter, Michael Ontkean, Alexandra Paul, Lance Guest, Timothy Daly, Patrick Cassidy; **D:** Edouard Molinaro; **M:** Vladimir Cosma. VHS, Beta **$14.95** *MGM* 🎬

Just William's Luck A precocious English brat sneaks into an old mansion, which just happens to be the headquarters for a gang of thieves. Based on British series of children's books.
1947 87m/B William A. Graham, Garry Marsh; **D:** Val Guest. VHS, Beta **$24.95** *VYY* 🎬🎬

Justice A crusading attorney tries to keep a waterfront kangaroo court from applying its harsh justice to an admitted killer. A television crime-drama also titled "Flight from Fear."
1955 26m/B William Prince, Jack Klugman, Biff McGuire, Jack Warden. VHS, Beta **$19.95** *VYY* 🎬🎬

Justice of the West The Lone Ranger and his sidekick, Tonto, perform good deeds in the Old West, including helping to retrieve stolen gold, helping to build an Indian school, and giving a blind man a fresh perspective on life.
1961 71m/C Clayton Moore, Jay Silverheels; **D:** Earl Bellamy. VHS, Beta **$29.95** *MGM* 🎬

Justice Rides Again Mix tries to uphold law and order, but he's up against some very tough outlaws.
193? 55m/B Tom Mix. VHS, Beta **$29.95** *VCN* 🎬 ½

Justicia para los Mexicanos A gang of outlaws make a big mistake when they try to blame Mexican citizens for their crimes. The righteous folks show they're not pushovers.
19?? ?m/C Tony Kendall. VHS, Beta *MAD* 🎬

Justin Morgan Had a Horse The true story of a colonial school teacher in post-Revolutionary War Vermont who first bred the Morgan horse, the first and most versatile American breed.
1981 91m/C Don Murray, Lana Wood, Gary Crosby; **D:** Hollingsworth Morse. VHS, Beta **$69.95** *DIS* 🎬🎬

Justine In the 1930s, a prostitute who marries an Egyptian banker becomes involved with a variety of men and a plot to arm Palestinian Jews in their revolt against English rule. A condensed film version of Lawrence Durrell's "The Alexandria Quartet."
1969 115m/C Anouk Aimee, Michael York, Dirk Bogarde, Philippe Noiret, Michael Constantine, John Vernon, Jack Albertson; **D:** George Cukor; **W:** Lawrence B. Marcus; **M:** Jerry Goldsmith. VHS, Beta **$59.98** *FOX, HHE* 🎬🎬

K-9 After having his car destroyed by a drug dealer, "I work alone" Belushi is forced to take on a partner—a German Shepherd. Together they work to round up the bad guys and maybe chew on their shoes a little. Sometimes amusing one-joke comedy done in by a paper-thin script. Both the dog and Belushi are good, however.

1989 (PG-13) 111m/C James Belushi, Mel Harris, Kevin Tighe, Ed O'Neill, Cotter Smith, James Handy, Jerry Lee; **D:** Rod Daniel; **W:** Steven Siegel, Scott Myers; **M:** Miles Goodman. **VHS, Beta $19.95** MCA ‍‍½

K-9000 The Hound salutes the idea behind this standard sci-fi crime-fighter; a cyberdog fights the forces of evil with the aid of a cop, a lady reporter, and the usual cliches. Made For television. 1989 96m/C Chris Mulkey, Catherine Oxenberg; **D:** Kim Manners; **M:** Jan Hammer. **VHS $64.95** FRH ‍

Kafka Disappointing and gloomy Soderbergh film that serves no purpose whatsoever. Irons plays Kafka, an insurance workers by day and a writer by night. The movie exists largely without interest until Kafka uncovers an office conspiracy and makes his way to the enemy's castle headquarters. From then on, "Kafka" is nothing but a conventional horror film. Irons is wasted in a role that requires nothing but an impeccable British accent. On the plus side, the film is exquisitely shot in black and white until the castle scenes, when the cinematography is switched to color. 1991 (PG-13) 100m/C Jeremy Irons, Theresa Russell, Joel Grey, Ian Holm, Jeroen Krabbe, Armin Mueller-Stahl, Alec Guinness, Brian Glover, Robert Flemyng; **D:** Steven Soderberg; **W:** Lem Dobbs. **VHS, Beta $89.00** PAR, ING, PMS ‍‍

Kagemusha A thief is rescued from the gallows because of his striking resemblance to a warlord in 16th Century Japan. When the ambitious warlord is fatally wounded, the thief is required to pose as the warlord. In Japanese with English subtitles. **AKA:** The Shadow Warrior; The Double. 1980 (PG) 160m/C Tatsuya Nakadai, Tsutomu Yamazaki, Kenichi Hagiwara; **D:** Akira Kurosawa. Academy Awards '80 Nominations: Best Art Direction/Set Decoration, Best Foreign Language Film; British Academy Awards '80: Best Director (Kurosawa); Cannes Film Festival '80: Best Film; Cesar Awards '81: Best Foreign Film; National Board of Review Awards '80: 5 Best Foreign Films of the Year. **VHS, Beta $19.98** FOX, APD, ING ‍‍½

Kalifornia "Badlands" meets the '90s in a road trip with the hitchhikers from hell. Early Grayce (Pitt) is your average slimeball who murders his landlord and hops a ride with his waifish girlfriend Adele (Lewis) from Kentucky to California with Brian (Duchovny), a yuppie writer interested in mass murderers, and his sultry photographer girlfriend Carrie (Forbes). Pitt and Lewis were still an item when they made this. Pitt reportedly wanted to play against type, and as pretty boy gone homicidal, he succeeds. Extremely violent and disturbing. Also available in an unrated version. 1993 (R) 117m/C Brad Pitt, Juliette Lewis, David Duchovny, Michele Forbes, Sierra Pecheur, Lois Hall, Gregory Mars Martin; **D:** Dominic Sena; **W:** Tim Metcalfe. **VHS $94.95** PGV, BTV ‍‍½

Kameradschaft A great, early German sound film about Germans struggling to free themselves and French miners trapped underground on the countries' border. In German and French with English subtitles. 1931 80m/B Ernst Busch, Alexander Granach, Fritz Kampers; **D:** G.W. Pabst. **VHS, Beta $29.98** SUE, MRV, IHF ‍‍½

Kamikaze A Japanese WWII action drama about suicide pilots. 1945 100m/B VHS, Beta $14.99 VCD, RXM ‍

Kamikaze '89 German director Fassbinder has the lead acting role (his last) in this offbeat story of a police lieutenant in Berlin, circa 1989, who investigates a puzzling series of bombings. In German with English subtitles. 1983 90m/C Rainer Werner Fassbinder, Gunther Kaufman, Boy Gobert; **D:** Wolf Gremm; **M:** Tangerine Dream. **VHS, Beta $59.95** MGM, FCT, GLV ‍

Kamikaze Hearts A quasi-documentary set in the world of two lesbian-junkies (Sharon the actress and Tina the director/producer) making underground X-rated movies. 1991 80m/C Sharon Mitchell, Tina "Tigr" Mennett; **D:** Juliet Bashore; **W:** Tina "Tigr" Mennett. **VHS $59.95** FCT ‍

Kanal Wajda's first major success, a grueling account of Warsaw patriots, upon the onset of the Nazis toward the end of the war, fleeing through the ruined city's sewers. Highly acclaimed. Part 2 of Wajda's "War Trilogy," preceded by "A Generation" and followed by "Ashes and Diamonds." In Polish with English subtitles or dubbed. **AKA:** They Loved Life. 1956 96m/B Teresa Izewska, Tadeusz Janczar; **D:** Andrzej Wajda. **VHS, Beta $24.95** ING, NLC, HMV ‍‍½

Kandyland An over-the-hill stripper takes a young innocent stripper under her wing. 1987 (R) 94m/C Sandahl Bergman, Kimberly Evenson, Charles Laulette, Bruce Baum; **D:** Robert Allen Schnitzer. **VHS, Beta $19.95** STE, NWV ‍

Kangaroo An Australian adaptation of the semi-autobiographical D.H. Lawrence novel. A controversial English novelist and his wife move to the Outback in 1922, and are confronted with all manner of prejudice and temptation. 1986 (R) 115m/C Judy Davis, Colin Friels, John Walton, Hugh Keays-Byrne, Julie Nihill; **D:** Tim Burstall; **W:** Evan Jones; **M:** Nathan Waks. **VHS, Beta $79.95** MCA ‍

The Kansan The marshall in a Kansas town won't rest until he's stamped out all traces of corruption. 1943 79m/B Richard Dix, Victor Jory, Albert Dekker; **D:** George Archainbaud. **VHS, Beta $19.95** NOS, MRV, HEG ‍‍

Kansas Two young men, one a lawless rebel, the other a rational loner, stage a bank heist, and then go on the lam. Lame plot and very weak acting combine to make this film a dud. 1988 (R) 111m/C Matt Dillon, Andrew McCarthy, Leslie Hope, Kyra Sedgwick; **D:** David Stevens; **M:** Pino Donaggio. **VHS, Beta $19.95** MED ‍

Kansas City Confidential An ex-cop on the wrong side of the law launches a sophisticated armored car heist. A disgruntled ex-con gets arrested for the crime on circumstantial evidence. When released, he scours the underworld for the real thieves. 1952 98m/B John Payne, Coleen Gray, Preston Foster, Neville Brand, Lee Van Cleef, Jack Elam; **D:** Phil Karlson. **VHS $16.95** NOS, MGM, RXM ‍‍

Kansas City Massacre A made-for-television film chronicling the efforts of Melvin Purvis, as he tracked down Depression-era hoods. First called "Melvin Purvis, G-Man." 1975 99m/C Dale Robertson, Sally Kirkland, Bo Hopkins, Scott Brady, Lynn Loring, Matt Clark, Mills Watson, Robert Walden; **D:** Dan Curtis. **VHS, Beta $59.95** VMK ‍½

Kansas Pacific A group of Confederate sympathizers try to stop the Kansas Pacific Railroad from reaching the West Coast in the 1860s. 1953 73m/C Sterling Hayden, Eve Miller, Barton MacLane, Reed Hadley, Douglas Hadley; **D:** Ray Nazarro. **VHS, Beta $14.95** NOS, MRV, DVT ‍‍

The Kansas Terrors The "Three Mesquiteers" head for the Caribbean to deliver a herd of horses and wind up in a battle against local despot. 1939 57m/B Bob Livingston, Raymond Hatton, Duncan Renaldo, Jacqueline Wells, Yakima Canutt, Richard Alexander, Maureen McCormack; **D:** George Sherman. **VHS $19.95** NOS ‍‍

Kaos The Taviani brothers adaptation of four stories by Luigi Pirandello ("The Other Son," "Moonstruck," "The Jar," and "Requiem"), which look at peasant life in Sicily, ranging from the comic to the tragic. A fictional epilog, "Conversing with Mother," has Pirandello talking with the spirit of his dead mother. As with any anthology some stories are stronger than others but all possess the Taviani's great visual style and some fine acting. In Italian with English subtitles. **AKA:** Chaos-Kaos. 1985 (R) 188m/C Margarita Lozano, Claudio Bigagli, Massimo Bonetti, Omero Antonutti, Enrica Maria Modugno, Ciccio Ingrassia, Franco Franchi, Biagio Barone, Salvatore Rossi, Franco Scaldati, Pasquale Spadola, Regina Bianchi; **D:** Paolo Taviani, Vittorio Taviani; **W:** Paolo Taviani, Vittorio Taviani, Tonino Guerra. **VHS $29.98** MGM, BTV ‍‍

Kapo A 14-year-old Jewish girl and her family are imprisoned by the Nazis in a concentration camp. There, the girl changes identities with the help of the camp doctor, and rises to the position of camp guard. She proceeds to become taken with her power until a friend commits suicide and jolts the girl back into harsh reality. An Academy Award nominee for Best Foreign Film (lost to "The Virgin Spring"). Primarily English dialogue, with subtitles for foreign language. 1959 116m/B Susan Strasberg, Laurent Terzieff, Emmanuelle Riva, Gianno Garko; **D:** Gillo Pontecorvo; **W:** Gillo Pontecorvo. **VHS** DVT, HEG ‍‍

Karate Cop In a future without law or order John Travis (Marchini) is the last cop on earth. He saves Rachel, a beautiful scientist, from a band of scavengers and together they hunt for a hidden crystal with mysterious powers. Only first John has to defeat a gladiator in a martial arts fight to the death. 1993 (R) ?m/C Ron Marchini, Carrie Chambers, David Carradine, Michael Bristow, D.W. Landingham, Michael Foley, Dana Bentley; **D:** Alan Roberts. **VHS $89.95** IMP, IME, VTR ‍‍

The Karate Kid A teen-age boy finds out that Karate involves using more than your fists when a handyman agrees to teach him martial arts. The friendship that they develop is deep and sincere; the Karate is only an afterthought. From the director of the original "Rocky," this movie is easy to like. 1984 (PG) 126m/C Ralph Macchio, Noriyuki "Pat" Morita, Elisabeth Shue, Randee Heller, Martin Kove, Chad McQueen; **D:** John G. Avildsen; **W:** Robert Mark Kamen; **M:** Bill Conti. **VHS, Beta, 8mm $19.95** COL ‍‍‍½

The Karate Kid: Part 2 Sequel to the first film wherein our high-kicking hero tests his mettle in real-life karate exchanges in Okinawa, and settles a long-standing score. Followed by a second sequel. 1986 (PG) 95m/C Ralph Macchio, Noriyuki "Pat" Morita, Danny Kamekona, Martin Kove, Tamlyn Tomita, Nobu McCarthy, Yuji Okumoto; **D:** John G. Avildsen; **W:** Robert Mark Kamen; **M:** Bill Conti. **VHS, Beta, 8mm $19.95** COL ‍‍½

The Karate Kid: Part 3 Second sequel takes a tired plot and doesn't do much to perk it up. Macchio again battles an evil nemesis and learns about himself, but this time Morita refuses to be a part of his training until, of course, Macchio desperately needs his help. Followed by "The Next

Karate Kid'' which introduces a new kid—a girl.
1989 (PG) 105m/C Ralph Macchio, Noriyuki ''Pat'' Morita, John G. Avildsen, Thomas Ian Griffith, Martin Kove, Sean Kanan, Robyn Elaine; **D:** John G. Avildsen; **W:** Robert Mark Kamen; **M:** Bill Conti. VHS, Beta, 8mm **$19.95** COL ⅐½

Karate Polish Style Polish painter duo paint, plaster and draw blood. A sort of ''Dances with Poles'' in Warsaw's Mazurian Lake District. In Polish with English subtitles. Not a Polish joke.
1982 91m/C D: Jerzy Wojcik. VHS **$49.95** FCT ⅐

Karate Warrior Young martial artist is beaten and left for dead by Filipino crime syndicate. Bones mended, he prescribes a dose of their medicine. Plenty of rest and retaliation.
19?? 90m/C Jared Martin, Ken Watanabe. VHS, Beta **$19.95** IMP ⅐½

Karate Warriors Chiba takes his battle against crime to the streets.
19?? 90m/C Sonny Chiba. VHS, Beta NO ⅐

Kashmiri Run Action adventure about trio on the lam from Chinese communists chasing them through Tibet.
1969 (R) 101m/C Pernell Roberts, Alexandra Bastedo, Julian Mateos, Gloria Gamata; **D:** John Peyser. VHS **$29.95** LIV ⅐⅐

Katherine A young heiress rejects her pampered lifestyle and becomes a violent revolutionary, rebelling against social injustices and the system that spawned them. Made for television. **AKA:** The Radical.
1975 98m/C Sissy Spacek, Art Carney, Jane Wyatt, Henry Winkler, Julie Kavner, Hector Elias, Jenny Sullivan; **D:** Jeremy Paul Kagan. VHS, Beta **$19.95** STE, NWV, IME ⅐

Kavik the Wolf Dog Heartwarming story of a courageous dog's love and suffering for the boy he loves. Made for television. **AKA:** The Courage of Kavik, the Wolf Dog.
1984 99m/C Ronny Cox, Linda Sorensen, Andrew Ian McMillan, Chris Wiggins, John Ireland; **D:** Peter Carter. VHS, Beta **$19.95** MED ⅐½

Keaton's Cop Another cheap cop comedy involving the mistaken identity of an important mob witness.
1990 (R) 95m/C Lee Majors, Abe Vigoda, Don Rickles; **D:** Bob Burge. VHS, Beta **$14.95** MGM, OM ⅐

The Keep At the height of the Nazi onslaught, several German soldiers unleash an unknown power from a medieval stone fortress. Technically impressive but lacking in all other aspects.
1983 (R) 96m/C Scott Glenn, Alberta Watson, Juergen Prochnow, Robert Prosky, Gabriel Byrne; **D:** Michael Mann; **W:** Michael Mann. VHS, Beta **$79.95** PAR ⅐⅐

Keep 'Em Flying Bud and Lou star in the this wartime morale-booster that hasn't aged well. The duo follow their barnstorming friend into flight academy; a not-too-taxing plot includes five musical numbers and two Martha Rayes (she plays twins). ♫Pig Foot Pete; Together; I'm Looking for the Boy with the Wistful Eyes; Let's Keep 'Em Flying; I'm Getting Sentimental Over You.
1941 86m/B Bud Abbott, Lou Costello, Martha Raye; **D:** Arthur Lubin. VHS **$14.95** MCA ⅐⅐

Keep My Grave Open A woman lives in an isolated house where a series of strange murders take place. She attributes them to her brother, but does he really exist? Made cheaply, but not without style; filmed in Harrison County, Texas. **AKA:** The House Where Hell Froze Over.

1980 (R) 85m/C Camilla Carr, Gene Ross, Stephen Tobolowsky, Ann Stafford, Sharon Bunn, Chelcie Ross; **D:** S.F. Brownrigg. VHS, Beta **$9.95** UNI ⅐

Keep Punching A gambler/boxer is almost destroyed by life in the fast lane, as well as by a seductive woman.
1939 80m/C Henry Armstrong, Mae Johnson; **Cameos:** Canada Lee; **D:** John Clein. VHS **$34.95** FCT ⅐

Keep Talking Baby Action-packed thriller that finds Eddie in prison after being framed for murder. He escapes and is out for revenge on the organization that put him there.
1961 ?m/C Eddie Constantine. VHS **$16.95** SNC ⅐⅐

Keep the Change Joe Starling is an artist with painter's block, living in California with his girlfriend Astrid. He decides to revisit the family ranch in Deadrock, Montana, and his crackpot Uncle Smitty and saintly Aunt Lureen. The family ranch is coveted by the evil Overstreet (typecasting for Palance), whose daughter was once loved by Joe but is now married to his ex-best friend. Character more than plot rules this moody, low-key story based on a novel by Thomas McGuane. Made for cable television.
1992 (PG-13) 95m/C William L. Petersen, Lolita Davidovich, Rachel Ticotin, Buck Henry, Jack Palance, Fred Dalton Thompson, Jeff Kober, Lois Smith; **D:** Andy Tennant. VHS **$9.98** TTC ⅐⅐

Keeper Wealthy patients at Underwood Asylum suffer unspeakable horrors while under the care of Lee. Detective Dick Driver investigates. Obscure horror spoof.
1984 96m/C Christopher Lee, Tell Schreiber, Sally Gray; **D:** Tom Drake; **W:** Tom Drake. VHS, Beta **$49.95** TWE, HHE ⅐⅐

Keeper of the City Gossett stars as a tough detective out to get a vigilante (LaPaglia) who is roaming the streets of Chicago. LaPaglia turns in a good performance as the son of a Mafia operative who wants to rid himself of the Mafia ties that have controlled him. As he pursues his deadly course of action, a newspaper journalist tags him ''The Gangster Killer.'' Coyote plays the crusading journalist who is always interfering in Gossett's business. Good performances and an intriguing story line combine to make this action-packed thriller worthwhile, although the script isn't as good as Di Pega's novel, which he adapted himself.
1992 (R) 95m/C Louis Gossett Jr., Peter Coyote, Anthony LaPaglia, Renee Soutendijk, Aeryk Egan, Tony Todd; **D:** Bobby Roth; **W:** Gerald Di Pega. VHS, Beta **$89.98** FXV, VTR ⅐⅐½

Keeping On Television movie with a pro-union stance. A preacher, who is also a millworker, teams up with an organizer to try to unionize the mill. Originally produced for the PBS ''American Playhouse'' series.
1981 93m/C Dick Anthony Williams, Carol Kane, James Broderick, Marcia Rodd, Rosalind Cash, Carl Lee, Danny Glover, Guy Boyd; **D:** Barbara Kopple. VHS **$59.95** TWE ⅐½

Keeping Track Two tourists witness a murder and robbery and find the stolen $5 million on a New York-bound train. The two are relentlessly pursued by everyone, including the CIA and Russian spies.
1986 (R) 102m/C Michael Sarrazin, Margot Kidder, Alan Scarfe, Ken Pogue, Vlasta Vrana, Donald Pilon; **D:** Robin Spry. VHS, Beta **$19.98** NLC ⅐

Keetje Tippei In 1881 Amsterdam, a young Dutch prostitute works her way out of poverty and enters a world of education and wealth. A Victorian tale of exploitation with a tough and intelligent Cinderella heroine. In Dutch with English subtitles. **AKA:** Katie's Passion; Cathy Tippel; Hot Sweat.
1975 (R) 104m/C Monique Van De Ven, Rutger Hauer, Eddie Brugman, Hannah De Leeuwe, Andrea Domburg; **D:** Paul Verhoeven. VHS, Beta **$79.95** TPV, CVC, IME ⅐⅐

Kelly the Second Slow-moving boxing comedy about a punch-drunk fighter trying to win again with the encouragement of his trainer and manager.
1936 70m/B Guinn Williams, Patsy Kelly, Charley Chase, Pert Kelton, Edward Brophy, Maxie ''Slapsie'' Rosenbloom, Harold Huber, DeWitt Jennings, Billy Gilbert, Syd Saylor; **D:** Gus Meins. VHS RXM ⅐½

Kelly's Heroes A misfit band of crooks are led by Eastwood on a daring mission: to steal a fortune in gold from behind enemy lines. In the process, they almost win WWII. Sutherland is superb, as is McLeod, in his pre-Love Boat days.
1970 (PG) 145m/C Clint Eastwood, Donald Sutherland, Telly Savalas, Gavin MacLeod, Don Rickles, Carroll O'Connor, Stuart Margolin, Harry Dean Stanton; **D:** Brian G. Hutton. VHS, Beta **$19.98** MGM, TLF ⅐⅐½

Kemek An eccentric chemical company owner has his mistress push a new mind-control drug on an American writer, and has them killed after discovering their subsequent affair. Unfortunately, he didn't count on the woman's ex-husband seeking revenge.
1988 (R) 82m/C David Hedison, Helmut Snider, Mary Woronov, Alexandra Stewart, Cal Haynes. VHS, Beta GHV ⅐

Kennedy The long television mini-series biography of JFK from his inauguration to assassination.
1983 278m/C Martin Sheen, Blair Brown, Vincent Gardenia, Geraldine Fitzgerald, E.G. Marshall, John Shea; **D:** Richard Hartley. VHS, Beta **$14.99** PSM ⅐⅐

The Kennedys Don't Cry A sensitive and detailed look at the triumphs and tragedies of the Kennedy clan. Rare footage and interviews trace the growth of Joseph P. Kennedy's children and their influence on American history. Some segments are in black and white.
1983 100m/C VHS, Beta **$59.95** MPI ⅐⅐

The Kennel Murder Case Debonair detective Philo Vance suspects that a clear-cut case of suicide is actually murder. Fourth Vance mystery starring Powell. Remade as ''Calling Philo Vance'' in 1940.
1933 73m/B William Powell, Mary Astor, Jack LaRue, Ralph Morgan, Eugene Pallette; **D:** Michael Curtiz. VHS, Beta **$16.95** SNC, NOS, HHT ⅐⅐

Kenny Rogers as the Gambler Rogers stars as Brady Hawkes, debonair gambler searching for a son he never knew he had. Based on the Rogers song of the same name. One of the highest rated TV movies ever. Followed by several sequels.
1980 94m/C Kenny Rogers, Christine Belford, Bruce Boxleitner, Harold Gould, Clu Gulager, Lance LeGault, Lee Purcell, Noble Willingham; **D:** Dick Lowry. VHS WKV ⅐½

Kenny Rogers as the Gambler, Part 2: The Adventure Continues The surprise success of the made-for-TV western based on the popular Kenny Rogers' song spawned this equally popular sequel. Rogers returns as Brady Hawkes, this time searching for his kidnapped son. Followed by two more sequels.

1983 195m/C Kenny Rogers, Bruce Boxleitner, Linda Evans, Harold Gould, David Hedison, Clu Gulager, Johnny Crawford; **D:** Dick Lowry. **VHS, Beta, 8mm** $24.95 *WKV* ♪ ½

Kenny Rogers as the Gambler, Part 3: The Legend Continues Roger's third attempt at humanizing the gambler from his hit '70s song. This time, the Gambler gives a hand with the mediating between the warring U.S. government and the Sioux nation. Sitting Bull and Buffalo Bill add credibility to this average undertaking. Made for TV.

1987 190m/C Kenny Rogers, Bruce Boxleitner, Linda Gray, Melanie Chartoff, Matt Clark, George Kennedy, Dean Stockwell, Charles Durning, Jeffrey Jones, George American Horse; **D:** Dick Lowry. **VHS, Beta** *WKV* ♪♪

Kent State Made-for-television drama recounts the tragic events that took place at Kent State University in 1970, when student demonstrators faced National Guardsmen. Goldstone won an Emmy for Outstanding Direction.

1981 120m/C Talia Balsam, Ellen Barkin, Jane Fleiss, John Getz, Keith Gordon; **D:** James Goldstone. **VHS, Beta** $39.95 *MCA* ♪♪

The Kentuckian Burt Lancaster stars as a rugged frontiersman who leaves with his son to go to Texas. On their journey the two are harassed by fighting mountaineers.

1955 104m/C Burt Lancaster, Walter Matthau, Diana Lynn, John McIntire, Dianne Foster, Una Merkel, John Carradine; **D:** Burt Lancaster. **VHS, Beta** $19.98 *MGM* ♪♪ ½

Kentucky Blue Streak Young jockey is framed for murder while riding at an "illegal" racetrack. Later, almost eligible for parole, he escapes from jail to ride "Blue Streak" in the Kentucky Derby.

1935 61m/B Eddie Nugent, Frank "Junior" Coghlan, Patricia Scott, Ben Carter. **VHS, Beta** $19.95 *VYY* ♪ ½

Kentucky Fried Movie A zany potpourri of satire about movies, television, commercials, and contemporary society. Written by Abrahams and the Zuckers, who were later known for "Airplane!"

1977 (R) 85m/C Bill Bixby, Jerry Zucker, Jim Abrahams, David Zucker, Donald Sutherland, Henry Gibson, George Lazenby; **D:** John Landis; **W:** Jerry Zucker, Jim Abrahams, David Zucker. **VHS, Beta** $59.95 *MED* ♪♪♪

Kentucky Jubilee At the jubilee, a movie director is kidnapped and the master of ceremonies, among others, decides to find him.

1951 67m/B Jerry Colonna, Jean Porter, James Ellison, Raymond Hatton, Fritz Feld. **VHS, Beta** *RXM* ♪ ½

Kentucky Kernels A pair of down and out magicians (thirties comic duo Wheeler and Woolsey) happen upon a young boy (Little Rascal Spanky) who happens to be heir to a fortune. The three head for the rascal's Kentucky home, where they're welcomed with southern inhospitality. *AKA:* Triple Trouble.

1934 75m/B Bert Wheeler, Robert Woolsey, Mary Carlisle, George "Spanky" McFarland, Noah Beery Sr., Lucille LaVerne, Willie Best; **D:** George Stevens. **VHS** $19.98 *TTC, FCT, GVV* ♪♪

Kentucky Rifle A Comanche Indian tribe will let a group of stranded pioneers through their territory only if they agree to sell the Kentucky rifles aboard their wagon.

1955 80m/C Chill Wills, Lance Fuller, Cathy Downs, Jess Barker, Sterling Holloway, Jeanne Cagney; **D:** Carl K. Hittleman. **VHS, Beta** $29.95 *MON, HHE* ♪♪

Kept Husbands A factory worker saves two lives in an industrial accident, and the boss invites him home to dinner. When he meets the boss' daughter, romance blooms. But their different backgrounds cause difficulties. A bit dull, and dated by its chauvinism.

1931 76m/B Dorothy Mackaill, Joel McCrea, Robert McWade, Florence Roberts, Clara Kimball Young, Mary Carr, Ned Sparks, Bryant Washburn; **D:** Lloyd Bacon. **VHS** $19.95 *NOS, HEG* ♪♪

Kerouac Documentary frames the life of the beat poet Jack Kerouac with excerpts from his appearance on the Steve Allen Show in 1959. The film includes interviews with many of Kerouac's contemporaries. *AKA:* Jack Kerouac's America.

1984 90m/C Lawrence Ferlinghetti, Allen Ginsberg, William S. Burroughs, Steve Allen, Jack Kerouac. **VHS, Beta** $39.95 *AHV* ♪♪

The Key A long, slow WWII drama about the key to an Italian girl's apartment that gets passed from tugboat skipper to tugboat skipper before dangerous missions. Ultimately she finds true love, or does she? Based on the novel "Stella" by Jan de Hartog.

1958 134m/B William Holden, Sophia Loren, Trevor Howard, Oscar Homolka, Kieron Moore; **D:** Carol Reed; **W:** Carl Foreman; **M:** Malcolm Arnold. **VHS, Beta** $69.95 *COL* ♪♪ ½

Key Exchange Kevin Scott and Paul Kurta based this contemporary look at love and commitments on Kevin Wade's popular play. Two New York City "yuppies" have reached a point in their relationship where an exchange of apartment keys commonly occurs—but they are hesitant.

1985 (R) 96m/C Brooke Adams, Ben Masters, Daniel Stern, Tony Roberts, Danny Aiello, Annie Golden, Nancy Mette; **D:** Barnet Kellman; **W:** Kevin Scott, Paul Kurta; **M:** Jonathan Elias. **VHS, Beta** $79.98 *FOX* ♪♪ ½

Key Largo A gangster melodrama set in Key West, Florida, where hoods take over a hotel in the midst of a hurricane. Based on a play by Maxwell Anderson.

1948 101m/B Humphrey Bogart, Lauren Bacall, Claire Trevor, Edward G. Robinson, Lionel Barrymore; **D:** John Huston; **W:** Richard Brooks, John Huston. **VHS, Beta** $19.98 *MGM, FOX, TLF* ♪♪♪ ½

The Key Man A radio show host manages to get mixed up with gangsters after recreating a crime on the air. He uses his knowledge of crime to thwart the crooks. *AKA:* Life at Stake.

1957 63m/B Lee Patterson, Hy Hazell, Colin Gordon, Philip Leaver, Paula Byrne; **D:** Montgomery Tully; **M:** Les Baxter. **VHS, Beta** $16.95 *NOS, SNC* ♪♪

The Key to Rebecca The Nazis and the British go head-to-head in war torn North Africa. As the Germans push their way across Egypt, they find an unexpected ally in a half-German/half-Arab killer behind the British lines. Tense, well made thriller, originally a mini-series. On two cassettes. Made for television.

1985 190m/C David Soul, Cliff Robertson, Robert Culp, Season Hubley, Lina Raymond, Anthony Quayle, David Hemmings; **D:** David Hemmings. **VHS** $89.95 *WOV* ♪♪ ½

Key to the City Light comedy featuring Gable and Young as two small town mayors who meet and fall in love at a convention in San Francisco. Throw in some sharp lines, a

little slapstick, and a bit of satire for an amusing picture. Based on the story by Albert Beich.

1950 99m/B Clark Gable, Loretta Young, Frank Morgan, Marilyn Maxwell, Raymond Burr, James Gleason, Lewis Stone, Raymond Walburn; **D:** George Sidney; **W:** Robert Riley Crutcher. **VHS** $19.98 *MGM* ♪♪ ½

Key to Vengeance Lone wolf battles bad guy with wealth of weapons. Vengeance is mine saith the guy with the most toys.

197? 90m/C Patrick L'Argent, Laura Yang. **VHS** *NO* ♪ ½

The Keys of the Kingdom An earnest adaptation of A.J. Cronin's novel about a young Scottish missionary spreading God's word in 19th Century China.

1944 137m/B Gregory Peck, Thomas Mitchell, Edmund Gwenn, Vincent Price, Roddy McDowall, Cedric Hardwicke, Peggy Ann Garner, James Gleason, Anne Revere, Rose Stradner, Sara Allgood, Abner Biberman, Arthur Shields; **D:** John M. Stahl; **W:** Joseph L. Mankiewicz, Nunnally Johnson. **VHS, Beta** $19.98 *FOX, IGP* ♪♪♪

The KGB: The Secret War Reheated Cold War fare. *AKA:* Lethal.

1986 (PG-13) 90m/C Sally Kellerman, Michael Ansara, Michael Billington. **VHS** *HHE* ♪ ½

Khartoum A sweeping but talky adventure epic detailing the last days of General "Chinese" Gordon as the title city is besieged by Arab tribes in 1884.

1966 134m/C Charlton Heston, Laurence Olivier, Ralph Richardson, Richard Johnson, Alexander Knox, Hugh Williams, Nigel Green, Michael Hordern, Johnny Sekka; **D:** Basil Dearden. **VHS, Beta** $19.98 *MGM, CCB* ♪♪ ½

The Kick Fighter Would you believe the hero has to kickbox to finance his kid sister's operation? Grungy, Bangkok-set chopsocky cheapie leaves no cliche untouched, but fights are well-staged. A strange end credit lauds real-life champ Urquidez, here a bad guy.

1991 92m/C Richard Norton, Benny "The Jet" Urquidez, Glen Ruehland, Franco Guerrero, Erica Van Wagener, Steve Rackman; **D:** Anthony Maharaj. **VHS** $79.95 *AIP* ♪

Kick of Death: The Prodigal Boxer A young boxer is accused of a murder he didn't commit, and fights a battle to the death to prove it.

1987 (R) 90m/C Mang Sei, Suma Wah Lung, Pa Hung; **D:** Chai Yang Min. **VHS, Beta** $19.95 *GEM* ♪

Kickboxer The brother of a permanently crippled kickboxing champ trains for a revenge match.

1989 (R) 97m/C Jean-Claude Van Damme, Rochelle Ashana, Dennis Chan, Dennis Alexio; **D:** Mark DiSalle; **W:** Jean-Claude Van Damme, Mark DiSalle. **VHS, Beta** $14.95 *HBO, WAR* ♪ ½

Kickboxer 2: The Road Back Mitchell takes over for Van Damme in this action sequel which finds our athletic hero seeking revenge on the kickboxer who murdered his brother.

1990 (R) 90m/C Sasha Mitchell, Peter Boyle, John Diehl; **D:** Albert Pyun. **VHS** $14.95 *WAR, MOV, HBO* ♪ ½

Kickboxer 3: The Art of War Mitchell returns in this second sequel. This time the American kickboxing champ flies to Rio for a big match which turns out to be fixed by a local mobster. For a little more fun our hero saves a kidnapped girl and fights a hired killer.

1992 (R) 92m/C Sasha Mitchell, Dennis Chan, Richard Comar, Noah Verduzco, Althea Miranda, Ian Jacklin; **D:** Rick King. **VHS** $89.98 *LIV* ♪ ½

Kickboxer the Champion The opium trade is in for a kick to the stomach when Archer challenges the big man in charge to a deathly duel.
1991 ?m/C Don Murray, Wayne Archer; *D:* Alton Cheung. VHS $79.95 *WLA* ✂

Kicks Two well-off San Francisco professionals play high-risk games with each other, culminating in a life-or-death hunt. Made for television.
1985 97m/C Anthony Geary, Shelley Hack, Tom Mason, Ian Abercrombie, James Avery; *D:* William Wiard. VHS, Beta *NO* ✂½

The Kid Sensitive and sassy film about a tramp who takes home an orphan. Chaplin's first feature. Also launched Coogan as the first child superstar.
1921 60m/B Charlie Chaplin, Jackie Coogan, Edna Purviance; *D:* Charlie Chaplin. VHS $29.98 *FCT, MLB* ✂✂✂

Kid Young guy carries grudge for the murder of his parents and seeks pound of flesh. Enter mysterious beautiful woman and copious complications. Good sound FX.
1990 (R) 94m/C C. Thomas Howell, R. Lee Ermey, Brian Austin Green, Sarah Trigger; *D:* John Mark Robinson. VHS, Beta $89.95 *LIV, IME* ✂✂½

Kid and the Killers Young orphan and a hardened criminal band together to pursue a villain.
198? (PG) 90m/C Jon Cypher. VHS, Beta *NO* ✂

The Kid Brother The shy, weak son of a tough sheriff, Harold fantasizes about being a hero like his father and big brothers, falls in love with a carnival lady, and somehow saves the day. Classic silent comedy.
1927 84m/B Harold Lloyd, Walter James, Jobyna Ralston; *D:* Ted Wilde. VHS, Beta *TLF* ✂✂✂½

Kid Colter Enjoyable family film about a city kid who goes to visit his dad in a remote wilderness area of the Pacific Northwest. While there he is abducted by two grizzly mountain men and left for dead, but survives and pursues his abductors relentlessly. Received the Film Advisory Board Award of Excellence and the Award of Merit from the Academy of Family Films.
1985 101m/C Jim Stafford, Jeremy Shamos, Hal Terrance, Greg Ward, Jim Turner; *D:* David O'Malley; *W:* David O'Malley. VHS, Beta $79.98 *FOX* ✂✂½

Kid Courageous An athlete goes west, tracks ore mine thieves and prevents a hot-blooded spitfire from marrying the wrong man.
1935 53m/B Bob Steele. VHS, Beta $19.95 *NOS* ✂

Kid Dynamite A Bowery Boys series episode. Gorcey is a boxer who is kidnapped to prevent his participation in a major fight. The real fighting occurs when his brother is substituted, and Gorcey is smitten. *AKA:* Queen of Broadway.
1943 73m/B Leo Gorcey, Huntz Hall, Bobby Jordan, Gabriel Dell, Pamela Blake; *D:* Wallace Fox. VHS $19.95 *NOS, HEG* ✂

A Kid for Two Farthings An episodic, sentimental portrait of the Jewish quarter in London's East End, centered on a boy with a malformed angora goat he thinks is a magic unicorn capable of granting wishes and bringing happiness to his impoverished 'hood. Acclaimed adaptation of a novel by screenwriter Wolf Mankowitz, also on tape in a shorter rehash as "The Unicorn."
1955 96m/C Jonathan Ashmore. VHS $39.95 *HMV, FCT* ✂✂½

Kid from Brooklyn A shy, musically inclined milkman becomes a middleweight boxer by knocking out the champ in a street brawl. Remake of "The Milky Way" by Harold Lloyd. Available with digitally remastered stereo and original movie trailer. ♫Sunflower Song; Hey, What's Your Name; You're the Cause Of It All; Welcome, Burleigh; I Love An Old-Fashioned Song; Josie.
1946 113m/C Danny Kaye, Virginia Mayo, Eve Arden, Fay Bainter, Walter Abel; *D:* Norman Z. McLeod. VHS, Beta $19.98 *HBO, SUE* ✂✂

Kid from Gower Gulch A singing, non-horse-riding cowboy enters a rodeo through a clever ruse.
1947 56m/B Spade Cooley. VHS, Beta $19.95 *NOS* ✂

The Kid from Left Field Bat boy for the San Diego Padres transforms the team from losers to champions when he passes on the advice of his father, a "has-been" ballplayer, to the team members. A made-for-television remake of the 1953 classic.
1979 80m/C Gary Coleman, Robert Guillaume, Ed McMahon, Tab Hunter; *D:* Adell Aldrich. VHS, Beta $69.95 *VES* ✂✂

Kid from Not-So-Big A family film that tells the story of Jenny, a young girl left to carry on her grandfather's frontier-town newspaper. When two con-men come to town, Jenny sets out to expose them.
1978 87m/C Jennifer McAllister, Veronica Cartwright, Robert Viharo, Paul Tulley; *D:* Bill Crain. VHS, Beta $39.98 *WAR, OM* ✂✂

Kid Galahad Well acted boxing drama with Robinson playing an honest promoter who wants to make Morris into a prize fighter. Davis plays the girl they both want. Remade as "The Wagons Roll at Night" and then made again as an Elvis Presley vehicle. Shown on television. *AKA:* The Battling Bellhop.
1937 101m/B Edward G. Robinson, Bette Davis, Humphrey Bogart, Wayne Morris, Jane Bryan, Harry Carey Sr., Veda Ann Borg; *D:* Michael Curtiz; *W:* Seton I. Miller. VHS $19.98 *MGM* ✂✂✂

Kid Galahad The King plays a young boxer who weathers the fight game, singing seven songs along the way. ♫King of the Whole Wide World; This Is Living; I Got Lucky; A Whistling Tune; Home Is Where The Heart Is; Riding the Rainbow; Love Is For Loves.
1962 95m/C Elvis Presley, Lola Albright, Charles Bronson, Ned Glass, Joan Blackman, Ed Asner, Gig Young; *D:* Phil Karlson. VHS, Beta $14.95 *MGM* ✂✂

The Kid/Idle Class The Little Tramp adopts a homeless orphan in "The Kid," Chaplin's first feature-length film. This tape also includes "The Idle Class," a rare Chaplin short.
1921 85m/B Charlie Chaplin, Jackie Coogan, Edna Purviance, Chuck Reisner, Lita Grey; *D:* Charlie Chaplin. VHS, Beta $19.98 *FOX* ✂✂✂

Kid Millions Vintage musical comedy in which a dull-witted Brooklyn boy must travel to exotic Egypt to collect an inherited fortune. The finale is filmed in early three-strip Technicolor. Lucille Ball appears as a Goldwyn Girl. ♫Your Head on My Shoulder; Ice Cream Fantasy; An Earful of Music; When My Ship Comes In; Okay Toots; I Want to be a Minstrel Man; Mandy.
1934 90m/B Eddie Cantor, Ethel Merman, Ann Sothern, George Murphy; *D:* Roy Del Ruth. VHS, Beta $19.98 *SUE* ✂✂½

Kid 'n' Hollywood and Polly Tix in Washington These two "Baby Burlesks" shorts star a cast of toddlers, featuring the most famous moppet of all time, Shirley Temple, in her earliest screen appearances.
1933 20m/B Shirley Temple. VHS, Beta $19.98 *CCB* ✂✂½

Kid Ranger A ranger shoots an innocent man, but later sets things straight by bringing the real culprit to justice.
1936 57m/B Bob Steele, William Farnum; *D:* Robert North Bradbury. VHS, Beta $19.95 *VYY* ✂

Kid Sister A young girl is determined to grab her sister's boyfriend for herself, and enlists the aid of a burglar to do it.
1945 56m/B Roger Pryor, Judy Clark, Frank Jenks, Constance Worth. VHS, Beta $19.95 *VYY* ✂½

Kid Vengeance After witnessing the brutal slaying of his family, a boy carries out a personal vendetta against the outlaws.
1975 (R) 90m/C Leif Garrett, Jim Brown, Lee Van Cleef, John Marley, Glynnis O'Connor; *D:* Joseph Manduke. VHS, Beta *NO* ✂✂

The Kid Who Loved Christmas After his adoptive mother is killed in a car accident, a young boy is taken from his adoptive father. The boy, upset about being removed from his new family, writes to Santa Claus for help. A touching yuletide drama. This was Sammy Davis, Jr.'s last film. Made for television.
1990 118m/C Cicely Tyson, Michael Warren, Sammy Davis Jr., Gilbert Lewis, Ken Page, Della Reese, Esther Rolle, Ben Vereen, Vanessa Williams, John Beal, Trent Cameron, Arthur Seidelman. VHS $14.95 *PAR* ✂✂

The Kid with the Broken Halo Coleman and Guillaume are paired again in this unsuccessful pilot for a TV series. A young angel, out to earn his wings, must try to help three desperate families, with the help of an experienced angel.
1982 100m/C Gary Coleman, Robert Guillaume, June Allyson, Mason Adams, Ray Walston, John Pleshette, Kim Fields, Georg Stanford Brown, Telma Hopkins; *D:* Leslie Martinson. VHS *NO* ✂✂

The Kid with the 200 I.Q. When an earnest boy genius enters college at age 13, predictable comic situations arise that involve his attempts at impressing his idolized astronomy professor (Guillaume), as well as an equally unrequited bout of first love. Harmless comedy, one of a series of squeaky-clean made-for-TV family fare starring Coleman.
1983 96m/C Gary Coleman, Robert Guillaume, Harriet Hilliard Nelson, Dean Butler, Karli Michaelson, Christina Murrull, Mel Stewart; *D:* Leslie Martinson. VHS, Beta $49.95 *LIV* ✂✂

Kidco The true story of a money-making corporation headed and run by a group of children ranging in age from nine to sixteen.
1983 (PG) 104m/C Scott Schwartz, Elizabeth Gorcey, Cinnamon Idles, Tristine Skyler; *D:* Ronald F. Maxwell. VHS, Beta $59.98 *FOX* ✂✂

Kidnap Syndicate Kidnappers swipe two boys, releasing one—the son of a wealthy industrialist who meets their ransom demands. When they kill the other boy, a mechanic's son, the father goes on a revengeful killing spree.
1976 (R) 105m/C James Mason, Valentina Cortese; *D:* Fernando Di Leo. VHS, Beta *NO* ✂½

Kidnapped A young boy is sold by his wicked uncle as a slave, and is helped by an outlaw. A Disney film based on the Robert Louis Stevenson classic.

1960 94m/C Peter Finch, James MacArthur, Peter O'Toole; *D:* Robert Stevenson. **VHS, Beta** $19.99 *DIS* ♂♂½

Kidnapped When a teenage girl is kidnapped by pornographers, her sister seeks help from a tough cop and together they go undercover to find her. Plot is flimsy cover for what is actually an exploitative piece.
1987 (R) 100m/C David Naughton, Barbara Crampton, Lance LeGault, Chick Vennera, Charles Napier; *D:* Howard (Hikmet) Avedis. **VHS, Beta** *NO Woof!*

Kidnapping of Baby John Doe Tragedy strikes a family's newborn, and they must make the terrifying decision between life and death. A doctor and nurse, however, take matters into their own hands to save the baby.
1988 90m/C Helen Hughes, Jayne Eastwood, Janet-Laine Green, Geoffery Boues, Peter Gerretsen. **VHS, Beta** *NO Woof!*

The Kidnapping of the President The U.S. president is taken hostage by Third World terrorists. The Secret Service is on the ball trying to recover the nation's leader. Well-integrated subplot involves the vice president in a scandal. Engrossing political thriller. Based on novel by Charles Templeton.
1980 (R) 113m/C William Shatner, Hal Holbrook, Van Johnson, Ava Gardner, Miguel Fernandez; *D:* George Mendeluk. **VHS, Beta** *NO* ♂♂½

Kid's Auto Race/Mabel's Married Life "Kid's Auto Race" (1914) concerns a kiddie-car contest; "Mabel's Married Life" (1915) is about flirtations in the park between married individuals. Piano and organ scores. *AKA:* Kid Auto Races at Venice.
1915 21m/B Charlie Chaplin, Mabel Normand, Mack Swain; *D:* Mack Sennett. **VHS, Beta** $19.98 *CCB, GVV* ♂

Kid's Last Ride Three tough guys come into town to settle a feud.
1941 55m/B Ray Corrigan, John "Dusty" King, Max Terhune, Luana Walters, Edwin Brian; *D:* S. Roy Luby. **VHS** $19.95 *NOS, DVT* ♂

The Kill A rough, cynical, hard-boiled, womanizing detective tracks down stolen cash in downtown Macao.
1973 81m/C Richard Jaeckel, Henry Duval, Judy Washington. **VHS, Beta** $19.95 *NWV* ♂♂½

Kill Alex Kill A Vietnam POW returns to find his family murdered, and uses the crime underworld to take revenge.
1983 88m/C Tony Zarindast, Tina Bowmann, Chris Ponti. **VHS, Beta** $59.95 *GEM Woof!*

Kill and Go Hide A young girl visits her mother's grave nightly to communicate with and command the ghoul-like creatures that haunt the surrounding woods. *AKA:* The Child.
1976 95m/C **VHS, Beta** *NO* ♂

Kill and Kill Again A martial arts champion attempts to rescue a kidnapped Nobel Prize-winning chemist who has developed a high-yield synthetic fuel. Colorful, tongue-in-cheek, and fun even for those unfamiliar with the genre.
1981 (PG) 100m/C James Ryan, Anneline Kriel, Stan Schmidt, Bill Flynn, Norman Robinson, Ken Gampu, John Ramsbottom; *D:* Ivan Hall. **VHS, Beta** $19.95 *MED* ♂♂½

Kill, Baby, Kill A small Transylvanian town is haunted by the ghost of a seven-year-old witchcraft victim, and the town's suicide victims all seem to have hearts of gold (coins, that is). Lots of style and atmosphere in this Transylvanian tale from horror tongue in cheekster Bava. Considered by many genre connoisseurs to be the B man's

finest, except that it bears early symptoms of the director's late onset infatuation with the zoom shot. *AKA:* Curse of the Living Dead; Operacione Paura.
1966 83m/C Erika Blanc, Giacomo "Jack" Rossi-Stuart, Fabienne Dali, Giana Vivaldi; *D:* Mario Bava. **VHS** $19.98 *SNC, FRG* ♂♂♂

Kill Castro Ever hear the one about the exploding cigar? Key West boat skipper is forced to carry a CIA agent to Cuba on a mission to assassinate Castro. Low-budget adventure that's deadly dull.
1980 (R) 90m/C Sybil Danning, Albert Salmi, Michael Gazzo, Raymond St. Jacques, Woody Strode, Stuart Whitman, Robert Vaughn, Caren Kaye; *D:* Chuck Workman. **VHS, Beta** *NO* ♂

Kill Cruise The depressed and alcoholic skipper of the yacht Bella Donna gives up sailing until he meets two beautiful young women who want to sail to Bermuda for a taste of the good life. The calm of the Atlantic is disturbed when they are plagued by bad weather and fierce storms, and tensions rise as the two women's jealousies erupt. Will it set the climate for murder?
1990 (R) 99m/C Juergen Prochnow, Patsy Kensit, Elizabeth Hurley; *D:* Peter Keglevic; *W:* Peter Keglevic. **VHS, Beta** *MCA* ♂♂

Kill Factor A spy thriller with a dash of martial arts. *AKA:* Death Dimension.
19?? (R) 91m/C Jim Kelly, George Lazenby, Aldo Ray, Harold Sakata, Terry Moore. **VHS, Beta** $19.95 *ACA* ♂

Kill Line Kim stars as Joe, a street fighter who seeks to clear his name after serving a 10-year prison sentence for a crime he didn't commit. When he finds his brother's family has been murdered by criminals looking for the millions he supposedly stole, Joe wages a one-man martial arts war against a corrupt police force and the gang of thugs who are looking for the money.
1991 (R) 93m/C Bobby Kim, Michael Parker, Marlene Zimmerman, H. Wayne Lowery, C.R. Valdez, Mark Williams, Ben Pfeifer; *D:* Richard H. Kim; *W:* Richard H. Kim. **VHS** $9.95 *HMD* ♂♂

Kill Me Again A woman hires a private detective to fake her death, which only gets him targeted by her boyfriend, the Mob, and the cops.
1989 (R) 93m/C Val Kilmer, Joanne Whalley-Kilmer, Michael Madsen, Jonathan Gries, Bibi Besch; *D:* John Dahl; *W:* John Dahl, David Warfield. **VHS, Beta** $89.95 *MGM* ♂♂

Kill My Wife...Please! Comic adventure of a despicable husband trying to bump off his wife in order to cash in on her insurance policy.
19?? 90m/C Bob Dishy, Joanna Barnes, Bill Dana; *D:* Steven Hilliard Stern. **VHS** $19.95 *HHE* ♂♂

Kill or Be Killed Martial arts champion is lured to a phony martial arts contest by a madman bent on revenge.
1980 (PG) 90m/C James Ryan, Charlotte Michelle, Norman Combes; *D:* Ivan Hall. **VHS, Beta** $54.95 *MED* ♂

Kill or Be Killed Michael Julian just spent eight years in jail for saving his brother Charlie's life. He must wonder why he bothered since Charlie has stolen his girl Beth and set up a drug empire. Michael ambushes Charlie's men and steals a million dollars to use as leverage but Charlie thinks rival drug lords are out to get him and starts a street war.
1993 97m/C David Heavener, Joseph Nuzzolo, Paulo Tocha, Lynn Levand; *D:* Joe Straw; *W:* Joseph Nuzzolo. **VHS** $89.95 *AIP* ♂½

The Kill Reflex A tough black cop and his beautiful rookie partner battle the mob and corruption.
1989 (R) 90m/C Maud Adams, Fred Williamson, Bo Svenson, Phyllis Hyman; *D:* Fred Williamson. **VHS, Beta** $79.95 *COL* ♂

Kill Slade When a United Nations food-aid diversion conspiracy is uncovered by a beautiful journalist, a plan to kidnap her is put into action. Romance follows.
1989 (PG-13) 90m/C Patrick Dollaghan, Lisa Brady, Anthony Fridjhon, Danny Keogh, Alfred Nowke; *D:* Bruce McFarlane. **VHS, Beta** $19.98 *SUE, NLC* ♂

Kill Squad Squad of martial arts masters follow a trail of violence and bloodshed to a vengeful, deadly battle of skills.
1981 (R) 85m/C Jean Claude, Jeff Risk, Jerry Johnson, Bill Cambra, Cameron Mitchell. **VHS, Beta** *VTR* ♂

Kill the Golden Goose Two martial arts masters work on opposite sides of a government corruption and corporate influence peddling case.
1979 (R) 91m/C Brad von Beltz, Ed Parker, Master Bong Soo Han; *D:* Elliot Hong. **VHS, Beta** $59.95 *GEM* ♂

Killcrazy On the way to a weekend camping trip, five Vietnam vets released from a mental hospital are slowly massacred by a group of dangerous killers until one of the vets decides to fight back.
1989 (R) 94m/C David Heavener, Danielle Brisebois, Burt Ward, Lawrence Hilton-Jacobs, Bruce Glover, Gary Owens, Rachelle Carson; *D:* David Heavener; *W:* David Heavener. **VHS** $89.98 *MED, IME* ♂

Killer An ex-convict sets up an ingenious bank robbery, and gets double-crossed himself.
1977 87m/C Henry Silva. **VHS, Beta** *NO* ♂

The Killer Jeffrey Chow is a gangster gunman who wants out. He's hired by his best friend to perform one last killing, but it doesn't go as smoothly as he wanted. He's almost caught by "Eagle" Lee, a detective who vows to hunt him down using Jennie, a singer blinded by Chow in crossfire. Lots of action and gunfights, but also pretty corny and sentimental. Very similar to American action movies, but using Chinese and Asian cultural conventions. A good introduction to the Chinese gangster-flick genre. Available with subtitles or dubbed in English. *AKA:* Die Xue Shuang Xiong.
1990 (R) 110m/C Chow Yun-fat, Sally Yeh, Danny Lee, Kenneth Tsang, Chu Kong; *D:* John Woo; *W:* John Woo. **VHS** $89.95 *FXL, ART, BTV* ♂♂♂½

Killer Bait Muddled drama about an innocent couple who find a large sum of money accidentally dropped into their car by mobsters. Possession of the money leads the greedy wife to ruin when she gets involved with gangsters, blackmail, and murder. Also known as "Killer Bait."
1949 99m/C Lizabeth Scott, Don DeFore, Dan Duryea, Arthur Kennedy, Kristine Miller, Barry Kelley; *D:* Byron Haskin. **VHS** $16.95 *SNC* ♂♂½

Killer Commandos Mercenaries go to the rescue of an oppressed African nation to overthrow the sinister white supremacy dictator.
19?? 87m/C Cameron Mitchell, Anthony Eisley. **VHS** *NO* ♂

Killer Dill Also killer dull. A meek salesman is misidentified as a death-dealing gangster, and the comic mixups begin.

1947 71m/B Stuart Erwin, Anne Gwynne, Frank Albertson, Mike Mazurki, Milburn Stone, Dorothy Granger; *D:* Lewis D. Collins. **VHS** $19.95 *NOS, VYY* 𝒵1/2

Killer Diller All-black musical revue featuring Nat King Cole and his Trio.
1948 70m/B Dusty Fletcher, Nat King Cole, Butterfly McQueen, Moms Mabley, George Wiltshire; *D:* Joe Binney. **VHS, Beta** $19.95 *MVD, NOS, DVT* 𝒵1/2

Killer Elephants A Thai man struggles to save his plantation, his wife, and his baby from the terrorists hired by a land baron to drive him away from his property.
1976 83m/C Sung Pa, Alan Yen, Nai Yen Ne, Yu Chien. **VHS, Beta** $29.95 *UNI* 𝒵𝒵

The Killer Elite Straight-ahead Peckinpah fare examining friendship and betrayal. Two professional assassins begin as friends but end up stalking each other when they are double-crossed. This minor Peckinpah effort is murky and doesn't have a clear resolution, but is plenty bloody. Lots of Dobermans roam through this picture too.
1975 (PG) 120m/C James Caan, Robert Duvall, Arthur Hill, Gig Young, Burt Young, Mako, Bo Hopkins, Helmut Dantine; *D:* Sam Peckinpah; *W:* Marc Norman, Sterling Silliphant. **VHS, Beta** $14.95 *MGM* 𝒵𝒵1/2

Killer Fish A scheme to steal and then hide a fortune in emeralds at the bottom of a tank full of piranhas backfires as the criminals find it impossible to retrieve them...as if that took a lot of foresight. Director Dawson is AKA Antonio Margheriti. Filmed in Brazil. *AKA:* Deadly Treasure of the Piranha.
1979 (PG) 101m/C Lee Majors, James Franciscus, Margaux Hemingway, Karen Black, Roy Brocksmith, Marisa Berenson; *D:* Anthony M. (Antonio Marghereti) Dawson. **VHS, Beta** $59.98 *FOX* 𝒵

Killer Force Predictable adventure involving international diamond smuggling.
1975 (R) 100m/C Telly Savalas, Peter Fonda, Maud Adams, Hugh O'Brian; *D:* Val Guest. **VHS, Beta** $69.98 *LIV, VES* 𝒵1/2

Killer Image A photographer unwittingly sees more than he should and becomes involved in a lethal political coverup. At the same time a wealthy senator targets him and he must fight for his life. Viewers might feel they have to fight their boredom.
1992 (R) 97m/C John Pyper-Ferguson, Michael Ironside, M. Emmet Walsh, Krista Errickson; *D:* David Winning. **VHS, Beta** *PAR* 𝒵

A Killer in Every Corner Three psychology students visit a loony professor and succumb to his hair-raising shenanigans.
1974 80m/C Joanna Pettet, Patrick Magee, Max Wall, Eric Flynn. **VHS, Beta** $29.95 *LIV* 𝒵

Killer Inside Me The inhabitants of a small western town are unaware that their mild-mannered deputy sheriff is actually becoming a crazed psychotic murderer. From the novel by Jim Thompson.
1976 (R) 99m/C Stacy Keach, Susan Tyrrell, Tisha Sterling, Keenan Wynn, John Dehner, John Carradine, Don Stroud; *D:* Burt Kennedy. **VHS, Beta** $59.95 *WAR, OM* 𝒵

Killer Instinct Two brothers do bloody warfare with notorious mobster kingpins in prohibition-era New York City.
1992 (R) 101m/C Christopher Bradley, Bruce Nozick, Rachel York; *D:* Greydon Clark, Ken Stein. **VHS** $89.95 *VMK* 𝒵

Killer Klowns from Outer Space Bozo-like aliens resembling demented clowns land on earth and set up circus tents to lure Earthlings in. Visually striking, campy but slick horror flick that'll make you think twice about your next visit to the big top.

Mood is heightened by a cool title tune by the Dickies. Definitely has cult potential!
1988 (PG-13) 90m/C Grant Cramer, Suzanne Snyder, John Allen Nelson, Royal Dano, John Vernon, Peter Licassi, Michael Siegel; *D:* Stephen Chiodo; *W:* Charles Chiodo, Stephen Chiodo; *M:* John Massari. **VHS, Beta** $19.95 *MED, CVS* 𝒵𝒵1/2

Killer Likes Candy An assassin stalks the King of Kafiristan, and a CIA operative tries to stop him.
1978 86m/C Kerwin Mathews, Marilu Tolo; *D:* Richard Owens. **VHS, Beta** $59.95 *GEM, MRV* 𝒵

Killer on Board Folks spending their holiday on a cruise ship are afflicted by a fatal virus and subsequently quarantined. Typical made-for-TV disaster flick.
1977 100m/C Claude Akins, Beatrice Straight, George Hamilton, Patty Duke, Frank Converse, Jane Seymour, William Daniels; *D:* Philip Leacock. **VHS, Beta** $49.95 *LIV* 𝒵𝒵

Killer Party Three coeds pledge a sorority and are subjected to a hazing that involves a haunted fraternity house. Standard horror plot; Paul Bartel ("Eating Raoul"; "Lust in the Dust") is the only significant element.
1986 (R) 91m/C Elaine Wilkes, Sherry Willis-Burch, Joanna Johnson, Paul Bartel, Martin Hewitt, Ralph Seymour; *D:* William Fruet. **VHS, Beta** $79.98 *FOX* Woof!

The Killer Shrews Lumet (Sidney's father) creates a serum that causes the humble shrew to take on killer proportions. The creatures are actually dogs in makeup. Goude was 1957's Miss Universe.
1959 70m/B James Best, Ingrid Goude, Baruch Lumet, Ken Curtis; *D:* Ray Kellogg. **VHS** $19.98 *SNC, MRV, HHT* 𝒵𝒵

Killer Tomatoes Eat France Professor Gangrene takes his tomato fetish to France, where the giant vegetables try to take over the streets. The fourth in the killer-vegetable series.
1991 94m/C John Astin, Marc Price, Steve Lundquist; *D:* John DeBello. **VHS** $92.98 *FXV* 𝒵1/2

Killer Tomatoes Strike Back The third "Killer Tomatoes" movie isn't in the league of "The Naked Gun" satires, but it's still bright parody for the Mad Magazine crowd, as tomato-mad scientist Astin harnesses the powers of trash-TV in a planned vegetable invasion. Perhaps due to a 'Killer Tomatoes' cartoon series at the time, this isn't as saucy as its predecessors and is acceptable for family audiences. Followed by "Killer Tomatoes Eat France."
1990 87m/C John Astin, Rick Rockwell, Crystal Carson, Steve Lundquist, John Witherspoon; *D:* John DeBello. **VHS** $39.98 *FXV, IME* 𝒵𝒵

Killer with Two Faces A woman is terrorized by the evil twin of her boyfriend. Made for television.
1974 70m/C Donna Mills, Ian Hendry, David Lodge, Roddy McMillian. **VHS, Beta** $12.95 *LIV* 𝒵

Killer Workout A murderer stalks the clients of a sweat/sex/muscle-filled gym. *AKA:* Aerobicide.
1986 (R) 89m/C David James Campbell, Ted Prior; *D:* David A. Prior. **VHS, Beta** $29.95 *ACA* 𝒵

The Killers After two hired assassins kill a teacher, they look into his past and try to find leads to a $1,000,000 robbery. Reagan's last film. Remake of 1946 film of the same name, which was loosely based on a short story by Ernest Hemingway. Originally intended for television, but released to theaters instead due to its violence. *AKA:* Ernest Hemingway's the Killers.

1964 95m/C Lee Marvin, Angie Dickinson, John Cassavetes, Ronald Reagan, Clu Gulager, Claude Akins, Norman Fell; *D:* Don Siegel; *M:* John Williams. **VHS, Beta** $39.95 *MCA* 𝒵𝒵

Killers Remote jungles of southern Africa are the scene of a military coup.
1988 83m/C Cameron Mitchell, Alicia Hammond, Robert Dix; *D:* Ewing Miles Brown. **VHS, Beta** $39.95 *GHV* 𝒵

The Killer's Edge Cop is caught between rock and hard place in L.A. when he's forced to confront criminal who once saved his life in 'Nam. Plenty of gut busting and soul wrenching. *AKA:* Blood Money.
1990 (R) 90m/C Wings Hauser, Robert Z'Dar, Karen Black. **VHS** $79.95 *PMH* 𝒵1/2

Killers from Space Cheap sci-fi flick in which big-eyed men from beyond Earth bring scientist Graves back to life to assist them with their evil plan for world domination.
1954 80m/B Peter Graves, Barbara Bestar, James Scay; *D:* W. Lee Wilder. **VHS, Beta** $9.95 *NOS, MRV, RHI* Woof!

Killer's Kiss A boxer and a dancer set out to start a new life together when he saves the woman from an attempted rape. Gritty, second feature from Kubrick was financed by friends and family and shows signs of his budding talent.
1955 67m/C Frank Silvera, Jamie Smith, Irene Kane, Jerry Jarret; *D:* Stanley Kubrick; *W:* Stanley Kubrick. **VHS** *FCT* 𝒵𝒵1/2

Killer's Moon Four sadistic psychopaths escape from a prison hospital and unleash their murderous rage on anyone who crosses their path.
1984 90m/C **VHS, Beta** *NO* 𝒵

The Killing The dirty, harsh, street-level big heist epic that established Kubrick and presented its genre with a new and vivid existentialist aura, as an ex-con engineers the rip-off of a racetrack with disastrous results. Displays characteristic nonsentimental sharp-edged Kubrick vision. Cinematography by Lucien Ballard. Based on the novel "Clean Break" by Lionel White.
1956 83m/B Sterling Hayden, Marie Windsor, Elisha Cook Jr., Jay C. Flippen, Vince Edwards, Timothy Carey, Coleen Gray, Joseph Sawyer, Ted de Corsia; *D:* Stanley Kubrick. **VHS, Beta** $19.95 *MGM, VYG* 𝒵𝒵𝒵

A Killing Affair Set in West Virginia, 1943, this is the story of a widow who takes in a drifter who she believes is the man who killed her husband. She begins to fall for him, but cannot be sure if she should trust him. Vague and melodramatic. From the novel "Monday, Tuesday, Wednesday" by Robert Houston. Saperstein's directorial debut.
1985 (R) 100m/C Peter Weller, Kathy Baker, John Glover, Bill Smitrovich; *D:* David Saperstein; *M:* John Barry. **VHS, Beta** $9.99 *STE, PSM* 𝒵

Killing at Hell's Gate A made-for-television movie about a group of whitewater rafters being picked off by snipers as they travel down river.
1981 96m/C Robert Urich, Deborah Raffin, Lee Purcell; *D:* Jerry Jameson. **VHS, Beta** $59.98 *FOX* 𝒵1/2

The Killing Beach Australian photojournalist Judith Wilkes (Scacchi) travels to Malaysia in the late 1970s to report on the plight of the Vietnamese boat people seeking refuge there. She befriends the wife of the Australian ambassador, a former callgirl from Saigon, who hopes to find her own children among the refugees. But the native Malays resent the foreign intrusion and are determined to stop the boat people—no matter what the cost in blood. Based on the novel

"Turtle Beach" by Blanche D'Alpuget. *AKA:* Turtle Beach.
1992 (R) 105m/C Greta Scacchi, Joan Chen, Jack Thompson, Art Malik, Norman Kaye; *D:* Stephen Wallace; *W:* Ann Turner. VHS $19.95 COL *♢♢*

Killing Cars A German car designer's pet project, a car that runs without gas, is halted by the influence of an Arab conglomerate. He nevertheless tries to complete it, and is hunted down.
1985 (R) 104m/C Juergen Prochnow, Senta Berger, William Conrad, Agnes Soral; *D:* Michael Verhoeven. VHS, Beta $79.95 VMK, HHE, STE *♢♢½*

The Killing Device Two government scientists lose their funding on a covert political assassination project and decide to eliminate the government officials responsible. When two journalists attempt to solve the murders they become the next targets.
1992 93m/C Clu Gulager, Antony Alda, Gig Rauch. VHS $59.95 VCI *♢½*

The Killing Edge In post-nuclear holocaust Earth, a lone warrior seeks justice, and his family, in a lawless land.
1986 85m/C Bill French, Marv Spencer; *D:* Lindsay Shonteff. VHS $39.98 VCD, HHE *♢½*

Killing 'em Softly Segal portrays a down-on-his-luck musician who accidentally murders a music manager during an argument. Cara's boyfriend is accused and to clear his name, the singer moonlights as a detective. She and Segal end up falling in love. Disappointing.
1985 90m/C George Segal, Irene Cara; *D:* Max Fischer. VHS, Beta $79.95 PSM, HHE *♢*

The Killing Fields Based on the New York Times' Sydney Schanberg's account of his friendship with Cambodian interpreter Dith Pran. They separated during the fall of Saigon, when Western journalists fled, leaving behind countless assistants who were later accused of collusion with the enemy by the Khmer Rouge and killed or sent to re-education camps during the bloodbath known as "Year Zero." Schanberg searched for Pran through the Red Cross and U.S. government, while Pran struggled to survive, finally escaping and walking miles to freedom. Ngor's own experiences echoed those of his character Pran. Malkovich's debut is intense. Joffe's directorial debut shows a generally sure hand, with only a bit of melodrama at the end.
1984 (R) 142m/C Sam Waterston, Haing S. Ngor, John Malkovich, Athol Fugard, Craig T. Nelson, Julian Sands, Spalding Gray, Bill Paterson; *D:* Roland Joffe; *W:* Bruce Robinson. Academy Awards '84: Best Cinematography, Best Film Editing, Best Supporting Actor (Ngor); Nominations: Best Actor (Waterston), Best Adapted Screenplay, Best Director (Joffe), Best Picture; Golden Globe Awards '85: Best Supporting Actor (Ngor). VHS, Beta $19.98 WAR, BTV, HMV *♢♢♢½*

Killing Floor A black sharecropper during WWI travels to Chicago to get work in the stockyards and becomes a voice in the growing labor movement. Made for television.
1985 (PG) 118m/C Damien Leake, Alfre Woodard, Moses Gunn, Clarence Felder, Bill Duke; *D:* William Duke. VHS, Beta $14.95 COL, SUE, FCT *♢♢*

The Killing Game A husband-wife cartoonist team link up with an unhinged playboy and act out a murder-mystery comic they produce together. In French with subtitles. *AKA:* All Weekend Lovers; Jeu de Massacre.
1967 90m/C Jean-Pierre Cassel, Claudine Auger, Michel Duchaussoy, Anna Gaylor; *D:* Alain Jessua. VHS, Beta $39.95 FCT *♢♢½*

The Killing Game A slew of Californians kill and betray each other for lustful reasons.
1987 90m/C Chad Hayward, Cynthia Killion, Geoffrey Sadwith; *D:* Joseph Merhi. VHS, Beta NO *♢*

Killing Heat An independent career woman living in South Africa decides to abandon her career to marry a struggling jungle farmer. Based on Doris Lessing's novel "The Grass is Singing." *AKA:* The Grass is Singing.
1984 (R) 104m/C Karen Black, John Thaw, John Kani, John Moulder-Brown; *D:* Michael Raeburn. VHS, Beta $59.98 FOX *♢♢½*

Killing Hour A psychic painter finds that the visions she paints come true in a string of grisly murders. Her ability interests a television reporter and a homicide detective. *AKA:* The Clairvoyant.
1984 (R) 97m/C Elizabeth Kemp, Perry King, Norman Parker, Kenneth McMillan; *D:* Armand Mastroianni. VHS, Beta $79.98 FOX, VTR *♢♢*

A Killing in a Small Town Candy Morrison seems like the perfect member of her small Texas community—but appearances can be deceiving, particularly after she's charged with killing a fellow churchgoer by striking her 41 times with an axe (shades of Lizzie Borden)! Dennehy is her skeptical lawyer who isn't sure if it was self-defense or a peculiar sort of revenge. Good performances by Hershey and Dennehy lift this above the usual tawdry made for TV level. Based on a true story; originally a television miniseries.
1990 (R) 95m/C Barbara Hershey, Brian Dennehy, Hal Holbrook, Richard Gilliland, John Terry, Lee Garlington; *D:* Stephen Gyllenhaal; *M:* Richard Gibbs. VHS $89.95 VMK *♢♢♢*

Killing in the Sun Gripping struggle for prosperous smuggling in the Mediterranean consume mobsters from three countries.
19?? (R) 90m/C Henry Silva, Michael Constantine. VHS NO *♢*

The Killing Kind Man released from prison is obsessed with wreaking vengeance on his daft lawyer and his accuser. His vendetta eventually draws his mother into the fray as well. Fine performance by Savage.
1973 95m/C Ann Sothern, John Savage, Ruth Roman, Luana Anders, Cindy Williams; *D:* Curtis Harrington. VHS NO *♢♢½*

The Killing Mind A young girl witnesses a grisly murder that is never solved. Twenty years later she (Zimbalist) becomes a cop who specializes in trapping psychos. Haunted by her memories, she and a reporter (Bill) team up to find the killer, never suspecting that she is his next victim. Originally made-for-cable-television.
1990 96m/C Stephanie Zimbalist, Tony Bill, Daniel Roebuck; *D:* Michael Rhodes. VHS $89.98 WOV *♢♢½*

Killing Obsession Albert (Savage) has been locked in the Parkview State Psychiatric Facility for 20 years, ever since he murdered 11-year-old Annie's mother. Annie is Albert's obsession and in his mind she's always remained a young girl. So when Albert is released, he goes looking for Annie—murdering along the way. Now that the real Annie is an adult will Albert finally accept the passage of time or will she be just another victim?
1994 95m/C John Savage, Kimberly Chase, John Saxon, Bernie White; *D:* Paul Leder; *W:* Paul Leder. VHS $89.95 TRI *♢½*

The Killing of a Chinese Bookie Gazzara runs a Sunset Strip nightclub and is in hock to loan sharks. When he can't come up with the cash, he's offered a deal—get rid of a troublesome Chinese bookie and all debts will be forgiven. But it turns out the bookie is highly connected in the Asian mob and nothing goes as planned. Cassavette's improv technique makes for a self-indulgent and endless film.
1976 (R) 109m/C Ben Gazzara, Jean-Pierre Cassel, Zizi Johari, Soto Joe Hugh, Robert Phillips, Timothy Carey, Morgan Woodward; *D:* John Cassavetes; *W:* John Cassavetes. VHS, Beta $89.95 TOU, FCT *♢♢*

Killing of Angel Street A courageous young woman unwittingly becomes the central character in an escalating nightmare about saving a community from corrupt politicians and organized crime.
1981 (PG) 101m/C Liz Alexander, John Hargreaves; *D:* Donald Crombie; *W:* Evan Jones. VHS, Beta $14.98 FCT *♢♢*

Killing of Randy Webster A father attempts to prove that his son did not die as a criminal when Texas policemen shot him after transporting a stolen van across state lines.
1981 90m/C Hal Holbrook, Dixie Carter, Sean Penn, Jennifer Jason Leigh; *D:* Sam Wanamaker. VHS, Beta NO *♢½*

The Killing of Sister George Racy, sensationalized film based on the Frank Marcus black comedy/melodrama about a lesbian love triangle between a television executive and two soap opera stars. Things get a little uncomfortable when they learn one of their characters is to be written out of the show. Shot in England.
1969 (R) 138m/C Beryl Reid, Susannah York, Coral Browne, Ronald Fraser, Patricia Medina, Hugh Paddick, Cyril Elaine Church, Brandan Dillon; *D:* Robert Aldrich. VHS, Beta $79.98 FOX *♢♢*

Killing Stone A freelance writer uncovers a small town sheriff's plot to cover up a scandalous homicide. Made for television.
1978 120m/C Gil Gerard, J.D. Cannon, Jim Davis, Nehemiah Persoff; *D:* Michael Landon; *W:* Michael Landon. VHS, Beta $49.95 PSM *♢♢*

Killing Streets A commando learns that his twin brother is being held hostage in Lebanon and plans a rescue mission. A standard farfetched actioner; noteworthy for a real sense of despair over the endless carnage in the Mideast. Some dialogue in Arabic with subtitles.
1991 109m/C Michael Pare, Lorenzo Lamas; *D:* Stephen Cornwell. VHS $89.98 VES, LIV *♢♢*

The Killing Time A minor, effective murder thriller about a quiet small resort town suddenly beset by a web of murder, double-crossings, blackmail, and infidelity. They seem to coincide with the appearance of a mysterious stranger posing as the town's deputy sheriff just as the new sheriff is about to take up the badge.
1987 (R) 94m/C Kiefer Sutherland, Beau Bridges, Joe Don Baker, Wayne Rogers; *D:* Rick King. VHS, Beta $19.95 NWV, STE *♢♢*

The Killing Zone Convict nephew of onetime Drug Enforcement agent rewrites zoning ordinances to hunt for Mexican drug lord south of the border.
1990 90m/C Daron McBee, James Dalesandro, Melissa Moore, Armando Silvestre, Augustine Beral, Sydne Squire, Deborah Dare; *D:* Addison Randall. VHS $29.95 PMH *♢½*

Killings at Outpost Zeta Earthmen investigate a barren planet where previous expeditions have disappeared, and find hordes of aliens.
1980 92m/C Gordon Devol, Jackie Ray, James A. Watson Jr. **VHS, Beta $69.95** VCI ⅃

Killjoy A sleazy surgeon's daughter is the prey in this television thriller. The plot twists are led by the array of people who become involved. A clever suspense mystery. Made for television. *AKA:* Who Murdered Joy Morgan?
1981 100m/C Kim Basinger, Robert Culp, Stephen Macht, Nancy Marchand, John Rubinstein, Ann Dusenberry, Ann Wedgeworth; *D:* John Llewellyn Moxey; *M:* Bruce Broughton. **VHS, Beta $49.95** LIV ⅃⅃½

Killpoint Special task force is assembled to catch the criminals who robbed a National Guard armory for its weapons.
1984 (R) 89m/C Leo Fong, Richard Roundtree, Cameron Mitchell; *D:* Frank Harris. **VHS, Beta $79.98** LIV, VES ⅃½

Killzone A brainwashed Vietnam vet breaks down during a training exercise and embarks on a psychotic killing spree.
1985 86m/C Ted Prior, David James Campbell, Richard Massery; *D:* David A. Prior. **VHS, Beta $69.98** VES ⅃

Kilma, Queen of the Amazons A shipwrecked sailor finds himself on an island populated by man-hating Amazons. When a shipload of lusty sailors arrive to rescue him, carnage ensues.
1986 90m/C **VHS, Beta** NO Woof!

Kim A colorful Hollywood adaptation of the Rudyard Kipling classic about an English boy disguised as a native in 19th Century India, and his various adventures.
1950 113m/C Errol Flynn, Dean Stockwell, Paul Lukas, Cecil Kellaway; *D:* Victor Saville. **VHS, Beta $19.98** MGM ⅃⅃⅃

Kind Hearts and Coronets Black comedy in which an ambitious young man sets out to bump off eight relatives in an effort to claim a family title. Guinness is wonderful in his role as all eight of the fated relations. Based on Roy Horiman's novel.
1949 104m/B Alec Guinness, Dennis Price, Valerie Hobson, Joan Greenwood; *D:* Robert Hamer. **VHS, Beta $19.98** FCT, HMV ⅃⅃⅃½

A Kind of Loving Two North English young people marry rashly as a result of pregnancy, find they really didn't like each other all that much, but manage to adjust.
1962 107m/B Alan Bates, Thora Hird, June Ritchie; *D:* John Schlesinger. **VHS, Beta** NO ⅃⅃⅃

Kindergarten Endearing tale based on a true story of a young Russian street violinist. During WWII, the boy meets a variety of interesting people as he travels throughout the Soviet Union. In Russian with English subtitles.
1984 143m/C Klaus Maria Brandauer; *D:* Yevgeny Yevtushenko. **VHS $59.99** KIV ⅃⅃⅃

Kindergarten Cop Pectoral perfect cop Kimble (Schwarzenegger) stalks mama's boy/criminal Crisp (Tyson) by locating the drug lord's ex and his six-year-old son. When the pec man's female partner succumbs to a nasty bout of food poisoning, he's forced to take her place as an undercover kindergarten teacher in the drowsy Pacific northwest community where mother and son reside incognito. A cover all the bases Christmas release, it's got romance, action, comedy and cute. Box office earnings to match Arnie's chest measurements. A bit violent for the milk and cookie set.
1990 (PG-13) 111m/C Arnold Schwarzenegger, Penelope Ann Miller, Pamela Reed, Linda Hunt, Richard Tyson, Carroll Baker, Cathy Moriarty, Park Overall, Richard Portnow, Jayne Brook; *D:* Ivan Reitman; *W:* Murray Salem, Herschel Weingrod, Timothy Harris; *M:* Randy Edelman. **VHS, Beta $19.95** MCA, CCB ⅃⅃½

The Kindred A young student discovers that his mother the biologist has created a hybrid creature using his body tissue. Naturally, he is horrified and begins to search for his test-tube brother; the problem is, this brother likes eating people. Not too bad; boasts some good acting.
1987 (R) 92m/C Rod Steiger, Kim Hunter, David Allan Brooks, Timothy Gibbs, Amanda Pays, Talia Balsam, Jeffrey Obrow, Peter Frechette, Julia Montgomery; *D:* Jeffrey Obrow, Stephen Carpenter; *W:* Jeffrey Obrow, Stephen Carpenter, Joseph Stefano, John Penney, Earl Ghaffari; *M:* David Newman. **VHS, Beta $14.98** LIV, VES ⅃⅃½

King Docudrama with terrific cast follows the life and career of one of the greatest non-violent civil rights leaders of all time, Martin Luther King. Made for television.
1978 272m/C Paul Winfield, Cicely Tyson, Roscoe Lee Browne, Ossie Davis, Art Evans, Ernie Banks, Howard E. Rollins Jr., William Jordan, Cliff DeYoung; *D:* Abby Mann; *W:* Abby Mann; *M:* Billy Goldenberg. **VHS, Beta** NO ⅃⅃⅃

The King and Four Queens Gable, on the run from the law, happens upon a deserted town, deserted, that is, except for a woman and her three daughters. Clark soon discovers that the women are looking for $100,000 in gold that one of their missing husbands had stolen. True to form, conniving Clark wastes no time putting the moves on each of them to find the whereabouts of the loot.
1956 86m/C Clark Gable, Eleanor Parker, Jo Van Fleet, Jean Wiles, Barbara Nichols, Sara Shane, Roy Roberts, Arthur Shields, Jay C. Flippen; *D:* Raoul Walsh. **VHS, Beta $19.98** MGM, CCB ⅃⅃½

The King and I Wonderful adaptation of Rogers and Hammerstein's Broadway play based on the novel "Anna and the King of Siam" by Margaret Landon. English governess Kerr is hired to teach the King of Siam's many children and bring them into the 20th century. She has more of a job than she realizes, for this is a king, a country, and a people who value tradition above all else. Features one of Rodgers and Hammerstein's best-loved scores. Brynner made this role his, playing it over 4,000 times on stage and screen before his death. Kerr's voice was dubbed when she sang; the voice you hear is Marni Nixon, who also dubbed the star's singing voices in "West Side Story" and "My Fair Lady." ♫Shall We Dance?; Getting To Know You; Hello, Young Lovers; We Kiss in a Shadow; I Whistle a Happy Tune; March of the Siamese Children; I Have Dreamed; A Puzzlement; Something Wonderful.
1956 133m/C Deborah Kerr, Yul Brynner, Rita Moreno, Martin Benson, Terry Saunders, Rex Thompson, Alan Mowbray, Carlos Rivas; *D:* Walter Lang; *W:* Ernest Lehman; *M:* Richard Rodgers, Oscar Hammerstein. Academy Awards '56: Best Actor (Brynner), Best Art Direction/Set Decoration (Color), Best Costume Design (Color), Best Sound, Best Score; Nominations: Best Actress (Kerr), Best Color Cinematography, Best Director (Lang), Best Picture; Golden Globe Awards '57: Best Actress—Musical/Comedy (Kerr), Best Film—Musical/Comedy. **VHS, Beta $19.98** FOX, BTV, RDG ⅃⅃⅃⅃

King Arthur, the Young Warlord The struggle that was the other side of Camelot—the campaign against the Saxon hordes. The early, somewhat violent years of King Art.
1975 (PG) 90m/C Oliver Tobias, Michael Gothard, Jack Watson, Brian Blessed, Peter Firth; *D:* Sidney Hayers, Pat Jackson, Peter Sasdy. **VHS, Beta $29.95** GEM ⅃⅃

King Boxer A famous martial arts school is taken over by a menacing gang. When a student-to-be finds this out, he enlists himself to take on the best individual of the gang in a deadly match.
1990 106m/C Lo Lieh, Wang Ping. **VHS $14.95** HMD ⅃

King Boxers Kurate stars in this tale of elephant hunts, warding off Triad Society gangs, and personal combat. Nainam is a former Thailand fists and kick boxing champion.
1980 (R) 90m/C Yasuka Kurata, Johnny Nainam. **VHS, Beta $59.95** GEM ⅃⅃

King Creole The King goes film noir as a teenager with a criminal record who becomes a successful pop singer in New Orleans but is threatened by his ties to crime, represented by Walter Matthau. One of the better Elvis films, based on Harold Robbins' "A Stone for Danny Fisher." Features Elvis' last film appearance before his service in the Army. ♫King Creole; Banana; New Orleans; Turtles, Berries and Gumbo; Crawfish; Don't Ask Me Why; As Long As I Have You; Trouble; Hard-Headed Woman.
1958 115m/B Elvis Presley, Carolyn Jones, Walter Matthau, Dean Jagger, Dolores Hart, Vic Morrow, Paul Stewart; *D:* Michael Curtiz. **VHS, Beta $19.95** MVD, FOX ⅃⅃½

King David The story of David, the legendary Biblical hero whose acts of bravery paved the way for him to become king of Israel.
1985 (PG-13) 114m/C Richard Gere, Alice Krige, Cherie Lunghi, Hurd Hatfield, Edward Woodward; *D:* Bruce Beresford; *W:* Andrew Birkin; *M:* Carl Davis. **VHS, Beta $14.95** PAR ⅃½

King Dinosaur A new planet arrives in the solar system, and a scientific team checks out its giant iguana-ridden terrain.
1955 63m/B Bill Bryant, Wanda Curtis, Patti Gallagher, Douglas Henderson. **VHS, Beta** MLB ⅃½

A King in New York Chaplin plays the deposed king of a European mini-monarchy who comes to the United States in hope of making a new life. Looks critically at 1950s-era America, including Cold War paranoia and over reliance on technology. Containing Chaplin's last starring performance, this film wasn't released in the U.S. until 1973. Uneven but interesting.
1957 105m/B Charlie Chaplin, Dawn Addams, Michael Chaplin, Oliver Johnston, Maxine Audley, Harry Green; *D:* Charlie Chaplin. **VHS, Beta $19.98** FOX ⅃⅃

King Kelly of the U.S.A. Robertson carries on a forgettable romance with a princess aboard a trans-Atlantic line.
1934 64m/B Guy Robertson, Irene Ware, Edgar Kennedy, Franklin Pangborn, Joyce Compton, Ferdinand Gottschalk, William von Brinken, Otis Harlan; *D:* Leonard Fields. **VHS $19.95** NOS ⅃

King Kong The original beauty and the beast film classic tells the story of Kong, a giant ape captured in Africa and brought to New York as a sideshow attraction. Kong falls for Wray, escapes from his captors and rampages through the city, ending up on top of the newly built Empire State Building. Moody Steiner score adds color, and Willis

O'Brien's stop-motion animation still holds up well. Remade numerous times with various theme derivations. Available in a colorized version. The laserdisc, produced from a superior negative, features extensive liner notes and running commentary by film historian Ronald Haver.
1933 105m/B Fay Wray, Bruce Cabot, Robert Armstrong, Frank Reicher, Noble Johnson, Sam Hardy, James Flavin; **D:** Ernest B. Schoedsack; **M:** Max Steiner. **VHS, Beta, 8mm $16.98** *TTC, RKO, MED* 🎬🎬🎬

King Kong Oil company official travels to a remote island to discover it inhabited by a huge gorilla. The transplanted beast suffers unrequited love in classic fashion: monkey meets girl, monkey gets girl and brandishes her while atop the World Trade Center. An updated remake of the 1933 movie classic that also marks the screen debut of Lange. Impressive sets and a believable King Kong romp around New York City in this film. Watch for Joe Piscopo, and quickly for Corbin Bernsen as a reporter.
1976 (PG) 135m/C Jeff Bridges, Charles Grodin, Jessica Lange, Rene Auberjonois, John Randolph, Ed Lauter, Jack O'Halloran; **D:** John Guillermin; **M:** John Barry. Academy Awards '76: Best Visual Effects; Nominations: Best Cinematography, Best Sound. **VHS, Beta, 8mm $24.95** *PAR, HMV* 🎬🎬

King Kong Lives Unnecessary sequel to the 1976 remake of "King Kong," in which two scientists set up the big ape, now restored after his asphalt-upsetting fall, together with a lady ape his size and type.
1986 (PG-13) 105m/C Brian Kerwin, Linda Hamilton, John Ashton, Peter Michael Goetz; **D:** John Guillermin; **W:** Steven Pressfield. **VHS, Beta $14.95** *MED, WAR* 🎬

King Kong Versus Godzilla The planet issues a collective shudder as the two mightiest monsters slug it out for reasons known only to themselves. Humankind can only stand by and watch in impotent horror as the tide of the battle sways to and fro, until one monster stands alone and victorious. *AKA:* King Kong Tai Godzilla.
1963 105m/C Inoshiro Honda, Michael Keith, Tadao Takashima; **D:** Thomas Montgomery. **VHS $9.95** *GKK* 🎬🎬½

King Kung Fu A karate master raises a gorilla, and sends it from Asia to the U.S. There, two out-of-work reporters decide to release it from captivity and then recapture it so they can get the story and some needed recognition. The background they don't have on the gorilla is that its master taught it kung fu.
1987 (G) 90m/C John Balee, Tom Leahy, Maxine Gray, Bill Schwartz; **D:** Bill Hayes. **VHS** *NO* 🎬

King Lear Brook's version of Shakespeare tragedy. The king drives away the only decent daughter he has, and when he realizes this, it is too late. Powerful performances and interesting effort at updating the bard.
1971 137m/B Paul Scofield, Irene Worth, Jack MacGowran, Alan Webb, Cyril Cusack, Patrick Magee; **D:** Peter Brook. **VHS $29.95** *NOS, DVT* 🎬🎬🎬½

King Lear Loosely adapted from Shakespeare's tragedy of a king who loses everything. A fragmented French existential reading with gangster undercurrent. This updated version is dark, ominous, wandering, strange, and quite unlike the other 1984 remake. Or any other remake, for that matter.

1987 91m/C Peter Sellers, Burgess Meredith, Molly Ringwald, Jean-Luc Godard, Woody Allen; **D:** Jean-Luc Godard; **W:** Norman Mailer. **VHS $59.95** *ING, CAN* 🎬½

The King Murder Case High-society sleuth Tearle tries to solve the mysterious death of a beautiful, yet dangerous extortionist. Looks a lot like murder, although no weapon can be found.
1932 67m/B Conway Tearle, Natalie Moorhead, Marceline Day, Dorothy Revier; **D:** Richard Thorpe; **W:** Charles Reed Jones. **VHS $12.95** *SNC* 🎬🎬

King of America A Greek sailor and a local labor agent battle over who will become King of America.
1980 90m/C D: Dezso Magyar. **VHS, Beta** *NO* 🎬

King of Comedy An unhinged would-be comedian haunts and eventually kidnaps a massively popular Johnny Carson-type television personality. A cold, cynical farce devised by Scorsese seemingly in reaction to John Hinckley's obsession with his film "Taxi Driver." Controlled, hard-hitting performances, especially by De Niro and Lewis.
1982 (PG) 101m/C Robert De Niro, Jerry Lewis, Sandra Bernhard, Tony Randall, Diahnne Abbott, Shelley Hack, Liza Minnelli; **D:** Martin Scorsese. **VHS, Beta $19.95** *COL, FCT* 🎬🎬🎬

The King of Hearts In WWI, a Scottish soldier finds a battle-torn French town evacuated of all occupants except a colorful collection of escaped lunatics from a nearby asylum. The lunatics want to make him their king, which is not a bad alternative to the insanity of war. Bujold is cute as ballerina wannabe; look for Serrault ("La Cage aux Folles") as, not surprisingly, a would-be effeminate hairdresser. Light-hearted comedy with a serious message; definitely worthwhile. *AKA:* Le Roi de Coeur.
1966 101m/C Alan Bates, Genevieve Bujold, Adolfo Celi, Francoise Christophe, Micheline Presle; **D:** Philippe de Broca; **M:** Georges Delerue. **VHS, Beta $19.95** *MGM, ING, TVC* 🎬🎬🎬

King of Jazz A lavish revue built around the Paul Whiteman Orchestra with comedy sketches and songs by the stars on Universal Pictures' talent roster. (Though billed as the King of Jazz, Whiteman was never as good as jazz's real royalty.) Filmed in two-color Technicolor with a cartoon segment by Walter Lantz. ♫Rhapsody in Blue; So the Bluebirds and the Blackbirds Got Together; Mississippi Mud; It Happened in Monterey; Ragamuffin Romeo; Happy Feet; Song of the Dawn; A Bench in the Park.
1930 93m/C Paul Whiteman, John Boles, Jeanette Loff, Bing Crosby; **D:** John Murray Anderson. **VHS, Beta $19.98** *MCA, MLB, RXM* 🎬🎬½

King of Kings DeMille depicts the life of Jesus Christ in this highly regarded silent epic. The resurrection scene appears in color. Remade by Nicholas Ray in 1961.
1927 115m/B H.B. Warner, Dorothy Cumming, Ernest Torrence, Joseph Schildkraut, Jacqueline Logan, Victor Varconi, William Boyd; **D:** Cecil B. DeMille. **VHS, Beta $69.95** *MSP* 🎬🎬½

The King of Kings The life of Christ is intelligently told, with an attractive visual sense and a memorable score. Remake of Cecil B. DeMille's silent film, released in 1927. Laserdisc format features a special letterboxed edition of this film.
1961 170m/C Jeffrey Hunter, Siobhan McKenna, Hurd Hatfield, Robert Ryan, Rita Gam, Viveca Lindfors, Rip Torn; **D:** Nicholas Ray; **W:** Philip Yordan; **M:** Miklos Rozsa. **VHS, Beta $29.98** *MGM, IGP* 🎬🎬🎬

King of Kong Island Intent on world domination, a group of mad scientists implant receptors in the brains of gorillas on Kong Island, and the monster apes run amok.
1978 92m/C Brad Harris, Marc Lawrence; **D:** Robert Morris. **VHS, Beta $54.95** *VCI Woof!*

The King of Marvin Gardens Nicholson stars as a Midwest radio jock who prefers to reminisce about his life and family back in Atlantic City, New Jersey to playing records. When Nicholson returns for a visit he finds brother Dern, king of the get-rich-quick schemers, working for a black crime syndicate. Dern is involved in another scheme which means embezzling money from his boss—not a smart idea although Nicholson can't disuade him. Talky drama also features Burstyn as Dern's neglected girlfriend.
1972 (R) 104m/C Jack Nicholson, Bruce Dern, Ellen Burstyn, Scatman Crothers, Julia Anne Robinson, Charles Lavine, Arnold Williams, Josh Mostel; **D:** Bob Rafelson; **W:** Jacob Brackman. **VHS $19.95** *COL, BTV* 🎬🎬½

King of New York Drug czar Frank White (Walken), recently returned from a prison sabbatical, regains control of his New York drug empire with the aid of a loyal network of black dealers. How? Call it dangerous charisma, an inexplicable sympatico. Headquartered in Manhattan's chic Plaza hotel, he ruthlessly orchestrates the drug machine, while funneling the profits into a Bronx hospital for the poor. As inscrutable as White himself, Walken makes the drug czar's power tangible, believable, yet never fathomable.
1990 (R) 106m/C Christopher Walken, Laurence "Larry" Fishburne, David Caruso, Victor Argo, Wesley Snipes, Janet Julian, Joey Chin, Giancarlo Esposito, Steve Buscemi; **D:** Abel Ferrara; **W:** Nicholas St. John; **M:** Joe Delia. **VHS $89.95** *LIV* 🎬🎬🎬

King of the Bullwhip Two undercover U.S. Marshals are sent to Tioga City to stop the killing and looting of a masked bandit, whose whip is as dangerous as his gun.
1951 59m/B Lash LaRue, Al "Fuzzy" St. John, Anne Gwynne, Tom Neal, Jack Holt, Dennis Moore, Michael Whalen, George Lewis; **D:** Ron Ormond. **VHS, Beta $19.95** *NOS, VCN, DVT* 🎬½

King of the Congo Crabbe, in his last serial, as a pilot who is frantically searching for an important piece of film. In 15 parts.
1952 ?m/B Buster Crabbe, Gloria Dee; **D:** Spencer Gordon Bennet, Wallace Grissell. **VHS** *MLB* 🎬½

King of the Cowboys Roy fights a gang of saboteurs and saves a defense installation.
1943 54m/B Roy Rogers, Smiley Burnette, James Bush. **VHS $9.99** *NOS, VCN, DVT* 🎬🎬

King of the Damned On an island prison Veidt leads a convict's revolt against the cruel administrator (Hallard), who gets killed. Before he dies, Hallard alerts a convenient warship, which begins shelling the island. Hallard's daughter, who has fallen for Veidt, pleads for the men and everyone is given a fair trial. Miscast and ineptly performed, although Veidt retains some dignity.
1936 81m/B Conrad Veidt, Helen Vinson, C.M. Hallard, Noah Beery Sr., Percy Walsh, Raymond Lovell, Cecil Ramage, Peter Croft; **D:** Walter Forde. **VHS** *HCV* 🎬

King of the Forest Rangers Ranger Steve King must stop an evil archaeologist from finding a treasure whose secret lies within an ancient Indian rug pattern. Edited from an original, 12 episode serial on two cassettes.

1946 167m/B Larry Thompson, Helen Talbot, Stuart Hamblen, Anthony Warde. **VHS, Beta** $29.98 *REP, MLB* 🎞

King of the Grizzlies
The mystical relationship between a Cree Indian and a grizzly cub is put to the real test when the full grown bear attacks a ranch at which the Indian is foreman.
1969 (G) 93m/C Chris Wiggins, John Yesno; *D:* Ron Kelly. **VHS, Beta** $69.95 *DIS* 🎞½

King of the Gypsies
Interesting drama. A young man, scornful of his gypsy heritage, runs away from the tribe and tries to make a life of his own. He is summoned home to his grandfather's deathbed where he is proclaimed the new king of the gypsies, thus incurring the wrath of his scorned father. From Peter Maas's best-selling novel.
1978 (R) 112m/C Sterling Hayden, Eric Roberts, Susan Sarandon, Brooke Shields, Shelley Winters, Annie Potts, Annette O'Toole, Judd Hirsch, Michael Gazzo, Roy Brocksmith; *D:* Frank Pierson; *W:* Frank Pierson. **VHS, Beta** $14.95 *PAR, CCB* 🎞🎞½

King of the Hill
Quiet depression-era drama focuses on Aaron, a 12-year-old who lives in a seedy hotel in St. Louis. The family is barely scraping by: his mother is in a tuberculosis sanitarium, his younger brother has been sent away to live with relatives, and Aaron must fend for himself when his father gets work as a traveling salesman. Aaron excels at school and his efforts there, as well as his hotel friends, manage to provide him with some semblance of a regular life. Soderbergh's third directorial effort is unsentimental but admiring of his character's resourcefulness and imagination during difficult times. Based on the book by A.E. Hochner describing his own childhood.
1993 (PG-13) 102m/C Jesse Bradford, Jeroen Krabbe, Lisa Eichhorn, Karen Allen, Spalding Gray, Elizabeth McGovern, Joseph Chrest, Adrien Brody, Cameron Boyd, Chris Samples, Katherine Heigl, Amber Benson, John McConnell, Ron Vawter, John Durbin, Lauryn Hill, David Jensen; *D:* Steven Soderberg; *W:* Steven Soderberg; *M:* Cliff Martinez. **VHS** *MCA* 🎞🎞🎞½

The King of the Kickboxers
The villains make kung-fu snuff movies with unwitting actors killed on camera. Otherwise, same old junk about a karate cop back in Bangkok to get the dude who squashed his brother. Pretty racist at times.
1991 (R) 90m/C Loren Avedon, Richard Jaeckel, Billy Blanks, Don Stroud, Keith Cooke; *D:* Lucas Lowe. **VHS** $89.95 *IMP Woof!*

King of the Kongo
A handsome young man is sent by the government to Nuhalla, deep in the jungle, to break up a gang of ivory thieves. Serial was made in silent and sound versions.
1929 213m/B Jacqueline Logan, Boris Karloff, Richard Tucker; *D:* Richard Thorpe. **VHS, Beta** $39.95 *VYY, NOS, MLB* 🎞🎞

King of the Mountain
The "Old King" and the "New King" must square off in this tale of daredevil road racers who zoom through the streets of Hollywood. Interesting cast trapped by tired script.
1981 (PG) 92m/C Richard Cox, Harry Hamlin, Dennis Hopper, Joseph Bottoms, Deborah Van Valkenburgh, Dan Haggerty; *D:* Noel Nosseck. **VHS, Beta** $24.98 *SUE* 🎞½

King of the Pecos
A young lawyer (who's also adept at the shootin' iron) exacts revenge on his parents' killers in the courtroom. Well made early Wayne outing, with good character development, taut pacing and beautiful photography.

1936 54m/B John Wayne, Muriel Evans, Cy Kendall, Jack Clifford, John Beck, Yakima Canutt; *D:* Joseph Kane. **VHS** $9.98 *REP, MLB* 🎞½

The King of the Roaring '20s: The Story of Arnold Rothstein
"True" story of infamous gangster, Arnold Rothstein, a brilliant and ruthless gambler who practically ran New York in the twenties. This version of his life focuses on his rise to power, the dealings with his enemies, and his crumbling personal life. Superficial due mostly to the weak screenplay. Adapted from the book "The Big Bankroll" by Leo Katcher. *AKA:* The Big Bankroll.
1961 106m/B David Janssen, Dianne Foster, Mickey Rooney, Jack Carson, Diana Dors, Dan O'Herlihy, Mickey Shaughnessy, Keenan Wynn; *D:* Joseph M. Newman. **VHS, Beta** $19.98 *FOX, FCT* 🎞🎞½

King of the Rocketmen
Jeff King thwarts an attempt by traitors to steal government scientific secrets. Serial in twelve episodes. Later released as a feature titled "Lost Planet Airmen."
1949 156m/B Tristram Coffin, Mae Clarke, I. Stanford Jolley; *D:* Fred Brannon. **VHS** $29.98 *MED, VCN, REP* 🎞🎞

King of the Rodeo
Cowpoke Hoot wins a rodeo and catches a thief in the Windy City. Hoot's final silent ride into the sunset.
1928 54m/B Hoot Gibson, Kathryn Crawford, Slim Summerville, Charles French, Monte Montague, Joseph Girard; *D:* Henry MacRae. **VHS, Beta** $14.95 *GPV* 🎞🎞

King of the Sierras
Bosworth tells his nephew the story of a white horse that protected his mares from a black stallion. The acting of the horses is better than that of the humans.
1938 58m/B Hobart Bosworth, Harry Harvey, Harry Harvey Jr., Jim Campeau; *D:* Samuel Diege; *W:* W. Scott Darling. **VHS** $11.95 *GPV* 🎞½

King of the Stallions
A dangerous stallion is a menacing threat to the herd and the cowboys and Indians and other scattered wildlife. Chief Thundercloud is the only one capable of tackling the matter. Largely Indian cast, including Iron Eyes Cody, famed for the anti-litter campaign.
1942 63m/B Chief Thundercloud, Princess Bluebird, Chief Yowlachie, Rick Vallin, Dave O'Brien, Barbara Felker, Iron Eyes Cody; *D:* Edward Finney. **VHS** $19.95 *NOS, DVT* 🎞½

King of the Texas Rangers
Tom King, Texas Ranger, finds that his father's killers are a group of saboteurs who have destroyed American oil fields. This twelve episode serial comes on two tapes.
1941 195m/B Sammy Baugh, Neil Hamilton; *D:* William Witney, John English. **VHS** $59.95 *REP, MRV, MLB* 🎞½

King of the Wild Horses
Engaging children's story about a wild stallion that comes to the rescue. Terrific action photography of Rex going through his paces. Look for Chase in a rare dramatic role. Silent.
1924 50m/B Rex, Edna Murphy, Leon Barry, Pat Hartigan, Frank Butler, Charley Chase; *D:* Fred Jackman. **VHS, Beta** *NO* 🎞🎞

King of the Wind
An epic adventure featuring the true story of a legendary Arabian horse and a poor stable boy who gave the most precious gift of all: love.
1993 (PG) 101m/C Richard Harris, Glenda Jackson. **VHS** $89.98 *FHE* 🎞🎞½

King of the Zombies
Mad scientist creates his own zombies without souls, to be used as the evil tools of a foreign government. Zombie nonsense.

1941 67m/B John Archer, Dick Purcell, Mantan Moreland, Henry Victor, Joan Woodbury; *D:* Jean Yarborough. **VHS, Beta** $19.95 *VYY, MRV, SNC Woof!*

The King on Main Street
A king on vacation in America finds romance.
1925 ?m/B Adolphe Menjou, Bessie Love. **VHS, Beta** *NO* 🎞🎞½

King, Queen, Knave
Sexy black comedy about a shy, awkward 19-year-old boy, keenly aware that his interest in girls is not reciprocated. He has to go live with his prosperous uncle and his much younger wife when his parents are killed. Based on the Vladimir Nabokov novel. *AKA:* Herzbube.
1972 94m/C Gina Lollobrigida, David Niven, John Moulder-Brown; *D:* Jerzy Skolimowski; *W:* David Seltzer. **VHS, Beta** $69.98 *SUE* 🎞🎞🎞

King Ralph
When the rest of the royal family passes away in a freak accident, lounge lizard Ralph finds himself the only heir to the throne. O'Toole is the long-suffering valet who tries to train him for the job. Funny in spots and Goodman is the quintessential good sport, making the whole outing pleasant. Sometimes too forced.
1991 (PG) 96m/C John Goodman, Peter O'Toole, Camille Coduri, Joely Richardson, John Hurt; *D:* David S. Ward; *W:* David S. Ward; *M:* James Newton Howard. **VHS, Beta** $19.95 *MCA, CCB* 🎞🎞

King Rat
Drama set in a WWII Japanese prisoner-of-war camp. Focuses on the effect of captivity on the English, Australian, and American prisoners. An American officer bribes his Japanese captors to live more comfortably than the rest. Based on James Clavell's novel.
1965 134m/B George Segal, Tom Courtenay, James Fox, James Donald, Denholm Elliott, Patrick O'Neal, John Mills; *D:* Bryan Forbes; *M:* John Barry. **VHS, Beta** $59.95 *COL* 🎞🎞🎞

King Richard and the Crusaders
Laughable costume epic with Sanders as Richard the Lionheart, who survives an assassination attempt during the Crusades. Harvey is a loyal knight sworn to find the traitors with Harrison as the noble leader of the Arab forces. Mayo plays Harvey's object of affection. Even the battle scenes are boring. Based on "The Talisman" by Sir Walter Scott.
1954 113m/C George Sanders, Rex Harrison, Laurence Harvey, Virginia Mayo, Robert Douglas, Michael Pate, Paula Raymond, Lester Matthews; *D:* David Butler; *W:* John Twist. **VHS** $19.98 *FCT, MOV, WAR* 🎞½

King Solomon's Mines
The search for King Solomon's Mines leads a safari through the treacherous terrain of the desert, fending off sandstorms, Zulus, and a volcanic eruption. Adapted from the novel by H. Rider Haggard and remade twice.
1937 80m/B Cedric Hardwicke, Paul Robeson, Roland Young, John Loder, Anna Lee; *D:* Robert Stevenson. **VHS, Beta** $16.95 *SNC, NOS, HMV* 🎞🎞🎞

King Solomon's Mines
A lavish version of the classic H. Rider Haggard adventures about African explorers searching out a fabled diamond mine. Remake of the 1937 classic; remade again in 1985.
1950 102m/C Stewart Granger, Deborah Kerr, Richard Carlson, Hugo Haas, Lowell Gilmore; *D:* Compton Bennett. Academy Awards '50: Best Color Cinematography, Best Film Editing; Nominations: Best Picture. **VHS, Beta** $14.98 *MGM* 🎞🎞🎞

King Solomon's Mines
The third remake of the classic H. Rider Haggard novel about a safari deep into Africa in search of an explorer who disappeared while searching

for the legendary diamond mines of King Solomon. Updated but lacking the style of the previous two films. Somewhat imperialistic, racist point of view.
1985 (PG-13) 101m/C Richard Chamberlain, John Rhys-Davies, Sharon Stone, Herbert Lom; *D:* J. Lee Thompson; *W:* Gene Quintano; *M:* Jerry Goldsmith. **VHS, Beta $14.98** MGM *✗½*

King Solomon's Treasure The great white adventurer takes on the African jungle, hunting for hidden treasure in the Forbidden City. Ekland stars as a Phoenician Queen— need we say more??
1976 90m/C David McCallum, Britt Ekland, Patrick Macnee, Wilfrid Hyde-White; *D:* Alvin Rakoff. **VHS, Beta $59.95** VCI *✗*

Kingdom of the Spiders A desert town is invaded by swarms of killer tarantulas, which begin to consume townspeople.
1977 (PG) 90m/C William Shatner, Tiffany Bolling, Woody Strode; *D:* John Cardos. **VHS, Beta $19.95** VCI, FCT *✗✗½*

Kingfisher Caper A power struggle between a businessman, his brother, and a divorced sister is threatening to rip a family-owned diamond empire apart.
1976 (PG) 90m/C Hayley Mills, David McCallum; *D:* Dirk DeVilliers. **VHS, Beta $9.95** MED *✗✗*

Kingfisher the Killer Charles, the Raging Titan of Ninja skill, stalks the bad gang that killed his mother and hits them with nunchakos.
198? 90m/C Sho Kosugi. **VHS, Beta $39.95** TWE *✗*

Kings and Desperate Men Apprentice terrorists plea their case at a public forum when they take a rakish talk show host hostage.
1983 118m/C Patrick McGoohan, Alexis Kanner, Andrea Marcovicci, Robin Spry, Frank Moore; *D:* Alexis Kanner. **VHS** NO *✗½*

Kings Go Forth Hormones and war rage in this love triangle set against the backdrop of WWII France. Sinatra loves Wood who loves Curtis. When Sinatra asks for her hand in marriage she refuses because she is mixed—half black, half white. He says it doesn't matter, but she still declines because she's in love with Curtis. When Sinatra tells Curtis that Wood is mixed, Curtis says that it doesn't matter to him either because he'd never planned on marrying her. Meanwhile, the war continues. Not particularly satisfying on either the war or race front. Based on a novel by Joe David Brown.
1958 109m/B Frank Sinatra, Tony Curtis, Natalie Wood, Leora Dana; *D:* Delmer Daves; *M:* Elmer Bernstein. **VHS, Beta $19.98** MGM *✗✗½*

Kings of the Road—In the Course of Time A writer and a film projectionist travel by truck across Germany. The film stands out for its simple and expressive direction, and truly captures the sense of physical and ideological freedom of being on the road. A landmark Wenders epic. In German with English subtitles.
1976 176m/B Ruediger Vogler, Hanns Zischler, Elisabeth Kreuzer; *D:* Wim Wenders; *W:* Wim Wenders. **VHS, Beta $29.95** FCT, GLV, ING *✗✗✗½*

Kings, Queens, Jokers Package includes a foolish lover and ghosts in "Haunted Spooks," an escaped convict in "Dangerous Females," and a search for lost jewels in "Stolen Jools."
193? 60m/B Harold Lloyd, Marie Dressler, Polly Moran, Edward G. Robinson, Gary Cooper, Joan Crawford. **VHS, Beta** NO *✗✗✗½*

King's Ransom When the Japanese Emperor's Pearl is stolen, the underworld is abuzz with excitement. But only the wealthiest individuals are invited to bid for the jewel at Cameron King's secret casino. There, untold pleasures, and dangers, await them.
1991 ?m/C Miles O'Keeffe, Dedee Pfeiffer, Christopher Atkins; *D:* Hugh Parks. **VHS** NO *Woof!*

The King's Rhapsody Flynn is an heir who abdicates his throne in order to be with the woman he loves. But when the king dies, Flynn sacrifices love for honor and goes back to marry a princess. Very dated and Flynn is long past his swashbuckling-romantic days.
1955 93m/C Errol Flynn, Anna Neagle, Patrice Wymore, Martita Hunt, Finlay Currie, Frank Wolff, Joan Benham, Reginald Tate, Miles Malleson; *D:* Herbert Wilcox. **VHS $29.95** FCT *✗✗*

Kings Row The Harry Bellamann best-selling Middle American potboiler comes to life. Childhood friends grow up with varying degrees of success, in a decidedly macabre town. All are continually dependent on and inspired by Parris (Cummings) a psychiatric doctor and genuine gentleman. Many cast members worked against type with unusual success. Warner held the film for a year after its completion, in concern for its dark subject matter, but it received wide acclaim. Shot completely within studio settings—excellent scenic design by William Cameron Menzies, and wonderful score.
1941 127m/B Ann Sheridan, Robert Cummings, Ronald Reagan, Betty Field, Charles Coburn, Claude Rains, Judith Anderson, Nancy Coleman, Karen Verne, Maria Ouspenskaya, Harry Davenport, Ernest Cossart, Pat Moriarity, Scotty Beckett; *D:* Sam Wood; *M:* Erich Wolfgang Korngold. **VHS, Beta $19.98** MGM, FOX, CCB *✗✗✗*

The King's Thief Costume swashbuckler with Niven as the bad guy. He's a duke at the court of 17th-century English King Charles II and is involved in a plot to steal the crown jewels.
1955 78m/C David Niven, Edmund Purdom, George Sanders, Ann Blyth, Roger Moore, John Dehner, Sean McClory, Melville Cooper, Alan Mowbray; *D:* Robert Z. Leonard; *W:* Christopher Knopf; *M:* Miklos Rozsa. **VHS $19.98** MGM *✗✗½*

The King's Whore Dalton stars as a 17th-century king who falls obsessively in love with the wife of one of his courtiers. His passions lead him to make a decision between the woman and the throne. Good-looking costume epic with obligatory sword fights.
1990 (R) 111m/C Timothy Dalton, Valeria Golino, Feodor Chaliapin, Margaret Tyzack; *W:* Daniel Vigne, Frederic Raphael. **VHS $92.95** VMK *✗✗*

Kinjite: Forbidden Subjects A cop takes on a sleazy pimp whose specialty is recruiting teenage girls, including the daughter of a Japanese business man. Slimy, standard Bronson fare.
1989 (R) 97m/C Charles Bronson, Juan Fernandez, Peggy Lipton; *D:* Lee Thompson. **VHS, Beta $14.95** MGM, CAN *✗✗*

A Kink in the Picasso MTV personality Daddo joins a cast of criminals who chase after a Picasso artwork and a counterfeit. Artless Australian production.
1990 84m/C Peter O'Brien, Jon Finlayson, Jane Clifton, Andrew Daddo; *D:* Marc Gracie. **VHS $79.95** ATL *✗*

Kino Pravda/Enthusiasm Two famous documentaries by Vertov, the first a prime example of his pioneering avant-garde newsreels that helped establish Soviet mon-tage aesthetic, and the second the famous portrait of Don Basin coal miners, augmented by the famous use of sound editing/montage. In Russian with English titles.
1931 120m/B *D:* Dziga Vertov. **VHS, Beta $69.95** FCT, FST *✗✗*

Kipperbang During the summer of 1948, a 13-year-old boy wishes he could kiss the girl of his dreams. Not unsatisfying, but falls short of being the bittersweet coming-of-age drama it could have been. *AKA:* Ptang, Yang, Kipperbang.
1982 (PG) 85m/C John Albasiny, Abigail Cruttenden, Alison Steadman; *D:* Michael Apted. **VHS, Beta $59.95** MGM *✗*

Kipps Based on H.G. Wells' satirical novel. A young British shopkeeper inherits a fortune and tries to join high society while neglecting his working-class girlfriend. Set the stage for the musical "Half a Sixpence." *AKA:* The Remarkable Mr. Kipps.
1941 95m/B Michael Redgrave, Phyllis Calvert, Michael Wilding; *D:* Carol Reed. **VHS, Beta $19.95** NOS, HHT, CAB *✗✗✗*

The Kirlian Witness A woman uses the power of telepathic communication with house plants to solve her sister's murder. *AKA:* The Plants Are Watching.
1978 (PG) 88m/C Nancy Snyder, Joel Colodner, Ted Leplat; *D:* Jonathan Sarno. **VHS, Beta** NO *✗*

Kismet Original screen version of the much filmed lavish Arabian Nights saga (remade in '30, '44 and '55). A beggar is drawn into deception and intrigue among Bagdad uppercrusters. Glorious sets and costumes; silent with original organ score.
1920 98m/B Otis Skinner, Elinor Fair, Herschel Mayall; *D:* Louis Gasnier. **VHS $24.95** VYY *✗✗✗*

Kismet A big budget Arabian Nights musical drama of a Baghdad street poet who manages to infiltrate himself into the Wazir's harem. The music was adapted from Borodin by Robert Wright and George Forrest. Original trailer and letterboxed screen available in special laserdisc edition. *♫*Fate; Not Since Ninevah; Baubles, Bangles, and Beads; Stranger in Paradise; Bored; Night of My Nights; The Olive Tree; And This Is My Beloved; Sands of Time.
1955 113m/C Howard Keel, Ann Blyth, Dolores Gray, Vic Damone; *D:* Vincente Minnelli. **VHS, Beta $19.98** MGM, FCT *✗✗*

The Kiss Garbo, the married object of earnest young Ayres' lovelorn affection, innocently kisses him nighty night since a kiss is just a kiss. Or so she thought. Utterly misconstrued, the platonic peck sets the stage for disaster, and murder and courtroom anguish follow. French Feyder's direction is stylized and artsy. Garbo's last silent and Ayres' first film.
1929 89m/B Greta Garbo, Conrad Nagel, Holmes Herbert, Lew Ayres, Anders Randolf; *D:* Jacques Feyder. **VHS $29.98** MGM, FCT *✗✗✗*

The Kiss A kind of "Auntie Mame from Hell" story in which a mysterious aunt visits her teen-age niece in New York, and tries to apprentice her to the family business of sorcery, demon possession, and murder. Aunt Felicity's kiss will make you appreciate the harmless cheek-pinching of your own aunt; your evening would be better spent with her, rather than this movie.
1988 (R) 98m/C Pamela Collyer, Peter Dvorsky, Joanna Pacula, Meredith Salenger, Mimi Kuzyk, Nicholas Kilbertus, Jan Rubes; *D:* Pen Densham; *W:* Tom Ropelewski. **VHS, Beta $19.95** COL, IME *✗*

Kiss and Be Killed Crazy guy with knife cuts short couple's wedding night. Shortchanged widow is mighty miffed. Will she have to return the wedding gifts?
1991 (R) 89m/C Caroline Ludvik, Crystal Carson, Tom Reilly, Chip Hall, Ken Norton, Jimmy Baio; **D:** Tom Milo. **VHS, Beta, 8mm $79.95** MNC *II½*

Kiss and Kill Lee returns in his fourth outing as Fu Manchu. This time the evil one has injected beautiful girls with a deadly poison that reacts upon kissing. They are then sent out to seduce world leaders. Not on par with the previous movies, but still enjoyable. Sequel to "Castle of Fu Manchu." **AKA:** Blood of Fu Manchu; Against All Odds.
1968 (R) 91m/C Christopher Lee, Richard Greene, Shirley Eaton, Tsai Chin, Maria Rohm, H. Marion Crawford; **D:** Jess (Jesus) Franco. **VHS $14.99** MRV *II*

A Kiss Before Dying Botched adaptation of Ira Levin's cunning thriller novel (filmed before in 1956). This flick serves up an exploded head in the first few minutes. So much for subtlety. The highlight is Dillon's chilly role as a murderous opportunist bent on marrying into a wealthy family. Young plays two roles (not very well) as lookalike sisters on his agenda. The ending was hastily reshot and it shows.
1991 (R) 93m/C Matt Dillon, Sean Young, Max von Sydow, Diane Ladd, James Russo, Martha Gehman, Ben Browder, Joy Lee, Adam Horovitz; **D:** James Dearden; **W:** James Dearden. **VHS, Beta $19.98** MCA *II*

Kiss Daddy Goodbye A widower keeps his two children isolated in order to protect their secret telekinetic powers. When he is killed by bikers, the kids attempt to raise him from the dead. Also on video as "Revenge of the Zombie" and "The Vengeful Dead."
1981 (R) 81m/C Fabian, Marilyn Burns, Jon Cedar, Marvin Miller; **D:** Patrick Regan. **VHS, Beta $59.95** MRV, GHV *II*

Kiss Daddy Goodnight A Danish-made thriller about a beautiful young girl who seduces men, drugs them and takes their money. One man turns the tables on her, however, and decides that she will only belong to him.
1987 89m/C Uma Thurman, Paul Dillon, Paul Richards, David Brisbin; **D:** P.I. Huemer. **VHS, Beta $29.95** ACA *I*

A Kiss for Mary Pickford A rare, hilarious cinematic oddity, a film formulated from Kuleshov montage techniques from footage of the famous American couple's visit to Russia in 1926, wherein a regular guy tries to win a girl through friendship with the stars. Fairbanks and Pickford didn't know of their role in this film, being spliced in later according to montage theory.
1927 70m/B Mary Pickford, Douglas Fairbanks Sr., Igor Ilinsky; **D:** Sergei Komarov. **VHS, Beta $49.95** FCT *II½*

Kiss Me a Killer The ancient thriller plot about a young wife and her lover who scheme to kill her middle-aged husband. It's set in L.A.'s Latino community, but extensive shots of salsa music and ethnic cooking hardly raise this above the mediocre.
1991 91m/C Julie Carmen, Robert Beltran, Guy Boyd, Ramon Franco, Charles Boswell; **D:** Marcus De Leon. **VHS $89.95** COL *II*

Kiss Me Deadly Aldrich's adaptation of Mickey Spillane's private eye tale takes pulp literature high concept. Meeker, as Mike Hammer, is a self interested rough and tumble all American dick (detective, that is). When a woman to whom he happened to give a ride is found murdered, he follows the mystery straight into a nuclear conspiracy. Aldrich, with tongue deftly in cheek, styles a message through the medium; topsy turvy camerawork and rat-a-tat-tat pacing tell volumes about Hammer, the world he orbits, and that special 50s kind of paranoia. Now a cult fave, it's considered to be the American grandaddy to French New Wave. Cinematography by Ernest Laszlo.
1955 105m/B Ralph Meeker, Albert Dekker, Paul Stewart, Wesley Addy, Cloris Leachman, Strother Martin, Marjorie Bennett; **D:** Robert Aldrich. **VHS, Beta $19.98** MGM, FCT *III½*

Kiss Me Goodbye Young widow Fields can't shake the memory of her first husband, a charismatic but philandering Broadway choreographer, who's the antithesis of her boring but devoted professor fiance. She struggles with the charming ghost of her first husband, as well as her domineering mother, attempting to understand her own true feelings. Harmless but two-dimensional remake of "Dona Flor and Her Two Husbands."
1982 (PG) 101m/C Sally Field, James Caan, Jeff Bridges, Paul Dooley, Mildred Natwick, Claire Trevor; **D:** Robert Mulligan; **W:** Charlie Peters; **M:** Ralph Burns. **VHS, Beta $59.98** FOX *II*

Kiss Me Kate A married couple can't separate their real lives from their stage roles in this musical-comedy screen adaptation of Shakespeare's "Taming of the Shrew," based on Cole Porter's Broadway show. Bob Fosse bursts from the screen—particularly if you see the 3-D version—when he does his dance number. ♫Out of This World; From This Moment On; Wunderbar; So In Love; I Hate Men; Were Thine That Special Face; I've Come To Wive It Wealthily In Padua; Where Is The Life That Late I Led?; Always True To You Darling In My Fashion.
1953 110m/C Kathryn Grayson, Howard Keel, Ann Miller, Tommy Rall, Bob Fosse, Bobby Van, Keenan Wynn, James Whitmore; **D:** George Sidney. **VHS, Beta $19.98** MGM, FCT *III*

Kiss Me, Kill Me Confused woman is on the run after she may have murdered someone..
1969 (R) 91m/C Carroll Baker, George Eastman, Isabelle DeFunes, Ely Gallo; **W:** Nick Castle. **VHS, Beta** NO *II½*

Kiss Me, Stupid! Once condemned as smut, this lesser Billy Wilder effort now seems no worse than an average TV sitcom. Martin basically plays himself as a horny Vegas crooner stranded in the boondocks. A local songwriter wants Dino to hear his tunes but knows the cad will seduce his pretty wife, so he hires a floozy to pose as the tempting spouse. It gets better as it goes along, but the whole thing suffers from staginess, being an adaptation of an Italian play "L'Ora Della Fantasia" by Anna Bonacci.
1964 (PG) 126m/B Dean Martin, Kim Novak, Ray Walston, Felicia Farr, Cliff Osmond, Barbara Pepper, Doro Merande, Howard McNear, Henry Gibson, John Fiedler, Mel Blanc; **D:** Billy Wilder; **W:** Billy Wilder, I.A.L. Diamond. **VHS, Beta $19.98** MGM *II*

KISS Meets the Phantom of the Park The popular '70s rock band is featured in this Dr. Jekyll-esque Halloween horror tale, interspersed with musical numbers. **AKA:** Attack of the Phantoms.
1978 96m/C Gene Simmons, Paul Stanley, Peter Criss, Ace Frehley, Anthony Zerbe, Deborah Ryan, John Dennis Johnston; **D:** Gordon Hessler. **VHS, Beta $10.98** MVD, WOV *II½*

Kiss My Grits A good ole boy hightails it to Mexico with his girlfriend and son, chased by mobsters and the law.

1982 (PG) 101m/C Bruce Davison, Anthony (Tony) Franciosa, Susan George, Bruno Kirby; **D:** Jack Starrett. **VHS, Beta $49.95** MED *I*

Kiss of a Killer O'Toole is a mousy miss living a dead-end life with her nagging mother. But she has a secret—she spends weekends in a hotel, dressed to entice and picking up strangers. Involved in an auto mishap she's aided by a handsome mechanic, who turns out to be a rapist. When he accidentally kills his latest victim, he realizes our mystery woman can identify him and tries to find her. Based on the novel "The Point of Murder" by Margaret Yorke. Made for television.
1993 93m/C Annette O'Toole, Brian Wimmer, Eva Marie Saint, Greg Henry, Vic Polizos; **D:** Larry Elikann; **W:** David Warfield. **VHS** ABC *II½*

Kiss of Death Paroled when he turns state's evidence, Mature must now watch his back constantly. Widmark, in his film debut, seeks to destroy him. Police chief Donlevy tries to help. Filmed on location in New York, this gripping and gritty film is a vision of the most terrifying sort of existence, one where nothing is certain, and everything is dangerous. Excellent.
1947 98m/B Victor Mature, Richard Widmark, Anne Grey, Brian Donlevy, Karl Malden, Coleen Gray; **D:** Henry Hathaway. **VHS $39.98** FOX, FCT *III*

Kiss of the Spider Woman From the novel by Manuel Puig, an acclaimed drama concerning two cell mates in a South American prison, one a revolutionary, the other a homosexual. Literate, haunting, powerful.
1985 (R) 119m/C William Hurt, Raul Julia, Sonia Braga, Jose Lewgoy, Milton Goncalves, Nuno Leal Maia, Denise Dumont; **D:** Hector Babenco; **W:** Leonard Schrader; **M:** John Neschling, Wally Badarou. Academy Awards '85: Best Actor (Hurt); Nominations: Best Adapted Screenplay, Best Director (Babenco), Best Picture; British Academy Awards '85: Best Actor (Hurt); Cannes Film Festival '85: Best Actor (Hurt); Independent Spirit Awards '86: Best Foreign Film. **VHS, Beta, 8mm $19.95** COL, BTV, NLC *II*

Kiss of the Tarantula Teen girl who lives with her family in a mortuary battles inner torment and vents anxiety by releasing her deadly pet spiders on those whom she despises. Eight-legged "Carrie" rip-off.
1975 (PG) 85m/C Eric Mason; **D:** Chris Munger; **W:** Warren Hamilton. **VHS, Beta $19.95** MPI, FCT *I*

Kiss Shot Goldberg is a struggling single mother who loses her job but still must make the mortgage payments. She takes a job as a waitress but realizes it isn't going to pay the bills so she tries her hand as a pool hustler. Frantz is the promoter who finances her bets and Harewood, the pool-shooting playboy whose romantic advances are destroying her concentration.
1989 88m/C Whoopi Goldberg, Dennis Franz, Dorian Harewood, David Marciano, Teddy Wilson; **D:** Jerry London; **M:** Stephen Dorff. **VHS, Beta $19.95** ACA, MOV *II*

Kiss the Night An unfortunate hooker falls head over heels for a man she had the pleasure of doing business with. To her chagrin, it is much harder to leave the street than she thought. A dramatic and timely presentation.
1987 (R) 99m/C Patsy Stephens, Warwick Moss, Gary Aron Cook; **D:** James Ricketson. **VHS $79.95** MCG *I*

Kiss Tomorrow Goodbye A brutal, murderous escaped convict rises to crimelord status before his inevitable downfall. Based on a novel by Horace McCoy.

1950 102m/B James Cagney, Barbara Payton, Ward Bond, Luther Adler, Helena Carter, Steve Brodie, Rhys Williams; **D:** Gordon Douglas. **VHS** $19.98 *REP* 🐾🐾

Kisses Lauren Bacall hosts an entertaining look at screen kisses from yesterday and today.
1991 47m/C VHS, Beta $14.98 *TTC* 🐾🐾

Kisses for My President Silly comedy about the first woman elected President and her trials and tribulations. MacMurray is the husband who has to adjust to the protocol of being "First Man." Bergen is miscast, but the other performances are just fine.
1964 113m/C Fred MacMurray, Polly Bergen, Arlene Dahl, Edward Andrews, Eli Wallach, Donald May; **D:** Curtis Bernhardt. **VHS** 🐾🐾½

Kissin' Cousins Air Force officer on a secluded base in the South discovers a local hillbilly is his double. Presley quickie that includes country tunes such as "Smokey Mountain Boy" and "Barefoot Ballad" as well as the title song.
1964 96m/C Elvis Presley, Arthur O'Connell, Jack Albertson, Glenda Farrell, Pam Austin, Yvonne Craig, Cynthia Pepper, Donald Woods, Tommy Farrell, Beverly Powers; **D:** Gene Nelson. VHS, Beta $19.95 *MGM* 🐾½

The Kissing Place A woman who abducted her "son" years ago tracks the boy to New York City to prevent him from finding his biological family.
1990 90m/C Meredith Baxter Birney, David Ogden Stiers; **D:** Tony Wharmby. **VHS, Beta** $29.95 *PAR* 🐾🐾

Kit Carson Frontiersman Kit Carson leads a wagon train to California, fighting off marauding Indians all the way.
1940 97m/B Jon Hall, Dana Andrews, Ward Bond, Lynn Bari; **D:** George B. Seitz. **VHS, Beta** $14.95 *MED, VTR* 🐾🐾

The Kitchen Toto Set in 1950 Kenya as British rule was being threatened by Mau Mau terrorists. A young black boy is torn between the British for whom he works and the terrorists who want him to join them. Complex and powerful story of the Kenyan freedom crusade.
1987 (PG-13) 96m/C Bob Peck, Phyllis Logan, Robert Urquhart, Edward Judd, Edwin Mahinda, Kirsten Hughes; **D:** Harry Hook; **W:** Harry Hook; **M:** John Keane. VHS, Beta $79.95 *WAR* 🐾🐾🐾

Kitty and the Bagman A comedy about two rival madames who ruled Australia in the 1920s.
1982 (R) 95m/C Liddy Clark; **D:** Donald Crombie. VHS, Beta $59.98 *SUE* 🐾🐾

Kitty Foyle From the novel by Christopher Morley, Rogers portrays the white-collar working girl whose involvement with a married man presents her with both romantic and social conflicts.
1940 108m/B Ginger Rogers, Dennis (Stanley Morner) Morgan, James Craig, Gladys Cooper, Ernest Cossart, Eduardo Ciannelli; **D:** Sam Wood. Academy Awards '40: Best Actress (Rogers); Nominations: Best Adapted Screenplay, Best Director (Wood), Best Picture, Best Sound. VHS, Beta $19.98 *MED, CCB, FCT* 🐾🐾🐾

The Klansman Race relations come out on the short end in this film about a sheriff trying to keep the lid on racial tensions in a southern town. Even the big-name cast can't save what comes off as a nighttime soaper rather than a serious drama. *AKA:* Burning Cross; KKK.

1974 (R) 112m/C Lee Marvin, Richard Burton, Cameron Mitchell, Lola Falana, Lucianna Paluzzi, Linda Evans, O.J. Simpson; **D:** Terence Young; **W:** Samuel Fuller. VHS $14.95 *PAR, FCT* 🐾

Klondike Annie West stars as a woman on the lam for a murder (self-defense) who heads out for the Yukon aboard McLaglen's ship. He falls for her, finds out about her problems, and helps her with a scam to pass herself off as a missionary, only she begins to take her saving souls seriously (although in her own risque style).
1936 77m/B Mae West, Victor McLaglen, Philip Reed, Helen Jerome Eddy, Harry Beresford, Harold Huber, Conway Tearle, Esther Howard; **D:** Raoul Walsh; **W:** Mae West. VHS $14.98 *MCA, BTV* 🐾🐾🐾

Klondike Fever Join the young Jack London as he travels from San Francisco to the Klondike fields during the Great Gold Rush of 1898. *AKA:* Jack London's Klondike Fever.
1979 (PG) 118m/C Rod Steiger, Angie Dickinson, Lorne Greene; **D:** Peter Carter; **M:** Hagood Hardy. VHS, Beta *NO* 🐾½

Klute A small-town policeman (Sutherland) comes to New York in search of a missing friend and gets involved with a prostitute/would-be actress (Fonda) being stalked by a killer. Intelligent, gripping drama.
1971 (R) 114m/C Jane Fonda, Donald Sutherland, Charles Cioffi, Roy Scheider, Rita Gam, Jean Stapleton; **D:** Alan J. Pakula. Academy Awards '71: Best Actress (Fonda); Nominations: Best Story & Screenplay; Golden Globe Awards '72: Best Actress—Drama (Fonda); New York Film Critics Awards '71: Best Actress (Fonda); National Society of Film Critics Awards '71: Best Actress (Fonda). VHS, Beta $19.98 *WAR, BTV* 🐾🐾🐾½

The Klutz A bumbling fool, on the way to visit his girlfriend, becomes accidentally embroiled in a bank robbery and other ridiculous mishaps. Light French comedy; dubbed.
1973 87m/C Claude Michaud, Louise Portal, Guy Provost; **D:** Pierre Rose. VHS, Beta $19.95 *NWV* 🐾🐾

The Knack Amusing, fast-paced adaptation of the play by Ann Jellicoe. Schoolteacher Crawford is baffled by his tenant Brooks' extreme luck with the ladies so Brooks decides to teach him the "knack" of picking up women. Crawford promptly falls for the first woman (Tushingham) he meets. Swinging London at its most mod. *AKA:* The Knack...and How to Get It.
1965 84m/B Michael Crawford, Ray Brooks, Rita Tushingham, Donal Donnelly; **D:** Richard Lester; **W:** Charles Wood; **M:** John Barry. VHS $19.98 *MGM* 🐾🐾🐾

Knife in the Head Biogeneticist Berthold Hoffman (Ganz) is meeting his wife (Winkler) at the left-wing youth centre where she works when there's a police raid and Berthold is shot in the head. He awakens in the hospital having lost both his memory and all physical co-ordination. Determined to battle his disabilities, Berthold also becomes the pawn in a political game between the police and political dissidents. In German with English subtitles. *AKA:* Messer Im Kopf.
1978 108m/C Bruno Ganz, Angela Winkler, Hans Honig, Hans Brenner, Udo Samel, Carla Egerer; **D:** Reinhard Hauff; **W:** Peter Schneider. VHS $79.95 *NYF* 🐾🐾

Knife in the Water A journalist, his wife and a hitchhiker spend a day aboard a sailboat. Sex and violence can't be far off. Tense psychological drama. Served as director Polanski's debut. In Polish with English subtitles. *AKA:* Noz w Wodzie.

1962 94m/B Leon Niemczyk, Jolanta Umecka, Zygmunt Malandowicz; **D:** Roman Polanski; **W:** Jerzy Skolimowski, Roman Polanski. Academy Awards '63 Nominations: Best Foreign Language Film; Venice Film Festival '62: International Critics Award. VHS, Beta $24.95 *VYY, FOX, BTV* 🐾🐾🐾🐾

Knight Moves Suspenseful thriller about a series of murders which take place at an international resort where a championship chess match is underway. The prime suspect is a chess master who has an unlikely affair with a beautiful police psychologist called in to decipher the mind of the murderer. Filmed in the Pacific Northwest.
1993 (R) 105m/C Christopher Lambert, Diane Lane, Tom Skerritt, Daniel Baldwin; **D:** Carl Schenkel; **W:** Brad Mirman; **M:** Anne Dudley. VHS $92.98 *REP* 🐾🐾

Knight Without Armour A journalist opposed to the Russian monarchy falls in love with the daughter of a czarist minister in this classic romantic drama.
1937 107m/B Marlene Dietrich, Robert Donat; **D:** Jacques Feyder; **M:** Miklos Rozsa. VHS, Beta $14.98 *SUE* 🐾🐾🐾

Knightriders The story of a troupe of motorcyclists who are members of a traveling Renaissance Fair and look and act like modern-day Knights of the Round Table. Their battles center around who is the bravest and strongest, and who deserves to be king.
1981 (R) 145m/C Ed Harris, Gary Lahti, Tom Savini, Amy Ingersoll; **D:** George A. Romero; **W:** George A. Romero. VHS, Beta $19.98 *FUS, MED* 🐾🐾½

Knights In a futuristic wasteland a young martial-arts warrior (Long) and a cyborg (Kristofferson) team up to battle rebel cyborgs that have discovered a new source of fuel—human blood.
1993 (R) 89m/C Kathy Long, Kris Kristofferson, Lance Henriksen, Scott Paulin, Gary Daniels; **D:** Albert Pyun; **W:** Albert Pyun. VHS, Beta *PAR* 🐾½

Knights & Emeralds Cross-cultural rivalries and romances develop between members of two high school marching bands in a British factory town as the national band championships draw near.
1987 (PG) 90m/C Christopher Wild, Beverly Hills, Warren Mitchell; **D:** Ian Emes. VHS, Beta $19.98 *WAR* 🐾½

Knights of the City Miami street gangs fight each other over their "turf." One leader decides to opt out, using music. ♫Let the Music Play; Cry of the City; Jailhouse Rap; T.K. and Jessie Rap; Kurtis Blow Rap; Bounce; My Part of Town; Can You Feel It; Love Goes Up and Down.
1985 (R) 87m/C Nicholas Campbell, John Mengatti, Wendy Barry, Stoney Jackson, The Fat Boys, Michael Ansara, Janine Turner; **D:** Leon Isaac Kennedy, Dominic Orlando; **W:** Leon Isaac Kennedy. VHS, Beta $14.95 *NWV, STE* 🐾

Knights of the Range Vintage western.
1940 66m/B Russell Hayden, Victor Jory, Jean Parker, Britt Wood, J. Farrell MacDonald, Eddie Dean; **D:** Lesley Selander. VHS, Beta $29.95 *VCN, MLB, GPV* 🐾½

Knights of the Round Table The story of the romantic triangle between King Arthur, Sir Lancelot and Guinevere during the civil wars of sixth century England.
1953 106m/C Robert Taylor, Ava Gardner, Mel Ferrer, Anne Crawford, Felix Aylmer, Stanley Baker; **D:** Richard Thorpe. VHS, Beta $19.95 *MGM* 🐾🐾½

Knock on Any Door A young hoodlum from the slums is tried for murdering a cop. He is defended by a prominent attorney who has known him from childhood.
1949 100m/B Humphrey Bogart, John Derek, George Macready; **D:** Nicholas Ray; **W:** Daniel Taradash, John Monks Jr. **VHS, Beta $9.95** COL ✗✗

Knock Outs Samantha not only loses her shirt at a sorority strip poker marathon but she loses her tuition money to a gang of biker chicks. Then Samantha and a bevy of bikini-clad friends decide to pose for a swimsuit calendar to earn some cash but are secretly videotaped in the nude by some local sleaze promoters. Tired of being taken advantage of these lovelies take up martial arts and challenge their nefarious girl biker rivals to a winner-take-all wrestling match, not forgetting about the purveyors of the not-so-secret videotape.
1992 90m/C Chona Jackson, Sindi Rome, Brad Zutaut; **D:** John Bowen. **VHS $14.95** HMD ✗

The Knockout/Dough and Dynamite Two Chaplin shorts: "The Knockout" (1914), in which Charlie referees a big fight; "Dough and Dynamite" (1914), in which a labor dispute at a bake shop leaves Charlie in charge when the regular baker walks out.
1914 54m/B Charlie Chaplin, Fatty Arbuckle, Mabel Normand, The Keystone Cops; **D:** Charlie Chaplin, Sydney Chaplin. **VHS, Beta $24.95** VYY ✗✗✗

Knute Rockne: All American Life story of Notre Dame football coach Knute Rockne, who inspired many victories with his powerful speeches. Reagan, as the dying George Gipp, utters that now-famous line, "Tell the boys to win one for the Gipper." **AKA:** A Modern Hero.
1940 96m/B Ronald Reagan, Pat O'Brien, Gale Page, Donald Crisp, John Qualen; **D:** Lloyd Bacon. **VHS, Beta $19.98** MGM, FHE ✗✗✗

Kojak: The Belarus File The bald-headed detective of prime-time television fame searches for a neo-Nazi who is killing Holocaust survivors in New York. Made for television.
1985 95m/C Telly Savalas, Suzanne Pleshette, Max von Sydow, George Savalas; **D:** Robert Markowitz. **VHS, Beta $39.95** MCA ✗✗

Kojiro A sprawling epic by prolific Japanese director Inagaki about a dashing rogue's bid for power in feudal times. With English subtitles.
1967 152m/C Kikunosuke Onoe, Tatsuya Nakadai; **D:** Hiroshi Inagaki. **VHS, Beta** VDA ✗✗✗

Kolberg The true story of a Prussian town heroically withstanding Napoleon. Produced by Joseph Goebbels in the last days of the Third Reich, it is best remembered as the film whose expensive production and momentous use of real German soldiers, supplies, and ammunition eventually helped to fell the Axis war machine. In German with English subtitles. **AKA:** Burning Hearts.
1945 118m/C Kristina Soderbaum, Heinrich George, Horst Caspar, Paul Wegener; **D:** Veit Harlan. **VHS, Beta $39.95** FCT, IHF, GLV ✗✗

Konrad Konrad, an "instant" child made in a factory, is accidentally delivered to an eccentric woman. The factory wants him back when the mistake is discovered, but Konrad stands up against it. Includes a viewers' guide. Part of the "Wonderworks" series.
199? 110m/C Ned Beatty, Polly Holliday, Max Wright, Huckleberry Fox. **VHS $29.95** PME, HMV, BTV ✗✗

Korczak Based on the life of Dr. Janusz Korczak, an outspoken critic of the Nazis, who ran the Jewish orphanage in Warsaw, Poland and accompanied 200 children to to the Treblinka concentration camp. Harshly poetic film quietly details Polish resistance to the Nazi terror. Criticized for end scenes of the children romping in the countryside, implying that they were somehow freed— since the director did not want to show the children actually entering the gas chambers he used this allegory to imply that their souls were freed. In Polish with English subtitles.
1990 118m/C Wojtek Pszoniak, Ewa Dalkowska, Piotr Kozlowski, Marzena Trybala, Wojciech Klata, Adam Siemion; **D:** Andrzej Wajda; **W:** Agnieszka Holland. **VHS $79.95** NYF, FCT ✗✗✗

Koroshi Secret Agent John Drake is dispatched to Hong Kong to disband a secret society who is killing off international political figures.
1967 100m/C Patrick McGoohan, Kenneth Griffith, Yoko Tani; **D:** Michael Truman, Peter Yates. **VHS, Beta $59.95** MPI ✗✗½

Kostas A migrant Greek taxi driver romantically pursues a wealthy Australian divorcee in England.
1979 (R) 88m/C Takis Emmanuel, Wendy Hughes; **D:** Paul Cox. **VHS, Beta $69.98** LIV, VES ✗

Kotch An elderly man resists his children's attempts to retire him. Warm detailing of old age with a splendid performance by Matthau. Lemmon's directorial debut.
1971 (PG) 113m/C Walter Matthau, Deborah Winters, Felicia Farr; **D:** Jack Lemmon; **M:** Marvin Hamlisch. Academy Awards '71 Nominations: Best Actor (Matthau), Best Film Editing, Best Song ("Life Is What You MaKe It"), Best Sound; Golden Globe Awards '72: Best Song ("Life Is What You Make It"). **VHS $59.98** FOX ✗✗✗

Kowloon Assignment Comic book superhero Golgo 13 comes to life in this action film dealing with a drug war in the Hong Kong underground.
1977 93m/C Sonny Chiba. **VHS, Beta** NO ✗

Koyaanisqatsi A mesmerizing film that takes an intense look at modern life (the movie's title is the Hopi word for "life out of balance"). Without dialogue or narration, it brings traditional background elements, landscapes and cityscapes, up front to produce a unique view of the structure and mechanics of our daily lives. Riveting and immensely powerful. A critically acclaimed score by Glass, and Reggio's cinematography prove to be the perfect match to this brilliant film. Followed by "Powaqqatsi."
1983 87m/C **D:** Godfrey Reggio; **M:** Philip Glass. **VHS, Beta $14.95** MVD, FCT, MLB ✗✗✗✗

Kramer vs. Kramer Highly acclaimed family drama about an advertising executive husband and child left behind when their wife and mother leaves on a quest to find herself, and the subsequent courtroom battle for custody when she returns. Hoffman and Streep give exacting performances as does young Henry. Successfully moves you from tears to laughter and back again. Based on the novel by Avery Corman.
1979 (PG) 105m/C Dustin Hoffman, Meryl Streep, Jane Alexander, Justin Henry, Howard Duff, JoBeth Williams; **D:** Robert Benton. Academy Awards '79: Best Actor (Hoffman), Best Adapted Screenplay, Best Director (Benton), Best Picture, Best Supporting Actress (Streep); Nominations: Best Cinematography, Best Film Editing, Best Supporting Actor (Henry); Golden Globe Awards '80: Best Actor—Drama (Hoffman), Best Film—Drama, Best Screenplay, Best Supporting Actress (Streep); National Board of Review Awards '79: 10 Best Films of the

Year, Best Supporting Actress (Streep); National Society of Film Critics Awards '79: Best Actor (Hoffman), Best Director (Benton), Best Supporting Actress (Streep). **VHS, Beta $19.95** COL, BTV ✗✗✗½

The Krays An account of British gangsters Reggie and Ronnie Kray, the brothers who ruled London's East End with brutality and violence, making them bizarre celebrities of the sixties. The leads are portrayed by Gary and Martin Kemp, founders of the British pop group Spandau Ballet.
1990 (R) 119m/C Gary Kemp, Martin Kemp, Billie Whitelaw, Steven Berkoff, Susan Fleetwood, Charlotte Cornwell; **D:** Peter Medak; **W:** Philip Ridley; **M:** Michael Kamen. **VHS, 8mm $19.95** COL, FCT ✗✗✗½

Kriemhilde's Revenge The second film, following "Siegfried," of Lang's "Die Nibelungen," a lavish silent version of the Teutonic legends Wagner's "Ring of the Nibelungen" was based upon. In this episode, Kriemhilde avenges Siegfried's death by her marriage to the Kings of the Huns, thus fulfilling a prophecy of destruction. **AKA:** Die Nibelungen.
1924 95m/B Paul Richter, Margareta Schoen, Theodore Loos, Hanna Ralph, Rudolf Klein-Rogge; **D:** Fritz Lang. **VHS $19.95** CCB, IHF, REP ✗✗✗✗

Kronos A giant robot from space drains the Earth of all its energy resources. A good example of this genre from the 50s. Includes previews of coming attractions from classic science fiction films.
1957 78m/B Jeff Morrow, Barbara Lawrence, John Emery; **D:** Kurt Neumann. **VHS, Beta $19.95** MED, MLB ✗✗½

Krull Likeable fantasy adventure set in a world peopled by creatures of myth and magic. A prince embarks on a quest to find the Glaive (a magical weapon) and then rescues his young bride, taken by the Beast of the Black Fortress.
1983 (PG) 121m/C Ken Marshall, Lysette Anthony, Freddie Jones, Francesca Annis, Liam Neeson; **D:** Peter Yates; **M:** James Horner. **VHS, Beta $14.95** GKK ✗✗

Krush Groove The world of rap music is highlighted in this movie, the first all-rap musical. ♫King of Rock; Don't You Dog Me; A Love Bizarre; Pick up the Pace; If I Ruled the World; Holly Rock; It's Like That; Feel the Spin; I Can't Live Without My Radio.
1985 (R) 95m/C Blair Underwood, Eron Tabor, Kurtis Blow, The Fat Boys, Sheila E; **D:** Michael A. Schultz. **VHS, Beta $14.95** WAR ✗

K2: The Ultimate High Two men, one a skirt-chasing lawyer, the other a happily married physicist, tackle the world's second largest mountain—the K-2 in Kashmir, northern Pakistan. They encounter a number of dangers, including an ascent of sheer rock face, an avalanche, and a fall down perpendicular mountain ice, but even the exciting mountain-climbing scenes can't hold up this watered down movie. The film was actually shot on Canada's Mount Waddington. Based on the play by Patrick Meyers.
1992 (R) 104m/C Michael Biehn, Matt Craven, Raymond J. Barry, Luca Bercovici, Patricia Charbonneau, Julia Nickson-Soul, Hiroshi Fujioka, Jamal Shah; **D:** Franc Roddam; **W:** Patrick Meyers, Scott Roberts. **VHS, Beta $19.95** PAR ✗✗

Kuffs Slater stars as George Kuffs, a young guy who reluctantly joins his brother's highly respected private security team in this original action comedy. After his brother is gunned down in the line of duty, George finds himself the new owner of the business. Out to avenge his brother, George pursues a

crooked art dealer as he battles crime on the streets of San Francisco. Worthwhile premise is hampered by a predictable plot and mediocre acting.
1992 (PG-13) 102m/C Christian Slater, Tony Goldwyn, Milla Jovovich, Bruce Boxleitner, Troy Evans, George de la Pena, Leon Rippy; *D:* Bruce A. Evans; *W:* Bruce A. Evans, Raynold Gideon; *M:* Harold Faltermeyer. VHS, Beta $19.98 *MCA* ⅛⅛

Kung Fu A fugitive Buddhist quasi-Asian martial arts master accused of murder in his native land, roams across the Old West fighting injustice. Served as a pilot for the successful television series and was reincarnated 14 years later in the sequel, "Kung Fu: The Movie."
1972 75m/C Keith Carradine, David Carradine, Barry Sullivan, Keye Luke; *D:* Jerry Thorpe. VHS, Beta $24.98 *WAR* ⅛⅛⅛½

Kung Fu Avengers On his way to a karate show at Madison Square Garden, our hero Li confronts the abominable Mr. Chin and his deadly henchman. Another footstomper.
1985 90m/C Bruce Li, Carl Scott, Jim James, Ku Feng. VHS, Beta $59.95 *PSM* ⅛

Kung Fu Commandos Five martial arts masters must face an evil warlord's army to rescue a captured agent.
1980 (R) 90m/C John Liu, Shangkuan Ling-Feng. VHS, Beta $59.95 *PSM, GEM* ⅛

Kung Fu from Beyond the Grave The ultimate warrior/zombies are summoned from the cold earth for evil purposes. Not for the brain-active.
19?? 90m/C Billy Chong, Sung Kam Shing, Lo Lieh, Hui Piu Wan. VHS, Beta $29.95 *OCE* ⅛

Kung Fu Massacre Farmers hire hard-handed mercenaries to fight evil war lords.
1982 (R) 90m/C Yangzi, Pi Li Lee. VHS, Beta $12.95 *LIV* ⅛

Kung Fu of Eight Drunkards Ching dynasty warriors battle it out using a karate technique that gives them the appearance of being drunk.
19?? 188m/C VHS, Beta *BFV* ⅛

Kung Fu Powerhouse No one dares to get in the way of a powerful kung fu drug lord. If they do, they die!
19?? 90m/C Kam Kong, Yasuka Kurata, Lee Ka Ting. VHS, Beta $49.95 *OCE* ⅛

Kung Fu Rebels Rebels are fearsome enough, but when they're kung fu masters, the establishment has real trouble on its hands.
1980 90m/C Wang Chung, Wen Ching Lung, Chang Mei. VHS, Beta *NO* ⅛½

Kung Fu Strongman A peace-loving blacksmith is forced to crush, kill, and destroy when he is framed for a robbery.
19?? 90m/C Lei Chen, Lung Fei, Kam Kong. VHS, Beta $49.95 *OCE* ⅛

Kung Fu Terminator A lady terminator proves that her fists are just as quick and deadly as any man's.
19?? 90m/C Wang Kuang Hsiung, Liu Hao Yi. VHS, Beta $49.95 *OCE* ⅛

Kung Fu: The Movie Carradine reprises his role as Kwai Chang Caine from the television show of the '70s. In this made-for-television fare he's hunted by evil warlord Mako, who's involved in the California opium trade. Mako sends assassin Lee (son of martial-arts star Bruce) after Caine. Luke appears in flashbacks as the young Grasshopper's blind mentor, Master Po.
1986 93m/C David Carradine, Mako, Brandon Lee, Keye Luke, Kerrie Keane, Martin Landau, William Lucking, Luke Askew, Benson Fong; *D:* Richard Lang. VHS, Beta $19.98 *WAR* ⅛⅛½

Kung Fu Vampire Buster Two Taoist kung fu priests take on coffins, cemeteries, and vampires. Good luck! The ultimate (tasteless) cross-genre flick.
19?? 90m/C Lu Fang, Wang Hsiao Feng, Chien Hsiao Hou. VHS, Beta $49.95 *OCE* Woof!

Kung Fu's Hero A detective must resort to killing with Kung Fu to stop a slave/drug ring.
19?? 90m/C VHS, Beta $49.95 *OCE* ⅛

Kuni Lemel in Tel Aviv The bungling folk-hero of the shtetl of 100 years ago is updated to the present. Grandpa Kuni is now 80 and living in Brooklyn. Anxious to see the family line continue, he offers five million dollars to the first of his twin grandsons to marry a nice Jewish girl and settle in Israel. However, the grandsons have plans of their own which conflict with Grandpa's. In Hebrew with English subtitles.
1977 90m/C Mike Burstyn, Mandy Rice-Davies; *D:* Yoel Silberg. VHS, Beta $79.95 *ERG* ⅛⅛½

Kurt Vonnegut's Monkey House Dramatization of four short stories from Vonnegut's "Welcome to the Monkey House" collection, including a twist on the familiar Frankenstein tale. Made for cable television.
1991 100m/C Frank Langella. VHS $29.95 *PBS* ⅛⅛

Kwaidan A haunting, stylized quartet of supernatural stories, each with a surprise ending. Adapted from the stories of Lafcadio Hearn, an American author who lived in Japan just before the turn of the century. The visual effects are splendid. In Japanese with English subtitles.
1964 164m/C Michiyo Aratama, Rentaro Mikuni, Katsuo Makamura, Keiko Kishi, Tatsuya Nakadai, Takashi Shimura; *D:* Masaki Kobayashi; *M:* Toru Takemitsu. VHS, Beta $39.95 *VYY, NOS, SNC* ⅛⅛⅛⅛

L.A. Bad A Puerto Rican street thug learns he has cancer, and must come to terms with his own impending death.
1985 (R) 101m/C Esai Morales, Janice Rule, John Phillip Law, Chuck Bail, Carrie Snodgress. VHS, Beta $9.99 *STE, PSM* ⅛

La Balance An underworld stool-pigeon is recruited by the Parisian police to blow the whistle on a murderous mob. Baye, as a prostitute in love with the pimp-stoolie, is a standout. Critically acclaimed in France; won many Caesar awards, including for Best Picture. In French with English subtitles.
1982 (R) 103m/C Philippe Leotard, Nathalie Baye, Bob Swaim; *D:* Reymond LePlont. VHS, Beta $79.95 *ING, FOX* ⅛⅛

La Bamba A romantic biography of the late 1950s pop idol Ritchie Valens, concentrating on his stormy relationship with his half-brother, his love for his WASP girlfriend, and his tragic, sudden death in the famed plane crash that also took the lives of Buddy Holly and the Big Bopper. Soundtrack features Setzer, Huntsberry, Crenshaw, and Los Lobos as, respectively, Eddie Cochran, the Big Bopper, Buddy Holly, and a Mexican bordello band.
1987 (PG-13) 99m/C Lou Diamond Phillips, Esai Morales, Danielle von Zernaeck, Joe Pantoliano, Brian Setzer, Marshall Crenshaw, Howard Huntsberry, Rosana De Soto, Elizabeth Pena, Rick Dees; *D:* Luis Valdez; *W:* Luis Valdez; *M:* Carlos Santana, Miles Goodman. VHS, Beta, 8mm $14.95 *COL* ⅛⅛⅛

La Bella Lola A poor singer falls in love with a rich politician in nineteenth century society.
1987 113m/C Sara Montiel, Antonio Charriello, Frank Villard, Luisa Mattiol. VHS, Beta $53.95 *MAD* ⅛⅛

La Belle Noiseuse The connections between art and life are explored in this beautiful (and long) drama. Creatively crippled, an aging painter has left unfinished a masterpiece work, entitled "La Belle Noiseuse," for ten years. When an admiring younger artist and his beautiful lover arrive for a visit, the painter is newly inspired by the young woman and makes her the model and muse for his masterwork. The film details every nuance of the work from the first to the last brushstroke and the battle of wills between artist and model over the symbiotic creative process. Based on a novella by Honore Balzac. In French with English subtitles.
1990 240m/C Michel Piccoli, Emmanuelle Beart, Jane Birkin, David Bursztein, Marianne Denicourt; *D:* Jacques Rivette. VHS $89.95 *NYF, FCT, ING* ⅛⅛⅛½

La Bete Humaine A dark, psychological melodrama about human passion and duplicity, as an unhinged trainman plots with a married woman to kill her husband. Wonderful performances and stunning photography. Based on the Emile Zola novel. In French with English subtitles. 1954 Hollywood remake, "Human Desire," was directed by Fritz Lang. *AKA:* The Human Beast.
1938 90m/B Jean Gabin, Simone Simon, Julien Carette, Fernand Ledoux; *D:* Jean Renoir. VHS, Beta, 8mm $24.95 *NOS, HHT, CAB* ⅛⅛⅛½

La Boca del Lobo Peru's civil strife inspired this sluggish drama about government troops occupying a jungle village. Tormented by unseen communist guerillas, the stressed-out soldiers reach the breaking point. *AKA:* The Lion's Den.
1989 111m/C *D:* Francisco J. Lombardi. VHS $68.00 *CCN, APD, TPV* ⅛⅛

La Boum A teenager's adjustment to the changes brought about by a move to Paris is compounded by her parents' marital problems. Followed by "La Boum 2."
1981 90m/C Sophie Marceau, Claude Brasseur, Brigitte Fossey, Denise Grey, Bernard Giraudeau; *D:* Claude Pinoteau; *M:* Vladimir Cosma. VHS, Beta $59.95 *COL* ⅛⅛½

L.A. Bounty A beautiful cop and a bounty hunter go after the same murderer. Hauser steals the show as a psychopath who has completely blown a gasket.
1989 (R) 85m/C Sybil Danning, Wings Hauser, Henry Darrow, Lenore Kasdorf, Robert Hanley; *D:* Worth Keeter. VHS, Beta *NO* ⅛½

La Cage aux Folles Adaption of the popular French play. A gay nightclub owner and his transvestite lover play it straight when Tognazzi's son from a long-ago liaison brings his fiancee and conservative parents home for dinner. Charming music and lots of fun. So successful, it was followed by two sequels, "La Cage Aux Folles II & III" and also a Broadway musical. In French with English subtitles.
1978 (R) 91m/C Ugo Tognazzi, Michel Serrault, Michel Galabru, Claire Maurier, Remy Laurent, Benny Luke; *D:* Edouard Molinaro; *W:* Francis Veber; *M:* Ennio Morricone. Academy Awards '79 Nominations: Best Adapted Screenplay, Best Costume Design, Best Director (Molinaro); Cesar Awards '79: Best Actor (Serrault); Golden Globe Awards '80: Best Foreign Film. VHS, Beta $19.98 *MGM, FOX, VYG* ⅛⅛⅛½

La Cage aux Folles 2 Albin sets out to prove to his companion that he still has sex appeal, and gets mixed up in some espionage antics. This sequel to the highly successful "La Cage aux Folles" loses some steam, but is still worth seeing. Followed by "La Cage Aux Folles 3: The Wedding."
1981 (R) 101m/C Ugo Tognazzi, Michel Serrault, Marcel Bozzuffi, Michel Galabru, Benny Luke; **D:** Edouard Molinaro; **W:** Francis Veber; **M:** Ennio Morricone. VHS, Beta $19.98 *MGM, FCT, FOX* ♂♂½

La Cage aux Folles 3: The Wedding The flamboyant drag queen Albin must feign normalcy by marrying and fathering a child in order to collect a weighty inheritance. Final segment of the trilogy; inferior to the previous films. In French with English subtitles.
1986 (PG-13) 88m/C Michel Serrault, Ugo Tognazzi, Michel Galabru, Benny Luke, Stephane Audran; **D:** Georges Lautner; **M:** Ennio Morricone. VHS, Beta $29.95 *COL, ING* ♂½

La Carcel de Laredo Two young lovers find they have made the biggest mistake of their lives when they have a baby out of wedlock.
1984 ?m/C Rodolfo de Anda, Eleazar Garcia Chelelo; **D:** Rodolfo de Anda. VHS, Beta NO ♂♂

La Casa de Madame Lulu A man who falls in love with a prostitute disrupts life in a brothel in this satire on the balance of power between men and women.
1965 90m/C Libertad Leblanc, Enzo Viena, Elena Lucena, Juan C. Altavista. VHS, Beta $39.95 *MAD* ♂♂

La Chamuscada A group of Mexican rebels fight against the army so they can live their lives freely.
1987 97m/C VHS, Beta $58.95 *MAD* ♂

La Chartreuse de Parme Nineteenth century period piece featuring an Archbishop willing to break his vows for the woman he loves, and the aunt who will make sure that if she can't have him only God will. French adaptation of the novel by Stendahl. Available dubbed. *AKA:* Charterhouse at Parma.
1948 ?m/C Gerard Philippe, Maria Casares, Rene Faure. VHS $59.95 *FRA, FCT* ♂♂½

La Chevre A screwball French comedy about two policemen (Richard and Depardieu—picture Nick Nolte and Gene Wilder with accents) stumbling along the path of a missing heiress who suffers from chronic bad luck. Contains a hilarious scene with chairs used to test the luck of the investigative team; based on one partner's ability to sit on the only broken chair in a rather large collection, he is judged to be sufficiently jinxed to allow them to recreate the same outrageous misfortunes that befell the heiress in her plight. In French with English subtitles. *AKA:* The Goat.
1981 91m/C Gerard Depardieu, Pierre Richard, Corynne Charbit, Michel Robin, Pedro Armendariz Jr.; **D:** Francis Veber; **M:** Vladimir Cosma. VHS, Beta $69.95 *FCT, ING, TPV* ♂♂♂½

La Chienne Dark, troubling tale of a bedraggled husband whose only excitement is his painting hobby until he becomes consumed by the ever-tempting prostitute Lulu. Director Renoir broke ground with his use of direct sound and Paris shooting locations, and the experiment was a hit. Portrays marriage with acidity; Renoir's own marriage broke up as a result of this film's casting. Mareze died shortly after the filming was complete in a car crash. Based on the novel by Georges de la Fouchardiere. Produced in 1931, but didn't reach American theaters until 1975. In French with English subtitles.

Remade in 1945 as "Scarlet Street." *AKA:* Isn't Life A Bitch?; The Bitch.
1931 93m/B Michel Simon, Janie Mareze, Georges Flament, Madeleine Berubet; **D:** Jean Renoir; **W:** Andre Girard, Jean Renoir. VHS, Beta $59.95 *INT, ING, TPV* ♂♂♂♂

La Choca A gang of smugglers deep in the jungle turn on a member and slaughter him. The victim's wife and child must struggle to survive and avenge their loved one's fate.
1973 94m/C Pilar Pellicer, Gregorio Casal, Armando Silvestre; **D:** Emilio Fernandez. VHS, Beta NO ♂

La Chute de la Maison Usher An expressionistic, abstracted adaptation of the Poe story "The Fall of the House of Usher" about an evil mansion and its ruined denizens. Epstein used slow motion, superimpressions, and weird camera angles to obtain the proper atmosphere. *AKA:* The Fall of the House of Usher.
1928 48m/B Marguerite Gance, Jean Debucourt, Charles Lamy; **D:** Jean Epstein. VHS, Beta $59.95 *FCT, GVV, ING* ♂♂♂

La Cicada The sparks fly when a woman and her seventeen-year-old daughter become rivals for the affections of the same man. *AKA:* The Cricket.
1983 90m/C Clio Goldsmith, Virna Lisi, Anthony (Tony) Franciosa, Renato Salvatori; **D:** Alberto Lattuada. VHS, Beta $29.98 *SUE* ♂½

La Corona de un Campeon A boxer and a wrestler attempt to beat each others brains in.
1987 90m/C Andres Garcia, Rogelio Guerra, Norma Lazarendo, Crox Alvarado. VHS, Beta $53.95 *MAD* ♂♂

L.A. Crackdown A ruthless yet compassionate policewoman goes after crack dealers and pimps who are exploiting women. Pretty trashy fare; followed by "L.A. Crackdown." Made for video.
1987 90m/C Pamela Dixon, Tricia Parks, Kita Harrison, Jeffrey Olson, Michael Coon; **D:** Joseph Merhi. VHS, Beta NO ♂

L.A. Crackdown 2 A woman cop goes undercover as a dancer in a dance hall to try to catch a psychotic killer who stalks hookers in this silly sequel to "L.A. Crackdown."
1988 90m/C Pamela Dixon, Anthony Gates, Joe Vance, Cynthia Miguel, Lisa Anderson, Bo Sabato; **D:** Joseph Merhi. VHS, Beta $79.95 *HHE* ♂

La Cucaracha A lavish production filled with Mexican songs and dances. The first three-strip, live-action Technicolor film ever made. Historically interesting.
1934 21m/C Steffi Duna. VHS, Beta $9.95 *VYY, GVV* ♂♂♂

La Diosa Arrodillada A marriage ends in divorce because the husband is in love with another woman. *AKA:* The Kneeling Goddess.
1947 89m/B Maria Felix, Arturo de Cordova, Rosario Granados; **D:** Roberto Gavaldon. VHS, Beta $39.95 *MAD* ♂

La Discrete Antoine (Luchini) is a cocky writer who is not the lothario he imagines himself to be—in fact his girlfriend has just dumped him. He and his publisher plan a sexist revenge with Antoine advertising for a young female typist whom he will seduce and abandon—all the while keeping a diary of the experience which will be published. The self-possessed Catherine (Henry) answers the ad and even though Antoine protests that she is not his type he finds himself falling in love. Then Catherine discovers Antoine's original scheme. Vincent's directorial debut. In

French with English subtitles. *AKA:* The Discreet.
1990 95m/C Fabrice Luchini, Judith Henry, Maurice Garrel, Marie Bunel, Francois Toumarkine; **D:** Christian Vincent; **W:** Jean-Pierre Ronssin, Christian Vincent; **M:** Jay Gottlieb. VHS $89.95 *NYF, FCT* ♂♂♂

La Dolce Vita In this influential and popular work a successful, sensationalistic Italian journalist covers the show-biz life in Rome, and alternately covets and disdains its glitzy shallowness. The film follows his dealings with the "sweet life" over a pivotal week. A surreal, comic tableaux with award-winning costuming; one of Fellini's most acclaimed films. In this film Fellini called his hungry celebrity photographers the Paparazzo—and it is as the paparazzi they have been ever since. In Italian with English subtitles.
1960 174m/B Marcello Mastroianni, Anita Ekberg, Anouk Aimee, Alain Cuny, Lex Barker, Yvonne Furneaux, Barbara Steele, Nadia Gray, Magali Noel, Walter Santesso, Jacques Sernas, Annabelle Ninchi; **D:** Federico Fellini; **W:** Tullio Pinelli, Ennio Flaino, Brunello Rondi, Federico Fellini; **M:** Nino Rota. Academy Awards '61: Best Costume Design (B & W); Nominations: Best Art Direction/Set Decoration (B & W), Best Director (Fellini), Best Story & Screenplay; Cannes Film Festival '60: Best Film; National Board of Review Awards '63: 5 Best Foreign Films of the Year; New York Film Critics Awards '63: Best Foreign Film. VHS $24.98 *ING, REP, APD* ♂♂♂♂

La Femme Nikita Stylish French noir version of Pygmalion. Having killed a cop during a drugstore theft gone awry, young French sociopath Nikita (Parillaud) is reprieved from a death sentence in order to enroll in a government finishing school, of sorts. Trained in etiquette and assasination, she's released after three years, and starts a new life with a new beau, all the while carrying out agency-mandated assassinations. Parillaud is excellent as the once-amoral street urchin transformed into a woman of depth and sensitivity—a bitterly ironic moral evolution for a contract killer. Remade as "Point of No Return."
1991 (R) 117m/C Anne Parillaud, Jean-Hughes Anglade, Tcheky Karyo, Jeanne Moreau, Jean Reno, Jean Bouise; **D:** Luc Besson; **W:** Luc Besson; **M:** Eric Serra. VHS $19.95 *VMK, FCT, BTV* ♂♂♂

La Fuerza Inutil A college professor tries to join the radical actions of his students.
1987 103m/C Rafael Baledon, Veronica Castro, Roberto Jordan, Silvia Mariscal. VHS, Beta $58.95 *MAD* ♂♂

La Fuga del Rojo An inmate is aided in his escape attempt so he can smuggle arms across the border.
1987 120m/C Mario Almada, Patricia Rivera, Carmen Del Valle, Noe Murayama. VHS, Beta $59.95 *MAD* ♂

L.A. Gangs Rising The streets of Los Angeles run red with blood as a gang war explodes into bloody fury.
1989 87m/C David Kyle, Steve Bond, John Ashton; **D:** John Bushelman. VHS, Beta $9.95 *SIM* ♂♂

La Generala A woman seeks vengeance for her brother's death after the Mexican Revolution.
1987 90m/C Maria Felix. VHS, Beta $59.95 *MAD* ♂

L.A. Goddess A hard-living, and drinking, movie star and her beautiful stunt double both fall for a studio head. Both of these women know what they want and the man in the middle hasn't got a clue. Also available in an unrated version.

1992 (R) 92m/C Kathy Shower, Jeff Conaway, David Heavener, Wendy McDonald, Joe Estevez, James Hong; D: Jag Mundhra; W: Jerry Davis. VHS $79.95 PSM ℐℐ½

La Grande Bourgeoise Historical romance about the clash of aristocratic society and the new bourgeoisie in 1897 Italy. Great cast tries to save the true tale of murder and political intrigue from film's slow pacing, but in the end it's the movie's visual polish that shines forth. In Italian with subtitles. *AKA:* The Murri Affair.
1974 115m/C Catherine Deneuve, Giancarlo Giannini, Fernando Rey, Tina Aumont; D: Mauro Bolognini; M: Ennio Morricone. VHS, Beta $69.95 FCT ℐℐ½

La Grande Vadrouille In 1943 German-occupied France, three Allied parachutists drop in on a Paris Opera conductor and a house painter. If the pair wish to find some peace, they must help the trio get to the free zone. France's number one box office hit for almost thirty years. Also available dubbed. *AKA:* Don't Look Now, We've Been Shot At.
1966 122m/C Louis de Funes, Bourvil, Terry-Thomas; D: Gerard Oury. VHS $59.95 FRA, FCT ℐℐℐ

L.A. Heat When a vice cop's partner is killed, he seeks revenge on the murderers, only to find that his own department may have been involved. Followed by "L.A. Vice."
1988 90m/C Jim Brown, Lawrence Hilton-Jacobs; D: Joseph Merhi. VHS, Beta $19.95 PAR, HHE ℐℐ½

La Hifa Sin Padre A country girl gains fame as a folk singer in Mexico City.
1987 90m/C Jaime Moreno, Mercedes Castro, Roberto "Flaco" Guzman, Dacia Gonzales. VHS, Beta $79.95 MAD ℐℐ½

La Hija del General Moving story of a young girl becoming a woman in revolutionary Spain. She loses her mother and friends to the brutal government which her father heads.
1984 101m/C Jorge Russek, Juan Ferrara, Rocio Brambilia, Patricia Aspillaga. VHS, Beta $69.95 MED ℐ

La Hora 24 A beggar with the power of premonition foresees dire consequences in the next 24 hours.
1987 102m/C Julio Aleman, Diana Ferreti, Jose Natera, Carlos Rotzinger; D: Fernando Duran. VHS, Beta $74.95 CCV ℐ

La Isla Encantada The new adventures of Robinson Crusoe and Man Friday, as they pursue wild beasts and cannibals and fight off pirates. *AKA:* The Enchanted Island.
1984 90m/C VHS, Beta $57.95 UNI ℐ½

La Justicia Tiene Doce Anos A twelve-year-old girl decides to rid the world of evil.
1987 88m/C Joaquin Cordero, Iran Eroy, Jorge Mistral, Sergio Guzik. VHS, Beta $57.95 MAD ℐℐ

L.A. Law The pilot episode of the acclaimed dramatic series, in which the staff of a Los Angeles law firm tries a variety of cases.
1986 97m/C Michael Tucker, Jill Eikenberry, Harry Hamlin, Richard Dysart, Jimmy Smits, Alan Rachins, Susan Ruttan, Susan Dey, Corbin Bernsen; D: Gregory Holbit. VHS, Beta $79.98 FOX ℐℐℐ

La Lectrice Artesian landscapes, Beethoven sonatas, and a Raymond Jean novel titled "La Lectrice" provide the backdrop for Constance (Miou-Miou) to read aloud to her boyfriend in bed, and from there she imagines herself the novel's heroine, who hires out her services as a reader to various odd characters. She reads from "L'Amant," "Al-

ice," "War and Peace," and "Les Fleurs du Mal." Richly textured and not overly intellectual. In French with English subtitles. *AKA:* The Reader.
1988 (R) 98m/C Miou-Miou, Christian Ruche, Sylvie Laporte, Michael Raskine, Brigitte Catillon, Regis Royer, Maria Casares, Pierre Dux, Patrick Chesnais; D: Michel DeVille; W: Rosalinde DeVille, Michel DeVille. VHS, Beta $14.98 ORI, ING ℐℐ½

La Ley del Revolver This is an Old West adventure where the law of the gun speaks for and against justice. In Spanish. *AKA:* The Law of the Gun.
1978 90m/C Michael Rivers, Angel Del Pozo, Lucia Gil Fernandez. VHS, Beta HHT ℐ

La Mansion de la Locura A journalist goes into a horrifying castle owned by a madman.
1987 83m/C Claudio Brook, Arthur Dansel, Ellen Sherman, Martin LaSalle. VHS, Beta $75.95 MAD ℐℐ½

La Marchanta A poor woman comes to Mexico City and becomes a street merchant.
1973 100m/C Lucha Villa, Adalberto "Resortes" Martinez, Antonio "Clavillazo" Espino; D: Arturo Martinez. VHS, Beta $59.95 MAD ℐℐ

La Marseillaise Sweeping epic by Renoir made before he hit his stride with "Grand Illusion." It details the events of the French Revolution in the summer of 1789 using a cast of thousands. The opulent lifestyle of the French nobility is starkly contrasted with the peasant lifestyle of poverty and despair. The focus is on two new recruits who have joined the Marseilles division of the revolutionary army as they begin their long march to Paris, the heart of France. As they travel, they adopt a stirring and passionate song that embodies the spirit and ideals of the revolution known as "La Marseillaise," now France's national anthem. In French with English subtitles.
1937 130m/B Pierre Renoir, Lisa Delamare, Louis Jouvet, Aime Clarimond, Andrex Andrisson, Paul Dullac; D: Jean Renoir; W: Jean Renoir. VHS, Beta $24.95 NOS, INT, HHT ℐℐℐ½

La Mentira A man falls in love with a woman he had previously wanted to kill. Based on the novel by Caridad Bravo Adams.
1987 107m/C Enrique Lizalde, Julissa, Blanca Sanchez, David Estuardo. VHS, Beta $73.95 MAD ℐℐ½

La Merveilleuse Visite Bittersweet fantasy about an angel that falls from the sky and is found unconcious by a priest. He's nursed back to health but causes problems for his host when he wanders into the nearby village and his curiosity is misunderstood. Adapted from a short story by H.G. Wells. In French with English subtitles. *AKA:* The Marvelous Visit.
1974 102m/C Gilles Kohler, Deborah Berger, Jean-Pierre Castaldi; D: Marcel Carne; W: Marcel Carne. VHS $59.95 HTV, FCT ℐℐ½

La Montana del Diablo Two men escape from slavery and then ask the superhero El Payo for help. *AKA:* The Devil's Mountain.
1987 89m/C Jorge Rivero, Ernesto Yanez, Carmen Vicarte, Miguel Garza. VHS, Beta $75.95 MAD ℐℐ½

La Notte Brava Italian drama focusing on the life of Rome's aimless youth in the late fifties. *AKA:* Lusty Night in Rome.
1959 96m/B VHS, Beta CIG ℐℐ

La Nueva Cigarra A brothel is quarantined with the bubonic plague, and the customers are caught with their proverbial pants down. In Spanish.

1986 90m/C Toco Gomez, Haydee Balsa, Gogo Andreu, Olga Zubarry. VHS, Beta $57.95 UNI ℐℐ

La Nuit de Varennes This semi-historical romp is based on an actual chapter in French history when King Louis XVI and Marie Antoinette fled from revolutionary Paris to Varennes in 1791. On the way they meet an unlikely group of characters, including Cassanova and Thomas Paine. At times witty and charming, the melange of history and fiction is full of talk, sometimes profane, punctuated by sex and nudity. Director Scola's imagination stretches to light up this night. In French with English subtitles.
1982 (R) 133m/C Marcello Mastroianni, Harvey Keitel, Jean-Louis Barrault, Hanna Schygulla, Jean-Claude Briely; D: Ettore Scola; W: Ettore Scola. VHS, Beta $59.95 COL, IME, APD ℐℐℐ

La Passante An otherwise peace-loving man murders the Paraguayan ambassador to France. In somewhat clumsy flashback style the murderer's orphaned childhood and other memories provide motives for the murder. Though posed more slowly than typical intrigue plots, the movie blends love and the legacy of Nazism, passion and politics in an engaging way, spiced with nudity and some violence. In her last screen appearance Schneider movingly portrays dual roles. In French with English subtitles. *AKA:* La Passante du Sans Souci; The Passerby.
1983 106m/C Romy Schneider, Michel Piccoli, Helmut Griem, Gerard Klein, Matthieu Carriere, Maria Schell; D: Jacques Rouffio; M: Georges Delerue. VHS, Beta $29.95 ING, TPV ℐℐℐ

La Pastorela An adaptation of the traditional Spanish Christmas play about the shepherds' journey to Bethlehem. Told through the eyes of a young Hispanic girl, using contemporary references to make this a modern-day story. Available in English and Spanish versions.
1992 80m/C Linda Ronstadt, Richard "Cheech" Marin, Paul Rodriguez, Karla Montana, Don Novello, Robert Beltran, Freddy Fender, Falco Jimenez; D: Luis Valdez; W: Luis Valdez; M: Los Lobos. VHS $19.98 BMG, MVD, RIN ℐℐℐ

La Petite Bande Seven little British schoolchildren run away from home and wind up in the French countryside, being chased by police and causing havoc wherever they go. Based on a true story.
1984 (PG) 91m/C D: Michel DeVille. VHS, Beta $59.95 COL, ING ℐℐ½

La Petite Sirene Isabelle is a 14-year-old schoolgirl, obsessed with the story of the Little Mermaid, who tries to ingratiate herself to Georges, a 40-year-old garage mechanic. Seeing him as her prince charming, she persists in trying to make him a part of her life, in spite of his resistance. In French with English subtitles. *AKA:* The Little Mermaid.
1980 104m/C Laura Alexis, Philippe Leotard, Evelyne Dress, Marie DuBois; D: Roger Andrieux; W: Roger Andrieux. VHS $59.95 WAC, FCT, ING ℐℐ

La Puritaine Before his planned reconciliation with his daughter, the artistic manager of a theater has young actresses portray different sides of the daughter's personality. In French with English subtitles.
1986 90m/C Michel Piccoli, Sandrine Bonnaire; D: Lou Doillon. VHS $49.95 FCT ℐℐ½

La Ronde A classic comedy of manners and sharply witty tour-de-farce in which a group of people in 1900 Vienna keep changing romantic partners until things wind up where they started. Ophuls' swirling direction creates a fast-paced farce of desire and regret with wicked yet subtle style. Based on

Arthur Schnitzler's play and remade as "Circle of Love." In French with English subtitles. **1951 97m/B** Simone Signoret, Anton Walbrook, Simone Simon, Serge Reggiani, Daniel Gelin, Danielle Darrieux, Jean-Louis Barrault, Fernand Gravet, Odette Joyeux, Isa Miranda, Gerard Philippe; *D:* Max Ophuls. Academy Awards '51 Nominations: Best Art Direction/Set Decoration (B & W), Best Screenplay; British Academy Awards '51: Best Film. **VHS, Beta $29.98** SUE, APD, ING ♪♪♪½

La Rupture Thriller about a wife trying to protect her child from her husband's unsavory family. Audran and her son are attacked by her husband (Drouot), who's high on drugs. She fights back and he winds up in the hospital. Her father-in-law (Bouquet), who wants his grandson to live with him, then hires a seedy investigator (Cassel) to spy on Audran. Based on the Charlotte Armstrong novel. In French with English subtitles. *AKA:* The Breakup. **1970 124m/C** Stephane Audran, Jean-Claude Drouot, Michel Bouquet, Jean-Pierre Cassel, Catherine Rouvel, Jean Carmet, Annie Cordy; *D:* Claude Chabrol; *W:* Claude Chabrol; *M:* Pierre Jansen. **VHS $79.95** CVC, FCT ♪♪½

La Signora di Tutti An early Italian biography of Gaby Doriot, a movie star whose professional success is paired by personal misery. Prestigious director Ophuls, working in exile from his native Germany, was unable to complete many projects in the years leading up to and during WWII. This is one of the few. Watch for innovative camera work intended to underscore the film's mood. In Italian with English subtitles. **1934 92m/B** Isa Miranda; *D:* Max Ophuls. **VHS, Beta $59.95** CVC, FCT, ING ♪♪♪

L.A. Story Livin' ain't easy in the city of angels. Harris K. Telemacher (Martin), a weatherman in a city where the weather never changes, wrestles with the meaning of life and love while consorting with beautiful people, distancing from significant other Henner, cavorting with valley girl Parker, and falling for newswoman Tennant (Martin's real life wife). Written by the comedian, the story's full of keen insights into the everyday problems and ironies of living in the Big Tangerine. (It's no wonder the script's full of so much thoughtful detail: Martin is said to have worked on it intermittently for seven years.) Charming, fault forgiving but not fault ignoring portrait. **1991 (PG-13) 98m/C** Steve Martin, Victoria Tennant, Richard E. Grant, Marilu Henner, Sarah Jessica Parker, Sam McMurray, Patrick Stewart, Iman, Kevin Pollak; *D:* Mick Jackson; *W:* Steve Martin; *M:* Peter Melnick. **VHS, Beta $92.95** LIV, WAR ♪♪♪

La Strada Simple-minded girl, played by Fellini's wife, Masina, is sold to a brutal, coarse circus strong-man and she falls in love with him despite his abuse. They tour the countryside and eventually meet up with a gentle acrobat, played by Basehart, who alters their fate. Fellini masterwork was the director's first internationally acclaimed film, and is, by turns, somber and amusing as it demonstrates the filmmaker's sensitivity to the underprivileged of the world and his belief in spiritual redemption. Subtitled in English. *AKA:* The Road. **1954 107m/B** Giulietta Masina, Anthony Quinn, Richard Basehart, Aldo Silvani; *D:* Federico Fellini; *W:* Ennio Flaino, Brunello Rondi, Tullio Pinelli, Federico Fellini; *M:* Nino Rota. Academy Awards '56: Best Foreign Language Film; Nominations: Best Original Screenplay; National Board of Review Awards '56: 5 Best Foreign Films of the Year; New York Film Critics Awards '56: Best Foreign Film. **VHS, Beta $29.98** SUE, IME, APD ♪♪♪♪

La Symphonie Pastorale A Swiss pastor takes in an orphan blind girl who grows up to be beautiful. The pastor then competes for her affections with his son. Quiet drama based on the Andre Gide novel, with breathtaking mountain scenery as the backdrop for this tragedy rife with symbolism. **1946 105m/B** Pierre Blanchar, Michele Morgan, Jean Desailly, Line Noro, Andree Clement; *D:* Jean Delannoy. **VHS** FLI ♪♪♪

La Terra Trema The classic example of Italian neo-realism, about a poor Sicilian fisherman, his family and their village. A spare, slow-moving, profound and ultimately lyrical tragedy, this semi-documentary explores the economic exploitation of Sicily's fishermen. Filmed on location with the villagers playing themselves; highly acclaimed though not commercially successful. In Sicilian with English subtitles. Some radically cut versions may be available, but are to be avoided. Franco Zefferelli was one of the assistant directors. *AKA:* Episoda Del Mare; The Earth Will Tremble. **1948 161m/B** Antonio Pietrangeli; *D:* Luchino Visconti. **VHS, Beta $89.95** FCT, ING ♪♪♪½

La Trinchera A Spanish western centering around the Mexican Revolution. **1987 91m/C** David Reynoso, Ignacio Lopez Tarso, Julio Aleman, Pilar Pellicer. **VHS, Beta $59.95** MAD ♪

La Truite A young woman leaves her family's rural trout farm and a loveless marriage to seek her fortune in high finance and corporate mayhem. The complicated plot, full of intrigue and sexual encounters, sometimes lacks focus. Slickly filmed. *AKA:* The Trout. **1983 (R) 80m/C** Isabelle Huppert, Jean-Pierre Cassel, Daniel Olbrychski, Jeanne Moreau, Jacques Spiesser, Ruggero Raimondi, Alexis Smith, Craig Stevens; *D:* Joseph Losey. **VHS, Beta $59.95** COL ♪♪♪

La Venganza del Rojo A doctor helps the rebels in a revolution. **1987 90m/C** Mario Almada, Ferdinando Almada, Carmen Del Valle, Noe Murayama, Jorge Patino. **VHS, Beta $59.95** MAD ♪

La Vengeance d'une Femme Refined Cecile and sultry Suzy are two sides of a love triangle whose third member, Cecile's husband, has just died. Cecile decides to get to know his mistress better, which naturally has Suzy worried. Is Cecile out for revenge or does she sincerely want to befriend the "other woman." Based on Dostoyevski's "The Eternal Husband." In French with English subtitles. *AKA:* A Woman's Revenge. **1989 133m/C** Isabelle Huppert, Beatrice Dalle; *D:* Jacques Doillon; *W:* Jean-Francois Goyet, Jacques Doillon. **VHS $79.95** ING, FCT ♪♪

L.A. Vice A detective is transferred to the vice squad, where he must investigate a series of murders. Sequel to "L.A. Heat." **1989 90m/C** Jim Brown, Lawrence Hilton-Jacobs, William Smith; *D:* Joseph Merhi. **VHS, Beta** PAR ♪½

La Vie Continue A middle-aged woman suddenly finds herself widowed after 20 years of marriage and tries to build a new life for herself and her children. Girardot's performance can't quite dispel melodramatic suds. Loosely and more effectively remade as "Men Don't Leave." In French with English subtitles or dubbed. **1982 93m/C** Annie Girardot, Jean-Pierre Cassel, Michel Aumont, Pierre Dux, Guilia Salvatori, Emmanuel Goyet, Rivera Andres; *D:* Moshe Mizrahi; *M:* Georges Delerue. **VHS, Beta $59.95** COL, ING ♪♪½

La Vie de Boheme Comedy takes a mocking look at art and romantic love. A trio of hapless but dedicated comrades, Rodolfo (Pellonpaa) the painter, Marcel (Wilms) the poet, and Schaunard (Vaananen), must scrounge around the mealy edges of modern Paris because their art isn't filling their stomachs. Meanwhile, they experience the pangs of love like everyone else, although each is devoutly committed to his art as well. Starkly different from the lush, operatic version by Puccini, but based on the same source, a 19th century novel by Henri Mullet. **1993 100m/C** Matti Pellonpaa, Andre Wilms, Kari Vaananen, Jean-Pierre Leaud, Samuel Fuller, Louis Malle, Evelyne Didi, Christine Murillo, Laika, Carlos Salgado, Alexis Nitzer, Sylvie van den Elsen, Gilles Charmant, Dominique Marcas; *D:* Aki Kaurismaki; *W:* Aki Kaurismaki. **VHS** ♪♪♪½

La Violetera A poor flower vendor falls in love with a rich diplomat despite their opposite positions in society. *AKA:* The Violet. **1971 90m/C** Sara Montiel, Raf Vallone, Frank Villard. **VHS, Beta $39.95** MAD ♪

La Virgen de Guadalupe A miracle occurs amidst fighting between the Aztecs and the Spaniards. **1987 82m/C** Fernando Allende, Valentin Trujillo, Angelica Chain. **VHS, Beta $75.95** MAD ♪♪½

L.A. Wars A Latin American drug dealer moves into the territory of an Italian mobster, causing a turf war. When a cop rescues the mobster's daughter from the scuzzball, his boss forces him to infiltrate the mobster's organization. Abundant body count, lots of T&A. **1994 (R) 94m/C** Vince Murdocco, Mary Zilba, A.J. Stevens, Rodrigo Obregon; *D:* Martin Morris, Tony Kandah. **VHS $89.95** MNC ♪½

Laboratory Things go awry when the earthling subjects of an alien experiment revolt against their captors. **1980 93m/C** Camille Mitchell, Corinne Michaels, Garnett Smith. **VHS, Beta $49.95** VCI ♪

Labyrinth While baby-sitting her baby brother Froud, Connelly is so frustrated she asks the goblins to take him away. When the Goblin King, played by Bowie, comes to answer her idle wish, she must try to rescue Froud by solving the fantastic labyrinth. If she does not find him in time, Froud will become one of the goblins forever. During her journey, Connelly is befriended by all sorts of odd creatures created by Henson, and she grows up a little along the way. A fascinating adventure movie for the whole family. **1986 (PG) 90m/C** David Bowie, Jennifer Connelly, Toby Froud; *D:* Jim Henson; *W:* Terry Jones; *M:* David Bowie, Trevor Jones. **VHS, Beta, 8mm $14.98** SUE, NLC ♪♪♪

Labyrinth of Passion A screwball farce, directed by Almodovar, featuring a host of strange characters running around Madrid in search of sex and laughter. They find plenty of both. An early film by an influential director. In Spanish with English subtitles. *AKA:* Laberinto de Pasiones. **1982 100m/C** Antonio Banderas, Imanol Arias, Celia Roth; *D:* Pedro Almodovar; *W:* Pedro Almodovar. **VHS, Beta $79.95** CCN, IME, ING ♪♪½

The Lacemaker Huppert's first shot at stardom, on videodisc with digital sound and a letterboxed print. A young beautician and a university student fall in love on vacation but soon begin to realize the differences in their lives. Adapted from the novel by Pascal Laine. In French with English subtitles. *AKA:* La Dentiellaire.

1977 107m/C Isabelle Huppert, Yves Beneyton, Florence Giorgetti, Anna Marie Duringer; **D:** Claude Goretta. $39.95 HMV, CRC, VYG ✂✂✂1/2

L'Addition According to some cinematic code, the male lead always gets in lots of trouble whenever he tries to help a beautiful stranger. This time, Berry, as Bruno Windler, winds up arrested for shoplifting when he attempts to help Abril. Jailed and on the verge of parole, Windler unwittingly becomes involved in a prison break and is accused of helping a crime don mastermind the escape and of shooting a guard. That's where that gallic flair for capturing the sado-masochistic underbelly of humanity comes in, as Windler is viciously pursued by the malevolent guard. **AKA:** The Patsy; Caged Heart.
1985 (R) 85m/C Richard Berry, Victoria Abril, Richard Bohringer, Farid Chopel, Fabrice Eberhard; **D:** Denis Amar; **W:** Jean Curtelin; **M:** Jean-Claude Petit. VHS, Beta $19.95 NWV, MOR ✂✂1/2

The Ladies Club A group of rape victims get together and begin to victimize rapists.
1986 (R) 86m/C Bruce Davison, Karen Austin, Diana Scarwid, Shera Danese, Beverly Todd; **D:** A.K. Allen. VHS, Beta $79.95 MED ✂1/2

The Ladies' Man Piecemeal Lewis farce, with Jerry playing a clutzy handyman working at a girls' boarding house. Some riotous routines balanced by slow pacing.
1961 106m/C Jerry Lewis, Helen Traubel, Jack Kruschen, Doodles Weaver, Gloria Jean; **D:** Jerry Lewis; **W:** Jerry Lewis. VHS, Beta $14.95 PAR ✂✂

Ladies Man Spy adventure with Constantine playing super sleuth/agent, Lemmy Caution, on the French Riviera.
1962 ?m/C Eddie Constantine. VHS $16.95 SNC ✂✂

Ladies of the Chorus Monroe stars as a burlesque chorus girl who shares the stage with her mom (Jergens) and a handful of other beauties. She meets and falls in love with a wealthy socialite (Brooks), but her mother completely disapproves of the relationship. Monroe later learns that her mother was in love with the same man several years before. Although only her second film appearance, Monroe's talents are already quite apparent in this low-budget musical romance. ♫Every Baby Nees a Da Da Daddy; Anyone Can Tell I Love You; Crazy For You; You're Never Too Old; Ladies of the Chorus.
1949 61m/B Adele Jergens, Marilyn Monroe, Rand Brooks, Nana Bryant, Steve Geray, Bill Edwards; **D:** Phil Karlson. VHS $19.95 COL ✂✂

Ladies of the Lotus Bloodthirsty Vancouver gangsters raid Lotus, Inc., a modeling agency, and sell beautiful young women into slavery. As bad as it sounds.
1987 120m/C Richard Dale, Angela Read, Patrick Bermel, Darcia Carnie; **D:** Lloyd A. Simandl, Douglas G. Nicolle. VHS, Beta NO ✂

Ladies on the Rocks Aspiring comediennes Micha and Laura pack up their van and take their bizarre cabaret act on the road through rural Denmark. They find their private lives disintegrating but turn each disaster into new material for their act. In Danish with English subtitles. **AKA:** Koks I Kulissen.
1983 100m/C Helle Ryslinge, Anne Marie Helger, Flemming Quist Moller; **D:** Christian Braad Thomsen. VHS $79.95 NYF, ING ✂✂1/2

Ladies They Talk About Stanwyck stars as a tough-talking gun moll who belongs to a gang of bank robbers. They get caught and Stanwyck is sent to the female division of San Quentin. The acting is great in this pre-Code prison movie, but the film gets

a bit punchy at times. Based on the true-life experiences of actress Dorothy Mackaye, who went to jail after her husband was killed in a fight with actor Paul Kelley, who was also sent to prison. Adapted from the play "Women in Prison" by Dorothy Mackaye and Carlton Miles. **AKA:** Women in Prison.
1933 69m/B Barbara Stanwyck, Preston Foster, Lyle Talbot, Dorothy Burgess, Lillian Roth, Maude Eburne, Harold Huber, Ruth Donnelly; **D:** Howard Bretherton, William Keighley. VHS $19.98 MGM ✂✂1/2

Lady and the Tramp The animated Disney classic about two dogs who fall in love. Tramp is wild and carefree; Lady is a spoiled pedigree who runs away from home after her owners have a baby. They just don't make dog romances like this anymore. ♫He's a Tramp; La La Lu; Siamese Cat Song; Peace on Earth; Bella Notte.
1955 (G) 76m/C **D:** Hamilton Luske; **M:** Peggy Lee, Sonny Burke; **V:** Larry Roberts, Peggy Lee, Barbara Luddy, Stan Freberg, Alan Reed, Bill Thompson, Bill Baucon, Verna Felton, George Givot, Dallas McKennon, Lee Millar. VHS, Beta $29.95 DIS, APD ✂✂✂✂

Lady Avenger A woman is bent on getting revenge on her brother's killers.
1989 (R) 90m/C Peggie Sanders. VHS, Beta NO ✂

Lady Be Good Adapted from the 1924 Gershwin Broadway hit, the plot's been revamped, much to the critics' distaste ("Variety" called it "molasses paced"). Sothern and Young play a tunesmith duo who excel at musical harmony and marital strife. Applauded for its music (the critics loved Hammerstein's and the Gershwins' tunes), the show's Academy Award winning song was, ironically, written by Jerome Kern. And if that's not enough, levity man Skelton and hoofer Powell are thrown in for good measure. ♫The Last Time I Saw Paris; So Am I; Oh Lady Be Good; Fascinating Rhythm; Hang On To Me; You'll Never Know; You're Words, My Music; Saudades.
1941 111m/B Eleanor Powell, Ann Sothern, Robert Young, Lionel Barrymore, John Carroll, Red Skelton, Dan Dailey, Virginia O'Brien, Tom Conway, Phil Silvers, Doris Day; **D:** Norman Z. McLeod; **M:** Oscar Hammerstein, George Gershwin, Ira Gershwin, Jerome Kern. VHS $19.98 MGM, TTC, FCT ✂✂1/2

Lady Beware A psychotic doctor becomes obsessed with a beautiful store-window dresser who specializes in steamy, erotic fantasies. When he wages a campaign of terror against her, she realizes that she must stop him before he kills her.
1987 (R) 108m/C Diane Lane, Michael Woods, Cotter Smith, Viveca Lindfors, Tyra Ferrell, Peter Nevargic, Edward Penn; **D:** Karen Arthur. VHS, Beta $14.95 LIV ✂✂

Lady by Choice Lombard stars as a beautiful young fan dancer who is arrested for a lewd public performance. Taking the advice of her press agent, she hires an old bag lady to pose as her mother on Mother's Day. Robson portrays her "mother" and comes to think of Lombard as her own daughter. Robson encourages Lombard to give up fan dancing and to strive for greater things in life. She also pushes her into romance with a wealthy young man (Pryor). Robson is excellent in her role as "mother" and Lombard shows great comic talent in this charming film.
1934 78m/C Carole Lombard, May Robson, Roger Pryor, Walter Connolly, Raymond Walburn, James Burke; **D:** David Burton; **W:** Jo Swerling. VHS $19.95 COL ✂✂1/2

Lady Caroline Lamb Lady Caroline is a passionate young lady in 19th-century England, who, although the wife of a member of Parliament, has an affair with Lord Byron and brings about her own downfall. Costume drama that never quite goes anywhere.
1973 123m/C Sarah Miles, Richard Chamberlain, Jon Finch, Laurence Olivier, John Mills, Ralph Richardson; **D:** Robert Bolt; **W:** Robert Bolt; **M:** Richard Rodney Bennett. Beta $14.95 PSM ✂✂

Lady Chatterley's Lover Englishwoman has bad luck to have husband shot up during WWI and sent home paralyzed. In her quest for sexual fulfillment, she takes a new lover, the estate's earthy gamekeeper. Limp adaptation of D.H. Lawrence's novel. In French with English subtitles. **AKA:** L'Amant de Lady Chatterley.
1955 102m/B Danielle Darrieux, Erno Crisa, Leo Genn; **D:** Marc Allegret. VHS, Beta $24.95 NOS, MRV, HHT ✂1/2

Lady Chatterley's Lover Remake of the 1955 film version of D.H. Lawrence's classic novel of an English lady who has an affair with the gamekeeper of her husband's estate. Basically soft-focus soft porn.
1981 (R) 107m/C Sylvia Kristel, Nicholas Clay, Shane Briant; **D:** Just Jaeckin. VHS, Beta $79.95 MGM ✂1/2

Lady Cocoa Routine story of a young woman who gets released from jail for 24 hours and sets out for Las Vegas to find the man who framed her.
1975 (R) 93m/C Lola Falana, Joe "Mean Joe" Greene, Gene Washington, Alex Dreier; **D:** Matt Cimber. VHS, Beta $49.95 UNI ✂1/2

The Lady Confesses Average mystery that involves Hughes trying to clear her boyfriend of murder. Independently produced. "Leave it to Beaver" fans will want to watch for "Ward Cleaver" Beaumont.
1945 66m/B Mary Beth Hughes, Hugh Beaumont, Edmund MacDonald, Claudia Drake, Emmett Vogan; **D:** Sam Newfield. VHS $16.95 NOS, SNC ✂✂

Lady Dragon A woman and her husband are viciously attacked and only she survives. Found by an old man, she learns a number of martial arts tricks and goes out to get her revenge.
1992 (R) 89m/C Cynthia Rothrock, Richard Norton, Robert Ginty, Bella Esperance, Hengko Tornado; **D:** David Worth; **W:** David Worth. VHS $89.95 IMP ✂✂

Lady Dragon 2 Martial arts queen Rothrock returns in another saga of kickboxing vengeance. Susan Morgan seeks revenge on the three killers who terrorized her family. When she unleashes the power of the dragon they don't stand a chance.
1993 (R) ?m/C Cynthia Rothrock, Billy Drago, Sam Jones, Greg Stuart, Bella Esperance, George Rudy, Adisoerya Abdi; **D:** David Worth; **W:** Clifford Mohr; **M:** Jim West. VHS $92.95 PSM ✂✂

The Lady Eve Two con artists, out to trip up wealthy beer tycoon Fonda, instead find themselves tripped up when one falls in love with the prey. Ridiculous situations, but Sturges manages to keep them believable and funny. With a train scene that's every man's nightmare. Perhaps the best Sturges ever. Based on the story "The Faithful Heart" by Monckton Hoffe. Later remade as "The Birds and the Bees."
1941 93m/B Barbara Stanwyck, Henry Fonda, Charles Coburn, Eugene Pallette, William Demarest, Eric Blore, Melville Cooper; **D:** Preston Sturges; **W:** Preston Sturges. Academy Awards '41 Nominations: Best Story; National Board of Review Awards '41: 10 Best Films of the Year. VHS, Beta $14.98 MCA, RKO ✂✂✂✂

Lady for a Day Delightful telling of the Damon Runyon story, "Madame La Gimp," about an apple peddler (Robson) down on her luck, who is transformed into a lady by a criminal with a heart. "Lady By Choice" is the sequel.
1933 96m/B May Robson, Warren William, Guy Kibbee, Glenda Farrell, Ned Sparks, Jean Parker, Walter Connolly; *D:* Frank Capra. **VHS, Beta** $29.95 *CVC, VYG, CRC* ᑊᑊᑊ½

Lady for a Night The female owner of a gambling riverboat does her best to break into high society, when murder threatens to spoil her plans. Cast and costumes burdened by pacing.
1942 88m/B John Wayne, Joan Blondell, Ray Middleton, Philip Merivale, Blanche Yurka, Edith Barrett, Leonid Kinskey, Montagu Love; *D:* Leigh Jason. **VHS** $14.98 *REP* ᑊᑊ

Lady Frankenstein Frankenstein's lovely daughter graduates from medical school and returns home. When she sees what her father's been up to, she gets some ideas of her own. Good fun for fans of the genre. *AKA:* La Figlia di Frankenstein; The Daughter of Frankenstein; Madame Frankenstein.
1972 (R) 84m/C Joseph Cotten, Rosalba (Sara Bay) Neri, Mickey Hargitay, Paul Muller; *D:* Mel Welles. **VHS, Beta** $9.98 *SNC, SUE, HEG* ᑊ½

Lady from Louisiana A lawyer in old New Orleans out to rid the city of corruption falls in love with the daughter of a big-time gambler. Great storm scene.
1942 84m/B John Wayne, Ona Munson, Dorothy Dandridge, Ray Middleton, Henry Stephenson, Helen Westley, Jack Pennick; *D:* Bernard Vorhaus. **VHS** $14.98 *REP* ᑊᑊ

Lady from Nowhere A woman is the only witness to a gangland rub-out and is subsequently pursued by both the mob and the police. Unfortunately for her, the gangsters catch up with her first.
1936 60m/B Mary Astor, Charles Quigley, Thurston Hall, Victor Kilian, Spencer Charters; *D:* Gordon Wiles. **VHS, Beta** $16.95 *SNC* ᑊᑊ

The Lady from Shanghai An unsuspecting seaman becomes involved in a web of intrigue when a woman hires him to work on her husband's yacht. Hayworth (a one-time Mrs. Orson Welles), in her only role as a villainess, plays a manipulative, sensual schemer. Wonderful and innovative cinematic techniques from Welles, as usual, including a tense scene in a hall of mirrors. Filmed on a yacht belonging to Errol Flynn.
1948 87m/B Orson Welles, Rita Hayworth, Everett Sloane, Glenn Anders, Ted de Corsia, Erskine Sanford, Gus Schilling; *D:* Orson Welles; *W:* Orson Welles. **VHS, Beta** $19.95 *COL, MLB* ᑊᑊᑊ½

Lady from Yesterday An American couple's life is shattered by the appearance of the husband's Vietnamese mistress and her 10-year-old son. Made for television.
1985 87m/C Wayne Rogers, Bonnie Bedelia, Pat Hingle, Barrie Youngfellow, Blue Deckert, Tina Chen; *D:* Robert Day. **VHS, Beta** NO ᑊ

Lady Godiva Rides A bad, campy version of the story of Lady Godiva. Godiva comes to the United States with a bevy of scantily clad maidens and winds up in the Old West. When the town villain threatens to compromise her, Tom Jones comes to the rescue. The film (of course) features Godiva's naked ride on horseback through the town.
1968 88m/C Marsha Jordan, Forman Shane; *D:* A.C. Stephen. **VHS** $19.95 *VDM* ᑊ

Lady Grey A poor farmer's daughter rises to the top of the country music charts, but at a price.
1982 111m/C Ginger Alden, David Allen Coe; *D:* Worth Keeter. **VHS, Beta** NO ᑊ

Lady Ice Sutherland, as an insurance investigator on the trail of jewel thieves, follows them to Miami Beach and the Bahamas. After stealing a diamond he enters into partnership with a crook's daughter. Worth seeing for the cast.
1973 (PG) 93m/C Donald Sutherland, Jennifer O'Neill, Robert Duvall, Eric (Hans Gudegast) Braeden; *D:* Tom Gries; *W:* Alan R. Trustman. **VHS, Beta** NO ᑊ

Lady in a Cage A wealthy widow is trapped in her home elevator during a power failure and becomes desperate when hoodlums break in. Shocking violence ahead of its time probably plays better than when first released. Young Caan is a standout among the star-studded cast.
1964 95m/B Olivia de Havilland, Ann Sothern, James Caan, Jennifer Billingsley, Jeff Corey, Scatman Crothers, Rafael Campos; *D:* Walter Grauman. **VHS, Beta** $49.95 *PAR* ᑊᑊᑊ

Lady in Cement The second Tony Rome mystery, in which the seedy Miami dick finds a corpse with cement shoes while swimming.
1968 (R) 93m/C Frank Sinatra, Raquel Welch, Richard Conte, Martin Gabel, Lainie Kazan, Pat Henry, Steve Peck, Joe E. Lewis, Dan Blocker; *D:* Gordon Douglas. **VHS, Beta** $59.98 *FOX* ᑊ½

Lady in Distress A British drama about an unhappily married man who witnesses an apparent murder. He discovers, however, it was actually the prank of an illusionist and his flirtatious wife. He soon finds himself becoming increasingly involved with their lives. *AKA:* A Window in London.
1939 59m/B Michael Redgrave, Paul Lukas, Sally Gray; *D:* Herbert Mason. **VHS, Beta** $16.95 *SNC, VYY, MLB* ᑊᑊ½

The Lady in Question A Parisian shopkeeper, played by Aherne, sits on a jury that acquits Hayworth of murder. His interest doesn't end with the trial, however, and matters heat up when his son also becomes involved. Remake of a melodramatic French release. *AKA:* It Happened in Paris.
1940 81m/B Rita Hayworth, Glenn Ford, Brian Aherne, Irene Rich, Lloyd Corrigan, George Coulouris, Evelyn Keyes, Curt Bois, Edward Norris; *D:* Charles Vidor. **VHS, Beta** $19.95 *COL, CCB* ᑊ½

Lady in Red A story of America in the '30s, and the progress through the underworld of the woman who was Dillinger's last lover. *AKA:* Guns, Sin and Bathtub Gin.
1979 90m/C Pamela Sue Martin, Louise Fletcher, Robert Conrad, Christopher Lloyd; *D:* Lewis Teague; *W:* John Sayles; *M:* James Horner. **VHS, Beta** $69.98 *LIV, VES* ᑊᑊ

Lady in the Death House A framed woman is set to walk the last mile, as a scientist struggles to find the real killer in time.
1944 57m/B Jean Parker, Lionel Atwill, Marcia Mae Jones. **VHS, Beta** $19.95 *VYY* ᑊᑊ

Lady in the Lake Why is it everyone wants to get artsy with pulp fiction? Actor Montgomery directs himself in this Philip Marlowe go-round, using a subjective camera style to imitate Chandler's first person narrative (that means the only time we get to see Marlowe/Montgomery's mug is in a mirror. That pretty well says it all). Having decided to give up eyeing privately, Marlowe turns to the pen to tell the tangled tale of the lady in the lake: once upon a time, a detec-

tive was hired to find the wicked wife of a paying client...Some find the direction clever. Others consider MGM chief Louis B. Mayer, who made sure this was Montgomery's last project with MGM, to be a wise man.
1946 103m/B Robert Montgomery, Lloyd Nolan, Audrey Totter, Tom Tully, Leon Ames, Jayne Meadows; *D:* Robert Montgomery. **VHS, Beta** $19.98 *MGM, FCT* ᑊᑊ½

The Lady in White Small-town ghost story about murder and revenge. Young Haas is accidentally locked in school one night and is visited by the ghost of a little girl; he is determined to find her murderer. Well-developed characters, interesting style, and suspenseful plot make for a sometimes slow but overall exceptional film.
1988 (PG-13) 92m/C Lukas Haas, Len Cariou, Alex Rocco, Katherine Helmond, Jason Presson, Renato Vanni, Angelo Bertolini, Jared Rushton; *D:* Frank Laloggia; *W:* Frank Laloggia; *M:* Frank Laloggia. **VHS, Beta** NO ᑊᑊᑊ

The Lady is Willing Dietrich is a stage star who longs for a baby and when an abandoned infant comes her way she decides to keep the child. Only she hasn't a clue about any of the practical aspects. Lucky for her MacMurray is a friendly pediatrician who gives her some advice. Dietrich finds out she can't adopt as a single parent and persuades MacMurray to marry her, in name only, but since this is a romantic comedy the two eventually fall in love.
1942 91m/B Marlene Dietrich, Fred MacMurray, Aline MacMahon, Stanley Ridges, Arline Judge, Roger Clark, Ruth Ford, Sterling Holloway, Harvey Stephens, Harry Shannon, Elisabeth Risdon, Charles Halton; *D:* Mitchell Leisen; *W:* James Edward Grant, Albert McCleery. **VHS** $19.95 *FCT* ᑊᑊ½

Lady Jane An accurate account of the life of 15-year-old Lady Jane Grey, who secured the throne of England for 9 days in 1553 as a result of political maneuvering by noblemen and the Church-of-England. A wonderful film even for non-history buffs. Carter's first film.
1985 (PG-13) 140m/C Helena Bonham Carter, Cary Elwes, Sara Kestelman, Michael Hordern, Joss Ackland, Richard Johnson, Patrick Stewart; *D:* Trevor Nunn. **VHS, Beta** $79.95 *PAR, TVC* ᑊᑊᑊ½

Lady Killer Racy, pre-Code comedy with mobster Cagney hiding out in Hollywood. He gets discovered and becomes a big star, but his old gang turns up to blackmail him. Lots of movie "in" jokes and Clarke (of "Public Enemy" fame) is great as a wisecracking moll. Based on the story "The Finger Man" by Rosalind Keating Shaffer.
1933 74m/B James Cagney, Mae Clarke, Leslie Fenton, Margaret Lindsay, Henry O'Neill, Raymond Hatton, George Chandler; *D:* Roy Del Ruth; *W:* Ben Markson, Lillie Hayward. **VHS** $19.98 *MGM* ᑊᑊᑊ

Lady L Silly turn-of-the-century farce about a sexy laundress (Loren), married to a French anarchist (Newman!), who also marries the aristocratic Niven (in name only). Elaborate sets and Paris and London backgrounds couldn't overcome the odd casting and weak script. Adapted from the novel by Romain Gary.
1965 107m/C Sophia Loren, Paul Newman, David Niven, Cecil Parker, Claude Dauphin, Marcel Dalio, Philippe Noiret, Michel Piccoli, Daniel Emilfork, Eugene Deckers; *Cameos:* Peter Ustinov; *D:* Peter Ustinov; *W:* Peter Ustinov. **VHS, Beta** $19.98 *MGM, FCT* ᑊ½

Lady Mobster When her parents are murdered a young girl is taken in by a Mafia family. She grows up to be a shrewd lawyer but winds up working in her adoptive family's crime syndicate in order to take revenge on her parents' murderers. Exaggerated and silly but watchable for its so-bad-it's-good qualities. Made for television.

1988 (PG-13) 94m/C Susan Lucci, Michael Nader, Roscoe Born, Joseph Wiseman; *D:* John Llewellyn Moxey. **VHS, Beta** $89.98 *TTC ℤ*

Lady of Burlesque Burlesque dancer is found dead, strangled with her own G-string. Clever and amusing film based on "The G-String Murders" by Gypsy Rose Lee. *AKA:* Striptease Lady.

1943 91m/B Barbara Stanwyck, Michael O'Shea, Janis Carter, Pinky Lee; *D:* William A. Wellman. **VHS, Beta** $9.95 *CNG, MRV, NOS ℤℤ½*

Lady of the Evening A prostitute and a crook team up to seek revenge against the mob.

1979 (PG) 110m/C Sophia Loren, Marcello Mastroianni. **VHS, Beta** *NO ℤℤ*

Lady of the House A true story about a madame who rose from operator of a brothel to become a political force in San Francisco.

1978 100m/C Dyan Cannon, Susan Tyrrell, Colleen Camp, Armand Assante; *D:* Ralph Nelson. **VHS, Beta** $49.95 *PSM ℤℤ*

Lady of the Lake Rare silent adventure film in which an exiled girl saves the king from outlaws in Scotland. Orchestra score.

1928 47m/B Percy Marmont, Benita Hume, Huddon Mason, Lawson Butt; *D:* James A. Fitzpatrick. **VHS** $14.95 *GPV, FCT, GVV ℤℤ*

Lady on the Bus Sexually frustrated newlywed bride rides the city buses looking for men to satisfy her. This bothers her husband. Shot in Rio de Janeiro. In Portuguese with English subtitles.

1978 (R) 102m/C Sonia Braga; *D:* Neville D'Almeida. **VHS, Beta** $69.98 *LIV, VES ℤℤ*

The Lady Refuses A stuffy Victorian father is disappointed in his wastrel son and decides a poor but honest young woman could be the making of him. Problems arise when the girl falls for the father instead.

1931 70m/B Betty Compson, John Darrow, Margaret Livingston, Gilbert Emery; *D:* George Archainbaud. **VHS, Beta** $24.95 *DVT, VYY ℤℤ*

The Lady Says No A photographer must photograph an attractive author who has written a book uncomplimentary toward the male sex.

1951 80m/B Joan Caulfield, David Niven, James Robertson Justice, Francis Bavier, Henry Jones, Jeff York, Robert Williams; *D:* Frank Ross. **VHS** $29.95 *FCT ℤℤ*

Lady Scarface Murderous mobster queen breaks the law, bats men around, and takes the cops on a merry chase. Cheap, fast-paced action.

1941 66m/B Mildred Coles, Dennis O'Keefe, Frances Neal, Judith Anderson, Eric Blore, Charles Halton; *D:* Frank Woodruff. **VHS, Beta** $34.95 *RKO ℤℤ*

Lady Scarface/The Threat A crime double feature: "Lady Scarface" (1941), a clever cop is on the trail of a dangerous gunwoman; and "The Threat" (1949), a ruthless killer escapes from prison intent on murdering those who convicted him.

1949 132m/B Dennis O'Keefe, Judith Anderson, Robert Knapp, Eric Blore, Charles McGraw, Michael O'Shea, Virginia Grey; *D:* Frank Woodruff. **VHS, Beta** $34.95 *RKO, TTC ℤℤ*

Lady Sings the Blues Jazz artist Billie Holiday's life becomes a musical drama depicting her struggle against racism and drug addiction in her pursuit of fame and romance. What could be a typical price-of-fame story is saved by Ross' inspired performance as the tragic singer. ♫My Man;

Strange Fruit; God Bless the Child; Don't Explain; T'Ain't Nobody's Business If I Do; Lady Sings the Blues; All Of Me; The Man I Love; Our Love Is Here to Stay.

1972 (R) 144m/C Diana Ross, Billy Dee Williams, Richard Pryor; *D:* Sidney J. Furie. **VHS, Beta** $29.95 *PAR, FCT ℤℤℤ*

Lady Stay Dead A gory Australian shocker about another faceless, knife-wielding psychotic chasing a girl.

1983 100m/C VHS, Beta $59.95 *VCD ℤ½*

Lady Street Fighter A well-armed female combat fighter battles an organization of assassins to avenge her sister's murder.

1986 73m/C Renee Harmon, Joel McCrea Jr. **VHS, Beta** $59.95 *UNI ℤ*

Lady Takes a Chance A romantic comedy about a New York working girl with matrimonial ideas and a rope-shy rodeo rider who yearns for the wide open spaces. Fine fun on the range.

1943 86m/B John Wayne, Jean Arthur, Phil Silvers, Charles Winninger; *D:* William A. Seiter. **VHS, Beta** *NO ℤℤ*

Lady Terminator A student on an anthropology expedition digs up more than she bargained for when she is possessed by an evil spirit and goes on a rampage.

1989 (R) 83m/C Barbara Constable, Christopher Hart, Joseph McGlynn, Claudia Rademaker; *D:* Jalil Jackson. **VHS, Beta** *NO ℤ½*

The Lady Vanishes When a kindly old lady disappears from a fast-moving train, her young friend finds an imposter in her place and a spiraling mystery to solve. Hitchcock's first real winner, a smarmy, wit-drenched British mystery that precipitated his move to Hollywood. Along with "39 Steps," considered an early Hitchcock classic. From the novel "The Wheel Spins," by Ethel Lina White. Special edition contains short subject on Hitchcock's cameos in his films. Remade in 1979.

1938 99m/B Margaret Lockwood, Paul Lukas, Michael Redgrave, May Whitty, Googie Withers, Basil Radford, Naunton Wayne, Cecil Parker, Linden Travers, Catherine Lacey, Sidney Gilliat; *Cameos:* Alfred Hitchcock; *D:* Alfred Hitchcock; *W:* Frank Launder, Louis Levy, Alma Reville. **VHS, Beta** $16.95 *SNC, NOS, SUE ℤℤℤℤ*

The Lady Vanishes In this reworking of the '38 Alfred Hitchcock film, a woman on a Swiss bound train awakens from a nap to find that the elderly woman seated next to her was kidnapped. Falls short of the original movie due to the "screwball" nature of the main characters, Gould and Shepherd. Based on Ethel Lina White's novel "The Wheel Spins."

1979 95m/C Elliott Gould, Cybill Shepherd, Angela Lansbury, Herbert Lom; *D:* Anthony Page; *W:* George Axelrod. **VHS, Beta** $9.95 *MED, MRV ℤ½*

Lady Windermere's Fan The silent, Lubitsch adaptation of the Oscar Wilde tale concerning an upper-class couple's marriage being almost destroyed by suspected adultery.

1926 66m/B Ronald Colman, May McAvoy, Bert Lytell; *D:* Ernst Lubitsch. **VHS, Beta, 8mm** $24.95 *VYY, GPV, GVV ℤℤ½*

The Lady with the Dog A bittersweet love story based on the Anton Chekhov story, about two married Russians who meet by chance in a park, fall in love, and realize they are fated to a haphazard, clandestine affair. In Russian with English titles.

1959 86m/B Iya Savvina, Alexei Batalov, Ala Chostakova, N. Alisova; *D:* Yosif Heifitz. **VHS, Beta** $29.95 *WST, FCT, ING ℤℤℤ*

The Lady Without Camelias A young woman is discovered by a film producer who casts her in a successful movie and eventually marries her. Convinced that she can sustain a career as a serious actress, the producer is dismayed by the job offers that come her way, usually of a sexually exploitive nature. What follows is a tragic decline for both.

1953 106m/C VHS, Beta *CIG ℤℤ½*

Ladybugs Hangdog salesman Dangerfield would like to move up the corporate ladder, but must first turn the company-sponsored girl's soccer team into winners. Routine Dangerfield vehicle exploits nearly everything for laughs, including dressing an athletic boy as a girl so he can play on the team. Obvious fluff.

1992 (PG-13) 91m/C Rodney Dangerfield, Jackee, Jonathan Brandis, Ilene Graff, Vinessa Shaw, Tom Parks, Jeanetta Arnetta, Nancy Parsons, Blake Clark, Tommy Lasorda; *D:* Sidney J. Furie; *M:* Richard Gibbs. **VHS, Beta** $19.95 *PAR ℤ½*

Ladyhawke In medieval times, a youthful pickpocket befriends a strange knight who is on a mysterious quest. This unlikely duo, accompanied by a watchful hawk, are enveloped in a magical adventure.

1985 (PG-13) 121m/C Matthew Broderick, Rutger Hauer, Michelle Pfeiffer, John Wood, Leo McKern, Alfred Molina, Ken Hutchison; *D:* Richard Donner; *W:* Edward Khmara, Michael Thomas, Tom Mankiewicz; *M:* Andrew Powell. **VHS, Beta** $19.98 *WAR ℤℤ½*

Ladykiller Rogers stars as a burned-out cop who goes to a dating service to find a man who'll give her the attention she craves. When she meets wealthy professional Shea she thinks he's the one but her cop's curiosity about her lover's past may cost her her life.

1992 (R) 92m/C Mimi Rogers, John Shea, Alice Krige, Tom Irwin; *D:* Michael Scott; *W:* Shelley Evans. **VHS** $89.98 *MCA ℤℤ*

Ladykillers A gang of bumbling bank robbers is foiled by a little old lady. Hilarious antics follow, especially on the part of Guinness, who plays the slightly demented-looking leader of the gang. *AKA:* The Lady Killers.

1955 87m/C Alec Guinness, Cecil Parker, Katie Johnson, Herbert Lom, Peter Sellers; *D:* Alexander MacKendrick; *W:* William Rose. **VHS, Beta** $19.98 *FCT, HMV ℤℤℤ½*

Ladykillers At the glitzy L.A. club Ladykillers, men strip as the women cheer. At the climax of the performance, one of the dancers is brutally murdered, live on stage. In this decadent world of glitter and sex, the women are the hunters and the men are the reward.

1988 97m/C Marilu Henner, Susan Blakely, Lesley-Anne Down, Thomas Calabro; *D:* Robert Lewis; *W:* Greg Dinallo. **VHS, Beta** $79.95 *PSM ℤℤ*

The Lady's Maid's Bell Based upon the story by Edith Wharton, this ghost story deals with the new maid in a family estate who discovers the ghost of another past maid.

1985 60m/C VHS, Beta $59.95 *PSM ℤℤ*

Lafayette Escadrille Action and romance in WWI via the famed flying unit manned by American volunteers. Hunter is banal in the lead role as his romance with a reformed prostitute (Choreau). Director Wellman actually was a member of the squadron and his son plays him in the film but the director regarded the film as a failure because of studio interference. *AKA:* Hell Bent for Glory.

L

1958 92m/B Tab Hunter, Etchika Choreau, William Wellman Jr., Joel McCrea, Dennis Devine, Marcel Dalio, David Janssen, Paul Fix, Will Hutchins, Clint Eastwood; **D:** William A. Wellman; **W:** A.S. Fleischman; **M:** Leonard Rosenman. VHS $19.98 WAR ♂♂½

L'Age D'Or Bunuel's first full-length film and his masterpiece of sex, repression, and of course, death. A hapless man is prevented from reaching his beloved by middle-class morality, forces of the establishment, the Church, government and every bastion of modern values. Banned for years because of its anti-religious stance. Co-scripted by Dali. A mercilessly savage, surreal satire, the purest expression of Bunuel's wry misanthropy. In French with English subtitles. **AKA:** Age of Gold.
1930 62m/B Gaston Modot, Lya Lys, Max Ernst, Pierre Prevert, Marie Berthe Ernst, Paul Eluard; **D:** Luis Bunuel; **W:** Salvador Dali, Luis Bunuel. VHS, Beta $59.95 FCT, IME, GVV ♂♂♂♂

Lagrimas de Amor A bank cashier, a night club singer, and her lover form an unusual love triangle.
1987 94m/C Ana Louisa Peluffo, Carlos Lopez Moctezuma, Sergio Bustamante. VHS, Beta $24.95 MAD ♂♂½

Laguna Heat A tired LA cop investigates a series of murders that are related to an old friend of his father's. Based on a novel by T. Jefferson Parker. Made for television.
1987 110m/C Harry Hamlin, Jason Robards Jr., Catherine Hicks, Rip Torn, Anne Francis; **D:** Simon Langton. VHS, Beta $79.95 LHV, WAR ♂♂

Lai Shi: China's Last Eunuch A starving Chinese child becomes a eunuch in order to garner wealth in the Emperor's palace. But he is castrated at a historically inopportune moment (as if there's a good time for such modification), just prior to the turbulent 1920s. In Cantonese with English subtitles.
1988 100m/C **D:** Chan Tsi-liang. VHS $39.95 FCT ♂♂½

The Lair of the White Worm Scottish archaeologist uncovers a strange skull, and then a bizarre religion to go with it, and then a very big worm. An unusual look at the effects of Christianity and paganism on each other, colored with sexual innuendo and, of course, giant worms. A cross between a morality play and a horror film. Adapted from Bram Stoker's last writings, done while he was going mad from Bright's disease. Everything you'd expect from Russell.
1988 (R) 93m/C Amanda Donohoe, Sammi Davis-Voss, Catherine Oxenberg, Hugh Grant, Peter Capaldi, Stratford Johns, Paul Brooke, Christopher Gable; **D:** Ken Russell; **W:** Ken Russell; **M:** Stanislas Syrewicz. VHS, Beta $14.95 VES, LIV, TPV ♂♂♂

Lake Consequence Severance plays a suburban housewife who accidentally gets locked in the camper of the tree-trimmer stud (Zane) she's been eyeing while he's been working in her neighborhood. Next thing she knows they wind up at a distant lake where the bored housewife is more than willing to give into her growing sexual fantasies. An unrated version at 90 minutes is also available.
1992 (R) 85m/C Joan Severance, Billy Zane, May Karasun; **D:** Rafael Eisenman; **W:** Zalman King, Melanie Finn, Henry Cobbold; **M:** George S. Clinton. VHS $89.98 REP ♂♂

The Lamb Intent on proving to his sweetheart that he's not the coward people say he is, a guy heads west to engage in various manly activities, including fisticuffs, karate

and Indian kidnapping. Fairbanks' debut on film (he was already an established Broadway star) set the mold for the American leading man: moral, cheerful, physical, and not hard to look at. A popular guy with the public, Fairbanks formed his own film company the following year. Story's based on D.W. Griffith's book, "The Man and the Test."
1915 60m/B Douglas Fairbanks Sr., Seena Owen, Lillian Langdon, Monroe Salisbury, Kate Toncray, Alfred Paget, William E. Lowery; **D:** Christy Cabanne. VHS, Beta $24.95 GPV, FCT ♂♂½

Lambada By day, he's a high school teacher in Beverly Hills; by night, a Latin dirty dancer cum tutor of ghetto teens. The very first of several films based on the short-lived dance craze.
1989 (PG) 92m/C J. Eddie Peck, Melora Hardin, Adolfo "Shabba Doo" Quinones, Ricky Paull Goldin, Basil Hoffman, Dennis Burkley; **D:** Joel Silberg. VHS, Beta $14.95 MGM ♂

Lamp at Midnight Presentation from "George Schaefer's Showcase Theatre" deals with three critical periods in the life of Italian astronomer Galileo Galilei, from his invention of the telescope, through his appearance at the Holy Office of the Inquisition, to the publication of his "Dialogue on the Two Systems of the World." For those in a planetary state of mind.
1966 76m/C Melvyn Douglas, David Wayne, Michael Hordern, Hurd Hatfield, Kim Hunter; **D:** George Schaefer. VHS, Beta FHS ♂♂½

Lana in Love A lonely woman places an ad in the personal section in hopes of finding her Mr. Right.
1992 90m/C Daphna Kastner, Clark Gregg. VHS, Beta NO ♂♂

The Land Before Time Lushly animated children's film about five orphaned baby dinosaurs who band together and try to find the Great Valley, a paradise where they might live safely. Works same parental separation theme as Bluth's "American Tail." Charming, coy, and shamelessly tearjerking; producers included Steven Spielberg and George Lucas.
1988 (G) 67m/C **D:** Don Bluth; **W:** Stu Krieger; **M:** James Horner; **V:** Pat Hingle, Helen Shaver, Gabriel Damon, Candice Houston, Burke Barnes, Judith Barsi, Will Ryan. VHS $19.98 MCA, FCT, APD ♂♂♂

The Land Before Time: The Great Valley Adventure Sequel to 1988's animated adventure finds dinsosaur pals Littlefoot, Cera, Ducky, Petrie, and Spike happily settled in the Great Valley. But their adventures don't stop as they chase two egg-stealing Struthiomimuses and retrieve an egg of unknown origin from the Mysterious Beyond.
1994 75m/C VHS $19.98 MCA ♂♂½

Land of Doom An amazon and a warrior struggle for survival in a post-holocaust fantasy setting.
1984 87m/C Deborah Rennard, Garrick Dowhen; **D:** Peter Maris. VHS, Beta $19.98 LIV ♂

The Land of Faraway A Swedish boy is whisked off to a magical land where he does battle with evil knights and flies on winged horses. Dubbed; based on a novel by Astrid Lindgren.
1987 (G) 95m/C Timothy Bottoms, Christian Bale, Susannah York, Christopher Lee, Nicholas Pickard; **D:** Vladimir Grammatikov. VHS, Beta $9.99 PSM ♂

Land of Fury British naval officer Hawkins steps on New Zealand's shore and into trouble when he accidently walks on sacred Maori burial ground. Very British, very dated

colonial saga, based on the novel "The Seekers" by John Guthrie. **AKA:** The Seekers.
1955 90m/C Jack Hawkins, Glynis Johns, Noel Purcell, Ian Fleming; **D:** Ken Annakin. VHS $19.95 NOS ♂♂

Land of Hunted Men The Range Busters are on the case as they track down the hideout of terrorizing gunmen.
1943 58m/B Ray Corrigan, Dennis Moore, Max Terhune. VHS, Beta $19.95 NOS, DVT ♂

Land of Promise At the turn of the century three men build a textile factory in Lodz, Poland. They each represent a particular ethnic group: a Pole (Olbrychski), a German (Seweryn), and a Jew (Pszoniak). Class conflicts threaten to overwhelm as their overworked and underpaid workers plan a revolt. Based on the novel by Wladyslav Reymont. In Polish with English subtitles. **AKA:** Ziemia Obiecana.
1974 178m/C Daniel Olbrychski, Wojciech Pszoniak, Andrzej Seweryn, Anna Nehrebecka; **D:** Andrzej Wajda; **W:** Andrzej Wajda; **M:** Wojciech Kilar. VHS $79.95 FCT ♂♂½

Land of the Lawless A group of outlaws rule over a barren wasteland. What's the point?
1947 54m/B Rachel Brown, Raymond Hatton, Christine McIntyre, Tristram Coffin; **D:** Lambert Hillyer. VHS $19.95 NOS, DVT ♂

Land of the Minotaur Small village is the setting for horrifying ritual murders, demons, and disappearances of young terrorists. Fans of Pleasence and Cushing won't want to miss this. **AKA:** The Devil's Men.
1977 (PG) 88m/C Donald Pleasence, Peter Cushing, Luan Peters; **D:** Costa Carayiannis; **M:** Brian Eno. VHS, Beta $29.95 VCI, MRV ♂♂

Land of the Pharaohs An epic about the building of Egypt's Great Pyramid. Hawkins is the extremely talkative pharoah and Collins plays his sugary-sweet yet villainous wife. Sort of campy, but worth watching for the great surprise ending.
1955 106m/C Jack Hawkins, Joan Collins, James Robertson Justice, Dewey Martin, Alexis Minotis, Sydney Chaplin; **D:** Howard Hawks. VHS $19.98 WAR, HBO ♂♂½

Land Raiders Savalas plays a man who hates Apaches and wants their land, but is distracted when his brother arrives on the scene, igniting an old feud.
1969 101m/C Telly Savalas, George Maharis, Arlene Dahl, Janet Landgard; **D:** Nathan Juran. VHS, Beta GKK ♂

The Land That Time Forgot A WWI veteran, a beautiful woman, and their German enemies are stranded in a land outside time filled with prehistoric creatures. Based on the 1918 novel by Edgar Rice Burroughs. Followed in 1977 by "The People that Time Forgot."
1975 (PG) 90m/C Doug McClure, John McEnery, Susan Penhaligon; **D:** Kevin Connor. VHS, Beta $59.98 LIV, VES ♂♂

The Land Unknown A Naval helicopter is forced down in a tropical land of prehistoric terror, complete with ferocious creatures from the Mesozoic Era. While trying to make repairs, the crew discovers the sole survivor of a previous expedition who was driven to madness by life in the primordial jungle. Good performances from cast, although monsters aren't that believable. Based on a story by Charles Palmer.
1957 78m/B Jock Mahoney, Shawn Smith, William Reynolds, Henry Brandon, Douglas Kennedy; **D:** Virgil W. Vogel; **W:** Laszlo Gorog; **M:** Henry Mancini. VHS $14.98 MCA ♂♂½

Landlord Blues A trashy slumlord without morals or a conscience goes one step too far, and a tenant retaliates with munitions.
1987 96m/C Mark Boone, Raye Dowell, Richard Litt, Bill Rice, Mary Schultz, Gigi Williams; **D:** Jacob Burckhardt. **VHS, Beta** $79.95 MNC ♫♫½

Landscape in the Mist A stark Greek landscape in a rainy winter sets the scene for a tragic search by two children for their unknown father. Relies heavily on symbolism to make its point about unfulfilled desire (including the film's imaginary German-Greek border). In Greek with English subtitles. **AKA:** Topio Stin Omichli.
1988 126m/C Tania Palaiologou, Michalis Zeke, Stratos Tzortzoglou, Eva Kotamanidou, Alika Georgouli; **D:** Theo Angelopoulos; **W:** Thanassis Valtinos, Tonino Guerra, Theo Angelopoulos. **VHS** $79.95 NYF, FCT, BTV ♫♫♫

Landslide As a geologist, suffering from memory loss, comes closer to discovering his identity his life is endangered by a sinister plot.
1992 (PG-13) 95m/C Anthony Edwards, Tom Burlinson, Joanna Cassidy, Melody Anderson, Ronald Lacey, Ken James, Lloyd Bochner; **D:** Jean-Claude Lord. **VHS** $89.98 REP ♫♫½

L'Anne Sainte In his last film, Gabin is an escaped convict returning to his hidden loot in Rome when his plane is hijacked by international terrorists. Available dubbed. **AKA:** Pilgrimage to Rome.
1978 ?m/C Jean Gabin, Jean-Claude Brialy, Paul Giusti, Danielle Darrieux. **VHS** $59.95 FRA, FCT ♫♫½

L'Annee des Meduses An 18-year-old girl tries to seduce the local Monsieur Beefcake she meets on her vacation. When he doesn't return her interest, she decides to teach him a lesson. In French with English subtitles, or dubbed. **AKA:** The Year of the Jellyfish.
1986 (R) 110m/C Valerie Kaprisky, Barnard Giradeau; **D:** Christopher Frank. **VHS, Beta** $69.95 FCT, TPV ♫½

Lantern Hill During the Depression, a 12-year-old girl attempts to fan the embers between her estranged parents. Made for cable Wonderworks production, filmed partly on Canada's Prince Edward Island. Based on a story by Lucy Maud Montgomery, whose "Anne of Green Gables" is also part of the Wonderworks series.
1990 (G) 112m/C Sam Waterston, Colleen Dewhurst, Sarah Polley, Marion Bennett, Zoe Caldwell; **D:** Kevin Sullivan. **VHS** $29.95 BVV, FCT ♫♫½

Laramie Kid A vintage Tyler sagebrush saga.
1935 60m/B Tom Tyler, Alberta Vaughn, Al Ferguson, Murdock McQuarrie, George Cheseboro; **D:** Harry S. Webb. **VHS, Beta** $19.95 NOS, DVT, RXM ♫

L'Argent When a young man's parents refuse to lend him any money a friend helps out by giving him a counterfeit 500-franc note. This sets off a chain of events, with every passing of the money leading to another lie, betrayal, and increasingly violent crime. Austere and stylized vision is not for all tastes. In French with English subtitles.
1983 82m/C Christian Patey, Sylvie van den Elsen, Michel Briguet, Caroline Lang; **D:** Robert Bresson; **W:** Robert Bresson. **VHS** $79.95 NYF, FCT ♫♫

Larks on a String Banned for 23 years, this wonderful film is Menzel's masterpiece, even better than his Oscar winning "Closely Watched Trains." Portrays the story of life in labor camps where men and women are re-educated at the whim of the government. No matter what the hardships, these people find humor, hope and love. Their individuality will not be lost, nor their humanity dissolved. Excellent performances, tellingly directed with a beautiful sense of composition and tone. Screenplay written by Menzel and Bohumil Hrabil, author of the short story on which it is based. In Czech with English subtitles.
1968 96m/C Vaclav Neckar, Jitka Zelenohorska, Jaroslav Satoransky, Rudolf Hrusinsky; **D:** Jiri Menzel; **W:** Jiri Menzel. **VHS** $79.95 FXL, ING ♫♫♫

Larry Based on the Nevada State Hospital case history of a 26-year-old man, institutionalized since infancy, who is discovered to be of normal intelligence and must learn to live the life he has always been capable of living. Made for television.
1974 80m/C Frederic Forrest, Tyne Daly, Katherine Helmond, Michael McGuire, Robert Walden; **D:** William A. Graham. **VHS, Beta** LCA ♫♫

Las Vegas Hillbillys A pair of country-singing hillbillies inherit a saloon in Las Vegas and enjoy wine, moonshine, and song. These two make the Clampetts look like high society. Followed, believe it or not, by "Hillbillys in a Haunted House." ♫Money Greases the Wheel. **AKA:** Country Music.
1966 85m/C Mamie Van Doren, Jayne Mansfield, Ferlin Husky, Sonny James; **D:** Arthur C. Pierce. **VHS, Beta** $29.95 NLC ♫

Las Vegas Lady Three shrewd casino hostesses plot a multi-million dollar heist in the nation's gambling capital. Non-captivating caper.
1976 (PG) 90m/C Stella Stevens, Stuart Whitman, George de Cecenzo, Andrew Stevens; **D:** Noel Nosseck. **VHS, Beta** $49.95 PSM ♫

Las Vegas Serial Killer A serial killer, let out of prison on a technicality, starts killing again. Made for video by Camp.
1986 90m/C Pierre Agostino, Ron Jason, Tara MacGowan, Kathryn Downey. **VHS, Beta** NO Woof!

The Las Vegas Story Gambling, colorful sights, and a murder provide the framework for this non-compelling fictional guided-tour of the city. Save your money for the slots.
1952 88m/B Victor Mature, Jane Russell, Vincent Price, Hoagy Carmichael, Brad Dexter; **D:** Robert Stevenson. **VHS, Beta** NO Woof!

Las Vegas Weekend A computer nerd goes to Las Vegas and discovers fun.
1985 83m/C Barry Hickey, Macka Foley, Ray Dennis Steckler; **D:** Dale Trevillion; **W:** Dale Trevillion. **VHS, Beta** $19.95 STE, NWV ♫

Laser Mission When it is discovered that the Soviets have laser weapon capabilities, an agent is given the task of destroying the weapon and kidnapping the scientist who developed it.
1990 83m/C Brandon Lee, Debi Monahan, Ernest Borgnine, Werner Pochat, Graham Clarke, Maureen Lahoud, Pierre Knoessen; **D:** Beau Davis. **VHS** $79.98 TTC ♫♫½

Laser Moon A serial killer uses a surgical laser beam to kill his beautiful victims, and he strikes at every full moon. When he announces his next attack on a late-night radio talk show the police call in a beautiful rookie cop (Lords) to use as bait.
1992 90m/C Traci Lords, Crystal Shaw, Harrison Leduke, Bruce Carter; **D:** Bruce Carter. **VHS** $9.95 HMD ♫♫

Laserblast Standard wimp-gets-revenge story in which a frustrated young man finds a powerful and deadly laser which was left near his home by aliens; upon learning of its devastating capabilities, his personality changes and he seeks revenge against all who have taken advantage of him.
1978 (PG) 87m/C Kim Milford, Cheryl "Rainbeaux" Smith, Keenan Wynn, Roddy McDowall; **D:** Michael Raye; **M:** Richard Band, Joel Goldsmith. **VHS, Beta** $29.95 MED Woof!

The Lash of the Penitents An explosive documentary about Southern fundamentalist cults.
1939 70m/B VHS, Beta $16.95 SNC, NOS, DVT Woof!

Lassie Everyone's favorite collie returns as the Turner family moves to Virginia's Shenandoah Valley to take up sheep ranching. However, because this is the '90s, Dad meets financial disaster, and junior can't stand his stepmom. Can Lassie meet the challenges of dysfunctional family living? "What is it girl? Call a therapist?" This Lassie is a direct descendant of Pal, the original 1943 star.
1994 ?m/C Helen Slater, Jon Tenney, Tom Guiry, Brittany Boyd, Richard Farnsworth, Frederic Forrest; **D:** Daniel Petrie; **W:** Matthew Jacobs, Gary Ross, Elizabeth Anderson. **VHS** NYR ♫♫½

Lassie: Adventures of Neeka America's best friend joins her Native American buddy, Neeka, for a journey through a forest in the Pacific Northwest. They camp out in a deserted settlement, pull an elderly gentleman out of a frigid pond, and risk their lives to release horses from a stable during a raging wildfire.
1968 75m/B Jed Allan, Mark Miranda, Robert Rockwell, Lassie; **D:** Richard Moder, Jack B. Hively. **VHS, Beta** NO ♫♫½

Lassie, Come Home In first of the Lassie series, the famed collie is reluctantly sold and makes a treacherous cross-country journey back to her original family.
1943 (G) 90m/C Roddy McDowall, Elizabeth Taylor, Donald Crisp, Edmund Gwenn, May Whitty, Nigel Bruce, Elsa Lanchester, J. Pat O'Malley, Lassie; **D:** Fred M. Wilcox. Academy Awards '43 Nominations: Best Color Cinematography; National Board of Review Awards '43: 10 Best Films of the Year. **VHS, Beta** $14.95 MGM ♫♫½

Lassie from Lancashire Not the famous Collie—but here, a Colleen. A pair of struggling lovebirds try to make it in show biz against all odds, including the girl's lunatic aunt, who locks her away before an audition.
1938 67m/B Marjorie Brown, Hal Thompson, Marjorie Sandford, Lassie, Mark Daly. **VHS, Beta** $24.95 VYY ♫½

Lassie: The Miracle A TV-movie featuring the faithful collie saving new-born pups and befriending a mute boy.
1975 90m/C Lassie. **VHS, Beta** $29.95 MGM ♫

Lassie: Well of Love Various installments of the classic television series featuring the heroic collie are combined to create a movie-length presentation for home video. Lassie takes two young pups under her paw and, in the process, loses her way. As she tries to get home, she brings joy back into the lives of two despondent children. Finally, the old girl faces death when she tumbles into an abandoned well and must depend on humans for rescue.
1990 76m/C Lassie, Mary Gregory, Robert Donner. **VHS, Beta** NO ♫

Lassie's Great Adventure Lassie and her master Timmy are swept away from home by a runaway balloon. After they land in the Canadian wilderness, they learn to rely on each other through peril and adventure. Made for television.
1962 104m/C June Lockhart, Jon Provost, Hugh Reilly, Lassie; *D:* William Beaudine. **VHS, Beta** $29.99 *MGM* 𝘐𝘐½

Lassiter Selleck plays a jewel thief who is asked to steal diamonds from the Nazis for the FBI. Supporting cast adds value to what is otherwise a fairly ordinary adventure drama.
1984 (R) 100m/C Tom Selleck, Jane Seymour, Lauren Hutton, Bob Hoskins, Joe Regalbuto, Ed Lauter, Warren Clarke; *D:* Roger Young. **VHS, Beta** $19.98 *WAR* 𝘐𝘐½

Last Action Hero Newcomer O'Brien finds himself in a movie starring his idol Jack Slater, the kind of guy who never loses a fight and is impervious to gunfire and explosions (and he has a really cool car and a really big gun). Disappointing action/spoof of movies within a movie (rumored to have cost over $80 million) was critically maimed and never recovered. The concept isn't new and has been done better before, though Ah-nold possesses his usual self-mocking charm, which is more than can be said for the movie. Look for lots of big stars in small roles and cameos. Cluttered with inside Hollywood gags, the script was given uncredited assistance from William Goldman.
1993 (PG-13) 131m/C Arnold Schwarzenegger, Austin O'Brien, Mercedes Ruehl, F. Murray Abraham, Charles Dance, Anthony Quinn, Robert Prosky, Tommy Noonan, Frank McRae, Art Carney, Brigitte Wilson; *Cameos:* Sharon Stone, M.C. Hammer, Chevy Chase, Jean-Claude Van Damme, Tori Spelling, Joan Plowright, Adam Ant, James Belushi, James Cameron, Tony Curtis, Timothy Dalton, Tony Danza, Edward Furlong, Little Richard, Damon Wayans, Robert Patrick; *D:* John McTiernan; *W:* Shane Black, David Arnott; *M:* Michael Kamen. **VHS, Beta, 8mm** $96.95 *COL, BTV* 𝘐𝘐

The Last American Hero The true story of how former moonshine runner Junior Johnson became one of the fastest race car drivers in the history of the sport. Entertaining slice of life chronicling whiskey running and stock car racing, with Bridges superb in the lead. Based on a series of articles written by Tom Wolfe. *AKA:* Hard Driver.
1973 (PG) 95m/C Jeff Bridges, Valerie Perrine, Gary Busey, Art Lund, Geraldine Fitzgerald, Ned Beatty; *D:* Lamont Johnson; *W:* William Roberts; *M:* Charles Fox. **VHS, Beta** $59.98 *FOX* 𝘐𝘐½

Last American Virgin Usual brainless teen sex comedy about three school buddies who must deal with a plethora of problems in their search for girls who are willing. Music by Blondie, The Cars, The Police, The Waitresses, Devo, U2, Human League, and Quincy Jones.
1982 (R) 92m/C Lawrence Monoson, Diane Franklin, Steve Antin, Louisa Moritz; *D:* Boaz Davidson. **VHS, Beta** $79.95 *MGM* 𝘐𝘐

The Last Angry Man An old, idealistic Brooklyn doctor attracts a television producer wanting to make a documentary about his life and career, and the two conflict. Muni was Oscar-nominated for this, his last film.
1959 100m/B Paul Muni, David Wayne, Betsy Palmer, Luther Adler, Dan Tobin; *D:* Daniel Mann. **VHS, Beta** $69.95 *COL* 𝘐𝘐𝘐½

The Last Bastion A WWII drama emphasizing the political struggle between Churchill, MacArthur, Roosevelt, and Australia's John Curtin.
1984 160m/C Robert Vaughn, Timothy West. **VHS, Beta** $19.95 *ACA* 𝘐𝘐

The Last Boy Scout This formula thriller stars Willis as a private eye and Wayans as an ex-quarterback teaming up against a pro-football team owner who will stop at nothing to get political backing for a bill promoting legalized gambling on sports. Another variation of the violent buddy-picture by "Lethal Weapon" screenwriter Black.
1991 (R) 105m/C Bruce Willis, Damon Wayans, Halle Berry, Chelsea Field, Noble Willingham, Taylor Negron, Danielle Harris, Bruce McGill; *D:* Tony Scott; *W:* Shane Black. **VHS** $19.98 *WAR* 𝘐𝘐

Last Bullet A young westerner chases after a band of outlaws to avenge the cold-blooded murder of his parents.
1950 55m/B James Ellison, Russell Hayden, John Cason. **VHS, Beta** *NO* 𝘐𝘐

Last Call Clearly, Joe Sixpack won't rent this bimbo fest for its subtle plot. Katt, a mafiosi-cheated real estate guy, decides to even the score with the assistance of gal pal/playmate of the year Tweed, who's more than willing to compromise her position. A direct to video release, it also features the talents of playboy emerita Stevens. Available in rated and unrated versions.
1990 (R) 90m/C William Katt, Shannon Tweed, Joseph Campanella, Stella Stevens, Matt Roe; *D:* Jag Mundhra. **VHS, Beta** $29.95 *PSM* 𝘐

The Last Chance A realistic look at the efforts of three WWII Allied officers to help a group of refugees escape across the Alps from Italy to Switzerland. The officers are played by former pilots who were shot down over Switzerland. In spite of this—or perhaps because of it—the acting is superb. Watch for inspirational scene of refugees singing.
1945 105m/B E.G. Morrison, John Hoy, Ray Reagan, Odeardo Mosini, Sigfrit Steiner, Emil Gerber; *D:* Leopold Lindtberg. **VHS** $19.95 *NOS* 𝘐𝘐𝘐

Last Chase Famed race car driver becomes a vocal dissenter against the sterile society that has emerged, in this drama set in the near future. Made for television. Screenplay written by Christopher Crowe under the pseudonym C.R. O'Cristopher.
1981 (PG) 106m/C Lee Majors, Burgess Meredith, Chris Makepeace, Alexandra Stewart; *D:* Martyn Burke; *W:* Christopher Crowe, Martyn Burke. **VHS, Beta** $69.95 *VES* 𝘐½

Last Command Famous powerful silent film by Sternberg about a expatriate Czarist general forging out a pitiful living as a silent Hollywood extra, where he is hired by his former adversary to reenact the revolution he just left. Next to "The Last Laugh," this is considered Jannings' most acclaimed performance. Deeply ironic, visually compelling film with a new score by Gaylord Carter.
1928 88m/B Emil Jannings, William Powell, Evelyn Brent, Nicholas Soussanin, Michael Visaroff, Jack Raymond, Fritz Feld; *D:* Josef von Sternberg; *W:* Warren Duff; *M:* Max Steiner, Gaylord Carter. Academy Awards '28: Best Actor (Jannings); Nominations: Best Original Screenplay, Best Picture. **VHS, Beta** $14.95 *PAR, FCT, BTV* 𝘐𝘐𝘐𝘐

The Last Command Jim Bowie and his followers sacrifice their lives in defending the Alamo. A good cast holds its own against a mediocre script; battle scenes are terrific.
1955 110m/C Sterling Hayden, Richard Carlson, Ernest Borgnine, J. Carroll Naish, Virginia Grey, Anna Maria Alberghetti; *D:* Frank Lloyd. **VHS** $14.95 *REP, PAR* 𝘐𝘐½

The Last Contract An artist who pays his bills by working as a hitman, kills the wrong man. As a result, he must fear for his life since a counterhit is inevitable.

1986 (R) 85m/C Jack Palance, Rod Steiger, Bo Svenson, Richard Roundtree, Ann Turkel; *D:* Allan A. Buckhantz. **VHS** $19.95 *ACA* 𝘐𝘐

Last Cry for Help A psychiatrist helps a seventeen-year-old high school coed who, fearing she has disappointed her parents, attempts suicide. Typical made-for-television melodrama that attempts to make a statement, but falls short. Definitely not the "Partridge Family."
1979 98m/C Linda Purl, Shirley Jones, Tony LoBianco, Murray Hamilton, Grant Goodeve; *D:* Hal Sitowitz; *M:* Miles Goodman. **VHS, Beta** $29.95 *UNI* 𝘐½

Last Dance Five scantily-clad exotic dancers are ready to compete for the title of Miss Dance-TV, but trouble ensues when the dancers start turning up dead.
1991 86m/C Cynthia Bassinet, Elaine Hendrix, Kurt T. Williams, Allison Rhea, Erica Ringston; *D:* Anthony Markes. **VHS, Beta** $79.95 *PSM* 𝘐½

Last Day of the War A German scientist is chased by Americans and Germans as WWII winds to its conclusion. Filmed in Spain.
1969 (PG) 96m/C George Maharis, Maria Perschy, James Philbrook, Gerard Herter; *D:* Juan Antonio Bardem. **VHS, Beta** $39.95 *LIV* 𝘐½

The Last Days of Chez Nous Armstrong's dramatic comedy about a family falling apart has Ganz as a homesick Frenchman married to controlling, successful Australian writer Harrow. Trouble starts when his wayward sister-in-law Fox returns home to live with them and his wife decides to take an extended holiday with her father. Ganz suddenly finds himself only too involved in Fox's complicated life. Self-involved characters with messy emotional lives leave viewers feeling rather distant, though cast, and particularly Ganz, strive for intimacy.
1992 (R) 96m/C Bruno Ganz, Lisa Harrow, Kerry Fox, Kiri Paramore, Bill Hunter, Miranda Otto; *D:* Gillian Armstrong; *W:* Helen Garner; *M:* Paul Grabowsky. Australian Film Insti Nominations: ute '92: Best Director (Armstrong), Best Film, Best Supporting Actor (Hunter); Australian Film Institute '92: Best Actress (Harrow). **VHS** $19.95 *NLC, IME, COL* 𝘐𝘐½

The Last Days of Dolwyn A man banned for thievery from his Welsh village returns bent upon revenge. He plans to buy the entire district when it is designated part of a water reservoir project, but finds plans thwarted by a dowager and her stepson. Burton's first film was based on a true story. *AKA:* Woman of Dolwyn; Dolwyn.
1949 95m/B Edith Evans, Emlyn Williams, Richard Burton, Anthony James, Barbara Couper, Alan Aynesworth, Hugh Griffith, Roddy Hughes, Tom Jones; *D:* Emlyn Williams; *W:* Emlyn Williams. **VHS** $29.95 *FCT* 𝘐𝘐½

Last Days of Frank & Jesse James A tired television-movie rehash of the well-known western legend in which the famous brothers try to be like others after their personal war against society ends.
1986 100m/C Johnny Cash, Kris Kristofferson, June Carter Cash, Willie Nelson, Margaret Gibson, Gail Youngs; *D:* William A. Graham. **VHS, Beta** $19.95 *VMK* 𝘐½

The Last Days of Patton A made-for-television movie depicting the aging general's autumn years as a controversial ex-Nazi defender and desk-bound WWII historian. Scott reprises his feature-film role.
1986 146m/C George C. Scott, Ed Lauter, Eva Marie Saint, Richard Dysart, Murray Hamilton, Kathryn Leigh Scott; *D:* Delbert Mann. **VHS, Beta** $89.98 *FOX* 𝘐½

Last Days of Pompeii Vintage DeMille-style epic based on Lord Lytton's book, where the eruption of Vesuvius threatens noblemen and slaves alike. State-of-the-art special effects still look fantastic today. Remade in 1960; available colorized.
1935 96m/B Preston Foster, Alan Hale, Basil Rathbone, John Wood, Louis Calhern, David Holt, Dorothy Wilson, Wryley Birch, Gloria Shea; *D:* Ernest B. Schoedsack. VHS, Beta TTC √√½

The Last Days of Pompeii Superman Reeves plays a gladiator trying to clean up the doomed town of Pompeii in this remake of the 1935 classic. Some spectacular scenes, including the explosive climax when the mountain blows its top. *AKA:* Ultimi Giorni di Pompeii.
1960 105m/C Steve Reeves, Christine Kaufmann, Barbara Carroll, Anne Marie Baumann, Mimmo Palmara; *D:* Mario Bonnard; *W:* Sergio Leone. VHS $9.95 GKK √√

The Last Detail Two hard-boiled career petty officers (Nicholson and Young) are commissioned to transfer a young sailor facing an eight-year sentence for petty theft from one brig to another. In an act of compassion, they attempt to show the prisoner a final good time. Nicholson shines in both the complexity and completeness of his character. Adapted from a Daryl Ponicsan novel.
1973 (R) 104m/C Jack Nicholson, Otis Young, Randy Quaid, Clifton James, Michael Moriarty, Carol Kane, Nancy Allen; *Cameos:* Gilda Radner; *D:* Hal Ashby; *W:* Robert Towne; *M:* Johnny Mandel. Academy Awards '73 Nominations: Best Actor (Nicholson), Best Adapted Screenplay, Best Supporting Actor (Quaid); British Academy Awards '74: Best Actor (Nicholson); Cannes Film Festival '74: Best Actor (Nicholson); National Board of Review Awards '74: 10 Best Films of the Year; New York Film Critics Awards '74: Best Actor (Nicholson); National Society of Film Critics Awards '74: Best Actor (Nicholson). VHS, Beta $14.95 COL, WME √√√√

The Last Dragon It's time for a Motown kung fu showdown on the streets of Harlem, for there is scarcely enough room for even one dragon. *AKA:* Berry Gordy's The Last Dragon.
1985 (PG-13) 108m/C Taimak, Vanity, Christopher Murney, Julius J. Carry III, Faith Prince; *D:* Michael A. Schultz. VHS, Beta $29.95 FOX √√½

The Last Embrace A feverish thriller in the Hitchcock style dealing with an ex-secret serviceman who is convinced someone is trying to kill him.
1979 (R) 102m/C Roy Scheider, Janet Margolin, Christopher Walken, John Glover, Charles Napier, Mandy Patinkin; *D:* Jonathan Demme. VHS, Beta $14.95 MGM, FOX √√√

The Last Emperor Deeply ironic epic detailing life of Pu Yi, crowned at the age of three as the last emperor of China before the onset of communism. Follows Pu Yi from childhood to manhood (sequestered away in the Forbidden City) to fugitive to puppet-ruler to party proletariat. O'Toole portrays the sympathetic Scot tutor who educates the adult Pu Yi (Lone) in the ways of the western world after Pu Yi abdicates power in 1912. Shot on location inside the People's Republic of China with a cast of thousands; authentic costumes. Rich, visually stunning movie. The Talking Heads' David Byrne contributed to the score. Cinematography by Vittorio Storaro.
1987 (PG-13) 140m/C John Lone, Peter O'Toole, Joan Chen, Victor Wong, Ryuichi Sakamoto, Dennis Dun, Maggie Han, Ying Ruocheng, Ric Young; *D:* Bernardo Bertolucci; *W:* Mark Peploe, Bernardo Bertolucci; *M:* Ryuichi

Sakamoto, David Byrne. VHS, Beta, 8mm $19.98 COL, FCT, BTV √√√√

Last Exit to Brooklyn Hubert Selby, Jr.'s shocking book comes to the screen in a vivid film. Leigh gives a stunning performance as a young Brooklyn girl caught between the Mafia, union men, and friends struggling for something better. Set in the 1950s. Fine supporting cast; excellent pacing.
1990 (R) 102m/C Jennifer Jason Leigh, Burt Young, Stephen Lang, Ricki Lake, Jerry Orbach, Maia Danzinger, Stephen Baldwin; *D:* Uli Edel. VHS $89.95 COL, FCT √√√½

The Last Fight Boxer risks his life and his girlfriend for a shot at the championship title. Watch and see if he could've been a contender.
1982 (R) 85m/C Fred Williamson, Willie Colon, Ruben Blades, Joe Spinell, Darlanne Fluegel; *D:* Fred Williamson. VHS, Beta $69.99 HBO √½

The Last Five Days Based on the true story of a girl and her brother who, in 1943 Munich, were arrested for distributing anti-Nazi propaganda. The film covers the five days between their capture and execution. In German with English subtitles.
1982 112m/C Lena Stolze, Irm Hermann; *D:* Percy Adlon. VHS $79.95 CVC, ING √√

The Last Flight of Noah's Ark Disney adventure concerns a high-living pilot, a prim missionary, and two stowaway orphans who must plot their way off a deserted island following the crash landing of their broken-down plane.
1980 (G) 97m/C Elliott Gould, Genevieve Bujold, Rick Schroder, Vincent Gardenia, Tammy Lauren; *D:* Charles Jarrott; *M:* Maurice Jarre. VHS, Beta $69.95 DIS √√½

Last Flight Out: A True Story Hours before Saigon fell to the Vietcong in 1975, Vietnamese and Americans rushed to board the last commercial flight out of Vietnam. Lukewarm account of a true story.
1990 99m/C James Earl Jones, Richard Crenna, Haing S. Ngor, Eric Bogosian. VHS, 8mm $39.95 MNC √√

Last Flight to Hell When a drug lord is kidnapped, Brown is sent to South America to rescue the slimeball. His interest in the job picks up when the drug lord's 11-on-a-scale-of-ten daughter joins him for the chase.
19?? 94m/C Reb Brown, Chuck Connors. VHS $79.98 AIP √√

The Last Fling When Selleca has her mind set on a romantic fling, Ritter is headed for trouble. She wants love for one night, he wants it forever. Will they solve this difference of opinion? Will true love prevail? Will Ritter consent to being used as a one-night stand? Weakly plotted and poorly acted comedy. Made for television.
1986 95m/C John Ritter, Connie Sellecca, Scott Bakula, Shannon Tweed, Paul Sand, John Bennett Perry; *D:* Corey Allen; *M:* Charles Bernstein. VHS $29.95 ACA √√½

Last Four Days A chronicle of the final days of Benito Mussolini.
1977 (PG) 91m/C Rod Steiger, Henry Fonda, Franco Nero; *D:* Carlo Lizzani. VHS, Beta $69.98 LIV √√

Last Frontier Serial of 12 chapters contains shades of spectacular figures in Western history: Custer, Hickok, and others in a background of grazing buffalo, boom towns, and covered wagon trails.
1932 216m/B Lon Chaney Jr., Yakima Canutt, Francis X. Bushman; *D:* Spencer Gordon Bennet, Thomas L. Story. VHS, Beta $14.95 VCN, VYY, DVT √√½

Last Game A college student is torn between his devotion to his blind father and going out for the college's football team.
1980 107m/C Howard Segal, Ed L. Grady, Terry Alden; *D:* Martin Beck. VHS, Beta NO √√

Last Gun A legendary gunman on the verge of retirement has to save his town from a reign of terror before turning his gun in.
1964 98m/C Cameron Mitchell. VHS, Beta NO √√

The Last Hit Michael Grant (Brown) is a professional assassin, working for the CIA, who's very good at his job. But now he's burned out and ready to retire to New Mexico for some peace and quiet. He buys a house from the widowed Anna (Adams), naturally falling in love with her. Then one last assignment comes along and, wouldn't you know, his target turns out to be Anna's father (Yulin). Based on the novel "The Large Kill" by Patrick Ruell.
1993 (R) 93m/C Bryan Brown, Brooke Adams, Harris Yulin; *D:* Jan Egleson; *W:* Walter Klenhard, Alan Sharp. VHS $89.98 MCA √√½

Last Holiday A man who is told he has a few weeks to live decides to spend them in a posh resort where people assume he is important.
1950 89m/B Alec Guinness, Kay Walsh, Beatrice Campbell, Wilfrid Hyde-White, Bernard Lee; *D:* Henry Cass; *W:* J.B. Priestly. VHS, Beta $39.95 HMV, RXM, LCA √√

The Last Horror Film Beautiful queen of horror films is followed to the Cannes Film Festival by her number one fan who, unbeknownst to her, is slowly murdering members of her entourage in a deluded and vain attempt to capture her attentions. Title refers to lack of plans for a sequel. *AKA:* The Fanatic.
1982 (R) 87m/C Caroline Munro, Joe Spinell, Judd Hamilton; *D:* David Winters. VHS, Beta $59.95 MED Woof!

The Last Hour A Wall Street crook crosses a Mafia punk, so the latter holds the former's wife hostage in an unfinished skyscraper. Fortunately the lady's first husband is a gung-ho cop eager to commence the DIE HARD-esque action. Undistinguished fare that gives away the climax in an opening flash-forward.
1991 (R) 85m/C Michael Pare, Shannon Tweed, Bobby DiCicco, Robert Pucci; *D:* William Sachs. VHS, Beta $19.95 ACA √

Last House on Dead End Street Gore galore as actors die for their art in this splatter flick about snuff films. *AKA:* The Fun House.
1977 (R) 90m/C Steven Morrison, Dennis Crawford, Lawrence Bornman, Janet Sorley; *D:* Victor Janos. VHS $54.95 SUN Woof!

Last House on the Left Two girls are kidnapped from a rock concert by a gang of escaped convicts when the girls' parents exact bloody revenge when the guilty parties pay an intended housecall. Controversial and grim low-budget shocker; loosely based on Bergman's "The Virgin Spring."
1972 (R) 83m/C David Hess, Lucy Grantham, Sandra Cassel, Mark Sheffler, Fred J. Lincoln; *D:* Wes Craven. VHS, Beta $19.98 LIV, VES, HHE Woof!

The Last Hunt Well-performed western starring Taylor as a seedy buffalo hunter who gains his identity from senseless acts of murder. When personalities clash, he seeks revenge on fellow buffalo hunter Granger. Shot in Custer National Park, the buffalo scenes were real-life attempts at keeping the

animals controlled. Based on the novel by Milton Lott.
1956 108m/C Robert Taylor, Stewart Granger, Lloyd Nolan, Debra Paget, Russ Tamblyn, Constance Ford, Ainslie Pryor, Ralph Moody, Fred Graham, Dan White, Bill Phillips, Roy Barcroft; *D:* Richard Brooks; *W:* Richard Brooks; *M:* Daniele Amfitheatrof. VHS $19.98 *MGM* 🎬🎬½

The Last Hunter A soldier fights for his life behind enemy lines during the Vietnam War. *AKA:* Hunter of the Apocalypse.
1980 (R) 97m/C Tisa Farrow, David Warbeck, Tony King, Bobby Rhodes, Margit Evelyn Newton, John Steiner, Alan Collins; *D:* Anthony M. (Antonio Marghereti) Dawson. VHS, Beta $69.98 *LIV, VES* 🎬

Last Hurrah An aging Irish-American mayor battles corruption and political back-biting in his effort to get re-elected for the last time. Semi-acclaimed heart warmer, based on the novel by Edwin O'Connor.
1958 121m/B Spencer Tracy, Basil Rathbone, John Carradine, Jeffrey Hunter, Dianne Foster, Pat O'Brien, Edward Brophy, James Gleason, Donald Crisp, Ricardo Cortez, Wallace Ford, Frank McHugh, Jane Darwell; *D:* John Ford. VHS, Beta $19.95 *COL* 🎬🎬½

The Last Innocent Man An attorney who quit law due to a guilty conscience is lured into defending a suspected murderer. Things become even more complicated when he begins having an affair with his client's seductive wife. A well-acted and suspense-filled flick. Made for cable television.
1987 113m/C Ed Harris, Roxanne Hart, Bruce McGill, Clarence Williams III, Rose Gregorio, David Suchet, Darrell Larson; *D:* Roger Spottiswoode; *W:* Dan Bronson; *M:* Brad Fiedel. VHS, Beta $79.95 *LHV, WAR* 🎬🎬½

The Last Laugh An elderly man, who as the doorman of a great hotel was looked upon as a symbol of "upper class," is demoted to washroom attendant due to his age. Important due to camera technique and consuming performance by Jannings. Silent with music score. A 91-minute version is also available. *AKA:* Der Letzte Mann.
1924 77m/B Emil Jannings, Maly Delshaft, Max Hiller; *D:* F.W. Murnau. VHS, Beta $19.95 *NOS, FCT, IHF* 🎬🎬🎬½

Last Light A prison guard (Whitaker) on death row forms a tenuous bond with an incorrigible inmate (Sutherland) who's about to be executed. Disturbing, especially the execution scene. Filmed on location at California's Soledad Prison. Sutherland's directorial debut. Made for cable television.
1993 (R) 95m/C Kiefer Sutherland, Forest Whitaker, Clancy Brown, Lynne Moody, Kathleen Quinlan, Amanda Plummer; *D:* Kiefer Sutherland. VHS $92.95 *VMK* 🎬🎬

The Last Man on Earth Price is the sole survivor of a plague which has turned the rest of the world into vampires, who constantly harass him. Uneven U.S./Italian production manages to convey a creepy atmosphere of dismay. *AKA:* L'Ultimo Uomo Della Terra.
1964 86m/B Vincent Price, Franca Bettoya, Giacomo "Jack" Rossi-Stuart, Emma Danieli; *D:* Ubaldo Ragona, Sidney Salkow. VHS $16.95 *SNC, MRV* 🎬🎬

Last Man Standing A cheap, gritty drama about bare-knuckle fist fighting. Wells stars as a down-on-his-luck prizefighter try-ing to find work that doesn't involve pugilism.
1987 (R) 89m/C William Sanderson, Vernon Wells, Franco Columbo; *D:* Damian Lee. VHS, Beta $29.95 *ACA* 🎬

The Last Married Couple in America A couple fight to stay happily married amidst the rampant divorce epidemic engulfing their friends.
1980 (R) 103m/C George Segal, Natalie Wood, Richard Benjamin, Valerie Harper, Dom DeLuise, Priscilla Barnes; *D:* Gilbert Cates; *M:* Charles Fox. VHS, Beta $69.95 *MCA* 🎬🎬

Last Mercenary An angry ex-soldier kills everyone who makes him mad.
1984 90m/C Tony Marsina, Malcolm Duff, Kitty Nichols, Louis Walser. VHS, Beta *NO Woof!*

The Last Metro Truffaut's alternately gripping and touching drama about a theater company in Nazi-occupied Paris. In 1942, Lucas Steiner (Bennent) is a successful Jewish theater director who is forced into hiding. He turns the running of the theater over to his wife, Marion (the always exquisite Deneuve), who must contend with a pro-Nazi theater critic (Richard) and her growing at-traction to the company's leading man (De-pardieu), who is secretly working with the Resistance. In French with English subtitles. *AKA:* Le Dernier Metro.
1980 135m/C Catherine Deneuve, Gerard Depardieu, Heinz Bennent, Jean-Louis Richard, Jean Poiret, Andrea Ferreol, Paulette Dubost, Sabine Haudepin; *D:* Francois Truffaut; *W:* Suzanne Schiffman; *M:* Georges Delerue. Academy Awards '80 Nominations: Best Foreign Language Film; Cesar Awards '81: Best Actor (Depardieu), Best Actress (Deneuve), Best Director (Truffaut), Best Film. VHS, Beta $39.95 *HMV, FOX, APD* 🎬🎬🎬

The Last Mile The staff of a prison prepares for the execution of a celebrated murderer.
1932 70m/B Preston Foster, Howard Phillips, George E. Stone; *D:* Sam Bischoff. VHS, Beta $19.95 *NOS, MRV, BAR* 🎬🎬

The Last Movie A movie stunt man stays in a small Peruvian town after his filming stint is over. Hopper's confused, pretentious follow-up to "Easy Rider," has a multitude of cameos but little else. Given an award by the Italians; nobody else under-stood it. Kristofferson's film debut; he also wrote the music. Based on a story by Hopper and Stern. *AKA:* Chinchero.
1971 (R) 108m/C Dennis Hopper, Julie Adams, Peter Fonda, Kris Kristofferson, Sylvia Miles, John Phillip Law, Russ Tamblyn, Rod Cameron; *D:* Dennis Hopper; *W:* Stewart Stern; *M:* Kris Kristofferson. VHS $79.95 *VCI* 🎬🎬

Last Night at the Alamo Patrons fight to stop the destruction of their Houston bar, the Alamo, which is about to be razed to make room for a modern skyscraper. Insight-ful comedy written by the author of "The Texas Chainsaw Massacre."
1983 80m/B Sonny Carl Davis, Lou Perry, Steve Matilla, Tina Hubbard, Doris Hargrave; *D:* Eagle Pennell; *W:* Kim Henkel. VHS *NO* 🎬🎬🎬

The Last of England A furious non-narrative film by avant-garde filmmaker Jar-man, depicting the modern British landscape as a funereal, waste-filled rubble-heap—as depleted morally as it is environmentally.
1987 87m/C Tilda Swinton, Spencer Leigh; *D:* Derek Jarman. VHS, Beta $29.95 *MFV, TPV, ING* 🎬🎬🎬½

The Last of His Tribe In 1911 an anthropologist befriends an Indian and dis-covers that Ishi is the last surviving member of California's Yahi tribe. Ishi then becomes a media and scientific society darling, spending the remainder of his remaining life in captivity to academia. A good portrayal of the Native American plight. Based on a true story; made for cable television.

1992 (PG-13) 90m/C Jon Voight, Graham Greene, David Ogden Stiers, Jack Blessing, Anne Archer, Daniel Benzali; *D:* Harry Hook. VHS $89.99 *WAR* 🎬🎬

The Last of Mrs. Cheyney Remake of Norma Shearer's 1929 hit, based on the play by Frederick Lonsdale, about a sophisti-cated jewel thief in England. Crawford stars as the jewel thief who poses as a wealthy woman to get into parties hosted by London bluebloods. Dripping with charm, she works her way into Lord Drilling's mansion where she plans a huge heist. The film is handled well, and the cast gives solid performances throughout. This chic comedy of high society proved to be one of Crawford's most popular films of the '30s.
1937 98m/B Joan Crawford, Robert Montgomery, William Powell, Frank Morgan, Nigel Bruce, Jessie Ralph; *D:* Richard Boleslawski, George Fitzmaurice. VHS $19.98 *MGM* 🎬🎬🎬

The Last of Mrs. Lincoln Intimate made for TV portrayal of the famous first lady. Film focuses on Mary Todd Lincoln's life from the assassination of her husband, through her autumn years, and her untimely downfall.
1976 118m/C Julie Harris, Robby Benson, Patrick Duffy. VHS, Beta *NO* 🎬🎬½

The Last of Philip Banter An alco-holic writer is terrified to learn events in his life exactly match a mysterious manuscript.
1987 (R) 105m/C Tony Curtis, Greg Henry, Irene Miracle, Scott Paulin, Kate Vernon; *D:* Herve Hachuel. VHS $79.95 *REP* 🎬½

The Last of Sheila A movie producer invites six big-star friends for a cruise aboard his yacht, the "Sheila." He then stages an elaborate "Whodunnit" parlor game to dis-cover which one of them murdered his wife.
1973 (PG) 119m/C Richard Benjamin, James Coburn, James Mason, Dyan Cannon, Joan Hackett, Raquel Welch, Ian McShane; *D:* Herbert Ross; *W:* Anthony Perkins, Stephen Sondheim; *M:* Billy Goldenberg. VHS, Beta $64.95 *WAR* 🎬🎬½

Last of the Clintons A range detec-tive tracks an outlaw gang amid spur jinglin', sharp shootin' and cow punchin'.
1935 64m/B Harry Carey Sr. VHS, Beta $19.95 *NOS* 🎬½

Last of the Comanches Cavalry and Indians fight for water when both are dying of thirst in the desert. *AKA:* The Sabre and the Arrow.
1952 85m/C Broderick Crawford, Barbara Hale, John Stewart, Lloyd Bridges, Mickey Shaughnessy, George Mathews; *D:* Andre de Toth. VHS, Beta $14.99 *GKK* 🎬🎬

The Last of the Finest Overzealous anti-drug task force cops break the rules in trying to put dealer-drug lords in prison; ostensibly a parallel on the Iran-Contra affair. *AKA:* Street Legal; Blue Heat.
1990 (R) 106m/C Brian Dennehy, Joe Pantoliano, Jeff Fahey, Bill Paxton, Deborra-Lee Furness, Guy Boyd, Henry Darrow, Lisa Jane Persky, Michael C. Gwynne; *D:* John MacKenzie; *M:* Jack Nitzsche. VHS, Beta $9.98 *ORI* 🎬½

The Last of the Mohicans Color tints enhance this silent version of the James Fenimore Cooper rouser. Beery is the villa-nious Magua, with Bedford memorable as the lovely Cora and Roscoe as the brave Uncas. Fine action sequences, including the Huron massacre at Fort Henry. Director credit was shared when Tourneur suffered an on-set injury and was off for 3 months.
1920 75m/B Wallace Beery, Barbara Bedford, Albert Roscoe, Lillian Hall, Henry Woodward, James Gordon, George Hackathorne, Harry Lorraine, Nelson McDowell, Theodore Lorch,

Boris Karloff; *D:* Maurice Tourneur, Clarence Brown; *W:* Robert Dillon. **VHS $40.00** *LUM, FCT, MIL* ♫♫♫

The Last of the Mohicans Serial based on James Fenimore Cooper's novel of the life-and-death struggle of the Mohican Indians during the French and Indian War. Twelve chapters, 13 minutes each. Remade as a movie in 1936 and 1992 and as a television movie in 1977.
1932 230m/B Edwina Booth, Harry Carey Sr., Hobart Bosworth, Frank ''Junior'' Coghlan; *D:* Ford Beebe, B. Reeves Eason. **VHS, Beta $39.95** *VYY, VCN, NOS* ♫♫

The Last of the Mohicans James Fenimore Cooper's classic about the French and Indian War in colonial America is brought to the screen. Remake of the 1932 serial was remade itself in 1977 for television.
1936 91m/B Randolph Scott, Binnie Barnes, Bruce Cabot, Henry Wilcoxon, Heather Angel, Hugh Buckler; *D:* George B. Seitz. **VHS, Beta $12.95** *LIV, MED, CCB* ♫♫½

The Last of the Mohicans The classic novel by James Fenimore Cooper about the scout Hawkeye and his Mohican companions, Chingachgook and Uncas during the French and Indian war, comes to life in this made-for-television film. Remake of a 1932 serial and a 1936 film.
1985 (R) 97m/C Steve Forrest, Ned Romero, Andrew Prine, Don Shanks, Robert Tessier, Jane Actman; *D:* James L. Conway. **VHS, Beta $19.95** *STE, VCI* ♫♫

The Last of the Mohicans It's 1757, at the height of the French and English war in the American colonies, with various Native American tribes allied to each side. Hawkeye (Day-Lewis), a white frontiersman raised by the Mohicans, wants nothing to do with either ''civilized'' side, until he rescues the beautiful Cora (Stowe) from the revenge-minded Huron Magua (Studi in a powerful performance). Graphically violent battle scenes are realistic, but not gratuitous. The real pleasure in this adaptation, which draws from both the James Fenimore Cooper novel and the 1936 film, is in its lush look and attractive stars. Means is terrific in his film debut as Hawkeye's foster-father. Released in a letterbox format to preserve the original integrity of the film.
1992 (R) 114m/C Daniel Day-Lewis, Madeleine Stowe, Wes Studi, Russell Means, Eric Schweig, Jodhi May, Steven Waddington, Maurice Roeves, Colm Meaney, Patrice Chereau; *D:* Michael Mann; *W:* Christopher Crowe, Michael Mann; *M:* Trevor Jones, Randy Edelman. **VHS $24.98** *FXV, BTV* ♫♫♫

Last of the Pony Riders When the telegraph lines linking the East and West Coasts are completed, Gene and the other Pony Express riders find themselves out of a job. Autry's final feature film.
1953 59m/B Gene Autry, Smiley Burnette, Kathleen Case; *D:* George Archainbaud. **VHS, Beta $37.50** *CCB* ♫♫½

Last of the Red Hot Lovers Not so funny adaptation of Neil Simon's Broadway hit. Middle-aged man decides to have a fling and uses his mother's apartment to seduce three very strange women.
1972 (PG) 98m/C Alan Arkin, Paula Prentiss, Sally Kellerman, Renee Taylor; *D:* Gene Saks; *W:* Neil Simon. **VHS, Beta $14.95** *PAR* ♫½

The Last of the Redmen An adaptation of James Fenimore Cooper's ''The Last of the Mohicans'' geared toward youngsters. Hall must lead three children of a British general through dangerous Indian territory. They have a number of adventures including meeting up with Uncas, the last of

the Mohicans, who's a villain in this mangled version.
1947 79m/B Jon Hall, Michael O'Shea, Evelyn Ankers, Julie Bishop, Buster Crabbe, Rick Vallin, Frederick Worlock, Guy Hedlund; *D:* George Sherman; *W:* Herbert Dalmas. **VHS $19.95** *COL* ♫½

Last of the Warrens A cowboy returns home after WWI to discover that an unscrupulous storekeeper has stolen his property.
1936 56m/C Bob Steele, Charles ''Blackie'' King, Lafe McKee, Margaret Marquis, Horace Murphy; *D:* Robert North Bradbury. **VHS, Beta $19.95** *NOS, DVT, GPV* ♫

Last of the Wild Horses Range war almost starts when ranch owner is accused of trying to force the small ranchers out of business.
1949 86m/B Mary Beth Hughes, James Ellison, Jane Frazee. **VHS, Beta NO** ♫½

The Last Outlaw Action-packed western with Cooper following his success of ''Wings'' with Paramount. Most excellent equine stunts.
1927 61m/B Gary Cooper, Jack Luden, Betty Jewel; *D:* Arthur Rosson. **VHS, Beta $19.95** *GPV, FCT* ♫♫

Last Outlaw The last of the famous badmen of the old West is released from jail and returns home to find that times have changed. The action climaxes in an old-time blazing shoot-out.
1936 79m/B Harry Carey Sr., Hoot Gibson, Henry B. Walthall, Tom Tyler, Russell Hopton, Alan Curtis, Harry Woods, Barbara Pepper; *D:* Christy Cabanne. **VHS, Beta $29.95** *VCN* ♫♫

The Last Outlaw Rourke stars as an ex-Confederate officer who leads a gang of outlaws until his violent excesses leave even them disgusted. The gang shoots Rourke but of course he doesn't die and then he sets out for revenge. Made for cable television.
1993 (R) 90m/C Mickey Rourke, Dermot Mulroney, Ted Levine, John C. McGinley, Steve Buscemi, Keith David; *D:* Geoff Murphy; *W:* Eric Red. **VHS $92.99** *HBO* ♫♫½

The Last Picture Show Slice of life/nostalgic farewell to an innocent age, based on Larry McMurtry's novel. Set in Archer City, a backwater Texas town, most of the story plays out at the local hangout run by ex-cowboy Sam the Lion. Bridges is hooked up with spoiled pretty girl Sheperd, while Bottoms, a sensitive guy, is having an affair with the coach's neglected wife (Leachman). Loss of innocence, disillusionment and confusion are played out against the backdrop of a town about to close its cinema. Shepherd's and Bottoms' film debut. Stunningly photographed in black and white (Bogdanovich claimed he didn't want to ''prettify'' the picture by shooting in color) by Robert Surtees. Available in a laserdisc special edition with 17 minutes restored. Followed by a weak sequel, ''Texasville.'' A boxed set featuring both films is also available.
1971 (R) 118m/B Jeff Bridges, Timothy Bottoms, Ben Johnson, Cloris Leachman, Cybill Shepherd, Ellen Burstyn, Eileen Brennan, Clu Gulager, Sharon Taggart, Randy Quaid, Sam Bottoms, John Hillerman; *D:* Peter Bogdanovich; *W:* Larry McMurtry, Peter Bogdanovich. Academy Awards '71: Best Supporting Actor (Johnson), Best Supporting Actress (Leachman); Nominations: Best Adapted Screenplay, Best Cinematography, Best Director (Bogdanovich), Best Picture, Best Supporting Actor (Bridges), Best Supporting Actress (Burstyn); Golden Globe Awards '72: Best Supporting Actor (Johnson). **VHS, 8mm $19.95** *COL, VYG, CRC* ♫♫♫♫

Last Plane Out A Texas journalist sent out on assignment to Nicaragua falls in love with a Sandanista rebel. Based on producer Jack Cox's real-life experiences as a journalist during the last days of the Samosa regime. Low-budget propaganda.
1983 (R) 90m/C Jan-Michael Vincent, Lloyd Batista, Julie Carmen, Mary Crosby, David Huffman, William Windom; *D:* David Nelson. **VHS, Beta $19.95** *STE, FOX* ♫½

The Last Polka SCTV vets Candy and Levy are Yosh and Stan Schmenge, polka kings interviewed for a ''documentary'' on their years in the spotlight and on the road. Hilarious spoof on Martin Scorsese's ''The Last Waltz,'' about The Band's last concert. Several fellow Second City-ers keep the laughs coming. If you liked SCTV or ''This is Spinal Tap,'' you'll like this. Made for cable (HBO).
1984 54m/C John Candy, Eugene Levy, Rick Moranis, Robin Duke, Catherine O'Hara; *D:* John Blanchard. **VHS, Beta $19.98** *LIV, VES* ♫♫♫

The Last Porno Flick A pornographic movie script winds up in the hands of a couple of goofy cab drivers. The twosome sneak the movie's genre past the producers, families, and police.
1974 (PG) 90m/C Michael Pataki, Marianna Hill, Carmen Zapata, Mike Kellin, Colleen Camp, Tom Signorelli, Antony Carbone; *D:* Ray Marsh. **VHS NO** ♫

The Last Prostitute Two teenage boys search for a legendary prostitute to initiate them into manhood, only to discover that she has retired. They hire on as laborers on her horse farm, and one of them discovers the meaning of love. Made for cable TV.
1991 (PG-13) 93m/C Sonia Braga, Wil Wheaton, David Kaufman, Woody Watson, Dennis Letts, Cotter Smith; *D:* Lou Antonio. **VHS $89.95** *MCA* ♫♫

The Last Radio Station A mini-musical with a largely Motown soundtrack about a failing radio station supported by old rock songs: ''Reflections,'' ''Nowhere to Run,'' ''Dancing in the Street'' and others.
1986 60m/C VHS, Beta $19.95 *MCA, MVD* ♫♫

The Last Remake of Beau Geste A slapstick parody of the familiar Foreign Legion story from the Mel Brooks-ish school of loud genre farce. Gary Cooper makes an appearance by way of inserted footage from the 1939 straight version.
1977 (PG) 85m/C Marty Feldman, Ann-Margret, Michael York, Peter Ustinov, James Earl Jones; *D:* Marty Feldman. **VHS, Beta $14.95** *MCA* ♫♫

Last Resort A married furniture executive unknowingly takes his family on vacation to a sex-saturated, Club Med-type holiday spot, and gets more than he anticipated. *AKA:* She Knew No Other Way.
1986 (R) 80m/C Charles Grodin, Jon Lovitz; *D:* Zane Buzby. **VHS, Beta $79.98** *LIV, VES* ♫♫

Last Reunion Rare British ghost story starring Gough.
1955 ?m/C Michael Gough. **VHS NO** ♫♫

The Last Reunion The only witness to a brutal killing of a Japanese official and his wife during WWII seeks revenge on the guilty American platoon, thirty-three years later. Violent.
1980 98m/C Cameron Mitchell, Leo Fong, Chanda Romero, Vic Silayan, Hal Bokar, Philip Baker Hall; *D:* Jay Wertz. **VHS $16.95** *SNC* ♫½

The Last Ride Another movie probing the dark side of hitchhiking. This time our hero thumbs a ride with a truck driver who plans to bypass the next city...for hell.

1991 84m/C Dan Ranger, Michael Hilow. **VHS** $79.98 AIP ✗

The Last Ride of the Dalton Gang A long-winded retelling of the wild adventures that made the Dalton gang legendary among outlaws.
1979 146m/C Larry Wilcox, Jack Palance, Randy Quaid, Cliff Potts, Dale Robertson, Don Collier; **D:** Dan Curtis. **VHS, Beta** $19.98 WAR, OM ✗✗

The Last Riders Motorcycle centaur Estrada revs a few motors fleeing from cycle club cronies and crooked cops. Full throttle foolishness.
1990 (R) 90m/C Erik Estrada, William Smith, Armando Silvestre, Kathrin Lautner; **D:** Joseph Merhi. **VHS** $19.95 PMH, HHE ✗

Last Rites A priest at St. Patrick's Cathedral in New York allows a young Mexican woman to seek sanctuary from the Mob, who soon come after both of them.
1988 (R) 103m/C Tom Berenger, Daphne Zuniga, Chick Vennera, Dane Clark, Carlo Pacchi, Anne Twomey, Paul Dooley, Vassili Lambrinos; **D:** Donald P. Bellisario; **M:** Bruce Broughton. **VHS, Beta** $19.98 FOX ✗✗

The Last Safari A young man on safari in Africa befriends a bitter professional guide in a drama hampered by a poor script. Granger and Garas set out to hunt the rampaging elephant which killed Granger's friend. Granger thinks killing the beast will restore his courage and help him overcome the guilt he feels. Based on the novel "Gilligan's Last Elephant" by Gerald Hanley.
1967 111m/C Stewart Granger, Kaz Garas, Gabriella Licudi, Johnny Sekka, Liam Redmond; **D:** Henry Hathaway; **W:** John Gay. **VHS** $14.95 PAR ✗✗½

The Last Season Shoot 'em up involving a bunch of hunters. Their aimless destruction provokes the good guy to save the forest they are demolishing. A battle ensues.
1987 90m/C Christopher Gosch, Louise Dorsey, David Cox; **D:** Raja Zahr. **VHS** NO Woof!

The Last Slumber Party A slumber party is beset by a homicidal maniac. Heavy metal soundtrack.
1987 89m/C Jan Jensen, Nancy Meyer. **VHS, Beta** $19.95 VCI Woof!

Last Song A singer's husband discovers a plot to cover up a fatal toxic-waste accident, and is killed because of it. It's up to her to warn the authorities before becoming the next victim.
1980 (PG) 96m/C Lynda Carter, Ronny Cox, Nicholas Pryor, Paul Rudd, Jenny O'Hara; **D:** Alan J. Levi. **VHS, Beta** $59.98 FOX ✗✗

The Last Starfighter A young man who becomes an expert at a video game is recruited to fight in an inter-galactic war. Listless adventure which explains where all those video games come from. Watch for O'Herlihy disguised as a lizard.
1984 (PG) 100m/C Lance Guest, Robert Preston, Barbara Bosson, Dan O'Herlihy, Catherine Mary Stewart, Cameron Dye, Kimberly Ross, Wil Wheaton; **D:** Nick Castle. **VHS, Beta** $19.95 MCA ✗✗

Last Summer Three teenagers discover love, sex, and friendship on the white sands of Fire Island, N.Y. The summer vacation fantasy world they create shatters when a sweet but homely female teenager joins their group. Based on a novel by Evan Hunter.
1969 (R) 97m/C Barbara Hershey, Richard Thomas, Bruce Davison, Cathy Burns; **D:** Frank Perry. **VHS, Beta** $59.98 FOX ✗✗½

The Last Supper A repentant Cuban slave-owner in the 18th-century decides to cleanse his soul and convert his slaves to Christianity by having twelve of them reenact the Last Supper. Based on a true story. In Spanish with English subtitles.
1976 110m/C Nelson Villagra, Silvano Rey, Lamberto Garcia, Jose Antonio Rodriguez, Samuel Claxton, Mario Balmasada, Thomas Gutierrez Alea. **VHS, Beta** $69.95 NYF, FCT, ING ✗✗✗

Last Tango in Paris Brando plays a middle-aged American who meets a French girl and tries to forget his wife's suicide with a short, extremely steamy affair. Bertolucci proves to be a master; Brando gives one of his best performances. Very controversial when made, still quite explicit. Visually stunning. The X-rated version, at 130 minutes, is also available.
1973 (R) 126m/C Marlon Brando, Maria Schneider, Jean-Pierre Leaud; **D:** Bernardo Bertolucci; **W:** Bernardo Bertolucci. Academy Awards '73 Nominations: Best Actor (Brando), Best Director (Bertolucci); New York Film Critics Awards '73: Best Actor (Brando); National Society of Film Critics Awards '73: Best Actor (Brando). **VHS, Beta** $29.98 MGM, FOX, VYG ✗✗✗½

The Last Temptation of Christ Scorcese's controversial adaptation of the Nikos Kazantzakis novel, portraying Christ in his last year as an ordinary Israelite tormented by divine doubt, human desires and the voice of God. The controversy engulfing the film, as it was heavily protested and widely banned, tended to divert attention from what is an exceptional statement of religious and artistic vision. Excellent score by Peter Gabriel.
1988 (R) 164m/C Willem Dafoe, Harvey Keitel, Barbara Hershey, Harry Dean Stanton, Andre Gregory, David Bowie, Verna Bloom, Juliette Caton, John Lurie, Roberts Blossom, Irvin Kershner, Barry Miller, Tomas Arana, Nehemiah Persoff, Paul Herman; **D:** Martin Scorsese; **W:** Paul Schrader; **M:** Peter Gabriel. **VHS, Beta** $19.95 MCA ✗✗✗½

The Last Time I Saw Paris A successful writer reminisces about his love affair with a wealthy American girl in post-WWII Paris.
1954 116m/C Elizabeth Taylor, Van Johnson, Walter Pidgeon, Roger Moore, Donna Reed, Eva Gabor; **D:** Richard Brooks; **W:** Richard Brooks, Julius J. Epstein, Philip C. Epstein. **VHS, Beta** $19.98 MGM, MRV, NOS ✗✗½

The Last Tomahawk Colorful and action packed reworking of Cooper's "Last of the Mohicans."
1965 ?m/C Anthony Steffen, Karin Dor, Dan Martin, Joachim Fuchsberger. **VHS** $16.95 SNC ✗✗

The Last Train Romance most hopeless in the heart of France during zee beeg war. French, very French.
1974 ?m/C Romy Schneider, Jean-Louis Trintignant. **VHS, Beta** NO ✗✗

Last Train from Gun Hill An all-star cast highlights this suspenseful story of a U.S. marshall determined to catch the man who raped and murdered his wife. Excellent action packed western.
1959 94m/C Kirk Douglas, Anthony Quinn, Carolyn Jones, Earl Holliman, Brad Dexter, Brian Hutton, Ziva Rodann; **D:** John Sturges. **VHS** $19.95 STE ✗✗✗

The Last Tycoon An adaptation of the unfinished F. Scott Fitzgerald novel about the life and times of a Hollywood movie executive of the 1920s. Confusing and slow moving despite a blockbuster conglomera-

tion of talent. Joan Collins introduces the film.
1976 (PG) 123m/C Robert De Niro, Tony Curtis, Ingrid Boulting, Jack Nicholson, Jeanne Moreau, Peter Strauss, Robert Mitchum, Theresa Russell, Donald Pleasence, Ray Milland, Dana Andrews, John Carradine, Anjelica Huston; **D:** Elia Kazan; **W:** Harold Pinter; **M:** Maurice Jarre. Academy Awards '76 Nominations: Best Art Direction/Set Decoration; National Board of Review Awards '76: 10 Best Films of the Year. **VHS, Beta** $19.95 PAR, FCT ✗✗✗

The Last Unicorn Peter Beagle's popular tale of a beautiful unicorn who goes in search of her lost, mythical "family."
1982 (G) 95m/C **D:** Jules Bass; **M:** Jim Webb; **V:** Alan Arkin, Jeff Bridges, Tammy Grimes, Angela Lansbury, Mia Farrow, Robert Klein, Christopher Lee, Keenan Wynn. **VHS, Beta** $14.98 FOX, KAR, WTA ✗✗½

The Last Valley A scholar tries to protect a pristine 17th century Swiss valley, untouched by the Thirty Years War, from marauding soldiers. Historical action with an intellectual twist.
1971 (PG) 128m/C Michael Caine, Omar Sharif, Florinda Bolkan, Nigel Davenport, Per Oscarsson, Arthur O'Connell; **D:** James Clavell; **W:** James Clavell; **M:** John Barry. **VHS** NO ✗✗

The Last Voyage Suspenseful disaster film in which Stack and Malone play a married couple in jeopardy while on an ocean cruise. To make the film more realistic, the French liner Ile de France was actually used in the sinking scenes. Although a bit far-fetched, film is made watchable because of fine performances and excellent camerawork.
1960 91m/C Robert Stack, Dorothy Malone, George Sanders, Edmond O'Brien, Woody Strode, Jack Kruschen; **D:** Andrew L. Stone; **W:** Andrew L. Stone. **VHS** $19.98 MGM ✗✗½

The Last Waltz Martin Scorsese filmed this rock documentary featuring the farewell performance of The Band, joined by a host of musical guests that they have been associated with over the years. Songs include: "Up On Cripple Creek," "Don't Do It," "The Night They Drove Old Dixie Down," "Stage Fright" (The Band), "Helpless" (Young), "Coyote" (Mitchell), "Caravan" (Morrison), "Further On Up the Road" (Clapton), "Who Do You Love" (Hawkins), "Mannish Boy" (Waters), "Evangeline" (Harris), "Baby, Let Me Follow You Down" (Dylan).
1978 (PG) 117m/C The Band, Bob Dylan, Neil Young, Joni Mitchell, Van Morrison, Eric Clapton, Neil Diamond, Emmylou Harris, Muddy Waters, Ronnie Hawkins; **D:** Martin Scorsese. **VHS, Beta** $19.95 MVD, MGM ✗✗½

Last War A nuclear war between the United States and Russia triggers Armageddon.
1968 79m/C Frankie Sakai, Nobuko Otowa, Akira Takarada, Yuriko Hoshi; **D:** Shue Matsubayashi. **VHS, Beta** $19.95 GEM ✗

The Last Warrior A good-looking but exploitive "Hell in the Pacific" rip-off, as an American and a Japanese soldier battle it out alone on a remote island during WWII. **AKA:** Coastwatcher.
1989 (R) 94m/C Gary Graham, Cary-Hiroyuki Tagawa, Maria Holvoe; **D:** Martin Wragge. **VHS, Beta** $14.95 COL ✗½

The Last Wave An Australian attorney takes on a murder case involving an aborigine and he finds himself becoming distracted by apocalyptic visions concerning tidal waves and drownings that seem to foretell the future. Weir's masterful creation and communication of time and place are marred by a somewhat pat ending.

1977 (PG) 109m/C Richard Chamberlain, Olivia Hamnett, David Gulpilil, Frederick Parslow; *D:* Peter Weir; *W:* Peter Weir. **VHS, Beta** *FCT, RHI* 🎬🎬🎬

The Last Winter An American woman fights to find her Israeli husband who has disappeared in the 1973 Yom Kippur War. Trouble is, an Israeli woman thinks the man she's looking for is really her husband too. **1984** (R) 92m/C Kathleen Quinlan, Yona Elian, Zipora Peled, Michael Schnider; *D:* Riki Shelach. **VHS, Beta** \$79.95 *COL* 🎬🎬

The Last Winters From Jean Charles Tacchella, writer-producer-director of "Cousin Cousine," comes his first short film about an old couple's bittersweet romance. In French with English subtitles. **1971** 23m/C *D:* Jean-Charles Tacchella. **VHS, Beta** \$79.98 *INT, MTI* 🎬🎬½

Last Witness A man on the run from the government claims that he is innocent and was unjustly persecuted, but the government sees him as a dangerous threat. Nothing will stop the hunt for the escaped man, no matter what it costs. **1988** 85m/C Jeff Henderson. **VHS, Beta** \$79.95 *TWE* 🎬

The Last Woman on Earth Two men vie for the affections of the sole surviving woman after a vague and unexplained disaster of vast proportions. Robert Towne, who appears herein under the pseudonym Edward Wain, wrote the script (his first screenwriting effort). You might want to watch this if it were the last movie on earth, although Corman fans will probably love it. **1961** 71m/C Antony Carbone, Edward Wain, Betsy Jones-Moreland; *D:* Roger Corman; *W:* Robert Towne. **VHS** \$16.95 *NOS, MRV, SNC* Woof!

The Last Word Comedy drama about struggling inventor Harris fighting to protect his home, family, and neighbors from a corrupt real estate deal involving shady politicians, angry policemen, and a beautiful television reporter. **1980** (PG) 103m/C Richard Harris, Karen Black, Martin Landau, Dennis Christopher, Bill McGuire, Christopher Guest, Penelope Milford, Michael Pataki; *W:* Michael Varhol, Kit Carson. **VHS, Beta** \$69.98 *SUE* 🎬🎬

Last Year at Marienbad A young man tries to lure a mysterious woman to run away with him from a hotel in France. Once a hit on the artsy circuit, it's most interesting for its beautiful photography. In French with English subtitles. *AKA:* L'Anee Derniere a Marienbad. **1961** 93m/B Delphine Seyrig, Giorgia Albertazzi, Sacha Pitoeff, Luce Garcia-Ville; *D:* Alain Resnais. **VHS, Beta, 8mm** \$24.95 *VYY, MRV, NOS* 🎬🎬🎬

L'Atalante Vigo's great masterpiece, a slight story about a husband and wife quarreling, splitting, and reuniting around which has been fashioned one of the cinema's greatest poetic films. In French with English subtitles. **1934** 82m/B Dita Parlo, Jean Daste, Michel Simon; *D:* Jean Vigo. **VHS, Beta** \$24.95 *NOS, HHT, PMS* 🎬🎬🎬½

Late Chrysanthemums A middle-aged geisha has settled into comfortable retirement as a money lender. When she hears a former lover wants to visit her, she tries to recapture her old glamour only to be disillusioned. Based on a short story by Fumiko Hayashi. In Japanese with English subtitles. *AKA:* Bangiku.

1954 101m/B Haruko Sugimura, Chikako Hosokawa, Sadako Sawahura; *D:* Mikio Naruse. **VHS** \$79.95 *WAC, ING* 🎬

Late Extra A novice reporter attempts to track down a notorious bank robber and gets some help from a savvy female journalist. Mason's first role of substance. **1935** 69m/B Virginia Cherrill, James Mason, Alastair Sim, Ian Colin, Clifford McLaglen, Cyril Cusack, David Horne, Antoinette Cellier, Donald Wolfit, Michael Wilding; *D:* Albert Parker. **VHS, Beta** \$16.95 *SNC* 🎬

Late for Dinner In 1962 Willie, a young, married man, and his best friend Frank are framed by a sleazy land developer. On the run, the two decide to become guinea pigs in a cryonics experiment and wind up frozen for 29 years. It's now 1991 and Willie wants to find his family—only his wife is middle-aged and his daughter is all grown-up. Can he make a life with them again or has time indeed passed him by? **1991** (PG) 93m/C Brian Wimmer, Peter Berg, Marcia Gay Harden, Peter Gallagher, Ross Malinger; *D:* W.D. Richter. **VHS** \$19.95 *COL, NLC* 🎬🎬

The Late Show A veteran private detective finds his world turned upside down when his ex-partner comes to visit and winds up dead, and a flaky woman whose cat is missing decides to become his sidekick. Carney and Tomlin are fun to watch in this sleeper, a tribute to the classic detective film noirs. **1977** (PG) 93m/C Art Carney, Lily Tomlin, Bill Macy, Eugene Roche, Joanna Cassidy, John Considine; *D:* Robert Benton. Academy Awards '77 Nominations: Best Original Screenplay; Edgar Allan Poe Awards '77: Best Screenplay; National Board of Review Awards '77: 10 Best Films of the Year. **VHS, Beta** \$64.95 *WAR* 🎬🎬🎬

Late Spring An exquisite Ozu masterpiece. A young woman lives with her widowed father for years. He decides to remarry so that she can begin life for herself. Highly acclaimed, in Japanese with English subtitles. Reworked in 1960 as "Late Autumn." **1949** 107m/B Setsuko Hara, Chishu Ryu, Jun Usami, Haruko Sugimura; *D:* Yasujiro Ozu. **VHS, Beta** \$49.95 *FCT* 🎬🎬🎬🎬

Late Summer Blues Experience the life and death decisions of seven teenagers who have finished their finals and face now a more difficult test: serving in the Israeli Armed Forces in the Suez Canal. In Hebrew with English subtitles. *AKA:* Blues La-Chofesh Ha-Godol. **1987** 101m/C Dor Zweigenbom, Shahar Segal, Yoav Zafir; *D:* Renen Schorr. **VHS** \$79.95 *ERG, AUD, HMV* 🎬🎬

Lathe of Heaven In a late twentieth century world suffocating from pollution, a young man visits a dream specialist. He then dreams of a world free from war, pestilence, and overpopulation. At times, these dreams have disastrous side effects. Based on futuristic novel by Ursula K. LeGuin; produced for PBS. **1980** 120m/C Bruce Davison, Kevin Conway, Margaret Avery; *D:* David Loxton. **VHS, Beta** *WNE* 🎬🎬½

Latin Lovers Turner plays a wealthy heiress who can't decide if men love her for herself or her money in this festive Brazilian romp. Lund and Montalban portray the suitors vying for her affection. Although not one of MGM's best musicals, the music is good because of the Brodszky-Robin tunes. ♪Night and You; Carlotta, You Gotta Be Mine; A Little More of Your Armor; Come To My Arms; I Had To Kiss You.

1953 104m/C Lana Turner, Ricardo Montalban, John Lund, Louis Calhern, Jean Hagen, Eduard Franz, Beulah Bondi; *D:* Mervyn LeRoy; *W:* Isobel Lennart. **VHS** \$19.98 *MGM* 🎬🎬½

Latino The self-tortured adventures of a Chicano Green Beret who, while fighting a covert U.S. military action in war-torn Nicaragua, begins to rebel against the senselessness of the war. **1985** 108m/C Robert Beltran, Annette Cardona, Tony Plana, James Karen, Ricardo Lopez, Luis Torrentes, Juan Carlos Ortiz, Julio Medina; *D:* Haskell Wexler; *W:* Haskell Wexler; *M:* Diane Louie. **VHS, Beta** \$79.98 *FOX, ING* 🎬🎬🎬

Lauderdale Two college schmoes hit the beach looking for beer and babes. Few laughs for the sober and mature. Surf's down in this woofer. **1989** (R) 91m/C Darrel Gilbeau, Michelle Kemp, Jeff Greenman, Lara Belmonte; *D:* Bill Milling. **VHS, Beta** \$19.95 *PSM* Woof!

Laugh with Linder! Compilation of Linder shorts, including "Max Learns to Skate" and "Max and His Dog." **1913** 70m/B Max Linder. **VHS, Beta** \$47.50 *GVV* Woof!

Laughfest Five classic slapstick shorts: "It's a Gift" (1923), with Snub Pollard, "Barney Oldfield's Race for a Life" (1913), "Kid Auto Races" and "Busy Day" (1914), both with Charlie Chaplin, and "Daredevil" (1923), starring Ben Turpin. **191?** 59m/B Ben Turpin, Barney Oldfield, Mabel Normand, Charlie Chaplin, Snub Pollard. **VHS, Beta** \$19.98 *CCB* Woof!

Laughing at Danger Talmadge is the supposedly playboy son of a Washington politician. In reality, he's the dashing "Mr. Pep" who comes to the rescue of a scientist who has invented a death ray and is being stalked by agents of a sinister foreign power. Talmadge was a fine silent-screen action star, though his heavy German action proved a barrier with sound films. **1924** 45m/B Richard Talmadge, Joseph Girard, Eva Novak, Joe Harrington, Stanhope Wheatcroft; *D:* James W. Horne. **VHS** \$16.95 *GPV* 🎬🎬½

Laughing at Life A mercenary leaves his family to fight in South America. Years later, when he is the leader of said country, he meets a man who turns out to be his son. Rehashed plot has been done better. **1933** 72m/B Victor McLaglen, William Boyd, Lois Wilson, Henry B. Walthall, Regis Toomey; *D:* Ford Beebe. **VHS** \$24.95 *NOS, DVT, HEG* 🎬½

The Laughing Policeman Two antagonistic cops embark on a vengeful hunt for a mass murderer through the seamy underbelly of San Francisco. Adapted from the Swedish novel by Per Wahloo and Maj Sjowallo. *AKA:* An Investigation of Murder. **1974** (R) 111m/C Walter Matthau, Bruce Dern, Louis Gossett Jr.; *D:* Stuart Rosenberg; *M:* Charles Fox. **VHS, Beta** \$59.98 *FOX* 🎬🎬½

Laughing Sinners Society girl Crawford attempts suicide after Hamilton dumps her and is rescued by Gable—a Salvation Army worker! Predictable drama with some unintentionally funny moments. Gable and Crawford were having an off-screen romance at the time which accounts for the sparks generated on-screen. Based on the play "Torch Song" by Kenyon Nicholson. **1931** 71m/B Joan Crawford, Neil Hamilton, Clark Gable, Marjorie Rambeau, Guy Kibbee, Cliff Edwards, Roscoe Karns; *D:* Harry Beaumont. **VHS** \$19.98 *MGM* 🎬🎬

Laura A detective assigned to the murder investigation of the late Laura Hunt finds himself falling in love with her painted portrait. Superb collaboration by excellent cast and fine director. Superior suspense yarn, enhanced by a love story. Based on the novel by Vera Caspary. Rouben Mamoulian was the original director, then Preminger finished the film.
1944 85m/B Gene Tierney, Dana Andrews, Clifton Webb, Lane Chandler, Vincent Price, Judith Anderson, Grant Mitchell, Dorothy Adams; **D:** Otto Preminger; **M:** David Raskin. Academy Awards '44: Best Black and White Cinematography; Nominations: Best Director (Preminger), Best Interior Decoration, Best Screenplay, Best Supporting Actor (Webb). **VHS, Beta** $19.98 *FXV, PMS, BTV* 🎬🎬🎬🎬

Laurel & Hardy and the Family Four zany comedies seeing the boys in all kinds of trouble involving homelife. Includes "Brats," "Perfect Day," "Their First Mistake," and "Twice Two."
1933 85m/B Stan Laurel, Oliver Hardy. **VHS** $14.98 *VTR, FCT* 🎬🎬🎬🎬

Laurel & Hardy: Another Fine Mess The boys find themselves the owners of a magnificent Beverly Hills mansion. Yeah right. Lots of physical comedy and hilarious dialogue with a "special appearance" by Laurel in drag as a maid. Based on a sketch written by Laurel's father. Colorized.
1930 25m/C Stan Laurel, Oliver Hardy. **VHS** $9.95 *CAF* 🎬🎬🎬🎬

Laurel & Hardy: At Work Three short films collected here. Includes "Towed in a Hole," "Busy Bodies," and "The Music Box."
1932 70m/B Oliver Hardy, Stan Laurel. **VHS** $14.98 *VTR, FCT* 🎬🎬🎬🎬

Laurel & Hardy: Be Big Stan and Ollie ditch their wives to go to a swinging stag party at their club. Of course everything goes wrong in their quest for lascivious fun. Filled with tons of sight gags. Colorized.
1931 25m/C Stan Laurel, Oliver Hardy. **VHS** $9.95 *CAF, MOV* 🎬🎬🎬🎬

Laurel & Hardy: Below Zero It's the Great Depression of 1929, and Laurel and Hardy are about as depressed as you can get, working for pennies as street musicians. Their luck changes when they find a full wallet lying in the snow. But, as the saying goes, a fool and his money are soon parted. Colorized.
1930 25m/C Stan Laurel, Oliver Hardy. **VHS** $9.95 *CAF, MOV* 🎬🎬🎬🎬

Laurel & Hardy: Berth Marks Laurel & Hardy take a hilarious train trip to Pottsville for a vaudeville performance. Colorized.
1929 25m/C Stan Laurel, Oliver Hardy. **VHS** $9.95 *CAF* 🎬🎬🎬🎬

Laurel & Hardy: Blotto Laurel and Hardy want to get drunk, but they can't get any alcohol and their wives won't let them get away. When they finally do escape, they wind up at the swanky Rainbow Club, where they're drastically out of their element. Colorized.
1930 25m/C Stan Laurel, Oliver Hardy. **VHS** $9.95 *CAF* 🎬🎬🎬🎬

Laurel & Hardy: Brats Stan and Ollie play not only themselves but also their children when their wives go away and they have to babysit. The children, of course, wreak havoc wherever they go, playing on the hilariously oversized props and sets. One of the few films in which only Laurel and Hardy appear. Colorized.

1930 25m/C Stan Laurel, Oliver Hardy. **VHS** $9.95 *CAF, MOV* 🎬🎬🎬🎬

Laurel & Hardy: Chickens Come Home Ollie is running for mayor, but things go crazy when an ex-girlfriend shows up and blackmails him with a compromising photo. Stan, acting as Ollie's campaign manager, tries to help, but things just get worse. A remake of their own film "Love 'Em and Weep." Colorized.
1931 25m/C Stan Laurel, Oliver Hardy, James Finlayson. **VHS** $9.95 *CAF, MOV* 🎬🎬🎬🎬

Laurel & Hardy Comedy Classics, Vol. 1 A collection of four classic comedy shorts starring Laurel and Hardy: "The Music Box," which won an Academy Award for Best Short Subject, "Country Hospital," "The Live Ghost," and "Twice Two," all from 1932-33.
1933 84m/B Stan Laurel, Oliver Hardy, Mae Busch, May Wallace, Charlie Hall, Billy Gilbert. **VHS, Beta** $9.95 *MED* 🎬🎬🎬🎬

Laurel & Hardy Comedy Classics, Vol. 2 A collection of four Laurel and Hardy shorts from 1930 including "Blotto," "Towed in a Hole," "Brats," and "Hog Wild."
1930 75m/B Stan Laurel, Oliver Hardy, Billy Gilbert, Tiny Sandford, Anita Garvin. **VHS, Beta** $9.95 *MED* 🎬🎬🎬🎬

Laurel & Hardy Comedy Classics, Vol. 3 Laurel and Hardy star in four separate comedy shorts, including "Oliver the 8th," "Busy Bodies," "Their First Mistake," and "Dirty Work," all from 1933-34.
1934 75m/B Stan Laurel, Oliver Hardy, Billy Gilbert, Mae Busch, Tiny Sandford. **VHS, Beta** $9.95 *MED* 🎬🎬🎬🎬

Laurel & Hardy Comedy Classics, Vol. 4 Laurel and Hardy star in four of their comedy shorts from 1931-32. Included are "Another Fine Mess," "Come Clean," "Laughing Gravy," and "Any Old Part."
1932 75m/B Stan Laurel, Oliver Hardy, Jacqueline Wells, James Finlayson, Thelma Todd. **VHS, Beta** $9.95 *MED* 🎬🎬🎬🎬

Laurel & Hardy Comedy Classics, Vol. 5 Four classic comedy shorts starring Laurel and Hardy. Included are "Be Big," "The Perfect Day," "Night Owls," and "Help Mates," from 1929-31.
1931 84m/B Stan Laurel, Oliver Hardy, Edgar Kennedy, James Finlayson, Blanche Payson. **VHS, Beta** $19.95 *MED* 🎬🎬🎬🎬

Laurel & Hardy Comedy Classics, Vol. 6 Laurel and Hardy comedy shorts are presented in this package: "Our Wife," "The Fixer Uppers," "Them Thar Hills," and "Tit for Tat," from 1932-35.
1935 75m/B Stan Laurel, Oliver Hardy, Charlie Hall, Billy Gilbert, Ben Turpin, Mae Busch, James Finlayson. **VHS, Beta** $19.95 *MED* 🎬🎬🎬🎬

Laurel & Hardy Comedy Classics, Vol. 7 Four Laurel and Hardy two-reelers are combined on this tape: "Me and My Pal" (1933), "The Midnight Patrol" (1933), "Thicker than Water" (1935), and the classic "Below Zero" (1930).
193? 90m/B Stan Laurel, Oliver Hardy, Mae Busch, Daphne Pollard, James Finlayson. **VHS, Beta** $19.95 *MED* 🎬🎬🎬🎬

Laurel & Hardy Comedy Classics, Vol. 8 Compilation of Laurel and Hardy shorts includes: "Men O' War" (1929), "Scram" (1932), "Laurel and Hardy Murder Case" (1930) and "One Good Turn" (1931).

193? 90m/B Stan Laurel, Oliver Hardy, Lewis R. Foster, James W. Horne, James Parrott. **VHS, Beta** $19.95 *MED* 🎬🎬🎬🎬

Laurel & Hardy Comedy Classics, Vol. 9 Includes the shorts: "Beau Hunks" (1931), "Chickens Come Home" (1931), "Going Bye-Bye" (1934), and "Berth Marks" (1929).
193? 100m/B Stan Laurel, Oliver Hardy. **VHS, Beta** $19.95 *MED* 🎬🎬🎬🎬

Laurel & Hardy: Hog Wild Hilarity ensues when Laurel and Hardy try to fix the radio antenna on Hardy's roof. It may sound easy, but come on, this is Laurel and Hardy. Colorized.
1930 25m/C Stan Laurel, Oliver Hardy. **VHS** $9.95 *CAF, MOV* 🎬🎬🎬🎬

Laurel & Hardy: Laughing Gravy The boys' pet dog, oddly named Laughing Gravy, gets them into trouble with their landlord who keeps trying to evict them. So funny even the mashed potatos will laugh. Colorized.
1931 25m/C Stan Laurel, Oliver Hardy. **VHS** $9.95 *CAF, MOV* 🎬🎬🎬🎬

Laurel & Hardy: Men O'War Laurel & Hardy star as two sailors on shore leave trying to impress the ladies. Things go from bad to worse when they take two ladies out on a date. Features the memorable soda fountain and canoe scenes. Colorized.
1929 25m/C Stan Laurel, Oliver Hardy, Gloria Greer, Anne Cornwall. **VHS** $9.95 *CAF* 🎬🎬🎬🎬

Laurel & Hardy: Night Owls When a cop needs to capture some crooks to save his job, he sets up a fake break-in and catches two bungling burglars—Laurel and Hardy. Lots of sight gags and slapstick. Colorized.
1930 25m/C Stan Laurel, Oliver Hardy, Edgar Kennedy. **VHS** $9.95 *CAF, MOV* 🎬🎬🎬🎬

Laurel & Hardy On the Lam Four Laurel & Hardy classics are collected, including "Scram," "Another Fine Mess," "One Good Turn," and "Going Bye-Bye."
1930 90m/B Oliver Hardy, Stan Laurel. **VHS** $14.98 *VTR, FCT* 🎬🎬🎬🎬

Laurel & Hardy: Perfect Day Laurel & Hardy plan a quiet picnic with their wives, but car trouble turns their day into a disaster. Colorized.
1929 25m/C Stan Laurel, Oliver Hardy, Edgar Kennedy. **VHS** $9.95 *CAF* 🎬🎬🎬🎬

Laurel & Hardy Special A unique program of Laurel and Hardy films including the first film they appeared in together—"Lucky Dog" (1918), "The Soilers," a wild Laurel spoof of The Spoilers, "Kill or Cure," "Near Dublin," "The Sleuths," "Laurel and Hardy's Trip to Britain," and "Stan Visits Ollie," a color home movie of their last visit together.
19?? 60m/B Stan Laurel, Oliver Hardy. **VHS, Beta** $57.95 *GVV* 🎬🎬½

Laurel & Hardy Spooktacular Stan and Ollie scream through four spooky comedies, including "The Live Ghost," "The Laurel-Hardy Murder Case," "Oliver the Eighth" and "Dirty Work."
1934 95m/B **VHS** $14.98 *VTR, FCT* 🎬🎬½

Laurel & Hardy: Stan "Helps" Ollie Four Stan and Ollie classics including "County Hospital," "Me and My Pal," "Hog Wild," and "Helpmates."
1933 85m/B Stan Laurel, Oliver Hardy. **VHS** $14.98 *VTR, FCT* 🎬🎬½

1930 25m/C Stan Laurel, Oliver Hardy. **VHS** $9.95 *CAF, MOV* 🎬🎬🎬🎬

Laurel & Hardy: The Hoose-Gow Laurel and Hardy are mistakenly picked up by the police and sent to prison to do hard labor. Hilarity ensues when they try to convince the warden that they're innocent. Colorized.
1929 25m/C VHS $9.95 CAF, MOV 🎬🎬½

Laurel Avenue Looks at the life of an extended working-class black family in St. Paul, Minnesota, over a busy weekend. Large cast includes family heads Jake and Maggie who live with their basketball coach son, teenage daughter, and elderly uncle. Other children include fraternal twin Yolanda, a cop married to a white man, who knows sister Rolanda's (a recovering drug addict) son is a dealer. Their brother Marcus manages a Mafia-controlled clothing store and is involved in some shady deals while brother Woody is an aspiring musician. The four households are all united at a disastrous Sunday afternoon party. Made for cable television.
1993 156m/C Mary Alice, Mel Winkler, Scott Lawrence, Malinda Williams, Jay Brooks, Juanita Jennings, Rhonda Stubbins White, Monte Russell, Vonte Sweet; **D:** Carl Franklin; **W:** Michael Henry Brown. **VHS $49.99** HBO 🎬🎬½

The Lavender Hill Mob A prim and prissy bank clerk schemes to melt the bank's gold down and re-mold it into miniature Eiffel Tower paper-weights for later resale. The foolproof plan appears to succeed, but then develops a snag. An excellent comedy that is still a delight to watch. Also available with "The Man in the White Suit" on laserdisc.
1951 78m/B Alec Guinness, Stanley Holloway, Sidney James, Alfie Bass, Marjorie Fielding, John Gregson; **Cameos:** Audrey Hepburn; **D:** Charles Crichton; **W:** T.E.B. Clarke. Academy Awards '52: Best Story & Screenplay; Nominations: Best Actor (Guinness); British Academy Awards '51: Best Film. **VHS, Beta $19.95** FCT, HMV 🎬🎬🎬½

L'Avventura A stark, dry and minimalist exercise in narrative by Antonioni, dealing with the search for a girl on an Italian island by her lethargic socialite friends who eventually forget her in favor of their own preoccupations. A highly acclaimed, innovative film; somewhat less effective now, in the wake of many film treatments of angst and amorality. Subtitled in English. Laser edition features the original trailer, commentary and a collection of still photographs from Antonioni's work. **AKA:** The Adventure.
1960 145m/C Monica Vitti, Gabriel Ferzetti, Lea Massari, Dominique Blanchar, James Addams; **D:** Michelangelo Antonioni; **W:** Tonino Guerra, Michelangelo Antonioni. **VHS, Beta $29.95** CVC, VDM, VYG 🎬🎬🎬½

Law and Disorder Two average Joes, fed up with the rate of rising crime, start their own auxiliary police group. Alternately funny and serious with good performances from the leads.
1974 (R) 103m/C Carroll O'Connor, Ernest Borgnine, Ann Wedgeworth, Anita Dangler, Leslie Ackerman, Karen Black, Jack Kehoe; **D:** Ivan Passer; **M:** Angelo Badalamenti. **VHS** COL 🎬🎬½

The Law and Jake Wade Gripping western starring Taylor as a former bank robber turned marshal. His old partner (Widmark) turns up and forces Taylor to lead him to buried loot.
1958 86m/C Robert Taylor, Richard Widmark, Patricia Owens, Robert Middleton, Henry Silva, DeForest Kelley, Burt Douglas, Eddie Firestone; **D:** John Sturges. **VHS $19.98** MGM 🎬🎬½

Law and Lawless A roving cowboy brings justice to a gang of cattle thieves in this film.
1933 58m/B Jack Hoxie. **VHS, Beta $19.95** NOS, DVT 🎬

Law and Order Billy the Kid impersonates a Cavalry lieutenant in order to swindle his aunt out of her money. Also called "Billy the Kid's Law and Order."
1942 58m/B Buster Crabbe, Al "Fuzzy" St. John. **VHS, Beta $9.95** VDM, MRV 🎬🎬

Law of Desire A wicked, Almodovarian attack-on-decency farce about a love-obsessed gay Madridian and his transsexual brother-sister, among others, getting hopelessly entangled in cross-gender relationships. Unlike the work of any other director; in Spanish with English subtitles. **AKA:** La Ley del Deseo.
1986 100m/C Carmen Maura, Eusebio Poncela, Antonio Banderas, Bibi Andersson; **D:** Pedro Almodovar; **W:** Pedro Almodovar. **VHS, Beta $79.95** CCN, ING, TPV 🎬🎬🎬½

Law of the Jungle A lady scientist and a fugitive team up to uncover a secret Nazi radio base in the jungle.
1942 61m/B Arline Judge, John "Dusty" King, Mantan Moreland, Martin Wilkins, Arthur O'Connell; **D:** Jean Yarborough. **VHS, Beta $16.95** SNC 🎬½

Law of the Land A made-for-television sagebrush epic with the author/artist of "Garfield" portraying an accused but innocent man searching for a murderer.
1976 100m/C Jim Davis, Don Johnson, Barbara Parkins, Charles Martin Smith. **VHS, Beta $14.98** WOV 🎬

Law of the Lash Cowboys and rustlers battle it out.
1947 54m/B Lash LaRue, Al "Fuzzy" St. John. **VHS, Beta $9.99** NOS, MRV, VCN 🎬

Law of the Pampas Boyd and Hayden ride off to South America to deliver some cattle, but the bad guys intervene. This is Toler's first outing as Hoppy's sidekick, briefly replacing "Gabby" Hayes.
1939 72m/B William Boyd, Russell Hayden, Steffi Duna, Sidney Toler, Sidney Blackmer, Pedro de Cordoba, Eddie Dean, Glenn Strange; **D:** Nate Watt. **VHS $19.95** NOS 🎬🎬

Law of the Saddle The Lone Rider pits himself against a gang of outlaws.
1945 60m/B Bob Livingston. **VHS, Beta $29.95** VCN, MLB 🎬½

Law of the Sea A family on a sinking ship is rescued by a lecherous sea captain who makes advances on the wife and blinds the husband in a fight. Twenty years later, the husband meets him again, recognizes his laugh and exacts revenge.
1938 63m/B Priscilla Dean, Sally Blane, Ralph Ince, Rex Bell, William Farnum. **VHS, Beta $24.95** VYY 🎬

Law of the Texan Jones goes undercover to stop Harlan and his gang from stealing a town's store of silver bullion.
1938 54m/B Buck Jones, Dorothy Fay, Kenneth Harlan, Don Douglas, Matty Kemp, Robert F. (Bob) Kortman, Dave O'Brien; **D:** Elmer Clifton. **VHS $11.95** GPV 🎬½

Law of the Underworld An innocent couple is framed for the robbery of a jewelry store which resulted in the death of a clerk. When they are arrested, their fate lies in the hands of the gangster responsible for the crime. Will he let them fry in the electric chair, or will his conscience get the better of him?
1938 58m/B Chester Morris, Anne Shirley, Eduardo Ciannelli, Walter Abel, Richard Bond, Lee Patrick, Paul Guilfoyle, Frank M. Thomas Sr., Eddie Acuff, Jack Arnold; **D:** Lew Landers. **VHS, Beta $16.95** SNC 🎬½

Law of the Wild The search for a magnificent stallion that was hijacked by race racketeers before a big sweepstakes race is shown in this 12 chapter serial.
1934 230m/B Bob Custer, Ben Turpin, Lucille Browne, Lafe McKee; **D:** B. Reeves Eason, Armand Schaefer. **VHS $24.95** GPV, NOS, VCN 🎬

The Law Rides Rush of gold claims causes an outbreak of murder and robbery.
1936 57m/B Bob Steele. **VHS, Beta $29.95** DVT 🎬

The Law Rides Again Prairie lawmen bring a cheating Indian agent to justice.
1943 56m/B Ken Maynard, Hoot Gibson, Betty Miles, Jack LaRue; **D:** William Castle. **VHS $19.95** NOS, MRV, DVT 🎬

Law West of Tombstone A former outlaw moves to a dangerous frontier town in order to restore the peace.
1938 73m/B Tim Holt, Harry Carey Sr., Evelyn Brent; **D:** Glenn Tryon. **VHS, Beta** MED 🎬🎬½

Lawless Frontier In the early West, the Duke fights for law and order.
1935 53m/B John Wayne, George "Gabby" Hayes, Sheila Terry, Earl Dwire; **D:** Robert North Bradbury. **VHS, Beta $9.98** REP, NOS, VYY 🎬½

The Lawless Land Post-holocaust America is ruled by a tyrant. Two young lovers who can't take it anymore go on the lam to escape the despotic rule.
1988 (R) 81m/C Leon Berkeley, Xander Berkeley, Nick Corri, Amanda Peterson; **D:** Jon Hess; **W:** Tony Cinciripini, Larry Leahy. **VHS, Beta $14.95** MGM 🎬🎬

The Lawless Nineties Wayne plays a government agent sent to guarantee honest elections in the Wyoming territory. Hayes is exceptional as the newspaper editor who backs him up. Re-made in 1940 as "The Dark Command."
1936 55m/B John Wayne, Ann Rutherford, Lane Chandler, Harry Woods, George "Gabby" Hayes, Charles "Blackie" King, Sam Flint; **D:** Joseph Kane. **VHS $12.98** REP 🎬

Lawless Range Wayne and the marshal's posse save the ranchers from trouble.
1935 56m/B John Wayne, Sheila Manners, Jack Curtis, Earl Dwire; **D:** Robert North Bradbury. **VHS $9.98** REP, NOS, MRV 🎬½

A Lawless Street Scott portrays a sheriff who rides the Colorado Territory cleaning up lawless towns. His dedication to duty has caused his wife to leave him and she won't come back until he lays downs his guns forever, which may come sooner than they think after he rides into the corrupt town of Medicine Bend. Based on the novel "Marshal of Medicine Bend" by Brad Ward.
1955 78m/B Randolph Scott, Angela Lansbury, Warner Anderson, Jean Parker, Wallace Ford, John Emery, James Bell, Ruth Donnelly, Michael Pate, Don Megowan, Jeanette Nolan; **D:** Joseph H. Lewis; **W:** Kenneth Gamet. **VHS $19.95** COL 🎬🎬½

Lawman Brutal western about a fanatical U.S. marshal (Lancaster) who rides into town after Cobb and his six ranch hands. The cowboys have accidentally killed a man and Lancaster is determined to bring them to justice no matter what the cost. Though the entire town is against his mission that doesn't stop his mission. Brooding and relentless with fine performances, particularly by Ryan as the local marshall living on past glories.
1971 (PG) 95m/C Burt Lancaster, Robert Ryan, Lee J. Cobb, Sheree North, Joseph Wiseman, Robert Duvall, Albert Salmi, J.D. Cannon, John McGiver, Richard Jordan, John Beck, Ralph Waite, John Hillerman, Richard Bull; **D:** Michael

Winner; **W:** Gerald Wilson. **VHS $19.98**
MGM *III*

A Lawman is Born A tough-as-nails marshal goes gunning for a pack of no-good, land-stealing varmits in this installment of the Johnny Mack Brown movie serials. Be sure to count the number of bullets each cowboy can fire from a six-shooter before being forced to reload; you may be surprised.
1937 58m/B Johnny Mack Brown, Iris Meredith, Warner Richmond, Mary MacLaren, Dick Curtis, Earle Hodgins, Charles "Blackie" King, Frank LaRue; **D:** Sam Newfield. **VHS, Beta $19.99**
NOS, MOV, MRV *III*

Lawmen Government agents fight to enforce the law in the badlands.
1944 55m/B Johnny Mack Brown, Raymond Hatton. **VHS, Beta $19.95** NOS, DVT *II½*

The Lawnmower Man Brosnan is a scientist who uses Fahey, a dim-witted gardener, as a guinea pig to test his experiments in "virtual reality," an artificial computer environment. With the use of drugs and high-tech equipment, Brosnan is able to increase Fahey's mental powers—but not necessarily for the better. Fantastic special effects and a memorable "virtual reality" sex scene. Available in an unrated version which contains 32 more minutes of footage. So minimally based on a short story by Stephen King that the author sued (and won) to have his name removed from the film.
1992 (R) 108m/C Jeff Fahey, Pierce Brosnan, Jenny Wright, Mark Bringleson, Geoffrey Lewis, Jeremy Slate, Dean Norris; **D:** Brett Leonard; **W:** Brett Leonard, Gimel Everett. **VHS $19.95** COL, FCT, MOV *II*

Lawrence of Arabia Exceptional biography of T.E. Lawrence, a British military "observer" who strategically aids the Bedouins battle the Turks during WWI. Lawrence, played masterfully by O'Toole in his first major film, is a hero consumed more by a need to reject British tradition than to save the Arab population. He takes on Arab costume and a larger-than-life persona. Stunning photography of the desert in all its harsh reality. Laser edition contains 20 minutes of restored footage and a short documentary about the making of the film. Available in letterboxed format.
1962 (PG) 221m/C Peter O'Toole, Omar Sharif, Anthony Quinn, Alec Guinness, Jack Hawkins, Claude Rains, Anthony Quayle, Arthur Kennedy, Jose Ferrer; **D:** David Lean; **W:** Robert Bolt; **M:** Maurice Jarre. Academy Awards '62: Best Art Direction/Set Decoration (Color), Best Color Cinematography, Best Director (Lean), Best Film Editing, Best Picture, Best Sound, Best Original Score; Nominations: Best Actor (O'Toole), Best Adapted Screenplay, Best Supporting Actor (Sharif); British Academy Awards '62: Best Actor (O'Toole), Best Film; Directors Guild of America Awards '62: Best Director (Lean); Golden Globe Awards '63: Best Director (Lean), Best Film—Drama, Best Supporting Actor (Sharif). **VHS, Beta $34.95** COL, VYG, CRC *IIIII*

The Lawrenceville Stories Chronicles the life and times of a group of young men at the prestigious Lawrenceville prep school in 1905. Galligan plays William Hicks, alias "The Prodigious Hickey," the ringleader of their obnoxious stunts. Based on the stories of Owen Johnson, which originally ran in the Saturday Evening Post. Shown on "American Playhouse" and The Disney Channel. Tapes are available separately or as a set.
198? 180m/C Zach Galligan, Edward Herrmann, Nicholas Rowe, Allan Goldstein, Robert Joy, Stephen Baldwin; **D:** Robert Iscove. **VHS $69.95** MON, BTV *II½*

Laws of Gravity Critically acclaimed debut film from 29-year-old writer/director Gomez is a three day slice of life set in Brooklyn. Hotheaded Jon (Trese) and married friend Jimmy (Greene) channel violent energy into their relationships and illegal activities. Camera follows "cinema verite" style and captures urban tension as it trails them through a gun heist and subsequent arrest.
1992 (R) 100m/C Peter Greene, Edie Falco, Adam Trese, Arabella Field, Paul Schulzie; **D:** Nick Gomez; **W:** Nick Gomez. **VHS $89.95** TRI *III*

The Lazarus Syndrome Astute doctor teams up with an ex-patient of the chief of surgery in an effort to expose the chief's unethical surgical procedures.
1979 90m/C Louis Gossett Jr., E.G. Marshall. **VHS, Beta** NO *III*

LBJ: A Biography Produced for the PBS series "The American Experience," this four-hour revisionist look at LBJ is one of the most critically acclaimed political documentaries of our time. Divided into four segments. "Beautiful Texas" chronicles Johnson's rise to power. "My Fellow Americans" focuses on his years as an unelected president. The Great Society and and the escalation of war in Vietnam are covered in "We Shall Overcome." "The Last Believer" highlights events leading to Johnson's withdrawal from politics.
1991 240m/C D: David Grubin; **W:** David Grubin. **VHS $39.95** PBS, SIG *III*

LBJ: The Early Years The early years of President Lyndon Baines Johnson's political career are dramatized in this made-for-television movie. Winning performances hoist this above other biographies.
1988 144m/C Randy Quaid, Patti LuPone, Morgan Brittany, Pat Hingle, Kevin McCarthy, Barry Corbin, Charles Frank; **D:** Peter Werner. **VHS, Beta $29.95** FRH *III*

Le Bal You won't find many films with the music of Paul McCartney and Chopin in the credits, and even fewer without dialogue. With only music and dancing the film uses a French dance hall to illustrate the changes in French society over a fifty-year period. Based on a French play. ♫La Vie en Rose; In the Mood; Michelle; Top Hat White Tie and Tails; Let's Face the Music and Dance; Harlem Nocturne; Shuffle Blues; Tutti Frutti; Only You.
1982 112m/C D: Ettore Scola; **M:** Irving Berlin, Paul McCartney, John Lennon, Frederick Chopin, Vladimir Cosma. Academy Awards '83 Nominations: Best Foreign Language Film; Cesar Awards '84: Best Director (Scola), Best Film. **VHS $79.99** WAR, FCT, ING *III*

Le Beau Mariage An award-winning comedy from the great French director about a zealous woman trying to find a husband and the unsuspecting man she chooses to marry. In French with English subtitles. *AKA:* A Good Marriage; The Well-Made Marriage.
1982 (R) 97m/C Beatrice Romand, Arielle Dombasle, Andre Dussollier; **D:** Eric Rohmer; **W:** Eric Rohmer. **VHS, Beta $59.95** ING *III*

Le Beau Serge A convalescing Frenchman returns to his home village and tries to help an old friend, who's become a hopeless drunkard, change his life. Chabrol's first film, and a major forerunner of the nouvelle vague. In French with English subtitles. *AKA:* Handsome Serge.
1958 97m/B Gerard Blain, Jean-Claude Brialy, Michele Meritz, Bernadette LaFont; **D:** Claude Chabrol; **W:** Claude Chabrol. **VHS, Beta $79.95** FCT *III*

Le Bonheur A seemingly happily married carpenter (Drouot) takes a vacation with his wife and children where he meets the local postal clerk and the two begin a passionate affair. Unwilling to leave his family, Drouot believes the two women can share him but when his wife discovers his infidelity she kills herself. His grief does not cause Drouot to stop the affair, instead he moves in with his mistress. An uninvolving, unbelievable tale with a lovely Mozart score. In French with English subtitles. *AKA:* Happiness.
1965 87m/C Jean-Claude Drouot, Claire Drouot, Marie-France Boyer; **D:** Agnes Varda; **W:** Agnes Varda. **VHS $29.95** FCT *II½*

Le Boucher In a provincial French town a sophisticated schoolmistress is courted by the shy local butcher—who turns out to be a sex murderer. A well-played thriller that looks at sexual frustration. In French with English subtitles. *AKA:* The Butcher.
1969 94m/C Stephane Audran, Jean Yanne, Antonio Passallia; **D:** Claude Chabrol; **W:** Claude Chabrol. **VHS $79.95** CVC, ING *III*

Le Bourgeois Gentilhomme Translated "The Would-Be Gentleman." A comedy-ballet in five acts in prose, performed by the Comedie Francaise. Subtitled in English.
1958 97m/C VHS, Beta $24.95 VYY, APD, ING *II*

Le Cas du Dr. Laurent A country doctor in a small French town tries to introduce methods of natural childbirth to the native women, but meets opposition from the superstitious villagers. Fine performance by Gabin.
1957 88m/B Jean Gabin, Nicole Courcel; **D:** Jean-Paul LeChanois. **VHS, Beta $29.95** NOS, VYY, DVT *III*

Le Cavaleur A light hearted comedy about a philandering concert pianist. *AKA:* Practice Makes Perfect.
1978 90m/C Jean Rochefort, Lila Kedrova, Nicole Garcia, Annie Girardot, Danielle Darrieux; **D:** Philippe de Broca; **M:** Georges Delerue. **VHS, Beta** NO *II*

Le Chat A middle-aged couple's marriage dissolves into a hate-filled battle of wits, centering around the husband's love for their cat. In French with English subtitles. *AKA:* The Cat.
1975 88m/C Jean Gabin, Simone Signoret, Annie Cordy, Jacques Rispal; **D:** Pierre Granier-Deferre. **VHS, Beta $59.95** FCT, LUM *III½*

Le Complot When de Gaulle announces his intention to abandon Algeria, several army officers, feeling that their service has been in vain, stage a coup. There's suspense aplenty as the Gaulists, the leftists, and the police spy and are spied upon. In French with English subtitles. *AKA:* The Conspiracy.
1973 120m/C Michel Bouquet, Jean Rochefort; **D:** Rene Gainville. **VHS $79.95** CVC, FCT, ING *III*

Le Corbeau A great, notorious drama about a small French village whose everyday serenity is ruptured by a series of poison pen letters that lead to suicide and despair. The film was made within Nazi-occupied France, sponsored by the Nazis, and has been subjected to much misdirected malice because of it. In French with English subtitles. *AKA:* The Raven.
1943 92m/B Pierre Fresnay, Noel Roquevort, Ginette LeClerc, Pierre Larquey, Antoine Belpetre; **D:** Henri-Georges Clouzot. **VHS, Beta $24.95** NOS, HHT, ING *III*

Le Crabe Tambour Rochefort plays a dying naval captain remembering his relationship with his first officer. Revealed via flashbacks, the recollections concern the adven-

tures which transpired on a North Atlantic supply ship. Great performances from all and award-winning cinematography by Raoul Coutard. Winner of several French Cesars. A French script booklet is available.
1977 120m/C Jean Rochefort, Claude Rich, Jacques Dufilho, Jacques Perrin, Odile Versois, Aurore Clement; *D:* Pierre Schoendoerffer. **VHS $59.95** *INT, IME, APD 𝄈𝄈𝄈*

Le Dernier Combat A stark film about life after a devastating nuclear war marks the directorial debut of Besson. The characters fight to survive in a now speechless world by staking territorial claims and forming new relationships with other survivors. An original and expressive film made without dialogue. *AKA:* The Last Battle.
1984 (R) 93m/B Pierre Jolivet, Fritz Wepper, Jean Reno, Jean Bouise, Christiane Kruger; *D:* Luc Besson; *W:* Luc Besson. **VHS, Beta** COL, OM 𝄈𝄈𝄈

Le Doulos Compelling story of an ex-convict and his buddy, a man who may be a police informant. Chronicles the efforts of the snitch (the "doulos" of the title) to bring the criminal element before the law. Melville blends in several plot twists and breathes a new-French life into the cliche-ridden genre.
1961 108m/B Serge Reggiani, Jean-Paul Belmondo, Michel Piccoli; *D:* Jean-Pierre Melville. **VHS, Beta $59.95** *INT, TPV, ING 𝄈𝄈𝄈*

Le Gendarme de Saint-Tropez Officer Ludovic Cruchot's plans for career advancement are on shaky ground after he is transferred to St. Tropez where his daughter has a little too much fun at the beach. Also available dubbed.
1967 ?m/C Louis de Funes, Michel Galabru, Genevieve Grad, Jean LeFevre, Christian Marin. **VHS $59.95** *FRA, FCT 𝄈𝄈½*

Le Gentleman D'Epsom A French comedy about a breezy con man who scams everyone around him in order to keep up his upwardly mobile appearance and to put his bets down at the racetrack. Subtitled in English.
1962 83m/B Jean Gabin, Paul Frankeur. **VHS, Beta $19.95** *ING, BAR 𝄈𝄈*

Le Grand Chemin A sweet, slice-of-life French film about a young boy's idyllic summer on a family friend's farm while his mother is having a baby. Hubert's son plays the boy Louis in this retelling of the director's own childhood. In French with English subtitles. Remade with an American setting in 1991 as "Paradise." *AKA:* The Grand Highway.
1987 107m/C Anemone, Richard Bohringer, Antoine Hubert, Vanessa Guedj, Christine Pascal, Raoul Billerey, Pascale Roberts; *D:* Jean-Loup Hubert; *W:* Jean-Loup Hubert; *M:* Georges Granier. **VHS, Beta $29.95** *FCT, ING, IME 𝄈𝄈𝄈*

Le Joli Mai A famous documentary that established Marker, depicting the everyday life of Paris denizens on the occasion of the end of the Algerian War, May 1962, when France was at peace for the first time since 1939. In French with English subtitles.
1962 180m/B *D:* Chris Marker. **VHS, Beta $29.95** *FCT 𝄈𝄈𝄈*

Le Jour Se Leve The dark, expressionist film about a sordid and destined murder/love triangle that starts with a police standoff and evolves into a series of flashbacks. The film that put Carne and Gabin on the cinematic map. Highly acclaimed. French with English subtitles. Remade in 1947 as "The Long Night." *AKA:* Daybreak.
1939 85m/B Jean Gabin, Jules Berry, Arletty, Jacqueline Laurent; *D:* Marcel Carne. **VHS, Beta $24.95** *VYY, HMV, APD 𝄈𝄈𝄈½*

Le Magnifique Belmondo is a master spy and novelist who mixes fantasy with reality when he chases women and solves cases. *AKA:* The Magnificent One.
1976 84m/C Jean-Paul Belmondo, Jacqueline Bisset; *W:* Francis Veber; *M:* Claude Bolling. **VHS, Beta $59.95** *PSM 𝄈𝄈*

Le Mans The famous 24-hour Grand Prix race sets the stage for this tale of love and speed. McQueen (who did his own driving) is the leading race driver, a man who battles competition, fear of death by accident, and emotional involvement. Excellent documentary-style race footage almost makes up for weak plot and minimal acting.
1971 (G) 106m/C Steve McQueen, Elga Andersen, Ronald Leigh-Hunt, Luc Merenda; *D:* Lee H. Katzin. **VHS $39.98** *FOX, FCT 𝄈𝄈𝄈*

Le Million A comedy/musical masterpiece of the early sound era which centers on an artist's adventures in searching for a winning lottery ticket throughout Paris. Highly acclaimed member of the Clair school of subtle French farce. In French with English subtitles.
1931 89m/B Annabella, Rene Lefevre, Paul Olivier, Louis Allibert; *D:* Rene Clair. **VHS, Beta $24.95** *VYY, NOS, DVT 𝄈𝄈𝄈½*

Le Petit Amour A popular French comedy about the fateful romance between a 40-year-old divorced woman and a 15-year-old boy obsessed with a kung fu video game. In French with English subtitles. *AKA:* Kung Fu Master.
1987 (R) 80m/C Jane Birkin, Mathieu Demy, Charlotte Gainsbourg, Lou Doillon; *D:* Agnes Varda. **VHS, Beta $79.95** *PSM 𝄈𝄈𝄈*

Le Plaisir An anthology of three Guy de Maupassant stories, "Le Masque," "Le Modele," and "La Maison Teillier," about the search for pleasure. In French with English subtitles. *AKA:* House of Pleasure.
1952 97m/B Claude Dauphin, Simone Simon, Jean Gabin, Danielle Darrieux; *D:* Max Ophuls. **VHS, Beta $24.95** *NOS, DVT, ING 𝄈𝄈*

Le Repos du Guerrier Star vehicle for Bardot in which she plays a respectable woman who abandons societal norms to pursue an unbalanced lover. In French with English subtitles. *AKA:* Warrior's Rest.
1962 100m/C Brigitte Bardot, Robert Hossein, James Robertson Justice, Jean-Mark Bory; *D:* Roger Vadim. **VHS, Beta $19.95** *BAR, ING 𝄈*

Le Secret This classic French thriller with a shocking ending finds an escaped convict seeking shelter with a reclusive couple in the mountains. His tales of abuse and torture create tension for the pair as one believes the woeful story and the other doesn't. Dubbed in English.
1974 103m/C Jean-Louis Trintignant, Philippe Noiret, Jean-Francois Adam; *D:* Robert Enrico; *M:* Ennio Morricone. **VHS, Beta** NO 𝄈𝄈

Le Sex Shop A man turns his little book store into a porn equipment palace, to make ends meet. When his relationship with his wife gets boring, they begin to use their erotic merchandise and adopt a swinging lifestyle.
1973 (R) 92m/C Claude Berri, Juliet Berto, Daniel Auteuil, Nathalie Delon; *D:* Claude Berri; *M:* Serge Gainsbourg. **VHS, Beta** COL 𝄈𝄈𝄈

Leader of the Band An out-of-work musician tries to train the world's worst high school band. Landesberg helps this attempted comedy along.
1987 (PG) 90m/C Steve Landesburg, Gailard Sartain, Mercedes Ruehl, James Martinez, Calvert Deforest; *D:* Nessa Hyams; *M:* Dick Hyman. **VHS, Beta $14.95** *LIV 𝄈𝄈*

The League of Gentlemen An ex-Army officer plots a daring bank robbery using specially skilled military personnel and irreproachable panache. Hilarious British humor fills the screen.
1960 115m/B Jack Hawkins, Nigel Patrick, Richard Attenborough, Roger Livesey, Bryan Forbes; *D:* Basil Dearden. **VHS, Beta $39.95** *HMV, FCT 𝄈𝄈𝄈½*

A League of Their Own Charming look at sports history and the Rockford Peaches, one of the teams in the real-life All American Girls Professional Baseball League, formed in the 40s when the men were off at war. Main focus is on sibling rivalry between Davis, the beautiful, crackerjack catcher, and Petty, the younger, insecure pitcher. Boozy coach Hanks is wonderful as he reluctantly leads the team; he also gets credit for the classic "There's no crying in baseball" scene. Great cast of supporting characters, including sarcastic talent scout Lovitz, opinionated, sleazy taxi dancer Madonna, loud-mouthed O'Donnell, and shy, homely Cavanagh. Lots of baseball for the sports fan.
1992 (PG) 127m/C Tom Hanks, Geena Davis, Madonna, Lori Petty, Jon Lovitz, David Strathairn, Garry Marshall, Bill Pullman, Rosie O'Donnell, Megan Cavanagh, Tracy Reiner, Bitty Schram, Ann Cusack, Anne Elizabeth Ramsay, Freddie Simpson, Renee Coleman; *D:* Penny Marshall; *W:* Lowell Ganz, Babaloo Mandel; *M:* Hans Zimmer. **VHS, Beta, 8mm $19.95** COL 𝄈𝄈𝄈

Lean on Me The romanticized version of the career of Joe Clark, a tough New Jersey teacher who became the principal of the state's toughest, worst school and, through controversial hard-line tactics, turned it around.
1989 (PG-13) 109m/C Morgan Freeman, Robert Guillaume, Beverly Todd, Alan North, Lynne Thigpen, Robin Bartlett, Michael Beach, Ethan Phillips, Regina Taylor; *D:* John G. Avildsen; *W:* Michael Schiffer; *M:* Bill Conti. **VHS, Beta, 8mm $19.98** *WAR, FCT 𝄈𝄈𝄈*

Leap of Faith Jonas Nightengale (Martin) is a traveling evangelist/scam artist whose tour bus is stranded in an impoverished farm town. Nevertheless he sets up his show and goes to work, aided by the technology utilized by accomplice Winger. Both Martin and Winger begin to have a change of heart after experiencing love—Winger with local sheriff Neeson and Martin after befriending a waitress (Davidovich) and her crippled brother (Haas). Martin is in his element as the slick revivalist with the hidden heart but the film is soft-headed as well as soft-hearted.
1992 (PG-13) 110m/C Steve Martin, Debra Winger, Lolita Davidovich, Liam Neeson, Lukas Haas, Meatloaf, Philip S. Hoffman, M.C. Gainey, La Chanze, Delores Hall, John Toles-Bey, Albertina Walker, Ricky Dillard; *D:* Richard Pearce; *W:* Janus Cercone; *M:* Cliff Eidelman. **VHS, Beta $19.95** *PAR, BTV 𝄈𝄈½*

Leap Year Made at the apex of the 300 pound comedian's career, "Leap Year" wasn't released in the States until the sixties. Tried for manslaughter in 1921 (with two hung juries), Fatty was forced off camera and his films were taken out of circulation (although he did return to cinema behind the camera using the pseudonym William Goodrich).
1921 60m/B Fatty Arbuckle. **VHS, Beta $24.95** *GPV, FCT 𝄈𝄈½*

The Learning Tree A beautifully photographed adaptation of Parks' biographical novel about a fourteen-year-old black boy in the 1920s South, living on the verge of manhood, maturity, love, and wisdom.
1969 (PG) 107m/C Kyle Johnson, Alex Clarke, Estelle Evans, Dana Elcar; **D:** Gordon Parks. VHS, Beta **$19.98** WAR, FCT, AFR ♫♫

Leather Boys A teen-aged girl marries a mechanic and then begins to look beyond the boundaries of marriage. Considered very controversial in the 60s, but less so now.
1963 103m/C Rita Tushingham, Dudley Sutton, Colin Campbell; **D:** Sidney J. Furie. VHS, Beta NO ♫♫

Leather Burners Hoppy goes under cover to get the goods on a suspected rustler. When his cover is blown, the bad guys frame him for murder. Look for Robert Mitchum in his third bit part in this series.
1943 66m/B William Boyd, Andy Clyde, Jay Kirby, Victor Jory, George Givot, Bobby Larson, George Reeves, Hal Taliaferro, Forbes Murray, Robert Mitchum; **D:** Joseph Henabery. VHS **$19.95** NOS, MRV ♫♫

Leather Jackets Sweeney plays a nice guy who lets involvement with a childhood pal destroy his life. Elwes is the friend, now gang member, in trouble with both the cops and members of a rival gang, who needs Sweeney's help to escape. Fonda plays Sweeney's girlfriend caught between the two men. Essentially a routine fugitive pic with an attractive cast.
1990 (R) 90m/C D.B. Sweeney, Bridget Fonda, Cary Elwes, Christopher Penn, Marshall Bell, James LeGros, Jon Polito, Craig Ng, Ginger Lynn Allen; **D:** Lee Drysdale; **W:** Lee Drysdale. VHS **$14.95** COL ♫♫

Leatherface: The Texas Chainsaw Massacre 3 The human-skin-wearing cannibal is at it again in this, the second sequel to the Tobe Hooper proto-mess. This one sports a bit more humor and is worth seeing for that reason.
1989 (R) 81m/C Kate Hodge, William Butler, Ken Foree, Tom Hudson, R.A. Mihailoff; **D:** Jeff Burr; **W:** David J. Schow. VHS, Beta **$19.95** COL ♫

The Leatherneck Love unrequited in a faraway place starring soon to be cowboy (Hopalong Cassidy) matinee idol Boyd and Hale, the real life dad of Gilligan Island's skipper.
1928 65m/B William Boyd, Alan Hale, Diane Ellis. VHS, Beta **$24.95** GPV, FCT ♫♫

Leave 'Em Laughing Rooney plays Chicago clown Jack Thum in this based-on-real-life TV movie. Thum takes in orphans even though he cannot find steady work, and then discovers he has cancer.
1981 103m/C Mickey Rooney, Anne Jackson, Allen (Gooritz) Garfield, Elisha Cook Jr., William Windom, Red Buttons, Michael Le Clair; **D:** Jackie Cooper. VHS, Beta **$14.95** FRH ♫♫

Leave It to the Marines A jerky guy wanders into a recruiting office instead of a marriage license bureau and unwittingly signs on for military service.
1951 66m/B Sid Melton, Mara Lynn. VHS, Beta NO ♫½

Leaves from Satan's Book Impressionistic episodes of Satan's fiddling with man through the ages, from Christ to the Russian Revolution. An early cinematic film by Dreyer, with ample indications of his later brilliance. Silent.
1919 165m/B Helge Milsen, Halvart Hoft, Jacob Texiere; **D:** Carl Theodor Dreyer. VHS, Beta **$24.95** GPV, FCT, GVV ♫♫½

Leaving Normal Darly, a fed-up waitress, and Marianne, an abused housewife, meet at a bus stop in Normal, Wyoming and decide to blow town. They travel across the American West, through Canada, and up to Alaska, where Lahti's ex-boyfriend has left her a house. Because both women have made bad choices all their lives, they decide to leave their futures to chance, and end up finding their nirvana. Plot is similar to "Thelma & Louise," but "Leaving Normal" doesn't come close to the innovativeness of the former. Sappy and sentimental to the point of annoyance at times.
1992 (R) 110m/C Christine Lahti, Meg Tilly, Lenny Von Dohlen, Maury Chaykin, James Gammon, Patrika Darbo, Eve Gordon, James Eckhouse, Brett Cullen, Rutanya Alda; **D:** Edward Zwick; **W:** Edward Solomon. VHS **$19.98** MCA ♫½

L'Ecole Buisoniere In a provincial French school a teacher with modern ideas inspires his students with a passion for learning until the suspicious parents are aroused. In French with English subtitles.
1951 108m/C Jean-Paul LeChanois. VHS **$29.95** FCT, ING, WBF ♫♫

The Leech Woman While in Africa, an older woman (Gray) discovers how to restore her youth through a tribal ritual. The only problem is it requires the pineal gland of males, which causes her to go on a killing spree to keep that youthful look. Based on a story by Ben Pivar and Francis Rosenwald.
1959 77m/B Coleen Gray, Grant Williams, Gloria Talbot, Phillip Terry; **D:** Edward Dein; **W:** David Duncan. VHS **$14.98** MCA ♫

Left for Dead A millionaire is accused of brutally killing his wife, and discovers in his search for an alibi that he is the victim of a conspiracy.
1978 82m/C Elke Sommer, Donald Pilon; **D:** Murray Markowitz. VHS, Beta **$69.98** LIV, VES ♫½

The Left Hand of God After an American pilot escapes from a Chinese warlord in post-WWII, he disguises himself as a Catholic priest and takes refuge in a missionary hospital. Bogie is great as the flyboy/cleric.
1955 87m/C Humphrey Bogart, E.G. Marshall, Lee J. Cobb, Agnes Moorehead, Gene Tierney; **D:** Edward Dmytryk. VHS, Beta **$19.98** FOX ♫♫♫

The Left-Handed Gun An offbeat version of the exploits of Billy the Kid, which portrays him as a 19th-century Wild West juvenile delinquent. Newman's role, which he method-acted, was originally intended for James Dean. Based on a 1955 Philco teleplay by Gore Vidal.
1958 102m/B Paul Newman, Lita Milan, John Dehner; **D:** Arthur Penn. VHS, Beta **$19.98** WAR, TLF ♫♫♫

The Legacy An American couple become privy to the dark secrets of an English family gathering in a creepy mansion to inherit an eccentric millionaire's fortune. Death and demons abound. *AKA:* The Legacy of Maggie Walsh.
1979 (R) 100m/C Katharine Ross, Sam Elliott, John Standing, Roger Daltrey, Ian Hogg; **D:** Richard Marquand. VHS, Beta **$19.95** MCA ♫½

A Legacy for Leonette A girl is led into a web of murder and love in this torrid romance novel brought to video.
1985 90m/C Loyita Chapel, Michael Anderson Jr., Dinah Anne Rogers. Beta **$14.95** PSM Woof!

Legacy of Horror A weekend at the family's island mansion with two unfriendly siblings sounds bad enough, but when terror, death, and a few family skeletons pop out of the closets, things go from bad to weird. All-round poor effort with substantial gore. A remake of the director's own "The Ghastly Ones."
1978 (R) 83m/C Elaine Boies, Chris Broderick, Marilee Troncone, Jeannie Cusik; **D:** Andy Milligan. VHS, Beta **$59.95** MPI Woof!

Legacy of Lies Zack Resnick is a serious, honest Chicago cop assigned to a murder investigation. He first discovers the killers got the wrong man and then finds out a lot of family secrets he wishes he didn't know. His cop-father is on the take to the Mob, which is really no surprise since Zack's grandfather turns out to be a retired gangland boss, all of which leaves Zack wondering where his loyalties lie. Too intricate plot hampers the story's flow but the cast performances are well worth watching. Made for cable television.
1992 (R) 94m/C Michael Ontkean, Martin Landau, Eli Wallach, Joe Morton, Patricia Clarkson, Gerry Becker, Chelcie Ross, Ron Dean; **D:** Jason Meshover-Iorg; **W:** David Black. VHS **$89.98** MCA ♫♫½

Legal Eagles An assistant D.A. faces murder, mayhem, and romance while prosecuting a girl accused of stealing a portrait painted by her father. Redford sparkles in this otherwise convoluted tale from Reitman, while Hannah lacks depth as the daffy thief.
1986 (PG) 116m/C Robert Redford, Debra Winger, Daryl Hannah, Brian Dennehy, Terence Stamp, Steven Hill, David Clennon, Roscoe Lee Browne, John McMartin, Jennie Dundas, Ivan Reitman; **D:** Ivan Reitman; **W:** Jim Cash, Jack Epps Jr.; **M:** Elmer Bernstein. VHS, Beta **$14.95** MCA ♫♫½

Legal Tender Rude talk-show host Downey as a corrupt S & L chief? Big, menacing Davi as a romantic hero? Give this often-inept thriller credit for creative casting, if little else. Roberts adds steamy sex appeal as a lovely saloon-keeper imperiled by deadly bank fraud.
1990 (R) 93m/C Robert Davi, Tanya Roberts, Morton Downey Jr.; **D:** Jag Mundhra. VHS, Beta **$89.95** PSM ♫½

Legend A colorful, unabashedly Tolkien-esque fantasy about the struggle to save an innocent waif from the Prince of Darkness. Set in a land packed with unicorns, magic swamps, bumbling dwarves and rainbows. Produced in Great Britain.
1986 (PG) 89m/C Tom Cruise, Mia Sara, Tim Curry, David Bennent, Billy Barty, Alice Playten; **D:** Ridley Scott; **M:** Jerry Goldsmith. VHS, Beta **$14.95** MCA ♫♫

Legend of Alfred Packer The true story of how a guide taking five men searching for gold in Colorado managed to be the sole survivor of a blizzard.
1980 87m/C Patrick Dray, Ron Haines, Bob Damon, Dave Ellingson; **D:** Jim Roberson. VHS, Beta NO ♫½

Legend of Big Foot Facing a spree of killings, a local town mobilizes to stop the legendary beast.
1982 92m/C Stafford Morgan, Katherine Hopkins. VHS, Beta NO ♫

Legend of Billie Jean Billie Jean believed in justice for all. When the law and its bureaucracy landed hard on her, she took her cause to the masses and inspired a generation.
1985 (PG-13) 92m/C Helen Slater, Peter Coyote, Keith Gordon, Christian Slater, Richard Bradford, Yeardley Smith, Dean Stockwell; **D:** Matthew Robbins; **W:** Mark Rosenthal. VHS, Beta **$79.98** FOX ♫♫

The Legend of Black Thunder Mountain A children's adventure in the mold of "Grizzly Adams" and "The Wilderness Family."
1979 (G) 90m/C Holly Beeman, Steve Beeman, Ron Brown, F.A. Milovich; *D:* Tom Beeman. VHS, Beta *NO* ♂½

The Legend of Blood Castle Another version of the Countess of Bathory legend, in which an evil woman bathes in the blood of virgins in an attempt to keep the wrinkles away. Released hot on the heels of Hammer's "Countess Dracula." *AKA:* The Female Butcher; Blood Ceremony; Ceremonia Sangrienta.
1972 (R) 87m/C Lucia Bose, Ewa Aulin; *D:* Jorge Grau. VHS, Beta *NO* ♂

Legend of Boggy Creek A dramatized version of various Arkansas Bigfoot sightings.
1975 (G) 87m/C Willie E. Smith, John P. Nixon, John W. Gates, Jeff Crabtree, Buddy Crabtree; *D:* Charles B. Pierce; *W:* Charles B. Pierce. VHS, Beta $59.98 *LIV, MRV* ♂½

Legend of Earl Durand In Wyoming 1939, a man spends his life searching for freedom and justice. His Robin Hood actions cause a manhunt of massive proportions.
1974 90m/C Martin Sheen, Peter Haskell, Keenan Wynn, Slim Pickens, Anthony Caruso; *D:* John D. Patterson. VHS *NO* ♂

The Legend of Frank Woods Gunslinger returns to the land of the free after an extended holiday south of the border. Mistaken for an expected preacher in a small town, he poses as the padre and signs on the dotted line to take out a new lease on life.
1977 88m/C Troy Donahue, Brad Steward, Kitty Vallacher, Michael Christian; *D:* Deno Paoli. VHS $9.95 *SIM* ♂♂

Legend of Frenchie King When prospectors discover oil on disputed land, two families feud over their conflicting claims to the property. Adult western still working out the kinks has Bardot heading a band of female outlaws. *AKA:* Petroleum Girls.
1971 96m/C Brigitte Bardot, Claudia Cardinale, Michael J. Pollard, Micheline Presle; *D:* Christian Jaque. VHS, Beta *NO* ♂½

The Legend of Hell House A multi-millionaire hires a team of scientists and mediums to investigate his newly acquired haunted mansion. It seems that the creepy house has been the site of a number of deaths and may hold clues to the afterlife. A suspenseful, scary screamfest. Matheson wrote the screenplay from his novel "Hell House."
1973 (PG) 94m/C Roddy McDowall, Pamela Franklin, Clive Revill, Gayle Hunnicutt; *D:* John Hough; *W:* Richard Matheson. VHS, Beta $19.98 *FOX* ♂♂♂

The Legend of Hillbilly John Hillbilly John holds off the devil with a strum of his six-string. When demons plague the residents of rural America, the hayseed messiah wanders about saving the day. *AKA:* Who Fears the Devil; My Name is John.
1973 (G) 86m/C Severn Darden, Denver Pyle, Susan Strasberg, Hedge Capers; *D:* John Newland. VHS, Beta $19.95 *NWV* ♂

The Legend of Jedediah Carver A rancher battles desert elements and hostile Indians in a desperate bid for survival.
197? 90m/C DeWitt Lee, Joshua Hoffman, Val Chapman, Richard Montgomery, David Terril; *D:* DeWitt Lee. VHS $39.95 *XVC* ♂♂

Legend of Lobo The story of Lobo, a crafty wolf who seeks to free his mate from the clutches of greedy hunters. A Disney wildlife adventure.
1962 67m/C VHS, Beta $69.95 *DIS* ♂½

The Legend of Sea Wolf A sadistic sea captain forcefully rules his crew in this weak version of Jack London's novel. Also known as "Wolf Larsen."
1975 (PG) 90m/C Chuck Connors, Barbara Bach, Joseph Palmer. VHS, Beta *NO* ♂

The Legend of Sleepy Hollow The story of Ichabod Crane and the legendary ride of the headless horseman by Washington Irving; narrated by Crosby. Also includes two classic short cartoons, "Lonesome Ghosts" (1932) with Mickey Mouse and "Trick or Treat" (1952) with Donald Duck.
1949 45m/C *D:* Jack Kinney, Clyde Geronomi, James Algar. VHS, Beta $12.99 *DIS, WTA* ♂♂

The Legend of Sleepy Hollow Washington Irving's classic tale of the Headless Horseman of Sleepy Hollow is brought to life on the screen. Made for television.
1979 (G) 100m/C Jeff Goldblum, Dick Butkus, Paul Sand, Meg Foster, James Griffith, John S. White. VHS, Beta $9.99 *STE, VCI* ♂♂½

The Legend of Sleepy Hollow Classic Washington Irving tale is given the Shelly Duvall treatment in her "Tall Tales and Legends" series. When a snooty teacher goes too far, the town blacksmith decides to play the ultimate Halloween trick on him. Made for cable television.
1986 51m/C Ed Begley Jr., Beverly D'Angelo, Charles Durning, Tim Thomerson. VHS $19.98 *FOX* ♂♂½

The Legend of Suram Fortress Based on a Georgian folktale about a medieval fortress that collapses as soon as it is built. The village soothsayer tells a young man he must sacrifice himself, by bricking himself up alive within the fortress walls, if the building is every to stand. In Russian with English subtitles. *AKA:* Legenda Suramskoi Kreposti.
1985 89m/C Levan Outchanechvili, Zourab Kipchidze; *D:* Sergei Paradjanov. VHS $59.95 *KIV* ♂♂

Legend of the Dinosaurs Slavering, teeth-gnashing dinosaurs are discovered on Mt. Fuji.
1983 92m/C VHS, Beta $39.95 *CEL* Woof!

Legend of the Lone Ranger The fabled Lone Ranger (whose voice is dubbed throughout the entire movie) and the story of his first meeting with his Indian companion, Tonto, are brought to life in this weak and vapid version of the famous legend. The narration by Merle Haggard leaves something to be desired as do most of the performances.
1981 (PG) 98m/C Klinton Spilsbury, Michael Horse, Jason Robards Jr., Richard Farnsworth, Christopher Lloyd, Matt Clark; *D:* William A. Fraker; *W:* William Roberts, Ivan Goff, Michael Kane; *M:* John Barry. VHS, Beta $29.98 *FOX* ♂♂

Legend of the Lost Two men vie for desert treasure and desert women. Interesting only because of Wayne, but certainly not one of his more memorable films.
1957 109m/C John Wayne, Sophia Loren, Rossano Brazzi, Kurt Kasznar, Sonia Moser; *D:* Henry Hathaway. VHS $19.98 *MGM* ♂♂

Legend of the Northwest The loyalty of a dog is evidenced in the fierce revenge he has for the drunken hunter who shot and killed his master.

1978 (G) 83m/C Denver Pyle. VHS, Beta $19.95 *STE, GEM, HHE* ♂♂

The Legend of the Sea Wolf Adaptation of Jack London's dramatic adventure novel, "The Sea Wolf." A slave driving ship captain rescues a shipwreck victim and sets to abusing him along with the rest of his crew. A rebellion ensues. Superb musical score benefits the strong acting and good pace. *AKA:* Wolf Larsen; Larsen, Wolf of the Seven Seas.
1958 83m/B Barry Sullivan, Peter Graves, Gita Hall, Thayer David; *D:* Harmon Jones; *W:* Jack DeWitt. VHS *NO* ♂♂½

Legend of the Werewolf A child who once ran with the wolves has forgotten his past, except when the moon is full.
1975 (R) 90m/C Peter Cushing, Hugh Griffith, Ron Moody, David Rintoul, Lynn Dalby; *D:* Freddie Francis. VHS, Beta *MRV* ♂♂

The Legend of the Wolf Woman The beautiful Daniella assumes the personality of the legendary wolfwoman, leaving a trail of gruesome killings across the countryside. Genre fans will find this one surprisingly entertaining. Also on video as "Werewolf Woman."
1977 (R) 84m/C Anne Borel, Fred Stafford, Tino Carey, Elliot Zamuto, Ollie Reynolds, Andrea Scotti, Karen Carter; *D:* Raphael D. Silver. VHS, Beta $19.95 *VIP, VCI* ♂♂½

Legend of Valentino Made-for-television docudrama traces the legendary exploits of one of the silver screen's greatest lovers, Rudolph Valentino. Typical TV-movie fare that lacks the power of the legend's life.
1975 96m/C Franco Nero, Suzanne Pleshette, Lesley Ann Warren, Yvette Mimieux, Judd Hirsch, Milton Berle, Harold J. Stone; *D:* Melville Shavelson. VHS, Beta $49.95 *PSM, MRV, NLC* ♂♂½

The Legend of Valentino A biographical documentary of perhaps the world's greatest lover, beginning with his immigration to America and ending at his unexpected, sudden death.
1983 71m/B VHS, Beta $24.98 *SUE* ♂♂½

Legend of Walks Far Woman A made for television film about a proud Sioux woman fighting for survival and her tribe during the American-Indian Wars. Welch is miscast. From Colin Stuart's novel.
1982 120m/C Raquel Welch, Nick Mancuso, Bradford Dillman; *D:* Mel Damski. VHS, Beta *NO* ♂

The Legend of Wolf Mountain Three children are held hostage by two prison escapees in the Utah mountains. They are aided in their escape by a Native American "wolf spirit." With the criminals on their trail will the three be able to survive in the wilderness until a search party can find them?
1992 (PG) 91m/C Mickey Rooney, Bo Hopkins, Don Shanks, Vivian Schilling, Robert Z'Dar, David Shark, Nicole Lund, Natalie Lund, Matthew Lewis, Jonathan Best; *D:* Craig Clyde. VHS $9.95 *HMD* ♂♂½

Legion of Iron Adventures in a computer-run, neo-Roman civilization where men and women battle for supremacy.
1990 (R) 85m/C Kevin T. Walsh, Erica Nann, Regie De Morton, Camille Carrigan; *D:* Yakov Bentsvi. VHS, Beta $79.95 *COL* ♂

Legion of Missing Men Professional soldiers of fortune, the French Foreign Legion, fight the evil sheik Ahmed in the Sahara.

1937 62m/B Ralph Forbes, Ben Alexander, Hala Linda, Roy D'Arcy, Paul Hurst, James Aubrey; *D:* Hamilton MacFadden. VHS, Beta $19.95 *VYY, GPV* 🎬 ½

Legion of the Lawless Group of outlaws band together in order to spread terror and confusion among the populace.
1940 59m/B George O'Brien, Virginia Vale. VHS, Beta *MED* 🎬 ½

Legs Backstage story of three girls who are competing for a job with Radio City Music Hall's Rockettes. Made for television.
1983 91m/C Gwen Verdon, John Heard, Sheree North, Shanna Reed, Maureen Teefy; *D:* Jerrold Freedman. VHS, Beta $59.95 *PSM* 🎬

The Lemon Drop Kid Second version of the Damon Runyon chestnut about a racetrack bookie who must recover the gangster's money he lost on a bet. As the fast-talking bookie, Hope sparkles. 🎵Silver Bells; It Doesn't Cost a Dime to Dream; They Obviously Want Me to Sing.
1951 91m/B Bob Hope, Lloyd Nolan, Fred Clark, Marilyn Maxwell, Jane Darwell, Andrea King, William Frawley, Jay C. Flippen, Harry Bellaver; *D:* Sidney Lanfield; *W:* Frank Tashlin, Edmund Hartman, Robert O'Brien. VHS, Beta $14.95 *COL* 🎬🎬 ½

The Lemon Sisters Three women, friends and performance partners since childhood, struggle to buy their own club. They juggle the men in their lives with less success. Great actresses like these should have done more with this interesting premise, and the excellent male cast has much more potential.
1990 (PG-13) 93m/C Diane Keaton, Carol Kane, Kathryn Grody, Elliott Gould, Ruben Blades, Aidan Quinn; *D:* Joyce Chopra. VHS $19.98 *HBO, FCT* 🎬🎬

Lemora, Lady Dracula A pretty young church singer is drawn into the lair of the evil Lady Dracula, whose desires include her body as well as her blood. Horror fans will enjoy some excellent atmosphere, particularly in a scene where the girl's church bus is attacked by zombie-like creatures; Smith remains a '70s "B" movie favorite. Perhaps a double feature with "Lady Frankenstein...?" *AKA:* The Lady Dracula; The Legendary Curse of Lemora.
1973 (PG) 80m/C Leslie Gilb, Cheryl "Rainbeaux" Smith, William Whitton, Steve Johnson, Monty Pyke, Maxine Ballantyne, Parker West, Richard Blackburn; *D:* Richard Blackburn. VHS $18.00 *FRG* 🎬

Lena's Holiday Fluffy comedy about a winsome East German girl visiting L.A. for the first time, and the culture-shock that ensues. Sharp script and performances.
1990 (PG-13) 97m/C Felicity Waterman, Chris Lemmon, Noriyuki "Pat" Morita, Susan Anton, Michael Sarrazin, Nick Mancuso, Bill Dana, Liz Torres; *D:* Michael Keusch. VHS, Beta $19.95 *PSM* 🎬🎬

Leningrad Cowboys Go America An outlandish Finnish band, the Leningrad Cowboys, pack up their electric accordians and their one dead member and go on tour in America. With matching front-swept pompadours and pointy shoes, the group's appearance is the picture's best joke—and one of its only jokes, as the road trip plods in deadpan fashion that may bore viewers. It's best appreciated by fans of comic minimalist Jim Jarmusch (who has a guest role). In Finnish with English subtitles.
1989 (PG-13) 78m/C Jim Jarmusch, Matti Pellonpaa, Kari Vaananen, Nicky Tesco; *D:* Aki Kaurismaki; *W:* Aki Kaurismaki. VHS $79.98 *ORI, FCT, ING* 🎬🎬 ½

Lenny Smokey nightclubs, drug abuse and obscenities abound in Hoffman's portrayal of the controversial comedian Lenny Bruce, whose use of street language led to his eventual blacklisting. Perrine is a gem as his stripper wife. Adapted from the Julian Barry play, this is a visually compelling piece that sharply divided critics upon release.
1974 (R) 111m/B Dustin Hoffman, Valerie Perrine, Jan Miner, Stanley Beck; *D:* Bob Fosse; *W:* Julian Barry; *M:* Ralph Burns. Academy Awards '74 Nominations: Best Actor (Hoffman), Best Actress (Perrine), Best Adapted Screenplay, Best Cinematography, Best Director (Fosse), Best Picture; Cannes Film Festival '75: Best Film; Cannes Film Festival '75: Best Actress (Perrine); National Board of Review Awards '74: 10 Best Films of the Year, Best Supporting Actress (Perrine). VHS, Beta $19.98 *MGM, FOX* 🎬🎬🎬

Lenny Bruce Performance Film A videotape of one of Lenny Bruce's last nightclub appearances at Basin Street West in San Francisco. Also included is "Thank You Masked Man," a color cartoon parody of the Lone Ranger legend, with Lenny Bruce providing all the character voices.
1968 72m/B Lenny Bruce. VHS, Beta $59.95 *VES, RHI, MVD* 🎬🎬🎬

Lensman In the 25th century space pirates known as the Boskande are threatening the civilized universe. Young Kimall Kenison is chosen by a higher power to become a lensman—and live or die for freedom. Based on the E.E. "Doc" Smith novels, this production is a combination of animation and computer graphics. Dubbed in English.
1984 107m/C VHS $29.95 *WTA, STP, FUS* 🎬🎬🎬

Leolo Deeply disturbing black-comedy about one of the screen's most dysfunctional families. Leo is a 12-year-old French Canadian from Montreal who is determined to remake himself. He's decided to be a Sicilian lad named Leolo, escaping from his horrific family into his fantasies (and potential madness). His parents are obsessed with toilet training, his cowardly brother with body-building, his sisters are demented, and his grandfather is a sadistic, dirty old man. Not for the faint of heart (or stomach). In French with English subtitles.
1992 107m/C Maxime Collin, Julien Guiomar, Ginette Reno, Pierre Bourgault, Yves Montmarquette, Roland Blouin, Giuditta del Vecchio; *D:* Jean-Claude Lauzon; *W:* Jean-Claude Lauzon. VHS *NLC, ING* 🎬🎬

Leon Morin, Priest A young priest and a widow, who happens to be a Communist, fall in love during the WWII German occupation of France. Based on the novel by Beatrix Beck. In French with English subtitles.
1961 118m/B Jean-Paul Belmondo, Emmanuelle Riva; *D:* Jean-Pierre Melville. VHS $59.95 *INT, ING, FCT* 🎬🎬

Leon the Pig Farmer Dry comedic satire about identity. Leon Geller has never quite fitted into his parents' comfortable Jewish society and no wonder—Leon accidentally discovers he is the product of artificial insemination. And what's more, the lab made a mistake and Leon isn't a true Geller after all. His father is actually a genial (and Gentile) Yorkshire pig farmer named Brian Chadwick, who cheerfully welcomes Leon as his long-lost son. All four parents try to cope while Leon moves bewilderedly amongst them. Film tends to be too timid in its satire but still has its witty moments.
1993 98m/C Mark Frankel, Janet Suzman, Brian Glover, Connie Booth, David DeKeyser, Maryam D'Abo, Gina Bellman; *D:* Vadim Jean, Gary Sinyor; *W:* Gary Sinyor, Michael Normand. VHS $89.98 *ORI* 🎬🎬 ½

Leonard Part 6 A former secret agent comes out of retirement to save the world from a crime queen using animals to kill agents. In the meantime, he tries to patch up his collapsing personal life. Wooden and disappointing; produced and co-written by Cosby, who himself panned the film.
1987 (PG) 83m/C Bill Cosby, Gloria Foster, Tom Courtenay, Joe Don Baker; *D:* Paul Weiland; *W:* Bill Cosby, Jonathan Reynolds; *M:* Elmer Bernstein. VHS, Beta $89.95 *COL* 🎬

Leonor Idiotic medieval drivel with Ullmann rising from the dead after husband Piccoli seals her in a tomb. Directed by the son of Luis Bunuel.
1975 90m/C Liv Ullmann, Michel Piccoli, Ornella Muti; *D:* Juan Bunuel; *M:* Ennio Morricone. VHS, Beta *FOX* 🎬

Leopard Fist Ninja A masked ninja whacks away at American hoodlums in a fit of Maoist, anti-capitalistic fury. Dubbed.
198? 88m/C Willie Freeman, Jack Lam, Chuck Horry. VHS, Beta *NO* 🎬

Leopard in the Snow The romance between a race car driver allegedly killed in a crash and a young woman is the premise of this film.
1978 (PG) 89m/C Keir Dullea, Susan Penhaligon, Kenneth More, Billie Whitelaw; *D:* Gerry O'Hara. VHS, Beta $59.98 *SUE* 🎬🎬

The Leopard Man An escaped leopard terrorizes a small town in New Mexico. After a search, the big cat is found dead, but the killings continue. Minor but effective Jacques Tourneur creepie. Based on Cornell Woolrich's novel "Black Alibi." Another Val Lewton Horror production.
1943 66m/B Jean Brooks, Isabel Jewell, James Bell, Margaret Landry, Dennis O'Keefe, Margo, Rita Corday; *D:* Jacques Tourneur. VHS, Beta $19.95 *MED* 🎬🎬 ½

The Leopard Woman Long before the cat lady cut her first claws, there was the leopard woman. Vamp Glaum finds much trouble to meow about on the Equator.
1920 66m/B Louise Glaum. VHS, Beta $19.95 *GPV, FCT, GVV* 🎬🎬

Leper A melodrama of forbidden love between a wealthy nobleman and a beautiful high school teacher. The townspeople try to destroy the love between the two because of their different social classes. In Polish with English subtitles. Also known as "Tredowata."
1976 100m/C Elzbieta Starostecka, Leszek Teleszynski; *D:* Jerzy Hoffman. VHS $49.95 *FCT* 🎬

Lepke The life and fast times of Louis "Lepke" Buchalter from his days in reform school to his days as head of Murder, Inc. and his execution in 1944.
1975 (R) 110m/C Tony Curtis, Milton Berle, Gianni Russo, Vic Tayback, Michael Callan; *D:* Menahem Golan. VHS, Beta $59.95 *WAR* 🎬🎬 ½

Leprechaun A sadistic 600-year-old leprechaun winds up wreaking havoc in North Dakota. If this makes no particular sense, neither does the film which is basic horror story excess. A man goes to Ireland for his mother's funeral, steals the gold belonging to the leprechaun, locks the creature up, and winds up accidentally taking the evil imp back to the States with him. When the leprechaun gets free, he wants a bloodthirsty revenge—and shoes. One of the so-called humorous bits is the leprechaun's shoe fetish. Irish eyes will not be smiling watching this mess.
1993 (R) 92m/C Warwick Davis, Jennifer Aniston, Ken Olandt, Mark Holton, John Sanderford, Robert Gorman; *D:* Mark Jones; *W:* Mark Jones. VHS $94.95 *VMK* Woof!

L

Leprechaun 2 Sequel to the Irish horror flick about a malevolent gnome. It seems one of his fairy entitlements is that he can possess any woman he wants if she sneezes three times. Thwarted in his attempt to snare a comely lass one thousand years earlier, he returns to present-day California to exact revenge on her descendant Durkin. Contrary to the popular legend that leprechauns are benign kind-hearted sprites, this nasty combines the treachery of a Gestapo officer with the firepower of a Rambo in his attempt to harass the unimpressed Durkin into his clutches.
1994 (R) 85m/C Warwick Davis, Sandy Baron, Adam Biesk, James Lancaster, Clint Howard, Kimmy Robertson, Charlie Heath, Shevonne Durkin; **D:** Rodman Flender; **W:** Turi Meyer, Al Septien; **M:** Jonathan Elias. **VHS $94.99** VMK ♫♫½

Les Assassins de L'Ordre A righteous French judge faces the case of an innocent man killed by police brutality. Subtitled in English. **AKA:** Law Breakers.
1971 100m/C Jacques Brel, Catherine Rouvel, Michael Lonsdale, Charles Denner; **D:** Marcel Carne; **M:** Michel Colombier. **VHS, Beta $29.95** ING ♫♫

Les Aventuriers Two friends find themselves swindled in an insurance scam and set out after the perpetrator who sent them off to Africa in search of a treasure. Available dubbed. **AKA:** The Last Adventure.
1977 ?m/C Alain Delon, Lino Ventura, Joanna Shimkus. **VHS $59.95** FRA, FCT ♫♫½

Les Biches An exquisite film that became a landmark in film history with its theme of bisexuality and upper class decadence. A rich socialite picks up a young artist drawing on the streets of Paris, seduces her, and then takes her to St. Tropez. Conflict arises when a suave architect shows up and threatens to come between the two lovers. In French with English subtitles. **AKA:** The Heterosexuals.
1968 (R) 95m/C Stephane Audran, Jean-Louis Trintignant, Jacqueline Sassard; **D:** Claude Chabrol; **W:** Claude Chabrol. **VHS $79.95** CVC, ING, LUM ♫♫♫½

Les Bons Debarras In French with English subtitles, this Canadian film follows a lonely 13-year-old's effort to win her mother's exclusive love.
1981 114m/C Marie Tifo, Charlotte Laurier, German Houde; **D:** Francis Mankiewicz. **VHS, Beta NO** ♫♫½

Les Carabiniers A cynical, grim anti-war tract, detailing the pathetic adventures of two young bums lured into enlisting with promises of rape, looting, torture and battle without justification. Controversial in its day, and typically elliptical and non-narrative. In French with English subtitles. **AKA:** The Soldiers.
1963 80m/B Anna Karina, Genevieva Galea, Marino Mase; **D:** Jean-Luc Godard. **VHS, Beta $29.95** FCT ♫♫♫

Les Comperes A woman suckers two former lovers into finding her wayward son by secretly telling each ex he is the natural father of the punk. Depardieu is a streetwise journalist who teams up with a suicidal hypochondriac/wimp (Richard) to find the little brat. Humorous story full of bumbling misadventures. In French with English subtitles.
1983 92m/C Pierre Richard, Gerard Depardieu, Anny Duperey, Michel Aumont; **D:** Francis Veber; **W:** Francis Veber; **M:** Vladimir Cosma. **VHS, Beta $59.99** MED, FCT, ING ♫♫♫

Les Enfants Terrible The classic, lyrical treatment of adolescent deviance adapted by Cocteau from his own play, wherein a brother and sister born into extreme wealth eventually enter into casual crime, self-destruction, and incest. In French with English subtitles. **AKA:** The Strange Ones.
1950 105m/B Edouard Dermithe, Nicole Stephane, Jean Cocteau; **D:** Jean-Pierre Melville. **VHS, Beta $59.98** FCT, ING ♫♫♫

Les Girls When one member of a performing troupe writes her memoirs, the other girls sue for libel. Told through a series of flashbacks, this story traces the girls' recollections of their relationships to American dancer Kelly. Cole Porter wrote the score for this enjoyable "Rashomon"-styled musical. Laserdisc features include the original trailer and letterboxed screen. ♫Les Girls; Flower Song; You're Just Too, Too; Ca C'est L'Amour; Ladies In Waiting; La Habanera; Why Am I So Gone (About That Gal?).
1957 114m/C Gene Kelly, Mitzi Gaynor, Kay Kendall, Taina Elg, Henry Daniell, Patrick Macnee; **D:** George Cukor. Academy Awards '57: Best Costume Design; Nominations: Best Art Direction/Set Decoration, Best Sound; Golden Globe Awards '58: Best Actress—Musical/Comedy (Kendall), Best Film—Musical/Comedy. **VHS, Beta $19.98** MGM ♫♫½

Les Grandes Gueules From the director of the classic "An Occurrence at Owl Creek Bridge," comes this comedy-drama about a sawmill owner dealing with two ex-convicts hired as lumberjacks. In French with English subtitles. **AKA:** Jailbirds' Vacation.
1965 125m/C Lino Ventura, Bourvil, Marie DuBois; **D:** Robert Enrico. **VHS, Beta $19.95** BAR, ING ♫♫½

Les Miserables Victor Hugo's classic novel about small-time criminal Jean Valjean and 18th-century France. After facing poverty and prison, escape and torture, Valjean is redeemed by the kindness of a bishop. As he tries to mend his ways, he is continually hounded by the policeman Javert, who is determined to lock him away. The final act is set during a student uprising in the 1730s. This version is the best of many, finely detailed and well-paced with excellent cinematography by Gregg Toland.
1935 108m/B Fredric March, Charles Laughton, Cedric Hardwicke, Rochelle Hudson, John Beal, Frances Drake, Florence Eldridge, John Carradine, Jessie Ralph, Leonid Kinskey; **D:** Richard Boleslawski; **W:** W.P. Lipscomb; **M:** Alfred Newman. Academy Awards '35 Nominations: Best Cinematography, Best Picture; Academy Awards '36: Best Film Editing; National Board of Review Awards '35: 10 Best Films of the Year. **VHS, Beta $59.98** FOX, APD ♫♫♫♫

Les Miserables Hugo's classic novel done up Italian style with lavish sets and spectacle. Dubbed in English.
1952 119m/B Gino Cervi, Valentina Cortese; **D:** Riccardo (Robert Hampton) Freda. **VHS $24.95** VYY, FCT ♫♫½

Les Miserables An epic French adaptation of the Victor Hugo standard about Valjean, Javert, and injustice. Although this doesn't reach the level of the 1935 classic, it is still worth watching. Dubbed in English.
1957 210m/C Jean Gabin, Daniele Delorme, Bernard Blier, Bourvil, Gianni Esposito, Serge Reggiani; **D:** Jean-Paul LeChanois. **VHS, Beta $29.95** FCT, VEC ♫♫♫

Les Miserables An excellent made-for-television version of the Victor Hugo classic about the criminal Valjean and the policeman Javert playing cat-and-mouse in 18th-century France. Dauphin's last film role.

1978 150m/C Richard Jordan, Anthony Perkins, John Gielgud, Cyril Cusack, Flora Robson, Celia Johnson, Claude Dauphin; **D:** Glenn Jordan. **VHS, Beta $59.98** FOX, FCT ♫♫♫½

Les Mistons This study of male adolescence finds five teen-age boys worshiping a beautiful girl from afar, following her everywhere, spoiling her dates, and finally reaching maturity in light of their mistakes.
1957 18m/C D: Francois Truffaut. **VHS, Beta** FLI ♫♫♫

Les Nuits Fauves Collard's semi-autobiographical film about the emotional and physical havoc an H.I.V.-positive filmmaker visits on the two objects of his violent affections—an innocent 18-year-old girl and a sadomasochistic 20-year-old boy. As Jean displays increasing desperation with his situation, the life around him shows an equally arbitrary violence and humor. In French with English subtitles. Collard died of AIDS shortly before his film won both best first film and best French film at the 1993 Cesars—a first in the ceremony's history. **AKA:** Savage Nights.
1992 129m/C Cyril Collard, Romane Bohringer, Carlos Lopez, Maria Schneider; **D:** Cyril Collard; **W:** Cyril Collard. **VHS** NYR ♫♫♫

Les Patterson Saves the World An obnoxious ambassador to an anonymous Middle Eastern country teams up with the singularly distastefully named Dr. Herpes to stop a new killer disease about to engulf the world.
1990 (R) 105m/C Barry Humphries, Pamela Stephenson, Thaao Penghlis, Andrew Clarke, Joan Rivers; **D:** George Miller. **VHS $14.95** HMD ♫½

Les Rendez-vous D'Anna An independent woman travels through Europe and comes face to face with its post-war modernism. In French with English subtitles. **AKA:** The Meetings of Anna.
1978 120m/C Aurore Clement, Helmut Griem, Magali Noel, Hanns Zischler, Lea Massari, Jean-Pierre Cassel; **D:** Chantal Akerman; **W:** Chantal Akerman. **VHS $29.95** WAC, ING ♫♫

Les Violons du Bal Follows the story of a young Jewish boy and his family's attempted escape from Nazi-occupied France during WWII. The boy grows up to be a filmmaker obsessed with making a movie about his childhood experiences. In French with English subtitles.
1974 110m/C Marie-Jose Nat, Jean-Louis Trintignant; **D:** Michael Drach. Cannes Film Festival Nominations: cs 74: Best Film; Cannes Film Festival '74: Best Actress (Nat). **VHS $79.95** CVC, ING, PMS ♫♫♫

Les Visiteurs du Soir A beautiful, charming fairy tale about the devil's intrepid interference with a particular love affair in 15th-century France, which he cannot squelch. Purportedly a parable about Hitler's invasion of France. Interestingly, this was released after the Nazi occupation of France, so one assumes that the Germans didn't make the connection. In French with English subtitles. **AKA:** The Devil's Envoys.
1942 110m/B Arletty, Jules Berry, Marie Dea, Alain Cuny, Fernand Ledoux, Marcel Herrand; **D:** Marcel Carne; **W:** Jacques Prevert, Pierre Laroche. **VHS, Beta $39.95** HMV, ING, FCT ♫♫♫½

Less Than Zero An adaptation of Bret Easton Ellis' popular, controversial novel about a group of affluent, drug-abusing youth in Los Angeles. McCarthy and Gertz play friends of Downey who try to get him off his self-destructive path—to no avail. Although it tries, the film fails to inspire any sort of sympathy for this self-absorbed and he-

donistic group. Mirrors the shallowness of the characters although Downey manages to rise above this somewhat. Music by the Bangles, David Lee Roth, Poison, Roy Orbison, Aerosmith and more.
1987 (R) 98m/C Andrew McCarthy, Jami Gertz, Robert Downey Jr., James Spader; **D:** Marek Kanievska. VHS, Beta $19.98 FOX *I*

Lesson in Love A gynecologist's philandering is discovered by his wife, who then starts an affair of her own. Change of pace for Bergman as he does this modest comedy. In Swedish with English subtitles. **AKA:** En Lekiton i Karlek.
1954 95m/B Gunnar Bjornstrand, Eva Dahlbeck, Harriet Andersson; **D:** Ingmar Bergman; **W:** Ingmar Bergman. VHS, Beta $29.98 SUE, ING, NLC *II*½

Let 'Em Have It Exciting action saga loosely based on the newly formed FBI and its bouts with John Dillinger. Car chases and tommy guns abound in this fairly ordinary film. **AKA:** False Faces.
1935 90m/B Richard Arlen, Virginia Bruce, Bruce Cabot, Harvey Stephens, Eric Linden, Joyce Compton, Gordon Jones; **D:** Sam Wood. VHS $19.95 MGM, NOS, HEG *II*½

Let 'er Go Gallegher A youngster sees a murder, tells his newspaper buddy about it, and the guy writes an article about the crime. It's a big hit, the guy's ego starts to overinflate, and his life starts to head downwind until he decides its time for him and the little guy to rope themselves a miscreant.
1928 57m/B Frank "Junior" Coghlan, Elinor Fair, Wade Boteler; **D:** Elmer Clifton. VHS, Beta $19.95 GPV, FCT *II*

Let Freedom Ring Sappy, yet enjoyable patriotism that has lawyer Eddy returning to small hometown and fighting corruption. Hokey, but it works largely due to Hecht's fine script. ♫Dusty Road; Love Serenade; Home Sweet Home; When Irish Eyes Are Smiling; America; Pat Sez He; Where Else But Here; Funiculi Funicula; Ten Thousand Cattle Straying.
1939 100m/B Nelson Eddy, Virginia Bruce, Victor McLaglen, Lionel Barrymore, Edward Arnold, Guy Kibbee, Charles Butterworth, H.B. Warner, Raymond Walburn; **D:** Jack Conway; **W:** Ben Hecht. VHS $19.98 MGM *II*½

Let Him Have It Compelling, controversial film about a miscarriage of British justice. In 1952 Christopher Craig, 16, and Derek Bentley, 19, climbed onto the roof of a warehouse in an apparent burglary attempt. The police arrived and captured Bentley; Craig shot and wounded one policeman and killed another. According to testimony Bentley shouted "Let him have it" but did he mean shoot or give the officer the gun? Bentley, whose IQ was 66, was sentenced to death by the British courts—though he didn't commit the murder. The uproar over the sentence was reignited by this release, leading to a request for a reexamination of evidence and sentencing by the British Home Office.
1991 (R) 115m/C Christopher Eccleston, Paul Reynolds, Tom Bell, Eileen Atkins, Clare Holman, Michael Elphick, Mark McGann, Tom Courtenay; **D:** Peter Medak. VHS $89.95 COL, NLC *III*½

Let It Be Documentary look at a Beatles recording session, giving glimpses of the conflicts which led to their breakup. Features appearances by Yoko Ono and Billy Preston.
1970 80m/C John Lennon, Paul McCartney, George Harrison, Ringo Starr, Billy Preston, Yoko Ono; **D:** Michael Lindsay-Hogg; **M:** The Beatles. VHS, Beta FOX *II*

Let It Ride Dreyfuss is a small-time gambler who finally hits it big at the track. Some funny moments but generally a lame script cripples the cast, although the horses seem unaffected. Garr is okay as his wife who slips further into alcoholism with each race.
1989 (PG-13) 91m/C Richard Dreyfuss, Teri Garr, David Johansen, Jennifer Tilly, Allen (Gooritz) Garfield, Ed Walsh, Michelle Phillips, Mary Woronov, Robbie Coltrane, Richard Edson, Cynthia Nixon; **D:** Joe Pytka. VHS, Beta, 8mm $14.95 PAR *II*

Let It Rock A maniacal promoter makes superstars out of his new band by staging publicity stunts. Not one of Hopper's better efforts. Filmed in Germany, but Roger Corman bought the U.S. rights and added clips from other movies before it was released here.
1986 75m/C Dennis Hopper, David Hess; **D:** Roland Klick. VHS, Beta $79.95 MED *I*

L'Etat Sauvage This French political thriller finds its heart in the middle of racism. The story unfolds around a newly independent African republic and a love affair between a black cabinet minister and a white Frenchwoman. Corruption abounds in this film based on George Conchon's award-winning novel. In French with English subtitles. **AKA:** The Savage State.
1978 111m/C Marie-Christine Barrault, Claude Brasseur, Jacques Dutronc, Doura Mane, Michel Piccoli; **D:** Francis Girod. VHS, Beta $59.95 INT, ING, TPV *III*½

Lethal Charm Two power-hungry journalists go head-to-head in the high stakes arena of Washington D.C.
1990 92m/C Barbara Eden, Heather Locklear. VHS LIV *II*

Lethal Games Stallone and Vaccaro lead a small community against a bloodthirsty band of criminals.
1990 83m/C Frank Stallone, Brenda Vaccaro, Dave Adams, Christopher Whalley, Heidi Paine, Karen Russell; **D:** John Bowen. VHS $79.95 AIP *II*

Lethal Lolita—Amy Fisher: My Story The only made-for-television Amy Fisher story of three whose cast members even remotely resemble the real people—except of course actress Parker is actually pretty. Minor details aside, this account is Amy's story, purchased by NBC for an undisclosed amount, portraying her as an incest victim who gets involved with an opportunistic married jerk who drags her into prostitution, leading her to take out her frustration on his wife. If this is true, the obvious question is "why?"...to which she answers, "He loves me. We have great sex. And he fixes my car." Oh. See also: "The Amy Fisher Story" and "Casualties of Love: The 'Long Island Lolita' Story." **AKA:** Amy Fisher: My Story.
1992 93m/C Noelle Parker, Ed Marinaro, Kathleen Lasky, Boyd Kestner, Mary Ann Pascal, Lawrence Dane, Kate Lynch; **D:** Bradford May. VHS $89.98 TTC *II*

Lethal Ninja Kickboxers Joe and Pete set out to rescue Joe's wife from some third-world country overrun by ninjas. Hackneyed but lots of action for martial arts fans.
1993 97m/C Ross Kettle, David Webb, Karyn Hill, Frank Notaro. VHS $92.95 VMK *I*

Lethal Obsession Two cops battle street crime and a powerful drug ring. Filmed in Germany. **AKA:** Der Joker.
1987 (R) 100m/C Michael York, Elliott Gould, Tahnee Welch, Peter Maffay, Armin Mueller-Stahl; **D:** Peter Patzak; **M:** Tony Carey. VHS, Beta $29.95 VMK *I*½

Lethal Pursuit A popular singer who returns to the town where she grew up is tormented by her ex-boyfriend, a criminal.
1988 90m/C Mitzi Donahue, Blake Gahner, John Wildman; **D:** Donald M. Jones. VHS, Beta $14.95 HMD *I*

Lethal Weapon In Los Angeles, a cop nearing retirement (Glover) unwillingly begins work with a new partner (Gibson), a suicidal, semi-crazed risk-taker who seems determined to get the duo killed. Both Vietnam vets, the pair uncover a vicious heroin smuggling ring run by ruthless ex-Special Forces personnel. Packed with plenty of action, violence, and humorous undertones. Clapton's contributions to the musical score are an added bonus. Gibson and Glover work well together and give this movie extra punch. Followed by (so far) two sequels.
1987 (R) 110m/C Mel Gibson, Danny Glover, Gary Busey, Mitchell Ryan, Tom Atkins, Darlene Love, Traci Wolfe, Steve Kahan; **D:** Richard Donner; **W:** Shane Black; **M:** Michael Kamen, Eric Clapton. VHS, Beta, 8mm $19.98 WAR *III*

Lethal Weapon 2 This sequel to the popular cop adventure finds Gibson and Glover taking on a variety of blond South African "diplomats" who try to use their diplomatic immunity status to thwart the duo's efforts to crack their smuggling ring. Gibson finally finds romance, and viewers learn the truth about his late wife's accident. Also features the introduction of obnoxious, fast-talking con artist Leo ("OK, OK") Getz, adeptly played by Pesci, who becomes a third wheel to the crime-fighting team. Followed by a second sequel.
1989 (R) 114m/C Mel Gibson, Danny Glover, Joe Pesci, Joss Ackland, Derrick O'Connor, Patsy Kensit, Darlene Love, Traci Wolfe, Steve Kahan, Mary Ellen Trainor; **D:** Richard Donner; **W:** Jeffrey Boam; **M:** Michael Kamen, Eric Clapton, David Sanborn. VHS, Beta, 8mm $19.98 WAR *III*

Lethal Weapon 3 Murtaugh and Riggs return for more action in another slam-bang adventure. Murtaugh hopes his last week before retirement will be a peaceful one, but partner Riggs isn't about to let him go quietly. Not many changes from the successful formula with bickering buddies, lots of adventure, exploding buildings, a little comic relief from Pesci, and the addition of Russo as an Internal Affairs cop who proves to be more than a match for Riggs.
1992 (R) 118m/C Mel Gibson, Danny Glover, Joe Pesci, Rene Russo, Stuart Wilson, Steve Kahan, Darlene Love, Traci Wolfe, Gregory Millar, Jason Meshover-Iorg, Delores Hall; **D:** Richard Donner; **W:** Jeffrey Boam, Robert Mark Kamen; **M:** Michael Kamen, Eric Clapton, David Sanborn. VHS, 8mm $19.98 WAR, PMS *II*½

Lethal Woman A group of beautiful women, all once victimized by rapes, is recruited to an island by the "Lethal Woman," who plots revenge on any man who dares to vacation on the island.
1988 96m/C Shannon Tweed, Merete Van Kamp. VHS, Beta NO *I*½

Let's Dance A young widow tries to protect her son from his wealthy, paternal grandmother, while Fred dances his way into her heart. More obscure Astaire vehicle, but as charming as the rest. Needless to say, great dancing. ♫Tunnel of Love; The Hyacinth; Piano Dance; Jack and the Beanstalk; Can't Stop Talking; Oh, Them Dudes; Why Fight the Feeling?
1950 112m/C Betty Hutton, Fred Astaire, Roland Young, Ruth Warrick, Sheppard Strudwick, Lucile Watson, Barton MacLane, Gregory Moffett, Melville Cooper; **D:** Norman Z. McLeod. VHS, Beta $14.95 PAR *II*½

Let's Do It Again Atlanta milkman and his pal, a factory worker, milk two big-time gamblers out of a large sum of money in order to build a meeting hall for their fraternal lodge. Lesser sequel to "Uptown Saturday Night."
1975 (PG) 113m/C Sidney Poitier, Bill Cosby, John Amos, Jimmie Walker, Ossie Davis, Denise Nicholas, Calvin Lockhart; *D:* Sidney Poitier; *W:* Richard Wesley. VHS, Beta $19.98 WAR 🎬🎬½

Let's Get Harry Americans led by mercenaries mix it up with a Columbian cocaine franchise in an attempt to rescue their friend, Harry. Never released theatrically, for good reason. *AKA:* The Rescue.
1987 (R) 107m/C Robert Duvall, Gary Busey, Michael Schoeffling, Tom Wilson, Glenn Frey, Rick Rossovich, Ben Johnson, Matt Clark, Mark Harmon, Gregory Sierra, Elpidia Carrillo; *D:* Alan Smithee; *W:* Samuel Fuller; *M:* Brad Fiedel. VHS, Beta $14.99 HBO 🎬½

Let's Get Lost Absorbing documentary of Chet Baker, the prominent '50s "cool" jazz trumpeter (and occasional vocalist) who succumbed, like many of his peers, to drug addiction. Weber's black-and-white, fashion photography style well suits his subject. Downbeat, but rarely less than worthy.
1988 125m/B Chet Baker; *D:* Bruce Weber. VHS $89.95 MVD, COL 🎬🎬½

Let's Get Married A young doctor's weakness under pressure brings him to the brink of babbling idiocy when his wife goes into early labor.
1963 90m/B Anthony Newley, Ann Aubrey. VHS, Beta NO 🎬

Let's Get Tough The East Side Kids, unable to enlist because of their age, harass local Oriental shopkeepers and eventually get involved with a murder.
1942 52m/B Leo Gorcey, Bobby Jordan, Huntz Hall, Gabriel Dell, Sammy Morrison; *D:* Wallace Fox. VHS, Beta, 8mm $24.95 VYY, NOS, RXM 🎬

Let's Go! The son of a cement company president sets out to prove his worth to the firm by landing a contract with the town of Hillsboro. For some unknown reason, he sets off on an amazing set of stunts. Silent with original organ music.
1923 79m/B Richard Talmadge, Hal Clements, Eileen Percy, Tully Marshall; *D:* W.K. Howard. VHS, Beta, 8mm $24.95 VYY, GPV, GVV 🎬½

Let's Go Collegiate Two college rowers promise their girlfriends that they'll win the big race, but their plans are almost frustrated when their best oarsman is drafted. Their only hope lies in replacing him with a truck driver. 🎵Look What You've Done To Me; Sweet 16; Let's Do A Little Dreaming.
1941 62m/B Frankie Darro, Marcia Mae Jones, Jackie Moran, Keye Luke, Mantan Moreland, Gale Storm; *D:* Jean Yarborough. VHS $19.95 NOS 🎬½

Let's Kill All the Lawyers Low-budget satire about one man's angst over whether to become a lawyer is witty, entertaining, and not just for legal eagles. Law-firm intern Foster Merkul (Frederick) is apprenticed to a sleazeball (Vezina) who teaches him that money—not justice—is the name of the game in the law biz. Growing increasingly disillusioned, Foster sets out to reform the system with the help of Satori, a beautiful and mysterious creature of his imagination. Shot at sites in and around Detroit, this independent production features lots of cameos by local media celebrities.
1993 ?m/C Rick Frederick, James Vezina, Michelle De Vuono, Maggie Patton, Marty Smith; *D:* Ron Senkowski; *W:* Ron Senkowski. VHS NYR 🎬🎬½

Let's Make it Legal Amusing comedy of a married couple who decide to get a divorce after 20 years of marriage. Colbert stars as the woman who decides to leave her husband, Carey, because he's a chronic gambler. They part as friends, but soon Colbert's old flame, Scott, is back in town and things get rather complicated. A solid cast serves as the main strength in this film.
1951 77m/B Claudette Colbert, MacDonald Carey, Zachary Scott, Barbara Bates, Robert Wagner, Marilyn Monroe; *D:* Richard Sale; *W:* Hugh Herbert. VHS $14.98 FXV 🎬🎬½

Let's Make Love An urbane millionaire discovers he is to be parodied in an off-Broadway play, and vows to stop it—until he falls in love with the star of the show. He then ends up acting in the play. 🎵My Heart Belongs to Daddy; Let's Make Love; Specialization; Incurably Romantic; Sing Me a Song That Sells; You With the Crazy Eyes; Give Me the Simple Life.
1960 118m/C Yves Montand, Marilyn Monroe, Tony Randall, Frankie Vaughan, Bing Crosby, Gene Kelly, Milton Berle; *D:* George Cukor. VHS, Beta $14.98 FOX 🎬🎬½

Let's Make Up When it comes to giving her heart, Neagle can't decide between two dashing men. *AKA:* Lilacs in the Spring.
1955 94m/C Errol Flynn, Anna Neagle, David Farrar, Kathleen Harrison, Peter Graves; *D:* Herbert Wilcox. VHS GKK, MLB, MRV 🎬🎬

Let's Scare Jessica to Death A young woman who was recently released from a mental hospital is subjected to unspeakable happenings at a country home with her friends. She encounters murder, vampires, and corpses coming out of nowhere. A supernatural thriller with quite a few genuine scares.
1971 (PG) 89m/C Zohra Lampert, Barton Heyman, Kevin J. O'Connor, Gretchen Corbett, Alan Manson; *D:* John Hancock. VHS, Beta $49.95 PAR 🎬🎬

Let's Sing Again Eight-year-old singing sensation Bobby Breen made his debut in this dusty musical vehicle, as a runaway orphan who becomes the pal of a washed-up opera star in a traveling show. 🎵Let's Sing Again; Lullaby; Farmer in the Dell; La Donna e Mobile.
1936 70m/B Bobby Breen, Henry Armetta, George Houston, Vivienne Osborne, Grant Withers, Inez Courtney, Lucien Littlefield; *D:* Kurt Neumann. VHS $15.95 NOS, LOO, DVT 🎬🎬

The Letter When a man is shot and killed on a Malaysian plantation, the woman who committed the murder pleads self-defense. Her husband and his lawyer attempt to free her, but find more than they expected in this tightly-paced film noir. Based on the novel by W. Somerset Maugham. Davis emulated the originator of her role, Jeanne Eagels, in her mannerisms and line readings, although Eagels later went mad from drug abuse and overwork.
1940 96m/B Bette Davis, Herbert Marshall, James Stephenson, Gale Sondergaard, Bruce Lester, Cecil Kellaway, Victor Sen Yung, Frieda Inescort; *D:* William Wyler; *W:* Howard Koch; *M:* Max Steiner. VHS, Beta $19.95 FOX, MGM 🎬🎬🎬🎬

Letter from an Unknown Woman A woman falls in love with a concert pianist on the eve of his departure. He promises to return but never does. The story is told in flashbacks as the pianist reads a letter from the woman. A great romantic melodrama.
1948 90m/B Joan Fontaine, Louis Jourdan, Mady Christians, Marcel Journet, Art Smith; *D:* Max Ophuls. VHS $14.98 REP 🎬🎬🎬

Letter of Introduction A struggling young actress learns that her father is really a well known screen star and agrees not to reveal the news to the public.
1938 104m/B Adolphe Menjou, Edgar Bergen, George Murphy, Eve Arden, Ann Sheridan; *D:* John M. Stahl. VHS, Beta $19.95 NOS, MRV, HHT 🎬🎬½

Letter to Brezhnev Acclaimed independent film about two working-class Liverpool girls who fall in love with two furloughed Russian sailors. When the men eventually return to the USSR, one of the girls contacts the Russian Secretary General in an effort to rejoin her lover. Amusing tale of different relationships.
1986 (R) 94m/C Margi Clarke, Alexandra Pigg, Peter Firth, Ken Campbell, Tracy Lea, Alfred Molina, Angela Clarke; *D:* Chris Bernard; *W:* Frank Clarke; *M:* Alan Gill. VHS, Beta $19.98 LHV, IME, WAR 🎬🎬🎬

A Letter to Three Wives Crain, Darnell, and Sothern star as three friends who, shortly before embarking on a Hudson River boat trip, each receive a letter from Holm (who's never shown), the fourth member in their set. The letter tells them that she has run off with one of their husbands but does not specify his identity. The women spend the rest of the trip reviewing their sometimes shaky unions which provides some of the funniest and most caustic scenes, including Douglas (as Sothern's husband) ranting against the advertising business which supports his wife's radio soap opera. Sharp dialogue, moving performances. Based on the novel by John Klempner. Remade for television in 1985.
1949 103m/B Jeanne Crain, Linda Darnell, Ann Sothern, Kirk Douglas, Paul Douglas, Jeffrey Lynn, Thelma Ritter, Barbara Lawrence, Connie Gilchrist, Florence Bates; *D:* Joseph L. Mankiewicz; *W:* Joseph L. Mankiewicz; *M:* Alfred Newman; *V:* Celeste Holm. Academy Awards '49: Best Director (Mankiewicz), Best Screenplay (Mankiewicz); Nominations: Best Picture. VHS, Beta $19.98 FXV 🎬🎬🎬🎬

Letters from My Windmill A series of three short stories: "The Three Low Masses," "The Elixir of Father Gaucher," and "The Secret of Master Cornille" from respected director Pagnol. This unique format only enhances this film. In French with English subtitles.
1954 116m/B Henri Velbert, Yvonne Gamy, Robert Vattier, Roger Crouzet; *D:* Marcel Pagnol. VHS $29.95 NOS, DVT, APD 🎬🎬🎬½

Letters from the Park In Cuba, 1913, two taciturn would be lovers hire a poet, Victor La Place, to write love letters to each other. Normal proboscis aside, the poet follows the fate of Cyrano, and finds himself the unhappy hypotenuse in a triangular romance. Made for Spanish television. In Spanish with English subtitles.
1988 85m/C Victor Laplace, Ivonne Lopez, Miguel Paneque; *D:* Thomas Gutierrez Alea; *W:* Gabriel Garcia Marquez, Thomas Gutierrez Alea. VHS $79.95 FXL, FCT, APD 🎬🎬🎬

Letters to an Unknown Lover During WWII, a man and woman engage in sexual and emotional combat. *AKA:* Les Louves.
1984 101m/C Cherie Lunghi, Mathilda May, Yves Beneyton, Ralph Bates; *D:* Peter Duffell. VHS, Beta $29.95 ACA 🎬🎬½

Letting Go Made for television comedy-drama about a broken-hearted career woman and a young widower who fall in love.
1985 (PG) 94m/C John Ritter, Sharon Gless, Joe Cortese; *D:* Jack Bender. VHS, Beta $79.95 AIP 🎬🎬

Letting the Birds Go Free When a stranger is caught stealing from a farmer's barn, the farmer and his son decide to let the villain work off his crime. Some very interesting relationships develop from this arrangement.
1986 60m/C Lionel Jeffries. VHS $11.95 PSM ��

Leviathan A motley crew of ocean-floor miners are trapped when they are accidentally exposed to a failed Soviet experiment that turns humans into insatiable, regenerating fish-creatures.
1989 (R) 98m/C Peter Weller, Ernie Hudson, Hector Elizondo, Amanda Pays, Richard Crenna, Daniel Stern, Lisa Eilbacher, Michael Carmine, Meg Foster; D: George P. Cosmatos; W: David Peoples, Jeb Stuart; M: Jerry Goldsmith. VHS, Beta $14.95 MGM ��

L'Homme Blesse A serious erotic film about an 18-year-old boy, cloistered by an overbearing family, and his sudden awakening to his own homosexuality. In French with English subtitles. **AKA:** The Wounded Man.
1983 90m/C Jean-Hughes Anglade, Roland Bertin, Vittorio Mezzogiorno; D: Patrice Chereau. VHS, Beta $79.95 TPV, ING, CCN ��

Liana, Jungle Goddess A variation on the Greystoke legend featuring a beautiful (and topless) jungle goddess who is discovered living in the wilds of Africa. Thinking that she may be the lost granddaughter of a wealthy English nobleman, she's brought back to London for a reunion. Will civilization prove to be as dangerous as the jungle?
1956 ?m/C Marion Michael, Hardy Kruger. VHS $16.95 SNC ��

Lianna Acclaimed screenwriter/director John Sayles wrote and directed this story of a woman's romantic involvement with another woman. Chronicles an unhappy homemaker's awakening to the feelings of love that she develops for a female professor. Sayles makes an appearance as a family friend.
1983 (R) 110m/C Jon DeVries, Linda Griffiths, Jane Hallaren, Jo Henderson, Jessica Wright MacDonald; **Cameos:** John Sayles; D: John Sayles; W: John Sayles; M: Mason Daring. VHS, Beta $69.95 VES ��

The Liars Mystery in which a Frenchman strikes it rich in Africa, then returns home to Paris in search of a wife. He advertises for a mate, but is set up by con artists instead. In French with English subtitles.
1964 92m/C Dawn Addams, Jean Servais; D: Edmond T. Greville. VHS $29.95 FCT, ING ��

Liar's Edge Tweed portrays a single mother whose teenaged son, Mark, is plagued by violent fantasies. When she remarries and her new husband and sleazy brother-in-law move in, Mark's hallucinations become stronger until he believes he's witnessed a murder. The murder turns out to be a fact and his new stepfather is involved but can Mark prove it. Filmed on location in Niagra Falls.
1992 (R) 97m/C Shannon Tweed, Nicholas Shields, David Keith, Joseph Bottoms, Christopher Plummer; D: Ron Oliver; W: Ron Oliver. VHS $89.95 NLC, IME ��

Liar's Moon A local boy woos and weds the town's wealthiest young lady, only to be trapped in family intrigue.
1982 (PG) 106m/C Cindy Fisher, Matt Dillon, Christopher Connelly, Susan Tyrrell; D: David Fisher. VHS, Beta $29.98 VES ��

Libeled Lady A fast, complicated screwball masterwork, dealing with a newspaper editor's efforts to get something on a bratty heiress with the help of his own fiancee and a

reporter he recently fired. One of the era's funniest Hollywood films. Remade in 1946 as "Easy to Wed."
1936 98m/B Myrna Loy, Spencer Tracy, Jean Harlow, William Powell, Walter Connolly, Charley Grapewin, Cora Witherspoon, E.E. Clive, Charles Trowbridge, Dennis O'Keefe, Hattie McDaniel; D: Jack Conway. VHS, Beta $19.98 MGM ���½

The Liberation of L.B. Jones A wealthy black undertaker wants a divorce from his wife, who is having an affair with a white policeman. Wyler's final film.
1970 (R) 101m/C Lee J. Cobb, Lola Falana, Barbara Hershey, Anthony Zerbe, Roscoe Lee Browne; D: William Wyler; W: Sterling Silliphant; M: Elmer Bernstein. VHS, Beta $59.95 COL, FCT ��

Liberators Kinski stars as a criminal soldier battling with the American authorities, German troops, and his fugitive partner.
1977 91m/C Klaus Kinski. VHS, Beta $9.95 UNI �

Liberty & Bash Two boyhood friends who served together in Vietnam reunite to rid their neighborhood of drug pushers and save the life of a friend.
1990 (R) 92m/C Miles O'Keeffe, Lou Ferrigno, Mitzi Kapture, Richard Eden, Cheryl Paris, Gary Conway; D: Myrl A. Schreibman. VHS, Beta $89.95 FRH �

License to Drive When teen Haim fails the road test for his all-important driver's license, he steals the family car for a hot date with the girl of his dreams. The evening starts out quietly enough, but things soon go awry. If Haim survives the weekend, he'll definitely be able to pass his driving test on Monday morning. Semi-funny in a demolition derby sort of way.
1988 (PG-13) 90m/C Corey Feldman, Corey Haim, Carol Kane, Richard Masur; D: Greg Beeman; M: Jay Michael Ferguson. VHS, Beta $19.98 FOX ��

License to Kill Constantine stars as Agent Nick Carter involved with Oriental spies and a new secret weapon.
1964 100m/C Eddie Constantine, Yvonne Monlaur, Paul Frankeur; D: Henri Decoin. VHS $16.95 SNC ��

License to Kill A young girl is killed by a drunk driver, devastating both families. A made-for-television movie with a strong message against drinking and driving.
1984 96m/C James Farentino, Don Murray, Penny Fuller, Millie Perkins, Donald Moffatt, Denzel Washington, Ari Meyers; D: Judd Taylor. VHS, Beta $59.95 GEM ��

License to Kill The 18th Bond film, and Dalton's second, in which drug lords try to kill 007's best friend and former CIA agent. Disobeying orders for the first time and operating without his infamous "license to kill," Bond goes after the fiends. Fine outing for Dalton (and Bond, too).
1989 (PG-13) 133m/C Timothy Dalton, Carey Lowell, Robert Davi, Frank McRae, Talisa Soto, David Hedison, Anthony Zerbe, Everett McGill, Wayne Newton, Benicio Del Toro, Desmond Llewelyn, Priscilla Barnes; D: John Glen; W: Michael G. Wilson, Richard Maibaum; M: Michael Kamen. VHS, Beta $19.98 FOX, MGM ���

Liebestraum An architectural expert, his old college friend and the friend's wife form a dangerous triangle of passion and lust that strangely duplicates a situation that led to a double murder forty years earlier. The unrated version clocks in at 116 minutes.
1991 (R) 109m/C Kevin Anderson, Bill Pullman, Pamela Gidley, Kim Novak; D: Mike Figgis; W: Mike Figgis. VHS $14.95 MGM ��

Lies Complicated mystery about a murder/thriller movie plot becoming reality as it is being filmed, revolving around a scam to collect an inheritance from a rich guy in a mental hospital.
1983 (PG) 93m/C Ann Dusenberry, Gail Strickland, Bruce Davison, Clu Gulager, Bert Remsen, Dick Miller; D: Ken Wheat, Jim Wheat. VHS, Beta $79.98 FOX ��½

Lies Before Kisses A woman finds out her loving husband has been spending time with a beautiful call girl. When the call girl is murdered the husband is accused. His wife decides to help him clear his name but she just may have her own type of revenge in mind.
1992 (PG-13) 93m/C Jaclyn Smith, Ben Gazzara, Nick Mancuso, Greg Evigan, Penny Fuller, James Karen; D: Lou Antonio; W: Ellen Weston. VHS, Beta $89.98 TTC, PMS ��

Lies My Father Told Me Simple drama about growing up in the 1920s in a Jewish ghetto. The story revolves around a young boy's relationship with his immigrant grandfather. Quiet and moving.
1975 (PG) 102m/C Yossi Yadin, Len Birman, Marilyn Lightstone, Jeffery Lynas; D: Jan Kadar; W: Ted Allan. Academy Awards '75 Nominations: Best Original Screenplay; Golden Globe Awards '76: Best Foreign Film. VHS NO ���

Lies of the Twins A beautiful model becomes involved with her therapist and his identical, and irresponsible, twin brother.
1991 93m/C Isabella Rossellini, Aidan Quinn, Iman, John Pleshette; D: Tim Hunter. VHS $79.95 MCA ��

Lt. Robin Crusoe, U.S.N. A lighthearted navy pilot crash lands amusingly on a tropical island, falls hard for an island babe and schemes intensely against the local evil ruler. Lackluster Disney debacle.
1966 (G) 113m/C Dick Van Dyke, Nancy Kwan, Akim Tamiroff; D: Byron Paul. VHS, Beta DIS, OM ��

The Life and Assassination of the Kingfish Recommended by the NEA, this story of Louisiana politician Huey Long is riveting. Asner gives a profound performance.
1976 96m/C Ed Asner, Nicholas Pryor, Diane Kagan; D: Robert Collins. VHS, Beta NO �

The Life and Death of Colonel Blimp Chronicles the life of a British soldier who survives three wars (Boer, WWI, and WWII), falls in love with three women (all portrayed by Kerr), and dances a fine waltz. Fine direction and performance abound. **AKA:** Colonel Blimp.
1943 115m/C Roger Livesey, Deborah Kerr, Anton Walbrook, Ursula Jeans, Albert Lieven; D: Michael Powell, Emeric Pressburger. VHS, Beta $19.98 VYG ����

The Life and Loves of Mozart Despite the title, this is really about the great composer's later life at the time of the premiere of "Die Zauberfloete" ("The Magic Flute"). This is only partly saved by a stellar performance from Werner, as well as the music. Other than that, it gets bogged down in titillation about W.A.M.'s romantic life. In German with English subtitles.
1959 87m/C Oskar Werner, Johanna Matz, Angelika Hauff; D: Karl Hartli; M: The Vienna State Opera, The Vienna Philharmonic Orchestra; V: Anton Dermota. VHS $24.95 NOS, VEC ��½

Life and Nothing But Two young women search for their lovers at the end of WWI. They're helped by a French officer brutalized by the war and driven to find all of France's casualties. Romantic, evocative,

and saddening. In French with English subtitles. *AKA:* La Vie est Rien d'Autre.
1989 (PG) 135m/C Philippe Noiret, Sabine Azema, Francoise Perrot; *D:* Bertrand Tavernier; *W:* Bertrand Tavernier. **VHS, Beta $79.98** ORI, FCT, ING 🐾🐾🐾½

Life & Times of Captain Lou Albano The long and illustrious career of wrestling's most notorious manager.
1985 97m/C Captain Lou Albano, Mr. Fuji, Mr. Saito. **VHS, Beta $59.95** CSM 🐾🐾🐾½

Life & Times of Grizzly Adams Lightweight family adventure film based on the rugged life of legendary frontiersman, Grizzly Adams, that served as the launching pad for the TV series. Grizzly is mistakenly chased for a crime he didn't commit and along the way befriends a big bear.
1974 (G) 93m/C Dan Haggerty, Denver Pyle, Lisa Jones, Marjorie Harper, Don Shanks; *D:* Richard Friedenberg. **VHS, Beta $19.95** VCI 🐾🐾

Life & Times of Judge Roy Bean Based on the life of the famed Texas "hanging judge," the film features Newman as the legendary Bean who dispenses frontier justice in the days of the Wild West. Filled with gallows humor. Gardner sparkles as actress Lily Langtry.
1972 (PG) 124m/C Paul Newman, Stacy Keach, Ava Gardner, Jacqueline Bisset, Anthony Perkins, Roddy McDowall, Victoria Principal; *D:* John Huston; *W:* John Milius; *M:* Maurice Jarre. **VHS, Beta $19.98** WAR 🐾🐾½

The Life & Times of the Chocolate Killer Police turn against the hand that's helped them save property and lives, by framing a good samaritan with deeds done by the "Chocolate Killer."
1988 75m/C Michael Adrian, Rod Browning, Tabi Cooper. **VHS $79.95** VMK 🐾½

Life Begins for Andy Hardy Andy gets a job in New York before entering college and finds the working world to be a sobering experience. Surprisingly downbeat and hard-hitting for an Andy Hardy film. Garland's last appearance in the series.
1941 100m/B Mickey Rooney, Judy Garland, Lewis Stone, Ann Rutherford, Fay Holden, Gene Reynolds, Ralph Byrd; *D:* George B. Seitz. **VHS, Beta $19.95** MGM 🐾🐾🐾

A Life in the Theater Life in the theater as a hammy stage veteran (Lemmon) shares his experiences (and his dressing room) with a callow newcomer (Broderick). Petty squabbles, missed cues, and rare candor are displayed as the two stage scenes from their various repertory. Gentle, slight Mamet play, written when he was 25. Made for television.
1993 78m/C Jack Lemmon, Matthew Broderick; *D:* Gregory Mosher; *W:* David Mamet. **VHS** TTC 🐾🐾½

Life is a Circus, Charlie Brown/ You're the Greatest, Charlie Brown Two Peanuts favorites appear on this tape. In the Emmy award-winning "Life Is a Circus, Charlie Brown," Snoopy falls in love with Fifi, a French poodle circus performer, and winds up as a member of the traveling circus. In "You're the Greatest, Charlie Brown," our hero has a chance to win a decathlon in the Junior Olympics. With Peppermint Patty coaching, anything can happen!
1980 60m/C *D:* Phil Roman. **VHS, Beta $14.95** SHV, VTR, WTA 🐾🐾½

Life Is a Long Quiet River Social comedy about a nurse who, infuriated with her married doctor employer/lover, switches two babies at birth. Twelve years later, after

her lover's wife has died and he still refuses to marry her, she reveals the swap. The children are returned to their rightful families causing a multitude of confusion and adjustment. Directorial debut of Chatiliez. In French with English subtitles. *AKA:* La Vie Est Une Longue Fleuve Tranquille.
1988 89m/C Benoit Magimel, Helene Vincent, Andre Wilms, Daniel Gelin, Catherine Hiegel, Christine Pignet, Patrick Bouchitey, Valerie Lalande, Tara Romer, Jerome Floch, Sylvie Cubertafon; *D:* Etienne Chatiliez; *W:* Florence Quentin, Etienne Chatiliez; *M:* Gerard Kawczynski. **VHS $79.95** NYF, FCT 🐾🐾🐾

Life is Beautiful A politically neutral man is arrested and tortured in pre-revolutionary Lisbon, and forced to make, and act on, a political commitment. Dubbed.
1979 102m/C Giancarlo Giannini, Ornella Muti; *D:* Grigorij Ciukhrai. **VHS, Beta $19.95** NWV 🐾🐾½

Life is Sweet The consuming passions of food and drink focus the lives of an oddball English working-class family beset by hopeless dreams and passions. Mother is always fixing family meals—in between helping her friend open a gourmet restaurant which features such revolting dishes as pork cyst and prune quiche. Dad is a chef who buys a snack truck and dreams of life on the road. Natalie and Nicola, the grown twins, eat their meals in front of the television but Nicola is also a bulimic who binges and purges on chocolate bars behind her bedroom door. (Note the chocolate scene between Nicola and her boyfriend.) An affectionate, if sometimes unattractive, look at a chaotic family.
1991 (R) 103m/C Alison Steadman, Jane Horrocks, Jim Broadbent, Claire Skinner, Timothy Spall, Stephen Rea, David Thewlis; *D:* Mike Leigh; *W:* Mike Leigh. **VHS $14.98** REP, BTV 🐾🐾🐾½

The Life of Emile Zola Writer Emile Zola intervenes in the case of Alfred Dreyfus who was sent to Devil's Island for a crime he did not commit. Well-crafted production featuring a handsome performance from Muni.
1937 117m/B Paul Muni, Gale Sondergaard, Gloria Holden, Joseph Schildkraut; *D:* William Dieterle. Academy Awards '37: Best Picture, Best Screenplay, Best Supporting Actor (Schildkraut); Nominations: Best Actor (Muni), Best Director (Dieterle), Best Interior Decoration, Best Sound, Best Story, Best Original Score. **VHS, Beta $19.98** MGM, BTV 🐾🐾🐾½

A Life of Her Own Turner stars as a farm girl who takes her dream of becoming a top model to the Big Apple. She signs with an agency and is befriended by Dvorak, an aging model, who acts as her mentor. Turner finds success and is soon the toast of the town until she gets involved with a married man (Milland) and her life starts to crumble. Average soap opera with flimsy script. Turner is good, but Dvorak steals the show in her role as an over-the-hill fashion plate.
1950 108m/B Lana Turner, Ray Milland, Tom Ewell, Louis Calhern, Ann Dvorak, Barry Sullivan, Jean Hagen, Phyllis Kirk, Sara Haden; *D:* George Cukor; *W:* Isobel Lennart. **VHS $19.98** MGM 🐾🐾½

Life of Oharu A near masterpiece rivaled only by "Ugetsu" in the Mizoguchi canon, this film details the slow and agonizing moral decline of a woman in feudal Japan, from wife to concubine to prostitute. A scathing portrait of social pre-destination based on a novel by Ibara Saikaku. In Japanese with English subtitles. *AKA:* Diary of Oharu; Saikaku Ichidai Onna.
1952 136m/B Kinuyo Tanaka, Toshiro Mifune; *D:* Kenji Mizoguchi. **VHS, Beta $39.95** VYY, APD, ING 🐾🐾🐾½

A Life of Sin Scandalous drama about an impoverished Caribbean girl who rises to wealth and power as a world-famous madame. Colon stars as the beautiful Isabel, who is betrayed by her childhood friend Paulo (Julia) and rejected by the Catholic bishop (Ferrer) in this tragic story of passion and greed.
1992 (R) 112m/C Raul Julia, Miriam Colon, Jose Ferrer; *D:* Efrain Lopez Neris; *W:* Emilio Diaz Valcarcel. **VHS $89.95** COL, PMS 🐾🐾

Life of Verdi Epic mini-series biography of the famous composer, with many excerpts of his music sung by Luciano Pavarotti, Renata Telbaldi, and Maria Callas. Made for television.
1984 600m/B Ronald Pickup, Carla Fracci. **VHS, Beta $124.95** HMV, KUL, MVD 🐾🐾

Life on a String Set in the distant past, this is a lyrical story of a young boy searching for a cure for his blindness. His possible cure involves a myth which requires him to devote his life to music and the breaking of 1000 strings on a banjo. Adapted from a story by Shi Tiesheng. In Chinese with English subtitles.
1990 110m/C *D:* Chen Kaige. **VHS $79.95** FCT, KIV 🐾🐾

Life Stinks So does the film. A grasping tycoon bets he can spend a month living on the street without money, resulting in cheap laughs, heavy-handed sentiment and one musical number. Those expecting the innovative, hilarious Brooks of "Young Frankenstein" or "Blazing Saddles" will be very disappointed—these jokes are stale and the timing is tedious. Those looking for a Chaplinesque tale for modern times should stick with Chaplin.
1991 (PG-13) 93m/C Mel Brooks, Jeffrey Tambor, Lesley Ann Warren, Stuart Pankin, Howard Morris, Teddy Wilson, Michael Ensign, Billy Barty, Carmine Caridi, Rudy DeLuca; *D:* Mel Brooks; *W:* Mel Brooks, Rudy DeLuca. **VHS, Beta $14.95** MGM 🐾

Life with Father Based on the writings of the late Clarence Day, Jr., this is the story of his childhood in New York City during the 1880s. A delightful saga about a stern but loving father and his relationship with his knowing wife and four red-headed sons.
1947 118m/C William Powell, Irene Dunne, Elizabeth Taylor, Edmund Gwenn, ZaSu Pitts, Jimmy Lydon, Martin Milner; *D:* Michael Curtiz. Academy Awards '47: Nominations: Best Actor (Powell), Best Art Direction/Set Decoration (Color), Best Color Cinematography; Golden Globe Awards '48: Best Score; New York Film Critics Awards '47: Best Actor (Powell). **VHS, Beta $9.95** CNG, MRV, NOS 🐾🐾🐾½

Life with Mikey Michael "Mikey" Chapman (Fox) is a washed-up former child star who now half-heartedly runs a minor talent agency for other pint-sized would-be thespians. Ever mindful of his previous glory, he believes he is doomed to obscurity when a 10-year-old Brooklyn pickpocket reanimates his taste for life. Light, sweet comedy is generally predictable, a typical Fox effort. Unbilled cameo from Reuben Blades as Vidal's father.
1993 (PG-13) 92m/C Michael J. Fox, Christina Vidal, Cyndi Lauper, Nathan Lane, David Huddleston, Victor Garber, David Krumholtz, Tony Hendra; *Cameos:* Ruben Blades; *D:* James Lapine; *W:* Marc Lawrence; *M:* Alan Menken. **VHS, Beta $39.99** TOU, BTV 🐾🐾½

Lifeboat When a German U-boat sinks a freighter during WWII, the eight survivors seek refuge in a tiny lifeboat. Tension peaks after the drifting passengers take in a stranded Nazi. Hitchcock saw a great challenge in

having the entire story take place in a lifeboat and pulled it off with his usual flourish. In 1989, the film "Dead Calm" replicated the technique. From a story by John Steinbeck. Bankhead shines.
1944 96m/B Tallulah Bankhead, John Hodiak, William Bendix, Canada Lee, Walter Slezak, Hume Cronyn, Henry Hull, Mary Anderson; *D:* Alfred Hitchcock. Academy Awards '44 Nominations: Best Director (Hitchcock); National Board of Review Awards '44: 10 Best Films of the Year; New York Film Critics Awards '44: Best Actress (Bankhead). **VHS, Beta $19.98** HMV, FOX ✐✐✐½

Lifeforce A beautiful female vampire from outer space drains Londoners and before long the city is filled with disintegrating zombies in this hi-tech thriller. Sex was never stranger.
1985 (R) 100m/C Steve Railsback, Peter Firth, Frank Finlay, Patrick Stewart, Michael Gothard, Nicholas Ball, Aubrey Morris, Nancy Paul, Mathilda May, John Hallam; *D:* Tobe Hooper; *W:* Dan O'Bannon, Don Jakoby; *M:* Henry Mancini, Michael Kamen. **VHS, Beta $9.99** FHE, LIV, VES ✐✐½

Lifeguard The lifeguard lives by the credo that work is for people who cannot surf. Aging, he questions whether he should give up the beach life and start selling Porsches. Made for television.
1975 (PG) 96m/C Sam Elliott, Anne Archer, Stephen Young, Parker Stevenson, Kathleen Quinlan; *D:* Daniel Petrie. **VHS, Beta $14.95** PAR ✐✐

Lifepod A group of intergalactic travelers is forced to evacuate a luxury space liner when a mad computer sabotages the ship.
1980 94m/C Joe Penny, Jordan Michaels, Kristine DeBell. **VHS, Beta $49.95** VCI ✐

Lifepod Trapped on a ship with a killer—only this time it's a space ship. In the year 2169 an interplanetary liner is sabotaged. Nine people escape in a damaged lifepod emergency craft. The survivors are perilously short of food and water and cannot contact Earth. They also face frightening evidence that the terrorist is among their group and is determined to kill the remaining survivors. Very loose adaptation of Alfred Hitchcock's 1944 film "Lifeboat." Made for television.
1993 120m/C Ron Silver, Robert Loggia, CCH Pounder, Stan Shaw, Adam Storke, Jessica Tuck, Kelli Williams, Ed Gate; *D:* Ron Silver; *W:* M. Jay Roach, Pen Densham. **VHS $89.95** CAF ✐✐½

Lifespan A young American scientist visiting Amsterdam discovers experiments involving a drug that halts aging.
1975 85m/C Klaus Kinski, Hiram Keller, Tina Aumont; *D:* Alexander Whitelaw. **VHS, Beta $69.95** VES ✐

The Lifetaker A woman lures an unsuspecting young man into her home where she seduces him. Violence and sex ensue.
1989 97m/C Lea Dregorn, Peter Duncan, Terence Morgan; *D:* Michael Papas. **VHS** NO Woof!

The Lift Unsuspecting passengers meet an unfortunate fate when they take a ride in a demonic elevator in a highrise. In this film the last stop isn't ladies' lingerie, but death. In Dutch with English subtitles.
1985 (R) 95m/C Huub Stapel, Willeke Van Ammelrooy; *D:* Dick Maas. **VHS, Beta $59.95** MED, ING ✐

The Light Ahead Lovers Fishke and Hodel dream of escaping the poverty and prejudices of their shtetl for the possibilities of big city life in Odessa. They're aided in their quest by enlightened bookseller Mendele who turns the town's superstitions to

their advantage. Based on the stories of social satirist Mendele Mokher Seforim. In Yiddish with English subtitles.
1939 94m/B David Opatoshu, Isadore Cashier, Helen Beverly; *D:* Edgar G. Ulmer. **VHS $72.00** NCJ, ERG ✐✐½

Light at the Edge of the World A band of pirates torments a lighthouse keeper near Cape Horn after he sees a shipwreck they caused.
1971 (PG) 126m/C Kirk Douglas, Yul Brynner, Samantha Eggar; *D:* Kevin Billington. **VHS, Beta $69.95** MED ✐

The Light in the Forest Disney adaptation of the classic Conrad Richter novel about a young man, kidnapped by Indians when he was young, who is forcibly returned to his white family.
1958 92m/C James MacArthur, Fess Parker, Carol Lynley, Wendell Corey, Joanne Dru, Jessica Tandy, Joseph Calleia, John McIntire; *D:* Herschel Daugherty. **VHS, Beta $69.95** DIS ✐✐½

The Light in the Jungle The biography of Nobel Peace Prize winner Dr. Albert Schweitzer. He established a hospital in Africa and had to overcome many obstacles, including tribal superstitions and European bureaucracy to make it successful and bring health care to the area.
1991 (PG) 91m/C Malcolm McDowell, Susan Strasberg, Andrew Davis; *D:* Gray Hof-meyr. **VHS $89.98** LIV ✐✐½

Light of Day A rock 'n roll semi-musical about a working class brother and sister who escape from their parents and aimless lives through their bar band. Script tends to fall flat although both Fox and Jett are believable. Title song written by Bruce Springsteen.
1987 (PG-13) 107m/C Michael J. Fox, Joan Jett, Gena Rowlands, Jason Miller, Michael McKean, Michael Rooker, Michael Dolan; *D:* Paul Schrader; *W:* Paul Schrader. **VHS, Beta $29.98** LIV, VES ✐✐

The Light of Faith A sick young woman is cured when she touches the Holy Grail, which a man stole from her former lover in order to help her. Silent.
1922 33m/C Lon Chaney Sr., Hope Hampton; *D:* Clarence Brown. **VHS, Beta $16.95** SNC, BFA, CNM ✐✐

The Light of Western Stars Brian plays a young woman from the east who comes to claim her late brother's ranch. She meets her murdered brother's best friend (Arlen) who is a drunken cowboy, and he falls madly in love with her. Wanting to impress her, he quickly sobers up and prevents a gang from taking over the ranch. This was Paramount's first talking adaptation of a Grey novel and the third version of this particular Grey novel; silent versions were made in 1918 and 1925.
1930 70m/B Richard Arlen, Mary Brian, Regis Toomey, Harry Green, Syd Saylor, George Chandler; *D:* Otto Brower, Edwin H. Knopf. **VHS $9.95** GPV ✐✐½

The Light of Western Stars A proper Eastern woman goes West and falls in love with a drunken lout.
1940 67m/B Victor Jory, Jo Ann Sayers, Russell Hayden, Morris Ankrum; *D:* Lesley Selander. **VHS $9.95** GPV, DVT, NOS ✐

Light Sleeper Schrader's moody look at upscale drug dealers in New York. Dafoe is John LaTour, a 40 year-old drug courier to the club scene. Since his boss (Sarandon) is giving up the drug business for the safer world of natural cosmetics, John must look to his own future. His life becomes even more complicated when he runs into a bitter ex-flame (Delany) and finds the attraction is

still overpowering. Cynical, contemplative, and menacing.
1992 (R) 103m/C Willem Dafoe, Susan Sarandon, Dana Delany, David Clennon, Mary Beth Hurt; *D:* Paul Schrader; *W:* Paul Schrader. **VHS $92.98** LIV ✐✐

Light Years Garish animated fantasy epic about an idyllic land suddenly beset by evil mutations and death rays. Based on the novel "Robots Against Gondohar" by Jean-Pierre Andrevan.
1988 83m/C *D:* Harvey Weinstein; *W:* Isaac Asimov; *M:* Gabriel Yared; *V:* Glenn Close, Jennifer Grey, Christopher Plummer, Penn Jillette, John Shea, David Johansen, Bridget Fonda, Paul Shaffer, Terrence Mann, Teller. **VHS, Beta $29.95** VMK, WTA, FUS ✐✐½

Lightblast A San Francisco policeman tries to stop a deadly explosive-wielding mad scientist from blowing the city to kingdom come.
1985 89m/C Erik Estrada, Michael Pritchard; *D:* Enzo G. Castellari. **VHS, Beta $69.98** LIV ✐

The Lighthorsemen Compelling WWI drama follows several battle-hardened men of the Australian Light-Horse mounted infantry stationed in the Middle Eastern desert and the new recruit who joins their ranks and craves acceptance. Superbly filmed, particularly the final battle scene which pits the Aussies against the Turks for control of the wells at Beersheba. Fine performance by Andrews in this epic which contains the essential elements of a good war movie—horses, guns, and more horses. Originally filmed at 140 minutes. Good companion film for another Aussie WWI saga: "Gallipoli."
1987 (PG-13) 110m/C Jon Blake, Peter Phelps, Tony Bonner, Bill Kerr, Nick Wateres, John Walton, Tim McKenzie, Sigrid Thornton, Anthony Andrews; *D:* Simon Wincer; *W:* Ian Jones; *M:* Mario Millo. **VHS, Beta $19.98** WAR, HBO ✐✐✐

Lightnin' Carson Rides Again A tough frontier lawman tracks down his pay-roll-carrying nephew who's been accused of murder and thievery.
1938 58m/B Tim McCoy, Joan Barclay, Ted Adams, Forrest Taylor; *D:* Sam Newfield. **VHS, Beta, 8mm $19.95** NOS, VYY ✐½

Lightning Bill Bill champions good in battling rustlers.
1935 46m/B Buffalo Bill Jr. **VHS, Beta** NO ✐

Lightning Bill Crandall Gunman heads south for the quiet life. Unfortunately, Arizona proves the scene of a fierce battle between various factions of cattlemen. The gunman aids the good guys, and tries to win the daughter's heart.
1937 60m/B Bob Steele, Lois January, Charles "Blackie" King, Frank LaRue, Ernie Adams, Earl Dwire, Dave O'Brien; *D:* Sam Newfield. **VHS $19.95** NOS, DVT ✐½

Lightning Bolt Someone is stealing moon rockets from Cape Kennedy, and secret agent Harry Sennet must find out who is doing this devilish deed. It leads him to an evil madman who plots to destroy the world from his underwater hideout. Cheap and unintentionally funny. *AKA:* Operazione Goldman.
1967 96m/C Anthony Eisley, Wandisa Leigh, Folco Lulli, Diana Lorys, Ursula Parker; *D:* Anthony M. (Antonio Marghereti) Dawson. **VHS $16.95** SNC ✐

The Lightning Incident McKeon plays a young Santa Fe sculptor whose worst nightmares come true when her baby is kidnapped by a devil-worshipping cult. Discovering she has a powerful psychic gift, she pursues the kidnappers across the country in a race to save her baby. Almost as bad as it sounds.

1991 (R) 90m/C Nancy McKeon, Polly Bergen, Tantoo Cardinal, Elpidia Carrillo, Tim Ryan; **D:** Michael Switzer; **W:** Michael J. Murray. **VHS, Beta** *PAR* ♫½

Lightning Jack Western comedy about Lightning Jack Kane (Hogan), an aging second-rate outlaw who desperately wants to become a western legend. Mute store clerk Ben (Gooding) winds up as his partner in crime, while barely eluding criticisms of Stepin Fetchitism. Cliches galore, the running gags (including Kane's surreptitious use of his eyeglasses so he can see his shooting targets) fall flat.

1994 (PG-13) 101m/C Paul Hogan, Cuba Gooding Jr., Beverly D'Angelo, Kamala Dawson, Pat Hingle, Richard Riehle, Frank McRae, Roger Daltrey, L.Q. Jones, Max Cullen; **D:** Simon Wincer; **W:** Paul Hogan; **M:** Bruce Rowland. **VHS** *HBO* ♫½

Lightning Over Water An odd, touching documentary co-arranged by Ray and Wenders, all about Ray's last months dying of cancer in his New York loft, his editing of his final film "We Can't Go Home Again," his film corpus and career in general.

1980 91m/C Nicholas Ray, Wim Wenders, Ronee Blakley, Tom Farrel, Gerry Bamman; **D:** Wim Wenders; **W:** Wim Wenders. **VHS, Beta** **$59.95** *IME, ING* ♫½

Lightning Raiders When a stage coach filled with mail gets robbed, Billy Carson (Crabbe) and Fuzzy (St. John) set off to avenge the postal system. One of the last Crabbe/St. John efforts; perhaps they should have called it quits a few films earlier.

1945 61m/C Buster Crabbe, Al "Fuzzy" St. John, Mady Lawrence, Henry Hall, Steve Darrell, I. Stanford Jolley, Karl Hackett, Roy Brent, Marin Sais, Al Ferguson; **D:** Sam Newfield; **W:** Elmer Clifton. **VHS** *HEG* ♫♫

Lightning Range Roosevelt stars as a U.S. Deputy Marshal who continually foils the nefarious plots of a gang of outlaws.

1933 50m/B Buddy Roosevelt, Lafe McKee. **VHS, Beta** **$19.95** *NOS, VYY* ♫

Lightning Strikes West U.S. Marshal trails an escaped convict, eventually catches him, and brings him in to finish paying his debt to society.

1940 57m/B Ken Maynard. **VHS, Beta** **$19.95** *VCN, VCI* ♫½

Lightning: The White Stallion An old gambler and his two young friends enter a horse race in order to win their beloved white stallion back from thieves.

1986 (PG) 93m/C Mickey Rooney, Susan George, Isabel Lorca; **D:** William A. Levey. **VHS, Beta** **$19.98** *MED* ♫½

Lightning Warrior Western suspense about pioneer life and the unraveling of a baffling mystery. Twelve chapters, 13 minutes each.

1931 156m/B George Brent, Frankie Darro; **D:** Armand Schaefer, Ben Kline. **VHS, Beta** **$27.95** *VCN* ♫½

Lights! Camera! Murder! When a twelve-year-old boy witnesses a filmed murder, he becomes the next target.

1989 89m/C John Barrett; **D:** Frans Nel. **VHS** **$79.95** *ATL* ♫♫

Lights of Old Santa Fe A cowboy rescues a beautiful rodeo owner from bankruptcy. The original, unedited version of the film.

1947 78m/B Roy Rogers, Dale Evans, George "Gabby" Hayes, Bob Nolan, The Pioneers. **VHS, Beta** **$19.95** *NOS, DVT, TIM* ♫½

The Lightship On a stationary lightship off the Carolina coast, the crew rescues three men from a disabled boat, only to find they are murderous criminals. Duvall as a flamboyant homosexual psychopath is memorable, but the tale is pretentious, overdone, and hackneyed. Based on Siegfried Lenz's story.

1986 (PG-13) 87m/C Robert Duvall, Klaus Maria Brandauer, Tom Bower, William Forsythe, Arliss Howard; **D:** Jerzy Skolimowski. **VHS, Beta** **$79.95** *FOX* ♫♫

Like Father, Like Son First and worst of a barrage of interchangeable switcheroo movies that came out in '87-'88. Moore is in top form, but the plot is contrived.

1987 (PG-13) 101m/C Dudley Moore, Kirk Cameron, Catherine Hicks, Margaret Colin, Sean Astin; **D:** Rod Daniel; **M:** Miles Goodman. **VHS, Beta** **$19.95** *COL* ♫

Like Water for Chocolate Magical Mexican fairytale set in the early 1900s about family, love, and the power of food. Formidable Mama Elena is left a widow with three daughters. The youngest, Tita, grows up in the kitchen surrounded by all the magic Nacha, the housekeeper, can impart to her about food. Doomed by tradition to spend her days caring for her mother, Tita escapes by cooking, releasing her sorrows and longings into the food, infecting all who eat it. Wonderfully sensuous and slyly exaggerated. Based on the novel by Esquival who also wrote the screenplay and whose husband, Arau, directed. In Spanish with English subtitles; also available dubbed. *AKA:* Como Agua para Chocolate.

1993 (R) 105m/C Lumi Cavazos, Marco Leonardi, Regina Torne, Mario Ivan Martinez, Ada Carrasco, Yareli Arizmendi, Caudette Maille, Pilar Aranda; **D:** Alfonso Arau; **W:** Laura Esquivel; **M:** Leo Brower. **VHS** *TOU* ♫♫♫½

Li'l Abner Al Capp's famed comic strip comes somewhat to life in this low-budget comedy featuring all of the Dogpatch favorites. *AKA:* Trouble Chaser.

1940 78m/C Cranville Owen, Martha Driscoll, Buster Keaton; **D:** Albert Rogell. **VHS, Beta** **$24.95** *NOS, MRV, DVT* ♫½

Li'l Abner High color Dogpatch drama adapted from the Broadway play (with most of the original cast) based on the Al Capp comic strip. When Abner's berg is considered as a site for atomic bomb testing, the natives have to come up with a reason why they should be allowed to exist. Choreography by Michael Kidd and Dee Dee Wood. ♫Jubilation T. Cornpone; Don't Take That Rag Off'n the Bush; A Typical Day; If I Had My Druthers; Room Enuff for Us; Namely You; The Country's in the Very Best of Hands; Unnecessary Town; I'm Past My Prime.

1959 114m/C Peter Palmer, Leslie Parrish, Stubby Kaye, Julie Newmar, Howard St. John, Stella Stevens, Billie Hayes, Joe E. Marks; **D:** Melvin Frank; **W:** Norman Panama; **M:** Johnny Mercer, Jean De Paul. **VHS, Beta** **$14.95** *PAR, FCT* ♫♫½

Lili Delightful musical romance about a 16-year-old orphan who joins a traveling carnival and falls in love with a crippled, embittered puppeteer. Heartwarming and charming, if occasionally cloying. Leslie Caron sings the films's song hit, "Hi-Lili, Hi-Lo."

1953 81m/C Leslie Caron, Jean-Pierre Aumont, Mel Ferrer, Kurt Kasznar, Zsa Zsa Gabor; **D:** Charles Walters; **M:** Bronislau Kaper. Academy Awards '53: Best Score; Nominations: Best Actress (Caron), Best Art Direction/Set Decoration (Color), Best Color Cinematography, Best Director (Walters), Best Screenplay; British Academy Awards '53: Best Actress (Caron);

Golden Globe Awards '54: Best Screenplay; National Board of Review Awards '53: 10 Best Films of the Year. **VHS, Beta** **$19.98** *MGM* ♫♫♫

Lilies of the Field Five East German nuns enlist the aid of a free-spirited U.S. Army veteran. They persuade him to build a chapel for them and teach them English. Poitier is excellent as the itinerant laborer, holding the saccharine to an acceptable level, bringing honesty and strength to his role. Actress Skala had been struggling to make ends meet in a variety of day jobs until this opportunity. Poitier was the first African-American man to win an Oscar, and the first African-American nominated since Hattie MacDaniel in 1939. Followed by "Christmas Lilies of the Field," (1979).

1963 94m/B Sidney Poitier, Lilia Skala, Lisa Mann, Isa Crino, Stanley Adams; **D:** Ralph Nelson; **M:** Jerry Goldsmith. Academy Awards '63: Best Actor (Poitier); Nominations: Best Adapted Screenplay, Best Black and White Cinematography, Best Picture, Best Supporting Actress (Skala); Berlin International Film Festival '63: Best Actor (Poitier); Golden Globe Awards '64: Best Actor—Drama (Poitier); National Board of Review Awards '63: 10 Best Films of the Year. **VHS, Beta** **$19.98** *MGM, FOX, BTV* ♫♫♫

Liliom Boyer goes to heaven and is put on trial to see if he is deserving of his wings. Lang's first film after leaving Nazi Germany is filled with wonderful ethereal imagery, surprising coming from the man responsible for such grim visions as "Metropolis." In French only.

1935 85m/B Charles Boyer, Madeleine Ozeray, Florelle, Roland Toutain; **D:** Fritz Lang. **VHS, Beta** **$16.95** *SNC, DVT, HEG* ♫♫♫

Lilith Therapist-in-training Beatty falls in love with beautiful mental patient Seberg and approaches madness himself. A look at the doctor-patient relationship among the mentally ill and at the nature of madness and love. Doesn't always satisfy, but intrigues. Rossen's swan song.

1964 114m/B Warren Beatty, Jean Seberg, Peter Fonda, Gene Hackman, Kim Hunter; **D:** Robert Rossen. **VHS, Beta** **$59.95** *COL, MLB* ♫♫♫

Lillie The life of Edwardian beauty Lillie Langtry, known as "The Jersey Lily," is portrayed in this British made-for-television drama. Defying the morals of the times, Lillie was the first publicly acknowledged mistress of the Prince of Wales, only one of her numerous lovers. On seven cassettes. Shown on "Masterpiece Theatre" on PBS.

1979 690m/C Francesca Annis, Cheryl Campbell, John Castle, Dennis Lili, Peter Egan, Anton Rodgers, Ann Firbank. **VHS** **$149.95** *SIG, TVC, HMV* ♫♫♫

Lily in Love An aging stage star disguises himself as a suave Italian to star in his playwright wife's new play, and woos her to test her fidelity. Charming, warm, and sophisticated. Loosely based on Molnar's "The Guardsman." Made for television. *AKA:* Playing for Keeps; Jatszani Kell.

1985 (PG-13) 100m/C Dame Maggie Smith, Christopher Plummer, Elke Sommer, Adolph Green; **D:** Karoly Makk; **W:** Frank Cucci. **VHS, Beta** **$79.98** *LIV, VES* ♫♫½

Lily of Killarney A musical comedy romance about a British lord who arranges to pay his debts via horse-races, arranged marriages and inheritances. *AKA:* The Bride of the Lake.

1934 82m/B Gina Malo, John Garrick, Stanley Holloway; **D:** Maurice Elvey. **VHS, Beta, 8mm** **$24.95** *VYY* ♫♫

Lily was Here After her fiancee is senselessly murdered, a young woman named Lily is forced to turn to a life of crime in order to survive. A series of petty thefts evolves into a huge crime wave and Lily soon finds herself the object of a massive manhunt. Lily must make the ultimate choice between freedom and motherhood in this shocking thriller. Soundtrack by Dave Stewart features hit instrumental theme "Lily was Here" by saxophonist Candy Dulfur.
1989 (R) 110m/C Marion Van Thijn, Thom Hoffman, Adrian Brine, Dennis Rudge; *W:* Ben Verbong, Sytze Van Der Laan, Willem Jan Otten. VHS ING ♪♪½

Limelight A nearly washed-up music hall comedian is stimulated by a young ballerina to a final hour of glory. A subtle if self-indulgent portrait of Chaplin's own life, featuring an historic pairing of Chaplin and Keaton.
1952 120m/B Charlie Chaplin, Claire Bloom, Buster Keaton, Nigel Bruce; *D:* Charlie Chaplin. VHS, Beta $19.98 FOX ♪♪♪

Limit Up An ambitious Chicago Trade Exchange employee makes a deal with the devil to corner the market in soybeans. Turgid attempt at supernatural comedy, featuring Charles as God. Catch Sally Kellerman in a cameo as a nightclub singer.
1989 (PG-13) 88m/C Nancy Allen, Dean Stockwell, Brad Hall, Danitra Vance, Ray Charles, Luana Anders; *Cameos:* Sally Kellerman; *D:* Richard Martini. VHS, Beta NO ♪♪

The Limping Man Bridges returns to post-WWII London to renew a wartime romance. On the way, he gets caught up in solving a murder. Unexceptional of-its-era thriller.
1953 76m/B Lloyd Bridges, Moira Lister, Leslie Phillips, Helene Cordet, Alan Wheatley; *D:* Charles De Latour. VHS, Beta $16.95 SNC, RXM, VYY ♪♪

Linchamiento Cattle ranchers and farmers battle it out again. Dubbed into Spanish. *AKA:* Lynching.
1968 90m/C Glen Saxson, Gordon Mitchell, Christine Schmidt, King MacQueen. VHS, Beta NO ♪

Lincoln County Incident A satiric western starring secondary-school children.
1980 47m/C VHS, Beta NO ♪½

Linda Linda, a young mountain girl, is forced to marry a much older man though her heart belongs to a young doctor. Her kind husband tries to make the best of the situation.
1929 75m/B Helen Foster, Warner Baxter, Noah Beery Sr., Mitchell Lewis, Kate Price, Alan Connor; *D:* Dorothy Davenport Reid. VHS $19.95 GPV ♪♪½

Linda Madsen in her femme fatale mode as treacherous wife Linda who wants to frame her schlump husband (Thomas) for murder. Whose murder? Why the inconvenient wife (Harrington) of her boyfriend (McGinley). The two homicidal lovebirds want to take the insurance money and run—leaving hubby to face the consequences. Based on the novella "Linda" by John D. MacDonald.
1993 (PG-13) 88m/C Virginia Madsen, Richard Thomas, Ted McGinley, Laura Harrington; *D:* Nathaniel Gutman; *W:* Nevin Schreiner; *M:* David Michael Frank. VHS, Beta PAR ♪♪

The Lindbergh Kidnapping Case The famous Lindbergh baby kidnapping in 1932 and the trial and execution of Bruno Hauptmann, convincingly portrayed by Hopkins. DeYoung as Lindbergh is blah, but the script is quite good. Made for TV.

1976 150m/C Anthony Hopkins, Joseph Cotten, Cliff DeYoung, Walter Pidgeon, Dean Jagger, Martin Balsam, Laurence Luckinbill, Tony Roberts; *D:* Buzz Kulik; *M:* Billy Goldenberg. VHS, Beta $69.95 COL ♪♪♪

The Line Not-so-hot anti-war drama about a sit-down strike at a military installation by Vietnam veteran prison inmates. Leans heavily on recycled footage from director Siegel's own "Parade" (1971).
1980 (R) 94m/C Russ Thacker, David Doyle, Erik Estrada; *D:* Robert Siegel. VHS, Beta NO ♪½

The Linguini Incident An inept escape artist, a pathological liar, a lingerie designer, a deaf restaurant hostess who throws out one-liners in sign language, and two sinister, yet chic, restaurant owners get together in this marginal comedy about magic and adventure.
1992 (R) 99m/C Rosanna Arquette, David Bowie, Eszter Balint, Andre Gregory, Buck Henry, Viveca Lindfors, Marlee Matlin, Lewis Arquette; *Cameos:* Julian Lennon, Iman; *D:* Richard Shepard; *W:* Richard Shepard, Tamar Brott. VHS $89.95 IME ♪♪

Link A primatologist and his nubile assistant find their experiment has gone—you guessed it—awry, and their hairy charges are running—yep, that's right—amok. Run for your life!
1986 (R) 103m/C Elisabeth Shue, Terence Stamp; *D:* Richard Franklin; *M:* Jerry Goldsmith. VHS, Beta NO Woof!

The Lion Has Wings The story of how Britain's Air Defense was set up to meet the challenge of Hitler's Luftwaffe during their "finest hour." Dated, now-quaint but stirring wartime period piece. "Docudrama" style was original at the time.
1940 75m/B Merle Oberon, Ralph Richardson, Flora Robson, June Duprez; *D:* Michael Powell, Brian Desmond Hurst. VHS, Beta SUE, RXM ♪♪½

The Lion in Winter Medieval monarch Henry II and his wife, Eleanor of Aquitane, match wits over the succession to the English throne and much else in this fast-paced film version of James Goldman's play. The family, including three grown sons, and visiting royalty are united for the Christmas holidays fraught with tension, rapidly shifting allegiances, and layers of psychological manipulation. Superb dialogue and perfectly realized characterizations. O'Toole and Hepburn are triumphant. Screen debuts for Hopkins and Dalton. Shot on location, this literate costume drama surprised the experts with its box-office success.
1968 (PG) 134m/C Peter O'Toole, Katharine Hepburn, Jane Merrow, Nigel Terry, Timothy Dalton, Anthony Hopkins, John Castle, Nigel Stock; *D:* Anthony Harvey; *W:* Jim Goldman; *M:* John Barry. Academy Awards '68: Best Actress (Hepburn), Best Adapted Screenplay, Best Score; Nominations: Best Actor (O'Toole), Best Costume Design, Best Director (Harvey), Best Picture; Directors Guild of America Awards '68: Best Director (Harvey); Golden Globe Awards '69: Best Actor—Drama (O'Toole), Best Film—Drama; National Board of Review Awards '68: 10 Best Films of the Year; New York Film Critics Awards '68: Best Film. VHS $19.95 COL, BTV, TVC ♪♪♪♪

A Lion is in the Streets Cagney stars as a backwoods politician in a southern state who fights on the side of the sharecroppers and wins their support when he exposes the corrupt practices of a powerful businessman. On his way up the political ladder, however, Cagney betrays and exploits the very people who support him. Although this is a familiar storyline, Cagney is

riveting as the corrupt politician, and Hale is wonderful as his patient wife.
1953 88m/C James Cagney, Barbara Hale, Anne Francis, Warner Anderson, John McIntire, Jeanne Cagney, Lon Chaney Jr., Frank McHugh, Larry Keating, Onslow Stevens; *D:* Raoul Walsh. VHS WAR ♪♪♪

The Lion King Epic animated African adventure once again does Disney proud. Lion cub Simba is destined to be king of the beasts, until evil uncle Scar (Irons) plots against him. Growing up in the jungles of Africa he learns about life and responsibility as he returns to reclaim his throne. Heartwarming combo of crowd-pleasing songs, a story with depth, emotion, and politically correct multiculturalism, and stunning animation created in painstaking detail with lifelike creatures and beautiful landscapes. 32nd Disney animated film is the first without human characters, the first based on an original story, and the first to use the voices of a well-known, ethnically diverse cast. Scenes of violence in the animal kingdom may be too much for younger viewers. ♫Can You Feel the Love Tonight; The Circle of Life; I Just Can't Wait to Be King; Be Prepared; Hakuna Matata.
1994 (G) 87m/C Jim Cummings; *D:* Rob Minkoff, Roger Allers; *W:* Jonathan Roberts, Irene Mecchi; *M:* Elton John, Hans Zimmer, Tim Rice; *V:* Matthew Broderick, Jeremy Irons, James Earl Jones, Madge Sinclair, Robert Guillaume, Jonathan Taylor Thomas, Richard "Cheech" Marin, Whoopi Goldberg, Rowan Atkinson, Nathan Lane, Ernie Sabella, Niketa Calame, Moira Kelly. VHS NYR ♪♪♪½

The Lion Man Arabian tale of a boy raised by lions.
1936 ?m/B Jon Hall, Ted Adams. VHS $15.95 LOO ♪♪

Lion Man Raised by wild animals, the son of King Solomon returns to his father's kingdom and roars his way to the throne.
1979 91m/C Steve Arkin. VHS, Beta $19.99 BFV ♪

The Lion of Africa A down-to-earth woman doctor and an abrasive diamond dealer share a truck ride across Kenya. Filmed on location in East Africa. Fine lead performances in otherwise nothing-special made-for-cable adventure.
1987 115m/C Brian Dennehy, Brooke Adams, Joseph Shiloal; *D:* Kevin Connor; *M:* George S. Clinton. VHS, Beta $19.98 LHV, WAR, HBO ♪♪

Lion of the Desert Bedouin horse militias face-off against Mussolini's armored terror in this epic historical drama. Omar Muktar (Quinn as the "Desert Lion") and his Libyan guerrilla patriots kept the Italian troops of Mussolini (Steiger) at bay for 20 years. Outstanding performances enhanced by the desert backdrop. A British-Libyan co-production. *AKA:* Omar Mukhtar.
1981 (PG) 162m/C Anthony Quinn, Oliver Reed, Irene Papas, Rod Steiger, Raf Vallone, John Gielgud; *D:* Moustapha Akkad; *M:* Maurice Jarre. VHS, Beta NO ♪♪

The Lion of Thebes A muscleman unhesitatingly jumps into the thick of things when Helen of Troy is kidnapped. A superior sword and sandal entry.
1964 ?m/C Mark Forest, Yvonne Furneaux. VHS, Beta $16.95 SNC ♪♪♪

The Lion of Venice A kid and an old Venetian gondolier see a stone lion move and uncover a legend of secret treasure.
1982 73m/C VHS, Beta $29.95 GEM ♪

Lionheart A romantic portrayal of the famous English King Richard the Lionheart's early years. Meant for kids, but no Ninja turtles herein—and this is just as silly, and slow to boot.
1987 (PG) 105m/C Eric Stoltz, Talia Shire, Nicola Cowper, Dexter Fletcher, Nicholas Clay, Deborah Barrymore, Gabriel Byrne; **D:** Franklin J. Schaffner; **W:** Richard Outten; **M:** Jerry Goldsmith. **VHS, Beta $19.98** WAR ⅆ½

Lionheart Van Damme deserts the foreign legion and hits the streets when he learns his brother has been hassled. Many fights ensue, until you fall asleep. **AKA:** A.W.O.L.; Wrong Bet.
1990 (R) 105m/C Jean-Claude Van Damme, Harrison Page, Deborah Rennard, Lisa Pelikan, Brian Thompson; **D:** Sheldon Lettich; **W:** Jean-Claude Van Damme, Sheldon Lettich. **VHS, Beta $19.98** MCA ⅆ½

Lion's Den A night club performer and a detective head west to fight crime in this film.
1936 59m/B Tim McCoy, Dave O'Brien. **VHS, Beta $19.95** NOS, DVT ⅆ½

The Lion's Share A gang of bank robbers have their loot stolen and go after the guy who ripped them off.
1979 105m/C Julio de Grazia, Luisina Brando, Fernanda Mistral, Ulises Dumont, Julio Chavez. **VHS, Beta** NO ⅆ

Lip Service Satirical comedy-drama about the TV news industry. An ambitious young newscaster befriends a veteran reporter. He then manipulates his way to replace him on the reporter's morning program. Dooley as the veteran and Dunne as the upstart are fun to watch in this well-done cable rip-off of "Broadcast News."
1988 67m/C Griffin Dunne, Paul Dooley; **D:** William H. Macy. **VHS, Beta $79.95** PSM ⅆⅆⅆ

Lipstick Fashion model Margaux seeks revenge on the man who brutally attacked and raped her, after he preys on her kid sister (real-life sis Mariel, in her debut). Exquisitely exploitative excuse for entertainment.
1976 (R) 90m/C Margaux Hemingway, Anne Bancroft, Perry King, Chris Sarandon, Mariel Hemingway; **D:** Lamont Johnson; **W:** David Rayfiel. **VHS, Beta $59.95** PAR Woof!

Lipstick Camera Keats wants a career in television news and seeks out a successful freelance cameraman (Wimmer) to help her out. She also asks to borrow her techno-friend Feldman's mini-camera and then goes after a story on an ex-spy and his sexy companion. Only no one expects what the camera captures. Weak plot but strong cast and high-end production.
1993 (R) 93m/C Ele Keats, Brian Wimmer, Corey Feldman, Sandahl Bergman, Terry O'Quinn; **D:** Mike Bonifer. **VHS $89.95** TRI ⅆ½

Liquid Dreams In this fast-paced, futuristic thriller, Daly goes undercover as an erotic dancer in a glitzy strip joint to try and solve her sister's murder. She finds that the owner and clientele deal not only in sexual thrills, but also in a strange brain-sucking ritual that provides the ultimate rush. Also available in an unrated version.
1992 (R) 92m/C Richard Steinmetz, Candice Daly, Barry Dennen, Juan Fernandez, Tracy Walter, Frankie Thorn, Paul Bartel, Mink Stole; **D:** Mark Manos. **VHS, Beta $89.95** ACA ⅆ½

Liquid Sky An androgynous bisexual model living in Manhattan is the primary attraction for a UFO, which lands atop her penthouse in search of the chemical nourishment that her sexual encounters provide. Low-budget, highly creative film may not be for everyone, but the audience for which it

was made will love it. Look for Carlisle also playing a gay male.
1983 (R) 112m/C Anne Carlisle, Paula Sheppard, Bob Brady; **D:** Slava Tsukerman. **VHS, Beta $59.95** MED ⅆⅆⅆ

Lisa A young girl develops a crush on the new guy in town and arranges a meeting with him in which she pretends to be her mother. Little does she realize he's a psychotic serial killer. Lock your doors! Don't let anyone in if they have this video!
1990 (PG-13) 95m/C Staci Keanan, Cheryl Ladd, D.W. Moffett, Tanya Fenmore, Jeffrey Tambor, Julie Cobb; **D:** Gary Sherman. **VHS $19.98** FOX ⅆ

Lisa and the Devil An unfortunate outing for Savalas and Sommer, about devil worship. Poor quality leaves little room for redemption. Just like on the telly, Telly's sucking on a sucker. A shortened version of the director's original 1972 release, re-edited and with additional footage added by producer Alfred Leone. **AKA:** The House of Exorcism; La Casa Dell' Exorcismo.
1975 (R) 93m/C Telly Savalas, Elke Sommer, Sylva Koscina, Robert Alda; **D:** Mario Bava. **VHS $19.95** VDM, MPI Woof!

Lisbon First film directed by Milland, shot in Portugal, details the adventures of a sea captain entangled in international espionage and crime while attempting to rescue damsel O'Hara's husband from communist doings. A familiar plot told with less-than-average panache.
1956 90m/C Ray Milland, Claude Rains, Maureen O'Hara, Francis Lederer, Percy Marmont; **D:** Ray Milland. **VHS, Beta $59.98** NO ⅆ

The List of Adrian Messenger A crafty murderer resorts to a variety of disguises to eliminate potential heirs to a family fortune. Solid Huston-directed thriller with a twist: you won't recognize any of the name stars.
1963 98m/B Kirk Douglas, George C. Scott, Robert Mitchum, Dana Wynter, Burt Lancaster, Frank Sinatra; **D:** John Huston; **M:** Jerry Goldsmith. **VHS, Beta $19.98** MCA ⅆⅆⅆ

Listen, Darling Garland is appealing in her first big screen role as Pinky Wingate, who decides to find the perfect husband for her widowed mother (Astor). Pinky and her friend Buzz (Bartholomew) manage to find Pidgeon and have him become the engaging objection of everyone's affections. ♫Zing! Went the Strings of My Heart; Ten Pins in the Sky; On the Bumpy Road to Love.
1938 70m/C Judy Garland, Freddie Bartholomew, Mary Astor, Walter Pidgeon, Alan Hale, Scotty Beckett; **D:** Edwin L. Marin. **VHS $19.98** MGM, FCT ⅆⅆ½

Listen to Me A small-town college debate team heads for the big time when they go to a national debate tournament. The usual mutual-distaste-turns-to-romance thing. Cheesy-as-all-get-out climactic abortion debate, in front of supposed real-life Supreme Court justices—yeah, right. And Kirk Cameron: get an accent, will ya?
1989 (PG-13) 109m/C Kirk Cameron, Jami Gertz, Roy Scheider, Amanda Peterson, Tim Quill, Christopher Atkins; **D:** Douglas Day Stewart; **M:** David Foster. **VHS, Beta $19.95** COL ⅆ½

Listen to Your Heart Office romance in the '80s! Sounds like a mediocre, forgettable made-for-TV comedy-drama—which is exactly what it is. If Jackson was the brainy one on "Charlie's Angels," why wasn't she smart enough to avoid this one?
1983 90m/C Tim Matheson, Kate Jackson; **D:** Don Taylor. **VHS, Beta $59.98** FOX ⅆ½

Lisztomania Russell's excessive vision of what it must have been like to be classical composer/musician Franz Liszt, who is depicted as the first pop star. Rock opera in the tradition of "Tommy" with none of the sense or music.
1975 (R) 106m/C Roger Daltrey, Sara Kestelman, Paul Nicholas, Fiona Lewis, Ringo Starr; **D:** Ken Russell; **W:** Ken Russell. **VHS, Beta $19.98** WAR Woof!

The Little American WWI drama sees a young woman sending her lover off to war. Silent.
1917 80m/B Mary Pickford, Jack Holt, Raymond Hatton, Walter Long. **VHS, Beta $32.95** GPV ⅆⅆ½

Little Annie Rooney A policeman's tomboy daughter spends her time mothering her father and brother while getting into mischief with street punks. Minor melodrama. Silent.
1925 60m/B Mary Pickford, William Haines, Walter James, Gordon Griffith, Vola Vale; **D:** William Beaudine. **VHS, Beta $19.95** NOS, CCB, IME ⅆⅆ

Little Ballerina A young dancer struggles against misfortune and jealousy to succeed in the world of ballet, under the auspices of Fonteyn.
1947 62m/B Margot Fonteyn, Anthony Newley, Martita Hunt, Yvonne Marsh. **VHS, Beta $19.95** VYY ⅆⅆ

Little Big Horn Low-budget depiction of Custer et al. at Little Big Horn actually has its gripping moments; solid acting all around helps. **AKA:** The Fighting Seventh.
1951 88m/B Marie Windsor, John Ireland, Lloyd Bridges, Reed Hadley, Hugh O'Brian, Jim Davis; **D:** Charles Marquis Warren. **VHS, Beta** MRV ⅆⅆ½

Little Big League 12-year-old inherits the Minnesota Twins baseball team from his grandfather, appoints himself manager when everyone else declines, and becomes the youngest owner-manager in history. Nothing new about the premise, but kids and America's favorite pastime add up to good clean family fun. Features real-life baseball players, including the Mariners' Griffey and O'Neil from the Yankees. Good cast features TV's Busfield at first base. Screenwriting debut from Pincus, and directorial debut from the executive producer of "Seinfeld," Scheinman.
1994 (PG) 119m/C Luke Edwards, Jason Robards Jr., Kevin Dunn, Dennis Farina, John Ashton, Jonathan Silverman, Wolfgang Bodison, Timothy Busfield, Ashley Crow, Scott Patterson, Billy L. Sullivan, Miles Feulner, Kevin Elster, Leon "Bull" Durham, Brad "The Animal" Lesley; **Cameos:** Don Mattingly, Ken Griffey Jr., Paul O'Neill; **D:** Andrew Scheinman; **W:** Gregory Pincus, Adam Scheinman. **VHS** NYR ⅆⅆ½

Little Big Man Based on Thomas Berger's picaresque novel, this is the story of 121-year-old Jack Crabb and his quixotic life as gunslinger, charlatan, Indian, ally to George Custer, and the only white survivor of Little Big Horn. Told mainly through flashbacks. Hoffman provides a classic portrayal of Crabb, as fact and myth are jumbled and reshaped.
1970 (PG) 135m/C Dustin Hoffman, Faye Dunaway, Chief Dan George, Richard Mulligan, Martin Balsam, Jeff Corey, Aimee Eccles; **D:** Arthur Penn; **W:** Calder Willingham. **VHS, Beta $19.98** FOX, HMV ⅆⅆⅆ½

Little Boy Lost The true story of the disappearance of a young boy in Australia.
1978 (G) 92m/C John Hargreaves, Tony Barry, Lorna Lesley; **D:** Alan Spires. **VHS, Beta** NO ⅆⅆ

Little Buddha Tibetan Lama Norbu informs the Seattle Konrad family that their 10-year-old son Jesse may be the reincarnation of a respected monk. He wants to take the boy back to Tibet to find out and, with some apparently minor doubts, the family head off on their spiritual quest. In an effort to instruct Jesse in Buddhism, this journey is interspersed with the story of Prince Siddhartha, who will leave behind his worldly ways to follow the path towards enlightenment and become the Buddha. The two stories are an ill-fit, the acting awkward (with the exception of Ruocheng as the wise Norbu), but boy, does the film look good (from cinematographer Vittorio Storaro). Filmed on location in Nepal and Bhutan.
1993 (PG) 123m/C Keanu Reeves, Alex Wiesendanger, Ying Ruocheng, Chris Isaak, Bridget Fonda; **D:** Bernardo Bertolucci; **W:** Mark Peploe, Rudy Wurlitzer; **M:** Ryuichi Sakamoto. **VHS** NYR ♫♫

Little Caesar A small-time hood rises to become a gangland czar, but his downfall is as rapid as his rise. Still thrilling. The role of Rico made Robinson a star and typecast him as a crook for all time.
1930 80m/B Edward G. Robinson, Glenda Farrell, Sidney Blackmer, Douglas Fairbanks Jr.; **D:** Mervyn LeRoy. **VHS, Beta $19.98** FOX, FCT ♫♫♫

Little Church Around the Corner Silent small town melodrama about a preacher who falls in love with a mine owner's daughter, but finds he isn't dad's favorite fella when he confronts him about poor mining conditions. When the mine caves in, the preacher man's caught between a rock and hard place when his sweetie's family needs protection from an angry mob.
1923 70m/B Kenneth Harlan, Hobart Bosworth, Walter Long, Pauline Starke, Alec B. Francis, Margaret Seddon, George Cooper; **D:** William A. Seiter. **VHS, Beta $19.95** GPV ♫♫½

The Little Colonel After the Civil War, an embittered Southern patriarch turns his back on his family, until his dimple-cheeked granddaughter softens his heart. Hokey and heartwarming. Shirley's first teaming with Bill "Bojangles" Robinson features the famous dance scene. Adapted by William Conselman from the Annie Fellows Johnston best-seller.
1935 80m/B Shirley Temple, Lionel Barrymore, Evelyn Venable, John Lodge, Hattie McDaniel, Bill Robinson, Sidney Blackmer; **D:** David Butler. **VHS, Beta $19.98** FOX ♫♫

Little Darlings Distasteful premise has summer campers Kristy and Tatum in a race to lose their virginity. Kristy is better (at acting, that is); but who cares? And just who is meant to be the market for this movie, anyway?
1980 (R) 95m/C Tatum O'Neal, Kristy McNichol, Matt Dillon, Armand Assante, Margaret Blye; **D:** Ronald F. Maxwell; **M:** Charles Fox. **VHS, Beta $14.95** PAR Woof!

Little Dorrit, Film 1: Nobody's Fault The mammoth version of the Dickens tome, about a father and daughter trapped interminably in the dreaded Marshalsea debtors' prison, and the good samaritan who works to free them. Told in two parts (on four tapes), "Nobody's Fault," and "Little Dorrit's Story."
1988 369m/C Alec Guinness, Derek Jacobi, Cyril Cusack, Sarah Pickering, Joan Greenwood, Max Wall, Amelda Brown, Daniel Chatto, Miriam Margolyes, Bill Fraser, Roshan Seth, Michael Elphick, Eleanor Bron, Patricia Hayes, Robert Morley, Sophie Ward; **D:** Christine Edzard; **W:** Christine Edzard; **M:** Giuseppe Verdi. Academy Awards '88 Nominations: Best Adapted Screenplay, Best Supporting Actor (Guinness);

Los Angeles Film Critics Association Awards '88: Best Film, Best Supporting Actor (Guinness). **VHS, Beta $29.98** WAR, SIG, TVC ♫♫♫

Little Dorrit, Film 2: Little Dorrit's Story The second half of the monumental adaptation of Dicken's most popular novel during his lifetime tells of Amy Dorrit's rise from debtor's prison to happiness.
1988 369m/C Alec Guinness, Derek Jacobi, Cyril Cusack, Sarah Pickering, Joan Greenwood, Max Wall, Amelda Brown, Daniel Chatto, Miriam Margolyes, Bill Fraser, Roshan Seth, Michael Elphick, Patricia Hayes, Robert Morley, Sophie Ward, Eleanor Bron; **D:** Christine Edzard; **W:** Christine Edzard; **M:** Giuseppe Verdi. **VHS, Beta $29.98** WAR, SIG, TVC ♫♫♫

Little Dragons A grandfather and two young karate students rescue a family held captive by a backwoods gang.
1980 90m/C Ann Sothern, Joe Spinell, Charles Lane, Chris Petersen, Pat Petersen, Sally Boyden, Rick Lenz, Sharon Weber, Tony Bill; **D:** Curtis Hanson; **W:** Alan Ormsby. **VHS, Beta $19.95** AHV ♫

The Little Drummer Girl An Israeli counter-intelligence agent recruits an actress sympathetic to the Palestinian cause to trap a fanatical terrorist leader. Solid performances from Keaton as the actress and Kinski as the Israli counter-intelligence office sustain interest through a puzzling, sometimes boring and frustrating, cinematic maze of espionage. Keaton is at or near her very best. Based on the bestselling novel by John Le Carre.
1984 (R) 130m/C Diane Keaton, Klaus Kinski, Yorgo Voyagis, Sami Frey, Michael Cristofer, Anna Massey, Thorley Walters; **D:** George Roy Hill; **M:** Dave Grusin. **VHS, Beta $19.98** WAR ♫♫♫

The Little Foxes A vicious southern woman will destroy everyone around her to satisfy her desire for wealth and power. Filled with corrupt characters who commit numerous revolting deeds. The vicious matriarch is a part made to fit for Davis, and she makes the most of it. Script by Lillian Hellman from her own play.
1941 116m/B Bette Davis, Herbert Marshall, Dan Duryea, Teresa Wright, Charles Dingle, Richard Carlson; **D:** William Wyler. **VHS, Beta $14.98** SUE ♫♫♫½

Little Giant The duo fly separately in this entry, which highlights Costello's comic talents and leaves Abbott in the supporting role. Costello is a country bumpkin come to the big city to get enough money to marry his sweetheart. He's hired to sell vacuum cleaners by Abbott and becomes the butt of everyone's jokes but the joke's on them when Lou becomes the company's top-selling salesman.
1946 92m/B Bud Abbott, Lou Costello, Brenda Joyce, Jacqueline De Wit, George Cleveland, Elena Verdugo, Mary Gordon, Pierre Watkin; **D:** William A. Seiter; **W:** Walter DeLeon. **VHS $14.98** MCA ♫♫½

Little Girl...Big Tease Teen society girl is kidnapped and exploited (along with the viewer) by a group which includes her teacher.
1975 (R) 86m/C Jody Ray, Rebecca Brooke; **D:** Roberto Mitrotti. **VHS, Beta** NO ♫

The Little Girl Who Lives Down the Lane Engrossing, offbeat thriller about a strange 13-year-old girl whose father is never home, and who hides something - we won't say what - in her basement. Very young Foster is excellent, as are her supporters. Then there's a child molester who knows what she's hiding. . .

1976 (PG) 90m/C Jodie Foster, Martin Sheen, Alexis Smith, Scott Jacoby; **D:** Nicolas Gessner. **VHS, Beta $29.98** LIV, VES ♫♫½

Little Gloria...Happy at Last Mini series based on the best-selling book about the custody battle over child heiress Gloria Vanderbilt, and her tumultuous youth. Lansberry leads a fine cast as the poor little rich girl's aunt Gertrude, the matriarchal family power broker. Made for television.
1984 180m/C Bette Davis, Angela Lansbury, Christopher Plummer, Maureen Stapleton, Martin Balsam, Barnard Hughes, John Hillerman; **D:** Waris Hussein. **VHS, Beta $79.95** PSM, PAR ♫♫½

Little Heroes An impoverished little girl gets through hard times with the aid of her loyal dog (the Hound can relate). A low-budget family tearjerker that nonetheless works, it claims to be based on a true story.
1991 (G) 78m/C Raeanin Simpson, Katherine Willis, Keith Christensen, Hoover the Dog; **D:** Craig Clyde; **W:** Craig Clyde; **M:** John McCallum. **VHS $14.95** HMD ♫♫½

Little Heroes of Shaolin Temple The "Prince of Blood" attacks the Shaolin temple, but the Master's Ninjas await him.
1972 90m/C Cheng Tain Syh, Hw-Luen, Li Shuen Hwa, Tang Chen Da. **VHS, Beta $29.95** TWE ♫

Little House on the Prairie The pilot for the television series based on the life of Laura Ingalls Wilder and her family's struggles on the American plains in the 1860s. Other episodes are also available on tape, including one in which Patricia Neal guest stars as a terminally ill widow seeking a home for her children. Neal's performance earned her a best actress Emmy in 1975.
1974 98m/C Michael Landon, Karen Grassle, Victor French, Melissa Gilbert, Melissa Sue Anderson; **D:** Michael Landon. **VHS, Beta $19.98** WAR, OM ♫♫♫

Little Johnny Jones George M. Cohan's classic musical is featured in a 1980 revival. Songs include "Yankee Doodle Dandy" and "Give My Regards to Broadway."
1980 93m/C **VHS, Beta $59.95** WAR, OM ♫♫♫

Little Ladies of the Night Former pimp tries to save Purl and other teenagers from the world of prostitution. Exploitation posing as "significant drama." **AKA:** Diamond Alley.
1977 96m/C Linda Purl, David Soul, Clifton Davis, Carolyn Jones, Louis Gossett Jr.; **D:** Marvin J. Chomsky. **VHS, Beta $49.95** PSM, VTR ♫

Little Laura & Big John The true-life exploits of the small-time Ashley Gang in the Florida everglades around the turn of the century. Fabian's comeback vehicle, for what it's worth.
1973 82m/C Fabian, Karen Black; **D:** Luke Moberly. **VHS, Beta** NO ♫♫

Little Lord Fauntleroy The vintage Hollywood version of the Frances Hodgson Burnett story of a fatherless American boy who discovers he's heir to a British dukedom. Also available in computer-colorized version. Well cast, charming, remade for TV in 1980. Smith is loveable as the noble tyke's crusty old guardian.
1936 102m/B Freddie Bartholomew, Sir C. Aubrey Smith, Mickey Rooney, Dolores Costello, Jessie Ralph, Guy Kibbee; **D:** John Cromwell. **VHS, Beta $19.95** NOS, MRV, VEC ♫♫♫½

Little Lord Fauntleroy A poor boy in New York suddenly finds himself the heir to his grandfather's estate in England. Lavish remake of the 1936 classic, adapted from Frances Hodgson Burnett's novel. Well-de-

L

served Emmy winner for photography; Guinness is his usual old-pro self. Made for TV.
1980 98m/C Rick Schroder, Alec Guinness, Victoria Tennant, Eric Porter, Colin Blakely, Connie Booth, Rachel Kempson; **D:** Jack Gold. **VHS, Beta $14.95** FHE, STE 𝘈𝘈½

Little Man Tate A seven-year-old genius is the prize in a tug of war between his mother, who wants him to lead a normal life, and a domineering school director who loves him for his intellect. An acclaimed directorial debut for Foster, with overtones of her own extraordinary life as a child prodigy.
1991 (PG) 99m/C Jodie Foster, Dianne Wiest, Harry Connick Jr., Adam Hann-Byrd, George Plimpton, Debi Mazar, Celia Weston, David Pierce, Danitra Vance, Josh Mostel, P.J. Ochlan; **D:** Jodie Foster; **W:** Scott Frank; **M:** Mark Isham. **VHS $19.98** ORI, CCB 𝘈𝘈𝘈

Little Marines Three young boys journey into the wilderness for three days of fun and instead embark on an incredible adventure.
1990 90m/C Stephen Baker, Steve Landers Jr., Noah Williams; **D:** A.J. Hixon. **VHS** MHF 𝘈𝘈𝘈

The Little Match Girl A musical version of the Hans Christian Andersen classic about a girl whose dying grandmother tells her of the magic in the matches she sells.
1984 54m/C Monica McSwain, Nancy Duncan, Matt McKim, Don Hays; **D:** Mark Hoeger. **VHS, Beta $14.98** SUE 𝘈𝘈

The Little Match Girl The Hans Christian Andersen Yuletide classic about an orphan selling magical matches this time set in the 1920's, with the littlest "Cosby" kid in the title role. Ain't she cute?
1987 90m/C John Rhys-Davies, Rue McClanahan, Roger Daltrey, Twiggy, Natalie Morse; **D:** Michael Lindsay-Hogg. **VHS, Beta $19.95** ACA 𝘈𝘈

Little Men A modern version of the classic juvenile story by Louisa May Alcott is too cute for words.
1940 86m/B Jack Oakie, Jimmy Lydon, Kay Francis, George Bancroft; **D:** Norman Z. McLeod. **VHS, Beta $19.95** NOS, MRV, VCN 𝘈𝘈½

The Little Mermaid An animated version of Hans Christian Andersen's tale about a little mermaid who rescues a prince whose boat has capsized. She immediately falls in love and wishes that she could become a human girl. Not to be confused with the 1989 Disney version.
1978 (G) 71m/C **D:** Tim Reid. **VHS, Beta $19.95** STE, GEM 𝘈𝘈½

The Little Mermaid From "Faerie Tale Theatre" comes an adaptation of the Hans Christian Andersen tale of a little mermaid who makes a big sacrifice to win the prince she loves.
1984 60m/C Karen Black, Brian Dennehy, Helen Mirren, Pam Dawber, Treat Williams; **D:** Robert Iscove. **VHS, Beta $14.98** KUI, FOX, FCT 𝘈𝘈½

The Little Mermaid Headstrong teenage mermaid falls in love with a human prince and longs to be human too. She makes a pact with the evil Sea Witch to trade her voice for a pair of legs; based on the famous Hans Christian Andersen tale. Charming family musical, which harks back to the days of classic Disney animation, and hails a new era of superb Disney animated musicals. Sebastian the Crab nearly steals the show with his wit and showstopping number "Under the Sea." ♫Under the Sea; Kiss the Girl; Daughters of Triton; Part of Your World; Poor Unfortunate Souls; Les Poissons.

1989 (G) 82m/C **D:** John Musker, Ron Clements; **M:** Alan Menken, Howard Ashman; **V:** Jodi Benson, Christopher Daniel Barnes, Pat Carroll, Rene Auberjonois, Samuel E. Wright, Buddy Hackett, Jason Marin, Edie McClurg, Kenneth Mars, Nancy Cartwright. Academy Awards '89: Best Song ("Under the Sea"), Best Original Score; Nominations: Best Song ("Kiss the Girl"); Golden Globe Awards '90: Best Song ("Under the Sea"), Best Score. **VHS, Beta, 8mm** DIS, OM 𝘈𝘈𝘈½

Little Minister An adaptation of the James Barrie novel about a prissy Scottish pastor who falls in love with a free-spirited gypsy...he thinks she is, in fact, the local earl's daughter, played to perfection by the young Hepburn.
1934 101m/B Katharine Hepburn, John Beal, Alan Hale, Donald Crisp; **D:** Richard Wallace. **VHS, Beta $19.98** RKO, TTC 𝘈𝘈𝘈

Little Miss Broadway Orphan Temple brings the residents of a theatrical boarding house together in hopes of getting them into show business. She and Durante give worthwhile performances. Also available in computer-colorized version. ♫Be Optimistic; How Can I Thank You; I'll Build a Broadway For You; If All the World Were Paper; Thank You For the Use of the Hall; We Should Be Together; Swing Me an Old-Fashioned Song; When You Were Sweet Sixteen; Happy Birthday to You.
1938 70m/B Shirley Temple, George Murphy, Jimmy Durante, Phyllis Brooks, Edna May Oliver, George Barbier, Donald Meek, Jane Darwell; **D:** Irving Cummings. **VHS, Beta $19.98** FOX 𝘈𝘈

Little Miss Innocence Recording executive tries to survive the amorous advances of the two attractive female hitchhikers that he drove home.
1973 79m/C John Alderman, Sandy Dempsey, Judy Medford; **D:** Chris Warfield. **VHS, Beta $24.95** AHV 𝘈

Little Miss Marker Heartwarming story starring Temple, who is the IOU for a gambling debt and steals her way into everyone's heart. Remade three times as "Sorrowful Jones," as "40 Pounds of Trouble," and in 1980 with the original title. **AKA:** Girl in Pawn.
1934 88m/B Adolphe Menjou, Shirley Temple, Dorothy Dell, Charles Bickford, Lynne Overman; **D:** Alexander Hall. **VHS $49.99** MCA 𝘈𝘈𝘈

Little Miss Marker Mediocre remake of the often retold story of a bookie who accepts a little girl as a security marker for a $10 bet. Disappointing performance from Curtis adds to an already dull film.
1980 (PG) 103m/C Walter Matthau, Julie Andrews, Tony Curtis, Bob Newhart, Lee Grant, Sara Stimson, Brian Dennehy; **D:** Walter Bernstein; **M:** Henry Mancini. **VHS, Beta $14.98** MCA 𝘈½

Little Miss Millions A 12-year-old has run away from her wicked stepmom who hires a bounty hunter to bring her back—for a half a million bucks. Only when he finds the girl stepmom doesn't want to pay up and she tells anyone who will listen that the bounty hunter actually kidnapped the girl. Bounty hunter turns to friends, including the 12-year-old who isn't a fool and knows stepmom is a lying witch, for help.
1993 (PG) 90m/C Howard Hesseman, Anita Morris, Love Hewitt; **D:** Roger Corman. **VHS $89.98** NHO 𝘈𝘈½

Little Monsters A young boy (Savage) discovers a monster (Mandel) under his bed and eventually befriends it. The pair embark on adventures that land them in trouble. Hardworking, talented cast hurdles the weak script, but can't save the film.

1989 (PG) 100m/C Fred Savage, Howie Mandel, Margaret Whitton, Ben Savage, Daniel Stern, Rick Ducommun, Frank Whaley; **D:** Richard Alan Greenberg; **W:** Ted Elliot, Terry Rossio. **VHS, Beta $14.95** MGM 𝘈𝘈

Little Moon & Jud McGraw A wronged Indian woman and a framed cowpoke take their revenge on a small, corrupt town, razing it overnight. Already-weak plot is disabled by too many flashbacks.
1978 92m/C James Caan, Sammy Davis Jr., Stefanie Powers, Aldo Ray; **D:** Bernard Girard. **VHS, Beta $59.95** PSM 𝘈½

Little Murders Black comedy set in New York City. A woman convinces a passive photographer to marry her. Gardenia gives an excellent performance as the woman's father. A shadow of crime, depression, and strife seem to hangs over the funny parts of this film; more often depressing than anything else. Adapted by Jules Feiffer from his own play.
1971 (PG) 108m/C Elliott Gould, Marcia Rodd, Vincent Gardenia, Elizabeth Wilson, Jon Korkes, Donald Sutherland, Alan Arkin, Lou Jacobi; **D:** Alan Arkin; **W:** Jules Feiffer. **VHS, Beta $59.98** FOX 𝘈𝘈𝘈

Little Nellie Kelly Garland plays both mother and daughter in a film based on a musical comedy by George M. Cohan. Garland is married to Irish cop Murphy but dies in childbirth. The film then advances twenty years to daughter Garland who is trying to make good on the stage and have a romance with a young man her father disapproves of. ♫Nellie Kelly I Love You; Nellie is a Darling; It's a Great Day For the Irish; A Pretty Girl Milking Her Cow; Danny Boy; Singing in the Rain.
1940 100m/B Judy Garland, George Murphy, Charles Winninger, Douglas McPhail; **D:** Norman Taurog. **VHS $19.98** MGM, FCT 𝘈𝘈½

Little Nemo: Adventures in Slumberland A bland animated tale of a young boy whose dreams take him to Slumberland. There, Nemo unwittingly unleashes a monster from Nightmare Land who kidnaps Slumberland's king. Nemo must then rescue the king—aided by the king's daughter, a comic squirrel sidekick, and a mischievous con-frog. Based on Winsor McCay's 1900 comic strip. Has some cute comic moments for the kiddies and, while the animation is better than Saturday-morning cartoon quality, it's not Disney.
1992 (G) 85m/C **D:** William T. Hurtz, Masami Hata; **W:** Chris Columbus, Richard Outten; **M:** Tom Chase, Steve Rucker; **V:** Gabriel Damon, Mickey Rooney, Rene Auberjonois, Daniel Mann, Laura Mooney, Bernard Erhard, William E. Martin. **VHS $24.95** HMD, WTA 𝘈𝘈½

A Little Night Music Features four interwoven, contemporary love stories adapted from the Broadway play, and based loosely on Bergman's "Smiles of a Summer Night." Taylor's pathetic rendition of "Send in the Clowns" should be banned. Filmed on location in Austria.
1977 (PG) 110m/C Elizabeth Taylor, Diana Rigg, Hermione Gingold, Len Cariou, Lesley-Anne Down; **D:** Harold Prince. Academy Awards '77: Best Adapted Score; Nominations: Best Costume Design. **VHS, Beta $9.98** SUE 𝘈½

Little Nikita A California boy (Phoenix) discovers that his parents are actually Soviet spies planted as American citizens for eventual call to duty. Poitier's performance as the FBI agent tracking the spies is about the only spark in this somewhat incoherent thriller.

1988 (PG) 98m/C River Phoenix, Sidney Poitier, Richard Bradford, Richard Lynch, Caroline Kava, Lucy Deakins; *D:* Richard Benjamin; *W:* Bo Goldman; *M:* Marvin Hamlisch. VHS, Beta $14.95 COL *III*

Little Ninjas Three topnotch ninja kids go up against the Sarak to rescue their friend who is being held hostage.
1992 85m/C Steven Nelson, Jon Anzaldo, Alan Godshaw; *D:* Emmett Alston. VHS $89.95 VMK *II ½*

Little Noises Glover stars as an artist who seeks not only fame and fortune, but also the love of his best friend (O'Neal). He finally creates a piece that his agent loves, but problems arise.
1991 91m/C Crispin Glover, Tatum O'Neal, Rik Mayall, Tate Donovan, John C. McGinley; *D:* Jane Spencer; *W:* Jane Spencer. VHS, Beta $89.95 PSM *III*

Little Orphan Annie The unjustly forgotten first sound adaptation of the comic strip. Fun score adds a lot, as does the good cast.
1932 60m/B May Robson, Buster Phelps, Mitzie Green, Edgar Kennedy; *D:* John S. Robertson; *M:* Max Steiner. VHS, Beta $29.98 CCB *II ½*

The Little Prince Disappointing adaptation of the classic children's story by Antoine de Saint-Exupery, about a little boy from asteroid B-612. Lousy Lerner and Loewe score underscores a general lack of magic or spontaneity. ♫It's a Hat; I Need Air; I'm On Your Side; Be Happy; You're a Child; I Never Met a Rose; Why Is the Desert (Lovely to See)?; Closer and Closer and Closer; Little Prince (From Who Knows Where).
1974 (G) 88m/C Richard Kiley, Bob Fosse, Steven Warner, Gene Wilder; *D:* Stanley Donen; *W:* Alan Jay Lerner; *M:* Frederick Loewe, Alan Jay Lerner. Academy Awards '74 Nominations: Best Song ("Little Prince"), Best Original Score; Golden Globe Awards '75: Best Score. VHS, Beta $14.95 PAR *II*

The Little Princess Based on the Frances Hodgson Burnett children's classic; perhaps the best of the moppet's films. Shirley is a young schoolgirl in Victorian London sent to a harsh boarding school when her Army officer father is posted abroad. When her father is declared missing, the penniless girl must work as a servant at the school to pay her keep, all the while haunting the hospitals, never believing her father has died. A classic tearjerker.
1939 91m/B Shirley Temple, Richard Greene, Anita Louise, Ian Hunter, Cesar Romero, Arthur Treacher, Sybil Jason, Miles Mander, Marcia Mae Jones, E.E. Clive; *D:* Walter Lang. VHS, Beta $9.95 CNG, MRV, NOS *III ½*

The Little Princess A three-cassette adaptation of Frances Hodgson Burnett's book. In Victorian England, kind-hearted Sara is forced into poverty when her father suddenly dies. Can his longtime friend find her and restore her happiness? Originally aired on PBS as part of the "Wonderworks" family movie series.
1987 180m/C Amelia Shankley, Nigel Havers, Maureen Lipman; *D:* Carol Wiseman. VHS $29.95 FCT, PME, SIG *III ½*

The Little Rascals Alfalfa runs afoul of the membership requirements for the "He-Man Woman Haters Club" when he starts to fall for Darla. Charming remake of the original television series, from Spheeris, who also redid another television favorite, "The Beverly Hillbillies."
1994 (PG) ?m/C Daryl Hannah, Courtland Mead, Travis Tedford, Brittany Ashton Holmes, Bug Hall, Zachary Mabry, Kevin Jamal Woods, Ross Bagley, Sam Saletta, Blake Collins, Jordan

Warkol, Blake Ewing, Juliette Brewer, Heather Karasek; *Cameos:* Whoopi Goldberg; *D:* Penelope Spheeris; *W:* Penelope Spheeris, Paul Guay, Steve Mazur; *M:* David Foster, Linda Thompson. VHS NYR *III*

Little Rascals, Book 1 Three "Our Gang" shorts: "Railroadin'" (1929), in which the gang takes off on a runaway train; "A Lad and a Lamp" (1932), wherein they find an Aladdin's lamp; and "Beginner's Luck" (1935), in which Spanky wins a dress for a young actress.
193? 59m/B Farina Hoskins, Joe Cobb, Matthew "Stymie" Beard, George "Spanky" McFarland, Carl "Alfalfa" Switzer, Mary Ann Jackson. VHS, Beta $29.98 CCB *III*

Little Rascals, Book 2 A second package of "Our Gang" two-reelers: "Bear Shooters" (1930), in which the Gang goes hunting but runs into some bootleggers; "Forgotten Babies" (1933), has Spanky baby-sitting for the gang's brothers and sisters; and "Teacher's Beau" (1935), where the gang cooks up a scheme to chase their teacher's fiance away.
193? 56m/B Matthew "Stymie" Beard, Wheezer Hutchins, George "Spanky" McFarland, Carl "Alfalfa" Switzer. VHS, Beta $29.98 CCB *III*

Little Rascals, Book 3 Three more "Our Gang" installments are packaged on this tape: "Dogs Is Dogs"(1931), "Anniversary Trouble" (1935) and "Three Men in a Tub" (1938).
1938 54m/B Wheezer Hutchins, Dorothy DeBorba, Matthew "Stymie" Beard, George "Spanky" McFarland, Carl "Alfalfa" Switzer, Darla Hood. VHS, Beta $29.98 CCB *III*

Little Rascals, Book 4 Another package of Our Gang favorites, including "Helping Grandma" (1931), "Little Papa" (1935) and "Bear Facts" (1938).
193? 52m/B Matthew "Stymie" Beard, George "Spanky" McFarland, Carl "Alfalfa" Switzer, Darla Hood. VHS, Beta $29.98 CCB *III*

Little Rascals, Book 5 The comic adventures of the Little Rascals continue in this package of three original shorts: "Readin' and Writin'", (1932), "Sprucin' Up" (1935) and "Reunion in Rhythm" (1937).
193? 49m/B Breezy Brisbane, Matthew "Stymie" Beard, George "Spanky" McFarland, Carl "Alfalfa" Switzer, Darla Hood. VHS, Beta $29.98 CCB *III*

Little Rascals, Book 6 Three more classic "Our Gang" comedy shorts are packaged on this tape: "Free Eats" (1932), "Arbor Day" (1936) and "Mail and Female" (1937).
193? 48m/B Matthew "Stymie" Beard, Breezy Brisbane, George "Spanky" McFarland, Carl "Alfalfa" Switzer, Darla Hood, Dorothy DeBorba, Billy Gilbert. VHS, Beta $29.98 CCB *III*

Little Rascals, Book 7 The "Our Gang" kids serve up another portion of comedy in these three shorts: "Hook and Ladder" (1932), "The Lucky Corner" (1936) and "Feed 'Em and Weep" (1938).
193? 47m/B George "Spanky" McFarland, Breezy Brisbane, Dickie Moore, Matthew "Stymie" Beard, Scotty Beckett, Carl "Alfalfa" Switzer, Darla Hood. VHS, Beta $29.98 CCB *III*

Little Rascals, Book 8 More fun and nuttiness with "Our Gang" in three original short comedies, "Bouncing Babies" (1929), "Two Too Young" (1936), and "The Awful Tooth" (1938).
193? 42m/B Mary Ann Jackson, Darla Hood, George "Spanky" McFarland, Carl "Alfalfa" Switzer. VHS, Beta $29.98 CCB *III*

Little Rascals, Book 9 The Little Rascals scamper into more mischief in these three original shorts: "Little Daddy" (1931), "Spooky Hooky" (1936), and "Hide and Shriek" (1938).
193? 48m/B Darla Hood, George "Spanky" McFarland, Carl "Alfalfa" Switzer, Matthew "Stymie" Beard, Mary Ann Jackson, Jackie Cooper. VHS, Beta $29.98 CCB *III*

Little Rascals, Book 10 The tenth compilation of original "Our Gang" comedies includes "The First Seven Years" (1929), "Bored of Education" (1936), and "Rushin' Ballet" (1937).
193? 41m/B Jackie Cooper, Mary Ann Jackson, George "Spanky" McFarland, Carl "Alfalfa" Switzer, Darla Hood. VHS, Beta $29.98 CCB *III*

Little Rascals, Book 11 The Little Rascals go dramatic in these three shorts, all with a "putting-on-a-show" theme: "Pay As You Exit" (1936), "Three Smart Boys" (1937) and "Our Gang Follies of 1938."
1938 42m/B George "Spanky" McFarland, Carl "Alfalfa" Switzer, Darla Hood. VHS, Beta $29.98 CCB *III*

Little Rascals, Book 12 The Little Rascals explore a haunted house, take a train ride and play football in these three original shorts: "Moan and Groan, Inc." (1929), "Choo-Choo!" (1932) and "The Pigskin Palooka" (1937).
1937 53m/B Jackie Cooper, Farina Hoskins, Mary Ann Jackson, George "Spanky" McFarland, Carl "Alfalfa" Switzer, Darla Hood. VHS, Beta $29.98 CCB *III*

Little Rascals, Book 13 The Our Gang kids return in three more original shorts: "Shivering Shakespeare" (1930), "The First Round-Up" (1934) and "Fishy Tales" (1937).
1937 48m/B Jackie Cooper, George "Spanky" McFarland, Edgar Kennedy, Carl "Alfalfa" Switzer. VHS, Beta $29.98 CCB *III*

Little Rascals, Book 14 Package of shorts leads off with Our Gang's first talkie, "Small Talk" (1929), a three-reeler. The other two entries are "Little Sinner" (1935) and "Hearts Are Thumps" (1937).
193? 52m/B Darla Hood, Mary Ann Jackson, George "Spanky" McFarland, Carl "Alfalfa" Switzer. VHS, Beta $29.98 CCB *III*

Little Rascals, Book 15 Those rascally imps return once again in three more original shorts: "When the Wind Blows" (1930), "For Pete's Sake" (1934) and "Glove Taps" (1937).
193? 50m/B Edgar Kennedy, Tommy "Butch" Bond, George "Spanky" McFarland, Wheezer Hutchins. VHS, Beta $29.98 CCB *III*

Little Rascals, Book 16 Three more charming episodes featuring the original brat pack. The urchins of yesteryear star in "Love Business," "Hi Neighbor," and "Came the Brawn."
193? 30m/B Matthew "Stymie" Beard, Carl "Alfalfa" Switzer, George "Spanky" McFarland, Darla Hood; *D:* Fred Wolf. VHS, Beta $19.95 REP, CCB *III*

Little Rascals, Book 17 Three classic shorts, "Boxing Gloves," "The Kid from Borneo," and "Roamin' Holiday."
1931 46m/B Jean Darling, George "Spanky" McFarland, Darla Hood. VHS, Beta $29.98 CCB *III*

Little Rascals, Book 18 Here are two early "Our Gang" comedies from the silent era: "Saturday's Lesson" (1929) and "Wiggle Your Ears" (1929).

1929 41m/B Farina Hoskins, Wheezer Hutchins, Mary Ann Jackson, Joe Cobb. VHS, Beta $29.98 CCB 🎞🎞🎞

Little Rascals: Choo Choo/Fishy Tales Spanky, Darla, Buckwheat, Stymie, and Alfalfa in two uncut installments of the groundbreaking children's comedy.
1932 30m/B George "Spanky" McFarland, Darla Hood, Carl "Alfalfa" Switzer, Matthew "Stymie" Beard. VHS $9.98 REP, CCB 🎞🎞🎞

Little Rascals Christmas Special Spanky and the Little Rascals attempt to raise enough money to buy a winter coat for Spanky's mom and learn the true meaning of Christmas along the way.
1979 60m/C Darla Hood, Matthew "Stymie" Beard; **D:** Fred Wolf, Charles Swenson. VHS, Beta $29.95 FHE 🎞🎞🎞

Little Rascals Collector's Edition, Vol. 1-6 A collection put together by Spotlight containing six individual two-reelers. Twelve episodes total featuring the rambunctious bunch of child stars.
19?? 180m/B George "Spanky" McFarland, Darla Hood, Carl "Alfalfa" Switzer, Matthew "Stymie" Beard. VHS, Beta $89.95 REP 🎞🎞🎞

Little Rascals Comedy Classics, Vol. 1 Vivacious collection of six of the gang's original episodes. This presentation contains "Railroadin'," "A Lad and a Lamp," "Beginner's Luck," "Bear Shooters," "Forgotten Babies," and "Teacher's Beau."
19?? 112m/B George "Spanky" McFarland, Darla Hood, Carl "Alfalfa" Switzer, Matthew "Stymie" Beard. VHS, Beta $19.95 REP, CCB 🎞🎞🎞

Little Rascals Comedy Classics, Vol. 2 Second volume of the mischievous gang's uncut, original shorts. The six episodes on this installment are "Pay as You Exit," "Three Smart Boys," "Our Gang Follies of 1938," "The First Round-Up," "Shivering Shakespeare," and "Fishy Tales."
19?? 90m/B George "Spanky" McFarland, Darla Hood, Carl "Alfalfa" Switzer, Matthew "Stymie" Beard. VHS $19.95 REP, CCB 🎞🎞🎞

Little Rascals: Fish Hooky/ Spooky Hooky Two uncut classics featuring those mischievous little pranksters.
1933 30m/B Carl "Alfalfa" Switzer, Darla Hood, George "Spanky" McFarland, Matthew "Stymie" Beard. VHS $9.98 REP, CCB 🎞🎞🎞

Little Rascals: Honkey Donkey/ Sprucin' Up The gang's comic capers continue in "Honky Donkey" and "Sprucin' Up."
1934 30m/B George "Spanky" McFarland, Darla Hood, Carl "Alfalfa" Switzer, Matthew "Stymie" Beard. VHS $9.95 REP, CCB 🎞🎞🎞

Little Rascals: Little Sinner/Two Too Young The gang stars in "Little Sinner" and "Two Too Young."
1935 30m/B George "Spanky" McFarland, Darla Hood, Carl "Alfalfa" Switzer, Matthew "Stymie" Beard. VHS $9.98 REP, CCB 🎞🎞🎞

Little Rascals: Mush and Milk/ Three Men in a Tub Two uncensored features starring those lovable urchins.
1933 30m/B George "Spanky" McFarland, Carl "Alfalfa" Switzer, Darla Hood, Matthew "Stymie" Beard. VHS $9.98 REP, CCB 🎞🎞🎞

Little Rascals on Parade A collection of six vintage "Our Gang" shorts from the '30s: "Free Eats," "Arbor Day," "Mail and Female," "Hook and Ladder," "The Lucky Corner," and "Feed 'Em and Weep."
1937 60m/B George "Spanky" McFarland, Carl "Alfalfa" Switzer, Darla Hood. VHS $19.95 REP, CCB 🎞🎞🎞

Little Rascals: Pups is Pups/ Three Smart Boys Two of the most hilarious features from the Little Rascals.
1930 30m/B George "Spanky" McFarland, Carl "Alfalfa" Switzer, Darla Hood, Matthew "Stymie" Beard. VHS $9.98 REP, CCB 🎞🎞🎞

Little Rascals: Readin' and Writin'/Mail and Female Two uncut features starring those delightful rapscallions.
1931 30m/B George "Spanky" McFarland, Carl "Alfalfa" Switzer, Darla Hood, Matthew "Stymie" Beard. VHS $9.98 REP, CCB 🎞🎞🎞

Little Rascals: Reunion in Rhythm/Mike Fright Join the gang in the outrageous episodes "Reunion in Rhythm" and "Mike Fright."
1937 30m/B George "Spanky" McFarland, Darla Hood, Carl "Alfalfa" Switzer, Matthew "Stymie" Beard. VHS $9.98 REP, CCB 🎞🎞🎞

Little Rascals: Spanky/Feed 'Em and Weep Two hilarious features with the antics of those crazy kids.
1932 30m/B George "Spanky" McFarland, Carl "Alfalfa" Switzer, Darla Hood, Matthew "Stymie" Beard. VHS $9.98 REP, CCB 🎞🎞🎞

Little Rascals: The Pinch Singer/Framing Youth Mischievous youngsters run amok in "The Pinch Singer" and "Framing Youth."
1936 30m/B George "Spanky" McFarland, Darla Hood, Carl "Alfalfa" Switzer, Matthew "Stymie" Beard. VHS $9.98 REP, CCB 🎞🎞🎞

Little Rascals Two Reelers, Vol. 1 Wacky youngsters two reeler containing "Lazy Days," and "Spooky Hooky."
1929 30m/B George "Spanky" McFarland, Carl "Alfalfa" Switzer, Darla Hood, Matthew "Stymie" Beard. VHS $14.95 REP 🎞🎞🎞

Little Rascals Two Reelers, Vol. 2 Comic two-reeler from those mischievous youngsters containing "Bedtime Worries," and "Glove Taps."
1933 30m/B George "Spanky" McFarland, Darla Hood, Carl "Alfalfa" Switzer, Matthew "Stymie" Beard. VHS $14.95 REP 🎞🎞🎞

Little Rascals Two Reelers, Vol. 3 Those troublesome youngsters are back in a two-reeler containing "Second Childhood" and "Hide and Shriek."
1936 30m/B George "Spanky" McFarland, Darla Hood, Carl "Alfalfa" Switzer, Matthew "Stymie" Beard. VHS $14.95 REP 🎞🎞🎞

Little Rascals Two Reelers, Vol. 4 Two reeler containing "When the Wind Blows," and "Hearts are Thumps."
1930 30m/B George "Spanky" McFarland, Darla Hood, Carl "Alfalfa" Switzer, Matthew "Stymie" Beard. VHS $14.95 REP 🎞🎞🎞

Little Rascals Two Reelers, Vol. 5 These two episodes of the gang feature "Hi Neighbor," and "Came the Brawn."
1934 30m/B George "Spanky" McFarland, Darla Hood, Carl "Alfalfa" Switzer, Matthew "Stymie" Beard. VHS $14.95 REP 🎞🎞🎞

Little Rascals Two Reelers, Vol. 6 The gang frolics in this two-reeler containing "Love Business," and "Pigskin Palooka."
1936 30m/B George "Spanky" McFarland, Darla Hood, Carl "Alfalfa" Switzer, Matthew "Stymie" Beard. VHS $14.95 REP 🎞🎞🎞

Little Rascals, Vol. 1 Here is a collection of three uncut "Little Rascals" short subjects. In "Boxing Gloves" (1929), Chubby and Joe decide two settle their differences over who should have Jean Darling's love by staging a winner-take-all boxing match. In "The Kid from Borneo" (1933), Spanky

thinks he's met a crazy relative when he confuses an untamed human from Borneo for his uncle from the circus. In "Roamin' Holiday" (1936), Alfalfa and Spanky lead the gang on a journey fit for a hobo.
1929 50m/B Darla Hood, George "Spanky" McFarland, Carl "Alfalfa" Switzer, Matthew "Stymie" Beard. VHS $14.95 REP, CCB 🎞🎞🎞

Little Rascals, Vol. 2 Another uncut compilation of three classic episodes featuring the goofy gang. In "The First Seven Years" (1930), Speck and Jackie battle for the attention of a beautiful Mary Ann. In the award-winning "Bored of Education" (1936), Spanky and Alfalfa devise a plan to play hooky from school by developing very acute tooth problems. In "Rushin' Ballet" (1937), Alfalfa and Spanky establish the Secret Revengers Club and liberate Buckwheat and Porky from the bonds of tyranny.
1930 50m/B George "Spanky" McFarland, Carl "Alfalfa" Switzer. VHS $9.95 REP, CCB 🎞🎞🎞

Little Red Riding Hood From "Faerie Tale Theatre" comes the retelling of the story about a girl (Mary Steenburgen) off to give her grandmother a picnic basket, only to get stopped by a wicked wolf McDowell. Not particularly faithful, but fun and scary.
1983 60m/C Mary Steenburgen, Malcolm McDowell; **D:** Graeme Clifford. VHS, Beta $14.98 FOX, FCT 🎞🎞🎞

Little Red Schoolhouse A hard-nosed schoolteacher hunts for a truant lad and both of them land in jail.
1936 64m/C Frank "Junior" Coghlan, Dickie Moore, Ann Doran. VHS, Beta $19.95 NOS, BAR, FCT 🎞🎞

A Little Romance An American girl living in Paris falls in love with a French boy; eventually they run away, to seal their love with a kiss beneath a bridge. Olivier gives a wonderful, if not hammy, performance as the old pickpocket who encourages her. Gentle, agile comedy based on the novel by Patrick Cauvin.
1979 (PG) 110m/C Laurence Olivier, Diane Lane, Thelonious Bernard, Sally Kellerman, Broderick Crawford; **D:** George Roy Hill; **M:** Georges Delerue. Academy Awards '79: Best Original Score; Nominations: Best Adapted Screenplay. VHS, Beta $14.95 WAR, ING 🎞🎞🎞

A Little Sex Capshaw, in her screen debut, finds herself the wife of womanizer Matheson. Harmless, but pointless, with a TV-style plot.
1982 (R) 94m/C Tim Matheson, Kate Capshaw, Edward Herrmann, Wallace Shawn, John Glover; **D:** Bruce Paltrow; **M:** Georges Delerue. VHS, Beta $59.95 MCA 🎞🎞

Little Shop of Horrors The landmark cheapie classic, which Roger Corman reputedly filmed in three days, about a nebbish working in a city florist shop who unknowingly cultivates an intelligent plant that demands human meat for sustenance. Notable for then-unknown Nicholson's appearance as a masochistic dental patient. Hilarious, unpretentious farce—if you liked this one, check out Corman's "Bucket of Blood" for more of the same. Inspired a musical of the same name, remade as a movie again in 1986. Available colorized.
1960 70m/B Jackie Joseph, Jonathan Haze, Mel Welles, Jack Nicholson, Dick Miller; **D:** Roger Corman. VHS, Beta $9.95 CNG, MRV, NOS 🎞🎞🎞½

Little Shop of Horrors During a solar eclipse, Seymour buys an unusual plant and takes it back to the flower shop where he works. The plant, Audrey 2, becomes a town attraction as it grows at an unusual rate, but Seymour learns that he must feed Audrey

L

fresh human blood to keep her growing. Soon, Audrey is giving the orders ("Feed me") and timid Seymour must find "deserving" victims. Martin's performance as the masochistic dentist is alone worth the price. Song, dance, gore, and more prevail in this outrageous musical comedy. Four Top Levi Stubbs is the commending voice of Audrey 2. Based on the off-broadway play, which was based on Roger Corman's 1960 horror spoof. ♫ Mean Green Mother From Outer Space; Some Fun Now; Your Day Begins Tonight.
1986 (PG-13) 94m/C Rick Moranis, Ellen Greene, Vincent Gardenia, Steve Martin, James Belushi, Christopher Guest, Bill Murray, John Candy; **D:** Frank Oz; **M:** Miles Goodman, Howard Ashman. **VHS, Beta $14.95** WAR, HMV, MVD ⅃⅃⅃

Little Sister Prankster Silverman, on a dare, dresses up as a girl and joins a sorority. Problems arise when he falls in love with his "big sister" (Milano) in the sorority. What will happen when she finds out the truth? Will we care?
1992 (PG-13) 94m/C Jonathan Silverman, Alyssa Milano. **VHS $89.98** LIV ⅃½

Little Sweetheart A reworking of "The Bad Seed," with a nine-year-old girl engaging in murder, burglary, and blackmail, ruining the adults around her. Based on "The Naughty Girls" by Arthur Wise.
1990 (R) 93m/C John Hurt, Karen Young, Barbara Bosson, John McMartin, Cassie Barasch; **D:** Anthony Simmons. **VHS, Beta, 8mm $79.98** SUE ⅃½

The Little Theatre of Jean Renoir A farewell by director Jean Renoir featuring three short films. In the first, Renoir's humanist beliefs are apparent in "The Last Christmas Dinner," a Hans Christian Andersen-inspired story. Next, "The Electric Floor Waxer" is a comic opera. The third piece is called "A Tribute to Tolerance." Slight but important late statement by a great director. In French with English subtitles.
1971 100m/C Jean Renoir, Fernand Sardou, Jean Carmet, Francoise Arnoul, Jeanne Moreau; **D:** Jean Renoir; **W:** Jean Renoir. **VHS, Beta $49.95** INT, FLI, IME ⅃⅃⅃

The Little Thief Touted as Francois Truffaut's final legacy, this trite mini-drama is actually based on a story he co-wrote with Claude de Givray about a post-WWII adolescent girl who reacts to the world around her by stealing and petty crime. In French with English subtitles. Truffaut's hand is markedly absent, but this film is a testament to his abruptly and sadly truncated career. Director Miller was Truffaut's longtime assistant.
1989 (PG-13) 108m/C Charlotte Gainsbourg, Simon de la Brosse, Didier Bezace, Raoul Billerey, Nathalie Cardone; **D:** Claude Miller; **W:** Annie Miller, Claude Miller; **M:** Alain Jonny. **VHS, Beta $89.99** HBO, ING ⅃⅃

Little Tough Guy The Little Tough Guys (a.k.a. Dead End Kids) come to the rescue of Halop, a young tough guy gone bad to avenge his father's unjust imprisonment. First of the "Little Tough Guys" series for the former Dead End Kids, who later became the East Side Kids before eventually evolving into the Bowery Boys.
1938 84m/B Helen Parrish, Billy Halop, Leo Gorcey, Marjorie Main, Gabriel Dell, Huntz Hall; **D:** Harold Young. **VHS, Beta $19.95** NOS, MRV, VYY ⅃⅃

Little Treasure A stripper heads for Mexico to search for her long-lost father, but ends up looking for treasure with an American guy. Disappointing effort of director Sharp.

1985 (R) 95m/C Burt Lancaster, Margot Kidder, Ted Danson, Joseph Hacker, Malena Doria; **D:** Alan Sharp; **W:** Alan Sharp. **VHS, Beta $79.95** COL ⅃½

The Little Valentino One day in the aimless life of a young punk who gets by on his wits and petty theft. Jeles' directorial debut. In Hungarian with English subtitles.
1979 102m/B **D:** Andras Jeles. **VHS $59.95** FCT, AUD ⅃⅃

Little Vegas Looks like easy street for a young man who inherits a bundle from his girlfriend, but he's forced to wake up and smell the cappucino when her family and the other residents of the tiny desert berg think there's a gigolo in the woodpile. Much strife with siblings as he wages a battle for the bucks while the son while wooing the woman's daughter, with a measure of mob inflicted plot twists. Mildly amusing, cut from vein of you can't get rich quick and get away with it.
1990 (R) 90m/C Michael Nouri, Jerry Stiller, John Sayles, Anthony John Denison, Catherine O'Hara, Bruce McGill, Anne Francis, Bob(cat) Goldthwait, Jay Thomas, Perry Lang; **D:** Perry Lang; **W:** Perry Lang; **M:** Mason Daring. **VHS $89.95** COL ⅃⅃½

Little Vera Extremely well-done Soviet film chronicles the life of a young working-class woman who loves rock music and who has been profoundly affected by Western Civilization. Post-glasnost Soviet production gives Westerners a glimpse into the Russian way of life. A box-office bonanza back home. In Russian with English subtitles. **AKA:** Malenkaya Vera.
1988 130m/C Natalia Negoda, Andrei Sokolov, Yuri Nazarov, Ludmila Zaisova, Alexander Niegreva; **D:** Vassili Pitchul. **VHS, Beta $34.95** FCT, LUM, WBF ⅃⅃

Little White Lies Jillian and Matheson meet and fall in love during an exotic vacation. But both are traveling under assumed identities—she's a policewoman tracking a jewel thief and he's an incognito doctor. When they reunite stateside they try to stick to their ruses in humdrum comedic fashion. Made for network TV.
1989 88m/C Ann Jillian, Tim Matheson; **D:** Anson Williams. **VHS $79.95** RHI ⅃⅃

Little Women Louisa May Alcott's Civil War story of the four March sisters—Jo, Beth, Amy, and Meg—who share their loves, their joys, and their sorrows. Everything about this classic film is wonderful, from the lavish period costumes to the excellent script, and particularly the captivating performances by the cast. A must-see for fans of Alcott and Hepburn, and others will find it enjoyable. Remade in 1949 and again in 1978 for television.
1933 107m/B Katharine Hepburn, Joan Bennett, Paul Lukas, Edna May Oliver, Frances Dee, Spring Byington, Jean Parker, Douglass Montgomery; **D:** George Cukor; **W:** Andrew Solt, Sarah Y. Mason, Victor Heerman; **M:** Adolph Deutsch. Academy Awards '33: Best Adapted Screenplay; Nominations: Best Director (Cukor), Best Picture; Venice Film Festival '34: Best Actress (Hepburn). **VHS, Beta, 8mm $19.98** MGM, KUI, IGP ⅃⅃⅃⅃

Little Women Stylized color remake of the George Cukor 1933 classic. Top-notch if too obvious cast portrays Louisa May Alcott's story of teenage girls growing up against the backdrop of the Civil War. Remade again, for television in 1978.
1949 121m/C June Allyson, Peter Lawford, Margaret O'Brien, Elizabeth Taylor, Janet Leigh, Mary Astor; **D:** Mervyn LeRoy. Academy Awards '49: Best Art Direction/Set Decoration (Color);

Nominations: Best Color Cinematography. **VHS $19.98** MGM ⅃⅃⅃

Little Women The third screen version of Louisa May Alcott's classic story. Lackluster compared to the previous attempts, particularly the sterling 1933 film, but still worthwhile. During the Civil War, four sisters share their lives as they grow up and find romance. Garson's television debut. Followed by a television series.
1978 200m/C Meredith Baxter Birney, Susan Dey, Ann Dusenberry, Eve Plumb, Dorothy McGuire, Robert Young, Greer Garson, Cliff Potts, William Shatner; **D:** David Lowell Rich; **M:** Elmer Bernstein. **VHS** NO ⅃⅃

Little World of Don Camillo A French-made farce based on the beloved novels of Giovanni Guareschi. Earthy priest Don Camillo clashes repeatedly with his friendly enemy, the communist mayor of a tiny Italian village. The hero talks directly to God, whose voice is provided by Orson Welles, also narrator of the English version. Charming, good-natured approach. **AKA:** Le Petit Monde de Don Camillo.
1951 106m/B Fernandel, Gino Cervi, Sylvia, Vera Talqui; **D:** Julien Duvivier. **VHS, Beta, 8mm $24.95** VYY, FCT ⅃⅃⅃

The Littlest Angel Musical about a shepherd boy who dies falling off a cliff and wants to become an angel. He learns a valuable lesson in the spirit of giving. Made for TV.
1969 77m/C Johnny Whitaker, Fred Gwynne, E.G. Marshall, Cab Calloway, Connie Stevens, Tony Randall. **VHS, Beta $14.98** SUE, CNG, KAR ⅃⅃

The Littlest Horse Thieves Good Disney film about three children and their efforts to save some ponies who work in mines. The children take it upon themselves to see that the animals escape the abuse and neglect they are put through. Filmed on location in England with excellent photography. **AKA:** Escape from the Dark.
1976 (G) 109m/C Alastair Sim, Peter Barkworth; **D:** Charles Jarrott. **VHS, Beta $69.95** DIS ⅃⅃½

The Littlest Outlaw A Mexican peasant boy steals a beautiful stallion to save it from being destroyed. Together, they ride off on a series of adventures. Disney movie filmed on location in Mexico.
1954 73m/C Pedro Armendariz Sr., Joseph Calleia, Andres Velasquez; **D:** Roberto Gavaldon. **VHS, Beta $69.95** DIS ⅃⅃½

The Littlest Rebel Temple stars in this well-done piece set during the Civil War in the Old South. She befriends a Union officer while protecting her father at the same time. She even goes to Washington to talk with President Lincoln. Nice dance sequences by Temple and Robinson. Available in computer-colored version.
1935 70m/B Shirley Temple, John Boles, Jack Holt, Bill Robinson, Karen Morley, Willie Best; **D:** David Butler. **VHS, Beta $19.98** FOX ⅃⅃½

Live a Little, Love a Little Itinerant photographer Elvis juggles two different jobs by running around a lot. Sexually more frank than earlier King vehicles. ♫ Almost in Love; A Little Less Conversation; Edge of Reality; Wonderful World.
1968 (PG) 90m/C Elvis Presley, Michele Carey, Rudy Vallee, Don Porter, Dick Sargent, Sterling Holloway, Eddie Hodges; **D:** Norman Taurog. **VHS, Beta $14.95** MGM ⅃⅃

Live and Let Die Agent 007 is out to thwart the villainous Dr. Kananga, a black mastermind who plans to control western powers with voodoo and hard drugs. Moore's first appearance as Bond. Can't we

have the real Bond back? Title song by Paul McCartney.
1973 (PG) 131m/C Roger Moore, Jane Seymour, Yaphet Kotto, Clifton James, Julius W. Harris, Geoffrey Holder, David Hedison, Gloria Hendry, Bernard Lee, Lois Maxwell, Madeleine Smith, Roy Stewart; *D:* Guy Hamilton; *W:* Tom Mankiewicz; *M:* George Martin. **VHS, Beta** **$19.98** *MGM, FOX, TLF* 🎬🎬

Live! From Death Row Cassidy plays a tabloid TV host who'll do anything to get ratings. She's set to do a live interview with a condemned serial killer (Davison) shortly before his execution. But Davison and his fellow death-row inmates take Cassidy and her crew hostage as he decides to use the show for his own media message.
1992 94m/C Joanna Cassidy, Bruce Davison, Art LaFleur, Calvin Levels, Michael D. Roberts; *D:* Patrick Duncan; *W:* Patrick Duncan. **VHS** **$79.95** *ABC, PSM* 🎬🎬

The Live Wire Stunt-ridden action fare featuring Talmadge at his most daring. This adventure is complete with desert island, lost treasure, stowaways, evil-doers, and a race against the clock.
1934 57m/B Richard Talmadge, George Walsh, Charles French, Alberta Vaughn; *D:* Harry S. Webb. **VHS, Beta** **$24.95** *NOS, DVT, GPV* 🎬🎬

Live Wire Brosnan is an FBI bomb expert who needs a new line of work. He's up against a terrorist psychopath who has his greedy hands on a new type of explosive. It's liquid, undetectable, looks as innocent as a glass of water, and is capable of blowing up Washington, D.C. Made for cable television. Also available in an unrated version.
1992 (R) 85m/C Pierce Brosnan, Ben Cross, Ron Silver, Lisa Eilbacher; *D:* Christian Duguay. **VHS** **$89.95** *COL, NLC* 🎬🎬½

The Lives of a Bengal Lancer One of Hollywood's greatest rousing adventures. Three British Lancers, of varying experience, encounter a vicious revolution against colonial rule. Rivaled only by "Gunga Din" as the ultimate 1930s swashbuckler. Swell plot, lotsa action, great comraderie. Based on the novel by Major Francis Yeats-Brown, and remade in 1939 as "Geronimo."
1935 110m/B Gary Cooper, Franchot Tone, Richard Cromwell, Guy Standing, Sir C. Aubrey Smith, Monte Blue, Kathleen Burke, Noble Johnson, Lumsden Hare, Akim Tamiroff, J. Carroll Naish, Douglass Dumbrille; *D:* Henry Hathaway; *W:* Waldemar Young, John Balderston; *M:* Milan Roder. Academy Awards '35 Nominations: Best Adapted Screenplay, Best Director (Hathaway), Best Film Editing, Best Interior Decoration, Best Picture, Best Sound; National Board of Review Awards '35: 10 Best Films of the Year. **VHS, Beta** **$14.98** *MCA* 🎬🎬🎬🎬

Livin' Large An African-American delivery boy gets the break of his life when a nearby newscaster is shot dead. Grabbing the microphone and continuing the story, he soon finds himself hired by an Atlanta news station as an anchorman, fulfilling a life-long dream. But problems arise when he finds himself losing touch with his friends, his old neighborhood and his roots. Comedy "deals" with the compelling issue of blacks finding success in a white world by trivializing the issue at every turn and resorting to racial stereotypes.
1991 (R) 96m/C Terrence "T.C." Carson, Lisa Arrindell, Blanche Baker, Nathaniel "Afrika" Hall, Julia Campbell; *D:* Michael A. Schultz; *M:* Herbie Hancock. **VHS** **$92.99** *HBO* 🎬🎬

The Living Coffin Woman has alarm rigged on her coffin in case she's buried alive. And they called her paranoid. Loosely based on Poe's "Premature Burial." *AKA:* El Grito de la Muerte.
1958 72m/C Gaston Santos, Maria Duval, Pedro de Aguillon; *D:* Fernando Mendez. **VHS** **$19.98** *SNC* 🎬½

The Living Daylights The 17th Bond film. After being used as a pawn in a fake Russian defector plot, our intrepid spy tracks down an international arms and opium smuggling ring. Fine debut by Dalton as 007 in a rousing, refreshing cosmopolitan shoot-em-up. Let's be frank: we were all getting a little fatigued of Roger Moore.
1987 (PG) 130m/C Timothy Dalton, Maryam D'Abo, Jeroen Krabbe, John Rhys-Davies, Robert Brown, Joe Don Baker, Desmond Llewelyn, Art Malik, Geoffrey Keen, Walter Gotell, Andreas Wisniewski; *D:* John Glen; *W:* Richard Maibaum, Michael G. Wilson; *M:* John Barry. **VHS, Beta** **$19.98** *MGM, TLF, FOX* 🎬🎬🎬

The Living Dead An English film about a mad, re-animating scientist. *AKA:* The Scotland Yard Mystery.
1936 76m/B Gerald du Maurier, George Curzan. **VHS, Beta** **$24.95** *NOS, SNC, DVT* 🎬🎬

The Living End Director Araki's radical lovers-on-the-lam story concerns freelance L.A. writer Jon (Gilmore) who has just learned he is H.I.V.-positive. He meets a handsome, violent, hustler named Luke (Dytri) and the two begin a desperate road trip along the California coast which can only end in tragedy. Araki not only wrote and directed the film but also served as cinematographer and editor—all on a $23,000 budget. Stylish, tragic, and filled with black humor and frank homoeroticism.
1992 92m/C Craig Gilmore, Mike Dytri, Darcy Marta; *D:* Gregg Araki; *W:* Gregg Araki. **VHS** **$89.95** *ACA* 🎬🎬

Living Free Sequel to "Born Free," based on the nonfictional books by Joy Adamson. Recounts the travails of Elsa the lioness, who is now dying, with three young cubs that need care. Nice and pleasant, but could you pick up the pace?
1972 (G) 91m/C Susan Hampshire, Nigel Davenport; *D:* Jack Couffer. **VHS, Beta** **$9.95** *COL, GKK* 🎬🎬½

The Living Head Archaeologists discover the ancient sepulcher of the great Aztec warrior, Acatl. Ignoring a curse, they steal his severed head and incur the fury of Xitsliapoli. They should have known better. Dubbed in English. *AKA:* La Cabeza Viviente.
1959 75m/B Mauricio Garces, Ana Louisa Peluffo, German Robles, Abel Salazar; *D:* Chano Urueto. **VHS, Beta** **$24.95** *VYY, SNC* 🎬½

Living on Tokyo Time Interesting but often dull, low budget independent comedy about a young Japanese woman who hitches up with a boorish Japanese-American man in order to stay in the United States. An Asian view of Asian-America, filmed on location in San Francisco.
1987 83m/C Minako Ohashi, Ken Nakagawa, Kate Connell, Mitzi Abe, Bill Bonham, Brenda Aoki; *D:* Steven Okazaki; *W:* Steven Okazaki, John McCormick. **VHS, Beta** **$19.98** *NLC, ING* 🎬🎬½

Living to Die Vegas gumshoe is assigned to investigate a blackmailed official, and discovers a woman believed to be dead is alive and beautiful and living incognito. This mystifies him.
1991 (R) 84m/C Wings Hauser, Darcy Demoss, Asher Brauner, Arnold Vosloo, Jim Williams; *D:* Wings Hauser. **VHS** **$19.95** *PMH, HHE* 🎬½

The Lizzies of Mack Sennett Three quick-paced, hilarious Sennett "Tin Lizzie" comedies: "Lizzies of the Field," "Leading Lizzie Astray" and "Love, Speed

and Thrills." Plenty of signature slapstick from the master.
1915 51m/C Billy Bevan, Fatty Arbuckle, Mack Swain, Chester Conklin; *D:* Mack Sennett. **VHS, Beta** **$19.95** *VYY* 🎬½

Loaded Guns Airline stewardess-cum-double agent must totally immobilize a top drug trafficking ring. Pathetic spy tale with plenty of unintended laughs.
1975 90m/C Ursula Andress, Woody Strode; *D:* Fernando Di Leo. **VHS, Beta** **$59.95** *LIV, MON* Woof!

Loaded Pistols Story set in the old West starring Gene Autry.
1948 80m/B Gene Autry, Jack Holt, Barbara Britton; *D:* John English. **VHS, Beta** **$19.95** *NOS, VCN, DVT* 🎬

Loan Shark An ex-convict gets a job at a tire company, working undercover to expose a loan shark ring. Hackneyed plot moves quickly.
1952 79m/B George Raft, John Hoyt; *D:* Seymour Friedman. **VHS, Beta** *NO* 🎬🎬

Lobster for Breakfast An Italian gag-fest about a toilet salesman infiltrating his friend's confused marital existence just to make a sale. With English subtitles; also available in a dubbed version.
1982 (R) 96m/C Enrico Montesano, Claude Brasseur, Claudine Auger; *D:* Giorgio Capitani. **VHS, Beta** **$39.98** *SUE* 🎬🎬½

Lobster Man from Mars When rich movie producer (Curtis) learns from his accountant that he must produce a flop or be taken to the cleaners by the IRS, he buys a homemade horror movie from a young filmmaker. The film is an ultra-low budget production featuring a kooky lobster man and a screaming damsel. The premise peters out about halfway through, but there are enough yuks to keep you going.
1989 (PG) 84m/C Tony Curtis, Deborah Foreman, Patrick Macnee. **VHS, Beta** **$14.95** *LIV* 🎬🎬

Local Badman A dim-witted cowhand saves the day in this rip-roaring tale of the old west.
1932 60m/B Hoot Gibson. **VHS, Beta** **$19.95** *NOS, VCI, RXM* 🎬

Local Hero Riegert is a yuppie representative of a huge oil company who endeavors to buy a sleepy Scottish fishing village for excavation, and finds himself hypnotized by the place and its crusty denizens. Back in Texas at company headquarters, tycoon Lancaster deals with a psycho therapist and gazes at the stars looking for clues. A low-key, charmingly offbeat Scottish comedy with its own sense of logic and quiet humor, poetic landscapes, and unique characters, epitomizing Forsyth's original style.
1983 (PG) 112m/C Peter Riegert, Denis Lawson, Burt Lancaster, Fulton Mackay, Jenny Seagrove, Peter Capaldi, Norman Chancer; *D:* Bill Forsyth; *W:* Bill Forsyth; *M:* Mark Knopfler. **VHS, Beta** **$19.98** *WAR* 🎬🎬🎬🎬

The Loch Ness Horror The famed monster surfaces and chomps on the local poachers—and with good reason. Would that it had munched this movie's producer in, say, 1981.
1982 93m/C Barry Buchanan, Miki McKenzie, Sandy Kenyon; *D:* Larry Buchanan. **VHS, Beta** **$39.95** *MON* Woof!

Lock 'n' Load Why are all the soldiers in the 82nd Airborne stealing vast sums, then committing suicide? One of the guys involved wants to know.
1990 (R) ?m/C Jack Vogel; *D:* David A. Prior. **VHS** **$14.95** *AIP* 🎬🎬

Lock Up Peaceful con Stallone, with only six months to go, is harassed and tortured by vicious prison warden Sutherland in retribution for an unexplained past conflict. Lackluster and moronic; semi-color; surely Sutherland can find better roles.
1989 (R) 115m/C Sylvester Stallone, Donald Sutherland, Sonny Landham, John Amos, Darlanne Fluegel, Frank McRae; **D:** John Flynn; **W:** Jeb Stuart; **M:** Bill Conti. **VHS, Beta $14.95** LIV ♪♪½

Lockdown Charged with his partner's murder, a detective is forced to ponder the perennial puzzle of life. Not a pretty sight.
1990 90m/C Joe Estevez, Mike Farrell, Richard Lynch. **VHS $89.95** VMK ♪½

L'Odeur des Fauves One of a cynical reporter's scandalous stories gets an innocent man killed, compelling the reporter somehow to make restitution. Subtitled in English.
1966 86m/C Maurice Ronet, Josephine Chaplin, Vittorio De Sica; **D:** Richard Balducci. **VHS, Beta** BAR ♪

The Lodger A mysterious lodger is thought to be a rampaging mass murderer of young women. First Hitchcock film to explore the themes and ideas that would become his trademarks. Silent. Climactic chase is memorable. Remade three times. Look closely for the Master in his first cameo. **AKA:** The Case of Jonathan Drew; The Lodger: A Case of London Fog.
1926 91m/B Ivor Novello, Marie Ault, Arthur Chesney, Malcolm Keen; **Cameos:** Alfred Hitchcock; **D:** Alfred Hitchcock; **W:** Alfred Hitchcock. **VHS, Beta $18.95** GPV, NOS, VYY ♪♪♪

The Lodger Based on the true story of the murderer (Jack the Ripper) who stalked the gloomy streets of Whitechapel in 1889, slashing the throats of prostitutes. Cregar has been called the most haunting of the screen Rippers. He lurkingly plays the houseguest who bewilders his hosts, the Burtons, with his bizarre ways. As the film proceeds, they truly become unhinged by the similarities between "Slade" and the killer. Considered by fans to be the classic of the Ripper genre. Adapted from the book of the same name by Marie Belloc Lowndes.
1944 84m/B Merle Oberon, George Sanders, Laird Cregar, Cedric Hardwicke, Sara Allgood, Aubrey Mather, Queenie Leonard; **D:** John Brahm. **VHS** ♪♪♪

Logan's Run In the 23rd century, a hedonistic society exists in a huge bubble and people are only allowed to live to the age of 30. Intriguing concepts and great futuristic sets prevail here. Based on the novel by William Nolan and George Clayton Johnson.
1976 120m/C Michael York, Jenny Agutter, Richard Jordan, Roscoe Lee Browne, Farrah Fawcett, Peter Ustinov, Camilla Carr, Ann Ford; **D:** Michael Anderson Sr.; **W:** David Zelag Goodman; **M:** Jerry Goldsmith. Academy Awards '76: Best Visual Effects; Nominations: Best Art Direction/Set Decoration, Best Cinematography. **VHS, Beta $19.98** MGM ♪♪½

Lois Gibbs and the Love Canal Mason's television movie debut as Lois Gibbs, a housewife turned activist, fighting the authorities over chemical-dumping in the Love Canal area of Niagara Falls, New York. The script doesn't convey the seriousness of developments in that region.
1982 100m/C Marsha Mason, Bob Gunton, Penny Fuller, Roberta Maxwell, Jeremy Licht, Louise Latham; **D:** Glenn Jordan. **VHS** NO ♪♪

Lola A wonderful tale of a nightclub dancer and her amorous adventures. Innovative film that marked the beginning of French New Wave. In French with English subtitles.
1961 90m/B Anouk Aimee, Marc Michel, Elina Labourdette, Jacques Harden; **D:** Jacques Demy. **VHS $59.95** INT, ING, TPV ♪♪♪

Lola A teenaged girl links up romantically with a considerably older writer of pornographic books. One would expect more from such a good cast, but the film never follows through. British release was originally 98 minutes. **AKA:** The Statutory Affair; Twinky.
1969 (PG) 88m/C Charles Bronson, Susan George, Trevor Howard, Michael Craig, Honor Blackman, Lionel Jeffries, Robert Morley, Jack Hawkins, Orson Bean, Kay Medford, Paul Ford; **D:** Richard Donner. **VHS $59.95** FCT, MRV ♪♪

Lola Montes Ophuls' final masterpiece recounts the life and sins of the famous courtesan, mistress of Franz Liszt and the King of Bavaria. Ignored upon release, but hailed later by the French as a cinematic landmark. Presented in its original widescreen format; in French with English subtitles. Also available in a 110 minute version. Adapted from an unpublished novel by Cecil Saint-Laurent.
1955 140m/C Martine Carol, Peter Ustinov, Anton Walbrook, Ivan Desny, Oskar Werner; **D:** Max Ophuls; **W:** Max Ophuls; **M:** Georges Auric. **Beta $69.95** CRC, ING, NLC ♪♪♪♪

Lolita A middle-aged professor is consumed by his lust for a teenage nymphet in this strange film considered daring in its time. Based on Vladimir Nabokov's novel. Watch for Winters' terrific portrayal as Lolita's sex-starved mother.
1962 152m/B James Mason, Shelley Winters, Peter Sellers, Sue Lyon; **D:** Stanley Kubrick. **VHS, Beta $19.98** MGM, CRC ♪♪♪

London Kills Me A slice-of-life story London-style. Set at the end of the Thatcher era, Clint is a homeless drifter dealing drugs to get by. He's trying to get enough money for a new pair of shoes which will enable him to get a job in a fancy restaurant and away from his aimless life. His friend Muffdiver leads the group of drug pushers and is obsessed with money and power. Sylvie is the sultry junkie who drifts between Clint, Muffdiver, and her drug needs. The directorial debut of Kureishi is more a collection of characters and situations than a complete film but there are moments of disturbing intensity and odd sweetness.
1991 (R) 105m/C Justin Chadwick, Steven Mackintosh, Emer McCourt, Roshan Seth, Fiona Shaw, Brad Dourif, Gordon Warnecke; **D:** Hanif Kureishi; **W:** Hanif Kureishi. **VHS $89.98** LIV, PMS ♪♪

London Melody Neagle is a spirited Cockney busker who meets a kindly Italian diplomat who decides to finance her musical education. He promptly also falls in love with her. **AKA:** Girl in the Street.
1937 71m/B Anna Neagle, Tullio Carminati, Robert Douglas, Horace Hodgers; **D:** Herbert Wilcox. **VHS, Beta, 8mm $24.95** VYY ♪½

The Lone Avenger Average oater centers around a bank panic, with two-gun Maynard clearing out the trouble.
1933 60m/B Ken Maynard, Muriel Gordon, James Marcus. **VHS, Beta $19.95** NOS, VCN, CAB ♪♪

Lone Bandit Vintage western starring Chandler.
1933 57m/B Lane Chandler, Doris Brook, Wally Wales; **D:** J.P. McGowan. **VHS, Beta $27.95** VCN ♪½

The Lone Defender A dozen episodes of the western serial starring the canine crusader, Rin Tin Tin.
1932 235m/B Rin Tin Tin, Walter Miller, June Marlowe, Buzz Barton, Josef Swickard, Frank Lanning, Robert F. (Bob) Kortman; **D:** Richard Thorpe. **VHS, Beta $19.95** VDM, GPV, MLB ♪½

Lone Justice Cowboy Ned Blessing has seen and done it all (from outlaw to sheriff) but his wild ways have caught up with him. Now, he's relating his exploits from a jail cell as he awaits his fate at the end of a rope. Beware—this looks like the first chapter of a series and there's no real ending.
1993 (R) 94m/C Daniel Baldwin, Luis Avalos, Chris Cooper, Sean Baca, Taylor Fry, Julia Campbell, Rene Auberjonois, Timothy Scott, Bob Gunton, Miguel Sandoval, Jeff Kober; **D:** Peter Werner; **W:** Bill Wittliff; **M:** Basil Poledouris. **VHS $92.95** ACA ♪♪½

The Lone Ranger Western serial about the masked man and his faithful Indian sidekick. From a long-sought print found in Mexico, this program is burdened by a noisy sound track, two completely missing chapters, an abridged episode #15, and Spanish subtitles.
1938 234m/B Lee Powell; **D:** William Witney, John English. **VHS, Beta $39.95** VYY, NOS, VCN ♪♪½

Lone Ranger Tonto and that strange masked man must prevent a war between ranchers and Indians in the first of the "Lone Ranger" series. "Hi-ho Silver!"
1956 87m/C Clayton Moore, Jay Silverheels, Lyle Bettger, Bonita Granville; **D:** Stuart Heisler. **VHS, Beta $29.95** MGM ♪♪½

Lone Ranger and the Lost City of Gold Three Indian men are found dead, and the Lone Ranger and Tonto set out to discover the killers.
1958 80m/C Clayton Moore, Jay Silverheels, Douglas Kennedy; **D:** Lesley Selander; **M:** Les Baxter. **VHS** NO ♪♪

The Lone Rider in Cheyenne One of the last in the "Lone Rider" series. The Lone Rider is out to clear the name of an innocent man accused of murder.
1942 59m/B George Houston, Al "Fuzzy" St. John; **D:** Sigmund Neufeld. **VHS $19.95** NOS, DVT, HEG ♪½

The Lone Rider in Ghost Town Outlaws "haunt" a ghost town to protect their hidden mine and the Lone Rider and his pal, Fuzzy, are out to solve the mystery. Installment in the short-lived "Lone Rider" series.
1941 64m/B George Houston, Al "Fuzzy" St. John, Budd Buster; **D:** Sigmund Neufeld. **VHS $19.95** NOS, DVT, HEG ♪½

The Lone Runner An adventurer rescues a beautiful heiress from Arab kidnappers in this dud.
1988 (PG) 90m/C Miles O'Keeffe, Ronald Lacey, Michael J. Aronin, John Steiner, Al Yamanouchi; **D:** Ruggero Deodato. **VHS, Beta $79.95** MED Woof!

Lone Star Big stars, big budget western in which Texas fights for independence as good guy Gable and badman Crawford fight each other. Gardner plays a fiery newspaper editor as well as Gable's love interest. Script is chock full of holes, but great action scenes make up for it. Based on the story by Borden Chase.
1952 94m/B Clark Gable, Ava Gardner, Broderick Crawford, Lionel Barrymore, Beulah Bondi, Ed Begley Sr., William Farnum, Lowell Gilmore; **D:** Vincent Sherman; **W:** Howard Estabrook, Borden Chase. **VHS $19.98** MGM ♪♪½

Lone Star Kid 11-year-old Brian Zimmerman lives in Crabb, Texas—population 400. After he witnesses a car accident death because there's no adequate emergency service, he decides to run for mayor and help modernize the town. Based on a true story. Includes a viewers' guide. Presented as part of the "Wonderworks" series.
199? 55m/C James Earl Jones, Chad Sheets; **M:** Charlie Daniels. VHS $29.95 *PME, HMV, BTV* ♫♫½

Lone Star Law Men A U.S. marshal has his hands full in a border town overrun with bandits. Keene stars as the deputy marshall who goes undercover and joins the gang in an attempt to foil their crooked plans.
1942 58m/B Tom Keene, Frank Yaconelli, Sugar Dawn, Betty Miles; **D:** Robert Tansey. VHS $19.95 *NOS, DVT* ♫

The Lone Star Ranger Former outlaw O'Brien is trying to go straight by helping to bring a gang of rustlers to justice. Interesting plot twist in the link between his girlfriend and the head of the gang.
1939 64m/B George O'Brien, Sue Carol, Walter McGrail, Warren Hymer, Russell Simpson; **D:** A.E. Erickson. VHS $19.95 *DVT, HEG* ♫½

Lone Wolf A werewolf terrorizes a high school, and a few computerniks track it down.
1988 97m/C Dyann Brown, Kevin Hart, Jamie Newcomb, Ann Douglas; **D:** John Callas. VHS, Beta $79.95 *PSM* ♫

Lone Wolf McQuade Martial arts action abounds in this modern-day Western which pits unorthodox Texas Ranger Norris against a band of gun-running mercenaries led by Carradine. Oh, and there's a conflict-ridden love interest as well. Violent (and not particularly literary) but worthy entry in chop-socky genre.
1983 107m/C Chuck Norris, Leon Isaac Kennedy, David Carradine, L.Q. Jones, Barbara Carrera; **D:** Steve Carver; **W:** H. Kaye Dyal. VHS, Beta $19.98 *VES* ♫♫½

The Loneliest Runner Based on the true story of an Olympic track star who, as a teenager, suffered humiliation as a bed-wetter. The real-life experiences of producer-director Landon are presented in a touching and sensitive manner. Made for television.
1976 74m/C Michael Landon, Lance Kerwin, DeAnn Mears, Brian Keith, Melissa Sue Anderson; **D:** Michael Landon. VHS, Beta $19.98 *WAR, OM* ♫♫

The Loneliness of the Long Distance Runner Courtenay, in his film debut, turns in a powerful performance as an angry young man infected by the poverty and hopelessness of the British slums. His first attempt at crime is a bust and lands him in a boys reformatory where he is recruited for the running team. While training for the big event with a rival school, Redgrave's obsession with winning the race and Courtenay's continued indifference to the outcome lock the two in an intriguing, seemingly one-sided power struggle. Though widely overlooked when first released, it has since been praised as one of the finest teenage angst films of the '60s. Riveting depiction on a boy's rite of passage into manhood. *AKA:* Rebel with a Cause.
1962 104m/B Tom Courtenay, Michael Redgrave, Avis Bunnage, Peter Madden, James Bolam, Julia Foster, Topsy Jane, Frank Finlay; **D:** Tony Richardson; **M:** John Addison. VHS, Beta $19.98 *WAR, SNC* ♫♫♫

Lonely are the Brave A free-spirited cowboy out of sync with the modern age tries to rescue a buddy from a local jail, and in his eventual escape is tracked relentlessly by modern law enforcement. A compelling, sorrowful essay on civilized progress and exploitation of nature. Adapted from the novel "Brave Cowboy" by Edward Abbey.
1962 107m/B Kirk Douglas, Walter Matthau, Gena Rowlands, Carroll O'Connor, George Kennedy; **D:** David Miller; **M:** Jerry Goldsmith. VHS, Beta $19.95 *MCA* ♫♫♫

The Lonely Guy Romantic comedy with Martin as a jilted writer who writes a best-selling book about being a lonely guy and finds stardom does have its rewards. Based on "The Lonely Guy's Book of Life" by Bruce Jay Friedman.
1984 (R) 91m/C Steve Martin, Charles Grodin, Judith Ivey, Steve Lawrence, Robyn Douglass, Merv Griffin, Dr. Joyce Brothers; **D:** Arthur Hiller; **M:** Jerry Goldsmith. VHS, Beta $19.95 *MCA* ♫♫½

Lonely Hearts An endearing Australian romantic comedy about a piano tuner, who at 50 finds himself alone after years of caring for his mother, and a sexually insecure spinster, whom he meets through a dating service. Wonderful performances and a good script make this a delightful film that touches the human heart.
1982 (R) 95m/C Wendy Hughes, Norman Kaye, Jon Finlayson, Julia Blake, Jonathon Hardy; **D:** Paul Cox; **W:** Paul Cox. VHS, Beta $24.98 *SUE* ♫♫♫

Lonely Hearts A handsome con man works his wiles on a lonely woman in this erotic thriller. Standard plot wastes a good cast.
1991 (R) 109m/C Eric Roberts, Beverly D'Angelo, Joanna Cassidy. VHS $89.98 *LIV* ♫½

Lonely in America Charming romantic comedy of a newcomer in New York City. Arun (Chowdhry) has just arrived from India and has quite a few things to learn about life in the Big Apple.
1990 96m/C Ranjit Chowdhry, Adelaide Miller, Robert Kessler, Melissa Christopher, David Toney, Tirlok Malik; **D:** Barry Brown; **W:** Barry Brown, Satyajit Joy Palit. VHS $89.95 *ACA* ♫♫½

The Lonely Lady Young writer comes to Hollywood with dreams of success, gets involved with the seamy side of movie-making, and is driven to a nervous breakdown. Pia needs acting lessons, yet it probably wouldn't have helped this trash. Adapted from the novel by Harold Robbins.
1983 (R) 92m/C Pia Zadora, Lloyd Bochner, Bibi Besch, Joseph Cali, Ray Liotta; **D:** Peter Sasdy. VHS, Beta $59.95 *MCA* Woof!

Lonely Man A gunfighter tries to end his career, but is urged into one last battle. Strong performances and tight direction make up for weak plot.
1957 87m/B Jack Palance, Anthony Perkins, Neville Brand, Elaine Aiken; **D:** Henry Levin. VHS, Beta $14.95 *PAR, BAR* ♫♫½

The Lonely Passion of Judith Hearne A self-effacing Dublin spinster meets a man who gives her his attention, but she must overcome her own self-doubt and crisis of faith. Adapted from Brian Moore's 1955 novel. Excellent performances from both Hoskins and Smith.
1987 (R) 116m/C Dame Maggie Smith, Bob Hoskins, Wendy Hiller, Marie Kean, Ian McNeice, Alan Devlin, Rudi Davies, Prunella Scales; **D:** Jack Clayton; **W:** Peter Nelson; **M:** Georges Delerue. VHS $79.98 *CAN* ♫♫♫

The Lonely Sex Creepy and bizarre film in which a maniac kidnaps a young girl and is then harassed by her psychotic housemate.
1959 ?m/C Jean Evans, Karl Light, Mary Gonzales. VHS $16.95 *SNC, TPV* ♫½

Lonely Trail/Three Texas Steers Double your pleasure with two early Duke operas. In "Lonely Trail," Wayne dukes it out with dastardly carpetbaggers after the Civil War, while "Three Texas Steers," part of the "Three Mesquiteers" series, has Wayne and company spare a gal rancher/major babe from certain peril.
1939 112m/B John Wayne, George "Gabby" Hayes, Ray Corrigan, Raymond Hatton; **D:** George Sherman. VHS $14.98 *REP* ♫½

Lonely Wives A lawyer hires an entertainer to serve as his double because of his marital problems.
1931 86m/B Edward Everett Horton, Patsy Ruth Miller, Laura La Plante, Esther Ralston; **D:** Russell Mack. VHS, Beta $19.95 *NOS, VYY* ♫♫

Lonelyhearts Clift plays a reporter who is assigned the lovelorn column of his paper and gets too immersed in the problems of his readers. Given the superior cast and excellent material, this is a somewhat disappointing adaptation of the brilliant Nathanael West novel "Miss Lonelyhearts." Film debuts of both Stapleton and director Donehue.
1958 101m/B Montgomery Clift, Robert Ryan, Myrna Loy, Dolores Hart, Maureen Stapleton, Frank Maxwell, Jackie Coogan, Mike Kellin; **D:** Vincent J. Donehue. VHS $19.98 *MGM, SUE* ♫♫½

Loners Three teenagers run from the Southwest police after they are accused of murdering a highway patrolman.
1972 (R) 80m/C Dean Stockwell, Gloria Grahame, Scott Brady, Alex Dreier, Pat Stich; **D:** Sutton Roley; **W:** Barry Sandler. VHS, Beta *NO* ♫♫

Lonesome Dove Classic western saga with Duvall and Jones in outstanding roles as two aging ex-Texas Rangers who decide to leave their quiet lives for a last adventure—a cattle drive from Texas to Montana. Along the way they encounter a new love (Lane), a lost love (Huston), and a savage renegade Indian (well-played by Forrest). Based on Larry McMurtry's Pulitzer Prize winning novel, this handsome television miniseries is a finely detailed evocation of the Old West, with a wonderful cast and an equally fine production. Available in a four volume boxed set. Followed by "Return to Lonesome Dove."
1989 480m/C Robert Duvall, Tommy Lee Jones, Anjelica Huston, Danny Glover, Diane Lane, Rick Schroder, Robert Urich, D.B. Sweeney; **D:** Simon Windsor; **W:** Bill Wittliff. VHS $99.95 *CAF, TVC, IME* ♫♫♫½

Lonesome Trail Routine Western that differs from the average oater by having the good guys use bows and arrows to fight their battles.
1955 73m/B Jimmy Wakely, Lee White, Lorraine Miller, John James; **D:** Richard Bartlett. VHS, Beta *NO* ♫½

Long Ago Tomorrow A paralyzed athlete enters a church-run home for the disabled rather than return to his family as the object of their pity. A love affair with a woman, who shares the same disability, helps the athlete to adapt. *AKA:* The Raging Moon.
1971 (PG) 90m/C Malcolm McDowell, Nanette Newman, Bernard Lee, Georgia Brown, Gerald Sim; **D:** Bryan Forbes. VHS, Beta $59.95 *COL* ♫♫

The Long Dark Hall Courtroom drama in which an innocent man is brought to trial when his showgirl mistress is found dead.
1951 86m/B Rex Harrison, Lilli Palmer, Denis O'Dea, Raymond Huntley, Patricia Wayne, Anthony M. (Antonio Marghereti) Dawson; **D:** Anthony Bushell, Reginald Beck. **VHS, Beta** $16.95 SNC 𝒜𝒜½

The Long Day Closes It's 1956 Liverpool and 11-year-old Bud (McCormack) is part of a working-class Catholic family who longs to escape from his humdrum life. And how? By going to the movies of course and filling his head with pop songs. Nostalgic view of family life filled with sweet, small everyday moments set in a dreary postwar England. Sequel to Davies's also autobiographical film "Distant Voices, Still Lives."
1992 (PG) 84m/C Leigh McCormack, Marjorie Yates, Anthony Watson, Ayse Owens; **D:** Terence Davies; **W:** Terence Davies. **VHS** $89.95 COL 𝒜𝒜𝒜

Long Day's Journey into Night A brooding, devastating film based on Eugene O'Neill's most powerful and autobiographical play. Depicts a day in the life of a family deteriorating under drug addiction, alcoholism, and imminent death. Hepburn's performance is outstanding. In 1988, the Broadway version was taped and released on video.
1962 174m/B Ralph Richardson, Katharine Hepburn, Dean Stockwell, Jeanne Barr, Jason Robards Jr.; **D:** Sidney Lumet; **W:** Eugene O'Neill; **M:** Andre Previn. Academy Awards '62 Nominations: Best Actress (Hepburn); Cannes Film Festival '62: Best Actress (Hepburn); National Board of Review Awards '62: 10 Best Films of the Year, Best Supporting Actor (Robards). **VHS** $39.98 REP 𝒜𝒜𝒜𝒜

Long Day's Journey into Night A taped version of the Broadway production of the epic Eugene O'Neill play about a Southern family deteriorating under the weight of terminal illness, alcoholism and drug abuse. In 1962 a movie adaptation of the play was released with outstanding performances from its cast.
1988 169m/C Jack Lemmon, Bethel Leslie, Peter Gallagher, Kevin Spacey, Jodie Lynne McLintock; **D:** Jonathan Miller. **VHS, Beta** $59.98 LIV, VES 𝒜𝒜

The Long Days of Summer Set in pre-WWII America, this film portrays a Jewish attorney's struggle against the prejudices of the New England town where he lives. Sequel to "When Every Day Is the Fourth of July." Made for television.
1980 105m/C Dean Jones, Joan Hackett, Louanne, Donald Moffatt, Andrew Duggan, Michael McGuire; **D:** Dan Curtis. **VHS** $49.95 LIV 𝒜𝒜

Long Gone In the fifties, an over-the-hill minor-league player/manager is given a last lease on life and the pennant with two talented rookies and a sexy baseball groupie. Made for cable television.
1987 113m/C William L. Petersen, Henry Gibson, Katy Boyer, Virginia Madsen; **D:** Martin Davidson. **VHS, Beta** $19.98 LHV, WAR 𝒜𝒜½

The Long Good Friday Set in London's dockland, this is a violent story of a crime boss who meets his match. Hoskin's world crumbles over an Easter weekend when his buildings are bombed and his men murdered. He thinks its the work of rival gangsters only to discover an even deadlier threat is behind his troubles. One of the best of the crime genre, with an exquisitely charismatic performance by Hoskins.
1979 109m/C Bob Hoskins, Helen Mirren, Dave King, Bryan Marshall, George Coulouris, Pierce Brosnan, Derek Thompson, Eddie Constantine; **D:** John MacKenzie. **VHS, Beta** NO 𝒜𝒜𝒜½

The Long Goodbye Raymond Chandler's penultimate novel with the unmistakable Altman touch—which is to say that some of the changes to the story have pushed purist noses out of joint. Gould is cast as an insouciant anti-Marlowe, the film noir atmosphere has been transmuted into a Hollywood film neon, genre jibing abounds, and the ending has been rewritten. But the revamping serves a purpose, which is to make Marlowe a viable character in a contemporary world. Handsomely photographed by Vilmos Zsigmond. Don't miss bulky boy Arnold's cameo (his second film appearance).
1973 (R) 112m/C Elliott Gould, Nina Van Pallandt, Sterling Hayden, Henry Gibson, Mark Rydell, David Arkin, Warren Berlinger; **Cameos:** Arnold Schwarzenegger, David Carradine; **D:** Robert Altman; **W:** Leigh Brackett; **M:** John Williams. **VHS, Beta** $19.98 MGM, FCT 𝒜𝒜𝒜

The Long Gray Line Power gives an outstanding performance as Marty Maher, a humble Irish immigrant who became an institution at West Point. This is the inspiring story of his rise from an unruly cadet to one of the academy's most beloved instructors. O'Hara does a fine job of playing his wife, who like her husband, adopts the young cadets as her own. Director Ford gracefully captures the spirit and honor associated with West Point in this affectionate drama.
1955 138m/C Tyrone Power, Maureen O'Hara, Robert Francis, Donald Crisp, Ward Bond, Betsy Palmer, Phil Carey; **D:** John Ford. **VHS** $19.95 COL 𝒜𝒜𝒜

The Long Haul A truck driver becomes involved with crooks as his marriage sours.
1957 88m/C Victor Mature, Diana Dors, Patrick Allen, G.M. Anderson; **D:** Ken Hughes. **VHS** GKK 𝒜𝒜

The Long, Hot Summer A tense, well-played adaptation of the William Faulkner story about a wanderer latching himself onto a tyrannical Mississippi family. The first on-screen pairing of Newman and Woodward, and one of the best. Remade for television in 1986.
1958 117m/C Paul Newman, Orson Welles, Joanne Woodward, Lee Remick, Anthony (Tony) Franciosa, Angela Lansbury, Richard Anderson; **D:** Martin Ritt; **W:** Harriet Frank Jr., Irving Ravetch; **M:** Alex North. **VHS, Beta** $19.98 FOX 𝒜𝒜𝒜½

The Long, Hot Summer A made-for-television version of the William Faulkner story, "The Hamlet," about a drifter taken under a Southern patriarch's wing. He's bribed into courting the man's unmarried daughter. Wonderful performances from the entire cast, especially Ivey and surprisingly, Johnson. Remake of the 1958 film with Paul Newman and Joanne Woodward that is on par with the original.
1986 172m/C Don Johnson, Cybill Shepherd, Judith Ivey, Jason Robards Jr., Ava Gardner, William Russ, Wings Hauser, William Forsythe, Albert Hall; **D:** Stuart Cooper; **M:** Charles Bernstein. **VHS, Beta** $59.98 FOX 𝒜𝒜𝒜½

The Long Island Four Four Nazi saboteurs are smitten by the decadent nightlife of the Big Apple in 1942. The late Grafstrom's Super-8 film, based on a true story, was an underground hit.
1980 100m/C **D:** Anders Grafstrom. **VHS** $59.95 MWF 𝒜𝒜½

Long John Silver Famed pirate John Silver plans a return trip to Treasure Island to search for the elusive treasure; unofficial sequel to "Treasure Island" by Disney. **AKA:** Long John Silver Returns to Treasure Island.
1953 106m/C Robert Newton, Connie Gilchrist, Kit Taylor, Grant Taylor, Rod Taylor; **D:** Byron Haskin. **VHS, Beta** $29.95 GEM, MRV, CAB 𝒜½

Long Journey Back The biographical story of a young woman's rehabilitation after her injury in a school bus accident. Produced for television.
1978 100m/C Mike Connors, Cloris Leachman, Stephanie Zimbalist, Katy Kurtzman; **D:** Mel Damski. **VHS** $39.95 LIV 𝒜𝒜

The Long, Long Trailer A couple on their honeymoon find that trailer life is more than they bargained for. Lots of fun with charming direction from Minelli, and Ball's incredible slapstick style.
1954 97m/C Desi Arnaz Sr., Lucille Ball, Marjorie Main, Keenan Wynn; **D:** Vincente Minnelli. **VHS** $19.98 BTV, MGM, FCT 𝒜𝒜½

The Long Riders Excellent mythic western in which the Jesse James and Cole Younger gangs raid banks, trains, and stagecoaches in post-Civil War Missouri. Stylish, meticulous and a violent look back, with one of the better slow-motion shootouts in Hollywood history. Notable for the portrayal of four sets of brothers by four Hollywood brother sets. Complimented by excellent Cooder score.
1980 (R) 100m/C Stacy Keach, James Keach, Randy Quaid, Dennis Quaid, David Carradine, Keith Carradine, Robert Carradine, Christopher Guest, Nicholas Guest, Pamela Reed, Savannah Smith, James Whitmore Jr., Harry Carey Jr.; **D:** Walter Hill; **M:** Ry Cooder. **VHS, Beta** $14.95 MGM 𝒜𝒜𝒜

Long Shadows An analysis of how the resonating effects of the Civil War can still be felt on society, via interviews with a number of noted writers, historians, civil rights activists and politicians.
1986 88m/C Robert Penn Warren, Studs Terkel, Jimmy Carter, Robert Coles, Tom Wicker. **VHS, Beta** JAF 𝒜½

Long Shot Two foosball enthusiasts work their way through local tournaments to make enough money to make it to the World Championships in Tahoe.
1981 100m/C Ian Giatti. **VHS, Beta** NO 𝒜½

Long Time Gone An over-the-hill detective tries to solve a murder while dealing with his bratty, alienated 11-year-old son. Made for television.
1986 97m/C Paul LeMat, Wil Wheaton, Ann Dusenberry, Barbara Stock; **D:** Robert Butler. **VHS, Beta** NO 𝒜

The Long Voyage Home A talented cast performs this must-see screen adaptation of Eugene O'Neill's play about crew members aboard a merchant steamer in 1939. Wayne plays a young lad from Sweden who is trying to get home and stay out of trouble as he and the other seaman get shore leave.
1940 105m/B John Wayne, Thomas Mitchell, Ian Hunter, Barry Fitzgerald, Mildred Natwick, John Qualen; **D:** John Ford. Academy Awards '40 Nominations: Best Black and White Cinematography, Best Film Editing, Best Picture, Best Screenplay, Best Original Score; National Board of Review Awards '40: 10 Best Films of the Year; New York Film Critics Awards '40: Best Director (Ford). **VHS, Beta** $19.98 WAR 𝒜𝒜𝒜½

The Long Walk Home In Montgomery Alabama, in the mid 1950s, sometime after Rosa Parks refused to sit in the black-designated back of the bus, Martin Luther

King Jr. led a bus boycott. Spacek is the affluent wife of a narrow-minded businessman while Goldberg is their struggling maid. When Spacek discovers that Goldberg is supporting the boycott by walking the nine-mile trek to work, she sympathizes and tries to help, antagonizing her husband. The plot marches inevitably toward a white-on-white showdown on racism while quietly exploring gender equality between the women. Outstanding performances by Spacek and Goldberg, and a great 50s feel.

1989 (PG) 95m/C Sissy Spacek, Whoopi Goldberg, Dwight Schultz, Ving Rhames, Dylan Baker; **D:** Richard Pearce; **M:** George Fenton. **VHS $14.98** *LIV, IME, FCT* 🎬🎬🎬

A Long Way Home A television movie about a grown man searching for his long-lost siblings, after the three of them were given up for adoption after birth.

1981 97m/C Timothy Hutton, Brenda Vaccaro, Rosanna Arquette, Paul Regina, George Dzundza, John Lehne, Bonnie Bartlett; **D:** Robert Markowitz; **M:** William Goldstein. **VHS, Beta $59.95** *LIV* 🎬🎬

The Long Weekend When a vacationing couple goes camping and carelessly destroys a forest, Mother Nature turns her powers of retribution on them.

1986 95m/C VHS, Beta $59.95 *TWE* 🎬

The Longest Day The complete story of the D-Day landings at Normandy on June 6, 1944, as seen through the eyes of American, French, British, and German participants. Exhaustively accurate details and extremely talented cast make this one of the all-time great Hollywood epic productions. The first of the big budget, all-star war productions; based on the book by Cornelius Ryan. Three directors share credit. Also available in a colorized version.

1962 179m/C John Wayne, Richard Burton, Red Buttons, Robert Mitchum, Henry Fonda, Robert Ryan, Paul Anka, Mel Ferrer, Edmond O'Brien, Fabian, Sean Connery, Roddy McDowall, Arletty, Curt Jurgens, Rod Steiger, Jean-Louis Barrault, Peter Lawford, Robert Wagner, Sal Mineo, Leo Genn, Richard Beymer, Jeffrey Hunter, Stuart Whitman, Eddie Albert, Tom Tryon, Alexander Knox, Ray Danton, Kenneth More, Richard Todd, Gert Frobe, Christopher Lee; **D:** Ken Annakin; **W:** Bernhard Wicki; **M:** Maurice Jarre. Academy Awards '62: Best Black and White Cinematography, Best Special Effects; Nominations: Best Art Direction/Set Decoration (B & W), Best Film Editing, Best Picture; National Board of Review Awards '62: 10 Best Films of the Year. **VHS, Beta $24.98** *FXV, TLF, HMV* 🎬🎬🎬½

The Longest Drive Two brothers comb the wildest parts of the West for their sister, whom they believe is living with Indians. A made for television movie originally titled "The Quest," which became a brief television series. Highlights include colorful performances from the veteran actors and a unique horse/camel race. A continuation of the series is available on video as "The Captive: The Longest Drive 2." **AKA:** The Quest.

1976 92m/C Kurt Russell, Tim Matheson, Brian Keith, Keenan Wynn, Neville Brand, Cameron Mitchell, Morgan Woodward, Iron Eyes Cody, Luke Askew; **D:** Lee H. Katzin. **VHS $89.95** *VMK* 🎬🎬

The Longest Yard A one-time pro football quarterback, now an inmate, organizes his fellow convicts into a football team to play against the prison guards. Filmed on location at Georgia State Prison.

1974 (R) 121m/C Burt Reynolds, Eddie Albert, Bernadette Peters, Ed Lauter, Richard Kiel; **D:** Robert Aldrich; **W:** Tracy Keenan Wynn. Academy Awards '74 Nominations: Best Film

Editing; Golden Globe Awards '75: Best Film—Musical/Comedy. **VHS, Beta $14.95** *PAR* 🎬🎬½

The Longshot Four bumblers try to raise cash to put on a sure-bet racetrack tip in this sorry comedy. Mike Nichols is the executive producer.

1986 (PG-13) 89m/C Tim Conway, Harvey Korman, Jack Weston, Ted Wass, Jonathan Winters, Stella Stevens, Anne Meara; **D:** Paul Bartel; **W:** Tim Conway, John Myhers; **M:** Charles Fox. **VHS, Beta $59.95** *HBO, CNG* Woof!

Longtime Companion Critically acclaimed film follows a group of gay men and their friends during the 1980s. The closely knit group monitors the progression of the AIDS virus from early news reports until it finally hits home and begins to take the lives of their loved ones. One of the first films to look at the situation in an intelligent and touching manner. Produced by the PBS "American Playhouse" company.

1990 (R) 100m/C Stephen Caffrey, Patrick Cassidy, Brian Cousins, Bruce Davison, John Dossett, Mark Lamos, Dermot Mulroney, Mary-Louise Parker, Michael Schoeffling, Campbell Scott, Robert Joy; **D:** Norman Rene. Academy Awards '90 Nominations: Best Supporting Actor (Davison); Golden Globe Awards '91: Best Supporting Actor (Davison); Independent Spirit Awards '91: Best Supporting Actor (Davison); New York Film Critics Awards '90: Best Supporting Actor (Davison); National Society of Film Critics Awards '90: Best Supporting Actor (Davison). **VHS $19.95** *VMK, FCT, BTV* 🎬🎬🎬½

Look Back in Anger Based on John Osborne's famous play, the first British "angry young man" film, in which a squalor-living lad takes out his anger on the world by seducing his friend's wife.

1958 99m/B Richard Burton, Claire Bloom, Mary Ure, Edith Evans, Gary Raymond; **D:** Tony Richardson; **W:** John Osborne; **M:** John Addison. **VHS, Beta $24.98** *SUE* 🎬🎬½

Look Back in Anger A working class man angered by society's hypocrisy lashes out at his upper class wife, his mistress, and the world. Inferior remake of 1958 film version starring Richard Burton, based on '50s stage hit.

1980 100m/C Malcolm McDowell, Lisa Banes, Fran Brill, Raymond Hardie, Lindsay Anderson. **VHS, Beta $19.98** *WAR, OM* 🎬🎬

Look Back in Anger There's something about John Osborne's play that brings out the angry young man in British leads. Richard Burton played Osborne's irascible guy in 1958, Malcom McDowell looked back angrily in '80, and now Branagh convincingly vents his spleen on wife and mistress in this made for British TV production. Director Jones earlier filmed "84 Charing Cross Road" and "Jacknife."

1989 114m/C Kenneth Branagh, Emma Thompson, Gerard Horan, Siobhan Redmond; **D:** David Jones. **VHS $29.99** *HBO* 🎬🎬🎬

Look for the Silver Lining Insipid musical biography of Broadway star Marilyn Miller (Haver). Bolger is the highlight as Miller's mentor from vaudeville to the Great White Way. 🎵Look for the Silver Lining; Whip-Poor-Will; A Kiss in the Dark; Pirouette; Just a Memory; Time On My Hands; Wild Rose; Shine On Harvest Moon; Back, Back, Back to Baltimore.

1949 100m/C June Haver, Ray Bolger, Gordon MacRae, Charlie Ruggles, Rosemary DeCamp, S.Z. Sakall; **D:** David Butler; **W:** Phoebe Ephron, Henry Ephron, Marian Spitzer. **VHS, Beta $19.98** *MGM, FCT, BTV* 🎬🎬½

Look Out Sister Jordan and an all-black cast star in this musical satire of westerns. "Two Gun" Jordan saves a dude ranch from foreclosure and wins the girl. Lots of black

culture, slang and music from the '40s. Broad but enjoyable humor. 🎵Caldonia; Don't Burn the Candle at Both Ends.

1948 64m/B Louis Jordan, Suzette Harbin, Monte Hawley, Maceo B. Sheffield; **D:** Bud Pollard. **VHS $24.95** *NOS* 🎬

Look Who's Laughing Bergen's plane lands in a town conveniently populated by radio stars. Not much plot here, but it might be worth a look to fans of the stars including Jim and Marion Jordan, better known as Fibber McGee and Molly.

1941 79m/C Edgar Bergen, Jim Jordan, Marion Jordan, Lucille Ball, Harold Peary, Lee Bonnell, Charles Halton; **D:** Allan Dwan. **VHS, Beta $19.98** *TTC, MLB* 🎬🎬

Look Who's Talking When Alley bears the child of a married, and quite fickle man, she sets her sights elsewhere in search of the perfect father; Travolta is the cabbie with more on his mind than driving Alley around and babysitting. All the while, the baby gives us his views via the voice of Bruce Willis. A very light comedy with laughs for the whole family.

1989 (PG-13) 90m/C John Travolta, Kirstie Alley, Olympia Dukakis, George Segal, Abe Vigoda; **D:** Amy Heckerling; **W:** Amy Heckerling; **M:** David Kitay; **V:** Bruce Willis. **VHS, Beta $19.95** *COL, RDG* 🎬🎬🎬

Look Who's Talking Now Continuing to wring revenue from a tired premise, the family dogs throw in their two cents in the second sequel to "Look Who's Talking." For anyone who thinks Diane Keaton's hair makes her look a little like a hound dog, here's a chance to visualize her as a similarly long-eared poodle with an attitude. DeVito is also cast in character as the voice of a rough street-smart mutt, who happens to get thrown into the same household as the bosses' pure-bred poodle. Sparks, Alpo, and butt jokes fly as the dogs mark their territory. Meanwhile, dimwit wife Alley is worried that husband Travolta is having an affair, and is determined to get him back.

1993 (PG-13) 95m/C John Travolta, Kirstie Alley, Olympia Dukakis, George Segal, Lysette Anthony; **D:** Tom Ropelewski; **W:** Tom Ropelewski, Leslie Dixon; **M:** William Ross; **V:** Diane Keaton, Danny DeVito. **VHS, 8mm** *COL* 🎬½

Look Who's Talking, Too If Academy Awards for Stupidest Sequel and Lamest Dialogue existed, this diaper drama would have cleaned up. The second go-round throws the now married accountant-cabbie duo into a marital tailspin when Alley's babysitting brother moves in and the Saturday Night dancer moves out. Meanwhile, Willis cum baby smartasses incessantly. A once-clever gimmick now unencumbered by plot; not advised for linear thinkers. The voice of Arnold, though, is a guarantee you'll get one laugh for your rental.

1990 (PG-13) 81m/C Kirstie Alley, John Travolta, Olympia Dukakis, Elias Koteas; **D:** Amy Heckerling; **V:** Bruce Willis, Mel Brooks, Damon Wayans, Roseanne (Barr) Arnold. **VHS, 8mm $19.95** *COL* 🎬

The Lookalike A made for cable adaptation of Kate Wilhelm's novel. Bereaved mother Gilbert questions her sanity when she thinks she sees her daughter after she was killed in an automobile accident. Could this girl provide answers to questions about her past?

1990 (PG-13) 88m/C Melissa Gilbert, Diane Ladd, Frances Lee McCain, Jason Scott Lee, Thaao Penghlis; **D:** Gary Nelson. **VHS $79.98** *MCA* 🎬🎬

Looker Stunning models are made even more beautiful by a plastic surgeon, but one by one they begin to die. Finney plays the Beverly Hills surgeon who decides to investigate when he starts losing all his clients.
1981 (PG) 94m/C Albert Finney, James Coburn, Susan Dey, Leigh Taylor-Young; **D:** Michael Crichton; **W:** Michael Crichton. VHS, Beta $64.95 WAR 𝄫 ½

Lookin' to Get Out Comedy about two gamblers running from their debts. They wind up at the MGM Grand in Las Vegas trying to get out of a mess.
1982 (R) 70m/C Ann-Margret, Jon Voight, Burt Young; **D:** Hal Ashby; **M:** Miles Goodman. VHS, Beta $59.98 FOX 𝄫𝄫 ½

Looking for Miracles Two brothers, separated during the Depression because of poverty, get a chance to cultivate brotherly love when they're reunited in 1935. A Wonderworks production based on the A.E. Hochner novel.
1990 (G) 104m/C Zachary Bennett, Greg Spottiswood, Joe Flaherty. VHS $29.95 BVV, DIS, FCT 𝄫𝄫 ½

Looking for Mr. Goodbar Young teacher Keaton seeks companionship and love by frequenting single's bars and furthers her self-destruction by her aimless intake of drugs and alcohol. In need of a father figure, she makes herself available to numerous men and eventually regrets her hedonistic behavior. Unpleasant, aimless characters do little for this dreary film, whose sexual theme sparked a bit of public conversation when first released. Based on the bestselling novel by Judith Rossner. Oscar nominations for supporting actress Weld, and cinematography.
1977 (R) 136m/C Diane Keaton, Tuesday Weld, Richard Gere, Tom Berenger, William Atherton, Richard Kiley; **D:** Richard Brooks; **W:** Richard Brooks. VHS, Beta $39.95 PAR 𝄫𝄫

The Looking Glass War Polish defector is sent behind the Iron Curtain on a final mission to photograph a rocket in East Berlin. He's guided by frustrated British security officers Rogers and Richardson, who both offer sly turns. An otherwise slow-moving adaptation of John Le Carre's bestselling spy novel.
1969 (PG) 108m/C Christopher Jones, Ralph Richardson, Pia Degermark, Anthony Hopkins, Susan George; **D:** Frank Pierson; **W:** Frank Pierson. VHS, Beta $59.95 COL, MLB 𝄫𝄫

Looney Looney Looney Bugs Bunny Movie A feature-length compilation of classic Warner Brothers cartoons tied together with new animation. Cartoon stars featured include Bugs Bunny, Elmer Fudd, Porky Pig, Yosemite Sam, Duffy Duck and Foghorn Leghorn. **AKA:** Friz Freleng's Looney Looney Looney Bugs Bunny Movie.
1981 (G) 80m/C **D:** Friz Freleng, Chuck Jones, Bob Clampett; **V:** Mel Blanc, June Foray. VHS, Beta $14.95 WAR, FCT, WTA 𝄫𝄫𝄫

Loophole An out-of-work architect, hard pressed for money, joins forces with an elite team of expert criminals, in a scheme to make off with millions from the most established holding bank's vault. **AKA:** Break In.
1983 105m/C Albert Finney, Martin Sheen, Susannah York, Robert Morley, Colin Blakely, Jonathan Pryce; **D:** John Quested. VHS, Beta $59.95 MED, HHE, MTX 𝄫𝄫

Loose Cannons Yet another mismatched-cop-partner comedy, wherein a mystery is ostensibly solved by a veteran cop and a schizophrenic detective.
1990 (R) 95m/C Gene Hackman, Dan Aykroyd, Dom DeLuise, Ronny Cox, Nancy Travis, David Alan Grier; **D:** Bob (Benjamin) Clark; **W:** Bob (Benjamin) Clark, Richard Matheson. VHS, Beta $14.95 COL 𝄫

Loose Connections A feminist driving to a convention in Europe advertises for a travelmate, and gets a hopeless chauvinist who is masquerading as a gay man in this offbeat cult comedy.
1987 90m/C Lindsay Duncan, Stephen Rea, Robbie Coltrane; **D:** Richard Eyre. VHS, Beta $79.95 TPV 𝄫𝄫

Loose in New York Much to her surprise, a cynical socialite begins to fall for her computer-arranged mate.
1987 91m/C Rita Tushingham, Aldo Maccione; **D:** Gian Polidoro. VHS, Beta NO 𝄫𝄫

Loose Screws Four perverted teenagers are sent to a restrictive academy where they continue their lewd ways in this stupid sequel to "Screwballs."
1985 (R) 75m/C Bryan Genesse, Karen Wood, Alan Deveau, Jason Warren; **D:** Rafal Zeilinski. VHS, Beta $79.98 LIV 𝄫

Loose Shoes A collection of vignettes that satirize movie trailers, teasers and special announcements. Murray's film debut. **AKA:** Coming Attractions.
1980 (R) 84m/C Bill Murray, Howard Hesseman, Jaye P. Morgan, Buddy Hackett, Misty Rowe, Susan Tyrrell; **D:** Ira Miller. VHS, Beta $39.98 FOX 𝄫𝄫

Loot...Give Me Money, Honey! Black comedy about a motley crew of greed-driven golddiggers who chase after a heisted fortune in jewels, which is hidden in a coffin belonging to one of the thieves' mother. From Joe Orton's play.
1970 101m/C Richard Attenborough, Lee Remick, Hywel Bennett, Milo O'Shea, Roy Holder; **D:** Silvio Narizzano. VHS, Beta NO 𝄫𝄫 ½

Lord Jim A ship officer (O'Toole) commits an act of cowardice that results in his dismissal and disgrace, which leads him to the Far East in search of self-respect. Excellent supporting cast. Based on Joseph Conrad's novel.
1965 154m/C Peter O'Toole, James Mason, Curt Jurgens, Eli Wallach, Jack Hawkins, Paul Lukas, Akim Tamiroff, Daliah Lavi, Andrew Keir, Jack MacGowran, Walter Gotell; **D:** Richard Brooks; **W:** Richard Brooks. VHS, Beta $19.95 COL, TVC 𝄫𝄫𝄫

Lord of the Flies Proper English schoolboys stranded on a desert island during a nuclear war are transformed into savages. A study in greed, power, and the innate animalistic/survivalistic instincts of human nature. Based on William Golding's novel, which he described as a journey to the darkness of the human heart. The laser disc version contains outtakes, the film trailer, and additional material.
1963 91m/B James Aubrey, Tom Chapin, Hugh Edwards, Roger Elwin, Tom Gamen; **D:** Peter Brook. VHS, Beta $29.95 HMV, FUS 𝄫𝄫𝄫 ½

Lord of the Flies Inferior second filming of the famed William Golding novel about schoolboys marooned on a desert island who gradually degenerate into savages. Lushly photographed, yet redundant and poorly acted.
1990 (R) 90m/C Balthazar Getty, Danuel Pipoly, Chris Furrh, Badgett Dale, Edward Taft, Andrew Taft; **D:** Harry Hook. VHS, Beta, 8mm $19.95 COL, SUE, TVC 𝄫𝄫

The Lord of the Rings An animated interpretation of Tolkien's classic tale of the hobbits, wizards, elves, and dwarfs who inhabit Middle Earth. Animator Ralph Bakshi used live motion animation (roto-scoping) to give his characters more life-like and human motion. Well done in spite of the difficulty of adapting from Tolkien's highly detailed and lengthy works.
1978 (PG) 128m/C **D:** Ralph Bakshi; **V:** Christopher Guard, John Hurt. VHS, Beta $14.98 REP, FCT, WTA 𝄫𝄫

The Lords of Discipline A military academy cadet is given the unenviable task of protecting a black freshman from racist factions at a southern school circa 1964. Based on Pat Conroy's autobiographical novel.
1983 (R) 103m/C David Keith, Robert Prosky, Barbara Babcock, Judge Reinhold, G.D. Spradlin, Rick Rossovich, Michael Biehn; **D:** Franc Roddam; **M:** Howard Blake. VHS, Beta $14.95 PAR 𝄫𝄫 ½

The Lords of Flatbush Four street toughs battle against their own maturation and responsibilities in 1950s Brooklyn. Winkler introduces the leather-clad hood he's made a career of and Stallone introduces a character not unlike Rocky. Interesting slice of life.
1974 (PG) 88m/C Sylvester Stallone, Perry King, Henry Winkler, Susan Blakely, Armand Assante, Paul Mace; **D:** Stephen Verona, Martin Davidson; **M:** Joseph Brooks. VHS, Beta $14.95 COL 𝄫𝄫 ½

Lords of Magick Two warriors chase an evil sorcerer and the princess he's kidnapped across time to the 20th century.
1988 (PG-13) 98m/C Jarrett Parker, Matt Gauthier, Brendan Dillon Jr.; **D:** David Marsh. VHS, Beta $79.95 PSM 𝄫

Lords of the Deep A Roger Corman cheapie about underwater technicians trapped on the ocean floor with a race of aliens. A film rushed out to capitalize on the undersea sci-fi subgenre highlighted by "The Abyss."
1989 (PG-13) 95m/C Bradford Dillman, Priscilla Barnes, Melody Ryane, Eb Lottimer, Daryl Haney; **D:** Mary Ann Fisher; **W:** Daryl Haney, Howard R. Cohen. VHS, Beta $14.95 MGM Woof!

Lorenzo's Oil Based on the true story of Augusto and Michaela Odone's efforts to find a cure for their 5-year-old, Lorenzo, diagnosed with the rare and incurable disease ALD (Adrenoleukodystrophy). Confronted by a slow-moving and clinically cold medical community, the Odones embark on their own quest for a cure. Sarandon delivers an outstanding and emotionally charged performance as Lorenzo's determined mother. Nolte is his equally devoted Italian father, complete with black hair and hand gestures. They are a powerful presence in a film which could have easily degenerated into a made-for-TV movie, but is instead a tribute to what love and hope can accomplish.
1992 (PG-13) 135m/C Nick Nolte, Susan Sarandon, Zach O'Malley-Greenberg, Peter Ustinov, Kathleen Wilhoite, Gerry Bamman, Margo Martindale, James Rebhorn, Ann Hearn; **D:** George Miller; **W:** Nick Enright, George Miller. VHS, Beta $19.98 MCA, MOV, BTV 𝄫𝄫𝄫

The Loretta Young Show Two enchanting episodes of the popular fifties series "The Loretta Young Show," entitled "Somebody Else's Dream" and "So Bright the Light." Other episodes are also available, two per tape.
1954 60m/C Loretta Young. VHS, Beta $19.95 MVC 𝄫𝄫

Lorna Doone A young girl of royal descent is kidnapped and raised by the bandit Doone family in the highlands of Scotland. Adapted from the novel by R.D. Blackmore.

1922 ?m/C Madge Bellamy, John Bowers; *D:* Maurice Tourneur. VHS, Beta, 8mm $55.95 *GVV* � III

Lorna Doone Classic romance set in 17th-century England and based on the novel by R.D. Blackmore. John Ridd (Bean) vows to destroy the land-grabbing Doone family, whom he blames for the death of his parents. Then he meets, and immediately falls in love with, the beautiful and innocent Lorna Doone (Walker). Made for British television.
1990 (PG) 90m/C Sean Bean, Polly Walker, Clive Owen, Billie Whitelaw; *D:* Andrew Grieve; *W:* Matthew Jacobs. VHS, Beta *PAR* �II½

Los Amores de Marieta Love and jealousy abound amidst the Mexican Revolution.
1987 100m/C Elvira Quintana, Joaquin Cordero, Gina Romand. VHS, Beta $59.95 *MAD* II

Los Apuros de Dos Gallos Four Mexican singing aces spend some time at a ranch serenading the ranch hands. *AKA:* The Troubles of Two Roosters.
1969 102m/C Miguel Aceves Mejia, Marco Antonio Muniz, Lilian de Celis. VHS, Beta $69.95 *MAD* II

Los Asesinos Two rival bandits arrive in a lawless town and fight for control. Dialogue in Spanish.
1968 95m/C Nick Adams, Regina Torne, Pedro Armendariz Jr., Elsa Cardenas. VHS, Beta $29.95 *UNI* II

Los Caciques A comic-book hero comes alive and stops an evil empire of crime.
1987 96m/C Jorge Rivero, Pedro Armendariz Sr., Carmen Vicarte, Mario Alberto Rodriquez. VHS, Beta $79.95 *MAD* II½

Los Cacos A group of eleven friends try to steal a large sum of money but they run into problems.
1987 80m/C Silvia Pinal, Milton Rodriguez. VHS, Beta $59.95 *MAD* II

Los Caifanes A group of men live life on the edge, challenging death at every minute.
1987 95m/C Julissa, Enrique Alvarez Felix, Sergio Jimenez, Oscar Chavez. VHS, Beta $55.95 *MAD* II

Los Dos Hermanos A woman causes two brothers to hate each other.
1987 92m/C Jorge Rivero, Gregorio Casal, Nadia Milton, Sergio Jimenez. VHS, Beta $75.95 *MAD* II½

Los Hermanos Centella Two brothers from Northern Mexico change from bandits to people who protect the oppressed.
1965 105m/C Dacia Gonzales, Jaime Fernandez, Dagoberto Rodriguez, Guillermo Rivas. VHS, Beta $39.95 *MAD* II

Los Hermanos Diablo Jose, Julio, and Juan are the Diablo brothers, and they are determined to keep outlaws and Indians off their ranch.
1965 90m/B Mauricio Garces, Abel Salazar, Rafael Baledon. VHS, Beta $39.95 *MAD* II

Los Jinetes de la Bruja A witch and her horsemen avenge the death of innocent puppeteers on a Frenchman's ranch. *AKA:* The Witch's Horsemen.
1976 93m/C Blanca Sanchez, Kitty De Hoyos, Ferdinando Almada, Mario Almada. VHS, Beta $69.95 *MAD* II

Los Olvidados From surrealist Bunuel, a powerful story of the poverty and violence of young people's lives in Mexico's slums. In Spanish with English subtitles. *AKA:* The Young and the Damned.
1950 81m/B Alfonso Mejias, Roberto Cobo; *D:* Luis Bunuel. VHS, Beta, 8mm $24.95 *VYY, HHT, DVT* III½

Los Sheriffs de la Frontera Two lawmen have to rid a town of mean bad guys.
1947 90m/B Fernando Casanova, Juan Gallardo. VHS, Beta $39.95 *MAD* II

Los Tres Amores de Losa A girl becomes friends with a famous actress in Madrid and then falls in love with her cousin.
1947 90m/B Lola Flores, Agustin Lara, Luis Aguilar, Abel Salazar. VHS, Beta $39.95 *MAD* II

Los Tres Calaveras The story of the Skeleton trio from its beginnings to the top of the international music charts. *AKA:* The Three Skeletons.
1964 105m/B Javier Solis, Lucha Villa, Joaquin Cordero, Manuel Lopez Ochoa, Ruben Zepeda Novelo; *D:* Fernando Cortes. VHS, Beta $44.95 *MAD* II

Los Vampiros de Coyacan Two wrestlers are summoned to help a girl who has fallen under the spell of a vampire.
1987 87m/C German Robles, Mil Mascaras, Superzan, Sasha Montenegro. VHS, Beta $69.95 *MAD* II

The Losers Four motorcyclists are hired by the U.S. Army to rescue a presidential advisor who is being held captive by Asian bad guys.
1970 (R) 96m/C William Smith, Bernie Hamilton, Adam Roarke, Houston Savage, Brad Johnson, Vernon Wells; *D:* Jack Starrett. VHS, Beta $29.95 *ACA* II½

Losin' It Four teens travel across the Mexican border to Tijuana on a journey to lose their virginity. Cruise meets a married woman who says she is in town for a divorce, while the others become caught up in frenzied undertakings of their own.
1982 (R) 104m/C Tom Cruise, John Stockwell, Shelley Long, Jackie Earle Haley; *D:* Curtis Hanson. VHS, Beta $9.98 *SUE, NLC* II

Lost A young girl runs away into the wilderness because of the resentment she feels toward her new stepfather.
1983 92m/C Sandra Dee, Don Stewart, Ken Curtis, Jack Elam, Sheila Newhouse. VHS, Beta $49.95 *PSM* II½

Lost When their boat capsizes in the Pacific, three sailors desperately cling to life, drifting aimlessly for 74 days. Based on a true story, this film is adult-fare.
1986 93m/C Michael Hogan, Helen Shaver, Kenneth Welsh; *D:* Peter Rowe. VHS, Beta *HHE, BMV* II

Lost and Found An American professor of English and an English film production secretary fall in love on a skiing vacation. Good cast but Segal and Jackson did romance better in "A Touch of Class."
1979 (PG) 104m/C George Segal, Glenda Jackson, Maureen Stapleton, Hollis McLaren, John Cunningham, Paul Sorvino, John Candy, Martin Short; *D:* Melvin Frank; *W:* Jack Rose. VHS, Beta $9.95 *GKK* II½

Lost Angels A glossy "Rebel Without a Cause" '80s reprise providing a no-holds-barred portrait of life in the fast lane. A wealthy, disaffected San Fernando Valley youth immerses himself in sex, drugs and rock 'n' roll. Ultimately he is arrested and sent by his parents to a youth home, where a dedicated therapist assists his tortuous road back to reality.
1989 (R) 116m/C Donald Sutherland, Adam Horovitz, Amy Locane, Kevin Tighe, John C. McGinley, Graham Beckel, Park Overall, Don Bloomfield, Celia Weston; *D:* Hugh Hudson; *W:* Michael Weller; *M:* Philippe Sarde. VHS, Beta $19.98 *ORI* II½

The Lost Boys Santa Cruz seems like a dull town when Michael, his younger brother, and their divorced mom move into their eccentric grandfather's home. But when Michael falls for a pretty girl with some hard-living friends he takes on more than he imagines—these partying teens are actually a group of vampires. Some humor, some bloodletting violence, and an attractive cast help out this updated vampire tale. Rock-filled soundtrack.
1987 (R) 97m/C Jason Patric, Kiefer Sutherland, Corey Haim, Jami Gertz, Dianne Wiest, Corey Feldman, Barnard Hughes, Edward Herrmann, Billy Wirth; *D:* Joel Schumacher; *W:* Jeffrey Boam. VHS, Beta, 8mm $14.95 *WAR, FUS* II

Lost Canyon Hoppy tries to help a fugitive who's been framed for bank robbery. This is the second installment distributed by United Artists. The song "Jingle, Jangle, Jingle" is sung by the Sportsman Quartet.
1943 61m/B William Boyd, Jay Kirby, Andy Clyde, Lola Lane, Douglas Fowley, Herbert Rawlinson; *D:* Lesley Selander. VHS $19.95 *NOS* II

The Lost Capone Made for cable TV version of the story of Al Capone's youngest brother, a clean living small town sheriff who struggles with his sibling's reputation at every turn.
1990 (PG-13) 93m/C Ally Sheedy, Eric Roberts, Adrian Pasdar, Titus Welliver, Jimmie F. Skaggs, Maria Pitillo, Anthony Crivello; *D:* John Gray; *W:* John Gray. VHS, Beta $79.95 *TTC* II

The Lost City A feature version of the rollicking vintage movie serial about a lost jungle city, adventurers and mad scientists.
1934 74m/B William Boyd, Kane Richmond, George "Gabby" Hayes, Claudia Dell; *D:* Harry Revier. VHS, Beta $19.95 *NOS, SNC, DVT* II

Lost City of the Jungle 13-chapter serial focusing on a crazed Atwill, in his last screen role, believing that he can rule the world from the heart of a deep, dark jungle by utilizing a special mineral. The final Universal serial.
1945 169m/B Russell Hayden, Lionel Atwill, Jane Adams; *D:* Ray Taylor, Lewis D. Collins. VHS, Beta $49.95 *NOS, GPV, DVT* II

The Lost Command A French colonel, relieved of his command, endeavors to regain power by battling a powerful Arab terrorist with his own specially trained platoon of soldiers. Crisp adventure set in post-WWII North Africa. Based on "The Centurions" by Jean Larteguy.
1966 129m/C Anthony Quinn, Michele Morgan, George Segal, Alain Delon, Maurice Ronet, Claudia Cardinale; *D:* Mark Robson. Beta $69.95 *COL* II½

The Lost Continent An expedition searching for a lost rocket on a jungle island discovers dinosaurs and other extinct creatures.
1951 82m/B Cesar Romero, Hillary Brooke, Chick Chandler, John Hoyt, Acquanetta, Sid Melton, Whit Bissell, Hugh Beaumont; *D:* Sam Newfield. VHS, Beta $19.98 *MRV, MLB* II½

Lost Diamond Bumbling spies search for a smuggled gem.
1974 83m/C Juan Ramon, Sonia Rivas, Ricardo Bauleo. VHS, Beta $39.95 *MED* II

The Lost Empire Three bountiful and powerful women team up to battle the evil Dr. Syn Do.
1983 (R) 86m/C Melanie Vincz, Raven De La Croix, Angela Aames, Paul Coufos, Robert Tessier, Angus Scrimm, Angelique Pettyjohn, Kenneth Tobey; *D:* Jim Wynorski; *W:* Jim Wynorski. VHS, Beta $69.98 *LIV* II

Lost Honeymoon Monkeyshines abound as a soldier marries a girl while in a state of amnesia, and then wakes up to find twin daughters.
1947 70m/B Franchot Tone, Ann Richards; **D:** Leigh Jason. **VHS, Beta $24.95** NOS, DVT, HEG 🎬🎬

The Lost Honor of Katharina Blum A woman becomes involved with a man who's under police surveillance and finds her life open to public scrutiny and abuse from the media and the government. Based on Heinrich Boll's Nobel Prize-winning novel. In German with English subtitles. Remade for television as "The Lost Honor of Kathryn Beck." **AKA:** Die Verlorene Ehre Der Katharina Blum.
1975 (R) 97m/C Angela Winkler, Mario Adorf, Dieter Laser, Juergen Prochnow; **D:** Volker Schlondorff, Margarethe von Trotta. **VHS, Beta $29.98** SUE, APD, GLV 🎬🎬🎬

Lost Horizon A group of strangers fleeing revolution in China are lost in the Tibetan Himalayas and stumble across the valley of Shangri La. The inhabitants of this Utopian community have lived for hundreds of years in kindness and peace—but what will the intrusion of these strangers bring? The classic romantic role for Colman. Capra's directorial style meshed perfectly with the pacifist theme of James Hilton's classic novel, resulting in one of the most memorable films of the 1930s. This version restores more than 20 minutes of footage which had been cut from the movie through the years.
1937 132m/B Ronald Colman, Jane Wyatt, H.B. Warner, Sam Jaffe, Thomas Mitchell, Edward Everett Horton, Isabel Jewell, John Howard, Margo; **D:** Frank Capra; **W:** Robert Riskin; **M:** Dimitri Tiomkin, Burt Bacharach. Academy Awards '37: Best Film Editing, Best Interior Decoration; Nominations: Best Picture, Best Sound, Best Supporting Actor (Warner), Best Original Score. **VHS, Beta $19.95** COL, RDG 🎬🎬🎬🎬

The Lost Idol/Shock Troop In "The Lost Idol," a lone soldier raids a sacred temple in order to retrieve a golden idol. "Shock Troop" tells of top secret mission to destroy a powerful computer that lies behind enemy lines.
198? 219m/C Danny Aiello, Lyle Alzado, Erik Estrada. **VHS** NO 🎬🎬🎬🎬

Lost in a Harem Abbott & Costello play magicians in a theatrical troupe stranded in a desert kingdom ruled by an evil sheik. The sheik's nephew (and rightful heir) hires the two to steal some magic rings and the pretty Maxwell to play footsie with his susceptible uncle in an attempt to regain his kingdom. Average comedy with musical numbers by Jimmy Dorsey and His Orchestra.
1944 89m/B Bud Abbott, Lou Costello, Marilyn Maxwell, John Conte, Douglass Dumbrille, Lottie Harrison; **D:** Charles Riesner. **VHS $19.98** MGM 🎬🎬½

Lost in Alaska Up in the Alaskan wilderness, Abbott & Costello save Ewell from a greedy saloon owner and his cohorts who are trying to get their hands on Ewell's fortune.
1952 87m/B Bud Abbott, Lou Costello, Tom Ewell, Mitzie Green, Bruce Cabot, Emory Parnell, Jack Ingram, Rex Lease; **D:** Jean Yarborough; **W:** Martin Ragaway, Leonard Stern; **M:** Henry Mancini. **VHS $14.98** MCA, FCT 🎬🎬½

Lost in America After deciding that he can't "find himself" at his current job, advertising executive David Howard and his wife sell everything they own and buy a Winnebago to travel across the country. This Albert Brooks comedy is a must-see for everyone who thinks that there is more in life than pushing papers at your desk and sitting on "Mercedes leather." Available in widescreen on laserdisc.
1985 (R) 91m/C Albert Brooks, Julie Hagerty, Michael Greene, Tom Tarpey, Garry Marshall, Art Frankel; **D:** Albert Brooks; **W:** Albert Brooks, Monica Johnson; **M:** Arthur B. Rubinstein. **VHS, Beta $19.98** WAR 🎬🎬🎬

Lost in the Barrens Two young boys, one a Canadian Indian and the other a rich white boy, get lost in the wilderness of the Canadian north. Out of necessity and common need they become close and form a lifelong friendship. Based on the book by Farley Mowat.
1991 95m/C Graham Greene, Nicholas Shields. **VHS** NO 🎬🎬

Lost in Yonkers Arty and Jay are two teenage brothers who, while their widowed father looks for work, are sent to live with their stern grandmother, small-time gangster uncle, and childlike aunt in 1942 New York. Ruehl reprises her Tony award-winning performance as Aunt Bella, who loses herself in the movies while trying to find a love of her own, out from under the oppressive thumb of her domineering mother (Worth). Performances by the adults are more theatrical than necessary but the teenagers do well in their observer roles. Based on the play by Neil Simon, which again chronicles his boyhood. **AKA:** Neil Simon's Lost in Yonkers.
1993 (PG) 114m/C Mercedes Ruehl, Irene Worth, Richard Dreyfuss, Brad Stoll, Mike Damus, David Strathairn, Robert Miranda, Jack Laufer, Susan Merson; **D:** Martha Coolidge; **W:** Neil Simon; **M:** Elmer Bernstein. **VHS, 8mm $95.95** COL, FCT 🎬🎬½

The Lost Jungle Circus legend Beatty searches for his girl and her dad in the jungle. Animal stunts keep it interesting. Serial in 12 chapters, 13 minutes each.
1934 156m/B Clyde Beatty, Cecilia Parker, Syd Saylor, Warner Richmond, Wheeler Oakman; **D:** Armand Schaefer, David Howard. **VHS, Beta $19.95** NOS, VCN, VDM 🎬🎬

The Lost Language of Cranes David Leavitt's novel is transported from New York to present-day London but the wrenching emotional drama remains the same. A family is in crisis as long-hidden secrets concerning homosexuality and infidelity are finally revealed. The title refers to one character's social worker's thesis on a young boy from a dysfunctional family who imitates the movements of the building cranes he sees. Fine performances by all. Adult sexual situations.
1992 90m/C Brian Cox, Eileen Atkins, Angus MacFadyen, Corey Parker, Cathy Tyson; **Cameos:** John Schlesinger, Rene Auberjonois; **D:** Nigel Finch. **VHS $19.98** FOX, BTV 🎬🎬🎬

Lost Legacy: A Girl Called Hatter Fox Tradition and technology are at odds in the life of a young Indian girl. Strong cast makes this work. Made for television and better than average.
1977 100m/C Ronny Cox, Joanelle Romero, Conchata Ferrell; **D:** George Schaefer. **VHS $59.95** GEM 🎬🎬½

Lost, Lonely, and Vicious Clayton is a suicidal Hollywood actor who spends much of his time indulging his penchant for women, figuring he may as well enjoy what little time he has left. Then he meets Wilson, a drugstore clerk who moves him to reconsider his self-destructive ways.

1959 73m/B Ken Clayton, Barbara Wilson, Lilyan Chauvin, Richard Gilden, Carole Nugent, Sandra Giles, Allen Fife, Frank Stallworth, Johnny Erben, Clint Quigley, T. Earl Johnson; **D:** Frank Myers; **W:** Norman Graham. **VHS $23.00** SMW, TPV 🎬

The Lost Missile A lost, alien missile circles the Earth, causing overheating and destruction on the planet's surface. A scientist works to find a way to save the planet before it explodes into a gigantic fireball. Director Burke's last film.
1958 70m/B Robert Loggia, Ellen Parker, Larry Kerr, Phillip Pine, Marilee Earle; **D:** William Berke. **VHS $18.00** FRG 🎬🎬

Lost Moment A publisher travels to Italy to search for a valuable collection of a celebrated author's love letters, but finds a neurotic woman in his way. Based on Henry James' "Aspern Papers."
1947 89m/B Robert Cummings, Agnes Moorehead, Susan Hayward; **D:** Martin Gabel. **VHS $14.98** REP 🎬🎬

The Lost One A German scientist's lover is suspected of selling his findings to England during WWII. Based on a true story; Lorre's only directorial outing. **AKA:** Der Verlone.
1951 97m/B Peter Lorre, Karl John, Renate Mannhardt; **D:** Peter Lorre. **VHS** NO 🎬🎬

The Lost Patrol WWI British soldiers lost in the desert are shot down one by one by Arab marauders as Karloff portrays a religious soldier convinced he's going to die. The usual spiffy Ford exteriors peopled by great characters with a stirring score. Based on the story, "Patrol" by Philip MacDonald.
1934 66m/B Victor McLaglen, Boris Karloff, Reginald Denny, Wallace Ford, Alan Hale; **D:** John Ford; **M:** Max Steiner. Academy Awards '34 Nominations: Best Score; National Board of Review Awards '34: 10 Best Films of the Year. **VHS, Beta $14.98** CCB, MED, RXM 🎬🎬🎬½

Lost Planet Airmen A feature-length condensation of the 12-part sci-fi serial "King of the Rocket Men." Rocket Man is pitted against the sinister Dr. Vulcan in this intergalactic battle of good and evil.
1949 65m/B Tristram Coffin, Mae Clarke, Dale Van Sickel; **D:** Fred Brannon. **VHS, Beta** AOV, DVT, RXM 🎬½

The Lost Platoon A troop of soldiers are transformed into vampires.
1989 (R) 120m/C David Parry, William Knight, Sean Heyman; **D:** David A. Prior. **VHS, Beta $14.95** AIP 🎬½

Lost Squadron A look at the dangers stuntmen go through in movie-making.
1932 79m/B Richard Dix, Erich von Stroheim; **D:** George Archainbaud. **VHS, Beta** RXM 🎬🎬½

The Lost Stooges From the trio's one year at MGM, rare clips of them performing their famous slapstick gags. In black and white and color.
1933 68m/B Moe Howard, Curly Howard, Larry Fine, Clark Gable, Joan Crawford, Jimmy Durante, Robert Montgomery. **VHS, Beta $14.98** TTC 🎬🎬½

The Lost Tribe A man takes his wife on a trek through the jungle to find his lost brother.
1989 96m/C John Bach, Darien Teakle; **D:** John Laing. **VHS, Beta** MED 🎬

The Lost Weekend The heartrending Hollywood masterpiece about alcoholism, depicting a single weekend in the life of a writer, who cannot believe he's addicted. Except for its pat ending, it is an uncompromising, startlingly harsh treatment, with Milland giving one of the industry's bravest lead performances ever. Acclaimed then and now.

1945 100m/B Ray Milland, Jane Wyman, Phillip Terry, Howard da Silva, Doris Dowling, Frank Faylen, Mary Young; *D:* Billy Wilder; *W:* Charles Brackett, Billy Wilder; *M:* Miklos Rozsa. Academy Awards '45: Best Actor (Milland), Best Director (Wilder), Best Picture, Best Screenplay; Nominations: Best Black and White Cinematography, Best Film Editing, Best Original Score; Cannes Film Festival '46: Best Actor (Milland), Best Film; Golden Globe Awards '46: Best Actor—Drama (Milland), Best Director (Wilder), Best Film—Drama; National Board of Review Awards '45: 10 Best Films of the Year, Best Actor (Milland). **VHS, Beta $14.95** *MCA, PAR, BTV ⅃⅃⅃⅃*

The Lost World A zoology professor leads a group on a South American expedition in search of the "lost world," where dinosaurs roam in this silent film. Based on a story by Sir Arthur Conan Doyle. A 90-minute version includes the film's original trailer and a recreation of some of the missing footage (the film was released at 108 minutes). 1925 62m/B Wallace Beery, Lewis Stone, Bessie Love, Lloyd Hughes; *D:* Harry Hoyt. **VHS, Beta $19.95** *NOS, MIL, VYY ⅃⅃½*

The Lost World "Land of the Lost"/ "Jurassic Park" themes, based on the story by Sir Arthur Conan Doyle. A scientific team ventures deep into uncharted African jungles where they find themselves confronted by dinosaurs and other dangers. 1992 99m/C John Rhys-Davies, David Warner; *D:* Timothy Bond. **VHS $89.95** *WOV ⅃⅃½*

Lost Zeppelin A dirigible becomes lost in the wastes of Antarctica, forcing its passengers to combat the elements. Impressive special effects and miniatures for its time. 1929 73m/B Conway Tearle, Virginia Valli, Ricardo Cortez, Duke Martin, Kathryn McGuire; *D:* Edward Sloman. **VHS, Beta $16.95** *SNC, GPV ⅃⅃*

Lots of Luck A knee-slapping comedy about a family that wins the million-dollar lottery and sees that money doesn't solve all problems. Disney made for cable. 1985 88m/C Martin Mull, Annette Funicello, Fred Willard, Polly Holliday; *D:* Peter Baldwin; *M:* William Goldstein. **VHS, Beta $69.95** *DIS ⅃⅃*

Lottery Bride In this charming musical, Jeanette MacDonald is the lottery bride who is won by the brother of the man she really loves. A fine outing for all involved, particularly the supporting cast. ♫You're an Angel; My Northern Lights; Come Drink to the Girl That You Love; Yubla; Round She Whirls; Shoulder to Shoulder; High and Low; Napoli; Two Strong Men. 1930 85m/B Jeanette MacDonald, Joe E. Brown, ZaSu Pitts, John Garrick, Carroll Nye; *D:* Paul Stein. **VHS, Beta** *NO ⅃⅃½*

Louisiana A belle of the Old South tries to get back the family plantation by romancing the new owner, even though she loves someone else. Oh, and then the Civil War breaks out. Made for television. 1987 130m/C Ian Charleson, Margot Kidder, Victor Lanoux, Len Cariou, Lloyd Bochner; *D:* Philippe de Broca. **VHS, Beta $9.99** *PSM ⅃*

Louisiana Purchase Successful screen adaptation of the Broadway musical features several performers from the original cast, lavish costumes, and great musical numbers. As usual, Hope's comedy is extremely funny, especially his famous filibuster scene in Congress. Based on the stage musical by Morrie Ryskind and B. G. DeSylva. 1941 95m/C Bob Hope, Vera Zorina, Victor Moore, Dona Drake, Irene Bordoni, Raymond Walburn, Maxie "Slapsie" Rosenbloom, Frank Albertson, Barbara Britton; *D:* Irving Cummings. **VHS $14.98** *MCA, BTV ⅃⅃½*

Louisiana Story The final effort by the master filmmaker, depicting the effects of oil industrialization on the southern Bayou country as seen through the eyes of a young boy. One of Flaherty's greatest, widely considered a premiere achievement. 1948 77m/B *D:* Robert Flaherty; *M:* Virgil Thompson. Academy Awards '48 Nominations: Best Story; National Board of Review Awards '48: 10 Best Films of the Year. **VHS, Beta $29.95** *HMV, VYY, DVT ⅃⅃⅃*

Loulou A woman leaves her middle-class husband for a leather-clad, uneducated jock who is more attentive. Romantic and erotic. In French with English subtitles. 1980 (R) 110m/C Isabelle Huppert, Gerard Depardieu, Guy Marchand; *D:* Maurice Pialat. **VHS, Beta $79.95** *NYF, ING ⅃⅃⅃½*

The Lovable Cheat Pretty lame adapatation of Balzac's play "Mercadet Le Falseur," about a father who cons money from his friends in order to line up a marriage suitable for his daughter. 1949 75m/B Charlie Ruggles, Peggy Ann Garner, Richard Ney, Alan Mowbray, Iris Adrian, Ludwig Donath, Fritz Feld; *D:* Richard Oswald. **VHS** *FCT ⅃⅃*

Love Torocsik, touted as Hungary's leading actress in the '70s, plays a young woman whose husband has been imprisoned for political crimes. Living in a cramped apartment with her mother-in-law, she keeps the news from the aged and dying woman (Darvas) by reading letters she's fabricated to keep alive the woman's belief that her son is a successful movie director in America. The story is punctuated by the older woman's dreamy remembrances of things past. Exceptional performances by both women, it was Darvas' final film. Based on two novellas by Tibor Dery, it won a special jury prize at the 1973 Cannes film festival. In Hungarian with English subtitles. 1971 100m/C Lili Darvas, Mari Torocsik, Ivan Darvas; *D:* Karoly Makk. **VHS $59.95** *CVC, IME, ING ⅃⅃⅃½*

Love Affair Dunn and Boyer fall in love while on a ship, but both are involved with others. They agree to meet later on the Empire State Building to see if their feelings hold true, but tragedy intervenes. Excellent comedy-drama is witty at first, more subdued later, with plenty of romance and melodrama. Remade by McCarey in 1957 with Cary Grant and Deborah Kerr as "An Affair to Remember." This is the better version, but "Affair" is remembered more often. Keep your eyes peeled for fleeting glimpses of Leslie, Beckett, and Mohr. Don't bother with the public domain video, which replaces the original music. 1939 87m/B Irene Dunne, Charles Boyer, Maria Ouspenskaya, Lee Bowman, Astrid Allwyn, Maurice Moscovich, Scotty Beckett, Joan Leslie, Gerald Mohr, Dell Henderson, Carol Hughes; *D:* Leo McCarey; *W:* Delmer Daves, Leo McCarey, Donald Ogden Stewart. **VHS $19.95** *NOS, MRV, TTC ⅃⅃⅃⅃*

The Love Affair, or The Case of the Missing Switchboard Operator Makavejev's second film, a dissertation on the relationship between sex and politics, involving an affair between a switchboard operator and a middle-aged ex-revolutionary, is told in the director's unique, farcically disjointed manner. In Serbian with English subtitles. *AKA:* Switchboard Operator; Case of the Missing Switchboard Operator; Ljubarni Slucaj; An Affair of the Heart. 1967 73m/B Eva Ras, Slobodan Aligrudic, Ruzica Sokic; *D:* Dusan Makavejev; *W:* Dusan Makavejev. **VHS, Beta $59.95** *FCT ⅃⅃⅃*

Love Affair: The Eleanor & Lou Gehrig Story The true story, told from Mrs. Gehrig's point of view, of the love affair between baseball great Lou Gehrig and his wife Eleanor from his glory days as a New York Yankee, to his battle with an incurable disease. A television drama that is supported by Herrmann and Danner's convincing portrayals. 1977 96m/C Blythe Danner, Edward Herrmann, Patricia Neal, Ramon Bieri, Lainie Kazan; *D:* Fielder Cook. **VHS, Beta $7.50** *WOV ⅃⅃⅃*

Love Among the Ruins A made-for-television romance about an aging, wealthy widow who, after being scandalously sued for breach of promise by her very young lover, turns for aid to an old lawyer friend who has loved her silently for more than forty years. 1975 100m/C Laurence Olivier, Katharine Hepburn, Leigh Lawson, Colin Blakely; *D:* George Cukor; *M:* John Barry. **VHS, Beta $59.98** *FOX ⅃⅃⅃*

Love and Anarchy An oppressed peasant vows to assassinate Mussolini after a close friend is murdered. Powerful drama about the rise of Italian fascism. In Italian with English subtitles. *AKA:* Film d'Amore et d'Anarchia. 1973 108m/C Giancarlo Giannini, Mariangela Melato; *D:* Lina Wertmuller; *W:* Lina Wertmuller. Cannes Film Festival Nominations: cs 73: Best Film; Cannes Film Festival '73: Best Actor (Giannini). **VHS, Beta $59.95** *COL, APD ⅃⅃⅃*

Love and Bullets An Arizona homicide detective is sent on a special assignment to Switzerland to bring a mobster's girlfriend back to the United States to testify against him in court. 1979 (PG) 95m/C Charles Bronson, Jill Ireland, Rod Steiger, Strother Martin, Bradford Dillman, Henry Silva, Michael Gazzo; *D:* Stuart Rosenberg; *W:* Wendell Mayes. **VHS, Beta $19.98** *FOX ⅃½*

Love and Death In 1812 Russia, a condemned man reviews the follies of his life. Woody Allen's satire on "War and Peace," and every other major Russian novel. 1975 (PG) 89m/C Woody Allen, Diane Keaton, Georges Adel, Despo Diamantidou, Frank Adu, Harold Gould; *D:* Woody Allen; *W:* Woody Allen. **VHS, Beta $14.95** *MGM, FOX ⅃⅃⅃*

Love and Faith Two lovers are torn between their love for each other and their faiths during sixteenth-century Japan. English subtitles. 1978 154m/C Toshiro Mifune, Takashi Shimura, Yoshiko Nakana; *D:* Kei Kumai. **VHS, Beta** *VDA ⅃⅃⅃*

Love and Hate: A Marriage Made in Hell Marital murder mystery based on a true Canadian case. Joanne (Nelligan), the wife of wealthy rancher-politico Colin (Walsh), leaves his publicly charismatic and privately abusive husband with two thirds of their brood. A bitter battle for custody is waged, and Joanne is soon found savagely slain. The number one suspect: philandering ex-spouse Colin. Based on Maggie Siggins' "A Canadian Tragedy," the faux biography originally aired in two parts on Canadian TV. *AKA:* Love and Hate: The Story of Colin and Joanne Thatcher. 1990 156m/C Kate Nelligan, Ken Walsh, Leon Pownall, John Colicos, Noam Zylberman, Victoria Snow, Cedric Smith, R.H. Thomson, Victoria Wauchope, Doris Petrie, Duncan Ollenenshaw; *D:* Francis Mankiewicz; *W:* Suzette Couture. **VHS, Beta $99.95** *PAR ⅃⅃½*

Love & Murder Poorly developed tale of a photographer and his bevy of with beautiful models involved with murder and love, not necessarily in that order.
1991 (R) 87m/C Todd Waring, Kathleen Lasky, Ron White, Wayne Robson; **D:** Steven Hilliard Stern. **VHS $9.95** HMD ♫ 1/2

Love and the Frenchwoman A French tale tracing the nature of love through stages. Deals with a story about where babies come from, puppy love, saving sex for marriage, and the way some men treat women. **AKA:** La Francaise et L'Amour.
1960 135m/B Jean-Paul Belmondo, Pierre-Jean Vaillard, Marie-Jose Nat, Annie Girardot; **D:** Jean Delannoy; **M:** Georges Delerue. **VHS, Beta $29.95** DVT, MRV, HEG ♫♫♫

Love at First Bite Intentionally campy spoof of the vampire film. Dracula is forced to leave his Transylvanian home as the Rumanian government has designated his castle a training center for young gymnasts. Once in New York, the Count takes in the night life and falls in love with a woman whose boyfriend embarks on a campaign to warn the city of Dracula's presence. Hamilton of the never-fading tan is appropriately tongue-in-cheek in a role which resurrected his career.
1979 (PG) 93m/C George Hamilton, Susan St. James, Richard Benjamin, Dick Shawn, Arte Johnson, Sherman Hemsley, Isabel Sanford; **D:** Stan Dragoti; **M:** Charles Bernstein. **VHS, Beta $9.98** ORI, WAR ♫♫ 1/2

Love at First Sight A pre-"Saturday Night Live" hack job for Aykroyd, playing a blind man who falls in love with a girl he bumps into. ♫Love at First Sight. **AKA:** Love is Blind; At First Sight.
1976 86m/C Dan Aykroyd, Mary Ann McDonald, George Murray, Barry Morse; **D:** Rex Bromfield. **VHS, Beta** NO ♫

Love at Large Hired by a beautiful woman, a private detective accidentally follows the wrong man and winds up being followed himself. He vies with a female detective in solving this case of mistaken identity.
1989 (R) 90m/C Tom Berenger, Elizabeth Perkins, Anne Archer, Ann Magnuson, Annette O'Toole, Kate Capshaw, Ted Levine, Kevin J. O'Connor, Ruby Dee, Neil Young, Barry Miller; **D:** Alan Rudolph; **W:** Alan Rudolph. **VHS, Beta $89.98** ORI, FCT ♫♫♫

Love at Stake It's condo owners versus the witches in this charming parody that features a hilarious cameo by Dr. Joyce Brothers and a very sexy performance from Carrera.
1987 (R) 83m/C Patrick Cassidy, Kelly Preston, Bud Cort, Barbara Carrera, Stuart Pankin, Dave Thomas, Georgia Brown, Annie Golden; **Cameos:** Dr. Joyce Brothers; **D:** John Moffitt; **M:** Charles Fox. **VHS $19.98** SUE, NLC ♫♫ 1/2

Love at the Top Ladies' foundation designer falls in love with her boss's son-in-law, jeopardizing her career.
1986 90m/C Janis Paige, Richard Young, Jim MacKrell; **D:** John Bowab. **Beta $14.95** PSM ♫♫ 1/2

The Love Boat All aboard! Love's waiting for you in this special movie presentation of the immensely popular television series. Captain Stuebing, Julie, Gopher, Isaac (your bartender) and a whole host of celebrities at the end of their careers, fall in and out of love as they sail back and forth between expensive resorts.
1977? ?m/C Gavin MacLeod, Bernie Kopell, Ted Lange, Lauren Tewes. **VHS** GKK ♫♫ 1/2

The Love Bug A race car driver (Jones) is followed home by Herbie, a white Volkswagen with a mind of its own. Eventually, Jones follows the "Love Bug" to a life of madcap fun. Followed by several sequels.
1968 (G) 110m/C Dean Jones, Michele Lee, Hope Lange, Robert Reed, Bert Convy; **D:** Robert Stevenson. **VHS, Beta $19.99** DIS ♫♫ 1/2

Love Butcher A crippled old gardener kills his female employers with his garden tools and cleans up neatly afterward.
1982 (R) 84m/C Erik Stern, Kay Neer, Robin Sherwood; **D:** Mikel Angel, Donald M. Jones. **VHS, Beta $39.95** MON ♫♫ 1/2

Love by Appointment An unlikely romantic comedy with a very unlikely cast has two businessmen meeting up with European prostitutes. Made for television.
1976 96m/C Ernest Borgnine, Robert Alda, Francoise Fabian, Corinne Clery. **VHS, Beta $59.98** NLC ♫

Love Camp A woman is invited to a swinger's holiday camp, frolics for a while, then is told she can never leave. Suspenseful hijinks ensue.
1976 100m/C Laura Gemser, Christian Anders, Gabriele Tinti. **VHS, Beta $29.95** AHV ♫

Love, Cheat & Steal Convicted murderer Reno Adams (Roberts) breaks out of prison when he hears that his luscious ex (Amick) has just married another man (Lithgow). He turns up on her door, threatening to destroy her new life, but things aren't exactly what they seem. Made for television.
1994 (R) 95m/C Eric Roberts, Madchen Amick, John Lithgow, Richard Edson, Donald Moffatt, David Ackroyd, Dan O'Herlihy; **D:** William Curran; **W:** William Curran. **VHS** COL ♫♫

Love Child The story of a young woman in prison who becomes pregnant by a guard and fights to have and keep her baby.
1982 (R) 97m/C Amy Madigan, Beau Bridges, MacKenzie Phillips, Albert Salmi; **D:** Larry Peerce; **M:** Charles Fox. **VHS, Beta $49.95** WAR ♫♫

Love Crazy Powell and Loy team once again for a non-"Thin Man" romp through a married-people farce. Via a nosy mother-in-law and a series of misunderstandings, Powell and Loy squabble almost to the point of divorce. Not the wry wit the team was known for, but zany, high-action comedy at its best.
1941 99m/B William Powell, Myrna Loy, Gail Patrick, Jack Carson, Florence Bates, Sidney Blackmer, Sig Rumann; **D:** Jack Conway. **VHS $19.98** MGM ♫♫♫ 1/2

Love Crimes A con man (Bergin) poses as a photographer who sexually intimidates women while playing on their erotic fantasies. Young is the Atlanta district attorney who sets out to nail him when none of his victims will testify against him, only she may be enjoying her undercover work more than she realizes. Implausible and sleazy. Also available in an unrated version.
1992 (R) 84m/C Sean Young, Patrick Bergin, Arnetia Walker, James Read; **D:** Lizzie Borden; **M:** Graeme Revell. **VHS $92.99** HBO ♫

Love Desperados Cowboys and ranchers' wives mix it up in a lot of softcore hay.
1986 99m/C Virginia Gordon, James Arena. **VHS, Beta $29.95** MED ♫

Love 'Em and Leave 'Em Two sisters, with opposite personalities, are department store sales clerks. Brent is the "good" girl and Brooks the "bad" flirt who, under the influence of Perkins, bets the store's welfare benefit money on the horses and loses it all. Brent manages to make things right, while keeping boyfriend Gray from her sister's clutches. Brooks' baby vamp (the actress was 19) stole the picture. Introduced the "Black Bottom" shimmy dance to the screen. Remade in 1929 as "The Saturday Night Kid" with Clara Bow and Jean Arthur.
1926 70m/B Louise Brooks, Evelyn Brent, Lawrence Gray, Osgood Perkins; **D:** Frank Tuttle. **VHS, Beta $24.95** GPV ♫♫♫

The Love Factor A secret agent tries to foil the plans of a race of topless female aliens in this sleazy softcore sci-fi film. Also known as "Zeta One."
1969 ?m/C Robin Hawdon, James Robertson Justice, Yutte Stensgaard. **VHS $16.95** SNC ♫

Love Field Pfeiffer is a Jackie Kennedy-obsessed hairdresser who decides to travel by bus to D.C. when she hears about President Kennedy's assassination. Along the way she gets involved in an interracial friendship with the secretive Haysbert, who's traveling with his young daughter. Pfeiffer's Lurene is basically a sweet dim bulb and Haysbert has an unfortunately written one-note character (mainly exasperation). The 6-year-old McFadden (in her debut) makes the most impact.
1991 (PG-13) 104m/C Michelle Pfeiffer, Dennis Haysbert, Stephanie McFadden, Brian Kerwin, Louise Latham, Peggy Rea, Beth Grant, Cooper Huckabee, Mark Miller, Johnny Rae McGhee; **D:** Jonathan Kaplan; **W:** Don Roos; **M:** Jerry Goldsmith. **VHS $89.99** ORI, MOV ♫♫ 1/2

Love Film A train trip from Budapest, Hungary to Lyon, France leads a young man to recall his past as he journeys to visit a childhood sweetheart. Jancsi and Kata's friendship has been disrupted by the 1956 uprising and Jancsi wonders if the love once developing between them has been broken by distance and time. In Hungarian with English subtitles.
1970 130m/C Andras Balint, Judit Halasz; **D:** Istvan Szabo. **VHS $39.95** ING, TPV ♫♫

Love Finds Andy Hardy Young Andy Hardy finds himself torn between three girls before returning to the girl next door. Garland's first appearance in the acclaimed Andy Hardy series features her singing "In Between" and "Meet the Best of my Heart." Also available with "Andy Hardy Meets Debutante" on Laser Disc.
1938 90m/B Mickey Rooney, Judy Garland, Lana Turner, Ann Rutherford, Fay Holden, Lewis Stone, Marie Blake, Cecilia Parker, Gene Reynolds; **D:** George B. Seitz. **VHS, Beta $19.95** MGM ♫♫♫

The Love Flower A man kills his second wife's lover and escapes with his daughter to a tropical island, pursued by a detective and a young adventurer. Interesting ending wraps things up nicely. Silent.
1920 70m/B Carol Dempster, Richard Barthelmess, George MacQuarrie, Anders Randolf, Florence Short; **D:** D.W. Griffith; **W:** D.W. Griffith. **VHS, Beta** NO ♫♫ 1/2

Love for Lydia Made for British television miniseries following wayward beauty Lydia, orphaned heiress to a manufacturing fortune, through the high-spirited 1920s. Set in the industrial Midlands and farming communities of England, Lydia dazzles every man she meets, often to an unhappy end. Based on the novel by H.E. Bates. Available as a seven cassette boxed set.
1979 657m/C Mel Martin, Christopher Blake, Peter Davison, Jeremy Irons, Michael Aldridge, Rachel Kempson, Beatrix Lehmmann. **VHS $199.95** FCT, SIG ♫♫♫

Love from a Stranger Thriller about a working woman who wins a lottery. Soon she is charmed by and marries a man whom she later suspects may be trying to kill her. Remade in 1947.
1937 90m/B Ann Harding, Basil Rathbone, Binnie Hale, Bruce Seton, Bryan Powley, Jean Cadell; **D:** Rowland V. Lee. **VHS $19.95** NOS, SNC, NWV ✂️✂️

Love from a Stranger In this remake of the 1937 film, a young newlywed bride fears that the honeymoon is over when she suspects that her husband is a notorious killer and that she will be his next victim. **AKA:** A Stranger Walked In.
1947 81m/B Sylvia Sidney, John Hodiak, John Howard, Ann Richards, Isobel Elsom, Ernest Cossart; **D:** Richard Whorf. **VHS, Beta $19.95** NWV ✂️✂️½

The Love Goddesses A sixty-year examination of some of the most beautiful women on the silver screen, reflecting with extraordinary accuracy the customs, manners and mores of the times. Released theatrically in 1972.
1965 83m/B Marlene Dietrich, Greta Garbo, Jean Harlow, Gloria Swanson, Mae West, Betty Grable, Rita Hayworth, Elizabeth Taylor, Marilyn Monroe, Theda Bara, Claudette Colbert, Dorothy Lamour; **D:** Saul J. Turell. **VHS, Beta $14.95** COL, SUE, VYG ✂️✂️½

Love Happy A group of impoverished actors accidentally gain possession of valuable diamonds. Unfortunately for them, detective Groucho is assigned to recover them!
1950 85m/B Groucho Marx, Harpo Marx, Chico Marx, Vera-Ellen, Ilona Massey, Marion Hutton, Raymond Burr, Marilyn Monroe; **D:** David Miller. **VHS $19.98** REP ✂️✂️

Love has Many Faces Judith Crist was too kind when she said this was for connoisseurs of truly awful movies. Playgal Turner marries beachboy Robertson and many faces come between them. Much melodrama. Filmed on location.
1965 104m/C Lana Turner, Cliff Robertson, Hugh O'Brian, Ruth Roman, Stefanie Powers, Virginia Grey, Ron Husmann; **D:** Alexander Singer. **VHS, Beta $9.95** GKK ✂️½

Love Hurts A guy looking for romance finds his hands full with a number of beautiful women. Will he find the love he craves, or will the pain be too much to bear?
1991 (R) 110m/C Jeff Daniels, Judith Ivey, John Mahoney, Cynthia Sikes, Amy Wright; **D:** Bud Yorkin; **W:** Ron Nyswaner. **VHS $14.98** LIV, VES ✂️✂️

A Love in Germany A tragic love affair develops between a German shopkeeper's wife and a Polish prisoner-of-war in a small German village during WWII. In German with English subtitles. **AKA:** Un Amour En Allemagne; Eine Liebe in Deutschland.
1984 (R) 110m/C Hanna Schygulla, Piotr Lysak, Elisabeth Trissenaar, Armin Mueller-Stahl; **D:** Andrzej Wajda; **W:** Andrzej Wajda, Agnieszka Holland, Boleslaw Michalek. **VHS, Beta $59.95** COL, APD, GLV ✂️✂️½

Love in the Afternoon A Parisian private eye's daughter (Hepburn) decides to investigate a philandering American millionaire (Cooper) and winds up falling in love with him. Cooper's a little old for the Casanova role but Hepburn is always enchanting.
1957 126m/B Gary Cooper, Audrey Hepburn, John McGiver, Maurice Chevalier; **D:** Billy Wilder; **W:** Billy Wilder, I.A.L. Diamond. **VHS, Beta $49.98** FOX, IME ✂️✂️½

Love in the City Five stories of life, love and tears in Rome. In Italian with English subtitles and narration.
1953 90m/B Ugo Tognazzi, Maresa Gallo, Caterina Rigoglioso, Silvia Lillo; **D:** Michelangelo Antonioni, Federico Fellini, Dino Risi, Carlo Lizzani, Alberto Lattuada, Francesco Maselli, Cesare Zavattini; **W:** Federico Fellini. **VHS, Beta $24.95** NOS, FCT, APD ✂️✂️✂️

Love in the Present Tense A woman's romantic novel on video, dealing with an affair that reawakens the torpid, tragic life of a beautiful ex-model.
1985 90m/C VHS, Beta $14.95 PSM ✂️

Love is a Many-Splendored Thing A married American war correspondent and a beautiful Eurasian doctor fall in love in post-WWII Hong Kong. They struggle with racism and unhappiness, until he's sent to Korea to observe the Army's activities there. Based on the novel by Han Suyin. The extensive LA Asian acting community got some work out of this film, although the leads are played by Caucasians. Oscar winning song was a very big popular hit.
1955 102m/C William Holden, Jennifer Jones, Torin Thatcher, Isobel Elsom, Jorja Curtright, Virginia Gregg, Richard Loo; **D:** Henry King; **M:** Alfred Newman. Academy Awards '55: Best Costume Design (Color), Best Song ("Love Is a Many-Splendored Thing"), Best Score; Nominations: Best Actress (Jones), Best Art Direction/Set Decoration (Color), Best Color Cinematography, Best Picture, Best Sound. **VHS, Beta $19.98** FXV, BTV ✂️✂️½

Love is Better Than Ever Lightweight romantic-comedy casts Taylor as a dancing instructor who travels to the Big Apple for a convention. Once there, she meets and falls for talent agent Parks. Carefree, bachelor Parks is too busy to be bothered by small town Taylor, but Liz is determined to land her man. Release of this picture was held back because of Parks' blacklisting by the McCarthy committee. **AKA:** The Light Fantastic.
1952 81m/B Larry Parks, Elizabeth Taylor, Josephine Hutchinson, Tom Tully, Ann Doran, Elinor Donahue, Kathleen Freeman; **Cameos:** Gene Kelly; **D:** Stanley Donen; **W:** Ruth Brooks Flippen. **VHS $19.98** MGM ✂️✂️½

Love Kills Is the man a beautiful heiress falls in love with actually an assassin hired by her husband to kill her? Find out in this steamy suspenser.
1991 (PG-13) 92m/C Virginia Madsen, Lenny Von Dohlen, Erich Anderson, Kate Hodge, Jim Metzler; **D:** Brian Grant. **VHS, Beta** PAR ✂️✂️

Love Laughs at Andy Hardy Andy Hardy, college boy, is in love and in trouble. Financial and romantic problems come to a head when Andy is paired with a six-foot tall blind date. One in the series.
1946 93m/B Mickey Rooney, Lewis Stone, Sara Haden, Lina Romay, Bonita Granville, Fay Holden; **D:** Willis Goldbeck. **VHS, Beta $19.95** NOS, MRV, HHT ✂️✂️

Love Leads the Way The true story of how Morris Frank established the seeing-eye dog system in the 1930s.
1984 99m/C Timothy Bottoms, Eva Marie Saint, Arthur Hill, Susan Dey, Ralph Bellamy, Ernest Borgnine, Patricia Neal; **D:** Delbert Mann. **VHS, Beta $69.95** DIS ✂️✂️

Love Letters A young disc jockey falls under the spell of a box of love letters that her mother left behind which detailed her double life. She, in turn, begins an affair with a married man. Thoughtful treatment of the psychology of infidelity. **AKA:** Passion Play; My Love Letters.
1983 (R) 102m/C Jamie Lee Curtis, Amy Madigan, Bud Cort, Matt Clark, Bonnie Bartlett, Sally Kirkland, James Keach; **D:** Amy Jones. **VHS, Beta $79.98** LIV, VES, IME ✂️✂️✂️

Love, Lies and Murder Shocking psychological thriller in which a businessman convinces his daughter and sister-in-law to murder his wife and then sends his daughter to prison for the crime. The "perfect murder" is not so perfect, however, when the daughter learns that her father has remarried and is now living an insurance-rich lifestyle. She decides to fight back in this true made-for-television story of bizarre murder and deception.
1991 (PG-13) 190m/C Clancy Brown, John Ashton, Sheryl Lee, Moira Kelly, Ramon Bieri, Ken Walsh, Tom Bower, John M. Jackson; **D:** Robert Markowitz. **VHS $89.98** REP ✂️✂️½

The Love Machine A power-hungry newscaster climbs the corporate ladder by sleeping with many, including the president's wife. An adaptation of Jacqueline Susann's novel.
1971 (R) 108m/C John Phillip Law, Dyan Cannon, Robert Ryan, Jackie Cooper, David Hemmings, Jodi Wexler, William Roerick, Maureen Arthur, Shecky Greene, Clinton Greyn, Sharon Farrell, Alexandra Hay, Eve Bruce, Greg Mullavey, Edith Atwater, Gene Baylos, Claudia Jennings, Mary Collinson, Madeleine Collinson, Ann Ford, Gayle Hunnicutt; **D:** Jack Haley Jr. **VHS, Beta $69.95** COL, MLB ✂️½

Love Matters Tom and Julie's fast-track marriage is hovering on the brink when Tom's best friend Geoff, who's also married, shows up on their doorstep with his sexy mistress and announces he's getting a divorce. Reluctantly, Tom and Julie allow the X-rated lovebirds to stay the night but all that heat only shows up the flaws in their own marriage even more. An unrated version at 103 minutes is also available.
1993 (R) 97m/C Griffin Dunne, Tony Goldwyn, Annette O'Toole, Gina Gershon, Kate Burton; **D:** Eb Lottimer; **W:** Eb Lottimer. **VHS** REP ✂️✂️

Love Me Deadly A young woman tries to get her husband interested in her new hobby-necrophilia.
1976 (R) 95m/C Mary Wilcox, Lyle Waggoner, Christopher Stone, Timothy Scott. **VHS, Beta $24.95** GEM ✂️

Love Me or Leave Me A hard-hitting biography of '20s torch singer Ruth Etting and her rise and fall at the hand of her abusive, gangster husband, a part just made for Cagney. Day emotes and sings expressively in one of the best performances of her career. ♫I'll Never Stop Loving You; Never Look Back; Shaking the Blues Away; Mean to Me; Love Me or Leave Me; Sam, the Old Accordian Man; At Sundown; Everybody Loves My Baby; Five Foot Two.
1955 122m/C Doris Day, James Cagney, Cameron Mitchell, Robert Keith, Tom Tully, Veda Ann Borg; **D:** Charles Vidor. Academy Awards '55: Best Story; Nominations: Best Actor (Cagney), Best Screenplay, Best Song ("I'll Never Stop Loving You"), Best Sound, Best Original Score. **VHS, Beta $19.98** MGM ✂️✂️✂️

Love Me Tender A Civil War-torn family is divided by in-fighting between two brothers who both seek the affections of the same woman. Presley's first film. Songs include "Poor Boy," "We're Gonna Move," and the title tune.
1956 89m/B Elvis Presley, Richard Egan, Debra Paget, Neville Brand, Mildred Dunnock, James Drury, Barry Coe; **D:** Robert D. Webb. **VHS, Beta $19.95** MVD, FOX ✂️✂️

Love Meetings Pasolini acts as director and interviewer to query a wide-range of individuals on their experiences at love, including homosexuality, prostitution, marital and non-marital interludes. In Italian with English subtitles. **AKA:** Comizi d'Amore.

1964 90m/B **D:** Pier Paolo Pasolini. VHS **$29.95** WBF, ING 🎞🎞

Love Nest Lundigan stars as Jim Scott, the landlord of an apartment building brimming with wacky tenants, including Monroe, Paar, and Fay. He dreams of becoming a famous writer, but his time is always filled with fixing up the building and trying to pay the mortgage. When one of the tenants ends up in jail because he was living off wealthy widows, Scott's luck changes. This moderately funny film is a good look at the early careers of Monroe and Paar.
1951 84m/B William Lundigan, June Haver, Frank Fay, Marilyn Monroe, Jack Paar; **D:** Joseph M. Newman. VHS **$14.98** FXV 🎞🎞

Love Notes Three short vignettes of soft core fantasy, in the life of an ordinary guy.
1988 60m/C Jeff Daniels, Christine Veronica. **VHS, Beta $29.95** AHV 🎞🎞

The Love of Three Queens The loves, on and off stage, of a beautiful actress in a European traveling theatre group.
1954 80m/C Gerard Oury, Massimo Serato, Robert Beatty, Cathy O'Donnell, Terence Morgan, Hedy Lamarr; **D:** Marc Allegret. **VHS, Beta** FCT, VDM 🎞½

Love on the Dole In a gloomy industrial section of England during the early '30s a family struggles to survive and maintain dignity. Grim Depression drama salvaged by great acting.
1941 89m/B Deborah Kerr, Clifford Evans, George Carney; **D:** John Baxter. **VHS, Beta $19.95** NOS, VYY 🎞🎞🎞

Love on the Run Enjoyable romantic comedy starring Crawford as a rich American heiress and Gable and Tone (Crawford's real husband at the time) as journalists stationed in Europe. Gable and Tone are assigned to cover an international aviator, who turns out to be an evil spy, as well as the upcoming wedding of flighty Crawford. When Crawford asks for help in getting out of her marriage, Gable and Tone steal a plane and the trio is chased across Europe by spies. Wild and farfetched plot, but the stars make it worthwhile. Based on the story "Beauty and the Beast" by Alan Green and Julian Brodie.
1936 80m/B Joan Crawford, Clark Gable, Franchot Tone, Reginald Owen, Mona Maris, Ivan Lebedeff, Charles Judels, William Demarest; **D:** Woodbridge S. Van Dyke; **W:** John Lee Mahin, Manuel Seff, Gladys Hurlbut. VHS **$19.98** MGM 🎞🎞½

Love on the Run The further amorous adventures of Antoine Doinel, hero of "The 400 Blows," "Stolen Kisses," and "Bed and Board." Doinel is now in his thirties and newly divorced. He renews affairs with several women from his past but, after his mother's death, must contend with his emotional immaturity and his inability to sustain a relationship. In French with English subtitles. **AKA:** L'Amour en Fuite.
1978 95m/C Jean-Pierre Leaud, Marie-France Pisier, Claude Jade; **D:** Francois Truffaut; **M:** Georges Delerue. **VHS, Beta $39.95** HMV, WAR 🎞🎞🎞

Love on the Run A beautiful lawyer helps a wrongly-accused convict escape from prison, then they both evade the law. Made for television.
1985 102m/C Stephanie Zimbalist, Adam Baldwin, Constance McCashin, Howard Duff; **D:** Gus Trikonis; **M:** Billy Goldenberg. **VHS, Beta $69.95** COL 🎞½

Love or Money? A small comedy about a yuppie who must choose between a woman and a real estate deal.

1988 (PG-13) 90m/C Timothy Daly, Haviland Morris, Kevin McCarthy, Shelley Fabares, David Doyle, Allen Havey; **D:** Todd Hallowell. **VHS, Beta** NO 🎞½

Love Potion #9 Two nerdy biochemists procure a love potion that they test on animals. Meeting with success they agree to test it on themselves. Predictably, the scientists are transformed and fall in love with each other. Features a talented young cast, with an amusing cameo by Bancroft, but the script is a real disappointment because of its shallow characters and lame gags. Inspired by the song by Jerry Leiber and Mike Stoller.
1992 (PG-13) 96m/C Tate Donovan, Sandra Bullock, Mary Mara, Dale Midkiff, Hillary Bailey Smith, Dylan Baker; **Cameos:** Anne Bancroft; **D:** Dale Launer; **W:** Dale Launer. VHS FXV 🎞½

Love Songs A mother of two is confronted with her husband's abandonment and a subsequent romance with a younger man. In French with English subtitles or dubbed. 🎵Leave It to Me; Psychic Flash; I Am With You Now; Human Race; We Can Dance; One More Moment; From the Heart; This Must Be Heaven.
1985 (R) 107m/C Catherine Deneuve, Christopher Lambert; **D:** Elie Chouraqui. **VHS, Beta $79.98** LIV, VES, ING 🎞🎞

Love Story Melodrama had enormous popular appeal. O'Neal is the son of Boston's upper crust at Harvard; McGraw's the daughter of a poor Italian on scholarship to study music at Radcliffe. They find happiness, but only for a brief period. Timeless story, simply told, with artful direction from Hiller pulling exceptional performances from the young duo (who have never done as well since). The end result is perhaps better than Segal's simplistic novel, which was produced after he sold the screenplay and became a best-seller before the picture's release—great publicity for any film. Remember: "Love means never having to say you're sorry."
1970 (PG) 100m/C Ryan O'Neal, Ali MacGraw, Ray Milland, John Marley, Tommy Lee Jones; **D:** Arthur Hiller; **W:** Erich Segal. Academy Awards '70: Best Original Score; Nominations: Best Actor (O'Neal), Best Actress (MacGraw), Best Director (Hiller), Best Picture, Best Story & Screenplay, Best Supporting Actor (Marley); Golden Globe Awards '71: Best Actress—Drama (MacGraw), Best Director (Hiller), Best Film—Drama, Best Screenplay, Best Score; National Board of Review Awards '70: 10 Best Films of the Year. **VHS, Beta $14.95** PAR 🎞🎞🎞

Love Strange Love A young boy develops a bizarre relationship with his mother who works in a luxurious bordello. Also available in an unedited 120-minute version.
1982 97m/C Vera Fischer, Mauro Mendonca. **VHS, Beta $79.98** LIV, VES 🎞½

Love Streams A quirky character drama about a writer and his sister who struggle to find love despite their personal problems.
1984 (PG-13) 122m/C Gena Rowlands, John Cassavetes, Diahnne Abbott, Seymour Cassel; **D:** John Cassavetes; **W:** Ted Allan. **VHS, Beta $79.95** MGM 🎞🎞½

Love Thrill Murders A film about a Mansonesque lunatic who is worshipped and obeyed by a mob of runaways and dropouts.
1971 (R) 89m/C Troy Donahue. **VHS, Beta $69.98** LIV, VES Woof!

Love Under Pressure Man and woman's marriage starts to evaporate when they realize their son is seriously disturbed.
1987 92m/C Karen Black, Keir Dullea. VHS **$19.99** ACA 🎞🎞

Love with a Perfect Stranger This Harlequin Romance takes place in Italy where a young widow meets a dashing Englishman. He changes her life forever.
1986 102m/C Marilu Henner, Daniel Massey; **M:** John Du Prez. **VHS, Beta $19.95** PAR 🎞🎞

Love with the Proper Stranger A quiet, gritty romance about an itinerant musician and a young working girl in Manhattan awkwardly living through the consequences of their one night stand. Moved Wood well into the realm of adult roles, after years playing teen-agers and innocents. Although the story is about an Italian neighborhood and family, an exceptional number of the cast members were Jewish, as was the screenwriter. Story does not conclude strongly, although this did not hamper the box office returns.
1963 102m/B Natalie Wood, Steve McQueen, Edie Adams, Herschel Bernardi, Tom Bosley, Harvey Lembeck, Penny Santon, Virginia Vincent, Nick Alexander, Augusta Ciolli; **D:** Robert Mulligan; **W:** Arnold Schulman; **M:** Elmer Bernstein. **VHS, Beta $19.95** PAR 🎞🎞🎞

Love Without Fear A dramatic, heart-rendering look at children with AIDS. Story focuses on the lives of three women from completely different backgrounds who adopt babies with AIDS and develop a special love for these children. Also shows their confrontations with a society which fears the disease and the women's strength to reach out and make a difference.
1990 ?m/C VHS NO 🎞🎞🎞

Love Without Pity Rochant's theatrical debut is a modern romance, with more distance and alienation than joy. A lovely, successful grad student loses her heart to a jobless, unambitious layabout who wants total commitment from her. Untypical, sardonic love story may be too cynical for sentimental types. In French with English subtitles.
1991 95m/C Hippolyte Girardot, Mireille Perrier, Jean Marie Rollin; **D:** Eric Rochant; **W:** Eric Rochant; **M:** Gerard Torikian. **VHS $79.98** ING, ORI 🎞🎞½

Love Your Mama An urban black drama about the strong Dorothy whose faith helps her cope with her many family complications, including her drunken husband, car thief son, and pregnant teenage daughter. Believable role models and good performances help out this amatuer filmmaking effort.
1989 (PG-13) 93m/C Audrey Morgan, Carol E. Hall, Andre Robinson, Ernest Rayford, Kearo Johnson, Jacqueline Williams; **D:** Ruby L. Oliver; **W:** Ruby L. Oliver. **VHS $89.95** HMD, BTV, FCT 🎞🎞½

The Loved One A famously outlandish, death-mocking farce based on Evelyn Waugh's satire about a particularly horrendous California funeral parlor/cemetery and how its denizens do business. A shrill, protracted spearing of American capitalism.
1965 118m/B Robert Morse, John Gielgud, Rod Steiger, Liberace, Anjanette Comer, Jonathan Winters, James Coburn, Dana Andrews, Milton Berle, Tab Hunter, Robert Morley, Lionel Stander, Margaret Leighton, Roddy McDowall, Bernie Kopell, Alan Napier; **D:** Tony Richardson; **W:** Terry Southern, Christopher Isherwood; **M:** John Addison. **VHS, Beta $19.95** MGM 🎞🎞🎞

Loveless A menacing glance into the exploits of an outcast motorcycle gang. In the 50s, a group of bikers on their way to the Florida Cycle Races stop for lunch in a small-town diner. While repairs are being made on their motorcycles, they decide to take full advantage of their situation.

1983 (R) 85m/C Robert Gordon, Willem Dafoe, J. Don Ferguson; **D:** Kathryn Bigelow. **VHS, Beta** $59.95 *MED ♪♪*

Lovelines Two rock singers from rival high schools meet and fall in love during a panty raid. Laughs uncounted ensue.
1984 (R) 93m/C Greg Bradford, Michael Winslow, Mary Beth Evans, Don Michael Paul, Tammy Taylor, Stacey Toten, Miguel Ferrer, Shecky Greene, Aimee Eccles, Sherri Stoner; **D:** Rod Amateau. **VHS, Beta** $79.98 *FOX ♪*

Lovely...But Deadly Young girl wages a war against the drug dealers in her school after her brother dies of an overdose.
1982 (R) 95m/C Lucinda Dooling, John Randolph, Richard Herd, Susan Mechsner, Mel Novak; **D:** David Sheldon. **VHS, Beta** $69.98 *LIV, VES ♪½*

Lovely to Look At Three wanna-be Broadway producers (Skelton, Keel, Champion) go to gay Paree to peddle Skelton's half interest in Madame Roberta's, a chi chi dress shop. There, they meet the shop's other half interest, two sisters (Champion and Miller), and together they stage a fashion show to finance the floundering hospice of haute couture. Lavish production, light plot. Filmed in Technicolor based on Kern's 1933 Broadway hit (inspired by Alice Duer Miller's ''Gowns by Roberta''). Vincent Minelli staged the fashion show, with gowns by Adrian (watch for cop-beater Zsa Zsa as a model). Laserdisc format features the original motion picture trailer. ♫Opening Night; Smoke Gets in Your Eyes; Lovely to Look At; The Touch of Your Hand; Yesterdays; I Won't Dance; You're Devastating; The Most Exciting Night; I'll Be Hard to Handle.
1952 105m/C Kathryn Grayson, Red Skelton, Howard Keel, Gower Champion, Marge Champion, Ann Miller, Zsa Zsa Gabor, Kurt Kasznar, Marcel Dalio, Diane Cassidy; **D:** Mervyn LeRoy; **M:** Jerome Kern. **VHS** $19.98 *MGM, TTC, FCT ♪♪♪*

The Lover Portrays the sexual awakening of a French teenager and her older Chinese lover in Indochina in 1929. The characters, who remain nameless, meet on a ferry where the man is smitten by the girl's beauty. Detached, determined, and unromantic (the opposite of her indolent lover), she allows herself to be seduced for the experience, and money, he offers. The film is equally detached, including the beautifully photographed but uninvolving sex scenes. Moreau narrates as an adult looking back on her life. March's debut; filmed on location in Vietnam. Based on the semi-autobiographical novel by Marguerite Duras who reputiated director Annuad's film when it was released in France. Also available in an unrated, letterbox version at 115 minutes.
1992 (R) 103m/C Jane March, Tony Leung, Frederique Meininger, Arnaud Giovanietti, Melvil Poupaud, Lisa Faulkner, Xiem Mang; **D:** Jean-Jacques Annaud; **W:** Gerard Brach, Jean-Jacques Annaud. **VHS, Beta** $19.98 *MGM, BTV ♪♪*

Lover Come Back More Day-Hudson antics in which an advertising executive falls in love with his competitor but that doesn't stop him from stealing her clients. Is there no shame?
1961 107m/C Rock Hudson, Doris Day, Tony Randall, Edie Adams, Joe Flynn, Ann B. Davis, Jack Oakie, Jack Albertson, Jack Kruschen, Howard St. John; **D:** Delbert Mann. **VHS, Beta** $14.95 *BAR, MOV ♪♪*

Loverboy A college schnook takes a summer job as a Beverly Hills pizza delivery boy and is preyed upon by many rich and sex-hungry housewives.

1989 (PG-13) 105m/C Patrick Dempsey, Kate Jackson, Barbara Carrera, Kirstie Alley, Carrie Fisher, Robert Ginty; **D:** Joan Micklin Silver; **W:** Tom Ropelewski, Leslie Dixon; **M:** Michel Colombier. **VHS, Beta** $19.95 *COL ♪*

The Lovers Chic tale of French adultery with Moreau starring as a provincial wife whose shallow life changes overnight when she meets a young man. Had a controversial American debut because of the film's tender eroticism and innocent view of adultery. In French with English subtitles.
1959 90m/B Jeanne Moreau, Alain Cuny, Jose-Luis De Villalonga, Jean-Mark Bory; **D:** Louis Malle; **W:** Louis Malle. **VHS** $69.95 *NYF, FCT, ART ♪♪♪*

Lovers: A True Story Erotic love triangle in 1950s Madrid, while Spain is under the suffocating dictatorship of Franco. Naive, young Paco has a virginal, hardworking fiancee named Trini. Things would seem to be headed for an average life until Paco rents a room from young widow Luisa and they embark on a sexual affair bordering on obsession. When Trini discovers what's going on she turns out to have a more passionate and violent nature than even Paco could imagine. Steamy and highly dramatic with excellent performances. Based on a true story. In Spanish with English subtitles. An unrated version is also available.
1990 (R) 105m/C Victoria Abril, Jorge Sanz, Maribel Verdu; **D:** Vicente Aranda. **VHS** $89.95 *WOV, ING ♪♪♪*

Lovers and Liars A romantic adventure in Rome turns into a symphony of zany mishaps when the man forgets to tell the woman that he is married!! **AKA:** Travels with Anita; A Trip with Anita.
1981 (R) 93m/C Goldie Hawn, Giancarlo Giannini, Laura Betti; **D:** Mario Monicelli; **M:** Ennio Morricone. **VHS, Beta** $24.98 *SUE ♪♪*

Lovers and Other Strangers Two young people decide to marry after living together for a year and a half. Various tensions surface between them and among their families as the wedding day approaches. Good comedy features some charming performances. Keaton's first film.
1970 (R) 106m/C Gig Young, Beatrice Arthur, Bonnie Bedelia, Anne Jackson, Harry Guardino, Michael Brandon, Richard Castellano, Bob Dishy, Marian Hailey, Cloris Leachman, Anne Meara, Diane Keaton; **D:** Cy Howard; **W:** Renee Taylor, Joseph Bologna, David Zelag Goodman. Academy Awards '70: Best Song (''For All We Know''); Nominations: Best Adapted Screenplay, Best Supporting Actor (Castellano). **VHS** *FOX ♪♪♪*

Lovers Like Us Two people each leave their spouses, meet one another, and fall in love. **AKA:** Le Sauvage; The Savage.
1975 103m/C Catherine Deneuve, Yves Montand, Luigi Vannucchi, Tony Roberts, Dana Wynter; **D:** Jean-Paul Rappeneau; **W:** Jean-Paul Rappeneau. **VHS, Beta** *NO ♪♪½*

Lovers' Lovers All sorts of bizarre and erotic adventures ensue when Blaire and the jilted narcissist meets Michael, who doesn't want to commit to girlfriend Teri. Michael plans an affair with Blaire without realizing that Teri is already having a fling with Ray, Blaire's ex. Some funny situations but too many talky scenes stop the film cold.
1994 90m/C Serge Rodnunsky, Jennifer Ciesar, Cindy Parker, Ray Bennett; **D:** Serge Rodnunsky; **W:** Serge Rodnunsky; **M:** Pierre Rodnunsky. **VHS** $89.95 *TRI ♪½*

Lovers of Their Time A romantic novel on tape, about forbidden love and other problems.

1985 60m/C Edward Petherbridge, Cheryl Prime, Lynn Farleigh; **D:** Robert Knights. **Beta** $11.95 *PSM ♪*

Loves & Times of Scaramouche Eighteenth-century rogue becomes involved in a plot to assassinate Napoleon and winds up seducing Josephine in the process. Dubbed. **AKA:** Scaramouche.
1976 92m/C Michael Sarrazin, Ursula Andress, Aldo Maccione; **D:** Enzo G. Castellari. **VHS, Beta** $19.95 *SUE, COL ♪½*

Loves of a Blonde A shy teenage factory girl falls in love with a visiting piano player when the reservist army comes to her small town. But when she goes to visit his family, she discovers things aren't as she imagined. Touching look at the complications of love and our expectations. In Czechoslovakian with English subtitles. **AKA:** A Blonde in Love; Lasky Jedne Plavovlasky.
1965 88m/B Jana Brejchova, Josef Sebanek, Vladimir Pucholt; **D:** Milos Forman. **VHS, Beta** $39.95 *HMV, ING, COL ♪♪♪½*

The Loves of Carmen Film version of the classic Prosper Merrimee novel about a tempestuous Spanish gypsy and the soldier who loves her. Hayworth is great to look at and the film's main selling point.
1948 98m/C Rita Hayworth, Glenn Ford, Ron Randell, Victor Jory, Arnold Moss, Luther Adler, Joseph Buloff; **D:** Charles Vidor. **VHS, Beta** $19.95 *COL ♪♪½*

The Loves of Edgar Allen Poe A bland biographical drama about young Poe's adoption, his treatment at the hands of his foster father, his rejection by a woman for a more well-off man, his marriage to his first cousin, and his early death from alcoholism.
1942 67m/B Linda Darnell, Sheppard Strudwick, Virginia Gilmore, Jane Darwell, Mary Howard; **D:** Harry Lachman. **VHS** *TCF ♪♪*

The Loves of Hercules The mythic mesomorph finds a mate with equiponderant chest measurements, and must save her from an evil queen. Somehow it eludes him that both queen and maiden are Miss Jayne in red and black wigs. Kudos for worst dubbing and special effects; a must see for connoisseurs of kitsch. **AKA:** Hercules and the Hydra.
1960 94m/C Jayne Mansfield, Mickey Hargitay; **D:** Carlo L. Bragaglia. **VHS** $19.98 *SNC, VDM Woof!*

The Loves of Irina Franco's dreamy, sanguine, produced-on-a-dime tale of a vampiress. She cruises the Riviera, seducing and nibbling on a variety of men and women. Spanish release known as ''Erotikill,'' not for most tastes.
1987 95m/C Lina Romay, Monica Swin, Jack Taylor, Alice Arno; **D:** Jess (Jesus) Franco. **VHS, Beta** $29.95 *MED ♪*

Love's Savage Fury Two escapees from a Union prison camp seek out a hidden treasure that could determine the outcome of the Civil War. A bad made-for-television ''Gone With the Wind'' rip-off.
1979 100m/C Jennifer O'Neill, Perry King, Robert Reed, Raymond Burr, Connie Stevens, Ed Lauter; **D:** Joseph Hardy. **VHS, Beta** $49.95 *PSM Woof!*

Lovesick A very-married New York psychiatrist goes against his own best judgment when he falls in love with one of his patients.
1983 (PG) 98m/C Dudley Moore, Elizabeth McGovern, Alec Guinness, John Huston, Ron Silver; **D:** Marshall Brickman; **W:** Marshall Brickman. **VHS, Beta** $19.98 *WAR ♪♪*

Lovespell A retelling of the legend of Isolde and Tristan. Stilted direction and writing, but another chance to reminisce on Richard Burton. *AKA:* Tristan and Isolde.
1979 91m/C Richard Burton, Kate Mulgrew, Nicholas Clay, Cyril Cusack, Geraldine Fitzgerald, Niall Toibin, Diana Van Der Vlis, Niall O'Brien; *D:* Tom Donovan. VHS *NO &*

Lovey: A Circle of Children 2 Teacher for special children takes in a terrified girl diagnosed as brain damaged or schizophrenic, and discovers love and intelligence in the girl as well as finding some important insights into her own life.
1982 120m/C Jane Alexander, Kris McKeon; *D:* Judd Taylor. VHS, Beta *TLF &&*

Loving The full-length, shot-on-video pilot for the daytime television soap opera, with various guest stars. Exteriors shot at C.W. Post Center on Long Island.
1984 120m/C Lloyd Bridges, Geraldine Page. VHS, Beta *NO &&*

Loving Couples Two happily married couples meet at a weekend resort...and switch partners. Tired and predictable but it has its moments.
1980 (PG) 120m/C Shirley MacLaine, James Coburn, Susan Sarandon, Stephen Collins, Sally Kellerman; *D:* Jack Smight. VHS, Beta $29.98 *VES &&*

Loving You A small town boy with a musical style all his own becomes a big success thanks to the help of a female press agent. Features many early Elvis hits. ♫Loving You; Teddy Bear; Lonesome Cowboy; Got a Lot of Livin' To Do; Party; Mean Woman Blues; Hot Dog.
1957 101m/C Elvis Presley, Wendell Corey, Lizabeth Scott, Dolores Hart, James Gleason; *D:* Hal Kanter; *W:* Hal Kanter. VHS, Beta $19.98 *WAR, OM &&*

Low Blow A kung fu expert tracks down a mind-bending cult.
1985 90m/C Cameron Mitchell, Leo Fong; *D:* Frank Harris. VHS, Beta $69.98 *LIV, VES &*

Low Down Dirty Shame A down-on-his-luck private eye (Wayans) is hired to find a missing person who turns out to be in the federal witness protection program.
1994 ?m/C Keenan Ivory Wayans, Jada Pinkett, Salli Richardson, Charles S. Dutton, Andrew Divoff, Corwin Hawkins; *D:* Keenan Ivory Wayans; *W:* Keenan Ivory Wayans. VHS *&&*

The Lower Depths Renoir's adaptation of the Maxim Gorky play about a thief and a financially ruined baron learning about life from one another. In French with English subtitles. *AKA:* Les Bas Fonds; Underground.
1936 92m/B Jean Gabin, Louis Jouvet, Vladimir Sokoloff, Robert Le Vigan, Suzy Prim; *D:* Jean Renoir. VHS, Beta $39.95 *FCT, DVT, GVV &&&*

The Lower Depths Kurosawa sets the Maxim Gorky play in Edo during the final Tokugawa period, using Noh theatre elements in depicting the lowly denizens of a low-rent hovel. In Japanese with English subtitles.
1957 125m/B Toshiro Mifune, Isuzu Yamada, Ganjiro Nakamura, Kyoko Kagawa, Bokuzen Hidari; *D:* Akira Kurosawa. VHS, Beta $24.95 *FCT, ING, COL &&&½*

Lower Level While working late, an attractive business woman becomes trapped in an office building by her psychotic secret admirer.
1991 (R) 88m/C David Bradley, Elizabeth Gracen, Jeff Yagher; *D:* Kristine Peterson. VHS $9.98 *REP &*

Loyalties A strong treatment of the issue of sexual abuse of girls by men, and of an upper-class woman's willingness to establish a true friendship with a woman of a so-called lower economic class.
1986 (R) 98m/C Kenneth Welsh, Tantoo Cardinal, Susan Wooldridge, Vera Martin, Christopher Barrington-Leigh; *D:* Anne Wheeler; *W:* Sharon Riis; *M:* Michael Conway Baker. VHS $9.95 *VTR &&½*

Loyola, the Soldier Saint A biography of the founder of the Jesuits from his years as a page in the Spanish court to his daring exploits on the battle field and, finally, his spiritual awakening at the University of Paris. Narrated by Father Alfred J. Barrett.
1952 93m/B Rafael Duran, Maria Rosa Jiminez; *D:* Jose Diaz Morales. VHS *IVY, KEP &&½*

Lucas A high school brain falls in love with the new girl in town, and tries to win her by trying out for the football team. Genuine film about the perils of coming of age. Thoughtful, non-condescending, and humorous.
1986 (PG-13) 100m/C Corey Haim, Kerri Green, Charlie Sheen, Winona Ryder, Courtney Thorne-Smith, Thomas E. Hodges; *D:* David Seltzer; *W:* David Seltzer; *M:* Dave Grusin. VHS, Beta $14.98 *FXV, FOX &&&*

The Lucifer Complex Nazi doctors are cloning exact duplicates of such world leaders as the Pope and the President of the United States on a remote South American island in the year 1996.
1978 91m/C Robert Vaughn, Merrie Lynn Ross, Keenan Wynn, Aldo Ray; *D:* David L. Hewitt, Kenneth Hartford. VHS, Beta $59.95 *VCI &*

Lucky Cisco Kid Romero takes over from Warner Baxter in the fourth entry in the series, with Martin as his loyal sidekick. This time a rustler and his gang are stealing cattle and using the Kid's name to place the blame. Fast-paced with Romero appropriately debonair. Andrews screen debut.
1940 67m/B Cesar Romero, Chris-Pin Martin, Mary Beth Hughes, Dana Andrews, Evelyn Venable, Joseph Sawyer, Francis Ford; *D:* H. Bruce Humberstone; *W:* Robert Ellis, Helen Logan. VHS $12.95 *GPV &&½*

Lucky Devil Lucky devil wins car and motors around the country to the tune of organ music.
1925 63m/B Richard Dix, Esther Ralston, Edna May Oliver, Tom Findley; *D:* Frank Tuttle. VHS, Beta $19.95 *GPV, FCT &½*

Lucky Jim A junior lecturer in history at a small university tries to get himself in good graces with the head of his department, but is doomed from the start by doing the wrong things at the worst possible times. Minus the social satire of the Kingsley Amis novel on which it was based; what's left is a cheerful comedy.
1958 91m/B Ian Carmichael, Terry-Thomas, Hugh Griffith; *D:* John Boulting; *M:* John Addison. VHS, Beta *NO &&½*

Lucky Luciano A violent depiction of the final years of Lucky Luciano, gangster kingpin. *AKA:* A Proposito Luciano; *RE:* Lucky Luciano.
1974 (R) 108m/C Edmond O'Brien, Rod Steiger, Vincent Gardenia, Gian Marie Volonte; *D:* Francesco Rosi. VHS, Beta $9.95 *NLC &&*

Lucky Luke: Daisy Town Full-length animated feature starring Lucky Luke, the all-American cowboy who saves the little community of Daisy Town from the hot-headed Dalton Brothers gang. A wacky western spoof.
1971 75m/C *M:* Claude Bolling. VHS, Beta $49.95 *DIS, WTA &&*

Lucky Luke: The Ballad of the Daltons Easygoing cowboy hero Lucky Luke gets involved in a wild feud with the bumbling Dalton Brothers gang in this animated feature.
1978 82m/C VHS, Beta $49.95 *DIS, WTA &&*

Lucky Me A group of theater entertainers are stranded in Miami and are forced to work in a hotel kitchen. They soon acquire the support of a wealthy oilman (Goodwin) who invests in their show, but not before his spoiled daughter tries to thwart all plans. ♫Lucky Me; Superstition Song; I Speak to the Stars; Take a Memo to the Moon; Love You Dearly; Bluebells of Broadway; Parisian Pretties; Wanna Sing Like an Angel; High Hopes.
1954 100m/C Doris Day, Robert Cummings, Phil Silvers, Eddie Foy Jr., Nancy Walker, Martha Hyer, Bill Goodwin, Marcel Dalio, James Burke, Jack Shea, William "Billy" Bakewell, Charles Cane, Ray Teal, Tom Powers, Angie Dickinson, Dolores Dorn; *D:* Jack Donohue. VHS $19.98 *WAR, CCB, MVD &&*

Lucky Partners When an artist and an errand girl share a winning lottery ticket, funny complications arise as they embark on a fantasy honeymoon. Although Rogers' innocence and Coleman's savoir faire provide an interesting contrast, the script isn't equal to the status of its stars.
1940 101m/B Ronald Colman, Ginger Rogers, Jack Carson, Spring Byington, Harry Davenport; *D:* Lewis Milestone. VHS, Beta $19.98 *RKO, TTC &&*

Lucky Stiff A fat, unpopular dweeb has the shock of his life when a radiant woman falls in love with him, the strangeness of which becomes evident when he meets her very weird family.
1988 (PG) 93m/C Donna Dixon, Joe Alaskey; *D:* Anthony Perkins; *W:* Pat Proft. VHS, Beta $89.95 *COL &&*

Lucky Terror Routine Hoot cowboy drama.
1936 60m/B Hoot Gibson, Kone Andre, Charles "Blackie" King; *D:* Alan James. VHS, Beta $19.95 *NOS, GPV, VCN &*

Lucky Texan Wayne plays a tough easterner who goes West and finds himself involved in a range war.
1934 61m/B John Wayne, George "Gabby" Hayes, Yakima Canutt; *D:* Robert North Bradbury. VHS, Beta $9.98 *REP, COL, MRV &½*

Lucy and Desi: Before the Laughter The meeting and early married life of actress/comedian Lucille Ball and Cuban bandleader Desi Arnaz is depicted in this routine biopic. Film depicts Desi's womanizing, their struggles with fame, and their efforts to get their television show on the air. Fisher does well as television's favorite redhead but this made-for-television effort is melodramatic. Daughter Lucy Arnaz vehemently opposed this depiction of her parents life.
1991 (PG-13) 95m/C Frances Fisher, Maurice Benard, John Wheeler, Robin Pearson Rose; *D:* Charles Jarrott; *W:* William Luce. VHS $89.98 *REP, PMS &&½*

L'Udienza A bizarre black comedy about a guy who does anything he can, at any criminal cost, to obtain an audience with the Pope. In Italian with subtitles.
1971 111m/C Claudia Cardinale, Ugo Tognazzi; *D:* Marco Ferreri. VHS, Beta $49.95 *FCT &&½*

Luggage of the Gods A lost tribe of cave people are confronted with civilization when suitcases fall from an airplane. Low-budget comedy reminiscent of "The Gods Must Be Crazy."

L

1987 (G) 78m/C Mark Stolzenberg, Gabriel Barre, Gwen Ellison; **D:** David Kendall. **VHS, Beta** $29.95 ACA 🎬🎬

Lullaby of Broadway Many songs highlight this flimsy musical about a girl (Day) who ventures from England to the Big Apple in search of an acting career. She soon discovers that her mom has become a has-been actress now performing in a Greenwich Village dive. Day struggles to gain her own success while coping with her mother's downfall. ♫Lullaby of Broadway; You're Getting to Be a Habit With Me; Just One of Those Things; Somebody Loves Me; I Love the Way You Say Goodnight; Fine and Dandy; Please Don't Talk About Me When I'm Gone; A Shanty in Old Shanty Town; We'd Like to Go On A Trip.
1951 93m/C Doris Day, Gene Nelson, S.Z. Sakall, Billy DeWolfe, Gladys George, Florence Bates; **D:** David Butler. **VHS** $19.98 WAR, CCB, MVD 🎬🎬½

Lumiere An acclaimed drama about four actresses who, during the course of one night together, make pivotal decisions about their lives and relationships. Moreau's first directorial effort; dubbed.
1976 (R) 101m/C Jeanne Moreau, Lucia Bose, Francine Racette, Caroline Cartier, Keith Carradine; **D:** Jeanne Moreau. **VHS, Beta** $29.98 SUE 🎬🎬½

Lunatic "Some minds should be wasted" according to the film promo and if you're in the mood for an amateur mind (and time) waster, this is for you. High schoolers in the woods encounter mayhem in the best horror tradition as the innocents are slaughtered by an escapee from the local lunatic asylum.
1991 90m/C Rocky Tucker, Ondrea Tucker, Brian D'Lawrence, Keith Vallot, Bronwyn St. John, Cameron Derrick, Ernest Jackson, Rookie Macpherson, Susan Spain; **D:** James Tucker; **W:** James Tucker. **VHS** $29.95 CTC 🎬

The Lunatic A robust, oversexed, and scheming German tourist travels to Jamaica where she meets the village idiot, a man who regularly holds conversations with the local plants. The two hook up with a butcher, and the three live happily in the hills, that is until the money is gone. The Jamaican scenery, a few bawdy laughs, and a great reggae soundtrack make this one worthwhile.
1992 (R) 93m/C Julie T. Wallace, Paul Campbell, Reggie Carter, Carl Bradshaw; **D:** Lol Creme; **M:** Wally Badarou. **VHS, Beta** $89.95 ACA 🎬

Lunatics: A Love Story Hank (Raimi) is an ex-mental patient poet suffering from hallucinations and afraid to leave his Los Angeles apartment. For companionship he dials a party-line until, one day, he misdials and insteads gets the number of a local pay telephone, which is answered by a naive woman dumped by her boyfriend. When Nancy (Foreman) decides to visit Hank you learn she's as crazy as he is—so it only makes sense they would fall in love. A well-acted fable of how love fragilely connects even the most unlikely of people.
1992 (PG-13) 87m/C Theodore Raimi, Deborah Foreman, Bruce Campbell, Brian McCree, Eddie Rosmaya, Michele Stacey; **D:** Josh Beck; **W:** Josh Beck; **M:** Joseph Lo Duca. **VHS** NO 🎬🎬🎬

Lunatics & Lovers Musician meets a bizarre nobleman who is in love with an imaginary woman.
1976 (PG) 92m/C Marcello Mastroianni, Lino Toffalo; **D:** Flavio Mogherini. **VHS, Beta** $59.98 FOX 🎬🎬½

Lunch Wagon Two co-eds are given a restaurant to manage during summer vacation and wind up involved in a hilarious diamond chase and sex romp. **AKA:** Come 'n' Get It; Lunch Wagon Girls.
1981 (R) 88m/C Rick Podell, Candy Moore, Pamela Bryant, Rosanne Katon; **D:** Ernie Pintoff. **VHS, Beta** $19.95 MED 🎬🎬

Lupo When threatened with the loss of his home and the separation of his family, an exuberant Greek man challenges the modern world.
1970 (G) 99m/C Yuda Barkan, Gabi Armoni, Esther Greenberg; **D:** Menahem Golan. **VHS, Beta** $59.95 MGM 🎬🎬

Lure of the Islands Federal agents track wanted criminals to an island retreat in this highly predictable low-budget thriller.
1942 61m/B Margie Hart, Robert Lowery, Guinn Williams, Warren Hymer, Gale Storm; **D:** Jean Yarborough. **VHS, Beta** $16.95 NOS, SNC 🎬

Lure of the Sila Italian melodrama about a young peasant girl infiltrating a landowner's home in order to avenge the death of her brother and mother. Dubbed and more interesting than it sounds.
1949 72m/B Silvana Mangano, Amadeo Nazzari, Vittorio Gassman; **D:** Duilio Coletti. **VHS, Beta, 8mm** $29.95 VYY 🎬🎬½

Lurkers An unappealing metaphysical morass about a woman who has been haunted throughout her life by...something.
1988 (R) 90m/C Christine Moore, Gary Warner, Marina Taylor, Carissa Channing, Tom Billett; **D:** Roberta Findlay. **VHS** $79.95 MED Woof!

Lurking Fear The town of Lefferts Corner has suffered from generations of horror thanks to man-eating ghouls that dwell beneath the local graveyard and arise whenever a storm breaks out. The inhabitants prepare to fight back but their plan is hindered by the arrival of a group of criminals who are after a fortune supposedly hidden in one of the graves. Based on a story by H.P. Lovecraft.
1994 78m/C Jon Finch, Blake Bailey, Ashley Lauren, Jeffrey Combs, Paul Mantee, Allison Mackie, Joe Leavengood, Vincent Schiavelli; **D:** C. Courtney Joyner; **W:** C. Courtney Joyner; **M:** Jim Manzie. **VHS, Beta** PAR 🎬

Lust for a Vampire The sanguine tale of a deadly vampire who indiscriminately preys on pupils and teachers when she enrolls at a British finishing school. Moody and erotically charged, with an impressive ending. Quasi-sequel to "The Vampire Lovers." **AKA:** To Love a Vampire.
1971 (R) 95m/C Ralph Bates, Barbara Jefford, Suzanna Leigh, Michael Johnson, Yutte Stensgaard, Pippa Steele; **D:** Jimmy Sangster. **VHS, Beta** $59.99 MLB 🎬🎬

Lust for Freedom An undercover cop decides to hit the road after she sees her partner gunned down. She winds up near the California-Mexico border, where she is wrongly imprisoned with a number of other young women in a white slavery business. This low-budget film includes lots of steamy women-behind-bars sex scenes.
1987 92m/C Melanie Coll, William J. Kulzer; **D:** Eric Louzil. **VHS** $89.95 AIP, MOV 🎬

Lust for Gold Ford battles against greedy former lover Lupino and her husband for control of the Lost Dutchman gold mine.
1949 90m/B Ida Lupino, Glenn Ford, Gig Young, William Prince, Edgar Buchanan, Will Geer, Paul Ford, Jay Silverheels; **D:** Sylvan Simon; **M:** George Duning. **VHS, Beta** GKK 🎬🎬

Lust for Life Absorbing, serious biography of Vincent Van Gogh, from his first paintings to his death. Remarkable for Douglas' furiously convincing portrayal. Featuring dozens of actual Van Gogh works from private collections. Based on an Irving Stone novel, produced by John Houseman.
1956 122m/C Kirk Douglas, Anthony Quinn, James Donald, Pamela Brown, Everett Sloane, Henry Daniell, Niall MacGinnis, Noel Purcell, Lionel Jeffries, Jill Bennett; **D:** Vincente Minnelli; **M:** Miklos Rozsa. Academy Awards '56: Best Supporting Actor (Quinn); Nominations: Best Actor (Douglas), Best Adapted Screenplay, Best Art Direction/Set Decoration (Color); Golden Globe Awards '57: Best Actor–Drama (Douglas); National Board of Review Awards '56: 10 Best Films of the Year; New York Film Critics Awards '56: Best Actor (Douglas). **VHS, Beta** $39.95 MGM, BTV 🎬🎬🎬½

Lust in the Dust When part of a treasure map is found on the derriere of none other than Divine, the hunt is on for the other half. This comedy western travels to a sleepy town called Chile Verde (green chili for those who don't speak Spanish) and the utterly ridiculous turns comically corrupt. Deliciously distasteful fun. Features Divine singing a bawdy love song in his/her break from John Waters.
1985 (R) 85m/C Tab Hunter, Divine, Lainie Kazan, Geoffrey Lewis, Henry Silva, Cesar Romero, Gina Gallego, Courtney Gains, Woody Strode, Pedro Gonzalez-Gonzalez; **D:** Paul Bartel; **W:** Philip John Taylor; **M:** Peter Matz. **VHS, Beta** $14.95 NWV, STE, HHE 🎬🎬🎬

The Lusty Men Two rival rodeo champions, both in love with the same woman, work the rodeo circuit until a tragic accident occurs. Mitchum turns in a fine performance as the has-been rodeo star trying to make it big again.
1952 113m/B Robert Mitchum, Susan Hayward, Arthur Kennedy, Arthur Hunnicutt; **D:** Nicholas Ray. **VHS, Beta** $15.95 VCI 🎬🎬🎬

Luther A well-acted characterization of Martin Luther's development from a young seminarian to his leadership of the Reformation Movement.
1974 (G) 112m/C Stacy Keach, Patrick Magee, Hugh Griffith, Robert Stephens, Alan Badel; **D:** Guy Green; **W:** Edward Anhalt; **M:** John Addison. **VHS** NO 🎬🎬

Luther the Geek Little Luther's visit to the circus is dramatically changed when he sees the geek, a sideshow freak. Since then Luther has taken to biting off chicken's heads and drinking their blood in his small Illinois town; the town will never be the same. (And neither will you if you watch this stupid film.)
1990 90m/C Edward Terry, Joan Roth, J. Jerome Clarke, Tom Mills; **D:** Carlton J. Albright. **VHS** NO Woof!

Luv Although good cast tries hard, they can't do much with this comic farce. Three intellectuals, including one that's suicidal, discuss the trials and tribulations of their middle-class New York existence.
1967 (PG) 95m/C Jack Lemmon, Peter Falk, Elaine May; **D:** Clive Donner; **W:** Murray Schisgal. **VHS, Beta** $9.95 GKK 🎬½

Luzia Ohana stars as a tough and sexy Brazilian cowgirl who is caught in the middle of a class struggle where the personal is definitely political. Her horseriding skills and beauty give her options in both lifestyles. Will she choose to side with the squatters or the wealthy landowners? In Portuguese with English subtitles.
1988 112m/C Claudia Ohana, Thales Pan Chacon, Jose de Abreu, Luiza Falcao; **D:** Fabio Barreto. **VHS** $79.95 FXL, ING 🎬🎬½

Lydia Sentimental drama in which an elderly lady (Oberon) gets to relive her romantic past when she has a reunion with four of her lost loves. Well acted and directed, Oberon

gives one of her best performances ever. Adapted from the highly regarded French film "Un Carnet de Bal."
1941 98m/B Merle Oberon, Joseph Cotten, Alan Marshal, George Reeves; **D:** Julien Duvivier; **M:** Miklos Rozsa. **VHS, Beta** SUE ♫♫♫

Lying Lips All-black detective mystery about a young nightclub singer framed for murder. Her boyfriend then turns detective to clear her name.
1939 60m/B Edna Mae Harris, Carmen Newsome, Earl Jones, Amanda Randolph; **D:** Oscar Micheaux. **VHS, Beta $24.95** FCT, VCN, DVT ♫ 1/2

M The great Lang dissection of criminal deviance, following the tortured last days of a child murderer, and the efforts of both the police and the underground to bring him to justice. Poetic, compassionate, and chilling. Inspired by real-life serial killer known as "Vampire of Dusseldorf," Lang also borrowed story elements from Jack the Ripper's killing spree. Lorre's screen debut. Lang's personal favorite among his own films. In German with English subtitles. Remade in 1951.
1931 99m/B Peter Lorre, Ellen Widmann, Inge Landgut, Gustav Grundgens; **D:** Fritz Lang; **W:** Fritz Lang. **VHS, Beta, 8mm $16.95** SNC, NOS, HHT ♫♫♫♫

M. Butterfly Disappointing adaptation of Hwang's award-winning play, which was based on a true story. Irons is Rene Gallimard, a minor French diplomat sent to China in 1964. Taken in by the exoticism of the mysterious east, he falls for a Chinese opera performer, Song Liling (Lone). Only she's no lady and the oblivious diplomat turns out to be a patsy as Song Liling uses him to gather information. The story only works if the passion, however deceptive, between Gallimard and Song Liling is believable, passion which is noticeably lacking between Irons and Lone. Irons comes across as too intelligent to be gullible and the usually excellent Lone does not make his role believable.
1993 (R) 101m/C Jeremy Irons, John Lone, Ian Richardson, Barbara Sukowa, Vernon Dobtcheff, Annabel Leventon, Shizuko Hoshi, Richard McMillan; **D:** David Cronenberg; **W:** David Henry Hwang; **M:** Howard Shore. **VHS, Beta** WAR ♫♫

Ma and Pa Kettle The hillbilly couple were supporting characters in "The Egg and I" but their popularity found them spun off into their own cornpone series. This first feature finds the couple and their 15 children about to be evicted only to have Pa win a tobacco slogan contest. The prize is a brand-new fully-automated house whose futuristic contraptions get the better of Pa. **AKA:** The Further Adventures of Ma and Pa Kettle.
1949 76m/B Marjorie Main, Percy Kilbride, Richard Long, Meg Randall, Esther Dale, Barry Kelley, Patricia Alphin; **D:** Charles Lamont; **W:** Al Lewis, Herbert Margolis, Louis Morheim. **VHS $14.98** MCA ♫♫ 1/2

Ma and Pa Kettle at the Fair The Kettle's eldest daughter Rosie wants to go to college so Ma enters the county fair baking contest to win some money and Pa buys a decrepit old nag to enter in the fair's horse race. Somehow things just have a way of working out for the Kettles.
1952 79m/B Marjorie Main, Percy Kilbride, Lori Nelson, James Best, Esther Dale, Russell Simpson, Emory Parnell; **D:** Charles T. Barton; **W:** John Grant, Richard Morris. **VHS $14.98** MCA ♫♫ 1/2

Ma and Pa Kettle Back On the Farm First-time grandparents, the Kettles have to deal with their daughter-in-law's snobby Bostonian parents and their parent-

ing ideas. The family's also moved back to their ramshackle farm where Pa thinks he's found uranium, leading to all sorts of problems.
1951 81m/B Marjorie Main, Percy Kilbride, Richard Long, Meg Randall, Ray Collins, Barbara Brown, Emory Parnell; **D:** Edward Sedgwick; **W:** Jack Henley. **VHS $14.98** MCA ♫♫ 1/2

Ma and Pa Kettle Go to Town Ma and Pa head off for New York City when Pa wins a jingle-writing contest, unknowingly leaving their brood in the care of on the lam mobster Mike, who asks the Kettles to deliver a package to his brother. This gets both the crooks and the cops trailing the hillbilly couple, whose backwoods ways are more than a match for any city slicker.
1950 80m/B Marjorie Main, Percy Kilbride, Richard Long, Meg Randall, Charles McGraw, Ray Collins, Esther Dale, Ellen Corby, Barbara Brown; **D:** Charles Lamont; **W:** Martin Ragaway, Leonard Stern. **VHS $14.98** MCA ♫♫ 1/2

Ma Barker's Killer Brood Biography of the infamous American criminal and her four sons, edited together from a television serial. The shoot-em-up scenes and Tuttle's performance keep the pace from slackening.
1960 82m/B Lurene Tuttle, Tristram Coffin, Paul Dubov, Nelson Leigh, Myrna Dell, Vic Lundin, Donald Spruance; **D:** Bill Karn. **VHS, Beta $16.95** SNC, DVT, HEG ♫♫

Mabel & Fatty Three silent shorts featuring the two stars, made with Mack Sennett: "He Did and He Didn't," "Mabel and Fatty Viewing The World's Fair at San Francisco" (with scenes of the actual 1914 World's Fair) and "Mabel's Blunder."
1916 61m/B Mabel Normand, Fatty Arbuckle, Al "Fuzzy" St. John. **VHS, Beta, 8mm $19.95** VYY ♫♫

Mac It's a family affair. Immigrant carpenter's funeral is the starting point for the story of his three sons, construction workers who live in Queens, New York in the 1950s. The passionate bros battle, bitch, and build, with Turturro as the eldest summing up the prevailing philosophy: "It's the doing, that's the thing." Turturro's directorial debut is a labor of love and a tribute to his own dad. Filmed on location in New York City. Fine performances from newcomers Badalucco and Capotorto are complemented by smaller roles from Amos, Barkin, and Turturro's real-life wife Borowitz and brother Nick.
1993 (R) 118m/C John Turturro, Carl Capotorto, Michael Badalucco, Katherine Borowitz, John Amos, Olek Krupa, Ellen Barkin, Joe Paparone, Nicholas Turturro, Dennis Farina; **D:** John Turturro; **W:** John Turturro, Brandon Cole; **M:** Richard Termini, Vin Tese. **VHS $19.95** COL, FCT ♫♫♫

Mac and Me Lost E.T.-like alien stranded on Earth befriends a wheelchair-bound boy. Aimed at young kids, it's full of continual product plugs, most notably for McDonald's. Make the kids happy and stick to the real thing.
1988 (PG) 94m/C Christine Ebersole, Jonathan Ward, Katrina Caspary, Lauren Stanley, Jade Calegory; **D:** Stewart Raffill; **W:** Stewart Raffill. **VHS, Beta $9.98** ORI ♫

Macabre A beautiful woman, lustful and precocious, kills her husband and his twin brother.
1977 89m/C Larry Ward, Teresa Gimpera, Giacomo "Jack" Rossi-Stuart. **VHS, Beta** NO ♫♫

Macao On the lam for a crime he didn't commit, an adventurer sails to the exotic Far East, meets a buxom cafe singer, and helps Interpol catch a notorious crime boss. A strong film noir entry. Russell sneers, Mitc-

hum wise cracks. Director von Sternberg's last film for RKO.
1952 81m/B Robert Mitchum, Jane Russell, William Bendix, Gloria Grahame; **D:** Josef von Sternberg. **VHS, Beta $19.95** MED ♫♫♫

Macario Traditional Mexican fable about a desperate farmer who makes a deal with the Devil for healing powers. His gift only leads to greater misfortunes, of course. In Spanish with English subtitles.
1958 91m/B Ignacio Lopez Tarso, Pina Pellicer, Enrique Lucero; **D:** Roberto Gavaldon. **VHS, Beta $59.95** CVC, MAD, ING ♫

Macaroni An uptight American businessman returns to Naples forty years after being stationed there in WWII. Comedic situations abound when he is reunited with his Italian war buddy, brother of his lover. Pleasant acting can't save irritating script. **AKA:** Maccheroni.
1985 (PG) 104m/C Jack Lemmon, Marcello Mastroianni, Daria Nicolodi, Isa Danieli; **D:** Ettore Scola; **W:** Ettore Scola. **VHS, Beta $79.95** PAR, ING ♫ 1/2

MacArthur General Douglas MacArthur's life from Corregidor in 1942 to his dismissal a decade later in the midst of the Korean conflict. Episodic sage with forceful Peck but weak supporting characters. Fourteen minutes were cut from the original version; intended to be Peck's "Patton," it falls short of the mark.
1977 (PG) 130m/C Gregory Peck, Ivan Bonar, Ward Costello, Nicholas Coster, Dan O'Herlihy; **D:** Joseph Sargent; **W:** Matthew Robbins; **M:** Jerry Goldsmith. **VHS, Beta $19.95** MCA, TLF ♫♫

MacArthur's Children A poignant evocation of life in a Japanese fishing village as it faces the end of WWII and American occupation. Not as good as some of the other Japanese films, but it is an interesting look at the changes in culture caused by their defeat in the war. In Japanese with English subtitles.
1985 115m/C Masako Natsume, Shima Iwashita, Hiromi Go, Takaya Yamamauchi, Shiori Sakura, Ken Watanabe, Juzo Itami, Yoshiyuka Omori; **D:** Masahiro Shinoda; **W:** Takeski Tamura. **VHS, Beta $29.95** FCT, ING, TPV ♫♫♫

Macbeth Shakespeare's classic tragedy is performed in this film with a celebrated lead performance by Welles, who plays the tragic king as a demonic leader of a barbaric society. A low budget adaptation with cheap sets, a 3-week shooting schedule, lots of mood, and an attempt at Scottish accents. After making this film, Welles took a ten-year break from Hollywood.
1948 111m/B Orson Welles, Jeanette Nolan, Dan O'Herlihy, Roddy McDowall, Robert Coote; **D:** Orson Welles. **VHS $19.98** REP, TVC ♫♫♫ 1/2

Macbeth Polanski's notorious adaptation of the Shakespearean classic, marked by realistic design, unflinching violence, and fatalistic atmosphere. Contains stunning fight scenes and fine acting. Polanski's first film following the grisly murder of his pregnant wife, actress Sharon Tate, was torn apart by critics. It is in fact a worthy continuation of his work in the horror genre. Very well made. First film made by Playboy Enterprises. Originally rated X.
1971 (R) 139m/C Jon Finch, Nicholas Selby, Martin Shaw, Francesca Annis, Terence Baylor; **D:** Roman Polanski. **VHS, Beta $19.95** COL, HMV, PBS ♫♫♫

Macbeth An extraordinary version of Shakespeare's "Macbeth" in which all the fire, ambition and doom of his text come brilliantly to life.
1976 137m/C Eric Porter, Janet Suzman. **$19.95** TLF ♫♫♫

M

VIDEOHOUND'S GOLDEN MOVIE RETRIEVER

▲ 605

Macbeth Another production of the classic tragedy by Shakespeare. Produced as part of HBO's Thames Collection.
1990 110m/C Michael Jayston, Leigh Hunt. **VHS, Beta $39.99** *HBO* 🐾🐾

Machine Gun Kelly Corman found Euro-appeal with this thirties style gangster bio. Bronson, who was just gaining a reputation as an action lead, stars as criminal Kelly, who's convinced by his moll to give up bank robbery for kidnapping. Amsterdam, the wisecracking writer from "The Dick Van Dyke Show," is the fink who turns him in.
1958 80m/B Charles Bronson, Susan Cabot, Morey Amsterdam, Barboura Morris, Frank De Kova, Jack Lambert, Wally Campo; *D:* Roger Corman; *W:* Mike Werb. **VHS $9.95** *COL, FCT* 🐾🐾

Macho Callahan A Civil War convict escapes from a frontier jail bent on tracking down the man who imprisoned him. (The escaped prisoner bit is a recurring theme in Janssen's oeuvre.) Confused script even has a one-armed Carradine!
1970 (R) 99m/C David Janssen, Jean Seberg, David Carradine, Lee J. Cobb; *D:* Bernard L. Kowalski. **VHS, Beta $9.95** *COL, NLC* 🐾🐾

Machoman The matchless, peerless, Machoman knows all the best killing methods including: Lizard Fists, Crane Kung Fu, and the Drunken Fist.
197? 94m/C Araujo, Enyaw Liew, Jerry Rages. **VHS, Beta** *NO* 🐾

Maciste in Hell Inexplicably living in 17th century Scotland, Italian hero Maciste pursues a witch into the depths of Hell. She's placed a curse on the world and he wants her to remove it. *AKA:* Witch's Curse.
1960 78m/C Kirk Morris, Helene Chanel, Vira Silenti, Andrea Bosic, Angelo Zanolli, John Karlsen; *D:* Riccardo (Robert Hampton) Freda. **VHS $19.98** *UNI, SNC* 🐾½

Mack The Mack is a pimp who comes out of retirement to reclaim a piece of the action in Oakland, California. Violent blaxploitation flick was a box office dynamite at time of release. Early Pryor appearance.
1973 (R) 110m/C Max Julien, Richard Pryor, Don Gordon, Roger E. Mosley, Carol Speed; *D:* Michael Campus. **VHS, Beta $9.98** *NLC* 🐾½

Mack & Carole Lombard began her screen career, in earnest, as a Mack Sennett comedienne. These three shorts represent her earliest screen work.
1928 60m/B Carole Lombard. **VHS, Beta $49.50** *GVV* 🐾½

Mack Sennett Comedies: Vol. 1 Four Sennett films are included: "The Eyes Have It," "The Cannon Ball," "The Desperate Scoundrel," and "Pride of Pikeville." Ben Turpin and the Keystone Cops at their manic best.
1921 85m/B Ben Turpin, Chester Conklin, Ford Sterling, Minta Durfee; *D:* Mack Sennett. **VHS $29.98** *REP* 🐾½

Mack Sennett Comedies: Vol. 2 Four more Sennett shorts are featured: "Mabel and Fatty Adrift," "Mabel, Fatty, and the Law," "Fatty's Tin-Type Tangle," and "Our Congressman." The last film features Will Rogers in a lampoon of Capitol Hill.
1916 84m/B Fatty Arbuckle, Mabel Normand, Will Rogers, Madge Hunt; *D:* Mack Sennett. **VHS $29.98** *REP* 🐾½

Mack the Knife Terrible adaptation of Brecht and Weill's "Threepenny Opera," detailing the adventures of a master thief in love with an innocent girl. Too much music, too much dancing, too much emoting. *AKA:* The Threepenny Opera.

1989 (PG-13) 121m/C Raul Julia, Roger Daltrey, Richard Harris, Julie Walters, Clive Revill, Erin Donovan, Rachel Robertson, Julia Migenes-Johnson; *D:* Menahem Golan. **VHS, Beta $89.95** *COL Woof!*

MacKenna's Gold Grim desperados trek through Apache territory to uncover legendary cache of gold in this somewhat inflated epic. Subdued stars Peck and Shariff vie for attention here with such overactors as Cobb, Meredith, and Wallach. Meanwhile, Newmar (Catwoman of TV's Batman) swims nude. A must for all earthquake buffs.
1969 (PG) 128m/C Gregory Peck, Omar Sharif, Telly Savalas, Julie Newmar, Edward G. Robinson, Keenan Wynn, Ted Cassidy, Eduardo Ciannelli, Eli Wallach, Raymond Massey, Lee J. Cobb, Burgess Meredith, Anthony Quayle, John David Garfield; *D:* J. Lee Thompson; *M:* Quincy Jones. **VHS, Beta $12.95** *GKK* 🐾🐾½

Mackintosh Man An intelligence agent must undo a communist who has infiltrated the free world's network in this solid but somewhat subdued thriller. Good cast keeps narrative rolling, but don't look here for nudity-profanity-violence fix.
1973 (PG) 100m/C Paul Newman, Dominique Sanda, James Mason, Ian Bannen, Nigel Patrick, Harry Andrews, Leo Genn, Peter Vaughan, Michael Hordern; *D:* John Huston; *W:* Walter Hill; *M:* Maurice Jarre. **VHS, Beta $19.98** *WAR* 🐾🐾½

Macon County Line A series of deadly mistakes and misfortunes lead to a sudden turn-around in the lives of three young people when they enter a small Georgia town and find themselves accused of brutally slaying the sheriff's wife. Sequelled by "Return to Macon County" in 1975, starring Don Johnson and Nick Nolte.
1974 (R) 89m/C Alan Vint, Jesse Vint, Cheryl Waters, Geoffrey Lewis, Joan Blackman, Max Baer Jr.; *D:* Richard Compton. **VHS, Beta $9.98** *SUE* 🐾🐾½

Macumba Love An author journeys to Brazil to prove a connection between mysterious murders and voodoo. A tedious suspense exploitation travelogue with generous servings of cheesecake and calypso music.
1960 86m/C Walter Reed, Ziva Rodann, William Wellman Jr., June Wilkinson, Ruth de Souza; *D:* Douglas Fowley. **VHS** *NO* 🐾

Mad About Money An early sound comedy about a bespectacled mild-mannered fellow who runs up against a Mexican spitfire. 🎵 Oh So Beautiful; Perpetual Motion; Little Lost Tune; Dustin' The Stars. *AKA:* He Loved an Actress; Stardust.
1930 80m/B Lupe Velez, Wallace Ford, Ben Lyon, Harry Langdon, Jean Colin; *D:* Melville Brown. **VHS, Beta $24.95** *NOS, DVT, HEG* 🐾🐾

Mad About You Millionaire helps his daughter measure prospective suitors. Adam West is not the fourth man in the Montgomery Clift-James Dean-Marlon Brando chain of American acting greats.
1990 (PG) 92m/C Claudia Christian, Joseph Gian, Adam West, Sharry Shattuck; *D:* Lorenzo Doumani. **VHS, Beta $29.95** *ACA Woof!*

Mad at the Moon Western thriller in which a young bride (Masterson) discovers that the man she married is less than human with the rising of the full moon. The only one who can protect her is her husband's half-brother played by Bochner. Masterson gives a great performance as a woman torn apart by a terrifying family secret out on the American plains.
1992 (R) 98m/C Mary Stuart Masterson, Hart Bochner, Fionnula Flanagan, Cec Verrell; *D:* Martin Donovan; *W:* Martin Donovan, Richard Pelusi. **VHS $89.98** *REP* 🐾🐾

The Mad Bomber Grim lawman Edwards tracks deranged bomber Connors, who is determined to blow up anyone who ever offended him. A must for all connoisseurs of acting that is simultaneously overblown and flat. *AKA:* Police Connection; Detective Geronimo.
1972 80m/C Vince Edwards, Chuck Connors, Neville Brand; *D:* Bert I. Gordon. **VHS, Beta $24.95** *MRV Woof!*

Mad Bull Sensitive wrestler finds meaning in life when he falls in love. If you ever cared about Karras, then you probably already saw this. If you never cared about Karras, then you probably never heard of this. If you ever cared about Anspach, rent "Five Easy Pieces" instead.
1977 96m/C Alex Karras, Susan Anspach, Nicholas Colasanto, Tracy Walter; *D:* Walter Doniger. **VHS, Beta** *NO* 🐾

The Mad Butcher Typically unhinged mental patient seeks teenage flesh for his various instruments of torture and death. Buono has never been more imposing.
1972 (R) 90m/C Victor Buono, Karin Field, Brad Harris; *D:* John Zuru. **VHS, Beta** *GHV, MRV* 🐾

Mad Death The British Isles take extreme steps to quarantine themselves against rabies from the European continent. This condensed TV miniseries preys on fears of the worst, as an outbreak of the virus spreads from dogs and other pets to humans, and special commandoes are mobilized.
1985 120m/C VHS $49.95 *FCT* 🐾🐾

Mad Doctor of Blood Island Dull band of travelers arrive on mysterious tropical island and encounter bloodthirsty creature. Warning: This film is not recognized for outstanding achievements in acting, dialogue, or cinematography. *AKA:* Tomb of the Living Dead; Blood Doctor.
1969 110m/C John Ashley; *D:* Gerardo (Gerry) De Leon. **VHS, Beta** *NO Woof!*

Mad Dog An escaped convict seeks revenge on the cop responsible for his imprisonment.
1984 90m/C Helmut Berger, Marisa Mell; *D:* Sergio Grieco. **VHS, Beta $24.95** *VDC Woof!*

Mad Dog and Glory Cast against type, Murray and De Niro play each other's straight man in this dark romantic comedy. Meek "Mad Dog" (De Niro) is an off-duty police photographer who happens upon a convenience store robbery and manages to save the life of Frank (Murray), obnoxious gangster by day, obnoxious stand-up comic by night. To settle up, Frank offers him Glory (Thurman), for a week. Eventually, Frank wants Glory back, forcing wimpy Mad Dog to either confront or surrender. Directed by McNaughton, who established himself with "Henry: Portrait of a Serial Killer." Uneven and not of the knee-slapper ilk, but the performances are tight, including "NYPD Blue" Caruso as a cop buddy of De Niro's.
1993 (R) 97m/C Robert De Niro, Uma Thurman, Bill Murray, David Caruso, Mike Starr, Tom Towles, Kathy Baker, Derek Anunciation, J.J. Johnston, Richard Belzer; *D:* John McNaughton; *W:* Richard Price. **VHS $95.95** *MCA, FCT* 🐾🐾🐾

Mad Dog Morgan Hopper delivers as engaging outlaw roaming outlands of nineteenth-century Australia. Quirky and violent G'day man. Based on a true story. *AKA:* Mad Dog.
1976 (R) 93m/C Dennis Hopper, David Gulpilil; *D:* Philippe Mora. **VHS, Beta $59.99** *SIM* 🐾🐾½

The Mad Executioners Scotland Yard inspector searches for a sex maniac who decapitates women. In the meantime, a group of vigilantes capture criminals and sentence them without a trial. Confusing film with a predictable ending. Based on the book "White Carpet" by Bryan Edgar Wallace. **AKA:** Der Henker Von London.
1965 92m/B Hansjorg Felmy, Maria Perschy, Dieter Borsche, Rudolph Forster, Chris Howland, Wolfgang Preiss; **D:** Edwin Zbonek. **VHS $16.95** *SNC* ✍✍

The Mad Ghoul Mad scientist (is there any other kind?) Dr. Morris (Zucco) is researching an ancient Egyptian gas that causes paralysis, turning victims into obedient zombies. Morris exposes his innocent assistant Ted (Bruce) to the gas, making Ted dependent on the antidote serum made from newly dead hearts. Poor Ted's fiance Isabel (Ankers) just can't understand what's the matter.
1943 66m/B George Zucco, David Bruce, Evelyn Ankers, Turhan Bey, Robert Armstrong, Milburn Stone, Charles McGraw, Rose Hobart; **D:** James Hogan; **W:** Brenda Weisberg, Paul Gangelin. **VHS $14.98** *MCA* ✍✍½

Mad Love A brilliant surgeon (Lorre) falls madly in love with an actress, but she rebuffs him. When her pianist husband's hands are cut off in a train accident, Lorre agrees to attach new hands, using those of a recently executed murderer. Lorre then kills the man's stepfather, and to drive him crazy uses psychological terror to make the pianist think he killed him. There's also an appearance by the supposedly executed murderer who shows up to reclaim his hands. A real chiller about obsessive love and psychological fear. The only downfall to this one is the unnecessary comic relief by Healy. Lorre's first American film. **AKA:** The Hands of Orlac.
1935 70m/B Peter Lorre, Colin Clive, Frances Drake, Ted Healy, Edward Brophy, Sara Haden, Henry Kolker; **D:** Karl Freund. **VHS $19.98** *MGM* ✍✍✍

Mad Max Set on the stark highways of the post-nuclear future, an ex-cop seeks personal revenge against a rovin' band of vicious outlaw bikers who killed his wife and child. Futuristic scenery and excellent stunt work make for an exceptionally entertaining action-packed adventure. Followed by "Road Warrior" (also known as "Mad Max 2") in 1981 and "Mad Max Beyond Thunderdome" in 1985.
1980 (R) 93m/C Mel Gibson, Joanne Samuel, Hugh Keays-Byrne, Steve Bisley, Tim Burns, Roger Ward; **D:** George Miller; **W:** George Miller. **VHS, Beta $29.98** *LIV, VES* ✍✍✍½

Mad Max: Beyond Thunderdome Max drifts into evil town ruled by Turner and becomes gladiator, then gets dumped in desert and is rescued by band of feral orphans. Third in a bleak, extremely violent, often exhilirating series.
1985 (PG-13) 107m/C Mel Gibson, Tina Turner, Helen Buday, Frank Thring, Bruce Spence, Robert Grubb, Angelo Rossitto, Angry Anderson, George Spartels, Rod Zuanic; **D:** George Miller; **W:** George Miller, Terry Hayes; **M:** Maurice Jarre. **VHS, Beta, 8mm $19.98** *WAR* ✍✍½

Mad Miss Manton A socialite turns detective to solve murder. Pleasant comedy-mystery provides occasional laughs and suspense.
1938 80m/B Barbara Stanwyck, Henry Fonda, Hattie McDaniel, Sam Levene, Miles Mander, Charles Halton; **D:** Leigh Jason. **VHS, Beta $39.95** *RKO, TTC* ✍✍

Mad Mission 3 Chinese man vacationing in Paris becomes involved in plot to recover precious jewels stolen from England's royal crown. Has there already been "Mad Mission" and "Mad Mission 2"?
1984 81m/C Richard Kiel, Sam Kui, Karl Muka, Sylvia Chang, Tsuneharu Sugiyama. **VHS, Beta** *NO* ✍✍½

The Mad Monster This "Wolf Man"-inspired cheapie looks like a misty relic today. A mad scientist furthers the war effort by injecting wolf's blood into a handyman, who becomes hairy and anti-social.
1942 77m/B Johnny Downs, George Zucco, Anne Nagel, Sarah Padden, Glenn Strange, Gordon DeMain, Mae Busch; **D:** Sam Newfield. **VHS $15.95** *NOS, LOO, VCN* ✍½

Mad Monster Party Frankenstein is getting older and wants to retire from the responsibilities of being senior monster, so he calls a convention of creepy creatures to decide who should take his place—The Wolfman, Dracula, the Mummy, the Creature, It, the Invisible Man, or Dr. Jekyll and Mr. Hyde. Animated feature using the process of "Animagic."
1968 94m/C **D:** Jules Bass; **V:** Boris Karloff, Ethel Ennis, Phyllis Diller. **VHS, Beta $9.95** *COL, SUE* ✍✍½

Mad Wax: The Surf Movie A flimsy plot about a window-cleaner who discovers a magical surfing wax serves as a framework for lots and lots of scenes of surfin' dudes.
1990 45m/C Richard Cram, Marvin Foster, Aaron Napolean, Tom Carroll, Bryce Andrews, Ross Clarke-Jones; **D:** Michael Hohensee. **VHS, Beta $14.95** *FCT* ✍

The Mad Whirl The Roarin' Twenties are a mad mad whirl in this silent silent piece of period period.
1925 80m/B Myrtle Stedman, Barbara Bedford, Alec B. Francis, George Fawcett, Joseph Singleton. **VHS, Beta $17.95** *GPV, FCT* ✍½

Mad Youth A teenage girl falls in love with a man whom her slutty, alcoholic mother had been chasing. Bottom of the barrel production provides many unintentional laughs. Extraneous South American dance sequences included as character development.
1940 61m/B Mary Ainslee, Betty Atkinson, Willy Castello, Betty Compson, Tommy Wonder; **D:** Willis Kent; **W:** Willis Kent. **VHS, Beta $16.95** *SNC* Woof!

Madam Satan Extremely bizarre DeMille film highlighted by lavish musical numbers and outrageous costumes. Wealthy socialite realizes she's losing her husband to a young showgirl, so she disguises herself as a sultry French tramp and entices her husband at a masquerade party aboard a zeppelin—surely one of the wildest party scenes ever captured on film. Chorus girls perform several exotic dance numbers inside the airship that are nothing short of fantastic. A storm breaks out and the floating dirigible is struck by lightning—leading viewers to wonder if the mad party-goers will make it to safety or crash and burn like this pic did at the box office.
1930 115m/B Kay Johnson, Reginald Denny, Lillian Roth, Roland Young, Boyd Irwin, Elsa Peterson; **D:** Cecil B. DeMille. **VHS $19.98** *MGM* ✍✍½

Madame Bovary A young adultress with delusions of romantic love finds only despair in this offbeat adaptation of Flaubert's masterpiece. In French with English subtitles.
1934 102m/B Pierre Renoir, Valentine Tessier, Max Dearly; **D:** Jean Renoir. **VHS, Beta $59.95** *HTV, ING* ✍✍✍

Madame Bovary Young adultress with delusions of romantic love finds only despair, even in this Hollywood version of Flaubert's classic. Mason/Flaubert is put on trial for indecency following publication of the novel, with the story told from the witness stand. While this device occasionally slows the narrative, astute direction helps the plot along. Minnelli's handling of the celebrated ball sequence is superb.
1949 115m/B Jennifer Jones, Van Heflin, Louis Jourdan, James Mason, Gene Lockhart, Gladys Cooper, George Zucco; **D:** Vincente Minnelli; **M:** Miklos Rozsa. **VHS, Beta $19.98** *MGM, CCB* ✍✍✍

Madame Bovary Provincial 19th century France is the setting for the tragedy of a romantic woman. Emma Bovary is bored by her marriage to an unsuccessful country doctor and longs for passion and excitement. She allows herself to be seduced (and abandoned) by a local aristocrat and herself seduces a young banker. She also struggles with an increasing burden of debt as she continues her quest for luxury. Realizing she will never find the passion she desires, Emma takes drastic, and tragic, measures. Sumptuous-looking film, with an extraordinary performance by Huppert. In French with English subtitles. Based on the novel by Gustave Flaubert.
1991 (PG-13) 130m/C Isabelle Huppert, Jean-Francois Balmer, Christophe MaLavoy, Jean Yanne; **D:** Claude Chabrol; **W:** Claude Chabrol; **M:** Matthieu Chabrol. **VHS $14.98** *REP, ING, BTV* ✍✍✍½

Madame Curie The film biography of Madame Marie Curie, the woman who discovered Radium. A deft portrayal by Garson, who is reteamed with her "Mrs. Miniver" co-star, Pidgeon. Certainly better than most biographies from this time period and more truthful as well.
1943 124m/B Greer Garson, Walter Pidgeon, Robert Walker, May Whitty, Henry Travers, Sir C. Aubrey Smith, Albert Basserman, Victor Francen, Reginald Owen, Van Johnson; **D:** Mervyn LeRoy. **VHS $19.98** *MGM, CCB* ✍✍✍

Madame Rosa An aging Jewish prostitute tends prostitutes' offspring in this warmhearted work. A survivor of the Holocaust, the old woman finds her spirit revived by one of her charges—an abandoned Arab boy. In French with English subtitles. **AKA:** La Vie Devant Soi.
1977 (PG) 105m/C Simone Signoret, Claude Dauphin; **D:** Moshe Mizrahi. **VHS, Beta $59.95** *HTV, VES* ✍✍✍

Madame Sin Aspiring world dominator enlists former CIA agent in scheme to obtain nuclear submarine. Davis is appealing as evil personified, in her first television movie.
1971 91m/C Bette Davis, Robert Wagner; **D:** David Greene; **M:** Michael Gibbs. **VHS, Beta $9.99** *CCB, FOX* ✍✍½

Madame Sousatzka Eccentric, extroverted piano teacher helps students develop spiritually as well as musically. When she engages a teenage Indian student, however, she finds herself considerably challenged. MacLaine is perfectly cast in this powerful, winning film.
1988 (PG-13) 113m/C Shirley MacLaine, Peggy Ashcroft, Shabana Azmi, Twiggy, Leigh Lawson, Geoffrey Bayldon, Navin Chowdhry, Lee Montague; **D:** John Schlesinger; **W:** Ruth Prawer Jhabvala, John Schlesinger; **M:** Gerald Gouriet. **VHS, Beta $19.95** *MCA* ✍✍✍

Madame X Fourth version of this classic tearjerker finds diplomat's wife George having a fling with a playboy. There's a murder and she turns to her nasty mother-in-law for aid. She arranges for daughter-in-law-dear-

est's "death" in order to prevent a scandal. Then George is on the slippery path to alcoholism and prostitution. Adapted from the play by Alexandre Bisson. Run-of-the-mill; Lana Turner's 1966 version is still the one to watch.
1937 96m/B Gladys George, John Beal, Warren William, Reginald Owen, William Henry, Henry Daniell, Philip Reed, Lynne Carver, Emma Dunn, Ruth Hussey; **D:** Sam Wood; **W:** John Meehan. **VHS $29.98** MGM ♫♫½

Madame X Turner is perfectly cast in this oft-filmed melodrama about a social outcast who is tried for murder and defended by her unknowing son, who believes her long dead. Bennett's last film. **AKA:** Absinthe.
1966 100m/C Lana Turner, John Forsythe, Ricardo Montalban, Burgess Meredith, Virginia Grey, Constance Bennett, Keir Dullea; **D:** David Lowell Rich. **VHS, Beta $14.95** MCA ♫♫

M.A.D.D.: Mothers Against Drunk Driving Emotionally gripping television movie recounts the story of Candy Lightner, who, after her daughter was killed in a drunk driving accident, founded M.A.D.D. and built it into a nationwide organization. Similar to "License to Kill," which dramatized the effect that a drunk driving accident can have on the families of those involved.
1983 97m/C Mariette Hartley, Paula Prentiss, Bert Remsen; **D:** William A. Graham; **M:** Bruce Broughton. **VHS, Beta $39.95** MCA ♫♫½

Made for Each Other Newlyweds must overcome meddlesome in-laws, poverty, and even serious illness in this classic melodrama. Dated but appealing.
1939 85m/B James Stewart, Carole Lombard, Charles Coburn, Lucile Watson; **D:** John Cromwell. **VHS, Beta $9.95** CNG, MRV, NOS ♫♫♫

Made for Love Couple journeys romantically in Egypt until disaster strikes: they fall into a tomb and can't get out.
1926 65m/B Leatrice Joy, Edmund Burns, Ethel Wales, Brandon Hurst, Frank Butler; **D:** Paul Sloane. **VHS, Beta $16.00** GPV, FCT ♫½

Made in America High-energy, lightweight comedy stars Whoopi Goldberg as a single mom whose daughter Long discovers her birth was the result of artifical insemination. More surprising is her biological dad: white, obnoxious, country-western car dealer Danson. Overwrought with obvious gags, basically a one-joke movie. Nonetheless, Goldberg and Danson chemically connect onscreen (and for a short time offscreen as well) while supporting actor Smith grabs comedic attention as Teacake, Long's best friend. Both Goldberg and Danson deserve better material.
1993 (PG-13) 111m/C Whoopi Goldberg, Ted Danson, Will Smith, Nia Long, Paul Rodriguez, Jennifer Tilly, Peggy Rea, Clyde Kusatsu; **D:** Richard Benjamin; **W:** Holly Goldberg Sloan; **M:** Mark Isham. **VHS, Beta $34.98** WAR ♫♫

Made in Argentina An Argentinean couple living in New York decide to return for a visit. Having left for political reasons, they still harbor bitterness.
1986 90m/C Luis Brandoni, Marta Bianchi, Leonor Manso; **D:** Juan Jose Jusid. **VHS, Beta $69.98** VES ♫♫

Made in Heaven Arid comedy in which British newlyweds try to sustain honeymoon for entire year. The bride, however, eventually suspects her husband of shenanigans with the maid. If this sounds good, then you may like it.
1952 90m/C Petula Clark, David Tomlinson, Sonja Ziemann, A.E. Matthews; **D:** John Paddy Carstairs. **VHS, Beta $29.98** HMV ♫♫

Made in Heaven Two souls in heaven fall in love and must find each other after being reborn on Earth if they are to remain eternal lovers. Contains ethereal interpretations of heaven and several cameo appearances by famous actors and musicians.
1987 (PG) 105m/C Timothy Hutton, Kelly McGillis, Maureen Stapleton, Mare Winningham, Ann Wedgeworth, Don Murray, Amanda Plummer, Timothy Daly, Marj Dusay; **Cameos:** Ellen Barkin, Neil Young, Tom Petty, Ric Ocasek, Tom Robbins, Debra Winger, Gary Larsen, David Rasche; **D:** Alan Rudolph; **W:** Raynold Gideon, Bruce A. Evans; **M:** Mark Isham. **VHS, Beta $14.95** WAR, LHV ♫♫

Made in USA Wayward dudes engage vixen while cruising Midwest. Trouble, however, awaits. Note: This is not Godard's midsixties classic.
1988 (R) 82m/C Adrian Pasdar, Lori Singer, Christopher Penn; **D:** Ken Friedman; **W:** Ken Friedman. **VHS, Beta $19.98** SUE, NLC ♫½

Madeleine Courtroom drama of woman charged with poisoning her French lover in 1850s Scotland. Directed by the same David Lean who made "Bridge on the River Kwai" and "Lawrence of Arabia". Here, though, he was merely trying to provide a vehicle for his wife, actress Todd. Intrigued? **AKA:** The Strange Case of Madeleine.
1950 114m/B Ann Todd, Leslie Banks, Ivan Desny; **D:** David Lean. **VHS, Beta $14.95** LCA ♫♫½

Mademoiselle Moreau is a psychotic, sexually repressed schoolteacher in a small village who manages to keep herself under control until studly woodcutter Manni and his son take up residence. The locals distrust the stranger but Moreau can't wait to get her hands on him. Suddenly, the village is battered by a rash of poisonings, fires, and floods, all of which are blamed on Manni, leading the locals to exact a terrible vengeance. In French with English subtitles.
1966 105m/B Jeanne Moreau, Ettore Manni, Umberto Orsini, Keith Skinner, Jane Berretta, Mony Rey; **D:** Tony Richardson; **W:** Jean Genet. **VHS $19.98** MGM, FCT ♫♫

Mademoiselle Fifi Simon stars as a French laundress in 1870 France who refuses to give in to her small town's Prussian oppressors. The film title is the nickname of the most brutal of the Prussian officers, played by Kreuger. An unsuccessful attempt at political allegory for the devastation of WWII.
1944 69m/B Simone Simon, John Emery, Kurt Kreuger, Alan Napier, Jason Robards Sr.; **D:** Robert Wise. **VHS, Beta $19.98** FCT ♫½

Mademoiselle Striptease Bardot stars as a young woman who finds a valuable stolen book. Her attempts to disassociate herself from the actual theft are supposed to be funny. Bardot is characteristically appealing. **AKA:** Please! Mr. Balzac; While Plucking the Daisy; En Effeuillant la Marguerite.
1957 100m/B Brigitte Bardot, Robert Hirsch, Daniel Gelin; **D:** Marc Allegret. **VHS, Beta $29.95** STV, MRV ♫♫½

Madhouse A troubled horror film star tries to bring his "Dr. Death" character to television, but during production people begin dying in ways remarkably similar to the script. A strong genre cast should hold the fans' attention during this mild adaptation of Angus Hall's novel "Devilday."
1974 92m/C Vincent Price, Peter Cushing, Robert Quarry, Adrienne Corri, Natasha Pyne, Linda Hayden, Michael Parkinson; **D:** Jim Clark. **VHS, Beta** HBO ♫♫

Madhouse A woman has bizarre recollections of her twin sister whom she finally meets when she escapes from a mental hospital. Lots of violence and gore, has definite cult potential.
1987 90m/C Trish Everly, Michael MacRae, Dennis Robertson, Morgan Hart; **D:** Ovidio G. Assonitis. **VHS, Beta** NO ♫♫

Madhouse New homeowners find themselves unable to expel loathsome, boorish guests. Presumably, a comedy cashing in on two of sitcom's brightest lights.
1990 (PG-13) 90m/C John Larroquette, Kirstie Alley, Alison La Placa, John Diehl, Jessica Lundy, Bradley Gregg, Dennis Miller, Robert Ginty; **D:** Tom Ropelewski; **W:** Tom Ropelewski. **VHS, Beta $9.98** ORI ♫♫

Madhouse Mansion A horror actor revives his career and becomes embroiled in murder. Plenty of in-jokes and clips from older movies. **AKA:** Ghost Story.
1974 (PG) 86m/C Marianne Faithfull, Leigh Lawson, Anthony Bate, Larry Dann, Sally Grace, Penelope Keith, Vivian Mackerell, Murray Melvin, Barbara Shelley; **D:** Stephen Weeks. **VHS** NO ♫♫½

Madigan Realistic and exciting and among the best of the behind-the-scenes urban police thrillers. Hardened NYC detectives (Widmark and Guardino) lose their guns to a sadistic killer and are given 72 hours to track him down. Fonda is the police chief none to pleased with their performance. Adapted by Howard Rodman, Abraham Polonsky, and Harry Kleiner from Richard Dougherty's "The Commissioner."
1968 101m/C Richard Widmark, Henry Fonda, Inger Stevens, Harry Guardino, James Whitmore, Susan Clark, Michael Dunn, Don Stroud; **D:** Don Siegel; **W:** Abraham Polonsky. **VHS, Beta $14.98** MCA ♫♫♫

Madigan's Millions Incompetent Treasury agent treks to Italy to recover funds swiped from deceased gangster. This is Hoffman's first film, and is to his career what "The Last Chalice" was to Paul Newman's and "Studs and Kitty" was Sylvester Stallone. Recommended only to the terminally foolhardy.
1967 (G) 89m/C Dustin Hoffman, Elsa Martinelli, Cesar Romero; **D:** Stanley Prager. **VHS, Beta $59.95** RHI Woof!

Madman Deranged Soviet Jew joins Israeli army to more effectively fulfill his desire to kill loathsome Soviets. Good date movie for those nights when you're home alone. Weaver's first starring role.
1979 (R) 95m/C Sigourney Weaver, Michael Beck, F. Murray Abraham; **D:** Dan Cohen. **VHS, Beta $19.95** CNG ♫

Madman Camp leader prompts terror when he revives legend regarding ax murderer. Seems that when you call his name, he appears. Buffoon does not believe story and calls out madman's name. Madman hears the call and emerges from forest, says hi, and hacks everyone to death. Lesson learned, case closed. Filmed on Long Island.
1982 (R) 89m/C Alexis Dubin, Tony Fish. **VHS, Beta $69.99** HHE ♫

Mado A middle-aged businessman's life is undone when he falls for a mysterious woman. Piccoli and Schneider are, as usual, convincing. Another of underrated director Sautet's effective, low-key works. In French with subtitles.
1976 130m/C Romy Schneider, Michel Piccoli, Charles Denner; **D:** Claude Sautet. **VHS, Beta $59.95** FCT ♫♫♫

Madron Road western filmed in the Israel desert, complete with menacing Apaches, wagon train massacre, a nun and a gunslinger.
1970 (PG) 93m/C Richard Boone, Leslie Caron, Paul Smith; *D:* Jerry Hopper. **VHS, Beta $59.95** *VCI* 🎬½

The Madwoman of Chaillot Four men conspire to drill for oil which they believe lurks under Paris. Hepburn finds out about their plot and tells each man that oil is bubbling up through her basement. Before the men can arrive at her house to confirm this, she and her three cronies hold a mock trial and sentence the men to death. Features a stellar cast, but this modern-day adaptation of Jean Giraudoux's play ''La Folle de Chaillot'' falls flat.
1969 (G) 142m/C Katharine Hepburn, Charles Boyer, Claude Dauphin, Edith Evans, John Gavin, Paul Henreid, Oscar Homolka, Margaret Leighton, Giulietta Masina, Nanette Newman, Richard Chamberlain, Yul Brynner, Donald Pleasence, Danny Kaye, Fernand Gravet; *D:* Bryan Forbes; *W:* Edward Anhalt. **VHS** *WAR* 🎬½

Mae West This made-for-television film details West's life from her humble beginnings to her racy film stardom. Jillian does a good job bringing the buxom legend back to life.
1984 97m/C Ann Jillian, James Brolin, Piper Laurie, Roddy McDowall; *D:* Lee Philips; *M:* Brad Fiedel. **VHS, Beta $59.95** *LHV* 🎬🎬½

Maedchen in Uniform A scandalous early German talkie about a rebellious schoolgirl who falls in love with a female teacher and commits suicide when the teacher is punished for the relationship. A controversial criticism of lesbianism and militarism that impelled the Nazis, rising to power two years later, to exile its director. It was also banned in the United States. In German with English subtitles. Remade in 1965. *AKA:* Girls in Uniform.
1931 90m/B Dorothea Wieck, Ellen Schwannecke, Hertha Thiele; *D:* Leontine Sagan. **VHS, Beta $29.98** *SUE, MRV, ING* 🎬🎬🎬½

Mafia la Ley Que Non Perdona A Mafia kingpin struggles to maintain his power through violence. Dubbed into Spanish.
1979 90m/C Gordon Mitchell, Antonella Lualdi. **VHS, Beta** *NO* 🎬½

Mafia Princess The daughter of a Mafia boss tries to discover her own identity despite her father's involvement in crime. Based on a best-selling autobiography by a real-life member of a Mob family, Antoinette Giancana. Made for television.
1986 100m/C Tony Curtis, Susan Lucci, Kathleen Widdoes, Chuck Shamata, Louie Dibianco; *D:* Robert Collins. **VHS** *NO* 🎬🎬

Mafia vs. Ninja The mob wants to control the city, but the Ninja has other ideas.
1984 90m/C Alexander Lou, Silvio Azzolini, Wang Hsia, Charlema Hsu, Eugene Trammel. **VHS, Beta** *NO* 🎬½

Magdalene Somewhere in medieval Europe, a violent Baron seeks revenge on a beautiful whore that spurned him. Small-budget costumer.
1988 (PG) 89m/C Steve Bond, Nastassia Kinski, David Warner, Gunter Meisner, Ferdinand ''Ferdy'' Mayne, Anthony Quayle, Franco Nero, Janet Agren; *D:* Monica Teuber. **VHS, Beta $89.99** *PAR, FCT* 🎬½

Magee and the Lady The crusty captain of a rusty ship must warm up to a spoiled debutante or lose his ship to a foreclosure firm. Could be better. Made for TV. *AKA:* She'll Be Sweet.

1978 (PG) 92m/C Tony LoBianco, Sally Kellerman; *D:* Gene Levitt. **VHS, Beta $19.95** *ACA* 🎬

Magic Ventriloquist Hopkins and his dummy, an all-too-human counterpart, get involved with a beautiful but impressionable woman lost between reality and the irresistible world of illusion. Spine-chilling psychodrama with a less-than-believable premise. Screenplay by Goldman from his novel.
1978 (R) 106m/C Anthony Hopkins, Ann-Margret, Burgess Meredith, Ed Lauter; *D:* Richard Attenborough; *W:* William Goldman; *M:* Jerry Goldsmith. **VHS, Beta $14.98** *SUE, NLC* 🎬🎬½

The Magic Bubble On her 40th birthday, Julia Cole finds the fountain of youth...inside a bottle of enchanted bubbles. Ageless and timeless, she begins to know the meaning of true happiness.
1993 (PG-13) 90m/C Diane Salinger, John Calvin, Priscilla Pointer, Colleen Camp, Tony Peck, Wallace Shawn; *D:* Alfredo Ringel, Deborah Taper Ringel; *W:* Meredith Baer, Geof Pryssir. **VHS $89.95** *MNC* 🎬🎬½

The Magic Christian A series of related skits about a rich man (Sellers) and his son (Starr) who try to prove that anyone can be bought. Raucous, now somewhat dated comedy; music by Badfinger, including Paul McCartney's ''Come and Get It.''
1969 (PG) 101m/C Peter Sellers, Ringo Starr, Isabel Jeans, Wilfrid Hyde-White, Graham Chapman, John Cleese, Peter Graves, John Lennon, Yoko Ono, Richard Attenborough, Leonard Frey, Laurence Harvey, Christopher Lee, Spike Milligan, Yul Brynner, Roman Polanski, Raquel Welch; *D:* Joseph McGrath; *W:* Terry Southern. **VHS, Beta $59.98** *REP, MRV* 🎬🎬🎬

The Magic Flute Bergman's acclaimed version of Mozart's famous comic opera, universally considered one of the greatest adaptations of opera to film ever made. Staged before a live audience for Swedish television. In Swedish with English subtitles.
1973 (G) 134m/C Josef Kostlinger, Irma Urrila, Hakan Hagegard, Elisabeth Erikson; *D:* Ingmar Bergman. **VHS, Beta $29.95** *HMV, PAR, MVD* 🎬🎬🎬

The Magic Fountain Three princes search for a magic fountain whose waters will cure their ailing father. Two of them, however, take the evil course and are turned into ravens by a wicked dwarf. Based on the fairy tale ''Das Wasser des Lebens'' by the Brothers Grimm.
1961 82m/C Peter Nestler, Helmo Kinderman, Josef Marz, Catherine Hansen, Cedric Hardwicke; *D:* Allan David. **VHS $16.95** *SNC* 🎬🎬

Magic Kid Thirteen-year-old martial-arts champ Kevin and his older sister vacation in L.A., staying with their shady Uncle Bob, a second-rate talent agent. Kevin wants to meet his martial arts movie idol and his sister her favorite soap opera hunk. But they wind up being chased by the mobsters Uncle Bob owes money to. *AKA:* Ninja Dragons.
1992 (PG) 91m/C Ted Jan Roberts, Shonda Whipple, Stephen Furst, Joseph Campanella, Billy Hufsey, Sondra Kerns, Pamela Dixon, Lauren Tewes, Don ''The Dragon'' Wilson; *D:* Joseph Merhi; *W:* Stephen Smoke; *M:* Jim Halfpenny. **VHS $89.95** *PMH* 🎬🎬

The Magic Legend of the Golden Goose A retelling of the familiar brothers Grimm chestnut.
1965 72m/C **VHS, Beta** *VCI* 🎬

Magic of Lassie Stewart is engaging as the nice grandpa who refuses to sell his land to mean rich guy Roberts. Innocuous, pleasant remake of ''Lassie Come Home.''

Stewart sings, as do Pat Boone and daughter Debby.
1978 (G) 100m/C James Stewart, Mickey Rooney, Stephanie Zimbalist, Alice Faye, Pernell Roberts, Lassie; *D:* Don Chaffey. **VHS, Beta $19.98** *MGM* 🎬🎬

Magic on Love Island Romantic misadventures ensue when eight ladies go on vacation to Love Island, a tropical paradise.
1980 96m/C Adrienne Barbeau, Bill Daily, Howard Duff, Dody Goodman, Dominique Dunne, Lisa Hartman, Janis Paige; *D:* Earl Bellamy. **VHS, Beta** *NO* 🎬

Magic Serpent Fantasy set in medieval Japan features a grand duel in magic between a good hero and evil sorcerer who transform into a giant dragon and a giant frog to do battle.
1966 ?m/C **VHS $20** *SMW* 🎬

The Magic Sword A family-oriented adventure film about a young knight who sets out to rescue a beautiful princess who is being held captive by an evil sorcerer and his dragon.
1962 80m/C Basil Rathbone, Estelle Winwood, Gary Lockwood; *D:* Bert I. Gordon. **VHS, Beta $14.95** *MGM, MRV, VYY* 🎬🎬

Magic Town An opinion pollster investigates a small town which exactly reflects the views of the entire nation, making his job a cinch. The publicity causes much ado in the town with ensuing laughs. Uneven but entertaining.
1947 103m/B Jane Wyman, James Stewart, Kent Smith, Regis Toomey, Donald Meek; *D:* William A. Wellman. **VHS $19.98** *REP* 🎬🎬

The Magic Voyage Animated tale of a friendly woodworm named Pico who voyages with Columbus to the new world and convinces him that the world is indeed round. He then comes to the aid of a magical firefly named Marilyn who helps Columbus find gold to bring back to Spain.
1993 (G) 82m/C *V:* Dom DeLuise, Mickey Rooney, Corey Feldman, Irene Cara, Dan Haggerty, Samantha Eggar. **VHS $19.95** *HMD* 🎬½

The Magic Voyage of Sinbad Sinbad embarks on a fantastic journey after promising the people of his Covasian home that he will find the elusive Phoenix, the bird of happiness. Unreleased in the U.S. until 1962; rewritten for the American screen by a young Coppola. *AKA:* Sadko.
1952 79m/C Sergey Stolyarov, Alla Larionova, Mark Troyanovsky; *D:* Alexander Ptushko; *W:* Francis Ford Coppola. **VHS, Beta $16.95** *SNC* 🎬🎬

Magical Mystery Tour On the road with an oddball assortment of people, the Beatles experience a number of strange incidents around the English countryside. Originally made for British television. ♫Magical Mystery Tour; Blue Jay Way; Your Mother Should Know; The Fool on the Hill.
1967 55m/C John Lennon, George Harrison, Ringo Starr, Paul McCartney, Victor Spinetti. **VHS, Beta $19.98** *MPI, MED, WFV* 🎬

Magical Wonderland Join a handsome prince and his fair young maiden as they venture through such fairy tale classics as ''Beauty and the Beast'' and ''Sleeping Beauty.''
1985 90m/C **VHS, Beta $39.95** *VCI* 🎬🎬

The Magician A master magician in 19th century Sweden (von Sydow) wreaks ill in this darkly comical, supernatural parable. Dark, well photographed early Bergman effort. In Swedish with English subtitles.

1958 101m/B Max von Sydow, Ingrid Thulin, Gunnar Bjornstrand, Bibi Andersson, Naima Wifstrand; **D:** Ingmar Bergman; **W:** Ingmar Bergman. VHS, Beta $29.95 SUE, MRV, HHT ℐℐℐ

The Magician of Lublin Based on an unusual story by Issac Bashevis Singer. Follows the exploits of a magician/con man in turn-of-the-century Poland whose personal flaws kill his career, until a chance emerges for one last trick. A good example of movie not as good as book; this rendering is superficial, badly acted and unsatisfying. Made soon after Singer won the Nobel Prize for literature in 1978.
1979 (R) 105m/C Alan Arkin, Valerie Perrine, Louise Fletcher, Lou Jacobi, Shelley Winters; **D:** Menahem Golan; **M:** Maurice Jarre. VHS, Beta NO ℐ ½

Magnificent Adventurer Ostensibly a biography of Benvenuto Cellini, the Florentine sculptor, with a concentration on his love life and swordplay.
1976 94m/C Brett Halsey. VHS, Beta $59.95 UNI ℐ

The Magnificent Ambersons Welles' second film. A fascinating, inventive translation of the Booth Tarkington novel about a wealthy turn of the century family collapsing under the changing currents of progress. Pure Welles, except the glaringly bad tacked-on ending that the studio shot (under the direction of the great Robert Wise and Fred Fleck), after taking the film from him. It seems they wanted the proverbial happy ending. Also available on laserdisc, with interviews and the original story boards.
1942 88m/B Joseph Cotten, Anne Baxter, Tim Holt, Richard Bennett, Dolores Costello, Erskine Sanford, Ray Collins, Agnes Moorehead; **D:** Freddie Fleck, Robert Wise, Orson Welles; **W:** Orson Welles; **M:** Bernard Herrmann, Roy Webb. Academy Awards '42 Nominations: Best Black and White Cinematography, Best Interior Decoration, Best Picture, Best Supporting Actress (Moorehead); New York Film Critics Awards '42: Best Actress (Moorehead). VHS, Beta $19.95 RKO, VYG, CRC ℐℐℐℐ

The Magnificent Dope Fonda is likeable, as usual, as the hapless yokel in the big city. A trip to New York to take a course on being successful is his prize for winning a "laziest man" contest. He falls for his teacher; she uses his crush to motivate him. Funny and entertaining.
1942 83m/B Henry Fonda, Lynn Bari, Don Ameche, Edward Everett Horton, Hobart Cavanaugh, Pierre Watkin; **D:** Walter Lang. VHS TCF ℐℐ ½

The Magnificent Matador The story of an aging matador who faces death in the bullring to win the love of a woman. Quinn is the bullfighter on the horns of a dilemma. Lots of bull in script carried by harried bull in ring. **AKA:** The Brave and the Beautiful.
1955 94m/C Anthony Quinn, Maureen O'Hara, Thomas Gomez; **D:** Budd Boetticher. VHS, Beta $29.95 VHE ℐℐ ½

Magnificent Obsession A drunken playboy (Hudson) kills a man and blinds his wife in an automobile accident. Plagued by guilt, he devotes his life to studying medicine in order to restore the widow's sight. Well-acted melodrama lifted Hudson to stardom. Faithful to the 1935 original, based on a novel by Lloyd C. Douglas.
1954 108m/C Jane Wyman, Rock Hudson, Barbara Rush, Agnes Moorehead; **D:** Douglas Sirk. VHS, Beta $14.95 MCA ℐℐ ½

The Magnificent Seven Western remake of Akira Kurosawa's classic "The Seven Samurai." Mexican villagers hire gunmen to protect them from the bandits who are destroying their town. Most of the actors were relative unknowns, though not for long. Sequelled by "Return of the Seven" in 1966, "Guns of the Magnificent Seven" in 1969, and "The Magnificent Seven Ride" in 1972. Excellent score. Uncredited writing by Walter Newman and Walter Bernstein.
1960 126m/C Yul Brynner, Steve McQueen, Robert Vaughn, James Coburn, Charles Bronson, Horst Buchholz, Eli Wallach, Brad Dexter; **D:** John Sturges; **W:** William Roberts; **M:** Elmer Bernstein. VHS, Beta $19.98 MGM, FOX, TLF ℐℐℐℐ

The Magnificent Yankee Adaptation of Emmet Lavery's Broadway play on the life of Supreme Court Justice Oliver Wendell Holmes, starring Calhern (who also did the stage version). America's foremost legal mind was well-served by Calhern, with Harding as his ever-patient wife. **AKA:** The Man with Thirty Sons.
1950 80m/B Louis Calhern, Ann Harding, Eduard Franz, Philip Ober, Ian Wolfe, Edith Evanson, Richard Anderson, Jimmy Lydon, Robert Sherwood, Hugh Sanders; **D:** John Sturges; **W:** Emmet Lavery. VHS, Beta $19.98 MGM, FCT, BTV ℐℐℐ

Magnum Force Eastwood's second "Dirty Harry" movie. Harry finds a trail leading from a series of gangland killings straight back to the P.D. Less gripping than "Dirty Harry" (1971); followed by "The Enforcer" (1976), "Sudden Impact" (1983), and "The Dead Pool" (1988). Holbrook is cast intriguingly against type, and the premise is good, but little else recommends this too-violent installment.
1973 (R) 124m/C Clint Eastwood, Hal Holbrook, Mitchell Ryan, David Soul, Robert Urich, Tim Matheson, Kip Niven; **D:** Ted Post; **W:** Michael Cimino, John Milius. VHS, Beta $19.98 WAR, TLF ℐℐ

Magnum Killers A young man becomes involved in a web of deadly intrigue when he sets out to find who cheated him out of a small fortune during a card game.
1976 92m/C Sombat Methance, Prichela Lee. VHS, Beta $29.95 UNI ℐ

The Mahabharata Adapted from the myths and folklore of ancient India, the screen version of the original 9 hour stage play is the story of a devastating war between two powerful clans. Initially broadcast on public television, the 6 hour movie is divided into three 2 hour tapes, "The Game of Dice," "Exile in the Forest," and "The War."
1989 318m/C Robert Langton-Lloyd, Antonin Stahly-Vishwanadan, Bruce Myers; **D:** Peter Brook; **W:** Jean-Claude Carriere; **M:** Toshi Tsuchitori. VHS $99.95 BTV, WSH, FCT ℐ

Mahler Strange Russell effort on the life of the great composer Gustav Mahler. Imperfect script is rescued by fine acting.
1974 (PG) 110m/C Robert Powell, Georgina Hale, Richard Morant, Lee Montague, Terry O'Quinn; **D:** Ken Russell; **W:** Ken Russell. VHS, Beta NO ℐℐℐ

Mahogany Poor girl becomes world-famous high fashion model and designer, ditches boyfriend in the old neighborhood, gets a career boost when she daringly appears in a dress of her own creation at a Roman fashion show, and still yearns for the boy back home. Motown attempt to make mainstream hit that's glossy and predictable.
1975 (PG) 109m/C Diana Ross, Billy Dee Williams, Jean-Pierre Aumont, Anthony Perkins, Nina Foch; **D:** Berry Gordy. VHS, Beta $14.95 PAR, CCB, FCT ℐ ½

The Maid An offbeat comedy romance with Sheen as the house husband to Bisset's female executive character. Nice acting; charming, if unoriginal, premise.
1990 (PG) 91m/C Martin Sheen, Jacqueline Bisset, Jean-Pierre Cassel, James Faulkner, Victoria Shalet; **D:** Ian Toynton. VHS, Beta $89.98 MED, VTR ℐℐ ½

Maid to Order Rich girl Sheedy's fairy godmother puts her in her place by turning her into a maid for a snooty Malibu couple. Good-natured and well-acted if rather mindless Cinderella story.
1987 (PG) 92m/C Ally Sheedy, Beverly D'Angelo, Michael Ontkean, Dick Shawn, Tom Skerritt, Valerie Perrine; **D:** Amy Jones; **W:** Perry Howze; **M:** Georges Delerue. VHS, Beta $14.95 LIV ℐ ½

Maid's Night Out Pleasant, simple-minded mistaken-identity comedy. Fontaine is an heiress; rich-guy posing-as-milkman Lane thinks she is a maid. They fall in love, of course.
1938 64m/B Joan Fontaine, Allan "Rocky" Lane, Hedda Hopper, George Irving, William Brisbane, Billy Gilbert, Cecil Kellaway; **D:** Ben Holmes. VHS RKO, MLB ℐℐ

Maids of Wilko Wajda's adaptation of Jaroslav Iwaszkiewicz's memoirs set in the late '20s. Viktor Ruben (Olbrychski) reexamines his life following the death of a friend. He returns to the home of his aunt and uncle in Wilko where he renews friendships with five sisters on a neighboring estate in an attempt to resurrect a happier past. Lots of fruitless romantic yearning. In French and Polish with English subtitles. **AKA:** The Young Ladies of Wilko; Panny z Wilka.
1979 118m/C Daniel Olbrychski, Christine Pascal, Maja Komorowska, Anna Seniuk, Krystyna Zachwatowicz, Stanislawa Celinska, Zofia Jaroszewska, Tadeusz Bialoszczynski; **D:** Andrzej Wajda; **W:** Zbigniew Kaminski. VHS $49.95 FCT ℐℐ

The Main Event Streisand plays a wacky—and bankrupt—cosmetic executive who must depend on the career of washed-up boxer O'Neal to rebuild her fortune. Desperate (and more than a little smitten), she badgers and bullies him back into the ring. Lame, derivative screwball comedy desperate to suggest chemistry of Streisand and O'Neal's "What's Up, Doc?" (1972). Streisand sings the title song.
1979 (PG) 109m/C Barbra Streisand, Ryan O'Neal; **D:** Howard Zieff. VHS, Beta $14.95 WAR ℐℐ

Main Street to Broadway Superficial story of a struggling playwright. Interesting mainly for abundant big-name cameos. Based on a story by Robert E. Sherwood.
1953 102m/B Tom Morton, Mary Murphy, Agnes Moorehead, Herb Shriner, Rosemary DeCamp, Clinton Sundberg; **Cameos:** Lionel Barrymore, Ethel Barrymore, Tallulah Bankhead, Shirley Booth, Cornel Wilde, Rex Harrison, Joshua Logan, Helen Hayes, Mary Martin; **D:** Tay Garnett. VHS, Beta $59.95 MPI, MLB ℐℐ

Maitresse An examination of the sexual underworld in the same vein as "Blue Velvet" and "Crimes of Passion." Director Scroeder also created "Reversal of Fortune." In French with English subtitles.
1976 112m/C Gerard Depardieu; **D:** Barbet Schroeder. VHS $59.99 WAR, BTV, FCT ℐℐ ½

Major Barbara A wealthy, idealistic girl joins the Salvation Army against her father's wishes. Based on the play by George Bernard Shaw. The excellent adaptation of the original and the cast make this film a winner. Deborah Kerr's film debut.

1941 90m/B Wendy Hiller, Rex Harrison, Robert Morley, Sybil Thorndike, Deborah Kerr; *D:* Gabriel Pascal. VHS, Beta $39.95 LCA, FCT, HMV *ℐℐℐ* ½

Major Dundee A Union army officer (Heston) chases Apaches into Mexico with a motley collection of prisoner volunteers. Too long and flawed; would have been better had Peckinpah been allowed to finish the project. Excellent cast.
1965 124m/C Charlton Heston, Richard Harris, James Coburn, Jim Hutton, Ben Johnson, Slim Pickens; *D:* Sam Peckinpah. VHS, Beta $12.95 GKK *ℐℐ* ½

Major League Comedy about a pathetic major league baseball team whose new owner schemes to lose the season and relocate the team to Miami. Sheen is okay as the pitcher with control problems (both on and off the field), while Bernsen seems to be gazing affectionately at "L.A. Law" from a distance. Predictable sports spoof is good for a few laughs, particularly those scenes involving Haysbert as a slugger with voodoo on his mind (and in his locker) and Snipes as a base stealer whose only problem is getting on base.
1989 (R) 107m/C Tom Berenger, Charlie Sheen, Corbin Bernsen, James Gammon, Margaret Whitton, Bob Uecker, Rene Russo, Wesley Snipes, Dennis Haysbert, Charles Cyphers; *D:* David S. Ward; *W:* David S. Ward; *M:* James Newton Howard. VHS, Beta, 8mm $14.95 PAR *ℐℐ* ½

Major League 2 It's been five years since they won the series, and this plodding sequel finds the wacky championship Cleveland Indians ruined by success and once again struggling in last place. Limited charm of original is lost; dull and filled with lame jokes that you won't care if they manage to make it to the top again. Cast returns with the exception of Wesley Snipes as Willie Mae Hays (now played by Epps).
1994 (PG) 105m/C Charlie Sheen, Tom Berenger, Corbin Bernsen, James Gammon, Dennis Haysbert, Omar Epps, David Keith, Bob Uecker, Alison Doody, Michelle Burke, Margaret Whitton, Eric Bruskotter, Takaaki Ishibashi; *D:* David S. Ward; *W:* R.J. Stewart; *M:* Michel Colombier. VHS WAR *ℐ* ½

The Majorettes Eek! Someone is lurking around a high school murdering the majorettes with their own batons. A barebones plot lurks within this otherwise worthless pic.
1987 (R) 93m/C Kevin Kindlan, Terrie Godfrey, Mark V. Jevicky; *D:* John Russo. VHS, Beta $69.98 LIV, VES, TEM *ℐ*

Make a Million The Depression is played (successfully) for yuks in this tale of an economics professor fired from his post for advocating radical income redistribution. He doesn't get mad, he gets even: he makes a million by advertising for money.
1935 66m/B Charles Starrett, Pauline Brooks. VHS, Beta $24.95 VYY *ℐℐ*

Make a Wish A noted composer goes stale in this colorful musical about backstage life. The comic relief provides the films best moments. ♫Music In My Heart; My Campfire Dreams; Make a Wish; Old Man Rip.
1937 80m/B Basil Rathbone, Leon Errol, Bobby Breen, Ralph Forbes; *D:* Kurt Neumann; *M:* Oscar Strauss. VHS, Beta $24.95 VYY *ℐℐ*

Make Haste to Live Good, scary thriller. A woman survives attempted murder by her husband; moves far away to raise their infant daughter. He does time, then returns for revenge. McGuire is good as the terrorized wife.

1954 90m/B Dorothy McGuire, Stephen McNally, Edgar Buchanan, John Howard; *D:* William A. Seiter; *M:* Elmer Bernstein. VHS $19.98 REP *ℐℐ* ½

Make Me an Offer Somewhat slow-moving comedy centering on an antique dealer who attempts to buy an expensive vase from an old man. From the novel by Wolf Mankowitz.
1955 88m/C Peter Finch, Adrienne Corri, Rosalie Crutchley, Finlay Currie; *D:* Cyril Frankel. VHS $59.98 SUE *ℐℐ*

Make Me an Offer Made-for-TV movie about selling real estate in Hollywood. Better than similar efforts.
1980 97m/C Susan Blakely, Stella Stevens, Patrick O'Neal; *D:* Jerry Paris; *M:* Ralph Burns. VHS, Beta $59.98 NLC *ℐℐ* ½

Make Mine Mink Oft-hilarious British comedy about guests at an elegant but run-down mansion who become unlikely thieves, stealing furs for charity. Good cast headed by Terry-Thomas.
1960 100m/C Terry-Thomas, Billie Whitelaw, Hattie Jacques; *D:* Robert Asher. VHS, Beta NO *ℐℐℐ*

Make Room for Tomorrow Subtle, somewhat funny French comedy about generations in a family. A man in mid-life crisis has to cope with his father, son, and grandfather on the grandfather's 90th birthday.
1981 (R) 106m/C Victor Lanoux, Jane Birkin, George Wilson; *D:* Peter Kassovitz. VHS, Beta $29.95 SUE *ℐℐ*

Make-Up A doctor turned circus clown uses his medical skills when an elephant renders a society girl unconscious. After she awakens the two become involved. The clown's daughter objects, but is soon caught up in an accusation that she murdered the lion tamer. Her father the clown tries to save the day. Predictable doctor/clown relationship.
1937 72m/B Nils Asther, June Clyde, Judy Kelly, Kenne Duncan, John Turnbull; *D:* Alfred Zeisler. VHS $24.95 NOS, DVT, HEG *ℐℐ*

Making Contact A small boy's telekinetic powers enable him to bring to life his favorite toys. The ridicule he endures because of this leads him to set off on terrifying adventures with only his toys and a friend for company.
1986 (PG) 83m/C Joshua Morrell, Eve Kryll; *D:* Roland Emmerich. VHS, Beta $14.95 NWV, STE *ℐ* ½

Making Love A closet homosexual risks his 8-year marriage by getting involved with a carefree writer. What could be a powerful subject gets bland treatment.
1982 (R) 112m/C Kate Jackson, Harry Hamlin, Michael Ontkean, Wendy Hiller, Arthur Hill, Nancy Olson, Terry Kiser, Camilla Carr, Michael Dudikoff; *D:* Arthur Hiller; *W:* Barry Sandler. VHS, Beta $69.98 FOX *ℐℐ*

Making Mr. Right Under-rated satire about a high-powered marketing and image consultant who falls in love with the android that she's supposed to be promoting. Unbelievable comedy is shaky at times, but Magnuson and Malkovich create some magic.
1986 (PG-13) 95m/C John Malkovich, Ann Magnuson, Glenne Headly, Ben Masters, Laurie Metcalf, Polly Bergen, Hart Bochner, Polly Draper, Susan Anton; *D:* Susan Seidelman. VHS, Beta $19.99 HBO *ℐℐ*

The Making of "A Brief History of Time" A behind-the-scenes look at Morris' film, based on the best-seller by physicist Stephen Hawking. Includes interviews with the director and producers.
1992 30m/C *D:* Errol Morris. VHS PAR *ℐℐ* ½

The Making of a Legend: "Gone With the Wind" An exhaustive tribute to the American classic on its 50th anniversary, featuring miles of film clips, wardrobe tests, interviews with surviving cast and crew members, and scads of production trivia.
1989 130m/C Clark Gable, Vivien Leigh, Carole Lombard, Laurence Olivier, David O. Selznick, Margaret Mitchell, Ann Rutherford, Butterfly McQueen, Evelyn Keyes, Leslie Howard, Olivia de Havilland, Thomas Mitchell, Ona Munson, Ward Bond, Hattie McDaniel, Victor Fleming, Sam Wood, George Cukor, Paulette Goddard, Lana Turner, Jean Arthur, Joan Bennett, Tallulah Bankhead, Melvyn Douglas, George Reeves, Fred Crane. VHS, Beta $29.95 MGM *ℐℐ* ½

The Making of The Hitchhiker's Guide to the Galaxy A behind-the-scenes look at the British science fiction comedy covering a year in the television production of author Douglas Adams' novels. Includes interviews with cast and crew.
1987 ?m/C Simon Jones, David Dixon, Sandra Dickinson, Mark Wing-Davey; *D:* Alan J.W. Bell. VHS $14.98 FOX *ℐℐ* ½

Making the Grade Jersey tough kid owes the mob; attends prep school in place of a rich kid who can't be bothered. Better than similar '80s teen flicks, but not by much. *AKA:* Preppies.
1984 (PG) 105m/C Judd Nelson, Joanna Lee, Dana Olsen, Ronald Lacey, Scott McGinnis, Gordon Jump, Carey Scott, Andrew Dice Clay; *D:* Dorian Walker; *W:* Gene Quintano. VHS, Beta $79.95 MGM *ℐℐ*

The Makioka Sisters Much praised drama centering around the lives of four Japanese sisters who are heiresses to the family fortune and, hence, must be found proper husbands. The efforts of the older sisters to "match" their younger siblings are entwined with a gradual realization on the part of the elders that the quiet way of life representative of their own formative years is passing away with the advent of WWII. The movie is as visually stunning as it is poignant. In Japanese with English subtitles.
1983 140m/C Keiko Kishi, Yoshiko Sakuma, Sayuri Yoshinaga; *D:* Kon Ichikawa. VHS $59.99 FCT, ING, TPV *ℐℐℐ*

Malarek Tough Montreal journalist Victor Malarek exposed abuse in that city's teen detention center in his book "Hey, Malarek." Compelling lead performance from Koteas in decent though not great screen adaptation.
1989 (R) 95m/C Michael Sarrazin, Elias Koteas, Al Waxman, Kerrie Keane; *D:* Roger Cardinal. VHS, Beta $14.95 COL *ℐℐ*

Malaya Hokey adventure tale set in WWII that's based on a true story. Stewart and Tracy are hired to smuggle a huge shipment of rubber out of Malaya to waiting U.S. ships without the Japanese finding out. Greenstreet does his usual shifty role. *AKA:* East of the Rising Sun.
1949 98m/B Spencer Tracy, James Stewart, Sydney Greenstreet, Valentina Cortese, John Hodiak, Lionel Barrymore, Gilbert Roland, Richard Loo, Roland Winters; *D:* Richard Thorpe; *W:* Frank Fenton; *M:* Bronislau Kaper. VHS $19.98 MGM *ℐℐ* ½

Malcolm An offbeat comedy about a slightly retarded young man who is mechanically inclined and his unusual entry into a life of crime. Directorial debut for actress Tass, whose husband Parker wrote the screenplay (and designed the Tinkertoys). Music score performed by The Penguin Cafe Orchestra.
1986 (PG-13) 86m/C Colin Friels, John Hargreaves, Lindy Davies, Chris Haywood, Charles Tingwell, Beverly Phillips, Judith Stratford; *D:* Nadia Tass; *W:* David Parker; *M:*

Penguin Cafe Orchestra. VHS, Beta $79.98 *LIV, VES* ✂✂½

Malcolm X Stirring tribute to the controversial black activist, a leader in the struggle for black liberation. Hitting bottom during his imprisonment in the 50s, he became a Black Muslim and then a leader in the Nation of Islam. His assassination in 1965 left a legacy of black nationalism, self-determination, and racial pride. Marked by strong direction from Lee and good performances (notably Freeman Jr. as Elijah Muhammad), it is Washington's convincing performance in the title role that truly brings the film alive. Based on "The Autobiography of Malcolm X" by Malcolm X and Alex Haley.
1992 (PG-13) 201m/C Denzel Washington, Angela Bassett, Albert Hall, Al Freeman Jr., Delroy Lindo, Spike Lee, Theresa Randle, Kate Vernon, Lonette McKee, Tommy Hollis, James McDaniel, Ernest Thompson, Jean LaMarre, Giancarlo Esposito, Craig Wasson, John Ottavino, David Patrick Kelly, Shirley Stoler; *Cameos:* Christopher Plummer, Karen Allen, Peter Boyle, William Kunstler, Bobby Seale, Al Sharpton; *D:* Spike Lee; *W:* Spike Lee, Arnold Perl, James Baldwin; *M:* Terence Blanchard. Academy Awards '92 Nominations: Best Actor (Washington), Best Costume Design; Chicago Film Critics Awards '93: Best Actor (Washington), Best Film; MTV Movie Awards '93: Best Actor (Washington); New York Film Critics Awards '93: Best Actor (Washington). **VHS, Beta, 8mm $24.98** *WAR, MOV, BTV* ✂✂✂

Male and Female A group of British aristocrats is shipwrecked on an island and must allow their efficient butler (Meighan) to take command for their survival. Swanson is the spoiled rich girl who falls for her social inferior. Their rescue provides a return to the rigid British class system. Based on the play "The Admirable Crichton" by James M. Barrie.
1919 110m/B Gloria Swanson, Thomas Meighan, Lila Lee, Raymond Hatton, Bebe Daniels; *D:* Cecil B. DeMille. **VHS, Beta $19.95** *GPV* ✂✂✂✂

Malibu Beach The California beach scene is the setting for this movie filled with bikini clad girls, tanned young men, and instant romances. For connoisseurs of the empty-headed teen beach movie.
1978 (R) 93m/C Kim Lankford, James Daughton; *D:* Robert J. Rosenthal. **VHS, Beta $9.99** *STE, PSM, VCI* ✂½

The Malibu Beach Vampires Three unscrupulous yuppies, Congressman Teri Upstart, Col. Ollie West and Rev. Timmy Fakker, keep beautiful mistresses in their Malibu beach house. What they don't know is, the girls are all really vampires who have injected them with a serum that compels them to tell the truth! Will our "heroes" continue to dupe the American Public, or will the sexy blood suckers cause their downfall?
1991 (R) 90m/C Angelyne, Becky Le Beau, Joan Rudelstein, Marcus A. Frishman, Rod Sweitzer, Francis Creighton, Anet Anatelle, Yvette Buchanan, Cherie Romaors, Kelly Galindo; *D:* Francis Creighton. **VHS** *NO* ✂½

Malibu Bikini Shop Two brothers manage a beachfront bikini shop in Malibu, and spend their time ogling the customers and arguing about running the "business." Just another excuse for parading babes in bathing suits across the naked screen.
1986 (R) 90m/C Michael David Wright, Bruce Greenwood, Barbara Horan, Debra Blee, Jay Robinson, Galyn Gorg, Ami Julius, Frank Nelson, Kathleen Freeman, Rita Jenrette; *D:* David Wechter; *W:* David Wechter. **VHS, Beta $19.98** *FOX* ✂

Malibu Express Mystery/adventure plot about a P.I. is the excuse; babes in swimsuits is the reason for this waste of time.
1985 (R) 101m/C Darby Hinton, Sybil Danning, Art Metrano, Shelley Taylor Morgan, Niki Dantine, Barbara Edwards; *D:* Andy Sidaris. **VHS, Beta $14.95** *MCA* ✂

Malibu High The accidental death of a young prostitute's client leads her to a new series of illegal activities of the "sex and hit" variety. Dark, sleazy, and antisocial; belies Beach Boys-esque title.
1979 (R) 92m/C Jill Lansing, Stuart Taylor; *D:* Irvin Berwick. **VHS, Beta $19.95** *VCI* ✂

Malibu Hot Summer Three aspiring young women combine their talents in acting, music, and athletics to find their careers as they spend a fun-filled summer in Malibu.
1981 89m/C Terry Congie, Leslie Brander, Roselyn Royce. **VHS, Beta $49.95** *VHE* ✂

Malice In a sleepy little college town, strange things sure do happen. Too bad rumpled college dean Andy Safian (Pullman) didn't see "Pacific Heights." If he did, he would know that sometimes roommates are more trouble than they're worth, even if renovation on that old Victorian is getting expensive. Routine thriller throws out an inventive twist to keep things moving, but manages to be fairly predictable anyway.
1993 (R) 107m/C Alec Baldwin, Nicole Kidman, Bill Pullman, Bebe Neuwirth, Anne Bancroft, George C. Scott, Peter Gallagher, Josef Sommer; *D:* Harold Becker; *W:* Aaron Sorkin, Scott Frank; *M:* Jerry Goldsmith. **VHS** *NLC* ✂✂½

Malicious A housekeeper hired for a widower and his three sons becomes the object of lusty affection from all four men. As Papa makes plans to court and marry her, his fourteen-year-old son plots to have her as a companion on his road to sensual maturity. Dubbed in English. *AKA:* Malizia.
1974 (R) 98m/C Laura Antonelli, Turi Ferro, Alessandro Momo, Tina Aumont; *D:* Salvatore Samperi. **VHS, Beta $49.95** *PAR* ✂✂

Malone A burnt-out secret agent stumbles into a real-estate swindle/murder plot in Oregon and sets out to stop it. Film tries hard but doesn't succeed in being believable.
1987 (R) 92m/C Burt Reynolds, Lauren Hutton, Cliff Robertson, Kenneth McMillan, Scott Wilson, Cynthia Gibb; *D:* Harley Cokliss. **VHS, Beta $14.98** *ORI* ✂½

Malou A young French woman tries to uncover the truth about her late mother's life, sifting through wildly contradictory evidence in the desire to discover her own identity and avoid her mother's mistakes. A feminist story. In German with English subtitles.
1983 (R) 95m/C Grischa Huber, Ingrid Caven, Helmut Griem; *D:* Jeanine Meerapfel. **VHS, Beta $34.95** *SUE, GLV* ✂✂

Malta Story A British WWII flier becomes involved with the defense of Malta.
1953 103m/B Alec Guinness, Jack Hawkins, Anthony Steel, Flora Robson, Muriel Pavlow; *D:* Brian Desmond Hurst. **VHS, Beta $14.95** *SUE* ✂✂½

The Maltese Falcon A good first screen version of the Dashiell Hammett story about private detective Sam Spade's search for the elusive Black Bird. Remade five years later as "Satan Met a Lady" with Bette Davis. Its most famous remake, however, occurred in 1941 with Humphrey Bogart in the lead. *AKA:* Dangerous Female.
1931 80m/B Bebe Daniels, Ricardo Cortez, Dudley Digges, Thelma Todd, Una Merkel, Dwight Frye, Robert Elliott; *D:* Roy Del Ruth. **VHS, Beta** *GPV* ✂✂✂

The Maltese Falcon After the death of his partner, detective Sam Spade finds himself enmeshed in a complicated, intriguing search for a priceless statuette. "It's the stuff dreams are made of," says Bogart of the Falcon. Excellent, fast-paced film noir with outstanding performances, great dialogue, and concentrated attention to details. Director Huston's first film and Greenstreet's talky debut. First of several films by Bogart and Astor. Based on the novel by Dashiell Hammett. Also available colorized.
1941 101m/B Humphrey Bogart, Mary Astor, Peter Lorre, Sydney Greenstreet, Ward Bond, Barton MacLane, Gladys George, Lee Patrick, Elisha Cook Jr., Jerome Cowan; *Cameos:* Walter Huston; *D:* John Huston; *W:* John Huston; *M:* Adolph Deutsch. **VHS, Beta $19.98** *MGM, FOX, TLF* ✂✂✂✂

Mama Dracula Fletcher stars in this poor satire of the horror genre. She's a vampire who needs the blood of virgins to stay young. Her son helps out—what good son wouldn't?
1980 90m/C Louise Fletcher, Bonnie Schneider, Maria Schneider, Marc-Henri Wajnberg, Alexander Wajnberg, Jess Hahn; *D:* Boris Szulzinger. **VHS $79.95** *TWE Woof!*

Mama, There's a Man in Your Bed When a powerful executive is framed for insider trading, the only witness to the crime and his only hope is an earthy cleaning woman named Juliette. Together they plot revenge and takeovers in her tiny apartment, filled with children. Soon, he regains his former position of power but realizes his life isn't complete without his co-conspirator. In French with English subtitles. *AKA:* Romuald et Juliette.
1989 (PG) 111m/C Daniel Auteuil, Firmine Richard, Pierre Vernier, Maxime LeRoux, Gilles Privat, Muriel Combeau, Catherine Salviat, Sambou Tati; *D:* Coline Serreau; *W:* Coline Serreau. **VHS, Beta $89.99** *HBO, FCT, ING* ✂✂✂

Mama Turns a Hundred A baronial family (a bizarre set of characters) is celebrating their mother's 100th birthday at her estate. One of the daughter's seduces her brother-in-law, another has a uniform fetish, a religious zealot is desperate to hang-glide, and several of them are trying to kill poor Mama. But of course she prevails, although sick and ailing. Slow-paced yet uproarious film full of inept characters who bumble along. In Spanish with English subtitles.
1979 (R) 100m/C Geraldine Chaplin, Fernando Gomez, Amparo Munoz; *D:* Carlos Saura. **VHS, Beta $59.95** *INT, AUD, ING* ✂✂✂

Mama's Dirty Girls A gangster mom's daughters take over where their mother left off and have the time of their lives.
1974 (R) 82m/C Gloria Grahame, Paul Lambert, Sondra Currie, Candice Rialson, Mary Stoddard; *D:* John Hayes. **VHS, Beta $69.95** *TWE* ✂✂✂

Mambo A poor young dancer inspires patronage and lust by dancing the Mambo. Although attracted to Gassman, she marries Rennie for his money. Technically weak but artistically interesting, though Rennie and Mangano have done their roles somewhat better elsewhere.
1955 94m/B Silvana Mangano, Michael Rennie, Vittorio Gassman, Shelley Winters, Katherine Dunham, Mary Clare, Eduardo Ciannelli; *D:* Robert Rossen. **VHS $19.95** *NOS, HTV, ING* ✂✂½

The Mambo Kings Armand and Banderas (in his first English speaking role) are Cesar and Nestor Castillo, two brothers who flee Cuba for New York City with dreams of hitting it big with their mambo music. Desi Arnaz Jr. gets to play his own dad in a funny and technical scene that leads to a climactic

confrontation between the brothers. Good cast and great music make this one worthwhile. Based on the Pulitzer prizewinning novel "The Mambo Kings Play Songs of Love" by Oscar Hijuelos.
1992 (R) 100m/C Armand Assante, Antonio Banderas, Cathy Moriarty, Maruschka Detmers, Desi Arnaz Jr., Celia Cruz, Roscoe Lee Browne, Vondie Curtis-Hall, Tito Puente, Talisa Soto; **D:** Arne Glimcher; **W:** Cynthia Cidre; **M:** Robert Kraft, Carlos Franzetti. **VHS, 8mm $19.98** *WAR, FCT, MVD ♫♫♫*

Mame In an adaptation of the Broadway musical "Auntie Mame" by Jerry Herman, Ball plays a dynamic woman who takes it upon herself to teach a group of eccentrics how to live life to the fullest. Arthur plays Mame's friend just as splendidly as she did in the Broadway version, but Ball in her last feature film is a lame Mame. Overly ambitious production avoids reaching goal. ♫Mame; We Need a Little Christmas; If He Walked Into My Life; Bosom Buddies; It's Today; Loving You; My Best Girl; What Do I Do Now? (Gooch's Sont); Open a New Window.
1974 (PG) 132m/C Lucille Ball, Beatrice Arthur, Robert Preston, Joyce Van Patten, Bruce Davison; **D:** Gene Saks. **VHS, Beta $19.98** *WAR, MVD ♫♫*

Mamele Picon prematurely becomes the "mother" of her seven siblings when their mother dies. Quintessential Yiddish musical with the usual shimmering performance from Picon. In Yiddish with English subtitles. **AKA:** Little Mother.
1938 95m/B Molly Picon, Max Bozyk, Edmund Zayenda; **D:** Joseph Green. **VHS, Beta $79.95** *ERG, ING, TPV ♫♫♫*

A Man, a Woman, and a Bank Two con-men plan to rob a bank by posing as workers during the bank's construction. An advertising agency woman snaps their picture for a billboard to show how nice the builders have been, then becomes romantically involved with one of the would-be thieves. Nice performances, but wacky touches aren't plentiful enough or well-timed to sustain comedy. Also called "A Very Big Weekend."
1979 (PG) 100m/C Donald Sutherland, Brooke Adams, Paul Mazursky; **D:** Noel Black; **W:** Bruce A. Evans, Raynold Gideon; **M:** Bill Conti. **VHS, Beta $9.98** *SUE, NLC ♫♫½*

A Man, a Woman and a Killer Unusual film within a film shows the actual making of a movie while unfolding a story of a hired killer. A joint project from the directors of the well-received "Emerald Cities" and "Chan is Missing."
19?? 75m/C Rick Schmidt, Wayne Wang. **VHS $59.95** *FCT ♫♫½*

A Man About the House Two unmarried English sisters move into the Italian villa they have inherited. There, one marries the caretaker, who secretly plans to regain the property that once belonged to his family. When the newly married sister is found dead, her sibling sets out to solve the murder.
1947 83m/B Kieron Moore, Margaret Johnston, Dulcie Gray, Guy Middleton, Felix Aylmer; **D:** Leslie Arliss. **VHS $16.95** *NOS, SNC ♫♫½*

A Man Alone Man falsely accused of robbing a stagecoach hides not alone but with comely sheriff's daughter. Milland's debut behind the camera.
1955 96m/C Ray Milland, Ward Bond, Mary Murphy, Raymond Burr, Lee Van Cleef; **D:** Ray Milland. **VHS $14.95** *REP ♫♫*

A Man and a Woman When a man and a woman, both widowed, meet and become interested in one another but experience difficulties in putting their past loves behind them. Intelligently handled emotional conflicts within a well-acted romantic drama, acclaimed for excellent visual detail. Remade in 1977 as "Another Man, Another Chance." Followed in 1986 with "A Man and A Woman: 20 Years Later." Dubbed. **AKA:** Un Homme et Un Femme.
1966 102m/C Anouk Aimee, Jean-Louis Trintignant, Pierre Barouh, Valerie Lagrange; **D:** Claude Lelouch; **W:** Claude Lelouch. Academy Awards '66: Best Foreign Language Film, Best Original Screenplay; Nominations: Best Actress (Aimee), Best Director (Lelouch); British Academy Awards '67: Best Actress (Aimee); Cannes Film Festival '66: Best Film; Golden Globe Awards '67: Best Actress—Drama (Aimee), Best Foreign Film. **VHS, Beta $19.98** *WAR, APD, ING ♫♫♫*

A Man and a Woman: 20 Years Later Slouchy sequel to the highly praised "A Man and a Woman" that catches up with a couple after a long separation. The sad romantic complications of the original are more mundane in this sequel, which is burdened by a film-within-a-film script as well as shots from the original. In French with English subtitles. **AKA:** Un Homme Et Une Femme: Vingt Ans Deja.
1986 (PG) 112m/C Jean-Louis Trintignant, Anouk Aimee, Richard Berry; **D:** Claude Lelouch; **W:** Claude Lelouch. **VHS, Beta $19.98** *WAR, ING ♫½*

Man & Boy A black Civil War veteran, played by Bill Cosby, encounters bigotry and prejudice when he tries to set up a homestead in Arizona. An acceptable family film, some might be disappointed that Cosby is not playing this one for laughs. **AKA:** Ride a Dark Horse.
1971 (G) 98m/C Bill Cosby, Gloria Foster, George Spell, Henry Silva, Yaphet Kotto; **D:** E.W. Swackhamer; **M:** Quincy Jones. **VHS, Beta $59.95** *COL ♫♫*

The Man and the Monster When a concert pianist sells his soul to the devil, he fails to realize that part of the deal has him turning into a hideous beast every time he hears a certain piece of music. Maybe it was "Stairway to Heaven."
1965 78m/B Enrique Rambal, Abel Salazar, Martha Roth; **D:** Rafael Baledon. **VHS $19.98** *SNC ♫½*

Man Bait A complex web of intrigue and mystery surrounds a blackmailed book dealer when he allows a blonde woman to catch his eye. A competently made film. **AKA:** The Last Page.
1952 78m/B George Brent, Marguerite Chapman, Diana Dors; **D:** Terence Fisher. **VHS, Beta** *RXM, MLB ♫♫½*

Man Beast The abominable snowman is sought and found in this grade-Z '50s monster movie.
1955 65m/B Rock Madison, Virginia Maynor, George Skaff, Lloyd Nelson, Tom Maruzzi; **D:** Jerry Warren. **VHS, Beta $19.95** *NOS, MRV, RHI ♫*

Man Bites Dog A pseudo-documentary about a serial killer, filled with ever-mounting violence. Ben is the killer being followed by a two-man camera/sound crew (which he's hired), who record his casual carnage without lifting a finger to stop him. Indeed his continued killing and robbing is to pay for financing the documentary about himself. This satire on film violence, as well as reality-based television shows, is both appalling and humorous in a sick way. In French with

English subtitles. Also available in an unrated edited version.
1991 (NC-17) 95m/B Benoit Poelvoorde, Remy Belvaux, Andre Bonzel; **D:** Benoit Poelvoorde, Remy Belvaux, Andre Bonzel; **W:** Benoit Poelvoorde, Remy Belvaux, Andre Bonzel, Vincent Tavier. **VHS $89.95** *FXL, FCT ♫♫*

A Man Called Adam A jazz musician is tortured by prejudice and the guilt created by his having accidentally killed his wife and baby years before. Davis is appropriately haunted, but the film is poorly produced.
1966 103m/B Sammy Davis Jr., Louis Armstrong, Ossie Davis, Cicely Tyson, Frank Sinatra Jr., Lola Falana, Mel Torme, Peter Lawford; **D:** Leonard Penn. **VHS, Beta $14.95** *COL, NLC ♫½*

A Man Called Horse After a wealthy Britisher is captured and tortured by the Sioux Indians in the Dakotas, he abandons his formal ways and discovers his own strength. As he passes their torture tests, he is embraced by the tribe. In this very realistic and gripping portrayal of American Indian life, Harris provides a strong performance. Sequelled by "Return of a Man Called Horse" (1976) and "Triumphs of a Man Called Horse" (1983).
1970 (PG) 114m/C Richard Harris, Judith Anderson, Jean Gascon, Stanford Howard, Manu Tupou, Dub Taylor; **D:** Elliot Silverstein; **W:** Jack DeWitt. **VHS, Beta $59.98** *FOX ♫♫♫*

A Man Called Peter A biographical epic about Peter Marshall, a Scottish chaplain who served the U.S. Senate. Todd does his subject justice by sensitively showing all that was human in Marshall, and a talented supporting cast makes for a thoroughly watchable film.
1955 119m/C Richard Todd, Jean Peters, Marjorie Rambeau, Jill Esmond, Les Tremayne, Robert Burton; **D:** Henry Koster. **VHS, Beta $19.98** *FOX ♫♫♫*

A Man Called Rage Rage is the only man capable of safely escorting a group of pioneers through a nuclear wasteland infested with mutants and cannibals.
1984 90m/C Stelio Candelli, Conrad Nichols; **D:** Anthony Richmond. **VHS, Beta $39.95** *LIV Woof!*

A Man Called Sarge Sophomoric comedy about a daffy WWII sergeant leading his squad against the Germans at Tobruk.
1990 (PG-13) 88m/C Gary Kroeger, Marc Singer, Gretchen German, Jennifer Runyon; **D:** Stuart Gillard. **VHS, Beta $79.95** *WAR, OM ♫½*

A Man Called Sledge Garner fans might be surprised to see the star play a villain in this violent story of a gang of outlaws who wind up fighting each over a cache of gold. This is mainstream Western entertainment.
1971 93m/C James Garner, Dennis Weaver, Claude Akins, John Marley, Laura Antonelli; **D:** Vic Morrow. **VHS, Beta** *GKK ♫♫*

Man Called Tiger A Chinese martial arts expert infiltrates a ruthless Japanese gang in order to find the man who murdered his father.
1981 (R) 97m/C **VHS, Beta $9.98** *SUE ♫*

A Man Escaped There's an excruciating realism about Bresson's account of a WWII Resistance fighter's escape from a Nazi prison just before he was to be executed by the Gestapo. It's the sounds and lingering camera shots, not the wham bam variety of action, that create and sustain the film's suspense. Bresson, who had been a Nazi prisoner, solicited the supervision of Andre Devigny, whose true story the film tells. Contributing to the realistic feel was the use of non professional actors. An award-

wiining film that fellow director Truffaut lauded as the most crucial French film of the previous ten years. In French with English subtitles. *AKA:* Un Condamne a Mort s'est Echappe; The Wind Bloweth Where it Listeth.
1957 102m/B Francois Leterrier; *D:* Robert Bresson. **VHS $59.95** ING, FST, NYF 🎬🎬🎬½

Man Facing Southeast The acclaimed Argentinean film about the sudden appearance of a strange man in an asylum who claims to be an extraterrestrial, and a psychologist's attempts to discover his true identity. The sense of mystery intensifies when the new patient indeed seems to have some remarkable powers. Although the pace at times lags, the story intriguingly keeps one guessing about the stranger right to the end. In Spanish, with English subtitles. *AKA:* Hombre Mirando Al Sudeste; Man Looking Southeast.
1986 (R) 105m/C Lorenzo Quinteros, Hugo Soto, Ines Vernengo; *D:* Eliseo Subiela. **VHS, Beta $19.95** STE, NWV, IME 🎬🎬🎬

A Man for All Seasons Sterling, heavily Oscar-honored biographical drama concerning the life and subsequent martyrdom of 16th-century Chancellor of England, Sir Thomas More (Scofield). Story revolves around his personal conflict when King Henry VIII (Shaw) seeks a divorce from his wife, Catherine of Aragon, so he can wed his mistress, Anne Boleyn—events that ultimately lead the King to bolt from the Pope and declare himself head of the Church of England. Remade for television in 1988 with Charlton Heston in the lead role.
1966 (G) 120m/C Paul Scofield, Robert Shaw, Orson Welles, Wendy Hiller, Susannah York, John Hurt, Nigel Davenport, Vanessa Redgrave; *D:* Fred Zinneman; *W:* Constance Willis, Robert Bolt; *M:* Georges Delerue. Academy Awards '66: Best Actor (Scofield), Best Adapted Screenplay, Best Color Cinematography, Best Costume Design (Color), Best Director (Zinneman), Best Picture; Nominations: Best Supporting Actor (Shaw), Best Supporting Actress (Hiller); British Academy Awards '67: Best Actor (Scofield), Best Film; Directors Guild of America Awards '66: Best Director (Zinneman); Golden Globe Awards '67: Best Actor—Drama (Scofield), Best Director (Zinneman), Best Film—Drama, Best Screenplay; National Board of Review Awards '66: 10 Best Films of the Year, Best Actor (Scofield), Best Director (Zinneman), Best Supporting Actor (Shaw). **VHS, Beta $19.95** COL, BTV, TVC 🎬🎬🎬🎬

A Man for All Seasons Fresh from the London stage, Heston directs and stars in this version of Robert Bolt's play depicting the conflict between Henry VIII and his chief advisor, Sir Thomas More. Strong supporting cast. Made for cable TV.
1988 150m/C Charlton Heston, Vanessa Redgrave, John Gielgud, Richard Johnson, Roy Kinnear, Martin Chamberlain; *D:* Charlton Heston. **VHS $79.98** TTC 🎬🎬🎬

Man Friday Stranded on a deserted island, a man forces a native from a neighboring island to be his slave. Based on the classic story "Robinson Crusoe" by Daniel Defoe, this adaptation charts the often-brutal treatment the native receives as his captor tries to civilize him. Through his intelligence, the enslaved man regains his freedom and returns home with his former captor, who then seeks acceptance from the native's tribe. A sometimes confusing story line and excessive blood and guts detract from this message-laden effort.
1975 (PG) 115m/C Peter O'Toole, Richard Roundtree, Peter Cellier, Christopher Cabot, Joel Fluellen; *D:* Jack Gold; *M:* Carl Davis. **VHS** FOX 🎬🎬

The Man from Atlantis Patrick Duffy stars as the water-breathing alien who emerges from his undersea home, the Lost City of Atlantis. The made-for-TV movie led to a brief television series.
1977 60m/C Patrick Duffy, Belinda J. Montgomery, Victor Buono; *D:* Lee H. Katzin. **VHS, Beta $19.95** WOV 🎬🎬

The Man from Beyond Frozen alive, a man returns 100 years later to try and find his lost love. Silent.
1922 50m/B Harry Houdini, Arthur Maude, Nita Naldi; *D:* Burton King. **VHS, Beta $16.95** SNC, VYY, DVT 🎬🎬½

Man from Button Willow Classic animated adventure is the story of Justin Eagle, a man who leads a double life. He is a respected rancher and a shrewd secret agent for the government, but in 1869 he suddenly finds himself the guardian of a four-year-old Oriental girl, leading him into a whole new series of adventures. Strictly for younger audiences.
1965 (G) 79m/C *V:* Dale Robertson, Edgar Buchanan, Barbara Jean Wong, Howard Keel. **VHS, Beta** NO 🎬

Man from Cairo An American in Algiers is mistaken for a detective in search of gold lost during WWII and decides to play along.
1954 82m/B George Raft, Giana Maria Canale; *D:* Ray Enright. **VHS, Beta** NO 🎬🎬

Man from Cheyenne Cowboy comes home to find his town under a siege of terror from a lawless gang of cattle rustlers. He gets mad and seeks some frontier justice.
1942 54m/B Roy Rogers, Gale Storm, George "Gabby" Hayes, Sally Payne. **VHS, Beta $19.95** NOS, DVT, RXM 🎬

Man from Clover Grove Hilarity takes over a town when a nutty boy inventor puts the sheriff in a spin.
1978 (G) 96m/C Ron Masak, Cheryl Miller, Jed Allan, Rose Marie. **VHS, Beta $19.95** MED 🎬½

Man from Colorado An odd Technicolor western about two Civil War vets at odds, one an honest marshall, the other a sadistic judge. Solid Western fare with a quirky performance by Ford.
1949 99m/C William Holden, Glenn Ford, Ellen Drew, Ray Collins, Edgar Buchanan, Jerome Courtland, James Millican, Jim Bannon; *D:* Henry Levin; *M:* George Duning. **VHS, Beta $14.95** COL 🎬🎬½

Man from Deep River A photographer is captured by a savage tribe in Thailand and forced to undergo a series of grueling initiation rites. Full of very violent and sickening tortures inflicted on both human and animal victims.
1977 (R) 90m/C Ivan Rassimov; *D:* Umberto Lenzi. **VHS, Beta** NO Woof!

The Man from Gun Town McCoy comes to the rescue of a woman who has been framed by an evil gang for the murder of her brother.
1936 58m/B Tim McCoy, Billie Seward, Rex Lease, Jack Clifford, Wheeler Oakman, Bob McKenzie; *D:* Ford Beebe. **VHS $19.95** NOS, DVT 🎬½

Man from Headquarters Good silent mystery in which a U.S. agent takes on a gang of foreign operatives.
1928 ?m/B Cornelius Keefe, Edith Roberts. **VHS $16.95** SNC 🎬

The Man from Hell Sheriff Russell goes undercover to expose the head of a gang of outlaws. Low-budget fare.
1934 55m/B Reb Russell, Fred Kohler Jr., Ann Darcy, George "Gabby" Hayes, Jack Rockwell, Charles French, Charles "Slim" Whitaker, Yakima Canutt; *D:* Lewis Collins. **VHS $19.95** DVT, HEG, GPV 🎬

Man from Hell's Edges An innocent cowpoke escapes from jail and brings the real baddy to justice.
1932 63m/B Bob Steele, Nancy Drexel, Julian Rivero, Robert E. Homans, George "Gabby" Hayes; *D:* Robert North Bradbury. **VHS, Beta $19.95** NOS, DVT 🎬½

The Man from Laramie A ranch baron who is going blind worries about which of his two sons he will leave the ranch to. Into this tension-filled familial atmosphere rides Stewart, a cow-herder obsessed with hunting down the men who sold guns to the Indians that killed his brother. Needless to say, the tension increases. Tough, surprisingly brutal western, the best of the classic Stewart-Mann films.
1955 104m/C James Stewart, Arthur Kennedy, Donald Crisp, Alex Nicol, Cathy O'Donnell, Aline MacMahon, Wallace Ford, Jack Elam; *D:* Anthony Mann; *W:* Philip Yordan. **VHS, Beta $14.95** COL 🎬🎬🎬½

Man from Montana Brown is a sheriff who battles outlaws trying to stir up trouble between ranchers and homesteaders. *AKA:* Montana Justice.
1941 56m/B Johnny Mack Brown, Fuzzy Knight, William Gould, Kermit Maynard, Nell O'Day, Billy Lenhart, Kenneth Brown, Murdock McQuarrie, Ray Taylor. **VHS $11.95** GPV 🎬½

Man from Monterey South-of-the-border Western has U.S. Army captain Wayne trying to get Mexican landowners to register their property under Spanish land grants or lose them to public domain. Wayne's last series western for Warner Bros.
1933 59m/B John Wayne, Ruth Hall, Luis Alberni, Francis Ford, Lafe McKee, Lillian Leighton, Charles "Slim" Whitaker; *D:* Mack V. Wright; *W:* Lesley Mason. **VHS $19.98** MGM 🎬

The Man from Music Mountain Worthless mining stock is sold in a desert mining town, but Gene and Smiley clear that up, with a little singing as well.
1938 54m/B Gene Autry, Smiley Burnette, Carol Hughes, Polly Jenkins. **VHS, Beta $19.95** NOS, VDM, HHT 🎬🎬

Man from Nowhere A henpecked man gets the break of his life when his domineering wife and mother-in-law believe he's dead. Based on the novel by Luigi Pirandello. In French with English subtitles.
1937 98m/B Pierre Blanchar, Ginette LeClerc; *D:* Pierre Chenal. **VHS, Beta $59.95** FCT, AUD 🎬🎬½

The Man from Painted Post Fairbanks plays a Cattlemen's Association detective who comes to the range to stop the cattle rustlers as well as to find the man who murdered his sister.
1917 ?m/B Douglas Fairbanks Sr., Eileen Percy, Frank Campeau, Monte Blue; *D:* Joseph Henabery. **VHS** GVV 🎬

The Man from Snowy River Stunning cinematography highlights this otherwise fairly ordinary adventure story set in 1880's Australia. A young man comes of age in the outback while taming a herd of wild horses. In a dual role, Douglas portrays battling brothers, one a rich landowner and the other a one-legged prospector. Based on the epic poem by A.B. "Banjo" Paterson and followed by "Return to Snowy River Part II." A big hit in Australia and not directed by "Mad Max's" Miller, but another Miller named George.

1982 (PG) 104m/C Kirk Douglas, Tom Burlinson, Sigrid Thornton, Terence Donovan, Tommy Dysart, Jack Thompson, Bruce Kerr; **D:** George Miller. **VHS, Beta** $14.98 FOX, TVC, HMV ✂✂ ½

Man from Texas Singing and gun-slinging Tex defends a kid accused of horse thieving until the kid turns bad and Tex must bring him in.
1939 55m/B Tex Ritter, Hal Price, Charles B. Wood, Vic Demourelle Sr.; **D:** Al Herman. **VHS, Beta** $19.95 NOS, VDM ✂✂

Man from the Alamo A soldier sent from the Alamo during its last hours to get help is branded as a deserter, and struggles to clear his name. Well acted, this film will satisfy those with a taste for action.
1953 79m/C Glenn Ford, Julie Adams, Chill Wills, Victor Jory, Hugh O'Brian; **D:** Budd Boetticher. **VHS, Beta** $14.95 BAR ✂✂✂

Man from Thunder River A group of cowboys uncover a plot to steal gold ore and wind up saving a young girl's life in the process. Standard western with lots of action.
1943 55m/B Wild Bill Elliott, George "Gabby" Hayes, Anne Jeffreys, Ian Keith, John James; **D:** John English. **VHS, Beta** $29.95 DVT ✂✂

The Man from U.N.C.L.E. Vaughn and McCallum star as Napoleon Solo and Illya Kuryakin, two super-cool super-agents battling the evil forces of THRUSH. The series ran from 1964-1968. Two epsiodes per tape; additional episodes available. On this tape: "The Project Strigas Affair" has Solo and Illya against a Balkan intelligence agent. In "The Never Never Affair" an innocent translator is captured by a ruthless THRUSH operator who's after some valuable microfilm.
1964 110m/B Robert Vaughn, David McCallum, Leo G. Carroll, Leonard Nimoy, William Shatner, Barbara Feldon, Cesar Romero. **VHS, Beta** $14.95 MGM, MOV ✂✂

Man from Utah The Duke tangles with the crooked sponsor of some rodeo events who has killed several of the participants. Also available with "Blue Steel" on laserdisc.
1934 55m/B John Wayne, George "Gabby" Hayes, Polly Ann Young, Yakima Canutt, Lafe McKee; **D:** Robert North Bradbury. **VHS, Beta** $8.95 CNG, NOS, MRV ✂½

The Man I Love Slick drama about nightclub singer Lupino falling for no-good mobster Alda. Enjoyable and well-acted, although script doesn't make sense. Great selection of tunes. This film inspired Scorsese's "New York, New York." Based on the novel "Night Shift" by Maritta Wolff. ♫Body and Soul; Why Was I Born; Bill; The Man I Love; Liza; If I Could Be With You.
1946 96m/B Ida Lupino, Robert Alda, Andrea King, Martha Vickers, Bruce (Herman Brix) Bennett, Alan Hale, Dolores Moran, John Ridgely, Don McGuire, Warren Douglas, Craig Stevens; **D:** Raoul Walsh, John Maxwell; **W:** Catherine Turney, Jo Pagano. **VHS** $19.98 MGM, FCT ✂✂✂

The Man in Grey In a story of romantic intrigue set in nineteenth-century England, a Marquis's wife is betrayed by her vile husband and the schoolmate she once befriended who has an affair with him. Stunning costumes and fine performances compensate for the overly extravagant production values in a work that helped bring stardom to Mason.
1945 116m/B James Mason, Margaret Lockwood, Stewart Granger, Phyllis Calvert; **D:** Leslie Arliss. **VHS, Beta** NO ✂✂✂

A Man in Love An international romantic melodrama set during the Italian filming of a biography of suicidal author Cesar Pavese. The self-important lead actor and a beautiful supporting actress (Coyote and Scacchi) become immersed in the roles and fall madly in love, oblivious to the fact that Coyote is married and Scacchi's engaged. The two make a steamy pair, to the detriment of friends, family, and the movie they're making. Kurys' first English-language film is visually appealing with a lush, romantic score, seamlessly weaving the story lines among vivid characters. **AKA:** Un Homme Amoureux.
1987 (R) 110m/C Peter Coyote, Greta Scacchi, Jamie Lee Curtis, Peter Riegert, Jean Pigozzi, John Berry, Claudia Cardinale, Vincent Lindon; **D:** Diane Kurys; **W:** Diane Kurys; **M:** Georges Delerue. **VHS, Beta** $14.95 COL, SUE ✂✂✂

The Man in the Gray Flannel Suit A very long and serious adaptation of the Sloan Wilson novel about a Madison Avenue advertising exec trying to balance his life between work and family while the Hollywood treatment falls short of the adaptation potential of the original story.
1956 152m/C Gregory Peck, Fredric March, Jennifer Jones, Ann Harding, Arthur O'Connell, Henry Daniell, Lee J. Cobb, Marisa Pavan, Gene Lockhart, Keenan Wynn, Gigi Perreau, Joseph Sweeney, Kenneth Tobey, DeForest Kelley; **D:** Nunnally Johnson. **VHS, Beta** $39.98 FOX ✂✂½

The Man in the Iron Mask Swashbuckling tale about twin brothers separated at birth. One turns out to be King Louis XIV of France, and the other a carefree wanderer and friend of the Three Musketeers. Their eventual clash leads to action-packed adventure and royal revenge. Remake of the "The Iron Mask" (1929) with Douglas Fairbanks. Remade for television in 1977 with Richard Chamberlain.
1939 110m/B Louis Hayward, Alan Hale, Joan Bennett, Warren William, Joseph Schildkraut, Walter Kingsford, Marion Martin; **D:** James Whale. **VHS, Beta** $9.99 CCB, MED ✂✂✂

The Man in the Iron Mask A tyrannical French king kidnaps his twin brother and imprisons him on a remote island. Chamberlain, the king of the miniseries, is excellent in a dual role in this big production swashbuckler. Adapted from the Dumas classic. Made for television.
1977 105m/C Richard Chamberlain, Patrick McGoohan, Louis Jourdan, Jenny Agutter, Ian Holm, Ralph Richardson; **D:** Mike Newell. **VHS, Beta** $19.98 LIV, FUS, FOX ✂✂✂

The Man in the Mist Private investigators Tommy and Tuppence Beresford find themselves trying to solve a murder while on vacation in a provincial hotel. Made for British television and based upon the Agatha Christie story.
1983 51m/C Francesca Annis, James Warwick. **VHS, Beta** $14.95 TPV ✂✂✂

The Man in the Moon Beautifully rendered coming-of-age tale. On a farm outside a small Louisiana town in the 1950s, 14 year-old Dani wonders if she will ever be as pretty and popular as her 17 year old sister Maureen. This becomes especially important as Dani is beginning to notice boys, particularly Court, the 17 year-old young man she meets when swimming. Although Dani and Maureen have always been especially close a rift develops between the sisters after Court meets Maureen. Intelligently written, excellent direction, lovely cinematography, and exceptional acting make this a particularly worthwhile and entertaining film.

1991 (PG-13) 100m/C Reese Witherspoon, Emily Warfield, Jason London, Tess Harper, Sam Waterston, Gail Strickland; **D:** Robert Mulligan. **VHS** $19.98 MGM ✂✂✂½

The Man in the Raincoat French film about a bumbling clarinet player who is erroneously tracked down as a murderer. Strenuous efforts to evoke laughter usually fail. Dubbed.
1957 97m/B Fernandel, John McGiver, Bernard Blier; **D:** Julien Duvivier. **VHS, Beta, 8mm** $24.95 VYY ✂✂

The Man in the Santa Claus Suit A costume shop owner has an effect on three people who rent Santa Claus costumes from him. Astaire plays seven different roles in this made for television film. Average holiday feel-good movie.
1979 96m/C Fred Astaire, Gary Burghoff, John Byner, Nanette Fabray, Bert Convy; **D:** Corey Allen. **VHS, Beta** $69.95 MED ✂✂

Man in the Silk Hat A collection of the nearly-forgotten French comic's early silent comedy shorts, made in France before his resettlement in America.
1915 96m/B Max Linder; **D:** Maud Linder. **VHS, Beta** $59.95 ING ✂✂

Man in the Silk Hat Gabriel-Maximilien Leuvielle, known in films as Max Linder, is now credited with developing the style of silent-movie slapstick comedy that Mack Sennett, Charlie Chaplin, and others became more famous for in their time. Here, Linder's daughter has done a fine job writing and directing a film full of historic footage of her father's work.
1983 99m/B Mack Sennett, Buster Keaton, Charlie Chaplin, Max Linder. **VHS, Beta** $24.95 XVC, MED ✂✂

The Man in the White Suit A humble laboratory assistant in a textile mill invents a white cloth that won't stain, tear, or wear out, and can't be dyed. The panicked garment industry sets out to destroy him and the fabric, resulting in some sublimely comic situations and a variety of inventive chases. Also available with "Lavender Hill Mob" on Laser Disc.
1951 82m/B Alec Guinness, Joan Greenwood; **D:** Alexander MacKendrick. Academy Awards '52 Nominations: Best Screenplay; National Board of Review Awards '52: 10 Best Films of the Year. **VHS, Beta** $19.98 HMV ✂✂✂½

Man in the Wilderness Harris is part of an expedition traveling through the Northwest Territory. He's mauled by a grizzly and left for dead by leader Huston. While Harris fights for survival, he also plots revenge. Blood and violence is somewhat offset by good lead performances.
1971 (PG) 108m/C Richard Harris, John Huston, Henry Wilcoxon, Percy Herbert, Dennis Waterman, Prunella Ransome, Norman Rossington, James Doohan; **D:** Richard Sarafian; **W:** Jack DeWitt; **M:** Johnny Harris. **VHS** $19.98 WAR ✂✂½

The Man Inside Undercover agent infiltrates a powerful underworld narcotics ring and finds his honesty tested when $2 million is at stake.
1976 96m/C James Franciscus, Stefanie Powers, Jacques Godin; **D:** Gerald Mayer. **VHS, Beta** $49.95 TWE ✂½

The Man Inside Lukewarm Cold War saga based on the true story of Gunther Wallraff, a West German journalist who risked all to expose the corruption behind a large European newspaper.
1990 (PG) 93m/C Juergen Prochnow, Peter Coyote, Nathalie Baye, Dieter Laser, Monique Van De Ven, Sylvie Granotier; **D:** Bobby Roth; **W:** Bobby Roth. **VHS** $89.95 COL ✂✂

Man is Not a Bird Follows the destructive love of a factory engineer and a hairdresser in a small Yugoslavian mining town. In Serbian with English subtitles.
1965 80m/B Eva Ras, Milena Dravic, Janez Urhovec; **D:** Dusan Makavejev; **W:** Dusan Makavejev. VHS, Beta $59.95 FCT 𝒵𝒵½

A Man Like Eva A weird, morbid homage to and portrait of Rainer Werner Fassbinder after his inevitable death, detailing his work-obsessed self-destruction. Mattes, one of Fassbinder's favorite actresses, plays him in drag, in an eerie gender-crossing transformation. In German with English subtitles. **AKA:** Ein Mann wie Eva.
1983 92m/C Eva Mattes, Elisabeth Kreuzer, Charles Regnier, Werner Stocker; **D:** Radu Gabrea. VHS, Beta $79.95 FCT, APD, GLV 𝒵𝒵𝒵

Man Made Monster Chaney stars as carnival performer "Dynamo" Dan McCormick, whose act has caused Dan to build up an immunity to electrical charges. Dan falls prey to the mad Dr. Rigas (Atwill) who seeks to create a race of electro-men who'll do his bidding. Experiments on the hapless Dan turn him into a glowing monster whose very touch can kill. Chaney's first role in the horror genre led to Universal's casting him in "The Wolf Man" and "The Ghost of Frankenstein."
1941 61m/B Lon Chaney Jr., Lionel Atwill, Anne Nagel, Frank Albertson, Samuel S. Hinds; **D:** George Waggner; **W:** Joseph West. VHS $14.98 MCA 𝒵𝒵½

Man of a Thousand Faces A tasteful and touching portrayal of Lon Chaney, from his childhood with his deaf and mute parents to his success as a screen star. Recreates some of Chaney's most famous roles, including the Phantom of the Opera and Quasimodo in "Notre Dame." Cagney is magnificent as the long-suffering film star who was a genius with makeup and mime.
1957 122m/B James Cagney, Dorothy Malone, Jane Greer, Marjorie Rambeau, Jim Backus, Roger Smith, Robert Evans; **D:** Joseph Pevney; **W:** Ivan Goff. VHS $14.98 MCA 𝒵𝒵𝒵½

Man of Action Texas Ranger McCoy is out to solve the mystery of what happened to money, recovered from a robbery, which has vanished once again.
1933 56m/B Tim McCoy, Wheeler Oakman, Walter Brennan, Stanley Blystone, Charles French; **D:** George Melford. VHS $11.95 GPV 𝒵½

Man of Aran Celebrated account of a fisherman's struggle for survival on a barren island near the west coast of Ireland, featuring amateur actors. Three years in the making, it's the last word in man against nature cinema, and a visual marvel. A former explorer, Flaherty became an influential documentarian. Having first gained fame with "Nanook of the North," he compiled an opus of documentaries made for commercial release.
1934 132m/B D: Robert Flaherty. VHS $29.95 HMV, GVV 𝒵𝒵𝒵

Man of Destiny Bonaparte (Keach) and a mysterious woman battle good-humoredly over a collection of love letters. From a Bernard Shaw story. Charming and well-acted.
1973 60m/C Stacy Keach, Samantha Eggar. VHS, Beta NO 𝒵𝒵½

Man of Evil The hard times of the illegitimate daughter of a member of the British Parliament in the early 1900s, told with an astonishing number of plot twists and a plodding melodramtic style. Based on the novel "Fanny by Gaslight." **AKA:** Fanny by Gaslight.
1948 108m/B Phyllis Calvert, James Mason, Wilfred Lawson, Stewart Granger, Margaretta Scott, Jean Kent, John Laurie, Stuart Lindsell, Nora Swinburne, Amy Veness, Ann Wilton, Helen Haye, Cathleen Nesbitt, Guy le Feuvre, John Turnbull, Peter Jones; **D:** Anthony Asquith. VHS $29.95 FCT 𝒵𝒵

Man of Flowers Because of his puritan upbringing, a reclusive art collector has trouble coping with his feelings of sexuality. He pays a woman to disrobe in front of him, but is never able to bring himself to see her naked. A moody piece with overtones of black humor, this work has limited audience appeal.
1984 91m/C Norman Kaye, Alyson Best, Chris Haywood, Sarah Walker, Julia Blake, Bob Ellis, Werner Herzog; **D:** Paul Cox; **W:** Bob Ellis, Paul Cox. VHS, Beta $69.98 LIV, VES 𝒵𝒵½

Man of Iron Director Wajda's follow-up to "Man of Marble" deals with a reporter (Odania) who is expected to tow the government line when writing about the Gdansk shipyard strike of 1980. He meets the harassed laborer son (Radziwilowicz) of worker-hero Birkut, against whom Odania is expected to conduct a smear campaign, and finds his loyalties tested. In Polish with English subtitles. **AKA:** Czlowiek z Zelaza.
1981 (PG) 116m/C Jerzy Radziwilowicz, Marian Opania, Krystyna Janda; **D:** Andrzej Wajda; **W:** Aleksander Scibor-Rylski; **M:** Andrzej Korzynski. VHS $19.98 MGM 𝒵𝒵𝒵

Man of La Mancha Arrested by the Inquisition and thrown into prison, Miguel de Cervantes relates the story of Don Quixote. Not nearly as good as the Broadway musical it is based on. ♫It's All the Same; The Impossible Dream; Barber's Song; Man of La Mancha; Dulcinea; I'm Only Thinking of Him; Little Bird, Little Bird; Life as It Really Is; The Dubbing.
1972 (PG) 129m/C Peter O'Toole, Sophia Loren, James Coco, Harry Andrews, John Castle, Brian Blessed; **D:** Arthur Hiller. Academy Awards '72 Nominations: Best Original Score; National Board of Review Awards '72: 10 Best Films of the Year, Best Actor (O'Toole). VHS, Beta $19.99 FOX, FCT 𝒵½

Man of Legend An adventure-romance filmed in Morocco; a WWI German soldier flees to the Foreign Legion and fights with nomadic rebels, ultimately falling in love with their chief's beautiful daughter. An unoriginal desert saga.
1971 (PG) 95m/C Peter Strauss, Tina Aumont, Pier Paola Capponi; **D:** Sergio Grieco. VHS, Beta $59.95 VCI 𝒵𝒵

Man of Marble A satire on life in post-WWII Poland. A young filmmaker sets out to tell the story of a bricklayer who, because of his exceptional skill, once gained popularity with other workers. He became a champion for worker rights, only to then find himself being persecuted by the government. The conclusion was censored by the Polish government. Highly acclaimed and followed by "Man of Iron" in 1981. In Polish with English subtitles.
1976 160m/C Krystyna Janda, Jerzy Radziwilowicz, Tadeusz Lomnicki, Jacek Lomnicki, Krystyna Zachwatowicz; **D:** Andrzej Wajda; **W:** Aleksander Scibor-Rylski; **M:** Andrzej Korzynski. VHS $79.95 NYF, FCT, ING 𝒵𝒵𝒵

A Man of Passion Quinn plays an aging artist living pleasurably on a Mediterranean isle. His summer guest is his uptight grandson, a classical pianist. Naturally, Gramps is about to teach the kid to loosen up, including appreciating one of his lovely artist's models. Another variation for Quinn on his "Zorba" personality but it works.
199? (R) 90m/C Anthony Quinn, Ramon Sheen, Maud Adams, Elizabeth Ashley, R.J. Williams, Ray Walston, Victoria Vera; **D:** J. Anthony Loma; **W:** J. Anthony Loma. VHS $89.95 ATV 𝒵𝒵

Man of the Forest A cowboy goes to the aid of a damsel in distress and he winds up being framed for murder for his efforts. Based on Zane Grey's novel.
1933 59m/B Randolph Scott, Verna Hillie, Harry Carey Sr., Noah Beery Sr., Barton MacLane; **D:** Henry Hathaway. VHS $19.95 NOS, DVT, MLB 𝒵𝒵

Man of the West Reformed bad guy Cooper is asked to deliver a tidy hunk of cash to another city to recruit a school marm. Ambushed en route by his former partners in crime (who are led by his wacko uncle) he's forced to revert to his wanton ways in order to survive and save innocent hostages. There's a raging debate among Cooper fans whether this late effort has been unduly overlooked or duly ignored. A number of things conspire to give it a bad rap: Cooper does little but look mournful until the very end; there's no hiding the fact that he's older than Cobb, who plays his uncle; and the acting is in general more befitting of a B-grade slice and dicer. You be the judge.
1958 100m/C Gary Cooper, Julie London, Lee J. Cobb, Arthur O'Connell, Jack Lord, John Dehner, Royal Dano, Guy Wilkerson, Emory Parnell; **D:** Anthony Mann; **W:** Reginald Rose. VHS, Beta $19.98 MGM, FCT 𝒵𝒵½

Man of Violence A vulgar, tasteless man spends the worthless hours of his wasted life lurking about the more wretched entrance-ways of his native land. **AKA:** The Sex Racketeers.
1971 107m/C Michael Latimer, Luan Peters; **D:** Pete Walker. VHS, Beta $39.95 MON 𝒵

Man on a String In order to bring down a Mob boss the feds first frame cop Peter King and send him to the pen. When he gets out, King uses his prison contacts to get in with the Mob and winds up pitting two rival gangs against each other in order to destroy them both. Made for television.
1971 (PG) 73m/C Christopher George, Jack Warden, Keith Carradine, Joel Grey, William Schallert, Kitty Winn; **D:** Joseph Sargent. VHS COL 𝒵𝒵½

Man on Fire Told via flashback, a cynical ex-CIA man is hired as a bodyguard for the daughter of a wealthy Italian couple, who is soon thereafter kidnapped by terrorists. He goes to her rescue with all the subtlety of a wrecking ball. Decent cast goes down the tubes in this botched thriller.
1987 (R) 92m/C Scott Glenn, Brooke Adams, Danny Aiello, Joe Pesci, Paul Shenar, Jonathan Pryce, Jade Malle; **D:** Elie Chouraqui. VHS, Beta $89.98 LIV, VES 𝒵

The Man on the Box Chaplin is a wealthy bachelor who takes a job as a gardener to be near his girl. He overhears a plot by the butler, who's an enemy agent, to steal the secret plans for a helicopter from his sweetie's father. In order to thwart the dastardedly scheme Chaplin dresses as a maid to infiltrate the household.
1925 58m/B Sydney Chaplin, David Butler, Alice Calhoun, Kathleen Calhoun, Helene Costello, Theodore Lorch; **D:** Charles F. Reisner. VHS $16.95 GPV, GVV 𝒵𝒵½

Man on the Eiffel Tower Laughton plays Inspector Maigret, the detective created by novelist Georges Simenon, in a highly suspenseful and cerebral mystery about a crazed killer who defies the police to discover his identity. This is the first film Meredith directed.

1948 82m/C Charles Laughton, Burgess Meredith, Franchot Tone, Patricia Roc; **D:** Burgess Meredith. **VHS, Beta** $19.95 NOS, MRV, GEM ✗✗✗

Man on the Run A robbery takes place in the store where an Army deserter is trying to sell his gun, and he ends up taking the rap. It's up to a lovely lady lawyer to prove his innocence. Efficiently told ''B'' crime drama. **1949** 82m/B Derek Farr, Joan Hopkins, Edward Chapman, Laurence Harvey, H. Marion Crawford, Alfie Bass, John Bailey, John Stuart, Edward Underdown, Leslie Perrins, Kenneth More, Martin Miller, Eleanor Summerfield; **D:** Lawrence Huntington; **W:** Lawrence Huntington. **VHS, Beta** $16.95 SNC ✗✗

Man on the Run After an unwitting involvement with a small robbery, a teenager finds himself the object of a police manhunt for a murder suspect. **1974** (R) 90m/C Kyle Johnson, James B. Sikking, Terry Carter; **D:** Herbert L. Strock. **VHS, Beta** $59.95 PSM ✗✗½

Man or Gun Standard western yarn involving a drifter who rides into a town operated by a powerful family and liberates the cowardly townsfolk. **1958** 79m/B MacDonald Carey, Audrey Totter, James Craig, James Gleason, Warren Stevens, Harry Shannon; **D:** Albert C. Gannaway; **W:** Vance Skarstedt, James C. Cassity. **VHS** $19.99 MOV ✗½

The Man Outside After a CIA agent is fired for allegedly assisting another agent in defecting to the East, he becomes involved in further intrigue. A Russian spy is looking to defect. In the process, the ex-agent is framed for murder. Straightforward espionage tale taken from Gene Stackleborg's novel ''Double Agent.'' **1968** (R) 98m/C Van Heflin, Heidelinde Weis, Pinkas Braun, Peter Vaughan, Charles Gray, Ronnie Barker; **D:** Samuel Gallu. **VHS** NO ✗✗

Man Outside Logan is an ex-lawyer who takes to the Arkansas outback after his wife dies. Anthropologist/teacher Quinlan takes a shine to him. He seems like an okay guy, but bad guy Dillman has made it look like he's a child snatcher. Slick on the outside but empty inside independent effort. Look for former members of The Band in supporting roles. **1988** (PG-13) 109m/C Robert F. Logan, Kathleen Quinlan, Bradford Dillman, Rick Danko, Levon Helm; **D:** Mark Stouffer. **VHS** NO ✗

The Man That Corrupted Hadleyburg Entertaining adaptation of a Mark Twain short story about a stranger's plot of revenge against the hypocritical residents of a small town. Originally made for television. **1980** 40m/C Robert Preston, Fred Gwynne, Frances Sternhagen; **D:** Ralph Rosenblum. **VHS, Beta** $24.95 MON, KAR ✗

The Man They Could Not Hang A good doctor tinkering with artificial hearts is caught by police while experimenting on a willing student. When the doctor is convicted and hanged for a murder, his assistant uses the heart to bring him back to life. No longer a nice guy, he vows revenge against the jurors that sentenced him. Karloff repeated the same story line in several films, and this one is representative of the type. **1939** 70m/B Boris Karloff, Lorna Gray, Roger Pryor, Robert Wilcox; **D:** Nick Grinde. **VHS, Beta** $9.95 GKK ✗✗

Man Trouble A divorcing opera singer (Barkin) seeks the help of a sleazy attack-dog trainer (Nicholson) when she becomes the victim of a stalker. Nicholson hits on her, first because that's one of his habits, and then because he is being paid to by a billionaire who wants him to steal the manuscript of a tell-all book about him written by Barkin's sister. Although both Nicholson and Barkin are excellent actors, they lack the electricity to make the romance credible, and the jokes are weak. Supporting cast, including D'Angelo, Stanton, and McKean, provide the funny parts in this otherwise dull film. **1992** (PG-13) 100m/C Jack Nicholson, Ellen Barkin, Harry Dean Stanton, Beverly D'Angelo, Michael McKean, Saul Rubinek, Viveka Davis, Veronica Cartwright, David Clennon, John Kapelos, Paul Mazursky; **D:** Bob Rafelson; **W:** Adrien (Carole Eastman) Joyce; **M:** Georges Delerue. **VHS** $19.98 FXV ✗✗

The Man Upstairs Escaped con Moony Polaski (O'Neal) hides out in the home of crotchety spinster Victoria Brown (Hepburn). When she finds the crook in her attic, instead of turning him in, Victoria befriends the slob and soon the two are sharing dinner and secrets. Meanwhile, the manhunt for Moony is intensifying and, oh yes, Christmas is coming as well. Made for television cornpone barely saved by some professional performances. Executive producer Burt Reynolds was hoping for a part until scheduling made it impossible. **1993** 95m/C Katharine Hepburn, Ryan O'Neal, Henry Beckman, Helen Carroll, Brenda Forbes; **D:** George Schaefer; **W:** James Prideaux. **VHS** $89.95 CAF ✗✗½

The Man Who Broke 1,000 Chains A made-for-television movie about a man who is committed to a chain gang after WWII for a petty crime, and his efforts, after escaping, in making a new life for himself. An unimaginative plot is occasionally highlighted by a good scene or two. **1987** 113m/C Val Kilmer, Charles Durning, Sonia Braga; **D:** Daniel Mann; **M:** Charles Bernstein. **VHS, Beta** $79.95 LHV, WAR ✗✗

The Man Who Came to Dinner Based on the Moss Hart-George S. Kaufman play, this comedy is about a bitter radio celebrity (Woolley) on a lecture tour (a character based on Alexander Woolcott). He breaks his hip and must stay in a quiet suburban home for the winter. While there, he occupies his time by barking orders, being obnoxious and generally just driving the other residents nuts. Woolley reprises his Broadway role in this film that succeeds at every turn, loaded with plenty of satiric jabs at the Algonquin Hotel Roundtable regulars. **1941** 112m/B Monty Woolley, Bette Davis, Ann Sheridan, Jimmy Durante, Reginald Gardiner, Richard Travis, Billie Burke, Grant Mitchell, Mary Wickes, George Barbier, Ruth Vivian, Elisabeth Fraser; **D:** William Keighley; **W:** Julius J. Epstein, Philip C. Epstein. **VHS, Beta** $19.95 MGM ✗✗✗½

The Man Who Could Work Miracles A mild-mannered draper's assistant becomes suddenly endowed with supernatural powers to perform any feat he wishes. Great special effects (for an early film) and fine performances result in a classic piece of science fiction. **1937** 82m/B Ralph Richardson, Joan Gardner, Roland Young; **D:** Lothar Mendes. **VHS, Beta** $14.98 SUE ✗✗✗½

The Man Who Envied Women The non-narrative feminist story of a smug womanizer: the man ''who knows almost too much about women.'' **1985** 125m/C Bill Raymond, Larry Loonin, Trisha Brown; **D:** Yvonne Rainer; **W:** Yvonne Rainer. **VHS, Beta** NO ✗½

The Man Who Fell to Earth Entertaining and technically adept cult classic about a man from another planet (Bowie, in a bit of typecasting) who ventures to earth in hopes of finding water to save his family and drought-stricken planet. Instead he becomes a successful inventor and businessman, along the way discovering the human vices of booze, sex, and television. Also available in a restored version at 138 minutes. Remade for television in 1987 and based on Walter Tevis' novel. **1976** (R) 118m/C David Bowie, Candy Clark, Rip Torn, Buck Henry, Bernie Casey; **D:** Nicolas Roeg. **VHS, Beta** $19.95 COL ✗✗✗½

The Man Who Guards the Greenhouse Tracy must come to terms with her attraction for Jeff as well as once again trying to write a meaningful novel. **1988** 150m/C Christopher Cazenove, Rebecca Dewey. **VHS** $79.95 LHV ✗✗✗½

Man Who Had Power Over Women Disappointing sex farce about the exploits of a carnally insatiable (and married) talent executive (Taylor) who has an affair with every woman he meets and creates problems aplenty. Adapted from a novel by Gordon Williams. **1970** (R) 89m/C Rod Taylor, James Booth, Carol White, Penelope Horner, Clive Francis; **D:** John Krish; **W:** Chris Bryant, Allan Scott. **VHS, Beta** $59.98 SUE ✗✗

The Man Who Haunted Himself While a man lies in critical condition on the operating table after a car accident, his alter-ego emerges and turns his ideal life into a nightmare until the man recovers and moves toward a fateful encounter. An expanded version of an episode of the television series ''Alfred Hitchcock Presents,'' this was Moore's first movie after having starred in the TV series ''The Saint,'' and it was Dearden's last film; he died in a car accident the following year. Appeals primarily to those fascinated by ''Hitchcock'' or ''The Twilight Zone''—where mystery matters most. Filmed in London. **1970** 94m/C Roger Moore, Hildegarde Neil, Olga Georges-Picot; **D:** Basil Dearden. **VHS, Beta** NO ✗✗

The Man Who Knew Too Much Hitchcock's first international success. A British family man on vacation in Switzerland is told of an assassination plot by a dying agent. His daughter is kidnaped to force his silence. In typical Hitchcock fashion, the innocent person becomes caught in a web of intrigue; the sticky situation culminates with surprising events during the famous shootout in the final scenes. Remade by Hitchcock in 1956. **1934** 75m/B Leslie Banks, Edna Best, Peter Lorre, Nova Pilbeam, Pierre Fresnay; **D:** Alfred Hitchcock; **W:** Emlyn Williams, Charles Bennett. **VHS, Beta** $16.95 SNC, MRV, NOS ✗✗✗

The Man Who Knew Too Much Hitchcock's remake of his 1934 film, this time about an American doctor and his family vacationing in Marrakech. They become involved in a complicated international plot involving kidnapping and murder. While Doris tries to save the day by singing ''Que Sera, Sera,'' Stewart tries to locate his abducted son. More lavish settings and forms of intrigue make this a less focused and, to some, inferior version. **1956** (PG) 120m/C James Stewart, Doris Day, Brenda de Banzie, Bernard Miles, Ralph Truman, Daniel Gelin, Alan Mowbray, Carolyn Jones, Hillary Brooke; **D:** Alfred Hitchcock. **VHS, Beta** $19.95 MCA, HHE ✗✗½

The Man Who Laughs Veidt's sensitive performance highlights this silent classic. He plays a young man whose features are surgically altered into a permanent smile because his family are political enemies of the current ruler. The man is befriended by the owner of a sideshow who first exhibits him as a freak but later finds Veidt gaining fame as a clown. A beautiful blind girl in the show loves Veidt for who he is and the two find happiness.
1927 110m/B Conrad Veidt, Mary Philbin, Olga Baclanova, Josephine Crowell, George Siegmann, Brandon Hurst; **D:** Paul Leni. **VHS** *GPV ♫♫♫½*

The Man Who Lived Again Boris strives to be a brain-switcher, and suspense builds around the question of whether or not he will change his mind. Shot in England with fine sets and a definite Anglo feel to the proceedings, with Karloff doing one of his better mad scientist routines. **AKA:** The Man Who Changed His Mind; The Brainsnatchers; Dr. Maniac.
1936 61m/B Boris Karloff, Anna Lee, John Loder, Frank Cellier, Lyn Harding, Cecil Parker; **D:** Robert Stevenson. **VHS, Beta, 8mm $14.95** *SNC, VYY, MLB ♫♫½*

Man Who Loved Cat Dancing Reynolds is an outlaw on the run after avenging his wife's murder and robbing a safe with pals Hopkins and Warden, and Miles has recently escaped from her abusive husband. It's love on the run as Burt and Sarah are pursued by bounty hunters and their tragic pasts—coming close to making us care, but close doesn't mean as much in movies as it does in dancing. Based on Marilyn Durham's novel.
1973 (PG) 114m/C Burt Reynolds, Sarah Miles, Jack Warden, Lee J. Cobb, Jay Silverheels, Robert Donner; **D:** Richard Sarafian; **M:** John Williams. **VHS, Beta $19.98** *MGM, FCT ♫♫*

The Man Who Loved Women An intelligent, sensitive bachelor writes his memoirs and recalls the many, many, many women he has loved. Truffaut couples sophistication and lightheartedness, the thrill of the chase and, when it leads to an accidental death, the wondering what-it's-all-about in the mourning after. In French with English subtitles. Remade in 1983. **AKA:** L'Homme Qui Aimait les Femmes.
1977 119m/C Charles Denner, Brigitte Fossey, Leslie Caron; **D:** Francois Truffaut; **W:** Suzanne Schiffman. **VHS, Beta $19.98** *MGM, ING, BTV ♫♫♫*

The Man Who Loved Women A remake of the 1977 French film, this is slower, tries to be funnier, and is less subtle than the original. Reynolds is a Los Angeles sculptor whose reputation as a playboy leads him to a psychoanalyst's couch, where a lot of talk slows the action—though Burt & Julie (the shrink) do share the couch.
1983 (R) 110m/C Burt Reynolds, Julie Andrews, Kim Basinger, Marilu Henner, Cynthia Sikes, Jennifer Edwards; **D:** Blake Edwards; **W:** Blake Edwards. **VHS, Beta $79.95** *COL ♫♫*

The Man Who Never Was Tense true story (with melodramatic embroidery) from WWII shows in step-by-step detail how Britain duped the Axis by letting them find an Allied corpse bearing phony invasion plans. Based on the book by the scheme's mastermind Ewen Montagu, played by Webb; Peter Sellers provides the voice of an offscreen Winston Churchill.
1955 102m/C Clifton Webb, Gloria Grahame, Robert Flemyng, Josephine Griffin, Stephen Boyd, Andre Morell, Laurence Naismith, Geoffrey Keen, Michael Hordern; **D:** Ronald Neame. **VHS, Beta $19.98** *FOX, FCT ♫♫♫*

The Man Who Shot Liberty Valance Tough cowboy Wayne and idealistic lawyer Stewart join forces against dreaded gunfighter Liberty Valance, played leatherly by Marvin. While Stewart rides to Senatorial success on his reputation as the man who shot the villain, he suffers moral crises about the act, but is toughened up by Wayne. Wayne's use of the word "pilgrim" became a standard for his impersonators. Strong character acting, great Western scenes, and value judgements to ponder over make this last of Ford's black and white westerns among his best.
1962 123m/B James Stewart, John Wayne, Vera Miles, Lee Marvin, Edmond O'Brien, Andy Devine, Woody Strode, Ken Murray, Jeanette Nolan, John Qualen, Strother Martin, Lee Van Cleef, John Carradine, Carleton Young; **D:** John Ford. **VHS, Beta $14.95** *PAR, HMV ♫♫♫½*

The Man Who Skied Down Everest Documentary about a Japanese athlete who undertakes a demanding downhill run, and the cost (human and financial) of getting there.
1975 (G) 86m/C **VHS** *NO ♫♫½*

The Man Who Wagged His Tail A mean slumlord is turned into a dog as the result of a curse cast upon him. In order to return to his human form, he must be loved by someone. Despite his attempts to be loved, the dog alienates his only friend and must try to redeem himself. Played for fun, this is a mildly amusing fantasy filmed in Spain and Brooklyn. Not released in the U. S. until 1961. **AKA:** An Angel Passed Over Brooklyn; Un Angelo e Sceso a Brooklyn.
1957 91m/B Peter Ustinov, Pablito Calvo, Aroldo Tieri, Silvia Marco; **D:** Ladislao Vajda. **VHS $16.95** *SNC, VYY ♫♫½*

The Man Who Wasn't There A member of the State department receives a formula from a dying spy that can render him invisible, see? He has to use the formula to protect himself from the police and other spies, becoming a comic "Invisible Man," see? Generally chaotic tale that's bad, but not so bad that it's worth seeing, though you might want to see what invisibility looks like in 3-D.
1983 (R) 111m/C Steve Guttenberg, Jeffrey Tambor, Art Hindle, Lisa Langlois; **D:** Bruce Malmuth; **M:** Miles Goodman. **VHS, Beta $59.95** *PAR ♫*

The Man Who Would Be King A grand, old-fashioned adventure based on the classic story by Rudyard Kipling about two mercenary soldiers who travel from India to Kafiristan in order to conquer it and set themselves up as kings. Splendid characterizations by Connery and Caine, and Huston's royal directorial treatment provides it with adventure, majestic sweep, and well-developed characters.
1975 (PG) 129m/C Sean Connery, Michael Caine, Christopher Plummer, Saeed Jaffrey, Shakira Caine; **D:** John Huston; **W:** Gladys Hill, John Huston; **M:** Maurice Jarre. **VHS, Beta $19.98** *FOX ♫♫♫*

The Man Who Would Not Die During his investigation of several deaths, a man discovers that all of the deceased were actually the same man. It seems the deaths were part of an intricate scheme to cover up a million dollar heist. Two of the top three actors are killed early on; it's not very suspenseful. It's more like the mystery that would not die. From Charles Williams' novel "The Sailcloth Shroud." **AKA:** Target in the Sun.

1975 (PG) 83m/C Dorothy Malone, Keenan Wynn, Aldo Ray; **D:** Robert Arkless. **VHS, Beta $59.95** *WAR, OM ♫♫*

Man with a Cross Archaeologists of the cinema may want to unearth this early Rossellini, made by the future father of neorealist cinema as a propaganda piece for the fascist war effort. A heroic Italian chaplain on the Russian front ministers to foe and friend alike, and even converts a few commies to Christ. Not as awful as it sounds—but never forget where this came from.
1943 88m/B **D:** Roberto Rossellini. **VHS $59.95** *FST ♫♫*

A Man with a Maid A bizarre British exploitation pic mixes spookhouse cliches and sex, as a young man finds his new bachelor pad haunted by Jack the Ripper. Originally shot in 3-D and known variously as "The Groove Room" and "What the Swedish Butler Saw." It didn't help.
1973 83m/C Sue Longhurst, Martin Long, Diana Dors; **D:** Vernon Becker. **VHS $19.95** *VDM ♫*

The Man with a Movie Camera A plotless, experimental view of Moscow through the creative eye of the cameraman Dziga Vertov, founder of the Kino Eye. The editing methods and camera techniques used in this silent film were very influential and still stand up to scrutiny today.
1929 69m/B **D:** Dziga Vertov. **VHS, Beta $35.95** *IHF, MRV, DVT ♫♫♫½*

The Man with Bogart's Face Sacchi is no Bogart, but he does imitate him well. Bogart fans will enjoy this fond tribute to the late great actor, but the story uncertainly wavers between genuine detective story and detective spoof. **AKA:** Sam Marlowe, Private Eye.
1980 (PG) 106m/C Robert Sacchi, Misty Rowe, Sybil Danning, Franco Nero, Herbert Lom, Victor Buono, Olivia Hussey; **D:** Robert Day; **W:** Andrew J. Fenady; **M:** George Duning. **VHS, Beta $59.98** *FOX ♫♫*

The Man with One Red Shoe Hanks is a lovable clod of a violinist who ensnares himself in a web of intrigue when CIA agents, both good and evil, mistake him for a contact by his wearing one red shoe. Sporadically funny remake of the French "The Tall Blond Man with One Black Shoe."
1985 (PG) 92m/C Tom Hanks, Dabney Coleman, Lori Singer, Carrie Fisher, James Belushi, Charles Durning, Edward Herrmann, Tommy Noonan, Gerrit Graham, David Lander, David Ogden Stiers; **D:** Stan Dragoti. **VHS, Beta $14.98** *FXV, FOX ♫♫*

The Man with the Golden Arm A gripping film version of the Nelson Algren junkie melodrama, about an ex-addict who returns to town only to get mixed up with drugs again. Considered controversial in its depiction of addiction when released. Sinatra's performance as Frankie Machine is a stand-out.
1955 119m/B Frank Sinatra, Kim Novak, Eleanor Parker, Arnold Stang, Darren McGavin, Robert Strauss, George Mathews, John Conte, Doro Merande; **D:** Otto Preminger; **M:** Elmer Bernstein. **VHS, Beta $9.95** *WAR, MRV, CNG ♫♫♫*

The Man with the Golden Gun Roger Moore is the debonair secret agent 007 in this ninth James Bond flick. Assigned to recover a small piece of equipment which can be utilized to harness the sun's energy, Bond engages the usual bevy of villains and beauties.
1974 (PG) 134m/C Roger Moore, Christopher Lee, Britt Ekland, Maud Adams, Herve Villechaize, Clifton James, Soon-Teck Oh, Richard Loo, Marc Lawrence, Bernard Lee, Lois Maxwell, Desmond Llewelyn; **D:** Guy Hamilton;

W: Tom Mankiewicz; **M:** John Barry. VHS, Beta $19.98 *MGM, FOX* ♫♫½

The Man with Two Brains Did you hear the one about the brilliant neuro-surgeon who falls in love with a woman in his laboratory? He only has two problems: dealing with his covetous wife and finding a body for his cerebral lover. Plenty of laughs in this spoof of mad scientist movies that is redeemed from potential idiocy by the cast's titillating performances. Listen closely and you'll recognize the voice of Spacek as the brain-in-the-jar of Martin's dreams.
1983 (R) 91m/C Steve Martin, Kathleen Turner, David Warner, Sissy Spacek; **D:** Carl Reiner; **W:** Steve Martin, George Gipp, Carl Reiner; **M:** Joel Goldsmith. VHS, Beta $34.98 *WAR* ♫♫♫

Man with Two Heads Doctor Jekyll gets in touch with his innermost feelings when his muffed experiments turn him into, gasp, Mr. Blood. Another forlorn addition to the Dr. Jekyll retread collection.
1972 (R) 80m/C D: Andy Milligan; **W:** Andy Milligan. VHS *NO* ♫

The Man with Two Lives Well done horror thriller about a wealthy young man who's killed in a car accident, then brought back to life by a mad scientist. At precisely the moment his life is restored, a murderous gangster is executed and his soul enters the young man's body.
1942 ?m/C Edward Norris, Addison Richards, Marlo Dwyer. VHS $16.95 *SNC* ♫♫

The Man Without a Face Gibson plays a badly scarred recluse in Maine who develops a mentor relationship with a lonely, fatherless boy. Chuck (Stahl) wants to go away to military school, but flunks the entrance exam, and enlists former teacher McLeod as a tutor. First foray for Gibson into the director's chair tends to be overly melodramatic. Adapted from a novel by Isabelle Holland.
1993 (PG-13) 115m/C Mel Gibson, Nick Stahl, Margaret Whitton, Fay Masterson, Richard Masur, Gaby Hoffman, Geoffrey Lewis, Jack DeMave; **D:** Mel Gibson; **W:** Malcolm MacRury; **M:** James Horner. VHS, Beta *WAR* ♫♫½

Man Without a Star A cowboy helps ranchers stop a ruthless cattle owner from taking over their land. The conflict between freedom in the wild west and the need for order and settlements is powerfully internalized in Douglas, whose fight for justice will tame the cowboy code he lives by. You'll shed a tear for the fading frontier.
1955 89m/B Kirk Douglas, Jeanne Crain, Claire Trevor, William Campbell; **D:** King Vidor. VHS, Beta $19.95 *MCA* ♫♫♫

Man, Woman & Child A close, upscale California family is shocked when a child from the husband's long-ago affair with a Frenchwoman appears at their door. Pure sentimentalism, as the family confronts this unexpected development. Two hankies—one each for fine performances by Sheen and Danner. Based on a sentimental novel by Erich Segal of "Love Story" fame, who co-wrote the script.
1983 (PG) 99m/C Martin Sheen, Blythe Danner, Craig T. Nelson, David Hemmings; **D:** Dick Richards; **W:** Erich Segal; **M:** Georges Delerue. VHS, Beta $59.95 *PAR* ♫♫

Manchurian Avenger Desperados have wrested control of a Colorado gold rush town from Joe Kim's family, and he'll put an end to that, chop chop.
1984 (R) 87m/C Bobby Kim, Bill Wallace; **D:** Ed Warnick. VHS, Beta *NO* ♫

The Manchurian Candidate Political thriller about an American Korean War vet who suspects that he and his platoon may have been brainwashed during the war, with his highly decorated, heroic friend programmed by commies to be an operational assassin. Loaded with shocks, conspiracy, inventive visual imagery, and bitter political satire of naivete and machinations of the left and right. Excellent performances by an all-star cast, with Lansbury and Gregory particularly frightening. Based on the Richard Condon novel. Featuring a special interview with Sinatra and Frankenheimer in which Sinatra is deified.
1962 126m/B Frank Sinatra, Laurence Harvey, Angela Lansbury, Janet Leigh, James Gregory, Leslie Parrish, John McGiver, Henry Silva, Khigh Deigh; **D:** John Frankenheimer; **W:** George Axelrod, John Frankenheimer; **M:** David Amram. Academy Awards '62 Nominations: Best Film Editing, Best Supporting Actress (Lansbury); Golden Globe Awards '63: Best Supporting Actress (Lansbury); National Board of Review Awards '62: Best Supporting Actress (Lansbury). VHS, Beta $19.98 *MGM* ♫♫♫

The Mandarin Mystery In the process of trying to retrieve a stolen Mandarin stamp, detective Ellery Queen uncovers a counterfeiting ring. Some fine performances, but a muddled script creates a mystery as to whether or not the action is played for laughs.
1937 65m/B Eddie Quillan, Charlotte Henry, Rita La Roy, Wade Boteler, Franklin Pangborn, George Irving, Kay Hughes, William Newell; **D:** Ralph Staub. VHS, Beta $16.95 *NOS, SNC* ♫♫

Mandela A gripping, powerful drama about human rights and dignity, tracing the real-life trials of Nelson and Winnie Mandela. The story focuses on the couple's early opposition to South African apartheid, as well as the events leading up to Nelson's life-imprisonment sentencing in 1964. Excellent, restrained performances from Glover and Woodard. Made for cable television.
1987 135m/C Danny Glover, Alfre Woodard, John Matshikiza, Warren Clarke, Allan Cordunner, Julian Glover; **D:** Philip Saville. VHS, Beta $79.99 *KUI, FCT* ♫♫♫

Mandinga A plantation owner develops an obsession for one of his female slaves. Made to cash in on the already exploitive "Mandingo"; two wrongs don't make a right.
1977 100m/C Anthony Gismondi; **D:** Mario Pinzauti. VHS, Beta $59.95 *PAR* ♫

Mandingo Overheated Southern-fried tale of slavery in the Deep South, circa 1840, dealing with the tangled loves and hates of a family and their slaves. Heavyweight boxer Norton made his screen debut in the title role as the slave who makes his master money with his boxing prowess. King is the wastrel son who makes Norton's wife, another slave, his mistress. Followed by 1975's "Drum." Based on the novel by Kyle Onstott.
1975 (R) 127m/C James Mason, Susan George, Perry King, Richard Ward, Ken Norton, Ben Masters, Brenda Sykes, Paul Benedict, Ji Tu Cambuka; **D:** Richard Fleischer; **M:** Maurice Jarre. VHS, Beta $59.95 *PAR* ♫♫

Mandroid Two scientists design a high-tech robot, Mandroid, to handle a powerful new element they've discovered. Dr. Zimmer and daughter Zanna want to use their creation to help mankind while mad scientist Dr. Drago wants the power Mandroid can give him. When a laboratory accident leaves Drago horribly disfigured it also gives him the chance to steal Mandroid and put his evil plan into action. Filmed on location in Romania.

1993 (R) 81m/C Brian Cousins, Jane Caldwell, Michael DellaFemina, Curt Lowens, Patrick Ersgard, Robert Symonds; **D:** Joakim Ersgard; **W:** Jackson Barr, Earl Kenton. VHS, Beta *PAR* ♫♫

Mandy Poignant drama of a deaf child and the family who must come to terms with her deafness. Well-developed plot and well performed; an intelligent treatment in all. *AKA:* Crash of Silence.
1953 93m/B Phyllis Calvert, Jack Hawkins, Mandy Miller; **D:** Alexander MacKendrick. VHS, Beta *LCA* ♫♫♫

Manfish Two men venture out in a boat, the Manfish, to hunt for sunken treasure in the Caribbean. Only one survives the trip, as his greed destroys the other. The scenes off the Jamaican coast are lovely, but the story fails to take hold. Though there is a star aboard in Chaney, you'll look astern and bow out with a sinking feeling. Derived from two Edgar Allan Poe stories, "The Gold Bug" and "The Tell-Tale Heart."
1956 76m/C John Bromfield, Lon Chaney Jr., Victor Jory, Barbara Nichols; **D:** W. Lee Wilder. VHS $16.95 *NOS, SNC* ♫½

The Mango Tree A young man comes of age in a small Australian town during the 1920s. Everything is well done, if not dramatic or fascinating.
1977 93m/C Geraldine Fitzgerald, Robert Helpmann, Diane Craig, Gerald Kennedy, Christopher Pate; **D:** Kevin Dobson. VHS, Beta *NO* ♫♫½

The Manhandlers After the uncle of a young woman is killed by the mob, she goes after them for revenge. For your entertainment pleasure, best stick with the soup commercial of the same name.
1973 (R) 87m/C Cara Burgess, Judy Brown, Vince Cannon, Rosalind Miles; **D:** Lee Madden. VHS, Beta $69.95 *TWE* ♫

Manhattan Successful TV writer Allen yearns to be a serious writer. He struggles through a series of ill-fated romances, including one with high school senior Hemingway, about 25 years younger, and another with Keaton, who's also having an on-again, off-again affair with Murphy, Allen's best friend. Scathingly serious and comic view of modern relationships in urban America and of the modern intellectual neuroses. Shot in black-and-white to capture the mood of Manhattan and mated with an excellent Gershwin soundtrack, the video version preserves the widescreen effect adding yet another impressive element to the overall production.
1979 (R) 96m/B Woody Allen, Diane Keaton, Meryl Streep, Mariel Hemingway, Michael Murphy, Wallace Shawn, Anne Byrne, Tisa Farrow, Mark Linn-Baker, David Rasche, Karen Allen; **D:** Woody Allen; **W:** Woody Allen, Marshall Brickman; **M:** George Gershwin. Academy Awards '79 Nominations: Best Original Screenplay, Best Supporting Actress (Hemingway); British Academy Awards '79: Best Film; Cesar Awards '80: Best Foreign Film; National Board of Review Awards '79: 10 Best Films of the Year; New York Film Critics Awards '79: Best Director (Allen); National Society of Film Critics Awards '79: Best Actress (Keaton), Best Director (Allen). VHS, Beta $14.95 *MGM* ♫♫♫♫

Manhattan Baby Unscary horror film about an archaeologist who digs up a relic that draws evil into the world and infects an American girl with powers that lead to many deaths. Advice to you that might have saved the archaeologist: don't dig this.
1982 90m/C Christopher Connelly, Martha Taylor; **D:** Lucio Fulci. VHS, Beta $69.98 *LIV* ♫

Manhattan Melodrama Powell and Gable are best friends from childhood, growing up together in an orphanage. Their adult lives take different paths, however, as Powell becomes a respected prosecuting attorney while Gable becomes a notorious gambler/racketeer. Lovely Loy is Gable's girl who comes between the two. Eventually, Powell must prosecute his life-long friend for murder in order to win the governorship. One of Gable's toughest roles; Powell's character, however, is a bit unbelievable as his ethics seem to extend beyond love and friendship. This is the first film to team Powell and Loy, who would go on to make 13 more films together, including the "Thin Man" series. **1934 93m/B** Clark Gable, William Powell, Myrna Loy, Leo Carrillo, Nat Pendleton, George Sidney, Isabel Jewell, Muriel Evans, Claudelle Kaye, Frank Conroy, Jimmy Butler, Mickey Rooney, Edward Van Sloan; **D:** Woodbridge S. Van Dyke. **VHS, Beta $19.98** MGM, CCB *♪♪♪½*

Manhattan Merry-Go-Round One of the movies where a corrupt boss—in this case a record producer—threatens a bunch of good people as a pretense for a plot when the movie simply serves as a showcase for stars. Features many singing stars of the thirties ("where have you gone Cab Calloway?") plus Joltin' Joe, who ended up having a hit-streak in another genre. ♫ Mama I Wanna Make Rhythm; Manhattan Merry-Go-Round; Heaven?; I Owe You; It's Round Up Time in Reno. **1937 89m/B** Cab Calloway, Louis Prima, Ted Lewis, Ann Dvorak, Phil Regan, Kay Thompson, Gene Autry, Joe DiMaggio; **D:** Charles Reisner. **VHS, Beta $19.95** NOS, VCN, HHT *♪♪*

Manhattan Murder Mystery Keaton and Allen team up again as two New Yorkers who get involved in a mystery when their neighbor dies under strange circumstances. Light, entertaining comedy steers clear of some of Allen's heavier themes and should keep audiences laughing till the end. Allen, writing with Brickman for the first time since "Annie Hall" and "Manhattan," makes viewers fall in love with the magic of NYC all over again. **1993 (PG) 105m/C** Woody Allen, Diane Keaton, Anjelica Huston, Alan Alda, Jerry Adler, Ron Rifkin, Joy Behar, Lynn Cohen, Melanie Norris; **D:** Woody Allen; **W:** Woody Allen, Marshall Brickman. **VHS, 8mm** COL *♪♪♪*

The Manhattan Project An exceptionally bright teenager decides to build a nuclear bomb for his project at the New York City science fair. He's out to prove how dangerously easy it is to build big bombs. When he steals plutonium from a local government installation, the feds attempt to nab the precocious youngster. Light moral overtones abound. Director Brickman co-wrote similarly titled "Manhattan." **AKA:** Manhattan Project: The Deadly Game. **1986 (PG-13) 112m/C** John Lithgow, Christopher Collet, Cynthia Nixon, Jill Eikenberry, John Mahoney, Sully Boyer, Richard Council, Robert Schenkkan, Paul Austin; **D:** Marshall Brickman; **W:** Marshall Brickman. **VHS, Beta $14.98** REP *♪♪*

Manhunt A man marked for execution by the mob launches his own assault on the organization's headquarters. Action and Italian food, but not much else. Dubbed. **AKA:** The Italian Connection; La Mala Ordina. **1973 (R) 93m/C** Henry Silva, Mario Adorf, Woody Strode, Lucianna Paluzzi; **D:** Fernando Di Leo. **VHS, Beta $59.95** MED, AIP *♪♪*

The Manhunt A framed cowhand escapes from prison to prove his innocence. Made-for-TV movie.

1986 89m/C Ernest Borgnine, Bo Svenson, John Ethan Wayne; **D:** Larry Ludman. **VHS, Beta $59.95** MED *♪♪*

Manhunt for Claude Dallas Mountain man uses game wardens for firing practice, ticks off local sheriff Torn, is tossed behind bars, checks out ahead of schedule and becomes a legend in his own time. Mediocre made-for-TV macho man melodrama. From the novel "Outlaw" by Jeff Long. **1986 93m/C** Matt Salinger, Rip Torn, Claude Akins, Pat Hingle, Lois Nettleton, Beau Starr, Frederick Coffin; **D:** Jerry London; **W:** John Gay; **M:** Stephen Dorff. **VHS, Beta $79.95** PSM *♪♪*

Manhunt in the African Jungle An American undercover agent battles Nazi forces in Africa. A serial in fifteen episodes. **1954 240m/B** Rod Cameron, Joan Marsh, Duncan Renaldo. **VHS $29.98** VCN, REP, MLB *♪♪*

Manhunt of Mystery Island Serial about the super-powered Captain Mephisto. **AKA:** Captain Mephisto and the Transformation Machine. **1945 100m/C** Linda Stirling, Roy Barcroft, Richard Bailey, Kenne Duncan; **D:** Spencer Gordon Bennet. **VHS, Beta** MED, MLB *♪♪*

Manhunter A made-for-television escapade about a WWI Marine who returns home from China in 1933 to track down a bunch of gangsters headed by his sister. **1974 78m/C** Ken Howard, Stefanie Powers, Gary Lockwood, Tim O'Connor, L.Q. Jones; **D:** Walter Grauman. **VHS, Beta $19.98** WAR, TWE *♪*

Manhunter A mercenary sets out to disengage organized crime from high-level politics. Produced by Owensby. **1983 92m/C** Earl Owensby, Johnny Popwell, Doug Hale, Elizabeth Upton; **D:** Earl Owensby. **VHS, Beta $49.95** MED *♪♪½*

Manhunter FBI forensic specialist—who retired after a harrowing pursuit of a serial killer—is called back to duty to find a psychotic family killer. His technique: to match the thought processes of serial killers and thus anticipate their moves. Intense thriller, based on the Thomas Harris novel "Red Dragon." Harris also wrote "The Silence of the Lambs," whose most notorious character Hannibal ("The Cannibal") Lecter, appears in this movie as well. Director Mann applies the slick techniques he introduced in the popular television series "Miami Vice," creating a quiet, moody intensity broken by sudden onslaughts of violence. Available in widescreen on laserdisc. **AKA:** Red Dragon. **1986 (R) 100m/C** William L. Petersen, Kim Greist, Joan Allen, Brian Cox, Dennis Farina, Stephen Lang, Tommy Noonan; **D:** Michael Mann; **W:** Michael Mann. **VHS, Beta $14.95** WAR *♪♪♪*

Mania Fine adaptation of the Burke and Hare grave robbing legend. Cushing is the doctor who needs corpses and Pleasence and Rose provide them by any means. Highly atmospheric representation of dismal, 19th century Edinburgh. Very graphic for its time. **AKA:** The Flesh and the Fiends; Fiendish Ghouls; Psycho Killers. **1960 87m/B** Peter Cushing, June Laverick, Donald Pleasence, George Rose, Dermot Walsh, Renee Houston, Billie Whitelaw, John Cairney, Michael Balfour; **D:** John Gilling. **VHS $16.95** SNC, DVT, MLB *♪♪½*

Mania Four suspense/murder stories set in a sleazy urban milieu. **198? 120m/C** Deborah Grover, Stephen Hunter, Lenore Zann, Wayne Robson. **Beta** NO *♪♪*

Maniac A scientist has designs on raising the dead and searches for victims on which to experiment. Bizarre "adults only" exploitation feature was considered very risque for

its time, and includes eaten eyeballs, a cat fight with syringes and a rapist who thinks he's an orangutan. A must for genre aficionados. **1934 67m/B** Bill Woods, Horace Carpenter, Ted Edwards, Phyllis Diller, Thea Ramsey, Jennie Dark, Marcel Andre, Celia McGann; **D:** Dwain Esper. **VHS, Beta $14.95** VDM, SNC, MRV Woof!

Maniac An American artist living in France becomes involved with the daughter of a cafe owner, not suspecting that murder will follow. Seems that her old man is locked up in an insane asylum for torching the daughter's rapist several years earlier. **1963 86m/B** Kerwin Mathews, Nadia Gray, Donald Houston, Liliane Brousse; **D:** Michael Carreras; **W:** Jimmy Sangster. **VHS, Beta $49.95** COL, MLB *♪♪*

Maniac A New York cop hunts down an arrow-shooting and obviously crazed Vietnam veteran who endeavors to hold an entire Arizona town for ransom. Which is entirely appropriate, since the cast is in it only for the money. **AKA:** Ransom; Assault on Paradise; The Town That Cried Terror. **1977 (PG) 87m/C** Oliver Reed, Deborah Raffin, Stuart Whitman, Jim Mitchum, Edward Brett, John Ireland, Richard Compton, Paul Koslo; **D:** Richard Compton. **VHS, Beta $24.98** SUE, LIV, VES *♪*

Maniac A psycho murderer slaughters and scalps his victims, adding the "trophies" to his collection. Carries a self-imposed equivalent "X" rating due to its highly graphic gore quotient. For extremely strong stomachs only. **1980 91m/C** Joe Spinell, Caroline Munro, Gail Lawrence, Kelly Piper, Tom Savini; **D:** William Lustig; **W:** William Lustig. **VHS, Beta $54.95** MED Woof!

Maniac Cop In New York city, a cop goes beyond the realm of sanity and turns vigilante. Low-budget slasher/thriller that too often sags. **1988 (R) 92m/C** Tom Atkins, Bruce Campbell, Laurene Landon, Richard Roundtree, William Smith, Robert Z'Dar, Sheree North; **D:** William Lustig; **W:** Larry Cohen. **VHS, Beta $19.98** TWE, HHE *♪*

Maniac Cop 2 Everyone thought he was dead but you can't keep a bad guy down so this grossly disfigured policeman forms a one-man vigilante squad, seeking revenge (why never matters—just the body count). Blood and guts fly as any plot shortcomings are cleverly disguised by an array of violent video deaths. Sequel to "Maniac Cop." **1990 (R) 90m/C** Robert Davi, Claudia Christian, Michael Lerner, Bruce Campbell, Laurene Landon, Robert Z'Dar, Clarence Williams III, Leo Rossi; **D:** William Lustig; **W:** Larry Cohen. **VHS $89.95** LIV *♪*

Maniac Cop 3 The grossly disfigured policeman returns yet again to exact gory vengeance as the good guys try to get rid of him once and for all. **1993 (R) 85m/C** Robert Z'Dar, Robert Davi, Gretchen Becker, Paul Gleason, Doug Savant, Caitlin Dulany; **D:** William Lustig, Joel Soisson; **W:** Larry Cohen; **M:** Jerry Goldsmith. **VHS $89.95** ACA *♪*

Maniac Warriors A nuclear apocalypse has caused some strange changes in the population—and not for the better. Blood-crazed mutants attack the heavily armed inhabitants of New State Idaho and there's lots of mayhem in store. **1992? 91m/C** Tom Schioler, Frank Wilson, Melanie Kilgour. **VHS $89.95** AIP, MOV *♪*

The Manions of America The long and sometimes interesting rags-to-riches tale of Rory O'Manion, a feisty Irish patriot who leaves his native land during the potato famine of 1845 to settle in America. Originally a television miniseries.
1981 290m/C Pierce Brosnan, Kate Mulgrew, Linda Purl, David Soul, Kathleen Beller, Simon MacCorkindale; *D:* Joseph Sargent, Charles S. Dubin. VHS, Beta $69.95 *PSM, PAR ⅔½*

Manipulator A deranged ex-movie make-up man (Rooney, playing to type) kidnaps a young actress and holds her prisoner in a deserted Hollywood sound stage.
1971 (R) 91m/C Mickey Rooney, Luana Anders, Keenan Wynn; *D:* Yabo Yablonsky. VHS, Beta $69.98 *LIV, VES ⅔*

The Manitou A San Francisco woman suffers from a rapidly growing neck tumor which eventually grows into a 400-year-old Indian witch doctor. (I hate when that happens.) Redeemed only by good special effects, especially those that kept Curtis, Strasberg, and Meredith from laughing.
1978 (PG) 104m/C Susan Strasberg, Tony Curtis, Stella Stevens, Ann Sothern, Burgess Meredith, Michael Ansara; *D:* William Girdler. VHS, Beta $9.95 *COL, NLC ⅔*

Mankillers A group of tough female convicts are enlisted to hunt down and rub out a psycho drug dealer, all the while displaying their feminine charms.
1987 90m/C Edd Byrnes, Gail Fisher, Edy Williams, Lynda Aldon, William Zipp, Christopher Lunde, Susanne Tegman, Marilyn Stafford, Paul Bruno, Byron Clark; *D:* David A. Prior. VHS, Beta $14.95 *COL ⅔*

Mannequin Tracy and Crawford star in this romantic story of a poor girl who finds temporary happiness by marrying a wealthy man after ditching her con-artist husband. Somewhat predictable, the movie reads like a "People" magazine story on The Donald and Ivana. Tracy and Crawford keep the story afloat (in their only film together), with an able assist from Curtis.
1937 95m/B Joan Crawford, Spencer Tracy, Alan Curtis, Ralph Morgan, Leo Gorcey, Elisabeth Risdon, Paul Fix; *D:* Frank Borzage; *W:* Joseph L. Mankiewicz. VHS $19.98 *MGM, MED ⅔½*

Mannequin A young artist creates a store window display using various mannequins, one of which contains the spirit of an ancient Egyptian woman. She comes to life when he is around, and naturally none of his co-workers believe him. Very light comedy, featuring two pretty stars and music by Jefferson Starship.
1987 (PG) 90m/C Andrew McCarthy, Kim Cattrall, Estelle Getty, James Spader, Meshach Taylor, Carole Davis, G.W. Bailey; *D:* Michael Gottlieb; *M:* Jefferson Starship. VHS, Beta $9.99 *CCB, MED, VTR ⅔*

Mannequin 2: On the Move Less of a sequel, more of a lame rehash proving that the first "Mannequin" could have been even dumber. At this rate part three will be off the scale. Now it's a lovesick Teutonic princess frozen for 1,000 years who revives in a department store. Taylor reprises his grotesque gay role.
1991 (PG) 95m/C Kristy Swanson, William Ragsdale, Meshach Taylor, Terry Kiser, Stuart Pankin; *D:* Stewart Raffill; *W:* Ed Rugoff. VHS $92.98 *LIV Woof!*

Mannikin A chilling supernatural short by Robert Bloch about a young singer who is possessed by a demon.
1977 28m/C Ronee Blakley, Keir Dullea; *D:* Donald W. Thompson. VHS, Beta *LCA Woof!*

Manny's Orphans An out-of-work teacher takes on a lovable home for orphaned boys. Dull remake of "Bad News Bears." *AKA:* Here Come the Tigers.
1978 (PG) 92m/C Richard Lincoln, Malachy McCourt, Sel Skolnick; *D:* Sean S. Cunningham. VHS, Beta $69.98 *LIV, VES, CNG ⅔*

Manon Tragic tale of a French woman condemned for her affair with a Resistance fighter. They flee to Paris, where her brother forces her into prostitution. Based on the novel "Manon Lescaut" by Abbe Antoine-Francois Prevost. In French with English subtitles.
1950 91m/B Cecile Aubry, Michel Auclair, Serge Reggiani, Henri Vilbert, Daniel Ivernel; *D:* Henri-Georges Clouzot. VHS $24.95 *NOS ⅔*

Manon of the Spring In this excellent sequel to "Jean de Florette," the adult daughter of the dead hunchback, Jean, discovers who blocked up the spring on her father's land. She plots her revenge, which proves greater than she could ever imagine. Montand is astonishing. Based on a Marcel Pagnol novel. In French with English subtitles. *AKA:* Manon des Sources; Jean de Florette 2.
1987 (PG) 113m/C Yves Montand, Daniel Auteuil, Emmanuelle Beart, Hippolyte Girardot; *D:* Claude Berri; *W:* Gerard Brach, Claude Berri. VHS, Beta $19.98 *ORI, APD, ING ⅔⅔½*

Manos, the Hands of Fate Horrible acting and laughable special effects elevate this story of a family ensnared by a satanic cult a notch above your average bad horror film. Highlights include a Satan-like character who can't stop laughing; the dreaded "hounds of hell" (or are those mangy dogs with big ears glued on?); and Torgo the monstrous henchman, who you know is evil because he has giant kneecaps (a sure sign of the devil's work). Notable as the one of the most often requested movies on Comedy Central's satiric "Mystery Science Theatre 3000," this one is good for a laugh.
1966 74m/C Tom Nayman, Diane Mahree, Hal P. Warren, John Reynolds; *D:* Hal P. Warren; *W:* Hal P. Warren. VHS $19.98 *SNC Woof!*

Manos Torpes A man who is left to die in the desert is rescued by someone who teaches him how to avenge his would-be killers.
1965 93m/C Peter Lee Lawrence, Alberto De Mendoza, Pilar Velasquez. VHS, Beta $45.95 *MAD ⅔*

Man's Best Friend A guard dog is the object of a genetic experiment that has given him the agressiveness of other creatures, including a cobra and a leopard. Since Max is an enormous Tibetan mastiff this means big trouble for everyone but the reporter (Sheedy) who rescued him—and even she better watch out.
1993 (R) 87m/C Ally Sheedy, Lance Henriksen, Frederic Lehne, Robert Costanzo, John Cassisi, J.D. Daniels; *D:* John Lafia; *W:* John Lafia; *M:* Joel Goldsmith. VHS *NLC ⅔*

Man's Country A rip-roarin' western saga filled with the usual action and danger, as ranger Randall leads the fight against a band of nasties headed by Long, in a dual role as twin brothers.
1938 55m/B Jack Randall, Ralph Peters, Marjorie Reynolds, Walter Long; *D:* Robert F. Hill. VHS, Beta $19.95 *NOS, DVT ⅔*

Man's Favorite Sport? A slapstick comedy about a renowned fishing expert author who actually hates fishing, but is forced to compete in a major tournament by a romantically inclined publicity agent. Very funny in spots.

1963 121m/C Rock Hudson, Paula Prentiss, Charlene Holt, Maria Perschy, John McGiver; *D:* Howard Hawks; *M:* Henry Mancini. VHS, Beta $14.95 *MCA, CCB ⅔½*

Man's Land A ranch needs savin', and Hoot's the guy to do it in this formulaic Gibson epic.
1932 65m/B Hoot Gibson, Marion Shilling, Skeeter Bill Robbins, Alan Bridge; *D:* Phil Rosen. VHS, Beta *VCI ⅔*

Mansfield Park Fanny is an impoverished young woman, snubbed by society, who earns the respect and love of her cousin in a BBC mini-series adaptation of the Jane Austen classic set in 19th century England.
1985 261m/C Sylvestria Le Touzel, Bernard Hepton, Anna Massey, Donald Pleasence; *D:* David Giles. VHS, Beta $29.98 *FOX, TVC, HMV ⅔*

The Manster Another masterpiece from the director who brought us "Monster from Green Hell." Womanizing, whiskey swilling American journalist receives mysterious injection from crazed scientist and sprouts unsightly hair and extra head. Although shot in the land of the rising sun, lips move in sync with dialogue. *AKA:* The Manster—Half Man, Half Monster; The Split.
1959 72m/B Peter Dyneley, Jane Hylton, Satoshi Nakamura, Terri Zimmern; *D:* Kenneth Crane. VHS $19.98 *SNC, MRV ⅔*

Mantis in Lace A go-go dancer slaughters men while tripping on LSD. Cinematography by pre-"Easy Rider" Laslo Kovacs. Watch it for the "hep" dialogue. *AKA:* Lila.
1968 (R) 68m/C Susan Stewart, Steve Vincent, M.K. Evans, Vic Lance, Pat Barrington, Janu Wine, Stuart Lancaster, John Carrol, Judith Crane, Cheryl Trepton; *D:* William Rotsler. VHS $24.95 *TPV ⅔*

Mantrap Early silent success by Fleming, who later directed "Gone with the Wind" and "The Wizard of Oz." Fabled flapper Bow tempts a lawyer on retreat in the woods.
1926 66m/B Clara Bow, Ernest Torrence, Percy Marmont, Eugene Pallette, Tom Kennedy; *D:* Victor Fleming. VHS, Beta $19.95 *GPV, FCT ⅔*

The Manxman Hitchcock's last silent film, a romantic melodrama about ambition and infidelity on the Isle of Man.
1929 129m/B Carl Brisson, Anny Ondra; *D:* Alfred Hitchcock. VHS, Beta $39.95 *VYY, MRV, MLB ⅔*

Many Faces of Sherlock Holmes A documentary look at the various incarnations of the famous sleuth from A. Conan Doyle's stories to various film portrayals.
1986 58m/C Christopher Plummer, Basil Rathbone, Christopher Lee. VHS, Beta $79.95 *PSM ⅔½*

Map of the Human Heart Thirty-year saga told in flashback. Young Eskimo Avik (Lee) and his Metis love interest Albertine (Parillaud) struggle with racism in a white world. They meet and become friends as children and years later meet again in Dresden during WWII, but now Albertine is married to Avik's once close friend, denying her heritage and living in the white world that he has been fighting for so long. Mediocre movie with extraordinary Arctic scenery. Cusack has a small role as a mapmaker.
1993 (R) 109m/C Jason Scott Lee, Anne Parillaud, Patrick Bergin, Robert Joamie, Annie Galipeau, John Cusack, Jeanne Moreau; *D:* Vincent Ward; *W:* Vincent Ward, Louis Nowra. VHS $19.98 *HBO, FCT, BTV ⅔*

Marat/Sade A theatrical production presented by patients at a mental institution is directed by the Marquis de Sade. Well directed and visually effective, featuring Jackson's first film performance. Based on a play by Peter Weiss. Some theaters were forced to add extensions to the marquee when the film was first released. *AKA:* Persecution and Assassination of Jean-Paul Marat as Performed by the Inmates of the Asylum of Charenton Under the Direction of the Marquis De Sade.
1966 (R) 115m/C Patrick Magee, Clifford Rose, Glenda Jackson, Ian Richardson, Brenda Kempner, Ruth Baker, Michael Williams; *D:* Peter Brook. **VHS $34.95** *WBF, MGM, LUM* 🐾🐾🐾½

Marathon When a middle-aged jogger's ego gets a boost through the attention of a beautiful young woman, he takes up marathon running. Light comedy. Made for television.
1980 100m/C Bob Newhart, Leigh Taylor-Young, Herb Edelman, Dick Gautier, Anita Gillette, John Hillerman; *D:* Jackie Cooper. **VHS $59.95** *LIV* 🐾🐾

Marathon Man Nightmarish chase-thriller in which a graduate student becomes entangled in a plot involving a murderous Nazi fugitive. As student Hoffman is preparing for the Olympic marathon, he is reunited with his secret-agent brother, setting the intricate plot in motion. Courtesy of his brother, Hoffman becomes involved with Olivier, an old crazed Nazi seeking jewels taken from concentration camp victims. Nonstop action throughout, including a torture scene sure to set your teeth on edge. Goldman adapted the screenplay from his novel.
1976 (R) 125m/C Dustin Hoffman, Laurence Olivier, Marthe Keller, Roy Scheider, William Devane, Fritz Weaver; *D:* John Schlesinger; *W:* William Goldman. Academy Awards '76 Nominations: Best Supporting Actor (Olivier); Golden Globe Awards '77: Best Supporting Actor (Olivier). **VHS, Beta $24.95** *PAR* 🐾🐾🐾

Marauder The prince of Venice leads a sea-faring onslaught against ransacking pirates and enemy fleets.
1965 90m/C Gordon Scott, Giana Maria Canale, Franca Bettoya; *D:* Luigi Capuano. **VHS, Beta** *NO* 🐾🐾

Marbella A luxury resort in Spain is the setting for a big caper heist of three million dollars from a monarchical tycoon.
1985 96m/C Rod Taylor, Britt Ekland; *D:* Miguel Hermoso. **VHS, Beta $29.98** *LIV* 🐾½

Marcados por el Destino Three Mexicans come into America looking for a better life, but they don't find it.
1987 95m/C Julio Aleman, Roberto "Flaco" Guzman, Alma Murillo. **VHS, Beta $77.95** *MAD* 🐾🐾½

March of the Wooden Soldiers The classic Mother Goose tale about the secret life of Christmas toys, with Laurel and Hardy as Santa's helpers who must save Toyland from the wicked Barnaby. A Yuletide "must see." Also available in a colorized version. *AKA:* Babes in Toyland.
1934 73m/B Stan Laurel, Oliver Hardy, Charlotte Henry, Henry Kleinbach (Brandon), Felix Knight, Jean Darling, Johnny Downs, Marie Wilson; *D:* Charles "Buddy" Rogers, Gus Meins. **VHS $29.95** *NOS, GKK, IME* 🐾🐾🐾

March or Die Great potential, unrealized. An American joins the French Foreign Legion during WWI after his dismissal from West Point. Following the brutality of training, he is assigned to guard an archeological expedition in Morocco, where he pulls together a rag-tag outfit for the mission. Hackman proves once again the wide range of his

acting abilities, surmounting the cliched and fairly sadistic plot. Shot on location in the Sahara Desert.
1977 (PG) 104m/C Gene Hackman, Terence Hill, Max von Sydow, Catherine Deneuve, Ian Holm; *D:* Dick Richards; *W:* David Zelag Goodman; *M:* Maurice Jarre. **VHS** *FOX* 🐾🐾½

Marciano A made-for-television version of the great boxer's life. Average fight movie.
1979 97m/C Tony LoBianco, Vincent Gardenia; *D:* Bernard L. Kowalski; *M:* Ernest Gold. **VHS, Beta $9.98** *SUE, NLC* 🐾🐾

Marco Entertaining musical adventure of Marco Polo's life casts Arnaz as Marco Polo and Mostel as Kublai Khan. A couple of cut-ups, right? One of the first films to combine animation with live action. Shot partially on location in the Orient. 🎵By Damn; Walls; A Family Man; Spaghetti.
1973 109m/C Desi Arnaz Jr., Zero Mostel, Jack Weston, Cie Cie Win; *D:* Seymour Robbie. **VHS, Beta $49.95** *PSM* 🐾🐾

Marco Polo, Jr. Marco Polo, Jr., the daring descendant of the legendary explorer, travels the world in search of his destiny in this song-filled, feature-length, but poorly animated, fantasy.
1972 82m/C *D:* Eric Porter; *V:* Bobby Rydell. **VHS, Beta $24.95** *FHE, WTA* 🐾🐾

Mardi Gras for the Devil Black magic and the occult combine as a New Orleans cop tries to catch a killer who strikes only at Mardi Gras. The cop's got his work cut out for him since the killer is no mere mortal but a demon who believes in human sacrifice.
1993 (R) 95m/C Robert Davi, Michael Ironside, Lesley-Anne Down, Lydie Denier, Mike Starr, Margaret Avery, John Amos; *D:* David A. Prior; *W:* David A. Prior. **VHS, Beta $89.95** *PSM* 🐾🐾

Mardi Gras Massacre Aztec priest arrives in New Orleans during Mardi Gras to revive the blood ritual of human sacrifice to an Aztec god. A police detective relentlessly pursues him. Much gore and gut-slicing, with no redeeming social value. *AKA:* Crypt of Dark Secrets.
1978 92m/C Curt Dawson, Gwen Arment, Wayne Mack, Laura Misch; *D:* Jack Weis. **VHS, Beta $49.95** *VHE* Woof!

Margin for Murder Mike Hammer investigates a mysterious accident that killed his best friend. Made for television. *AKA:* Mickey Spillane's Margin for Murder.
1981 98m/C Kevin Dobson, Cindy Pickett, Donna Dixon, Charles Hallahan; *D:* Daniel Haller. **VHS, Beta $59.95** *PSM* 🐾🐾

Maria A young man returns to his hometown to rekindle a romance with his childhood sweetheart. *AKA:* Marie.
1971 102m/C Fernando Allende, Taryn Power, Alicia Caro, Jose Suarez; *D:* Tito Davison. **VHS, Beta $67.45** *MAD* 🐾🐾

Maria Candelaria Society rejects a woman because people don't like her mother. (She posed nude for an artist, and the town responds by stoning her to death, proving that going against small-town morals can be lethal). Eventually, time and circumstance push daughter onto mother's path in this tragic soaper. Del Rio portrays the scorned young woman, although she was 40 years old. *AKA:* Portrait of Maria; Xochimilco.
1946 96m/B Dolores Del Rio, Pedro Armendariz Sr., Margarita Cortes; *D:* Emilio Fernandez. **VHS, Beta $44.95** *MAD, AUD* 🐾🐾🐾

Maria Chapdelaine An early film from the renowned French director, in which a brutish trapper and a sophisticate battle for the love of a girl in the Canadian wilderness. English subtitles. Remade in 1984.

1934 75m/B Jean Gabin, Jean-Pierre Aumont, Madeleine Renaud; *D:* Julien Duvivier. **VHS, Beta $44.95** *HHT* 🐾🐾🐾

Maria Chapdelaine Around the turn of the century, a young girl in the Northern Canadian wilderness endures a year of passion, doomed love, and tragedy. In French with subtitles. Remake of a 1935 French film.
1984 108m/C Nick Mancuso, Carole Laure, Claude Rich, Pierre Curzi; *D:* Gilles Carle. **VHS, Beta $59.95** *MED* 🐾🐾½

Mariachis Mexican folklore and music are included in this Western.
1949 90m/B Antonio Badu, Isobel Del Puerto, Fernando Casanova, Beatriz Aguirre, Jose Angel "Ferrusquilla" Espinosa; *D:* Adolfo Fernandez Bustamante. **VHS, Beta $54.95** *MAD* 🐾🐾

Marianela A disfigured peasant girl cares for a blind man, and the two fall in love. She doesn't tell him about her appearance until the day comes that he regains his sight. In Spanish.
197? 113m/C Pierre Orcel, Rocio Durcal; *D:* Angelino Fons. **VHS, Beta** *MED* 🐾🐾

Maria's Child Light comedy about a dancer who becomes pregnant and must decide whether or not to keep the baby. When her live-in boyfriend (not the father) admits he cheated on her, she kicks him out. Unable to make up her mind, she imagines a dialogue with the fetus. Second of a trilogy by British television screenwriter Malcolm McKay on the subject of forgiveness.
1993 97m/C Yolanda Vasquez, David O'Hara, Fiona Shaw, Alec McCowen, Sophie Okenado, Linda Davidson, Rudi Davies, Nicholas Woodeson, Anita Zagaria; *D:* Malcolm McKay; *W:* Malcolm McKay; *M:* Philip Appleby. **VHS** *NYR* 🐾🐾½

Maria's Day Chronicles the plague-riddled downfall of a formerly aristocratic and wealthy Hungarian family in the years following the failed 1849 Revolution. In Hungarian with English subtitles.
1984 113m/C *D:* Judit Elek. **VHS, Beta $59.95** *FCT, AUD* 🐾🐾🐾

Maria's Lovers The wife (Kinski) of an impotent WWII veteran (Savage) succumbs to the charms of a rakish lady-killer (Spano). Savage turns to the charms of an older woman, finds love again with Kinski, but is still impotent; she gets pregnant by a wandering minstrel (Carradine) and on we go to film climax. Offbeat and uneven, representing Russian director Konchalovsky's first American film and one of Kinski's better roles.
1984 (R) 103m/C Nastassia Kinski, John Savage, Robert Mitchum, Keith Carradine, Anita Morris, Bud Cort, Karen Young, Tracy Nelson, John Goodman, Vincent Spano; *D:* Andrei Konchalovsky; *W:* Marjorie David, Andrei Konchalovsky. **VHS, Beta $14.95** *MGM* 🐾🐾½

Maricela Young Maricela Flores and her mother have come to the U.S. from El Salvador to escape the fighting. Living with a Southern Californian family, Maricela has a hard time adjusting to American life and, in particular, dealing with prejudice. An entry in the PBS "Wonderworks" series.
1988 55m/C Linda Lavin, Carlina Cruz. **VHS $29.95** *PME, HMV, BTV* 🐾🐾

Marie In this true story, a divorced (and battered) mother works her way through school and the system to become the first woman to head the Parole Board in Tennessee. Finding rampant corruption, she blows the whistle on her bosses, who put her life in jeopardy. Spacek gives a powerful performance, as does first-time actor Thompson, portraying himself as the abused woman's attorney. Based on the book by Peter Maas. **1985 (PG-13) 113m/C** Sissy Spacek, Jeff Daniels, Keith Szarabajka, John Cullum, Morgan Freeman, Fred Dalton Thompson, Don Hood, Lisa Banes, Vincent Irizarry; *D:* Roger Donaldson; *W:* John Briley; *M:* Francis Lai. VHS, Beta $79.95 MGM 🐾🐾🐾

Marie Antoinette An elephantine costume drama chronicling the French queen's life from princesshood to her final days before the Revolution. A Shearer festival all the way, and a late example of MGM's overstuffed period style and star-power. Overlong, but engrossing for the wrong reasons. Morley, in his first film, plays Louis XVI. Power's only MGM loan-out casts him as a Swedish count and Marie's romantic dalliance. Based on a book by Stephan Zweig, with script assistance from (among others) F. Scott Fitzgerald. **1938 160m/B** Norma Shearer, Tyrone Power, John Barrymore, Robert Morley, Gladys George, Anita Louise, Joseph Schildkraut, Henry Stephenson, Reginald Gardiner, Peter Bull, Albert Dekker, Joseph Calleia, George Zucco, Cora Witherspoon, Barry Fitzgerald, Mae Busch, Harry Davenport, Scotty Beckett; *D:* Woodbridge S. Van Dyke; *W:* F. Scott Fitzgerald. VHS, Beta $19.98 MGM 🐾🐾½

Marie Galante Fine spy drama has Tracy running into Gallien in Panama (years earlier she had been left there after a kidnapping). He finds her most helpful in his attempt to thwart the bombing of the Panama Canal. It's the performances that raise this otherwise standard thriller up a few notches. **1934 88m/B** Spencer Tracy, Katie Galian, Ned Sparks, Helen Morgan, Sig Rumann, Leslie Fenton, Jay C. Flippen; *D:* Henry King. VHS, Beta $16.95 NOS, SNC, HEG 🐾🐾🐾

Marihuana An unintentionally hilarious, "Reefer Madness"-type cautionary film about the exaggerated evils of pot smoking. A real dopey film favored by right-winger zealots. *AKA:* Marijuana: The Devil's Weed. **1936 57m/B** Harley Wood, Hugh McArthur, Pat Carlyle; *D:* Dwain Esper. VHS, Beta $16.95 SNC, VYY, HEG 🐾

Marilyn Rock Hudson narrates this documentary on the life of Marilyn Monroe. **1963 83m/B** VHS NO 🐾

Marilyn: The Untold Story Nominated for an Emmy, Hicks elevates what could easily have been a dull made-for-TV movie with her remarkable performance as Marilyn Monroe. Based on the book by Norman Mailer. **1980 156m/C** Catherine Hicks, Richard Basehart, Frank Converse, John Ireland, Sheree North, Anne Ramsey, Viveca Lindfors, Jason Miller, Bill Vint; *D:* Jack Arnold, John Flynn; *W:* Lawrence Schiller; *M:* William Goldstein. VHS ABC 🐾🐾🐾

Marine Raiders Marines train and then fight at Guadalcanal. A typical flag-waver, watchable but not particularly engaging. **1943 90m/B** Pat O'Brien, Robert Ryan, Ruth Hussey, Frank McHugh, Barton MacLane; *D:* Harold Schuster. VHS, Beta $19.98 TTC 🐾🐾

Marius This is the first of Marcel Pagnol's trilogy ("Fanny" and "Cesar" followed), about the lives and adventures of the people of Provence, France. Marius is a young man who dreams of going away to sea. When he acts on those dreams, he leaves behind his girlfriend, Fanny. Realistic dialogue and vivid characterizations. Adapted by Pagnol from his play. The musical play and film "Fanny" (1961) were adapted from this trilogy.

1931 125m/B Raimu, Pierre Fresnay, Charpin, Orane Demazis; *D:* Alexander Korda; *W:* Marcel Pagnol; *M:* Francis Gromon. VHS, Beta $24.95 NOS, MRV, INT 🐾🐾🐾🐾

Marjoe Documentary follows the career of rock-style evangelist Marjoe Gortner, who spent 25 years of his life touring the country as a professional preacher. Marjoe later went on to become an actor and professional fundraiser. **1972 (PG) 88m/C** Marjoe Gortner; *D:* Howard Smith, Sarah Kernochan. VHS, Beta $59.95 COL 🐾🐾🐾🐾

Marjorie Morningstar A temperate Hollywood adaptation of the Herman Wouk story of a young actress who fails to achieve stardom and settles on being a housewife. Wood slipped a bit in this story. **1958 123m/C** Natalie Wood, Gene Kelly, Martin Balsam, Claire Trevor, Ed Wynn, Everett Sloane, Carolyn Jones; *D:* Irving Rapper. VHS $14.98 REP 🐾🐾

The Mark Story of a convicted child molester who cannot escape his past upon his release from prison. Whitman gives a riveting performance as the convict. **1961 127m/B** Stuart Whitman, Maria Schell, Rod Steiger, Brenda de Banzie, Maurice Denham, Donald Wolfit, Paul Rogers, Donald Houston; *D:* Guy Green; *M:* Richard Rodney Bennett. VHS, Beta VTR 🐾🐾🐾½

Mark of Cain Twin brothers, one normal, the other a raving lunatic with murderous tendencies, confuse the authorities who imprison the nice guy, allowing the nutcase to chase after his beautiful sister-in-law. **1984 90m/C** Robin Ward, Wendy Crewson, August Schellenberg; *D:* Bruce Pittman. VHS, Beta $69.98 LIV, VES 🐾🐾½

Mark of the Beast Two students inadvertently videotape an assassination, and are then relentlessly pursued by the killer. **19?? 90m/C** James Gordon, Carolyn Guillet, David Smulker; *D:* Robert Stewart. VHS NO 🐾

Mark of the Devil Witchcraft and romance don't mix, as a Medieval witch hunter and a sexy girl accused of witchery discover. Notoriously graphic torture scenes add to the mayhem but the weird part is that this is based on true stories. *AKA:* Burn, Witch, Burn; Brenn, Hexe, Brenn. **1969 (R) 96m/C** Herbert Lom, Olivera Vuco, Udo Kier, Reggie Nalder, Herbert Fux, Michael Maien, Ingeborg Schoener, Johannes Buzalski, Gaby Fuchs; *D:* Michael Armstrong. VHS, Beta $69.98 VES, LIV, TPV 🐾🐾🐾

Mark of the Devil 2 Sadistic witch-hunters torture satan's servants and torch sisters of mercy, whilst trying to horn in on a nobleman's fortune. It's just not as gross without the vomit bags. **1972 (R) 90m/C** Erika Blanc, Anton Diffring, Reggie Nalder; *D:* Adrian Hoven. VHS $29.98 VDM 🐾

The Mark of the Hawk A uniquely told story of African nations struggling to achieve racial equality after gaining independence. Songs include "This Man Is Mine," sung by Kitt. *AKA:* The Accused. **1957 83m/C** Sidney Poitier, Eartha Kitt, Juano Hernandez, John McIntire; *D:* Michael Audley. VHS MRV 🐾🐾🐾

Mark of the Spur A cowboy must find out who left a mysterious spur mark on his horse. **1932 60m/B** Bob Custer, Lillian Rich, Franklin Farnum, Bud Osborne; *D:* J.P. McGowan. VHS, Beta $19.95 NOS, DVT 🐾½

Mark of the Vampire A murder in a small town is solved through the use of vaudeville actors who pose as vampires. Great cast, surprise ending. **1935 61m/B** Lionel Barrymore, Bela Lugosi, Elizabeth Allan; *D:* Tod Browning. VHS, Beta $19.95 MGM, MLB 🐾🐾🐾

Mark of Zorro Fairbanks plays a dual role as the hapless Don Diego and his dashing counterpart, Zorro, the hero of the oppressed. Silent film. **1920 80m/B** Douglas Fairbanks Sr., Marguerite de la Motte, Noah Beery Sr.; *D:* Fred Niblo. VHS $19.95 REP, MRV, GPV 🐾🐾🐾

The Mark of Zorro The dashing Power swashbuckles his way through this wonderfully acted and directed romp. He plays the foppish son of a 19th-century California aristocrat who is secretly the masked avenger of the oppressed peons. Bromberg plays the wicked governor, with the beautiful niece (Darnell) beloved by Power, and Rathbone is supremely evil as his cruel minion. Lots of swordplay with a particularly exciting duel to the death between Rathbone and Power. Based on the novel "The Curse of Capistrano" by Johnston McCulley. Remake of the 1921 silent film and followed by a number of other Zorro incarnations. **1940 93m/B** Tyrone Power, Linda Darnell, Basil Rathbone, Gale Sondergaard, Eugene Pallette, J. Edward Bromberg, Montagu Love, Janet Beecher; *D:* Rouben Mamoulian; *W:* John Taintor Foote; *M:* Alfred Newman. VHS $19.98 FXV, BTV 🐾🐾🐾½

Mark Twain and Me Robards portrays the aging and irascible Mark Twain, attended by a neglected but devoted daughter, and befriended by 11-year-old Dorothy Quick, as they travel on the same ship. Based on a true story. Made for television. **1991 93m/C** Jason Robards Jr., Talia Shire, Amy Stewart, Chris Wiggins, R.H. Thomson, Fiona Reid; *D:* Daniel Petrie. VHS $19.99 DIS, BTV 🐾🐾½

Marked for Death Having killed a prostitute, DEA agent Seagal decides it's time to roll out the white picket fence in the 'burbs with the little woman and brood. Trouble is, a bunch of guys with dreadlocks don't approve of his early retirement, and the Jamaican gangsters plan to send him and his family to the great Rasta playground in the sky. Whereupon the Stevester kicks and punches and wags his ponytail. Much blood flows, mon. Tunes by Jimmy Cliff. *AKA:* Screwface. **1990 (R) 93m/C** Steven Seagal, Joanna Pacula, Basil Wallace, Keith David, Tom Wright, Danielle Harris, Arlen Dean Snyder, Teri Weigel; *D:* Dwight Little; *W:* Mark Victor, Michael Grais. VHS $14.98 FXV, CCB 🐾½

Marked for Murder Another in the Texas Ranger series. In this entry, the Rangers come to the rescue when a rancher war appears inevitable. **1945 58m/B** Tex Ritter, Dave O'Brien, Guy Wilkerson; *D:* Elmer Clifton; *W:* Elmer Clifton. VHS $79.95 VMK 🐾½

Marked for Murder Two TV station employees are framed for murder after being sent out to find a missing videocassette. Renee Estevez is part of the Sheen/Estevez dynasty. **1989 (R) 88m/C** Renee Estevez, Wings Hauser, Jim Mitchum, Ross Hagen, Ken Abraham; *D:* Rick Sloane. VHS, Beta $79.95 VMK 🐾½

Marked Money Amiable captain takes in boy who'll soon roll in the dough and swindlers show up on the scene. The captain's courageous girl and her pilot beau step in to right the rookery.

1928 61m/B Frank "Junior" Coghlan, George Duryea, Tom Kennedy, Bert Woodruff, Virginia Bradford, Maurice Black, Jack Richardson; **D:** Spencer Gordon Bennet. **VHS, Beta** $19.95 *GPV, FCT* ✗✗

Marked Trails One clue stamps out the guilty parties in this wild west saga.
1944 59m/B Hoot Gibson, Bob Steele, Veda Ann Borg. **VHS, Beta** $19.95 *NOS, DVT* ✗

Marked Woman Gangster drama about crusading District Attorney who persuades a group of clipjoint hostesses to testify against their gangster boss. A gritty studio melodrama loosely based on a true story.
1937 97m/B Bette Davis, Humphrey Bogart, Eduardo Ciannelli, Isabel Jewell, Jane Bryan, Mayo Methot, Allen Jenkins, Lola Lane; **D:** Lloyd Bacon. **VHS, Beta** $19.95 *MGM* ✗✗✗

Marlon Brando Documentary recounting the life and career of Hollywood's most rebellious superstar.
1985 120m/C Marlon Brando; **D:** Claudio Masenza. **VHS, Beta** *BAR* ✗✗✗

Marlowe Updated telling by Stirling Silliphant of Chandler's "The Little Sister" sports retro guy Garner as Philip Marlowe, gumshoe. Hired by a mystery blonde to find her misplaced brother, rumpled sleuth Marlowe encounters kicking Bruce Lee in his first film. Slick looking, but the story's a bit slippery.
1969 (PG) 95m/C James Garner, Gayle Hunnicutt, Carroll O'Connor, Rita Moreno, Sharon Farrell, William Daniels, Bruce Lee; **D:** Paul Bogart; **W:** Sterling Silliphant. **VHS, Beta** $19.98 *MGM, FCT* ✗✗½

Marnie A lovely blonde with a mysterious past robs her employers and then changes her identity. When her current boss catches her in the act and forces her to marry him, he soon learns the puzzling aspects of Marnie's background. Criticized at the time of its release, the movie has since been accepted as a Hitchcock classic.
1964 130m/C Tippi Hedren, Sean Connery, Diane Baker, Bruce Dern; **D:** Alfred Hitchcock; **W:** Jay Presson Allen. **VHS, Beta** $19.95 *MCA* ✗✗✗½

Maroc 7 Slow story of a secret agent after a thief suffering from a split personality.
1967 92m/C Gene Barry, Elsa Martinelli, Cyd Charisse, Leslie Phillips; **D:** Gerry O'Hara. *PAR* ✗

Marooned Tense thriller casts Crenna, Hackman, and Franciscus as astronauts stranded in space after a retro-rocket misfires and their craft is unable to return to earth.
1969 (G) 134m/C Gregory Peck, David Janssen, Richard Crenna, James Franciscus, Gene Hackman, Lee Grant; **D:** John Sturges. Academy Awards '69: Best Visual Effects; Nominations: Best Cinematography, Best Sound. **VHS, Beta** $9.95 *GKK* ✗✗

The Marquise In 1735, in a beautiful chateau outside Paris, the Compte De Vriac is celebrating the betrothal of his son with a few old friends. Then an unexpected visitor arrives, the Marquise De Kestournel. She's the Compte's former mistress and she announces she is staying for good. Based on a comedy by Noel Coward.
19?? 55m/C Diana Rigg, Richard Johnson, James Villers. **VHS** $24.98 *BFS, FCT* ✗✗½

The Marriage Circle A pivotal silent comedy depicting the infidelity of several married couples in Vienna. Director Lubitsch's first American comedy. Remade as a musical, "One Hour With You," in 1932. Silent.
1924 90m/B Florence Vidor, Monte Blue, Marie Prevost, Creighton Hale, Adolphe Menjou, Harry Myers, Dale Fuller; **D:** Ernst Lubitsch. **VHS** $19.95 *NOS, MOV, GVV* ✗✗✗

Marriage is Alive and Well A wedding photographer reflects on the institution of marriage from his unique perspective. Made for television.
1980 100m/C Joe Namath, Jack Albertson, Melinda Dillon, Judd Hirsch, Susan Sullivan, Fred McCarren, Swoosie Kurtz; **D:** Russ Mayberry. **VHS** $59.95 *LIV* ✗

Marriage Italian Style When an engaged man hears that his mistress is on her death bed, he goes to her side and, in an emotional gesture, promises to marry her if she survives. She does, and holds him to his promise. After they're married, however, she gives him a big surprise—three grown sons. A silly film, but DeSica's direction keeps it from being too fluffy. Lots of fun. Based on the play "Filumena Marturano" by Eduardo De Filippo.
1964 102m/C Sophia Loren, Marcello Mastroianni, Aldo Puglisi, Tecla Scarano, Marilu Tolo; **D:** Vittorio De Sica. Academy Awards '64 Nominations: Best Actress (Loren), Best Foreign Language Film; Golden Globe Awards '65: Best Foreign Film. **VHS** *STE* ✗✗

The Marriage of Maria Braun In post-WWII Germany, a young woman uses guile and sexuality to survive as the nation rebuilds itself into an industrial power. The first movie in Fassbinder's trilogy about German women in Germany during the post war years, it is considered one of the director's finest films, and an indispensable example of the New German Cinema. In German with English subtitles. *AKA:* Die Ehe Der Maria Braun.
1979 (R) 120m/C Hanna Schygulla, Klaus Lowitsch, Ivan Desny, Gottfried John, Gisela Uhlen; **D:** Rainer Werner Fassbinder; **W:** Rainer Werner Fassbinder; **M:** Peer Raben. **VHS, Beta** $79.95 *NYF, COL, GLV* ✗✗✗

Married? Couple endures 365 days of marital bliss in order to inherit big bucks. Some do it for less.
1926 65m/B Owen Moore, Constance Bennett; **D:** George Terwilliger. **VHS, Beta** $16.00 *GPV, FCT* ✗½

A Married Man Story focusing on a bored British lawyer who begins cheating on his wife. Amid the affair, someone gets murdered. Made for television.
1984 200m/C Anthony Hopkins, Ciaran Madden, Lise Hilboldt, Yvonne Coulette, John Le Mesurier, Sophie Ashton; **D:** John Davies. **VHS, Beta** $69.95 *LIV* ✗✗

Married People, Single Sex Three couples decide to spread their sexual wings. Shelly takes a new lover; Artie makes obscene phone calls; and Beth and Mike, who end their relationship, still can't keep out of bed. An unrated version is also available.
1993 (R) 110m/C Chase Masterson, Joseph Pilato, Darla Slavens, Shelley Michelle, Wendi Westbrook, Robert Zachar, Samuel Mongiello, Teri Thompson; **D:** Mike Sedan; **W:** Catherine Tavel. **VHS** $89.95 *TRI* ✗✗

Married to It Three vastly different couples work together to plan a pageant at a private school. The oil and water group includes struggling hippie leftovers Bridges and Channing, '80s-era corporate cutthroats Shepherd and Silver, and starry-eyed newlyweds Masterson and Leonard. Contrived plot offers few humourous moments, with the main focus revolving around coping rather than comedy. And the coping is slow business, done by characters you don't really care about with problems that don't really matter.
1993 (R) 112m/C Beau Bridges, Stockard Channing, Robert Sean Leonard, Mary Stuart Masterson, Cybill Shepherd, Ron Silver; **D:** Arthur Hiller; **W:** Janet Kovalcik; **M:** Henry Mancini. **VHS** *ORI* ✗✗

Married to the Mob After the murder of her husband, an attractive Mafia widow tries to escape "mob" life, but ends up fighting off amorous advances from the current mob boss while being wooed by an undercover cop. A snappy script and a spry performance by Pfeiffer pepper this easy-to-watch film.
1988 (R) 102m/C Michelle Pfeiffer, Dean Stockwell, Alec Baldwin, Matthew Modine, Mercedes Ruehl, Anthony J. Nici, Joan Cusack, Ellen Foley, Chris Isaak, Trey Wilson, Charles Napier, Tracey Walter, Al Lewis, Nancy Travis, David Johansen, Jonathan Demme; **D:** Jonathan Demme; **W:** Mark Burns, Barry Strugatz; **M:** David Byrne. **VHS, Beta** $9.98 *ORI* ✗✗✗

Married Too Young High school honeys elope, despite disapproval from the parental units. When the boy groom trades his med school plans for a monkey wrench in order to support the little missus, he finds much trouble with the hot rod heavies. *AKA:* I Married Too Young.
1962 76m/B Harold Lloyd Jr., Jana Lund, Anthony Dexter, Marianna Hill, Trudy Marshall, Brian O'Hara, Nita Loveless; **D:** George Moskov. **VHS** $59.98 *HHT, SNC* ✗✗

A Married Woman Dramatizes a day in the life of a woman who has both a husband and a lover. One of Godard's more mainstream efforts. *AKA:* La Femme Mariee.
1965 94m/B Macha Meril, Phillippe LeRoy, Bernard Noel; **D:** Jean-Luc Godard; **W:** Jean-Luc Godard. **VHS, Beta, 8mm** $24.95 *VYY, MRV, DVT* ✗✗✗

Marry Me, Marry Me While in Paris, a Jewish encyclopedia salesman falls in love with a pregnant Belgian woman. A sensitive story about European Jewish families. Berri wrote, produced, directed, and starred in this romantic comedy. *AKA:* Mazel Tov Ou le Mariage.
1969 (R) 87m/C Elisabeth Wiener, Regine, Claude Berri, Louisa Colpeyn; **D:** Claude Berri. **VHS** *LHV* ✗✗✗

The Marrying Man Young man meets his match when his buddies take him to Las Vegas for his bachelor party. He falls like a ton of bricks for the singer, not knowing she belongs to the local crime lord, who catches them together and forces them to marry. They immediately divorce, can't forget each other and eventually re-marry, again and again and again. Silly story supposedly based on the story of Harry Karl (eventual husband of Debbie Reynolds) and Marie MacDonald. Basinger and Baldwin's off-stage romance created quite a stir but their chemistry onscreen is zilch. Ineffective, not funny, poorly paced and acted: a good example of what happens when egotistical stars get their way.
1991 (R) 116m/C Alec Baldwin, Kim Basinger, Robert Loggia, Armand Assante, Elisabeth Shue, Paul Reiser, Fisher Stevens, Peter Dobson, Gretchen Wyler; **D:** Jerry Rees; **W:** Neil Simon. **VHS** $19.99 *HPH* ✗½

Mars Needs Women When the Martian singles scene starts to drag, Mars boys cross the galaxy in search of fertile earth babes to help them repopulate the planet. Seems Batgirl Craig, the go-go dancing lady scientist, is at the top of their dance cards.
1966 80m/C Tommy Kirk, Yvonne Craig; **D:** Larry Buchanan; **W:** Larry Buchanan. **VHS** $19.98 *SNC* ✗

Marshal of Cedar Rock Marshal Rocky Lane sets a prisoner free, thinking the guy will lead him to a stash of stolen bank funds. Seems he miscalculates, but by way of consolation, he routs a rotten railroad agent who's rooking innocent people. Features the equine talent of Black Jack.
1953 54m/B Allan "Rocky" Lane, Phyllis Coates, Roy Barcroft, William Henry, Robert Shayne, Eddy Waller; **D:** Harry Keller. **VHS $19.99** *HEG, DVT, NOS* 🎬🎬

Marshal of Heldorado An outlaw-infested town needs an injection of law and order.
1950 53m/B James Ellison, Russell Hayden, Raymond Hatton, Fuzzy Knight; **D:** Thomas Carr. **VHS $19.95** *NOS, DVT* 🎬

The Marshal's Daughter A father and daughter team up to outwit an outlaw. Features many cowboy songs, including the title track by Tex Ritter.
1953 71m/B Tex Ritter, Ken Murray, Laurie Anders, Preston Foster, Hoot Gibson; **D:** William Berke. **VHS $19.95** *NOS, MOV, HEG* 🎬½

Martial Law A film solely for martial arts fans. Two cops use their hands, feet, and other body parts to fight crime.
1990 (R) 90m/C Chad McQueen, Cynthia Rothrock, David Carradine, Andy McCutcheon; **D:** S.E. Cohen. **VHS $89.98** *MED, FOX, VTR* 🎬½

Martial Law 2: Undercover Two cops, martial arts experts and part of an elite police force called Martial Law, go undercover to investigate the murder of a colleague. They uncover a fast-growing crime ring headed by a bad cop and a nightclub owner. The nightclub is host to the city's rich and powerful, who are treated to a bevy of beautiful women, protected by martial arts experts, and entertained by martial arts fights to the death. Lots of high-kicking action.
1991 (R) 92m/C Jeff Wincott, Cynthia Rothrock, Paul Johansson, Evan Lurie, L. Charles Taylor, Sherrie Rose, Billy Drago; **D:** Kurt Anderson; **W:** Richard Brando, Jiles Fitzgerald. **VHS $19.98** *MCA* 🎬½

Martial Outlaw DEA man Kevin White (Wincott) has been following a drug-dealing ex-KGB kingpin from Moscow to San Francisco. The Russian's latest move takes him to Los Angeles where Kevin meets up with his older brother Jack (Hudson), a maverick LA cop. Jack persuades Kevin to let him in on the action but Kevin begins to suspect Jack is playing both sides and their sibling rivalry could lead to death.
1993 (R) 89m/C Jeff Wincott, Gary Hudson, Richard Jaeckel, Krista Errickson, Vladimir Skomarovsky, Liliana Komorowska, Gary Wood; **D:** Kurt Anderson; **W:** Thomas Ritz. **VHS $92.98** *REP* 🎬

The Martian Chronicles: Part 1 Series episode "The Explorers." Adapted from Ray Bradbury's critically acclaimed novel. Futuristic explorations of the planet Mars. Strange fates of the discovery teams make everything more curious. Made for television.
1979 120m/C Rock Hudson, Bernie Casey, Nicholas Hammond, Darren McGavin; **D:** Michael Anderson Sr. **VHS, Beta $14.95** *FRH* 🎬½

The Martian Chronicles: Part 2 Episode following the television movie. This part is called "The Settlers." The planet Mars meets with its first colonization and the settlers watch the Earth explode.
1979 97m/C Rock Hudson, Fritz Weaver, Roddy McDowall, Bernie Casey, Darren McGavin, Gayle Hunnicutt, Barry Morse, Bernadette Peters; **D:** Michael Anderson Sr. **VHS, Beta $14.95** *FRH* 🎬½

The Martian Chronicles: Part 3 In the final chapter of this space saga, the Martian's secrets become known and will forever change man's destiny. Adapted from Ray Bradbury's classic novel; made-for-television.
1979 97m/C Rock Hudson, Bernadette Peters, Christopher Connelly, Fritz Weaver, Roddy McDowall, Bernie Casey, Nicholas Hammond, Darren McGavin, Gayle Hunnicutt, Barry Morse; **D:** Michael Anderson Sr. **VHS, Beta $14.95** *FRH* 🎬🎬½

Martians Go Home! Joke-loving Martians come to earth and pester a nerdy composer.
1990 (PG-13) 89m/C Randy Quaid, Margaret Colin, Anita Morris, John Philbin, Ronny Cox, Gerrit Graham, Barry Sobel, Vic Dunlop; **D:** David Odell. **VHS, Beta** *NO* 🎬½

Martin Martin is a charming young man, though slightly mad. He freely admits of the need to drink blood. Contemporary vampire has found a new abhorrent means of killing his victims.
1977 (R) 96m/C John Amplas, Lincoln Maazel; **D:** George A. Romero; **W:** George A. Romero. **VHS, Beta** *NO* 🎬🎬

Martin Luther French-made biography of the 16th century reformer who began the Protestant Reformation.
1953 105m/B Niall MacGinnis, John Ruddock, Pierre Leeavre, Guy Verney. **VHS, Beta $19.95** *NOS, VCI, VGD* 🎬½

Martin's Day An unusual friendship develops between an escaped convict and the young boy he kidnaps.
1985 (PG) 99m/C Richard Harris, Lindsay Wagner, James Coburn, Justin Henry, Karen Black, John Ireland; **D:** Alan Gibson; **W:** Chris Bryant, Allan Scott. **VHS, Beta $14.95** *MGM, FOX* 🎬🎬

Marty The empty life of a Bronx butcher is forever altered when he meets an equally lonely young woman. The original television version of the famous story, later filmed in 1955, starring Ernest Borgnine.
1953 58m/B Rod Steiger, Nancy Marchand; **D:** Delbert Mann; **W:** Paddy Chayefsky. **VHS, Beta $14.95** *RHI, BTV* 🎬🎬

Marty Marty is a painfully shy bachelor who feels trapped in a pointless life of family squabbles. When he finds love, he also finds the strength to break out of what he feels is a meaningless existence. A sensitive and poignant film from the writer of "Altered States." Remake of a television version that originally aired in 1953. Notable for Borgnine's sensitive portrayal, one of his last quality jobs before sinking into the B-Movie sludge pit.
1955 91m/B Ernest Borgnine, Betsy Blair, Joe De Santis, Ester Minciotti, Jerry Paris, Karen Steele; **D:** Delbert Mann; **W:** Paddy Chayefsky. Academy Awards '55: Best Actor (Borgnine), Best Picture (Mann), Best Director, Best Screenplay; Nominations: Best Art Direction/Set Decoration (B & W), Best Black and White Cinematography, Best Supporting Actor (Mantell), Best Supporting Actress (Blair); British Academy Awards '55: Best Actor (Borgnine), Best Actress (Blair); Golden Globe Awards '56: Best Actor—Drama (Borgnine); National Board of Review Awards '55: 10 Best Films of the Year, Best Actor (Borgnine). **VHS, Beta $14.95** *MGM, FOX, BTV* 🎬🎬🎬½

Marvelous Stunts of Kung Fu Beautiful woman, fortune teller, and martial arts hero team up to seek vengeance against the evil empire.
1983 86m/C Ling Yun, Wei Ping Line, Lung Fei. **VHS, Beta $39.95** *TWE* 🎬

Marvin & Tige A deep friendship develops between an aging alcoholic and a streetwise 11-year-old boy after they meet one night in an Atlanta park.
1984 (PG) 104m/C John Cassavetes, Gibran Brown, Billy Dee Williams, Fay Hauser, Denise Nicholas-Hill; **D:** Eric Weston. **VHS, Beta $24.98** *SUE* 🎬🎬½

The Marx Brothers in a Nutshell A tribute to the Marx Brothers, narrated by Gene Kelly. Contains clips from "Duck Soup," "Horse Feathers," "Animal Crackers," "Cocoanuts," and "Room Service." Also contains rare outakes and interviews with the brothers, plus guest appearances by Dick Cavett, Robert Klein, David Steinberg, and others. Indispensible.
1990 100m/B Groucho Marx, Chico Marx, Harpo Marx, Zeppo Marx, Robert Klein, David Steinberg, George Fenneman, Dick Cavett. **VHS $19.98** *FCT* 🎬🎬🎬½

Mary and Joseph: A Story of Faith A speculative look at the experiences and courtship of Mary and Joseph before the birth of Jesus. Made for television.
1979 100m/C Blanche Baker, Jeff East, Colleen Dewhurst, Stephen McHattie, Lloyd Bochner, Paul Hecht; **D:** Eric Till. **VHS, Beta $19.98** *LIV, WAR* 🎬½

Mary, Mary, Bloody Mary Young beautiful artist ravages Mexico with her penchant for drinking blood. Turns out she's a bisexual vampire. When even her friends become victims, her father steps in to end the bloodbath.
1976 (R) 85m/C Christina Ferrare, David Young, Helena Rojo, John Carradine; **D:** Carlos Lopez Moctezuma; **M:** Tom Bahler. **VHS, Beta** *NO* 🎬

Mary of Scotland The historical tragedy of Mary, Queen of Scots and her cousin, Queen Elizabeth I of England is enacted in this classic film. Traces Mary's claims to the throne of England which ultimately led to her execution. Based on the Maxwell Anderson play.
1936 123m/B Katharine Hepburn, Fredric March, Florence Eldridge, Douglas Walton, John Carradine, Robert Barratt, Gavin Muir, Ian Keith, Moroni Olsen, William Stack, Alan Mowbray; **D:** John Ford. **VHS, Beta** *RKO, TTC* 🎬🎬🎬

Mary Poppins Magical English nanny arrives one day on the East Wind and takes over the household of a very proper London banker. She introduces her two charges to her friends and family, including Bert, the chimney sweep (Van Dyke), and eccentric Uncle Albert (Wynn). She also changes the lives of everyone in the family. From her they learn that life can always be happy and joyous if you take the proper perspective. Film debut of Andrews. Based on the books by P.L. Travers. A Disney classic that hasn't lost any of its magic. Look for the wonderful sequence where Van Dyke dances with animated penguins. ♫Chim Chim Cheree; A Spoonful of Sugar; The Perfect Nanny; Sister Suffragette; The Life I Lead; Stay Awake; Feed the Birds; Fidelity Feduciary Bank; Let's Go Fly a Kite.
1964 139m/C Ed Wynn, Hermione Baddeley, Julie Andrews, Dick Van Dyke, David Tomlinson, Glynis Johns; **D:** Robert Stevenson. Academy Awards '64: Best Actress (Andrews), Best Film Editing, Best Song ("Chim Chim Cher-ee"), Best Visual Effects, Best Score; Nominations: Best Adapted Screenplay, Best Art Direction/Set Decoration (Color), Best Color Cinematography, Best Costume Design (Color), Best Director (Stevenson), Best Picture, Best Sound, Best Original Score; Golden Globe Awards '65: Best Actress—Musical/Comedy (Andrews). **VHS, Beta $24.99** *DIS, APD, BTV* 🎬🎬🎬½

Mary White The true story of Mary White, the sixteen-year-old daughter of a newspaper editor who rejects her life of wealth and sets out to find her own identity. 1977 102m/C Ed Flanders, Kathleen Beller, Tim Matheson, Donald Moffatt, Fionnula Flanagan; D: Judd Taylor. **VHS, Beta $29.95** PAR 🐾🐾

Masada Based on Ernest K. Gann's novel "The Antagonists," this dramatization recreates the first-century A.D. Roman siege of the fortress Masada, headquarters for a group of Jewish freedom fighters. Abridged from the original television presentation. 1981 131m/C Peter O'Toole, Peter Strauss, Barbara Carrera, Anthony Quayle, Giulia Pagano, David Warner; D: Boris Sagal; M: Jerry Goldsmith. **VHS, Beta $59.95** MCA 🐾🐾🐾

Masala An experiment in a variety of genres, including glitzy musical-comedy numbers, erotic fantasy sequences, and all manner of kitsch. Krishna (who both stars and directs in his feature film debut) is a violence-prone, ex-junkie still trying to recover from the deaths of his family in a plane crash as they travelled from their home in Toronto to a vacation in India. Jaffrey has multi-roles as Krishna's unscrupulous uncle and cousin as well as the blue-skinned Indian deity, Lord Krishna, who appears to an Indian grandmother on her television set. Multicultural confusion. 1991 105m/C Srinivas Krishna, Saeed Jaffrey, Zohra Segal, Sakina Jaffrey; D: Srinivas Krishna; W: Srinivas Krishna. **VHS $89.95** FXL, FCT 🐾🐾

Mascara A group inspecting a transvestite's death are led into the seedy underground world of Belgian nightlife. 1987 (R) 99m/C Derek De Lint, Charlotte Rampling, Michael Sarrazin; D: Patrick Conrad. **VHS, Beta $79.95** WAR 🐾🐾

Masculine Feminine A young Parisian just out of the Army engages in some anarchistic activities when he has an affair with a radical woman singer. Hailed as one of the best French New Wave films. In French with English subtitles. AKA: Masculin Feminin. 1966 103m/B Jean-Pierre Leaud, Chantal Goya, Marlene Jobert; D: Jean-Luc Godard. **VHS, Beta $69.95** NYF, DVT, VDM 🐾🐾🐾½

M*A*S*H Hilarious, irreverent, and well-cast black comedy about a group of surgeons and nurses at a Mobile Army Surgical Hospital in Korea. The horror of war is set in counterpoint to their need to create havoc with episodic late-night parties, practical jokes, and sexual antics. An all-out anti-war festival, highlighted by scenes that starkly uncover the chaos and irony of war, and establish Altman's influential style. Watch for real-life football players Fran Tarkenton, Ben Davidson, and Buck Buchanan in the game. Loosely adapted from the novel by the pseudonymous Richard Hooker (Dr. H. Richard Hornberger and William Heinz). Subsequent hit TV series moved even further from the source novel. 1970 (R) 116m/C Donald Sutherland, Elliott Gould, Tom Skerritt, Sally Kellerman, JoAnn Pflug, Robert Duvall, Rene Auberjonois, Roger Bowen, Gary Burghoff, Fred Williamson, John Schuck, Bud Cort, G. Wood; D: Robert Altman; W: Ring Lardner Jr.; M: Johnny Mandel. Academy Awards '70: Best Adapted Screenplay; Nominations: Best Director (Altman), Best Film Editing, Best Picture, Best Supporting Actress (Kellerman); Cannes Film Festival '70: Best Film; Golden Globe Awards '71: Best Film—Musical/Comedy. **VHS, Beta $19.98** FOX 🐾🐾🐾🐾

M*A*S*H: Goodbye, Farewell & Amen The final two-hour special episode of the television series "M*A*S*H" follows Hawkeye, B.J., Colonel Potter, Charles, Margaret, Klinger, Father Mulcahy, and the rest of the men and women of the 4077th through the last days of the Korean War, the declaration of peace, the dismantling of the camp, and the fond and tearful farewells. 1983 120m/C Alan Alda, Mike Farrell, Harry Morgan, David Ogden Stiers, Loretta Swit, Jamie Farr, William Christopher. **VHS, Beta** FOX, OM 🐾🐾🐾½

M*A*S*H: The Collector's Edition Join Hawkeye, Trapper John, Radar, Klinger, and the rest of the loonies of the 4077th Mobile Army Surgical Hospital, located three miles from the frontline of the Korean conflict, as they battle military regulations (and sometimes each other). Three episodes per cassette from the television series which lasted 11 seasons. Additional episodes available. 1972 ?m/C Alan Alda, Wayne Rogers, McLean Stevenson, Gary Burghoff, Loretta Swit, Larry Linville, Jamie Farr, William Christopher. **VHS** CMB 🐾🐾🐾½

The Mask A deservedly obscure gory horror film about a masked killer, filmed mostly in 3-D. With special 3-D packaging and limited edition 3-D glasses. AKA: Eyes of Hell; The Spooky Movie Show. 1961 85m/B Paul Stevens, Claudette Nevins, Bill Walker, Anne Collings, Martin Lavut; D: Julian Roffman. **VHS, Beta $12.95** RHI, MLB 🐾🐾

Mask A dramatization of the true story of a young boy afflicted with craniodiaphyseal dysplasia (Elephantitis). The boy overcomes his appearance and revels in the joys of life in the California bikers' community. Well acted, particularly the performances of Stoltz and Cher. A touching film, well-directed by Bogdanovich, that only occasionally slips into maudlin territory. 1985 (PG-13) 120m/C Cher, Sam Elliott, Eric Stoltz, Estelle Getty, Richard Dysart, Laura Dern, Harry Carey Jr., Lawrence Monoson, Marsha Warfield, Barry Tubb, Andrew (Andy) Robinson, Alexandra Powers; D: Peter Bogdanovich; W: Anna Hamilton Phelan. **VHS, Beta $19.95** MCA 🐾🐾🐾

The Mask Adolescent supernatural horror comedy with lollapalooza special effects is Carrey's follow-up to "Ace Ventura." Mild-mannered bank clerk Carrey discovers an ancient mask that has supernatural powers. Based on the Dark Horse comic book series and originally conceived as a horror flick, director Russell, who gave Freddy Krueger a sense of humor, recast this one as a cartoon-action black comedy. Carrey's rubber face is an asset combined with the breakthrough special effects courtesy of Industrial Light and Magic. 1994 (PG-13) 100m/C Jim Carrey, Peter Riegert, Peter Greene, Amy Yasbeck; D: Chuck Russell; W: Mike Werb. **VHS** NYR 🐾🐾🐾

The Mask of Dijon A mad magician suspects that his wife is cheating on him and tries to hypnotize her into killing her supposed paramour. The plan goes awry when the wife uses a gun loaded with blanks. Von Stroheim's performance makes it worthwhile. 1946 73m/B Erich von Stroheim, Jeanne Bates, William Wright, Edward Van Sloan, Denise Vernac; D: Lew Landers. **VHS, Beta** NOS 🐾🐾½

The Mask of Fu Manchu The evil Dr. Fu Manchu and his equally evil daughter set out to capture the scimitar and golden mask of Genghis Khan. With them, they will be able to destroy all white men and rule the world. Although a detective from Scotland Yard tries to stop them, the pair obtain the treasures and begin sadistically torturing their victims to death. Can they be stopped before they destroy the earth? One of the creepiest entries in the Fu Manchu series, and Loy's last oriental role. Based on the novel by Sam Rohmer. 1932 72m/B Boris Karloff, Lewis Stone, Karen Morley, Charles Starrett, Myrna Loy, Jean Hersholt, Lawrence Grant, David Torrence; D: Charles Brabin. **VHS $19.98** MGM 🐾🐾½

Mask of the Dragon A soldier's friend and girlfriend track down his killer after he delivers a golden curio to a shop in Los Angeles. 1951 54m/B Richard Travis, Sheila Ryan, Richard Emory, Jack Reitzen. **VHS, Beta** NO 🐾

The Masked Marvel The Masked Marvel saves America's war industries from sabotage. Serial in twelve episodes. AKA: Sakima and the Masked Marvel. 1943 195m/B William Forrest, Louise Currie, Johnny Arthur; D: Spencer Gordon Bennet. **VHS $29.98** VCN, REP, MLB 🐾🐾

The Masked Rider Drifters Brown and Knight head south of the border and find themselves trying to solve crimes committed by a mysterious masked rider. Latin American dancers and singers provide a nice change of pace from the usual cowpoke musical relief. Based on a story by Sam Robins. 1941 57m/B Johnny Mack Brown, Fuzzy Knight, Nell O'Day, Grant Withers; D: Ford Beebe; W: Sherman Lowe, Victor McLeod. **VHS $19.99** MOV 🐾🐾½

Masks of Death New adventure for Sherlock Holmes, as he is pulled from retirement to find the murderer of three unidentified corpses found in London's East End. 1986 80m/C Peter Cushing, John Mills, Anne Baxter, Ray Milland; D: Roy Ward Baker. **VHS, Beta $19.98** LHV, IME, WAR 🐾🐾

Mason of the Mounted Harmless enough western in which a Canadian Mountie tracks down a murderer in the U.S. 1932 58m/B Bill Cody, Nancy Drexel, Art Mix, Nelson McDowell; D: Harry Fraser. **VHS $19.95** NOS, DVT, HEG 🐾½

Masque of the Red Death An integral selection in the famous Edgar Allan Poe/Roger Corman canon, it deals with an evil prince who traffics with the devil and playfully murders any of his subjects not already dead of the plague. Photographed by Nicholas Roeg. Remade in 1989 with Corman as producer. 1965 88m/C Vincent Price, Hazel Court, Jane Asher, Patrick Magee; D: Roger Corman. **VHS, Beta $14.98** ORI, LIV, MLB 🐾🐾🐾

Masque of the Red Death Roger Corman's second attempt at Edgar Allan Poe's horror tale pales compared to his Vincent Price version made 25 years earlier. Under-aged cast adds youth appeal but subtracts credibility from the fable of a sadistic prince and his sycophants trying to ignore the plague outside castle walls. Only late in the plot does veteran actor Macnee add proper note of doom. 1989 (R) 90m/C Patrick Macnee, Jeffery Osterhage, Adrian Paul, Tracy Reiner, Maria Ford; D: Larry Brand; W: Larry Brand, Daryl Haney. **VHS, Beta $14.95** MGM, IME 🐾🐾

Masque of the Red Death Unrecognizable Poe mutation has guests invited to the mansion of a dying millionaire, only to be murdered by an unknown stalker. One scene features a pendulum, and that's it for literary faithfulness.

1990 (R) 94m/C Frank Stallone, Brenda Vaccaro, Herbert Lom, Michelle McBride, Christine Lunde; **D:** Alan Birkinshaw. VHS COL ⅃½

Masque of the Red Death/Premature Burial
Double feature of horror classics adapted from Edgar Allan Poe's work. Price stars in "Masque of the Red Death" as a satan worshipper. Millard plays a man obsessed with the fear of catastrophe in "Premature Burial."
1965 175m/C Vincent Price, Hazel Court, Jane Asher, Patrick Magee, Nigel Green, Ray Milland; **D:** Roger Corman. VHS $44.95 IME ⅃½

Masquerade
A lonely young heiress meets a handsome "nobody" with a mysterious background and it is love at first sight. The romance distresses everyone in the circle of the elite because they assume that he is after her money and not her love. At first it seems decidedly so, then definitely not, and then nothing is certain. A real romantic thriller, with wonderful scenes of the Hamptons.
1988 (R) 91m/C Rob Lowe, Meg Tilly, John Glover, Kim Cattrall, Doug Savant, Dana Delany, Eric Holland; **D:** Bob Swaim; **W:** Dick Wolf; **M:** John Barry. VHS, Beta $14.95 FOX ⅃⅃⅃

Mass Appeal
An adaptation of the Bill C. Davis play about the ideological debate between a young seminarian and a complacent but successful parish pastor. Lemmon has had better roles and done better acting.
1984 (PG) 99m/C Jack Lemmon, Zeljko Ivanek, Charles Durning, Louise Latham, James Ray, Sharee Gregory, Talia Balsam; **D:** Glenn Jordan; **M:** Bill Conti. VHS, Beta $19.95 MCA ⅃⅃

Massacre at Central High
A new student takes matters into his own hands when gang members harass other students at a local high school. Other than some silly dialogue, this low-budget production is above average.
1976 (R) 85m/C Derrel Maury, Andrew Stevens, Kimberly Beck, Robert Carradine, Roy Underwood, Steve Bond; **D:** Renee Daalder; **W:** Renee Daalder. VHS $79.95 MPI ⅃⅃½

Massacre in Dinosaur Valley
A dashing young paleontologist and his fellow explorers go on a perilous journey down the Amazon in search of the Valley of the Dinosaur.
1985 98m/C Michael Sopkiw, Suzanne Carvall. VHS, Beta $69.98 LIV ⅃½

Massacre in Rome
A priest opposes a Nazi colonel's plan to execute Italian civilians in retaliation for the deaths of 33 German soldiers. Strong drama based on a real event.
1973 (PG) 110m/C Richard Burton, Marcello Mastroianni, Leo McKern, John Steiner, Anthony Steel; **D:** George P. Cosmatos; **M:** Ennio Morricone. VHS, Beta NO ⅃⅃½

Massive Retaliation
Hordes of pesky villagers seek refuge within the secluded safety of a family's country house as WWIII approaches.
1985 90m/C Tom Bower, Peter Donat, Karlene Crockett, Jason Gedrick, Michael Pritchard; **D:** Thomas A. Cohen. VHS, Beta $19.98 LIV, VES ⅃

Master Blaster
Friendly game of survival with paintball guns goes awry when one of the contestants exchanges the play guns for deadly weapons.
1985 (R) 94m/C Jeff Moldovan, Donna Rosae, Joe Hess, Peter Lunblad; **D:** Glenn Wilder. VHS $13.95 MVD, PSM ⅃½

Master Harold and the Boys
Stagey cable presentation of South African Athol Fugard's play about relationship between white man and two black servants. Occasionally provocative.

1984 90m/C Matthew Broderick; **D:** Michael Lindsay-Hogg. VHS, Beta $19.98 LHV, WAR ⅃⅃⅃

Master Key
Federal agents battle Nazis in this action-packed 12-chapter serial.
1944 169m/B Jan Wiley, Milburn Stone, Lash LaRue, Dennis Moore; **D:** Ray Taylor, Lewis D. Collins. VHS, Beta $49.95 NOS, DVT, MLB ⅃½

Master Killer
Master Killers are made, not born. Liu trains as he readies himself for an attack on the brutal Manchu assassins. **AKA:** The Thirty-Sixth Chamber.
1984 (R) 109m/C Liu Chia Hui; **D:** Liu Chia Liang. VHS, Beta $9.98 SUE, FXL ⅃

Master Mind
A renowned Japanese super sleuth attempts to solve the theft of a sophisticated midget android.
1973 86m/C Zero Mostel, Keiko Kishi, Bradford Dillman, Herbert Berghof, Frankie Sakai; **D:** Alex March. VHS, Beta $9.95 UNI ⅃⅃

Master Minds
The Bowery Boys run into trouble when Hall gets a toothache and can suddenly predict the future. He takes a job at a carnival where a mad scientist wants to transplant his brain into that of a monster ape man.
1949 64m/B Leo Gorcey, Huntz Hall, Glenn Strange, Gabriel Dell, Alan Napier, Billy Benedict, Bennie Bartlett, David Gorcey; **D:** Jean Yarborough. VHS $11.95 GPV ⅃½

Master Ninja
First in the continuing adventures of the Master and Max (Van Cleef and Van Patten) follow the pair across the US in their search for the Master's long-lost daughter. They're pursued by Kosugi. Originally filmed for television; each tape includes two programs. **AKA:** The Master.
1978 93m/C Lee Van Cleef, Sho Kosugi, Timothy Van Patten. VHS, Beta $9.99 QVD, TWE ⅃½

The Master of Ballantrae
Flynn plays James Durrisdear, the heir to a Scottish title, who gets involved in a rebellion with Bonnie Prince Charlie against the English crown. When the rebellion fails, Flynn heads for the West Indies where he and his partner amass quite a fortune through piracy. Flynn eventually returns to Scotland where he finds that his brother has taken over his title as well as his longtime love. Based on the novel by Robert Louis Stevenson. Flynn's riotous life had put him long past his peak swashbuckling days, as this film unfortunately demonstrates.
1953 89m/C Errol Flynn, Roger Livesey, Anthony Steel, Beatrice Campbell, Yvonne Furneaux, Jacques Berthier, Felix Aylmer, Mervyn Johns; **D:** William Keighley. VHS, Beta $19.98 WAR ⅃⅃

Master of Dragonard Hill
A low-rent swashbuckling romance-novel pastiche.
1989 92m/C Oliver Reed, Eartha Kitt; **W:** R.J. Marx. VHS, Beta $79.95 MED ⅃½

Master of Kung Fu
A Kung Fu instructor calls upon his former teacher to help him fend off loan sharks who want to take over his school.
1977 88m/C Yu Chan Yuan, Chi Hsiao Fu. VHS, Beta $59.98 FOX ⅃

Master of the House
Story of a spoiled husband, a type extinct in this country but still in existence abroad. Silent with titles in English. **AKA:** Thou Shalt Honour Thy Wife.
1925 118m/B **D:** Carl Theodor Dreyer. VHS, Beta $39.95 VYY, ING, FCT ⅃⅃⅃

Master of the World
Visionary tale of a fanatical 19th century inventor who uses his wonderous flying fortress as an antiwar weapon. Adapted from "Robur, the Conqueror" and "Master of the World," both by Jules Verne.

1961 95m/C Vincent Price, Charles Bronson, Henry Hull; **D:** William Witney; **W:** Richard Matheson; **M:** Les Baxter. VHS, Beta $14.98 ORI, WAR ⅃⅃½

Master Race
Absorbing cautionary tale of a German officer who escapes retribution when the Nazis collapse, continuing to hold control over the inhabitants of a small town through intimidation.
1944 98m/B George Coulouris, Lloyd Bridges, Osa Massen, Nancy Gates, Stanley Ridges; **D:** Herbert Biberman. VHS, Beta $29.95 RKO, TTC ⅃⅃½

Master Touch
When a legendary safecracker is released from prison, he attempts one last heist at a Hamburg insurance company. **AKA:** Hearts and Minds; Un Uomo da Rispettare.
1974 (PG) 96m/C Kirk Douglas, Florinda Bolkan, Giuliano Gemma; **D:** Michele Lupo; **M:** Ennio Morricone. VHS, Beta $59.95 PSM ⅃½

The Masters of Menace
The men in blue are mighty miffed when a bunch of bikers break parole to pay their last respects to a comrade in leather. Comic bits by Candy, Belushi, Aykroyd and Wendt provide little relief.
1990 (PG-13) 97m/C David Rasche, Catherine Bach, Dan Aykroyd, James Belushi, John Candy, George Wendt, Tino Insana; **D:** Daniel Raskov; **W:** Tino Insana. VHS $89.95 COL ⅃½

Masters of the Universe
A big-budget live-action version of the cartoon character's adventures, with He-Man battling Skeletor for the sake of the universe.
1987 (PG) 109m/C Dolph Lundgren, Frank Langella, Billy Barty, Courteney Cox, Meg Foster; **D:** Gary Goddard; **M:** Bill Conti. VHS, Beta $19.98 WAR ⅃⅃

Masters of Venus
Eight-part serial about spaceships, space maidens and the like.
1959 121m/B Ferdinand "Ferdy" Mayne. VHS, Beta $24.95 SNC, VDM ⅃½

Master's Revenge
When a girl is kidnapped by a violent motorcycle gang, martial artists are called in to rescue her. Originally released as "Devil Rider."
1971 78m/C Sharon Mahon, Ridgely Abele, Johnny Pachivas. VHS $19.95 ACA ⅃½

Mata Hari
During WWI, a lovely German spy steals secrets from the French through her involvement with two military officers. Lavish production and exquisite direction truly make this one of Garbo's best. Watch for her exotic pseudo-strip tease.
1932 90m/B Greta Garbo, Ramon Novarro, Lionel Barrymore, Lewis Stone, C. Henry Gordon, Karen Morley, Alec B. Francis; **D:** George Fitzmaurice. VHS, Beta $19.98 MGM, FCT ⅃⅃⅃

Mata Hari
Racy, adventure-prone story of WWI's most notorious spy, Mata Hari, who uses her seductive beauty to seduce the leaders of Europe. Stars "Emmanuelle" Kristel.
1985 (R) 105m/C Sylvia Kristel, Christopher Cazenove, Oliver Tobias, Gaye Brown, Gottfried John; **D:** Curtis Cunningham. VHS, Beta $79.95 MGM ⅃⅃

Matador
Bizarre, entertaining black comedy about a retired matador who satiates his desire to kill by appearing in snuff films. He meets his match in an equally deadly woman and the two are drawn closer together by a young bullfighting student who confesses to a series of murders. Not for all tastes, but fine for those who like the outrageous. In Spanish with English subtitles.

1986 90m/C Assumpta Serna, Antonio Banderas, Nacho Martinez, Eva Cobo, Carmen Maura, Julieta Serrano, Chus Lampreave; *D:* Pedro Almodovar; *W:* Pedro Almodovar, Jesus Ferrere; *M:* Bernardo Bonazzi. VHS, Beta $79.95 CCN, ING, TPV *✓✓½*

The Match Factory Girl Kaurismak's final segment of his "working class" trilogy. Iris, a plain, shy outsider shares a drab dwelling with her one-dimensional mother and stepfather, works in a match factory, and hopes desperately for romantic love. Her world is transformed when the extraordinary occurs—she spots a brightly colored party dress in a shop window, buys it, wears it to a bar, and meets the Scandinavian creep who will soon get her pregnant and dump her. Angry at the world, Iris seeks revenge, and in so doing the audience learns that she has become very real and human. Kaurismaki makes his point that beauty can exist in ugly places. In Finnish with English subtitles. *AKA:* Tulitkkutehtaan Tytto.
1990 70m/C Kati Outinen, Elina Salo, Esko Nikkari, Vesa Vierikko; *D:* Aki Kaurismaki; *W:* Aki Kaurismaki. VHS $79.95 KIV, BTV, FCT *✓✓✓*

The Matchmaker An adaptation of the Thornton Wilder play concerning two young men in search of romance in 1884 New York. Later adapted as "Hello Dolly." An amusing diversion.
1958 101m/B Shirley Booth, Anthony Perkins, Shirley MacLaine, Paul Ford, Robert Morse, Perry Wilson, Wallace Ford, Russell Collins, Rex Evans, Gavin Gordon, Torben Meyer; *D:* Joseph Anthony. VHS, Beta $19.95 PAR, FCT *✓✓✓*

Matewan An acclaimed dramatization of the famous Matewan massacre in the 1920s, in which coal miners in West Virginia, reluctantly influenced by a young union organizer, rebelled against terrible working conditions. Complex and imbued with myth, the film is a gritty, moving, powerful drama with typically superb Sayles dialogue and Haskell Wexler's beautiful and poetic cinematography. Jones delivers an economical yet intense portrayal of the black leader of the miners. The director makes his usual on-screen appearance, this time as an establishment-backed reactionary minister. Partially based on the Sayles novel "Union Dues."
1987 (PG-13) 130m/C Chris Cooper, James Earl Jones, Mary McDonnell, William Oldham, Kevin Tighe, David Strathairn; *D:* John Sayles; *W:* John Sayles; *M:* Mason Daring. Academy Awards '87 Nominations: Best Cinematography; Independent Spirit Awards '88: Best Cinematography. VHS, Beta $79.95 LHV, WAR *✓✓✓½*

Matilda Family fare about a entrepreneur who decides to manage a boxing kangaroo, which nearly succeeds in defeating the world heavyweight champion. Uneven and occasionally engaging. Based on Paul Gallico's novel.
1978 (PG) 103m/C Elliott Gould, Robert Mitchum, Harry Guardino, Clive Revill; *D:* Daniel Mann. VHS, Beta $69.98 LIV, VES *✓✓*

Matinee "MANT: Half-man, Half-ant, All Terror!" screams from the movie marquee after Lawrence Woolsey, promoter extraordinaire, and Ruth Corday, his leading lady, roll into Key West circa 1962. Meanwhile, teen Gene Loomis listens to his health teacher push the benefits of red meat and his girlfriend question life, while worrying about his dad, stationed in Cuba. Builds sly parallels between real life and movie horror by juxtaposing Woolsey (modeled after B-movie king William Castle) hyping his schlock, shown in "Atomo-Vision," against JFK solemnly announcing the Russian's approach. Fun, nostalgic look at days gone by—and the matinees that died with them.

1992 (PG) 98m/C John Goodman, Cathy Moriarty, Simon Fenton, Omri Katz, Lisa Jakub, Kellie Martin, Jesse Lee, Lucinda Jenney, James Villemaire, Robert Picardo, Dick Miller, John Sayles, Mark McCracken, Jesse White, David Clennon, Luke Halpin; *D:* Joe Dante; *M:* Jerry Goldsmith. VHS, Beta $19.98 MCA, BTV *✓✓½*

The Mating Game A fast-paced comedy about a tax collector, a beautiful girl, and a wily farm couple. Randall is the straitlaced IRS agent who finds out that the farming Larkins have never paid taxes and use a complicated barter system to get along. Randall falls for farm daughter Reynolds, gets drunk with her Pa, and decides to help the family out of their government dilemma—to the dismay of his superiors. Randall has a terrific drunk scene among his many comedic capers and Reynolds is a highlight.
1959 96m/C Tony Randall, Debbie Reynolds, Paul Douglas, Una Merkel, Fred Clark, Philip Ober, Charles Lane; *D:* George Marshall; *W:* William Roberts. VHS $19.98 MGM *✓✓✓*

Mating Season Successful female attorney Arnaz meets good-natured laundromat owner Luckinbill at a bird-watching retreat. Romance ensues. Made for television.
1981 96m/C Lucie Arnaz, Laurence Luckinbill; *D:* John Llewellyn Moxey. VHS, Beta $14.95 LCA *✓✓½*

Matrimaniac A man goes to great lengths to marry a woman against her father's wishes. Silent with music score.
1916 48m/B Douglas Fairbanks Sr., Constance Talmadge. VHS, Beta $24.95 VYY, GPV *✓✓*

A Matter of Degrees Weeks before his graduation, a beatnik-type college senior finally acquires a goal: romancing a mystery girl...or maybe saving the student radio station...or not. The hero's aimlessness permeates the script, which never goes anywhere in its exploration of campus ennui. Good photography and a great stratum of alternative music groups on the soundtrack: Dream Syndicate, Pere Ubu, Schooly D, Pixies, Poi Dog Pondering, Minutemen, and Throwing Muses.
1990 (R) 89m/C Arye Gross, Judith Hoag, Tom Sizemore, John Doe; *Cameos:* John F. Kennedy Jr., Fred Schneider, Kate Pierson; *D:* W.T. Morgan. VHS, Beta $89.95 PSM *✓✓*

A Matter of Dignity Young girl, forced into marriage with millionaire, eventually brings ruin to the entire family. Why? In Greek with English subtitles.
1957 104m/B Georges Pappas, Ellie Lambetti, Athena Michaelidou, Eleni Zafirou; *D:* Michael Cacoyannis. VHS, Beta $59.95 FCT *✓✓*

A Matter of Life and Death True story follows the real-life experiences of nurse Joy Ufema who has devoted her life to helping terminally ill patients. Exceptional work from Lavin. Made for television.
1981 98m/C Linda Lavin, Salome Jens, Gail Strickland, Gerald S. O'Loughlin, Ramon Bieri, Tyne Daly, Larry Breeding, John Bennett Perry; *D:* Russ Mayberry. VHS NO *✓✓*

A Matter of Love Two couples indulge in spouse swapping while vacationing at the beach.
1978 (R) 89m/C Michelle Harris, Mark Anderson, Christy Neal, Jeff Alin; *D:* Chuck Vincent. VHS, Beta $69.98 LIV, VES *✓*

A Matter of Principle The perennial Christmas special about a Scrooge-like character's yuletide change of heart. He decides it's time to shape up when he realizes he may lose his family permanently.
1983 60m/C Alan Arkin, Barbara Dana, Tony Arkin; *D:* Gwen Arner. VHS, Beta $19.95 ACA *✓*

A Matter of Time Maid is taught to enjoy life by an eccentric, flamboyant contessa, then finds the determination to become an aspiring actress. Often depressing and uneven, arguably Minnelli's worst directing job and his last film. Also Boyer's last appearance and first bit for Bergman's daughter Rosellini, in a small part as a nun.
1976 (PG) 97m/C Liza Minnelli, Ingrid Bergman, Charles Boyer, Tina Aumont, Spiros Andros, Anna Proclemer, Isabella Rossellini; *D:* Vincente Minnelli. VHS, Beta $69.95 VES Woof!

A Matter of WHO A detective for the World Health Organization, or WHO, investigates the disease related deaths of several oil men. Travelling to the Middle East, he uncovers a plot by an unscrupulous businessman to control the oil industry by killing off its most powerful members. Although intended as a comedy, the subject matter is too grim to be taken lightly.
1962 92m/B Terry-Thomas, Alex Nicol, Sonja Ziemann, Richard Briers, Clive Morton, Vincent Ball, Honor Blackman, Carol White, Martin Benson, Geoffrey Keen; *D:* Don Chaffey. VHS, Beta $16.95 SNC *✓✓*

Matters of the Heart Young pianist searches for an opportunity to display his talents, much to the disapproval of his veteran father. He meets a successful but embittered musician who takes him under her wing and passion between the two soon flares. Made for cable TV and based on "The Country of the Heart" by Barbara Wershba.
1990 94m/C Jane Seymour, Christopher Gartin, James Stacy, Geoffrey Lewis, Nan Martin, Allen Rich, Clifford David, Kathy Cannon; *D:* Michael Rhodes. VHS $89.95 MCA *✓✓*

Maurice Based on E.M. Forster's novel about a pair of Edwardian-era Cambridge undergraduates who fall in love, but must deny their attraction and abide by British society's strict norms regarding homosexuality. Maurice finds, however, that he cannot deny his nature, and must come to a decision regarding family, friends, and social structures. A beautiful and stately film of struggle and courage.
1987 (R) 139m/C James Wilby, Hugh Grant, Rupert Graves, Mark Tandy, Ben Kingsley, Denholm Elliott, Simon Callow, Judy Parfitt, Helena Bonham Carter, Billie Whitelaw, Phoebe Nicholls, Barry Foster; *D:* James Ivory; *W:* James Ivory, Kit Hesketh-Harvey; *M:* Richard Robbins. VHS, Beta $79.95 LHV, IME, WAR *✓✓✓*

Mausoleum Only one man can save a woman from eternal damnation.
1983 (R) 96m/C Marjoe Gortner, Bobbie Bresee, Norman Burton, LaWanda Page, Shari Mann; *D:* Michael Dugan. VHS, Beta $14.98 SUE *✓✓*

Maverick Entertaining remake of the popular ABC series is fresh and funny, with sharp dialogue and a good cast. Everybody looks like they're having a great time, not difficult for the charming Gibson, but a refreshing change of pace for the usually serious Foster and Greene. In a fun bit of casting, Garner, the original Maverick, shows up as Marshal Zane Cooper. Lightweight, fast-paced comedy was reportedly highly improvised, though Donner retained enough control to keep it coherent. The end is left wide open so a sequel seems likely. Keep your eyes peeled for cameos from country stars, old time Western actors, and an unbilled appearance from Glover.
1994 (PG) 129m/C Mel Gibson, Jodie Foster, James Garner, Graham Greene, James Coburn, Alfred Molina, Paul Smith, Geoffrey Lewis, Max Perlich; *Cameos:* Dub Taylor, Dan Hedaya, Robert Fuller, Doug McClure, Bert Remsen, Denver Pyle, Will Hutchins, Waylon Jennings, Kathy Mattea, Danny Glover, Clint Black; *D:*

Richard Donner; **W:** William Goldman; **M:** Randy Newman. VHS *NYR* 🎬🎬½

Maverick Queen Barbara Stanwyck, owner of a gambling casino and a member of the "Wild Bunch" outlaw gang, is torn between going straight for the love of a lawman or sticking with the criminals. Stanwyck is perfectly cast in this interesting Western.
1955 90m/C Barbara Stanwyck, Barry Sullivan, Wallace Ford, Scott Brady, Jim Davis, Mary Murphy; **D:** Joseph Kane. VHS **$14.95** *REP* 🎬🎬½

Maverick: The Collector's Edition Offbeat television western starring Garner as conniving gambler Bret Maverick. The premiere show, "War of the Silver Kings," finds Maverick falling out with the richest man in town over a card game. "Point Blank" features Connors as a conniving bank clerk. Additional episodes are available.
195? 100m/B James Garner, Mike Connors. VHS **$19.98** *WAR, MOV* 🎬🎬½

Max Compilation of hilarious Linder shorts plus two features, "Seven Years Bad Luck" and "The Three Must-Get-Theres"
1922 90m/B Max Linder. VHS, Beta **$49.50** *GVV* 🎬🎬

Max A night watchman watches an aspiring actress who is working on her performance in a Broadway play. He tells her she would be better off marrying a doctor.
1979 20m/C Jack Gilford, Lynn Lipton; **D:** Joseph Gilford, Jennifer Lax. VHS, Beta *CFV* 🎬

Max and Helen Uneven, but sensitive and at times highly moving made for TV story of two lovers who are victims of the holocaust. Max (Williams) survives both Nazi and Stalinist camps out of both love for his fiancee and guilt for having lived while she did not.
1990 94m/C Treat Williams, Alice Krige, Martin Landau, Jodhi May, John Phillips, Adam Kotz; **D:** Philip Saville; **W:** Corey Blechman. VHS, Beta **$9.98** *TTC* 🎬🎬½

Max Dugan Returns A Simon comedy about an ex-con trying to make up with his daughter by showering her with presents bought with stolen money. Sweet and light, with a good cast.
1983 (PG) 98m/C Jason Robards Jr., Marsha Mason, Donald Sutherland, Matthew Broderick, Kiefer Sutherland; **D:** Herbert Ross; **W:** Neil Simon. VHS, Beta **$59.98** *FOX* 🎬🎬

Max Fleischer's Documentary Features Two scientific films, "Evolution" and "Einstein's Theory of Relativity," from Fleischer's early studio were made to finance their cartoons. Features animated sequences.
1923 60m/B D: Max Fleischer. VHS, Beta *GVV* 🎬🎬

Max Headroom, the Original Story The computer-generated, British Channel-4 comedy personality stars in his first film, actually a shot-on-video feature about an innocent reporter who is transformed by an evil futuristic TV station into Headroom, the perfect (read: artificial) talk show host.
1986 60m/C Matt Frewer, Nickolas Grace, Hilary Tindall, Amanda Pays, Rocky Morton, Annabel Jankel. VHS, Beta **$29.95** *LHV, WAR* 🎬🎬

Max Maven's Mindgames Magician Max Maven performs mindgames with the use of playing cards, signs and symbols, and magic with money in such settings as Las Vegas, a tropical jungle, the moon and an operating room.
1984 56m/C VHS, Beta **$29.95** *MCA* 🎬🎬

Max, Mon Amour A very refined British diplomat in Paris discovers his bored wife has become involved with Max, who happens to be a chimpanzee. Instead of being upset, the husband decides Max should live with them. Very strange menage a trois manages to avoid the obvious vulgarities. In French with English subtitles. **AKA:** Max, My Love.
1986 97m/C Anthony Higgins, Charlotte Rampling, Victoria Abril, Christopher Hovik, Anne-Marie Besse, Pierre Etaix; **D:** Nagisa Oshima; **W:** Jean-Claude Carriere; **M:** Michel Portal. VHS **$89.95** *CVC, ING* 🎬🎬

Maxie Highly predictable, and forgettable, comedy where a ghost of a flamboyant flapper inhabits the body of a modern-day secretary, and her husband is both delighted and befuddled with the transformations in his spouse. Close is okay, but the film is pretty flaky.
1985 (PG) 98m/C Glenn Close, Ruth Gordon, Mandy Patinkin, Barnard Hughes, Valerie Curtin, Harry Hamlin; **D:** Paul Aaron; **W:** Patricia Resnick; **M:** Georges Delerue. VHS, Beta **$19.99** *HBO* 🎬🎬

Maxim Xul A professor of the occult is forced to tangle with a beast from Hell that possesses enormous strength and an insatiable appetite for human blood.
1991 90m/C Adam West, Jefferson Leinberger, Hal Strieb, Mary Schaeffer; **D:** Arthur Egeli. VHS *NO* 🎬🎬

Maximum Breakout A beautiful and wealthy girl is kidnapped, her boyfriend left for dead. But he recovers and leads a posse of mercenaries to the rescue.
1991 93m/C Sydney Coale Phillips; **D:** Tracy Lynch Britton. VHS **$56.96** *AIP* 🎬½

Maximum Force Three renegade cops join together to infiltrate the underworld and bring to justice both the city's leading crime king and their own corrupt chief of police.
1992 (R) 90m/C Sam Jones, Sherrie Rose, Jason Lively, John Saxon, Richard Lynch, Mickey Rooney, Jeff Langton; **D:** Joseph Merhi. VHS **$89.95** *PMH* 🎬½

Maximum Overdrive Based upon King's story "Trucks," recounts what happens when a meteor hits Earth and machines run by themselves, wanting only to kill people. Score by AC/DC.
1986 (R) 97m/C Emilio Estevez, Pat Hingle, Laura Harrington, Christopher Murney, Yeardley Smith; **D:** Stephen King; **W:** Stephen King; **M:** AC/DC. VHS, Beta **$19.98** *LHV, WAR* 🎬🎬

Maximum Security A small-budget prison film detailing the tribulations of a model prisoner struggling to resist mental collapse.
1987 113m/C Geoffrey Lewis, Jean Smart, Robert Desiderio; **D:** Bill Duke. VHS **$19.95** *STE, NWV* 🎬

Maximum Thrust A few white men confront a deadly Caribbean voodoo tribe.
1987 80m/C Rick Gianasi, Joe Derrig, Jennifer Kanter, Mizan Nunes. Beta *NO* Woof!

May Fools Malle portrays individuals collectively experiencing personal upheaval against the backdrop of unrelated social upheaval. An upper-crust family gathers at a country estate for the funeral of the clan's matriarch, while the May of '68 Parisian riots unfold. Few among the family members mourn the woman's passing, save her son Milou (Piccoli) who leads a pastoral existence tending grapes on the estate. Milou's daughter (Miou-Miou), like the others, is more concerned with her personal gain, suggesting, to her father's horror, that they divide the estate in three. Touching, slow, keenly ob-

served. In French with English subtitles. **AKA:** Milou en Mai; Milou in May.
1990 (R) 105m/C Michel Piccoli, Miou-Miou, Michael Duchaussoy, Dominique Blanc, Harriet Walter, Francois Berleand, Paulette Dubost, Bruno Carette, Martine Gautier; **D:** Louis Malle; **W:** Jean-Claude Carriere, Louis Malle; **M:** Stephane Grappelli. VHS **$79.95** *ORI, FXL, FCT* 🎬🎬🎬

May Wine A sexy, romantic comedy starring "Twin Peaks" alumna, Boyle.
1990 (R) 85m/C Guy Marchand, Lara Flynn Boyle, Joanna Cassidy. VHS **$89.98** *MED, VTR* 🎬🎬

Maya After the death of his mother, young Terry (North) goes to join his big-game hunting father in India. After a quarrel Terry runs off and meets an Indian boy who has promised his dying father he will deliver a sacred white elephant to a jungle temple. The two lads join forces for the trek and have all sorts of adventures along the way. Basis for a short-lived television series.
1966 91m/C Jay North, Clint Walker, Sajid Kahn, I.S. Johar; **D:** John Berry; **W:** John Fante. VHS **$14.95** *MGM, FCT* 🎬🎬

Maya A teacher of fashion in a high school becomes the object of a student's devotion and another teacher's insane jealousy.
1982 114m/C Berta Dominguez, Joseph D. Rosevich; **D:** Agust Agustsson. VHS, Beta *NO* Woof!

Mayalunta A young artist is emotionally tortured by a dying older couple.
1986 90m/C Federico Luppi, Miguel Angel Sola, Barbara Mujica. VHS **$59.98** *VES* Woof!

Maybe I'll Be Home in the Spring Denise (Field) is estranged from her family and decides to leave home for life on a commune where she becomes involved with drugs. When she decides to return home everyone finds it hard to adjust. Made for television. **AKA:** Deadly Desire.
1970 (PG) 90m/C Sally Field, Jackie Cooper, Eleanor Parker, David Carradine, Lane Bradbury; **D:** Joseph Sargent. VHS **$9.99** *VTR* 🎬🎬½

Mayerling Considered one of the greatest films about doomed love. Story of the tragic and hopeless affair between Crown Prince Rudolf of Hapsburg and young Baroness Marie Vetsera. Heart wrenching and beautiful, with stupendous acting. Remade in 1968. In French with English subtitles.
1936 95m/B Charles Boyer, Danielle Darrieux; **D:** Anatole Litvak. VHS, Beta **$24.95** *VYY, MRV, FCT* 🎬🎬🎬½

Mayflower Madam Fairly unsexy and uninteresting made-for-TV movie recounting the business dealings and court battles of the real-life Sydney Biddle Barrows. Barrows/Bergen is a prominent New York socialite and madam of an exclusive escort service whose clientele includes businessmen and dignitaries.
1987 (R) 93m/C Candice Bergen, Chris Sarandon, Chita Rivera; **D:** Lou Antonio. VHS, Beta **$19.95** *STE, VMK* 🎬🎬

Mayhem Two loners in Hollywood confront all types of urban low-life murderers, drug pushers, and child molesters.
1987 90m/C Raymond Martino, Pamela Dixon, Robert Gallo, Wendy MacDonald. VHS, Beta *NO* 🎬

Maytime Lovely story of an opera star (MacDonald) and penniless singer (Eddy) who fall in love in Paris, but her husband/teacher (Barrymore) interferes. One of the best films the singing duo ever made. ♫Maytime Finale; Virginia Ham and Eggs; Vive l'Opera; Student Drinking Song; Carry

Me Back to Old Virginny; Reverie; Jump Jim Crow; Road to Paradise; Page's Aria.
1937 132m/B Jeanette MacDonald, Nelson Eddy, John Barrymore, Herman Bing, Tom Brown, Lynne Carver; **D:** Robert Z. Leonard; **W:** Noel Langley. **VHS $19.98** MGM ⅃⅃⅃

Maytime in Mayfair A dress shop owner's rival is getting all the goodies first, for which he takes the heat from his partner. When he finds out how the rival is doing it, the partners up and head for a vacation in the south of France. Overly simplistic but charming kitsch, helped along by Technicolor shots of the fashions and sets.
1952 94m/C Anna Neagle, Michael Wilding, Peter Graves, Nicholas Phipps, Tom Walls, Tom Walls Jr.; **D:** Herbert Wilcox. **VHS $19.95** NOS ⅃⅃

The Maze Made-for-British-television mystery about a young girl who meets the ghost of her mother's first love in her garden estate.
1985 60m/C Francesca Annis, James Bolam, Sky McCatskill. **Beta $59.95** PSM ⅃⅃⅃

Mazes and Monsters A group of university students becomes obsessed with playing a real life version of the fantasy roleplaying game, Dungeons & Dragons (known in the film as Mazes & Monsters since D&D is trademarked). Early Hanks appearance is among the film's assets. Adapted for television from the book by Rona Jaffe. **AKA:** Rona Jaffe's Mazes & Monsters; Dungeons and Monsters.
1982 100m/C Tom Hanks, Wendy Crewson, David Wallace, Chris Makepeace, Lloyd Bochner, Peter Donat, Murray Hamilton, Vera Miles, Louise Sorel, Susan Strasberg, Anne Francis; **D:** Steven Hilliard Stern; **M:** Hagood Hardy. **VHS, Beta $19.98** LHV, HHE, WAR ⅃⅃½

McBain In this exciting fast-paced action-thriller, POW Robert McBain (Walken) leads a group of veterans into battle against the Columbian drug cartel. Stunning cinematography and superb performances combine to make this a riveting action film you won't soon forget.
1991 (R) 104m/C Christopher Walken, Maria Conchita Alonso, Michael Ironside, Steve James, Jay Patterson, Thomas G. Waites; **D:** James Glickenhaus; **W:** James Glickenhaus. **VHS $19.98** MCA ⅃⅃½

McCabe & Mrs. Miller Altman's characteristically quirky take on the Western casts Beatty as a self-inflated entrepreneur who opens a brothel in the Great North. Christie is the madame who helps stabilize the haphazard operation. Unfortunately, success comes at a high price, and when gunmen arrive to enforce a business proposition, Beatty must become the man he has, presumably, merely pretended to be. A poetic, moving work, and a likely classic of the genre. Based on the novel by Edmund Naughton.
1971 (R) 121m/C Warren Beatty, Julie Christie, William Devane, Keith Carradine, John Schuck, Rene Auberjonois, Shelley Duvall, Bert Remsen, Michael Murphy, Hugh Millais, Jack Riley; **D:** Robert Altman; **W:** Robert Altman; **M:** Leonard Cohen. **VHS, Beta $19.98** WAR ⅃⅃⅃⅃

The McConnell Story True story of ace flyer McConnell, his heroism during WWII and the Korean conflict, and his postwar aviation pioneer efforts. Fine acting from Allyson and Ladd, with good support from Whitmore and Faylen. **AKA:** Tiger in the Sky.
1955 107m/C Alan Ladd, June Allyson, James Whitmore, Frank Faylen; **D:** Gordon Douglas; **M:** Max Steiner. **VHS, Beta $19.98** WAR, FCT ⅃⅃½

The McGuffin A film critic's inquisitiveness about the activities of his neighbors gets him caught up in murder and a host of other problems. A takeoff of Alfred Hitchcock's 1954 classic "Rear Window."
1985 95m/C Charles Dance, Ritza Brown, Francis Matthews, Brian Glover, Phyllis Logan, Jerry Stiller, Anna Massey; **D:** Colin Bucksey. **VHS** NO ⅃⅃

McKenzie Break Irish intelligence agent John Connor (Keith) is sent to Scotland to Camp McKenzie, a prison for German POWs during WWII. Captured U-boat commander Schluetter (Griem) is suspected of planning a mass escape and Connor is supposed to stop the action. The battle of wills between the hard-headed Connor and wily Schluetter provides taut, suspenseful drama. Adapted from "The Bowmanville Break" by Sidney Shelley.
1970 106m/C Brian Keith, Helmut Griem, Ian Hendry, Jack Watson, Horst Janson, Patrick O'Connell; **D:** Lamont Johnson; **W:** William W. Norton Sr. **VHS $19.98** MGM ⅃⅃⅃

McLintock! Rowdy western starring Wayne as a tough cattle baron whose refined wife (O'Hara) returns from the east after a two-year separation. She wants a divorce and custody of their 17-year-old daughter (Powers), who's been away at school. In the meantime, he's hired a housekeeper (De Carlo), whose teenage son (real-life son Patrick) promptly falls for Powers. It's a battle royal between the feisty wife and cantankerous husband but no one out-dukes the Duke. Other Wayne family members involved in the production include daughter Aissa (as the housekeeper's daughter) and son Michael who produced the film.
1963 127m/C John Wayne, Maureen O'Hara, Yvonne De Carlo, Patrick Wayne, Stefanie Powers, Jack Kruschen, Chill Wills, Jerry Van Dyke, Edgar Buchanan, Bruce Cabot, Perry Lopez, Michael Pate, Strother Martin, Gordon Jones; **D:** Andrew V. McLaglen; **W:** James Edward Grant. **VHS $14.99** MPI, GKK, ING ⅃⅃⅃

The McMasters Set shortly after the Civil War, the film tells the story of the prejudice faced by a black soldier who returns to the southern ranch on which he was raised. Once there, the rancher gives him half of the property, but the ex-soldier has difficulty finding men who will work for him. When a group of Native Americans assist him, a band of bigoted men do their best to stop it. The movie was released in two versions with different endings: in one, prejudice prevails; in the other, bigotry is defeated. **AKA:** The Blood Crowd; The McMasters...Tougher Than the West Itself.
1970 (PG) 89m/C Burl Ives, Brock Peters, David Carradine, Nancy Kwan, Jack Palance, Dane Clark, L.Q. Jones, Alan Vint, John Carradine; **D:** Alf Kjellin. **VHS $19.95** STE, XVC ⅃⅃

McQ After several big dope dealers kill two police officers, a lieutenant resigns to track them down. Dirty Harry done with an aging Big Duke.
1974 (PG) 116m/C John Wayne, Eddie Albert, Diana Muldaur, Clu Gulager, Colleen Dewhurst, Al Lettieri, Julie Adams, David Huddleston; **D:** John Sturges; **M:** Elmer Bernstein. **VHS, Beta $19.98** WAR ⅃⅃½

McVicar A brutish and realistic depiction of crime and punishment based on the life of John McVicar, who plotted to escape from prison. From the book by McVicar.
1980 (R) 90m/C Roger Daltrey, Adam Faith, Cheryl Campbell; **D:** Tom Clegg. **VHS, Beta $29.98** VES ⅃⅃½

Me and Him An unsuspecting New Yorker finds himself jockeying for position with his own instincts when his libido decides it wants a life of its own. **AKA:** Ich und Er.
1989 (R) 94m/C Griffin Dunne, Carey Lowell, Ellen Greene, Craig T. Nelson; **D:** Doris Dorrie; **M:** Klaus Doldinger; **V:** Mark Linn-Baker. **VHS $79.95** COL ⅃½

Me and the Kid A con man, trying to go straight, hooks up with a neglected rich kid and the two hit the road, with the cops on their trail.
1993 (PG) 97m/C Danny Aiello, Joe Pantoliano, Cathy Moriarty, Alex Zuckerman; **D:** Dan Curtis. **VHS** ORI ⅃⅃½

Me & Veronica Two estranged sisters try to come to terms with each other and their dead end lives. Good sister Fanny (McGovern) is a divorced waitress living in a run-down seaside town in New Jersey. One day bad sister Veronica (Wettig) shows up, announcing she's about to be sent to jail for welfare fraud. Veronica asks Fanny to look after her two kids while she's in jail and it is while visiting Veronica in prison that Fanny comes to realize her seemingly flamboyant sister is actually mentally ill and possibly suicidal. Grim little film with good lead performances.
1993 (R) 97m/C Elizabeth McGovern, Patricia Wettig, Michael O'Keefe, John Heard; **D:** Don Scardino; **W:** Leslie Lyles; **M:** David Mansfield. **VHS $89.95** COL ⅃⅃

Me, Myself & I Segal is a successful New York writer who falls in love with next-door neighbor Williams. But the road to romance is never smooth—particularly when your paranoid gal suffers from multiple personality disorder. Fun leads, dumb movie.
1992 (R) 97m/C George Segal, JoBeth Williams, Shelley Hack, Don Calfa, Bill Macy, Betsey Lynn George, Sharon McNight, Ruth Gilbert; **D:** Pablo Fero; **W:** Julian Barry. **VHS** COL ⅃⅃½

The Meal During a dinner party held by a wealthy woman, the rich and powerful guests divulge each others' secrets with reckless disregard for the consequences. **AKA:** Deadly Encounter.
1975 (R) 90m/C Dina Merrill, Carl Betz, Leon Ames, Susan Logan, Vicki Powers, Steve Potter; **D:** R. John Hugh. **VHS $19.95** VCI, MOV ⅃⅃

Mean Dog Blues A musician is convicted of hit-and-run driving after hitching a ride with an inebriated politician.
1978 (PG) 108m/C George Kennedy, Kay Lenz, Scatman Crothers, Greg Henry, Gregory Sierra, Tina Louise, William Windom; **D:** Mel Stuart. **VHS, Beta $69.98** LIV, VES ⅃⅃½

Mean Frank and Crazy Tony A mobster and the man who idolizes him attempt a prison breakout in this fun, action-packed production.
1975 (R) 92m/C Lee Van Cleef, Tony LoBianco, Jean Rochefort, Jess Hahn; **D:** Michele Lupo. **VHS, Beta $39.95** LIV ⅃⅃

Mean Johnny Barrows When Johnny Barrows returns to his home town after being dishonorably discharged from the Army he is offered a job as a gang hitman.
1975 83m/C Fred Williamson, Roddy McDowall, Stuart Whitman, Luther Adler, Jenny Sherman, Elliott Gould; **D:** Fred Williamson. **VHS, Beta $49.95** UNI ⅃½

Mean Machine A man and his beautiful cohort plot revenge on organized crime for the murder of his father.
1973 (R) 89m/C Chris Mitchum, Barbara Bouchet, Arthur Kennedy. **VHS, Beta** MON ⅃⅃

Mean Season A vicious mass murderer makes a Miami crime reporter his confidante in his quest for publicity during his killing spree. In time, the madman's intentions become clear as the tensions and headlines grow with each gruesome slaying. Then the reporter must come to terms with the idea that he is letting himself be used due to the success that the association is bringing him. Suspenseful story with a tense ending. Good performance from Russell as the reporter. Screenplay written by Christopher Crowe under the pseudonym Leon Piedmont.
1985 (R) 106m/C Kurt Russell, Mariel Hemingway, Richard Jordan, Richard Masur, Andy Garcia, Joe Pantoliano, Richard Bradford, William Smith; **D:** Phillip Borsos; **W:** Christopher Crowe. **VHS, Beta** *NO* ✶✶

Mean Streets A grimy slice of street life in Little Italy among lower echelon Mafiosos, unbalanced punks, and petty criminals. A riveting, free-form feature film, marking the formal debut by Scorsese (five years earlier he had completed a student film, "Who's That Knocking At My Door?"). Unorthodox camera movement and gritty performances by De Niro and Keitel, with underlying Catholic guilt providing the moral conflict. Excellent early '60s soundtrack.
1973 (R) 112m/C Harvey Keitel, Robert De Niro, David Proval, Amy Robinson, Richard Romanus, David Carradine, Robert Carradine, Cesare Danova, George Memmoli; **D:** Martin Scorsese; **W:** Mardik Martin, Martin Scorsese. **VHS, Beta $19.98** *WAR* ✶✶✶✶

The Meanest Men in the West Two criminal half-brothers battle frontier law and each other.
1976 (PG) 92m/C Charles Bronson, Lee Marvin, Lee J. Cobb, James Drury, Albert Salmi, Charles Grodin; **D:** Samuel Fuller; **W:** Charles S. Dubin. **VHS, Beta $14.98** *MCA* ✶

Meatballs The Activities Director at a summer camp who is supposed to organize fun for everyone prefers his own style of "fun." If you enjoy watching Murray blow through a movie, you'll like this one even as it lapses into box office sentimentality.
1979 (PG) 92m/C Bill Murray, Harvey Atkin, Kate Lynch; **D:** Ivan Reitman; **W:** Len Blum, Harold Ramis; **M:** Elmer Bernstein. **VHS, Beta $24.95** *PAR* ✶✶

Meatballs 2 The future of Camp Sasquatch is in danger unless the camp's best fighter can beat Camp Patton's champ in a boxing match. The saving grace of Bill Murray is absent in this one.
1984 (PG) 87m/C Archie Hahn, John Mengatti, Tammy Taylor, Kim Richards, Ralph Seymour, Richard Mulligan, Hamilton Camp, John Larroquette, Paul (Pee Wee Herman) Reubens, Misty Rowe, Elayne Boosler; **D:** Ken Wiederhorn. **VHS, Beta, 8mm $79.95** *COL* ✶½

Meatballs 3 Second sequel to the teenage sex/summer camp comedy. Enough is enough!
1987 (R) 95m/C Sally Kellerman, Shannon Tweed, George Buza, Isabelle Mejias, Al Waxman, Patrick Dempsey; **D:** George Mendeluk. **VHS, Beta $19.95** *LIV* Woof!

Meatballs 4 Feldman stars as a water skier hired to serve as recreation director of Lakeside Water Ski Camp. His enemy is Monica (Douglas) of a nearby rival camp who wants to buy out Lakeside's owner and use the land for real estate development. Lame plot only serves to showcase some good water skiing stunts.
1992 (R) 87m/C Corey Feldman, Jack Nance, Sarah Douglas, Bojesse Christopher; **D:** Bob Logan. **VHS $89.99** *HBO* ✶½

The Meateater Disgusting horror flick of a disfigured hermit who inhabits a closed-up movie house. When it is reopened he turns into a stereotypical slasher. Vegetarians beware: references throughout about eating meat.
1979 84m/C Arch Jaboulian, Diane Davis, Emily Spendler; **D:** Derek Savage. **VHS, Beta** *NO* Woof!

The Mechanic Bronson stars as Arthur Bishop, a wealthy professional killer for a powerful organization. He has innumerable ways to kill. **AKA:** Killer of Killers.
1972 (R) 100m/C Charles Bronson, Jan-Michael Vincent, Keenan Wynn, Jill Ireland, Linda Ridgeway; **D:** Michael Winner. **VHS, Beta $14.95** *MGM, FOX* ✶✶

Mechanical Crabs A scientist develops the ultimate war weapon: giant mechanical crabs, strong enough to crush anything in their path and devour metal, grow, and multiply. They eventually turn on the scientist and eliminate him.
1977 10m/C VHS, Beta *BFA* Woof!

The Medal of Honor Features 17 segments which highlight amazing and daring aerial feats, in tribute to the flying Medal of Honor recipients.
1985 100m/B VHS, Beta $29.95 *FGF* Woof!

Medea Medea, who betrayed her homeland for Jason, is becoming wary of his boredom with her. The classic story of love and revenge ensues thereafter in unbridled fury and passion.
1959 107m/B Colleen Dewhurst, Zoe Caldwell, Judith Anderson; **D:** Jose Quintero. **VHS** *IVY, FHS* Woof!

Medea Cinema poet Pasolini directs opera diva Callas in this straightforward adaptation of Euripides's classic about a sorceress whose escapades range from assisting in the theft of the Golden Fleece to murdering her own children. Not Pasolini at his best, but still better than most if what you're looking for is something arty. In Italian with English subtitles.
1970 118m/C Maria Callas, Guiseppi Gentile, Laurent Terzieff; **D:** Pier Paolo Pasolini. **VHS, Beta $49.95** *HMV, VAI, APD* Woof!

Medic Boone stars as Dr. Konrad Stuner, the protagonist in this controversial series, ranked as television's first realistic medical show and based on real-life incidents. Featured are two episodes "My Brother Joe" and "Flash of Darkness." Additional episodes available.
1954 55m/B Richard Boone. **VHS, Beta $19.95** *HEG, MOV* Woof!

Medicine Man Benny stars as a con-man who fronts a medicine show in this early talkie comedy.
1930 57m/B Jack Benny, Betty Bronson, E. Allen Warren, George E. Stone, Tom Dugan; **D:** Scott Pembroke. **VHS, Beta $19.95** *NOS, DVT, VYY* ✶½

Medicine Man Connery's usual commanding presence and the beautiful scenery are the only things to recommend in this lame effort. Dr. Robert Campbell (Connery) is a biochemist working in the Amazon rain forest on a cancer cure. Bracco is Dr. Rae Crane, a fellow researcher sent by the institute sponsoring Campbell to see how things are going. Although Crane is uptight and Campbell is gruff, they fall in love (supposedly), but they're sorely lacking in chemistry. Oh, Campbell's cancer cure is made from a rare flower being eradicated by the destruction of the rain forest. This politically correct cause

meets romance falls short of ever being truly entertaining.
1992 (PG-13) 105m/C Sean Connery, Lorraine Bracco, Jose Wilker, Rodolfo de Alexandra, Francisco Tsirene Tsere Rereme, Elias Monteiro da Silva; **D:** John McTiernan; **M:** Jerry Goldsmith. **VHS, Beta $94.95** *HPH* ✶✶

The Mediterranean in Flames In Nazi-occupied Greece, a small but brave resistance is formed to fight its captors. One of the women within the group is forced to seduce a Nazi officer in an attempt to learn enemy secrets.
1972 85m/C Costas Karras, Costas Precas; **D:** Dimis Dadiras. **VHS, Beta** *NO* ✶✶½

Mediterraneo Languid, charming comedy based on the premise that love does make the world go 'round—especially in wartime. In 1941, eight misfit Italian soldiers are stranded on a tiny Greek island and are absorbed into the life of the island, finding love and liberty in the idyllic setting. Lighthearted fun. In Italian with English subtitles.
1991 (R) 90m/C Diego Abatantuono, Giuseppe Cederna, Claudio Bigagli, Vanna Barba, Claudio Bisio, Luigi Alberti, Ugo Conti, Memo Dini, Vasco Mirandola, Luigi Montini, Irene Grazioli, Antonio Catania; **D:** Gabriele Salvatores. **VHS, Beta $94.95** *TOU, IME* ✶✶✶

The Medium A phony medium is done in by her own trickery in this filmed version of the Menotti opera.
1951 80m/B Marie Powers, Anna Maria Alberghetti, Leo Coleman; **D:** Gian-Carlo Menotti; **W:** Gian-Carlo Menotti. **VHS, Beta $49.95** *MVD, VAI* ✶

Medium Cool Commentary on life in the '60s focuses on a television news cameraman and his growing apathy with the events around him. Shot during the riots of 1968. A frightening depiction of detachment in modern society.
1969 111m/C Robert Forster, Verna Bloom, Peter Bonerz, Marianna Hill; **D:** Haskell Wexler; **W:** Haskell Wexler. **VHS, Beta** *PAR, OM* ✶✶✶½

Medusa A bizarre series of events occur when an abandoned yacht containing two lifeless bodies is found on the Aegean Sea. Also released on video as "Twisted."
1974 103m/C George Hamilton, Cameron Mitchell, Lucianna Paluzzi, Theodore Roubanis; **D:** Gordon Hessler. **VHS, Beta $16.95** *SNC, PSM* ✶

Medusa Against the Son of Hercules This time the strongman takes on the evil Medusa and her deadly army of rock men. **AKA:** Perseus the Invincible.
1962 ?m/C Richard Harrison. **VHS, Beta $16.95** *SNC* ✶

The Medusa Touch A man is struck over the head and is admitted to a hospital. Meanwhile, strange disasters befall the surrounding city. It seems that despite his unconscious state, the man is using his telekinetic powers to will things to happen....
1978 (R) 110m/C Richard Burton, Lino Ventura, Lee Remick, Harry Andrews, Alan Badel, Marie-Christine Barrault, Michael Hordern, Derek Jacobi, Jeremy Brett; **D:** Jack Gold. **VHS** *FOX* ✶

Meet Danny Wilson Talented New York singer Wilson (Siantra) and his pianist buddy Mike Ryan (Nicol) head out to Hollywood to try their luck. Danny meets club singer Joy Carroll (Winters) who introduces him to gangster owner Nick Driscoll (Burr). Nick manages Danny for a hefty percentage and makes him a star at his club but Danny's lovelife goes south when Joy picks Mike over him. Then Driscoll demands his money. Sinatra gets to croon some great tunes. ♫I've Got a Crush on You; How Deep Is the

Ocean; When You're Smiling; All of Me; She's Funny That Way; That Old Black Magic; You're a Sweetheart; Lonesome Man Blues; A Good Man Is Hard to Find. **1952 88m/B** Frank Sinatra, Alex Nicol, Shelley Winters, Raymond Burr, Tommy Farrell, Vaughn Taylor, Jack Kruschen, Donald MacBride; **D:** Joseph Pevney; **W:** Don McGuire. **VHS $19.98** *MCA* ♫♫½

Meet Dr. Christian The good old doctor settles some problems. Part of a series. **1939 72m/B** Jean Hersholt, Robert Baldwin, Paul Harvey; **D:** Bernard Vorhaus. **VHS, Beta $19.95** *NOS, DVT, VYY* ♫♫½

Meet John Doe A social commentary about an unemployed, down-and-out man selected to be the face of a political goodwill campaign. Honest and trusting, he eventually realizes that he is being used to further the careers of corrupt politicians. Available in colorized version. **1941 123m/B** Gary Cooper, Barbara Stanwyck, Edward Arnold, James Gleason, Walter Brennan, Spring Byington, Gene Lockhart, Regis Toomey, Ann Doran, Rod La Rocque; **D:** Frank Capra. **VHS $14.95** *NOS, MRV, PSM* ♫♫♫

Meet Me in Las Vegas Compulsive gambler/cowboy Dailey betters his luck when he hooks up with hoofer girlfriend Charisse. Much frolicking and dancing and cameo appearances by a truckload of stars. A little more entertaining than a game of solitaire. ♫The Girl With the Yaller Shoes; If You Can Dream; Hell Hath No Fury; Lucky Charm; I Refuse to Rock 'n Roll; Rehearsal Ballet; Sleeping Beauty Ballet; Frankie and Johnny. **1956 112m/C** Dan Dailey, Cyd Charisse, Agnes Moorehead, Lili Darvas, Jim Backus, Cara Williams, Betty Lynn, Oscar Karlweis, Liliane Montevecchi, Jerry Colonna, Frankie Laine; *Cameos:* Debbie Reynolds, Frank Sinatra, Peter Lorre, Vic Damone, Tony Martin, Elaine Stewart; **D:** Roy Rowland; **W:** Isobel Lennart. **VHS $19.98** *MGM, TTC, FCT* ♫♫

Meet Me in St. Louis Wonderful music in this charming tale of a St. Louis family during the 1903 World's Fair. One of Garland's better musical performances. ♫You and I; Skip to My Lou; Over the Bannister; Meet Me In St. Louis; Brighten the Corner; Summer In St. Louis; All Hallow's Eve; Ah, Love; The Horrible One. **1944 113m/C** Judy Garland, Margaret O'Brien, Mary Astor, Lucille Bremer, Tom Drake, June Lockhart, Harry Davenport; **D:** Vincente Minnelli. Academy Awards '44 Nominations: Best Color Cinematography, Best Screenplay, Best Song ("The Trolley Song"), Best Original Score; National Board of Review Awards '44: 10 Best Films of the Year. **VHS, Beta, 8mm $19.98** *MGM, TLF, HMV* ♫♫♫½

Meet Sexton Blake A detective is hired to find a ring and some secret papers that were stolen from the corpse of a man killed in an air raid. He discovers that the papers contained the plans for a new metal alloy to be used in planes. Entertaining for its melodramatic elements. **1944 80m/B** David Farrar, John Varley, Magda Kun, Gordon McLeod, Manning Whiley; **D:** John Harlow; **W:** John Harlow. **VHS, Beta $16.95** *SNC* ♫♫

Meet the Hollowheads Family situation comedy set in a futuristic society. **1989 (PG-13) 89m/C** John Glover, Nancy Mette, Richard Portnow, Matt Shakman, Juliette Lewis, Anne Ramsey; **D:** Tom Burman. **VHS $39.95** *MED, IME* ♫½

Meet the Mob A country spinster visits her son in the big city and is mistaken for a notorious murderess. Complications arise when she tries to keep the boy honest. Could have worked better.

1942 62m/B ZaSu Pitts, Roger Pryor, Warren Hymer, Gwen Kenyon, Douglas Fowley, Elizabeth Russell, Tristram Coffin, Lester Dorr, Wheeler Oakman, Bud McTaggart; **D:** Jean Yarborough. **VHS $19.95** *NOS* ♫♫

Meet the Navy Post-war musical revue about a pianist and a dancer. **1946 81m/B** Joan Pratt, Margaret Hurst, Lionel Murton. **VHS, Beta $24.95** *VYY* ♫♫

Meet the Parents A young man visits his fiance's parents and every nightmare, every tragedy that can possibly happen, does. From the minds of "National Lampoon," with an appearance by beyond-bizarre comedian Emo Phillips. **1991 ?m/C** Greg Glionna, Jacqueline Cahill, Dick Galloway, Carol Wheeler, Mary Ruth Clarke, Emo Phillips; **D:** Greg Glionna. **VHS** *NO* ♫♫

Meeting at Midnight Charlie Chan is invited to a seance to solve a perplexing mystery. Chan discovers that they use mechanical figures and from there on solving the murder is easy. **1944 67m/B** Sidney Toler, Joseph Crehan, Mantan Moreland, Frances Chan, Ralph Peters, Helen Beverly; **D:** Phil Rosen. **VHS, Beta $19.98** *MGM, VCN, MRV* ♫♫

The Meeting: Eddie Finds a Home Ben Davidson finds an orphan pup rummaging through the trash and cautiously begins a relationship of trust. **1990 ?m/C VHS $14.95** *SPW* ♫♫

Meeting Venus Backstage drama featuring Close as Karin Anderson, a world-famous Swedish opera diva. An international cast of characters adds to this sophisticated film of romance, rivalry and political confrontation set amidst a newly unified Europe. **1991 (PG-13) 121m/C** Glenn Close, Niels Arestrup, Erland Josephson, Johanna Ter Steege, Maria De Medeiros, Victor Poletti, Ildiko Bansagi, Macha Meril, Dorottya Udvaros, Jay O. Sanders; **D:** Istvan Szabo; **W:** Istvan Szabo, Michael Hirst; **M:** Richard Wagner; **V:** Kiri Te Kanawa. **VHS, Beta $92.99** *WAR* ♫♫½

Meetings with Remarkable Men An acclaimed, visually awesome film version of the memoir by Gurdjieff, about his wanderings through Asia and the Middle East searching for answers and developing his own spiritual code. Mildly entertaining but only of true interest to those familiar with the subject. **1979 108m/C** Terence Stamp, Dragan Maksimovic, Mikica Dmitrijevic; **D:** Peter Brook. **VHS, Beta $69.95** *ING, WSH* ♫♫½

Megaforce Futuristic thriller directed by stuntman Needham follows the adventures of the military task force, Megaforce, on its mission to save a small democratic nation from attack. Bostwick leads the attack. 'Nuff said. **1982 (PG) 99m/C** Barry Bostwick, Persis Khambatta, Edward Mulhare, Henry Silva, Michael Beck, Ralph Wilcox; **D:** Hal Needham. **VHS, Beta $19.98** *FOX* Woof!

Megaville Set in the not too distant future, corrupt politician Travanti struggles to corner the market on the evil technology "Dream-a-Life," which aims to control the rebellious "riff-raff" of Megaville. He does all of his dealings while up against a hitman who has a defective memory chip in his brain. **1991 (R) 96m/C** Billy Zane, Daniel J. Travanti, J.C. Quinn, Grace Zabriskie; **D:** Peter Lehner; **W:** Peter Lehner. **VHS $89.98** *LIV* ♫♫

Mein Kampf The rise and fall of German fascism and its impact upon the world is examined in this documentary. **1960 120m/C** **D:** Erwin Leiser. **VHS, Beta $39.95** *SUE, MRV, CAM* ♫♫

Melanie Drama tells the tale of one poor woman's courage, determination, and optimism, as she tries to regain her child from her ex-husband. She befriends musician Cummings (a founding member of "Guess Who" rock band) who helps. Usual cliches balanced by good performances. **1982 (PG) 109m/C** Glynnis O'Connor, Paul Sorvino, Don Johnson, Burton Cummings; **D:** Rex Bromfield. **VHS, Beta $69.95** *VES* ♫♫½

Melodie en Sous-Sol Two ex-convicts, one old and one young, risk their lives and freedom for one last major heist: a gambling casino. In French with English subtitles. *AKA:* Any Number Can Win. **1963 118m/B** Jean Gabin, Alain Delon, Viviane Romance; **D:** Henri Verneuil. **VHS, Beta $19.95** *BAR, ING* ♫♫

Melody Sensitive but slow study of a special friendship which enables two preteens to survive in a regimented and impersonal world. Features music by the Bee Gees. **1971 (G) 106m/C** Tracy Hyde, Jack Wild, Mark Lester, Colin Barrie, Roy Kinnear; **D:** Waris Hussein; **W:** Alan Parker. **VHS, Beta $69.98** *SUE* ♫♫

Melody Cruise Boring musical romantic comedy that can't stay with any one of those three things for more than a minute without careening into one of the other two. ♫I Met Her at a Party; He's Not the Marrying Kind; Isn't This a Night For Love; This is the Hour. **1932 75m/B** Phil Harris, Charlie Ruggles, Greta Nissen, Helen Mack, Chick Chandler; **D:** Mark Sandrich. **VHS, Beta $19.98** *TTC* ♫♫

Melody for Three In the tradition of matchmaker, Doctor Christian aids in the reuniting of music-teacher mother and great-conductor father, who have been divorced for years, in order to help the couple's son, a violin prodigy. **1941 69m/B** Jean Hersholt, Fay Wray; **D:** Erle C. Kenton. **VHS, Beta, 8mm $19.95** *NOS, VYY, DVT* ♫♫

Melody in Love A young girl visits her cousin and her swinging friends on a tropical island. Dubbed. **1978 90m/C** Melody O'Bryan, Sasha Hehn; **D:** Hubert Frank. **VHS, Beta $59.98** *FOX* ♫

Melody Master Romanticized biography of composer Franz Schubert, chronicling his personal life and loves, along with performances of his compositions. If you just have to know what drove the composer of "Ave Maria" it may hold your interest, but otherwise not very compelling. *AKA:* New Wine. **1941 80m/B** Alan Curtis, Ilona Massey, Binnie Barnes, Albert Basserman, Billy Gilbert, Sterling Holloway; **M:** Miklos Rozsa. **VHS, Beta $19.95** *NOS, VYY, DVT* ♫♫

Melody of the Plains Singing cowpoke teams up with a young girl for some cattle-rustlin' adventure. Substandard horse opry due to poor direction and haphazard lensing. **1937 53m/B** Fred Scott, Louise Small, Al "Fuzzy" St. John, David Sharpe, Lafe McKee, Charles "Slim" Whitaker, Hal Price, Lew Meehan; **D:** Sam Newfield; **W:** Bennett Cohen. **VHS $19.99** *MOV* ♫

Melody Ranch Gene returns to his home town as an honored guest and appointed sheriff. But gangster MacLane is determined to drive him out of town. ♫Melody Ranch; Call of the Canyon; We Never Dream the Same Dream Twice; Vote for Autry; My Gal Sal; Torpedo Joe; What Are Cowboys Made Of?; Rodeo Rose; Back in the Saddle Again.

1940 84m/C Gene Autry, Jimmy Durante, George "Gabby" Hayes, Ann Miller, Barton MacLane, Joseph Sawyer, Horace McMahon, Veda Ann Borg; *D:* Joseph Santley. **VHS, Beta $19.95** *CCB, VCN ♂½*

Melody Trail Autry wins $1000 in a rodeo, loses the money to a gypsy, gets a job, falls for his employer's daughter...and in the end captures a kidnapper and cattle rustlers. ♫ Hold On, Little Doggie, Hold On; On the Prairie; Lookin for the Lost Chord; The Hurdy Gurdy Man; My Prayer For Tonight; End of the Trail; I'd Love a Home in the Mountains.
1935 60m/B Gene Autry, Smiley Burnette, Ann Rutherford; *D:* Joseph Kane. **VHS, Beta $37.95** *CCB, VCN ♂*

Melvin and Howard Story of Melvin Dummar, who once gave Howard Hughes a ride. Dummar later claimed a share of Hughes's will. Significant for Demme's direction and fine acting from Steenburgen/Le-Mat, and Robards in a small role as Hughes. Offbeat and very funny.
1980 (R) 95m/C Paul LeMat, Jason Robards Jr., Mary Steenburgen, Michael J. Pollard, Dabney Coleman, Elizabeth Cheshire, Pamela Reed, Cheryl "Rainbeaux" Smith; *D:* Jonathan Demme; *W:* Bo Goldman. Academy Awards '80: Best Original Screenplay, Best Supporting Actress (Steenburgen); Nominations: Best Supporting Actor (Robards); Los Angeles Film Critics Association Awards '80: Best Supporting Actress (Steenburgen); National Board of Review Awards '80: 10 Best Films of the Year; New York Film Critics Awards '80: Best Director (Demme), Best Supporting Actress (Steenburgen). **VHS, Beta $14.95** *MCA, BTV ♂♂♂½*

Melvin Purvis: G-Man Mediocre action film has dedicated federal agent tracking killer Machine Gun Kelly across American Midwest during Depression. Made for television. *AKA:* The Legend of Machine Gun Kelly.
1974 78m/C Dale Robertson, Harris Yulin, Margaret Blye, Matt Clark, Elliot Street, Dick Sargent, John Karlen, David Canary; *D:* Dan Curtis. **VHS $69.95** *HBO ♂♂*

The Member of the Wedding While struggling through her adolescence, a twelve-year-old girl growing up in 1945 Georgia seeks solace from her family's cook. Based on Carson McCullers's play, this story of family, belonging, and growth is well acted and touching.
1952 90m/C Ethel Waters, Julie Harris, Brandon de Wilde, Arthur Franz; *D:* Fred Zinneman; *W:* Edward Anhalt. **VHS, Beta** *NO ♂♂♂*

The Member of the Wedding TV rehash of Carson McCuller's play about a young girl who finds she's got some growing up to do when big brother marries. No match for Zinnemann's '52 version, or for Mann's earlier "All Quiet on the Western Front" and "Marty."
1983 90m/C Dana Hill, Pearl Bailey, Howard E. Rollins Jr.; *D:* Delbert Mann. **VHS $49.95** *VHE ♂♂*

Memoirs of an Invisible Man Nick Halloway, a slick and shallow stock analyst, is rendered invisible by a freak accident. When he is pursued by a CIA agent-hit man who wants to exploit him, Nick turns for help to Alice, a documentary filmmaker he has just met. Naturally, they fall in love along the way. Effective sight gags, hardworking cast can't overcome pitfalls in script, which indecisively meanders between comedy and thrills.
1992 (PG-13) 99m/C Chevy Chase, Daryl Hannah, Sam Neill, Michael McKean, Stephen Tobolowsky, Jim Norton, Patricia Heaton, Rosalind Chao; *D:* John Carpenter. **VHS $19.98** *WAR ♂½*

Memorial Day Good cast highlights this made-for-television outing covering a Vietnam veterans reunion. With the old memories come new problems for the men and their families.
1983 120m/C Mike Farrell, Shelley Fabares, Keith Mitchell, Bonnie Bedelia, Robert Walden, Edward Herrmann, Danny Glover; *D:* Joseph Sargent; *M:* Billy Goldenberg. **VHS** *NO ♂♂*

Memorial Valley Massacre When campers settle for a weekend in a new, unfinished campground, they're slaughtered in turn by a nutty hermit.
1988 (R) 93m/C Cameron Mitchell, William Smith, John Kerry, Mark Mears, Lesa Lee, John Caso; *D:* Robert C. Hughes. **VHS, Beta $19.98** *SUE, NLC ♂*

Memories of a Marriage A nostalgic look at a couple's many years of marriage, from the husband's point of view, as they face their most trying times. Touchingly reminiscent as it spans the youthful years of new love and marriage to the more quiet, solid years of matured love. In Danish with English subtitles.
1990 90m/C Ghita Norby, Frits Helmuth, Rikke Bendsen, Henning Moritzen; *D:* Kaspar Rostrup. **VHS $79.95** *FXL, ING ♂♂♂*

Memories of Hell Examines the special bonds of friendship that have been maintained among the New Mexicans who survived one of WWII's most brutal battles and subsequent prisoner experiences.
1987 57m/C Beta *CEN ♂♂♂*

Memories of Me A distraught doctor travels to L.A. to see his ailing father and make up for lost time. Both the doctor and his father learn about themselves and each other. Story of child/parent relationships attempts to pull at the heartstrings but only gets as far as the liver. Co-written and co-produced by Crystal, this film never quite reaches the potential of its cast.
1988 (PG-13) 103m/C Billy Crystal, Alan King, JoBeth Williams, David Ackroyd, Sean Connery, Janet Carroll; *D:* Henry Winkler; *W:* Billy Crystal, Eric Roth; *M:* Georges Delerue. **VHS, Beta $14.95** *FOX ♂♂*

Memories of Murder A woman suffering from amnesia is stalked by a merciless killer, apparently seeking revenge. Can she regain her memory and understand why she is being hunted, before it's too late?
1990 104m/C Vanity, Nancy Allen, Robin Thomas; *D:* Robert Lewis; *W:* John Kent Harrison, Nevin Schreiner. **VHS, Beta $79.98** *PSM ♂♂*

Memories of Underdevelopment Set in the early 1960s. An anti-revolutionary, Europeanized intellectual takes a stand against the new government in Cuba. In Spanish with English subtitles.
1968 97m/B Sergio Corrieri, Daisy Granados; *D:* Thomas Gutierrez Alea; *W:* Thomas Gutierrez Alea. **VHS $69.95** *NYF, FCT, ING ♂♂½*

Memory of Us Still-relevant story of a married, middle-aged woman who starts to question her happiness as a wife and mother. Written by its star Geer, whose father, Will, plays a bit part.
1974 (PG) 93m/C Ellen Geer, Jon Cypher, Barbara Colby, Peter Brown, Robert Hogan, Rose Marie, Will Geer; *D:* H. Kaye Dyal. **VHS $19.95** *ACA ♂♂*

Memphis In 1957 three white drifters (two men and a woman) decide to secure some easy money by kidnapping the young grandson of the richest black businessman in Memphis. They think it's an easy job since, given the prejudice of the times, the police will do little or nothing but they reckon

without the resources of the black community itself. Based on the novel "September, September" by Shelby Foote. Originally made for cable.
1991 (PG-13) 92m/C Cybill Shepherd, John Laughlin, J.E. Freeman, Richard Brooks, Moses Gunn, Vanessa Bell, Martin C. Gardner; *D:* Yves Simoneau; *W:* Cybill Shepherd, Larry McMurtry. **VHS, Beta $89.98** *TTC ♂♂½*

Memphis Belle Satisfying Hollywood version of the documentary of the same name captures the true story of the final mission of a WWII bomber crew stationed in England. The boys of the Memphis Belle were the first group of B-17 crewmen to complete a 25 mission tour—no small feat in an air war that claimed many lives. Good ensemble cast of up and coming young actors; Lithgow has a nice turn as an army PR guy determined to exploit their boyish good looks on the homefront. Caton-Jones effectively uses 1940s film techniques and some original footage, making up for a rather hokey script. Film debut of singer Connick. Produced by Catherine Wyler, whose father made the original.
1990 107m/C Matthew Modine, John Lithgow, Eric Stoltz, Sean Astin, Harry Connick Jr., Reed Edward Diamond, Tate Donovan, D.B. Sweeney, Billy Zane, David Strathairn, Jane Horrocks, Courtney Gains, Neil Giuntoli; *D:* Michael Caton-Jones; *W:* Monte Merrick; *M:* George Fenton. **VHS, Beta, 8mm $19.98** *WAR, VYY, FCT ♂♂♂*

Memphis Belle: A Story of a Flying Fortress The entire final mission of the B-25 bomber "Memphis Belle" and its daring daylight attack on the submarine pens at Wilhelmshaven, Germany is captured through newsreel footage. The crew was the first to complete a 25 run mission. A film version of the story was released in 1990 as "Memphis Belle." Produced by William Wyler.
1944 43m/C VHS, Beta $24.95 *TPV, NOS, HHT ♂♂♂*

The Men A paraplegic WWII veteran sinks into depression until his former girlfriend manages to bring him out of it. Marlon Brando's first film. A thoughtful story that relies on subtle acting and direction. *AKA:* Battle Stripe.
1950 85m/B Marlon Brando, Teresa Wright, Everett Sloane, Jack Webb; *D:* Fred Zinneman. Academy Awards '50 Nominations: Best Story & Screenplay; National Board of Review Awards '50: 10 Best Films of the Year. **VHS $19.98** *REP ♂♂♂½*

Men... A funny and insightful satire about a man who discovers his loving wife has been having an affair with a young artist. In a unique course of revenge, the husband ingratiates himself with the artist and gradually turns him into a carbon copy of himself. In German with English subtitles or dubbed.
1985 96m/C Heiner Lauterbach, Uwe Ochsenknecht, Ulrike Kriener, Janna Marangosoff; *D:* Doris Dorrie. **VHS $79.95** *ING, NYF ♂♂♂½*

Men are not Gods Verbose film (precursor to "A Double Life") about an actor playing Othello who nearly kills his wife during Desdemona's death scene.
1937 90m/B Rex Harrison, Miriam Hopkins, Gertrude Lawrence; *D:* Walter Reisch. **VHS, Beta** *SUE ♂♂½*

Men at Work Garbage collectors Sheen and Estevez may not love their work, but at least it's consistent from day to day. That is, until they get wrapped up in a very dirty politically-motivated murder. And who will clean up the mess when the politicians are

through trashing each other? A semi-thrilling semi-comedy that may leave you semi-satisfied.
1990 (PG-13) 98m/C Charlie Sheen, Emilio Estevez, Leslie Hope, Keith David; *D:* Emilio Estevez; *W:* Emilio Estevez. **VHS, Beta $19.95** COL, FOX 🐾🐾

Men Don't Leave A recent widow tries to raise her kids single-handedly, suffers big city life and regains her love life. Good performances by all, especially Cusack. By the director of ''Risky Business.''
1989 (PG-13) 115m/C Jessica Lange, Arliss Howard, Joan Cusack, Kathy Bates, Charlie Korsmo, Corey Carrier, Chris O'Donnell, Tom Mason, Jim Haynie; *D:* Paul Brickman; *W:* Barbara Benedek, Paul Brickman. **VHS, Beta, 8mm $19.98** WAR 🐾🐾½

Men in Love A young San Franciscan travels to Hawaii with the cremated remains of his lover, who has succumbed to AIDS. There he encounters a supportive group of men who nurse him back to sexual and spiritual wholeness.
1990 93m/C Doug Self, Joe Tolbe, Emerald Starr, Kutira Decosterd; *D:* Marc Huestis; *W:* Starr Emerald Catamas Scott. **VHS $29.95** WBF, FCT, ING 🐾🐾

Men in War Korean War drama about a small platoon trying to take an enemy hill by themselves. A worthwhile effort with some good action sequences.
1957 100m/B Robert Ryan, Robert Keith, Aldo Ray, Vic Morrow; *D:* Anthony Mann; *W:* Philip Yordan; *M:* Elmer Bernstein. **VHS, Beta $19.95** FGF, MRV, BMV 🐾🐾½

Men of Boys Town Sequel to 1938's ''Boys Town'' has the same sentimentality, even more if that's possible. Father Flanagan's reformatory faces closure, while the kids reach out to an embittered new inmate. Worth seeing for the ace cast reprising their roles.
1941 106m/B Spencer Tracy, Mickey Rooney, Darryl Hickman, Henry O'Neill, Lee J. Cobb, Sidney Miller; *D:* Norman Taurog. **VHS $19.98** MGM, FCT 🐾🐾½

Men of Ireland A Dublin medical student cavorts with islanders off the Irish coast. Uninspired programmer with authentic native folk of the Blasket Islands, plus their songs and dances.
1938 62m/B Cecil Ford, Eileen Curran, Brian O'Sullivan, Gabriel Fallon; *D:* Dick Bird. **VHS, Beta, 8mm $19.95** VYY 🐾🐾

Men of Respect Shakespeare meets the mafia in this misbegotten gangster yarn. Turturro, a gangster MacBeth, is prodded by wife and psychic to butcher his way to the top o' the mob. Well acted but ill conceived, causing Bard's partial roll over in grave.
1991 (R) 113m/C John Turturro, Katherine Borowitz, Peter Boyle, Dennis Farina, Chris Stein, Steven Wright, Stanley Tucci; *D:* William Reilly; *W:* William Reilly. **VHS, 8mm $19.95** COL 🐾🐾

Men of Sherwood Forest Robin Hood and his band take it to the sheriff et al in this colorful Hammer version of the timeless legend.
1957 77m/C Don Taylor, Reginald Beckwith, Eileen Moore, Davis King-Wood, Patrick Holt, John Van Eyssen, Douglas Wilmer; *D:* Val Guest. **VHS $16.95** NOS, SNC, DVT 🐾🐾½

Men of Steel Two Canadian military officers, one French and one English, must struggle to survive when their plane crashes in the wilderness. Besides contending with the surroundings, they must deal with one another's instilled bitterness and underlying prejudices.

1988 (PG) 91m/C Allan Royal, Robert Lalonde, David Ferry, Mavor Moore, Yvan Ponton; *D:* Donald Shebib. **VHS, Beta** TWE 🐾

Men of the Fighting Lady Action-adventure offers plenty of exciting battle footage. Features the stories of selected pilots stationed on a U.S. aircraft carrier in the Pacific during the Korean War. The stories, told to Calhern as writer James A. Michener, center around the lead pilot Johnson. Dramatic airflights include a scene in which Johnson helps a blinded Martin land his plane safely on the carrier deck. Gene Ruggerio's editing of the war footage was so expertly done that he was questioned by the Pentagon when they had a hard time believing the scenes were achieved by skillful editing and painted backdrops. Look for ''Beaver'' Mathers as one of Wynn's sons.
1954 81m/C Van Johnson, Walter Pidgeon, Louis Calhern, Dewey Martin, Keenan Wynn, Frank Lovejoy, Robert Horton, Bert Freed, Jerry Mathers; *D:* Andrew Marton. **VHS, Beta $19.98** MGM 🐾🐾🐾½

Men of Two Worlds Classical musician raised in Africa is the toast of Europe until he finds out he's got a voodoo curse, and suddenly he's got the heebie jeebies too bad to play chopsticks. *AKA:* Witch Doctor; Kisenga, Man of Africa.
1946 90m/C Robert Adams, Eric Portman, Orlando Martins, Phyllis Calvert, Arnold Marle, Cathleen Nesbitt, David Horne, Cyril Raymond; *D:* Thorold Dickinson. **VHS, Beta $16.95** SNC 🐾🐾

The Men Who Tread on the Tiger's Tail Twelfth-century Japan is the setting for this struggle of power between two brothers, one a reigning shogun, the other on the run. English subtitles.
1945 60m/B *D:* Akira Kurosawa. **VHS, Beta $29.95** IHF 🐾🐾

Menace on the Mountain Family-oriented drama about a father and son who battle carpetbagging Confederate deserters during the Civil War.
1970 (G) 89m/C Patricia Crowley, Albert Salmi, Charles Aidman. **VHS, Beta $69.95** DIS 🐾🐾

Menace II Society Portrayal of black teens lost in inner-city hell is realistically captured by 21-year-old twin directors, in their big-screen debut. Caine (Turner) lives with his grandparents and peddles drugs for spending money, from the eve of his high school graduation to his decision to escape south-central Los Angeles for Atlanta. Bleak and haunting, with some of the most unsettling, bloodiest violence ever shown in a commercial film. Disturbing to watch, but critically acclaimed. The Hughes' make their mark on contemporary black cinema with intensity, enhanced by an action-comics visual flair. Based on a story by the Hughes' and Tyger Williams.
1993 (R) 104m/C Tyrin Turner, Larenz Tate, Samuel L. Jackson, Glenn Plummer, Julian Roy Doster, Bill Duke, Charles S. Dutton; *D:* Allen Hughes, Albert Hughes; *W:* Tyrin Turner. Independent Spirit Aw Nominations: rds '94: Best Actor (Turner), Best Cinematography, Best First Feature; MTV Movie Awards '94: Best Film. **VHS** COL, NLC, IME 🐾🐾🐾

Menage Depardieu is the homosexual crook who breaks into the home of an impoverished couple—the dominating Miou-Miou and her submissive husband, Blanc. An unrepentant thief, he begins to take over their lives, introducing them to the wonderful world of crime, among other, more kinky, pastimes. Gender-bending farce that doesn't hold up to the end but is worth watching for sheer outrageousness. In French with English subtitles. *AKA:* Tenue de Soiree.

1986 84m/C Gerard Depardieu, Michel Blanc, Miou-Miou, Bruno Cremer, Jean-Pierre Marielle; *D:* Bertrand Blier; *W:* Bertrand Blier; *M:* Serge Gainsbourg. **VHS $89.95** TRI, ING, FCT 🐾🐾🐾

The Men's Club Seven middle-aged buddies get together for a single night, and bare their respective souls and personal traumas, talking about women and eating and drinking. Banal. Based on novel by Leonard Michael.
1986 (R) 100m/C Harvey Keitel, Roy Scheider, Craig Wasson, Frank Langella, David Dukes, Richard Jordan, Treat Williams, Stockard Channing, Jennifer Jason Leigh, Ann Dusenberry, Cindy Pickett, Gwen Welles; *D:* Peter Medak. **VHS, Beta $19.95** PAR 🐾🐾

Menschenfrauen A philandering journalist is put in his place by the four women with whom he is simultaneously having relationships. In German with English subtitles.
1980 100m/C *D:* Valie Export. **VHS, Beta $59.95** FCT 🐾🐾½

Mephisto An egomaniacal actor, compellingly played by Brandauer, sides with the Nazis to further his career, with disastrous results. The first of three brilliant films by Szabo and Brandauer exploring the price of power and personal sublimation in German history. Critically hailed. In German with English subtitles. From the novel by Klaus Mann. Followed by ''Colonel Redl'' and ''Hanussen.''
1981 144m/C Klaus Maria Brandauer, Krystyna Janda, Ildiko Bansagi, Karin Boyd, Rolf Hoppe, Christine Harbort, Gyorgy Cserhalmi, Christiane Graskoff, Peter Andorai, Ildiko Kishonti; *D:* Istvan Szabo. Academy Awards '81: Best Foreign Language Film; Nominations: s 81: Best Film. **VHS, Beta $14.98** REP, ING, SWC 🐾🐾🐾½

The Mephisto Waltz Journalist gets more than a story when he is granted an interview with a dying pianist. It turns out that he is a satanist and the cult he is a part of wants the journalist. Chilling adaptation of the Fred Mustard Stewart novel features a haunting musical score.
1971 (R) 108m/C Alan Alda, Jacqueline Bisset, Barbara Parkins, Curt Jurgens, Bradford Dillman, William Windom, Kathleen Widdoes; *D:* Paul Wendkos; *M:* Jerry Goldsmith. **VHS $59.98** FOX 🐾🐾🐾

The Mercenaries Romantic warrior fights to save the lives and honor of his people who are under attack from mercenaries murdering and raping their way across Europe.
1965 98m/C Debra Paget. **Beta $39.95** AIP 🐾½

The Mercenaries A tough guy, given the assignment to kill Fidel Castro, encounters all sorts of adversity along the way. Key West scenery is the only thing of interest. *AKA:* Cuba Crossing; Kill Castro; Assignment: Kill Castro; Key West Crossing; Sweet Dirty Tony.
1980 92m/C Stuart Whitman, Robert Vaughn, Caren Kaye, Raymond St. Jacques, Woody Strode, Sybil Danning, Albert Salmi, Michael Gazzo; *D:* Chuck Workman. **VHS, Beta $59.95** ACA, JEF, VTR 🐾

Mercenary Fighters An American soldier-of-fortune fights for both sides of an African revolution. Shot in South Africa.
1988 (R) 90m/C Peter Fonda, Reb Brown, Ron O'Neal, Jim Mitchum; *D:* Riki Shelach. **VHS, Beta $79.95** MED, VTR 🐾½

The Merchant of Four Seasons Story focuses on the depression and unfulfilled dreams of an average street merchant. Direction from Fassbinder is slow, deliberate, and mesmerizing. In German with English subtitles.

1971 88m/C Hans Hirschmuller, Irm Hermann, Hanna Schygulla, Andrea Schober, Gusti Kreissl; *D:* Rainer Werner Fassbinder; *W:* Rainer Werner Fassbinder. VHS, Beta $79.95 NYF, ING 𝆕𝆕𝆕

The Merchant of Venice Shakespeare's tragedy of prejudice, vengeance, and sacrifice stars Olivier as the persecuted money lender Shylock, who demands his payment of a pound of flesh for a defaulted loan.
1973 131m/C Laurence Olivier, Joan Plowright, Jeremy Brett. VHS $19.98 FUS, FCT 𝆕𝆕𝆕

Merchants of War Sent out by the CIA on a mission, two best friends are soon the target of one of the most dangerous terrorists in the world. The fanatical Islamic terrorist soon casts his wrath upon the two men.
1990 (R) 100m/C Asher Brauner, Jesse Vint, Bonnie Beck; *D:* Peter M. MacKenzie. VHS $89.95 VMK 𝆕

Mere Jeevan Saathi A bizarre, unclassifiable Indian film with music, fantasy, special effects, violence, and flamboyant mise-en-scene. In Hindi with English subtitles. English title: "My Life Partner."
1965 126m/C Lata Mangeskar. VHS, Beta $24.95 VYY, AUD 𝆕𝆕½

Meridian: Kiss of the Beast A beautiful heiress is courted, kidnapped and loved by a demonic man-beast.
1990 90m/C Sherilyn Fenn, Malcom Jamieson, Hilary Mason, Alex Daniels, Phil Fondacaro; *D:* Charles Band; *W:* Dennis Paoli; *M:* Pino Donaggio. VHS, Beta $19.95 PAR 𝆕½

Merlin In a remote California town reporter Christy Lake is stunned to discover her ancient heritage. Turns out she's the reincarnated daughter of legendary Merlin the magician and it is her duty to protect the Sword of Power from the evil sorcerer Pendragon. And aided by a handsome warrior and an ancient sage, that's just what she intends to do.
1993 (PG-13) 112m/C Nadia Cameron, Peter Phelps, Richard Lynch, James Hong, Ted Markland, Desmond Llewelyn; *D:* Paul Hunt; *W:* Nick McCarty. VHS $92.95 HMD 𝆕𝆕½

Merlin and the Sword Poor use of a good cast in this treatment of the legend of Merlin, Arthur and Excalibur. *AKA:* Arthur the King.
1985 94m/C Malcolm McDowell, Edward Woodward, Candice Bergen, Dyan Cannon; *D:* Clive Donner. VHS, Beta $69.98 LIV, VES 𝆕

Merlin of the Crystal Cave Depicts the adventures of the young boy Merlin as he learns the ways of magic in the days before Camelot and King Arthur. Made for British television.
1991 159m/C VHS $19.98 FOX 𝆕𝆕½

Mermaids Mrs. Flax (Cher) is the flamboyant mother of two who hightails out of town every time a relationship threatens to turn serious. Having moved some eighteen times, her daughters, Charlotte (Ryder), 15, and Kate (Ricci), 8, are a little worse for the wear, psychologically speaking. One aspires to be a nun though not Catholic, and the other holds her breath under water. Now living in Massachusetts, Mrs. Flax starts having those "I got you, babe" feelings for Hoskins, a shoestore owner. Amusing, well-acted multi-generational coming of ager based on a novel by Patty Dann.
1990 (PG-13) 110m/C Cher, Winona Ryder, Bob Hoskins, Christina Ricci, Michael Schoeffling, Caroline McWilliams, Jan Miner; *D:* Richard Benjamin; *W:* June Roberts; *M:* Jack Nitzsche. VHS, Beta $9.98 ORI 𝆕𝆕𝆕

The Mermaids of Tiburon A marine biologist and a criminal travel to a remote island off Mexico in search of elusive, expensive "fire pearls." There they encounter a kingdom of lovely mermaids who promptly liven things up. Filmed in "Aquascope" for your viewing pleasure. *AKA:* The Aqua Sex.
1962 77m/C Diane Webber, George Rowe, Timothy Carey, Jose Gonzalez-Gonzalez, John Mylong, Gil Baretto, Vicki Kantenwine, Nani Morrissey, Judy Edwards, Jean Carroll, Diana Cook, Karen Goodman, Nancy Burns; *D:* John Lamb; *W:* John Lamb. VHS $18.00 FRG 𝆕

Merrill's Marauders Chandler is the commander of a battle-hardened regiment fighting in the jungles of Burma in 1944. The exhausted unit gains their latest objective and expects to be relieved, only to be continuously pushed into more fighting down the line. Director Fuller excels at showing the confusion of battle; Chandler's last film role (he died before the film was released).
1962 98m/C Jeff Chandler, Ty Hardin, Peter Brown, Andrew Duggan, Will Hutchins, Claude Akins; *D:* Samuel Fuller; *W:* Milton Sperling, Samuel Fuller; *M:* Howard Jackson. VHS $19.98 WAR 𝆕𝆕½

Merry Christmas, Mr. Lawrence An often overlooked drama about a WWII Japanese POW camp. Taut psychological drama about clashing cultures and physical and emotional survival focusing on the tensions between Bowie as a British POW and camp commander Sakamato, who also composed the outstanding score. A haunting and intense film about the horrors of war. Based on the novel by Laurens van der Post.
1983 (R) 124m/C David Bowie, Tom Conti, Ryuichi Sakamoto, Takeshi, Jack Thompson; *D:* Nagisa Oshima. VHS, Beta $59.95 MCA 𝆕𝆕𝆕

Merry-Go-Round A handsome Austrian count is engaged to a woman of his class when he meets the beautiful Agnes, who works as an organ grinder for the local merry-go-round. He disguises himself to woo her but finally decides to marry his fiance, although Agnes continues to love him. But the story doesn't end for the two lovers who are destined to be together. Producer Thalberg and director von Stroheim battled over the expense and length of the film until Thalberg had the director replaced. However, much of the film still shows the von Stroheim brilliance and attention to lavish detail.
1923 110m/B Norman Kerry, Mary Philbin, Cesare Gravina, Edith Yorke, George Hackathorne; *D:* Rupert Julian, Erich von Stroheim. VHS $29.95 FCT, HEG 𝆕𝆕𝆕

The Merry Widow The first sound version of the famous Franz Lehar operetta, dealing with a playboy from a bankrupt kingdom who must woo and marry the land's wealthy widow or be tried for treason. A delightful musical comedy, with a sterling cast and patented Lubitschian gaiety. Made as a silent in 1912 and 1925; remade in color in 1952. 𝄞 Girls, Girls, Girls; Vilia; Tonight Will Teach Me to Forget; Melody of Laughter; Maxim's; The Girls at Maxim's; The Merry Widow Waltz; If Widows are Rich; Russian Dance. *AKA:* The Lady Dances.
1934 99m/B Maurice Chevalier, Jeanette MacDonald, Edward Everett Horton, Una Merkel, George Barbier, Minna Gombell, Ruth Channing, Sterling Holloway, Henry Armetta, Barbara Leonard, Donald Meek, Akim Tamiroff, Herman Bing; *D:* Ernst Lubitsch; *M:* Franz Lehar, Lorenz Hart. VHS, Beta $19.98 MGM 𝆕𝆕𝆕½

The Merry Widow Rich widow Turner travels to her husband's homeland of Marshovia to dedicate a statue to his memory. The country is deeply in debt and the king would like the widow to marry a local count and remain (along with her fortune). Lamas is charming as the intended bridegroom but Turner, though lovely looking, is miscast; her singing was dubbed by Erwin. Uninspired remake of the 1934 film only benefits from being shot in color and the lavish production values. Based on the operetta by Lehar. 𝄞 The Merry Widow Waltz; Can-Can; Girls, Girls, Girls; I'm Going to Maxim's.
1952 105m/C Lana Turner, Fernando Lamas, Una Merkel, Richard Haydn, Thomas Gomez, John Abbott, Marcel Dalio, King Donovan, Robert Coote, Joi Lansing; *Cameos:* Gwen Verdon; *D:* Curtis Bernhardt; *W:* Sonya Levien, William Ludwig; *M:* Franz Lehar; *V:* Trudy Erwin. VHS $19.98 MGM 𝆕𝆕½

Merton of the Movies Skelton stars as star-struck, small town theater usher Merton Gill who wins a trip to Hollywood. He's befriended by stunt double Phyllis (O'Brien) who recognizes his comedic talents and works to get him that big break. Based on the play by George S. Kaufman and Marc Connelly and previously filmed in 1924 and 1932 (as "Make Me a Star").
1947 82m/B Red Skelton, Virginia O'Brien, Gloria Grahame, Leon Ames, Alan Mowbray, Charles D. Brown, Hugo Haas, Harry Hayden; *D:* Robert Alton; *W:* George Wells, Lou Breslow. VHS, Beta $19.98 MGM, FCT 𝆕𝆕½

Mesa of Lost Women Mad scientist creates brave new race of vicious women with long fingernails. So bad it's a wanna-B. Addams Family buffs will spot the Fester in Coogan. *AKA:* Lost Women; Lost Women of Zarpa.
1952 70m/B Jackie Coogan, Richard Travis, Allan Nixon, Mary Hill, Robert Knapp, Tandra Quinn, Lyle Talbot, Katherine Victor, Angelo Rossitto, Herbert Tevos; *D:* Ron Ormond. VHS $16.95 NOS, MRV, SNC Woof!

Mesmerized Based on the work by Jerzy Skolimowski, the film is a dramatization of the Victoria Thompson murder case in 1880's New Zealand. A teenaged orphaned girl marries an older man and decides after years of abuse to kill him through hypnosis. An unengaging drama, though the lovely New Zealand landscape serves as a fitting contrast to the film's ominous tone. *AKA:* Shocked.
1984 90m/C John Lithgow, Jodie Foster, Michael Murphy, Dan Shor, Harry Andrews; *D:* Michael Laughlin. VHS, Beta $89.98 LIV, VES, VTR 𝆕𝆕

Mesquite Buckaroo Two cowboys bet over who is the better bronco buster, but one of them gets kidnapped.
1939 59m/B Bob Steele, Carolyn Curtis, Frank LaRue, Juanita Fletcher, Charles "Blackie" King; *D:* Harry S. Webb. VHS, Beta $19.95 NOS, DVT 𝆕

Messalina, Empress of Rome Ancient Rome is torn to bits in the zaniest manner possible in this Italian-French coproduction.
1980 100m/C VHS, Beta VCD 𝆕

Messalina vs. the Son of Hercules A Roman slave leads a rebellion against the emperor Messalina. Italian; dubbed into English.
1964 105m/C Richard Harrison, Marilu Tolo, Lisa Gastoni; *D:* Umberto Lenzi. VHS, Beta $16.95 SNC, NLC 𝆕

The Messenger A man right out of prison sets out to avenge his wife's murder by an Italian drug syndicate.
1987 (R) 95m/C Fred Williamson, Sandy Cummings, Christopher Connelly, Cameron Mitchell. VHS, Beta NO 𝆕

Messenger of Death A tough detective investigates the slaughter of a Mormon family, and uncovers a conspiracy centering around oil-rich real estate.
1988 (R) 90m/C Charles Bronson, Trish Van Devere, Laurence Luckinbill, Daniel Benzali, Marilyn Hassett, Jeff Corey, John Ireland, Penny Peyser, Gene Davis; *D:* J. Lee Thompson; *W:* Paul Jarrice; *M:* Robert O. Ragland. VHS, Beta $89.95 MED, VTR ✱✱½

The Messiah Rossellini's final film, a rarely-seen version of the life of Christ, completely passed over any notions of divinity to portray him as a morally perfect man. In Italian with subtitles.
1975 145m/C *D:* Roberto Rossellini. VHS, Beta $39.95 FCT, MVD ✱✱✱½

Messiah of Evil California coastal town is invaded by zombies. Confusing low-rent production from the writers of "American Graffiti." *AKA:* Dead People; Return of the Living Dead; Revenge of the Screaming Dead; The Second Coming.
1974 (R) 90m/C Marianna Hill, Joy Bang, Royal Dano, Elisha Cook Jr., Michael Greer; *D:* Gloria Katz, Willard Huyck; *W:* Gloria Katz, Willard Huyck. VHS, Beta $24.95 GEM, MRV ✱

Metallica Alien warmongers endeavor to conquer Earth and scientists try to stop them.
1985 90m/C Anthony Newcastle, Sharon Baker; *D:* Al Bradley. VHS, Beta NO ✱

Metalstorm It's the science fiction battle of the ages with giant cyclops and intergalactic magicians on the desert planet of Lemuria.
1983 (PG) 84m/C Jeffrey Byron, Mike Preston, Tim Thomerson, Kelly Preston, Richard Moll; *D:* Charles Band; *M:* Richard Band. VHS, Beta $59.95 MCA ✱

Metamorphosis Novice scientist foolishly uses himself as the guinea pig for his anti-aging experiments. He quickly loses control of the project.
1990 (R) 90m/C Gene Le Brock, Catherine Baranov, Stephen Brown, Harry Cason, Jason Arnold; *D:* G.L. Eastman. VHS, Beta $89.95 IMP, VMK ✱

Metamorphosis: The Alien Factor Gerard is a genetic engineer who is bitten by a frog injected with a mutation sample from outer space. He turns into a slimy virus that infects everything he touches.
1993 (R) 92m/C George Gerard, Tony Gigante, Katharine Romaine; *D:* Glen Takakjian. VHS $92.95 VMK ✱✱½

Meteor American and Soviet scientists attempt to save the Earth from a fast-approaching barrage of meteors from space in this disaster dud. Destruction ravages parts of Hong Kong and the Big Apple.
1979 (PG) 107m/C Sean Connery, Natalie Wood, Karl Malden, Brian Keith, Martin Landau, Trevor Howard, Henry Fonda, Joseph Campanella, Richard Dysart; *D:* Ronald Neame. VHS, Beta $19.98 WAR, OM Woof!

The Meteor Man Townsend is a school teacher who reluctantly becomes a hero when he acquires semi-super powers after being hit by a meteor. Meteor Man flies only four feet off the ground (because he's afraid of heights) and wears costumes fashioned by his mother. Funny premise satires "superhero" movies, but is inconsistent with some hilarious gags and others that fall flat. Includes interesting cameos by Cosby, Sinbad, Vandross, and Page.

1993 (PG) 100m/C Robert Townsend, Robert Guillaume, Marla Gibbs, James Earl Jones, Frank Gorshin; *Cameos:* Bill Cosby, Sinbad, Luther Vandross, LaWanda Page; *D:* Robert Townsend; *W:* Robert Townsend. VHS $94.99 MGM ✱✱½

Meteor Monster A young boy is hit by a meteor and is somehow transformed into a raving, slime-covered maniac. *AKA:* Teenage Monster.
1957 73m/C Anne Gwynne, Stuart Wade, Gloria Castillo, Chuck Courtney; *D:* Jacques Marquette. VHS, Beta $39.95 SNC Woof!

Metropolis Now a classic meditation on futurist technology and mass mentality, this fantasy concerns mechanized society. Original set design and special effects made this an innovative and influential film in its day. Is now considered one of the hippest films of the sci-fi genre. Silent, with musical score. The 1984 re-release features some color tinting, reconstruction, and a digital score with songs by Pat Benatar, Bonnie Tyler, Giorgio Moroder, and Queen.
1926 115m/B Brigitte Helm, Alfred Abel, Gustav Froehlich, Rudolf Klein-Rogge, Fritz Rasp; *D:* Fritz Lang. VHS, Beta $16.95 SNC, NOS, MRV ✱✱✱✱

Metropolitan The Izod set comes of age on Park Avenue during Christmas break. Tom Townsend (Clements), a member of the middle class, finds himself drawn into a circle of self-proclaimed urban haute bourgeoisie types. They're embarrassingly short on male escorts for the holiday season's parties so he stands in and gets an inside look at life with the rat pack. Intelligently written and carefully made, it transcends the flirting-with-adulthood genre.
1990 (PG-13) 98m/C Carolyn Farina, Edward Clements, Taylor Nichols, Christopher Eigeman, Allison Rutledge-Parisi, Dylan Hundley, Isabel Gillies, Bryan Leder, Will Kempe, Elizabeth Thompson; *D:* Whit Stillman; *W:* Whit Stillman; *M:* Mark Suozzi, Mark Suozzi. Academy Awards '90 Nominations: Best Original Screenplay; Independent Spirit Awards '91: Best First Feature; New York Film Critics Awards '90: Best Director (Stillman). VHS $19.95 COL, FCT ✱✱✱

Mexican Bus Ride A good-natured Bunuel effort about a newlywed peasant who travels to the big city to attend to his mother's will. While en route, he encounters a diversity of people on the bus and some temptation. In Spanish with English subtitles. *AKA:* Ascent to Heaven; Subida Al Cielo.
1951 85m/B Lilia Prado, Esteban Marquez, Carmelita Gonzalez; *D:* Luis Bunuel. VHS, Beta $39.95 FCT, APD, AUD ✱✱½

Mexican Hayride Bud heads a gang of swindlers and Lou is the fall guy. When things up north get too hot, the boys head south of the border to cool off and start a mining scam. Watch for the hilarious bullfighting scene. Believe it or not, this is based on a Cole Porter musical—minus the music.
1948 77m/B Bud Abbott, Lou Costello, Virginia Grey, Luba Malina, John Hubbard, Pedro de Cordoba, Fritz Feld, Tom Powers, Pat Costello, Frank Fenton; *D:* Charles T. Barton; *W:* Oscar Brodney. VHS $14.98 MCA ✱✱

Mexican Spitfire at Sea The feisty wife from South of the Border heads for Hawaii to close a deal for her husband. She goes along to help her, impersonating nobility. The thin story line keeps it from being quite as good as the first "Mexican Spitfire" film. Most of the action takes place aboard ship.
1942 73m/B Lupe Velez, Leon Errol, Charles "Buddy" Rogers, ZaSu Pitts, Elisabeth Risdon, Florence Bates, Marion Martin, Eddie Dunn, Harry Holman; *D:* Leslie Goodwins. VHS $19.95 NOS ✱½

Mexican Spitfire/Smartest Girl in Town A comedy double feature: In "Mexican Spitfire," a man impersonates an English lord in order to save a contract for the spitfire's husband. In "The Smartest Girl in Town," a photographer's model mistakes a millionaire for a fellow magazine model.
1940 125m/B Lupe Velez, Leon Errol, Donald Woods, Ann Sothern, Gene Raymond. VHS, Beta $34.95 RKO, TTC ✱½

MGM: When the Lion Roars Three-part documentary covers the history and films of the Metro-Goldwyn-Mayer (MGM) studio from its beginnings in 1924 with the release of the studio's first film ("He Who Gets Slapped"), through its glory years, to the studio's gradual decline and ever-changing leadership. MGM brought out such films as "The Wizard of Oz," "Gone With the Wind," the Andy Hardy series, and the Thin Man films. Features clips of films and stars as well as footage of studio executives, including Louis B. Mayer and legendary studio chief and producer Irving Thalberg. Tapes are also available individually for $19.98. Originally made for cable TV.
1992 360m/C VHS $69.98 MGM ✱½

MGM's The Big Parade of Comedy An anthology of more than 50 of MGM's stars and comedians in some of their funniest screen moments. Looks at Laurel & Hardy, the Marx Brothers, W.C. Fields, Clark Gable, Jean Harlow, Greta Garbo, and others.
1992 100m/C VHS $19.98 MGM ✱½

Mi Vida Loca Looks at the lives of Latina gang members from L.A.'s Echo Park. The women talk about their romantic dreams, friendships, families, and raising children amidst the pervasive violence and despair of their tough neighborhood. Small budget and some unpolished performances don't lessen film's impact—about the stupidity of violence and how "average" the hopes and dreams of these women are. *AKA:* My Crazy Life.
1994 (R) 92m/C Angel Aviles, Jacob Vargas, Jesse Borrego, Seidy Lopez, Mario Marron, Neilida Lopez, Bertilla Damas, Art Esquer, Christina Solis, Salma Hayek, Magali Alvarado, Julian Reyes, Panchito Gomez; *D:* Allison Anders; *W:* Allison Anders; *M:* John Taylor. VHS NYR ✱✱✱

Miami Blues Cold-blooded killer plays cat-and-mouse with bleary cop while diddling with an unflappable prostitute. Violent and cynical, with appropriate performances from three leads. Based on the novel by Charles Willeford.
1990 (R) 97m/C Fred Ward, Alec Baldwin, Jennifer Jason Leigh, Nora Dunn, Charles Napier, Jose Perez, Paul Gleason, Obba Babatunde, Martine Beswick; *D:* George Armitage; *W:* George Armitage; *M:* Gary Chang. VHS, Beta $14.98 ORI, IME ✱✱½

Miami Cops When a cop's father is killed by a drug smuggler, he and his partner pursue the murderer over two continents. Italian-made adventure is a bit drawn-out.
1989 103m/C Richard Roundtree, Harrison Muller, Dawn Baker, Michael J. Aronin; *D:* Al Bradley. VHS, Beta $79.95 CAN ✱

Miami Horror A Florida scientist is experimenting with bacteria from space, trying to recreate a human only to have his efforts stolen by a crook. His intentions for the use of the experiment are not exactly for the furtherance of science.
1987 85m/C David Warbeck, Laura Trotter, Lawrence Loddi, John Ireland; *D:* Martin Herbert. VHS, Beta NO ✱

Miami Supercops Two goofy policemen strike out against such threats as a gang that hassles buses, the attempted kidnapping of an Orange Bowl quarterback, and a multi-million-dollar robbery.
1985 97m/C Terence Hill, Bud Spencer, Jackie Castellano, C.V. Wood Jr.; **D:** Bruno Corbucci. **VHS, Beta $19.98** WAR *Il ½*

Miami Vendetta L.A. vice cop risks it all to avenge his friend's death at the hands of Cuban drug smugglers.
1987 90m/C Sandy Brooke, Frank Gargani, Maarten Goslins, Barbara Pilavin; **D:** Steven Seemayer. **VHS, Beta** NO *Il*

Miami Vice Pilot for the popular television series paired Crockett and Tubbs for the first time on the trail of a killer in Miami's sleazy underground. Music by Jan Hammer and other pop notables.
1984 99m/C Don Johnson, Philip Michael Thomas, Saundra Santiago, Michael Talbott, John Diehl, Gregory Sierra; **D:** Thomas Carter. **VHS, Beta $14.95** MCA *Il Il ½*

Miami Vice 2: The Prodigal Son The second full-length television movie spawned by the popular series, following the laconic Floridians to the gritty streets of New York.
1985 99m/C Don Johnson, Philip Michael Thomas, Edward James Olmos, Penn Jillette. **VHS, Beta $14.95** MCA *Il Il*

The Michigan Kid Two boys fight for the same girl in this silent love triangle set in Alaska. Film's most notable scene is of a raging forest fire, considered a classic even today.
1928 62m/B Conrad Nagel, Renee Adoree, Fred Esmelton, Virginia Grey, Adolph Milar, Lloyd Whitlock; **D:** Irwin Willat. **VHS, Beta** GPV *Il*

Mickey Spoof on high society as a penniless young woman moves in with relatives and works as the family's maid. Silent film.
1917 105m/B Mabel Normand, Lew Cody, Minta Durfee; **D:** Mack Sennett. **VHS, Beta $19.95** NOS, VYY, DVT *Il Il*

Mickey A tomboy becomes a woman even as she plays matchmaker for her own father and sings a few songs. Not too exciting; you may fall asleep if you're slipped this "Mickey." Based on the novel "Clementine," by Peggy Goodin.
1948 87m/C Lois Butler, Bill Goodwin, Irene Hervey, John Sutton, Hattie McDaniel; **D:** Ralph Murphy. **VHS $19.95** NOS *Il*

Mickey Rooney in the Classic Mickey McGuire Silly Comedies The classic boyhood series starring Rooney is also hosted by the actor. Three volumes available.
19?? 40m/C VHS $9.99 SUM *Il*

Mickey the Great Stitched together from several late 20's Mickey McGuire shorts, starring 10-year-old Rooney.
1939 70m/B Billy Barty, Mickey Rooney. **VHS, Beta $19.95** VYY, DVT, NOS *Il*

Mickey's Christmas Carol Mickey Mouse returns along with all the other Disney characters in this adaptation of the Charles Dickens classic. Includes a documentary on how the featurette was made.
1983 (G) 25m/C VHS, Beta $12.99 DIS, MTI, DSN *Il*

Micki & Maude When a man longs for a baby, he finds that his wife, Micki, is too busy for motherhood. Out of frustration, he has an affair with Maude that leads to her pregnancy. Still shocked by the news of his upcoming fatherhood, the man learns that his wife is also expecting.
1984 (PG-13) 117m/C Dudley Moore, Amy Irving, Ann Reinking, Richard Mulligan, Wallace Shawn, George Gaynes, Andre the Giant; **D:** Blake Edwards; **W:** Jonathan Reynolds. **VHS, Beta $79.95** COL *Il Il*

Microwave Massacre Killer kitchen appliances strike again as late lounge comic Vernon murders nagging wife and 'waves her. Overcome by that Betty Crocker feeling, he goes on a microwave murdering/feeding spree of the local ladies. Lots of Roger Corman copying.
1983 (R) 80m/C Jackie Vernon, Loren Schein, Al Troupe; **D:** Wayne Berwick. **VHS $59.95** RHI, FCT *Il*

Mid-Channel A married couple become bored with each other and the wife seeks diversion with other men. Surprise ending.
1920 70m/B Clara Kimball Young, J. Frank Glendon, Edward M. Kimball, Bertram Grassby, Eileen Robinson, Helen Sullivan, Katherine Griffith, Jack Livingston; **D:** Harry Garson. **VHS, Beta $16.95** NOS, MRV, GPV *Il Il ½*

Mid Knight Rider Penniless actor becomes a male prostitute at the service of bored, rich women. At an all-night orgy, he suddenly goes on a rampage, nearly killing one of his customers.
1984 76m/C Michael Christian, Keenan Wynn. **VHS, Beta $49.95** TWE *Il*

The Midas Touch A flea market merchant in 1956 Budapest has the ability to turn items into gold. In Hungarian with English subtitles.
1989 100m/C D: Geza Beremenyi; **W:** Geza Beremenyi. **VHS, Beta $79.95** EVD, FCT, ING *Il*

Middle Age Crazy Story of a Texas building contractor who takes life pretty lightly until his own father dies. Then he becomes immersed in a mid-life crisis and has an affair with a Dallas Cowboys' cheerleader. Ann-Margaret plays the victim wife of the middle aged swingin' guy.
1980 (R) 95m/C Bruce Dern, Ann-Margret, Graham Jarvis, Eric Christmas, Deborah Wakeham; **D:** John Trent. **VHS $59.98** FOX *Il ½*

Midnight A jury foreman's daughter is romantically involved with a gangster who is interested in a particular case before it appears in court. The foreman, who sentenced a girl to death, faces a dilemma when his own daughter is arrested for the same crime. An early Bogart appearance in a supporting role led to a re-release of the film as "Call it Murder" after Bogart made it big. Weak melodrama. **AKA:** Call it Murder.
1934 74m/B Humphrey Bogart, Sidney Fox, O.P. Heggie, Henry Hull, Richard Whorf, Margaret Wycherly, Lynne Overman; **D:** Chester Erskine. **VHS, Beta $34.98** CCB, DVT, BAR *Il Il ½*

Midnight Russo, who cowrote the original "Night of the Living Dead," wrote and directed this film about a runaway girl who is driven out of her home by a lecherous stepfather and meets two young thieves and then a family of cultists. Russo adapted his own novel. He also attains some of "Night of the Living Dead's" low-budget ambience. **AKA:** Backwoods Massacre.
1981 (R) 88m/C Lawrence Tierney, Melanie Verliin, John Hall, John Amplas; **D:** John Russo. **VHS, Beta $79.95** VMK *Il*

Midnight Murder-thriller involving the vampirish hostess of a television horror movie showcase and a fanatical fan.
1989 (R) 90m/C Lynn Redgrave, Tony Curtis, Steve Parrish, Rita Gam, Gustav Vintas, Karen Witter, Frank Gorshin, Wolfman Jack; **D:** Norman Thaddeus Vane. **VHS, Beta** VTR *Il*

Midnight 2: Sex, Death, and Videotape Sequel to "Midnight" finds the sole surviving member of the crazed family stalking a beautiful unsuspecting teller with a video camera. Only she's teamed up with a detective to solve the murder of her best friend—even if it means she's bait for a psycho.
1993 70m/C Matthew Jason Walsh, Jo Norcia; **D:** John Russo. **VHS $30.00** TEM, MOV *Il*

Midnight at the Wax Museum A man attempts to spend an evening in a wax museum's chamber of horrors, only to find that he is the target of a murder plot. **AKA:** Midnight at Madame Tussaud's.
1936 66m/B Lucille Lisle, James Carew, Charles Oliver, Kim Peacock; **D:** George Pearson. **VHS $24.95** NOS, DVT, SNC *Il*

Midnight Auto Supply Dealers in hot car parts, working out of the garage behind the local brothel, become persuaded to donate some of their profits to the cause of Mexican farm workers. Also called "Love and the Midnight Auto Supply."
1978 91m/C Michael Parks, Rory Calhoun, Scott Jacoby, Rod Cameron, Colleen Camp, Linda Cristal, John Ireland; **D:** James Polakof. **VHS $79.95** MNC *Il ½*

Midnight Cabaret A New York nightclub-based Satanic cult selects a child actress to bear Satan's child.
1990 (R) 94m/C Michael Des Barres, Thom Mathews, Carolyn Seymour, Leonard Termo, Norbert Weisser, Lydie Denier; **D:** Pece Dingo; **W:** Pece Dingo; **M:** Michel Colombier. **VHS, Beta $19.98** WAR Woof!

A Midnight Clear Sensitive war drama that takes place in the Ardennes Forest, near the French-German border in December 1944. It's Christmastime and six of the remaining members of a 12-member squad are sent on a dangerous mission to an abandoned house to locate the enemy. Filmed in a dreamy surreal style, the setting is somewhat reminiscent of a fairytale, although a sense of anguish filtrates throughout the picture. A solid script, excellent direction, and a good cast make this a worthwhile film that pits the message of peace against the stupidity of war. Adapted from the novel by William Wharton.
1992 (PG) 107m/C Peter Berg, Kevin Dillon, Arye Gross, Ethan Hawke, Gary Sinise, Frank Whaley, John C. McGinley, Larry Joshua, Curt Lowens; **D:** Keith Gordon; **W:** Keith Gordon; **M:** Mark Isham. **VHS $19.95** COL, PMS *Il Il Il*

Midnight Cop A young woman gets tangled up in a web of murder, intrigue, prostitution and drugs, and she enlists the aid of a cop to help get her out of it.
1988 (R) 100m/C Michael York, Morgan Fairchild, Frank Stallone, Armin Mueller-Stahl; **D:** Peter Patzak. **VHS, Beta $29.95** VMK, HHE *Il*

Midnight Cowboy Drama about the relationship between a naive Texan hustler and a seedy derelict, set in the underbelly of New York City. Graphic and emotional character study is brilliantly acted and engaging. Shocking and considered quite risque at the time of its release, this film now carries an "R" rating. It is the only film carrying an "X" rating ever to win the Best Picture Oscar. From James Leo Herlihy's novel. Laserdisc version features: audio commentary by director John Schlesinger and producer Jereome Hellman, behind the scenes production photos, and original movie trailer.
1969 (R) 113m/C Dustin Hoffman, Jon Voight, Sylvia Miles, Brenda Vaccaro, John McGiver, Bob Balaban, Barnard Hughes; **D:** John Schlesinger; **W:** Waldo Salt; **M:** John Barry. Academy Awards '69: Best Adapted Screenplay,

Best Director (Schlesinger), Best Picture; Nominations: Best Actor (Hoffman), Best Actor (Voight), Best Film Editing, Best Supporting Actress (Miles); British Academy Awards '69: Best Actor (Hoffman), Best Director (Schlesinger), Best Film; Directors Guild of America Awards '69: Best Director (Schlesinger); New York Film Critics Awards '69: Best Actor (Voight); National Society of Film Critics Awards '69: Best Actor (Voight), Best Film. **VHS, Beta $19.98** *MGM, VYG, CRC* ✏✏✏½

Midnight Crossing Two married couples are subjected to jealousy, betrayal and uncloseted-skeletons as their pleasure cruise on a yacht turns into a ruthless search for sunken treasure.
1987 (R) 96m/C Faye Dunaway, Daniel J. Travanti, Kim Cattrall, John Laughlin, Ned Beatty; **D:** Roger Holzberg. **VHS, Beta $89.98** *LIV, VES* ✏✏

Midnight Dancer A young ballerina is forced to work as an erotic dancer.
1987 97m/C Deanne Jeffs, Mary Regan; **D:** Pamela Gibbons. **VHS, Beta $29.95** *ACA* ✏✏

Midnight Express Gripping and powerful film based on the true story of Billy Hayes. Davis plays Hayes as a young American in Turkey who is busted trying to smuggle hashish. He is sentenced to a brutal and nightmarish prison for life. After enduring tremendous mental and physical torture, he seeks escape along the "Midnight Express." Not always easy to watch, but the overall effect is riveting and unforgettable.
1978 (R) 120m/C John Hurt, Randy Quaid, Brad Davis, Paul Smith, Bo Hopkins, Oliver Stone; **D:** Alan Parker; **W:** Oliver Stone; **M:** Giorgio Moroder. Academy Awards '78: Best Adapted Screenplay, Best Score; Nominations: Best Director (Parker), Best Film Editing, Best Picture, Best Supporting Actor (Hurt); British Academy Awards '78: Best Director (Parker), Best Supporting Actor (Hurt); National Board of Review Awards '78: 10 Best Films of the Year. **VHS, Beta, 8mm $14.95** *COL* ✏✏✏

Midnight Faces Mysterious doings abound in a house in the Florida bayous, recently inherited by Bushman. Silent, with original organ music.
1926 72m/B Francis X. Bushman, Rocky Aoki, Jack Perrin, Kathryn McGuire. **VHS, Beta, 8mm $16.95** *SNC, VYY, LSV* ✏

Midnight Fear When a sexually demented killer skins a woman alive, Sheriff Hanley sets out to find whodunit. He suspects two weird brothers, who turn out to be holding a woman hostage, but the situation may not be so simple. Carradine plays the good-guy sheriff in this creeper.
1990 90m/C John Carradine, Craig Wasson; **D:** Bill Crain. **VHS $79.95** *RHI* ✏½

Midnight Girl A fading opera impresario plots to steal a family's fortune. Lugosi before he became Dracula. Silent.
1925 84m/B Bela Lugosi, Lila Lee. **VHS, Beta, 8mm $16.95** *GPV, VYY, DVT* ✏½

The Midnight Hour A group of high schoolers stumbles upon a vintage curse that wakes up the dead. Made for television. More humor than horror.
1986 97m/C Shari Belafonte-Harper, LeVar Burton, Lee Montgomery, Dick Van Patten, Kevin McCarthy, Jonelle Allen, Peter DeLuise, Dedee Pfeiffer, Mark Blankfield; **D:** Jack Bender; **M:** Brad Fiedel. **VHS $89.95** *VMK* ✏½

Midnight Kiss When a woman police detective investigates a mysterious series of deaths—women whose blood has been drained—she gets more than she bargains for. She's attacked by a vampire and is herself turned into a reluctant bloodsucker. Quick moving and some gross special effects. Also available in an unrated version.

1993 (R) 85m/C Michelle Owens, Gregory A. Greer; **D:** Joel Bender; **W:** John Weidner, Ken Lamplugh. **VHS $89.95** *ACA* ✏✏½

Midnight Lace Acceptable thriller about a woman in London who is being harassed by a telephone creep. Day is at her frantic best, and Harrrison is suitably charming. Handsome Gavin later became American ambassador to Mexico. Adapted from the play "Matilda Shouted Fire."
1960 108m/C Doris Day, Rex Harrison, John Gavin, Myrna Loy, Roddy McDowall; **D:** David Miller; **W:** Ivan Goff. **VHS, Beta $59.95** *MCA* ✏✏½

Midnight Limited A detective sets out to thwart the criminals who would rob the "Midnight Limited" train on its route from New York to Montreal.
1940 61m/B John "Dusty" King, Marjorie Reynolds, George Cleveland, Edward Keane, Pat Flaherty, Monty Collins, I. Stanford Jolley; **D:** Howard Bretherton. **VHS, Beta $16.95** *SNC* ✏✏

Midnight Madness Five teams of college students search the city of Los Angeles for clues leading to hundreds and thousands of dollars in buried treasure.
1980 (PG) 110m/C David Naughton, Stephen Furst, Debra Clinger, Eddie Deezen, Michael J. Fox, Maggie Roswell; **D:** David Wechter; **W:** David Wechter. **VHS, Beta** *BVV, OM* ✏

Midnight Movie Massacre Retro splatterama has really gross alien land outside a movie theater in 1956, and the really weird movie patrons try to terminate it.
1988 86m/C Robert Clarke, Ann Robinson; **D:** Mark Stock. **VHS $19.95** *VCI* ✏✏½

The Midnight Phantom Incredibly rare horror film featuring a bizarre murder at a midnight lecture.
1935 ?m/B Reginald Denny. **VHS $12.95** *SNC* ✏✏

Midnight Run An ex-cop, bounty hunter must bring in an ex-mob accountant who has embezzled big bucks from his former boss. After he catches up with the thief, the hunter finds that bringing his prisoner from New York to Los Angeles will be very trying, especially when it is apparent that the Mafia and FBI are out to stop them. The friction between the two leads—De Niro and Grodin—is fun to watch, while the action and comic moments are enjoyable.
1988 (R) 125m/C Robert De Niro, Charles Grodin, Yaphet Kotto, John Ashton, Dennis Farina, Joe Pantoliano, Richard Foronjy, Wendy Phillips; **D:** Martin Brest; **W:** George Gallo; **M:** Danny Elfman. **VHS, Beta $14.98** *MCA* ✏✏✏

Midnight Warning A woman thinks she's going off the deep-end when her brother and all records of his existence disappear. Based on an urban legend that appeared somewhere around the time of the 1893 World's Fair. Remade in 1952 as "So Long at the Fair."
1932 84m/B William Boyd, Claudia Dell, Henry Hall, John Harron, Hooper Atchley; **D:** Spencer Gordon Bennet. **VHS $12.95** *SNC, NOS, DVT* ✏✏½

Midnight Warrior A reporter strikes it big when he investigates the underside of L.A. nightlife, but things go terribly wrong when he becomes wrapped up in the sleaze.
1989 90m/C Bernie Angel, Michelle Berger, Kevin Bernhardt, Lilly Melgar; **D:** Joseph Merhi. **VHS, Beta $29.95** *PAR* ✏

Midnight Witness A young couple videotapes (why—they have nothing better to do?) a routine traffic stop but then find themselves witnesses to the brutal murder of the motorist by several of the cops. But when the rogue cops find out they go after

the tape—and the couple. Can you say "Rodney King" rip-off?
1993 (R) 90m/C Maxwell Caulfield, Jan-Michael Vincent, Paul Johansson, Karen MonGrieff; **D:** Peter Foldy; **W:** Peter Foldy; **M:** Graydon Hillock. **VHS $89.95** *ACA* ✏½

Midnight's Child Another Nanny-from-Hell story, only this time it's literal. D'Abo is the Nanny in question, who belongs to a Satanic cult. Her mission is to select the young daughter in her care as a bride for the devil, even if the girl's parents don't approve of the match.
1993 89m/C Olivia D'Abo, Marcy Walker, Cotter Smith, Elissabeth Moss, Jim Norton, Judy Parfitt, Roxann Biggs, Mary Larkin; **D:** Colin Bucksey; **W:** David Chaskin. **VHS, Beta $79.95** *PSM* ✏½

Midnite Spares A young man's search for the men who kidnapped his father leads him into the world of car thieves and chop-shops.
1985 90m/C Bruce Spence, Gia Carides, James Laurie; **M:** Cameron Allan. **VHS, Beta** *NO* ✏✏

A Midsummer Night's Dream Famed Reinhardt version of the Shakespeare classic, featuring nearly every star on the Warner Brothers lot. The plot revolves around the amorous battle between the king and queen of a fairy kingdom, and the humans who are drawn into their sport. Features de Havilland's first film role. Classic credit line: Dialogue by William Shakespeare.
1935 117m/B James Cagney, Dick Powell, Joe E. Brown, Hugh Herbert, Olivia de Havilland, Ian Hunter, Mickey Rooney, Victor Jory, Arthur Treacher, Billy Barty; **D:** Max Reinhardt, William Dieterle. Academy Awards '35: Best Cinematography, Best Film Editing; Nominations: Best Picture. **VHS, Beta $19.98** *MGM, FOX, FCT* ✏✏✏

A Midsummer Night's Dream Fine acting from the Royal Shakespeare Company cast in this filmed version of the play. Makes very little use of the Athens, Greece scenery.
1968 124m/C David Warner, Diana Rigg, Ian Richardson, Judi Dench, Ian Holm, Barbara Jefford, Nicholas Selby, Helen Mirren, Michael Jayston, Derek Godfrey, Hugh Sullivan, Paul Rogers, Sebastian Shaw, Bill Travers; **D:** Peter Hall. **VHS $24.95** *WBF, WAR, BTV* ✏✏½

A Midsummer Night's Sex Comedy Allen's homage to Shakespeare, Renoir, Chekhov, Bergman, and who knows who else is an engaging ensemble piece about hijinks among friends and acquaintances gathered at a country house at the turn of the century. Standouts include Ferrer as pompous professor and Steenburgen as Allen's sexually repressed wife. Mia's first for the Woodman.
1982 (PG) 88m/C Woody Allen, Mia Farrow, Mary Steenburgen, Tony Roberts, Julie Hagerty, Jose Ferrer; **D:** Woody Allen; **W:** Woody Allen. **VHS, Beta $14.95** *WAR* ✏✏✏½

Midway The epic WWII battle of Midway, the turning point in the war, is retold through Allied and Japanese viewpoints by a big all-star cast saddled with dumpy dialogue and enough weaponry to seize Hollywood on any given Wednesday.
1976 (PG) 132m/C Charlton Heston, Henry Fonda, James Coburn, Glenn Ford, Hal Holbrook, Robert Mitchum, Cliff Robertson, Robert Wagner, Kevin Dobson, Christopher George, Toshiro Mifune, Tom Selleck; **D:** Jack Smight; **M:** John Williams. **VHS, Beta $19.95** *MCA, TLF* ✏✏

The Mighty Ducks Bad News Bears on skates. Selfish yuppie lawyer is arrested for drunk driving and as part of his community service sentence, he is forced to coach an

inner-city hockey team full of the usual misfits and underachievers. Although sarcastic and skeptical, Coach Gordon Bombay (Estevez) eventually bonds with the Ducks and learns to treat them with respect. Dual themes of teamwork and redemption are repeated constantly, and it gets a bit hokey at times, but the kids won't mind with this fun Disney film, while adults will appreciate the sarcasm. Followed by "D2: The Mighty Ducks."
1992 (PG) 114m/C Emilio Estevez, Joss Ackland, Lane Smith, Heidi Kling, Josef Sommer, Matt Doherty, Steven Brill, Joshua Jackson, Elden Ratliff, Shaun Weiss; *D:* Stephen Herek; *W:* Steven Brill, Brian Hohlfield; *M:* David Newman. VHS, Beta $94.95 *TOU, BTV* ♪♪½

Mighty Joe Young Tongue-in-cheek King Kong variation features giant ape brought to civilization and exploited in a nightclub act, whereupon things get darned ugly. Bullied and given the key to the liquor cabinet, mild-mannered Joe goes on a drunken rampage, but eventually redeems himself by rescuing orphans from a fire. Special effects (courtesy of Willis O'Brien and the great Ray Harryhausen) probably film's greatest asset. Also available colorized.
1949 94m/B Terry Moore, Ben Johnson, Robert Armstrong, Frank McHugh; *D:* Ernest B. Schoedsack. VHS, Beta $19.95 *TTC* ♪♪½

Mighty Jungle Lost in the Amazon jungle, a hunter must fight off killer iguanas, man-eating crocodiles and bloodthirsty natives who perform human sacrifices.
1964 90m/C Marshall Thompson, David Dalie. VHS, Beta *NO* ♪♪

The Mighty Pawns Inner-city kids turn to chess when their teacher inspires them to stay off the streets. Originally aired on PBS as part of the "Wonderworks" family movie series.
1987 58m/C Paul Winfield, Alfonso Ribeiro, Terence Knox, Rosalind Cash, Teddy Wilson; *D:* Eric Laneuville. VHS $29.95 *PME, HMV, FCT* ♪♪

The Mighty Quinn While investigating the local murder of a rich white guy, the black Jamaican head of police becomes convinced that the prime suspect, a childhood friend, is innocent. As the police chief, Denzel is good in this off-beat comedy mystery.
1989 (R) 98m/C Denzel Washington, Robert Townsend, James Fox, Mimi Rogers, M. Emmet Walsh, Sheryl Lee Ralph, Esther Rolle, Art Evans, Norman Beaton, Keye Luke; *D:* Carl Schenkel; *W:* Hampton Fancher; *M:* Anne Dudley. VHS, Beta $19.98 *MGM, FOX* ♪♪½

Mike's Murder Disjointed drama about a shy bank teller who falls for a slick tennis player. When he is murdered, she investigates the circumstances, placing herself in dangerously close contact with his seedy, drug-involved buddies. The twists and confused plot leave the viewer bewildered.
1984 (R) 109m/C Debra Winger, Mark Keyloun, Paul Winfield, Darrell Larson, Dan Shor, William Ostrander; *D:* James Bridges; *W:* James Bridges; *M:* John Barry. VHS, Beta $79.95 *WAR* ♪½

Mikey Mikey seems like such a sweet little boy—but these awful things keep happening all around him. At every foster home and every school people have such dreadful, and deadly, accidents. But innocent Mikey couldn't be to blame—or could he.
1992 (R) 92m/C Brian Bonsall, John Diehl, Lyman Ward, Josie Bisset; *D:* Dennis Dimster. VHS $89.95 *IMP* ♪½

Mikey & Nicky Quirky, uneven film about longtime friends dodging a hit man during one long night. Bears little evidence of time and money invested. Cassavetes and Falk, however, provide some salvation.

1976 (R) 105m/C John Cassavetes, Peter Falk, Ned Beatty, Oliver Clark, William Hickey; *D:* Elaine May; *W:* Elaine May. VHS, Beta $69.95 *WAR, OM* ♪♪½

The Milagro Beanfield War Redford's endearing adaptation of John Nichols's novel about New Mexican townfolk opposing development. Seemingly simple tale provides plenty of insight into human spirit. Fine cast, with especially stellar turns from Blades, Braga, and Vennera.
1988 (R) 118m/C Chick Vennera, John Heard, Ruben Blades, Sonia Braga, Daniel Stern, Julie Carmen, Christopher Walken, Richard Bradford, Carlos Riqueline, James Gammon, Melanie Griffith, Freddy Fender, M. Emmet Walsh; *D:* Robert Redford; *W:* David S. Ward; *M:* Dave Grusin. VHS, Beta $14.98 *MCA* ♪♪½

Mildred Pierce Gripping melodrama features Crawford as hard-working divorcee rivaling daughter for man's love. Things, one might say, eventually get ugly. Adaptation of James M. Cain novel is classic of its kind.
1945 113m/B Joan Crawford, Jack Carson, Zachary Scott, Eve Arden, Ann Blyth, Bruce (Herman Brix) Bennett; *D:* Michael Curtiz; *W:* Ranald MacDougall. Academy Awards '45: Best Actress (Crawford); Nominations: Best Black and White Cinematography, Best Picture, Best Screenplay, Best Supporting Actress (Arden, Blyth). VHS, Beta $19.98 *MGM, FOX, BTV* ♪♪♪½

Miles from Home Times are tough for farmers Frank and Terry Roberts. The brothers are about to have another bad harvest and the bank is threatening to foreclose. In a symbolic last ditch effort to save their pride, they decide to burn the farm and leave. On their journey, they meet strangers who recognize the pair and help them escape the police. A melodrama with many members of Chicago's Steppenwolf Theater. *AKA:* Farm of the Year.
1988 (R) 113m/C Richard Gere, Kevin Anderson, John Malkovich, Brian Dennehy, Judith Ivey, Penelope Ann Miller, Laurie Metcalf, Laura San Giacomo, Daniel Roebuck, Helen Hunt; *D:* Gary Sinise; *W:* Chris Gerolmo; *M:* Robert Folk. VHS, Beta $19.98 *WAR* ♪♪

Miles to Go A successful businesswoman tries to enjoy her last days after learning she has terminal cancer.
1986 88m/C Mimi Kuzyk, Tom Skerritt, Jill Clayburgh; *D:* David Greene. VHS, Beta *NO* ♪½

Miles to Go Before I Sleep A retired, lonely man and a delinquent girl distrust each other but eventually reach out in mutual need.
1974 78m/C Martin Balsam, MacKenzie Phillips, Kitty Winn, Elizabeth Wilson; *D:* Fielder Cook. VHS, Beta *LCA* ♪♪½

Militant Eagle Usual good vs. evil, complete with nobles, warriors, and villains who fight to the death.
19?? 90m/C Choi Yue, Lu Ping, Pai Ying. VHS, Beta *NO* ♪

Milk Money Twelve year-old Frank (Carter) talks his pals into pooling their milk money and heading to the big city so they can get a look at a naked woman. They find a prostitute (Griffith) for the job, whom Frank decides would be perfect to bring home to his widower dad (Harris). Although Griffith is well-cast, overall, it's sappy and completely implausible Cinderella sop.
1994 (PG-13) ?m/C Michael Patrick Carter, Melanie Griffith, Ed Harris, Malcolm McDowell, Casey Siemaszko; *D:* Richard Benjamin. VHS *NYR* ♪♪

Milky Way Loopy comedy about milkman who finds unhappiness after accidentally knocking out champion boxer. Adequate, but not equal to Lloyd's fine silent productions.

1936 89m/B Harold Lloyd, Adolphe Menjou, Verree Teasdale, Helen Mack, William Gargan; *D:* Leo McCarey. VHS, Beta $24.95 *VYY, MRV, NOS* ♪♪½

The Milky Way Wicked anti-clerical farce. Two bums team on religious pilgrimage and encounter seemingly all manner of strangeness and sacrilege in this typically peculiar Bunuel work. Perhaps the only film in which Jesus is encouraged to shave. In French with English subtitles.
1968 102m/C Laurent Terzieff, Paul Frankeur, Delphine Seyrig, Alain Cuny, Bernard Verley, Michel Piccoli, Edith Scob; *D:* Luis Bunuel; *W:* Jean-Claude Carriere. VHS, Beta $24.95 *XVC, MED, FCT* ♪♪♪

Mill of the Stone Women Sculpture-studying art student encounters strange carousel with beautiful babes rather than horsies, and soon finds out that the statues contain shocking secrets. Filmed in Holland, it's offbeat and creepy. *AKA:* Il Mulino Delle Donne di Pietra; Horror of the Stone Women; The Horrible Mill Women.
1960 94m/C Pierre Brice, Scilla Gabel, Danny Carrel, Wolfgang Preiss, Herbert Boenne, Liana Orfei; *D:* Giorgio Ferroni. VHS $16.95 *SNC* ♪♪½

The Mill on the Floss Based on George Eliot's classic novel, this film follows the course of an ill-fated romance and family hatred in rural England. Underwhelming, considering the source.
1937 77m/B James Mason, Geraldine Fitzgerald, Frank Lawton, Victoria Hopper, Fay Compton, Griffith Jones, Mary Clare; *D:* Tim Whelan. VHS, Beta $19.95 *NOS, MRV, DVT* ♪♪

Millenium The Earth of the future is running out of time. The people are sterile and the air is terrible. To keep the planet viable, Ladd and company must go back in time and yank people off planes that are doomed to crash. Great special effects and well-thought out script make this a ball of fun.
1989 (PG-13) 108m/C Kris Kristofferson, Cheryl Ladd, Daniel J. Travanti, Lloyd Bochner, Robert Joy, Brent Carver, Maury Chaykin, David McIlwraith, Al Waxman; *D:* Michael Anderson Sr.; *W:* John Varley; *M:* Eric N. Robertson. VHS, Beta *CCB* ♪♪½

Miller's Crossing From the Coen brothers (makers of "Blood Simple" and "Raising Arizona") comes this extremely dark entry in the gangster movie sweepstakes of 1990. Jewish, Italian, and Irish mobsters spin webs of deceit, protection, and revenge over themselves and their families. Byrne is the protagonist, but no hero, being as deeply flawed as the men he battles. Harden stuns as the woman who sleeps with Byrne and his boss, Finney, in hopes of a better life and protection for her small-time crook brother. Visually exhilarating, excellently acted and perfectly paced.
1990 (R) 115m/C Albert Finney, Gabriel Byrne, Marcia Gay Harden, John Turturro, Jon Polito, J.E. Freeman; *D:* Joel Coen; *W:* Joel Coen, Ethan Coen. VHS, Beta $14.98 *FXV, FCT* ♪♪♪½

Millie Creaky melodrama about a divorcee who wants every man but one. He pursues her teenage daughter instead, leading to tragedy and courtroom hand-wringing. Twelvetrees still stands out in this hokum, based on a Donald Henderson novel considered daring in its day.
1931 85m/B Helen Twelvetrees, Robert Ames, Lilyan Tashman, Joan Blondell, Peter Halliday, James Hall, Anita Louise, Frank McHugh; *D:* John Francis Dillon. VHS $19.95 *NOS* ♪½

Million Dollar Duck A family duck is doused with radiation and begins to lay gold eggs. Okay Disney family fare, especially for youngsters.
1971 (G) 92m/C Dean Jones, Sandy Duncan, Joe Flynn, Tony Roberts; *D:* Vincent McEveety; *M:* Buddy Baker. **VHS, Beta** DIS, OM *ℐ*½

Million Dollar Haul Tarzan sniffs out a ring of warehouse thieves.
1935 60m/B Reed Howes, Janet Chandler, William Farnum. **VHS, Beta** NO *ℐ*

Million Dollar Kid When a group of thugs wreak havoc in the neighborhood, the East Side Kids try to help a wealthy man put a stop to it. They face an even greater dilemma when they discover that the man's son is part of the gang. Part of the "Bowery Boys" series.
1944 65m/B Leo Gorcey, Huntz Hall, Gabriel Dell, Louise Currie, Noah Beery Jr., Iris Adrian, Mary Gordon; *D:* Wallace Fox. **VHS $19.95** VYY, DVT, NOS *ℐℐ*

Million Dollar Mermaid The prototypical Williams aquashow, with the requisite awesome Berkeley dance numbers. As a biography of swimmer Annette Kellerman it isn't much, but as an MGM extravaganza, it fits the bill.
1952 115m/C Esther Williams, Victor Mature, Walter Pidgeon, Jesse White, David Brian, Maria Tallchief, Howard Freeman, Busby Berkeley; *D:* Mervyn LeRoy. **VHS, Beta $19.98** MGM *ℐℐ*

Million Dollar Mystery Silent suspense film involving an old house, a secret society, and a million dollars in missing money.
1927 ?m/B VHS $16.95 SNC *ℐℐ*

Million Dollar Mystery A dying man's last words indicate that several million dollars have been stashed near a diner. Chaos breaks out as nearly everyone in town tries to dig up the loot.
1987 (PG) 95m/C Eddie Deezen, Penny Baker, Tom Bosley, Rich Hall, Wendy Sherman, Rick Overton, Mona Lyden; *D:* Richard Fleischer; *W:* Rudy DeLuca, Tim Metcalfe. **VHS $79.95** HBO, CNG *ℐ*½

A Million to One An athlete trains for the Olympic decathlon, and catches the eye of an upper-class woman in the process. The lead Bennett was actually a shot-putter in the 1932 Olympic Games.
1937 60m/B Bruce (Herman Brix) Bennett, Joan Fontaine, Monte Blue, Kenneth Harlan, Reed Howes; *D:* Lynn Shores. **VHS $19.95** VYY *ℐ*½

Millions To a family of millionaires, money is everything, and the heir to the family fortune is willing to do anything to get his hands on all that money. Even if it means sleeping with his sister-in-law and cousin! Lucky for him they happen to be beautiful models.
1990 (R) 118m/C Billy Zane, Lauren Hutton, Carol Alt, Alexandra Paul, Catherine Hickland, Donald Pleasence; *D:* Carlo Vanzina. **VHS, Beta $89.95** PSM *ℐ*½

Milo & Otis Charming tale of a kitten named Milo and his best friend, a puppy named Otis. The two live on a farm and, when exploring the countryside, Milo is swept down a rushing river. Otis goes after to rescue his friend and the two begin a series of adventures as they try to return home.
19?? (G) 76m/C VHS $19.95 COL *ℐℐ*½

Milo Milo Comedy about some very silly French people who propose to steal the Venus de Milo from the Louvre.
1967 110m/C Antonio Fargas, Joe Higgins. **VHS, Beta $39.95** VCD *ℐℐ*

The Milpitas Monster Creature spawned in a Milpitas, California, waste dump terrorizes the town residents.
1975 (PG) 80m/C Doug Hagdahl, Scott A. Henderson, Scott Parker; *D:* Robert L. Burrill. **VHS, Beta $19.98** VCI *ℐ*

Mimi Melodrama with a down-on-his-luck playwright falling for a poor lass who provides him with the needed inspiration to be a winner. The question is, will she die before he hits the big time? Loosely based on "La Vie de Boheme" by Henri Murger.
1935 98m/B Douglas Fairbanks Jr., Gertrude Lawrence, Diana Napier, Harold Warrender, Carol Goodner, Richard Bird, Austin Trevor, Lawrence Hanray, Paul Graetz, Martin Walker; *D:* Paul Stein. **VHS $19.95** VYY, FCT *ℐℐ*

Min & Bill Patchy early talkie about two houseboat dwellers fighting to preserve their waterfront lifestyle and keep their daughter from being taken to a "proper" home.
1930 66m/B Marie Dressler, Wallace Beery, Marjorie Rambeau, Dorothy Jordan; *D:* George Roy Hill. **VHS, Beta** MGM, BTV, FHE *ℐℐ*

Mind, Body & Soul When a woman witnesses a human sacrifice performed by her boyfriend's satanic cult, she goes to the police. The cops, however, believe she is part of the cult, so she is forced to rely on the public defender to protect her from angry cult members. Pretty dull, but Hauser and Allen add some spice to this hokey thriller.
1992 (R) 93m/C Wings Hauser, Ginger Lynn Allen, Jay Richardson, Ken Hill, Jesse Kaye, Tami Bakke; *D:* Rick Sloane. **VHS $89.95** AIP *ℐℐ*

Mind Games A young couple and their ten-year-old son pick up a hitcher in their mobile home, never suspecting that he's a deranged psychology student ready to pit the family against each other as an experiment.
1989 (R) 93m/C Edward Albert, Shawn Weatherly, Matt Norero, Maxwell Caulfield; *D:* Bob Yari. **VHS, Beta $79.98** FOX, HHE *ℐℐ*

Mind Snatchers An American G.I. becomes involved in U.S. Army experimental psychological brain operations when he is brought into a western European hospital for treatment. Also know as "The Happiness Cage."
1972 (PG) 94m/C Christopher Walken, Ronny Cox, Ralph Meeker, Joss Ackland; *D:* Bernard Girard. **VHS, Beta $59.95** PSM *ℐℐ*½

Mind Trap A beautiful movie star's family is killed due to her father's involvement with naval research. The government wants no part of her troubles so she is forced to take the law into her own hands.
1991 90m/C Dan Haggerty, Lyle Waggoner, Martha Kincare, Thomas Elliot, Samuel Steven; *D:* Eames Demetrios. **VHS** NO *ℐℐ*½

Mind Twister Erotic thriller finds a tough police detective on the trail of a sadistic killer with a twist. An unrated version is available at 94 minutes.
1993 (R) 87m/C Telly Savalas, Gary Hudson, Richard Roundtree, Erica Nann, Suzanne Slater; *D:* Fred Olen Ray. **VHS $59.95** VCI *ℐ*½

Mind Warp A future society exercises mental control and torture over its citizens.
AKA: Grey Matter; The Brain Machine.
1972 (R) 92m/C James Best, Barbara Burgess, Gil Peterson, Gerald McRaney, Marcus J. Grapes, Doug Collins, Anne Latham; *D:* Joy Houck Jr. **VHS, Beta $19.95** ACA *ℐ*½

Mindfield An innocent man gets trapped by the CIA and is used by them in mind control experiments.

1989 (R) 91m/C Michael Ironside, Lisa Langlois, Christopher Plummer, Stefan Wodoslowsky, Sean McCann; *D:* Jean-Claude Lord. **VHS, Beta** NO *ℐ*½

Mindkiller A tongue-in-cheek gore-fest about a shy young guy who develops his brain in an effort to be socially accepted. Unfortunately, he overdoes it and his brain mutates, bursts from his head and runs around on its own. An aspiring cult classic.
1987 84m/C Joe McDonald, Christopher Wade, Shirley Ross, Kevin Hart; *D:* Michael Krueger. **VHS, Beta $79.95** PSM *ℐ*½

Mindwalk: A Film for Passionate Thinkers A feature-length intellectual workout; a physicist, poet and politician stroll the ancient grounds of Mont St. Michel monastery in France and discuss the need to change mankind's view of the universe. Uncinematic? Perhaps, but it entertainingly conveys the epochal ideas of scientist/author Fritjof Capra (whose book was adapted for the screen by younger brother Bernt).
1991 102m/C Burgess Meredith, Sam Waterston, John Heard, Ione Skye; *D:* Bernt Capra; *W:* Fritjof Capra, Floyd Byars; *M:* Philip Glass. **VHS, Beta $19.95** PAR, WSH *ℐℐℐ*

Mindwarp After an ecological disaster, residents of Earth move to a sterile haven known as "Inworld." When survivor Judy (Alicia) seeks answers about her missing father (accidentally killing her mother in the process), she is cast from "Inworld" into Earth's wasteland, where she and human compatriot Stover (Campbell) are left to fight the elements and learn the awful truth about Judy's father.
1991 (R) 91m/C Marta Alicia, Bruce Campbell, Angus Scrimm, Elizabeth Kent, Mary Becker; *D:* Steve Barnett; *W:* Henry Dominick. **VHS** COL *ℐℐ*

Mine Own Executioner Determined but unstable psychologist in postwar London struggles to treat schizophrenic who suffered torture by Japanese while wartime prisoner. Strong, visually engrossing fare.
1947 102m/B Burgess Meredith, Kieron Moore, Dulcie Gray, Christine Norden, Barbara White, John Laurie, Michael Shepley; *D:* Anthony Kimmins. **VHS, Beta $19.95** NOS, DVT, HHT *ℐℐℐ*

Mines of Kilimanjaro An archaeology student heads for Africa to investigate his professor's murder and comes up with a heap of trouble.
1987 (PG-13) 88m/C Christopher Connelly, Tobias Hoels, Gordon Mitchell, Elena Pompei; *D:* Mino Guerrini. **VHS, Beta $79.95** IMP *ℐ*½

Ministry of Vengeance A psychotic murderer who hates grapes of any kind finds the woman of his dreams—she's a psychotic murderer who hates grapes! Together they find bliss—until the plumber discovers their secret!
1989 (R) 90m/C John Schneider, Ned Beatty, George Kennedy, Yaphet Kotto, James Tolkan, Apollonia. **VHS, Beta $89.95** LIV, VTR *ℐ*

The Miniver Story Weepy sequel to "Mrs. Miniver" reunites the family in post-WWII England, but clearly lacks the inspiration of the original. Garson is again Mrs. Miniver and she's secretly suffering from a never-named fatal disease. She decides to straighten out the family troubles before her time is up, including her daughter's love life and her husband's plan to move to Brazil. Depressing and glum.
1950 104m/B Greer Garson, Walter Pidgeon, John Hodiak, Leo Genn, Cathy O'Donnell, Reginald Owen, Anthony Bushell; *D:* H.C. Potter; *W:* Ronald Millar, George Froeschel; *M:* Miklos Rozsa. **VHS $19.98** MGM *ℐℐ*

Minnelli on Minnelli: Liza Remembers Vincente One of MGM's best directors, Vincente Minnelli, is profiled in this tribute.
1987 88m/C **VHS, Beta** $19.98 *MGM, FCT, BTV* ♫♫

Minnesota Clay A blind gunman, who aims by sound and smell, is marked by two rival gangs and a tempestuous tramp. *AKA:* L'Homme du Minnesota.
1965 89m/C Cameron Mitchell, Diana Martin; *D:* Sergio Corbucci. **VHS, Beta** *NO* ♫½

A Minor Miracle Tender family fare about a group of orphaned children who band together under the loving guidance of their guardian (Huston) to save St. Francis School for boys from the town planners. Warms the cockles.
1983 (G) 100m/C John Huston, Pele, Peter Fox; *D:* Terrell Tannen. **VHS, Beta** $9.95 *COL, SUE* ♫

Minsky's Follies Recreation of an old time burlesque revue complete with strippers.
1983 60m/C Phyllis Diller, Rip Taylor, Stubby Kaye. **VHS, Beta** $39.95 *RKO* ♫♫

A Minute to Pray, A Second to Die A notorious, wanted-dead-or-alive gunman retreats to the amnesty of the New Mexico Territory, but finds he cannot shake his past. *AKA:* Un Minuto Per Pregare, Un Istante Per Morire; Dead or Alive; Outlaw Gun.
1967 100m/C Robert Ryan, Arthur Kennedy, Alex Cord; *D:* Franco Giraldi. **VHS, Beta** $19.98 *FOX* ♫♫

The Miracle An innocent peasant woman is seduced by a shepherd and becomes convinced that her pregnancy will produce a second Christ. Controversial, compelling film derived from a story by Federico Fellini. In Italian with English subtitles. *AKA:* Ways of Love.
1948 43m/B Anna Magnani, Federico Fellini; *D:* Roberto Rossellini. **VHS, Beta** $24.95 *NOS, FCT, APD* ♫♫♫

The Miracle Irish teens, whose strong friendship is based upon their equally unhappy home lives, find both tested when a secretive American woman turns up in town. Excellent debuts from Byrne and Pilkington but tedious pacing in a dreamy script that tells too much too soon. Worth watching just for D'Angelo's smouldering rendition of "Stardust."
1991 (PG) 97m/C Beverly D'Angelo, Donal McCann, Niall Byrne, Lorraine Pilkington, J.G. Devlin; *D:* Neil Jordan; *W:* Neil Jordan; *M:* Anne Dudley. **VHS** $89.98 *LIV* ♫♫½

Miracle at Moreaux Three Jewish children fleeing from Nazis find sanctuary with a nun and her wards. Based on Clare Huchet Bishop's book "Twenty and Ten." Originally aired on PBS as part of the "Wonderworks" family movie series.
1986 58m/C Loretta Swit, Marsha Moreau, Robert Joy, Ken Pogue, Robert Kosoy, Talya Rubin; *D:* Paul Shapiro. **VHS** $29.95 *PME, HMV, IGP* ♫♫½

Miracle Beach Scotty McKay has lost his job, his apartment, and his girl. Then he gets rejected by Dana, the super model he's secretly adored. Can things get any worse? Scotty decides to take a walk along the beach and sort things out when he stumbles across a girl genie, named Jeanie, who has been sent to Earth on a good will mission. Scotty gets Jeanie to grant his every material wish in order to dazzle model Dana. But when Jeanie falls in love with Scotty can she

get him to recognize the difference between true love and fantasy?
1992 (PG-13) 88m/C Dean Cameron, Felicity Waterman, Ami Dolenz, Alexis Arquette, Martin Mull, Noriyuki "Pat" Morita, Vincent Schiavelli; *D:* Skott Snider. **VHS** $89.95 *COL* ♫½

Miracle Down Under A family endures arduous times in 1890s Australia before a Christmas miracle changes their fortunes. Inoffensive Disney-produced drama. Australia has two directors named George Miller—one directs Mad Max movies; the other directs family fare such as "The Man from Snowy River." This Miller is the latter.
1987 101m/C Dee Wallace Stone, John Waters, Charles Tingwell, Bill Kerr, Andrew Ferguson; *D:* George Miller. **VHS, Beta** $29.95 *BVV, IGP* ♫♫

Miracle in Harlem A gang tries to take over a candy shop and when the gang leader is killed, the evidence points to the foster daughter of the shop owner. The script suffers from cliched dialog and less-than-believable situations, but the all-black cast turns in good performances.
1948 69m/B Sheila Guyse, Stepin Fetchit, Hilda Offley, Lawrence Criner, Monte Hawley; *D:* Jack Kemp. **VHS** $24.95 *NOS* ♫♫

Miracle in Milan An innocent, child-like fantasy about heavenly intervention driving capitalists out of a Milanese ghetto and helping the poor to fly to a new Utopia. Happy mixture of whimsy and neo-realism. In Italian with English subtitles. *AKA:* Miracolo a Milano.
1951 95m/B Francesco Golisano, Brunella Bova, Emma Gramatica, Paolo Stoppa; *D:* Vittorio De Sica; *W:* Cesare Zavattini. **VHS, Beta** $39.95 *HMV, FCT, VYG* ♫♫♫

Miracle in Rome Man digs up dead daughter and finds her body in perfect condition despite 12-year interment. Attempting to convince the local clergy that she's miracle material, he finds them less than eager to elect her to sainthood. Made for Spanish TV. In Spanish with English subtitles. *AKA:* Milagro en Roma.
1988 76m/C Frank Ramirez, Gerardo Arellano, Amalia Duque Garcia, Lisandro Duque, Daniel Priolett; *D:* Lisandro Duque Naranjo; *W:* Lisandro Duque Naranjo, Gabriel Garcia Marquez. **VHS** $79.95 *FXL, FCT, APD* ♫♫½

Miracle in the Wilderness A Christmas western based on Paul Gallico's novella, "The Snow Goose." Kristofferson stars as Jericho Adams, a former Indian fighter, who turns to farming to support his wife and child. When they are captured by a raiding party of Blackfeet, Adams discovers they have never heard the story of the Nativity.
1991 88m/C Kris Kristofferson, Kim Cattrall, John Dennis Johnston, Joanelle Romero, Dennis Olvers, Sheldon Peters Wolfchild; *D:* Kevin Dobson. **VHS** $14.98 *TTC, FCT* ♫♫½

Miracle Kid Standard story of a young boxer who'd rather be something else. His romance is interrupted when he becomes successful in the ring.
1942 66m/B Tom Neal, Carol Hughes, Betty Blythe, Minta Durfee, Gertrude Messinger; *D:* William Beaudine. **VHS** $19.95 *NOS* ♫♫

Miracle Mile A riveting, apocalyptic thriller about a mild-mannered misfit who, while inadvertently standing on a street corner at 2 a.m., answers a ringing pay phone. The caller is a panicked missile-silo worker who announces that the bombs have been launched for an all-out nuclear war. With about an hour left before the end, he decides to head into the city and rendezvous with his new girlfriend. A surreal, wicked farce sadly overlooked in theatrical release. Music by Tangerine Dream.

1989 (R) 87m/C Anthony Edwards, Mare Winningham, John Agar, Denise Crosby, Lou Hancock, Mykel T. Williamson, Kelly Jo Minter, Kurt Fuller, Robert DoQui, Danny De La Paz; *D:* Steve DeJarnatt; *W:* Steve DeJarnatt; *M:* Tangerine Dream. **VHS, Beta** $89.99 *HBO* ♫♫♫

Miracle of Morgan's Creek The breakneck comedy that stands as Sturges' premier achievement. Details the misadventures of a wartime floozy who gets drunk, thinks she marries a soldier on leave, gets pregnant by him, forgets the whole thing, and then tries to evade scandal by getting a local schnook to marry her again. And she's expecting sextuplets. Hilarious, out-to-make-trouble farce that shouldn't have, by all rights, made it past the censors of the time. Sturges' most scathing assault on American values earned him an Oscar nomination for writing. Remade as "Rock-A-Bye Baby" in 1958.
1944 98m/B Eddie Bracken, Betty Hutton, Diana Lynn, Brian Donlevy, Akim Tamiroff, Porter Hall, Emory Parnell, Alan Bridge, Julius Tannen, Victor Potel, Almira Sessions, Chester Conklin, William Demarest, Jimmy Conlin; *D:* Preston Sturges; *W:* Preston Sturges; *M:* Leo Shuken, Charles Bradshaw. **VHS, Beta** $14.95 *PAR, CCB* ♫♫♫♫

Miracle of Our Lady of Fatima Slick cold-war version of the supposedly true events surrounding the sighting of a holy vision by three children in Portugal during WWI. *AKA:* The Miracle of Fatima.
1952 102m/C Gilbert Roland, Susan Whitney, Sherry Jackson, Sammy Ogg, Angela Clark, Frank Silvera, Jay Novello; *D:* John Brahm. **VHS, Beta** $19.98 *WAR, IGP, KEP* ♫♫

The Miracle of the Bells A miracle occurs after a dead movie star is buried in the cemetary of her modest hometown. Given the premise, the casting is all the more peculiar. Adapted by Ben Hecht from Russell Janney's novel.
1948 120m/B Fred MacMurray, Alida Valli, Frank Sinatra, Lee J. Cobb; *D:* Irving Pichel. **VHS, Beta** $19.98 *REP, IGP* ♫♫

Miracle of the Heart: A Boys Town Story A television movie based on the story of Boys Town, and an old priest who sticks up for Boys Town's principles in the face of a younger priest with rigid ideas.
1986 100m/C Art Carney, Casey Siemaszko, Jack Bannon; *D:* Georg Stanford Brown. **VHS, Beta** $19.95 *COL* ♫♫

The Miracle of the White Stallions A disappointing Disney adventure about the director of a Viennese riding academy who guides his prized Lipizzan stallions to safety when the Nazis occupy Austria in WWII. *AKA:* The Flight of the White Stallions.
1963 92m/C Robert Taylor, Lilli Palmer, Eddie Albert, Curt Jurgens; *D:* Arthur Hiller. **VHS, Beta** $69.95 *DIS* ♫½

Miracle on Ice Occasionally stirring television film recounts the surprise triumph of the American hockey team over the touted Soviet squad during the 1980 Winter Olympics at Lake Placid.
1981 150m/C Karl Malden, Steve Guttenberg, Andrew Stevens, Lucinda Dooling, Jessica Walter; *D:* Steven Hilliard Stern. **VHS, Beta** *NO* ♫♫½

Miracle on 34th Street The actual Kris Kringle is hired as Santa Claus for the Macy's Thanksgiving parade but finds difficulty in proving himself to the cynical parade sponsor. When the boss's daughter also refuses to acknowledge Kringle, he goes to extraordinary lengths to convince her. Holiday classic equal to "It's a Wonderful Life," with Gwenn and Wood particularly engaging. Also available colorized. *AKA:* The Big Heart. **1947 97m/B** Maureen O'Hara, John Payne, Edmund Gwenn, Natalie Wood, William Frawley, Porter Hall, Gene Lockhart, Thelma Ritter, Jack Albertson; **D:** George Seaton; **W:** George Seaton; **M:** Cyril Mockridge. Academy Awards '47: Best Story & Screenplay, Best Supporting Actor (Gwenn); Nominations: Best Picture. **VHS, Beta $9.98** *CCB, FOX, HMV* 🐾🐾🐾🐾

The Miracle Rider A 15-chapter serial finds the bad guys trying to run the Indians off their lands in this saga of the old west. **1935 295m/B** Tom Mix, Joan Gale, Charles Middleton, Jason Robards Sr., Pat O'Malley, Robert Frazer, Wally Wales, Tom London, George Cheseboro, Lafe McKee; **D:** B. Reeves Eason, Armand Schaefer. **VHS $29.95** *GPV, MRV, VCN* 🐾🐾🐾

The Miracle Worker Depicts the unconventional methods that teacher Anne Sullivan used to help the deaf and blind Helen Keller adjust to the world around her and shows the relationship that built between the two courageous women. An intense, moving experience. William Gibson adapted his own play for the screen. **1962 107m/B** Anne Bancroft, Patty Duke, Victor Jory, Inga Swenson, Andrew Prine, Beah Richards; **D:** Arthur Penn. Academy Awards '62: Best Actress (Bancroft), Best Supporting Actress (Duke); Nominations: Best Adapted Screenplay, Best Costume Design (B & W), Best Director (Penn); National Board of Review Awards '62: 10 Best Films of the Year, Best Actress (Bancroft). **VHS, Beta $19.98** *MGM, BTV, CCB* 🐾🐾🐾½

The Miracle Worker Remade for television story of blind, deaf and mute Helen Keller and her teacher, Annie Sullivan, whose patience and perseverance finally enable Helen to learn to communicate with the world. Duke was Keller in the 1962 original, but plays the teacher in this version. **1979 98m/C** Patty Duke, Melissa Gilbert; **D:** Paul Aaron; **M:** Billy Goldenberg. **VHS, Beta $59.95** *WAR, OM* 🐾🐾🐾

Miracles Comedic misfire pairs a recently divorced couple as reluctant adventurers dodging jewel thieves and peculiar tribes in South America. In a desperate move to create a plot, Mexican jewel thieves, strange tribal rites, and some outrageously unlikely coincidences reunite the family. If this sounds good, see "Romancing the Stone" instead. **1986 (PG) 90m/C** Tom Conti, Teri Garr, Paul Rodriguez, Christopher Lloyd, Jorge Russek, Charles Rocket, Bob Nelson; **D:** Jim Kouf; **M:** Peter Bernstein. **VHS, Beta $79.99** *HBO, IME* 🐾½

Mirage An amnesiac finds himself the target of a dangerous manhunt in New York City in this offbeat thriller. Peck is particularly sympathetic in the lead, and McCarthy, Matthau, and Kennedy all shine in supporting roles. Worth it just to hear thug Kennedy grunt, "I owe this man some pain!" **1966 108m/B** Gregory Peck, Diane Baker, Walter Matthau, Jack Weston, Kevin McCarthy, Walter Abel, George Kennedy; **D:** Edward Dmytryk; **M:** Quincy Jones. **VHS, Beta $14.95** *BAR, MLB* 🐾🐾🐾

Mirele Efros A widowed but successful businesswoman finds herself at odds with her daughter-in-law in this film set in the turn of the century. In Yiddish with English subtitles. **1938 80m/B** Berta Gersten, Michael Rosenberg, Ruth Elbaum, Albert Lipton, Sarah Krohner, Moishe Feder; **D:** Joseph Berne. **VHS, Beta $79.95** *ERG, ING* 🐾🐾½

The Mirror Wonderful child's view of life in Russia during WWII. Black and white flashbacks of important events in the country's history are interspersed with scenes of day-to-day family life. In Russian with English subtitles. *AKA:* Zerkalo; A White White Boy. **1975 106m/C** Margarita Terekhova, Philip Yankovsky, Ignat Daniltsev, Oleg Yankovsky; **D:** Andrei Tarkovsky. **VHS $39.95** *ING, TPV, KIV* 🐾🐾🐾

The Mirror Crack'd While filming a movie in the English countryside, an American actress is murdered and Miss Marple must discover who the killer is. Based on the substantially better Agatha Christie novel. **1980 (PG) 105m/C** Elizabeth Taylor, Rock Hudson, Kim Novak, Tony Curtis, Edward Fox, Geraldine Chaplin, Charles Gray, Pierce Brosnan; **D:** Guy Hamilton; **W:** Barry Sandler. **VHS, Beta $14.98** *REP* 🐾🐾

Mirror Images Although sexy twins Kaitlin and Shauna may look alike, they couldn't have more diverse personalities. Yet the gorgeous twins find their lives thrown together in a mad tornado of passion and danger when they each encounter a handsome, mysterious stranger. Could it be that this guy has something more on his mind than love, something like... murder? Also available in an even steamier unrated version. **1991 (R) 94m/C** Delia Sheppard, Jeff Conaway, Richard Arbolino, John O'Hurley, Korey Mall, Julie Strain, Nels Van Patten; **D:** Alexander Gregory Hippolyte. **VHS $89.95** *ACA* 🐾½

Mirror Images 2 Direct-to-video erotic thriller features identical twins Carrie and Terrie (Whirry in a dual role). Carrie's Miss Goody Two-Shoes and Terrie's a murderous nympho who likes Carrie's guys. Terrie dies in a mysterious fire and Carrie sets out to investigate. Sex and nudity sells. **1993 92m/C** Shannon Whirry, Luca Bercovici, Tom Reilly; **D:** Alexander Gregory Hippolyte. **VHS $92.95** *ACA* 🐾🐾

Mirror, Mirror The prolific Ms. Black turns on the ol' black magic when her daughter's classmates decide it's open season for taunting shrinking violets. Thanks to a magical mirror on the wall, the cheerleading classmates are willed to the great pep rally in the sky. **1990 (R) 105m/C** Karen Black, Rainbow Harvest, Kristin Datillo, Ricky Paull Goldin, Yvonne De Carlo, William Sanderson; **D:** Marina Sargenti. **VHS $19.95** *ACA* 🐾🐾

Mirror of Death A woman subject to physical abuse gets more than she bargains for when she seeks revenge by unleashing the gruesome Queen of Hell. Watch this if you dare! **1987 85m/C** Julie Merrill, Kuri Browne, John Reno, Deryn Warren. **VHS, Beta** *NO* 🐾

Mirrors Woman finds that her dreams lead to death and destruction in New Orleans. **1978 83m/C** Kitty Winn, Peter Donat, William Swetland, Mary-Robin Redd, William Burns; **D:** Noel Black. **VHS, Beta** *NO* 🐾

Mirrors A Detroit-born ballerina goes to the Big Apple in search of fame and glory, leaving behind her journalist boyfriend. This upbeat love story features some spectacular dance routines and a behind-the-scenes look at a Broadway dancer's lifestyle. Originally made for television. **1985 99m/C** Timothy Daly, Marguerite Hickey, Antony Hamilton; **D:** Harry Winer. **VHS $89.95** *VMK* 🐾🐾½

The Misadventures of Merlin Jones A pair of college sweethearts become embroiled in a rollicking chimp-napping scandal. Disney pap done appropriately. A sequel, "The Monkey's Uncle," followed. **1963 (G) 90m/C** Tommy Kirk, Annette Funicello, Leon Ames, Stuart Erwin, Connie Gilchrist; **D:** Robert Stevenson; **M:** Buddy Baker. **VHS, Beta $69.95** *DIS* 🐾½

The Misadventures of Mr. Wilt Bumbling college lecturer has to convince inept inspector that he murdered a blowup doll, not his mean missing wife. Based on Tom Sharpe's bestseller. *AKA:* Wilt. **1990 (R) 84m/C** Griff Rhys Jones, Mel Smith, Alison Steadman, Diana Quick; **D:** Michael Tuchner; **M:** Anne Dudley. **VHS** *VMK* 🐾🐾

Mischief Alienated youths form a friendship during James Dean's heydey. Warning: this film offers a fairly convincing recreation of the 1950s. **1985 (R) 97m/C** Doug McKeon, Catherine Mary Stewart, Kelly Preston, Chris Nash, D.W. Brown, Jami Gertz, Margaret Blye, Graham Jarvis, Terry O'Quinn; **D:** Mel Damski. **VHS, Beta $79.98** *FOX* 🐾🐾

Misery Author Caan decides to chuck his lucrative but unfulfilling pulp novels and write seriously by finishing off his most popular character, Misery Chastain. However, fate intervenes when he crashes his car near the home of Bates, his "biggest fan ever," who saves his life, but then tortures him into resurrecting his favorite character. Bates is chillingly glib and and calmly brutal—watch your ankles. Based on the novel by Stephen King. **1990 (R) 107m/C** James Caan, Kathy Bates, Lauren Bacall, Richard Farnsworth, Frances Sternhagen, Graham Jarvis; **D:** Rob Reiner; **W:** William Goldman; **M:** Marc Shaiman. **VHS, Beta $19.95** *COL, NLC, BTV* 🐾🐾🐾

The Misfit Brigade Variation on the "Dirty Dozen" finds German misfits recruited for warfare by desperate Nazis during WWII. *AKA:* Wheels of Terror. **1987 (R) 99m/C** Bruce Davison, Oliver Reed, David Carradine, David Patrick Kelly, D.W. Moffett, Keith Szarabajka; **D:** Gordon Hessler. **VHS, Beta $19.98** *TWE* 🐾🐾

The Misfits A cynical floozy befriends grim cowboys in this downbeat drama. Compelling performances from leads Clift, Monroe (screenwriter Miller's wife), and Gable. Last film for the latter two performers, and nearly the end for Clift. **1961 124m/B** Clark Gable, Marilyn Monroe, Montgomery Clift, Thelma Ritter, Eli Wallach, James Barton, Estelle Winwood; **D:** John Huston; **W:** Arthur Miller. **VHS, Beta $19.98** *MGM, FOX, FCT* 🐾🐾🐾

Misfits of Science Pilot for a failed television series about a group of teens with special powers who fight to save the world. **1985 96m/C** Dean Paul Martin, Kevin Peter Hall, Mark Thomas Miller, Kenneth Mars, Courteney Cox; **D:** Philip DeGuere. **VHS, Beta $39.95** *MCA* 🐾

Mishima: A Life in Four Chapters Somewhat detached account and indulgent portrayal of the narcissistic Japanese author (and actor, filmmaker, and militarist) alternates between stylized interpretations of his books and a straightforward account of his life. Culminates in a pseudo-military operation that, in turn, resulted in Mishima's ritualistic suicide. A U.S./Japanese production. Innovative design by Eiko Ishioka. In Japanese with English subtitles. **1985 (R) 121m/C** Ken Ogata, Kenji Sawada, Yasosuke Bando; **D:** Paul Schrader; **W:** Leonard Schrader, Paul Schrader; **M:** Philip Glass. **VHS, Beta $79.95** *WAR, ING* 🐾🐾🐾

Mision Suicida Santo joins forces with a beautiful Interpol agent in his quest to break a spy ring.

1987 90m/C Santo, Lorena Velasquez, Elsa Cardenas, Dagoberto Rodriguez. **VHS, Beta** $49.95 *MAD* 🎬🎬

Miss A & Miss M A young girl is shocked when she realizes that two teachers she has befriended also live together. 1986 60m/C Kika Markham, Jennifer Hilary. **VHS** $11.95 *PSM* 🎬🎬

Miss All-American Beauty A behind-the-scenes look at a smalltime Texas beauty pageant. Lane stars as a contestant who comes to realize her self-respect is more important than winning an award. Meadow's mean pageant director adds an ironic edge that the movie as a whole lacks. Made for television. 1982 96m/C Diane Lane, Cloris Leachman, David Dukes, Jayne Meadows, Alice Hirson, Brian Kerwin; *D:* Gus Trikonis. **VHS, Beta** $39.95 *LIV* 🎬 ½

Miss Annie Rooney Intended to bill the child star in a more mature role, Temple receives her first screen kiss in this story about a poor Irish girl who falls in love with a wealthy young man. The well-worn plot is weighed down by lifeless dialogue. 1942 (G) 86m/B Shirley Temple, Dickie Moore, William Gargan, Guy Kibbee, Peggy Ryan, June Lockhart; *D:* Edwin L. Marin. **VHS, Beta** $12.95 *LIV, MED* 🎬🎬

Miss Firecracker Hunter, longing for love and self-respect, decides to change her promiscuous image by entering the local beauty pageant in her conservative southern hometown. The somewhat drippy premise is transformed by a super script and cast into an engaging and upbeat film. Henley's script was adapted from her own Off-Broadway play where Hunter created the role. Actress Lahti, wife of director Schlamme, makes a brief appearance. 1989 (PG) 102m/C Holly Hunter, Scott Glenn, Mary Steenburgen, Tim Robbins, Alfre Woodard, Trey Wilson, Bert Remsen, Ann Wedgeworth, Christine Lahti, Amy Wright; *D:* Thomas Schlamme; *M:* Beth Henley; *M:* David Mansfield. **VHS, Beta** $89.99 *HBO* 🎬🎬🎬

Ms. 45 Rough, bristling cult favorite about a mute girl who, in response to being raped and beaten twice in one night, goes on a man-killing murder spree. Wild ending. *AKA:* Angel of Vengeance. 1981 (R) 84m/C Zoe Tamerlis, Steve Singer, Jack Thibeau, Peter Yellen, Darlene Stuto, Editta Sherman, Albert Sinkys, Jimmy Laine; *D:* Abel Ferrara. **VHS, Beta** $19.95 *LIV, FCT* 🎬🎬🎬

Miss Grant Takes Richmond Zipperhead secretary finds herself in hot water a la Lucy when she finds out the company she's been working for is really the front for a gambling getup. Only Lucy fans need apply. *AKA:* Innocence is Bliss. 1949 87m/B Lucille Ball, William Holden, Janis Carter, James Gleason, Gloria Henry, Frank McHugh, George Cleveland, Arthur Space, William Wright, Jimmy Lloyd; *D:* Lloyd Bacon. **VHS** $19.95 *COL, FCT* 🎬🎬

Miss Julie Melodramatic stew adapted from from the August Strindberg play about a confused noblewoman who disgraces herself when she allows a servant to seduce her. In Swedish with English subtitles. 1950 90m/B Anita Bjork, Ulf Palme, Anders Henrikson; *D:* Alf Sjoberg. **VHS, Beta** $19.95 *COL, SUE, ING* 🎬🎬

Miss Mary A compassionate English governess in Buenos Aires conflicts with the honor-obsessed family she works for and Argentina's tumultuous history. Christie gives a wonderful performance. Some profanity and nudity.

1986 (R) 100m/C Julie Christie, Donald McIntire, Sofia Viruboff; *D:* Maria-Luisa Bemberg. **VHS, Beta** $9.99 *STE, NWV* 🎬🎬 ½

Miss Melody Jones A beautiful young black woman's dreams of stardom unravel as she is forced to pander to prurient men by disrobing publicly for financial recompense. 1973 86m/C Philomena Nowlin, Ronald Warren, Jacqueline Dalya, Peter Jacob; *D:* Bill Brame; *W:* Bill Brame. **VHS** $39.95 *XVC* 🎬

Miss Right A young man determines to find the ideal woman for himself and casts aside his other romantic interests. Sputtering lightweight comedy. 1981 (R) 98m/C William Tepper, Karen Black, Virna Lisi, Margot Kidder, Marie-France Pisier; *D:* Paul Williams. **VHS** $14.95 *IME* 🎬

Miss Rose White Sedgwick is Rose, a modern young career woman in post-WWII New York, as American as apple pie, who lives two very separate lives. Born Rayzel Weiss, a Polish Jew, she immigrated to the U.S. with her father as a very young girl, before the holocaust devastated her remaining family in Poland. After the war her older sister, thought dead, comes to America. The haunted Luisa causes Rose to question whether she can ever leave her past behind. Above average Hallmark Hall of Fame presentation has a good cast, particularly Plummer as Luisa. Based on the play "A Shayna Maidel" by Barbara Lebow. 1992 (PG) 95m/C Kyra Sedgwick, Amanda Plummer, Maximilian Schell, D.B. Sweeney, Penny Fuller, Milton Selzer, Maureen Stapleton; *D:* Joseph Sargent; *W:* Anna Sandor. **VHS** $89.98 *REP, BTV* 🎬🎬

Miss Sadie Thompson Based on the novel "Rain" by W. Somerset Maugham. Promiscuous tart Hayworth arrives on a Pacific island occupied by a unit of Marines and a sanctimonious preacher played by Ferrer While Hayworth parties with the Marines and becomes involved with Ray's Sgt. O'Hara, Ferrer moralizes and insists she return to the mainland to face moral charges. Quasi-musical with a scattering of dubbed songs by Hayworth includes a memorable erotic dance scene complete with tight dress and dripping sweat. Hayworth's strong performance carries the picture with Ferrer and Ray turning in cardboard versions of their Maugham characters. Originally filmed in 3-D. 1953 91m/C Rita Hayworth, Jose Ferrer, Aldo Ray, Charles Bronson; *D:* Curtis Bernhardt. **VHS, Beta** $19.95 *COL* 🎬🎬

Missile to the Moon First expedition to the moon encounters not acres of dead rock but a race of gorgeous women in lingerie and high heels. A bad but entertaining remake of "Cat Women of the Moon," featuring a bevy of beauty contest winners from New Hampshire to Yugoslavia. Who says truth is stranger than fiction. 1959 78m/B Gary Clarke, Cathy Downs, K.T. Stevens, Laurie Mitchell, Michael Whalen, Nina Bara, Richard Travis, Tommy Cook, Marjorie Hellen; *D:* Richard Cunha. **VHS, Beta** $9.95 *RHI, SNC, CNM* 🎬 ½

Missiles of October Telling the story of the October 1962 Cuban Missile crisis, this made-for-TV drama keeps you on the edge of your seat while unfolding the sequence of events within the U.S. Government. Well written, with a strong cast including Devane, who turns in a convincing performance as-guess who-J.F.K. 1974 155m/C William Devane, Ralph Bellamy, Martin Sheen, Howard da Silva; *D:* Anthony Page. **VHS, Beta** $59.95 *MPI, LCA* 🎬🎬🎬

Missing At the height of a military coup in Chile (never named in the movie), a young American writer (Shea) disappears. His rightwing father Lemon tries to get to the bottom of his disappearance while bickering with Shea's wife, played by Spacek, a bohemian who is the political opposite of her father-in-law. Outstanding performances by Spacek and Lemon along with excellent writing and direction result in a gripping and thought-provoking thriller. Based on the book by Thomas Hauser from the true story of Charles Horman. 1982 (PG) 122m/C Jack Lemmon, Sissy Spacek, John Shea, Melanie Mayron, David Clennon, Charles Cioffi, Joe Regalbuto, Richard Venture, Janice Rule; *D:* Constantin Costa-Gavras; *W:* Constantin Costa-Gavras, Donald Stewart. Academy Awards '82: Best Adapted Screenplay; Nominations: Best Actor (Lemmon), Best Actress (Spacek), Best Picture; Cannes Film Festival '82: Best Actor (Lemmon), Best Film. **VHS, Beta** $19.95 *MCA* 🎬🎬🎬 ½

The Missing Corpse When a newspaper publisher's worst rival is murdered, he fears that he will be implicated. He decides the only thing to do is hide the body to prevent its being discovered. Enjoyable, light comedy/mystery. 1945 62m/B J. Edward Bromberg, Eric Sinclair, Frank Jenks, Isabelle Randolph, Paul Guilfoyle, John Shay, Lorell Sheldon; *D:* Albert Herman. **VHS** $16.95 *NOS, MRV, SNC* 🎬

Missing in Action An army colonel returns to the Vietnam jungle to settle some old scores and rescue some POWs while on an MIA fact-finding mission. Box office smash. 1984 (R) 101m/C Chuck Norris, M. Emmet Walsh; *D:* Joseph Zito. **VHS, Beta** $14.95 *MGM, TLF* 🎬 ½

Missing in Action 2: The Beginning Set in Vietnam, this prequel to the original "Missing in Action" provides some interesting background on Norris's rocky relationship with communism. Packed with violence, bloodshed and torture. 1985 97m/C Chuck Norris, Soon-Teck Oh, Cosie Costa, Steven Williams; *D:* Lance Hool; *W:* Steve Bing. **VHS, Beta** $14.95 *MGM* 🎬

Missing Link A strange, meditative quasi-documentary depicting the singular adventures of a humanoid silently transversing the African wilderness and confronting various natural phenomena. Beautifully photographed. Make-up by Rick Baker. 1988 (PG) 92m/C Peter Elliott, Michael Gambon; *D:* David Hughes. **VHS, Beta** $89.95 *MCA* 🎬🎬 ½

Missing Pieces A woman takes a job as a private investigator in order to find her journalist husband's killer. Effective made-for-television mystery taken from the novel "A Private Investigation" by Karl Alexander. 1983 96m/C Elizabeth Montgomery, Louanne, John Reilly, Ron Karabatsos, Robin Gammell, Julius W. Harris; *D:* Mike Hodges. **VHS** *LIV* 🎬🎬 ½

The Mission Sweeping, cinematically beautiful historical drama about an 18th-century Jesuit mission in the Brazilian jungle. The missionaries struggle against the legalized slave trade of Portugal and political factions within the church. Written by Bolt (of "A Man for All Seasons" fame), its visual intensity is marred by length and so much overt symbolism that an emotional coolness surfaces when the action slows. Nonetheless, epic in ambition and nearly in quality. Magnificent musical score. 1986 (PG) 125m/C Robert De Niro, Jeremy Irons, Ray McAnally, Philip Bosco, Aidan Quinn, Liam Neeson, Cherie Lunghi, Rev. Daniel Berrigan, Ronald Pickup; *D:* Roland Joffe; *W:*

Robert Bolt; **M:** Ennio Morricone. Academy Awards '86: Best Cinematography; Nominations: Best Art Direction/Set Decoration, Best Costume Design, Best Director (Joffe), Best Film Editing, Best Picture, Best Original Score; British Academy Awards '86: Best Supporting Actor (McAnally); Cannes Film Festival '86: Best Film; Golden Globe Awards '87: Best Screenplay, Best Score. **VHS, Beta, 8mm $19.98** WAR 🐾🐾🐾

Mission Batangas Unremarkable adventure-war-heist movie tells the story of a shallow American WWII pilot (Weaver) and a missionary nurse (Miles), who team up to steal the Philippine government's entire stock of gold bullion from the Japanese who captured it. Beautiful scenery, shot in the Philippines, adds something to an otherwise vacant effort.
1969 100m/C Dennis Weaver, Vera Miles, Keith Larsen; **D:** Keith Larsen. **VHS, Beta $19.95** STE, NWV 🐾½

Mission Corbari One heavily armed and ill-tempered hombre takes on the Nazis, with indifferent results.
197? 88m/C VHS, Beta NO 🐾

Mission Galactica: The Cylon Attack Spaceship Battlestar Galactica is stranded in space without fuel and open to attack from the chrome-plated Cylons. Adama (Greene) is forced to stop Commander Cain's (Bridges) efforts to launch an attack against the Cylons, while countering the attacks of the Cylon leader. Warmed over made-for-television sci-fi.
1979 108m/C Lorne Greene, Lloyd Bridges, Richard Hatch, Dirk Benedict. **VHS, Beta $19.95** MCA 🐾🐾

Mission in Morocco When an oilman scouting for oil fields in the Sahara is killed, his partner, Barker, hops a jet to Morocco to find the whereabouts of a microfilm that gives the location of a valuable oil deposit. The search for the secret microfilm is complicated by competing parties also interested in the black gold. Ho-hum action adventure.
1959 79m/C Lex Barker, Juli Reding. **VHS $19.98** REP 🐾

Mission Inferno The ups and downs of a hot-blooded Korean War commando taking revenge, escaping prison, fighting and just plain making war.
1984 90m/C VHS, Beta $39.95 VCD 🐾

Mission Kiss and Kill Enchanting title. A movie filled with martial arts, beautiful girls, and exotic settings that takes place in the early days of the Chinese Republic.
19?? 90m/C Lung Fei, Lu I Lung, Yuan Lung. **VHS, Beta $29.95** OCE 🐾

Mission Manila An ex-CIA operative and Manila-based drug addict is called by his ex-lover to return to Manila to help his brother, who has gotten in much the same trouble he had.
1987 (R) 98m/C Larry Wilcox. **VHS, Beta** NO 🐾

Mission Mars American astronauts McGavin and Adams, on a mission to the red planet, discover the bodies of two cosmonauts floating in space. After landing on the planet's surface, they find a third cosmonaut, this one in a state of suspended animation. While putting the viewer to sleep, they proceed to revive the third cosmonaut and have at it with the sinister alien force responsible for all the trouble.
1967 87m/C Darren McGavin, Nick Adams, George DeVries; **D:** Nicholas Webster. **VHS, Beta $29.95** UNI 🐾

Mission: Monte Carlo An episode from the television series "The Persuaders," wherein our two vacationing adventurers discover a girl's drowned body and try to solve the case.
1975 102m/C Roger Moore, Tony Curtis, Susan George, Annette Andre, Alfred Marks, Laurence Naismith; **D:** Basil Dearden, Roy Ward Baker. **VHS, Beta $59.98** FOX 🐾🐾

Mission of Justice Revel in non-stop martial arts action with this tale of a cop who goes undercover to get the goods on a corrupt female politico, who also happens to run her own ruthless private army.
1992 (R) ?m/C Jeff Wincott, Brigitte Nielsen, Matthias Hues, Luca Bercovici, Cyndi Pass, Billy "Sly" Williams, Tony Burton; **D:** Steve Barnett. **VHS $89.94** REP 🐾

Mission of the Shark A top secret naval mission leads to a scandal-ridden court martial in this true WWII saga, based on the worst sea disaster in naval history. The U.S.S. Indianapolis has just completed a secret mission when it is torpedoed by enemy subs. The survivors spend five days in shark-infested waters awaiting rescue and, when the Navy points fingers, the ship's highly decorated and well-respected Captain McVay accepts responsibility for the good of the service. Contains some harrowing scenes of sailors versus sharks. Made for television.
1991 92m/C Stacy Keach, Richard Thomas, Steve Landesburg, Carrie Snodgress, Bob Gunton, Andrew Prine, Stacy Keach Sr., Don Harvey; **D:** Robert Iscove. **VHS $89.95** TRI 🐾🐾🐾

Mission Phantom A group of spies on a mission in Russia plans to steal some diamonds and help a woman get to the United States.
1979 90m/C Andrew Ray, Ingrid Sholder, Peter Martell; **D:** James Reed. **VHS, Beta $59.95** VCI 🐾

Mission Stardust An internationally produced but thoroughly unambitious adaptation of the once-popular Perry Rhodan sci-fi serial, in which Rhodan and his team bring ill aliens back to Earth and defend them against evil spies. Dubbed. **AKA:** 4...3...2...1...Morte.
1968 90m/C Essy Persson, Gianni Rizzo, Lang Jeffries, Pinkas Braun; **D:** Primo Zeglio. **VHS, Beta $9.95** RHI 🐾🐾

Mission to Death An adventure extravaganza in which a group of friends must risk their very lives.
1966 76m/C Jim Brewer, James E. McLarty, Jim Westerbrook, Robert Stolper, Dudley Hafner, Jerry Lasater. **VHS** LBD 🐾½

Mission to Glory This dozer tells the story of Father Francisco "Kino" Kin, a tough, seventeenth-century priest in California who took on the Apaches and murderous Conquistadors in defense of his people. **AKA:** The Father Kino Story.
1980 (PG) 100m/C Richard Egan, John Ireland, Cesar Romero, Ricardo Montalban, Rory Calhoun, Michael Ansara, Keenan Wynn, Aldo Ray; **D:** Ken Kennedy. **VHS, Beta** IGP 🐾🐾

Mission to Kill An American demolitions expert, Ginty, joins a Latin American guerrilla force in battling tyrannical junta forces. This action-packed, fast-paced thriller is big on revenge and violence but not much else.
1985 (R) 97m/C Robert Ginty, Olivia D'Abo, Cameron Mitchell; **D:** David Winters. **VHS, Beta $79.95** MED 🐾½

Mission to Venice Flynn plays a sleuth attempting to find a missing husband when he accidentally stumbles upon a ring of spies.
1963 ?m/C Sean Flynn, Madeleine Robinson. **VHS $16.95** SNC 🐾🐾

The Missionary A mild-mannered English missionary returns to London from his work in Africa and is recruited into saving the souls of a group of prostitutes. Aspiring to gentle comedy status, it's often formulaic and flat, with Palin and Smith fighting gamely to stay above script level. Still, good for some laughs, particularly during the near classic walking butler sequence.
1982 (R) 86m/C Michael Palin, Dame Maggie Smith, Trevor Howard, Denholm Elliott, Michael Hordern; **D:** Richard Loncraine; **W:** Michael Palin. **VHS, Beta $19.95** PAR, TVC, FCT 🐾🐾½

Mississippi Burning Hard-edged social drama centers around the civil rights movement in Mississippi in 1964. When three activists turn up missing, FBI agents Hackman and Dafoe are sent to head up the investigation. Unfortunately, this is another example of a "serious" film about racial conflict in which white characters predominate and blacks provide background.
1988 (R) 127m/C Gene Hackman, Willem Dafoe, Frances McDormand, Brad Dourif, R. Lee Ermey, Gailard Sartain, Stephen Tobolowsky, Michael Rooker, Pruitt Taylor Vince, Badja Djola, Kevin Dunn, Frankie Faison, Tom Mason, Park Overall; **D:** Alan Parker; **W:** Chris Gerolmo; **M:** Trevor Jones. Academy Awards '88: Best Cinematography; Nominations: Best Actor (Hackman), Best Director (Parker), Best Film Editing, Best Picture, Best Sound, Best Supporting Actress (McDormand); Berlin International Film Festival '88: Best Actor (Hackman); National Board of Review Awards '88: 10 Best Films of the Year, Best Actor (Hackman), Best Director (Parker), Best Supporting Actress (McDormand). **VHS, Beta $9.98** ORI 🐾🐾🐾

Mississippi Masala "Masala" is an Indian seasoning blending different-colored spices, as this film is a blend of romance, comedy, and social conscience. An interracial romance sets off a cultural collision and escalates racial tensions in a small Southern town when Mina, a sheltered young Indian woman, falls in love with Demetrius, an ambitious black man with his own carpet-cleaning business. Washington and Choudhury are engaging as the lovers with Seth, as Mina's unhappy father, especially watchable.
1992 (R) 118m/C Denzel Washington, Sarita Choudhury, Roshan Seth, Sharmila Tagore, Charles S. Dutton, Joe Seneca, Ranjit Chowdhry; **Cameos:** Mira Nair; **D:** Mira Nair; **W:** Sooni Taraporevala; **M:** L. Subramaniam. **VHS $92.95** COL, FCT 🐾🐾🐾

Mississippi Mermaid Truffaut generally succeeds in merging his own directorial style with Hitchcockian suspense, but this is not considered one of his best. Millionaire tobacco planter Belmondo looks for a bride in the personals and finds Deneuve. Belmondo feels lucky landing this beauty until she leaves him and takes his money with her. A lookalike, also played by Deneuve, takes over his wife's role and attempts to poison Belmondo. Look for numerous references to the movies, including Bogart, Balzac and Cocteau. In French with English subtitles.
1969 (PG) 110m/C Jean-Paul Belmondo, Catherine Deneuve, Michel Bouquet, Nelly Borgeaud, Marcel Berbert, Martine Ferriere; **D:** Francois Truffaut; **W:** Francois Truffaut; **M:** Antoine Duhamel. **VHS $19.99** MGM, FCT, ING 🐾🐾🐾

Missouri Breaks Thomas McGuane wrote the screenplay for this offbeat tale of Montana ranchers and rustlers fighting over land and livestock in the 1880s. Promising combination of script, cast and director unfortunately yields rather disappointing results, though both Brando and Nicholson chew up scenery to their hearts' content.

1976 (PG) 126m/C Jack Nicholson, Marlon Brando, Randy Quaid, Kathleen Lloyd, Frederic Forrest, Harry Dean Stanton; **D:** Arthur Penn; **W:** Thomas McGuane; **M:** John Williams. **VHS, Beta $19.98** *FOX* 🎬🎬

Missouri Traveler An orphan boy struggles to get his own farm in Missouri. Family fare based on John Buress' novel.
1958 103m/C Lee Marvin, Gary Merrill, Brandon de Wilde, Paul Ford. **VHS, Beta** *MRV* 🎬🎬🎬

Missourians Small-town sheriff Hale helps a Polish rancher overcome ethnic prejudice among the townspeople. The situation worsens with the arrival in town of the rancher's outlaw brother. Strong direction and engaging storyline.
1950 60m/B Monte Hale, Paul Hurst. **VHS, Beta $29.95** *DVT* 🎬🎬½

Mrs. Amworth E.F. Benson's classic tale of the occult, in which a mysterious and deadly epidemic attacking a quiet English village is diagnosed to be the work of a vampire.
1977 29m/C Glynis Johns; **D:** Alvin Rakoff. **VHS, Beta $14.95** *LCA* 🎬🎬½

Mrs. Brown, You've Got a Lovely Daughter The Herman's Hermits gang inherits a greyhound and attempts to make a racer out of him while singing their songs. For the Brit group's diehard fans only. 🎵It's Nice To Be Out in the Morning; Ooh, She's Done It Again; Lemon and Lime; The World is for the Young; Holiday Inn; The Most Beautiful Thing in My Life; Daisy Chain; Mrs. Brown, You've Got a Lovely Daughter; There's a King of Hush.
1968 (G) 95m/C Peter Noone, Stanley Holloway, Mona Washbourne; **D:** Saul Swimmer. **VHS, Beta $59.95** *MGM* 🎬½

Mrs. Doubtfire Williams is an unemployed voiceover actor going through a messy divorce. When his wife gets custody, the distraught father decides to dress up as a woman and become a nanny to his own children. He also has to deal with the old flame who re-enters his ex-wife's life. Williams schtick extraordinaire with more than a little sugary sentimentality. Based on the British children's book "Madame Doubtfire" by Anne Fine.
1993 (PG-13) 120m/C Robin Williams, Sally Field, Pierce Brosnan, Harvey Fierstein, Robert Prosky, Mara Wilson; **D:** Chris Columbus; **W:** Randi Mayem Singer, Leslie Dixon; **M:** Howard Shore. Academy Awards '93: Best Makeup; Nominations: : Best Actor (Williams); Golden Globe Awards '94: Best Actor—Musical/Comedy (Williams), Best Film—Musical/Comedy; MTV Movie Awards '94: Best Comedic Performance (Williams). **VHS $19.98** *FXV* 🎬🎬

Mrs. Miniver A moving tale of a courageous, gentle middle-class British family and its struggle to survive during WWII. A classic that garnered six Academy Awards, it's recognized for contributions to the Allied effort. Contains one of the most powerful orations in the film history, delivered by Wilcoxon, who portrayed the vicar. Followed by "The Miniver Story." Adapted from Jan Struther's book.
1942 134m/B Greer Garson, Walter Pidgeon, Teresa Wright, May Whitty, Richard Ney, Henry Travers, Reginald Owen, Henry Wilcoxon, Helmut Dantine, Aubrey Mather, Rhys Williams, Tom Conway, Peter Lawford; **D:** William Wyler; **W:** George Froeschel, James Hilton, Arthur Wimperis, Claudine West; **M:** Herbert Stothart. Academy Awards '42: Best Actress (Garson), Best Black and White Cinematography, Best Director (Wyler), Best Picture, Best Screenplay, Best Supporting Actress (Wright); Nominations: Best Actor (Pidgeon), Best Film Editing, Best Sound, Best Supporting Actor (Travers), Best

Supporting Actress (Whitty). **VHS, Beta $19.98** *MGM, BTV* 🎬🎬🎬🎬

Mrs. Parkington Overblown epic drama spanning six decades tells the story of the rise and fall of an American dynasty made on easy money. Garson plays the woman who goes from working as a maid in a boarding house to living a life of luxury when she marries a multimillionaire. This was the fifth pairing of Garson and Pidgeon and although it's not one of their best, it proved to be a big hit with audiences. Lavish costumes and good performances by Garson and Moorehead. Based on the novel by Louis Bromfield.
1944 124m/B Greer Garson, Walter Pidgeon, Edward Arnold, Frances Rafferty, Agnes Moorehead, Selena Royle, Gladys Cooper, Lee Patrick; **D:** Tay Garnett; **W:** Robert Thoeren, Polly James. Academy Awards '44 Nominations: Best Actress (Garson), Best Supporting Actress (Moorehead); Golden Globe Awards '45: Best Supporting Actress (Moorehead). **VHS $19.98** *MGM* 🎬🎬½

Mrs. R's Daughter An outraged mother fights the judicial systems in order to bring her daughter's rapist to trial. Based on a true story and made for television.
1979 97m/C Cloris Leachman, Season Hubley, Donald Moffatt, John McIntire, Stephen Elliott, Ron Rifkin; **D:** Dan Curtis. **VHS, Beta $19.98** *WAR, OM* 🎬🎬

Mrs. Silly Romance novel on tape, following the exploits of an aging woman who in losing material wealth, gains contentment.
1985 60m/C Dame Maggie Smith, James Villers, Cyril Luckham. **Beta $11.95** *PSM* 🎬

Mrs. Soffel Falling in love with a convicted murderer and helping him flee confinement occupies the time of the prison warden's wife. Effectively captures the 1901 setting, yet a dark pall fairly strangles any emotion. Based on a true story.
1984 (PG-13) 110m/C Diane Keaton, Mel Gibson, Matthew Modine, Edward Herrmann, Trini Alvarado, Terry O'Quinn, Jennie Dundas, Danny Corkill, Maury Chaykin, Dana Wheeler-Nicholson; **D:** Gillian Armstrong; **W:** Ron Nyswaner; **M:** Mark Isham. **VHS, Beta $14.95** *MGM* 🎬🎬

Mrs. Wiggs of the Cabbage Patch A warm, funny, and altogether overdone story of a mother whose husband abandons her, leaving the woman to raise their four children alone. It's Thanksgiving, so the rich visit the poor household to deliver a turkey dinner, and in the end all live happily ever after. Not one of Fields' larger roles; he doesn't even make an appearance until midway through the schmaltz.
1942 80m/B Pauline Lord, ZaSu Pitts, W.C. Fields, Evelyn Venable, Donald Meek, Barbara Britton; **D:** Norman Taurog. **VHS $9.95** *GKK* 🎬🎬½

Mistaken Identity A swank hotel is the setting for this so-so comedy about three con men who wind up conning each other as much as their supposed victims. A couple of light romances are also thrown in for good measure.
1936 75m/B Chick Chandler, Evelyn Knapp, Berton Churchill, Patricia Farr, Richard Carle, Bradley Page, Lew Kelly; **D:** Phil Rosen. **VHS $24.95** *VYY* 🎬½

Mistaken Identity All-black mystery set against the background of a nightclub, and featuring a production number, "I'm a Bangi from Ubangi."
1941 60m/B Nellie Hill, George Oliver. **VHS, Beta $29.95** *VCN, DVT, RXM* 🎬½

Mr. Ace A congresswoman decides to run for governor without the approval of the loyal political kingpin, Mr. Ace.

1946 85m/B George Raft, Sylvia Sidney, Sara Haden, Stanley Ridges; **D:** Edwin L. Marin. **VHS, Beta $14.95** *COL* 🎬½

Mr. & Mrs. Bridge Set in the thirties and forties in Kansas City, Ivory's adaptation of Evan S. Connell's novels painstakingly portrays an upper middle-class family struggling to survive within an emotional vacuum. Newman and Woodward, together for the first time in many years as Walter and Ivory Bridge, bring a wealth of experience and insight to their characterizations. Many consider this to be Newman's best, most subtle and nuanced performance.
1991 (PG-13) 127m/C Joanne Woodward, Paul Newman, Kyra Sedgwick, Blythe Danner, Simon Callow, Diane Kagan, Robert Sean Leonard, Saundra McClain, Margaret Welsh, Austin Pendleton, Gale Garnett, Remak Ramsay; **D:** James Ivory; **W:** Ruth Prawer Jhabvala. **VHS $92.99** *HBO, FCT* 🎬🎬🎬🎬

Mr. & Mrs. Smith Hitchcock's only screwball comedy, an underrated, endearing farce about a bickering but happy modern couple who discover their marriage isn't legitimate and go through courtship all over again. Vintage of its kind, with inspired performances and crackling dialogue.
1941 95m/B Carole Lombard, Robert Montgomery, Gene Raymond, Jack Carson, Lucile Watson, Charles Halton; **D:** Alfred Hitchcock; **W:** Norman Krasna. **VHS, Beta $19.95** *MED, TTC* 🎬🎬🎬½

Mr. Arkadin Screenwriter, director, star Welles, adapting from his own novel, gave this plot a dry run on radio during early 1950s. Welles examines the life of yet another ruthless millionaire, but this one can't seem to remember the sordid source of all that cash. Investigator Arden follows the intriguing and descending trail to a surprise ending. As in "Citizen Kane," oblique camera angles and layered dialogue prevail, but this time only serve to confuse the story. Shot over two years around Europe, required seven years of post production before finding distribution in 1962. **AKA:** Confidential Report.
1955 99m/B Orson Welles, Akim Tamiroff, Michael Redgrave, Patricia Medina, Mischa Auer; **D:** Orson Welles. **VHS, Beta $24.95** *VDM, HTV, HEG* 🎬🎬🎬

Mr. Baseball Washed-up American baseball player tries to revive his career by playing in Japan and experiences cultures clashing under the ballpark lights. Semi-charmer swings and misses often enough to warrant return to minors. Film drew controversy during production when Universal was bought by the Japanese Matsushita organization and claims of both Japan- and America-bashing were thrown about.
1992 (PG-13) 109m/C Tom Selleck, Ken Takakura, Toshi Shioya, Dennis Haysbert, Aya Takanashi; **D:** Fred Schepisi; **W:** Gary Ross, Kevin Wade, Monte Merrick; **M:** Jerry Goldsmith. **VHS, Beta $19.98** *MCA* 🎬🎬

Mr. Billion Engaging chase adventure comedy about an Italian mechanic who stands to inherit a billion dollar fortune if he can travel from Italy to San Francisco in twenty days. Of course, things get in his way. Hill made his American debut in this film.
1977 (PG) 89m/C Jackie Gleason, Terence Hill, Valerie Perrine, Slim Pickens, Chill Wills; **D:** Jonathan Kaplan; **W:** Jonathan Kaplan, Ken Friedman; **M:** Dave Grusin. **VHS, Beta $59.98** *FOX* 🎬🎬

Mr. Bill's Real Life Adventures A made-for-television live-action adventure for the "Saturday Night Live" clay star, portrayed by Scolari, who is victimized as usual by his nemesis, Mr. Sluggo.
1986 43m/C Peter Scolari, Valerie Mahaffey, Lenore Kasdorf, Michael McManus; **D:** Jim Drake. VHS, Beta $29.95 PAR ♫♫

Mr. Blandings Builds His Dream House Classic comedy features Grant as an adman who tires of city life and moves his family to the country, where his troubles really begin. Grant is at his funniest. Loy and Douglas provide strong backup. A must for all homeowners.
1948 93m/B Cary Grant, Myrna Loy, Melvyn Douglas, Lex Barker, Reginald Denny, Louise Beavers; **D:** H.C. Potter; **W:** Norman Panama. VHS, Beta $14.95 TTC, MED, MLB ♫♫ 1/2

Mr. Boggs Steps Out A pencil-pusher wins a bundle and invests it in a barrel factory. Trouble arises when a slickster tries to close it down. Even with the usual romantic entanglements, the film has trouble staying interesting.
1938 68m/B Stuart Erwin, Helen Chandler, Toby Wing, Tully Marshall, Spencer Charters, Otis Harlan, Walter Byron, Milburn Stone; **D:** Gordon Wiles. VHS $19.95 NOS, VYY ♫♫ 1/2

Mr. Corbett's Ghost A young man, displeased with his boss's managerial finesse, cuts a deal with a soul collector who pink slips the guy to the great unemployment line in the sky. Once a boss always a boss, and the guy's ghost stops in to say boo, while the soul collector is hot to get his hands on his part of the bargain. Huston's final film appearance. Made for television.
1990 60m/C John Huston, Paul Scofield, Burgess Meredith. VHS $24.95 MON, KAR ♫♫

Mr. Deeds Goes to Town Typical Capra fare offers Cooper as philanthropic fellow who inherits $20 million and promptly donates it to the needy. He also manages to find time to fall in love with a beautiful reporter. Arthur is the hard-edged reporter determined to fathom the good guy's motivation. Superior entertainment. Based on Clarence Budington Kelland's play "Opera Hut."
1936 118m/B Gary Cooper, Jean Arthur, Raymond Walburn, Walter Catlett, Lionel Stander, George Bancroft, H.B. Warner, Ruth Donnelly, Douglass Dumbrille, Margaret Seddon, Margaret McWade; **D:** Frank Capra; **W:** Robert Riskin. Academy Awards '36: Best Director (Capra); Nominations: Best Actor (Cooper), Best Picture, Best Screenplay, Best Sound; National Board of Review Awards '36: 10 Best Films of the Year; New York Film Critics Awards '36: Best Film. VHS, Beta $19.95 COL, BTV ♫♫♫ 1/2

Mr. Destiny Mid-level businessman Belushi has a mid-life crisis of sorts when his car dies. Wandering into an empty bar, he encounters bartender Caine who serves cocktails and acts omniscient before taking him on the ten-cent tour of life as it would've been if he hadn't struck out in a high school baseball game. Less than wonderful rehash of "It's a Wonderful Life."
1990 (PG-13) 110m/C James Belushi, Michael Caine, Linda Hamilton, Jon Lovitz, Bill McCutcheon, Hart Bochner, Rene Russo, Jay O. Sanders, Maury Chaykin, Pat Corley, Douglas Seale, Courteney Cox, Kathy Ireland; **D:** James Orr; **W:** James Orr, Jim Cruickshank. VHS, Beta $19.99 TOU, FCT ♫♫

Mr. Emmanuel An elderly Jewish widower leaves his English home in 1935 in quest of the mother of a German refugee boy, and is subjected to shocking treatment in Germany.
1944 97m/B Felix Aylmer, Greta Gynt, Walter Rilla, Jean Simmons. VHS, Beta LCA ♫♫ 1/2

Mr. Frost Goldblum feigns fascination in this lackluster tale of the devil incarnate, who is imprisoned after owning up to a series of grisly murders, and who hides his true identity until approached by a woman psychiatrist.
1989 (R) 92m/C Jeff Goldblum, Kathy Baker, Alan Bates, Roland Giraud, Jean-Pierre Cassel; **D:** Phillip Setbon; **W:** Phillip Setbon, Brad Lynch. VHS $39.95 FCT, IME ♫

Mister Halpren & Mister Johnson Gleason attends the funeral of a longtime friend and one time flame, and becomes acquainted with the woman's husband (Olivier). Heavyweight cast wasted on flimsy script...and away we go!
1983 57m/C Laurence Olivier, Jackie Gleason; **D:** Alvin Rakoff. VHS, Beta NO ♫♫

Mr. Hobbs Takes a Vacation Good-natured comedy in which beleagured parents try to resolve family squabbles while the entire brood is on a seaside vacation. Stewart and O'Hara are especially fine and funny as the well-meaning parents.
1962 116m/C James Stewart, Maureen O'Hara, Fabian, John Saxon, Marie Wilson, John McGiver, Reginald Gardiner; **D:** Henry Koster; **M:** Henry Mancini. VHS, Beta $19.98 FOX, HMV ♫♫♫

Mr. Horn Based on the William Goldman western novel, this slow-paced film about folk-hero Scott Tom Horn capturing the famous Apache warrior, Geronimo, is average at best.
1979 200m/C David Carradine, Richard Widmark, Karen Black, Jeremy Slate, Enrique Lucero, Jack Starrett; **D:** Jack Starrett. VHS $59.95 LIV ♫♫

Mr. Hulot's Holiday Superior slapstick details the misadventures of a dullard's seaside holiday. Inventive French comedian Tati at his best. Light-hearted and natural, with magical mime sequences. Followed by "Mon Oncle." **AKA:** Les Vacances de Monsieur Hulot; Monsieur Hulot's Holiday.
1953 86m/B Jacques Tati, Natalie Pascaud, Michelle Rolla; **D:** Jacques Tati. Academy Awards '55 Nominations: Best Story & Screenplay; National Board of Review Awards '54: 5 Best Foreign Films of the Year. VHS, Beta, 8mm $24.95 NOS, MRV, VYY ♫♫♫ 1/2

Mr. Inside, Mr. Outside A television movie about two New York City cops, one undercover, one not, trying to infiltrate a tough diamond-smuggling ring.
1974 74m/C Tony LoBianco, Hal Linden; **D:** William A. Graham. VHS, Beta $59.95 VMK ♫ 1/2

Mister Johnson In 1923 Africa, an educated black man working for the British magistrate constantly finds himself in trouble, thanks to backfiring schemes. This highly enjoyable film from the director of "Driving Miss Daisy" suffers only from the underdevelopment of the intriguing lead character. Based on the novel by Joyce Cary.
1991 (PG-13) 105m/C Pierce Brosnan, Edward Woodward, Maynard Eziashi, Beatie Edney, Denis Quilley, Nick Reding; **D:** Bruce Beresford; **W:** Bruce Beresford, William Boyd; **M:** Georges Delerue. VHS $89.98 VES, LIV ♫♫♫

Mr. Jones Psychiatrist (Olin) falls in love with her manic-depressive patient (Gere). Head case Mr. Jones (Gere) is a charmer who gets a rush from tightrope walking a high beam on a construction site, yet is prone to bad moods when he fails to remember his own name. He can't resist flirting with the seductive Dr. Bowen, who eagerly leaps past professional boundaries while trying to coax him out of his illness. Wastes the talents of its stars with Gere showy, Olin brittle, and the whole story as contrived as their prefunctory love affair. Psychiatrists are getting as

bad a rep professionally as lawyers in their recent film appearances.
1993 (R) 110m/C Richard Gere, Lena Olin, Anne Bancroft, Tom Irwin, Delroy Lindo, Bruce Altman, Lauren Tom; **D:** Mike Figgis; **W:** Michael Cristofer, Eric Roth; **M:** Maurice Jarre. VHS COL ♫ 1/2

Mr. Kingstreet's War An idealistic game warden and his wife defend the wildlife of Africa against the fighting Italian and British armies at the dawn of WWII. **AKA:** Heroes Die Hard.
1971 92m/C John Saxon, Tippi Hedren, Rossano Brazzi, Brian O'Shaughnessy; **D:** Percival Rubens. VHS, Beta VCI ♫♫ 1/2

Mr. Klein Cleverly plotted script and fine direction in this dark and intense film about a French-Catholic merchant who buys valuables from Jews trying to escape Nazi occupied France in 1942, paying far less than what the treasures are worth. Ironically, he is later mistaken for a Jew by the same name who has been using this man's reputation as a cover.
1975 (PG) 122m/C Alain Delon, Jeanne Moreau; **D:** Joseph Losey. VHS, Beta $59.95 COL, SWC ♫♫♫

Mr. Love A meek gardener is perceived by neighbors as a fool until he dies and numerous women arrive for his funeral. Is it his cologne? The radishes?
1986 (PG-13) 91m/C Barry Jackson, Maurice Denham, Margaret Tyzack, Linda Marlowe; **D:** Roy Battersby; **M:** Willy Russell. VHS, Beta $19.98 WAR ♫♫ 1/2

Mr. Lucky Likeable wartime drama about a gambler who hopes to swindle a philanthropic organization, but then falls in love and determines to help the group in a fundraising effort. Grant is, no surprise, excellent as the seemingly cynical con artist who actually has a heart of gold. Cliched, but nonetheless worthwhile. Later developed into a television series.
1943 99m/B Cary Grant, Laraine Day, Charles Bickford, Gladys Cooper, Paul Stewart, Henry Stephenson, Florence Bates; **D:** H.C. Potter. VHS, Beta $19.98 MED, RXM, TTC ♫♫♫

Mr. Majestyk When a Vietnam veteran's attempt to start an honest business is thwarted by Mafia hitmen and the police, he goes after them with a vengeance.
1974 (PG) 103m/C Charles Bronson, Al Lettieri, Linda Cristal, Lee Purcell; **D:** Richard Fleischer; **W:** Elmore Leonard; **M:** Charles Bernstein. VHS, Beta $14.95 MGM ♫♫ 1/2

Mister Mean A man who once worked for a mafia don is now given the task of rubbing him out. For Cosa Nostra diehards and gluttons for Roman scenery.
1977 98m/C Fred Williamson; **D:** Fred Williamson. VHS, Beta NO ♫

Mr. Mike's Mondo Video A bizarre, outrageous comedy special declared too wild for television conceived by the "Saturday Night Live" alumnus Mr. Mike.
1979 (R) 75m/C Michael O'Donoghue, Dan Aykroyd, Jane Curtin, Carrie Fisher, Teri Garr, Joan Haskett, Deborah Harry, Margot Kidder, Bill Murray, Laraine Newman, Gilda Radner, Julius LaRosa, Paul Shaffer, Sid Vicious; **W:** Mitch Glazer. VHS, Beta NO ♫♫

Mr. Mom A tireless auto exec loses his job and stays home with the kids while his wife becomes the breadwinner. He's forced to cope with the rigors of housework and child care, resorting to drugs, alcohol and soap operas. Keaton's hilarious as the homebound dad chased by killer appliances and poker buddy to the ladies in the neighborhood.

1983 (PG) 92m/C Michael Keaton, Teri Garr, Christopher Lloyd, Martin Mull, Ann Jillian, Jeffrey Tambor, Edie McClurg, Valri Bromfield; **D:** Stan Dragoti; **W:** John Hughes. **VHS, Beta** $29.98 *LIV, VES* 🐾🐾🐾

Mr. Moto's Last Warning One of the better in the series of Mr. Moto, the wily detective! Lorre is convincing in the title role and gets good support from character villains Carradine and Sanders in this story of saboteurs converging on the Suez Canal plotting to blow up the French Fleet.
1939 71m/B Peter Lorre, George Sanders, Ricardo Cortez, John Carradine, Virginia Field, Robert Coote; **D:** Norman Foster. **VHS, Beta** $16.95 *SNC, NOS, CAB* 🐾🐾🐾

Mr. Moto's Last Warning/ Meeting at Midnight The first film finds Moto at the Suez Canal trying to save France's flotilla from a deadly conspiracy. The second feature is classic Charlie Chan fare. This time his driver, Birmingham, gets Chan caught in the midst of the occult.
1944 130m/B Sidney Toler, Peter Lorre, Mantan Moreland. **VHS, Beta** *AOV* 🐾🐾🐾

Mr. Music Crosby is a successful songwriter who would rather enjoy life on the golf course than pen any more tunes. He's persuaded by his secretary to help out an old-time producer who's fallen on hard times by writing a new Broadway show. Light-hearted fluff. Based on the play "Accent on Youth" by Samson Raphaelson which had been filmed in 1935. ♫Life is So Precious; Accidents Will Happen; High on the List; Wouldn't It Be Funny; Wasn't I There?; Mr. Music; Once More the Blue and White; Milady; Then You'll Be Home.
1950 113m/B Bing Crosby, Nancy Olson, Charles Coburn, Robert Stack, Tom Ewell, Ruth Hussey, Charles Kemper, Donald Woods, Gower Champion, Marge Champion; *Cameos:* Groucho Marx, Peggy Lee; **D:** Richard Haydn. **VHS** $14.95 *PAR* 🐾🐾½

Mr. Nanny For those who fear change, this predictable plot should serve as comforting assurance that Hollywood will still sacrifice substance for the quick buck. Basic story line has the child-hating Hulkster playing nanny/bodyguard to a couple of bratty kids. Meanwhile, his arch rival (Johansen) hatches a scheme to gain world dominance by kidnapping the kids for the ransom of their father's top secret computer chip. Never fear—in this world, the good guys kick butt, naturally, and everyone learns a lesson.
1993 (PG) 85m/C Hulk Hogan, Sherman Hemsley, Austin Pendleton, Robert Gorman, Madeline Zima, Mother Love, David Johansen; **D:** Michael Gottlieb; **W:** Ed Rugoff, Michael Gottlieb; **M:** David Johansen, Brian Koonin. **VHS** *NLC, COL* 🐾🐾

Mr. Nice Guy In the near future, a hired gun strives for national recognition as the best of his now legitimate profession. Comedy with few laughs.
1986 (PG-13) 92m/C Michael MacDonald, Jan Smithers, Joe Silver. **VHS, Beta** $19.95 *STE, NWV* 🐾

Mr. North Capra-corn fable about a charming, bright Yale graduate who encounters admiration and disdain from upper-crust Rhode Island residents when news of his miraculous "cures" spreads. Marks the directorial debut of Danny Huston, son of John Huston, who co-wrote the script and served as executive producer before dying several weeks into shooting. Set in the 1920s and adapted from Thornton Wilder's "Theophilus North."

1988 (PG) 90m/C Anthony Edwards, Robert Mitchum, Lauren Bacall, Harry Dean Stanton, Anjelica Huston, Mary Stuart Masterson, Virginia Madsen, Tammy Grimes, David Warner, Hunter Carson, Christopher Durang, Mark Metcalf, Katherine Houghton; **D:** Danny Huston; **W:** John Huston, Janet Roach; **M:** David McHugh. **VHS, Beta** *NO* 🐾🐾½

Mr. Peabody & the Mermaid Lightweight fish story about a middle-aged married man who hooks a beautiful mermaid while fishing in the Caribbean and eventually falls in love with her. Powell is smooth as always, though hampered by the unrestrained absurdity of it all. Based on the novel by Guy and Constance Jones. Also available colorized.
1948 89m/B William Powell, Ann Blyth, Irene Hervey, Andrea King, Clinton Sundberg, Art Smith; **D:** Irving Pichel; **W:** Nunnally Johnson. **VHS** $14.98 *REP* 🐾🐾½

Mr. Peek-A-Boo A French clerk discovers he has the ability to walk through walls. Although friends try to coax him into a life of crime, he instead comes to the aid of an English girl who is being blackmailed. Good-natured French comedy was shot with English dialogue for the American market. *AKA:* Garou Garou le Passe Muraille.
1950 74m/B Joan Greenwood, Bourvil, Marcel Arnold, Roger Treville; **D:** Jean Boyer. **VHS, Beta** $16.95 *SNC* 🐾🐾½

Mr. Reeder in Room 13 Based on the mystery stories created by Edgar Wallace, Mr. Reeder (a cultured English gentleman who fights crime) enlists the aid of a young man to get evidence on a gang of counterfeiters.
1938 66m/B Gibb McLaughlin. **VHS, Beta** $24.95 *VYY* 🐾🐾

Mister Roberts Crew of a Navy cargo freighter in the South Pacific during WWII relieves the boredom of duty with a series of elaborate practical jokes, mostly at the expense of their long-suffering and slightly crazy captain, who then determines that he will get even. The ship's cargo officer, Mr. Roberts, longs to be transferred to a fighting vessel and see some action. Originally a hit Broadway play (based on the novel by Thomas Heggen) which also featured Fonda in the title role. Great performance from Lemmon as Ensign Pulver. Powell's last film. Sequelled in 1964 by "Ensign Pulver," and later a short-lived TV series as well as a live TV special. Newly transferred in 1988 from a pristine stereo print.
1955 120m/C Henry Fonda, James Cagney, Jack Lemmon, William Powell, Betsy Palmer, Ward Bond, Harry Carey Jr., Nick Adams, Phil Carey, Ken Curtis, Martin Milner, Jack Pennick, Perry Lopez, Patrick Wayne; **D:** John Ford, Mervyn LeRoy; **W:** Frank Nugent, Joshua Logan; **M:** Franz Waxman. Academy Awards '55: Best Supporting Actor (Lemmon); Nominations: Best Picture; Academy Awards '55: Best Sound; National Board of Review Awards '55: 10 Best Films of the Year. **VHS, Beta** $19.98 *WAR, BTV* 🐾🐾🐾🐾

Mr. Robinson Crusoe Rollicking adventure in the South Seas as Fairbanks makes a bet that he can live on a desert island for a year without being left any refinements of civilization. Lucky for him, a woman arrives. Also written by Fairbanks.
1932 76m/B Douglas Fairbanks Sr., William Farnum, Maria Alba, Earle Brown; **D:** Edward Sutherland; **W:** Douglas Fairbanks Sr.; **M:** Alfred Newman. **VHS, Beta** $19.95 *NOS, GPV, CCB* 🐾🐾½

Mr. Saturday Night Crystal, in his directorial debut, stars as Buddy Young, Jr., a self-destructive comedian whose career spans five decades. His nasty one-liners and witty jokes combine with poignancy in this satisfying comedy/drama. Paymer is excellent as Young's long-suffering, faithful brother and manager. Watch for Lewis in a cameo role. Expectations were very high and the box office results were disappointing, but fans of Crystal shouldn't miss this one. The video also includes additional footage and outtakes selected and hosted by Crystal.
1992 (R) 118m/C Billy Crystal, David Paymer, Julie Warner, Helen Hunt, Mary Mara, Jerry Orbach, Ron Silver, Sage Allen, Jackie Gayle, Carl Ballantine, Slappy White, Conrad Janis; *Cameos:* Jerry Lewis; **D:** Billy Crystal; **W:** Billy Crystal, Babaloo Mandel, Lowell Ganz; **M:** Marc Shaiman. **VHS** $19.95 *COL, IME, MOV* 🐾🐾½

Mr. Scarface A young man searches for the man who murdered his father years earlier in a dark alley.
1977 (R) 85m/C Jack Palance, Edmund Purdom, Al Cliver, Harry Baer, Gisela Hahn; **D:** Fernando Di Leo. **VHS, Beta** $19.95 *CNG* 🐾

Mr. Skeffington A super-grade soap opera spanning 26 years in the life of a ravishing, spoiled New York socialite. The beauty with a fondness for bedrooms marries for convenience, abuses her husband, then enjoys a highly equitable divorce settlement. Years later when diphtheria leaves her totally deformed and no man will have her, she is saved by her former husband. Based on the novel by "Elizabeth" (Mary Annette Beauchamp Russell) and adapted by "Casablanca's" Julius and Philip Epstein.
1944 147m/B Bette Davis, Claude Rains, Walter Abel, Richard Waring, George Coulouris, John Alexander; **D:** Vincent Sherman. **VHS, Beta** $19.95 *MGM* 🐾🐾🐾

Mr. Skitch Weak Rogers offering. Couple loses their farm and begins cross country jaunt with mishaps at every turn. All ends well when their daughter meets an Army cadet, but few laughs and lots of loose ends.
1933 70m/B Will Rogers, ZaSu Pitts, Rochelle Hudson, Charles Starrett; **D:** James Cruze. **VHS** $19.98 *FOX, FCT* 🐾🐾

Mr. Smith Goes to Washington Another classic from Hollywood's golden year of 1939. Jimmy Stewart is an idealistic and naive young man selected to fill in for an ailing Senator. Upon his arrival in the Capitol, he is inundated by a multitude of corrupt politicians. He takes a stand for his beliefs and tries to denounce many of those he feels are unfit for their positions, meeting with opposition from all sides. Great cast is highlighted by Stewart in one of his most endearing performances. Quintessential Capra tale sharply adapted from Lewis Foster's story. Outstanding in every regard.
1939 130m/B James Stewart, Jean Arthur, Edward Arnold, Claude Rains, Thomas Mitchell, Beulah Bondi, Eugene Pallette, Guy Kibbee, Harry Carey Sr., H.B. Warner, Porter Hall, Jack Carson, Charles Lane; **D:** Frank Capra; **W:** Sidney Buchman; **M:** Dimitri Tiomkin. Academy Awards '39: Best Story; Nominations: Best Actor (Stewart), Best Director (Capra), Best Interior Decoration, Best Picture, Best Screenplay, Best Sound, Best Supporting Actor (Rains, Carey), Best Score; National Board of Review Awards '39: 10 Best Films of the Year; New York Film Critics Awards '39: Best Actor (Stewart). **VHS, Beta** $19.95 *COL, HMV* 🐾🐾🐾🐾

Mr. Superinvisible Searching to cure the common cold, a bumbling scientist invents a bizarre virus, then strives with his loyal (of course) sheepdog to keep it from falling into the wrong hands. The Disney-like

plot, featuring enemy agents and invisibilty may appeal to youngsters. *AKA:* Mr. Invisible; L'Inafferrabile Invincible.
1973 (G) 90m/C Dean Jones, Ingeborg Schoener, Gastone Moschin; *D:* Anthony M. (Antonio Margheretti) Dawson. **VHS, Beta** NO ♫♫

Mr. Sycamore A sappy mail carrier escapes his badgering wife by sprouting into a tree. A potentially whimsical piece that wilts.
1974 90m/C Jason Robards Jr., Jean Simmons, Sandy Dennis; *D:* Pancho Kohner; *M:* Maurice Jarre. **VHS, Beta $39.95** WOV ♫1/2

Mr. Walkie Talkie Tired of a sargeant's jabber-jaws, a soldier requests to be relocated to the front lines, only to find his catty comrade has followed. Set during the Korean War and featuring some truly amusing escapades set between the lulls in the war.
1952 65m/B William Tracy, Joseph Sawyer; *D:* Fred Guiol. **VHS, Beta** NO ♫♫

Mr. Winkle Goes to War A weak, nerdy former banker is drafted for service during WWII and proves himself a hero by bulldozing a Japanese foxhole. Bits of genuine war footage add a measure of realism to an otherwise banal flag-waving comedy that is based on a novel by Theodore Pratt.
1944 80m/B Edward G. Robinson, Ruth Warrick, Richard Lane, Robert Armstrong; *D:* Alfred E. Green. **VHS, Beta $59.95** COL ♫♫

Mr. Wise Guy The East Side Kids break out of reform school to clear one of the Kids' brother of a murder charge. Typical pre-Bowery Boys vehicle.
1942 70m/B Leo Gorcey, Huntz Hall, Billy Gilbert, Guinn Williams, Benny Rubin, Douglas Fowley, Ann Doran, Jack Mulhall, Warren Hymer, David Gorcey; *D:* William Nigh. **VHS, Beta $19.95** NOS, DVT, HEG ♫♫

Mr. Wonderful Bittersweet (rather than purely romantic) look at love and romance. Divorced Con Ed worker Gus (Dillon) is hard up for cash and tries to marry off ex-wife Lee (Sciorra) so he can use her alimony to invest in a bowling alley with his buddies. Routine flick's saved by the cast, who manage to bring a small measure of believability to a transparent plot. Minghella was a hit with his first film "Truly, Madly, Deeply" but may find that fame can be fleeting with this second effort.
1993 (PG-13) 99m/C Matt Dillon, Annabella Sciorra, William Hurt, Mary-Louise Parker, Luis Guzman, Dan Hedaya, Vincent D'Onofrio; *D:* Anthony Minghella; *W:* Amy Schor, Vicki Polon; *M:* Michael Gore. **VHS, Beta** WAR ♫♫1/2

Mr. Wong, Detective The first in the Mr. Wong series, the cunning detective traps a killer who feigns guilt to throw suspicion away from himself. The plot is loaded with the usual twists and villains. However, Karloff is a standout.
1938 69m/B Boris Karloff, Grant Withers; *D:* William Nigh. **VHS, Beta $19.95** NOS, MRV, HHT ♫♫

Mr. Wong in Chinatown Third of the Mr. Wong series finds James Lee Wong investigating the murder of a wealthy Chinese woman. She had been helping to fund the purchase of airplanes to equip China in its 1930s' struggle with Japan.
1939 70m/B Boris Karloff, Grant Withers, William Royle, Marjorie Reynolds, Peter George Lynn, Lotus Long, Richard Loo; *D:* William Nigh. **VHS $14.95** VYY, MRV, SNC ♫1/2

Mistral's Daughter Frothy miniseries, based on the Judith Krantz novel, about a French artist and his relationship with three beautiful women. Formulaic TV melodrama offers sexual scenes and revealing glimpses.

Produced, like other Krantz miniseries, by author's hubby, Steve.
1984 390m/C Stefanie Powers, Lee Remick, Stacy Keach, Robert Urich, Timothy Dalton; *D:* Douglas Hickox; *M:* Vladimir Cosma. **VHS, Beta $79.95** LIV ♫1/2

Mistress A classic Japanese period piece about an innocent woman who believes she's married to a ruthless industrialist, only to find he is already married and she is but his mistress. Her love for a medical student unleashes tragedy. Subtly moving in a low-key way; starkly beautiful in black and white. In Japanese, with English subtitles. *AKA:* Wild Geese.
1953 106m/B Hideko Takamine, Hiroshi Akutagawa; *D:* Shiro Toyoda. **VHS, Beta $79.95** SUE, ING ♫♫♫

Mistress Weepy made-for-television melodrama about a woman who makes a living as a mistress. When her lover dies, she must learn to stand on her own two feet.
1987 96m/C Victoria Principal, Alan Rachins, Don Murray; *D:* Michael Tuchner; *M:* Michael Convertino. **VHS $79.98** REP ♫1/2

Mistress A weak script does in a formidable cast in a behind-the-scenes look at movie making. Wuhl plays Marvin Landisman, a failed director/screenwriter, who's approached by has-been producer Jack Roth (Landau) who says he's found a backer to finance a movie from one of Marvin's old scripts. It turns out Roth has three men (De Niro, Aiello, and Wallach) ready to finance the film as long as each of their mistresses, who all have acting ambitions, gets the starring role. Double-dealing at a bargain basement level sets up the rest of this lifeless comedy.
1991 (R) 100m/C Robert Wuhl, Martin Landau, Robert De Niro, Eli Wallach, Danny Aiello, Sheryl Lee Ralph, Jean Smart, Tuesday Weld, Jace Alexander, Laurie Metcalf; *Cameos:* Christopher Walken, Ernest Borgnine; *D:* Barry Primus; *W:* J.F. Lawton, Barry Primus. **VHS $92.98** LIV, PMS ♫♫

Mistress of the Apes A woman searches for her missing husband in Africa with a group of scientists and discovers a tribe of near-men, who may be the missing link in evolution (or perhaps, a professional football team). Into their little group she is accepted, becoming their queen. Buchanan earned his reputation as a maker of horrible films honestly. Includes the songs "Mistress of the Apes" and "Ape Lady."
1979 (R) 88m/C Jenny Neumann, Barbara Leigh, Garth Pillsbury, Walt Robin, Stuart Lancaster, Suzy Mandel; *D:* Larry Buchanan; *W:* Larry Buchanan. **VHS, Beta $39.95** MON Woof!

Mistress of the World A scientist, aided by Swedish Intelligence agent Ventura, works to protect his gravity-altering invention from Chinese agents. Partly based on a German serial from the silent film era, but not up to director Dieterle's usual fare. A must-see for Ventura fans and Mabuse mavens.
1959 107m/C Martha Hyer, Micheline Presle, Gino Cervi, Lino Ventura, Sabu, Wolfgang Preiss; *D:* William Dieterle. **VHS, Beta** VMK ♫♫

Mistress Pamela When young Pamela goes to work in the household of handsome Lord Devonish, he sets about in wild pursuit of her virginity. Loosely based on the 1740 work "Pamela" by Samuel Richardson, considered the first modern English novel. Read the book unless you only have 95 minutes to spend finding out who gets what.
1974 (R) 95m/C Anne Michelle, Julian Barnes, Anna Quayle, Rosemary Dunham; *D:* Jim O'Connor. **VHS, Beta** NO ♫1/2

Misty Ladd and Smith are two kids who capture a wild pony and teach it to run around in circles and step over things. Based on Marguerite Henry's bestselling "Misty of Chincoteague," and filmed on an island off the coast of Virginia.
1961 92m/C David Ladd, Arthur O'Connell, Pam Smith; *D:* James B. Clark. **VHS $14.95** PAR, WAX, FCT ♫♫

Misunderstood A former black market merchant has to learn how to relate to his sons after his wife dies. The father, now a legitimate businessman, is more concerned with running his shipping business than growing closer to his boys. Fine acting can't overcome a transparent plot.
1984 (PG) 92m/C Gene Hackman, Susan Anspach, Henry Thomas, Rip Torn, Huckleberry Fox; *D:* Jerry Schatzberg. **VHS, Beta $79.95** MGM ♫♫1/2

Misunderstood A father learns his lonely son is full of love and sensitivity when a tragedy reveals that it is this son who takes the blame for all the wrongs his brother commits.
1987 101m/C Anthony Quayle, Stefano Colagrande, Simone Gianozzi, John Sharp; *D:* Luigi Comencini. **VHS, Beta $59.95** IMP ♫♫1/2

Mitchell Tough cop battles drug traffic and insipid script. Big screen release with that certain TV look.
1975 (R) 90m/C Joe Don Baker, Linda Evans, Martin Balsam, John Saxon, Merlin Olsen, Harold J. Stone; *D:* Andrew V. McLaglen. **VHS $9.95** SIM, VTR ♫

Mixed Blood From the renowned underground film-maker, a dark comedy that examines the seedy drug subculture in New York. Violent, fast, and funny.
1984 (R) 98m/C Marilia Pera, Richard Vlacia, Linda Kerridge, Geraldine Smith, Angel David; *D:* Paul Morrissey; *W:* Paul Morrissey. **VHS, Beta $59.95** MED ♫♫1/2

M'Lady's Court A lawyer searching for an heiress in a convent of lusty maidens has loads of fun. None too captivating.
198? 92m/C Sonia Jeanine, Maja Hoppe. **VHS, Beta $29.95** MED ♫

Mo' Better Blues Not one of his more cohesive or compelling works, Lee's fourth feature is on the surface a backstage jazz biopic. But all Lee features are vitally concerned with complicated racial issues, and though subtle, this is no exception. Bleek Gilliam is a handsome, accomplished jazz trumpeter who divides his limited extra-curricular time between Clarke (newcomer Williams) and Indigo (junior Lee sibling Joie). What's interesting is not so much the story of self-interested musician and ladies' man Gilliam, but the subtle racial issues his life draws into focus. The Branford Marsalis Quartet provides the music for Bleek's group, scored by Lee's dad Bill (on whose life the script is loosely based).
1990 (R) 129m/C Denzel Washington, Spike Lee, Joie Lee, Wesley Snipes, Cynda Williams, Giancarlo Esposito, Robin Harris, Bill Nunn, John Turturro, Dick Anthony Williams, Ruben Blades, Nicholas Turturro, Samuel L. Jackson, Abbey Lincoln, Tracy C. Johns, Joe Seneca; *D:* Spike Lee; *W:* Spike Lee; *M:* Branford Marsalis, Bill Lee. **VHS, Beta $19.95** MCA, FCT ♫♫1/2

Mo' Money Damon Wayans is a small-time con-artist who is inspired to go straight by a beautiful woman (Dash). He lands a job at the credit card company she works for, but temptation overcomes him, he swipes some plastic, and the scamming begins anew. With the help of his younger brother (played by real-life younger brother Marlon), they get involved in an even bigger, more

dangerous scam being operated by the credit card company's head of security. Crude formula comedy driven by energetic, inventive performances by the brothers Wayans. Needless to say, will be especially enjoyed by fans of TV's "In Living Color."
1992 (R) 97m/C Damon Wayans, Marlon Wayans, Stacey Dash, Joe Santos, John Diehl, Harry J. Lennix, Mark Beltzman, Quincy Wong, Larry Brandenburg, Almayvonne; **D:** Peter Macdonald; **W:** Damon Wayans; **M:** Jay Gruska. **VHS, Beta, 8mm $19.95** *COL* ♫♫½

Moana, a Romance of the Golden Age An early look through American eyes at the society of the people of Samoa, in the Pacific Islands. Picturesque successor to Flaherty's "Nanook of the North."
1926 76m/B Ta'avale, Fa'amgase, Moana; **D:** Robert Flaherty. **VHS $29.95** *GPV, FCT* ♫♫♫½

Mob Boss Gangster films spoof starring Hickey as the head of a successful California crime ring. When his beautiful wife conspires to have him killed, he is left just breaths away from his demise. He calls his nerdy son to his bedside to ask him to take over the family business. But this kid thinks that money laundering requires detergent! Take this one down for a walk by the river in its new cement shoes.
1990 (R) 93m/C Eddie Dezen, Morgan Fairchild, William Hickey, Stuart Whitman; **D:** Fred Olen Ray. **VHS $89.95** *VMK* ♫

Mob Story Vernon stars as a big-wig mob boss on the run from the government and a few of his "closest" friends. He plans to disappear into Canada, but if his girl (Kidder) and best friend (Waxman) find him first he'll be traveling in a body-bag. Very silly, but fun.
1990 98m/C John Vernon, Margot Kidder, Al Waxman, Kate Vernon; **D:** Gabriel Markiw, Jancarlo Markiw. **VHS, Beta** *IME* ♫½

Mob War A bloody Mafia adventure in which a sausage factory plays a large role.
1978 102m/C VHS, Beta $79.98 *VCD* Woof!

Mob War A war breaks out between the head of New York's underworld and a media genius. After deciding to become partners, the "family" tries to take over. For fun, count how many times the word "respect" pops up in the script. Tries hard but fails.
1988 (R) 96m/C John Christian, David Henry Keller, Jake La Motta, Johnny Stumper; **D:** J. Christian Ingvordsen. **VHS, Beta $79.98** *MCG* ♫½

Mobsters It sounded like a great idea, casting the hottest young actors of the '90s as youthful racketeers "Lucky" Luciano, Meyer Lansky, Bugsy Siegel, and Frank Costello. But it would take an FBI probe to straighten out the blood-choked plot, as the pals' loyalties get tested the hard way in a dismembered narrative. Sicker than the violence is a seeming endorsement of the glamorous hoods.
1991 (R) 104m/C Christian Slater, Patrick Dempsey, Richard Grieco, Costas Mandylor, Anthony Quinn, F. Murray Abraham, Lara Flynn Boyle, Michael Gambon, Christopher Penn; **D:** Michael Karbelnikoff; **W:** Nicholas Kazan. **VHS, Beta $19.98** *MCA, CCB* ♫½

Moby Dick This adaptation of Herman Melville's high seas saga features Peck as Captain Ahab. His obsession with desire for revenge upon the great white whale, Moby Dick, isn't always believable, but the moments that click, however, make the film more than worthwhile.

1956 116m/C Gregory Peck, Richard Basehart, Orson Welles, Leo Genn, Harry Andrews, Friedrich Ledebur; **D:** John Huston; **W:** Ray Bradbury, John Huston. **VHS, Beta $19.95** *FOX, BMV, HMV* ♫♫♫

Mockery Chaney plays a peasant working for a Russian countess. He becomes involved in a peasant revolution against the rich and threatens the countess but eventually saves her from the mob.
1927 75m/B Lon Chaney Sr., Barbara Bedford, Ricardo Cortez, Emily Fitzroy; **D:** Benjamin Christiansen. **VHS $29.95** *FCT* ♫♫½

The Mod Squad The ultimate sixties series features a trio of young misfits who are recruited by a gruff police captain in Southern California. Their undercover assignments take them into the counter-culture. The series was created by former L.A. police officer Bud Ruskin, and was based on his own experiences. Two episodes per tape: "Teeth of the Barracuda" explains the formation of the Mod Squad, while "Mother of Sorrow" finds a generation gap leading to murder. Additional episodes are available.
1968 60m/C Michael Cole, Clarence Williams III, Peggy Lipton, Tige Andrews, Lee Grant, Richard Dreyfuss. **VHS $19.99** *MOV* ♫♫½

Model Behavior Fresh from college, an aspiring photographer pines for a glamorous model.
1982 86m/C Richard Bekins, Bruce Lyons, Cindy Harrel; **D:** Bud Gardner. **VHS, Beta $79.98** *LIV* ♫½

Model by Day When New York model Janssen's father is murdered, she takes up martial arts training and becomes the vengeful "Lady X." Then she becomes the prime suspect in a murder and finds herself falling for a plainclothes cop. Fair amount of action, somewhat less exploitive than usual for the genre.
1994 (R) 89m/C Famke Janssen, Stephen Shellan, Shannon Tweed, Sean Young; **D:** Christian Duguay. **VHS, Beta $92.95** *ACA* ♫½

Modern Girls Teen comedy about three bubble-headed LA rock groupies and their various wild adventures during a single night on the town. Surprising in that the three lead actresses waste their talents in this lesson in exploitation. Bruce Springsteen's younger sister portrays a drug user.
1986 (PG-13) 82m/C Cynthia Gibb, Daphne Zuniga, Virginia Madsen; **D:** Jerry Kramer. **VHS, Beta $19.95** *PAR* ♫½

Modern Love An average slob realizes that marriage, fatherhood and in-law-ship isn't quite what he expected. Benson stars, directs and produces as well as co-starring with real-life family DeVito. A plotless hodge-podge of bits that were more successful in "Look Who's Talking" and "Parenthood."
1990 90m/C Robby Benson, Karla DeVito, Rue McClanahan, Kaye Ballard, Frankie Valli, Cliff Bemis, Louise Lasser, Burt Reynolds, Lyric Benson; **D:** Robby Benson. **VHS, Beta** NO ♫

Modern Problems A man involved in a nuclear accident discovers he has acquired telekinetic powers, which he uses to turn the tables on his professional and romantic rivals. A fine cast but an unsuccessful fission trip.
1981 (PG) 93m/C Chevy Chase, Patti D'Arbanville, Mary Kay Place, Brian Doyle-Murray, Nell Carter, Dabney Coleman; **D:** Ken Shapiro. **VHS, Beta $14.98** *FOX* ♫♫

Modern Romance The romantic misadventures of a neurotic film editor who is hopelessly in love with his girlfriend but can't seem to maintain a normal relationship with her. Smart and hilarious at times and always

simmering with anxiety. Offers an honest look at relationships as well as an accurate portrait of filmmaking.
1981 (R) 102m/C Albert Brooks, Kathryn Harrold, Bruno Kirby, George Kennedy, James L. Brooks, Bob Einstein; **D:** Albert Brooks; **W:** Albert Brooks, Monica Johnson. **VHS, Beta $14.95** *COL* ♫♫♫

Modern Times This "mostly" silent film finds Chaplin playing a factory worker who goes crazy from his repetitious job on an assembly line and his boss' demands for greater speed and efficiency. Ultimately encompassing the tyranny of machine over man, this cinematic masterpiece has more relevance today than ever. Chaplin wrote the musical score which produced the tune "Smile." Look for a young Gloria De Haven as one of Goddard's sisters; she's the real-life daughter of Chaplin's assistant director.
1936 87m/B Charlie Chaplin, Paulette Goddard, Henry Bergman, Stanley Sandford, Gloria De Haven, Chester Conklin; **D:** Charlie Chaplin; **W:** Charlie Chaplin; **M:** Charlie Chaplin. **VHS, Beta $19.98** *FOX, HMV* ♫♫♫♫

The Moderns One of the quirkier directors around, this time Rudolph tries a comedic period piece about the avant-garde art society of 1920s Paris. Fleshed out with some familiar characters (Ernest Hemingway, Gertrude Stein) and some strange art-world types. The tone is not consistently funny but, instead, romantic as the main characters clash over art and love.
1988 (R) 126m/C Keith Carradine, Linda Fiorentino, John Lone, Genevieve Bujold, Geraldine Chaplin, Wallace Shawn, Kevin J. O'Connor; **D:** Alan Rudolph; **W:** Alan Rudolph; **M:** Mark Isham. **VHS, Beta, 8mm $14.98** *SUE, NLC* ♫♫♫

Modigliani Life of dissolute 19th-century painter Modigliani (Philipe), which tracks his affairs with British poet Beatrice Hastings (Palmer) and later mistress Jeanne (Aimee), who commits suicide shortly before his death. Female performances make up for the lackluster lead. Becker inherited the film from director Max Ophuls, who co-wrote the screenplay but who died before the start of production. In French with English subtitles. **AKA:** Montparnasse 19; The Lovers of Montparnasse; Modigliani of Montparnasse.
1958 110m/B Gerard Philippe, Lilli Palmer, Anouk Aimee, Gerard Sety, Lino Ventura, Lila Kedrova, Lea Padovani; **D:** Jacques Becker; **W:** Max Ophuls, Henri Jeanson, Jacques Becker. **VHS $59.95** *FCT* ♫♫½

Mogambo Remake of "Red Dust," this is the steamy story of a love triangle between an African game hunter, a proper British lady, and an American showgirl in the jungles of Kenya.
1953 115m/C Clark Gable, Ava Gardner, Grace Kelly; **D:** John Ford. Academy Awards '53 Nominations: Best Actress (Gardner), Best Supporting Actress (Kelly); Golden Globe Awards '54: Best Supporting Actress (Kelly); National Board of Review Awards '53: 10 Best Films of the Year. **VHS, Beta $19.98** *MGM, FCT, CCB* ♫♫♫

Mohammed: Messenger of God Sprawling saga of the genesis of the religion of Islam, with Quinn portraying Mohammad's uncle, Hamza, an honored warrior. The story behind the movie might prove much more successful as a sequel than did the movie itself. The filming itself created a religious controversy. **AKA:** The Message; Al-Ris-Alah.

1977 (PG) 180m/C Damien Thomas, Anthony Quinn, Irene Papas, Michael Ansara, Johnny Sekka, Michael Forest, Neville Jason; D: Moustapha Akkad; M: Maurice Jarre. VHS NO ✔✔

Mohawk A cowboy and his Indian maiden try to stop a war between Indian tribes and fanatical landowners.
1956 80m/C Rita Gam, Neville Brand, Scott Brady, Lori Nelson; D: Kurt Neumann. VHS, Beta $19.95 NOS, MRV, GEM ✔✔½

Mole Men Against the Son of Hercules Italian muscleman Maciste battles the pale-skinned denizens of an underground city.
1961 ?m/C Mark Forest. VHS, Beta $16.95 SNC ✔½

The Mole People A really bad fifties creature feature which finds two archeologists accidentally discovering an underground civilization of albinos who shun all forms of light. They've also enslaved the local populace of half-human, half-mole creatures who decide to help the good guys escape by rising up in a revolt against their evil masters. When the weapon of choice is a flashlight you know not to expect much.
1956 78m/B John Agar, Cynthia Patrick, Hugh Beaumont, Alan Napier, Nestor Paiva, Phil Chambers; D: Virgil W. Vogel; W: Laszlo Gorog. VHS $14.98 MCA ✔

Molly and Gina The very different lives of Molly and Gina intersect suddenly when their boyfriends are killed in the street by gunfire. They are drawn into the underworld of gun-runners and violence, as they seek justice for the men they loved.
1994 (R) 90m/C Frances Fisher, Natasha Gregson Wagner, Bruce Weitz, Stella Stevens, Peter Fonda; D: Paul Leder; W: Reuben Leder; M: Dana Walden. VHS $92.95 APX ✔✔

Molly & Lawless John Average western, with Miles the wife of a sadistic sheriff who helps a prisoner escape the gallows so they can run away together. Enough cliches for the whole family to enjoy.
1972 90m/C Sam Elliott, Vera Miles; D: Gary Nelson. VHS, Beta NO ✔✔

Molly Maguires Dramatization based on a true story, concerns a group of miners called the Molly Maguires who resort to using terrorist tactics in their fight for better working conditions during the Pennsylvania Irish coal mining rebellion in the 1870s. During their reign of terror, the Mollies are infiltrated by a Pinkerton detective who they mistakenly believe is a new recruit. It has its moments but never fully succeeds. Returned less than fifteen percent of its initial eleven million dollar investment.
1970 (PG) 123m/C Sean Connery, Richard Harris, Samantha Eggar, Frank Finlay; D: Martin Ritt; M: Henry Mancini. VHS, Beta $14.95 PAR, CCB ✔✔½

Mom When his mother is bitten by a flesh-eater, Clay Dwyer is at a loss as to what to do. How do you tell your own mother that she must be destroyed, lest she continue to devour human flesh? A campy horror/comedy.
1989 (R) 95m/C Mark Thomas Miller, Art Evans, Mary McDonough, Jeanne Bates, Brion James, Stella Stevens, Claudia Christian; D: Patrick Rand. VHS $79.95 COL ✔✔½

Mom & Dad An innocent young girl's one night of passion leads to an unwanted pregnancy. Stock footage of childbirth and a lecture on the evils of syphilis concludes this campy schlock that features the national anthem. Banned or denied release for years, this movie is now a cult favorite for its time-

capsule glimpse at conventional 1940s sexual attitudes.
1947 97m/B Hardie Albright, Sarah Blake, George Eldridge, June Carlson, Jimmy Clark, Bob Lowell; D: William Beaudine. VHS, Beta $19.95 VDM

Mom and Dad Save the World A suburban housewife (Garr) is transported along with her husband in the family station wagon to the planet Spengo, ruled by King Tod Spengo (Lovitz), who has fallen in love with her and wants to save her from his plans to blow up Earth. While trying to prevent the king from marrying her and killing him, Garr and Jones wind up in many goofy situations and wind up saving the Earth from its imminent doom. Uninspired comedy just isn't funny, and the excellent cast is misused, especially Idle and Shawn. Save this one for the kiddies.
1992 (PG) 87m/C Teri Garr, Jeffrey Jones, Jon Lovitz, Eric Idle, Wallace Shawn, Dwier Brown, Kathy Ireland, Thalmus Rasulala; D: Greg Beeman; M: Jerry Goldsmith. VHS $92.99 HBO ✔½

Mom, the Wolfman and Me An 11-year-old girl arranges and manages the love affair of her mother, an ultra-liberated photographer, and an unemployed teacher, who is also the owner of an Irish wolfhound. Charming adaptation of a novel by Norma Klein.
1980 100m/C Patty Duke, David Birney, Danielle Brisebois, Keenan Wynn, Viveca Lindfors, John Lithgow; D: Edmond Levy. VHS, Beta TLF ✔✔½

Moment in Time A romantic novel on tape, about a guy, a girl, and their various troubles.
1984 60m/C Jean Simmons. Beta $11.95 PSM ✔

Mommie Dearest Film based on Christina Crawford's memoirs of her incredibly abusive and violent childhood at the hands of her adoptive mother, actress Joan Crawford. The story is controversial and sometimes trashy, but fairly well done nevertheless.
1981 (PG) 129m/C Faye Dunaway, Diana Scarwid, Steve Forrest, Mara Hobel, Rutanya Alda, Harry Goz, Howard da Silva; D: Frank Perry; W: Robert Getchell. VHS, Beta $59.95 PAR ✔✔

Mon Oncle Tati's celebrated comedy contrasts the simple life of Monsieur Hulot with the technologically complicated life of his family when he aids his nephew in war against his parents' ultramodern, push-button home. An easygoing, delightful comedy, this is the director's first piece in color. Sequel to "Mr. Hulot's Holiday," followed by "Playtime." In French with English subtitles. AKA: My Uncle; My Uncle, Mr. Hulot.
1958 110m/C Jacques Tati, Jean-Pierre Zola, Adrienne Serrantie, Alain Bacourt; D: Jacques Tati. VHS, Beta, 8mm $24.95 NOS, MRV, SUE ✔✔✔✔

Mon Oncle Antoine A splendid tale of young Benoit, who learns about life from a surprisingly compassionate uncle, who works as everything from undertaker to grocer in the depressed area where they live.
1971 104m/C Jean Duceppe, Olivette Thibault; D: Claude Jutra. VHS $39.95 HMV, FLI, APD ✔✔✔½

Mon Oncle D'Amerique Three French characters are followed as they try to find success of varying kinds in Paris, interspersed with ironic lectures by Prof. Henri Laborit about the biology that impels human behavior. Their disappointments lead them to dream of a legendary American uncle, who could make their desires come true. An acclaimed, witty comedy by former Nouvelle

Vague filmmaker, dubbed into English. AKA: Les Somnambules.
1980 (PG) 123m/C Gerard Depardieu, Nicole Garcia, Roger-Pierre, Marie DuBois; D: Alain Resnais; W: Jean Gruault. Academy Awards '80 Nominations: Best Original Screenplay; Cannes Film Festival '80: Best Film; New York Film Critics Awards '80: Best Foreign Film. VHS, Beta $79.95 NYF, BTV ✔✔✔½

Mona Lisa Jordan's wonderful, sad, sensitive story of a romantic, small-time hood who gets personally involved with the welfare and bad company of the high-priced whore he's been hired to chauffeur. Hoskins is especially touching and Caine is chilling as a suave gangster. Fine film debut for Tyson. Brilliantly filmed and critically lauded.
1986 (R) 104m/C Bob Hoskins, Cathy Tyson, Michael Caine, Clarke Peters, Kate Hardie, Robbie Coltrane, Zoe Nathenson, Sammi Davis-Voss, Rod Bedall, Joe Brown, Pauline Melville; D: Neil Jordan; W: Neil Jordan; M: Michael Kamen. Academy Awards '86 Nominations: Best Actor (Hoskins); British Academy Awards '86: Best Actor (Hoskins); Cannes Film Festival '86: Best Actor (Hoskins); Golden Globe Awards '87: Best Actor—Drama (Hoskins); Los Angeles Film Critics Association Awards '86: Best Actor (Hoskins); New York Film Critics Awards '86: Best Actor (Hoskins); National Society of Film Critics Awards '86: Best Actor (Hoskins). VHS, Beta NO ✔✔✔½

Monaco Forever An enigmatic American meets a mysterious Frenchwoman and they set off on a string of unusual romantic adventures. Set around the 1956 marriage of Grace Kelly to Prince Rainier of Monaco. Film debut of Van Damme.
1983 79m/C Charles Pitt, Martha Farris, Sydney Lassick, Jean-Claude Van Damme; D: William A. Levey; W: C. William Pitt, William A. Levey. VHS $39.95 VHE, FCT ✔

Mondo Balardo Translated as "Crazy World," this is crude sensationalism masked as a horror story. Karloff guides the viewer through a curious mixture of society's fringe elements. A loosely connected series of sketches includes portraits of a reincarnated Rudolph Valentino, practitioners of transvestism, Roman coke whores, and an Italian-Japanese rock 'n roll midget (Drago) in director Montero's unusual vision of an antiparadise. Includes standard lesbian club scene. Volume 11 of Frank Henenlotter's Sexy Shockers.
1964 86m/C Franz Drago; D: Robert Montero; W: Albert T. Viola. VHS $23.00 SMW, TPV ✔

Mondo Cane A documentary showcasing the eccentricities of human behavior around the world, including cannibalism, pig killing and more. Dubbed in English. Inspired a rash of "shockumentaries" over the next several years. The song "More" made its debut in this film.
1963 (R) 105m/C D: Gualtiero Jacopetti. VHS, Beta $16.95 SNC, VDC, VDM ✔✔

Mondo Cane 2 More documentary-like views of the oddities of mankind and ethnic rituals around the world. Enough, already. AKA: Mondo Pazzo.
1964 90m/C D: Gualtiero Jacopetti. VHS, Beta $19.95 VDC, HHE, TPV ✔

Mondo Magic A compilation of tribal rituals offering viewers a look on the darker side of matters magical.
1976 100m/C D: Melvin Ashford. VHS, Beta NO ✔½

Mondo Trasho A major trasho film of the last day in the life of a most unfortunate woman, complete with sex and violence. First full length effort from cult filmmaker

Waters, who was also writer, producer, and editor.
1969 95m/B Divine, Mary Vivian Pearce, John Leisenring, Mink Stole, David Lochary, Chris Atkinson; **D:** John Waters; **W:** John Waters. **VHS, Beta** *NO Woof!*

The Money The quest for money drives a young man to kidnap the child that his girlfriend is baby-sitting. Average but Workman's direction is right on the money.
1975 (R) 88m/C Laurence Luckinbill, Elizabeth Richards, Danny DeVito, Graham Beckel; **D:** Carl Workman. **VHS $59.95** *GHV, VTR* ✍✍

Money for Nothing $1.2 million falls off a truck in the warehouse district of Philadelphia where a simple-minded unemployed longshoreman (Cusack) finds the chance of a lifetime. Indiscreetly leaving behind a trail of spending, he soon has a detective (Madsen) snooping around dangerously close. But he only digs himself deeper by enlisting the assistance of the mob to help him launder the money. At this point the film disintegrates into a limp diatribe on the injustice of capitalism on society's downtrodden. Mazar plays Joey's ex-girlfriend who double-times it back to the fold after his find. Based on a true story.
1993 (R) 100m/C John Cusack, Michael Madsen, Benicio Del Toro, Michael Rappaport, Debi Mazar, Fionnula Flanagan, Maury Chaykin, James Gandolfini, Elizabeth Bracco, Ashleigh Dejon, Lenny Venito; **D:** Ramon Menendez; **W:** Ramon Menendez, Carol Sobieski, Tom Musca; **M:** Craig Safan. **VHS** *BVV* ✍✍

Money Madness Beaumont (Ward Cleaver) plays a taxi driver turned thief in this curiosity.
1947 ?m/C Hugh Beaumont, Frances Rafferty. **VHS $16.95** *SNC* ✍✍

Money Movers Aussie thieves plan megabuck bank robbery but heist and plot go sour. An oft told tale based on a true story. Features early appearance from burly boy Brown.
1978 94m/C Terence Donovan, Ed Devereaux, Tony Bonner, Lucky Grills, Charles Tingwell, Candy Raymond, Bryan Brown, Alan Cassell; **D:** Bruce Beresford; **W:** Bruce Beresford. **VHS $79.95** *IMP* ✍✍

The Money Pit A young yuppie couple encounter sundry problems when they attempt to renovate their newly purchased, seemingly self-destructive, Long Island home. However, the collapse of their home leads directly to the collapse of their relationship as well. Somewhat modeled after "Mr. Blandings Builds His Dream House." Hanks and Long fail to jell as partners and the many sight gags are on the predictable side. A Spielberg production.
1986 (PG) 91m/C Tom Hanks, Shelley Long, Alexander Godunov, Maureen Stapleton, Philip Bosco, Joe Mantegna, Josh Mostel; **D:** Richard Benjamin; **M:** Michel Colombier. **VHS, Beta $14.95** *MCA* ✍✍

Money to Burn Aging high school counselor and two senior citizens develop a plan to steal $50 million dollars from the Federal Reserve Bank. Harmless bit of fun.
1983 90m/C Jack Kruschen, Meegan King, David Wallace, Phillip Pine; **D:** Virginia Lively Stone. **VHS, Beta** *NO* ✍

Money to Burn Two buddies go off on a wild spending spree when $2 million in cash falls into their laps. Only one problem—a crazy cop who's determined to stop them squandering the money.
1994 96m/C Chad McQueen, Don Swayze, Joe Estevez, Julie Strain, Sydney Lassick; **D:** John Sjogren; **W:** John Sjogren, Scott Ziehl. **VHS** *NLC, COL* ✍ 1/2

The Mongols Splashy Italian production has Genghis Khan's son repelling invading hordes while courting buxom princess. Pairing of Palance and Ekberg makes this one worthy of consideration. *AKA:* Les Mongols.
1960 105m/C Jack Palance, Anita Ekberg, Antonella Lualdi, Franco Silva, Gianni Garko, Roldano Lupi, Gabriella Pallotti; **D:** Andre de Toth, Leopoldo Savona, Riccardo (Robert Hampton) Freda. **VHS $16.95** *SNC* ✍✍ 1/2

Mongrel El-cheapo kennel horror about a man who dreams he's a wild murderous mutt. His relief upon waking up is short-lived, however, when he discovers the people he killed in his dreams are actually dead. Flick will make you want to gnaw on a bone.
1983 90m/C Aldo Ray, Terry Evans; **D:** Robert Burns. **VHS, Beta** *NO Woof!*

Monika Two teenagers who run away together for the summer find the winter brings more responsibility than they can handle when the girl becomes pregnant and gives birth. Lesser, early Bergman, sensitively directed, but dull. Adapted by Bergman from a Per Anders Fogelstrom novel. In Swedish with English subtitles. *AKA:* Summer with Monika.
1952 96m/B Harriet Andersson, Lars Ekborg, John Harryson, Georg Skarstedt, Dagmar Ebbesen, Ake Gronberg; **D:** Ingmar Bergman; **W:** Ingmar Bergman; **M:** Les Baxter. **VHS $29.95** *HMV, CVC, TPV* ✍✍ 1/2

Monique A sophisticated career woman is about to unleash a terrifying secret on her new husband.
1983 96m/C Florence Giorgetti, John Ferris. **VHS, Beta** *NO* ✍

Monkey Boy Decent sci-fi horror from Britain, about a cunning human-ape hybrid that escapes from a genetics lab after massacring the staff. Not excessively gruesome or vulgar, and some sympathy is aroused for the killer mutant. Based on the novel "Chimera."
1990 104m/C John Lynch, Christine Kavanagh, Kenneth Cranham; **D:** Lawrence Gordon Clark. **VHS, Beta $79.95** *PSM* ✍✍ 1/2

Monkey Business Marx Brothers run amok as stowaways on ocean liner. Fast-paced comedy provides seemingly endless amount of gags, quips, and pratfalls, including the fab four imitating Maurice Chevalier at Immigration. This film, incidentally, was the group's first to be written—by noted humorist Perelman—directly for the screen.
1931 77m/B Groucho Marx, Harpo Marx, Chico Marx, Zeppo Marx, Thelma Todd, Ruth Hall, Harry Woods; **D:** Norman Z. McLeod. **VHS, Beta $14.98** *MCA* ✍✍✍ 1/2

Monkey Business A scientist invents a fountain-of-youth potion, a lab chimpanzee mistakenly dumps it into a water cooler, and then grown-ups start turning into adolescents. Top-flight crew occasionally labors in this screwball comedy, though comic moments shine. Monroe is the secretary sans skills, while absent-minded Grant and sexy wife Rogers race hormonally as teens.
1952 97m/B Cary Grant, Ginger Rogers, Charles Coburn, Marilyn Monroe, Hugh Marlowe, Larry Keating, George Winslow; **D:** Howard Hawks; **W:** Ben Hecht, Charles Lederer, I.A.L. Diamond. **VHS, Beta $14.98** *FOX* ✍✍✍

Monkey Grip An unmarried woman copes with parenthood and a drug-addicted boyfriend while working on the fringe of Australia's music business. Grim but provocative, based on Helen Graham's novel.
1982 101m/C Noni Hazlehurst, Colin Friels, Alice Garner, Harold Hopkins, Candy Raymond; **D:** Ken Cameron; **W:** Ken Cameron. **VHS $24.98** *SUE* ✍✍✍

Monkey Hustle Vintage blaxploitation has trouble hustling laffs. The Man plans a super freeway through the ghetto, and law abiding do gooders join forces with territorial lords of vice to fight the project. Shot in the Windy City.
1977 (PG) 90m/C Yaphet Kotto, Rudy Ray Moore, Rosalind Cash, Debbi Morgan, Thomas Carter; **D:** Arthur Marks. **VHS $59.95** *ORI, FCT* ✍

Monkey Shines Based on the novel by Michael Stuart, this is a sick, scary yarn about a quadriplegic who is given a specially trained capuchin monkey as a helpmate. However, he soon finds that the beast is assuming and acting on his subconscious rages. *AKA:* Monkey Shines: An Experiment in Fear.
1988 (R) 108m/C Jason Beghe, John Pankow, Melanie Parker, Christine Forrest, Stephen Root, Kate McNeil, Joyce Van Patten, Stanley Tucci, Janine Turner; **D:** George A. Romero; **W:** George A. Romero. **VHS, Beta $19.98** *ORI* ✍✍

Monkey Trouble Lonely schoolgirl Birch is feeling abandoned when mom and stepdad shower attention on her new baby brother. Then a monkey trained as a pickpocket enters her life. Keitel is the organ grinder turned bad who must answer to the mob when the monkey scampers off to suburbia. Stakes a lot of its entertainment wallop on the considerable talents of the slippery-fingered monkey, who steals the show. Birch is amusing as the youngster caught in all sorts of uncomfortable situations. Formula abounds, but the milk and cookies set won't notice; fine family fare.
1994 (PG) 95m/C Thora Birch, Finster, Harvey Keitel, Mimi Rogers, Christopher McDonald; **D:** Franco Amurri; **W:** Franco Amurri, Stu Krieger; **M:** Mark Mancina. **VHS** *NYR* ✍✍ 1/2

Monkeys, Go Home! Dumb Disney yarn about young American who inherits a badly neglected French olive farm. When he brings in four chimpanzees to pick the olives, the local townspeople go on strike. People can be so sensitive. Based on "The Monkeys" by G. K. Wilkinson. Chevalier's last film appearance.
1966 89m/C Dean Jones, Yvette Mimieux, Maurice Chevalier, Clement Harari, Yvonne Constant; **D:** Andrew V. McLaglen. **VHS, Beta $69.95** *DIS* ✍ 1/2

Monkey's Uncle A sequel to Disney's "The Misadventures of Merlin Jones" and featuring more bizarre antics and scientific hoopla, including chimps and a flying machine.
1965 90m/C Tommy Kirk, Annette Funicello, Leon Ames, Arthur O'Connell; **D:** Robert Stevenson; **M:** Buddy Baker. **VHS, Beta $69.95** *DIS* ✍ 1/2

The Monocle Steele plays a seductive villainess in this rare, spy/comedy thriller.
1964 ?m/C Paul Meurisse, Barbara Steele, Marcel Dalio. **VHS $16.95** *SNC* ✍✍

Monolith Tucker (Paxton) and Flynn (Frost) are unlikely partners on the LAPD. But they're teamed up on an unlikely case: a Russian scientist commits a seemingly senseless murder and is taken away by a mystery man (Hurt) before she can be interrogated. What the curious duo discover is a lethal alien force capable of possessing any living creature and whose objective is the destruction of the planet.
1993 (R) 96m/C Bill Paxton, Lindsay Frost, John Hurt, Louis Gossett Jr.; **D:** John Eyres; **W:** Stephen Lister. **VHS** *MCA* ✍✍ 1/2

The Monolith Monsters A geologist investigates a meteor shower in Arizona and discovers strange crystals. The crystals attack humans and absorb their silicone, causing them to grow into monsters. Good "B" movie fun.
1957 76m/B Grant Williams, Lola Albright, Les Tremayne, Trevor Bardette; **D:** John Sherwood; **W:** Norman Jolley, Robert M. Fresco; **M:** Henry Mancini. **VHS $14.98** MCA, MLB, FRG ♫♫

Monsieur Beaucaire The Duke of Chartres ditches France posing as a barber, and once in Britain, becomes a lawman. Not a classic Valentino vehicle.
1924 100m/B Rudolph Valentino, Bebe Daniels, Lois Wilson, Doris Kenyon, Lowell Sherman, John Davidson; **D:** Sidney Olcott. **VHS, Beta $19.95** GPV ♫ ½

Monsieur Beaucaire Entertaining Hope vehicle that casts him as a barber impersonating a French nobleman in the court of Louis XV. He's set to wed a Spanish princess in order to prevent a full-scale war from taking place. However, he really wants to marry social-climber chambermaid Caulfield. Director Marshall was at his best here. Based on the novel by Booth Tarkington.
1946 93m/B Bob Hope, Joan Caulfield, Patric Knowles, Marjorie Reynolds, Cecil Kellaway, Joseph Schildkraut, Reginald Owen, Constance Collier; **D:** George Marshall; **W:** Melvin Frank, Norman Panama. **VHS $14.98** MCA, BTV ♫♫♫

Monsieur Hire The usual tale of sexual obsesssion and suspense. Mr. Hire spends much of his time trying to spy on his beautiful young neighbor woman, alternately alienated and engaged by her love affairs. The voyeur soon finds his secret desires have entangled him in a vicious intrigue. Political rally setpiece is brilliant. Excellent acting, intense pace, elegant photography. Based on "Les Fiancailles de M. Hire" by Georges Simenon and adapted by Leconte and Patrick Dewolf. In French with English subtitles. **AKA:** M. Hire.
1989 (PG-13) 81m/C Michel Blanc, Sandrine Bonnaire, Luc Thuillier, Eric Berenger, Andre Wilms; **D:** Patrice Leconte; **W:** Patrice Leconte. **VHS $39.95** FXL, FCT, IME ♫♫♫ ½

Monsieur Verdoux A thorough Chaplin effort, as he produced, directed, wrote, scored and starred. A prim and proper bank cashier in Paris marries and murders rich women in order to support his real wife and family. A mild scandal in its day, though second-thought pacifism and stale humor date it. A bomb upon release (leading Chaplin to shelve it for 17 years) and a cult item today, admired for both its flaws and complexity. Raye fearlessly chews scenery and croissants. Initially based upon a suggestion from Orson Welles.
1947 123m/B Charlie Chaplin, Martha Raye, Isobel Elsom, Mady Correll, Marilyn Nash, Irving Bacon, William Frawley, Allison Roddan, Robert Lewis; **D:** Charlie Chaplin; **W:** Charlie Chaplin. Academy Awards '47 Nominations: Best Original Screenplay; National Board of Review Awards '47: 10 Best Films of the Year. **VHS, Beta $19.98** FOX ♫♫♫

Monsieur Vincent True story of 17th century French priest who became St. Vincent de Paul. He forsakes worldly possessions and convinces members of the aristocracy to finance his charities for the less fortunate. Inspirational. In French with English subtitles or dubbed.
1948 100m/B Pierre Fresnay, Lisa Delamare, Aime Clairmond; **D:** Maurice Cloche. **VHS, Beta $29.95** HTV, MRV, DVT ♫♫♫

Monsignor Callow, ambitious priest befriends mobsters and even seduces a nun while managing Vatican's business affairs. No sparks generated by Reeve and Bujold (who appears nude in one scene), and no real conviction related by most other performers. Absurd, ludicrous melodrama best enjoyed as unintentional comedy. Based on Jack Alain Leger's book.
1982 (R) 121m/C Christopher Reeve, Fernando Rey, Genevieve Bujold, Jason Miller; **D:** Frank Perry; **W:** Abraham Polonsky, Wendell Mayes; **M:** John Williams. **VHS, Beta $59.98** FOX Woof!

Monsignor Quixote A small town priest takes on the persona of his ancestor, Don Quixote, and prepares to battle the evil he sees around him. Based on the novel by Graham Greene.
1991 118m/C Alec Guinness, Ian Richardson, Graham Crowden, Maurice Denham, Philip Stone, Rosalie Crutchley, Valentine Pelka, Don Fellows, Leo McKern; **D:** Rodney Bennett. **VHS $59.99** FCT, ING ♫♫ ½

The Monster This silent horror film has all the elements that would become genre standards. A mad scientist (Chaney), working in an asylum filled with lunatics, abducts strangers to use in his fiendish experiments to bring the dead back to life. There's the obligatory dungeon and even a lovely heroine that needs rescuing. Great atmosphere and Chaney's usual spine-tingling performance.
1925 86m/B Lon Chaney Sr., Gertrude Olmsted, Johnny Arthur, Charles Sellon; **D:** Roland West. **VHS $29.95** FCT ♫♫♫

Monster Bloodthirsty alien indiscriminately preys on gaggle of teens in wilds of civilization. Performers struggle with dialogue and their own self-esteem.
1978 (R) 98m/C Jim Mitchum, Diane McBain, Roger Clark, John Carradine, Phil Carey, Anthony Eisley, Keenan Wynn; **D:** Herbert L. Strock. **VHS, Beta $24.95** GHV, MRV ♫

Monster a Go-Go! Team of go-go dancers battle a ten-foot monster from outerspace whose mass is due to a radiation mishap. He can't dance, either.
1965 70m/B Phil Morton, June Travis, Bill Rebane, Sheldon Seymour; **D:** Herschell Gordon Lewis. **VHS, Beta $39.95** VCI Woof!

The Monster and the Girl It's the mob vs. the ape in this tale of revenge. Scott (Terry) discovers innocent sister Susan (Drew) is being lead down the path to prostitution by suave mobster Reed (Paige). But Reed manages to frame Scott for murder and he's executed, although not before donating his brain to science. Then scientist Parry (Zucco) decides to transplant the brain into the body of an ape who goes on a rampage aimed at the mobster.
1941 65m/B Ellen Drew, Robert Paige, Phillip Terry, Paul Lukas, Joseph Calleia, Onslow Stevens, Rod Cameron, George Zucco, Marc Lawrence, Gerald Mohr; **D:** Stuart Heisler; **W:** Stuart Anthony. **VHS $14.98** MCA ♫♫ ½

The Monster and the Stripper A bayou creature is pursued by a gangster who foolishly hopes to realize considerable profits from the venture.
1973 (R) 90m/C **VHS, Beta** NO ♫

The Monster Club Price and Carradine star in this music-horror compilation, featuring songs by Night, B.A. Robertson, The Pretty Things and The Viewers. Soundtrack music by John Williams, UB 40 and The Expressos.
1985 104m/C Vincent Price, Donald Pleasence, John Carradine, Stuart Whitman, Britt Ekland, Simon Ward, Patrick Magee; **D:** Roy Ward Baker. **VHS, Beta $39.95** LIV ♫♫

The Monster Demolisher Nostradamus' descendent shares the family penchant for sanguine cocktails, and threatens a professor who protects himself with an electronic wonder of modern technology. Edited from a sombrero serial; if you make it through this one, look up its Mexican siblings, "Curse of Nostradamus" and "Genie of Darkness."
1960 ?m/B German Robles; **D:** Frederick Curiel. **VHS $19.98** NOS, LOO ♫

Monster Dog A rock band is mauled, threatened, and drooled upon by an untrainable mutant canine. Rock star Cooper plays the leader of the band. No plot, but the German shepherd is worth watching.
1982 88m/C Alice Cooper, Victoria Vera; **D:** Clyde Anderson. **VHS, Beta $69.95** TWE Woof!

Monster from Green Hell An experimental rocket containing radiation-contaminated wasps crashes in Africa, making giant killer wasps that run amok. Stinging big bug horror.
1958 71m/B Jim Davis, Robert Griffin, Barbara Turner, Eduardo Ciannelli; **D:** Kenneth Crane. **VHS, Beta $14.95** NOS, MRV, SNC ♫

Monster from the Ocean Floor An oceanographer in a deep-sea diving bell is threatened by a multi-tentacled creature. Roger Corman's first production. **AKA:** It Stalked the Ocean Floor; Monster Maker.
1954 66m/C Anne Kimball, Stuart Wade; **D:** Wyott Ordung. **VHS, Beta $29.98** VMK ♫

Monster High Bloodthirsty alien indiscriminately preys on gaggle of teens in wilds of civilization. Even the people who made this one may not have seen it all the way through.
1989 (R) 89m/C David Marriott, Dean Iandoli, Diana Frank, D.J. Kerzner; **D:** Rudiger Poe. **VHS, Beta $89.95** COL ♫

Monster in a Box Master storyteller Gray spins a wonderful tale about his life, including stories about his adventures at a Moscow film festival, a trip to Nicaragua, and his first experience with California earthquakes. Filled with wit, satire, and hilarity. Filmed before an audience, this is based on Gray's Broadway show of the same title. By the way, the monster in the box is a 1,900-page manuscript of his autobiography and the box in which he lugs it around.
1992 (PG-13) 88m/C Spalding Gray; **D:** Nick Broomfield; **W:** Spalding Gray; **M:** Laurie Anderson. **VHS $89.95** NLC, COL, BTV ♫♫♫

Monster in the Closet A gory horror spoof about a rash of San Francisco murders that all take place inside closets. A news reporter and his scientist friend decide they will be the ones to protect California from the evil but shy creatures. From the makers of "The Toxic Avenger."
1986 (PG) 87m/C Donald Grant, Claude Akins, Denise DuBarry, Stella Stevens, Howard Duff, Henry Gibson, Jesse White, John Carradine; **D:** Bob Dahlin. **VHS, Beta $19.98** LHV, WAR ♫♫

The Monster Maker Low-budget gland fest in which deranged scientist develops serum that inflates heads, feet, and hands. He recklessly inflicts others with this potion, then must contend with deformed victims while courting a comely gal.
1944 65m/B J. Carroll Naish, Ralph Morgan, Wanda McKay, Terry Frost; **D:** Sam Newfield. **VHS, Beta $19.95** NOS, MRV, SNC ♫

The Monster of London City During a stage play about Jack the Ripper, murders occur paralleling those in the production. The lead actor finds himself to be the prime suspect. Lightweight horror from Germany. **AKA:** Das Ungeheuer von London City.

1964 87m/B Hansjorg Felmy, Marianne Koch, Dietmar Schoenherr, Hans Nielsen; *D:* Edwin Zbonek. VHS, Beta $16.95 SNC *Z ½*

The Monster of Piedras Blancas During a seaside festival, two fisherman are killed by a bloodthirsty oceanic critter with no respect for holidays. The fishing village is determined to find it and kill it. Low-budget, with amateurish effects and poor acting.
1957 72m/B Les Tremayne, Jeanne Carmen, Forrest Lewis; *D:* Irvin Berwick. VHS $14.98 VDM, MRV, REP Woof!

Monster on the Campus Science-fiction thriller about the blood of a prehistoric fish turning college professor into murderous beast. Will the halls of Dunsfield University ever be safe again?
1959 76m/B Arthur Franz, Joanna Moore, Judson Pratt, Nancy Walters, Troy Donahue; *D:* Jack Arnold; *W:* David Duncan. VHS $14.98 MCA *ZZ ½*

The Monster Squad Youthful monster enthusiasts find their community inundated by Dracula, Frankenstein creature, Wolf Man, Mummy, and Gill Man(!?!), who are all searching for a life-sustaining amulet. Somewhat different, but still somewhat mediocre.
1987 (PG-13) 82m/C Andre Gower, Stephen Macht, Tommy Noonan, Duncan Regehr; *D:* Fred Dekker; *W:* Fred Dekker, Shane Black; *M:* Bruce Broughton. VHS, Beta $19.98 LIV, VES *Z ½*

The Monster that Challenged the World Huge, ancient eggs are discovered in the Salton Sea and eventually hatch into killer, crustaceous caterpillars. Superior monster action.
1957 83m/B Tim Holt, Audrey Dalton, Hans Conried, Harlen Ward, Casey Adams, Mimi Gibson, Gordon Jones; *D:* Arnold Laven. VHS $14.95 MGM, FRG, MLB *ZZ ½*

The Monster Walks A whodunit thriller, complete with stormy nights, suspicious cripples, weird servants, a screaming gorilla, and a spooky house. Not unique but entertaining. *AKA:* The Monster Walked.
1932 60m/B Rex Lease, Vera Reynolds, Mischa Auer, Willie Best; *D:* Frank Strayer. VHS, Beta $12.95 SNC, NOS, CCB *ZZ*

Monsters Crash the Pajama Party Mad scientist is discovered conducting weird experiments by a group of teens who enter a supposedly haunted house. This one was much better in the theater, because "monsters" would run through the audience and select a victim. Then the monsters and the victim would magically appear on the screen. Weird.
1965 ?m/C Don Brandon. VHS $16.95 SNC *ZZ*

Montana Hoyce and Bess Guthrie are long-married and strong-willed ranchers who are at odds over the family ranch in Montana. He wants to sell the land to a power company for oil drilling but she wants to keep the land in the family. Made for cable television.
1990 (PG) 91m/C Gena Rowlands, Richard Crenna, Lea Thompson, Justin Deas, Elizabeth Berridge, Scott Coffey, Darren Dalton; *D:* William A. Graham; *W:* Larry McMurtry. VHS, Beta $9.98 TTC, FCT *ZZ ½*

Montana Belle A buxom bandit teams with the notorious Dalton Brothers before embarking on a life of reform. In the card-game of life, Russell is always holding a pair.
1952 81m/C Jane Russell, George Brent, Scott Brady, Forrest Tucker, Andy Devine, Jack Lambert, John Litel, Ray Teal; *D:* Allan Dwan. VHS, Beta $19.98 TTC *ZZ*

Monte Carlo A sexy Russian woman aids the Allies by relaying important messages during WWII. Fun, made for television production featuring Collins at her seductive best.
1986 200m/C Joan Collins, George Hamilton, Lisa Eilbacher, Lauren Hutton, Robert Carradine, Malcolm McDowell; *D:* Anthony Page. VHS, Beta $29.95 STE, NWV *ZZ*

Monte Carlo Nights Wrongly convicted murderer determines to prove his innocence even as he is tracked by police.
1934 60m/B Mary Brian, John Darrow, Kate Campbell, Robert Frazer, Astrid Allwyn, George "Gabby" Hayes, George Cleveland; *D:* William Nigh. VHS, Beta $16.95 SNC *Z ½*

Monte Walsh Aging cowboy sees declining of Old West, embarks on mission to avenge best friend's death. Subdued, moving western worthy of genre greats Marvin and Palance. Cinematographer Fraker proves himself a proficient director in this, his first venture. Based on Jack Schaefer's novel.
1970 (PG) 100m/C Lee Marvin, Jack Palance, Jeanne Moreau, Jim Davis, Mitchell Ryan; *D:* William A. Fraker; *W:* David Zelag Goodman; *M:* John Barry. VHS, Beta $59.98 FOX *ZZ*

Montenegro Offbeat, bawdy comedy details experiences of bored, possibly mad housewife who lands in a coarse, uninhibited ethnic community. To its credit, this film remains unpredictable to the end. And Anspach, an intriguing, resourceful—and attractive—actress, delivers what is perhaps her greatest performance. *AKA:* Montenegro—Or Pigs and Pearls.
1981 97m/C Susan Anspach, Erland Josephson; *D:* Dusan Makavejev; *W:* Dusan Makavejev. VHS, Beta NO *ZZZ ½*

Monterey Pop This pre-Woodstock rock 'n roll festival in Monterey, California features landmark performances by some of the most popular sixties rockers. Compelling for the performances, and historically important as the first significant rock concert film. Appearances by Jefferson Airplane, Janis Joplin, Jimi Hendrix, Simon and Garfunkel, The Who, and Otis Redding.
1968 72m/C The Jefferson Airplane, Janis Joplin, Jimi Hendrix, Art Garfunkel, Paul Simon, Pete Townshend, Roger Daltrey, Keith Moon, John Entwistle; *D:* James Desmond. VHS, Beta, 8mm $29.95 VYG, MVD, COL *ZZZ ½*

A Month in the Country The reverently quiet story of two British WWI veterans, one an archeologist and the other a church painting restorer, who are working in a tiny village while trying to heal their emotional wounds. Based on the novel by J.L. Carr.
1987 92m/C Colin Firth, Natasha Richardson, Kenneth Branagh, Patrick Malahide, Tony Haygarth, Jim Carter; *D:* Pat O'Connor; *W:* Simon Gray; *M:* Howard Blake. VHS, Beta $79.95 LHV, WAR *ZZZ*

Monty Python and the Holy Grail Britain's famed comedy band assaults the Arthurian legend in a cult classic replete with a Trojan rabbit and an utterly dismembered, but inevitably pugnacious, knight. Fans of manic comedy—and graphic violence—should get more than their fill here.
1975 (PG) 90m/C Graham Chapman, John Cleese, Terry Gilliam, Eric Idle, Terry Jones, Michael Palin, Carol Cleveland, Connie Booth, Neil Innes, Patsy Kensit; *D:* Terry Gilliam, Terry Jones; *W:* Graham Chapman, John Cleese, Terry Gilliam, Eric Idle, Terry Jones, Michael Palin. VHS, Beta, 8mm $19.95 COL, SIG, TVC *ZZZ ½*

Monty Python Live at the Hollywood Bowl The revered comedy group perform many of their most celebrated routines in this uproarious performance documentary. A must-see for all Python aficionados.
1982 78m/C Eric Idle, Michael Palin, John Cleese, Terry Gilliam, Terry Jones, Graham Chapman; *D:* Terry Hughes; *W:* John Cleese, Terry Gilliam; *M:* John Du Prez. VHS, Beta $14.95 PAR *ZZZ*

Monty Python Meets Beyond the Fringe More fine British humor is featured in this compendium of skits, sketches, routines, and sequences. Those who know, will know. Those who don't probably won't enjoy it anyway.
19?? 85m/C Graham Chapman, John Cleese, Terry Gilliam, Eric Idle, Terry Jones, Michael Palin. VHS VCI *ZZZ*

Monty Python's Flying Circus The original classic irreverant BBC comedy series that introduced the gang of six comics to the world. Two episodes per tape. Four skits: "The Architect's Sketch," "The Naughty Chemist," "Ministry of Silly Walks," and "The Piranha Brothers."
1971 60m/C Michael Palin, Graham Chapman, Eric Idle, John Cleese, Terry Jones, Terry Gilliam, Carol Cleveland, Connie Booth, Neil Innes; *D:* Ian MacNaughton. VHS, Beta $19.99 MOV, PAR *ZZZ*

Monty Python's Life of Brian Often riotous spoof of Christianity tracks hapless peasant mistaken for the messiah in 32 A.D. Film reels from routine to routine, and only the most pious will remain unmoved by a chorus of crucifixion victims. Probably the group's most daring, controversial venture. *AKA:* Life of Brian.
1979 (R) 94m/C Graham Chapman, John Cleese, Terry Gilliam, Eric Idle, Terry Jones, Michael Palin, George Harrison; *D:* Terry Jones; *W:* Graham Chapman, John Cleese, Terry Gilliam, Eric Idle, Terry Jones, Michael Palin. VHS, Beta $14.95 PAR, SIG *ZZZ ½*

Monty Python's Parrot Sketch Not Included To celebrate their 20th anniversary, the crazy guys of Monty Python put together this collection of some of their funniest sketches. The parrot was pretty disappointed that he wasn't included.
1990 75m/C Graham Chapman, John Cleese, Terry Gilliam, Eric Idle, Terry Jones, Michael Palin. VHS $19.95 PAR, SIG, TVC *ZZZ ½*

Monty Python's The Meaning of Life Funny, technically impressive film conducts various inquiries into the most profound questions confronting humanity. Notable among the sketches here are a live sex enactment performed before bored schoolboys, a student-faculty rugby game that turns quite violent, and an encounter between a physician and a reluctant, untimely organ donor. Another sketch provides a memorable portrait of a glutton prone to nausea. And at film's end, the meaning of life is actually revealed.
1983 (R) 107m/C Graham Chapman, John Cleese, Terry Gilliam, Eric Idle, Terry Jones, Michael Palin, Carol Cleveland; *D:* Terry Jones; *W:* Graham Chapman, John Cleese, Terry Gilliam, Eric Idle, Terry Jones, Michael Palin; *M:* John Du Prez. VHS, Beta $14.95 MCA, CCB, SIG *ZZZ*

The Moon and Sixpence Stockbroker turns ambitious painter in this adaptation of W. Somerset Maugham's novel that was, in turn, inspired by the life of artist Paul Gaugin. Fine performance from Sanders. Filmed mainly in black and white, but uses color sparingly to great advantage. Compare

this one to "Wolf at the Door," in which Gaugin is played by Donald Sutherland.
1943 89m/B George Sanders, Herbert Marshall, Steve Geray, Doris Dudley, Eric Blore, Elena Verdugo, Florence Bates, Albert Basserman, Heather Thatcher; **D:** Albert Lewin. **VHS** *MGM, IVY* 🎬🎬🎬

Moon 44 A space prison is overrun by thugs who terrorize their fellow inmates. Fine cast, taut pacing. Filmed in Germany.
1990 (R) 102m/C Malcolm McDowell, Lisa Eichhorn, Michael Pare, Stephen Geoffreys, Roscoe Lee Browne, Brian Thompson, Dean Devlin, Mechmed Yilmaz, Leon Rippy; **D:** Roland Emmerich. **VHS $89.95** *LIV, IME, BTV* 🎬½

Moon in Scorpio Three Vietnam-vet buddies go sailing and are attacked by the back-from-the-dead victims of a bloody war crime.
1986 90m/C John Phillip Law, Britt Ekland, William Smith; **D:** Gary Graver. **VHS, Beta $79.95** *TWE* 🎬½

Moon in the Gutter In a ramshackle harbor town, a man searches despondently for the person who killed his sister years before. Various sexual liaisons and stevedore fights intermittently spice up the action. Nasty story that doesn't have much sense on film. In French with English subtitles. *AKA:* La Lune Dans le Caniveau.
1983 (R) 109m/C Gerard Depardieu, Nastassia Kinski, Victoria Abril, Vittorio Mezzogiorno, Dominique Pinon; **D:** Jean-Jacques Beineix; **W:** Jean-Jacques Beineix. **VHS, Beta $59.95** *COL* 🎬½

Moon is Blue A young woman flaunts her virginity in this stilted adaptation of F. Hugh Herbert's play. Hard to believe that this film was once considered risque. Good performances, though, from Holden and Niven.
1953 100m/B William Holden, David Niven, Maggie McNamara; **D:** Otto Preminger. Academy Awards '53 Nominations: Best Actress (McNamara), Best Film Editing, Best Song ("The Moon is Blue"); Golden Globe Awards '54: Best Actor—Musical/Comedy (Niven). **Beta $19.98** *WAR* 🎬🎬

Moon of the Wolf A small town in bayou country is terrorized by a modern-day werewolf that rips its victims to shreds. Made-for-television.
1972 74m/C David Janssen, Barbara Rush, Bradford Dillman, John Beradino; **D:** Daniel Petrie. **VHS, Beta $49.95** *WOV, GKK* 🎬

Moon Over Harlem A musical melodrama about a widow who unwittingly marries a fast-talking gangster involved in the numbers racket. The film features 20 chorus girls, a choir, and a 60-piece orchestra.
1939 67m/B Bud Harris, Cora Green, Alec Lovejoy, Sidney Bechet; **D:** Edgar G. Ulmer. **VHS, Beta $24.95** *FCT, DVT, NOS* 🎬½

Moon Over Miami Manhunting trio meet their match in this engaging musical. A remake of 1938's "Three Blind Mice," this was later remade in 1946 as "Three Little Girls in Blue." 🎵 Moon Over Miami; I've Got You All To Myself; What Can I Do For You?; Kindergarten Congo; You Started Something; Oh Me Oh Mi-Am-Mi; Solitary Seminole; Is That Good?; Loveliness and Love.
1941 91m/C Don Ameche, Betty Grable, Robert Cummings, Carole Landis, Charlotte Greenwood, Jack Haley; **D:** Walter Lang; **W:** Mitch Glazer. **VHS, Beta $19.95** *FOX* 🎬🎬🎬

Moon Over Parador An uneven comedy about a reluctant American actor who gets the role of his life when he gets the chance to pass himself off as the recently deceased dictator of a Latin American country. A political strongman wants to continue the charade until he can take over, but the

actor begins to enjoy the benefits of dictatorship. Look for a cameo by director/writer Mazursky in drag.
1988 (PG-13) 103m/C Richard Dreyfuss, Sonia Braga, Raul Julia, Jonathan Winters, Fernando Rey, Ed Asner, Dick Cavett, Michael Greene, Sammy Davis Jr., Polly Holliday, Charo, Marianne Sagebrecht, Dana Delany, Ike Pappas; **Cameos:** Paul Mazursky; **D:** Paul Mazursky; **W:** Leon Capetanos, Paul Mazursky; **M:** Maurice Jarre. **VHS, Beta $19.95** *MCA* 🎬🎬

Moon Pilot An astronaut on his way to the moon encounters a mysterious alien woman who claims to know his future.
1962 98m/C Tom Tryon, Brian Keith, Edmond O'Brien, Dany Saval, Tommy Kirk; **D:** James Neilson. **VHS, Beta $69.95** *DIS* 🎬🎬

The Moon-Spinners Lightweight Disney drama featuring Mills as a young tourist traveling through Crete who meets up with a young man, accused of being a jewel thief, and the two work together to find the real jewel thieves. Watch for silent film star Pola Negri.
1964 (PG) 118m/C Hayley Mills, Peter McEnery, Eli Wallach, Pola Negri; **D:** James Neilson. **VHS, Beta** *DIS, OM* 🎬🎬

The Moon Stallion A charming tale of mystery and fantasy for children and adults. Professor Purwell is researching King Arthur. His blind daughter soon becomes involved with supernatural events and a white horse that appears to lead her into adventures not of this age.
19?? 95m/C VHS $29.95 *BFS, HMV* 🎬🎬½

Mooncussers A children's film detailing the exploits of a precocious 12-year-old determined to exact revenge upon a band of ruthless pirates.
1962 85m/C Kevin Corcoran, Rian Garrick, Oscar Homolka; **D:** James Neilson. **VHS, Beta $69.95** *DIS* 🎬½

Moonfleet Follows the adventures of an 18th century buccaneer who tries to swindle a young lad in his charge of a valuable diamond. From J. Meade Falkner's novel.
1955 89m/C Stewart Granger, Jon Whiteley, George Sanders, Viveca Lindfors, Joan Greenwood, Ian Wolfe; **D:** Fritz Lang. **VHS $34.98** *MGM* 🎬🎬½

Moonlight Sonata Professional concert pianist Paderewski performs his way through a confusing soap-opera of a film. Includes performances of Franz Liszt's "Second Hungarian Rhapsody" and Frederic Chopin's "Polonaise."
1938 80m/B Ignace Jan Paderewski, Charles Farrell, Marie Tempest, Barbara Greene, Eric Portman; **D:** Lothar Mendes. **VHS $19.95** *NOS, DVT* 🎬🎬½

Moonlighting Compelling drama about Polish laborers illegally hired to renovate London flat. When their country falls under martial law, the foreman conceals the event and pushes workers to complete project. Unlikely casting of Irons as foreman is utterly successful.
1982 (PG) 97m/C Jeremy Irons, Eugene Lipinski, Jiri Stanislav, Eugeniusz Haczkiewicz; **D:** Jerzy Skolimowski. **VHS, Beta $49.95** *MCA* 🎬🎬½

Moonlighting The television-pilot for the popular detective show, where Maddie and David, the daffy pair of impetuous private eyes, meet for the first time and solve an irrationally complex case.
1985 93m/C Cybill Shepherd, Bruce Willis, Allyce Beasley; **D:** Robert Butler. **VHS, Beta $19.95** *WAR, OM* 🎬🎬½

The Moonraker Compelling action scenes highlight this tale set at the end of the English Civil War, as the Royalists attempt to sneak the king out of England and into France.
1958 82m/C George Baker, Sylvia Syms, Peter Arne, Marius Goring, Clive Morton, Gary Raymond, Richard Leech, Patrick Troughton; **D:** David MacDonald. **VHS $19.95** *NOS* 🎬🎬½

Moonraker Uninspired Bond fare has 007 unraveling intergalactic hijinks. Bond is aided by a female CIA agent, assaulted by a giant with jaws of steel, and captured by Amazons when he sets out to protect the human race. Moore, Chiles, and Lonsdale all seem to be going through the motions only.
1979 (PG) 136m/C Roger Moore, Lois Chiles, Richard Kiel, Michael Lonsdale, Corinne Clery, Geoffrey Keen, Emily Bolton, Walter Gotell, Bernard Lee, Lois Maxwell, Desmond Llewelyn; **D:** Lewis Gilbert; **M:** John Barry. **VHS, Beta $19.98** *MGM, TLF* 🎬🎬

Moonrise A melodramatic tale about the son of an executed murderer who becomes the object of derision in the small town where he lives. One tormentor finally attacks him, and the young man must make a split-second decision that may affect his own mortality.
1948 90m/B Dane Clark, Gail Russell, Ethel Barrymore, Allyn Joslyn, Harry Morgan, Lloyd Bridges, Selena Royle, Rex Ingram, Harry Carey Jr.; **D:** Frank Borzage. **VHS $19.98** *REP* 🎬🎬

Moon's Our Home A fast-paced, breezy, screwball comedy about an actress and adventurer impulsively marrying and then bickering through the honeymoon. Silliness at its height. Fonda and Sullavan were both married and then divorced before filming this movie.
1936 80m/B Margaret Sullavan, Henry Fonda, Beulah Bondi, Charles Butterworth, Margaret Hamilton, Walter Brennan; **D:** William A. Seiter. **VHS, Beta $14.95** *BAR* 🎬🎬½

Moonshine County Express Three sexy daughters of a hillbilly moonshiner set out to run the still and avenge their father's murder.
1977 (PG) 97m/C John Saxon, Susan Howard, William Conrad, Morgan Woodward, Claudia Jennings, Jeff Corey, Dub Taylor, Maureen McCormick, Albert Salmi, Candice Rialson; **D:** Gus Trikonis. **VHS, Beta $39.98** *WAR* 🎬½

Moonshine Mountain A country-western star travels with his girlfriend to the singer's home in backwoods Carolina. When the girl is killed by a lusting resident, all hell breaks loose. One of gore-meister Lewis' excursions into the dramatic. *AKA:* White Trash on Moonshine Mountain.
1964 90m/C Chuck Scott, Adam Sorg, Jeffrey Allen, Bonnie Hinson, Carmen Sotir, Ben Moore, Pat Patterson, Mark Douglas; **D:** Herschell Gordon Lewis. **VHS, Beta $16.95** *SNC* Woof!

Moonstruck Winning romantic comedy about widow engaged to one man but falling in love with his younger brother in Little Italy. Excellent performances all around, with Cher particularly fetching as attractive, hapless widow. Unlikely casting of usually dominating Aiello, as unassuming mama's boy also works well, and Cage is at his best as a tormented one-handed opera lover/baker.
1987 (PG-13) 103m/C Cher, Nicolas Cage, Olympia Dukakis, Danny Aiello, Vincent Gardenia, Julie Bovasso, Louis Guss, Anita Gillette, Feodor Chaliapin, John Mahoney; **D:** Norman Jewison; **W:** John Patrick Shanley. Academy Awards '87: Best Actress (Cher), Best Original Screenplay, Best Supporting Actress (Dukakis); Nominations: Best Director (Jewison), Best Picture, Best Supporting Actor (Gardenia); Golden Globe Awards '88: Best Actress—Musical/Comedy

(Cher), Best Supporting Actress (Dukakis). **VHS, Beta** $19.98 *MGM, BTV, HMV* 🐾🐾🐾½

Moontrap An astronaut discovers an alien frozen in space and returns to Earth with it. Once thawed, the creature reveals its horrible secret.
1989 92m/C Walter Koenig, Bruce Campbell, Leigh Lombardi; *D:* Robert Dyke. **VHS** $89.99 *MOV, IME* 🐾🐾

Morals for Women This soap-opera's so old it almost predates soap. A secretary becomes the Kept Woman of her boss in the Big Bad City. She escapes, but not for long.
1931 65m/B Bessie Love, Conway Tearle, John Holland, Natalie Moorhead, Emma Dunn, June Clyde; *D:* Mort Blumenstock. **VHS** $15.95 *NOS, LOO* 🐾½

Moran of the Lady Letty Seaweed saga of Ramon Laredo (Valentino), a high society guy who's kidnapped aboard a pirate barge. When the salty dogs rescue/capture Moran (a theme ahead of its time?) from a ship fuming with burning coal, Ramon is smitten in a big way with the boyish girl and battles contagiously to prevent the pirates from selling her as a slave. Excellent fight scenes with much hotstepping over gangplanks and swinging from masts, with a 60-foot death dive from above. Little known Dalton was a celluloid fave in the 'teens and twenties, and Valentino is atypically cast as a man's man. The sheik himself is said not to have like this one because it undermined his image as a ladies' man.
1922 71m/B Dorothy Dalton, Rudolph Valentino, Charles Brinley, Walter Long, Emil Jorgenson; *D:* George Melford. **VHS, Beta** $32.95 *GPV, FCT* 🐾🐾½

More Smells like teen angst in the sixties when a German college grad falls for an American in Paris, to the tune of sex, drugs, and Pink Floyd. Schroeder's first effort as director, it's definitely a sixties pic. In French with English subtitles.
1969 110m/C Mimsy Farmer, Klaus Grunberg, Heinz Engelmann, Michel Chanderli; *D:* Barbet Schroeder. **VHS, Beta** $59.99 *WAR, BTV, FCT* 🐾🐾½

More American Graffiti Sequel to 1973's acclaimed '50s homage ''American Graffiti'' charts various characters' experiences in the more radical '60s. George Lucas didn't direct, Richard Dreyfuss didn't reprise. Ron Howard doesn't direct, he acts. B.W.L. Norton doesn't direct either, though he's credited. Pass on this one and have that root canal done instead.
1979 (PG) 111m/C Candy Clark, Bo Hopkins, Ron Howard, Paul LeMat, MacKenzie Phillips, Charles Martin Smith, Anna Bjorn, Richard Bradford, Cindy Williams, Scott Glenn; *D:* B.W.L. Norton. **VHS** $14.98 *MCA* 🐾½

More! Police Squad More episodes from the seminal spoof of television cop shows, episodes entitled ''Revenge and Remorse,'' ''The Butler Did It'' and ''Testimony of Evil.''
1982 75m/C Leslie Nielsen, Alan North, Rex Hamilton, Peter Lupus; *D:* George Stevens. **VHS, Beta** $19.95 *PAR* 🐾½

The More the Merrier Likeable romantic comedy in which working girl must share apartment with two bachelors in Washington, D.C., during WWII. Arthur is especially endearing as a young woman in male company.
1943 104m/B Joel McCrea, Jean Arthur, Charles Coburn, Richard Gaines, Bruce (Herman Brix) Bennett, Ann Savage, Ann Doran, Frank Tully, Grady Sutton; *D:* George Stevens. Academy Awards '43: Best Supporting Actor (Coburn); Nominations: Best Actress (Arthur), Best Director

(Stevens), Best Picture, Best Story; New York Film Critics Awards '43: Best Director (Stevens). **VHS, Beta** $19.95 *COL, BTV* 🐾🐾🐾

More Wild, Wild West Another feature-length continuation of the satirical television western series, with Winters taking on Conrad and Martin. Made for television.
1980 94m/C Robert Conrad, Ross Martin, Jonathan Winters, Victor Buono; *D:* Burt Kennedy. **VHS, Beta** $59.98 *FOX* 🐾🐾

Morgan! Offbeat comedy in which deranged artist copes with divorce by donning ape suit. Some laughs ensue. Based on David Mercer's play. *AKA:* Morgan: A Suitable Case for Treatment; A Suitable Case for Treatment.
1966 93m/B Vanessa Redgrave, David Warner, Robert Stephens, Irene Handl; *D:* Karel Reisz. Academy Awards '66 Nominations: Best Actress (Redgrave), Best Costume Design (B & W); Cannes Film Festival '66: Best Actress (Redgrave). **VHS, Beta** *NO* 🐾🐾½

Morgan Stewart's Coming Home When Dad needs a good family image in his political race, he brings Morgan home from boarding school. Fortunately, Morgan can see how his parents are using him and he doesn't approve at all. He decides to turn his family's life upside down while pursuing the love of his life. *AKA:* Home Front.
1987 (PG-13) 96m/C Jon Cryer, Lynn Redgrave, Nicholas Pryor, Viveka Davis, Paul Gleason, Andrew Duncan, Savely Kramorov, John Cullum, Robert Sedgwick, Waweru Njenga, Sudhir Rad; *D:* Alan Smithee; *M:* Peter Bernstein. **VHS, Beta** $34.95 *HBO* 🐾🐾

Morgan the Pirate Steve Reeves is at his finest as Morgan, an escaped slave who becomes a notorious pirate in the Caribbean and is wrongly condemned to death in this brisk, sea-going adventure. *AKA:* Capitaine Morgan; Morgan il Pirata.
1960 93m/C Steve Reeves, Valerie Lagrange; *D:* Andre de Toth. **VHS, Beta** $39.98 *SUE, FCT* 🐾🐾

Morituri Gripping wartime drama in which an Allied spy tries to persuade German gunboat captain to surrender his vessel. Brando is—no surprise—excellent. *AKA:* Saboteur: Code Name Morituri; The Saboteur.
1965 123m/C Marlon Brando, Yul Brynner, Trevor Howard, Janet Margolin, Wally Cox, William Redfield; *D:* Bernhard Wicki; *W:* Daniel Taradash; *M:* Jerry Goldsmith. **VHS, Beta** $19.98 *FOX* 🐾🐾🐾

A Mormon Maid Young woman and her family, after being saved from an Indian attack by a Mormon group, come to live among them without converting to their beliefs. Considered a shocking expose of controversial Mormon practices, including polygamy.
1917 78m/B Mae Murray, Frank Borzage, Hobart Bosworth, Noah Beery Sr.; *D:* Robert Z. Leonard. **VHS, Beta** $24.95 *VYY, GVV* 🐾½

The Morning After A predictable suspense-thriller about an alcoholic actress who wakes up one morning with a corpse in bed next to her, but cannot remember anything about the night before. She evades the police, accidentally meets up with an ex-cop, and works with him to unravel an increasingly complicated mystery.
1986 (R) 103m/C Jane Fonda, Jeff Bridges, Raul Julia, Diane Salinger, Richard Foronjy, Geoffrey Scott, Kathleen Wilhoite, Frances Bergen, Rick Rossovich, Kathy Bates; *D:* Sidney Lumet. **VHS, Beta** $19.98 *LHV, WAR* 🐾🐾

Morning Glory Small-town girl finds love and fame in the big city. Predictable fare nonetheless boasts fine performances from Hepburn and Fairbanks. Adapted from Zoe Atkins' stage play.
1933 74m/B Katharine Hepburn, Douglas Fairbanks Jr., Adolphe Menjou, Mary Duncan; *D:* Lowell Sherman. **VHS, Beta** $19.98 *RKO, CCB, MED* 🐾🐾½

Morning Glory Sappy romance, set during the Depression, about a pregnant widow (Raffin) trying to survive on her hardscrabble farm in Georgia. Elly Dinsmore advertises for a husband, not for romance but to help with the work, and is answered by Will Parker (Reeve), an ex-con trying to live down his past. When a local floozy who has been eyeing Will is killed the sheriff (Walsh) is only too happy to go after the stranger in town. Light-weight with some unbelievable plot twists. Based on the novel ''Morning Glory'' by LaVyrle Spencer.
1993 (PG-13) 90m/C Deborah Raffin, Christopher Reeve, Lloyd Bochner, Nina Foch, Helen Shaver, J.T. Walsh; *D:* David Hillard Stern; *W:* Deborah Raffin, Charles Jarrott; *M:* Jonathan Elias. **VHS** *ACA* 🐾🐾½

Morocco A foreign legion soldier falls for a world-weary chanteuse along the desert sands. Cooper has never been more earnest, and Dietrich has never been more blase and exotic. In her American film debut, Dietrich sings ''What am I Bid?'' A must for anyone drawn to improbable, gloriously well-done kitsch. Based on Benno Vigny's novel, ''Amy Jolly.''
1930 92m/B Marlene Dietrich, Gary Cooper, Adolphe Menjou, Ullrich Haupt, Francis McDonald, Eve Southern, Paul Porcasi; *D:* Josef von Sternberg. **VHS, Beta** $14.95 *MCA, FCT* 🐾🐾🐾½

Morons from Outer Space Slow-witted aliens from elsewhere in the universe crash onto Earth, but unlike other sci-fis, these morons become internationally famous, despite them acting like intergalactic stooges. Plenty of sight gags.
1985 (PG) 87m/C Griff Rhys Jones, Mel Smith, James B. Sikking, Dinsdale Landen, Jimmy Nail, Joanne Pearce, Paul Brown; *D:* Mike Hodges; *M:* Peter Brewis. **VHS** $14.95 *MGM* 🐾🐾

Mortal Passions Another ''Double Indemnity'' rip-off, with a scheming tramp manipulating everyone around her with betrayal, sex, and murder. Her dead husband's brother eventually ignites old flames to steer her away from his money.
1990 (R) 96m/C Zach Galligan, Krista Errickson, Michael Bowen, Luca Bercovici, Sheila Kelley, David Warner; *D:* Andrew Lane. **VHS, Beta** $89.98 *FOX* 🐾½

Mortal Sins A TV evangelist finds more than salvation at the altar, when bodies begin to turn up. The detective he hires is close-mouthed, but more than a little interested in the preacher's daughter. A tense psychosexual thriller.
1990 (R) 85m/C Brian Benben, Anthony LaPaglia, Debrah Farentino; *D:* Yuri Sivo. **VHS** $29.95 *ACA, FXV* 🐾

Mortal Sins Reeve stars as parish priest Thomas Cusack, who hears the confession of a serial killer. What's worse is that the killer is preying on the women of Cusack's parish. Since he can't break the seal of the confessional, the good Father tries to stop the killer himself before another murder takes place.
1992 (PG-13) 93m/C Christopher Reeve; *D:* Bradford May. **VHS** $89.98 *FXV* 🐾🐾

The Mortal Storm Phyllis Bottome's famous novel comes to life in this extremely well acted film about the rise of the Nazi regime. Stewart and Sullavan are young lovers who risk everything to escape the country after their families are torn apart by the Nazi takeover. Although Germany is never identified as the country, it is obvious in this story about the early days of WWII. Hitler took one look at this and promptly banned all MGM movies in Nazi Germany.
1940 100m/B Margaret Sullavan, James Stewart, Robert Young, Frank Morgan, Robert Stack, Bonita Granville, Irene Rich; **D:** Frank Borzage; **W:** Claudine West, George Froeschel, Anderson Ellis. **VHS $19.98** MGM ☆☆☆½

Mortal Thoughts Best friends find their relationship tested when the brutal husband of one of them is murdered. Moore and Headly are exceptional, capturing the perfect inflections and attitudes of the hard-working New Jersey beauticians sure of their friendship. Excellent pacing, fine supporting cast, with Keitel and Willis stand-outs.
1991 (R) 104m/C Demi Moore, Bruce Willis, Glenne Headly, Harvey Keitel, John Pankow, Billie Neal; **D:** Alan Rudolph; **W:** William Reilly, Claude Kerven; **M:** Mark Isham. **VHS, Beta, 8mm $19.95** COL ☆☆☆

Mortuary Young woman's nightmares come startlingly close to reality.
1981 (R) 91m/C Christopher George, Lynda Day George, Paul Smith; **D:** Howard (Hikmet) Avedis. **VHS, Beta $79.98** LIV, VES ☆

Mortuary Academy To win an inheritance two brothers must attend the family mortician school, a situation paving the way for aggressively tasteless jokes on necrophilia. An attempt to recapture the successful black humor of the earlier Bartel/Woronov teaming "Eating Raoul," this one's dead on arrival.
1991 (R) 86m/C Christopher Atkins, Perry Lang, Paul Bartel, Mary Woronov, Tracy Walter, Lynn Danielson, Cesar Romero, Wolfman Jack; **D:** Michael Schroeder. **VHS $79.95** COL ☆

Mosby's Marauders A young boy joins a Confederate raiding company during the Civil War and learns about bravery, war, and love.
1966 79m/C Kurt Russell, James MacArthur, Jack Ging, Peggy Lipton, Nick Adams; **D:** Michael O'Herlihy. **VHS, Beta $69.95** DIS ☆☆

Moscow Does Not Believe in Tears Three Soviet women realize very different fates when they pursue their dreams in 1950's Moscow. Bittersweet, moving fare that seems a somewhat surprising production from pre-Glasnost USSR. Brief nudity and violence. In Russian with English subtitles. A 150-minute version has also been released. **AKA:** Moscow Distrusts Tears; Moskwa Sljesam Nje Jerit.
1980 115m/C Vera Alentova, Irina Muravyova, Raisa Ryazanova, Natalie Vavilova, Alexei Batalov; **D:** Vladimir Menshov. **VHS, Beta $59.98** COL, IME, ING ☆☆☆

Moscow on the Hudson Good-natured comedy has Williams as Soviet defector trying to cope with new life of freedom in fast-paced, freewheeling melting pot of New York City. Williams is particularly winning as naive jazzman, though Alonso also scores as his Hispanic love interest. Be warned though, it's not just played for laughs.
1984 (R) 115m/C Robin Williams, Maria Conchita Alonso, Cleavant Derricks, Alejandro Rey, Elya Baskin; **D:** Paul Mazursky; **W:** Leon Capetanos, Paul Mazursky. **VHS, Beta, 8mm $14.95** COL ☆☆☆

Moses Lancaster goes biblical as Moses, the man with the tablets. Edited from the 360-minute British television series, with no improvement obvious from the economy, except that the bad parts are shorter. Poor chatter and scattered bouts of acting are surpassed in inadequacy only by special effects.
1976 (PG) 141m/C Burt Lancaster, Anthony Quayle, Ingrid Thulin, Irene Papas, William Lancaster; **D:** Gianfranco DeBosio; **W:** Anthony Burgess, Vittorio Bonicelli; **M:** Ennio Morricone. **VHS, Beta $19.98** FOX, LIV, VES Woof!

The Mosquito Coast Ambitious adaptation of Paul Theroux's novel about an asocial inventor who transplants his family to a rainforest to realize his utopian dream. A nightmare ensues. Ford tries hard, but supporters Mirren and Phoenix are main appeal of only intermittently successful drama.
1986 (PG) 119m/C Harrison Ford, Helen Mirren, River Phoenix, Andre Gregory, Martha Plimpton, Conrad Roberts, Butterfly McQueen, Jadrien Steele, Hilary Gordon, Rebecca Gordon, Dick O'Neill, Jason Alexander; **D:** Peter Weir; **W:** Paul Schrader; **M:** Maurice Jarre. **VHS, Beta $19.98** WAR ☆☆½

The Most Dangerous Game Shipwrecked McRae washed ashore on the island of Banks's Count Zaroff, a deranged sportsman with a flair for tracking humans. Guess who becomes the mad count's next target. Oft-told tale is compellingly related in this, the first of many using Richard Connell's famous short story. If deja vu sets in, don't worry. This production uses most of the scenery, staff, and cast from its studio cousin, "King Kong." Remade in 1945 as "A Game of Death" and in 1956 as "Run for the Sun." **AKA:** The Hounds of Zaroff.
1932 78m/B Joel McCrea, Fay Wray, Leslie Banks, Robert Armstrong; **D:** Ernest B. Schoedsack, Irving Pichel. **VHS, Beta $16.95** SNC, NOS, MED ☆☆☆

Most Wanted A psychopath with a penchant for raping nuns and collecting crucifixes is tracked down by a special police unit in this made-for-television film. Became a TV series.
1976 78m/C Robert Stack, Shelly Novack, Leslie Charleson, Tom Selleck, Sheree North; **D:** Walter Grauman. **VHS, Beta $49.95** WOV ☆½

Motel Hell A completely tongue-in-cheek gore-fest about a farmer who kidnaps tourists, buries them in his garden, and reaps a human harvest to grind into his distinctive brand of smoked, preservative-free sausage.
1980 (R) 102m/C Rory Calhoun, Nancy Parsons, Paul Linke, Nina Axelrod, Wolfman Jack, Elaine Joyce, Dick Curtis; **D:** Kevin Connor. **VHS, Beta $14.95** MGM ☆½

Mother Pudovkin's innovative classic about a Russian family shattered by the uprising in 1905. A masterpiece of Russian cinema that established Pudovkin, and rivaled only Eisenstein for supremacy in montage, poetic imagery, and propagandistic ideals. Based on Maxim Gorky's great novel, it's one of cinematic history's seminal works. Striking cinematography, stunning use of montage make this one important. Silent with English subtitles.
1926 70m/B Vera Baranovskaya, Nikolai Batalov; **D:** Vsevolod Pudovkin. **VHS, Beta $24.95** NOS, IHF, DVT ☆☆☆½

Mother A Japanese family is undone after the devastation of WWII. An uncharacteristically dramatic, and thus more accessible, film from one of the Japanese cinema's greatest masters. In Japanese with English subtitles. **AKA:** Okasan.

1952 98m/B Kinuyo Tanaka, Kyoko Kagawa, Eiji Okada, Akihiko Katayama; **D:** Mikio Naruse. **VHS, Beta** FCT, IME, ING ☆☆☆½

Mother & Daughter: A Loving War A made-for-television film about three women experiencing motherhood. Special appearance by Harry Chapin as himself.
1980 96m/C Tuesday Weld, Frances Sternhagen, Kathleen Beller, Jeanne Lang, Ed Winter; **D:** Burt Brinckerhoff. **VHS, Beta $59.98** NLC ☆½

Mother and Son Melodrama finds the wayward Young shielding her son from the fact that she runs a gambling hall. He grows up to be a society lad before discovering the devastating truth.
1931 67m/B Clara Kimball Young, Bruce Warren, Mildred Golden, John Elliott, Gordon Wood, Ernest Hilliard q; **D:** John P. McCarthy. **VHS $11.95** GPV ☆

Mother Doesn't Always Know Best A strange relationship between a young count and his widowed mother initiates a strange series of events.
1967 95m/C Senta Berger; **D:** Alfredo Gianelli. **VHS, Beta** NO ☆½

Mother Goose Rock 'n' Rhyme Duvall follows the success of her "Faerie Tale Theatre" series with a new comedic fable, starring some of Hollywood's top names. Great fun for the whole family.
1990 96m/C Shelley Duvall, Teri Garr, Howie Mandel, Jean Stapleton, Ben Vereen, Bobby Brown, Art Garfunkel, Dan Gilroy, Deborah Harry, Cyndi Lauper, Little Richard, Paul Simon, Stray Cats, ZZ Top, Harry Anderson, Elayne Boosler, Woody Harrelson, Richard "Cheech" Marin, Garry Shandling. **VHS, Beta $79.98** MED ☆½

Mother, Jugs and Speed Black comedy about the day-to-day tragedies encountered by a group of ambulance drivers. Interesting mix of stars.
1976 (PG) 95m/C Bill Cosby, Raquel Welch, Harvey Keitel, Allen (Gooritz) Garfield, Larry Hagman, Bruce Davison, Dick Butkus, L.Q. Jones, Toni Basil; **D:** Peter Yates; **W:** Tom Mankiewicz. **VHS $79.98** FOX ☆½

Mother Kusters Goes to Heaven Mrs. Kusters's husband is a frustrated factory worker who goes over the edge and kills the factory owner's son and himself. Left alone, she learns that everyone is using her husband's death to further their own needs, including her daughter, who uses the publicity to enhance her singing career. A statement that you should trust no one, not even your family and friends. This film was banned from the Berlin Film Festival because of its political overtones. In German with English subtitles. **AKA:** Mutter Kusters Fahrt Zum Himmel.
1976 108m/C Brigitte Mira, Ingrid Caven, Armin Meier, Irm Hermann, Gottfried John, Margit Carstensen; **D:** Rainer Werner Fassbinder; **W:** Rainer Werner Fassbinder. **VHS $79.95** NYF ☆☆☆

Mother Lode The violent conflict between twin brothers (played by Heston) is intensified by greed, near madness, and the all-consuming lust for gold in this action-adventure. Heston's son, Fraser Clarke Heston, wrote as well as produced the film. **AKA:** Search for the Mother Lode; The Last Great Treasure.
1982 (PG) 101m/C Charlton Heston, Nick Mancuso; **D:** Charlton Heston. **VHS, Beta $79.95** VES ☆½

Mother of Kings Livin' ain't easy for a widowed charwoman thanks to WWII and Stalinism. Innovative use of newsreel scenes. In Polish with English subtitles.
1982 126m/C Magda Teresa Wojcik. **VHS $49.99** FCT ☆☆

Mother's Boys Estranged mother Curtis attempts to reunite with the family she abandoned only to be snubbed, inspiring in her a ruthless effort to win back the children and oust father Gallagher's new live-in girlfriend Whalley-Kilmer. With an almost psychotic devotion, she terrorizes everyone in the family, including enticing her 12-year-old son Edwards into a nude bathtub game of peek-a-boo. Film lacks the tension necessary to carry suspense. Based on the novel by Bernard Taylor.
1994 (R) 95m/C Jamie Lee Curtis, Peter Gallagher, Joanne Whalley-Kilmer, Luke Edwards, Vanessa Redgrave, Colin Ward, Joss Ackland, Paul Guilfoyle, John C. McGinley, J.E. Freeman, Ken Lerner, Lorraine Toussaint, Joey Zimmerman, Jill Freedman; **D:** Yves Simoneau; **W:** Richard Hawley, Barry Schneider; **M:** George S. Clinton. **VHS** *✶✶*

Mother's Day Three women who were former college roommates plan a reunion together in the wilderness. All goes well until they are dragged into an isolated house by two insane boys who constantly watch television, ardently consume the products advertised, and then terrorize and torture people to please their mom. Sanitized gore with black satiric intentions.
1980 98m/C Tiana Pierce, Nancy Hendrickson, Deborah Luee, Holden McGuire, Billy Ray McQuade, Rose Ross; **D:** Charles Kaufman; **W:** Warren Leight, Charles Kaufman. **VHS, Beta** **$49.95** *MED ✶½*

Mothra Classic Japanese monster shenanigans about an enraged giant caterpillar that invades Tokyo while searching for the Alilenas, a set of very tiny, twin princesses who've been kidnapped by an evil nightclub owner in the pursuit of big profits. After tiring of crushing buildings and wreaking incidental havoc, the enormous crawly thing zips up into a cocoon and emerges as Mothra, a moth distinguished by both its size and bad attitude. Mothra and the wee babes make appearances in later Godzilla epics.
1962 101m/C Yumi Ito, Frankie Sakai, Lee Kresel, Emi Ito; **D:** Inoshiro Honda. **VHS, Beta** **$9.95** *GKK ✶✶✶*

Motor Patrol A cop poses as a racketeer to infiltrate a car-stealing ring.
1950 66m/B Don Castle, Jane Nigh, Charles Victor. **VHS, Beta** *NO ✶½*

Motor Psycho When a motorcycle gang rapes a woman, she and her husband pursue them into the desert to seek their brutal revenge.
1965 73m/B Haji, Alex Rocco, Stephen Oliver, Holle K. Winters, Joseph Cellini, Thomas Scott, Coleman Francis, Sharon Lee; **D:** Russ Meyer. **VHS** *RMF ✶½*

Motorama A 10-year-old juvenile delinquent becomes obsessed with winning a gas station contest which involves collecting game cards. So he steals a car and hits the road where he gets his first tattoo and encounters a beautiful "older" woman (Barrymore) and lots of trouble.
1991 (R) 89m/C Jordan Christopher Michael, Martha Quinn, Flea, Michael J. Pollard, Meatloaf, Drew Barrymore, Garrett Morris, Robin Duke, Sandy Baron, Mary Woronov, Susan Tyrrell, John Laughlin, John Diehl, Robert Picardo, Jack Nance, Vince Edwards, Dick Miller, Allyce Beasley, Shelley Berman; **D:** Barry Shils; **W:** Joe Minion; **M:** Andy Summers. **VHS $89.95** *COL, BTV ✶✶*

Motorcycle Gang It's the summer of '57, and Randy plans to bring home the title at the Pacific Motorcycle Championships for his club, the "Skyriders." But first his old rival Nick, who's just out of jail, turns up and challenges Randy to an illegal street race.

Will Randy succumb to peer pressure and race? Lame plot + lame acting = lame movie.
1957 78m/B Steven Terrell, John Ashley, Anne Neyland, Carl "Alfalfa" Switzer, Raymond Hatton; **D:** Edward L. Cahn; **W:** Lou Rusoff. **VHS $9.95** *COL ✶*

Motorcycle Squad A policeman is dishonorably discharged so he can get the "inside" dope on a gang of crooks in this 'B' thriller.
1937 ?m/C Kane Richmond, Wynne Gibson. **VHS $16.95** *SNC ✶½*

Motown's Mustang Eleven old Motown hits are used as the framework for this new musical drama featuring cameos by various artists, about a '64 Mustang passing through various owners' hands and cultural changes.
1986 43m/C Clyde Jones, Christi Shay, Louis Carr Jr., Billy Preston, The Temptations. **VHS, Beta $19.95** *MCA ✶½*

Mouchette A lonely 14-year-old French girl, daughter of a drunk father and dying mother, eventually finds spiritual release by committing suicide. Typically somber, spiritual fare from unique master filmmaker Bresson. Perhaps the most complete expression of Bresson's austere, Catholic vision. In French with English subtitles.
1960 80m/B Nadine Nortier, Maria Cardinal, Paul Hebert; **D:** Robert Bresson. **VHS, Beta $59.95** *FCT, ING, TPV ✶✶✶½*

Moulin Rouge Colorful, entertaining portrait of acclaimed Impressionist painter Toulouse-Lautrec, more famous for its production stories than on-screen drama. Ferrer delivers one of his most impressive performances as the physically stunted, cynical artist who basked in the seamy Montmartre nightlife.
1952 119m/C Jose Ferrer, Zsa Zsa Gabor, Christopher Lee, Peter Cushing, Colette Marchand, Katherine Kath, Michael Balfour, Eric Pohlmann; **D:** John Huston. Academy Awards '52: Best Art Direction/Set Decoration (Color), Best Costume Design (Color); Nominations: Best Actor (Ferrer), Best Director (Huston), Best Film Editing, Best Picture, Best Supporting Actress (Marchand); National Board of Review Awards '53: 5 Best Foreign Films of the Year. **VHS, Beta $19.95** *MGM ✶✶✶½*

The Mountain A man and his shady younger brother set out to inspect a Paris-routed plane that crashed in the French Alps. After some harrowing experiences in climbing the peak, it becomes evident that one brother has designs to save whatever he can, while the other intends to loot it. Many real, as well as staged, climbing scenes. Based on Henri Troyat's novel.
1956 105m/C Spencer Tracy, Robert Wagner, Claire Trevor, William Demarest, Richard Arlen, E.G. Marshall; **D:** Edward Dmytryk. **VHS, Beta $19.95** *PAR ✶✶*

Mountain Charlie Mountain girl's life is destroyed by three drifters.
1980 96m/C Denise Neilson, Dick Robinson, Rick Guinn, Lynn Seus; **D:** George Stapleford. **VHS, Beta** *NO ✶½*

Mountain Family Robinson An urban family, seeking escape from the hassles of city life, moves to the Rockies, determined to get back to nature. They soon find that nature may be more harsh than rush-hour traffic and nasty bosses when a bear comes calling. More "Wilderness Family"-type adventures.
1979 (G) 102m/C Robert F. Logan, Susan Damante Shaw, Heather Rattray, Ham Larsen, William Bryant, George Flower; **D:** John Cotter. **VHS, Beta $9.98** *MED, VTR ✶✶*

Mountain Fury A spoof based on the novel by Alexandre Dumas wherein two brothers separated at birth are reunited and battle against an evil French baron.
1990 (R) 90m/C VHS *NO ✶✶*

Mountain Justice Maynard's first all-talkie western finds our hero in search of his father's murderer. Good action sequences (with stunts performed by Maynard), including those aboard a moving train and a buckboard. **AKA:** Kettle Creek.
1930 73m/B Ken Maynard, Otis Harlan, Kathryn Crawford, Paul Hurst; **D:** Harry Joe Brown. **VHS $12.95** *GPV ✶✶½*

Mountain Man Historically accurate drama about Galen Clark's successful fight in the 1860s to save the magnificent wilderness area that is now Yosemite National Park. Together with naturalist John Muir, he fought a battle against the lumber companies who wanted the timber and won President Lincoln's support for his cause. **AKA:** Guardian of the Wilderness.
1977 96m/C Denver Pyle, John Dehner, Ken Berry, Cheryl Miller, Don Shanks, Cliff Osmond, Jack Kruschen, Ford Rainey; **D:** David O'Malley; **W:** David O'Malley. **VHS, Beta** *LME ✶✶½*

The Mountain Men Dull adventure drama set in the American West of the 1880s. Two trappers argue about life and have trouble with Indians.
1980 (R) 102m/C Charlton Heston, Brian Keith, John Glover, Seymour Cassel, Victor Jory; **D:** Richard Lang. **VHS, Beta $9.95** *COL ✶½*

The Mountain Road Listless drama of an American squadron stationed in China during the last days of WWII. Only Stewart makes this drab film worthwhile.
1960 102m/B James Stewart, Harry Morgan, Glenn Corbett, Mike Kellin; **D:** Daniel Mann. **VHS $14.99** *COL ✶½*

Mountains of the Moon Sprawling adventure detailing the obsessive search for the source of the Nile conducted by famed Victorian rogue/explorer Sir Richard Burton and cohort John Hanning Speke in the late 1800s. Spectacular scenery and images. Director Rafelson, better known for overtly personal films such as "Five Easy Pieces" and "The King of Marvin Gardens," shows considerable skill with this epic. Cinematography by Roger Deakins. From William Harrison's novel "Burton and Speke."
1990 (R) 140m/C Patrick Bergin, Iain Glen, Fiona Shaw, Richard E. Grant, Peter Vaughan, Roger Rees, Bernard Hill, Anna Massey, Leslie Phillips, John Savident, James Villers, Delroy Lindo, Roshan Seth; **D:** Bob Rafelson; **W:** Bob Rafelson. **VHS, Beta $89.95** *LIV ✶✶✶½*

Mountaintop Motel Massacre A resort motel's hostess is a raving lunatic who regularly slaughters her guests.
1986 95m/C Bill Thurman, Anna Chappell, Will Mitchell; **D:** Jim McCullough. **VHS, Beta $19.95** *STE, NWV* Woof!

Mouse and His Child A gentle animated fantasy adventure about a toy wind-up mouse and his child who fall into the clutches of a villainous rat when they venture into the outside world.
1977 83m/C D: Fred Wolf; **V:** Peter Ustinov, Cloris Leachman, Andy Devine. **VHS, Beta $19.95** *COL, WTA ✶✶*

The Mouse That Roared With its wine export business going down the drain, a tiny, desperate country decides to declare war on the United States in hopes that the U.S., after its inevitable triumph, will revive the conquered nation. So off to New York go 20 chain-mail clad warriors armed with bow and arrow. Featured in three roles, Sellers is great as the duchess, less effective (though still funny) as the prime minister, and a military leader. A must for Sellers' fans; maintains a sharp satiric edge throughout. Based on the novel by Leonard Wibberley. **1959 83m/C** Peter Sellers, Jean Seberg, Leo McKern; *D:* Jack Arnold. **VHS, Beta $19.95** COL *ɪɪ*

Movers and Shakers An irreverent spoof of Hollywood depicting a filmmaker's attempt to render a best-selling sex manual into a blockbuster film. Fails to live up to its potential and wastes a star-studded cast. **1985 (PG) 100m/C** Walter Matthau, Charles Grodin, Gilda Radner, Vincent Gardenia, Bill Macy, Tyne Daly, Steve Martin, Penny Marshall, Luana Anders; *D:* William Asher; *W:* Charles Grodin. **VHS, Beta $79.95** MGM *ɪ* 1/2

The Movie House Massacre A psychopath runs rampant in a theatre killing and maiming moviegoers. No refunds are given. **1978 80m/C** Mary Woronov. **VHS, Beta $24.95** AHV, MRV *ɪ*

Movie...In Your Face Japanese mobsters want to take over a movie studio. This supposed comedy comes with a "PU-13" rating—"Stinks to anyone with an I.Q. over 13," make of that what you will and be forewarned that it's also sophomoric and tasteless. **1990 85m/C** Tommy Sledge. **VHS $89.95** HTV *ɪ*

Movie Maker A young filmmaker ineptly raises money for his next film. *AKA:* Smart Alec. **1986 87m/C** Zsa Zsa Gabor, Antony Alda, Orson Bean, Bill Henderson; *D:* Jim Wilson. **VHS, Beta $79.98** LIV *ɪ*

Movie, Movie Acceptable spoof of 1930s films features Scott in twin-bill of black and white "Dynamite Hands," which lampoons boxing dramas, and "Baxter's Beauties," a color send-up of Busby Berkeley musicals. There's even a parody of coming attractions. Wholesome, mildly entertaining. **1978 (PG) 107m/B** Stanley Donen, George C. Scott, Trish Van Devere, Eli Wallach, Red Buttons, Barbara Harris, Barry Bostwick, Harry Hamlin, Art Carney; *D:* Stanley Donen; *W:* Larry Gelbart; *M:* Ralph Burns. **VHS** FOX *ɪɪ* 1/2

A Movie Star's Daughter The daughter of a famous movie star moves to a new town and school. She is afraid her popularity is due to her famous father. She must make choices and learn the real meaning of friendship. Also available in a 33-minute edited version. **1979 46m/C** Frank Converse, Trini Alvarado; *D:* Robert Fuest. **VHS, Beta $14.95** LCA *ɪ*

Movie Stuntmen A retired Hollywood stunt man takes a job for a dead friend so that the friend's widow can receive the fee. Good stunt work taken mostly from old Richard Taldmadge movies almost makes up for poor production. *AKA:* Hollywood Thrillmakers; Hollywood Stunt Man. **1953 56m/B** James Gleason, William Henry; *D:* Bernard B. Ray. **VHS $19.95** NOS *ɪ*

Moving An engineer must relocate his family from New Jersey to Idaho in order to get his dream job. Predictable calamities ensue. Not apt to move you. **1988 (R) 89m/C** Richard Pryor, Randy Quaid, Dana Carvey, Dave Thomas, Rodney Dangerfield, Stacey Dash; *D:* Alan Metter. **VHS, Beta, 8mm $19.98** WAR *ɪ*

Moving Out Adolescent migrant Italian boy finds it difficult to adjust to his new surroundings in Melbourne, Australia. **1983 91m/C** Vince Colosimo, Sally Cooper, Maurice Devincentis, Tibor Gyapjas; *D:* Michael Pattinson. **VHS, Beta** NO *ɪɪ*

Moving Target A young woman witnesses the brutal murder of her boyfriend by mobsters and flees to Florida. Unbeknownst to her, the thugs are still after her. Although top-billed, Blair's role is actually a supporting one. **1989 (R) 85m/C** Linda Blair, Ernest Borgnine, Stuart Whitman, Charles Pitt, Jainine Linde, Kurt Woodruff; *D:* Marius Mattei. **VHS, Beta $14.95** HMD *ɪ* 1/2

Moving Targets A young girl and her mother find themselves tracked by a homicidal maniac. **1987 95m/C** Michael Aitkens, Carmen Duncan, Annie Jones, Shane Briant; *D:* Chris Langman. **VHS, Beta $29.95** ACA *ɪɪ*

Moving Violation Crooked cops chase two young drifters who have witnessed the local sheriff commit a murder. Corman car chase epic. **1976 (PG) 91m/C** Eddie Albert, Kay Lenz, Stephen McHattie, Will Geer, Loni Chapman; *D:* Charles S. Dubin; *W:* William W. Norton Sr. **VHS, Beta $59.98** FOX *ɪɪ*

Moving Violations This could be entitled "Adventures in Traffic Violations School." A wise-cracking tree planter is sent to traffic school after accumulating several moving violations issued to him by a morose traffic cop. Bill Murray's little brother in feature role. **1985 (PG-13) 90m/C** John Murray, Jennifer Tilly, James Keach, Brian Backer, Sally Kellerman, Fred Willard, Clara Peller, Wendie Jo Sperber; *D:* Neal Israel; *W:* Pat Proft; *M:* Ralph Burns. **VHS, Beta $79.98** FOX *ɪɪ*

Mozart: A Childhood Chronicle An experimental, semi-narrative portrait of the immortal composer, from the ages of seven to twenty, filmed on authentic locations and with the original instruments of the era. Entire soundtrack is composed of Mozart's music. In German with English subtitles. **1976 224m/B** *D:* Klaus Kirschner. **VHS, Beta $99.95** KIV, IME, GLV *ɪɪɪ*

The Mozart Brothers An angst-ridden Swedish opera director decides to break all the rules while doing an innovative production of Mozart's "Don Giovanni." At first he horrifies his conservative opera company but as his vision is gradually realized their resistance breaks down. A wonderful look at behind-the-scenes chaos and not just for opera aficionados. In Swedish with English subtitles. **1986 111m/C** Etienne Glaser, Philip Zanden, Henry Bronett; *D:* Suzanne Osten. **VHS $59.95** TPV, ING *ɪɪɪ*

The Mozart Story After Mozart's death, music minister to the Emperor, Antonio Salieri, reflects on how his jealousy and hatred of the musical genius held the great composer back and contributed to his death. Originally filmed in Austria in 1937, scenes were added for the U.S. release in 1948. **1948 91m/B** Hans Holt, Winnie Markus, Irene von Meyendorf, Rene Deltgen, Edward Vedder, Wilton Graff, Walther Jansson, Curt Jurgens, Paul Hoerbiger; *D:* Karl Hartl. **VHS, Beta $24.95** VYY, GLV *ɪɪ*

Much Ado About Nothing Shakespeare for the masses details romance between two sets of would-be lovers—the battling Beatrice and Benedick (Thompson and Branagh) and the ingenuous Hero and Claudio (Beckinsdale and Leonard). Washington is the noble warrior leader, Reeves his evil half-dressed half-brother, and Keaton serves comic relief as the officious, bumbling Dogberry. Sunlit, lusty, and revealing about all the vagaries of love, Branagh brings passion to his quest of making Shakespeare more approachable. His second attempt after "Henry V" at breaking the stuffy Shakespearean tradition. Filmed on location in Tuscany, Italy. **1993 (PG-13) 110m/C** Kenneth Branagh, Emma Thompson, Robert Sean Leonard, Kate Beckinsale, Denzel Washington, Keanu Reeves, Michael Keaton, Brian Blessed, Phyllida Law, Imelda Staunton, Gerard Horan, Jimmy Yuill, Richard Clifford, Ben Elton; *D:* Kenneth Branagh; *W:* Kenneth Branagh; *M:* Patrick Doyle. **VHS** COL *ɪɪɪ* 1/2

Mugsy's Girls A messy comedy about six sorority women, educated in the refined skills of bar mud wrestling, who wallow in a Las Vegas championship tournament. Features pop singer Laura Branigan. *AKA:* Delta Pi. **1985 (R) 87m/C** Ruth Gordon, Laura Branigan, Eddie Deezen; *D:* Kevin Brodie. **VHS, Beta $79.98** LIV, VES *ɪ*

Multiple Maniacs Waters at his most perverse. Divine's travelling freak show, filled with disgusting side-show sex acts, is the vehicle used for robbing and killing hapless spectators. One of the best scenes of a sordid lot is Divine being raped by Lobstora, a 15-foot broiled lobster. **1970 90m/B** Divine, David Lochary, Mary Vivian Pearce, Edith Massey, Mink Stole; *D:* John Waters. **VHS** NO *ɪ*

The Mummy Eerie chills mark this classic horror tale of an Egyptian priest, buried alive nearly 4000 years earlier, who comes back to life after a 1921 archeological dig. Eight hours of extraordinary makeup transformed Karloff into the macabre mummy, who believes the soul of the long-deceased (and probably long-decayed) lover resides in the body of a young woman. Marked the directing debut of famed German cinematographer Freund. **1932 72m/B** Boris Karloff, Zita Johann, David Manners, Edward Van Sloan; *D:* Karl Freund. **VHS, Beta $14.95** MCA, TLF *ɪɪɪ* 1/2

The Mummy A group of British archaeologists discover they have made a grave mistake when a mummy kills off those who have violated his princess' tomb. A summation of all the previous "mummy" films, this one has a more frightening mummy (6'4" Lee) who is on screen much of the time. Additionally, there is pathos in this monster, not merely murder and revenge. An effective remake of the 1932 classic. **1959 88m/C** Peter Cushing, Christopher Lee, Felix Aylmer, Yvonne Furneaux; *D:* Terence Fisher; *W:* Jimmy Sangster. **VHS, Beta $14.95** WAR, MLB *ɪɪɪ*

Mummy & Curse of the Jackal Upon opening the tomb of female mummy, a man is cursed to roam the streets of Las Vegas as a werejackal. Impossibly inept. **1967 86m/C** Anthony Eisley, Martina Pons, John Carradine, Saul Goldsmith; *D:* Oliver Drake. **VHS $19.95** ACA Woof!

The Mummy's Curse Sequel to "The Mummy's Ghost" and Chaney's last outing as Kharis. Construction by a government order causes Kharis and Ananka to be dug up in a Louisiana bayou and taken to Cajun country for study by archaeologists. The usual havoc ensues. Includes lots of stock footage from earlier mummy movies. Based on a story by Leon Abrams and Dwight V. Babcock.

1944 61m/B Lon Chaney Jr., Peter Coe, Virginia Christine, Kay Harding, Dennis Moore, Martin Kosleck, Kurt Katch; **D:** Leslie Goodwins; **W:** Bernard Shubert. **VHS $14.98** MCA, FCT ⅛⅛

The Mummy's Ghost Sequel to "The Mummy's Tomb" has Chaney, Jr. searching for the reincarnation of his ancient love, Princess Ananka. The least interesting entry in the series. Based on a story by Griffith Jay and Henry Sucher.
1944 61m/B Lon Chaney Jr., John Carradine, Ramsay Ames, Robert Lowery, Barton MacLane, George Zucco; **D:** Reginald LeBorg; **W:** Griffin Jay, Henry Sucher, Brenda Weisberg. **VHS $14.98** MCA, FCT ⅛⅛

The Mummy's Hand Two archaeologists (Foran and Ford) searching for the tomb of ancient Egyptian Princess Ananka discover more than they bargained for when they find that an evil and deadly mummy is the tomb's guardian. From there the plot unravels, but the good cast and a mix of scares and comedy make this worth watching.
1940 70m/B Dick Foran, Wallace Ford, Peggy Moran, Cecil Kellaway, George Zucco, Tom Tyler, Eduardo Ciannelli, Charles Trowbridge; **D:** Christy Cabanne. **VHS $14.98** MCA ⅛⅛½

The Mummy's Revenge A fanatic revives a mummy with virgin blood. The first mummy movie to feature open gore.
1973 91m/C Paul Naschy, Jack Taylor, Maria Silva, Helga Line; **D:** Carlos Aured; **W:** Paul Naschy. **VHS, Beta $49.95** UNI ⅛

The Mummy's Tomb Chaney, Jr. is in wraps for the first time in this sequel to "The Mummy's Hand." Kharis is transported to America by a crazed Egyptian high priest to kill off surviving members of the expedition. Weakened by a lame script and too much stock footage. Based on a story by Neil P. Varnick.
1942 71m/B Lon Chaney Jr., Dick Foran, John Hubbard, Elyse Knox, George Zucco, Wallace Ford, Turhan Bey; **D:** Harold Young; **W:** Griffin Jay, Henry Sucher. **VHS $14.98** MCA, FCT ⅛⅛

Munchie A forgotten alien critter is discovered in a mine shaft by young Gage. Munchie turns out to be a good friend, protecting Gage from bullies and granting other wishes. Frequent sight gags help keep the film moving but it's still awfully slow. Sequel to "Munchies" (1987).
1992 (PG) 80m/C Loni Anderson, Andrew Stevens, Arte Johnson, Jamie McEnnan; **D:** Jim Wynorski; **V:** Dom DeLuise. **VHS $89.98** NHO ⅛½

Munchies "Gremlins" rip-off about tiny aliens who love beer and fast food, and invade a small town. Lewd and ribald.
1987 (PG) 83m/C Harvey Korman, Charles Stratton, Nadine Van Der Velde; **D:** Bettina Hirsch. **VHS, Beta $14.98** MGM ⅛

Munster's Revenge Television movie based on the continuing adventures of the 1960s comedy series characters. Herman, Lily, and Grandpa have to contend with robot replicas of themselves that were created by a flaky scientist.
1981 96m/C Fred Gwynne, Yvonne De Carlo, Al Lewis, Jo McDonnel, Sid Caesar, Ezra Stone, Howard Morris, Bob Hastings, K.C. Martel; **D:** Don Weis. **VHS, Beta $14.98** MCA ⅛

The Muppet Christmas Carol Christmas classic features all the muppet favorites together and in Victorian garb. Storyline is more or less faithful to Dickens original, with pleasant special effects. Gonzo the Great as Dickens narrates the tale as Scrooge (Caine) takes his legendary Christmas Eve journey escorted by three (flannel) spirits. The Cratchits are led by Kermit and Miss Piggy. Directed by Brian Henson, Jim's

son, the film is as heartwarming as the Cratchit's crackling fire, but doesn't quite achieve the former muppet magic. Also features some sappy songs by Williams, including "Love is Like a Heatwave" and "Island in the Sun."
1992 (G) 120m/C Michael Caine; **D:** Brian Henson; **M:** Paul Williams, Miles Goodman; **V:** Dave Goelz, Steve Whitmire, Jerry Nelson, Frank Oz. **VHS, Beta $22.99** JHV ⅛⅛½

The Muppet Movie Seeking fame and footlights, Kermit the Frog and his pal Fozzie Bear travel to Hollywood, and along the way are joined by sundry human and muppet characters, including the lovely Miss Piggy. A delightful cult favorite filled with entertaining cameos, memorable (though somewhat pedestrian) songs and crafty special effects—Kermit rides a bike and rows a boat! A success for the late Jim Henson. ♫The Rainbow Connection; Frog's Legs So Fine; Movin Right Along; Can You Picture That?; Never Before; Something Better; This Looks Familiar; I'm Going Back There Someday.
1979 (G) 94m/C Jim Henson's Muppets; **Cameos:** Edgar Bergen, Milton Berle, Mel Brooks, Madeline Kahn, Steve Martin, Carol Kane, Paul Williams, Charles Durning, Bob Hope, James Coburn, Dom DeLuise, Elliott Gould, Cloris Leachman, Telly Savalas, Orson Welles; **D:** James Frawley; **V:** Jim Henson, Frank Oz. **VHS, Beta $22.99** JHV, FOX ⅛⅛⅛½

The Muppets Take Manhattan Following a smashing success with a college musical, the Muppets take their show and talents to Broadway, only to face misfortune in the form of an unscrupulous producer. A less imaginative script than the first two Muppet movies, yet an enjoyable experience with numerous major stars making cameo appearances.
1984 (G) 94m/C Jim Henson's Muppets; **Cameos:** Dabney Coleman, James Coco, Art Carney, Joan Rivers, Gregory Hines, Linda Lavin, Liza Minnelli, Brooke Shields, John Landis; **D:** Frank Oz; **M:** Ralph Burns; **V:** Jim Henson, Frank Oz. **VHS, Beta $14.98** FOX, HMV ⅛⅛⅛

Murder Believing in a young woman's innocence, one jurist begins to organize the pieces of the crime in order to save her. Fine early effort by Hitchcock based on play "Enter Sir John," by Clemense Dane and Helen Simpson.
1930 92m/B Herbert Marshall, Nora Baring, Phyllis Konstam, Miles Mander; **D:** Alfred Hitchcock; **W:** Alfred Hitchcock. **VHS, Beta $9.98** REP, NOS, HHT ⅛⅛⅛

Murder Ahoy Miss Marple looks perplexed when dead bodies surface on a naval cadet training ship. Dame Marge is the dottie detective in the final, and least appealing, of her four Agatha Christie films of the sixties (although it was released in the States prior to "Murder Most Foul").
1964 74m/B Margaret Rutherford, Lionel Jeffries, Charles Tingwell, William Mervyn, Francis Matthews; **D:** George Pollock. **VHS, Beta $19.98** MGM, FCT ⅛⅛½

Murder at 45 R.P.M. A singer and her lover suspect each other of her husband's murder. Things become sticky when she receives a recorded message from her dead husband. Average. **AKA:** Meurtre en 45 Tours.
1965 98m/C Danielle Darrieux, Michel Auclair, Jean Servais, Henri Guisol; **D:** Etienne Perier. **VHS $16.95** SNC ⅛⅛

Murder at Midnight The killings begin with a game of charades in which the gun wasn't supposed to be loaded, and continue as members of English high society die one by one. "Blondie" director Strayer still working on his change of pace.

1931 69m/B Alice White, Leslie Fenton, Aileen Pringle, Hale Hamilton, Robert Elliott, Clara Blandick, Brandon Hurst; **D:** Frank Strayer. **VHS, Beta, 8mm $12.95** SNC, NOS, DVT ⅛⅛

Murder at the Baskervilles Sherlock Holmes is invited to visit Sir Henry Baskerville at his estate, but then finds that Baskerville's daughter's fiance is accused of stealing a race horse and murdering its keeper. Based on Sir Arthur Conan Doyle's story "Silver Blaze." **AKA:** Silver Blaze.
1937 67m/B Arthur Wontner, Ian Fleming, Lyn Harding; **D:** Thomas Bentley. **VHS, Beta $16.95** SNC, CCB, REP ⅛⅛

Murder at the Gallop Snooping Miss Marple doesn't believe a filthy rich oldtimer died of natural causes, despite the dissenting police point of view. Wheedling her way into the police investigation, she discovers the secret of the Gallop club, a place where people bounce up and down on top of horses. Much mugging between Dame Margaret and Morley. Marple's assistant, Mr. Stringer, is the real life Mr. Dame Margaret. Based on Christy's Poirot mystery "After the Funeral."
1963 81m/B Margaret Rutherford, Robert Morley, Flora Robson, Charles Tingwell, Duncan Lamont; **D:** George Pollock. **VHS, Beta $19.98** MGM, FCT ⅛⅛⅛½

Murder at the Vanities Vintage murder mystery set against a musical revue format, in which a tough detective must find a killer before the Earl Carroll-based cabaret ends and he or she will escape with the exiting crowd. Also featured is a mind-boggling production number based on the song "Marijuana." ♫Marijuana; Lovely One; Where Do They Come From Now; Live and Love Tonight; Cocktails for Two; Ebony Rhapsody.
1934 91m/B Victor McLaglen, Kitty Carlisle Hart, Jack Oakie, Duke Ellington, Carl Brisson; **D:** Mitchell Leisen. **VHS, Beta $59.95** MCA ⅛⅛½

Murder by Death Capote is an eccentric millionaire who invites the world's greatest detectives to dinner, offering one million dollars to the one who can solve the evening's murder. Entertaining and hammy spoof of Agatha Christie's "And Then There Were None" and the earlier "Ten Little Indians."
1976 (PG) 95m/C Peter Falk, Alec Guinness, David Niven, Dame Maggie Smith, Peter Sellers, Eileen Brennan, Elsa Lanchester, Nancy Walker, Estelle Winwood, Truman Capote, James Coco; **D:** Robert Moore; **W:** Neil Simon; **M:** Dave Grusin. **VHS, Beta $19.95** COL, TVC ⅛⅛½

Murder by Decree Realistic and convincing version of the Jack the Ripper story. Sherlock Holmes and Dr. Watson find a vast web of conspiracy when they investigate the murders of Whitechapel prostitutes. Based partially on facts, it's a highly detailed suspenser with interesting camera work and fine performances.
1979 (PG) 120m/C Christopher Plummer, James Mason, Donald Sutherland, Genevieve Bujold, Susan Clark, David Hemmings, Frank Finlay, John Gielgud, Anthony Quayle; **D:** Bob (Benjamin) Clark; **W:** John Hopkins. **VHS, Beta $19.98** SUE, NLC ⅛⅛⅛

Murder by Moonlight Rival agents investigate a mysterious murder in a prosperous mining colony on the moon. Not only do they discover a dastardly trail that leads all the way back to Earth, but a strange romantic attraction for each other. Originally broadcast on British TV.
1991 (PG-13) 94m/C Julian Sands, Brigitte Nielsen, Gerald McRaney, Jane Lapotaire, Brian Cox; **D:** Michael Lindsay-Hogg; **M:** Trevor Jones. **VHS $89.95** VMK ⅛⅛

Murder by Natural Causes A made-for-TV brain teaser in which a woman and her lover plot to kill her mind-reader husband. Lots of twists make this fun for viewers who enjoy a challenge.
1979 96m/C Hal Holbrook, Barry Bostwick, Katharine Ross, Richard Anderson; **D:** Robert Day. **VHS, Beta** NO *ďďď*

Murder by Night Amnesia victim Urich is found next to a dead body, the result of a gruesome murder. Urich is the only witness and thinks he may be the next victim. Others think he's the killer. Made for cable mystery with enough twists to make it worthwhile.
1989 (PG-13) 95m/C Robert Urich, Kay Lenz, Jim Metzler, Richard Monette, Michael Ironside, Michael Williams; **D:** Paul Lynch. **VHS, Beta** **$79.95** MCA *ďď½*

Murder by Numbers Murder in the art world stumps a detective. What might have been a good suspense story is ruined by bad editing and a lack of continuity, resulting in confusion rather than suspense.
1989 (PG-13) 91m/C Sam Behrens, Shari Belafonte-Harper, Ronee Blakley, Stanley Kamel, Jayne Meadows, Debra Sandlund, Dick Sargent, Cleavon Little; **D:** Paul Leder; **W:** Paul Leder. **VHS, Beta** NO *ď½*

Murder by Phone A deranged technician has turned his phone into an instrument of electronic death. Chamberlain is the visiting professor trying to discover who's permanently disconnecting the numbers of his students. Good cast decides to test schlock meter. **AKA:** Bells; The Calling.
1982 (R) 79m/C Richard Chamberlain, John Houseman, Sara Botsford; **D:** Michael Anderson Sr.; **W:** Michael Butler, John Kent Harrison; **M:** John Barry. **VHS, Beta** **$19.98** WAR *ďď*

Murder by Television Low-budget murder mystery with Lugosi in a dual role as twins—one good, one not so. When a professor and the evil twin are murdered, the instrument of death suspected is...television. Still an exotic and misunderstood invention when this was made, TV sometimes invoked fear and suspicion in the general public. Historically interesting and Lugosi fans will appreciate seeing him in a non-vampiric role. **AKA:** The Houghland Murder Case.
1935 55m/B Bela Lugosi, George Meeker; **D:** Clifford Sandforth. **VHS, Beta** **$19.95** VYY, SNC, NOS *ď½*

Murder by the Book A mystery writer finds that his fictional character, a hard-boiled private eye, has taken control of his life. With his new macho persona the writer solves a crime and saves the obligatory dame. Based on the novel "Alter Ego" by Mel Arrighi. Made for television. **AKA:** Alter Ego.
1987 100m/C Robert Hays, Catherine Mary Stewart, Celeste Holm, Fred Gwynne, Christopher Murney; **D:** Mel Damski. **VHS, Beta** NO *ďď½*

Murder Elite A murdering maniac terrorizes the rural English countryside, where MacGraw has returned after losing all her money in America. Poor acting and direction make this one a dust-gatherer.
1986 98m/C Ali MacGraw, Billie Whitelaw, Hywel Bennett; **D:** Claude Whatham. **VHS, Beta** **$69.98** LIV, VES *ď½*

Murder for Sale Secret Agent 117 stages an elaborate scam in order to infiltrate a ring of terrorists and criminals. Ask for Bond next time.
1970 90m/C John Gavin, Margaret Lee, Curt Jurgens. **VHS, Beta** **$59.95** MED *ď*

Murder in Coweta County Griffith and Cash are strong in this true-crime drama based on the book by Margaret Anne Barnes. Griffith is a Georgia businessman who thinks he's gotten away with murder; Cash is the lawman who tenaciously pursues him. Based on an actual 1948 case. Made for television.
1983 100m/C Johnny Cash, Andy Griffith, Earl Hindman, June Carter Cash, Cindi Knight, Ed Van Nuys; **D:** Gary Nelson; **M:** Brad Fiedel. **VHS, Beta** **$39.95** LIV *ďď½*

Murder-in-Law Graphic slasher flick about a mother-in-law from hell who escapes from an insane asylum and terrorizes her son-in-law (Estevez) and his family in a series of gruesome killings.
1992 (R) 97m/C Marilyn Adams, Joe Estevez, Sandy Snyder, Darrel Guilbeau; **D:** Tony Jiti Gill. **VHS** **$79.95** MNC *ď*

Murder in New Hampshire: The Pamela Smart Story A sleazy true story about a young high school teacher who seduces an impressionable student into murdering her husband. Hunt's fine as the seductress but this made-for-television fare is just average.
1991 (PG-13) 93m/C Helen Hunt, Chad Allen, Larry Drake, Howard Hesseman, Ken Howard, Michael Learned; **D:** Joyce Chopra. **VHS, Beta** **$89.98** TTC, PMS *ďď½*

Murder in Space Nine multinational astronauts are stranded aboard a space station when they discover one of them is a murderer. This creates anxiety, particularly since the killer's identity is unknown. Oatmeal salesman Brimley is the earth-bound mission control chief trying desperately to finger a spaceman while the bodies pile up. Made for television.
1985 95m/C Wilford Brimley, Martin Balsam, Michael Ironside; **D:** Steven Hilliard Stern. **VHS, Beta** **$79.95** VMK *ď½*

Murder in Texas Made for television docudrama looks at the strange but true events surrounding the death of society woman Joan Robinson Hill, first wife of prominent plastic surgeon, Dr. John Hill, and daughter of wealthy oilman Ash Robinson. Well-crafted script and effective performances keep your interest. Griffith was Emmy nominated. From the book "Prescription Murder," written by the doctor's second wife.
1981 200m/C Farrah Fawcett, Katharine Ross, Andy Griffith, Sam Elliott, Craig T. Nelson, Barbara Sammeth; **D:** William Hale. **VHS, Beta** **$59.95** VHE, HHE *ďďď*

Murder in the Doll House Private detective must find out who is systematically killing off the family of a Japanese toy executive. With English subtitles.
1979 92m/C Yusaku Matsuda, Hiroko Shino, Yoko Nosaki. **VHS, Beta** **$59.95** VDA *ď½*

Murder in the Footlights Murder drama involving a socialite and a vaudeville team.
1951 ?m/C Lesley Brook, David Hutcheson. **VHS** **$16.95** SNC *ďď*

Murder in the Old Red Barn Based on the real murder of an unassuming girl by a randy squire. Stiff, melodramatic performances are bad enough, but the play-style production, unfamiliar to modern viewers, is the last nail in this one's coffin. **AKA:** Maria Marten.
1936 67m/B Tod Slaughter, Sophie Stewart, D.J. Williams, Eric Portman; **D:** Milton Rosmer. **VHS, Beta** **$16.95** NOS, MRV, SNC *ď*

A Murder is Announced From the critically acclaimed BBC television series. While on holiday, super-sleuth Marple encounters a murder that was advertised in the local newspaper one week prior to its occurrence. Based on the 1952 Agatha Christie novel, Hickson shines once again as Christie's detective extraordinaire.
1987 155m/C Joan Hickson; **D:** David Giles. **VHS, Beta** **$29.98** FOX, HMV *ď*

Murder Mansion Some decent scares ensue when a group of travelers is stranded in an old haunted mansion.
1970 84m/C Evelyn Stewart, Analia Gade; **D:** Francisco Lara Polop. **VHS, Beta** **$59.98** UNI, SNC, FCT *ď½*

Murder Most Foul Erstwhile school marm Dame Margaret is excellent as the only jury member to believe in the accused's innocence. Posing as a wealthy actress to insinuate herself into the local acting troupe, she sniffs out the true culprit. Based on the Poirot mystery "Mr. McGinty's Dead."
1965 90m/B Margaret Rutherford, Ron Moody, Charles Tingwell, Megs Jenkins, Dennis Price, Ralph Michael; **D:** George Pollock. **VHS, Beta** **$19.98** MGM, FCT *ďďď*

Murder Motel Inept made-for-television spine-tingler about a motel keeper who makes a practice of killing his customers. There's always a vacancy at the Murder Motel, at least until the fiancee of one of his victims decides to look into the matter.
1974 80m/C Robyn Millan, Derek Francis, Ralph Bates, Edward Judd. **VHS, Beta** **$29.95** LIV *ď*

Murder, My Sweet Down-on-his-luck private detective Philip Marlowe (Powell) searches for a ex-convict's missing girlfriend through a dark world of murder, mayhem and ever-twisting directions. Classic film noir screen version of Raymond Chandler's tense novel "Farewell, My Lovely," which employs flashback fashion using that crisp Chandler narrative. A breakthrough dramatically for singer Powell; Chandler's favorite version. Remade using the novel's title in 1975. **AKA:** Farewell, My Love.
1944 95m/B Dick Powell, Claire Trevor, Mike Mazurki, Otto Kruger, Anne Shirley, Miles Mander; **D:** Edward Dmytryk. **VHS, Beta** **$19.95** MED, CCB *ďďď½*

Murder of a Moderate Man An Interpol agent sets out for the Alps to apprehend an assassin gunning down political leaders. A British-made effort based on a novel by John Howlett.
197? 165m/C Denis Quilley, Susan Fleetwood. **VHS** **$49.95** FCT, MOV *ď½*

The Murder of Mary Phagan Lemmon stars as John Slaton, governor of Georgia during one of America's most notorious miscarriages of justice. In 1913, timid, Jewish factory manager Leo Frank is accused of the brutal murder of a female worker. Prejudice and a power hungry prosecuting attorney conspire to seal the man's fate at the end of the hangman's noose. Sensing the injustice, Slaton re-opens the case, causing riots in Atlanta. Top notch television drama, featuring a superb recreation of turn of the century atmosphere and a compelling, true story which was not finally resolved until the 1970s.
1987 (PG) 251m/C Jack Lemmon, Peter Gallagher, Richard Jordan, Robert Prosky, Paul Dooley, Rebecca Miller, Kathryn Walker, Charles S. Dutton, Kevin Spacey, Wendy J. Cooke; **D:** Billy Hale; **M:** Maurice Jarre. **VHS** **$79.98** ORI *ďďď½*

Murder on Approval Conway is a carbon-copy Sherlock Holmes, called in to verify the authenticity of a stamp and finds himself involved in murder. Slow-paced, weak and transparent. *AKA:* Barbados Quest.
1956 70m/B Tom Conway, Delphi Lawrence, Brian Worth, Michael Balfour, John Colicos; *D:* Bernard Knowles. **VHS $19.95** *NOS* 🎬

Murder on Flight 502 A crisis arises on a 747 flight from New York to London when a terrorist runs amuck. Big cast of TV stars and Stack as the pilot keep this stale television flick from getting lost in the ozone.
1975 97m/C Farrah Fawcett, Sonny Bono, Ralph Bellamy, Theodore Bikel, Dane Clark, Polly Bergen, Laraine Day, Fernando Lamas, George Maharis, Hugh O'Brian, Molly Picon, Walter Pidgeon, Robert Stack; *D:* George McCowan. **VHS, Beta $49.95** *PSM* 🎬

Murder on Lenox Avenue When the leader of the Harlem Better Business Bureau is overthrown, he swears revenge.
1941 60m/C Alec Lovejoy. **VHS $29.99** *BBE, MOV* 🎬🎬½

Murder on Line One A London murderer films his crimes for his later viewing pleasure. The police arrest a suspect, but the killings continue. Both the police and viewer are soon aware that they've made a mistake.
1990 103m/C Emma Jacobs, Peter Blake, Simon Shepherd, Allan Surtees, Andrew Wilde, Dirkan Tulane, Neil Duncan, Brett Forrest; *D:* Anders Palm; *W:* Anders Palm. **VHS, Beta $29.95** *ACA, TTC* 🎬

Murder on the Bayou Down on the L'siana bayou, a white guy who thinks civil rights are color coded is murdered, and an elderly black man is accused of the crime. Made for TV, well performed, engaging. From the novel by Ernest J. Gaines. *AKA:* A Gathering of Old Men.
1991 (PG) 91m/C Louis Gossett Jr., Richard Widmark, Holly Hunter, Woody Strode, Joe Seneca, Papa John Creach, Julius W. Harris, Will Patton; *D:* Volker Schlondorff. **VHS $89.95** *VMK* 🎬🎬🎬

Murder on the Campus A reporter investigates the apparant suicide of his brother at Cambridge University. He discovers that a number of other mysterious deaths have occurred as well. Interesting characterizations hampered by predictability. *AKA:* Out of the Shadow.
1952 61m/B Terence Longden, Donald Gray, Diane Clare, Robertson Hare, Dermot Walsh; *D:* Michael Winner; *W:* Michael Winner. **VHS, Beta $16.95** *NOS, MRV, SNC* 🎬

Murder on the High Seas Infidelity and murder aboard a cruise ship.
1932 ?m/C Natalie Moorhead, Jack Mulhall. **VHS $16.95** *SNC* 🎬

Murder on the Midnight Express Made-for-television mystery about spies, thieves, honeymooners and a corpse aboard an all-night train. All aboard.
1974 70m/C Judy Geeson, James Smilie, Charles Gray. **VHS, Beta $12.95** *LIV* 🎬½

Murder on the Orient Express An Agatha Christie mystery lavishly produced with an all-star cast. In 1934, a trainful of suspects and one murder victim make the trip from Istanbul to Calais especially interesting. Super-sleuth Hercule Poirot sets out to solve the mystery. An entertaining whodunit, ably supported by the remarkable cast. Followed by "Death on the Nile."
1974 (PG) 128m/C Albert Finney, Martin Balsam, Ingrid Bergman, Lauren Bacall, Sean Connery, Richard Widmark, Anthony Perkins, John Gielgud, Jacqueline Bisset, Jean-Pierre Cassel, Wendy Hiller, Rachel Roberts, Vanessa

Redgrave, Michael York, Colin Blakely, George Coulouris; *D:* Sidney Lumet; *M:* Richard Rodney Bennett. Academy Awards '74: Best Supporting Actress (Bergman); Nominations: Best Actor (Finney), Best Adapted Screenplay, Best Cinematography, Best Costume Design, Best Original Score; British Academy Awards '74: Best Supporting Actor (Gielgud), Best Supporting Actress (Bergman). **VHS, Beta $69.95** *PAR, BTV* 🎬🎬🎬

Murder on the Yukon An installment in the "Renfrew of the Royal Mounted" series. Newill and O'Brien's vacation plans are ruined when they find a corpse in a canoe and must investigate. Lots of action, but a somewhat threadbare production. Based on "Renfrew Rides North" by Lauri York Erskine.
1940 57m/B James Newill, Dave O'Brien, Polly Ann Young; *D:* Louis Gasnier. **VHS, Beta $12.95** *VDM* 🎬½

Murder Once Removed A private eye discovers that a respectable doctor has a bedside manner that women are dying for. Made for television.
1971 74m/C John Forsythe, Richard Kiley, Barbara Bain, Joseph Campanella; *D:* Charles S. Dubin. **VHS, Beta $59.95** *LHV* 🎬½

Murder One Two half-brothers escape from a Maryland prison and go on a killing spree, dragging their younger brother with them. Low-budget and it shows. Based on a true story.
1988 (R) 83m/C Henry Thomas, James Wilder, Stephen Shellan, Errol Slue; *D:* Graeme Campbell. **VHS, Beta $19.98** *SUE, NLC* 🎬

Murder 101 Brosnan plays Charles Lattimore, an author and English professor who specializes in murder mysteries. He gives his students a rather unique assignment of planning the perfect murder. When a student is killed right before his eyes and a fellow teacher turns up dead, Lattimore realizes he's being framed for murder. Surprising twists abound in this stylish thriller.
1991 (PG-13) 93m/C Pierce Brosnan, Dey Young, Raphael Sbarge, Kim Thomson; *D:* Bill Condon. **VHS $89.98** *MCA* 🎬🎬

Murder or Mercy Still timely story of a famous doctor accused of killing his terminally ill wife. Focuses on the morality of mercy killing. Made for television.
1974 78m/C Melvyn Douglas, Bradford Dillman, David Birney, Denver Pyle, Mildred Dunnock; *D:* Harvey Hart. **VHS $49.95** *WOV* 🎬🎬½

Murder Ordained Yet another true-crime network miniseries, this time about a Kansas minister and her lover plotting the demise of their spouses. Good acting for this sort of thing. In two-cassette package.
1987 183m/C Keith Carradine, JoBeth Williams, Terry Kinney, Guy Boyd, Terence Knox, Darrell Larson, M. Emmet Walsh, Kathy Bates; *D:* Mike Robe. **VHS $79.95** *FRH* 🎬🎬½

Murder Over New York Episode in the Charlie Chan mystery series. Chan visits New York City and becomes involved in an investigation at the airport. With the aid of his klutzy son, he sleuths his way through a slew of suspects until the mystery is solved. Standard fare for the Chan fan.
1940 65m/B Sidney Toler, Marjorie Weaver, Robert Lowery, Ricardo Cortez, Donald MacBride, Melville Cooper, Sen Yung; *D:* Harry Lachman. **VHS, Beta $19.98** *FOX* 🎬

Murder Rap An aspiring musician/sound technologist becomes involved with a mysterious woman and her plot to kill her husband. Complications galore, especially for the viewer.
1987 90m/C John Hawkes, Seita Kathleen Feigny; *D:* Kliff Keuhl. **VHS, Beta $79.95** *VCI* 🎬

Murder She Said Dame Margaret, playing the benign Miss M for the first time, witnesses a murder on board a train, but the authorities don't seem inclined to believe her. Posing as a maid at an estate near where she thought the body was dropped, she solves the murder and lands three more Miss Marple movies. Based on Christy's "4:50 From Paddington," it features Marple-to-be Hickson as the cook. *AKA:* Meet Miss Marple.
1962 87m/B Margaret Rutherford, Arthur Kennedy, Nadia Pavlova, James Robertson Justice, Thorley Walters, Charles Tingwell, Conrad Phillips; *D:* George Pollock. **VHS, Beta $19.98** *MGM, FCT* 🎬🎬½

Murder So Sweet Hamlin stars as a slick small-town loser, with an apparently limitless appeal to women. He marries five of them but two wives and his mother mysteriously die of poisoning. Then an ex gets suspicious and tries to make certain it'll never happen again. Based on a true story. Made for television. *AKA:* Poisoned by Love: The Kern County Murders.
1993 94m/C Harry Hamlin, Helen Shaver, Faith Ford, Daphne Ashbrook, Eileen Brennan, K.T. Oslin, Terence Knox, Ed Lauter. **VHS $92.95** *ACA* 🎬🎬½

Murder Story An aspiring mystery writer finds himself mixed up in a real murder and winds up involving his mentor as well. An overdone story, but a reasonably enjoyable film.
1989 (PG) 90m/C Christopher Lee, Bruce Boa; *D:* Eddie Arno, Markus Innocenti. **VHS, Beta $29.95** *FHS, ACA* 🎬🎬½

Murder: Ultimate Grounds for Divorce A quiet weekend of camping turns into a night of horror for two couples when one of them plans an elaborate murder scheme.
1985 90m/C Roger Daltrey, Toyah Wilcox, Leslie Ash, Terry Raven. **VHS, Beta $59.95** *LHV, WAR* 🎬

Murder with Music A musical drama featuring an all-black cast.
1945 60m/B Bob Howard, Noble Sissle, Nellie Hill; *D:* George P. Quigley. **VHS, Beta $29.95** *NOS, DVT, VDM* 🎬

Murderer in the Hotel An inspector is lead to a remote hotel run by a peculiar couple while investigating the murder of a wealthy woman. In Spanish.
1983 99m/C Jose Alonso, Blanca Guerra; *D:* Luis Mandoki. **VHS, Beta** *NO* 🎬

Murderers Among Us: The Simon Wiesenthal Story Powerful re-enactment of concentration camp survivor Simon Wiesenthal's search for war criminals. Kingsley's gripping performance drives this made-for-cable film. Be prepared for disturbing death camp scenes.
1989 157m/C Ben Kingsley, Renee Soutendijk, Craig T. Nelson, Paul Freeman, Louisa Haigh, Jack Shepherd; *D:* Brian Gibson; *W:* Abby Mann; *M:* Bill Conti. **VHS $89.99** *HBO, FCT* 🎬🎬🎬

Murderer's Keep Secret ingredients used in the Central Meat Market's hamburger are discovered by a young, deaf girl. Beware of filler, she learns, particularly if it's someone you know.
1988 89m/C Vic Tayback, Talia Shire, Robert Walden; *D:* Paulmichel Miekhe. **VHS, Beta $24.95** *GHV* Woof!

Murderers' Row Daredevil bachelor and former counter-espionage agent Matt Helm is summoned from his life of leisure to ensure the safety of an important scientist. Martin's attempt as a super-spy doesn't wash, and Margret is implausible as the kidnaped

scientist's daughter. Unless you want to hear Martin sing "I'm Not the Marrying Kind," don't bother. Second in the "Matt Helm" series.
1966 108m/C Dean Martin, Ann-Margret, Karl Malden, Beverly Adams, James Gregory; **D:** Henry Levin. **VHS, Beta $14.95** COL *✝️½*

Murderer's Wife A teacher at a private school seeks to prevent one of her students from making the same mistakes she did in her youth. An episode from the 1950's television drama series, "Fireside Theatre."
19?? 24m/B Audrey Totter, John Howard, June Kennedy, Michael Chapin. **VHS, Beta $19.98** CCB *✝️½*

Murderlust Employers in search of a security guard make a poor choice in offering the position to a sexually frustrated man whose hobbies include strangling prostitutes. Poor hiring decisions come into play later when he secures a job at an adolescent crisis center.
1986 90m/C Eli Rich, Rochelle Taylor, Dennis Gannon, Bonnie Schneider, Lisa Nichols; **D:** Donald M. Jones. **VHS, Beta $79.95** PSM Woof!

Murderous Vision Television fixture Boxleitner is a bored detective in this outing. But one day, while tracking a young mother in the missing persons bureau, he stumbles upon the trail of a serial killer. Enter a beautiful psychic who wants to help, add a race to catch the murderer, and Bruce suddenly has his hands full. Made for television.
1991 (R) 93m/C Bruce Boxleitner, Laura Johnson, Robert Culp; **D:** Gary Sherman. **VHS** PAR *✝️✝️*

Murders at Lynch Cross Made-for-British-television mystery about a weird, isolated hotel on the Yorkshire moors.
1985 60m/C Jill Bennett, Joanna David, Barbara Jefford, Sylvia Syms. **VHS, Beta $59.95** PSM *✝️✝️*

Murders in the Rue Morgue Lugosi stars as a deranged scientist (what a stretch) who wants to find a female companion for his pet gorilla. He kidnaps a beautiful woman and prepares to make her the gorilla's bride. Very loosely based on the story by Edgar Allan Poe, which has been remade several times.
1932 61m/B Bela Lugosi, Sidney Fox, Leon Ames, Brandon Hurst, Arlene Francis; **D:** Robert Florey. **VHS $14.98** MCA *✝️✝️½*

Murders in the Rue Morgue A young woman has frightening dreams inspired by a play that her father is producing in Paris at the turn of the century. After many people associated with the production become murder victims, the girl becomes involved with one of her father's former associates, a man who killed her mother years ago and then faked his own suicide. The fourth film based on Edgar Allan Poe's classic horror story.
1971 (PG) 87m/C Jason Robards Jr., Lilli Palmer, Herbert Lom, Michael Dunn, Christine Kaufmann, Adolfo Celi; **D:** Gordon Hessler. **VHS, Beta** NO *✝️✝️½*

The Murders in the Rue Morgue The fifth filmed version of the Edgar Allan Poe story. Set in 19th-century Paris; actors in a mystery play find their roles coming to life. Scott is terrific, with good supporting help. Made for television.
1986 (PG) 92m/C George C. Scott, Rebecca DeMornay, Val Kilmer, Ian McShane, Neil Dickson; **D:** Jeannot Szwarc. **VHS $89.95** VMK *✝️✝️✝️*

Muriel A complex, mosaic drama about a middle-aged woman who meets an old lover at Boulogne, and her stepson who cannot forget the needless suffering he caused a

young woman named Muriel while he was a soldier at war. Throughout, director Alain Resnais plumbs the essential meanings of memory, age, and the anxieties created from the tension between personal and public actions. Acclaimed; in French with subtitles. **AKA:** Muriel, Ou le Temps d'Un Retour; The Time of Return; Muriel, Or the Time of Return.
1963 115m/C Delphine Seyrig, Jean-Pierre Kerien, Nita Klein, Jean-Baptiste Thierree; **D:** Alain Resnais; **M:** Georges Delerue. **VHS, Beta $59.95** HTV, FCT *✝️✝️✝️½*

Murmur of the Heart Honest treatment of a fourteen-year-old's coming of age. After his older brothers take him to a prostitute for his first sexual experience, he comes down with scarlet fever. He then travels to a health spa with his mom to recover. There they find that their mother-son bond is stronger than most. Music by Charlie Parker is featured in the score. In French with English subtitles.
1971 (R) 118m/C Benoit Ferreux, Daniel Gelin, Lea Massari, Corinne Kersten, Jacqueline Chauveau, Marc Wincourt, Michael Lonsdale; **D:** Louis Malle; **W:** Louis Malle. **VHS, Beta $79.98** ORI, ING *✝️✝️✝️½*

Murph the Surf Fact-based, engrossing story of two beach bums turned burglars who grow bored with small-time robbery and plan a trip to New York City to steal the Star of Africa sapphire. Notable among the many action scenes is a boat chase through the inland waterways of Miami, Florida. **AKA:** Live a Little, Steal a Lot; You Can't Steal Love.
1975 (PG) 102m/C Robert Conrad, Don Stroud, Donna Mills, Luther Adler, Robyn Millan, Paul Stewart; **D:** Marvin J. Chomsky. **VHS, Beta** WAR, OM *✝️✝️½*

Murphy's Fault Dark comedy about a night watchman/writer plagued by a series of bad luck incidents.
1988 (PG-13) 94m/C Patrick Dollaghan, Anne Curry, Stack Pierce; **D:** Robert J. Smawley. **VHS, Beta $89.95** VMK *✝️✝️*

Murphy's Law A hard-headed cop gets framed for his ex-wife's murder and embarks on a mission to find the actual killer. He is slowed down by a smart-mouthed prostitute who is handcuffed to him during his search. Casting a female in the role of a psycho-killer is unique to the genre.
1986 (R) 101m/C Charles Bronson, Carrie Snodgress, Kathleen Wilhoite, Robert F. Lyons, Richard Romanus, Angel Tompkins, Bill Henderson, James Luisi, Janet MacLachlan, Lawrence Tierney; **D:** J. Lee Thompson; **M:** Mark Donohue. **VHS, Beta $19.95** MED, VTR *✝️*

Murphy's Romance A young divorced mother with an urge to train horses pulls up the stakes and heads for Arizona with her son. There she meets a pharmacist who may be just what the doctor ordered to help her build a new life.
1985 (PG-13) 107m/C James Garner, Sally Field, Brian Kerwin, Corey Haim, Dennis Burkley, Charles Lane, Georgann Johnson; **D:** Martin Ritt; **W:** Harriet Frank Jr., Irving Ravetch; **M:** Carole King. **VHS, Beta $14.95** COL, HMV *✝️✝️✝️*

Murphy's War In WWII, the Germans sink an English ship and gun down most of its crew. An Irishman, however, survives and returns to health with the help of a nurse. He then seeks revenge on those who killed his crewmates, even after he learns the war has ended. O'Toole is interesting as the revenge-minded seaman though saddled with a mediocre script.

1971 (PG) 106m/C Peter O'Toole, Sian Phillips, Philippe Noiret; **D:** Peter Yates; **W:** Sterling Silliphant; **M:** John Barry. **VHS, Beta $9.99** CCB, PAR *✝️✝️*

Murrow A cable television biography of the renowed chain-smoking journalist who changed broadcasting history by fearlessly voicing his liberal ideas on the air waves. His life was more interesting though Travanti does his best to breathe some life into the script.
1986 114m/C Daniel J. Travanti, Dabney Coleman, Edward Herrmann, David Suchet, John McMartin, Robert Vaughn, Kathryn Leigh Scott; **D:** Jack Gold; **W:** Ernest Kinoy; **M:** Carl Davis. **VHS, Beta $9.98** FCT, LIV *✝️✝️½*

Muscle Beach Party Sequel to "Beach Party" finds Frankie and Annette romping in the sand again. Trouble invades teen nirvana when a new gym opens and the hardbodies try to muscle in on surfer turf. Meanwhile, Paluzzi tries to muscle in on Funicello's turf. Good clean corny fun, with the usual lack of script and plot. Lorre appeals in a cameo, his final screen appearance. Watch for "Little" Stevie Wonder in his debut. Rickles' first appearance in the "BP" series; Lupus was credited as Rock Stevens. Followed by "Bikini Beach." ♫ Muscle Beach Party; Runnin' Wild; Muscle Bustle; My First Love; Surfin' Woodie; Surfer's Holiday; Happy Street; A Girl Needs a Boy; A Boy Needs a Girl.
1964 94m/C Frankie Avalon, Annette Funicello, Buddy Hackett, Lucianna Paluzzi, Don Rickles, John Ashley, Jody McCrea, Morey Amsterdam, Peter Lupus, Candy Johnson, Dolores Wells, Stevie Wonder, Donna Loren, Amadee Chabot; **Cameos:** Peter Lorre; **D:** William Asher; **W:** Robert Dillon; **M:** Les Baxter. **VHS, Beta $29.95** VTR *✝️✝️*

Muse Concert: No Nukes Concert film of performances held at New York's Madison Square Garden for the benefit of the anti-nuclear power movement. Features Jackson Browne, Crosby, Stills and Nash, James Taylor, Bruce Springsteen, the Doobie Brothers, Bonnie Raitt, Carly Simon, and John Hall. Excellent editing keeps the joint hopping, while Bruce steals the show.
1980 (PG) 103m/C D: Julian Schlossberg; **Performed by:** Jackson Browne, David Crosby, Stephen Stills, Graham Nash, James Taylor, Bruce Springsteen, The Doobie Brothers, Bonnie Raitt, Carly Simon, John Hall. **VHS, Beta** FOX *✝️✝️✝️*

Music Box An attorney defends her father against accusations that he has committed inhumane Nazi war crimes. If she loses, her father faces deportation. As the case progresses, she must struggle to remain objective in the courtroom and come to terms with the possibility that her father is guilty. Lange's portrayal of an ethnic character is highly convincing.
1989 (R) 126m/C Jessica Lange, Frederic Forrest, Lukas Haas, Armin Mueller-Stahl, Michael Rooker, Donald Moffatt, Cheryl Lynn Bruce; **D:** Constantin Costa-Gavras; **W:** Joe Eszterhas; **M:** Philippe Sarde. **VHS, Beta $19.95** JCF *✝️✝️½*

Music Box/Helpmates These two classic, award-winning comedy shorts by the dynamic duo have been color-enhanced by Colorization.
1932 50m/B Stan Laurel, Oliver Hardy. **VHS, Beta** VTR *✝️✝️½*

Music in My Heart Two taxi cabs crash and spur the love of Martin and Hayworth. She proceeds to break off her engagement to save Martin from deportation. Hayworth's last low-budget film before becoming a Hollywood goddess.

1940 69m/B Rita Hayworth, Tony Martin, Edith Fellows, Alan Mowbray, Eric Blore, George Tobias, Joseph Crehan, George Humbert, Phil Tead; *D:* Joseph Santley; *M:* Andre Kostelanetz. VHS $19.95 COL, CCB *ℐℐ* ½

The Music Lovers Russell's version of Tchaikovsky's tormented life and glorious achievements is a shocker, a movie that infuriates professed music lovers but, nonetheless, has introduced many a neophyte to the world of classical music via its sensationalism. Homosexual Tchaikovsky marries an admirer to appease the Russian government and his financial benefactor. Stunned when he discovers his wife is a nymphomaniac, he banishes her to a netherworld of prostitution and eventual insanity which Russell mercilessly explores. Tchaikovsky's own squalid life is hardly better, though he does enjoy success before the bottom falls out.
1971 (R) 122m/C Richard Chamberlain, Glenda Jackson, Max Adrian, Christopher Gable, Kenneth Colley, Izabella Telezynska, Maureen Pryor; *D:* Ken Russell. VHS $19.99 MGM, MLB, FCT *ℐℐ* ½

The Music Man Con man in the guise of a traveling salesman gets off the train in River City, Iowa. After hearing about plans to build a pool hall, he argues it would be the gateway to hell for the young, impressionable males of the town. He then convinces the River Cityians to look toward the future of the community and finance a wholesome children's marching band. Although the huckster plans to take their money and run before the instruments arrive, his feelings for the town librarian cause him to think twice about fleeing the Heartland. This isn't just a slice of Americana; it's a whole pie. Acting and singing are terrific "with a capital 'T' and that rhymes with 'P' and that stands for" Preston, who epitomizes the charismatic pitchman. ♫Seventy-six Trombones; Trouble; If You Don't Mind; Till There Way You; The Wells Fargo Wagon; Being in Love; Goodnight, My Someone; Rock Island; Iowa Stubborn.
1962 (G) 151m/C Robert Preston, Shirley Jones, Buddy Hackett, Hermione Gingold, Paul Ford, Pert Kelton, Ron Howard; *D:* Morton DaCosta; *W:* Marion Hargrove. Academy Awards '62: Best Adapted Score; Nominations: Best Art Direction/Set Decoration (Color), Best Costume Design (Color), Best Film Editing, Best Picture, Best Sound; Golden Globe Awards '63: Best Film—Musical/Comedy. VHS, Beta $19.98 WAR, MVD, TLF *ℐℐℐℐ*

The Music of Chance Convoluted story about a smalltime gambler (Spader) and a drifter (Patinkin) who wind up involved in a bizarre high stakes poker game with a Laurel and Hardyish pair (Durning and Grey) who live in an isolated mansion. When Spader and Patinkin lose, their debt forces them into an indentured servitude where they must construct a brick wall around their new masters' estate. Bloated with symbolism, this adaptation from cult fave novelist Auster (who has a small part), loses its eclectic significance in the translation to the big screen. Nonetheless, valiant effort by rookie director Haas.
1993 (R) 98m/C James Spader, Mandy Patinkin, Joel Grey, Charles Durning, M. Emmet Walsh, Samantha Mathis, Christopher Penn, Pearl Jones, Paul Auster; *D:* Philip Haas; *W:* Philip Haas; Belinda Haas; *M:* Philip Johnston. VHS COL, BTV *ℐℐ* ½

Music Shoppe Four teenagers form a rock band with the assistance of the local music store proprietor. Interesting cast.

1982 (G) 93m/C Gary Crosby, Nia Peeples, Benny Medina, Stephen Schwartz, David Jackson, Jesse White, Doug Kershaw, Giselle MacKenzie. VHS, Beta GEM *ℐℐ*

The Music Teacher A Belgian costume drama dealing with a famed singer who retires to devote himself to teaching two students exclusively. In time, he sees his prized pupils lured into an international competition by an old rival of his. Although the singing is sharp, the story is flat. In French with yellow English subtitles. *AKA:* Le Maitre de Musique.
1988 (PG) 95m/C Patrick Bauchau, Sylvie Fennec, Phillipe Volter, Jose Van Dam, Johan Leysen, Anne Roussel; *D:* Gerard Corbiau. VHS, Beta $79.98 ORI, ING *ℐℐ* ½

Musica Proibita A serious opera-spiced drama about a young romance crushed by adultery in the teenage couple's ancestry. In Italian with English subtitles.
1943 93m/B Tito Gobbi, Maria Mercader. VHS, Beta $24.95 VYY, APD, ING *ℐℐ* ½

Musico, Poeta y Loco Wild and crazy antics abound in this film.
1947 90m/B Tin Tan. VHS, Beta $48.95 MAD *ℐℐ*

Mussolini & I Docudramatization of the struggle for power between Italy's Benito Mussolini and his son-in-law, Galeazzo Ciano. Narrated by Sarandon in the role of Il Duce's daughter. Made for cable television. *AKA:* Mussolini: The Decline and Fall of Il Duce.
1985 130m/C Bob Hoskins, Anthony Hopkins, Susan Sarandon, Annie Girardot, Barbara DeRossi, Fabio Testi, Kurt Raab; *D:* Alberto Negrin. VHS, Beta $19.95 NLC *ℐℐ* ½

Mutant Another argument for the proper disposal of toxic waste. Hazardous materials transform the people of a southern town into monsters. *AKA:* Night Shadows.
1983 (R) 100m/C Wings Hauser, Bo Hopkins, Jennifer Warren, Lee Montgomery; *D:* John Cardos; *M:* Richard Band. VHS, Beta $19.98 LIV, VES *ℐℐ* ½

Mutant Hunt Made for video movie about a battle between robots gone haywire and an all-American hero. The detective cyborgs are set free while high on a sexual stimulant called Euphoron to wreak their technological havoc on a rampage in Manhattan. *AKA:* Matt Riker.
1987 90m/C Rick Gianasi, Mary-Anne Fahey; *D:* Tim Kincaid; *W:* Tim Kincaid. VHS, Beta $69.95 VCI Woof!

Mutant on the Bounty A musician, lost in space as a beam of light for 23 years, is transported aboard a spaceship. Once he materializes, it becomes apparent that he has undergone some incredible physical changes. As if that's not enough, the crew then must flee from a couple of thugs who are trying to steal a vial of serum they have on board. A space spoof that never gets into orbit.
1989 93m/C John Roarke, Deborah Benson, John Furey, Victoria Catlin, John Fleck, Kyle T. Heffner; *D:* Robert Torrance. VHS $14.95 HMD *ℐℐ* ½

Mutant Video Six comedic, award-winning short-subject films from Jim Belushi and Rob Riley. Outrageous humor.
1976 60m/B James Belushi, Rob Riley. VHS, Beta $19.95 LIV *ℐℐ* ½

Mutants In Paradise Comedy about a human guinea-pig who always gets involved in some sort of mishap.
1988 78m/C Brad Greenquist, Robert Ingham, Anna Nicholas. VHS, Beta $59.95 TWE Woof!

Mutator A corporation makes a tiny genetic mistake and winds up creating a new life form...a demonic pussycat who preys on humans.
1990 (R) 91m/C Brion James, Carolyn Ann Clark, Milton Raphiel Murrill; *D:* John R. Bowey; *W:* Lynn Rose Higgins. VHS, Beta $89.98 PSM *ℐℐ*

The Muthers Women prisoners escape from their confinement in a South American jungle.
1976 (R) 101m/C Jeanne Bell, Rosanne Katon, Jayne Kennedy, Trina Parks; *D:* Cirio H. Santiago. VHS, Beta $24.95 NO *ℐ*

The Mutilator After accidentally bumping off his mother, a young man stalks five high school students wanting to cut them up into tiny bits. An unedited version is also available. Bloody boredom. *AKA:* Fall Break.
1985 (R) 85m/C Jack Chatham, Trace Cooper, Frances Raines, Bill Hitchcock; *D:* Buddy Cooper. VHS, Beta $79.98 LIV, VES Woof!

Mutiny In the War of 1812, the crew of an American ship carrying $10 million in gold fight among themselves for a part of France's donation to the war effort. The beautiful photography doesn't make up for the predictability of the storyline.
1952 76m/C Mark Stevens, Gene Evans, Angela Lansbury, Patric Knowles; *D:* Edward Dmytryk; *W:* Philip Yordan. VHS, Beta $19.95 NOS, VCI *ℐℐ*

Mutiny in the Big House A man is sent to prison for writing a bad ten dollar check and must choose between seeking salvation with the prison chaplain or toughing it out with a hardened convict. Suprisingly good low-budget programmer.
1939 83m/B Charles Bickford, Barton MacLane, Pat Moriarity, Dennis Moore, William Royle, Charles Foy, George Cleveland; *D:* Grant Withers. VHS, Beta $16.95 SNC *ℐℐ* ½

The Mutiny of the Elsinore A writer on board an old sailing ship fights mutineers and wins back both the helm and the captain's daughter. Tedious British flotsam that made hash of an oft-filmed Jack London tale, and made news even in 1939 for its use of modern-day slang and clothing in the period setting.
1939 74m/B Paul Lukas, Lyn Harding, Kathleen Kelly, Clifford Evans, Ben Soutten, Jiro Soneya; *D:* Roy Lockwood. VHS $19.95 NOS *ℐ*

Mutiny on the Bounty Compelling adaptation of the true story of sadistic Captain Bligh, Fletcher Christian and their turbulent journey aboard the HMS Bounty. No gray here: Laughton's Bligh is truly a despicable character and extremely memorable in this MGM extravaganza. Remade twice, in 1962 and again in 1984 as "The Bounty." Much, much better than the 1962 remake.
1935 132m/B Clark Gable, Franchot Tone, Charles Laughton, Donald Crisp, Dudley Digges, Spring Byington, Henry Stephenson, Eddie Quillan, Herbert Mundin, Movita, Ian Wolfe; *D:* Frank Lloyd; *W:* Talbot Jennings, Jules Furthman, Carey Wilson; *M:* Herbert Stothart. Academy Awards '35: Best Picture; Nominations: Best Actor (Gable), Best Actor (Tone, Laughton), Best Adapted Screenplay, Best Director (Lloyd), Best Film Editing, Best Score; National Board of Review Awards '35: 10 Best Films of the Year; New York Film Critics Awards '35: Best Actor (Laughton). VHS, Beta, 8mm $19.98 MGM, BMV, BTV *ℐℐℐℐ*

Mutiny on the Bounty Based on the novel by Charles Nordhoff and James Norman Hall, this account of the 1789 mutiny led by Fletcher Christian against Captain Bligh of the Bounty is highlighted by lavish photography. Can't navigate the same perfect course

M

set by the 1935 classic. Marlon Brando seems miscast, giving a choppy performance as the mutiny leader.
1962 177m/C Marlon Brando, Trevor Howard, Richard Harris, Hugh Griffith; **D:** Lewis Milestone. **VHS, Beta $29.98** *MGM ♫♫*

Mutual Respect A dying wealthy man sets out to find the son he never knew.
1977 (PG) 88m/C Lloyd Bridges, Beau Bridges. **VHS, Beta $9.95** *ACA ♫½*

My African Adventure Silly tale of an ambassador's son discovering a talking monkey in Africa and meeting a slew of opportunistic misfits in his travels. A comedy unfortunately short on laughs. Based on Tamar Burnstein's book.
1987 93m/C Dom DeLuise, Jimmie Walker; **D:** Sam Firstenberg. **VHS, Beta** *MED Woof!*

My American Cousin Award-winning Canadian coming-of-age comedy about a 12-year-old girl who falls for her rebellious, fun-loving 17-year-old American cousin over summer vacation. Followed by "American Boyfriends."
1985 (PG) 94m/C Margaret Langrick, John Wildman, Richard Donat, Jane Mortifee; **D:** Sandy Wilson; **W:** Sandy Wilson. **VHS, Beta $19.95** *MED, VTR ♫♫*

My Apprenticeship The second film of Donskoi's trilogy on Maxim Gorky has the writer earning his living, at the age of eight, as an apprentice to a bourgeois family. Although they promise him an education, Gorky is forced to learn to read on his own and eventually sets off on a series of land and sea voyages. He recognizes that the poverty and abuse he has suffered is typical of the lives of most Russians and he encounters the beginnings of revolution. In Russian with English subtitles. Preceded by "My Childhood" and followed by "My Universities."
1939 100m/C D: Mark Donskoi. **VHS $39.95** *FCT ♫♫♫*

My Beautiful Laundrette Omar (Warnecke), the nephew of a Pakistani businessman, is given the opportunity to better himself by turning his uncle's run-down laundry into a profitable business. He reunites with Johnny (Day Lewis), a childhood friend and a working-class street punk, and they go into the business together. They find themselves battling the prejudice of each other's families and friends in order to succeed. An intelligent look at the sexuality, race relations and economic problems of Thatcher's London. Great performances by a relatively unknown cast (for contrast, note Day Lewis' performance in "Room with a View," released in the same year).
1985 (R) 93m/C Gordon Warnecke, Daniel Day-Lewis, Saeed Jaffrey, Roshan Seth, Shirley Anne Field, Derrick Branche; **D:** Stephen Frears; **W:** Hanif Kureishi; **M:** Ludus Tonalis. **VHS, Beta $79.95** *LHV, WAR ♫♫♫*

My Best Friend Is a Vampire Another teenage vampire story, about trying to cope with certain changes that adolescence and bloodsucking bring. Good supporting cast.
1988 (PG) 90m/C Robert Sean Leonard, Evan Mirand, Cheryl Pollak, Rene Auberjonois, Cecilia Peck, Fannie Flagg, Kenneth Kimmins, David Warner, Paul Wilson; **D:** Jimmy Huston; **M:** Stephen Dorff. **VHS $14.99** *HBO ♫♫*

My Best Friend's Girl Coy, sardonic French romance about a woman who slaloms between two buddies working at a ski resort. Despite fine performances from all, it never quite makes it to the top of the hill. In French with English subtitles. **AKA:** La Femme De Mon Pote.
1984 99m/C Isabelle Huppert, Thierry Lhermitte, Coluche, Francoise Perrot; **D:** Bertrand Blier; **W:** Bertrand Blier, Gerard Brach. **VHS, Beta $19.95** *COL, ING, SUE ♫♫½*

My Best Girl Mary attempts to bring her new sweetheart home for dinner, with disastrous results. A gentle satire on middle-American life in the 1920s. Includes organ score.
1927 78m/B Mary Pickford, Charles "Buddy" Rogers; **D:** Sam Taylor; **M:** Gaylord Carter. **VHS, Beta $19.95** *CCB ♫♫*

My Bloody Valentine Psychotic coal miner visits the peaceful little town of Valentine Bluffs on the night of the yearly Valentine Ball. Many of the townspeople have their hearts removed with a pick axe and sent to the sheriff in candy boxes. The bloodiest scenes were cut out to avoid an X-rating.
1981 (R) 91m/C Paul Kelman, Lori Hallier; **D:** George Mihalka. **VHS, Beta $19.95** *PAR ♫♫*

My Blue Heaven After agreeing to rat on the Mafia, Martin is dropped into suburbia as part of the witness protection program. Moranis plays the FBI agent assigned to help the former mobster become an upstanding citizen. Adjusting to life in the slow lane isn't easy for an ex con who has grown accustomed to the big time. Not the typical role for Martin, who plays a brunette with a New York accent and is handcuffed by bad writing.
1990 (PG-13) 96m/C Steve Martin, Rick Moranis, Joan Cusack, Melanie Mayron, Carol Kane, Bill Irwin, William Hickey, Daniel Stern; **D:** Herbert Ross; **W:** Nora Ephron. **VHS, Beta $92.95** *WAR, BTV ♫♫*

My Bodyguard An undersized high school student fends off attacking bullies by hiring a king-sized, withdrawn lad as his bodyguard. Their "business" relationship, however, develops into true friendship. An adolescent coming of age with more intelligence and sensitivity than most of its ilk, and a pack of up and coming stars as well as old stand-bys Houseman and Gordon.
1980 96m/C Chris Makepeace, Adam Baldwin, Martin Mull, Ruth Gordon, Matt Dillon, John Houseman, Joan Cusack, Craig Richard Nelson; **D:** Tony Bill; **W:** Alan Ormsby; **M:** Dave Grusin. **VHS, Beta $14.98** *FOX ♫♫♫*

My Boy Coogan stars as a foreign orphan who faces deportation. Instead he escapes and follows an old man home. This rare film includes an organ score.
1921 56m/B Jackie Coogan, Claude Gillingwater, Mathilde Brundage; **D:** Victor Herman, Albert Austin. **VHS, Beta $14.95** *GPV ♫♫½*

My Boyfriend's Back Embarrassingly dumb flick about a teenage boy who wants to take the prettiest girl in the school to the prom. The only problem is that he's become a zombie. Bits of him keep falling off (his girl thoughtfully glues them back on) and if he wants to stay "alive" long enough to get to the dance he has to munch on human flesh. Yuck. **AKA:** Johnny Zombie.
1993 (PG-13) 85m/C Andrew Lowery, Traci Lind, Edward Herrmann, Mary Beth Hurt, Danny Zorn, Austin Pendleton, Jay O. Sanders, Paul Dooley, Bob Dishy, Matthew Fox, Paxton Whitehead; **D:** Bob Balaban; **W:** Dean Lorey. **VHS** *BVV ♫*

My Boys are Good Boys A young foursome steal from an armored car and have to face the consequences. Quirky with an implausible storyline.
1978 (PG) 90m/C Ralph Meeker, Ida Lupino, Lloyd Nolan, David Doyle; **D:** Bethel Buckalew. **VHS, Beta** *NO ♫*

My Breakfast with Blassie Kaufman and professional wrestler Blassie meet for breakfast and carry on a comical dialogue.
1983 60m/C Andy Kaufman, Freddie Blassie; **D:** Johnny Legend, Linda Lautrec. **VHS, Beta $39.95** *RHI ♫*

My Brilliant Career A headstrong young woman spurns the social expectations of turn-of-the-century Australia and pursues opportunities to broaden her intellect and preserve her independence. Davis is wonderful as the energetic and charismatic community trendsetter. Based on an autobiographical novel by Miles Franklin which has been marvelously transferred to the screen. Armstrong deserves credit for her fine direction.
1979 (G) 101m/C Judy Davis, Sam Neill, Wendy Hughes; **D:** Gillian Armstrong. Academy Awards '80 Nominations: Best Costume Design; Cannes Film Festival '79: Best Film; Australian Film Institute '79: Best Film; British Academy Awards '80: Best Actress (Davis). **VHS, Beta $69.95** *VES ♫♫♫½*

My Brother has Bad Dreams Young man with sibling tosses and turns in bed.
1988 97m/C Nick Kleinholz, Marlena Lustic. **VHS $29.98** *VCI ♫*

My Brother's Wife Barney (Ritter), the black sheep of a wealthy family, spends two decades pursuing Eleanor (Harris), the woman of his dreams. Unfortunately, she's already married—to the brother he despises. Adapted from the play "The Middle Ages" by A.R. Gurney. Made for television.
1989 (PG) 94m/C John Ritter, Mel Harris, Polly Bergen, Dakin Matthews, David Byron, Lee Weaver; **D:** Jack Bender; **W:** Percy Granger. **VHS $92.95** *APX, TPV ♫♫½*

My Champion Chance meeting propels Mike Gorman and Miki Tsuwa into a relationship based on the strong bonds of love and athletic competition.
1984 101m/C Yoko Shimada, Chris Mitchum. **VHS, Beta $59.95** *MED ♫*

My Chauffeur When a wise-cracking female is hired on as a chauffeur at an all-male chauffeur service, sparks fly. And when the owner takes a definite liking to her work, things take a turn for the worse. As these sort of sexploitation flicks go, this is one of the better ones.
1986 (R) 94m/C Deborah Foreman, Sam Jones, Howard Hesseman, E.G. Marshall, Sean McClory; **D:** David Beaird; **W:** David Beaird. **VHS, Beta $79.98** *LIV, VES ♫♫½*

My Childhood The first of director Donskoi's trilogy on the life of Maxim Gorky, based on Gorky's autobiographical stories. In this first film, Donskoi depicts Gorky's childhood of abuse and poverty with his grandparents in the 1870s. Eventually, Gorky is forced into the streets and he becomes a wandering beggar. In Russian with English subtitles. Followed by "My Apprenticeship" and "My Universities."
1938 100m/C D: Mark Donskoi. **VHS $39.95** *FCT ♫♫♫*

My Cousin Vinny Vinny Gambini (Pesci), a lawyer who took the bar exam six times before passing, goes to Wahzoo City, Alabama to get his cousin and a friend off the hook when they're accused of killing a store clerk. Leather jackets, gold chains, Brooklyn accents, and his fiancee Tomei's penchant for big hair and bold clothing don't go over well with conservative judge Gwynne, causing plenty of misunderstandings. Surprising hit with simplistic story reaches popular heights via entertaining performances by the

entire cast. Tomei in particular steals every scene she's in and has an Oscar to prove it.
1992 (R) 120m/C Joe Pesci, Ralph Macchio, Marisa Tomei, Mitchell Whitfield, Fred Gwynne, Lane Smith, Austin Pendleton, Bruce McGill; *D:* Jonathan Lynn; *W:* Dale Launer; *M:* Randy Edelman. **VHS $94.98** FXV, MOV, PMS *∄∄∄*

My Darlin' Clementine Shelly Duvall gives the famous song about a miner who bemoans the loss of his daughter and her size nine shoes her own touch in this entry from the "Tall Tales and Legends" series. Made for cable television.
1986 49m/C Shelley Duvall, Ed Asner, David Dukes, John Matuszak. **VHS $19.98** FOX *∄∄∄*

My Darling Clementine One of the best Hollywood westerns ever made, this recounts the precise events leading up to and including the gunfight at the O.K. Corral. Ford allegedly knew Wyatt Earp and used his stories to recount the details vividly, though not always accurately. Remake of 1939's "Frontier Marshal."
1946 97m/B Henry Fonda, Victor Mature, Walter Brennan, Linda Darnell, Tim Holt, Ward Bond, John Ireland; *D:* John Ford. **VHS, Beta $19.98** FOX, TLF *∄∄∄ ½*

My Daughter's Keeper The apparently perfect nanny of an unsuspecting family reveals her deadly agenda of murder, adultery, and more.
1993 (R) 94m/C Nicholas Guest, Jocelyn Broderick, Ana Padrao. **VHS $89.98** LIV *∄∄*

My Dear Secretary After she marries her boss, a woman grows jealous of the secretary that replaces her. Comedic dialogue and antics result.
1949 94m/C Kirk Douglas, Laraine Day, Keenan Wynn, Rudy Vallee, Florence Bates, Alan Mowbray, Charles Halton; *D:* Charles Martin; *W:* Charles Martin. **VHS, Beta $19.95** NOS, MRV, BAR *∄∄ ½*

My Demon Lover This sex comedy is complicated by the hero's transformation into a demon whenever he is aroused. Saved from complete mediocrity by Family Ties's Valentine in a likable performance.
1987 (PG-13) 90m/C Scott Valentine, Michelle Little, Arnold Johnson; *D:* Charles Loventhal. **VHS, Beta $14.95** COL *∄∄*

My Dinner with Andre Two friends talk about their lives and philosophies for two hours over dinner one night. A wonderful exploration into storytelling, the conversation juxtaposes the experiences and philosophies of nerdish, bumbling Shawn and the globe-trotting spiritual pilgrimage of Gregory, in this sometimes poignant, sometimes comic little movie that starts you thinking.
1981 110m/C Andre Gregory, Wallace Shawn; *D:* Louis Malle. **VHS, Beta $19.95** ING, HMV, TPV *∄∄∄ ½*

My Dog Shep An orphan and his dog run away and are pursued diligently when it is discovered that he is a wealthy heir.
1946 71m/B Tom Neal, William Farnum, Lannie Rees, Flame; *D:* Ford Beebe. **VHS, Beta $19.95** NOS, VYY *∄ ½*

My Dog, the Thief A helicopter weatherman is unaware that the lovable St. Bernard he has adopted is a kleptomaniac. When the dog steals a valuable necklace from a team of professional jewel thieves, the fun begins.
1969 88m/C Joe Flynn, Elsa Lanchester, Roger C. Carmel, Mickey Shaughnessy, Dwayne Hickman, Mary Ann Mobley; *D:* Robert Stevenson. **VHS, Beta $69.95** DVT *∄*

My Dream is Yours Day plays an up and coming radio star in this Warner Brothers musical comedy with a cameo from Bugs Bunny in a dream sequence. This fresh, fun remake of "Twenty Million Sweethearts" is often underrated, but is well worth a look. ♫My Dream is Yours; Some Like You; Tic, Tic, Tic; Love Finds a Way; I'll String Along with You; Canadian Capers; Freddie Get Ready; You Must Have Been a Beautiful Baby; Jeepers, Creepers.
1949 101m/C Jack Carson, Doris Day, Lee Bowman, Adolphe Menjou, Eve Arden, S.Z. Sakall, Selena Royle, Edgar Kennedy; *D:* Michael Curtiz. **VHS $29.98** FOX, FCT, MLB *∄∄ ½*

My Fair Lady Colorful production of Lerner and Loewe's musical version of "Pygmalion," about an ill-mannered cockney girl who is plucked from her job as a flower girl by Professor Henry Higgins. Higgins makes a bet with a colleague that he can turn this rough diamond into a "lady." Winner of eight Academy Awards. Hepburn's singing voice is dubbed by Marni Nixon, who was also responsible for the singing in "The King and I" and "West Side Story;" the dubbing may have undermined her chance at an Oscar nomination. Typecasting role for Harrison as the crusty, egocentric Higgins. A timeless classic. ♫Why Can't the English?; Wouldn't It Be Loverly?; I'm an Ordinary Man; With a Little Bit of Luck; Just You Wait, 'Enry 'Iggins; The Servant's Chorus; The Rain in Spain; I Could Have Danced all Night; Ascot Gavotte.
1964 (G) 170m/C Audrey Hepburn, Rex Harrison, Stanley Holloway, Wilfrid Hyde-White, Theodore Bikel, Mona Washbourne, Jeremy Brett, Robert Coote, Gladys Cooper; *D:* George Cukor; *M:* Frederick Loewe, Alan Jay Lerner. Academy Awards '64: Best Actor (Harrison), Best Adapted Score, Best Art Direction/Set Decoration (Color), Best Color Cinematography, Best Costume Design (Color), Best Director (Cukor), Best Picture, Best Sound; Nominations: Best Adapted Screenplay, Best Film Editing, Best Supporting Actor (Holloway), Best Supporting Actress (Cooper); British Academy Awards '65: Best Film; Directors Guild of America Awards '64: Best Director (Cukor); Golden Globe Awards '65: Best Actor—Musical/Comedy (Harrison), Best Director (Cukor), Best Film—Musical/Comedy; National Board of Review Awards '64: 10 Best Films of the Year; New York Film Critics Awards '64: Best Actor (Harrison), Best Film. **VHS, Beta $19.98** FOX, FCT, BTV *∄∄∄ ½*

My Father is Coming German immigrant, Vicky, is trying to get an acting career off the ground in New York. She shares her apartment with Ben, a gay man, and generally does more work as a waitress than actress. Vicky's alarmed when her father, Hans, arrives for a visit. She's told him she's married (Vicky's also gay), so Ben agrees to pose as her husband. The rest of the film details Vicky's complicated love life, unsuccessful career tryouts, and her father's increasing bewilderment. It's meant as a sort of reverse, and perverse, innocents abroad, with the two Germans adrift in zany New York but this only works fitfully.
1991 82m/C Shelley Kastner, Alfred Edel, David Bronstein, Mary Lou Graulau, Michael Massee, Annie Sprinkle, David Benderson; *D:* Monika Treut; *W:* Monika Treut. **VHS** NO *∄*

My Father, My Rival A high school student's crush on his teacher leads to emotional complications when his widowed father becomes romantically involved with her.
1985 60m/C Lance Guest. **VHS, Beta** NO *∄*

My Father the Hero Another adaptation of a French film ("Mon Pere, Ce Heroes") finds 14-year-old Heigl on an island paradise with divorced dad Depardieu, passing him off as her boyfriend (without his knowledge) to impress a cute boy, causing obvious misunderstandings. Depardieu shows a flair for physical comedy, but his talent is wasted in a role that's vaguely disturbing; one of the few funny moments finds him unwittingly singing "Thank Heaven For Little Girls" to a horrified audience. For the pre-teen set only, others will probably find it a waste of time. Top notch actress Thompson's surprising (uncredited) cameo is due to her friendship with Depardieu.
1993 (PG) 90m/C Gerard Depardieu, Katherine Heigl, Dalton James, Lauren Hutton, Faith Prince; *Cameos:* Emma Thompson; *D:* Steve Miner; *W:* Francis Veber, Charlie Peters; *M:* David Newman. **VHS** TOU *∄∄*

My Father's Glory Based on Marcel Pagnol's tales of his childhood, this is a sweet, beautiful memory of a young boy's favorite summer in the French countryside of the early 1900s. Not much happens, yet the film is such a perfect evocation of the milieu that one is carried swiftly into the dreams and thoughts of all the characters. One half of a duo, followed by "My Mother's Castle." In French with English subtitles. *AKA:* La Gloire de Mon Pere.
1991 (G) 110m/C Julien Ciamaca, Philippe Caubere, Nathalie Roussel, Therese Liotard, Didier Pain; *D:* Yves Robert; *W:* Lucette Andrei; *M:* Vladimir Cosma. **VHS $19.98** ING, ORI, BTV *∄∄∄*

My Father's House Magazine editor recounts his youth while recovering from a heart attack. He measures his own quality of life against the life that his father led and begins to question his own choices with regard to his family.
1975 96m/C Cliff Robertson, Robert Preston, Eileen Brennan, Rosemary Forsyth. **VHS, Beta $49.95** WOV *∄∄*

My Father's Nurse While father convalesces upstairs, the family frolics about the house and plots his dispatch. When his new nurse secretly cures him, he takes to a wheelchair and mounts a comedic covert counter offensive.
1985 97m/C VHS, Beta $39.95 VCD, MOV *∄*

My Favorite Blonde Beautiful British spy Carroll convinces Hope to aid her in carrying out a secret mission. Lots of fun as Hope and his trained penguin, along with Carroll, embark on a cross-country chase to elude the Nazis. Hope's behavior is hilarious and the pacing of the film is excellent. Based on a story by Melvin Frank and Norman Panama.
1942 78m/B Bob Hope, Madeleine Carroll, Gale Sondergaard, George Zucco, Lionel Royce, Walter Kingsford, Victor Varconi; *Cameos:* Bing Crosby; *D:* Sidney Lanfield; *W:* Frank Butler, Don Hartman. **VHS $14.98** MCA, BTV *∄∄∄*

My Favorite Brunette Detective parody starring Hope as a photographer turned grumbling private eye. He becomes involved with a murder, a spy caper, and a dangerous brunette (Lamour).
1947 85m/B Bob Hope, Dorothy Lamour, Peter Lorre, Lon Chaney Jr., Alan Ladd, Reginald Denny, Bing Crosby; *D:* Elliott Nugent. **VHS, Beta $9.95** CNG, MRV, NOS *∄*

My Favorite Wife Handsome widower Grant remarries only to discover that first wife Dunne, shipwrecked seven years earlier and presumed dead, has reappeared. Eventually, a judge must decide what to do in this most unusual situation, completely lacking

precedent. Farcical and hilarious story filled with a clever cast. The 1963 remake "Move Over Darling" lacks the style and wit of this presentation. Also available colorized.
1940 88m/B Irene Dunne, Cary Grant, Randolph Scott, Gail Patrick, Scotty Beckett; *D:* Garson Kanin; *W:* Samuel Spewack, Bella Spewack, Leo McCarey. **VHS, Beta $19.98** *MED, MLB, TTC* ⅃⅃⅃

My Favorite Year A young writer on a popular live television show in the 1950s is asked to keep a watchful eye on the week's guest star—his favorite swashbuckling movie hero. Through a series of misadventures, he discovers his matinee idol is actually a drunkard and womanizer who has trouble living up to his cinematic standards. Sterling performance from O'Toole, with memorable portrayal from Bologna as the show's host, King Kaiser (a take-off of Sid Caesar from "Your Show of Shows"). *AKA:* My Favourite Year.
1982 (PG) 92m/C Peter O'Toole, Mark Linn-Baker, Joseph Bologna, Jessica Harper, Lainie Kazan, Bill Macy, Anne DeSalvo, Lou Jacobi, Adolph Green, Cameron Mitchell, Gloria Stuart; *D:* Richard Benjamin; *W:* Norman Steinberg; *M:* Ralph Burns. **VHS, Beta $19.95** *MGM* ⅃⅃⅃

My First Wife Strong drama about a self-indulgent man's devastation when his wife abruptly leaves him after ten years of marriage. Realistic and well-acted.
1984 (PG) 95m/C John Hargreaves, Wendy Hughes, Lucy Angwin, Anna Jemison, David Cameron; *D:* Paul Cox; *W:* Paul Cox, Bob Ellis. **VHS** *NO* ⅃⅃½

My Forbidden Past Melodrama set in 1890 New Orleans centers on a young woman (Gardner) with an unsavory past who unexpectedly inherits a fortune and vows to break up the marriage of the man (Mitchum) she loves. His wife is murdered and he is charged with doing the deed until Gardner, exposing her past, wins his love and helps to extricate him.
1951 81m/B Ava Gardner, Melvyn Douglas, Robert Mitchum; *D:* Robert Stevenson. **VHS, Beta $19.95** *MED* ⅃⅃½

My Friend Flicka Boy makes friends with four-legged beast. Dad thinks the horse is full of wild oats, but young Roddie trains it to be the best gosh darned horse in pre-Disney family faredom. Based on Mary O'Hara book, followed by "Thunderhead, Son of Flicka," and TV series.
1943 89m/C Roddy McDowall, Preston Foster, Rita Johnson, James Bell, Jeff Corey; *D:* Harold Schuster. **VHS, Beta $14.98** *FXV, FCT, HMV* ⅃⅃⅃

My Friend Irma An adaptation of the radio series, featuring Wilson as the dumb blonde with boyfriend trouble and Lynn as her sensible pal. The film debut of Martin (singing) and Lewis (mugging) as juice-bar operators. Followed by a sequel, "My Friend Irma Goes West," and later by a television series.
1949 103m/B Marie Wilson, Diana Lynn, John Lund, Don DeFore, Dean Martin, Jerry Lewis, Hans Conried; *D:* George Marshall. **VHS $14.95** *PAR* ⅃½

My Friend Walter Bess Throckmorten attends a family reunion in London with her Aunt Ellie and discovers one of her ancestors is Sir Walter Raleigh. Visiting the Tower of London, Bess finds Sir Walter's ghost who wants to follow her home to Devon to see how the family is doing. He finds that the Throckmorten's are about to lose the family farm but Sir Walter comes up with a plan to restore their fortunes. Shot on location in England and based on the book by Michael Morpurgo.

1993 87m/C Polly Grant, Ronald Pickup, Prunella Scales, Louise Jameson, James Hazeldine, Lawrence Cooper, Constance Chapman; *D:* Gavin Millar. **VHS $29.95** *PME, BTV* ⅃⅃½

My Geisha MacLaine and husband experience bad karma because she wants to be in his new film. In pancake makeup and funny shoes, she poses as a geisha girl and is cast as Madame Butterfly. Her husband, however, is one sharp cookie. Filmed in Japan.
1962 120m/C Shirley MacLaine, Yves Montand, Edward G. Robinson, Robert Cummings; *D:* Jack Cardiff. **VHS $14.95** *PAR, WAX, FCT* ⅃⅃½

My Girl Chlumsky is delightful in her film debut as an 11-year old tomboy who must come to grips with the realities of life. Culkin plays her best friend Thomas, who understands her better than anyone else, including her father, a mortician, and his girlfriend, the makeup artist at the funeral parlor. Some reviewers questioned whether young children would be able to deal with some unhappy occurrences in the film, but most seemed to classify it as a movie the whole family would enjoy.
1991 (PG) 102m/C Dan Aykroyd, Jamie Lee Curtis, Macaulay Culkin, Anna Chlumsky, Griffin Dunne, Raymond Buktenica, Richard Masur, Ann Nelson, Peter Michael Goetz, Tom Villard; *D:* Howard Zieff; *W:* Laurice Elehwany; *M:* James Newton Howard. **VHS, 8mm $19.95** *COL* ⅃⅃½

My Girl 2 Chlumsky is back as Vada (this time without Culkin) in this innocent coming-of-ager. Portly Ackroyd and flaky Curtis return as parental window dressing who encourage Vada's search for information on her long-dead mother. She tracks down old friends of her mom's (Masur and Rose) who are having difficulties with their obnoxious adolescent son (O'Brien). Predictable, but enjoyable. Certain to fail the credibility test of nit-pickers who may wonder why the only thing Ackroyd can remember of his first wife is that she left behind a paper bag with a date scribbled on it. Set in 1974.
1994 (PG) 99m/C Anna Chlumsky, Dan Aykroyd, Jamie Lee Curtis, Austin O'Brien, Richard Masur, Christine Ebersole; *D:* Howard Zieff; *W:* Janet Kovalcik; *M:* Cliff Eidelman. **VHS, 8mm** *COL* ⅃⅃⅃

My Girl Tisa Chronicles the experiences of a young immigrant woman who struggles to survive in the U.S. at the turn of the century and hopes to bring her father over from their home country. Based on a play by Lucille S. Prumbs and Sara B. Smith.
1948 95m/B Lilli Palmer, Sam Wanamaker, Akim Tamiroff, Alan Hale, Hugo Haas, Gale Robbins, Stella Adler; *D:* Elliott Nugent. **VHS $19.98** *REP* ⅃⅃

My Grandpa is a Vampire When 12 year-old Lonny and his pal visit Grandpa Cooger in New Zealand Lonny discovers a long-hidden family secret—Grandpa's a vampire! This doesn't stop either boy from joining with Grandpa in lots of scary adventures.
1992 (PG) 90m/C Al Lewis, Justin Gocke, Milan Borich, Noel Appleby; *D:* David Blyth. **VHS $89.98** *REP* ⅃½

My Heroes Have Always Been Cowboys An aging rodeo rider returns to his hometown to recuperate and finds himself forced to confront his past. His ex-girlfriend, his dad and his sister all expect something from him. He learns how to give it, and gains the strength of purpose to get back on the bull that stomped him. Excellent rodeo footage, solid performances, but the story has been around the barn too many times to hold much interest.

1991 (PG) 106m/C Scott Glenn, Kate Capshaw, Ben Johnson, Balthazar Getty, Mickey Rooney, Gary Busey, Tess Harper, Clarence Williams III, Dub Taylor, Clu Gulager, Dennis Fimple; *D:* Stuart Rosenberg; *W:* Joel Don Humphreys; *M:* James Horner. **VHS, Beta $9.99** *VTR, FXV, COL* ⅃⅃½

My Lady of Whims Clara Bow's dad disapproves of debutante daughter's desire to hang out with the girls who just want to have fun.
1925 42m/B Clara Bow, Betty Baker, Carmelita Geraghty, Donald Keith, Lee Moran. **VHS, Beta $19.95** *GPV, FCT* ⅃

My Left Foot A gritty, unsentimental drama based on the life and autobiography of cerebral-palsy victim Christy Brown. Considered an imbecile by everyone but his mother (Fricker, in a stunning award-winning performance) until he teaches himself to write. He survives his impoverished Irish roots to become a painter and writer using his left foot, the only appendage over which he has control. He also falls in love and finds some heartaches along the way. Day-Lewis is astounding; the supporting cast, especially Shaw and Cusack, match him measure for measure.
1989 (R) 103m/C Daniel Day-Lewis, Brenda Fricker, Ray McAnally, Cyril Cusack, Fiona Shaw, Hugh O'Conor, Adrian Dunbar, Ruth McCabe, Alison Whelan; *D:* Jim Sheridan; *W:* Shane Connaughton, Jim Sheridan; *M:* Elmer Bernstein. Academy Awards '89: Best Actor (Day-Lewis), Best Supporting Actress (Fricker); Nominations: Best Adapted Screenplay, Best Director (Sheridan), Best Picture; Independent Spirit Awards '90: Best Foreign Film; Los Angeles Film Critics Association Awards '89: Best Actor (Day-Lewis), Best Supporting Actress (Fricker); New York Film Critics Awards '89: Best Actor (Day-Lewis); National Society of Film Critics Awards '89: Best Actor (Day-Lewis). **VHS, Beta $89.99** *HBO, BTV, HMV* ⅃⅃⅃

My Life Maudlin, sometimes depressing production preaches the power of a well-examined life. Public relations exec Keaton is diagnosed with cancer and the doctors predict he will most likely die before the birth of his first child. Film follows his transition from uncommunicative and angry to acceptance, a role to which Keaton brings a sentimental strength. Kidman is window dressing as the ever-patient, nobly suffering wife, a cardboard character notable mainly for her beauty.
1993 (PG-13) 114m/C Michael Keaton, Nicole Kidman, Haing S. Ngor, Bradley Whitford, Queen Latifah, Michael Constantine, Toni Sawyer, Rebecca Schull, Lee Garlington; *D:* Bruce Joel Rubin; *W:* Bruce Joel Rubin; *M:* John Barry. **VHS, 8mm** *COL* ⅃⅃½

My Life as a Dog A troublesome boy is separated from his brother and is sent to live with relatives in the country when his mother is taken ill. Unhappy and confused, he struggles to understand sexuality and love and tries to find security and acceptance. Remarkable Swedish film available with English subtitles or dubbed. *AKA:* Mitt Liv Som Hund.
1985 101m/C Anton Glanzelius, Tomas Van Bromssen, Anki Liden, Melinda Kinnaman, Kicki Rundgren, Ing-mari Carlsson; *D:* Lasse Hallstrom. Academy Awards '87 Nominations: Best Adapted Screenplay, Best Director (Hallstrom); Golden Globe Awards '88: Best Foreign Film; Independent Spirit Awards '88: Best Foreign Film. **VHS, Beta $79.95** *PAR, ING, HMV* ⅃⅃⅃⅃

My Life to Live A woman turns to prostitution in this probing examination of sexual, and social, relations. Idiosyncratic Godard has never been more starstruck than in this vehicle for the endearing Karina, his

wife at the time. A classic. In French with English subtitles. *AKA:* Vivre Savie; It's My Life.
1962 85m/B Anna Karina, Sady Rebbot, Andre S. Labarthe, Guylaine Schlumberger; *D:* Jean-Luc Godard; *W:* Jean-Luc Godard; *M:* Michel Legrand. VHS, Beta $24.95 *NOS, NYF, DVT* 🎞🎞🎞🎞

My Little Chickadee Classic comedy about a gambler and a fallen woman who marry for convenience so they can respectably enter an unsuspecting town. Sparks fly in their adventures together. Fields and West are both at their best playing their larger-than-life selves.
1940 91m/B W.C. Fields, Mae West, Joseph Calleia, Dick Foran, Margaret Hamilton, Donald Meek; *D:* Eddie Cline. VHS, Beta $14.98 *MCA, MLB, BTV* 🎞🎞🎞

My Little Girl A rich Philadelphia girl idealistically volunteers her time to help local institutionalized orphans, but meets with opposition.
1987 (R) 118m/C Mary Stuart Masterson, James Earl Jones, Geraldine Page, Anne Meara, Peter Gallagher, George Newbern; *D:* Connie Kaiserman. VHS, Beta $9.99 *STE, PSM* 🎞🎞

My Little Pony: The Movie Animated tale about the siege of Ponyland by malevolent witches.
1986 87m/C *D:* Michael Joens; *V:* Danny DeVito, Cloris Leachman, Tony Randall, Madeline Kahn. VHS, Beta $9.99 *VTR, WTA* 🎞🎞

My Love For Yours The romantic tale of a young man hoping to win the love of a beautiful but icy girl. A tad silly in parts, but the clever dialogue moves the story along. *AKA:* Honeymoon in Bali.
1939 99m/B Fred MacMurray, Madeleine Carroll; *D:* Edward H. Griffith. VHS, Beta $19.95 *NOS, CAB* 🎞🎞½

My Lucky Star Skating star Henie plays a department store clerk that gets sent off to college to model clothes from the store's sports line. She somehow manages to convince school officials to stage their winter ice show in the department store, where she gets to show off her stuff. Don't miss the grand finale, a performance of "Alice in Wonderland Ice Ballet." Based on the story "They Met in Chicago" by Karl Tunberg and Don Ettlinger. ♫I've Got a Date With a Dream; Could You Pass in Love; This May Be the Night; The All-American Swing; Plymouth University Song.
1938 81m/B Sonja Henie, Richard Greene, Joan Davis, Cesar Romero, Buddy Ebsen, Arthur Treacher, George Barbier, Gypsy Rose Lee; *D:* Roy Del Ruth; *W:* Harry Tugend, Jack Yellen. VHS $19.98 *FXV* 🎞🎞½

My Man Adam A dreamy, Mitty-esque high schooler falls in love with a girl (Daryl's auburn-haired sister, Page Hannah), and becomes ensnared in a real life crime, leaving his friend to bail him out. Typical boy-meets-girl, boy-gets-in-trouble yarn.
1986 (R) 84m/C Raphael Sbarge, Veronica Cartwright, Page Hannah, Larry B. Scott, Charlie Barnett, Arthur Pendleton, Dave Thomas; *D:* Roger L. Simon. VHS, Beta $79.98 *FOX* 🎞

My Man Godfrey A spoiled rich girl picks up someone she assumes is a bum as part of a scavenger hunt and decides to keep him on as her butler. In the process, he teaches her about life, money, and happiness. Top-notch screwball comedy defines the genre. Lombard is a stunner alongside the equally charming Powell. Watch for Jane Wyman as an extra in the party scene. Remade in 1957 with June Allyson and David Niven. From the novel by Eric Hatch, who also co-scripted.
1936 95m/B William Powell, Carole Lombard, Gail Patrick, Alice Brady, Mischa Auer, Eugene Pallette, Alan Mowbray, Franklin Pangborn, Jane Wyman; *D:* Gregory La Cava; *W:* Morrie Ryskind, Gregory La Cava. VHS, Beta $9.95 *CNG, MRV, NOS* 🎞🎞🎞

My Man Godfrey Inferior remake of the sophisticated screwball comedy of the 30's about a butler who brings a touch of the common man to the filthy rich. Niven stars as the butler and Allyson plays the rich girl, but nothing compares to the original roles created by Powell and Lombard.
1957 92m/C June Allyson, David Niven, Martha Hyer, Jessie Royce Landis, Robert Keith, Eva Gabor, Jay Robinson, Jeff Donnell; *D:* Henry Koster; *W:* Everett Freeman, Peter Berneis, William Bowers. VHS $19.98 *MCA* 🎞🎞½

My Michael Sensitive adaptation of Amos Oz's novel set in Jerasalem in the late 1950s. A young woman is stifled by marriage and the conventions of her bourgeois life and her fantasies begin to take over. In Hebrew with English subtitles.
1975 90m/C Efrat Lavie, Oded Kotler; *D:* Dan Wolman. VHS, Beta $79.95 *ERG, FCT, ING* 🎞🎞🎞

My Mom's a Werewolf An average suburban mother gets involved with a dashing stranger and soon, to her terror, begins to turn into a werewolf. Her daughter and companion must come up with a plan to regain dear, sweet mom.
1989 (PG) 90m/C Susan Blakely, John Saxon, John Schuck, Katrina Caspary, Ruth Buzzi, Marilyn McCoo, Marcia Wallace, Diana Barrows; *D:* Michael Fischa; *W:* Mark Pirro. VHS, Beta $79.95 *PSM* 🎞½

My Mother's Castle The second half of the two part film series based on the autobiography of Marcel Pagnol. Picking up where "My Father's Glory" left off, the family begins a series of vacations in a beautiful country home. Dynamically acted and tenderly directed, charming and suitable for the entire family. In French with English subtitles. *AKA:* Le Chateau de Ma Mere.
1991 (PG) 98m/C Philippe Caubere, Nathalie Roussel, Didier Pain, Therese Liotard, Julien Ciamaca, Victorien Delmare; *D:* Yves Robert; *M:* Vladimir Cosma. VHS $19.98 *ING, ORI, BTV* 🎞🎞🎞½

My Mother's Secret Life Dull drama focusing on a long-forgotten daughter who suddenly appears on her mother's doorstep and discovers that mom makes a living as a high-priced hooker.
1984 100m/C Loni Anderson, Paul Sorvino, Amanda Wyss, James Sutorius, Sandy McPeak; *D:* Robert Markowitz; *M:* Brad Fiedel. VHS, Beta $79.95 *PSM* 🎞½

My Name Called Bruce When the unstoppable "Bruce" is teamed with a sexy secret agent, the criminals of Hong Kong issue a collective shudder.
1987 90m/C Bruce Le. VHS, Beta $19.99 *BFV* 🎞½

My Name is Ivan Tarkovsky's first feature film is a vivid, wrenching portrait of a young Soviet boy surviving as a spy behind enemy lines during WWII. Technically stunning, heralding the coming of modern cinema's greatest formalist. In Russian with English subtitles. *AKA:* Ivan's Childhood; The Youngest Spy.
1962 84m/B Kolya Burlyayev, Valentin Zubkov, Ye Zharikov, S. Krylov; *D:* Andrei Tarkovsky. VHS, Beta $79.95 *FXL, FCT, ING* 🎞🎞🎞

My Name is Nobody Fast-paced spaghetti-western wherein a cocky, soft-hearted gunfighter is sent to kill the famous, retired outlaw he reveres, but instead they band together. *AKA:* Il Mio Nome e Nessuno.
1974 (PG) 115m/C Henry Fonda, Terence Hill, R.G. Armstrong; *D:* Tonino Valerii; *M:* Ennio Morricone. VHS, Beta $14.95 *BAR, HHE* 🎞½

My Neighbor Totoro Rather gooey Japanese animated movie about Satsuki and her younger sister Lucy, whose new house in the country is filled with magic, including a friendly creature named Totoro. Totoro is a cuddly, if weird, mix of bear, owl, and seal, with whiskers and a gentle roar. He can fly, has a magic bus, and can only be seen by children. Naturally, every time the two girls get into mischief Totoro is there to rescue them. Dubbed into English.
1993 (G) 76m/C *D:* Hayao Miyazaki; *W:* Hayao Miyazaki. VHS $19.98 *FXV* 🎞🎞½

My Neighborhood A debonair bar-owner leads a double life as a knife wielding psychopath.
1984 35m/C VHS, Beta *NO* 🎞🎞½

My New Gun Uneven, restless dark comedy about Debbie and Gerald Bender, yuppified suburban couple whose lives are disrupted by a gun. When their newly engaged friends get a gun, Gerry decides they need a gun as well. Debbie is very uncomfortable about having a weapon in the house and doesn't want anything to do with it. When mysterious neighbor LeGros steals the gun, it sets off a bizarre chain of events that culminate at the wedding of their friends. Impressive first effort for writer/director Cochran.
1992 97m/C Diane Lane, Stephen Collins, James LeGros, Tess Harper, Bill Raymond, Bruce Altman, Maddie Corman; *D:* Stacy Cochran; *W:* Stacy Cochran; *M:* Pat Irwin. VHS *COL* 🎞🎞½

My New Partner Amiable French comedy in which cynical veteran cop is saddled with straight arrow rookie partner. French Cesars for best film and best director, but remember: They like Jerry Lewis too. In French with English subtitles. *AKA:* Les Ripoux.
1984 (R) 106m/C Philippe Noiret, Thierry Lhermitte, Regine, Grace de Capitani, Claude Brosset, Julien Guiomar; *D:* Claude Zidi; *W:* Claude Zidi. VHS, Beta $29.95 *MED, IME* 🎞🎞½

My Night at Maud's Typically subtle Rohmer entry concerns quandary of upright fellow who finds himself drawn to comparatively carefree woman. Talky, somewhat arid film is one of director's Six Moral Tales. You'll either find it fascinating or wish you were watching "Rocky XXIV" instead. Cinematography by Nestor Almendros; in French with English subtitles. *AKA:* My Night with Maud; Ma Nuit Chez Maud.
1969 111m/B Jean-Louis Trintignant, Francoise Fabian, Marie-Christine Barrault, Antoine Vitez; *D:* Eric Rohmer; *W:* Eric Rohmer. VHS, Beta $29.98 *MED, ING, APD* 🎞🎞🎞

My Old Man Plucky teen and her seedy horsetrainer father come together over important horse race. Oates makes this one worth watching on a slow evening. A Hemingway story made for television.
1979 102m/C Kristy McNichol, Warren Oates, Eileen Brennan; *D:* John Erman. VHS, Beta $9.95 *CAF* 🎞½

My Old Man's Place A veteran, with two war buddies and a girl, returns to his father's run-down farm, hoping to fix it up. Sexual tensions arise and violence erupts.
1971 (R) 93m/C Arthur Kennedy, Michael Moriarty, Mitchell Ryan, William Devane, Topo Swope; *D:* Edwin Sherin. VHS, Beta $79.95 *PSM* 🎞½

My Other Husband A woman has two husbands and families, one in Paris and one in Trouville, who eventually meet each other. Seems silly but grows into a sensitive and sad portrait of married life. In French with English subtitles. *AKA:* Attention! Une Femme Peut en Cacher une Autre.
1985 (PG-13) 110m/C Miou-Miou, Rachid Ferrache, Roger Hanin; *D:* Georges Lautner. VHS, Beta $59.95 COL, ING ♂♂½

My Outlaw Brother A man travelling West to visit his brother in Mexico meets a Texas Ranger on the train. The man discovers that his brother is an outlaw, and teams up with the Ranger to capture him. *AKA:* My Brother, the Outlaw.
1951 82m/B Mickey Rooney, Wanda Hendrix, Robert Preston, Robert Stack, Jose Torvay; *D:* Elliott Nugent. VHS $19.98 MOV, MRV, VYY ♂♂

My Own Private Idaho Director Van Sant of "Drugstore Cowboy" returns to the underworld to examine another group of outsiders, this time young, homosexual hustlers. On the streets of Seattle, narcoleptic hustler Mike meets slumming rich boy Scott, and together they begin a search for Mike's lost mother, which leads them to Idaho and Italy. Stunning visuals, an elliptical plot, and a terrific performance by Phoenix highlight this search for love, the meaning of life, and power. Van Sant couples these activities with scenes from Shakespeare's "Henry IV" for a sometimes inscrutable, but always memorable film. Look for director Richert's Falstaff role as an aging chickenhawk.
1991 (R) 105m/C River Phoenix, Keanu Reeves, James Russo, William Richert, Rodney Harvey, Michael Parker, Flea, Chiara Caselli, Udo Kier, Grace Zabriskie, Tom Troupe; *D:* Gus Van Sant; *W:* Gus Van Sant. VHS $19.95 COL, NLC ♂♂♂

My Pal, The King Amusing western with Rooney as the boy king of Ruritania, who's bored with his official duties. He meets Mix, the proprietor of a traveling wild west show which just happens to be performing in the country. Good thing too because Rooney has an evil prime minister who wants the throne for himself and kidnaps the kid. Naturally, Mix and his friends arrive to save him in the nick of time.
1932 62m/B Tom Mix, Mickey Rooney, Stuart Holmes, Paul Hurst, Noel Francis, James Kirkwood, Jim Thorpe; *D:* Kurt Neumann. VHS $12.95 GPV ♂♂½

My Pal Trigger Roy is unjustly imprisoned in this high adventure on the plains. Better than usual script and direction makes this is one of the more entertaining of the singing cowboy's films.
1946 79m/B Roy Rogers, George "Gabby" Hayes, Dale Evans, Jack Holt; *D:* Frank McDonald. VHS, Beta $19.95 NOS, MRV, HHT ♂♂

My Pleasure Is My Business Cinematic autobiography of Xaveria Hollander, the world's most renowned prostitute of the seventies, and the zany occurrences which abound in her profession.
1974 (R) 85m/C Xaviera Hollander, Henry Ramer, Colin Fox, Ken Lynch, Jayne Eastwood; *D:* Al Waxman. VHS NO ♂♂

My Samurai When young Peter McCrea witnesses a gang murder he turns to his martial-arts expert friend Young Park to help him. On the run from both the gang and the police Peter learns self-defense and the courage to face his fears.
1992 (R) 87m/C Julian Lee, Mako, Terry O'Quinn, Bubba Smith, Jim Turner, Carlos Palomino, John Kallo; *D:* Fred Dresch. VHS $89.95 IMP ♂½

My Science Project Teenager Stockwell stumbles across a crystal sphere with a funky light. Unaware that it is an alien time-travel device, he takes it to school to use as a science project in a last-ditch effort to avoid failing his class. Chaos follows and Stockwell and his chums find themselves battling gladiators, mutants, and dinosaurs. Plenty of special effects and a likeable enough, dumb teenage flick.
1985 (PG) 94m/C John Stockwell, Danielle von Zernaeck, Fisher Stevens, Raphael Sbarge, Richard Masur, Barry Corbin, Ann Wedgeworth, Dennis Hopper, Candace Silvers, Beau Dremann, Pat Simmons, Pamela Springsteen; *D:* Jonathan Betuel; *M:* Peter Bernstein. VHS, Beta $79.95 TOU ♂♂

My Side of the Mountain A thirteen-year-old boy decides to emulate his idol, Henry David Thoreau, and gives up his home and his family to live in the Canadian mountains.
1969 (G) 100m/C Teddy Eccles, Theodore Bikel; *D:* James B. Clark. VHS, Beta $29.95 KUI, PAR ♂♂½

My Sister Eileen Ruth and Eileen are two small-town Ohio sisters who move to Manhattan seeking excitement. They live in a basement apartment in Greenwich Village with an assortment of oddball tenants as they pursue success and romance. Everyone is daffy and charming, as is the film. Fun, but unmemorable songs, however the terrific choreography is by Fosse, who also appears as one sister's suitor. Remake of a 1942 film which was based on a Broadway play, which was based on a series of autobiographical stories published in the New Yorker. The play was later turned into a Broadway musical known as "Wonderful Town," which has nothing to do with this version of the original stories. ♫Give Me a Band and My Baby; It's Bigger Than You and Me; There's Nothing Like Love; As Soon As They See Eileen; I'm Great; Conga; Atmosphere.
1955 108m/C Janet Leigh, Betty Garrett, Jack Lemmon, Bob Fosse, Kurt Kasznar, Dick York, Lucy Marlow, Tommy Rall, Barbara Brown, Horace McMahon; *D:* Richard Quine; *W:* Blake Edwards, Richard Quine; *M:* Jules Styne. VHS $19.95 COL, MOV, MVD ♂♂♂

My Sister, My Love Odd tale of two sisters' incestuous relationship and what happens when one of them takes another lover. The cage of the alternate titles refers to the place where their pet apes are kept and seems to symbolize the confining nature of their life together. *AKA:* The Cage; The Mafu Cage.
1978 (R) 102m/C Lee Grant, Carol Kane, Will Geer, James Olson; *D:* Karen Arthur. VHS $59.95 VCI ♂½

My Son, the Vampire Last of Britain's Old Mother Riley series in which Lucan plays the Irish housekeeper in drag. Lugosi is a crazed scientist who thinks he's a vampire and wants to take over the world with his giant robot. Mother Riley interferes. Theme song by Alan Sherman. *AKA:* Old Mother Riley Meets the Vampire; The Vampire and the Robot; Vampire Over London; Mother Riley Meets the Vampire.
1952 72m/B Bela Lugosi, Arthur Lucan, Dora Bryan, Richard Wattis; *D:* John Gilling. VHS $19.98 NOS, SNC ♂½

My Song Goes Round the World Chronicles the romantic foibles of a singing trio and the one girl they decide they all love.
1934 68m/B Joseph Schmidt, John Loder, Charlotte Ander; *D:* Richard Oswald. VHS $29.95 NOS, DVT ♂½

My Stepmother Is an Alien When eccentric physicist Aykroyd sends a message beam to another galaxy on a stormy night, the last thing he expects is a visit from beautiful alien Basinger. Unfortunately, he does not realize that this gorgeous blonde is an alien and he continues to court her despite her rather odd habits. Only the daughter seems to notice the strange goings on, and her dad ignores her warnings, enabling Basinger's evil sidekick to continue in its plot to take over the Earth.
1988 (PG-13) 108m/C Dan Aykroyd, Kim Basinger, Jon Lovitz, Alyson Hannigan, Joseph Maher, Seth Green, Wesley Mann, Adrian Sparks, Juliette Lewis, Tanya Fenmore; *D:* Richard Benjamin; *W:* Herschel Weingrod, Timothy Harris, Jonathan Reynolds. VHS, Beta $14.95 COL ♂♂

My Sweet Charlie Unwed, pregnant white woman hides out with black lawyer in backwater Texas. Better than it sounds, with nice performances by Duke and Freeman. Made for television.
1970 97m/C Patty Duke, Al Freeman Jr., Ford Rainey, William Hardy, Chris Wilson, Archie Moore, Noble Willingham; *D:* Lamont Johnson. VHS, Beta $39.95 MCA ♂♂½

My Sweet Victim A young couple who recently moved to the United States from Poland try to make a go of their own business. The business fails, and so does their marriage. Will it end in murder?
1985 92m/C Candice Bergen, Juergen Prochnow. VHS $9.99 QVD ♂♂

My Therapist A sex therapist's boyfriend cannot bear the thought of her having intercourse with other men as part of her work. Soft core.
1984 81m/C Marilyn Chambers; *D:* Gary Legon. VHS, Beta NO Woof!

My Tutor When a high school student is in danger of flunking French, his parents hire a private tutor to help him learn the lessons. It becomes clear that his studies will involve many more subjects, however. Standard teen sex comedy.
1982 (R) 97m/C Caren Kaye, Matt Lattanzi, Kevin McCarthy, Clark Brandon, Bruce Bauer, Arlene Golonka, Crispin Glover, Shelley Taylor Morgan, Francesca "Kitten" Natavidad, Jewel Shepard, Marilyn Tokuda; *D:* George Bowers. VHS, Beta $14.95 MCA ♂½

My Twentieth Century This quirky gem of a movie is a charming, sentimental journey through the early 1900s. Twins Dora and Lili are separated in early childhood. They reunite as grown, very different women on the Orient Express after they both (unknowingly) have sex with the same man. Dora is a sex kitten, while Lili is a radical equipped with explosives. When the two sisters come together, they both lose their destructive, dependent selves (Dora on men, Lili on politics) and become independent women. Lots of sidelights and subplots that are sure to amuse the viewer. In Hungarian with English subtitles. *AKA:* Az en XX. Szazadom.
1990 104m/B Dortha Segda, Oleg Jankowski, Peter Andorai, Gabor Mate, Paulus Manker, Laszlo Vidovszky; *D:* Ildiko Enyedi; *W:* Ildiko Enyedi. VHS $89.95 FXL, ING ♂♂♂

My Universities In the final part of Donskoi's trilogy on Maxim Gorky, Gorky is a young man at university who is introduced to radical politics by several liberal intellectuals. He makes his first attempts at writing and joins the revolution as he leaves his painful past behind. In Russian with English subtitles. Preceded by "My Childhood" and "My Apprenticeship."

1940 100m/C *D:* Mark Donskoi. VHS $39.95 *FCT 𝄞𝄞𝄞*

My Wicked, Wicked Ways Cleverly cast, low-budget television drama based on the autobiography of Errol Flynn.
1984 95m/C Duncan Regehr, Barbara Hershey, Hal Linden, Darren McGavin; *D:* Don Taylor. VHS, Beta $59.98 *FOX 𝄞𝄞 ½*

My Wonderful Life Softcore gristle about a beautiful tramp climbing the social ladder via the boudoir.
1990 (R) 107m/C Pierre Cosso, Jean Rochefort, Massimo Venturiello, Carol Alt, Elliott Gould; *D:* Carlo Vanzina. VHS, Beta $79.95 *COL 𝄞*

Myra Breckinridge A tasteless version of the Gore Vidal novel. An alleged satire of a film critic who undergoes a sex change operation and then plots the destruction of the American male movie star stereotype. Created an outcry from all sides, and hung out to dry by studio where it's reportedly still blowing in the wind.
1970 (R) 94m/C Mae West, John Huston, Raquel Welch, Rex Reed, Farrah Fawcett, Jim Backus, John Carradine, Andy Devine, Tom Selleck; *D:* Michael Sarne. VHS, Beta *FOX, MLB* Woof!

The Mysterians A race of gigantic scientific intellects from a doomed planet attempts to conquer Earth. They want to rebuild their race by reproducing with earth women. Earth fights back. From the director of "Godzilla." Dubbed in English from Japanese. *AKA:* Earth Defense Forces; Chikyu Boelgun.
1958 85m/C Kenji Sahara, Yumi Shirakawa, Takashi Shimura; *D:* Inoshiro Honda. VHS, Beta $29.95 *VCI, MLB 𝄞𝄞 ½*

Mysteries A rich tourist becomes obsessed by a beautiful local girl. As his obsession grows, his behavior becomes stranger. Interesting and well-acted. The film is an adaptation of the famous love story by Nobel-laureate Knut Hamsun. Suffers from poor dubbing.
1984 100m/C Rutger Hauer, Sylvia Kristel, David Rappaport, Rita Tushingham; *D:* Paul de Lussanet. VHS, Beta *NO 𝄞 ½*

Mysterious Desperado Young man, about to inherit a large estate, is framed on a murder charge by land grabbers.
1949 61m/B Tim Holt, Richard Martin. VHS, Beta $39.95 *RKO 𝄞*

Mysterious Desperado/Rider From Tucson A western double feature. In "Mysterious Desperado," a young man is framed for a crime he did not commit. In "Rider From Tucson," evil claim jumpers will resort to murder to gain control of a gold mine.
1949 121m/B Tim Holt, Richard Martin. VHS, Beta $39.95 *RKO, TTC 𝄞𝄞 ½*

Mysterious Doctor Satan A mad satanic scientist builds an army of mechanical robots to rob and terrorize the nation. In 15 episodes.
1940 250m/B Eduardo Ciannelli, Robert Wilcox, Ella Neal; *D:* William Witney. VHS $29.95 *REP, VCN, MLB 𝄞𝄞*

Mysterious Island Exhilarating sci-fi classic adapted from Jules Verne's novel about escaping Civil War soldiers who go up in Verne balloon and come down on a Pacific island populated by giant animals. They also encounter two shipwrecked English ladies, pirates, and Captain Nemo (and his sub). Top-rate special effects by master Ray Harryhausen.

1961 101m/C Michael Craig, Joan Greenwood, Michael Callan, Gary Merrill, Herbert Lom, Beth Rogan, Percy Herbert, Dan Jackson, Nigel Green; *D:* Cy Endfield; *M:* Bernard Herrmann. VHS, Beta $19.95 *COL, MLB 𝄞𝄞𝄞 ½*

Mysterious Island of Beautiful Women A male sextet is stranded on a South Sea island, where they must endure the trials of an angry tribe of conveniently bikini-clad women.
1979 100m/C Jamie Lyn Bauer, Jayne Kennedy, Kathryn Davis, Deborah Shelton, Susie Coelho, Peter Lawford, Steven Keats, Clint Walker; *D:* Joseph Pevney. VHS $39.95 *LIV 𝄞*

Mysterious Jane Amid soft-focus nudity, a husband and his lover conspire to institutionalize his wife.
198? 90m/C Amber Lee, Sandy Carey. VHS, Beta $29.95 *MED 𝄞*

The Mysterious Lady Pre-Ninotchka Garbo plays Russian spy who betrays her mother country because she does not want to be alone.
1928 99m/B Greta Garbo, Conrad Nagel, Gustav von Seyffertitz, Richard Alexander, Albert Pollet, Edward Connelly. VHS $29.99 *MGM, FCT 𝄞𝄞 ½*

The Mysterious Magician Entertaining suspense story of the mad murderer known as "The Wizard," who was thought by Scotland Yard to be dead, but the current murderwave in London suggests otherwise. Based on an Edgar Wallace story.
1965 95m/C Joachim Fuchsberger, Eddi Arent, Sophie Hardy, Karl John, Heinz Drache; *D:* Alfred Vohrer. VHS $16.95 *SNC 𝄞𝄞*

Mysterious Mr. Wong The Thirteen Coins of Confucius put San Francisco's Chinatown in a state of terror until Mr. Wong arrives.
1935 56m/B Arline Judge, Wallace Ford; *D:* William Nigh. VHS, Beta $24.95 *VYY, MRV, SNC 𝄞𝄞*

Mysterious Planet Humans fight off alien hordes in this space flick.
1984 90m/C VHS, Beta $59.95 *VCD 𝄞*

The Mysterious Rider A cowboy tries to prevent unscrupulous homesteaders from cheating farmers out of their land. *AKA:* The Fighting Phantom.
1933 59m/B Kent Taylor, Lona Andre, Gail Patrick, Warren Hymer, Berton Churchill; *D:* Fred Allen. VHS $12.95 *SNC, DVT 𝄞𝄞 ½*

The Mysterious Rider A man framed for murder must help innocent homesteaders from being cheated out of their land. *AKA:* Mark of the Avenger.
1938 75m/B Douglass Dumbrille, Sidney Toler, Russell Hayden, Charlotte Field; *D:* Lesley Selander. VHS $19.95 *NOS, DVT, RXM 𝄞*

The Mysterious Rider Routine oater has Crabbe and St. John helping a couple of kids protect their inheritance.
1942 56m/B Buster Crabbe, Al "Fuzzy" St. John, Caroline Burke, John Merton, Kermit Maynard, Jack Ingram, Charles "Slim" Whitaker; *D:* Sherman Scott. VHS $19.95 *DVT, HEG 𝄞𝄞*

The Mysterious Stranger Printer's apprentice is given to bouts of daydreaming about a magic castle in Austria. Based on Twain tale.
1982 89m/C Chris Makepeace, Lance Kerwin, Fred Gwynne; *D:* Peter Hunt. VHS $19.95 *MCA 𝄞𝄞*

Mysterious Two Two aliens visit the Earth in an effort to enlist converts to travel the universe with them.
1982 100m/C John Forsythe, Priscilla Pointer, Noah Beery Jr., James Stephens, Karen Werner, Robert Englund, Robert Pine; *D:* Gary Sherman. VHS, Beta $59.95 *LIV 𝄞𝄞 ½*

Mystery at Castle House Three precocious children stumble onto a mystery when their friends disappear at a neighborhood castle.
1982 80m/C VHS, Beta *NO 𝄞𝄞 ½*

Mystery at Fire Island A clever young girl and her cousin encounter some strange people as they try to find out why their fisherman friend mysteriously vanished.
1981 52m/C Frank Converse, Barbara Byrne, Beth Ehlers, Eric Gurry. VHS, Beta *NO 𝄞*

Mystery Date A sort of teen version of "After Hours," in which a shy college guy gets a date with the girl of his dreams, only to be mistaken for a master criminal and pursued by gangsters, police and a crazed florist. Not terrible, but if you're old enough to drive you're probably too old to watch with amusement.
1991 (PG-13) 98m/C Ethan Hawke, Teri Polo, Brian McNamara, Fisher Stevens, B.D. Wong; *D:* Jonathan Wacks; *W:* Terry Runte; *M:* John Du Prez. VHS $92.98 *ORI 𝄞*

Mystery in Swing An all-black mystery with music, about a trumpet player who has snake venom put on his mouthpiece.
1940 66m/B F.E. Miller, Monte Hawley, Marguerite Whitten, Tom Moore, Ceepee Johnson; *D:* Arthur Dreifuss. VHS, Beta $24.95 *VYY 𝄞𝄞*

Mystery Island Beautifully filmed underwater scenes in this children's film about four youths who discover a deserted island which they name Mystery Island, and a retired pirate who lives there. When the children find counterfeit money and the bad guys return for it, the old pirate's clever plans keep the kids safe.
1981 75m/C VHS, Beta *NO 𝄞𝄞 ½*

Mystery Liner Dead bodies are found aboard ocean liner and passengers are concerned about it. Slow-moving sea cruise. *AKA:* The Ghost of John Holling.
1934 62m/B Noah Beery Sr., Astrid Allwyn, Cornelius Keefe, Gustav von Seyffertitz, Edwin Maxwell, Booth Howard, George "Gabby" Hayes; *D:* William Nigh. VHS, Beta $16.95 *NOS, SNC 𝄞𝄞 ½*

The Mystery Man A Chicago reporter goes on a drinking binge and ends up in St. Louis. There he stumbles upon a mystery which may involve the paper for which he works. He teams up with a beautiful woman to try to crack the case.
1935 65m/B Robert Armstrong, Maxine Doyle, Henry Kolker, Leroy Mason, James Burke; *D:* Ray McCarey. VHS, Beta $16.95 *SNC 𝄞𝄞 ½*

Mystery Man Below-average episode has rancher Hoppy being bothered by rustlers. Boyd solves things in the usual way, while Clyde provides the laughs.
1944 58m/B William Boyd, Andy Clyde, Jimmy Rogers, Don Costello, Francis McDonald, Forrest Taylor, Eleanor Stewart; *D:* George Archainbaud. VHS $19.95 *NOS 𝄞 ½*

Mystery Mansion Fortune in gold and a hundred-year-old mystery lead three children into an exciting treasure hunt. Family fare.
1983 (PG) 95m/C Dallas McKennon, Greg Wynne, Jane Ferguson. VHS, Beta $19.95 *MED 𝄞𝄞*

Mystery Mountain Twelve episodes depict the villain known as the "Rattler" attempting to stop the construction of a railroad over Mystery Mountain.
1934 156m/B Ken Maynard, Gene Autry, Smiley Burnette; *D:* Otto Brower, B. Reeves Eason. VHS, Beta $39.95 *NOS, VCN, CAB 𝄞 ½*

The Mystery of Alexina True story of Herculine Adelaide Barbin, a 19th-century French hermaphrodite, who, after growing up a woman, fell in love with another woman and was actually revealed to be a man. Subtitled. *AKA:* Mystere Alexina.
1986 86m/C Vuillemin, Valeri Stroh; *D:* Rene Feret; *W:* Jean Gruault. **VHS, Beta $29.98** SUE, NLC 𝄢𝄢½

Mystery of Mr. Wong The largest star sapphire in the world, the "Eye of the Daughter of the Moon," is stolen from a museum in its home country of China. Mr. Wong becomes involved in trying to trace its trail and the perpetrator of the murders that follow in its wake. One in the series of detective films.
1939 67m/B Boris Karloff, Grant Withers, Dorothy Tree, Lotus Long; *D:* William Nigh. **VHS $14.95** VYY, MRV, DVT 𝄢½

Mystery of the Hooded Horseman Tex finds himself pitted against a very strange adversary.
1937 61m/B Tex Ritter, Iris Meredith, Charles "Blackie" King, Joseph Girard, Lafe McKee; *D:* Ray Taylor. **VHS, Beta $19.95** NOS, VDM, DVT 𝄢𝄢

Mystery of the Leaping Fish/ Chess Fever Two silent shorts. The first, filmed in 1916, is a surreal comedy-mystery about a doped-up detective named Coke Ennyday and his hallucinatory, sped-up adventures. The second, made in 1925 during the Moscow Chess Tournament, is a parody of professional chess playing and the fever with which it grips a country. Pudovkin's second directorial credit.
1925 64m/B Douglas Fairbanks Sr., Bessie Love, Alma Rubens; *D:* John Emerson, Vsevolod Pudovkin; *W:* Tod Browning. **VHS, Beta, 8mm $24.95** VYY, MRV 𝄢𝄢½

The Mystery of the Mary Celeste Tale of terror based on the bizarre case of the "Marie Celeste," an American ship found adrift off the coast of England with her sails set but minus any of her crew on December 5, 1872. *AKA:* The Phantom Ship; The Mystery of the Marie Celeste.
1937 64m/B Bela Lugosi, Shirley Grey, Edmund Willard, Arthur Margetson. **VHS, Beta $19.95** NOS, MRV, VYY 𝄢𝄢

Mystery of the Million Dollar Hockey Puck Sinister diamond smugglers learn a lesson on ice from a pair of orphan lads. Features the National Hockey League's Montreal Canadiens in one of their few film appearances.
1987 88m/C Michael MacDonald, Angele Knight, The Montreal Canadiens; *D:* Jean LaFleur, Peter Svatek. **VHS, Beta** NO 𝄢½

Mystery of the Riverboat Louisiana and the Mississippi River are the background for these 13 episodes of mystery and murder.
1944 90m/B Robert Lowery, Eddie Quillan, Lyle Talbot, Francis McDonald, Arthur Hohl; *D:* Ray Taylor, Lewis D. Collins. **VHS, Beta $29.95** VCI, MLB, GPV 𝄢𝄢½

Mystery of the Wax Museum Rarely seen, vintage horror classic about a wax-dummy maker who, after a disfiguring fire, resorts to murder and installs the wax-covered bodies of his victims in his museum. Famous for its pioneering use of two-strip Technicolor. Remade in 1953 in 3-D as "House of Wax."
1933 77m/C Lionel Atwill, Fay Wray, Glenda Farrell; *D:* Michael Curtiz. **VHS, Beta $19.98** MGM, MLB 𝄢𝄢𝄢

Mystery Plane An inventor devises a new bomb-dropping mechanism, and must evade secret agents on his way to deliver it to the government.
1939 60m/B John Trent, Marjorie Reynolds, Milburn Stone, Peter George Lynn, Polly Ann Young; *D:* George Waggner. **VHS, Beta $19.95** NOS, DVT, HEG 𝄢½

Mystery Ranch A cowboy finds himself in strange predicaments out on the range.
1934 52m/B George O'Brien, Charles Middleton, Cecilia Parker; *D:* David Howard. **VHS, Beta $19.95** NOS, DVT 𝄢½

Mystery Squadron Twelve chapters, 13 minutes each. Daredevil air action in flight against the masked pilots of the Black Ace.
1933 240m/B Bob Steele, Guinn Williams, Lucille Browne, Jack Mulhall, J. Carroll Naish, Jack Mower; *D:* Colbert Clark. **VHS, Beta $24.95** GPV, VCN, DVT 𝄢½

Mystery Train A run down hotel in Memphis is the scene for three vignettes concerning the visit of foreigners to the U.S. Themes of mythic Americana, Elvis, and life on the fringe pervade this hip and quirky film. The three vignettes all tie together in clever and funny overlaps. Waits fans should listen for his performance as a DJ.
1989 (R) 110m/C Masatoshi Nagase, Youki Kudoh, Jay Hawkins, Cinque Lee, Joe Strummer, Nicoletta Braschi, Elizabeth Bracco, Steve Buscemi, Tommy Noonan, Rockets Redglare, Rick Aviles, Rufus Thomas; *D:* Jim Jarmusch; *W:* Jim Jarmusch; *M:* John Lurie; *V:* Tom Waits. **VHS $79.98** ORI 𝄢𝄢𝄢

Mystery Trooper Adventures in the great wilderness full of prospecting, greed, and Indians all being observed by the Royal Mounties. Ten chapters of the serial at 20 minutes each. *AKA:* Trail of the Royal Mounted.
1932 200m/B Robert Frazer, Buzz Barton. **VHS, Beta $24.95** GPV, NOS, CAB 𝄢𝄢

Mystic Circle Murder Reporter sets out to uncover phony mediums, particularly the Great La Gagge, whose fake apparitions are so convincing that it caused one of his clients to have a heart attack. Cheaply made, and it's obvious. Watch for a cameo by Harry Houdini's wife, who talks about life after death. Also known as "Religious Racketeers." Based on a story by director O'Connor.
1939 69m/B Betty Compson, Robert Fiske, Helene Le Berthon, Arthur Gardner; *D:* Frank O'Connor. **VHS $16.95** SNC 𝄢

Mystic Pizza Intelligent coming of age drama centers on two sisters and their best friend as they struggle with their hopes, loves, and family rivalries in the small town of Mystic, Connecticut. At times predictable, there are enough unexpected moments to keep interest high; definite appeal to young women, but others may not relate. The relatively unknown Roberts got most of the attention, but is the weakest of the three leads, so watch this one for the strong performances from Gish and Taylor.
1988 (R) 101m/C Annabeth Gish, Julia Roberts, Lili Taylor, Vincent D'Onofrio, William R. Moses, Adam Storke, Conchata Ferrell, Joanna Merlin; *D:* Daniel Petrie; *W:* Amy Jones, Perry Howze, Alfred Uhry; *M:* David McHugh. **VHS, Beta** NO 𝄢𝄢𝄢

Nabonga The daughter of an embezzler, whose plane crashes in the jungle, befriends a gorilla who protects her. Soon a young man comes looking for the embezzler's cash, meets the woman and the ape, and together they go on a wonderful journey. *AKA:* Gorilla; Jungle Woman.

1944 72m/B Buster Crabbe, Fifi d'Orsay, Barton MacLane, Julie London, Herbert Rawlinson; *D:* Sam Newfield. **VHS $16.95** SNC, NOS, MOV 𝄢𝄢

Nadia Entertaining account of the life of Nadia Comaneci, the Romanian gymnast who earned six perfect tens with her stunning performance at the 1976 Olympic Games. Made for television.
1984 100m/C Talia Balsam, Jonathan Banks, Simone Blue, Johann Carlo, Carrie Snodgress; *D:* Alan Cooke. **VHS, Beta $19.95** FHE, STP 𝄢𝄢½

Nadine In Austin circa 1954, an almost divorced beautician witnesses a murder and goes undercover with her estranged husband to track down the murderer, before he finds her. Plenty of low-key humor. Well-paced fun; Basinger is terrific.
1987 (PG) 83m/C Jeff Bridges, Kim Basinger, Rip Torn, Gwen Verdon, Glenne Headly, Jerry Stiller, Jay Patterson; *D:* Robert Benton; *W:* Robert Benton; *M:* Howard Shore. **VHS, Beta $19.98** FOX 𝄢𝄢½

Nail Gun Massacre A crazed killer with a penchant for nailing bodies to just about anything goes on a hammering spree. In horrific, vivid color.
1986 90m/C Rocky Patterson, Ron Queen, Beau Leland, Michelle Meyer; *D:* Bill Lesley. **VHS, Beta** NO Woof!

Nails Harry "Nails" Niles (Hopper) is a tough, experienced cop whose partner has been killed by drug dealers. Harry doesn't take this well and decides to go on a violent search for revenge. Archer is wasted as Harry's estranged wife and Hopper can sleepwalk through this type of cliched wild-man role. Made for cable television.
1992 (R) 96m/C Dennis Hopper, Anne Archer, Tomas Milian, Cliff DeYoung; *D:* John Flynn. **VHS, Beta $89.98** FXV, VTR 𝄢½

Nairobi Affair Savage and Heston fight poachers and each other in Kenya, when the father has an affair with his son's ex-wife. Mediocre, derivative script, but beautiful scenery. Made for television.
1988 (PG) 95m/C Charlton Heston, John Savage, Maud Adams, John Rhys-Davies, Connie Booth; *D:* Marvin J. Chomsky. **VHS, Beta $79.95** VMK 𝄢𝄢

Nais Vintage Pagnolian peasant drama. A hunchback sacrifices himself for the girl he loves. She escapes to another man's arms. Adapted from the Emile Zola novel "Nais Micoulin." In French with English subtitles.
1945 105m/B Fernandel; *D:* Fernand Lauterier; *W:* Marcel Pagnol. **VHS, Beta, 8mm $24.95** VYY, FCT, DVT 𝄢𝄢𝄢

Naked Existential angst in a '90s London filled with Leigh's usual eccentrics. The unemployed Johnny (Thewlis) comes to London and bunks with former girlfriend Louise (Sharp). After seducing her flatmate Sophie (Cartlidge), Johnny leaves to wander the streets, exchanging philosophical, if foul-mouthed, dialogues with a variety of odd characters. Thewlis gives an explosive performance as the calculatingly brutal and desolate Johnny. Chaotic shifts in mood from comedy to violence to love prove a challenge and the pervasive abuse of all the women characters is very disturbing. Critically acclaimed; see it as a reflection on the mess of modern England. *AKA:* Mike Leigh's Naked.
1993 (R) 131m/C David Thewlis, Lesley Sharp, Katrin Cartlidge, Greg Cruttwell, Claire Skinner, Peter Wight, Ewen Bremmer, Susan Vidler; *D:* Mike Leigh; *W:* Mike Leigh; *M:* Andrew Dickson. British Academy Award Nominations: '93: Best Film; Cannes Film Festival '93: Best Film; Independent Spirit Awards '94: Best Foreign Film; Cannes Film Festival '93: Best Actor (Thewlis), Best Director (Leigh); National Society

of Film Critics Awards '93: Best Actor (Thewlis). **VHS** *COL, IME* 🎞🎞🎞

The Naked and the Dead Sanitized adaptation of Norman Mailer's bestselling novel about army life in the Pacific during WWII. Resentment between officers and enlisted men proves to be almost as dangerous as the Japanese. Uneven acting and cliched characterizations make this an average outing. Don't expect to hear the profane language that sensationalized the book, because most of it was edited out of the screenplay. **1958** 131m/C Aldo Ray, Cliff Robertson, Joey Bishop, Raymond Massey, Lili St. Cyr, James Best; **D:** Raoul Walsh. **VHS, Beta $15.95** *VCI* 🎞🎞½

The Naked Angels Rape, mayhem, beatings, and road-hogging streetbikes highlight this biker film, acted, in part, by actual bikers, and in part by others who were actually (almost) actors. The gang war rages from Los Angeles to Las Vegas. Roger Corman was the executive producer. **1969 (R)** 83m/C Michael Greene, Richard Rust, Felicia Guy; **D:** Bruce Clark; **W:** Bruce Clark. **VHS, Beta $39.95** *CRV* 🎞

Naked Cage Brutal women's prison film that is borderline soft-core, about an innocent country woman, a horseriding fanatic, who is framed for a robbery and sent to the slammer. There, she contends with lesbian wardens and inmates. Disgusting. **1986 (R)** 97m/C Shari Shattuck, Angel Tompkins, Lucinda Crosby, Christina Whitaker; **D:** Paul Nicholas. **VHS, Beta $19.95** *COL Woof!*

The Naked City Film noir classic makes spectacular use of its NYC locations. Beautiful playgirl is murdered and police detectives Fitzgerald and Taylor are left without clues. They spend most of their time running down weak leads and interviewing various suspects and witnesses. When they finally get a break, it leads to playboy Duff. Spectacular ending on the Brooklyn Bridge between cops and killer. Producer Hellinger provided the hard-boiled narration, patterned after the tabloid newspaper stories he once wrote. Served as the impetus for the TV show of the same name, where Hellinger's film postscript also became the show's noted tagline: "There are eight million stories in the naked city, this has been one of them." **1948** 96m/B Barry Fitzgerald, Don Taylor, Howard Duff, Ted de Corsia, Dorothy Hart; **D:** Jules Dassin; **M:** Miklos Rozsa. Academy Awards '48: Best Black and White Cinematography, Best Film Editing; Nominations: Best Story. **VHS $29.95** *IVY* 🎞🎞🎞½

The Naked Civil Servant Remarkable film, based on the life of flamboyant homosexual Quentin Crisp, who came out of the closet in his native England, long before his lifestyle would be tolerated by Britains. For mature audiences. **1975** 80m/C John Hurt; **D:** Jack Gold; **M:** Carl Davis. **VHS, Beta $19.99** *HBO* 🎞🎞🎞½

The Naked Country In the untamed frontier of Australia rancher bigoted Lance Dillion and his sensual wife Mary are determined to make their way. But when Lance finds out that the neglected Mary is fooling around with a local cop, he goes on a killing spree on land sacred to the Aborigines. Plodding plot. **1985 (R)** 90m/C John Stanton, Rebecca Gilling, Ivar Kants; **D:** Tim Burstall. **VHS $89.95** *HMD* 🎞½

The Naked Edge Cooper stars as a middle-aged businessman whose wife suspects him of murder after she begins snooping into his business affairs. Cooper's last film and far from his best. Poor direction and holes in the screenplay divert from what could have been a tight thriller. **1961** 99m/C Gary Cooper, Deborah Kerr, Eric Portman, Diane Cilento, Hermione Gingold, Peter Cushing, Michael Wilding, Ronald Howard; **D:** Michael Anderson Sr.; **W:** Joseph Stefano. **VHS $19.98** *MGM, MOV* 🎞🎞

The Naked Face A psychiatrist tries to find out why his patients are being killed. He gets no help from police, who suspect he is the murderer. A dull affair featuring unusual casting of Moore, while Steiger's suspicious police captain character provides spark. From the novel by Sidney Sheldon. **1984 (R)** 105m/C Roger Moore, Rod Steiger, Elliott Gould, Art Carney, Anne Archer, David Hedison; **D:** Bryan Forbes. **VHS, Beta $79.95** *MGM* 🎞🎞

The Naked Flame O'Keefe plays an investigator in a strange town inhabited by weird, religious fanatics. After he arrives, the womenfolk shed their clothes in this pitiful, pathetic hilarity. **1968 (R)** ?m/C Dennis O'Keefe, Linda Bennett, Kasey Rogers. **VHS $16.95** *SNC Woof!*

The Naked Gun: From the Files of Police Squad More hysterical satire from the creators of "Airplane!" The short-lived television cop spoof "Police Squad" moves to the big screen and has Lt. Drebin uncover a plot to assassinate Queen Elizabeth while she is visiting Los Angeles. Nearly nonstop gags and pratfalls provide lots of laughs. Nielsen is perfect as Drebin and the supporting cast is strong; cameos abound. **1988 (PG-13)** 85m/C Leslie Nielsen, Ricardo Montalban, Priscilla Presley, George Kennedy, O.J. Simpson, Nancy Marchand, John Houseman; **Cameos:** Weird Al Yankovic, Reggie Jackson, Dr. Joyce Brothers; **D:** David Zucker; **W:** Jerry Zucker, Jim Abrahams, Pat Proft, David Zucker; **M:** Ira Newborn. **VHS, Beta, 8mm $14.95** *PAR* 🎞🎞🎞

Naked Gun 33 1/3: The Final Insult Ever dumb, crass, and crude, Lt. Drebin returns to the force from retirement to lead an investigation into terrorist activities in Hollywood. Lots of current events jokes—dated as soon as they hit the screen. Sure to satisfy genre fans with a taste for bad puns. Watch for the cameos, especially at the "Oscars." **1994 (PG-13)** 90m/C Leslie Nielsen, Priscilla Presley, O.J. Simpson, Fred Ward, George Kennedy, Gary Cooper, Kathleen Freeman, Raquel Welch; **Cameos:** Pia Zadora, James Earl Jones, Weird Al Yankovic, Ann B. Davis; **D:** Peter Segal; **W:** Pat Proft, Robert Locash, David Zucker; **M:** Ira Newborn. **VHS** *NYR* 🎞🎞

Naked Gun 2 1/2: The Smell of Fear Lt. Drebin returns to rescue the world from a faulty energy policy devised by the White House and oil-lords. A notch down from the previous entry but still hilarious cop parody. Nielsen has this character down to a tee, and there's a laugh every minute. Laserdisc version is letterboxed and features dolby surround sound. **1991 (PG-13)** 85m/C Leslie Nielsen, Priscilla Presley, George Kennedy, O.J. Simpson, Robert Goulet, Richard Griffiths, Jacqueline Brookes, Lloyd Bochner, Tim O'Connor, Peter Mark Richman; **Cameos:** Mel Torme, Eva Gabor, Weird Al Yankovic; **D:** David Zucker; **W:** David Zucker, Pat Proft; **M:** Ira Newborn. **VHS, Beta, 8mm, CDV $14.95** *PAR* 🎞🎞½

Naked Hills Meandering tale about a man (Wayne) who, suffering from gold fever, searches for 40 years in 19th Century California and ends up out of luck, losing his wife and family. **1956** 72m/C David Wayne, Keenan Wynn, James Barton, Marcia Henderson, Jim Backus, Denver Pyle, Myrna Dell, Frank Fenton, Fuzzy Knight; **D:** Josef Shaftel; **W:** Josef Shaftel. **VHS** *NO* 🎞🎞

Naked in New York Aspiring New York playwright Jake Briggs (Stoltz) and his girlfriend Joanne (Parker), an aspiring photographer, find their relationship in jeopardy when their respective careers start to take off. Offspring from the "Annie Hall" school of neurotic romance examines a number of issues, including ambition, commitment, and the societal dynamics of theatre and art. Celebrity appearances abound, including Styron as himself and Goldberg as a tragedy mask on a wall. Directorial debut of Scorsese protege Algrant is uneven but charming. Parker is particularly strong, and Turner's a riot as a sexpot soap star on the prowl for Jake. **1993 (R)** 91m/C Eric Stoltz, Mary-Louise Parker, Ralph Macchio, Jill Clayburgh, Tony Curtis, Kathleen Turner, Timothy Dalton, Lynne Thigpen, Roscoe Lee Browne; **Cameos:** Whoopi Goldberg, William Styron, Eric Bogosian, Quentin Crisp; **D:** Dan Algrant; **W:** Dan Algrant, John Warren; **M:** Angelo Badalamenti; **V:** David Johansen. **VHS** *NYR* 🎞🎞½

Naked in the Night Cheap German exploitation film about the dangers of promiscuous women. Dubbed in English. **1958** ?m/C Eva Bartok, Alexander Kerst. **VHS $16.95** *SNC, TPV* 🎞

Naked in the Sun The true story of events leading to the war between the Osceola and Seminole Indians and a slave trader. Somewhat slow. **1957** 95m/C James Craig, Lita Milan, Barton MacLane, Tony Hunter; **D:** R. John Hugh. **VHS $19.98** *REP* 🎞🎞

Naked Is Better A couple of buffoons pose as hospital workers so they can play doctor with a hospitalized actress. **1973** 93m/C Alberto Olmedo, Jorge Porcel, Jorge Barreiro, Maria Casan. **VHS, Beta $39.95** *MED* 🎞

Naked Jungle Suspenseful, well-done jungle adventure of a plantation owner (Heston) in South America and his North American mail-order bride (Parker), who do battle with a deadly, miles-long siege of red army ants. Realistic and worth watching. Produced by George Pal, shot by Ernest Laszlo and based on the story "Leiningen vs. the Ants" by Carl Stephenson. **1954** 95m/C Charlton Heston, Eleanor Parker, Abraham Sofaer, William Conrad; **D:** Byron Haskin; **W:** Philip Yordan. **VHS, Beta $19.95** *PAR* 🎞🎞🎞

Naked Killer Kitty (Ching) turns to a female assassin to learn the art of killing so that she may avenge her father's death. When her teacher is herself unceremoniously murdered, Kitty and her policeman boyfriend (Yam) have two scores to settle. Sex and violence. Subtitled in English. **1992** 86m/C My Yau Ching, Simon Yam; **D:** Clarence Fok Yiu Leung. **VHS** *WVE* 🎞

Naked Kiss Fuller's most savage, hysterical film noir. A brutalized prostitute escapes her pimp and tries to enter respectable small-town society. She finds even more perversion and sickness there. **AKA:** The Iron Kiss.

1964 92m/B Constance Towers, Anthony Eisley, Michael Dante, Virginia Grey, Patsy Kelly, Betty Bronson; *D:* Samuel Fuller. **VHS** $59.95 *HMV, VYG* 🐾🐾½

Naked Lie A District Attorney and a judge engage in an ultra-steamy affair and inevitably clash when she is assigned as a prosecutor on the politically explosive case over which he is presiding.
1989 89m/C Victoria Principal, James Farentino, Glenn Withrow, William Lucking, Dakin Matthews; *D:* Richard A. Colla. **VHS** $79.95 *ING* 🐾🐾

Naked Lunch Whacked-out movie based on William S. Burroughs's autobiographical account of drug abuse, homosexuality, violence, and weirdness set in the drug-inspired land called Interzone. Hallucinogenic images are carried to the extreme: typewriters metamorphose into beetles, bloblike creatures with sex organs scurry about, and characters mainline insecticide. Some of the characters are clearly based on writers of the Beat generation, including Jane and Paul Bowles, Allen Ginsberg, and Jack Kerouac.
1991 (R) 117m/C Peter Weller, Judy Davis, Ian Holm, Julian Sands, Roy Scheider, Monique Mercure, Nicholas Campbell, Michael Zelniker, Robert A. Silverman, Joseph Scorsiani; *D:* David Cronenberg; *W:* David Cronenberg; *M:* Howard Shore. **VHS** $94.98 *TCF, ING* 🐾🐾🐾

The Naked Maja Elaborate, yet dull drama about the tumultous romance between a Spanish duchess and the legendary painter Francisco Goya. Even the gorgeous costumes and spectacular sets can't overcome the weak script and poor direction that plague the film. Based on a story by Oscar Saul and Talbot Jennings.
1959 111m/C Ava Gardner, Anthony (Tony) Franciosa, Amadeo Nazzari, Gino Cervi, Lea Padovani, Massimo Serato, Carlo Rizzo, Renzo Cesana; *D:* Henry Koster, Maria Russo; *W:* Norman Corwin, Giorgio Prosperi. **VHS** $19.98 *MGM, FCT* 🐾🐾

Naked Massacre A maniac kills nurses, leaving no clues for the police to follow.
1987 90m/C Matthieu Carriere, Carol Laurie; *D:* Denis Heroux. **VHS, Beta** $19.98 *VDC* 🐾

Naked Obsession A city councilman running for mayor is mugged in one of the seedier parts of the city. He's found by a homeless man who takes him to a kinky nightclub where the councilman is promptly seduced by a topless bar hostess with secrets of her own. Also available in an unrated version.
1991 (R) 93m/C William Katt, Maria Ford, Rick Dean; *D:* Dan Golden. **VHS** $89.98 *VES, MOV* 🐾½

Naked Paradise A young woman moves in with her mother and step-sister and finds difficulty in adjusting.
1978 (R) 86m/C Laura Gemser, Annie Belle. **VHS, Beta** *VCI* 🐾½

The Naked Prey Unnerving African adventure which contains some unforgettably brutal scenes. A safari guide (Wilde), leading a hunting party, must watch as an indigenous tribe murders all his companions, and according to their customs, allows him to be set free, sans clothes or weapons, to be hunted by the best of the tribe.
1966 96m/C Cornel Wilde, Gertrude Van Der Berger, Ken Gampu; *D:* Cornel Wilde. **VHS, Beta** $19.95 *PAR* 🐾🐾🐾

The Naked Spur A compulsive bounty hunter tracks down a vicious outlaw and his beautiful girlfriend. An exciting film from the Mann-Stewart team and considered one of their best, infusing the traditional western

with psychological confusion. Wonderful use of Rockies locations.
1953 93m/C James Stewart, Robert Ryan, Janet Leigh, Millard Mitchell; *D:* Anthony Mann. **VHS, Beta** $19.98 *MGM, TLF* 🐾🐾½

Naked Sun Beguiling mystery set during the Carnival at Rio chock full of suspense, romance, and just a touch of the supernatural.
19?? 100m/C David Brandon. **VHS** *NO* 🐾🐾

The Naked Sword of Zorro Deadly Don Luis taxes the town by day and violates the women by night, but Zorro takes a stand and saves the town. When he's not dressed as Zorro, he is Don Diego, an inept fool, but when he puts that suit on, look out. The ladies can't keep their hands off of him. There are more lusty females than villains, but there's still lots of swordplay and action.
1969 94m/C **VHS** $19.95 *VDM* 🐾

The Naked Truth A greedy publisher tries to get rich quick by publishing a scandal magazine about the "lurid" lives of prominent citizens. Well-drawn characters in an appealing offbeat comedy. *AKA:* Your Past is Showing.
1958 92m/C Peter Sellers, Terry-Thomas, Shirley Eaton, Dennis Price; *D:* Mario Zampi. **VHS, Beta** $59.95 *SUE* 🐾🐾½

Naked Vengeance A woman's husband is murdered, she is beaten and raped, and she becomes a vengeful, vicious killing machine. Gratuitous violence, distasteful to the max. *AKA:* Satin Vengeance.
1985 (R) 97m/C Deborah Tranelli, Kaz Garas, Bill McLaughlin; *D:* Cirio H. Santiago. **VHS, Beta** $79.98 *LIV* Woof!

Naked Venus Ulmer's last film is a slow-paced tale about an American artist, married to a model who poses in the nude and belongs to a nudist camp, whose wealthy mother tries to tear the marriage apart. Discrimination and intolerance of nudist camps is explored.
1958 80m/B Patricia Conelle; *D:* Edgar G. Ulmer. **VHS, Beta** $19.95 *VDM, TPV* 🐾½

Naked Warriors Ancient Romans capture beautiful women from around the world and force them to compete in gladiatorial games. New World exploitation gem featuring mostly Italian cast, including Bay, who starred in the previous years "Lady Frankenstein." *AKA:* The Arena.
1973 (R) 75m/C Margaret Markov, Pam Grier, Lucretia Love, Paul Muller, Daniel Vargas, Marie Louise, Mary Count, Rosalba (Sara Bay) Neri, Vic Karis, Sid Lawrence, Peter Cester, Anna Melita; *D:* Steve Carver. **VHS, Beta** $79.95 *MGM* 🐾🐾

The Naked Witch College student researching witchcraft digs up the grave of a long-dead witch. She comes back to life and takes revenge on the village that killed her years earlier. The nude shots feature someone's finger over the camera lens to cover the witch's vital organs. *AKA:* The Naked Temptress.
1964 60m/C Beth Porter, Robert Burgos, Bryarly Lee, Lee Forbes; *D:* Andy Milligan. **VHS** $16.95 *SNC* 🐾

Naked Youth Seedy drive-in cheapie about two punks breaking out of juvenile prison and heading south of the border on a trail filled with crime, drugs, and loose women. *AKA:* Wild Youth.
1959 80m/B Robert Hutton, John Goddard, Carol Ohmart, Jan Brooks, Robert Arthur, Steve Rowland, Clancy Cooper; *D:* John F. Schreyer. **VHS, Beta** $9.95 *RHI, SNC* Woof!

Nam Angels Hell's Angels enter Southeast Asia and rescue POWs.

1988 (R) 91m/C Brad Johnson, Vernon Wells, Kevin Duffis; *D:* Cirio H. Santiago. **VHS, Beta** $79.95 *MED* 🐾

A Name for Evil Having grown tired of city living, a couple moves to an old family estate out in the country near the Great Lakes. Strange sounds in the night are the first signs of the terror to come.
1970 (R) 74m/C Robert Culp, Samantha Eggar, Sheila Sullivan, Mike Lane; *D:* Bernard Girard. **VHS, Beta** *NO* 🐾🐾

The Name of the Rose An exhaustive, off-center adaptation of the bestselling Umberto Eco novel about violent murders in a 14th-century Italian abbey. An English monk struggles against religious fervor in his quest to uncover the truth.
1986 (R) 128m/C Sean Connery, F. Murray Abraham, Christian Slater, Ron Perlman, William Hickey, Feodor Chaliapin, Elya Baskin, Michael Lonsdale; *D:* Jean-Jacques Annaud; *W:* Andrew Birkin, Gerard Brach, Howard Franklin; *M:* James Horner. **VHS, Beta** $14.95 *NLC* 🐾🐾½

Namu, the Killer Whale Based on the true story of a marine biologist (Lansing) who gets the perfect opportunity to study killer whales when one is confined to a small cove. The local fisherman want to kill the creature because it feeds on the salmon they catch but they are persuaded against their baser instincts. Filmed on location in the San Juan Islands of Puget Sound. The real Namu lived at the Seattle Public Aquarium.
1966 89m/C Robert Lansing, John Anderson, Robin Mattson, Richard Erdman, Lee Meriwether, Joe Higgins; *D:* Laslo Benedek. **VHS** $14.95 *MGM, FCT* 🐾🐾

Nana French version of Emile Zola's novel about an actress-prostitute who seduces the high society of Paris in the late 1880s, and suffers a heart-breaking downfall and death. Film has three remakes of the original 1926 version.
1955 118m/C Charles Boyer, Martine Carol. **VHS, Beta** $24.95 *NOS, DVT, HEG* 🐾🐾🐾

Nana A lavishly photographed, graphic adaptation of the Emile Zola novel about a Parisian whore who acquires power by seducing the richest and politically formidable men. Dubbed.
1982 92m/C Katya Berger, Jean-Pierre Aumont; *D:* Dan Wolman; *M:* Ennio Morricone. **VHS, Beta** $79.95 *FCT, MGM* 🐾½

Nancy Astor A portrait of the beautiful, spirited Virginian who became a member of the British Parliament.
1982 55m/C Lisa Harrow, James Fox, Dan O'Herlihy, Sylvia Syms. **VHS, Beta** *TLF* 🐾🐾

Nancy Drew, Reporter The young sleuth gets to play reporter after winning a newspaper contest. In no time at all, she's involved in a murder mystery.
1939 68m/B Bonita Granville, John Litel, Frankie Thomas Jr., Mary Lee, Sheila Bromley, Betty Amann, Dick Jones, Olin Howland, Charles Halton; *D:* William Clemens. **VHS** $19.95 *HTV, NOS* 🐾🐾

Nancy Goes to Rio Actresses Powell and Sothern compete for the same part in a play and for the same man. Catch is, they're mother and daughter. Zany consequences ensue. Sothern's last film for MGM. ♫Time and Time Again; Shine On Harvest Moon; Cha Bomm Pa Pa; Yipsee-I-O; Magic is the Moonlight; Musetta's Waltz; Love is Like This; Nancy Goes to Rio.
1950 99m/C Ann Sothern, Jane Powell, Barry Sullivan, Carmen Miranda, Louis Calhern, Scotty Beckett, Hans Conried, Glenn Anders; *D:* Robert Z. Leonard; *W:* Sidney Sheldon. **VHS** $19.98 *MGM, MLB, CCB* 🐾🐾½

Napoleon A vivid, near-complete restoration of Gance's epic silent masterpiece about the famed conqueror's early years, from his youth through the Italian Campaign. An innovative, spectacular achievement with its use of multiple split screens, montage, color, and triptychs. Given a gala theatrical re-release in 1981. Remade in 1955.
1927 235m/B Albert Dieudonne, Antonin Artaud, Pierre Batcheff, Gina Manes, Armand Bernard, Harry Krimer, Albert Bras, Abel Gance, Georges Cahuzac; *D:* Abel Gance; *M:* Carmine Coppola. **VHS, Beta** $29.95 MCA, ING ✰✰✰✰

Napoleon Depicts life story of Napoleon from his days as a soldier in the French army to his exile on the Island of Elba. Falls short of the fantastic 1927 silent classic as it attempts to delve into Napoleon the man, as opposed to his conquests. Some might find it too slow for their tastes.
1955 123m/C Raymond Pellegrin, Orson Welles, Maria Schell, Yves Montand, Erich von Stroheim, Jean Gabin, Jean-Pierre Aumont; *D:* Sacha Guitry. **VHS, Beta** $19.95 NOS, MRV, MPI ✰✰

Napoleon and Samantha Disney adventure about Napoleon, an orphan (Whitaker), who is befriended by Danny, a college student (Douglas). After the death of his grandfather, Napoleon decides to take Major, his elderly pet lion, and follow Danny, who is herding goats for the summer, across the American northwest mountains and they are joined by Samantha (Foster in her film debut). Worth watching.
1972 91m/C Jodie Foster, Johnny Whitaker, Michael Douglas, Will Geer, Henry Jones; *D:* Bernard McEveety; *W:* Stewart Raffill; *M:* Buddy Baker. **VHS, Beta** $69.95 DIS ✰✰✰

The Narcotics Story Bad film on the same vein as "Reefer Madness." Originally intended as a police training film, this shows the evils and destruction of heroin addiction. Portrayals of drug addicts are hilarious. *AKA:* The Dreaded Persuasion.
1958 75m/C Sharon Strand, Darlene Hendricks, Herbert Crisp, Fred Marratto; *D:* Robert W. Larsen. **VHS** $16.95 SNC, TPV *Woof!*

Narda or The Summer Two young men decide they will share a girlfriend during a summer romance, only Narda has other plans. She decides that both men will belong to her rather than the other way around. In Spanish with English subtitles.
1976 96m/C Hector Bonilla, Enrique Alvarez Felix; *D:* Juan Guerreo. **VHS** $24.98 ING ✰✰

The Narrow Margin Well-made, harrowing adventure about a cop who is in charge of transporting a gangster's widow to a trial where she is to testify. On the train he must try to keep her safe from the hit-men who would murder her. A real cat and mouse game—one of the best suspense movies of the '50s.
1952 71m/B Charles McGraw, Marie Windsor, Jacqueline White, Queenie Leonard, Gordon Gebert, Don Beddoe, Harry Harvey; *D:* Alfred E. Green. **VHS** $19.98 TTC, MLB, TTC ✰✰✰

Narrow Margin Archer reluctantly agrees to testify against the mob after witnessing a murder, and Los Angeles D.A. Hackman is assigned to protect her on the train through the Rockies back to L.A. Bad idea, she finds out. No match for its '52 predecessor.
1990 (R) 99m/C Gene Hackman, Anne Archer, James B. Sikking, J.T. Walsh, M. Emmet Walsh; *D:* Peter Hyams; *W:* Peter Hyams. **VHS** $19.95 LIV ✰✰

Narrow Trail A silent classic that still stands as one of the best Westerns ever made. A tough cowboy with a troubled past hopes a good woman can save him. But

she's seen trouble, too. They meet up again in San Francisco's Barbary Coast. A horse race might hold the answer.
1917 56m/B William S. Hart, Sylvia Bremer, Milton Ross; *D:* William S. Hart. **VHS, Beta** $15.95 NOS, GPV, CCB ✰✰✰ ½

Nashville Altman's stunning, brilliant film tapestry that follows the lives of 24 people during a political campaign/music festival in Nashville. Seemingly extemporaneous vignettes, actors playing themselves (Elliott Gould and Julie Christie), funny, touching, poignant character studies concerning affairs of the heart and despairs of the mind. Repeatedly blurs reality and fantasy. ♫I'm Easy; Two Hundred Years; Keep A'Goin'; One, I Love You; Let Me Be the One; The Day I Looked Jesus in the Eye; For the Sake of the Children; I Never Get Enough; It Don't Worry Me.
1975 (R) 159m/C Keith Carradine, Lily Tomlin, Henry Gibson, Ronee Blakley, Keenan Wynn, David Arkin, Geraldine Chaplin, Lauren Hutton, Shelley Duvall, Barbara Harris, Allen (Gooritz) Garfield, Karen Black, Christina Raines, Michael Murphy, Ned Beatty, Barbara Baxley, Scott Glenn, Jeff Goldblum, Gwen Welles, Bert Remsen, Robert DoQui; *Cameos:* Elliott Gould, Julie Christie; *D:* Robert Altman; *W:* Joan Tewkesbury; *M:* Richard Baskin. Academy Awards '75: Best Song ("I'm Easy"); Nominations: Best Director (Altman), Best Picture, Best Supporting Actress (Blakley, Tomlin); Golden Globe Awards '76: Best Song ("I'm Easy"); National Board of Review Awards '75: 10 Best Films of the Year, Best Director (Altman), Best Supporting Actress (Blakley); National Society of Film Critics Awards '75: Best Director (Altman), Best Film, Best Supporting Actor (Gibson), Best Supporting Actress (Tomlin). **VHS, Beta** $79.95 PAR ✰✰✰✰

Nashville Beat Gang targets the citizens of Nashville, Tennessee, until two tough cops stomp the gang's delusion that Southern folk are easy marks.
1989 110m/C Kent McCord, Martin Milner; *D:* Bernard L. Kowalski. **VHS** NO ✰✰

Nashville Girl Innocent country girl who wants to make good in the country music scene, rises to the top of the Nashville success ladder, by compromising everything and hanging out with stereotyped no-goods in the show biz world. It's as good as a yawn. *AKA:* Country Music Daughter; New Girl in Town.
1976 (R) 90m/C Monica Gayle, Johnny Rodriguez; *D:* Gus Trikonis. **VHS, Beta** $59.98 NLC ✰

The Nasty Girl A bright young German model plans to enter a national essay contest on the topic of her hometown's history during the Third Reich. While researching the paper, she's harassed and even brutalized, but refuses to cease her sleuthing. Excellent performances, tight direction, with comedic touches that charmingly imparts an important message. Based on a true story. In German with English subtitles.
1990 (PG-13) 93m/C Lena Stolze, Monika Baumgartner, Michael Gahr; *D:* Michael Verhoeven; *W:* Michael Verhoeven. **VHS** $89.99 ING, HBO ✰✰✰½

Nasty Habits Broad farce depicting a corrupt Philadelphia convent as a satiric parallel to Watergate, with nuns modeled on Nixon, Dean and Mitchell. Includes cameo appearances by various media personalities. Based on the British novel "The Abbess of Crewe" by Muriel Spark.
1977 (PG) 92m/C Glenda Jackson, Geraldine Page, Anne Jackson, Melina Mercouri, Sandy Dennis, Susan Penhaligon, Anne Meara, Edith Evans, Rip Torn, Eli Wallach, Jerry Stiller; *Cameos:* Mike Douglas, Bill Jorgensen, Jessica

Savitch, Howard K. Smith; *D:* Michael Lindsay-Hogg. **VHS, Beta** $69.95 MED ✰✰

Nasty Hero Hard-boiled ex-con comes to Miami to avenge the car thieves who framed him and got him sent to the slammer. This is car-chase scene heaven—little plot or drama.
1989 (PG-13) 79m/C Robert Sedgwick, Carlos Palomino, Scott Feraco, Mike Starr, Rosanna DaVon; *D:* Nick Barwood. **VHS, Beta** $79.95 COL ✰½

Nasty Rabbit Ridiculous spoof about Soviet spies intent on releasing a rabbit with a hideous Communist disease into the U.S. Everyone gets in on the chase: Nazi forces, cowboys and indians, sideshow freaks, banditos—what is the point? *AKA:* Spies-A-Go-Go.
1964 88m/C Arch Hall Jr., Micha Terr, Melissa Morgan, John Akana; *D:* James Landis. **VHS, Beta** $59.95 RHI ✰

Natas...The Reflection A reporter persists in validating an Indian demon myth.
1983 (PG) 90m/C Randy Mulkey, Pat Bolt, Craig Hensley, Kelli Kuhn. **VHS, Beta** $29.95 LIV ✰

Nate and Hayes Set during the mid-1800s in the South Pacific, the notorious real-life swashbuckler Captain "Bully" Hayes ("good pirate") helps young missionary Nate recapture his fiancee from a cutthroat gang of evil slave traders. Entertaining "jolly rogers" film.
1983 (PG) 100m/C Tommy Lee Jones, Michael O'Keefe, Max Phipps, Jenny Seagrove; *D:* Ferdinand Fairfax; *M:* Trevor Jones. **VHS, Beta** $14.95 PAR ✰✰½

A Nation Aflame Anti-Klan film is based on a story by Thomas L. Dixon, the author of "The Clansman," from which D.W. Griffith made "The Birth of a Nation." In this story, a con man gains control of the state's government through an ultra-nationalistic secret society, and eventually pays for his corruption.
1937 70m/B Lila Lee, Noel Madison, Snub Pollard; *D:* Norma Trelvar. **VHS, Beta** $16.95 SNC, NOS, GVV ✰½

National Lampoon Goes to the Movies Parodies of popular Hollywood genres, including cop thrillers, melodramas, and inspirational biographies, done in goofy "Lampoon" style.
1981 89m/C Robby Benson, Candy Clark, Diane Lane, Christopher Lloyd, Peter Riegert, Richard Widmark, Henny Youngman; *D:* Henry Jaglom. **VHS** $14.99 MOV ✰

National Lampoon's Animal House Classic Belushi vehicle running amuck. Set in 1962 and responsible for launching Otis Day and the Knights and defining cinematic food fights. Every college tradition from fraternity rush week to the homecoming pageant is irreverently and relentlessly mocked in this wild comedy about Delta House, a fraternity on the edge. Climaxes with the homecoming parade from hell. Sophomoric, but very funny, with a host of young stars who went on to more serious work. Remember: "Knowledge is good." *AKA:* Animal House.
1978 (R) 109m/C John Belushi, Tim Matheson, John Vernon, Donald Sutherland, Peter Riegert, Stephen Furst, Bruce McGill, Mark Metcalf, Verna Bloom, Karen Allen, Tom Hulce, Mary Louise Weller, Kevin Bacon; *D:* John Landis; *W:* Harold Ramis; *M:* Elmer Bernstein. **VHS, Beta** $14.95 MCA ✰✰✰½

National Lampoon's Christmas Vacation The third vacation for the Griswold family finds them hosting repulsive relatives for Yuletide. The sight gags, al-

though predictable, are sometimes on the mark. Quaid is a standout as the slovenly cousin. *AKA:* Christmas Vacation.
1989 (PG-13) 93m/C Chevy Chase, Beverly D'Angelo, Randy Quaid, Diane Ladd, John Randolph, E.G. Marshall, Doris Roberts, Julia Louis-Dreyfus, Mae Questel, William Hickey, Brian Doyle-Murray, Juliette Lewis, Johnny Galecki, Nicholas Guest, Miriam Flynn; *D:* Jeremiah S. Chechik; *W:* John Hughes; *M:* Angelo Badalamenti. **VHS, Beta, 8mm $19.98** WAR ⱮⱮ½

National Lampoon's Class of '86 This is a live stage comedy show written and sponsored by the infamous adult humor magazine, featuring a new cast of comics. *AKA:* Class of '86.
1986 86m/C Rodger Bumpass, Veanne Cox, Annie Golden, John Michael Higgins, Tommy Koenig. **VHS, Beta $29.95** PAR ⱮⱮ½

National Lampoon's Class Reunion Class reunion with some very wacky guests and a decided lack of plot or purpose. Things go from bad to worse when a crazed killer decides to join in on the festivities. Disappointing with very few laughs. *AKA:* Class Reunion.
1982 (R) 85m/C Shelley Smith, Gerrit Graham, Michael Lerner; *D:* Michael Miller; *W:* John Hughes; *M:* Peter Bernstein. **VHS, Beta $29.98** LIV, VES Woof!

National Lampoon's European Vacation Sappy sequel to "Vacation" that has witless Chase and his family bumbling around in the land "across the pond." The Griswolds nearly redefine the term "ugly American." Stonehenge will never be the same. *AKA:* European Vacation.
1985 (PG-13) 94m/C Chevy Chase, Beverly D'Angelo, Dana Hill, Jason Lively, Victor Lanoux, John Astin; *D:* Amy Heckerling; *W:* John Hughes, Robert Klane, Eric Idle; *M:* Charles Fox. **VHS, Beta, 8mm $19.98** WAR Ɽ½

National Lampoon's Loaded Weapon 1 Cop Jack Colt (Estevez) and partner Wes Luger (Jackson) attempt to recover a microfilm which contains a formula for turning cocaine into cookies. Essentially a sendup of the popular "Lethal Weapon" series, although other movies and themes make an appearance, well sort of. Short on plot and long on slapstick, but that's the whole point. Tired formula creates nostalgia for the granddaddy of them all, "Airplane." Lots of cameos, including one from sibling spoof star Sheen. The magazine folded while the movie was in production, an ominous sign. *AKA:* Loaded Weapon 1.
1993 (PG-13) 83m/C Emilio Estevez, Samuel L. Jackson, Jon Lovitz, Tim Curry, Kathy Ireland, William Shatner; *Cameos:* Dr. Joyce Brothers, James Doohan, Richard Moll, F. Murray Abraham, Denis Leary, Corey Feldman, Phil Hartman, J.T. Walsh, Erik Estrada, Larry Wilcox, Allyce Beasley, Charlie Sheen; *D:* Gene Quintano; *W:* Gene Quintano, Don Holley. **VHS** NLC, IME Ɽ½

National Lampoon's Vacation The Clark Griswold (Chase) family of suburban Chicago embarks on a westward cross-country vacation via car to the renowned "Wally World." Ridiculous and hysterical misadventures, including a falling asleep at the wheel sequence and the untimely death of Aunt Edna. *AKA:* Vacation.
1983 (R) 98m/C Chevy Chase, Beverly D'Angelo, Imogene Coca, Randy Quaid, Christie Brinkley, James Keach, Anthony Michael Hall, John Candy, Eddie Bracken, Brian Doyle-Murray, Eugene Levy; *D:* Harold Ramis; *W:* John Hughes, Harold Ramis; *M:* Ralph Burns. **VHS, Beta $19.98** WAR ⱮⱮⱮ

National Velvet A young English girl wins a horse in a raffle and is determined to train it to compete in the famed Grand National race. Taylor, only 12 at the time, is superb in her first starring role. Rooney also gives a fine performance. Filmed with a loving eye on lushly decorated sets, this is a masterpiece version of the story of affection between a girl and her pet. Based on the novel by Enid Bagnold and followed by "International Velvet" in 1978.
1944 124m/C Elizabeth Taylor, Mickey Rooney, Arthur Treacher, Donald Crisp, Anne Revere, Angela Lansbury, Reginald Owen, Norma Varden, Jackie "Butch" Jenkins, Terence Kilburn; *D:* Clarence Brown; *W:* Helen Deutsch, Theodore Reeves; *M:* Herbert Stothart. Academy Awards '45: Best Film Editing, Best Supporting Actress (Revere); Nominations: Best Color Cinematography, Best Director (Brown). **VHS, Beta, 8mm $19.98** MGM, KUI, TLF ⱮⱮⱮⱮ

Native Son A young black man from the ghettos of Chicago is hired as a chauffeur by an affluent white family. His job is to drive their head-strong daughter anywhere she wants to go. Unintentionally, he kills her, tries to hide, and is ultimately found guilty. Based on the classic novel by Richard Wright, who also stars. Remade in 1986. Unprofessional direction and low budget work against the strong story.
1951 91m/B Richard Wright, Jean Wallace, Nicholas Joy, Gloria Madison, Charles Cane; *D:* Pierre Chenal. **VHS $24.95** NOS, XVC, FCT ⱮⱮ½

Native Son This second film adaptation of the classic Richard Wright novel is chock full of stars and tells the story of a poor black man who accidentally kills a white woman and then hides the body. Changes in the script soft-soap some of the novel's disturbing truths and themes—so-so drama for those who have not read the book.
1986 (R) 111m/C Geraldine Page, Oprah Winfrey, Matt Dillon, John Karlen, Elizabeth McGovern, Akosua Busia, Carroll Baker, Victor Love, John McMartin, Art Evans, Willard Pugh, David Rasche; *D:* Jerrold Freedman; *W:* Richard Wesley; *M:* James Mtume. **VHS, Beta $14.98** LIV, KUI, FCT ⱮⱮ½

Nativity Unmemorable, made-for-TV portrayal of the romance between Mary and Joseph (of the Bible story), Joseph's response to Mary's pregnancy, and the birthing of Jesus. Not exactly a Bible epic, the direction and acting are uninspired.
1978 97m/C John Shea, Madeleine Stowe, Jane Wyatt, John Rhys-Davies, Kate O'Mara; *D:* Bernard L. Kowalski. **VHS, Beta $14.98** FOX ⱮⱮ

The Natural A beautifully filmed movie about baseball as myth. A young man, whose gift for baseball sets him apart, finds that trouble dogs him, particularly with a woman. In time, as an aging rookie, he must fight against his past to lead his team to the World Series, and win the woman who is meant for him. From the Bernard Malamud story.
1984 (PG) 134m/C Robert Redford, Glenn Close, Robert Duvall, Kim Basinger, Wilford Brimley, Barbara Hershey, Richard Farnsworth, Robert Prosky, Darren McGavin, Joe Don Baker, Michael Madsen; *D:* Barry Levinson; *M:* Randy Newman. **VHS, Beta $14.95** COL ⱮⱮⱮ

Natural Born Killers An old script by (Graphic Screen Violence) Tarantino is resurrected by (Damn the Torpedoes) Stone and invested with its own unique subtle nuance and style. Controversial (natch, considering the director and writer) look at the way the media portrays criminals. Harrelson and Lewis are the lovestruck, white-trash serial killers who become tabloid-TV darlings, thanks to a sensationalistic press led by

Downey, Jr. Stone's dark comment on America's fascination and revulsion with violence is strictly of the love it or leave it variety.
1994 (R) ?m/C Woody Harrelson, Robert Downey Jr., Juliette Lewis, Tommy Lee Jones, Ashley Judd, Tom Sizemore, Rodney Dangerfield, Rachel Ticotin, Arliss Howard, Russell Means, Denis Leary, Steven Wright; *D:* Oliver Stone; *W:* Quentin Tarantino. **VHS**

Natural Enemies A successful publisher begins to consider suicide and murder as the cure for his family's increasing alienation and despair. Dark and depressing drama.
1979 (R) 100m/C Hal Holbrook, Louise Fletcher, Jose Ferrer, Viveca Lindfors; *D:* Jeff Kanew; *W:* Jeff Kanew. **VHS, Beta $59.95** COL ⱮⱮ½

Nature's Playmates A beautiful private eye tours Florida nudist camps in search of a missing man with a distinctive tattoo on his posterior. One of H.G. Lewis' obscure "nudie" flicks, sexually tame by modern standards, awful by any standards.
1962 56m/B Vicki Miles, Scott Osborne; *D:* Herschell Gordon Lewis. **VHS $19.95** VDM, TPV Ɽ

Naughty Knights Soft-core romp in a medieval setting. Toss it in the moat. *AKA:* Up the Chastity Belt.
1971 (PG) 94m/C Frankie Howerd, Graham Crowden, Bill Fraser, Roy Hudd, Hugh Paddick, Anna Quayle, Eartha Kitt, Dave King, Fred Emney; *D:* Bob Kellett; *M:* Carl Davis. **VHS, Beta $19.95** ACA Ɽ

Naughty Marietta A French princess switches identities with a mail-order bride to escape from her arranged marriage, and is captured by pirates. When she's saved by a dashing Indian scout, it's love at first sight. The first MacDonald-Eddy match-up and very popular in its day. ♫Italian Street Song; Chansonette; Antoinette and Anatole; Prayer; Tramp, Tramp, Tramp; The Owl and the Bobcat; Neath the Southern Moon; Mon Ami Pierrot; Ship Ahoy.
1935 106m/B Jeanette MacDonald, Nelson Eddy, Frank Morgan, Elsa Lanchester, Douglass Dumbrille, Cecilia Parker; *D:* Woodbridge S. Van Dyke. Academy Awards '35: Best Sound; Nominations: Best Picture. **VHS, Beta $19.95** MGM ⱮⱮ½

The Naughty Nineties Bud and Lou help a showboat owner fend off crooks in the 1890s. Usual slapstick shenanigans, but highlighted by verbal banter. Includes the first on-screen rendition of the classic "Who's on First?" routine. ♫Rolling Down the River; Uncle Tom's Cabin; I Can't Get You Out of My Mind; On a Sunday Afternoon; I'd Leave My Happy Home for You; Nora Malone; Ma Blushin' Rosie; The Showboat's Comin' to Town; A Blarney from Killarney.
1945 72m/B Bud Abbott, Lou Costello, Henry Travers, Alan Curtis, Joseph Sawyer, Rita Johnson, Joe Kirk, Lois Collier; *D:* Jean Yarborough. **VHS, Beta $14.95** MCA, MLB ⱮⱮ

Navajo Joe The sole survivor of a massacre single-handedly kills each person involved in the atrocity, and aids a terrorized, though unappreciative, town in the process. Low-budget Spanish-Italian western only worth watching because of Reynolds. Filmed in Spain.
1967 89m/C Burt Reynolds, Aldo Sambrel, Tanya Lopert, Fernando Rey; *D:* Sergio Corbucci; *M:* Ennio Morricone. **VHS $14.95** MGM Ɽ½

The Navigator Ever the quick thinker, Keaton actually bought a steamer headed for the scrap heap and used it to film an almost endless string of sight gags. Rejected by a socialite, millionaire Keaton finds himself alone with her on the abandoned boat. As he saves her from various and sundry perils, the gags and thrills abound—including one stunt that was inspired by a near-accident on the set. Too bad they don't make 'em like this anymore. Silent.

1924 60m/B Buster Keaton, Kathryn McGuire, Frederick Vroom, Noble Johnson, Clarence Burton, H. M. Clugston; *D:* Buster Keaton, Donald Crisp. VHS *NO* ♫♫♫

The Navigator A creative time-travel story of a 14th-century boy with visionary powers who leads the residents of his medieval English village away from a plague by burrowing through the earth's core and into late 20th-Century New Zealand. Quite original and refreshing.

1988 (PG) 92m/C Hamish McFarlane, Bruce Lyons, Chris Haywood, Marshall Napier, Noel Appleby, Paul Livingston, Sarah Pierse; *D:* Vincent Ward; *W:* Vincent Ward. VHS *NO* ♫♫♫

Navy Blue and Gold Three football-playing midshipmen (Young, Stewart, and Brown) at Annapolis share a friendship. Stewart has registered under a false name since his dad was unfairly cashiered from the service. When he hears some slander about his old man he stands up and tells the truth and gets suspended, just before the big game with Army. Naturally, he's reinstated just in time to make the big play and carry the team to victory. Well-done, old-fashioned hokum.

1937 94m/B James Stewart, Robert Young, Tom Brown, Lionel Barrymore, Florence Rice, Billie Burke, Samuel S. Hinds, Paul Kelly, Frank Albertson, Minor Watson; *D:* Sam Wood; *W:* George Bruce. VHS $29.98 MGM, MOV ♫♫½

The Navy Comes Through Salty sailors aboard a mangy freighter beat the odds and sink Nazi warships and subs with the greatest of ease. Boy meets girl subplot is added for good measure. Morale booster includes newsreel footage.

1942 81m/B Pat O'Brien, George Murphy, Jane Wyatt, Jackie Cooper, Carl Esmond, Max Baer Sr., Desi Arnaz Sr., Ray Collins, Lee Bonnell, Frank Jenks, Helmut Dantine; *D:* Edward Sutherland. VHS $19.98 TTC ♫♫

Navy SEALS A group of macho Navy commandos, whose regular work is to rescue hostages from Middle Eastern underground organizations, finds a stash of deadly weapons. They spend the balance of the movie attempting to destroy the arsenal. Sheen chews the scenery as a crazy member of the commando team. Lots of action and violence, but simplistic good guys - bad guys philosophy and plot weaknesses keep this from being more than below average.

1990 (R) 113m/C Charlie Sheen, Michael Biehn, Joanne Whalley-Kilmer, Rick Rossovich, Cyril O'Reilly, Bill Paxton, Dennis Haysbert, Paul Sanchez, Ron Joseph, Nicholas Kadi; *D:* Lewis Teague; *W:* Gary Goldman. VHS, Beta $14.98 ORI ♫½

Navy vs. the Night Monsters When horrifying, acid-secreting plant monsters try to take over the world, Van Doren and the Navy must come to the rescue, with the action taking place in a tropical South Pole setting. Amazing deployment of talents.

1966 87m/C Mamie Van Doren, Anthony Eisley, Pamela Mason, Bobby Van, Russ Bender; *D:* Michael Hoey; *W:* Michael Hoey. VHS, Beta *NO Woof!*

Navy Way Hurriedly produced war propaganda film in which a boxer gets inducted into the Navy just before his title shot.

1944 74m/B Robert Lowery, Jean Parker; *D:* William H. Pine, William C. Thomas. VHS $24.95 NOS, DVT, HEG ♫

Nazarin Bunuel's scathing indictment of Christianity finds its perfect vehicle in the adventures of a defrocked priest attempting to relive Christ's life. Gathering a group of disciples, he wanders into the Mexican desert as a cross between Christ and Don Quixote. Filmed in Mexico, this is Bunuel at his grimmest. In Spanish with English subtitles.

1958 92m/B Francesco Rabal, Rita Macedo, Margo Lopez, Rita McLedo, Ignacio Lopez Tarso, Jesus Fernandez; *D:* Luis Bunuel. VHS, Beta $69.95 MAD, ING, CVC ♫♫♫

Nea Comic drama about a young girl from a privileged home who writes a best selling pornographic novel anonymously. When her book writing talents are made public through betrayal, she gets even in a most unique way. Subtitled "A Young Emmanuelle." Kaplan also performs. Appealing and sophisticated.

1978 (R) 101m/C Sami Frey, Ann Zacharias, Heinz Bennent; *D:* Nelly Kaplan. VHS, Beta $59.95 COL ♫♫½

Near Dark A farm boy falls in unwillingly with a family of thirsty, outlaw-fringe vampires who roam the West in a van. The first mainstream effort by Bigelow, and a rollicking, blood-saturated, slaughterhouse of a movie, with enough laughs and stunning imagery to revive the genre.

1987 (R) 95m/C Adrian Pasdar, Jenny Wright, Bill Paxton, Jenette Goldstein, Lance Henriksen, Tim Thomerson, Joshua Miller; *D:* Kathryn Bigelow; *W:* Kathryn Bigelow, Eric Red; *M:* Tangerine Dream. VHS, Beta $19.99 HBO, IME ♫♫♫

Near Misses Missable farce with Reinhold as a bigamist in the foreign service. To make time for a mistress he swaps identities with a young Marine in Paris, but then the KGB kidnaps the imposter. Doors slam in hallways all over the place as the performers crank up the mixups to maximum frenzy, but with little effect since you really don't care much about these fools.

1991 93m/C Judge Reinhold, Casey Siemaszko; *D:* Baz Taylor. VHS, Beta $89.98 FXV, VTR ♫½

Near the Rainbow's End Cattle rancher Steele (in his first talking western) finds out that rustlers are aggravating the trouble between the cattlemen and the sheep herders. So he goes after the bad guys and then settles the feud by marrying a sheep herder's daughter.

1930 57m/B Bob Steele, Lafe McKee, Louise Lorraine, Al Ferguson, Al Hewston; *D:* J.P. McGowan. VHS $11.95 GPV ♫½

'Neath Brooklyn Bridge The Boys from the Bowery get tangled up in crime when they try to help a young girl whose guardian was murdered.

1942 61m/B Leo Gorcey, Huntz Hall, Bobby Jordan, Sammy Morrison, Anne Gillis, Noah Beery Jr., Marc Lawrence, Gabriel Dell; *D:* Wallace Fox. VHS $19.95 NOS, MRV, PME ♫♫

'Neath Canadian Skies Mounted lawman who says "eh" a lot tracks murdering gang of mine looters.

1946 41m/B Russell Hayden, Inez Cooper, Cliff Nazarro, Kermit Maynard, Jack Mulhall. VHS, Beta, 8mm $19.95 VYY ♫

'Neath the Arizona Skies Low budget oater epic about a cowhand who finds all the action he and his friends can handle as they try to rescue a young Indian girl (and oil heiress) who has been kidnapped. 'Nuff said.

1934 54m/B John Wayne, George "Gabby" Hayes, Sheila Terry; *D:* Harry Fraser. VHS $9.98 REP, NOS, COL ♫♫

Necessary Parties Based on Barbara Dana's book that has a 15-year-old boy filing a lawsuit to stop his parents' divorce. Originally aired on PBS as part of the "Wonderworks" family movie series.

1988 10m/C Alan Arkin, Mark Paul Gosselaar, Barbara Dana, Adam Arkin, Donald Moffatt, Julie Hagerty, Geoffrey Pierson, Taylor Fry; *D:* Gwen Arner. VHS $29.95 PME, WNE, HMV ♫♫

Necessary Roughness After losing their NCAA standing, the Texas Southern University (passing for the real Texas State) Armadillos football team looks like it's headed for disaster. The once proud football factory is now composed of assorted goofballs instead of stud players. But hope arrives in the form of a 34-year-old farmer with a golden arm, ready to recapture some lost dreams as quarterback. Can this unlikely team rise above itself and win a game, or will their hopes be squashed all over the field?

1991 (PG-13) 108m/C Scott Bakula, Robert Loggia, Harley Jane Kozak, Sinbad, Hector Elizondo, Kathy Ireland, Jason Bateman; *D:* Stan Dragoti; *M:* Bill Conti. VHS, Beta $14.95 PAR ♫

Necromancer: Satan's Servant After a woman is brutally raped, she contacts a sorceress and makes a pact with the devil to ensure her successful revenge. Plenty of graphic violence and nudity.

1988 (R) 90m/C Elizabeth Cayton, Russ Tamblyn, Rhonda Dorton; *D:* Dusty Nelson. VHS, Beta $79.98 MCG, IME ♫

Necropolis A witch burned at the stake 300 years ago is brought back to life as a motorcycle punkette in New York searching for a sacrificial virgin (in New York?). New wave horror should have been watchable.

1987 (R) 77m/C Leeanne Baker, Michael Conte, Jacquie Fritz, William Reed, Paul Ruben; *D:* Bruce Hickey. VHS, Beta $79.98 LIV, VES ♫

Ned Kelly Dramatizes the life of Australia's most notorious outlaw. Kelly (Jagger) and his family start off as horse thieves and proceed from there. A manhunt results in death and the eventual capture and execution of Kelly. The very contemporary British Jagger was miscast as a period Australian and British director Richardson seems to have lacked an empathy for the material, given his lethargic direction. *AKA:* Ned Kelly, Outlaw.

1970 (PG) 100m/C Mick Jagger, Allen Bickford, Geoff Gilmour, Mark McManus, Serge Lazareff, Peter Sumner, Ken Shorter, James Elliott, Diane Craig, Sue Lloyd, Clarissa Kaye; *D:* Tony Richardson; *W:* Ian Jones, Tony Richardson; *M:* Shel Silverstein. VHS $14.95 MGM ♫♫½

Needful Things Stephen King film adaptations are becoming as prolific as his novels, though few seem to improve in the transition from page to screen. This time a scheming Maine shopkeeper (Von Sydow) sells unsuspecting small towners peculiar items that, not surprisingly, begin to cause horror and mayhem. Harris is the town sheriff who tries to warn everyone that he's the devil in disguise. Big screen directorial debut for Heston (yes, Charlton's son).

1993 (R) 120m/C Ed Harris, Bonnie Bedelia, Max von Sydow, Amanda Plummer, J.T. Walsh; *D:* Fraser Heston; *W:* W.D. Richter; *M:* Patrick Doyle. VHS $95.95 COL ♫♫½

Nefertiti, Queen of the Nile Woman, married against her will, turns into Nefertiti. For fans of Italo-Biblical epics only.

1964 97m/C Jeanne Crain, Vincent Price, Edmund Purdom, Amadeo Nazzari, Liana Orfei; *D:* Fernando Cerchio. VHS *NO* ♫♫

Negatives A couple indulge in sexual fantasies to dangerous extremes, with the man first impersonating Dr. Crippen, the early 1900s murderer, and later a WWI flying ace. When a photographer friend joins the fun, the action careens off the deep end.
1968 90m/C Peter McEnery, Diane Cilento, Glenda Jackson, Maurice Denham, Norman Rossington; *D:* Peter Medak. **VHS** *NO ⚼⚼*

The Neighbor See nice city couple John and Mary move to small town Vermont. See their nice retired obstetrician neighbor Myron welcome them. See Mary get pregnant and Myron take an obsessional interest. See John arrested for murder. See Mary left alone—except for Myron's tender care.
1993 (R) 93m/C Linda Kozlowski, Ron Lea, Rod Steiger, Francis Bay, Bruce Boa, Jane Wheeler; *D:* Rodney Gibbons; *W:* Kurt Wimmer. **VHS** *ACA ⚼⚼ ½*

The Neighborhood Thief Two thieves team up for the heist of their lives, but can they trust each other?
1983 84m/C Alfonso Zayas, Alberto Rojas, Angelica Chain. **VHS, Beta $74.95** *VVC ⚼⚼*

Neighbors The Keeses (Belushi and Walker) live in a quiet, middle-class suburban neighborhood where life is calm and sweet. But their new neighbors, Ramona and Vic (Aykroyd and Moriarty), prove to be loud, obnoxious, crazy, and freeloading. Will Earl and Enid Keese mind their manners as their neighborhood disintegrates? Some funny moments, but as the script fades, so do the laughs. Belushi's last waltz is based on Thomas Berger's novel.
1981 (R) 90m/C John Belushi, Dan Aykroyd, Kathryn Walker, Cathy Moriarty; *D:* John G. Avildsen; *W:* Larry Gelbart; *M:* Bill Conti. **VHS, Beta $14.95** *GKK ⚼⚼*

Nemesis Futuristic thriller that combines cybernetics and cyborgs in post-nuclear Los Angeles. Gruner plays a human (although he's mostly composed of mechanical replacement parts) in a world overwrought with system cowboys, information terrorists, bio-enhanced gangsters, and cyborg outlaws. Film's biggest flaw is the extremely confusing script that makes no attempt at logic whatsoever. Special visual effects are good despite the obviously low f/x budget.
1993 (R) 95m/C Olivier Gruner, Tim Thomerson, Cary-Hiroyuki Tagawa, Merele Kennedy, Yuji Okumoto, Marjorie Monaghan, Nicholas Guest, Vincent Klyn; *D:* Albert Pyun; *W:* Rebecca Charles; *M:* Michael Rubini. **VHS $94.95** *IMP, UND ⚼ ½*

Neon City Title refers to a rumored city of refuge in the year 2053, where eight misfit adventurers in an armored transport seek safety from the Earth's toxic environment and "Mad Max" cliches.
1991 (R) 99m/C Michael Ironside, Vanity, Lyle Alzado, Valerie Wildman, Nick Klar, Juliet Landau, Arsenio "Sonny" Trinidad, Richard Sanders; *D:* Monte Markham. **VHS $89.95** *VMK ⚼⚼*

The Neon Empire Tepid tale of two gangsters battling inner mob opposition and backstabbing to build Las Vegas. Ostensibly based on the story of Bugsy Siegel and Meyer Lansky. Made for cable.
1989 (R) 120m/C Martin Landau, Ray Sharkey, Gary Busey, Harry Guardino, Julie Carmen, Linda Fiorentino, Dylan McDermott; *D:* Larry Peerce; *W:* Pete Hamill. **VHS, Beta $39.95** *FRH ⚼ ½*

Neon Maniacs An even half-dozen fetish-ridden zombies stalk the streets at night, tearing their victims into teensy weensy bits. Brave teenagers try to stop the killing. Brave viewers will stop the tape.
1986 (R) 90m/C Allan Hayes, Leilani Sarelle Ferrer, Bo Sabato, Donna Locke, Victor Elliot Brandt; *D:* Joseph Mangine. **VHS, Beta $79.98** *LIV, VES* Woof!

Neptune Factor Scientists board a special new deep-sea sub to search for their colleagues lost in an undersea earthquake. Diving ever deeper into the abyss that swallowed their friend's Ocean Lab II, they end up trapped themselves. The plot's many holes sink it. *AKA:* The Neptune Disaster; An Underwater Odyssey.
1973 (G) 94m/C Ben Gazzara, Yvette Mimieux, Walter Pidgeon, Ernest Borgnine; *D:* Daniel Petrie; *W:* Jack DeWitt. **VHS, Beta $59.98** *FOX ⚼*

Neptune's Daughter A swim-happy bathing suit designer finds romance and deep pools of studio water to dive into. Typically lavish and ridiculous Williams aquaparade. ♫Baby, It's Cold Outside; I Love Those Men; My Heart Beats Faster.
1949 92m/C Esther Williams, Red Skelton, Ricardo Montalban, Betty Garrett, Keenan Wynn, Xavier Cugat, Ted de Corsia, Mike Mazurki, Mel Blanc, Juan Duvall, George Mann, Joi Lansing; *D:* Edward Buzzell. **VHS, Beta $19.98** *MGM ⚼⚼*

Nervous Ticks Ninety minutes in the life of airline employee York Daley. All he needs to do is get off work, go home, grab his luggage, pick up his married girrlfiend, and get back to the airport for a flight to Rio De Janeiro. Simple, right? Not in this movie.
1993 (R) 95m/C Bill Pullman, Julie Brown, Peter Boyle, James LeGros, Brent Jennings; *D:* Rocky Lang; *W:* David Frankel. **VHS $89.95** *COL ⚼⚼ ½*

The Nervous Wreck Harrison Ford (not the one from "Indiana Jones") heads West, seeking a cure for what he believes is a terminal illness. Once there, he becomes romantically entangled with the sheriff's fiancee, uses a wrench to hold up a gas station, and gets involved in other shenanigans. And then he discovers he's going to live after all.
1926 70m/B Harrison Ford, Phyllis Haver, Chester Conklin, Mack Swain, Hobart Bosworth, Charles Gerrard; *D:* Scott Sidney. **VHS, Beta** *NO ⚼⚼*

The Nest Tragic romance of an elderly man and a 13-year-old girl is helped along by superior script and directing.
1980 109m/C Ana Torrent, Hector Alterio, Patricia Adriani; *D:* Jaime de Arminan. **VHS, Beta $68.00** *SUE, APD ⚼⚼ ½*

The Nest A small island is overcome by giant cockroaches created by, you guessed it, a scientific experiment gone wrong. Special effects make it watchable.
1988 (R) 89m/C Robert Lansing, Lisa Langlois, Franc Luz, Terri Treas, Stephen Davies, Diana Bellamy, Nancy Morgan; *D:* Terence H. Winkless; *W:* Robert King; *M:* Rick Conrad. **VHS, Beta $14.95** *MGM ⚼⚼ ½*

The Nesting Too-long tale of a neurotic author who rents a haunted Victorian manor and finds herself a pawn in a ghostly plan for revenge. Features Grahame's last performance.
1980 (R) 104m/C Robin Groves, John Carradine, Gloria Grahame, Christopher Loomis, Michael Lally; *D:* Armand Weston. **VHS, Beta $59.95** *WAR ⚼ ½*

Netherworld A young man investigating his mysterious, dead father travels to his ancestral plantation in the bayou. To his horror, he discovers that his father was involved in the black arts. Now two beautiful young witches are after him. Can he possibly survive this madness?
1991 (R) 87m/C Michael C. Bendetti, Denise Gentile, Anjanette Comer, Holly Floria, Robert Burr; *D:* David Schmoeller; *M:* Edgar Winter. **VHS** *PAR ⚼ ½*

Network As timely now as it was then; a scathing indictment of the television industry and its propensity towards self-prostitution. A television newscaster's mental breakdown turns him into a celebrity when the network tries to profit from his illness. The individual characters are startlingly realistic and the acting is excellent.
1976 (R) 121m/C Faye Dunaway, Peter Finch, William Holden, Robert Duvall, Wesley Addy, Ned Beatty, Beatrice Straight; *D:* Sidney Lumet; *W:* Paddy Chayefsky. Academy Awards '76: Best Actor (Finch), Best Actress (Dunaway), Best Original Screenplay, Best Supporting Actress (Straight); Nominations: Best Actor (Holden), Best Cinematography, Best Director (Lumet), Best Film Editing, Best Picture, Best Supporting Actor (Beatty); Golden Globe Awards '77: Best Actor—Drama (Finch), Best Actress—Drama (Dunaway), Best Director (Lumet), Best Screenplay; Los Angeles Film Critics Association Awards '76: Best Director (Lumet), Best Film; National Board of Review Awards '76: 10 Best Films of the Year. **VHS, Beta $19.98** *MGM, BTV ⚼⚼⚼ ½*

Neurotic Cabaret Would-be actress dances exotically and finds more exotic ways to roll in dough.
1990 90m/C Edwin Neal, Tammy Stone. **VHS $79.95** *AIP ⚼ ½*

Neutron and the Black Mask Man wears mask with lightning bolts and gains comic book style powers to do deathly battle with a scientist with a neutron bomb up his sleeve. First Neutron feature.
1961 80m/B Wolf Ruvinskis, Julio Aleman, Armando Silvestre, Rosita Arenas, Claudio Brook; *D:* Frederick Curiel. **VHS $19.98** *SNC ⚼*

Neutron vs. the Amazing Dr. Caronte Dr. Caronte from "Neutron and the Black Mask" just won't give up that neutron bomb and let the series die.
1961 80m/B Wolf Ruvinskis, Julio Aleman, Armando Silvestre, Rosita Arenas, Rodolfo Landa; *D:* Frederick Curiel. **VHS $19.98** *SNC ⚼*

Neutron vs. the Death Robots Guy with a mask takes on army of killer robots and neutron bomb to protect the world from future sequels.
1962 80m/B Wolf Ruvinskis, Julio Aleman, Armando Silvestre, Rosita Arenas; *D:* Frederick Curiel. **VHS $19.98** *SNC ⚼*

Neutron vs. the Maniac Man in mask hunts guys who kill people.
1962 80m/B Wolf Ruvinskis. **VHS $19.98** *SNC ⚼*

Nevada Cowpoke Mitchum is mistaken for the killer of a homesteader and narrowly escapes the rope by finding the real killer. First leading role for Mitchum as the tough but laconic hero. Based on a story by Zane Grey.
1944 62m/B Robert Mitchum, Anne Jeffreys, Nancy Gates, Craig Reynolds, Guinn Williams, Richard Martin, Harry Woods; *D:* Edward Killy. **VHS $12.95** *GPV ⚼⚼ ½*

Nevada City Roy outwits a financier who is trying to monopolize transportation in California.
1941 54m/B Roy Rogers. **VHS, Beta $27.95** *VCN ⚼ ½*

Nevada Smith The half-breed Nevada Smith (previously introduced in Harold Robbins' story "The Carpetbaggers" and film of same name) seeks the outlaws who killed his parents. Standard western plot, characters. Later remade as a TV movie.

1966 135m/C Steve McQueen, Karl Malden, Brian Keith, Arthur Kennedy, Raf Vallone, Suzanne Pleshette; *D:* Henry Hathaway. **VHS, Beta $14.95** *PAR ᒪᒪ*

The Nevadan A marshal goes in search of an outlaw's gold cache, only to be opposed by a crooked rancher. Good scenery and action, but not one of Scott's best. *AKA:* The Man From Nevada.
1950 81m/C Randolph Scott, Dorothy Malone, Forrest Tucker, Frank Faylen, George Macready, Charles Kemper, Jeff Corey, Tom Powers, Jock Mahoney; *D:* Gordon Douglas. **VHS, Beta** *GKK ᒪ½*

Never a Dull Moment New York songwriter falls for rodeo Romeo, moves out West, and finds welcome wagon deficient. Mediocre songs; many dull moments. ♫Once You Find Your Guy; Sagebrush Lullaby; The Man With the Big Felt Hat.
1950 89m/B Irene Dunne, Fred MacMurray, William Demarest, Andy Devine, Gigi Perreau, Natalie Wood, Philip Ober, Jack Kirkwood, Ann Doran, Margaret Gibson; *D:* George Marshall. **VHS $19.98** *TTC, FCT ᒪᒪ*

Never a Dull Moment Mobsters mistake an actor for an assassin in this gag-filled adventure. They threaten the thespian into thievery, before the trouble really starts when Ace, the actual assassin, arrives.
1968 (G) 90m/C Dick Van Dyke, Edward G. Robinson, Dorothy Provine, Henry Silva, Joanna Moore, Tony Bill, Slim Pickens, Jack Elam; *D:* Jerry Paris. **VHS, Beta $39.95** *DIS ᒪᒪ*

Never Cry Wolf A young biologist is sent to the Arctic to study the behavior and habitation of wolves, then becomes deeply involved with their sub-society. Based on Farley Mowat's book. Beautifully photographed.
1983 (PG) 105m/C Charles Martin Smith, Brian Dennehy, Samson Jorah; *D:* Carroll Ballard; *W:* Curtis Hanson, Sam Hamm. **VHS, Beta $19.99** *DIS ᒪᒪᒪ½*

Never Forget Made-for-cable-TV true story of California resident Mel Mermelstein (played by Nimoy), a survivor of Hitler's death camps who accepted a pro-Nazi group's challenge to prove in court that the Holocaust of six million Jews really happened. A sincere, well-meaning courtroom drama that just can't surmount the uncinematic nature of the source material.
1991 94m/C Leonard Nimoy, Blythe Danner, Dabney Coleman; *D:* Joseph Sargent; *M:* Henry Mancini. **VHS, Beta $89.98** *TTC ᒪᒪ*

Never Give a Sucker an Even Break An almost plotless comedy, based on an idea reputedly written on a napkin by Fields (he took screenplay credit as Otis Criblecoblis), and features Fields at his most unleashed. It's something of a cult favorite, but not for all tastes. Classic chase scene ends it. Fields' last role in a feature-length film. *AKA:* What a Man.
1941 71m/B W.C. Fields, Gloria Jean, Franklin Pangborn, Leon Errol, Margaret Dumont; *D:* Eddie Cline. **VHS, Beta $14.95** *MCA, BAR ᒪᒪᒪ½*

Never Let Go A man unwittingly tracks down the mastermind of a gang of racketeers. Sellers sheds his comedic image to play the ruthless and brutal gang boss, something he shouldn't have done.
1960 91m/C Peter Sellers, Richard Todd, Elizabeth Sellars, Carol White; *D:* John Guillermin; *M:* John Barry. **VHS, Beta** *SUE ᒪᒪ*

Never Let Me Go Implausible yet entertaining account of American newsman Gable trying to smuggle ballerina wife Tierney out of Russia. Hard to believe Gable as a one-man assault force infiltrating Russia, but

enjoyable nonetheless. Based on the novel "Came the Dawn" by Roger Bax.
1953 94m/B Clark Gable, Gene Tierney, Richard Haydn, Bernard Miles, Kenneth More, Karel Stepanek, Theodore Bikel; *D:* Delmer Daves; *W:* Ronald Millar, George Froeschel. **VHS $19.98** *MGM ᒪᒪ½*

Never Love a Stranger A young man becomes a numbers runner for a mobster and ultimately winds up heading his own racket. Later he finds himself in conflict with his old boss and the district attorney. No surprises here. Based on the Harold Robbins' novel.
1958 93m/B John Blythe Barrymore Jr., Steve McQueen, Lita Milan, Robert Bray; *D:* Robert Stevens. **VHS $19.98** *REP ᒪᒪ*

Never on Sunday An American intellectual tries to turn a Greek prostitute into a refined woman. Fine performances and exhilarating Greek photography. Fun all around.
1960 91m/B Melina Mercouri, Tito Vandis, Jules Dassin, Mitsos Liguisos; *D:* Jules Dassin; *W:* Jules Dassin; *M:* Manos Hadjidakis. Academy Awards '60: Best Song ("Never on Sunday"); Nominations: Best Actress (Mercouri), Best Costume Design (B & W), Best Director (Dassin), Best Story & Screenplay; Cannes Film Festival '60: Best Actress (Mercouri). **VHS, Beta $19.98** *MGM, HMV ᒪᒪᒪ*

Never on Tuesday Two jerks from Ohio head to California and find themselves stuck midway in the desert with a beautiful girl, who has plans of her own.
1988 (R) 90m/C Claudia Christian, Andrew Lauer, Peter Berg; *Cameos:* Charlie Sheen, Emilio Estevez; *D:* Adam Rifkin; *W:* Adam Rifkin. **VHS, Beta $14.95** *PAR ᒪᒪ½*

Never Pick Up a Stranger When a local hooker is murdered, her cop boyfriend, who never gives up on a case, hunts her killer with a vengeance. Extremely graphic. Also on video as "Bloodrage."
1979 82m/C Ian Scott, Judith-Marie Bergan, James Johnston, Lawrence Tierney; *D:* Joseph Bigwood. **VHS, Beta $49.95** *LIV, BFV ᒪᒪ½*

Never Say Die Two innocents are thrown into a web of international intrigue and acquit themselves rather well. Lots of explosions and car crashes for a film shot in New Zealand.
1990 98m/C George Wendt, Lisa Eilbacher; *D:* Geoff Murphy. **VHS, Beta $29.95** *JTC ᒪᒪ½*

Never Say Never Again James Bond matches wits with a charming but sinister tycoon who is holding the world nuclear hostage as part of a diabolical plot by SPECTRE. Connery's return to the world of Bond after 12 years is smooth in this remake of "Thunderball" hampered by an atrocious musical score. Carrera is stunning as Fatima Blush.
1983 (PG) 134m/C Sean Connery, Klaus Maria Brandauer, Max von Sydow, Barbara Carrera, Kim Basinger, Edward Fox, Bernie Casey, Pamela Salem, Rowan Atkinson, Valerie Leon, Prunella Gee, Saskia Cohen Tanugi; *D:* Irvin Kershner. **VHS, Beta $19.98** *WAR, TLF ᒪᒪ½*

Never So Few A military commander and his outnumbered troops overcome incredible odds against the Japanese. There is a lot of focus on romance, but the script and acting make a strong impression nonetheless. Based on the novel by Tom T. Chamales.
1959 124m/C Frank Sinatra, Gina Lollobrigida, Peter Lawford, Steve McQueen, Richard Johnson, Paul Henreid, Charles Bronson; *D:* John Sturges. **VHS $29.95** *MGM ᒪᒪ½*

Never Steal Anything Small A tough union boss pushes everyone as he battles the mob for control of the waterfront. A strange musical-drama combination that will be of interest only to the most ardent Cagney and Jones fans. Based on the Maxwell Anderson/Rouben Mamoulian play "The Devil's Hornpipe." Largely forgettable songs. ♫I'm Sorry, I Want a Ferrari; I Haven't a Thing to Wear; It Takes Love to Make a Home; Never Steal Anything Small; Helping Out Friends.
1959 94m/C James Cagney, Shirley Jones, Cara Williams; *D:* Charles Lederer; *M:* Henry Mancini. **VHS, Beta $59.95** *MCA ᒪᒪ½*

Never Too Late to Mend Victorian British play about the abuses of the penal system which had, upon its initial London West End run, caused Queen Victoria to institute a sweeping program of prison reform. The movie caused considerably less stir.
1937 67m/B Tod Slaughter, Marjorie Taylor, Jack Livesey, Ian Colin; *D:* David MacDonald. **VHS, Beta, 8mm $24.95** *VYY, MRV, SNC ᒪᒪ*

Never Too Young to Die A young man is drawn into a provocative espionage adventure by his late father's spy associates. Together they try to discover who killed the young man's father. High point may be Simmons as a crazed hermaphrodite plotting to poison L.A.
1986 (R) 97m/C John Stamos, Vanity, Gene Simmons, George Lazenby; *D:* Gil Bettman; *M:* James Newton Howard. **VHS, Beta $14.95** *COL, NLC ᒪ*

Never Wave at a WAC A Washington socialite joins the Women's Army Corps hoping for a commission that never comes. She has to tough it out as an ordinary private. A reasonably fun ancestor of "Private Benjamin," with a cameo by Gen. Omar Bradley as himself. *AKA:* The Private Wore Skirts.
1952 87m/B Rosalind Russell, Paul Douglas, Marie Wilson, William Ching, Arleen Whelan, Leif Erickson, Hillary Brooke, Regis Toomey; *Cameos:* Omar Bradley; *D:* Norman Z. McLeod; *M:* Elmer Bernstein. **VHS $19.95** *NOS, DVT, HEG ᒪᒪ½*

Never Weaken/Why Worry? Silent comedy shorts from Harold. In "Never Weaken" (1921), Lloyd hustles customers. In "Why Worry?" (1923), he plays a wealthy young man who journeys to South America for his health and gets caught in the middle of a revolution.
1923 78m/B Harold Lloyd. **VHS, Beta** *TLF ᒪᒪᒪ*

The NeverEnding Story A lonely young boy helps a warrior save the fantasy world in his book from destruction by the Nothing. A wonderful, intelligent family movie about imagination, with swell effects and a sweet but not overly sentimental script. Petersen's first English-language film, based on the novel by Michael Ende.
1984 (PG) 94m/C Barret Oliver, Noah Hathaway, Gerald McRaney, Moses Gunn, Tami Stronach, Patricia Hayes, Sydney Bromley; *D:* Wolfgang Petersen; *W:* Wolfgang Petersen; *M:* Klaus Doldinger, Giorgio Moroder. **VHS, Beta, 8mm $14.95** *WAR, GLV, APD ᒪᒪᒪ½*

NeverEnding Story 2: The Next Chapter Disappointing sequel to the first story that didn't end. Boy Oliver staves off life of couch potatodom reading books and escaping into fantasy land. Even the kids may wander away. But wait: contains the first Bugs Bunny theatrical cartoon in 26 years, "Box Office Bunny."

1991 (PG) 90m/C Jonathan Brandis, Kenny Morrison, Clarissa Burt, John Wesley Shipp, Martin Umbach; *D:* George Miller; *M:* Robert Folk. VHS, 8mm $14.95 *WAR, APD 🐾🐾*

Nevil Shute's The Far Country Carl Zlintner (York), once a doctor in Hitler's army, escapes to Australia from postwar Europe to begin a new life with a new identity. Falling in love with the beautiful Jennifer Morton (Thornton), Carl hopes he's left his past behind. But nothing is every that simple. Made-for-television adaptation of the Shute novel. *AKA:* The Far Country.
1985 120m/C Michael York, Sigrid Thornton; *D:* George Miller. VHS, Beta *NO 🐾🐾½*

The New Adventures of Pippi Longstocking Decent cast is trapped in another musical rehashing of the Astrid Lindgren children's books about a precocious red-headed girl and her fantastic adventures with horses, criminals, and pirates.
1988 (G) 100m/C Tami Erin, Eileen Brennan, Dennis Dugan, Dianne Hull, George DiCenzo, John Schuck, Dick Van Patten; *D:* Ken Annakin. VHS, Beta $19.95 *COL, TVC 🐾🐾*

The New Adventures of Tarzan Twelve episodes, each 22 minutes long, depict the adventures of Edgar Rice Burrough's tree-swinging character—Tarzan. Also known as "Tarzan and the Green Goddess."
1935 260m/B Bruce (Herman Brix) Bennett, Ula Holt, Frank Baker, Dale Walsh, Lewis Sargent; *D:* Edward Kull. VHS, Beta $26.95 *SNC, NOS, VCN 🐾½*

The New Centurions Rookies training for the Los Angeles Police Department get the inside info from retiring cops. Gritty and realistic drama based on the novel by former cop Joseph Wambaugh. Tends to be disjointed at times, but overall is a good adaptation of the bestseller. Scott, excellent as the retiring beat-walker, is supported well by the other performers.
1972 (R) 103m/C George C. Scott, Stacy Keach, Jane Alexander, Scott Wilson, Erik Estrada, James B. Sikking; *D:* Richard Fleischer; *W:* Sterling Silliphant; *M:* Quincy Jones. VHS, Beta $14.95 *COL, FCT 🐾🐾½*

New Faces of 1952 Based on the hit Broadway revue. The plot revolves around a Broadway show that is about to be closed down, and the performers who fight to keep it open. Lots of hit songs. Mel Brooks is credited as a writer, under the name Melvin Brooks. ♫C'est Si Bon; Santa Baby; Uskadara; Monotonous; Bal Petit Bal; Boston Beguine; I'm in Love with Miss Logan; Penny Candy; Time for Tea.
1954 98m/C Ronny Graham, Eartha Kitt, Robert Clary, Alice Ghostley, June Carroll, Carol Lawrence, Paul Lynde; *D:* Harry Horner. VHS, Beta $29.95 *FCT, NOS, VAI 🐾🐾½*

New Fist of Fury During WWII, a former pickpocket becomes a martial arts whiz with the assistance of his fiancee, and fights the entire Imperial Army.
1985 120m/C Jackie Chan; *D:* Jackie Chan. VHS, Beta *NO 🐾*

The New Frontier Wayne is a small-town sheriff whose predecessor, his father, was murdered. The local saloon-keeper and his gang do everything they can to prevent Wayne from bringing the culprit to justice.
1935 59m/B John Wayne, Muriel Evans, Murdock McQuarrie, Mary MacLaren, Warner Richmond; *D:* Carl Pierson. VHS $19.95 *NOS, MLB 🐾½*

The New Gladiators In the future, criminals try to kill each other on television for public entertainment. Two such gladiators discover that the network's computer is using the games in order to take over mankind, and they attempt to stop it. Even if the special effects were any good, they couldn't save this one.
1987 90m/C Jared Martin, Fred Williamson, Eleanor Gold, Howard Ross, Claudio Cassinelli; *D:* Lucio Fulci. VHS, Beta $79.95 *MED Woof!*

The New Invisible Man A so-so Mexican adaptation of the popular H.G. Wells novel has a prisoner receiving a vanishing drug from his brother, who created it—perhaps to aid an escape attempt. Also called "H.G. Wells' New Invisible Man."
1958 95m/B Arturo de Cordova, Ana Louisa Peluffo, Jorge Mondragon; *D:* Alfredo B. Crevenna. VHS $16.95 *SNC 🐾🐾*

New Jack City Just say no ghetto-melodrama. Powerful performance by Snipes as wealthy Harlem drug lord sought by rebel cops Ice-T and Nelson. Music by Johnny Gill, 2 Live Crew, Ice-T and others. Available with Spanish subtitles.
1991 (R) 101m/C Wesley Snipes, Ice-T, Mario Van Peebles, Chris Rock, Judd Nelson, Tracy C. Johns, Allen Payne, Kim Park, Vanessa Williams, Nick Ashford, Thalmus Rasulala, Michael Michele, Bill Nunn, Russell Wong; *D:* Mario Van Peebles; *W:* Keith Critchlow, Barry Michael Cooper; *M:* Roger Bourland, Michel Colombier. VHS $19.98 *WAR, CCB 🐾🐾½*

The New Kids An orphaned brother and sister find out the limitations of the good neighbor policy. A sadistic gang terrorizes them after their move to a relatives' home in Florida. They go after expected revenge.
1985 (R) 90m/C Shannon Presby, Lori Loughlin, James Spader, Eric Stoltz; *D:* Sean S. Cunningham; *W:* Brian Taggert, Stephen Gyllenhaal. VHS, Beta $79.95 *COL 🐾🐾*

A New Kind of Love Romantic fluff starring real-life couple Newman and Woodward who meet en route to Paris and end up falling in love. Newman plays a reporter and Woodward is a fashion designer in this light comedy set amidst the sights of Paris.
1963 110m/C Paul Newman, Joanne Woodward, Thelma Ritter, Eva Gabor, Maurice Chevalier, George Tobias; *D:* Melville Shavelson; *W:* Melville Shavelson. VHS, Beta $14.95 *PAR 🐾🐾½*

The New Land Sequel to "The Emigrants" follows Von Sydow and his family as they struggle to make their new home in the new world. Hardships include severe weather which devastates the farm, a Sioux indian uprising, and a disastrous trek to the Southwest to search for gold. Sensitive performances and direction. Based on the novels by Vilhelm Moberg. Dubbed into English. *AKA:* Nybyggarna.
1973 (PG) 161m/C Max von Sydow, Liv Ullmann, Allan Edwall, Eddie Axberg, Hans Alfredson, Halvar Bjork, Peter Lindgren, Monica Zetterlund, Pierre Lindstedt, Per Oscarsson; *D:* Jan Troell; *W:* Jan Troell, Bengt Forslund; *M:* Bengt Ernryd, George Oddner. VHS $29.99 *WAR, MOV 🐾🐾🐾*

A New Leaf A playboy who has depleted his financial resources tries to win the hand of a clumsy heiress. May was the first woman to write, direct and star in a movie. She was unhappy with the cuts that were made by the studio, but that didn't seem to affect its impact with the public. Even with the cuts, the film is still funny and May's performance is worth watching.
1971 (G) 102m/C Walter Matthau, Elaine May, Jack Weston, George Rose, William Redfield, James Coco; *D:* Elaine May; *W:* Elaine May. VHS $14.95 *PAR, CCB 🐾🐾½*

A New Life An uptight stockbroker is abandoned by his wife. The New York singles scene beckons both of them to a new chance at life. Appealing performances cannot completely mask the old story line, but it's definitely worth a look.
1988 (PG-13) 104m/C Alan Alda, Ann-Margret, Hal Linden, Veronica Hamel, John Shea, Mary Kay Place, Cynthia Belliveau, Beatrice Alda; *D:* Alan Alda; *W:* Alan Alda; *M:* Joseph Turrin. VHS, Beta $89.95 *PAR 🐾🐾½*

New Mafia Boss Italian-made plodder has Savalas taking over a huge Mafia family and all hell breaking loose. *AKA:* Crime Boss.
1972 (PG) 90m/C Telly Savalas, Lee Van Cleef, Antonio Sabato, Paolo Tedesco; *D:* Alberto De Martino. VHS, Beta $59.95 *VCD 🐾½*

New Moon An adaptation of the operetta by Sigmund Romberg and Oscar Hammerstein II. A French heiress traveling on a boat that is captured by pirates falls in love with their leader. Remake of the 1930 film. Includes the 1935 Robert Benchley MGM short "How to Sleep." ♫Dance Your Cares Away; Stranger in Paris; The Way They Do It in Paris; Lover Come Back; Shoes; Softly as in a Morning Sunrise; One Kiss; Troubles of the World; No More Weeping.
1940 106m/B Jeanette MacDonald, Nelson Eddy, Buster Keaton, Joe Yule, Jack Perrin, Mary Boland; *D:* Robert Z. Leonard. VHS, Beta $19.95 *MGM 🐾🐾*

New Orleans After Dark A pair of New Orleans detectives tour the city, crimebuster style, and bag a dope ring. Average crime tale, shot on location in the Big Easy.
1958 69m/B Stacy Harris, Louis Sirgo, Ellen Moore; *D:* John Sledge. VHS $15.95 *NOS, LOO 🐾🐾*

New Pastures Three ex-convicts run into some humorous situations when they go back to their small hometown. A semi-acclaimed Czech comedy, with subtitles.
1962 92m/B *D:* Vladimir Cech. VHS, Beta $39.95 *IHF 🐾🐾½*

New Year's Day Jaglom continues his look at modern relationships in this story of a man reclaiming his house from three female tenants. Introspective character study lightened by humor and insight.
1989 (R) 90m/C Maggie Jakobson, Gwen Welles, Melanie Winter, Milos Forman, Michael Emil, David Duchovny, Tracy Reiner, Henry Jaglom; *D:* Henry Jaglom; *W:* Henry Jaglom. VHS, Beta $79.98 *PAR, BTV, FCT 🐾🐾🐾*

New Year's Evil Every hour during a New Year's Eve concert, a madman kills an unsuspecting victim. After each killing, the murderer informs a local disc jockey of his deed. Little does the disc jockey know that she will soon be next on his list. No suspense, bad music makes this slash and crash a holiday wrecker.
1978 (R) 88m/C Roz Kelly, Kip Niven, Chris Wallace, Louisa Moritz, Grant Kramer, Jed Mills; *D:* Emmett Alston. VHS, Beta *CAN Woof!*

New York, New York Tragic romance evolves between a saxophonist and an aspiring singer/actress in this salute to the big-band era. A love of music isn't enough to hold them together through career rivalries and life on the road. Fine performances by De Niro and Minnelli and the supporting cast. Re-released in 1981 with the "Happy Endings" number, which was cut from the original. Look for "Big Man" Clarence Clemons on sax. ♫New York, New York; There Goes the Ball Game; Happy Endings; But the World Goes 'Round; Night in Tunisia; Opus One; Avalon; You Brought a New Kind of

Love to Me; I'm Getting Sentimental Over You.
1977 (PG) 163m/C Robert De Niro, Liza Minnelli, Lionel Stander, Barry Primus, Mary Kay Place, Dick Miller, Diahnne Abbott; **D:** Martin Scorsese; **W:** Mardik Martin; **M:** Ralph Burns. **VHS, Beta $29.98** FOX 🌑🌑🌑

New York Nights The lives of nine New Yorkers intertwine in a treacherous game of passion and seduction. Liberal borrowing from plot of "La Ronde."
1984 (R) 104m/C Corinne Alphen, George Auyer, Bobbi Burns, Peter Matthey, Cynthia Lee, Willem Dafoe; **D:** Simon Nuchtern. **VHS, Beta $79.98** LIV 🌑

New York Ripper A New York cop tracks down a rampaging murderer in this dull, mindless slasher flick.
1982 88m/C Fred Williamson; **D:** Lucio Fulci. **VHS, Beta $49.95** VMK Woof!

New York Stories Entertaining anthology of three separate short films by three esteemed directors, all set in New York. In "Life Lessons" by Scorsese, an impulsive artist tries to prevent his live-in girlfriend from leaving him. "Life Without Zoe" by Coppola involves a youngster's fantasy about a wealthy 12-year-old who lives mostly without her parents. Allen's "Oedipus Wrecks," generally considered the best short, is about a 50-year-old man who is tormented by the specter of his mother.
1989 (PG) 124m/C Nick Nolte, Rosanna Arquette, Woody Allen, Mia Farrow, Mae Questel, Julie Kavner, Talia Shire, Giancarlo Giannini, Don Novello, Patrick O'Neal, Peter Gabriel, Paul Herman, Deborah Harry, Steve Buscemi, Heather McComb, Chris Elliott, Carol Bouquet, Edward I. Koch; **D:** Woody Allen, Martin Scorsese, Francis Ford Coppola; **W:** Woody Allen, Francis Ford Coppola, Richard Price, Sofia Coppola; **M:** Carmine Coppola, Kid Creole & the Coconuts. **VHS, Beta $19.99** TOU 🌑🌑🌑

New York's Finest Three prostitutes are determined to leave their calling and marry very eligible millionares. But becoming society ladies is more difficult than they thought. Would-be sophisticated comedy misfires.
1987 (R) 80m/C Ruth Collins, Jennifer Delora, Scott Thompson Baker, Heidi Paine, Jane Hamilton, Alan Naggar, John Altamura, Alan Fisler, Josey Duval; **D:** Chuck Vincent. **VHS, Beta $29.95** ACA 🌑

The Newlydeads An uptight, conservative, honeymoon resort owner murders one of his guests and finds out that "she" is really a he. Fifteen years later, on his wedding night, all of his guests are violently murdered by the transvestite's vengeful ghost. Oddball twist to the usual slasher nonsense.
1987 84m/C Scott Kaske, Jim Williams, Jean Levine, Jay Richardson; **D:** Joseph Merhi. **VHS, Beta** NO 🌑½

Newman's Law A city detective is implicated in a corruption investigation. While on suspension, he continues with his own investigation of a large drug ring and finds corruption is closer than he thought. Director Heffron's first feature film.
1974 (PG) 98m/C George Peppard, Roger Robinson, Eugene Roche, Gordon Pinsent, Louis Zorich, Abe Vigoda; **D:** Richard T. Heffron. **VHS, Beta $59.95** MCA 🌑🌑

News at Eleven A fading news anchorman is pressured by his ambitious young boss to expose a touchy local sex scandal, forcing him to consider the public's right to know versus the rights of the individual. About average for made-for-television drama.

1986 95m/C Martin Sheen, Peter Riegert, Barbara Babcock, Sheree J. Wilson, Sydney Penny, David S. Sheiner, Christopher Allport; **D:** Mike Robe. **VHS, Beta $9.98** TTC 🌑🌑

News from Home Scenes of life in New York are juxtaposed with voiceover from the letters of a mother to her young daughter. Plotless narrative deals with the small details of life.
1976 85m/C D: Chantal Akerman; **W:** Chantal Akerman. **VHS $79.95** WAC, FCT 🌑🌑

Newsfront A story about two brothers, both newsreel filmmakers, and their differing approaches to life and their craft in the 1940s and '50s. Tribute to the days of newsreel film combines real stories and fictionalized accounts with color and black and white photography. Noyce's feature film debut.
1978 110m/C Bill Hunter, Gerard Kennedy, Angela Punch McGregor, Wendy Hughes, Chris Haywood, John Ewart, Bryan Brown; **D:** Phillip Noyce. **VHS $59.98** SUE 🌑🌑🌑

Newsies An unfortunate attempt at an old-fashioned musical with a lot of cute kids and cardboard characters and settings. The plot, such as it is, concerns the 1899 New York newsboys strike against penny-pinching publisher Joseph Pulitzer. Bale plays the newsboy's leader and at least shows some charisma in a strictly cartoon setting. The songs are mediocre but the dancing is lively. However, none of it moves the story along. Strictly for the kids. Choreographer Ortega's feature-film directorial debut.
1992 (PG) 121m/C Christian Bale, Bill Pullman, Robert Duvall, Ann-Margret, Michael Lerner, Kevin Tighe, Charles Cioffi, Luke Edwards, Max Casella, David Moscow; **D:** Kenny Ortega; **M:** Alan Menken, Jack Feldman. **VHS, Beta $19.99** DIS 🌑½

The Next Karate Kid Fourth installment in the "Kid" series finds martial arts expert Miyagi (Morita) training Julie Pierce (Swank), the orphaned tomboy daughter of an old war buddy who saved his life 50 years earlier. He even teaches her the waltz, just in time for the prom, but she's still tough enough to scrap with a guy. A must-see for "Karate Kid" fans, if there are any left.
1994 (PG) ?m/C Noriyuki "Pat" Morita, Hilary Swank; **D:** Christopher Cain; **W:** Mark Lee; **M:** Bill Conti. **VHS** 🌑🌑½

Next of Kin A daughter moves into her dead mother's retirement home and discovers an unspeakable evil that lurks there. Typical horror stuff has some very creepy moments; filmed in New Zealand.
1982 90m/C Jackie Kerin, John Jarratt, Gerida Nicholson, Alex Scott; **D:** Tony Williams. **VHS, Beta, 8mm** NO 🌑

Next of Kin A young man experiencing familial difficulties undergoes experimental video therapy where he views a videotape of an Armenian family who gave their son up for adoption. When he discovers the actual family he insinuates himself into their life, determined to be their long-lost son.
1984 72m/C Patrick Tierney; **D:** Atom Egoyan; **W:** Atom Egoyan. **VHS $29.95** CVC, FCT, ING 🌑🌑

Next of Kin A Chicago cop returns to his Kentucky home to avenge his brother's brutal murder. Swayze's return to action films after his success in "Dirty Dancing" is unimpressive.
1989 (R) 108m/C Patrick Swayze, Adam Baldwin, Bill Paxton, Helen Hunt, Andreas Katsulas, Ben Stiller, Michael J. Pollard, Liam Neeson; **D:** John Irvin; **M:** Jack Nitzsche. **VHS, Beta, 8mm $19.98** WAR 🌑🌑

Next One Mysterious visitor from another time winds up on an isolated Greek island as the result of a magnetic storm. The local inhabitants are amazed when the visitor displays some Christ-like characteristics.
1984 105m/C Keir Dullea, Adrienne Barbeau, Jeremy Licht, Peter Hobbs; **D:** Nico Mastorakis. **VHS, Beta $69.95** VES 🌑½

Next Stop, Greenwich Village An affectionate, autobiographical look by Mazursky at a Brooklyn boy with acting aspirations, who moves to Greenwich Village in 1953. Good performances, especially by Winters as the overbearing mother.
1976 (R) 109m/C Lenny Baker, Christopher Walken, Ellen Greene, Shelley Winters, Lou Jacobi, Mike Kellin; **D:** Paul Mazursky; **W:** Paul Mazursky; **M:** Bill Conti. **VHS $59.98** FXV 🌑🌑🌑

Next Summer A large, character-studded French family pursues power, love and beauty. Excellent performances. In French with English subtitles. **AKA:** L'Ete Prochain.
1984 120m/C Jean-Louis Trintignant, Claudia Cardinale, Fanny Ardant, Philippe Noiret, Marie Trintignant; **D:** Nadine Trintignant. **VHS, Beta $69.95** TPV, FCT, ING 🌑🌑🌑

Next Time I Marry Lucy fraternizes with ditch digger Ellison because she needs to hitch a Yankee in order to inherit $20 mill. Seems she really loves a foreigner, though. Not much to bobaloo about. Director Kanin's second effort.
1938 65m/B Lucille Ball, James Ellison, Lee Bowman, Granville Bates, Mantan Moreland, Florence Lake; **D:** Garson Kanin. **VHS $19.98** TTC, FCT, MLB 🌑½

The Next Victim The unfaithful wife of an Austrian diplomat attempts to find out who has been slicing up beautiful jet-setters. Tepid mystery. **AKA:** Lo Strano Vizio Della Signora Wardh.
1971 (PG) 87m/C George Hilton, Edwige French, Christina Airoldi, Ivan Rassimov; **D:** Sergio Martino. **VHS, Beta $19.95** GEM, CNG 🌑

Next Victim A beautiful woman confined to a wheelchair is stalked by a lunatic killer. You've seen it before, and done better.
1974 80m/C Carroll Baker, T.P. McKenna, Ronald Lacey, Maurice Kaufman; **D:** James Ormerod. **VHS, Beta $29.95** LIV 🌑

The Next Voice You Hear Lives are changed forever when a group of people hear the voice of God on the radio. Interesting premise presented seriously.
1950 84m/B James Whitmore, Nancy Davis, Gary Gray, Lillian Bronson, Art Smith, Tom D'Andrea, Jeff Corey, George Chandler; **D:** William A. Wellman. **VHS, Beta $19.98** MGM 🌑🌑½

Next Year If All Goes Well Two young lovers struggle to overcome insecurities while establishing a relationship. Dubbed.
1983 95m/C Isabelle Adjani, Thierry Lhermitte, Mariann Chazel; **D:** Jean-Loup Hubert. **VHS, Beta $19.95** STE 🌑🌑½

Ni Chana Ni Juana A girl gets herself into lots of wacky situations on her trip to the capitol in search of her family.
1987 102m/C Maria Elena Velasco, Armando Calvo, Carmen Montejo. **VHS, Beta $79.95** MAD 🌑½

Niagara During their honeymoon in Niagara Falls, a scheming wife (Monroe) plans to kill her crazed war-vet husband (Cotten). Little does she know that he is plotting to double-cross her. Steamy, quasi-Hitchcockian mystery ably directed, with interesting performances. Monroes sings "Kiss."

N

1952 89m/B Joseph Cotten, Jean Peters, Marilyn Monroe, Casey Adams, Don "The Dragon" Wilson; *D:* Henry Hathaway. **VHS, Beta** $14.98 *FOX* 🎬🎬½

Nice Girl Like Me An orphaned young girl roams Europe, getting pregnant twice by two different men. She eventually finds love in the form of a kind caretaker. Harmless fluff. Based on Anne Piper's novel "Marry At Leisure."
1969 (PG) 91m/C Harry Andrews, Barbara Ferris, Gladys Cooper, Bill Hinnant, James Villers; *D:* Desmond Davis. **VHS, Beta** $59.98 *NLC* 🎬🎬

Nice Girls Don't Explode A girl telekinetically starts fires when sexually aroused. This puts a bit of a damper on her relationship with O'Leary, much to her mother's delight. Matchless entertainment.
1987 (PG) 92m/C Barbara Harris, Wallace Shawn, Michelle Meyrink, William O'Leary; *D:* Chuck Martinez. **VHS, Beta** $19.95 *STE, NWV* 🎬🎬

Nice Neighbor An acclaimed film about an outwardly self-sacrificing neighbor who cold-bloodedly manipulates his fellow rooming house tenants for his own ends. In Hungarian with English subtitles.
1979 90m/C Laszlo Szabo, Margit Dayka, Agi Margittay; *D:* Zsolt Kedzi-Kovacs. **VHS, Beta** $59.95 *FCT* 🎬🎬🎬

Nicholas and Alexandra Epic chronicling the final years of Tsar Nicholas II, Empress Alexandra and their children. Their lavish royal lifestyle gives way to imprisonment and eventual execution under the new Lenin government. Beautiful, but overlong costume epic that loses steam in the second half. Based on the biography by Robert Massie. Available in widescreen format on laserdisc.
1971 (PG) 183m/C Michael Jayston, Janet Suzman, Tom Baker, Laurence Olivier, Michael Redgrave, Harry Andrews, Jack Hawkins, Alexander Knox, Curt Jurgens; *D:* Franklin J. Schaffner; *M:* Richard Rodney Bennett. Academy Awards '71: Best Art Direction/Set Decoration, Best Costume Design; Nominations: Best Actress (Suzman), Best Cinematography, Best Picture, Best Original Score; National Board of Review Awards '71: 10 Best Films of the Year. **VHS, Beta** $29.95 *COL, TVC* 🎬🎬

Nicholas Nickleby An ensemble cast works hard to bring to life Charles Dickens' novel about an impoverished family dependent on their wealthy but villainous uncle. Young Nicholas is an apprentice at a school for boys, and he and a student run away to a series of exciting adventures. An enjoyable film, though it is hard to tell the entire story in such a small amount of time. *AKA:* The Life and Adventures of Nicholas Nickleby.
1946 108m/B Cedric Hardwicke, Stanley Holloway, Derek Bond, Alfred Drayton, Sybil Thorndike, Sally Ann Howes, Bernard Miles, Mary Merrall, Cathleen Nesbitt; *D:* Alberto Cavalcanti. **VHS, Beta** $19.98 *MRV, PSM, DVT* 🎬🎬

Nick Knight An L.A. cop on the night beat is really a good-guy vampire, who quaffs cattle blood as he tracks down another killer who's draining humans of their plasma. A gimmicky pilot for a would-be TV series that never bit.
1987 92m/C Rick Springfield, Michael Nader, Laura Johnson. **VHS** $19.95 *STE* 🎬🎬

Nickel & Dime A con artist's luck turns bad when the IRS catches up with him, impounds all his worldly goods, and sticks him with an officious auditor. But if Jack can find the heiress to a fortune, within 48 hours, he can claim a hefty finder's fee and his money worries will be a thing of the past.
1992 (PG) 96m/C C. Thomas Howell, Wallace Shawn, Lise Cutter, Lynn Danielson, Roy Brocksmith; *D:* Ben Moses; *W:* Seth Front, Eddy Polon, Ben Moses. **VHS** $89.95 *COL* 🎬🎬

Nickel Mountain Heartwarming story of a suicidal 40-year-old man who finds a new reason to live when he falls in love with a pregnant 16-year-old girl who works at his diner. Langenkamp particularly appealing. Based on a John Gardner novel.
1985 88m/C Michael Cole, Heather Langenkamp, Ed Lauter, Brian Kerwin, Patrick Cassidy, Grace Zabriskie, Don Beddoe; *D:* Drew Denbaum. **VHS, Beta** $59.95 *LHV* 🎬🎬½

Nicole The downfall of a wealthy woman who is able to buy everything she wants except love.
1972 (R) 91m/C Leslie Caron, Catherine Bach, Ramon Bieri; *D:* Itsvan Ventilia. **VHS, Beta** *GHV* 🎬

Nido de Aguilas Two brothers stripped of their ranch search for the band of thieves who killed their parents. *AKA:* Eagle's Nest.
1976 93m/C Mario Almada, Martha Elena Cervantes. **VHS, Beta** $55.95 *MAD* 🎬

The Night After Halloween A young woman gets the shock of her life when she discovers that her boyfriend is a crazed killer.
1983 (R) 90m/C Chantal Contouri, Robert Bruning, Sigrid Thornton. **VHS, Beta** *NO* 🎬

Night After Night West's screen debut finds her in an unaccustomed secondary role, although a prime scene-stealer. In Raft's first starring role, he's a monied lowlife who opens a fancy nightclub and becomes infatuated with Park Avenue beauty Cummings. His problems are compounded by the arrival of raucous ex-flames West and Gleason. When a hatcheck girl cries "Goodness!" over West's diamonds, she replies, in suggestive West-style, "Goodness had nothing to do with it, dearie." Adapted from the novel "Single Night" by Louis Bromfield.
1932 73m/B George Raft, Constance Cummings, Mae West, Wynne Gibson, Alison Skipworth, Roscoe Karns, Louis Calhern; *D:* Archie Mayo; *W:* Mae West, Kathryn Scola, Vincent Lawrence. **VHS** $14.98 *MCA* 🎬🎬½

Night Ambush A Nazi general is kidnapped on Crete by British agents, who embark on a dangerous trip to the coast where a ship awaits to take them to Cairo. The general tries to thwart their plans, but they outwit him at every turn. Based on a novel by W. Stanley Moss that details a similar real-life event. *AKA:* Ill Met By Moonlight.
1957 100m/B Dirk Bogarde, Marius Goring, David Oxley, Cyril Cusack, Christopher Lee; *D:* Michael Powell, Emeric Pressburger. **VHS** *NO* 🎬🎬½

Night and Day Sentimental musical about the life of bon-vivant composer-extraordinaire Cole Porter. His intensity and the motivations for his music are dramatized, but this film succeeds best as a fabulous showcase for Porter's songs. ♫Begin the Beguine; My Heart Belongs to Daddy; You're the Top; I've Got You Under My Skin; Just One of Those Things; I Get a Kick Out of You; Night and Day; What Is This Thing Called Love; Do I Love You.
1946 128m/C Cary Grant, Alexis Smith, Jane Wyman, Eve Arden, Mary Martin, Alan Hale, Monty Woolley, Ginny Simms, Dorothy Malone; *D:* Michael Curtiz. **VHS, Beta** $19.98 *MGM, FCT* 🎬🎬½

Night and Day Charming adult romance about Jack and Julie, young lovers newly arrived in Paris. When Jack gets a night job driving a cab, Julie finds her evenings lonely. But not for long. She meets Joseph, a cab driver on the day shift. Soon, Julie is juggling sexual affairs with both men and everything gets increasingly complicated. Her lovers find out about each other but Julie doesn't want to fully commit to either of them. In French with English subtitles. *AKA:* Nuit et Jour.
1991 90m/C Guilaine Londez, Thomas Langmann, Francois Negret; *D:* Chantal Akerman; *W:* Pascal Bonitzer, Chantal Akerman; *M:* Marc Herouet. **VHS** $89.98 *FXL, ORI, FCT* 🎬🎬🎬

Night and the City A film noir classic about a hustler's money-making schemes. Widmark is Harry Fabian, a small-time promoter working for slimy nightclub owner Sullivan, whose job is to hustle the marks into the club where his girlfriend Tierney is the singer. Widmark also happens to be romancing Sullivan's wife, Withers, and wants her to back his latest con. But his schemes go awry and Fabian's on the run for his life. Widmark gives a riveting performance of a lowlife whose brains don't match his ambitions. Filmed in London with appropriate brooding tawdriness. Adapted from the novel by Gerald Kersh; remade in 1992.
1950 95m/B Richard Widmark, Gene Tierney, Googie Withers, Francis L. Sullivan, Hugh Marlowe, Herbert Lom, Mike Mazurki, Charles Farrell; *D:* Jules Dassin; *W:* Joe Eisinger; *M:* Franz Waxman. **VHS** $19.99 *FXV, MOV, RXM* 🎬🎬🎬½

Night and the City Harry Fabian (De Niro), a con-artist/ambulance-chaser, concocts a scheme to make it big, and approaches an old boxing great (Warden) to come out of retirement and revive a local boxing night. Problem is, although Harry has energy and ambition, he also has a talent for making enemies out of the wrong people, like the boxer's brother (King), a neighborhood mobster. Filled with details more interesting than the plot; more about fast-living, fast-talking New Yorkers, a fine showcase for De Niro's talent. Winkler's remake of the 1950 Jules Dassin film.
1992 (R) 98m/C Robert De Niro, Jessica Lange, Cliff Gorman, Alan King, Jack Warden, Eli Wallach, Barry Primus, Gene Kirkwood, Pedro Sanchez; *Cameos:* Regis Philbin, Joy Philbin, Richard Price; *D:* Irwin Winkler; *W:* Richard Price; *M:* James Newton Howard. **VHS** $19.98 *FXV* 🎬🎬🎬

Night Angel A beautiful seductress lures men into a deadly trap from which only true love can free them.
1990 (R) 90m/C Isa Anderson, Linda Ashby, Debra Feuer, Helen Martin, Karen Black; *D:* Dominique Othenin-Girard; *W:* Joe Augustyn. **VHS, Beta** $89.95 *FRH* 🎬

A Night at the Opera The Marx Brothers get mixed up with grand opera in their first MGM-produced epic and their first without Zeppo. Jones, as a budding opera singer warbles "Alone" and "Cosi Cosa." One of their best films, blessed with a big budget—used to reach epic anarchic heights. Some scenes were tested on live audiences before inclusion, including the Groucho/Chico paper-tearing contract negotiation and the celebrated stateroom scene, in which the boys are joined in a small closet by two maids, the ship's engineer, his assistant, a manicurist, a young woman, a cleaning lady, and four food-laden waiters. Laserdisc includes letterboxing, digital sound, original trailers, production photos, memorabilia, and soundtrack commentary by film critic Leonard Maltin.

1935 92m/B Groucho Marx, Chico Marx, Harpo Marx, Allan Jones, Kitty Carlisle Hart, Sig Rumann, Margaret Dumont, Walter Woolf King; **D:** Sam Wood; **W:** George S. Kaufman, Morrie Ryskind, Bert Kalmar, Harry Ruby, Al Boasberg; **M:** Herbert Stothart. **VHS, Beta** $19.95 *MGM, VYG, CRC* ⍟⍟⍟⍟

Night Beast Alien creature lands his spaceship near a small town and begins a bloody killing spree. Recycled plot.
1983 90m/C Tom Griffith, Dick Dyszel, Jaimie Zemarel. **VHS, Beta** *NO* ⍟

Night Beat A labored crime drama from postwar Britain. Two army pals pursue diverging careers. One becomes a cop, the other a crook. Want to bet that they meet again?
1948 95m/B Anne Crawford, Maxwell Reed, Ronald Howard, Christine Norden; **D:** Harold Huth. **VHS** $15.95 *LOO* ⍟½

The Night Before Snobby high school beauty Loughlin loses a bet and has to go to the prom with the school geek Reeves. On the way, they get lost on the wrong side of the tracks, and become involved with pimps, crime and the police. A drunken Reeves loses Loughlin as well as his father's car. Typical teen farce.
1988 (PG-13) 90m/C Keanu Reeves, Lori Loughlin, Trinidad Silva, Michael Greene, Theresa Saldana, Suzanne Snyder, Morgan Lofting, Gwil Richards; **D:** Thom Eberhardt; **W:** Gregory Scherick, Thom Eberhardt. **VHS, Beta** $79.99 *HBO* ⍟⍟½

Night Birds Early British thriller about a notorious crook named "Flash Jack," who heads a gang of top-hatted criminals that rob the wealthy. Poor production quality and Raine's standoffish screen presence contribute to this below-average film.
1931 76m/B Jameson Thomas, Jack Raine, Muriel Angelus, Eve Gray; **D:** Richard Eichberg; **W:** Miles Malleson. **VHS** $12.95 *SNC* ⍟

Night Breed A teenager flees a chaotic past to slowly become a member of a bizarre race of demons that live in a huge, abandoned Canadian graveyard; a place where every sin is forgiven. Based on Barker's novel "Cabal," and appropriately gross, nonsensical and strange. Good special effects almost save this one.
1990 (R) 102m/C Craig Sheffer, Anne Bobby, David Cronenberg, Charles Haid; **D:** Clive Barker; **W:** Clive Barker. **VHS, Beta** $89.98 *MED* ⍟½

The Night Brings Charlie A disfigured tree surgeon is the prime suspect in some grisly murders committed with a tree trimming saw. Obviously, everyone in the town fears him as a result. Not a sequel to "Roots."
1990 90m/C Kerry Knight, Joe Fishback, Aimee Tenalia, Monica Simmons; **D:** Tom Logan. **VHS** *NO* ⍟½

Night Call Nurses Three gorgeous nurses find danger and intrigue on the night shift at a psychiatric hospital. Third in the "nurse" quintet is back on target, shrugging off the previous film's attempts at "serious" social commentary. Miller provides comic relief. Preceded by "The Student Nurses" and "Private Duty Nurses" and followed by "The Young Nurses," and "Candy Stripe Nurses." Also on video as "Young L.A. Nurses 2."
1972 (R) 85m/C Patricia T. Byrne, Alana Collins, Mittie Lawrence, Clinton Kimbrough, Felton Perry, Stack Pierce, Richard Young, Dennis Dugan, Dick Miller; **D:** Jonathan Kaplan. **VHS, Beta** $59.98 *NLC* ⍟⍟

Night Caller from Outer Space When a woman-hunting alien arrives in London, women begin to disappear. At first, incredibly, no one makes the connection, but then the horrible truth comes to light. *AKA:* Blood Beast from Outer Space; The Night Caller.
1966 84m/B John Saxon, Maurice Denham, Patricia Haines, Alfred Burke, Jack Watson, Aubrey Morris; **D:** John Gilling. **VHS, Beta** $14.95 *COL* ⍟½

Night Children Tough L.A. cop teams with a parole officer to battle a nasty gang leader. The battle is quite violent and senseless.
1989 (R) 90m/C David Carradine, Nancy Kwan, Griffin O'Neal, Tawny Fere; **D:** Norbert Meisel. **VHS, Beta** $79.95 *VMK* ⍟

The Night Club Swinging single stands to gain fortune if he weds a certain girl, and, as luck would have it, he falls for her. When the usual hearts and roses don't convince her he's earnest, he tries to prove his love is true by attempting suicide and hiring a hit man.
1925 62m/B Raymond Griffith, Vera Reynolds, Wallace Beery, Louise Fazenda; **D:** Frank Urson. **VHS, Beta** $19.95 *GPV* ⍟⍟½

Night Creature A tough, Hemingway-type writer is determined to destroy the man-eating black leopard which nearly killed him once before. Filmed in Thailand. *AKA:* Out of the Darkness; Fear.
1979 (PG) 83m/C Donald Pleasence, Nancy Kwan, Ross Hagen; **D:** Lee Madden. **VHS, Beta** $19.95 *VCI* ⍟

Night Cries After a woman's baby dies at birth, she has persistent dreams that he is alive and in trouble. No one will believe her when she tells them that something is wrong. Made for television.
1978 100m/C Susan St. James, Michael Parks, William Conrad; **D:** Richard Lang. **VHS, Beta** *WOV* ⍟⍟½

Night Crossing The fact-based story of two East German families who launch a daring escape to the West in a homemade hot air balloon. Exciting action for the whole family.
1981 (PG) 106m/C John Hurt, Jane Alexander, Glynnis O'Connor, Doug McKeon, Beau Bridges; **D:** Delbert Mann; **W:** John McGreevey; **M:** Jerry Goldsmith. **VHS, Beta** $69.95 *DIS* ⍟⍟½

The Night Cry Silent canine melodrama has sheep-murdering dog sentenced to death row until he saves little girl from unbelievably big bird.
1926 65m/B Rin Tin Tin, John Harron, June Marlowe, Mary Louise Miller; **D:** Herman C. Raymaker. **VHS, Beta** *GPV, GVV* ⍟⍟

The Night Evelyn Came Out of the Grave A wealthy Italian playboy, obsessed with his dead, flame-haired wife, lures living redheads into his castle, where he tortures and kills them. Standard '70s Euro/horror/sex stuff enlivened by the presence of the incredible Erika Blanc as a stripper who works out of a coffin. *AKA:* La Notte Che Evelyn Usca Dalla Tomba.
1971 (R) 99m/C Anthony Steffen, Marina Malfatti, Rod Murdock, Erika Blanc, Giacomo "Jack" Rossi-Stuart, Umberto Raho; **D:** Emilio P. Miraglio. **VHS** $18.00 *FRG* ⍟½

Night Eyes Surveillance can be a dangerous profession, especially when your boss happens to be the jealous husband of a very sexy woman. Watching turns to yearning for this professional peeper, but he may just get more than he bargained for. Roberts is worth watching. *AKA:* Hidden Vision.

1990 (R) 95m/C Andrew Stevens, Tanya Roberts, Warwick Sims, Cooper Huckabee; **D:** Emilio P. Miraglio. **VHS, Beta** $29.95 *PSM* ⍟

Night Eyes 2 A security expert assigned to protect the sultry wife of a foreign diplomat finds himself spending a little too much time eyeing her through his hidden cameras. Soon he can no longer control his desire and he makes a move on her that may have international implications. Also available in an unrated version.
1991 (R) 97m/C Andrew Stevens, Shannon Tweed, Tim Russ, Richard Chaves, Geno Silva; **D:** Rodney McDonald. **VHS, Beta** $29.95 *PSM* ⍟½

Night Eyes 3 Night Eyes Security boss Stevens' latest assignment is to protect the superstar lead (Shannon Tweed) of a top TV cop show from a stalker. They wind up in very close contact but someone is videotaping their private moments which don't stay private for long. Maybe on-screen partner Tracy (Shannon's sister) has something to do with it. Also available in an unrated version.
1993 (R) 97m/C Andrew Stevens, Shannon Tweed, Tracy Tweed, Tristan Rogers; **D:** Andrew Stevens; **W:** Andrew Stevens, Michael W. Potts. **VHS, Beta** $92.95 *PSM* ⍟⍟

Night Flight from Moscow A Soviet spy defects with a fistful of secret documents that implicate every free government. Then the CIA must decide if he's telling the truth. Complex espionage thriller. *AKA:* The Serpent.
1973 (PG) 113m/C Yul Brynner, Henry Fonda, Dirk Bogarde, Virna Lisi, Philippe Noiret, Farley Granger, Robert Alda, Marie DuBois, Elga Andersen; **D:** Henri Verneuil; **M:** Ennio Morricone. **VHS, Beta** $59.98 *NLC* ⍟⍟

A Night for Crime A movie star disappears during the filming of a movie. When she turns up dead, a bumbling cop suspects everyone on the set.
1942 75m/B Glenda Farrell, Lyle Talbot, Lena Basquette, Donald Kirke, Ralph Sanford; **D:** Alexis Thurn-Taxis. **VHS** $24.95 *NOS, DVT, HEG* ⍟⍟

Night Friend A priest sets out to help a young woman caught up in a world of drug abuse and prostitution. Exploitation morality flick.
1987 (R) 94m/C Art Carney, Chuck Shamata, Jayne Eastwood, Heather Kjollesdal; **D:** Peter Gerretsen. **VHS, Beta** $79.95 *PSM* ⍟

A Night Full of Rain Italian communist tries unsuccessfully to seduce vacationing American feminist. They meet again in San Francisco and wedding bells chime. They argue. They argue more. They put all but rabid Wertmuller fans to sleep. The director's first English-language film. *AKA:* End of the World (in Our Usual Bed in a Night Full of Rain).
1978 (R) 104m/C Giancarlo Giannini, Candice Bergen, Anne Byrne, Flora Carabella; **D:** Lina Wertmuller; **W:** Lina Wertmuller. **VHS** $59.98 *WAR, FCT* ⍟½

Night Gallery Serling is the tour guide through an unusual art gallery consisting of portraits that reflect people's greed, desire and guilt. Made for television pilot for the series, which ran from 1969 to 1973. Three stories, including "Eyes," which saw novice Spielberg directing veteran Crawford.
1969 95m/C Joan Crawford, Roddy McDowall, Tom Bosley, Barry Sullivan, Ossie Davis, Sam Jaffe, Kate Greenfield; **D:** Steven Spielberg, Boris Sagal. **VHS, Beta** $59.95 *MCA* ⍟⍟⍟

Night Game A cop links a string of serial killings to the night games won by the Houston Astros. Brave cast tries hard, but is retired without a hit.

1989 (R) 95m/C Roy Scheider, Karen Young, Paul Gleason, Lane Smith, Carlin Glynn; *D:* Peter Masterson; *M:* Pino Donaggio. VHS, Beta $89.99 *HBO* 🎬½

Night Games Raped as a child, California girl Pickett has trouble relating to her husband. To overcome her sexual anxieties, she engages in a number of bizarre fantasies.
1980 (R) 100m/C Cindy Pickett, Joanna Cassidy, Barry Primus, Gene Davis; *D:* Roger Vadim; *M:* John Barry. VHS, Beta $69.98 *SUE* 🎬

The Night God Screamed A fanatical cult leader is convicted of murder and the cult goes wild. *AKA:* Scream.
198? (PG) 85m/C Michael Sugich, Jeanne Crain, James B. Sikking; *D:* Lee Madden. VHS, Beta $19.98 *TWE* Woof!

The Night Has Eyes Tense melodrama concerns a young teacher who disappears on the Yorkshire moors at the same spot where her girlfriend had vanished the previous year. Early film appearance for Mason. *AKA:* Terror House.
1942 79m/B James Mason, Joyce Howard, Wilfred Lawson, Mary Clare; *D:* Leslie Arliss. VHS, Beta $19.95 *NOS, SNC, DVT* 🎬🎬½

A Night in Casablanca Groucho, Harpo and Chico find themselves in the luxurious Hotel Casablanca, going after some leftover Nazis searching for treasure. One of the later Marx Brothers' films, but still loaded with the familiar wisecracks and mayhem.
1946 85m/B Groucho Marx, Harpo Marx, Chico Marx, Charles Drake, Dan Seymour, Sig Rumann; *D:* Archie Mayo. VHS, Beta *NO* 🎬🎬🎬

A Night in Heaven A college teacher gets involved with one of her students, who moonlights as a male stripper. Will he earn that extra credit he needs to pass? Uninspired, overly explicit. Look for Denny Terrio of "Dance Fever" fame.
1983 (R) 85m/C Christopher Atkins, Lesley Ann Warren, Carrie Snodgress, Andy Garcia; *D:* John G. Avildsen; *W:* Joan Tewkesbury. VHS, Beta $59.98 *FOX* Woof!

A Night in the Life of Jimmy Reardon A high school Casanova watches his friends leave for expensive schools while he contemplates a trip to Hawaii with his rich girlfriend, a ruse to avoid the dull business school his father has picked out. Well photographed, but acting leaves something to be desired. Based on Richert's novel "Aren't You Even Going to Kiss Me Good-bye?"
1988 (R) 95m/C River Phoenix, Meredith Salenger, Matthew L. Perry, Louanne, Ione Skye, Ann Magnuson, Paul Koslo, Jane Hallaren, Jason Court; *D:* William Richert; *M:* Elmer Bernstein, Bill Conti. VHS, Beta $19.98 *FOX* 🎬½

Night Is My Future A young musician, blinded in an accident, meets a girl who tries to bring him happiness. Usual somber Bergman, but unimportant story. In Swedish with English subtitles. *AKA:* Music in Darkness.
1947 89m/B Mai Zetterling, Birger Malmsten, Naima Wifstrand, Olof Winnerstrand, Hilda Borgstrom; *D:* Ingmar Bergman. VHS, Beta $24.95 *VYY, DVT, ING* 🎬🎬

Night Life A teenager gets the all-out, high-stakes ride of his life when four cadavers are re-animated in his uncle's mortuary.
1990 (R) 92m/C Scott Grimes, John Astin, Cheryl Pollak, Alan Blumenfeld; *D:* David Acomba; *M:* Keith Critchlow; *M:* Roger Bourland. VHS $79.95 *COL* 🎬🎬

Night Life in Reno When a man leaves his wife, she sets out for Reno and falls in love with a married man. When her new love is killed by his jealous wife, the

woman returns to her husband and they begin their marriage anew. Watchable melodrama.
1931 58m/B Jameson Thomas, Dorothy Christy, Virginia Valli, Carmelita Geraghty. VHS, Beta *NO* 🎬🎬

Night Master A handful of karate students practice their homework with much higher stakes away from the classroom. For them, deadly Ninja games are the only way to study.
1987 87m/C Tom Jennings, Nicole Kidman, Vince Martin; *D:* Mark Joffe. VHS, Beta $79.95 *ACA* 🎬

Night Monster A maniac wears artifical limbs to hunt down and murder the doctors responsible for amputating his legs. Picture was shot in 11 days. Fire scene was stock footage from "The Ghost of Frankenstein." *AKA:* House of Mystery.
1942 80m/B Ralph Morgan, Lionel Atwill, Leif Erickson, Don Porter, Irene Hervey, Nils Asther, Bela Lugosi; *D:* Ford Beebe. VHS $12.95 *GPV* 🎬🎬½

'night, Mother A depressed woman, living with her mother, announces one evening that she is going to kill herself. Her mother spends the evening reliving their lives and trying to talk her out of it, but the outcome seems inevitable. Well acted, though depressing. Based on Marsha Norman's Pulitzer Prize-winning novel.
1986 (PG-13) 97m/C Sissy Spacek, Anne Bancroft, Ed Berke, Carol Robbins, Jennifer Roosendahl; *D:* Tom Moore; *W:* Marsha Norman; *M:* David Shire. VHS, Beta $79.95 *MCA* 🎬🎬½

Night Moves While tracking down a missing teenager, a Hollywood detective uncovers a bizarre smuggling ring in the Florida Keys. Hackman is realistic as the detective whose own life is unraveling and in one of her early roles, Griffith plays the teenager. The dense, disjointed plot reaches a shocking end. Underrated when released and worth a view.
1975 (R) 100m/C Gene Hackman, Susan Clark, Jennifer Warren, Melanie Griffith, Harris Yulin, Edward Binns, Kenneth Mars, James Woods, Dennis Dugan, Max Gail; *D:* Arthur Penn. VHS, Beta $19.98 *WAR* 🎬🎬🎬

Night Nurse Stanwyck is a nurse who uncovers a sordid plot involving the murder of two young children for an inheritance. An entertaining, overlooked crime-drama, initially notorious for Stanwyck and roommate Blondell's continual onscreen dressings and undressings. Gable is compelling in an early, villainous role.
1931 72m/B Barbara Stanwyck, Ben Lyon, Joan Blondell, Charles Winninger, Charlotte Merriam, Eddie Nugent, Blanche Frederici, Allan "Rocky" Lane, Walter McGrail, Ralf Harolde, Clark Gable; *D:* William A. Wellman. VHS $19.98 *MGM* 🎬🎬🎬

Night Nurse Young nurse signs on to care for an aging, wheelchair-ridden opera star, only to find that the house is haunted.
1977 80m/C Davina Whitehouse, Kay Taylor, Gary Day, Kate Fitzpatrick; *D:* Igor Auzins. VHS, Beta *NO* 🎬

Night of a Thousand Cats A reclusive playboy cruises Mexico City in his helicopter, searching for beautiful women. It seems he needs their bodies for his cats who, for some reason, eat only human flesh. He keeps the heads, for some reason, for his private collection. A really odd '70s cannibal cat entry, but it moves along nicely and features some truly groovy fashions (floppy hats, translucent blouses, etc.). Not to be confused with the 1963 film of the same name. From the director of "Night of the

Bloody Apes" and "Survive!" *AKA:* La Noche de Los Mil Gatos; Blood Feast.
1972 (R) 83m/C Anjanette Comer, Zulma Faiad, Hugo Stiglitz, Christa Linder, Teresa Velasquez, Barbara Ange; *D:* Rene Cardona Jr. VHS, Beta *ACA, JEF* 🎬

Night of Bloody Horror Tale of a former mental patient who is believed to be responsible for the brutal murders of his ex-girlfriends. A night of bloody horror indeed, as the gore is liberally spread.
1976 (R) 89m/C Gaye Yellen, Evelyn Hendricks, Gerald McRaney. VHS, Beta *NO* 🎬½

Night of Dark Shadows An abominable film which even fans of the TV show have a hard time liking. The last of the Collins family and his new bride are sent 150 years into the past. Sequel to "House of Dark Shadows." *AKA:* Curse of Dark Shadows.
1971 (PG) 97m/C David Selby, Lara Parker, Kate Jackson, Grayson Hall, John Karlen, Nancy Barrett, James Storm; *D:* Dan Curtis. VHS, Beta $19.98 *MGM* Woof!

Night of Evil Girl is released from reform school and promptly wins a beauty contest. Her bid to win the Miss America title is blown to smithereens however, when it is discovered that she has been secretly married all along. From there she resorts to working in strip joints and attempts to pull off an armed robbery. As exploitation fare goes, a winner.
1962 88m/B Lisa Gaye, William Campbell; *D:* Richard Galbreath. VHS, Beta $16.95 *SNC* 🎬½

Night of Horror Zombies attack four young people stranded in the wilderness.
198? (R) 76m/C Steve Sandkuhler, Gae Schmitt, Rebecca Bach, Jeff Canfield. VHS, Beta *GHV, MRV* 🎬½

Night of Terror A swami, a couple of Hindu servants, a pretty heroine, a reporter, and all stalked by a killer who's after a formula that can put people in a state of suspended animation. Lame chiller. *AKA:* He Lived to Kill.
1933 64m/B Bela Lugosi, Sally Blane, Wallace Ford, Tully Marshall, George Meeker, Edwin Maxwell; *D:* Ben Stoloff. VHS $11.95 *GPV* 🎬½

Night of Terror A bizarre family conducts brain experiments on themselves and then begins to kill each other. Bloodshed for the whole family.
1987 105m/C Renee Harmon, Henry Lewis. VHS $49.95 *IME* 🎬½

Night of the Assassin Priest leaves his pulpit to become a terrorist. He plans a surprise for a U.N. secretary visiting Greece that would put the U.S. and Greek governments in the palm of his hand. Hard to believe.
1977 98m/C Klaus Kinski, Michael Craig, Eva Renzi; *D:* Robert McMahon. VHS, Beta $69.98 *LIV* 🎬

Night of the Blood Beast An astronaut comes back from space with an alien growing inside his body. The low budget defeats a valiant attempt at a story. Alternative title: "Creature from Galaxy 27."
1958 65m/B Michael Emmet, Angela Greene, John Baer, Ed Nelson; *D:* Bernard L. Kowalski. VHS $16.95 *SNC, MRV* 🎬½

Night of the Bloody Apes When a doctor transplants an ape's heart into his dying son's body, the son goes berserk. Gory Mexican-made horror at its finest. *AKA:* Gomar the Human Gorilla; La Horriplante Bestia Humana.
1968 (R) 84m/C Jose Elias Moreno, Carlos Lopez Moctezuma, Armando Silvestre, Norma Lazarendo, Agustin Martinez Solares, Gina Moret, Noelia Noel, Gerard Zepeda; *D:* Rene Cardona Jr. VHS, Beta $59.95 *MPI* Woof!

Night of the Bloody Transplant A lunatic scientist switches hearts from one person to another in this bloody gorefest. Footage of real surgery adds authenticity, but not believeability.
1986 (R) 90m/C Dick Grimm; **D:** David W. Hanson. **VHS, Beta** $24.95 *VCI Woof!*

Night of the Cobra Woman A woman who can turn herself into a cobra needs constant sex and snake venom to keep her eternally young. Shot on location in the Philippines. One-time underground filmmaker Meyer co-wrote the script, for the Corman factory.
1972 (R) 85m/C Joy Bang, Marlene Clark, Roger Garrett, Slash Marks, Vic Diaz; **D:** Andrew Meyer; **W:** Andrew Meyer. **VHS, Beta** *NO 𝙸*

Night of the Comet After surviving the explosion of a deadly comet, two California girls discover that they are the last people on Earth. When zombies begin to chase them, things begin to lose their charm. Cute and funny, but the script runs out before the movie does.
1984 (PG-13) 90m/C Catherine Mary Stewart, Kelli Maroney, Robert Beltran, Geoffrey Lewis, Mary Woronov, Sharon Farrell, Michael Bowen; **D:** Thom Eberhardt; **W:** Thom Eberhardt. **VHS, Beta** $19.98 *FOX 𝙸𝙸½*

Night of the Creeps In 1958 an alien organism lands on earth and infects a person who is then frozen. Thirty years later he is accidentally unfrozen and starts spreading the infection throughout a college town. B-movie homage contains every horror cliche there is. Director Dekker's first film.
1986 89m/C Jason Lively, Jill Whitlow, Tom Atkins, Dick Miller, Steve Marshall; **D:** Fred Dekker; **W:** Fred Dekker. **VHS, Beta** $14.99 *HBO 𝙸𝙸½*

Night of the Cyclone A complex but not overly interesting thriller about a big city cop who goes to an island paradise in search of his missing daughter and finds murder.
1990 (R) 90m/C Kris Kristofferson, Jeffrey Meek, Marisa Berenson, Winston Ntshona, Gerrit Graham; **D:** David Irving. **VHS, Beta** $89.94 *REP 𝙸𝙸*

Night of the Death Cult After moving to a quiet seaside community, a young couple is plagued by cult practising human sacrifice in order to appease the Templars, a zombie-like pack of ancient clergymen who rise from the dead and torture the living. Last in a four film series about the Templars. *AKA:* Night of the Seagulls.
1975 90m/C Victor Petit, Julie James, Maria Kosti, Sandra Mozarowsky; **D:** Armando de Ossorio. **VHS, Beta** *NO 𝙸𝙸*

Night of the Demon Anthropology students are attacked by the legendary Bigfoot. Later they discover that he has raped and impregnated a young woman. Gore and sex prevail.
1980 97m/C Jay Allen, Michael J. Cutt, Bob Collins, Jodi Lazarus; **D:** James C. Watson. **VHS, Beta** $49.95 *VHE Woof!*

Night of the Demons A gory, special-effects-laden horror farce about teenagers calling up demons in a haunted mortuary. On Halloween, of course.
1988 92m/C Linnea Quigley, Cathy Podewell, Alvin Alexis, William Gallo, Mimi Kinkade, Lance Fenton; **D:** Kevin S. Tenney; **W:** Joe Augustyn. **VHS** $89.98 *REP 𝙸𝙸*

Night of the Demons 2 Some humor and reasonable special effects help this rise above the usual teen-slasher horror sequels. The demonic Angela (complete with her skull-shaped lollipops) lives on in legend, handily haunting her creepy old house where a group of dumb teens end up on Halloween (and

soon wind up dead). With each casualty, a new victim also joins the ranks of the undead. Funniest parts come with heroic rescuer, yardstick-wielding Sister Gloria, who's not about to let any of Satan's helpers get the better of her.
1994 (R) 96m/C Amelia Kinkade, Jennifer Rhodes, Merele Kennedy, Bobby Jacoby, Rod McCary, Zoe Trilling, Cristi Harris, Johnny Moran, Rick Peters, Christine Taylor, Ladd York, Darin Heames; **D:** Brian Trenchard-Smith; **W:** Joe Augustyn; **M:** Jim Manzie. **VHS** *REP 𝙸𝙸*

The Night of the Following Day Four professional criminals kidnap a young girl at France's Orly airport, demanding a large ransom from her wealthy father. One kidnapper turns out to be beset by personal demons, hindering their plans and leading to a bloody climax. Then, there's a final twist to the entire story. Brando and Boone are properly chilling but the plot is muddled and melodramatic. From the novel "The Snatchers" by Lionel White.
1969 (R) 93m/C Marlon Brando, Richard Boone, Rita Moreno, Pamela Franklin, Jess Hahn, Jacques Marin, Gerard Buhr, Hughes Wanner; **D:** Hubert Cornfield; **W:** Robert Phippeny, Hubert Cornfield. **VHS** $89.94 *MCA, FCT 𝙸𝙸*

Night of the Fox An American officer with top secret knowledge is captured by Germans on the brink of D-day. His home team plans to kill him if he cannot be rescued before spilling the beans. On-location filming adds much. Made for cable.
1990 (R) 95m/C Michael York, Deborah Raffin, George Peppard; **D:** Charles Jarrott. **VHS** $89.95 *VMK 𝙸𝙸*

Night of the Generals A Nazi intelligence officer is pursuing three Nazi generals who may be involved in the brutal murder of a Warsaw prostitute. Dark and sinister, may be too slow for some tastes. Based on Hans Helmut Kirst's novel. *AKA:* La Nuit de Generaux.
1967 (R) 148m/C Peter O'Toole, Omar Sharif, Tom Courtenay, Joanna Pettet, Donald Pleasence, Christopher Plummer, Philippe Noiret, John Gregson; **D:** Anatole Litvak; **M:** Maurice Jarre. **VHS, Beta** $9.95 *COL 𝙸𝙸𝙸*

Night of the Ghouls Second to last in Wood's celebrated series of inept horror films that began with "Bride of the Monster" and "Plan 9 from Outer Space." This one tells of a phony spiritualist who swindles the grieving by pretending to raise the dead. To his great surprise he actually does enliven some cadavers, who then go after him. Unreleased for over 20 years because Wood couldn't pay the film lab. Not quite as classically bad as his other films, but still a laugh riot. *AKA:* Revenge of the Dead.
1959 69m/B Paul Marco, Tor Johnson, Duke Moore, Kenne Duncan, John Carpenter, Criswell; **D:** Edward D. Wood Jr. **VHS, Beta** $9.95 *RHI, SNC, MED Woof!*

Night of the Grizzly An ex-lawman's peaceful life as a rancher is threatened when a killer grizzly bear goes on a murderous rampage terrorizing the residents of the Wyoming countryside.
1966 99m/C Clint Walker, Martha Hyer; **D:** Joseph Pevney. **VHS, Beta** $29.95 *PAR 𝙸𝙸*

Night of the Howling Beast The selling point of this one is an epic, first-time battle between a werewolf and a Yeti. Unfortunately it lasts about fifteen seconds. Naschy's eighth stint as the wolfman. *AKA:* The Werewolf and the Yeti.
1975 (R) 87m/C Paul Naschy, Grace Mills, Castillo Escalona, Silvia Solar, Gil Vidal; **D:** Miguel Iglesias Bonns. **VHS, Beta** *REP 𝙸*

The Night of the Hunter The nightmarish story of a psychotic preacher who marries a lonely widow with two children in the hopes of finding the cache of money her thieving husband had stashed. A dark, terrifying tale, completely unique in Hollywood's history. Mitchum is terrific. From novel by Davis Grubb and, sadly, Laughton's only directorial effort.
1955 93m/B Robert Mitchum, Shelley Winters, Lillian Gish, Don Beddoe, Evelyn Varden, Peter Graves, James Gleason, Billy Chapin, Sally Jane Bruce; **D:** Charles Laughton; **W:** James Agee. **VHS, Beta** $19.98 *MGM, VYG 𝙸𝙸𝙸𝙸*

The Night of the Iguana An alcoholic ex-minister acts as a tour guide in Mexico, becoming involved with a spinster and a hotel owner. Based on Tennessee Williams' play. Excellent performances from Burton and Gardner.
1964 125m/B Richard Burton, Deborah Kerr, Ava Gardner, Grayson Hall, Sue Lyon; **D:** John Huston. Academy Awards '64: Best Costume Design (B & W); Nominations: Best Art Direction/Set Decoration (B & W), Best Black and White Cinematography, Best Supporting Actress (Hall). **VHS, Beta** $19.98 *MGM 𝙸𝙸𝙸*

Night of the Juggler An ex-cop encounters countless obstacles in trying to track down his daughter's kidnapper in New York City. Just a tad too complicated for some tastes.
1980 (R) 101m/C James Brolin, Cliff Gorman, Richard Castellano, Mandy Patinkin, Julie Carmen; **D:** Robert Butler; **W:** William W. Norton Sr. **VHS, Beta** $49.95 *MED 𝙸𝙸½*

Night of the Kickfighters A mighty band of martial artists takes on a terrorist group that has in their possession a secret weapon that could destroy the world.
1991 87m/C Andy Bauman, Adam West, Marcia Karr; **D:** Buddy Reyes. **VHS** $89.98 *AIP 𝙸*

Night of the Laughing Dead Veteran British comedy cast perform unthinkable spoof. Man stands to inherit lotsa money as his family members kick the bucket one by one. *AKA:* Crazy House; House in Nightmare Park.
1975 90m/C Ray Milland, Frankie Howerd, Rosalie Crutchley, Kenneth Griffith; **D:** Peter Sykes. **VHS** *MGM 𝙸½*

Night of the Living Babes Two yuppie men go looking for fun at a brothel. They get their just deserts in the form of sex-seeking female zombies.
1987 60m/C Michelle (McClellan) Bauer, Connie Woods, Andrew Nichols, Louie Bonanno; **D:** Jon Valentine. **VHS** *NO Woof!*

Night of the Living Dead Cult favorite is low budget but powerfully frightening. Space experiments set off a high level of radiation that makes the newly dead return to life, with a taste for human flesh. Handful of holdouts find shelter in a farmhouse. Claustrophobic, terrifying, gruesome, extreme, and yes, humorous. Followed by "Dawn of the Dead" (1979) and "Day of the Dead" (1985). Romero's directorial debut. Available in a colorized version. *AKA:* Night of the Flesh Eaters.
1968 90m/B Judith O'Dea, Duane Jones, Russell Streiner, Karl Hardman; **D:** George A. Romero. **VHS** $19.95 *REP, MRV, NOS 𝙸𝙸𝙸½*

Night of the Living Dead A bunch of people are trapped in a farmhouse and attacked by ghouls with eating disorders. Remake of the '68 classic substitutes high tech blood 'n' guts for bona fide frights.
1990 (R) 92m/C Tony Todd, Patricia Tallman, Tom Towles; **D:** Tom Savini; **W:** George A. Romero. **VHS** $19.95 *COL 𝙸𝙸*

Night of the Living Dead, 25th Anniversary Documentary Features behind the scenes look at low-budget 1968 classic film about legions of dead people who stalk the earth looking for live humans to feed on.
1993 83m/C VHS $29.95 MTH ✍✍

Night of the Sharks Mercenaries in a downed plane go after a jewel-ridden shipwreck despite a plethora of sharks.
1989 87m/C Treat Williams, Christopher Connelly, Antonio Fargas, Janet Agren; D: Anthony Richmond. VHS, Beta $79.95 LIV, VTR Woof!

The Night of the Shooting Stars Set in an Italian village during the last days of WWII, this film highlights the schism in the village between those who support the fascists and those who sympathize with the Allies. This division comes to a head in the stunning final scene. A poignant, deeply moving film. AKA: The Night of San Lorenzo.
1982 (R) 106m/C Omero Antonutti, Margarita Lozano, Claudio Bigagli, Massimo Bonetti, Norma Martel; D: Paolo Taviani, Vittorio Taviani; W: Tonino Guerra, Giuliani G. De Negri, Paolo Taviani, Vittorio Taviani; M: Nicola Piovani. Cannes Film Festival Nominations: cs 82: Best Film; National Society of Film Critics Awards '83: Best Film. VHS, Beta $29.95 MGM, APD, AUD ✍✍✍✍

Night of the Sorcerers An expedition to the Congo uncovers a bizarre tribe of vampire leopard women who lure young girls to their deaths.
1970 85m/C Jack Taylor, Simon Andrew, Kali Hansa; D: Armando de Ossorio. VHS, Beta $49.95 UNI Woof!

Night of the Strangler A love affair between a white society girl and a young black man causes a chain of events that end with brutal murders in New Orleans.
1973 (R) 88m/C Mickey Dolenz, James Ralston, Susan McCullough; D: Joy Houck Jr. VHS, Beta NO ✍✍

Night of the Warrior Music videos and martial arts don't mix...not here, anyway. A hunky exotic-dance-club owner pays his disco bills by fighting in illegal, underground blood matches, but not enough to make it exciting. Lamas stars with real life wife Kinmont and mom Dahl.
1991 (R) 96m/C Lorenzo Lamas, Anthony Geary, Kathleen Kinmont, Arlene Dahl. VHS $89.95 VMK ✍

Night of the Wilding Very, very loosely based on the story of the female jogger who was gang-raped and left for dead in New York's Central Park. Made for television, soon after the actual incident occurred.
1990 90m/C Erik Estrada, Kathrin Lautner; D: Joseph Merhi. VHS, Beta NO ✍

Night of the Zombies WWII soldiers with eating disorders shuffle through 88 minutes of gratuitous gore, while pursued by porn star cum intelligence agent. From the director of "Bloodsucking Freaks." AKA: Gamma 693; Night of the Wehrmacht Zombies.
1981 (R) 88m/C James Gillis, Ryan Hilliard, Samantha Grey, Joel M. Reed; D: Joel M. Reed; W: Joel M. Reed. VHS $49.99 PSM ✍

Night of the Zombies Staff of a scientific research center are killed and then resurrected as cannibals who prey on the living. The living will suffer again if trapped into watching. Mattel is pseudonym for director Vincent Dawn. Cheap, dubbed, and possessing minimal coherence. AKA: Apocalipsis Canibal; Hell of the Living Dead; Zombie Creeping Flesh.
1983 101m/C Margit Evelyn Newton, Frank Garfield, Selan Karay; D: Bruno Mattei. VHS, Beta $49.95 VES, PSM Woof!

Night on Earth Jarmusch's "road" movie comprises five different stories taking place on the same night in five different cities—Los Angeles, New York, Paris, Rome, and Helsinki—between cabbies and their passengers. As with any anthology some stories work better than others but all have their moments in this ambitious film with its outstanding international cast. Subtitled in English for the three foreign segments.
1991 (R) 125m/C Winona Ryder, Gena Rowlands, Giancarlo Esposito, Armin Mueller-Stahl, Rosie Perez, Beatrice Dalle, Roberto Benigni, Paolo Bonacelli, Matti Pellonpaa, Kari Vaananen, Sakari Kuosmanen, Tomi Salmela; D: Jim Jarmusch; W: Jim Jarmusch; M: Tom Waits. VHS $19.95 NLC, ING, FFF ✍✍✍

Night Partners Bored housewives assist the police to patrol the streets after the kids have gone to bed. Originally made for television with the intention of turning it into a series, but the script doesn't hold water.
1983 100m/C Yvette Mimieux, Diana Canova, Arlen Dean Snyder, M. Emmet Walsh, Patricia Davis, Larry Linville; D: Noel Nosseck. VHS, Beta $39.95 NWV ✍½

The Night Patrol Talmadge is a cop who winds up arresting his girlfriend's brother for murder. Convinced the boy is innocent, Talmadge disguises himself in order to infiltrate the gang he thinks is actually responsible for the crime. Lots of derring-do and a last-minute rescue from the electric chair.
1926 53m/B Richard Talmadge, Mary Carr, Rose Blossom, Josef Swickard, Gardner James; D: Noel Mason Smith. VHS $16.95 GPV ✍✍½

Night Patrol The streets of Hollywood will never be the same after the night patrol runs amuck in the town. Crude imitation of "Police Academy."
1985 (R) 87m/C Linda Blair, Pat Paulsen, Jaye P. Morgan, Jack Riley, Murray Langston, Billy Barty, Noriyuki "Pat" Morita, Sydney Lassick, Andrew Dice Clay; D: Jackie Kong. VHS, Beta $9.95 NWV, STE Woof!

The Night Porter Max, an ex-SS concentration camp officer, unexpectedly meets his former lover-victim at the Viennese hotel where he works as the night porter. After they get reacquainted, the couple must hide from the porter's ex-Nazi friends who want the women dead because they fear she will disclose their past. A sado-masochistic voyage not for the faint-hearted. AKA: Il Portiere de Notte.
1974 (R) 115m/C Dirk Bogarde, Charlotte Rampling, Phillipe LeRoy, Gabriel Ferzetti, Isa Miranda; D: Liliana Cavani. VHS, Beta $19.98 SUE, GLV, ING ✍✍

Night Rhythms Nick West is a radio talk show host with a sexy voice that causes his women listeners to reveal their most intimate fantasies and problems to him on the air. When one listener goes too far, it's murder, and Nick must work to prove his innocence in the crime if he intends to save his career—and his life. Also available in an unrated version.
1992 (R) ?m/C Martin Hewitt, Delia Sheppard, David Carradine, Terry Tweed, Sam Jones, Deborah Driggs, Julie Strain; D: Alexander Gregory Hippolyte. VHS $89.95 IMP, MOV ✍½

Night Rider A cowboy posing as a gunman ends a trail of murder and violence in a small western town.
1932 54m/B Harry Carey Sr., George "Gabby" Hayes. VHS, Beta $19.95 NOS, DVT ✍

Night Riders of Montana A state ranger helps a group of ranchers to fight off a band of rustlers.
1950 60m/B Allan "Rocky" Lane. VHS, Beta $24.95 DVT ✍

Night Ripper A psychopathic killer stalks high fashion models and kills them by carving them up. Lots of violence.
1986 88m/C James Hansen, April Anne, Larry Thomas; D: Jeff Hathcock. VHS, Beta NO ✍

Night School A police detective must find out who has been decapitating the women attending night school at Wendell College. Ward's first film. AKA: Terror Eyes.
1981 (R) 89m/C Edward Albert, Rachel Ward, Leonard Mann, Drew Snyder, Joseph R. Sicari; D: Ken Hughes; M: Brad Fiedel. VHS, Beta $19.98 FOX ✍

Night Screams Violent scare-monger about two escaped convicts who crash a high school house party. Kids and convicts start getting killed, one by one.
1987 85m/C Joe Manno, Ron Thomas, Randy Lundsford, Megan Wyss; D: Allen Plone. VHS, Beta $79.95 PSM ✍

Night Shadow A woman, returning home after being away for years, picks up a hitchhiker. Soon after her arrival, terrible serial killings begin, and only she has the nerve to track down the killer.
1990 (R) 90m/C Brenda Vance, Dana Chan, Tom Boylan; D: Randolph Cohlan; W: Randolph Cohlan. VHS NO ✍

Night Shift Two morgue attendants, dull Winkler and manic Keaton, decide to spice up their latenight shift by running a call-girl service on the side. Keaton turns in a fine performance in his film debut, and Howard's sure-handed direction almost overcome the silly premise.
1982 (R) 106m/C Henry Winkler, Michael Keaton, Shelley Long, Kevin Costner, Pat Corley, Bobby DiCicco, Nita Talbot, Richard Belzer, Shannen Doherty; D: Ron Howard; W: Babaloo Mandel, Lowell Ganz; M: Burt Bacharach. VHS, Beta $19.98 WAR ✍✍

Night Slasher A madman enjoys spilling the innards of London prostitutes with his dagger.
1984 87m/C Jack May, Linda Marlowe. VHS, Beta $49.95 UNI ✍

Night Stage to Galveston Autry leads his Texas Rangers on a mission to uncover corruption in the Texas State Police during the turbulent post-Civil War era.
1952 61m/B Gene Autry, Pat Buttram, Virginia Huston, Thurston Hall; D: George Archainbaud. VHS, Beta $29.98 CCB ✍½

Night Stalker A bloodthirsty serial killer is tracked by a detective through the streets in New York. The usual mararole of fisticuffs, gunplay, and car chases ensure. Impressive acting from Napier raises the film from the run-of-the-mill.
1987 (R) 91m/C Charles Napier, John Goff, Robert Viharo, Robert Z'Dar, Joseph Gian, Gary Crosby, Joan Chen, Michelle Reese; D: Max Cleven. VHS, Beta $79.98 VES ✍✍

The Night Stalker: Two Tales of Terror Two episodes from the television series "Kolchak: The Night Stalker" in which McGavin plays a nosy newspaper reporter who constantly stumbles upon occult phenomenon. Episodes are "Jack the Ripper" and "The Vampire."
1974 98m/C Darren McGavin, Simon Oakland. VHS, Beta MCA ✍✍

Night Terror Everyone's after a hausfrau who saw a highway patrolman murdered on an expressway...including the psychotic murderer. Pretty standard fare. Made for television.
1976 73m/C Valerie Harper, Richard Romanus, Michael Tolan, Beatrice Manley, John Quade, Quinn Cummings, Nicholas Pryor; **D:** E.W. Swackhamer. **VHS, Beta $59.95** WOV ℐ

Night Terror A man wakes up from a nightmare only to find that his terrors are still present.
1989 90m/C Lloyd B. Mote, Jeff Keel, Guy Ecker, Jon Hoffman, Michael Coopet; **D:** Michael Weaver, Paul Howard. **VHS, Beta** NO ℐ

The Night the City Screamed It's the hottest day of the year, the city experiences a massive blackout, and nighttime brings out less-than-noble emotions amongst the citizenry. Made for television.
1980 (PG) 96m/C Raymond Burr, Georg Stanford Brown, Linda Purl, Robert Culp, Clifton Davis, David Cassidy, George DiCenzo, Gary Frank, Don Meredith, Shelley Smith, Vic Tayback, Dick Anthony Williams; **D:** Harry Falk; **W:** Larry Brody. **VHS $59.95** COL ℐℐ½

The Night the Lights Went Out in Georgia Loosely based on the popular hit song, the film follows a brother and sister as they try to cash in on the country music scene in Nashville. McNichol is engaging.
1981 (PG) 112m/C Kristy McNichol, Dennis Quaid, Mark Hamill, Don Stroud; **D:** Ronald F. Maxwell. **VHS, Beta $69.95** SUE, TWE ℐℐ

The Night They Raided Minsky's Chaotic but interesting period comedy about a young Amish girl who leaves her tyrannical father to come to New York City in the 1920s. She winds up at Minsky's Burlesque and accidentally invents the striptease. Lahr's last performance—he died during filming. ♫The Night They Raided Minsky's; Take Ten Terrific Girls But Only 9 Costumes; How I Love Her; Perfect Gentleman; You Rat, You; Penny Arcade; Wait For Me. *AKA:* The Night They Invented Striptease.
1969 (PG) 97m/C Jason Robards Jr., Britt Ekland, Elliott Gould, Bert Lahr, Norman Wisdom, Denholm Elliott; **D:** William Friedkin; **W:** Norman Lear, Arnold Schulman. **VHS, Beta $19.98** FOX ℐℐℐ

The Night They Robbed Big Bertha's Bungling burglar attempts to knock off Big Bertha's massage parlor.
1983 83m/C Robert Nichols. **VHS, Beta** NO ℐ

The Night They Saved Christmas A Christmas special in which Santa's North Pole headquarters are endangered by the progress of an expanding oil company. Will the attempts of three children be enough to save the day?
1987 94m/C Art Carney, Jaclyn Smith, Paul Williams, Paul LeMat; **D:** Jackie Cooper. **VHS, Beta $9.95** CAF, PSM ℐ½

Night Tide Hopper in another off the wall character study, this time as a lonely sailor. He falls for a mermaid (Lawson) who works at the dock. She may be a descendent of the man-killing Sirens. Interesting and different little love story, sometimes advertised as horror, which it is not.
1963 84m/B Dennis Hopper, Gavin Muir, Luana Anders, Marjorie Eaton, Tom Dillon; **D:** Curtis Harrington. **VHS $16.95** SNC, FRG, TPV ℐℐ½

Night Time in Nevada Young woman heads West to claim $50,000 trust left by dear old dad, but her crooked lawyer and associate have their hands in the pot. Cowboy Roy rides horse and flexes dimples while helping helpless girl.
1948 67m/B Roy Rogers, Adele Mara, Andy Devine, Grant Withers, Joseph Crehan; **D:** William Witney. **VHS, Beta, 8mm $19.95** NOS, HEG, VYY ℐℐ½

A Night to Remember A murder-mystery writer's wife convinces him to move to a new apartment because she thinks the change might help him finish a novel he started long ago. When they find a dead body behind their new building, they try their hands at sleuthing. A clever and witty mystery, indeed, supported by likeable performances.
1942 91m/B Loretta Young, Brian Aherne, Sidney Toler, Gale Sondergaard, William Wright, Donald MacBride, Blanche Yurka; **D:** Richard Wallace. **VHS $69.95** COL ℐℐℐ

A Night to Remember Gripping tale of the voyage of the Titanic with an interesting account of action in the face of danger and courage amid despair. Large cast is effectively used. Adapted by Eric Ambler from the book by Walter Lord.
1958 119m/B Kenneth More, David McCallum, Anthony Bushell, Honor Blackman, Michael Goodliffe, George Rose, Laurence Naismith, Frank Lawton, Alec McCowen; **D:** Roy Ward Baker; **W:** Eric Ambler. **VHS, Beta $19.95** PAR, HMV ℐℐℐ

The Night Train to Kathmandu A young girl accompanies her parents on a research expedition to Nepal, where her head is turned by an exotically handsome young Sherpa. Old story without much help from actors or director. Made for cable.
1988 102m/C Milla Jovovich, Pernell Roberts, Eddie Castrodad; **D:** Robert Wiemer. **VHS, Beta $14.95** PAR ℐℐ

Night Train to Munich There's Nazi intrigue galore aboard a big train when a scientist's daughter joins allied intelligence agents in retrieving some secret documents. From the book "Report on a Fugitive" by Gordon Wellesley. *AKA:* Night Train; Gestapo.
1940 93m/B Margaret Lockwood, Rex Harrison, Paul Henreid; **D:** Carol Reed. **VHS, Beta $24.95** NOS, DVT, HEG ℐℐℐ

Night Train to Terror Strange things start happening on the train where a rock band makes its last appearance. Clips from other horror flicks were pieced together to make this film that's so bad it's almost good.
1984 (R) 98m/C John Phillip Law, Cameron Mitchell, Marc Lawrence, Charles Moll, Ferdinand "Ferdy" Mayne; **D:** Jay Schlossberg-Cohen. **VHS, Beta $79.95** PSM *Woof!*

Night Vision A young writer in the big city is given a video monitor by a street thief which is equipped with some remarkable features, including the ability to present scenes of future murders and demon worship.
1987 102m/C Ellie Martins, Stacy Carson, Shirley Ross, Tony Carpenter; **D:** Michael Krueger. **VHS, Beta $79.95** PSM ℐ

The Night Visitor A man in a prison for the criminally insane seeks violent vengeance on those he believes have set him up. Heavily detailed, slow moving. Ullman and von Sydow can do better.
1970 (PG) 106m/C Max von Sydow, Liv Ullmann, Trevor Howard, Per Oscarsson, Andrew Keir; **D:** Laslo Benedek; **M:** Henry Mancini. **VHS, Beta $59.95** VCI ℐℐ½

Night Visitor A retired police detective teams up with a teenage peeping tom to disclose the identity of a satanic serial killer. The killer, of course, is one of the youth's teachers. *AKA:* Never Cry Devil.

1989 (R) 95m/C Derek Rydell, Shannon Tweed, Elliott Gould, Allen (Gooritz) Garfield, Michael J. Pollard, Richard Roundtree, Henry Gibson; **D:** Rupert Hitzig. **VHS, Beta $14.95** MGM ℐ

The Night Walker Stanwyck is always worth watching and she has the best moments in this psycho-thriller which suffers from a low-budget and confused script. The basic story has Stanwyck as a rich widow with a recurring nightmare featuring a faceless lover. There's also a too-helpful lawyer (Taylor), a suspicious private detective (Bochner)—and maybe her husband isn't so dead after all. Taylor and Stanwyck, who had once been married, worked together for the first time in 27 years.
1964 86m/B Barbara Stanwyck, Robert Taylor, Lloyd Bochner, Hayden Rorke, Judith Meredith, Rochelle Hudson; **D:** William Castle; **W:** Robert Bloch. **VHS $14.98** MCA, GPV ℐℐ½

Night Warning A slasher gorefest redeemed by Tyrrell's go-for-broke performance. She plays a sexually repressed aunt who makes up for her problems by going on murderous rampages. Hide the kitchen knives! *AKA:* Nightmare Maker; Butcher Baker (Nightmare Maker).
1982 (R) 96m/C Bo Svenson, Jimmy McNichol, Susan Tyrrell, Julia Duffy; **D:** William Asher. **VHS, Beta** NO ℐ

Night Wars Two ex-POWs who are plagued by their memories turn to dream therapy to relive their escape. Eventually, they rescue a buddy they left behind.
1988 90m/C Dan Haggerty, Brian O'Connor, Cameron Smith; **D:** David A. Prior. **VHS, Beta $14.95** COL ℐ½

Night Watch A woman recovering from a nervous breakdown witnesses a murder, but no one will believe her. *AKA:* Le Trou; Il Buco.
1972 100m/C Elizabeth Taylor, Laurence Harvey, Billie Whitelaw; **D:** Brian G. Hutton. **VHS, Beta $9.95** MED ℐ½

The Night We Never Met Three yuppies bring different visions of romance and a case of mistaken identity to a time-share apartment in New York's Greenwich Village. Sam (Broderick) needs a quiet space to get over being dumped by a flaky performance artist (Tripplehorn). Ellen (Sciorra) is looking for space to paint away from the confines of her thick-headed spouse (Mantell). Brian, the organizer of the living arrangement, wants a space where he can be one of the boys and escape from his cloying fiancee (Bateman). Fairly predictable but enjoyable romantic comedy.
1993 (R) 98m/C Matthew Broderick, Jeanne Tripplehorn, Kevin Anderson, Justine Bateman, Annabella Sciorra, Christine Baranski, Doris Roberts, Dominic Chianese, Michael Mantell, Tim Guinee, Greg Germann, Dana Wheeler-Nicholson, Louise Lasser, Bill Campbell, Ranjit Chowdhry, Garry Shandling, Katherine Houghton, Brooke Smith; **D:** Warren Leight; **W:** Warren Leight; **M:** Evan Lurie. **VHS** HBO ℐℐ½

Night Zoo A confusing story about a father/son reconciliation and the lurid underworld of drugs and sex in Montreal. The graphic sex and violence undermines the sensitive aspects of the film. *AKA:* Un Zoo, La Nuit.
1987 115m/C Gilles Maheu, Roger Le Bel, Lynne Adams, German Houde; **D:** Jean-Claude Lauzon. **VHS, Beta $9.99** STE, NWV, IME ℐℐ

Nightbreaker Revelation of the U.S. government's deliberate exposure of servicemen to atomic bomb tests and the resulting radiation, in order to observe the effects on humans. Sheen and his son, Estevez, portray

a U.S. doctor in the 1980s and the 1950s, respectively.
1989 100m/C Martin Sheen, Emilio Estevez, Lea Thompson, Melinda Dillon, Nicholas Pryor, Joe Pantoliano; **D:** Peter Markle; **W:** T.S. Cook; **M:** Peter Bernstein. **VHS** $9.98 *TTC* ✱✱

The Nightcomers A pretend "prequel" to Henry James's "The Turn of the Screw," wherein an Irish gardener trysts with the nanny of two watchful children who believe that lovers unite in death. Don't be fooled: stick to the original.
1972 (R) 96m/C Marlon Brando, Stephanie Beacham, Thora Hird; **D:** Michael Winner. **VHS, Beta** $14.95 *COL, NLC* ✱

Nightfall Ray, accused of a crime he didn't commit, is forced to flee from both the law and the underworld. Classic example of film noir, brilliantly filmed by Tourneur.
1956 78m/B Aldo Ray, Brian Keith, Anne Bancroft, Jocelyn Brando, James Gregory, Frank Albertson; **D:** Jacques Tourneur; **W:** Sterling Silliphant. **VHS** *GKK* ✱✱

Nightfall Television adaptation of the classic Isaac Asimov short story. A planet that has two suns (and therefore no night) experiences an eclipse and its inhabitants go mad.
1988 (PG-13) 87m/C David Birney, Sarah Douglas, Alexis Kanner, Andra Millian; **D:** Paul Mayersberg. **VHS, Beta** $79.95 *MGM* ✱✱

Nightflyers Aboard a weathered space freighter, the crew experience a series of deadly accidents caused by an unknown evil presence. From a novella by George R.R. Martin; T.C. Blake is better known as Robert Collector.
1987 (R) 88m/C Michael Praed, Michael Des Barres, Catherine Mary Stewart, John Standing, Lisa Blount; **D:** T.C. Blake. **VHS, Beta** *NO* ✱✱½

Nightforce Five buddies plunge into Central American jungles to rescue a young girl held by terrorists.
1986 (R) 87m/C Linda Blair, James Van Patten, Chad McQueen, Richard Lynch, Cameron Mitchell; **D:** Lawrence Foldes. **VHS, Beta** *NO* ✱

Nighthawks New York City cops scour Manhattan to hunt down an international terrorist on the loose. They race from disco to subway to an airborne tramway. Exciting and well paced. Hauer's American film debut.
1981 (R) 100m/C Sylvester Stallone, Billy Dee Williams, Rutger Hauer, Lindsay Wagner, Nigel Davenport, Persis Khambatta, Catherine Mary Stewart, Joe Spinell; **D:** Bruce Malmuth; **M:** Keith Emerson. **VHS, Beta** $19.98 *MCA* ✱✱½

The Nightingale From "Faerie Tale Theatre" comes the story of an Emperor who discovers the value of true friendship and loyalty from his palace kitchen maid who gives him a nightingale.
1983 60m/C Mick Jagger, Barbara Hershey, Bud Cort, Mako; **D:** Ivan Passer. **VHS, Beta** $14.98 *KUI, FOX, FCT* ✱✱½

Nightkill Simple love affair turns into a deadly game of cat and mouse when a bored wife plots to do away with her wealthy, powerful husband with the aid of her attractive lover. Mitchum is the reluctant investigator pulled into the game.
1980 (R) 104m/C Jaclyn Smith, Mike Connors, James Franciscus, Robert Mitchum, Sybil Danning; **D:** Ted Post. **VHS, Beta** $24.98 *SUE, NLC* ✱✱½

Nightlife An ancient vampiress who rises from the dead spends her time haunting a blood clinic, where the Jewish hematologist starts to fall for her. Made for cable.
1990 93m/C Ben Cross, Maryam D'Abo, Keith Szarabajka, Jesse Corti, Oliver Clark, Glenn Shadix, Camille Saviola; **D:** Daniel Taplitz. **VHS, Beta** $79.95 *MCA* ✱✱½

The Nightman Ex-soldier Marcoux becomes the night manager of a failing southern resort, run by sexy, and lonely, Kerns. They begin an affair, which turns sour when Roberston, Kerns' teenaged daughter, also falls for the stud. Then mom is murdered and Marcoux goes to prison. But 18 years later Robertson's past comes back to haunt her. Just what did happen all those years ago? Made for television thriller with additional footage.
1993 (R) 96m/C Ted Marcoux, Jenny Robertson, Joanna Kerns; **D:** Charles Haid; **W:** James Poe; **M:** Gary Chang. **VHS** *APX* ✱✱

Nightmare Boring splatterthon has a young boy hacking his father and his aggressive mistress to pieces when he discovers them in bed. He grows up to be a psycho who continues along the same lines. Humorless and dreadful, the original ads claimed Tom Savini did the special effects. He had nothing to do with it. *AKA:* Blood Splash.
1982 (R) 97m/C Baird Stafford, Sharon Smith, C.J. Cooke, Mik Cribben, Kathleen Ferguson, Danny Ronan; **D:** Romano Scavolini; **W:** Romano Scavolini. **VHS, Beta** *NO Woof!*

Nightmare at Bittercreek Four babes and a tour guide are pursued by psycho gang in the Sierra mountains. Made for television nightmare in your living room.
1991 (PG-13) 92m/C Tom Skerritt, Joanna Cassidy, Lindsay Wagner, Constance McCashin, Janne Mortil; **D:** Tim Burstall. **VHS** $89.95 *VMK* ✱✱

Nightmare at 43 Hillcrest A family's life becomes a living hell when the police mistakenly raid their house. Based on a true story.
1974 72m/C Jim Hutton, Mariette Hartley. **VHS, Beta** *NO* ✱✱

Nightmare at Noon Watered-down thriller about a small desert town beset by violent terrorists (who are really locals gone mad from a chemical experiment dumped into the water system). Only the sheriff's small staff is there to stop them.
1987 (R) 96m/C Wings Hauser, George Kennedy, Bo Hopkins, Brion James, Kimberly Beck, Kimberly Ross; **D:** Nico Mastorakis. **VHS** $79.98 *REP* ✱

The Nightmare Before Christmas Back when he was a animator trainee at Disney, Burton came up with this adventurous idea but couldn't get it made; subsequent directorial success brought more clout. Relies on a painstaking stop-motion technique that took more than two years to film and is justifiably amazing. The story revolves around Jack Skellington, the Pumpkin King of the dangerously weird Halloweentown. Suffering from ennui, he accidentally discovers the wonders of Christmastown and decides to kidnap Santa and rule over this peaceable holiday. Fast pace is maintained by the equally breathless score. Not cuddly, best appreciated by those with a feel for the macabre. *AKA:* Tim Burton's The Nightmare Before Christmas.
1993 (PG) 75m/C D: Henry Selick; **M:** Danny Elfman; **V:** Danny Elfman, Chris Sarandon, Catherine O'Hara, William Hickey, Ken Page, Ed Ivory. **VHS** *BVV* ✱✱✱

Nightmare Castle Jealous mad scientist murders his wife and her lover. Then he conducts a bizarre experiment, using the dead couple's blood to rejuvenate an old servant. Not quite satisfied with his revenge, he then seeks to marry his late wife's sister after realizing that she has been left the inheritance. In time, the perturbed ghosts of the late lovers appear and seek revenge. A

real nightmare. *AKA:* Amanti d'Oltretomba; Night of the Doomed; The Faceless Monsters; Lovers From Beyond the Tomb.
1965 90m/B Barbara Steele, Paul Muller, Helga Line; **D:** Allan Grunewald; **M:** Ennio Morricone. **VHS, Beta** $44.95 *SNC, HHT* ✱✱

Nightmare in Badham County Two girls get arrested on trumped-up charges in a small backwoods town. They soon discover that the prison farm is a front for a slavery ring. Made for television. *AKA:* Nightmare.
1976 100m/C Deborah Raffin, Lynne Moody, Chuck Connors, Della Reese, Robert Reed, Ralph Bellamy, Tina Louise; **D:** John Llewellyn Moxey; **M:** Charles Bernstein. **VHS, Beta** $19.95 *VMK* ✱

Nightmare in Blood Vampires lurk in San Francisco and wreak havoc on the night life. *AKA:* Horror Convention.
1975 90m/C Kerwin Mathews, Jerry Walter, Barrie Youngfellow; **D:** John Stanley. **VHS, Beta** $59.95 *VCD* ✱½

Nightmare in Red China A campy film examining life in communist China with an all-Indian cast.
1955 67m/B **VHS, Beta** *NO Woof!*

Nightmare in Wax After suffering disfigurement in a fight with a studio boss, a former make-up man starts a wax museum. For fun, he injects movie stars with a formula that turns them into statues. *AKA:* Crimes in the Wax Museum.
1969 91m/C Cameron Mitchell, Anne Helm; **D:** Bud Townsend. **VHS, Beta** $29.95 *VCI, MRV* ✱½

A Nightmare on Elm Street Feverish, genuinely frightening horror film about Freddy Krueger (Englund), a scarred maniac in a fedora and razor-fingered gloves who kills neighborhood teens in their dreams and, subsequently, in reality. Of the children-fight-back genre, in which the lead victim (Langenkamp) ingeniously goes to great lengths to destroy Freddy. In the tradition of "Friday the 13th" and "Halloween;" spawned a "Freddy" phenomenon: five sequels (to date); a TV series ("Freddy's Nightmares;" a horror anthology show hosted by Englund capitalized on his character); and an army of razor-clawed trick or treaters at Halloween.
1984 (R) 92m/C John Saxon, Heather Langenkamp, Ronee Blakley, Robert Englund, Amanda Wyss, Nick Corri, Johnny Depp, Charles Fleischer; **D:** Wes Craven; **W:** Wes Craven; **M:** Charles Bernstein. **VHS, Beta** $24.95 *MED, CVS, IME* ✱✱½

A Nightmare on Elm Street 2: Freddy's Revenge Mediocre sequel to the popular horror film. Freddy, the dream-haunting psychopath with the ginsu knife hands, returns to possess a teenager's body in order to kill again. Nothing new here, however praise is due for the stunning high-tech dream sequence.
1985 (R) 87m/C Mark Patton, Hope Lange, Clu Gulager, Robert Englund, Kim Myers; **D:** Jack Sholder; **W:** David Chaskin. **VHS, Beta** $34.95 *MED, CVS, IME* ✱½

A Nightmare on Elm Street 3: Dream Warriors Chapter three in this slice and dice series. Freddy Krueger is at it again, haunting the dreams of unsuspecting suburban teens. Langenkamp, the nightmare-freaked heroine from the first film, returns to counsel the latest victims of Freddy-infested dreams. Noted for the special effects wizardry but little else, Part Three was produced on a $4.5 million shoe string and took in more than $40 million, making it one of the most successful independently

produced films in Hollywood. Followed by "Nightmare on Elmstreet 4: Dream Master."
1987 (R) 96m/C Patricia Arquette, Robert Englund, John Saxon, Craig Wasson, Heather Langenkamp, Dick Cavett, Priscilla Pointer, Laurence "Larry" Fishburne; *D:* Chuck Russell; *W:* Chuck Russell, Bruce Wagner, Wes Craven, Frank Darabont; *M:* Angelo Badalamenti. **VHS, Beta $36.95** *MED, CVS, IME* ⅟₂⅟₂⅟₂

A Nightmare on Elm Street 4: Dream Master Freddy Krueger is still preying on people in their dreams, but he may have met his match as he battles for supremacy with a telepathically talented girl. What Part 4 lacks in substance, it makes up for in visual verve, including scenes of a kid drowning in his waterbed, and a pizza covered with pepperoni-like faces of Freddy's previous victims. This box office bonanza set a new record as the most successful opening weekend of any independently released film. Followed by "A Nightmare on Elm Street: A Dream Child."
1988 (R) 99m/C Robert Englund, Rodney Eastman, Danny Hassel, Andras Jones, Tuesday Knight, Lisa Wilcox, Ken Sagoes, Toy Newkirk, Brooke Theiss, Brooke Bundy; *D:* Renny Harlin; *W:* Scott Pierce, Brian Helgeland; *M:* Craig Safan. **VHS, Beta $36.95** *MED, CVS, IME* ⅟₂⅟₂

A Nightmare on Elm Street 5: Dream Child The fifth installment of Freddy Krueger's never-ending adventures. Here, America's favorite knife-wielding burn victim, unable to best the Dream Master from the previous film, haunts the dreams of her unborn fetus. Gore fans may be disappointed to discover that much of the blood and guts ended up on the cutting room floor.
1989 (R) 90m/C Robert Englund, Lisa Wilcox, Kelly Jo Minter, Danny Hassel; *D:* Stephen Hopkins; *M:* Jay Michael Ferguson. **VHS, Beta $89.95** *IME, MED, VTR* ⅟₂⅟₂

Nightmare on the 13th Floor A travel writer at an old hotel glimpses murder on a supposedly non-existent floor. Nasty devil-worshippers are afoot, but the chills in this mild made-for-cable throwaway seldom dip below room temperature.
1990 (PG-13) 85m/C Michael Greene, John Karlen, Louise Fletcher, Alan Fudge, James Brolin; *D:* Walter Grauman. **VHS, Beta** *PAR* ⅟

Nightmare Sisters Three sorority sisters become possessed by a demon and then sexually ravage a nearby fraternity.
1987 (R) 83m/C Brinke Stevens, Michelle (McClellan) Bauer, Linnea Quigley; *D:* David DeCoteau. **VHS, Beta $79.95** *TWE Woof!*

Nightmare Weekend A professor's evil assistant lures three young women into his lab and performs cruel and vicious experiments that transform the girls and their dates into crazed zombies.
1986 86m/C Dale Midkiff, Debbie Laster, Debra Hunter, Lori Lewis; *D:* Henry Sala. **VHS, Beta $79.98** *LIV* ⅟

The Nightmare Years An American reporter in Nazi Germany dares to report the truth to an unbelieving world. Based on a true story. Two cassettes.
1989 237m/C Sam Waterston, Marthe Keller, Kurtwood Smith; *D:* Anthony Page; *M:* Vladimir Cosma. **VHS, Beta $89.98** *TTC* ⅟

Nightmares A less-than-thrilling horror anthology featuring four tales in which common, everyday occurrences take on the ingredients of a nightmare. In the same vein as "Twilight Zone" and "Creepshow."
1983 (PG) 99m/C Christina Raines, Emilio Estevez, Moon Zappa, Lance Henriksen, Richard Masur, Veronica Cartwright; *D:* Joseph Sargent; *W:* Jeffrey Bloom, Christopher Crowe. **VHS, Beta $59.95** *MCA* ⅟⅟

Nights and Days Adaptation of writer Maria Dabrowska's tale about a Polish family chronicles the persecution, expulsions, and land grabbing that occurred after the unsuccessful Uprising of 1864. In Polish with English subtitles.
1976 255m/C Jadwiga Baranska, Jerzy Binczycki; *D:* Jerzy Antczak. **VHS $69.95** *FCT* ⅟⅟½

Nights in White Satin A made-for-video Cinderella story about the growing love between a fashion photographer and a young model whose boyfriend has just been murdered.
1987 96m/C Kenneth Gilman, Priscilla Harris; *D:* Michael Bernard. **VHS, Beta $79.95** *PSM, PAR* ⅟½

Nights of Cabiria Fellini classic which details the personal decline of a naive prostitute who thinks she's found true love. In Italian with English subtitles or dubbed. Basis for the musical "Sweet Charity." *AKA:* Le Nottie de Cabiria; Cabiria.
1957 111m/B Giulietta Masina, Amadeo Nazzari; *D:* Federico Fellini; *W:* Federico Fellini, Tullio Pinelli, Ennio Flaino. **VHS, Beta $29.95** *NOS, VYY, APD* ⅟⅟⅟½

Nightstalker A brother and sister who were condemned to eternal death 12,000 years ago must eat virgins to keep their bodies from rotting. Trouble is, while they search for dinner, the movie decomposes. For mature audiences with no fantasies of celluloid nirvana.
1979 90m/C Aldo Ray. **VHS, Beta $39.95** *LIV Woof!*

Nightstick New York vigilante cop fights nasties who threaten to blow the lid off the city. Worse, they kidnap super cop's girl forcing him to save her along with the city. Lots of violence, predictable plot, and mediocre acting leave this one without much bang. *AKA:* Calhoun.
1987 (R) 90m/C Bruce Fairbairn, Kerrie Keane, John Vernon, Robert Vaughn, Isaac Hayes, Leslie Nielsen; *D:* Joseph L. Scanlan. **VHS, Beta $79.95** *COL* ⅟½

Nightwing Suspense drama about three people who risk their lives to exterminate a colony of plague-carrying vampire bats in New Mexican Indian community. From the novel by Martin Cruz Smith and adapted by Smith, Steve Shagan, and Bud Shrake. OK viewing for the undiscriminating palate.
1979 (PG) 103m/C Nick Mancuso, David Warner, Kathryn Harrold, Strother Martin; *D:* Arthur Hiller; *M:* Henry Mancini. **VHS, Beta $39.95** *COL* ⅟½

Nightwish Students do more than homework when a professor leads them into their own horrifying dreams. Soon it becomes impossible to distinguish dreams from reality.
1989 (R) 96m/C Jack Starrett, Robert Tessier; *D:* Bruce Cook Jr. **VHS $89.95** *VES* ⅟½

Nijinsky An opulent biography of the famous ballet dancer. His exciting and innovative choreography gets little attention. The film concentrates on his infamous homosexual lifestyle and his relationship with impresario Sergei Diaghilev (Bates, in a tour-de-force performance). Lovely to look at, but slow and unconvincing.
1980 (R) 125m/C Alan Bates, George de la Pena, Leslie Browne, Alan Badel, Carla Fracci, Colin Blakely, Ronald Pickup, Ronald Lacey, Vernon Dobtcheff, Jeremy Irons, Frederick Jaeger, Janet Suzman, Sian Phillips; *D:* Herbert Ross. **VHS, Beta $29.95** *PAR* ⅟⅟

Nikki, the Wild Dog of the North When a Malemute pup is separated from his Canadian trapper master, he teams up with a bear cub for a series of adventures. Later the pup is reunited with his former master for still more adventures. Adapted from a novel by James Oliver Curwood for Disney.
1961 (G) 73m/C Jean Coutu; *D:* Jack Couffer, Don Haldane. **VHS, Beta $69.95** *DIS* ⅟½

Nine Ages of Nakedness The story of a man whose ancestors have been plagued by a strange problem: beautiful, naked women who create carnal chaos.
1969 88m/C Harrison Marks. **VHS, Beta $19.95** *VDM, MED, MRV* ⅟

9 1/2 Ninjas A cautious and disciplined martial artist trains a young and flirtatious woman in the ways of the ninja. His life becomes exciting in more ways than one, when he realizes she's being followed by ninjas with more on their minds than her training—they want to assassinate her! Crazy mixture of sex, kung fu and humor make this film one surprise after another.
1990 88m/C Michael Phenicie, Andee Gray, Tiny Lister; *D:* Aaron Worth. **VHS, Beta $9.98** *REP* ⅟⅟½

9 1/2 Weeks Chance meeting between a Wall Street exec and an art gallery employee evolves into an experimental sexual relationship bordering on sado-masochism. Video version is more explicit than the theatrical release, but not by much. Strong characterizations by both actors prevent this from being strictly pornography. Well-written, with strength of male and female personalities nicely balanced. Intriguing, but not for all tastes.
1986 (R) 114m/C Mickey Rourke, Kim Basinger, Margaret Whitton, Karen Young, David Margulies, Christine Baranski, Roderick Cook, Dwight Weist; *D:* Adrian Lyne; *W:* Patricia Louisianna Knop, Zalman King; *M:* Jack Nitzsche. **VHS, Beta $19.95** *MGM* ⅟⅟½

Nine Days a Queen An historical drama based on the life of Lady Jane Grey, proclaimed Queen of England after the death of Henry VIII of England and summarily executed for treason by Mary Tudor after a nine-day reign. An obscure tragedy with good performances and absorbing storyline. Remade as "Lady Jane" (1985). *AKA:* Lady Jane Grey; Tudor Rose.
1934 80m/B John Mills, Cedric Hardwicke, Nova Pilbeam, Sybil Thorndike, Leslie Perrins, Felix Aylmer, Miles Malleson; *D:* Robert Stevenson. **VHS, Beta $44.95** *HHT, DVT* ⅟⅟⅟

Nine Deaths of the Ninja Faceless ninja warrior Kosugi leads a team of commandos on a mission to rescue a group of political prisoners held captive in the Philippine jungles. Features Ozone-depleted plot, incongruous performances, and inane dialogue, not to mention two main villains—a neurotic Nazi in a wheelchair and a black lesbian amazon—who chew jungle and bring bad art to a new level of appreciation. Amazing in its total badness. Produced by Cannon.
1985 (R) 93m/C Sho Kosugi, Brent Huff, Emelia Lesniak, Regina Richardson; *D:* Emmett Alston; *W:* Emmett Alston. **VHS, Beta $69.95** *MED Woof!*

The Nine Lives of Elfego Baca Venerable Western hero Loggia faces a veritable army of gunfighters and bandits. Action-packed but not too violent; family fun.
1958 78m/C Robert Loggia, Robert Simon, Lisa Montell, Nestor Paiva; *D:* Norman Foster. **VHS, Beta $69.95** *DIS* ⅟⅟

Nine Lives of Fritz the Cat Fritz feels that life's too square in the 70's, so he takes off into some of his other lives for more adventure. Cleaner but still naughty sequel to the X-rated "Fritz the Cat," featuring neither the original's writer/director Ralph Bakshi nor cartoonist Robert Crumb. Tame and lame. Animated.
1974 77m/C D: Robert Taylor. **VHS** $19.98 VES ♂♂

9 to 5 In this caricature of large corporations and women in the working world, Coleman plays the male chauvinist boss who calls the shots and keeps his employees, all female, under his thumb. Three of the office secretaries daydream of Coleman's disposal and rashly kidnap him after a silly set of occurrences threaten their jobs. While they have him under lock and key, the trio take office matters into their own hands and take a stab at running things their own way, with amusing results. The basis for a television series.
1980 (PG) 111m/C Jane Fonda, Lily Tomlin, Dolly Parton, Dabney Coleman, Sterling Hayden; **D:** Colin Higgins; **W:** Patricia Resnick; **M:** Charles Fox. **VHS, Beta** $19.98 FOX ♂♂½

976-EVIL Englund (the infamous Freddy from the Nightmare on Elm Street epics) directs this horror movie where a lonely teenager dials direct to demons from hell.
1988 (R) 102m/C Stephen Geoffreys, Jim Metzler, Maria Rubell, Sandy Dennis, Robert Picardo, Leslie Deane, Pat O'Bryan; **D:** Robert Englund; **M:** Tom Chase, Steve Rucker. **VHS, Beta** $14.95 COL ♂♂

976-EVIL 2: The Astral Factor Satan returns the call in this supernatural thriller that sequels the original film.
1991 (R) 93m/C Pat O'Bryan, Rene Assa, Debbie James; **D:** Jim Wynorski; **W:** Erik Anjou. **VHS** $14.98 LIV, VES ♂½

984: Prisoner of the Future A shocking, futuristic tale of human self-destruction.
1984 70m/C Don Francks, Stephen Markle. **VHS, Beta** NO ♂½

1900 Bertolucci's impassioned epic about two Italian families, one land-owning, the other, peasant. Shows the sweeping changes of the 20th century begun by the trauma of WWI and the onslaught of Italian socialism. Edited down from its original 360-minute length and dubbed in English from three other languages, the film suffers somewhat from editing and from its nebulous lack of commitment to any genre. Elegantly photographed by Vittorio Storaro. Also titled "Novecento."
1976 (R) 255m/C Robert De Niro, Gerard Depardieu, Burt Lancaster, Donald Sutherland, Dominique Sanda, Sterling Hayden, Laura Betti, Francesca Bertini, Werner Bruhns, Stefania Sandrelli, Anna Henkel, Alida Valli; **D:** Bernardo Bertolucci; **W:** Giuseppe Bertolucci. **VHS, Beta** $29.95 PAR, ING ♂♂♂

1918 An adaptation of the Horton Foote play about the effects of WWI and an influenza epidemic on a small Texas town. Slow-moving but satisfying. Score by Willie Nelson. Originally produced for PBS's "American Playhouse." Prequelled by "On Valentine's Day."
1985 89m/C Matthew Broderick, Hallie Foote, William Converse-Roberts, Rochelle Oliver, Michael Higgins, Horton Foote Jr., William Bill McGhee, Jeannie McCarthy; **D:** Ken Harrison; **W:** Horton Foote; **M:** Willie Nelson. **VHS, Beta** $79.98 FOX ♂♂½

1931: Once Upon a Time in New York Prohibition-era gangsters war, beat each other up, make headlines, and drink bathtub gin.
1972 90m/C Richard Conte, Adolfo Celi, Lionel Stander, Irene Papas. **VHS, Beta** $59.95 VCD ♂♂

1939, The Movies' Vintage Year: Trailers on Tape A compilation of coming attractions from such classics as "Gunga Din," "Idiot's Delight," "Juarez," "Dark Victory" and "Gone With The Wind." Some segments are in color.
1939 60m/B Cary Grant, Clark Gable, Vivien Leigh. **VHS, Beta** $34.95 SFR ♂♂

1941 Proved to be the most expensive comedy of all time with a budget exceeding $35 million. The depiction of Los Angeles in the chaotic days after the bombing of Pearl Harbor combines elements of fantasy and black humor.
1979 (PG) 120m/C John Belushi, Dan Aykroyd, Patti LuPone, Ned Beatty, Slim Pickens, Murray Hamilton, Christopher Lee, Tim Matheson, Toshiro Mifune, Warren Oates, Robert Stack, Nancy Allen, Elisha Cook Jr., Lorraine Gary, Treat Williams, Mickey Rourke, John Candy; **D:** Steven Spielberg; **W:** Robert Zemeckis, Bob Gale; **M:** John Williams. **VHS, Beta** $14.95 MCA, CCB ♂♂½

1969 Three teenage friends during the 1960s become radicalized by the return of one of their friends from Vietnam in a coffin. Critically lambasted directorial debut for "On Golden Pond" author Ernest Thompson.
1989 (R) 96m/C Kiefer Sutherland, Robert Downey Jr., Winona Ryder, Bruce Dern, Joanna Cassidy, Mariette Hartley; **D:** Ernest Thompson. **VHS, Beta** $19.98 MED ♂♂♂½

1984 A very fine adaptation of George Orwell's infamous novel, this version differs from the overly simplistic and cautionary 1954 film because of fine casting and production design. The illegal love affair of a government official becomes his attempt to defy the crushing inhumanity and lack of simple pleasures of an omniscient government. Filmed in London, it skillfully visualizes our time's most central prophetic nightmare.
1984 (R) 117m/C John Hurt, Richard Burton, Suzanna Hamilton, Cyril Cusack, Gregory Fisher, Andrew Wilde, Rupert Baderman; **D:** Michael Radford. **VHS, Beta** $19.95 LIV ♂♂♂½

1990: The Bronx Warriors Good street gang members combat evil corporate powers in a semi-futuristic South Bronx. Lame copy of "Escape from New York." **AKA:** 1990 I Guerrieri del Bronx; Bronx Warriors.
1983 (R) 86m/C Vic Morrow, Christopher Connelly, Fred Williamson; **D:** Enzo G. Castellari. **VHS, Beta** $59.95 MED Woof!

1991: The Year Punk Broke Documents a grunge rock tour of European festivals in 1991 when the alternative bands were largely unknown to all but hardcore fans. Follows Sonic Youth, Nirvana, Dinosaur Jr., Babes in Toyland, Gumball, and grandaddy punk idols, The Ramones, behind-the-scenes and through their performances.
1992 95m/C D: David Markey. **VHS** $19.99 MOV Woof!

90 Days Charming independently made Canadian comedy about two young men handling their respective romantic dilemmas—one awaiting an oriental fiancee he's never met, the other who is being kicked out of his house by his wife.
1986 99m/C Stefan Wodoslowsky, Sam Grana, Christine Pak; **D:** Giles Walker. **VHS, Beta** $79.98 FOX ♂♂♂

92 in the Shade Based upon McGuane's novel, the film deals with a bored, wealthy rogue who becomes a fishing guide in the Florida Keys, and battles against the competition of two crusty, half-mad codgers. Sloppy, irreverent comedy as only a first-time writer-turned-director can fashion.
1976 (R) 91m/C Peter Fonda, Warren Oates, Margot Kidder, Burgess Meredith, Harry Dean Stanton; **D:** Thomas McGuane; **W:** Thomas McGuane. **VHS, Beta** $59.98 FOX ♂♂♂

99 & 44/100 Dead Frankenheimer falters with this silly gangster flick. Harris is hired to kill Dillman, by local godfather O'Brien. Originally written as a satirical look at gangster movies, but it doesn't stick to satire, and as a result is disappointing. **AKA:** Call Harry Crown.
1974 (PG) 98m/C Richard Harris, Chuck Connors, Edmond O'Brien, Bradford Dillman, Ann Turkel; **D:** John Frankenheimer; **W:** Robert Dillon; **M:** Henry Mancini. **VHS** FOX ♂

99 Women Sympathetic prison warden attempts to investigate conditions at a women's prison camp. Thin and exploitative view of lesbianism behind bars that sensationalizes the subject. **AKA:** Isle of Lost Women.
1969 (R) 90m/C Maria Schell, Herbert Lom, Mercedes McCambridge, Lucianna Paluzzi; **D:** Jess (Jesus) Franco. **VHS, Beta** $39.98 NO ♂½

Ninja 3: The Domination Ninja master must remove the spirit of a deadly ninja assassin from a young woman intent on wreaking havoc among the Phoenix police department. Extremely silly super ninja epic utterly uninhibited by the usual plot conventions.
1984 (R) 92m/C Lucinda Dickey, Sho Kosugi; **D:** Sam Firstenberg; **W:** James R. Silke. **VHS, Beta** $14.95 MGM ♂♂

Ninja Academy Seven wimps, losers, and spoiled brats come to the Ninja Academy to learn the art. Will they make it?
1990 (R) 93m/C Will Egan, Kelly Randall, Gerald Okomura, Michael David, Robert Factor, Jeff Robinson; **D:** Nico Mastorakis. **VHS** NO ♂½

Ninja: American Warrior An evil ninja takes on the U.S. Drug Enforcement Agency when the authorities threaten to shut him down.
1990 90m/C Joff Houston, John Wilford; **D:** Tommy Cheng. **VHS, Beta** $59.95 IMP ♂½

Ninja Brothers of Blood A guy falls for a rival gang member's girl. Neither the gang nor the guy's former girlfriend take kindly to this!
1989 90m/C Marcus Gibson, Fonda Lynn, Brian McClave, Jonathan Soper; **D:** Raymond Woo. **VHS, Beta** $59.95 IMP ♂

Ninja Champion White-clad and masked ninja heros come to the aid of some Interpol agents tracking down a sleazy diamond smuggler. Invisible storyline features very little actual ninja. Extremely unconvincing and poorly dubbed.
198? 90m/C Bruce Baron, Richard Harrison; **D:** Godfrey Ho; **W:** Godfrey Ho. **VHS, Beta** $39.95 TWE Woof!

Ninja Checkmate An evil ninja seems indestructible, but finally he meets his match.
1990 90m/C Simon Lee, Jack Long, Jeanie Chang. **VHS, Beta** $49.95 OCE ♂

Ninja Commandments Everything is at stake when an evil warrior takes on the greatest fighter in the land: the winner will rule the empire!
1987 90m/C Richard Harrison, Dave Wheeler; **D:** Joseph Lai. **VHS, Beta** $59.95 IMP ♂

Ninja Condors A young man grows up to avenge the murder of his father.

1987 85m/C Alexander Lou, Stuart Hugh; *D:* James Wu. **VHS, Beta** $59.95 *TWE* 🎬

Ninja Connection Ninja terrorism is employed as a scare tactic to deter a group who wants to break up an international drug ring.
1990 90m/C Patricia Greenford, Jane Kingsly, Joe Nelson, Louis Roth, Henry Steele, Stuart Steen; *D:* York Lam. **VHS, Beta** $59.95 *IMP*

Ninja Death Squad A team specializing in political assassinations is hunted down by a special agent.
1987 89m/C Glen Carson, Patricia Goodman, Joff Houston, Billy Jones, Wallace Jones, John Wilford; *D:* Tommy Cheng. **VHS, Beta** $59.95 *IMP* 🎬

Ninja Demon's Massacre Ninja named Willie responds to federal investigations into his spying business by wearing a black robe and slashing feds with long swords.
198? 89m/C Ted Brooke, James Lear. **VHS, Beta** $59.95 *TWE*

Ninja Destroyer Ninja warriors battle over an emerald mine.
197? (R) 92m/C Bruce Baron, Stuart Smith; *D:* Godfrey Ho; *W:* Godfrey Ho. **VHS, Beta** $19.98 *TWE* 🎬

Ninja Dragon Two Ninjas are hired in a gang war and dazzle all those who watch by kicking their enemies to death.
198? 92m/C Richard Harrison. **VHS, Beta** $59.95 *TWE* 🎬

Ninja Exterminators Low-grade kung-fu antics mascarading as ninja rib-kicking bonanza. Dubbed.
1981 85m/C Jacky Cheng, Ko Shou Liang, Tai Chen. **VHS, Beta** *NO Woof!*

Ninja Fantasy Ninja drug smugglers and government officials battle over a large drug shipment. Everybody go chop socky. Not much in way of ninja fantasy. Dubbed.
1986 95m/C Adam Nell, Ian Frank, Jordan Heller, Ken Ashley, Jenny Mills, Jack Rodman; *D:* Bruce Lambert; *W:* Anthony Green. **VHS, Beta** $59.95 *TWE Woof!*

Ninja Hunt This time, ninjas kick international terrorists in the head while searching for secret formula. Poorly dubbed pseudo ninja developed by Godfrey Ho.
198? 92m/C Bruce Baron, Stuart Smith; *D:* Joseph Lai; *W:* Stephen Saul. **VHS, Beta** $59.95 *TWE Woof!*

Ninja Massacre Gangsters covet a secret manual of kung fu techniques. Heel-splintering battles break out as a result.
1984 87m/C Lo Lieh, Pai Ying, Lung Jun Ehr, Tiki Shirtee. **VHS, Beta** *GEM, MRV* 🎬

Ninja Masters of Death Terrorists reign supreme until the white ninja saves the city.
1985 90m/C Mick Jones, Chris Petersen, Daniel Wells, Richard Young; *D:* Bruce Lambert. **VHS, Beta** $59.95 *IMP* 🎬

Ninja Mission First Scandinavian ninja epic follows CIA agent and his group of ninja fighters as they embark on a hazardous mission to rescue two people from a Soviet prison. They use their fighting skills (Swedish ninjas favor guns more than ninjutsu) against Russian soldiers. Dubbed.
1984 (R) 95m/C Christopher Kohlberg, Curt Brober, Hanna Pola; *D:* Mats Helge. **VHS, Beta** $59.95 *MED* 🎬 ½

Ninja Nightmare A man seeks revenge for his family's death.
1988 (R) 98m/C Leo Fong. **VHS, Beta** $9.99 *PSM* 🎬

Ninja of the Magnificence When the ninja master is killed, factions within his group battle for control.
1989 90m/C Sam Baker, Patrick Frbezar, Clive Hadwen, Tim Michael, Renato Sala; *D:* Charles Lee. **VHS, Beta** $59.95 *IMP* 🎬 ½

Ninja Operation: Licensed to Terminate Two warriors risk broken noses and twisted limbs to take on the Black Ninja Empire.
1987 89m/C Richard Harrison, Paul Marshall, Jack McPeat, Grant Temple; *D:* Joseph Lai. **VHS, Beta** $59.95 *IMP* 🎬

Ninja Phantom Heroes Two Vietnam vets are imprisoned for war crimes. One escapes and forms his own secret ninja society.
1987 90m/C Glen Carson, George Dickson, Allen Leung, Christine Wells; *D:* Bruce Lambert. **VHS, Beta** $59.95 *TWE* 🎬

The Ninja Pirates In the Sung Dynasty, a group of bloodthirsty pirates are hunted down after stealing a golden treasure.
1990 90m/C Chi Lan, Lo Lieh, Carter Wong, Nancy Yan. **VHS, Beta** $49.95 *OCE* 🎬 ½

Ninja Powerforce Two childhood friends end up as members of rival ninja gangs in the midst of a bloody war. Usual assortment of ninja-inflicted injuries result.
1990 90m/C Jonathan Bould, Richard Harrison; *D:* Joseph Lai. **VHS, Beta** $59.95 *IMP* 🎬 ½

Ninja Showdown A warrior must take on a number of vicious bandits in order to defend his small town. He vows revenge on anyone who threatens his people.
1990 92m/C Richard Harrison; *D:* Joseph Lai. **VHS, Beta** $59.95 *TWE* 🎬

Ninja Squad Empires, families, and honor or are at stake in a fierce battle of heel-to-head action.
198? 92m/C Dave Wheeler, Richard Harrison, Timalden. **VHS, Beta** $59.95 *TWE* 🎬

Ninja Strike Force The Black Ninjas steal the powerful "spirit sword," and go on a bloody rampage.
1988 89m/C Richard Harrison, Gary Carter; *D:* Joseph Lai. **VHS, Beta** $59.95 *IMP* 🎬 ½

Ninja Supremo A rebellious teenager studies Kung-fu, and then returns to his village a hero after he gains expertise in his chosen field.
1990 100m/C David Tao, Yueh Wah, Sun Yueh. **VHS, Beta** $49.95 *OCE* 🎬 ½

Ninja Swords of Death A noble warrior challenges a vicious assassin who uses a spur-sword. He is nearly decapitated in the process.
1990 90m/C Chang Ying Chun, Chia Ling, Tien Pang, Kong Pun. **VHS, Beta** $29.95 *OCE* 🎬 ½

Ninja Terminator Possession of all three pieces of the Golden Warrior turns the holder into the magically super-powered "Ninja Terminator." Three students battle for that honor. Very bad indeed.
1969 92m/C **VHS** $59.95 *TWE, VTR Woof!*

Ninja the Battalion Agents from America, the Soviet Union, and China try to recover germ warfare secrets stolen by the Japanese secret service.
1990 90m/C Roger Crawford, Sam Huxley, Alexander Lou, Dickson Warn; *D:* Victor Sears. **VHS, Beta** $59.95 *TWE* 🎬

Ninja the Protector A ninja tracks down and kicks the ninja head of a counterfeiting ring.
198? 92m/C Richard Harrison. **VHS, Beta** $19.98 *TWE* 🎬

Ninja, the Violent Sorcerer Murderer, with the help of Chinese vampires, does battle with the ghost of a dead gambling lord's wife and the gambling lord's living brother. Often tedious even with above average production and incredible plot.
1986 90m/C *D:* Bruce Lambert; *W:* Daniel Clough. **VHS, Beta** $59.95 *TWE* 🎬 ½

Ninja Turf Teenage kick artists rip off a Hollywood drug dealer and are pursued by a swarm of ninja hitmen. *AKA:* L.A. Streetfighters.
1986 (R) 83m/C Jun Chong, Bill Wallace, Rosanna King, James Lew, Phillip Rhee. **VHS, Beta** $79.95 *COL* 🎬

Ninja Vengeance The corrupt sheriff of a small Texas town, who also leads the KKK, is terrorizing a young African-American local. Then our lone hero rides into town on his trusty motorcycle to save the day. Only this time instead of your average gunman, he's a ninja.
1993 (R) 87m/C Stephen K. Hayes, Janet K. Pawlak, Craig Boyett, David Paul Lord; *D:* Karl Armstrong; *W:* Carrie Armstrong, Karl Armstrong. **VHS** $89.95 *COL* 🎬 ½

Ninja vs. Bruce Lee Lee investigates a secret ninja sect involved in smuggling.
1990 90m/C **VHS, Beta** $49.95 *OCE* 🎬

Ninja vs. Ninja A scientist has found a cure for heroin addiction, but ninja drug lords won't let his discovery see the light of day!
1990 90m/C Hui Hsiao Chiang, Callan Leong. **VHS, Beta** $49.95 *OCE* 🎬 ½

Ninja vs. the Shaolin Savage fighting between priests and ninjas results in one of the bloodiest pages in history.
1984 90m/C Alexander Lou, John Wu; *D:* Jacky Hwong. **VHS, Beta** *OCE* 🎬 ½

Ninja Wars One ninja takes on five ninja assassins who, along with an evil ninja sorcerer, have kidnapped his ninja girlfriend. Medieval ninja nonsense that's essentially incoherent. In Japanese with English dubbing.
1984 95m/C **VHS, Beta** $79.95 *PSM Woof!*

Ninja's Extreme Weapons Blue Ninja takes it to the streets when his brother is killed by the underworld.
1990 90m/C James Gray, Donald Muir; *D:* Victor Sears. **VHS, Beta** $59.95 *TWE, HHE* 🎬 ½

Ninotchka Delightful romantic comedy. Garbo is a cold Russian agent sent to Paris to check up on her comrades, who are being seduced by capitalism. She inadvertently falls in love with a playboy, who melts her communist heart. Garbo talks and laughs. Satirical, energetic, and witty. Later a Broadway musical called "Silk Stockings."
1939 (R) 110m/B Greta Garbo, Melvyn Douglas, Ina Claire, Sig Rumann, Felix Bressart, Bela Lugosi; *D:* Ernst Lubitsch; *W:* Billy Wilder. Academy Awards '39 Nominations: Best Actress (Garbo), Best Picture, Best Screenplay, Best Story; National Board of Review Awards '39: 10 Best Films of the Year. **VHS, Beta, 8mm** $24.95 *MGM* 🎬🎬🎬 ½

The Ninth Configuration Based on Blatty's novel "Twinkle, Twinkle, Killer Kane" (also the film's alternate title), this is a weird and surreal tale of a mock rebellion of high-ranking military men held in a secret base hospital for the mentally ill. Keach is good as the commander who is just as insane as the patients. Available in many different lengths, this is generally considered to be the best. *AKA:* Twinkle, Twinkle, Killer Kane.

1979 (R) 115m/C Stacy Keach, Scott Wilson, Jason Miller, Ed Flanders, Neville Brand, Alejandro Rey, Robert Loggia, George DiCenzo; *D:* William Peter Blatty. **VHS, Beta $19.95** *NWV* 🐾🐾🐾

Nitti: The Enforcer Made-for-TV saga about Al Capone's brutal enforcer and right hand man, Frank Nitti. Diversified cast, (Moriarty in particular) do their best to keep things moving along, and the atmosphere is consistently and appropriately violent. Made to capitalize on the success of 1987's "The Untouchables."
1988 (PG-13) 94m/C Anthony LaPaglia, Vincent Guastaferro, Trini Alvarado, Michael Moriarty, Michael Russo, Louis Guss, Bruno Kirby; *D:* Michael Switzer. **VHS $89.95** *ACA* 🐾🐾

No Big Deal Dillon is a streetwise teenager who makes friends at his new school. Blah promise; bad acting makes this no big deal.
1983 (PG-13) 86m/C Kevin Dillon, Sylvia Miles, Tammy Grimes, Jane Krakowski, Christopher Gartin, Mary Joan Negro; *D:* Robert Charlton. **VHS $79.95** *BTV* 🐾 1/2

No Comebacks Two British mysteries, made for television from stories by Frederick Forsyth: "A Careful Man," about a dying millionaire who cheats his heirs, and "Privilege," about a clever stamp dealer who exacts revenge upon a libelous gossip columnist.
1985 60m/C Milo O'Shea, Cyril Cusack, Dan O'Herlihy, Gayle Hunnicutt. **VHS, Beta $59.95** *PSM* 🐾 1/2

No Dead Heroes Green Beret Vietnam war hero succumbs to Soviet scheming when they plant a computer chip in his brain. Unoriginal and unworthy.
1987 86m/C Max Thayer, John Dresden, Toni Nero; *D:* J.C. Miller. **VHS, Beta** *NO* 🐾

No Deposit, No Return Tedious, silly, pointless Disney action comedy. Rich brats persuade bumbling crooks to kidnap them, offer them for ransom to millionaire grandfather. *AKA:* Double Trouble.
1976 (G) 115m/C David Niven, Don Knotts, Darren McGavin, Barbara Feldon, Charles Martin Smith; *D:* Norman Tokar; *M:* Buddy Baker. **VHS, Beta $69.95** *DIS* 🐾🐾

No Drums, No Bugles A West Virginia farmer and conscientious objector leaves his family to live alone in a cave for three years during the Civil War. Bad direction spoils Sheen's good performance.
1971 (G) 85m/C Martin Sheen, Davey Davidson, Denine Terry, Rod McCary; *D:* Clyde Ware. **VHS, Beta $39.95** *CNG, VTR* 🐾 1/2

No End The ghost of a dead lawyer watches as his wife and young son struggle to survive without him, including the widow getting involved in her husband's last case about a worker arrested for organizing a strike. Well-acted but overly solemn and slow; set during Poland's martial law in 1982. In Polish with English subtitles. *AKA:* Bez Konca.
1984 108m/C Grazyna Szapolowska, Jerzy Radziwilowicz, Maria Pakulnis, Aleksander Bardini, Artur Barcis, Michal Bajor; *D:* Krzysztof Kieslowski; *W:* Krzysztof Piesiewicz, Krzysztof Kieslowski. **VHS $79.95** *NYF, FCT, ING* 🐾🐾

No Escape In 2022, Captain Robbins (Liotta) has been banished to a prison colony island inhabited by the most dangerous criminals. With no walls and no guards, the prisoners are left to kill each other. Then Robbins discovers a relatively peaceful community of prisoners who help each other. But this group is soon bedeviled by the evil nasties on the other side of the island.

Attempts at escape define the plot, so the film is filled with superhuman feats of sheer courage, determination, and guts. Adapted from the book "The Penal Colony" by Richard Herley.
1994 (R) 118m/C Ray Liotta, Lance Henriksen, Stuart Wilson, Kevin Dillon, Kevin J. O'Connor, Michael Lerner, Ernie Hudson, Ian McNeice, Jack Shepherd; *D:* Martin Campbell; *W:* Joel Gross, Joel Gross; *M:* Graeme Revell. **VHS** 🐾🐾 1/2

No Escape, No Return An FBI agent (Nouri) and a police captain (Saxon) force three renegade cops (Nguyen, Caulfield, and Loveday) to infiltrate a drug syndicate. But things go from bad to worse when a war breaks out between rival drug gangs, leaving a lot of bodies, and a large chunk of money gone missing. Now the trio is sought by both the cops and the crooks.
1993 (R) 93m/C Maxwell Caulfield, Dustin Nguyen, Denise Loveday, John Saxon, Michael Nouri, Kevin Benton; *D:* Charles Kanganis; *W:* Charles Kanganis; *M:* Jim Halfpenny. **VHS $89.95** *PMH* 🐾🐾 1/2

No Fear, No Die To make some quick cash two black immigrants in France train and sell birds for illegal cockfights at a roadside restaurant. Jocelyn, who trains the cocks, pays them lavish, obsessive attention. But cultural conflicts and repressed passions are just waiting to explode. In French with English subtitles.
1990 97m/C Alex Descas, Isaach de Bankole, Jean-Claude Brialy, Solveig Dommartin, Christopher Buchholz; *D:* Claire Denis; *W:* Claire Denis, Jean-Pol Fargeau; *M:* Abdullah Ibrahim. **VHS $79.95** *ICA* 🐾🐾

No Greater Love Capraesque Soviet war movie. A peasant woman mobilizes her village against the Nazis to avenge her family's death. Dubbed into English by the Soviets for Western circulation during WWII.
1943 74m/B Vera Maretskaya; *D:* Frederic Ermler. **VHS, Beta $35.95** *FCT, IHF* 🐾🐾 1/2

No Grumps Allowed! A package of episodes of the children's fantasy series.
1969 90m/C **VHS, Beta $19.98** *SUE* 🐾🐾 1/2

No Holds Barred Cheesy, campy remake of cheesy, campy 1952 wrestling movie. Hulk Hogan on the big screen, at last.
1989 (PG-13) 98m/C Hulk Hogan, Kurt Fuller, Joan Severance, Tiny Lister; *D:* Thomas J. Wright. **VHS, Beta $19.95** *COL* 🐾 1/2

No Love for Johnnie Well acted if unoriginal political drama. Finch is a British M.P. who fails in both public and private life. Based on the novel by Wilfred Fienburgh.
1960 105m/B Peter Finch, Stanley Holloway, Donald Pleasence, Mary Peach, Mervyn Johns, Dennis Price, Oliver Reed, Billie Whitelaw; *D:* Ralph Thomas; *W:* Mordecai Richler; *M:* Malcolm Arnold. **VHS, Beta** *NO* 🐾🐾🐾

No Man of Her Own Gable and Lombard in their only screen pairing. A gambler marries a local girl on a bet and attempts to hide his secret life from her. Neither star's best film.
1932 81m/B Carole Lombard, Clark Gable, Grant Mitchell, Elizabeth Patterson, Dorothy Mackaill; *D:* Wesley Ruggles. **VHS, Beta $14.95** *MCA, BAR* 🐾🐾 1/2

No Man's Land Undercover cop Sweeney tails playboy Sheen but is seduced by wealth and glamour. Flashy surfaces, shiny cars, little substance.
1987 (R) 107m/C Charlie Sheen, D.B. Sweeney, Lara Harris, Randy Quaid; *D:* Peter Werner; *W:* Dick Wolf. **VHS, Beta $19.98** *ORI* 🐾🐾

No Man's Law Hardy plays the depraved villian desperate to get the goldmine owned by an old prospector and his beautiful daughter. But the mine is protected by Rex the Wonder Horse!
1921 ?m/B Oliver Hardy, Barbara Kent, James Finlayson, Theodore von Eltz; *D:* Fred Jackman. **VHS** *NO* 🐾🐾 1/2

No Man's Range Unremarkable, typical, predictable Western: good guys, bad guys, guns, bullets, horses. *AKA:* No Man's Land.
1935 56m/B Bob Steele. **VHS, Beta** *NO* 🐾

No Mercy A Chicago cop (Gere) plunges into the Cajun bayou in order to avenge the murder of his partner. He falls for a beautiful girl enslaved by the killer, but that doesn't stop him from using her to flush out the powerful swamp-inhabiting crime lord. Absurd story without much plot.
1986 (R) 108m/C Richard Gere, Kim Basinger, Jeroen Krabbe, George Dzundza, William Atherton, Ray Sharkey, Bruce McGill; *D:* Richard Pearce; *W:* Jim Carabatsos. **VHS, Beta $19.95** *COL* 🐾🐾

No, No Nanette Lackluster filming of the Broadway production which fared better on the stage. Stock story of a young woman (Neagle) who rescues her uncle from financial ruin and finds romance in the process.
1940 96m/B Anna Neagle, Richard Carlson, Victor Mature, Roland Young, ZaSu Pitts, Eve Arden, Billy Gilbert, Keye Luke; *D:* Herbert Wilcox. **VHS $19.95** *NOS* 🐾🐾

No One Cries Forever When a prostitute breaks away from a gangster-madam after finding love, she is tracked down and disfigured. Swedish; dubbed.
1985 96m/C Elke Sommer, Howard Carpendale, Zoli Marks; *D:* Jans Rautenbach. **Beta** *NO* Woof!

No Place to Hide A girl's father drowns and she blames herself. Her mother and psychologist try to convince the girl that her father's spirit isn't stalking her. She doesn't believe them. Made for television.
1981 120m/C Keir Dullea, Mariette Hartley, Kathleen Beller, Arlen Dean Snyder, Gary Graham, John Llewellyn Moxey; *D:* John Llewellyn Moxey. **VHS, Beta $59.95** *PSM* 🐾 1/2

No Place to Run An elderly man fights for custody of his grandson, then kidnaps him and flees with him to Canada. Made for TV.
1972 78m/C Herschel Bernardi, Larry Hagman, Stefanie Powers, Neville Brand; *D:* Delbert Mann. **VHS, Beta $59.95** *VMK* 🐾🐾

No Prince for My Cinderella A schizophrenic girl who has turned to prostitution is sought desperately by her social worker.
1978 100m/C Robert Reed. **VHS, Beta $49.95** *WOV* 🐾🐾

No Problem A man is pursued, shot, and drops dead in the apartment of an unsuspecting man who doesn't know what to do with the body. Dubbed in English.
1977? 94m/C Miou-Miou. **VHS, Beta** *NO* 🐾🐾

No Regrets for Our Youth A feminist saga depicting the spiritual growth of a foolish Japanese girl during the tumultuous years of WWII. In Japanese with English subtitles.
1946 110m/B Setsuko Hara; *D:* Akira Kurosawa. **VHS $29.95** *CVC, ING* 🐾🐾🐾

No Retreat, No Surrender A young American kick-boxer battles a formidable Russian opponent and wins, quite improbably, after having been tutored by the ghost of Bruce Lee in an abandoned house. Notable as Van Damme's debut, but little else recommends this silly "Rocky" rehash. Followed by "No Retreat, No Surrender II." **1986** (PG) 85m/C Kurt McKinney, J.W. Fails, Jean-Claude Van Damme; **D:** Corey Yuen. **VHS, Beta $14.95** NWV, STE ✍

No Retreat, No Surrender 2 With help from two karate experts, a man sets out to find his girlfriend who has been kidnapped by Soviets. Has little or nothing to do with the movie to which it is ostensibly a sequel. High level kick-boxing action sequences. **1989** (R) 92m/C Loren Avedon, Max Thayer, Cynthia Rothrock; **D:** Corey Yuen. **VHS, Beta $79.98** MCG ✍

No Retreat, No Surrender 3: Blood Brothers Sibling martial arts rivals decide to bond in a manly way when CIA agent dad is most heinously slain by terrorists. Answers the burning question: "Whatever became of Joseph Campanella?" **1991** (R) 97m/C Keith Vitali, Loren Avedon, Joseph Campanella. **VHS $19.95** IMP ✍

No Room to Run Concert promoter's life turns into a nightmare of deadly corporate intrigue when he arrives in Australia. Luckily, he finds time to fall in love. Made for television hokum. **1978** 101m/C Richard Benjamin, Paula Prentiss, Barry Sullivan; **D:** Robert Lewis. **VHS, Beta $9.95** ACA ✍½

No Safe Haven A government agent seeks revenge for his family's death. **1987** (R) 92m/C Wings Hauser, Marina Rice, Robert Tessier; **D:** Ronnie Rondell; **M:** Joel Goldsmith. **VHS, Beta $79.98** MCG ✍

No Secrets A young man on the run seeks refuge with three girls in an isolated house. His dread secret isn't so dread, leaving this mild teen-oriented thriller starved for lack of menace. **1991** (R) 92m/C Adam Coleman Howard, Amy Locane, Heather Fairfield, Traci Lin; **D:** Dezso Magyar. **VHS $89.98** COL ✍½

No Small Affair A 16-year-old aspiring photographer becomes romantically involved with a sultry 22-year-old rock star. **1984** (R) 102m/C Jon Cryer, Demi Moore, George Wendt, Peter Frechette, Elizabeth Daily, Tim Robbins, Jennifer Tilly, Rick Ducommun, Ann Wedgeworth; **D:** Jerry Schatzberg; **M:** Rupert Holmes. **VHS, Beta $19.95** COL ✍✍

No Surrender An unpredictable, darkly charming comedy about a Liverpool nightclub newly managed by Angelis. On New Year's Eve, a small drunken war is triggered when two groups of irate senior citizens are booked into the club and clash over their beliefs. The group is made up of Protestants and Catholics and the fight resembles the ongoing conflicts in modern-day Northern Ireland, although most of the action takes place in the loo. Watch for Costello as an inept magician. **1986** (R) 100m/C Ray McAnally, Michael Angelis, Avis Bunnage, James Ellis, Tom Georgeson, Mark Mulholland, Joanne Whalley-Kilmer, Elvis Costello, Bernard Hill, Michael Ripper; **D:** Peter Smith; **W:** Alan Bleasdale; **M:** Daryl Runswick. **VHS, Beta $79.95** PSM ✍✍✍

No Survivors, Please Aliens from Orion take over politicians in order to rule the Earth. Bizarre, obscure, based on true story. **AKA:** Der Chef Wuenscht Keine Zeugen; The Chief Wants No Survivors. **1963** 92m/B Maria Perschy, Uwe Friedrichsen, Robert Cunningham, Karen Blanguernon, Gustavo Rojo; **D:** Hans Albin, Peter Berneis. **VHS $19.98** MOV ✍½

No Time for Romance A sprightly musical with an all-black cast. First such film to be shot in color.

1948 ?m/C Bill Walker. **VHS $39.95** FCT ✍✍

No Time for Sergeants Hilarious film version of the Broadway play by Ira Levin. Young Andy Griffith is excellent as the Georgia farm boy who gets drafted into the service and creates mayhem among his superiors and colleagues. Story also told on an earlier television special and later in a series. Note Don Knotts and Benny Baker in small roles along with Jameel Farah who went on to star in TV's M*A*S*H after changing his name to Jamie Farr. **1958** 119m/B Andy Griffith, Nick Adams, Murray Hamilton, Don Knotts, Jamie Farr, Myron McCormick; **D:** Mervyn LeRoy. **VHS, Beta $19.98** WAR ✍✍✍

No Time to Die In Indonesia, two corporate pawns and a beautiful reporter battle for the possession of a new laser cannon. **1978** 87m/C Chris Mitchum, John Phillip Law, Grazyna Dylong. **VHS, Beta $59.95** TWE ✍

No Trace A writer who broadcasts his crime stories as part of a radio show is the victim of blackmail. It seems a former associate is aware that the stories are all based in fact. A Scotland Yard detective investigates when murder rears its ugly head. **1950** 76m/B Hugh Sinclair, Dinah Sheridan, John Laurie, Barry Morse, Michael Brennan, Dora Bryan; **D:** John Gilling. **VHS, Beta $16.95** SNC ✍✍

No Way Back Way. Writer, director, and producer Williamson portrays Jess Crowder, a man-for-hire who is an expert with guns, fists, and martial arts. An angry look at the white establishment. **1974** (R) 92m/C Fred Williamson, Charles Woolf, Tracy Reed, Virginia Gregg, Don Cornelius; **D:** Fred Williamson. **VHS, Beta $49.95** UNI ✍✍

No Way Out Career Navy man Costner is involved with a beautiful, sexy woman who is murdered. Turns out she was also the mistress of the Secretary of Defense, Costner's boss. Assigned to investigate the murder, he suddenly finds himself the chief suspect. A tight thriller based on 1948's "The Big Clock," with a new surprise ending. **1987** (R) 114m/C Kevin Costner, Sean Young, Gene Hackman, Will Patton, Howard Duff, George Dzundza, Iman, Chris D, Marshall Bell, Jason Bernard, Fred Dalton Thompson, David Paymer; **D:** Roger Donaldson; **W:** Robert Garland; **M:** Maurice Jarre. **VHS, Beta $14.95** HBO ✍✍✍

No Way to Treat a Lady Steiger is a psychotic master of disguise who stalks and kills various women in this suspenseful cat-and-mouse game. Segal, as the detective assigned to the case, uncovers clues, falls in love, and discovers that his new girl may be the killer's next victim. **1968** 108m/C Rod Steiger, Lee Remick, George Segal, Eileen Heckart, Murray Hamilton; **D:** Jack Smight; **W:** John Gay. **VHS, Beta $49.95** PAR ✍✍✍

Noa at Seventeen The political/social turmoil of Israel in 1951 is allegorically depicted by the school vs. kibbutz debate within a young girl's middle-class family. In Hebrew with English subtitles. **1982** 86m/C Dalia Shimko, Idit Zur, Shmuel Shilo, Moshe Havazelet; **D:** Isaac Yeshurun. **VHS, Beta $79.95** ERG, FCT, ING ✍✍✍

The Noble Ninja In a fantastic prehistoric world, a ninja does battle with foes both real and supernatural. **1990** 90m/C Tsui Fung, Lo Lieh. **VHS, Beta** OCE ✍✍

Nobody's Daughter The tragedy of an eight-year-old orphan shuttled from one family to another, all of whom are only interested in the money the government will pay for her care. In Hungarian with English subtitles. **1976** 90m/C Zsuzsi Czinkoczi; **D:** Lazlo Ranody. **VHS $59.95** EVD, ING ✍✍½

Nobody's Fool Another entry in the genre of quirky Americana, this romantic comedy concerns a hapless Midwestern waitress suffering from low-self esteem who falls in love with a traveling stage-hand. **1986** (PG-13) 107m/C Rosanna Arquette, Eric Roberts, Mare Winningham, Louise Fletcher, Jim Youngs; **D:** Evelyn Purcell; **W:** Beth Henley; **M:** James Newton Howard. **VHS, Beta $19.98** LHV, WAR ✍✍

Nobody's Perfect Where "Tootsie" and "Some Like it Hot" collide (or more likely crash and burn). A lovesick teenager masquerades as a girl and joins the tennis team to be near his dream girl. Takes its title from Joe E. Brown's famous last line in "Some Like it Hot." **1990** (PG-13) 90m/C Chad Lowe, Gail O'Grady, Patrick Breen, Kim Flowers, Robert Vaughn; **D:** Robert Kaylor. **VHS, Beta $89.98** MED, VTR ✍

Nobody's Perfekt Supposed comedy about three psychiatric patients who decide to extort $650,000 from the city of Miami when their car is wrecked. Lacks laughs and generally considered a turkey. **1979** (PG) 95m/C Gabe Kaplan, Robert Klein, Alex Karras, Susan Clark; **D:** Peter Bonerz. **VHS, Beta $69.95** COL Woof!

Nocturna Hard times have fallen upon the house of Dracula. To help pay the taxes on the castle, the owners have converted it to the Hotel Transylvania. In order to increase business and the blood supply at the hotel, Nocturna books a disco group to entertain the guests. Hard times fell on this script, too. It's no wonder that director Tampa hid behind the alias Harry Hurwitz. **AKA:** Nocturna, Granddaughter of Dracula. **1979** (R) 82m/C Yvonne De Carlo, John Carradine, Tony Hamilton, Nai Bonet; **D:** Harry Tampa. **VHS, Beta $44.95** MED Woof!

Nocturne A police lieutenant investigates the supposed suicide of a famous composer and uncovers dark secrets that suggest murder is afoot. An overlooked RKO production shines thanks to Raft's inimitable tough guy performance and some offbeat direction. For film noir completists. **1946** 88m/B George Raft, Lynn Bari, Virginia Huston, Joseph Pevney, Myrna Dell, Edward Ashley, Walter Sande, Mabel Paige; **D:** Edwin L. Marin. **VHS, Beta $19.98** TTC ✍✍½

Noises Off An Americanization of a British farce about a group of second-rate actors touring in a sex comedy and their convoluted private lives. Wretched rehearsals and equally disasterous preformances, backstage sniping, lovers' quarrels, and a beleaguered director all bumble along together. It worked better on stage, where it was a Broadway hit, but the actors at least have some fun with the material. Based on the play by Michael Frayn. **1992** (PG-13) 101m/C Michael Caine, Carol Burnett, Denholm Elliott, Julie Hagerty, Marilu Henner, Mark Linn-Baker, Christopher Reeve, John Ritter, Nicollette Sheridan; **D:** Peter Bogdanovich; **W:** Marty Kaplan; **M:** Phil Marshall. **VHS, Beta $19.99** TOU, PMS ✍✍½

Nomad Riders A la "Mad Max," (though with an even smaller budget and a decided lack of originality) one rugged man goes after the bikers who killed his wife and daughter.

1981 82m/C Wayne Chema, Richard Cluck, Ron Gregg; *D:* Frank Roach. VHS, Beta $69.98 *LIV, VES ◻*

Nomads A supernatural thriller set in Los Angeles about a French anthropologist who is mysteriously killed, and the woman doctor who investigates and becomes the next target of a band of strange street people with nomadic spirits. Nomad notables include pop stars Adam Ant and Josie Cotton. 1986 (R) 91m/C Pierce Brosnan, Lesley-Anne Down, Adam Ant, Anna Maria Monticelli, Mary Woronov; *D:* John McTiernan; *M:* Bill Conti. VHS, Beta $29.95 *IME, PAR ◻◻½*

Nomads of the North Vintage silent melodrama set in the North Woods with the requisite young girl beset by evil villians, a climactic forest fire, and a dashing Mountie who allows a man wrongly sought by the law to be reunited with the woman he secretly loves. 1920 109m/B Lon Chaney Sr., Lewis Stone, Betty Blythe. VHS, Beta, 8mm $16.95 *SNC, GPV, VYY ◻½*

Nomugi Pass A young woman working in a Japanese silk mill in the early 1900s must endure hardship and abuse. English subtitles. 1979 154m/C Shinobu Otake, Meiko Harada, Rentaro Mikuni, Takeo Jii. VHS, Beta *VDA ◻◻½*

Non-Stop New York Mystery tale with interesting twist. A wealthy woman can give an alibi for a murder suspect, but no one will listen, and she is subsequently framed. Pays homage to Hitchcock with its photography and humor. Quick and charming. 1937 71m/B Anna Lee, John Loder, Francis L. Sullivan, Frank Cellier; *D:* Robert Stevenson. VHS $16.95 *NOS, SNC ◻◻½*

None But the Brave During WWII, an American bomber plane crash-lands on an island already inhabited by stranded Japanese forces. After a skirmish, the two groups initiate a fragile truce, with the understanding that fighting will resume if one or the other sends for help. The Americans repair their radio unit and must decide on their next actions. Sinatra's directorial debut is a poor effort. 1965 105m/C Frank Sinatra, Clint Walker, Tommy Sands, Brad Dexter, Tony Bill, Tatsuya Mihashi, Takeshi Kato, Sammy Jackson; *D:* Frank Sinatra; *M:* John Williams. VHS, Beta $59.95 *WAR, FCT ◻◻*

None But the Lonely Heart In the days before WWII, a Cockney drifter (Grant) wanders the East End of London. When his get-rich-quick schemes fail, his dying shopkeeper-mother tries to help and lands in prison. Interesting characterization of life in the slums. Odets not only directed, but wrote the screenplay. 1944 113m/B Cary Grant, Ethel Barrymore, Barry Fitzgerald, Jane Wyatt, Dan Duryea, George Coulouris, June Duprez; *D:* Clifford Odets; *W:* Clifford Odets. Academy Awards '44: Best Supporting Actress (Barrymore); Nominations: Best Actor (Grant), Best Film Editing, Best Original Score; National Board of Review Awards '44: 10 Best Films of the Year. VHS, Beta $19.95 *MED, BTV ◻◻◻*

Noon Sunday A cold war situation in the Pacific islands explodes into an orgy of death. 1971 (PG) 104m/C Mark Lenard, John Russell, Linda Avery, Keye Luke. VHS, Beta $19.95 *ACA ◻*

Noon Wine Dramatization of Katherine Anne Porter's classic story about a Swedish worker on a Texas farm who becomes the center of a family battle. Made for PBS' American Playhouse. 1984 60m/C Fred Ward, Lise Hilboldt, Stellan Skarsgard, Jon Cryer; *D:* Michael Fields. VHS, Beta $24.95 *MON, FCT, KAR ◻◻◻*

The Noose Hangs High This broad comedy has our heroes as window washers mistaken for gamblers and getting involved with a bunch of gangsters. Much physical and verbal shenanigans as only these two can do it. The bits may be a bit old, but they're done with a fresh twist. Some good word play with the phrase "You can't be here" runs in the same vein as their classic "Who's on first?" routine. Genuinely funny. 1948 77m/B Bud Abbott, Lou Costello, Cathy Downs, Joseph Calleia, Leon Errol, Mike Mazurki, Jack Overman, Fritz Feld, Vera Martin, Joe Kirk, Matt Willis, Benny Rubin; *D:* Charles T. Barton. VHS $19.98 *MGM, NOS ◻◻◻*

Norma Rae A poor, uneducated textile worker joins forces with a New York labor organizer to unionize the reluctant workers at a Southern mill. Field was a surprise with her fully developed character's strength, beauty, and humor; her Oscar was well-deserved. Ritt's direction is top-notch. Jennifer Warnes sings the theme song, "It Goes Like It Goes," which also won an Oscar. 1979 (PG) 114m/C Sally Field, Ron Leibman, Beau Bridges, Pat Hingle; *D:* Martin Ritt; *W:* Harriet Frank Jr., Irving Ravetch. Academy Awards '79: Best Actress (Field), Best Song ("It Goes Like It Goes"); Nominations: Best Adapted Screenplay, Best Picture; Cannes Film Festival '79: Best Film; Golden Globe Awards '80: Best Actress—Drama (Field); Los Angeles Film Critics Association Awards '79: Best Actress (Field); National Board of Review Awards '79: Best Actress (Field); New York Film Critics Awards '79: Best Actress (Field). VHS, Beta $19.98 *FOX, BTV ◻◻◻*

Norman Conquest Conway finds himself drugged and framed for murder in this bargain-basement thriller. Bartok is the leader of a diamond-smuggling operation who may be involved. *AKA:* Park Plaza. 1953 75m/B Tom Conway, Eva Bartok, Joy Shelton, Sidney James, Richard Wattis, Robert Adair, Ian Fleming; *D:* Bernard Knowles; *W:* Bernard Knowles. VHS $19.95 *NOS, SNC ◻*

The Norman Conquests, Part 1: Table Manners Part one of playwright Alan Ayckbourn's comic trilogy of love unfulfilled, as the charmingly unreliable Norman (Conti) works his amorous wiles on three women. 1980 108m/C Tom Conti, Richard Briers, Penelope Keith. VHS, Beta $59.99 *TVC ◻◻◻*

The Norman Conquests, Part 2: Living Together Part two concerns the happenings in the living room during Norman's disastrous weekend of unsuccessful seduction. 1980 93m/C Tom Conti, Penelope Keith, Richard Briers. VHS, Beta $59.99 *TVC ◻◻◻*

The Norman Conquests, Part 3: Round and Round the Garden Part three concerns Norman's furtive appearance in the garden, which suggests that the weekend is going to misfire. 1980 106m/C Tom Conti, Penelope Keith, Richard Briers. VHS, Beta $59.99 *TVC ◻◻◻*

Norman, Is That You? Unsuccessful film adaptation based on the unsuccessful Broadway play about one family's sexual revolution. Revamped by a host of black stars, it's basically a one-joke affair when Foxx discovers his son is gay and living with his white lover. Shot on videotape and transferred to film. 1976 91m/C Redd Foxx, Pearl Bailey, Dennis Dugan, Michael Warren, Tamara Dobson, Vernee Watson, Jayne Meadows, George Furth; *D:* George Schlatter; *W:* George Schlatter, Ron Clark, Sam Bobrick; *M:* William Goldstein. VHS $19.98 *MGM ◻½*

Norman Loves Rose A precocious 13-year-old and his married sister-in-law join forces in this substandard comedy. When Rose tries to help Norman by teaching him about sex, she learns a little too—she's pregnant. 1982 (R) 95m/C Carol Kane, Tony Owen, Warren Mitchell, Myra de Groot; *D:* Henri Safran. VHS, Beta $69.98 *LIV, VES ◻½*

Norman's Awesome Experience Three adolescents are transported back in time to the Roman Empire. Bill and Ted, anyone? 1988 (PG-13) 90m/C Tom McCamus, Laurie Paton, Jaques Lussier; *D:* Paul Donovan. VHS, Beta *NO Woof!*

Norseman Leader of a band of Norsemen sets sail for the New World in search of his missing royal father. Low-budget Viking adventure. 1978 (PG) 90m/C Lee Majors, Cornel Wilde, Mel Ferrer, Christopher Connelly, Jack Elam; *D:* Charles B. Pierce; *W:* Charles B. Pierce. VHS, Beta $69.98 *LIV, VES ◻½*

North Some laughs with a message in family fare from Reiner. Eleven-year old ace kid actor Wood divorces his workaholic parents Alexander and Louis-Dreyfus and searches the world for a functional family (good luck). Willis, who's a treat in a pink bunny suit, acts as guardian angel/narrator and shows the kid what's really important. Illustrious comedic cast inhabits story based on a book by original "Saturday Night Live" screenwriter (and "Gary Shandling Show" co-creator) Zweibel, who put things in motion ten years ago when he asked Reiner to write a book jacket quote for the novel. 1994 (PG) ?m/C Elijah Wood, Jason Alexander, Julia Louis-Dreyfus, Bruce Willis, Jon Lovitz, Alan Arkin, Dan Aykroyd, Kathy Bates, Faith Ford, Graham Greene, Reba McEntire, John Ritter, Abe Vigoda, Kelly McGillis, Alexander Godunov, Noriyuki "Pat" Morita; *D:* Rob Reiner; *W:* Andrew Scheinman, Alan Zweibel; *M:* Marc Shaiman. VHS *NYR ◻◻◻*

North and South Book 1 Lavish spectacle about a friendship tested by the turbulent times leading up to Civil War. Orry Main (Swayze) is a South Carolina plantation owner while his best friend George Hazard (Read) comes from a Pennsylvania industrial family. Orry is also involved in a doomed romance with the beautiful Madeline (Down), who's forced to marry the odious Justin LaMotte (Carradine). Lots of intrigue and excitement. Based on the novel by John Jakes. Filmed on location in Charleston, South Carolina. Originally broadcast as a six-part TV miniseries. Available on six cassettes. 1985 561m/C Patrick Swayze, James Read, Lesley-Anne Down, David Carradine, Kirstie Alley, Jean Simmons, Inga Swenson, Jonathon Frakes, Genie Francis, Terri Garber, Georg Stanford Brown, Olivia Cole, David Ogden Stiers, Robert Guillaume, Hal Holbrook, Gene Kelly, Robert Mitchum, Johnny Cash, Elizabeth Taylor; *M:* Bill Conti. VHS, Beta $119.95 *WAR, FUS ◻◻◻*

North and South Book 2 Equally dramatic sequel follows the southern Main clan and the northern Hazard family into the Civil War as friendship and romance struggle to survive the fighting. Casnoff is a notable presence as the aptly-named Bent, who will go to any length to settle old scores with both families. Based on the John Jakes novel

"Love and War." Originally broadcast as a six-part TV miniseries; on six cassettes. The last of the Jakes trilogy, "Heaven and Hell," was finally filmed for TV in '94 but proved a major disappointment.
1986 570m/C Patrick Swayze, James Read, Lesley-Anne Down, Terri Garber, Genie Francis, Jean Simmons, Kirstie Alley, Philip Casnoff, Hal Holbrook, Lloyd Bridges, James Stewart, Morgan Fairchild, Nancy Marchand, Parker Stevenson, Lewis Smith; **M:** Bill Conti. **VHS $119.95** *WAR ✂✂✂*

The North Avenue Irregulars Slapstick Disney comedy along the same lines as some of their earlier laugh-fests. A priest and three members of the local ladies' club try to bust a crime syndicate. Though the premise is silly, there are still lots of laughs in this family film.
1979 (G) 99m/C Edward Herrmann, Barbara Harris, Susan Clark, Karen Valentine, Michael Constantine, Cloris Leachman, Melora Hardin, Alan Hale Jr., Ruth Buzzi, Patsy Kelly, Virginia Capers; **D:** Bruce Bilson. **VHS $69.95** *DIS ✂✂½*

North by Northwest Self-assured Madison Avenue ad exec Grant inadvertently gets involved with international spies when they mistake him for someone else. His problems are compounded when he's framed for murder. The movie where Grant and Saint dangle from the faces of Mount Rushmore and a plane chases Grant through farm fields. Exceptional performances, particularly Grant's. Plenty of plot twists are mixed with tongue-in-cheek humor. Considered by many to be one of Hitchcock's greatest films. Laserdisc includes letterboxing, digital soundtrack, Hitchcock interview, production and publicity photos, storyboards, and the original trailer.
1959 136m/C Cary Grant, Eva Marie Saint, James Mason, Leo G. Carroll, Martin Landau, Jessie Royce Landis, Philip Ober, Adam Williams, Josephine Hutchinson, Edward Platt; **D:** Alfred Hitchcock; **W:** Ernest Lehman; **M:** Bernard Herrmann. Academy Awards '59 Nominations: Best Art Direction/Set Decoration (Color), Best Film Editing, Best Story & Screenplay; Edgar Allan Poe Awards '59: Best Screenplay. **VHS, Beta $19.98** *MGM, VYG, CRC ✂✂✂*

North Dallas Forty Based on the novel by former Dallas Cowboy Peter Gent, the film focuses on the labor abuses in pro-football. One of the best football movies ever made, it contains searing commentary and very good acting, although the plot is sometimes dropped behind the line of scrimmage.
1979 (R) 119m/C Nick Nolte, Mac Davis, Charles Durning, Bo Svenson, Brian Dennehy, John Matuszak, Dayle Haddon, Steve Forrest, Dabney Coleman, G.D. Spradlin; **D:** Ted Kotcheff. **VHS, Beta $14.95** *PAR ✂✂✂½*

North of the Border A cowboy in Canada gets involved with back-stabbing and treachery in and around Alberta.
1946 40m/B Russell Hayden, Lyle Talbot, Inez Cooper, Douglas Fowley, Jack Mulhall; **D:** B. Reeves Eason. **VHS, Beta $19.95** *VYY ✂½*

North of the Great Divide Standard Rogers programmer, with Roy as a half-breed mediator between salmon fisherman and Indians.
1950 67m/C Roy Rogers, Penny Edwards, Gordon Jones, Roy Barcroft, Jack Lambert, Douglas Evans, Noble Johnson; **D:** William Witney. **VHS $12.98** *REP ✂½*

North Shore A young surfer from Arizona hits the beaches of Hawaii and discovers love, sex, and adventure. Only redeeming quality is surfing footage.
1987 (PG) 96m/C Matt Adler, Nia Peeples, John Philbin, Gregory Harrison, Christina Raines; **D:** Will Phelps. **VHS, Beta $79.95** *MCA ✂½*

The North Star Gripping war tale of Nazis over-running an eastern Russian city, with courageous villagers fighting back. Colorized version available. **AKA:** Armored Attack.
1943 108m/B Dana Andrews, Walter Huston, Anne Baxter, Farley Granger, Walter Brennan, Erich von Stroheim, Jack Perrin, Dean Jagger; **D:** Lewis Milestone; **M:** Aaron Copland. **VHS, Beta $19.95** *NOS, MRV, VYY ✂✂✂*

North to Alaska A gold prospector encounters many problems when he agrees to pick up his partner's fiancee in Seattle to bring her home to Nome, Alaska, in the 1890s. Overly slapstick at times, but great fun nonetheless. Loosely based on Laszlo Fodor's play "The Birthday Gift."
1960 120m/C John Wayne, Stewart Granger, Ernie Kovacs, Fabian, Capucine; **D:** Henry Hathaway. **VHS, Beta $19.98** *FOX ✂✂✂*

Northanger Abbey Catherine is a young woman whose head is turned by her romance readings of dark secrets, sinister castles, dashing heroes, and helpless women. When the handsome Henry Tilney invites her to visit his ancestral home, Northanger Abbey, it seems all her fancies have come to life. A somewhat tepid adaptation of Jane Austen's parody of the popular Gothic romances of her day.
198? 90m/C Peter Firth, Katherine Schlesinger, Googie Withers, Robert Hardy. **VHS $29.95** *TVC, BFS, FUS ✂✂½*

Northeast of Seoul Three people will stop at nothing to steal a legendary jewel-encrusted sword out of Korea.
1972 (PG) 84m/C Anita Ekberg, John Ireland, Victor Buono; **D:** David Lowell Rich. **VHS, Beta $59.95** *MGM ✂*

Northern Extremes Silly comedy about an eccentric Canadian island village whose fishing livelihood is threatened. So the town mayor captures an errant nuclear submarine and uses it as a big bargaining chip. Filmed in Nova Scotia, Canada.
1993 (PG) 80m/C Paul Gross, Denise Virieux, Henry Czerny, Jeff Leder, Tommy Sexton, Louis Del Grande, Maury Chaykin; **D:** Paul Donovan; **W:** Bill Flemming. **VHS $89.95** *ACA ✂½*

Northern Lights A small, black-and-white independent drama depicting the struggle of a lowly farmer combating governmental forces in the 1915 heartland. Subtitled.
1979 85m/B Robert Behling, Susan Lynch, Joe Spano, Rob Nilsson, Henry Martinson, Marianne Astrom-DeFina, Ray Ness, Helen Ness; **D:** Rob Nilsson, John Hanson; **W:** Rob Nilsson. **VHS, Beta $19.95** *STE, NWV ✂✂✂*

Northern Pursuit A Canadian Mountie disguises himself to infiltrate a Nazi spy ring in this exciting adventure film. Based on Leslie White's "Five Thousand Trojan Horses."
1943 94m/B Errol Flynn, Helmut Dantine, Julie Bishop, Gene Lockhart, Tom Tully; **D:** Raoul Walsh. **VHS, Beta $19.98** *MLB ✂✂½*

Northville Cemetery Massacre Gang of bikers comes to town and all hell breaks loose. The result is a horribly bloody war between the townsfolk and the gang. Yup, it was a massacre. **AKA:** The Northfield Cemetery Massacre.
1976 (R) 81m/C David Hyry, Craig Collicott, Jan Sisk. **VHS, Beta** *NO ✂*

Northwest Outpost Eddy is a California cavalry officer in this lightweight operetta. He helps a young woman who is trying to free her husband from jail, and after his death they are able to pursue their relationship. Eddy's last film. ♫Weary; Raindrops on a Drum; Tell Me With Your Eyes; One More

Mile to Go; Russian Easter Hymn; Love is the Time; Nearer and Dearer. **AKA:** End of the Rainbow.
1947 91m/B Nelson Eddy, Ilona Massey, Hugo Haas, Elsa Lanchester, Lenore Ulric; **D:** Allan Dwan. **VHS $19.98** *REP ✂½*

Northwest Passage The lavish first half of a projected two-film package based on Kenneth Roberts' popular novel, depicting the troop of Rogers' Rangers fighting the wilderness and hostile Indians. Beautifully produced; the second half was never made and the passage itself is never seen.
1940 126m/C Spencer Tracy, Robert Young, Ruth Hussey, Walter Brennan, Nat Pendleton, Robert Barrat, Lumsden Hare; **D:** King Vidor. **VHS, Beta $19.98** *MGM ✂✂✂*

Northwest Trail Royal Canadian Mountie Steele's assignment is to escort Woodbury across the wilderness. She's carrying a large sum of money to save her uncle's business. Problem is, killers are on their trail.
1946 75m/C Bob Steele, Joan Woodbury, John Litel, Raymond Hatton, Madge Bellamy, Charles Middleton; **D:** Derwin Abrahams. **VHS, Beta $19.95** *NOS, HHT, VCN ✂✂*

A Nos Amours Craving the attention she is denied at home, a young French girl searches for love and affection from numerous boyfriends in hopes of eradicating her unhappy home. Occasional lapses in quality and slow pacing hamper an otherwise excellent effort. The characterization of the girl Suzanne is especially memorable. In French with English subtitles.
1984 (R) 99m/C Sandrine Bonnaire, Dominique Besnehard, Maurice Pialat, Evelyne Ker; **D:** Maurice Pialat. **VHS, Beta $59.95** *COL, ING ✂✂✂*

Nosferatu The first film adaptation of Bram Stoker's "Dracula" remains one of the creepiest and most atmospheric versions. Murnau knew how to add just the right touches to make this one of the best vampire films ever made. All it lacks is the name of Dracula, which was changed due to copyright problems with Stoker's widow. Filmed in Bavaria. Silent with music and English titles. Remade by Werner Herzog in 1979. **AKA:** Nosferatu, Eine Symphonie des Grauens; Nosferatu, A Symphony of Terror; Nosferatu, A Symphony of Horror; Nosferatu, The Vampire.
1922 63m/B Max Schreck, Alexander Granach, Gustav von Wagenheim, Greta Schroeder; **D:** F.W. Murnau. **VHS, Beta $19.95** *GPV, MRV, NOS ✂✂*

Nosotros A thief tries to straighten up his life so he can win the love of a pretty girl. **AKA:** We.
1944 87m/B Ricardo Montalban, Emilia Guiu, Esther Luquin, Carlos M. Baena; **D:** Fernando A. Rivero. **VHS, Beta $34.95** *MAD ✂*

Not as a Stranger Glossy film about the medical profession and the varying degrees of dedication shown by doctors. Mitchum stars as an medical student who can't afford to pay his tuition, so he marries nurse de Havilland and continues going to school on her money, although their relationship is far from being a loving one. Producer Kramer's directorial debut. Based on the book by Morton Thompson.
1955 135m/B Olivia de Havilland, Robert Mitchum, Frank Sinatra, Gloria Grahame, Broderick Crawford, Charles Bickford, Myron McCormick, Lon Chaney Jr.; **D:** Stanley Kramer; **W:** Edward Anhalt. **VHS $19.98** *MGM ✂✂½*

Not for Publication A woman working as both a tabloid reporter and a mayoral campaign worker uncovers governmental corruption with the help of a shy photographer and a midget. Meant to be on par with

older screwball comedies but lacking the wit and subtlety.
1984 (R) 87m/C Nancy Allen, David Naughton, Richard Paul, Alice Ghostley, Laurence Luckinbill; **D:** Paul Bartel. **VHS, Beta $69.99** HBO *&&*

Not My Kid The 15-year-old daughter of a surgeon brings turmoil to her family when she becomes heavily involved in drugs. Producer Polson, along with Dr. Miller Newton, wrote the original book for this emotional story that is one of the better treatments of this important subject. Made for television.
1985 120m/C George Segal, Stockard Channing, Viveka Davis, Andrew (Andy) Robinson, Gary Bayer, Nancy Cartwright, Tate Donovan; **D:** Michael Tuchner; **W:** Christopher Knopf. **VHS, Beta $79.95** SVE *&&½*

Not of This Earth In a remake of the 1957 Roger Corman quickie, an alien wearing sunglasses makes an unfriendly trip to Earth. In order to save his dying planet he needs major blood donations from unsuspecting Earthlings. Not a match for the original version, some may nevertheless want to see ex-porn star Lords in her role as the nurse.
1988 (R) 92m/C Traci Lords, Arthur Roberts, Lenny Juliano, Rebecca Perle; **D:** Jim Wynorski; **W:** Jim Wynorski, R.J. Robertson. **VHS, Beta $14.95** MGM *&½*

Not Quite Human When Jonas Carson builds himself an android teenage son, he must keep the technology from falling into the hands of an evil toy manufacturer with plans of his own. Humorous hijinks abound. Based on the book series "Not Quite Human" by Seth McEvoy. Made for cable television; followed by two sequels.
1987 91m/C Alan Thicke, Robin Lively, Robert Harper, Joseph Bologna, Jay Underwood; **D:** Steven Hilliard Stern. **VHS, Beta $39.99** DIS *&&*

Not Quite Human 2 In this sequel, Dr. Jonas Carson sends his cyber-son off to college where Chip meets the not-quite-human girl of his dreams. Followed by "Still Not Quite Human." Made for cable television.
1989 91m/C Alan Thicke, Jay Underwood, Robin Lively, Greg Mullavey, Katie Barberi, Mark Arnott; **D:** Eric Luke. **VHS, Beta $39.99** DIS *&&½*

Not Quite Love Pre-pubescent ghetto waif and a self-appointed prophet seek love in uncaring city. Much music, singing and foot-stomping.
1988 30m/C D: David Scmidlapp. **VHS $29.95** FCT, MWF *&&*

Not Quite Paradise A young American medical student falls in love with a young Israeli girl on an Israeli kibbutz. Also called "Not Quite Jerusalem."
1986 (R) 106m/C Sam Robards, Joanna Pacula; **D:** Lewis Gilbert. **VHS, Beta $19.95** STE, NWV *&*

Not Tonight Darling A bored suburban housewife becomes involved with a fast-talking businessman who leads her into a web of deceit and blackmail.
1972 (R) 70m/C Luan Peters, Vincent Ball, Jason Twelvetrees. **VHS, Beta $59.95** GEM *&*

Not Without My Daughter Overwrought drama shot in Israel about American Field, who travels with her Arab husband and their daughter to his native Iran, where (he must have forgotten to tell her) she has no rights. He decides the family will stay, using beatings and confinement to persuade his uncooperative wife, but she risks all to escape with daughter. Based on the true story of Betty Mahmoody.

1990 (PG-13) 116m/C Sally Field, Alfred Molina, Sheila Rosenthal, Roshan Seth, Sarah Badel, Mony Rey, Georges Corraface; **D:** Brian Gilbert. **VHS, Beta, 8mm $14.95** MGM, FCT *&&½*

Notes for an African Orestes Director Pasolini's insight into how a filmmaker works and what motivates him, as the camera reveals his plans to film a modern day version of Aeschylus' "Orestes" in Africa.
1970 75m/B D: Pier Paolo Pasolini; **M:** Gato Garbieri. **VHS $29.95** MFV, CIG, ING *&&*

Nothing But a Man Duff Anderson (Dixon) is a black laborer trying to make a life in a small Alabama town. He falls for the daughter of a minster, they marry, and he gets a job at a local sawmill. When he won't bend to his racist white employers, he's fired and labeled a troublemaker. Unsentimental depiction of the times.
1964 95m/B Ivan Dixon, Abbey Lincoln, Gloria Foster, Julius W. Harris, Martin Priest, Yaphet Kotto; **D:** Michael Roemer; **W:** Michael Roemer. **VHS $89.95** NEW, BTV *&&*

Nothing But the Night Lee's company produced this convoluted story of orphans who are victims of a cult that uses them in their quest for immortality. **AKA:** The Devil's Undead; The Resurrection Syndicate.
1972 (PG) 90m/C Christopher Lee, Peter Cushing, Diana Dors, Georgia Brown, Keith Barron, Fulton Mackay, Gwyneth Strong; **D:** Peter Sasdy. **VHS** SNC *&½*

Nothing But Trouble Laurel & Hardy's last film for MGM is a complicated tale of two servants who wind up protecting an exiled boy king from the machinations of his power-mad uncle.
1944 70m/B Stan Laurel, Oliver Hardy, Henry O'Neill, Mary Boland, David Leland, John Warburton, Connie Gilchrist, Philip Merivale; **D:** Sam Taylor. **VHS $19.98** MGM *&&½*

Nothing But Trouble Yuppie couple out for weekend drive find themselves smoldering in small town hell thanks to a traffic ticket. Horror and humor mix like oil and water in Aykroyd's debut as director.
1991 (PG-13) 93m/C Dan Aykroyd, Demi Moore, Chevy Chase, John Candy, Taylor Negron, Bertila Demas, Valri Bromfield; **D:** Dan Aykroyd. **VHS, Beta, 8mm $92.99** WAR *&*

Nothing in Common In his last film, Gleason plays the abrasive, diabetic father of immature advertising agency worker Hanks. After his parents separate, Hanks learns to be more responsible and loving in caring for his father. Comedy and drama are blended well here with the help of satirical pokes at the ad business and Hanks turns in a fine performance, but the unorganized, lengthy plot may lose some viewers.
1986 (PG) 119m/C Tom Hanks, Jackie Gleason, Eva Marie Saint, Bess Armstrong, Hector Elizondo, Barry Corbin, Sela Ward, John Kapelos, Jane Morris, Dan Castellaneta, Tracy Reiner; **D:** Garry Marshall; **W:** Rick Podell; **M:** Patrick Leonard. **VHS, Beta $19.98** WAR, HBO *&&½*

Nothing Personal Confused mix of romantic comedy and environmental themes. Lawyer (?) Somers attempts to help college professor Sutherland prevent the slaughter of seals. Enter romance (hey, but what about the baby seals?). Enlivened by appearances of Canadian SCTV vets and Somers's first starring theatrical role.
1980 (PG) 96m/C Donald Sutherland, Suzanne Somers, Dabney Coleman, John Dehner, Roscoe Lee Browne, Catherine O'Hara; **D:** George Bloomfield. **VHS, Beta $69.98** LIV, VES *&½*

Nothing Sacred Slick, overzealous reporter takes advantage of a small-town girl's situation. As a publicity stunt, his newspaper brings her to the Big Apple to distract her from her supposedly imminent death in order to manipulate the public's sentiment as a means to sell more copy. Innocent young Lombard, however, is far from death's door, and deftly exploits her exploitation. Scathing indictment of the mass media and bovine mentality of the masses. Both hysterically funny and bitterly cynical; boasts Lombard's finest performance as the small-town rube who orchestrates the ruse. Remade in 1954 as "Living It Up."
1937 75m/C Fredric March, Carole Lombard, Walter Connolly, Sig Rumann, Charles Winninger, Margaret Hamilton; **D:** William A. Wellman; **W:** Ben Hecht; **M:** Oscar Levant. **VHS, Beta $19.95** NOS, MRV, VYY *&&&*

Nothing Underneath An American guy goes to Rome to search for his model twin sister, who may be one of the victims of a series of scissor killings.
1985 95m/C Tom Schanley, Renee Simonsen, Nicola Perring, Donald Pleasence; **D:** Carlo Vanzina. **VHS, Beta** NO *&½*

Notorious Post-WWII story of a beautiful playgirl sent by the US government to marry a suspected spy living in Brazil. Grant is the agent assigned to watch her. Duplicity and guilt are important factors in this brooding, romantic spy thriller. Suspenseful throughout, with a surprise ending. The acting is excellent all around and Hitchcock makes certain that suspense is maintained throughout this classy and complex thriller. Laser edition contains original trailer, publicity photos, and additional footage.
1946 101m/B Cary Grant, Ingrid Bergman, Claude Rains, Louis Calhern, Madame Konstantin, Reinhold Schunzel, Moroni Olsen; **D:** Alfred Hitchcock; **W:** Ben Hecht. **VHS, Beta $19.98** FOX, VYG, CRC *&&&&*

Nous N'Irons Plus au Bois On the outskirts of a forest held by the Germans, a small group of French resistance fighters capture a German soldier during WWII. He actually wants to join forces with them, however, after falling in love with a lovely young French girl. In French; subtitled in English.
1969 98m/C Marie-France Pisier, Siegfried Rauch, Richard Leduc; **D:** Georges Dumoulin. **VHS, Beta** NO *&&*

Nouvelle Vague Delon is a philosopher king and Giordano a wealthy countess involved in Godard's usual sexual and political themes, which has society geared toward support of the rich. Dialogue is composed entirely of quotations. In French with English subtitles. **AKA:** New Wave.
1990 89m/C Alain Delon, Domiziana Giordano, Roland Amstutz, Laurence Cote, Christophe Odent; **D:** Jean-Luc Godard; **W:** Jean-Luc Godard. **VHS $79.95** ING, FCT *&&½*

Novel Desires Brian Freedman is a best-selling author who teams up with his writing rival, Vicky Chance. But it isn't just their imaginations they give free reign to, it's all their desires as well.
1992 (R) 80m/C Tyler Gains, Caroline Monteith, Mitchell Clark, Lisa Hayland; **D:** Lawrence Unger. **VHS $79.95** CEL *&½*

Now and Forever Young wife's life is shattered when her unfaithful husband is wrongly accused and convicted of rape. After he is sent to prison, she begins drinking and taking drugs. From the novel by Danielle Steel, it will appeal most to those who like their romances a la Harlequin.

1982 (R) 93m/C Cheryl Ladd, Robert Coleby, Carmen Duncan, Christine Amor, Aileen Britton; **D:** Adrian Carr. **VHS, Beta** $59.95 MCA 🎬½

Now, Voyager Davis plays a lonely spinster who is transformed into a vibrant young woman by therapy. She comes out of her shell to have a romantic affair with a suave European (who turns out to be married) but still utters the famous phrase "Oh, Jerry, we have the stars. Let's not ask for the moon." Definitely melodramatic, but an involving story nonetheless. Based on a novel by Olive Higgins Prouty.
1942 117m/B Bette Davis, Gladys Cooper, Claude Rains, Paul Henreid, Bonita Granville; **D:** Irving Rapper; **M:** Max Steiner. Academy Awards '42: Best Score; Nominations: Best Actress (Davis), Best Supporting Actress (Cooper). **VHS, Beta** $19.95 MGM 🎬🎬🎬½

Now You See Him, Now You Don't Light Disney comedy involving a gang of crooks who want to use a college student's invisibility formula to rob a local bank. Sequel to Disney's "The Computer Wore Tennis Shoes."
1972 (G) 85m/C Kurt Russell, Joe Flynn, Cesar Romero, Jim Backus; **D:** Robert Butler. **VHS, Beta** $69.95 DIS 🎬🎬

Nowhere to Hide A widow whose Marine officer husband has been assassinated is chased by some bad guys who are after a helicopter part (say what?) and she must fight for survival for herself and her 6-year-old son.
1987 (R) 91m/C Amy Madigan, Daniel Hugh-Kelly, Michael Ironside; **D:** Mario Azzopardi; **M:** Brad Fiedel. **VHS, Beta** $79.95 LHV, HHE, WAR 🎬🎬

Nowhere to Hide A hitman is hired to kill a young boy who witnesses a brutal murder. The hitman, however, decides he's already killed too many people and wants to get out of the business. Will he become the next murder target?
19?? 80m/C Paul Winfield, Rod Taylor. **VHS** $9.99 QVD 🎬🎬

Nowhere to Run Slipshod version of a true story about a series of murders in Caddo, Texas in 1960. Carradine, paroled from prison, murders for revenge while six high school seniors get involved in the chase and in the seedy side of politics, police, and their own puberty.
1988 (R) 87m/C David Carradine, Jason Priestly, Kieran Mulroney, Henry Jones; **D:** Carl Franklin. **VHS, Beta** $14.95 MGM 🎬

Nowhere to Run Kickboxer with heart seeks cross-over movie to establish real acting career. Unfortunately, even if such a movie existed, Van Damme wouldn't know what to do with it. Arquette plays the damsel in distress, facing eviction from the family farm with her two small children. Fortunately for Van Damme's escaped convict character, she is also a very lonely widow (nudge, nudge). He saves the day by abusing the daylights out of the big bad bankers, yet also finds time to play surrogate dad. Whatta guy.
1993 (R) 95m/C Jean-Claude Van Damme, Rosanna Arquette, Kieran Culkin, Tiffany Taubman, Joss Ackland, Ted Levine; **D:** Robert Harmon; **W:** Joe Eszterhas, Leslie Boehm, Randy Feldman; **M:** Mark Isham. **VHS, 8mm** $19.95 COL 🎬½

Nuclear Conspiracy A reporter disappears while investigating a huge nuclear waste shipment, and his wife searches for him.
1985 115m/C Birgit Doll, Albert Fortell. **VHS, Beta** $69.95 VMK 🎬½

The Nude Bomb Proof that old TV shows never die—they just get made into big screen movies. Maxwell Smart from "Get Smart" (would you believe?) tries to save the world from a bomb intended to destroy clothing and leave everyone in the buff. Old hat lines. Followed by the TV movie "Get Smart, Again!" **AKA:** The Return of Maxwell Smart.
1980 (PG) 94m/C Don Adams, Dana Elcar, Pamela Hensley, Sylvia Kristel, Norman Lloyd, Rhonda Fleming, Joey Forman; **D:** Clive Donner. **VHS** $14.98 MCA 🎬🎬½

Nude on the Moon Lunar expedition discovers moon inhabited by people who bare skin as hobby. Groovy theme song, "I'm Mooning Over You, My Little Moon Doll." Part of Joe Bob Brigg's "Sleaziest Movies in the History of the World" series.
1961 83m/C **D:** Doris Wishman. **VHS** $19.98 SVI Woof!

Nudity Required Two pals use the casting couch, pretending to be Hollywood producers, to seduce young women. Silly comedy with gratuitous nudity (Ms. Newmar included). Hardly a laugh to be found.
1990 90m/C Julie Newmar, Troy Donahue, Brad Zutaut, Billy Frank, Ty Randolph, Alvin Silver, Eli Rich, Phil Hock; **D:** John Bown. **VHS** NO 🎬

Nudo di Donna A witty comedy about a Venetian bookseller who is becoming tired of marital struggles with his sexy wife of 16 years. He wanders into a fashion photography shop, sees a backside nude photo of a model who looks like his wife, and he takes off in fiery pursuit to find the subject of the photo. Venetian location photography is quite nice. In Italian with English subtitles. **AKA:** Portrait of a Woman, Nude.
1983 112m/C Nino Manfredi, Jean-Pierre Cassel, George Wilson, Elenora Giorgi; **D:** Nino Manfredi. **VHS, Beta** $29.95 APD, TPV 🎬🎬🎬

Nukie Brothers from another planet crash land on Earth. The first one is subjected to a dizzying array of scientific experiments in Florida involving electric cattle prods. The other one, Nukie, lands in Africa and is befriended by twins from a remote tribal village. They join him in his quest to free his brother from the sadistic clutches of suntanned professionals who have lost all compassion. Important message for our youth about the dangers of a runaway technocracy.
1993 (G) 99m/C Glynis Johns, Steve Railsback; **D:** Sias Odendal. **VHS, Beta** $92.95 VMK 🎬🎬

Number 1 of the Secret Service A handsome secret agent must foil the plans of a millionaire industrialist to destroy the economy. Spy spoof that's marginally interesting.
1977 (PG) 87m/C Nicky Henson, Geoffrey Keen, Sue Lloyd, Aimi MacDonald, Richard Todd; **D:** Lindsay Shontoff. **VHS, Beta** $79.95 MGM 🎬🎬

Number One with a Bullet Two unorthodox "odd couple" detectives are demoted after losing a key witness, but still set out on their own to unearth a drug czar. Carradine and Williams are better than this standard action material.
1987 (R) 103m/C Robert Carradine, Billy Dee Williams, Peter Graves, Valerie Bertinelli; **D:** Jack Smight. **VHS, Beta** $14.95 MGM 🎬🎬

No. 17 A humorous early thriller by the Master Hitchcock, filmed before the likes of "The 39 Steps." An unsuspecting hobo accidentally finds a jewel thief's cache. The chase is on—superb final chase sequence involving a bus and a train. Based on the play by J. Jefferson Farjeon.

1932 64m/B Leon M. Lion, Anne Grey, John Stuart, Donald Calthrop; **D:** Alfred Hitchcock; **W:** Alfred Hitchcock. **VHS, Beta, 8mm** $9.98 REP, NOS, HHT 🎬½

Numero Deux Godard explores politics, sex, and the trials of the modern family. A dissatisfied wife suffers from chronic constipation, her exhausted husband is impotent, they, their children, and grandparents all try to cope with daily life. For nine-tenths of the film Godard only used small portions of the screen (the upper left and lower right corners) to manipulate his message of frustration. It's only at the end that the full-screen is used to offer some sort of relief. In French with English subtitles. **AKA:** Number Two.
1975 90m/C Sandrine Battistella, Pierre Oudry, Alexandre Rignault, Rachel Stefanopol; **D:** Jean-Luc Godard; **W:** Anne-Marie Mieville, Jean-Luc Godard. **VHS** $59.95 FCT 🎬🎬

The Nun A young woman, unable to meet financial obligations, is forced into a convent. Victimized by the mother superior and betrayed by a clergyman who befriends her, she escapes from the convent and eventually ends up in a bordello, despairing and suicidal. Not a cheery story. Banned in France for two years. In French with English subtitles.
1966 155m/C Anna Karina, Lilo (Liselotte) Pulver, Micheline Presle, Christine Lenier, Francine Berge, Francesco Rabal, Wolfgang Reichmann, Catherine Diamant, Yori Bertin; **D:** Jacques Rivette. **VHS** $59.95 INT, FCT, ING 🎬🎬½

Nuns on the Run Idle and Coltrane are two nonviolent members of a robbery gang who double-cross their boss during a hold-up and disguise themselves as nuns while on the run from both the Mob and the police. Catholic humor, slapstick, and much fun with habits dominate. Idle and Coltrane do their best to keep the so-so script moving with its one-joke premise.
1990 (PG-13) 95m/C Eric Idle, Robbie Coltrane, Janet Suzman, Camille Coduri, Robert Patterson, Tom Hickey, Doris Hare, Lila Kaye; **D:** Jonathan Lynn; **W:** Jonathan Lynn. **VHS, Beta** $89.98 FOX 🎬🎬

The Nun's Story The melancholy tale of a young nun working in the Congo and Belgium during WWII, and struggling to reconcile her free spirit with the rigors of the order. Highly acclaimed; from the Kathryn Hulme novel.
1959 152m/C Audrey Hepburn, Peter Finch, Edith Evans, Peggy Ashcroft, Mildred Dunnock, Dean Jagger, Beatrice Straight, Colleen Dewhurst; **D:** Fred Zinneman; **W:** Robert Anderson. Academy Awards '59 Nominations: Best Actress (Hepburn), Best Adapted Screenplay, Best Color Cinematography, Best Director (Zinneman), Best Film Editing, Best Picture, Best Sound, Best Original Score; British Academy Awards '59: Best Actress (Hepburn); National Board of Review Awards '59: 10 Best Films of the Year, Best Director (Zinneman), Best Supporting Actress (Evans). **VHS, Beta** $19.98 WAR 🎬🎬🎬½

Nurse A recently widowed woman resumes her career as a nurse in a large urban hospital, after her son leaves for college. Based on Peggy Anderson's book. Made for television; became a weekly series.
1980 105m/C Michael Learned, Robert Reed, Antonio Fargas; **D:** David Lowell Rich. **VHS, Beta** $59.95 LIV 🎬🎬½

Nurse Edith Cavell Fine performances in this true story of Britain's famous nurse who aided the Belgian underground during WWI, transporting wounded soldiers out of the German-occupied country. Decidedly opposes war and, ironically, was released just as WWII began to heat up in 1939.

1939 95m/B George Sanders, Edna May Oliver, ZaSu Pitts, Robert Coote, May Robson, Anna Neagle; *D:* Herbert Wilcox. VHS, Beta $19.95 NOS, CAB, BAR ✗✗✗

Nurse on Call A bevy of trampy nurses cavort throughout a big city hospital. Softcore.
1988 80m/C Anne Tilson, Jennie Martinez, Christopher Floyd. VHS, Beta $29.95 MED ✗

Nutcase A trio of young children in New Zealand attempt to thwart a group of terrorists who threaten to reactivate a large city's volcanoes unless they are given a large sum of money. Novel twist there.
1983 49m/C Nevan Rowe, Ian Watkin, Michael Wilson; *D:* Roger Donaldson. VHS, Beta NO ✗

Nutcracker, A Fantasy on Ice An ice-skating version of the famed story and Tchaikovsky ballet aired as a television special in 1983.
1983 85m/C Dorothy Hamill. VHS, Beta $19.95 VMK ✗

The Nutcracker Prince The classic children's Christmas tale comes alive in this feature-length animated special.
1991 75m/C *D:* Paul Schibli; *V:* Kiefer Sutherland, Megan Follows, Michael MacDonald, Phyllis Diller, Peter O'Toole. VHS, 8mm $19.98 WAR, WTA ✗✗

Nutcracker Sweet Ridiculous drama about a beautiful and powerful socialite (Collins) who runs a renowned ballet company with an iron fist. A Russian ballerina defects and infiltrates Collins's company to try out her own treacherous motives.
1984 101m/C Joan Collins, Finola Hughes, Paul Nicholas; *D:* Anwar Kawadri. VHS, Beta $69.98 LIV, VES ✗

Nutcracker: The Motion Picture A lavish, stage-bound filmization of the Tchaikovsky ballet, designed by Maurice Sendak.
1986 82m/C Pacific Northwest Ballet; *D:* Carroll Ballard. VHS, Beta $14.95 PAR, BAR, KAR ✗✗½

Nuts A high-priced prostitute attempts to prove her sanity when she's accused of manslaughter. Ashamed of her lifestyle, and afraid of her reasons for it, her parents attempt to institutionalize her. A filmed version of Tom Topor's play that manages to retain its mesmerizing qualities. Fine performances, although the funnygirl goes over the top on several occasions.
1987 (R) 116m/C Barbra Streisand, Richard Dreyfuss, Maureen Stapleton, Karl Malden, James Whitmore, Robert Webber, Eli Wallach, Leslie Nielsen, William Prince, Dakin Matthews, Hayley Taylor Block; *D:* Martin Ritt; *W:* Tom Topor, Darryl Ponicsan, Alvin Sargent; *M:* Barbra Streisand. VHS, Beta, 8mm $19.98 WAR ✗✗✗

Nuts in May Two smug, middle-aged, middle-class vegetarians go on a camping trip and totally alienate their cynical, working-class fellow campers.
1976 84m/C Alison Steadman; *D:* Mike Leigh. VHS $79.95 WBF, BTV ✗✗

The Nutty Professor A mild-mannered chemistry professor creates a potion that turns him into a suave, debonair, playboy type with an irresistible attraction to women. Lewis has repeatedly denied the slick character is a Dean Martin parody, but the evidence is quite strong. Easily Lewis's best film.
1963 107m/C Jerry Lewis, Stella Stevens, Howard Morris, Kathleen Freeman; *D:* Jerry Lewis; *W:* Jerry Lewis. VHS, Beta $14.95 PAR ✗✗✗

Nyoka and the Tigermen The adventures of the jungle queen Nyoka and her rival Vultura in their search for the lost tablets of Hippocrates. In 15 episodes. *AKA:* Nyoka and the Lost Secrets of Hippocrates; Perils of Nyoka.
1942 250m/B Kay Aldridge, Clayton Moore; *D:* William Witney. VHS $29.98 VCN, REP, MLB ✗✗✗

O Lucky Man! Surreal, black comedy following the rise and fall and eventual rebirth of a modern British coffee salesman. Several actors play multiple roles with outstanding performances throughout. Price's excellent score combines with the hilarity for an extraordinary experience.
1973 (R) 178m/C Malcolm McDowell, Ralph Richardson, Rachel Roberts, Arthur Lowe, Alan Price, Helen Mirren, Mona Washbourne, Warren Clarke; *D:* Lindsay Anderson; *M:* Alan Price. Cannes Film Festival Nominations: cs 73: Best Film; British Academy Awards '73: Best Supporting Actor (Lowe); National Board of Review Awards '73: 10 Best Films of the Year. VHS, Beta $29.95 WAR ✗✗✗✗

O Pioneers! Lange plays Alexandra Bergson, an unmarried woman at the turn of the century, who inherits her family's Nebraska homestead because her father knows how much she loves the land. Although the family has prospered through Alexandra's smart investments, her brothers come to resent her influence. When her first love returns after fifteen years and the romance is rekindled, family resentments surface once again. Based on the novel by Willa Cather. A Hallmark Hall of Fame presentation.
1991 (PG) 99m/C Jessica Lange, David Strathairn, Tom Aldredge, Reed Edward Diamond, Anne Heche, Heather Graham, Josh Hamilton, Leigh Lawson, Graham Beckel; *D:* Glenn Jordan; *W:* Glenn Jordan. VHS $14.98 REP, FCT ✗✗½

O Youth and Beauty Film dealing with one of author Cheever's favorite themes, the American male's fear of losing his identity. Frustrated by the onset of age, a man tries to recapture his college years and athletic ability by hurdling furniture. From the "Cheever Short Stories" series.
1979 60m/C Michael Murphy, Kathryn Walker. VHS, Beta FLI ✗

The Oak Morgenstern grieves over the loss of her father until she realizes she can't get rid of the body. Her difficulties in locating adequate medical facilities reflect the nightmarish realities of pre-1990 communist Romania. Potentially farcical aspects of storyline are successfully removed by violence in following scene involving Morgenstern and a band of roaming soldiers. A tragicomic look at obstinate communist bureaucrats and the wily, willful peasants who overcome them. Based on a novel by Ion Baiesu. In Romanian with English subtitles.
1993 105m/C Maia Morgenstern, Razvan Vasilescu, Victor Rebengiuc, Dorel Visan, Mariana Mihut, Dan Condurache, Virgil Andriescu, Leopoldina Balanuta, Matei Alexandru, Gheorghe Visu, Magda Catone, Ionel Mahailescu; *D:* Lucian Pintilie; *W:* Lucian Pintilie. VHS $89.95 NYF ✗✗½

Oasis of the Zombies European students set out to find buried treasure in Saharan oasis but instead find bevy of hungry Nazis with eating disorders.
1982 75m/C Manuel Gelin, France Jordan, Jeff Montgomery, Miriam Landson, Eric Saint-Just, Caroline Audret, Henry Lambert; *D:* A.M. Frank. VHS, Beta $59.95 VCI ✗

Oath of Vengeance Billy the Kid rides the West once more.
1944 50m/B Buster Crabbe, Al "Fuzzy" St. John, Jack Ingram, Charles "Blackie" King; *D:* Sam Newfield. VHS, Beta $27.95 VCN, RXM ✗½

The Object of Beauty Two Americans, trapped in Europe by their love of pleasure and their lack of money, bicker over whether to sell their one object of value - a tiny Henry Moore sculpture. When it disappears, their relationship is challenged. Excellent acting and telling direction. Forces an examination of one's own value placement.
1991 (R) 105m/C Andie MacDowell, John Malkovich, Joss Ackland, Lolita Davidovich, Peter Riegert, Bill Paterson, Rudi Davies, Ricci Harnett; *D:* Michael Lindsay-Hogg; *M:* Tom Bahler. VHS $89.95 LIV ✗✗✗

Objective, Burma! Deemed by many to be the greatest and most moving WWII production released during the war. American paratroopers are dropped over Burma where their mission is to destroy a Japanese radar station. The Americans led by Flynn are successful in wiping out the station, but they are spotted and descended upon by Japanese forces. Impeded from returning to Allied lines, the American soldiers must try to survive enemy encounters, exhaustion, starvation, and the elements until they are rescued. Splendid performance by Flynn and exceptional direction from Walsh; excellent performances enhanced by energetic score.
1945 142m/B Errol Flynn, James Brown, William Prince, George Tobias, Henry Hull, Warner Anderson, Richard Erdman, Mark Stevens, Anthony Caruso, Hugh Beaumont; *D:* Raoul Walsh; *W:* Ranald MacDougall, Lester Cole; *M:* Franz Waxman. VHS, Beta $19.98 MGM ✗✗✗✗

Oblomov A production of the classic Goncharov novel about a symbolically inert Russian aristocrat whose childhood friend helps him find a reason for action. Well made, with fine performances. In Russian with English subtitles. *AKA:* A Few Days in the Life of I.I. Oblomov; Neskolko Dnel iz Zhizni I.I. Oblomov.
1981 145m/C Oleg Tabakov, Elena Solovei; *D:* Nikita Mikhalkov. VHS, Beta $59.95 TPV, KIV, AUD ✗✗✗½

The Oblong Box Coffins, blood, and live corpses fill drawn-out and lifeless adaptation of Edgar Allan Poe story. English aristocrat Price attempts to hide his disfigured brother in an old tower. Brother predictably escapes and rampages through town before being killed. *AKA:* Edgar Allen Poe's The Oblong Box.
1969 (PG) 91m/C Vincent Price, Christopher Lee, Alastair Williamson, Hilary Dwyer, Peter Arne, Harry Baird, Carl Rigg, Sally Geeson, Maxwell Shaw; *D:* Gordon Hessler. VHS, Beta NO ✗✗

The Obsessed Uninspiring story with Farrar suspected of murdering his wife. Competent performances, but this mystery isn't developed with any sense of style and the killer's real identity will be obvious to anyone watching. Cliches and stereotyped situations don't add anything. *AKA:* The Late Edwina Black.
1951 77m/B David Farrar, Geraldine Fitzgerald, Roland Culver, Jean Cadell, Mary Merrall; *D:* Maurice Elvey. VHS $16.95 SNC, NOS, MOV ✗✗

Obsessed Semi-realistic tale of a woman's exhausting desire for revenge against hit-and-run driver who killed her son. Cast acceptable but lack of psychological foundation weakens plot.
1988 (PG-13) 100m/C Kerrie Keane, Alan Thicke, Colleen Dewhurst, Saul Rubinek, Daniel Pilon, Lynne Griffin; *D:* Robin Spry. VHS, Beta NO ✗½

Obsession A rich, lonely businessman meets a mysterious young girl in Italy, the mirror image of his late wife who was killed by kidnappers. Intriguing suspense film that's

not quite up to comparisons with Hitchcock thrillers. Music by Hitchcock-collaborator Herrmann.
1976 (PG) 98m/C Cliff Robertson, Genevieve Bujold, John Lithgow; *D:* Brian DePalma; *W:* Paul Schrader; *M:* Bernard Herrmann. Academy Awards '76 Nominations: Best Original Score; National Board of Review Awards '76: 10 Best Films of the Year. **VHS, Beta $12.95** *COL, HHE* 🎬🎬½

Obsession: A Taste for Fear Diane's high fashion models are being killed and although there are plenty of suspects, she can't find the killer.
1989 (R) 90m/C Virginia Hey, Gerard Darmon, Carlo Mucari; *D:* Piccio Raffanini. **VHS, Beta $89.95** *IMP* 🎬½

Obsessive Love A lonely, mentally unstable typist (Mimieux) becomes obsessed with her soap opera hero and decides to go to Hollywood to seduce him. She transforms herself into a sleek and stunning Hollywood temptress to woo him, and at first he goes along with her—until he realizes that she is insane. An average made-for-TV movie of the older woman/younger man genre.
1984 97m/C Yvette Mimieux, Simon MacCorkindale, Kin Shriner, Constance McCashin, Allan Miller, Lainie Kazan; *D:* Steven Hilliard Stern. **VHS $59.98** *LIV* 🎬🎬½

O.C. and Stiggs Two teens spend a summer harassing a neighbor and his family. Flimsy attempts at comedy fall flat. A failed adaptation of a National Lampoon short story, it was held for three years before release.
1987 (R) 109m/C Daniel H. Jenkins, Neill Barry, Jane Curtin, Tina Louise, Jon Cryer, Dennis Hopper, Paul Dooley, Ray Walston, Louis Nye, Martin Mull, Melvin Van Peebles; *D:* Robert Altman. **VHS, Beta $79.98** *FOX* 🎬½

The Occult Experience An engrossing study into the world of devil-worshippers, shamans, and the like. This documentary actually records exorcisms and other rituals. Not for the faint hearted.
1984 87m/C VHS $14.95 *COL* 🎬½

The Occultist Satan worshippers do the dance of death as they skin men alive for their evil purposes.
1989 82m/C Rick Gianasi; *D:* Tim Kincaid; *W:* Tim Kincaid. **VHS, Beta $79.95** *UNI Woof!*

An Occurrence at Owl Creek Bridge A man is about to be hanged when the rope snaps, and he is able to swim to safety. He entertains thoughts of his family while making his way home. Suddenly, his new-found sweetness of life comes to a halt. Based on a short story by Ambrose Bierce. Telecast on "The Twilight Zone" in 1963.
1962 27m/B *D:* Robert Enrico. **VHS, Beta $19.95** *FST, VYY, HEG* 🎬🎬½

An Occurrence at Owl Creek Bridge/Coup de Grace "Occurrence at Owl Creek Bridge" (1962), from a story by Ambrose Bierce documents the last moments of a man about to be hanged for sabotage. "Coup de Grace" (1978) tells the story of a group of friends who are caught up amongst the turmoil of the Bolshevik revolution.
1962 123m/B Margarethe von Trotta, Matthias Habich, Rudiger Kirschstein, Matthieu Carriere, Valeska Gert; *D:* Volker Schlondorff, Robert Enrico. **VHS, Beta** *HEG* 🎬🎬🎬½

Ocean Drive Weekend Several college students congregate at "Ocean Drive" for a weekend of beer, sex, and dancing. Stereotyped characters, lack of plot, and poor versions of 1960 classics combine for boring and inane comedy.

1985 (PG-13) 98m/C Robert Peacock, Charles Redmond, Tony Freeman; *D:* Brian Thomas Jones. **VHS, Beta $69.98** *LIV, VES Woof!*

Ocean's 11 A gang of friends plans to rob five Las Vegas casinos simultaneously. Part of the "A Night at the Movies" series, this tape simulates a 1960 movie evening, with Bugs Bunny cartoon, "Person to Bunny;" a newsreel; and coming attractions for "The Sundowners" and "Sunrise at Campobello."
1960 148m/C Frank Sinatra, Dean Martin, Sammy Davis Jr., Angie Dickinson, Peter Lawford; *D:* Lewis Milestone. **VHS, Beta $19.98** *WAR* 🎬🎬½

Oceans of Fire Average rehash of the tension-filled world of oil riggers. Lives of two ex-cons are threatened when they hire on as divers for world's deepest undersea oil rig.
1986 (PG) 100m/C Gregory Harrison, Billy Dee Williams, Cynthia Sikes, Lyle Alzado, Tony Burton, Ray "Boom Boom" Mancini, David Carradine, Ken Norton; *D:* Steve Carver. **VHS, Beta $79.95** *VMK* 🎬

Octagon Norris protects a woman from threatening Ninja warriors in average kung-fu adventure. Enough action and violence for fans of the genre.
1980 (R) 103m/C Chuck Norris, Karen Carlson, Lee Van Cleef, Kim Lankford, Art Hindle, Jack Carter; *D:* Eric Karson. **VHS, Beta $19.95** *MED* 🎬🎬

Octaman Comical thriller featuring non-threatening octopus-man discovered by scientists in Mexico. Rip-off of director Essex's own "Creature from the Black Lagoon." Not without its curiosity factor: young Rick Baker designed the octopus man, while actress Angeli died of a drug overdose during filming.
1971 79m/C Kerwin Mathews, Pier Angeli, Harry Guardino, David Essex, Jeff Morrow, Norman Fields; *D:* Harry Essex. **VHS, Beta $19.95** *GEM, CNG, PSM* 🎬½

Octavia A contemporary fable about a blind girl who befriends a convict and learns about life and love.
1982 (R) 93m/C Susan Curtis; *D:* David Beaird; *W:* David Beaird. **VHS, Beta $59.98** *NLC* 🎬

October Man When a model is found murdered, a stranger with mental problems must prove his innocence to others and himself. Strong characters make good, suspenseful mystery reminiscent of Hitchcock.
1948 95m/B John Mills, Joan Greenwood, Edward Chapman, Joyce Carey, Kay Walsh, Felix Aylmer, Juliet Mills; *D:* Roy Ward Baker. **VHS, Beta** *LCA* 🎬🎬🎬

Octopussy The Bond saga continues as Agent 007 is on a mission to prevent a crazed Russian general from launching a nuclear attack against the NATO forces in Europe. Lots of special effects and gadgets keep weak plot moving.
1983 (PG) 140m/C Roger Moore, Maud Adams, Louis Jourdan, Kristina Wayborn, Kabir Bedi; *D:* John Glen; *W:* Michael G. Wilson; *M:* John Barry. **VHS, Beta $19.98** *MGM, FOX, TLF* 🎬🎬🎬

The Odd Angry Shot Australian soldiers fighting in Vietnam discover the conflict is not what they expected. Ironic perspective of men struggling with their feelings about the war. More of an unremarkable drama with comic overtones than a combat film, it will appeal to those who prefer good direction to bloodshed.
1979 90m/C *D:* Tom Jeffrey. **VHS, Beta $69.98** *LIV, VES* 🎬🎬½

Odd Birds Coming of age drama set in 1965 California. Shy 15 year old Joy Chan is a Chinese-American dreaming of becoming an actress. Her widowed immigrant mother

wants Joy to have a practical profession—like nursing. Longing for someone to understand Joy meets Brother Murphy, a math teacher at the local boys school. Murphy's been trying to reconcile his religious commitment with his unorthodox views. It isn't long before these two individualists recognize a fellow kindred spirit.
1985 87m/C Michael Moriarty, Donna Lai Ming Lew, Nancy Lee, Bruce Gray, Karen Maruyama, Scott Crawford; *D:* Jeanne Collachia; *W:* Jeanne Collachia. **VHS $79.95** *WAC* 🎬🎬

The Odd Couple Two divorced men with completely opposite personalities move in together. Lemmon's obsession with neatness drives slob Matthau up the wall, and their inability to see eye-to-eye results in many hysterical escapades. A Hollywood rarity, it is actually better in some ways than Neil Simon's original Broadway version. Basis for the hit television series.
1968 (G) 106m/C Jack Lemmon, Walter Matthau; *D:* Gene Saks; *W:* Neil Simon. **VHS, Beta $14.95** *PAR* 🎬🎬🎬½

The Odd Job Insurance salesman Chapman, depressed after his wife leaves him, hires a hit man to kill him. Chapman then has a hard time shaking his stalker after deciding he wants to live. Monty Python fans will enjoy seeing ex-troupe member Chapman again, but the comic's heart isn't in this unoriginal story.
1978 100m/C Graham Chapman; *D:* Peter Medak; *M:* Howard Blake. **VHS, Beta $69.95** *VES* 🎬🎬

Odd Jobs When five college friends look for jobs during summer break, they wind up running their own moving business with the help of the mob. Good comic talent, but a silly slapstick script results in only a passable diversion.
1985 (PG-13) 89m/C Paul Reiser, Scott McGinnis, Rick Overton, Robert Townsend; *D:* Mark Story; *M:* Robert Folk. **VHS, Beta $79.95** *HBO* 🎬🎬

Odd Man Out An Irish revolutionary is injured during a robbery attempt. Suffering from gunshot wounds and closely pursued by the police, he must rely on the help of others who could betray him at any moment. A gripping tale of suspense and intrigue that will keep the proverbial seat's edge warm until the final credits. Adapted from F.L. Green's novel, previously filmed as "The Last Man." *AKA:* Gang War.
1947 111m/B James Mason, Robert Newton, Dan O'Herlihy, Kathleen Ryan, Cyril Cusack; *D:* Carol Reed. Academy Awards '47 Nominations: Best Film Editing; British Academy Awards '47: Best Film; National Board of Review Awards '47: 10 Best Films of the Year. **VHS, Beta $19.95** *PAR* 🎬🎬🎬½

Odd Obsession One of Ichikawa's first films, about an elderly Japanese gentleman with a young wife whose feelings of jealousy and impotence eventually wreak havoc on the marriage. In Japanese with English subtitles. *AKA:* The Key.
1960 96m/C Machiko Kyo, Ganjiro Nakamura; *D:* Kon Ichikawa. **VHS, Beta $19.95** *COL, SUE, ING* 🎬🎬½

The Odd Squad Five GIs in WWII defend a bridge from the enemy, and manage in doing so to have loads of laughs.
1986 (R) 82m/C Johnny Dorelli, Vincent Gardenia; *D:* E.B. Clucher. **VHS, Beta $9.99** *STE, PSM* 🎬

Oddball Hall Two aging jewel thieves hide out in the African wilds, masquerading as powerful "wizards." When they head back to civilization, an African tribe be-

seeches the phony sorcerers to cure their long drought.
1991 (PG) 87m/C Don Ameche, Burgess Meredith; **D:** Jackson Hunsicker; **W:** Jackson Hunsicker. **VHS $89.98** *WAR, CAN* 🎬🎬

Oddballs In another attempt to capitalize on the success of Bill Murray's "Meatballs," this summer camp story follows three campers and their pathetic attempts to lose their virginity. Brooks has his moments, but there is little else to recommend here.
1984 (PG-13) 92m/C Foster Brooks, Jason Sorokin, Wally Wodchis, Konnie Krome; **D:** Miklos Lente. **VHS, Beta $79.98** *LIV Woof!*

Odds and Evens Italian supercops pretend they don't have badges in order to clean up illegal betting and gambling rings in sunny Miami. Odds are this spaghetti cop-o-rama won't keep Morpheus at bay.
1978 (PG) 109m/C Terence Hill, Bud Spencer; **D:** Sergio Corbucci. **VHS, Beta $79.95** *WAR* 🎬½

Ode to Billy Joe The 1967 Bobby Gentry hit song of the same title is expanded to tell why a young man jumped to his death off the Tallahatchie Bridge. The problems of growing up in the rural South and teenage romance do not match the appeal of the theme song. Benson and O'Connor, however, work well together.
1976 (PG) 106m/C Robby Benson, Glynnis O'Connor, Joan Hotchkis, Sandy McPeak, James Best; **D:** Max Baer Jr. **VHS, Beta $19.98** *CCB, WAR* 🎬🎬

The Odessa File During 1963, a German journalist attempts to track down some SS war criminals who have formed a secret organization called ODESSA. The story, from Frederick Forsyth's novel, drags in some places, but the scene where bad guy Schell and reporter Voight finally confront each other is a high point.
1974 (PG) 128m/C Jon Voight, Mary Tamm, Maximilian Schell, Maria Schell, Derek Jacobi; **D:** Ronald Neame; **M:** Andrew Lloyd Webber. **VHS, Beta $9.95** *GKK* 🎬🎬½

The Odyssey of the Pacific Three young Cambodian refugees encounter retired train engineer Rooney living in the woods where a railway station once thrived. Together they work to restore an old locomotive. The ordinary, inoffensive script will not endanger quality family time. *AKA:* The Emperor of Peru.
1982 82m/C Mickey Rooney, Monique Mercure; **D:** Fernando Arrabal. **VHS, Beta $39.95** *MCA* 🎬🎬½

Oedipus Rex Contained, and highly structured rendering of Sophocles' Greek tragedy, by the Stratford (Ontario) Festival Players; this production belongs on the stage, not the screen. Rain went on to be the voice of the Hal 9000 computer in Stanley Kubrick's "2001: A Space Odyssey." *AKA:* King Oedipus.
1957 87m/C Douglas Campbell, Douglas Rain, Eric House, Eleanor Stuart; **D:** Tyrone Guthrie. **VHS** *HMV, WBF* 🎬🎬½

Oedipus Rex A new twist on the famous tragedy as Pasolini gives the story a modern prologue and epilogue. The classic plot has Oedipus spiraling downward into moral horror as he tries to avoid fulfilling the prophecy that he will murder his father and sleep with his mother. Cross-cultural curiosities include Japanese music and Lenin-inspired songs, some written by Pasolini, who also stars as the high priest. In Italian with English subtitles. *AKA:* Edipo Re.
1967 110m/C Franco Citti, Silvana Mangano, Alida Valli, Julian Beck, Pier Paolo Pasolini; **D:** Pier Paolo Pasolini. **VHS $29.95** *FST, ING, FCT* 🎬🎬🎬

Of Cooks and Kung-Fu A martial arts culinary adventure.
198? 90m/C Jacky Cheng, Chia Kai, Lee Kuen. **VHS, Beta $57.95** *OCE* 🎬🎬

Of Human Bondage The first movie version of W. Somerset Maugham's classic novel in which a young, handicapped medical student falls in love with a crude cockney waitress, in a mutually destructive affair. Established Davis's role as the tough, domineering woman. Remade in 1946 and 1964.
1934 84m/B Bette Davis, Leslie Howard, Frances Dee, Reginald Owen, Reginald Denny, Alan Hale; **D:** John Cromwell. **VHS, Beta $9.95** *CNG, MRV, NOS* 🎬🎬🎬

Of Human Bondage An essentially decent man falls fatally in love with an alluring but heartless waitress, who subtly destroys him. Based on the W. Somerset Maugham novel. Miscast and least interesting of the three film versions, although Novak gives a good performance.
1964 100m/B Kim Novak, Laurence Harvey, Robert Morley, Roger Livesey, Siobhan McKenna; **D:** Henry Hathaway, Ken Hughes; **W:** Bryan Forbes. **VHS, Beta $24.95** *MGM* 🎬🎬

Of Human Hearts Rural life just before the Civil War sets up this cornpone tale of family strife. Huston is a stern preacher who has his family living in near poverty as an example of sacrifice to his flock. Son Stewart wants to study medicine and Bondi, defying her husband, manages to fund his dream. Only Stewart becomes so engrossed by his ambitions that he ignores the family, even after his father dies and his mother is left poor and alone. Then Stewart joins the Civil War as a doctor where he meets President Lincoln (Carradine), who tells him he should never neglect his mother. Oy. Well, the cast is good. Adapted from the story "Benefits Forgot" by Honore Morrow.
1938 100m/B James Stewart, Beulah Bondi, Walter Huston, John Carradine, Guy Kibbee, Charles Coburn, Ann Rutherford, Charley Grapewin, Gene Lockhart; **D:** Clarence Brown; **W:** Bradbury Foote. **VHS $29.98** *MGM, MOV* 🎬🎬½

Of Mice and Men A powerful adaptation of the classic Steinbeck tragedy about the friendship between two itinerant Southern ranch hands during the Great Depression. Chaney is wonderful as the gentle giant and mentally retarded Lenny, cared for by migrant worker Meredith. They both get into an irreversible situation when a woman is accidentally killed.
1939 107m/C Lon Chaney Jr., Burgess Meredith, Betty Field, Bob Steele, Noah Beery Jr., Charles Bickford; **D:** Lewis Milestone; **M:** Aaron Copland. **VHS, Beta $59.95** *NO* 🎬🎬🎬🎬

Of Mice and Men Made-for-television remake of the classic Steinbeck tale, casting TV's Baretta (Blake) as George and Quaid as Lenny. Worth watching.
1981 150m/C Robert (Bobby) Blake, Randy Quaid, Lew Ayres, Mitchell Ryan, Ted Neeley, Cassie Yates, Pat Hingle, Whitman Mayo, Dennis Fimple, Pat Corley; **D:** Reza Badiyi. **VHS, Beta $14.99** *PSM, KUI* 🎬🎬

Of Mice and Men Set on the migratory farms of California, John Steinbeck's novel covers the friendship of the simple-minded Lennie, his protector George, and a flirtatious farm wife who doesn't know Lennie's strength. Director Sinise got permission from Steinbeck's widow to film the novel (actually the third adaptation).

1992 (PG-13) 110m/C John Malkovich, Sherilyn Fenn, Casey Siemaszko, Joe Morton, Ray Walston, Gary Sinise, John Terry, Richard Riehle; **D:** Gary Sinise; **W:** Horton Foote. **VHS $19.98** *MGM, PMS, BTV* 🎬🎬🎬½

Of Unknown Origin Weller encounters a mutated rampaging rat in his New York townhouse while his family is away on vacation. His house becomes the battleground in a terror-tinged duel of survival. A well-done rat thriller not for those with a delicate stomach.
1983 (R) 88m/C Peter Weller, Jennifer Dale, Lawrence Dane, Kenneth Welsh, Louis Del Grande, Shannon Tweed; **D:** George P. Cosmatos; **W:** Brian Taggert. **VHS, Beta $19.98** *WAR* 🎬🎬½

Off Beat A shy librarian unluckily wins a spot in a police benefit dance troupe, and then falls in love with a tough police woman. With a screenplay by playwright Medoff, and a good supporting cast, it still manages to miss the mark.
1986 (PG) 92m/C Judge Reinhold, Meg Tilly, Cleavant Derricks, Fred Gwynne, John Turturro, Jacques D'Amboise, James Tolkan, Joe Mantegna, Harvey Keitel, Amy Wright; **D:** Michael Dinner; **W:** Medoff; **M:** James Horner. **VHS, Beta $79.95** *TOU* 🎬🎬½

Off Limits When a boxing manager is drafted into the Army, he freely breaks regulations in order to train a fighter as he sees fit. Hope and Rooney, while not in peak form, make a snappy duo in this amusing romp.
1953 89m/B Bob Hope, Mickey Rooney, Marilyn Maxwell, Marvin Miller; **D:** George Marshall. **VHS, Beta $19.98** *BAR* 🎬🎬½

Off Limits A spree of murders involving Vietnamese hookers draws two cops from the Army's Criminal Investigation Department into the sleazy backstreets of 1968 Saigon. There is little mystery as to who the killer is in this tale that seems written more for the sake of foul language and gratuitous gunfights than actual plot.
1987 (R) 102m/C Willem Dafoe, Gregory Hines, Fred Ward, Scott Glenn, Amanda Pays, Keith David, David Alan Grier; **D:** Christopher Crowe; **W:** Christopher Crowe, Jack Thibeau; **M:** James Newton Howard. **VHS, Beta $14.98** *FOX* 🎬½

Off on a Comet An animated adaptation of the Jules Verne story about a group of people carried through the cosmos on a comet. In HiFi.
1979 52m/C VHS, Beta $19.95 *MGM* 🎬½

Off the Mark Neely is a young athlete suffering from a childhood affliction that causes spasms in his legs. Facing the ultimate challenge, he must overcome his handicap and defeat a talented woman athlete and a Russian student in a triathalon competition. An unremarkable effort, it had a limited one-week run in theaters.
1987 (R) 89m/C Mark Neely, Terry Farrell, Jon Cypher, Clarence Gilyard Jr.; **D:** Bill Berry. **VHS, Beta** *FRH* 🎬

Off the Wall Two hitchhikers wind up in a southern maximum security prison after being accused of a crime they did not commit. What follows is a series of shenanigans as they try to escape. This supposed comedy falls flat in every way with the possible exception of Arquette's portrayal of the governor's daughter.
1982 (R) 86m/C Paul Sorvino, Rosanna Arquette, Patrick Cassidy, Billy Hufsey, Monte Markham, Mickey Gilley; **D:** Rick Friedberg. **VHS, Beta $29.98** *LIV, VES* 🎬

Off Your Rocker Representatives of a corporate conglomerate find that the residents of Flo Adler's Mapleview Nursing Home can still muster stiff resistance to a threatened takeover.
1980 99m/C Milton Berle, Red Buttons, Lou Jacobi, Dorothy Malone, Helen Shaver, Sharon Acker, Helen Hughes; **D:** Morley Markson, Larry Pall. VHS, Beta **NO** 🎞🎞½

The Offence Connery plays a London detective who beats a suspected child molester to death during a police interrogation. Turns out he's reacting to a long-buried molestation incident from his own childhood. A chilling psycho-drama highlighted by a strong lead performance by Connery. **AKA:** Something Like the Truth.
1973 (R) 108m/C Sean Connery, Trevor Howard, Vivien Merchant, Ian Bannen, Derek Newark, John Hallam, Peter Bowles; **D:** Sidney Lumet; **W:** John Hopkins. VHS **$14.95** MGM 🎞🎞🎞

Offerings After a boy is tormented by a gang of children who cause him to fall down a well, his resulting brain injuries turn him into a psychopathic killer. Seeking revenge ten years later, he systematically murders his oppressors, offering bits of their anatomy to the one girl who treated him kindly. A typical slasher movie, the plot is only slightly better than the worst examples of the genre.
1989 (R) 96m/C G. Michael Smith, Loretta L. Bowman; **D:** Christopher Reynolds. VHS, Beta **$14.95** HMD 🎞

Office Romances A woman who has moved to London from the country is seduced by her employer. Because of her plain appearance, she is flattered by his attention even though he is married and has no real feelings for her. Competently made, nonetheless hard to watch because of the slow pace.
1986 60m/C Judy Parfitt, Ray Brooks, Suzanne Burden. VHS, Beta **$11.95** PSM 🎞🎞

An Officer and a Gentleman Young drifter Gere, who enters Navy Officer Candidate School because he doesn't know what else to do with his life, becomes a better person almost despite himself. Winger is the love interest who sets her sights on marrying Gere, and Gossett is the sergeant who whips him into shape. Strong performances by the whole cast made this a must-see in 1982 that is still appealing, despite the standard Hollywood premise.
1982 (R) 126m/C Richard Gere, Louis Gossett Jr., David Keith, Lisa Eilbacher, Debra Winger, David Caruso, Robert Loggia, Lisa Blount; **D:** Taylor Hackford; **M:** Jack Nitzsche. Academy Awards '82: Best Song ("Up Where We Belong"), Best Supporting Actor (Gossett); Nominations: Best Actress (Winger), Best Film Editing, Best Original Screenplay, Best Original Score. VHS, Beta, 8mm **$14.95** PAR, FCT, BTV 🎞🎞🎞

Official Denial A victim of an alien abduction becomes the only hope for a captured space being. Can Paul help the alien escape from a special Air Force UFO group and what secrets will he uncover if he does? Made for television.
1993 86m/C Parker Stevenson, Erin Gray, Dirk Benedict, Chad Everett; **D:** Brian Trenchard-Smith; **W:** Bruce Zabel; **M:** Garry McDonald, Laurie Stone. VHS, Beta PAR 🎞🎞½

The Official Story A devastating drama about an Argentinian woman who realizes her young adopted daughter may be a child stolen from one of the thousands of citizens victimized by the country's repressive government. A powerful, important film. In Spanish with English subtitles or dubbed. **AKA:** La Historia Oficial; The Official History; The Official Version.
1985 (R) 112m/C Norma Aleandro, Hector Alterio, Chunchuna Villafane, Patricio Contreras; **D:** Luis Puenzo; **W:** Luis Puenzo, Aida Bortnik. Academy Awards '85: Best Foreign Language Film; Nominations: Best Original Screenplay; Cannes Film Festival '85: Best Actress (Aleandro); Golden Globe Awards '86: Best Foreign Film. VHS, Beta **$19.95** APD, AUD, ING 🎞🎞🎞

Offnight When a man is put on the day shift for the first time in fifteen years, his life turns to chaos.
1984 47m/C VHS, Beta **NO** 🎞½

The Offspring In four stories of past evils Price reveals his hometown can force folks to kill. Not the usual Price material: dismemberment, cannibalism, and necrophilia clash with his presence. Strong yuk factor. **AKA:** From a Whisper to a Scream.
1987 (R) 99m/C Vincent Price, Cameron Mitchell, Clu Gulager, Terry Kiser, Susan Tyrrell, Harry Caesar, Rosalind Cash, Martine Beswick, Angelo Rossitto, Lawrence Tierney; **D:** Jeff Burr; **W:** C. Courtney Joyner. VHS, Beta **$14.95** LIV 🎞🎞

Oh, Alfie In every man's life, there comes a time to settle down... but never when you're having as much fun as Alfie! Inadequate sequel to "Alfie." **AKA:** Alfie Darling.
1975 (R) 99m/C Joan Collins, Alan Price, Jill Townsend; **D:** Ken Hughes; **W:** Ken Hughes. VHS, Beta **$59.95** MON, HHE 🎞🎞

Oh, Bloody Life! Young actress faces deportation during the Stalin era in Hungary because of her aristocratic family ties. In Hungarian with English subtitles.
1988 115m/C Udvaros Dorottya, Szacsvay Laszlo, Kern Andras, Bezeredi Zoltan, Oze Lajos, Lukacs Margit; **D:** Peter Bacso; **W:** Peter Bacso. VHS **$49.95** EVD, ING, TPV 🎞🎞½

Oh! Calcutta! Film version of the first nude musical to play on Broadway, which caused a sensation in the late 1960s. It's really a collection of skits, some of which were written by such notables as John Lennon, Sam Shepard, and Jules Feiffer. And it's really not that funny or erotic.
1972 105m/C Bill Macy, Mark Dempsey, Raina Barrett, Samantha Harper, Patricia Hawkins, Mitchell McGuire; **D:** Guillaume Martin Aucion. VHS, Beta **NO** 🎞½

Oh Dad, Poor Dad (Momma's Hung You in the Closet & I'm Feeling So Sad) Cult fave black comedy about a bizarre family on a vacation in Jamaica. The domineering mother travels with a coffin containing the stuffed body of her late husband. Additional corpses abound. Based on the play by Arthur L. Kopit.
1967 86m/C Rosalind Russell, Robert Morse, Barbara Harris, Hugh Griffith, Lionel Jeffries, Jonathan Winters; **D:** Richard Quine. VHS, Beta **$49.95** PAR 🎞

Oh, God! God, in the person of Burns, recruits Denver as his herald in his plan to save the world. Despite initial skepticism, Denver, in his film debut, keeps faith and is rewarded. Sincere performances and optimistic end make for satisfying story. Followed by "Oh God! Book 2" and "Oh God! You Devil."
1977 (PG) 104m/C George Burns, John Denver, Paul Sorvino, Ralph Bellamy, Teri Garr, William Daniels, Donald Pleasence, Barnard Hughes, Barry Sullivan, Dinah Shore, Jeff Corey, David Ogden Stiers; **D:** Carl Reiner; **W:** Larry Gelbart. VHS, Beta **$19.98** WAR 🎞🎞½

Oh, God! Book 2 Burns returns as the "Almighty One" in strained sequel to "Oh God!" This time he enlists the help of a young girl to remind others of his existence. The slogan she concocts saves God's image,

but not the movie. Followed by "Oh, God! You Devil."
1980 (PG) 94m/C George Burns, Suzanne Pleshette, David Birney, Louanne, Conrad Janis, Wilfrid Hyde-White, Hans Conried, Howard Duff; **D:** Gilbert Cates; **M:** Charles Fox. VHS, Beta **$19.98** WAR 🎞

Oh, God! You Devil During his third trip to earth, Burns plays both the Devil and God as he first takes a struggling musician's soul, then gives it back. A few zingers and light atmosphere save unoriginal plot. The second sequel to "Oh, God!"
1984 (PG) 96m/C George Burns, Ted Wass, Roxanne Hart, Ron Silver, Eugene Roche, Robert Desiderio; **D:** Paul Bogart; **W:** Andrew Bergman. VHS, Beta **$19.98** WAR 🎞🎞

Oh, Heavenly Dog! A private eye returns from the dead as a dog to solve his own murder. Man's best friend and intelligent to boot. The famous dog Benji's third film, and his acting improves with each one. Adults may find this movie slow, but kids will probably love it.
1980 (PG) 104m/C Chevy Chase, Jane Seymour, Omar Sharif, Robert Morley, Susan Kellerman; **D:** Joe Camp. VHS, Beta **$19.98** FOX 🎞🎞

Oh, Mr. Porter Billeted at an obscure railway post, the stationmaster hero renovates the place and hires a special train to transport the area soccer team. Trouble arises when the train is hijacked by gun smugglers.
1937 85m/B Will Hay, Moore Marriot, Graham Moffatt, Frederick Piper; **D:** Marcel Varnel. VHS **$19.95** NOS 🎞🎞

Oh Susannah Robbed and thrown from a train, Autry and the two drifters who rescue him follow the thieves to Mineral Springs. Their journey is plagued by too many songs and the bad guys are predictably punished in the end.
1938 59m/B Gene Autry, Booth Howard, Smiley Burnette, Frances Grant, Donald Kirke, Clara Kimball Young; **D:** Joseph Cane. VHS, Beta **$19.95** NOS, VDM, HHT 🎞½

Oh, What a Night Bittersweet coming of age tale about a lonely 17-year-old (Haim) who has moved with his father and stepmother to a chicken farm in 1955 Ontario. After struggling with the untimely death of his mother, Haim falls in love with an older woman who has a husband and two kids. Features a great fifties soundtrack and beautiful scenes of the Canadian countryside.
1992 (PG-13) 93m/C Corey Haim, Barbara Williams, Keir Dullea, Genevieve Bujold, Robbie Coltrane; **D:** Eric Till. VHS **$89.95** COL, NLC 🎞🎞

O'Hara's Wife Loving wife Harley continues to care for her family even after her untimely death. Only husband Asner, however, can see her ghost. Lightweight, made-for-television drama traps good cast.
1982 87m/C Ed Asner, Mariette Hartley, Jodie Foster, Tom Bosley, Perry Lang, Ray Walston; **D:** William S. Bartman. VHS, Beta **$69.95** VES 🎞½

O.H.M.S. Convoluted story about a New York hood (Ford) who flees to England where he joins the British Army by posing as a Canadian. He buddies up with Mills and they both fall for Lee. His regiment is sent to China, via ship, and Lee just happens to be a stowaway. In China, Ford manages to prove his worth by saving Lee from bandits. Maybe it's not supposed to make sense.
1937 71m/B Wallace Ford, John Mills, Anna Lee, Frank Cellier, Frederick Leister, Peter Croft; **D:** Raoul Walsh. VHS HCV 🎞🎞½

Oil Seven men fight a raging oil fire that threatens to destroy an entire country. Unfortunately, the movie is unable to ignite any interest at all.
1978 (PG) 95m/C Ray Milland, Woody Strode, Stuart Whitman, Tony Kendall, William Berger; **D:** Mircea Dragan. **VHS, Beta $19.95** VCI ℐ

Oklahoma! Jones's film debut; a must-see for musical fans. A cowboy and country girl fall in love, but she is tormented by another unwelcomed suitor. At over two hours, cuteness wears thin for some. Actually filmed in Arizona. Adapted from Rodgers and Hammerstein's broadway hit with original score; choreography by Agnes de Mille. ♫Oh, What a Beautiful Morning; Surrey with the Fringe on Top; I Cain't Say No; Many a New Day; People Will Say We're in Love; Poor Jud Is Dead; All 'Er Nuthin'; Everything's Up to Date in Kansas City; The Farmer and the Cowman.
1955 (G) 145m/C Gordon MacRae, Shirley Jones, Rod Steiger, Gloria Grahame, Eddie Albert, Charlotte Greenwood, James Whitmore, Gene Nelson, Barbara Lawrence, Jay C. Flippen; **D:** Fred Zinneman; **W:** Sonya Levien, William Ludwig; **M:** Richard Rodgers, Oscar Hammerstein. Academy Awards '55: Best Sound, Best Score; Nominations: Best Color Cinematography, Best Film Editing. **VHS, Beta $19.98** FOX, RDG, HMV ℐℐℐ½

Oklahoma Annie Storekeeper Canova joins the new sheriff in booting undesirables out of town, and tries to sing her way into his heart. Amazingly, it works—not for delicate ears.
1951 90m/C Judy Canova, Fuzzy Knight, Grant Withers, John Russell, Denver Pyle, Allen Jenkins, Almira Sessions; **D:** R.G. Springsteen. **VHS, Beta** MLB ℐ

Oklahoma Badlands Lane and his horse outsmart a corrupt newspaper publisher trying to steal land from a female rancher. An early directorial work for veteran stuntman Canutt.
1948 59m/B Allan "Rocky" Lane, Mildred Coles; **D:** Yakima Canutt. **VHS, Beta $29.95** DVT ℐ½

Oklahoma Bound A feisty farmer tries to save his failing farm through a series of ostensibly comedic, unsuccessful schemes.
1981 92m/C F.E. Bowling, Dan Jones; **D:** Patrick C. Poole. **VHS, Beta $19.95** VCI ℐ

Oklahoma Crude Sadistic oil trust rep Palence battles man-hating Dunaway for her well. Drifter Scott helps her resist on the promise of shared profits. In this 1913 setting, Dunaway tells Scott she wishes she could avoid men altogether, but later settles for him.
1973 (PG) 108m/C George C. Scott, Faye Dunaway, John Mills, Jack Palance, Harvey Jason, Woodrow Parfrey; **D:** Stanley Kramer; **W:** Marc Norman; **M:** Henry Mancini. **VHS** FOX ℐℐ½

Oklahoma Cyclone A group of bronco busters find action and adventure on the prairie. Second of eight talkies in Steele series; includes his first of few singing roles.
1930 64m/B Bob Steele, Al "Fuzzy" St. John, Nita Ray, Charles "Blackie" King; **D:** John P. McCarthy. **VHS $19.95** NOS, GPV, DVT ℐ½

Oklahoma Kid Offbeat, hilarious western with Bogie as the villain and gunfighter Cagney seeking revenge for his father's wrongful death. Highlight is Cagney's rendition of "I Don't Want To Play In Your Yard," complete with six-shooter accompaniment.
1939 82m/B James Cagney, Humphrey Bogart, Rosemary Lane, Ward Bond, Donald Crisp, Charles Middleton, Harvey Stephens; **D:** Lloyd Bacon. **VHS, Beta $19.98** MGM, FCT ℐℐℐ

The Oklahoman A routine western with some trivia value. Town doc McCrea helps Indian Pate keep his land. Talbott plays Indian maiden in same year as her title role in Daughter of Jekyll. Continuity buffs will note Hale wears the same outfit in most scenes.
1956 80m/C Joel McCrea, Barbara Hale, Brad Dexter, Gloria Talbott, Verna Felton, Douglas Dick, Michael Pate, Scotty Beckett; **D:** Francis D. Lyon. **VHS, Beta $19.98** FOX ℐℐ

Okoge Rueful sexual comedy about a triangular friendship. Sayoko is a single young working woman living in a tiny Tokyo apartment. She meets the gay Noh and his older married lover Tochi and when they become friendly, Sayoko lets them use her apartment as their love nest—to the complications of all concerned. Title is a slang term used to refer to women who prefer the company of gay men. In Japanese with English subtitles.
1993 120m/C Misa Shimizu, Takehiro Murata, Takeo Nakahara, Masayuki Shionoya, Noriko Songoku, Kyozo Nagatsuka, Toshie Nogishi; **D:** Takehiro Nakajima; **W:** Takehiro Nakajima. **VHS $79.95** FCT ℐℐ

Old Barn Dance Autry and his singing cowboys are selling horses until a crooked tractor company puts them out of business. They join a radio program, discovers that it is owned by the same company that put them out of the horse-selling business, and runs the crooks out of town.
1938 54m/B Gene Autry, Smiley Burnette, Roy Rogers; **D:** Joseph Kane. **VHS, Beta $19.95** NOS, VCN, DVT ℐ½

Old Boyfriends Shire is weak as a psychologist searching for old boyfriends in order to analyze her past. Strange combination of Carradine and Belushi may draw curious fans.
1979 (R) 103m/C Talia Shire, Richard Jordan, John Belushi, Keith Carradine, John Houseman, Buck Henry; **D:** Joan Tewkesbury; **W:** Leonard Schrader, Paul Schrader. **VHS, Beta $9.95** NLC ℐ

Old Corral Sheriff Autry protects his love interest, a girl fleeing the Mob. **AKA:** Texas Serenade.
1936 54m/B Gene Autry, Roy Rogers, Smiley Burnette; **D:** Joseph Kane. **VHS, Beta $19.95** NOS, MRV, VTR ℐℐ

The Old Curiosity Shop Webster and Benson are an old gambler and his daughter in this well-made film adaptation of the Dickens tale. Their miserly landlord tries to ruin their lives by evicting them and forcing them into a life of poverty. Remade as "Mr. Quilp" in 1957.
1935 90m/B Ben Webster, Elaine Benson, Hay Petrie, Beatrix Thompson, Gibb McLaughlin, Reginald Purdell; **D:** Thomas Bentley. **VHS $19.95** NOS ℐℐ½

The Old Curiosity Shop Flat musical version of the Charles Dickens story about an evil man who wants to take over a small antique shop run by an elderly man and his granddaughter. ♫When a Felon Needs a Friend; Somewhere; Love Has the Longest Memory; Happiness Pie; The Sport of Kings; What Shouldn't Happen to a Dog; Quilp. **AKA:** Mr. Quilp.
1975 (G) 118m/C Anthony Newley, David Hemmings, David Warner, Jill Bennett, Peter Duncan, Michael Hordern; **D:** Michael Tuchner; **M:** Elmer Bernstein. **VHS, Beta $14.98** REP, SUE ℐℐ

The Old Curiosity Shop An animated adaptation of the classic Dickens story about a young girl and her grandfather who are evicted from their curiosity shop by an evil man.

1984 (G) 72m/C VHS, Beta $19.98 LIV ℐℐ

The Old Dark House An atmospheric horror film, with more than a touch of comedy, well-directed by Whale. In an old haunted house live the bizarre Femm family: the 102 year-old patriarch, an atheist son, a religious fanatic daughter, and a crazed pyromanic son, all watched over by the mute, scarred, and psychotic butler (Karloff's first starring role). Into this strange group wander five unsuspecting, stranded travelers who set all sorts of dastardly plots in motion. Based on the novel "Benighted" by J.B. Priestley.
1932 71m/B Boris Karloff, Melvyn Douglas, Charles Laughton, Gloria Stuart, Ernest Thesiger, Raymond Massey, Lillian Bond, Eva Moore, Brember Wills, John Dudgeon; **D:** James Whale; **W:** Robert Dillon. **VHS $29.95** FCT ℐℐℐ

Old Enough Slow-moving coming-of-age comedy on the rich kid-poor kid friendship theme. Silver's directing debut.
1984 (PG) 91m/C Sarah Boyd, Rainbow Harvest, Neill Barry, Danny Aiello, Susan Kingsley, Roxanne Hart, Alyssa Milano, Fran Brill, Anne Pitoniak; **D:** Marisa Silver; **W:** Marisa Silver. **VHS, Beta $59.95** MED ℐℐ

Old Explorers Two old friends refuse to let old age lessen their want for excitement, so they get together on a regular basis to set out on dangerous, imaginary adventures. They search for Atlantis, explore the Himalayan Mountains, and visit the Bermuda Triangle. After one of the men survives a stroke, the two set out on a real-life adventure on a tugboat cruising down the Mississippi River. Although the leads put in strong performances, they can't hide the slow-moving plot or the thin action sequences. Based on the play by James Cada and Mark Keller.
1990 (PG) 91m/C Jose Ferrer, James Whitmore, Jeffrey Gadbois, Caroline Kaiser, William Warfield, Christopher Pohlad, Storm Richardson, William M. Pohlad. **VHS $19.95** ACA ℐℐ½

Old Gringo Adapted from Carlos Fuentes' novelization of writer Ambrose Bierce's mysterious disappearance in Mexico during the revolution of 1913. Features Fonda in the unlikely role of a virgin schoolteacher, Smits as her revolutionary lover, and Peck as her hero. Soggy acting by all but Peck, whose presence is wasted in a sketchy character. Technical problems and cheesy sets and costumes—look for the dusk backdrop in the dance scene and Smits' silly moustache. Better to read the book.
1989 (R) 119m/C Jane Fonda, Gregory Peck, Jimmy Smits, Patricio Contreras, Jenny Gago, Gabriela Roel, Sergio Calderon, Guillermo Rios, Anne Pitoniak, Pedro Armendariz Jr., Jim Metzler; **D:** Luis Puenzo; **W:** Aida Bortnik, Luis Puenzo; **M:** Lee Holdridge. **VHS, Beta, 8mm $14.95** COL ℐℐ½

Old Gun A grief-plagued doctor finds he must seek out and kill each Nazi involved in the slaughter of his wife and child to ease his pain. Excellent directing and a fully formed main character.
1976 141m/C Philippe Noiret, Romy Schneider, Jean Bouise; **D:** Robert Enrico. **VHS, Beta $49.95** MED ℐℐ

Old Ironsides Silent, black-and-white version of the big budget/important director and stars action-adventure. Merchant marines aboard the famous Old Ironsides battle 19th century Barbary pirates in rousing action scenes. Home video version features an engaging organ score by Gaylord Carter. Based on the poem "Constitution" by Oliver Wendell Holmes.

1926 111m/B Esther Ralston, Wallace Beery, Boris Karloff, Charles Farrell, George Bancroft; *D:* James Cruze; *M:* Gaylord Carter. **VHS, Beta** $29.95 PAR 🐾🐾🐾

The Old Maid After her beau is killed in the Civil War, a woman allows her cousin to raise her illegitimate daughter, and therein begins a years-long struggle over the girl's affections. High grade soaper based on Zoe Adkin's stage adaptation of Edith Wharton's novel.
1939 96m/B Bette Davis, Miriam Hopkins, George Brent, Donald Crisp, Jane Bryan, Louise Fazenda, Henry Stephenson; *D:* Edmund Goulding. **VHS, Beta** $19.95 MGM 🐾🐾🐾

Old Mother Riley's Ghosts A group of spies "haunt" Mother Riley's castle home in a futile attempt to scare her out; she turns the tables. Some good scares and laughs. Part of the Old Mother Riley series. Look for similarities to later Monty Python films.
1941 82m/B Arthur Lucan, Kitty McShane, John Stuart; *D:* John Baxter. **VHS, Beta** $16.95 NOS, SNC 🐾🐾

Old Spanish Custom Only a Keaton fan could love this comedy, set in Spain and filmed in England. One of his rarest—and poorest—sound films. He plays a bumbling rich yachtsman smitten with Tovar, a Spanish maiden who uses him to make her lover jealous. *AKA:* The Invader.
1936 58m/B Buster Keaton, Lupita Tova, Lyn Harding, Esme Percy; *D:* Adrian Brunel. **VHS, Beta** $14.95 VYY, GPV, VDM 🐾

Old Swimmin' Hole Small-town friends Moran and Jones try to bring their single parents together; his mother can't afford to finance his dream to be a doctor. Dull, melodramatic ode to heartland America, reminiscent of "Our Town." *AKA:* When Youth Conspires.
1940 78m/B Marcia Mae Jones, Jackie Moran, Leatrice Joy, Charles D. Brown; *D:* Robert McGowan. **VHS, Beta** $24.95 VYY 🐾🐾

Old Yeller Disney Studios' first and best boy-and-his-dog film. Fifteen-year-old Kirk is left in charge of the family farm while Parker is away. When his younger brother brings home a stray dog, Kirk is displeased but lets him stay. Yeller saves Kirk's life, but contracts rabies in the process. Kirk is forced to kill him. Keep tissue handy, especially for the kids. Stong acting, effective scenery—all good stuff. Based on the novel by Fred Gipson. Sequel "Savage Sam" released in 1963.
1957 (G) 84m/C Dorothy McGuire, Fess Parker, Tommy Kirk, Kevin Corcoran, Jeff York, Beverly Washburn, Chuck Connors; *D:* Robert Stevenson. **VHS, Beta** $19.99 DIS 🐾🐾🐾½

Oldest Living Graduate Fonda is memorable in his last stage role as the oldest graduate of a Texas military academy. He and his son clash when Fonda refuses to give up his land. Teleplay features strong performances from Leachman and other big-name cast members.
1982 75m/C Cloris Leachman, Henry Fonda, John Lithgow, Timothy Hutton, Harry Dean Stanton, David Ogden Stiers, George Grizzard, Penelope Milford. **VHS, Beta** $49.95 VHE 🐾🐾🐾½

Oldest Profession A study of prostitution from prehistoric times to the future. Generally unexciting and unfunny. In six segments meant as vehicles for their directors. *AKA:* Le Plus Vieux Metier du Monde.
1967 97m/C Raquel Welch, Jeanne Moreau, Elsa Martinelli, Michele Mercier; *D:* Jean-Luc Godard, Philippe de Broca, Claude Autant-Lara, Franco Indovina, Mauro Bolognini, Michael Pfleghar; *W:* Jean-Luc Godard. **VHS, Beta** $19.95 NWV, IME 🐾

Oliver! Splendid big-budget musical adaptation of Dickens' "Oliver Twist." An innocent orphan is dragged into a life of crime when he is befriended by a gang of pickpockets. ♫Food, Glorious Food; Oliver; Boy For Sale; Where Is Love?; Consider Yourself; Pick a Pocket or Two; I'd Do Anything; Be Back Soon; As Long As He Needs Me.
1968 (G) 145m/C Mark Lester, Jack Wild, Ron Moody, Shani Wallis, Oliver Reed, Hugh Griffith; *D:* Carol Reed. Academy Awards '68: Best Art Direction/Set Decoration, Best Director (Reed), Best Picture, Best Sound, Best Score; Nominations: Best Actor (Moody), Best Adapted Screenplay, Best Cinematography, Best Costume Design, Best Film Editing, Best Supporting Actor (Wild); Golden Globe Awards '69: Best Actor—Musical/Comedy (Moody), Best Film—Musical/Comedy; National Board of Review Awards '68: 10 Best Films of the Year. **VHS, Beta** $19.95 COL, BTV, HMV 🐾🐾🐾½

Oliver Twist Silent version of the Dickens classic is a vehicle for young Jackie Coogan. As orphan Oliver Twist, he is subjected to many frightening incidents before finding love and someone to care for him. Remade numerous times, most notably in 1933 and 1948 and as the musical "Oliver!" in 1968.
1922 77m/B Jackie Coogan, Lon Chaney Sr., Gladys Brockwell, George Siegmann, Esther Ralston; *D:* Frank Lloyd. **VHS, Beta** $19.95 NOS, CCB 🐾🐾🐾

Oliver Twist The first talking version of Dickens' classic about an ill-treated London orphan involved with youthful gang of pickpockets. Moore was too young—at five—to be very credible in the lead role. The 1948 version is much more believable.
1933 70m/B Dickie Moore, Irving Pichel, William Boyd, Barbara Kent; *D:* William J. Cowan. **VHS, Beta** $19.95 NOS, MRV, HHT 🐾🐾

Oliver Twist Charles Dickens' immortal story of a workhouse orphan who is forced into a life of crime with a gang of pickpockets. The best of many film adaptations, with excellent portrayals by the cast.
1948 116m/B Robert Newton, John Howard Davies, Alec Guinness, Francis L. Sullivan, Anthony Newley, Kay Walsh, Diana Dors, Henry Stephenson; *D:* David Lean; *W:* David Lean. **VHS, Beta** $19.95 PAR, DVT, FHS 🐾🐾🐾🐾

Oliver Twist Good made-for-television version of the classic Dicken's tale of a boy's rescue from a life of crime. Scott's Fagin is a treat, and period details are on the mark.
1982 72m/C George C. Scott, Tim Curry, Michael Hordern, Timothy West, Lysette Anthony, Eileen Atkins, Cherie Lunghi; *D:* Clive Donner; *W:* James Goldman; *M:* Nick Bicat. **VHS, Beta** $14.98 REP, VES 🐾🐾🐾

Oliver Twist A British television miniseries adaptation of the Charles Dickens classic about an orphan boy plunging into the underworld of 19th-century London. On two tapes.
1985 333m/C Ben Rodska, Eric Porter, Frank Middlemass, Gillian Martell. **VHS, Beta** $29.98 FOX, SIG, HMV 🐾🐾🐾

Oliver's Story A "not so equal" sequel to "Love Story", where widower O'Neal wallows in grief untils rich heiress Bergen comes along. He falls in love again, this time with money.
1978 (PG) 90m/C Ryan O'Neal, Candice Bergen, Ray Milland, Edward Binns, Nicola Pagetti, Charles Haid; *D:* John Korty; *W:* Erich Segal. **VHS, Beta** $14.95 PAR 🐾

Olivia Abused housewife moonlights as a prostitute and begins killing her customers. She falls in love with an American businessman and flees to America when her husband finds out about the affair. Revenge and murder are the result.

1983 90m/C Suzanna Love, Robert Walker Jr., Jeff Winchester; *D:* Ulli Lommel. **VHS, Beta** $49.95 VHE 🐾½

Olivier, Olivier Holland's directorial follow-up to "Europa, Europa" is based on a 1984 French newspaper story and evokes "The Return of Martin Guerre" and its update, "Sommersby." Beloved nine-year-old boy disappears from his home in a small French town and his dysfunctional family falls apart. Mom obsesses and falls into trances, dad escapes to North Africa, and sister Nadine develops telekinetic powers in order to cope. Six years later a detective brings an amnesiac teenager, who has been working as a hustler in Paris, to the boy's family. Is it the missing Olivier? Spooky, provocative, and emotionally resonate. In French with English subtitles.
1992 (R) 110m/C Francois Cluzet, Brigitte Rouan, Gregoire Colin, Marina Golovine, Jean-Francois Stevenin, Emmanuel Morozof, Faye Gatteau, Frederic Quiring; *D:* Agnieszka Holland); *W:* Agnieszka Holland. **VHS** $89.95 COL 🐾🐾🐾

Ollie Hopnoodle's Haven of Bliss Humorist Jean Shepherd (of "A Christmas Story" fame) spins another tale of frantic family life with his alter ego, Ralphie. This time the family is off on a summer vacation—with all its inherent problems. Made for cable television.
1988 90m/C James B. Sikking, Dorothy Lyman, Jerry O'Connell; *D:* Dick Bartlett. **VHS, Beta** $39.99 DIS 🐾🐾½

Olly Olly Oxen Free Junkyard owner Hepburn helps two boys fix up and fly a hot-air balloon, once piloted by McKenzie's grandfather, as a surprise for the man's birthday. Beautiful airborne scenes over California and a dramatic landing to the tune of the "1812 Overture," but not enough to make the whole film interesting. *AKA:* The Great Balloon Adventure.
1978 89m/C Katharine Hepburn, Kevin McKenzie, Dennis Dimster, Peter Kilman; *D:* Richard A. Colla. **VHS, Beta** TLF 🐾🐾

Olongape: The American Dream A young woman works in a cheap bar while waiting for the chance to come to America.
1989 97m/C Jacklyn Jose, Susan Africa, Chanda Romero, Joel Torre, Marilou Sadiua; *D:* Chito Rono. **VHS, Beta** $59.95 TWE 🐾½

Omar Khayyam In medieval Persia, Omar (Wilde) becomes involved in a romance with the Shah of Persia's fiancee, while trying to fight off a faction of assassins trying to overthrow the Shah. Although this film has a great cast, the script is silly and juvenile, defeating the cast's fine efforts.
1957 101m/C Cornel Wilde, Michael Rennie, Debra Paget, Raymond Massey, John Derek, Yma Sumac, Margaret Hayes, Joan Taylor, Sebastian Cabot; *D:* William Dieterle. **VHS** PAR 🐾🐾

Omega Cop In a post-apocalyptic future, there's only one cop left. He uses his martial arts skills and tons of guns attempting to rescue three women, but the violence doesn't cover the poor acting and shoddy production. Fans of TV's Batman might enjoy this for West's presence.
1990 (R) 89m/C Ron Marchini, Adam West, Stuart Whitman, Troy Donahue, Meg Thayer, Jennifer Jostyn, Chrysti Jimenez, D.W. Landingham, Chuck Katzakian; *D:* Paul Kyriazi. **VHS** $14.95 HMD 🐾

Omega Man In post-holocaust Los Angeles, Heston is immune to the effects of a biologically engineered plague and battles those who aren't—an army of albino victims bent on destroying what's left of the world. Strong suspense with considerable violence,

despite the PG rating. Based on the science fiction thriller "I Am Legend" by Richard Matheson, which is also the basis for the film "The Last Man on Earth."
1971 (PG) 98m/C Charlton Heston, Anthony Zerbe, Rosalind Cash, Paul Koslo; **D:** Boris Sagal. **VHS, Beta $14.95** WAR ♫♫½

Omega Syndrome Neo-Nazis kidnap Wahl's daughter. He and Vietnam buddy DiCenzo get her back. Ho hum. DiCenzo's is the best performance. Tolerable for vigilante film fans.
1987 (R) 90m/C Ken Wahl, Ron Kuhlman, George DiCenzo, Doug McClure; **D:** Joseph Manduke. **VHS, Beta $14.95** NWV, STE ♫½

The Omen American diplomat's family adopts a young boy who always seems to be around when bizarre and inexplicable deaths occur. Of course, what else would you expect of Satan's son? The shock and gore prevalent in "The Exorcist" is replaced with more suspense and believable effects. Well-done horror film doesn't insult the viewer's intelligence. Followed by two sequels: "Damien: Omen 2" and "The Final Conflict." *AKA:* Birthmark.
1976 (R) 111m/C Gregory Peck, Lee Remick, Billie Whitelaw, David Warner, Holly Palance, Richard Donner; **D:** Richard Donner; **W:** David Seltzer; **M:** Jerry Goldsmith. Academy Awards '76: Best Original Score; Nominations: Best Song ("Ave Satani"). **VHS, Beta $19.98** FOX ♫♫½

Omen 4: The Awakening It turns out Damien of Omens past had a daughter, Delia, who takes up where dear old devilish Dad left off. Delia is adopted by your basic clueless couple and proceeds to wreak havoc wherever she goes, including getting rid of several interfering adults. She also plans to make her adoptive father, a U.S. senator, President, so that this delightful child anti-Christ can have him carry out all her evil plans.
1991 97m/C Faye Grant, Michael Woods, Michael Lerner, Asia Vieira; **D:** Jorge Montesi, Dominique Othenin-Girard. **VHS $89.98** FXV ♫♫

Omoo Omoo, the Shark God A sea captain is cursed when he removes the black pearls from a stone shark god in this extremely cheap adventure.
1949 58m/B Ron Randell, Devera Burton, Trevor Bardette, Pedro de Cordoba, Richard Benedict, Rudy Robles, Michael Whalen, George Meeker; **D:** Leo Leonard. **VHS $16.95** SNC ♫

On a Clear Day You Can See Forever A psychiatric hypnotist helps a girl stop smoking and finds that in trances she remembers previous incarnations. He falls in love with one of the women she used to be. Alan Jay Lerner of "My Fair Lady" and "Camelot" wrote the lyrics and the book. Based on a musical by Lerner and Burton Lane. ♫On a Clear Day, You Can See Forever; Come Back to Me; What Did I Have That I Don't Have?; He Isn't You; Hurry, It's Lovely Up Here; Go To Sleep; Love with All the Trimmings; Melinda.
1970 (G) 129m/C Barbra Streisand, Yves Montand, Bob Newhart, Jack Nicholson, Simon Oakland; **D:** Vincente Minnelli. **VHS, Beta $14.95** PAR ♫♫

On an Island with You Williams plays a movie star who finds romance on location in Hawaii in this musical extravaganza. Contains many of Williams' famous water ballet scenes and a bevy of bathing beauties. ♫On an Island with You; If I Were You; Taking Miss Mary to the Ball; Dog Song; Buenas Noches, Buenos Aires; Wedding Samba; I Can Do Without Broadway, But Can Broadway Do Without Me?.

1948 107m/C Esther Williams, Peter Lawford, Ricardo Montalban, Jimmy Durante, Cyd Charisse, Leon Ames; **D:** Richard Thorpe. **VHS $19.98** MGM ♫♫½

On Approval Hilarious British farce in which two women trade boyfriends. Lillie's performace provides plenty of laughs. Brook runs the show as leading man, co-author, director, and co-producer. Based on the play by Frederick Lonsdale.
1944 80m/B Clive Brook, Beatrice Lillie, Googie Withers, Roland Culver; **D:** Clive Brook. **VHS, Beta $19.95** NOS, MRV, HHT ♫♫♫

On Borrowed Time Engrossing tale of Death (Hardwicke) coming for an old man (Barrymore) who isn't ready to die so he traps him in his backyard apple tree. Performances are first rate in this good adaptation of the stage success (originally by Eugene O'Neill). Hardwicke is especially a standout; he gave up theatre for Hollywood after making this film.
1939 99m/B Lionel Barrymore, Cedric Hardwicke, Beulah Bondi, Una Merkel, Bobs Watson, Henry Travers; **D:** Harold Bucquet. **VHS $19.98** MGM ♫♫♫

On Dangerous Ground A world-weary detective is sent to the countryside to investigate a murder. He encounters the victim's revenge-hungry father and the blind sister of the murderer. In the hateful father the detective sees a reflection of the person he has become, in the blind woman, he learns the redeeming qualities of humanity and compassion. A well-acted example of film noir that features the composer Herrman's favorite score.
1951 82m/B Robert Ryan, Ida Lupino, Ward Bond, Ed Begley Sr., Cleo Moore, Charles Kemper; **D:** Nicholas Ray; **M:** Bernard Herrmann. **VHS, Beta $39.95** TTC ♫♫♫

On Deadly Ground Seagal nearly destroys Alaska in an effort to save it in this inane, preachy story of an oil-rig roughneck out to protect the landscape from an evil oil company's drilling habits. Directorial debut for Seagal lumbers from scene to scene. Violence is expected, as is silly dialogue—just try to keep from laughing when stoney-faced Steven intones "What does it take to change the essence of man?" A better script, for one.
1994 (R) 102m/C Steven Seagal, Michael Caine, Joan Chen, John C. McGinley; **D:** Steven Seagal; **W:** Ed Horowitz; **M:** Basil Poledouris. **VHS** WAR Woof!

On Golden Pond Henry Fonda won his first, and long overdue, Oscar for his role as the curmudgeonly patriarch of the Thayer family. He and his wife have grudgingly agreed to look after a young boy while at their summer home in Maine. Through his gradually affectionate relationship with the boy, Fonda learns to allay his fears of mortality. He also gains an understanding of his semi-estranged daughter. Jane Fonda plays his daughter and Hepburn is his loving wife in this often funny adaptation of Ernest Thompson's 1978 play. Predictable but deeply moving. Henry Fonda's final screen appearance.
1981 (PG) 109m/C Henry Fonda, Jane Fonda, Katharine Hepburn, Dabney Coleman, Doug McKeon, William Lanteau; **D:** Mark Rydell; **W:** Ernest Thompson; **M:** Dave Grusin. Academy Awards '81: Best Actor (Fonda), Best Actress (Hepburn), Best Adapted Screenplay; Nominations: Best Actor (Fonda), Best Cinematography, Best Director (Rydell), Best Film Editing, Best Sound, Best Supporting Actress (Fonda), Best Original Score; British Academy Awards '82: Best Actress (Hepburn); Golden Globe Awards '82: Best Actor—Drama (Fonda),

Best Film—Drama, Best Screenplay. **VHS, Beta $14.95** FHE, SUP, KAR ♫♫♫½

On Her Majesty's Secret Service In the sixth 007 adventure, Bond again confronts the infamous Blofeld, who is planning a germ-warfare assault on the entire world. Australian Lazenby took a crack at playing the super spy, with mixed results. Many feel this is the best-written of the Bond films and might have been the most famous, had Sean Connery continued with the series. Includes the song "We Have All the Time In the World," sung by Louis Armstrong.
1969 (PG) 144m/C George Lazenby, Diana Rigg, Telly Savalas, Gabriel Ferzetti, Ilse Steppat, Bernard Lee, Lois Maxwell, Desmond Llewelyn, Catherine Schell, Julie Ege, Joanna Lumley, Mona Chong, Anouska Hempel, Jenny Hanley; **D:** Peter Hunt; **M:** John Barry. **VHS, Beta $19.98** MGM, FOX, TLF ♫♫♫

On Moonlight Bay Set in small-town Indiana in 1917 with Day as the tomboyish Marjorie who falls for college man MacRae. Her father (Ames) doesn't approve but the trouble really begins when Marjorie's younger brother gets into trouble at school. The incorrigible Wesley (Gray) blames everything on dear old dad and MacRae feels he must come to Marjorie's rescue! Gray steals the movie as the bratty brother—otherwise its business as usual. Based on Booth Tarkington's "Penrod" stories and followed by "By the Light of the Silvery Moon." ♫Love Ya; On Moonlight Bay; Till We Meet Again; Pack Up Your Troubles In Your Old Kit Bag; I'm Forever Blowing Bubbles; Christmas Story; Tell Me Why Nights Are Lonely; Cuddle Up a Little Closer; Every Little Movement Has a Meaning All Its Own.
1951 95m/C Doris Day, Gordon MacRae, Leon Ames, Billy Gray, Rosemary DeCamp, Mary Wickes, Ellen Corby, Esther Dale; **D:** Roy Del Ruth; **W:** Melville Shavelson, Jack Rose; **M:** Max Steiner. **VHS $19.98** WAR, MVD ♫♫

On the Air Live with Captain Midnight Socially challenged teen finds hipness as a rebel DJ operating an illegal radio station from his van. Leading actor is the son of the director/writer/producer but nepotism does not a good film make. *AKA:* Captain Midnight.
1979 90m/C Tracy Sebastian; **D:** Ferd Sebastian. **VHS, Beta** NO ♫½

On the Avenue Broadway showman Powell opens up a new musical, starring Faye as the richest girl in the world, in this musical-comedy satirizing upper-crust society. Debutante Carroll is outraged because she realizes it's mocking her actual life. Carroll tries to get Powell to change the show, they fall in love, Faye gets her nose out of joint, and after lots of fuss everything ends happily. Fine Berlin score. ♫He Ain't Got Rhythm; You're Laughing at Me; This Year's Kisses; Slumming on Park Avenue; The Girl on the Police Gazette; I've Got My Love to Keep Me Warm.
1937 90m/B Dick Powell, Madeleine Carroll, Alice Faye, George Barbier, The Ritz Brothers, Alan Mowbray, Cora Witherspoon, Walter Catlett, Stepin Fetchit, Sig Rumann, Douglas Fowley, Joan Davis; **D:** Roy Del Ruth; **W:** Gene Markey; **M:** Irving Berlin. **VHS $19.98** FXV ♫♫

On the Beach A group of survivors attempt to live normal lives in post-apocalyptic Australia, waiting for the inevitable arrival of killer radiation. Astaire is strong in his first dramatic role. Though scientifically implausible, still a good anti-war vehicle. Based on the best-selling novel by Nevil Shute.

1959 135m/B Gregory Peck, Anthony Perkins, Donna Anderson, Ava Gardner, Fred Astaire; *D:* Stanley Kramer; *M:* Ernest Gold. Academy Awards '59 Nominations: Best Film Editing, Best Original Score; Golden Globe Awards '60: Best Score; National Board of Review Awards '59: 10 Best Films of the Year. VHS, Beta $19.98 FOX, FCT *ⅡⅡ*½

On the Comet Zeman's fourth fantasy based on Jules Verne stories, about a chunk of the Earth's crust suddenly becoming a comet and giving its passengers a ride through the galaxy. Complete with Zeman's signature animation fantasias. In English. *AKA:* Na Komete; Hector Servadac's Ark.
1968 76m/C Emil Horvath Jr., Magda Vasarykova, Frantisek Filipovsky; *D:* Karel Zeman. VHS, Beta $19.99 FCT, MRV *ⅡⅡⅡ*

On the Edge A narcotics agent tracks down a wealthy Brazilian drug kingpin.
1982 82m/C Anthony Steffen. VHS, Beta NO *Ⅱ*

On the Edge A drama about the inevitable Rocky-esque triumph of Dern as an aging marathon runner. Simultaneous to his running endeavor, Dern is trying to make up for lost time with his father. Available in two versions, one rated, the other unrated with a racy appearance by Pam Grier as the runner's interracial lover.
1986 (PG-13) 86m/C Bruce Dern, John Marley, Bill Bailey, Jim Haynie, Pam Grier; *D:* Rob Nilsson; *W:* Rob Nilsson. VHS, Beta NO *ⅡⅡ*½

On the Edge: The Survival of Dana Another entry from the world of low-quality made-for-TV films. A young girl moves with her family to a new town. When she falls in with the "bad" crowd, her ethical standards are challenged. A stinker that may appeal to those with campy tastes. Not for the discriminating palate.
1979 92m/C Melissa Sue Anderson, Robert Carradine, Marion Ross, Talia Balsam, Michael Pataki, Kevin Breslin, Judge Reinhold, Barbara Babcock; *D:* Jack Starrett. VHS, Beta GEM Woof!

On the Line Two Mexico-US border guards, one hard-bitten, the other sympathetic to the illegal immigrants' plight, battle it out over a beautiful Mexican whore. Disjointed and confusing.
1983 95m/C David Carradine, Victoria Abril, Scott Wilson, Sam Jaffe, Jesse Vint; *D:* Jose Luis Borau. VHS, Beta $19.98 SUE, NLC *Ⅱ*½

On the Nickel An ex-alcoholic returns to Fifth Street in Los Angeles to save his friend from a life of despair. Waits' musical score enhances this sentimental skid row drama. Scripted, directed and produced by "The Waltons'" Waite.
1980 (R) 96m/C Ralph Waite, Donald Moffatt, Hal Williams, Jack Kehoe; *D:* Ralph Waite; *W:* Ralph Waite; *M:* Tom Waits. VHS, Beta $69.95 VES *ⅡⅡ*

On the Night Stage Gruff bandit (legendary Hart) loses his girl-of-questionable-values to town preacher. One of the first feature length westerns.
1915 83m/B William S. Hart, Robert Edeson, Rhea Mitchell, Shorty Hamilton; *D:* Reginald Barker. VHS, Beta, 8mm $18.95 GPV, VYY *ⅡⅡ*

On the Old Spanish Trail Rogers becomes a singing cowboy with a traveling tent show in order to pay off a note signed by the Sons of the Pioneers.
1947 56m/B Roy Rogers, Jane Frazee, Andy Devine, Tito Guizar; *D:* William Witney. VHS, Beta $9.95 NOS, MRV, VCN *Ⅱ*

On the Right Track Young orphan living in Chicago's Union Station has the gift of being able to pick winning race horses. May be appealing to fans of Coleman and

"Different Strokes" television show, but lacks the momentum to keep most viewers from switching tracks.
1981 (PG) 98m/C Gary Coleman, Lisa Eilbacher, Michael Lembeck, Norman Fell, Maureen Stapleton, Herb Edelman; *D:* Lee Philips. VHS, Beta $59.95 FOX *Ⅱ*½

On the Run An ex-con and his gal cut a law-defying swath through the Bayou.
1985 (R) 96m/C Jack Conrad, Rita George, Dub Taylor, David Huddleston. VHS, Beta $59.95 GEM *Ⅱ*

On the Third Day A headmaster finds a mysterious stranger in his house who turns out to be his long-lost illegitimate son.
1983 101m/C Richard Marant, Catherine Schell, Paul Williamson. VHS, Beta $59.95 LHV *Ⅱ*

On the Town Kelly's directorial debut features three sailors on a one day leave search for romance in the Big Apple. Filmed on location in New York City, with uncompromisingly authentic flavor. Based on the successful Broadway musical, with a score composed by Leonard Bernstein, Betty Comden, and Adolph Green. Additional songs by Roger Edens. Available in a deluxe collector's laserdisc edition. ♫New York, New York; I Feel Like I'm Not Out of Bed Yet; Come Up to My Place; Miss Turnstiles Ballet; Main Street; You're Awful; On the Town; You Can Count on Me; Pearl of the Persian Sea.
1949 98m/C Gene Kelly, Frank Sinatra, Vera-Ellen, Ann Miller, Betty Garrett; *D:* Gene Kelly, Stanley Donen; *W:* Betty Comden, Adolph Green. VHS, Beta $19.98 MGM *ⅡⅡⅡ*½

On the Town Bernstein's first big Broadway success in 1944, recorded in a live performance June 1992, at London's Barbican Centre. Follows the story of three sailors on a 24-hour leave in New York City during WWII. This version includes numbers which never made it into the original Broadway show.
1991 110m/C Frederica von Stade, Tyne Daly, Marie McLaughlin, David Garrison, Thomas Hampson, Kurt Ollman, Evelyn Lear, Samuel Ramey, Cleo Laine; *M:* Leonard Bernstein, Betty Comden, Adolph Green. VHS $29.95 PGV, FCT *ⅡⅡ*½

On the Waterfront A trend-setting, gritty portrait of New York dock workers embroiled in union violence. Cobb is the gangster union boss, Steiger his crooked lawyer, and Brando, Steiger's ex-fighter brother who "could've been a contender!" Intense performances and excellent direction stand up well today. The picture was a huge financial success.
1954 108m/B Marlon Brando, Rod Steiger, Eva Marie Saint, Lee J. Cobb, Karl Malden, Pat Henning, Leif Erickson, Tony Galento, John Hamilton, Nehemiah Persoff; *D:* Elia Kazan; *W:* Budd Schulberg; *M:* Leonard Bernstein. Academy Awards '54: Best Actor (Brando), Best Art Direction/Set Decoration (B & W), Best Black and White Cinematography, Best Director (Kazan), Best Film Editing, Best Picture, Best Story & Screenplay, Best Supporting Actress (Saint); Nominations: Best Supporting Actor (Cobb), Best Supporting Actor (Malden, Steiger), Best Original Score; Directors Guild of America Awards '54: Best Director (Kazan); Golden Globe Awards '55: Best Actor—Drama (Brando), Best Director (Kazan), Best Film—Drama; National Board of Review Awards '54: 10 Best Films of the Year; New York Film Critics Awards '54: Best Actor (Brando), Best Director (Kazan), Best Film. VHS, Beta $19.95 COL, BTV *ⅡⅡⅡⅡ*

On the Yard An attempt to realistically portray prison life. Focuses on a murderer who runs afoul of the leader of the prisoners and the system. A fairly typical prison drama

with above average performances from Heard and Kellin.
1979 (R) 102m/C John Heard, Thomas G. Waites, Mike Kellin, Joe Grifasi; *D:* Raphael D. Silver. VHS, Beta $69.95 MED *ⅡⅡ*

On Top of Old Smoky Autry and the Cass County Boys are mistaken for Texas Rangers by a gang of land poachers.
1953 59m/B Gene Autry, Smiley Burnette, Gail Davis, Sheila Ryan; *D:* George Archainbaud. VHS, Beta $29.98 CCB *ⅡⅡ*

On Top of the Whale Two scholars move onto the estate of strange but wealthy benefactor to conduct research on the few survivors of a disappearing clan of Indians. Two tribesmen speak bizarre dialect which utilizes only one word while others confound the researchers with stories of ghosts and graveyards. Dutch comedy subtitled in English.
1982 93m/C *D:* Raul Ruiz. VHS $59.95 KIV, FCT, ING *ⅡⅡ*

On Valentine's Day Author Horton Foote based this story loosely on his parents' lives. A wealthy young Southern girl marries a poor but decent young man and finds herself ostracized from her family. A prequel to the same author's "1918." Produced with PBS for "American Playhouse." *AKA:* Story of a Marriage.
1986 (PG) 106m/C Hallie Foote, Matthew Broderick, Michael Higgins, Steven Hill, William Converse-Roberts, Rochelle Oliver, Richard Jenkins, Horton Foote Jr., Carol Goodheart; *D:* Ken Harrison; *W:* Horton Foote; *M:* Jonathan Sheffer. VHS, Beta $19.98 LHV *ⅡⅡ*

On Wings of Eagles During the 1979 Iranian revolution two American executives are imprisoned by Islamic radicals. Help arrives in the form of covert agents of their boss—Texas tycoon H. Ross Perot (played by Crenna). Don't expect strict historical veracity or insight from this network miniseries (based on the "nonfiction novel" by Ken Follett), an okay but lengthy "mission impossible." It came out in a two-cassette set, just in time for Perot's 1992 presidential campaign.
1986 221m/C Burt Lancaster, Richard Crenna, Paul LeMat, Esai Morales, Constance Towers, Jim Metzler, James Sutorius, Lawrence Pressman, Karen Carlson, Cyril O'Reilly; *D:* Andrew V. McLaglen. VHS $89.95 WOV *ⅡⅡ*½

Onassis Romanticized biography of Greek shipping magnate Aristotle Onassis, from the poverty of his youth to his later wealth and family and romantic liaisons and tragedies. Julia is adequate as the title character but English actress Annis is badly miscast as Jackie Kennedy Onassis. However, Seymour is terrific as Onassis' lover, opera star Maria Callas. Quinn, who played Onassis in "The Greek Tycoon," plays Onassis' father in this one. Based on the novel by Peter Evans. Originally a made for television miniseries known as "The Richest Man in the World: The Story of Aristotle Onassis."
1988 120m/C Raul Julia, Jane Seymour, Francesca Annis, Anthony Quinn, Anthony Zerbe, Lorenzo Quinn; *D:* Waris Hussein. VHS $89.98 TTC *Ⅱ*½

Once a Hero The dregs of society, the Cicero Gang, have taken Captain Justice's number one fan and his mother hostage. Is it really curtains for rosy cheeks, bubble gum, and apple pie? But wait, it's Captain Justice, the man, the myth, to the rescue!
1988 74m/C Jeff Lester, Robert Forster, Milo O'Shea; *D:* Claudia Weill. VHS $9.99 NWV, STE *ⅡⅡ*

Once Around 30ish, lonely Renata Bella (Hunter) meets boisterous, self-assured (read utterly obnoxious) Lithuanian salesman Sam Sharpe (Dreyfuss). He sweeps her off her feet, showers her with affection and gifts, and then tries hard—too hard—to please her close-knit Italian family. Casting doesn't get much better than the group assembled here and Hallstrom steers everyone to wonderful performances in his American directorial debut. The major flaw is the script, a light romantic comedy that sometimes swerves into heavy drama, so much so that you may need kleenex.
1991 (R) 115m/C Richard Dreyfuss, Holly Hunter, Danny Aiello, Gena Rowlands, Laura San Giacomo, Roxanne Hart, Danton Stone, Tim Guinee, Greg Germann, Griffin Dunne; **D:** Lasse Hallstrom; **W:** Malia Scotch Marmo, **M:** James Horner. **VHS, Beta $19.98** MCA, FCT ♫♫½

Once Before I Die Army soldiers caught in the Philippines during WWII struggle to survive and elude the Japanese. A single woman traveling with them becomes the object of their spare time considerations. A brutal, odd, and gritty war drama. Director/actor Derek was Andress' husband at the time.
1965 97m/C Ursula Andress, John Derek, Richard Jaeckel, Rod Lauren, Ron Ely; **D:** John Derek. **VHS** MOV ♫♫½

Once Bitten Centuries-old though still remarkably youthful vampiress comes to LA to stalk male virgins. That may be the wrong city, but she needs their blood to retain her young countenance. Vampire comedy theme was more effectively explored in 1979s "Love at First Bite," notable, however for the screen debut of comic Carrey who would later gain fame for TV's "In Living Color" and "Ace Ventura, Pet Detective."
1985 (PG-13) 94m/C Lauren Hutton, Jim Carrey, Cleavon Little, Karen Kopins, Thomas Balltore, Skip Lackey; **D:** Howard Storm; **W:** Jonathan Roberts; **M:** John Du Prez. **VHS, Beta $79.98** LIV, VES ♫♫

Once in Paris... A bittersweet romance about a scriptwriter working in Paris, the chauffeur who befriends him, and the aristocratic British woman with whom the writer falls in love. Beautiful French scenery and the engaging performance of Lenoir as the chauffeur make this film a diverting piece of entertainment.
1979 (PG) 100m/C Wayne Rogers, Gayle Hunnicutt, Jack Lenoir; **D:** Frank D. Gilroy; **W:** Frank D. Gilroy. **VHS, Beta $9.95** SUE, MED ♫♫½

Once is Not Enough Limp trash-drama concerning the young daughter of a has-been movie producer who has a tempestuous affair with a writer who reminds her of her father. Based on the novel by Jacqueline Susann. **AKA:** Jacqueline Susann's Once is Not Enough.
1975 (R) 121m/C Kirk Douglas, Deborah Raffin, David Janssen, George Hamilton, Brenda Vaccaro, Alexis Smith, Melina Mercouri; **D:** Guy Green; **W:** Julius J. Epstein, Philip C. Epstein; **M:** Henry Mancini. Academy Awards '75 Nominations: Best Supporting Actress (Vaccaro); Golden Globe Awards '76: Best Supporting Actress (Vaccaro). **VHS, Beta $59.95** PAR ♫½

Once Upon a Brothers Grimm An original musical fantasy in which the Brothers Grimm meet a succession of their most famous storybook characters including Hansel and Gretel, the Gingerbread Lady, Little Red Riding Hood, and Rumpelstiltskin.
1977 102m/C Dean Jones, Paul Sand, Cleavon Little, Ruth Buzzi, Chita Rivera, Teri Garr. **VHS, Beta $39.95** VCI ♫♫

Once Upon a Crime Extremely disappointing comedy featuring a high profile cast set in Europe. The plot centers around Young and Lewis finding a dachshund and travelling from Rome to Monte Carlo to return the stray and collect a $5,000 reward. Upon arrival in Monte Carlo, they find the dog's owner dead and they end up getting implicated for the murder. Other prime suspects include Belushi, Candy, Hamilton, and Shepherd. Weak script is made bearable only by the comic genius of Candy.
1992 (PG) 94m/C John Candy, James Belushi, Cybill Shepherd, Sean Young, Richard Lewis, Ornella Muti, Giancarlo Giannini, George Hamilton, Joss Ackland, Elsa Martinelli; **D:** Eugene Levy; **M:** Richard Gibbs. **VHS $14.95** MGM ♫½

Once Upon a Forest Animated tale of three woodland creatures in a daring race against time when their young friend's life is at stake. Ecologically correct story by "American Tail" creator David Kirschner is light on humor and heavy on gloom, as little animals encounter oppressive human society and their big, bad machines. Servicable animation, though not up to Don Bluth standards (and a long, long way from Disney). Crawford, the voice of the wise old uncle, has a song, while Vereen breaks into a fervent gospel number as a marsh bird with a yen for preaching. For an evening of anti-pollution, treat the earth kindly animation, see it with "Ferngully."
1993 (G) 80m/C **D:** Charles Grosvenor; **W:** Mark Young, Kelly Ward; **V:** Michael Crawford, Ben Vereen. **VHS $24.98** FXV, FUS, WTA ♫♫

Once Upon a Honeymoon Set in 1938, Grant is an American radio broadcaster reporting on the oncoming war. Rogers is the ex-showgirl who unknowingly marries a Nazi. In this strange, uneven comedy, Grant tries to get the goods on him and also rescue Rogers. The plot is basic and uneven with Grant attempting to expose the Nazi and save Rogers. However, the slower moments are offset by some fairly surreal pieces of comedy.
1942 116m/B Ginger Rogers, Cary Grant, Walter Slezak, Albert Dekker; **D:** Leo McCarey. **VHS, Beta $19.98** CCB, TTC, FCT ♫♫½

Once Upon a Midnight Scary Price narrates a collection of three tales of terror, "The Ghost Belonged to Me," "The Legend of Sleepy Hollow," and "The House with a Clock in Its Walls." Aimed at the kiddies.
1990 50m/C Rene Auberjonois, Severn Darden; **D:** Neil Cox. **VHS** GEM, MRV ♫♫

Once Upon a Scoundrel A ruthless Mexican land baron arranges to have a young woman's fiancee thrown in jail so he can have her all to himself.
1973 (G) 90m/C Zero Mostel, Katy Jurado, Tito Vandis, Priscilla Garcia, A. Martinez; **D:** George Schaefer. **VHS, Beta $9.99** PSM ♫♫½

Once Upon a Time A pretty girl, her puppy, a charming prince, and a grinch combine for a magical, wondrous animated fantasy.
1976 (G) 83m/C **VHS, Beta $29.95** GEM ♫♫½

Once Upon a Time Two rival tribes spoil the love of a prince and princess in ancient times. Animated.
1987 92m/C **VHS, Beta $39.95** MED ♫♫½

Once Upon a Time in America The uncut original version of director Leone's saga of five young men growing up in Brooklyn during the '20s who become powerful mob figures. Also available in a 143-minute version. Told from the perspective of De Niro's Noodles as an old man looking back at 50 years of crime, love, and death, told with a sweeping and violent elegance.
1984 (R) 225m/C Robert De Niro, James Woods, Elizabeth McGovern, Treat Williams, Tuesday Weld, Burt Young, Joe Pesci, Danny Aiello, Darlanne Fluegel, Jennifer Connelly; **D:** Sergio Leone; **M:** Ennio Morricone. **VHS, Beta $19.98** WAR ♫♫♫½

Once Upon a Time in the West The uncut version of Leone's sprawling epic about a band of ruthless gunmen who set out to murder a mysterious woman waiting for the railroad to come through. Filmed in John Ford's Monument Valley, it's a revisionist western with some of the longest opening credits in the history of the cinema. Fonda is cast against type as an extremely cold-blooded villain. Brilliant musical score.
1968 (PG) 165m/C Henry Fonda, Jason Robards Jr., Charles Bronson, Claudia Cardinale, Keenan Wynn, Lionel Stander, Woody Strode, Jack Elam; **D:** Sergio Leone; **W:** Sergio Leone, Bernardo Bertolucci, Dario Argento; **M:** Ennio Morricone. **VHS, Beta $24.95** PAR ♫♫♫½

Once Upon a Time in Vietnam This politically irksome drama about Vietnam was filmed in Georgia. **AKA:** How Sleep the Brave.
198? 90m/C **VHS, Beta** VCD ♫

One Against the Wind A true story of one woman's courage against great odds. British Mary Liddell and her children are living in Paris during the WWII Nazi occupation. Mary's secret agenda is to smuggle downed Allied pilots out of the country to safety without arousing Nazi suspicions. Great performances by Davis as the resourceful Mary and Neill as one of the pilots she rescues. A Hallmark Hall of Fame presentation.
1991 (PG) 96m/C Judy Davis, Sam Neill, Denholm Elliott, Anthony Higgins, Christien Anholt, Kate Beckinsale, Frank Middlemass; **D:** Larry Elikann. **VHS $14.98** REP ♫♫

One A.M. Charlie is a drunk who must first battle a flight of stairs in order to get to bed. Silent with music track.
1916 20m/B Charlie Chaplin. **VHS, Beta** CAB, GVV ♫♫♫

The One and Only An egotistical young man is determined to make it in show business. Instead, he finds himself in the world of professional wrestling. Most of the humor comes from the wrestling scenes, with Winkler and Darby's love story only serving to dilute the film.
1978 (PG) 98m/C Henry Winkler, Kim Darby, Gene Saks, William Daniels, Harold Gould, Herve Villechaize; **D:** Carl Reiner. **VHS, Beta $69.95** PAR ♫♫½

The One and Only, Genuine, Original Family Band A harmonious musical family becomes divided when various members take sides in the presidential battle between Benjamin Harrison and Grover Cleveland, a political era that has been since overlooked.
1968 (G) 110m/C Walter Brennan, Buddy Ebsen, Lesley Ann Warren, Kurt Russell, Goldie Hawn, Wally Cox, Richard Deacon, Janet Blair; **D:** Michael O'Herlihy. **VHS, Beta $9.99** DIS ♫♫♫

One Arabian Night When an exotic dancer in a traveling carnival troupe is kidnapped into a harem, a dwarf acts on his unrequited love and avenges her death by murdering the sheik who killed her. Secured a place in American filmmaking for director Lubitsch. **AKA:** Sumurun.
1921 85m/B Pola Negri, Ernst Lubitsch, Paul Wegener; **D:** Ernst Lubitsch. **VHS, Beta $24.95** VYY, GPV, GLV ♫♫♫

The One Arm Swordsmen Many one-armed men are persecuted for the murder committed by one fugitive one-armed man, and they decide to group together to track him down themselves.
1972 109m/C VHS, Beta $39.95 *UNI* 🐾

One Armed Executioner An Interpol agent seeks revenge on his wife's murderers.
1980 (R) 90m/C Franco Guerrero, Jody Kay; *D:* Bobby A. Auarez. **VHS, Beta** *NO* 🐾🐾

One Away Gypsy escapes from a South African prison and the police are in hot pursuit.
1980 (PG) 83m/C Elke Sommer, Bradford Dillman, Dean Stockwell. **VHS, Beta $39.95** *MON* 🐾

One Body Too Many A mystery spoof about a wacky insurance salesman who's mistaken for a detective. The usual comedy of errors ensues. A contrived mish-mash—but it does have Lugosi going for it.
1944 75m/B Jack Haley, Jean Parker, Bela Lugosi, Lyle Talbot; *D:* Frank McDonald. **VHS, Beta $19.95** *NOS, SNC, HHT* 🐾🐾

One Brief Summer Love triangles and intrigues abound on a spectacular country manor. An aging woman is mortified by her father's interest in a young seductress, who finds herself attracted to the old man, but not only him.
1970 (R) 86m/C Clifford Evans, Felicity Gibson, Jennifer Hilary, Jan Holden, Peter Egan; *D:* John MacKenzie. **VHS $14.95** *LPC Woof!*

One Cooks, the Other Doesn't A most unlikely story of a man's ex-wife and his son moving back into his house, where he's now living with his new wife. Made for television.
1983 96m/C Suzanne Pleshette, Joseph Bologna, Rosanna Arquette, Oliver Clark; *D:* Richard Michaels. **VHS, Beta $39.95** *LIV* 🐾🐾

One Crazy Summer A group of wacky teens spend a fun-filled summer on Nantucket Island in New England. This follow-up to "Better Off Dead" is offbeat and fairly charming, led by Cusack's perplexed cartoonist and with comic moments delivered by Goldthwait.
1986 (PG) 94m/C John Cusack, Demi Moore, William Hickey, Curtis Armstrong, Bob(cat) Goldthwait, Mark Metcalf, Joel Murray, Tom Villard, Joe Flaherty; *D:* Steve Holland; *W:* Steve Holland; *M:* Cory Lerios. **VHS, Beta $19.98** *WAR* 🐾🐾½

One Dark Night Two high school girls plan an initiation rite for one of their friends who is determined to shed her "goody-goody" image. West is the caped crusader of TV series "Batman" fame.
1982 94m/C Meg Tilly, Adam West, David Mason Daniels, Robin Evans; *D:* Tom McLoughlin. **VHS, Beta $69.95** *HBO* 🐾½

One Day in the Life of Ivan Denisovich The film version of Nobel Prize-winner Alexander Solzhenitsyn's novel about a prisoner's experiences in a Soviet labor camp. A testament to human endurance. Photography be Sven Nykvist.
1971 105m/C Tom Courtenay, Alfred Burke, Espen Skjonberg, James Maxwell, Eric Thompson; *D:* Caspar Wrede; *W:* Ronald Harwood. **VHS $79.95** *ING* 🐾🐾🐾

One Deadly Owner A made-for-television film about a possessed Rolls-Royce torturing its new owner. Quite a vehicle for the usually respectable set of wheels.
1974 80m/C Donna Mills, Jeremy Brett, Robert Morris, Laurence Payne. **VHS, Beta $29.95** *LIV* 🐾

One Deadly Summer Revenge drama about a young girl who returns to her mother's home village to ruin three men who had assaulted her mother years before. Very well acted. From the novel by Sebastien Japrisot. In French with English subtitles. *AKA:* L'Ete Meurtrier.
1983 (R) 134m/C Isabelle Adjani, Alain Souchon, Suzanne Flon; *D:* Jean Becker; *M:* Georges Delerue. Cannes Film Festival Nominations: cs 83: Best Film; Cesar Awards '84: Best Actress (Adjani), Best Supporting Actress (Flon). **VHS, Beta $59.95** *MCA, ING* 🐾🐾🐾

One Down, Two to Go! When the mob is discovered to be rigging a championship karate bout, two dynamic expert fighters join in a climactic battle against the hoods. Example of really bad "blaxploitation" that wastes talent, film, and the audience's time.
1982 (R) 84m/C Jim Brown, Fred Williamson, Jim Kelly, Richard Roundtree; *D:* Fred Williamson. **VHS, Beta $59.95** *MED, RHI, HHE Woof!*

One-Eyed Jacks An often engaging, but lengthy, psychological western about an outlaw who seeks to settle the score with a former partner who became a sheriff. Great acting by all, particularly Brando, who triumphed both as star and director. Stanley Kubrick was the original director, but Brando took over mid-way through the filming. The photography is wonderful and reflects the effort that went into it.
1961 141m/C Marlon Brando, Karl Malden, Katy Jurado, Elisha Cook Jr., Slim Pickens, Ben Johnson, Pina Pellicer, Timothy Carey; *D:* Marlon Brando; *W:* Calder Willingham. **VHS, Beta $79.95** *PAR* 🐾🐾🐾½

One-Eyed Soldiers Young woman, criminal, and dwarf follow trail to mysterious key to unlock $15 million treasure. Much cheesy intrigue.
1967 83m/C Dale Robertson, Lucianna Paluzzi; *D:* Jean Christopher. **VHS** *NO* 🐾

One-Eyed Swordsman A handicapped samurai battles shogun warriors. With English subtitles.
1963 95m/C Tetsuro Tamba, Haruko Wanibuchi; *D:* Seiichiro Uchikawa. **VHS, Beta** *VDA* 🐾

One False Move Black psycho Pluto, his white-trash partner Ray, and Ray's biracial lover Fantasia are three low-level drug dealers on the streets of Los Angeles who get involved in murder. Fleeing the city for Fantasia's small hometown in Arkansas, they come up against the local sheriff and two L.A. cops sent to bring them back. Not a typical crime thriller, first-time feature director Franklin is more interested in a psychological character study of racism and smalltown mores than in your average shoot 'em up action picture. Good performances, especially by Williams as the deceptive bad girl.
1991 (R) 105m/C Bill Paxton, Cynda Williams, Michael Beach, Jim Metzler, Earl Billings, Billy Bob Thornton, Natalie Canderday, Robert Ginnaven, Robert Anthony Bell, Kevin Hunter; *D:* Carl Franklin; *W:* Billy Bob Thornton, Tom Epperson. **VHS $89.95** *COL, FCT* 🐾🐾🐾

One Flew Over the Cuckoo's Nest Touching, hilarious, dramatic, and completely effective adaptation of Ken Kesey's novel. Nicholson is a two-bit crook, who, facing a jail sentence, feigns insanity to be sentenced to a cushy mental hospital. The hospital is anything but cushy, with a tyrannical head nurse out to squash any vestige of the patients' independence. Nicholson proves to be a crazed messiah and catalyst for these mentally troubled patients and a

worthy adversary for the head nurse. Classic performs superbly on numerous levels.
1975 (R) 129m/C Jack Nicholson, Brad Dourif, Louise Fletcher, Will Sampson, William Redfield, Danny DeVito, Christopher Lloyd, Scatman Crothers, Vincent Schiavelli, Michael Berryman, Peter Brocco, Louisa Moritz; *D:* Milos Forman; *W:* Ken Kesey, Bo Goldman; *M:* Jack Nitzche. Academy Awards '75: Best Actor (Nicholson), Best Actress (Fletcher), Best Adapted Screenplay, Best Director (Forman), Best Picture; Nominations: Best Cinematography, Best Film Editing, Best Supporting Actor (Dourif), Best Original Score; British Academy Awards '76: Best Actor (Nicholson), Best Actress (Fletcher), Best Director (Forman), Best Film, Best Supporting Actor (Dourif); Golden Globe Awards '76: Best Actor—Drama (Nicholson), Best Actress—Drama (Fletcher), Best Director (Forman), Best Film—Drama, Best Screenplay; National Board of Review Awards '75: 10 Best Films of the Year, Best Actor (Nicholson); National Society of Film Critics Awards '75: Best Actor (Nicholson); People's Choice Awards '77: Best Film. **VHS, Beta $14.98** *REP, BTV, FCT* 🐾🐾🐾🐾

One Frightened Night An eccentric millionaire informs his family members that he is leaving each of them one million dollars...as long as his long-lost granddaughter doesn't reappear. Guess who comes to dinner.
1935 69m/B Mary Carlisle, Wallace Ford, Hedda Hopper, Charley Grapewin; *D:* Christy Cabanne. **VHS, Beta $19.95** *NOS, BAR, VYY* 🐾🐾½

One from the Heart The film more notable for sinking Coppola's Zoetrope Studios than for its cinematic context. Garr and Forrest are a jaded couple who seek romantic excitement with other people. An extravagant (thus Coppola's finance problems) fantasy Las Vegas set, pretty to look at but does little to enhance the weak plot. Score by Waits, a much-needed plus.
1982 (R) 100m/C Teri Garr, Frederic Forrest, Nastassia Kinski, Raul Julia, Lainie Kazan, Rebecca DeMornay, Harry Dean Stanton; *D:* Francis Ford Coppola; *W:* Francis Ford Coppola, Armyan Bernstein; *M:* Tom Waits. **VHS, Beta $79.95** *COL* 🐾🐾

One Good Cop A noble, inconsistent attempt to do a police thriller with a human face, as a young officer and his wife adopt the three little daughters of his slain partner from the force. But it reverts to a routine action wrapup, with 'Batman' Keaton even donning a masked-avenger getup to get revenge.
1991 (R) 105m/C Michael Keaton, Rene Russo, Anthony LaPaglia, Kevin Conway, Rachel Ticotin, Grace Johnston, Blair Swanson, Rhea Silver-Smith, Tony Plana, Benjamin Bratt, Charlaine Woodard; *D:* Heywood Gould; *W:* Heywood Gould; *M:* William Ross. **VHS, Beta $19.99** *HPH* 🐾🐾½

100 Rifles Native American bank robber and Black American lawman join up with a female Mexican revolutionary to help save the Mexican Indians from annihilation by a despotic military governor. What it lacks in political correctness it makes up for in fits of action. Although quite racy in its day for its interracial sex sizzle of Brown and Rachel, it's tame and overblown by today's standards.
1969 (R) 110m/C Jim Brown, Raquel Welch, Burt Reynolds, Fernando Lamas; *D:* Tom Gries; *M:* Jerry Goldsmith. **VHS, Beta $19.98** *FOX, FXV* 🐾🐾

101 Dalmations Disney classic is one of the highest-grossing animated films in the history of Hollywood. Dogowners Roger and Anita, and their spotted pets Pongo and Perdita are shocked when their puppies are kidnapped by Cruella de Vil, villainess ex-

traordinaire, to make a simply fabulous spotted coat. The aid of various animals including a dog named Colonel, a horse, a cat, and a goose is enlisted to rescue the doomed pups. Imagine their surprise when they find not only their own puppies, but 84 more as well. You can expect a happy ending and lots of spots—6,469,952 to be exact. Based on the children's book by Dodie Smith. Technically notable for the first time use of the Xerox process to transfer the animator's drawings onto celluloid, which made the film's opening sequence of dots evolving into 101 barking dogs possible. ♫Remember When; Cruella de Vil; Dalmation Plantation; Kanine Krunchies Kommercial.
1961 (G) 79m/C D: Clyde Geronomi, Wolfgang Reitherman, Hamilton Luske; **V:** Rod Taylor, Betty Lou Gerson, Lisa Davis, Ben Wright, Frederick Worlock, J. Pat O'Malley. **VHS, Beta $24.99** *DIS, OM 𝔏𝔏½*

125 Rooms of Comfort A mental patient has bizarre fantasies that create havoc among those who stand in his way.
1983 82m/C Tim Henry, Jackie Burroughs, Bob Warner, Bob Silverman, Les Barker; **D:** Patrick Loubert; **W:** Patrick Loubert, Bill Freut. **VHS, Beta** *TWE 𝔏𝔏*

One in a Million Debut film of Norwegian skating star Henie centers around a Swiss girl whose father is training her for the Olympics. Features good comedy by the Ritz Brothers and Sparks, as well as the beautiful skating of Henie. ♫One in a Million; We're Back in Circulation Again; Who's Afraid of Love; Lovely Lady in White; The Moonlight Waltz.
1936 95m/B Sonja Henie, Adolphe Menjou, Jean Hersholt, The Ritz Brothers, Arline Judge, Don Ameche, Ned Sparks, Montagu Love, Leah Ray; **D:** Sidney Lanfield; **W:** Leonard Praskins, Mark Kelly. **VHS $19.98** *FXV 𝔏𝔏𝔏*

One in a Million: The Ron LaFlore Story The true story of Detroit Tigers' star Ron LeFlore, who rose from the Detroit ghetto to the major leagues. Adaptation of LeFlore's autobiography, "Breakout." A well-acted and compelling drama with Burton in a standout performance.
1978 90m/C LeVar Burton, Madge Sinclair, Billy Martin, James Luisi; **D:** William A. Graham. **VHS, Beta** *NO 𝔏𝔏½*

One Last Run It's drama on the slopes as a variety of individuals confront their pasts/fears/personal demons via extreme skiing. Features the performances of champion skiers Franz Weber and Scot Schmidt.
1989 82m/C Russell Todd, Ashley Laurence, Craig Branham, Jimmy Aleck, Tracy Scoggins, Nels Van Patten, Chuck Connors; **D:** Peter Winograd, Glenn Gebhard; **W:** Peter Winograd, Glenn Gebhard. **VHS, Beta $79.95** *PSM 𝔏½*

One Little Indian An AWOL cavalry man and his Indian ward team up with a widow and her daughter in an attempt to cross the New Mexican desert. A tepid presentation from the usually high quality Disney studio.
1973 90m/C James Garner, Vera Miles, Jodie Foster, Clay O'Brien, Andrew Prine, Bernard McEveety; **D:** Bernard McEveety; **M:** Jerry Goldsmith. **VHS, Beta $69.95** *DIS 𝔏𝔏*

One Magic Christmas Disney feel-good film about a disillusioned working woman whose faith in Christmas is restored when her guardian angel descends to Earth and performs various miracles. Somewhat cliched and tiresome, but partially redeemed by Stanton and Steenburgen's presence.

1985 (G) 88m/C Mary Steenburgen, Harry Dean Stanton, Gary Basaraba, Michelle Meyrink, Arthur Hill, Elisabeth Harnois, Robbie Magwood; **D:** Phillip Borsos; **M:** Michael Conway Baker. **VHS, Beta $14.99** *DIS 𝔏𝔏½*

One Man Force L.A. narcotics cop Jake Swan goes on a vigilante spree. Huge in body and vengeful in spirit, he makes his partner's murderers pay!
1989 (R) 92m/C John Matuszak, Ronny Cox, Charles Napier, Sharon Farrell, Sam Jones, Chance Boyer, Richard Lynch, Stacey Q; **D:** Dale Trevillion; **W:** Dale Trevillion; **M:** Charles Fox. **VHS, Beta $29.95** *ACA 𝔏𝔏*

One Man Jury LAPD lieutenant, wearied by an ineffective justice system, becomes a one-man vigilante avenger. Pale Dirty Harry rip-off with over acting and an overdose of violence.
1978 (R) 95m/C Jack Palance, Chris Mitchum, Joe Spinell, Pamela Shoop; **D:** Charles Martin. **VHS, Beta $19.95** *VCI 𝔏*

One Man Out An ex-CIA agent diverts his psychological problems into his new job: assassin for a South American despot. His jaded view of life changes when he meets and falls in love with an American journalist. Trouble in paradise when he is ordered to kill her. One man out was not enough, they should have done away with the entire crew of this stinker.
1989 (R) 90m/C Stephen McHattie, Deborah Van Valkenburgh, Aharon Ipale, Ismael Carlo, Michael Champion, Dennis A. Pratt; **D:** Michael Kennedy. **VHS, Beta $14.95** *COL 𝔏*

One Man's War A human-rights crusader in repressive Paraguay won't be silenced, even after government thugs torture and murder his son. He fights obsessively to bring the killers to justice. The true story of the Joel Filartiga family is heartfelt but ultimately a dramatic letdown; an epilogue proves that full story hasn't been told.
1990 (PG-13) 91m/C Anthony Hopkins, Norma Aleandro, Fernanda Torres, Ruben Blades; **D:** Sergio Toledo. **VHS $89.99** *HBO 𝔏𝔏½*

One Man's Way Murray is appropriately devout as charasmatic religious leader Norman Vincent Peale. With the support of his wife (Hyland), he survives the adulations and accusations of blasphemy for his rather unorthodox theological ideas and his book, "The Power of Positive Thinking." Based on the book "Norman Vincent Peale: Minister to Millions" by Arthur Gordon.
1963 105m/B Don Murray, Diana Hyland, William Windom, Virginia Christine, Carol Ohmart, Veronica Cartwright, Liam Sullivan, June Dayton, Ian Wolfe; **D:** Denis Sanders; **W:** Eleanore Griffin, John W. Bloch. **VHS, Beta $19.98** *MGM, FCT, BTV 𝔏𝔏½*

One Million B.C. The strange saga of the struggle of primitive cavemen and their battle against dinosaurs and other monsters. Curiously told in flashbacks, this film provided stock footage for countless dinosaur movies that followed. Portions of film rumored to be directed by cinematic pioneer D. W. Griffith. **AKA:** The Cave Dwellers; Cave Man; Man and His Mate.
1940 80m/B Victor Mature, Carole Landis, Lon Chaney Jr.; **D:** Hal Roach, Hal Roach Jr. **VHS, Beta $9.95** *MED, RXM 𝔏𝔏½*

One Minute Before Death A woman is buried in a catatonic state, and returns from the grave to exact retribution. Supposedly based loosely on Poe.
1988 87m/C Giselle MacKenzie. **VHS, Beta** *NO 𝔏*

One Minute to Zero Korean War action film divides its time between an army romance and war action. The lukewarm melodrama features Mitchum as a colonel in charge of evacuating American civilians but who ends up bombing refugees.
1952 105m/B Robert Mitchum, Ann Blyth, William Talman, Charles McGraw, Margaret Sheridan, Richard Egan, Eduard Franz, Robert Osterloh, Robert Gist; **D:** Tay Garnett. **VHS, Beta** *RKO, TTC 𝔏𝔏*

One More Chance While he was in jail, an ex-con's family moves away without leaving a forwarding address. When he's released he strikes up a friendship with a woman from the neighborhood who knows where they've gone.
1990 102m/C Kirstie Alley, John Lamotta, Logan Clarke, Michael Pataki, Hector Maisonette; **D:** Sam Firstenberg. **VHS, Beta $59.95** *WAR, OM 𝔏½*

One More Saturday Night Franken and Davis, "Saturday Night Live" alumni, wrote this film about a small town going wild on the weekend. Dry, taxing, and unfunny. Averages about 1 laugh per 1/2 hour—at 1 1/2 hours, it's way too long.
1986 (R) 96m/C Al Franken, Tom Davis, Nan Woods, Dave Reynolds; **D:** Dennis Klein; **W:** Al Franken. **VHS, Beta** *NO 𝔏*

One Night in the Tropics The film debut of radio stars Abbott & Costello who play secondary roles to a love triangle (set to music). Jones is an insurance salesman who falls in love with Kelly, the fiance of Cummings. Based on the novel "Love Insurance" by Earl Derr Biggers. ♫Back in My Shell; Remind Me; You and Your Kiss; Your Dream is the Same as My Dream.
1940 83m/B Allan Jones, Robert Cummings, Nancy Kelly, Bud Abbott, Lou Costello, Mary Boland, Peggy Moran, William Frawley, Leo Carrillo; **D:** Edward Sutherland; **W:** Kathryn Scola, Gertrude Purcell, Charles Grayson, Francis Martin. **VHS $14.98** *MCA, FCT 𝔏𝔏½*

One Night of Love Moore's best quasi-operetta, about a young American diva rebelling in response to her demanding Italian teacher. "Pygmallion"-like story has her falling in love with her maestro. Despite being nearly 60 years old, this film is still enchanting and fresh. ♫One Night of Love; Ciri-Biri-Bin; Sempre Libera; Sextet; Indian Love Call; Tis the Last Rose of Summer; Habanera; Un bel di; None But the Lonely Heart.
1934 95m/B Grace Moore, Tullio Carminati, Lyle Talbot, Jane Darwell, Nydia Westman, Mona Barrie, Jessie Ralph, Luis Alberni; **D:** Victor Schertzinger. Academy Awards '34: Best Sound, Best Score; Nominations: Best Actress (Moore), Best Director (Schertzinger), Best Film Editing, Best Picture. **VHS, Beta $19.95** *COL 𝔏𝔏𝔏½*

One Night Only A gorgeous law student decides to make big money by hiring herself and her friends out as hookers to the school football team.
1984 87m/C Lenore Zann, Jeff Braunstein, Grant Alianak; **D:** Timothy Bond. **VHS, Beta $59.98** *FOX 𝔏𝔏𝔏½*

One Night Stand Woman's chance encounter with a man in a singles bar leads to an evening of unexpected terror. Adapted from a play for Canadian television. Billed as a horror flick, it is really more of a drama.
1977 90m/C Chapelle Jaffe, Brent Carver. **VHS, Beta $49.95** *TWE 𝔏*

One Night Stand Four young people attempt to amuse themselves at the empty Sydney Opera House on the New Year's Eve, that night WWIII begins. An odd commentary on nuclear war that sees the bomb as the ultimate bad joke. Features an appearance by alternative rock group Midnight Oil. 1984 94m/C Tyler Coppin, Cassandra Delaney, Jay Hackett, Saskia Post; *D:* John Duigan. **VHS, Beta** $59.98 *SUE* ✁✁✁

One of My Wives Is Missing An ex-New York cop tries to solve the mysterious disappearance of a newlywed socialite. Things become strange when she reappears but is discovered as an imposter. Above average acting in a film adapted from the play, "The Trap for a Lonely Man." 1976 97m/C Jack Klugman, Elizabeth Ashley, James Franciscus; *D:* Glenn Jordan. **VHS, Beta** $59.95 *LHV* ✁✁ ½

One of Our Aircraft Is Missing The crew of an R.A.F. bomber downed in the Netherlands, struggle to escape Nazi capture. A thoughtful study of wars and the men who fight them, with an entertaining melodramatic plot. Look for the British version, which runs 106 minutes. Some of the American prints only run 82 minutes. 1941 103m/B Godfrey Tearle, Eric Portman, Hugh Williams, Pamela Brown, Googie Withers, Peter Ustinov; *D:* Emeric Pressburger, Michael Powell. Academy Awards '42 Nominations: Best Original Screenplay; National Board of Review Awards '42: 10 Best Films of the Year. **VHS** $19.95 *NOS, MRV, REP* ✁✁✁½

One of Our Dinosaurs Is Missing An English nanny and her cohorts help British Intelligence retrieve a microfilm—concealing dinosaur fossil from the bad guys that have stolen it. Disney film was shot on location in England. 1975 (G) 101m/C Peter Ustinov, Helen Hayes, Derek Nimmo, Clive Revill, Robert Stevenson, Joan Sims; *D:* Robert Stevenson. **VHS, Beta** $69.95 *DIS* ✁✁

One on One A Rocky-esque story about a high school basketball star from the country who accepts an athletic scholarship to a big city university. He encounters a demanding coach and intense competition. Light weight drama that is economically entertaining. 1977 (PG) 100m/C Robby Benson, Annette O'Toole, G.D. Spradlin, Gail Strickland, Melanie Griffith; *D:* Lamont Johnson; *M:* Charles Fox. **VHS, Beta** $39.98 *WAR* ✁✁½

One Plus One A dramatization, believe it or not, of the Kinsey sex survey of the 1950s. Participants in a sex lecture talk about and demonstrate various "risque" practices, such as premarital sex and extramarital affairs. Despite this film, the sexual revolution went on as planned. *AKA:* Exploring the Kinsey Report. 1961 114m/B Leo G. Carroll, Hilda Brawner, William Traylor, Kate Reid, Ernest Graves; *D:* Arch Oboler; *W:* Arch Oboler. **VHS, Beta** $16.95 *SNC* ✁

One-Punch O'Day Boxing boy tries to buy back hometown's oil livelihood by winning prizefight. Much patient waiting by his honey. 1926 60m/B Billy Sullivan, Jack Herrick, Charlotte Merriam; *D:* Harry Joe Brown. **VHS, Beta** $19.95 *GPV, FCT, GVV* ✁

One Rainy Afternoon A bit-player kisses the wrong girl in a Paris theater causing a massive uproar that brands him as a notorious romantic "monster." Patterned after a German film, the story lacks depth and zest. 1936 80m/B Francis Lederer, Ida Lupino, Hugh Herbert, Roland Young, Donald Meek; *D:* Rowland V. Lee. **VHS, Beta** $19.95 *NOS, MRV, VYY* ✁✁

One Russian Summer During the Russian Revolution, a cripple seeks revenge on the corrupt land baron who murdered his parents. An unfortunate attempt to dramatize a novel by M. Lermontov. 1973 (R) 112m/C Oliver Reed, Claudia Cardinale, John McEnery, Carole Andre, Ray Lovelock; *D:* Antonio Calenda. **VHS, Beta** $59.95 *VCI* *Woof!*

One Shoe Makes It Murder A shady casino owner hires ex-cop Mitchum to investigate the disappearance of his unfaithful wife. Adapted from Eric Bercovici's novel, the story does little to enhance Mitchum's TV debut. 1982 100m/C Robert Mitchum, Angie Dickinson, Mel Ferrer, Howard Hesseman, Jose Perez; *D:* William Hale; *M:* Bruce Broughton. **VHS, Beta** $89.95 *LIV* ✁✁

One Sings, the Other Doesn't Seeking contentment, a conservative widow and a liberal extrovert help each other cope in a man's world. Endearing characters, but a superficial treatment of dated feminist issues. In French with English subtitles. *AKA:* L'Une Chante L'Autre Pas. 1977 105m/C Valerie Mairesse, Therese Liotard; *D:* Agnes Varda; *W:* Agnes Varda. **VHS, Beta** $59.95 *COL, ING* ✁✁½

One Step Beyond This creepy anthology series featured stories of the occult and supernatural which were supposedly based on true incidents. Two episodes per tape. Includes "Message from Clara" starring Barbara Baxley and Robert Ellenstein and "The Sorcerer" with Christopher Lee and Martin Benson. 1959 60m/B *D:* John Newland. **VHS** $19.99 *MOV, HEG* ✁✁½

One Step to Hell Good cop rescues gold-miner's widow from three escaped convicts. Beautiful African scenery helps save an otherwise mediocre film. *AKA:* Caccia Ai Violenti; King of Africa. 1968 90m/C Ty Hardin, Rossano Brazzi, Pier Angeli, George Sanders, Tab Hunter, Sandy Howard. **VHS, Beta** $39.95 *NO* ✁½

One Summer Love Man checks out from loony bin, searches for family ties and befriends beautiful woman who works in a moviehouse. *AKA:* Dragonfly. 1976 95m/C Beau Bridges, Susan Sarandon, Mildred Dunnock, Ann Wedgeworth, Michael B. Miller, Linda Miller, James Noble, Frederick Coffin; *D:* Gilbert Cates; *W:* N. Richard Nash. **VHS** $79.99 *HBO* ✁½

One That Got Away A loyal German Luftwaffe pilot captured by the British becomes obsessed with escape. Fast paced and exciting. Based on a true story. 1957 111m/B Hardy Kruger, Colin Gordon, Alec Gordon; *D:* Roy Ward Baker. **VHS, Beta** *NO* ✁✁✁

One Third of a Nation Depression era film contrasts the conditions of slum life with those in high society. A young entrepreneur inherits a city block in ruins, only to fall in love with a young woman who lives there and help her crippled brother. Timely social criticism. 1939 79m/M Sylvia Sidney, Leif Erickson, Myron McCormick, Sidney Lumet; *D:* Dudley Murphy. **VHS** $19.95 *NOS, PAR, MLB* ✁✁½

1001 Arabian Nights In this Arabian nightmare, the nearsighted Mr. Magoo is known as "Azziz" Magoo, lamp dealer and uncle of Aladdin. 1959 76m/C *D:* Jack Kinney; *M:* George Duning; *V:* Jim Backus, Kathryn Grant, Hans Conried, Herschel Bernardi. **VHS, Beta** $19.95 *COL* ✁✁½

One Too Many Exploitation film depicting the evils of alcoholism. Campy, but slick. *AKA:* The Important Story of Alcoholism; Killer With a Label. 1951 ?m/C Ruth Warrick, Richard Travis, Victor Kilian, Onslow Stevens, Lyle Talbot. **VHS** $16.95 *SNC* ✁

One Touch of Venus Love fills a department store when a window dresser kisses a statue of the goddess Venus—and she comes to life. Appealing adaptation of the Broadway musical. ♫Speak Low; The Trouble with Women; That's Him; Don't Look Now But My Heart Is Showing; My Week. 1948 82m/B Ava Gardner, Robert Walker, Eve Arden, Dick Haymes, Olga San Juan, Tom Conway; *D:* William A. Seiter; *M:* Kurt Weill, Ogden Nash. **VHS** $14.98 *REP, MLB* ✁✁½

One Trick Pony Once-popular rock singer/songwriter struggles to keep his head above water in a turbulent marriage and in the changing currents of popular taste. Simon wrote the autobiographical screenplay and score, but let's hope he is more sincere in real life. A good story. 1980 (R) 100m/C Paul Simon, Blair Brown, Rip Torn, Joan Hackett, Mare Winningham, Lou Reed, Harry Shearer, Allen (Gooritz) Garfield, Daniel Stern; *D:* Robert M. Young. **VHS, Beta** $14.95 *WAR* ✁✁½

One, Two, Three Cagney, an American Coca-Cola exec in Germany, zealously pursues any opportunity to run Coke's European operations. He does the job too well and loses his job to a Communist hippy turned slick capitalist. Fast-paced laughs, wonderful cinematography, and a fine score. 1961 110m/B James Cagney, Horst Buchholz, Arlene Francis; *D:* Billy Wilder; *W:* Billy Wilder, I.A.L. Diamond. Academy Awards '61 Nominations: Best Black and White Cinematography; National Board of Review Awards '61: 10 Best Films of the Year. **VHS, Beta** $19.98 *MGM* ✁✁✁½

One Wild Moment Comic complications arise when a divorced man is seduced by his best friend's daughter while vacationing. Warm and charming. Later re-made as "Blame It on Rio." In French with English subtitles. 1978 (R) 88m/C Jean-Pierre Marielle, Victor Lanoux, Agnes Soral, Christine Dejoux, Martine Sarcey; *D:* Claude Berri; *W:* Claude Berri. **VHS, Beta** $59.95 *COL, ING* ✁✁½

One Wish Too Many A young boy finds a marble that grants wishes. He has the time of his life with his teachers and the school bullies, but runs into trouble when he creates a giant steam roller which overruns London. Winner of Best Children's Film, 1956 Venice Film Festival, but it is hard to say why. 1955 55m/B Anthony Richmond, Rosalind Gourgey, John Pike; *D:* John Durst. **VHS, Beta** $16.95 *SNC* ✁✁½

One Woman or Two Paleontologist Depardieu is duped by beautiful ad-exec who plans to use his findings to push perfume. Remake of "Bringing Up Baby," this screwball comedy has a few screws loose. Dubbed. *AKA:* Une Femme ou Deux. 1985 (PG-13) 100m/C Gerard Depardieu, Sigourney Weaver, Dr. Ruth Westheimer, Michel Aumont, Zabou; *D:* Daniel Vigne; *W:* Elisabeth Rappeneau, Daniel Vigne. **VHS, Beta** $19.98 *LIV, VES, ING* ✁✁½

Onibaba A brutal parable about a mother and her daughter-in-law in war-ravaged medieval Japan who subsist by murdering stray soldiers and selling their armor. One soldier beds the daughter, setting the mother-in-law on a vengeful tirade. Review of the film

varied widely, hailed by some as a masterpiece and by others as below average; in Japanese with subtitles. *AKA:* The Demon; The Devil Woman.
1964 103m/B Nobuko Otowa, Yitsuko Yoshimura, Kei Sato; *D:* Kaneto Shindo. **VHS, Beta** $29.95 *CVC, ING, TPV &*

The Onion Field True story about the mental breakdown of an ex-cop who witnessed his partner's murder. Haunted by the slow process of justice and his own feelings of insecurity, he is unable to get his life together. Based on the novel by Joseph Wambaugh, who also wrote the screenplay. Compelling script and excellent acting.
1979 (R) 126m/C John Savage, James Woods, Ronny Cox, Franklyn Seales, Ted Danson; *D:* Harold Becker. **VHS, Beta** $14.98 *SUE, NLC &&&½*

Only Angels Have Wings Melodramatic adventure about a broken-down Peruvian air mail service. Large cast adds to the love tension between Grant, a pilot, and Arthur, a showgirl at the saloon. Nominated for special effects, a category recognized by the academy that year for the first time. William Rankin and Eleanor Griffin are uncredited writers.
1939 121m/B Cary Grant, Thomas Mitchell, Richard Barthelmess, Jean Arthur, Noah Beery Jr., Rita Hayworth, Sig Rumann, John Carroll, Allyn Joslyn; *D:* Howard Hawks; *W:* Jules Furthman; *M:* Dimitri Tiomkin. **VHS, Beta** $19.95 *COL &&&&*

Only Once in a Lifetime A love story about an Hispanic immigrant painter looking for success in America.
1983 90m/C Miguel Robelo, Estrellita Lopez, Sheree North. **VHS, Beta** $49.95 *VHE, MOV &*

Only One Night Upon finding out that he's the illegitimate son of an aristocrat, a happy-go-lucky carousel operator in a circus joins high society and is promptly matched with a beautiful but repressed woman. In Swedish with English subtitles. *AKA:* En Enda Natt.
1942 87m/B Ingrid Bergman, Edvin Adolphson, Aino Taube, Olof Sandborg, Erik Berglund, Marianne Lofgren, Magnus Kesster; *D:* Gustaf Molander. **VHS, Beta** $29.95 *WAC, LUM, ING &&*

Only the Lonely Middle-aged cop, Candy, falls in love with a shy undertaker's assistant, Sheedy, and is torn between love and dear old Mom, O'Hara, in her first role in years. Candy is an unlikely leading man and even the jokes are forced. But the restaurant scene makes the whole thing well worth seeing.
1991 (PG) 104m/C John Candy, Ally Sheedy, Maureen O'Hara, Anthony Quinn, Kevin Dunn, James Belushi, Milo O'Shea, Bert Remsen, Macaulay Culkin, Joe V. Greco; *D:* Chris Columbus; *W:* Chris Columbus; *M:* Maurice Jarre. **VHS, Beta** $19.98 *FXV &&½*

Only the Strong Louis (Dacascos) is a special forces officer who has mastered capoeira, a Brazilian form of kung fu. In Miami, he works with his old teacher (Lewis) to instill discipline in the 12 toughest punks in school by teaching them his martial arts skills. A neighborhood drug lord, related to two of the students, decides to cause trouble for Louis. Dacascos displays some charm along with his physical abilities but the story's ridiculous and the movie hastily put together.
1993 (PG-13) 96m/C Mark Dacascos, Stacy Travis, Todd Susman, Geoffrey Lewis, Paco Christian Prieto; *D:* Sheldon Lettich; *W:* Sheldon Lettich, Luis Esteban; *M:* Harvey W. Mason. **VHS** *FXV &½*

Only the Valiant Action-packed story of a cavalry officer who struggles to win his troops respect while warding off angry Apaches. Fast-paced Western fun requires little thought.
1950 105m/B Gregory Peck, Ward Bond, Gig Young, Lon Chaney Jr., Barbara Payton, Neville Brand; *D:* Gordon Douglas. **VHS** $14.95 *REP &&*

Only Two Can Play Sellers is a hilarious Casanova librarian who puts the moves on a society lady to get a promotion. Funny, of course, and based on Kingsley Amis' novel "That Uncertain Feeling."
1962 106m/C Peter Sellers, Virginia Maskell, Mai Zetterling, Richard Attenborough; *D:* Sidney Gilliat; *M:* Richard Rodney Bennett. **VHS, Beta** $69.95 *COL &&&*

The Only Way A semi-documentary account of the plight of the Jews in Denmark during the Nazi occupation. Despite German insistence, the Danes succeeded in saving most of their Jewish population from the concentration camps.
1970 (G) 86m/C Jane Seymour, Martin Potter, Benjamin Christiansen; *M:* Carl Davis. **VHS, Beta** $19.95 *VCI &&½*

The Only Way Home Two bikers end up in big trouble when one of them kills a wealthy man, and they kidnap his wife. Filmed entirely in Oklahoma.
1972 (PG) 86m/C Bo Hopkins, Beth Brickell, Steve Sandor, G.D. Spradlin; *D:* G.D. Spradlin. **VHS, Beta** *NO &&*

Only When I Laugh Neil Simon reworked his Broadway flop "The Gingerbread Lady" to produce this poignant comedy about the relationship between an aging alcoholic actress and her teenage daughters. *AKA:* It Hurts Only When I Laugh.
1981 (R) 120m/C Marsha Mason, Kristy McNichol, James Coco, Joan Hackett, David Dukes, Kevin Bacon, John Bennett Perry; *D:* Glenn Jordan; *W:* Neil Simon. Academy Awards '81 Nominations: Best Actress (Mason), Best Supporting Actor (Coco), Best Supporting Actress (Hackett); Golden Globe Awards '82: Best Supporting Actress (Hackett). **VHS, Beta** $19.95 *COL &&&*

Only with Married Men Carne's hassle-free dating routine is disrupted when a sly bachelor pretends that he's married to get a date. A middle-aged persons answer to a teenage sex comedy. Pretty bad.
1974 74m/C David Birney, Judy Carne, Gavin MacLeod, John Astin; *D:* Jerry Paris. **VHS, Beta** $59.95 *LHV &*

Only You A shy guy has always searched for true romance. But his cup runneth over when he meets, and must choose between, two beautiful women—your basic beach babe and a sensible beauty. What's a guy to do?
1992 (PG-13) 85m/C Andrew McCarthy, Kelly Preston, Helen Hunt. **VHS** $89.98 *LIV &½*

Only You Romantic comedy follows Faith (Tomei) on her journey to Italy in search of her soul mate when her ouija board promises that she'll find her true love there. On the way over she meets charming shoe salesman Peter (Downey, Jr.) and wonders if ouija got things wrong. Coming between the couple is piggish hunk Zane. Jewison creates satisfactory chemistry with talented Downey and Tomei. *AKA:* Him; Just in Time.
1994 (PG) ?m/C Marisa Tomei, Robert Downey Jr., Bonnie Hunt, Fisher Stevens, Billy Zane, Joaquim de Almeida; *D:* Norman Jewison; *W:* Diane Drake. **VHS** *&&&*

Open All Hours A British television comedy about a small corner shop and its viciously greedy, opportunistic owner.

1983 85m/C Ronnie Barker, Lynda Baron, David Jason, Stephenie Cole. **VHS, Beta** $14.98 *FOX &*

Open City A leader in the Italian underground resists Nazi control of the city. A stunning film, making Rossellini's realistic style famous. In Italian with English subtitles. *AKA:* Roma, Citta Aperta; Rome, Open City.
1945 103m/B Anna Magnani, Aldo Fabrizi, Marcel Pagliero, Maria Michi, Vito Annicchiarico, Nando Bruno, Harry Feist; *D:* Roberto Rossellini; *W:* Federico Fellini, Sergio Amidei. Academy Awards '46 Nominations: Best Screenplay; National Board of Review Awards '46: 5 Best Foreign Films of the Year; New York Film Critics Awards '46: Best Foreign Film. **VHS, Beta, 8mm** $24.95 *VYY, MRV, NOS &&&&*

Open Doors Bitter review of Fascist rule and justice. The Fascist regime promises security, safety, and tranquility. So, on the morning that a white collar criminal murders his former boss, murders the man who got his job, and then rapes and murders his wife, tensions rise and the societal structures are tested. The people rally for his death. A judge and a juror struggle to uphold justice rather than serve popular passions. Winner of 4 Donatello Awards, Italian Golden Globes for Best Film, Best Actor, and Best Screenplay, and many international film awards. In Italian with English subtitles. *AKA:* Porte Aperte.
1989 (R) 109m/C Gian Marie Volonte, Ennio Fantastichini, Lidia Alfonsi; *D:* Gianni Amelio. **VHS** $79.98 *ORI, FCT, ING &&&½*

Open House Radio psychologist and beautiful real estate agent search for the killer of real estate agents and their clients. A mystery-thriller for the very patient.
1986 95m/C Joseph Bottoms, Adrienne Barbeau, Mary Stavin, Rudy Ramos; *D:* Jag Mundhra. **VHS, Beta** $79.95 *PSM &*

Open Secret Jewish residents are plagued by a gang of anti-semitic thugs. Violence and destruction escalate until a fed up police lieutenant, tenaciously played by Ireland, and a victimized shop owner (Tyne) join forces to just say no more. When the gang learns the shopkeeper has caught their dastardly deeds on camera, the battle begins in earnest. Fast-paced and intriguing suspense.
1948 70m/B John Ireland, Jane Randolph, Roman Bohnen, Sheldon Leonard, George Tyne, Morgan Farley, Ellen Lowe, Anne O'Neal, Arthur O'Connell; *D:* John Reinhardt. **VHS, Beta** $16.95 *SNC &&*

Opening Night Very long study about an actress (Rowlands) and the play she's about to open in on Broadway. Backstage turmoil increases her own insecurities and the bad luck persists when an adoring fan dies in an accident on opening night. Performances carry this neurotic epic along, including Cassavetes as Rowland's co-star and Blondell as the playwright.
1977 (PG-13) 144m/C Gena Rowlands, John Cassavetes, Joan Blondell, Ben Gazzara, Paul Stewart, Zohra Lampert, Laura Johnson; *D:* John Cassavetes; *W:* John Cassavetes. **VHS, Beta** $89.95 *TOU, BTV &&½*

Opera do Malandro A lavish Brazilian take off of "The Threepenny Opera." Married hustler falls for a beautiful entrepreneur longing to get rich off of American goods. Based on Chico Buarque's musical play. In Portuguese, with subtitles.
1987 106m/C Edson Celulari, Claudia Ohana, Elba Ramalho, Ney Latorraca; *D:* Ruy Guerra. **VHS, Beta** *NO &&½*

Operation Amsterdam Four agents have fourteen hours to snare $10 million in diamonds from under the noses of local Nazis. Based on a true story. Full of 1940s wartime action and suspense.
1960 103m/B Peter Finch, Eva Bartok, Tony Britton, Alexander Knox; *D:* Michael McCarthy. **VHS, Beta** $59.95 SUE *✗✗*

Operation C.I.A. A plot to assassinate the U.S. ambassador in Saigon inspires brave CIA agent Reynolds to wipe out the bad guys. Action-packed and somewhat exciting. *AKA:* Last Message From Saigon.
1965 90m/C Burt Reynolds, John Hayt, Kieu Chinh, Danielle Aubry; *D:* Christian Nyby. **VHS, Beta** $59.98 FOX, DVT, HEG *✗✗*

Operation Cross Eagles Routine WWII military thriller with Conte and Calhoun on a mission to rescue an American general in exchange for their German prisoner. Their mission is complicated by a traitor in the group. Conte's only directorship. *AKA:* Unakrsna Vatra.
1969 90m/C Richard Conte, Rory Calhoun, Aili King, Phil Brown; *D:* Richard Conte. **VHS** NO *✗✗*

Operation Crossbow Action-packed espionage tale in which a trio of agents are assigned to destroy a Nazi munitions installation. Exciting ending and sensational pyrotechnics. *AKA:* The Great Spy Mission; Code Name: Operation Crossbow.
1965 116m/C Sophia Loren, George Peppard, Trevor Howard, John Mills, Richard Johnson, Tom Courtenay, Jeremy Kemp, Anthony Quayle, Helmut Dantine; *D:* Michael Anderson Sr. **VHS** $19.98 MGM *✗✗✗*

Operation Dames A squadron of soldiers must go behind Korean enemy lines to locate a missing U.S.O. troupe and bring them to safety. Low budget and not very funny for a supposed comedy.
1959 73m/B Eve Meyer, Chuck Henderson, Don Devlin, Ed Craig, Cindy Girard; *D:* Louis Clyde Stouman. **VHS** $9.95 COL *✗1/2*

Operation Haylift The true story of the U.S. Air Force's efforts to rescue starving cattle and sheep herds during Nevada's blizzards of 1949. The Air Force provided realism for the film with planes, equipment, and servicemen.
1950 73m/B Bill Williams, Tom Brown, Ann Rutherford, Jane Nigh; *D:* William Berke. **VHS, Beta** NO *✗✗*

Operation Inchon A foreign film depicting the battle in Devil Ridge during the Korean War.
1981 90m/C **VHS, Beta** $39.95 VCD *✗*

Operation Julie A detective searches out a huge drug ring that manufactures LSD.
1985 100m/C Colin Blakely, Lesley Nightingale, Clare Powney; *D:* Bob Mahoney. **VHS, Beta** $59.98 LIV *✗1/2*

Operation 'Nam A group of bored Vietnam vets return to 'Nam to rescue their leader from a POW camp. Nothing special, but features John Wayne's son.
1985 85m/C Oliver Tobias, Christopher Connelly, Manfred Lehman, John Steiner, Ethan Wayne, Donald Pleasence; *D:* Larry Ludman. **VHS** $79.95 IMP *✗*

Operation Orient A statue laden with drugs is stolen when an international drug smuggler tries to bring it to the U.S.
19?? 94m/C Gianni Gori, Gordon Mitchell; *D:* Elia Milonakos. **VHS, Beta** MED *✗✗*

Operation Petticoat Submarine captain Grant teams with wheeler-dealer Curtis to make his sub seaworthy. They're joined by a group of Navy women, and the gags begin. Great teamwork from Grant and Curtis

keeps things rolling. Jokes may be considered sexist these days. Later remake and TV series couldn't hold a candle to the original.
1959 120m/C Cary Grant, Tony Curtis, Joan O'Brien, Dina Merrill, Gene Evans, Arthur O'Connell, Virginia Gregg; *D:* Blake Edwards. **VHS** $14.98 REP *✗✗✗1/2*

Operation Thunderbolt Israeli-produced depiction of Israel's July 14, 1976 commando raid on Entebbe, Uganda to rescue the passengers of a hijacked plane. Better than the American versions "Raid on Entebbe" and "Victory at Entebbe" in its performances as well as the information provided, much of it unavailable to the American filmmakers. *AKA:* Entebbe: Operation Thunderbolt.
1977 120m/C Yehoram Gaon, Assaf Dayan, Ori Levy, Klaus Kinski, Menahem Golan. **VHS, Beta** $59.95 MGM *✗✗1/2*

Operation War Zone A platoon of soldiers uncovers a plot by corrupt officers to continue the Vietnam war and sell weapons.
1989 86m/C Joe Spinell. **VHS, Beta** AIP *✗*

The Oppermann Family On two tapes, the long epic made for German television about a family trying to survive in Berlin during the rise of Hitler. In German with subtitles.
1982 238m/C *D:* Egon Monk. **VHS, Beta** $99.95 FCT, APD *✗✗1/2*

The Opponent A young boxer saves a young woman's life, not realizing that she has mob connections, thus embroiling him in a world of crime.
1989 (R) 102m/C Daniel Greene, Ernest Borgnine, Julian Gemma, Mary Stavin, Kelly Shaye Smith; *D:* Sergio Martino. **VHS** $89.95 VMK *✗✗*

Opportunity Knocks Carvey's first feature film has him impersonating a friend of a rich suburbanite's family while hiding from a vengeful gangster. They buy it, and give him a job and the daughter. Not hilarious, but not a dud either.
1990 (PG-13) 105m/C Dana Carvey, Robert Loggia, Todd Graff, Milo O'Shea, Julia Campbell, James Tolkan, Doris Belack, Sally Gracie, Del Close; *D:* Donald Petrie; *W:* Mitchel Katlin, Nat Bernstein; *M:* Miles Goodman. **VHS, Beta** $19.95 MCA *✗✗*

Opposing Force The commander of an Air Force camp simulates prisoner-of-war conditions for realistic training, but he goes too far, creating all too real torture situations. He preys on the only female in the experiment, raping her as part of the training. A decent thriller. *AKA:* Hellcamp.
1987 (R) 97m/C Tom Skerritt, Lisa Eichhorn, Anthony Zerbe, Richard Roundtree, Robert Wightman, John Considine, George Kee Cheung, Paul Joynt, Jay Louden, Ken Wright, Dan Hamilton; *D:* Eric Karson; *W:* Gil Cowan; *M:* Mark Donohue. **VHS, Beta** $19.99 HBO *✗✗1/2*

The Opposite Sex Bevy of women battle mediocre script in adaptation of 1939's "The Women." Laserdisc includes original trailer and letterboxed screen. ♫The Opposite Sex; Dere's Yellow Gold on de Trees (De Banana); A Perfect Love; Rock and Roll Tumbleweed; Now! Baby, Now!; Jungle Red; Young Man with a Horn.
1956 115m/C June Allyson, Joan Collins, Dolores Gray, Ann Sheridan, Ann Miller, Leslie Nielsen, Agnes Moorehead, Joan Blondell; *D:* David Miller; *W:* Fay Kanin, Michael Kanin. **VHS** $19.98 MGM, FCT *✗1/2*

The Opposite Sex and How to Live With Them Yuppies (Gross and Cox) from different backgrounds (he's Jewish, she's a WASP) meet, fall in love, fight,

break up, and reunite, inspiring yawning disinterest. All this while their two best buddies (Pollak and Brown) offer what are meant to be "candid insights" delivered directly to the camera. Flat and formulaic romantic comedy wants to sparkle, but script lacks both purpose and point, and worse, takes way too much time not getting there. Winner of the annual Grammar Police award for the worst example of a semantically incorrect title in recent years.
1993 (R) 86m/C Arye Gross, Courteney Cox, Kevin Pollak, Julie Brown, Mitchell Ryan, Philip Bruns, Mitzi McCall, B.J. Ward; *D:* Matthew Meshekoff; *W:* Noah Stern; *M:* Ira Newborn. **VHS** HBO *✗*

Options Nerdy Hollywood agent Salinger treks to Africa to "option" a princess's life story—hence the title. He gets mixed up with her kidnapping and with her. Misplaced cameos by Roberts and Anton drag down the overall comedy content, which isn't to high to begin with.
1988 (PG) 105m/C Matt Salinger, Joanna Pacula, John Kani, James Keach; *Cameos:* Susan Anton, Eric Roberts; *D:* Camilo Vila. **VHS** $89.98 LIV, VES *✗✗*

The Oracle A woman takes a new apartment only to find that the previous occupant's spirit is still a resident. The spirit tries to force her to take revenge on his murderers. Not bad for a low-budget thriller, but bad editing is a distraction.
1985 94m/C Caroline Capers Powers, Roger Neil; *D:* Roberta Findlay. **VHS, Beta** $59.95 LIV *✗*

Orca Ridiculous premise has a killer whale chasing bounty hunter Harris to avenge the murder of its pregnant mate. Great for gore lovers, especially when the whale chomps Derek's leg off. *AKA:* Orca—Killer Whale.
1977 (PG) 92m/C Richard Harris, Charlotte Rampling, Bo Derek, Keenan Wynn, Will Sampson; *D:* Michael Anderson Sr.; *M:* Ennio Morricone. **VHS, Beta** $19.95 PAR *Woof!*

Orchestra Wives A drama bursting with wonderful Glenn Miller music. A woman marries a musician and goes on the road with the band and the other wives. Trouble springs up with the sultry singer who desperately wants the woman's new husband. The commotion spreads throughout the group. ♫People Like You and Me; At Last; Serenade in Blue; I've Got a Gal in Kalamazoo.
1942 98m/B George Montgomery, Glenn Miller, Lynn Bari, Carole Landis, Jackie Gleason, Cesar Romero, Ann Rutherford, Virginia Gilmore, Mary Beth Hughes, Harry Morgan; *D:* Archie Mayo. **VHS, Beta** $19.98 FXV, FCT *✗✗✗*

Ordeal by Innocence Sutherland is an amateur sleuth in 1950s England convinced he has proof that a convicted murderer is innocent, but no one wishes to reopen the case. Big-name cast is essentially wasted. Based on an Agatha Christie story.
1984 (PG-13) 91m/C Donald Sutherland, Christopher Plummer, Faye Dunaway, Sarah Miles, Ian McShane, Diana Quick, Annette Crosbie, Michael Elphick; *D:* Desmond Davis; *M:* Pino Donaggio. **VHS, Beta** $79.95 MGM *✗1/2*

The Ordeal of Dr. Mudd His name was Mudd—a fitting moniker after he unwittingly aided President Lincoln's assassin. Dr. Mudd set John Wilkes Boothe's leg, broken during the assassination, and was jailed for conspiracy. He became a hero in prison for his aid during yellow fever epidemics and was eventually released. A strong and intricate performance by Weaver keeps this made-for-television drama interesting. Mudd's descendants are still trying to com-

pletely clear his name of any wrongdoing in the Lincoln assassination.
1980 143m/C Dennis Weaver, Susan Sullivan, Richard Dysart, Michael McGuire, Nigel Davenport, Arthur Hill; **D:** Paul Wendkos. **VHS, Beta $39.95** LIV *III*

Order of the Black Eagle A Bondish spy and his sidekick, Typhoon the Baboon, battle neo-Nazis planning to bring Hitler back to life in this silly tongue-in-cheek thriller.
1987 (R) 93m/C Ian Hunter, Charles K. Bibby, William T. Hicks, Jill Donnellan; **D:** Worth Keeter. **VHS, Beta $19.95** CEL *II*½

Order of the Eagle An innocent scouting trip turns into a non-stop nightmare when an Eagle Scout uncovers some dangerous information.
1989 88m/C Frank Stallone. **VHS, Beta $9.95** AIP *II*½

Order to Kill A gambling boss puts out a contract on a hit man.
1973 110m/C Jose Ferrer, Helmut Berger, Sydne Rome, Kevin McCarthy; **D:** Jose Maesso. **VHS, Beta** NO *II*½

Ordet A man who believes he is Jesus Christ is ridiculed until he begins performing miracles, which result in the rebuilding of a broken family. A statement on the nature of religious faith vs. fanaticism by the profoundly religious Dreyer, and based on the play by Kaj Munk. In Danish with English subtitles. **AKA:** The Word.
1955 126m/B Henrik Malberg; **D:** Carl Theodor Dreyer. **VHS, Beta $24.95** NOS, WFV, ING *III*½

Ordinary Heroes The story is familiar but the leads make it worthwhile. Anderson is strong as a blinded Vietnam vet readjusting to life at home. Bertinelli's portrayal of his former girlfriend is eloquent. Nice work on an overdone story.
1985 105m/C Richard Dean Anderson, Doris Roberts, Valerie Bertinelli; **D:** Peter H. Cooper. **VHS $79.99** HBO *II*½

Ordinary Magic Teenaged Jeffrey was raised in India, picking up more than a little eastern wisdom along the way. After the death of his parents Jeffrey comes to the U.S. to live with his aunt where he sticks out not only as the new kid but as a decided oddball. But he manages to make some new friends and teach a few lessons about individuality along the way. Adapted from the novel by Malcolm Bosse.
1993 96m/C David Fox, Glenne Headly, Heath Lamberts, Ryan Reynolds; **Cameos:** Paul Anka; **D:** Giles Walker; **W:** Jefferson Lewis. **VHS $89.95** TRI *II*½

Ordinary People Powerful, well-acted story of a family's struggle to deal with one son's accidental death and the other's subsequent guilt-ridden suicide attempt. Features strong performances by all, but Moore is especially believable as the cold and rigid mother. McGovern's film debut as well as Redford's directorial debut. Based on the novel by Judith Guest.
1980 (R) 124m/C Mary Tyler Moore, Donald Sutherland, Timothy Hutton, Judd Hirsch, M. Emmet Walsh, Elizabeth McGovern, Adam Baldwin, Dinah Manoff, James B. Sikking; **D:** Robert Redford; **W:** Alvin Sargent; **M:** Marvin Hamlisch. Academy Awards '80: Best Adapted Screenplay, Best Director (Redford), Best Picture, Best Supporting Actor (Hutton); Nominations: Best Actress (Moore), Best Supporting Actor (Hirsch); Golden Globe Awards '81: Best Actress—Drama (Moore), Best Director (Redford), Best Film—Drama, Best Supporting Actor (Hutton); National Board of Review Awards '80: 10 Best Films of the Year, Best Director (Redford). **VHS, Beta $14.95** PAR, BTV *III*½

Oregon Trail A western serial in 15 chapters, each 13 minutes long.
1939 195m/B Johnny Mack Brown, Fuzzy Knight; **D:** Ford Beebe. **VHS, Beta $29.95** VCN, DVT, MLB *III*½

The Organization Poitier's third and final portrayal of Detective Virgil Tibbs, first seen in "In the Heat of the Night." This time around he battles a drug smuggling ring with a vigilante group. Good action scenes and a realistic ending.
1971 (PG) 108m/C Sidney Poitier, Barbara McNair, Sheree North, Raul Julia; **D:** Don Medford. **VHS, Beta $14.95** MGM, FOX *III*

Orgy of the Dead Classic anti-canon film scripted by Ed Wood, Jr. from his own novel. Two innocent travelers are forced to watch an even dozen nude spirits dance in a cardboard graveyard. Hilariously bad.
1965 90m/C Criswell, Fawn Silver, William Bates, Pat Barringer; **D:** A.C. Stephen; **W:** Edward D. Wood Jr. **VHS, Beta $19.95** RHI Woof!

Orgy of the Vampires Tourists wander into village during cocktail hour. **AKA:** Vampire's Night Orgy.
1973 (R) 86m/C Jack Taylor, Charo Soriano, Dianik Zurakowska, John Richard; **D:** Leon Klimovsky. **VHS $19.99** SNC *II*

Oriane A troubled Venezuelan woman must leave France for her native soil when her aunt dies. Once there, in the place where she spent youthful summers, she begins to recall her incestuous past.
1985 88m/C Deniela Sliverio, Doris Wells, Philippe Rouleau, David Crotto; **D:** Fina Torres. **VHS** NO *II*

The Original Fabulous Adventures of Baron Munchausen An adventure fantasy that takes the hero all over, from the belly of a whale, eventually landing him on the surface of the moon. **AKA:** The Fabulous Baron Munchausen.
1961 84m/C Milos Kopecky, Jana Brejchova, Rudolph Jelinek, Jan Werich; **D:** Karel Zeman. **VHS** NO *II*

The Original Flash Gordon Collection Four vintage Flash Gordon serials from the 1930s were recently re-edited into feature length films and released as this collection. Great stuff, including "Spaceship to the Unknown," "Deadly Ray From Mars," "Peril From Planet Mongo," and "Purple Death From Outer Space."
1991 366m/B Buster Crabbe. **VHS $79.95** QHV, FCT *II*½

Original Intent A successful lawyer, facing a mid-life crisis, jeopardizes both his family and career when he decides to defend a homeless shelter from eviction proceedings. What might have been a powerful drama about one man's crusade to help the homeless instead merely melodramtic. Actor/activist Sheen appears briefly as a homeless man.
1991 (PG) 97m/C Jay Richardson, Candy Clark, Kris Kristofferson, Vince Edwards, Cindy Pickett, Robert DoQui, Joseph Campanella; **Cameos:** Martin Sheen; **D:** Robert Marcarelli; **W:** Robert Marcarelli. **VHS, Beta** PAR *II*

Orion's Belt Three Norwegian adventurers must flee through the wilderness when they discover a secret Soviet base on the Europe/Russia/Greenland border.
1985 (PG) 87m/C VHS, Beta $19.95 STE, NWV *II*

Orlak, the Hell of Frankenstein The monster of Frankenstein is revived for the purposes of revenge. The monster is forced to wear a helmet, as his face melted

during the obligatory electrification. In Spanish only, no English subtitles. **AKA:** Orlak, El Infierno de Frankenstein.
1960 103m/B Joaquin Cordero, Andres Soler, Rosa de Castilla, Irma Dorante, Armando Calvo, Pedro de Aguillon, David Reynoso; **D:** Rafael Baledon. **VHS, Beta $16.95** SNC *II*

Orlando Potter's sumptuous film adaptation of Virginia Woolf's 1928 novel, which covers 400 years in the life of an English nobleman, who not only defys death but evolves from a man to a woman in the intervening years. Orlando (Swinton) is first seen as a young man in the court of Queen Elizabeth I (Crisp) but after a deep sleep it's suddenly 40 years later. Things like this just keep happening and by 1750 he is now a she (and remains so), finding and losing love, and eventually gaining fulfillment in the 20th century. Elaborate productions never overwhelm Swinton's serene, self-assured performance.
1992 (PG-13) 93m/C Tilda Swinton, Charlotte Valandrey, Billy Zane, Lothaire Bluteau, John Wood, Quentin Crisp, Heathcote Williams, Dudley Sutton, Thom Hoffman; **D:** Sally Potter; **W:** Sally Potter. COL *III*

The Orphan A young orphaned boy seeks revenge against his cruel aunt who is harassing him with sadistic discipline.
1979 80m/C Mark Evans, Joanna Miles, Peggy Feury; **D:** John Ballard. **VHS, Beta $49.95** PSM, RHI *II*½

An Orphan Boy of Vienna A homeless street urchin with a beautiful singing voice is accepted into the wonderful world of the Choir, but is later unjustly accused of stealing. Performances by the Vienna Boys' Choir redeem the melodramatic plot. In German with English subtitles.
1937 87m/B The Vienna Boys Choir; **D:** Max Neufeld. **VHS, Beta $24.95** VYY, IHF, GLV *II*½

Orphan Train A woman realizes her New York soup kitchen can't do enough to help the neighborhood orphans, so she takes a group of children out West in hopes of finding families to adopt them. Their journey is chronicled by a newspaper photographer and a social worker. Based on the actual "orphan trains" of the mid- to late 1800s. From the novel by Dorothea G. Petrie. Made for television.
1979 150m/C Jill Eikenberry, Kevin Dobson, Glenn Close, Linda Manz; **D:** William A. Graham. **VHS $14.95** PSM, KAR, HHE *III*

Orphans A sensitive edge-of-glasnost portrait of a young boy's discovery of love, friendship, and literature. In Russian with English subtitles.
1983 97m/C D: Nikolai Gubenko. **VHS, Beta $79.95** FCT *III*

Orphans A gangster on the run is kidnapped by a tough New York orphan but soon takes control by befriending his abductor's maladjusted brother. Eventually each brother realizes his need for the older man, who has become a father figure to them. This very quirky film is salvaged by good performances. Based on the play by Lyle Kessler.
1987 (R) 116m/C Albert Finney, Matthew Modine, Kevin Anderson; **D:** Alan J. Pakula; **W:** Lyle Kessler; **M:** Michael Small. **VHS, Beta $19.95** LHV, WAR *III*

Orphans of the North The story of Bedrock Brown's search for gold and his lost partner. Filmed on location in Alaska with non-professional actors. Impressive footage of America's "last frontier," including the flora and fauna.
1940 56m/C D: Norman Dawn; **W:** Norman Dawn. **VHS, Beta, 8mm $19.95** VYY *I*

Orphans of the Storm Two sisters are separated and raised in opposite worlds—one by thieves, the other by aristocrats. Gish's poignant search for her sister is hampered by the turbulent maelstrom preceding the French Revolution. Silent. Based on the French play "The Two Orphans."
1921 190m/B Lillian Gish, Dorothy Gish, Monte Blue, Joseph Schildkraut; *D:* D.W. Griffith. **VHS** $19.98 *NOS, MRV, CCB* ♦♦♦1/2

Orpheus Cocteau's fascinating, innovative retelling of the Orpheus legend in a modern, though slightly askew, Parisian setting. Classic visual effects and poetic imagery. In French with English subtitles. *AKA:* Orphee.
1949 95m/B Jean Marais, Francois Perier, Maria Casares; *D:* Jean Cocteau. **VHS, Beta, 8mm** $16.95 *SNC, NOS, SUE* ♦♦1/2

Orpheus Descending Lust and hatred in small Southern town. Confusing, poorly paced, but interesting for Anderson as Elvis-style drifter and Redgrave as woman addicted to love. Made-for-cable version of the 1989 Broadway revival of Tennessee Williams play.
1991 117m/C Vanessa Redgrave, Kevin Anderson, Anne Twomey, Miriam Margolyes, Brad Sullivan, Sloane Shelton, Patti Allison; *D:* Peter Hall; *W:* Peter Hall, Tennessee Williams. **VHS** $79.95 *TTC, FCT* ♦♦1/2

Osa Yet another post-nuke flick with the usual devastated landscape, leather-clad survivors, and hokey dialog. It's sometimes funny, despite everyone's effort to make it dramatic. The supposed plot centers on one woman's efforts to break up a man's monopoly on clean water.
1985 94m/C Kelly Lynch, Daniel Grimm, Phillip Vincent, Etienne Chicot, John Forristal, Pete Walker, David Hausman, Bill Moseley; *D:* Oleg Egorov; *M:* Mason Daring. **VHS** *CNG* ♦1/2

Osaka Elegy A study of Japanese cultural rules when society condemns a woman for behavior that is acceptable for a man. In Japanese with English subtitles. *AKA:* Woman of Osaka.
1936 71m/B Isuzu Yamada; *D:* Kenji Mizoguchi. **VHS** $39.95 *ING* ♦♦1/2

The Oscar Unless you enjoy razzing bad acting, this is not for you. Meant as a comeuppance for Hollywood, by Hollywood, this story of a star climbing the ladder of success and squashing fingers on every rung is too schlocky to succeed. The climax, when the scumbag star thinks he's won an Oscar and stands up, only to find it's for someone else, was based on Frank Capra's embarrassing experience with the same situation.
1966 (R) 119m/C Stephen Boyd, Elke Sommer, Jill St. John, Tony Bennett, Milton Berle, Eleanor Parker, Joseph Cotten, Edie Adams, Ernest Borgnine, Ed Begley Sr., Walter Brennan, Broderick Crawford, James Dunn, Peter Lawford, Merle Oberon, Bob Hope, Frank Sinatra; *D:* Russel Rouse. **VHS, Beta** $19.95 *SUE* ♦1/2

Oscar The improbable casting of Stallone in a 1930s style crime farce (an attempt to change his image) is hard to imagine, and harder to believe. Stallone has little to do as he plays the straight man in this often ridiculous story of a crime boss who swears he'll go straight. Cameos aplenty, with Curry's the most notable. Based on a French play by Claude Magnier.
1991 (PG) 109m/C Sylvester Stallone, Ornella Muti, Peter Riegert; *Cameos:* Tim Curry, Chazz Palminteri; *D:* John Landis; *M:* Elmer Bernstein. **VHS** $19.99 *COL, IME, TOU* ♦♦

Oscar's Greatest Moments: 1971-1991 Collection of highlights from the Oscar ceremonies, featuring footage from the past 21 years. Proceeds from video sales benefit the Center for Motion Picture Study.
1992 110m/C *D:* Jeff Margolis. **VHS, 8mm** $19.95 *COL, BTV* ♦♦

Ossessione An adaptation of "The Postman Always Rings Twice," transferred to Fascist Italy, where a drifter and an innkeeper's wife murder her husband. Visconti's first feature, which initiated Italian neo-realism, was not released in the U.S. until 1975 due to a copyright dispute. In Italian with English subtitles.
1942 135m/B Massimo Girotti, Clara Calamai, Juan deLanda, Elio Marcuzzo; *D:* Luchino Visconti. **VHS, Beta** $79.95 *FCT, ING, TPV* ♦♦♦1/2

The Osterman Weekend Peckinpah was said to have disliked the story and the script in this, his last film, which could account for the convoluted and confusing end result. Adding to the problem is the traditional difficulty of adapting Ludlum's complex psychological thrillers for the screen. The result: cast members seem to not quite "get it" as they portray a group of friends, one of whom has been convinced by the CIA that the others are all Soviet spies.
1983 (R) 102m/C Burt Lancaster, Rutger Hauer, Craig T. Nelson, Dennis Hopper, John Hurt, Chris Sarandon, Meg Foster, Helen Shaver; *D:* Sam Peckinpah. **VHS, Beta** *NO* ♦

Otaku no Video Fictionalized animated history of the famed Japanese animation studio Gainax, including strange interviews with rabid fans who want to "Otakunize" the human race. Contains both episodes: "Otaku no Video" (1982) and "More Otaku no Video" (1985). In Japanese with English subtitles. *AKA:* Fan's Video.
1991 100m/C VHS *ANI* ♦♦

Otello An uncommon film treat for opera fans, with a stellar performance by Domingo as the trouble Moor who murders his wife in a fit of jealous rage and later finds she was never unfaithful. Be prepared, however, for changes from the Shakespeare and Verdi stories, necessitated by the film adaptation. Highly acclaimed and awarded; in Italian with English subtitles.
1986 (PG) 123m/C Placido Domingo, Katia Ricciarelli, Justino Diaz; *D:* Franco Zeffirelli. **VHS, Beta** $79.95 *HMV, MED, MVD* ♦♦♦1/2

Othello A silent version of Shakespeare's tragedy, featuring Jannings as the tragic Moor. Titles are in English; with musical score.
1922 81m/B Emil Jannings, Lya de Putti, Werner Krauss; *D:* Dimitri Buchowetzki. **VHS, Beta** $24.95 *VYY, NOS, DVT* ♦♦1/2

Othello Welles' striking adaptation of the Shakespeare tragedy casts him as the self-deluding Moor, with MacLiammoir as the despicable Iago and Cloutier as innocent victim, Desdemona. Welles filmed his epic over a four-year period due to budget difficulties, which also resulted in his filming in a number of different countries and settings. The film underwent a $1 million restoration, supervised by Welles' daughter, prior to its limited theatrical re-release in 1992.
1952 90m/B Orson Welles, Michael MacLiammoir, Suzanne Cloutier, Robert Coote, Hilton Edwards, Michael Lawrence, Nicholas Bruce, Fay Compton, Doris Dowling, Jean Davis, Joseph Cotten, Joan Fontaine; *D:* Orson Welles. **VHS** $89.95 *ACA* ♦♦♦♦

The Other Eerie, effective thriller adapted by Tyron from his supernatural novel. Twin brothers represent good and evil in a 1930s Connecticut farm town beset with gruesome murders and accidents. A good scare.
1972 (PG) 100m/C Martin Udvarnoky, Chris Udvarnoky, Uta Hagen, Diana Muldaur, Christopher Connelly, Victor French, John Ritter; *D:* Robert Mulligan; *M:* Jerry Goldsmith. **VHS, Beta** $59.98 *FOX* ♦♦♦

Other Hell Schlocky Italian-made chiller has the devil inhabiting a convent where he does his damnest to upset the nuns. Gross, but not scary—lots of cliche dark-hallway scenes and fright music.
1985 (R) 88m/C Carlo De Meyo, Francesca Carmeno; *D:* Stefan Oblowsky. **VHS, Beta** $69.98 *LIV, VES* ♦

Other People's Money DeVito is "Larry the Liquidator," a corporate raider with a heart of stone and a penchant for doughnuts. When he sets his sights on a post-smokestack era, family-owned cable company, he gets a taste of love for the first time in his life. He and Miller, the daughter of the company president and also its legal advisor, court one another while sparring over the fate of the company. Unbelievably clipped ending mars otherwise enterprising comedy about the triumph of greed in corporate America. Based on the off-Broadway play by Jerry Sterner.
1991 (R) 101m/C Danny DeVito, Penelope Ann Miller, Dean Jones, Gregory Peck, Piper Laurie, Tom Aldredge, R.D. Call; *D:* Norman Jewison; *W:* Alvin Sargent; *M:* David Newman. **VHS, 8mm** $19.98 *WAR, CCB* ♦♦1/2

The Other Side of Midnight The dreary, depressingly shallow life story of a poor French girl, dumped by an American GI who sleeps her way to acting stardom and a profitable marriage, then seeks revenge for the jilt. Based on Sidney Sheldon's novel, it's not even titillating—just a real downer.
1977 (R) 160m/C Susan Sarandon, Marie-France Pisier, John Beck, Raf Vallone, Clu Gulager, Sorrell Booke; *D:* Charles Jarrott; *W:* Daniel Taradash. **VHS, Beta** $59.98 *FOX* Woof!

The Other Side of the Mountain Tear-jerking true story of Olympic hopeful skier Jill Kinmont, paralyzed in a fall. Bridges helps her pull her life together. A sequel followed two years later. Based on the book "A Long Way Up" by E.G. Valens. *AKA:* A Window to the Sky.
1975 (PG) 102m/C Marilyn Hassett, Beau Bridges, Dabney Coleman, John David Garfield, Griffin Dunne; *D:* Larry Peerce; *W:* David Seltzer; *M:* Charles Fox. **VHS, Beta** $14.98 *MCA* ♦♦

The Other Side of the Mountain, Part 2 Quadriplegic Jill Kinmont, paralyzed in a skiing accident that killed her hopes for the Olympics, overcomes depression and the death of the man who helped her to recover. In this chapter, she falls in love again and finds happiness. More tears are jerked.
1978 (PG) 99m/C Marilyn Hassett, Timothy Bottoms; *D:* Larry Peerce. **VHS, Beta** $14.98 *MCA* ♦♦

Oubliette A peripheral version of Francois Villon, in what is a recently discovered and restored film, the earliest Chaney film.
1914 35m/B Lon Chaney Sr. **VHS, Beta** $39.50 *GVV, LSV* ♦♦

Our Daily Bread Vidor's sequel to the 1928 "The Crowd." A young couple inherit a farm during the Depression and succeed in managing the land. A near-classic, with several sequences highly influenced by directors Alexander Dovshenko and Sergei Eisenstein. Director Vidor also co-scripted this film, risking bankruptcy to finance it. *AKA:* Miracle of Life.
1934 80m/B Karen Morley, Tom Keene, John Qualen, Barbara Pepper, Addison Richards; *D:* King Vidor; *W:* King Vidor. **VHS, Beta** $19.95 *NOS, SUE, BAR* ♦♦♦

Our Dancing Daughters Flapper (Crawford on the brink of stardom) falls hard for millionaire who's forced into arranged marriage, but obliging little missus kicks bucket so Crawford can step in.
1928 98m/B Joan Crawford, Johnny Mack Brown, Nils Asther, Dorothy Sebastian, Anita Page; **D:** Harry Beaumont. **VHS, Beta $19.98** MGM, FCT 𝒵𝒵½

Our Family Business Made for television and meant as a series pilot, this generally plodding "Godfather"-type story is saved by good performances by Wanamaker and Milland.
1981 74m/C Sam Wanamaker, Vera Miles, Ray Milland, Ted Danson, Chip Mayer; **D:** Robert Collins. **VHS $59.95** LIV 𝒵𝒵

Our Gang Two silent "Our Gang" comedies, including "Thundering Fleas" and "Shivering Spooks."
1926 57m/B Joe Cobb, Farina Hoskins, Mary Kornman, Mickey Daniels, Scooter Lowry. **VHS, Beta, 8mm $19.95** VYY 𝒵𝒵

Our Gang Comedies The five shorts on this cassette show the gang at their comedic best. They include "The Big Premiere," "Bubbling Troubles," "Clown Princes," "Don't Lie" and "Farm Hands."
194? 53m/B Robert (Bobby) Blake, Billie "Buckwheat" Thomas, George "Spanky" McFarland, Darla Hood, Carl "Alfalfa" Switzer, Tommy "Butch" Bond, Eugene "Porky" Lee, Shirley "Muggsy" Coates, Joe "Corky" Geil, Billy "Froggy" Lauglin. **VHS, Beta $29.95** MGM, VTR 𝒵𝒵

Our Gang Comedy Festival A 20-year span of comedy from the Little Rascals, including rare silent features.
1988 45m/B Joe Cobb, Farina Hoskins, Mary Kornman, Mickey Daniels, Scooter Lowry. **VHS** GKK 𝒵𝒵

Our Gang Comedy Festival 2 More riotous good times with The Little Rascals, including silent footage.
1989 45m/B Joe Cobb, Farina Hoskins, Mary Kornman, Mickey Daniels, Scooter Lowry. **VHS** GKK 𝒵𝒵

Our Hospitality One of Keaton's finest silent films, with all the elements in place. William McKay (Keaton) travels to the American South on a quaint train (a near-exact replica of the Stephenson Rocket), to claim an inheritance as the last survivor of his family. En route, a young woman traveler informs him that her family has had a long, deadly feud with his, and that they intend to kill him. McKay resolves to get the inheritance, depending on the Southern rule of hospitality to guests to save his life until he can make his escape. Watch for the river scene where, during filming, Keaton's own life was really in danger. By the way, Keaton married his leading lady in real life.
1923 74m/B Buster Keaton, Natalie Talmadge, Joe Keaton, Buster Keaton Jr., Kitty Bradbury, Joe Roberts; **D:** Buster Keaton, John Blystone. **VHS $49.95** HBO 𝒵𝒵𝒵𝒵

Our Little Girl A precocious little tyke tries to reunite her estranged parents by running away to their favorite vacation spot. Sure to please Shirley Temple fans, despite a lackluster script.
1935 63m/B Shirley Temple, Joel McCrea, Rosemary Ames, Lyle Talbot, Erin O'Brien Moore; **D:** John S. Robertson. **VHS, Beta $19.98** FOX 𝒵𝒵

Our Man Flint James Bond clone Derek Flint uses gadgets and his ingenuity to save the world from an evil organization, GAL-AXY, that seeks world domination through control of the weather. The plot moves

quickly around many bikini-clad women, but still strains for effect. Spawned one sequel: "In Like Flint."
1966 107m/C James Coburn, Lee J. Cobb, Gila Golan, Edward Mulhare, Benson Fong, Shelby Grant, Sigrid Valdis, Gianna Serra, James Brolin, Helen Funai, Michael St. Clair; **D:** Daniel Mann; **M:** Jerry Goldsmith. **VHS, Beta $19.98** FOX 𝒵𝒵

Our Miss Brooks Quietly pleasing version of the television series. Miss Brooks pursues the "mother's boy" biology professor. The father of the child she begins tutoring appears taken with her. The professor takes notice.
1956 85m/B Eve Arden, Gale Gordon, Nick Adams, Richard Crenna, Don Porter; **D:** Al Lewis. **VHS** WAR 𝒵𝒵½

Our Modern Maidens Scandalous jazz-age drama in which Crawford and Fairbanks both fall in love with other people before their wedding is to take place. This sequel to "Our Dancing Daughters" features beautiful gowns and lush, opulent Art Deco interiors. Based on a story by Josephine Lovett.
1929 75m/B Joan Crawford, Rod La Rocque, Douglas Fairbanks Jr., Anita Page, Josephine Dunn; **D:** Jack Conway; **W:** Josephine Lovett. **VHS $19.98** MGM 𝒵𝒵½

Our Relations Confusion reigns when Stan and Ollie meet the twin brothers they never knew they had, a pair of happy-go-lucky sailors. Laurel directs the pair through madcap encounters with their twins' wives and the local underworld. One of the pair's best efforts, though not well-remembered. Based on a story by W.W. Jacobs.
1936 94m/B Stan Laurel, Oliver Hardy, Alan Hale, Sidney Toler, James Finlayson, Daphne Pollard; **D:** Harry Lachman. **VHS, Beta $19.95** MED, CCB, MLB 𝒵𝒵𝒵½

Our Time An exclusive girls finishing school in the fifties is the setting for the friendship of Abby (Martin) and Muffy (Slade) and their first stirrings of romance. But when Muffy gets pregnant, tragedy awaits. Sappy. **AKA:** Death of Her Innocence.
1974 91m/C Pamela Sue Martin, Betsey Slade, Parker Stevenson, George O'Hanlon Jr., Roderick Cook, Edith Atwater, Meg Wyllie, Debralee Scott, Nora Heflin, Kathryn Holcomb, Robert Walden; **D:** Peter Hyams; **W:** Jane C. Stanton. **VHS $29.99** WAR 𝒵𝒵½

Our Town Small-town New England life in Grover's Corners in the early 1900s is celebrated in this well-performed and directed adaptation of the Pulitzer Prize-winning play by Thornton Wilder. Film debut of Scott.
1940 90m/B Martha Scott, William Holden, Thomas Mitchell, Fay Bainter, Guy Kibbee, Beulah Bondi, Frank Craven; **D:** Sam Wood; **M:** Aaron Copland. Academy Awards '40 Nominations: Best Actress (Scott), Best Interior Decoration, Best Picture, Best Sound, Best Original Score; National Board of Review Awards '40: 10 Best Films of the Year. **VHS, Beta $9.95** CNG, MRV, NOS 𝒵𝒵𝒵

Our Town Television version of Thornton Wilder's classic play about everyday life in Grovers Corners, a small New England town at the turn of the century. It hews more closely to the style of the stage version than the earlier film version.
1977 120m/C Ned Beatty, Sada Thompson, Ronny Cox, Glynnis O'Connor, Robby Benson, Hal Holbrook, John Houseman; **D:** Franklin J. Schaffner. **VHS, Beta $74.95** MAS 𝒵𝒵𝒵

Our Vines Have Tender Grapes A change of pace role for the volatile Robinson who plays a kind Norwegian widower, living in Wisconsin with his daughter, the spunky O'Brien. The film is made-up of small-town moments as O'Brien learns a few of life's

lessons, eased by the thoughtful compassion of Robinson. Based on the novel "For Our Vines Have Tender Grapes" by George Victor Martin.
1945 105m/B Edward G. Robinson, Margaret O'Brien, James Craig, Agnes Moorehead, Jackie "Butch" Jenkins, Morris Carnovsky, Frances Gifford, Sara Haden, Louis Jean Heydt; **D:** Roy Rowland; **W:** Dalton Trumbo. **VHS $19.98** MGM, MOV, BTV 𝒵𝒵𝒵½

Out A drifter's travels throughout the U.S. from the sixties to the eighties. Successfully manages to satirize just about every conceivable situation but keeps from posturing by not taking itself too seriously. Adapted from an experimental novel by Ronald Sukenick.
1988 88m/C Peter Coyote, Danny Glover, O-Lan Shepard, Jim Haynie, Scott Beach, Semu Haute; **D:** Eli Hollander; **W:** Eli Hollander; **M:** David Cope. **VHS** NO 𝒵𝒵½

Out Cold Black comedy follows the misadventures of a butcher who believes he has accidentally frozen his business partner; the iced man's girlfriend, who really killed him; and the detective who tries to solve the crime. Too many poor frozen body jokes may leave the viewer cold.
1989 (R) 91m/C John Lithgow, Teri Garr, Randy Quaid, Bruce McGill; **D:** Malcolm Mowbray; **M:** Michel Colombier. **VHS, Beta $89.98** HBO 𝒵½

Out for Blood Attorney John Decker is living a happy life until his family is murdered by drug dealers. He turns vigilante, dubbed "Karateman" by the press, and finds himself hunted by the cops and the criminals.
1993 (R) ?m/C Don "The Dragon" Wilson, Shari Shattuck, Michael Delano, Kenneth McLeod, Todd Curtis, Timothy Baker, Howard Jackson, Bob Schott, Eric Lee; **D:** Richard W. Munchkin; **W:** David S. Green. **VHS $89.95** PMH 𝒵𝒵

Out for Justice A psycho Brooklyn hood goes on a murder spree, and homeboy turned lone-wolf cop Seagal races other police and the mob to get at him. Bloodthirsty and profane, it does try to depict N.Y.C.'s Italian-American community—but 90 percent of them are dead by the end so what's the point? Better yet, why does it open with a quote from Arthur Miller? Better still, what's Daffy Duck doing on this tape peddling Warner Brothers T-shirts to kid viewers?!
1991 (R) 91m/C Steven Seagal, William Forsythe, Jerry Orbach. **VHS, Beta, 8mm $19.98** WAR 𝒵½

Out of Africa An epic film of the years spent by Danish authoress Isak Dinesen (her true name is Karen Blixen) on a Kenya coffee plantation. She moved to Africa to marry, and later fell in love with Denys Finch-Hatten, a British adventurer. Based on several books, including biographies of the two lovers. Some critics loved the scenery and music; others despised the acting and the script. A definite "no" for those who love action.
1985 (PG) 161m/C Meryl Streep, Robert Redford, Klaus Maria Brandauer, Michael Kitchen, Malick Bowens, Michael Gough, Suzanna Hamilton, Rachel Kempson, Graham Crowden, Shane Rimmer, Donal McCann, Iman, Joseph Thiaka, Stephen Kinyanjui; **D:** Sydney Pollack; **W:** Kurt Luedtke; **M:** John Barry. Academy Awards '85: Best Adapted Screenplay, Best Art Direction/Set Decoration, Best Cinematography, Best Director (Pollack), Best Picture, Best Sound, Best Original Score; Nominations: Best Actress (Streep), Best Costume Design, Best Supporting Actor (Brandauer); Golden Globe Awards '86: Best Film—Drama, Best Supporting Actor (Brandauer), Best Score. **VHS, Beta $19.98** MCA, BTV 𝒵𝒵𝒵

Out of Bounds An Iowa farmboy picks up the wrong bag at the Los Angeles airport, and is plunged into a world of crime, drugs, and murder. Plenty of action, but the fast pace can't hide huge holes in the script or the silliness of Hall playing a tough kid on the run from the law.
1986 (R) 93m/C Anthony Michael Hall, Jenny Wright, Jeff Kober; **D:** Richard Tuggle; **M:** Stewart Copeland. **VHS, Beta $79.95** COL �️✓½

Out of Control A plane full of rich teenagers crash on a secluded island and must battle a gang of vicious smugglers to survive. A teen sex theme keeps working its way in, leaving the viewer as confused as the actors and actresses appear to be.
1985 (R) 78m/C Betsy Russell, Martin Hewitt, Claudia Udy, Andrew J. Lederer; **D:** Allan Holzman. **VHS, Beta $9.95** NWV, STE ✓

Out of Order A German-made film about people stuck in an office building's malevolent, free-thinking elevator. Dubbed.
1984 87m/C Renee Soutendijk, Goetz George, Wolfgang Kieling, Hannes Jaenicke; **D:** Carl Schenkel. **VHS, Beta $69.98** LIV, VES ✓½

Out of Season Mother and teenage daughter compete for the attentions of the mother's mysterious ex-lover. We never know who wins the man in this enigmatic drama set in an English village, and hints of incest make the story even murkier. Had only a short run in the U.S. **AKA:** Winter Rates.
1975 (R) 90m/C Cliff Robertson, Vanessa Redgrave, Susan George; **D:** Alan Bridges. **VHS, Beta $19.95** VCI ✓✓

Out of Sight, Out of Her Mind After witnessing her daughter burned alive, Alice is released from a mental institution. She tries to start a new life, but her daughter won't let her—she keeps appearing, crying out for help.
1989 (R) 94m/C Susan Blakely, Eddie Albert, Wings Hauser. **VHS, Beta** PSM, PAR ✓✓

Out of the Blue There's trouble in paradise for a married man when a shady lady passes out in his apartment. Thinking she is dead, he tries to get rid of the body. The antics with his neighbor and wife provide plenty of laughs.
1947 86m/B George Brent, Virginia Mayo, Carole Landis, Turhan Bey, Ann Dvorak; **D:** Leigh Jason. **VHS, Beta $19.95** NWV ✓✓½

Out of the Blue A harsh, violent portrait of a shattered family. When an imprisoned father's return fails to reunite this Woodstock-generation family, the troubled teenage daughter takes matters into her own hands. "Easy Rider" star Hopper seems to have reconsidered the effects of the 1960s.
1980 (R) 94m/C Dennis Hopper, Linda Manz, Raymond Burr; **D:** Dennis Hopper. **VHS, Beta $59.95** MED ✓✓✓

Out of the Body A man is possessed by a spirit that likes to kill young, beautiful women. This makes him (and the viewer) uncomfortable.
1988 (R) 91m/C Mark Hembrow, Tessa Humphries; **D:** Brian Trenchard-Smith. **VHS** NO ✓

Out of the Dark The female employees of a telephone-sex service are stalked by a killer wearing a clown mask in this tongue-in-cheek thriller. A few laughs amid the slaughter. Look for Divine.
1988 (R) 98m/C Cameron Dye, Divine, Karen Black, Bud Cort, Lynn Danielson, Geoffrey Lewis, Paul Bartel, Tracy Walter, Silvania Gallardo, Starr Andreeff, Lainie Kazan, Tab Hunter; **D:** Michael Schroeder. **VHS, Beta $89.95** COL ✓½

Out of the Darkness A television movie about the personal life of the New York detective who hunted and arrested sexual killer Son of Sam. Sheen shines in a tight suspenser.
1985 (R) 96m/C Martin Sheen, Hector Elizondo, Matt Clark, Jennifer Salt, Eddie Egan, Robert Trebor; **D:** Jud Taylor; **W:** T.S. Cook. **VHS, Beta $19.95** STE, VMK ✓

Out of the Past A private detective gets caught in a complex web of love, murder, and money in this film noir classic. The plot is torturous but clear thanks to fine directing. Mitchum became an overnight star after this film, which was overlooked but now considered one of the best in its genre. Based on Geoffrey Homes' novel "Build My Gallows High." Remade in 1984 as "Against All Odds." **AKA:** Build My Gallows High.
1947 97m/B Robert Mitchum, Kirk Douglas, Jane Greer, Rhonda Fleming, Steve Brodie, Dickie Moore; **D:** Jacques Tourneur; **W:** Geoffrey Homes. **VHS, Beta $19.98** MED, TTC ✓✓✓½

Out of the Rain A small town becomes a hotbed of deceit and lies due to the influence of drugs. A man and and a woman engage in a passionate struggle to free themselves from the town's grip.
1990 (R) 91m/C Bridget Fonda, Michael O'Keefe, John E. O'Keefe, John Seitz, Georgine Hall, Al Shannon; **D:** Gary Winick; **W:** Shem Bitterman. **VHS, Beta $9.99** CCB, LIV ✓✓

The Out-of-Towners A pair of Ohio rubes travels to New York City and along the way everything that could go wrong does. Lemmon's performance is excellent and Simon's script is, as usual, both wholesome and funny.
1970 (G) 98m/C Jack Lemmon, Sandy Dennis, Anne Meara, Sandy Baron, Billy Dee Williams; **D:** Arthur Hiller; **W:** Neil Simon. **VHS, Beta $14.95** PAR ✓✓✓

Out on a Limb MacLaine plays herself in this made-for-television miniseries based on her best-selling book by the same name. In the midst of love affairs with an unnamed British politician and a mysterious teacher, she learns about her past, present, and future through meditation and her beliefs in reincarnation. Features footage of psychics performing spiritual channeling. Beautiful scenery filmed on location in California, Hong Kong, London, Hawaii, Sweden, and Perú, but the acting is just average, and the movie is slow in some parts. A 234-minute special collector's edition is also available.
1987 160m/C Shirley MacLaine, Charles Dance, John Heard, Anne Jackson, Jerry Orbach; **D:** Robert Butler. **VHS, Beta $89.95** PSM, WSH ✓

Out on a Limb Lame comedy follows the misadventures of financial whiz Bill Campbell (Broderick). His young sister is convinced their stepfather is a criminal and persuades her brother to return home. On his way, Bill is robbed and abandoned by a woman hitchhiker, then found by two moronic brothers. It also turns out his stepfather has a twin brother who wants revenge for past crimes. Frantic chase scenes and lots of noise do not a comedy make. Broderick and Jones also appeared together in "Ferris Bueller's Day Off."
1992 (PG) 82m/C Matthew Broderick, Jeffrey Jones, Heidi Kling, John Reilly, Marian Mercer, Larry Hankin, David Margulies; **D:** Francis Veber. **VHS, Beta $19.98** MGM ✓

Out on Bail A law-abiding citizen witnesses a murder, only to discover the crooked town council is behind the slaying.
1989 (R) 102m/C Robert Ginty, Kathy Shower, Tom Badal, Sydney Lassick; **D:** Gordon Hessler. **VHS, Beta $89.95** TWE ✓½

Outcast A young tough heads west to seize the family ranch wrongfully held by a conniving uncle. Of course he finds love as well, and enjoys gun and fistfights in this exciting though unspectacular western.
1954 90m/C John Derek, Jim Davis, Joan Davis; **D:** William Witney. **VHS $19.98** REP ✓✓

The Outcast Story of three brothers who live by the ax, love from the heart, hate with passion, and die violently. Trouble is they have to recite from a script written in crayon.
1984 86m/C Ben Dekker, Sandra Prinsloo. **VHS $19.95** REP ✓½

The Outcasts A Taiwanese film about young gay boys in an urban jungle who are given shelter and protection by an aging photographer. In Chinese with English subtitles.
1986 102m/C D: Yu Kan-Ping. **VHS, Beta $79.95** FCT ✓✓✓

Outcasts of the City The sort of negligible film filler that TV killed off. An American officer in post-WWII Germany romances a German girl, then gets blamed for the death of her Boche beau.
1958 61m/B Osa Massen, Robert Hutton, Maria Palmer, Nestor Paiva, John Hamilton, George Neise, Norbert Schiller, George Sanders; **D:** Boris L. Petroff. **VHS $19.95** NOS ✓

The Outer Limits: Galaxy Being "There is nothing wrong with your TV set..." in this sci-fi series which ran from 1963-1965. In the show's pilot episode an obsessed scientist transmits a pure-energy being from Andromeda into our universe, and chaos ensues. Additional episodes are available.
1963 53m/B Cliff Robertson, Jacqueline Scott, Lee Phillips, William O. Douglas Jr.; **D:** Leslie Stevens. **VHS, Beta $12.98** MGM, MOV ✓✓

The Outfit It's the 1930s and a mob war is brewing between Lucky Luciano, Legs Diamond and Dutch Schultz. A maverick FBI agent gets in good with Diamond and works to end their reign of crime—only he winds up being the spark to light a war between the rival bosses.
1993 (R) 92m/C John Christian, Billy Drago, Lance Henriksen, Martin Kove, Josh Moby, Rick Washburne; **D:** J. Christian Ingvordsen; **W:** J. Christian Ingvordsen, Steven Kaman, Whitney Ransick. **VHS $89.98** MCA, SGE ✓✓½

The Outing A group of high school kids sneaks into a museum at night to party, and get hunted down by a 3,000-year-old genie-in-a-lamp. The genie idea is original enough to make things interesting. Mediocre special effects and run-of-the-mill acting. **AKA:** The Lamp.
1987 (R) 87m/C Deborah Winters, James Huston; **D:** Tom Daley. **VHS, Beta $14.95** LIV ✓✓

Outland On a volcanic moon of Jupiter, miners begin suffering from spells of insanity. A single federal marshal begins an investigation that threatens the colony's survival. No more or less than a western in space, and the science is rather poor. Might make an interesting double feature with "High Noon," though.
1981 (R) 109m/C Sean Connery, Peter Boyle, Frances Sternhagen, James B. Sikking; **D:** Peter Hyams; **W:** Peter Hyams; **M:** Jerry Goldsmith. **VHS, Beta $19.98** WAR ✓✓

The Outlaw Hughes's variation on the saga of Billy the Kid, which spends more time on Billy's relationship with girlfriend Rio than the climactic showdown with Pat Garrett. The famous Russell vehicle isn't as steamy as it must have seemed to viewers of the day, but the brouhaha around it served to

keep it on the shelf for six years. Also available colorized.
1943 123m/B Jane Russell, Jack Beutel, Walter Huston, Thomas Mitchell; *D:* Howard Hughes. **VHS, Beta $8.95** *CNG, MRV, NOS 💿*

The Outlaw and His Wife An early silent film about a farmer, accused of a petty crime, who flees with his wife into the mountains to escape the police. This powerful drama was a breakthrough film for the early Swedish movie industry.
1917 73m/B Victor Sjostrom, Edith Erastoff; *D:* Victor Sjostrom. **VHS, Beta $29.95** *KIV, FCT, ING 💿💿½*

The Outlaw Bikers—Gang Wars The original road warriors take it to the streets as rival biker gangs square off.
1970 90m/C Clancy Syrko, Des Roberts, King John III, Linda Jackson; *D:* Lawrence Merrick. **VHS, Beta $59.95** *PSM 💿💿½*

Outlaw Blues An ex-convict becomes a national folk hero when he sets out to reclaim his stolen hit song about prison life. St. James is charming in her first major movie role. A grab bag of action, drama, and tongue-in-cheek humor.
1977 (PG) 101m/C Peter Fonda, Susan St. James, Johnny Crawford, Michael Lerner, James Callahan; *D:* Richard T. Heffron; *M:* Charles Bernstein. **VHS, Beta $19.98** *WAR 💿💿*

Outlaw Country LaRue has a dual role as the marshal who is after a band of counterfeiters and an outlaw who's part of the gang.
1949 72m/B Lash LaRue, Al "Fuzzy" St. John, House Peters, Ted Adams, Steve Dunhill; *D:* Ray Taylor. **VHS $11.95** *GPV 💿💿½*

The Outlaw Deputy The law-abiding McCoy as an outlaw! It's really a mistake and Lane helps him clear his name. Based on the story "King of Cactusville" by Johnston McCulley.
1935 55m/B Tim McCoy, Nora Lane, Bud Osborne, Si Jenks, George Offerman Jr.; *D:* Otto Brower. **VHS $11.95** *GPV 💿½*

Outlaw Express After the annexing of California, a U.S. marshall is sent to stop a gang of outlaws who have been raiding Spanish landowners.
1938 57m/B Bob Baker, Cecilia Callejo, Leroy Mason, Don Barclay, Carleton Young; *D:* George Waggner. **VHS, Beta $24.95** *DVT 💿½*

Outlaw Force A Vietnam veteran country singer tracks down the vicious rednecks that kidnapped his daughter and raped and killed his wife. Heavener did all the work in this low-budget, low-quality take-off on "Death Wish."
1987 (R) 95m/C David Heavener, Frank Stallone, Paul Smith, Robert Bjorklund, Devin Dunsworth; *D:* David Heavener. **VHS, Beta $19.98** *TWE 💿*

Outlaw Fury Another Shamrock Ellison epic, this time dealing with a coward proving himself by killing the bad guys.
1950 55m/B James Ellison, Russell Hayden. **VHS, Beta** *NO 💿½*

Outlaw Gang A marshal investigates a rash of rancher killings, leading to a conflict between Indians and local land and water companies.
1949 59m/B Donald (Don "Red") Barry, Robert Lowery, Betty Adams. **VHS, Beta** *NO 💿½*

The Outlaw Josey Wales Eastwood plays a farmer with a motive for revenge—his family was killed and for years he was betrayed and hunted. His desire to play the lone killer is, however, tempered by his need for family and choice. He kills plenty, but in the end finds happiness. Considered one of the last great Westerns, with many superb

performances. Eastwood took over directorial chores during filming from Kaufman, who co-scripted. Adapted from "Gone To Texas" by Forest Carter.
1976 (PG) 135m/C Clint Eastwood, Chief Dan George, Sondra Locke, Matt Clark, John Vernon, Bill McKinney, Sam Bottoms; *D:* Clint Eastwood, Philip Kaufman; *W:* Philip Kaufman. **VHS, Beta $19.98** *WAR, TLF 💿💿💿½*

Outlaw Justice Worn oater plot has our hero infiltrating a gang of outlaws to bring them to justice and save the heroine.
1932 56m/C Jack Hoxie, Dorothy Gulliver, Donald Keith, Kermit Maynard, Charles "Blackie" King, Tom London; *D:* Armand Schaefer. **VHS, Beta** *GPV 💿💿*

Outlaw of Gor Once again, the mild professor is transported to Gor, where he has new, improved, bloody adventures. Lots of sword-play, but no magic. Sequel to "Gor." From the novel by John Norman.
1987 (PG) 89m/C Rebecca Ferratti, Urbano Barberini, Jack Palance, Donna Denton; *D:* John Cardos; *W:* R.J. Marx. **VHS, Beta $19.98** *WAR 💿*

Outlaw of the Plains Another of Crabbe's cowboy pictures in which he played hero Billy Carson, now bailing his trouble-prone sidekick out of a land swindle. Very plain indeed.
1946 56m/B Buster Crabbe, Al "Fuzzy" St. John, Patti McCarty, Charles "Blackie" King, Karl Hackett, John Cason, Bud Osborne, Budd Buster, Charles "Slim" Whitaker; *D:* Sam Newfield. **VHS $19.95** *NOS 💿*

Outlaw Riders Three outlaw bikers take it on the lam after committing a series of disastrous bank robberies.
1972 (PG) 84m/C Sonny West, Darlene Duralia, Bambi Allen, Bill Bonner; *D:* Tony Houston. **VHS, Beta** *NO 💿*

Outlaw Roundup The Texas Rangers battle an outlaw gang. Guess who wins.
1944 51m/B Tex O'Brien, James Newill, Guy Wilkerson, Helen Chapman, Jack Ingram, I. Stanford Jolley; *D:* Harry Fraser. **VHS, Beta $19.95** *NOS, MRV, VDM 💿*

Outlaw Rule Standard action-packed western adventure pitting outlaws against the law of the West.
1936 61m/B Reb Russell, Betty Mack, Yakima Canutt, Jack Rockwell, John McGuire, Alan Bridge; *D:* S. Roy Luby. **VHS, Beta $19.95** *NOS, VCN, HEG 💿½*

The Outlaw Tamer Even though Chandler is on the run he still helps capture some horse thieves.
1933 56m/B Lane Chandler, J.P. McGowan, Janet Morgan, George "Gabby" Hayes; *D:* J.P. McGowan. **VHS, Beta $11.95** *GPV, VCN 💿*

Outlaw Trail The Trail Blazers put an end to a counterfeiter's evil ways.
1944 53m/B Hoot Gibson, Bob Steele, Chief Thundercloud, Jennifer Holt, Cy Kendall; *D:* Robert Tansey. **VHS, Beta $19.95** *NOS, DVT 💿½*

Outlaw Women A western town is run by a woman who won't let male outlaws in—until one wins her heart.
1952 76m/C Marie Windsor, Jackie Coogan, Carla Balenda; *D:* Sam Newfield. **VHS, Beta $59.95** *MON 💿*

Outlaws of Sonora A man transports money to a neighboring town while his outlaw double tries to steal it from him.
1938 58m/B Bob Livingston, Ray Corrigan, Max Terhune, Jack Mulhall, Otis Harlan; *D:* George Sherman. **VHS $19.95** *NOS, DVT 💿½*

Outlaws of the Desert Having run out of bad guys in the Old West, Hoppy and his pals head to Arabia to buy some horses. Once there, they get involved in a kidnap-

ping. Russell Hayden is replaced as Hoppy's sidekick by Brad King. Duncan ("The Cisco Kid") Renaldo plays the sheik.
1941 66m/B William Boyd, Brad King, Andy Clyde, Forrest Stanley, Jean Phillips, Duncan Renaldo, George Lewis; *D:* Howard Bretherton. **VHS $19.95** *NOS 💿½*

Outlaws of the Range Action western featuring outlaws who terrorize the countryside.
1936 60m/B Bill Cody, Catherine Cotter, William McCall, Gordon Griffith; *D:* Al Herman. **VHS, Beta** *VCN 💿*

Outlaw's Paradise Cowboy hero McCoy plays not only a lawman out to catch mail thieves, but also the chief outlaw he's hunting! That's one way to keep the budget low.
1939 62m/B Tim McCoy, Benny Corbett, Joan Barclay, Ted Adams, Forrest Taylor, Bob Terry; *D:* Sam Newfield. **VHS $15.95** *NOS, LOO, RXM 💿*

Outpost in Morocco A desert soldier is sent to quiet the restless natives and falls for the rebel leader's daughter. The good guys win, but the love interest is sacrificed. Glory before love boys, and damn the story.
1949 92m/B George Raft, Marie Windsor, Akim Tamiroff, John Litel, Eduard Franz; *D:* Robert Florey. **VHS $19.95** *NOS, MRV, MGM 💿½*

Outrage! An upstanding citizen guns down his daughter's killer and turns himself in to police. His ambitious lawyer fights an open-and-shut homicide case with both fair and foul means. Not a shootout like the cassette box suggests, but an okay courtroom drama attacking excesses of the legal system. From a novel by Henry Denker, made for TV by producer Irwin Allen.
1986 96m/C Robert Preston, Beau Bridges, Anthony Newley, Mel Ferrer, Burgess Meredith, Linda Purl, William Allen Young; *D:* Walter Grauman. **VHS $89.95** *VMK 💿💿½*

Outrageous! An offbeat, low-budget comedy about the strange relationship between a gay female impersonator and his pregnant schizophrenic friend. The pair end up in New York, where they feel right at home. Russell's impersonations of female film stars earned him the best actor prize at the Berlin Film Festival.
1977 (R) 100m/C Craig Russell, Hollis McLaren, Richard Easley, Allan Moyle, Helen Shaver; *D:* Richard Benner. **VHS, Beta $64.95** *COL 💿💿💿*

Outrageous Fortune Two would-be actresses - one prim and innocent and one wildly trampy - chase after the same two-timing boyfriend and get involved in a dangerous CIA plot surrounding a deadly bacteria. Tired plot. Mediocre acting and formula jokes, but somehow still funny. Disney's first foray into comedy for grown-ups.
1987 (R) 112m/C Shelley Long, Bette Midler, George Carlin, Peter Coyote; *D:* Arthur Hiller; *W:* Leslie Dixon. **VHS, Beta $19.95** *TOU 💿💿*

Outside Chance A soapy, sanitized remake of Mimieux's film, "Jackson County Jail," wherein an innocent woman is persecuted in a small Southern jail. Made for television.
1978 92m/C Yvette Mimieux, Royce D. Applegate; *D:* Michael Miller. **VHS, Beta $59.98** *NLC 💿*

Outside Chance of Maximillian Glick A sentimental Canadian comedy about a boy's dreams and his tradition-bound Jewish family.
1988 (G) 94m/C Noam Zylberman, Fairuza Balk, Saul Rubinek; *D:* Allan Goldstein. **VHS, Beta $14.95** *HMD 💿💿*

The Outside Man A French hit man is called to Los Angeles to knock off a crime boss, which he does. But then an American hit man is hired to do in the Frenchman. The climatic showdown is set around the crime boss' body, which happens to be embalmed in a sitting position. Decidely offbeat. *AKA:* Un Homme Est Mort.
1973 (PG) 104m/C Jean-Louis Trintignant, Roy Scheider, Ann-Margret, Angie Dickinson, Georgia Engel, Carlo De Meyo, Umberto Orsini, Ted de Corsia, Felice Orlandi, John Hillerman; *D:* Jacques Deray. **VHS $14.95** MGM ♫♫

Outside the Law Lon Chaney plays dual roles of the underworld hood in "Black Mike Sylva," and a Chinese servant in "Ah Wing." Silent.
1921 77m/B Lon Chaney Sr., Priscilla Dean, Ralph Lewis, Wheeler Oakman; *D:* Tod Browning. **VHS, Beta $16.95** SNC, CCB, VYY ♫♫

The Outsiders Based on the popular S.E. Hinton book, the story of a teen gang from the wrong side of the tracks and their conflicts with society and each other. Melodramatic and over-done, but teen-agers still love the story. Good soundtrack and cast ripples with up and coming stars. Followed by a television series. Coppola adapted another Hinton novel the same year, "Rumble Fish."
1983 (PG) 91m/C C. Thomas Howell, Matt Dillon, Ralph Macchio, Patrick Swayze, Diane Lane, Tom Cruise, Emilio Estevez, Rob Lowe, Tom Waits, Leif Garrett; *D:* Francis Ford Coppola; *W:* Kathleen Rowell; *M:* Carmine Coppola. **VHS, Beta $19.98** WAR ♫♫♫

Outtakes A piecemeal compilation of comedy skits, concentrating on sex and genre parody.
1985 (R) 85m/C Forrest Tucker, Bobbi Wexler, Joleen Lutz; *D:* Jack M. Sell. **VHS, Beta** NO ♫♫

The Oval Portrait An adaptation of the Edgar Allan Poe suspense tale about a Civil War-era maiden, her illicit love for a Confederate soldier and her eventual death.
1988 89m/C Giselle MacKenzie, Barry Coe; *D:* Regelio A. Gonzalez Jr. **VHS, Beta** NO ♫½

Over Indulgence A young woman witnesses a murder in an affluent society in British East Africa.
1987 (R) 95m/C Denholm Elliott, Holly Aird, Michael Byrne, Kathryn Pogson; *D:* Ross Devenish. **VHS, Beta $79.98** MCG ♫♫

Over the Brooklyn Bridge A young Jewish man (Gould) must give up his Catholic girlfriend (Hemingway) in order to get his uncle (Caesar) to lend him the money he needs to buy a restaurant in Manhattan. Nowhere near as funny as it should be, and potentially offensive to boot. *AKA:* My Darling Shiksa.
1983 (R) 100m/C Elliott Gould, Sid Caesar, Shelley Winters, Margaux Hemingway, Carol Kane, Burt Young; *D:* Menahem Golan; *M:* Pino Donaggio. **VHS, Beta $79.95** MGM ♫♫

Over the Edge The music of Cheap Trick, The Cars, and The Ramones highlights this realistic tale of alienated suburban youth on the rampage. Dillon makes his screen debut in this updated, well-done "Rebel Without a Cause." Shelved for several years, the movie was finally released after Dillon made it big. Sleeper with excellent direction and dialogue.
1979 (PG) 91m/C Michael Kramer, Matt Dillon, Pamela Ludwig, Vincent Spano; *D:* Jonathan Kaplan. **VHS, Beta $19.98** WAR ♫♫♫½

Over the Hill Dukakis stars as Alma, an eccentric widow who decides to leave her well-meaning son's restrictive home in Maine to visit her estranged daughter Elizabeth in Sydney, Australia. Embarassed by her peculiarities Elizabeth arranges a holiday away but Mom has her own plans. She wants to "loop the loop," and make a complete circuit around the Australian continent. Soon Alma is on the road, meeting fellow eccentrics and experiencing a variety of adventures.
1993 (PG) 102m/C Olympia Dukakis, Sigrid Thornton, Derek Fowlds, Pippa Grandison; *D:* George Miller. **VHS** NLC, COL, IME ♫♫½

Over the Summer Strong drama about a troubled teen who escapes the city for a summer with her grandparents. No cliches here—the grandfather lusts after the granddaughter and eventually kills himself, and problems remain at the end. Intelligent and entertaining, though marred by needless nude scenes.
1985 97m/C Laura Hunt, Johnson West, Catherine Williams, David Romero; *D:* Teresa Sparks. **VHS, Beta $69.98** LIV, VES ♫♫½

Over the Top The film that started a nationwide arm-wrestling craze. A slow-witted trucker decides the only way he can retain custody of his estranged son, as well as win the boy's respect, is by winning a big arm-wrestling competition. Stallone is an expert at grinding these movies out by now, and the kid (General Hospital's Mikey) is all right, but the end result is boredom, as it should be with an arm-wrestling epic.
1986 (PG) 94m/C Sylvester Stallone, Susan Blakely, Robert Loggia, David Mendenhall; *D:* Menahem Golan; *W:* Sylvester Stallone, Gary Conway, Sterling Silliphant. **VHS, Beta $19.98** WAR ♫½

Overboard A wealthy, spoiled woman falls off of her yacht and into the arms of a low-class carpenter who picks her up and convinces her she is in fact his wife, and mother to his four brats. Just when she learns to like her life, the tables are turned again. Even though it's all been done before, you can't help but laugh at the screwy gags.
1987 (PG) 112m/C Goldie Hawn, Kurt Russell, Katherine Helmond, Roddy McDowall, Edward Herrmann; *D:* Garry Marshall; *W:* Leslie Dixon. **VHS, Beta $14.95** MGM, HMV, FOX ♫♫

The Overcoat An adaptation of Nikolai Gogol's classic story about the dehumanizing life endured in 20th-century bureaucracy. All a menial civil servant wants is a new overcoat. When he finally gets one, this treasured article not only keeps him warm but makes him feel self-satisfied as well. In Russian with English subtitles.
1959 93m/B Rolan Bykov; *D:* Alexei Batalov. **VHS, Beta $59.95** HTV, ING ♫♫½

Overdrawn at the Memory Bank In a futuristic tyranny, a romantic rebel becomes somehow fused with the spirit of Humphrey Bogart in the milieu of "Casablanca," and lives out a cliched version of the film character's adventures.
1983 84m/C Raul Julia, Linda Griffiths; *D:* Douglas Williams. **VHS, Beta $19.95** STE, NWV ♫♫

Overexposed All the wackos love the sultry soap star Oxenburg; one is a killer. Eighty minutes and a bunch of bodies later the killer is unmasked. Plenty of suspense and some original gore. Based on the true stories of fans who stalk celebrities.
1990 (R) 83m/C Catherine Oxenberg, David Naughton, Jennifer Edwards, Karen Black; *D:* Larry Brand. **VHS $14.95** MGM ♫♫

Overkill A detective and the vengeance-minded brother of a dead Japanese-American fight back against the controlling Yakuza in Little Tokyo.
1986 (R) 81m/C Steve Rally, John Nishio, Laura Burkett, Roy Summerset; *D:* Ulli Lommel. **Beta** NO ♫

Overland Mail Fifteen episodes of the vintage serial filled with western action.
1941 225m/B Lon Chaney Jr., Helen Parrish. **VHS, Beta $49.95** NOS, VCN, MLB ♫

Overland Stage Raiders The "Three Mesquiteers" ride again, this time to guard a Greyhound bus! The trio must protect a shipment of gold from hijackers. This is the last film for Brooks, who had starred in the German masterpiece "Pandora's Box" in 1929.
1938 55m/B John Wayne, Ray Corrigan, Max Terhune, Louise Brooks, John Archer, Frank LaRue, Yakima Canutt; *D:* George Sherman. **VHS $9.95** REP, NOS ♫♫

Overlanders The Japanese may invade, but rather than kill 1,000 head of cattle, these Aussies drive the huge herd across the continent, facing danger along the way. Beautifully photographed, featuring the "Australian Gary Cooper" and a stampede scene to challenge "Dances with Wolves."
1946 91m/B Chips Rafferty, Daphne Campbell, Jean Blue, John Nugent Hayward; *D:* Harry Watt. **VHS, Beta $19.95** NOS, DVT, HEG ♫♫♫

The Overlanders A group of nine men, two women and a boy challenge the forbidding Canadian Northwest circa 1862.
1979 76m/C VHS, Beta $59.95 TWE ♫♫

Overnight Sensation A modern adaptation of the W. Somerset Maugham story about a traditional marriage being tested by the wife's sudden literary success.
1983 30m/C Louise Fletcher, Robert Loggia, Shari Belafonte-Harper. **VHS, Beta $225.00** PYR ♫♫

Overseas: Three Women with Man Trouble Three beautiful sisters in French colonial Algeria surround themselves in a life of luxury to avoid the incredible social changes going on around them. Each sister has a different perspective on her life, and the perspectives are graphically revealed. Lush photography set in the Mediterranean. In French with English subtitles.
1990 96m/C Nicole Garcia, Marianne Basler, Philippe Galland, Pierre Doris, Brigitte Rouan; *D:* Brigitte Rouan; *W:* Brigitte Rouan. **VHS $89.95** FXL, ART, BTV ♫♫

Overthrow American sportswriter finds himself caught up in violence and intrigue in Buenos Aires.
1982 (R) 90m/C John Phillip Law, Lewis Van Bergen, Roger Wilson; *D:* Larry Ludman. **VHS, Beta $79.95** IMP, HHE, VTR ♫½

Overture An episode of "The Persuaders." Brett and Danny are tricked into helping a retired judge. This adventure leads them to the Mediterranean and a gorgeous gal.
1975 52m/C Roger Moore, Tony Curtis. **VHS** NO ♫½

Overture to Glory A Jewish cantor longs for the world of opera. He leaves his wife and son to fulfill his passion, but eventually he loses his voice and humbly returns home on Yom Kippur, the Jewish Day of Atonement. He learns that his son has passed away. Grief-stricken, he goes to the synagogue. There, the cantor regains his voice as he performs Kol Nidre in a passionate and melodious rendering. In Yiddish with English subtitles. *AKA:* Der Vilner Shtot Khazn.
1940 85m/B Helen Beverly, Florence Weiss. **VHS, Beta $79.95** ERG, ING, TPV ♫♫½

The Owl and the Pussycat Nerdy author gets the neighborhood hooker evicted from her apartment. She returns the favor, and the pair hit the street—and the sack—in Buck Henry's hilarious adaptation of the Broadway play. Streisand's first non-singing role.
1970 (PG) 96m/C Barbra Streisand, George Segal, Robert Klein, Allen (Gooritz) Garfield; *D:* Herbert Ross; *W:* Buck Henry. VHS, Beta $9.95 GKK &&&

The Ox Slow-moving, simple tale, set in rural Sweden in the 1860's during a famine. Desperate to feed his family a tenant farmer kills his employer's ox. Consumed by guilt, the man is quickly found out and sentenced to life imprisonment. Pardoned after six years, the farmer returns to his family, to find out his wife has survived by doing things he finds difficult to forgive. Based on a true story. Directorial debut of Nykvist, the long-time cinematographer for Ingmar Bergman, well displays his familiarity with composition and lighting to heighten mood. In Swedish with English subtitles.
1991 93m/C Stellan Skarsgard, Ewa Froling, Lennart Hjulstrom, Max von Sydow, Liv Ullmann, Bjorn Granath, Erland Josephson; *D:* Sven Nykvist; *W:* Lasse Summanen, Sven Nykvist. VHS $89.95 ACA, ICA, FCT &&½

The Ox-Bow Incident A popular rancher is murdered, and a mob of angry townspeople can't wait for the sheriff to find the killers. They hang the young man, despite the protests of Fonda, a cowboy with a conscience. Excellent study of mob mentality with strong individual characterizations. A brilliant western based on a true story by Walter Van Tilburg Clark. Also see "Twelve Angry Men"—less tragic but just as moving. *AKA:* Strange Incident.
1943 75m/B Henry Fonda, Harry Morgan, Dana Andrews, Anthony Quinn, Frank Conroy, Harry Davenport, Jane Darwell, William Eythe, Mary Beth Hughes; *D:* William A. Wellman; *W:* Lamar Trotti; *M:* Cyril Mockridge. Academy Awards '43 Nominations: Best Picture; National Board of Review Awards '43: 10 Best Films of the Year, Best Director (Wellman). VHS, Beta $19.98 FOX &&&

The Ox-Bow Incident Usually called "Lynch Mob," this is a television play based upon the famous book and 1943 film about mob ethics.
1955 45m/B Cameron Mitchell, Robert Wagner, Raymond Burr. VHS, Beta $19.98 NOS, DVT &&&

Oxford Blues An American finagles his way into England's Oxford University and onto the rowing team in pursuit of the girl of his dreams. Beautiful scenery, but the plot is wafer-thin. Remake of "Yank at Oxford."
1984 (PG-13) 98m/C Rob Lowe, Ally Sheedy, Amanda Pays, Julian Sands, Michael Gough, Gail Strickland; *D:* Robert Boris; *M:* John Du Prez. VHS, Beta $19.98 FOX &&

Ozzie & Harriet Meet television's Nelson family in this 7-volume series, which contains two episodes of the sitcom per tape. In "The Pancake Mix," Ricky wants to get a refund from the baking company. In "The New Chairs," the department store sends the Nelsons more chairs than they had bargained for.
1967 55m/B Ozzie Nelson, Harriet Hilliard Nelson, David Nelson, Ricky Nelson. VHS $19.99 NOS, MOV &&

Pace That Kills An anti-drug cautionary drama from the Roaring '20s, one of many now marketed on cassette as campy fun. Beware, though, a little bit of this stuff goes a long way. A young man goes to the big city to find his missing sister and winds up hooked on heroin.
1928 87m/B Owen Gorin, Virginia Roye, Florence Turner. VHS, Beta, 8mm $24.95 GVV &

Pacific Heights Young San Francisco couple takes on mammoth mortgage assuming tenants will write their ticket to the American dream, but psychopathic tenant Keaton moves in downstairs and redecorates. He won't pay the rent and he won't leave. Creepy psycho-thriller has lapses but builds to effective climax. It's a treat to watch mother/daughter actresses Hedren and Griffith work together. Watch for Beverly D'Angelo as Keaton's lover.
1990 (R) 103m/C Melanie Griffith, Matthew Modine, Michael Keaton, Mako, Nobu McCarthy, Laurie Metcalf, Carl Lumbly, Dorian Harewood, Luca Bercovici, Tippi Hedren, Sheila McCarthy, Dan Hedaya, Beverly D'Angelo, Nicholas Pryor, Miriam Margolyes; *D:* John Schlesinger; *W:* Daniel Pyne; *M:* Hans Zimmer. VHS $19.98 FOX &&&

Pacific Inferno During WWII, American POWs endeavor to break out of a Japanese prison camp in the Philippines. Their goal is to prevent their captors from retrieving millions of dollars worth of sunken U.S. gold. Made for cable television.
1985 90m/C Jim Brown, Richard Jaeckel, Tim Brown; *D:* Rolf Bayer. VHS, Beta NO &&

The Pack A group of dogs become wild when left on a resort island. A marine biologist leads the humans who fight to keep the dogs from using vacationers as chew toys. Fine production valves keep it from going to the dogs. Made with the approval of the American Humane Society who helped with the treatment of stage hands. *AKA:* The Long, Dark Night.
1977 (R) 99m/C Joe Don Baker, Hope Alexander-Willis, R.G. Armstrong, Richard B. Shull; *D:* Robert Clouse. VHS, Beta $19.98 WAR &&½

Pack Up Your Troubles Laurel and Hardy make good on a promise to help find the grandfather of a girl whose father was killed in WWI. All they know is the grandfather's last name though—Smith. Wholesome R and R. *AKA:* We're In the Army Now.
1932 68m/B Stan Laurel, Oliver Hardy, James Finlayson, Jacquie Lyn; *D:* George Marshall. VHS, Beta $14.98 MED, FCT, MLB &&½

The Package An espionage thriller about an army sergeant who loses the prisoner he escorts into the U.S. When he tries to track him down, he uncovers a military plot to start WWIII. Hackman is believable in his role as the sergeant.
1989 (R) 108m/C Gene Hackman, Tommy Lee Jones, Joanna Cassidy, Dennis Franz, Pam Grier, John Heard, Reni Santoni, Thalmus Rasulala, Ike Pappas, Kevin Crowley; *D:* Andrew Davis; *W:* John Bishop; *M:* James Newton Howard. VHS, Beta $19.98 ORI &&½

Packin' It In A Los Angeles family is in for a rude awakening when they leave the city for a quieter life in the Oregon woods. There they encounter a band of survivalists with semi-comedic results.
1983 92m/C Richard Benjamin, Paula Prentiss, Molly Ringwald, Tony Roberts, Andrea Marcovicci; *D:* Judd Taylor. VHS, Beta NO &&

Paco A young, South American boy heads for the city, where he meets his uncle. He discovers his uncle is the leader of a gang of youthful thieves. Predictable and sluggish.
1975 (G) 89m/C Jose Ferrer, Panchito Gomez, Allen (Gooritz) Garfield, Pernell Roberts, Andre Marquis; *D:* Robert Vincent O'Neil. VHS, Beta GHV &½

Paddy A young Irish lad realizes his sexual potential by seducing every woman he can find. Freudians will have a field day. *AKA:* Goodbye to the Hill.
1970 (PG) 97m/C Des Cave, Milo O'Shea, Darbnia Molloy, Peggy Cass; *D:* Daniel Haller. VHS, Beta $59.98 NO &&

Padre Nuestro Religious satire about a dying priest who wishes to reunite his family, who include an atheist brother, a mistress from his youth, and his illegitimate daughter who's a notorious prostitute. In Spanish with English subtitles.
1985 91m/C Fernando Rey, Francesco Rabal, Victoria Abril; *D:* Francisco Regueiro. VHS $79.95 CVC, FCT &&½

Padre Padrone The much acclaimed adaptation of the Gavino Ledda autobiography about his youth in agrarian Sardinia with a brutal, tyrannical father. Eventually he overcomes his handicaps, breaks the destructive emotional ties to his father and successfully attends college. Highly regarded although low budget; in an Italian dialect (Sardinian) with English subtitles. *AKA:* Father Master; My Father, My Master.
1977 113m/C Omero Antonutti, Saverio Marconi, Marcella Michelangeli, Fabrizio Forte, Salverio Marioni; *D:* Paolo Taviani, Vittorio Taviani; *W:* Paolo Taviani, Vittorio Taviani. VHS, Beta $59.95 COL, ING &&&½

Pagan Island A man is stranded on a desert island with 30 beautiful girls who tie him up and abandon him. Maki, to be sacrificed by the rest, saves Dew and they fall in love. They go off in search of a reputed treasure, which they find, but at a deadly cost.
1960 67m/B Eddie Dew, Nani Maka; *D:* Barry Mahon; *W:* Clelle Mahon. VHS $23.00 SMW, TPV &

Pagan Love Song A dull musical which finds Keel in Tahiti taking over his uncle's coconut plantation and falling in love with Williams. Surprise! Williams performs one of her famous water ballets, which is the only saving grace in this lifeless movie. ♫The House of Singing Bamboo; Singing in the Sun; Etiquette; Why is Love So Crazy; Tahiti; The Sea of the Moon; Pagan Love Song; Coconut Milk.
1950 76m/C Esther Williams, Howard Keel, Minna Gombell, Rita Moreno; *D:* Robert Alton. VHS $19.98 MGM &&

Paid to Kill A failing businessman hires a thug to kill him in order to leave his family insurance money, but when the business picks up, he can't contact the thug to cancel the contract. The actors' lack of talent is matched only by the characters' lack of motivation. *AKA:* Five Days.
1954 71m/B Dane Clark, Paul Carpenter, Thea Gregory; *D:* Montgomery Tully. VHS, Beta RXM &&

Pain in the A— A hit man helps a suicidal shirt salesman solve his marital problems in this black comedy that was later Americanized as "Buddy, Buddy." Not for all tastes, but has acquired a reputation for its dark wit. In French with English subtitles.
1977 (PG) 90m/C Lino Ventura, Jacques Brel, Caroline Cellier; *D:* Edouard Molinaro; *W:* Francis Veber, Edouard Molinaro. VHS, Beta $59.95 COL, ING &&&

Paint It Black A violent/steamy mystery and action flick from the director of "River's Edge," in which a young man from the silver-spoon set develops a fascination for an artist.

O

1989 (R) 101m/C Sally Kirkland, Rick Rossovich, Martin Landau, Doug Savant, Peter Frechette, Julie Carmen, Jason Bernhard, Monique Van De Ven; **D:** Tim Hunter. **VHS, Beta $89.98** LIV, VES ⅋⅋½

The Paint Job Wesley, the lonely house painter, falls in love with his neighbor, Margaret. Unfortunately, Margaret is married—to Wesley's boss Willy. Margaret is drawn to Wesley and bored with Willy. But one of the men turns out to be a serial killer. What's a gal in love to do?
1993 (R) 90m/C Will Patton, Bebe Neuwirth, Robert Pastorelli; **D:** Micheal Taav; **W:** Micheal Taav; **M:** John Wesley Harding. **VHS** COL ⅋⅋

Paint Your Wagon Big-budget western musical-comedy about a gold mining boom town, and two prospectors sharing the same Mormon wife complete with a classic Lerner and Lowe score. Marvin chews up the sagebrush and Eastwood attempts to sing, although Seberg was mercifully dubbed. Overlong, with patches of interest, pretty songs, and plenty of panoramic scenery. Adapted from the L & L play. ♫I Talk To The Trees; I Still See Elisa; I'm On My Way; Hand Me Down That Can O' Beans; Whoop-Ti-Ay; They Call the Wind Maria; There's a Coach Comin' In; Wandrin' Star; Best Things.
1969 (PG) 164m/C Lee Marvin, Clint Eastwood, Jean Seberg, Harve Presnell; **D:** Joshua Logan; **W:** Paddy Chayefsky; **M:** Frederick Loewe, Andre Previn, Alan Jay Lerner. **VHS, Beta $29.95** PAR ⅋⅋½

Painted Desert Gable's first film role of any consequence came in this early sound western. Gable plays a villain opposite "good guy" William Boyd.
1931 80m/B William Boyd, Helen Twelvetrees, George O'Brien, Clark Gable, William Farnum; **D:** Howard Higgin. **VHS, Beta $19.95** NOS, MRV, HHT ⅋⅋

The Painted Hills Lassie outsmarts crooked miners and rescues her friends. Surprise, Surprise! Overly sentimental, but action packed and beautifully shot. Lassie's last outing with MGM.
1951 (G) 70m/C Paul Kelly, Bruce Cowling, Gary Gray, Art Smith, Ann Doran, Lassie; **D:** Harold F. Kress. **VHS, Beta $14.95** MGM, BPG, FCT ⅋⅋½

The Painted Stallion This 12-chapter serial features a mysterious figure on a painted stallion who attempts to maintain peace between Mexicans and Indians.
1937 212m/B Ray Corrigan, Hoot Gibson, Duncan Renaldo, Leroy Mason, Yakima Canutt; **D:** William Witney, Ray Taylor. **VHS $29.98** NOS, VDM, REP ⅋⅋½

The Painted Veil Adaptation of a W. Somerset Maugham story. Garbo, once again the disillusioned wife turning to the affections of another man, is magnificent, almost eclipsing the weak script. Lost money at the box office, but for Garbo fans, an absolute must.
1934 83m/B Greta Garbo, Herbert Marshall, George Brent, Warner Oland, Jean Hersholt; **D:** Richard Boleslawski. **VHS, Beta $19.98** MGM, FCT ⅋⅋½

Pair of Aces Kristofferson is a Texas Ranger who's on the trail of a serial killer. His only other problem is being saddled with Nelson, a philosophical safecracker who's awaiting trial and in the reluctant cop's custody. Low-key western with good buddy pairing of Nelson and Kristofferson. Made for television.
1990 94m/C Willie Nelson, Kris Kristofferson, Rip Torn, Helen Shaver, Jane Cameron, Sonny Carl Davis, Lash LaRue, Emily Warfield, Michael Marich; **D:** Aaron Lipstadt. **VHS** WAR ⅋⅋½

Paisan Six episodic tales of life in Italy, several featuring Allied soldiers and nurses during WWII. One of the stories tells of a man who tries to develop a relationship without being able to speak Italian. Another focuses on a young street robber who is confronted by one of his victims. Strong stories that covers a wide range of emotions. In Italian with English subtitles.
1946 90m/B Maria Michi, Carmela Sazio, Gar Moore, William Tubbs, Harriet White, Robert Van Loon, Dale Edmonds, Carla Pisacane, Dots Johnson; **D:** Roberto Rossellini; **W:** Federico Fellini, Roberto Rossellini. Academy Awards '49 Nominations: Best Story & Screenplay; National Board of Review Awards '48: 5 Best Foreign Films of the Year, Best Director (Fellini). **VHS, Beta, 8mm $24.95** NOS, HHT, CAB ⅋⅋⅋

Pajama Game A spritely musical about the striking workers of a pajama factory and their plucky negotiator, who falls in love with the boss. Based on the hit Broadway musical, which was based on Richard Bissell's book "Seven and a Half Cents" and adapted for the screen by Bisell and Abbott. Bob Fosse choreographed the dance numbers. ♫I'm Not at All in Love; Small Talk; There Once Was a Man; Steam Heat; Hernando's Highway; Hey There; Once-a-Year Day; Seven and a Half Cents; I'll Never Be Jealous Again.
1957 101m/C Doris Day, John Raitt, Eddie Foy Jr., Reta Shaw, Carol Haney; **D:** Stanley Donen, George Abbott. **VHS, Beta $19.95** WAR ⅋⅋⅋½

Pajama Party Followup to "Bikini Beach" takes the party inside in this fourth entry in the popular "Beach Party" series. Plot is up to beach party realism. Funicello is Avalon-less (although he does have a cameo) so she falls for Martian Kirk instead. He's scouting for an alien invasion, but after he falls into Annette's lap decides to save the planet instead. Typical fluff with the usual beach movie faces present; look for a young Garr as a dancer. Followed by the classic "Beach Blanket Bingo." ♫It's That Kind of Day; There Has to Be a Reason; Where Did I Go Wrong?; Pajama Party; Beach Ball; Among the Young; Stuffed Animal.
1964 82m/C Tommy Kirk, Annette Funicello, Elsa Lanchester, Harvey Lembeck, Jesse White, Jody McCrea, Donna Loren, Susan Hart, Bobbi Shaw, Cheryl Sweeten, Luree Holmes, Candy Johnson, Dorothy Lamour, Toni Basil, Teri Garr, Ben Lessy; **Cameos:** Buster Keaton, Frankie Avalon, Don Rickles; **D:** Don Weis; **W:** Louis M. Heyward; **M:** Les Baxter. **VHS** NO ⅋⅋

Pajama Tops A stage production of the classic French bedroom farce, taped live at the Music Hall Theatre in Toronto, Canada. Includes all the trials of marriage including adultery and deceit.
1983 105m/C Robert Klein, Susan George, Pia Zadora. **VHS** NO ⅋⅋½

Pal Joey Musical comedy about an opportunistic singer who courts a wealthy socialite in hopes that she will finance his nightclub. His play results in comedic complications. Stellar choreography, fine direction, and beautiful costumes complement performances headed by Hayworth and Sinatra. Oscar overlooked his pal Joey when awards were handed out. Songs include some of Rodgers and Hart's best. Based on John O'Hara's book and play. ♫Zip; Bewitched, Bothered and Bewildered; I Could Write a Book; That Terrific Rainbow; Whad Do I Care for a Dame?; Happy Hunting Horn; Plant You Now, Dig You Later; Do It the Hard Way; Take Him.

1957 109m/C Frank Sinatra, Rita Hayworth, Kim Novak; **D:** George Sidney; **M:** Richard Rodgers, Lorenz Hart. Academy Awards '57 Nominations: Best Art Direction/Set Decoration, Best Costume Design, Best Film Editing, Best Sound; Golden Globe Awards '58: Best Actor—Musical/Comedy (Sinatra). **VHS, Beta $19.95** COL ⅋⅋⅋

Palais Royale Craven plays an ad exec who gets involved in the world of gangsters in the late 50s.
1988 100m/C Matt Craven, Kim Cattrall, Dean Stockwell; **D:** Martin Lavut. **VHS** REP ⅋½

Pale Blood A serial killer in Los Angeles is leaving his victims drained of blood. Could it be that a vampire is stalking the modern American metropolis, or is this merely the workings of a bloodthirsty psychopath?
1991 (R) 93m/C George Chakiris, Wings Hauser, Pamela Ludwig, Diana Frank, Darcy Demoss; **D:** VV Dachin Hsu. **VHS** NO ⅋½

Pale Rider A mysterious nameless stranger rides into a small California gold rush town to find himself in the middle of a feud between a mining syndicate and a group of independent prospectors. Christlike Eastwood evokes comparisons to "Shane." A classical western theme treated well complemented by excellent photography and a rock-solid cast.
1985 (R) 116m/C Clint Eastwood, Michael Moriarty, Carrie Snodgress, Sydney Penny, Richard Dysart, Richard Kiel, Christopher Penn, John Russell, Charles Hallahan, Douglas McGrath, Fran Ryan; **D:** Clint Eastwood; **W:** Michael Butler, Dennis Shryack; **M:** Lennie Niehaus. **VHS, Beta, 8mm $19.98** WAR, TLF ⅋⅋⅋

The Paleface A cowardly dentist becomes a gunslinging hero when Calamity Jane starts aiming for him. A rip-roarin' good time as the comventions of the Old West are turned upside down. Includes the Oscar-winning song "Buttons and Bows." The 1952 sequel is "Son of Paleface." Remade in 1968 as "The Shakiest Gun in the West."
1948 91m/C Jane Russell, Bob Hope, Robert Armstrong, Iris Adrian, Robert Watson; **D:** Norman Z. McLeod. **VHS, Beta $14.95** MCA ⅋⅋⅋

The Palermo Connection Not the action-thriller the cassette box claims, but a cynical study of a crusading N.Y.C. mayoral candidate who honeymoons in Mafia-haunted Sicily and learns that the war on crime has already been lost. Remote adaptation of "To Forget Palermo" by Edmonde Charles-Roux.
1991 (R) 100m/C James Belushi, Mimi Rogers, Joss Ackland, Philippe Noiret, Vittorio Gassman, Caroline Rosi; **D:** Francesco Rosi; **W:** Gore Vidal. **VHS $89.95** LIV ⅋⅋

Palm Beach The lives of two petty thieves, a runaway, and a private detective intertwine at Palm Beach Down Under. Best appreciated by fans of things Aussie.
1979 90m/C Bryan Brown, Nat Young, Ken Brown, Amanda Berry; **D:** Albie Thomas. **VHS, Beta $19.95** AHV ⅋⅋

The Palm Beach Story Colbert and McCrea play a married couple who have everything—except money. The wife decides to divorce her current husband, marry a rich man, and finance her former husband's ambitions. She decides the best place to husband-hunt is Palm Beach. A Sturges classic screwball comedy.
1942 88m/B Claudette Colbert, Joel McCrea, Mary Astor, Rudy Vallee, William Demarest, Franklin Pangborn; **D:** Preston Sturges. **VHS, Beta $14.98** MCA ⅋⅋⅋

Palm Springs Weekend A busload of love-hungry kids head south and get involved in routine hijinks. Actually shot in Palm Springs with adove average performances by a handful of stars.
1963 100m/C Troy Donahue, Ty Hardin, Connie Stevens, Stefanie Powers, Robert Conrad, Jack Weston, Andrew Duggan; **D:** Norman Taurog. **VHS, Beta $19.98** WAR ♪♪½

Palombella Rossa Political comedy about the fate of Italian communism. When communist politician Michele loses his memory in a car crash, he finds himself trying to reconstruct his life during a game of water polo as well as trying to answer political questions and keep track of the people from his life who randomly appear and disappear. In Italian with English subtitles.
1989 87m/C **D:** Nanni Moretti. **VHS $89.98** FXL, ORI, FCT ♪♪

Palooka Based on the comic strip, this film portrays a fast-talking boxing manager and his goofy, lovable protege. The young scrapper fights James Cagney's little brother. Durante sings his classic tune, "Inka-Dinka-Doo," and packs a punch in the lead. A two-fisted comedy with a witty dialogue and fine direction. Not a part of the Palooka series of the 1940s. **AKA:** Joe Palooka; The Great Schnozzle.
1934 (G) 86m/B Jimmy Durante, Stuart Erwin, Lupe Velez, Robert Armstrong, Thelma Todd, William Cagney; **D:** Ben Stoloff. **VHS, Beta $19.95** NOS, RXM, VYY ♪♪½

Pals Old friends stumble across $3 million in cash and learn the predictable lesson that money can't buy happiness. A terribly trite TV-movie with an exceptional cast.
1987 90m/C Don Ameche, George C. Scott, Sylvia Sidney, Susan Rinell, James Greene; **D:** Lou Antonio. **VHS $89.95** VMK ♪♪

Pals of the Range A framed ranch owner breaks out of jail in order to catch the real cattle thieves. Ho hum in the Old West.
1935 55m/B Rex Lease. **VHS, Beta $19.95** NOS ♪

Pals of the Saddle The intrepid trio go after enemy agents who are trying to smuggle chemicals for poisonous gas into Mexico. This is the first of the series in which the Duke played the part of Stony Brooke. Somewhat convoluted plot, but nevertheless enjoyable.
1938 55m/B John Wayne, Ray Corrigan, Max Terhune, Doreen McKay, Josef Forte, Ted Adams, Curly Dresden; **D:** George Sherman. **VHS $19.95** NOS ♪♪½

The Pamela Principle A bored, middle-aged man thinks his prayers are answered when he meets a sexy 20-year-old model and begins a sordid affair with her. Soon, however, he finds himself in a tense situation when he must choose between his family or his fantasy. Also available in an unrated version.
1991 (R) ?m/C J.K. Dumont, Veronica Cash, Shelby Lane, Troy Donahue, Frank Pesce; **D:** Toby Phillips. **VHS $89.95** IMP ♪♪

Panama Hattie Screen adaptation of Cole Porter's delightful Broadway musical. Unfortunately, something (like a plot) was lost in transition. Southern runs a saloon for our boys down in Panama. Among the musical numbers and vaudevillian acts some spies show up. Several screenwriters, including Vincente Minnelli, worked uncredited on this picture, to no avail. Horne's second screen appearance. ♪It Was Just One of Those Things; Fresh as a Daisy; I've Still Got My Health; Let's Be Buddies; Make It Another Old Fashioned;

Hattie from Panama; Good Neighbors; I'll Do Anything for You; The Son of a Gun Who Pick on Uncle Sam.
1942 79m/B Ann Sothern, Dan Dailey, Red Skelton, Virginia O'Brien, Rags Ragland, Alan Mowbray, Ben Blue, Carl Esmond, Lena Horne, Roger Moore; **D:** Norman Z. McLeod; **M:** Cole Porter. **VHS $19.98** MGM, CCB ♪♪

Panama Lady Ball stars as the sexy, sultry "Panama Lady" in this old-fashioned romance. She gets involved in some shady business south of the border. A lackluster remake of "Panama Flo."
1939 65m/B Lucille Ball, Evelyn Brent. **VHS, Beta** NO ♪½

Panama Menace An agent heads to Panama to thwart spies who are after a special paint that makes things invisible. Poor effort all around, in spite of Beaumont's presence. **AKA:** South of Panama.
1941 68m/B Roger Pryor, Virginia Vale, Lionel Royce, Lucien Prival, Duncan Renaldo, Lester Dorr, Hugh Beaumont; **D:** Jean Yarborough. **VHS, Beta $16.95** SNC, VYY ♪

Panama Patrol Just as they are about to be married, two Army officers are called to duty in Panama. It seems that the Chinese have infiltrated the area with spies and something's got to be done. Too much attention to minor parts of the plot slows the story occasionally, but performances and photography compensate for some of the sluggishness.
1939 67m/B Leon Ames, Charlotte Wynters, Weldon Heyburn, Adrienne Ames, Abner Biberman, Hugh McArthur, Donald (Don "Red") Barry; **D:** Charles Lamont. **VHS, Beta $16.95** SNC ♪♪½

Panamint's Bad Man Ballaw is a poor man's Gary Cooper fighting for justice against stagecoach robbers. Almost as much flavor as tumbleweed.
1938 59m/B Smith Ballew, Evelyn Daw, Noah Beery Sr.; **D:** Ray Taylor. **VHS, Beta $19.95** NOS, VDM, DVT ♪

Pancho Barnes Routine biography of one of the first female pilots of the 1920s. Barnes is a bored debutante who finds her challenge in life when she learns to fly, becoming a barnstormer and movie stunt pilot. Her ambitions naturally get in the way of her romantic life. Good flying scenes. Made for television.
1988 (PG) 150m/C Valerie Bertinelli, Ted Wass, Sam Robards, James Stephens, Cynthia Harris, Geoffrey Lewis; **D:** Richard T. Heffron; **W:** John Hayes. **VHS** ORI ♪♪½

Pancho Villa Savalas has the lead in this fictional account of the famous Mexican, He leads his men in a raid on an American fort after being hoodwinked in an arms deal. Connors tries to hold the fort against him. The finale, in which two trains crash head on, is the most exciting event in the whole darn movie.
1972 (PG) 92m/C Telly Savalas, Clint Walker, Anne Francis, Chuck Connors, Angel Del Pozo, Luis Davila; **D:** Eugenio Martin. **VHS** NO ♪½

Pancho Villa Returns It's 1913, and noble Mexican General Pancho Villa leads his merry men against the assassins of President Madera. This Mexican production (filmed in English) paints a partisan portrait of title character as a good-hearted revolutionary folk hero, not the roving bandit later notorious north of the border.
1950 95m/B Leo Carrillo, Esther Fernandez, Jeanette Comber, Rodolfa Acosta; **D:** Miguel Contreras Torres; **W:** Miguel Contreras Torres. **VHS $15.95** NOS, LOO ♪♪

Pandemonium A spoof of teen slasher films involving murder at Bambi's Cheerleading School. Seems that nationwide, cheerleaders have been brutally eliminated from their squads, leaving Bambi's as the last resort for the terminally perky. Smothers is interesting and more intelligent than his TV persona (although not by much) as the Mountie hero, assisted by Paul Reubens in a pre-Pee-Wee role. Kane steals the show as Candy, a pleasant lass with hyperkinetic powers. **AKA:** Thursday the 12th.
1982 (PG) 82m/C Tom Smothers, Carol Kane, Miles Chapin, Paul (Pee Wee Herman) Reubens, Judge Reinhold, Tab Hunter, Marc McClure, Donald O'Connor, Eve Arden, Eileen Brennan, Edie McClurg; **D:** Alfred Sole. **VHS, Beta $79.95** MGM ♪♪½

Pandora's Box This silent classic marked the end of the German Expressionist era and established Brooks as a major screen presence. She plays the tempestuous Lulu, who destroys everyone she comes in contact with, eventually sinking to prostitution and a fateful meeting with Jack the Ripper. Silent with orchestral score. **AKA:** Die Buechse Der Pandora.
1928 110m/B Louise Brooks, Fritz Kortner, Francis Lederer, Carl Goetz; **D:** G.W. Pabst; **W:** G.W. Pabst. **VHS, Beta $19.95** GPV, MRV, VDM ♪♪♪♪

Panic A scientist terrorizes a small town when he becomes hideously deformed by one of his bacteria experiments. He should have known better.
1983 90m/C David Warbeck, Janet Agren. **VHS, Beta $59.95** MPI ♪½

Panic Button Mel Brooks took the plot from this film and made "The Producers," which was much better. Italian gangsters produce a television show and stack the deck so that it will fail. Unbeknownst to them, the star has figured out what they are doing and works to make it a success. Shot in Italy, mainly in Venice and Rome.
1962 90m/B Maurice Chevalier, Eleanor Parker, Jayne Mansfield, Mike Connors, Akim Tamiroff; **D:** George Sherman. **VHS** NO ♪½

Panic in Echo Park A doctor races against time to find the cause of an epidemic that is threatening the health of a city. Good performances compensate for a predictable plot. Made for television.
1977 78m/C Dorian Harewood, Robin Gammell, Catlin Adams, Ramon Bieri, Movita; **D:** John Llewellyn Moxey. **VHS** NO ♪♪

Panic in Needle Park Drugs become an obsession for a young girl who goes to New York for an abortion. Her new boyfriend is imprisoned for robbery in order to support both their habits. She resorts to prostitution to continue her drug habit, and trouble occurs when her boyfriend realizes she was instrumental in his being sent to jail. Strikes a vein in presenting an uncompromising look at drug use. May be too much of a depressant for some. Pacino's first starring role.
1975 (R) 90m/C Al Pacino, Kitty Winn, Alan Vint, Richard Bright, Kiel Martin, Warren Finnerty, Raul Julia, Paul Sorvino; **D:** Jerry Schatzberg; **W:** Joan Didion, Gregory Dunne. Cannes Film Festival Nominations: cs 71: Best Film; Cannes Film Festival '71: Best Actress (Winn). **VHS** FOX ♪♪♪

Panic in the Streets The Black Death threatens New Orleans in this intense tale. When a body is found on the water front, a doctor (Widmark) is called upon for a diagnosis. The carrier proves to be deadly in more ways than one. Fine performances, taut direction (this was one of Kazan's favorite movies). Filmed on location in New Orleans.

1950 96m/B Richard Widmark, Jack Palance, Barbara Bel Geddes, Paul Douglas, Zero Mostel; **D:** Elia Kazan; **W:** Edward Anhalt. VHS **$39.98** FOX, FCT ♦♦♦

Panic in the Year Zero! Milland and family leave Los Angeles for a fishing trip just as the city is hit by a nuclear bomb. Continuing out into the wilderness for safety, the family now must try to survive as their world crumbles around them. Generally considered the best of Milland's five directorial efforts. **AKA:** End of the World.
1962 92m/B Ray Milland, Jean Hagen, Frankie Avalon, Mary Mitchell, Joan Freeman, Richard Garland, Rex Holman; **D:** Ray Milland; **M:** Les Baxter. VHS **$18.00** FRG ♦♦ 1/2

Panic on the 5:22 Wealthy commuters are kidnapped and held hostage by terrorist hoodlums in a suburban train club car. Standard made for television vehicle.
1974 78m/C Lynda Day George, Laurence Luckinbill, Ina Balin, Bernie Casey; **D:** Harvey Hart. VHS, Beta **$14.95** WOV ♦♦

Panic Station Two guys get lonely at remote satellite relay station. **AKA:** The Plains of Heaven.
1982 90m/C Richard Moir, Reg Evans, Gerard Kennedy; **D:** Ian Pringle. VHS **$19.95** ACA ♦♦

Panique A study of mob psychology in slums of post-WWII Paris. Two lovers frame a stranger for murder. Dark and tautly paced thriller taken from the novel by Georges Simenon. In French with English subtitles. **AKA:** Panic.
1947 87m/B Michel Simon, Viviane Romance; **D:** Julien Duvivier. VHS, Beta **$24.95** NOS, HHT, CAB ♦♦♦

Pantaloons A man who fancies himself to be irresistible chases women for sport. A quaint and lively period film.
1957 93m/C Fernandel, Carmen Sevilla, Fernando Rey; **D:** John Berry. VHS **$24.95** VYY ♦♦

Panther Squad Litter of sex kittens led by Danning get into major scraps to save world.
1984 77m/C Sybil Danning. VHS NO ♦

The Panther's Claw Murder befalls an opera troupe, but a sleuth with the memorable name of Thatcher Colt is on the case. A quick-moving mystery quickie that delivers on its own modest terms.
1942 72m/B Sidney Blackmer, Byron Foulger, Rick Vallin, Herbert Rawlinson; **D:** William Beaudine. VHS **$15.95** NOS, LOO ♦♦

Papa's Delicate Condition Based on the autobiographical writings of silent screen star Corinne Griffith. Gleason is Papa whose "delicate condition" is a result of his drinking. His antics provide a constant headache to his family. A paean to turn-of-the-century family life. No I.D.s required as the performances are enjoyable for the whole family. Features the Academy Award-winning song "Call Me Irresponsible."
1963 98m/C Jackie Gleason, Glynis Johns, Charlie Ruggles, Laurel Goodwin, Elisha Cook Jr., Murray Hamilton; **D:** George Marshall; **W:** Jack Rose. VHS, Beta **$14.95** BAR ♦♦♦

The Paper Another crowd pleaser from director Howard follows a red letter day in the life of an editor at the tabloid New York Sun (modeled on the trashy Post). Fresh, fast-moving script by the Koepp brothers (who appear as reporters) offers a fairly accurate portrait of the business of journalism (including the "brisk" language), with a few Hollywood exceptions. Pace suffers from cutaways to life outside, while script and direction sometimes coast past targets. Propelled by a fine cast, with Keaton the

focus as he juggles his personal and professional lives. Close is strong as a managing editor married to her work, while Duvall is solid as the old newsroom warhorse. Tons of cameos, though those outside of the business may not notice them.
1994 (R) 112m/C Michael Keaton, Robert Duvall, Marisa Tomei, Glenn Close, Randy Quaid, Jason Robards Jr., Jason Alexander, Spalding Gray, Catherine O'Hara, Lynne Thigpen; **D:** Ron Howard; **W:** David Koepp, Steven Koepp; **M:** Randy Newman. VHS NYR ♦♦♦

The Paper Chase Students at Harvard Law School suffer and struggle through their first year. A realistic, sometimes acidly humorous look at Ivy League ambitions, with Houseman stealing the show as the tough professor. Wonderful adaptation of the John Jay Osborn novel which later became the basis for the acclaimed television series.
1973 (PG) 111m/C Timothy Bottoms, Lindsay Wagner, John Houseman, Graham Beckel, Edward Herrmann, James Naughton, Craig Richard Nelson, Bob Lydiard; **D:** James Bridges; **W:** James Bridges; **M:** John Williams. Academy Awards '73: Best Supporting Actor (Houseman); Nominations: Best Adapted Screenplay, Best Sound; Golden Globe Awards '74: Best Supporting Actor (Houseman); National Board of Review Awards '73: Best Supporting Actor (Houseman). VHS, Beta **$19.98** FOX, BTV ♦♦♦

Paper Lion A comedy "documentary" about bestselling writer George Plimpton's tryout game as quarterback with the Detroit Lions. Film debut of Alan Alda. Helped Karras make the transition from the gridiron to the silver screen. Moves into field goal range but doesn't quite score.
1968 107m/C Alan Alda, Lauren Hutton, Alex Karras, Ann Turkel, John Gordy, Roger Brown, "Sugar Ray" Robinson, Roy Scheider, David Doyle; **D:** Alex March. VHS, Beta NO ♦♦ 1/2

Paper Man A group of college students create a fictitious person in a computer for a credit card scam. The scheme snowballs, resulting in murder and hints of possible artificial intelligence. But it's just standard network TV fare, with a creepy performance by Stockwell as a computer whiz.
1971 90m/C Dean Stockwell, Stefanie Powers, James Stacy, Elliot Street, Tina Chen, James Olson, Ross Elliott; **D:** Walter Grauman. VHS **$39.95** XVC, VTR ♦♦

Paper Marriage In Canada, a less than successful Chinese boxer agrees to marry a Hong Kong girl for a promise of payment in order that she may become a citizen. The money never comes, but the nearly betrothed pair discover that they love each other, after all. In Cantonese with English subtitles.
1988 102m/C Samo Hung, Maggie Cheung; **D:** Alfred Cheung. VHS **$39.95** FCT, MOV, ACA ♦ 1/2

Paper Marriage Yet another variation on the marriage in order to gain citizenship but yes we're going to fall in love films. A young Polish woman has fallen for an upper-crust English doctor she's met in Warsaw. When Alicja arrives in England, she's promptly dumped by the cad. She's ambitious and wants to stay in England so Alicja arranges a marriage of convenience with small-time crook Aiden, who finds his new bride is more than he bargained for.
1993 88m/C Gary Kemp, Joanna Trepechinska, Rita Tushingham, Richard Hawley, David Horovitch, William Ilkley, Mark McKellen, Ann Mitchell, Sadie Frost; **D:** Krzysztof Lang; **W:** Marek Kreutz, Krzysztof Lang. VHS **$89.95** ACA ♦♦ 1/2

Paper Mask When a promising young doctor is killed in an auto accident, an unscrupulous, psychotic porter assumes his identity. He uses said identity to, among other things, initiate an affair with a sultry coworker. How long will this madman play his unholy game, and at what cost?
1991 (R) 105m/C Paul McGann, Amanda Donohoe, Frederick Treves, Barbara Leigh-Hunt, Jimmy Yuill, Tom Wilkinson; **D:** Christopher Morahan; **W:** John Collee; **M:** Richard Harvey. VHS **$89.95** ACA ♦♦ 1/2

Paper Moon Award-winning story set in depression-era Kansas with Ryan O'Neal as a Bible-wielding con who meets up with a nine-year-old orphan. During their travels together, he discovers that the orphan (his daughter, Tatum) is better at "his" game than he is. Irresistible chemistry between the O'Neals, leading to Tatum's Oscar win (she is the youngest actor ever to take home a statue). Cinematically picturesque and cynical enough to keep overt sentimentalism at bay. Based on Joe David Brown's novel, "Addie Pray."
1973 (PG) 102m/B Ryan O'Neal, Tatum O'Neal, Madeline Kahn, John Hillerman, Randy Quaid; **D:** Peter Bogdanovich; **W:** Alvin Sargent. Academy Awards '73: Best Supporting Actress (O'Neal); Nominations: Best Adapted Screenplay, Best Sound, Best Supporting Actress (Kahn); National Board of Review Awards '73: 10 Best Films of the Year. VHS, Beta **$49.95** PAR, BTV ♦♦♦ 1/2

Paper Tiger Niven plays an imaginative English tutor who fabricates fantastic yarns fictionalizing his past in order to impress his student, the son of the Japanese ambassador to a Southeast Asian country. Poorly executed karate, misdirection, and a simplistic storyline work against it.
1974 104m/C David Niven, Toshiro Mifune, Eiko Ando, Hardy Kruger; **D:** Ken Annakin. VHS, Beta SUE, OM ♦♦

A Paper Wedding A middle-aged literature professor with a dead-end career and equally dead-end romance with a married man is persuaded by her lawyer sister to marry a Chilean political refugee to avoid his deportation. Of course, they must fool an immigration official and their fake marriage does turn into romance, but this is no lighthearted "Green Card." Bujold shines. In French and Spanish with English subtitles. **AKA:** Les Noces de Papier.
1989 90m/C Genevieve Bujold, Manuel Aranguiz, Dorothee Berryman; **D:** Michel Brault. VHS **$79.95** CTL, ING, LUM ♦♦♦

Paperback Hero A hot-shot hockey player turns to crime when his team loses its financial backing. Choopy storyline could use a Zamboni, while Dullea should be penalized for occasionally losing his rustic accent. Still the supporting actors skate through their roles and, for periods, it works. A slapshot that ultimately clangs off the goal post.
1973 94m/C Keir Dullea, Elizabeth Ashley, John Beck, Dayle Haddon; **D:** Peter Pearson. VHS NO ♦♦

Paperhouse An odd fantasy about a young girl plagued by recurring dreams that begin to influence real life. Very obtuse, British-minded film with "Twilight Zone" feel that manages to capture genuine dreamness. Not for all audiences, but intriguing nontheless. Based on the novel "Marianne Dreams" by Catherine Storr.
1989 92m/C Glenne Headly, Ben Cross, Charlotte Burke, Elliott Spiers, Gemma Jones, Sarah Newbold; **D:** Bernard Rose; **W:** Matthew Jacobs; **M:** Hans Zimmer, Stanley Myers. VHS, Beta **$89.98** LIV, VES ♦♦♦

Papillon McQueen is a criminal sent to Devil's Island in the 1930s determined to escape from the Lemote prison. Hoffman is the swindler he befriends. A series of escapes and recaptures follow. Box-office winner based on the autobiographical writings of French thief Henri Charriere. Excellent portrayal of prison life and fine performances from the prisoners. Certain segments would have been better left on the cutting room floor. The film's title refers to the lead's butterfly tattoo.
1973 (PG) 150m/C Steve McQueen, Dustin Hoffman, Victor Jory, George Coulouris, Anthony Zerbe; **D:** Franklin J. Schaffner; **M:** Jerry Goldsmith. **VHS, Beta $19.98** *FOX, WAR* 𝘫𝘫𝘫

Para Servir a Usted A waiter gets mixed in with the high society crowd that he works for.
1987 95m/C Enrique Rambal, Claudia Islas, Norma Lazarendo, Ofelia Guillman. **VHS, Beta $55.95** *MAD* 𝘫𝘫

Parade A series of vignettes in a circus, "Parade" is actually a play within a play, meshing the action with events offstage. The laser disc edition includes Rene Clement's 1936 "Soigne Ton Gauche," Tati's inspiration.
1974 85m/C Jacques Tati; **D:** Jacques Tati; **W:** Jacques Tati. **VHS $29.95** *HMV, VYG, CRC* 𝘫𝘫𝘫

The Paradine Case A passable Hitchcock romancer about a young lawyer who falls in love with the woman he's defending for murder, not knowing whether she is innocent or guilty. Script could be tighter and more cohesive. Seventy thousand dollars of the three million budget were spent recreating the original Bailey courtroom. Based on the novel by Robert Hichens.
1947 125m/B Gregory Peck, Alida Valli, Ann Todd, Louis Jourdan, Charles Laughton, Charles Coburn, Ethel Barrymore, Leo G. Carroll; **D:** Alfred Hitchcock. **VHS, Beta $19.98** *FOX* 𝘫𝘫½

Paradise Young American boy and beautiful English girl on a 19th-century jaunt through the Middle East are the sole survivors when their caravan is massacred. Left to their own devices, they discover a magnificent oasis and the joys of frolicking naked and experience (surprise) their sexual awakening. Do a double-take: it's the "Blue Lagoon" all over, with a bit more nudity and a lot more sand.
1982 (R) 96m/C Phoebe Cates, Willie Aames, Richard Curnock, Tuvio Tavi; **D:** Stuart Gillard. **VHS, Beta $19.95** *COL* 𝘫𝘫

Paradise Young boy is sent to the country to live with his pregnant mother's married friends (real life husband and wife Johnson and Griffith). From the outset it is clear that the couple are experiencing marital troubles, making the boy's assimilation all the more difficult. Help arrives in the form of a sprightly ten-year-old girl, with whom he forms a charming relationship. Largely predictable, this remake of the French film "Le Grand Chemin" works thanks to the surprisingly good work of its ensemble cast, and the gorgeous scenery of South Carolina, where the movie was filmed.
1991 (PG-13) 112m/C Melanie Griffith, Don Johnson, Elijah Wood, Thora Birch, Sheila McCarthy, Eve Gordon, Louise Latham, Greg Travis, Sarah Trigger; **D:** Mary Agnes Donoghue; **W:** Mary Agnes Donoghue; **M:** David Newman. **VHS, Beta $92.95** *TOU* 𝘫𝘫𝘫

Paradise Alley Rocky tires of boxing, decides to join the WWF. Three brothers brave the world of professional wrestling in an effort to strike it rich and move out of the seedy Hell's Kitchen neighborhood of New York, circa 1946. Stallone wrote, stars in,

and makes his directorial debut in addition to singing the title song. He makes a few good moves as director, but is ultimately pinned to the canvas.
1978 (PG) 109m/C Sylvester Stallone, Anne Archer, Armand Assante, Lee Canalito, Kevin Conway; **D:** Sylvester Stallone; **W:** Sylvester Stallone; **M:** Bill Conti. **VHS, Beta $19.98** *MCA* 𝘫𝘫

Paradise Canyon Early Wayne "B" thriller, in which he plays an undercover government agent sent to track down a group of counterfeiters.
1935 59m/B John Wayne, Yakima Canutt, Marion Burns. **VHS $9.98** *REP, NOS, VCN* 𝘫½

Paradise, Hawaiian Style Out-of-work pilot returns to Hawaii, where he and a buddy start a charter service with two helicopters. Plenty of gals are wooed by "the Pelvis." Filmed four years after Elvis's first Pacific piece, "Blue Hawaii." Presley, showing the first signs of slow-down, displays no surprises here. ♫Paradise, Hawaiian Style; Scratch My Back (Then I'll Scratch Yours); Stop Where You Are; This Is My Heaven; House of Sand; Queenie Wahine's Papaya; Datin'; Drums of the Islands; A Dog's Life.
1966 91m/C Elvis Presley, Suzanna Leigh, James Shigeta, Donna Butterworth, Irene Tsu, Julie Parrish, Philip Ahn, Mary Treen, Marianna Hill, John Doucette, Grady Sutton; **D:** Michael Moore. **VHS, Beta $14.98** *FOX, MVD* 𝘫½

Paradise in Harlem All-black musical in which a cabaret performer witnesses a gangland murder, sees his sick wife die, and is pressured into leaving town by the mob. Have a nice day.
1940 83m/B Frank Wilson, Mamie Smith, Edna Mae Harris, Juanita Hall; **D:** Joseph Seiden. **VHS, Beta $24.95** *VYY, FCT, VCN* 𝘫½

Paradise Island Down-scale musical romance about an ingenue on her way to join her fiance in the South Seas, only to find that he has gambled away his money. The opportunistic saloon owner tries to put the moves on her. Will the two lovers be reunited? ♫I've Got a Girl In Every Port; Drinking Song; Lazy Breezes; Just Another Dream.
1930 68m/B Kenneth Harlan, Marceline Day, Thomas Santschi, Paul Hurst, Victor Potel, Gladden James, Will Stanton; **D:** Bert Glennon. **VHS $12.95** *GPV, NOS* 𝘫

Paradise Motel Teen exploitation film centered around a local motel predominantly used for one-night rendezvous. High school heroes and jocks battle for the affections of a beautiful classmate.
1984 (R) 87m/C Bob Basso, Gary Hershberger, Jonna Leigh Stack, Robert Krantz; **D:** Cary Medoway. **VHS, Beta $19.98** *FOX* 𝘫½

Paradisio Dying inventor wills Oxford professor an authentic pair of X-ray specs. Spies come gunning for the professor, chasing him through Europe. Doc keeps forgetting he's being chased while using the special specs to see (sometimes in 3-D) through the clothing of young women. Meager plot does not get in way of 3-D nudie exploitation.
1961 (R) 82m/C Arthur Howard, Eva Waegner. **VHS, Beta $19.95** *NWV, VDM* 𝘫½

Parallax View A reporter tries to disprove a report which states that a presidential candidate's assassination was not a conspiracy. As he digs deeper and deeper, he uncovers more than he bargained for and becomes a pawn in the conspirators' further plans. Beatty is excellent and the conspiracy is never less than believable. A lesser-known, compelling political thriller that deserves to be more widely seen.

1974 (R) 102m/C Warren Beatty, Hume Cronyn, William Daniels, Paula Prentiss, Kenneth Mars, Bill McKinney, Anthony Zerbe, Walter McGinn; **D:** Alan J. Pakula. **VHS, Beta $14.95** *PAR* 𝘫𝘫½

Parallel Corpse A mortuary attendant finds a murder victim hidden in a coffin and blackmails the remorseless killer.
1983 89m/C Buster Larsen, Jorgen Kiil, Agneta Ekmanner, Masja Dessau. **VHS, Beta $49.95** *MED* 𝘫

Paralyzed An unconscious journalist, mistaken for dead in a hospital emergency room, flashes back to the investigation that embroiled him in his predicament.
1977 90m/C Ingrid Thulin, Jean Sorel, Mario Adorf; **D:** Aldo Lado; **W:** Aldo Lado. **VHS, Beta $59.95** *MPI* 𝘫

Paramedics A motley crew of cavorting paramedics battle their evil captain. Another parody of people in uniform. A comedy with little pulse.
1988 (PG-13) 91m/C George Newbern, Christopher McDonald, John P. Ryan, Ray Walston, Lawrence Hilton-Jacobs; **D:** Stuart Margolin. **VHS, Beta $79.98** *LIV, VES* 𝘫½

Paranoia Beautiful jet-set widow is trapped in her own Italian villa by a young couple who drug her to get her to perform in various sex orgies, which are probably the most interesting part of this muddled affair. **AKA:** Orgasmo; A Beautiful Place to Kill; A Quiet Place to Kill.
1969 94m/C Carroll Baker, Lou Castel, Colette Descombes; **D:** Umberto Lenzi. **VHS, Beta** *REP* 𝘫

Parasite A small town is beset by giant parasites. An "Alien" ripoff originally filmed in 3-D, during that technique's brief return in the early '80s. Bad films like this killed it both the first and second times. An unpardonable mess that comes off as a stinky sixth-grade film project.
1981 (R) 90m/C Demi Moore, Gale Robbins, Luca Bercovici, James Davidson, Al Fann, Cherie Currie, Cheryl "Rainbeaux" Smith, Vivian Blaine; **D:** Charles Band; **M:** Richard Band. **VHS, Beta $89.95** *PAR* Woof!

Pardners Spoiled New York millionaire (Lewis) becomes the sheriff of small western town, with Martin as a ranch foreman. The two team up to rid the town of bad guys and romance two local cuties. Western spoof (with music) is a remake of 1936's "Rhythm on the Range." ♫Buckskin Beauty; Pardners; The Wind! The Wind!; Me 'N You 'N the Moon.
1956 88m/C Jerry Lewis, Dean Martin, Lori Nelson, Jackie Loughery, Jeff Morrow, John Baragrey, Agnes Moorehead, Lon Chaney Jr., Milton Frome, Lee Van Cleef, Jack Elam, Bob Steele, Emory Parnell; **D:** Norman Taurog; **W:** Sidney Sheldon, Jerry Davis. **VHS $14.95** *PAR* 𝘫𝘫½

Pardon Mon Affaire When a middle-aged civil servant gets a look at a model in a parking garage, he decides it's time to cheat on his wife. Enjoyable French farce. Re-made as in the United States "The Woman in Red" and followed by "Pardon Mon Affair, Too!" Subtitled. **AKA:** Un Elephant a Trompe Enormement.
1976 (PG) 107m/C Jean Rochefort, Claude Brasseur, Guy Bedos, Victor Lanoux, Daniele Delorme, Martine Sarcey, Anny Duperey; **D:** Yves Robert; **M:** Vladimir Cosma. **VHS, Beta $29.98** *SUE* 𝘫𝘫

Pardon Mon Affaire, Too! Pale sequel to the first popular French comedy, "Pardon Mon Affair." This time the four fantasy-minded buddies withstand the trials of marriage and middle-class life. With En-

glish subtitles or dubbed. *AKA:* We Will All Meet in Paradise.
1977 105m/C Jean Rochefort, Claude Brasseur, Guy Bedos; *D:* Yves Robert; *M:* Vladimir Cosma. **VHS, Beta** $29.98 *SUE* �½

Pardon My Gun Cowpoke falls for the boss' daughter but has a rival in a wealthy rancher, who isn't above sabotage to get the girl.
1930 64m/B George Duryea, Harry Woods, Sally Starr, Lee Moran, Mona Ray; *D:* Robert De Lacy; *W:* Hugh Cummings. **VHS** $12.95 *GPV* ½

Pardon My Sarong Bud and Lou star as Chicago bus drivers who end up shipwrecked on a South Pacific island when they get involved with notorious jewel thieves. The island natives think Lou is a god! Standard Abbott & Costello fare.
1942 83m/B Bud Abbott, Lou Costello, Virginia Bruce, Robert Paige, Lionel Atwill, Leif Erickson, William Demarest, Samuel S. Hinds; *D:* Erle C. Kenton. **VHS** $14.98 *MCA* ½

Pardon My Trunk Struggling against poverty on his teacher's salary, a man and his family receive a gift from a Hindu prince—an elephant. De Sica carries this silly premise beyond mere slapstick. Dubbed. *AKA:* Hello Elephant; Bvongiorno, Elefante.
1952 85m/B Sabu, Vittorio De Sica; *D:* Gianni Franciolini. **VHS, Beta** $24.95 *VYY* ½

Pardon Us Laurel and Hardy are thrown into prison for bootlegging. Plot meanders along aimlessly, but the duo have some inspired moments. The first Laurel and Hardy feature. *AKA:* Jail Birds.
1931 78m/B Stan Laurel, Oliver Hardy, June Marlowe, James Finlayson; *D:* James Parrott. **VHS, Beta** $19.95 *MED, CCB, MLB* ½

The Parent Trap Mills plays a dual role in this heartwarming comedy as twin sisters who conspire to bring their divorced parents together again. Well-known Disney fluff. Followed by several made-for-television sequels featuring the now grown-up twins.
1961 127m/C Hayley Mills, Maureen O'Hara, Brian Keith, Charlie Ruggles, Una Merkel, Leo G. Carroll; *D:* David Swift. **VHS, Beta** $19.99 *DIS* ½

Parenthood Four grown siblings and their parents struggle with various levels of parenthood. From the college drop-out, to the nervous single mother, to the yuppie couple raising an overachiever, every possibility is explored, including the perspective from the older generation, portrayed by Robards. Genuinely funny with dramatic moments that work most of the time, with an affecting performance from Martin and Wiest. Director Howard has four kids and was inspired to make this film when on a European jaunt with them.
1989 (PG-13) 124m/C Steve Martin, Mary Steenburgen, Dianne Wiest, Martha Plimpton, Keanu Reeves, Tom Hulce, Jason Robards Jr., Rick Moranis, Harley Jane Kozak, Leaf (Joaquin Rafael) Phoenix, Paul Linke, Dennis Dugan; *D:* Ron Howard; *W:* Lowell Ganz, Babaloo Mandel, Ron Howard; *M:* Randy Newman. **VHS, Beta** $19.95 *MCA* ½

Parents Dark satire of middle class suburban life in the '50s, centering on a young boy who discovers that his parents aren't getting their meat from the local butcher. Gives new meaning to leftovers and boasts a very disturbing barbecue scene. Balaban's debut is a strikingly visual and creative gorefest with definite cult potential. The eerie score is by Badalamenti, who also composed the music for "Blue Velvet," "Wild at Heart," and the television series "Twin Peaks."

1989 (R) 81m/C Randy Quaid, Mary Beth Hurt, Sandy Dennis, Kathryn Grody, Deborah Rush, Graham Jarvis, Bryan Madorsky, Juno Mills-Cockell; *D:* Bob Balaban; *W:* Christopher Hawthorne; *M:* Angelo Badalamenti, Jonathan Elias. **VHS, Beta** $14.98 *LIV, VES, HHE* ½

Paris Belongs to Us An early entry in the French "new wave" of naturalistic cinema, this psychological mystery drama has a woman investigating a suicide linked to a possible worldwide conspiracy. Interesting, if somewhat dated by Cold War elements. *AKA:* Paris Nous Appartient; Paris is Ours.
1960 120m/B Jean-Claude Brialy, Betty Schneider, Gianni Esposito, Francoise Prevost; *D:* Jacques Rivette; *W:* Jacques Rivette, Jean Gruault. **VHS** $29.95 *VDM* ½

Paris Blues Two jazz musicians, one white, one black, strive for success in Paris and become involved with American tourists who want to take them back to the States. Score by Duke Ellington and an appearance by Armstrong make it a must-see for jazz fans.
1961 100m/B Paul Newman, Sidney Poitier, Joanne Woodward, Diahann Carroll, Louis Armstrong, Barbara Lange; *D:* Martin Ritt; *W:* Jack Sher, Walter Bernstein; *M:* Duke Ellington. **VHS, Beta** $19.98 *MGM, FCT, RHP* ½

Paris Express When a man steals money from his employer, he boards the Paris Express to escape from the police. A bit convoluted, but well acted. Based on the George Simenon novel. *AKA:* The Man Who Watched Trains Go By.
1953 82m/C Claude Rains, Herbert Lom, Felix Aylmer, Marius Goring, Anouk Aimee, Marta Toren; *D:* Harold French. **VHS, Beta** $16.95 *SNC, NOS, MRV* ½

Paris Holiday An actor heading for Paris to buy a noted author's latest screenplay finds mystery and romance. Entertaining chase scenes as the characters try to find the elusive script.
1957 100m/C Bob Hope, Fernandel, Anita Ekberg, Martha Hyer, Preston Sturges; *D:* Gerd Oswald. **VHS, Beta** $9.95 *UNI* ½

Paris is Burning Livingston's documentary portrayal of New York City's transvestite balls where men dress up, dance, and compete in various categories. Filmed between 1985 and 1989, this is a compelling look at a subculture of primarily black and Hispanic men and the one place they can truly be themselves. Madonna noted this look and attitude (much watered down) in her song "Vogue."
1991 (R) 71m/C Dorian Corey, Pepper Labeija, Venus Xtravaganza, Octavia St. Laurant, Willi Ninja, Anji Xtravaganza, Freddie Pendavis, Junior Labeija; *D:* Jennie Livingston. **VHS** $89.95 *ACA, FCT* ½

Paris, Texas After four years a drifter returns to find his son is being raised by his brother because the boy's mother has also disappeared. He tries to reconnect with the boy. Introspective script acclaimed by many film critics, but others found it to be too slow.
1983 (PG) 145m/C Harry Dean Stanton, Nastassia Kinski, Dean Stockwell, Hunter Carson, Aurore Clement; *D:* Wim Wenders; *W:* Sam Shepard; *M:* Ry Cooder. **VHS, Beta** $19.98 *FOX* ½

Paris Trout Believing himself above the law, southern Trout (Hopper) shoots the mother and sister of a young black man who reneged on his IOU. Lawyer Harris is forced to defend a man he knows deserves to be punished, and wife Hershey suffers long. Adapted by Pete Dexter from his National Book Award-winning novel. Made for cable.

1991 (R) 98m/C Dennis Hopper, Barbara Hershey, Ed Harris, Tina Lifford, Darnita Henry, Eric Ware, Ray McKinnon; *D:* Stephen Gyllenhaal; *W:* Pete Dexter. **VHS, Beta** $89.98 *MED, FXV, FCT* ½

Paris When It Sizzles A screenwriter and his secretary fall in love while working on a film in Paris, confusing themselves with the script's characters. Star-studded cast deserves better than this lame script. Shot on location in Paris. Holden's drinking—he ran into a brick wall while under the influence—and some unresolved romantic tension between him and Hepburn affected shooting. Dietrich, Sinatra, Astaire, Ferrer, and Curtis show up for a party on the set.
1964 110m/C William Holden, Audrey Hepburn, Gregoire Aslan, Raymond Bussieres, Tony Curtis, Fred Astaire, Frank Sinatra, Noel Coward, Marlene Dietrich, Mel Ferrer; *D:* Richard Quine; *W:* George Axelrod. **VHS, Beta** $29.95 *PAR* ½

The Park is Mine A deranged and desperate Vietnam vet takes hostages in Central Park. Semi-infamous film, notable for being the first movie made for HBO on cable and for being filmed in Toronto, before the inexpensive practice of filming in Canada became widespread.
1985 102m/C Tommy Lee Jones, Yaphet Kotto, Helen Shaver; *D:* Steven Hilliard Stern. **VHS, Beta** $59.98 *FOX* ½

Parker An executive is kidnapped, then released, but does not know why. Unable to live with the mystery, he tracks his kidnappers down into a world of blackmail, drugs, and intrigue.
1984 100m/C Bryan Brown, Kurt Raab. **VHS, Beta** $59.95 *LHV* ½

Parlor, Bedroom and Bath A family tries to keep a young woman from seeing that her love interest is flirting with other prospects. Doesn't live up to the standard Keaton set in his silent films. Keaton spoke French and German for foreign versions. *AKA:* Romeo in Pyjamas.
1931 75m/B Buster Keaton, Charlotte Greenwood, Cliff Edwards, Reginald Denny; *D:* Edward Sedgwick. **VHS, Beta** $19.95 *NOS, VYY, VDM* ½

Parole, Inc. FBI takes on the underground in this early crime film. Criminals on parole have not served their sentences, and the mob is responsible. A meagerly financed yawner.
1949 71m/B Michael O'Shea, Evelyn Ankers, Turhan Bey, Lyle Talbot; *D:* Alfred Zeisler. **VHS** $16.95 *NOS, SNC* ½

Paroled to Die A man frames a young rancher for a bank robbery and a murder he committed in this wild west saga. Predictable and bland.
1937 66m/B Bob Steele, Kathleen Elliott. **VHS, Beta** $19.95 *NOS, DVT* ½

Parrish Parrish McLean (Donohue) is a very ambitious young man, determined to make it in the rich world of the tobacco growers of the Connecticut River Valley. But his ruthless tobacco king stepfather (Malden) would like to thwart his plans. As befits Donohue's teen idol status, he also gets to romance three beautiful girls. Very silly and much too long. Based on the novel by Mildred Savage.
1961 138m/C Troy Donahue, Claudette Colbert, Karl Malden, Dean Jagger, Diane McBain, Connie Stevens, Sharon Hugueny, Dub Taylor, Hampton Fancher, Bibi Osterwald, Madeline Sherwood, Sylvia Miles, Carroll O'Connor, Vincent Gardenia; *D:* Delmer Daves; *W:* Delmer Daves. **VHS** $29.99 *WAR* ½

Parting Glances Low-budget but acclaimed film shows the relationship between two gay men and how they deal with a close friend's discovery of his exposure to the AIDS virus. Touching and realistic portrayals make this a must see. In 1990 Sherwood died of AIDS without completing any other films.
1986 (R) 90m/C John Bolger, Richard Ganoung, Steve Buscemi, Adam Nathan, Patrick Tull; *D:* Bill Sherwood; *W:* Bill Sherwood. **VHS, Beta** $79.98 *FOX, ING* 🎬🎬🎬

Partner An extremely shy young man invents a strong alter ego to cope with the world but this second personality comes to dominate—with tragic results. In Italian with English subtitles.
1968 110m/C Pierre Clementi, Stefania Sandrelli, Tina Aumont; *D:* Bernardo Bertolucci; *M:* Ennio Morricone. **VHS** $39.95 *ING, TPV* 🎬🎬🎬

Partners A straight, macho cop must pose as the lover of a gay cop to investigate the murder of a gay man in Los Angeles' homosexual community. Sets out to parody "Cruising"; unfortunately, the only source of humor the makers could find was in ridiculous homosexual stereotypes that are somewhat offensive and often unfunny.
1982 (R) 93m/C Ryan O'Neal, John Hurt, Kenneth McMillan, Robyn Douglass, Jay Robinson, Rick Jason; *D:* James Burrows; *W:* Francis Veber; *M:* Georges Delerue. **VHS, Beta** $79.95 *PAR* 🎬🎬

Partners of the Trail U.S. marshals Brown and Hatton try to find out who's murdering ranchers which leads them to gunplay with Ingraham's band of outlaws.
1944 57m/B Johnny Mack Brown, Raymond Hatton, Lloyd Ingraham, Christine McIntyre, Robert Frazer; *D:* Lambert Hillyer. **VHS** $11.95 *GPV* 🎬 ½

The Party Disaster-prone Indian actor wreaks considerable havoc at a posh Hollywood gathering. Laughs come quickly in this quirky Sellers vehicle.
1968 99m/C Peter Sellers, Claudine Longet, Marge Champion, Sharron Kimberly, Denny Miller, Gavin MacLeod, Carol Wayne; *D:* Blake Edwards; *W:* Blake Edwards; *M:* Henry Mancini. **VHS** $14.95 *MGM, TVC* 🎬🎬🎬

Party Animal A college stud teaches a shy farm boy a thing or two about the carnal aspects of campus life.
1983 (R) 78m/C Timothy Carhart, Matthew Causey, Robin Harlan; *D:* David Beaird; *W:* David Beaird. **VHS, Beta** $79.98 *LIV* 🎬

Party Camp A rowdy summer camp counselor endeavors to turn a tame backwoods camp into a non-stop party. Late entry in the "Meatballs"-spawned genre fails to do anything of even minor interest.
1987 (R) 96m/C Andrew Ross, Billy Jacoby, April Wayne, Kirk Cribb; *D:* Gary Graver. **VHS, Beta** $79.98 *LIV* 🎬

Party Favors Erotic dancing, strip tease acts, and general hilarity are featured in this party tape.
1989 (R) 83m/C Jeannie Winters, Marjorie Miller, Gail Thackray; *D:* Ed Hansen. **VHS, Beta** $79.98 *LIV, VES* Woof!

Party Girl A crime drama involving an attorney representing a 1920s crime boss and his henchmen when they run afoul of the law. The lawyer falls in love with a nightclub dancer who successfully encourages him to leave the mob, but not before he is wounded in a gang war attack, arrested, and forced to testify against the mob as a material witness. The mob then takes his girlfriend hostage to prevent his testifying, leading to an exciting

climax. Must-see viewing for Charisse's steamy dance numbers.
1958 99m/C Robert Taylor, Cyd Charisse, Lee J. Cobb, John Ireland, Kent Smith, Claire Kelly, Corey Allen; *D:* Nicholas Ray. **VHS, Beta** $19.98 *MGM* 🎬🎬🎬 ½

Party Girls Escort service girls run afoul of the law in this hokey melodrama.
1929 67m/B Douglas Fairbanks Jr., Jeanette Loff, Judith Barrie, Marie Prevost, John St. Polis, Lucien Prival; *D:* Victor Halperin. **VHS, Beta** $16.95 *NOS, LOO, SNC* 🎬 ½

Party Girls for Sale Mystery thriller in which a young girl's body is found on the beach in Rio de Janeiro. Also known as "Violated."
1954 ?m/C Raymond Burr, Scott Brady, Johanna Matz. **VHS** $16.95 *SNC* 🎬

Party Incorporated Marilyn Chambers (of "Behind the Green Door" fame) stars as a young widow with a huge tax load who gives parties to pay it off. Also known as "Party Girls." *AKA:* Party Girls.
1989 (R) 80m/C Marilyn Chambers, Kurt Woodruff, Christine Veronica, Kimberly Taylor; *D:* Chuck Vincent. **VHS** $19.95 *STE, NWV, IME* 🎬

Party Line A veteran police captain and a district attorney team up to track down a pair of killers who find their victims through party lines.
1988 (R) 90m/C Richard Hatch, Shawn Weatherly, Richard Roundtree, Leif Garrett, Greta Blackburn; *D:* William Webb. **VHS, Beta** *NO* 🎬

Party! Party! A bunch of kids go nuts and have a party when their parents leave.
1983 100m/C *M:* Sting, David Bowie, The Clash, Joe Jackson, Elvis Costello. **VHS** $29.95 *ACA* 🎬

Party Plane Softcore fun-fest about a plane full of oversexed stewardesses.
1990 81m/C Kent Stoddard, Karen Annarino, John Goff, Jill Johnson; *D:* Ed Hansen. **VHS, Beta** $79.98 *VES* 🎬

Pascali's Island A Turkish spy becomes involved with an adventurer's plot to steal rare artifacts, then finds himself ensnared in political and personal intrigue. Superior tragedy features excellent performances from Kingsley, Dance, and Mirren.
1988 (PG-13) 106m/C Ben Kingsley, Helen Mirren, Charles Dance, Sheila Allen, Vernon Dobtcheff; *D:* James Dearden; *W:* James Dearden; *M:* Loek Dikker. **VHS, Beta** $14.95 *LIV* 🎬🎬🎬 ½

Pass the Ammo Entertaining comedy about a young couple who attempt to steal back $50,000 of inheritance money that a televangelist swindled from the family. One of the more creative satires on this religious TV phenomenon.
1988 (R) 93m/C Bill Paxton, Tim Curry, Linda Kozlowski, Annie Potts, Anthony Geary, Dennis Burkley, Glenn Withrow, Richard Paul; *D:* David Beaird; *W:* Neil Cohen, Joel Cohen; *M:* Carter Burwell. **VHS, Beta** $89.95 *LIV* 🎬🎬 ½

A Passage to India An ambitious adaptation of E.M. Forster's complex novel about relations between Brits and Indians in the 1920s. Drama centers on a young British woman's accusations that an Indian doctor raped her while serving as a guide in some rather ominous caves. Film occasionally flags, but is usually compelling. Features particularly strong performances from Bannerjee, Fox, and Davis.
1984 (PG) 163m/C Peggy Ashcroft, Alec Guinness, James Fox, Judy Davis, Victor Banerjee, Nigel Havers; *D:* David Lean; *M:* Maurice Jarre. Academy Awards '84: Best Supporting Actress (Ashcroft), Best Original Score; Nominations: Best Adapted Screenplay, Best Art Direction/Set Decoration, Best Cinematography, Best Costume Design, Best

Director (Lean), Best Film Editing, Best Picture, Best Sound; Academy Awards '87: Best Actress (Davis); British Academy Awards '85: Best Actress (Ashcroft); Golden Globe Awards '85: Best Foreign Film, Best Supporting Actress (Ashcroft), Best Score; New York Film Critics Awards '84: Best Film. **VHS, Beta** $19.95 *COL, BTV, HMV* 🎬🎬🎬

Passage to Marseilles Hollywood propaganda in which convicts escape from Devil's Island and help French freedom fighters combat Nazis. Routine but entertaining. What else could it be with Bogart, Raines, Greenstreet, and Lorre, who later made a pretty good film set in Casablanca?
1944 110m/B Humphrey Bogart, Claude Rains, Sydney Greenstreet, Peter Lorre, Helmut Dantine, George Tobias, John Loder, Eduardo Ciannelli, Michele Morgan; *D:* Michael Curtiz. **VHS, Beta** *FOX* 🎬🎬🎬

Passed Away Family patriarch Jack Scanlan dies and his entire family gets together for the funeral and a big Irish wake. The family, of course, is made up of a weird group of characters, good steadfast son Hoskins, dim-witted but good-looking son Petersen, rebellious daughter Reed, and a left-wing nun who works in Central America and is accompanied by an illegal alien (McDormand). Throw in a mysterious female mourner and a pregnant granddaughter who goes into labor at the graveside and you come up with a movie that manages to use every comic death cliche ever imagined. Talented cast is wasted in a movie that should have passed away.
1992 (PG-13) 96m/C Bob Hoskins, Jack Warden, William L. Petersen, Helen Lloyd Breed, Maureen Stapleton, Pamela Reed, Tim Curry, Peter Riegert, Blair Brown, Patrick Breen, Nancy Travis, Teri Polo, Frances McDormand; *D:* Charlie Peters; *W:* Charlie Peters; *M:* Richard Gibbs. **VHS, Beta** $19.99 *HPH* 🎬 ½

The Passenger A dissatisfied television reporter changes identities with a dead man while on assignment in Africa, then learns that he is posing as a gunrunner. Mysterious, elliptical production from Italian master Antonioni, who co-wrote. Nicholson is fine in the low-key role, and Schneider is surprisingly winning as the woman drawn to him. The object of much debate, hailed by some as quintessential cinema and by others as slow and unrewarding. *AKA:* Profession: Reporter.
1975 (PG) 119m/C Jack Nicholson, Maria Schneider, Ian Hendry, Jenny Runacre, Steven Berkoff; *D:* Michelangelo Antonioni; *W:* Mark Peploe, Michelangelo Antonioni, Mark Peploe; *M:* Claude Bolling. **VHS, Beta** $19.98 *WAR* 🎬🎬🎬 ½

Passenger 57 Classic movie-of-the-week fare. Anti-terrorist specialist John Cutter (Snipes) leaves his profession because of his wife's murder, and coincidentally boards the same plane as Charles Rane (Payne), an apprehended evil terrorist headed to trial in L.A. Somehow, Rane's thugs have also sneaked aboard with plans to hijack the plane, and it's up to Cutter to use his skills and save the day. Athletic Snipes is convincing in his role but can't make up for the plot's lack of premise.
1992 (R) 84m/C Wesley Snipes, Bruce Payne, Tom Sizemore, Alex Datcher, Bruce Greenwood, Robert Hooks, Elizabeth Hurley, Michael Horse; *D:* Kevin Hooks; *W:* David Loughery, Dan Gordon; *M:* Stanley Clarke. **VHS** $19.98 *WAR* 🎬

The Passing Two men find themselves trapped in the darker vicissitudes of life. The two lead almost parallel lives until an extraordinary event unites them.

1988 96m/C James Plaster, Welton Benjamin Johnson, Lynn Dunn, Albert B. Smith; *D:* John Huckert. VHS *NO ♂♂½*

The Passing of Evil
Bisset is a star-struck Canadian undone by the bright lights and big cities of America. By age 22, she's a burnt-out prostitute in Las Vegas. Cheerless but compelling. *AKA:* The Grasshopper; Passions.
1970 (R) 96m/C Jacqueline Bisset, Jim Brown, Joseph Cotten, Corbett Monica, Ramon Bieri, Christopher Stone, Roger Garrett, Stanley Adams, Dick Richards, Tim O'Kelly, Ed Flanders; *D:* Jerry Paris; *M:* Billy Goldenberg. VHS $29.98 *WAR ♂♂½*

The Passing of the Third Floor Back
Boarding house tenants improve their lives after being inspired by a mysterious stranger. They revert, though, when he leaves. Now you know. Based on a Victorian morality play.
1936 80m/B Conrad Veidt, Rene Ray, Frank Cellier, Anna Lee, John Turnbull, Cathleen Nesbitt; *D:* Berthold Viertel. VHS, Beta $16.95 *SNC ♂♂*

Passion
Paris, and the decadent Louis XV falls for the lovely Jeanne, making her his mistress, much to the scandal of the nation. Respectable silent version of "Madame DuBarry" is a relatively realistic costume drama, but it doesn't rate with the best German films of this period.
1919 135m/B Pola Negri, Emil Jannings, Harry Liedtke; *D:* Ernst Lubitsch. VHS, Beta $39.95 *VYY, GLV, GVV ♂♂½*

Passion
When a rancher's young family falls victim to rampaging desperadoes, he enlists an outlaw's aid to avenge the murders of his loved ones.
1954 84m/C Raymond Burr, Cornel Wilde, Yvonne De Carlo, Lon Chaney Jr., John Qualen; *D:* Allan Dwan. VHS, Beta *NO ♂♂*

Passion Fish
McDonnell plays May-Alice, a soap opera actress who is paralyzed after a taxi accident in New York. Confined to a wheelchair, the bitter woman moves back to her Louisiana home and alienates a number of live-in nurses until Chantelle (Woodard), who has her own problems, comes along. Blunt writing and directing by Sayles overcome the story's inherent sentimentality as do the spirited performances of the leads, including Curtis-Hall as the rogue romancing Chantelle and Strathairn as the Cajun bad boy McDonnell once loved. The laserdisc is available in letterbox format.
1992 (R) 136m/C Mary McDonnell, Alfre Woodard, David Strathairn, Vondie Curtis-Hall, Nora Dunn, Sheila Kelley, Angela Bassett, Mary Portser, Maggie Renzi, Leo Burmester; *D:* John Sayles; *W:* John Sayles; *M:* Mason Daring. Academy Awards '92 Nominations: Best Actress (McDonnell), Best Original Screenplay; Independent Spirit Awards '93: Best Supporting Actress (Woodard). VHS $19.95 *COL, MOV, BTV ♂♂♂*

Passion Flower
A tropical romantic melodrama made for network TV and set in Singapore, where an ambitious banker falls in love with the daughter of island's wealthiest smuggler. The mixture of high finance, low-dealing and lust only proves moderately passionate.
1986 (PG-13) 95m/C Bruce Boxleitner, Barbara Hershey, Nicol Williamson; *D:* Joseph Sargent; *M:* Miles Goodman. VHS $89.95 *VMK ♂♂*

Passion for Life
A new teacher uses revolutionary methods to engage students, but draws ire from staid parents in rural France. Worthwhile drama. In French with English subtitles. *AKA:* L'Ecole Buissonniere; I Have a New Master.

1948 89m/B Bernard Blier, Julliette Faber, Edouard Delmont; *D:* Jean-Paul LeChanois. VHS, Beta $59.95 *FCT ♂♂½*

Passion for Power
Two men involved in a drug-smuggling syndicate attempt to take over the business. Complications arise when they both fall for a beautiful, deceitful woman who turns them against one another.
1985 94m/C Hector Suarez, Sasha Montenegro, Manuel Capetillo, Alejandra Peniche. VHS *NO ♂♂½*

Passion in Paradise
Fact-based mystery set in the Bahamas in 1943. Stewart is a spoiled rich girl who marries a handsome gigolo (Assante), much to daddy big bucks' (Steiger) displeasure. Then daddy is murdered and the son-in-law becomes the key suspect. Trashy, but Assante's fine. Made for television.
1989 100m/C Armand Assante, Catherine Mary Stewart, Rod Steiger, Mariette Hartley, Wayne Rogers; *D:* Harvey Hart. VHS *APX ♂♂½*

The Passion of Anna
A complicated psychological drama about four people on an isolated island. Von Sydow is an ex-con living a hermit's existence when he becomes involved with a crippled widow (Ullmann) and her two friends—all of whom have secrets in their pasts. Brutal and disturbing. Wonderful cinematography by Sven Nykvist. Filmed on the island of Faro. In Swedish with English subtitles.
1970 (R) 101m/C Max von Sydow, Liv Ullmann, Bibi Andersson, Erland Josephson, Erik Hell; *D:* Ingmar Bergman; *W:* Ingmar Bergman. VHS $19.98 *MGM, BTV ♂♂♂*

The Passion of Joan of Arc
Masterful silent film relates the events of St. Joan's trial and subsequent martyrdom. Moving, eloquent work features legendary performace by Falconetti. Also rates among master Dreyer's finest efforts. A classic. Silent with music.
1928 114m/B Maria Falconetti, Eugena Sylvaw, Maurice Schultz, Antonin Artaud; *D:* Carl Theodor Dreyer. VHS, Beta $24.95 *VYY, MRV, NOS ♂♂♂♂*

Passion of Love
Military captain becomes the obsession of his commander's mysterious cousin when he reports to an outpost far from home. Daring and fascinating. An unrelentingly passionate historical romance guaranteed to heat up the VCR. Available dubbed or with subtitles. *AKA:* Passione d'Amore.
1982 117m/C Laura Antonelli, Bernard Giraudeau, Valeria D'Obici, Jean-Louis Trintignant; *D:* Ettore Scola; *W:* Ettore Scola. VHS, Beta $69.95 *VES, ING, CIG ♂♂♂*

Passionate Thief
Two pickpockets and a bumbling actress plan to rip off the guests at a posh New Year's Eve party with slightly comic results. Not much to recommend in this slow moving flick. *AKA:* Risate de Gioia.
1960 100m/C Anna Magnani, Ben Gazzara, Toto, Fred Clark; *D:* Mario Monicelli. VHS, Beta $19.95 *NLC ♂♂½*

The Passover Plot
A controversial look at the crucifixion of Christ which depicts him as a Zealot leader who, aided by his followers, faked his death and then "rose" to win new converts.
1975 (PG) 105m/C Harry Andrews, Hugh Griffith, Zalman King, Donald Pleasence, Scott Wilson; *D:* Michael Campus. VHS, Beta $59.95 *CAN ♂♂*

Passport to Pimlico
Farce about a London neighborhood's residents who discover an ancient charter proclaiming their right to form their own country within city limits. Passable comedy.

1949 81m/B Stanley Holloway, Margaret Rutherford, Hermione Baddeley, Naunton Wayne, Basil Radford; *D:* Henry Cornelius. VHS, Beta $19.95 *NOS, PSM, DVT ♂♂½*

Past Midnight
Richardson plays a social worker who believes recently paroled killer Hauer was wrongly convicted. She attempts to prove his innocence while also falling in love—a dangerous combination. Richardson's beautiful and Hauer's making a successful career out of playing handsome psychos.
1992 (R) 100m/C Natasha Richardson, Rutger Hauer, Clancy Brown, Guy Boyd; *D:* Jan Eliasberg; *W:* Frank Norwood. VHS $19.95 *COL ♂♂*

Pastime
A bittersweet baseball elegy set in the minor leagues in 1957. A boyish 41-year-old pitcher can't face his impending retirement and pals around with the team pariah, a 17-year-old black rookie. Splendidly written and acted, it's a melancholy treat whether you're a fan of the game or not, and safe for family attendance. The only drawback is a grungy, low-budget look. *AKA:* One Cup of Coffee.
1991 (PG) 94m/C William Russ, Scott Plank, Glenn Plummer, Noble Willingham, Jeffrey Tambor, Deidre O'Connell; *D:* Robin B. Armstrong. VHS $19.95 *COL ♂♂♂*

Pat and Mike
War of the sexes rages in this comedy about a leathery sports promoter who futilely attempts to train a woman for athletic competition. Tracy and Hepburn have fine chemistry, but supporting players contribute too. Watch for the first on-screen appearance of Bronson (then Charles Buchinski) as a crook.
1952 95m/B Spencer Tracy, Katharine Hepburn, Aldo Ray, Jim Backus, William Ching, Sammy White, Phyllis Povah, Charles Bronson, Chuck Connors, Mae Clarke, Carl "Alfalfa" Switzer; *D:* George Cukor; *W:* Ruth Gordon, Garson Kanin. VHS, Beta $19.98 *MGM ♂♂♂*

Pat Garrett & Billy the Kid
Coburn is Garrett, one-time partner of Billy the Kid (Kristofferson), turned sheriff. He tracks down and eventually kills the outlaw. The uncut director's version which was released on video is a vast improvement over the theatrically released and television versions. Dylan's soundtrack includes the now famous "Knockin' on Heaven's Door."
1973 106m/C Kris Kristofferson, James Coburn, Bob Dylan, Richard Jaeckel, Katy Jurado, Chill Wills, Charles Martin Smith, Slim Pickens, Harry Dean Stanton; *D:* Sam Peckinpah; *W:* Rudy Wurlitzer; *M:* George Duning. VHS, Beta $19.95 *MGM ♂♂♂*

A Patch of Blue
A kind-hearted blind girl falls in love with a black man without acknowledging racial differences. Good performances from Hartman and Poitier are film's strongest assets.
1965 108m/C Sidney Poitier, Elizabeth Hartman, Shelley Winters, Wallace Ford, Ivan Dixon, John Qualen, Elisabeth Fraser, Kelly Flynn; *D:* Guy Green; *M:* Jerry Goldsmith. Academy Awards '65: Best Supporting Actress (Winters); Nominations: Best Actress (Hartman), Best Art Direction/Set Decoration (B & W), Best Black and White Cinematography. VHS, Beta $19.98 *MGM, BTV ♂♂½*

Patchwork Girl of Oz
A very early silent film production by Baum that brought his own Oz books to the screen.
1914 80m/B *D:* L. Frank Baum. VHS, Beta $19.95 *NOS, DVT, VYY ♂♂*

Paternity
Routine comedy about middle-aged manager of Madison Square Gardens (Reynolds) who sets out to find a woman to bear his child, no strings attached. The

predictability of the happy ending makes this a yawner. Steinberg's directorial debut.

1981 (PG) 94m/C Burt Reynolds, Beverly D'Angelo, Lauren Hutton, Norman Fell, Paul Dooley, Elizabeth Ashley; *D:* David Steinberg; *W:* Charlie Peters. **VHS, Beta $14.95** PAR *ℐℐ*

Pather Panchali Somber, moving story of a young Bengali boy growing up in impoverished India. Stunning debut from India's master filmmaker Ray, who continued the story in "Aparajito" and "World of Apu." A truly great work. In Bengali with English subtitles. *AKA:* The Song of the Road; The Saga of the Road; The Lament of the Path.

1954 112m/B Kanu Banerjee, Karuna Banerjee, Uma Das Gupta, Subir Banerji, Runki Banerji, Chunibala Devi; *D:* Satyajit Ray; *W:* Satyajit Ray; *M:* Ravi Shankar. **VHS, Beta $24.95** NOS, FCT, MRV *ℐℐℐℐ*

Pathfinder A young boy in Lapland of 1,000 years ago comes of age prematurely after he falls in with cutthroat nomads who already slaughtered his family and now want to wipe out the rest of the village. Gripping adventure in the ice and snow features stunning scenery. In Lappish with English subtitles and based on an old Lapp fable.

1987 88m/C Mikkel Gaup, Nils Utsi, Svein Scharffenberg, Helgi Skulason, Sara Marit Gaup, Sverre Porsanger; *D:* Nils Gaup; *W:* Nils Gaup. **VHS $79.95** FXL, FCT, ING *ℐℐℐ½*

Paths of Glory Classic anti-war drama set in WWI France. A vain, ambitious officer imposes unlikely battle strategy on his hapless troops, and when it fails, he demands that three soldiers be selected for execution as cowards. Menjou is excellent as the bloodless French officer, with Douglas properly heroic as the French officer who knows about the whole disgraceful enterprise. Fabulous, wrenching fare from filmmaking great Kubrick, who co-wrote. Based on a true story from Humphrey Cobb's novel of the same name.

1957 86m/B Kirk Douglas, Adolphe Menjou, George Macready, Ralph Meeker, Richard Anderson, Wayne Morris, Timothy Carey, Susanne Christian, Bert Freed; *D:* Stanley Kubrick; *W:* Calder Willingham, Stanley Kubrick. **VHS, Beta $19.98** MGM, FOX *ℐℐℐℐ*

Paths to Paradise Compson and Griffith share criminal past, reunite at gala event to snatch priceless necklace and head south of the border. World-class chase scene.

1925 78m/B Raymond Griffith, Betty Compson, Thomas Santschi, Bert Woodruff, Fred Kelsey; *D:* Clarence Badger. **VHS, Beta $19.95** GPV *ℐℐℐ*

Patrick Coma patient suddenly develops strange powers and has a weird effect on the people he comes in contact with.

1978 (PG) 115m/C Robert Helpmann, Susan Penhaligon, Rod Mullinar; *D:* Richard Franklin. **VHS, Beta** NO *ℐ½*

The Patriot An action film about an ex-Navy commando who battles a band of nuclear-arms smuggling terrorists. Edited via George Lucas's electronic editor, Edit Droid.

1986 (R) 88m/C Jeff Conaway, Michael J. Pollard, Leslie Nielsen, Greg Henry, Simone Griffeth; *D:* Frank Harris; *W:* Andy Ruben, Katt Shea Ruben; *M:* Jay Michael Ferguson. **VHS, Beta $79.98** LIV, VES *ℐ½*

Patriot Games Jack Ryan, retired CIA analyst, takes his wife and daughter to England on a holiday and ends up saving a member of the Royal Family from assassination by IRA extremists. Ryan, who has killed one of the terrorists, then becomes the target of revenge by the dead man's brother. Good action sequences but otherwise predictable adaptation of the novel by Tom Clancy. Companion to "The Hunt for Red October," with Ford taking over the role of Ryan from Alec Baldwin. Since this movie did well, we can probably expect two more from Ford, who's becoming the king of trilogies. Followed by "Clear and Present Danger."

1992 (R) 117m/C Harrison Ford, Anne Archer, Patrick Bergin, Thora Birch, Sean Bean, Richard Harris, James Earl Jones, James Fox, Samuel L. Jackson, Polly Walker; *D:* Phillip Noyce; *W:* W. Peter Iliff, Donald Stewart; *M:* James Horner. **VHS, Beta, CDV $19.95** PAR *ℐℐℐ*

The Patriots A German prisoner works as a shoemaker in a small village during WWI. A lyrical drama in German and Russian with English titles.

1933 82m/B *D:* Boris Barnett. **VHS, Beta $29.95** FCT, IHF *ℐℐℐ*

The Patsy Shady producers attempt to transform a lowly bellboy into a comedy superstar. Not one of Lewis's better efforts; Lorre's last film.

1964 101m/C Jerry Lewis, Ina Balin, Everett Sloane, Phil Harris, Keenan Wynn, Peter Lorre, John Carradine, Hans Conried, Richard Deacon, Scatman Crothers, Del Moore, Neil Hamilton, Buddy Lester, Nancy Kulp, Norman Alden, Jack Albertson; *D:* Jerry Lewis; *W:* Jerry Lewis. **VHS, Beta $59.95** IME *ℐℐ*

Patsy, Mi Amor A modern woman eventually chooses to give herself to an older man, and finds life with him powerful and adventurous.

1987 94m/C Julio Aleman, Ofelia Medina, Joaquin Cordero, Leticia Robles, Carlos Cortes, Julian Pastor. **VHS, Beta $55.95** MAD *ℐℐ*

Patterns Realistic depiction of big business. Heflin starts work at a huge New York office that is under the ruthless supervision of Sloane. Serling's astute screenplay (adapted from his TV play) is adept at portraying ruthless, power-struggling executives and the sundry workings of a large corporation. Film has aged slightly, but it still has some edge to it. Originally intended for television. *AKA:* Patterns of Power.

1956 83m/B Van Heflin, Everett Sloane, Ed Begley Sr., Beatrice Straight, Elizabeth Wilson; *D:* Fielder Cook; *W:* Rod Serling. **VHS $19.95** NOS, MGM, MRV *ℐℐℐ*

Pattes Blanches A reclusive aristocrat always wears white spats, causing ridicule in the small fishing village where he lives. Trouble comes when a local saloon-keeper becomes resentful of the rich man's advances on his girlfriend. Moody, sensual French melodrama exploring class, money and sex. Adaptation of a play by Jean Anouilh. In French with English subtitles. *AKA:* White Paws.

1949 92m/B Suzy Delair, Fernand Ledoux, Paul Bernard, Michel Bouquet; *D:* Jean Gremillon. **VHS** INT, FCT *ℐℐ½*

Patti Rocks Offbeat, realistic independent effort concerns a foul chauvinist who enlists a friend to accompany him on a visit to a pregnant girlfriend who turns out to be less than the bimbo she's portrayed as en route. Mulkey shines as the sexist. Same characters featured earlier in "Loose Ends."

1988 (R) 86m/C Chris Mulkey, John Jenkins, Karen Landry, David L. Turk, Stephen Yoakam; *D:* David Burton Morris; *W:* Chris Mulkey, John Jenkins, Karen Landry, John Jenkins, David Burton Morris; *M:* Doug Maynard. **VHS, Beta** NO *ℐℐℐ*

Patton Lengthy but stellar bio of the vain, temperamental American general who masterminded significant combat triumphs during WWII. "Old Blood and Guts," who considered himself an 18th-century commander living in the wrong era, produced victory after victory in North Africa and Europe, but not without a decided impact upon his troops. Scott is truly magnificent in the title role, and Malden shines in the supporting role of General Omar Bradley. Not a subtle film, but neither is its subject. Interesting match-up with the 1986 made-for-TV movie "The Last Days of Patton," also starring Scott. *AKA:* Patton—Lust for Glory; Patton: A Salute to a Rebel.

1970 (PG) 171m/C George C. Scott, Karl Malden, Stephen Young, Michael Strong, Frank Latimore, James Edwards, Lawrence Dobkin, Michael Bates, Tim Considine; *D:* Franklin J. Schaffner; *W:* Francis Ford Coppola, Edmund H. North; *M:* Jerry Goldsmith. Academy Awards '70: Best Actor (Scott), Best Art Direction/Set Decoration, Best Director (Schaffner), Best Film Editing, Best Picture, Best Sound, Best Story & Screenplay; Nominations: Best Original Score; Directors Guild of America Awards '70: Best Director (Schaffner); Golden Globe Awards '71: Best Actor—Drama (Scott); National Board of Review Awards '70: 10 Best Films of the Year, Best Actor (Scott); National Society of Film Critics Awards '70: Best Actor (Scott). **VHS, Beta $29.98** FXV, TLF, BTV *ℐℐℐ½*

Patty Hearst Less than fascinating, expressionistic portrait of Hearst from her kidnapping through her brainwashing and eventual criminal participation with the SLA. An enigmatic film that seems to only make Hearst's transformation into a Marxist terrorist all the more mysterious. Based on Hearst's book, "Every Secret Thing."

1988 (R) 108m/C Natasha Richardson, William Forsythe, Ving Rhames, Frances Fisher, Jodi Long, Dana Delany; *D:* Paul Schrader; *W:* Nicholas Kazan. **VHS, Beta $19.98** MED *ℐ½*

Paul and Michelle The equally dull sequel to "Friends" finds the two lovers a little older but no wiser. Paul has graduated from his British school and returns to France to seek out Michelle and their child. They try to rekindle their romance but the stresses of everyday life cause them problems.

1974 (R) 102m/C Sean Bury, Anicee Alvina, Keir Dullea, Ronald Lewis, Catherine Allegret, Georges Beller; *D:* Lewis Gilbert; *M:* Michel Colombier. **VHS $14.95** PAR *ℐ*

Paul Bartel's The Secret Cinema A woman cannot determine whether her life is real or a film by a maniacal director. Offbeat, creative, and a little disturbing. Followed by Bartel's short "Naughty Nurse."

1969 37m/B *D:* Paul Bartel. **VHS, Beta $29.95** RHI *ℐℐ½*

Paul Robeson Major events in the life of the popular actor are recounted in this one-man performance. Originally staged by Charles Nelson Reilly.

197? 118m/C James Earl Jones; *D:* Lloyd Richards. **VHS, Beta $39.95** KAR *ℐℐ*

Pauline at the Beach A young woman accompanies her more experienced cousin to the French coast for a summer of sexual hijinks. Contemplative, not coarse, though the leads look great in—and out—of their swimsuits. Breezy, typically talky fare from small-film master Rohmer. Cinematography by Nester Almendro. In French with English subtitles. *AKA:* Pauline a la Plage.

1983 95m/C Amanda Langlet, Arielle Dombasle, Pascal Greggory, Rosette; *D:* Eric Rohmer; *W:* Eric Rohmer. **VHS, Beta $24.95** XVC, MED, ING *ℐℐℐ½*

Paul's Case In turn-of-the-century Pittsburgh, an ambitious young man enters the upper crust of New York society through deceiving pretenses. Based on a story by Willa Cather. Made for television.

1980 52m/C Eric Roberts, Michael Higgins, Lindsay Crouse; *D:* Lamont Johnson. **VHS, Beta $24.95** MON, MTI, KAR *ℐℐ½*

P

The Pawnbroker A Jewish pawnbroker in Harlem is haunted by his grueling experiences in a Nazi camp during the Holocaust. Powerful and well done. Probably Steiger's best performance. Adapted from a novel by Edward Lewis Wallant.
1965 120m/B Rod Steiger, Brock Peters, Geraldine Fitzgerald, Jaime Sanchez, Thelma Oliver; **D:** Sidney Lumet; **M:** Quincy Jones. Academy Awards '65 Nominations: Best Actor (Steiger); Berlin International Film Festival '65: Best Actor (Steiger); British Academy Awards '66: Best Actor (Steiger). **VHS $14.98** REP ♊♊♊½

Pawnshop Charlie is employed as a pawnbroker's assistant. Silent with music track.
1916 20m/B Charlie Chaplin. **VHS, Beta** CAB, GVV ♊♊♊½

Pay Off A lunatic psychiatrist seeks murderous revenge on his ex-patient/girlfriend and her family.
1989 87m/C Michael Fitzpatrick, Veronika Mattson, Margareta Krook; **D:** George Tirl. **VHS, Beta $59.95** TWE ♊

Pay or Die A crime boss' men turn on him and kidnap his daughter.
1983 (R) 92m/C Dick Adair, Johnny Wilson; **D:** Bobby Suarez. **VHS, Beta $29.95** LIV ♊

Payback A brawny young man uses firepower to avenge those who have wronged him.
1989 90m/C Jean Carol. **VHS, Beta** NO ♊

Payback A convict sets out to avenge his brother's death, and creates all sorts of mayhem in the process. Produced by Bob "Newlywed Game" Eubanks and scored by Daryl "Captain and Tennille" Dragon.
1990 (R) 94m/C Corey Michael Eubanks, Michael Ironside, Teresa Blake, Bert Remsen, Vincent Van Patten, Don Swayze; **D:** Russell Solberg; **M:** Daryl Dragon. **VHS $89.98** REP ♊

Payday Torn stars as a declining country music star on tour in this portrayal of the seamy side of show business, from groupies to grimy motels. Well-written script and fine performances make this an engaging, if rather draining, drama not easily found on the big screen.
1972 98m/C Rip Torn, Anna Capri, Michael C. Gwynne, Jeff Morris; **D:** Daryl Duke. **VHS, Beta** NO ♊♊♊½

The Payoff The old-fashioned newspaper-reporter-as-crime-fighter routine. When the city's special prosecutor is murdered a daring newshawk investigates and tracks the bad guys. But will he spell their names right?
1943 74m/B Lee Tracy, Tom Brown, Tina Thayer, Evelyn Brent, Jack La Rue, Ian Keith, John Maxwell; **D:** Arthur Dreifuss. **VHS $19.95** NOS, LOO ♊½

Payoff An ex-cop discovers the identity of gangsters who killed his parents. He traces them to a Lake Tahoe resort and plots revenge. Familiar crime story with a good cast.
1991 (R) 111m/C Keith Carradine, Kim Greist, Harry Dean Stanton, John Saxon, Jeff Corey; **D:** Stuart Cooper. **VHS, Beta $89.98** FXV ♊

P.C.U. Satire on campus political correctness follows freshman Tom Lawrence's (Young) adventures as he navigates the treacherous waters of Port Chester University (PCU). He falls in with the gang from the Pit, the militantly non-PC dorm, who encourage bizarre and offensive behavior. Essentially a modern update of "National Lampoon's Animal House," but without the brilliance; add half a bone for tackling the thorny sensitivity issue in a humorous way that parodies, but shouldn't offend. Actor Bochner's directorial debut.
1994 (PG-13) 81m/C Jeremy Piven, Chris Young, David Spade, Sarah Trigger, Jessica Walter, Jon Favreau, Megan Ward, Jake Busey; **Cameos:** George Clinton; **D:** Hart Bochner; **W:** Adam Leff, Zak Penn; **M:** Steve Vai. **VHS** NYR ♊♊

Peacekillers A mean bunch of bikers visit a commune to kidnap a young woman. The gang has a big surprise in store for them when the girl escapes.
1971 86m/C Michael Ontkean, Clint Ritchie, Paul Krokop; **D:** Douglas Schwartz. **VHS, Beta $19.95** NWV, STE ♊½

Peacemaker Two aliens masquerading as human cops stalk each other through a major city.
1990 (R) 90m/C Robert Forster, Lance Edwards, Hilary Shepard, Bert Remsen, Robert Davi; **D:** Kevin S. Tenney; **W:** Kevin S. Tenney. **VHS, Beta $89.95** FRH ♊

The Peacock Fan The Peacock Fan is protected by a deadly curse, with certain death to anyone who possesses it.
1929 50m/B Lucian Preval. **VHS, Beta $16.95** SNC, VYY ♊½

The Peanut Butter Solution An imaginative 11-year-old boy investigates a strange old house which is haunted by friendly ghosts who are in possession of a magic potion.
1985 (PG) 96m/C Matthew Mackay, Siluck Saysanasy, Alison Podbrey, Michael Maillot, Griffith Brewer, Michael Hogan, Helen Hughes; **D:** Michael Rubbo; **W:** Michael Rubbo; **M:** Lewis Furey. **VHS, Beta $14.95** NWV, STE, HHE ♊♊½

The Pearl Based on a John Steinbeck story, a Mexican fisherman, living in poverty, finds a magnificent pearl and he thinks it will improve the lives of his family. He is bewildered by what this pearl really brings—liars and thieves. Simple, yet larger-than-life film, beautifully photographed; a timeless picture capturing human nature.
1948 77m/B Pedro Armendariz Sr., Maria Elena Marques, Fernando Wagner, Charles Rooner; **D:** Emilio Fernandez. **VHS, Beta $69.95** FCT, MAS ♊♊

The Pearl of Death Holmes and Watson investigate the theft of a precious pearl.
1944 69m/B Basil Rathbone, Nigel Bruce, Dennis Hoey, Miles Mander, Rondo Hatton, Evelyn Ankers; **D:** Roy William Neill. **VHS, Beta $14.98** FOX ♊♊½

Pearl of the South Pacific A trio of adventurers destroy a quiet and peaceful island when they ransack it for pearl treasures. **AKA:** South Sea Woman.
1955 85m/C Dennis (Stanley Morner) Morgan, Virginia Mayo, David Farrar; **D:** Allan Dwan. **VHS, Beta** NO ♊♊

The Peasants Poignant rural Polish saga pits father against son due to the passion they share for one woman. In two tapes, based on Wladyslaw Reymont's Nobel prize-winning novel. In Polish with English subtitles.
19?? 184m/C VHS $69.99 FCT ♊♊½

Peck's Bad Boy Impudent, precocious brat causes his parents considerable grief. Someone should lock this kid in a room with W.C. Fields or the Alien. Silent film based on the stories by George Wilbur Peck.
1921 51m/B Jackie Coogan, Thomas Meighan, Raymond Hatton, Wheeler Oakman, Lillian Leighton; **D:** Sam Wood. **VHS, Beta $19.95** NOS, MRV, CCB ♊♊

Peck's Bad Boy A wedge is driven between a young boy and his adoptive father when the man's sister and her son move in. The aunt wants her son to be number one, causing much discord. Cooper is excellent in his role as the adopted son.
1934 70m/B Thomas Meighan, Jackie Cooper, Dorothy Peterson, Jackie Searl, O.P. Heggie, Harvey Clark, Lloyd Ingraham; **D:** Eddie Cline. **VHS $19.95** NOS, MLB ♊♊½

Peck's Bad Boy with the Circus The circus will never be the same after the mischievous youngster and his buddies get done with it. Gilbert and Kennedy provide the high points.
1938 67m/B Tommy Kelly, Anne Gillis, George "Spanky" McFarland, Edgar Kennedy, Billy Gilbert; **D:** Eddie Cline. **VHS, Beta $19.95** NOS, VYY, DVT ♊♊

Pecos Bill Meet the man who used the Grand Canyon for a swimmin' hole, dug the Rio Grande and used the Texas panhandle for a fryin' pan. From Shelly Duvall's "Tall Tales and Legends" series. Originally made for cable television.
1986 50m/C Steve Guttenberg, Martin Mull, Claude Akins, Rebecca DeMornay. **VHS $19.98** FOX, COL ♊♊

Pecos Kid A child has his parents killed, and grows up embittered, vengeful and thirsty for blood.
1935 56m/B Fred Kohler Jr. **VHS, Beta $19.95** NOS ♊

Peddlin' in Society A fruit vendor makes it big on the black market and lives the good life, until poor investments force her back to her old means. Strong perfomances by Magnani and De Sica. In Italian with English subtitles. **AKA:** Da Bancarella a Bancarotta.
1947 85m/B Anna Magnani, Vittorio De Sica, Virgilio Riento, Laura Gore; **D:** Gennaro Righelli. **VHS** DVT, HEG ♊♊

The Pedestrian A prominent German industrialist is exposed as a Nazi officer who supervised the wholesale devastation of a Greek village during WWII. Impressive debut for director Schell, who also appears in a supporting role. **AKA:** Der Fussgaenger.
1973 (PG) 97m/C Maximilian Schell, Peggy Ashcroft, Lil Dagover, Francoise Rosay, Elisabeth Bergner; **D:** Maximilian Schell; **M:** Manos Hadjidakis. Academy Awards '73 Nominations: Best Foreign Language Film; Golden Globe Awards '74: Best Foreign Film; National Board of Review Awards '74: 5 Best Foreign Films of the Year. **VHS, Beta $69.98** SUE, GLV, SWC ♊♊♊½

The Pee Wee Herman Show The original HBO special which introduced Pee Wee to the world. Hilarious stuff, with help from Captain Carl (Hartman), Miss Yvonne, and other assorted pals. Warning: Not to be confused with Pee Wee's children's show.
1982 60m/C Paul (Pee Wee Herman) Reubens, Phil Hartman, John Paragon. **VHS** NO ♊♊½

Pee Wee's Big Adventure Zany, endearing comedy about an adult nerd's many adventures while attempting to recover his stolen bicycle. Chock full of classic sequences, including a barroom encounter between Pee Wee and several ornery bikers, and a tour through the Alamo. A colorful, exhilerating experience.
1985 (PG) 92m/C Paul (Pee Wee Herman) Reubens, Elizabeth Daily, Mark Holton, Diane Salinger, Judd Omen, Cassandra Peterson, James Brolin, Morgan Fairchild, Tony Bill, Jan Hooks; **D:** Tim Burton; **W:** Paul (Pee Wee Herman) Reubens, Phil Hartman, Michael Varhol; **M:** Danny Elfman. **VHS, Beta $19.98** WAR ♊♊♊½

Pee Wee's Playhouse Christmas Special Pee Wee does an extended Playhouse episode for Christmas, with a load of guest stars.

P

VIDEOHOUND'S GOLDEN MOVIE RETRIEVER

▲ 725

1988 49m/C Paul (Pee Wee Herman) Reubens, Whoopi Goldberg, Zsa Zsa Gabor, Grace Jones, Dinah Shore, Frankie Avalon, Annette Funicello, Joan Rivers, Oprah Winfrey, Charo, Earle Johnson, k.d. lang, Kareem Abdul-Jabbar, Del Rubio Triplets, Little Richard. **VHS, Beta $9.99** VTR ✗✗✗½

Pee Wee's Playhouse Festival of Fun Five fun-filled episodes of the playhouse!
1988 123m/C Paul (Pee Wee Herman) Reubens. **VHS, Beta $79.95** MED ✗✗✗½

Peeping Tom Controversial, unsettling thriller in which a psychopath lures women before his film camera, then records their deaths at his hand. Unnerving subject matter is rendered impressively by British master Powell. A classic of its kind, but definitely not for everyone. This is the original uncut version of the film, released in the U.S. in 1979 with the assistance of Martin Scorsese.
1963 88m/C Karl-Heinz Boehm, Moira Shearer, Anna Massey, Maxine Audley, Esmond Knight, Shirley Anne Field, Brenda Bruce, Pamela Green, Jack Watson, Nigel Davenport, Susan Travers, Veronica Hurst; **D:** Michael Powell. **VHS, Beta $39.95** HMV, AOV ✗✗✗½

Peg O' My Heart Taylor portrays the motherless Irish charmer sent to live with her mother's English relatives during the Irish rebellion. Of course, she must overcome their upper-class English snobbery to become part of the family.
1922 85m/B Laurette Taylor, Mahlon Hamilton, Russell Simpson, Ethel Grey; **D:** King Vidor. **VHS** GPV ✗✗

Peggy Sue Got Married Uneven but entertaining comedy about an unhappily married woman seemingly unable to relive her life when she falls unconscious at a high school reunion and awakens to find herself back in school. Turner shines, but the film flags often, and Cage isn't around enough to elevate entire work. O'Connor scores, though, as a sensitive biker. Look for musician Marshall Crenshaw as part of the reunion band.
1986 (PG-13) 103m/C Kathleen Turner, Nicolas Cage, Catherine Hicks, Maureen O'Sullivan, John Carradine, Helen Hunt, Lisa Jane Persky, Barbara Harris, Joan Allen, Kevin J. O'Connor, Barry Miller, Don Murray, Leon Ames, Sofia Coppola, Sachi Parker, Jim Carrey; **D:** Francis Ford Coppola; **W:** Jerry Leichtling, Arlene Sarner; **M:** John Barry. **VHS, Beta $19.98** FOX ✗✗½

The Peking Blond French-fried spyfilm boasts lousy acting unencumbered by plot. Amnesiac may or may not hold secrets coveted by Americans, Russians and Chinese. **AKA:** The Blonde From Peking; Le Blonde de Pekin.
1968 80m/C Mireille Darc, Claudio Brook, Edward G. Robinson, Pascale Roberts; **D:** Nicolas Gessner. **VHS** MRV ✗½

The Pelican Brief Tulane law student Darby Shaw (Roberts) writes a speculative brief on the murders of two Supreme Court justices that results in more murder and sends her running for her life. Fairly faithful to the Grisham bestseller, but the multitude of characters is confusing. Pakula adds style and star-power, but much will depend on your tolerance for paranoid political thrillers and ability to accept Roberts as the smart cookie who hits on the right answer and then manages to keep herself alive while bodies are dropping all around her. Washington is sharp as reporter Gray Grantham, the guy Roberts looks like she tried hard for (but the book's romance is nowhere to be seen).

1993 (PG-13) 141m/C Julia Roberts, Denzel Washington, John Heard, Tony Goldwyn, Stanley Tucci, James B. Sikking, William Atherton, Robert Culp, John Lithgow, Sam Shepard; **Cameos:** Hume Cronyn; **D:** Alan J. Pakula; **W:** Alan J. Pakula; **M:** James Horner. **VHS, 8mm** WAR ✗✗✗

Pelle the Conqueror Overpowering tale of a Swedish boy and his widower father who serve landowners in late 19th-century Denmark. Compassionate saga of human spirit contains numerous memorable sequences. Hvenegaard is wonderful as young Pelle, but von Sydow delivers what is probably his finest performance as a sympathetic weakling. American distributors foolishly trimmed the film by some 20 minutes (140 minute version). From the novel by Martin Anderson Nexo. In Swedish with English subtitles.
1988 160m/C Max von Sydow, Pelle Hvenegaard, Erik Paaske, Bjorn Granath, Axel Strobye, Astrid Villaume, Troels Asmussen, John Wittig, Anne Lise Hirsch Bjerrum, Kristina Tornqvist, Morten Jorgensen; **D:** Bille August; **W:** Bille August. Academy Awards '88: Best Foreign Language Film; Nominations: Best Actor (von Sydow); Cannes Film Festival '88: Best Film; Golden Globe Awards '89: Best Foreign Film. **VHS, Beta $19.98** HBO, ING ✗✗✗✗

Penalty Phase An up-for-election judge must decide a murder case in which his future, as well as the defendant's, is in question. Made for television.
1986 94m/C Peter Strauss, Melissa Gilbert, Jonelle Allen; **D:** Tony Richardson; **M:** Ralph Burns. **VHS, Beta $19.95** STE, NWV ✗✗

Pendulum A police captain struggles to prove himself innocent of his wife's—and his wife's lover's—murders. Wow.
1969 (PG) 106m/C George Peppard, Jean Seberg, Richard Kiley, Madeline Sherwood, Charles McGraw, Marj Dusay; **D:** George Schaefer. **VHS, Beta $59.95** COL ✗✗

The Penitent A remote village's annual reenactment of the crucifixion of Christ serves as the backdrop for Assante's affair with his friend's (Julia) wife. Quirky little tale that focuses a shade too much on the romantic problems of the trio rather than the intriguing religious practices going on around them.
1988 (PG-13) 94m/C Raul Julia, Armand Assante, Rona Freed, Julie Carmen; **D:** Cliff Osmond. **VHS, Beta $29.95** LIV ✗✗

Penitentiary A realistic story of a black fighter who survives his prison incarceration by winning bouts against the other prisoners. Well-made and executed, followed by two progressively worse sequels.
1979 (R) 99m/C Leon Isaac Kennedy, Jamaa Fanaka; **D:** Jamaa Fanaka; **W:** Jamaa Fanaka. **VHS, Beta $59.95** UNI, FCT ✗✗½

Penitentiary 2 A welterweight fighter is after the man who murdered his girlfriend, who, luckily, is incarcerated in the same prison as Our Hero. Sometimes things just work out right.
1982 (R) 108m/C Leon Isaac Kennedy, Mr. T, Leif Erickson, Ernie Hudson, Glynn Turman; **D:** Jamaa Fanaka; **W:** Jamaa Fanaka. **VHS, Beta $14.95** MGM, HHE ✗

Penitentiary 3 Once again, Kennedy as the inmate boxer extraordinaire punches his way out of various prison battles. Another punch-drunk sequel.
1987 (R) 91m/C Leon Isaac Kennedy, Anthony Geary, Steve Antin, Ric Mancini, Kessler Raymond, Jim Bailey; **D:** Jamaa Fanaka; **W:** Jamaa Fanaka. **VHS, Beta $19.98** WAR ✗½

Penn and Teller Get Killed The comedy team with a cult following are pursued by an assassin through dozens of pratfalls in this dark comedy.
1990 91m/C Penn Jillette, Teller, Caitlin Clarke, Leonardo Cimino, David Patrick Kelly; **D:** Arthur Penn. **VHS, Beta $89.95** WAR ✗✗

Pennies From Heaven Underrated, one-of-a-kind musical about a horny sheet-music salesman in Chicago and his escapades during the Depression. Extraordinary musical sequences have stars lip-synching to great effect. Martin is only somewhat acceptable as the hapless salesman, but Peters and Harper deliver powerful performances as the women whose lives he ruins. Walken brings down the house in a stunning song-and-dance sequence. Adapted by Dennis Potter from his British television series. ♫The Clouds Will Soon Roll By; Did You Ever See A Dream Walking?; Yes, Yes; Pennies From Heaven; Love Is Good for Anything That Ails You; I Want to Be Bad; Let's Misbehave; Life Is Just a Bowl of Cherries; Let's Face the Music and Dance.
1981 (R) 107m/C Steve Martin, Bernadette Peters, Christopher Walken, Jessica Harper, Vernel Bagneris; **D:** Herbert Ross; **W:** Dennis Potter; **M:** Ralph Burns, Marvin Hamlisch. Academy Awards '81 Nominations: Best Adapted Screenplay, Best Costume Design, Best Sound; Golden Globe Awards '82: Best Actress—Musical/Comedy (Peters). **VHS, Beta $19.99** MGM, FCT ✗✗✗½

Penny Serenade Newlyweds adopt a child, but tragedy awaits. Simplistic story nonetheless proves to be a moving experience. They don't make 'em like this anymore, and no one plays Grant better than Grant. Dunne is adequate. Also available colorized.
1941 120m/B Cary Grant, Irene Dunne, Beulah Bondi, Edgar Buchanan; **D:** George Stevens. **VHS $9.95** CNG, NOS, PSM ✗✗✗

Penthouse Baxter is a corporation lawyer who, for a change of pace, defends a gangland boss (Pendleton). His success loses him his high-society clientele but wins him Pendleton's respect and protection. But Baxter then gets involved in a further series of gang-related crimes, which nearly cost him his life. Also aiding Baxter is Loy, playing a smart-cookie gun moll, who would take her wisecracks to "The Thin Man" the following year. Good combo of melodrama, suspense, and humor. **AKA:** Crooks in Clover.
1933 90m/B Warner Baxter, Myrna Loy, Nat Pendleton, C. Henry Gordon, Mae Clarke, Charles Butterworth, Phillips Holmes; **D:** Woodbridge S. Van Dyke.MGM ✗✗✗

The Penthouse Givens stars as a wealthy young woman stalked by an old boyfriend who just happens to have escaped from a mental institution. When he traps her in her home, she has two choices—love him or die. Based on the novel by Elleston Trevor.
1992 93m/C Robin Givens, David Hewlett, Cedric Smith, Donnelly Rhodes, Robert Guillaume; **D:** David Greene. **VHS $89.98** TTC ✗✗

The People A young teacher takes a job in a small town and finds out that her students have telepathic powers and other strange qualities. Adapted from a novel by Zenna Henderson. Good atmosphere, especially for a TV movie.
1971 74m/C Kim Darby, Dan O'Herlihy, Diane Varsi, William Shatner; **D:** John Korty; **M:** Carmine Coppola. **VHS, Beta $59.95** PSM ✗✗½

People Are Funny Battling radio producers vie to land the big sponsor with an original radio idea. Comedy ensues when one of them comes up with a great idea—stolen from a local station.
1946 94m/B Jack Haley, Rudy Vallee, Ozzie Nelson, Art Linkletter, Helen Walker; D: Sam White. VHS, Beta $29.95 NO ♫♫

The People Next Door Seventies attempt at exposing the drug problems of suburban youth. Typical middle-class parents Wallach and Harris are horrified to discover that daughter Winters is strung out on LSD. They fight to expose the neighborhood pusher while struggling to understand their now-alien daughter. Based on J.P. Miller's television play.
1970 93m/C Deborah Winters, Eli Wallach, Julie Harris, Stephen McHattie, Hal Holbrook, Cloris Leachman, Nehemiah Persoff; D: David Greene. VHS NO ♫♫

The People That Time Forgot Sequel to "The Land That Time Forgot," based on the Edgar Rice Burroughs novel. A rescue team returns to a world of prehistoric monsters to rescue a man left there after the first film.
1977 (PG) 90m/C Doug McClure, Patrick Wayne, Sarah Douglas, Dana Gillespie, Thorley Walters, Shane Rimmer; D: Kevin Connor. VHS, Beta $9.98 SUE ♫♫½

The People Under the Stairs Adams is part of a scheme to rob a house in the slums owned by a mysterious couple (Robie and McGill, both of "Twin Peaks" fame). After his friends are killed off in a gruesome fashion, he discovers that the couple aren't the house's only strange inhabitants—homicidal creatures also lurk within.
1991 (R) 102m/C Everett McGill, Wendy Robie, Brandon Adams, Ving Rhames, A.J. Langer, Sean Whalen; D: Wes Craven; W: Wes Craven; M: Don Peake. VHS, Beta $19.98 MCA ♫♫½

The People vs. Jean Harris Follows the trial of Jean Harris. Shortly before this film was released, she had been convicted of murder in the death of Dr. Herman Tarnower, the author of "The Scarsdale Diet." Harris was a head mistress in a private school all the while. Made for television. Burstyn was nominated for an Emmy Award for best actress.
1981 147m/C Ellen Burstyn, Martin Balsam, Richard Dysart, Peter Coyote, Priscilla Morrill, Sarah Marshall, Millie Slavin; D: George Schaefer; M: Brad Fiedel. VHS, Beta NO ♫♫♫

People Who Own the Dark A group of wealthy men and a coterie of call girls are having an orgy in the basement of an old home when a nuclear war breaks out. Everyone outside is blinded by the blast but some survivors manage to make their way to the house where they try to attack the inhabitants. Don't bother.
1975 (R) 87m/C Paul Naschy, Tony Kendall, Maria Perschy, Terry Kemper, Tom Weyland, Anita Brock, Paul Mackey; D: Armando de Ossorio; W: Armando de Ossorio. VHS $19.95 SUN, MRV Woof!

People Will Talk Grant plays Dr. Noah Praetorius, a doctor and educator who believes that the mind is a better healer than medicine. Arch enemy Cronyn is the fellow instructor with a vengeance. Sickened by Grant's goodwill and the undying attention he receives, Cronyn reports Grant's unconventional medical practices to the higher-ups in hopes of ruining his reputation as doctor/educator. Witty and satirical, this well-crafted comedy-drama is chock full of interesting characters and finely-tuned dialog. Adapted

from the play "Dr. Praetorius" by Curt Goetz.
1951 110m/B Cary Grant, Jeanne Crain, Finlay Currie, Hume Cronyn, Walter Slezak, Sidney Blackmer, Basil Ruysdael, Katherine Locke, Margaret Hamilton, Carleton Young, Billy House, Stuart Holmes; D: Joseph L. Mankiewicz; W: Joseph L. Mankiewicz. VHS $19.99 FXV ♫♫♫½

People's Choice A small town boy suffers laryngitis, becomes a radio personality via his new huskiness, and claims he's a notorious criminal.
1946 68m/B Drew Kennedy, Louise Arthur, George Meeker, Rex Lease, Fred Kelsey. VHS, Beta NO ♫♫

Pepe Le Moko An influential French film about a notorious gangster holed up in the Casbah, emerging at his own peril out of love for a beautiful woman. Stirring film established Gabin as a matinee idol. Cinematography is particularly fine too. Based upon the D'Ashelbe novel. The basis for both "Algiers," the popular Boyer-Lamarr melodrama, and the musical "The Casbah." In French with English subtitles.
1937 87m/B Jean Gabin, Mireille Balin, Gabriel Gabrio, Lucas Gridoux; D: Julien Duvivier. VHS, Beta, 8mm $24.95 VYY, NOS, HHT ♫♫♫

Pepi, Luci, Bom and Other Girls on the Heap Almodovar's low-budget directorial debut will be of interest primarily to the director's aficionados. Pepi (Maura's debut role) is a Madrid heiress who gets in trouble when her neighbor, a policeman, notices her marijuana plants. She offers sexual favors in return for silence but is raped instead. Pepi later decides on revenge by seducing Luci, the policeman's wife, aided by her girlfriend, Bom. There's lots of partying, drugs, promiscuity, and violence, none of it very involving. In Spanish with English subtitles. AKA: Pepi, Luci, Bom y Otras Chicas del Monton.
1980 80m/C Carmen Maura, Eva Siva, Olivido Gara, Felix Rotaeta; D: Pedro Almodovar; W: Pedro Almodovar. VHS $79.95 FCT, ING, CCN ♫½

Pepper International intrigue and super spying abound in fast-paced, sexy, and not altogether intelligent adventure featuring Pepper, a female secret agent in the James Bond tradition.
1982 88m/C VHS, Beta $69.95 VES ♫½

Pepper and His Wacky Taxi Father of four buys a '59 Cadillac and starts a cab company. Time-capsule fun.
1972 (G) 79m/C John Astin, Frank Sinatra Jr., Jackie Gayle, Alan Sherman; D: Alex Grasshof. VHS, Beta $19.95 UNI ♫½

Peppermint Soda Kury's affecting directorial debut is a semi-autobiographical tale of two teenaged sisters set in 1963 Paris. Seen through the eyes of the 13-year-old Anne, who lives with 15-year-old sister Frederique and their divorced mother, this is the year of first loves, strict teachers, dreaded family vacations, and a general awareness of growing up. Sweet look at adolescence and all its embarassing tribulations. In French with English subtitles.
1977 97m/C Eleonore Klarwein, Odile Michel, Anouk Ferjac, Tsilla Chelton, Coralie Clement, Marie-Veronique Maurin, Puterflam; D: Diane Kurys; W: Diane Kurys. VHS $79.95 NYF, BTV, FCT ♫♫♫

Perfect A "Rolling Stone" reporter goes after the shallowness of the Los Angeles health club scene, and falls in love with the aerobics instructor he is going to write about. "Rolling Stone" publisher Wenner plays himself. As bad as it sounds.

1985 (R) 120m/C John Travolta, Jamie Lee Curtis, Carly Simon, Marilu Henner, Laraine Newman, Jann Wenner, Anne DeSalvo; D: James Bridges; W: James Bridges, Aaron Latham; M: Ralph Burns. VHS, Beta $14.95 COL ♫½

The Perfect Bride A pretty young nurse prepares to marry her fiance, but his sister thinks she is hiding a secret. Could the bride-to-be have murder on her mind? Made for cable.
1991 (R) 95m/C Sammi Davis-Voss, Kelly Preston, Linden Ashby, Marilyn Rockafellow, Ashley Tillman; D: Terrence O'Hara. VHS, Beta $89.98 FXV, VTR ♫½

Perfect Crime A Scotland Yard inspector must find out who has been killing off executives of a powerful world trust.
1978 90m/C Joseph Cotten, Anthony Steel, Janet Agren. VHS, Beta NO ♫♫

Perfect Family Standard woman-and-kids-in-peril-from-psycho tale. Maggie is a recent widow with two young daughters who's looking for a nanny and a handyman. She hires brother and sister combo Janice and Alan, who, of course, are too good to be true. One is a sociopath who has murdered a family once before. Guess along with Maggie who the nut might be.
1992 (R) 92m/C Jennifer O'Neill, Bruce Boxleitner, Joanna Cassidy, Juliana Hansen, Shiri Appleby; D: E.W. Swackhamer; W: Christian Stoianovich, Phoebe Dorin; M: Nicholas Pike. VHS, Beta PAR ♫♫

Perfect Furlough A corporal wins a week in Paris with a movie star, accompanied by a female Army psychologist. Pretty bizarre, but it works. AKA: Strictly for Pleasure.
1959 93m/C Tony Curtis, Janet Leigh, Keenan Wynn, Linda Cristal, Elaine Stritch; D: Blake Edwards. VHS, Beta $14.95 BAR, MLB ♫♫

Perfect Harmony Racial conflict at an exclusive Southern boys school in 1950s South Carolina is overcome through friendship and the love of music in this sentimental tale. Made for cable television.
1991 93m/C Peter Scolari, Darren McGavin, Catherine Mary Stewart, Moses Gunn, Cleavon Little, Justin Whalin, David Faustino, Richie Havens, Eugene Boyd; D: Will MacKenzie. VHS, Beta $39.99 DIS ♫½

Perfect Killer Van Cleef stars as a world weary Mafia hit-man who is double-crossed by his girl, set up by his best friend, and hunted by another hired assassin. AKA: Satanic Mechanic.
1977 (R) 85m/C Lee Van Cleef, Tita Barker, John Ireland, Robert Widmark; D: Marlon Sirko. VHS, Beta PSM ♫♫

A Perfect Little Murder Marsha is expecting an uneventful life of barbecues and Little League when her family settles down in the suburbs. But then she overhears a murder plot and someone finds out she knows. Made for television. AKA: A Quiet Little Neighborhood, A Perfect Little Murder.
1990 94m/C Teri Garr, Robert Urich, Susan Ruttan, Jeffrey Tambor, Tom Poston, Florence Stanley, Gail Edwards, Alex Rocco; D: Anson Williams; W: Mark Stein. VHS $89.98 TTC ♫♫½

The Perfect Marriage Tired comedy about a perfect couple who decide they can't stand each other anymore after ten years of marriage. Good cast makes the most of weak script. Based on the play by Samuel Raphaelson.
1946 88m/B Loretta Young, David Niven, Eddie Albert, Charlie Ruggles, ZaSu Pitts, Jerome Cowan, Rita Johnson; D: Lewis Allen; W: Leonard Spigelgass. VHS $19.98 MCA ♫♫

Perfect Match A timid young woman and an unambitious young man meet each other through the personal ads and then lie to each other about who they are and what they do for a living.
1988 (PG) 93m/C Marc McClure, Jennifer Edwards, Diane Stilwell, Rob Paulsen, Karen Witter; *D:* Mark Deimel. **VHS, Beta $79.98** *MCG* 🎬🎬

A Perfect Spy In this BBC miniseries, John le Carre takes a break from the world of George Smiley to take a look at spying from a personal view. Magnus Pym (Evan) would seem to be the perfect English gentleman; having gone to the right schools he proceeds to join the covert world of espionage. But Magnus hides the secret that his estranged father is a con man par excellence and it leads him to his own betrayals. Adapted from the novel, which le Carre is said to have drawn from his own past. On three cassettes. *AKA:* John le Carre's A Perfect Spy.
1988 360m/C Peter Egan, Ray McAnally, Frances Tomelty, Benedict Taylor, Tim Healy; *W:* Arthur Hopcraft. **VHS $79.98** *FOX, SIG* 🎬🎬½

Perfect Strangers Thriller develops around a murder and the child who witnesses it. The killer attempts to kidnap the young boy, but problems arise when he falls in love with the lad's mother. *AKA:* Blind Alley.
1984 (R) 90m/C Anne Carlisle, Brad Rijn, John Woehrle, Matthew Stockley, Ann Magnuson, Stephen Lack; *D:* Larry Cohen; *W:* Larry Cohen. **VHS, Beta $24.98** *SUE, NLC* 🎬

Perfect Timing Soft-core film about a fledgling photographer who can't turn his orgy-like photo sessions into anything profitable.
1984 87m/C Stephen Markle, Michelle Scarabelli; *D:* Rene Bonniere. **VHS, Beta $69.98** *LIV* Woof!

Perfect Victims Beautiful models are being hunted by a killer, and a police officer wants to catch the psychopath before he strikes again.
1987 (R) 100m/C Deborah Shelton, Clarence Williams III, Lyman Ward, Tom Dugan; *D:* Shuki Levy. **VHS, Beta $29.95** *ACA* 🎬

The Perfect Weapon Kenpo karate master Speakman severs family ties and wears funny belt in order to avenge underworld murder of his teacher.
1991 (R) 85m/C Jeff Sanders, Jeff Speakman; *D:* Mark DiSalle; *W:* David Wilson; *M:* Gary Chang. **VHS, Beta $14.95** *PAR* 🎬🎬

Perfect Witness A restaurant owner witnesses a mob slaying and resists testifying against the culprit to save his family and himself. Made for cable television. Filmed in New York City.
1989 104m/C Brian Dennehy, Aidan Quinn, Stockard Channing, Laura Harrington, Joe Grifasi; *D:* Robert Mandel; *M:* Brad Fiedel. **VHS, Beta $89.99** *HBO* 🎬🎬½

A Perfect World Butch Haynes (Costner) is an escaped con who takes 8-year-old fatherless Phillip (Lowther) as a hostage in 1963 Texas and is pursued by Texas Ranger Red Garnett (Eastwood). Butch is a bad guy and the film never tries to make him heroic but it also allows him to grow attached to Phillip and acknowledge him as a surrogate son. Costner gives a quiet and strong performance and the remarkable Lowther never goes wrong in his role as the needy little boy. Eastwood's role is strictly secondary as the well-tested lawman who understands justice without seeking vengeance. Somewhat draggy—especially the protracted final scene.

1993 (PG-13) 138m/C Kevin Costner, T.J. Lowther, Clint Eastwood, Laura Dern, Keith Szarabajka, Leo Burmester, Paul Hewitt, Bradley Whitford, Ray McKinnon, Wayne Dehart, Jennifer Griffin, Linda Hart; *D:* Clint Eastwood; *W:* John Lee Hancock; *M:* Lennie Niehaus. **VHS $96.03** *WAR* 🎬🎬

Perfectly Normal Two friends end up in hilarious situations when one opens an eccentric restaurant with a mysterious, newly found fortune.
1991 (R) 106m/C Michael Riley, Robbie Coltrane, Kenneth Welsh, Eugene Lipinski; *D:* Yves Simoneau; *W:* Eugene Lipinski, Paul Quarrington. **VHS, Beta $19.95** *ACA* 🎬🎬

Performance Grim and unsettling psychological account of a criminal who hides out in a bizarre house occupied by a peculiar rock star and his two female companions. Entire cast scores high marks, with Pallenberg especially compelling as a somewhat mysterious and attractive housemate to mincing Jagger. A cult favorite, with music by Nitzsche under the direction of Randy Newman.
1970 (R) 104m/C James Fox, Mick Jagger, Anita Pallenberg; *D:* Donald Cammell, Nicolas Roeg; *W:* Donald Cammell; *M:* Jack Nitzsche. **VHS, Beta $19.98** *WAR* 🎬🎬🎬½

Perfume Five beautiful, black childhood friends join together to conquer the cosmetics industry with their new perfume, Sassy. But can they resist all the temptations success brings and keep both their company and their friendship?
1991 98m/C Cheryl Francis Harrington, Kathleen Bradley Overton, Shy Jefferson, Lynn Marlin, Eugina Wright, Ted Lange; *D:* Roland S. Jefferson. **VHS $89.95** *XVC* 🎬½

Perfumed Nightmare Unique, appealing fable about a Filipino youth who discovers the drawbacks of social and cultural progress when he moves to Paris. Director Tahimik also plays the lead role. Imaginative, yet remarkably economical, this film was produced for $10,000 and received the International Critics Award at the Berlin Film Festival. In Tagalog with English dialogue and subtitles.
1989 93m/C Kidlat Tahimik, Dolores Santamaria, Georgette Baudry, Katrin Muller, Harmut Lerch; *D:* Kidlat Tahimik. **VHS $17.00** *UWA* 🎬🎬🎬

Peril From the novel "Sur La Terre Comme Au Ciel" by Rene Belletto. Deals with a music teacher's infiltration into a wealthy family and the sexually motivated, back-stabbing murder plots that ensue. DeVille does poorly with avant-garde technique. In French with English subtitles. *AKA:* Peril en la Demeure.
1985 (R) 100m/C Michel Piccoli, Christophe MaLavoy, Richard Bohringer, Nicole Garcia, Anais Jeanneret; *D:* Michel DeVille; *W:* Michel DeVille. **VHS, Beta $59.95** *ING* 🎬🎬½

The Perils of Gwendoline A young woman leaves a convent to search for her long-lost father, in this adaptation of a much funnier French comic strip of the same name. What ends up on the screen is merely a very silly rip-off of the successful "Raiders of the Lost Ark," and of primary interest for its numerous scenes of amply endowed Kitaen in the buff. *AKA:* Gwendoline; The Perils of Gwendoline in the Land of the Yik-Yak.
1984 (R) 88m/C Tawny Kitaen, Brent Huff, Zabou, Bernadette LaFont, Jean Rougerie; *D:* Just Jaeckin. **VHS, Beta $79.98** *LIV, VES* 🎬🎬½

The Perils of Pauline All 12 episodes of this classic melodrama/adventure serial in one package, featuring dastardly villains, cliff-hanging predicaments, and worldwide chases.

1934 238m/B Evelyn Knapp, Robert Allen, James Durkin, Sonny Ray, Pat O'Malley; *D:* Ray Taylor. **VHS, Beta $29.95** *NOS, VYY, MLB* 🎬🎬½

The Perils of Pauline A musical biography of Pearl White, the reigning belle of silent movie serials. Look for lots of silent film stars.
1947 96m/C Betty Hutton, John Lund, Constance Collier, William Demarest, Billy DeWolfe; *D:* George Marshall; *M:* Frank Loesser. **VHS, Beta $19.95** *CNG, NOS, PSM* 🎬🎬

Perils of the Darkest Jungle Tiger Woman battles money-mad oil profiteers to protect her tribe. This twelve episode serial comes on two tapes. *AKA:* The Tiger Woman; Jungle Gold.
1944 180m/B Linda Stirling, Allan "Rocky" Lane, Duncan Renaldo, George Lewis; *D:* Spencer Gordon Bennet. **VHS $29.95** *REP, MLB* 🎬🎬½

Period of Adjustment Heartwarming comedy about young newlyweds adjusting to the pressures of domestic life and trying to help the troubled marriage of an older couple. Based on the play by Tennessee Williams.
1962 112m/B Anthony (Tony) Franciosa, Jane Fonda, Jim Hutton, Lois Nettleton, John McGiver, Jack Albertson; *D:* George Roy Hill; *W:* Isobel Lennart. **VHS $19.98** *MGM* 🎬🎬

Periphery Shot in Berlin, this fictional narrative tells the story of a group of refugees from WWII who build their own society in which they communicate telepathically. They are hunted down by the press and the police. The film raises questions about the inability of society to deal with alternative lifestyles.
1986 29m/C VHS *NO* 🎬🎬½

Permanent Record Hyper-sincere drama about a popular high schooler's suicide and the emotional reactions of those he left behind. Great performance from Reeves. Cinematography by Frederick Elmes.
1988 (PG-13) 92m/C Alan Boyce, Keanu Reeves, Michelle Meyrink, Jennifer Rubin, Pamela Gidley, Michael Elgart, Richard Bradford, Barry Corbin, Kathy Baker; *D:* Marisa Silver; *W:* Jarre Fees, Alice Liddle, Larry Ketron; *M:* Joe Strummer. **VHS, Beta $89.95** *PAR* 🎬🎬½

Permanent Vacation A young man disenchanted with New York City decides to escape to Europe to forget about his problems.
1984 80m/C John Lurie, Chris Parker; *D:* Jim Jarmusch; *W:* Jim Jarmusch; *M:* John Lurie. **VHS, Beta** *NO* 🎬🎬½

Permission To Kill Grim spy drama features Bogard as an agent determined to prevent the return of a third-world radical to a totalitarian state.
1975 (PG) 96m/C Dirk Bogarde, Ava Gardner, Timothy Dalton, Frederic Forrest; *D:* Cyril Frankel; *M:* Richard Rodney Bennett. **VHS, Beta $39.98** *SUE* 🎬🎬½

Permissive Stride teaches Singleton how to live along the edges of the underground music world with the other groupies and flunkies.
19?? ?m/C Maggie Stride, Gay Singleton, Gilbert Wynne; *D:* Lindsay Shonteff; *W:* Jeremy Craig Dryden. **VHS $79.95** *NMD* 🎬🎬

Perry Mason Returns Perry Mason returns to solve another baffling mystery. This time he must help his longtime assistant, Della Street, when she is accused of killing her new employer.
1985 95m/C Raymond Burr, Barbara Hale, William Katt, Patrick O'Neal, Richard Anderson, Cassie Yates, Al Freeman Jr.; *D:* Ron Satlof. **VHS, Beta $29.98** *MCG* 🎬🎬🎬

Perry Mason: The Case of the Lost Love Super-lawyer Mason defends the husband of a former lover he hadn't seen in 30 years. The solution to the mystery may catch viewer off guard.
1987 98m/C Raymond Burr, Barbara Hale, William Katt, Jean Simmons, Gene Barry, Robert Walden, Stephen Elliott, Robert Mandan, David Ogden Stiers; **D:** Ron Satlof. **VHS $19.95** *STE* 🐾🐾½

Persona A famous actress turns mute and is treated by a talkative nurse at a secluded cottage. As their relationship turns increasingly tense, the women's personalitites begin to merge. Memorable, unnerving—and atypically avant garde—fare from cinema giant Bergman. First of several collaborations between the director and leading lady Ullman. In Swedish with English subtitles.
1966 100m/C Bibi Andersson, Liv Ullmann, Gunnar Bjornstrand, Margareta Krook; **D:** Ingmar Bergman; **W:** Ingmar Bergman. **VHS, Beta, 8mm $19.98** *MGM, VYY, VDM* 🐾🐾🐾🐾

Personal Best Lesbian lovers compete while training for the 1990 Olympics. Provocative fare often goes where few films have gone before, but overly stylized direction occasionally overwhelms characterizations. It gleefully exploits locker-room nudity, with Hemingway in her pre-implant days. Still, an ambitious, often accomplished production. Towne's directorial debut.
1982 (R) 126m/C Mariel Hemingway, Scott Glenn, Patrice Donnelly; **D:** Robert Towne; **W:** Robert Towne; **M:** Jack Nitzsche. **VHS, Beta $69.95** *WAR* 🐾🐾🐾

Personal Exemptions In this stock comedy a frenzied IRS auditor learns that her daughter is smuggling aliens into the country, her son is brokering with some businessmen she's targeted for tax fraud, and her husband is having an affair with a high-school girl.
1988 (PG) 100m/C Nanette Fabray, John Cotton; **D:** Peter Rowe. **VHS, Beta $14.95** *HMD* 🐾½

Personal Property Taylor tries every trick in the book to win Harlow over in this MGM romantic fluff. Not that big on laughs, but plenty of good shots of Harlow and a beefcake scene of Taylor in a bathtub, who was the darling of the MGM lot and worked with every leading lady. This was the only film Harlow and Taylor made together. Remake of the 1931 film "The Man in Possession." **AKA:** The Man in Possession.
1937 84m/B Robert Taylor, Jean Harlow, Reginald Owen, Una O'Connor, E.E. Clive, Henrietta Crosman, Cora Witherspoon; **D:** Woodbridge S. Van Dyke; **W:** Hugh Mills. **VHS $19.98** *MGM* 🐾🐾½

Personal Services A bawdy satire loosely based on the life and times of Britain's modern-day madam, Cynthia Payne, and her rise to fame in the world of prostitution. Payne's earlier years were featured in the film "Wish You Were Here."
1987 (R) 104m/C Julie Walters, Alec McCowen, Shirley Stelfox, Tim Woodward, David Atkins, Danny Schiller, Victoria Hardcastle; **D:** Terry Jones; **W:** David Leland; **M:** John Du Prez. **VHS, Beta $29.98** *LIV, VES* 🐾🐾½

The Personals A recently divorced young man takes out a personal ad in a newspaper to find the woman of his dreams. But it isn't quite that simple in this independent comedy shot entirely in Minneapolis.
1983 (PG) 90m/C Bill Schoppert, Karen Landry, Paul Eiding, Michael Laskin, Vickie Dakil; **D:** Peter Markle. **VHS, Beta $29.98** *SUE* 🐾🐾½

Personals Chilling drama that casts O'Neill as an unnoticed librarian, until she begins to meet (and kill) the men who answer her ads. Zimbalist is a widow who is determined to learn the truth. Made for television.
1990 93m/C Stephanie Zimbalist, Jennifer O'Neill, Robin Thomas, Clark Johnson, Gina Gallego, Rosemary Dunsmore, Colm Feore; **D:** Steven Hilliard Stern. **VHS, Beta $79.95** *PAR* 🐾🐾

The Persuaders The first two episodes of Moore and Curtis as international playboy crime fighters.
1971 52m/C Roger Moore, Tony Curtis, Alex Scott, Joan Collins, Robert Hutton; **D:** Basil Dearden. **VHS, Beta** *NO* 🐾🐾

The Perverse Countess Romay is a bored tourist who spends a free weekend on a fling with Woods, who procures human flesh for the cannibalistic Count and Countess Zaroff (Vernon and Arno). Romay accompanies her lover to the haunted castle on a delivery, not realizing she is the package. When the Countess sees what a succulent bon-bon Romay is, she faces difficult choices. Subtitled in English. **AKA:** La Comtesse Perverse.
1973 86m/C Lina Romay, Robert Woods, Howard Vernon, Alice Arno, Caroline Riviere; **D:** Jess (Jesus) Franco. **VHS $27.90** *VSM* 🐾

Pet Sematary A quirky adaptation of Stephen King's bestseller about a certain patch of woods in the Maine wilderness that rejuvenates the dead, and how a newly located college MD eventually uses it to restore his dead son. Mildly creepy.
1989 (R) 103m/C Dale Midkiff, Fred Gwynne, Denise Crosby, Stephen King; **D:** Mary Lambert; **W:** Stephen King; **M:** Elliot Goldenthal. **VHS, Beta, 8mm $14.95** *PAR* 🐾🐾

Pet Sematary 2 Lame sequel to original Stephen King flick. After seeing his mother electrocuted, a teen and his veterinarian father move to the Maine town where the legendary Pet Sematary is located. Horror begins when the boy's friend's dog is shot by his stepfather, and the boys bury the dog in the "sematary." King wasn't involved with this film, so the story isn't very coherent, but shock value and special effects are great. Not recommended for those with a weak stomach.
1992 (R) 102m/C Anthony Edwards, Edward Furlong, Clancy Brown, Jared Rushton, Darlanne Fluegel, Lisa Waltz, Jason McGuire, Sarah Trigger; **D:** Mary Lambert; **W:** Richard Outten. **VHS, Beta** *PAR* 🐾½

Pete Kelly's Blues A jazz musician in a Kansas City speakeasy is forced to stand up against a brutal racketeer. The melodramatic plot is brightened by a nonstop flow of jazz tunes sung by Lee and Fitzgerald and played by an all-star lineup that includes Dick Cathcart, Matty Matlock, Eddie Miller and George Van Eps. ♫Sugar; Sombody Loves Me; Bye Bye Blackbird; What Can I Say After I Say I'm Sorry?; He Needs Me; Sing a Rainbow; Pete Kelly's Blues.
1955 96m/C Jack Webb, Janet Leigh, Edmond O'Brien, Lee Marvin, Martin Milner, Peggy Lee, Ella Fitzgerald, Jayne Mansfield; **D:** Jack Webb. **VHS, Beta $19.98** *WAR* 🐾🐾

Pete 'n' Tillie Amiable comedy turns to less appealing melodrama as couple meets, marries, and endures tragedy. Film contributes little to director Ritt's hitt-and-miss reputation, but Matthau and Burnett shine in leads. Adapted by Julius J. Epstein from a Peter de Vries' story.
1972 (PG) 100m/C Walter Matthau, Carol Burnett, Geraldine Page, Barry Nelson, Rene Auberjonois, Lee Montgomery, Henry Jones, Kent Smith; **D:** Martin Ritt; **W:** Julius J. Epstein;

M: John Williams. Academy Awards '72 Nominations: Best Adapted Screenplay, Best Supporting Actress (Page); British Academy Awards '73: Best Actor (Matthau). **VHS, Beta $14.98** *MCA* 🐾🐾½

Pete Townshend: White City The Who guitarist portrays a musician who helps bring a close friend and and his estranged wife back together. This semi-autobiographical film includes music from Townsend.
1985 60m/C Pete Townshend, Andrew Wilde, Frances Barber; **D:** Richard Lowenstein. **VHS, Beta $19.95** *MVD, VES* 🐾🐾½

Peter Gunn Detective Peter Gunn returns, only to find himself being hunted by both the mob and the Feds. A TV movie reprise of the vintage series that has none of the original cast members.
1989 97m/C Peter Strauss, Barbara Williams, Jennifer Edwards, Charles Cioffi, Pearl Bailey, Peter Jurasik, David Rappaport; **D:** Blake Edwards. **VHS $19.95** *STE* 🐾🐾

Peter Lundy and the Medicine Hat Stallion A teenaged Pony Express rider must outrun the Indians and battle the elements in order to carry mail from the Nebraska Territory to the West Coast in this made-for-television film. Good family entertainment. **AKA:** The Medicine Hat Stallion; Pony Express.
1977 85m/C Leif Garrett, Mitchell Ryan, Bibi Besch, John Quade, Milo O'Shea; **D:** Michael O'Herlihy. **VHS, Beta $69.98** *LIV, VES, VTR* 🐾🐾½

Peter Pan Disney classic about a boy who never wants to grow up. Based on J.M. Barrie's book and play. Still stands head and shoulders above any recent competition in providing fun family entertainment. Terrific animation and lovely hummable music.
1953 (G) 76m/C D: Hamilton Luske; **V:** Bobby Driscoll, Kathryn Beaumont, Hans Conried, Heather Angel, Candy Candido. **VHS, Beta $24.99** *DIS, APD, HMV* 🐾🐾🐾

Peter Pan A TV classic, this videotape of a performance of the 1954 Broadway musical adapted from the J.M. Barrie classic features Mary Martin in one of her most famous incarnations, as the adolescent Peter Pan. Songs include "I'm Flying," "Neverland," and "I Won't Grow Up."
1960 100m/C Mary Martin, Cyril Ritchard, Sondra Lee, Heather Halliday, Luke Halpin; **D:** Vincent J. Donehue. **VHS, Beta $24.99** *GKK, COL, MLT* 🐾🐾🐾½

Peter the First: Part 1 The first half of Petrov's Soviet epic about the early years of Tsar Peter I's reign. Lavish, in Russian with English subtitles.
1937 95m/B D: Vladimir Petrov. **VHS, Beta $29.95** *FCT, ING* 🐾🐾

Peter the First: Part 2 The second half of Petrov's epic, also titled "The Conquests of Peter the Great," covering the triumphs and final years of the famous Tsar. In Russian with English subtitles.
1938 104m/B D: Vladimir Petrov. **VHS, Beta $29.95** *FCT, ING* 🐾🐾

Peter the Great Dry but eye-pleasing TV mini-series follows the life of Russia's colorful, very tall ruler from childhood on. Much of the interesting cast is wasted in tiny roles.
1986 371m/C Maximilian Schell, Laurence Olivier, Omar Sharif, Vanessa Redgrave, Ursula Andress. **VHS $29.95** *STE* 🐾🐾🐾

Peter's Friends Peter has recently inherited a grand manor house located outside London and invites some chums to celebrate a New Year's Eve weekend, ten years after they've been at university together. So begins another nostalgic trip down memory

lane ala "The Big Chill," but unlike other clones, this one can stand on its own, with a lightweight and sly script by talented comedienne Rudner (in her film debut) and her husband Bergman. If the script sometimes falls a little flat, the fine cast will make up for it. Thompson's mother, actress Law, plays the housekeeper.
1992 (R) 102m/C Kenneth Branagh, Rita Rudner, Emma Thompson, Stephen Fry, Hugh Laurie, Imelda Staunton, Alphonsia Emmanuel, Tony Slattery, Alex Lowe, Alex Scott, Phyllida Law, Richard Briers; **D:** Kenneth Branagh; **W:** Rita Rudner, Martin Bergman; **M:** Jacques Offenbach. **VHS** $92.99 HBO, BTV ♫♫½

Pete's Dragon Elliot, an enormous, bumbling dragon with a penchant for clumsy heroics, becomes friends with poor orphan Pete. Combines brilliant animation with the talents of live actors for an interesting effect.
1977 (G) 128m/C Helen Reddy, Shelley Winters, Mickey Rooney, Jim Dale, Red Buttons, Sean Marshall, Jim Backus, Jeff Conaway; **D:** Don Chaffey; **W:** Malcolm Marmorstein; **V:** Charlie Callas. **VHS, Beta** $24.99 DIS, FCT, WTA ♫♫½

Petit Con A live-action version of the popular French comic strip wherein a young rebel drops out of society to live with aging hippies. With English subtitles.
1984 (R) 90m/C Guy Marchand, Michel Choupon, Caroline Cellier, Bernard Brieux, Soudad Amidou; **D:** Gerard Lauzier. **VHS, Beta** $59.95 LHV ♫♫½

Petrified Forest Patrons and employees are held captive by a runaway gangster's band in a desert diner. Often gripping, with memorable performances from Davis, Howard, and Bogart. Based on the play by Robert Sherwood with Howard and Bogart recreating their stage roles.
1936 83m/B Bette Davis, Leslie Howard, Humphrey Bogart, Dick Foran, Charley Grapewin, Porter Hall; **D:** Archie Mayo. **VHS, Beta** $19.95 FOX, MGM ♫♫♫

Petulia Overlooked, offbeat drama about a flighty woman who spites her husband by dallying with a sensitive, recently divorced surgeon. Classic '60s document and cult favorite offers great performance from the appealing Christie, with Scott fine as the vulnerable surgeon. On-screen performances by the Grateful Dead and Big Brother. Among idiosyncratic director Lester's best. Photographed by Nicholas Roeg. From the novel "Me and the Arch Kook Petulia" by John Haase.
1968 (R) 105m/c George C. Scott, Richard Chamberlain, Julie Christie, Shirley Knight, Arthur Hill, Joseph Cotten, Richard Dysart, Kathleen Widdoes, Austin Pendleton, Rene Auberjonois; **D:** Richard Lester; **W:** Lawrence B. Marcus; **M:** John Barry. **VHS, Beta** $19.98 WAR ♫♫♫♫

Peyton Place Passion, scandal, and deception in a small New England town set the standard for passion, scandal, and deception in soap operadom. Shot on location in Camden, Maine. Performances and themes now seem dated, but produced a blockbuster in its time. Adapted from Grace Metalious' popular novel and followed by "Return to Peyton Place."
1957 157m/C Lana Turner, Hope Lange, Lee Phillips, Lloyd Nolan, Diane Varsi, Lorne Greene, Russ Tamblyn, Arthur Kennedy, Terry Moore, Barry Coe, David Nelson, Betty Field, Mildred Dunnock, Leon Ames, Alan Reed Jr.; **D:** Mark Robson; **W:** John Michael Hayes. **VHS** $39.98 FOX, FCT ♫♫♫

Phaedra Loose and updated adaptation of Euripides' "Hipploytus." Mercouri, the second wife of a rich Greek shipping magnate, is dispatched to London to convince her hus-

band's adult son (Perkins) to come home to Greece. Mercouri and Perkins immediately begin a steamy affair but their return home brings problems for all. Dubbed.
1961 116m/B Melina Mercouri, Anthony Perkins, Raf Vallone, Elizabeth Ercy; **Cameos:** Jules Dassin; **D:** Jules Dassin; **W:** Jules Dassin, Margarita Liberki; **M:** Mikis Theodorakis. **VHS** $29.95 FCT ♫♫

Phantasm A small-budgeted, hallucinatory horror fantasy about two parentless brothers who discover weird goings-on at the local funeral parlor, including the infamous airborne, brain-chewing chrome ball. Creepy, unpredictable nightmare fashioned on a shoestring by young independent producer Coscarelli. Scenes were cut out of the original film to avoid "X" rating. Followed by "Phantasm II."
1979 (R) 90m/C Michael Baldwin, Bill Thornbury, Reggie Bannister, Kathy Lester, Terrie Kalbus, Ken Jones, Susan Harper, Lynn Eastman, David Arntzen, Angus Scrimm, Bill Cone; **D:** Don A. Coscarelli. **VHS, Beta** $14.95 COL, SUE ♫♫½

Phantasm II Teen psychic keeps flashing on villainous Tall Man. A rehash sequel to the original, cultishly idiosyncratic fantasy, wherein more victims are fed into the interdimensional abyss and Mike discovers that the horror is not all in his head. Occasional inspired gore; bloodier than its predecessor. More yuck for the buck.
1988 (R) 97m/C James LeGros, Reggie Bannister, Angus Scrimm; **D:** Don A. Coscarelli. **VHS, Beta** $14.98 MCA ♫♫

The Phantom Rare cheapie of a hooded killer terrorizing a group of people in a haunted house.
1931 62m/C Guinn Williams, Wilfrid Lucas, Sheldon Lewis, Tom O'Brien, William Gould; **D:** Alvin J. Neitz. **VHS** $12.95 SNC, GPV ♫♫

The Phantom Broadcast A popular radio crooner is murdered. The main suspect is his hunchbacked accompanist and manager, who had all along secretly pre-recorded his own velvet voice for the crooner to lip-sync along with. A tightly plotted minor thriller that holds up surprisingly well. **AKA:** Phantom of the Air.
1933 63m/B Ralph Forbes, Gail Patrick, Vivienne Osborne, Guinn Williams, George "Gabby" Hayes; **D:** Phil Rosen. **VHS, Beta, 8mm** $24.95 VYY, NOS, FCT ♫♫½

Phantom Brother A semi-spoof about a teenager left orphaned by a car crash that wiped out his entire family, and who is subsequently haunted by his dead brother. Even thinner than it sounds.
1988 92m/C Jon Hammer, Patrick Molloy, John Gigante, Mary Beth Pelshaw; **D:** William Szarka. **VHS, Beta** $14.95 HMD ♫½

The Phantom Bullet Hoot wants to holler at his father's murderers.
1926 60m/B Hoot Gibson. **VHS, Beta** $16.95 GPV ♫½

The Phantom Chariot A fantasy depicting the Swedish myth about how Death's coach must be driven by the last man to die each year. Silent.
1920 89m/B D: Victor Sjostrom. **VHS, Beta** $16.95 SNC, FCT, GVV ♫♫½

The Phantom Creeps Evil Dr. Zorka, armed with a meteorite chunk which can bring an army to a standstill, provides the impetus for this enjoyable serial in 12 episodes.
1939 235m/B Bela Lugosi, Dorothy Arnold, Robert Kent, Regis Toomey; **D:** Ford Beebe, Saul Goodkind. **VHS, Beta** $19.95 NOS, SNC, VCN ♫♫½

The Phantom Empire Autry faces the futuristic "Thunder Riders" from the subterranean city of Murania, located 20,000 feet beneath his ranch. A complete serial in twelve episodes. If you only see one science fiction western in your life, this is the one. Also available in an edited theatrical version at 80 minutes. **AKA:** Radio Ranch.
1935 245m/B Gene Autry, Frankie Darro, Betsy King Ross, Smiley Burnette; **D:** B. Reeves Eason, Otto Brower. **VHS, Beta** $19.95 NOS, SNC, VYY ♫♫

Phantom Empire A woman who rules over a lost city takes a bunch of scientists prisoner and forces them to be slaves.
1987 (R) 85m/C Ross Hagen, Jeffrey Combs, Dawn Wildsmith, Robert Quarry, Susan Stokey, Michelle (McClellan) Bauer, Russ Tamblyn, Sybil Danning; **D:** Fred Olen Ray. **VHS, Beta** $79.95 PSM ♫♫

Phantom Express Experienced old engineer is dismissed from his job because no one believes his explanation that a mysterious train caused the wreck of his own train. He aims to find justice.
1932 65m/B J. Farrell MacDonald, Sally Blane, William Collier Jr., Hobart Bosworth; **D:** Emory Johnson. **VHS, Beta** $12.95 SNC, NOS, IUF ♫♫

Phantom Fiend A gentle musician becomes a suspect when a series of Jack-the-Ripper type murders terrorize London. Is he the nice guy known by his girlfriend and the people in his lodging house, or is the musician really JTR? Based on the novel "The Lodger" by Marie Belloc-Lowndes.
1935 70m/B Ivor Novello, Elizabeth Allan, A.W. Baskcomb, Jack Hawkins, Barbara Everest, Peter Gawthorne, P. Kynaston Reeves; **D:** Maurice Elvey. **VHS** $29.95 FCT, RXM ♫½

The Phantom Flyer Stunt pilot helps out a cattle-owning frontier family bedeviled by rustlers. Silent.
1928 54m/B Al Wilson. **VHS, Beta, 8mm** $19.95 VYY, GPV, RXM ♫½

Phantom from Space An invisible alien lands on Earth, begins killing people, and is pursued by a pair of scientists.
1953 72m/B Ted Cooper, Rudolph Anders, Noreen Nash, James Seay, Harry Landers; **D:** W. Lee Wilder. **VHS, Beta** $14.95 VYY, SNC, NOS ♫½

The Phantom from 10,000 Leagues Slimy sea monster attacks swimmers and fishermen; investigating oceanographer pretends not to notice monster is hand puppet. Early AIP release, when still named American Releasing Company.
1956 80m/B Kent Taylor, Cathy Downs, Michael Whalen, Helene Stanton, Phillip Pine; **D:** Dan Milner. **VHS** $14.95 VYY, SNC, MLB ♫♫

Phantom Gold The wicked Whitaker claims to have struck it rich but it's really a scam to lure unsuspecting miners to the claim and then rob and murder them. Luden's suspicious and proves Whitaker's a bad guy.
1938 56m/B Jack Luden, Charles "Slim" Whitaker, Beth Marion, Hal Taliaferro, Art Davis; **D:** Joseph Levering. **VHS** $11.95 GPV ♫½

The Phantom in the House A woman commits a murder and has her inventor husband take the rap. While he's in prison, she gets rich off of his work. Things get hairy when he is released thirteen years later and is introduced to his daughter as a friend of the family. Melodramatic film was originally made with and without sound.
1929 64m/B Ricardo Cortez, Nancy Welford, Henry B. Walthall, Grace Valentine; **D:** Phil Rosen. **VHS, Beta** $16.95 SNC ♫♫

Phantom Killer A district attorney tries to hang a murder rap on a most improbable suspect. When the man is aquitted, the DA quits his job to find the truth, which takes a disturbing twist. The plot is a thinly veiled rehash of "The Sphinx" (1933).
1942 61m/B Dick Purcell, Joan Woodbury, John Hamilton, Warren Hymer, Kenneth Harlan, J. Farrell MacDonald, Mantan Moreland; **D:** William Beaudine. **VHS $19.95** *NOS* 🎞🎞

The Phantom Light A lighthouse keeper is murdered under strange circumstances and a mysterious light keeps appearing at the scene. Detective Hale joins up with a navy man and another lighthouse keeper to solve the crime. A low-budget mystery with good atmosphere and some humor.
1935 75m/B Binnie Hale, Gordon Harker, Ian Hunter, Donald Calthrop; **D:** Michael Powell. **VHS** *HCV* 🎞🎞½

Phantom of Chinatown Mr. Wong is called in to solve another murder in the final entry in the series. The first to have an Asian actor portray the lead, as Luke replaced Boris Karloff.
1940 61m/B Keye Luke, Lotus Long, Grant Withers, Paul McVey, Charles Miller; **D:** Phil Rosen. **VHS $16.95** *NOS, SNC, HEG* 🎞

Phantom of Death A brilliant pianist, stricken by a fatal disease that causes rapid aging, goes on a murderous rampage.
1987 (R) 95m/C Michael York, Donald Pleasence, Edwige Fenech; **D:** Ruggero Deodato; **M:** Pino Donaggio. **VHS, Beta $79.95** *VMK* 🎞½

The Phantom of 42nd Street An actor and a cop team up to find the killer of a wealthy uncle.
1945 58m/B Dave O'Brien, Kay Aldridge, Alan Mowbray, Frank Jenks; **D:** Martin Mooney. **VHS $16.95** *SNC, NOS, MRV* 🎞🎞

Phantom of Liberty Master surrealist Bunuel's episodic film wanders from character to character and from event to event. Animals wander through a man's bedroom, soldiers conduct military exercises in an inhabited area, a missing girl stands before her parents even as they futilely attempt to determine her whereabouts, and an assassin is found guilty, then applauded and led to freedom. They don't get much more surreal than this. If you think you may like it, you'll probably love it. Bunuel, by the way, is among the firing squad vicitms in the film's opening enactment of Goya's May 3, 1808. In French with English subtitles. **AKA:** Le Fantome de la Liberte; The Specter of Freedom.
1968 104m/C Adrianna Asti, Jean-Claude Brialy, Michel Piccoli, Adolfo Celi, Monica Vitti; **D:** Luis Bunuel. **VHS, Beta $24.95** *XVC, ING, APD* 🎞🎞🎞½

The Phantom of Soho A Scotland Yard detective investigates the murders of several prominent businessmen and is assisted by a beautiful mystery writer. **AKA:** Das Phantom von Soho.
1964 92m/B Dieter Borsche, Barbara Rutting, Hans Sohnker, Peter Vogel, Helga Sommerfeld, Werner Peters; **D:** Franz Gottlieb. **VHS, Beta $16.95** *SNC* 🎞🎞

Phantom of the Air Twelve chapters of high-flying adventure with Tom Tyler!
1933 230m/B Tom Tyler, Gloria Shea, William Desmond, Leroy Mason, Walter Brennan; **D:** Ray Taylor. **VHS $24.95** *GPV, VCI, MLB* 🎞🎞

Phantom of the Mall: Eric's Revenge A murderous spirit haunts the local mall. Gore flows like water.
1989 91m/C Morgan Fairchild, Kari Whitman, Jonathan Goldsmith, Derek Rydell; **D:** Richard S. Friedman. **VHS, Beta $19.95** *FRH* 🎞

The Phantom of the Opera Deranged, disfigured music lover haunts the sewers of a Parisian opera house and kills to further the career of an unsuspecting young soprano. First of many film versions still packs a wallop, with fine playing from Chaney, Sr. Silent with two-color Technicolor "Bal Masque" sequence. An 88-minute version with an introduction by Christopher Lee is also available.
1925 79m/B Lon Chaney Sr., Norman Kerry, Mary Philbin, Gibson Gowland; **D:** Rupert Julian. **VHS, Beta, 8mm $9.95** *CNG, NOS, FUS* 🎞🎞🎞

The Phantom of the Opera Second Hollywood version—the first with talking—of Gastron Leroux novel about a madman who promotes fear and mayhem at a Paris opera house. Raines is good in lead; Eddy warbles away.
1943 92m/C Claude Rains, Nelson Eddy, Susanna Foster, Edgar Barrier, Leo Carrillo, Hume Cronyn, J. Edward Bromberg; **D:** Arthur Lubin. Academy Awards '43: Best Color Cinematography, Best Interior Decoration; Nominations: Best Sound. **VHS, Beta $14.95** *MCA* 🎞🎞🎞

The Phantom of the Opera A gory, "Elm Street"-ish version of the Gaston Leroux classic, attempting to cash in on the success of the Broadway musical.
1989 (R) 93m/C Robert Englund, Jill Schoelen, Alex Hyde-White, Bill Nighy, Terence Harvey, Stephanie Lawrence; **D:** Dwight Little. **VHS, Beta $14.95** *COL* 🎞½

Phantom of the Paradise A rock 'n roll parody of "Phantom of the Opera." Splashy, only occasionally horrific spoof in which cruel music executive Williams, much to his everlasting regret, swindles a songwriter. Violence ensues. Not for most, or even many, tastes. Graham steals the film as rocker Beef. A failure at the box office, and now a cult item (small enthusiastic cult with few outside interests) for its oddball humor and outrageous rock star parodies. Williams also wrote the turgid score. ♫Goodbye, Eddie, Goodbye; Faust; Upholstery; Special to Me; Old Souls; Somebody Super Like You; Life At Last; The Hell of It; The Phantom's Theme (Beauty and the Beast).
1974 (PG) 92m/C Paul Williams, William Finley, Jessica Harper, Gerrit Graham; **D:** Brian DePalma; **W:** Brian DePalma; **M:** Paul Williams. **VHS, Beta $14.98** *FOX* 🎞🎞

The Phantom of the Range Marion is trying to sell her grandfather's ranch only his "ghost" is scaring everyone away. She and cowpoke Tyler find out a group of evil treasure hunters are searching the property for hidden gold.
1938 59m/B Tom Tyler, Beth Marion, Charles "Blackie" King, Forrest Taylor, John Elliott, Soledad Jiminez, Sammy Cohen; **D:** Bob Hill. **VHS $11.95** *GPV* 🎞½

Phantom of the Ritz Bizarre accidents begin to take place when Ed Blake and his girlfriend start renovating the old Ritz Theater. It seems the theater is inhabited by a rather angry ghost and somebody's got to deal with it before the Ritz can rock and roll. Featuring the fabulous sounds of the Fifties.
1988 (R) 89m/C Peter Bergman, Deborah Van Valkenburgh, The Coasters; **D:** Allen Plone. **VHS, Beta $79.95** *PSM* 🎞🎞

Phantom of the West Ten-episode serial about a rancher who becomes "The Phantom of the West" in order to smoke out his father's killer.
1931 166m/B William Desmond, Thomas Santschi, Tom Tyler; **D:** David Ross Lederman. **VHS, Beta $39.95** *VYY, NOS, VCN* 🎞🎞

Phantom Patrol A mystery writer is kidnapped and someone impersonates him. Mountie Maynard must come to the rescue.
1936 60m/B Kermit Maynard, Joan Barclay, Paul Fix, Julian Rivero, Eddie Phillips, Roger Williams; **D:** Charles Hutchinson. **VHS, Beta $24.95** *DVT, NOS* 🎞½

The Phantom Planet An astronaut crash-lands on an asteroid and discovers a race of tiny people living there. Having breathed the atmosphere, he shrinks to their dimunitive size and aids them in their war against brutal invaders. Infamously peculiar.
1961 82m/B Dean Fredericks, Coleen Gray, Tony Dexter, Dolores Faith, Francis X. Bushman, Richard Kiel; **D:** William Marshall. **VHS, Beta $16.95** *NOS, SNC* 🎞½

Phantom Rancher Roaring melodrama finds Maynard donning a mask to find the real Phantom, who is causing havoc.
1939 61m/B Ken Maynard. **VHS, Beta** *VCI, VCN* 🎞½

Phantom Ranger A federal agent masquerades as a crook to catch a band of counterfeiters.
1938 54m/B Tim McCoy, Suzanne Kaaren, Karl Hackett, John St. Polis, John Merton, Harry Strang; **D:** Sam Newfield. **VHS $19.95** *NOS, DVT* 🎞½

The Phantom Rider Mystery fills the old West in this serial composed of fifteen chapters.
1937 152m/B Buck Jones, Maria Shelton. **VHS, Beta $29.98** *REP, MLB, VCN* 🎞½

The Phantom Rider The masked do-gooder rides the plains protecting the local Indians from some surly settlers. A 12-episode serial.
1946 167m/C Robert Kent, Peggy Stewart, Leroy Mason, Chief Thundercloud. **VHS $29.99** *MOV* 🎞½

Phantom Thunderbolt A man who has falsely spread the rumor that he's a gunfighter is hired to chase away some good-for-nothings.
1933 62m/B Ken Maynard, Frances Lee, Frank Rice, William Gould, Robert F. (Bob) Kortman; **D:** Alan James. **VHS, Beta $19.95** *NOS, DVT, MTX* 🎞½

Phantom Tollbooth A young boy drives his car into an animated world, where the numbers are at war with the letters and he has been chosen to save Rhyme and Reason, to bring stability back to the Land of Wisdom. Completely unique and typically Jonesian in its intellectual level and interests. Bright children will be interested, but this is really for adults who will understand the allegory. Based on Norman Justers' metaphorical novel.
1969 (G) 89m/C **D:** Chuck Jones; **V:** Mel Blanc, Hans Conried. **VHS, Beta $19.95** *MGM, WTA* 🎞🎞🎞

Phar Lap Saga of a legendary Australian racehorse who rose from obscurity to win nearly 40 races in just three years before mysteriously dying in 1932. American version runs 10 minutes shorter than the Aussie one. **AKA:** Phar Lap: Heart of a Nation.
1984 (PG) 107m/C Ron Leibman, Tom Burlinson, Judy Morris, Celia de Burgh; **D:** Simon Wincer; **W:** David Williamson. **VHS, Beta $14.98** *FOX* 🎞🎞½

Pharaoh An expensive Polish epic about the power plays of royalty in ancient Egypt. Dubbed.
1966 125m/B Jerzy Zelnick; **D:** Jerzy Kawalerowicz. **VHS, Beta** *FCT* 🎞🎞

Pharmacist A day in the life of a hapless druggist undone by disgruntled customers and robbers. Typical Fields effort.
1932 19m/B Elise Cavanna, Babe Kane, W.C. Fields, Grady Sutton. **VHS, Beta** $24.98
CCB 🐾🐾 ½

Phase 4 A tale of killer ants retaliating against the humans attempting to exterminate them.
1974 (PG) 84m/C Nigel Davenport, Michael Murphy, Lynne Frederick; **D:** Saul Bass. **VHS, Beta** $39.95 PAR 🐾🐾

Phedre Jean Racine's adaptation of the Greek legend involving Phedre, Theseus, and Hippolyte. Bell is the only one worth watching in this weak and stagy picture. In French with English subtitles.
1968 93m/C Marie Bell; **D:** Pierre Jourdan. **VHS, Beta** $24.95 VYY, APD, ING 🐾🐾 ½

Phenomenal and the Treasure of Tutankamen Fiendish criminal genius steals priceless golden mask of King Tut. Superhero Phenomenal is less than dry spaghetti sci-fi.
197? (R) 90m/C Mauro Parenti, Lucretia Love. **VHS** $29.99 VCI 🐾

Phffft! Holliday and Lemmon are a bored couple who decide to divorce, date others, and take mambo lessons. By no stretch of plausibility, they constantly run into each other and compete in the same mambo contest.
1954 91m/B Judy Holliday, Jack Lemmon, Jack Carson, Kim Novak, Luella Gear, Merry Anders; **D:** Mark Robson; **W:** George Axelrod. **VHS** GKK 🐾🐾 ½

Philadelphia AIDS goes Hollywood as hot-shot corporate attorney Andrew Beckett (Hanks), fired because he has the disease, hires brilliant but homophobic personal injury attorney Washington as his counsel when he sues for discrimination. Box office winner was criticized by some gay activists as too mainstream, which is the point. It doesn't probe deeply into the gay lifestyle, focusing instead on justice and compassion. Boasts a good script, make-up that transforms Hanks, sure direction, great soundtrack, and a strong supporting cast, but all would mean little without Hanks' superb performance, his best to date.
1993 (PG-13) 125m/C Tom Hanks, Denzel Washington, Antonio Banderas, Jason Robards Jr., Joanne Woodward, Mary Steenburgen, Ron Vawter, Robert Ridgely, Obba Babatunde, Robert Castle, Daniel Chapman, Roger Corman, John Bedford Lloyd, Roberta Maxwell, Warren Miller, Anna Deavere Smith, Kathryn Witt, Andre B. Blake, Ann Dowd, Bradley Whitford, Chandra Wilson, Charles Glenn, Peter Jacobs, Paul Lazar, Dan Olmstead, Joey Perillo, Lauren Roselli, Bill Rowe, Lisa Talerico, Daniel von Bargen, Tracey Walter; **Cameos:** Karen Finley, David Drake, Quentin Crisp; **D:** Jonathan Demme; **W:** Ron Nyswaner; **M:** Howard Shore. Academy Awards '93: Best Actor (Hanks), Best Song ("Streets of Philadelphia"); Nominations: Best Makeup, Best Original Screenplay, Best Song ("Philadelphia"); MTV Movie Awards '94: Best Film, Best On-Screen Duo (Tom Hanks/Denzel Washington), Best Song ("Streets of Philadelphia"); Golden Globe Awards '94: Best Actor—Drama (Hanks), Best Song ("Streets of Philadelphia"). **VHS, 8mm** COL 🐾🐾🐾 ½

The Philadelphia Experiment A WWII sailor falls through a hole in time and lands in the mid-1980s, whereupon he woos a gorgeous woman. Sufficient chemistry between Pare and Allen, but PG rating is an indication of the film's less-than-graphic love scenes.

1984 (PG) 101m/C Michael Pare, Nancy Allen, Eric Christmas, Bobby DiCicco; **D:** Stewart Raffill; **W:** Don Jakoby. **VHS, Beta** $19.99 STE 🐾🐾 ½

Philadelphia Experiment 2 Melodramatic sci-fi what-ifer has Germany winning WWII by dropping a bomb on Washington. So southern California is now one big labor camp with an evil mad scientist (Graham) and a beleaguered hero (Johnson) who must time-travel back to 1943 to prevent the Germans from dropping that bomb.
1993 (PG-13) 98m/C Brad Johnson, Gerrit Graham, Marjean Holden, James Greene, Geoffrey Blake, John Christian Grass, Cyril O'Reilly; **D:** Stephen Cornwell; **W:** Kevin Rock, Nick Paine; **M:** Gerald Gouriet. **VHS** $94.95 VMK 🐾🐾 ½

The Philadelphia Story A woman's plans to marry again go awry when her dashing ex-husband arrives on the scene. Matters are further complicated when a loopy reporter—assigned to spy on the nuptials—falls in love with the blushing bride. Classic comedy, with trio of Hepburn, Grant, and Stewart all serving aces. Based on the hit Broadway play by Philip Barry, and remade as the musical "High Society" in 1956 (stick to the original). Also available colorized.
1940 112m/B Katharine Hepburn, Cary Grant, James Stewart, Ruth Hussey, Roland Young, John Howard, John Halliday, Virginia Weidler, Henry Daniell, Hillary Brooke, Mary Nash; **D:** George Cukor; **W:** Donald Ogden Stewart; **M:** Franz Waxman. Academy Awards '40: Best Actor (Stewart), Best Screenplay; Nominations: Best Actress (Hepburn), Best Director (Cukor), Best Picture, Best Supporting Actress (Hussey). **VHS, Beta** $19.98 MGM, BTV, HMV 🐾🐾🐾🐾

Philby, Burgess and MacLean: Spy Scandal of the Century The true story of the three infamous British officials who defected to the Soviet Union in 1951, after stealing some vital British secrets for the KGB.
1984 83m/C Derek Jacobi, Anthony Bate, Michael Culver; **D:** Gordon Flemyng. **VHS, Beta** $59.95 MTI 🐾🐾 ½

Phobia Patients at a hospital are mysteriously being murdered. Stupid and unpleasant story that lasts too long and probably should never have started.
1980 (R) 91m/C Paul Michael Glaser, Susan Hogan; **D:** John Huston; **W:** Peter Bellwood, Lew Lehman, Gary Sherman, Ronald Shusett, Jimmy Sangster. **VHS, Beta** $69.95 PAR Woof!

Phoenix Aging queen summons her marksman to find the Phoenix, a mythical bird that she believes will bring her eternal life. With English subtitles.
1978 137m/C Tatsuya Nakadai, Tomisaburo Wakayama, Raoru Yumi, Reiko Ohara. **VHS, Beta** $29.95 VDA 🐾 ½

Phoenix Team Two agents discover their mutual attraction can be deadly in the spy business.
1980 90m/C Don Francks, Elizabeth Shepherd. **VHS, Beta** $49.95 TWE 🐾

Phoenix the Ninja A young girl grows up to be a ninja warrior and battles everyone who would deign to impede her.
198? 92m/C Sho Kosugi. **VHS, Beta** $59.95 TWE 🐾

Phoenix the Warrior Sometime in the future, female savages battle each other for control of the now ravaged earth. A newcomer seeks the tribe most worthy of receiving the last man on the planet, thereby continuing the human race.
1988 90m/C Persis Khambatta, James H. Emery, Peggy Sands, Kathleen Kinmont; **D:** Robert Hayes. **VHS** NO 🐾

The Phone Call 900-number morality tale about high-powered executive who calls phone sex line and is connected with an escaped homicidal maniac who takes a toll on him and his family.
1989 (R) 95m/C Michael Sarrazin, Linda Smith, Ron Lea, Lisa Jakub; **D:** Allan Goldstein. **VHS** $79.95 MNC 🐾🐾

Phone Call from a Stranger After a plane crash, a survivor visits the families of three of the victims whom he met during the flight.
1952 96m/B Bette Davis, Gary Merrill, Michael Rennie, Shelley Winters, Hugh Beaumont, Keenan Wynn, Eve Arden, Craig Stevens; **D:** Jean Negulesco; **W:** Nunnally Johnson. **VHS, Beta** $19.98 FOX 🐾🐾🐾

Photographer A photographer turns into a murderer, showing the negative side of his personality.
1975 (PG) 94m/C Michael Callan; **D:** William B. Hillman. **VHS, Beta** $59.98 NLC 🐾

Physical Evidence A lawyer finds herself falling for an ex-cop turned murder suspect while she tries to defend him for a crime he doesn't remember committing.
1989 (R) 99m/C Burt Reynolds, Theresa Russell, Ned Beatty, Kay Lenz, Ted McGinley; **D:** Michael Crichton; **W:** Bill Phillips. **VHS, Beta** $89.98 LIV, VES, HHE 🐾🐾

P.I. Private Investigations Corrupt, drug-dealing cops stalk another cop who can finger them.
1987 (R) 91m/C Martin Balsam. **VHS, Beta** FOX 🐾

Piaf Musical drama chronicles the life of Edith Piaf, France's legendary singer of the Roaring '20s. Her rise from the streets, bout with temporary blindness, and many self-destructive attempts at experiencing life are retold in music.
1981 (PG) 114m/C Jane Lapotaire. **VHS, Beta** FOX 🐾

The Piano In the 1850s, Ada (Hunter), a mute Scottish widow with a young daughter, agrees to an arranged marriage with Stewart (Neill), a colonial landowner in New Zealand. The way she expresses her feelings is by playing her cherished piano, left behind on the beach by her new husband. Another settler, George, (Keitel) buys it, arranges for lessons with Ada, and soon the duo begin a grand passion leading to a cruelly calculated revenge. Fiercely poetic and well acted (with Keitel in a notably romantic role), though the film may be too dark and intense for some. Fine original score with Hunter doing her own piano playing.
1993 (R) 120m/C Holly Hunter, Harvey Keitel, Sam Neill, Anna Paquin, Kerry Walker, Genevieve Lemon; **D:** Jane Campion; **W:** Jane Campion; **M:** Michael Nyman. Academy Awards '93: Best Actress (Hunter), Best Original Screenplay, Best Supporting Actress (Paquin); Nominations: Best Cinematography, Best Costume Design, Best Director (Campion), Best Film Editing, Best Picture; British Academy Awards '94: Best Director (Campion), Best Film, Best Original Screenplay, Best Original Score; Directors Guild of America Awards '93: Best Director (Campion); Golden Globe Awards '94: Best Director (Campion), Best Film—Drama, Best Screenplay, Best Supporting Actress (Paquin), Best Original Score; British Academy Awards '94: Best Actress (Hunter); Cannes Film Festival '93: Best Actress (Hunter), Best Film; Golden Globe Awards '94: Best Actress—Drama (Hunter); Independent Spirit Awards '94: Best Foreign Film; Los Angeles Film Critics Association Awards '93: Best Actress (Hunter), Best Cinematography, Best Director (Campion), Best Supporting Actress (Paquin); New York Film Critics Awards '93: Best Actress (Hunter), Best Director (Campion), Best Screenplay; National

Society of Film Critics Awards '93: Best Actress (Hunter), Best Screenplay. **VHS $94.95** *LIV ↗↗↗↗½*

A Piano for Mrs. Cimino
Declared senile and incompetent, a widowed woman fights for control of her own life. Good script helps this made for TV soaper.
1982 100m/C Bette Davis, Keenan Wynn, Alexa Kenin, Penny Fuller, Christopher Guest, George Hearn; **M:** James Horner. **VHS, Beta $59.95** *GEM ↗↗↗*

Picasso Trigger
An American spy tries to catch an elusive murderer. The sequel to "Hard Ticket to Hawaii" and "Malibu Express."
1989 (R) 99m/C Steve Bond, Dona Speir, John Aprea, Hope Marie Carlton, Guich Koock, Roberta Vasquez, Bruce Penhall; **D:** Andy Sidaris. **VHS $19.98** *WAR ↗↗*

Pick a Star
Lawrence is a small-town girl who wins a contest and is off to Hollywood. Only no one pays any attention to her except for publicity man Haley, who arranges her screen test. Naturally, she knocks the studio bosses for a loop and becomes a star. Laurel & Hardy are featured in a couple of comedy segments showing the newcomer some backstage silliness and movie business on the set of a Western they're filming (with Finlayson, better known as a director, cast as the duo's director). **AKA:** Movie Struck.
1937 70m/B Rosina Lawrence, Jack Haley, Patsy Kelly, Mischa Auer, Stan Laurel, Oliver Hardy, Charles Halton, Tom Dugan, Russell Hicks, James Finlayson; **D:** Edward Sedgwick. **VHS $19.98** *MGM, NOS, CAB ↗↗*

The Pick-Up Artist
The adventures of a compulsive Don Juan who finds he genuinely loves the daughter of an alcoholic who's in debt to the mob. Standard story with no surprises.
1987 (PG-13) 81m/C Robert Downey Jr., Molly Ringwald, Dennis Hopper, Harvey Keitel, Danny Aiello, Vanessa Williams, Robert Towne, Mildred Dunnock, Lorraine Bracco, Joe Spinell, Victoria Jackson, Polly Draper, Brian Hamill; **D:** James Toback; **W:** James Toback; **M:** Georges Delerue. **VHS, Beta $19.98** *FOX ↗↗½*

Pick-Up Summer
Two suburban boys cruise their town after school lets out, chasing a pair of voluptuous sisters. **AKA:** Pinball Summer; Pinball Pick-Up.
1979 (R) 99m/C Michael Zelniker, Carl Marotte; **D:** George Mihalka. **VHS, Beta $59.95** *NWV ↗*

The Pickle
Self-indulgent comedy about a midlife crisis. Aiello stars as a middle-aged manic-depressive director certain that his new film is going to be an abysmal flop (as have all his recent pictures). He seeks comfort and reassurance from various ex-wives, children, lovers, and others, though he abuses them all. This dispirited tale also shows clips of the director's dreadful film about children who launch a giant pickle into space. It couldn't possibly be worse than what Mazursky actually put up on the screen.
1993 (R) 103m/C Danny Aiello, Dyan Cannon, Clothilde Courau, Shelley Winters, Barry Miller, Jerry Stiller, Christopher Penn, Rebecca Miller; **Cameos:** Ally Sheedy, Little Richard, Spalding Gray, Griffin Dunne, Isabella Rossellini, Dudley Moore; **D:** Paul Mazursky; **W:** Paul Mazursky; **M:** Michel Legrand. **VHS $19.95** *COL ↗*

Pickpocket
Slow moving, documentary-like account of a petty thief's existence is a moral tragedy inspired by "Crime and Punishment." Ending is particularly moving. Classic filmmaking from Bresson, France's master of austerity. In French with English subtitles.

1959 75m/B Martin LaSalle, Marika Green, Pierre Leymarie; **D:** Robert Bresson. **VHS, Beta $59.95** *FCT, ING, TPV ↗↗↗*

Pickup on South Street
Petty thief Widmark lifts woman's wallet only to find it contains top secret Communist micro-film for which pinko agents will stop at nothing to get back. Intriguing look at the politics of the day. The creme of "B" movies.
1953 80m/B Richard Widmark, Jean Peters, Thelma Ritter, Murvyn Vye, Richard Kiley, Milburn Stone; **D:** Samuel Fuller; **W:** Samuel Fuller. **VHS, Beta $19.98** *FOX, FCT ↗↗↗*

The Pickwick Papers
Comedy based on the Dickens classic wherein Mrs. Bardell sues the Pickwick Club for breach of promise.
1954 109m/B James Hayter, James Donald, Nigel Patrick, Hermione Gingold, Hermione Baddeley, Kathleen Harrison; **D:** Noel Langley. **VHS, Beta $19.98** *VCI ↗↗½*

Picnic
A wanderer arrives in a small town and immediately wins the love a his friend's girl. The other women in town seem interested too. Strong, romantic work, with Holden excelling in the lead. Novak provides a couple pointers too. Lavish Hollywood adaptation of the William Inge play, including the popular tune "Moonglow/Theme from Picnic."
1955 113m/C William Holden, Kim Novak, Rosalind Russell, Susan Strasberg, Arthur O'Connell, Cliff Robertson, Betty Field, Verna Felton, Reta Shaw, Nick Adams, Phyllis Newman, Raymond Bailey; **D:** Joshua Logan; **W:** Daniel Taradash; **M:** George Duning. Academy Awards '55: Best Art Direction/Set Decoration (Color), Best Film Editing; Nominations: Best Picture, Best Supporting Actor (O'Connell); Golden Globe Awards '56: Best Director (Logan); National Board of Review Awards '55: 10 Best Films of the Year. **VHS, Beta $19.95** *COL ↗↗↗½*

Picnic at Hanging Rock
School outing in 1900 into a mountainous region ends tragically when three girls disappear. Eerie film is strong on atmosphere, as befits mood master Weir. Lambert is extremely photogenic—and suitable subdued—as one of the girls to disappear. Otherwise beautifully photographed on location. From the novel by Joan Lindsey.
1975 (PG) 110m/C Margaret Nelson, Rachel Roberts, Dominic Guard, Helen Morse, Jacki Weaver; **D:** Peter Weir. **VHS, Beta** *VES, OM ↗↗↗*

Picnic on the Grass
A strange, whimsical fantasy heavily evocative of the director's Impressionist roots; a science-minded candidate for the president of Europe throws a picnic as public example of his earthiness, and falls in love with a peasant girl. In French with English subtitles. **AKA:** Le Dejeuner Sur l'Herbe; Lunch on the Grass.
1959 92m/C Paul Meurisse, Catherine Rouvel, Fernand Sardou, Jacqueline Morane, Jean-Pierre Granval; **D:** Jean Renoir. **VHS, Beta $49.95** *FCT, INT, ING ↗↗↗*

Picture Mommy Dead
Well acted melodrama involving a scheming shrew who struggles to drive her mentally disturbed stepdaughter insane for the sake of cold, hard cash.
1966 85m/C Don Ameche, Zsa Zsa Gabor, Martha Hyer, Susan Gordon; **D:** Bert I. Gordon. **VHS, Beta $9.98** *NLC ↗↗*

Picture of Dorian Gray
Hatfield plays the rake who stays young while his portrait ages in this adaptation of Oscar Wilde's classic novel. Lansbury steals this one.
1945 110m/B Hurd Hatfield, George Sanders, Donna Reed, Angela Lansbury, Peter Lawford, Lowell Gilmore; **D:** Albert Lewin. Academy Awards '45: Best Black and White

Cinematography; Nominations: Best Interior Decoration, Best Supporting Actress (Lansbury); Golden Globe Awards '46: Best Supporting Actress (Lansbury). **VHS, Beta $19.98** *MGM, FHE, TVC ↗↗↗*

Picture of Dorian Gray
Another version of Wilde's renowned novel about a man who retains his youthful visage while his portrait shows the physical ravages of aging. Davenport is particularly appealing in the lead. Made for television.
1974 130m/C Shane Briant, Nigel Davenport, Charles Aidman, Fionnula Flanagan, Linda Kelsey, Vanessa Howard; **D:** Glenn Jordan. **VHS, Beta $29.95** *LIV, MPI ↗↗↗*

Pictures
The silent-film era in England is spoofed in this look at ambitious waitress Ruby Sears, who's determined to be a film star, and writer Bill Trench, who winds up a novice screenwriter. Bill's first movie script is based on Ruby's life and she desperately wants to star in the production, if only she can convince the producer and the drunken male lead that she has the talent. Made for British television; 7 episodes on 4 cassettes.
1987 208m/C Wendy Morgan, Peter McEnery, Harry Towb, Anton Rodgers, Annette Badland, Malcom Jamieson, Marc Smith; **W:** Roy Clarke. **VHS $99.95** *TVC, SIG ↗↗½*

Piece of Cake
Adaptation of the Derek Robinson novel follows the flyboys of the RAF Hornet Squadron during the early years of WWII. They have trouble taking the war seriously but tangles with the Luftwaffe and increasing casualties put a strain on everyone. Great aerial photography and the British planes are vintage Spitfires not repros. Made for television miniseries on 6 cassettes.
1990 312m/C Tom Burlinson, Tim Woodward, Boyd Gaines, Nathaniel Parker, Neil Dudgeon, David Horovitch, Richard Hope, Jeremy Wortham, Michael Elwyn, Corinne Dacla, Helena Michell. **VHS $129.95** *SIG ↗↗½*

A Piece of Pleasure
Marriage declines due to a domineering husband in this familiar domestic study from French master Chabrol. Good, but not among the director's best efforts. In French with English subtitles.
1970 100m/C D: Claude Chabrol. **VHS, Beta** *FCT ↗↗↗*

Piece of the Action
An ex-cop beats two con men at their own game when he convinces them to work for a Chicago community center.
1977 (PG) 135m/C Sidney Poitier, Bill Cosby, James Earl Jones, Denise Nicholas, Hope Clarke, Tracy Reed, Tito Vandis, Ja'net DuBois; **D:** Sidney Poitier; **M:** Curtis Mayfield. **VHS, Beta $19.98** *WAR ↗↗½*

Pieces
Chain-saw wielding madman roams a college campus in search of human parts for a ghastly jigsaw puzzle. Gory and loathsome.
1983 (R) 90m/C Christopher George, Lynda Day George, Paul Smith; **D:** J.P. Simon. **VHS, Beta $79.98** *VES* Woof!

Pied Piper of Hamelin
The evergreen classic of the magical piper who rids a village of rats and then disappears with the village children into a mountain when the townspeople fail to keep a promise.
1957 90m/C Van Johnson, Claude Rains, Jim Backus, Kay Starr, Lori Nelson; **D:** Bretaigne Windust. **VHS, Beta $14.95** *KAR, NOS, MED ↗↗*

The Pied Piper of Hamelin
From Shelley Duvall's "Faerie Tale Theatre" comes the story of how a man with a magic flute charmed the rats out of Hamelin.
1984 60m/C Eric Idle; **D:** Nicholas Meyer. **VHS, Beta $14.98** *FOX, FCT ↗↗*

Pier 23 A private eye is hired to bring a lawless ex-convict to a priest's custody, but gets an imposter instead. A web of intrigue follows.
1951 57m/B Hugh Beaumont, Ann Savage, David Bruce, Raymond Greenleaf, Joi Lansing. **VHS, Beta** NO ⅔⅔

Pierrot le Fou A woman fleeing a gangster joins a man leaving his wife in this stunning, occasionally confusing classic from iconoclast Godard. A hallmark in 1960s improvisational filmmaking, with rugged Belmondo and always-photogenic Karina effortlessly excelling in leads. In French with English subtitles.
1965 110m/C Samuel Fuller, Jean-Pierre Leaud, Jean-Paul Belmondo, Anna Karina, Dirk Sanders; **D:** Jean-Luc Godard; **M:** Antoine Duhamel. **VHS** $59.95 INT, FCT, IME ⅔⅔⅔½

Pigeon Feathers A young man realizes a greater understanding of life in this adaptation of a John Updike tale.
1988 45m/C Christopher Collet, Caroline McWilliams; **W:** John Updike. **VHS** $24.95 MON, KAR ⅔⅔½

Pigs Young woman who has escaped from a mental hospital teams up with an evil old man to go on a murdering spree. They complement each other beautifully. She kills them and he disposes of the bodies by making pig slop out of them. **AKA:** Daddy's Deadly Darling; The Killers.
1973 90m/C Toni Lawrence, Marc Lawrence, Jesse Vint, Katharine Ross; **D:** Marc Lawrence; **W:** Marc Lawrence. **VHS, Beta** MRV ⅔½

Pilgrim, Farewell Dramatic story about a dying woman who needs to tie up loose ends before her death and goes looking for her estranged teenage daughter. Made for television for PBS' "American Playhouse."
1982 110m/C Elizabeth Huddle, Christopher Lloyd, Laurie Pranage, Lesley Paxton, Shelley Wyant, Robert Brown; **D:** Michael Roemer. **VHS, Beta** FLI ⅔⅔½

Pillow Talk Sex comedy in which a man woos a woman who loathes him. By the way, they share the same telephone party line. Narrative provides minimal indication of the film's strengths, which are many. Classic '50's comedy with masters Day and Hudson exhibiting considerable rapport, even when fighting. Lighthearted, constantly funny.
1959 102m/C Rock Hudson, Doris Day, Tony Randall, Thelma Ritter, Nick Adams, Lee Patrick; **D:** Michael Gordon. Academy Awards '59: Best Story & Screenplay; Nominations: Best Actress (Day), Best Art Direction/Set Decoration (Color), Best Supporting Actress (Ritter). **VHS, Beta** $14.95 MCA, CCB ⅔⅔½

Pilot Young girl discovers the debilitating effects of dishonesty when she becomes a break-dancing champion.
1984 27m/C Kelly Jo Minter, Adolph "Oz" Alvarez, Katie Rich. **VHS, Beta** PAU ⅔½

Pimpernel Smith Seemingly scatter-brained archaeology professor is actually a dashing agent rescuing refugees from evil Nazis in WWII France. Howard is well cast, but the film is somewhat predictable, and it's too long. Wonderful scene, though, in which a Nazi officer champions Shakespeare as Aryan. **AKA:** Mister V.
1942 121m/B Leslie Howard, Mary Morris, Francis L. Sullivan, David Tomlinson; **D:** Leslie Howard. **VHS, Beta** $24.95 VYY ⅔⅔½

Pin A boy's imaginary friend assists in the slaying of various enemies. Horror effort could be worse.
1988 (R) 103m/C Cyndy Preston, David Hewlett, Terry O'Quinn; **D:** Sandor Stern. **VHS, Beta** $19.95 STE, NWV, IME ⅔⅔½

Pin Down Girls Great schlock about girl wrestlers. Also known as "Racket Girls."
1951 ?m/C Clara Mortensen, Rita Martinez. **VHS** $16.95 SNC ⅔

Pin-Up Girl Grable plays a secretary who becomes an overnight sensation during WWII. Loosely based on her famous pinup poster that was so popular at the time, the movie didn't even come close to being as successful. The songs aren't particularly memorable, although Charlie Spivak and his Orchestra perform. ♫ Once Too Often; Yankee Doodle Dandy; I'll Be Marching to a Love Song; You're My Little Pin Up Girl; Story of the Very Merry Widow; Time Alone Will Tell; Don't Carry Tales Out of School; Red Robins, Bob Whites and Blue Birds.
1944 83m/C Betty Grable, Martha Raye, Joe E. Brown, Eugene Pallette, Mantan Moreland; **D:** H. Bruce Humberstone. **VHS** $19.98 FOX, FXV

The Pinchcliffe Grand Prix Master inventor designs the ultimate race car.
1981 (G) 88m/C **VHS, Beta** $19.95 STE, GEM ⅔

Ping Pong A Chinese patriarch drops dead in London's Chinatown, leaving a young law student to disentangle his will, and get mixed up with his cross-cultured family.
1987 (PG) 100m/C David Yip, Lucy Sheen, Robert Lee, Lam Fung, Victor Kan, Ric Young; **D:** Po Chich Leong. **VHS, Beta** NO ⅔½

Pink Cadillac A grizzled, middle-aged bondsman is on the road, tracking down bail-jumping crooks. He helps the wife and baby of his latest target escape from her husband's more evil associates. Eastwood's performance is good and fun to watch, in this otherwise lightweight film.
1989 (PG-13) 121m/C Clint Eastwood, Bernadette Peters, Timothy Carhart, Michael Des Barres, William Hickey, John Dennis Johnston, Geoffrey Lewis, Jim Carrey, Tiffany Gail Robinson, Angela Louise Robinson; **D:** Buddy Van Horn; **W:** John Eskow; **M:** Stephen Dorff. **VHS, Beta, 8mm** $19.98 WAR ⅔⅔½

The Pink Chiquitas Sci-fi spoof about a detective battling a mob of meteorite-traveling Amazons.
1986 (PG-13) 86m/C Frank Stallone, Eartha Kitt, Bruce Pirrie, McKinlay Robinson, Elizabeth Edwards, Claudia Udy; **D:** Anthony Currie. **VHS, Beta** $9.99 PSM ⅔

Pink Flamingos Divine, the dainty 300-pound transvestite, faces the biggest challenge of his/her career when he/she competes for the title of World's Filthiest Person. Tasteless, crude, and hysterical film; this one earned Waters his title as "Prince of Puke." If there are any doubts about this honor—or Divine's rep—watch through to the end to catch Divine chewing real dog excrement, all the time wearing a you-know-what grin.
1972 95m/C Divine, David Lochary, Mary Vivian Pearce, Danny Mills, Mink Stole, Edith Massey; **D:** John Waters; **W:** John Waters. **VHS, Beta** NO ⅔⅔

Pink Floyd: The Wall Film version of Pink Floyd's 1979 LP, "The Wall." A surreal, impressionistic tour-de-force about a boy who grows up numb from society's pressures. The concept is bombastic and overwrought, but Geldof manages to remain somewhat likeable as the cynical rock star and the Gerald Scarfe animation perfectly complements the film. Laserdisc edition includes the original theatrical trailer and the letterboxed format of the film.
1982 (R) 95m/C Bob Geldof, Christine Hargreaves, Bob Hoskins; **D:** Alan Parker; **M:** Michael Kamen. **VHS, Beta** $19.95 MVD, MGM ⅔⅔½

Pink Motel Several people spend a night meant to be romantic at a pink stucco motel which caters to couples. Comic stiff with Diller and Pickens as the owners of said pink motel. **AKA:** Motel.
1982 (R) 90m/C Phyllis Diller, Slim Pickens, Terri Berland, Squire Fridell; **D:** Mike MacFarland. **VHS, Beta** NO Woof!

Pink Nights A high school nebbish is suddenly pursued by three beautiful girls, and his life gets turned upside-down.
1987 (PG) 87m/C Shaun Allen, Kevin Anderson, Larry King, Johnathan Jamcovic Michaels; **D:** Philip Koch. **VHS, Beta** $19.95 STE, NWV ⅔

The Pink Panther Bumbling, disaster-prone inspector invades a Swiss ski resort and becomes obsessed with capturing a jewel thief hoping to lift the legendary "Pink Panther" diamond. Said thief is also the inspector's wife's lover, though the inspector doesn't know it. Slick slapstick succeeds on strength of Sellers' classic portrayal of Clouseau, who accidentally destroys everything in his path while speaking in a funny French accent. Followed by "A Shot in the Dark," "Inspector Clouseau" (without Sellers), "The Return of the Pink Panther," "The Pink Panther Strikes Again," "Revenge of the Pink Panther," "Trail of the Pink Panther," and "Curse of the Pink Panther." Memorable theme supplied by Mancini.
1964 113m/C Peter Sellers, David Niven, Robert Wagner, Claudia Cardinale, Capucine, Brenda de Banzie; **D:** Blake Edwards; **W:** Blake Edwards; **M:** Henry Mancini. **VHS, Beta** $19.98 MGM, FOX, TVC ⅔⅔⅔

The Pink Panther Strikes Again Fifth in the series has the incompetent inspector tracking his former boss, who has gone insane and has become preoccupied with destroying the entire world. A must for Sellers buffs and anyone who appreciates slapstick.
1976 (PG) 103m/C Peter Sellers, Herbert Lom, Lesley-Anne Down, Colin Blakely, Leonard Rossiter, Burt Kwouk; **D:** Blake Edwards; **W:** Edwards Waldman, Frank Waldman; **M:** Henry Mancini. **VHS, Beta** $19.95 FOX, TVC ⅔⅔⅔

Pink Strings and Sealing Wax A brutish pub owner in Victorian England is poisoned by his abused wife. She tries to involve the son of a chemist with the idea of blackmailing the father. Fine period flavor.
1945 75m/B Mervyn Johns, Mary Merrall, Gordon Jackson, Googie Withers, Sally Ann Howes, Catherine Lacey, Garry Marsh; **D:** Robert Hamer. **VHS, Beta** $16.95 SNC ⅔⅔

Pinky Early Hollywood treatment of the tragic choice made by some black Americans to pass as white in order to attain a better life for themselves and their families. The story is still relevant today. Waters and Barrymore also star, but the lead black character is portrayed by a white actress. Based on the novel "Quality" by Cyd Ricketts Sumner.
1949 102m/B Jeanne Crain, Ethel Barrymore, Ethel Waters, Nina Mae McKinney, William Lundigan; **D:** Elia Kazan; **W:** Philip Dunne, Dudley Nichols; **M:** Alfred Newman. **VHS** $19.98 FXV ⅔⅔⅔

Pinocchio Second Disney animated film featuring Pinocchio, a little wooden puppet, made with love by the old woodcarver Geppetto, and brought to life by a good fairy. Except Pinocchio isn't content to be just a puppet—he wants to become a real boy. Lured off by a sly fox, Pinocchio undergoes a number of adventures as he tries to return safely home. Has some scary scenes, including Geppetto, Pinocchio, and their friend Jiminy Cricket getting swallowed by a whale, and Pleasure Island, where naughty boys are

turned into donkeys. An example of animation at its best and a Disney classic that has held up over time. ♫When You Wish Upon a Star; Give a Little Whistle; Turn on the Old Music Box; Hi-Diddle-Dee-Dee (An Actor's Life For Me); I've Got No Strings.
1940 (G) 87m/C D: Ben Sharpsteen; **V:** Dick Jones, Cliff Edwards, Evelyn Venable, Walter Catlett, Frankie Darro, Charles Judels, Don Brodie, Christian Rub. **VHS, Beta $24.99** DIS, WTA �⅛

Pinocchio Classic Pinocchio story in musical form.
1976 76m/C Danny Kaye, Sandy Duncan. **VHS, Beta $14.98** VCI ⅛

Pinocchio Pee Wee Herman is the puppet who wants to be a real little boy in this "Faerie Tale Theatre" adaptation of this children's classic.
1983 60m/C Paul (Pee Wee Herman) Reubens, James Coburn, Carl Reiner, Lainie Kazan; **D:** Peter Medak. **VHS, Beta $14.98** FOX, FCT ⅛⅛

Pinocchio's Storybook Adventures Pinocchio takes over for an ailing puppet master and puts on a show for a group of children.
1979 80m/C D: Ron Merk. **VHS, Beta $9.99** VTR ⅛⅛

Pinto Canyon An honest sheriff does away with a band of cattle rustlers.
1940 55m/B Bob Steele, Louise Stanley, Kenne Duncan, Ted Adams, Steve Clark, Budd Buster; **D:** Raymond K. Johnson. **VHS $19.95** NOS, DVT ⅛⅛

Pinto Rustlers A cowboy left orphaned by a gang of rustlers seeks revenge.
1936 57m/B Tom Tyler, Catherine Cotter. **VHS, Beta $19.95** NOS, DVT ⅛⅛

Pioneer Marshal Lawman Hale disguises himself as a criminal to track down an embezzler.
1949 60m/B Monte Hale, Paul Hurst. **VHS, Beta $29.95** DVT ⅛

Pioneer Woman A family encounters hostility when they set up a frontier homestead in Nebraska in 1867. Told from the feminine perspective, the tale is strewn with hurdles, both personal and natural. **AKA:** Pioneers.
1973 74m/C Joanna Pettet, William Shatner, David Janssen; **D:** Buzz Kulik. **VHS, Beta $14.98** WOV ⅛⅛

The Pioneers Ritter sets out to protect a wagon train.
1941 59m/B Tex Ritter. **VHS, Beta** VCN ⅛⅛

Pipe Dreams A couple tries to repair their broken marriage against the backdrop of the Alaskan pipeline's construction.
1976 (PG) 89m/C Gladys Knight, Barry Hankerson, Bruce French, Sally Kirkland, Sherry Bain; **D:** Stephen Verona. **VHS, Beta $14.95** COL, SUE ⅛⅛

Pippi Goes on Board The fourth and last film in the Swedish series finds Pippi's father arriving one day to take her sailing to Taka-Kuka, his island kingdom. She can't bear to leave her friends and jumps off the ship to return home. The series is poorly dubbed and technically flawed, which the kids probably won't notice. Based on the books by Astrid Lindgren. Preceded by "Pippi Longstocking," "Pippi in the South Seas," and "Pippi on the Run."
1975 (G) 83m/C Inger Nilsson; **D:** Olle Hellbron. **VHS, Beta $19.95** GEM, MOV, TPV ⅛⅛

Pippi in the South Seas Pippi, a fun-loving, independent, red haired little girl, and her two friends decide to rescue her father, who is being held captive by a band of pirates on a South Sea island. Naturally,

clever Pippi saves the day. Poorly dubbed and edited. Based on the children's book by Astrid Lindgren. Follows "Pippi Longstocking" and precedes "Pippi on the Run" and "Pippi Goes on Board." **AKA:** Pippi Langstrump Pa de Sju Haven.
1974 (G) 99m/C Inger Nilsson; **D:** Olle Hellbron. **VHS, Beta $19.95** GEM, MOV, TPV ⅛⅛½

Pippi Longstocking This little red-headed, pigtailed terror is left alone by her sailor father as he heads out to sea. Not that Pippi minds, since it gives her the chance to create havoc in her town through the antics of her pets, a monkey and a horse. Pippi's antics may amuse the kiddies but adults will find her obnoxious. Poorly dubbed and technically somewhat shaky. Based on the children's book by Astrid Lindgren. Followed by "Pippi in the South Seas," "Pippi on the Run," and "Pippi Goes on Board."
1973 (G) 99m/C Inger Nilsson; **D:** Olle Hellbron. **VHS, Beta $19.95** GEM, MOV, TPV ⅛⅛

Pippi on the Run The third film in the series finds Pippi on the trail of two friends who have run away from home. The three have many adventures before deciding home is best. Preceded by "Pippi Longstocking" and "Pippi in the South Seas," followed by "Pippi Goes on Board." Films lacks technical and dubbing skills. Based on the children's book by Astrid Lindgren.
1974 (G) 99m/C VHS, Beta $19.99 GEM, MOV, TPV ⅛⅛½

Pippin Video version of the stage musical about the adolescent son of Charlemagne finding true love. Adequate record of Bob Fosse's Broadway smash. Features Vereen recreating his original Tony Award-winning role.
1981 120m/C Ben Vereen, William Katt, Martha Raye, Chita Rivera. **VHS, Beta $29.95** VCI, FHE, FCT ⅛⅛½

Piranha A rural Texas resort area is plagued by attacks from ferocious man-eating fish which a scientist created to be used as a secret weapon in the Vietnam War. Spoofy horror film features the now-obligatory Dante film in-jokes in the background.
1978 (R) 90m/C Bradford Dillman, Heather Menzies, Kevin McCarthy, Keenan Wynn, Barbara Steele, Dick Miller, Paul Bartel; **D:** Joe Dante; **W:** John Sayles; **M:** Pino Donaggio. **VHS, Beta $39.98** WAR, OM ⅛⅛½

Piranha 2: The Spawning Diving instructor and a biochemist seek to destroy piranha mutations that are murdering tourists at a club. Early Cameron exercise in gore tech that's a step down from original "Piranha." **AKA:** Piranha 2: Flying Killers.
1982 (R) 88m/C Steve Marachuk, Lance Henriksen, Ricky Paul; **D:** James Cameron. **VHS, Beta $14.95** SUE, NLC ⅛½

The Pirate A traveling actor poses as a legendary pilot to woo a lonely woman on a remote Caribbean island. Minnelli always scores with this type of fare, and both Garland and Kelly make the most of the Cole Porter score. ♫Be a Clown; Nina; Mack the Black; You Can Do No Wrong; Sweet Ices, Papayas, Berry Man; Sea Wall; Serafin; The Ring; Judy Awakens.
1948 102m/C Judy Garland, Gene Kelly, Walter Slezak, Gladys Cooper, George Zucco, Reginald Owen, Nicholas Brothers; **D:** Vincente Minnelli. **VHS, Beta $19.98** MGM ⅛⅛⅛

Pirate Movie Gilbert and Sullivan's "The Pirates of Penzance" is combined with new pop songs in this tale of fantasy and romance. Feeble attempt to update a musical that was fine the way it was.

1982 (PG) 98m/C Kristy McNichol, Christopher Atkins, Ted Hamilton, Bill Kerr, Garry McDonald; **D:** Ken Annakin. **VHS, Beta $59.95** FOX ⅛⅛½

Pirate Warrior Grade-B pirate flick about slavery and the evil Tortuga.
1964 86m/C Ricardo Montalban, Vincent Price, Liana Orfei; **D:** Mary Costa. **VHS, Beta NO** ⅛⅛

Pirates Blustery, confused effort at a big-budgeted retro-adventure, about a highly regarded pirate and his gains and losses on the high seas. Broad comedy, no story to speak of.
1986 (PG-13) 124m/C Walter Matthau, Cris Campion, Damien Thomas, Richard Pearson, Charlotte Lewis, Olu Jacobs, David Patrick Kelly, Roy Kinnear, Bill Fraser, Jose Santamaria; **D:** Roman Polanski; **W:** Gerard Brach, Roman Polanski. **VHS, Beta $19.95** LIV ⅛⅛

The Pirates of Penzance Gilbert and Sullivan's comic operetta is the story of a band of fun-loving pirates, their reluctant young apprentice, the "very model of a modern major general," and his lovely daughters. An adaptation of Joseph Papp's award-winning Broadway play.
1983 (G) 112m/C Kevin Kline, Angela Lansbury, Linda Ronstadt, Rex Smith, George Rose; **D:** Wilford Leach. **VHS, Beta $19.98** MCA, FOX ⅛⅛

Pirates of the Coast A Spanish naval commander teams up with a group of pirates to even the score with an evil governor during the 1500s.
1961 102m/C Lex Barker, Estella Blain, Livio Lorenzon, Liana Orfei; **D:** Domenico Paolella. **VHS, Beta $29.95** UNI ⅛½

Pirates of the High Seas Crabbe helps a friend save his shipping line from sabotage. A serial in fifteen chapters.
1950 ?m/C Buster Crabbe, Lois Hall, Tommy Farrell, Gene Roth, Tristram Coffin; **D:** Spencer Gordon Bennet, Thomas Carr. **VHS** MLB ⅛½

Pirates of the Seven Seas In the further tales of "Sandokan the Great," the pirate hero helps save the heroine's father from an evil English Imperialist.
1962 90m/C Steve Reeves, Jacqueline Sassard, Andrea Bosic; **D:** Umberto Lenzi. **VHS, Beta NO** ⅛½

Pistol: The Birth of a Legend Biography of "Pistol" Pete Maravich, the basketball star who defied age limitations in the 1960s to play on his varsity team.
1990 (G) 104m/C Adam Guier, Nick Benedict, Boots Garland, Millie Perkins; **D:** Frank C. Schroeder. **VHS, Beta $19.95** COL ⅛⅛½

Pistoleros Asesinos Plenty of action, plus a little romance, when a man falls in love with a crooked landowner's daughter and must battle her father's henchmen for her hand.
1987 83m/C Maria de Lourdes, Federico Villa, Victor Alcocer, Arturo Benavides, Polo Ortin, Rosa Gloria. **VHS, Beta $79.95** MAD ⅛⅛

The Pit Autistic boy gets his chance for revenge. The townspeople who humiliate him are in for a surprise after he stumbles across a huge hole in the forest, at the bottom of which are strange and deadly creatures.
1981 (R) 96m/C Sammy Snyders, Sonja Smits, Jeannie Elias, Laura Hollingsworth; **D:** Lew Lehman. **VHS, Beta $19.95** STE, SUE ⅛½

The Pit and the Pendulum A woman and her lover plan to drive her brother mad, and he responds by locking them in his torture chamber, which was built by his loony dad, whom he now thinks he is. Standard Corman production only remotely derived from the classic Poe tale, with the cast chewing on a loopy script. A landmark in Gothic horror.

1961 80m/C Vincent Price, John Kerr, Barbara Steele, Luana Anders; *D:* Roger Corman; *W:* Richard Matheson; *M:* Les Baxter. **VHS, Beta** $19.98 *WAR, OM ⅋⅋⅋*

The Pit & the Pendulum Retelling of the classic Poe short story, mixed with his "A Cask of Amantillado" and set during the Spanish Inquisition. Great special effects and professional scary guy, Lance Henriksen. **1991 (R)** 97m/C Lance Henriksen, Rona De Ricci, Jonathan Fuller, Jeffrey Combs, Tom Towles, Stephen Lee, Francis Bay, Oliver Reed; *D:* Stuart Gordon; *W:* Dennis Paoli; *M:* Richard Band. **VHS** $19.95 *PAR ⅋⅋½*

Pitfall Gritty tale in which an insurance salesman, bored with his routine suburban life and family, follows his less noble instincts—and finds himself up to his ears in stolen goods, adultery and murder. **1948** 85m/B Dick Powell, Jane Wyatt, Lizabeth Scott, Raymond Burr, John Litel, Byron Barr, Ann Doran; *D:* Andre de Toth. **VHS** $19.98 *REP, FCT ⅋⅋⅋*

Pittsburgh Slow-moving drama about a love triangle combined with class differences. Dietrich loves Wayne, but he's more interested in the coal and steel business, so rival Scott steps in. Although limited by standard plot, picture works because of excellent performances by leads. Based on a screen story by George Owen and Tom Reed. **1942** 98m/B Marlene Dietrich, Randolph Scott, John Wayne, Frank Craven, Louise Allbritton, Shemp Howard, Thomas Gomez, Ludwig Stossel; *D:* Lewis Seiler; *W:* Kenneth Gamet, Tom Reed, John Twist. **VHS** $14.98 *MCA, FCT ⅋⅋*

Pixote Wrenching, documentary-like account of an orphan-boy's life on the streets in a Brazil metropolis. Graphic and depressing, it's not for all tastes but nonetheless masterfully done. In Portuguese with English subtitles. **1981** 127m/C Fernando Ramos Da Silva, Marilia Pera, Jorge Juliao, Gilberto Moura, Jose Nilson dos Santos, Edilson Lino; *D:* Hector Babenco; *W:* Hector Babenco; *M:* John Neschling. **VHS, Beta** $59.95 *COL ⅋⅋⅋*

Pizza Man Pizza deliveryman Elmo Bunn is minding his own business, delivering an extra large with anchovies and sausage, when he finds himself mixed up in a political scandal. Lawton directed under alias "J.D. Athens." **1991 (PG-13)** 90m/C Bill Maher, Annabelle Gurwitch; *D:* J.F. Lawton; *W:* J.F. Lawton. **VHS** $79.95 *MNC ⅋½*

P.K. and the Kid A runaway kid meets up with a factory worker on his way to an arm wrestling competition and they become friends. **1985** 90m/C Molly Ringwald, Paul LeMat, Alex Rocco, John Madden, Esther Rolle; *D:* Lou Lombardo; *M:* James Horner. **VHS, Beta** $79.95 *LHV, WAR ⅋⅋*

A Place Called Glory Barker comes to the aid of the local townsfolk in Glory city who have their hands full with a gang of bloodthirsty outlaws. *AKA:* Die Holle von Manitoba. **1966** 92m/C Lex Barker, Pierre Brice, Marianne Koch. **VHS** $16.95 *SNC ⅋⅋*

A Place Called Today Sordid tale of big city politics where violence and fear in the streets is at the heart of the campaign. Also called "City in Fear." **1972** 105m/C Cheri Caffaro, J. Herbert Kerr Jr., Lana Wood, Richard Smedley, Tim Brown; *D:* Don Schain. **VHS, Beta** $39.95 *MON ⅋*

Place in Hell The Japanese armed forces camouflage a Pacific island beach which they are holding and invite the American forces to invade it during WWII. **1965** 106m/C Guy Madison, Helene Chanel, Monty Greenwood. **VHS, Beta** $49.95 *UNI ⅋½*

A Place in the Sun Melodramatic adaptation of "An American Tragedy," Theodore Dreiser's realist classic about an ambitious laborer whose aspirations to the high life with a gorgeous debutante are threatened by his lower-class lover's pregnancy. Clift is magnificent in the lead, and Taylor and Winters also shine in support. Burr, however, grossly overdoes his role of the vehement prosecutor. Still, not a bad effort from somewhat undisciplined director Stevens. **1951** 120m/B Montgomery Clift, Elizabeth Taylor, Shelley Winters, Raymond Burr, Anne Revere; *D:* George Stevens; *M:* Franz Waxman. Academy Awards '51: Best Black and White Cinematography, Best Costume Design (B & W), Best Director (Stevens), Best Film Editing, Best Screenplay, Best Score; Nominations: Best Actor (Clift), Best Actress (Winters), Best Picture; Directors Guild of America Awards '51: Best Director (Stevens); Golden Globe Awards '52: Best Film—Drama; National Board of Review Awards '51: 10 Best Films of the Year. **VHS, Beta** $19.95 *PAR, BTV ⅋⅋⅋*

Place of Weeping Early entry in the anti-apartheid sweepstakes (made in South Africa, no less). A South African woman opposes her nation's racist policies. A reporter supports her. **1986 (PG)** 88m/C James Whylie, Geini Mhlophe; *D:* Darrell Roodt. **VHS, Beta** $19.95 *STE, NWV, FCT ⅋½*

Places in the Heart A young widow determines to make the best of a bad situation on a small farm in Depression-era Texas, fighting poverty, racism, and sexism while enduring back-breaking labor. Support group includes a blind veteran and a black drifter. Hokey but nonetheless moving film is improved significantly by strong performances by virtually everyone in the cast. In his debut, Malkovich shines through this stellar group. Effective dust-bowl photography by Nestor Almendros. **1984 (PG)** 113m/C Sally Field, John Malkovich, Danny Glover, Ed Harris, Lindsay Crouse, Amy Madigan, Terry O'Quinn; *D:* Robert Benton; *W:* Robert Benton. Academy Awards '84: Best Actress (Field), Best Original Screenplay; Nominations: Best Costume Design, Best Director (Benton), Best Picture, Best Supporting Actor (Malkovich), Best Supporting Actress (Crouse); Golden Globe Awards '85: Best Actress—Drama (Field). **VHS, Beta** $19.98 *FOX, BTV, HMV ⅋⅋⅋*

The Plague An outbreak of bubonic plague has turned the South American city of Oran into a prison, with no one permitted to leave until the disease has run its course. Hurt is the doctor trying to balance his duties with his own fears. Necessarily bleak adaptation of the Albert Camus novel is also slow-moving and long-winded—an equally deadly combination for the viewer. **1992 (R)** 105m/C William Hurt, Robert Duvall, Raul Julia, Sandrine Bonnaire, Jean-Marc Barr; *D:* Luis Puenzo. **VHS** $92.98 *LIV, FCT, BTV ⅋½*

The Plague Dogs Two dogs carrying a plague escape from a research center and are tracked down in this unlikely animated film. A bit ponderous. And yes, that is Hurt's voice. From the novel by Richard Adams, author of "Watership Down." **1982** 99m/C *D:* Martin Rosen; *W:* Martin Rosen; *M:* Patrick Gleeson; *V:* John Hurt, Christopher Benjamin, Judy Geeson, Barbara Leigh-Hunt, Patrick Stewart. **VHS, Beta** $9.98 *NLC ⅋⅋½*

Plain Clothes An undercover cop masquerades as a high school student to solve the murder of a teacher. He endures all the trials that made him hate high school the first time around. **1988 (PG)** 98m/C Arliss Howard, George Wendt, Suzy Amis, Diane Ladd, Seymour Cassel, Larry Pine, Jackie Gayle, Abe Vigoda, Robert Stack; *D:* Martha Coolidge; *M:* Scott Wilk. **VHS, Beta** $14.95 *PAR ⅋⅋½*

The Plainsman Western legends Wild Bill Hickock, Buffalo Bill, and Calamity Jane team up for adventure in this big, empty venture. Just about what you'd expect from splashy director DeMille. **1937** 113m/B Gary Cooper, Jean Arthur, Charles Bickford, Anthony Quinn, George "Gabby" Hayes, Porter Hall, James Mason; *D:* Cecil B. DeMille; *M:* John Williams. **VHS, Beta** $14.98 *MCA, MLB ⅋⅋½*

Plan 9 from Outer Space Two or three aliens in silk pajamas conspire to resurrect several slow-moving zombies from a cardboard graveyard in order to conquer the Earth. Spaceships that look suspiciously like paper plates blaze across the sky. Pitiful, inadvertently hilarious fright worth a look if you're desperate to kill time since it's in the running for the "dumbest movie ever made" award. Lugosi's actual screen time is under two minutes, since he had the good sense to die before the film was complete. Enjoy the taller and younger replacement (the chiropractor of Wood's wife) they found for Lugosi, who remains hooded to protect his identity. *AKA:* Grave Robbers from Outer Space. **1956** 78m/B Bela Lugosi, Tor Johnson, Lyle Talbot, Vampira, Gregory Walcott; *D:* Edward D. Wood Jr. **VHS, Beta** $19.95 *NOS, SNC, MED* Woof!

Planes, Trains & Automobiles One-joke Hughes comedy saved by Martin and Candy. A straight-laced businessman (played straight by Martin) on the way home for Thanksgiving meets up with a oafish, bad-luck-ridden boor who turns his efforts to get home upside down. Martin and Candy both turn in fine performances, and effectively straddle a thin line between true pathos and hilarious buffoonery. Bacon and McClurg, both Hughes alumni, have small but funny roles. **1987 (R)** 93m/C Steve Martin, John Candy, Edie McClurg, Kevin Bacon, Michael McKean, William Windom, Laila Robins, Martin Ferrero, Charles Tyner, Dylan Baker; *D:* John Hughes; *W:* John Hughes; *M:* Ira Newborn. **VHS, Beta, 8mm** $19.95 *PAR ⅋⅋½*

Planet Burg A classic Soviet sci-fi flick about a space exploration team landing on Venus. Their job becomes a rescue mission when one of the crew is stranded. Although there are some silly moments, some good plot twists and acting make up for them. In Russian with English subtitles. **1962** 90m/C Vladimir Temelianov, Gennadi Vernov, Kyunna Ignatova; *D:* Pavel Klushantsev. **VHS, Beta** $16.95 *SNC ⅋⅋½*

Planet Busters Japanimation feature. Haphazardly developed swift-paced science fiction adventure about a magic sword, a royal heir apparent, a couple of bounty hunters, and evil robots. **1985** 80m/C **VHS** $29.95 *STP, TPV ⅋*

Planet Earth In the year 2133, a man who has been in suspended animation for 154 years is revived to lead the troops against a violent group of women (and mutants, too!).

1974 78m/C John Saxon, Janet Margolin, Ted Cassidy, Diana Muldaur, Johana DeWinter, Christopher Gary; **D:** Marc Daniels. VHS $59.95 UNI 🐾🐾½

Planet of Blood Space opera about an alien vampire discovered on Mars by a rescue team. If you've ever seen the Soviet film "Niebo Zowiet," don't be surprised if some scenes look familiar; the script was written around segments cut from that film. **AKA:** Queen of Blood.
1966 81m/C John Saxon, Basil Rathbone, Judi Meredith, Dennis Hopper, Florence Marly; **D:** Curtis Harrington. VHS $16.95 SNC, NOS, MRV 🐾🐾

Planet of the Apes Astronauts crash land on a planet where apes are masters and humans are merely brute animals. Superior science fiction with sociological implications marred only by unnecessary humor. Heston delivers one of his more plausible performances. Superb ape makeup creates realistic pseudo-simians of McDowall, Hunter, Evans, Whitmore, and Daly. Adapted from Pierre Boulle's novel "Monkey Planet." Followed by four sequels and two television series.
1968 (G) 112m/C Charlton Heston, Roddy McDowall, Kim Hunter, Maurice Evans, Linda Harrison, James Whitmore, James Daly; **D:** Franklin J. Schaffner; **W:** Rod Serling, Michael G. Wilson; **M:** Jerry Goldsmith. Academy Awards '68 Nominations: Best Costume Design, Best Original Score; National Board of Review Awards '68: 10 Best Films of the Year. VHS, Beta $19.98 FOX, FUS 🐾🐾🐾½

Planet of the Dinosaurs Survivors from a ruined spaceship combat huge savage dinosaurs on a swampy uncharted planet.
1980 (PG) 85m/C James Whitworth; **D:** James K. Shea. VHS, Beta $39.95 AHV, VTR 🐾½

Planet of the Vampires Astronauts search for missing comrades on a planet dominated by mind-bending forces. Acceptable atmospheric filmmaking from genre master Bava, but it's not among his more compelling ventures. **AKA:** Terror in Space; Terreur dans l'Espace; Space Mutants; The Demon Planet.
1965 86m/C Barry Sullivan, Norman Bengell, Angel Aranda, Evi Marandi; **D:** Mario Bava. VHS, Beta $9.98 ORI, HBO 🐾🐾½

Planet on the Prowl A fiery planet causes earthly disasters, so a troop of wily astronauts try to destroy it with the latest technology. They fail, leading one sacrificial soul to do it himself. **AKA:** War Between the Planets.
1965 80m/C Giacomo "Jack" Rossi-Stuart, Amber Collins, Peter Martell, John Bartha, Halina Zalewska, James Weaver; **D:** Anthony M. (Antonio Marghereti) Dawson. VHS, Beta NO 🐾

Planets Against Us Science fiction tale of escaped alien humanoid robots who take refuge on Earth, but whose touch is fatal. Good special effects. **AKA:** I Pianeti Contro di Noi; The Man with the Yellow Eyes; Hands of a Killer; The Monster with Green Eyes.
1961 85m/B Michel Lemoine, Maria Pia Luzi, Jany Clair; **D:** Romano Ferrara. VHS $16.95 SNC 🐾½

Platinum Blonde Screwball comedy in which a newspaper journalist (Williams) marries a wealthy girl (Harlow) but finds that he doesn't like the restrictions and confinement of high society. Yearning for a creative outlet, he decides to write a play and hires a reporter (Young) to collaborate with him. The results are funny and surprising when Young

shows up at the mansion flanked by a group of hard-drinking, fun-loving reporters.
1931 86m/B Loretta Young, Robert Williams, Jean Harlow, Louise Closser Hale; **D:** Frank Capra; **W:** Jo Swerling, Dorothy Howell. VHS $19.95 COL 🐾🐾🐾

Platinum High School Divorced father Rooney is appalled when his son is "accidentally" killed while off at an exclusive military academy. His suspicions are aroused by the prevaricating school commander and he discovers some horrible truths about his son's death and life at the school. **AKA:** Trouble at 16; Rich, Young, and Deadly.
1960 91m/B Mickey Rooney, Terry Moore, Dan Duryea, Conway Twitty, Warren Berlinger, Yvette Mimieux, Jimmy Boyd, Richard Jaeckel, Harold Lloyd Jr., Elisha Cook Jr., Jimmy Murphy; **D:** Charles Haas; **W:** Robert Smith. VHS $9.98 REP 🐾½

Platoon A grunt's view of the Vietnam War is provided in all its horrific, inexplicable detail. Sheen is wooden in the lead, but both Dafoe and Berenger are resplendent as, respectively, good and bad soldiers. Strong, visceral filmmaking from fearless director Stone, who based the film on his own GI experiences. Highly acclaimed; considered by many to be the most realistic portrayal of the war on film.
1986 (R) 113m/C Charlie Sheen, Willem Dafoe, Tom Berenger, Francesco Quinn, Forest Whitaker, John C. McGinley, Kevin Dillon, Richard Edson, Reggie Johnson, Keith David, Johnny Depp; **D:** Oliver Stone; **W:** Oliver Stone; **M:** Georges Delerue. Academy Awards '86: Best Director (Stone), Best Film Editing, Best Picture, Best Sound; Nominations: Best Cinematography, Best Original Screenplay, Best Supporting Actor (Berenger, Dafoe); British Academy Awards '87: Best Director (Stone); Directors Guild of America Awards '86: Best Director (Stone); Golden Globe Awards '87: Best Director (Stone), Best Film—Drama, Best Supporting Actor (Berenger); National Board of Review Awards '86: 10 Best Films of the Year. VHS, Beta $14.98 LIV, BTV 🐾🐾🐾½

Platoon Leader A battle-drenched portrait of a West Point lieutenant in Vietnam. When he first arrives, he must win the trust of his men, who have been on their tours for a much longer time. As time goes on, he slowly becomes hardened to the realities of the brutal life in the field. Made on the heels of the widely acclaimed "Platoon," but it doesn't have the same power. Norris is martial arts king Chuck Norris' brother.
1987 (R) 97m/C Michael Dudikoff, Brian Libby, Robert F. Lyons, Rick Fitts, Jesse Dabson, William Smith, Michael De Lorenzo; **D:** Aaron Norris; **W:** R.J. Marx; **M:** George S. Clinton. VHS, Beta $19.98 MED, VTR 🐾🐾

Platoon the Warriors The underworld rages with violence when two kingpins, Rex and Bill, become bitter and declare war over a botched drug deal.
1988 90m/C David Coley, Dick Crown, James Miller, Don Richard, Alex Sylvian; **D:** Philip Ko. VHS, Beta NO 🐾

Platypus Cove An adopted boy tracks down the culprits responsible for the sabotage of his family's boat, a crime for which he was suspected. Australian.
1986 82m/C Paul Smith; **D:** Peter Maxwell. VHS, Beta $59.98 SUE 🐾

Play Dead Poor Yvonne De Carlo plays a psychotic woman who trains a dog to rip people to shreds. **AKA:** Satan's Dog.
1981 89m/C Yvonne De Carlo, Stephanie Dunham, David Cullinane, Glenn Kezer, Ron Jackson, Carolyn Greenwood; **D:** Peter Wittman. VHS $19.95 ACA 🐾

Play It Again, Charlie Brown The Peanuts gang goes bananas when Lucy enlists Schroeder to play rock music at a PTA meeting.
1970 25m/C Charles M. Schulz. VHS, Beta $14.95 SHV, VTR, WTA 🐾

Play It Again, Sam Allen is—no surprise—a nerd, and this time he's in love with his best friend's wife. Modest storyline provides a framework of endless gags, with Allen borrowing heavily from "Casablanca." Bogey even appears periodically to counsel Allen on the ways of wooing women. Superior comedy isn't hurt by Ross directing instead of Allen, who adapted the script from his own play.
1972 (PG) 85m/C Woody Allen, Diane Keaton, Tony Roberts, Susan Anspach, Jerry Lacy, Jennifer Salt, Joy Bang, Viva, Herbert Ross; **D:** Herbert Ross; **M:** Billy Goldenberg. VHS, Beta, 8mm $19.95 PAR 🐾🐾🐾½

Play Misty for Me A radio deejay obliges a psychotic woman's song request and suddenly finds himself the target of her obsessive behavior, which rapidly turns from seductive to murderous. Auspicious directorial debut for Eastwood, borrowing from the Siegel playbook (look for the director's cameo as a barkeep). Based on a story by Heims.
1971 (R) 102m/C Clint Eastwood, Jessica Walter, Donna Mills, John Larch, Irene Hervey, Jack Ging; **Cameos:** Don Siegel; **D:** Clint Eastwood; **W:** Jo Heims, Dean Reisner. VHS, Beta $19.95 MCA, TLF 🐾🐾🐾

Play Murder for Me Saxophonist performing in a seedy Buenos Aires nightclub has his world turned upside down when a former lover suddenly re-enters his life. She still has her eye on him, but she's now the woman of a notorious mobster. Soon the musician finds himself drawn into the usual deadly world of crime, deceit, and unharnessed passion.
1991 (R) 80m/C Jack Wagner, Tracy Scoggins; **D:** Hector Olivera. VHS $89.98 NHO 🐾

Play Nice A detective hunts down a murderous psychopath but is shocked when he discovers his suspect is a woman—and someone he knows. Also available in an unrated version.
1992 (R) 90m/C Ed O'Ross. VHS $89.95 VMK 🐾½

Playboy of the Western World An innkeeper's daughter is infatuated with a young man who says he murdered his father. Adapted from the classic play by John Millington Synge.
1962 96m/C Siobhan McKenna, Gary Raymond; **D:** Brian Desmond Hurst. VHS, Beta NO 🐾🐾½

The Playboys In 1957 in a tiny Irish village, unmarried Tara Maguire causes a scandal by having a baby. Her beauty attracts lots of men—there's a former beau who kills himself, the obsessive, middle-aged Sergeant Hegarty, and the newest arrival, Tom Castle, an actor with a rag-tag theatrical troupe called the Playboys. Slow-moving and simple story with particularly good performances by Wright as the strong-willed Tara and Finney as Hegarty, clinging to a last chance at love and family. The Playboys' hysterically hammy version of "Gone With the Wind" is a gem. Directorial debut of Mackinnon. Filmed in the village of Redhills, Ireland, the hometown of co-writer Connaughton.
1992 (PG-13) 114m/C Albert Finney, Aidan Quinn, Robin Wright, Milo O'Shea, Alan Devlin, Niamh Cusack, Ian McElhinney, Niall Buggy, Adrian Dunbar; **D:** Gilles Mackinnon; **W:** Shane Connaughton, Kerry Crabbe; **M:** Jean-Claude Petit. VHS $92.99 HBO, FCT 🐾🐾🐾

The Player Clever, entertaining, and biting satire of the movie industry and the greed that controls it. Robbins is dead-on as Griffin Mill, a young studio exec who becomes the chief suspect in a murder investigation. He personifies Hollywood's ethics (or lack thereof) in a performance both cold and vulnerable, as he looks for the right buttons to push and the proper back to stab. Strong leading performances are supplemented by 65 star cameos. Some viewers may be put off by the inside-Hollywood jokes, but Altman fans will love it. The laserdisc version includes commentary by Altman, interviews with 20 screenwriters, and celebrity cameos that didn't make the final cut.
1992 (R) 123m/C Tim Robbins, Greta Scacchi, Fred Ward, Whoopi Goldberg, Peter Gallagher, Brion James, Cynthia Stevenson, Vincent D'Onofrio, Dean Stockwell, Richard E. Grant, Dina Merrill, Sydney Pollack, Lyle Lovett, Randall Batinkoff, Gina Gershon; *Cameos:* Burt Reynolds, Cher, Nick Nolte, Jack Lemmon, Lily Tomlin, Marlee Matlin, Julia Roberts, Bruce Willis, Anjelica Huston, Elliott Gould, Sally Kellerman, Steve Allen, Richard Anderson, Harry Belafonte, Shari Belafonte-Harper, Karen Black, Gary Busey, Robert Carradine, James Coburn, Cathy Lee Crosby, John Cusack, Brad Davis, Peter Falk, Teri Garr, Leeza Gibbons, Scott Glenn, Jeff Goldblum, Joel Grey, Buck Henry, Kathy Ireland, Sally Kirkland, Andie MacDowell, Martin Mull, Mimi Rogers, Jill St. John, Susan Sarandon, Rod Steiger, Joan Tewkesbury, Robert Wagner, Michael Tolkin; *D:* Robert Altman; *W:* Michael Tolkin; *M:* Thomas Newman. Academy Awards '92 Nominations: Best Adapted Screenplay, Best Director (Altman), Best Film Editing; Cannes Film Festival '92: Best Film; Cannes Film Festival '92: Best Actor (Robbins), Best Director (Altman); Golden Globe Awards '93: Best Actor—Musical/Comedy (Robbins), Best Film—Musical/Comedy; Independent Spirit Awards '93: Best Film; New York Film Critics Awards '93: Best Film, Best Director (Altman), Best Film. **VHS $19.95** *NLC, CRC, MOV* 🎞️🎞️🎞️½

Players Young tennis hustler touring Mexico hooks up with beautiful and mysterious older woman. They seem to be from different worlds yet their love grows. She inspires him enough to enter Wimbledon. Several tennis pros appear, including Guillermo Vilas, John McEnroe, and Ilie Nastase. Almost as boring as watching a real tennis game.
1979 (PG) 120m/C Ali MacGraw, Dean Paul Martin, Maximilian Schell, Pancho Gonzales; *D:* Anthony Harvey; *W:* Arnold Schulman; *M:* Jerry Goldsmith. **VHS, Beta $49.95** *PAR* 🎞️

Playgirl Killer After impulsively murdering a restless model, an artist continues to kill indiscriminately, keeping his spoils on ice. Sedaka croons between kills and luxuriates poolside—seemingly oblivious to the plot of the film—while a female decoy is sent to bait the killer for the police. For adult viewers. *AKA:* Decoy for Terror.
1966 86m/C William Kerwin, Jean Christopher, Andree Champagne, Neil Sedaka; *D:* Erick Santamaria. **VHS, Beta $19.95** *NWV* 🎞️

Playing Away A team of Caribbean cricket players meet a team of stuffy Brits on the field in a clash of the cultures.
1987 100m/C Norman Beaton, Robert Urquhart; *D:* Horace Love. **VHS, Beta $19.98** *NLC* 🎞️

Playing Dead Drew and his wife portray a married couple in this silent farce. The insecure husband decides to fake his death so his wife can be with the man he thinks she loves.
1915 58m/B Sidney Drew, Lucille Drew, Alice Lake, Donald Hall, Harry English, Isadore Marcil; *D:* Sidney Drew. **VHS $16.95** *GPV* 🎞️🎞️½

Playing for Keeps Three high school grads turn a dilapidated hotel into a rock 'n roll resort. Music by Pete Townshend, Peter Frampton, Phil Collins, and others.
1986 (PG-13) 103m/C Daniel Jordano, Matthew Penn, Leon Grant, Harold Gould, Jimmy Baio; *D:* Bob Weinstein. **VHS, Beta $79.95** *MCA* 🎞️

Playing for Time Compelling, award-winning television drama based on actual experiences of a Holocaust prisoner who survives by leading an inmate orchestra. Strong playing from Redgrave and Mayron. Pro-Palestinian Redgrave's political beliefs made her a controversial candidate for the role of Jewish Fania Fenelon, but her stunning performance is on the mark.
1980 148m/C Vanessa Redgrave, Jane Alexander, Maud Adams, Verna Bloom, Melanie Mayron; *D:* Daniel Mann; *M:* Brad Fiedel. **VHS, Beta** *NO* 🎞️🎞️🎞️

Playing with Fire A young girl gets caught up in drugs, casual sex, and murder.
197? 87m/C Karen Tungay, Danny Keogh, Sam Marais; *D:* Alan Nathanson. **VHS, Beta** *NO* 🎞️

Playmates Barrymore is practically wasted in his last film as a down-on-his-luck actor who agrees to turn bandleader Kyser into a Shakespearean actor. Bizarre comedy is funny at times, but leaves the audience wondering what Barrymore thought he was doing. ♫Humpty Dumpty Heart; How Long Did I Dream?; Que Chica?; Romeo Smith and Juliet Jones; Thank Your Lucky Stars and Stripes.
1941 96m/B Kay Kyser, John Barrymore, Ginny Simms, Lupe Velez, May Robson, Patsy Kelly, Peter Lind Hayes, George Cleveland; *D:* David Butler. **VHS, Beta $19.98** *TTC* 🎞️

Playmates Two divorced buddies fall in love with each other's ex-wives in this made for television flick. Typical Alda vehicle isn't bad.
1972 78m/C Doug McClure, Alan Alda, Connie Stevens, Barbara Feldon, Eileen Brennan, Tiger Williams, Severn Darden; *D:* Theodore J. Flicker. **VHS, Beta $19.98** *VMK* 🎞️🎞️½

Playroom Archaeologist McDonald is completing his father's search for the tomb of a medieval boy-prince. But someone, or something, has been waiting for him for a long, long time. When he finally reaches the long-sought-after tomb, he discovers that it is a torture chamber where his worst nightmares become realities. The demonic prince who was buried in the tomb has picked Chris as his playmate, and the rest of the staff as his personal toys.
1990 (R) 87m/C Lisa Aliff, Aron Eisenberg, Christopher McDonald, James Purcell, Jamie Rose, Vincent Schiavelli; *D:* Manny Coto. **VHS $89.98** *REP* 🎞️🎞️

Playtime Occasionnally enterprising comedy in which the bemused Frenchman Hulot tries in vain to maintain an appointment in an urban landscape of glass and steel. The theme of cold, unfeeling civilization is hardly unique, but the film is nonetheless enjoyable. The third in the Hulot trilogy, preceded by "Mr. Hulot's Holiday" and "Mon Oncle." In French with English subtitles.
1967 108m/C Jacques Tati, Barbara Dennek, Jacqueline Lecomte, Jack Gautier; *D:* Jacques Tati. **VHS, Beta $29.98** *SUE, ING, NLC* 🎞️🎞️🎞️

Plaza Suite Three alternating skits from Neil Simon's play about different couples staying at the New York hotel. Matthau shines in all three vignettes. Some of Simon's funnier stuff, with the first sketch being the best: Matthau and Stapleton are a couple celebrating their 24th anniversary. She's sentimental, while he's yearning for his mistress.

Number two has producer Matthau putting the make on old flame Harris, while the finale has father Matthau coaxing his anxious daughter out of the bathroom on her wedding day.
1971 (PG) 114m/C Walter Matthau, Maureen Stapleton, Barbara Harris, Lee Grant, Louise Sorel; *D:* Arthur Hiller; *W:* Neil Simon; *M:* Maurice Jarre. **VHS, Beta $14.95** *PAR* 🎞️🎞️🎞️

Please Don't Eat My Mother A softcore remake of "Little Shop of Horrors" in which a lonely voyeur plays host to a human-eating plant. *AKA:* Hungry Pets; Glump.
1972 95m/C Buck Kartalian, Renee Bond; *D:* Carl Monson. **VHS $19.98** *MOV, VDM, TPV* Woof!

Please Don't Eat the Daisies City couple and kids leave the Big Apple for the country and are traumatized by flora and fauna. Goofy sixties fluff taken from Jean Kerr's book and the basis for the eventual TV series.
1960 111m/C Doris Day, David Niven, Janis Paige, Spring Byington, Richard Haydn, Patsy Kelly, Jack Weston, Margaret Lindsay; *D:* Charles Walters. **VHS, Beta $19.98** *MGM, FCT* 🎞️🎞️½

Pleasure A saga of love, treachery, and melodrama in English society where self-indulgence held priority and good manners were the rule.
1931 53m/B Conway Tearle, Roscoe Karns, Carmel Myers, Lena Basquette. **VHS, Beta $19.95** *NOS* 🎞️🎞️

A Pleasure Doing Business Three high school buddies, now in their 40s, are reunited at a stag party, where they decide to go into business as managers in "the oldest profession."
1979 (R) 86m/C Conrad Bain, John Byner, Alan Oppenheimer, Misty Rowe, Phyllis Diller, Tom Smothers; *D:* Steve Vagnino. **VHS, Beta $49.95** *VHE* 🎞️

Pleasure Palace A gambling lady's-man (Sharif) meets his match when he helps a woman casino owner (Lange). Made for television.
1980 96m/C Omar Sharif, Victoria Principal, J.D. Cannon, Gerald S. O'Loughlin, Jose Ferrer, Hope Lange, Alan King; *D:* Walter Grauman. **VHS, Beta $29.95** *LIV* 🎞️🎞️

Pledge Night Tale of horror and revenge. Killed years before in a fraternity hazing, Sid returns for the brothers who did him in. Gory and violent.
1990 (R) 90m/C Will Kempe, Shannon McMahon, Todd Eastland, Paul Ziller; *M:* Anthrax. **VHS $89.95** *IMP* 🎞️🎞️

Plenty Difficult but worthwhile film with Streep in top form as a former member of the French Resistance, who upon returning to England finds life at home increasingly tedious and banal and begins to fear her finest hours may be behind her. Gielgud is flawless as the aging career diplomat. Adapted by David Hare from his play, an allegory to British decline.
1985 (R) 119m/C Meryl Streep, Tracey Ullman, Sting, John Gielgud, Charles Dance, Ian McKellan, Sam Neill, Burt Kwouk; *D:* Fred Schepisi; *W:* David Hare; *M:* Bruce Smeaton. **VHS, Beta $14.98** *REP* 🎞️🎞️½

The Plot Against Harry Jewish racketeer Harry Plotnik checks out of prison, and finds the outside world ain't what it used to be. Attempting to lead an honest life only makes matters worse. Completely overlooked when first released in 1969 (and quickly shelved) because it was considered to have no commercial potential, Roemer's crime comedy found an enthusiastic audience when it was rediscovered twenty years later.

1969 81m/B Martin Priest, Ben Lang, Maxine Woods, Henry Nemo; **D:** Michael Roemer; **W:** Michael Roemer. **VHS $79.95** *NYF, FCT ♔♔♔*

The Ploughman's Lunch A BBC news reporter claws and lies his way to the top. He then discovers that he is the victim of a far more devious plan. Engrossing and well made, although some of the political views are simplistic.

1983 107m/C Jonathan Pryce, Charlie Dore, Tim Curry, Rosemary Harris, Frank Finlay, Bill Paterson; **D:** Richard Eyre. **VHS, Beta $59.98** *SUE ♔♔♔*

Plumber A plumber who makes a house call extends his stay to psychologically torture the woman of the house. Originally made for Australian television.

1979 76m/C Judy Morris, Ivar Kants, Robert Coleby; **D:** Peter Weir; **W:** Peter Weir. **VHS, Beta $59.95** *MED ♔♔1/2*

Plunder Road A pair of crooks cook up a plan to rob a train bound for the San Francisco Mint that's carrying a fortune in gold bullion. Top notch B-film noir.

1957 76m/B Gene Raymond, Jeanne Cooper, Wayne Morris, Elisha Cook Jr.; **D:** Hubert Cornfield. **VHS $19.98** *REP ♔♔1/2*

Plunge Into Darkness Quiet weekend in the mountains turns into a nightmare for an ex-Olympic runner and his family.

1977 77m/C Bruce Barry, Olivia Hamnett, Ashley Greenville, Wallace Eaton, Tom Richards; **D:** Peter Maxwell. **VHS, Beta** *NO ♔1/2*

Plutonium Baby A mutated kid, whose mother was killed by the same radiation exposure that infected him, tracks down the guilty party in New York in this comic-book style film.

1987 85m/C Patrick Molloy, Danny Guerra; **D:** Ray Hirschman. **VHS, Beta $79.95** *TWE ♔*

Plutonium Incident A female technician at a nuclear power plant suspects the facility to be less safe than it appears, and faces a diabolical plan of harassment when she attempts to bring attention to the hazards.

1982 90m/C Janet Margolin, Powers Boothe, Bo Hopkins, Joseph Campanella; **D:** Richard Michaels. **VHS, Beta** *TLF ♔♔*

The Pocatello Kid Maynard stretches in a dual role as the wrongly convicted Kid and the Kid's no-good sheriff brother.

1931 60m/B Ken Maynard, Marceline Day, Charles "Blackie" King, Lafe McKee; **D:** Phil Rosen. **VHS, Beta $19.95** *NOS, VCN, VDM ♔1/2*

Pocket Money Down-on-their-luck cowpokes foolishly do business with crooked rancher in attempt to make comeback in faltering acting careers. Star-powered, moderately entertaining modern western-comedy based on the novel "Jim Kane" by J.K.S. Brown.

1972 (PG) 100m/C Paul Newman, Lee Marvin, Strother Martin, Christine Belford, Wayne Rogers, Hector Elizondo, Gregory Sierra; **D:** Stuart Rosenberg; **W:** Terence Malick. **VHS, Beta $59.95** *WAR, FCT ♔♔*

Pocketful of Miracles Capra's final film, a remake of his 1933 "Lady for a Day," is just as corny and sentimental but doesn't work quite as well. Davis is delightful as Apple Annie, a down-on-her-luck street vendor who will go to any extreme to hide her poverty from the well-married daughter she adores. Ford is terrific as the man who transforms Annie into a lady in time for her daughter's visit. Touching. Maybe too touching. Also marks Ann-Margret's film debut.

1961 136m/C Bette Davis, Glenn Ford, Peter Falk, Hope Lange, Arthur O'Connell, Ann-Margret, Thomas Mitchell, Jack Elam, Edward Everett Horton, David Brian, Mickey Shaughnessy; **D:** Frank Capra. Academy Awards '61 Nominations: Best Costume Design (Color), Best Song ("Pocketful of Miracles"), Best Supporting Actor (Falk); Golden Globe Awards '62: Best Actor—Musical/Comedy (Ford). **VHS, Beta $14.98** *MGM, FOX, CCB ♔♔♔*

A Pocketful of Rye Based on Agatha Christie's novel featuring the sleuthing Miss Marple. She faces another murderous puzzle, this one based on an old nursery rhyme. Made for British television.

1987 101m/C Joan Hickson; **D:** Guy Slater. **VHS, Beta $29.98** *FOX, HMV ♔♔*

Poco The story of Poco, a shaggy little dog who travels across the country to search for the young girl who owns him.

1977 88m/C Chill Wills, Michelle Ashburn, John Steadman. **VHS, Beta $69.98** *LIV, VES ♔*

Poetic Justice Justice (Jackson in her movie debut, for better or worse) gives up college plans to follow a career in cosmetology after her boyfriend's brutal murder. She copes with her loss by dedicating herself to poetry writing (provided by no less than poet Maya Angelou) and meets postal worker Shakur. Singleton's second directorial effort is about the girlz n the hood and boasts a lighter script (well, it is about a hairdresser) focusing less on the Boyz-style morality and more on the trials and tribulations of Justice. Production stopped on the South Central L.A. set during the '92 riots, but the aftermath provided poignant pictures for later scenes.

1993 (R) 109m/C Janet Jackson, Tupac Shakur, Tyra Ferrell, Regina King, Joe Torry; **D:** John Singleton; **M:** Stanley Clarke. Academy Awards '93 Nominations: Best Song ("Again"); Golden Globe Awards '94: Best Song ("Again"); MTV Movie Awards '94: Best Actress (Jackson), Most Desirable Female (Jackson). **VHS, 8mm** *COL, BTV ♔♔1/2*

Pogo for President: "I Go Pogo" Animated adventure with Walt Kelly's Pogo Possum becoming an unlikely presidential candidate when Howland Owl proclaims him the winner of a election.

1984 (PG) 120m/C V: Jonathan Winters, Vincent Price, Ruth Buzzi, Stan Freberg, Jimmy Breslin. **VHS, Beta $49.95** *DIS, WTA ♔♔1/2*

Poil de Carotte A semi-famous French melodrama about a young boy harassed by his overbearing mother to the point of disaster, redeemed finally by the love of his father. In French with English subtitles. **AKA:** The Red Head.

1931 90m/B Harry Baur, Robert Lynen, Catherine Fontenoy; **D:** Julien Duvivier. **VHS, Beta $24.95** *NOS, FCT, MRV ♔♔1/2*

The Point Charming and sincere made-for-television animated feature about the rejection and isolation of a round-headed child in a world of pointy-headed people. Excellent score.

1971 74m/C D: Fred Wolf; **M:** Harry Nilsson. **VHS, Beta $14.98** *FHE, VES, WTA ♔♔1/2*

Point Blank Adapted from Stark's "The Hunter." The film's techniques are sometimes compared to those of Resnais and Godard. Double-crossed and believed dead, gangster Marvin returns to claim his share of the loot from the Organization. Hard-nosed examination of the depersonalization of a mechanized urban world.

1967 92m/C Lee Marvin, Angie Dickinson, Keenan Wynn, Carroll O'Connor, Lloyd Bochner, Michael Strong, James B. Sikking; **D:** John Boorman. **VHS, Beta $19.98** *MGM ♔♔1/2*

Point Break If you can suspend your disbelief—and you'd need a crane—then this crime adventure is just dandy. Reeves is a young undercover FBI kid sent to infiltrate a gang of bank-robbing surfer dudes. Swayze is the leader of the beach subculture, a thrillseeker who plays cat-and-mouse with the feds in a series of excellent action scenes. Silly brain candy.

1991 (R) 117m/C Patrick Swayze, Keanu Reeves, Gary Busey, Lori Petty, John C. McGinley, Chris Pederson, Bojesse Christopher, Julian Reyes, Daniel Beer, Sydney Walsh, Vincent Klyn, James LeGros, John Philbin; **D:** Kathryn Bigelow; **W:** W. Peter Iliff; **M:** Mark Isham. **VHS $19.98** *FXV ♔♔1/2*

Point of Impact A Miami customs officer is killed in an explosion and his partner is blamed. He knows a Cuban crime boss was actually behind it and goes undercover to bring the criminal organization down. But there's also the temptation of the the criminal's sexy ladyfriend. Also available in an unrated version.

1993 (R) 96m/C Michael Pare, Barbara Carrera, Michael Ironside. **VHS $92.95** *VMK ♔♔*

Point of No Return Fonda is Maggie, a drugged-out loser condemned to death for her part in a murder spree, but if she agrees to work as a government assassin, she'll be given a reprieve. Fonda displays a certain perkiness as the assassin and is better in her early surly scenes; Keitel is creepy as another assassin. Flashy, exacting, but ultimately innocuous remake of the 1990 French thriller "La Femme Nikita."

1993 (R) 108m/C Bridget Fonda, Gabriel Byrne, Dermot Mulroney, Miguel Ferrer, Anne Bancroft, Olivia D'Abo, Harvey Keitel, Richard Romanus, Lorraine Toussaint, Geoffrey Lewis, Calvin Levels; **D:** John Badham; **W:** Robert Getchell, Alexandra Seros; **M:** Hans Zimmer. **VHS, Beta $19.98** *WAR ♔♔1/2*

Point of Terror A handsome rock singer seduces a record company executive's wife in order to further his career.

1971 (R) 88m/C Peter Carpenter, Dyanne Thorne, Lory Hansen, Leslie Simms; **D:** Alex Nicol. **VHS, Beta $39.95** *VCI ♔*

The Pointsman A quirky, small film based on the novel by Jean Paul Franssens. A beautiful Scandinavian woman accidentally gets off a train in Northern Scotland, where the only shelter is a small railway outpost, and the only company is a mysterious pointsman who lives by the comings and goings of the trains. The couple's increasing isolation as winter falls and their lack of a common language persists is portrayed with both humor and poignancy. **AKA:** De Wisselwachter.

1986 (R) 95m/C Jim Van Der Woude, Stephane Excoffier, John Kraaykamp, Josse De Pauw, Ton Van Dort; **D:** Jos Stelling. **VHS, Beta $79.98** *LIV, VES ♔♔1/2*

Poison A controversial, compelling drama weaving the story of a seven year-old boy's murder of his father with two other tales of obsessive, fringe behavior. From the director of the underground hit "Superstar: The Karen Carpenter Story," which was shot using only a cast of "Barbie" dolls.

1991 (R) 85m/C Edith Meeks, Larry Maxwell, Susan Norman, Scott Renderer, James Lyons; **D:** Todd Haynes; **W:** Todd Haynes; **M:** James Bennett. **VHS $89.95** *FXL, ING ♔♔♔*

Poison Ivy A routine, made for television comedy about a chaotic and lusty summer camp.

1985 97m/C Michael J. Fox, Nancy McKeon, Robert Klein, Caren Kaye; **D:** Larry Elikann; **M:** Miles Goodman. **VHS, Beta** *NO ♔♔*

Poison Ivy Barrymore is right on target as a junior femme fatale in this trashy tale of a wayward teenager and her takeover of her best friend's family. Ivy has no discernable family life and quickly attaches herself to the lonely, neglected Cooper (Gilbert) who ends up watching as she systematically seduces both her mother (emotionally) and her father (physically). But when Ivy's homewrecking turns lethal, Cooper must fight her "friend" to save herself. Glossy, over-done pulp. An unrated version is also available.
1992 (R) 91m/C Drew Barrymore, Sara Gilbert, Tom Skerritt, Cheryl Ladd; *D:* Katt Shea Ruben; *W:* Katt Shea Ruben, Andy Ruben. **VHS** *COL, NLC, PMS* 🎬🎬

Poker Alice A lively Western starring Elizabeth Taylor as a sometime gambler who wins a brothel in a poker game.
1987 100m/C Elizabeth Taylor, George Hamilton, Tom Skerritt, Richard Mulligan, David Wayne, Susan Tyrrell, Pat Corley; *D:* Arthur Seidelman; *W:* James Lee Barrett. **VHS, Beta $19.95** *STE, NWV* 🎬🎬

The Polar Bear King When a handsome prince refuses to marry the evil witch of Summerland, the wicked woman uses her power to turn him into a polar bear. The polar bear prince embarks on a journey to Winterland where he meets and falls in love with a beautiful princess. Together they return to Summerland and try to break the witch's spell. Filmed on location in Norway and Sweden.
1994 (PG) 87m/C Maria Bonnerie, Jack Fjeldstad, Tobias Hoesl, Anna-Lotta Larsson; *D:* Ola Solum. **VHS $19.95** *HMD* 🎬🎬½

Poldark Tempestuous love, political intrigue, and family struggles all set in 18th-century Cornwall, then the copper-producing center of England. Heroic Ross Poldark has just returned from fighting upstart Americans in the Revolutionary War only to discover that his father has died and the family mines are about to be sold to the scheming Warleggan family. Ross struggles to pay off family debts, reclaim his heritage, resolve his feelings for an old love, and fight his attraction to the beguiling, but completely unsuitable, Demelza. Adapted from the novels by Winston Graham. Made for British television; 12 episodes on 6 cassettes.
1975 720m/C Robin Ellis, Angharad Rees, Jill Townsend, Judy Geeson, Ralph Bates, Richard Morant, Clive Francis, John Baskcomb, Paul Curran, Tilly Tremayne, Mary Wimbush; *D:* Paul Annett, Christopher Barry, Kenneth Ives; *W:* Paul Wheeler, Jack Russell, Peter Draper, Jack Pulman. **VHS $149.95** *TVC, SIG* 🎬🎬🎬

Police French police drama with the intense Depardieu as a cop hunting an Algerian drug boss. Matters grow complicated when he falls for the elusive crook's girlfriend. Sometimes gripping, but uneven; the actors were encouraged to improvise. Inspired by the novel "Bodies Are Dust" by P.J. Wolfson. In French with English subtitles.
1985 113m/C Gerard Depardieu, Sophie Marceau, Sandrine Bonnaire, Richard Anconina, Pascale Rocard; *D:* Maurice Pialat; *W:* Catherine Breillat. **VHS $79.95** *NYF, FCT, ING* 🎬🎬½

Police Academy In an attempt to recruit more cops, a big-city police department does away with all its job standards. The producers probably didn't know that they were introducing bad comedy's answer to the "Friday the 13th" series, but it's hard to avoid heaping the sins of its successors on this film. Besides, it's just plain dumb.
1984 (R) 96m/C Steve Guttenberg, Kim Cattrall, Bubba Smith, George Gaynes, Michael Winslow, Leslie Easterbrook, Georgina Spelvin, Debralee Scott; *D:* Hugh Wilson; *W:* Hugh Wilson, Pat

Proft, Neal Israel; *M:* Robert Folk. **VHS, Beta, 8mm $19.98** *WAR* 🎬½

Police Academy 2: Their First Assignment More predictable idiocy from the cop shop. This time they're determined to rid the precinct of some troublesome punks. No real story to speak of, just more high jinks in this mindless sequel.
1985 (PG-13) 87m/C Steve Guttenberg, Bubba Smith, Michael Winslow, Art Metrano, Colleen Camp, Howard Hesseman, David Graf, George Gaynes; *D:* Jerry Paris; *W:* Barry W. Blaustein. **VHS, Beta $19.98** *WAR* 🎬

Police Academy 3: Back in Training In yet another sequel, the bumbling cops find their alma mater is threatened by a budget crunch and they must compete with a rival academy to see which school survives. The "return to school" plot allowed the filmmakers to add new characters to replace those who had some scruples about picking up yet another "Police Lobotomy" check. Followed by three more sequels.
1986 (PG) 84m/C Steve Guttenberg, Bubba Smith, David Graf, Michael Winslow, Marion Ramsey, Art Metrano, Bob(cat) Goldthwait, Leslie Easterbrook, Tim Kazurinsky, George Gaynes, Shawn Weatherly; *D:* Jerry Paris; *W:* Gene Quintano; *M:* Robert Folk. **VHS, Beta $19.98** *WAR* 🎬

Police Academy 4: Citizens on Patrol The comic cop cutups from the first three films aid a citizen's patrol group in their unnamed, but still wacky, hometown. Moronic high jinks ensue. Fourth in the series of five (or is it six?) that began with "Police Academy".
1987 (PG) 88m/C Steve Guttenberg, Bubba Smith, Michael Winslow, David Graf, Tim Kazurinsky, George Gaynes, Colleen Camp, Bob(cat) Goldthwait, Sharon Stone; *D:* Jim Drake; *W:* Gene Quintano; *M:* Robert Folk. **VHS, Beta $19.98** *WAR* 🎬

Police Academy 5: Assignment Miami Beach The fourth sequel, wherein the misfits-with-badges go to Miami and bumble about in the usual manner. It's about time these cops were retired from the force.
1988 (PG) 89m/C Bubba Smith, David Graf, Michael Winslow, Leslie Easterbrook, Rene Auberjonois, Marion Ramsey, Janet Jones, George Gaynes, Matt McCoy; *D:* Alan Myerson; *M:* Robert Folk. **VHS, Beta $19.98** *WAR* Woof!

Police Academy 6: City Under Siege In what is hoped to be the last in a series of bad comedies, the distinguished graduates pursue three goofballs responsible for a crime wave.
1989 (PG) 85m/C Bubba Smith, David Graf, Michael Winslow, Leslie Easterbrook, Marion Ramsey, Matt McCoy, Bruce Mahler, G.W. Bailey, George Gaynes; *D:* Peter Bonerz; *M:* Robert Folk. **VHS $89.95** *WAR* 🎬

Police Court The son of a faded, alcoholic screen star tries to bring the old fellow back to prominence.
1937 62m/B Nat Barry, Henry B. Walthall, Leon Janney. **VHS, Beta** *NO* 🎬

Police Squad! Help Wanted! Three episodes from the brilliant, short-lived television spoof, with the patented pun-a-second style of humor typical of the makers of "Airplane!" and "The Naked Gun," which was based on this show. Episodes included: "A Substantial Gift," "Ring of Fear," and "Rendezvous at Big Gulch." See also "More! Police Squad."
1982 75m/C Leslie Nielsen, Alan North, Ed Williams, William Duell; *D:* Jerry Zucker, David Zucker, Jim Abrahams; *W:* Jerry Zucker, David Zucker, Jim Abrahams. **VHS, Beta $19.95** *PAR* 🎬🎬

Policewoman Centerfold Exploitative rendering based on the true story of a cop who posed for a pornographic magazine. Anderson is appealing in the lead.
1983 100m/C Melody Anderson, Ed Marinaro, Donna Pescow, Bert Remsen, David Spielberg; *D:* Reza Badiyi. **VHS, Beta** *NO* 🎬

Policewomen Female undercover agent must stop a ring of gold smugglers.
1973 (R) 99m/C Sondra Currie, Tony Young, Phil Hoover, Elizabeth Stuart, Jeanne Bell; *D:* Lee Frost. **VHS, Beta** *NO* 🎬½

A Polish Vampire in Burbank A shy vampire in Burbank tries again and again to find blood and love. Wacky.
1980 84m/C Mark Pirro, Lori Sutton, Eddie Deezen; *D:* Mark Pirro. **VHS, Beta** *SIM* 🎬🎬

Pollyanna A young orphan girl is adopted by her cold, embittered aunt and does her best to bring joy and gladness to all the new people she meets. Silent with music score.
1920 60m/B Mary Pickford. **VHS, Beta $19.95** *CCB* 🎬🎬½

Pollyanna Based on the Eleanor Porter story about an enchanting young girl whose contagious enthusiasm and zest for life touches the hearts of all she meets. Mills is perfect in the title role and was awarded a special Oscar for outstanding juvenile performance. A distinguished supporting cast is the icing on the cake in this delightful Disney confection. Original version was filmed in 1920 with Mary Pickford.
1960 134m/C Hayley Mills, Jane Wyman, Richard Egan, Karl Malden, Nancy Olson, Adolphe Menjou, Donald Crisp, Agnes Moorehead, Kevin Corcoran; *D:* David Swift. **VHS, Beta $19.99** *DIS, BTV* 🎬🎬🎬

Poltergeist This production has Stephen Spielberg written all over it. A young family's home becomes a house of horrors when they are terrorized by menacing spirits who abduct their five-year-old daughter...through the TV screen! Roller-coaster thrills and chills, dazzling special effects, and perfectly timed humor highlight this stupendously scary ghost story.
1982 (PG) 114m/C JoBeth Williams, Craig T. Nelson, Beatrice Straight, Heather O'Rourke, Zelda Rubinstein, Dominique Dunne, Oliver Robbins, Richard Lawson, James Karen; *D:* Tobe Hooper; *W:* Steven Spielberg, Michael Grais, Mark Victor; *M:* Jerry Goldsmith. **VHS, Beta $19.98** *MGM* 🎬🎬🎬

Poltergeist 2: The Other Side Adequate sequel to the Spielburg-produced venture into the supernatural, where demons follow the Freeling family in their efforts to recapture the clairvoyant young daughter Carol Anne. The film includes sojourns into Indian lore and a four-foot long agave worm designed by H.R. Giger. The movie was followed by "Poltergeist 3" in 1988.
1986 (PG-13) 92m/C Craig T. Nelson, JoBeth Williams, Heather O'Rourke, Will Sampson, Julian Beck, Geraldine Fitzgerald, Oliver Robbins, Zelda Rubinstein; *D:* Brian Gibson; *W:* Mark Victor, Michael Grais; *M:* Jerry Goldsmith. **VHS, Beta $14.95** *MGM* 🎬🎬½

Poltergeist 3 Wrestling with the supernatural has finally unnerved Carol Ann and she's sent to stay with her aunt and uncle in Chicago where she attends a school for gifted children with emotional disorders. Guess who follows her? Uninspired acting, threadbare premise, and one ghastly encounter too many. Oddly, O'Rourke died suddenly four months before the film's release.
1988 (PG-13) 97m/C Tom Skerritt, Nancy Allen, Heather O'Rourke, Lara Flynn Boyle, Zelda Rubinstein; *D:* Gary Sherman; *W:* Brian Taggert. **VHS, Beta $14.95** *MGM* 🎬½

Polyester Amusing satire on middle-class life, described by producer, director and writer Waters as "'Father Knows Best' gone berserk." Forlorn housewife Divine pines for the man of her dreams while the rest of her life is falling apart at the seams. Filmed in "Odorama," a hilarious gimmick in which theatre goers were provided with scratch-n-sniff cards, containing specific scents corresponding to key scenes. Video watchers will have to use their imagination in experiencing a wide range of smells. The first of Waters' more mainstream films. Features songs by Murray and Harry.
1981 (R) 86m/C Divine, Tab Hunter, Edith Massey, Mink Stole, Stiv Bators, David Samson, Mary Garlington, Kenneth King, Joni-Ruth White; *D:* John Waters; *W:* John Waters; *M:* Bill Murray, Deborah Harry, Michael Kamen. VHS, Beta $19.95 COL 𝄫𝄫½

Pom Pom Girls High school seniors, intent on having one last fling before graduating, get involved in crazy antics, clumsy romances, and football rivalries.
1976 (R) 90m/C Robert Carradine, Jennifer Ashley, Michael Mullins, Cheryl "Rainbeaux" Smith, Dianne Lee Hart, Lisa Reeves, Bill Adler; *D:* Joseph Ruben. VHS, Beta $9.99 STE, VCI 𝄫½

The Pony Express Melodramatic western about an evil senator (Hart) who's out to establish his own empire. His scheme is thwarted by pony express rider Cortez. Based on the novel by Henry James Forman and Walter Woods.
1925 60m/B Ricardo Cortez, Al Hart, Betty Compson, Ernest Torrence, Wallace Beery, George Bancroft, Frank Lackteen; *D:* James Cruze; *W:* Walter Woods. VHS $14.95 GPV 𝄫𝄫½

Pony Express Buffalo Bill Cody and Wild Bill Hickok join forces to extend the Pony Express mail route west to California through rain and sleet, snow and hail. Far from a factual account but good for extending the myth of the Old West.
1953 101m/C Charlton Heston, Rhonda Fleming, Jan Sterling, Forrest Tucker; *D:* Jerry Hopper. VHS, Beta $14.95 PAR, BAR, HHE 𝄫𝄫𝄫

Pony Express Rider Young man with a mission joins up with the Pony Express hoping to bag the male responsible for killing his pa. The well-produced script boasts a bevy of veteran western character actors, all lending, solid, rugged performances.
1976 (G) 100m/C Stewart Peterson, Henry Wilcoxon, Buck Taylor, Maureen McCormick, Joan Caulfield, Ken Curtis, Slim Pickens, Dub Taylor, Jack Elam; *D:* Robert Totten. VHS TPI 𝄫𝄫𝄫

Pony Post Standard horse opera has Brown running a pony express station where he battles Indians and typical villains.
1940 59m/B Johnny Mack Brown, Fuzzy Knight, Nell O'Day, Dorothy Short, Kermit Maynard, Lane Chandler; *D:* Ray Taylor; *W:* Sherman Lowe. VHS $11.95 GPV 𝄫½

Pool Hustlers A romantic comedy about an amateur billiards whiz who finds love and successfully defeats the national champ. In Italian with English subtitles.
1983 101m/C Francesco Nuti, Guiliana de Sio, Marcello Loti; *D:* Maurizio Ponzi. VHS, Beta $24.95 XVC, MED, ING 𝄫½

Pool Sharks W.C. Fields' first film features the comedian's antics while playing a pool game to win the love of a woman. Silent.
1915 10m/B W.C. Fields. VHS, Beta FLI, GVV 𝄫𝄫½

Poor Girl, A Ghost Story A young girl takes a job as a governess at an English mansion and is besieged by all manner of strange goings-on.
1974 52m/C Lynn Miller, Angela Thorne; *D:* Michael Apted. VHS, Beta $59.95 PSM 𝄫𝄫

A Poor Little Rich Girl Mary Pickford received raves in this film, in which she portrayed Gwendolyn, with everything money could buy, except the attention of her family. Gwendolyn has a bizarre dream in which she sees a number of horrors and is tempted by death. Elaborate sets and special effects, as well as Pickford's delicate performance, make this one special. Organ score.
1917 64m/B Mary Pickford, Madeline Traverse, Charles Wellesley, Gladys Fairbanks; *D:* Maurice Tourneur. VHS, Beta $19.98 CCB, VYY 𝄫𝄫𝄫

The Poor Little Rich Girl A motherless rich girl wanders away from home and is "adopted" by a pair of struggling vaudevillians. With her help, they rise to the big time. Also available with "Heidi" on laserdisc. ♫Oh My Goodness; Buy a Bar of Barry's; Wash Your Neck With a Cake of Peck's; Military Man; When I'm with You; But Definitely; You've Gotta Eat Your Spinach, Baby.
1936 79m/B Shirley Temple, Jack Haley, Alice Faye, Gloria Stuart, Michael Whalen, Sara Haden, Jane Darwell; *D:* Irving Cummings. VHS, Beta $19.95 FOX 𝄫𝄫½

Poor Little Rich Girl: The Barbara Hutton Story Bio-drama of the one-time richest woman in America, Woolworth heiress Hutton (Fawcett), and her extravagant lifestyle. She married seven times (including actor Cary Grant) until falling into self-destructive alcohol and drug addictions. Lavishly presented but superficial. Based on the book by C. David Heymann. Originally a two-part television movie.
1987 98m/C Farrah Fawcett, Bruce Davison, Kevin McCarthy, Burl Ives, James Read, Stephane Audran, Anne Francis, David Ackroyd, Tony Peck, Zoe Wanamaker, Amadeus August; *D:* Charles Jarrott; *W:* Dennis Turner; *M:* Richard Rodney Bennett. VHS $59.98 LIV 𝄫𝄫½

Poor Pretty Eddie A young black singer gets waylaid and taken in by a twisted white Southern clan. An incredibly sleazy movie which boasts Shelly Winters performing a strip act. Also on video as "Black Vengeance," "Redneck County," and "Heartbreak Motel."
1973 (R) 90m/C Leslie Uggams, Shelley Winters, Michael Christian, Ted Cassidy, Slim Pickens, Dub Taylor; *D:* Richard Robinson. Beta MRV 𝄫½

Poor White Trash An architect arrives in bayou country with plans to design a new building. He meets with resistance from the locals but falls for the sensual daughter of one of his staunchest detractors. *AKA:* Bayou.
1957 83m/B Peter Graves, Lita Milan, Douglas Fowley, Timothy Carey, Jonathan Haze; *D:* Harold Daniels. VHS, Beta NO 𝄫½

Poor White Trash 2 A young couple, vacationing in Louisiana's bayou country, are introduced to an unusual brand of southern hospitality by the eponymous group of locals. *AKA:* Scum of the Earth.
1975 (R) 90m/C Gene Ross, Ann Stafford, Norma Moore, Camilla Carr; *D:* S.F. Brownrigg. VHS, Beta $24.95 TPV 𝄫

Pop Always Pays A father gets in a jam when he has to make good on a bet with his daughter's boyfriend.
1940 67m/B Walter Catlett, Dennis O'Keefe, Leon Errol, Adele Pearce; *D:* Leslie Goodwins. VHS, Beta RKO, MLB 𝄫

Pop Goes the Cork Three films by the man Chaplin referred to as his "professor," Max Linder: "Be My Wife," "Seven Years Bad Luck," and "The Three Must-Get-Theres." Linder was the foremost film comedian in early twentieth-century France, and made these three films during a stay in America.
1922 87m/B Max Linder. VHS, Beta CCB 𝄫𝄫

Popcorn A killer stalks a movie audience who is unaware that his crimes are paralleling those in the very film they are watching.
1989 (R) 93m/C Jill Schoelen, Tom Villard, Dee Wallace Stone, Derek Rydell, Elliott Hurst, Kelly Jo Minter, Malcolm Danare, Ray Walston, Tony Roberts; *D:* Mark Herrier; *W:* Alan Ormsby. VHS, 8mm $89.95 COL 𝄫𝄫

Pope John Paul II A made-for-television biography of the Pontiff, from childhood to world eminence.
1984 150m/C Albert Finney, Michael Crompton, Nigel Hawthorne, John McEnery, Brian Cox; *D:* Herbert Wise. VHS, Beta $19.98 PSM, IGP 𝄫𝄫

The Pope Must Diet Coltrane stars as a misfit who accidentally becomes Pope Dave I. Living up to the benevolence suggested by his title, Pope Dave proposes to use Vatican money to create a children's fund. But there are those in the organization who have different, less noble plans for the cash, and soon Dave finds himself the target of a mob hit. Frantic comedy caused a stir with its original title "The Pope Must Die," with many newspapers refusing to run ads for the film. This, coupled with lukewarm critical reviews, led to a very brief stint at the box office. *AKA:* The Pope Must Die.
1991 (R) 87m/C Robbie Coltrane, Alex Rocco, Beverly D'Angelo, Herbert Lom, Paul Bartel, Salvatore Cascio, Balthazar Getty; *D:* Peter Richardson; *M:* Jeff Beck, Anne Dudley. VHS, Beta $92.98 MED, VTR 𝄫½

The Pope of Greenwich Village A film about two Italian-American cousins who struggle to escape the trap of poverty in New York's Greenwich Village. When a small crime goes wrong in a big way, the two must learn about deception and loyalty. Mostly character study; Page is exceptional. Inferior re-run of the "Mean Streets" idea.
1984 (R) 122m/C Eric Roberts, Mickey Rourke, Daryl Hannah, Geraldine Page, Tony Musante, M. Emmet Walsh, Kenneth McMillan, Burt Young; *D:* Stuart Rosenberg; *W:* Vincent Patrick; *M:* Dave Grusin. VHS, Beta $19.98 CCB, MGM 𝄫½

Popeye The cartoon sailor brought to life is on a search to find his long-lost father. Along the way, he meets Olive Oyl and adopts little Sweet Pea. Williams accomplishes the near-impossible feat of physically resembling the title character, and the whole movie does accomplish the maker's stated goal of "looking like a comic strip," but it isn't anywhere near as funny as it should be.
1980 (PG) 114m/C Robin Williams, Shelley Duvall, Ray Walston, Paul Dooley, Bill Irwin, Paul Smith, Linda Hunt, Ray Libertini; *D:* Robert Altman; *W:* Jules Feiffer; *M:* Harry Nilsson. VHS, Beta $19.95 PAR 𝄫𝄫

Popi Arkin is the heart and soul of this poignant charmer in his role as a Puerto Rican immigrant hell-bent on securing a better life outside the ghetto for his two sons. His zany efforts culminate in one outrageous scheme to set them adrift off the Florida coast in hopes they will be rescued and raised by a wealthy family. Far fetched, but ultimately heartwarming.
1969 (G) 115m/C Alan Arkin, Rita Moreno, Miguel Alejandro, Ruben Figueroa; *D:* Arthur Hiller. VHS, Beta NO 𝄫𝄫𝄫

The Poppy is also a Flower A star-laden, antidrug drama produced by the United Nations. Filmed on location in Iran, Monaco, and Italy. Based on a drug trade thriller by Ian Fleming that explains how poppies, converted into heroin, are brought into the United States. Made for television. *AKA:* Poppies Are Also Flowers; Opium Connection.
1966 (PG) 100m/C E.G. Marshall, Trevor Howard, Gilbert Roland, Eli Wallach, Marcello Mastroianni, Angie Dickinson, Rita Hayworth, Yul Brynner, Trini Lopez, Bessie Love; *D:* Terence Young. **VHS, Beta** *NO ♫ ½*

Porcile Pasolini intertwines the story of a soldier cannibal living in a medieval age with the son of an ex-Nazi industrialist in present day Germany. Both the soldier and the young German (who prefers pigs to his fiance) become sacrificial victims of their differing societies. A grotesque fable on Pasolini's hatred of middle class mores and the 20th century. In Italian with English subtitles. *AKA:* Pigsty.
1969 90m/C Pierre Clementi, Franco Citti, Jean-Pierre Leaud, Anna Wiazemsky, Ugo Tognazzi, Alberto Lionello; *D:* Pier Paolo Pasolini; *W:* Pier Paolo Pasolini. **VHS** $79.95 *WBF ♫♫*

Pork Chop Hill A powerful, hard-hitting account of the last hours of the Korean War. Peck is totally believable as the man ordered to hold his ground against the hopeless onslaught of Chinese Communist hordes. A chilling, stark look in the face of a no-win situation. Top notch cast and masterful directing.
1959 97m/B Gregory Peck, Harry Guardino, Rip Torn, George Peppard, James Edwards, Bob Steele, Woody Strode, Robert (Bobby) Blake, Martin Landau, Norman Fell, Bert Remsen; *D:* Lewis Milestone. **VHS, Beta** $14.95 *MGM ♫♫♫*

Porky's Investigation of teen horniness set in South Florida during the fab '50s. Irreverent comedy follows the misadventures of six youths imprisoned in Angel Beach High School who share a common interest: girls. Their main barrier to sexual success: the no-touch babes they lust after and the incredibly stupid adults who run the world. Fairly dumb and tasteless with occasional big laughs that earned mega bucks at the drive-in and created perceived popular outcry for more porky: "Porky's II: The Next Day" (1983) and "Porky's Revenge" (1985).
1982 (R) 94m/C Dan Monahan, Wyatt Knight, Scott Colomby, Tony Ganios, Mark Herrier, Cyril O'Reilly, Roger Wilson, Bob (Benjamin) Clark, Kim Cattrall, Kaki Hunter; *D:* Bob (Benjamin) Clark; *W:* Bob (Benjamin) Clark. **VHS, Beta** $14.98 *FXV, FOX ♫♫ ½*

Porky's 2: The Next Day More tame tomfoolery about teenage sex drives, Shakespeare, fat high school teachers, the Ku Klux Klan, and streaking in the Florida high school where it all began. Outright caricature shares the stage with juvenile humor, some of which may induce laughter.
1983 (R) 100m/C Bill Wiley, Dan Monahan, Wyatt Knight, Cyril O'Reilly, Roger Wilson, Tony Ganios, Mark Herrier, Scott Colomby; *D:* Bob (Benjamin) Clark; *W:* Alan Ormsby, Bob (Benjamin) Clark. **VHS, Beta** $29.98 *FOX ♫♫*

Porky's Revenge The Angel Beach High School students are out to get revenge against Porky who orders the school basketball coach to throw the championship game. The second of the "Porky's" sequels.
1985 (R) 95m/C Dan Monahan, Wyatt Knight, Tony Ganios, Nancy Parsons, Chuck "Porky" Mitchell, Kaki Hunter, Kimberly Evenson, Scott Colomby; *D:* James Komack. **VHS, Beta** $29.98 *FOX ♫*

The Pornographers Bizzare, black comedy focuses on a part-time porno filmmaker lusting after the daughter of the widow he lives with and trying to cope with his family, the world, and himself. A perversely fascinating exploration of contemporary Japenses society and the many facets of sexual emotion. In Japanese with English subtitles.
1966 128m/B Shoichi Ozawa, Massaomi Konda, Sumiko Sakamota, Haruo Tanaka, Keiko Sagowa; *D:* Shohei Imamura. **VHS** $29.95 *CVC, ING, TPV ♫♫♫*

Porridge A British comedy inspired by the popular BBC situation comedy of the title, about a habitual criminal and convict who makes the most of his time in prison. *AKA:* Doing Time.
1991 105m/C Ronnie Barker, Fulton Mackay, Peter Vaughan, Julian Holloway, Geoffrey Bayldon; *D:* Dick Clement. **VHS** $29.95 *BFS ♫♫*

Port Arthur A sweeping Japanese film describing the Russo-Japanese Wars in the early 1900's.
1983 140m/C VHS, Beta $69.95 *VCD ♫♫ ½*

Port of Call Early Bergman drama about a seaman on the docks who falls for a troubled woman whose wild, unhappy past has earned her an unsavory reputation. The hopeful, upbeat tone seems incongruous with the grim harbor/slum setting. It's minor Bergman but the seeds of his trademark themes can be seen taking shape, making it a must-see for avid fans. In Swedish with English subtitles.
1948 100m/B Ivine-Christine Jonsson, Bengt Eklund, Erik Hell, Berta Hall, Mimi Nelson; *D:* Ingmar Bergman. **VHS, Beta** $29.98 *SUE, ING, NLC ♫♫♫*

The Port of Missing Girls A young woman implicated in a murder stows away on a freighter. There she becomes caught up in a waterfront world of pirates, smugglers and other assorted undesirables.
1938 56m/B Harry Carey Sr., Judith Allen, Milburn Stone, Betty Compson; *D:* Karl Brown. **VHS, Beta, 8mm** $19.95 *VYY ♫*

Port of New York A narcotics gang is smuggling large quantities of drugs into New York. A government agent poses as a gang member in order to infiltrate the mob and get the goods on them. Brynner's film debut.
1949 82m/B Scott Brady, Yul Brynner, K.T. Stevens; *D:* Laslo Benedek. **VHS, Beta** $19.95 *NOS, VYY, DVT ♫♫*

Portfolio Real-life models star in this gritty drama about rising to the top of the fashion heap. Music by Eurythmics, Fun Boy Three and others.
1988 (R) 83m/C Paulina Porizkova, Julie Wolfe, Carol Alt, Kelly Emberg. **VHS** *NO ♫♫*

Portnoy's Complaint Limp screen adaptation of Philip Roth's novel follows the frustrating experiences of a sexually obsessed young man as he relates them to his psychiatrist.
1972 (R) 101m/C Richard Benjamin, Karen Black, Lee Grant, Jeannie Berlin, Jill Clayburgh; *D:* Ernest Lehman; *W:* Ernest Lehman. **VHS, Beta** $19.98 *WAR ♫ ½*

The Portrait Longtime real-life friends Bacall and Peck on-screen together for the first time in 37 years prove they are still shining stars as they play aging parents to Peck's real-life daughter, Cecilia Peck. The younger Peck is an artist preparing for a exhibition and asks her parents to sit for a portrait. This is the pole around which their relationships and reconciliations swing in this emotional made-for-cable-tv drama based loosely on Tina Howe's 1983 off-Broadway play, "Painting Churches."
1993 89m/C Lauren Bacall, Gregory Peck, Cecilia Peck, Paul McCrane, Joyce O'Connor, Donna Mitchell, Mitchell Laurance, William Prince, Augusta Dabney; *D:* Arthur Penn; *W:* Lynn Roth. **VHS** $89.98 *TTC, BTV ♫♫♫*

Portrait in Terror A master thief and a deranged artist plan a heist of a Titian painting in an oddball suspense piece. Not a great success, but atmospheric and weird.
1966 81m/B Patrick Magee, William Campbell, Anna Pavane; *D:* Jack Hill. **VHS** $20.00 *SMW ♫♫*

Portrait of a Hitman Aspiring painter leads a double life as a professional hitman. Ragged feature feels more abandoned than finished, as if most of the movie had been shot and then the money ran out. All leads turn in paycheck performances, no more. *AKA:* Jim Buck.
1977 85m/C Jack Palance, Rod Steiger, Richard Roundtree, Bo Svenson, Ann Turkel; *D:* Allan A. Buckhantz. **VHS, Beta** $49.95 *STE ♫*

Portrait of a Lady A spirited young American woman is taken to England and insists on complete freedom to choose her own future and make her own choices. Based on the 1881 novel by Henry James. On 2 cassettes.
1967 240m/C Richard Chamberlain, Suzanne Neve, Edward Fox. **VHS** $34.98 *BFS, TVC ♫♫ ½*

Portrait of a Rebel: Margaret Sanger TV docudrama about the struggle of Margaret Sanger to repeal the Comstock Act of 1912, which prohibited the distribution of birth control information.
1982 96m/C Bonnie Franklin, David Dukes, Milo O'Shea; *D:* Virgil W. Vogel. **VHS, Beta** *TLF ♫♫ ½*

Portrait of a Showgirl Inexperienced showgirl learns the ropes of Las Vegas life from a veteran of the Vegas stages. Made for television.
1982 100m/C Lesley Ann Warren, Rita Moreno, Tony Curtis, Dianne Kay, Howard Morris; *D:* Steven Hilliard Stern. **VHS, Beta** $59.95 *PSM ♫♫*

Portrait of a Stripper A widowed mother works part-time as a stripper to support her son. Trouble arises when her father-in-law attempts to prove that she is an unfit mother.
1979 100m/C Lesley Ann Warren, Edward Herrmann, Vic Tayback, Sheree North; *D:* John Alonzo. **VHS, Beta** $69.95 *VES ♫*

Portrait of a White Marriage An extended made-for-cable comedy special revamping certain old "Mary Hartman, Mary Hartman" and "Fernwood 2-Night" conventions; a moronic talk show host moves his cheap show to his hometown of Hawkins Falls in order to boost the ratings.
1988 81m/C Martin Mull, Mary Kay Place, Fred Willard, Michael McKean, Harry Shearer, Jack Riley, Conchata Ferrell; *D:* Harry Shearer. **VHS, Beta** $39.95 *MCA ♫♫*

Portrait of Grandpa Doc As a young artist prepares for his first one-man show, he struggles to complete a painting which he especially wants to have ready for the show—a portrait of his grandfather, who died seven years earlier. Well, okay.
1977 28m/C Melvyn Douglas, Bruce Davison, Barbara Rush, Anne Seymour, Keith Blanchard. **VHS, Beta** *BFA, ECU ♫♫*

Portrait of Jennie In this haunting, romantic fable, a struggling artist is inspired by and smitten with a strange and beautiful girl who he also suspects may be the spirit of a dead woman. A fine cast works wonders with what could have been a forgettable story. The last reel was tinted green in the

original release with the last scene shot in technicolor. Oscar-winning special effects. **AKA:** Jennie; Tidal Wave.
1948 86m/B Joseph Cotten, Jennifer Jones, Cecil Kellaway, Ethel Barrymore, David Wayne, Lillian Gish, Henry Hull, Florence Bates, Felix Bressart, Anne Francis; *D:* William Dieterle. Academy Awards '48: Best Special Effects; Nominations: Best Black and White Cinematography; Venice Film Festival '49: Best Actor (Cotten). **VHS, Beta $39.98** *FOX* 🎬🎬🎬½

Portrait of Teresa Havana housewife has to balance motherhood, textile job, and cultural group activities without the cooperation of her husband. Vega skillfully portrays the lingering archaic attitudes and insulting assumptions that still confront post-revolution women. A fine eye for the revealing moments and movements of everyday life. In Spanish with English subtitles.
1979 115m/C Daisy Granados, Aldolfo Llaurado, Alina Sanchez, Alberto Molina; *D:* Pastor Vega. **VHS $69.95** *NYF, FCT, ING* 🎬🎬🎬

Posed For Murder A young centerfold is stalked by a psycho who wants her all for himself.
1989 (R) 90m/C Charlotte J. Helmkamp, Carl Fury, Rick Gianasi, Michael Merrins; *D:* Brian Thomas Jones. **VHS, Beta $79.95** *ACA* 🎬🎬

The Poseidon Adventure The cruise ship Poseidon is on its last voyage from New York to Athens on New Year's Eve when it is capsized by a tidal wave. The ten survivors struggle to escape the water-logged tomb. Oscar-winning special effects, such as Shelley Winters floating in a boiler room. Created an entirely new genre of film making—the big cast disaster flick.
1972 (PG) 117m/C Gene Hackman, Ernest Borgnine, Shelley Winters, Red Buttons, Jack Albertson, Carol Lynley, Roddy McDowall; *D:* Ronald Neame; *W:* Wendell Mayes, Sterling Silliphant; *M:* John Williams. Academy Awards '72: Best Song ("The Morning After"), Best Visual Effects; Nominations: Best Art Direction/ Set Decoration, Best Cinematography, Best Costume Design, Best Film Editing, Best Sound, Best Supporting Actress (Winters), Best Original Score; Golden Globe Awards '73: Best Supporting Actress (Winters). **VHS, Beta $19.98** *FOX* 🎬🎬½

Positive I.D. A troubled housewife learns that the man who raped her years before is getting released on parole. She devises a second persona for herself with which to entrap him and get her revenge.
1987 (R) 96m/C Stephanie Rascoe, John Davies, Steve Fromholz; *D:* Andy Anderson. **VHS, Beta $79.95** *MCA* 🎬🎬

The Positively True Adventures of the Alleged Texas Cheerleader-Murdering Mom Satirical melodrama about Texas housewife Wanda Holloway (Hunter), accused of hiring a hitman to murder the mother of her daughter's chief cheerleading rival. She figures the girl will be so distraught that her own daughter can easily replace her. Ruthless and hilarious, this fact-based made-for-cable movie goes way over the top in satirizing suburban life-style excess and media overkill. Hunter, complete with whiney Texas twang, is perfect in her role as self-absorbed Wanda and Bridges is great as her loopy ex-brother-in-law and partner in planned homicide. A riot compared to the usual dramatic movies served up by the networks.
1993 (R) 99m/C Holly Hunter, Beau Bridges, Swoosie Kurtz, Greg Henry, Matt Frewer, Frankie Ingrassia, Elizabeth Ruscio, Megan Berwick; *D:* Michael Ritchie; *W:* Jane Anderson; *M:* Lucy Simon. **VHS $92.99** *HBO, FCT, BTV* 🎬🎬🎬½

Posse There's a hidden agenda, fueled by political ambition, in a lawman's (Douglas) dauntless pursuit of an escaped bandit (Dern). An interesting contrast between the evil of corrupt politics and the honesty of traditional lawlessness. Well performed, well photographed, and almost insightful.
1975 (PG) 94m/C Kirk Douglas, Bruce Dern, James Stacy, Bo Hopkins, Luke Askew, David Canary, Alfonso Arau, Kate Woodville, Mark Roberts; *D:* Kirk Douglas; *W:* William Roberts; *M:* Maurice Jarre. **VHS, Beta $14.95** *PAR* 🎬🎬🎬

Posse Big, brawny western shot with MTV in mind that tells the tale in part of how more than 8,000 black cowboys helped tame the American frontier. Or, as the advertising put it, "The untold story of the wild West." Or, spaghetti western meets blaxploitation meets the magnificent seven meets the L.A. riots, with characters actually saying, "No justice, no peace" and "Can't we all get along." However categorized, the intent is to show a side of Americana seldom seen, a goal realized. Strode, perhaps the greatest black Western star, appears at both the beginning and ending, while several other veteran black performers, including Russell, appear in cameos. Hunky Van Peebles is the leader of the usual misfits in the "Dirty Dozen" tradition, infantry deserters holding a load of gold. Between them and freedom is a gang of goons led by Zane. Lots of flash and dash, but lacking soul.
1993 (R) 113m/C Mario Van Peebles, Stephen Baldwin, Charles Lane, Tiny Lister, Big Daddy Kane, Billy Zane, Blair Underwood, Tone Loc, Salli Richardson, Reginald Hudlin, Richard Edson, Reginald Vel Johnson, Warrington Hudlin; *Cameos:* Melvin Van Peebles, Pam Grier, Isaac Hayes, Robert Hooks, Richard Jordan, Paul Bartel, Nipsey Russell, Woody Strode, Aaron Neville, Stephan J. Cannell; *D:* Mario Van Peebles; *W:* Sy Richardson, Dario Scardapane; *M:* Michel Colombier. **VHS $94.95** *PGV, FCT* 🎬🎬🎬

Possessed A poor factory girl becomes a wealthy Park Avenue sophisticate when she falls in love with a rich lawyer who wants to be governor. Not to be confused with Crawford's 1947 movie of the same name, but worth a look. Gable and Crawford make a great couple!
1931 77m/B Joan Crawford, Clark Gable, Wallace Ford, Richard "Skeets" Gallagher, John Miljan; *D:* Clarence Brown. **VHS, Beta $19.98** *MGM* 🎬🎬½

The Possessed Crawford is at her melodramatic best as a crazed gal who can't find happiness with either hunk Heflin or bland Massey. First film for Brooks. From the story "One Man's Secret" by Rita Weiman.
1947 109m/B Joan Crawford, Van Heflin, Raymond Massey, Geraldine Brooks, Stanley Ridges, John Ridgely, Nana Bryant, Moroni Olsen; *D:* Curtis Bernhardt. **VHS $19.98** *MGM* 🎬🎬🎬

The Possessed Farentino is a priest who loses his faith, but regains it after an apparently fatal auto accident. Hackett is the headmistress of a private girls' school which is in need of an exorcist, since one of her student's appears to be possessed, and Farentino seems just the man for the job. Fairly tame, since originally made for TV.
1977 (PG-13) 75m/C James Farentino, Joan Hackett, Diana Scarwid, Claudette Nevins, Eugene Roche, Ann Dusenberry, Dinah Manoff, P.J. Soles; *D:* Jerry Thorpe. **VHS, Beta $59.95** *UNI* 🎬½

Possession Returned from a long mission, a secret agent notices that his wife is acting very strangely. She's about to give birth to a manifestation of the evil within her! Gory, hysterical, over-intellectual and often

unintelligible. Originally shown in a longer version in Europe.
1981 (R) 97m/C Isabelle Adjani, Sam Neill, Heinz Bennent, Margit Carstensen, Shaun Lawtor; *D:* Andrzej Zulawski. Cannes Film Festival Nominations: cs 81: Best Film; Cesar Awards '82: Best Actress (Adjani). **VHS, Beta $69.98** *LIV, VES* 🎬

The Possession of Joel Delaney Blend of occult horror and commentary on social mores works for the most part, but some viewers may be put off by the low production values and spottiness of the script. MacLaine is a wealthy divorcee who must deal with the mysterious transformations affecting her brother. Skeptical at first, she begins to suspect he is the victim of Caribbean voodoo.
1972 (R) 105m/C Shirley MacLaine, Perry King, Michael Hordern, David Elliott, Robert Burr; *D:* Waris Hussein. **VHS $19.95** *PAR* 🎬🎬½

Possession: Until Death Do You Part When one man's attraction for a beautiful young woman becomes an obsession, a bizarre series of inexplicable events unravels a terrifying account of passion and revenge.
1990 93m/C Monica Marko, John R. Johnston, Sharlene Martin, Cat Williamson; *D:* Michael Mazo, Lloyd A. Simandl. **VHS** *NO* 🎬

Postal Inspector An extraordinary tale of a postal inspector's life. Crime, romance, and natural disaster all overtake this civil servant. Catch the song "Let's Have Bluebirds On All Our Wallpaper."
1936 58m/B Carlos Cortez, Patricia Ellis, Michael Loring, Bela Lugosi, David Oliver, Wallis Clark; *D:* Otto Brower. **VHS $16.95** *SNC, LSV* 🎬🎬

Postcards from the Edge Fisher adapted her best-selling novel, tamed and tempered, for the big screen with a tour-de-force of talent. Streep very fine as a delightfully harried actress struggling with her career, her drug dependence, and her competitive, overwhelming show-biz mother. Autobiographical script is bitingly clever and filled with refreshingly witty dialogue. Lots of cameos by Hollywood's hippest.
1990 (R) 101m/C Meryl Streep, Shirley MacLaine, Dennis Quaid, Gene Hackman, Richard Dreyfuss, Rob Reiner, Mary Wickes, Conrad Bain, Annette Bening, Michael Ontkean, Dana Ivey; *Cameos:* Robin Bartlett, Anthony Heald, Oliver Platt, CCH Pounder; *D:* Mike Nichols; *W:* Carrie Fisher. **VHS, Beta, 8mm $19.95** *COL, FCT* 🎬🎬½

The Postman Always Rings Twice Even without the brutal sexuality of the James M. Cain novel, Garfield and Turner sizzle as the lust-laden lovers in this lurid tale of fatal attraction. Garfield steals the show as the streetwise drifter who blows into town and lights a fire in Turner. As their affair steams up the two conspire to do away with her husband and circumstances begin to spin out of control. Tense and compelling. A classic.
1946 113m/B Lana Turner, John Garfield, Cecil Kellaway, Hume Cronyn, Leon Ames, Audrey Totter, Alan Reed; *D:* Tay Garnett. **VHS, Beta $19.98** *MGM* 🎬🎬🎬½

The Postman Always Rings Twice It must be true because he's ringing again in Mamet's version of James M. Cain's depression-era novel. This time Nicholson plays the drifter and Lange the amoral wife with an aged husband. Truer to the original story than the 1946 movie in its use of brutal sex scenes, it nevertheless lacks the power of the original. Nicholson works well in this time era and Lange adds depth and realism

to the character of Cora. But in the end it remains dreary and easily forgettable.
1981 (R) 123m/C Jack Nicholson, Jessica Lange, John Colicos, Anjelica Huston, Michael Lerner, John P. Ryan, Christopher Lloyd; **D:** Bob Rafelson; **W:** David Mamet. **VHS, Beta** $19.98 FOX, WAR ⅋⅋

Postmark for Danger Detectives do their best to smash a diamond smuggling ring that operates between Britain and the U.S. Along the way a number of people are killed. **AKA:** Portrait of Alison.
1956 84m/B Terry Moore, Robert Beatty, William Sylvester, Josephine Griffin, Geoffrey Keen, Henry Oscar; **D:** Guy Green. **VHS, Beta** $16.95 SNC ⅋⅋½

Postmark for Danger/Quicksand A "film noire" double feature. In "Postmark for Danger," a young actress returns from the dead to find a criminal, while in "Quicksand," a mechanic becomes indebted to the mob when he borrows extra money for a date.
1956 155m/B Terry Moore, Robert Beatty, Mickey Rooney, Jeanne Cagney, Peter Lorre; **D:** Guy Green. **VHS, Beta** SNC ⅋⅋

Pot O' Gold Stewart plays a wealthy young man who signs on with a struggling band. He convinces his uncle, who has a radio program, to let the band perform during a radio giveaway show he has concocted. Slight comedy, Stewart notwithstanding. **AKA:** The Golden Hour.
1941 87m/B Paulette Goddard, James Stewart, Art Carney; **D:** George Marshall. **VHS, Beta** $19.95 NOS, CCB, VYY ⅋⅋

Pot, Parents, and Police A 13-year-old boy goes crazy when his dog dies and soon gets in with a hippie crowd, drops acid, and gets in trouble with the cops.
1971 m/C Phillip Pine, Robert Mantell, Madelyn Keen; **D:** Phillip Pine. **VHS** $23.00 SMW, MOV, TPV ⅋

Pound Puppies and the Legend of Big Paw The Pound Puppies, known for breaking dogs out of pounds and delivering them to safe and secure homes, are featured in their first full-length musical (and merchandising effort). Fifties music.
1988 76m/C **D:** Pierre de Celles; **V:** Nancy Cartwright, George Rose, B.J. Ward, Ruth Buzzi, Brennan Howard. **VHS** $19.95 FHE, WTA ⅋

Pouvoir Intime What happens when robbers of an armored car lock the guard in the vehicle, and he decides to fight back? This film offers one possible scenario. Available in dubbed or subtitled versions.
1987 (PG-13) 86m/C Marie Tifo, Pierre Curzi, Yvan Ponton, Jaques Lussier; **D:** Yves Simoneau. **VHS** $59.98 YYY ⅋½

P.O.W. Deathcamp A combat unit is captured and tortured by the Vietcong in this typical Vietnam story.
1989 92m/C Charles Black, Bill Balbridge, Rey Malonzo; **D:** Jett C. Espiritu. **VHS** $79.95 ATL ⅋⅋

The P.O.W. Escape The adventures of a surly American commander captured as a POW during the final days of the Vietnam War. **AKA:** Behind Enemy Lines.
1986 (R) 90m/C David Carradine, Mako, Charles R. Floyd, Steve James; **D:** Gideon Amir. **VHS, Beta** VTR ⅋½

Powaqqatsi: Life in Transformation Director Reggio's follow-up to "Koyaanisqatsi" doesn't pack the wallop of its predecessor. Still, the cinematography is magnificent and the music of Philip Glass is exquisitely hypnotic as we are taken on a spellbinding video collage of various third world countries and see the price they've paid in the name of progress. Part 2 of a planned trilogy.
1988 (G) 95m/C **D:** Godfrey Reggio; **M:** Philip Glass. **VHS, Beta** $89.95 CAN ⅋⅋⅋½

Powder Keg Railroad company hires a rowdy team of investigators to retrieve a hijacked train. Action never quits. The idea for the television pilot "The Bearcats" came from this movie.
1970 93m/C Rod Taylor, Dennis Cole, Michael Ansara, Fernando Lamas, Tisha Sterling; **D:** Douglas Heyes. **VHS, Beta** $7.95 SIM, WOV ⅋⅋

Powdersmoke Range Crooked frontier politician plots to steal valuable ranch property. The new owners, however, have other ideas. First in "The Three Mesquiteer" series.
1935 71m/B Harry Carey Sr., Hoot Gibson, Tom Tyler, Guinn Williams, Bob Steele, Sam Hardy, Patricia "Boots" Mallory, Franklin Farnum, William Desmond, William Farnum, Buzz Barton, Wally Wales, Art Mix, Buffalo Bill Jr., Buddy Roosevelt; **D:** Wallace Fox. **VHS, Beta** MED, RXM ⅋½

Power Two dam-building construction workers vie with each other for the local girls. Silent.
1928 60m/B William Boyd, Alan Hale, Carole Lombard, Joan Bennett; **D:** Howard Hughes. **VHS, Beta** $24.95 FCT, GPV, GVV ⅋⅋½

Power A Jewish ghetto inhabitant in 18th-century Wurtemburg works his way out of the gutter and into some authority by pleasing the whims of an evil duke. Based on the novel by Leon Fuechtwangler. **AKA:** Jew Suss.
1934 105m/B Conrad Veidt, Benita Hume, Frank Vosper, Cedric Hardwicke, Gerald du Maurier, Pamela Ostrer, Joan Maude, Paul Graetz, Mary Clare, Percy Parsons, Dennis Hoey, Gibb McLaughlin, Francis L. Sullivan; **D:** Lothar Mendes. **VHS** DVT, HEG ⅋⅋

The Power An ancient clay idol that was created by the Aztecs and possesses incredible destructive power is unleashed on modern man.
1980 (R) 87m/C Warren Lincoln, Susan Stokey, Lisa Erickson, Jeffrey Obrow; **D:** Stephen Carpenter; **W:** Stephen Carpenter, John Penney. **VHS** $69.98 LIV, VES ⅋½

Power A study of corporate manipulations. Gere plays a ruthless media consultant working for politicians. Fine cast can't find the energy needed to make this great, but it's still interesting. Lumet did better with same material in "Network."
1986 (R) 111m/C Richard Gere, Julie Christie, E.G. Marshall, Gene Hackman, Beatrice Straight, Kate Capshaw, Denzel Washington, Fritz Weaver, Michael Learned, E. Katherine Kerr, Polly Rowles, Matt Salinger, J.T. Walsh; **D:** Sidney Lumet; **W:** David Himmelstein; **M:** Cy Coleman. **VHS, Beta** $19.98 LHV, WAR ⅋⅋½

The Power of One Good cast is generally wasted in liberal white look at apartheid. Set in South Africa during the 1940s, P.K. is a white orphan of British descent who is sent to a boarding school run by Afrikaaners (South Africans of German descent). Humiliated and bullied, particularly when England and Germany go to war, P.K. is befriended by a German pianist and a black boxing coach who teach him to box and stand up for his rights. Preachy and filled with stereotypes. Based on the novel by Bryce Courtenay.
1992 (PG-13) 126m/C Stephen Dorff, Armin Mueller-Stahl, Morgan Freeman, John Gielgud, Fay Masterson, Marius Weyers, Tracy Brooks Swope, John Osborne, Daniel Craig, Dominic Walker, Alois Mayo, Ian Roberts, Maria Marais; **D:** John G. Avildsen; **W:** Robert Mark Kamen. **VHS** $19.98 WAR ⅋⅋

The Power of the Ninjitsu A young man inherits the leadership of a martial arts crime gang, the Scorpions, but the elder members muscle him out of his place. He returns for revenge and has the old ones running scared. Power to the Ninjitsu!
1988 90m/C Britton Lee, Adam Frank, Peter Ujaer; **D:** Joseph Lai. **VHS, Beta** $59.95 IME ⅋

Power, Passion & Murder A young, glamorous movie star has an affair with a married man which begins the end of her career in 1930s Hollywood.
1983 104m/C Michelle Pfeiffer, Darren McGavin, Stella Stevens; **D:** Paul Bogart, Leon Ichaso. **VHS, Beta** $79.95 VMK, IME, HHE ⅋½

Power Play Young army colonel from a small European country joins forces with rebels to overthrow the government. After the coup, the group discovers that in their midst is a traitor. So who is it? Suspense never builds adequately. **AKA:** Operation Overthrow.
1981 95m/C Peter O'Toole, David Hemmings, Donald Pleasence, Barry Morse; **D:** Martyn Burke. **VHS, Beta** $49.95 MED ⅋½

The Power Within An electrified stuntman finds he can send electrical shocks from his hands and becomes the victim of a kidnapping plot.
1979 90m/C Eric (Hans Gudegast) Braeden, David Hedison, Susan Howard, Art Hindle; **D:** John Llewellyn Moxey. **VHS, Beta** $59.95 PSM ⅋½

Powwow Highway Remarkably fine performances in this unusual, thought-provoking, poorly-titled foray into the plight of Native Americans. Farmer shines as the unassuming, amiable Cheyenne traveling to New Mexico in a beat-up Chevy with his Indian activist buddy, passionately portrayed by Martinez. On the journey they are constantly confronted with the tragedy of life on a reservation. A sobering look at government injustice and the lingering spirit of a people lost inside their homeland.
1989 (R) 105m/C Gary Farmer, A. Martinez, Amanda Wyss, Rene Handren-Seals, Graham Greene; **D:** Joanelle Romero, Jonathan Wacks; **M:** Barry Goldberg. **VHS, Beta** $89.95 WAR, OM ⅋⅋⅋½

The Practice of Love A woman journalist's investigation of a murder casts suspicion on her two male lovers. The film raises the question of whether love is even possible in a world dominated by men's struggles for power. In German with English subtitles.
1984 90m/C **D:** Valie Export. **VHS** $59.95 FCT, MOV ⅋⅋

Prairie Badmen Outlaws are after a treasure map in the possession of the owner of a medicine show. It's up to our hero to stop them. One of the "Billy Carson" western series.
1946 55m/B Buster Crabbe. **VHS, Beta** VCN ⅋½

The Prairie King Will grants three people the same gold mine but stipulates only one may own it. Silent quandary.
1927 58m/B Hoot Gibson, Barbara Worth, Charles Sellon, Albert Priscoe. **VHS, Beta** $17.95 GPV ⅋½

Prairie Moon Autry becomes the guardian of three tough kids from Chicago after they inherit a ranch. The kids help Autry round up a gang of rustlers.
1938 58m/B Gene Autry, Smiley Burnette. **VHS, Beta** CCB, VCN, DVT ⅋½

Prairie Pals Deputies go undercover to rescue a kidnapped scientist.

1942 60m/B William Boyd, Lee Powell, Art Davis, Charles "Blackie" King, John Merton, Kermit Maynard, Al "Fuzzy" St. John; *D:* Sam Newfield. **VHS, Beta** $11.95 *GPV, VCN* 🎞 ½

The Prairie Pirate Carey is the western hero tracking down the dirty dogs who murdered his sister. Fast-paced.
1925 59m/B Harry Carey Sr., Lloyd Whitlock, Jean Dumas, Trilby Clark; *D:* Edmund Mortimer. **VHS** $16.95 *GPV* 🎞🎞 ½

Prancer An eight-year-old girl whose mother has recently died thinks an injured reindeer she has found belongs to Santa. She lovingly nurses him back to health. Harmless family entertainment.
1989 (G) 102m/C Sam Elliott, Rebecca Harrell, Cloris Leachman, Rutanya Alda, John Joseph Duda, Abe Vigoda, Michael Constantine, Ariana Richards, Mark Rolston; *D:* John Hancock; *M:* Maurice Jarre. **VHS, Beta, 8mm** $19.95 *COL, ORI, FCT* 🎞🎞

Pray for Death When a mild-mannered Japanese family is victimized by a crime syndicate in L.A., a master ninja comes to the rescue. Higher quality production than most ninja adventures.
1985 (R) 93m/C James Booth, Robert Ito, Sho Kosugi, Shane Kosugi, Kane Kosugi, Donna Kei Benz; *D:* Gordon Hessler; *W:* James Booth. **VHS, Beta** *NO* 🎞🎞

Pray for the Wildcats Three advertising executives' promotional trip from (or to?) Hell. Anything to please a client.
1974 96m/C Andy Griffith, William Shatner, Angie Dickinson, Janet Margolin, Marjoe Gortner, Lorraine Gary; *D:* Robert Lewis. **VHS, Beta** $69.95 *REP* 🎞 ½

Pray TV A sly con man turns a failing television station into a profitable one when the station starts to broadcast around-the-clock religious programming. Made for television. *AKA:* KGOD.
1980 (PG) 92m/C Dabney Coleman, Archie Hahn, Joyce Jameson, Nancy Morgan, Roger E. Mosley, Marcia Wallace; *D:* Rick Friedberg; *W:* Nick Castle. **VHS, Beta** $69.95 *VES* 🎞🎞

Pray TV A television movie expose of broadcast religion in which a young preacher chooses between orthodox religion and lots of money. Not as cutting an indictment as it could have been.
1982 100m/C John Ritter, Ned Beatty, Madolyn Smith, Richard Kiley, Louise Latham, Jonathan Prince, Michael Currie, Lois Areno; *D:* Robert Markowitz. **VHS, Beta** $9.98 *SUE* 🎞🎞

A Prayer for Katarina Horovitzova Stunning tale of a Polish singer who struggles to find the meaning and beauty of life while working to trade Nazi prisoners in U.S. jails for Jews hoping to emigrate. Based on the Arnost Lustig novel. Confiscated by the Czech Communist government and kept from the screen for 21 years. In Czechoslovakian with English subtitles.
1969 60m/C Jiri Adamira, Lenka Fiserova, Cestmir Randa. **VHS** $59.95 *FCT* 🎞🎞🎞 ½

Prayer for the Dying An IRA hitman longs to quit, but he has to complete one last assignment. The hit is witnessed by a priest who becomes an unwitting associate when the hitman hides out at the church. Fine performances from Bates and Rourke, though Hodges and Rourke were not satisfied with finished film.
1987 (R) 104m/C Mickey Rourke, Alan Bates, Bob Hoskins, Sammi Davis-Voss, Liam Neeson, Alison Doody, Christopher Fulford; *D:* Mike Hodges; *W:* Edmund Ward, Martin Lynch; *M:* Bill Conti. **VHS, Beta** *NO* 🎞🎞 ½

Prayer of the Rollerboys Violent, futuristic, funky action as Haim infiltrates a criminal gang of syncopated roller-blading neo-nazi youth with plans for nationwide domination. Though routinely plotted and predictable, it's got great skating stunts and a wry vision of tomorrow's shattered USA—broke, drug-soaked, homeless, foreign-owned; even sharper when you realize this is a Japanese-American co-production.
1991 (R) 94m/C Corey Haim, Patricia Arquette, Christopher Collet, Julius W. Harris, J.C. Quinn, Jake Dengel, Devin Clark, Mark Pellegrino, Morgan Weisser; *D:* Rick King. **VHS** $19.95 *ACA* 🎞🎞 ½

Praying Mantis The professor's scheming nurse murdered his family and plans to marry him for his money. She enlists the aid of the professor's assistant in her evil plot.
1983 (PG-13) 119m/C Jonathan Pryce, Cherie Lunghi, Ann Cropper, Carmen Du Sautoy, Pinkas Braun; *D:* Jack Gold; *M:* Carl Davis. **VHS, Beta** *NO* 🎞🎞

Praying Mantis Seymour stars as a femme fatale who likes to get married and then, in a rage against her own abusive childhood, kill her new husbands off. So far her total is five dead hubbies with number six (Bostwick) in her sights. Only this time, her almost-sister-in-law (Fisher) is very suspicious of the bride-to-be. Made for cable television.
1993 (PG-13) 90m/C Jane Seymour, Barry Bostwick, Frances Fisher, Chad Allen; *D:* James Keach; *W:* Duane Poole, William Delligan; *M:* John Debney. **VHS, Beta** *PAR* 🎞🎞 ½

Preacherman Phony preacher travels through the South, fleecing gullible congregations wherever he goes.
1983 (R) 90m/C Amos Huxley, Marian Brown, Adam Hesse. **VHS, Beta** *NO* 🎞 ½

Predator Schwarzenegger leads a team of CIA-hired mercenaries into the Central American jungles to rescue hostages. They encounter an alien force that begins to attack them one by one. Soon it's just Arnold and the Beast in this attention-grabbing, but sometimes silly, suspense film.
1987 (R) 107m/C Arnold Schwarzenegger, Jesse Ventura, Sonny Landham, Bill Duke, Elpidia Carrillo, Carl Weathers, R.G. Armstrong, Richard Chaves, Shane Black, Kevin Peter Hall; *D:* John McTiernan; *W:* Jim Thomas, John Thomas; *M:* Alan Silvestri. **VHS, Beta** $14.98 *FXV* 🎞🎞 ½

Predator 2 Tough cop takes time away from battling drug dealers to deal with malicious extraterrestrial who exterminated Arnold's band of commandos in "Predator." Miss-billed as sequel, its only resemblance to the original is that the predator has inexplicably returned (this time to the thick of L.A.). Gory action aplenty, little logic. Fine cast dominated by minority performers can't save this one.
1990 (R) 105m/C Danny Glover, Gary Busey, Ruben Blades, Maria Conchita Alonso, Bill Paxton, Robert Davi, Adam Baldwin, Kent McCord, Morton Downey Jr., Calvin Lockhart, Teri Weigel; *D:* Stephen Hopkins; *W:* John Thomas, Jim Thomas. **VHS, Beta** $14.98 *FXV, CCB* 🎞🎞

Prehistoric Bimbos in Armageddon City Trianna and her tribe of Prehistoric Bimbos must prevent post-nuclear domination in Old Chicago City, the last remaining civilization after WWIII, by defeating the evil ruler Nemesis and his cyborgs. "Enough bimbos to fill two post-nuclear action comedies." So bad its gotta be good.
1993 70m/C Robert Vollrath, Tonia Monahan, Deric Bernier. **VHS** *TEM* Woof!

Prehistoric Women A tribe of prehistoric women look for husbands the old-fashioned way—they drag them back to their caves from the jungle. So bad it's almost good. *AKA:* Slave Girls.
1950 74m/C Laurette Luez, Allan Nixon, Mara Lynn, Joan Shawlee, Judy Landon; *D:* Greg Tallas. **VHS, Beta** $9.99 *FHE, NOS, RHI* Woof!

Prehysteria Fantasy/adventure about a widower, his 11-year-old son and teenage daughter, and what happens when some mysterious eggs from South America accidentally wind up at their farm. Imagine their surprise when the eggs hatch and out pop a brood of pygmy dinosaurs. The dinosaurs are cute (as is the family), the villain is dumb, and the violence minimal.
1993 (PG) 86m/C Brett Cullen, Austin O'Brien, Samantha Mills, Colleen Morris, Tony Longo, Stuart Fratkin, Stephen Lee; *D:* Albert Band, Charles Band; *W:* Greg Suddeth, Mark Goldstein. **VHS, Beta** *PAR* 🎞🎞 ½

Prelude to a Kiss Disappointing screen adaptation of Craig Lucas' hit play features Baldwin and Ryan as young lovers in this romantic fantasy. Ryan is Rita, a free-spirited bartender and Baldwin is Peter, a conservative writer, who decide to marry after a whirlwind courtship. At their wedding reception, Rita obligingly kisses one of their guests, an old man (Walker). Then, on their honeymoon, Peter begins to notice a number of changes to Rita's character and comes to realize this is truly not the girl he married. The delicate fantasy which worked on stage struggles to survive the "opening up" of the screen adaptation though Baldwin (who reprises his stage role) and Ryan are appealing.
1992 (PG-13) 106m/C Alec Baldwin, Meg Ryan, Sydney Walker, Ned Beatty, Patty Duke, Kathy Bates, Stanley Tucci; *D:* Norman Rene. **VHS** $19.98 *FXV, PMS* 🎞🎞

Prelude to War A compact look at the events of 1931-39; includes a series of contrasts between free societies and totalitarian governments. From the "Why We Fight" series.
1942 53m/B *D:* Frank Capra. **VHS, Beta** $19.95 *REP, MPI, HHT* 🎞🎞

Premature Burial A cataleptic Englishman's worst fears come true when he is buried alive. He escapes and seeks revenge on his doctor and his greedy wife. Based upon the story by Edgar Allan Poe.
1962 81m/C Ray Milland, Richard Ney, Hazel Court, Heather Angel; *D:* Roger Corman. **VHS, Beta** $69.98 *LIV, VES, MLB* 🎞🎞

Premonition Three drug-riddled '60s college students experience similar premonitions of death, and subsequently either die or become tormented.
1971 (PG) 83m/C Carl Crow, Tim Ray, Winfrey Hester Hill, Victor Izay; *D:* Alan Rudolph; *W:* Alan Rudolph. **VHS, Beta** *NO* 🎞 ½

The Premonition Parapsychologist searching for a missing child is drawn into a frightening maze of dream therapy and communication with the dead. Well-done paranorm tale filmed in Mississippi.
1975 (PG) 94m/C Richard Lynch, Sharon Farrell, Jeff Corey, Ellen Barber, Edward Bell, Danielle Brisebois; *D:* Robert Allen Schnitzer; *W:* Anthony Mahon. **VHS, Beta** $24.98 *SUE* 🎞🎞 ½

Prep School A very proper New England prep school is turned topsy-turvy by two rambunctious co-eds. They're determined to break every one of the school's cardinal rules.
1981 (PG-13) 97m/C Leslie Hope, Andrew Sabiston; *D:* Paul Almond. **VHS, Beta** $79.95 *PSM* 🎞

The Preppie Murder Made for TV crime drama based on the killing of Jennifer Levin in New York City's Central Park in 1987, with Baldwin cast as prep school grad Robert Chambers. Amid sensational headlines, the story told of drugs, sexual games, and idle and disaffected youth.
1989 100m/C William Baldwin, Lara Flynn Boyle, Danny Aiello, Joanna Kerns, Dorothy Fielding, James Handy, William Devane; **D:** John Herzfeld. **VHS** *$92.98* TTC ♫♫½

Preppies Yet another teen sex comedy, but this time Ivy Leaguer Drake must pass his exams to receive his $50 million inheritance. Lots of skirt chasing as his conniving cousin leads him astray.
1982 (R) 83m/C Dennis Drake, Peter Brady Reardon, Steven Holt, Nitchie Barrett, Cindy Manion, Katt Shea Ruben, Lynda Wiesmeier; **D:** Chuck Vincent. **VHS, Beta** *$29.98* LIV, VES ♫½

Presenting Lily Mars A small-town girl comes to New York to make it on Broadway. Based on the Booth Tarkington novel. ♫When I Look at You; Three O'Clock in the Morning; Kulebiaka; Is It Love? (Or The Gypsy in Me); Broadway Rhythm; Sweethearts of America; Where There's Music; Every Little Movement Has a Meaning All Its Own; Tom, Tom the Piper's Son.
1943 105m/B Judy Garland, Van Heflin, Fay Bainter, Richard Carlson, Tommy Dorsey, Bob Crosby & His Orchestra; **D:** Norman Taurog. **VHS, Beta** *$19.98* MGM ♫½

The President's Analyst A superbly written, brilliantly executed satire from the mind of Theodore J. Flicker, who wrote as well as directed. Coburn steals the show as a psychiatrist who has the dubious honor of being appointed "secret shrink" to the President of the U.S. Pressures of the job steadily increase his paranoia until he suspects he is being pursued by agents and counter agents alike. Is he losing his sanity or...? Vastly entertaining.
1967 104m/C James Coburn, Godfrey Cambridge, Severn Darden, Joan Delaney, Pat Harrington, Will Geer, William Daniels; **D:** Theodore J. Flicker; **W:** Theodore J. Flicker. **VHS** *$14.95* PAR ♫♫♫½

President's Mistress A security agent searches for his sister's murderer, while trying to obscure the fact that she was having an affair with the President.
1978 97m/C Beau Bridges, Susan Blanchard, Larry Hagman, Joel Fabiani, Karen Grassle; **D:** John Llewellyn Moxey. **VHS, Beta** NO ♫½

The President's Mystery A lawyer decides to turn his back on society by giving up his practice and his marriage. Eventually he meets and falls in love with another woman. The most interesting aspect of the film is that it is based on a story by Franklin D. Roosevelt, which was published in "Liberty" magazine. The story was supposedly better than its screen adaptation. *AKA:* One For All.
1936 80m/B Henry Wilcoxon, Betty Furness, Sidney Blackmer, Evelyn Brent; **D:** Phil Rosen. **VHS, Beta** *$16.95* SNC ♫½

The President's Plane is Missing When Air Force One disappears, the less than trustworthy Vice President takes control. Could there be a dire plot in the making? Based on a novel by Rod Serling's brother Robert J. Serling.
1971 100m/C Buddy Ebsen, Peter Graves, Arthur Kennedy, Rip Torn, Louise Sorel, Raymond Massey, James Wainwright, Mercedes McCambridge, Dabney Coleman, Joseph Campanella; **D:** Daryl Duke. **VHS** *$69.98* REP ♫♫

President's Target An anti-drug mission in South America is ambushed and CIA operative Peter Caine is the only survivor. Now he's out to see who planned the double-cross and how best to get his revenge.
1993 82m/C John Coleman, Martin Kove, Bo Hopkins, Brigitte Audrey; **D:** Yvan Chiffre. **VHS** *$89.95* HMD ♫♫

The Presidio An easy going police detective must investigate a murder on a military base where he and the base commander have sparred before. The commander becomes downright nasty when his daughter shows an interest in the detective. Good action scenes in San Francisco almost covers up script weaknesses, but not quite.
1988 (R) 97m/C Sean Connery, Mark Harmon, Meg Ryan, Jack Warden, Mark Blum, Jenette Goldstein; **D:** Peter Hyams; **W:** Larry Ferguson; **M:** Bruce Broughton. **VHS, Beta, 8mm** *$89.95* PAR ♫♫

Pressure Point Poitier stars as a prison psychiatrist treating an inmate who is a racist and a member of the Nazi party. Darin gives an excellent performance as the Nazi patient in this intelligent drama based on a true case.
1962 87m/B Sidney Poitier, Bobby Darin, Peter Falk, Carl Benton Reid, Barry Gordon, Howard Caine, Mary Munday; **D:** Hubert Cornfield; **M:** Ernest Gold. **VHS** *$19.98* MGM ♫♫♫

Presumed Guilty An innocent man is released from prison only to find he is once again a wanted man! So he gets his gal, who happens to be the sheriff's daughter, is beaten up and in the end winds up living happily ever after.
1991 91m/C Jack Vogel, Holly Floria, Sean Holton, Wayne Zanelotti, Bradley Rockwell, Sharon Young, Al Schuerman; **D:** Lawrence L. Simeone; **W:** Lawrence L. Simeone. **VHS** *$79.98* AIP ♫

Presumed Innocent Assistant district attorney is the prime suspect when a former lover turns up brutally murdered. Cover-ups surround him, the political climate changes, and friends and enemies switch sides. Slow-paced courtroom drama with excellent performances from Ford, Julia, and Bedelia. Skillfully adapted from the best-seller by Chicago attorney Scott Turow.
1990 (R) 127m/C Harrison Ford, Brian Dennehy, Bonnie Bedelia, Greta Scacchi, Raul Julia, Paul Winfield, John Spencer, Joe Grifasi, Anna Maria Horsford, Sab Shimono, Christine Estabrook, Michael Tolan, Tom Mardirosian; **D:** Alan J. Pakula; **W:** Frank Pierson, Alan J. Pakula; **M:** John Williams. **VHS, Beta, 8mm** *$19.98* WAR, FCT ♫♫♫

Pretty Baby Shield's launching pad and Malle's first American film is a masterpiece of cinematography and style, nearly upstaged by the plodding storyline. Carradine manages to be effective but never succeeds at looking comfortable as the New Orleans photographer besotted with, and subsequently married to, an 11-year old prostitute (Shields). Low key, disturbingly intriguing story, beautifully photographed by Sven Nykist.
1978 (R) 109m/C Brooke Shields, Keith Carradine, Susan Sarandon, Barbara Steele, Diana Scarwid, Antonio Fargas; **D:** Louis Malle. Academy Awards '78 Nominations: Best Original Score; Cannes Film Festival '78: Best Film; National Board of Review Awards '78: 10 Best Films of the Year. **VHS, Beta** *$69.95* PAR ♫♫♫

Pretty in Pink More teen angst from the pen of Hughes. Poor girl falls for a rich guy. Their families fret, their friends are distressed, and fate conspires against them. If you can suspend your disbelief that a teenager with her own car and answering machine is financially inferior, then you may very well be able to accept the entire premise.

Slickly done and adequately, if not enthusiastically, acted. In 1987, Hughes essentially remade this film and put himself in the director's chair with "Some Kind of Wonderful," the same story with the rich/pauper characters reversed by gender.
1986 (PG-13) 96m/C Molly Ringwald, Andrew McCarthy, Jon Cryer, Harry Dean Stanton, James Spader, Annie Potts, Andrew Dice Clay, Margaret Colin, Alexa Kenin, Gina Gershon, Dweezil Zappa; **D:** Howard Deutch; **W:** John Hughes; **M:** Michael Gore. **VHS, Beta, 8mm** *$14.95* PAR ♫♫½

Pretty Poison You won't need an antidote for this one. Original, absorbing screenplay, top-notch acting, and on target direction combine to raise this low-budget, black comedy above the crowd. Perkins at his eerie best as a burned-out arsonist who cooks up a crazy scheme and enlists the aid of a hot-to-trot high schooler, only to discover too late she has some burning desires of her own. Weld is riveting as the turbulent teen.
1968 89m/C Anthony Perkins, Tuesday Weld, Beverly Garland, John Randolph, Dick O'Neill; **D:** Noel Black. **VHS** ING, MLB ♫♫♫½

Pretty Smart Two diametrically opposed sisters at a European finishing school team up against a drug-dealing, voyeuristic teacher. Pretty lame.
1987 (R) 84m/C Tricia Leigh Fisher, Patricia Arquette, Dennis Cole, Lisa Lorient; **D:** Dimitri Logothetis. **VHS, Beta** *$19.95* STE, NWV Woof!

Pretty Woman An old story takes a fresh approach as a successful but stuffy business man hires a fun-loving, energetic young hooker to be his companion for a week. The film caused some controversy over its upbeat portrayal of prostitution, but its popularity at the box office catapulted Roberts to stardom.
1990 (R) 117m/C Richard Gere, Julia Roberts, Ralph Bellamy, Jason Alexander, Laura San Giacomo, Hector Elizondo, Alex Hyde-White, Elinor Donahue, Larry Miller, Jane Morris; **D:** Garry Marshall; **W:** J.F. Lawton; **M:** James Newton Howard. Academy Awards '90 Nominations: Best Actress (Roberts); Golden Globe Awards '91: Best Actress—Musical/Comedy (Roberts); People's Choice Awards '91: Best Film, Best Film—Musical/Comedy. **VHS, Beta** *$19.99* TOU ♫♫♫

Prettykill A confusing storyline with numerous subplots involves detective with a paramour/prostitute (Hubley) attempting to stalk a mad killer while contending with her split personality.
1987 (R) 95m/C David Birney, Susannah York, Season Hubley, Yaphet Kotto, Suzanne Snyder, Germane Honde; **D:** George Kaczender. **VHS, Beta** *$19.98* WAR Woof!

The Prey Poorly done horror show about a predator who is looking for a mate in the Colorado Rockies and kills five campers in the process.
1980 (R) 80m/C Debbie Thureson, Steve Bond, Lori Lethin, Jackie Coogan; **D:** Edwin Scott Brown. **VHS, Beta** *$19.99* STE ♫

Prey for the Hunter Four businessmen on a big-game hunt decide they're bored with their usual prey. They persuade a photojournalist to join them in a game with paint pellet guns except they decide to use real bullets and the journalist becomes their new target. An old and tired plot with nothing new to distinguish it.
1992 (R) 90m/C Todd Jensen, Andre Jacobs, Michelle Bestbier, Evan J. Klisser, David Butler, Allan Granville; **D:** John H. Parr. **VHS** *$89.95* COL ♫

Prey of the Chameleon A female serial killer escapes from her asylum, ready to rip more men to shreds. However a tough lady cop has other ideas and goes all out to put an end to the madwoman's doings. Can she stop this fiend before the man she loves becomes the next victim?
1991 (R) **91m/C** Daphne Zuniga, James Wilder, Alexandra Paul, Don Harvey; *D:* Fleming Fuller. **VHS, Beta** $89.95 *PSM* ✗

Priceless Beauty Musician Lambert was only looking when he spotted the bottle which changed his life. Beautiful genie (Lane) lives inside, and is waiting just for him! Fun premise, good score, nice chemistry between the actors.
1990 (R) **94m/C** Christopher Lambert, Diane Lane, Francesco Quinn, J.C. Quinn, Claudia Ohana, Monica Scattini, Joaquin D'Almeida; *D:* Charles Finch. **VHS** $89.98 *REP* ✗✗½

Prick Up Your Ears Film biography of popular subversive playwright Joe Orton depicts his rise to fame and his eventual murder at the hands of his homosexual lover in 1967. Acclaimed for its realistic and sometimes humorous portrayal of the relationship between two men in a society that regarded homosexuality as a crime, the film unfortunately pays scant attention to Orton's theatrical success. The occasional sluggishness of the script detracts a bit from the three leads' outstanding performances.
1987 (R) **110m/C** Gary Oldman, Alfred Molina, Vanessa Redgrave, Julie Walters, Lindsay Duncan, Wallace Shawn, James Grant, Frances Barber, Janet Dale, David Atkins; *D:* Stephen Frears; *W:* Alan Bennett; *M:* Stanley Myers. **VHS, Beta** *NO* ✗✗✗

Pride and Prejudice Classic adaptation of Austen's classic novel of manners as a young marriageable woman spurns the suitor her parents choose for her. Excellent cast vividly recreates 19th century England, aided by the inspired set design that won the film an Oscar.
1940 **114m/B** Greer Garson, Laurence Olivier, Edmund Gwenn, Edna May Oliver, Mary Boland, Maureen O'Sullivan, Ann Rutherford, Frieda Inescort; *D:* Robert Z. Leonard. **VHS, Beta** $24.95 *MGM* ✗✗✗½

Pride and Prejudice BBC mini-series adaptation of Jane Austen's novel about 19th century British mores and the attempts of five sisters to get married.
1985 **226m/C** Elizabeth Garvie, David Rintoul; *D:* Cyril Coke. **VHS, Beta** $29.98 *KUI, FOX, SIG* ✗✗½

The Pride and the Passion A small group of resistance fighters battling for Spanish independence in 1810 must smuggle a 6-ton cannon across the rugged terrain of Spain. Miscasting, especially of Sinatra as a Spanish peasant, hurts this film.
1957 **132m/C** Cary Grant, Frank Sinatra, Sophia Loren; *D:* Stanley Kramer; *W:* Edward Anhalt. **VHS, Beta** $19.98 *MGM* ✗✗

Pride of Jesse Hallum A made-for-television film about an illiterate man, played by country singer Cash, who learns, after much trial and tribulation, to read.
1981 **105m/C** Johnny Cash, Brenda Vaccaro, Eli Wallach; *D:* Gary Nelson. **VHS, Beta** $59.98 *FOX* ✗½

Pride of St. Louis A romanticized and humorous portrait of famed baseball player-turned-commentator Dizzy Dean.
1952 **93m/B** Dan Dailey, Joanne Dru, Richard Crenna, Richard Haydn, Hugh Sanders; *D:* Harmon Jones; *W:* Herman J. Mankiewicz. **VHS, Beta** $19.98 *FOX* ✗✗

Pride of the Bowery The Dead End Kids versus a boxing hopeful in training camp. *AKA:* Here We Go Again.
1941 **60m/B** Leo Gorcey, David Gorcey, Huntz Hall, Gabriel Dell, Billy Halop, Bobby Jordan; *D:* Joseph H. Lewis. **VHS, Beta** $19.95 *NOS, CAB, DVT* ✗

Pride of the Clan Silent drama with Pickford and Moore as Scottish sweethearts battling a bit of adversity. When Pickford's father is lost at sea, she moves onto his fishing boat. She meets Moore, a fishing boy, and falls in love. But, he inherits a fortune and his parents forbid him to see Pickford. He goes off to live the good life but comes back to dramatically rescue Pickford.
1918 **80m/B** Mary Pickford, Matt Moore; *D:* Maurice Tourneur. **VHS, Beta** $19.95 *GPV* ✗✗

The Pride of the Yankees Excellent portrait of baseball great Lou Gehrig. Beginning as he joined the Yankees in 1923, the film follows this great American through to his moving farewell speech as his career was tragically cut short by the disease that bears his name. Cooper is inspiring in the title role.
1942 **128m/B** Gary Cooper, Teresa Wright, Babe Ruth, Walter Brennan, Dan Duryea; *D:* Sam Wood. Academy Awards '42: Best Film Editing; Nominations: Best Actress (Wright); Academy Awards '42: Best Actor (Cooper), Best Black and White Cinematography, Best Interior Decoration, Best Picture, Best Sound, Best Story, Best Original Score. **VHS, Beta** $19.98 *FOX* ✗✗✗½

Priest of Love Arty account of the final years of the life of then-controversial author D.H. Lawrence, during which time he published "Lady Chatterly's Lover." A slow-moving but interesting portrayal of this complex man and his wife as they grapple with his imminent death from tuberculosis.
1981 (R) **125m/C** Ian McKellan, Janet Suzman, John Gielgud, Helen Mirren, Jorge Rivero; *D:* Christopher Miles; *W:* Alan Plater. **VHS, Beta** $79.99 *HBO* ✗✗½

Primal Impulse An astronaut, stranded on the moon because of a sinister experimental double-cross, unleashes a mental scream which possesses a young woman's mind back on earth.
1974 **90m/C** Klaus Kinski. **VHS, Beta** *NO* ✗½

Primal Rage A student is bitten by an experimental monkey, and begins to manifest his primal urges physically. Special effects by Carlo Rimbaldi.
1990 (R) **92m/C** Bo Svenson, Patrick Lowe, Mitch Watson, Cheryl Arutt, Sarah Buxton; *D:* Vittoria Rambaldi. **VHS, Beta** $19.98 *WAR* ✗

Primal Scream The Year is 1993. Earth's fuel sources are rapidly decaying and the top secret project to mine a revolutionary new energy source is underway—independently managed by a corrupt corporation.
1987 (R) **95m/C** Kenneth John McGregor, Sharon Mason, Julie Miller, Jon Maurice, Mickey Shaughnessy; *D:* William Murray. **VHS** *NO* ✗½

Primary Motive Taut political thriller with Nelson as Andy Blumenthal, a press secretary who finds that an opposing candidate's campaign is covered by a web of lies. Blumenthal exposes the lies, but the candidate denies them and pulls further ahead in the polls. When the candidate's wife gives Blumenthal an extremely damaging piece of information, will the polls finally turn against him?
1992 (R) **93m/C** Judd Nelson, Richard Jordan, Sally Kirkland, Justine Bateman, John Savage; *D:* Daniel Adams; *W:* Daniel Adams, William Snowden III. **VHS, Beta** $89.98 *FXV, VTR* ✗✗

Primary Target A mercenary reunites his 'Nam guerilla unit to rescue a diplomat's wife kidnapped by a Laotian jungle lord.
1989 (R) **85m/C** John Calvin, Miki Kim, Joey Aresco, Chip Lucio, John Ericson, Colleen Casey; *D:* Clark Henderson. **VHS, Beta** $14.95 *MGM* ✗

Prime Cut Veritable orgy of drug trafficking, prostitution, extortion, loan sharking, fisticuffs and gangsters getting ground into mincemeat. Sleazy but well-made crime melodrama has its followers, but is best known as Spacek's film debut.
1972 (R) **86m/C** Lee Marvin, Gene Hackman, Sissy Spacek, Angel Tompkins, Gregory Walcott; *D:* Michael Ritchie; *W:* Robert Dillon. **VHS, Beta** $59.98 *FOX* ✗✗½

Prime Evil A brave and determined nun infiltrates a sect of devil worshipping monks in an attempt to end their demonic sacrifices. The question is, will this sister slide beneath Satan's cleaver?
1988 (R) **87m/C** William Beckwith, Christine Moore; *D:* Roberta Findlay. **VHS** $19.95 *STE* ✗✗

The Prime of Miss Jean Brodie Oscar-winning performance by Smith as a forward-thinking teacher in a Scottish Girls' school during the 1920s. She captivates her impressionable young students with her fascist ideals and free-thinking attitudes in this adaptation of the play taken from Muriel Spark's novel.
1969 (PG) **116m/C** Dame Maggie Smith, Pamela Franklin, Robert Stephens, Celia Johnson, Gordon Jackson, Jane Carr; *D:* Ronald Neame; *W:* Jay Presson Allen. Academy Awards '69: Best Actress (Smith); Nominations: Best Song ("Jean"); Cannes Film Festival '69: Best Film; British Academy Awards '69: Best Actress (Smith), Best Supporting Actress (Johnson). **VHS, Beta** $79.98 *FOX, BTV* ✗✗✗

Prime Risk A young engineer who discovers an electronic method to break into automated teller machines finds that it leads to more trouble when she discovers that foreign agents are hot on her trail.
1984 (PG-13) **98m/C** Toni Hudson, Lee Montgomery, Sam Bottoms; *D:* W. Farkas. **VHS, Beta** $79.98 *LIV* ✗½

Prime Suspect An honest citizen becomes the prime suspect after the coverage of a murder by an over-ambitious television reporter.
1982 **100m/C** Mike Farrell, Teri Garr, Veronica Cartwright, Lane Smith, Barry Corbin, James Sloyan, Charles Aidman; *D:* Noel Black. **VHS, Beta** *NO* ✗✗

Prime Suspect A young man escapes from a mental institution to clear his name after being wrongfully accused of murdering his girlfriend.
1988 **89m/C** Susan Strasberg, Frank Stallone, Billy Drago, Doug McClure; *D:* Mark Rutland. **VHS** *NO* ✗½

Prime Suspect Mirren stars as Detective Chief Inspector Jane Tennison in this British television police procedural. When a male inspector dies of a heart attack while investigating a rape-murder, Tennison, the only women of senior police status, wants the case. But she runs into multiple obstructions, not the least being the smug male police system. Then the case really takes a turn when it appears Tennison is searching for a serial killer. But Jane is no quitter and she has both the brains and the guts to back up her orders. Adapted from the book by Lynda La Plante, who also wrote the teleplay.

1992 240m/C Helen Mirren, Tom Bell, Zoe Wanamaker, John Bowe, Tom Wilkinson, Ralph Fiennes; *D:* Christopher Menaul; *W:* Lynda La Plante. VHS $79.95 *SIG, FXL* 🎬🎬🎬

Prime Suspect 2 DCI Jane Tennison (Mirren) returns in another British made for TV police drama. Jane has been off at a police seminar where she has a brief liaison with a black police detective, Robert Oswalde (Salmon). She is recalled to investigate the decomposed body of a young woman found in one of London's Afro-Caribbean neighborhoods and must deal with their resentment of the police. When detective Oswalde is reassigned to Jane's department, she begins having trouble separating her public and private feelings, while trying to obtain a confession from her most likely suspect. Based on a story by Lynda La Plante.
1993 240m/C Helen Mirren, Colin Salmon, Tom Watson, Ian Fitzgibbon, Philip Wright, Jack Ellis, Craig Fairbrass; *D:* John Strickland; *W:* Allan Cubitt. VHS $79.95 *SIG, FXL* 🎬🎬🎬

Prime Target Small-town cop John Bloodstone (Heavener) is recruited by the FBI to transfer a mafia boss (Curtis) from a safehouse to the courthouse. He has to keep the former mobster alive long enough to testify against the "family." Their cross-country adventure is heightened by a murderous confrontation with evil forces that want them both dead.
1991 (R) 87m/C David Heavener, Tony Curtis, Isaac Hayes, Jenilee Harrison, Robert Reed, Andrew (Andy) Robinson, Don Stroud; *D:* David Heavener; *W:* David Heavener. VHS $9.95 *HMD* 🎬🎬

The Prime Time Horrid film about a teen girl who leaves home and gets involved with a teen gang and a slimy detective. She's also kidnapped by a weird beatnik artist who forces her to pose nude. Black's film debut. Also known as "Hellkitten."
1960 76m/B JoAnn LeCompte, Frank Roche, James Brooks, Ray Gronwold, Maria Pavelle, Robert Major, Karen Black; *D:* Herschell Gordon Lewis. VHS $16.95 *SNC Woof!*

Prime Time Forgotten satirical comedy about what would happen if the censors took a day off from American television.
1980 (R) 73m/C Warren Oates, David Spielberg. VHS, Beta *NO* 🎬½

The Primitive Lover Early silent comedy about young wife who decides she deserves more than her marriage is giving her.
1916 67m/B Constance Talmadge, Kenneth Harlan, Harrison Ford; *D:* Sidney Franklin. VHS, Beta $19.95 *GPV* 🎬🎬

Primo Baby A troublesome 15-year-old girl learns responsibility when she must care for a crippled racehorse. They both have a chance at success when she enters the thoroughbred in a race.
1988 97m/C VHS $89.95 *WOV* 🎬🎬½

Primrose Path Melodramatic soaper with comedic touches about a wrong-side-of-the-tracks girl falling for and then losing an ambitious young go-getter running a hamburger stand.
1940 93m/B Ginger Rogers, Joel McCrea, Marjorie Rambeau, Henry Travers, Miles Mander, Queenie Vasser, Joan Carroll, Vivienne Osborne; *D:* Gregory La Cava. VHS, Beta $19.98 *RKO, TTC* 🎬🎬½

Prince and the Great Race Three Australian children search the outback to find their kidnapped horse who is scheduled to run in the big New Year's Day Race.
1983 91m/C John Ewart, John Howard, Nicole Kidman. VHS, Beta $14.98 *LIV* 🎬🎬

The Prince and the Pauper Satisfying adaptation of the classic Mark Twain story of a young street urchin who trades places with the young king of England. Wonderful musical score by noted composer Korngold who provided the music for many of Flynn's adventure films. Also available in a computer-colorized version.
1937 118m/B Errol Flynn, Claude Rains, Alan Hale, Billy Mauch, Montagu Love, Henry Stephenson, Barton MacLane; *D:* William Keighley; *M:* Erich Wolfgang Korngold. VHS, Beta $19.95 *FOX, MLB, CCB* 🎬🎬🎬

The Prince and the Pauper A prince and a poor young boy swap their clothes and identities, thus causing a lot of confusion for their families. Based on the story by Mark Twain.
1962 93m/C Guy Williams, Laurence Naismith, Donald Houston, Jane Asher, Walter Hudd. VHS, Beta $12.99 *DIS* 🎬🎬

The Prince and the Pauper Remake of the 1937 Errol Flynn film employing lavish sets and a tongue-in-cheek attitude among the all-star cast, who occasionally wander adrift when the director stops for tea. When an English prince and a pauper discover that they have identical appearances, they decide to trade places with each other. From Mark Twain's classic. *AKA:* Crossed Swords.
1978 (PG) 113m/C Oliver Reed, Raquel Welch, Mark Lester, Ernest Borgnine, George C. Scott, Rex Harrison, Charlton Heston, Sybil Danning; *D:* Richard Fleischer; *M:* Maurice Jarre. VHS, Beta $19.98 *MED* 🎬🎬½

The Prince and the Showgirl An American showgirl in 1910 London is wooed by the Prince of Carpathia. Part of the "A Night at the Movies" series, this tape simulates a 1957 movie evening, with a Sylvester the Cat cartoon, "Greedy for Tweety," a newsreel and coming attractions for "Spirit of St. Louis."
1957 127m/C Laurence Olivier, Marilyn Monroe, Sybil Thorndike; *D:* Laurence Olivier. VHS, Beta $19.98 *WAR* 🎬🎬½

Prince Jack Profiles the turbulent political career of President John F. Kennedy.
1983 100m/C Lloyd Nolan, Dana Andrews, Robert Guillaume, Cameron Mitchell; *D:* Bert Lovitt; *M:* Elmer Bernstein. VHS, Beta $69.98 *LIV* 🎬🎬

Prince of Bel Air A pool-cleaning playboy who makes a habit of one night stands meets a woman and starts falling in love with her. Originally a made-for-television movie.
1987 (R) 95m/C Mark Harmon, Kirstie Alley, Robert Vaughn, Patrick Laborteaux, Deborah Harmon; *D:* Charles Braverman; *M:* Robert Folk. VHS, Beta $89.95 *ACA* 🎬½

The Prince of Central Park Two young orphans are forced by circumstance to live in a tree in New York's Central Park until they are befriended by a lonely old woman. An above-average made for television adaptation of the novel by Evan H. Rhodes, the story was later used for a Broadway play.
1977 76m/C Ruth Gordon, T.J. Hargrave, Lisa Richards, Brooke Shields, Marc Vahanian, Dan Hedaya; *D:* Harvey Hart. VHS, Beta $59.95 *LIV* 🎬🎬

Prince of Darkness University students release Satan, in the form of a mysterious chemical, unwittingly on the world. Written by Martin Quatermass (a pseudonym of Carpenter). Strong personnel does not save this dreary and slow-moving cliche plot.

1987 (R) 102m/C Donald Pleasence, Lisa Blount, Victor Wong, Jameson Parker, Dennis Dun; *D:* John Carpenter; *W:* John Carpenter; *M:* John Carpenter. VHS, Beta $14.98 *MCA* 🎬½

Prince of Pennsylvania A mild comedy about a spaced-out youth who kidnaps his own father in hopes of nabbing a family inheritance.
1988 (R) 113m/C Keanu Reeves, Fred Ward, Amy Madigan, Bonnie Bedelia, Jeff Hayenga; *D:* Ron Nyswaner; *W:* Ron Nyswaner. VHS, Beta $29.95 *COL* 🎬½

Prince of the City Docu-drama of a police officer who becomes an informant in an effort to end corruption within his narcotics unit, but finds he must pay a heavy price. Based on the true story told in Robert Daly's book, the powerful script carries the tension through what would otherwise be an overly long film. Excellent performances make this a riveting character study.
1981 (R) 167m/C Treat Williams, Jerry Orbach, Richard Foronjy, Don Billett, Kenny Marino, Lindsay Crouse, Lance Henriksen; *D:* Sidney Lumet; *W:* Jay Presson Allen, Sidney Lumet. VHS, Beta $29.98 *WAR* 🎬🎬🎬

The Prince of Thieves Robin Hood helps Lady Marian extricate herself from a forced marriage in this adventure made with younger audiences in mind.
1948 72m/C Jon Hall, Patricia Morison, Adele Jergens, Alan Mowbray, Michael Duane; *D:* Howard Bretherton. VHS *COL* 🎬🎬

The Prince of Tides Conroy's sprawling southern-fried saga is neatly pared down to essentials in this tale of the dysfunctional Wingo family, whose dark tragedies are gradually revealed as twins Tom and Savannah come to grips with personal demons under the ministering aid of psychiatrist Streisand. Bravura performance by Nolte in what may be his best role to date; Streisand is restrained in both her performance and direction although a subplot dealing with her bad marriage and rebellious son is a predictable distraction. The South Carolina low country, and even New York City, never looked better. Conroy adapted the screenplay from his novel of the same name with Johnston's help.
1991 (R) 132m/C Nick Nolte, Barbra Streisand, Blythe Danner, Kate Nelligan, Jeroen Krabbe, Melinda Dillon, George Carlin, Jason Gould, Brad Sullivan; *D:* Barbra Streisand; *W:* Pat Conroy, Becky Johnston; *M:* James Newton Howard. Academy Awards '91 Nominations: Best Actor (Nolte), Best Adapted Screenplay, Best Art Direction/Set Decoration, Best Cinematography, Best Picture, Best Supporting Actress (Nelligan), Best Original Score; Golden Globe Awards '92: Best Actor—Drama (Nolte); Los Angeles Film Critics Association Awards '91: Best Actor (Nolte). VHS, Beta, 8mm $19.95 *COL* 🎬🎬🎬½

Prince Valiant When his royal dad is exiled by an evil tyrant, brave young Wagner brushes aside bangs and journeys to Camelot to seek the help of King Arthur. Based on Harold Foster's classic comic strip.
1954 100m/C James Mason, Janet Leigh, Robert Wagner, Debra Paget, Sterling Hayden, Victor McLaglen, Donald Crisp, Brian Aherne, Barry Jones, Mary Philips; *D:* Henry Hathaway; *W:* Dudley Nichols. VHS $14.98 *FXV, FCT* 🎬🎬½

Princes in Exile Young people struggle with their life-threatening illnesses at a special summer camp. They find that love and friendship hold the key to dreams about the future. Excellent cast of newcomers. Based on a novel of the same name by Mark Schreiber.

1990 (PG-13) 103m/C Zachary Ansley, Nicholas Shields, Stacy Mistysyn, Alexander Chapman, Chuck Shamata; **D:** Giles Walker. **VHS, Beta** $89.95 *FRH, FCT ♂♂½*

Princess Academy A self-respecting young debutante battles the ways of her elitist finishing school.
1987 (R) 91m/C Eva Gabor, Lu Leonard, Richard Paul, Lar Park Lincoln, Carole Davis; **D:** Bruce Block. **VHS, Beta** $79.98 *LIV ♂*

The Princess & the Call Girl A call girl asks her look-alike roommate to take her place in Monaco for a lavishly erotic weekend.
1984 90m/C Carol Levy, Shannah Hall, Victor Bevine; **D:** Radley Metzger. **VHS, Beta** $59.95 *MON ♂*

The Princess and the Goblin Little kiddies may enjoy this animated adventure but it's a bland story with mediocre animation. Groups of ugly, underground-dwelling goblins like nothing better than to scare humans, especially castle-dwelling Princess Irene. Brave working-class Curdie helps to save the day. Based on a book by George MacDonald.
1994 (G) 82m/C **V:** Sally Ann Marsh, Peter Murray, Claire Bloom. **VHS** $24.95 *HMD ♂♂½*

The Princess and the Pea From "Faerie Tale Theatre" comes the story of a princess who tries to prove that she's a blueblood by feeling the bump of a tiny pea under the thickness of twenty mattresses.
1983 60m/C Liza Minnelli, Tom Conti, Tim Kazurinsky, Pat McCormick, Beatrice Straight; **D:** Tony Bill. **VHS, Beta** $14.98 *KUI, FOX, FCT ♂♂♂*

The Princess and the Pirate Hope at his craziest as a vaudevillian who falls for a beautiful princess while on the run from buccaneers on the Spanish Main. Look for Crosby in a closing cameo performance. Available in digitally remastered stereo with original movie trailer.
1944 94m/C Bob Hope, Walter Slezak, Walter Brennan, Virginia Mayo, Victor McLaglen; **Cameos:** Bing Crosby; **D:** David Butler. **VHS, Beta** $19.98 *HBO, SUE ♂♂♂*

The Princess and the Swineherd A German adaptation of the Brothers Grimm fairy tale about a young suitor who tries to please a materialistic princess.
1960 82m/B **VHS, Beta** $24.95 *VYY ♂½*

The Princess Bride A modern update of the basic fairy tale crammed with all the cliches, this adventurously irreverent love story centers around a beautiful maiden and her young swain as they battle the evils of the mythical kingdom of Florin to be reunited with one another. Great dueling scenes and offbeat satire of the genre make this fun for adults as well as children. Based on William Goldman's cult novel.
1987 (PG) 98m/C Cary Elwes, Mandy Patinkin, Robin Wright, Wallace Shawn, Peter Falk, Andre the Giant, Chris Sarandon, Christopher Guest, Billy Crystal, Carol Kane, Fred Savage, Peter Cook, Mel Smith; **D:** Rob Reiner; **W:** William Goldman; **M:** Mark Knopfler. **VHS, Beta, 8mm** $14.95 *COL, SUE, SUP ♂♂♂½*

Princess Cinderella A live-action dramatization of the famous fantasy. Dubbed in English.
193? 75m/B Silvana Jachino, Roberto Villa. **VHS, Beta** $59.95 *JEF ♂♂*

Princess Daisy Made for television movie about a beautiful model who claws her way to the top of her profession while trying to find true love and avoid the clutches of her rotten half-brother. Adapted from Judith Krantz's glitzy best-selling novel.

1983 200m/C Merete Van Kamp, Lindsay Wagner, Claudia Cardinale, Stacy Keach, Ringo Starr, Barbara Bach; **D:** Waris Hussein. **VHS, Beta** $14.95 *STE, FOX, MOV ♂*

Princess Tam Tam Pleasing French adaptation of Shaw's "Pygmalion," as a beautiful native African woman is "westernized" by a handsome writer and then introduced to high society as an exotic princess. A musical notable for its spectacular choreography and on-location Tunisian scenery. Story by Pepito Abatino, who was then Baker's husband. In French with English subtitles.
1935 77m/B Josephine Baker, Albert Prejean, Germaine Aussey, Viviane Romance; **D:** Edmond T. Greville. **VHS, Beta** $29.95 *MVD, TPV, KIV ♂♂♂*

The Princess Who Never Laughed A stern king holds a laugh-off contest to make his morose daughter happy in this adaptation of the Brothers Grimm story from the "Faerie Tale Theatre" series.
1984 60m/C Ellen Barkin, Howard Hesseman, Howie Mandel, Mary Woronov. **VHS, Beta** $14.98 *KUI, FOX, FCT ♂♂♂*

Princess Yang Kwei Fei Set in 8th-century China and based on the life of the last T'ang emperor and the beautiful servant girl he loves and makes his bride. She falls victim to court jealousies and he to his greedy family, though even death cannot end their love. Beautifully filmed and acted romantic tragedy. In Japanese with English subtitles. **AKA:** Yokihi; The Empress Yang Kwei Fei.
1955 91m/C Machiko Kyo, Masayuki Mori, Sakae Ozawa, So Yamamura; **D:** Kenji Mizoguchi. **VHS** $79.95 *NYF ♂♂♂*

The Principal A tough, down-on-his-luck high school teacher is hired as the principal of a relentlessly violent, uncontrollable high school. Naturally he whips it into shape.
1987 (R) 109m/C James Belushi, Louis Gossett Jr., Rae Dawn Chong, Michael Wright, Esai Morales, J.J. Cohen, Troy Winbush; **D:** Christopher Cain; **W:** Frank Deese; **M:** Jay Gruska. **VHS, Beta** $14.95 *COL ♂♂½*

Prison The zombified body of an unjustly executed inmate haunts Creedmore Prison, stalking the guard that killed him. His search is aided by the terrified inmates.
1988 (R) 102m/C Lane Smith, Chelsea Field, Viggo Mortensen, Lincoln Kilpatrick, Tom Everett, Tiny Lister; **D:** Renny Harlin; **W:** C. Courtney Joyner; **M:** Richard Band. **VHS, Beta** $19.95 *NWV ♂½*

Prison Break A convict plans a daring prison escape in order to clear his name for a murder he did not commit.
1938 72m/B Barton MacLane, Glenda Farrell, Ward Bond. **VHS, Beta** $16.95 *SNC, NOS, MRV ♂♂*

Prison Planet In the year 2200 Earth is under the dictatorship of an evil king, with only a band of intrepid rebels to oppose him. Blaine, one of the rebels, gets himself arrested and sent to prison in search of the true ruler, the king's brother. But the prison is protected by a brutal warlord and his equally sadistic warriors, whom Blaine must battle if he ever hopes to find truth and justice.
1992 (R) 90m/C James Phillips, Jack Willcox, Michael Foley, Deborah Thompson-Carlin; **D:** Armand Gazarian; **W:** Armand Gazarian. **VHS** *COL ♂½*

Prison Shadows Contrived programmer about a fighter (Nugent) who attempts to make a comeback after having served three years of a five-year sentence for killing an opponent in the boxing ring. He makes his comeback, but deals yet another mortal

blow. Turns out that a gambling ring is behind the bizarre murders of the fighters and Nugent is their next victim.
1936 67m/B Eddie Nugent, Lucille Lund, Joan Barclay, Forrest Taylor, Syd Saylor, Monte Blue; **D:** Robert F. Hill; **W:** Al Martin. **VHS** $16.95 *SNC ♂*

Prison Stories: Women on the Inside Three short dramatic stories depict the life of women inside prison walls. "New Chicks," directed by Spheeris, tells the story of two lifelong friends and partners in crime. "Esperanza," directed by Deitch, tells the story of a woman on the inside trying to prevent her family from following the same destructive path. Silver's "Parole Board" features Davidovich as a murderess up for parole but reluctant to leave the security of the prison. Blunt and gritty portrayal of prison gangs, the lifestyle of female inmates, and their fears of returning to life on the outside. Originally produced for cable TV.
1991 94m/C Rae Dawn Chong, Annabella Sciorra, Lolita Davidovich, Talisa Soto, Rachel Ticotin, Grace Zabriskie, Silvania Gallardo, Francesca Roberts; **D:** Donna Deitch, Penelope Spheeris, Joan Micklin Silver. **VHS, Beta** *PSM ♂♂♂*

Prison Train Travelogue of a convicted murderer's cross-country journey to begin his prison sentence at Alcatraz. **AKA:** People's Enemy.
1938 84m/B Fred Keating, Linda (Dorothy Comingore) Winters, Clarence Muse, Faith Bacon, Alexander Leftwich, Nestor Paiva, Franklin Farnum; **D:** Gordon Wiles. **VHS** $24.95 *VYY, MOV ♂♂½*

The Prisoner Gritty drama about a Cardinal imprisoned in a Soviet bloc country as his captors attempt to break his determination not to be used as a propaganda tool. Interactions between the prisoner and his interogator are riveting. Based on the real-life experiences of Cardinal Mindszenty, a Hungarian activist during and after WWII.
1955 91m/B Alec Guinness, Jack Hawkins, Raymond Huntley, Wilfred Lawson; **D:** Peter Glenville. **VHS** $69.95 *COL ♂♂♂*

The Prisoner: Arrival Introductory episode of the cult television series. McGoohan stars as a former British spy abducted and held captive in a mysterious village where everyone is assigned a number. As Number 6 he tries to figure out what's going on and how he can get out. Additional episodes available.
1968 52m/C Patrick McGoohan, Virginia Maskell, Guy Doleman, Paul Eddington, George Baker, Angelo Muscat, Barbara Yu Ling, Stephanie Randall; **D:** Don Chaffey. **VHS, Beta** $29.95 *MPI, MOV, TVC ♂♂♂*

Prisoner Cell Block H Popular Australian television soap opera set in Wentworth Detention Center, a women's prison. Primary characters include Franky, a violent lesbian biker in for armed robbery; Karen, who murdered her husband and is the object of Franky's affection; and naive Lynn, accused of kidnapping and attempted murder. Two episodes per cassette.
1980 95m/C Carol Burns, Kerry Armstrong, Patsy King, Gerard Maguire, Barry Quin, Mary Ward, Monica Maughan, Fiona Spence, Val Lehman, Pieta Tommano. **VHS** $19.98 *MPI, MOV ♂♂♂*

Prisoner in the Middle Janssen is the only man who can stop a nuclear warhead from falling into the hands of rival Middle East factions. Originally released as "Warhead."

1974 (PG) 87m/C David Janssen, Karin Dor, Christopher Stone, Turia Tan, David Semadar, Art Metrano; **D:** John O'Conner. **VHS, Beta, 8mm** $69.95 *ACA, MTX, QVD* 🐾🐾

Prisoner of Honor A made-for-cable-TV retelling of notorious Dreyfus Affair, in which a Jewish officer in the 19th-century French military was accused of treason based on little evidence and lots of bigotry. George Piquart (Dreyfuss), the anti-semitic counterintelligence head, grows to realize Dreyfus' innocence and fights zealously for the truth. Russell's flamboyant direction takes the heroic tale into the realm of the surreal; this may not be a thoroughly accurate account, but it's one of the more eye-filling.
1991 (PG) 90m/C Richard Dreyfuss, Oliver Reed, Peter Firth, Jeremy Kemp, Brian Blessed, Peter Vaughan, Kenneth Colley, Lindsay Anderson; **D:** Ken Russell. **VHS** $89.99 *HBO* 🐾🐾🐾

Prisoner of Rio The made-for-cable-TV satire about scruple-less television evangelists and their nefarious schemes at acquiring their audience's money.
1989 90m/C Steven Berkoff, Paul Freeman; **D:** Lech Majewski. **VHS, Beta** $89.95 *MOV* 🐾🐾

Prisoner of Second Avenue A New Yorker in his late forties faces the future, without a job or any confidence in his ability, with the help of his understanding wife. Based on the Broadway play by Neil Simon.
1974 (PG) 98m/C Jack Lemmon, Anne Bancroft, Gene Saks, Elizabeth Wilson, Sylvester Stallone, F. Murray Abraham; **D:** Melvin Frank; **W:** Neil Simon; **M:** Marvin Hamlisch. **VHS, Beta** $19.98 *WAR* 🐾🐾½

Prisoner of Zenda An excellent cast and splendid photography make this the definitive film adaptation of Anthony Hope's swashbuckling novel. A British commoner is forced to pose as his cousin, the kidnapped king of a small European country, to save the throne. Complications of the romantic sort ensue when he falls in love with the queen. Excellent acting, robust sword play, and beautifully designed costumes make this an enjoyable spectacle.
1937 101m/B Ronald Colman, Douglas Fairbanks Jr., Madeleine Carroll, David Niven, Raymond Massey, Mary Astor, Sir C. Aubrey Smith, Montagu Love, Byron Foulger, Alexander D'Arcy, Charles Halton; **D:** John Cromwell; **W:** Donald Ogden Stewart, John Balderston, Wills Root. **VHS, Beta** $19.98 *MGM* 🐾🐾🐾½

Prisoner of Zenda Less-inspired remake of the 1937 version of Anthony Hope's novel, of a man resembling the monarch of a small country who is forced to pose as King during the coronation ceremony, becomes enamored with the queen, and finds himself embroiled in a murder plot. Worth watching for the luxurious costumes and lavish sets. Cast as a Cardinal here, Stone starred in the 1922 version.
1952 101m/C Stewart Granger, Deborah Kerr, Louis Calhern, James Mason, Jane Greer, Lewis Stone; **D:** Richard Thorpe. **VHS, Beta** $19.98 *MGM* 🐾🐾½

Prisoner of Zenda Flat comedic interpretation of Anthony Hope's swashbuckling tale of two identical men who switch places, only to find things complicated by a murder. Sellers stars in the double role of Prince Rudolph of Ruritania and Syd, the cockney cab driver who doubles for Rudolph when the Prince is imprisoned by his jealous brother Michael.

1979 (PG) 108m/C Peter Sellers, Jeremy Kemp, Lynne Frederick, Lionel Jeffries, Elke Sommer; **D:** Richard Quine; **W:** Dick Clement, Ian LaFrenais; **M:** Henry Mancini. **VHS, Beta** $14.98 *MCA* 🐾🐾

Prisoners of Inertia Two newlyweds travel to New York city and find themselves caught up in a whirlwind adventure in this well-acted but lazily scripted comedy drama.
1989 (R) 92m/C Amanda Plummer, Christopher Rich, John C. McGinley; **D:** Jay Noyles Seles. **VHS** $79.95 *BTV* 🐾🐾

Prisoners of the Lost Universe Talk-show hostess and her buddy are transported to a hostile universe by a renegade scientist. The two terrified humans search desperately for the dimensional door that is their only hope of escape. Made for television.
1984 94m/C Richard Hatch, Kay Lenz, John Saxon; **D:** Terry Marcel. **VHS, Beta** *NO* 🐾½

Prisoners of the Sun Right after WWII an Australian captain fights to convict Japanese officers for atrocities against Allied POWs, but he's stonewalled by both the U.S. military and still-defiant enemy prisoners. This fiery drama from Down Under packs a punch as it questions whether wartime justice even exists; similar in that way to Brown's earlier "Breaker Morant." Takei (Sulu of the original "Star Trek") makes an imposing Japanese admiral. *AKA:* Blood Oath.
1991 (R) 109m/C Bryan Brown, George Takei, Terry O'Quinn, John Back, Toshi Shioya, Deborah Unger; **D:** Stephen Wallace. **VHS, Beta** $92.98 *PAR* 🐾🐾🐾

Private Affairs The mistress of a well-known surgeon becomes jealous when the doctor decides to have a fling with a gorgeous young swim instructor. Italian-made cheapie.
1989 (R) 83m/C Guiliana de Sio, Kate Capshaw, David Naughton, Luca Barbareschi, Michele Placido; **D:** Francesco Massaro. **VHS, Beta** $29.95 *ACA* 🐾

The Private Affairs of Bel Ami "This is the story of a scoundrel," proclaims the opening. Sanders is ideally cast as a suave cad who rises in 1880s Parisian society, largely through stategic seduction of prominent women. Moralistically minded Old Hollywood toned down the talky adaptation of the Guy de Maupassant novel, but it's still drama of a high order.
1947 112m/B George Sanders, Angela Lansbury, Ann Dvorak, Frances Dee, John Carradine, Susan Douglas, Hugo Haas, Marie Wilson, Albert Basserman, Warren William, Katherine Emery, Richard Fraser; **D:** Albert Lewin; **W:** Albert Lewin. **VHS** $19.98 *REP, FCT* 🐾🐾

Private Benjamin Lighthearted fare about a pampered New York Jewish princess who impulsively enlists in the U.S. Army after her husband dies on their wedding night. Hawn, who also produced, creates a character loveable even at her worst moments and brings a surprising amount of depth to this otherwise frivolous look at high society attitudes. The basis for the television series.
1980 (R) 110m/C Goldie Hawn, Eileen Brennan, Albert Brooks, Robert Webber, Armand Assante, Barbara Barrie, Mary Kay Place, Sally Kirkland, Craig T. Nelson, Harry Dean Stanton, Sam Wanamaker; **D:** Howard Zieff; **W:** Nancy Meyers, Charles Shyer; **M:** Bill Conti. **VHS, Beta** $19.98 *WAR* 🐾🐾½

Private Buckaroo War time entertainment in which Harry James and his orchestra get drafted. They decide to put on a show for the soldiers and get help from the Andrews

Sisters. ♫Don't Sit Under the Apple Tree with Anyone Else But Me; Three Little Sisters; Private Buckaroo; Johnny Get Your Gun Again; We've Got a Job to Do; You Made Me Love You; Six Jerks in a Jeep; That's the Moon My Son; I Love the South.
1942 70m/B The Andrews Sisters, Harry James, Joe E. Lewis, Dick Foran, Shemp Howard, Mary Wickes, Donald O'Connor; **D:** Eddie Cline. **VHS, Beta** $19.95 *NOS, HEG, CAB* 🐾🐾

Private Contentment This is a drama about a young soldier's experiences before he goes off to war in 1945.
1983 90m/C Trini Alvarado, Peter Gallagher, John McMartin, Kathryn Walker; **D:** Vivian Matalon. **VHS, Beta** *FLI* 🐾🐾

Private Duty Nurses Three nurses take on racism, war wounds, and a menage-a-trois (between one nurse, a doctor, and a drug addict). Second in Roger Corman's "nurse" quintet takes itself too seriously to be entertaining, but the gals make good use of those exciting new inventions, waterbeds. Preceded by "The Student Nurses" and followed by "Night Call Nurses," "The Young Nurses," and "Candy Stripe Nurses." Also on video as "Young L.A. Nurses 1."
1971 (R) 80m/C Kathy Cannon, Joyce Williams, Pegi Boucher, Joseph Kaufmann, Dennis Redfield, Herbert Jefferson Jr., Paul Hampton, Paul Gleason; **D:** George Armitage; **W:** George Armitage. **VHS, Beta** $59.98 *NLC, SUE* 🐾½

The Private Eyes Light and uneven comedic romp with Knotts and Conway as bungling sleuths engaged to investigate two deaths. They're led on a merry chase through secret passages to a meeting with a ghostly adversary.
1980 (PG) 91m/C Don Knotts, Tim Conway, Trisha Noble, Bernard Fox; **D:** Lang Elliott; **W:** Tim Conway, John Myhers. **VHS, Beta** $29.98 *VES* 🐾½

The Private Files of J. Edgar Hoover Scandal-mongering "biography" of J. Edgar Hoover's private, sex-filled life.
1977 (PG) 112m/C Broderick Crawford, Dan Dailey, Jose Ferrer, Rip Torn, Michael Parks, Raymond St. Jacques, Ronee Blakley; **D:** Larry Cohen; **W:** Larry Cohen. **VHS** $69.99 *HBO* 🐾🐾½

A Private Function A ribald gag-fest dealing with Palin as a Yorkshireman who steals and fattens a wily contraband pig against the backdrop of post-WWII rationing. The satire ranges from biting to downright nasty, but Palin is always likeable in the center of it all.
1984 (PG) 96m/C Michael Palin, Dame Maggie Smith, Denholm Elliott, Bill Paterson, Liz Smith; **D:** Malcolm Mowbray; **W:** Alan Bennett; **M:** John Du Prez. **VHS, Beta** $19.95 *PAR, TVC, FCT* 🐾🐾½

Private Hell 36 Two detectives become guilt-ridden after keeping part of some stolen money recovered after a robbery. Co-produced by Lupino.
1954 81m/B Ida Lupino, Howard Duff, Steve Cochran; **D:** Don Siegel; **W:** Ida Lupino. **VHS** $19.95 *REP* 🐾🐾

The Private History of a Campaign That Failed Adaptation of the Mark Twain story about a cowardly troop of Confederate soldiers.
1987 89m/C Pat Hingle, Edward Herrmann. **VHS, Beta** $19.95 *MCA* 🐾½

Private Investigations A made-for-video thriller about a nosey reporter who gets himself and his adult son in trouble while investigating drug-pushing cops.
1987 (R) 91m/C Ray Sharkey, Clayton Rohner, Talia Balsam, Anthony Zerbe, Paul LeMat; **D:** Nigel Dick; **W:** John Dahl, David Warfield. **VHS, Beta** $14.95 *MGM, FOX* 🐾½

Private Lessons Teenage boy is left alone for the summer in the care of an alluring maid and a scheming chauffeur.
1981 (R) 83m/C Eric Brown, Sylvia Kristel, Howard Hesseman; *D:* Alan Myerson. **VHS, Beta $24.95** *MCA* ✍✍

Private Lessons A boy can't concentrate on his piano lessons when he gets a beautiful new teacher. You won't be able to concentrate on anything but comedy.
19?? 90m/C Carroll Baker. **VHS, Beta $79.95** *JEF* ✍✍

Private Life Suddenly with time on his hands, a Soviet official scrutinizes his relationships. After a number of revelations, he is forced to make new choices based on what he has learned. Oscar nominee in 1983. In Russian with English subtitles. *AKA:* Chastnaya Zhizn.
1982 103m/C Mikhail Ulyanov, Ita Sanvina, Irina Gubanova; *D:* Edgar Ryazanov. **VHS $59.95** *KIV, FCT* ✍✍½

Private Life of Don Juan Appropriately slow-moving British costume drama set in 17th-century Spain finds an aging Don Juan struggling to maintain his usual antics in the pursuit of beautiful women. Furthermore, his reputation is being upstaged by a young imposter. Notable only as the last film appearance by Douglas Fairbanks Sr., and based on the play by Henri Bataille. *AKA:* Don Juan.
1934 87m/B Douglas Fairbanks Sr., Merle Oberon, Binnie Barnes, Melville Cooper, Joan Gardner, Benita Hume, Athene Seyler; *D:* Alexander Korda. **VHS, Beta $9.95** *CNG, NOS, GPV* ✍✍

The Private Life of Henry VIII Lavish historical spectacle lustily portraying the life and lovers of notorious British Monarch, King Henry VIII. A tour de force for Laughton as the robust 16th-century king, with outstanding performances by the entire cast.
1933 97m/B Charles Laughton, Binnie Barnes, Elsa Lanchester, Robert Donat, Merle Oberon, Miles Mander, Wendy Barrie, John Loder; *D:* Alexander Korda. *W:* Arthur Wimperis, Lajos Biro. Academy Awards '33: Best Actor (Laughton); Nominations: Best Picture. **VHS, Beta $19.98** *HBO, NOS, PSM* ✍✍✍✍

The Private Life of Sherlock Holmes A unique perspective on the life of the famous detective reveals a complex character. Beautifully photographed, with fine performances by the supporting cast, the film boasts a haunting musical score but received suprisingly little recognition despite Wilder's high caliber direction.
1970 (PG-13) 125m/C Robert Stephens, Colin Blakely, Genevieve Page, Irene Handl, Stanley Holloway, Christopher Lee, Clive Revill; *D:* Billy Wilder; *W:* I.A.L. Diamond, Billy Wilder. **VHS $19.98** *FOX* ✍✍✍½

Private Lives Stylish adaptation of Noel Coward play starring Shearer and Montgomery as a couple with a tempestuous relationship. Although once married, they have since divorced and married other mates. While honeymooning at the same french hotel (Quelle coincidence!), they have trouble showing affection to their new spouses and realize they still feel passionately about one another. Excellent acting combined with Coward's witty dialogue makes this film a treat.
1931 92m/B Norma Shearer, Robert Montgomery, Reginald Denny, Una Merkel, Jean Hersholt; *D:* Sidney Franklin. **VHS $19.98** *MGM* ✍✍✍½

The Private Lives of Elizabeth & Essex Cast reads like a Who's Who in Hollywood in this lavishly costumed dramatization of the love affair between Queen Elizabeth I and the Second Earl of Essex. Forced to choose between her Kingdom and her lover, Davis' monarch is the epitome of a regal women. Fobray made her first film appearance as an adult in the adaptation of Maxwell Anderson's "Elizabeth the Queen."
1939 106m/C Bette Davis, Errol Flynn, Vincent Price, Nanette Fabray, Olivia de Havilland, Alan Hale, Donald Crisp, Leo G. Carroll; *D:* Michael Curtiz. **VHS, Beta $19.98** *FOX* ✍✍✍

Private Manoeuvres A comely Swiss military adviser gives her all to uplift the morale of the men at Camp Samantha.
1983 79m/C Zachi Noy, Yoseph Shiloah, Dvora Bekon. **VHS, Beta $59.95** *MGM* Woof!

A Private Matter Based on the true story of Sherri Finkbine (hostess of TV's "Romper Room") and the controversy surrounding her decision to terminate her pregnancy in 1962. Pregnant with her fifth child, she discovered her sleeping medication contained thalidomide, known to cause severe birth defects. Although technically illegal, her doctor agreed to quietly perform an abortion. Sherri warned a local newspaper reporter about the drug's dangers and her identity was mistakenly revealed. A storm of adverse publicity forced her to Sweden for the abortion. Great performances highlight this complex and traumatic issue. Made for cable television.
1992 (PG-13) 89m/C Sissy Spacek, Aidan Quinn, Estelle Parsons, Sheila McCarthy, Leon Russom, William H. Macy; *D:* Joan Micklin Silver; *W:* William Nicholson. **VHS $89.99** *HBO* ✍✍✍

Private Parts A bizarre first attempt at feature length for Bartel. Black comedy featuring a runaway, a voyeuristic photographer and a hotel full of strange people who participate in murder and a variety of freakish sexual acts.
1972 (R) 87m/C Ayn Ruymen, Lucille Benson, John Ventantonio, Laurie Main, Stanley Livingston, Charles Woolf; *D:* Paul Bartel. **VHS $18.00** *FRG, MGM* ✍✍

Private Passions A sultry woman gives her teenaged cousin a lesson in love during his European vacation.
1985 86m/C Sybil Danning. **VHS, Beta $59.95** *PSM* ✍

Private Resort Curious house detective and a bumbling thief interrupt the highjinks of two girl-crazy teens on a quest for fun at an expensive Miami hotel. Occasionally funny plodder.
1984 (R) 82m/C Johnny Depp, Rob Morrow, Karyn O'Bryan, Emily Longstreth, Tony Azito, Hector Elizondo, Dody Goodman, Leslie Easterbrook, Andrew Dice Clay; *D:* George Bowers. **VHS, Beta $14.95** *COL* ✍✍

Private Road: No Trespassing A stock car racer and a top engineer compete over a military project, cars and a rich heiress.
1987 (R) 90m/C George Kennedy, Greg Evigan, Mitzi Kapture; *D:* Raphael Nussbaum. **VHS, Beta $79.95** *TWE* ✍✍

Private School Two high school girls from the exclusive Cherryvale Academy for Women compete for the affections of a young man from nearby Freemount Academy for Men, while Cherryvale's headmistress is trying to raise funds to build a new wing. Banal teen sexploitation comedy with better-than-average cast.

1983 (R) 89m/C Phoebe Cates, Betsy Russell, Kathleen Wilhoite, Sylvia Kristel, Ray Walston, Matthew Modine, Michael Zorek, Fran Ryan, Jonathan Prince, Kari Lizer, Richard Stahl; *D:* Noel Black. **VHS, Beta $14.95** ✍✍½

The Private Secretary Horton is a mild-mannered clergyman who finds out his identity has been usurped by a young man with a great many angry creditors. Horton has some amusing comic bits but the film, based on a popular Victorian farce "Der Bibliotheker" by Van Moser, did not translate well to the screen.
1935 70m/B Edward Everett Horton, Barry Mackay, Oscar Asche, Judy Gunn, Michael Shepley, Alastair Sim; *D:* Henry Edwards. **VHS** *HCV* ✍½

Private War Training for an elite force turns deadly when the commanding officer makes the rules. Now it's a private war between two brutal fighting machines. Adapted from a Jan Guillou story.
1990 (R) 95m/C Martin Hewitt, Joe Dallesandro, Kimberly Beck; *D:* Frank De Palma; *W:* Frank De Palma. **VHS $89.98** *REP* ✍

Private Wars A law-abiding community falls victim to gangland violence until the inhabitants hire a down-and-out private eye (Railsback) to show them how to fight back. He finds out that a greedy land developer (Whitman) has bribed the Chief of Police (Champion) to let his goons do anything to get the people out so he can redevelop the land.
1993 (R) 94m/C Steve Railsback, Michael Champion, Stuart Whitman, Holly Floria, Dan Tullis Jr., Michael Delano, James Lew, Brian Patrick Clark; *D:* John Weidner; *W:* Ken Lamplugh, John Weidner. **VHS $89.95** *PMH, IME* ✍✍

Privates on Parade Film centering around the comic antics of an Army song-and-dance unit entertaining the troops in the Malayan jungle during the late '40s. Occasionally-inspired horseplay based on Peter Nichols play.
1984 (R) 107m/C John Cleese, Denis Quilley, Simon Jones, Joe Melia, Nicola Pagetti, Julian Sands; *D:* Michael Blakemore. **VHS, Beta $19.95** *PAR, TVC* ✍✍½

Prix de Beaute A woman's boyfriend does not know that she has won a beauty contest. Brooks' last starring role and the only film she did in France. In French with English subtitles. *AKA:* Miss Europe.
1930 93m/B Louise Brooks, Jean Bradin, George Charlia, Gaston Jacquet; *D:* Augusto Genina. **VHS, Beta $59.95** *INT, ING* ✍½

The Prize Gripping spy story laced with laughs based on a novel by Irving Wallace (adapted by Lehman). In Stockholm, writer accepts the Nobel prize for dubious reasons and then finds himself in the midst of political intrigue. Newman and Sommer turn in great performances in this action drama.
1963 136m/C Paul Newman, Edward G. Robinson, Elke Sommer, Leo G. Carroll, Diane Baker, Micheline Presle, Gerard Oury, Sergio Fantoni; *D:* Mark Robson; *W:* Ernest Lehman; *M:* Jerry Goldsmith. **VHS $19.98** *MGM, REP, MLB* ✍✍✍

Prize Fighter Comedy team of Knotts and Conway take on Depression-era boxing. Fight manager Knotts and his pugilistic protege Conway unknowingly get involved with a powerful gangster, who convinces them to fight in a fixed championship match. Most enjoyable if intelligence is suspended at onset.
1979 (PG) 99m/C Tim Conway, Don Knotts; *D:* Michael Preece; *W:* Tim Conway. **VHS, Beta $9.95** *MED* ✍✍

Prize of Peril A French television game show rewards its winners with wealth and its losers with execution. Not always the best policy to learn what's behind Door #1.
1984 95m/C Michel Piccoli, Marie-France Pisier; **D:** Yves Boisset. **VHS, Beta** $79.98 *LIV* 🐾🐾

The Prize Pulitzer Watered-down, made-for-television account of the scandalous divorce between publishing heir Herbert "Pete" Pulitzer and his young wife Roxanne. Based on the book "The Prize Pulitzer" by Roxanne Pulitzer. Also known as "Roxanne: The Prize Pulitzer."
1989 95m/C Perry King, Chynna Phillips, Courteney Cox, Betsy Russell, Sondra Blake, Caitlin Brown; **D:** Richard A. Colla. **VHS** *CAF* 🐾🐾

The Prizefighter and the Lady In his first film role boxer Baer (who won the heavyweight boxing crown in 1934) is a natural as a fighter who falls for a beautiful nightclub singer (Loy). Baer and Loy get, but don't stay, together but she does turn out to be his lucky charm in the big fight finale. Fellow professional boxer Carnera, Baer's opponent in the climatic fight scene, refused to lose as the script indicated and the film ending was eventually rewritten. The likeable Baer later earned his living as an actor. *AKA:* Every Woman's Man.
1933 102m/B Max Baer Sr., Myrna Loy, Otto Kruger, Primo Carnera, Walter Huston, Vince Barnett, Muriel Evans; **D:** Woodbridge S. Van Dyke. *MGM* 🐾🐾🐾

Prizzi's Honor Highly stylized, sometimes leaden black comedy about an aging and none-to-bright hit man from a New York mob family who breaks with family loyalties when he falls for an upwardly mobile tax consultant who's also a hired killer. Skirting caricature in every frame, Nicholson is excellent in his portrayal of the thick-skulled mobster, as are Angelica Huston as the hot-to-trot Mafia daughter and Hickey as the Don. Adapted by Richard Condon and Janet Roach from Condon's novel.
1985 (R) 130m/C Jack Nicholson, Kathleen Turner, Robert Loggia, John Randolph, Anjelica Huston, Lawrence Tierney, William Hickey, Lee Richardson, Michael Lombard, Joseph Ruskin, CCH Pounder; **D:** John Huston; **W:** Richard Condon, Janet Roach; **M:** Alx North. Academy Awards '85: Best Supporting Actress (Huston); Nominations: Best Actor (Nicholson), Best Adapted Screenplay, Best Costume Design, Best Director (Huston), Best Film Editing, Best Picture, Best Supporting Actor (Hickey); Golden Globe Awards '86: Best Actor—Musical/Comedy (Nicholson), Best Actress—Musical/Comedy (Turner), Best Director (Huston), Best Film—Musical/Comedy; New York Film Critics Awards '85: Best Film. **VHS, Beta** $29.98 *LIV, VES, BTV* 🐾🐾🐾

Probation A dashing young man in trouble with the law receives an unusual sentence; he must become a chauffeur for a spoiled society girl. Grable's first film role is a small one. *AKA:* Second Chances.
1932 60m/B Sally Blane, J. Farrell MacDonald, Eddie Phillips, Clara Kimball Young, Betty Grable; **D:** Richard Thorpe. **VHS, Beta** $16.95 *NOS, SNC* 🐾🐾

Probe A detective uses computer-age technology to apprehend criminals. Pilot for the television series "Search."
1972 95m/C Hugh O'Brian, Elke Sommer, John Gielgud, Burgess Meredith, Angel Tompkins, Lilia Skala, Kent Smith, Alfred Ryder, Jaclyn Smith; **D:** Russ Mayberry; **W:** Leslie Stevens. $59.95 *UNI* 🐾🐾½

Problem Child Ritter decides to adopt Oliver out of the goodness of his heart, but it seems young Oliver's already got a father figure named Beelzebub. Potential for laughs is unmet.
1990 (PG) 81m/C John Ritter, Michael Oliver, Jack Warden, Amy Yasbeck, Gilbert Gottfried, Michael Richards, Peter Jurasik; **D:** Dennis Dugan; **W:** Scott Alexander, Larry Karaszewski; **M:** Miles Goodman. **VHS** $14.98 *MCA* 🐾½

Problem Child 2 Ritter and his nasty adopted son are back, but this time there's an equally malevolent little girl. They team up to prevent Ritter's upcoming marriage to a socialite. Low slapstick junk.
1991 (PG-13) 91m/C John Ritter, Michael Oliver, Laraine Newman, Amy Yasbeck, Jack Warden, Ivyann Schwan, Gilbert Gottfried, James Tolkan, Charlene Tilton, Alan Blumenfeld; **D:** Brian Levant; **W:** Scott Alexander, Larry Karaszewski. **VHS, Beta** $19.98 *MCA* 🐾

The Prodigal Luke's New Testament Bible story of the son seduced by greed slickly transfered to the silver screen by MGM. A colorful cast is the main attraction.
1955 113m/C Lana Turner, Edmund Purdom, Louis Calhern, Audrey Dalton, Neville Brand, Walter Hampden, Taina Elg, Francis L. Sullivan, Joseph Wiseman, Sandy Descher, John Dehner, Cecil Kellaway, Henry Daniell, Paul Cavanagh, Tracey Roberts, Jay Novello, Dorothy Adams, Richard Devon; **D:** Richard Thorpe. $19.98 *MGM* 🐾🐾½

The Prodigal A born-again family drama in which a sundered family is brought together by the return of a once-estranged son.
1983 (PG) 109m/C John Hammond, Hope Lange, John Cullum, Morgan Brittany, Ian Bannen, Arliss Howard, Joey Travolta, Billy Graham; **M:** Bruce Broughton. **VHS, Beta** $59.95 *LIV* 🐾🐾

Prodigal Boxer: The Kick of Death A son must avenge his father's death by facing two kung fu masters.
1973 (R) 90m/C Meng Fei, Pa Hung, Suma Wah Lung. **VHS, Beta** $19.95 *GEM, MRV* 🐾

The Prodigal Planet Small group of believers continue their struggle against the world government UNTIE by disrupting their communication network. Sequel to "Thief in the Night," "A Distant Thunder," and "Image of the Beast."
1988 67m/C William Wellman Jr., Linda Beatie, Cathy Wellman, Thom Rachford; **D:** Donald W. Thompson. **VHS, Beta** *MIV, HHE* 🐾

The Producers Considered one of Brooks' best films, this hilarious farce follows an attempted swindle by a con artist and his accountant who attempt to stage a Broadway flop only to have it backfire. Achieving cult status, the film is known for musical interlude "Springtime for Hitler." The phony play was later actually produced by Alan Johnson.
1968 90m/C Zero Mostel, Gene Wilder, Dick Shawn, Kenneth Mars, Estelle Winwood; **D:** Mel Brooks; **W:** Mel Brooks. Academy Awards '68: Best Story & Screenplay; Nominations: Best Supporting Actor (Wilder). **VHS, Beta, 8mm** $14.95 *COL, VYG, CRC* 🐾🐾🐾½

The Professional: Golgo 13 Animated mystery & suspense film. Leonard Dawson vows revenge for his son's death and must battle Duke Togo, a professional hitman better known as "Golgo 13." Dubbed.
1983 94m/C **VHS** $29.95 *WTA* 🐾🐾🐾½

Professional Killers 1 Trio of hired assassins wanders about the countryside killing people during Japan's Feudal Era.
1973 87m/C Jiro Tamiya, Koji Takahashi. **VHS, Beta** *NO* 🐾

The Professionals Action and adventure count for more than a storyline in this exciting western about four mercenaries hired by a wealthy cattle baron to rescue his young wife from Mexican kidnappers. Breathtaking photography recreates turn-of-the-century Mexico in this adaptation of the Frank O'Rourke novel.
1966 (PG) 117m/C Burt Lancaster, Lee Marvin, Claudia Cardinale, Jack Palance, Robert Ryan, Woody Strode, Ralph Bellamy; **D:** Richard Brooks; **W:** Richard Brooks; **M:** Maurice Jarre. **VHS, Beta** $69.95 *COL* 🐾🐾🐾½

Professionals When the daily rigors of cocaine smuggling begin to dampen their spirits, the "Professionals" plan an exciting plutonium heist. From the British Action Show.
1976 104m/C Gordon Jackson, Martin Shaw, Lewis Collins. **VHS, Beta** $59.95 *TWE* 🐾🐾

The Professor Rare sci-fi thriller featuring a werewolf, an eccentric scientist and a communist plot. Also includes several 'were-wolf' oriented movie trailers.
1958 30m/C Doug Hobart, John Copeland, Irene Barr. **VHS** $16.95 *SNC* 🐾🐾

Profile A newsman gets an editorial job for a magazine called "Profile," and promptly falls in love with the boss's daughter. Complications arise when the boss's wife puts the moves on him. As if that isn't trouble enough, he finds himself accused of embezzlement. Average entertainment with some notable performances and an interesting chase scene.
1954 65m/B John Bentley, Kathleen Byron, Thea Gregory, Stuart Lindsell; **D:** Francis Searle. **VHS, Beta** $16.95 *SNC* 🐾🐾

The Program Sensitive tearjerker about college football players getting caught up in the drive for a championship. As the season takes its toll on both mind and body, players prepare for the Big Game. Caan is the team's gruff coach, who's willing to look the other way as long as his boys are winning. Film sparked controversy when the Disney studio pulled and recut it after release because one scene, where Sheffer's character lies down in traffic, sparked copy-cat actions and several deaths. The scene was not restored for the video version.
1993 (R) 110m/C James Caan, Craig Sheffer, Kristy Swanson, Halle Berry, Omar Epps, Duane Davis, Abraham Benrubi, Jon Maynard Pennell, Andrew Bryniarski; **D:** David S. Ward; **W:** Aaron Latham, David S. Ward; **M:** Michel Colombier. **VHS, Beta** $96.03 *TOU* 🐾🐾½

Programmed to Kill A beautiful terrorist is captured by the CIA and transformed into a buxom bionic assassin. *AKA:* Retaliator.
1986 (R) 91m/C Robert Ginty, Sandahl Bergman, James Booth, Louise Caire Clark; **D:** Allan Holzman. **VHS, Beta** $79.95 *MED* 🐾🐾

Project A-ko Set in the near future, this Japanese animated feature, which is intended for adults, concerns teenagers with strange powers, an alien spaceship, and lots of action. Seventeen year-old A-ko possesses superhuman strength and a ditzy sidekick, C-ko. B-ko, the spoiled and rich daughter of a business tycoon, decides to fight A-ko for C-ko's companionship. Meanwhile, an alien spaceship is headed toward Earth with unknown intentions. Somehow, everything ties together—watch and see how. In Japanese with English subtitles.
1986 86m/C **VHS** $39.95 *CPM, ING, WTA* 🐾🐾

Project A-ko 2: Plot of the Daitokuji Financial Group Summer vacation sees A-ko, B-ko, and C-ko all involved in relaxation while B-ko's father, Mr. Daitokuji, uses her designs to create an attack weapon to help his company seize technological secrets from a disabled spaceship. Subtitled from the Japanese, also available dubbed.
1994 70m/C VHS **$29.95** *CPM* 🎬🎬

Project A-ko 3: Cinderella Rhapsody A-ko falls for K but B-ko saw him first. Fortuneately, A-ko's hot little dress settles the question. Meanwhile, C-ko narrowly avoids being crushed by K's motorcycle. Subtitled from the Japanese; also available dubbed.
1994 50m/C VHS **$29.95** *CPM* 🎬🎬

Project: Alien Science fiction fans in search of a good extraterrestrial flick should avoid this teaser, for it has nothing to do with aliens. As the film begins, Earth is allegedly being attacked by beings from space, and a vast array of scientists, militia and journalists track the aliens. What's actually happening revolves around the testing of deadly biological weapons. Filmed in Yugoslavia.
1989 (R) 92m/C Michael Nouri, Darlanne Fluegel, Maxwell Caulfield, Charles Durning; *D:* Frank Shields; *W:* Anthony Able. VHS **$89.95** *VMK* 🎬🎬

Project: Eliminator A group of terrorists kidnap a designer of "smart" weapons, and it's up to a hard-hitting special forces unit to get him back. Filmed in New Mexico.
1991 (R) 89m/C David Carradine, Frank Zagarino, Drew Snyder, Hilary English, Vivian Schilling; *D:* H. Kaye Dyal; *W:* H. Kaye Dyal. VHS **$14.95** *HMD* 🎬½

Project: Genesis Pascal and a beautiful Alien Woman are shipwrecked on a desolate planet in the 23rd century. As they watch the worlds around them clash in war, they know it is up to them to create a new beginning at the end of the Universe.
1993 79m/C David Ferry, Olga Prokhorova; *D:* Philip Jackson; *W:* Philip Jackson; *M:* Andy McNeill. VHS **$79.95** *PSM* 🎬🎬½

Project: Kill! Head of a murder-for-hire squad suddenly disappears and his former assistant is hired to track him down dead or alive.
1977 94m/C Leslie Nielsen, Gary Lockwood, Nancy Kwan. VHS, Beta *QVD* 🎬

Project Moon Base Espionage runs rampant on a spaceship headed by a female officer. Eventually the ship is stranded on the moon. Actually filmed for a television series "Ring Around the Moon." A cold-war sexist relic.
1953 64m/C Donna Martell, Hayden Rourke; *D:* Richard Talmadge. VHS, Beta *VMK* 🎬½

Project: Nightmare Seems not all dreams are wish fulfillment, when these nightmares start coming t rue.
19?? 75m/C Charles Miller, Elly Koslo, Lance Dickson; *D:* Donald M. Jones. VHS **$19.99** *ACA, MOV* 🎬½

Project: Shadowchaser Action-packed would-be thriller about a billion dollar android who escapes from a top secret government laboratory. Programmed with superhuman strength and no human emotions the android and five terrorists take over a hospital (located in a skyscraper no less). Their hostages include the President's daughter and the terrorists demand a $50 million ransom. With a four-hour deadline the FBI calls in the hospital architect to advise them—only they've got the wrong man—and the android's creator, who wants his

creation back—no matter what the cost. A low budget Terminator clone.
1992 (R) 97m/C Martin Kove, Meg Foster, Frank Zagarino, Paul Koslo, Joss Ackland; *D:* John Eyres. VHS **$19.95** *PSM* 🎬½

Project X A bemused Air Force pilot is assigned to a special project involving chimpanzees. He must decide where his duty lies when he realizes the semi-intelligent chimps are slated to die.
1987 (PG) 107m/C Matthew Broderick, Helen Hunt, William Sadler, Johnny Rae McGhee, Jonathan Stark, Robin Gammell, Stephen Lang, Jean Smart, Dick Miller; *D:* Jonathan Kaplan; *W:* Stanley Weiser, Lawrence Lasker; *M:* James Horner. VHS, Beta **$19.98** *FOX* 🎬🎬½

The Projectionist A must-see for movie buffs, Dangerfield made his screen debut in this story about a projectionist in a seedy movie house whose real-life existence begins to blur into the films he continuously watches. Made on a limited budget, this creative effort by Hurwitz was the first film to utilize the technique of superimposition.
1971 (PG) 84m/C Rodney Dangerfield, Chuck McCann, Ina Balin; *D:* Harry Hurwitz; *W:* Harry Hurwitz. VHS, Beta **$69.98** *LIV, VES* 🎬🎬🎬

Prom Night A masked killer stalks four high school girls during their senior prom as revenge for a murder which occurred six years prior. Sequelled by "Hello Mary Lou: Prom Night II" and "Prom Night III: The Last Kiss."
1980 (R) 91m/C Jamie Lee Curtis, Leslie Nielsen; *D:* Paul Lynch. VHS, Beta **$19.95** *NLC* 🎬🎬

Prom Night 3: The Last Kiss The second sequel, in which the reappearing high school ghoul beguiles a lucky teenager.
1989 (R) 97m/C Tim Conlon, Cyndy Preston, Courtney Taylor; *D:* Ron Oliver, Peter Simpson. VHS, Beta **$14.98** *LIV* 🎬

Prom Night 4: Deliver Us From Evil Yet another gory entry in the Prom series (one would hope it will be the last). Another group of naive teens decide that they can have more fun at a private party than at the prom. They host the party in a summer home that was once a monastery, but the festive affair soon turns into a night of terror when an uninvited guest crashes the party. For true fans of slasher flicks.
1991 (R) 95m/C Nikki DeBoer, Alden Kane, Joy Tanner, Alle Ghadban; *D:* Clay Borris. VHS **$89.98** *LIV* 🎬

The Promise Weepie outdated story about star-crossed lovers Michael (Collins) and Nancy (Quinlan). A car accident leaves Michael comatose and Nancy badly disfigured. Michael's mother (Straight), who loathes Nancy, sees her chance to finally break them up. She offers to pay for Nancy's plastic surgery if she'll leave Michael forever, then Mom tells her son his girlfriend's dead. A year later Nancy, with her new face and new identity, and Michael meet. From the novel by Danielle Steele. *AKA:* Face of a Stranger.
1978 (PG) 97m/C Stephen Collins, Kathleen Quinlan, Beatrice Straight, Laurence Luckinbill, William Prince, Michael O'Hare; *D:* Gilbert Cates; *W:* Garry Michael White. VHS **$89.98** *MCA* 🎬½

Promise Her Anything A widow (Caron) with a baby decides to make her boss (Cummings), a child psychologist who hates kids, her new husband. So she stashes the kid with her upstairs neighbor (Beatty), a would-be filmmaker who earns his living making blue movies. But the filmmaker has romantic designs on the widow and decides the baby may be the way to make a good

impression. Beatty isn't very believable in this type of light-romantic comedy and the farcical situations are forced.
1966 98m/C Warren Beatty, Leslie Caron, Robert Cummings, Hermione Gingold, Lionel Stander, Keenan Wynn, Cathleen Nesbitt; *D:* Arthur Hiller; *W:* William Peter Blatty. VHS **$14.95** *PAR* 🎬🎬

Promise to Murder An early murder-drama episode from the "Climax" television series.
1956 60m/B Peter Lorre, Louis Hayward, Ann Harding. VHS, Beta **$24.95** *NOS, DVT* 🎬½

Promised a Miracle Based on the true story of a religious couple who sought help for their diabetic son through prayer rather than conventional medical means. Following the boy's death in 1974 the couple were charged with manslaughter. From the nonfiction account "We Let Our Son Die" by Larry Parker. Made for television.
1988 (PG) 94m/C Rosanna Arquette, Judge Reinhold, Tom Bower, Gary Bayer, Maria O'Brien, Vonni Ribisi; *D:* Stephen Gyllenhaal; *W:* David Hill. VHS **$89.98** *REP* 🎬🎬½

Promised Land Two high school friends from the rural northwestern U.S. come together several years after graduation under tragic circumstances. Writer Hoffman's semi-autobiographical, disillusioned look at the American Dream was re-discovered by movie goers due to its excellent dramatic performances, notable also as the first film produced by Robert Redford's Sundance Institute. *AKA:* Young Hearts.
1988 (R) 110m/C Kiefer Sutherland, Meg Ryan, Tracy Pollan, Jason Gedrick, Googy Gress, Deborah Richter, Sandra Seacat, Jay Underwood, Oscar Rowland; *D:* Michael Hoffman; *W:* Michael Hoffman; *M:* James Newton Howard. VHS, Beta **$29.98** *LIV, VES* 🎬🎬🎬

Promises in the Dark Drama focusing on the complex relationship between a woman doctor and her 17-year-old female patient who is terminally ill with cancer. Hellman's directorial debut.
1979 (PG) 118m/C Marsha Mason, Ned Beatty, Kathleen Beller, Susan Clark, Paul Clemens, Donald Moffatt, Michael Brandon; *D:* Jerome Hellman. VHS, Beta **$59.95** *WAR* 🎬🎬½

Promises! Promises! Having difficulty getting pregnant, a woman goes on a cruise with her husband. While on board, they meet another couple, all get drunk, and change partners. Of course, both women find themselves pregnant, leaving the paternity in doubt. Famous primarily as the movie Mansfield told "Playboy" magazine she appeared "completely nude" in. *AKA:* Promise Her Anything.
1963 90m/B Jayne Mansfield, Marie McDonald, Tommy Noonan, Fritz Feld, Claude Stroud. VHS, Beta *NO* 🎬🎬

The Promoter Horatio Alger comedy stars Guinness as an impoverished student who gives himself a surrepticious leg up in life by altering his school entrance exam scores. Outstanding performances enliven this subtle British comedy of morals. *AKA:* The Card.
1952 87m/B Alec Guinness, Glynis Johns, Petula Clark, Valerie Hobson, Michael Hordern; *D:* Ronald Neame. VHS, Beta **$39.95** *HMV* 🎬🎬🎬

Proof Directorial debut of Moorhouse tells a tale of manipulation, friendship, and obsessive love between a blind photographer, Martin, his housekeeper, and the young man he befriends. Martin, mistrustful of the world around him, takes photographs as "proof" of the reality of his life. A chance meeting with Andy provides Martin with his "eyes"

and the opportunity to expand his world and emotions—something his housekeeper, Celia, would be only too happy to help him with. Unhealthy triangle leads all three to a re-evaluation of their lives. Propelled by terrific performances and enough humor to balance its emotional content.
1991 (R) 90m/C Hugo Weaving, Genevieve Picot, Russell Crowe, Heather Mitchell, Jeffrey Walker, Frank Gallacher; **D:** Jocelyn Moorhouse; **W:** Jocelyn Moorhouse. **VHS $89.95** *NLC, COL, ING* 🎬🎬🎬

Proof of the Man A Japanese co-production about a murder in Tokyo that takes on international importance.
1984 100m/C George Kennedy, Broderick Crawford, Toshiro Mifune. **VHS, Beta $69.95** *VCD* 🎬

Property A comedy about a group of leftover '60s radicals adjusting to 1970s corporate America.
1978 92m/C VHS *NO* 🎬½

Prophecy A doctor and his wife travel to Maine to research the effects of pollution caused by the lumber industry. They encounter several terrifying freaks of nature and a series of bizarre human deaths. Laughable horror film.
1979 (PG) 102m/C Talia Shire, Robert Foxworth, Armand Assante, Victoria Racimo, Richard Dysart; **D:** John Frankenheimer; **W:** David Seltzer. **VHS, Beta $19.95** *PAR* 🎬½

A Propos de Nice First film by French director Vigo, the silent film parodies French travelogues in a manner that indicates the director's later brilliance.
1929 25m/B D: Jean Vigo. **VHS, Beta** *FST, MRV* 🎬🎬🎬

Prospero's Books Greenaway's free-ranging adaptation of Shakespeare's "The Tempest" has all his usual hallmarks of the bizarre. Gielgud is the aged Propsero, exiled to a magical island with his innocent daughter Miranda, and 24 beloved books containing the magician's recipe for life, each of which becomes a separate chapter in the film. Greenaway mixes film and high-definition video to create, with cinematographer Sacha Vierny, dazzling visuals that threaten to overwhelm but don't quite, thanks to both Greenaway's skill and the astonishing performance of the then 87-year-old Gielgud.
1991 (R) 129m/C John Gielgud, Michel Blanc, Erland Josephson, Isabelle Pasco, Tom Bell, Kenneth Cranham, Michael Clark, Mark Rylance; **D:** Peter Greenaway; **W:** Peter Greenaway; **M:** Michael Nyman. **VHS, Beta $89.98** *FXV, FCT, VTR* 🎬🎬🎬

Protect Your Daughters Hilarious schlock featuring good girls getting involved with sex and alcohol. Also known as "Reckless Decision."
1932 ?m/B VHS $16.95 *SNC* 🎬

Protector A semi-martial arts cops 'n' robbers epic about the cracking of a Hong Kong-New York heroin route.
1985 (R) 94m/C Jackie Chan, Danny Aiello; **D:** James Glickenhaus. **VHS, Beta $79.95** *WAR* 🎬

Protocol A series of comic accidents lead a Washington cocktail waitress into the U.S. State Department's employ as a protocol official. Once there she is used as a pawn to make an arms deal with a Middle Eastern country. Typical Hawn comedy with an enjoyable ending.
1984 (PG) 100m/C Goldie Hawn, Chris Sarandon, Andre Gregory, Cliff DeYoung, Ed Begley Jr., Gail Strickland, Richard Romanus, Keith Szarabajka, James Staley, Kenneth Mars, Kenneth McMillan, Archie Hahn, Amanda Bearse;

D: Herbert Ross; **W:** Charles Shyer, Buck Henry. **VHS, Beta $19.98** *WAR* 🎬🎬

Prototype Made-for-television revision of the Frankenstein legend has award-winning scientist Plummer as the creator of the first android. Fearful of the use the military branch of government has in mind for his creation, he attempts to steal back his discovery, in this suspenseful adventure.
1983 100m/C Christopher Plummer, David Morse, Frances Sternhagen, James Sutorius; **D:** David Greene; **M:** Billy Goldenberg. **VHS $14.95** *LIV* 🎬🎬🎬

Prototype X29A The year is 2057 in a desolate, lawless Los Angeles. A research scientist is conducting experiments on a crippled ex-soldier named Hawkins when they suddenly go awry, turning him into a half-man, half-machine robot. Known as Prototype, the creature goes on a hunting and killing spree. Lame "Terminator" & "Robocop" takeoff.
1992 (R) 98m/C Brenda Swanson. **VHS $89.95** *VMK* 🎬½

The Proud and the Damned Five Civil-War-veteran mercenaries wander into a Latin American war and get manipulated by both sides. *AKA:* Proud, Damned, and Dead.
1972 (PG) 95m/C Chuck Connors, Aron Kincaid, Cesar Romero; **D:** Ferde Grofe Jr. **VHS, Beta $19.95** *NOS, VCI, MRV* 🎬

Proud Men A cattle rancher and his expatriate son are separated by bitterness toward each other. Good acting from Heston and Strauss, and good action sequences, but ordinary script.
1987 95m/C Charlton Heston, Peter Strauss, Nan Martin, Alan Autry, Belinda Balaski, Red West; **D:** William A. Graham. **VHS $9.98** *TTC* 🎬🎬

The Proud Ones An aristocratic French woman and her husband are traveling through Mexico when he suddenly dies of a mysterious illness. Left penniless in a decaying seaside town, she falls for the local doctor who is mourning the death of his wife. Adaptation of the Satre novel "L'Amour Redempteur." In French with English subtitles. *AKA:* Les Orgueilleux.
1953 105m/B Gerard Philippe, Michele Morgan, Carlos Lopez Moctezuma, Victor Manuel Mendoza; **D:** Yves Allegret. **VHS $59.95** *FCT, INT* 🎬🎬½

Proud Rebel A character study of a stubborn widower who searches for a doctor to aid him in dealing with the problems of his mute son, and of the woman who helps to tame the boy. Ladd's real-life son makes his acting debut.
1958 99m/C Alan Ladd, Olivia de Havilland, Dean Jagger, Harry Dean Stanton; **D:** Michael Curtiz. **VHS, Beta $69.98** *SUE* 🎬🎬🎬

Providence An interesting score highlights this British fantasy drama of a dying writer envisioning his final novel as a fusion of the people from his past with the circumstances he encounters on a daily basis. The first English-language effort by French director Resnais.
1977 (R) 104m/C John Gielgud, Dirk Bogarde, Ellen Burstyn, David Warner, Elaine Stritch; **D:** Alain Resnais; **M:** Miklos Rozsa. **VHS, Beta $59.95** *COL* 🎬🎬🎬

Provoked What would you do if your husband were being held hostage by a gang of ruthless, but stupid, escaped cons? Well, Maranne actually wants her husband back (maybe 'cause they're newlyweds) and no by-the-book police chief (Jones) is gonna stop her. This bride gets her hands on some automatic weaponry and look out! Shot in eight days with a $130,000 budget.

1989 90m/C Cindy Maranne, McKeiver Jones III, Harold W. Jones, Sharon Blair, Bob Fall, Joe Sprosty, Phyllis Durant, Tara Untiedt; **D:** Rick Pamplin; **W:** Tara Untiedt, Steve Pake. **VHS, Beta $69.95** *VTR, HHE* 🎬🎬

Prowler Heflin is a cop who responds to a prowler scare and finds the beautiful married Keyes worried about an intruder. He learns she will inherit a lot of money if anything happens to her husband so he seduces her and then "accidentally" kills her husband, supposedly mistaking him for a prowler. Keyes then marries Heflin but when she learns the truth her own life is in danger. Tidy thriller with Heflin doing a good job as the unpredictable villain.
1951 92m/B Van Heflin, Evelyn Keyes, Katherine Warren, John Maxwell; **D:** Joseph Losey. **VHS, Beta** *NO* 🎬🎬½

The Prowler A soldier returns from duty during WWII, only to find his girl in bed with another guy. He kills them, and for unclear reasons, returns to the same town 35 years later to kill more people. An effects-fest for Tom Savini. *AKA:* Rosemary's Killer.
1981 (R) 87m/C Vicky Dawson, Christopher Goutman, Cindy Weintraub, Farley Granger, John Seitz, Lawrence Tierney; **D:** Joseph Zito; **M:** Richard Einhorn. **VHS $49.95** *VHE* 🎬

Prudential Family Playhouse Presentation of Sinclair Lewis' "Dodsworth." Tells the story of a wealthy American couple who travel from their small town to Europe.
1950 53m/B Ruth Chatterton, Walter Abel, Cliff Hall, Eva Marie Saint. **VHS, Beta $24.95** *VYY* 🎬

Prurient Interest A video play revolving around a movie producer's battle with the Board of Censors for approval of his feature "Eat Me in St. Louis."
1974 20m/B VHS, Beta *EAI* 🎬

PSI Factor A civilian researcher working at the NASA space track station observes and records signals coming from planet Serius B.
1980 91m/C Peter Mark Richman, Gretchen Corbett, Tommy Martin; **D:** Quentin Masters. **VHS $79.95** *MNC* 🎬🎬½

Psych-Out A deaf girl searches Haight-Ashbury for her runaway brother. She meets hippies and flower children during the Summer of Love. Psychedelic score with Strawberry Alarm Clock and The Seeds. Somewhere in the picture, Nicholson whangs on lead guitar.
1968 95m/C Jack Nicholson, Bruce Dern, Susan Strasberg, Dean Stockwell, Henry Jaglom; **D:** Richard Rush; **W:** Richard Rush. **VHS, Beta $19.99** *HBO* 🎬🎬½

Psychedelic Fever A swinging look at the free-love decade of the 1960s.
1990 (R) 80m/C D: William Rotsler. **VHS** *NO* 🎬

The Psychic An ad executive gains psychic powers after he falls off a ladder and tries to conquer the world. A later effort by gore-king Lewis, notable only for sex scenes inserted by Lewis to make the movie salable.
1968 90m/C Dick Genola, Robin Guest, Bobbi Spencer; **D:** Herschell Gordon Lewis. **VHS, Beta** *NO* Woof!

The Psychic A psychic envisions her own death and attempts to alter the prediction.
1978 (R) 90m/C Jennifer O'Neill, Marc Porel, Evelyn Stewart, Gabriel Ferzetti, Gianno Garko; **D:** Lucio Fulci. **VHS, Beta** *NO* 🎬

Psychic A college student with psychic powers believes he knows who the next victim of a demented serial killer will be. The problem is: no one will believe him. And the victim is the woman he loves.

1991 (R) 92m/C Michael Nouri, Catherine Mary Stewart, Zach Galligan. **VHS $89.95** VMK *½

Psychic Killer A wrongfully committed asylum inmate acquires psychic powers and decides to use them in a deadly revenge. Good cast in cheapie horror flick.
1975 (PG) 89m/C Jim Hutton, Paul Burke, Julie Adams, Neville Brand, Aldo Ray, Rod Cameron, Della Reese; *D:* Ray Danton. **VHS, Beta $14.98** SUE *½

Psycho Hitchcock counted on his directorial stature and broke all the rules in this story of violent murder, transvestism, and insanity. Based on Robert Bloch's novelization of an actual murder, Leigh plays a fleeing thief who stops at the secluded Bates Motel where she meets her death in Hitchcock's classic "shower scene." Shot on a limited budget in little more than a month, "Psycho" changed the Hollywood horror film forever. Followed by "Psycho II" (1983), "Psycho III" (1986), and a made-for-television movie.
1960 109m/B Anthony Perkins, Janet Leigh, Vera Miles, John Gavin, John McIntire, Martin Balsam, Simon Oakland, Ted Knight, John Anderson, Frank Albertson, Patricia Hitchcock; *D:* Alfred Hitchcock; *W:* Joseph Stefano; *M:* Bernard Herrmann. Academy Awards '60 Nominations: Best Art Direction/Set Decoration (B & W), Best Black and White Cinematography, Best Director (Hitchcock), Best Supporting Actress (Leigh); Edgar Allan Poe Awards '60: Best Screenplay; Golden Globe Awards '61: Best Supporting Actress (Leigh). **VHS, Beta $19.95** MCA, TLF ****

Psycho 2 This sequel to the Hitchcock classic finds Norman Bates returning home after 22 years in an asylum to find himself haunted by "mother" and caught up in a series of murders. In a surprisingly good horror film, Perkins and Miles reprise their roles from the original "Psycho." Perkins went on to direct yet another sequel, "Psycho 3."
1983 (R) 113m/C Anthony Perkins, Vera Miles, Meg Tilly, Robert Loggia, Dennis Franz; *D:* Richard Franklin; *W:* Tom Holland; *M:* Jerry Goldsmith. **VHS, Beta $14.98** MCA **

Psycho 3 The second sequel to Hitchcock's "Psycho" finds Norman Bates drawn into his past by "mother" and the appearance of a woman who reminds him of his original victim. Perkins made his directorial debut in this film that stretches the plausibility of the storyline to its limits, but the element of parody throughout makes this an entertaining film for "Psycho" fans.
1986 (R) 93m/C Anthony Perkins, Diana Scarwid, Jeff Fahey, Roberta Maxwell, Robert Alan Browne; *D:* Anthony Perkins; *W:* Charles Edward Pogue; *M:* Carter Burwell. **VHS, Beta $14.98** MCA **

Psycho 4: The Beginning Prequels "Psycho" when, at the behest of a radio talk show host, Norman Bates recounts his childhood and reveals the circumstances that aided in the development of his peculiar neuroses. Stefano wrote the original screenplay and the original score is used, but this doesn't even come close to the original.
1990 (R) 96m/C Anthony Perkins, Henry Thomas, Olivia Hussey, CCH Pounder, Warren Frost, Donna Mitchell; *D:* Mick Garris; *W:* Joseph Stefano; *M:* Bernard Herrmann. **VHS $14.98** MCA **

Psycho Cop Six college undergrads on a weekend retreat are menaced and picked off one at a time by a crazed local cop.
1988 89m/C Bobby Ray Shafer; *D:* Wallace Potts. **VHS, Beta** NO *½

Psycho Cop 2 Four buddies plan a raunchy bachelor party, commandeering the company conference room for an after-hours orgy. Only Psycho Cop is on their case. Gore.
1994 (R) 80m/C Bobby Ray Shafer, Barbara Lee Alexander, Julie Strain; *D:* Rif Coogan. **VHS** COL *½

Psycho from Texas Quiet Southern town is disrupted by the kidnapping of a wealthy oil man, followed by a string of meaningless murders. *AKA:* The Butcher.
1983 (R) 85m/C King John III, Candy Dee, Janel King. **VHS, Beta** NO *

Psycho Girls Very low budget horror flick redeemed by spurts of weird black humor. Crazed woman is released from institution to seek out sister who should have been put away in the first place. She crashes anniversary celebration and, well, let's just say she's not the life of the party. Never released theatrically.
1986 (R) 87m/C John Haslett Cuff, Darlene Mignacco, Agi Gallus, Rose Graham, Silvio Oliviero, Michael Hoole, Pier Giorgia DiCicco, Fernne Kane; *D:* Gerard Ciccoritti; *W:* Gerard Ciccoritti, Michael Boekner. **VHS, Beta $79.95** MGM *

Psychomania Semi-limpid mystery thriller about a former war hero and painter who is suspected of being the demented killer stalking girls on campus. To prove his innocence, he tracks the killer himself. *AKA:* Violent Midnight.
1963 95m/C Lee Phillips, Sheppard Strudwick, Jean Hale, Dick Van Patten, Sylvia Miles, James Farentino; *D:* Richard Hilliard. **VHS, Beta $24.95** SNC, HHT *½

Psychomania A drama of the supernatural, the occult, and the violence which lies just beyond the conventions of society for a group of dead motorcyclists, the Living Dead, who all came back to life after committing suicide with the help of the devil. *AKA:* The Death Wheelers.
1973 89m/C George Sanders, Beryl Reid, Nicky Henson, Mary Laroche, Patrick Holt; *D:* Don Sharp. **VHS, Beta $29.95** MED, MRV **

Psychopath A film about a modern-day, slightly unhinged, Robin Hood and his escapades, stealing from other thieves and giving to the victimized.
1968 90m/C Klaus Kinski, George Martin, Ingrid Schoeller; *D:* Guido Zurli. **VHS, Beta** NO *½

Psychopath A nutso children's television personality begins to murder abusive parents. Fairly gory, and definitely not for family viewing. *AKA:* An Eye for an Eye.
1973 (PG) 85m/C Tom Basham, Gene Carlson, Gretchen Kanne; *D:* Larry G. Brown; *M:* John Williams. **VHS, Beta $69.95** MED *

Psychos in Love A psychotic murderer who hates grapes of any kind finds the woman of his dreams—she's a psychotic murderer who hates grapes! Together they find bliss—until the plumber discovers their secret!
1987 90m/C Carmine Capobianco, Debi Thibeault, Frank Stewart; *D:* Gorman Bechard. **VHS, Beta $69.95** VCI Woof!

The Psychotronic Man An innocent man suddenly finds he possesses amazing and dangerous powers, enabling him to control outside events with a thought.
1991 88m/C Peter Spelson, Christopher Carbis, Curt Colbert, Robin Newton, Paul Marvel; *D:* Jack M. Sell. **VHS** UNI *½

PT 109 The WWII exploits of Lieutenant (j.g.) John F. Kennedy in the South Pacific. Part of the "A Night at the Movies" series, this tape simulates a 1963 movie evening, with a Foghorn Leghorn cartoon ("Banty Raids"), a newsreel on the JFK assassination, and coming attractions for "Critic's Choice" and "Four for Texas."
1963 159m/C Cliff Robertson, Ty Hardin, Ty Hardin, Robert (Bobby) Blake, Robert Culp, James Gregory; *D:* Leslie Martinson. **VHS, Beta $19.98** WAR **

Puberty Blues Two Australian girls become part of the local surfing scene in order to be accepted by the "in crowd" at their high school.
1981 (R) 86m/C Neil Schofield, Jad Capelja; *D:* Bruce Beresford. **VHS, Beta $59.95** MCA **½

A Public Affair Exposes the evils and abuses of collection agencies without even a shred of humor. Certainly gets its point across, but will bore any audience to tears or spontaneous naps.
1962 71m/B Myron McCormick, Edward Binns, Harry Carey Jr., Rocky Aoki. **VHS, Beta $24.95** VYY *½

Public Cowboy No. 1 Cattle thieves use a radio, airplanes, and refrigerator trucks in their updated rustling schemes.
1937 54m/B Gene Autry, William Farnum. **VHS, Beta $19.95** NOS, VCN, DVT *½

Public Enemy Cagney's acting career was launched by this story of two Irish boys growing up in a Chicago shantytown to become hoodlums during the prohibition era. Cagney and Woods hook up with molls Clarke and Blondell and their rise to the top. Considered the most realistic "gangster" film, Wellman's movie is also the most grimly brutal due to its release prior to Hollywood censorship. The scene where Cagney smashes a grapefruit in Clarke's face was credited with starting a trend in abusing film heroines. *AKA:* Enemies of the Public.
1931 85m/B James Cagney, Edward Woods, Leslie Fenton, Joan Blondell, Mae Clarke, Jean Harlow; *D:* William A. Wellman. **VHS, Beta $19.95** MGM, FOX ***½

The Public Eye Underappreciated film noir homage casts Pesci as a crime photographer with an unsuspected romantic streak. It's 1942 in NYC and cynical freelancer Leon "Bernzy" Bernstein's always looking for the perfect shot. Hershey's the recent widow whose nightclub-owner husband had mob ties and decides Pesci would be a likely patsy for helping her out. Hershey seems decorative and the romantic angle never quite develops, but Pesci delivers a rich, low-key performance as the visionary, hard-boiled artist. Climatic mob shootout is cinematic bullet ballet. Based loosely on the career of '40s photog Weegee, who defined New York and its times in his work.
1992 (R) 98m/C Joe Pesci, Barbara Hershey, Stanley Tucci, Richard Foronjy, Richard Riehle, Jared Harris, Jerry Adler, Dominic Chianese, Gerry Becker; *D:* Howard Franklin; *W:* Howard Franklin; *M:* John Barry. **VHS, Beta $19.98** MCA ***½

Pucker Up and Bark Like a Dog A young artist and his inspirationally lovely actress girl-friend find themselves in strange and crazy situations. Good cast gives this potential.
1989 (R) 94m/C Lisa Zane, Jonathan Gries, Paul Bartel, Robert Culp; *D:* Paul S. Parco. **VHS $79.95** FRH, BTV *½

Pudd'nhead Wilson An adaptation of a Mark Twain story about a small-town lawyer who discovers the illicit exchange of a white infant for a light-skinned negro infant by a slave woman. Made for television as an "American Playhouse" presentation on PBS.
1987 87m/C Ken Howard; *D:* Alan Bridges. **VHS, Beta $19.95** MCA *½

Pueblo Affair A dramatization of the capture of the American spy ship "Pueblo" by the North Koreans, during which time the crew was tortured, imprisoned, and all intelligence documents were confiscated.
1973 99m/C Hal Holbrook, Andrew Duggan, Richard Mulligan, George Grizzard, Gary Merrill, Mary Fickett; **D:** Anthony Page. **VHS, Beta** *ЛЛЛ*

Pulp Caine, playing a mystery writer, becomes a target for murder when he ghostwrites the memoirs of a movie gangster from the 1930s, played deftly by Rooney.
1972 (PG) 95m/C Michael Caine, Mickey Rooney, Lionel Stander, Lizabeth Scott, Nadia Cassini, Dennis Price, Al Lettieri; **D:** Mike Hodges; **W:** Mike Hodges. **VHS, Beta** NO *ЛЛ ½*

Pulp Fiction Tarantino moves into the cinematic mainstream and beats the sophomore jinx with a crime trilogy as stylish as it is clever. Presenting an insider's view of a community of criminals, the action shifts unexpectedly from funny, outrageous dialogue to terrifying extremes, so one never knows what to expect. Further enhanced by solid storytelling and superb performances by an offbeat cast, most notably those of Travolta, Jackson, and Willis. Although Tarantino's trademark violence is not for everyone, the unpredictably entertaining "Pulp Fiction" is a wild success. Inspired by "Black Mask" magazine.
1994 153m/C John Travolta, Samuel L. Jackson, Uma Thurman, Harvey Keitel, Tim Roth, Amanda Plummer, Maria De Medeiros, Ving Rhames, Eric Stoltz, Rosanna Arquette, Christopher Walken, Bruce Willis; **D:** Quentin Tarantino; **W:** Quentin Tarantino, Roger Roberts Avary. **VHS** *ЛЛЛ ½*

Pulse Electricity goes awry in this science-fiction thriller about appliances and other household devices that become supercharged and destroy property and their owners.
1988 (PG-13) 90m/C Cliff DeYoung, Roxanne Hart, Joey Lawrence, Charles Tyner, Dennis Redfield, Robert Romanus, Myron Healey; **D:** Paul Golding; **M:** Jay Michael Ferguson. **VHS, Beta** $19.95 COL *ЛЛ*

Pulsebeat Flick about warring health club owners. As boring as it sounds unless you're in the mood for lots of on-screen aerobics. If so, rent Jane Fonda instead. Dubbed.
1985 92m/C Daniel Greene, Lee Taylor Allen, Bob Small, Alice Moore, Helga Line, Alex Intriago, Peter Lupus; **D:** Marice Tobias. **VHS, Beta** $69.95 LIV Woof!

The Puma Man Puma Man is a super hero who must stop the evil Dr. Kobras from using an ancient mask in his attempt to become ruler of the world. Unreleased theatrically in the U.S., this low budget Sci fi/horror mix is so bad one wonders why an actor like Pleasence would sign on. Special effects these days are so extraordinary that the ones employed here are laughable.
1980 80m/C Donald Pleasence, Walter George Alton, Sydne Rome, Miguel Angel Fuentes; **D:** Alvin J. Neitz, Alberto De Martino. **VHS, Beta** $59.95 PSM Woof!

Pump Up the Volume High school newcomer leads double life as Hard Harry, sarcastic host of an illegal radio broadcast and Jack Nicholson soundalike. Anonymously popular with his peers, he invites the wrath of the school principal due to his less than flattering comments about the school administration. Slater seems to enjoy himself as defiant deejay while youthful cast effectively supports.

1990 (R) 105m/C Christian Slater, Scott Paulin, Ellen Greene, Samantha Mathis, Cheryl Pollak, Annie Ross, Lala, Mimi Kennedy; **D:** Allan Moyle; **W:** Allan Moyle. **VHS, 8mm** $14.95 COL, FCT, MVD *ЛЛ ½*

Pumping Iron A widely acclaimed documentary look at the sport of bodybuilding, following the behind-the-scenes action surrounding the competition for the Mr. Olympia title. The grueling training ritual and the constant striving for perfection are all explored.
1976 (PG) 90m/C Arnold Schwarzenegger, Mike Katz, Franco Columbo, Lou Ferrigno; **D:** George Butler. **VHS, Beta** $24.95 COL, SCH, RHI *ЛЛ ½*

Pumping Iron 2: The Women This sequel to "Pumping Iron" takes an in-depth look at the world of female body building. The documentary also follows the ladies to a competition held at Caesar's Palace in Las Vegas.
1985 107m/C Lori Bowen, Bev Francis, Rachel McLish, Carla Dunlap, Lydia Cheng; **D:** George Butler. **VHS, Beta** $79.95 VES *ЛЛ ½*

Pumpkinhead A farmer evokes a demon from the earth to avenge his son's death. When it continues on its murdering rampage, the farmer finds he no longer has any control over the vicious killer.
1988 (R) 89m/C Lance Henriksen, John DiAquino, Kerry Remsen, Matthew Hurley, Jeff East, Kimberly Ross, Cynthia Bain, Joel Hoffman, Florence Schauffler, Buck Flower, Tom Woodruff Jr.; **D:** Stan Winston; **W:** Gary Gerani, Mark Patrick Carducci; **M:** Richard Stone. **VHS, Beta** $14.95 MGM *ЛЛ ½*

Punch the Clock Attractive female thief finds her bail bondsman very exciting; he's ready to help her any way he can.
1990 (R) 88m/C Michael Rogan, Chris Moore, James Lorinz; **D:** Eric L. Schlagman. **VHS** NO *ЛЛ*

Punchline A look at the lives of stand-up comics, following the career ups-and-downs of an embittered professional funny-man and a frustrated housewife hitting the stage for the first time. Some very funny and touching moments and some not-so-funny and touching as the movie descends into melodrama without a cause.
1988 (R) 100m/C Tom Hanks, Sally Field, John Goodman, Mark Rydell, Kim Greist, Barry Sobel, Paul Mazursky, Pam Matteson, George Michael McGrath, Taylor Negron, Damon Wayans; **D:** David Seltzer; **W:** David Seltzer. **VHS, Beta** $19.95 COL *ЛЛ*

The Punisher Lundgren portrays Frank Castle, the Marvel Comics anti-hero known as the Punisher. When his family is killed by the mob Castle set his eyes on revenge. Filmed in Australia.
1990 (R) 92m/C Dolph Lundgren, Louis Gossett Jr., Jeroen Krabbe, Kim Miyori; **D:** Mark Goldblatt. **VHS, Beta** $92.95 LIV *Л*

Punk Rock Movie The musical explosion known as punk rock is documented here in its early days (circa 1977) at the Roxy in England. Includes a look at leading punk rock artists such as the Sex Pistols, the Clash, Slits, and others, and at the entire counter-culture that was punk.
1978 80m/C **VHS, Beta** $19.95 MVD, SUN *Л*

Punk Vacation A gang of motorcycle mamas terrorize a small town. The usual biker stuff.
1990 90m/C Stephen Falchi, Roxanne Rogers, Don Martin, Sandra Bogan; **D:** Stanley Lewis. **VHS, Beta** NO *Л*

Puppet Master Four psychics are sent to investigate a puppet maker who they think may have discovered the secret of life. Before they know it, they are stalked by evil puppets. Great special effects, not-so-great script.
1989 (R) 90m/C Paul LeMat, Jimmie F. Skaggs, Irene Miracle, Robin Rates, Barbara Crampton, William Hickey; **D:** David Schmoeller; **M:** Richard Band. **VHS, Beta** $14.95 PAR *ЛЛ ½*

Puppet Master 2 Puppets on a rampage turn hotel into den of special effects. Less effective string pulling than in original. Long live Pinocchio.
1991 (R) 90m/C Elizabeth MacLellan, Collin Bernsen, Greg Webb, Charlie Spradling, Nita Talbot, Steve Welles, Jeff Weston; **D:** David Allen; **W:** David Pabian; **M:** Richard Band. **VHS, Beta** $14.95 PAR *ЛЛ*

Puppet Master 3: Toulon's Revenge Prequel about the origin of the whole gory Puppet Master shebang, set in Nazi Germany. The weapon-hungry Third Reich tries to wrest secrets of artificial life from sorceror Andre Toulon, who sics his deadly puppets on them. Toulon's a good guy here, one of many contradictions in the series. Fine cast, but strictly for the followers.
1991 (R) 86m/C Guy Rolfe, Ian Abercrombie, Sarah Douglas; **D:** David DeCoteau; **M:** Richard Band. **VHS** $14.95 PAR *ЛЛ*

Puppet Master 4 It's the puppets versus the totems, equally loathsome midget creatures who derive their power from the same eternal force as the puppets. No one wants to share and there's lots of gore while they battle for supremacy.
1993 (R) 80m/C Gordon Currie, Chandra West, Jason Adams, Teresa Hill, Guy Rolfe; **D:** Jeff Burr; **W:** Todd Henschell, Steven E. Carr, Jo Duffy, Dough Aarniokoski, Keith Payson; **M:** Richard Band. **VHS, Beta** PAR *ЛЛ*

Puppet on a Chain American narcotics officer busts an Amsterdam drug ring and the leader's identity surprises him. Slow-moving thriller based on the Alistair MacLean novel.
1972 (PG) 97m/C Sven-Bertil Taube, Barbara Parkins, Alexander Knox, Patrick Allen, Geoffrey Reeve; **D:** Geoffrey Reeve. **VHS, Beta** $59.95 PSM *ЛЛ*

The Puppetoon Movie A compilation of George Pal's famous Puppetoon cartoons from the 1940s, marking his stature as an animation pioneer and innovator. Hosted by Gumby, Pokey, Speedy Alka Seltzer and Arnie the Dinosaur in newly directed scenes.
1987 (G) 80m/C **M:** Arnold Leibovit; **D:** Buddy Baker. **VHS, Beta** $19.95 FHE, WTA *ЛЛ*

The Purchase Price After a less than amorous beginning, farmer Brent and mail order bride Stanwyck fall into love and financial despair in this drama bordering on comedy. Good neighbor Landau is willing to help the poor agriculturalist out in exchange for Stanwyck. Tragedy strikes again when Stanwyck's bootlegger ex-boyfriend shows up and further disasters continue to test the couple's commitment. Based on the story "The Mud Lark" by Arthur Stringer.
1932 70m/B Barbara Stanwyck, George Brent, Lyle Talbot, Hardie Albright, David Landau; **D:** William A. Wellman; **W:** Robert Lord. **VHS** $19.98 MGM *ЛЛ*

Pure Country An easygoing movie about a familiar subject is held together by the charm of Strait (in his movie debut) and the rest of the cast. Strait plays a country music superstar, tired of the career glitz, who decides to get out and go back to his home in Texas. He falls in love with the spunky

Glasser and decides to run his career his own way. Warren is effective as his tough manager and old-time cowboy Calhoun is finely weathered as Glasser's gruff dad.
1992 (PG) 113m/C George Strait, Isabel Glasser, Lesley Ann Warren, Rory Calhoun, Kyle Chandler, Molly McClure, John Doe; **D:** Christopher Cain; **W:** Rex McGee; **M:** Stephen Dorff. **VHS, Beta $19.98** *WAR, MVD ♂♂½*

The Pure Hell of St. Trinian's In this sequel to "Blue Murder at St. Trinian's," a sheik who desires to fill out his harem tries recruiting at a rowdy girls' school. Although it isn't as funny as the first, due to the lack of Alistair Sim, it is still humorous. Followed by "The Great St. Trinian's Train Robbery." Based on the cartoon by Ronald Searle.
1961 94m/B Cecil Parker, Joyce Grenfell, George Cole, Thorley Walters; **D:** Frank Launder; **M:** Malcolm Arnold. **VHS** *FCT ♂♂½*

Pure Luck A who-asked-for-it remake of a 1981 Franco-Italian film called "La Chevre." The premise is the same: an accident-prone heiress disappears in Mexico, and her father tries to locate her using an equally clumsy accountant. The nebbish and an attendant tough private eye stumble and bumble south of the border until the plot arbitrarily ends. Pure awful.
1991 (PG) 96m/C Martin Short, Danny Glover, Sheila Kelley, Scott Wilson, Sam Wanamaker, Harry Shearer; **D:** Nadia Tass; **W:** Herschel Weingrod, Timothy Harris. **VHS, Beta $19.98** *MCA ♂½*

Purgatory While travelling abroad, two innocent women find themselves unjustly jailed. During their confinement they are tortured and raped.
1989 90m/C Tanya Roberts, Julie Pop; **D:** Ami Artzi. **VHS, Beta** *NO ♂*

Purlie Victorious Presentation of the award-winning Broadway hit, which takes a look at racial integration.
1963 93m/C Ossie Davis, Ruby Dee, Godfrey Cambridge, Alan Alda; **D:** Nicholas Webster. **VHS, Beta** *NO ♂♂*

The Purple Heart An American Air Force crew is shot down over Tokyo and taken into brutal POW camps. Intense wartime melodramatics.
1944 99m/B Dana Andrews, Richard Conte, Farley Granger, Donald (Don "Red") Barry, Sam Levene, Kevin O'Shea, Tala Birell, Nestor Paiva, Benson Fong, Marshall Thompson, Richard Loo; **D:** Lewis Milestone. **VHS, Beta $19.98** *FOX ♂♂½*

Purple Hearts Wahl stars as a Navy doctor who falls in love with nurse Ladd against the backdrop of the Vietnam war. Overlong and redundant.
1984 (R) 115m/C Cheryl Ladd, Ken Wahl, Stephen Lee, Annie McEnroe, Paul McCrane, Cyril O'Reilly; **D:** Sidney J. Furie; **W:** Sidney J. Furie, Ron Nyswaner; **M:** Robert Folk. **VHS, Beta $19.98** *WAR ♂½*

The Purple Monster Strikes A martian plots to conquer Earth to save his dying planet. Serial in fifteen episodes.
1945 188m/B Dennis Moore, Linda Stirling, Roy Barcroft; **D:** Spencer Gordon Bennet. **VHS $29.98** *REP, VCN, MLB ♂♂*

Purple People Eater The alien of the title descends to earth to mix with young girls and rock 'n roll. Based on the song of the same name whose performer, Sheb Wooley, appears in the film. Harmless, stupid fun for the whole family.
1988 (PG) 91m/C Ned Beatty, Shelley Winters, Neil Patrick Harris, Kareem Abdul-Jabbar, Little Richard, Chubby Checker, Peggy Lipton; **D:** Linda Shayne. **VHS, Beta $79.95** *MED, VTR ♂*

Purple Rain A quasi-autobiographical video showcase for the pop-star Prince. Film tells the tale of his struggle for love, attention, acceptance, and popular artistic recognition in Minneapolis. Not a bad film, for such a monumentally egotistical movie.
1984 (R) 113m/C Prince, Apollonia, Morris Day, Olga Karlatos, Clarence Williams III; **D:** Albert Magnoli; **M:** Michel Colombier. **VHS, Beta $19.98** *MVD, WAR ♂♂½*

The Purple Rose of Cairo A diner waitress, disillusioned by the Depression and a lackluster life, escapes into a film playing at the local movie house where a blond film hero, tiring of the monotony of his role, makes a break from the celluloid to join her in the real world. The ensuing love story allows director-writer Allen to show his knowledge of old movies and provide his fans with a change of pace. Farrow's film sister is also her real-life sister Stephanie, who went on to appear in Allen's "Zelig."
1985 (PG) 82m/C Mia Farrow, Jeff Daniels, Danny Aiello, Dianne Wiest, Van Johnson, Zoe Caldwell, John Wood, Michael Tucker, Edward Herrmann, Milo O'Shea, Glenne Headly, Karen Akers, Deborah Rush; **D:** Woody Allen; **W:** Woody Allen; **M:** Dick Hyman. Academy Awards '85 Nominations: Best Original Screenplay; British Academy Awards '85: Best Film; Cesar Awards '86: Best Foreign Film; Golden Globe Awards '86: Best Screenplay. **VHS, Beta $19.98** *LIV, VES, HMV ♂♂♂*

The Purple Taxi Romantic drama revolving around several wealthy foreigners who have taken refuge in beautiful southern Ireland. From Michel Deon's bestselling novel.
1977 (R) 93m/C Fred Astaire, Charlotte Rampling, Peter Ustinov, Philippe Noiret, Edward Albert; **D:** Yves Boisset. **VHS, Beta $59.95** *COL ♂♂½*

Purple Vigilantes The Three Mesquiteers uncover a gang of vigilantes. Part of the series. **AKA:** The Purple Riders.
1938 54m/B Bob Livingston, Ray Corrigan, Max Terhune. **VHS, Beta** *VCN, DVT ♂½*

Pursued Excellent performances by Mitchum and Wright mark this suspenseful Western drama of a Spanish-American war veteran in search of his father's killer.
1947 101m/B Teresa Wright, Robert Mitchum, Judith Anderson, Dean Jagger, Alan Hale, Harry Carey Jr., John Rodney; **D:** Raoul Walsh. **VHS $14.95** *REP, HEG ♂♂♂*

Pursuit A terrorist threatens to release a toxic nerve gas throughout a city hosting a political convention. Tension mounts as federal agents must beat the extremists' countdown to zero. Based on the novel by Crichton.
1972 73m/C Ben Gazzara, E.G. Marshall, Martin Sheen, Joseph Wiseman, William Windom; **D:** Michael Crichton; **M:** Jerry Goldsmith. **VHS, Beta $69.95** *REP ♂♂♂*

Pursuit A mercenary comes out of retirement to join a renegade team recovering stolen gold. But they turn on him, stealing the treasure and taking a hostage. Now he must track them down, or there's no movie.
1990 (R) 94m/C James Ryan, Andre Jacobs; **D:** John H. Parr. **VHS $89.99** *HBO ♂*

The Pursuit of D.B. Cooper Based on an actual hijacking that occurred on Thanksgiving Eve in 1971 in which J.R. Meade (alias D.B. Cooper) parachuted out of an airliner with $200,000 of stolen money. Although his fate and whereabouts have remained a mystery, this story speculates about what may have happened.
1981 (PG) 100m/C Robert Duvall, Treat Williams, Kathryn Harrold, Ed Flanders; **D:** Roger Spottiswoode; **M:** James Horner. **VHS, Beta $29.98** *LIV, VES ♂♂*

The Pursuit of Happiness An idealistic man is convicted of manslaughter after accidentally running down a woman. Once in prison, he's faced with the decision to try to escape.
1970 (PG) 85m/C Michael Sarrazin, Arthur Hill, E.G. Marshall, Barbara Hershey, Robert Klein; **D:** Robert Mulligan. **VHS, Beta** *NO ♂♂½*

Pursuit of the Graf Spee Three small British ships destroy the mighty Graf Spee, a WWII German battleship. **AKA:** The Battle of the River Plate.
1957 106m/C Anthony Quayle, Peter Finch, Ian Hunter; **D:** Michael Powell. **VHS, Beta** *NO ♂♂½*

Pursuit to Algiers The modernized Holmes and Watson guard over the King of fictional Rovenia during a sea voyage, during which assassins close in.
1945 65m/B Basil Rathbone, Nigel Bruce, Martin Kosleck, Marjorie Riordan, Rosalind Iven, John Abbott; **D:** Roy William Neill. **VHS, Beta $14.98** *FOX ♂♂½*

Pushed to the Limit Harry Lee, the most feared gangster in Chinatown, is about to meet his match in martial-arts queen Lesseos. She's out for revenge when she learns that Lee is responsible for her brother's murder but first she must get by Lee's lethal bodyguard, the equally skilled Inga.
1992 (R) 88m/C Mimi Lesseos. **VHS $89.95** *IMP ♂½*

Puss 'n Boots From "Faerie Tale Theatre" comes the story of a cat who makes his poor master a rich land-owning nobleman.
1984 60m/C Ben Vereen, Gregory Hines; **D:** Robert Iscove. **VHS, Beta $14.98** *KUI, FOX, FCT ♂½*

Putney Swope Comedy about a token black ad man mistakenly elected Chairman of the board of a Madison Avenue ad agency who turns the company upside-down. A series of riotous spoofs on commercials is the highpoint in this funny, though somewhat dated look at big business.
1969 (R) 84m/B Arnold Johnson, Laura Greene, Stanley Gottlieb, Mel Brooks; **D:** Robert Downey. **VHS, Beta $14.95** *COL ♂♂♂*

Puzzle Franciscus searches for the urn that contains the remains of Buddha but instead finds danger and intrigue. Made for television.
1978 90m/C James Franciscus, Wendy Hughes, Robert Helpmann, Peter Gwynne, Gerald Kennedy, Kerry McGuire; **D:** Gordon Hessler. **VHS $19.95** *ACA ♂♂*

Pygmalion Oscar-winning film adaptation of Shaw's play about a cockney flower-girl who is transformed into a "lady" under the guidance of a stuffy phonetics professor. Shaw himself aided in writing the script in this superbly acted comedy that would be adapted into the musical, "My Fair Lady," first on Broadway in 1956 and for the screen in 1964.
1938 96m/B Leslie Howard, Wendy Hiller, Wilfred Lawson, Marie Lohr; **D:** Leslie Howard, Anthony Asquith. Academy Awards '38: Best Adapted Screenplay; Nominations: Best Actor (Howard), Best Actress (Hiller), Best Picture; Venice Film Festival '38: Best Actor (Howard). **VHS, Beta $14.95** *COL, NOS, SUE ♂♂♂½*

Pyrates Real life husband-wife team of Bacon and Sedgwick try to provide fireworks as hot, hot lovers in the forgettable one. For the price of this one you can buy a newspaper and chewing gum instead. Use both at

the same time and you'll be ahead of everyone involved in this senseless hoot.
1991 (R) 98m/C Kevin Bacon, Kyra Sedgwick, Bruce Martyn Payne, Kristin Datillo; **D:** Noah Stern. **VHS $89.98** VES, LIV ♫

Python Wolf It's non-stop action in South Africa as a counter-terrorist group sets out to thwart a drug smuggler's plans to export plutonium. As usual, intense pacing from director Friedkin. Made for television. Sequel to "C.A.T. Squad" (1986). **AKA:** C.A.T. Squad: Python Wolf.
1988 (R) 100m/C Joe Cortese, Jack Youngblood, Steve James, Deborah Van Valkenburgh, Miguel Ferrer, Alan Scarfe; **D:** William Friedkin; **M:** Ennio Morricone. **VHS $19.95** STE, VMK ♫

The Pyx Canadian suspense thriller about the murder of a prostitute with satanic overtones. Poice sergeant investigates the crime and enters a world of devil worship and decadence. Based on the novel by John Buell. **AKA:** The Hooker Cult Murders.
1973 (R) 111m/C Karen Black, Christopher Plummer, Donald Pilon; **D:** Harvey Hart. **VHS $39.95** PSM ♫♫♫

Q & A Semi-taut thriller with Nolte playing a totally corrupt, hair-trigger cop trying to make his murder of a drug dealer look like self-defense. Assigned to the case is an ex-cop turned assistant DA (Hutton) who's supposed to sweep the case under the rug. Then he finds out another dealer (Assante) is a witness and he happens to be romancing Hutton's former girlfriend (film debut of director Lumet's daughter). Lots of violence and raw language.
1990 (R) 132m/C Nick Nolte, Timothy Hutton, Armand Assante, Patrick O'Neal, Lee Richardson, Luis Guzman, Charles S. Dutton, Jenny Lumet, Paul Calderone, Fyvush Finkel; **D:** Sidney Lumet; **W:** Sidney Lumet; **M:** Ruben Blades. **VHS, Beta $14.95** HBO, WAR ♫♫

Q Ships Silent German drama about a submarine commander who has inner conflicts with his country's war effort.
1928 78m/B J.P. Kennedy, Roy Travers, Johnny Butt, Philip Hewland; **D:** Geoffrey Barkas. **VHS, Beta $19.95** NOS, DVT, GLV ♫♫½

Q (The Winged Serpent) A cult of admirers surrounds this goony monster flick about dragonlike Aztec god Quetzlcoatl, summoned to modern Manhattan by gory human sacrifices, and hungry for rooftop sunbathers and construction teams. Direction and special effects are pretty ragged, but witty script helps the cast shine, especially Moriarty as a lowlife crook who's found the beast's hidden nest. Also called "Q: The Winged Serpent."
1982 (R) 92m/C Michael Moriarty, Candy Clark, David Carradine, Richard Roundtree; **D:** Larry Cohen; **W:** Larry Cohen. **VHS, Beta $14.98** MCA ♫♫♫

QB VII A knighted physician brings a suit for libel against a novelist for implicating him in war crimes. Hopkins as the purportedly wronged doctor and Gazzara as the writer are both superb. Ending is stunning. Adapted from the novel by Leon Uris. Over five hours long; made for TV. Available only as a three-cassette set.
1974 313m/C Anthony Hopkins, Ben Gazzara, Lee Remick, Leslie Caron, Juliet Mills, John Gielgud, Anthony Quayle; **D:** Tom Gries; **M:** Jerry Goldsmith. **VHS, Beta $139.95** COL, SWC ♫♫♫½

Quackser Fortune Has a Cousin in the Bronx An Irish fertilizer salesman meets an exchange student from the U.S., who finds herself attracted to this unlearned, but not unknowing, man. An original love

story with drama and appeal. **AKA:** Fun Loving.
1970 (R) 88m/C Gene Wilder, Margot Kidder; **D:** Waris Hussein. **VHS, Beta $19.95** VCI ♫♫♫

Quadrophenia Pete Townshend's excellent rock opera about an alienated youth looking for life's meaning in Britain's rock scene circa 1963. Music by The Who is powerful and apt. Fine performance by Sting in his acting debut.
1979 (R) 115m/C Phil Daniels, Mark Wingett, Philip Davis, Leslie Ash, Sting; **D:** Franc Roddam. **VHS, Beta $19.95** MVD, COL, RHI ♫♫♫

Quake Railsback stars as a stalker who takes advantage of the 1990 San Francisco earthquake to finally obtain the woman of his dreams. A surveillance expert, he's after a beautiful lawyer (Anderson) and when the earthquake leaves her trapped he rushes to rescue her—only to hold her captive himself.
1992 (R) 83m/C Steve Railsback, Erika Anderson, Eb Lottimer, Dick Miller; **D:** Louis Morneau; **W:** Mark Evan Schwartz. **VHS $89.95** COL ♫½

Quality Street English lovers Tone and Hepburn are separated when he leaves to fight in the Napoleonic Wars. When Tone returns years later, he's forgotten his erstwhile heartthrob. He also fails to recognize that the 16-year old coquette who's caught his eye is his old beloved in disguise. Cast works hard to overcome the absurd premise, based on the play by Sir James Barrie.
1937 84m/B Katharine Hepburn, Franchot Tone, Fay Bainter, Eric Blore, Cora Witherspoon, Estelle Winwood, Florence Lake, Bonita Granville; **D:** George Stevens; **W:** Sir James Barrie. **VHS $19.98** NOS, FCT, TTC ♫♫

Quarantine Quarantine camps for carriers of a fatal virus are the serious measures taken by the nation. The solution is clear to a rebel and an inventor; all must be liberated or exterminated.
1989 (R) 92m/C Beatrice Boepple, Garwin Sanford, Jerry Wasserman, Charles Wilkinson; **D:** Charles Wilkinson; **W:** Charles Wilkinson. **VHS $89.96** REP ♫♫½

Quarterback Princess Workaday made-for-TV telling of the real-life girl who goes out for football and becomes homecoming queen. Heartwarming, if you like that kinda stuff, but not exciting.
1985 96m/C Helen Hunt, Don Murray, John Stockwell, Daphne Zuniga; **D:** Noel Black. **VHS, Beta $59.98** FOX ♫♫

Quartet A young French woman is taken in by an English couple after her husband goes to prison. The husband seduces her, and she becomes trapped emotionally and socially. Superbly acted, claustrophobic drama based on a Jean Rhys novel.
1981 (R) 101m/C Isabelle Adjani, Alan Bates, Dame Maggie Smith, Anthony Higgins; **D:** James Ivory; **W:** Ruth Prawer Jhabvala. Cannes Film Festival Nominations: cs 81: Best Film; Cannes Film Festival '81: Best Actress (Adjani). **VHS, Beta $19.98** WAR ♫♫♫

Quatermass 2 In the well-made sequel to "Quatermass Experiment," (also known as "The Creeping Unknown") Professor Quatermass battles blobs and brainwashed zombies to rescue government officials whose bodies have been invaded by aliens. "Five Million Years to Earth" concluded the trilogy. **AKA:** Enemy from Space.
1957 84m/B Brian Donlevy, John Longden, Sidney James, Bryan Forbes, William Franklyn, Vera Day, John Van Eyssen, Michael Ripper, Michael Balfour; **D:** Val Guest. **VHS, Beta $54.95** FCT, CTH, SNC ♫♫♫

Quatermass Conclusion An elderly British scientist comes out of retirement to stop an immobilizing death ray from outer space from destroying Earth. Edited version of a television miniseries continues earlier adventures of Quatermass on film and television.
1979 105m/C John Mills, Simon MacCorkindale, Barbara Kellerman, Margaret Tyzack; **D:** Piers Haggard. **VHS, Beta $59.99** HBO ♫♫

The Quatermass Experiment Excellent British production about an astronaut who returns to Earth carrying an alien infestation that causes him to turn into a horrible monster. Competent acting and tense direction. Followed by "Enemy From Space." **AKA:** The Creeping Unknown.
1956 78m/B Brian Donlevy, Margia Dean, Jack Warner, Richard Wordsworth; **D:** Val Guest. **VHS $19.95** NOS, SNC ♫♫♫

Quatorze Juliet A taxi driver and a flower girl meet on Bastille Day and fall in love. When he becomes involved with gangsters, she steers him back to virtue in this minor French relic from director Clair.
1932 85m/B Anabella Rigaud, Jorge Rigaud; **D:** Rene Clair. **VHS $29.95** VDM, FCT ♫♫½

Que Viva Mexico Eisenstein's grand unfinished folly on the history of Mexico, reconstructed and released in 1979 by his protege, Grigori Alexandrov. Divided into four sections: "Sandunga" covers the Tehuantepec jungles and its inhabitants; "Manguei" is about a peasant and his bride; "Fiesta" devotes itself to bullfighting and romance; and "Soldadera" depicts the 1910 Mexican revolution through frescoes. Along with "Greed" and "Napoleon," it remains as one of cinema's greatest irrecoverable casualties. Russian narration with English subtitles.
1932 85m/B D: Sergei Eisenstein, Grigori Alexandrov. **VHS, Beta $59.95** KIV ♫♫♫

Queen Boxer A female kick-boxer beats up those who reprehensibly enslaved her family.
1973 (R) 92m/C Judy Lee, Peter Yang Kwan. **VHS, Beta $12.95** LIV ♫

Queen Christina A stylish, resonant star vehicle for Garbo, portraying the 17th-century Swedish queen from ascension to the throne to her romance with a Spanish ambassador. Alternately hilarious and moving, it holds some of Garbo's greatest and most memorable moments. Gilbert's second to last film and his only successful outing after the coming of sound.
1933 101m/B Greta Garbo, John Gilbert, Lewis Stone, Sir C. Aubrey Smith, Ian Keith, Reginald Owen, Elizabeth Young; **D:** Rouben Mamoulian. **VHS, Beta $19.98** MGM ♫♫♫½

Queen for a Day Three differing vignettes, based on a rather notorious radio/TV game show of the time, in which "deserving" (or sufficiently pathetic) working-class women were rewarded for their selflessness. Part one concerns a perfect suburban family whose son contracts polio. Part two has a teen spooking his immigrant parents by working as a carnival high diver to earn college cash. The finale is a Dorothy Parker farce about a homely but kindhearted nurse caring for the child of an unappreciative couple. So popular was this segment that the film was retitled after the main character. Overall, not bad considering the source. **AKA:** Horsie.
1951 107m/B Phyllis Avery, Darren McGavin, Tristram Coffin, Adam Williams, Tracey Roberts, Jack Bailey, Jim Morgan, Fort Pearson; **D:** Arthur Lubin. **VHS $19.95** NOS ♫♫½

Queen Kelly The popularly known, slap-dash version of von Stroheim's famous final film, in which an orphan goes from royal marriage to white slavery to astounding wealth. Never really finished, the film is the edited first half of the intended project, prepared for European release after von Stroheim had been fired. Even so, a campy, extravagant and lusty melodrama. Silent.
1929 113m/B Gloria Swanson, Walter Byron, Seena Owen, Tully Marshall, Madame Sul Te Wan; **D:** Erich von Stroheim. **VHS, Beta, 8mm** **$19.95** *NOS, KIV, VYY* 🎞️🎞️🎞️

Queen of Diamonds A woman pulls off the biggest diamond heist of all time.
198? 90m/C Claudia Cardinale, Stanley Baker, Henri Charriere. **VHS, Beta** *NO* 🎞️🎞️

Queen of Diamonds The "Queen of Diamonds" is an alienated blackjack dealer in Vegas who, in between dealing cards, casually searches for her missing husband and looks after an old man in a motel.
1991 77m/C Tinka Menkes; **D:** Nina Menkes; **W:** Nina Menkes. **VHS** **$59.95** *FCT* 🎞️🎞️

Queen of Hearts Excellent, original romantic comedy is a directorial triumph for Amiel in his first feature. An Italian couple defy both their families and marry for love. Four children later, we find them running a diner in England. Humorous, dramatic, sad—everything a move can and should be. Fine performances.
1989 (PG) 112m/C Anita Zagaria, Joseph Long, Eileen Way, Vittorio Duse, Vittorio Amandola, Ian Hawkes; **D:** Jon Amiel; **M:** Michael Convertino. **VHS, Beta** *NO* 🎞️🎞️🎞️½

The Queen of Mean Tabloid TV-movie based on Ransdell Pierson's scandal-sheet bio of the hotel magnate and convicted tax cheat. See Leona connive. See Leona bitch. See Leona get hers. What's the point? If you ask that you're too bright to watch. *AKA:* Leona Helmsley: The Queen of Mean.
1990 94m/C Suzanne Pleshette, Lloyd Bridges, Bruce Weitz, Joe Regalbuto; **D:** Richard Michaels. **VHS** **$64.95** *FRH* 🎞️½

Queen of Outer Space Notorious male-chauvinist sci-fi cheapie starts out slow, but then the laughs keep coming as the cast plays the hyperdumb material straight. Space cadets crash on Venus, find it ruled by women—and the dolls have wicked plans in store for mankind. Don't be surprised if you've seen the sets before since they were borrowed from "Forbidden Planet," "World Without End," and "Flight to Mars."
1958 80m/C Zsa Zsa Gabor, Eric Fleming, Laurie Mitchell, Paul Birch, Barbara Darrow, Dave Willcock, Lisa Davis, Patrick Waltz, Marilyn Buferd, Marjorie Durant, Lynn Cartwright, Gerry Gaylor; **D:** Edward L. Bernds. **VHS, Beta** **$14.98** *FXV* Woof!

The Queen of Spades Mystical drama about a Russian soldier who ruins his life searching for winning methods of card playing. Well-made version of the Pushkin story.
1949 95m/B Anton Walbrook, Edith Evans, Ronald Howard, Mary Jerrold, Yvonne Mitchell, Anthony M. (Antonio Margheret) Dawson; **D:** Thorold Dickinson. **VHS** *NO* 🎞️🎞️½

Queen of the Amazons A girl searches for her fiance and finds him reluctantly held captive by a tribe of women who rule the jungle.
1947 60m/B Robert Lowery, Patricia Morison, J. Edward Bromberg, John Miljan. **VHS, Beta** **$16.95** *SNC, NOS* 🎞️½

Queen of the Jungle Re-edited adventure serial featuring a white woman cast off in a hot-air balloon and landing in Africa, where she is hailed as a Queen. High camp, starring ex-Our Ganger Kornman.
1935 85m/B Mary Kornman, Reed Howes; **D:** Robert F. Hill. **VHS, Beta, 8mm** **$24.95** *VYY, NOS, MLB* 🎞️

Queen of the Road A feisty Aussie schoolteacher starts a new life as a tractor-trailer driver.
1984 96m/C Joanne Samuel, Amanda Muggleton; **D:** Bruce Best. **VHS, Beta** **$69.98** *LIV, VES* 🎞️🎞️

Queen of the Stardust Ballroom Well-made television drama about a lonely widow who goes to a local dance hall, where she meets a man and begins an unconventional late love.
1975 98m/C Maureen Stapleton, Charles Durning, Michael Strong, Charlotte Rae, Sam O'Steen; **D:** Michael Brandon; **M:** Billy Goldenberg. **Beta** **$11.95** *PSM* 🎞️🎞️

Queenie Television miniseries loosely based on the life of actress Merle Oberon, exploring her rise to stardom. Based on the best-selling novel by Michael Korda, Oberon's nephew by marriage. Many long, dry passages fit for leaving the room for snacks.
1987 233m/C Mia Sara, Kirk Douglas, Martin Balsam, Claire Bloom, Chaim Topol, Joel Grey, Sarah Miles, Joss Ackland; **D:** Larry Peerce; **M:** Georges Delerue. **VHS** **$29.95** *STE, NWV* 🎞️🎞️½

Queens Logic Ensemble comedy in the tradition of "The Big Chill" featuring the trials and tribulations of the "old-neighborhood" gang, who gather again on hometurf and reminisce. Most of the film centers around Olin and girlfriend Webb and whether or not he will chicken out of their wedding. Not bad comedy, with Mantegna delivering most of the good lines.
1991 (R) 116m/C John Malkovich, Kevin Bacon, Jamie Lee Curtis, Linda Fiorentino, Joe Mantegna, Ken Olin, Tom Waits, Chloe Webb, Ed Marinaro, Kelly Bishop, Tony Spiridakis; **D:** Steve Rash; **W:** Tony Spiridakis; **M:** Joe Jackson. **VHS** **$92.98** *LIV* 🎞️🎞️½

Querelle Querelle, a handsome sailor, finds himself involved in a bewildering environment of murder, drug smuggling, and homosexuality in the port of Brest. Highly stylized and erotic sets, along with a dark look, give the film an interesting feel. Nice performances by Davis, Nero, and Moreau. Fassbinder's controversial last film, based on the story by Jean Genet. Strange, difficult narrative (such as it is), alternately boring and engrossing.
1983 (R) 106m/C Brad Davis, Jeanne Moreau, Franco Nero, Laurent Malet; **D:** Rainer Werner Fassbinder; **M:** Peer Raben. **VHS, Beta** **$59.95** *COL, APD, GLV* 🎞️🎞️

The Quest Australian film never released theatrically in the United States. A young boy (Thomas, of "E.T." fame) raised in the outback investigates a local Aboriginal superstition about a monster living in an ancient cemetery. Not bad, just dull.
1986 (PG) 94m/C Henry Thomas, Tony Barry, John Ewart, Rachel Friend, Tamsin West, Dennis Miller, Katya Manning; **D:** Brian Trenchard-Smith. **VHS, Beta** **$9.98** *NLC* 🎞️🎞️

Quest for Fire An interesting story sans the usual dialogue thing. A group of men during the Ice Age must wander the land searching for fire after they lose theirs fending off an attack. During their quest, they encounter and battle various animals and tribesmen in order to survive. The special language they speak was developed by Anthony Burgess, while the primitive move-

ments were Desmond "The Naked Ape" Morris. Perlman went on to become the Beast in TV's "Beauty and the Beast"; Chong is the daughter of Tommy Chong of the comic duo Cheech and Chong.
1982 (R) 75m/C Everett McGill, Ron Perlman, Nameer El-Kadi, Rae Dawn Chong; **D:** Jean-Jacques Annaud; **W:** Gerard Brach. **VHS, Beta** **$69.98** *FOX, ING* 🎞️🎞️

Quest for Love Quirky sci-fi story of a man who passes through a time warp and finds himself able to maintain two parallel lives. Based on John Wyndham's short story.
1971 90m/C Joan Collins, Tom Bell, Denholm Elliott, Laurence Naismith; **D:** Ralph Thomas. **VHS, Beta** *NO* 🎞️🎞️½

Quest for the Mighty Sword A warrior battles dragons, demons and evil wizards.
1990 (PG-13) 94m/C Eric Allen Kramer, Margaret Lenzey, Donald O'Brien, Dina Marrone, Chris Murphy; **D:** David Hills. **VHS, Beta** **$79.95** *COL* 🎞️🎞️

Quest of the Delta Knights Swashbuckling fantasy about a kingdom suffering under an evil ruler and his equally sinister queen. They are opposed by the heroic Delta Knights whose only chance to defeat the fiendish powers of darkness is by unearthing a legendary storehouse containing technology from the age of Atlantis and all the powers of the Ancients.
1993 (PG) 97m/C David Warner, Olivia Hussey, Corbin Allred, Brigid Conley Walsh, David Kriegel; **D:** James Dodson. **VHS** **$89.95** *HMD* 🎞️🎞️½

A Question of Attribution Sir Anthony Blunt (Fox) is an internationally respected art expert who also serves as an art adviser to Queen Elizabeth II. His life unravels when an on-going British Intelligence investigation reveals him to be the fourth man in the Burgess-Maclean-Philby scandal involving Englishmen who spied for, and eventually defected to, the USSR. The investigation of Blunt's covert past is paralleled with his own art investigation of a painting attributed to Titian. Three men are depicted in the artwork—with a fourth male figure discovered to have been painted over. Alan Bennett adapted his play for the television drama.
1991 90m/C James Fox, David Calder, Geoffrey Palmer, Prunella Scales, Mark Payton, Jason Flemyng, Edward De Souza, Ann Beach; **D:** John Schlesinger; **W:** Alan Bennett. **VHS** *FOX* 🎞️🎞️½

Question of Faith A happily married woman is diagnosed with a rare form of cancer. Much to her family's dismay, she turns to some unconventional medical therapies in order to heal herself. Based on a true story. Basically noble, Archer and Neill lift this tearjerker out of most of its maudlin aspects.
1993 90m/C Anne Archer, Sam Neill, Frances Lee McCain, James Tolkan, James Hong, CCH Pounder, Louis Giambalvo, Norman Parker, Michael Constantine; **D:** Stephen Gyllenhaal; **W:** Bruce Hart. **VHS** **$89.95** *WOV* 🎞️🎞️½

A Question of Guilt When her child turns up dead, a free-wheeling divorcee is the prime suspect. Made-for-television soaper.
1978 100m/C Tuesday Weld, Ron Leibman, Peter Masterson, Alex Rocco, Viveca Lindfors, Lana Wood; **D:** Robert Butler. **VHS** **$39.95** *LIV* 🎞️🎞️

Question of Honor Under governmental pressures, an honest narcotics cop decides to inform on his department's corruption. Co-written and produced by ex-cop Sonny Grosso, on whom "The French Connection" was based. Made for television and

Q

based on the book, ''Point Blank,'' by Grosso and Philip Rosenberg.
1980 134m/C Ben Gazzara, Paul Sorvino, Robert Vaughn, Tony Roberts, Danny Aiello, Anthony Zerbe; **D:** Judd Taylor; **W:** Budd Schulberg. **VHS, Beta** NO 🐾🐾½

A Question of Love Fine performances in this well-done television movie about two lesbians—one of whom is fighting her ex-husband for custody of their child.
1978 100m/C Gena Rowlands, Jane Alexander, Ned Beatty, Clu Gulager, Bonnie Bedelia, James Sutorius, Jocelyn Brando; **D:** Jerry Thorpe; **M:** Billy Goldenberg. **VHS** 🐾🐾🐾

Question of Silence Three women, strangers to each other, stand trial for a murdering a man. Intricately analyzed courtroom drama with much to say about male domination. In Dutch with English subtitles or dubbed. **AKA:** De Stilte Rond Christine M.
1983 (R) 92m/C Cox Habrema, Nelly Frijda, Henriette Tol, Edda Barends; **D:** Morleen Gorris. **VHS, Beta** $59.95 SUE, ING 🐾🐾

Question 7 The fifteen-year-old son of a pastor who lives behind the iron curtain faces a dilemma: should he answer a political question the way his teacher wants or the way he believes? **AKA:** Frage 7.
1963 107m/B **VHS, Beta** VGD 🐾🐾🐾

Qui Etes Vous, Mr. Sorge? The story of German journalist Richard Sorge, who was hanged by the Japanese in 1944 for being a Soviet spy. Uninteresting docudrama which focuses on the opinions of various witnesses as to the accuracy of the espionage charge. In French with English subtitles.
1961 130m/B Thomas Holtzman, Keiko Kishi; **D:** Andre Girard. **VHS, Beta** $19.95 BAR, ING 🐾🐾

Quick Polo stars as Quick, a professional assassin whose latest job is Herschel (Donovan), a mob accountant turned federal witness. When Quick is double-crossed, she takes off with Herschel as her insurance and a couple of bad guys (Fahey and Davi) on her trail. Not too much sex and lots of violence to go along with the fast pacing.
1993 (R) 99m/C Teri Polo, Martin Donovan, Jeff Fahey, Robert Davi, Tia Carrere; **D:** Rick King; **W:** Frederick Bailey; **M:** Robert Springberry. **VHS** $92.95 ACA 🐾🐾½

The Quick and the Dead Based on a Louis L'Amour story, this made-for-cable western features a lone gunslinger who protects a defenseless settler's family from the lawless West, only to become a source of sexual tension for the wife.
1987 91m/C Sam Elliott, Tom Conti, Kate Capshaw, Kenny Morrison, Matt Clark; **D:** Robert Day; **M:** Stephen Dorff. **VHS, Beta** $79.95 LHV, WAR 🐾🐾

The Quick and the Dead Stone is a tough gal, out to avenge the murder of her father, who winds up defending the frontier town of Redemption. Hackman is arch-villain Herod with DiCaprio as his quick-on-the-draw son. Filmed on location in Tucson, Arizona. One of the many women action films in the Hollywood pipeline, and one of many westerns as well, contributing to the screen release being delayed until spring 1995. At least Stone has proven chutzpah.
1994 ?m/C Sharon Stone, Gene Hackman, Leonardo DiCaprio, Russell Crowe, Kevin Conway, Lance Henriksen, Roberts Blossom, Pat Hingle, Keith David, Michael Stone; **D:** Sam Raimi; **W:** Simon Moore, John Sayles. **VHS** NYR 🐾🐾½

Quick Change Murray, Davis, and Quaid form bumbling trio of New York bank robbers who can't seem to exit the Big Apple with loot. Based on Jay Cronley's book, it's Murray's directing debut (with help from screenwriter Franklin). Engaging minor caper comedy displaying plenty of NYC dirty boulevards.
1990 (R) 89m/C Bill Murray, Geena Davis, Randy Quaid, Jason Robards Jr., Bob Elliott, Victor Argo, Kathryn Grody, Philip Bosco, Phil Hartman, Kurtwood Smith, Jamey Sheridan; **D:** Bill Murray, Howard Franklin; **W:** Howard Franklin; **M:** Randy Edelman, Howard Shore. **VHS, Beta, 8mm** $19.98 WAR 🐾🐾½

Quick, Let's Get Married Quick, let's not watch this movie. Even the people who made it must have hated it: they waited seven years to release it. Rogers runs a whorehouse; Eden is a gullible, pregnant prostitute; Gould in his big-screen debut(!) is a deaf-mute. A must-not see. Also known as ''Seven Different Ways.'' **AKA:** Seven Different Ways; The Confession.
1971 96m/C Ginger Rogers, Ray Milland, Barbara Eden, Carl Schell, Michael Ansara, Walter Abel, Scott Meyer, Cecil Kellaway, Elliott Gould; **D:** William Dieterle. **VHS, Beta** NO Woof!

Quicker Than the Eye When a magician gets mixed up in an assassination plot, he must use his wit, cunning, and magic to get out of it.
1988 94m/C Ben Gazzara, Mary Crosby, Catherine Jarrett, Ivan Desny, Eb Lottimer, Sophie Carle, Wolfram Berger, Dinah Hinz, Jean Yanne; **D:** Nicolas Gessner. **VHS, Beta** $79.95 ACA 🐾🐾

Quicksand Mechanic Rooney borrows $20 from his boss's cash register, intending to return it. One thing leads to another, the plot thickens, and it's downhill (for Rooney) from there. Good, tense suspense drama.
1950 79m/B Mickey Rooney, Peter Lorre, Jeanne Cagney; **D:** Irving Pichel. **VHS, Beta** $14.95 NOS, MRV, SNC 🐾🐾½

Quicksand: No Escape Scott Reinhardt (Matheson) is a successful architect whose partner decides to secure a building contract by bribing a city official. When his partner is murdered Reinhardt is approached by a former cop (Sutherland) asking a lot of money for some incriminating evidence. Reinhardt is then drawn ever deeper into the illicit dealings, endangering his life.
1991 (PG-13) 93m/C Tim Matheson, Donald Sutherland, Jay Acovone, Timothy Carhart, John Finn, Marc Alaimo, Felicity Huffman, Al Pugliese; **D:** Michael Pressman. **VHS, Beta** $89.98 MCA 🐾🐾

Quicksilver A young stockbroker loses all, then quits his job to become a city bicycle messenger. Pointless, self-indulgent yuppie fantasy.
1986 (PG) 106m/C Kevin Bacon, Jami Gertz, Paul Rodriguez, Rudy Ramos, Andrew Smith, Gerald S. O'Loughlin, Laurence ''Larry'' Fishburne, Louie Anderson; **D:** Tom Donnelly; **W:** Tom Donnelly; **M:** Roger Daltrey, Ray Parker Jr. **VHS, Beta** $79.95 COL 🐾🐾½

Quiet Cool When his former girlfriend's family is killed, a New York cop travels to a sleepy California town run by a pot-growing tycoon. He subsequently kills the bad guys in a Rambo-like fit of vengeance. Dopey exercise in sleepy-eyed bloodshed.
1986 (R) 80m/C James Remar, Daphne Ashbrook, Adam Coleman Howard, Jared Martin, Fran Ryan; **D:** Clay Borris; **M:** Jay Michael Ferguson. **VHS, Beta** $79.95 COL 🐾

Quiet Day In Belfast Tragedy occurs when northern Irish patriots and British soldiers clash in an Irish betting parlor. Kidder plays a duel role: an Irish woman in love with a British soldier and the woman's twin sister. Convincingly adapted from a Canadian stage play.
1974 92m/C Barry Foster, Margot Kidder; **D:** Milad Bessada. **VHS, Beta** $59.95 MED 🐾🐾🐾

The Quiet Earth Serious science fiction film about a scientist who awakens to find himself seemingly the only human left on earth as the result of a misfired time/space government experiment. He later finds two other people, a girl and a Maori tribesman, and must try to repair the damage in order to save what's left of mankind.
1985 (R) 91m/C Bruno Lawrence, Alison Routledge, Peter Smith; **D:** Geoff Murphy; **W:** Bruno Lawrence, Sam Pillsbury, Bill Baer; **M:** John Charles. **VHS, Beta** $19.98 FOX 🐾🐾🐾

Quiet Fire A health-club owner tries to get the goods on the arms-dealing congressman who killed his best friend. Hilton-Jacobs looks properly pumped up since his sweathog days on TV's ''Welcome Back Kotter.''
1991 (R) 100m/C Lawrence Hilton-Jacobs, Robert Z'Dar, Nadia Marie, Karen Black, Lance Lindsay; **D:** Lawrence Hilton-Jacobs. **VHS** $79.95 PMH 🐾½

The Quiet Man The classic incarnation of Hollywood Irishness, and one of Ford's best, and funniest films. Wayne is Sean Thornton, a weary American ex-boxer who returns to the Irish hamlet of his childhood and tries to take a spirited lass as his wife, despite the strenuous objections of her brawling brother (McLaglen). Thornton's aided by the leprechaun-like Fitzgerald and the local parish priest, Bond. A high-spirited and memorable film filled with Irish stew, wonderful banter, and shots of the lush countryside. Listen for the Scottish bagpipes at the start of the horse race, a slight geographic inaccuracy.
1952 129m/C John Wayne, Maureen O'Hara, Barry Fitzgerald, Victor McLaglen, Arthur Shields, Jack MacGowran, Ward Bond, Mildred Natwick, Ken Curtis, Mae Marsh, Sean McClory, Francis Ford; **D:** John Ford; **W:** Frank Nugent; **M:** Victor Young. Academy Awards '52: Best Color Cinematography, Best Director (Ford); Nominations: Best Art Direction/Set Decoration (Color), Best Picture, Best Screenplay, Best Sound, Best Supporting Actor (McLaglen); National Board of Review Awards '52: 10 Best Films of the Year; Venice Film Festival '52: Best Director (Ford). **VHS** $19.98 REP, TLF, CCB 🐾🐾🐾🐾

Quiet Thunder A hard-drinking bush pilot in Africa and a beautiful senator's wife are thrown together on the run after both witness an assassination. Mindless, thoroughly derivative ''adventure.''
1987 (PG-13) 94m/C Wayne Crawford, June Chadwick, Victor Steinbach; **D:** David Rice. **VHS, Beta** $79.95 LIV 🐾

Quigley Down Under A Western sharpshooter moves to Australia in search of employment. To his horror, he discovers that he has been hired to kill aborigines. Predictable action is somewhat redeemed by the terrific chemistry between Selleck and San Giacomo and the usual enjoyable theatrics from Rickman as the landowner heavy.
1990 (PG-13) 121m/C Tom Selleck, Laura San Giacomo, Alan Rickman, Chris Haywood, Ron Haddrick, Tony Bonner, Roger Ward, Ben Mendelsohn, Jerome Ehlers, Conor McDermottroe; **D:** Simon Wincer; **W:** John Hill; **M:** Basil Poledouris. **VHS, Beta, 8mm** $19.98 MGM 🐾🐾½

The Quiller Memorandum An American secret agent travels to Berlin to uncover a deadly neo-Nazi gang. Refreshingly different from other spy tales of its era. Good screenplay adapted from Adam Hall's novel, "The Berlin Memorandum."
1966 103m/C George Segal, Senta Berger, Alec Guinness, Max von Sydow, George Sanders; *D:* Michael Anderson Sr.; *W:* Harold Pinter; *M:* John Barry. VHS, Beta $59.98 *FOX* 🎞🎞🎞

Quilombo The title refers to a legendary settlement of runaway slaves in 17th-century Brazil; an epic chronicles its fortunes as leadership passes from a wise ruler to a more militant one who goes to war against the government. Stunning scenery, tribal images, and folk songs, but the numerous characters seldom come to life as personalities. One of Brazil's most expensive films, in Portuguese with English subtitles.
1984 114m/C Vera Fischer, Antonio Pompeo, Zeze Motta, Toni Tornado; *D:* Carlos Diegues; *W:* Carlos Diegues. VHS $79.95 *NYF, FCT, ING* 🎞🎞½

Quintet Atypical Altman sci-fi effort. The stakes in "Quintet," a form of backgammon, are high—you bet your life. Set during the planet's final ice age, Newman and wife Fossey wander into a dying city and are invited to play the game, with Fossey losing quickly. Bizarre and pretentious, with heavy symbolic going.
1979 118m/C Paul Newman, Bibi Andersson, Fernando Rey, Vittorio Gassman, David Langton, Nina Van Pallandt, Brigitte Fossey; *D:* Robert Altman; *W:* Lionel Chetwynd, Patricia Resnick, Robert Altman. VHS, Beta $19.98 *FOX* 🎞🎞

Quo Vadis One of the first truly huge Italian silent epics. The initial adaptation of the Henryk Sienkiewicz novel about Nero and ancient Rome. Probably the cinema's first great financial success.
1912 45m/B *D:* Enrico Guazzoni. VHS, Beta $89.95 *FCT* 🎞🎞½

Quo Vadis Larger-than-life production about Nero and the Christian persecution. Done on a giant scale: features exciting fighting scenes, romance, and fabulous costumes. Definitive version of the classic novel by Henryk Siekiewicz. Remade for Italian television in 1985.
1951 171m/C Robert Taylor, Deborah Kerr, Peter Ustinov, Patricia Laffan, Finlay Currie, Abraham Sofaer, Marina Berti, Buddy Baer, Felix Aylmer, Nora Swinburne; *Cameos:* Sophia Loren, Elizabeth Taylor; *D:* Mervyn LeRoy; *M:* Miklos Rozsa. Academy Awards '51 Nominations: Best Art Direction/Set Decoration (Color), Best Color Cinematography, Best Costume Design (Color), Best Film Editing, Best Picture, Best Supporting Actor (Genn, Ustinov), Best Original Score; Golden Globe Awards '52: Best Supporting Actor (Ustinov). VHS, Beta $29.98 *MGM, APD, IGP* 🎞🎞🎞

Quo Vadis Third screen version of Henryk Sienkiewicz's book. See the other two first. This one is slow and perfunctory. Brandauer is memorable as Nero; Quinn (in the lead) is the son of Anthony.
1985 (R) 122m/C Klaus Maria Brandauer, Frederic Forrest, Christina Raines, Maria Therese Relin, Francesco Quinn, Barbara DeRossi, Phillipe LeRoy, Max von Sydow, Gabriel Ferzetti, Massimo Girotti, Leopoldo Trieste; *D:* Franco Rossi. VHS, Beta $89.95 *PSM, APD* 🎞🎞½

Rabbit Test In Rivers' first directorial effort, a clumsy virginal guy becomes the world's first pregnant man. So irreverent it's almost never in good taste, and so poorly written it's almost never funny.
1978 (PG) 86m/C Billy Crystal, Roddy McDowall, Imogene Coca, Paul Lynde, Alex Rocco, George Gobel; *D:* Joan Rivers. VHS, Beta $9.95 *COL, SUE* 🎞½

Rabid A young girl undergoes a radical plastic surgery technique and develops a strange and unexplained lesion in her armpit. She also finds she has an unusual craving for human blood. *AKA:* Rage.
1977 (R) 90m/C Marilyn Chambers, Frank Moore, Joe Silver; *D:* David Cronenberg; *W:* David Cronenberg. VHS, Beta $29.98 *WAR* 🎞🎞½

Rabid Grannies Wicked satire about two aging sisters who receive a surprise birthday gift from their devilworshiping nephew. The gift turns their party into a gorefest as they rip into various family members—literally. Any humor will be lost on any but the most diehard Troma fans. Dubbed.
1989 (R) 89m/C Catherine Aymerie, Caroline Brackman, Danielle Daven, Raymond Lescot, Anne Marie Fox, Richard Cotica, Patricia Davie; *D:* Emmanuel Kervyn; *W:* Emmanuel Kervyn. VHS, Beta $79.95 *MED, VTR Woof!*

Race for Glory A young motorcyclist builds a super-bike he hopes will help him win a world championship race. Will he win? Can you stand the suspense? Let's just say there's a happy ending.
1989 (R) 102m/C Alex McArthur, Peter Berg, Pamela Ludwig; *D:* Rocky Lang; *M:* Jay Michael Ferguson. VHS, Beta $89.99 *HBO* 🎞½

Race for Life A race car driver attempts to make a comeback despite objections from his wife. He races around Europe (great scenery); she leaves him; he tries to win her back and salvage his career. Standard, ungripping story. Car scenes are great. *AKA:* Mask of Dust.
1955 69m/B Richard Conte, Mari Aldon, George Coulouris; *D:* Terence Fisher. VHS, Beta *NO* 🎞½

Race for Your Life, Charlie Brown Another in the popular series of "Peanuts" character films. This one features Charlie Brown, Snoopy, and all the gang spending an exciting summer in the American wilderness.
1977 (G) 76m/C *W:* Charles M. Schulz. VHS, Beta $14.95 *PAR, WTA* 🎞🎞½

Race with the Devil Vacationers are terrorized by devil worshippers after they witness a sacrificial killing. Heavy on car chases; light on plot and redeeming qualities. Don't waste your time.
1975 (PG) 88m/C Peter Fonda, Warren Oates, Loretta Swit, Lara Parker; *D:* Jack Starrett. VHS, Beta $14.98 *FOX, FCT* 🎞½

The Racers Douglas brings power to the role of a man determined to advance to the winners' circle. Exciting European location photography, but not much plot. *AKA:* Such Men are Dangerous.
1955 112m/C Gilbert Roland, Kirk Douglas, Lee J. Cobb, Cesar Romero, Bella Darvi; *D:* Henry Hathaway. VHS, Beta $39.98 *FOX, FCT* 🎞🎞½

Rachel and the Stranger A Godfearing farmer declares his love for his wife when a handsome stranger (Mitchum) nearly woos her away. Well-cast, well-paced, charming Western comedy-drama.
1948 93m/B Loretta Young, Robert Mitchum, William Holden, Gary Gray; *D:* Norman Foster. VHS, Beta $19.95 *MED, TTC* 🎞🎞🎞

The Rachel Papers Based on the Martin Amis novel, this is the funny/sad tale of an Oxford youth who plots via his computer the seduction of a beautiful American girl. For anyone who has ever loved someone just out of their reach.
1989 (R) 92m/C Dexter Fletcher, Ione Skye, James Spader, Jonathan Pryce, Bill Paterson, Michael Gambon, Lesley Sharp; *D:* Damien Harris; *W:* Damien Harris; *M:* Chaz Jankel. VHS, Beta $79.98 *FOX* 🎞🎞🎞

Rachel, Rachel Rachel teaches by day, wearing simple, practical dresses and her hair up. By night she caters to her domineering mother by preparing refreshments for her parties. This sexually repressed, spinster schoolteacher, however, gets one last chance at romance in her small Connecticut town. Woodward mixes just the right amounts of loneliness and sweetness in the leading role. A surprising award-winner that was an independent production of Newman. Based on Margaret Laurence's "A Jest of God."
1968 (R) 102m/C Joanne Woodward, James Olson, Estelle Parsons, Geraldine Fitzgerald, Donald Moffatt; *D:* Paul Newman; *W:* Stewart Stern. Academy Awards '68 Nominations: Best Actress (Woodward), Best Adapted Screenplay, Best Picture, Best Supporting Actress (Parsons); Golden Globe Awards '69: Best Actress—Drama (Woodward), Best Director (Newman); New York Film Critics Awards '68: Best Actress (Woodward), Best Director (Newman). VHS, Beta $19.98 *WAR* 🎞🎞🎞½

Rachel River A divorced radio personality struggles to make something of her life in her small Minnesota town.
1989 (PG-13) 88m/C Pamela Reed, Craig T. Nelson, Viveca Lindfors, James Olson, Zeljko Ivanek, Jo Henderson, Alan North, Jon DeVries; *D:* Sandy Smolan; *W:* Judith Guest; *M:* Arvo Part. VHS $19.95 *ACA* 🎞🎞½

Rachel's Man A big-screen version of the Biblical love story of Jacob and Rachel.
1975 115m/C Mickey Rooney, Rita Tushingham, Leonard Whiting; *D:* Moshe Mizrahi. VHS, Beta $59.95 *LIV* 🎞

Racing Luck While working at a race track, a man is framed and forced to work for another stable. *AKA:* Red Hot Tires.
1935 56m/B William Boyd, Barbara Worth, George Ernest, Esther Muir, Dick Curtis; *D:* Sam Newfield. VHS, Beta $9.95 *GPV* 🎞

Racing with the Moon Sweet, nostalgic film about two buddies awaiting induction into the Marines in 1942. They have their last chance at summer romance. Benjamin makes the most of skillful young actors and conventional story. Great period detail. Keep your eyes peeled for glimpses of many rising young stars including Hannah and Carvey.
1984 (PG) 108m/C Sean Penn, Elizabeth McGovern, Nicolas Cage, John Karlen, Rutanya Alda, Max Showalter, Crispin Glover, Suzanne Adkinson, Page Hannah, Michael Madsen, Dana Carvey, Carol Kane, Michael Talbott; *D:* Richard Benjamin; *W:* Steven Kloves; *M:* Dave Grusin. VHS, Beta $14.95 *PAR* 🎞🎞🎞

The Racket Police captain Mitchum tries to break up mob racket of gangster Ryan. Internecine strife on both sides adds complexity. Mitchum and especially Ryan are super; fine, tense melodrama.
1951 88m/B Robert Ryan, Robert Mitchum, Lizabeth Scott, Ray Collins, William Conrad, Don Porter; *D:* John Cromwell. VHS, Beta $19.98 *MED, TTC* 🎞🎞🎞

The Racketeer A racketeer falls in love with a pretty girl and attempts to win her over. As part of his plan, the gangster arranges to help the girl's boyfriend begin his musical career in exchange for the girl's promise to marry him.
1929 68m/B Carole Lombard, Robert Armstrong, Hedda Hopper; *D:* Howard Higgin. VHS, Beta $16.95 *SNC, NOS, CAB* 🎞🎞½

Racketeers of the Range Cattleman fights a crooked attorney who wants to sell his client's stock to a large meat packing company.
1939 62m/B George O'Brien, Marjorie Reynolds, Chill Wills, Ray Whitley; *D:* David Ross Lederman. **VHS, Beta** *MED* ♂♂½

Racquet Tennis pro Convy searches for true love and a tennis court of to call his own in Beverly Hills. Lame, sophomoric, and unfunny.
1979 87m/C Bert Convy, Edie Adams, Lynda Day George, Phil Silvers, Bobby Riggs, Bjorn Borg, Tanya Roberts; *D:* David Winters. **VHS, Beta** *NO* ♂

Rad Teenage drama revolving around BMX racing and such dilemmas as: can the good guys beat the bad guys, who's got the fastest bike, must you cheat to win, and should our hero miss his SAT tests to compete in "the big race.." Directed by stunt-expert Needham.
1986 (PG) 94m/C Bill Allen, Bart Conner, Talia Shire, Jack Weston, Lori Loughlin; *D:* Hal Needham. **VHS, Beta $9.98** *SUE, NLC* ♂♂½

Radar Men from the Moon Commando Cody, with his jet-pack, fights to defend the earth from invaders from the moon. Twelve-episode serial on two tapes. Silly sci-fi. *AKA:* Retik, the Moon Menace.
1952 152m/B George Wallace, Aline Towne, Roy Barcroft, William "Billy" Bakewell, Clayton Moore; *D:* Fred Brannon. **VHS $49.95** *NOS, REP, SNC* ♂½

Radar Secret Service Two servicemen witness the hijacking of a truck loaded with nuclear material.
1950 59m/B John Howard, Adele Jergens, Tom Neal, Ralph Byrd. **VHS, Beta** *NO* ♂♂½

Radio Days A lovely, unpretentious remembrance of the pre-television radio culture. Allen tells his story in a series of vignettes centering around his youth in Brooklyn, his eccentric extended family, and the legends of radio they all followed. The ubiquitous Farrow is a young singer hoping to make it big.
1987 (PG) 96m/C Mia Farrow, Dianne Wiest, Julie Kavner, Michael Tucker, Wallace Shawn, Josh Mostel, Tony Roberts, Jeff Daniels, Kenneth Mars, Seth Green, William Magerman, Diane Keaton, Renee Lippin, Danny Aiello, Gina DeAngelis, Kitty Carlisle Hart, Mercedes Ruehl, Tito Puente; *D:* Woody Allen; *W:* Woody Allen. **VHS, Beta $19.95** *HBO* ♂♂♂

Radio Flyer It's 1969 and Mike and Bobby have just moved to northern California with their divorced mom. Everything would be idyllic if only their mother hadn't decided to marry a drunken child abuser who beats Bobby whenever the mood strikes him. Mike decides to help Bobby escape by turning their Radio Flyer wagon into a magic rocketship that will carry Bobby to safety, but ultimately proves tragic. Appealing version of childhood dreams sans the child abuse angle (toned down though it was), which is abruptly and unsatisfactorily handled.
1992 (PG-13) 114m/C Elijah Wood, Joseph Mazzello, Lorraine Bracco, Adam Baldwin, John Heard, Ben Johnson; *D:* Richard Donner. **VHS $19.95** *COL* ♂♂

Radio Patrol Plenty of action and thrills abound in this 12-chapter serial. Pinky Adams, radio cop, is assisted by his trusty canine partner, Irish (Silverwolf). A cop's best friend is his dog.
1937 235m/B Mickey Rentschler, Adrian Morris, Monte Montague, Jack Mulhall, Grant Withers, Catherine Hughes; *D:* Ford Beebe, Cliff Smith. **VHS, Beta $21.95** *NOS, VDM, MLB* ♂♂½

Radioactive Dreams Surreal, practically senseless fantasy wherein two men, trapped in a bomb shelter for 15 years with nothing to read but mystery novels, emerge as detectives into a post-holocaust world looking for adventure.
1986 (R) 94m/C John Stockwell, Michael Dudikoff, Lisa Blount, George Kennedy, Don Murray, Michelle Little; *D:* Albert Pyun; *W:* Albert Pyun. **VHS, Beta $79.98** *LIV, VES* ♂♂

Rafferty & the Gold Dust Twins Two women kidnap a motor vehicle inspector at gunpoint in Los Angeles and order him to drive to New Orleans. En route, they become pals. Wandering, pointless female buddy flick. *AKA:* Rafferty and the Highway Hustlers.
1975 (R) 91m/C Alan Arkin, Sally Kellerman, MacKenzie Phillips, Charles Martin Smith, Harry Dean Stanton; *D:* Dick Richards. **VHS, Beta $19.98** *WAR* ♂♂½

Rage Scott's directorial debut. A military helicopter sprays peace-loving rancher Scott and his son with nerve gas. The son's death is covered up; the rancher embarks on a vengeful rampage. Scott's sudden transformation to avenging killer is implausible and overwrought.
1972 (PG) 100m/C George C. Scott, Richard Basehart, Martin Sheen, Barnard Hughes, Kenneth Tobey, Ed Lauter, Nicholas Beauvy, Dabbs Greer; *D:* George C. Scott. **VHS, Beta $19.98** *WAR* ♂♂

Rage Well-acted, well-written, nerve-wracking drama about a convicted rapist who finds help through difficult therapy. Focuses on how the sex-offender discovers the "whys" behind his assaults. Made for television.
1980 100m/C David Soul, James Whitmore, Yaphet Kotto, Caroline McWilliams, Vic Tayback, Sharon Farrell, Craig T. Nelson, Garry Walberg; *D:* William A. Graham. **VHS, Beta $59.95** *WAR* ♂♂♂

Rage and Honor Rothrock stars as Kris Fairfield, a high-school teacher who spends her spare time tutoring students in the martial-arts. Her present students are a group of cops, including Aussie visitor Preston Michaels. When Michaels witnesses a drug deal, he gets set-up by the dealers for a murder he didn't commit and only Kris can help him prove his innocence.
1992 (R) 93m/C Cynthia Rothrock, Richard Norton, Brian Thompson, Terri Treas, Catherine Bach, Alex Datcher; *D:* Terence H. Winkless; *W:* Terence H. Winkless. **VHS $89.95** *COL, PMS* ♂♂

Rage and Honor 2: Hostile Takeover Rothrock returns as black-belt CIA operative Kris Fairfield, whose latest assignment takes her to Jakarta where a banker is involved in a large-scale drug money laundering operation. She teams up with Preston Michaels (Norton), a renegade Australian cop, and winds up following a trail that leads to a fortune in diamonds and lots of trouble.
1993 (R) 98m/C Cynthia Rothrock, Richard Norton, Patrick Muldoon, Frans Tumbuan, Ron Vreeken, Alex Tumundo; *D:* Guy Norris; *W:* Louis Sun, Steven Reich. **VHS $93.65** *COL* ♂♂½

Rage at Dawn An outlaw gang is tracked by a special agent who must "bend" the rules a little in order to get the bad guys. Not surprisingly, he gets his girl as well. A solid standard of the genre, with some clever plot twists. *AKA:* Seven Bad Men.
1955 87m/C Randolph Scott, Forrest Tucker, Mala Powers, J. Carroll Naish, Edgar Buchanan; *D:* Tim Whelan. **VHS $13.95** *NOS, GHV, MRV* ♂♂½

A Rage in Harlem The crime novels of Chester A. Himes were translated into the best movies of the early '70s blaxploitation era. Now, a Himes story gets the big budget Hollywood treatment with juice and aplomb. A voluptuous lady crook enters Harlem circa 1950 with a trunkful of stolen gold sought by competing crooks, and the chase is on, with one virtuous soul (Whitaker) who only wants the girl. Great cast and characters, much humor, but unsparing in its violence.
1991 (R) 108m/C Forest Whitaker, Gregory Hines, Robin Givens, Zakes Mokae, Danny Glover, Tyler Collins, Ron Taylor, T.K. Carter, Willard Pugh, Samm-Art Williams, Jay Hawkins, Badja Djola, John Toles-Bey, Stack Pierce, George Wallace; *D:* Bill Duke; *W:* John Toles-Bey, Bobby Crawford; *M:* Elmer Bernstein. **VHS $19.98** *HBO, FCT* ♂♂♂

Rage of Angels Lengthy television miniseries adaptation of the Sidney Sheldon novel about an ambitious female attorney, her furs, and her men. Followed by "Rage of Angels: The Story Continues" (1986).
1983 192m/C Jaclyn Smith, Ken Howard, Armand Assante, Ronald Hunter, Kevin Conway, George Coe, Deborah May; *D:* Buzz Kulik; *M:* Billy Goldenberg. **VHS, Beta $19.95** *COL* ♂♂

Rage of Angels: The Story Continues In this sequel to the Sidney Sheldon trash-with-flash television miniseries, Smith reprises her role as the beautiful lady lawyer who always gets involved with the wrong men. This time she tries to hide the fact of her illegitimate son from his father, who's about to become Vice President of the United States.
1986 200m/C Jaclyn Smith, Ken Howard, Michael Nouri, Susan Sullivan, Brad Dourif, Angela Lansbury, Mason Adams; *D:* Paul Wendkos; *M:* Billy Goldenberg. **VHS** *STE* ♂♂½

Rage of Honor A high-kicking undercover cop seeks vengeance on bad guys for his partner's murder. Standard of its type; why bother?
1987 (R) 92m/C Sho Kosugi, Lewis Van Bergen, Robin Evans, Gerry Gibson; *D:* Gordon Hessler. **VHS, Beta $19.95** *MED, VTR* ♂

The Rage of Paris Scheming ex-actress and head waiter hope to gain by helping a beautiful French girl (Darrieux) snag a rich hubby. She comes to her senses, realizing that love, true love, matters more than wealth. Well-acted, quaint comedy.
1938 78m/B Danielle Darrieux, Douglas Fairbanks Jr., Mischa Auer, Helen Broderick; *D:* Henry Koster. **VHS, Beta $19.95** *NOS, DVT, CAB* ♂♂♂

Rage of Wind Master boxer seeks revenge on a Japanese commandant who kidnaps his wife during WWII.
1982 97m/C Chen Hsing, Yasuka Kurata, Irene Ryder. **VHS, Beta** *WVE* ♂

Rage to Kill Jingoistic retelling of the 1982 Grenada invasion, complete with helpless American med students. Good-guy race car driver whips them into shape to fight the Soviet-supplied general (he's the bad guy). Guess who wins.
1988 (R) 94m/C Oliver Reed, James Ryan, Henry Cele, Cameron Mitchell; *D:* David Winters. **VHS, Beta $29.95** *AIP* ♂½

Raggedy Ann and Andy: A Musical Adventure Here are the fun-filled exploits of America's favorite fictional dolls, transformed into an enchanting animated musical. Includes 16 songs by Joe Raposo.
1977 (G) 87m/C *D:* Richard Williams; *V:* Didi Conn, Joe Silver. **VHS, Beta $14.98** *FOX* ♂½

Raggedy Man Spacek in her signature role as a lonely small-town woman. Here she's raising two sons alone in a small Texas town during WWII. Spacek's strong acting carries a well-scripted story, unfortunately marred by an overwrought ending.
1981 (PG) 94m/C Sissy Spacek, Eric Roberts, Sam Shepard, Tracy Walter, William Sanderson, Henry Thomas; D: Jack Fisk; W: Bill Wittliff; M: Jerry Goldsmith. VHS, Beta $59.95 MCA *ℑℑℑ*

The Raggedy Rawney A young Army deserter dresses in women's clothing and hides out as a mad woman with a band of gypsies. Good first directing effort by English actor Bob Hoskins. Unpretentious and engaging.
1990 (R) 102m/C Bob Hoskins, Dexter Fletcher, Zoe Nathenson, David Hill, Ian Dury, Zoe Wanamaker, J.G. Devlin, Perry Fenwick; D: Bob Hoskins; W: Bob Hoskins, Nicole De Wilde; M: Michael Kamen. VHS $19.95 CAN *ℑℑ*½

Ragin' Cajun Retired kickboxer is forced into a death match to save his girlfriend.
1990 91m/C David Heavener, Charlene Tilton, Sam Bottoms, Samantha Eggar, Dr. Death; D: William B. Hillman. VHS $79.95 AIP, HHE *ℑ*

Raging Bull Scorsese's depressing but magnificent vision of the dying American Dream and suicidal macho codes in the form of the rise and fall of middleweight boxing champ Jake LaMotta, a brutish, dull-witted animal who can express himself only in the ring and through violence. A photographically expressive, brilliant drama, with easily the most intense and brutal boxing scenes ever filmed. De Niro provides a vintage performance, going from the young LaMotta to the aging has-been, and is ably accompanied by Moriarty as his girl and Pesci as his loyal, much beat-upon bro.
1980 (R) 128m/B Robert De Niro, Cathy Moriarty, Joe Pesci, Frank Vincent, Nicholas Colasanto, Theresa Saldana; D: Martin Scorsese; W: Paul Schrader, Mardik Martin. Academy Awards '80: Best Actor (De Niro), Best Film Editing; Nominations: Best Cinematography, Best Director (Scorsese), Best Picture, Best Sound, Best Supporting Actor (Pesci), Best Supporting Actress (Moriarty); Golden Globe Awards '81: Best Actor—Drama (De Niro); Los Angeles Film Critics Association Awards '80: Best Actor (De Niro), Best Film; National Board of Review Awards '80: Best Actor (De Niro), Best Supporting Actor (Pesci). VHS, Beta, 8mm $14.95 MGM, FOX, VYG *ℑℑℑℑ*

Rags to Riches A wealthy Beverly Hills entrepreneur decides to improve his public image by adopting six orphan girls. TV pilot.
1987 96m/C Joseph Bologna, Tisha Campbell. VHS, Beta $19.95 STE, NWV *ℑ*

Ragtime The lives and passions of a middle class family weave into the scandals and events of 1906 America. A small, unthinking act represents all the racist attacks on one man, who refuses to back down this time. Wonderful period detail. From the E.L. Doctorow novel, but not nearly as complex. Features Cagney's last film performance.
1981 (PG) 156m/C Howard E. Rollins Jr., Kenneth McMillan, Brad Dourif, Mary Steenburgen, James Olson, Elizabeth McGovern, Pat O'Brien, James Cagney, Debbie Allen, Jeff Daniels, Moses Gunn, Donald O'Connor, Mandy Patinkin, Norman Mailer; D: Milos Forman; W: Michael Weller; M: Randy Newman. VHS, Beta $29.95 PAR, FCT *ℑℑℑ*

Raid on Entebbe Dramatization of the Israeli rescue of passengers held hostage by terrorists at Uganda's Entebbe Airport in 1976. A gripping actioner all the more compelling because true. Finch received an Emmy nomination in this, his last film. Made for television.
1977 (R) 113m/C Charles Bronson, Peter Finch, Horst Buchholz, John Saxon, Martin Balsam, Jack Warden, Yaphet Kotto, Sylvia Sidney; D: Irvin Kershner. VHS, Beta NO *ℑℑℑ*

Raid on Rommel A British soldier (Burton) poses as a Nazi and tries to infiltrate Rommel's team with his rag-tag brigade of misfits. Predictable drivel. Contains action footage from the 1967 film "Tobruk."
1971 (PG) 98m/C Richard Burton, John Colicos, Clinton Greyn, Wolfgang Preiss; D: Henry Hathaway. VHS, Beta $19.95 MCA *ℑ*½

Raiders in Action Tale following the activities of a band of allied commandos in the closing days of the war.
1971 89m/C Paul Smith. VHS, Beta $59.95 HHE *ℑ*

Raiders of Atlantis Battles break out when the lost continent surfaces in the Caribbean. The warriors in these apocalyptic frays deploy atomic arsenals.
1983 100m/C Christopher Connelly; D: Roger Franklin. VHS, Beta $69.95 PSM *ℑ*

Raiders of Ghost City Serial in 13 chapters involves a Union Secret Service Agent after a ring of gold robbers who are posing as Confederate soldiers during the end of the Civil War.
1944 ?m/C Dennis Moore, Lionel Atwill, Regis Toomey, Wanda McKay. VHS $29.99 MOV *ℑ*½

Raiders of Red Gap A cattle company tries running homesteaders off their land to get control of it. The Lone Rider saves the day.
1943 56m/B Al "Fuzzy" St. John, Bob Livingston. VHS, Beta $19.98 DVT, VYY, VCN *ℑ*½

Raiders of Sunset Pass Wartime western quickie makes an interesting novelty today. With most cowboys off fighting the Axis, the ladies form the Women's Army of the Plains to watch out for 4-F rustlers.
1943 57m/B Eddie Dew, Smiley Burnette, Jennifer Holt, Roy Barcroft, Mozelle Cravens, Beverly Aadland, Nancy Worth, Kenne Duncan, Jack Rockwell, Budd Buster, Jack Ingram; D: John English. VHS $19.95 NOS, HEG *ℑℑ*

Raiders of the Border A white-hatted cowboy must prevent the takeover of a trading post.
1944 55m/B Johnny Mack Brown, Raymond Hatton, Ellen Hall. VHS, Beta $19.95 VDM *ℑ*

Raiders of the Lost Ark Classic '30s-style adventure reminiscent of early serials spawned two sequels and numerous rip-offs. Made Ford a household name as dashing hero and intrepid archeologist Indiana Jones. He battles mean Nazis, decodes hieroglyphics, fights his fear of snakes, and even has time for a little romance in his quest for the biblical Ark of the Covenant. Allen is perfectly cast as his feisty ex-flame, more than a little irritated with the smooth talker who dumped her years earlier. Asks viewers to suspend belief as every chase and stunt tops the last. Unrelated opening sequence does a great job of introducing the character. Followed by "Indiana Jones and the Temple of Doom."
1981 (PG) 115m/C Harrison Ford, Karen Allen, Wolf Kahler, Paul Freeman, John Rhys-Davies, Denholm Elliott, Ronald Lacey, Anthony Higgins, Alfred Molina; D: Steven Spielberg; W: George Lucas, Philip Kaufman; M: John Williams. Academy Awards '81: Best Art Direction/Set Decoration, Best Film Editing, Best Sound, Best Visual Effects; Nominations: Best Cinematography, Best Director (Spielberg), Best Picture, Best Original Score; People's Choice Awards '82: Best Film. VHS, Beta, 8mm $14.95 PAR *ℑℑℑℑ*

Raiders of the Sun After the Earth has been ruined in a biological disaster, a futuristic warrior arrives to help restore world peace and order. Cheap "Mad Max" ripoff.
1992 (R) 80m/C Richard Norton, Rick Dean, William Steis, Blake Boyd, Brigitta Stenberg; D: Cirio H. Santiago. VHS $89.98 NHO *ℑ*

Railroaded The police seek a demented criminal who kills his victims with perfumed-soaked bullets. Tense, excellent noir Anothony Mann crime drama.
1947 72m/B John Ireland, Sheila Ryan, Hugh Beaumont, Ed Kelly; D: Anthony Mann. VHS, Beta $19.95 NOS, NWV, DVT *ℑℑ*

Railrodder Buster Keaton as the railroader in this slapstick short fumbles his way across Canada. As in the days of the silents, he speaks not a word.
1965 25m/C Buster Keaton. VHS, Beta NFB *ℑℑℑ*

Railway Children At the turn of the century in England, the father of three children is framed and sent to prison during Christmas. The trio and their mother must survive on a poverty stricken farm near the railroad tracks. They eventually meet a new friend who helps them prove their father's innocence. Wonderfully directed by Jeffries. From the classic Edith Nesbitt children's novel.
1970 104m/C Jenny Agutter, William Mervyn, Bernard Cribbins, Dinah Sheridan, Iain Cuthbertson; D: Lionel Jeffries. VHS, Beta NO *ℑℑℑ*½

The Railway Station Man Set in present-day Ireland. Christie plays a widowed artist struggling to put her life back together after her husband's death in a terrorist bombing. She meets a mysterious American (Sutherland) who's working on restoring the local railway station and finds herself falling in love. When she stumbles upon an IRA bombing plot she also finds out some unpleasant truths about her new lover. Wonderful performances, tragic story. Shot on location in County Donegal, Northern Ireland. Based on the novel by Jennifer Johnston. Made for cable television.
1992 93m/C Julie Christie, Donald Sutherland, John Lynch, Mandy Tandy, Frank McCusker, Niall Cusack; D: Michael Whyte; W: Shelagh Delaney. VHS, Beta $89.98 TTC *ℑℑℑ*

Rain W. Somerset Maugham's tale of a puritanical minister's attempt to reclaim a "lost woman" on the island of Pago Pago. Crawford and Huston work up some static. Remake of the 1928 silent film "Sadie Thompson." Remade again in 1953 as "Miss Sadie Thompson."
1932 92m/B Joan Crawford, Walter Huston, William Gargan, Guy Kibbee, Beulah Bondi, Walter Catlett; D: Lewis Milestone. VHS, Beta $8.95 CNG, NOS, VCI *ℑℑ*½

The Rain Killer Big city cop and fed don goloshes to track serial killer who slays rich ladies during heavy precipitation. Soggy story.
1990 (R) 94m/C Ray Sharkey, David Beecroft, Maria Ford, Woody Brown, Tania Coleridge; D: Ken Stein; W: Ray Cunneff. VHS $89.95 COL *ℑ*

Rain Man When his father dies, ambitious and self-centered Charlie Babbit finds he has an older autistic brother who's been institutionalized for years. Needing him to claim an inheritance, he liberates him from the institution and takes to the road, where both brothers undergo subtle changes. The Vegas montage is wonderful. Critically acclaimed drama and a labor of love for the entire cast. Cruise's best performance to date as he goes from cad to recognizing something wonderfully human in his brother and himself. Hoffman is exceptional.

1988 (R) 128m/C Dustin Hoffman, Tom Cruise, Valeria Golino, Jerry Molen, Jack Murdock, Michael D. Roberts, Ralph Seymour, Lucinda Jenney, Bonnie Hunt, Kim Robillard, Beth Grant; **D:** Barry Levinson; **W:** Ronald Bass. Academy Awards '88: Best Actor (Hoffman), Best Director (Levinson), Best Original Screenplay, Best Picture; Nominations: Best Art Direction/Set Decoration, Best Cinematography, Best Film Editing, Best Original Score; Berlin International Film Festival '88: Golden Berlin Bear; Directors Guild of America Awards '88: Best Director (Levinson); Golden Globe Awards '89: Best Actor—Drama (Hoffman), Best Film—Drama; People's Choice Awards '89: Best Film—Drama. **VHS, Beta, 8mm $19.98** MGM, BTV, JCF ✓✓✓½

The Rain People Pregnant housewife Knight takes to the road in desperation and boredom; along the way she meets retarded ex-football player Caan. Well directed by Coppola from his original script. Pensive drama.

1969 (R) 102m/C Shirley Knight, James Caan, Robert Duvall; **D:** Francis Ford Coppola; **W:** Francis Ford Coppola. **VHS, Beta $19.98** WAR ✓✓✓

Rainbow Broadway's "Annie" is badly miscast as Judy Garland from her early years in vaudeville to her starring years at M.G.M. Based on the book by Christopher Finch. Made for television; directed by sometime Garland flame Jackie Cooper.

1978 100m/C Andrea McArdle, Jack Carter, Don Murray; **D:** Jackie Cooper; **M:** Charles Fox. **VHS, Beta** NO ✓✓

The Rainbow Mature, literate rendering of the classic D.H. Lawrence novel about a young woman's sexual awakening. Beautiful cinematography. Companion/prequel to director Russell's earlier Lawrence adaptation, "Women in Love" (1969).

1989 (R) 104m/C Sammi Davis-Voss, Amanda Donohoe, Paul McGann, Christopher Gable, David Hemmings, Glenda Jackson, Kenneth Colley; **D:** Ken Russell; **W:** Vivian Russell, Ken Russell; **M:** Carl Davis. **VHS $49.95** VES, IME ✓✓✓

Rainbow Bridge The adventures of a group of hippies searching for their consciousness in Hawaii. Features concert footage from Jimi Hendrix's final performance.

1971 (R) 74m/C D: Chuck Wein. **VHS, Beta $19.95** RHI, FCT ✓

Rainbow Drive Made for cable tv cop thriller promises great things but fails to deliver. Weller is a good cop trapped in the political intrigues of Hollywood. He discovers five dead bodies; when the official count is four, he detects funny business. From the novel by Roderick Thorp.

1990 (R) 93m/C Peter Weller, Sela Ward, Bruce Weitz, David Caruso, James Laurenson, Chris Mulkey, Kathryn Harrold; **D:** Bobby Roth; **W:** Roderick Thorp, Bill Phillips, Bennett Cohen; **M:** Tangerine Dream. **VHS $89.95** BTV, VMK ✓✓½

The Rainbow Gang A trio of unlikely prospectors heads into a legendary mine in search of riches and fame.

1973 90m/C Donald Pleasence, Don Calfa, Kate Reid. **VHS, Beta $19.95** NWV ✓

Rainbow Ranch A Navy boxer returns home to his ranch to find murder and corruption. Needless to say, he rides off to seek revenge.

1933 54m/B Rex Bell, Cecilia Parker, Robert F. (Bob) Kortman, Henry Hall, Gordon DeMain; **D:** Harry Fraser. **VHS, Beta $19.95** NOS, DVT, HEG ✓½

Rainbow's End Gibson must defend Gale, the female rancher, from an evil adversary who is trying to run Gale and her invalid father off of their land. Things get complicat-

ed when Gibson discovers that Stark works for his father!

1935 54m/B Hoot Gibson, June Gale, Oscar Apfel, Ada Ince, Charles Hill, Warner Richmond; **D:** Norman Spencer. **VHS $19.95** NOS, DVT ✓✓

The Rainmaker Reminiscent of "Elmer Gantry" in his masterful performance, Lancaster makes it all believable as a con man who comes to a small midwestern town and works miracles not only on the weather but on spinster Hepburn, although both were a little long in the tooth for their roles. Written by Nash from his own play.

1956 121m/C Burt Lancaster, Katharine Hepburn, Wendell Corey, Lloyd Bridges, Earl Holliman, Cameron Prudhomme, Wallace Ford; **D:** Joseph Anthony; **W:** N. Richard Nash. Academy Awards '56 Nominations: Best Actress (Hepburn), Best Original Score; Golden Globe Awards '57: Best Supporting Actor (Holliman). **VHS $14.95** PAR, CCB ✓✓✓

The Rains Came Living within a loveless marriage in the mythical Indian city of Ranchipur, English socialite Loy pursues extramarital love interests, including the compassionate doctor Power, potential heir to the maharajah's throne. When an earthquake hits and brings major destruction to the city, Loy aids the doctor in helping the injured. Hankies should be kept handy. Adapted from the Louis Bromfield novel.

1939 104m/B Myrna Loy, Tyrone Power, George Brent, Brenda Joyce, Nigel Bruce, Maria Ouspenskaya, Joseph Schildkraut, Laura Hope Crews, Marilyn Nash, Jane Darwell, Marjorie Rambeau, Henry Travers, H.B. Warner, William Royle, Montague Shaw, Harry Hayden, Abner Biberman, George Regas; **D:** Clarence Brown; **W:** Philip Dunne, Julien Josephson; **M:** Alfred Newman. **VHS $19.99** FXV ✓✓½

Raintree County A lavish, somewhat overdone epic about two lovers caught up in the national turmoil of the Civil War. An Indiana teacher (Clift) marries a southern belle (Taylor) just after the outbreak of war. The new wife battles mental illness. Producers had hoped this would be another "Gone With the Wind." Adapted from the novel by Ross Lockridge, Jr. Film was delayed in mid-production by Clift's near-fatal and disfiguring car crash.

1957 175m/C Elizabeth Taylor, Montgomery Clift, Eva Marie Saint, Lee Marvin, Nigel Patrick, Rod Taylor, Agnes Moorehead, Walter Abel; **D:** Edward Dmytryk. **VHS, Beta $29.98** MGM ✓✓½

Rainy Day A successful actress' return home for her father's funeral brings back unpleasant childhood memories that force her to face the truth about herself.

1979 35m/C Mariette Hartley. **VHS, Beta** LCA ✓✓

Raise the Red Lantern Set in 1920s China, Zhang explores its claustrophobic world of privilege and humiliation. Songlian, an educated 19-year-old beauty, is forced into marriage as the fourth wife of a wealthy and powerful old man. She discovers that the wives have their own separate quarters and servants, and spend most of their time battling to attract their husband's attention. Over the course of a year, Songlian's fury and resentment grow until self-defeating rebellion is all she has. Gong Li is exquisite as the young woman struggling for dignity in a portrayal which is both both haunting and tragic.

1991 (PG) 125m/C Gong Li, Ma Jingwu, He Caifei, Cao Cuifeng, Jin Shuyuan, Kong Lin, Ding Weimin; **D:** Zhang Yimou. Academy Awards '91 Nominations: Best Foreign Language Film; New York Film Critics Awards '92: Best Foreign Film. **VHS $79.98** ORI, ING, BTV ✓✓✓½

Raise the Titanic A disaster about a disaster. Horrible script cannot be redeemed by purported thrill of the ship's emergence from the deep after 70 years. It's a shame, because the free world's security hangs in the balance. Based on Clive Cussler's best seller.

1980 (PG) 112m/C Jason Robards Jr., Richard Jordan, Anne Archer, Alec Guinness, J.D. Cannon; **D:** Jerry Jameson; **M:** John Barry. **VHS, Beta $29.98** FOX Woof!

A Raisin in the Sun Outstanding story of a black family trying to make a better life for themselves in an all-white neighborhood in Chicago. The characters are played realistically and make for a moving story. Each person struggles with doing what he must while still maintaining his dignity and sense of self. Based on the Broadway play by Hansberry, who also wrote the screenplay.

1961 128m/B Diana Sands, John Fiedler, Ivan Dixon, Louis Gossett Jr., Sidney Poitier, Claudia McNeil, Ruby Dee; **D:** Daniel Petrie; **W:** Lorraine Hansberry. **VHS, Beta $14.95** COL, HMV ✓✓✓✓

A Raisin in the Sun An "American Playhouse," made for television presentation of the Lorraine Hansberry play about a black family threatened with dissolution by the outside forces of racism and greed when they move into an all-white neighborhood in the 1950s.

1989 171m/C Danny Glover, Esther Rolle, Starletta DuPois; **D:** Bill Duke. **VHS, Beta $69.95** FRH ✓✓✓

Raising Arizona Hi's an ex-con and the world's worst hold-up man. Ed's a police-woman. They meet, fall in love, marry, and kidnap a baby (one of a family of quints). Why not? Ed's infertile and the family they took the baby from has "more than enough," so who will notice? But unfinished furniture tycoon Nathan Arizona wants his baby back, even if he has to hire an axe-murderer on a motorcycle to do it. A brilliant, original comedy narrated in notorious loopy deadpan style by Cage. Innovative camerawork by Barry Sonnenfeld. Wild, surreal and hilarious.

1987 (PG-13) 94m/C Nicolas Cage, Holly Hunter, John Goodman, William Forsythe, Randall "Tex" Cobb, Trey Wilson, M. Emmet Walsh, Frances McDormand; **D:** Joel Coen; **W:** Ethan Coen, Joel Coen; **M:** Carter Burwell. **VHS, Beta $19.98** FOX ✓✓✓½

Raising Cain Thriller evoking poor man's Hitchcock about a child psychiatrist who just happens to be nuts features Lithgow in five roles. Seems his supposedly dead Norwegian father has come to the United States and needs his son's help to steal babies for a child development experiment, so the son's alter ego, Cain, shows up to commit the nasty deed. Unfortunately Lithgow also catches his wife with another man, and that's when the bodies start piling up.

1992 (R) 95m/C John Lithgow, Lolita Davidovich, Steven Bauer, Frances Sternhagen, Cindy Girard, Tom Bower, Mel Harris, Gabrielle Carteris, Barton Heyman; **D:** Brian DePalma; **W:** Brian DePalma; **M:** Pino Donaggio. **VHS, Beta** MCA ✓✓

Rambling Rose Dern is Rose, a free-spirited, sexually liberated before her time young woman taken in by a Southern family in 1935. Rose immediately has an impact on the male members of the clan, father Duvall and son Haas, thanks to her insuppressible sexuality. This causes consternation with the strait-laced patriarch, who attempts to control his desire for the girl. Eventually Rose decides she must try to stick to one man, but this only causes further problems. Dern gives her best performance yet in this excellent

period piece, and solid support is offered from the rest of the cast, in particular Duvall and Dern's real-life mother Ladd.
1991 (R) 115m/C Laura Dern, Diane Ladd, Robert Duvall, Lukas Haas, John Heard, Kevin Conway, Robert Burke, Lisa Jakub, Evan Lockwood; *D:* Martha Coolidge; *W:* Calder Willingham; *M:* Elmer Bernstein. Academy Awards '91 Nominations: Best Actress (Dern), Best Supporting Actress (Ladd); Independent Spirit Awards '92: Best Director (Coolidge), Best Film, Best Supporting Actress (Ladd). **VHS $19.98** *LIV* 🐾🐾🐾

Rambo: First Blood, Part 2 If anyone can save Our Boys still held prisoner in Asia it's John Rambo. Along the way he's tortured, flexes biceps, grunts, and then disposes of the bad guys by the dozen in one of filmdom's bigger dead body parades. Mindless action best enjoyed by testosterone-driven fans of the genre. Sequel to "First Blood" (1982); followed by "Rambo 3" (1988).
1985 (R) 93m/C Sylvester Stallone, Richard Crenna, Charles Napier, Steven Berkoff, Julia Nickson-Soul, Martin Kove; *D:* George P. Cosmatos; *W:* Sylvester Stallone; *M:* Jerry Goldsmith. **VHS, Beta $14.95** *LIV* 🐾🐾

Rambo 3 John Rambo, the famous Vietnam vet turned Buddhist monk, this time invades Afghanistan to rescue his mentor. Meets up with orphan and fights his way around the country. Typically exploitative, kill now, ask questions later Rambo attack, lacking the sheer volume of no-brainer action of the first two Rambos. At the time, the most expensive film ever made, costing $58 million. Filmed in Israel.
1988 (R) 102m/C Sylvester Stallone, Richard Crenna, Marc De Jonge, Kurtwood Smith, Spiros Focas; *D:* Peter McDonald; *W:* Sylvester Stallone; *M:* Jerry Goldsmith. **VHS, Beta $14.95** *LIV* 🐾½

Rampage Seemingly all-American guy Charles Reece (McArthur) goes on a murder spree, killing and then mutiliating his victims. Fraser (Biehn) is a liberal district attorney who questions his own views as he argues during the trial that Reece was sane when he committed the murders and deserves the death penalty. Director Friedkin makes no bones about his concerns that the criminal insanity defense often spares the perpetrator while denying justice to the victims. Adapted from the book by William P. Wood and loosely based on killer Richard Chase. Filmed in 1987, the movie wasn't released until 1992 due to the production company's financial difficulties.
1987 (R) 92m/C Michael Biehn, Alex McArthur, Nicholas Campbell, Deborah Van Valkenburgh, John Harkins, Art LaFleur; *D:* William Friedkin; *W:* William Friedkin; *M:* Ennio Morricone. **VHS, Beta $92.95** *PAR, BTV* 🐾🐾

Ramparts of Clay A young woman in Tunisia walks the line between her village's traditional way of life and the modern world just after her country's independence from France. Brilliantly shot on location; exquisitely poignant. In Arabic with English subtitles.
1971 (PG) 87m/C *D:* Jean-Louis Bertucelli. **VHS, Beta $59.95** *COL, ING* 🐾🐾🐾

Ramrod Lake is a tough ranch owner at odds with her father, who is being manipulated by a big-time cattleman into trying to put them out of business. She fights back, and McCrea is caught in the middle as the only good guy. Nothing special.
1947 94m/B Veronica Lake, Joel McCrea, Arleen Whelan, Don DeFore, Preston Foster, Charlie Ruggles, Donald Crisp, Lloyd Bridges; *D:* Andre de Toth. **VHS $14.95** *REP* 🐾🐾

The Ramrodder An adult western spoof. *AKA:* Ramrodders.
1969 92m/C VHS, Beta $19.95 *VDM, TPV* 🐾

Ran The culmination of Kurosawa's career stands as his masterpiece. Loosely adapting Shakespeare's "King Lear," with plot elements from "Macbeth," he's fashioned an epic, heartbreaking statement about honor, ambition, and the futility of war. Aging medieval warlord Hidetora gives control of his empire to his oldest son, creating conflict with two other sons. Soon he's an outcast, as ambition and greed seize the two sons. Stunning battle scenes illuminate the full-blown tragedy of Kurosawa's vision. Superb acting with a scene-stealing Harada as the revenge-minded Lady Kaede; period costumes took three years to create. Japanese with English subtitles.
1985 (R) 160m/C Tatsuya Nakadai, Akira Terao, Jinpachi Nesu, Daisuke Ryu, Meiko Harada, Hisashi Igawa, Peter; *D:* Akira Kurosawa; *W:* Akira Kurosawa, Hideo Oguni, Masato Ide; *M:* Toru Takemitsu. Academy Awards '85: Best Costume Design; Nominations: Best Art Direction/Set Decoration, Best Cinematography, Best Director (Kurosawa); New York Film Critics Awards '85: Best Foreign Film; National Society of Film Critics Awards '85: Best Film. **VHS, Beta $19.98** *FOX, APD, ING* 🐾🐾🐾🐾

Rana: The Legend of Shadow Lake Gold at the bottom of a lake is guarded by a frog-monster, but treasure hunters try to retrieve it anyway.
1975 96m/C Alan Ross, Karen McDiarmid, Jerry Gregoris. VHS, Beta $24.95 *AHV* 🐾

The Ranch An executive who loses everything inherits a dilapidated ranch and renovates it into a health spa.
1988 (PG-13) 97m/C Andrew Stevens, Gary Fjelgaard, Lou Ann Schmidt, Elizabeth Keefe; *D:* Stella Stevens. **VHS, Beta $14.95** *HMD* 🐾

Rancho Deluxe Off-beat western spoof starring Bridges and Waterston as two carefree cowpokes. Cult favorite featuring music by Buffett, who also appears in the film.
1975 93m/C Jeff Bridges, Sam Waterston, Elizabeth Ashley, Charlene Dallas, Clifton James, Slim Pickens, Harry Dean Stanton, Richard Bright, Jimmy Buffett; *D:* Frank Perry; *W:* Thomas McGuane; *M:* Jimmy Buffett. **VHS $19.98** *MGM* 🐾🐾🐾

Rancho Notorious Kennedy, on the trail of his girlfriend's murderer, falls for dance hall girl Dietrich. Fine acting. A "period" sample of 50's westerns, but different. A must for Dietrich fans.
1952 89m/C Marlene Dietrich, Arthur Kennedy, Mel Ferrer, William Frawley, Jack Elam, George Reeves; *D:* Fritz Lang; *W:* Daniel Taradash. **VHS, Beta $15.95** *VCI* 🐾🐾🐾

Random Harvest A masterful, tearjerking film based on the James Hilton novel. A shell-shocked WWI amnesiac meets and is made happy by a beautiful music hall dancer. He regains his memory and forgets about the dancer and their child. This is Garson's finest hour, and a shamelessly potent sobfest.
1942 126m/B Greer Garson, Ronald Colman, Reginald Owen, Philip Dorn, Susan Peters, Henry Travers, Margaret Wycherly, Bramwell Fletcher; *D:* Mervyn LeRoy. **VHS, Beta $19.98** *MGM* 🐾🐾🐾

Randy Rides Alone Very young Wayne is good in this slappable but pleasant B effort. Wayne single-handedly cleans up the territory and rids the land of a passel o'bad guys.
1934 53m/B John Wayne, Alberta Vaughn, George "Gabby" Hayes; *D:* Harry Fraser. **VHS, Beta $9.98** *REP, NOS, VCN* 🐾🐾

Range Busters Range Busters are called in to find the identity of the phantom killer.
1940 55m/B Ray Corrigan, Max Terhune. **VHS, Beta $19.95** *NOS, VCN, DVT* 🐾

Range Feud Wayne is a ranch owner's son falsely accused of murder. Just as he's about to hang, Jones, as the heroic sheriff, saves the day and reveals the real killer's identity.
1931 58m/B Buck Jones, John Wayne, Susan Fleming, William Walling, Wallace MacDonald, Harry Woods, Ed LeSaint; *D:* David Ross Lederman. **VHS $14.95** *COL* 🐾½

The Range Feud/Two Fisted Law Two early, short Wayne oaters which reveal the Duke developing the drawl, gait and pleasingly profane style that would carry him to fame. In "Feud" he is a young rancher accused of murdering a cattle rustler. "Law" finds him playing a character named Duke who loses his land and girl to a neighboring land grabber.
1931 112m/C Buck Jones, Tim McCoy, John Wayne, Susan Fleming, Alice Faye, Walter Brennan; *D:* David Ross Lederman. **VHS $19.95** *COL* 🐾🐾

Range Law Another entry in the infamous Maynard series of horseplay, cliche, and repetitive plot elements.
1931 60m/B Ken Maynard, Charles "Blackie" King, Lafe McKee. **VHS, Beta $9.95** *GPV, VCI, DVT* 🐾

Range Law Ranchers are being terrorized for their silver mine and its up to Brown and Hatton to catch the villains.
1944 59m/B Johnny Mack Brown, Raymond Hatton, Lloyd Ingraham, Sarah Padden, Ellen Hall, Steve Clark, Jack Ingram, Bud Osborne; *D:* Lambert Hillyer. **VHS $11.95** *GPV* 🐾½

Range Renegades Sheriff Wakely and his pals have their hands full when his deputy gets involved with the leader of a gang of outlaw women. Predictable B oater reflects the then developing trend of using wicked female characters in westerns. Paved the way for films like "Johnny Guitar" and "Rancho Notorious."
1948 54m/B Jimmy Wakely, Dub Taylor, Dennis Moore, Jennifer Holt, John James, Steve Clark, Frank LaRue; *D:* Lambert Hillyer; *W:* Ronald Davidson, William Lively. **VHS $19.99** *MOV* 🐾½

Range Rider Eight episodes of the series are on four tapes, including "Greed Rides the Range," "Silver Blade," and "Fatal Bullet."
1952 60m/B Jock Mahoney. **VHS, Beta** *DVT* 🐾½

Range Riders A gunman poses as a wimp and cleans out an outlaw gang.
1935 46m/B Buddy Roosevelt. **VHS, Beta** *NO* 🐾½

Rangeland Empire Shamrock and Lucky are at it again, implicated as being members of an outlaw gang until that gang attacks them.
1950 59m/B James Ellison, Russell Hayden, Stanley Price, John Cason. **VHS, Beta** *NO* 🐾

Rangeland Racket The Lone Rider (Houston) has been wrongly accused of a crime.
1941 60m/B George Houston, Hillary Brooke, Al "Fuzzy" St. John. **VHS, Beta $19.95** *VYY* 🐾½

Ranger and the Lady Texas Ranger Rodgers romances the woman who is the leader of a wagon train.
1940 54m/B Roy Rogers, George "Gabby" Hayes; *D:* Joseph Kane. **VHS, Beta $19.95** *NOS, DVT* 🐾½

Ranger's Roundup The Rangers prove their courage by rounding up an outlaw gang.

1938 57m/B Fred Scott, Al ''Fuzzy'' St. John. VHS, Beta $19.95 NOS, DVT 𝒵

The Rangers Step In Allen leaves the Texas Rangers when a feud between his family and that of the girl he loves heats up again. Turns out rustlers are stirring things up in order to get some of the disputed land.
1937 56m/B Robert Allen, Eleanor Stewart, John Merton, Hal Taliaferro, Jack Ingram, Jack Rockwell, Lafe McKee, Robert F. (Bob) Kortman; **D:** Spencer Gordon Bennet. VHS $11.95 GPV 𝒵½

Rangers Take Over Gunlords are driven out by the Texas Rangers.
1943 62m/B Dave O'Brien, James Newill. VHS, Beta $19.95 NOS, VYY, DVT 𝒵½

Ransom Money A kidnapping scheme involving millions of dollars, in and around the Grand Canyon, backfires.
1988 87m/C Broderick Crawford, Rachel Romen, Gordon Jump, Randy Whipple; **D:** DeWitt Lee. VHS, Beta $9.95 SIM 𝒵½

Ranson's Folly Barthelmess makes a wager that he can impersonate a famous outlaw well enough to rob a stage with only a pair of scissors. When the army paymaster is killed, guess who gets caught with his swash unbuckled?
1926 80m/B Richard Barthelmess, Dorothy Mackaill, Anders Randolf, Pat Hartigan, Brooks Benedict; **D:** Sidney Olcott. VHS, Beta $19.95 GPV 𝒵𝒵½

Rap Master Ronnie Reagan-era social phenomena are targeted in a series of musical sketches/parodies. Based on an off-Broadway hit.
1988 60m/C Jim Morris, Carol Kane, Jon Cryer, Dick Smothers, Tom Smothers; **D:** Jay Dubin. VHS, Beta $39.99 HBO, TLF 𝒵½

Rape Two guys investigate a third pal's mysterious death. They discover that his supernatural-power-imbued girlfriend is at the root of the matter.
198? 90m/C Rick Joss, Gil Vidal. VHS, Beta NO 𝒵

Rape and Marriage: The Rideout Case The true story of an Oregon wife who accused her husband of rape. Thoughtfully explores the legal and moral questions raised by the case. Interpreted well enough, though not superbly, by a decent cast. although Rourke is a little too intense. Made for television.
1980 96m/C Mickey Rourke, Linda Hamilton, Rip Torn, Eugene Roche, Conchata Ferrell, Gail Strickland, Bonnie Bartlett, Alley Mills; **D:** Peter Levin. VHS, Beta $49.95 LIV 𝒵𝒵½

Rape of Love The story begins with one of the most chilling rape scenes on film and then attempts to analyze the emotional impact of rape on its victim. Well-acted and directed. In French with English subtitles.
1979 117m/C Nathalie Nell, Alain Foures; **D:** Yannick Bellon. VHS, Beta $59.95 COL, ING 𝒵𝒵½

The Rape of the Sabines The story of Romulus, king of Rome, and how he led the Romans to capture the women of Sabina. The battles rage, the women plot, and Romulus fights and lusts. Dubbed in English. **AKA:** El Rapto de las Sabinas; The Mating of the Sabine Women; Shame of the Sabine Women.
1961 101m/C Roger Moore, Mylene Demongeot, Jean Marais; **D:** Richard Pottier. VHS, Beta $29.95 UNI Woof!

Rapid Fire Cheap, made-for-video quickie about a good guy U.S. agent who battles terrorists. Easy to skip.

1989 90m/C Joe Spinell, Michael Wayne, Ron Waldron; **D:** David A. Prior. VHS, Beta $79.95 AIP 𝒵

Rapid Fire Lee (son of martial arts cult film star Bruce Lee) is a Chinese-American art student who also happens to be a martial arts expert. He's tapped by the police to help stem the violence between the Asian and Italian gangs fighting for control over Chicago's drug trade. Typical martial arts movie is made better by uniquely choreographed action sequences and Lee's attractive presence.
1992 (R) 96m/C Brandon Lee, Powers Boothe, Nick Mancuso, Raymond J. Barry, Kate Hodge, Tzi Ma, Tony Longo, Michael Paul Chan, Dustin Nguyen, John Vickery; **D:** Dwight Little; **W:** Alan B. McElroy, Cindy Cirile, Paul Attanasio; **M:** Christopher Young. VHS $19.98 FXV 𝒵𝒵½

Rappaccini's Daughter Adaptation of a Nathaniel Hawthorne short story about a doctor's daughter who is cursed with the ability to kill anything she touches. Made for television.
1980 59m/C Kathleen Beller, Kristopher Tabori, Michael Egan; **D:** Dezso Magyar. VHS, Beta $24.95 MON, MTI, KAR 𝒵½

Rappin' Ex-con Van Peebles gets into it with the landlord and a street gang leader. Forgettable action/music drivel. ♫Rappin'; Two of a Kind; Call Me; Born to Love; Killer; Itching for a Scratch; Snack Attack; Dodge; Golly Gee.
1985 (PG) 92m/C Mario Van Peebles, Tasia Valenza, Harry Goz, Charles Flohe; **D:** Joel Silberg. VHS, Beta $14.95 MGM 𝒵

The Rapture A beautiful telephone operator engages in indiscrimate sexual adventures to relieve the boredom of her job and life. She becomes curious by, and eventually converted to, evangelical Christianity, which leads her to a contented marriage and the birth of a daughter. When her husband is tragically killed she becomes convinced that she and her child will be taken by God into heaven if she only waits for the proper sign.
1991 (R) 100m/C Mimi Rogers, David Duchovny, Patrick Bauchau, Will Patton; **D:** Michael Tolkin; **W:** Michael Tolkin. VHS $19.95 COL 𝒵𝒵

Rapunzel A beautiful young woman locked in a tall tower is saved by the handsome prince who climbs her golden tresses. Part of Shelly Duvall's ''Faerie Tale Theatre'' series.
1982 60m/C Shelley Duvall, Gena Rowlands, Jeff Bridges. VHS, Beta $14.95 KUI, FOX, FCT 𝒵𝒵

The Rare Breed Plodding but pleasant Western. A no-strings ranch hand (Stewart) agrees to escort a Hereford Bull to Texas, where the widow of an English breeder plans to crossbreed the bull with longhorn cattle. The widow (O'Hara) insists that she and her daughter accompany Stewart on the trip, which features every kind of western calamity imaginable. When all others believe the attempt to crossbreed has failed, Stewart sets out to prove them wrong.
1966 97m/C James Stewart, Maureen O'Hara, Brian Keith, Juliet Mills, Jack Elam, Ben Johnson; **D:** Andrew V. McLaglen; **M:** John Williams. VHS, Beta $19.95 MCA 𝒵𝒵½

A Rare Breed Real-life story of a kidnapped horse in Italy and a young girl's quest to retrieve it. Directed by David Nelson of television's ''Ozzie and Harriet'' fame, this movie is cute and old-fashioned.
1981 (PG) 94m/C George Kennedy, Forrest Tucker, Tracy Vaccaro, Tom Hallick, Don DeFore; **D:** David Nelson. VHS, Beta $19.95 STE, LIV 𝒵½

Rascal Dazzle Montage-like tribute to that best-loved group of children, the Our Gang kids. Narrated by Jerry Lewis. Includes scenes with Spanky, Alfalfa, Darla and the rest of the gang.
1981 100m/B VHS, Beta $39.98 SUE 𝒵½

The Rascals An irrepressible youth at a rural Catholic boys' school comes of age.
1981 (R) 93m/C Thomas Chabrol; **D:** Bernard Revon. VHS, Beta $29.98 SUE 𝒵𝒵½

Rashomon In 12th century Japan, two travelers attempt to discover the truth about an ambush/rape/murder. They get four completely different versions of the incident from the three people involved in the crime and the single witness. An insightful masterpiece that established Kurosawa and Japanese cinema as major artistic forces. Fine performances, particularly Mifune as the bandit. Visually beautiful and rhythmic. Remade as a western, ''The Outrage,'' in 1964. In Japanese with English subtitles. **AKA:** In the Woods.
1951 83m/B Machiko Kyo, Toshiro Mifune, Masayuki Mori, Takashi Shimura; **D:** Akira Kurosawa; **W:** Akira Kurosawa. Academy Awards '51: Best Foreign Language Film; Nominations: Best Art Direction/Set Decoration (B & W); National Board of Review Awards '51: 5 Best Foreign Films of the Year, Best Director (Kurosawa). VHS, Beta $29.98 SUE, CRC, VYG 𝒵𝒵𝒵𝒵

Rasputin The long-censored and banned film of the story of the mad monk and his domination of the royal family before the Russian Revolution. Petrenko is superb. First released in the United States in 1988. In Russian with English subtitles. **AKA:** Agoniya.
1985 104m/C Alexei Petrenko, Anatoly Romashin, Velta Linne, Alice Freindlikh; **D:** Elem Klimov; **W:** Semyon Lunghin, Ilya Nusinov; **M:** Alfred Shnitke. VHS, Beta $79.95 WBF, ING 𝒵𝒵𝒵

Rasputin and the Empress Lavish historical epic teamed the three Barrymore sibs for the first and only time, as they vied for scene-stealing honors. Ethel is Empress Alexandra of Russia, tied to the weak-willed Nicholas II (Morgan) and under the spell of Rasputin, played by Lionel. John is a nobleman who seeks to warn the Russian rulers of their perilous perch on the throne, made only worse by Rasputin's spreading power and corruption. Ethel's first talkie and Wyngard's first film role. Uncredited director Charles Brabin was replaced by Boleslawski due to his incompatability with the imperious Ethel. **AKA:** Rasputin: The Mad Monk.
1932 123m/B Ethel Barrymore, John Barrymore, Lionel Barrymore, Ralph Morgan, Diana Wynyard, Tad Alexander, C. Henry Gordon, Edward Arnold, Gustav von Seyffertitz, Anne Shirley, Jean Parker, Henry Kolker; **D:** Richard Boleslawski; **W:** Charles MacArthur. VHS $19.98 MGM, MOV 𝒵𝒵𝒵

Rat Pfink a Boo-Boo Parody on ''Batman'' in which a bumbling superhero and his sidekick race around saving people. Notoriously inept. Title story is legendary—it was misspelled accidentally and Steckler didn't have the cash to fix it.
1966 72m/B Vin Saxon, Carolyn Brandt, Titus Moede, Mike Kannon; **D:** Ray Dennis Steckler. VHS, Beta NO Woof!

The Rat Race A dancer and a musician venture to Manhattan to make it big, and end up sharing an apartment. Their relationship starts pleasantly and becomes romantic. Enjoyable farce. Well photographed and scripted, with the supporting characters stealing the show.

1960 105m/C Tony Curtis, Debbie Reynolds, Jack Oakie, Kay Medford, Don Rickles, Joe Bushkin; **D:** Robert Mulligan; **M:** Elmer Bernstein. **VHS** PAR ⅋⅋⅋

Ratboy An unscrupulous woman attempts to transform a boy with a rat's face into a celebrity, with tragic results. First directorial effort by Locke that gradually loses steam. 1986 (PG-13) 105m/C Sondra Locke, Sharon Baird, Robert Townsend; **D:** Sondra Locke; **W:** Rob Thompson; **M:** Stephen Dorff. **VHS, Beta** $79.95 WAR ⅋⅋½

Rate It X Sexism in a variety of national institutions, from pornography to consumerism, is revealed through the average man on the street via microphone interviews. 1986 (R) 95m/C **D:** Lucy Winer, Paula de Koenigsberg. **VHS, Beta** $59.95 LIV ⅋⅋½

Ratings Game A bitter, out-of-work actor and a woman who works at the ratings service manage to mess up the television industry. Early directorial effort by DeVito is uneven but funny. Made for cable television. **AKA:** The Mogul. 1984 102m/C Danny DeVito, Rhea Perlman, Gerrit Graham, Kevin McCarthy, Jayne Meadows, Steve Allen, Ronny Graham, George Wenolt; **D:** Danny DeVito. **VHS, Beta** $79.95 PAR, VTR ⅋⅋

Rats In 2225, the beleaguered survivors of a nuclear holocaust struggle with a mutant rodent problem. 1983 100m/C Richard Raymond, Richard Cross; **D:** Vincent Dawn. **VHS, Beta** NO ⅋⅋

The Rats are Coming! The Werewolves are Here! Low budget schlock revolves around a family of werewolves and the daughter who decides to put an end to the curse. Imaginative title promises much more than movie delivers. The killer rats were thrown in as an afterthought to increase the run time. 1972 (R) 92m/C Hope Stansbury, Jackie Skarvellis, Noel Collins, Joan Ogden, Douglas Phair, Bernard Kaler; **D:** Andy Milligan; **W:** Andy Milligan. **VHS, Beta** NO Woof!

Rattle of a Simple Man A naive, chaste, middle-aged bachelor (Corbett) who lives in London must spend the night with a waitress (Cilento) to win a bet. She knows of the bet and kindly obliges. Enjoyable sex comedy. 1964 91m/B Harry H. Corbett, Diane Cilento, Michael Medwin, Thora Hird; **D:** Muriel Box. **VHS, Beta** NO ⅋⅋½

Rattler Kid Cavalry sergeant wrongly accused of murdering his commanding officer escapes from prison and finds the real killer. 197? 86m/C Richard Wyler, Brad Harris. **VHS, Beta** $49.95 UNI ⅋

Rattlers Made for television movie featuring poisonous rattlesnakes who attack at random. 1976 (PG) 82m/C Sam Chew, Elizabeth Chauvet, Dan Priest; **D:** John McCauley. **VHS, Beta** NO ⅋

The Raven An early, eccentric pseudo-biography of author Edgar Allan Poe. The film opens with a look at Poe's ancestors and follows the author to maturity when he turns to alcohol for solace. His drunken stupor produces hallucinations that lead to his tale of "The Raven." Silent with added music track. 1915 80m/B Henry B. Walthall, Wanda Howard; **D:** Charles Brabin. **VHS** $14.95 GPV, HEG, GVV ⅋⅋

The Raven A lunatic surgeon (Lugosi), who has a dungeon full of torture gadgets inspired by Edgar Allan Poe's stories, is begged by a man to save his daughter's life. The surgeon does, and then falls in love with the girl. But when she rejects his love (she's already engaged), he plans revenge in his chamber of horrors. Karloff plays the criminal who winds up ruining the mad doctor's plans. Lugosi is at his prime in this role, and any inconsistencies in the somewhat shaky script can be overlooked because of his chilling performance. 1935 62m/B Boris Karloff, Bela Lugosi, Irene Ware, Lester Matthews, Samuel S. Hinds; **D:** Lew Landers. **VHS** $14.98 MCA ⅋⅋⅋

The Raven This could-have-been monumental teaming of horror greats Karloff, Lorre and Price is more of a satire than a true horror film. One of the more enjoyable of the Corman/Poe adaptations, the movie takes only the title of the poem. As for the storyline: Price and Karloff play two rival sorcerers who battle for supremacy, with Lorre as the unfortunate associate turned into the bird of the title. 1963 86m/C Vincent Price, Boris Karloff, Peter Lorre, Jack Nicholson, Hazel Court; **D:** Roger Corman; **W:** Richard Matheson; **M:** Les Baxter. **VHS, Beta** MLB ⅋⅋⅋

Ravishing Idiot An unemployed bank clerk becomes mixed up with Soviet spies. **AKA:** Agent 38-24-36; Adorable Idiot; The Warm-Blooded Spy; Bewitching Scatterbrain. 1964 99m/B Brigitte Bardot, Anthony Perkins; **D:** Edouard Molinaro. **VHS, Beta** NO ⅋⅋

Raw Courage Three long-distance runners relax in New Mexico, but are kidnapped by vigilantes. Loosely based on a James Dickey novel. **AKA:** Courage. 1984 90m/C Ronny Cox, Lois Chiles, Art Hindle, Tim Maier, M. Emmet Walsh; **D:** Robert L. Rosen. **VHS, Beta** $9.95 NWV, STE ⅋

Raw Deal Don't ever give Schwarzenegger a raw deal! FBI agent Schwarzie infiltrates the mob and shoots lots of people. 1986 (R) 106m/C Arnold Schwarzenegger, Kathryn Harrold, Darren McGavin, Sam Wanamaker, Paul Shenar, Steven Hill; **D:** John Irvin; **W:** Gary De Vore, Patrick Edgeworth. **VHS, Beta** $14.95 HBO, TLF ⅋½

Raw Force Three karate buffs visit an island inhabited by a sect of cannibalistic monks who have the power to raise the dead (it could happen). They fix the villains by kicking them all in the head. **AKA:** Shogun Island. 1981 (R) 90m/C Cameron Mitchell, Geoffrey Binney, John Dresden, John Locke, Ralph Lombardi; **D:** Edward Murphy. **VHS, Beta** $49.95 MED ⅋

Raw Justice When the daughter of a powerful Southern mayor is murdered, tough ex-cop Mace (Keith) is hired to get the killer. Mace enlists the reluctant help of call girl Sarah (Anderson) to help him trap Mitch (Hayes), his prime suspect. Only things don't work out as Mace planned and the wary threesome must work together to save themselves from certain death. 1993 (R) 92m/C David Keith, Pamela Anderson, Robert Hayes, Leo Rossi, Charles Napier, Stacy Keach; **D:** David A. Prior; **W:** David A. Prior. **VHS** REP ⅋⅋

Raw Nerve A cast with possibilities can't overcome this poorly reasoned suspenser. A young man has visions of the local serial killer, but when he reports them to police he becomes the suspect. There are a few twists beyond that, none too thrilling.

1991 (R) 91m/C Glenn Ford, Traci Lords, Sandahl Bergman, Randall "Tex" Cobb, Ted Prior, Jan-Michael Vincent; **W:** David A. Prior. **VHS, Beta** $89.98 AIP ⅋

Raw Power Two thrill-seeking rich kids get their greedy hands on a super-car that defies any known power and gets them in loads of trouble. Some kids never learn. 19?? (R) 90m/C **VHS** PMH ⅋

Rawhead Rex An ancient demon is released from his underground prison in Ireland by a plowing farmer, and begins to decapitate and maim at will. Adapted by Clive Barker from his own short story. But Barker later disowned the film, so make your own judgment. 1987 (R) 89m/C David Dukes, Kelly Piper; **D:** George Pavlou; **W:** Clive Barker. **VHS, Beta** $19.98 LIV, VES ⅋½

Rawhide Rancher's Protection Association forces landowners to knuckle under resulting in friction. Lou Gehrig plays a rancher in a western released the year before he died. Bandleader Ballew could be more gripping in the lead. 1938 60m/B Lou Gehrig, Smith Ballew, Evelyn Knapp; **D:** Ray Taylor. **VHS, Beta** $19.98 NOS, CCB, DVT ⅋⅋

Rawhide Four escaped convicts hijack a stagecoach way station and hold hostages while waiting for a shipment of gold. A suspenseful B-grade western with a bang-up ending. Well paced and cast with an abundance of good talent. A remake of "Show Them No Mercy" (1938). **AKA:** Desperate Siege. 1950 86m/B Tyrone Power, Susan Hayward, Hugh Marlowe, Jack Elam, Dean Jagger, George Tobias, Edgar Buchanan, Jeff Corey; **D:** Henry Hathaway. **VHS, Beta** $19.98 FOX ⅋⅋⅋

Rawhide Mail Extremely rare "B" western. 193? ?m/C Jack Perrin. **VHS** $15.95 LOO ⅋⅋

Rawhide Romance Bill finds justice and love in this chap-slappin' opus, which finds him neglecting the thieves operating on the ranch as he romances his girl. Naturally he comes to his senses and goes after the crooks. 1934 47m/B Buffalo Bill Jr., Genee Boutell, Lafe McKee, Si Jenks; **D:** Victor Adamson. **VHS, Beta** $19.95 VYY ⅋

Razorback Young American travels to the Australian outback in search of his missing journalist wife. During his quest, he encounters a giant killer pig that has been terrorizing the area. Firmly establishes that pigs, with little sense of natural timing, make lousy movie villains. 1984 (R) 95m/C Gregory Harrison, Bill Kerr, Arkie Whiteley, Judy Morris, Chris Haywood; **D:** Russell Mulcahy. **VHS, Beta** $19.98 WAR ⅋

The Razor's Edge Adaptation of the W. Somerset Maugham novel. A rich young man spends his time between WWI & WWII searching for essential truth, eventually landing in India. A satisfying cinematic version of a difficult novel, supported by an excellent cast. Remade in 1984 with Bill Murray in the lead role. 1946 146m/B Tyrone Power, Gene Tierney, Anne Baxter, Clifton Webb, Herbert Marshall, John Payne, Elsa Lanchester; **D:** Edmund Goulding. Academy Awards '46: Best Supporting Actress (Baxter); Nominations: Best Interior Decoration, Best Picture, Best Supporting Actor (Webb); Golden Globe Awards '47: Best Supporting Actor (Webb), Best Supporting Actress (Baxter). **VHS, Beta** $59.98 FOX, BTV ⅋⅋⅋

The Razor's Edge A beautifully filmed but idiosyncratic version of the W. Somerset Maugham novel. WWI-ravaged Larry Darrell combs the world in search of the meaning of life. Murray is a little too old and sardonic to seem really tortured. Russell is great as the loser he rescues. Subtly unique, with real shortcomings.
1984 (PG-13) 129m/C Bill Murray, Catherine Hicks, Theresa Russell, Denholm Elliott, James Keach, Peter Vaughan, Saeed Jaffrey, Brian Doyle-Murray; **D:** John Byrum; **M:** Jack Nitzsche. VHS, Beta $79.95 COL *ZZ* ½

The Re-Animator Based on an H.P. Lovecraft story, this grisly film deals with a medical student who re-animates the dead. It has quickly turned into a black humor cult classic. Also available in an "R" rated version, and followed by "Bride of Re-Animator."
1985 86m/C Jeffrey Combs, Bruce Abbott, Barbara Crampton, David Gale, Robert Sampson; **D:** Stuart Gordon; **W:** Stuart Gordon, Dennis Paoli, William J. Norris; **M:** Richard Band. VHS, Beta $19.98 LIV, VES *ZZZ*

Reach for the Sky WW II flying ace loses both legs in an accident and learns to fly again. He becomes a hero during the Battle of Britain, then is shot down over France and held prisoner by the Germans. At war's end he returns to England to lead 3,000 planes over London in a victory flight. Inspirationally told true story.
1956 136m/B Kenneth More, Alexander Knox, Nigel Green; **D:** Lewis Gilbert; **M:** John Addison. VHS, Beta NO *ZZ* ½

Reaching for the Moon A daydreaming department store employee finds himself in the unlikely position of ruling a kingdom. Vintage Fairbanks fun, based on a story by Anita Loos. Silent.
1917 62m/B Douglas Fairbanks Sr., Eileen Percy, Millard Webb; **D:** John Emerson. VHS, Beta $24.95 VYY, GPV, GVV *ZZ* ½

Reaching for the Moon Fairbanks is a businessman who falls for liquor and Daniels on a transatlantic cruise. Dull and cruel; not as light-hearted as it intends. One Irving Berlin song sung by Crosby.
1931 62m/B Douglas Fairbanks Sr., Bebe Daniels, Bing Crosby, Edward Everett Horton; **D:** Edmund Goulding. VHS, Beta, 8mm $19.95 NOS, VYY, CAB *ZZ* ½

Reactor A low-budget sci-fi film about kidnapped scientists, alien ships and an activated nuclear reactor.
1985 90m/C Yanti Somer, Melissa Long, James R. Stuart, Robert Barnes, Nick Jordan. VHS, Beta NO *Z*

A Real American Hero Made for television story of Tennessee sheriff Buford Pusser, the subject of three "Walking Tall" films. Here, he battles moonshiners with the usual violence. **AKA:** Hard Stick.
1978 94m/C Brian Dennehy, Brian Kerwin, Forrest Tucker; **D:** Lou Antonio. VHS, Beta $9.99 STE, PSM *Z* ½

Real Bruce Lee Contains actual early films of Bruce Lee, once feared lost but recently discovered in the Chinese film archives, (the movies, not Bruce).
1979 (R) 108m/C Bruce Lee. VHS, Beta $24.95 GEM, SUN, VTR *Z* ½

The Real Buddy Holly Story Documentary serves as a tribute to the rock 'n' roll legend who met an untimely death in 1959.
1987 90m/C VHS, Beta $14.95 SMV, IME, MVD *Z* ½

Real Bullets Stunt team performs the real thing when two members get imprisoned in a bad guy's desert castle.

1990 86m/C John Gazarian, Martin Landau; **D:** Lance Lindsay. VHS, Beta $89.95 VMK *Z*

Real Genius Brainy kids in California work with lasers on a class project that is actually intended for use as an offensive military weapon. When they learn of the scheme, they use their brilliant minds to mount an amusingly elaborate strategic defense initiative of their own. Eccentric characters and an intelligent script provide a bevy of laughs for the family.
1985 (PG) 108m/C Val Kilmer, Gabe Jarret, Jonathan Gries, Michelle Meyrink, William Atherton, Patti D'Arbanville, Severn Darden; **D:** Martha Coolidge; **W:** Peter Torokvei, Neal Israel, Pat Proft. VHS, Beta $14.95 COL *ZZZ*

The Real Glory After the U.S. capture of the Philippine islands during the Spanish-American war, an uprising of Moro tribesmen spreads terror. After most of the islands are evacuated only a small group of Army officers is left to lead the Filipino soldiers against the rebels. Cooper plays the heroic doctor, who is not afraid to fight, especially when he comes to the rescue of the beseiged Army fort. Great action sequences and paticularly good performances by Cooper and Niven.
1939 95m/B Gary Cooper, Andrea Leeds, David Niven, Reginald Owen, Broderick Crawford; **D:** Henry Hathaway. VHS $19.98 MGM, WAR *ZZZ*

Real Life Writer/comedian Brooks's first feature sags in places, but holds its own as a vehicle for his peculiar talent. Brooks plays a pompous director whose ambition is to make a documentary of a "typical" American family. Good, intelligent comedy.
1979 (R) 99m/C Charles Grodin, Frances Lee McCain, Albert Brooks; **D:** Albert Brooks; **W:** Monica Johnson, Harry Shearer, Albert Brooks. VHS, Beta $19.95 PAR *ZZZ*

The Real McCoy Generally awful crime-caper film about female bank robber Karen McCoy (Basinger). Just out of prison, all Karen wants to do is go straight and raise her young son but her plans are thwarted by former associates who kidnap the child to force her into one last heist. Kilmer is the small-time thief, with a crush on Karen, who tries to help her out. Dumb, slow-moving story with a vapid performance by Basinger.
1993 (PG-13) 104m/C Kim Basinger, Val Kilmer, Terence Stamp, Zach English, Gailard Sartain; **D:** Russell Mulcahy; **W:** William Davies, William Osborne. VHS MCA *Z* ½

Real Men The junior Belushi brother is a spy forced to recruit ordinary guy Ritter to help him negotiate with aliens to save the world. Bizarre premise shows promise, but spy spoof doesn't fire on all comedic pistons. Nice try.
1987 (PG-13) 86m/C James Belushi, John Ritter, Barbara Barrie; **D:** Dennis Feldman; **M:** Miles Goodman. VHS, Beta $79.98 FOX *Z* ½

The Real Patsy Cline The story of Patsy Cline's brilliant rise to stardom and her tragic death at the pinnacle of her career.
1990 60m/C Patsy Cline, Loretta Lynn, Carl Perkins, Dottie West. VHS $14.95 MVD, CAF *Z* ½

Reality Bites Humorous look at four recent college grads living, working, and slacking in Houston. Script by newcomer Childress is at its best when highlighting the trends: 7-Eleven Big Gulps, tacky '70s memorabilia, and games revolving around episodes of old TV shows like "Good Times," to name a few. Definite appeal for those in their early 20s, but anyone over 25 may encounter a "Generation X-er" gap, a noticeable problem since "Reality" claims to speak for the entire twentysomething generation.

Decent directorial debut for Stiller; good cast, particularly Garofalo, in her film debut.
1994 (PG-13) 99m/C Winona Ryder, Ethan Hawke, Ben Stiller, Janeane Garofalo, Steve Zahn, Swoosie Kurtz, Joe Don Baker, John Mahoney; **Cameos:** David Pirner, Anne Meara, Jeanne Tripplehorn, Karen Duffy, Evan Dando; **D:** Ben Stiller; **W:** Helen Childress; **M:** Karl Wallinger. VHS MCA *ZZZ*

Really Weird Tales Several SCTV alumni highlight this three-story movie, which is science fiction with a satirical edge.
1986 85m/C John Candy, Martin Short, Joe Flaherty, Catherine O'Hara. VHS, Beta $7.00 VTR *ZZ* ½

Reap the Wild Wind DeMille epic about salvagers off the Georgia coast in the 1840s featuring Wayne as the captain and Massey and a giant squid as the villains. Good cast, lesser story, fine underwater photography.
1942 123m/C Ray Milland, John Wayne, Paulette Goddard, Raymond Massey, Robert Preston, Lynne Overman, Susan Hayward, Charles Bickford, Walter Hampden, Louise Beavers, Martha O'Driscoll, Elisabeth Risdon, Hedda Hopper, Raymond Hatton, Barbara Britton; **D:** Cecil B. DeMille. Academy Awards '42: Best Special Effects; Nominations: Best Color Cinematography, Best Interior Decoration. VHS, Beta $14.98 MCA *ZZ* ½

Rear Window A newspaper photographer with a broken leg (Stewart) passes the time recuperating by observing his neighbors through the window. When he sees what he believes to be a murder, he decides to solve the crime himself. With help from his beautiful girlfriend and his nurse, he tries to catch the murderer without getting killed himself. Top-drawer Hitchcock blends exquisite suspense with occasional on-target laughs. Based on the story by Cornell Woolrich.
1954 112m/C James Stewart, Grace Kelly, Thelma Ritter, Wendell Corey, Raymond Burr, Judith Evelyn; **D:** Alfred Hitchcock; **W:** John Michael Hayes; **M:** Franz Waxman. Academy Awards '54 Nominations: Best Director (Hitchcock), Best Screenplay, Best Sound; Edgar Allan Poe Awards '54: Best Screenplay. VHS, Beta $19.95 MCA, TLF, HMV *ZZZZ*

Reason to Die Bounty hunter uses his own girlfriend as a decoy to trap a psychotic prostitute killer.
1990 (R) 86m/C Liam Cundill, Wings Hauser, Anneline Kriel, Arnold Vosloo; **D:** Tim Spring. VHS $89.95 VMK *Z*

A Reason to Live, A Reason to Die A bland Italian-French-German-Spanish western in which a group of condemned men attempt to take a Confederate fort. **AKA:** Massacre at Fort Holman; Una Ragione Per Vivere e Una Per Morire.
1973 90m/C James Coburn, Telly Savalas, Bud Spencer, Robert Burton; **D:** Tonino Valerii. VHS, Beta NO *ZZ*

Rebecca Based on Daphne Du Maurier's best-selling novel about a young unsophisticated girl who marries a moody and prominent country gentleman haunted by the memory of his first wife. Fontaine and Olivier turn in fine performances as the unlikely couple. Suspenseful and surprising. Hitchcock's first American film and only Best Picture Oscar. Laserdisc features: rare screen tests of Vivien Leigh, Anne Baxter, Loretta Young, and Joan Fontaine, footage from Rebecca's winning night at the Academy Awards, original radio broadcasts of film by Orson Welles and David O. Selznick, and commentary of film with interview excerpts with Hitchcock.

1940 130m/B Joan Fontaine, Laurence Olivier, Judith Anderson, George Sanders, Nigel Bruce, Florence Bates, Gladys Cooper, Reginald Denny, Leo G. Carroll, Sir C. Aubrey Smith, Melville Cooper; **D:** Alfred Hitchcock; **W:** Joan Harrison, Robert E. Sherwood; **M:** Franz Waxman. Academy Awards '40: Best Black and White Cinematography, Best Picture; Nominations: Best Actor (Olivier), Best Actress (Fontaine), Best Adapted Screenplay, Best Director (Hitchcock), Best Film Editing, Best Interior Decoration, Best Supporting Actress (Anderson), Best Original Score; National Board of Review Awards '40: 10 Best Films of the Year. **VHS, Beta $19.98** FOX, VYG, HMV ✓✓✓✓

Rebecca of Sunnybrook Farm The original film version of the tale about an orphan who spreads sunshine and good cheer to all those around her. Silent with organ score. Based on the popular novel by Kate Douglas Wiggin; remade with Shirley Temple in 1938.
1917 77m/B Mary Pickford, Eugene O'Brien, Marjorie Daw, Helen Jerome Eddy; **D:** Marshall Neilan; **M:** Gaylord Carter. **VHS, Beta $19.98** CCB ✓✓

Rebecca of Sunnybrook Farm Temple becomes a radio star over her aunt's objections in this bouncy musical that has nothing to do with the famous Kate Douglas Wiggin novel. Temple sings a medley of her hits, and dances the finale with Bill "Bojangles" Robinson. ♫On the Good Ship Lollipop/When I'm With You/Animal Crackers medley; Crackly Corn Flakes; Alone With You; Happy Ending; Au Revoir; An Old Straw Hat; Come and Get Your Happiness; Parade of the Wooden Soldiers.
1938 80m/B Shirley Temple, Randolph Scott, Jack Haley, Phyllis Brooks, Gloria Stuart, Slim Summerville, Bill Robinson, Helen Westley, William Demarest; **D:** Allan Dwan. **VHS, Beta $19.98** FOX, MLB, MLT ✓✓½

Rebel Mumbling student radical must decide between his love for a country girl and his loyalty to an underground terrorist organization. Notable (or not) for display of early Stallone.
1973 (PG) 80m/C Sylvester Stallone, Anthony Page, Rebecca Grimes. **VHS, Beta** NO ✓✓½

Rebel A U.S. Marine falls in love with a Sydney nightclub singer and goes AWOL during WWII. Stylish but empty and badly cast.
1985 (R) 93m/C Matt Dillon, Debbie Byrne, Bryan Brown, Bill Hunter, Ray Barrett; **D:** Michael Jenkins. **VHS, Beta $79.98** LIV, VES ✓✓½

Rebel High Hijinks occur at a high school where youngsters study guerilla warfare and teachers wear bullet-proof vests.
1988 (R) 92m/C Harvey Berger, Stu Trivax, Larry Gimple, Shawn Goldwater; **D:** Harry Jacobs. **VHS, Beta $29.95** ACA ✓½

Rebel Love Love grows between a northern widow and a Confederate spy. In better hands it might have been a good story. Here, it's overwrought and embarrassing historical melodrama.
1985 84m/C Terence Knox, Jamie Rose, Fred Ryan; **D:** Milton Bagby Jr. **VHS, Beta $79.98** LIV, VES ✓

Rebel Rousers A motorcycle gang wreaks havoc in a small town where a drag-race is being held to see who will get the pregnant girlfriend of Dern's high-school buddy as the prize. Young Nicholson in striped pants steals the show.
1969 81m/C Jack Nicholson, Cameron Mitchell, Diane Ladd, Bruce Dern, Harry Dean Stanton; **D:** Martin B. Cohen. **VHS, Beta $29.95** MED ✓✓

The Rebel Set The owner of a beat generation coffeehouse plans an armed robbery with the help of some buddies. Genuinely suspenseful, competently directed. **AKA:** Beatsville.
1959 72m/B Gregg Palmer, Kathleen Crowley, Edward Platt, John Lupton, Ned Glass, Don Sullivan, Vicki Dougan, I. Stanford Jolley; **D:** Gene Fowler. **VHS, Beta $16.95** SNC ✓✓½

Rebel Storm A group of freedom fighters team up to rescue America from the totalitarian rulers that are in charge in 2099 A.D.
1990 (R) 99m/C Zach Galligan, Wayne Crawford, June Chadwick, Rod McCary, John Rhys-Davies, Elizabeth Kiefer; **D:** Francis Schaeffer. **VHS, Beta $29.95** ACA ✓

Rebel Vixens Even though the war is over, ex-confederate soldiers continue looting and raping, until a brothel-full of prostitutes concoct a plan that has a lot to do with softcore sex.
1985 94m/C Maria Lease, Roda Spain. **VHS, Beta $29.95** MED Woof!

Rebel Without a Cause James Dean's most memorable screen appearance. In the second of his three films, he plays a troubled teenager from the right side of the tracks. Dean's portrayal of Jim Stark, a teen alienated from both his parents and peers, is excellent. He befriends outcasts Wood and Mineo in a police station and together they find a commonground. Superb young stars carry this in-the-gut story of adolescence. All three leads met with real-life tragic ends.
1955 111m/C James Dean, Natalie Wood, Sal Mineo, Jim Backus, Nick Adams, Dennis Hopper, Ann Doran, William Hopper, Rochelle Hudson, Corey Allen, Edward Platt; **D:** Nicholas Ray; **W:** Stewart Stern; **M:** Leonard Rosenman. **VHS, Beta $19.98** WAR ✓✓✓✓

The Rebellious Reign In an effort to resurrect the Ming Dynasty, a single soldier seeks to unseat the sovereign power, the Ching Dynasty.
19?? (R) 100m/C Jimmy Lee, Tsui Siu Keung. **VHS, Beta $49.95** OCE ✓

The Rebels In the sequel to the television mini series "The Bastard," Philip Kent (Stevens) continues his Revolutionary War battle on the side of American independence. He is assisted by Southerner Judson Fletcher (Johnson) in thwarting an assassination attempt on George Washington. In addition to Bosley's Ben Franklin, "The Rebels" offers Backus as John Hancock. Followed by "The Seekers;" based on the novel by John Jakes.
1979 190m/C Andrew Stevens, Don Johnson, Doug McClure, Jim Backus, Richard Basehart, Joan Blondell, Tom Bosley, Rory Calhoun, MacDonald Carey, Kim Cattrall, William Daniels, Anne Francis, Peter Graves, Pamela Hensley, Wilfrid Hyde-White, Nehemiah Persoff, William Smith, Forrest Tucker, Tanya Tucker, Robert Vaughn, Deborah Richter; **D:** Russ Mayberry. **VHS $29.98** MCA ✓✓

Reborn A faith healer and a talent scout hire actors to be cured of fake ailments.
1978 91m/C Dennis Hopper, Michael Moriarty, Francesco Rabal, Antonella Murgia. **VHS, Beta $69.95** VES ✓✓

Reckless Harlow, in a role originally intended for Joan Crawford, plays a showgirl coveted by a millionaire and secretly loved by her manager. Unfortunately, Harlow couldn't pull off the acting (much less the singing and dancing), although the plot strangely paralleled her own life. Songs include "Reckless," "Ev'rything's Been Done Before," "Trocadero," "Hear What My Heart Is Saying" and "Cyclone."
1935 96m/B Jean Harlow, William Powell, Franchot Tone, May Robson, Ted Healy, Nat Pendleton, Rosalind Russell; **D:** Victor Fleming. **VHS $19.98** MGM ✓✓

Reckless A sincere movie about a "good" girl who finds herself obsessed with a rebel from the wrong side of her small town. Differs from 1950s' wrong-side-of-the-track flicks only in updated sex and music.
1984 (R) 93m/C Aidan Quinn, Daryl Hannah, Kenneth McMillan, Cliff DeYoung, Lois Smith, Adam Baldwin, Dan Hedaya, Jennifer Grey, Pamela Springsteen; **D:** James Foley; **W:** Chris Columbus. **VHS, Beta $14.95** MGM ✓✓½

Reckless Disregard A doctor whose career is ruined by a news report accusing him of involvement in a drug scam sues the newscaster. Made for television saga based on Dan Rather's "60 Minutes" story and ensuing lawsuit.
1984 92m/C Leslie Nielsen, Tess Harper, Ronny Cox, Kate Lynch; **D:** Harvey Hart. **VHS, Beta $69.98** LIV, VES ✓½

Reckless Moment A mother commits murder to save her daughter from an unsavory older man, and finds herself blackmailed. Gripping, intense thriller.
1949 82m/B James Mason, Joan Bennett, Geraldine Brooks; **D:** Max Ophuls. **VHS, Beta** LCA ✓✓✓

The Reckless Way A young woman struggles for her big break into the movies.
1936 72m/B Marion Nixon, Kane Richmond, Inez Courtney, Malcolm McGregor, Harry Harvey, Arthur Howard; **D:** Raymond K. Johnson. **VHS, Beta $12.95** GPV ✓½

Recruits Sophomoric gagfest about an inept Californian police force. Typical 80's-style mindless "comedy:" dumb gags ensue from perfunctory premise.
1986 81m/C Alan Deveau, Annie McAuley, Lolita David; **D:** Rafal Zielinski. **VHS, Beta $79.98** LIV, VES ✓

Red Alert Good, suspenseful, topical made for television thriller about nuclear meltdown. Will Minneapolis be saved? Usually Barbeau's name in the credits is a red alert, but this one is better than most.
1977 95m/C William Devane, Ralph Waite, Michael Brandon, Adrienne Barbeau; **D:** Billy Hale. **VHS, Beta $19.95** PAR ✓✓½

The Red and the Black A big budgeted French adaptation of the classic Stendhal novel. A young man from the country seeks success, first in the Church and later in the employment and seduction of the gentry. In French with English subtitles. **AKA:** Le Rouge et le Noir.
1957 134m/B Danielle Darrieux, Gerard Philippe; **D:** Claude Autant-Lara. **VHS, Beta $69.95** ING, IVY, MRV ✓✓✓

The Red and the White Epic war drama about the civil war between the Red Army and the non-communist Whites in Russia in 1918. Told from the perspective of Hungarians who fought alongside the Reds. Little dialogue. In Hungarian with English subtitles. **AKA:** Csillagosok, Katonak.
1968 92m/B **D:** Miklos Jancso. **VHS $79.95** KIV, ING ✓✓✓

The Red Badge of Courage John Huston's adaptation of the Stephen Crane Civil War novel is inspired, despite cutting room hatchet job by the studio. A classic study of courage and cowardice. Sweeping battle scenes and intense personal drama.
1951 69m/B Audie Murphy, Bill Mauldin, Douglas Dick, Royal Dano, Andy Devine; **D:** John Huston. **VHS, Beta $24.95** KUI, MGM, HMV ✓✓✓½

The Red Balloon The story of Pascal, a lonely French boy who befriends a wondrous red balloon which follows him everywhere. Lovely, finely done parable of childhood, imagination and friendship.
1956 34m/C Pascal Lamorisse; *D:* Albert Lamorisse. **VHS, Beta, 8mm $14.95** *COL, HHT, DVT* 🎞🎞🎞

Red Balloon/Occurrence at Owl Creek Bridge Two classic award-winning shorts have been combined on one tape: ''The Red Balloon'' (color, 1956) and ''An Occurrence at Owl Creek Bridge.'' The former is a children's story about a balloon on the loose; the latter is a perfectly rendered adaptation of the Ambrose Bierce short story of the same title, a taut narration of a Civil War hanging.
1962 60m/C Pascal Lamorisse, Roger Jacquet; *D:* Robert Enrico, Albert Lamorisse. **VHS, Beta** *SUE, VYY, WFV* 🎞🎞🎞½

Red Balloon/White Mane The two classic, award-winning children's films by the French master, released only on laserdisc in pristine transfers.
1956 72m/C *D:* Albert Lamorisse. **Beta** *CRC* 🎞🎞🎞½

Red Barry A comic strip detective tries to track down criminals who threaten the world. Thirteen episodes on one videotape.
1938 ?m/B Buster Crabbe, Frances Robinson, Edna Sedgwick, Cyril Delevanti, Frank Lackteen; *D:* Ford Beebe, Alan James. **VHS $49.95** *NOS, MLB* 🎞🎞🎞½

Red Beard An uncharacteristic drama by Kurosawa, about a young doctor in Japan awakening to life and love under the tutelage of a compassionate old physician. Highly acclaimed; in Japanese with English subtitles. *AKA:* Akahige.
1965 185m/B Toshiro Mifune, Yuzo Kayama, Yoshio Tsuchiya, Reiko Dan; *D:* Akira Kurosawa. **VHS, Beta $59.95** *ING, VYG, CRC* 🎞🎞🎞

Red Blooded American Girl A scientist develops a virus that turns people into vampires. Those infected hit the streets in search of blood.
1990 (R) 89m/C Christopher Plummer, Andrew Stevens, Heather Thomas, Kim Coates; *D:* David Blyth. **VHS, Beta $29.95** *PSM* 🎞

Red Dawn During WWIII, Russian invaders overrun America's heartland and take over the country. Eight small-town teenagers, calling themselves the Wolverines, hide out in the rugged countryside and fight the Russians. Swayze and Grey met again in ''Dirty Dancing.''
1984 (PG-13) 114m/C Patrick Swayze, C. Thomas Howell, Harry Dean Stanton, Powers Boothe, Lea Thompson, Charlie Sheen, Ben Johnson, Jennifer Grey, Ron O'Neal, William Smith; *D:* John Milius; *W:* John Milius, Kevin Reynolds. **VHS, Beta $19.95** *MGM* 🎞½

Red Desert The Pecos Kid is sent to track down the theft of a shipment of gold.
1950 60m/B Jack Holt, Donald (Don ''Red'') Barry, Tom Neal, Joseph Crehan, Tom London; *D:* Charles Marquis Warren. **VHS, Beta** *NO* 🎞

The Red Desert Antonioni's first color film, depicting an alienated Italian wife who searches for meaning in the industrial lunar landscape of northern Italy, to no avail. Highly acclaimed, and a masterpiece of visual form. Cinematography by Carlo di Palma. In Italian with English subtitles.
1964 120m/C Monica Vitti, Richard Harris, Carlos Chionetti; *D:* Michelangelo Antonioni; *W:* Michelangelo Antonioni, Tonino Guerra. **VHS, Beta $79.95** *FCT, ING, CVC* 🎞🎞🎞

Red Desert Penitentiary A spoof of movie-making featuring caricatures of industry-types.
1983 104m/C James Michael Taylor, Cathryn Bissell, Will Rose; *D:* George Sluizer. **VHS, Beta** *NO* 🎞🎞🎞

Red Dust The overseer of a rubber plantation in Indochina causes all kinds of trouble when he falls in love with a young engineer's wife. Filled with free-spirited humor and skillfully directed; remarkably original. Remade in 1940 as ''Congo Maisie'' and in 1954 as ''Mogambo.''
1932 83m/B Clark Gable, Jean Harlow, Mary Astor, Gene Raymond, Donald Crisp; *D:* Victor Fleming. **VHS, Beta $19.98** *MGM* 🎞🎞🎞

Red Earth A satire about life under Hungarian socialism. Szanto is a bauxite mixer whose pigs have rooted out high quality bauxite from his backyard. Only the local bauxite prospectors don't want to believe in luck (and pigs) and credit, instead, careful planning. When Szanto's village is turned into a vast open mine, he's blamed. In Hungarian with English subtitles.
19?? 105m/C Imre Nemeth, Sandor Kocsis, Kalman Toronyi, Ferenc Togh, Vilmos Gadori; *D:* Laszlo Vitezy; *W:* Istvan Darday. **VHS $59.95** *FCT* 🎞🎞

Red Flag: The Ultimate Game Pilots rival for success in battle simulation training with terrible consequences. Fine performances cover plot weaknesses. Well-written dialogue. Made for television.
1981 100m/C Barry Bostwick, William Devane, Joan VanArk, Fred McCarren, Debra Feuer, George Coe, Linden Chiles, Arlen Dean Snyder; *D:* Don Taylor. **VHS, Beta $39.95** *LIV* 🎞🎞½

The Red Fury Young Indian boy struggles to overcome prejudice and caring for his horse shows him the way. Good family viewing.
197? 105m/C William Jordan, Kathy Cannon. **VHS $59.95** *TPV, HHE, BPG* 🎞🎞

Red Garters A musical parody of old-time westerns which doesn't quite come off. Mitchell palys the cowpoke who comes to town to avenge the death of his brother with Clooney as the saloon singer who uses him to make boyfriend Carson jealous. The adequate songs include ''Red Garters,'' ''Man and Woman,'' ''A Dime and a Dollar,'' and ''Vaquero.''
1954 91m/C Guy Mitchell, Rosemary Clooney, Jack Carson, Gene Barry, Pat Crowley, Joanne Gilbert, Frank Faylen, Reginald Owen, Buddy Ebsen; *D:* George Marshall; *W:* Michael Fessier; *M:* Jay Livingston, Ray Evans. **VHS $14.95** *PAR* 🎞🎞½

The Red Half-Breed A lonely half-breed Indian, wrongly accused of murder, discovers the real killer while running from the law.
1970 103m/C Daniel Pilon, Genevieve Deloir; *D:* Gilles Carle. **VHS, Beta $59.95** *NWV* 🎞½

Red Headed Stranger Willie Nelson vehicle based on his 1975 album. Nelson is a gun-totin' preacher who kills his wife and is led to salvation by a good farm woman. But honestly: Morgan Fairchild as Willie Nelson's wife? Please.
1987 (R) 108m/C Willie Nelson, Katharine Ross, Morgan Fairchild; *D:* Bill Wittliff; *W:* Bill Wittliff. **VHS, Beta $9.98** *NLC* 🎞½

Red Headed Woman Harlow plays an unscrupulous woman who charms her way into the lives of influential men. She causes her boss to divorce his wife and marry her while she sleeps with the chauffeur (Boyer) and others. Audiences loved the scandalous material, but the Hays Office objected to the fact that the immoral woman goes unpunished. Boyer's small but important role salvaged his floundering American film career. Harlow is sultry and funny.
1932 79m/B Jean Harlow, Chester Morris, Lewis Stone, Leila Hyams, Una Merkel, Henry Stephenson, May Robson, Charles Boyer, Harvey Clark; *D:* Jack Conway. **VHS, Beta $19.98** *MGM, FCT* 🎞🎞🎞

Red Heat Blair is a tourist in East Germany mistakenly arrested and sent to a rough women's prison. Her fiance tries to free her. Meanwhile, she has to deal with tough-lady fellow jail bird Kristel. Familiar and marginal.
1985 104m/C Linda Blair, Sylvia Kristel, Sue Kiel, William Ostrander; *D:* Robert Collector. **VHS, Beta $19.98** *LIV, VES* 🎞½

Red Heat Two cops—one from the Soviet Union, one from Chicago—team up to catch the Eastern Bloc's biggest drug czar. Lots of action, but at times it seems too similar to Hill's earlier hit ''48 Hours.'' Film claims to be the first major U.S. production shot in Red Square, Moscow.
1988 (R) 106m/C Arnold Schwarzenegger, James Belushi, Peter Boyle, Ed O'Ross, Laurence ''Larry'' Fishburne, Gina Gershon, Richard Bright; *D:* Walter Hill; *W:* Walter Hill; *M:* James Horner. **VHS, Beta $14.95** *LIV, TLF* 🎞🎞

The Red House Robinson plays a crippled farmer who, after his daughter brings home a suitor, attempts to keep everyone from a mysterious red house located on his property. Madness and murder prevail. Strange film noir about tangled relationships and unsuccessful attempts to bury the horrid past. Based on the novel by George Agnew Chamberlain.
1947 100m/B Edward G. Robinson, Lon McCallister, Judith Anderson, Allene Roberts, Rory Calhoun, Ona Munson, Julie London; *D:* Delmer Daves; *M:* Miklos Rozsa. **VHS, Beta $9.95** *CNG, NOS, SNC* 🎞🎞🎞

Red Kimono Exploitative silent melodrama about a young woman ditched by her husband. She becomes a prostitute, but is redeemed by true love. Interesting slice of its period.
1925 95m/B Tyrone Power Sr., Priscilla Boner, Nellie Bly Baker, Mary Carr; *D:* Walter Lang. **VHS, Beta $19.95** *NOS, VYY, DVT* 🎞🎞

Red King, White Knight An assassin tries to kill Mikhail Gorbachev during superpower peace talks. Ex-s pook Skerritt returns to duty to thwart him. Better than most ''topical'' thrill ers. Made for cable television.
1989 (R) 106m/C Tom Skerritt, Max von Sydow, Helen Mirren; *D:* Geoff Murphy. **VHS, Beta $89.99** *HBO* 🎞🎞

Red Kiss In 1952 Paris, Nadia, a 15-year-old French-Jewish Stalinist of Polish descent falls in love with Stephane, an older, apolitical photographer. She's torn between love and politics; he's worried (rightly) about her being under-age; and to make matters more complicated, her Polish mother has been reunited with her first love and Nadia's family may be split apart. The sensual Valandrey is a real find in her difficult coming-of-age role. In French with English subtitles. *AKA:* Rouge Baiser.
1985 110m/C Charlotte Valandrey, Lambert Wilson, Marthe Keller, Gunter Lamprecht, Laurent Terzieff; *D:* Vera Belmont. **VHS $79.95** *FXL, FCT, ING* 🎞🎞🎞

The Red Light Sting A Justice Department rookie (Bridges) and a call girl (Fawcett) reluctantly team up to con the Mafia in order to convict a San Francisco rackets czar. Goes down easy, but also easily forgotten or skipped.

1984 96m/C Farrah Fawcett, Beau Bridges, Harold Gould, Paul Burke, Sunny Johnson; **D:** Rod Holcomb. **VHS, Beta $39.95** *MCA ♂♂*

Red Line 7000 High stakes auto racers drive fast cars and date women. Excellent racing footage in otherwise routine four-wheel fest.
1965 110m/C James Caan, Laura Devon, Gail Hire, Charlene Holt, John Crawford, Marianna Hill, George Takei; **D:** Howard Hawks. **VHS $39.95** *PAR, FCT ♂♂½*

Red Lion A bumbling horse-tender in feudal Japan impersonates a military officer to impress his family, only to be swept into leading a liberating revolution. In Japanese with English subtitles. *AKA:* Akage.
1969 115m/C Toshiro Mifune, Shima Iwashita; **D:** Kihachi Okamoto. **VHS, Beta $49.95** *ING, VDA ♂♂½*

The Red Menace Anti-Communist propaganda, made with unknown actors in documentary style has little to offer today's viewers other than unintentional laughs. Picture the Commies offering naive Americans money and sex to join the party, and you'll have an idea of the intellectual talent that went into this one.
1949 87m/B Robert Rockwell, Hanne Axman, Shepard Menken, Betty Lou Gerson, Barbara Fuller; **D:** R.G. Springsteen. **VHS $19.98** *REP, FCT Woof!*

Red Nightmare Anti-communist propaganda produced for the Department of Defense by Warner Brothers features the cast of "Dragnet." The story dramatizes the Red Menace, with communists conspiring to take over America, and shows what would happen to life in a small American town if the Commies took over.
1962 30m/B Jack Webb, Jack Kelly, Jeanne Cooper, Peter Brown. **VHS, Beta $19.95** *VYY, IHF ♂♂½*

Red Nights A country boy goes to Hollywood seeking success and finds instead corruption, decadence, and dishonesty. Excellent soundtrack by Tangerine Dream.
1987 90m/C Christopher Parker, Jack Carter, Brian Matthews; **D:** Izhak Hanooka. **VHS, Beta $19.98** *TWE ♂*

Red Planet Mars Anti-communist, pro-Christianity story about scientists discovering that the Voice of Radio Free Mars belongs to God. Incoherent film overburdened with messages about politics, religion, and science was ahead of its time. Based on the play "Red Planet" by John L. Balderson and John Hoare.
1952 87m/B Peter Graves, Andrea King, Marvin Miller, Herbert Berghof, House Peters, Vince Barnett; **D:** Harry Horner; **W:** Anthony Veiller, John Balderston. **VHS $14.95** *MGM, FCT ♂♂*

The Red Pony A young boy escapes from his family's fighting through his love for a pet pony. Based on the novel by John Steinbeck. Remade for television in 1976. Timeless classic that the whole family can enjoy.
1949 89m/C Myrna Loy, Robert Mitchum, Peter Miles, Louis Calhern, Sheppard Strudwick, Margaret Hamilton, Beau Bridges; **D:** Lewis Milestone; **M:** Aaron Copland. **VHS $14.98** *REP, KUI ♂♂♂*

The Red Pony Excellent TV remake of a classic 1949 adaptation of John Steinbeck. Fonda is superb as a troubled young boy's difficult father.
1976 101m/C Henry Fonda, Maureen O'Hara; **D:** Robert Totten. **VHS, Beta $19.98** *BFA ♂♂♂*

The Red Raven Kiss-Off A seedy Hollywood detective becomes the key suspect in a movie-making murder. Based on the 1930s' Dan Turner mystery stories. Made for video.
1990 (R) 93m/C Marc Singer, Tracy Scoggins, Nicholas Worth, Arte Johnson; **D:** Christopher Lewis. **VHS, Beta $19.95** *FRH ♂*

Red Riding Hood Musical version of story of wolf who has little girl fetish.
1988 81m/C Isabella Rossellini, Craig T. Nelson, Rocco Sisto. **VHS, Beta $14.95** *MGM, CAN ♂♂½*

Red River The classic Hawks epic about a gruelling cattle drive and the battle of wills between father and son. Generally regarded as one of the best westerns ever made, and Wayne's shining moment as a reprehensible, obsessive man. Featuring Clift in his first film. Restored version has eight minutes of previously edited material. Remade for television in 1988 with James Arness and Bruce Boxleitner.
1948 133m/B John Wayne, Montgomery Clift, Walter Brennan, Joanne Dru, John Ireland, Noah Beery Jr., Paul Fix, Coleen Gray, Harry Carey Jr., Harry Carey Sr., Chief Yowlachie, Hank Worden; **D:** Howard Hawks; **W:** Borden Chase, Charles Schnee; **M:** Dimitri Tiomkin. **VHS, Beta $19.98** *MGM, TLF, RDG ♂♂♂♂*

Red River Valley Autry and partner Burnette go undercover to find out who's plaguing a dam construction site with explosions. Not to be confused with a 1941 Roy Rogers pic bearing the same title. *AKA:* Man of the Frontier.
1936 60m/B Gene Autry, Smiley Burnette, Frances Grant, Booth Howard, Sam Flint, George Cheseboro, Charles "Blackie" King, Eugene Jackson, Frank LaRue, Lloyd Ingraham; **D:** B. Reeves Eason. **VHS $19.95** *NOS, VDM, VCN ♂♂*

Red Rock Outlaw A sleazy character tries to kill his twin brother and takes his place as an honest rancher.
1947 56m/B Lee White. **VHS, Beta** *NO ♂*

Red Rock West Nothing is what it seems in this stylish and entertaining film noir set in a desolate Wyoming town. Perennial loser and nice guy Michael (Cage) is headed to a job at oil rig, but blows his chance by admitting he has a bad leg. Landing in the tiny burg of Red Rock, he's mistaken for the hit man hired by local barkeep Walsh to kill his pretty wife (Boyle). Then Boyle doubles Walsh's offer—what's a film noir boy to do? And Hopper, the real killer, strides into town. Full of twists, turns, and shades of "El Mariachi," this enjoyable, well-acted thriller is a real gem that escaped directly to cable before being rescued by a San Francisco exhibitor.
1993 (R) 98m/C Nicolas Cage, Dennis Hopper, Lara Flynn Boyle, J.T. Walsh, Timothy Carhart, Dan Shor, Dwight Yoakam, Bobby Joe McFadden; **D:** John Dahl; **W:** John Dahl; **M:** William Orvis. **VHS $89.95** *COL ♂♂♂½*

The Red Rope A Western hero cuts his honeymoon short to track down some villains.
1937 56m/B Bob Steele, Lois January, Forrest Taylor, Charles "Blackie" King, Karl Hackett, Bobby Nelson; **D:** S. Roy Luby. **VHS $19.95** *NOS, DVT ♂½*

Red Scorpion A Soviet soldier journeys to Africa where he is to assassinate the leader of a rebel group. Will he succeed or switch allegiances? Poor acting and directing abound.
1989 (R) 102m/C Dolph Lundgren, M. Emmet Walsh, Al White, T.P. McKenna, Carmen Argenziano, Brion James, Regopstann; **D:** Joseph Zito; **W:** Arne Olsen. **VHS $89.95** *STE ♂*

Red Shoe Diaries After a woman's suicide her grieving lover discovers her diaries and finds out she led a secret erotic life, revolving around her shoe-salesman lover and a pair of sexy red shoes. Made for cable television; also available in an unrated version.
1992 (R) 105m/C David Duchovny, Billy Wirth, Brigitte Bako; **D:** Zalman King. **VHS $14.98** *REP ♂♂*

Red Shoe Diaries 2: Double Dare The erotic sequel to "Red Shoe Diaries" follows the libidinous fancies of three women. Severance begins a sexual affair with a stranger only be torn between love and lust. Johnson gets naked to tease an office worker in the building next door. Crosby is a cop who is rejected by the man she desires—so she arrests and handcuffs him in order to play some kinky games. Also available in an unrated version.
1992 (R) 92m/C Joan Severance, Laura Johnson, Denise Crosby, Steven Bauer, Arnold Vosloo, David Duchovny; **D:** Zalman King, Tibor Takacs. **VHS $89.98** *REP, PMS ♂♂*

Red Shoe Diaries 3: Another Woman's Lipstick Another sexual anthology focusing on three stories of desire from the made for cable television series. In "Another Woman's Lipstick" Zoey finds out her husband is having an affair and follows him to his liaison—only to become intrigued with his lover herself. "Just Like That" finds the up-tight Trudie falling for two very opposite men. "Talk to Me Baby" finds Ida and her lover Bud caught up in a very obsessional relationship. Also available in an unrated version.
1993 (R) 90m/C Nina Siemaszko, Matthew LeBlanc, Tcheky Karyo, Maryam D'Abo, Richard Tyson, Lydie Denier, Christina Fulton, Kevin Haley, David Duchovny; **D:** Ted Kotcheff, Rafael Eisenman, Zalman King; **W:** Zalman King, Chloe King. **VHS $92.95** *REP ♂*

Red Shoe Diaries 4: Auto Erotica Yet another compilation of erotic tales courtesy of the Zalman King series. The first story finds a maid finding her employer's secret chamber and uncovering a very private fantasy. The second has an architect lured by a mystery woman into a game of seduction and the third finds a couple engaged in competitive obsessions. Also available in an unrated version.
1993 (R) 83m/C Ally Sheedy, Scott Plank, David Duchovny, Sheryl Lee, Nicholas Chinlund; **D:** Zalman King. **VHS** *REP ♂♂*

The Red Shoes British classic about a young ballerina torn between love and success. Inspired by the Hans Christian Andersen fairy tale. Noted for its lavish use of Technicolor.
1948 136m/C Anton Walbrook, Moira Shearer, Marius Goring, Leonide Massine, Robert Helpmann, Albert Basserman, Ludmila Tcherina, Esmond Knight, Emeric Pressburger; **D:** Michael Powell; **W:** Emeric Pressburger, Michael Powell. Academy Awards '48: Best Art Direction/Set Decoration (Color), Best Score; Nominations: Best Film Editing, Best Picture, Best Story; Golden Globe Awards '49: Best Score; National Board of Review Awards '48: 10 Best Films of the Year. **VHS, Beta $19.95** *PAR, HMV ♂♂♂♂*

The Red Shoes The Children's Theatre Company and School of Minneapolis perform their own unique interpretation of the Hans Christian Andersen story.
1983 79m/C **VHS, Beta $39.95** *MCA ♂♂♂♂*

Red Signals Mystery criminal makes trains collide.

1927 70m/B Wallace MacDonald, Earl Williams, Eva Novak, J.P. McGowan, Frank Rice; *D:* J.P. McGowan. VHS, Beta $24.95 *GPV, FCT* ♫♫

Red Snow High in the Cascade Mountains, Kyle Lewis is the new snowboard instructor for the Hurricane Ridge Ski Resort. The job is fine in the beginning, until Kyle learns of the tragic fate of the last instructor. Before he knows it, Kyle is the next target and is framed for two murders. He secures the help of his fellow snowboard buddies in hopes of solving the mystery and getting the girl, too. High speed ski scenes and dangerous stunts are the film's only redeeming qualities.
1991 86m/C Carlo Scandiuzzi, Scott Galloway, Darla Slavens, Mitch Cox, Tamar Tibbs, Brian Mahoney; *D:* Phillip J. Roth. VHS $79.95 *VHE* ♫

Red Sonja Two warriors join forces against an evil queen in this sword and sorcery saga. Big, beautiful bodies everywhere, with Bergman returning from her Conan adventures. Little humor, few special effects, and weak acting make this a poor outing.
1985 (PG-13) 89m/C Arnold Schwarzenegger, Brigitte Nielsen, Sandahl Bergman, Paul Smith; *D:* Richard Fleischer. *M:* Ennio Morricone. VHS, Beta $19.95 *MGM, FOX* ♫ 1/2

Red Sorghum A stunning visual achievement, this new wave Chinese film (and Yimou's directorial debut) succeeds on many levels—as an ode to the color red, as dark comedy, and as a sweeping epic with fairy tale overtones. Set in rural China in the 1920s, during the period of the Japanese invasion. The sorghum plot nearby is a symbolic playing field in the movie's most stunning scenes. Here, people make love, murder, betray, and commit acts of bravery, all under the watchful eye of nature. In Mandarin with English subtitles.
1987 91m/C Gong Li, Jiang Wen, Ji Cun Hua; *D:* Zhang Yimou. VHS $79.95 *NYF, ING* ♫♫♫ 1/2

The Red Stallion Good film for animal lovers, but it loses something when it comes to human relationships. A young boy raises his pony into an award-winning racehorse that saves the farm when it wins the big race. Good outdoor photography.
1947 82m/B Robert Paige, Noreen Nash, Ted Donaldson, Jane Darwell; *D:* Lesley Selander. VHS $19.95 *NOS, MOV, HEG* ♫ 1/2

Red Sun A gunfighter, a samurai, and a French bandit fight each other in various combinations in the 1860s. Ludicrous and boring.
1971 115m/C Charles Bronson, Toshiro Mifune, Alain Delon, Ursula Andress; *D:* Terence Young; *W:* William Roberts; *M:* Maurice Jarre. VHS, Beta $24.95 *GEM* ♫♫

Red Surf Action abounds in this surfer film. A couple of hard-nosed wave-riders get involved with big money drug gangs and face danger far greater than the tide.
1990 (R) 104m/C George Clooney, Doug Savant, Dedee Pfeiffer, Gene Simmons, Rick Najera, Philip McKeon; *D:* H. Gordon Boos. VHS, Beta $29.95 *ACA* ♫♫

Red Tent A robust, sweeping man-versus-nature epic based on the true story of the Arctic stranding of Italian explorer Umberto Nobile's expedition in 1928. A Russian-Italian co-production. *AKA:* Krasnaya Palatka.
1969 (G) 121m/C Sean Connery, Claudia Cardinale, Peter Finch, Hardy Kruger, Massimo Girotti, Luigi Vannucchi; *D:* Mikhail Kalatozov; *M:* Ennio Morricone. Beta $19.95 *PAR* ♫♫♫

Red, White & Busted Amnesty or prison? That is the scorching, virtually unanswerable question asked by indictment of America. We follow three friends during the Vietnam War and see how they were affected by the events, whether or not they went. *AKA:* Outside In.
1975 85m/C Darrell Larson, Heather Menzies, Dennia Oliveri, John Bill. VHS, Beta *NO* ♫

Red Wind Kris Morrow is a psychotherapist whose latest patient, Lila, has a number of disturbing sadomasochistic fantasies. When Kris feels she's getting too close to the situation, she refers Lila to another therapist. But Lila calls and tells Kris she's already acted out one of her fantasies by killing her husband. In order to stop Lila from killing again, Kris goes on a dangerous search for her deadly patient.
1991 (R) 93m/C Lisa Hartman, Deanna Lund, Philip Casnoff, Christopher McDonald; *D:* Alan Metzger. VHS *MCA* ♫♫

The Redeemer Group of adults at their high school reunion play the children's game of hide-and-seek, with deadly results.
1976 80m/C F.G. Finkbinder, Damien Knight, Jeanetta Arnetta; *D:* Constantine S. Gochis. VHS, Beta *GHV* ♫

Redneck Implausible, distasteful purported "thriller" about criminals on the run.
1973 92m/C Telly Savalas, Franco Nero, Mark Lester, Ely Galleani, Dulio Del Prete, Maria Michi; *D:* Silvio Narizzano. VHS, Beta *NO* ♫

Redneck Zombies A bunch of backwoods rednecks become zombies after chug-a-lugging some radioactive beer. Eating local tourists becomes a hard habit to break. Betcha can't have just one!
1988 (R) 83m/C Floyd Piranha, Lisa DeHaven, W.E. Benson, William W. Decker, James Housely, Zoofoot, Tyrone Taylor, Perieles Lewnes. VHS, Beta $79.95 *TWE* ♫

Reds The recreation of the life of author John Reed ("Ten Days that Shook the World"), his romance with Louise Bryant, his efforts to start an American Communist party, and his reporting of the Russian Revolution. A sweeping, melancholy epic using dozens of "witnesses" who reminisce about what they saw. See director Sergei Eisenstein's silent masterpiece "Ten Days that Shook the World," based on Reed's book, for the Russian view of some of the events depicted in Beatty's film.
1981 (PG) 195m/C Warren Beatty, Diane Keaton, Jack Nicholson, Edward Herrmann, Maureen Stapleton, Gene Hackman, Jerzy Kosinski, George Plimpton, Paul Sorvino, William Daniels, M. Emmet Walsh, Dolph Sweet, Josef Sommer; *D:* Warren Beatty; *W:* Warren Beatty, Warren Beatty; *M:* Dave Grusin. Academy Awards '81: Best Cinematography, Best Director (Beatty), Best Supporting Actress (Stapleton); Nominations: Best Actor (Beatty), Best Actress (Keaton), Best Art Direction/Set Decoration, Best Costume Design, Best Film Editing, Best Original Screenplay, Best Picture, Best Sound, Best Supporting Actor (Nicholson); Directors Guild of America Awards '81: Best Director (Beatty); Golden Globe Awards '82: Best Director (Beatty); New York Film Critics Awards '81: Best Film. VHS, Beta $29.95 *PAR, BTV* ♫♫

Redwood Forest Trail Environmental-themed oater about a camp for underprivileged city boys. The boys of the camp are blamed for the death of a landowner whose daughter then refuses to renew the camp's mortgage. Allen and Switzer set out to prove that the real culprits are sawmill workers out to control the area timber. Smokey the Bear also makes an appearance to lecture about careless forest fires and the need to preserve the woods.

1950 67m/B Rex Allen, Jeff Donnell, Carl "Alfalfa" Switzer, Jane Darwell, Marten Lamont, Pierre Watkin; *D:* Philip Ford; *W:* Bradford Ropes. VHS $19.99 *MOV* ♫♫

Reefer Madness Considered serious at the time of its release, this low-budget depiction of the horrors of marijuana has become an underground comedy favorite. Overwrought acting and lurid script contribute to the fun. *AKA:* Tell Your Children.
1938 (PG) 67m/B Dave O'Brien, Dorothy Short, Warren McCollum, Lillian Miles, Thelma White, Carleton Young; *D:* Louis Gasnier. VHS, Beta $16.95 *SNC, NOS, HHT* ♫♫

Reet, Petite and Gone All-Black musical featuring the music of neglected jive singer Louis Jordan, and his band, The Tympany Five. A girl's mother dies; sneaky lawyer tries to cheat her. Slick and enjoyable.
1947 75m/B Louis Jordan, June Richmond; *D:* William Forest Crouch. VHS, Beta $19.95 *MVD, NOS, VYY* ♫♫

The Ref Burglur Gus (Leary) picks the wrong house to rob at exactly the wrong time (Christmas Eve) and winds up holding the bickering, obnoxious married homeowners as hostages. Caroline (Davis) and Lloyd (Spacey) take delight in insulting each other and their equally loathsome relatives. Gus plots his getaway while masquerading as the couple's marriage counselor, hence the film's title. Darkly mean-spirited insults offer lots of laughs; any repetitive humor is saved by the three leads.
1993 (R) 97m/C Denis Leary, Judy Davis, Kevin Spacey, Glynis Johns, Robert J. Steinmiller Jr., Christine Baranski; *D:* Ted Demme; *W:* Richard LaGravenese, Marie Weiss; *M:* David A. Stewart. VHS *TOU* ♫♫♫

The Reflecting Skin In a 1950s prairie town a small boy sees insanity, child-murder, and radiation sickness, leading him to fantasize that the tormented young widow next door is a vampire. The pretentious drama/freak show rationalizes its ghastly events as symbolizing the hero's loss of youthful innocence. But the Hound knows the score; this is "Faces of Death" for the arts crowd, a grotesque menagerie that dares you to watch. The exploding-frog opener is already notorious. Beautiful photography, with vistas inspired by the painting of Andrew Wyeth.
1991 116m/C Viggo Mortensen, Lindsay Duncan, Jeremy Cooper; *D:* Philip Ridley; *W:* Philip Ridley; *M:* Nick Bicat. VHS *NO* ♫♫

A Reflection of Fear Lame psycho-thriller about a young girl's jealousy of her father's girlfriend, with family members dying of supernatural causes. *AKA:* Labyrinth.
1972 (PG) 90m/C Robert Shaw, Sally Kellerman, Sondra Locke, Mary Ure; *D:* William A. Fraker. VHS, Beta $69.95 *COL* ♫♫

Reflections in a Golden Eye Huston's film adaptation of Carson McCullers novel about repressed homosexuality, madness, and murder at a Southern Army base in 1948. Star-studded cast cannot consistently pull off convoluted lives of warped characters; not for everyone, though it holds some interest.
1967 109m/C Elizabeth Taylor, Marlon Brando, Brian Keith, Julie Harris; *D:* John Huston. VHS, Beta $19.98 *WAR* ♫♫ 1/2

Reflections of Murder Evil schoolteacher's wife and mistress decide to kill him off and then are plagued by his phantom. Well done made for television remake of the French film "Diabolique." Suspenseful, with a great ending.

1974 97m/C Tuesday Weld, Joan Hackett, Sam Waterston, Lucille Benson, R.G. Armstrong, Michael Lerner, Ed Bernard, Lance Kerwin; *D:* John Badham; *M:* Billy Goldenberg. **VHS $14.98** *REP √√½*

Reform School Girl A young girl ends up behind bars when her boyfriend steals a car to go joy-riding and is involved in a hit-and-run murder. Extremely cheap production and incredulous story. Look for Kellerman in a bit part in her first screen appearance.
1957 71m/B Gloria Castillo, Ross Ford, Edward Byrnes, Ralph Reed, Jack Kruschen, Sally Kellerman; *D:* Edward L. Bernds; *W:* Edward L. Bernds. **VHS $9.95** *NLC √*

Reform School Girls Satiric raucous women's prison film, complete with tough lesbian wardens, brutal lesbian guards, sadistic lesbian inmates, and a single, newly convicted heterosexual heroine. Wendy O. Williams as a teenager? Come on. Overdone, over-campy, exploitative.
1986 (R) 94m/C Linda Carol, Wendy O. Williams, Pat Ast, Sybil Danning, Charlotte McGinnis, Sherri Stoner; *D:* Tom De Simone. **VHS, Beta $19.95** *STE, NWV √*

The Refrigerator Filmed on a miniscule budget, this comic/horror flick tells the story of the innocent Batemans of Ohio who move into a grubby New York apartment where they discover their battered Norge refrigerator is actually a doorway to hell. The fridge has a taste for flesh and tends to eat the unwary visitor as well as defrosting blood (very messy). All the previous tenants disappeared without a trace—will the Batemans be next? Cartoon satire is too amateurish to be successful.
1993 86m/C David Simonds, Julia McNeal, Angel Caban, Nena Segal, Jaime Rojo, Michelle DeCosta; *D:* Nicholas A.E. Jacobs; *W:* Nicholas A.E. Jacobs. **VHS $89.95** *MNC √½*

Refuge of Fear Drama set in a post-nuclear-holocaust world.
198? 90m/C VHS, Beta *NO √*

Regarding Henry A cold-hearted lawyer gets shot in the head during a holdup and survives with memory and personality erased. During recovery the new Henry displays compassion and conscience the old one never had. Though too calculated in its yuppie-bashing ironies, the picture works thanks to splendid acting and low-key, on-target direction.
1991 (PG-13) 107m/C Harrison Ford, Annette Bening, Bill Nunn, Mikki Allen, Elizabeth Wilson, Robin Bartlett, John Leguizamo, Donald Moffatt, Nancy Marchand; *D:* Mike Nichols; *W:* Jeffrey Abrams; *M:* Hans Zimmer. **VHS, Beta $14.95** *PAR √√√*

Reggie Mixes In Wealthy man brawls in bar room and falls for barmaid. Taking a job to be near his beloved, he wipes out local thugs while tending to her welfare. Exhilarating fight scenes in which Fairbanks fists it out with real life boxers.
1916 58m/B Douglas Fairbanks Sr., Bessie Love, Joseph Singleton, William E. Lowery, Wilbur Higby, Frank Bennett; *D:* Christy Cabanne. **VHS, Beta $24.95** *GPV, FCT √√√*

Regina A woman controls all the activities of her husband and son. At age 36, her son is ready to leave home and she refuses to let him. Fine performances in this strange and disturbing film.
1983 86m/C Anthony Quinn, Ava Gardner, Ray Sharkey, Anna Karina; *D:* Jean-Yves Prate. **VHS, Beta $69.95** *NWV √√½*

Reg'lar Fellers A gang of kids save the town and soften the heart of their grandmother, too. Production is sloppy. Based on a comic strip by Gene Byrnes.

1941 66m/B Billy Lee, Carl "Alfalfa" Switzer, Buddy Boles, Janet Dempsey, Sarah Padden, Roscoe Ates; *D:* Arthur Dreifuss. **VHS $19.95** *NOS, FMT, VYY √√*

Rehearsal for Murder Movie star Redgrave is murdered on the night of her Broadway debut. Seems it might have been someone in the cast. Brought to you by the creative team behind "Columbo." Challenging made for television whodunit a twist. Good cast.
1982 96m/C Robert Preston, Lynn Redgrave, Patrick Macnee, Lawrence Pressman, Madolyn Smith, Jeff Goldblum, William Daniels; *D:* David Greene; *M:* Billy Goldenberg. **VHS, Beta $59.95** *REP √√½*

Reign of Terror British-made adventure set during the French Revolution, with everyone after the black book that holds the names of those arch-fiend Robespierre plans to guillotine in his ruthless bid for power. Well-mounted, but historical personages and events are reduced to cartoon form. *AKA:* The Black Book.
1949 89m/B Robert Cummings, Arlene Dahl, Richard Hart, Arnold Moss, Richard Basehart; *D:* Anthony Mann; *W:* Philip Yordan. **VHS $19.95** *NOS, MRV, VEC √√*

Reilly: Ace of Spies Covers the exploits of the real-life superspy and womanizer Sydney Reilly who uncovers Russian secrets in 1901, allowing the Japanese to sink the Russian fleet and invade China. After a lively spying career for the British, Reilly eventually plots against the Bolsheviks and comes close to overthrowing Lenin and installing himself as the new leader of the Russian government. Eleven episodes on four cassettes.
1987 572m/C Sam Neill, Sebastian Shaw, Jeananne Crowley; *D:* Jim Goddard. **VHS, Beta $179.00** *SIG, HBO, FCT √√√*

The Reincarnate Cult guarantees lawyer will live forever if he can find a new body. Enter gullible sculptor; lawyer uses skill at persuasion.
1971 (PG) 89m/C Jack Creley, Jay Reynolds, Trudy Young, Terry Tweed; *D:* Don Haldane. **VHS, Beta** *NO √*

The Reincarnation of Golden Lotus In this highly erotic story of love and revenge, Wong escapes China for decadent Hong Kong by marrying a wealthy but foolish man. She has numerous sadomasochistic affairs and begins having flashbacks, revealing her to be the reincarnation of Golden Lotus, a courtesan of ancient China. In Mandarin Chinese with English subtitles.
1989 99m/C Joi Wong, Eric Tsang, Lam Chen Yen; *D:* Clara Law. **VHS $79.95** *CVC, ING √√√√*

The Reincarnation of Peter Proud A college professor has nightmares which lead him to believe the spirit of a murdered man is now possessing him. Kinda scary, but predictable. Screenplay by Ehrlich from his novel.
1975 (R) 105m/C Michael Sarrazin, Jennifer O'Neill, Margot Kidder, Cornelia Sharpe; *D:* J. Lee Thompson; *W:* Max Ehrlich; *M:* Jerry Goldsmith. **VHS, Beta $29.98** *LIV, VES √√*

The Reivers Young boy and two adult pals journey from small town Mississippi (circa 1905) to the big city of Memphis in a stolen car. Picaresque tale is delightful on-screen, as in William Faulkner's enjoyable last novel.
1969 (PG) 107m/C Steve McQueen, Sharon Farrell, Will Geer, Michael Constantine, Rupert Crosse; *D:* Mark Rydell; *W:* Harriet Frank Jr., Irving Ravetch; *M:* John Williams. **VHS, Beta $14.98** *FOX √√√½*

The Rejuvenator Also known as "Rejuvenatrix." An oft-told film story: an aging actress discovers a "youth" serum but finds out that the serum affects things other than her aging. Well-done. *AKA:* Rejuvenatrix.
1988 (R) 90m/C Marcus Powell, John MacKay, James Hogue, Vivian Lanko, Jessica Dublin; *D:* Brian Thomas Jones; *W:* Simon Nuchtern; *M:* Larry Juris. **VHS** *NO √√½*

Relentless Twisted psycho Nelson, once rejected by the LAPD Academy on psychological grounds takes his revenge by murdering people and using his police training to cover his tracks. Good acting keeps sporadically powerful but cliched thriller afloat.
1989 (R) 92m/C Judd Nelson, Robert Loggia, Meg Foster, Leo Rossi, Pat O'Bryan, Mindy Seeger, Angel Tompkins, Ken Lerner, George Flower; *D:* William Lustig. **VHS, Beta $19.95** *COL √√*

Relentless 2: Dead On Rossi, the detective from the first film, tracks yet another murderer whose occult-style mutilations mask an international political conspiracy. So-so slaughter with artsy camerawork. Honestly, how many "Relentless" fans can you name who've been waiting with anticipation?
1991 (R) 93m/C Leo Rossi, Ray Sharkey, Meg Foster, Miles O'Keeffe; *D:* Michael Schroeder. **VHS $19.95** *COL √√*

Relentless 3 A serial killer (Forsythe) likes to carve up his women victims and send various body parts to taunt the police. Then this sicko decides to really drive the cops crazy by stalking the beautiful girlfriend of the detective (Rossi) investigating the crimes.
1993 (R) 84m/C William Forsythe, Leo Rossi, Tom Bower, Robert Costanzo, Signy Coleman; *D:* James Lemmo; *W:* James Lemmo. **VHS $19.95** *COL √√*

The Reluctant Debutante Harrison and Kendall are the urbane parents of Dee who are trying to find a suitable British husband for their girl. It seems their choices just won't do however, and Dee falls for American bad boy musician Saxon. A very lightweight yet extremely enjoyable romantic comedy thanks to Harrison and in particular his real-life wife Kendall, who unfortunately died the following year.
1958 96m/C Rex Harrison, Kay Kendall, John Saxon, Sandra Dee, Angela Lansbury, Diane Clare; *D:* Vincente Minnelli. **VHS, Beta $19.98** *MGM √√√*

The Reluctant Dragon Classic Disney short about a fun-loving dragon, based on the Kenneth Grahame story; accompanied also by the Disney short "Morris, the Midget Moose." Not to be confused with the full-length 1941 Disney feature film.
1941 28m/C *D:* Alfred Werker. **VHS, Beta $12.99** *DIS, KUI, WTA √√√*

The Remains of the Day If repression is your cup of tea then this is the film for you. Others may want to shake British butler par excellence Stevens (Hopkins) and tell him to express an emotion. In the 1930s, Stevens is the rigidly traditional butler to Lord Darlington (Fox). When Miss Kenton (Thompson) the almost vivacious new housekeeper expresses a quietly personal interest in Stevens his loyalty to an unworthy master prevents him from a chance at happiness. A quiet movie, told in flashback. Hopkins' impressive performance gets by strictly on nuance with Thompson at least allowed a small amount of natural charm. Based on the novel by Kazuo Ishiguro.

1993 (PG) 135m/C Anthony Hopkins, Emma Thompson, James Fox, Christopher Reeve, Peter Vaughan, Hugh Grant, Michael Lonsdale, Tim Pigott-Smith; *D:* James Ivory; *W:* Ruth Prawer Jhabvala; *M:* Richard Robbins. Academy Awards '93 Nominations: Best Actor (Hopkins), Best Actress (Thompson), Best Adapted Screenplay, Best Art Direction/Set Decoration, Best Costume Design, Best Director (Ivory), Best Original Screenplay, Best Picture; British Academy Awards '94: Best Actress (Thompson), Best Adapted Screenplay, Best Director (Ivory), Best Film; Directors Guild of America Awards '93: Best Director (Ivory); Golden Globe Awards '94: Best Actor—Drama (Hopkins), Best Actress—Drama (Thompson), Best Director (Ivory), Best Film—Drama, Best Screenplay; British Academy Awards '94: Best Actor (Hopkins); Los Angeles Film Critics Association Awards '93: Best Actor (Hopkins); National Board of Review Awards '93: Best Actor (Hopkins). **VHS, 8mm** *COL* ✍✍✍

Rembrandt Necessarily very visual biography of the great Dutch painter, Rembrandt. Superb acting by Laughton.
1936 86m/B Charles Laughton, Elsa Lanchester, Gertrude Lawrence, Walter Hudd; *D:* Alexander Korda. **VHS, Beta $14.98** *SUE* ✍✍✍

Rembrandt—1669 A recreation of the controversial artist's last year, with his egotism clashing with his artistic impulses. In Dutch with English subtitles.
1977 114m/C Frans Stelling, Tom de Koff, Aye Fil; *D:* Jos Stelling. **VHS $79.95** *CVC, ING* ✍✍

Remedy for Riches The fourth "Dr. Christian" comedy, has the small-town doctor trying to uncover a real estate fraud before it bankrupts his community. Mildly funny.
1940 66m/B Jean Hersholt, Dorothy Lovett, Edgar Kennedy, Jed Prouty, Walter Catlett; *D:* Erle C. Kenton. **VHS, Beta, 8mm $19.95** *NOS, VYY* ✍✍

Remember Me Just as a woman is starting to gain control of her life, her husband returns home from the mental hospital.
1985 95m/C Robert Grubb, Wendy Hughes, Richard Moir; *D:* Lex Marinos. **VHS, Beta $59.95** *MNC* ✍

Remington Steele, Vol. 1: License to Steele Pilot episode to the light-hearted detective TV series starring Zimbalist as Laura Holt, a female PI who sets up her agency under the name of her fictitious male boss. Then a mystery man appears claiming to be the real Remington Steele (Brosnan) and the two decide to join forces. Also in the first episode are Read as Laura's suspicious assistant, Murphy Michaels, and DeMay as Bernice Fox, the agency secretary.
1982 60m/C Stephanie Zimbalist, Pierce Brosnan, James Read, Janet DeMay. **VHS $14.99** *MOV, MTM* ✍

Remo Williams: The Adventure Begins Adaptation of "The Destroyer" adventure novel series with a Bond-like hero who can walk on water and dodge bullets after being instructed by a Korean martial arts master. Funny and diverting, and Grey is excellent (if a bit over the top) as the wizened oriental. The title's assumption is that the adventure will continue.
1985 (PG-13) 121m/C Fred Ward, Joel Grey, Wilford Brimley, Kate Mulgrew; *D:* Guy Hamilton. **VHS, Beta $14.99** *HBO* ✍✍

Remolina de Pasiones A young woman is driven to suicide after succumbing to her mother's persistent lover.
1987 89m/C Amparo Rivelles, Carlos Pinar, Susana Dosamantes. **VHS, Beta** *MAD* ✍✍

Remote Thirteen-year-old Randy is a whiz designing high-tech remote-control gadgets. When one of his toys wipes out a friend's science project, Randy's parents try to put a halt to his tinkering but the kid has other plans. Innocuous rip-off of "Honey, I Shrunk the Kids" with some "Home Alone" thrown in as well.
1993 (PG) 80m/C Chris Carrara, Jessica Bowman, John Diehl, Derya Ruggles, Tony Longo, Stuart Fratkin; *D:* Ted Nicolaou; *W:* Mike Farrow; *M:* Richard Band. **VHS, Beta** *PAR* ✍✍½

Remote Control A circulating videotape of a 1950's sci-fi flick is turning people into murderous zombies, thanks to some entrepreneurial aliens. Silly, but performed by young actors with gusto.
1988 (R) 88m/C Kevin Dillon, Deborah Goodrich, Christopher Wynne, Jennifer Tilly; *D:* Jeff Lieberman; *M:* Peter Bernstein. **VHS, Beta $79.95** *LIV, HHE* ✍½

Renaissance Man Skeptical new teacher inspires a classroom of underachievers and finds his true calling. Based loosely on the experiences of screenwriter Burnstein at a base in Michigan. Civilian Bill Rago (DeVito) is an unemployed ad exec assigned to teach Shakespeare to a group of borderline Army recruits led by Hardison. Add half a bone for the recruits and their Hamlet rap, a breath of fresh air in an otherwise stale plot. Some funny moments, reminiscent of "Stripes," but not quite as wacky. On the other hand, Marshall does endearing well. Look for rapper Marky Mark with his shirt on (hard to recognize). Shot with the cooperation of the Army.
1994 (PG-13) 124m/C Danny DeVito, Gregory Hines, James Remar, Stacey Dash, Ed Begley Jr., "Marky" Mark Wahlberg, Lillo Brancato, Kadeem Hardison, Richard T. Jones, Khalil Kain, Peter Simmons, Jenifer Lewis; *Cameos:* Cliff Robertson; *D:* Penny Marshall; *W:* Jim Burnstein, Ned Mauldin; *M:* Hans Zimmer. **VHS** *NYR* ✍✍½

Rendez-Moi Ma Peau A modern-day witch transposes two people's personalities with comic results. In French with subtitles.
1981 82m/C *D:* Patrick Schulmann. **VHS, Beta** *FCT* ✍✍½

Rendez-vous A racy, dark film about the sensitive balance between sex and exploitation, the real world and the stage world. Some may be disturbed by chillingly explicit scenes. Impressive tour de force of imagination, direction, and cinematography. In French with English subtitles.
1985 (R) 82m/C Juliette Binoche, Lambert Wilson, Wadeck Stanczak, Jean-Louis Trintignant; *D:* Andre Techine. **VHS $29.95** *CVC, ING, TPV* ✍✍✍

Renegade Girl A special agent is sent west to capture the female head of a band of outlaws.
1946 65m/B Alan Curtis, Ann Savage, Edward Brophy, Ray Corrigan, Jack Holt; *D:* William Berke. **VHS, Beta $19.95** *NOS, RXM, VYY* ✍

Renegade Monk Invincible warrior-monk dispenses his own brand of justice with his fists of aluminum foil.
1982 (R) 90m/C Liu Chang Liang, Huang Hsing Shaw, Ko Shou Liang, Lang Shih Chia, Hsu Chung Hsing. **VHS, Beta $59.95** *GEM* ✍½

Renegade Ninja A man whose father was murdered kicks everyone within reach in his quest for revenge.
1983 109m/C Kensaku Marita; *D:* Sadao Nakajima. **VHS, Beta $79.95** *PSM* ✍

Renegade Ranger/Scarlet River A western double feature: A Texas Ranger and his singing sidekick attempt to help out a woman accused of murder in the "The Renegade Ranger," and a cowboy tries to free his sweetheart from a band of cattle rustlers in "Scarlet River."
1938 113m/B Rita Hayworth, Tim Holt, George O'Brien, Ray Whitley, Tom Keene, Lon Chaney Jr., Myrna Loy, Bruce Cabot, Betty Furness; *D:* David Howard. **VHS, Beta $34.95** *RKO, TTC* ✍½

Renegade Trail Hopalong Cassidy helps a marshall and a pretty widow round up ex-cons and rustlers. The King's Men, radio singers of the era, perform a fistful of songs.
1939 61m/B William Boyd, George "Gabby" Hayes, Russell Hayden, Charlotte Wynters, Russell Hopton, Sonny Bupp, Jack Rockwell, Roy Barcroft, Eddie Dean; *D:* Lesley Selander. **VHS $19.95** *NOS* ✍✍

Renegades A young cop from Philadelphia and a Lakota Indian begrudgingly unite to track down a gang of ruthless crooks. Good action, and lots of it; not much story.
1989 (R) 105m/C Kiefer Sutherland, Lou Diamond Phillips, Rob Knepper, Jami Gertz, Bill Smitrovich; *D:* Jack Sholder; *M:* Michael Kamen. **VHS, Beta $19.95** *MCA* ✍✍

Renfrew of the Royal Mounted A Canadian Mountie goes after counterfeiters and sings a few songs in this mild adaptation of a popular kids' radio serial. Newill was a popular tenor of the day, but the Hound thinks Renfrew's dog 'Lightning' should have been the star.
1937 57m/B Carol Hughes, James Newill, Kenneth Harlan; *D:* Al Herman. **VHS, Beta** *DVT, GPV, HEG* ✍✍

Renfrew on the Great White Trail A frustrated fur trader takes off after a pack of thieves. *AKA:* On the Great White Trail; Renfrew of the Royal Mounted on the Great White Trail.
1938 58m/B James Newill, Terry Walker, Robert Frazer, Richard Alexander; *D:* Al Herman. **VHS $19.95** *NOS, DVT* ✍½

Reno and the Doc Enjoyable comedy about two endearingly cranky middle-aged men battling mid-life crises join together and test their mettle in the world of professional skiing.
1984 88m/C Ken Walsh, Henry Ramer, Linda Griffiths; *D:* Charles Dennis. **VHS, Beta $19.95** *NWV* ✍✍½

Renoir Shorts Two early silent Renoir fantasies: "The Little Matchgirl," a lyrical adaptation of the Hans Christian Anderson fairy tale, and "Charleston," in which a space-traveling African and Parisian girl dance comically.
1927 50m/B Catherine Hessling; *D:* Jean Renoir. **VHS, Beta $24.95** *NOS, FCT* ✍✍✍

Rent-A-Cop A cop (Reynolds) is bounced from the force after he survives a drug-bust massacre under suspicious circumstances. He becomes a security guard and continues to track down the still-at-large killer with help from call girl Minnelli.
1988 (R) 95m/C Burt Reynolds, Liza Minnelli, James Remar, Richard Masur, Bernie Casey, John Stanton, John P. Ryan, Dionne Warwick, Robby Benson; *D:* Jerry London; *M:* Jerry Goldsmith. **VHS, Beta $14.99** *HBO* ✍✍

Rentadick A precursor to the Monty Python masterpieces, written by future members Chapman and Cleese. Private eye spoof isn't as funny as later Python efforts; but it is an indication of what was yet to come and fans should enjoy it.
1972 94m/C James Booth, Julie Ege, Ronald Fraser, Donald Sinden, Michael Bentine, Richard Briers, Spike Milligan; *D:* Jim Clark; *W:* Graham Chapman, John Cleese; *M:* Carl Davis. **VHS** *NO* ✍✍

Rented Lips Two documentary film makers sell out, taking over the production of a porno film at the request of a public television producer who promises to help their careers. Mull and Shawn are well supported by an impressive cast, but everyone's effort is wasted in unfunny attempt at comedy.
1988 (R) 82m/C Martin Mull, Dick Shawn, Jennifer Tilly, Kenneth Mars, Edy Williams, Robert Downey Jr., June Lockhart, Shelley Berman, Mel Welles, Pat McCormick, Eileen Brennan; **D:** Robert Downey. **VHS, Beta** *NO* ✗

Repentance A popular, surreal satire of Soviet and Communist societies. A woman is arrested for repeatedly digging up a dead local despot, and put on trial. Wickedly funny and controversial; released under the auspices of glasnost. In Russian with English subtitles. **AKA:** Pokayaniye; Confession.
1987 (PG) 151m/C Avtandil Makharadze, Zeinab Botsvadze, Ia Ninidze, Edisher Giorgobiani, Ketevan Abuladze, Kakhi Kavsadze; **D:** Tengiz Abuladze. **VHS, Beta $79.95** *MED* ✗✗✗

Repo Jake Jake Baxter learns the myth of the carefree life of a repossession man in this action thriller. His illusion is destroyed by angry clients, pornography, a deadly underworld racetrack, and a sinister crime boss.
1990 90m/C Dan Haggerty, Robert Axelrod. **VHS $19.95** *PMH* ✗½

Repo Man An inventive, perversely witty portrait of sick modern urbanity, following the adventures of a punk rocker taking a job as a car repossessor in a barren city. The landscape is filled with pointless violence, no-frills packaging, media hypnosis and aliens. Executive producer: none other than ex-Monkee Michael Nesmith.
1983 (R) 93m/C Emilio Estevez, Harry Dean Stanton, Sy Richardson, Tracy Walter, Olivia Barash, Fox Harris, Jennifer Balgobin, Vonetta McGee, Angelique Pettyjohn; **D:** Alex Cox. **VHS, Beta $14.98** *MCA* ✗✗✗½

The Report on the Party and the Guests A controversial, widely banned political allegory, considered a masterpiece from the Czech new wave. A picnic/lawn party deteriorates into brutality, fascist intolerance and persecution. Many Czech film makers, some banned at the time, appear. Based on a story by Ester Krumbachova, who also co-wrote the screenplay. In Czech with English subtitles.
1966 71m/B Jiri Nemec, Evald Schorm, Ivan Vyskocil, Jan Klusak, Zdena Skvorecka, Pavel Bosek; **D:** Jan Nemec; **W:** Jan Nemec. **VHS, Beta $59.95** *FCT* ✗✗✗✗

Report to the Commissioner A rough, energetic crime-in-the-streets cop thriller. A young detective accidentally kills an attractive woman who turns out to have been an undercover cop, then is dragged into the bureaucratic cover-up. **AKA:** Operation Undercover.
1974 (R) 112m/C Michael Moriarty, Yaphet Kotto, Susan Blakely, Hector Elizondo, Richard Gere, Tony King, Michael McGuire, Stephen Elliott; **D:** Milton Katselas; **W:** Abby Mann; **M:** Elmer Bernstein. **VHS, Beta $29.95** *MGM* ✗✗✗

Repossessed A corny, occasionally funny takeoff on the human-possessed-by-the-devil films with Blair, as usual, as the afflicted victim. Nielsen, in another typecast role, plays the goofy man of the cloth who must save the day. Numerous actors appear in brief comedy sequences which lampoon current celebrities and constitute the film's highlights. For fans of ''Airplane'' and ''The Naked Gun''; not necessarily for others.
1990 (PG-13) 89m/C Linda Blair, Ned Beatty, Leslie Nielsen, Anthony Starke, Jesse Ventura; **D:** Bob Logan; **W:** Bob Logan; **M:** Charles Fox. **VHS $89.95** *LIV* ✗✗

Repulsion Character study of a young French girl who is repulsed and attracted by sex. Left alone when her sister goes on vacation, her facade of stability begins to crack, with violent and bizarre results. Polanski's first film in English and his first publicly accepted full-length feature. Suspenseful, disturbing and potent.
1965 105m/B Catherine Deneuve, Yvonne Furneaux, Ian Hendry, John Fraser, Patrick Wymark, James Villers; **D:** Roman Polanski; **W:** Roman Polanski, Gerard Brach. **VHS, Beta $29.95** *VDM, VCN, MRV* ✗✗✗½

Requiem for a Heavyweight The original television version of the story about an American Indian heavyweight boxer played by Palance who risks blindness in order to help his manager pay off bookies. Highly acclaimed teleplay written for ''Playhouse 90.''
1956 90m/B Jack Palance, Keenan Wynn, Ed Wynn, Kim Hunter, Ned Glass; **D:** Ralph Nelson; **W:** Rod Serling. **VHS, Beta $14.95** *WKV, FUS, BTV* ✗✗✗

Requiem for Dominic A Communist-bloc country in the midst of revolution accuses a man of terrorist activities. Can his friend, exiled for years, help him discover the truth? Interesting and timely premise matched with outstanding ensemble acting make for a superior thriller. Amnesty International receives partial proceeds from all sales of this video. In German with English subtitles. **AKA:** Requiem fur Dominic.
1991 (R) 88m/C Felix Mitterer, Viktoria Schubert, August Schmolzer, Angelica Schutz; **D:** Robert Dornhelm. **VHS $79.95** *HMD, ING* ✗✗✗½

The Rescue An elite team of U.S. Navy Seals is captured after destroying a disabled submarine. When the U.S. government writes off the men, their children decide to mount a rescue. Puerile, empty-headed trash for teens.
1988 (PG) 97m/C Marc Price, Charles Haid, Kevin Dillon, Christina Harnos, Edward Albert; **D:** Ferdinand Fairfax; **W:** Jim Thomas, John Thomas; **M:** Bruce Broughton. **VHS, Beta $89.95** *TOU, HHE* ✗½

Rescue Force A crack team of anti-terrorists, led by Lt. Col. Steel, takes on the kidnappers of an American ambassador. Action filled excitement.
1990 85m/C Richard Harrison. **VHS** *NO* ✗✗

Rescue Me Geek photographer Fraser carries a torch for high school honey Ginny and just happens to be on the scene (with camera) when she's kidnapped. So he persuades a scruffy Vietnam vet to help him rescue his damsel in distress. Likeable adventure with lots of chases.
1993 (PG-13) 99m/C Michael Dudikoff, Stephen Dorff, Peter DeLuise, Ami Dolenz, William Lucking, Dee Wallace Stone; **D:** Arthur Seidelman; **W:** Michael Snyder; **M:** Al Kasha, Joel Hirschhorn, David Waters. **VHS** *WAR* ✗✗½

The Rescuers Bernard and Miss Bianca, two mice who are members of the Rescue Aid Society, attempt to rescue an orphan named Penny from the evil Madame Medusa, who's after the world's biggest diamond. They are aided by comic sidekick, Orville the albatross, and a group of lovable swamp creatures. Very charming in the best Disney tradition. Based on the stories of Margery Sharp. Followed by ''The Rescuers Down Under.''

1977 (G) 76m/C **D:** Wolfgang Reitherman, John Lounsbery, John Newhart; **V:** Bob Newhart, Eva Gabor, Geraldine Page, Jim Jordan, Jeanette Nolan, Pat Buttram. **VHS $24.99** *DIS, OM* ✗✗✗

The Rescuers Down Under ''Crocodile'' Dundee goes Disney; the followup to ''The Rescuers'' places its characters in Australia with only mild results for a Magic Kingdom product. Heroic mice Bernard and Bianca protect a young boy and a rare golden eagle from a poacher. The great bird closely resembles the logo of Republic Pictures.
1990 (G) 77m/C **D:** Hendel Butoy, Mike Gabriel; **W:** Jim Cox, Karey Kirkpatrick, Joe Ranft, Byron Simpson; **M:** Bruce Broughton; **V:** Bob Newhart, Eva Gabor, John Candy, Tristan Rogers, George C. Scott, Frank Welker, Adam Ryen. **VHS, Beta $29.99** *DIS, OM* ✗✗½

Reservoir Dogs Ultraviolent tale of honor among thieves. Six professional criminals known by code names to protect their identities (Misters Pink, White, Orange, Blonde, Blue, and Brown) are assembled by Tierney to pull off a diamond heist. But two of the gang are killed in a police ambush. The survivors regroup in an empty warehouse and try to discover the informer in their midst. In probably the most stomach-churning scene (there is some competition here), a policeman is tortured just for the heck of it to the tune of the Stealers Wheel ''Stuck in the Middle with You.'' Unrelenting; auspicious debut for Tarantino with strong ensemble cast anchored by Keitel as the very professional Mr. White.
1992 (R) 100m/C Harvey Keitel, Tim Roth, Michael Madsen, Steve Buscemi, Christopher Penn, Lawrence Tierney, Kirk Baltz, Quentin Tarantino; **D:** Quentin Tarantino; **W:** Quentin Tarantino. **VHS $19.98** *LIV, BTV* ✗✗✗½

The Respectful Prostitute Sartre's tale of hooker who is cajoled into providing false testimony as a witness in the trial of a member of a prominent family. English language version of French drama.
1952 75m/B Ivan Desny, Barbara Laage, Walter Bryan; **D:** Marcel Pagliero, Charles Brabant; **W:** Jean-Paul Sartre. **VHS $19.95** *XVC, FCT, ING* ✗✗½

Rest In Pieces A young woman inherits a Spanish mansion, and weird things begin to happen. It seems a cult of Satan worshippers is already living on the estate. As one might infer from the title, quite a bit of hacking and slashing ensues.
1987 (R) 90m/C Scott Thompson Baker, Lorin Jean, Dorothy Malone; **D:** Joseph Braunstein. **VHS, Beta $14.95** *LIV* ✗

Restless A restless homemaker begins an affair with a childhood friend. Director Cosmatos later oversaw ''Rambo.'' **AKA:** The Beloved.
1972 75m/C Raquel Welch, Richard Johnson, Jack Hawkins, Flora Robson; **D:** George P. Cosmatos. **VHS, Beta $79.95** *VMK* ✗

The Restless Breed Son is restless after dad, a secret service agent, is slain by gunrunners. Routine oater-revenge epic done in by listless script.
1958 81m/C Scott Brady, Anne Bancroft, Jay C. Flippen, Rhys Williams, Jim Davis; **D:** Allan Dwan. **VHS $19.95** *FRH, IME* ✗

The Resurrected One of the best recent H.P. Lovecraft horror adaptations, a fairly faithful try at ''The Case of Charles Dexter Ward.'' Ward learns he has a satanic ancestor who possessed the secret of resurrection and eternal life—but, as the warlock says, it is very messy. Surprisingly tasteful even with occasional gore and truly ghastly monsters; in fact this pic could have used a bit more intensity.

1991 (R) 108m/C John Terry, Jane Sibbet, Chris Sarandon; **D:** Dan O'Bannon; **M:** Richard Band. **VHS $14.98** *LIV* 🎬🎬½

Resurrection After a near-fatal car accident, a woman finds she has the power to heal others by touch. She denies that God is responsible, much to her Bible Belt community's dismay. Acclaimed and well-acted.

1980 (PG) 103m/C Ellen Burstyn, Sam Shepard, Roberts Blossom, Eva LeGallienne, Clifford David, Richard Farnsworth, Pamela Payton-Wright; **D:** Daniel Petrie; **M:** Maurice Jarre. Academy Awards '80 Nominations: Best Actress (Burstyn), Best Supporting Actress (LeGallienne); National Board of Review Awards '80: 10 Best Films of the Year, Best Supporting Actress (LeGallienne). **VHS, Beta $59.95** *MCA* 🎬🎬½

Resurrection of Zachary Wheeler A presidential candidate, who narrowly escaped death in an auto crash, is brought to a mysterious clinic in New Mexico. A reporter sneaks into the clinic and discovers the horrors of cloning.

1971 (G) 100m/C Angie Dickinson, Bradford Dillman, Leslie Nielsen, Jack Carter, James Daly; **D:** Bob Wynn. **VHS, Beta $29.95** *VCI* 🎬🎬½

Retreat, Hell! Korean War drama about the retreat from the Changjin Reservoir. Standard gun-ho military orientation with dismal results.

1952 95m/B Frank Lovejoy, Richard Carlson, Russ Tamblyn, Anita Louise; **D:** Joseph H. Lewis. **VHS $19.98** *REP* 🎬🎬

Retribution Struggling artist survives suicide attempt only to find himself possessed by the spirit of a criminal who was tortured to death. Seeing the hood's gruesome demise in his dreams, the survivor sets out to bring his murderers face-to-face with their maker.

1988 (R) 106m/C Dennis Lipscomb, Hoyt Axton, Leslie Wing, Suzanne Snyder; **D:** Guy Magar. **VHS, Beta** *NO* 🎬½

Retrievers Young man and a former CIA agent team up to expose the unsavory practices of the organization.

1982 90m/C Max Thayer, Roselyn Royce. **VHS, Beta $69.98** *VES* 🎬

The Return Vincent and Shepherd meet as adults and discover that they had both, as children, been visited by aliens who had given technology to a cattle-mutilating prospector. A mess with no idea of what sort of film it wants to be. **AKA:** The Alien's Return.

1980 (PG) 91m/C Cybill Shepherd, Raymond Burr, Jan-Michael Vincent, Martin Landau, Vincent Schiavelli, Zachary Vincent, Farah Bunch, Neville Brand, Susan Kiger; **D:** Greydon Clark. **VHS, Beta** *NO* Woof!

Return A woman believes that the man she loves is the reincarnation of her dead grandfather. Interesting concept, but overall, a disappointing mystery.

1988 (R) 78m/C Frederic Forrest, Anne Francis, Karlene Crockett, John Walcutt, Lisa Richards; **D:** Andrew Silver. **VHS, Beta $79.95** *ACA* 🎬🎬

Return Engagement A lonely middle-aged ancient history professor falls in love with one of her students.

1978 76m/C Elizabeth Taylor, Joseph Bottoms, Peter Donat, James Ray; **D:** Joseph Hardy. **VHS, Beta** *NO* 🎬½

Return Fire A former employee of the government finds that he must now fight the system if he wants to save his son. Trivial action fare.

1991 (R) 97m/C Adam West, Ron Marchini. **VHS $79.95** *AIP* 🎬½

Return from Witch Mountain A pair of evil masterminds use a boy's supernatural powers to place Los Angeles in nuclear jeopardy. Sequel to Disney's ever-popular "Escape to Witch Mountain."

1978 (G) 93m/C Christopher Lee, Bette Davis, Ike Eisenmann, Kim Richards, Jack Soo; **D:** John Hough; **W:** Malcolm Marmorstein. **VHS, Beta** *DIS* 🎬½

The Return of a Man Called Horse Sequel to "A Man Called Horse" tells the story of an English aristocrat who was captured and raised by Sioux Indians, and then returned to his native homeland. Contains more of the torture scenes for which this series is famous, but not much of Harris.

1976 (PG) 125m/C Richard Harris, Gale Sondergaard, Geoffrey Lewis; **D:** Irvin Kershner; **W:** Jack DeWitt. **VHS, Beta $59.98** *FOX* 🎬🎬

The Return of Boston Blackie The oft-filmed crook/detective tries to retrieve an heiress's stolen jewels. Silent.

1927 77m/B Raymond Glenn, Corliss Palmer, Strongheart, Rosemary Cooper, Coit Albertson; **D:** Harry Hoyt. **VHS, Beta, 8mm $24.95** *VYY* 🎬½

Return of Captain Invincible Arkin is a derelict super-hero persuaded to fight crime again in this unique spoof. One liners fly faster than a speeding bullet. Lee gives one of his best performances as the mad scientist. Musical numbers by Rocky Horror's O'Brien and Hartley sporadically interrupt. Made on a shoe-string budget, offbeat film is entertaining but uneven. **AKA:** Legend in Leotards.

1983 (PG) 90m/C Alan Arkin, Christopher Lee, Kate Fitzpatrick, Bill Hunter, Graham Kennedy, Michael Pate, Hayes Gordon, Max Phipps, Noel Ferrier; **D:** Philippe Mora; **W:** Steven E. de Souza. **VHS, Beta** *NO* 🎬🎬½

The Return of Casey Jones Early adventure film featuring lots of great railroad action. **AKA:** Train 2419.

1934 64m/B Charles Starrett, Ruth Hall, George "Gabby" Hayes, Robert Elliott, Margaret Seddon, Jackie Searl; **D:** John P. McCarthy. **VHS $12.95** *GPV* 🎬🎬

Return of Chandu This serial in 12 chapters features Bela Lugosi as Chandu, who exercises his magical powers to conquer a religious sect of cat worshippers inhabiting the island of Lemuria. In the process, he fights to save the Princess Nadji from being sacrificed by them.

1934 156m/B Bela Lugosi, Maria Alba, Clara Kimball Young; **D:** Ray Taylor. **VHS, Beta $24.95** *DVT, NOS, SNC* 🎬🎬

The Return of Count Yorga The vampire Count returns, taking up residence in a decrepit mansion nearby an orphanage. There he spies the toothsome Cynthia and Yorga decides to make her a vampiric bride. But the Count reckons without Cynthia's noble boyfriend who wants to keep his honey on this side of the grave. Preceded by "Count Yorga, Vampire."

1971 (R) 97m/C Robert Quarry, Mariette Hartley, Roger Perry, Yvonne Wilder, Rudy DeLuca, George Macready, Walter Brooke; **D:** Bob Kelljan; **W:** Yvonne Wilder, Bob Kelljan. **VHS $9.98** *ORI* 🎬

The Return of Dr. Mabuse The evil doctor is back, this time sending his entranced slaves to attack a nuclear power plant. Frobe, the inspector, and Barker, the FBI man, team up to thwart him. Fun for fans of serial detective stories. **AKA:** Im Stahlnetz Des Dr. Mabuse; Phantom Fiend.

1961 88m/B Gert Frobe, Lex Barker, Daliah Lavi, Wolfgang Preiss, Fausto Tozzi, Rudolph Forster; **D:** Harald Reinl. **VHS, Beta $16.95** *SNC* 🎬½

Return of Dracula Low-budget film about the Count killing a Czech artist and assuming his identity as he makes his way to the States. Once there, he moves in with the dead man's family and begins acting rather strangely. Retitled "The Curse of Dracula" for TV. **AKA:** The Curse of Dracula.

1958 77m/C Francis Lederer, Norma Eberhardt, Ray Stricklyn, Jimmie Baird; **D:** Paul Landres. **VHS $14.95** *MGM, FCT* 🎬🎬

Return of Draw Egan Vintage silent western wherein Hart is an outlaw-turned-greenhorn sheriff of a lawless town. Music score.

1916 64m/B William S. Hart, Louise Glaum; **D:** William S. Hart. **VHS, Beta, 8mm $24.95** *VYY, GPV, GVV* 🎬½

The Return of Eliot Ness Ness comes out of retirement in 1947 Chicago to track down a friend's killer. And with Al Capone dead, Chicago mob bosses are fighting for their piece of illegal turf. Stack reprises his "The Untouchables" TV role from the early '60s in this made for TV movie.

1991 94m/C Robert Stack, Charles Durning, Philip Bosco, Jack Coleman, Lisa Hartman, Anthony De Sando; **D:** James A. Contner. **VHS $92.95** *APX* 🎬🎬½

Return of Frank Cannon Portly private eye Frank Cannon comes out of retirement to investigate the alleged suicide of an old friend. Made for television.

1980 96m/C William Conrad, Diana Muldaur, Joanna Pettet, Allison Argo, Arthur Hill, Ed Nelson; **D:** Corey Allen; **M:** Bruce Broughton. **VHS, Beta $39.95** *WOV* 🎬🎬

Return of Frank James One of Lang's lesser Hollywood works, this is nonetheless an entertaining sequel to 1939's "Jesse James." Brother Frank tries to go straight, but eventually has to hunt down the culprits who murdered his infamous outlaw sibling. Tierney's first film.

1940 92m/C Henry Fonda, Gene Tierney, Jackie Cooper, Henry Hull, John Carradine, Donald Meek, J. Edward Bromberg; **D:** Fritz Lang. **VHS, Beta $19.98** *FOX* 🎬🎬🎬

The Return of Grey Wolf A wild dog must fight for survival in Northern Quebec and is befriended by a fur trapper. An intelligent hound, he repays the trapper's generosity by helping him put the moves on some fur thieves. Silent.

1922 62m/B Helen Lynch, Henry Pierce. **VHS, Beta, 8mm $19.95** *VYY* 🎬🎬

The Return of Jafar Clumsy thief Abis Mal inadvertently releases evil sorcerer Jafar from his lamp prison and now the powerful "genie Jafar" plots his revenge. So it's up to Aladdin and friends to save the Sultan's kingdom once again. Contains five new songs. ♪Just Forget About Love; Nothing In the World (Quite Like a Friend); I'm Looking Out for Me; You're Only Second Rate; Arabian Nights.

1994 (G) 66m/C **V:** Scott Weinger, Linda Larkin, Gilbert Gottfried, Val Bettin, Dan Castellaneta. **VHS $22.99** *DIS* 🎬🎬

Return of Jesse James Look-alike of dead outlaw Jesse James joins in with some former members of the James Gang, leading townsfolk to believe the notorious bank robber never died. It's up to brother Frank James, now an upstanding citizen, to set the record straight. A little slow moving at times, but still worth viewing.

1950 77m/B John Ireland, Ann Dvorak, Reed Hadley, Henry Hull, Hugh O'Brian, Tommy Noonan, Peter Marshall; **D:** Arthur Hilton. **VHS, Beta** NO ✍✍

The Return of Josey Wales No match for the original featuring Clint Eastwood, the title character is played woodenly by Parks. This installment finds Wales pitted against a bumbling lawman. Sequel to 1976's "The Outlaw Josey Wales."
1986 (R) 90m/C Michael Parks, Rafael Campos, Bob Magruder, Paco Vela, Everett Sifuentes, Charlie McCoy; **D:** Michael Parks. **VHS** HHE ✍

The Return of Martin Guerre In this medieval tale, a dissolute village husband disappears soon after his marriage. Years later, someone who appears to be Martin Guerre returns, allegedly from war, and appears much kinder and more educated. Starring in a love story of second chances, Depardieu does not disappoint, nor does the rest of the cast. In French with English subtitles. Based on an actual court case. Remade in 1993 as "Sommersby."
1983 111m/C Gerard Depardieu, Roger Planchon, Maurice Jacquemont, Barnard Pierre Donnadieu, Nathalie Baye; **D:** Daniel Vigne; **W:** Daniel Vigne, Jean-Claude Carriere. **VHS, Beta** $29.98 SUE, APD, HMV ✍✍✍ ½

The Return of Our Gang Contains three vintage silent Pathe "Our Gang" shorts: "The School Play (Stage Fright)," "Summer Daze (The Cobbler)," and "Dog Days."
1925 57m/B Joe Cobb, Ernie Morrison, Mickey Daniels, Farina Hoskins, Mary Kornman, Jackie Condon, Jack Davis, Jannie Hoskins, Andy Samuels, Eugene Jackson, Pete the Pup. **VHS, Beta, 8mm** $24.95 VYY ✍ ½

The Return of Peter Grimm Man returns from death to try to tidy up the mess he left behind. Enjoyable if trite fantasy based on a play by David Belasco.
1935 82m/B Lionel Barrymore, Helen Mack, Edward Ellis, Donald Meek, George Breakston, James Bush; **D:** George Nichols. **VHS** $19.98 TTC, FCT ✍✍ ½

The Return of Spinal Tap Cult-fave mock rock group Spinal Tap is back with a feature-length video of performance and backstage footage from its recent reunion concert tour promoting their album "Break Like the Wind." Sequel to "This is Spinal Tap" features lots of heavy metal songs including the title track, "Majesty of Rock," "Bitch School," "Diva Fever," "Clam Caravan," and "Stinkin' Up the Great Outdoors." Not as great as the original satire, but will appeal to Spinal Tap fans.
1992 110m/C Christopher Guest, Michael McKean, Harry Shearer, Rick Parnell, C.J. Vanston; **Cameos:** Paul Anka, Jeff Beck, Jamie Lee Curtis, Richard Lewis, Martha Quinn, Kenny Rogers, Martin Short, Mel Torme; **W:** Christopher Guest, Michael McKean, Harry Shearer. **VHS** $19.98 MPI, MVD ✍✍ ½

Return of Superfly Man with insect moniker pesters drug dealers and cops in Harlem. Long-awaited sequel to urban epic "Superfly," scored again by Mayfield.
1990 (R) 94m/C Margaret Avery, Nathan Purdee, Sam Jackson; **M:** Ice-T, Curtis Mayfield. **VHS** $92.95 VMK ✍

The Return of Swamp Thing The DC Comics creature rises again out of the muck to fight mutants and evil scientists. Tongue-in-cheek, and nothing at all like the literate, ecologically-oriented comic from which it was derived.
1989 (PG-13) 95m/C Louis Jourdan, Heather Locklear, Sarah Douglas, Dick Durock; **D:** Jim Wynorski. **VHS, Beta** $14.95 COL ✍ ½

Return of the Aliens: The Deadly Spawn Aliens infect the earth and violently destroy humans. Extremely violent and gory. Watch out for those officious offspring.
1983 (R) 90m/C Charles George Hildebrandt; **D:** Douglas McKeown. **VHS** NO ✍

Return of the Ape Man Campy fun with Carradine and Lugosi. A mad scientist transplants Carradine's brain into the body of the "missing link." Hams galore.
1944 51m/B Bela Lugosi, John Carradine, George Zucco, Judith Gibson, Michael Ames, Frank Moran, Mary Currier; **D:** Phil Rosen. **VHS** $59.95 MED ✍✍

Return of the Bad Men Scott is a retired marshall who must fight against a gang of outlaws lead by the Sundance Kid. Sequel to "Badman's Territory."
1948 90m/C Randolph Scott, Robert Ryan, Anne Jeffreys, George "Gabby" Hayes, Jason Robards Sr., Jacqueline White; **D:** Ray Enright. **VHS, Beta** $19.98 RKO, CCB, MED ✍✍

Return of the Chinese Boxer Samurai and ninja warriors fight, usually to the death.
1974 93m/C Jimmy Wang Yu, Lung Fei, Cheung Ying Chen, Chin Kang. **VHS, Beta** $39.95 UNI ✍

Return of the Dinosaurs A comet is about to collide with the Earth. Never fear! The dinosaur patrol will interfere (and ultimately save the planet).
1983 82m/C **VHS, Beta** $39.95 TWE ✍

Return of the Dragon In Lee's last picture, a Chinese restaurant in Rome is menaced by gangsters who want to buy the property. On behalf of the owners, Lee duels an American karate champ in the Roman forum. The battle scenes between Lee and Norris are great and make this a must-see for martial arts fans.
1973 (R) 91m/C Bruce Lee, Nora Miao, Chuck Norris; **D:** Bruce Lee. **VHS, Beta** $19.98 FOX, GEM ✍✍ ½

Return of the Evil Dead The sightless dead priests return to attack still more 1970s' Europeans in this second installment of the "blind dead" trilogy. Preceded by "Tombs of the Blind Dead" and followed by "Horror of the Zombies." Not to be confused with Raimi's "Evil Dead" slasher flicks. **AKA:** Return of the Blind Dead.
1975 85m/C Tony Kendall, Esther Roy, Frank Blake; **D:** Armando de Ossorio. **VHS** $59.95 JEF ✍

Return of the Family Man A mass murderer seems unstoppable as he continues to slash whole families at a time...the family man is redefined in this bloody gorefest.
1989 90m/C Ron Smerczak, Liam Cundill, Terence Reis, Michelle Constant; **D:** John Murlowski. **VHS** NO ✍

Return of the Fly The son of the scientist who discovered how to move matter through space decides to continue his father's work, but does so against his uncle's wishes. He soon duplicates his dad's experiments with similar results. This sequel to "The Fly" doesn't buzz like the original. Followed by "Curse of the Fly."
1959 80m/B Vincent Price, Brett Halsey, John Sutton, Dan Seymour, David Frankham; **D:** Edward L. Bernds. **VHS, Beta** $14.98 FOX, FCT ✍

Return of the Jedi Third film in George Lucas' popular space saga. Against seemingly fearsome odds, Luke Skywalker battles such worthies as Jabba the Hut and heavy-breathing Darth Vader to save his comrades and triumph over the evil Galactic Empire. Han and Leia reaffirm their love and team up with C3PO, R2-D2, Chewbacca, Calrissian, and a bunch of furry Ewoks to aid in the annihilation of the Dark Side. The special effects are still spectacular, even the third time around. Sequel to "Star Wars" (1977) and "The Empire Strikes Back" (1980).
1983 (PG) 132m/C Mark Hamill, Carrie Fisher, Harrison Ford, Billy Dee Williams, David Prowse, James Earl Jones, Kenny Baker, Denis Lawson, Anthony Daniels, Peter Mayhew; **D:** Richard Marquand; **W:** George Lucas, Lawrence Kasdan; **M:** John Williams; **V:** Alec Guinness, Frank Oz. Academy Awards '83: Best Visual Effects; Nominations: Best Art Direction/Set Decoration, Best Sound, Best Original Score; People's Choice Awards '84: Best Film. **VHS, Beta** $19.98 FOX, RDG, HMV ✍✍✍

Return of the Killer Tomatoes The man-eating plant-life from 1977's "Attack of the Killer Tomatoes" is back, able to turn into people due to the slightly larger budget. Astin is mad as the scientist. Not as bad as "Attack," representing a small hurdle in the history of filmdom. Followed by "Killer Tomatoes Strike Back."
1988 (PG) 98m/C Anthony Starke, George Clooney, Karen Mistal, Steve Lundquist, John Astin, Charlie Jones, Rock Peace, Frank Davis, C.J. Dillon, Teri Weigel; **D:** John DeBello. **VHS, Beta** $19.95 STE, NWV ✍

The Return of the King The third and final animated episode of J.R.R Tolkien's Middle Earth Trilogy. This saga features Frodo, relative to Hobbit Bilbo Baggins, and his faithful servant, making middle Earth safe from Orcs, Gollums and other ooky creatures.
1980 120m/C **D:** Arthur Rankin Jr., Jules Bass; **V:** Orson Bean, Roddy McDowall, John Huston, Theodore Bikel, William Conrad, Glen Yarborough, Paul Frees, Casey Kasem, Sonny Melendrez. **VHS** $9.99 XVC, VTR, FFF ✍

Return of the Lash Lash LaRue once again defends settlers' rights from ruthless outlaws.
1947 53m/B Lash LaRue, Al "Fuzzy" St. John, Mary Maynard, George Cheseboro; **D:** Ray Taylor. **VHS, Beta** $12.95 COL ✍

Return of the Living Dead Poisonous gas revives a cemetery and a morgue rendering an outrageous spoof on the living-dead sub-genre with fast-moving zombies, punk humor, and exaggerated gore. Its humor does not diminish the fear factor, however. Sequel follows. Directed by "Alien" writer O'Bannon.
1985 (R) 90m/C Clu Gulager, James Karen, Linnea Quigley, Don Calfa, Jewel Shepard; **D:** Dan O'Bannon. **VHS, Beta** NO ✍✍ ½

Return of the Living Dead 2 An inevitable sequel to the original Dan O'Bannon satire about George Romero-esque brain-eating zombies attacking suburbia with zest and vigor.
1988 (R) 89m/C Dana Ashbrook, Marsha Dietlein, Philip Bruns, James Karen, Thom Mathews; **D:** Ken Weiderhorn. **VHS, Beta** $14.95 LHV, WAR ✍ ½

Return of the Living Dead 3 When Curt's girlfriend Julie dies in a motorcycle accident you'd think that would be the end of romance. But not when your dad heads a secret project that involves reviving corpses. Only problem is now Julie's a zombie with long metal claws and glass spikes sticking out of various body parts. Hey, if it's true love Curt will get over it. Macabre special effects. Also available unrated.

1993 (R) 97m/C Mindy Clarke, J. Trevor Edmond, Kent McCord, Basil Wallace, Fabio Urena; **D:** Brian Yuzna; **W:** John Penney; **M:** Barry Goldberg. **VHS** $94.95 *VMK* ⅟₂

Return of the Man from U.N.C.L.E. Those dashing super agents Napoleon Solo and Illya Kuryakin come out of retirement to settle an old score with their nemesis THRUSH. Made for television. **1983** 96m/C Robert Vaughn, David McCallum, Patrick Macnee, Gayle Hunnicutt, Geoffrey Lewis; **D:** Ray Austin. **VHS, Beta** $69.95 *TWE* ⅔⅔

The Return of the Musketeers Lester's third Musketeers film (after his successful double-act in the '70s) is a good-natured but average costume/comedy/buddy film. Twenty years after D'Artagnan, Athos, Porthos, and Aramis saved the French queen from scandal it's time to do it all over again. Milady DeWinter, who hatched the first plot, is dead but her equally devious daughter Justine is more than able to take mama's scheming place. Just to add a little more excitement Athos' adopted son Raoul meets Justine and passions fly amidst the sword-play. Based on the Alexandre Dumas novel "Twenty Years After." **1989** (PG) 103m/C Michael York, Oliver Reed, Frank Finlay, Richard Chamberlain, Kim Cattrall, C. Thomas Howell, Geraldine Chaplin, Roy Kinnear, Christopher Lee, Philippe Noiret, Jean-Pierre Cassel, Billy Connolly, Eusebio Lazaro; **D:** Richard Lester; **W:** George MacDonald Fraser. **VHS** $89.98 *MCA, BTV, FCT* ⅔⅔⅟₂

Return of the Pink Panther Bumbling Inspector Clouseau is called upon to rescue the Pink Panther diamond stolen from a museum. Sellers manages to produce mayhem with a vacuum cleaner and other devices that, in his hands, become instruments of terror. Clever opening credits. Fourth installment in the Pink Panther series but the first with Sellers since 1964's "A Shot In The Dark." **1974** (G) 113m/C Peter Sellers, Christopher Plummer, Catherine Schell, Herbert Lom, Victor Spinetti; **D:** Blake Edwards; **W:** Frank Waldman, Blake Edwards; **M:** Henry Mancini. **VHS, Beta** $14.98 *FOX, FHE, FCT* ⅔⅔⅟₂

Return of the Rebels Made for television fluff with Eden as a motorcycle matron whose campground is rid of riff-raff by the crow-lined participants in a 25-year reunion of a biker gang. **1981** 100m/C Barbara Eden, Robert Mandan, Jamie Farr, Patrick Swayze, Don Murray, Christopher Connelly; **D:** Noel Nosseck. **VHS** *NO* ⅟₂

Return of the Scorpion Big trouble abounds as that crazy kung fu guy, the "Scorpion," comes back to town. **1980** 90m/C Yang Pan Pan, Lam Men Wei, Philip Ko. **VHS, Beta** *NO* ⅟

Return of the Secaucus 7 Centers around a weekend reunion of seven friends who were activists during the Vietnam War in the turbulent '60s. Now turning 30, they evaluate their present lives and progress. Writer and director Sayles plays Howie in this excellent example of what a low-budget film can and should be. A less trendy predecessor of "The Big Chill" (1983) which, perhaps, was a few years ahead of its time. **1980** 110m/C Mark Arnott, Gordon Clapp, Maggie Cousineau-Arndt, David Strathairn; **D:** John Sayles; **W:** John Sayles; **M:** Mason Daring. **VHS, Beta** $59.95 *COL* ⅔⅔⅟₂

Return of the Seven The first sequel to "The Magnificent Seven" features the group liberating a compatriot who is held hostage. Yawn. **AKA:** Return of the Magnificent Seven.

1966 97m/C Yul Brynner, Warren Oates, Robert Fuller, Claude Akins; **D:** Burt Kennedy; **W:** Larry Cohen; **M:** Elmer Bernstein. **VHS, Beta** $19.98 *MGM* ⅔⅔

Return of the Soldier A shell-shocked WWI veteran has no memory of his marriage, leaving his wife, his childhood flame, and an unrequited love to vie for his affections. Adapted from the novel by Rebecca West. **1982** 101m/C Glenda Jackson, Julie Christie, Ann-Margret, Alan Bates, Ian Holm, Frank Finlay; **D:** Alan Bridges; **M:** Richard Rodney Bennett. **VHS, Beta** *NO* ⅔⅔⅔

Return of the Tall Blond Man With One Black Shoe Sequel to 1972's "The Tall Blond Man With One Black Shoe." Again a "klutz" is mistaken for a master spy and becomes unknowingly involved in the world of international intrigue. In French with English subtitles. Not quite as good as the original. **1974** 84m/C Pierre Richard, Mireille Darc, Michael Duchaussoy, Jean Rochefort, Jean Carmet; **D:** Yves Robert; **W:** Francis Veber; **M:** Vladimir Cosma. **VHS, Beta** $29.95 *CVC, PSM, ING* ⅔⅔⅟₂

Return of the Tiger The Hovver Night Club in Bangkok fronts the operations of an international narcotics group headed by an American. When a rival Chinese gang tries to dominate the drug market, conflict and lots of kicking ensue. **1978** 95m/C Bruce Li, Paul Smith, Chaing I, Angela Mao; **D:** Jimmy Shaw. **VHS, Beta** $29.95 *MED* ⅔⅟₂

Return of the Vampire A Hungarian vampire and his werewolf servant seek revenge on the family who drove a spike through his heart two decades earlier. **1943** 69m/B Bela Lugosi, Nina Foch, Miles Mander, Matt Willis, Frieda Inescort, Roland Varno; **D:** Lew Landers, Kurt Neumann. **VHS, Beta** $9.95 *GKK, MLB* ⅔⅔

Return of Wildfire Two sisters are left to run the family horse ranch when their brother is killed. A drifter aids the sisters in bringing the murderer to justice. **1948** 83m/B Richard Arlen, Patricia Morison, Mary Beth Hughes. **VHS, Beta** *NO* ⅔⅟₂

Return to Africa Rebels threaten the familial paradise of the tightknit Mallory clan. **1989** 95m/C Stan Brock, Anne Collings, David Tors, Ivan Tors, Peter Tors, Steven Tors; **D:** Leslie Martinson. **VHS, Beta** $59.95 *PSM* ⅔⅔

Return to Boggy Creek Townspeople in a small fishing village learn from a photographer that a "killer" beast, whom they thought had disappeared, has returned and is living in Boggy Creek. Some curious children follow the shutterbug into the marsh, despite hurricane warnings, and the swamp monster reacts with unusual compassion. OK for the kiddies. Fictitious story unlike other "Boggy Creek" films, which are billed as semi-documentaries. Sequel to "Legend of Boggy Creek" and features Mary Ann from "Gilligan's Island." **1977** (PG) 87m/C Dawn Wells, Dana Plato, Louise Belaire, John Hofeus; **D:** Tom Moore. **VHS, Beta** $19.98 *FOX* ⅔⅔

Return to Earth Made for television drama deals with the self-doubts faced by Apollo 11 astronaut Buzz Aldrin after his triumphant return to Earth. Based on Aldrin's own novel. **1976** 74m/C Cliff Robertson, Shirley Knight, Ralph Bellamy, Stefanie Powers, Charles Cioffi; **D:** Judd Taylor. **VHS, Beta** $19.98 *TWE* ⅔⅔

Return to Eden A young woman falls in love with her philosophy tutor, but he can't return her affections. An interesting comparison between the passion of the primitive and the tangle of modern-day romance. **1989** 90m/C Sam Bottoms, Edward Binns, Renee Coleman; **D:** William Olsen. **VHS** *NO* ⅔⅔

Return to Fantasy Island Boss, boss, it's da plane! The second full-length television treatment of the once popular series wherein three couples get their most cherished fantasy fulfilled by Mr. Roarke. and company. **1977** 100m/C Ricardo Montalban, Herve Villechaize, Adrienne Barbeau, Pat Crowley, Joseph Campanella, Karen Valentine, Laraine Day, George Maharis, Horst Buchholz, France Nuyen, Joseph Cotten, Cameron Mitchell, George Chakiris; **D:** George McCowan. **VHS, Beta** $79.95 *PSM* ⅔⅟₂

Return to Horror High A horror movie producer makes a film in an abandoned and haunted high school, where a series of murders occurred years earlier. As in most "return" flicks, history repeats itself. **1987** (R) 95m/C Alex Rocco, Vince Edwards, Philip McKeon, Brendan Hughes, Lori Lethin, Scott Jacoby; **D:** Bill Froehlich. **VHS, Beta** $19.95 *STE, NWV* ⅔

Return to Lonesome Dove Routine sequel to successful western saga "Lonesome Dove" picks up after the burial of Gus McCrae in Texas by his friend, ex-Texas Ranger Woodrow F. Call (now played by Voight). The original dealt with a cattle drive, this one with horses. Along the way you'll run into the usual sidewinders as well as McCrae's lost love Clara (now Hershey) and Schroder, returning as Call's unacknowledged son Newt. Filmed on loction in Montana. TV production was already underway when author Larry McMurtry gave the producers his then unpublished sequel "Streets of Laredo" which differed from the script. Some changes were made but the book and miniseries don't match. **1993** 330m/C Jon Voight, William L. Petersen, Rick Schroder, Barbara Hershey, Louis Gossett Jr., Oliver Reed, Reese Witherspoon, Nia Peeples, Dennis Haysbert, Timothy Scott, Barry Tubb, Chris Cooper, CCH Pounder, William Sanderson; **D:** Mike Robe; **W:** John Wilder. **VHS** $99.95 *CAF, FUS* ⅔⅔⅟₂

Return to Macon County Tale of three young, reckless youths who become involved with drag racing and a sadistic law enforcement officer. Nolte turns in a good performance in his first film, as does Johnson, despite a mediocre script and dialogue. Sequel to 1974's "Macon County Line." **1975** 90m/C Nick Nolte, Don Johnson, Robin Mattson; **D:** Richard Compton. **VHS, Beta** $69.98 *LIV, VES* ⅔⅔

Return to Mayberry Andy Taylor returns to Mayberry after 20 years to obtain his old job as sheriff. Sixteen of the original actors reappeared for this nostalgia-fest. Made for television. **1985** 95m/C Andy Griffith, Ron Howard, Don Knotts, Jim Nabors, Aneta Corseaut, Jack Dodson, George Lindsey, Betty Lynn; **D:** Bob Sweeney. **VHS, Beta** $29.98 *MCG* ⅔⅔

Return to Oz Picking up where "The Wizard of Oz" left off, Auntie Em and Uncle Ed place Dorothy in the care of a therapist to cure her "delusions" of Oz. A natural disaster again lands her in the land of the yellow brick road, where the evil Nome King and Princess Mombi are spreading terror and squalor. Based on a later L. Frank Baum book. Enjoyable for the whole family al-

though some scenes may frighten very small children.
1985 (PG) 109m/C Fairuza Balk, Piper Laurie, Matt Clark, Nicol Williamson, Jean Marsh; **D:** Walter Murch. **VHS, Beta** $29.95 DIS 🎞🎞½

Return to Paradise Cooper is a soldier of fortune wandering through the Polynesian islands in the late 1920s. On a remote atoll he comes across a crazy missionary intent upon subduing the native population. Cooper falls in love with a native beauty (Haynes in her screen debut) and leads the natives in a revolt against authority. Cliched but with nice scenery from the location shoot in Samoa. Loose adaptation of the short story "Mr. Morgan" by James Michener.
1953 100m/C Gary Cooper, Roberta Haynes, Barry Jones, John Hudson, Moira MacDonald; **D:** Mark Robson; **W:** Charles Kaufman. **VHS, Beta** $19.98 MGM, FCT 🎞🎞

Return to Peyton Place A young writer publishes novel exposing town as virtual Peyton Place, and the townsfolk turn against her and her family. Sequel to the scandalously popular '50s original and inspiration for the just-as-popular soap opera. Astor is excellent as the evil matriarch.
1961 122m/C Carol Lynley, Jeff Chandler, Eleanor Parker, Mary Astor, Robert Sterling, Lucianna Paluzzi, Tuesday Weld, Brett Halsey, Bob Crane; **D:** Jose Ferrer. **VHS** $39.98 FOX, FCT 🎞🎞½

Return to Salem's Lot Enjoyable camp sequel to the Stephen King tale, this time involving a cynical scientist and his son returning to the town only to find it completely run by vampires.
1987 (R) 101m/C Michael Moriarty, Ricky Addison Reed, Samuel Fuller, Andrew Duggan, Evelyn Keyes, Jill Gatsby, June Havoc, Ronee Blakley, James Dixon, David Holbrook; **D:** Larry Cohen; **W:** James Dixon, Larry Cohen. **VHS, Beta** $14.95 WAR 🎞🎞

Return to Snowy River Continues the love story of the former ranch hand and the rancher's daughter in Australia's Victoria Alps that began in "The Man From Snowy River." Dennehy takes over from Kirk Douglas as the father who aims to keep the lovers apart. The photography of horses and the scenery is spectacular, making the whole film worthwhile.
1988 (PG) 99m/C Tom Burlinson, Sigrid Thornton, Brian Dennehy, Nicholas Eadie, Mark Hembrow, Bryan Marshall; **D:** Geoff Burrowes. **VHS, Beta** $19.99 DIS, TVC 🎞🎞🎞

Return to the Blue Lagoon Neither the acting nor the premise has improved with age. Another photogenic adolescent couple experiences puberty on that island; for continuity, the young woman is the daughter of the lovers in the first "Blue Lagoon." Breathtaking scenery—just turn down the sound.
1991 (PG-13) 102m/C Milla Jovovich, Brian Krause, Lisa Pelikan; **D:** William A. Graham. **VHS** $19.95 COL 🎞

Return to the Lost World Rival scientists Challenger and Summerlee set out for the Lost World and find it threatened by oil prospectors. With a volcano about to explode the scientists set out to save their prehistoric paradise and its dinosaur inhabitants. Based on a story by Sir Arthur Conan Doyle. Sequel to "The Lost World."
1993 (PG) 99m/C John Rhys-Davies, David Warner. **VHS** WOV 🎞🎞½

Return to Two Moon Junction New York supermodel Savannah (Clarke) returns to her family's riverfront home in Georgia and promptly sheds her clothing for local sculptor Jake (Schafer). Must be something about the southern heat. This sequel

should have the same video success as its predecessor since it keeps to the minimal plot/maximum teasing sex scenes outline.
1993 (R) 96m/C Mindy Clarke, John Clayton Schafer, Louise Fletcher; **D:** Ferhad Mann. **VHS** $94.95 VMK 🎞½

Return to Waterloo A psychological mystery concerning the fantasies and flashbacks of a businessman traveling by train to London. He may be cheating on his wife, he may be abusing his daughter, he may be a rapist wanted by the police. Surreal musical interludes highlight the ambiguity of the story. Written and directed by "Kinks" frontman, Davies.
1985 57m/C Kenneth Colley; **D:** Ray Davies; **W:** Ray Davies. **VHS** $12.98 LTY 🎞🎞

Reuben, Reuben Brilliant, but drunken poet Conti turns himself around when he falls in love with earthy college girl McGillis in her film debut. The student's dog Reuben unwittingly alters Conti's progress, however, in the film's startling conclusion. Based on the writings of Peter DeVries.
1983 (R) 100m/C Tom Conti, Kelly McGillis, Roberts Blossom, E. Katherine Kerr, Cynthia Harris, Joel Fabiani, Kara Wilson, Lois Smith; **D:** Robert Ellis Miller; **W:** Julius J. Epstein; **M:** Billy Goldenberg. **VHS, Beta** $59.98 FOX 🎞🎞

Reunion Robards stars as a Jewish businessman, living in the U.S., who returns to his boyhood home of Stuttgart, Germany some 50 years after his leaving in 1933. He hopes to find out what happened to a boyhood school chum—the son of an aristocratic (and Aryan) German family. Film uses extensive flashbacks to show the rise of anti-Semitism and how it affects the friendship of both youths. Thoughtfull and well-acted though occasionally plodding drama based on Fred Uhlman's novel.
1988 (PG-13) 120m/C Jason Robards Jr., Christien Anholt, Sam West, Francoise Fabian, Maureen Kerwin, Barbara Jefford, Alexander Trauner; **D:** Jerry Schatzberg; **W:** Harold Pinter. **VHS, Beta** $29.95 FRH, IME, FCT 🎞🎞

Reunion in France Parisian dress designer sacrifices her lifestyle to help an American flier flee France after the Nazis invade. Dated patriotic flag-waver. *AKA:* Mademoiselle France; Reunion.
1942 104m/B Joan Crawford, John Wayne, Philip Dorn, Reginald Owen, Albert Basserman, John Carradine, Anne Ayars, J. Edward Bromberg, Henry Daniell, Moroni Olsen, Howard da Silva, Ava Gardner, John Considine; **D:** Jules Dassin. **VHS, Beta** $19.98 MGM 🎞🎞

Revenge The parents of a girl who was brutally killed take the law into their own hands in this bloody, vengeful thriller. *AKA:* Terror under the House; After Jenny Died; Inn of the Frightened People.
1971 89m/C Joan Collins, James Booth, Ray Barrett, Sinead Cusack, Kenneth Griffith; **D:** Sidney Hayers. **VHS, Beta** $29.95 SUE, MRV 🎞½

Revenge Sequel to "Blood Cult" about a cult led by horror king Carradine. Seems these dog worshippers want McGowan's land and Senator Carradine will stop at nothing to get it. Woofer filled with gratuitous violence.
1986 (R) 104m/C Patrick Wayne, John Carradine, Bennie Lee McGowan, Josef Hanet, Stephanie Kropke; **D:** Christopher Lewis. **VHS, Beta** $19.95 VCI Woof!

Revenge Retired pilot Costner makes the mistake of falling in love with another man's wife. Quinn gives a first-rate performance as the Mexican crime lord who punishes his spouse and her lover, beginning a cycle of vengeance. Sometimes contrived, but artfully

photographed with tantalizing love scenes. Based on the Jim Harrison novel.
1990 (R) 123m/C Kevin Costner, Anthony Quinn, Madeleine Stowe, Sally Kirkland, Joe Santos, Miguel Ferrer, James Gammon, Tomas Milian; **D:** Tony Scott; **W:** Jim Harrison; **M:** Jack Nitzsche. **VHS, Beta, 8mm** $19.95 COL 🎞🎞

Revenge in the House of Usher House holds grudge.
1982 90m/C Howard Vernon, Dan Villers; **D:** Jess (Jesus) Franco. **VHS** $29.99 MOV 🎞🎞

Revenge of a Kabuki Actor When Kabuki actor Kazuo Hasegawa's parents are viciously murdered, he seeks their killer with a vengeance. In Japanese with English subtitles.
1963 114m/C **D:** Kon Ichikawa. **VHS** $59.95 FST, FCT 🎞🎞

Revenge of Doctor X A man/beast lies waiting for the pretty reporter who seeks her shipwrecked father in the jungles of an uncharted island.
198? 90m/C John Ashley, Ronald Remy, Angelique Pettyjohn. **VHS, Beta** NO Woof!

Revenge of the Barbarians As the barbarians descend on Rome, Olympus must decide whether to save the empire or the beautiful Gallo, the woman he loves. Decisions, decisions.
1964 99m/C Robert Alda, Anthony Steele. **Beta** $39.95 AIP 🎞

Revenge of the Barbarians A Scandinavian adventure about a young Celt seeking revenge against the Viking hordes that killed his family.
1985 95m/C **D:** Hrafn Gunnlaugsson. **Beta** NO 🎞

Revenge of the Cheerleaders The cheerleaders pull out all the stops to save their school from a ruthless land developer. What spirit.
1976 (R) 86m/C Jerii Woods, Cheryl "Rainbeaux" Smith, Helen Lang, Patrice Rohmer, Susie Elene, Eddra Gale, William Bramley, Carl Ballantine, David Hasselhoff; **D:** Richard Lerner. **VHS, Beta** $69.98 LIV 🎞

Revenge of the Creature In this follow up to "The Creature From the Black Lagoon," the Gill-man is captured in the Amazon and taken to a Florida marine park. There he is put on display for visitors and subjected to heartless experiments. Growing restless in his captive surroundings, the creature breaks free and makes for the ocean. Includes screen debut of Clint Eastwood as a lab technician. Originally shot in 3-D. Based on a story by William Alland. Available on laserdisc as part of a special Encore Edition Double Feature with "The Creature Walks Among Us."
1955 82m/B John Agar, Lori Nelson, John Bromfield, Robert Williams, Nestor Paiva, Clint Eastwood; **D:** Jack Arnold; **W:** Martin Berkeley. **VHS** $14.98 MCA, FCT 🎞🎞

Revenge of the Dead European archeological team discovers the existence of a powerful force that allows the dead to return to life.
1984 (R) 100m/C Gabriele Lavia, Anne Canoras; **D:** Pupi Avati. **VHS, Beta** $69.98 LIV 🎞

Revenge of the Living Zombies Teens on a Halloween hayride run headlong into flesh-craving zombies. Available in a slightly edited version.
1988 (R) 85m/C Bill Hinzman, John Mowod, Leslie Ann Wick, Kevin Kindlan; **D:** Bill Hinzman. **VHS, Beta** NO 🎞

Revenge of the Nerds When nerdy college freshmen are victimized by jocks, frat boys and the school's beauties, they start their own fraternity and seek revenge. Carra-

dine and Edwards team well as the geeks in this better than average teenage sex comedy. Guess who gets the girls? Sequel was much worse.
1984 (R) 89m/C Robert Carradine, Anthony Edwards, Timothy Busfield, Andrew Cassese, Curtis Armstrong, Larry B. Scott, Brian Tochi, Julia Montgomery, Michelle Meyrink, Ted McGinley, John Goodman, Bernie Casey; **D:** Jeff Kanew; **W:** Tim Metcalfe. **VHS, Beta $14.98** FOX 🐾🐾½

Revenge of the Nerds 2: Nerds in Paradise The nerd clan from the first film (minus Edwards who only makes a brief appearance) travels to Fort Lauderdale for a fraternity conference. They fend off loads of bullies and jocks with raunchy humor. Boy can Booger belch. Not as good as the first Nerds movie; a few laughs nonetheless.
1987 (PG-13) 89m/C Robert Carradine, Curtis Armstrong, Timothy Busfield, Andrew Cassese, Ed Lauter, Larry B. Scott, Courtney Thorne-Smith, Anthony Edwards, James Hong; **D:** Joe Roth. **VHS, Beta $89.98** FOX 🐾

Revenge of the Nerds 3: The Next Generation Adams College has nerd-loathing trustee Downey, Jr. mobilizing those frat boys against the bespectacled geeks, who turn to founding nerd Carradine to save them. Cookie-cutter characters and the gags won't hold your attention. Let's hope this is the last in the series.
1992 ?m/C Robert Carradine, Curtis Armstrong, Ted McGinley, Morton Downey Jr., Julia Montgomery. **VHS** FXV 🐾½

Revenge of the Ninja Ninja Kosugi hopes to escape his past in Los Angeles. A drug trafficker, also ninja-trained, prevents him. The two polish off a slew of mobsters before their own inevitable showdown. Better-than the standard chop-socky fest from Cannon with amusing surreal touches like a battling grandma ninja. Sequel to "Enter the Ninja," followed by "Ninja III."
1983 (R) 90m/C Sho Kosugi, Arthur Roberts, Keith Vitali, Virgil Frye, Ashley Ferrare, Kane Kosugi, John Lamotta, Grace Oshita, Melvin C. Hampton, Mario Gallo; **D:** Sam Firstenberg; **W:** James R. Silke; **M:** Rob Walsh. **VHS, Beta $14.95** MGM 🐾🐾½

Revenge of the Pink Panther Inspector Clouseau survives his own assassination attempt, but allows the world to think he is dead in order to pursue an investigation of the culprits in his own unique, bumbling way. The last "Pink Panther" film before Sellers died, and perhaps the least funny.
1978 (PG) 99m/C Peter Sellers, Herbert Lom, Dyan Cannon, Robert Webber, Burt Kwouk, Robert Loggia; **D:** Blake Edwards; **W:** Blake Edwards, Ron Clark, Frank Waldman; **M:** Henry Mancini. **VHS, Beta $19.98** FOX, FCT 🐾🐾½

Revenge of the Radioactive Reporter Nuclear plant honchos don't like journalist who's about to hang their dirty laundry, so they toss him into vat of nuclear waste. He returns as a reporter with a cosmetic peel.
1991 90m/C David Scammell, Kathryn Boese, Randy Pearlstein, Derrick Strange; **D:** Craig Pryce. **VHS** NO 🐾🐾

Revenge of the Red Baron Jim Spencer (Rooney) is the WWI pilot who shot down Germany's fearsome Red Baron. Now aged and infirm he's tormented by what he thinks is his enemy's ghost. A vengeful ghost who takes after Spencer's family.
1993 (PG-13) 90m/C Mickey Rooney, Toby Maguire, Laraine Newman, Cliff DeYoung; **D:** Robert Gordon. **VHS** NHO 🐾🐾½

Revenge of the Stepford Wives Made for television sequel to the Ira Levin fantasy about suburban husbands who create obedient robot replicas of their wives. In this installment, the wives are not robots, but are simply made docile by drugs. Strange casting pairs Johnson and Kavner as husband and stepford wife. Begat "The Stepford Children."
1980 95m/C Sharon Gless, Julie Kavner, Don Johnson, Audra Lindley, Mason Adams, Arthur Hill; **D:** Robert Fuest. **VHS, Beta $9.98** SUE, NLC 🐾½

Revenge of the Teenage Vixens from Outer Space A low-budget film about three sex starved females from another planet who come to earth to find men. When the ones they meet do not live up to their expectations, the frustrated females turn the disappointing dudes are turned into vegetables.
1986 84m/C Lisa Schwedop, Howard Scott; **D:** Jeff Ferrell. **VHS, Beta** NO 🐾🐾

Revenge of the Virgins A tribe of topless 'Indian' women protect their sacred land from the white men. Exhumed exploitation for bad-film junkies, narrated by Kenne Duncan, an Ed Wood cohort.
1962 53m/B Jewell Morgan, Charles Veltman, Jodean Russo, Stanton Pritchard; **D:** Paul Perri. **VHS $19.95** NOS, SMW, VDM 🐾

Revenge of the Zombies In this sequel of sorts to "King of the Zombies," Carradine is creating an army of the undead for use by an evil foreign entity.
1943 61m/B John Carradine, Robert Lowery, Gale Storm, Veda Ann Borg, Mantan Moreland; **D:** Steve Sekely. **VHS** MLB 🐾½

Revenge of the Zombies Kung-fu exploitation film featuring man-eating alligators, zombies, mad magicians, and more.
1981 (R) ?m/C Ti Lung, Lily Tu. **VHS $15.95** LOO 🐾½

The Revenge Rider Orphan McCoy goes after the villains who killed his parents. Good performance from McCoy in an otherwise average film.
1935 60m/B Tim McCoy, Robert Allen, Billie Seward, Edward Earle, Jack Clifford, Lafe McKee; **D:** David Selman. **VHS $19.95** DVT, HEG 🐾🐾

The Revenger A framed man returns from prison and finds that a mobster has kidnapped his wife and wants $50,000 to give her back.
1990 91m/C Oliver Reed, Frank Zagarino; **D:** Cedric Sundstrom. **VHS, Beta $79.95** AIP 🐾

Reversal of Fortune True tale of wealthy socialite Claus von Bulow (Irons) accused of deliberately giving his wife Sunny (Close) a near-lethal overdose of insulin. Comatose Close narrates history of the couple's courtship and married life, a saga of unhappiness and substance abuse, while Silver (as lawyer Dershowitz) et al prepare von Bulow's defense. An unflattering picture of the idle rich that never spells out what really happened. Irons is excellent as the eccentric and creepy defendant and richly deserved his Best Actor Oscar. From the novel by Dershowitz.
1990 (R) 112m/C Jeremy Irons, Glenn Close, Ron Silver, Annabella Sciorra, Uta Hagen, Fisher Stevens, Julie Hagerty, Jack Gilpin, Christine Baranski; **D:** Barbet Schroeder; **W:** Nicholas Kazan. Academy Awards '90: Best Actor (Irons); Nominations: Best Adapted Screenplay, Best Director (Schroeder); Golden Globe Awards '91: Best Actor—Drama (Irons). **VHS, Beta, 8mm $19.98** WAR, FCT, BTV 🐾🐾🐾½

The Revolt of Job An elderly Jewish couple adopts an 8-year-old Gentile boy although it is illegal in WWII-torn Hungary and against the beliefs of the orthodox community. Moving story with fine performances. **AKA:** Job Lazadasa.
1984 98m/C Fereno Zenthe, Hedi Tenessy; **D:** Imre Gyongyossy, Barna Kabay. **VHS, Beta $79.95** MGM, SWC 🐾🐾🐾

The Revolt of Mother Mary E. Wilkins Freeman story of two hard-working farmers. Set in 1890 New England.
1988 60m/C Amy Madigan, Jay O'Saunders. **VHS $24.95** MON, KAR 🐾🐾🐾½

Revolt of the Barbarians Ancient Rome is plagued by barbarian invasion and piracy. A consul travels to Gaul to try to put an end to their misdeeds.
1964 ?m/C Roland Carey, Grazia Maria Spina, Mario Feliciani. **VHS, Beta $16.95** SNC 🐾

Revolt of the Dragon Martial arts expert visits friends in his hometown and finds himself battling a ruthless gang that terrorizes the people.
1975 (R) 90m/C **VHS, Beta $54.95** HHT 🐾

Revolt of the Zombies A mad scientist learns the secret of bringing the dead to life and musters the zombies into an unique, gruesome military unit during WWI. Strange early zombie flick looks silly by today's standards.
1936 65m/B Dorothy Stone, Dean Jagger, Roy D'Arcy, Robert Noland, George Cleveland; **D:** Victor Halperin; **W:** Howard Higgin. **VHS, Beta $14.95** SNC, MLB, MRV 🐾

Revolution Documentary of hippie life in San Francisco during the turbulent '60s.
1969 90m/C Today Malone; **D:** Jack O'Connell. **VHS** WAR 🐾

Revolution The American Revolution is the setting for this failed epic centering on an illiterate trapper and his son who find themselves caught up in the fighting. Long and dull, which is unfortunate, because the story had some potential. The cast is barely believable in their individual roles. Where did you get that accent, Al?
1985 (R) 125m/C Al Pacino, Donald Sutherland, Nastassia Kinski, Annie Lennox, Joan Plowright, Steven Berkoff, Dave King; **D:** Hugh Hudson; **W:** Robert Dillon. **VHS, Beta $19.98** WAR 🐾

Revolution! A Red Comedy A group of students are lured away from their revolutionary tendencies by materialistic indulgences. This satirical comedy is in color and black and white.
1991 84m/B Kimberly Flynn, Christopher Renstrom, Georg Osterman; **D:** Jeff Kahn; **W:** Jeff Kahn. **VHS $69.95** ING 🐾🐾🐾

Revolver FBI agent Nick Sastro is paralyzed by an assassin's bullet when he tries to stop Aldo Testi, an arms and drug smuggler. But Nick decides to come out of retirement when a chance to nail Testi comes his way.
1992 (R) 96m/C Robert Urich, Dakin Matthews, Steven Williams, Assumpta Serna; **D:** Gary Nelson. **VHS $79.95** COL 🐾🐾

Rhapsody Taylor plays a wealthy woman torn between a famous young violinist and an equally talented pianist in this long and overdrawn soap opera. Although Taylor gives a superb performance, it's not enough to save this sugarcoated musical romance. Includes lush European scenery and sequences of classical music dubbed in by Claudio Arrau and Michael Rabin. Based on the adaptation of the Henry Handel Richardson novel "Maurice Guest."

1954 115m/C Elizabeth Taylor, Vittorio Gassman, John Ericson, Louis Calhern, Michael Chekhov, Barbara Bates, Celia Lovsky; *D:* Charles Vidor; *W:* Michael Kanin, Fay Kanin. **VHS** $19.98 *MGM* 🎬🎬½

Rhapsody in August Talky family drama has four children spending the summer with their grandmother Kane in Nagasaki. They become obsessed with the memorials and bomb sites commemorating the dropping of the atomic bomb in 1945 and their grandmother's experiences. Then Kane's Eurasian nephew (Gere) comes for a visit, inciting more family discussions. Adapted from the novel "Nabe-no-Naka" by Kiyoko Murata. Minor Kurosawa; in Japanese with English subtitles.
1991 (PG) 98m/C Sachiko Murase, Narumi Kayashima, Hisashi Igawa, Richard Gere; *D:* Akira Kurosawa; *W:* Akira Kurosawa. **VHS** $79.98 *ORI* 🎬🎬½

Rhapsody in Blue Standard Hollywood biography of the great composer features whitewashed and non-existent characters to deal with the spottier aspects of Gershwin's life. Still, the music is the main attraction and it doesn't disappoint. 🎵Rhapsody in Blue; Concerto in F; The Cuban Overture; Fascinatin' Rhythm; The Man I Love; Yankee Doodle Blues; Somebody Loves Me; Swanee; Mine.
1945 139m/B Robert Alda, Joan Leslie, Alexis Smith, Charles Coburn, Julie Bishop, Albert Basserman, Morris Carnovsky, Rosemary DeCamp, Herbert Rudley, Charles Halton, Robert Shayne, Johnny Downs, Al Jolson; *D:* Irving Rapper; *W:* Howard Koch; *M:* George Gershwin, Ira Gershwin. **VHS** $19.98 *MGM, FCT* 🎬🎬🎬

Rhinestone A country singer claims she can turn anyone, even a cabbie, into a singing sensation. Stuck with Stallone, Parton prepares her protege to sing at New York City's roughest country-western club, The Rhinestone. Only die-hard Dolly and Rocky fans need bother with this bunk. Some may enjoy watching the thick, New York accented Stallone learn how to properly pronounce dog ("dawg") in country lingo. Yee-haw.
1984 (PG) 111m/C Sylvester Stallone, Dolly Parton, Ron Leibman, Richard Farnsworth, Tim Thomerson; *D:* Bob (Benjamin) Clark; *W:* Sylvester Stallone, Phil Alden Robinson. **VHS, Beta** $79.98 *FOX* 🎬

Rhodes The story of Cecil Rhodes, a man who was instrumental in the Boer War in Africa and established the Rhodes Scholarships with $10 million, is told in this biography. Fine performance by Huston and Homolka. *AKA:* Rhodes of Africa.
1936 91m/B Walter Huston, Oscar Homolka, Basil Sydney, Frank Cellier, Peggy Ashcroft, Renne De Vaux, Percy Parsons, Bernard Lee, Ndanisa Kumalo; *D:* Berthold Viertel. **VHS** $19.95 *NOS, SNC* 🎬🎬½

Rhythm Parade A woman takes off for Hawaii, leaving her infant in the care of an L.A. nightclub singer. A jealous rival of the singer takes the opportunity to cause problems. The thin plot serves as a vehicle for lots of singing. 🎵Tootin' My Own Horn; Petticoat Army; Mimi From Tahiti; You're Drafted; Wait Till the Sun Shines Nellie; Sweet Sue; 'Neath the Yellow Moon In Old Tahiti.
1943 68m/B Nils T. Granlund, Gale Storm, Robert Lowery, Margaret Dumont, Chick Chandler, Cliff Nazarro, Jan Wiley, Candy Candido, Yvonne De Carlo; *D:* Howard Bretherton. **VHS** $19.95 *NOS, MLB* 🎬🎬

Ricco A young man swears vengeance against the mobsters who killed his father. He kidnaps the daughter of a mafia kingpin and the battle begins. *AKA:* Summertime Killer.

1974 (PG) 90m/C Chris Mitchum, Karl Malden, Olivia Hussey, Raf Vallone, Claudine Auger, Gerard Tichy; *D:* Antonio Isasi. **VHS, Beta** *NO* 🎬🎬

Rich and Famous The story of the 25-year friendship of two women, through college, marriage, and success. George Cukor's last film.
1981 (R) 117m/C Jacqueline Bisset, Candice Bergen, David Selby, Hart Bochner, Meg Ryan, Steven Hill, Michael Brandon, Matt Lattanzi; *D:* George Cukor; *M:* Georges Delerue. **VHS, Beta** $79.95 *MGM* 🎬🎬

Rich and Strange Early Hitchcock movie is not in the same class as his later thrillers. A couple inherits a fortune and journeys around the world. Eventually the pair gets shipwrecked. *AKA:* East of Shanghai.
1932 92m/B Henry Kendall, Joan Barry, Betty Amann, Percy Marmont, Elsie Randolph; *D:* Alfred Hitchcock; *W:* Alfred Hitchcock. **VHS** $9.98 *REP, SNC, MLB* 🎬🎬½

Rich Girl A winsome, wealthy wench hides her millions by going to work in a rock'n'roll bar and falls in love with the local Bruce Springsteen wannabee. Despite the thick coating of music, sex, drugs and profanity, this consists of cliches that were old before talkies. Too earnestly-acted to be campy fun. Poor movie.
1991 (R) 96m/C Jill Schoelen, Don Michael Paul, Ron Karabatsos, Sean Kanan, Willie Dixon, Paul Gleason; *D:* Joel Bender. **VHS** $89.95 *COL* 🎬

Rich Hall's Vanishing America Funnyman Hall travels across the country looking for the mail-order company that promised to give him a genuine Wilt Chamberlain basketball hoop.
1986 50m/C Rich Hall, M. Emmet Walsh, Peter Isacksen, Harry Anderson, Wilt Chamberlain; *D:* Steve Rash. **VHS, Beta** $29.95 *PAR* 🎬

Rich in Love Light-hearted look at the changes in a Southern family after matriarch Helen Odom leaves to pursue her own life, shattering the peaceful existence of those around her. Seen through the eyes of 17-year-old daughter Lucille who assumes the role of "mother" for her sister and father while trying to come to terms with her own confused feelings. Nice performances by newcomer Erbe and Finney can't overcome a mediocre script. Based on the novel by Josephine Humphreys.
1993 (PG-13) 105m/C Albert Finney, Jill Clayburgh, Kathryn Erbe, Kyle MacLachlan, Piper Laurie, Ethan Hawke, Suzy Amis, Alfre Woodard; *D:* Bruce Beresford; *W:* Alfred Uhry; *M:* Georges Delerue. **VHS** $19.98 *MGM, BTV, FCT* 🎬🎬½

Rich Kids A young girl trying to cope with the divorce of her parents is aided by a boyfriend whose parents have already split.
1979 (PG) 97m/C John Lithgow, Kathryn Walker, Trini Alvarado, Paul Dooley, David Selby, Jill Eikenberry, Olympia Dukakis; *D:* Robert M. Young. **VHS, Beta** $59.95 *MGM* 🎬½

Rich Man, Poor Man Classic television miniseries covers 20, sometimes bitter, years in the lives of the two Jordache brothers. It's 1945 in quiet Port Phillip, New York with embittered German baker Axel (Asner), his unfulfilled wife Mary (McGuire), and sons Tom (Nolte) and Rudy (Strauss). Tom is wild and irresponsible, Rudy is ambitious and college-bound, and Julie Prescott (Blakely), Rudy's girl, overshadows both their lives. Based on the novel by Irwin Shaw. The first series contained 12 episodes. A second series, of 21 episodes, primarily followed the tribulations of the next generation, although Strauss returned as Rudy.

1976 720m/C Peter Strauss, Nick Nolte, Susan Blakely, Ed Asner, Dorothy McGuire, Bill Bixby, Robert Reed, Ray Milland, Kim Darby, Talia Shire, Lawrence Pressman, Kay Lenz. **VHS** *CMB* 🎬🎬🎬

Rich, Young and Pretty Light-hearted, innocuous musical starring Powell as a Texas gal visiting Paris with her rancher father (Corey). Powell finds romance with Damone (in his screen debut) and a secret—the mother she has never known (Darrieux). Lamas (in his American screen debut) plays Darrieux's new heartthrob. 🎵Dark is the Night; L'Amour Toujours, Tonight For Sure; Wonder Why; I Can See You; Paris; We Never Talk Much; How Do You Like Your Eggs in the Morning?; There's Danger in Your Eyes, Cherie; The Old Piano Roll Blues.
1951 95m/C Jane Powell, Danielle Darrieux, Wendell Corey, Vic Damone, Fernando Lamas, Marcel Dalio, Una Merkel, Richard Anderson, Jean Murat, Hans Conried; *D:* Norman Taurog; *W:* Sidney Sheldon, Dorothy Cooper; *M:* Sammy Cahn, Nicholas Brodszky. **VHS** $19.98 *MGM, FCT* 🎬🎬

Richard III This landmark film version of the Shakespearean play features an acclaimed performance by Laurence Olivier, who also directs. The plot follows the life of the mentally and physically twisted Richard of Gloucester and his schemes for the throne of England.
1955 138m/C Laurence Olivier, Cedric Hardwicke, Ralph Richardson, John Gielgud, Stanley Baker, Michael Gough, Claire Bloom; *D:* Laurence Olivier. Academy Awards '56 Nominations: Best Actor (Olivier); British Academy Awards '55: Best Actor (Olivier), Best Director (Olivier), Best Film; Golden Globe Awards '57: Best Foreign Film. **VHS, Beta** $14.95 *COL, SUE, HMV* 🎬🎬🎬½

Richard Petty Story The biography of race car driver Petty, played by himself, and his various achievements on the track.
1972 (G) 83m/C Richard Petty, Darren McGavin, Kathie Browne, Lynn Marta, Noah Beery Jr., L.Q. Jones. **VHS, Beta** $59.95 *GEM* 🎬

Richard's Things A man's wife and his girlfriend find love and comfort in each other after his death. Screenplay by Frederic Raphael, from his novel. Very slow and dreary, with a weak performance from Ullman.
1980 (R) 104m/C Liv Ullmann, Amanda Redman; *D:* Anthony Harvey; *W:* Frederic Raphael; *M:* Georges Delerue. **VHS, Beta** $69.98 *SUE* 🎬🎬

Ricky 1 Mumbling pugilist spoof. Da Mob wants to make Ricky da fall guy, but uh, he's not as dumb as he looks.
1988 90m/C Michael Michaud, Maggie Hughes, James Herbert, Lane Montano; *D:* Bill Naud; *M:* Joel Goldsmith. **VHS** $69.99 *TPV, HHE* 🎬½

Ricochet Rookie cop Washington causes a sensation when he singlehandedly captures notorious psychopath Lithgow. But this particular criminal is a twisted genius, and from his prison cell he comes up with a plan to destroy the young cop. Teaming up with old friend Ice-T, the rookie tries to outwit his evil arch-nemesis, but to do so may cost him his very life. A genuinely scary, tense and violent thriller.
1991 (R) 104m/C Denzel Washington, John Lithgow, Ice-T, Jesse Ventura, Kevin Pollak, Lindsay Wagner, Mary Ellen Trainor, Josh Evans, Victoria Dillard, John Amos, John Cothran Jr.; *D:* Russell Mulcahy; *W:* Steven DeSouza; *M:* Alan Silvestri. **VHS, 8mm** $19.98 *HBO, CCB* 🎬🎬🎬

Riddance The second of Meszaros' trilogy, about a Hungarian couple, an upper-class male student, and a factory-working young woman, and their difficulties in meshing their lives together. In Hungarian with English subtitles.

1973 84m/B **D:** Marta Meszaros. **VHS, Beta** $69.95 KIV, ING 🎦🎦🎦

The Riddle of the Sands Two English yachtsmen in 1903 inadvertently stumble upon a German plot to invade England by sea. British film based on the Erskine Childers spy novel.
1979 99m/C Michael York, Jenny Agutter, Simon MacCorkindale, Alan Badel; **D:** Tony Maylam; **M:** Howard Blake. **VHS, Beta** $39.95 MOV, BMV 🎦🎦½

Ride a Wild Pony A poor Australian farmer's son is allowed to pick a horse of his own from a neighboring rancher's herd. After he trains and grows to love the pony, the rancher's daughter, a handicapped rich girl, decides to claim it for herself. Enjoyable Disney story is based on the tale ''Sporting Proposition,'' by James Aldridge.
1975 (G) 86m/C John Meillon, Michael Craig, Robert Bettles, Eva Griffith, Graham Rouse; **D:** Don Chaffey; **M:** John Addison. **VHS, Beta** $69.95 DIS 🎦🎦🎦

Ride 'Em Cowboy Two peanut and hotdog vendors travel west to try their hand as cowpokes. Usual Abbott and Costello fare with a twist—there are lots of great musical numbers. ♫A Tisket, A Tasket; I'll Remember April; Wake Up Jacob; Beside the Rio Tonto; Rock 'n' Reelin'; Give Me My Saddle; Cow Boogie.
1942 86m/B Bud Abbott, Lou Costello, Anne Gwynne, Samuel S. Hinds, Dick Foran, Richard Lane, Johnny Mack Brown, Ella Fitzgerald, Douglass Dumbrille; **D:** Arthur Lubin. **VHS** $14.98 MCA 🎦🎦½

Ride 'Em Cowgirl Singing cowgirl, Page, enters a horse race to expose the crook who cheated her father.
1941 51m/B Dorothy Page, Vince Barnett, Milton Frome; **D:** Samuel Diege. **VHS** VCN 🎦🎦

Ride Him, Cowboy Entertaining oater has Wayne saving horse Duke from being sentenced to death. This was the first of six series films Wayne made for Warner's, all of which costarred his white wonder horse, Duke. Remake of the 1926 Ken Maynard silent ''The Unknown Cavalier.'' Based on the story by Kenneth Perkins.
1932 55m/B John Wayne, Ruth Hall, Henry B. Walthall, Harry Gribbon, Otis Harlan, Charles Sellon; **D:** Fred Allen; **W:** Scott Mason. **VHS** $19.98 MGM, GPV 🎦🎦🎦

Ride in a Pink Car When a Vietnam vet returns home, he discovers that his welcoming committee is really a lynch mob.
1974 (R) 83m/C Glenn Corbett, Morgan Woodward, Ivy Jones; **D:** Robert Emery. **VHS, Beta** $19.95 ACA 🎦

Ride in the Whirlwind Three cowboys are mistaken for members of a gang by a posse. Screenplay for the offbeat western by Nicholson.
1967 83m/C Jack Nicholson, Cameron Mitchell, Millie Perkins, Katherine Squire, Harry Dean Stanton; **D:** Monte Hellman; **W:** Jack Nicholson. **Beta** $19.99 MED, HHT, DVT 🎦🎦½

Ride Lonesome The heroic Scott is a bounty hunter looking for a killer (Best). It's not just the money, Scott hopes Best will lead him to the man who murdered Scott's wife. Along the trail he meets a pretty widow and two outlaws who hope if they capture Best, they'll get a pardon. A well-done example of a ''B'' western with good performances; Coburn's film debut.
1959 73m/C Randolph Scott, James Best, Karen Steele, Pernell Roberts, Lee Van Cleef, James Coburn; **D:** Budd Boetticher; **W:** Burt Kennedy. **VHS** $12.99 MOV 🎦🎦½

Ride, Ranger, Ride Texas Ranger Autry is out to stop a group of Comanches from raiding a wagon train.
1936 56m/B Gene Autry, Smiley Burnette, Kay Hughes, Max Terhune, Monte Blue, Chief Thundercloud; **D:** Joseph Kane. **VHS, Beta** $19.95 NOS, MED, VYY 🎦½

Ride the High Country The cult classic western about two old friends who have had careers on both sides of the law. One, Joel McCrea, is entrusted with a shipment of gold, and the other, Randolph Scott, rides along with him to steal the precious cargo. Although barely promoted by MGM, became a critics' favorite. Grimacing and long in the tooth, McCrea and Scott enact a fitting tribute and farewell to the myth of the grand ol' West. Wonderfully photographed by Lucien Ballard. The laserdisc edition carries the film in widescreen format along with the original movie trailer. **AKA:** Guns in the Afternoon.
1962 93m/C Randolph Scott, Joel McCrea, Mariette Hartley, Edgar Buchanan, R.G. Armstrong, Ronald Starr, John Anderson, James Drury, L.Q. Jones, Warren Oates; **D:** Sam Peckinpah. **VHS, Beta** $19.98 MGM 🎦🎦🎦🎦

Ride the Man Down Story of a murderous land war between neighboring land-owners tells the same old story: Greed knows no boundaries.
1953 90m/C Brian Donlevy, Chill Wills, Jack LaRue, Rod Cameron, Ella Raines, Barbara Britton; **D:** Joseph Kane. **VHS** $19.98 REP 🎦½

Ride the Wild Surf It's fun in the sun when surfers Fabian, Hunter, and Brown head to Hawaii in search of the ultimate waves. Throw in a little romance and a cool title song by Jan and Dean and you've got your better than average beach movie. The surfing footage is excellent. Cowabunga!
1964 101m/C Fabian, Tab Hunter, Barbara Eden, Peter Brown, Susan Hart, Shelley Fabares, Jim Mitchum; **D:** Don Taylor. **VHS** $19.95 COL 🎦🎦½

Ride the Wind ''Bonanza'' gang goes to the aid of the Pony Express.
1966 120m/C Michael Landon, Lorne Greene, Dan Blocker. **VHS, Beta** $14.95 REP 🎦🎦

Ride to Glory In 1886, a cavalry officer deserts his troops to seek revenge on the Apaches that brutally killed his family. Hearing this, a general offers to pardon him if he will lead a dangerous group of men on a mission against the Apaches. Fast-paced and very bloody. **AKA:** The Deserter; La Spina Dorsale del Diavolo.
1971 90m/C Bekim Fehmiu, Richard Crenna, Chuck Connors, Ricardo Montalban, Ian Bannen, Slim Pickens, Woody Strode, Patrick Wayne, John Huston; **D:** Burt Kennedy. **VHS** $19.95 SIM, PAR, HHE 🎦🎦

Rider from Tucson Two rodeo riders head out to Colorado for a friend's wedding. They find out the bride has been kidnapped by a bunch of claim jumpers after control of a gold mine.
1950 60m/B Tim Holt, Richard Martin, Elaine Riley, Douglas Fowley, Veda Ann Borg; **D:** Lesley Selander. **VHS, Beta** RKO 🎦🎦

Rider of the Law A government agent poses as a greenhorn easterner to nab a gang of outlaws.
1935 56m/B Bob Steele. **VHS, Beta** NO 🎦

Rider on the Rain A young housewife is viciously raped by an escaped sex maniac. She kills and disposes of his body, not knowing that he is being relentlessly pursued by mysterious American Bronson. Suspenseful, French-made thriller featuring one of

Bronson's best performances. **AKA:** Lepassäger de la Pluie.
1970 115m/C Marlene Jobert, Charles Bronson, Jill Ireland; **D:** Rene Clement. **VHS, Beta** $19.95 MON 🎦🎦🎦

Riders of Death Valley Splendid western action serial in 15 episodes. Foran, Jones, and Carillo head a passel o'men watching for thieves and claim jumpers in a mining area.
1941 320m/B Dick Foran, Buck Jones, Leo Carrillo, Lon Chaney Jr.; **D:** Ford Beebe, Ray Taylor. **VHS, Beta** $49.95 NOS, VCN, DVT 🎦🎦½

Riders of Destiny Wayne plays a government agent sent to find out who is stealing water from the local farmers. Very early Wayne has the Duke looking awfully young as an agent securing water rights for ranchers.
1933 59m/B John Wayne, George ''Gabby'' Hayes, Cecilia Parker, Forrest Taylor, Al ''Fuzzy'' St. John; **D:** Robert North Bradbury. **VHS** $9.98 REP, NOS, COL 🎦🎦½

Riders of Pasco Basin Outlaws are tricking ranchers out of their money by falsely promising to build a dam. So Brown and his cohorts come to set things right.
1940 56m/B Johnny Mack Brown, Fuzzy Knight, Bob Baker, Frances Robinson, Arthur Loft, Frank LaRue, Lafe McKee, Kermit Maynard; **D:** Ray Taylor; **W:** Ford Beebe. **VHS** $11.95 GPV 🎦½

Riders of the Desert Steele tracks down the loot from a stagecoach robbery.
1932 57m/B Bob Steele. **VHS, Beta** $19.95 VYY, VCN 🎦½

Riders of the Purple Sage When Texas Ranger Jim Lassiter's (Mix) sister and niece are kidnapped by the evil Walters (Oland), he devotes his life to finding them. While working on a ranch (and falling in love with the beautiful ranch owner), he learns Walters has changed his name and is passing himself off as a judge. Promptly shooting the skunk dead, Lassiter and his sweetie must run from a posse. Based on the Zane Grey novel.
1925 63m/B Tom Mix, Warner Oland, Mabel Ballin, Beatrice Burnham, Arthur Morrison, Fred Kohler Sr.; **D:** Lynn F. Reynolds; **W:** Edfrid Bingham. **VHS** $19.95 GPV 🎦🎦½

Riders of the Range Sheep invade the cattle range and a range war flares up between those who would herd and the ranchers. Silent flick of interest because of the stars.
1924 62m/B Edmund Cobb, Helen Hayes, Dolly Dale; **D:** Otis Thayer. **VHS, Beta** GPV 🎦🎦

Riders of the Range Cowboy rides into town just in time to save a girl's brother from gamblers.
1949 60m/B Tim Holt, Richard Martin. **VHS, Beta** RKO 🎦

Riders of the Range/Storm Over Wyoming A double feature package of Tim Holt Westerns.
1950 120m/B Tim Holt, Richard Martin, Jacqueline Wells. **VHS, Beta** $39.95 RKO, TTC 🎦½

Riders of the Rockies An honest cowboy turns rustler in order to trap a border gang. One of Ritter's very best cowboy outings; good fun, and a very long fistfight with King.
1937 60m/B Tex Ritter, Yakima Canutt, Louise Stanley, Charles ''Blackie'' King, Snub Pollard; **D:** Robert North Bradbury. **VHS, Beta** $19.95 NOS, VCI, VCN 🎦🎦½

Riders of the Storm A motley crew of Vietnam vets runs a covert television broadcasting station from an in-flight B-29, jamming America's legitimate airwaves. Interesting premise with boring result. *AKA:* The American Way.
1988 (R) 92m/C Dennis Hopper, Michael J. Pollard, Eugene Lipinski, James Aubrey, Nigel Pegram; *D:* Maurice Phillips; *W:* Scott Roberts. VHS, Beta $19.98 SUE, NLC ♪♪½

Riders of the Timberline Unusual for a Hopalong Cassidy programmer in that it puts him in timber country. Yes, he's a lumberjack and he's okay, as he fights against land-grabbing crooks all day.
1941 59m/B William Boyd, Brad King, Andy Clyde, J. Farrell MacDonald, Elaine Stewart, Anna Q. Nilsson, Hal Taliaferro, Tom Tyler, Victor Jory; *D:* Lesley Selander. VHS $19.95 NOS ♪♪

Riders of the West An honest cowpoke fights off a band of rustlers.
1942 58m/B Buck Jones, Tim McCoy, Raymond Hatton, Sarah Padden, Harry Woods; *D:* Howard Bretherton. VHS $19.95 NOS, DVT ♪

Riders of the Whistling Pines Our ever-so-bland hero solves a murder perpetrated by a passel of lumber thieves and saves the day for yet another damsel in distress.
1949 70m/B Gene Autry, Patricia White, Jimmy Lloyd; *D:* John English. VHS, Beta $19.95 NOS, MED, DVT ♪♪

Riders of the Whistling Skull The Three Mesquiteers are guiding an expedition to an ancient Indian city. A gang of rustlers looting the city are holding an archeology professor hostage, and the Mesquiteers must rescue him. Swell cast; nifty, creepy plot; solid-as-usual leads. *AKA:* The Golden Trail.
1937 58m/B Bob Livingston, Ray Corrigan, Max Terhune, Yakima Canutt, Roland Winters; *D:* Mack V. Wright. VHS, Beta $12.95 SNC, NOS, VCN ♪♪½

Riders to the Sea A mother envisions the death of her last son in the same manner her other sons died—by drowning. Based on the play by Irish dramatist John Millington Synge.
1988 90m/C Geraldine Page, Amanda Plummer, Sachi Parker, Barry McGovern; *D:* Ronan O'Leary. VHS, Beta NO ♪♪½

Ridin' Down the Canyon Standard but entertaining entry in Rogers' popular series. It's Rogers to the rescue when a gang of outlaws are rustling cattle and selling to the government for wartime profits. Roy, along with the Sons of the Pioneers, also manages to croon a few tunes. Based on a story by Robert Williams and Norman Houston.
1942 54m/B Roy Rogers, George "Gabby" Hayes, Linda Hayes, Addison Richards, Lorna Gray, James Seay; *D:* Joseph Kane; *W:* Albert De Mond. VHS $19.99 MOV ♪♪½

Ridin' on a Rainbow Has-been performer on a steamboat decides to rob a bank in the hopes of starting a new life for himself and his daughter. The money he robs had just been deposited by some cattlemen, one of whom joins the steamboat's crew, wins the daughter's heart, and gets to the father. Slow and dull, with too much singing, and too little plot and scenery.
1941 79m/B Gene Autry, Smiley Burnette, Mary Lee; *D:* Lew Landers. VHS, Beta $39.98 REP, CCB, VCN ♪♪

Ridin' the California Trail The Cisco Kid is wanted dead or alive in several states.

1947 40m/B Gilbert Roland. VHS, Beta $24.95 DVT ♪♪½

Ridin' the Lone Trail Steele attempts to stop some criminals who've been harassing a stagecoach line. Republic was better than this weak western would lead us to believe. Steele, who went on to better things, is a bright spot in a film that sounds and looks bad. Keep your ears open for the sound of airplanes—apparently Newfield forgot they hadn't been invented in the time of the wild west. From a story by E.B. Mann.
1937 56m/B Bob Steele, Claire Rochelle, Charles "Blackie" King, Ernie Adams, Lew Meehan, Julian Rivero; *D:* Sam Newfield; *W:* Charles Francis Royal. VHS $19.95 NOS, DVT Woof!

Ridin' the Trail Scott stars as a cowboy out to rid the countryside of bad guys in this western.
1940 60m/B Fred Scott, Iris Lancaster, Harry Harvey, Jack Ingram, John Ward; *D:* Raymond K. Johnson. VHS, Beta $19.95 NOS, DVT ♪

Ridin' Thru Another Tom Tyler western, in which the hero does battle with unscrupulous villains.
1935 60m/B Tom Tyler, Ruth Hiatt, Lafe McKee, Philo McCullough, Lew Meehan, Bud Osborne; *D:* Harry S. Webb. VHS, Beta $16.95 NOS, DVT, HEG ♪♪

The Riding Avenger To gain the love of a beautiful lady, a cowboy vows never to fight again, but is forced to break his promise when the town is terrorized. Aw, shucks.
1936 56m/B Hoot Gibson, Ruth Mix, Buzz Barton. VHS, Beta $19.95 VCN ♪♪½

Riding High It's a battle for supremacy between the kings of the motorcycle stunt world. Made for television movie's soundtrack includes songs from The Police, Dire Straits, Jerry Lee Lewis, and more.
1978 92m/C Murray Salem, Marella Oppenheim, Eddie Kidd, Irene Handl; *D:* Ross Cramer. VHS, Beta $39.95 LIV ♪

Riding On Hayseed falls for the daughter of his father's arch rival. While his father battles it out over cattle, he pines for his enemy's daughter. Lots of action which is typical fare in mediocre western production.
1937 59m/B Tom Tyler, Germaine Greer, Rex Lease, John Elliott, Earl Dwire; *D:* Harry S. Webb. VHS $19.95 NOS, DVT ♪♪

Riding on Air Small-town newspaper editor Brown discovers that his bumbling methods get him the right results. Smugglers and crazy inventions in a ho-hum Brown entry.
1937 58m/B Joe E. Brown; *D:* Edward Sedgwick. VHS, Beta $19.95 NOS, BAR, FCT ♪♪

Riding Speed Our hero breaks up a gang of smugglers along the Mexican border.
1935 50m/B Buffalo Bill Jr. VHS, Beta NO ♪

Riding the Edge Teenage motocross rider rescues his scientist dad from Middle Eastern terrorists. Thoroughly unoriginal.
1990 (R) 100m/C VHS $89.99 HBO ♪

Riding the Sunset Trail Top-notch tale of Keene trying to stop a con from cashing in on his dead half-brother's fortune. Solid production values and an enthusiastic performance by Keene make this one of his best films after a string of flops.
1941 56m/B Tom Keene, Betty Miles, Frank Yaconelli, Sugar Dawn, Slim Andrews, Kenne Duncan; *D:* Robert Tansey; *W:* Robert Emmett, Frances Kavanaugh. VHS $19.99 MOV ♪♪♪

The Riding Tornado Bronc rider McCoy takes a job on Grey's ranch, promptly falling for her. Ranch foreman Oakman, who's really the leader of a gang of rustlers, kidnaps Grey and McCoy goes after them.
1932 63m/B Tim McCoy, Shirley Grey, Wheeler Oakman, Wallace MacDonald, Russell Simpson, Montagu Love, Lafe McKee, Bud Osborne; *D:* David Ross Lederman. VHS $11.95 GPV ♪♪½

Riding with Death A man who can become invisible, thanks to a military experiment, uses his power to uncover a dastardly plot by a mad scientist. So-so TV pilot.
1976 97m/C Ben Murphy, Andrew Prine, Katherine Crawford, Richard Dysart; *D:* Alan J. Levi. VHS, Beta $39.95 MCA ♪♪½

Riel The story of Louis Riel, a half-French, half-Indian visionary who challenged the Canadian army in his fight for equality and self-rule.
1979 150m/C Raymond Cloutier, Arthur Hill, William Shatner, Christopher Plummer, Leslie Nielsen; *D:* George Bloomfield. VHS, Beta $49.95 PSM ♪♪

Riff Raff Melodramatic story about the relationship of two waterfront workers in the tuna fishing business. Confusing script saddled with too many characters, but there is some good sharp dialogue between the leads. Also features the scenic California waterfront. *AKA:* Riffraff.
1935 80m/B Jean Harlow, Spencer Tracy, Joseph Calleia, Una Merkel, Mickey Rooney, Victor Kilian, J. Farrell MacDonald, Roger Imhof; *D:* J. Walter Ruben. VHS $19.98 MGM ♪♪

Riff-Raff Various dramatic and comic complications arise when a dying man gives Panama City con man O'Brien a map to oil deposits. Interesting and quick-moving melodrama.
1947 80m/B Pat O'Brien, Walter Slezak, Anne Jeffreys, Jason Robards Sr., Percy Kilbride, Jerome Cowan; *D:* Ted Tetzlaff. VHS, Beta $19.98 TTC ♪♪½

Riff Raff Unsparing black comedy about the British working-class by director Loach. Ex-con Stevie comes to London from Scotland to look for work and escape his thieving past. He finds a nonunion job on a construction site, takes up squatter's rights in an abandoned apartment, and finds a girlfriend in equally struggling singer Susie, who turns out to be a junkie. Loach's characters deal with their unenviable lot in life through rough humor and honest sentiment. Regional accents are so thick that the film is subtitled.
1992 96m/C Robert Carlyle, Emer McCourt, Jimmy Coleman, George Moss, Ricky Tomlinson, David Finch, Bill Jesse; *D:* Ken Loach; *W:* Bill Jesse; *M:* Stewart Copeland. VHS NLC, COL, IME ♪♪♪

Rififi Perhaps the greatest of all "heist" movies. Four jewel thieves pull off a daring caper, only to fall prey to mutual distrust. The long scene of the actual theft, completely in silence, will have your heart in your throat. In French with English subtitles. *AKA:* Du Rififi Chez les Hommes.
1954 115m/B Jean Servais, Carl Mohner, Robert Manuel, Jules Dassin; *D:* Jules Dassin. VHS, Beta $24.95 VYY, NOS, HHT ♪♪♪½

The Right Hand Man A brother and sister must deal with their crusty patriarch's demise in the Victorian-era Australian outback. Disappointing and overwrought.
1987 (R) 101m/C Rupert Everett, Hugo Weaving, Arthur Dignam; *D:* Di Drew. VHS, Beta $9.99 STE, NWV ♪½

Right of Way Stewart plays an elderly man who makes a suicide pact with his wife (Davis) when he learns of her terminal illness. Davis and Stewart's first film together is disappointing and stodgy, with an abrupt ending that looks like bad editing by a frightened studio. Made for TV.
1984 102m/C James Stewart, Bette Davis, Priscilla Morrill, Melinda Dillon; **D:** George Schaefer; **M:** Brad Fiedel. VHS, Beta NO ♂♂½

The Right Stuff A rambunctious adaptation of Tom Wolfe's nonfiction book about the beginnings of the U.S. space program, from Chuck Yeager's breaking of the sound barrier to the last of the Mercury missions. Featuring an all-star cast and an ambitious script. Rowdy, imaginative, and thrilling, though broadly painted and oddly uninvolving. Former astronaut John Glenn was running for president when this was out.
1983 (PG) 193m/C Ed Harris, Dennis Quaid, Sam Shepard, Scott Glenn, Fred Ward, Charles Frank, William Russ, Kathy Baker, Barbara Hershey, Levon Helm, David Clennon, Kim Stanley, Mary Jo Deschanel, Veronica Cartwright, Pamela Reed, Jeff Goldblum, Harry Shearer, Donald Moffatt, Scott Paulin, Lance Henriksen, Scott Wilson, John P. Ryan, Royal Dano; **D:** Philip Kaufman; **W:** Philip Kaufman; **M:** Bill Conti. Academy Awards '83: Best Film Editing, Best Sound, Best Original Score; Nominations: Best Art Direction/Set Decoration, Best Cinematography, Best Picture, Best Supporting Actress (Shepard). VHS, Beta $29.98 WAR ♂♂♂

Rikisha-Man A tragic melodrama about a rickshaw puller who helps raise a young boy after his father has died, and loves the boy's mother from afar. Also called "Rickshaw Man" and "Muhomatsu no Issho." Inagaki's remake of his original 1943 version. In Japanese with English subtitles.
1958 105m/B Toshiro Mifune; **D:** Hiroshi Inagaki. VHS, Beta $59.95 FCT ♂♂♂½

Rikky and Pete An engaging Australian comedy about a bizarre, precociously eccentric brother and sister. He's a Rube Goldberg-style mentor; she's a scientist-cum-country singer. They move together to the outback and meet a score of weird characters. A worthy follow-up to director Tass's "Malcolm."
1988 (R) 103m/C Nina Landis, Stephen Kearney, Tetchie Agbayani, Bruce Spence, Bruno Lawrence, Bill Hunter, Dorothy Allison, Don Reid, Lewis Fitzgerald; **D:** Nadia Tass; **W:** David Parker; **M:** Phil Judd. VHS, Beta $79.98 MGM, FOX ♂♂½

Rikyu Set in 16th century Japan, Rikyu is a Buddhist priest who elevated the tea ceremony to an art form. To him it is a spiritual experience, to his master, Lord Hideyoshi Toilyotomi, the ruler of Japan, mastery of the ceremony is a matter of prestige. Conflict arises between Rikyu's ideal of profound simplicity, symbolized by the ceremony, and Toilyotomi's planned conquest of China, which Rikyu opposes. In Japanese with English subtitles.
1990 116m/C Rentaro Mikuni, Tsutomu Yamazaki; **D:** Hiroshi Teshigahara. VHS $79.95 CTL, ING, LUM ♂♂♂

Rim of the Canyon Autry has a dual role as a lawman tracking villains who were jailed by his father years before.
1949 70m/B Gene Autry, Nan Leslie, Thurston Hall, Clem Bevans, Walter Sande, Jock Mahoney, Alan Hale Jr., Denver Pyle; **D:** John English. VHS, Beta $19.95 NOS, DVT, TIM ♂♂

Rimfire An undercover agent tracks down some stolen U.S. Army gold, aided by the ghost of a wrongly-hanged gambler. Fun B western.

1949 65m/B Mary Beth Hughes, Henry Hull, Fuzzy Knight, James Millican, Victor Kilian, Margia Dean, Jason Robards Sr., Reed Hadley; **D:** B. Reeves Eason. VHS, Beta NO ♂♂½

Rin Tin Tin, Hero of the West In one of his last adventures, the famous German Shepherd proves his courage and hyper-canine intelligence. Colorized.
1955 75m/C James Brown, Lee Aaker, Rin Tin Tin. VHS, Beta $24.95 MON ♂♂

The Ring Very early Hitchcock about boxer who marries carnival girl, loses carnival girl, and wins carnival girl back again. Standard romantic punch and roses yarn interesting as measure of young director's developing authority.
1927 82m/B Carl Brisson, Lillian Hall-Davies, Ian Hunter, Gordon Harker; **D:** Alfred Hitchcock; **W:** Alfred Hitchcock. VHS $19.98 VEC, MLB ♂♂½

The Ring Poignant early movie that gives a lesson in prejudice against Chicanos. The main character feels that the only way to get respect from the world is to fight for it. Well-directed and perceptive.
1952 79m/B Gerald Mohr, Rita Moreno, Kiri Te Kanawa, Robert Arthur, Art Aragon, Jack Elam; **D:** Kurt Neumann. VHS, MOV, DVT, HEG ♂♂½

Ring of Bright Water Well done story of a pet otter from Gavin Maxwell's autobiography. The film stars the couple that made the delightful "Born Free." Beautiful Scottish Highlands photography adds to this captivating and endearing tale of a civil servant who purchases an otter from a pet store and moves to the country.
1969 (G) 107m/C Bill Travers, Virginia McKenna, Peter Jeffrey, Archie Duncan; **D:** Charles Lamont. VHS, Beta FCT, SIG, TVC ♂♂♂

Ring of Death A tough cop investigating a routine case becomes a hunted man after someone kills the man he is following.
1972 93m/C Franco Nero, Florinda Bolkan, Adolfo Celi. VHS, Beta $14.95 CNG, MRV, GEM ♂½

Ring of Fire Wilson is one of very few modern American kung-fu heroes of Asian descent, and he works messages against prejudice into this interracial Romeo-and-Juliet chopsocky tale. What foot through yonder window breaks?
1991 (R) 100m/C Don "The Dragon" Wilson, Maria Ford, Vince Murdocco, Dale Jacoby, Michael Delano, Eric Lee; **D:** Richard W. Munchkin. VHS $89.95 IMP, HMV ♂½

Ring of Fire 2: Blood and Steel Wilson returns as Dr. Johnny Wu in this martial-arts actioner which finds the good doctor the witness to a robbery. When one of the robbers is killed, the gang's leader kidnaps Johnny's fiance and holds her for ransom. He decides to bypass the police and use his own expertise to rescue her.
1992 (R) 94m/C Don "The Dragon" Wilson, Maria Ford, Sy Richardson, Michael Delano, Dale Jacoby, Vince Murdocco, Evan Lorie, Gary Robbins, Charlie Ganis, Ron Yuan; **D:** Richard W. Munchkin. VHS $89.95 PMH ♂½

Ring of Steel Alex, a one-time Olympic hopeful in fencing, is enticed into combat by the mysterious owner of a decadent nightclub where gladiator-type matches are staged for the thrill of the bored and jaded super-rich. Unaware of the high stakes, Alex wins a duel and is showered with money and the attention of a beautiful, yet dangerous woman. When Alex discovers the club's dark secret, he no longer wants to fight, but blackmail draws him in even deeper.

1994 (R) 94m/C Joe Don Baker, Carol Alt, Robert Chapin, Gary Kasper, Darlene Vogel; **D:** David Frost; **W:** Robert Chapin; **M:** Jeff Beal. VHS MCA ♂♂

Ring of Terror College boy who wants to join a fraternity must survive the initiation rights, which include stealing a ring from a corpse. Unfortunately, this seemingly invincible guy has a deadly terror of the dead. Cheaply made flop alledgedly based on a composite of actual hazing incidents.
1962 72m/B George Mather, Esther Furst, Austin Green, Joseph Conway; **D:** Clark Paylow. VHS $16.95 NOS, SNC ♂

Ring of the Musketeers Contemporary spoof of the Musketeers saga finds three descendants of the swashbuckling heroes carrying on the family tradition of protecting the weak and innocent. They even get stuck with a Musketeer-wannabe when they come to the resuce of a young boy who is kidnapped to prevent his dad from testifying against mobsters.
1993 (PG-13) 86m/C David Hasselhoff, Alison Doody, Thomas Gottschalk, Richard "Cheech" Marin, Corbin Bernsen, John Rhys-Davies; **D:** John Paragon; **W:** Joel Surnow. VHS COL ♂♂½

Ringside A concert pianist turns boxer to avenge his brother who was blinded in a fight.
1949 64m/B Donald (Don "Red") Barry, Sheila Ryan, Tom Brown. VHS, Beta $16.95 SNC ♂½

The Rink Chaplin plays a waiter who spends his lunch hour on roller skates. Silent with musical soundtrack added.
1916 20m/B Charlie Chaplin; **D:** Charlie Chaplin. VHS, Beta CAB, GVV ♂♂♂

Rink/Immigrant Two Chaplin shorts: "The Rink" (1916), in which Charlie defends his girlfriend's honor at a local roller skating rink; "The Immigrant" (1917), features Charlie as a newcomer to America.
191? 56m/B Charlie Chaplin, Mack Swain, Edna Purviance. VHS, Beta $24.95 VYY ♂♂♂

Rio Bravo The sheriff of a Texas border town (Wayne) takes a brutal murderer into custody and faces a blockade of hired gunmen determined to keep his prisoner from being brought to justice. Long, but continually entertaining. Generally regarded as an American film classic, with an all-star cast, didn't impress the critics at the time. Sequel: "El Dorado." Semi-remake was called "Assault on Precinct 13."
1959 140m/C John Wayne, Dean Martin, Angie Dickinson, Ricky Nelson, Walter Brennan, Ward Bond, Claude Akins, Bob Steele, John Russell; **D:** Howard Hawks. VHS, Beta $19.98 WAR, TLF ♂♂♂♂

Rio Conchos Nifty nonstop action in this western set in Texas after the Civil War. Three Army buddies search for 2,000 stolen rifles. Boone is understated, O'Brien is good, and Brown memorable in his debut.
1964 107m/C Richard Boone, Stuart Whitman, Edmond O'Brien, Anthony (Tony) Franciosa, Jim Brown; **D:** Gordon Douglas; **M:** Jerry Goldsmith. VHS, Beta $19.98 FOX ♂♂♂

Rio Diablo Country Western singers abound in—what else—a made-for-TV Western movie. A bounty hunter (Rogers) and newlywed groom (Tritt) set off after a gang of thieving kidnappers who have snatched the young bride (Harring). Judd shows up as the owner of a desert hostelry, who happens to cross paths with the hunters. Watch out—this could be more fun than a Partridge Family reunion.
1993 120m/C Kenny Rogers, Travis Tritt, Naomi Judd, Stacy Keach, Brion James, Bruce Greenwood, Laura Harring. VHS CAF, MVD ♂♂½

Rio Grande The last entry in Ford's cavalry trilogy following ''Fort Apache'' and ''She Wore a Yellow Ribbon.'' A U.S. cavalry unit on the Mexican border conducts an unsuccessful campaign against marauding Indians. The commander (Wayne) faces an unhappy wife and is estranged from his son, a new recruit. Featuring an excellent Victor Young score and several songs by the Sons of the Pioneers.
1950 105m/B John Wayne, Maureen O'Hara, Ben Johnson, Claude Jarman Jr., Harry Carey Jr., Victor McLaglen, Chill Wills, J. Carroll Naish; **D:** John Ford. VHS $9.98 REP, TLF, RXM ⅔⅔⅔

Rio Grande Raiders A Stagecoach driver discovers that his kid brother is working for a crooked rival stage company.
1946 54m/B Sunset Carson, Linda Stirling, Bob Steele. VHS, Beta $29.95 DVT, RXM ⅔

Rio Hondo An ex-gunfighter comes back to his home town only to find it filled with outlaws.
1947 90m/B Carlos Cortez, Elsa Cardenas, Alfonso Mejias, Alfredo Leal. VHS, Beta $39.95 MAD ⅔⅔

Rio Lobo Hawks's final film takes place after the Civil War, when Union Colonel Wayne goes to Rio Lobo to take revenge on two traitors. Disappointing. The Duke has to carry weak supporting performances on his brawny shoulders—and nearly does.
1970 (G) 114m/C John Wayne, Jorge Rivero, Jennifer O'Neill, Jack Elam, Chris Mitchum, David Huddleston, George Plimpton; **D:** Howard Hawks; **M:** Jerry Goldsmith. VHS, Beta $19.98 FOX ⅔⅔½

Rio Rattler A vintage fast-shooting matinee western.
1935 60m/B Tom Tyler, Marion Shilling, Eddie Gribbon, William Gould, Tom London; **D:** Bernard B. Ray. VHS, Beta $27.95 VCN ⅔½

Rio Rita Abbott & Costello are working on a ranch and somehow become involved with Nazi spies. Provides a few original comic bits for the duo but is otherwise mediocre. An updated remake of the 1929 Wheeler & Woolsey comedy.
1942 91m/B Bud Abbott, Lou Costello, Kathryn Grayson, John Carroll, Patricia Dane, Tom Conway, Peter Whitney; **D:** Sylvan Simon. VHS $19.98 MGM ⅔⅔½

Riot Men in cages throw tantrums until warden returns from vacation. Filmed in Arizona State Prison with real convicts as extras. Strong performances by fullback Brown and durable Hackman. Based on story by ex-con Frank Elli. Too oft-played theme song sung by Bill Medley of the Righteous Brothers.
1969 (R) 97m/C Gene Hackman, Jim Brown, Mike Kellin, Ben Carruthers, Frank Eyman; **D:** Buzz Kulik; **W:** James Poe. VHS $14.95 PAR ⅔⅔½

Riot in Cell Block 11 A convict leads four thousand prisoners in an uprising to improve prison conditions. Based on producer/ex-con Walter Wanger's own experience. Powerful and still timely. Filmed at Folsom Prison.
1954 80m/B Neville Brand, Leo Gordon, Emile Meyer, Frank Faylen; **D:** Don Siegel. VHS, Beta $19.98 REP ⅔⅔⅔

Riot Squad An intern poses as a doctor in order to find out who was responsible for putting a mob hit on a police captain.
1941 55m/B Richard Cromwell, Rita Quigley, John Miljan, Mary Ruth, Herbert Rawlinson, Mary Gordon, Arthur Space; **D:** Edward Finney. VHS, Beta $16.95 SNC, RXM ⅔⅔

Rip-Off Two Greek wanderers enter the American way of life via sex, drugs, syndicated crime, and terrorism.
1977 78m/C Michael Benet, Michelle Simone, James Masters, Johnny Dark; **D:** Manolis Tsafos. VHS, Beta $49.95 UNI ⅔

The Rip Off A colorful gang of hoodlums goes for the biggest heist of their lives—six million bucks in diamonds!
1978 (R) 99m/C Lee Van Cleef, Karen Black, Robert Alda, Edward Albert; **D:** Anthony M. (Antonio Marghereti) Dawson. VHS, Beta $49.95 WOV ⅔

Rip Roarin' Buckaroo A fighter sets out to avenge himself when he is framed in a dishonest fight.
1936 51m/B Tom Tyler, B.J. Quinn Jr., Beth Marion, Charles ''Blackie'' King; **D:** Robert F. Hill. VHS, Beta $19.95 NOS, DVT, RXM ⅔

Rip van Winkle Sleepy Coppola adaptation of the Washington Irving story about a man who falls asleep for twenty years after a group of ghosts get him drunk. From the ''Faerie Tale Theatre'' series.
1985 60m/C Harry Dean Stanton, Talia Shire; **D:** Francis Ford Coppola. VHS, Beta $14.95 KUI, FOX, FCT ⅔⅔

Ripley's Believe It or Not! Each episode of this series outlines incredible facts based on the long-running newspaper feature. New volumes are being added to this on-going series on a regular basis. Volumes are available separately.
1985 80m/C VHS, Beta NO ⅔

The Ripper The spirit of Jack-the-Ripper possesses a university professor's body. Ultra-violent. Shot on videotape for the video market.
1986 90m/C Wade Tower, Tom Schreir, Mona Van Pernis, Andrea Adams; **D:** Christopher Lewis. VHS, Beta $24.95 CNG *Woof!*

Ripping Yarns Three episodes of the popular British comedy series written by Monty Python's Terry Jones and Michael Palin: ''Tomkinson's Schooldays,'' ''Escape from Stalag Luft 112B,'' and ''Golden Gordon.'' The subsequent episodes are released as ''More Ripping Yarns'' and ''Even More Ripping Yarns.''
1975 90m/C Michael Palin, Gwen Watford, Ian Ogilvy, Roy Kinnear, Bill Fraser; **D:** Terry Hughes, Jimmy Franklin, Alan Bell; **W:** Michael Palin, Terry Jones. VHS, Beta $14.98 FOX *Woof!*

Riptide Shearer is a carefree American married to stuffy English lord Marshall. He goes off to America on a business trip, she's bored and goes to a costume party (everyone dresses as insects!) where she meets old flame Montgomery. He gets drunk, follows her home in an effort to rekindle their passion, and winds up in the hospital after a drunken fall. The returning Marshall is appalled by the scandalous press and instigates divorce proceedings. Eventually, they come to their senses and decide they do love each other. Quality production with an entertaining cast.
1934 90m/B Norma Shearer, Herbert Marshall, Robert Montgomery, Richard ''Skeets'' Gallagher, Ralph Forbes, Lilyan Tashman; **D:** Edmund Goulding; **W:** Edmund Goulding. VHS $29.98 MGM ⅔⅔⅔

The Rise and Fall of Legs Diamond Not quite historically accurate but fast-paced and entertaining gangster bio of legendary booze trafficker Legs Diamond. Danton's debut.
1960 101m/B Ray Danton, Karen Steele, Jesse White, Simon Oakland, Robert Lowery, Elaine Stewart; **D:** Budd Boetticher. VHS $59.99 WAR, FCT ⅔⅔½

Rise and Fall of the Third Reich A pictorial record which tracks Adolf Hitler's path through the years between 1920 and 1945. Some segments are in black and white.
1968 120m/C VHS, Beta $59.95 MGM ⅔⅔½

The Rise & Rise of Daniel Rocket A exceptional young boy believes he can fly without the aid of a flying machine. From the ''American Playhouse'' series.
1986 90m/C Tom Hulce, Timothy Daly, Valerie Mahaffey; **D:** Emile Ardolino. VHS, Beta $59.95 ACA, PBS ⅔⅔

The Rise of Louis XIV A masterful docudrama detailing the life and court intrigues of Louis XIV of France. Successfully captures the attitudes and mores of the royalty at the time. One of a series of historical films directed by Rossellini. Made for French television. In French with English subtitles. *AKA:* La Prise de Pouvoir Par Louis XIV.
1966 100m/C Jean-Marie Patte, Raymond Jourdan, Dominique Vincent, Silvagni, Pierre Barrat; **D:** Roberto Rossellini. VHS $59.95 HTV, ING, FCT ⅔⅔⅔

Rising Damp Episodes from the caustic British comedy television series. Rigsby is the landlord of a crumbling boarding house filled with unhappy tenants. And no wonder, Rigsby is mean-spirited, miserly, prejudiced, greedy, and stupid. Two episodes per tape.
19?? 150m/C Leonard Rossiter. VHS $22.98 FCT ⅔⅔⅔

Rising Son A family man who loves his job faces trauma when his factory closes at the same time his son informs him he's quitting medical school. Solid family drama and parable of economic hard times of the early '80s, sustained by top-drawer performances by Dennehy, Damon, and Laurie. Well directed by Coles. Made for cable.
1990 92m/C Brian Dennehy, Matt Damon, Piper Laurie, Graham Beckel, Ving Rhames, Jane Adams, Richard Jenkins, Emily Longstreth; **D:** John David Coles; **W:** Bill Phillips. VHS, Beta $79.98 TTC ⅔⅔⅔

Rising Sun When a prostitute is found murdered in the boardroom of a powerful Japanese-owned corporation, seasoned cop (and Japanese expert) Connery and new partner Snipes are sent to investigate. Complicated yarn about business, prejudice, cops, and the differences between east and west. Filmed with stylized camera techniques, quick action, and good rapport between the two leads. Based on the book by Crichton, which offered ominous theories about international politics and business. These aspects had the film labeled as Japan-bashing, one of the reasons the script was rewritten to focus more on the murder mystery.
1993 (R) 129m/C Sean Connery, Wesley Snipes, Tia Carrere, Harvey Keitel, Kevin Anderson, Stan Egi, Mako, Cary-Hiroyuki Tagawa, Ray Wise, Tatjana Patitz; **D:** Philip Kaufman; **W:** Michael Backes, Michael Crichton, Philip Kaufman; **M:** Toru Takemitsu. VHS $96.98 FXV, BTV, FCT ⅔⅔⅔

Risky Business Fortune-seeking mother disapproves of daughter's doctor fiance, and educates girl in marital woes. Video includes early Pollard short ''Sold at Auction.''
1928 104m/B Vera Reynolds, ZaSu Pitts, Ethey Clayton; **D:** Alan Hale. VHS, Beta $18.95 GPV, FCT, WAR ⅔⅔

Risky Business With his parents out of town and awaiting word from the college boards, a teenager becomes involved in unexpected ways with a quick-thinking pros-

titute, her pimp, and assorted others. Cruise is likeable, especially when dancing in his underwear. Funny, well-paced, stylish prototypical '80s teen flick reintroduced Ray-Bans as the sunglasses for the wannabe hip. What a party!
1983 (R) 99m/C Tom Cruise, Rebecca DeMornay, Curtis Armstrong, Bronson Pinchot, Joe Pantoliano, Kevin Anderson, Richard Masur, Raphael Sbarge, Nicholas Pryor, Janet Carroll; **D:** Paul Brickman; **W:** Paul Brickman. **VHS, Beta, 8mm $19.98** *WAR* 🐾🐾🐾

Rita Hayworth: The Love Goddess Made for television drama details the tragic life of the beautiful film star. Carter, lovely though she is, plays Rita weakly and without depth.
1983 100m/C Lynda Carter, Michael Lerner, Alejandro Rey, John Considine; **D:** James Goldstone. **VHS, Beta $39.95** *LIV* 🐾🐾½

Rita, Sue & Bob Too A middle-aged Englishman gets involved in a menage a trois with two promiscuous teenagers, until the whole town gets wind of it. A raunchy, amoral British comedy.
1987 (R) 94m/C Michelle Holmes, George Costigan, Siobhan Finneran, Lesley Sharp, Willie Ross, Patti Nicholls, Kulvinder Ghir; **D:** Alan Clarke; **W:** Andrea Dunbar; **M:** Michael Kamen. **VHS, Beta $79.95** *LHV, WAR* 🐾🐾🐾

Rituals Group of five calm, rational men suddenly turn desperate after a chain of nightmarish events on a camping trip. Yet another low-budget "Deliverance" rip off. *AKA:* The Creeper.
1979 100m/C Hal Holbrook, Lawrence Dane; **D:** Peter Carter. **VHS, Beta $24.98** *SUE, VTR* 🐾½

The Ritz Weston tries to get away from his gangster brother-in-law by hiding out in a gay bathhouse in New York. Moreno plays a talentless singer Googie Gomez, who performs in the bathhouse while waiting for her big break. Moreno is great reprising her Tony-winning stage role, and Lester's direction is spiffy. Written by Terence McNally from his play.
1976 (R) 91m/C Rita Moreno, Jack Weston, Jerry Stiller, Kaye Ballard, Treat Williams, F. Murray Abraham; **D:** Richard Lester. **VHS, Beta $19.98** *WAR* 🐾🐾🐾

Rivals Shallow, unconvincing drama about a stepfather challenged by his stepson, who wants to kill this new contender for his mother's love. Nice handling of cast credits, but other details—like acting, directing and photography—leave much to be desired. *AKA:* Deadly Rivals.
1972 (R) 103m/C Robert Klein, Joan Hackett, Scott Jacoby; **D:** Krishna Shah. **VHS, Beta $54.95** *TPI* 🐾½

Rivals of the Silver Fox Young kickers prove no match for their hoary, hard-chopping elder.
1980 90m/C Casanova Wong, Barry Lam, Chen Shao Ping, Lee Fat Yuen. **VHS, Beta** *NO* 🐾½

The River A massively lauded late film by Renoir about three British girls growing up in Bengal, India, all developing crushes on a one-legged American vet. Lyrical and heartwarming, with hailed cinematography by Claude Renoir. Rumer Godden wrote the novel, and co-scripted the screenplay with director Renoir. Satyajit Ray, one of India's greatest filmmakers, assisted Renoir.
1951 99m/C Patricia Walters, Adrienne Corri, Nora Swinburne, Radha, Arthur Shields, Thomas E. Breen, Esmond Knight; **D:** Jean Renoir; **W:** Jean Renoir. **VHS, Beta $29.95** *HMV, VYG, CRC* 🐾🐾🐾🐾

The River Farmers battle a river whose flood threatens their farm. Spacek, as always, is strong and believable as the wife and mother, but Gibson falters. Beautiful photography. The third in an onslaught of films in the early '80s that dramatized the plight of the small American farmer. "The River" isn't as strong as "Country" and "Places in the Heart" which managed to convey important messages less cloyingly.
1984 (PG) 124m/C Mel Gibson, Sissy Spacek, Scott Glenn, Billy Green Bush; **D:** Mark Rydell; **W:** Julian Barry, Robert Dillon; **M:** John Williams. **VHS, Beta $14.98** *MCA* 🐾🐾

River Beat A woman aboard an American freighter is unwittingly used as diamond smuggler, and is arrested when the ship docks in London. An inspector does his best to clear the hapless woman.
1954 70m/B Phyllis Kirk, John Bentley, Robert Ayres, Lenny White, Glyn Houston, Charles Lloyd Pack; **D:** Guy Green. **VHS, Beta $16.95** *SNC* 🐾🐾

The River Niger Jones is riveting, and Tyson is good in an otherwise muddling adaptation of the Tony-award winning play about black ghetto life. Realistic emotions and believable characters.
1976 (R) 105m/C James Earl Jones, Cicely Tyson, Glynn Turman, Louis Gossett Jr., Roger E. Mosley, Jonelle Allen; **D:** Krishna Shah. **VHS** *NO* 🐾🐾½

River of Death Absurd adventure, based on an Alistair McLean novel, about a white man entering the Amazon jungle world of a forgotten tribe in search of wealth, tripping over Neo-Nazi scientists and war criminals. Too complex to be harmlessly enjoyable; too mindless for the complexity to be worth unraveling.
1990 (R) 103m/C Michael Dudikoff, Robert Vaughn, Donald Pleasence, Herbert Lom, L.Q. Jones, Cynthia Erland, Sarah Maur-Thorp; **D:** Steve Carver. **VHS, Beta $14.95** *MGM, WAR* 🐾½

River of Diamonds A daring adventurer, with the standard beautiful woman at his side, battles evil curses and Nazis buried alive to find a fortune in diamonds. Yeah, sure. Another miserable "Indiana Jones" rip off.
1990 88m/C Dack Rambo, Angela O'Neill, Ferdinand "Ferdy" Mayne, Graham Clark, David Sherwood, Tony Caprari, Dominique Tyawa; **D:** Robert J. Smawley. **VHS, Beta $79.98** *TTC* 🐾

River of Evil Action/adventure in which a young girl travels through the Amazon jungle searching for clues to her father's death.
1964 ?m/C Barbara Rutting, Harald Leipnitz. **VHS $16.95** *SNC* 🐾½

River of No Return During the gold rush, an itinerant farmer and his young son help a heart-of-gold saloon singer search for her estranged husband. Rather crummy script is helped by the mere presence of Mitchum and Monroe. Marilyn sings the title song, "Down in the Meadow," and "I'm Going to File My Claim."
1954 91m/C Robert Mitchum, Marilyn Monroe, Tommy Rettig, Rory Calhoun, Murvyn Vye, Douglas Spencer; **D:** Otto Preminger. **VHS, Beta $14.98** *FOX* 🐾🐾½

River of Unrest Remarkable visual expressiveness and emotional power mark this depiction of terrorism and open warfare during the Irish Rebellion. Based on a play, hence slow; but good acting pulls it up half a bone. *AKA:* Ourselves Alone.
1937 69m/B John Lodge, John Loder, Antoinette Cellier. **VHS, Beta $24.95** *VYY* 🐾🐾½

The River Rat Ex-con Jones is reunited with his daughter after spending thirteen years in prison. There's something in there about stashed loot that should have been jettisonned in favor of more getting-to-know-you father-daughter drama, which is good.
1984 (PG) 93m/C Tommy Lee Jones, Brian Dennehy, Martha Plimpton, Shawn Smith, Melissa Davis; **D:** Tom Rickman. **VHS, Beta $14.95** *PAR* 🐾🐾½

A River Runs Through It Contemplative exploration of family ties and coming of age with impact falling just short of the novel's is another well-crafted American tale directed by Redford. Set in Montana during the early part of the century, a Presbyterian minister teaches his two sons, one troubled and one on his way to success, about life and religion via fly-fishing. Based on the novel by Norman Maclean. The laser disc version includes commentary by Redford.
1992 (PG) 123m/C Craig Sheffer, Brad Pitt, Tom Skerritt, Brenda Blethyn, Emily Lloyd, Edie McClurg, Stephen Shellan, Susan Taylor; **D:** Robert Redford; **W:** Richard Friedenberg; **M:** Mark Isham. Academy Awards '92: Best Cinematography; Nominations: Best Adapted Screenplay, Best Original Score. **VHS, 8mm $19.95** *COL, CRC, BTV* 🐾🐾🐾½

Riverbend A renegade black Army major escapes a rigged court martial only to be persecuted by racist whites in a small Southern town. Made for television.
1989 (R) 106m/C Steve James, Tony Frank, Julius Tennon, Margaret Avery; **D:** Sam Firstenberg. **VHS, Beta $89.95** *PAR* 🐾🐾

River's Edge Drug-addled high school student strangles his girlfriend and casually displays the corpse to his apathetic group of friends, who leave the murder unreported for days. Harrowing and gripping; based on a true story. Aging biker Hopper is splendid.
1987 (R) 99m/C Keanu Reeves, Crispin Glover, Daniel Roebuck, Joshua Miller, Dennis Hopper, Ione Skye, Roxana Zal, Tom Bower, Constance Forslund, Leo Rossi, Jim Metzler; **D:** Tim Hunter; **W:** Neal Jimenez; **M:** Jurgen Knieper. **VHS, Beta, 8mm $14.98** *SUE, NLC* 🐾🐾🐾

Road Agent Hoxie is the Kansas Kid, a fugitive hired by a crooked lawyer to pose as the long-lost heir to a ranching fortune. Only the Kid develops a soft spot for his "family" and may not be able to go through with the evil plot. *AKA:* Texas Road Agent.
1926 70m/B Al Hoxie; **D:** J.P. McGowan. **VHS, Beta $19.95** *NOS, DVT, MLB* 🐾½

Road Games Trucker Keach is drawn into a web of intrigue surrounding a series of highway "Jack the Ripper"-style murders. Curtis is a hitchhiker. Nothing special. Director Franklin later helmed "Psycho II."
1981 (PG) 100m/C Stacy Keach, Jamie Lee Curtis; **D:** Richard Franklin. **VHS, Beta $9.95** *COL, SUE, NLC* 🐾🐾

Road House Nightclub singer Lupino inspires noir feelings between jealous road house owner Widmark and his partner Wilde. Widmark sets up Wilde to take the fall for a faked robbery, convinces the law to release him into his custody, then dares him to escape.
1948 95m/B Richard Widmark, Ida Lupino, Cornel Wilde, Celeste Holm, O.Z. Whitehead; **D:** Jean Negulesco. **VHS, Beta $19.98** *FOX, FCT* 🐾🐾½

Road House Bouncer Swayze is hired to do the impossible: clean up the toughest bar in Kansas City. When he lays down his rules he makes a lot of enemies, including ex-bar employees and local organized crime. Ample violence; an example of formula filmmaking at its most brain-numbing, with a rock sound-track.

1989 (R) 115m/C Patrick Swayze, Sam Elliott, Kelly Lynch, Ben Gazzara, Kevin Tighe, Marshall Teague, Julie Michaels, Jeff Healey; **D:** Rowdy Herrington; **M:** Michael Kamen. **VHS, Beta, 8mm** $19.98 MGM ♫♫ ½

Road Lawyers and Other Briefs Several recent comedic shorts. "Road Lawyers," the title short, is a hilarious look at lawyers in a post-apocalyptic world that won major awards at film festivals in New York, Houston, Australia, and Chicago. Also included are: "Escape from Heaven," about a nun with an attitude problem; "Radar Men on the Moon," a comic reworking of an old "Commander Cody" serial; and "Hairline."

1989 79m/C VHS $79.95 AIP ♫♫ ½

Road Racers The roar of the engine, fast cars, and family ties combine in this movie about the thrill of speed.

1959 73m/B Joel Lawrence, Marian Collier, Skip Ward; **D:** Arthur Swerdloff; **W:** Stanley Kalis, Ed Lasko. **VHS** $9.95 COL ♫♫

Road Show Menjou stars as a young man wrongfully committed to an insane asylum. He escapes and joins a bankrupt carnival owned by Landis. Some really zany stuff keeps this from being just standard fare. Co-written by silent film comic Langdon.

1941 87m/B Adolphe Menjou, Carole Landis, John Hubbard, Charles Butterworth, Patsy Kelly, George E. Stone, Polly Ann Young, Edward Norris, Marjorie Woodworth, Florence Bates; **D:** Hal Roach; **W:** Harry Langdon. **VHS** $19.95 NOS ♫♫ ½

The Road to Bali Sixth Bob-n-Bing road show, the only one in color, is a keeper. The boys are competing for the love of—that's right—Lamour. She must be some gal, cuz they chase her all the way to Bali, where they meet cannibals and other perils, including the actual Humphrey Bogart. Jones's debut, in a bit role. ♫Moonflowers; Chicago Style; Hoots Mon; To See You; The Merry-Go-Runaround; Chorale for Brass, Piano, and Bongo (instrumental).

1953 90m/C Bob Hope, Bing Crosby, Dorothy Lamour, Murvyn Vye, Ralph Moody, Jane Russell, Jerry Lewis, Dean Martin, Carolyn Jones; **D:** Hal Walker. **VHS, Beta** $29.95 UNI, DVT, MLB ♫♫♫

The Road to Hong Kong Last of the Crosby/Hope team-ups shows some wear, but still manages charm and humor. Lamour appears only briefly in this twisted comedy of hustlers caught in international espionage and cosmic goings-on. ♫Teamwork; Let's Not Be Sensible; It's The Only Way to Travel; We're On the Road to Hong Kong; Warmer Than a Whisper.

1962 91m/B Bob Hope, Bing Crosby, Joan Collins, Dorothy Lamour, Peter Sellers; **D:** Norman Panama; **W:** Norman Panama. **VHS** $14.95 MGM, BTV, FCT ♫♫ ½

The Road to Lebanon An original musical comedy featuring many stars, spoofing the famous Hope-Crosby "Road" films.

1960 50m/B Danny Thomas, Bing Crosby, Bob Hope, Hugh Downs, Claudine Auger, Sheldon Leonard. **VHS, Beta** $24.95 NOS, VYY, DVT ♫♫

The Road to Morocco The third in the road movie series finds Hope and Crosby in Morocco, stranded and broke. To get some money, Crosby sells Hope into slavery to be the princess' (Lamour) personal plaything. Feeling guilty, Crosby returns to the palace to rescue Hope, only to find that he and the princess are getting married because the royal astrologer said it was in the stars. Crosby then tries to woo Lamour and, when the astrologer discovers the stars were mis-

taken, those two decide to marry. Quinn, however, also wants her and hilarious scenes ensue when the boys rescue Lamour from him. One of the funniest in the series. Watch for the camel at the end. ♫Constantly; Moonlight Becomes You; Ain't Got a Dime to My Name; Road to Morocco.

1942 83m/C Bing Crosby, Bob Hope, Dorothy Lamour, Anthony Quinn, Dona Drake, Vladimir Sokoloff, Yvonne De Carlo; **D:** David Butler. **VHS** $14.98 MCA ♫♫♫ ½

Road to Nashville An agent travels to Nashville to enlist talent for a new musical. Why do so many of these semi-musicals insist on having a plot? Good music.

1967 (G) 110m/C Marty Robbins, Johnny Cash, Doodles Weaver, Connie Smith, Richard Arlen; **D:** Robert Patrick. **VHS, Beta** $29.95 VCI ♫♫

Road to 1984 Biodrama about futuristic author George Orwell centers on his classic "1984."

19?? 86m/C Edward Fox. **VHS** $19.99 PAR ♫♫ ½

The Road to Rio The wisecracking duo travel to Rio De Janeiro to prevent Spanish beauty Lamour (there she is again) from going through with an arranged marriage. Top-notch entry; fifth in the "Road" series. ♫But Beautiful; You Don't Have To Know the Language; For What?; Experience; Apalachicola, Florida; Cavaquinho; Brazil.

1947 100m/B Bing Crosby, Bob Hope, Dorothy Lamour, Gale Sondergaard, Frank Faylen, The Andrews Sisters, The Wiere Brothers; **D:** Norman Z. McLeod; **W:** Jack Rose. **VHS, Beta** $14.95 COL ♫♫♫ ½

The Road to Ruin The evils of smoking and drinking plummet a girl into a life of prostitution in this melodramatic, moralistic tale. An unintentional laugh-riot right up there with "Reefer Madness." Silent.

1928 45m/B Helen Foster, Grant Withers, Virginia Roye; **D:** Norton S. Parker; **W:** Erik Anjou. **VHS, Beta** $16.95 SNC, NOS, VYY ♫♫

Road to Ruin A rich playboy pretends to lose all his money to see if his girlfriend loves him for himself or for his wealth. But when his business partner embezzles his fortune, he must regain both his money and his girlfriend's trust.

1991 (R) 94m/C Peter Weller, Carey Lowell, Michael Duchaussoy; **D:** Charlotte Brandstrom. **VHS** $89.95 LIV ♫♫

Road to Salina A drifter is mistaken for (and might actually be) a desert-restaurant owner's long-lost son. He plays along, eventually seducing the family's daughter, who might be his sister.

1968 (R) 97m/C Robert Walker Jr., Rita Hayworth, Mimsy Farmer, Ed Begley Sr.; **D:** Georges Lautner. **VHS, Beta** $59.95 NLC ♫♫♫

The Road to Singapore This is the movie that started it all. Crosby and Hope decide to swear off women and escape to Singapore to enjoy the free life. There they meet Lamour, a showgirl who is abused by Quinn. The boys rescue Lamour, but soon find they are both falling for her. She's in love with one of them, but won't reveal her feelings. Who will get the girl? Not as funny as some of the other road movies, but it's great for a first try. ♫Captain Custard; The Moon and the Willow Tree; Sweet Potato Piper; Too Romantic; Kaigoon.

1940 84m/C Bing Crosby, Bob Hope, Dorothy Lamour, Charles Coburn, Judith Barrett, Anthony Quinn, Jerry Colonna, Johnny Arthur, Pierre Watkin; **D:** Victor Schertzinger. **VHS** $14.98 MCA ♫♫ ½

The Road to Utopia Fourth of the "Road" films, wherein the boys wind up in Alaska posing as two famous escaped killers in order to locate a secret gold mine. One of the series' funniest and most spontaneous entries, abetted by Benchley's dry, upper-crust comments. ♫Put It There, Pal; Welcome to My Dreams; Would You?; Personality; Sunday, Monday, or Always?; Goodtime Charlie; It's Anybody's Spring.

1946 90m/B Bing Crosby, Bob Hope, Dorothy Lamour, Jack LaRue, Robert Benchley, Douglass Dumbrille, Hillary Brooke; **D:** Hal Walker; **W:** Norman Panama. **VHS, Beta** $29.95 MCA ♫♫♫

The Road to Yesterday Two couples together on a crashing train are somehow thrown into the eighteenth century in roles parallel to their own lives. DeMille's first independent film; intriguing action/melodrama. Silent with musical soundtrack.

1925 136m/B Joseph Schildkraut, William Boyd, Jetta Goudal, Vera Reynolds, Iron Eyes Cody; **D:** Cecil B. DeMille. **VHS, Beta** $19.95 GPV, VYY ♫♫ ½

Road to Yesterday/The Yankee Clipper Four train passengers are transported back to previous lives in "The Road to Yesterday." "The Yankee Clipper" races the British Lord of the Isles from China to New England to capture the tea trade. Both of these pictures are abridged versions. Silent.

1927 56m/B William Boyd, Elinor Fair, Joseph Schildkraut, Jetta Goudal, Vera Reynolds; **D:** Cecil B. DeMille. **VHS, Beta** $29.95 CCB ♫♫ ½

The Road to Zanzibar After selling a fake diamond mine to a criminal, Crosby and Hope flee to Zanzibar, where they meet up with Lamour and Merkel. The guys put up the money for a safari, supposedly to look for Lamour's brother, but they soon discover that they too have been tricked. Deciding to head back to Zanzibar, Crosby and Hope find themselves surrounded by hungry cannibals. Will they survive, or will they be someone's dinner? Not as funny as the other road movies, but amusing nonetheless. ♫It's Always You; You're Dangerous; On the Road to Zanzibar; You Lucky People You; Birds of a Feather; African Etude.

1941 92m/C Bing Crosby, Bob Hope, Dorothy Lamour, Una Merkel, Eric Blore, Iris Adrian, Lionel Royce; **D:** Victor Schertzinger. **VHS** $14.98 MCA ♫♫♫

The Road Warrior The first sequel to "Mad Max" takes place after nuclear war has destroyed Australia. Max helps a colony of oil-drilling survivors defend themselves from the roving murderous outback gangs and escape to the coast. The climactic chase scene is among the most exciting ever filmed; this film virtually created the "action-adventure" picture of the 1980s.

1982 (R) 95m/C Mel Gibson, Bruce Spence, Emil Minty, Vernon Wells; **D:** George Miller; **W:** George Miller. **VHS, Beta** $19.98 WAR ♫♫♫ ½

Roadhouse Girl A sexy woman kindles a romance with one of her husband's employees and the result is murder. Reminiscent of "The Postman Always Rings Twice," but with poor production values and performances. **AKA:** Marilyn.

1953 70m/B Maxwell Reed, Sandra Dorne, Leslie Dwyer, Vida Hope, Ferdinand "Ferdy" Mayne; **D:** Wolf Rilla; **W:** Wolf Rilla. **VHS, Beta** $16.95 SNC ♫

Roadhouse 66 Utterly unoriginal broke-down-in-a-hick-town nonsense. Snooty Reinhold and scruffy Dafoe go through the motions, and of course find a pair of female companions. Soundtrack features Los Lobos, the Pretenders, and Dave Edmunds.

1984 (R) 90m/C Willem Dafoe, Judge Reinhold, Karen Lee, Kate Vernon, Stephen Elliott; **D:** John Mark Robinson. **VHS, Beta** $79.98 *FOX* 🐕🐕½

Roadie Supposedly a look at the backstage world of rock n' roll, but the performances and direction leave a lot to be desired. Meatloaf is a roadie who desperately wants to meet Alice Cooper, and spends the movie trying to do so. Features Art Carney, and musical names like Blondie, Roy Orbison, Hank Williams, Jr. and Don Cornelius (of "Soul Train" fame).
1980 (PG) 105m/C Meatloaf, Kaki Hunter, Alan Carney, Art Carney, Gailard Sartain, Alice Cooper, Blondie, Roy Orbison, Hank Williams Jr., Ramblin' Jack Elliot; **D:** Alan Rudolph; **W:** Alan Rudolph, Michael Ventura. **VHS** $14.95 *MVD* 🐕 ½

Roadkill Cheap thriller about Ramona (Buhagiar), a concert promoter who tries to find a lost band, "The Children of Paradise," in the Canadian north woods. Along the way, she meets a would-be serial killer and other assorted weirdos.
1989 85m/B Valerie Buhagiar, Don McKellar, Bruce McDonald; **D:** Bruce McDonald; **W:** Don McKellar. **VHS** *NO* 🐕

Roads to the South One-time Spanish revolutionary turned screenwriter returns to his homeland to fight fascism, but finds himself attracted to his son's beautiful girlfriend. Much soul searching. In French with English subtitles.
1978 100m/C Yves Montand, Miou-Miou; **D:** Joseph Losey. **VHS** $59.95 *CVC, IME, FCT* 🐕🐕½

Roadside Prophets Counter-culture road trip, striving to be the '90s version of "Easy Rider," follows factory worker/biker Joe (Doe) on his mission to transport the ashes of a fellow biker to Nevada. He is accompanied by the pesky younger Sam (Horovitz), and together they meet up with lots of eccentrics and stay at lots of cheap motels. Interesting cast meanders through sentimental and slow-moving buddy flick from debut director Wool, who wrote "Sid and Nancy." Cusack completes the cameo hat trick, with appearances here and in 1992's "The Player" and "Shadows and Fog."
1992 (R) 96m/C John Doe, Adam Horovitz, David Carradine, Timothy Leary, Arlo Guthrie, Barton Heyman, Jennifer Balgobin; **Cameos:** John Cusack; **D:** Abbe Wool; **W:** Abbe Wool. **VHS** *NLC* 🐕🐕

The Roamin' Cowboy In a town where the local ranchers are being threatened, a drifter comes to their rescue and wins both a girl and a job.
1937 56m/B Fred Scott, Al "Fuzzy" St. John, Lois January, Forrest Taylor, Roger Williams; **D:** Robert F. Hill. **VHS** $19.95 *NOS, DVT* 🐕🐕

Roamin' Wild Exciting, action-packed early western with marshal Tyler saving a lady's stagecoach line from unsavory varmints.
1936 60m/B Tom Tyler, Carol Wyndham, Al Ferguson, George Cheseboro, Max Davidson, Fred Parker; **D:** Bernard B. Ray. **VHS, Beta** $19.95 *NOS, DVT* 🐕🐕

Roanoak A dramatization in three parts of the mysterious fate of the early English settlement of Roanoak in North Carolina, which disappeared without a trace. Long, but intriguing. Made for PBS: "American Playhouse."
1986 180m/C Will Sampson, Victoria Racimo, Porky White, Adrian Sparks, Patrick Kilpatrick; **D:** Jan Egleson. **Beta** $150.00 *PBS* 🐕🐕

Roarin' Lead Three Mesquiteers fight with a gang of rustlers while helping the orphans' and cattlemen's associations.

1937 54m/B Bob Livingston, Ray Corrigan, Max Terhune. **VHS, Beta** $19.95 *VCN* 🐕½

Roaring City A hard-boiled detective searches for the person behind the murders of gangsters and prize fighters.
1951 58m/B Hugh Beaumont, Edward Brophy, Richard Travis; **D:** William Berke. **VHS, Beta** *NO* 🐕½

Roaring Guns An unflappable McCoy rides in to thwart a despicable landowner trying to drive all the small ranchers out of business. Low-budget fun.
1936 66m/B Tim McCoy, Rex Lease, Wheeler Oakman; **D:** Sam Newfield. **VHS, Beta** $19.95 *NOS, VCN, DVT* 🐕🐕½

Roaring Ranch Gibson is trying to protect his ranch from the evil Oakman while attempting to care for a baby as well.
1930 65m/B Hoot Gibson, Wheeler Oakman, Sally Eilers, Bobby Nelson, Frank Clark; **D:** B. Reeves Eason; **W:** B. Reeves Eason. **VHS** $12.95 *GPV* 🐕½

The Roaring Road Romantic comedy about a car salesman named Toodles, who drives for his company in a big race. Vintage racing footage; silent with original organ music.
1919 57m/B Wallace Reid, Ann Little, Theodore Roberts; **D:** James Cruze. **VHS, Beta, 8mm** $19.95 *VYY, GPV, GVV* 🐕🐕½

Roaring Roads An heir to a fortune acquires a lust for race car driving, and his family thinks, a reckless death wish.
1935 60m/B Gertrude Messinger, David Sharpe. **VHS, Beta** *NO* 🐕

Roaring Six Guns Maynard protects his property against his crooked partner and his fiancee's father.
1937 60m/B Kermit Maynard, Mary Hayes, John Merton, Edward Cassidy. **VHS, Beta** $19.95 *NOS, DVT, VCN* 🐕½

Roaring Speedboats Bakewell is a speedboat racer up against crooks who want to con him out of his money by tinkering with his invention. *AKA:* Mile a Minute Love.
1937 62m/B William "Billy" Bakewell, Arletta Duncan, Duncan Renaldo, Vivien Oakland, Wilfrid Lucas; **D:** Elmer Clifton. **VHS, Beta, 8mm** $19.95 *VYY* 🐕

The Roaring Twenties Three WWI buddies find their lives intersecting unexpectedly in Prohibition-era New York. Cagney becomes a bootlegger and vies with Bogart for status as crime boss. Lynn is the attorney working to prosecute them. Greatest of all gangster flicks. Cheesy script delivered with zest by top pros.
1939 106m/B James Cagney, Humphrey Bogart, Jeffrey Lynn, Priscilla Lane, Gladys George, Frank McHugh; **D:** Raoul Walsh. **VHS, Beta** $19.98 *MGM, FOX* 🐕🐕🐕½

Rob Roy—The Highland Rogue In the early 18th century, Scottish Highlander Rob Roy must battle against the King of England's secretary, who would undermine the MacGregor clan to enact his evil deeds. Dull Disney drama. *AKA:* Rob Roy.
1953 84m/C Richard Todd, Glynis Johns, James Robertson Justice, Michael Gough; **D:** Harold French. **VHS, Beta** $69.95 *DIS* 🐕½

Robbers of the Sacred Mountain TV rip-off of "Raiders of the Lost Ark," loosely based on Arthur Conan Doyle's story "Challenger's Gold." Adventurers seek meteorites in the Mexican jungle. Billed as the first made for cable movie. *AKA:* Falcon's Gold.
1983 95m/C John Marley, Simon MacCorkindale, Louise Vallance, George Touliatos; **D:** Bob Schulz. **VHS, Beta** $49.95 *PSM* 🐕🐕

Robbery Unoriginal but competent rendition of the hackneyed British Royal Mail robbery. Thieves plan and execute a heist of a late-night mail train carrying $10 million.
1967 113m/C Stanley Baker, James Booth, Joanna Pettet, Frank Finlay, Barry Foster; **D:** Peter Yates. **VHS, Beta** $9.98 *NLC* 🐕🐕½

Robbery A six-man platoon of Vietnam war veterans endeavors to assault and rob a mob of shiftless bookies.
1985 91m/C John Sheerin, Tony Rickards, Tim Hughes; **D:** Michael Thornhill. **VHS, Beta** $69.98 *LIV* 🐕

Robbery Under Arms From Australia in the 1800s, similar to the American wild west, comes a tale of love and robbery. Finch is the leader of a band of outlaws. Rather dull story redeemed by excellent photography of beautiful landscape.
1957 83m/C Peter Finch, Ronald Lewis, Laurence Naismith, Maureen Swanson, David McCallum, Jill Ireland; **D:** Jack Lee. **VHS** $79.95 *IMP* 🐕🐕½

Robby A young white boy and a young black boy shipwrecked on an island form a strong friendship that sees them through a series of adventures.
1968 60m/C Warren Raum, Ryp Siani, John Garces; **D:** Ralph Blumke. **VHS, Beta** *FCT* 🐕🐕

The Robe This moving, religious portrait follows the career and religious awakening of drunken and dissolute Roman tribune Marcellus (Burton), after he wins the robe of the just-crucified Christ in a dice game. Mature plays Burton's slave surprisingly well, and reprised the role in the sequel, "Demetrius and the Gladiators"; Burton is wooden. "The Robe" was the first movie to be filmed in CinemaScope. Based on the novel by Lloyd C. Douglas.
1953 133m/C Richard Burton, Jean Simmons, Victor Mature, Michael Rennie, Richard Boone, Dean Jagger, Jeff Morrow, Jay Robinson, Dawn Addams, Ernest Thesiger; **D:** Henry Koster. Academy Awards '53: Best Art Direction/Set Decoration (Color), Best Costume Design (Color); Nominations: Best Actor (Burton), Best Color Cinematography, Best Picture; Golden Globe Awards '54: Best Film—Drama; National Board of Review Awards '53: 10 Best Films of the Year, Best Actress (Simmons). **VHS, Beta** $19.98 *FOX, IGP* 🐕🐕🐕½

Robert et Robert Two 'ineligible' bachelors resort to using a computerized matrimonial agency to find the girls of their dreams. They become friends while they wait for their dates. Sensitive tale of loneliness and friendship. Warm and witty with fine performances throughout. French with English subtitles.
1979 95m/C Charles Denner, Jacques Villeret, Jean-Claude Brialy; **D:** Claude Lelouch; **W:** Claude Lelouch. **VHS, Beta** $59.95 *COL* 🐕🐕🐕

Robert Kennedy and His Times Another look at the Kennedy clan, this time from the Bobby angle. Good acting. Based on the book by Arthur Schlesinger.
1990 335m/C Brad Davis, Veronica Cartwright, Cliff DeYoung, Ned Beatty, Beatrice Straight, Jack Warden; **D:** Marvin J. Chomsky. **VHS** $59.95 *COL* 🐕🐕½

Roberta A football player inherits his aunt's Parisian dress shop and finds himself at odds with an incognito Russian princess. Dumb plot aside, this is one of the best Astaire-Rogers efforts. A later remake was titled "Lovely to Look At." ♫Let's Begin; Yesterdays; Smoke Gets in Your Eyes; I'll Be Hard to Handle; I Won't Dance; Lovely to Look At; Back Home Again in Indiana; The Touch of Your Hand; You're Devasting.

1935 85m/B Fred Astaire, Ginger Rogers, Irene Dunne, Lucille Ball, Randolph Scott; **D:** William A. Seiter. **VHS, Beta $19.98** *MGM &&&*

Robin and Marian After a separation of twenty years, Robin Hood is reunited with Maid Marian, who is now a nun. Their dormant feelings for each other are reawakened as Robin spirits her to Sherwood Forest. In case you wanted to see Robin Hood robbed of all magic, spontaneity, and fun. Connery is dull, dull, dull, working with an uninspired script.
1976 (PG) 106m/C Sean Connery, Audrey Hepburn, Robert Shaw, Richard Harris; **D:** Richard Lester; **M:** John Barry. **VHS, Beta $19.95** *COL, FOX &&*

Robin and the Seven Hoods Runyon-esque Rat Pack version of 1920s Chicago, with Frank and the boys as do-good gangsters in their last go-round. Fun if not unforgettable. ♫Bang! Bang!; Style; Mister Booze; Don't Be a Do-Badder; My Kind of Town.
1964 124m/C Frank Sinatra, Bing Crosby, Dean Martin, Sammy Davis Jr., Peter Falk, Barbara Rush, Allen Jenkins; **D:** Gordon Douglas. **VHS, Beta $19.98** *WAR &&1/2*

Robin Hood Extravagant production casts Fairbanks as eponymous gymnastic swashbuckler who departs for Crusades as Earl of Huntington and returns as the hooded one to save King Richard's throne from the sinister Sheriff of Nottingham. Best ever silent swashbuckling.
1922 110m/B Douglas Fairbanks Sr., Wallace Beery, Sam DeGrasse, Enid Bennett, Paul Dickey, William E. Lowery, Roy Coulson, Bill Bennett, Merrill McCormick, Wilson Benge, Willard Louis, Alan Hale, Maine Geary, Lloyd Talman; **D:** Allan Dwan. **VHS, Beta $19.95** *NOS, GPV, FCT &&&1/2*

Robin Hood This time the Sherwood Forest crew are portrayed by appropriate cartoon animals, hence, Robin is a fox, Little John a bear, etc. Good family fare, but not as memorable as other Disney features.
1973 83m/C **D:** Wolfgang Reitherman; **V:** Roger Miller, Brian Bedford, Monica Evans, Phil Harris, Andy Devine, Carol Shelley, Peter Ustinov, Terry-Thomas, Pat Buttram, George Lindsey, Ken Curtis. **VHS, Beta $24.99** *DIS, FCT, RDG &&&*

Robin Hood Dark version of the medieval tale. Bergin's Prince of Thieves is well developed and Thurman is a graceful Marion. Three studios announced plans to remake "Robin Hood" in 1990 and two were completed, including this one which was scaled down for cable television.
1991 116m/C Patrick Bergin, Uma Thurman, Juergen Prochnow, Edward Fox, Jeroen Krabbe, Jeff Nuttal, David Morrisey, Owen Teale; **D:** John Irvin. **VHS, Beta $89.98** *FXV, FCT &&&*

Robin Hood: Men in Tights Brooksian rendition of the classic legend inspires guffaws, but doesn't hit the bullseye on all it promises. Hood afficionados will appreciate the painstaking effort taken to spoof the 1938 Errol Flynn classic while leaving plenty of room to poke fun at the more recent Costner non-classic "Robin Hood: Prince of Thieves." Elwes, last seen swinging swords in "The Princess Bride," is well cast as the Flynn look-alike. Expect the usual off-color humor that's so prevalent in all Brooks outings. **AKA:** Men in Tights.
1993 (PG-13) 105m/C Cary Elwes, Richard Lewis, Roger Rees, Amy Yasbeck, Dave Chappelle, Isaac Hayes, Tracey Ullman, Mark Blankfield, Megan Cavanagh, Eric Allen Kramer, Tony Griffin, Dick Van Patten, Mel Brooks; **D:** Mel Brooks; **W:** Mel Brooks, J. David Shapiro; **M:** Hummie Mann. **VHS** *FXV &&1/2*

Robin Hood of Texas Autry finds his calm life disturbed when he is falsely accused of robbing a bank. Pretty good plot for once, in Autry's last Republic western, and plenty of action.
1947 71m/B Gene Autry, Lynn (Mary Hart) Roberts, Sterling Holloway, Adele Mara; **D:** Lesley Selander. **VHS, Beta** *NO &&1/2*

Robin Hood of the Pecos Ex-Confederate soldier takes on northern post-war politicians and carpetbaggers. Decent Rogers/Hayes outing.
1941 56m/B Roy Rogers, George "Gabby" Hayes, Marjorie Reynolds, Jay Novello, Roscoe Ates; **D:** Joseph Kane. **VHS, Beta $19.95** *NOS, DVT, VYY &&1/2*

Robin Hood: Prince of Thieves Costner is the politically correct Rebel with a Cause, but a thinker, not a doer—and therein lies the problem. His quiet thoughtfulness doesn't add up to leadership and Rickman easily overpowers him as the wicked, crazed Sheriff of Nottingham. Freeman is excellent as a civilized Moor who finds England, and its people, inhospitable, dangerous, and not a little stupid. Mastrantonio, a last minute choice, excels as the lovely Lady Marian. Great action sequences, a gritty and morbid picture of the Middle Ages, and some fun scenes with the Merry Men. Revisionist in its ideas about the times and people, critics generally disapproved of the changes in the story and Costner's performance, though their comments about his lack of an English accent seem nitpicky in light of some basic plot problems. Still has lots of fun for lovers of action, romance and fairy tales.
1991 (PG-13) 144m/C Kevin Costner, Morgan Freeman, Mary Elizabeth Mastrantonio, Christian Slater, Alan Rickman, Geraldine McEwan, Micheal McShane, Brian Blessed, Michael Wincott, Nick Brimble, Jack Wild, Harold Innocent, Jack Wild; **Cameos:** Sean Connery; **D:** Kevin Reynolds; **W:** Pen Densham, John Watson; **M:** Michael Kamen. Academy Awards '91 Nominations: Best Song ("(Everything I Do) I Do It for You"); British Academy Awards '92: Best Supporting Actor (Rickman); MTV Movie Awards '92: Best Song ("(Everything I Do) I Do for You"). **VHS $19.98** *WAR, RDG &&1/2*

Robin Hood: The Movie A colorized and re-mixed version of several episodes of the British television series adds up to a fine version of the classic tale. Excellent cast, clever editing and stunning colorization.
1955 90m/C Richard Greene, Bernadette O'Farrell, Alan Wheatley; **D:** Ralph Smart, Daniel Birt, Terence Fisher. **VHS $14.99** *GKK &&1/2*

Robin Hood...The Legend: Herne's Son When Robin Hood is killed by the Sheriff of Nottingham, he begs Robert of Huntington (Connery) to continue his work. Connery refuses, the band dissolves, Maid Marion is kidnapped, and they reunite to save her. Good entry in the BBC series.
1985 101m/C Jason Connery, Oliver Cotton, Michael Craig, Nickolas Grace, George Baker; **D:** Robert M. Young. **VHS, Beta $14.98** *FOX, FCT, TVC &&1/2*

Robin Hood...The Legend: Robin Hood and the Sorcerer Robin Hood is chosen by the mystical Herne the Hunter to thwart the evil Sheriff of Nottingham and protect the English peasantry. He must defeat the supernatural powers of a sorcerer and gather together his men in this introduction to the made for British television series.
1983 115m/C Michael Praed, Anthony Valentine, Nickolas Grace, Clive Mantle, Peter Williams; **D:** Ian Sharp. **VHS $14.98** *FOX, FCT, TVC &&1/2*

Robin Hood...The Legend: The Swords of Wayland A wicked sorceress provides a supernatural threat to Robin and his merry men. Second entry in the BBC series. Convoluted, breathless plot makes for swashbuckling fun and much derring-do.
1983 115m/C Michael Praed, Rula Lenska, Nickolas Grace; **D:** Robert M. Young. **VHS, Beta $14.98** *FOX, FCT &&1/2*

Robin Hood...The Legend: The Time of the Wolf Robin Hood finds out that an old enemy is about to release his evil doings on the world and only he can stop him, while Maid Marian comes to a momentous decision.
1985 105m/C Jason Connery, Nickolas Grace, Richard O'Brien; **D:** Syd Roberson. **VHS, Beta $14.98** *FOX, FCT, TVC &&1/2*

Robinson Crusoe A real oddity: a British silent film originally made in 1927, re-edited ten years later. Music and sound effects were added, along with a narration by children's radio personality Carney. Follows the plot of the famous adventure story by Daniel Defoe.
1936 34m/B **VHS, Beta $11.98** *VYY &&*

Robinson Crusoe & the Tiger A tiger tells the famous story of how Robinson Crusoe became stranded on a desert island.
1972 (G) 109m/C Hugo Stiglitz, Ahui; **D:** Rene Cardona Jr. **VHS, Beta $29.98** *SUE &1/2*

Robinson Crusoe of Clipper Island Fourteen-episodes serial featuring the investigative expertise of Mala, a Polynesian in the employ of the U.S. Intelligence Service. Each episode runs 16 minutes. Shortened version titled "Robinson Crusoe of Mystery Island."
1936 256m/B Mala, Rex, Buck, Kate Greenfield, John Ward, Tracy Lane, Robert F. (Bob) Kortman, Herbert Rawlinson; **D:** Mack V. Wright. **VHS $26.95** *SNC, NOS, REP &&*

Robinson Crusoe of Mystery Island A Polynesian employed by the U.S. Intelligence Service investigates saboteurs on a mysterious island. Would-be cliffhanger is a yawner; where are the chills and thrills? Edited from the serial "Robinson Crusoe of Clipper Island."
1936 100m/B Mala, Rex, Buck, Herbert Rawlinson, Ray Taylor; **D:** Mack V. Wright. **VHS, Beta $27.95** *VCN &&*

Robinson Crusoe on Mars Sci-fi interpretation of Defoe classic. West is one of two daring scientists who take a monkey with them on a mission to outer space. When a meteor strikes their ship, it hurtles out of control towards the red planet and only Mantee and Mona survive the wreckage. They meet Lundin, an escaped slave and teach him English until evil slave traders spoil the fun.
1964 109m/C Adam West, Vic Lundin, Paul Mantee, Mona (the Woolly Monkey); **D:** Byron Haskin; **W:** Ib Melchoir, John C. Higgins; **M:** Nathan Van Cleave. **$49.95** *IME &*

Robo-Chic A woman who is part cop, part machine, becomes a defender of justice.
1989 90m/C Kathy Shower, Jack Carter, Julie Newmar, Burt Ward, Lyle Waggoner. **VHS, Beta** *AIP &*

RoboCop A nearly dead Detroit cop is used as the brain for a crime-fighting robot in this bleak vision of the future. Humor, satire, action, and violence keep this moving in spite of its underlying sadness. Slick animation techniques from Phil Tippet. Verhoeven's first American film.

1987 (R) 103m/C Peter Weller, Nancy Allen, Ronny Cox, Kurtwood Smith, Ray Wise, Miguel Ferrer, Dan O'Herlihy, Robert DoQui, Felton Perry, Paul McCrane, Del Zamora; *D:* Paul Verhoeven; *W:* Michael Miner, Edward Neumeier; *M:* Basil Poledouris. **VHS, Beta $14.98** *ORI, SUP* ♪♪♪

RoboCop 2 Grimer, more violent sequel to the initial fascinating look at the future, where police departments are run by corporations hungry for profit at any cost. A new and highly addictive drug has made Detroit more dangerous than ever. Robocop is replaced by a stronger cyborg with the brain of a brutal criminal. When the cyborg goes berserk, Robocop battles it and the drug lords for control of the city. Dark humor and graphic savagery, with little of the tenderness and emotion of the original. **1990 (R) 117m/C** Peter Weller, Nancy Allen, Belinda Bauer, Dan O'Herlihy, Tommy Noonan, Gabriel Damon, Galyn Gorg, Felton Perry, Patricia Charbonneau; *D:* Irvin Kershner; *W:* Walon Green. **VHS, Beta $14.98** *ORI* ♪♪

RoboCop 3 Robocop's new Japanese owners plan to build a huge, new, ultra-modern city (in place of the decrepit 21st-century Detroit) but first must evict thousands of people in this third installment of the "Robocop" films (which sat on the studio shelf before finally being released in 1993). There's an android Ninja warrior to do battle with Robo who's gone over to the rebel underground but the plot and action sequences are rehashed from better films. Watch the original. **1991 (PG-13) 104m/C** Robert Burke, Nancy Allen, John Castle, CCH Pounder, Bruce Locke, Rip Torn, Remi Ryan, Felton Perry; *D:* Fred Dekker; *W:* Fred Dekker, Frank Miller; *M:* Basil Poledouris. **VHS** *ORI* ♪ ½

Roboman American scientist gets in car crash in Soviet Union. When he returns to the States as a cyborg, his friends seem to notice a change. *AKA:* Who?. **1975 (PG) 91m/C** Elliott Gould, Trevor Howard, Joe Bova, Ed Grover, James Noble, John Lehne; *D:* Jack Gold. **VHS** *ACE, MTX* ♪♪ ½

Robot Holocaust Somewhere in the doomed future, after the Earth is laid waste by robots with superior intelligence, a human survivor dares to challenge them. If you're doomed to watch this, you just might survive; it's so-so, unsurprisingly sci-fi. **1987 79m/C** Norris Culf, Nadine Hart, Joel von Ornsteiner, Jennifer Delora, Andrew Howarth, Angelika Jager, Rick Gianasi; *D:* Tim Kincaid; *W:* Tim Kincaid. **VHS, Beta $69.95** *VCI* ♪

Robot Jox Two futuristic warriors battle to the finish in giant mechanical robots. Preteen fare. **1989 (PG) 84m/C** Gary Graham, Anne-Marie Johnson, Paul Koslo, Robert Sampson, Danny Kamekona, Hilary Mason, Michael Alldredge; *D:* Stuart Gordon; *W:* Stuart Gordon. **VHS $14.95** *COL* ♪ ½

Robot Monster Ludicrous cheapie is widely considered one of the worst films of all time, as a single alien dressed in a moth-eaten gorilla suit and diving helmet conspires to take over the Earth from his station in a small, bubble-filled California cave. Available in original 3-D format. *AKA:* Monsters From the Moon. **1953 62m/B** George Nader, Claudia Barrett, Gregory Moffett, Selena Royle; *D:* Phil Tucker; *M:* Elmer Bernstein. **VHS, Beta $12.95** *RHI, FCT, COL* ♪♪ ½

Robot Pilot Tucker stars as a WWII test pilot trying to promote a friend's invention. Along the way, he's involved in a subplot with enemy agents who steal a bomber. He also finds time to become romantically entangled with the boss' spoiled daughter. *AKA:* Emergency Landing. **1941 68m/B** Forrest Tucker, Carol Hughes, Evelyn Brent, Emmett Vogan, William Halligan; *D:* William Beaudine. **VHS, Beta, 8mm $24.95** *VYY, SNC* ♪

The Robot vs. the Aztec Mummy Grade-Z Mexican horror film pits a jealous mummy who guards a tomb against tomb robbers and the robot they invent. Special effects are laughable today—the robot's ears are lightbulbs—but true mummy movie fans might want to watch this one. Everyone else will probably be better off skipping it. *AKA:* El Robot Humano; La Momia Azteca Contra el Robot Humano. **1959 65m/B** Ramon Gay, Rosita Arenas, Crox Alvarado, Luis Aceves Cantaneda, Emma Rolden; *D:* Rafael Portillo; *W:* Alfredo Salazar. **VHS, Beta $19.98** *SNC, AOV, MRV* Woof!

Robot Wars When what seems to be the last mega-robot on earth falls into enemy hands, a renegade pilot unearths another with the help of an engineer and archeologist to fight for the future of mankind. **1993 (PG) 106m/C** Don Michael Paul, Barbara Crampton, James Staley, Lisa Rinna, Danny Kamekona, Yuji Okumoto, J. Downing, Peter Haskell; *D:* Albert Band. **VHS, Beta** *PAR* ♪♪

Rocco and His Brothers A modern classic from top director Visconti, about four brothers who move with their mother from the Italian countryside to Milan. Very long, sometimes ponderous, but engrossing, complex drama. Available shortened to 90 minutes, but the unedited version is much more rewarding. In Italian with English subtitles. *AKA:* Rocco et Ses Freres. **1960 175m/B** Alain Delon, Renato Salvatori, Annie Girardot, Katina Paxinou, Claudia Cardinale, Roger Hanin; *D:* Luchino Visconti. **VHS $29.95** *VDM, CVC, ING* ♪♪♪ ½

Rock-a-Doodle Little Edmond is knocked out during a storm and has an Elvis-influenced vision. He sees Chanticleer, the sun-raising rooster, tricked into neglecting his duties by an evil barnyard owl. Humiliated and scorned, the earnest young fowl leaves the farm and winds up in a Las Vegas-like city as an Elvis-impersonating singer (complete with pompadour) where he meets with success and all its trappings. Mildly amusing, but bland by today's standards of animation, with music which is certainly nothing to crow about. **1992 (G) 77m/C** *D:* Don Bluth; *W:* David A. Weiss; *M:* Robert Folk; *V:* Glen Campbell, Christopher Plummer, Phil Harris, Sandy Duncan, Ellen Greene, Charles Nelson Reilly, Eddie Deezen, Toby Scott Granger, Sorrell Booke. **VHS $24.98** *HBO, MVD* ♪♪ ½

Rock All Night Typically trashy Corman quickie (filmed in five days on one set) about some wild fifties teens and, in this case, a couple of murderers. Someone called Cloud Nine, the local teen hangout, is invaded by a couple of murderers who hold the kids hostage. It's up to the hipster bartender, known as Shorty because he's five-foot-one, to save the day. Unrelated concert footage of The Platters and The Blockbusters opens the film. **1957 62m/B** Dick Miller, Abby Dalton, Russell Johnson, Jonathan Haze, Robin Morse; *D:* Roger Corman. **VHS $9.95** *COL, MOV, MVD* ♪♪

Rock & Roll Cowboys Set in the near-future. Mickey LaGrange is a roadie who has dreams of playing his own songs and becoming a rock and roll star himself. When he meets the mysterious Damien Shard he just may get the opportunity and a lot more besides. Shard is the inventor of an instrument that taps directly into the brain to transform thought into music. When Mickey uses the instrument he becomes an instant success—until he notices some horrifying side effects. **1992 83m/C** Peter Phelps, David Franklin, John Doyle; *D:* Robert Stewart. **VHS $59.95** *MOV* ♪

Rock & Rule Animated sword & sorcery epic with a rock soundtrack. Voices are provided by Deborah Harry, Cheap Trick, Lou Reed, and Iggy Pop. **1983 85m/C** *D:* Clive A. Smith; *M:* Deborah Harry, Cheap Trick, Lou Reed, Iggy Pop; *V:* Paul LeMat, Catherine O'Hara. **VHS, Beta $79.95** *MGM* ♪♪

Rock & the Money-Hungry Party Girls A struggling musician battles against Gabor-sister-worshiping bimbos in an effort to find unpublished songs by a '50s music legend. **1989 90m/C** Paul Sercu, Adam Small, Judi Durand, Mary Baldwin, Debra Lamb; *D:* Kurt MacCarley. **VHS, Beta** *NO* ♪

Rock, Baby, Rock It Weak and silly rock-and-roll crime drama about teens trying to fight the Mafia in Dallas in 1957. Features performances by many regional bands including Kay Wheeler, the Cell Block Seven, Johnny Carroll, Preacher Smith and the Deacons, and the Five Stars. If you grew up in Dallas in the '50s, the musical groups may bring back some fond memories; otherwise, this obscure film probably isn't worth your time. **1957 84m/B** Kay Wheeler, John Carroll; *D:* Murray Douglas Sporup. **VHS, Beta $59.95** *RHI* ♪

Rock House When an L.A. narcotics officer's wife is murdered by drug runners he goes on an obsessive revenge mission to destroy the city's cocaine operations. **1992 (R) 98m/C** Joseph Jennings, Michael Robbin, Alan Shearer; *D:* Jack Vacek; *W:* Jack Vacek. **VHS $9.95** *HMD* ♪♪

Rock Hudson's Home Movies Farr re-creates the character of the late actor over numerous film clips use to suggest homoerotic themes in Hudson's movies. Low-budget and high camp. **1992 63m/C** Eric Farr; *D:* Mark Rappaport; *W:* Mark Rappaport. **VHS $39.95** *WBF* ♪♪

Rock 'n' Roll High School The music of the Ramones highlights this non-stop high-energy cult classic about a high school out to thwart the principal at every turn. If it had been made in 1957, it would have been the ultimate rock 'n' roll teen movie. As it is, its 1970s' milieu works against it, but the performances are perfect for the material and the Ramones are great. Songs include "Teenage Lobotomy," "Blitzkrieg Bop," "I Wanna Be Sedated" and the title track, among others. Followed less successfully by "Rock 'n' Roll High School Forever." **1979 (PG) 94m/C** The Ramones, P.J. Soles, Vincent Van Patten, Clint Howard, Dey Young, Mary Woronov, Alix Elias, Dick Miller, Paul Bartel; *D:* Allan Arkush. **VHS, Beta $64.95** *MVD* ♪♪♪

Rock 'n' Roll High School Forever Jesse Davis and his band just want to rock 'n' roll, but the new principal doesn't share their enthusiasm. Way late, way lame sequel to "Rock 'n' Roll High School" doesn't come close to the originality that made it a cult classic. Soundtrack includes music from The Divinyls, Dee Dee Ramone, Mojo Nixon, Will and the Bushmen, The Pursuit of Happiness, and more.

1991 (PG-13) 94m/C Corey Feldman, Mary Woronov, Mojo Nixon, Evan Richards, Michael Ceveris, Patrick Malone, Larry Linville, Sarah Buxton; *D:* Deborah Brock; *W:* Deborah Brock. VHS, Beta $89.95 *LIV, IME* ♫♫

Rock 'n' Roll Nightmare
A rock band is pursued by demons from another dimension. The usual lame garbage. *AKA:* The Edge of Hell.
1985 (R) 89m/C Jon Mikl Thor, Paula Francescatto, Rusty Hamilton; *D:* John Fasano. VHS, Beta $29.95 *ACA* ♫♫½

Rock, Pretty Baby
Early rock-'n'-roll movie about a teenage band and high school riots.
1956 89m/B Sal Mineo, John Saxon, Rod McKuen, Luanna Patten, Fay Wray, Edward Platt, Alan Reed Jr.; *D:* Richard Bartlett; *M:* Henry Mancini. VHS, Beta $14.95 *BAR* ♫

Rock River Renegades
The Range Busters capture a band of renegades and restore peace to the territory once more.
1942 59m/B Ray Corrigan, John "Dusty" King. VHS, Beta $19.95 *NOS, DVT* ♫

Rock, Rock, Rock
A young girl tries to earn enough money for a prom gown after her father closes her charge account. Screen debut of Tuesday Weld. Ultra-low-budget, but a classic after a fashion. Includes classic musical numbers performed by Chuck Berry and other rock'n'roll pioneers.
1956 78m/B Alan Freed, Chuck Berry, Fats Domino, Tuesday Weld, Frankie Lymon & the Teenagers; *D:* Will Price. VHS, Beta $12.95 *MVD, MED, MRV* ♫♫½

Rocket Attack U.S.A.
Antiquated and ridiculous tale of nuclear warfare about the time of Sputnik, with Russia's first strike blowing up New York City and environs. Mercifully short, with time for a little romance. Everything about this movie is so bad it's good for a laugh.
1958 70m/B Monica Davis, John McKay, Dan Kern, Edward Czerniuk, Art Metrano; *D:* Barry Mahon. VHS, Beta *NO Woof!*

Rocket Gibraltar
On the occasion of a crusty patriarch's birthday, a large family unites on his remote estate to carry out his special birthday wish. Fine performance by Lancaster. Supported by a solid cast, overcomes a slim story, Culkin, later of "Home Alone," is loveable as the precocious five-year-old. Picturesque Long Island scenery.
1988 (PG) 92m/C Burt Lancaster, Bill Pullman, John Glover, Suzy Amis, Macaulay Culkin, Patricia Clarkson, Frances Conroy, Sinead Cusack, Bill Martin, Kevin Spacey; *D:* Daniel Petrie; *W:* Amos Poe; *M:* Andrew Powell. VHS, Beta $14.95 *COL* ♫♫♫

Rocket to the Moon
An adaptation of the Clifford Odets story about the mundane life of a 30-year-old Manhattan dentist and how he comes to terms with his life. From the PBS "American Playhouse" series.
1986 118m/C Judy Davis, John Malkovich, Eli Wallach; *D:* John Jacobs. VHS, Beta $59.95 *ACA, PBS* ♫♫

The Rocketeer
Lightheaded fun. A stunt flyer in the 1930s finds a prototype jet backpack sought by Nazi spies. Donning a mask, he becomes a flying superhero. Breezy family entertainment with stupendous effects; even better if you know movie trivia, as it brims with Hollywood references, like a great villain (Dalton) clearly based on Errol Flynn.
1991 (PG) 109m/C Bill Campbell, Jennifer Connelly, Alan Arkin, Timothy Dalton, Paul Sorvino, Melora Hardin, Tiny Ron, Terry O'Quinn, Ed Lauter, James Handy; *D:* Joe Johnston; *W:* Danny Bilson, Paul DeMeo; *M:* James Horner. VHS, Beta $19.99 *DIS, CCB, IME* ♫♫♫

Rocketship
Flash Gordon battles sea monsters, ray guns, and robots in this sci-fi adventure, which is an edited version of a Flash serial.
1936 ?m/B Buster Crabbe, Jean Rogers, Charles Middleton. VHS $15.95 *LOO, HEG* ♫♫

Rocketship X-M
A lunar mission goes awry and the crew lands on Mars, where they discover ancient ruins. Well acted and nicely photographed. Contains footage, a tinted sequence and previews of coming attractions from classis science fiction files. *AKA:* Expedition Moon.
1950 77m/B Lloyd Bridges, Osa Massen, John Emery, Hugh O'Brian, Noah Beery Jr.; *D:* Kurt Neumann. VHS, Beta $19.95 *MED, RXM* ♫♫½

Rockin' Road Trip
A guy meets a girl in a Boston bar, and finds himself on a drunken, slapstick road trip down the Eastern seaboard with a rock band.
1985 (PG-13) 101m/C Garth McLean, Katherine Harrison, Margeret Currie, Steve Boles. VHS, Beta $79.98 *FOX* ♫

Rockin' Ronnie
A rough, sophomoric, uproarious send-up of President Reagan, using news footage of him and of Queen Elizabeth, Ayatollah Khomeini, Jayne Mansfield, and other figures.
1987 45m/C VHS, Beta $19.98 *MPI* ♫♫½

The Rocking Horse Winner
Poignant tale of a young boy who discovers he can predict racehorse winners by riding his rocking horse. His spendthrift mother's greed leads to tragedy. Based on the short story by D.H. Lawrence.
1949 91m/B John Howard Davies, Valerie Hobson, Hugh Sinclair; *D:* Anthony Pelissier. VHS $39.95 *HMV* ♫♫½

Rocktober Blood
A convicted and executed rock star comes back from the grave and starts killing people all over again. Yet another gorefest.
1985 (R) 88m/C Donna Scoggins, Tray Loren, Nigel Benjamin, Beverly Sebastian; *D:* Ferd Sebastian. VHS, Beta $19.98 *LIV, VES* ♫½

Rockula
Teen rock comedy about a young-yet-300-year-old vampire looking to lose his virginity. Recommended only for hard-core Diddley fans.
1990 (PG-13) 90m/C Dean Cameron, Bo Diddley, Tawny Fere, Susan Tyrrell, Thomas Dolby, Toni Basil; *D:* Luca Bercovici. VHS, Beta $14.95 *MGM, WAR* ♫♫

Rockwell: A Legend of the Wild West
Black heroics in the wild west. U.S. Marshall Porter Rockwell and his posse of sharp shooters are after a vicious gang murdering supposed claim jumpers who just happen to be Rockwell's friends.
1993 ?m/C Randy Gleave, Karl Malone, Michael Rudd, George Sullivan. VHS $89.95 *IMP* ♫♫½

Rocky
Box office smash about a young man from the slums of Philadelphia who dreams of becoming a boxing champion. Stallone plays Rocky, the underdog hoping to win fame and self-respect. Rags-to-riches story seems to parallel Stallone's life; he had been previously virtually unknown before this movie. Intense portrayal of the American Dream; loses strength in the subsequent (and numerous) sequels.
1976 (PG) 125m/C Sylvester Stallone, Talia Shire, Burgess Meredith, Burt Young, Carl Weathers; *D:* John G. Avildsen; *W:* Sylvester Stallone; *M:* Bill Conti. Academy Awards '76: Best Director (Avildsen), Best Film Editing, Best Picture; Nominations: Best Actor (Stallone), Best Actress (Shire), Best Original Screenplay, Best Song ("Gonna Fly Now"), Best Sound, Best Supporting Actor (Meredith, Young); Directors Guild of America Awards '76: Best Director

(Avildsen); Golden Globe Awards '77: Best Film—Drama; Los Angeles Film Critics Association Awards '76: Best Film; National Board of Review Awards '76: 10 Best Films of the Year, Best Supporting Actress (Shire). VHS, Beta, 8mm $14.95 *MGM, FOX, BTV* ♫♫½

Rocky 2
Time-marking sequel to the box office smash finds Rocky frustrated by the commercialism which followed his match to Apollo, but considering a return bout. Meanwhile, his wife fights for her life. The overall effect is to prepare you for the next sequel.
1979 (PG) 119m/C Sylvester Stallone, Talia Shire, Burt Young, Burgess Meredith, Carl Weathers; *D:* Sylvester Stallone; *W:* Sylvester Stallone; *M:* Bill Conti. VHS, Beta $14.95 *MGM, FOX* ♫♫

Rocky 3
Rocky is beaten by big, mean Clubber Lang (played to a tee by Mr. T). He realizes success has made him soft, and has to dig deep to find the motivation to stay on top. Amazingly, Stallone regains his underdog persona here, looking puny next to Mr. T, who is the best thing about the second-best "Rocky" flick.
1982 (PG) 103m/C Sylvester Stallone, Talia Shire, Burgess Meredith, Carl Weathers, Mr. T, Leif Erickson, Burt Young; *D:* Sylvester Stallone; *W:* Sylvester Stallone; *M:* Bill Conti. VHS, Beta $14.95 *MGM, FOX* ♫♫½

Rocky 4
Rocky travels to Russia to fight the Soviet champ who killed his friend during a bout. Will Rocky knock the Russkie out? Will Rocky get hammered on the head a great many times and sag around the ring? Will Rocky ever learn? Lundgren isn't nearly as much fun as some of Rocky's former opponents and Stallone overdoes the hyper-patriotism and relies too heavily on uplifting footage from earlier "Rocky" movies.
1985 (PG) 91m/C Sylvester Stallone, Talia Shire, Dolph Lundgren, Brigitte Nielsen, Michael Pataki, Burt Young, Carl Weathers; *D:* Sylvester Stallone; *W:* Sylvester Stallone; *M:* Bill Conti. VHS, Beta $14.95 *MGM, FOX* ♫½

Rocky 5
Brain damaged and broke, Rocky finds himself back where he started on the streets of Philadelphia. Boxing still very much in his blood, Rocky takes in a protege, training him in the style that made him a champ (take a lickin' and keep on tickin'). However an unscrupulous promoter has designs on the young fighter and seeks to wrest the lad from under the former champ's wing. This eventually leads to a showdown between Rocky and the young boxer in a brutal streetfight. Supposedly the last "Rocky" film, it's clear the formula has run dry.
1990 (PG) 105m/C Sylvester Stallone, Talia Shire, Burt Young, Sage Stallone, Tom Morrison, Burgess Meredith; *D:* John G. Avildsen; *W:* Sylvester Stallone; *M:* Bill Conti. VHS, Beta, 8mm $14.95 *MGM* ♫♫

The Rocky Horror Picture Show
When a young couple take refuge in a haunted castle, they find themselves the unwilling pawns in a warped scientist's experiment. Cult camp classic has been a midnight movie favorite for years and has developed an entire subculture built around audience participation. The tape includes a seven-minute short detailing the story behind the movie's popularity. May not be as much fun watching it on the little screen unless you bring the rice and squirt guns. ♫The Time Warp; Science Fiction Double Feature; Wedding Song; Sweet Transvestite; The Sword of Damocles; Charles Atlas Song; Whatever Happened to Saturday Night; Touch-a Touch-a Touch-a Touch Me; Eddie's Teddy.

1975 (R) 105m/C Tim Curry, Susan Sarandon, Barry Bostwick, Meatloaf, Little Nell, Richard O'Brien; **D:** Jim Sharman; **M:** John Barry. **VHS** $19.98 FOX, FCT, PMS *III*

Rocky Jones, Space Ranger This syndicated space series followed the adventures of Rocky Jones, commander of the spaceship Orbit Jet, who worked for the United Worlds. The first three half-hour television episodes chronicle the story of how Rocky met his beautiful assistant Vena. Entitled "Beyond the Curtain of Space." Additional episodes available.
1954 78m/B Richard Crane, Sally Mansfield, Scotty Beckett. **VHS, Beta** $22.50 MVC, MOV *III*

Rocky Jones, Space Ranger: Renegade Satellite Nostalgia freaks may embrace this revived edition of the infamous early live-TV space cadet show. Rocky squares off against enemies of the United Solar System like Dr. Reno and Rudy DeMarco. Really cheap.
1954 69m/B Richard Crane, Sally Mansfield, Maurice Cass. **VHS** $19.95 VDM *I 1/2*

Rocky Mountain Rangers The Three Mesquiteers do what they best: save a town from bad guys.
1940 58m/B Bob Livingston, Raymond Hatton, Duncan Renaldo, Leroy Mason, Dennis Moore, John St. Polis; **D:** George Sherman. **VHS** $19.95 NOS *II*

Rodan A gigantic prehistoric bird is disturbed from his slumber by H-bomb tests. He awakens to wreak havoc on civilization. Big bugs also run amok. From the director of "Godzilla" and a host of other nuclear monster movies. *AKA:* Radon; Radon the Flying Monster.
1956 74m/C Kenji Sahara, Yumi Shirakawa; **D:** Inoshiro Honda. **VHS, Beta** PAR, MLB, VES *II*

Rodeo Girl Ross is a restless housewife who joins the rodeo in this television drama based on the life of cowgirl Sue Pirtle. Particularly strong supporting cast of Hopkins, Clark, and Brimley.
1980 100m/C Katharine Ross, Bo Hopkins, Candy Clark, Jacqueline Brookes, Wilford Brimley, Parley Baer; **D:** Jackie Cooper. **VHS, Beta** $39.95 LIV *II*

Rodrigo D.: No Future Gritty, realistic portrayal of the youth-killing culture of Medellin, Columbia. Minimal plot involves a young drummer and his drug-running friends. The actors used as actual untrained street kids, several of whom died after the film's completion. In Spanish with English subtitles.
1991 92m/C Ramiro Meneses, Carlos Mario Restrepo; **D:** Victor Gaviria. **VHS** $79.95 KIV, ING *II*

Roe vs. Wade Hunter is excellent as the single woman from Texas who successfully challenged the nation's prohibitive abortion laws in a landmark Supreme Court case. Television drama based on the actual 1973 case of Norma McCorvey.
1989 92m/C Holly Hunter, Amy Madigan, Terry O'Quinn, Stephen Tobolowsky, Dion Anderson, Kathy Bates, James Gammon, Chris Mulkey; **D:** Gregory Holbit. **VHS, Beta** $14.95 PAR *III*

Roger & Me The hilarious, controversial and lauded atypical semi-documentary. Details Moore's protracted efforts to meet General Motors president Roger Smith and confront him with the poverty and despair afflicting Flint, Michigan, after GM closed its plants there. Includes some emotionally grabbing scenes: a Flint family is evicted just before Christmas; a woman makes a living by selling rabbits for food or pets; and a then soon-to-be Miss America addresses the so-

cioeconomic impact of GM's decision. One of the highest-grossing non-fiction films ever released, and Moore's first.
1989 (R) 91m/C Michael Moore, Bob Eubanks, Pat Boone, Anita Bryant; **D:** Michael Moore. **VHS, Beta** $19.95 WAR *III 1/2*

Rogue The Rogue is a ruthless man who can make beautiful women do anything that he desires; so, of course, he does.
1976 (R) 87m/C Milan Galvonic, Barbara Bouchet, Margaret Lee; **D:** Gregory Simpson. **VHS, Beta** NO *II*

Rogue Lion A quasi-incompetent game warden more than meets his match when a voraciously carnivorous lion begins stalking an African community.
1975 89m/C **VHS, Beta** $59.95 VCI *II 1/2*

Rogue of the Range A lawman pretends that he is a bandit in order to track down an outlaw gang.
1936 60m/B Johnny Mack Brown. **VHS, Beta** $19.95 NOS, DVT, RXM *II*

Rogue of the Rio Grande Musical western in which the renowned bandit El Malo arrives in the peace-loving town of Sierra Blanca. One of Loy's earlier films. ♫Argentine Moon; Carmita; Song of the Bandoleros.
1930 60m/B Myrna Loy, Jose Bohr, Raymond Hatton, Carmelita Geraghty. **VHS, Beta** $27.95 VCN *II 1/2*

Rogue's Gallery A reporter and photographer covering the story of an inventor and his latest device are caught up in intrigue when he is found murdered.
1944 60m/B Frank Jenks, Robin Raymond, H.B. Warner, Ray Walker, Davison Clark, Robert E. Homans, Frank McGlynn, Pat Gleason, Edward Keane; **D:** Albert Herman. **VHS, Beta** $16.95 SNC, RXM *II*

Rogue's Tavern In this grade B curio, a blood-thirsty killer stalks the occupants of a country inn, bodies are found with their throats crushed, and a psycho psychic is on the loose. Surprise ending.
1936 70m/B Wallace Ford, Joan Woodbury, Clara Kimball Young, Barbara Pepper, Jack Mulhall, John Elliott; **D:** Bob Hill. **VHS, Beta** $24.95 NOS, DVT, HEG *II*

Rogue's Yarn An investigator probes the death of a woman, ostensibly the result of a boating accident. Gradually he uncovers a plot involving the woman's husband and his mistress in this semi-entertaining British mystery.
1956 80m/B Nicole Maurey, Derek Bond, Elwyn Brook-Jones, Hugh Latimer; **D:** Vernon Sewell. **VHS, Beta** $16.95 SNC *II*

Roland the Mighty Muscular, Herculeanesque hero takes on all comers in this sword and sandal epic set in the Asian steppes.
1958 ?m/C Rick Battaglia. **VHS, Beta** $16.95 SNC *II 1/2*

Roll Along Cowboy A vintage sagebrush saga about a cowboy caught by love. Based on Zane Grey's "The Dude Ranger."
1937 55m/B Smith Ballew, Cecilia Parker, Buster Fite & his Saddle Tramps; **D:** Gus Meins. **VHS, Beta** $19.95 NOS, CCB, VDM *II 1/2*

Roll of Thunder, Hear My Cry A black family struggles to survive in Depression-era Mississippi in this inspiring, if somewhat predictable, television production. Look for the always impressive Freeman in a supporting role. Set in the South of 1933 and based on the novels of Mildred Taylor.
1978 110m/C Claudia McNeil, Janet MacLachlan, Morgan Freeman; **D:** Jack Smight. **VHS, Beta** $14.98 LIV, LCA *II 1/2*

Roll on Texas Moon A cowpoke is hired to prevent a feud between the sheep men and the cattle ranchers.
1946 68m/B Roy Rogers, George "Gabby" Hayes, Dale Evans, Dennis Hoey; **D:** William Witney. **VHS** $19.95 NOS, DVT, MTX *II*

Roll, Wagons, Roll Tex Ritter leads a wagon train to Oregon.
1939 52m/B Tex Ritter; **D:** Al Herman. **VHS, Beta** $19.95 NOS, VCN *II 1/2*

Roller Blade In a post-holocaust world a gang of Amazon-style nuns, who worship a "have a nice day" happy face, battle the forces of evil with martial arts and mysticism. Has to be seen to be believed. Extremely low-budget outing.
1985 88m/C Suzanne Solari, Jeff Hutchinson, Shaun Mitchelle; **D:** Donald G. Jackson. **VHS, Beta** $19.95 NWV *I*

Roller Blade Warriors: Taken By Force Roller babes battle evil mutant while balancing on big boots with small wheels.
1990 90m/C Kathleen Kinmont, Rory Calhoun, Abby Dalton, Elizabeth Kaitan. **VHS** NO *II*

Roller Boogie A truly awful film made at the time of the mercifully brief roller-disco craze. Blair runs away from home and winds up helping some friends thwart a businessman looking to close the local roller rink. Everything about this one reeks amateur.
1979 (PG) 103m/C Linda Blair, Jim Bray, Beverly Garland, Roger Perry, James Van Patten, Kimberly Beck, Mark Goddard, Stoney Jackson, Sean McClory; **D:** Mark L. Lester; **W:** Barry Schneider. **VHS** $14.95 MGM Woof!

Rollerball Caan is utterly convincing in this futuristic tale in which a brutal sport assumes alarming importance to a sterile society. Flashy, violent, sometimes exhilirating.
1975 (R) 123m/C James Caan, John Houseman, Maud Adams, Moses Gunn; **D:** Norman Jewison. **VHS, Beta** $14.95 MGM *II 1/2*

Rollercoaster A deranged extortionist threatens to sabotage an amusement park ride. Plucky Segal must stop him. Video renters will be spared the nauseating effects of film's original "Sensurround."
1977 (PG) 119m/C George Segal, Richard Widmark, Timothy Bottoms, Henry Fonda, Susan Strasberg, Harry Guardino; **D:** James Goldstone; **W:** William Link. **VHS, Beta** $59.95 MCA *II*

Rollin' Plains A Texas Ranger tries to settle a feud between cattlemen and sheepmen over water rights.
1938 60m/B Tex Ritter; **D:** Al Herman. **VHS, Beta** $19.95 NOS, VCN, VCI *II*

Rolling Home Tame tale about aging cowpoke, his grandson, and a really swell horse. Saddle up and snooze.
1948 71m/B Jean Parker, Russell Hayden, Pamela Blake, Buss Henry, Raymond Hatton. **VHS, Beta** $24.95 VYY *II*

Rolling Thunder Vietnam vet turns vigilante when he arrives home from POW camp and sees his family slaughtered. Graphically violent, potentially cathartic. Typical of screenwriter Paul Schrader.
1977 (R) 99m/C William Devane, Tommy Lee Jones, Linda Haynes; **D:** John Flynn; **W:** Paul Schrader, Heywood Gould. **VHS, Beta** $79.98 LIV, VES *II 1/2*

Rolling Vengeance Enterprising fellow constructs powerful truck to better facilitate the extermination of gang members who earlier slaughtered his family. Keep on truckin'.
1987 (R) 90m/C Don Michael Paul, Ned Beatty, Lawrence Dane, Lisa Howard; **D:** Steven Hilliard Stern. **VHS, Beta** $19.98 NLC *II 1/2*

Rollover Turgid big-budget drama about Arab undermining of American economy. Kristofferson is lifeless, Fonda is humorless. Supporting players Sommer and Cronyn fare better.
1981 (R) 117m/C Jane Fonda, Kris Kristofferson, Hume Cronyn, Bob Gunton, Josef Sommer, Martha Plimpton; **D:** Alan J. Pakula. **VHS, Beta** $39.98 WAR ♫ ½

Roman Holiday Hepburn's first starring role is a charmer as a princess bored with her official visit to Rome who slips away and plays at being an "average Jane." A reporter discovers her little charade and decides to cash in with an exclusive story. Before they know it, love calls. Blacklisted screenwriter Trumbo was "fronted" by Ian McLellan Hunter, who accepted screen credit and the Best Story Oscar in Trumbo's stead. The Academy voted to posthumously award Trumbo his own Oscar in 1993.
1953 118m/B Audrey Hepburn, Gregory Peck, Eddie Albert, Tullio Carminati; **D:** William Wyler; **W:** Dalton Trumbo. Academy Awards '53: Best Actress (Hepburn), Best Costume Design (B & W), Best Story; Nominations: Best Art Direction/Set Decoration (B & W), Best Black and White Cinematography, Best Director (Wyler), Best Film Editing, Best Picture, Best Screenplay, Best Supporting Actor (Albert); British Academy Awards '53: Best Actress (Hepburn); Golden Globe Awards '54: Best Actress—Drama (Hepburn); New York Film Critics Awards '53: Best Actress (Hepburn). **VHS, Beta, 8mm** $14.95 PAR, BTV, HMV ♫♫♫ ½

Roman Scandals A penniless young man daydreams himself back to ancient Rome with uproarious results. Lucille Ball appears as one of the Goldwyn Girls. Dance sequences were choreographed by Busby Berkeley. ♫No More Love; Build A Little Home; Keep Young and Beautiful; Rome Wasn't Built in a Day; Put a Tax on Love.
1933 91m/B Eddie Cantor, Ruth Etting, Gloria Stuart, Edward Arnold, Lucille Ball, Busby Berkeley; **D:** Frank Tuttle. **VHS, Beta** $19.98 SUE, HBO ♫♫ ½

Roman Spring of Mrs. Stone An aging actress determines to revive her career in Rome but finds romance with a gigolo instead in this adaptation of Tennessee Williams's novella. Leigh and Beatty are compelling, but Lenya nearly steals the show as Leigh's distinctly unappealing confidant. *AKA:* The Widow and the Gigolo.
1961 104m/C Warren Beatty, Vivien Leigh, Lotte Lenya, Bessie Love, Jill St. John; **D:** Jose Quintero; **W:** Gavin Lambert. **VHS, Beta** $19.98 WAR, FHE ♫♫♫

Romance In only her second talkie, Garbo stars as an Italian opera star who seduces a young priest. Poor story and weak acting from everyone with the exception of Garbo. Even she can't save this one. Adapted from the play "Signora Cacllini."
1930 77m/B Greta Garbo, Lewis Stone, Gavin Gordon, Elliott Nugent, Florence Lake, Clara Blandick; **D:** Clarence Brown. **VHS** $19.98 MGM ♫♫

Romance in Manhattan Recent immigrant to New York struggles to build new life, in spite of unemployment, language barriers, and loneliness. He meets Broadway chorine Rogers and song and dance ensues. America, ain't it a great place?
1934 78m/B Ginger Rogers, Francis Lederer, J. Farrell MacDonald; **D:** Pandro S. Berman. **VHS** $19.98 TTC, FCT ♫♫

Romance of a Horsethief Brynner leads this entertaining but slow-paced "Fiddler on the Roof" comedic romp without the music. In 1904 Poland, a Cossack captain takes horses for the Russo-Japanese war.

The residents of the town rise up, goaded on by Birkin.
1971 (PG) 100m/C Yul Brynner, Eli Wallach, Jane Birkin, Oliver Tobias, Lainie Kazan, David Opatoshu; **D:** Abraham Polonsky. **VHS** ACE, MOV ♫♫ ½

Romance on the High Seas A woman is scheduled to take a cruise vacation but skips the boat when she believes her husband is cheating on her. Her husband believes she is taking the cruise to cheat on him and hires a private detective to follow her. Pleasant comedy features the film debut of Doris Day. ♫It's Magic; It's You or No One; The Tourist Trade; Put 'Em in a Box, Tie 'Em with a Ribbon, and Throw 'Em in the Deep Blue Sea; Two Lovers Met in the Night; Run, Run, Run; I'm in Love; Cuban Rhapsody.
1948 99m/C Jack Carson, Janis Paige, Don DeFore, Doris Day, Oscar Levant, S.Z. Sakall, Eric Blore, Franklin Pangborn, Leslie Brooks, William "Billy" Bakewell; **W:** Julius J. Epstein. **VHS** $29.98 FOX, FCT ♫♫♫

Romance on the Orient Express Sparks fly when former lovers meet again on the Orient Express. Don't expect any flesh, though, as film was made for television.
1989 96m/C Cheryl Ladd, Stuart Wilson, John Gielgud; **D:** Lawrence Gordon Clark. **VHS, Beta** $9.98 TTC ♫ ½

Romance on the Range Rogers sets out to trap a gang of fur thieves and finds romance.
1942 60m/B Roy Rogers, George "Gabby" Hayes, Sally Payne. **VHS** $19.95 NOS, VCN, REP ♫ ½

Romance with a Double Bass When a musician and a princess take a skinny dip in the royal lake and get their clothes stolen, comic complications arise. Reminiscent of Cleese's sojourn as a Monty Python member, with surreal, frequently raunchy humor.
1974 40m/C John Cleese, Connie Booth, Graham Crowden, Desmond Jones, Freddie Jones, Andrew Sachs; **D:** Robert Young. **VHS, Beta** $19.95 FCT, SIG ♫♫♫

Romancing the Stone Uptight romance novelist lives out her fantasies after she receives a mysterious map from her murdered brother-in-law and her sister is kidnapped in South America—the ransom being the map. Out to rescue her sister, she's helped and hindered by an American soldier of fortune (Douglas) whose main concern is himself and the hidden treasure described in the map. Great chemistry between the stars and loads of clever dialogue in this appealing adventure comedy. First outing with Turner, Douglas, and DeVito. Followed by "The Jewel of the Nile."
1984 (PG) 106m/C Michael Douglas, Kathleen Turner, Danny DeVito, Zack Norman, Alfonso Arau, Ron Silver; **D:** Robert Zemeckis. Academy Awards '84 Nominations: Best Film Editing; Golden Globe Awards '85: Best Actress—Musical/Comedy (Turner), Best Film—Musical/Comedy. **VHS, Beta** $19.98 FOX, HMV ♫♫♫

Romantic Comedy Writing duo never seem to synchronize their desires for each other in this dull comedy. Engaging stars don't inspire each other much, and supporting cast can't make up the difference. Adapted from the Bernard Slade play.
1983 (PG) 102m/C Dudley Moore, Mary Steenburgen, Frances Sternhagen, Ron Leibman; **D:** Arthur Hiller; **M:** Marvin Hamlisch. **VHS, Beta** $14.95 MGM, FOX ♫♫

Romantic Englishwoman Literate comedy-drama about the intertwined lives of several sophisticated and restrained Brits. Caine is a successful novelist with writer's block whose wife falls for another man while on a trip alone. He then invites his wife's lover to stay with them in order to generate ideas for his writing until his jealousy begins to surface.
1975 (R) 117m/C Glenda Jackson, Michael Caine, Helmut Berger, Kate Nelligan; **D:** Joseph Losey; **W:** Tom Stoppard, Thomas Wiseman. **VHS, Beta** WAR, OM ♫♫♫

Rome Adventure Spinster librarian Pleshette takes Roman vacation hoping to meet handsome prince. Donahue takes shine to her while girlfriend Dickinson is away, as does suave Roman Brazzi. Soapy, ill-paced romance. *AKA:* Lovers Must Learn.
1962 119m/C Troy Donahue, Angie Dickinson, Suzanne Pleshette, Rossano Brazzi, Constance Ford, Al Hirt, Chad Everett; **D:** Delmer Daves; **W:** Delmer Daves; **M:** Max Steiner. **VHS** $59.99 PAR, FCT, WAR ♫♫

Rome '78 Acclaimed underground film centered around Caligula and the Queen of Sheba in ancient Rome.
1978 60m/C Eric Mitchell; **D:** James Nares. **VHS** $59.95 MWF ♫♫ ½

Romeo and Juliet One of MGM producer Irving Thalberg's pet projects (and starring Thalberg's wife, Norma Shearer), this Shakespeare classic was given the spare-no-expense MGM treatment. Physically too old to portray teen-age lovers, both Howard and Shearer let their acting ability supply all necessary illusions. Also notable is Barrymore's over-the-top portrayal of Mercutio.
1936 126m/B Leslie Howard, Norma Shearer, John Barrymore, Basil Rathbone, Edna May Oliver; **D:** George Cukor. **VHS** $19.98 MGM, CCB ♫♫♫ ½

Romeo and Juliet Unfulfilling adaptation of Shakespeare's timeless drama of young love cast against family antagonisms. Peculiar supporting cast features both Cabot and ubiquitous master Gielgud.
1954 138m/C Laurence Harvey, Susan Shantall, Aldo Zollo, Sebastian Cabot, Flora Robson, Mervyn Johns, Bill Travers, John Gielgud; **D:** Renato Castellani. **VHS, Beta** $29.95 SUE, LCA ♫♫♫

Romeo and Juliet Young couple share love despite prohibitive conflict between their families in this adaptation of Shakespeare's classic play. Director Zeffirelli succeeds in casting relative novices Whiting and Hussey in the leads, but is somewhat less proficient in lending air of free-wheeling sixties appeal to entire enterprise. Kudos, however, to cinematographer Pasquale de Santis and composer Nina Rota. Also available in a 45-minute edited version.
1968 (PG) 138m/C Olivia Hussey, Leonard Whiting, Michael York, Milo O'Shea; **D:** Franco Zeffirelli; **M:** Nino Rota. Academy Awards '68: Best Cinematography, Best Costume Design; Nominations: Best Director (Zeffirelli), Best Picture; Golden Globe Awards '69: Best Foreign Film; National Board of Review Awards '68: 10 Best Films of the Year, Best Director (Zeffirelli). **VHS, Beta** $19.95 PAR, HMV, PBC ♫♫♫ ½

Romeo Is Bleeding Jack (Oldman) is a police detective accepting mobster payoffs from boss Falcone (Scheider) for fingering federally protected witnesses. But the next target proves Jack's undoing—hitwoman Mona (Olin), who's more than a match for any man. Oldman's character is played for a patsy by everyone while Olin's is a kinky psycho-villainess with an enjoyment of vio-

lence, red lipstick, and a constant, maniacal laugh. Sciorra is generally wasted as Jack's unhappy wife while Lewis is annoying as his young and vacuous mistress. Part homage, part satire of film noir is overly stylized with intrusive narration but some effective shocks.
1993 (R) 110m/C Gary Oldman, Lena Olin, Annabella Sciorra, Juliette Lewis, Roy Scheider, Michael Wincott, David Proval, Paul Butler, Will Patton, Larry Joshua, James Cromwell, Ron Perlman; **D:** Peter Medak; **W:** Hilary Henkin; **M:** Mark Isham. VHS *PGV ♫♫½*

Romero Julia is riveting as the Salvadoran archbishop who championed his destitute congregation despite considerable political opposition. A stirring biography financed by the United States Roman Catholic Church.
1989 102m/C Raul Julia, Richard Jordan, Ana Alicia, Eddie Velez, Alejandro Bracho, Tony Plana, Lucy Reina, Harold Gould, Al Ruscio, Robert Viharo; **D:** John Duigan; **W:** John Sacret Young; **M:** Gabriel Yared. VHS, Beta $29.95 *VMK ♫♫½*

Romola Silent adventure. After Powell and his father are attacked by pirates, Powell escapes. But instead of rescuing his father, he opts for a life of corruption. Dad eventually escapes and returns to exact vengeance. A rather expensive film in its day, troubled by modern-day sights in what was supposed to be old Florence. Gish's drowning scene had to be re-shot because she wouldn't sink. Colman arranged for his then-wife Raye to have a bit part, but they were divorced soon after the film was finished.
1925 120m/B Lillian Gish, Dorothy Gish, William H. Powell, Ronald Colman, Charles Lane, Herbert Grimwood, Bonaventure Ibanez, Frank Puglia, Thelma Raye; **D:** Henry King. VHS, Beta *NO ♫♫½*

Romper Stomper Violent confrontations between Australian skinheads and the Vietnamese community mixed in with a disturbed love story. Suburban rich girl Gabe (McKenzie) is drawn to the charasmatic Hando (Crowe), the certifiably loony leader of a group of Melbourne's skinheads. Any romance takes a backseat to the carnage brought by the skinheads' attacks on the local Asian community, who fight back with equal force. Disquieting look at a brutal world which can't be ignored. Film caused a furor upon its Australian release with debates about whether the extreme violence was intended to titilate or explicate the plot. An unrated version at 89 minutes is also available.
1992 (R) 85m/C Russell Crowe, Jacqueline McKenzie, Daniel Pollock; **D:** Geoffrey Wright; **W:** Geoffrey Wright. VHS $92.95 *ACA, FCT ♫♫*

The Roof Uninteresting outing about a young couple who married against their families' wishes and find that setting up a home of their own is more difficult than they thought. In Italian with English subtitles.
1956 98m/B Gabriella Pallotti, Giorgio Listuzzi; **D:** Vittorio De Sica. VHS, Beta $24.95 *NOS, HHT, APD ♫♫*

Rooftops Peculiar but predictable, centering on love between Hispanic girl and white youth who has mastered martial arts dancing. Director Wise is a long way from his earlier "West Side Story." See this one and be the only person you know who has.
1989 (R) 108m/C Jason Gedrick, Troy Beyer, Eddie Velez, Tisha Campbell; **D:** Robert Wise; **W:** Allan Goldstein; **M:** Michael Kamen. VHS, Beta $19.95 *LIV ♫½*

The Rookie Routine cop drama has worldly veteran and wide-eyed newcomer team to crack stolen-car ring managed by Germans. Eastwood and Sheen are reliable, but Hispanics Julia and Braga, though miscast, nonetheless steal this one as the German villains.
1990 (R) 121m/C Clint Eastwood, Charlie Sheen, Raul Julia, Sonia Braga, Lara Flynn Boyle, Pepe Serna, Marco Rodriguez, Tom Skerritt, Roberta Vasquez; **D:** Clint Eastwood. VHS, Beta, 8mm $19.98 *WAR ♫♫*

Rookie of the Year Kid's fluff fantasy come true. Twelve-year-old baseball fanatic Henry has dreams of making it to the big league. He falls, breaks his arm, and when it heals strangely is blessed with a pitching arm so spectacular he finds himself not only playing for the Chicago Cubs, but leading them to the World Series. Enjoyable family outing for first-time director Stern (who also plays a seasoned and very incredulous ballplayer). Keep your eyes peeled for appearances by real-live sluggers Pedro Guerrero, Barry Bonds, and others.
1993 (PG) 103m/C Thomas Ian Nicholas, Daniel Stern, Gary Busey, Dan Hedaya; **D:** Daniel Stern; **W:** Sam Harper; **M:** Bill Conti. VHS *FXV ♫♫½*

The Room Altman takes on Pinter in this brooding mini-play about two young strangers who try to rent the room already occupied by a disconnected woman and her semicatatonic husband. Made for television.
1987 48m/C Julian Sands, Linda Hunt, Annie Lennox, David Hemblen, Donald Pleasence; **D:** Robert Altman; **W:** Harold Pinter. VHS, Beta $79.95 *PSM ♫♫*

Room at the Top Ambitious factory man forsakes true love and marries boss's daughter instead in this grim drama set in industrial northern England. Cast excels, with Harvey and Sears as the worker and his wife. Signoret is also quite compelling as the abandoned woman. Adapted from John Braine's novel and followed by "Life at the Top" and "Man at the Top."
1959 118m/B Laurence Harvey, Simone Signoret, Heather Sears, Hermione Baddeley, Anthony Elgar, Donald Wolfit; **D:** Jack Clayton. Academy Awards '59: Best Actress (Signoret), Best Adapted Screenplay; Nominations: Best Actor (Harvey), Best Director (Clayton), Best Picture, Best Supporting Actress (Baddeley); British Academy Awards '58: Best Actress (Signoret), Best Film; Cannes Film Festival '59: Best Actress (Signoret). VHS *NO ♫♫♫½*

Room 43 Campy fable about a British cab driver who falls in love with a French girl, and stumbles onto a white-slavery ring when she falls victim to it. Features a young Caine and future novelist Collins in bit parts. *AKA:* Passport to Shame.
1958 93m/B Diana Dors, Herbert Lom, Eddie Constantine, Michael Caine, Jackie Collins; **D:** Alvin Rakoff. VHS, Beta $19.95 *VDM, TPV ♫½*

Room Service The Marx Brothers provide less than the usual mayhem here with Groucho as penniless theatrical producer determined to remain in his hotel room until he can secure funds for his next play. Ball doesn't help matters much either. Not bad, but certainly not up to the zany Marx clan's usual stuff.
1938 78m/B Groucho Marx, Harpo Marx, Chico Marx, Lucille Ball, Ann Miller, Frank Albertson, Donald MacBride, Charles Halton; **D:** William A. Seiter. VHS, Beta $19.95 *RKO, CCB, MED ♫♫½*

Room to Let An elderly woman and her daughter take in boarders in Victorian England. They rent a room to a man who claims to be a doctor, but the two women eventually become prisoners of fear, believing the man

is actually Jack the Ripper. Will there be a vacancy soon? Somewhat disturbing and suspenseful.
1949 68m/B Jimmy Hanley, Valentine Dyall, Christine Silver, Merle Tottenham, Charles Hawtrey, Connie Smith, Laurence Naismith; **D:** Godfrey Grayson. VHS, Beta $16.95 *NOS, SNC ♫♫*

A Room with a View Engaging adaptation of E.M. Forster's novel of requited love. Carter stars as the feisty British idealist who rejects dashing Sands for superficious Day Lewis, then repents and finds (presumably) eternal passion. A multi-Oscar nominee, with great music (courtesy of Puccini), great scenery (courtesy of Florence), and great performances (courtesy of practically everybody, but supporters Smith, Dench, Callow, and Elliott must be particularly distinguished). Truly romantic, and there's much humor too.
1986 117m/C Helena Bonham Carter, Julian Sands, Denholm Elliott, Dame Maggie Smith, Judi Dench, Simon Callow, Daniel Day-Lewis, Rupert Graves, Rosemary Leach; **D:** James Ivory; **W:** Ruth Prawer Jhabvala. Academy Awards '86: Best Adapted Screenplay, Best Art Direction/Set Decoration, Best Costume Design; Nominations: Best Cinematography, Best Director (Ivory), Best Picture, Best Supporting Actor (Elliott), Best Supporting Actress (Smith); British Academy Awards '86: Best Actress (Smith), Best Film, Best Supporting Actress (Dench); Independent Spirit Awards '87: Best Foreign Film; National Board of Review Awards '86: 10 Best Films of the Year. VHS, Beta $19.98 *FOX, HMV ♫♫♫♫*

Roommate A valedictorian church-goer and a rebellious iconoclast room together at Northwestern University in 1952, with the expected humorous results. Public television presentation based on a John Updike story.
1984 96m/C Lance Guest, Barry Miller, Elaine Wilkes, Melissa Ford, David Bachman; **D:** Neil Cox. VHS, Beta $69.98 *LIV, VES ♫♫♫♫*

Rooster Cogburn A Bible-thumping schoolmarm joins up with a hard-drinking, hard-fighting marshal in order to capture a gang of outlaws who killed her father. Tired sequel to "True Grit" but the chemistry between Wayne and Hepburn is right on target.
1975 (PG) 107m/C John Wayne, Katharine Hepburn, Richard Jordan, Anthony Zerbe, John McIntire, Strother Martin, Paul Koslo; **D:** Stuart Millar. VHS, Beta $19.95 *MCA, TLF ♫♫½*

Rooster: Spurs of Death! An expose on cock fighting, in which a young idealist tries to stop the thriving sport in a small southern town. Dog of a movie that (not surprisingly) went straight to video.
1983 (PG) 90m/C Vincent Van Patten, Ty Hardin, Kristine DeBell, Ruta Lee; **D:** NO Woof!

Rootin' Tootin' Rhythm All's not quiet on the range, but Autry comes along to sing things back to normal. Goofy, clumsy, ubiquitous sidekick Burnette is a symbol for this whole effort. *AKA:* Rhythm on the Ranch.
1938 55m/B Gene Autry, Smiley Burnette, Monte Blue; **D:** Mack V. Wright. VHS, Beta $19.95 *NOS, VYY, DVT ♫*

Roots The complete version of Alex Haley's made for television saga following a black man's search for his heritage, revealing an epic portrait of America's past. Available on six tapes, complete at 570 minutes.
1977 90m/C Ed Asner, Lloyd Bridges, LeVar Burton, Chuck Connors, Lynda Day George, Lorne Greene, Burl Ives, O.J. Simpson, Cicely Tyson, Ben Vereen, Sandy Duncan; **D:** David Greene; **M:** Quincy Jones. VHS, Beta $64.95 *WAR, KUI, MOV ♫♫♫♫*

Roots of Evil This erotic thriller follows a cop on the trail of a murderer who specializes in killing Hollywood's most beautiful prostitutes. Also available in unrated and Spanish-language versions.
1991 (R) ?m/C Alex Cord, Delia Sheppard, Charles Dierkop, Jillian Kesner; *D:* Gary Graver. VHS $89.99 CAN ♫1/2

Roots: The Gift It's Christmas, 1770, and Kunte Kinte (Burton) and Fiddler (Gossett) try to escape slavery via the Underground Railroad. In their attempt, they wind up giving the gift of freedom to several of their fellow slaves. A made for television movie based on the Alex Haley characters.
1988 94m/C Louis Gossett Jr., LeVar Burton, Michael Learned, Avery Brooks, Kate Mulgrew, Shaun Cassidy, John McMartin; *D:* Kevin Hooks. VHS $19.98 WAR, FCT ♫♫

Roots: The Next Generation Sequel to the landmark television miniseries continuing the story of author Alex Haley's ancestors from the Reconstruction era of the 1880s to 1967, culminating with Haley's visit to West Africa where he is told the story of Kunta Kinte. On seven tapes.
1979 685m/C Georg Stanford Brown, Lynne Moody, Henry Fonda, Richard Thomas, Marc Singer, Olivia de Havilland, Paul Koslo, Beah Richards, Stan Shaw, Harry Morgan, Irene Cara, Dorian Harewood, Ruby Dee, Paul Winfield, James Earl Jones, Debbie Allen; *Cameos:* Al Freeman Jr., Marlon Brando. VHS $149.99 MOV ♫♫♫

Rope In New York City, two gay college students murder a friend for kicks and store the body in a living room trunk. They further insult the dead by using the trunk as the buffet table and inviting his parents to the dinner party in his honor. Very dark humor is the theme in Hitchcock's first color film, which he innovatively shot in uncut ten-minute takes, with the illusion of a continuous scene maintained with tricky camera work. Based on the Patrick Hamilton play and on the Leopold-Laeb murder case.
1948 (PG) 81m/C James Stewart, John Dall, Farley Granger, Cedric Hardwicke, Constance Collier; *D:* Alfred Hitchcock; *W:* Arthur Laurents. VHS, Beta $19.95 MCA ♫♫♫1/2

Rorret "Rorret" is "terror" spelled backwards—a good indication of the psychological and physical terror Mr. Rorret, the owner of the Peeping Tom Cinema, inflicts upon his female patrons. The Cinema is devoted to the horror film and Rorret himself dresses like Peter Lorre in "M;" lives behind the movie screen, watching the films in mirror image; and enjoys the frightened reactions of his female patrons. He enjoys their reactions so much that he later stalks the women for real. Highlighted by recreated sequences from such psycho-terror classics as "Psycho," "Dial M for Murder," "Strangers on a Train," and "Peeping Tom." In Italian with English subtitles.
1987 105m/C Lou Castel, Anna Galiena, Massimo Venturiello; *D:* Fulvio Wetzl; *W:* Fulvio Wetzl. VHS $79.95 NYF, ING ♫♫♫

Rosa Luxemburg Based on the life of the Jewish political radical, murdered in 1919. Involving herself with the German Social Democratic Party, Luxemburg undergoes numerous imprisonments and maintains a tempestuous personal life. Based primarily on Luxemburg's letters and speeches; charismatic performance by Sukowa. In German with English subtitles.
1986 122m/C Barbara Sukowa, Daniel Olbrychski, Otto Sander, Adelheid Arndt; *D:* Margarethe von Trotta; *W:* Margarethe von Trotta. VHS $79.95 NYF, FCT ♫♫

Rosalie A gridiron great from West Point falls for a mysterious beauty from Vassar. He soon learns that her father reigns over a tiny Balkan nation. Expensive, massive, imperfect musical; exotic romantic pairing fails to conceal plot's blah-ness. Oh well, at least Porter's music is good. ♫I've a Strange New Rhythm in My Heart; Why Should I Care?; Spring Love Is in the Air; Rosalie; It's All Over But the Shouting; Who Knows?; In the Still of the Night; To Love or Not to Love; Close (instrumental).
1938 118m/B Nelson Eddy, Eleanor Powell, Frank Morgan, Ray Bolger, Ilona Massey, Reginald Owen, Edna May Oliver, Jerry Colonna; *D:* Woodbridge S. Van Dyke; *M:* Cole Porter. VHS, Beta $19.98 MGM ♫♫1/2

Rosalie Goes Shopping Satire about American consumerism hiding behind slapstick comedy, and it works, most of the time. Misplaced Bavarian (Sagebrecht) moves to Arkansas and begins spending wildly and acquiring "things." Twisty plot carried confidently by confident wackiness from Sagebrecht and supporters.
1989 (PG-13) 94m/C Marianne Sagebrecht, Brad Davis, Judge Reinhold, Willie Harlander, Alex Winter, Erika Blumberger, Patricia Zehentmayr; *D:* Percy Adlon; *W:* Percy Adlon; *M:* Bob Telson. VHS $89.95 VMK, ING ♫♫

The Rosary Murders Based on the William X. Kienzle mystery about a serial killer preying on nuns and priests. Father Koesler (Sutherland) must betray the confessional to stop him. Interesting, though sometimes muddled and too rarely tense. Filmed on location in Detroit.
1987 (R) 105m/C Donald Sutherland, Charles Durning, Belinda Bauer, Josef Sommer; *D:* Fred Walton; *W:* Elmore Leonard, Fred Walton. VHS, Beta VTR ♫♫

The Rose Modeled after the life of Janis Joplin, Midler plays a young, talented and self-destructive blues/rock singer. Professional triumphs don't stop her lonely restlessness and confused love affairs. The best exhibition of the rock and roll world outside of documentaries. Electrifying film debut for Midler features an incredible collection of songs. ♫Fire Down Below; I've Written A Letter to Daddy; Let Me Call You Sweetheart; The Rose; Stay With Me; Camellia; Sold My Soul To Rock 'n' Roll; Keep On Rockin'; When A Man Loves a Woman.
1979 (R) 134m/C Bette Midler, Alan Bates, Frederic Forrest, Harry Dean Stanton, David Keith; *D:* Mark Rydell. Academy Awards '79 Nominations: Best Actress (Midler), Best Film Editing, Best Sound, Best Supporting Actor (Forrest); Golden Globe Awards '80: Best Actress—Musical/Comedy (Midler), Best Song ("The Rose"). VHS, Beta $19.98 FOX ♫♫♫

The Rose and the Jackal Fun, intriguing fictionalization about the founder of the Pinkerton detective agency. During the Civil War, bearded, Scottish Reeve tries to persuade a wealthy Southern lady to help save the Union. Made for cable television.
1990 94m/C Christopher Reeve, Madolyn Smith, Granville Van Dusen, Carrie Snodgress, Kevin McCarthy; *D:* Jack Gold. VHS, Beta $79.98 TTC ♫♫

The Rose Garden In modern Germany, a Holocaust survivor is put on trial for assaulting an elderly man. The victim, it turns out, was a Nazi guilty of heinous war crimes. Ullmann and Schell lend substance, though treatment of a powerful theme is inadequate.
1989 (PG-13) 112m/C Liv Ullmann, Maximilian Schell, Peter Fonda, Jan Niklas, Kurt Hubner; *D:* Fons Rademakers; *W:* Paul Hengge; *M:* Egisto Mocchi. VHS, Beta $89.95 CAN ♫♫1/2

Rose Marie An opera star falls in love with the mountie who captured her escaped convict brother. Hollywood legend has it that when a British singer was presented with the first line in "Indian Love Song," which is "When I'm calling you-oo-oo-oo-oo-oo-oo," the confused performer sang, "When I'm calling you, double oh, double oh, double oh..." Maybe true, maybe not, but funny anyway. Classic MacDonald-Eddy operetta. Remade in 1954. ♫Indian Love Call; Pardon Me, Madame; The Mounties; Rose Marie; Totem Tom Tom; Just for You; Tex Yeux; St. Louis Blues; Dinah. *AKA:* Indian Love Call.
1936 112m/B Jeanette MacDonald, Nelson Eddy, James Stewart, Allan Jones, David Niven, Reginald Owen; *D:* Woodbridge S. Van Dyke; *M:* Rudolf Friml. VHS, Beta $19.95 MGM ♫♫♫

Rose Marie Blyth is a lonely Canadian woman wooed by a mean spirited fur trapper and a gallant mountie. Unremarkable remake of the Eddy/MacDonald musical is saved by spectalur technicolor and CinemaScope photography. Choreography by Busby Berkeley. ♫Rose Marie; Indian Love Call; Totem Tom Tom; The Mounties; I Have the Love; The Right Place For A Girl; Free to be Free; The Mountie Who Never Got His Man.
1954 (G) 115m/C Ann Blyth, Howard Keel, Fernando Lamas, Bert Lahr, Marjorie Main, Joan Taylor, Chief Yowlachie, Abel Fernandez, Al Ferguson, Dabbs Greer, Lumsden Hare; *D:* Mervyn LeRoy. VHS MGM, MLB ♫♫

Rose of Rio Grande A western musical about a Mexican gang that avenges the deaths of members of the upper strata.
1938 60m/B John Carroll, Movita, Antonio Moreno, Lena Basquette, Duncan Renaldo; *D:* William Nigh. VHS, Beta GPV ♫

Rose of Washington Square Singer Faye gets involved with the no-account Power, much to the dismay of her friend Jolson. They marry, and she becomes a singing sensation in the Ziegfeld Follies while he becomes an embarrassment, eventually winding up on the wrong side of the law. Jolson stole the movie, singing some of his best numbers. This thinly-disguised portrait of Fanny Brice caused the performer to sue for defamation of character; she eventually settled out of court. ♫California, Here I Come; My Mammy; Pretty Baby; Toot Toot Tootsie Goodbye; Rock-A-Bye Your Baby with a Dixie Melody; My Man; I'm Just Wild About Harry; I Never Knew Heaven Could Speak; Rose of Washington Square.
1939 86m/A Alice Faye, Tyrone Power, Al Jolson, William Frawley, Joyce Compton, Hobart Cavanaugh, Moroni Olsen; *D:* Gregory Ratoff; *W:* Nunnally Johnson. VHS $19.98 FXV ♫♫1/2

The Rose Tattoo Magnani, in her U.S. screen debut, is just right as a Southern widow who cherishes her husband's memory, but falls for virile trucker Lancaster. Williams wrote this play and screenplay specifically for Magnani, who was never as successful again. Interesting character studies, although Lancaster doesn't seem right as an Italian longshoreman.
1955 117m/B Anna Magnani, Burt Lancaster, Marisa Pavan, Ben Cooper, Virginia Grey, Jo Van Fleet; *D:* Daniel Mann; *W:* Tennessee Williams, Hal Kanter, John Michael Hayes. Academy Awards '55: Best Actress (Magnani), Best Art Direction/Set Decoration (B & W), Best Black and White Cinematography; Nominations: Best Costume Design (B & W), Best Film Editing, Best Picture, Best Supporting Actress (Pavan); British Academy Awards '56: Best Actress (Magnani); Golden Globe Awards '56: Best Actress—Drama (Magnani), Best Supporting Actress (Pavan). VHS, Beta $19.95 PAR, FCT, BTV ♫♫♫1/2

Rosebud Embarassingly dull film finds a group of PLO terrorists kidnapping five young women who were vacationing aboard O'Toole's yacht. He's supposedly a journalist but actually works for the CIA. Action ping-pongs between the plight of the victims and what's being done to rescue them but it's so boring you won't care. "Rosebud" is the name of the yacht. Based on a novel by Joan Hemingway and Paul Bonnecarrere.
1975 (PG) 126m/C Peter O'Toole, Richard Attenborough, Kim Cattrall, Brigitte Ariel, Isabelle Huppert, Lalla Ward, Deborah Berger, Cliff Gorman, Claude Dauphin, Peter Lawford, Raf Vallone, Adrienne Corri; *D:* Otto Preminger; *W:* Eric Lee Preminger, Marjorie Kellogg. **VHS** $19.98 *MGM &*

Rosebud Beach Hotel Wimpy loser tries his hand at managing a run-down hotel in order to please his demanding girlfriend. Camp is okay, but this soft-porn excuse is horrible in every other way. *AKA:* The Big Lobby; The No-Tell Hotel.
1985 (R) 82m/C Colleen Camp, Peter Scolari, Christopher Lee, Fran Drescher, Eddie Deezen, Chuck McCann, Hank Garrett, Hamilton Camp, Cherie Currie; *D:* Harry Hurwitz. **VHS, Beta** $79.98 *LIV, VES &*

Roseland Three interlocking stories, set at New York's famous old Roseland Ballroom, about lonely people who live to dance. Not fully successful, but strong characters, especially in the second and third stories, make it worth watching, although it lacks energy.
1977 (PG) 103m/C Christopher Walken, Geraldine Chaplin, Joan Copeland, Teresa Wright, Lou Jacobi; *D:* James Ivory; *W:* Ruth Prawer Jhabvala. **VHS, Beta** $59.95 *VES, CVC, ING &&&*

Rosemary's Baby A young woman, innocent and religious, and her husband, ambitious and agnostic, move into a new apartment. Soon the woman is pregnant, but she begins to realize that she has fallen into a coven of witches and warlocks, and that they claim the child as the antichrist. Gripping and powerful, subtle yet utterly horrifying, with luminous performances by all. Polanski's first American film; from Levin's best-seller.
1968 (R) 134m/C Mia Farrow, John Cassavetes, Ruth Gordon, Maurice Evans, Patsy Kelly, Elisha Cook Jr., Charles Grodin, Sidney Blackmer, William Castle, Ralph Bellamy; *D:* Roman Polanski; *W:* Roman Polanski; *M:* Krzysztof Komeda. Academy Awards '68: Best Supporting Actress (Gordon); Nominations: Best Adapted Screenplay; Golden Globe Awards '69: Best Supporting Actress (Gordon). **VHS, Beta** $14.95 *PAR, MLB, BTV &&&&*

Rosencrantz & Guildenstern Are Dead Playwright Stoppard adapted his own absurdist 1967 play to film—which makes as much sense as a "Swan Lake" ballet on radio. Two tragicomic minor characters in "Hamlet" squabble rhetorically and misperceive Shakespeare's plot tightening fatally around them. Uprooted from the stage environment, it's affected, arcane and pointless for all but fervent Stoppard fans and Bard completists.
1990 (PG) 118m/C Gary Oldman, Tim Roth, Richard Dreyfuss, Iain Glen; *D:* Tom Stoppard; *W:* Tom Stoppard. **VHS, Beta** $92.95 *BVV, FCT &*

Roses Bloom Twice When a middle-aged widow decides to make up for some of the wild living that she missed during her marriage, she shocks her children.
1977 87m/C Glynis McNicoll, Michael Craig, Diane Craig, John Allen, Jennifer West; *D:* David Stevens. **VHS, Beta** *NO & ½*

Rosie: The Rosemary Clooney Story Above average biography of Clooney's up-and-down career. Locke lip-synches Clooney's voice in songs. Orlando doesn't help matters portraying Jose Ferrer. Made for television.
1982 100m/C Sondra Locke, Tony Orlando, Penelope Milford, Katherine Helmond, Kevin McCarthy, John Karlen, Cheryl Anderson, Robert Ridgely, Joey Travolta; *D:* Jackie Cooper; *Performed by:* Rosemary Clooney. **VHS, Beta** $39.95 *LIV && ½*

R.O.T.O.R. R.O.T.O.R. (Robotic Officer of Tactical Operations Research) is a law enforcement robot that is supposed to stop criminals. But watch out! It might go beserk and wreck your town.
1988 90m/C Richard Gesswein, Margaret Trigg, Jayne Smith; *D:* Cullen Blaine. **VHS** $79.95 *IMP &*

Rouge A young prostitute enlists the aid of a journalist in helping her find her lover, who recovered from their attempted double suicide years before. Set in China of the 1930s. In Cantonese with English subtitles. *AKA:* Yanzhi Kou.
1987 99m/C Anita Mui, Leslie Cheung; *D:* Stanley Kwan. **VHS** $39.95 *FCT &*

Rough Cut American diamond thief Reynolds lives in London, pursued by an aging Scotland Yard detective who wants to end his career in a blaze of glory. A beautiful lady is the decoy. Good chemistry; lousy script.
1980 (PG) 112m/C Burt Reynolds, Lesley-Anne Down, David Niven, Timothy West, Joss Ackland, Patrick Magee; *D:* Don Siegel; *W:* Larry Gelbart. **VHS, Beta** $14.95 *PAR &&*

Rough Justice Spaghetti western about a lone gunfighter tracking down three killers. Kinski is a sexually aroused bad guy in this miserable excuse. What could he have been thinking?
1987 95m/C Klaus Kinski, Steven Tedd; *D:* Mario Costa. **VHS, Beta** $59.95 *TWE & ½*

Rough Night in Jericho Martin plays unredeemable scum in this cliched western. He's an ex-lawman trying to take over the town of Jericho and all that's left to own is the stagecoach line run by Simmons and McIntire. Coming to Simmons aid is Peppard, a former deputy marshall turned gambler. Predicatably violent.
1967 104m/C Dean Martin, Jean Simmons, George Peppard, John McIntire, Slim Pickens, Don Galloway; *D:* Arnold Laven; *W:* Sydney Boehm, Marvin H. Albert. **VHS** $14.98 *MCA, FCT & ½*

Rough Riders of Cheyenne Sunset Carson ends the feud between the Carsons and the Sterlings.
1945 54m/B Sunset Carson, Peggy Stewart. **VHS, Beta** *MED & ½*

Rough Riders' Roundup Roy and the boys rid a mining town of its crooked manager. Less yodeling than later Roger's outings; also better all around.
1939 54m/B Roy Rogers, Raymond Hatton, Lynn (Mary Hart) Roberts, Dorothy Sebastian, Duncan Renaldo, George Montgomery; *D:* Joseph Kane. **VHS, Beta** $9.95 *NOS, VDM, DVT &&*

Rough Ridin' Rhythm Wallace is kidnapped to care for the orphaned child of a bandit's sister with Maynard being accused of having murdered the woman. But he's innocent and fights the gang to clear his name. Based on the story "Getting a Start in Life" by James Oliver Curwood.
1937 58m/B Kermit Maynard, Beryl Wallace, Ralph Peters, Betty Mack, Curly Dresden; *D:* J.P. McGowan. **VHS** $11.95 *GPV & ½*

Rough Riding Rangers Threatening letters plague a western ranch family. *AKA:* The Secret Stranger.
1935 57m/B Rex Lease, Janet Chandler. **VHS, Beta** $27.95 *VCN & ½*

Roughnecks A team of Texas oil drillers attempt to dig the deepest oil well in history and chase women on the side. Too long, and not particularly action-packed or gripping. Made for television.
1980 240m/C Sam Melville, Cathy Lee Crosby, Vera Miles, Harry Morgan, Steve Forrest, Stephen McHattie, Wilford Brimley; *D:* Bernard McEveety. **VHS, Beta** $69.95 *PSM & ½*

Round Midnight An aging, alcoholic black American jazz saxophonist comes to Paris in the late 1950s seeking an escape from his self-destructive existence. A devoted young French fan spurs him to one last burst of creative brilliance. A moody, heartfelt homage to such expatriate bebop musicians as Bud Powell and Lester Young. In English and French with English subtitles. Available in a Spanish-subtitled version.
1986 (R) 132m/C Dexter Gordon, Lonette McKee, Francois Cluzet, Martin Scorsese, Herbie Hancock, Sandra Reaves-Phillips; *D:* Bertrand Tavernier; *W:* Bertrand Tavernier, David Rayfiel; *M:* Herbie Hancock. Academy Awards '86: Best Original Score; Nominations: Best Actor (Gordon). **VHS, Beta** $19.98 *MVD, WAR, ING &&&*

Round Numbers Judith Schweitzer believes her husband "Big Al the Muffler King" is having an affair with the gorgeous Muffler Mate of the Month, Mitzi (Playboy Playmate Hope Marie Carlton). Determined to get revenge, Judith books herself into the same health spa that Mitzi attends and the result is pure comedy.
1991 (R) 98m/C Kate Mulgrew, Samantha Eggar, Marty Ingels, Hope Marie Carlton, Shani Wallis, Natalie Barish, Debra Christofferson; *D:* Nancy Zala; *W:* Nancy Zala. **VHS** $9.95 *HMD & ½*

Round Trip to Heaven Party guy Larry (Feldman) and his innocent cousin (Galligan) take off in a borrowed Rolls Royce to go meet Larry's dream centerfold in a super model contest. Unfortunately, the Rolls' trunk is loaded with stolen money and Stoneface (Sharkey), the felon who stashed the cash, wants the money back. With Stoneface in pursuit these guys are in for the ride of their lives. For the teen set only. Also available with Spanish subtitles.
1992 (R) 97m/C Corey Feldman, Zach Galligan, Julie McCullough, Rowanne Brewer, Ray Sharkey; *D:* Alan Roberts. **VHS** $19.95 *PSM &&*

The Round Up Brutal tale spins a realistic political web of fear. Set in 1868 in a prison camp, suspected Hungarian subversives, largely peasants and herdsmen, are thrown into jail and tortured. A direct and shocking exploration of life under dehumanizing, totalitarian rule. In Hungarian with English subtitles. *AKA:* Szegenylegenyek Nehezeletuck; The Hopeless Ones; The Poor Outlaws.
1966 90m/B Janos Gorbe, Tibor Molnar, Andras Kozak; *D:* Miklos Jancso; *W:* Gyula Hernadi. **VHS** $59.95 *FST, HTV && ½*

Round-Up Time in Texas Autry delivers a herd of horses to his diamond-prospector brother in South Africa and has to deal with bandits after the jewels. Typical early Autry entry, with singin' on the side.
1937 54m/B Gene Autry, Smiley Burnette; *D:* Joseph Kane. **VHS, Beta** $19.95 *NOS, VCN, VYY &&*

The Rounders Two aging, no-account cowboys (Ford and Fonda) dream of giving up their bronco-busting ways to open a bar in Tahiti where they can watch the world go by. But they have a habit of blowing all their money on women, whiskey, and bad bets. An ornery unbreakable horse may be the key to changing their luck. Mild-mannered comedy with beautiful Arizona scenery.
1965 85m/C Glenn Ford, Henry Fonda, Sue Ane Langdon, Hope Holiday, Chill Wills, Edgar Buchanan, Kathleen Freeman, Joan Freeman, Denver Pyle; *D:* Burt Kennedy; *W:* Burt Kennedy. VHS $19.98 *MGM* 🎞🎞½

Rounding Up the Law Good guy dupes bad guy while organ plays.
1922 62m/B Russell Gordon, Chet Ryan, Patricia Palmer, William McCall, Guinn Williams; *D:* Charles Seeling. VHS, Beta, 8mm $19.95 *VYY, GPV* 🎞🎞½

Roustabout A roving, reckless drifter joins a carnival and romances the owner's daughter. Elvis rides on good support from Stanwyck et al. Welch has a bit part in her film debut; look for Terri Garr as a dancer. 🎵Roustabout; Poison Ivy League; One Track Heart; Little Egypt; Wheels on My Heels; It's a Wonderful World; It's Carnival Time; Hard Knocks; There's a Brand New Day on the Horizon.
1964 101m/C Elvis Presley, Barbara Stanwyck, Joan Freeman, Leif Erickson, Sue Ane Langdon, Pat Buttram, Joan Staley, Dabbs Greer, Steve Brodie, Jack Albertson, Marianna Hill, Beverly Adams, Billy Barty, Richard Kiel, Raquel Welch; *D:* John Rich. VHS, Beta $14.98 *FOX, MVD* 🎞🎞½

The Rousters Descendants of Wyatt Earp run a carnival in a small Western town. Comic misadventures arise when a modern varmint named Clayton comes looking for action. Cannell (of "The A-Team" and "Riptide" fame) co-wrote and produced—with his usual extraordinary mix of the absurd and the dangerous. Unusual vehicle for Rogers, but she keeps her style and humor. Made for TV.
1990 (PG) 72m/C Jim Varney, Mimi Rogers, Chad Everett, Maxine Stuart, Hoyt Axton; *D:* E.W. Swackhamer; *W:* E.W. Swackhamer, Stephan J. Cannell. VHS $79.95 *VMK* 🎞🎞½

Rover Dangerfield Lovable Las Vegas hound Rover Dangerfield searches for respect but finds none. The results are hilarious. Quality animation from a project developed by Rodney Dangerfield and Harold Ramis.
1991 (G) 78m/C *W:* Harold Ramis; *V:* Rodney Dangerfield. VHS, 8mm $19.98 *WAR* 🎞🎞

Roxanne A modern comic retelling of "Cyrano de Bergerac." The romantic triangle between a big nosed, small town fire chief, a shy fireman and the lovely astronomer they both love. Martin gives his most sensitive and believable performance. Don't miss the bar scene where he gets back at a heckler. A wonderful adaptation for the modern age.
1987 (PG) 107m/C Steve Martin, Daryl Hannah, Rick Rossovich, Shelley Duvall, Michael J. Pollard, Fred Willard, John Kapelos, Max Alexander, Damon Wayans, Matt Lattanzi, Kevin Nealon; *D:* Fred Schepisi; *W:* Steve Martin; *M:* Bruce Smeaton. VHS, Beta, 8mm $14.95 *COL* 🎞🎞

The Royal Bed King Eric's queen really wears the pants in the family, and when she leaves on a trip, he's left helpless and hapless. A revolution erupts, and his daughter announces she plans to marry a commoner. What's a king to do? *AKA:* The Queen's Husband.

1931 74m/B Lowell Sherman, Nance O'Neill, Mary Astor, Anthony Bushell, Gilbert Emery, Robert Warwick, J. Carroll Naish; *D:* Lowell Sherman. VHS, Beta $24.95 *VYY* 🎞🎞½

Royal Wedding Astaire and Powell play a brother-and-sister dance team who go to London during the royal wedding of Princess Elizabeth, and find their own romances. Notable for the inspired songs and Astaire's incredible dancing on the ceiling and walls; Lerner's first screenplay. The idea came from Adele Astaire's recent marriage to a British Lord. 🎵Too Late Now; Sunday Jumps; How Can You Believe Me When I Said I Love You When You Know I've Been A Liar All My Life?; You're All The World To Me; The Happiest Day of My Life; Open Your Eyes; Ev'ry Night at Seven; I Left My Hat in Haiti; What A Lovely Day For A Wedding. *AKA:* Wedding Bells.
1951 93m/C Fred Astaire, Jane Powell, Peter Lawford, Keenan Wynn, Sarah Churchill; *D:* Stanley Donen; *W:* Alan Jay Lerner. VHS, Beta $19.98 *MGM, NOS, CAB* 🎞🎞🎞

R.P.M.* **(*Revolutions Per Minute)** Another chance to relive the sixties. Student activists force the university hierarchy to appoint their favorite radical professor president. Hip prof-turned-prez Quinn is between a rock and a hard place, and allows police to crack down. Could have been intriguing, but loses steam; in any case, the script and direction both stink.
1970 (R) 90m/C Anthony Quinn, Paul Winfield, Gary Lockwood, Ann-Margret; *D:* Stanley Kramer; *W:* Erich Segal. VHS, Beta $59.95 *COL* 🎞½

R.S.V.P. Hollywood party honoring a writer turns tragic when a body is found in the guest of honor's pool. Most interesting part is watching the porn stars who make up most of the cast fail at acting while dressed.
1984 (R) 87m/C Harry Reems, Lynda Wiesmeier; *D:* Lem Amero. VHS, Beta $69.98 *LIV, VES* 🎞½

Rub a Dub Dub A jazzy score backs this modernization of classic Mother Goose tales. Animated.
1983 60m/C VHS, Beta $29.95 *MED* 🎞½

Rub a Dub Dub—There's a Zoo in This Tub!, Vol. 2 Another volume of songs & rhymes animated for children.
1987 60m/C VHS, Beta $29.95 *MED* 🎞½

Rubdown An ex-baseball player, turned Beverly Hills masseur, finds himself the victim of a frame-up when one of his clients is murdered.
1993 88m/C Jack Coleman, Michelle Phillips, Kent Williams, Alan Thicke, Catherine Oxenberg, William Devane; *D:* Stuart Cooper; *W:* Clyde Allen Hayes; *M:* Gerald Gouriet. VHS, Beta *PAR* 🎞🎞

Rubin & Ed Ed is a real estate groupie who bribes the eccentric Rubin to attend a get-rich-quick seminar. Rubin decides to cash in on the favor by taking Ed on the road in search of the perfect gravesite for Rubin's long-dead feline. If that sounds wacky, just wait—the fun really begins when the duo is stranded in Death Valley and begins to suffer from sunstroke and hallucinations. Those who dream of weirdos bonding in the desert may be enthused but other viewers may thirst for something more.
1992 (PG-13) 82m/C Crispin Glover, Howard Hesseman, Karen Black, Michael Greene, Brittney Lewis; *D:* Trent Harris; *W:* Trent Harris. VHS $89.95 *COL, FCT* 🎞🎞

Ruby A young woman, christened in blood and raised in sin, has a love affair with the supernatural and murders up a storm at a drive-in. Confused, uneven horror a step up from most similar flicks.
1977 (R) 85m/C Roger Davis, Janet Baldwin, Piper Laurie, Stuart Whitman; *D:* Curtis Harrington; *W:* Barry Schneider. VHS, Beta $14.95 *CNG* 🎞🎞

Ruby Another in the increasing number of Kennedy assassination and conspiracy dramas—this one told from the viewpoint of Jack Ruby, Lee Harvey Oswald's killer. Confusing plot, somewhat redeemed by the performances of Aiello and Fenn. Combines actual footage of Ruby shooting Oswald with black-and-white filmed scenes. Based on the play "Love Field" by Stephen Davis.
1992 (R) 111m/C Danny Aiello, Sherilyn Fenn, Arliss Howard, Tobin Bell, David Duchovny, Richard Sarafian, Joe Cortese, Marc Lawrence; *D:* John MacKenzie; *W:* Stephen Davis; *M:* John Scott. VHS $19.95 *COL* 🎞🎞½

Ruby Gentry White-trash girl Jones, cast aside by man-she-loves Heston, marries wealthy Malden to spite him, then seeks revenge. Classic Southern theme of comeuppance, good direction and acting lift it a notch.
1952 82m/B Charlton Heston, Jennifer Jones, Karl Malden; *D:* King Vidor. VHS, Beta $59.98 *FOX* 🎞🎞½

Ruby in Paradise Leaving her dead-end life in Tennessee, Gissing (Judd) moves to Panama City, Florida and lands a job selling souvenirs for no-nonsense Mildred Chambers (Lyman). Although pursued by two very different men, Ruby concentrates more on self-exploration, recording her thoughts in a journal. A seemingly effortless portrayal of Ruby Lee by Judd (daughter of Naomi and sister of Wynonna Judd) makes for a pleasurable character study of a young woman on her own.
1993 (R) 115m/C Ashley Judd, Todd Field, Bentley Mitchum, Allison Dean, Dorothy Lyman, Betsy Dowds; *D:* Victor Nunez; *W:* Victor Nunez; *M:* Charles Engstrom. Independent Spirit Aw Nominations: rds '94: Best Cinematography, Best Director (Nunez), Best Film, Best Screenplay, Best Supporting Actor (Field); Independent Spirit Awards '94: Best Actress (Judd). VHS *REP* 🎞🎞🎞

Ruby's Dream A bowling alley and nightclub owner dreams of making it big in Las Vegas. After his dreams crash to the ground, however, he realizes what is truly important in life.
19?? 100m/C Joe Pesci. VHS $9.99 *QVD* 🎞🎞

Ruckus A Vietnam vet uses his training to defend himself when he runs into trouble in a small Alabama town. Less obnoxious than "First Blood," (which came later), but basically the same movie. *AKA:* The Loner.
1981 (PG) 91m/C Dirk Benedict, Linda Blair, Ben Johnson, Richard Farnsworth, Matt Clark; *D:* Max Kleven. VHS, Beta *NO* 🎞

Ruddigore The Lords of Ruddigore have been bound for centuries by a terribly inconvenient curse; they must commit a crime every day or die a horribly painful death. When the Lord of Ruddigore passes his mantle on to the new heir, the young heir loses both his good reputation and his very proper fiancee. A new version of Gilbert and Sullivan's opera.
197? 112m/C Vincent Price, Keith Michell, Sandra Dugdale. VHS, Beta $49.98 *FOX* 🎞🎞

Rude Awakening A real estate agent is tortured by bizarre nightmares which lead to an unusual series of events. Part of the "Thriller Video" series.

1981 60m/C Denholm Elliott, James Laurenson, Pat Heywood; *D:* Peter Sasdy. VHS, Beta $29.95 *LIV* 🎗🎗½

Rude Awakening Hippies Cheech and Roberts (where's Chong?) settled in a South American commune 20 years ago. Now they're back, and don't know what to make of old pals Carradine and Hagerty who have become - that's right - yuppies. Rip Van Winkle-ian farce draws a few yuks, but could have been much funnier. Points for trying.
1989 (R) 100m/C Eric Roberts, Richard "Cheech" Marin, Julie Hagerty, Robert Carradine, Buck Henry, Louise Lasser, Cindy Williams, Andrea Martin, Cliff DeYoung; *D:* Aaron Russo, David Greenwalt; *W:* Richard LaGravenese; *M:* Jonathan Elias. VHS, Beta $89.99 *HBO* 🎗🎗

Rudolph & Frosty's Christmas in July More animated adventures of Rudolph and friends. This time they are transported to a glittering, sunny seashore for a magical summer weekend that almost turns into tragedy.
1982 97m/C *V:* Red Buttons, Ethel Merman, Mickey Rooney, Jackie Vernon, Shelley Winters. VHS, Beta $12.95 *LIV, TLF, WTA* 🎗

Rudolph the Red-Nosed Reindeer The durable Christmas story of the nasally enhanced reindeer who saved the holiday; colorful stop-motion animation and character voices bring it to life, with a memorable guest visit from an abominable snowman. Made for television.
1964 53m/C *D:* Larry Roemer. VHS, Beta, 8mm $12.98 *FHE, WTA, LME* 🎗🎗

Rudy Likeable, true story about a little guy who triumphs over big odds. Daniel "Rudy" Ruettiger (Astin) dreams of playing football for Notre Dame, no matter how farfetched the dream. He's a mediocre student, physically unsuitable for big time college ball, but sheer determination helps him attain his dream. Astin delivers an engaging performance and is backed up by a good supporting cast. Sentimental story stretches the truth with typical shameless Hollywood manipulation, but is still entertaining. From the director and writer of another David beats Goliath sports film, "Hoosiers."
1993 (PG) 112m/C Sean Astin, Ned Beatty, Charles S. Dutton, Lili Taylor, Robert Prosky, Jason Miller, Ron Dean, Chelcie Ross, Jon Favreau, Greta Lind, Scott Benjaminson, Christopher Reed; *D:* David Anspaugh; *W:* Angelo Pizzo; *M:* Jerry Goldsmith. VHS, 8mm *COL* 🎗🎗½

Rudyard Kipling's Classic Stories Three Kipling stories come to animated life: "How the Elephant Got His Trunk," "How the Whale Got His Throat" and "How the First Letter Was Written."
1970 25m/C VHS, Beta $14.95 *NWV* 🎗🎗½

The Rue Morgue Massacres A modern reprise of the Poe story with touches of Frankensteinia thrown in; plenty of gore.
1973 (R) 90m/C Paul Naschy, Rossana Yanni, Maria Perschy, Vic Winner, Mary Ellen Arpon; *D:* Javier Aguirre. VHS, Beta *NO* 🎗½

The Ruggles of Red Gap Classic comedy about an uptight British butler who is "won" by a barbarous American rancher in a poker game. Laughton as the nonplussed manservant is hilarious; supporting cast excellent. Third and far superior filming of Harry Leon Wilson story. One of the all-time great comedies, the film was remade musically with Bob Hope and Lucille Ball as "Fancy Pants" (1950).

1935 90m/B Charles Laughton, Mary Boland, Charlie Ruggles, ZaSu Pitts, Roland Young, Leila Hyams, James Burke, Maude Eburne; *D:* Leo McCarey; *W:* Walter DeLeon; *M:* Ralph Rainger. Academy Awards '35 Nominations: Best Picture; National Board of Review Awards '35: 10 Best Films of the Year; New York Film Critics Awards '35: Best Actor (Laughton). VHS, Beta $14.98 *MCA* 🎗🎗🎗

Rulers of the City Young gangster avenges his father's death.
1971 91m/C Jack Palance, Edmund Purdom, Al Cliver, Harry Baer. VHS, Beta $19.98 *VDC* 🎗

The Rules of the Game Renoir's masterpiece, in which a group of French aristocrats, gathering for a weekend of decadence and self-indulgence just before WWII, becomes a metaphor for human folly under siege. The film was banned by the French government, pulled from distribution by the Nazis, and not restored to its original form until 1959, when it premiered at the Venice Film Festival. A great, subtle, ominous film landmark. In French with English subtitles. The laserdisc version includes a commentary by director Peter Bogdanovich. Heavily copied and poorly remade in 1989 as "Scenes from the Class Struggle in Beverly Hills." *AKA:* Le Regle du Jeu.
1939 110m/B Marcel Dalio, Nora Gregor, Jean Renoir, Mila Parely, Julien Carette, Gaston Modot, Roland Toutain, Paulette Dubost, Odette Talazac; *D:* Jean Renoir; *W:* Jean Renoir. VHS, Beta, 8mm $19.95 *NOS, SUE, HHT* 🎗🎗🎗🎗

The Ruling Class The classic cult satire features O'Toole as the unbalanced 14th Earl of Gurney, who believes that he is either Jesus Christ or Jack the Ripper. Tongue-in-cheek look, complete with dance and music, at eccentric upper-class Brits and their institutions. Uneven, chaotic, surreal and noteworthy.
1972 (PG) 154m/C Peter O'Toole, Alastair Sim, Arthur Lowe, Harry Andrews, Coral Browne, Nigel Green; *D:* Peter Medak. Academy Awards '72 Nominations: Best Actor (O'Toole); Cannes Film Festival '72: Best Film; National Board of Review Awards '72: 10 Best Films of the Year, Best Actor (O'Toole). VHS, Beta $19.98 *SUE, NLC* 🎗🎗🎗½

Rumble Fish A young street punk worships his gang-leading older brother, the only role model he's known. Crafted by Coppola into an important story of growing up on the wrong side of town, from the novel by S.E. Hinton. Ambitious and experimental, with an atmospheric music score; in black and white.
1983 (R) 94m/B Matt Dillon, Mickey Rourke, Dennis Hopper, Diane Lane, Vincent Spano, Nicolas Cage, Diana Scarwid, Christopher Penn, Tom Waits; *D:* Francis Ford Coppola; *W:* Francis Ford Coppola; *M:* Stewart Copeland. VHS, Beta $59.95 *MCA* 🎗🎗🎗

The Rumor Mill The careers and titanic rivalry of influential Hollywood gossip writer Hedda Hopper and Louella Parsons, played with verve by Taylor and Alexander. Fictionalized script based on the book "Hedda and Louella" by George Eels. Made for TV. *AKA:* Malice in Wonderland.
1986 94m/C Elizabeth Taylor, Jane Alexander, Richard Dysart, Joyce Van Patten; *D:* Gus Trikonis; *W:* Jaqueline Feather, David Seidler; *M:* Charles Bernstein. VHS, Beta $79.95 *VMK* 🎗🎗½

A Rumor of War The first big Vietnam drama for TV is a triumph, portraying the real-life experience of author Philip Caputo (based on his bestseller), from naive youth to seasoned soldier to bitter murder suspect at court martial. Succeeds where Stone's later, much-ballyhooed "Born on the Fourth of July" fails. Adapted by John Sacret Young.

1980 195m/C Brad Davis, Keith Carradine, Michael O'Keefe, Stacy Keach, Steve Forrest, Richard Bradford, Brian Dennehy, John Friedrich, Perry Lang, Chris Mitchum, Dan Shor, Jeff Daniels; *D:* Richard T. Heffron. VHS, Beta $14.95 *FRH* 🎗🎗🎗½

Rumpelstiltskin From "Faerie Tale Theatre" comes the story of a woman who can spin straw into gold (Duvall) and the strange man who saves her life (Villechaize). Enjoyable for the whole family.
1982 60m/C Bud Cort, Ned Beatty, Shelley Duvall, Herve Villechaize, Paul Dooley; *D:* David Irving. VHS, Beta $14.98 *KUI, FOX, FCT* 🎗🎗🎗½

Rumpelstiltskin Musical retelling of the classic Brother Grimm fairy tale. Irving plays a young girl who says she can spin straw into gold. Barty is a dwarf who helps her. The catch: she must give up her first born to pay him. Lackluster direction and uninspired acting make this version a yawner. Irving's real-life mother (Pointer) and brother have roles too.
1986 (G) 84m/C Amy Irving, Billy Barty, Robert Symonds, Priscilla Pointer, Clive Revill, John Moulder-Brown; *D:* David Irving. VHS, Beta $19.98 *MED* 🎗🎗

Rumpole of the Bailey John Mortimer's famed British barrister comes to life in McKern's portrait in two episodes taken from the television series. In "Rumpole and the Genuine Article," Rumpole is called on to defend an embittered artist in a forgery case. "Rumpole and the Old Boy Network" has the barrister drawn into blackmail and deception when a brothel is discovered in a respectable London neighborhood. Additional episodes available.
198? 104m/C Leo McKern. VHS $49.95 *MOV, SIG, TVC* 🎗🎗

Rumpole of the Bailey: Rumpole's Return A feature-length film based on the popular British television series. A middle aged barrister refuses to settle for less than justice. Based on the character created by John Mortimer.
1990 106m/C Leo McKern. VHS $59.99 *FCT, ING* 🎗🎗🎗

Run A high energy action cartoon, with little plot but lots of stunts. Dempsey is a supersmart law student hired to drive a car to Atlantic City. A stop on the way starts trouble. Instant romance with a local girl balances mayhem from crime boss. Expect no more than physical feats and you'll be happy with this lightweight fare.
1991 (R) 91m/C Patrick Dempsey, Kelly Preston, Ken Pogue, Alan C. Peterson, Sean McCann; *D:* Geoff Burrowes. VHS, Beta $19.99 *HPH* 🎗½

Run, Angel, Run! Ex-biker Angel is on the run from his former gang after he helps expose them in a magazine article. He settles on a sheep ranch with his girl and then the gang shows up with revenge in mind. Prime drive-in fare with title song sung by none other than Ms. Tammy Wynette.
1969 (R) 90m/C William Smith, Margaret Markov, Valerie Starrett; *D:* Jack Starrett. VHS, Beta *NO* 🎗½

Run for the Roses "National Velvet" clone about a young Puerto Rican boy and a champion race horse in Kentucky. Cheery family fare. *AKA:* Thoroughbred.
1978 (PG) 93m/C Lisa Eilbacher, Vera Miles, Stuart Whitman, Sam Groom; *D:* Henry Levin. VHS, Beta $59.98 *LIV* 🎗½

Run If You Can A woman sees a brutal murderer killing his victims on her television. Will she be next?

1987 (R) 92m/C Martin Landau, Yvette Nipar, Jerry Van Dyke; **D:** Virginia Lively Stone. **Beta** $79.95 ALL *Z*

Run of the Arrow Rather than surrender to the North at the end of the Civil War, an ex-Confederate soldier (Steiger) joins the Sioux nation, engaged in war against the white man. Steiger's Irish brogue is weird and distracting, and the intriguing premise fails to satisfy, but the cast is competent and interesting. **AKA:** Hot Lead.
1956 85m/C Rod Steiger, Brian Keith, Charles Bronson, Ralph Meeker, Tim McCoy; **D:** Samuel Fuller; **W:** Samuel Fuller. VHS, Beta $54.95 VCI *ZZ*

Run, Rebecca, Run Interesting family adventure yarn for the family about a South American refugee who tries to stop a young girl from leaving from an Australian island where they are both stranded. She eventually befriends him, and attempts to get permission for him to enter the country.
1981 90m/C Simone Buchanan, Henri Szeps; **D:** Peter Maxwell. VHS, Beta NO *ZZ½*

Run Silent, Run Deep Submarine commander Gable battles his officers, especially the bitter Lancaster who vied for the same command, while stalking the Japanese destroyer that sunk his former command. Top-notch WWII sub action, scripted from Commander Edward L. Beach's novel.
1958 93m/B Burt Lancaster, Clark Gable, Jack Warden, Don Rickles, Brad Dexter; **D:** Robert Wise; **W:** John Gay. VHS, Beta $19.95 FOX, FCT, MGM *ZZZ*

Run, Stranger, Run The inhabitants of a seaside house in Nova Scotia are paralyzed with fear when a number of brutal murders occur. A couple of sicko slasher scenes, but hard to swallow. **AKA:** Happy Mother's Day, Love, George.
1973 (PG) 110m/C Ron Howard, Patricia Neal, Cloris Leachman, Bobby Darin; **D:** Darren McGavin. VHS $59.95 COL *ZZ*

Runaway A cop and his sidekick track down a group of killer robots wreaking havoc. Self-serious, sorry sci-fi. Features Simmons of the rock group KISS.
1984 (PG-13) 100m/C Tom Selleck, Cynthia Rhodes, Gene Simmons, Stan Shaw, Kirstie Alley; **D:** Michael Crichton; **W:** Michael Crichton; **M:** Jerry Goldsmith. VHS, Beta $14.95 COL *Z½*

Runaway A boy blames himself for his friend's accidental death and runs away to live in the subway tunnels of New York City. After four months of life underground, a disabled veteran and a waitress lend the boy a hand. Adapted from the novel ''Slake's Limbo'' by Felice Holman. Made for PBS and aired as part of the ''Wonderworks'' series.
1989 58m/C Charles S. Dutton, Jasmine Guy, Gavin Allen; **D:** Gilbert Moses. VHS $29.95 PME, HMV, COL *Z½*

The Runaway Barge Tiresomely ordinary TV yarn about three adventurers earning their living on a riverboat. The usual cliches are present, including a gang of bad guys.
1975 78m/C Bo Hopkins, Tim Matheson, Jim Davis, Nick Nolte, Devon Ericson, Christina Hart, James Best; **D:** Boris Sagal. VHS $29.95 LIV *ZZ*

The Runaway Bus Filled with the requisite motley crew of passengers, including a gold-carrying thief and the ever-befuddled Margaret Rutherford, a bus gets lost between airports and ends up in a deserted village. Would-be wacky comedy.
1954 78m/B Frankie Howerd, Margaret Rutherford, Petula Clark, George Coulouris; **D:** Val Guest. VHS, Beta $24.95 VYY, FCT *ZZ*

Runaway Father Pat Bennett's husband fakes his own death in an attempt to abandon his family. When Bennett discovers he's alive she works to set a legal precedent—17 years worth of back child support. Based on a true story. Made for television.
1991 94m/C Donna Mills, Jack Scalia, Chris Mulkey, Jenny Lewis; **D:** John Nicolella. VHS $89.95 WOV *ZZ½*

Runaway Island, Part 1 Episode: ''Quest for Jamie McLeod.'' In 1830's Australia, two youths battle corruption when their father leaves for England.
19?? 96m/C Miles Buchanan, Simone Buchanan. VHS, Beta NO *ZZ½*

Runaway Island, Part 2 Episode: ''The Exiles.'' When their father dies, the McLeod children realize their only hope of obtaining their property is to find his hidden will.
19?? 103m/C Miles Buchanan, Simone Buchanan. VHS, Beta NO *ZZ½*

Runaway Island, Part 3 Episode: ''The Bushranger.'' Jamie and Jemma McLeod continue the search for their father's will, but are captured by a gang of terrorists.
19?? 101m/C Miles Buchanan, Simone Buchanan. VHS, Beta NO *ZZ½*

Runaway Island, Part 4 Episode: ''Treasure of the Conquistadors.'' Having found the missing portion of the map that will lead them to their father's will, the McLeod children encounter a band of pirates, Aborigines and other dangers that might prevent them from staking their claim.
19?? 104m/C Miles Buchanan, Simone Buchanan. VHS, Beta NO *ZZ½*

Runaway Nightmare Two western worm ranchers are kidnapped by a female gang whose members torture and initiate them, then talk about their plan to steal from organized criminals. Just another typical worm rancher flick.
1984 104m/C Michael Cartel, Al Valletta; **D:** Michael Cartel. VHS NO *Z*

Runaway Train A tough jailbird and his sidekick break out of the hoosegow and find themselves trapped aboard a brakeless freight train heading for certain derailment in northwestern Canada. Harrowing existential action drama based on a screenplay by Akira Kurosawa. Voigt is superb.
1985 (R) 112m/C Jon Voight, Eric Roberts, Rebecca DeMornay, John P. Ryan, T.K. Carter, Kenneth McMillan; **D:** Andrei Konchalovsky; **W:** Andrei Konchalovsky, Djordje Milicevic; **M:** Trevor Jones. Academy Awards '85 Nominations: Best Actor (Voight), Best Film Editing, Best Supporting Actor (Roberts); Golden Globe Awards '86: Best Actor—Drama (Voight). VHS, Beta $14.98 MGM *ZZZ*

The Runaways A boy runs away from an unhappy foster home situation and becomes friends with a leopard that has escaped from an animal park. Sentimental but well-done family fun.
1975 76m/C Dorothy McGuire, John Randolph, Neva Patterson, Josh Albee; **D:** Harry Harris. VHS, Beta NO *Z*

Runaways A corrupt politician's wife falls in love with the man who saved her when she attempted suicide. The two try to escape her husband's wrathful vengeance.
1984 95m/C Steve Oliver, Sondra Currie, John Russell. VHS, Beta NO *Z*

The Runestone After the eponymous viking relic is unearthed, an archaeologist's meddling frees a long-imprisoned wolf-beast that terrorizes New York. An adequate horror flick that taps the seldom-explored vein of

Norse mythology. Based on a novel by Mark E. Rogers.
1991 (R) 105m/C Peter Riegert, Joan Severance, William Hickey, Tim Ryan, Chris Young, Alexander Godunov; **D:** Willard Carroll. VHS $14.98 LIV *ZZ*

The Runner Stumbles Dated melodrama about a priest who goes on trial for murdering the nun with whom he fell in love in a mining town in the 1920s. Based on a true incident, from the play by Milan Stiff. Van Dyke in an unwanted serious role is miserably grim and wooden.
1979 (R) 109m/C Dick Van Dyke, Kathleen Quinlan, Maureen Stapleton, Ray Bolger, Beau Bridges, Tammy Grimes; **D:** Stanley Kramer; **M:** Ernest Gold. VHS, Beta $59.98 FOX *Z½*

The Runnin' Kind A yuppie expecting to inherit his father's Ohio law firm goes on a wild spree with an all-girl rock band. Sexy drummer Howard shows him the sights of certain parts of L.A. Original, fun comedy. Independent.
1989 (R) 89m/C David Packer, Pleasant Gehman, Brie Howard, Susan Strasberg; **D:** Max Tash. VHS, Beta $79.98 FOX *Z½*

Running Against Time A teacher tries to change history (and erase his brother's Vietnam War death) by time-warping back to 1963 and preventing JFK's murder. The made for cable TV movie takes an offhanded gee-whiz approach to a tantalizing premise, as temporal paradoxes multiply in ''Back to the Future'' style. No assassination-conspiracy theories, by the way, but Lyndon Johnson fans may not like his portrayal here. Based on the novel ''A Time to Remember'' by Stanley Shapiro.
1990 (PG) 93m/C Robert Hays, Catherine Hicks, Sam Wanamaker, James DiStefano, Brian Smiar; **D:** Bruce Seth Green; **W:** Robert Glass. VHS $79.95 MCA *ZZ½*

Running Away Bittersweet story of WWII romance, with a twist of adventure. Strong cast creates good chemistry, but somehow the story is not engaging. Loren and Penny are mother and daughter, leaving Rome for the hills and encountering dangers.
1989 (PG-13) 101m/C Sophia Loren, Sydney Penny, Robert Loggia, Andrea Occhipinti; **D:** Dino Risi. VHS $89.95 PSM, PAR, FCT *ZZ*

Running Blind Espionage/adventure thriller has a double agent and a beautiful woman on the run in Iceland.
197? 120m/C Stuart Wilson, Heidi Steindorsottir. VHS $49.95 FCT *ZZ*

Running Brave The true story of Billy Mills, a South Dakota Sioux Indian who won the Gold Medal in the 10,000 meter run at the 1964 Tokyo Olympics. Not bad, but hokey in the way of many of these plodding true-story flicks.
1983 (PG) 90m/C Robby Benson, Claudia Cron, Pat Hingle, Denis Lacroix; **D:** D.S. Everett. VHS, Beta DIS *ZZ*

Running Cool Two easy-going bikers join up with an old friend to protect his wetlands property from a lowlife developer and his stooges. Chicks (there's a romance with a local biker babe), motorcyles, fighting, and saving the environment—what more could you want?
1993 (R) 106m/C Andrew Divoff, Tracy Sebastian, Dedee Pfeiffer, James Gammon, Paul Gleason, Arlen Dean Snyder, Bubba Baker; **D:** Beverly Sebastian, Ferd Sebastian; **W:** Beverly Sebastian, Ferd Sebastian. VHS, Beta PAR *Z*

Running Delilah Delilah (Cattrall) is a secret agent who is apparently killed by a vicious arms dealer. Only her fellow agent (Zane) resurrects her and Delilah is trans-

formed into a cybernetic super agent. And her assignment is to go after a terrorist who's building a nuclear weapon with plutonium supplied by Delilah's killer.
1993 85m/C Kim Cattrall, Billy Zane, Diana Rigg. **VHS** ABC ♪♪½

Running Hot Seventeen-year-old convicted murderer Stoltz gets love letter in prison from older woman Carrico. When he escapes, they flee the law together. Quick-paced and entertaining. *AKA:* Highway to Hell; Lucky 13.
1983 (R) 88m/C Monica Carrico, Eric Stoltz, Stuart Margolin, Virgil Frye, Richard Bradford, Sorrels Pickard, Juliette Cummins; *D:* Mark Griffiths; *W:* Mark Griffiths. **VHS, Beta $69.98** LIV, VES ♪♪½

The Running Man Special-effects-laden adaptation of the Stephen King novel about a futuristic television game show. Convicts are given a chance for pardon—all they have to do is survive an on going battle with specially-trained assassins in the bombed-out sections of Los Angeles. Sci-fi with an attitude.
1987 (R) 101m/C Arnold Schwarzenegger, Richard Dawson, Maria Conchita Alonso, Yaphet Kotto, Mick Fleetwood, Dweezil Zappa, Jesse Ventura; *D:* Paul Michael Glaser; *W:* Steven E. de Souza; *M:* Harold Faltermeyer. **VHS, Beta $14.98** LIV, VES ♪♪½

Running Mates Occasionally intriguing drama of two teens who fall in love, but are kept apart by their fathers' local political rivalry. Could have been better, but cardboard characters abound.
1986 (PG-13) 90m/C Greg Webb, Barbara Howard, J. Don Ferguson, Clara Dunn; *D:* Thomas L. Neff. **VHS, Beta $19.95** STE, NWV ♪♪♪

Running Mates Cynically amusing political satire about a bachelor politician and his too intelligent lady love. Harris is Hugh, a U.S. senator looking forward to the presidential primaries when he meets widowed children's novelist Aggie (Keaton). She hates politics and he's Mr. Slick, although decent enough behind the political expediency. Aggie, however, has a potentially damaging secret in her past which causes the scandal-scenting pack of press hounds to bay in salivating anticipation. Will Hugh stick by Aggie and will Aggie overcome her natural political distaste for everything to end happily? A well-played romp. Made for cable television.
1992 (PG-13) 88m/C Ed Harris, Diane Keaton, Ed Begley Jr., Ben Masters, Robert Harper, Brandon Maggart, Russ Tamblyn; *D:* Michael Lindsay-Hogg; *W:* A.L. Appling. **VHS $89.99** HBO ♪♪♪

Running on Empty Two 1960s radicals are still on the run in 1988 for a politically motivated Vietnam War-era crime. Though they have managed to stay one step ahead of the law, their son wants a "normal" life, even if it means never seeing his family again. Well-performed, quiet, plausible drama.
1988 (PG-13) 116m/C Christine Lahti, River Phoenix, Judd Hirsch, Martha Plimpton, Jonas Arby, Ed Crowley, L.M. Kit Carson, Steven Hill, Augusta Dabney, David Margulies, Sidney Lumet; *D:* Sidney Lumet; *W:* Naomi Foner; *M:* Tony Mottola. Academy Awards '88 Nominations: Best Original Screenplay, Best Supporting Actor (Phoenix); Golden Globe Awards '89: Best Screenplay; National Board of Review Awards '88: Best Supporting Actor (Phoenix). **VHS, Beta, 8mm $19.95** WAR ♪♪♪

Running Out of Luck A light, song-packed story about a rock star very much like Jagger who is abandoned in South America and believed dead, until he returns to his world. Features songs from Jagger's solo album "She's the Boss".
1986 (R) 88m/C Mick Jagger, Dennis Hopper, Jerry Hall, Rae Dawn Chong; *D:* Julien Temple. **VHS, Beta $19.95** MVD, FOX ♪½

Running Scared Two young men, returning from military service as stowaways aboard an Army cargo plane, are caught by an intelligence agent and thought to be spies, because Reinhold has unknowingly photographed a secret US base wire his stolen Army-issue camera. Not-bad spy thriller with a twist - the "spies" are hapless nobodies, now on the lam.
1979 (PG) 92m/C Ken Wahl, Judge Reinhold, John Saxon, Annie McEnroe, Bradford Dillman, Pat Hingle; *D:* Paul Glickler. **VHS, Beta** NO ♪♪

Running Scared Hip, unorthodox Chicago cops Hines and Crystal have to handle an important drug arrest before taking an extended vacation in Key West. Not as relentless as "48 Hrs," but more enjoyable in some ways. Ever wonder what it's like to ride in a car at high speed on the tracks? Find out here.
1986 (R) 107m/C Gregory Hines, Billy Crystal, Dan Hedaya, Jimmy Smits, Darlanne Fluegel, Joe Pantoliano, Steven Bauer; *D:* Peter Hyams; *W:* Gary De Vore. **VHS, Beta $14.98** MGM ♪♪½

Running Wild Early silent comedy starring mustachioed Fields as an eternal coward who suddenly turns into a lion by hypnosis. Odd, often unfunny Fields entry sometimes hits the mark. He's awfully mean, though.
1927 68m/B W.C. Fields, Mary Brian, Claud Buchanan; *D:* Gregory La Cava; *M:* Gaylord Carter. **VHS, Beta $29.95** PAR ♪♪

Running Wild A free-lance photographer becomes involved in a dispute to save a corral of wild mustang horses. The usual great Colorado scenery enhances a good, family-view story.
1973 (G) 102m/C Lloyd Bridges, Dina Merrill, Pat Hingle, Gilbert Roland, Morgan Woodward; *D:* Robert McCahon; *W:* Robert McCahon. **VHS, Beta $19.95** MED ♪♪½

Rush A post-nuclear world war movie in which a rebel named Rush battles the rulers of a slave colony.
1984 83m/C Conrad Nichols, Gordon Mitchell, Laura Trotter, Rita Furlan; *D:* Tonino Ricci. **VHS** NO ♪

Rush Texas drug culture, circa 1975, is portrayed in this bleak cop drama. Rookie narcotics officer Kristen Cates (Leigh) goes undercover with the experienced Raynor (Patric) to catch a big-time dealer, menacingly played by Allman, and their bosses don't much care how they do it. Cates falls in love with Raynor and is drawn ever deeper into the drug-addicted world they are supposed to destroy. Fine performances and a great blues score by Clapton. The directorial debut of Zanuck. Based on ex-narcotics cop Kim Wozencraft's autobiographical novel.
1991 (R) 120m/C Jason Patric, Jennifer Jason Leigh, Gregg Allman, Max Perlich, Sam Elliott, Tony Frank, William Sadler; *D:* Lili Fini Zanuck; *W:* Pete Dexter; *M:* Eric Clapton. **VHS $19.98** MGM ♪♪♪

Rush It Scriptwriters ponder possible plots over capucino: "I've got it! 'Bike Messengers in Love'!" "Nah. The title's too obvious. Why don't we call it 'Rush It'?" Much hard work and many months later, the result is forgettable.
1977 78m/C Tom Berenger, Jill Eikenberry. **VHS, Beta $49.95** UNI ♪½

Rush Week Dead coeds populate campus during frat week. Greg Allman has bit part and the Dickies perform two songs.
1988 (R) 93m/C Dean Hamilton, Gregg Allman, Kathleen Kinmont, Roy Thinnes, Pamela Ludwig; *D:* Bob Bralver. **VHS $79.95** COL ♪

The Russia House Russian scientist Brandauer attempts to publish book debunking Soviet Union's claims of military superiority by passing it through ex-lover Pfeiffer to British editor Connery, apparently unaware of impending glasnost. Star-studded spy thriller aspires to heights it never quite reaches. Adapted from John Le Carre's novel, Stoppard's screenplay is very fine, actually making some aspects of the novel work better.
1990 (R) 122m/C Sean Connery, Michelle Pfeiffer, Roy Scheider, James Fox, John Mahoney, Klaus Maria Brandauer, Ken Russell, J.T. Walsh, Michael Kitchen, David Threlfall, Ian McNeice, Christopher Lawford; *D:* Fred Schepisi; *M:* Tom Stoppard; *M:* Jerry Goldsmith. **VHS, 8mm $14.95** MGM, FCT ♪♪½

Russian Roulette The Russian premier is visiting Vancouver in 1970, and the Mounties must prevent a dissident KGB terrorist from assassinating him. Un-thrilling spy yarn fails to deliver on intriguing premise.
1975 100m/C George Segal, Christina Raines, Bo Brundin, Denholm Elliott, Louise Fletcher; *D:* Lou Lombardo. **VHS, Beta $59.98** FOX ♪♪

Russian Roulette Routine story about an American woman on vacation in Russia who finds herself in the middle of a plot to locate a hidden Czarist artifact and smuggle it out of the country. Everyone on her tour group is suspect, an American businessman becomes involved, and a killer starts eliminating the number of players. Great location scenery.
1993 89m/C Susan Blakely, Barry Bostwick, E.G. Marshall, Jeff Altman; *D:* Greydon Clark. **VHS $89.95** MNC ♪♪½

The Russian Terminator An FBI agent is up against a one-man "death squad."
1990 (R) 90m/C Helena Michaelson, Frederick Offrein, Harley Melin, Tina Tjung; *D:* Mats Helge; *W:* Mats Helge. **VHS $79.95** XVC, PHX ♪

The Russians are Coming, the Russians are Coming Based on the comic novel "The Off-Islanders" by Nathaniel Benchley, this is the story of a Russian sub which accidentally runs aground off the New England coast. The residents falsely believe that the nine-man crew is the beginning of a Soviet invasion, though the men are only looking for help. A memorable set of silly events follows the landing, engineered by a gung-ho police chief and a town filled with overactive imaginations.
1966 126m/C Alan Arkin, Carl Reiner, Theodore Bikel, Eva Marie Saint, Brian Keith, Paul Ford, Jonathan Winters, Ben Blue, Tessie O'Shea, Doro Merande, John Phillip Law; *D:* Norman Jewison. Academy Awards '66 Nominations: Best Actor (Arkin), Best Picture, Best Story & Screenplay; Golden Globe Awards '67: Best Actor—Musical/Comedy (Arkin), Best Film—Musical/Comedy; National Board of Review Awards '66: 10 Best Films of the Year. **VHS, Beta $19.95** FOX, MLB ♪♪♪

Russkies A jolly comedy about three adorable American kids who capture, and eventually grow to like, a stranded Russian sailor. Friendly and peace-loving, but dull.
1987 (PG) 98m/C Leaf (Joaquin Rafael) Phoenix, Whip Hubley, Peter Billingsley, Stefan DeSalle; *D:* Rick Rosenthal; *M:* James Newton Howard. **VHS, Beta $14.95** LHV, WAR ♪½

Rustler's Hideout One of numerous westerns starring Crabbe as cowboy do-gooder Billy Carson, here plodding through standard histrionics against rustlers, a card-sharp, and a business fraud. *AKA:* Rustler's Roundup.
1944 60m/C Buster Crabbe, Al ''Fuzzy'' St. John, Charles ''Blackie'' King, John Merton, Lane Chandler, Hal Price, Edward Cassidy, Bud Osborne; *D:* Sam Newfield. **VHS, Beta** *GPV* ♂

Rustlers of Red Dog A 12-chapter western serial about Indian wars and cattle rustlers.
1935 235m/B Johnny Mack Brown, Raymond Hatton, Joyce Compton, Walter Miller, Harry Woods, William Desmond, Wally Wales, Chief Thundercloud, Art Mix, Bill Patton, Bud Osborne, Lafe McKee; *D:* Lew Landers. **VHS $24.95** *GPV* ♂♂½

Rustler's Paradise Carey seeks revenge on the man who stole his wife and daughter.
1935 59m/B Harry Carey Sr., Gertrude Messinger, Edmund Cobb; *D:* Harry Fraser. **VHS, Beta $19.95** *NOS* ♪

Rustler's Rhapsody A singing cowboy rides into a small western town and encounters all kinds of desperados in this earnest would-be satire of '40s B-movie westerns.
1985 (PG) 89m/C Tom Berenger, Patrick Wayne, G.W. Bailey, Andy Griffith, Marilu Henner; *D:* Hugh Wilson; *W:* Hugh Wilson; *M:* Stephen Dorff. **VHS, Beta $14.95** *PAR* ♂♂

Rustler's Valley Hopalong Cassidy is a ranch foreman who tries to save his employer from the clutches of a crooked lawyer. Pretty fun ordinary range-ridin' saga.
1937 59m/B William Boyd, George ''Gabby'' Hayes, Lee J. Cobb; *D:* Nate Watt. **VHS, Beta $19.95** *VYY* ♂♂

The Rutanga Tapes Soviet bloc country has representatives in Africa producing deadly chemicals used for war and a dissident has taped evidence of native deaths. Reporter babe Simpson wants an exclusive, Petersen wants the dissident, Libyan agents want the tapes, and you'll want to fast forward to the end.
1990 (R) 88m/C Henry Cele, Arnold Vosloo, Wilson Dunster, David Dukes, Susan Anspach; *D:* David Lister. **VHS** *NO* ♂½

The Rutherford County Line A tough small-town sheriff searches for the killer of his deputies.
1987 98m/C Earl Owensby; *D:* Thom McIntyre. **VHS, Beta $59.95** *MCA* ♂

The Ruthless Four Quartet of unlikely mining partners match wills and wits and battle the elements. Not-so-hot spaghetti western, with good lead from Heflin. *AKA:* Every Man For Himself; Each One For Himself; Sam Cooper's Gold; Each Man For Himself.
1970 97m/C Van Heflin, Klaus Kinski, Gilbert Roland, George Hilton; *D:* Giorgio Capitani. **VHS, Beta $24.95** *MON* ♂♂

Ruthless People DeVito and his mistress spend a romantic evening plotting his obnoxious wife's untimely demise. Before he can put his plan into action, he's delighted to discover she's been kidnapped by some very desperate people—who don't stand a chance with Bette. High farcical entertainment is a variation on the story ''The Ransom of Red Chief,'' by O. Henry.
1986 (R) 93m/C Bette Midler, Danny DeVito, Judge Reinhold, Helen Slater, Anita Morris, Bill Pullman; *D:* David Zucker, Jerry Zucker, Jim Abrahams; *W:* Dale Lanner; *M:* Michel Colombier. **VHS, Beta $19.95** *TOU* ♂♂♂

Ryan's Daughter Irish woman (Miles) marries a man she does not love and then falls for a shell-shocked British major who arrives during the 1916 Irish uprising to keep the peace. Not surprisingly, she is accused of betraying the local IRA gunrunners to her British lover. Tasteful melodrama with lots of pretty scenery that goes on a bit too long.
1970 (PG) 194m/C Sarah Miles, Robert Mitchum, John Mills, Trevor Howard, Christopher Jones, Leo McKern; *D:* David Lean; *W:* Robert Bolt; *M:* Maurice Jarre. Academy Awards '70: Best Cinematography, Best Supporting Actor (Mills); Nominations: Best Actress (Miles), Best Sound; National Board of Review Awards '70: 10 Best Films of the Year. **VHS, Beta $29.98** *MGM, BTV* ♂♂½

Ryder P.I. P.I Ryder and his sidekick fight crime and solve weird cases in the big city.
1988 (PG-13) 92m/C Bob Nelson. **VHS, Beta $19.99** *MOV, VTR* ♂♂½

Sabaka Adventure set in India about a scary religious cult. Karloff and the cast of stalwart ''B'' movie performers have fun with this one, and you should, too. *AKA:* The Hindu.
1955 81m/C Boris Karloff, Reginald Denny, Victor Jory, Lisa Howard, Jeanne Bates, Jay Novello, June Foray; *D:* Frank Ferrin. **VHS $16.95** *SNC* ♂♂

Sabotage Early Hitchcock thriller based on Conrad's ''The Secret Agent.'' A woman who works at a movie theater (Sidney) suspects her quiet husband (Homolka) might be the terrorist planting bombs around London. Numerous sly touches of the Master's signature humor. *AKA:* Woman Alone.
1936 81m/B Oscar Homolka, Sylvia Sidney, John Loder; *D:* Alfred Hitchcock; *W:* Charles Bennett. **VHS, Beta, 8mm $16.95** *SNC, NOS, HHT* ♂♂♂

Saboteur A man wrongly accused of sabotaging an American munitions plant during WWII sets out to find the traitor who framed him. Hitchcock uses his locations, including Boulder Dam, Radio City Music Hall, and the Statue of Liberty, to greatly intensify the action. Stunning resolution.
1942 108m/B Priscilla Lane, Robert Cummings, Otto Kruger, Alan Baxter, Norman Lloyd, Charles Halton; *D:* Alfred Hitchcock; *W:* Alfred Hitchcock, Peter Viertel. **VHS, Beta $19.95** *MCA* ♂♂♂

Sabre Jet Run-of-the-mill wartime drama of hubbies flying combat missions in Korea and long-suffering spouses on the home front.
1953 90m/C Robert Stack, Amanda Blake, Louis King; *D:* Louis King. **VHS, Beta** *NO* ♂♂

Sabrina Two wealthy brothers, one an aging businessman and the other a dissolute playboy, vie for the attention of their chauffeur's daughter, who has just returned from a French finishing school. Typically acerbic, in the Wilder manner, with Bogart and Holden cast interestingly against type. Based on the play ''Sabrina Fair'' by Samuel Taylor. *AKA:* Sabrina Fair.
1954 113m/B Audrey Hepburn, Humphrey Bogart, William Holden, Walter Hampden, Francis X. Bushman, John Williams, Martha Hyer, Marcel Dalio; *D:* Billy Wilder; *W:* Billy Wilder, Ernest Lehman. Academy Awards '54: Best Costume Design (B & W); Nominations: Best Actress (Hepburn), Best Art Direction/Set Decoration (B & W), Best Black and White Cinematography, Best Director (Wilder), Best Screenplay; Directors Guild of America Awards '54: Best Director (Wilder); Golden Globe Awards '55: Best Screenplay; National Board of Review Awards '54: 10 Best Films of the Year, Best Supporting Actor (Williams). **VHS, Beta $19.95** *PAR* ♂♂♂

S

Sacco & Vanzetti Two Italian immigrants and acknowledged anarchists are caught amidst communist witch-hunts and judicial negligence when they are tried and executed for murder in 1920s America. Based on the true-life case, considered by some a flagrant miscarriage of justice and political martyrdom, by others, honest American judicial-system proceedings. Well-made and acted. Joan Baez sings the title song ''The Ballad of Sacco and Vanzetti.'' *AKA:* Sacco e Vanzetti.
1971 (PG) 120m/C Gian Marie Volonte, Riccardo Cucciolla, Milo O'Shea, Cyril Cusack, Geoffrey Keen; *D:* Guiliano Montaldo; *M:* Ennio Morricone. Cannes Film Festival Nominations: cs 71: Best Film; Cannes Film Festival '71: Best Actor (Cucciolla). **VHS, Beta** *NO* ♂♂

The Sacketts Follows the adventures of three Tennessee brothers who migrate to the West after the Civil War. Based on two Louis L'Amour novels. Made for television.
1979 198m/C Jeffery Osterhage, Tom Selleck, Sam Elliott, Glenn Ford, Ben Johnson, Mercedes McCambridge, Ruth Roman, Jack Elam, Gilbert Roland; *D:* Robert Totten. **VHS, Beta $14.98** *WAR, HHE* ♂♂½

Sacred Ground A trapper and his pregnant Apache wife unknowingly build shelter on the Paiute Indians' sacred burial ground. When the wife dies in childbirth, the pioneer is forced to kidnap a Paiute woman who has just buried her own deceased infant. Average western drama.
1983 100m/C Tim McIntire, Jack Elam, L.Q. Jones, Mindi Miller; *D:* Charles B. Pierce; *W:* Charles B. Pierce. **VHS, Beta $59.98** *FOX* ♂♂

Sacred Mountain/White Flame Two short films starring Riefenstahl, featuring mostly fluid dance sequences and Teutonic mountain boy/girl plots. Silent.
1931 60m/B Leni Riefenstahl. **VHS, Beta $34.95** *FCT, GLV, MRV* ♂♂♂

The Sacrifice Tarkovsky's enigmatic final film, released after his death. Deals with a retired intellectual's spiritually symbolic efforts at self-sacrifice in order to save his family on the eve of a nuclear holocaust. Stunning cinematography by Sven Nykvist. Acclaimed, but sometimes slow going; not everyone will appreciate Tarkovsky's visionary spiritualism. In Swedish with English subtitles.
1986 (PG) 145m/C Erland Josephson, Susan Fleetwood, Valerie Mairesse, Allan Edwall, Gudrun Gisladottir, Sven Wollter, Filippa Franzen; *D:* Andrei Tarkovsky. **VHS, Beta $29.95** *ING, TPV* ♂♂♂

Sacrilege A nun and a nobleman engage in a hot love affair that fosters scandal, murder and revenge. Cynical use of religious theme masks otherwise ordinary sex/romance flick. Controversial Italian-made erotic drama.
1986 104m/C Myriem Roussel, Alessandro Gassman; *D:* Luciano Odorisio. **VHS, Beta $79.95** *PSM* ♂½

The Sad Sack A bumbling hero with a photographic memory winds up in Morocco as a member of the French Foreign Legion. Although a success at the box office, Lewis's second movie (without partner Dean Martin) seems jerky and out of sorts today. Based on the comic strip character by George Baker, but not effectively.
1957 98m/B Jerry Lewis, Phyllis Kirk, David Wayne, Peter Lorre, Gene Evans, Mary Treen; *D:* George Marshall; *M:* Burt Bacharach, Hal David. **VHS** *COL* ♂♂

Sadat Gossett, Jr. well plays his title role of Egyptian leader and Nobel Peace Prize winner, Anwar el Sadat. But the controversial life and peace efforts of the president (assassinated in 1981) are given a quick overview in this average drama. Made for television.
1983 (PG) 191m/C Louis Gossett Jr., John Rhys-Davies, Jeremy Kemp, Nehemiah Persoff, Madolyn Smith, Anne Heywood, Jeffrey Tambor, Barry Morse; **D:** Richard Michaels; **M:** Charles Bernstein. VHS **$59.95** COL ♫♫½

Saddle Buster A rodeo cowboy loses his nerve after being thrown by a tough horse, but gets it back again by the end of the hour. Actual rodeo footage is incorporated into this low-budget bronco saga.
1932 59m/B Tom Keene, Helen Foster, Charles Quigley, Marie Quillen, Robert Frazer, Charles "Slim" Whitaker; **D:** Fred Allen. VHS **$19.95** NOS, HEG ♫

Saddle Mountain Round-Up The Range Busters are on the trail again as they smoke out a murderer.
1941 61m/B Ray Corrigan, John "Dusty" King, Max Terhune. VHS, Beta **$19.95** NOS, DVT, RXM ♫

Sadie McKee A melodrama with Crawford as a maid searching for love in the big city. She falls for a self-destructive ne'er-do-well, marries an alcoholic millionaire, and eventually finds true love with the wealthy Tone (who would become Crawford's third husband). Professional acting and directing elevate the story.
1934 90m/B Joan Crawford, Franchot Tone, Gene Raymond, Edward Arnold; **D:** Clarence Brown. VHS **$19.98** BTV ♫♫♫

Sadie Thompson Swanson plays a harlot with a heart of gold, bawdy and good-natured, in the South Seas. A zealot missionary (Barrymore) arrives and falls in love with her. The last eight minutes of footage have been recreated by using stills and the original title cards, to replace the last reel which had decomposed. Remade as "Rain," "Dirty Gertie From Harlem," and "Miss Sadie Thompson." Based on W. Somerset Maugham's "Rain."
1928 97m/B Gloria Swanson, Lionel Barrymore, Raoul Walsh, Blanche Frederici, Charles Lane, James Marcus; **D:** Raoul Walsh. VHS **$29.95** KIV, MOV ♫♫♫

The Sadist Three teachers on their way to Dodger Stadium find themselves stranded at a roadside garage and terrorized by a snivelling lunatic. Tense and plausible. Cinematography by Vilmos Zsigmond. **AKA:** The Profile of Terror.
1963 95m/B Arch Hall Jr., Helen Hovey, Richard Alden, Marilyn Manning; **D:** James Landis; **W:** James Landis. Beta **$16.95** SNC, RHI ♫♫½

Safari 3000 "Playboy" writer is assigned to do a story on a three-day, 3,000 kilometer car race in Africa. Doesn't take itself too seriously, and neither should we. Dumb, dull, and disjointed.
1982 (PG) 91m/C Stockard Channing, David Carradine, Christopher Lee; **D:** Harry Hurwitz; **M:** Ernest Gold. VHS, Beta **$59.95** MGM ♫½

Saga of Death Valley Rogers battles a band of outlaws and discovers that their leader is his own brother. Exciting and likeable early Rogers western.
1939 56m/B Roy Rogers, George "Gabby" Hayes, Donald (Don "Red") Barry, Doris Day; **D:** Joseph Kane. VHS, Beta **$19.95** NOS, VDM, VCN ♫♫½

The Saga of the Draculas An aging vampire wishes to continue his bloodline and seeks to convert his niece's baby to his bloodsucking ways. **AKA:** Dracula Saga;

Dracula: The Bloodline Continues...; The Saga of Dracula.
1972 (R) 90m/C Narciso Ibanez Menta, Tina Sainz, Tony Isbert, Maria Koski, Cristina Suriani, Helga Line; **D:** Leon Klimovsky. VHS **$19.98** SNC ♫

Saga of the Vagabond Arranged by master director Akira Kurosawa. A band of ruthless outlaws career across a civil war-torn countryside. With English subtitles. **AKA:** Sengoku Gunto-Den.
1959 115m/C Toshiro Mifune, Michiyo Aratama; **D:** Toshio Sugie. VHS, Beta **$59.95** VDA ♫♫½

Sagebrush Law Western yarn has Holt playing a young man trying to clear the name of his bank president father. Barclay serves as the love interest and "Ukulele Ike" Edwards provides needed comic and music relief.
1943 56m/B Tim Holt, Cliff Edwards, Joan Barclay, Edward Cassidy, Karl Hackett, Roy Barcroft, Ernie Adams; **D:** Sam Nelson; **W:** Bennett Cohen. VHS **$19.99** MOV ♫½

Sagebrush Trail Wayne's second-ever western, complete with all sorts of tumbleweed and white-hat cliches. Our hero is wrongly accused of killin' a man, and busts out of the hoosegow to clear his name. Interesting plot twists makes for fun, compelling viewing.
1933 53m/B John Wayne, Yakima Canutt, Wally Wales; **D:** Armand Schaefer. VHS **$8.95** CNG, REP, NOS ♫♫♫

Sahara A British-American unit must fight the Germans for their survival in the Libyan desert during WWII. Plenty of action and suspense combined with good performances makes this one a step above the usual war movie.
1943 97m/B Humphrey Bogart, Dan Duryea, Bruce (Herman Brix) Bennett, Lloyd Bridges, Rex Ingram, J. Carroll Naish, Richard Nugent, Miklos Rozsa; **D:** Zoltan Korda. VHS, Beta **$9.95** COL ♫♫♫

Sahara Disappointing "Perils of Pauline" type adventure. Shields disguises herself as a man (sure) to complete a race across the desert in honor of her late father, and a sheik captures her.
1983 (PG) 111m/C Brooke Shields, Lambert Wilson, Horst Buchholz, John Rhys-Davies, Ronald Lacey, John Mills, Steve Forrest, Perry Lang, Cliff Potts; **D:** Andrew V. McLaglen; **W:** James R. Silke; **M:** Ennio Morricone. VHS, Beta **$14.95** MGM Woof!

Saigon Commandos Commandos, on the eve of the fall of Saigon in the 1970s, attempt to prevent heroin dealers from toppling the already-shaky government. So-so war/action flick.
1988 (R) 84m/C Richard Young, P.J. Soles, John Allen Nelson, Jimi B Jr.; **D:** Clark Henderson. VHS, Beta **$79.95** MED ♫

Saigon: Year of the Cat A made for British television drama about an American ambassador, a CIA operative, and a British bank clerk who try to leave Saigon in 1974 before the Vietcong enter the city.
1987 106m/C Frederic Forrest, E.G. Marshall, Judi Dench; **D:** Stephen Frears; **W:** David Hare; **M:** George Fenton. VHS, Beta **$89.99** HBO ♫

Sailing Along British musical about a young starlet who sacrifices her career for true love.
1938 80m/B Jessie Matthews, Barry Mackay, Jack Whiting, Roland Young, Noel Madison, Athene Seyler, Patrick Barr; **D:** Sonnie Hale. VHS **$29.95** FCT ♫♫

Sailor-Made Man/Grandma's Boy Silent comedy shorts. In "A Sailor-Made Man" (1921) Lloyd joins the Navy. As shy "Grandma's Boy" (1922), he is given courage and good advice to win the hand of a girl and defeat a bully.
192? 83m/B Harold Lloyd. VHS, Beta TLF ♫♫♫

The Sailor Who Fell from Grace with the Sea Perverse tale of a disillusioned sailor who rejects the sea for the love of a lonely young widow and her troubled son. Graphic sexual scenes. Based on the novel by Yukio Mishima, the film suffers from the transition of Japanese culture to an English setting.
1976 (R) 105m/C Sarah Miles, Kris Kristofferson, Jonathan Kahn, Margo Cunningham; **D:** Lewis John Carlino. VHS, Beta FOX, SUE ♫♫

The Saint Moore is Simon Templar, Leslie Charteris' mysterious British detective/hero in this adventure tale that takes him to Naples. Revival of and improvement on earlier movie series, and based on the very popular British television show.
1968 98m/C Roger Moore, Ian Hendry. VHS **$59.98** FOX ♫♫

St. Benny the Dip Three con-men evade police by posing as clergymen, and end up going straight after a series of adventures in a skid row mission. Funny in parts but extremely predictable. Still, good for a few laughs. **AKA:** Escape If You Can.
1951 80m/B Dick Haymes, Nina Foch, Roland Young, Lionel Stander, Freddie Bartholomew; **D:** Edgar G. Ulmer. VHS **$19.95** NOS, FCT, HEG ♫♫

St. Elmo's Fire Seven Georgetown graduates confront adult problems during their first post-graduate year. Reminiscent of "The Big Chill," but a weak story wastes lots of talent and time.
1985 (R) 110m/C Rob Lowe, Demi Moore, Andrew McCarthy, Judd Nelson, Ally Sheedy, Emilio Estevez, Mare Winningham, Martin Balsam, Joyce Van Patten, Andie MacDowell, Anna Maria Horsford, Jenny Wright; **D:** Joel Schumacher; **W:** Joel Schumacher; **M:** David Foster. VHS, Beta **$12.95** COL ♫♫½

St. Helen's, Killer Volcano A young man and an old man develop a deep friendship amid the devastation, fear, greed, and panic surrounding the eruption of the Mt. St. Helen's volcano. Based on the true story of Harry Truman (!), who refused to leave his home. Pretty good.
1982 95m/C Art Carney, David Huffman, Cassie Yates, Bill McKinney, Ron O'Neal, Albert Salmi, Cesare Danova; **D:** Ernie Pintoff. VHS, Beta **$69.95** VES ♫♫½

Saint in London The Saint investigates a gang trying to pass counterfeit banknotes. The third in "The Saint" series.
1939 72m/B George Sanders, Sally Gray; **D:** John Paddy Carstairs. VHS, Beta MED ♫♫

The Saint in New York The Saint, Simon Templar, turns Robin Hood to help the Civic Committee clean up a gang of desperados. First of "The Saint" series.
1938 71m/B Louis Hayward, Kay Sutton, Jack Carson, Charles Halton; **D:** Ben Holmes. VHS, Beta MED ♫♫

St. Ives Former police reporter Bronson agrees to recover some stolen ledgers and finds himself dealing with betrayal and murder. Bisset is sultry and the tale is slickly told, but dumb. Co-stars Travanti, later of TV's "Hill Street Blues."

1976 (PG) 94m/C Charles Bronson, Jacqueline Bisset, John Houseman, Harry Guardino, Maximilian Schell, Harris Yulin, Elisha Cook Jr., Daniel J. Travanti; **D:** J. Lee Thompson. **VHS, Beta $59.95** *WAR* ✗✗

Saint Jack The story of a small-time pimp with big dreams working the pleasure palaces of late-night Singapore. Engrossing and pleasant. Based on Paul Theroux's novel.
1979 (R) 112m/C Ben Gazzara, Denholm Elliott, Joss Ackland, George Lazenby; **D:** Peter Bogdanovich; **W:** Peter Bogdanovich. **VHS, Beta $69.98** *LIV, VES* ✗✗✗

Saint Joan Film of the George Bernard Shaw play, adapted by Graham Greene, about the French Maid of Orleans at her trial. Otto Preminger went on a nationwide talent hunt for his leading actress and chose the inexperienced Seberg (her screen debut). A good thing for her career, but not for this ill-begotten, overambitious opus. Seberg doesn't fit. Also available colorized.
1957 131m/B Jean Seberg, Anton Walbrook, Richard Widmark, John Gielgud, Harry Andrews, Felix Aylmer, Richard Todd; **D:** Otto Preminger. **VHS, Beta $19.98** *WAR* ✗✗

The Saint of Fort Washington Sweetly naive and schizophrenic Matthew (Dillon) is homeless and through government screw-ups is sent to the Fort Washington Armory, which houses more than 700 homeless men. Harassed by others, Matthew is befriended by Jerry, a kindly Vietnam vet, who tries to care for him. Subject is taken seriously but slips into mawkishness; good performances by the leads.
1993 (R) 104m/C Danny Glover, Matt Dillon, Rick Aviles, Nina Siemaszko, Ving Rhames, Joe Seneca; **D:** Tim Hunter; **W:** Lyle Kessler; **M:** James Newton Howard. **VHS, Beta** *WAR* ✗✗ 1/2

The Saint Strikes Back Sanders debuts as the mysterious Simon Templar in this competent series. On a trip to San Francisco, the Saint aims to clear the name of a murdered man. The second in the series.
1939 67m/B George Sanders, Wendy Barrie, Jonathan Hale, Jerome Cowan, Neil Hamilton, Barry Fitzgerald, Edward Gargan, Robert Strange; **D:** John Farrow. **VHS $19.95** *MOV* ✗✗

The Saint Strikes Back: Criminal Court A suspense double feature: The Saint helps a daughter clear the name of her murdered father, a San Francisco police commissioner in ''The Saint Strikes Back,'' and a young lawyer becomes involved in murder in ''Criminal Court.''
1946 127m/B George Sanders, Wendy Barrie, Barry Fitzgerald, Tom Conway, Steve Brodie; **D:** John Farrow. **VHS, Beta $34.95** *RKO, TTC* ✗✗

The Saint Takes Over More adventures with the British mystery man; this time involving racetrack gambling. An original story that wasn't based on a Leslie Charteris novel as were the others.
1940 69m/B George Sanders, Jonathan Hale, Wendy Barrie, Paul Guilfoyle, Morgan Conway, Cy Kendall; **D:** Jack Hively. **VHS** *MOV* ✗✗

The St. Valentine's Day Massacre Corman's big studio debut recreates the events leading to one of the most violent gangland shootouts in modern history: the bloodbath between Chicago's Capone and Moran gangs on February 14, 1929. Uninspired and unremittingly violent. Watch for Jack Nicholson's bit part.
1967 100m/C Jason Robards Jr., Ralph Meeker, Jean Hale, Joseph Campanella, Bruce Dern, Clint Ritchie, Richard Bakalayan, George Segal; **D:** Roger Corman. **VHS, Beta $14.98** *FOX, FCT* ✗✗ 1/2

The Saint's Double Trouble Leslie Charteris' suave detective becomes embroiled in another mystery, this one involving jewel thieves. Sanders plays a dual role as the hero and the crook. The fourth in the series.
1940 68m/B George Sanders, Helene Whitney, Jonathan Hale, Bela Lugosi, Donald MacBride, John Hamilton; **D:** Jack Hively. **VHS** *MED* ✗✗

The Saint's Vacation/The Narrow Margin A mystery double feature. In ''The Saint's Vacation,'' Simon Templar prevents a valuable secret from getting into the wrong hands, and in ''The Narrow Margin,'' strange things happen to a detective when he takes a train ride with a witness to Chicago. Sinclair took over the sleuth's role from George Sanders in this series.
1952 148m/B Hugh Sinclair, Sally Gray, Charles McGraw, Marie Windsor, Jacqueline White. **VHS, Beta $34.95** *RKO, TTC* ✗✗

Sakharov The true story of the Russian physicist who designed the H-bomb and then rose to lead the Soviet dissident movement and win the Nobel Peace Prize. Robards is excellent. Made for cable; topical and powerful.
1984 120m/C Glenda Jackson, Jason Robards Jr., Michael Bryant; **D:** Jack Gold; **M:** Carl Davis. **VHS, Beta $69.95** *PSM* ✗✗

Sakura Killers Killer Ninjas steal a valuable gene-splicing formula and are hunted down by an American colonel.
1986 87m/C Chuck Connors, Mike Kelly, Brian Wong, Thomas Lung; **D:** Richard Ward. **VHS, Beta $59.98** *FOX* ✗

Salaam Bombay! A gritty film about a child street beggar in the slums of Bombay trying to raise enough money to return to his mother's house in the country. The boy experiences every variety of gutter life imaginable, from humiliation to love. Moving and searing. Filmed on location, with actual homeless children; Nair's first feature. In Hindi with subtitles.
1988 114m/C Shafiq Syed, Hansa Vithal, Chanda Sharma, Nana Patekar, Aneeta Kanwar, Sarfuddin Quarassi, Raju Barnad, Raghubir Yadav; **D:** Mira Nair; **W:** Sooni Taraporevala; **M:** L. Subramaniam. **VHS, Beta** *NO* ✗✗✗

The Salamander A French detective tries to find the assassin of the leaders of a neo-fascist underground movement in Italy and follows clues that lead back to WWII. Disappointing, overwrought adaptation of a Morris West novel.
1982 (R) 101m/C Franco Nero, Anthony Quinn, Martin Balsam, Sybil Danning, Christopher Lee, Cleavon Little, Paul Smith, Claudia Cardinale, Eli Wallach; **D:** Peter Zinner; **M:** Jerry Goldsmith. **VHS, Beta $59.95** *NLC* ✗ 1/2

Salammbo An early silent epic in the grand Italian tradition. Loosely based on Flaubert's novel about ancient Carthage.
1914 49m/B Ernesto Pagani; **D:** Giovanni Pastrone. **VHS, Beta $49.95** *FCT* ✗✗ 1/2

Salem's Lot Based on Stephen King's novel about a sleepy New England village which is infiltrated by evil. A mysterious antiques dealer takes up residence in a forbidding hilltop house—and it becomes apparent that a vampire is on the loose. Generally creepy; Mason is good, but Soul only takes up space in the lead as a novelist returning home. Also available in the original television miniseries version at 190 minutes on two cassettes. **AKA:** Blood Thirst.
1979 (PG) 112m/C David Soul, James Mason, Lance Kerwin, Bonnie Bedelia, Lew Ayres, Bo Fanders, Elisha Cook Jr., Reggie Nalder, Fred Willard, Kenneth McMillan, Marie Windsor; **D:** Tobe Hooper. **VHS, Beta $14.95** *WAR* ✗✗ 1/2

Sallah A North African Jew takes his family to Israel in 1949 in hopes of making his fortune. He finds himself in a transit camp and runs up against the local bureaucracy in a quest for permanent housing as well as the European work ethic. Amusing and enjoyable satire. In Hebrew with English subtitles.
1963 105m/B Chaim Topol, Geula Noni, Gila Almagor, Arik Einstein, Shraga Friedman, Esther Greenberg; **D:** Ephraim Kishon. Academy Awards '64 Nominations: Best Foreign Language Film; Golden Globe Awards '65: Best Foreign Film. **VHS, Beta $79.95** *MOV, ERG, NCJ* ✗✗✗

Sally of the Sawdust W. C. Fields' first silent feature; he is a carnival barker who adopts a young woman. Allows him to demonstrate his talent for juggling, conning customers, and car chasing. Interesting movie caught director Griffith on the decline and Fields on the verge of stardom. Remade as a talkie in 1936 entitled ''Poppy.'' Includes musical score.
1925 124m/B W.C. Fields, Carol Dempster, Alfred Lunt; **D:** D.W. Griffith. **VHS, Beta $19.95** *NOS, VYY, CCB* ✗✗ 1/2

Salmonberries East German Roswitha (Zech) is devastated when her lover is killed trying to scale the Berlin Wall. She manages to escape and finds herself stuck in a remote Eskimo community in Alaska where she becomes involved with a sexually ambivalent woman (lang in her film debut).
1991 94m/C Rosel Zech, k.d. lang; **D:** Percy Adlon. **VHS $69.95** *FCT* ✗✗

Salo, or the 120 Days of Sodom Extremely graphic film follows sixteen children (eight boys and eight girls) who are kidnapped by a group of men in Fascist Italy. On reaching a secluded villa in the woods, the children are told to follow strict rules and then subjected to incredible acts of sadomasochism, rape, violence, and mutilation. This last film of Pasolini's was taken from a novel by the Marquis de Sade. Viewers are strongly recommended to use their utmost discretion when watching this controversial film. In Italian with English subtitles.
1975 117m/C Giorgio Cataldi, Umberto P. Quinavalle, Paolo Bonacelli; **D:** Pier Paolo Pasolini; **M:** Ennio Morricone. **VHS $89.95** *ING, FCT, HHE* ✗✗

Salome Garish silent rendition of Oscar Wilde's scandalous tale.
1922 54m/B Alla Nazimova, Rose Dione, Mitchell Lewis, Earl Schenck; **D:** Charles Bryant. **VHS, Beta $14.95** *GPV, FCT, VYY* ✗✗ 1/2

Salome An over-costumed version of Oscar Wilde's Biblical story about King Herod's lascivious stepdaughter who danced her way to stardom and tried to save the life of John the Baptist. Talented cast can't overcome hokey script.
1953 103m/C Rita Hayworth, Stewart Granger, Charles Laughton, Judith Anderson, Cedric Hardwicke, Basil Sydney, Maurice Schwartz; **D:** William Dieterle; **M:** George Duning. **VHS, Beta $19.95** *COL, CCB* ✗✗

Salome An updated and graphic version of the Oscar Wilde historical fantasy about the temptress Salome who helped topple Herod's Biblical kingdom with her dance of the Seven Veils. Photographed by Pasqualino De Santis. Not really a remake of the 1953 film since this is set during the 1940s.
1985 (R) 100m/C Jo Ciampa, Tomas Milian, Pamela Salem; **D:** Claude D'Anna. **VHS, Beta $79.95** *MGM* ✗ 1/2

Salome/Queen Elizabeth Two famous silent shorts: ''Salome,'' (1923), an atmospheric adaptation of Oscar Wilde's tale, with sets designed after Aubrey Beardsley; and ''Queen Elizabeth,'' (1912), Bern-

hardt's famous, and famously stilted, singular film appearance.
1923 91m/B Alla Nazimova, Sarah Bernhardt, Lou Tellegen, Mitchell Lewis, Nigel de Brulier; **D:** Charles Bryant, Henri Desfontaines, Louis Mercanton. **VHS, Beta, 8mm** $29.95 *VYY* ✕✕½

Salome, Where She Danced Set during the Franco-Prussian war. A European dancer helps an American reporter in a spy scheme. She eventually relocates to America and becomes the toast of San Francisco. Somehow, De Carlo managed to spring from this ridiculous camp outing to stardom.
1945 90m/C Yvonne De Carlo, Rod Cameron, David Bruce, Walter Slezak; **D:** Charles Lamont. **VHS, Beta** $19.95 *NOS, BAR, DVT* ✕

Salome's Last Dance A theatrical, set-surreal adaptation of the Wilde story. Typically flamboyant Russell.
1988 (R) 113m/C Glenda Jackson, Stratford Johns, Nickolas Grace, Douglas Hodge, Imogen Millais Scott; **D:** Ken Russell; **W:** Ken Russell. **VHS, Beta** $89.98 *LIV, IME, VES* ✕✕

Salsa An auto repairman would rather dance in this "Dirty Dancing" clone. Rosa was formerly a member of the pop group Menudo.
1988 (PG) 97m/C Robby Rosa, Rodney Harvey, Magali Alvarado, Miranda Garrison, Moon Orona; **D:** Boaz Davidson. **VHS, Beta** $14.95 *MGM, CAN* ✕✕

Salt of the Earth Finally available in this country after being suppressed for thirty years, this controversial film was made by a group of blacklisted filmmakers during the McCarthy era. It was deemed anti-American, communist propaganda. The story deals with the anti-Hispanic racial strife that occurs in a New Mexico zinc mine when union workers organize a strike.
1954 94m/B Rosaura Revueltas, Will Geer, David Wolfe; **D:** Herbert Biberman. **VHS, Beta, CDV** $19.95 *IHF, NOS, VYG* ✕✕✕½

Salty A lovable but mischievous sea lion manages to complicate two brothers' lives when they volunteer to help a friend renovate a Florida marina, which is threatened by a mortgage foreclosure. Straightforward and inoffensive tale.
1973 93m/C Clint Howard, Mark Slade, Nina Foch; **D:** Ricou Browning. **VHS, Beta** *NO* ✕✕

Salut l'Artiste Two bad actors try to make it in the industry. Delightfully funny with an excellent cast, especially Mastroianni. Snide and irreverant, yet loving and comic look at the world of acting. In French with English subtitles.
1974 96m/C Marcello Mastroianni, Jean Rochefort, Francoise Fabian, Carla Gravina; **D:** Yves Robert; **M:** Vladimir Cosma. **VHS** $79.95 *FCT, ING, CVC* ✕✕✕

Salute John Citizen The life of an average English family during the early days of WWII is depicted, focusing on the deprivation and horror of the Nazi blitzkrieg.
1942 74m/B Peggy Cummins, Stanley Holloway, Dinah Sheridan, Jimmy Hanley. **VHS, Beta** $19.98 *VYY* ✕✕

Salute to the "King of the Cowboys," Roy Rogers Glimpses of Roy from song clips, home movies, trailers, out-takes, and other sources.
197? 60m/B Roy Rogers. **VHS, Beta** $29.95 *DVT* ✕✕✕

Salvador Photo journalist Richard Boyle's unflinching and sordid adventures in war-torn El Salvador. Boyle (Woods) must face the realities of social injustice. Belushi and Woods are hard to like, but excellent. Early critical success for director Stone.
1986 (R) 123m/C James Woods, James Belushi, John Savage, Michael Murphy, Elpidia Carrillo, Cynthia Gibb; **D:** Oliver Stone; **W:** Oliver Stone; **M:** Georges Delerue. Academy Awards '86 Nominations: Best Actor (Woods), Best Original Screenplay; Independent Spirit Awards '87: Best Actor (Woods). **VHS, Beta** $29.98 *LIV, IME, VES* ✕✕✕½

Salvation! A mean-tempered, timely satire about a money-hungry television evangelist beset by a family of fervent, equally money-hungry followers, who proceed to cheat, seduce and blackmail him. Occasionally quite funny, but sloppy and predictable. Underground director Beth B's first above-ground film. **AKA:** Salvation! Have You Said Your Prayers Today?.
1987 (R) 80m/C Stephen McHattie, Exene Cervenka, Dominique Davalos, Viggo Mortensen, Rockets Redglare, Billy Bastiani; **D:** Beth B; **W:** Beth B. **Beta** *NO* ✕✕½

The Salzburg Connection A list of Nazi collaborators is discovered in Austria. A vacationing American lawyer is caught up in the battle for its possession. Filmed on location, it's still a poor, cheesy adaptation of the Helen MacInnes novel.
1972 (PG) 94m/C Barry Newman, Anna Karina, Klaus Maria Brandauer, Karen Jensen, Lee H. Katzin; **D:** Lee H. Katzin. **VHS, Beta** $59.98 *FOX* ✕½

Samantha Twenty-one year-old Samantha discovers she was left on her parents' doorstep in a basket and decides to find out where she came from. Good cast and high charm quotient help this film along.
1992 (PG) 101m/C Martha Plimpton, Dermot Mulroney, Hector Elizondo, Mary Kay Place, Ione Skye; **D:** Steven La Rocque; **W:** John Golden, Steven La Rocque. **VHS, Beta** $89.95 *ACA* ✕✕½

Samar A liberal penal colony commandant rebels against his superiors by leading his prisoners through the Philippine jungles to freedom. Original action drama with an interesting premise.
1962 (PG) 89m/C George Montgomery, Gilbert Roland, Joan O'Brien, Ziva Rodann; **D:** George Montgomery. **VHS, Beta** $19.95 *NOS* ✕✕½

Samaritan: The Mitch Snyder Story Effective television drama based upon the true story of Vietnam vet Mitch Snyder (Sheen) who battles various government agencies and ultimately fasts to call national attention to his crusade against homelessness. Tyson appears as bag lady; Snyder eventually committed suicide.
1986 90m/C Martin Sheen, Roxanne Hart, Joe Seneca, Stan Shaw, Cicely Tyson; **D:** Richard T. Heffron. **VHS, Beta** $14.95 *FRH* ✕✕✕

Same Time, Next Year A chance meeting between an accountant and a housewife results in a sometimes tragic, always sentimental 25-year affair in which they meet only one weekend each year. Well-cast leads carry warm, touching story based on the Broadway play by Bernard Slade.
1978 119m/C Ellen Burstyn, Alan Alda; **D:** Robert Mulligan; **M:** Marvin Hamlisch. Academy Awards '78 Nominations: Best Actress (Burstyn), Best Adapted Screenplay, Best Cinematography, Best Song ("The Last Time I Felt Like This"); Golden Globe Awards '79: Best Actress—Musical/Comedy (Burstyn). **VHS, Beta** $14.98 *MCA* ✕✕✕

Sammy & Rosie Get Laid An unusual social satire about a sexually liberated couple living in London whose lives are thrown into turmoil by the arrival of the man's father - a controversial politician in India. Provides a confusing look at sexual and class collisions. From the makers of "My Beautiful Launderette."
1987 97m/C Shashi Kapoor, Frances Barber, Claire Bloom, Ayub Khan Din, Roland Gift, Wendy Gazelle, Meera Syal; **D:** Stephen Frears; **W:** Hanif Kureishi; **M:** Stanley Myers. **VHS, Beta** $79.95 *LHV, WAR* ✕✕✕

Sammy, the Way-Out Seal Two young boys bring a mischievous seal to live in their beach house and try to keep it a secret from their parents. Disney in its early '60s phase.
1962 89m/C Michael McGreevey, Billy Mumy, Patricia Barry, Robert Culp; **D:** Norman Tokar. **VHS, Beta** $69.95 *DIS* ✕✕

Sam's Son Sentimental, autobiographical tale about how a young man's athletic prowess opens the door for an acting career in Hollywood. Good performance by Wallach as the boy's father. Self-indulgent, though entertaining.
1984 (PG) 107m/C Eli Wallach, Anne Jackson, Timothy Patrick Murphy, Hallie Todd, James Karen, Allan Hayes, Joanna Lee, Michael Landon; **D:** Michael Landon; **W:** Michael Landon. **VHS, Beta** $59.95 *WOV* ✕✕

Samson Samson attempts to keep wits and hair about him.
1961 90m/C Brad Harris, Brigitte Corey, Alan Steel, Serge Gainsbourg, Mara Berni; **D:** Gianfranco Parolini. **VHS** $14.99 *SNC, MRV* ✕

Samson Against the Sheik Samson survives long enough to battle a sheik in the Middle Ages.
1962 ?m/C Ed Fury. **VHS, Beta** $16.95 *SNC* ✕

Samson and Delilah The biblical story of the vindictive Delilah, who after being rejected by the mighty Samson, robbed him of his strength by shearing his curls. Delivered in signature DeMille style. Wonderfully fun and engrossing. Mature is excellent.
1950 128m/C Victor Mature, Hedy Lamarr, Angela Lansbury, George Sanders, Henry Wilcoxon, Olive Deering, Fay Holden; **D:** Cecil B. DeMille. Academy Awards '50: Best Art Direction/Set Decoration (Color), Best Costume Design (Color); Nominations: Best Color Cinematography, Best Original Score. **VHS, Beta** $29.95 *PAR* ✕✕✕

Samson and Delilah A made for television version of the Biblical romance, semi-based on DeMille's 1950 version. Original Samson (Mature) plays Samson's father. Too long but inoffensive; see the DeMille version instead.
1984 95m/C Antony Hamilton, Belinda Bauer, Max von Sydow, Jose Ferrer, Victor Mature, Maria Schell; **D:** Lee Philips; **M:** Maurice Jarre. **VHS, Beta** $9.99 *PSM* ✕✕

Samson and His Mighty Challenge In this rarely seen muscle epic, Hercules, Maciste, Samson and Ursus all take part in a battle royale.
1964 ?m/C Alan Steel. **VHS, Beta** $16.95 *SNC* ✕

Samson and the 7 Miracles of the World This time the hero known as Maciste (renamed Samson for Americans) is in the 13th century battling brutal Tartar warlords. The very Earth itself shakes when our hero goes into battle! **AKA:** Maciste Alla Corte Del Gran Khan; Maciste at the Court of the Great Khan; Goliath and the Golden City.
1962 80m/C Gordon Scott, Yoko Tani, Gabriele Antonini, Leonardo Severini, Valeri Inkizhinov, Helene Chanel; **D:** Riccardo (Robert Hampton) Freda; **M:** Les Baxter. **VHS, Beta** $16.95 *SNC* ✕✕

Samson in the Wax Museum Masked Mexican wrestling hero Santo (here called Samson) does battle with a scientist who has discovered a way to make wax

monsters come to life. **AKA:** Santo en el Museo de Cera; Santo in the Wax Museum.
1963 92m/B Santo, Claudio Brook, Rueben Rojo, Norma Mora, Roxana Bellini; **D:** Alfonso Corona Blake. **VHS $19.98** SNC, HHT ₰₰ ½

Samson vs. the Vampire Women
Santo (here called Samson) the masked hero and athlete, battles the forces of darkness as a horde of female vampires attempt to make an unsuspecting girl their next queen.
1961 89m/B Santo, Lorena Velasquez, Jaime Fernandez, Maria Duval; **D:** Alfonso Corona Blake. **VHS, Beta $19.98** SNC, HHT ₰₰ ½

Samurai
Truly bad spy-exploitation film about a Japanese orphan who was raised in America, turns traitor, and helps plot the invasion of California.
1945 ?m/C Paul Fung, Luke Chan, David Chow. **VHS $16.95** SNC, TPV ₰

The Samurai
An unstoppable ninja warrior seeks revenge against a sadistic clan of martial arts experts for the murder of his fiance's father. He will settle for nothing less than the decapitation of those who have destroyed his life.
19?? 90m/C Chung Wong, Tien Pang. **VHS $49.95** OCE ₰

Samurai 1: Musashi Miyamoto
The first installment in the film version of Musashi Miyamoto's life, as he leaves his 17th century village as a warrior in a local civil war only to return beaten and disillusioned. Justly award-winning. In Japanese with English subtitles.
1955 92m/C Toshiro Mifune; **D:** Hiroshi Inagaki. **VHS, Beta $19.95** NLC, SUE, ING ₰₰₰ ½

Samurai 2: Duel at Ichijoji Temple
Inagaki's second film depicting the life of Musashi Miyamoto, the 17th century warrior, who wandered the disheveled landscape of feudal Japan looking for glory and love. In Japanese with English subtitles.
1955 102m/C Toshiro Mifune; **D:** Hiroshi Inagaki. **VHS, Beta $19.95** NLC, SUE, ING ₰₰₰ ½

Samurai 3: Duel at Ganryu Island
The final film of Inagaki's trilogy, in which Musashi Miyamoto confronts his lifelong enemy in a climactic battle. Depicts Miyamoto's spiritual awakening and realization that love and hatred exist in all of us. In Japanese with English subtitles.
1956 102m/C Toshiro Mifune, Koji Tsurata; **D:** Hiroshi Inagaki. **VHS, Beta $29.98** SUE, ING, NLC ₰₰₰ ½

Samurai Blood, Samurai Guts
The wooden hag offers The Book of 9 Yin to the man who will retrieve the Devil Knight's head. Yet the man who would do so will risk his very blood, guts, and brains.
19?? 90m/C Kong Pun, Ng Pun, Lee Shue. **VHS, Beta $29.95** OCE ₰

Samurai Cowboy
Sato (Go) is a successful Japanese businessman who worships the American western ideal so he decides to give up the rat race by moving to Running Moose, Montana, and buying a cattle ranch. Talk about culture shock! Inoffensive fish-out-of-water comedy. Go is a popular singer in his native Japan.
1993 101m/C Hiromi Go, Catherine Mary Stewart, Robert Conrad, Conchata Ferrell, Matt McCoy; **D:** Michael Keusch; **W:** Michael Keusch; **M:** Osamu Kitajima. **VHS $92.95** MNC ₰₰

Samurai Death Bells
Gory samurai sword fighting flick full of conspiracy and deceit.
19?? 90m/C Chung Wong, Lee Le Le, Miao Ko Sou. **VHS, Beta $49.95** OCE ₰

Samurai Reincarnation
After the Shogunate government kills 18,000 Christian rioters in the revolt of 1638, and publicly beheads the leader Shiro Amakusa, Shiro reincarnates during a monstrous thunderstorm. Consumed with hatred, he discards the teachings of Jesus Christ and seeks revenge. In Japanese with English subtitles.
1981 122m/C D: Kinji Fukasaku. **VHS $59.95** FCT ₰

Samurai Sword of Justice
A pair of gruelling samurai warriors seek and destroy their evil nemesis Chi. When they finally meet up with him, you can bet some guts and brains will be splattered about.
19?? 90m/C Kam Hon, Wong Kuan Hung, Mo Si Shing, Lee Shue. **VHS, Beta $49.95** OCE ₰

San Antonio
A bad girl working in a dance hall turns over a new leaf on meeting the good guy. Trite plot, but good production.
1945 105m/C Errol Flynn, Alexis Smith, S.Z. Sakall, Victor Francen, Florence Bates, John Litel, Paul Kelly; **D:** David Butler. **VHS, Beta $19.98** MGM, FCT, MLB ₰₰

San Demetrio, London
Set in 1940, the crew of a crippled tanker endures harrowing situations to reach port. A decent anti-war movie in its time, it's now showing its age. Based on a true story, the plot sags with unbelievable scenes and holes on the plot side.
1947 76m/B Walter Fitzgerald, Mervyn Johns, Ralph Michael, Robert Beatty, Charles Victor, Frederick Piper; **D:** Charles Frend. **VHS $19.95** NOS ₰₰ ½

San Fernando Valley
Also called "San Fernando". Another lawman-in-evil-town epic. Rogers received his first on-screen kiss in 1944's biggest western. Fairly typical, pleasant cowboy tale.
1944 54m/B Roy Rogers, Dale Evans. **VHS, Beta $19.95** NOS, DVT ₰₰

San Francisco
The San Francisco Earthquake of 1906 serves as the background for a romance between an opera singer and a Barbary Coast saloon owner. Somewhat overdone but gripping tale of passion and adventure in the West. Wonderful special effects. Finale consists of historic earthquake footage. Also available colorized. ♫San Francisco; A Heart That's Free; Would You?; Air des Bijoux; Sempre Libera.
1936 116m/B Jeanette MacDonald, Clark Gable, Spencer Tracy, Jack Holt, Jessie Ralph, Al Shear; **D:** Woodbridge S. Van Dyke; **W:** Anita Loos. Academy Awards '36: Best Sound; Nominations: Best Actor (Tracy), Best Director (Van Dyke), Best Picture, Best Story. **VHS, Beta $19.98** MGM ₰₰₰ ½

Sanctuary of Fear
A priest in New York City helps an actress subjected to a series of terrorizing incidents. Uninspired would-be TV pilot based on Chesterton's "Father Brown" series. **AKA:** Girl in the Park.
1979 98m/C George Hearn, Barnard Hughes, Kay Lenz, Michael McGuire, Robert Schenkkan, David Rasche, Fred Gwynne, Elizabeth Wilson; **D:** John Llewellyn Moxey. **VHS, Beta $29.98** FOX ₰ ½

Sand and Blood
A young matador who wishes to escape poverty and a young, cultivated doctor who despises bullfighting, meet and eventually become friends. A woman enters the picture and completes the love triangle. Widely praised by critics. Interesting and moving. In French with English subtitles. **AKA:** Blood and Sand; De Sable et de Sang.

1987 101m/C Sami Frey, Andre Dussollier, Clementine Celarie, Patrick Catalifo, Maria Casares, Catherine Rouvel; **D:** Jeanne Labrune; **W:** Jeanne Labrune. **VHS, Beta $29.95** NYF, FCT, ING ₰₰ ½

The Sand Pebbles
An American expatriate engineer, transferred to a gunboat on the Yangtze River in 1926, falls in love with a missionary teacher. As he becomes aware of the political climate of American imperialism, he finds himself at odds with his command structure; the treatment of this issue can be seen as commentary on the situation in Vietnam at the time of the film's release. Considered one of McQueen's best performances, blending action and romance.
1966 193m/C Steve McQueen, Richard Crenna, Richard Attenborough, Candice Bergen, Marayat Andriane, Gavin MacLeod, Larry Gates, Mako, Simon Oakland; **D:** Robert Wise; **W:** Robert Anderson; **M:** Jerry Goldsmith. Academy Awards '66 Nominations: Best Actor (McQueen), Best Art Direction/Set Decoration (Color), Best Color Cinematography, Best Film Editing, Best Picture, Best Sound, Best Supporting Actor (Mako), Best Original Score; Golden Globe Awards '67: Best Supporting Actor (Attenborough). **VHS, Beta $29.98** FOX, FCT ₰₰₰ ½

Sandakan No. 8
A Japanese woman working as a journalist befriends an old woman who was sold into prostitution in Borneo in the early 1900s. Justly acclaimed feminist story dramatizes the role of women in Japanese society. Japanese with English subtitles. **AKA:** Brothel 8; Sandakan House 8.
1974 121m/C Kinuyo Tanaka, Yoko Takakashi, Komake Kurihara, Eitaro Ozawa; **D:** Kei Kumai. Academy Awards '75 Nominations: Best Foreign Language Film; Berlin International Film Festival '75: Best Actress. **VHS, Beta $59.95** FCT ₰₰₰

Sanders of the River
A British officer in colonial Africa must work with the local chief to quell a rebellion. Tale of imperialism. Dated but still interesting and of value. Robeson is very good; superb location cinematography. **AKA:** Bosambo.
1935 80m/B Paul Robeson, Leslie Banks, Robert Cochran; **D:** Zoltan Korda. **VHS, Beta $19.95** NOS, SUE, VYY ₰₰₰

Sandflow
Well-made Western with Jones playing a man whose father has cheated many ranchers. Jones is out to avenge all of his father's misdeeds and build a new life for himself in this above-average oater.
1937 58m/B Buck Jones, Lita Chevret, Robert F. (Bob) Kortman, Arthur Aylsworth, Robert Terry, Enrique DeRosas; **D:** Lesley Selander. **VHS $9.95** GPV ₰₰ ½

The Sandlot
Young Scotty (Guiry) moves to a new neighborhood in California in 1962 and tries to make friends despite not knowing anything about playing baseball. His scrappy teammates include the friendly Benny (Vitar), a chubby loud-mouthed catcher named Ham (Renna), and Squints (Leopardi), a would-be Lothario before his time. Action revolves around Scotty's attempt to get baseball autographed by Babe Ruth out of the clutches of giant killer junkyard dog owned by Jones before dad Leary discovers it missing. Small wonder is nostalgic without being sentimental, and tells its tale with grace and humor, supported by a period soundtrack.
1993 (PG) 101m/C Tom Guiry, Mike Vitar, Patrick Renna, Chauncey Leopardi, Marty York, Brandon Adams, Karen Allen, James Earl Jones, Maury Wills, Art LaFleur, Marlee Shelton; **Cameos:** Denis Leary, Brooke Adams; **D:** David Mickey Evans; **W:** Robert Gunter, David Mickey Evans; **M:** David Newman; **V:** Arliss Howard. **VHS $19.98** FXV ₰₰₰

The Sandpiper Free-spirited artist Taylor falls in love with Burton, the married headmaster of her son's boarding school. Muddled melodrama offers little besides starpower. Filmed at Big Sur, California.
1965 117m/C Elizabeth Taylor, Richard Burton, Charles Bronson, Eva Marie Saint, Robert Webber, Morgan Mason; *D:* Vincente Minnelli. **VHS, Beta $19.98** *MGM* ♂♂

Sands of Iwo Jima Wayne earned his first Oscar nomination as a tough Marine sergeant, in one of his best roles. He trains a squad of rebellious recruits in New Zealand in 1943. Later they are responsible for the capture of Iwo Jima from the Japanese—one of the most difficult campaigns of the Pacific Theater. Includes striking real war footage.
1949 109m/B John Wayne, Forrest Tucker, John Agar, Richard Jaeckel; *D:* Allan Dwan. **VHS $9.98** *REP, TLF, RDG* ♂♂♂ ½

Sands of Sacrifice Hart, a Northwest Mountie, seeks an unscrupulous promoter who's selling worthless mining stock. *AKA:* Tangled Trails.
1921 56m/B Neal Hart, Violet Palmer, Gladys Hampton, Jules Cowles, Jean Bary, Ed Roseman; *D:* Charles Bartlett. **VHS $16.95** *GPV* ♂♂ ½

Sanjuro In this offbeat, satiric sequel to "Yojimbo," a talented but lazy samurai comes to the aid of a group of naive young warriors. The conventional ideas of good and evil are quickly tossed aside; much less earnest than other Kurosawa Samurai outings. In Japanese with English subtitles. *AKA:* Tsubaki Sanjuro.
1962 96m/B Toshiro Mifune, Tatsuya Nakadai; *D:* Akira Kurosawa. **VHS, Beta $29.95** *NOS, SUE, HHT* ♂♂♂

Sans Soleil A female narrator reads and comments on the letters she receives from a friend, a freelance cameraman traveling through Japan, West Africa, and Iceland. The cameraman meditates on the cultural dislocation he feels and the meaning of his work and of life itself. Both narrator and cameraman remain unseen with the visuals being the cameraman's work in progress. *AKA:* Sunless.
1982 100m/C *D:* Chris Marker; *W:* Chris Marker. **VHS $69.95** *NYF, BTV* ♂♂♂

Sanshiro Sugata Kurosawa's first film. A young man learns discipline in martial arts from a patient master. Climactic fight scene is early signature Kurosawa. In Japanese with English subtitles.
1943 82m/B Denjiro Okochi, Yukiko Todoroki, Ranko Hanai, Ryonosuke Tsukigata, Sugisaku Aoyama, Kokuten Kodo, Susumo Fusuita, Takashi Shimura; *D:* Akira Kurosawa. **VHS $59.95** *FCT, ING, COL* ♂♂♂

Sansho the Bailiff A world masterpiece by Mizoguchi about feudal society in 11th century Japan. A woman and her children are sold into prostitution and slavery. As an adult, the son seeks to right the ills of his society. Powerful and tragic, and often more highly esteemed than "Ugetsu." In Japanese with English subtitles. *AKA:* The Bailiff; Sansho Dayu.
1954 132m/B Kinuyo Tanaka, Yoshiaki Hanayagi, Kyoko Kagawa, Eitaro Shindo, Ichiro Sugai; *D:* Kenji Mizoguchi; *W:* Yoshikata Yoda; *M:* Fumio Hayasaka. **VHS, Beta $39.95** *HMV, ING* ♂♂♂♂

Santa Claus Santa Claus teams up with Merlin the Magician to fend off an evil spirit who would ruin everyone's Christmas. Mexican camp classic.
1959 94m/C Jose Elias Moreno, Cesareo Quezadas; *D:* Rene Cardona Sr. **VHS, Beta $16.95** *SNC, MLB* Woof!

Santa Claus Conquers the Martians A Martian spaceship comes to Earth and kidnaps Santa Claus and two children. Martian kids, it seems, are jealous that Earth tykes have Christmas. Features then-child star Pia Zadora. *AKA:* Santa Claus Defeats the Aliens.
1964 80m/C John Call, Pia Zadora, Leonard Hicks, Vincent Beck, Victor Stiles, Donna Conforti; *D:* Nicholas Webster. **VHS, Beta $19.95** *COL, SNC, SUE* ♂

Santa Claus is Coming to Town Kris Kringle takes you along on his quest to give toys to the citizens of Sombertown. An animated classic.
1970 53m/C *D:* Arthur Rankin Jr., Jules Bass; *V:* Mickey Rooney, Keenan Wynn, Paul Frees. **VHS, Beta $12.98** *FHE, WTA, LME* ♂

Santa Claus: The Movie A big-budgeted spectacle about an elf who falls prey to an evil toy maker and almost ruins Christmas and Santa Claus. Boring, 'tis-the-season fantasy-drama meant to warm our cockles.
1985 (PG) 112m/C Dudley Moore, John Lithgow, David Huddleston, Judy Cornwell, Burgess Meredith; *D:* Jeannot Szwarc; *W:* David Newman. **VHS, Beta $9.98** *MED* ♂♂

Santa Fe Bound Tyler must work to clear his name when he is falsely accused of having murdered a man.
1937 58m/B Tom Tyler, Jeanne Martel, Richard Cramer, Charles "Slim" Whitaker, Edward Cassidy, Lafe McKee, Dorothy Woods, Charles "Blackie" King; *D:* Harry S. Webb. **VHS $19.95** *DVT, HEG* ♂♂

Santa Fe Marshal The 27th Hopalong Cassidy movie, if anyone's counting. In the title job the Hopster goes undercover with a medicine show to smash a criminal gang. A little different than usual, right up to the surprise identity of the crooked mastermind.
1940 66m/B William Boyd, Russell Hayden, Marjorie Rambeau, Bernadene Hayes, Earle Hodgins, Kenneth Harlan, Eddie Dean; *D:* Lesley Selander. **VHS $19.95** *NOS* ♂♂

Santa Fe Stampede The Three Mesquiteers join an old prospector in his claim but when he is killed, one of them (Wayne) is framed. The photography makes up for the weak story line and direction.
1938 58m/B John Wayne, Ray Corrigan, Max Terhune, William Farnum, June Martel, Leroy Mason, Yakima Canutt, Curly Dresden; *D:* George Sherman. **VHS $19.95** *NOS* ♂♂ ½

Santa Fe Trail Historically inaccurate but entertaining tale about the pre-Civil War fight for "bloody Kansas." The action-adventure depicts future Civil War Generals J.E.B. Stuart (Flynn) and George Armstrong Custer (Reagan!) as they begin their military career (although Custer was really just a youth at this time). Good action scenes. Also available colorized.
1940 110m/B Errol Flynn, Olivia de Havilland, Ronald Reagan, Van Heflin, Raymond Massey, Alan Hale; *D:* Michael Curtiz. **VHS, Beta $19.98** *MGM, NOS, PSM* ♂♂ ½

Santa Fe Uprising Red Ryder has to save Little Beaver from kidnappers. Good first entry for Lane in the "Red Ryder" series.
1946 54m/B Allan "Rocky" Lane, Robert (Bobby) Blake. **VHS, Beta** *MED* ♂♂ ½

Santa Sangre A circus in Mexico City, a temple devoted to a saint without arms, and a son who faithfully dotes upon his armless mother are just a few of the bizarre things in this wildly fantastic film. Fenix acts as his mother's arms, plays the piano for her, and carries out any wish she desires—including murder. Visually intoxicating but strange outing may prove too graphic for some viewers. Not as rigorous as other Jodorowsky outings. Also available in an NC-17 version.
1990 (R) 123m/C Axel Jodorowsky, Sabrina Dennison, Guy Stockwell, Blanca Guerra, Thelma Tixou, Adan Jodorowsky, Faviola Tapia, Jesus Juarez; *D:* Alejandro Jodorowsky; *W:* Robert Leoni, Claudio Argento, Alejandro Jodorowsky; *M:* Simon Boswell. **VHS $19.95** *REP, FCT, ING* ♂♂♂

Santee A father-son relationship develops between a bounty hunter and the son of a man he killed. Good, but not great, Western.
1973 (PG) 93m/C Glenn Ford, Dana Wynter, Jay Silverheels, John Larch; *D:* Gary Nelson. **VHS, Beta $49.95** *PSM, HHE* ♂♂

The Saphead Keaton's first outing as the rich playboy has him playing the none-to-bright son of a Wall Street mogul. Some great moments provide a glimpse of cinematic greatness to come from the budding comedic genius. Based on the play "The New Henrietta" by Winchell Smith and Victor Mapes. Silent.
1921 70m/B William H. Crane, Buster Keaton, Carol Holloway, Edward Connelly, Irving Cummings; *D:* Herbert Blache. **VHS** *NO* ♂♂ ½

Sapphire Two Scotland Yard detectives seek the killer of a beautiful black woman who was passing for white. Good mystery and topical social comment; remains interesting and engrossing. Superbly acting all around.
1959 92m/C Nigel Patrick, Yvonne Mitchell, Michael Craig, Paul Massie, Bernard Miles; *D:* Basil Dearden. **VHS, Beta** *NO* ♂♂♂

Saps at Sea A doctor advises Ollie to take a rest away from his job at a horn factory. He and Stan rent a boat, which they plan to keep tied to the dock, until an escaped criminal happens by and uses the boys (and their boat) for his getaway. Cramer is a good bad guy; Stan and Ollie cause too much trouble, as always.
1940 57m/B Stan Laurel, Oliver Hardy, James Finlayson, Ben Turpin, Richard Cramer; *D:* Gordon Douglas. **VHS, Beta $12.98** *CCB, MED, VTR* ♂♂ ½

Sara Dane A strong young woman in the 18th century rises in the world through marriage and business acumen. Interesting but imperfect and slow.
1981 150m/C Harold Hopkins, Brenton Whittle, Barry Quin, Sean Scully; *D:* Rod Hardy, Gary Conway. **VHS, Beta $79.95** *PSM* ♂♂

Sarafina! Part coming-of-age saga, part political drama, part musical, and all emotionally powerful. Sarafina is a young girl in a township school in Soweto, South Africa in the mid-'70s, gradually coming into a political awakening amid the Soweto riots. Khumalo recreates her stage role as the glowing and defiant Sarafina with both Goldberg and Makeba good in their roles as Sarafina's outspoken and inspirational teacher and her long-suffering mother, respectively. Adapted from Ngema's stage musical.
1992 (PG-13) 98m/C Leleti Khumalo, Whoopi Goldberg, Miriam Makeba, John Kani, Mbongeni Ngema; *D:* Darrell Roodt; *W:* Mbongeni Ngema, William Nicholson; *M:* Stanley Myers. **VHS, Beta $94.95** *TOU* ♂♂♂

Sarah, Plain and Tall New England school teacher (Close) travels to Kansas circa 1910 to care for the family of a widowed farmer who has advertised for a wife. Superior entertainment for the whole family. Adapted for television from Patricia MacLachlan's novel of the same name by MacLachlan and Carol Sobieski. Nominated for nine Emmy Awards. A "Hallmark Hall of Fame" presentation.

1991 (G) 98m/C Glenn Close, Christopher Walken, Lexi Randall, Margaret Sophie Stein, Jon DeVries, Christopher Bell; *D:* Glenn Jordan. VHS $14.98 *REP* 🐾🐾🐾

Saratoga Gable plays a bookie and Harlow the daughter of an impoverished horse breeder in this romantic comedy centered around the race tracks. This was the final film appearance for Harlow, who died before the film's completion. Mary Dees was chosen as her stand-in and had to finish many of the scenes. "Saratoga" was released just a month after Harlow's death and became one of the biggest moneymakers of the year. 1937 94m/B Jean Harlow, Clark Gable, Lionel Barrymore, Walter Pidgeon, Frank Morgan, Una Merkel, Cliff Edwards, George Zucco, Hattie McDaniel, Jonathan Hale; *D:* Jack Conway; *W:* Anita Loos, Robert Hopkins. VHS $19.98 *MGM* 🐾🐾½

Sardinia Kidnapped A beautiful girl is trapped in a clash between two powerful families while on vacation in Sardinia, where the peasants' custom is to kidnap a member of a rival family and then exchange the victim for land. Former documentary maker Mingozzi creates a realistic and uncompromising look at culture and change. In Italian; dubbed. 1975 95m/C Charlotte Rampling, Franco Nero; *D:* Gianfranco Mingozzi. VHS, Beta $24.95 *AHV* 🐾🐾½

Sartana's Here...Trade Your Pistol for a Coffin A soldier of fortune searches for a missing shipment of gold in the Old West. 1970 92m/C George Hilton, Charles Southwood, Erika Blanc, Linda Sini. VHS, Beta $49.95 *UNI* 🐾

S.A.S. San Salvador A CIA agent tries to prevent a psychotic from running amok in El Salvador. 1984 95m/C Miles O'Keeffe, Dagmar Lassander, Catherine Jarrett. VHS, Beta $69.98 *LIV, VES* 🐾

Sasquatch Purported "documentary" about the mythical creature Bigfoot. Includes pictures of the "actual" monster. For those real stupid moods. 1976 94m/C George Lauris; *D:* Ed Ragozzini. VHS, Beta $19.95 *VCI Woof!*

Satan in High Heels Sordid show-biz tale of a carnival dancer (Myles) who dreams of making it big on Broadway. First she finagles her way into a position as a nightclub singer and the mistress of a convenient millionaire. But she loses it all for love when she falls for the millionaire's misbehaving son. Flamboyant performance by Hall as the lesbian nightclub owner. 1962 90m/C Meg Myles, Grayson Hall, Del Tenney; *D:* Jerald Intrator; *W:* John T. Chapman. VHS $23.00 *SMW, TPV* 🐾½

The Satan Killer A vicious serial killer is targeted by two tough police detectives. What makes it personal is Detective Stephen's fiance is one of the killer's victims and he's not going to let justice stand in the way of his revenge. 1993 90m/C Steve Sayre, Billy Franklin, James Westbrook, Belinda Creason, Cindy Healy; *D:* Stephen Calamari. VHS $89.95 *AIP* 🐾½

Satan Met a Lady A weak adaptation of Dashiell Hammett's "Maltese Falcon." This version has Davis employing a private detective to track down a mysterious woman. The hunted woman is herself searching for a valuable collectible. 1936 74m/B Bette Davis, Warren William, Alison Skipworth, Arthur Treacher, Marie Wilson, Porter Hall, Olin Howland; *D:* William Dieterle. VHS $19.98 *MGM, FCT* 🐾🐾½

The Satanic Rites of Dracula Count Dracula is the leader of a satanic cult of prominent scientists and politicians who develop a gruesome plague virus capable of destroying the human race. Preceded by "Dracula A.D. 1972" and followed by "The 7 Brothers Meet Dracula." *AKA:* Count Dracula and His Vampire Bride. 1973 88m/C Christopher Lee, Peter Cushing, Michael Coles, William Franklyn, Freddie Jones, Joanna Lumley, Richard Vernon, Patrick Barr, Barbara Yo Ling; *D:* Alan Gibson. VHS $14.95 *MLB* 🐾🐾

Satanik A hideous old hag is turned into a lovely young woman by a stolen potion, but it doesn't last long and she becomes a monster. 1969 (R) 85m/C Magda Konopka, Julio Pena, Luigi Montini, Armando Calvo, Umberto Raho; *D:* Piero Vivarelli. VHS $16.95 *SNC* 🐾

Satan's Black Wedding The ghouls arrive at a Monterey monastery in their Sunday best to celebrate devildom's most diabolical ritual, the "Black Wedding." 1975 (R) 61m/C Greg Braddock, Ray Miles, Lisa Milano. VHS, Beta *NO* 🐾

Satan's Blade The owner of an ancient talisman goes on a killing rampage at a remote mountain lodge. 1984 87m/C VHS, Beta $9.99 *STE, PSM Woof!*

Satan's Cheerleaders A demonic high school janitor traps a bevy of buxom cheerleaders at his Satanic altar for sacrificial purposes. The gals use all of their endowments to escape the clutches of the evil sheriff and his fat wife. Is it ever campy! 1977 (R) 92m/C John Carradine, John Ireland, Yvonne De Carlo, Kerry Sherman, Jacqulin Cole, Hilary Horan, Alisa Powell, Sherry Marks, Jack Kruschen, Sydney Chaplin; *D:* Greydon Clark. VHS, Beta $24.95 *VCI Woof!*

Satan's Harvest American detective inherits estate in Johannesburg, only to find the place is being used by drug smugglers. Sidesteps the political climate and shows the beauty of the land. And a good thing: the story is virtually nonexistent. 1965 88m/C George Montgomery, Tippi Hedren; *D:* Ferde Grofe Jr. VHS, Beta *NO* 🐾

Satan's Princess Satanic cult with a female leader runs amuck. Sloppy and forgettable. 1990 90m/C Robert Forster, Caren Kaye, Lydie Denier; *D:* Bert I. Gordon. VHS, Beta $29.95 *PAR* 🐾

Satan's Sadists Tamblyn and his biker gang terrorize folks in the Southern California desert, including a retired cop, a Vietnam vet and a trio of vacationing coeds. Violent film will probably be best appreciated by Adamson completists. 1969 (R) 88m/C Russ Tamblyn, Regina Carrol, Gary Kent, Jackie Taylor, John Cardos, Kent Taylor, Robert Dix, Scott Brady, Evelyn Frank, Greydon Clark, Bill Bonner, Bobby Clark, Yvonne Stewart, Cheryl Anne, Randee Lynn, Bambi Allen, Breck Warwick; *D:* Al Adamson. VHS *NO* 🐾

Satan's School for Girls When a young woman investigates the circumstances that caused her sister's suicide, it leads her to a satanic girl's academy. Dumb and puerile made for TV "horror." 1973 74m/C Pamela Franklin, Roy Thinnes, Kate Jackson, Lloyd Bochner, Jamie Smith-Jackson, Jo Van Fleet, Cheryl Ladd; *D:* David Lowell Rich. VHS, Beta $19.99 *PSM* 🐾½

Satan's Touch A simpleton worships the Devil and gets burned for his trouble. 1984 (R) 86m/C James Lawless, Shirley Venard. VHS, Beta *NO Woof!*

Satanwar A fictional look at various forms of Satan worship. 1979 95m/C Bart LaRue, Sally Schermerhorn, Jimmy Drankovitch. VHS, Beta $59.95 *VCI Woof!*

Satisfaction An all-girl, high school rock band play out the summer before college. The Keatons should have sent Bateman to her room for this stunt. 1988 (PG-13) 93m/C Justine Bateman, Trini Alvarado, Britta Phillips, Julia Roberts, Scott Coffey, Liam Neeson, Deborah Harry; *D:* Joan Freeman; *W:* Charles Purpura; *M:* Michel Colombier. VHS, Beta $19.98 *FOX* 🐾

Saturday Night Fever Brooklyn teenager (Travolta), bored with his daytime job, becomes the nighttime king of the local disco. Based on a story published in "New York Magazine" by Nik Cohn. Acclaimed for its disco dance sequences, memorable soundtrack by the Bee Gees, and carefree yet bleak script; extremely dated, although it made its mark on society in its time. Followed by the sequel "Staying Alive." Also available in a 112-minute "PG" rated version. 🎵Staying Alive; Night Fever; More Than a Woman; How Deep Is Your Love?. 1977 (R) 118m/C John Travolta, Karen Gorney, Barry Miller, Donna Pescow; *D:* John Badham. Academy Awards '77 Nominations: Best Actor (Travolta); National Board of Review Awards '77: 10 Best Films of the Year, Best Actor (Travolta). VHS, Beta $29.95 *PAR* 🐾🐾½

Saturday Night Live Premiere episode of the late night classic, SNL. Guests Steve Martin and Elliott Gould join in these "best of" skits which feature the Killer Bees, the Blues Brothers, and a parody of "Star Trek," among other bits. Additional episodes are available. 197? 90m/C Dan Aykroyd, John Belushi, Jane Curtin, Garrett Morris, Chevy Chase, Gilda Radner, Laraine Newman. VHS, Beta $14.99 *COL, MOV* 🐾🐾½

Saturday Night Live: Best of Robin Williams The unpredictable Williams featured in "Proud Dad," "I Wuv You," "Shakespeare," "The Sweeney Sisters," and more. 197? 90m/C VHS $14.99 *STE, MOV* 🐾🐾½

Saturday Night Serials A compilation of excerpts from four serials: "The Phantom Creeps," "The Phantom Empire," "Undersea Kingdom," and "Junior G-Men." 1940 90m/B Bela Lugosi, Gene Autry, Ray Corrigan, Lon Chaney Jr. VHS, Beta $29.98 *RHI* 🐾🐾½

Saturday Night Shockers Each volume in this series is comprised of two full-length horror flicks, featuring twisted twins, barbarous butchers and sinister snow creatures. Terror abounds. 1950 150m/B Daisy Hilton. VHS, Beta $49.95 *RHI* 🐾🐾½

Saturday Night Shockers, Vol. 2 Two horror film compilations, each with copious cartoons, film clips and trailers added. Volume 2 has "Human Gorilla" and "Manbeast" and some added clips and attractions. 1958 150m/B Tod Slaughter, Eric Portman, Richard Carlson. VHS, Beta $49.95 *RHI* 🐾🐾½

Saturday Night Shockers, Vol. 3 A double feature with "Murders in the Red Barn," and "Face at the Window," plus some added classic previews and shocking shorts. 19?? 150m/B VHS $39.95 *RHI* 🐾🐾½

Saturday Night Shockers, Vol. 4 Features "The Monsters of Piedras Blancas" and "Mesa of Lost Women."

19?? 145m/B VHS $39.95 *RHI* ♫♫½

Saturday Night Sleazies, Vol. 1
Two sleazy films. "College Girl Confidential" (1968) and "Suburban Confidential" (1966) are each directed by the man who helmed "Orgy of the Dead." Also includes sleazy short subjects.
1966 150m/B Marsha Jordan, Harvey Shane; **D:** A.C. Stephen; **W:** A.C. Stephen. **VHS, Beta** $49.95 *RHI* ♫♫½

Saturday the 14th A parody of the popular axe-wielding-maniac genre, about a family inheriting a haunted mansion. Poorly made; not funny or scary. Followed by even worse sequel: "Saturday the 14th Strikes Back".
1981 (PG) 91m/C Richard Benjamin, Paula Prentiss, Severn Darden; **D:** Howard R. Cohen. **VHS, Beta** $19.98 *SUE* ♫½

Saturday the 14th Strikes Back
Pathetic sequel to the horror film spoof of the "Friday the 13th" series.
1988 91m/C Ray Walston, Avery Schreiber, Patty McCormack, Julianne McNamara, Jason Presson; **D:** Howard R. Cohen. **VHS, Beta** $79.95 *MGM* ♫

Saturn 3 Two research scientists create a futuristic Garden of Eden in an isolated sector of our solar system, but love story turns to horror story when a killer robot arrives. Sporadically promising, but ultimately lame; dumb ending. For Farrah fans only.
1980 (R) 88m/C Farrah Fawcett, Kirk Douglas, Harvey Keitel, Ed Bishop; **D:** Stanley Donen; **M:** Elmer Bernstein. **VHS, Beta** $19.98 *FOX* ♫½

Saul and David Beautifully filmed story of David's life with King Saul, the battle with Goliath, and the tragic end of Saul. From the "Bible" series. **AKA:** Saul e David.
1968 120m/C Norman Wooland, Gianno Garko. **VHS, Beta** $19.95 *VCI, MOV, KEP* ♫½

Savage! A savage foreign mess with ex-baseball star Iglehardt killing people with grenades and guns, abetted by an army full of murderous models. Also on video as "Black Valor."
1973 (R) 81m/C James Inglehart, Lada Edmund, Carol Speed, Rossana Ortiz, Sally Jordan, Aura Aurea, Vic Diaz; **D:** Cirio H. Santiago. **VHS, Beta** $59.98 *NLC* Woof!

Savage Abduction Two girls visiting Los Angeles are kidnapped by a bizarre man.
1973 (R) 84m/C Tom Drake, Stephen Oliver, Sean Kenney; **D:** John Lawrence. **VHS, Beta** $24.95 *GHV* ♫

Savage Attraction True story of a 16-year-old girl forced to marry an ex-Nazi, and her hellish life thereafter. Frustrating because it could have been much better. **AKA:** Hostage: The Christine Maresch Story; Hostage.
1983 (R) 93m/C Kerry Mack, Ralph Schicha; **D:** Frank Shields. **VHS, Beta** $19.95 *STE, SUE* ♫½

Savage Beach A pair of well-endowed female federal agents battle assorted buccaneers on a remote Pacific isle over a rediscovered cache of gold from WWII. Exploitative, pornographic, and degrading to watch. Sequel to "Picasso Trigger."
1989 (R) 90m/C Dona Speir, Hope Marie Carlton, Bruce Penhall, Rodrigo Obregon, John Aprea, Teri Weigel, Lisa London; **D:** Andy Sidaris. **VHS, Beta** $79.95 *COL* ♫

The Savage Bees A South American ship harbored at New Orleans during Mardi Gras unleashes killer bees into the celebratory crowds. Not bad, relatively exciting, TV thriller.
1976 90m/C Ben Johnson, Michael Parks, Paul Hecht, Horst Buchholz, Gretchen Corbett; **D:** Bruce Geller. **VHS, Beta** $49.95 *LIV* ♫♫

Savage Dawn In yet another desert town, yet another pair of combat-hardened vets are confronted by yet another vicious motorcycle gang. Haven't we seen this one before?
1984 (R) 102m/C George Kennedy, Karen Black, Richard Lynch, Lance Henriksen, William Forsythe; **D:** Simon Nuchtern. **VHS, Beta** $59.95 *MED, VTR* ♫½

Savage Drums Sabu returns to his South Seas island to help end tribal warfare there. Dated and dumb, but fun-to-watch melodrama/action.
1951 70m/B Sabu, Lita Baron; **D:** William Berke. **VHS, Beta** *NO* ♫½

Savage Fury Feature-length version of the popular movie serial. **AKA:** Call of the Savage.
1933 80m/B Noah Beery Jr., Dorothy Short. **VHS, Beta** $19.95 *NOS, DVT, HEG* ♫

The Savage Girl A hunter journeys through the darkest jungle in search of prey. Instead, he stumbles across a beautiful white jungle girl, falls in love with her and attempts to take her back with him.
1932 64m/B Rochelle Hudson, Walter Byron, Harry Myers, Ted Adams, Adolph Milar, Floyd Schackleford; **D:** Harry Fraser. **VHS** $16.95 *SNC, NOS, DVT* ♫

Savage Guns A gunslinger goes after his brother's murderer. **AKA:** Tierra Bru Tal.
1968 85m/C VHS, Beta $39.95 *TWE* ♫♫½

Savage Hunger Ten plane crash survivors struggle to survive in the Baja desert.
1984 90m/C Chris Makepeace, Scott Hylands, Anne Lockhart; **D:** Sparky Green. **VHS, Beta** $69.95 *VES* ♫

Savage Instinct A woman stumbles across a drug ring and becomes a target when they fear she could expose them. Only Mongo and his crew are even more surprised when she decides to fight back.
1991 95m/C Debra Sweaney, Brian Oldfield. **VHS** $89.95 *AIP, MOV* ♫

Savage Intruder A wandering opportunist worms his way into the heart and home of a rich ex-movie star. She soon discovers that he's a sexual deviant who mutilates and murders for fun. Twisted doings with Hopkins in her final role.
1968 (R) 90m/C John David Garfield, Miriam Hopkins, Gale Sondergaard, Florence Lake, Joe Besser, Minta Durfee; **D:** Donald Wolfe. **VHS** $59.95 *UNI* ♫

Savage is Loose Drivel about a scientist, his wife, and their son stranded on a deserted island for 20 years. Not surprisingly, as junior matures he realizes there isn't a woman for him—or is there? Completely lacking in redeeming qualities. Absurd pseudo-Freudian claptrap produced by Scott.
1974 (R) 114m/C George C. Scott, Trish Van Devere, John David Carson, Lee Montgomery; **D:** George C. Scott. **VHS, Beta** $29.95 *MLB* Woof!

Savage Island Women's prison in the tropics sets the scene for the usual exploitative goings-on. Blair is actually in the film only for a few minutes. Chopped-up, even worse version of "Escape From Hell."
1985 (R) 74m/C Nicholas Beardsley, Linda Blair, Anthony Steffen, Ajita Wilson, Christina Lai, Leon Askin; **D:** Edward Muller. **VHS** *NO* ♫½

Savage Journey A wagon train of pioneers has difficulty on its westward journey. Simple story with no real appeal.
1983 (PG) 99m/C Richard Moll, Maurice Grandmaison, Faith Clift; **D:** Tom McGowan. **VHS, Beta** $79.95 *PSM, SIM* ♫½

Savage Justice A young woman seeks revenge against leftist rebels (boo, hiss) in a Southeast Asian country who killed her parents and raped her. She hooks up with an ex-Green Beret, and they fight and love their way through the jungle. The usual nudity and violence; derivative and dumb.
1988 90m/C Julia Montgomery, Steven Memel. **Beta** *VTR* ♫

Savage Messiah Bio of young French sculptor Henri Gaudier and his intense, though platonic, affair with a refined Polish woman 20 years his senior. Stylized drama is spared most of director Russell's noted excesses but he manages to believably show their magnetic attraction. Gaudier was killed in WWI at the age of 24. Based on the biography by H.S. Ede.
1972 (R) 96m/C Scott Antony, Dorothy Tutin, Helen Mirren, Lindsay Kemp, Peter Vaughan, Michael Gough; **D:** Ken Russell; **W:** Christopher Logue. **VHS** $19.98 *MGM* ♫♫♫

Savage Run Reynolds is Papago Indian framed and imprisoned for his brother's murder. Sprung from the pen, he heads back to the reservation to find the real killers and to avenge his brother's death. Convincing made for televisiondrama. Stevens' last role before her suicide. **AKA:** Run, Simon, Run.
1970 73m/C Burt Reynolds, Inger Stevens, James Best, Rodolfa Acosta, Don Dubbins, Joyce Jameson, Barney Phillips, Eddie Little Sky; **D:** George McCowan. **VHS** $9.95 *SIM* ♫♫♫

Savage Sam Intended as a sequel to "Old Yeller." Sam, the offspring of the heroic dog named Old Yeller, tracks down some children kidnapped by Indians. Fun, but not fully successful.
1963 103m/C Tommy Kirk, Kevin Corcoran, Brian Keith, Dewey Martin, Jeff York, Marta Kristen; **D:** Norman Tokar. **VHS, Beta** $69.95 *DIS* ♫♫

The Savage Seven An underground classic where everyone loses. A motorcycle gang rides into an Indian town which is at the mercy of corrupt businessmen. The gang's leader becomes involved in the Indians' problems but the businessmen and the cops cause trouble for all concerned. Less than memorable. Produced by Dick Clark.
1968 96m/C Larry Bishop, Joanna Frank, Adam Roarke, Robert Walker Jr.; **D:** Richard Rush. **VHS** *NO* ♫♫

Savage Streets Blair seeks commando-style revenge on the street gang that raped her deaf sister. Extended rape scene betrays the exploitative intentions, though other bits are entertaining, in a trashy kind of way.
1983 (R) 93m/C Linda Blair, John Vernon, Sal Landi, Robert Dryer, Debra Blee, Linnea Quigley; **D:** Danny Steinmann; **M:** John D'Andrea. **VHS, Beta** $29.98 *LIV, VES* ♫½

Savage Weekend A killer behind a ghoulish mask stalks human prey in the boonies, of couse. Astoundingly, there is one interesting role—William Sanderson's looney. Otherwise, throw this one no bones. **AKA:** The Killer Behind the Mask; The Upstate Murders.
1980 (R) 88m/C Christopher Allport. **VHS, Beta** *NO* Woof!

Savage Wilderness When a trio of fur trappers lose a year's worth of skins to a band of marauding Indians, they decide to take scouting jobs at a cavalry outpost. But they find the new commander (Preston) hasn't gotten his nickname as the "Butcher of Shiloh" without reason. Adapted from the novel "The Gilded Rooster" by Richard Emery Roberts. **AKA:** The Last Frontier.

1955 98m/C Victor Mature, Robert Preston, Guy Madison, James Whitmore, Anne Bancroft, Russell Collins, Peter Whitney, Pat Hogan, Manuel Donde, Guy Williams; **D:** Anthony Mann; **W:** Philip Yordan, Russell S. Hughes; **M:** Leigh Harline. VHS $14.95 COL ✇✇½

The Savage Woman Marianna escapes from a desperate situation and is found unconscious in the woods by Elysee. He nurses her back to health, learns her terrible secret, and tries to help Marianna decides whether to turn herself into the police or keep running. In French with English subtitles.
1991 100m/C Patricia Tulasne, Matthias Habich; **D:** Lea Pool. VHS $79.95 WBF ✇✇

Savages A group of savages descend on a palatial mansion, and after living there for some time, become refined ladies and gentlemen. The moral savages and "civilized" men are really the same.
1972 106m/C Lewis J. Stadlen, Anne Francine, Thayer David, Salome Jens, Susan Blakely, Kathleen Widdoes, Sam Waterston; **D:** James Ivory. VHS $59.95 CVC, FCT ✇✇

Savages Griffith as a demented nut-case stalking another man in the desert? That's right, Opie. "The Most Dangerous Game" remade-sort of-for TV.
1975 74m/C Andy Griffith, Sam Bottoms, Noah Beery Jr.; **D:** Lee H. Katzin. VHS, Beta $49.95 PSM ✇✇½

Savages from Hell Greasy biker dude beats up a young black guy because he was flirting with the biker's woman. The biker also tries to rape a migrant farmworker's daughter because he lusts after her. Trashy exploitation film. **AKA:** Big Enough and Old Enough.
1968 (R) 79m/C Bobbie Byers, Cyril Poitier, Diwaldo Myers, Viola Lloyd, William P. Kelley; **D:** Joseph Prieto; **W:** Joseph Prieto. VHS $16.95 SNC, TPV ✇

Savannah Smiles Poor little rich girl Anderson runs away from home, into the clutches of two ham-handed crooks. She melts their hearts, and they change their ways. Decent, sentimental family drama.
1982 (PG) 104m/C Bridgette Anderson, Mark Miller, Donovan Scott, Peter Graves, Chris Robinson, Michael Parks; **D:** Pierre De Moro. VHS, Beta $14.98 SUE, NLC ✇✇½

Save Me Jim Stevens' (Hamlin) wife has left him and his boss is involved in some dirty deals that could cost Jim his job. So things couldn't get worse, could they? Well, of course they could—and do. Because Jim meets Ellie (Anthony), a sexual adventuress just destined to bring trouble to a lonely guy. Also available in an unrated version.
1993 (R) 89m/C Harry Hamlin, Lysette Anthony, Michael Ironside, Olivia Hussey, Bill Nunn, Steve Railsback; **D:** Alan Roberts; **W:** Neil Ronco; **M:** Rick Marvin. VHS $19.95 COL ✇✇

Save the Lady Plucky kids fight city hall to save an old ferry, the Lady Hope, from the scrap heap. Nothing offensive here—just a pleasant family flick.
1982 76m/C Matthew Excell, Robert Clarkson, Miranda Cartledge, Kim Clifford; **D:** Leon Thau. VHS, Beta NO ✇✇

Save the Tiger A basically honest middle-aged man sees no way out of his failing business except arson. The insurance settlement will let him pay off his creditors, and save face. David, as the arsonist, and Gilford, as Lemmon's business partner, are superb. Lemmon is also excellent throughout his performance.

1973 (R) 100m/C Jack Lemmon, Jack Gilford, Laurie Heineman, Patricia Smith, Norman Burton, Thayer David; **D:** John G. Avildsen; **M:** Marvin Hamlisch. Academy Awards '73: Best Actor (Lemmon); Nominations: Best Story & Screenplay, Best Supporting Actor (Gilford). VHS, Beta $14.95 PAR, BTV ✇✇✇

Saving Grace A tale of the fictional youngest Pope of modern times, Pope Leo XIV (Conti). Beset by duty, he decides to shed his robes and get in touch with the world's peasantry. Improbable, but that's okay; the mortal sin is that it's improbable and slow and boring.
1986 (PG) 112m/C Tom Conti, Fernando Rey, Giancarlo Giannini, Erland Josephson, Donald Hewlett, Edward James Olmos; **D:** Robert M. Young; **W:** David S. Ward; **M:** William Goldstein. VHS, Beta, 8mm $14.98 SUE, NLC ✇✇

Sawdust & Tinsel Early Bergman film detailing the grisly, humiliating experiences of a traveling circus rolling across the barren Swedish countryside. Lonely parable of human relationships. In Swedish with English subtitles. **AKA:** The Naked Night; Sunset of a Clown; Gycklarnas Afton.
1953 87m/B Harriet Andersson, Ake Gronberg; **D:** Ingmar Bergman; **W:** Ingmar Bergman. VHS, Beta $29.95 HMV, ING, NLC ✇✇✇

Sawmill/The Dome Doctor Two silent comedies starring the inimitable klutz of the golden era, Larry Semon, whose name has been nearly forgotten today.
1922 71m/B Larry Semon, Dorothy Dwan. VHS, Beta $24.95 VYY ✇✇½

Say Anything A semi-mature, successful teen romance about an offbeat loner interested in the martial arts (Cusack, in a winning performance) who goes after the beautiful class brain of his high school. Things are complicated when her father is suspected of embezzling by the IRS. Joan Cusack, John's real-life sister, also plays his sister in the film. Works well on the romantic level without getting too sticky.
1989 (PG-13) 100m/C John Cusack, Ione Skye, John Mahoney, Joan Cusack, Lili Taylor, Richard Portnow, Pamela Segall, Jason Gould, Loren Dean, Pamela Neuwirth, Aimee Brooks, Eric Stoltz, Chynna Phillips, Joanna Frank; **D:** Cameron Crowe; **W:** Cameron Crowe; **M:** Anne Dudley, Richard Gibbs, Nancy Wilson. VHS, Beta $19.98 FOX ✇✇✇

Say Goodbye, Maggie Cole A widow goes to work as a doctor in a Chicago street clinic and becomes emotionally involved with a dying child. Hayward's final role in moving made-for-TV drama.
1972 78m/C Susan Hayward, Darren McGavin, Michael Constantine, Nichelle Nichols, Dane Clark; **D:** Judd Taylor. VHS, Beta $69.95 VMK ✇✇½

Say Hello to Yesterday A May-December romance that takes place entirely in one day. An unhappy housewife meets an exciting young traveler while both are in London. Cast and director try hard but fail to get the point across to the audience.
1971 (PG) 91m/C Jean Simmons, Leonard Whiting, Evelyn Laye; **D:** Alvin Rakoff. VHS, Beta $59.95 PSM ✇½

Say Yes! A nutty millionaire (Winters) bets $250 million that his inept nephew cannot get married within 24 hours. Three times the length of usual wacky sitcom, alas.
1986 (PG-13) 87m/C Jonathan Winters, Art Hindle, Logan Ramsey, Lissa Layng; **D:** Larry Yust. VHS, Beta NO ✇½

Sayonara An Army major is assigned to a Japanese airbase during the Korean conflict at the behest of his future father-in-law. Dissatisfied with his impending marriage, he

finds himself drawn to a Japanese dancer and becomes involved in the affairs of his buddy who, against official policy, marries a Japanese woman. Tragedy surrounds the themes of bigotry and interracial marriage. Based on the novel by James Michener.
1957 147m/C Marlon Brando, James Garner, Ricardo Montalban, Patricia Owens, Red Buttons, Miyoshi Umeki, Martha Scott; **D:** Joshua Logan. Academy Awards '57: Best Art Direction/Set Decoration, Best Sound, Best Supporting Actor (Buttons), Best Supporting Actress (Umeki); Nominations: Best Actor (Brando), Best Adapted Screenplay, Best Cinematography, Best Director (Logan), Best Film Editing, Best Picture. VHS, Beta $19.98 FOX, BTV ✇✇✇

The Scalawag Bunch Yet another retelling of Robin Hood and his Merry Men and their adventures in Sherwood Forest.
1975 100m/C Mark Damon, Luis Davila, Silvia Dionisio; **D:** George Ferron. VHS, Beta HHE ✇

Scalp Merchant Private investigator Cliff Rowan hunts for a missing payroll. Someone would rather see him dead than successful.
1977 108m/C Cameron Mitchell, John Waters, Elizabeth Alexander, Margaret Nelson; **D:** Howard Rubie. VHS, Beta NO ✇

Scalpel After his daughter's death, a plastic surgeon creates her image on another woman to get an inheritance. Violent and graphic, with a surprise ending. Not too bad; interesting premise. **AKA:** False Face.
1976 (R) 95m/C Robert Lansing, Judith Chapman, Arlen Dean Snyder; **D:** John Grissmer. VHS, Beta $9.95 NLC ✇✇

The Scalphunters Semi-successful, semi-funny western about an itinerant trapper (Lancaster) who is forced by Indians to trade his pelts for an educated black slave (Davis); many chases and brawls ensue. Good performances.
1968 102m/C Burt Lancaster, Ossie Davis, Telly Savalas, Shelley Winters, Nick Cravat, Dabney Coleman, Paul Picerni; **D:** Sydney Pollack; **W:** William W. Norton Sr.; **M:** Elmer Bernstein. VHS, Beta $19.98 MGM ✇✇

Scalps Hunted Indian princess and man whose family was killed by Indians form uneasy alliance in old West.
1983 (R) 90m/C Karen Wood, Albert Farley, Benny Cardosa, Charlie Bravo, Vassili Garis; **D:** Werner Knox. VHS, Beta $19.95 IMP, HHE ✇✇

Scam Maggie and her partner Barry are con artists making their living scamming high rollers in Miami Beach. Then Maggie tries to pull a con on the wrong man. Jack Shanks is an ex-FBI agent with a score to settle and he blackmails Maggie into helping him.
1993 (R) 102m/C Christopher Walken, Lorraine Bracco, Miguel Ferrer; **D:** John Flynn. VHS $89.98 FXV ✇✇½

Scandal A dramatization of Britain's Profumo government sex scandal of the 1960s. Hurt plays a society doctor who enjoys introducing pretty girls to his wealthy friends. One of the girls, Christine Keeler, takes as lovers both a Russian government official and a British Cabinet Minister. The resulting scandal eventually overturned an entire political party, and led to disgrace, prison, and death for some of those concerned. Also available in an unedited 115-minute version which contains more controversial language and nudity. Top-notch performances make either version well worth watching.
1989 (R) 105m/C John Hurt, Joanne Whalley-Kilmer, Ian McKellan, Bridget Fonda, Jeroen Krabbe, Britt Ekland, Roland Gift, Daniel Massey, Leslie Phillips, Roland Gift; **D:** Michael Caton-Jones; **W:** Michael Thomas; **M:** Carl Davis. VHS, Beta $19.95 HBO ✇✇✇

Scandal in a Small Town A cocktail waitress in a small town has to defend herself and her daughter from the town's critical eye and hateful actions. Self-righteous made for TV drama rehashes several earlier plots.
1988 90m/C Raquel Welch, Christa Denton, Peter Van Norden, Ronny Cox; **D:** Anthony Page. **VHS $9.99** *STE, VMK* ✂✂

Scandal Man A French photographer gets in over his head when he snaps the daughter of an American KKK leader embracing a black man in a nightclub. In French with English subtitles.
1967 86m/C Maurice Ronet; **D:** Richard Balducci. **VHS, Beta $19.95** *FCT, ING* ✂✂½

Scandalous A bumbling American television reporter becomes involved with a gang of British con artists. Starts well but peters out. Look for the scene where Gielgud attends a Bow Wow Wow concert.
1984 (PG) 93m/C Robert Hays, Pamela Stephenson, John Gielgud, Jim Dale, M. Emmet Walsh; **D:** Rob Cohen; **W:** Rob Cohen, Larry Cohen, John Byrum; **M:** Dave Grusin. **VHS, Beta $29.98** *LIV, VES* ✂½

Scandalous A duke and his uncle work together to find a secretary who disappeared after witnessing a murder.
1988 90m/C Albert Fortell, Lauren Hutton, Ursula Carven, Capucine; **D:** Robert W. Young. **VHS, Beta $9.99** *STE, PSM* ✂

Scandalous John Comedy western about a last cattle drive devised by an aging cowboy (Keith) in order to save his ranch. Keith's shrewd acting as the ornery cattle man who won't sell to developers carries this one.
1971 (G) 113m/C Brian Keith, Alfonso Arau, Michele Carey, Rick Lenz, John Ritter, Harry Morgan; **D:** Robert Butler. **VHS, Beta $69.95** *DIS* ✂✂

Scanner Cop When deranged scientist Sigmund Glock escapes from prison, he's determined to take revenge on Peter Harrigan, the cop who put him behind bars. With the aid of an evil assistant and a mind-altering drug, Glock kidnaps and programs innocent citizens into cop-killing maniacs. Harrigan's only weapon is a rookie cop with the Scanner power to read minds—and then destroy them.
1994 (R) 94m/C Daniel Quinn, Darlanne Fluegel, Richard Lynch, Mark Rolston, Hilary Shepard, Gary Hudson, Cyndi Pass, Luca Bercovici, Brion James; **D:** Pierce David; **W:** John Bryant, George Saunders. **VHS** *REP* ✂½

Scanners "Scanners" are telepaths who can will people to explode. One scanner in particular harbors Hitlerian aspirations for his band of psychic gangsters. Gruesome but effective special effects.
1981 (R) 102m/C Stephen Lack, Jennifer O'Neill, Patrick McGoohan, Lawrence Dane; **D:** David Cronenberg; **W:** David Cronenberg. **VHS, Beta $14.95** *COL, SUE, SUP* ✂✂½

Scanners 2: The New Order This not-bad sequel to the 1981 cult classic finds a power-mad police official out to build a psychic militia of captured Scanners. More story than last time, plus more and better special effects.
1991 (R) 104m/C David Hewlett, Deborah Raffin, Yvan Ponton, Isabelle Mejias, Valentin Trujillo, Tom Butler, Vlasta Vrana, Dorothee Berryman, Raoul Trujillo; **D:** Christian Duguay; **W:** B.J. Nelson; **M:** Marty Simon. **VHS, Beta $92.98** *MED, IME, VTR* ✂✂½

Scanners 3: The Takeover The third sequel in which Scanner siblings battle for control of the world. Lacks the creativity and storyline of the first two films.

1992 (R) 101m/C Steve Parrish, Liliana Komorowska, Valerie Valois; **D:** Christian Duguay. **VHS $14.98** *REP* ✂✂½

The Scar A cunning criminal robs the mob, then hides by "stealing" the identity of a lookalike psychologist. But he's overlooked one thing...or two. Farfetched film noir showcases a rare villainous role for Henreid (who also produced). Based on a novel by Murray Forbes. **AKA:** Hollow Triumph.
1948 83m/B Paul Henreid, Joan Bennett, Eduard Franz, Leslie Brooks, John Qualen, Mabel Paige, Herbert Rudley; **D:** Steve Sekely. **VHS $19.98** *REP, FCT, NOS* ✂✂

Scar of Shame Explores the ill-fated romance between a successful black concert pianist and the lower-class woman he marries. Gives a look at the color caste system and divisions within the black community of the era.
1927 90m/B Harry Henderson, Lucia Lynn Moses, Ann Kennedy, Norman Johnstone; **D:** Frank Peregini. **VHS $39.95** *FCT, BTV* ✂✂

Scaramouche Thrilling swashbuckler about a nobleman (Granger, very well cast) searching for his family during the French Revolution. To avenge the death of a friend, he joins a theater troupe where he learns swordplay and becomes the character "Scaramouche." Features a rousing six-and-a-half-minute sword battle.
1952 111m/C Stewart Granger, Eleanor Parker, Janet Leigh, Mel Ferrer, Henry Wilcoxon, Nina Foch, Richard Anderson, Robert Coote, Lewis Stone, Elisabeth Risdon, Howard Freeman; **D:** George Sidney. **VHS** *VYG, FCT* ✂✂✂½

Scarecrow Two homeless drifters (Hackman and Pacino) walk across America, heading toward a car wash business they never reach. An oft-neglected example of the early 70s extra-realistic subgenre initiated by "Midnight Cowboy." Engrossing until the end, when it falls flat. Filmed on location in Detroit.
1973 (R) 112m/C Gene Hackman, Al Pacino, Ann Wedgeworth, Eileen Brennan, Richard Lynch; **D:** Jerry Schatzberg. **VHS, Beta $19.98** *WAR* ✂✂½

Scared Stiff Fleeing a murder charge, Martin and Lewis find gangsters and ghosts on a Caribbean island. Funny and scary, a good remake of "The Ghost Breakers," with cameos by Hope and Crosby. ♫San Domingo; Song of the Enchilada Man; Mama Yo Quiero; You Hit the Spot; I Don't Care If the Sun Don't Shine; I'm Your Pal; When Somebody Thinks You're Wonderful.
1953 108m/B Dean Martin, Jerry Lewis, Lizabeth Scott, Carmen Miranda, Dorothy Malone; **Cameos:** Bob Hope, Bing Crosby; **D:** George Marshall. **VHS $14.95** *PAR, MLB, REP* ✂✂✂

Scared Stiff Three people move into a mansion once owned by a sadistic slave trader. Once there, they become unwilling victims of a voodoo curse. Bad special effects and script, not redeemed by decent but unoriginal story.
1987 (R) 85m/C Andrew Stevens, Mary Page Keller; **D:** Richard S. Friedman; **W:** Richard S. Friedman, Mark Frost. **VHS $14.95** *REP* ✂

Scared to Death Begins with a woman dying of fright when shown the death mask of the man she framed. Dead woman then proceeds to narrate remainder of the story, which focuses on events leading up to her unfortunate, untimely, and fairly uninteresting demise. Memorable as Lugosi's only color film.
1947 70m/C Bela Lugosi, George Zucco, Douglas Fowley, Nat Pendleton, Joyce Compton; **D:** Walt Mattox. **VHS, Beta $19.95** *NOS, SNC, MWP* ✂½

Scared to Death A scientific experiment goes awry as a mutation begins killing off the residents of Los Angeles.
1980 (R) 93m/C John Stinson, Diana Davidson, David Moses, Kermit Eller; **D:** William Malone; **M:** Tom Chase. **VHS, Beta $49.95** *MED* ✂

Scared to Death/Dick Tracy's Dilemma On one tape, two 40's programmers-Lugosi's only color film, about a psychotic magician who tortures a young girl, and a standard black-and-white Tracy entry.
1947 125m/C Bela Lugosi, George Zucco, Ralph Byrd, Kay Christopher, Ian Keith. **VHS, Beta** *AOV* ✂✂

Scarface The violent rise and fall of a 1930s Chicago crime boss (based on the life of notorious gangster Al Capone). Release was held back by censors due to the amount of violence and its suggestion of incest between the title character and his sister. Producer Howard Hughes recut and filmed an alternate ending, without director Hawks' approval, to pacify the censors, and both versions of the film were released at the same time. Almost too violent and intense at the time. Remains brilliant and impressive. Remade in 1983. **AKA:** Scarface: The Shame of a Nation.
1931 93m/B Paul Muni, Ann Dvorak, Karen Morley, Osgood Perkins, George Raft, Boris Karloff; **D:** Howard Hawks. **VHS, Beta $19.95** *MCA* ✂✂✂

Scarface Al Pacino is a Cuban refugee who becomes powerful in the drug trade until the life gets the better of him. A remake of the 1932 classic gangster film of the same name, although the first film has more plot. Extremely violent, often unpleasant, but not easily forgotten.
1983 (R) 170m/C Al Pacino, Steven Bauer, Michelle Pfeiffer, Robert Loggia, F. Murray Abraham, Mary Elizabeth Mastrantonio, Harris Yulin, Paul Shenar, Oliver Stone; **D:** Brian DePalma; **W:** Oliver Stone. **VHS, Beta $29.95** *MCA* ✂✂✂

Scarface Mob This is the original television pilot film for the popular series "The Untouchables," about Eliot Ness's band of good guys battling Chicago's crime lord, Al Capone. Still strong stuff. Narrated by Walter Winchell. **AKA:** Tueur de Ch Icago.
1962 120m/B Robert Stack, Neville Brand, Barbara Nichols; **D:** Phil Karlson; **W:** Paul Monash. **VHS, Beta** *PAR* ✂✂

The Scarlet & the Black A priest clandestinely works within the shield of the Vatican's diplomatic immunity to shelter allied soldiers from the Nazis in occupied Rome. His efforts put him at odds with the Pope and target him for Gestapo assassination. Swashbuckling adventure at its second-best. Made for television. Based on the nonfiction book "The Scarlet Pimpernel of the Vatican" by J.P. Gallagher.
1983 145m/C Gregory Peck, Christopher Plummer, John Gielgud, Raf Vallone; **D:** Jerry London; **M:** Ennio Morricone. **VHS, Beta $59.98** *FOX, FCT, IGP* ✂✂½

The Scarlet Car Chaney is a bank cashier who discover his boss has been embezzling funds. A fight causes Chaney to believe he has killed his employer and he hides out in a remote cabin where guilt preys on his mind.
1917 50m/B Lon Chaney Sr., Franklin Farnum, Edith Johnson, Sam DeGrasse; **D:** Joseph DeGrasse. **VHS, Beta $16.95** *SNC, GPV, FCT* ✂✂

Scarlet Claw Holmes and Watson solve the bloody murder of an old lady in the creepy Canadian village of Le Mort Rouge. The best and most authentic of the Sherlock

Holmes series. *AKA:* Sherlock Holmes and the Scarlet Claw.
1944 74m/B Basil Rathbone, Nigel Bruce, Miles Mander, Gerald Hamer, Kay Harding; **D:** Roy William Neill. **VHS, Beta $14.98** FOX ⅍⅍⅍

The Scarlet Clue A better script and faster pacing improved this Monogram entry in the Chan series. Charlie investigates a series of mysterious deaths which lead to a plot to steal secret government radar plans.
1945 65m/B Sidney Toler, Benson Fong, Mantan Moreland, Robert E. Homans, Helen Devereaux; **D:** Phil Rosen. **VHS $19.98** MGM ⅍⅍

Scarlet Dawn Lavish sets and costumes abound in this romantic drama starring Fairbanks as a Russian aristocrat and Carroll as his maid servant. Together they flee Russia during the Revolution, marry, and settle into the life of the common working class. Restless under his new status, Fairbanks pursues Tashman and tries his hand at swindling. A slow but interesting love story. Adapted from the novel "Revolt" by Mary McCall.
1932 58m/B Douglas Fairbanks Jr., Nancy Carroll, Lilyan Tashman, Sheila Terry, Guy Kibbee, Richard Alexander, Frank Reicher; **D:** William Dieterle; **W:** Douglas Fairbanks Jr., Niven Busch, Edwin Gelsey. **VHS $19.98** MGM ⅍⅍½

Scarlet Empress One of Von Sternberg's greatest films tells the story of Catherine the Great and her rise to power. Dietrich stars as the beautiful royal wife who outwits her maniacal husband to become empress of Russia. Incredibly rich decor is a visual feast for the eye, as perfectionist von Sternberg fussed over every detail. Dietrich is excellent as Catherine, and von Sternberg's mastery of lighting and camerawork makes for a highly extravagant film. Based on the diary of Catherine the Great.
1934 110m/B Marlene Dietrich, John Lodge, Sam Jaffe, Louise Dresser, Maria Sieber, Sir C. Aubrey Smith, Ruthelma Stevens, Olive Tell; **D:** Josef von Sternberg; **W:** Manuel Komroff. **VHS $14.98** MCA, FCT ⅍⅍⅍½

The Scarlet Letter Unlikely comic relief provides only measure of redemption for this poorly rendered version of Hawthorne's classic novel about sin and Hester Prynne. Actor Hale is Skipper from "Gilligan's Island".
1934 69m/B Colleen Moore, Hardie Albright, Henry B. Walthall, Alan Hale, Cora Sue Collins, Betty Blythe; **D:** Robert G. Vignola. **VHS, Beta $19.95** NOS, BAR, VYY ⅍⅍

The Scarlet Letter A studied, thoughtful, international production of the Nathaniel Hawthorne classic about a woman's adultery which incites puritanical violence and hysteria in colonial America. Fine modernization by Wenders. In German with English subtitles.
1973 90m/C Senta Berger, Lou Castel, Yella Rottlaender, William Layton, Yelena Samarina, Hans-Christian Blech; **D:** Wim Wenders. **VHS, Beta $59.95** FCT, GLV, ING ⅍⅍⅍

The Scarlet Pimpernel "The Scarlet Pimpernel," supposed dandy of the English court, assumes a dual identity to outwit the French Republicans and aid innocent aristocrats during the French Revolution. Classic rendering of Baroness Orczy's novel, full of exploits, 18th century costumes, intrigue, damsels, etc. Produced by Alexander Korda, who fired the initial director, Rowland Brown. Remade for television in 1982. Available in colorized version.
1934 95m/B Leslie Howard, Joan Gardner, Merle Oberon, Raymond Massey, Anthony Bushell; **D:** Harold Young. **VHS, Beta $9.95** CNG, NOS, PSM ⅍⅍⅍½

The Scarlet Pimpernel Remake of the classic about a British dandy who saved French aristocrats from the Reign of Terror guillotines during the French Revolution. Made for British television version is almost as good as the original 1935 film, with beautiful costumes and sets and good performances from Seymour and Andrews.
1982 142m/C Anthony Andrews, Jane Seymour, Ian McKellan, James Villers, Eleanor David; **D:** Clive Donner; **M:** Nick Bicat. **VHS, Beta $19.98** LIV, VES, FUS ⅍⅍⅍

Scarlet Spear Filmed in Nairobi National Park in Kenya. A great white hunter convinces a young African chief that the ancient practices of his people are uncivilized. Pathetically stated and culturally offensive by today's standards.
1954 78m/C John Bentley, Martha Hyer, Morasi; **D:** George Breakston, Roy Stahl. **VHS, Beta $39.95** MSP Woof!

Scarlet Street A mild-mannered, middle-aged cashier becomes an embezzler when he gets involved with a predatory, manipulating woman. Lang remake of Jean Renoir's "La Chienne" (1931). Set apart from later attempts on the same theme by excellent direction by Lang and acting. Also available Colorized.
1945 95m/B Edward G. Robinson, Joan Bennett, Dan Duryea, Samuel S. Hinds; **D:** Fritz Lang. **VHS, Beta $9.95** CNG, NOS, HHT ⅍⅍⅍

Scarred Unwed teenage mother becomes prostitute to support baby. Predictable plot and acting pull this one down. *AKA:* Street Love; Red on Red.
1984 (R) 85m/C Jennifer Mayo, Jackie Berryman, David Dean; **D:** Rosemarie Turko; **W:** Rosemarie Turko. **VHS, Beta $69.98** LIV, VES ⅍½

The Scars of Dracula A young couple tangles with Dracula in their search for the man's missing brother. Gory, creepy, violent, sexy tale from the dark side. Don't see it late at night. Preceded by "Taste the Blood of Dracula" and followed by "Dracula A.D. 1972." Available on Laserdisc with "The Horror of Frankenstein."
1970 (R) 96m/C Christopher Lee, Jenny Hanley, Dennis Waterman, Wendy Hamilton, Patrick Troughton, Michael Gwynn, Anouska Hempel, Michael Ripper; **D:** Roy Ward Baker. **VHS, Beta $59.99** MLB ⅍⅍½

Scavenger Hunt Action begins when a deceased millionaire's will states that his 15 would-be heirs must compete in a scavenger hunt, and whoever collects all the items first wins the entire fortune. Big cast wanders about aimlessly.
1979 (PG) 117m/C Richard Benjamin, James Coco, Ruth Buzzi, Cloris Leachman, Cleavon Little, Roddy McDowall, Scatman Crothers, Tony Randall, Robert Morley, Richard Mulligan, Dirk Benedict, Willie Aames, Vincent Price; **D:** Michael A. Schultz; **W:** Billy Goldenberg. **VHS, Beta $59.98** FOX ⅍

Scavengers A man and a woman become involved in a spy plot and wind up in all sorts of danger. Pathetic excuse for a "thriller."
1987 (PG-13) 94m/C Kenneth Gilman, Brenda Bakke, Ken Gampu, Norman Anstey, Crispin De Nys; **D:** Duncan McLachlan. **VHS, Beta $29.95** ACA ⅍

Scenario du Film Passion A classically self-analyzing video piece by Godard, in which he recreates on tape the scenario for his film "Passion," resulting in a reflexive, experimental essay on the process of image-making and conceptualizing films, especially Godard's. In French with English subtitles.
1982 54m/C D: Jean-Luc Godard, Anne-Marie Mieville, Barnard Menoud. **VHS, Beta** EAI ⅍⅍⅍

Scene of the Crime Three short mysteries, which the audience is asked to solve: "The Newlywed Murder," "Medium Is the Murder" and "Vote for Murder." Made for television.
1985 74m/C Markie Post, Alan Thicke, Ben Piazza; **D:** Walter Grauman. **VHS, Beta $39.95** MCA ⅍⅍½

Scene of the Crime Beautiful widow, trapped in small French town, is sexually awakened by escaped convict hiding out near her home. Acclaimed, but sometimes distracting camera technique and slow pace undermine the film. In French with English subtitles.
1987 90m/C Catherine Deneuve, Danielle Darrieux, Wadeck Stanczak, Victor Lanoux, Nicolas Giraudi, Jean Bousquet, Claire Nebout; **D:** Andre Techine. **Beta** NO ⅍⅍⅍

Scenes from a Mall Conspicuous consumers spend sixteenth wedding anniversary waltzing in mall while marriage unravels with few laughs. Surprisingly superficial comedy given the depth of talent of Allen and Midler.
1991 (R) 87m/C Woody Allen, Bette Midler, Bill Irwin, Daren Firestone, Rebecca Nickels; *Cameos:* Fabio Lanzoni; **D:** Paul Mazursky; **W:** Paul Mazursky. **VHS, Beta $19.99** TOU, IME ⅍⅍

Scenes from a Marriage Originally produced in six one-hour episodes for Swedish television, this bold and sensitive film excruciatingly portrays the painful, unpleasant, disintegration of a marriage. Ullman is superb. Realistic and disturbing. Dubbed.
1973 (PG) 168m/C Liv Ullmann, Erland Josephson, Bibi Andersson, Jan Malmsjo, Anita Wall; **D:** Ingmar Bergman; **W:** Ingmar Bergman. **VHS, Beta $89.95** COL ⅍⅍⅍⅍

Scenes from a Murder A killer (Savalas) stalks a beautiful actress (Heywood). Dull excuse for a suspense flick.
1972 91m/C Telly Savalas, Anne Heywood, Giorgio Piazza; **D:** Alberto De Martino. **VHS, Beta** NO ⅍½

Scenes from the Class Struggle in Beverly Hills Social satire about the wealthy, their servants, and their hangers-on in two Hollywood households. Two chauffeurs spend their spare time lusting after their lovely employers, and bet to see who can accomplish reality first. All kinds of erotic capers result. Usually funny and irreverent; occasionally misfires or takes itself too seriously. Reunites the trio from cult classic "Eating Raoul": Bartel, Woronov, and Beltran. Remake of Renoir's "The Rules of the Game."
1989 (R) 103m/C Jacqueline Bisset, Ray Sharkey, Mary Woronov, Robert Beltran, Ed Begley Jr., Wallace Shawn, Paul Bartel, Paul Mazursky, Arnetia Walker, Rebecca Schaeffer; *Cameos:* Little Richard; **D:** Paul Bartel; **W:** Bruce Wagner; **M:** Stanley Myers. **VHS, Beta** NO ⅍⅍½

Scenes from the Goldmine A young woman joins a rock band and falls in love with its lead singer. Realistic but bland; music not memorable (performed mostly by the actors themselves).
1987 (R) 99m/C Catherine Mary Stewart, Cameron Dye, Joe Pantoliano, John Ford Coley, Steve Railsback, Timothy B. Schmit, Jewel Shepard, Alex Rocco, Lee Ving, Lesley-Anne Down; **D:** Marc Rocco. **VHS, Beta $19.98** NLC ⅍½

The Scent of a Woman An acclaimed dark comedy that may be an acquired taste for some. A blinded military officer and his valet take a sensual tour of Italy, the sightless man seducing beautiful women on the way. But at the end of the journey awaits a shock, and the real point of

the tale, based on a novel by Giovanni Arpino. In Italian with English subtitles. Remade in 1992 as "Scent of a Woman." *AKA:* Sweet Smell of Woman; Profumo di Donna.
1975 103m/C Vittorio Gassman; *D:* Dino Risi. VHS *NO 𝄢𝄢½*

Scent of a Woman Pacino is a powerhouse (verging on caricature) in a story that, with anyone else in the lead, would be your run-of-the-mill, overly sentimental coming of age/redemption flick. Blind, bitter, and semi-alcoholic Pacino is a retired army colonel under the care of his married niece. He's home alone over Thanksgiving, under the watchful eye of local prep school student Charlie (O'Donnell). Pacino's abrasive (though wonderfully intuitive and romantic) colonel makes an impact on viewers that lingers like a woman's scent long after the last tango. O'Donnell is competently understated in key supporting role, while the tango lesson between Pacino and Anwar dances to the tune of "classic." Box-office winner is a remake of 1975 Italian film "Profumo di Donna." The laserdisc version is available in letterbox format.
1992 (R) 157m/C Al Pacino, Chris O'Donnell, James Rebhorn, Gabrielle Anwar, Philip S. Hoffman, Richard Venture, Bradley Whitford, Rochelle Oliver, Margaret Eginton, Tom Riis Farrell, Frances Conroy; *D:* Martin Brest; *W:* Bo Goldman; *M:* Thomas Newman. Academy Awards '92: Best Actor (Pacino); Nominations: Best Adapted Screenplay, Best Director (Brest), Best Picture; British Academy Awards '93: Best Adapted Screenplay; Golden Globe Awards '93: Best Actor—Drama (Pacino), Best Film—Drama. VHS $19.98 *MCA, MOV, BTV 𝄢𝄢𝄢*

The Scent of Green Papaya Tranquil film, set in 1951 Vietnam, follows 10-year-old peasant girl Mui as she spends the next 10 years as a servant in a troubled family, gracefully accommodating herself to the small changes in her life. At 20, she finds a fairy-tale romance with her next employer, a young pianist. Presents a romanticized view of the stoicism of Vietnamese women but is visually beautiful. Directorial debut of Hung is based on his childhood memories of Vietnam, which he re-created on a soundstage outside Paris. In Vietnamese with English subtitles.
1993 100m/C Tran Nu Yen-Khe, Lu Man San, Truong Thi Loc, Vuong Hoa Hoi; *D:* Tran Anh Hung; *W:* Tran Anh Hung, Patricia Petit. VHS *NYR 𝄢𝄢𝄢*

Scherzo One of McLaren's earliest films, an abstract meditation lost in 1939 and subsequently found and reconstructed in 1984.
1939 2m/C *D:* Norman McLaren. VHS, Beta *NFB 𝄢𝄢𝄢*

Schindler's List Spielberg's staggering evocation of the Holocaust finds its voice in Oscar Schindler (Neeson), womanizing German businessman and aspiring war profiteer, who cajoled, bribed, and bullied the Nazis into allowing him to employ Jews in his Polish factories during WWII. By doing so he saved over 1,000 lives. The atrocities are depicted matter of factly as a by-product of sheer Nazi evil. Shot in black and white and powered by splendid performances. Neeson uses his powerful physique as a protective buffer; Kingsley is watchful as his industrious Jewish accountant; and Fiennes personifies evil as Nazi Amon Goeth. Based on the novel by Thomas Keneally, which itself was based on survivor's memories. Filmed on location in Cracow, Poland; due to the sensitive nature of the story, sets of the Auschwitz concentration camp were reconstructed directly outside the camp after protests about filming on the actual site. A tour de force and labor of love for Spielberg, who finally garnered the attention and respect as a filmmaker he deserves.
1993 (R) 195m/B Liam Neeson, Ben Kingsley, Ralph Fiennes, Embeth Davidtz, Caroline Goodall, Jonathan Sagalle, Mark Ivanir; *D:* Steven Spielberg; *W:* Steven Zaillian; *M:* John Williams. Academy Awards '93: Best Adapted Screenplay, Best Art Direction/Set Decoration, Best Cinematography, Best Director (Spielberg), Best Film Editing, Best Picture, Best Original Score; Nominations: Best Actor (Neeson), Best Costume Design, Best Makeup, Best Sound, Best Supporting Actor (Fiennes); Golden Globe Awards '94: Best Actor—Drama (Neeson), Best Supporting Actor (Fiennes), Best Original Score; MTV Movie Awards '94: Best Film, Breakthrough Performance (Fiennes); British Academy Awards '94: Best Director (Spielberg), Best Film, Best Supporting Actor (Fiennes); Golden Globe Awards '94: Best Director (Spielberg), Best Film—Drama, Best Screenplay; Los Angeles Film Critics Association Awards '93: Best Cinematography, Best Film; National Board of Review Awards '93: Best Film; New York Film Critics Awards '93: Best Cinematography, Best Film, Best Supporting Actor (Fiennes). VHS $99.98 *MCA 𝄢𝄢𝄢𝄢*

Schizo Devious intentions abound as a middle-aged man is overcome by weird scenes and revelations, caused by the impending wedding of the figure skater he adores. Confusing tale of insanity, obsession, and skating. *AKA:* Amok; Blood of the Undead.
1977 (R) 109m/C Lynne Frederick, John Layton; *D:* Pete Walker. VHS, Beta $24.95 *VCI, MED 𝄢*

Schizoid Advice-to-the-lovelorn columnist Hill receives a series of threatening letters causing her to wonder whether psychiatrist Kinski is bumping off his own patients. Boring blood dripper that's difficult to follow. *AKA:* Murder by Mail.
1980 (R) 91m/C Klaus Kinski, Marianna Hill, Craig Wasson; *D:* David Paulsen. VHS, Beta $19.98 *MCA 𝄢*

Schlock Accurately titled horror parody is first directorial effort for Landis, who does double duty as a missing link who kills people and falls in love with blind girl. Look for cameo appearance by Forrest J. Ackerman; ape-makeup by Rick Baker. *AKA:* The Banana Monster.
1973 (PG) 78m/C John Landis, Saul Kahan, Joseph Piantadosi, Eliza Garrett; *Cameos:* Forrest J. Ackerman; *D:* John Landis; *W:* John Landis. VHS *NO 𝄢𝄢*

Schnelles Geld A mild-mannered guy gets involved with a prostitute, and is plunged into a world of crime and drugs. In German with English subtitles.
1984 90m/C VHS, Beta $39.95 *VCD, GLV 𝄢½*

School Daze Director/writer/star Lee's second outing is a rambunctious comedy (with a message, of course) set at an African-American college in the South. Skimpy plot revolves around the college's homecoming weekend and conflict among frats and sororities and African-Americans who would lose their racial identity and others who assert it. Entertaining and thought provoking. A glimpse at Lee's "promise," fulfilled in "Do the Right Thing."
1988 (R) 114m/C Spike Lee, Laurence "Larry" Fishburne, Giancarlo Esposito, Tisha Campbell, Ossie Davis, Joe Seneca, Art Evans, Ellen Holly, Branford Marsalis, Bill Nunn, Kadeem Hardison, Darryl M. Bell, Joie Lee, Tyra Ferrell, Jasmine Guy, Gregg Burge, Kasi Lemmons, Samuel L. Jackson, Phyllis Hyman; *D:* Spike Lee; *W:* Spike Lee; *M:* Bill Lee. VHS, Beta $14.95 *COL, FCT 𝄢𝄢𝄢*

School for Scandal British television adaptation of Richard Sheridan's comedic play of the morals and manners of 18th century England.
1965 100m/B Joan Plowright, Felix Aylmer. VHS, Beta $29.95 *VYY 𝄢𝄢*

School Spirit A hormonally motivated college student is killed during a date. He comes back as a ghost to haunt the campus, disrupt the stuffy president's affair, and fall in love. Forgettable, lame, low-grade teen sex flick.
1985 (R) 90m/C Tom Nolan, Elizabeth Foxx, Larry Linville; *D:* Allan Holleb. VHS, Beta $79.95 *MED 𝄢*

School Ties Encino man Fraser does a dramatic turn as a talented 1950's quarterback who gets a scholarship to the elite St. Matthew prep school. To conform with the closed-mindedness of the McCarthy era, both his father and coach suggest that he hide his Jewish religion. Fraser's compliance results in his big-man-on-campus status, until his rival in football and his love interest both find out that he is Jewish, creating an ugly rift in the school. What easily could have been just another teen hunk flick looks at much more than just Fraser's pretty face in successful, unflinching treatment of anti-Semitism.
1992 (PG-13) 110m/C Brendan Fraser, Matt Damon, Chris O'Donnell, Randall Batinkoff, Andrew Lowery, Cole Hauser, Ben Affleck, Anthony Rapp, Amy Locane, Peter Donat, Zeljko Ivanek, Kevin Tighe, Michael Higgins, Ed Lauter; *D:* Robert Mandel; *W:* Dick Wolf, Darryl Ponicsan; *M:* Maurice Jarre. VHS, Beta $19.95 *PAR 𝄢𝄢𝄢*

Science Crazed A scientist creates a monster who could conceivably destroy the world.
19?? 90m/C Cameron Klein; *D:* Ron Switzer. VHS, Beta *NO 𝄢½*

Scissors Yes, this Hitchcock imitation needs trimming. An unstable young woman contends with a rapist, devious lookalikes, birds, and a prison-like apartment, not all of which are relevant to the plot. An unsharp stab at suspense from novelist/filmmaker DeFelitta.
1991 (R) 105m/C Sharon Stone, Steve Railsback, Michelle Phillips, Ronny Cox; *D:* Frank de Felitta; *W:* Frank de Felitta. VHS, Beta $14.95 *PAR 𝄢½*

Scorchers Back in the bayou, Splendid (Lloyd), a newlywed who won't sleep with her husband, and her cousin Talbot (Tilly), a preacher's daughter whose husband prefers the town whore Thais (Dunaway), find their lives intertwined because of their marital and sexual problems. A real "scorcher."
1992 81m/C Faye Dunaway, Denholm Elliott, James Earl Jones, Emily Lloyd, Jennifer Tilly, Leland Crooke, James Wilder, Anthony Geary; *D:* David Beaird; *W:* David Beaird. VHS, Beta $89.98 *FXV, VTR 𝄢𝄢*

Scorchy Low-budget female cop action flick about a narcotics agent (Stevens) on the trail of a drug kingpin. Blood and guts, guns, and violence. Poor casting.
1976 (R) 100m/C Connie Stevens, William Smith, Cesare Danova, Marlene Schmidt; *D:* Howard (Hikmet) Avedis; *W:* Howard (Hikmet) Avedis. VHS, Beta $29.98 *LIV 𝄢*

Scorned Seductive Patricia Langley loves her husband Truman so much that she'll do anything to help him get that promotion, including seducing another man. Too bad Alex Weston gets the promotion instead. Really too bad, since Patricia decides Alex has ruined her life and she's going to get

revenge by ruining his. Also available in an unrated version.
1993 (R) 100m/C Shannon Tweed, Andrew Stevens, Stephen Young, Daniel McVicar; **D:** Andrew Stevens; **W:** Barry Avrich. **VHS** *PSM* 🎬🎬

Scorpio Okay cat-and-mouse espionage tale about a wily, veteran CIA agent (Lancaster) who may have turned traitor. He's set-up to be killed by a CIA boss but the assassin, code-name Scorpio (Delon), has some trouble fulfilling his assignment. Cross- and double-cross abound.
1973 (PG) 114m/C Burt Lancaster, Alain Delon, Paul Scofield, John Colicos, Gayle Hunnicutt, J.D. Cannon, Joanne Linville, Melvin Stewart, James B. Sikking, Vladek Sheybal, William Smithers, Celeste Yarnall; **D:** Michael Winner. **VHS $14.95** *MGM* 🎬🎬½

The Scorpio Factor Murder and mayhem follow microchip heist.
1990 87m/C Attila Bertalan, David Nerman, Wendy Dawn Wilson. **VHS** *NO* 🎬🎬

Scorpion A karate-master and anti-terrorist expert defuses a skyjacking and infiltrates international assassination conspiracies. Ex-real life karate champ Tulleners is a ho-hum hero, and the story is warmed over.
1986 (R) 98m/C Tonny Tulleners, Allen Williams, Don Murray; **D:** William Reed. **VHS, Beta $79.95** *COL, HHE* 🎬

Scorpion with Two Tails In an underworld of terror, people die grotesque deaths that a woman dreams of.
1982 99m/C John Saxon, Van Johnson. **VHS** *NO* 🎬

The Scorpion Woman A female Viennese judge becomes entwined in an unusual case which partially parallels her own life. Her new young lover turns out to be bisexual. Not gripping. In German with English subtitles.
1989 101m/C Angelica Domrose, Fritz Hammel; **D:** Susanne Zanke. **VHS, Beta** *NO* 🎬🎬

The Scorpion's Tail Graphic murder scenes rev up this early thriller by Martino filmed with plot twists and visual games. Dubbed in English.
1971 90m/C Evelyn Stewart, Anita Strindberg, George Hilton, Luigi Pistilli, Janine Reynaud; **D:** Sergio Martino; **W:** Sauro Scavolini, Ernesto Gastaldi; **M:** Bruno Nicolai. **VHS** *VSM* 🎬

Scotland Yard Inspector An American newspaperman (Romero) in London looks for a killer. Nothing special. **AKA:** Lady in the Fog.
1952 73m/B Cesar Romero, Bernadette O'Farrell; **D:** Sam Newfield. **VHS, Beta $24.95** *MLB* 🎬🎬

Scott of the Antarctic Drama of doomed British expedition of 1911 struggling to be the first group to reach the South Pole. Much of the stunning location filming was shot in the Swiss Alps. Story is authentic, but oddly uninvolving, as though seen from afar.
1948 111m/C John Mills, Christopher Lee, Kenneth More, Derek Bond; **D:** Charles Frend. **VHS, Beta $24.95** *NOS, DVT, MRV* 🎬🎬½

Scoumoune The local "fixer" and heavy gets into trouble and no one comes to help. A movie that searches for honesty. Dubbed in English.
1974 87m/C Jean-Paul Belmondo, Claudia Cardinale. **VHS, Beta** *NO* 🎬🎬½

The Scout Brooks is an about-to-be-canned scout for the New York Yankees who discovers a weird, though genuine, phenom pitcher (Fraser) on a trip to Mexico. He gets him on the team but nobody is sure whether Fraser is playing with a full deck—but with a 100 mph fast ball, who cares?

Brooks rewrote part of the script, adding much needed biting humor. Fraser, whether playing the Encino Man or someone more articulate, is one of the better young actors out there. Bombastic real-life team owner Steinbrenner plays himself.
1994 ?m/C Albert Brooks, Brendan Fraser, Dianne Wiest, Lane Smith, Michael Rappaport, Steve Garvey, Bob Costas, Roy Firestone, Anne Twomey, Tony Bennett; **D:** Michael Ritchie; **W:** Albert Brooks, Andrew Bergman, Monica Johnson; **M:** Bill Conti. **VHS** *NYR* 🎬🎬🎬

Scout's Honor An orphan (Coleman) is determined to become the best Cub Scout ever when he joins a troop led by an executive who dislikes children. Harmless, enjoyable family tale includes several former child stars as Scout parents. Made for television.
1980 96m/C Gary Coleman, Katherine Helmond, Wilfrid Hyde-White, Pat O'Brien, Joanna Moore, Meeno Peluce, Jay North, Harry Morgan, Angela Cartwright; **D:** Henry Levin. **VHS, Beta** *NO* 🎬🎬

Scrambled Feet An uninhibited satire of the world of show business.
1983 100m/C Madeline Kahn. **VHS, Beta $39.95** *RKO, TTC* 🎬🎬½

Scream Vacationers on a raft trip down the Rio Grande are terrorized by a mysterious murderer. Hopelessly dull.
1983 86m/C Pepper Martin, Hank Warden, Alvy Moore, Woody Strode, John Ethan Wayne; **D:** Byron Quisenberry. **VHS, Beta $69.98** *LIV, VES* 🎬

Scream and Scream Again Price is a sinister doctor who tries to create a super race of people devoid of emotions. Cushing is the mastermind behind the plot. Lee is the agent investigating a series of murders. Three great horror stars, a psychedelic disco, great '60s fashions; it's all here.
1970 (PG) 95m/C Vincent Price, Christopher Lee, Peter Cushing, Judy Huxtable, Alfred Marks, Anthony Newlands, Uta Levka, Judi Bloom, Yutte Stensgaard; **D:** Gordon Hessler. **VHS, Beta $69.98** *LIV, VES, ORI* 🎬🎬½

Scream, Baby, Scream An unsuccessful artist switches from sculpting clay to carving young models' faces into hideous deformed creatures. **AKA:** Nightmare House.
1969 86m/C Ross Harris, Eugenie Wingate, Chris Martell, Suzanne Stuart, Larry Swanson, Brad Grinter; **D:** Joseph Adler. **VHS, Beta** *NO* 🎬

Scream Blacula Scream Blacula returns from his dusty undoing in the original movie to once again suck the blood out of greater Los Angeles. A voodoo priestess (Grier) is the only person with the power to stop him. A weak follow up to the great "Blacula," but worth a look for Marshall and Grier.
1973 (R) 96m/C William Marshall, Don Mitchell, Pam Grier, Michael Conrad, Richard Lawson, Lynne Moody, Janee Michelle, Barbara Rhoades, Bernie Hamilton; **D:** Bob Kelljan. **VHS $59.98** *ORI, FCT* 🎬🎬

Scream Bloody Murder A young boy grinds his father to death with a tractor but mangles his own hand trying to jump off. After receiving a steel claw and being released from a mental institution he continues his murderous ways in and around his home town. Inspiring.
1972 (R) 90m/C Fred Holbert, Leigh Mitchell, Robert Knox, Suzette Hamilton; **D:** Robert Emery. **VHS, Beta $19.95** *VCI* Woof!

Scream Dream A beautiful rock star uses her supernatural powers to control her fans, turning them into revenge-seeking monsters when she wants to. Heavy on the blood and skin; heavily exploitative.

1989 (R) 80m/C Melissa Moore, Carole Carr, Nikki Riggins, Jesse Ray; **D:** Donald Farmer; **W:** Donald Farmer. **VHS** *NO* 🎬

Scream for Help A young girl discovers that her cheating stepfather is plotting to murder her mother, but no one will believe her. Is she paranoid? So bad it's funny; otherwise, it's just bad, and far from suspenseful.
1986 (R) 95m/C Rachael Kelly, David Brooks, Marie Masters; **D:** Michael Winner; **W:** Tom Holland. **VHS, Beta $19.95** *LHV, WAR* 🎬

Scream of Fear A wheelchair-bound young woman goes to visit her father and new stepmother only to find her father is away on business. But she believes she sees her father's corpse. Is someone trying to drive her mad? Abounds in plot twists and mistaken identities. A truly spooky film, suspenseful, and well-made. **AKA:** Taste of Fear.
1961 81m/B Susan Strasberg, Ronald Lewis, Ann Todd, Christopher Lee; **D:** Seth Holt; **W:** Jimmy Sangster. **VHS, Beta $69.95** *COL, MLB* 🎬🎬🎬

Scream of the Demon Lover A young biochemist has a busy day as she works for a reclusive Baron. She fantasizes about him, tries to track down a murderer, and eventually discovers a mutant in the cellar. About as bad as they come, but short!
1971 (R) 75m/C Jennifer Hartley, Jeffrey Chase; **D:** J.L. Merino. **VHS, Beta $59.98** *NLC* Woof!

Screamer A woman wants revenge after she is viciously attacked and raped. Now every man she sees is her attacker as she becomes more and more unbalanced.
1974 71m/C Pamela Franklin, Donal McCann. **VHS, Beta** *NO* 🎬

Screamers A mad scientist on a desert island gleefully turns escaped convicts into grotesque monstrosities. Gory and gratuitous. **AKA:** L'Isola Degli Uomini Pesce; Island of the Fishmen; Something Waits in the Dark.
1980 (R) 83m/C Richard Johnson, Joseph Cotten, Barbara Bach; **D:** Dan T. Miller; Sergio Martino. **VHS, Beta $19.98** *SUE* 🎬

The Screaming Dead Monsters rise from the tomb to do battle with planet Earth and each other. Not to be confused with the Al Adamson epic "Dracula vs. Frankenstein." **AKA:** Dracula vs. Frankenstein.
1972 84m/C Dennis Price, Howard Vernon, Alberto Dalbes, Mary Francis, Genevieve Deloir, Josianne Gibert, Fernando Bilbao; **D:** Jess (Jesus) Franco. **VHS $69.95** *VCI* 🎬

The Screaming Skull Man redecorates house with skulls in attempt to drive already anxious wife insane.
1958 68m/B William Hudson, Peggy Webber, Toni Johnson, Russ Conway, Alex Nicol; **D:** Alex Nicol; **M:** Ernest Gold. **VHS $19.98** *NOS, SNC* 🎬½

Screams of a Winter Night Ghostly tale of an evil monster from the lake and the terror he causes.
1979 (PG) 92m/C Matt Borel, Gil Glasco. **VHS, Beta $54.95** *VCI* 🎬

Screamtime Two fiendish friends filch a trilogy of horror tapes for home viewing. After the show, real scary things happen.
1983 (R) 89m/C Jean Anderson, Robin Bailey, Dora Bryan, David Van Day; **D:** Al Beresford. **VHS, Beta $69.98** *LIV* 🎬

Screen Test Oversexed silly teenagers arrange fake screen tests in order to meet girls.
1985 (R) 84m/C Michael Allan Bloom, Robert Bundy, Paul Lueken, David Simpatico; **D:** Sam Auster. **VHS, Beta $79.95** *COL* Woof!

Screwball Academy A beautiful female director makes a soft-core film on a secluded island, and gets trouble from thugs, evangelists, horny crew members and others. Former "SCTV" director John Blanchard understandably used a pseudonym to direct this lame effort.
1986 (R) 90m/C Colleen Camp, Kenneth Welsh, Christine Cattall; **D:** Reuben Rose. **VHS, Beta** $69.95 TWE ♂½

Screwballs Freewheeling group of high school boys stirs up trouble for their snooty and virginal homecoming queen. Another inept teen sex comedy with no subtlety whatsoever. Sequel: "Loose Screws."
1983 (R) 80m/C Peter Keleghan, Lynda Speciale; **D:** Rafal Zeilinski; **W:** Jim Wynorski. **VHS, Beta** $19.98 WAR ♂

Scrooge On Christmas Eve a miser changes his ways after receiving visits from the ghosts of Christmas past, present, and future. Co-scripter Hicks gives an interesting performance as Ebeneezer Scrooge. Based on the classic novel "A Christmas Carol" by Charles Dickens.
1935 61m/B Seymour Hicks, Maurice Evans, Robert Cochran, Donald Calthrop, Mary Glynne, Oscar Asche; **D:** Henry Edwards; **W:** Seymour Hicks. **VHS, Beta** $19.95 VYY, CCB, DVT ♂♂♂

Scrooge Well-done musical version of Charles Dickens' classic "A Christmas Carol," about a miserly old man who is faced with ghosts on Christmas Eve. Finney is memorable in the title role. ♫The Beautiful Day; Happiness; Thank You Very Much; A Christmas Carol; Christmas Children; I Hate People; Farver Chris'mas; See the Phantoms; December the 25th.
1970 (G) 86m/C Albert Finney, Alec Guinness, Edith Evans, Kenneth More; **D:** Ronald Neame; **M:** Leslie Bricusse. Academy Awards '70 Nominations: Best Art Direction/Set Decoration, Best Costume Design, Best Song ("Thank You Very Much"), Best Original Score; Golden Globe Awards '71: Best Actor—Musical/Comedy (Finney). **VHS, Beta** $14.98 FOX, FUS ♂♂½

Scrooged Somewhat disjointed big-budgeted version of the hallowed classic. A callous television executive staging "A Christmas Carol" is himself visited by the three ghosts and sees the light. Kane is terrific as one of the ghosts. Film is heavy-handed, Murray too sardonic to be believable.
1988 (PG-13) 101m/C Bill Murray, Carol Kane, John Forsythe, David Johansen, Bob(cat) Goldthwait, Karen Allen, Michael J. Pollard, Brian Doyle-Murray, Alfre Woodard, John Glover, Robert Mitchum, Buddy Hackett, Robert Goulet, Jamie Farr, Mary Lou Retton, Lee Majors; **D:** Richard Donner; **W:** Mitch Glazer, Michael O'Donoghue; **M:** Danny Elfman. **VHS, Beta, 8mm** $89.95 PAR ♂♂

Scrubbers Young girl is sent to reform school where she's forced to survive in a cruel and brutal environment. Low-budget "reform school" movie with no point, but lots of lesbianism.
1982 (R) 93m/C Amanda York, Chrissie Cotterill, Elizabeth Edmonds, Kate Ingram, Debbie Bishop, Dana Gillespie; **D:** Mai Zetterling. **VHS, Beta** NO ♂

Scruffy An orphan and his dog survive with the help of two crooks who are reformed through their love for the little boy. Animated.
1980 72m/C V: Alan Young, June Foray, Hans Conried, Nancy McKeon. **VHS, Beta** $19.95 WOV, GKK, WTA ♂

Scruples Set in the glamorous, jet-setting world of Beverly Hills, this top-rated miniseries follows the career of Billy Ikehorn (Wagner) as she weds a wealthy industrialist and opens a clothing boutique named "Scruples." She caters to high society's haute couture, and encounters unscrupulous individuals who threaten to dethrone her from her position of power and privilege. Based on the best-selling novel by Judith Krantz.
1980 279m/C Lindsay Wagner, Barry Bostwick, Kim Cattrall, Gavin MacLeod, Connie Stevens, Efrem Zimbalist Jr., Gene Tierney; **M:** Charles Bernstein. **VHS, Beta** $29.98 WAR ♂♂½

Scum Adapted from Roy Minton's acclaimed play, this British production looks at the struggle among three young men in a British Borstal (a prison for young convicts.) Portrays the physical, sexual, and psychological violence committed. Horrifying and powerful.
1979 96m/C Phil Daniels, Mick Ford, Ray Winstone; **D:** Alan Clarke. **VHS, Beta** $59.95 PSM ♂♂♂

Sea Chase An odd post-war sea adventure, wherein a renegade German freighter captain is pursued by British and German navies as he leaves Australia at the outbreak of WWII. A Prussian Wayne rivaled only by his infamous Genghis Khan in "The Conqueror" for strange character selection. Turner is on board as Wayne's girlfriend.
1955 117m/C John Wayne, Lana Turner, Tab Hunter, James Arness, Lyle Bettger, David Farrar, Richard Davalos, Claude Akins, John Qualen; **D:** John Farrow. **VHS, Beta** $19.98 WAR ♂♂½

Sea Devils Sentenced to prison for a crime he didn't commit, a man escapes and joins a boatload of treasure hunters, but mutiny is afoot. Don't get soaked by this cheapie.
1931 77m/B Walter Long, Edmund Burns, Henry Otto, James Donnelly; **D:** Joseph Levering. **VHS** $16.95 SNC, NOS ♂

Sea Devils The tale of a sea captain and his lovely daughter who have differing opinions on whom she should marry. While her father would like her to marry a tame gentlemen under his command, she has her heart set on another beau. Sound predictable? It is, but fun.
1937 88m/B Victor McLaglen, Preston Foster, Ida Lupino, Donald Woods, Gordon Jones; **D:** Ben Stoloff. **VHS** $9.95 MED ♂♂

Sea Devils A smuggler and a beautiful spy come together during the Napoleonic Wars in this sea romance filled with intrigue and adventure.
1953 86m/C Rock Hudson, Yvonne De Carlo, Maxwell Reed; **D:** Raoul Walsh. **VHS, Beta** $9.95 MED ♂♂

Sea Gypsies A sailing crew of five is shipwrecked off the Aleutian Islands. They must escape before winter or learn to survive. Passable family drama.
1978 (G) 101m/C Robert F. Logan, Mikki Jamison-Olsen, Heather Rattray, Cjon Damitri; **D:** Stewart Raffill; **W:** Stewart Raffill. **VHS, Beta** $14.95 WAR ♂♂

The Sea Hawk An English privateer learns the Spanish are going to invade England with their Armada. After numerous adventures, he is able to aid his queen and help save his country, finding romance along the way. One of Flynn's swashbuckling best. Available colorized.
1940 128m/B Errol Flynn, Claude Rains, Donald Crisp, Alan Hale, Flora Robson, Brenda Marshall, Henry Daniell, Gilbert Roland, James Stephenson, Una O'Connor; **D:** Michael Curtiz; **W:** Howard Koch. **VHS, Beta** $19.98 MGM, TTC, FOX ♂♂♂½

Sea Hound A 15-part series set in the late 1940s that charts the voyage of a group of pirates searching for buried treasure. Everything goes well until Crabbe emerges to wreck their hopes.
1947 ?m/B Buster Crabbe, Jimmy Lloyd, Pamela Blake, Ralph Hodges, Robert Barron; **D:** Walter B. Eason, Mack V. Wright. **VHS** MLB, GPV ♂♂

Sea Lion A vicious sea captain, embittered by a past romance, becomes sadistic and intolerable, until the truth emerges. Lots of action, but plodding, rehashed plot. Silent.
1921 50m/B Hobart Bosworth. **VHS, Beta** $24.95 VYY ♂♂

Sea of Dreams Don't expect much in the way of a script from this soft-core production.
1990 80m/C Jon Rodgers, Chad Scott, Jacky Peel, Renee O'Neil. **VHS, Beta** $39.95 AHV, HHE ♂

Sea of Love A tough, tightly wound thriller about an alcoholic cop with a mid-life crisis. While following the track of a serial killer, he begins a torrid relationship with one of his suspects. Pacino doesn't stand a chance when Barkin heats up the screen.
1989 (R) 113m/C Al Pacino, Ellen Barkin, John Goodman, Michael Rooker, William Hickey, Richard Jenkins; **D:** Harold Becker; **W:** Richard Price; **M:** Trevor Jones. **VHS, Beta** $19.95 MCA ♂♂♂½

Sea Prince and the Fire Child Japanese animated film follows two young lovers who set off on an adventure to escape the disapproval of their parents.
1982 70m/C VHS, Beta $19.95 COL ♂♂

Sea Racketeers Soggy old tribute to the Coast Guard inadvertently makes them look like a bunch of bumblers, as they belatedly uncover a fur-smuggling racket working under their noses from a floating nightclub.
1937 64m/B Weldon Heyburn, Jeanne Madden, Warren Hymer, Dorothy McNulty, J. Carroll Naish, Joyce Compton, Charles Trowbridge, Syd Saylor, Lane Chandler, Benny Burt; **D:** Hamilton MacFadden. **VHS, Beta** $16.95 SNC ♂½

The Sea Serpent A young sea captain and a crusty scientist unite to search out a giant sea monster awakened by atomic tests. Not one of Millan's better films.
1985 92m/C Timothy Bottoms, Ray Milland, Jared Martin; **D:** Gregory Greens. **VHS, Beta** $69.98 LIV ♂½

The Sea Shall Not Have Them A British bomber crashes into the North Sea during WWII. Film tells of the survivors' rescue by the Air-Sea Rescue Unit. Decent drama/adventure.
1955 92m/B Michael Redgrave, Dirk Bogarde; **D:** Lewis Gilbert; **M:** Malcolm Arnold. **VHS** $39.98 REP ♂♂½

The Sea Wolf Jack London's adventure novel about brutal, canny Captain Wolf Larsen (Robinson), his rebellious crew, and some unexpected passengers. Knox and Lupino are shipwreck survivors, picked up by Robinson and forced into working aboard his ship, the aptly named "Ghost." Crewman Garfield falls for Lupino and tries to rally his shipmates into resisting the meglomaniacal Robinson. Fine performances by all, especially Robinson as the personification of malevolent ego. Screen debut of Knox. Director Curtiz filmed entirely in studio tanks, sets, and pervasive fog machines. Previously filmed three times; later remade as "Barricade" and "Wolf Larsen."

1941 90m/C Edward G. Robinson, Alexander Knox, John Garfield, Ida Lupino, Gene Lockhart, Barry Fitzgerald, Stanley Ridges, Francis McDonald, David Bruce, Howard da Silva, Frank Lackteen, Ralf Harolde; **D:** Michael Curtiz; **W:** Robert Rossen. **VHS $19.98** *MGM, MOV, BTV* ⬥⬥⬥½

The Sea Wolf Yet another adaptation of Jack London's classic battle of wills tale. Captain Wolf Larsen (Bronson) commands a surly ship of seal hunters through sheer ruthlessness and ego. He rescues snobbish theater critic Van Weyden (Reeve) and pretty scam artist Flaxen (Stewart) from a capsized ferry. The self-educated captain wants to test out his theories about survival of the fittest by making the rich Van Weyden his cabin boy (Flaxen gets leered at). Lots of teeth-gnashing and bellowing in this turgid TV remake, although Revill has fun as the sniveling Cookie. See the Edward G. Robinson version instead.
1993 120m/C Charles Bronson, Christopher Reeve, Catherine Mary Stewart, Clive Revill; **D:** Michael Anderson Jr.; **W:** Andrew J. Fenady. **VHS $89.98** *TTC* ⬥⬥

Sea Wolves True WWII story about a commando-style operation undertaken by a group of middle-aged, retired British calvarymen in India in 1943. Decent acting, though Peck's British accent fades in and out, with Moore as Bond.
1981 (PG) 120m/C Gregory Peck, Roger Moore, David Niven, Trevor Howard, Patrick Macnee; **D:** Andrew V. McLaglen; **W:** Reginald Rose. **VHS, Beta $59.98** *FOX, WAR* ⬥⬥½

The Seagull A pensive, sensitive adaptation of the famed Chekhov play about the depressed denizens of an isolated country estate. In Russian with English subtitles.
1971 99m/B Alla Demidova, Lyudmila Savelyeva, Yuri Yakovlev; **D:** Yuri Karasik. **VHS, Beta $29.95** *FCT, MRV, AUD* ⬥⬥⬥

Seance on a Wet Afternoon Dark, thoughtful film about a crazed pseudo-psychic who coerces her husband into a kidnapping so she can gain recognition by divining the child's whereabouts. Directed splendidly by Forbes, and superb acting from Stanley and Attenborough, who co-produced with Forbes.
1964 111m/B Kim Stanley, Richard Attenborough, Margaret Lacey, Maria Kazan, Mark Eden, Patrick Magee; **D:** Bryan Forbes; **M:** John Barry. Academy Awards '64 Nominations: Best Actress (Stanley); British Academy Awards '64: Best Actor (Attenborough); National Board of Review Awards '64: 10 Best Films of the Year, Best Actress (Stanley). **VHS, Beta $29.95** *HMV, BTV* ⬥⬥⬥½

The Search Clift, an American soldier stationed in post-WWII Berlin, befriends a homeless nine-year-old amnesiac boy (Jandl) and tries to find his family. Meanwhile, his mother has been searching the Displaced Persons camps for her son. Although Clift wants to adopt the boy, he steps aside, and mother and son are finally reunited. "The Search" was shot on location in the American Occupied Zone of Germany. Jandl won a special juvenile Oscar in his first (and only) film role. This was also Clift's first screen appearance, although this movie was actually filmed after his debut in "Red River," it was released first.
1948 105m/B Montgomery Clift, Aline MacMahon, Ivan Jandl, Jarmila Novotna, Wendell Corey; **D:** Fred Zinneman. Academy Awards '48: Best Original Screenplay; Nominations: Best Actor (Clift), Best Director (Zinneman), Best Screenplay; Golden Globe Awards '49: Best Screenplay. **VHS $19.98** *MGM* ⬥⬥⬥½

Search and Destroy Deadly vendetta is begun by a Vietnamese official during the war. It is continued in the U.S. as he hunts down the American soldiers he feels betrayed him. Sub-par, forgettable war/action flick. **AKA:** Striking Back.
1981 (PG) 93m/C Perry King, Don Stroud, Park Jong Soo, George Kennedy, Tisa Farrow; **D:** William Fruet. **VHS, Beta $69.95** *VES* ⬥

Search and Destroy Sci-fi action flick about the capture of a secret biological warfare research station. Lotsa action, that's for sure - where's the plot?
1988 (R) 87m/C Stuart Garrison Day, Dan Kuchuck, Peggy Jacobsen; **D:** J. Christian Ingvordsen. **VHS, Beta $19.95** *MCG* ⬥

The Search for Bridey Murphy Long before channelers, Ramtha and New-Age profiteers, there was a Colorado housewife who under hypnosis described a previous life as an Irish girl. Her famous claim was never proven—but that didn't stop this well-acted but dull dramatization. Neither sensationalist, nor likely to persuade skeptics. Based on the book by Morey Bernstein, hypnotist in the case.
1956 84m/B Teresa Wright, Louis Hayward, Nancy Gates, Kenneth Tobey, Richard Anderson; **D:** Noel Langley; **W:** Noel Langley. **VHS $14.95** *PAR, FCT* ⬥⬥

Search for Signs of Intelligent Life in the Universe Tomlin's brilliant one-woman show has been expanded into a wonderful film. As Tomlin's cast of 12 female and male characters meet and interact, they show every viewer his/her own humanity.
1991 (PG-13) 120m/C Lily Tomlin; **D:** John Bailey; **W:** Jane Wagner; **M:** Jerry Goodman. **VHS $89.98** *WLF, BTV* ⬥⬥⬥

Search for the Gods A dig in the Southwest turns interesting when one of the archeologists comes across an exquisite ancient medallion that could answer questions about alien visitors. Pilot for a television series that didn't make it.
1975 100m/C Kurt Russell, Stephen McHattie, Ralph Bellamy, Victoria Racimo, Raymond St. Jacques; **D:** Judd Taylor. **VHS $59.95** *UNI, HHE* ⬥½

The Searchers The classic Ford western, starring John Wayne as a hard-hearted frontiersman who spends years doggedly pursuing his niece, who was kidnapped by Indians. A simple western structure supports Ford's most moving, mysterious, complex film. Many feel this is the best western of all time.
1956 119m/C John Wayne, Jeffrey Hunter, Vera Miles, Natalie Wood, Ward Bond, John Qualen, Harry Carey Jr., Olive Carey, Antonio Moreno, Henry Brandon, Hank Worden, Lana Wood, Dorothy Jordan, Patrick Wayne; **D:** John Ford; **W:** Frank Nugent; **M:** Max Steiner. **VHS, Beta $19.98** *WAR, TLF* ⬥⬥⬥⬥

Searching for Bobby Fischer 7-year-old Josh Waitzkin (Pomeranc, in his debut) shows an amazing gift for chess, stunning his parents, who must then try to strike the delicate balance of developing his abilities while also allowing him a "normal" childhood. Excellent cast features Mantegna and Allen as his parents, Kingsley as demanding chess teacher Pandolfini, and Fishburne as an adept speed-chess hustler. Pomeranc is great, and his knowledge of chess (he's a ranked player) brings authenticity to his role. Title comes from Pandolfini's belief that Josh may equal the abilities of chess whiz Bobby Fischer. Underrated little gem based on a true story and adapted from the book by Waitzkin's father.
1993 (PG) 111m/C Joe Mantegna, Max Pomeranc, Joan Allen, Ben Kingsley, Laurence "Larry" Fishburne, Robert Stephens, David Paymer, Robert Stephens, William H. Macy; **D:** Steven Zaillian; **W:** Steven Zaillian; **M:** James Horner. Academy Awards '93 Nominations: Best Cinematography; MTV Movie Awards '94: Best New Filmmaker Award (Zaillian). **VHS, Beta** *PAR* ⬥⬥⬥½

Seaside Swingers A group of teenagers at a seaside resort work to win a talent competition on television. But where is the talent? Dumb teen romance comedy with accidental plot. ♫All I Want Is You; A Girls Needs a Boy; Second Time Around; Indubitably Me; Love Me, Please; Now, Ain't That Somethin'—Caw Blimey; Romeo Jones; What's Cookin. **AKA:** Every Day's a Holiday.
1965 94m/C Michael Sarne, Grazina Frame, John Leyton, Freddie & the Dreamers; **D:** James Hill. **VHS, Beta $59.98** *NLC* ⬥½

Season for Assassins Police commissioner Castroni is the only man who can stop a wave of violence enveloping Rome.
1971 102m/C Joe Dallesandro, Martin Balsam. **VHS, Beta $29.95** *LIV* ⬥½

Season of Fear A young man visits his estranged father's home. Abandoned as a child, he's embroiled in a murder scheme engineered by his father's beautiful young wife. Intriguing premise, forgettable execution.
1989 (R) 89m/C Michael Bowen, Clancy Brown, Clare Wren, Ray Wise, Michael J. Pollard; **D:** Douglas Campbell. **VHS, Beta $79.98** *FOX* ⬥½

Season of the Witch A frustrated housewife becomes intrigued with a neighboring witch and begins to practice witchcraft herself, through murder and seduction. Meant to be suspenseful, thrilling, and topical, it is none of these. Poorly acted at best. Originally 130 minutes! **AKA:** Hungry Wives; Jack's Wife.
1973 (R) 89m/C Jan White, Ray Laine, Bill Thunhurst, Joedida McClain, Virginia Greenwald; **D:** George A. Romero; **W:** George A. Romero. **Beta** *NO* ⬥½

Sebastian Mathematics whiz is employed by the British to decipher codes. He falls in love with York, another code breaker, and becomes involved in international intrigue. A bit too fast-paced and busy, but enjoyable spy drama. Sutherland has a small role. **AKA:** Mr. Sebastian.
1968 100m/C Dirk Bogarde, Susannah York, Lilli Palmer, John Gielgud, Margaret Johnston, Nigel Davenport, Donald Sutherland; **D:** David Greene; **M:** Jerry Goldsmith. **VHS** *MOV* ⬥⬥½

Sebastiane An audacious film version of the legend of St. Sebastian, packed with homoerotic imagery and ravishing visuals. Honest, faithful rendering of the Saint's life and refusal to obey Roman authorities. Jarman's first film, in Latin with English subtitles.
1979 90m/C Leonardo Treviglio, Barney James, Richard James, Neil Kennedy; **D:** Derek Jarman; **M:** Brian Eno. **VHS, Beta $29.95** *FCT, ING* ⬥⬥⬥

Second Best Secret Agent in the Whole Wide World A klutzy agent attempts to prevent a Swedish anti-gravity formula from falling into Russian hands. Surprisingly good early spoof of the James Bond genre. **AKA:** Licensed to Kill.
1965 93m/C Tom Adams, Veronica Hurst, Peter Bull, Karel Stepanek, John Arnatt; **D:** Lindsay Shonteff. **VHS, Beta $59.98** *NLC* ⬥⬥½

Second Chance A former prizefighter (Mitchum) travels to Mexico where he protects a gangster's moll (Darnell) targeted for murder. But Palance are on their tail. Originally

S

released theatrically on a wide screen in 3-D. Good melodrama. **1953 82m/C** Robert Mitchum, Linda Darnell, Jack Palance, Reginald Sheffield, Roy Roberts; **D:** Rudolph Mate. VHS, Beta $19.95 MED ☆☆½

Second Chance When a woman finds her husband is in love with another, her marital happiness is shattered. She leaves her betrayer and struggles to adapt to life as a single mother. Made for British television. **1980 270m/C** Susannah York, Ralph Bates; **D:** Gerry Mill, Richard Handford. VHS NO ☆☆

Second Chorus Rivalry of two trumpet players for a girl and a job with Artie Shaw Orchestra. Music, dance, and romance. Nothing great, but pleasant. ♫Would You Like to Be the Love of My Life?; Poor Mr. Chisholm; (I Ain't Help to That Step) But I'll Dig It; Swing Concerto; Sweet Sue; I'm Yours. **1940 83m/B** Fred Astaire, Paulette Goddard, Burgess Meredith, Artie Shaw, Charles Butterworth; **D:** H.C. Potter. VHS, Beta $19.95 NOS, HHT, CAB ☆☆½

Second City Insanity The famed Second City improvisational troupe performs their unique brand of humor. **1981 60m/C** Fred Willard, John Candy. VHS, Beta LHV ☆☆½

Second Coming of Suzanne Young actress encounters a hypnotic film director. Her role: to star in a crucifixion—which may be more real than she imagines. Winner of two international film festivals. **1980 90m/C** Sondra Locke, Richard Dreyfuss, Gene Barry; **D:** Michael Barry. VHS, Beta $19.95 GEM ☆☆½

Second Fiddle Power is a studio flack who's hired to mount a huge talent search for a girl to star in a new film epic (very clear parallels to the Scarlet O'Hara "Gone With the Wind" hunt). He's sent to smalltown Minnesota where he meets Henie, who lives with her forbidding aunt (Oliver), who doesn't want her niece to go to wicked Hollywood. Nevertheless, Henie gets the part, becomes a success, and falls for her co-star Vallee. But it's all a publicity stunt on his part and Power is the one who really loves the girl. Henie gets to do some skating. ♫Back to Back; I'm Sorry for Myself; I Poured My Heart Into Song; An Old-Fashioned Tune Is Always New; When Winter Comes; Song of the Metronome. **AKA:** Irving Berlin's Second Fiddle. **1939 86m/B** Sonja Henie, Tyrone Power, Rudy Vallee, Edna May Oliver, Mary Healy, Lyle Talbot, Alan Dinehart, Minna Gombell; **D:** Sidney Lanfield; **W:** Harry Tugend; **M:** Irving Berlin, Irving Berlin. VHS $19.98 FXV ☆☆½

Second Sight A detective (Larroquette) and a goofy psychic (Pinchot) set out to find a kidnapped priest. Flick is sidetracked along the way by such peculiarities as a pixieish nun for romantic, not religious, intrigue. Remember this one? No? That's because you blinked when it was released to theaters. Eminently missable. **1989 (PG) 84m/C** John Larroquette, Bronson Pinchot, Bess Armstrong, James Tolkan, Christine Estabrook, Cornelia Guest, Stuart Pankin, William Prince, John Schuck; **D:** Joel Zwick; **W:** Patricia Resnick, Tom Schulman. VHS, Beta $19.95 WAR ☆

Second Thoughts Frustrated woman attorney divorces her stuffy husband and takes up with an aging hippie. She comes to regret her decision when it becomes obvious that her new man has his head firmly stuck in the 60s. Comedy-drama lacking real laughs or drama.

1983 (PG) 109m/C Lucie Arnaz, Craig Wasson, Ken Howard, Joe Mantegna; **D:** Lawrence Turman. VHS, Beta $59.99 CNG ☆

Second Time Lucky The devil makes a bet with God that if the world began all over again Adam and Eve would repeat their mistake they made in the Garden of Eden. Bites off a lot, but has no teeth nor laughs. **1984 98m/C** Diane Franklin, Roger Wilson, Robert Morley, Jon Gadsby, Bill Ewens; **D:** Michael Anderson Sr. VHS, Beta $14.95 LHV ☆

Second Victory Major Mark Hanlon has been appointed an Occupation Officer in the winter of 1945. He expects this will be his chance to work for peace but when a good friend is brutally murdered all his thoughts turn to revenge. Based on the novel by Morris West. **1987 (PG) 95m/C** Anthony Andrews, Max von Sydow, Renee Soutendijk; **D:** Gerald Thomas. VHS $89.95 AIP ☆☆½

Second Wind Wagner and Naughton are trying to settle into their new life together, but find they must make a variety of difficult choices. **1990 (PG) 93m/C** Lindsay Wagner, James Naughton. VHS NO ☆☆

Second Woman An architect, suffering from blackouts and depression, believes himself responsible for the death of his fiancee. Well-done psycho-drama. **AKA:** Here Lies Love; Twelve Miles Out. **1951 91m/B** Robert Young, Betsy Drake, John Sutton; **D:** James V. Kern. VHS, Beta $14.95 NOS, VCI, VDM ☆☆½

The Secret Businessman and political candidate Mike Dunsmore (Douglas) comes to terms with his lifelong battle with dyslexia when his grandson begins to show signs of the same affliction. Set in picturesque New England fishing village. **1993 92m/C** Kirk Douglas, Bruce Boxleitner, Brock Peters, Laura Harrington; **D:** Karen Arthur. VHS $89.95 CAF ☆☆½

Secret Admirer A teenager's unsigned love letter keeps falling into the wrong hands. Intends to be funny, and sometimes is; too often, though, it surrenders to obviousness and predictability. **1985 (R) 98m/C** C. Thomas Howell, Cliff DeYoung, Kelly Preston, Dee Wallace Stone, Lori Loughlin, Fred Ward, Casey Siemaszko, Corey Haim, Leigh Taylor-Young; **D:** David Greenwalt. VHS, Beta NO ☆☆

The Secret Adversary Set in 1920s London. Ace detectives Tommy and Tuppence Beresford must find a secret treaty before it falls into the wrong hands. Pilot for the "Partners in Crime" series. Based on the characters created by Agatha Christie. **1983 120m/C** Francesca Annis, James Warwick. VHS, Beta $19.95 TPV ☆☆

The Secret Agent Presumed dead, a British intelligence agent (Gielgud) reappears and receives a new assignment. Using his faked death to his advantage, he easily journeys to Switzerland where he is to eliminate an enemy agent. Strange Hitchcockian melange of comedy and intrigue; atypical, but worthy offering from the Master. **1936 83m/B** Madeleine Carroll, Peter Lorre, Robert Young, John Gielgud, Lilli Palmer; **D:** Alfred Hitchcock; **W:** Charles Bennett. VHS, Beta $16.95 SNC, NOS, HHT ☆☆☆

Secret Agent Secret agent John Drake embarks upon dangerous and exciting assignments around the world in this mystery-adventure series, which ran during 1965 and 1966. All but two episodes are in black and white.

1964 60m/B Patrick McGoohan, Niall MacGinnis, Dawn Addams, Lelia Goldoni; **D:** Don Chaffey. VHS, Beta $19.99 MPI, MOV ☆☆☆

Secret Agent 00 A master criminal plans to blackmail the western world and only special Secret Agent 00 can stop him. Bad spy genre ripoff, interesting only as the screen debut of Sean Connery's brother. **AKA:** Operation Kid Brother. **1967 (R) 97m/C** Neil Connery, Daniela Bianchi, Adolfo Celi; **D:** Alberto De Martino; **M:** Ennio Morricone. VHS NO ☆

Secret Agent Super Dragon The CIA calls in the agent known as "Super Dragon" when it is discovered that a Venezuelan drug czar plans to spike U.S. gum and candy with an LSD-like drug. Less than competent production offers some unintended laughter. **AKA:** Super Dragon. **1966 95m/C** Ray Danton, Marisa Mell, Margaret Lee, Jess Hahn, Carlo D'Angelo, Andriana Ambesi; **D:** Calvin Jackson Padget. VHS, Beta $16.95 SNC ☆

Secret Beyond the Door A wealthy heiress marries a widower and soon discovers that he murdered his first wife. Understandably, she wonders what plans he might have for her. Capably done chiller, but the plot is hackneyed pseudo-Hitchcock. **1948 99m/B** Joan Bennett, Michael Redgrave, Barbara O'Neil, Anne Revere; **D:** Fritz Lang; **M:** Miklos Rozsa. VHS $19.98 REP ☆☆

Secret Ceremony An aging prostitute and a young, aimless waif resemble each other's dead mother and dead daughter, respectively, and the relationship goes on, strangely, from there. This original big-screen version is very good Freudian psycho-drama; 101-minute TV version is unfortunately greatly diluted. **1969 109m/C** Elizabeth Taylor, Robert Mitchum, Mia Farrow, Pamela Brown, Peggy Ashcroft; **D:** Joseph Losey; **M:** Richard Rodney Bennett. VHS, Beta $14.95 BAR ☆☆½

The Secret Cinema A woman is caught between reality and a cinematic nightmare in this bizarre first film by famed cult director Bartel. **19?? 37m/C D:** Paul Bartel. VHS $19.95 RHI ☆

The Secret Code A 15-chapter serial with the Black Commando (Kelly) thwarting the Nazis' attempts at sabotage. After each chapter's cliffhanger ending a new form of secret code is explained and decoded. **1942 315m/B** Paul Kelly, Anne Nagel, Clancy Cooper, Trevor Bardette, Gregory Gay, Ludwig Donath, Ed Parker; **D:** Spencer Gordon Bennet. VHS $26.95 GPV ☆☆½

The Secret Diary of Sigmund Freud Spoofy look at the early years of Sigmund Freud, the father of modern psychoanalysis. Freud (Cort) has an affair with lisping nurse Kane while tending to patient Shawn and answering to mama Baker, who's carrying on with mad doctor Kinski. Talented cast falls asleep on couch. **1984 129m/C** Bud Cort, Carol Kane, Carroll Baker, Klaus Kinski, Marisa Berenson, Dick Shawn, Ferdinand "Ferdy" Mayne; **D:** Danford B. Greene. VHS, Beta $79.98 FOX ☆☆

Secret File of Hollywood A down-and-out private eye gets a job taking photos for a sleazy Hollywood scandal sheet and finds himself in the midst of a blackmail plot masterminded by his editor. An often childish potboiler, perhaps inspired by the once-feared Confidential Magazine. **AKA:** Secret File: Hollywood. **1962 85m/B** Robert Clarke, Francine York, Syd Mason, Maralou Gray, John Warburton; **D:** Ralph Cushman. VHS $15.95 NOS, LOO, TPV ☆½

The Secret Four Three young men seek to avenge the death of their friend at the hands of British traitors, and become involved in a plot to sabotage the Suez canal. Poorly adapted from the novel by Edgar Wallace. *AKA:* The Four Just Men.
1940 79m/B Hugh Sinclair, Griffith Jones, Francis L. Sullivan, Frank Lawton, Anna Lee, Alan Napier, Basil Sydney; *D:* Walter Forde. VHS, Beta $16.95 *SNC ♂♂*

Secret Games An unhappily married woman (Brin) is searching for relief from her restrictive marriage. At the "Afternoon Demitasse," an exclusive brothel where women are paid for fulfilling their ultimate fantasies, she meets a man (Hewitt) who pushes her beyond her sexual limits and threatens to totally possess her.
1992 (R) 90m/C Martin Hewitt, Michele Brin, Delia Sheppard, Billy Drago; *D:* Alexander Gregory Hippolyte. VHS $89.95 *IMP ♂ ½*

Secret Games 2: The Escort A performance artist (Hewitt) learns how to seduce women from a beautiful escort (Rochelle). However, he falls for his trainer despite being a star pupil who could have anyone he wanted. Plot conveniently lends itself to lots of steamy love scenes. Also available in an unrated version.
1993 (R) ?m/C Martin Hewitt, Amy Rochelle, Sara Suzanne Brown, Marie Leroux; *D:* Alexander Gregory Hippolyte; *W:* Russell Lavalle; *M:* Ashley Irwin. VHS $89.95 *IMP ♂ ½*

The Secret Garden The well-loved Frances Hodgson Burnett story has been remade and even revamped as a Broadway musical, but this is considered the definitive version. An orphan girl arrives at her uncle's somber Victorian estate. She starts tending a long-forgotten garden, and with its resurrection joy returns to the household. O'Brien leads an outstanding cast in one of her final juvenile roles. In black and white, with Technicolor for later garden scenes.
1949 92m/B Margaret O'Brien, Herbert Marshall, Dean Stockwell, Gladys Cooper, Elsa Lanchester, Brian Roper; *D:* Fred M. Wilcox. VHS, Beta $19.98 *MGM ♂♂♂*

The Secret Garden Orphaned Mary Lennox is sent to live with her mysterious uncle after her parents die. Mary is willful and spoiled and her uncle's house holds a number of secrets, including a crippled cousin. When Mary discovers a mysteriously abandoned locked garden she makes it her mission to restore the garden to life. Based on the children's classic by Frances Hodgson Burnett. Made for British television.
1984 107m/C Sarah Hollis Andrews, David Patterson; *D:* Katrina Murray. VHS $19.95 *MOV, SIG, TVC ♂♂½*

The Secret Garden Lonely orphan Mary Lennox is sent to live with her uncle in England after her parent's deaths. Mary, who has grown up in India, is selfish and unhappy until she discovers two secrets on her uncle's estate. Class production of the children's classic by Frances Hodgson Burnett with wonderful performances; added prologue and afterword showing Mary as an adult are unnecessary, but don't detract either. Made for television as a "Hallmark Hall of Fame" special.
1987 (PG) 100m/C Gennie James, Barret Oliver, Jadrien Steele, Michael Hordern, Derek Jacobi, Billie Whitelaw, Lucy Gutteridge, Julian Glover, Colin Firth, Alan Grint. VHS $14.98 *REP ♂♂♂*

The Secret Garden Rekindled interest in Frances Hodgson Burnett's classic tale has prompted a Broadway musical, two TV movies, and this latest big screen version. Mary Lennox is an orphan sent to live in her

reclusive uncle's forbidding mansion filled with secrets, including a crippled cousin she didn't know she had. She discovers a secret neglected garden and becomes determined to bring it back to life. Befitting director Holland's reputation this version is beautiful but dark, with children prey to very adult anxieties.
1993 (G) 102m/C Kate Maberly, Dame Maggie Smith, Haydon Prowse, Andrew Knott, John Lynch; *D:* Agnieszka Holland; *W:* Caroline Thompson; *M:* Zbigniew Preisner. VHS, Beta $24.96 *WAR, BTV ♂♂½*

Secret Honor Idiosyncratic, single-set, one-man film version adapted by Donald Freed and Arnold Stone from their stage play about Richard Nixon coping with the death of his presidency on the night he's decided to blow his brains out. Made with students at the University of Michigan, and carried by the ranting and raving of Hall as a tragic Shakespearean Nixon with plenty of darkly humorous lines. *AKA:* Lords of Treason; Secret Honor: The Last Testament of Richard M. Nixon; Secret Honor: A Political Myth.
1985 90m/C Philip Baker Hall; *D:* Robert Altman; *M:* George Burt. VHS, Beta $29.98 *LIV, VES, CRC ♂♂♂*

Secret Ingredient A legendary cognac recipe is the secret formula of the monks of St. Celare, whose monastery is located in the mountains of Yugoslavia. A wealthy American sends his flighty heiress daughter to pry the secret recipe from the monks but she runs into more than she bargains for when she falls for a handsome friar and gets caught up with a band of bumbling gypsies and the inept state police.
1992 95m/C Rick Rossovich, Catherine Hicks, Gary Kroeger, Jeff Corey, Brad Dexter, Sam Wanamaker; *D:* Slobodan Shijan. VHS $14.95 *HMD ♂ ½*

Secret Life of an American Wife A bored housewife (Jackson) tries to seduce a client of her husband's, with less than hilarious results. Too much dialogue, not enough genuine humor. Disappointing inversion of director Axelrod's "The Seven Year Itch."
1968 97m/C Walter Matthau, Anne Jackson, Patrick O'Neal, Edy Williams; *D:* George Axelrod; *W:* George Axelrod. VHS, Beta $59.98 *FOX ♂♂*

The Secret Life of Walter Mitty An entertaining adaptation of the James Thurber short story about a meek man (Kaye) who lives an unusual secret fantasy life. Henpecked by his fiancee and mother, oppressed at his job, he imagines himself in the midst of various heroic fantasies. While Thurber always professed to hate Kaye's characterization and the movie, it scored at the box office and today stands as a comedic romp for Kaye. Available with digitally remastered stereo and original movie trailer.
1947 110m/C Danny Kaye, Virginia Mayo, Boris Karloff, Ann Rutherford, Fay Bainter, Florence Bates; *D:* Norman Z. McLeod. VHS, Beta $19.98 *HBO, SUE ♂♂♂*

Secret Obsession A love triangle among a father, his illegitimate son, and the woman they both love, set in North Africa in 1955. Sounds intriguing, but don't be fooled. Slow, dull, and poorly acted.
1988 (PG) 82m/C Julie Christie, Ben Gazzara, Patrick Bruel, Jean Carmet; *D:* Henri Vart. VHS, Beta $79.95 *VMK ♂*

The Secret of El Zorro Don Diego's friend, Don Ricardo, threatens to unmask Zorro's secret identity when he challenges the legendary swordsman to a duel.
1957 75m/B Guy Williams. VHS, Beta $39.95 *DIS ♂ ½*

The Secret of My Success Country bumpkin Fox goes to the Big Apple to make his mark. He becomes the corporate mailboy who rises meteorically to the top of his company (by impersonating an executive) in order to win the love of an icy woman executive. He spends his days running frantically between his real job in the mailroom and his fantasy position, with various sexual shenanigans with the boss's wife thrown in to keep the viewer alert. Fox is charismatic while working with a cliche-ridden script that ties up everything very neatly at the end.
1987 (PG-13) 110m/C Michael J. Fox, Helen Slater, Richard Jordan, Margaret Whitton; *D:* Herbert Ross; *W:* Jim Cash, Jack Epps Jr.; *M:* David Foster. VHS, Beta $19.95 *MCA ♂♂*

The Secret of Navajo Cave Fair family adventure. Two young friends explore the mysterious Navajo cave, where one can be assured that a secret awaits. *AKA:* Legend of Cougar Canyon.
1976 (G) 84m/C Holger Kasper, Steven Benally Jr., Johnny Guerro; *D:* James T. Flocker. VHS $39.95 *XVC, VCI ♂♂*

The Secret of NIMH Animated tale, produced by a staff of Disney-trained artists led by "American Tail's" Bluth; concerns a newly widowed mouse who discovers a secret agency of superintelligent rats (they've escaped from a science lab) who aid her in protecting her family. As is usually the case with Bluth films, the animation is superb while the socially aware plot struggles to keep pace. That aside, it's still an interesting treat for the youngsters. Adapted from Robert C. O'Brien's "Mrs. Frisby and the Rats of N.I.M.H."
1982 (G) 84m/C *D:* Don Bluth; *W:* Don Bluth; *M:* Jerry Goldsmith; *V:* John Carradine, Derek Jacobi, Dom DeLuise, Elizabeth Hartman, Peter Strauss, Aldo Ray, Edie McClurg, Wil Wheaton. VHS, Beta, 8mm $14.95 *MGM, WTA ♂♂♂*

Secret of Tai Chi A young man uses his wits and martial arts to battle an evil Chinese general.
19?? 90m/C VHS, Beta $49.95 *OCE ♂*

Secret of the Black Trunk Chilling Edgar Wallace story about a series of murders at a famed English hotel. Filmed in Great Britain.
1962 96m/C Joachim Hansen, Senta Berger, Hans Reiser, Leonard Steckel, Peter Carsten; *D:* Werner Klinger. VHS $16.95 *SNC ♂♂½*

The Secret of the Golden Eagle A boy and his new adventurer friend are on a quest to find the strange "Golden Statue" that causes people to grow old before their time. They must take it from criminals who are using it for evil purposes. A good adventure/fantasy for the entire family.
1991 90m/C Michael Berryman, Brandon McKay; *D:* Cole McKay. VHS $79.95 *WLA ♂♂*

Secret of the Ice Cave A motley band of explorers, hijackers and mercenaries go after a secret treasure in the remote mountains.
1989 (PG-13) 106m/C Michael Moriarty, Sally Kellerman, David Mendenhall, Virgil Frye, Gerald Anthony, Norbert Weisser; *D:* Radu Gabrea. VHS, Beta $14.99 *MOV ♂*

The Secret of the Loch Scottish scientist claims to have seen Loch Ness Monster but everyone thinks his bagpipe's blown a reed.
1934 80m/B Seymour Hicks, Nancy O'Neil, Gibson Gowland, Frederick Peisley; *D:* Milton Rosmer. VHS $19.98 *NOS, SNC ♂ ½*

The Secret of the Telegian Rare Japanese sci-fi flick about a soldier who uses a teleportation device to kill fellow soldiers who tried to kill him. He could find his victims wherever they hid. Also known as "The Telegian."
1961 85m/C Koji Tsurata, Yumi Shirakawa, Akihiko Hirata, Tadao Nakamura; **D:** Jun Fukuda. VHS $16.95 SNC ℤℤ½

Secret of Yolanda Steamy romance about a young deaf-mute whose guardian and riding instructor both fall for her.
1982 (R) 90m/C Aviva Ger, Asher Zarfati, Shraga Harpaz. VHS, Beta $59.95 MGM ℤ

The Secret Passion of Robert Clayton When Robert Clayton Jr. (Valentine) returns to his home town to take the position of D.A., he is forced to go head to head in a lurid murder trial with the defense attorney (Mahoney), who also happens to be his own father.
1992 (R) 92m/C John Mahoney, Scott Valentine, Eve Gordon, Kevin Conroy; **D:** E.W. Swackhamer; **W:** Brian Ross. VHS $58.03 PAR ℤℤ

Secret Passions A young couple are haunted by a dark, romance-novel-type secret. Made for television.
1978 99m/C John James, Susan Lucci; **D:** Michael Pressman. VHS, Beta NO ℤ½

Secret Places On the brink of WWII, a German girl in an English school finds friendship with a popular classmate. Touching and involving, but somehow unsatisfying.
1985 (PG) 98m/C Maria Therese Relin, Tara MacGowan, Claudine Auger, Jenny Agutter; **D:** Zelda Barron. VHS, Beta $79.98 FOX ℤℤ½

The Secret Policeman's Other Ball Engaging live performance by most of the Monty Python troupe and guest rock artists, staged for Amnesty International. Follows 1979's "The Secret Policeman's Ball," and followed by 1987's "The Secret Policeman's Third Ball."
1982 (R) 101m/C John Cleese, Graham Chapman, Michael Palin, Terry Jones, Pete Townshend, Sting, Billy Connolly, Bob Geldof, Jeff Beck, Eric Clapton; **D:** Julien Temple; **W:** Michael Palin. VHS, Beta $14.95 MGM ℤℤℤ

Secret Policeman's Private Parts Various sketches and performances from the various Secret Policeman occasions, featuring classic Python sketches including "I'm a Lumberjack and I'm OK." Also featured are performances by Phil Collins, Pete Townshend, Donovan, and Bob Geldof. Thank you very much.
1981 77m/C John Cleese, Michael Palin, Terry Jones, Pete Townshend, Julien Temple; **D:** Roger Graef. VHS, Beta $59.95 MED ℤℤ½

A Secret Space Story of a young man, born of secular parents, searching for the meaning of his Jewish roots as he nears his Bar Mitzvah. He is helped along by a group of Jews who are also searching for this meaning.
1988 80m/C Robert Klein, Phyllis Newman, John Matthews, Sam Schacht, Virginia Graham; **D:** Roberta Hodes. VHS, Beta $79.95 ERG ℤℤ½

The Secret War of Harry Frigg Non-conformist WWII Private Harry Frigg is promoted to general as part of a scheme to help five Allied generals escape from the custody of the Germans. Rare Newman bomb; dismal comedy.
1968 123m/C Paul Newman, Sylva Koscina, John Williams, Tom Bosley, Andrew Duggan; **D:** Jack Smight. VHS, Beta $49.95 MCA ℤ½

Secret Weapon An Israeli technician flees his country with atomic secrets and a beautiful government agent is sent to induce him to return. Based on the true case of Mordecai Vanunu. Slow-paced and not very suspenseful. Made for cable.
1990 95m/C Griffin Dunne, Karen Allen, Stuart Wilson, Jeroen Krabbe, Brian Cox, John Rhys-Davies, Ian Mitchell; **D:** Ian Sharp. VHS, Beta $19.98 TTC ℤℤ

Secret Weapons Sexy Russian babes are KGB-trained to get any secret from any man. Strains credibility as well as patience. Made for TV. **AKA:** Secrets of the Red Bedroom.
1985 100m/C Linda Hamilton, Sally Kellerman, Hunt Block, Viveca Lindfors, Christopher Atkins, Geena Davis, James Franciscus; **D:** Don Taylor; **M:** Charles Bernstein. VHS NO ℤ½

Secrets A wife, her husband, and her daughter each have a sexual experience which they must keep secret. Bisset's nude love scene is an eye-opener. Fast forward through the rest of this dull, overwrought drama.
1971 (R) 86m/C Jacqueline Bisset, Per Oscarsson, Shirley Knight Hopkins, Robert Powell, Tarka Kings, Martin C. Thurley; **D:** Philip Saville; **M:** Michael Gibbs. VHS $59.95 PSM ℤ½

Secrets An unhappy young bride starts having numerous affairs when her mother dies. Made for television. Hardly worth the effort.
1977 100m/C Susan Blakely, Roy Thinnes, Joanne Linville, John Randolph, Anthony Eisley, Andrew Stevens; **D:** Paul Wendkos. VHS MGM ℤ

Secrets British drama about the confused life of an innocent schoolgirl who's the victim of a mess of authoritative misunderstandings. One of David Puttnam's "First Love" series.
1982 79m/C Helen Lindsay, Anna Campbell-Jones, Daisy Cockburn; **D:** Gavin Millar. VHS, Beta $59.95 MGM ℤℤ

Secrets of a Married Man A married man's philandering ways are his ruination when he falls hard for a beautiful prostitute. Shatner and Shepherd contain their laughter as they make their way through this hyper-earnest family drama.
1984 96m/C William Shatner, Cybill Shepherd, Michelle Phillips, Glynn Turman; **D:** William A. Graham. VHS, Beta $29.98 LIV ℤ

Secrets of a Soul A visually impressive presentation of Freudian psychoanalytic theory, in which a professor, wanting a child and jealous of his wife's childhood sweetheart, moves toward madness (we did say Freudian) and is cured through dream interpretation. Great dream sequences bring out the arm-chair psychoanalyst. Silent.
1925 94m/B Werner Krauss, Ruth Weyher, Jack Trevor; **D:** G.W. Pabst. VHS, Beta $49.95 FCT ℤℤ½

Secrets of Sweet Sixteen Gag-fest about budding sexuality in high school.
1974 (R) 84m/C Suzie Atkins. VHS, Beta NO Woof!

Secrets of Three Hungry Wives When a multi-millionaire is killed, the women with whom he was having affairs are suspected. Tacky made for television flick.
1978 97m/C Jessica Walter, Gretchen Corbett, Eve Plumb, Heather MacRae, James Franciscus, Craig Stevens; **D:** Gordon Hessler. VHS NO ℤ

Secrets of Women A rare Bergman comedy about three sisters-in-law who tell about their affairs and marriages as they await their husbands at a lakeside resort. His first commercial success, though it waited nine years for release (1961). In Swedish

with English subtitles. **AKA:** Kvinnors Vantan; Waiting Women.
1952 114m/B Anita Bjork, Karl Arne Homsten, Eva Dahlbeck, Maj-Britt Nilsson, Jarl Kulle; **D:** Ingmar Bergman; **W:** Ingmar Bergman. VHS, Beta $39.95 HMV, NLC, SUE ℤℤℤ

The Secrets of Wu Sin A suicidal news writer in Chinatown is given a reason to live by a news editor who gives her a job. She starts investigating a ring smuggling Chinese workers, with the trail leading to, of course, Chinatown. Low-budget crime thriller.
1932 65m/B Lois Wilson, Grant Withers, Dorothy Revier, Robert Warwick, Toschia Mori; **D:** Richard Thorpe. VHS $12.95 SNC, NOS, DVT ℤℤ

Seduced When a rich businessman turns up dead, the ambitious politician who was involved with his wife must find the killer. Not memorable or exceptional, but not boring or offensive either. Made for television.
1985 100m/C Gregory Harrison, Cybill Shepherd, Jose Ferrer, Adrienne Barbeau, Michael C. Gwynne, Karmin Murcelo, Paul Stewart; **D:** Jerrold Freedman. VHS $9.99 STE, PSM ℤℤ

Seduced and Abandoned A lothario seduces his fiancee's young sister. When the girl becomes pregnant, he refuses to marry her. Family complications abound. A comic look at the Italian code of honor. In Italian with English subtitles. **AKA:** Sedotta e Abbandonata.
1964 118m/B Saro Urzi, Stefania Sandrelli, Aldo Puglisi; **D:** Pietro Germi. VHS, Beta $24.95 NOS, HHT, HEG ℤℤ

The Seducer Things get dangerous when a playboy's goals turn from love to death.
1982 (R) 72m/C Christopher Mathews; **D:** Donovan Winters. VHS NO ℤℤ

The Seducers An acid-dropping mother takes her shy, withdrawn son on a Mediterranean cruise and asks along some of her girlfriends in the hopes of stoking his libido. However, she finds it difficult to control her own impulses. The boy gets a chance when the ship runs aground on a remote island and he meets an innocent native girl. His mother, though, has designs of her own. Dubbed from Italian.
1970 84m/C Rosalba (Sara Bay) Neri, Edwige Fenech, Maud de Belleroche, Maurizio Bonuglia, Ruggero Miti, Ewa Thulin; **D:** Ottavio Alessi. VHS $23.00 SMW, TPV ℤ

Seducers Wealthy, middle-aged man unsuspectingly allows two young lesbians to use his telephone. A night of bizarre mayhem and brutal murder begins. They tease him, tear apart his house, and generally make him miserable. Why? Good question. **AKA:** Death Game.
1977 (R) 90m/C Sondra Locke, Colleen Camp, Seymour Cassel, Beth Brickell; **D:** Peter S. Traynor. VHS, Beta $19.95 VCI, GEM ℤ

The Seduction Superstar television anchorwoman is harassed by a psychotic male admirer. Usual run of the mill exploitive "B" thriller with no brains behind the camera.
1982 (R) 104m/C Morgan Fairchild, Michael Sarrazin, Vince Edwards, Andrew Stevens, Colleen Camp, Kevin Brophy; **D:** David Schmoeller; **W:** David Schmoeller. VHS, Beta $9.98 MED, VTR ℤ

The Seduction of Joe Tynan Political drama about a young senator (Alda) torn between his family, his political career, and his mistress (Streep). Alda also wrote the thin screenplay, which reportedly is loosely based on the remarkable life of Ted Kennedy. Relatively shallow treatment of the meaty

themes of power, hypocrisy, sex, and corruption in our nation's capital.
1979 (R) 107m/C Alan Alda, Meryl Streep, Melvyn Douglas, Barbara Harris, Rip Torn; *D:* Jerry Schatzberg; *W:* Alan Alda; *M:* Bill Conti. **VHS, Beta $69.95** MCA 🐾🐾½

Seduction of Mimi Comic farce of politics and seduction about a Sicilian laborer's escapades with the Communists and the local Mafia. Giannini is wonderful as the stubborn immigrant to the big city who finds himself in trouble. One of the funniest love scenes on film. Basis for the later movie "Which Way is Up?"
1972 (R) 92m/C Giancarlo Giannini, Mariangela Melato; *D:* Lina Wertmuller; *W:* Lina Wertmuller. **VHS, Beta** FOX, OM 🐾🐾🐾

Seduction: The Cruel Woman A curiously uninvolving look at sexual games and fantasies. Wanda is a dominatrix, who also owns a sado-masochistic gallery where her various friends and current and formers lovers act out their basest desires. Stylized, with some graphic sex. Based on the novel "Venus in Furs" by Leopold Sacher-Masoch. In German with English subtitles.
1989 84m/C Mechthild Grossmann, Carola Regnier, Udo Kier, Sheila McLaughlin; *D:* Elfi Mikesch, Monika Treut; *W:* Elfi Mikesch, Monika Treut. **VHS $59.95** ING 🐾🐾

See How She Runs Running becomes a central and redefining experience for a 40-year-old divorced schoolteacher (Woodward). Her training culminates with a run in the Boston marathon. Her loved ones, though concerned for her health and sanity, cheer her on. Excellent made for TV drama. Screen daughter Newman is also Woodward's real-life daughter.
1978 92m/C Joanne Woodward, John Considine, Lissy Newman, Barbara Manning; *D:* Richard T. Heffron. **VHS, Beta** NO 🐾🐾🐾

See No Evil A blind girl gradually discovers the murdered bodies of her uncle's family. Trapped in the family mansion, she finds herself pursued by the killer. Chilling and well crafted. *AKA:* Blind Terror.
1971 (PG) 90m/C Mia Farrow, Dorothy Allison, Robin Bailey; *D:* Richard Fleischer; *W:* Brian Clemens; *M:* Elmer Bernstein. **VHS, Beta $39.95** COL 🐾🐾🐾

See No Evil, Hear No Evil Another teaming for Pryor and Wilder, in which they portray a blind man and a deaf man both sought as murder suspects. Pryor and Wilder deserve better.
1989 (R) 103m/C Gene Wilder, Richard Pryor, Joan Severance, Anthony Zerbe; *D:* Arthur Hiller; *W:* Gene Wilder; *M:* Stewart Copeland. **VHS, Beta, 8mm $14.95** COL 🐾🐾

See You in the Morning Ill-conceived romantic comedy-drama about a divorced psychiatrist and a widow, both of whom had unhappy marriages, who meet and marry. They must cope with their respective children, family tragedies, and their own expectations, in order to make this second marriage work.
1989 (PG-13) 119m/C Jeff Bridges, Alice Krige, Farrah Fawcett, Drew Barrymore, Lukas Haas, Macaulay Culkin, David Dukes, Frances Sternhagen, Theodore Bikel, George Hearn, Linda Lavin; *D:* Alan J. Pakula; *W:* Alan J. Pakula. **VHS, Beta $14.95** WAR 🐾½

Seedpeople Mindless horror flick has bloodthirsty plants inhabiting peaceful Comet Valley after their seeds fall from outer space and germinate. These "seedpeople" possess tremendous powers and soon have the rural residents transformed into zombies. Bears an uncanny resemblance to "Invasion of the Bodysnatchers," and is so bad it's

almost good. Also available with Spanish subtitles.
1992 87m/C Sam Hennings, Andrea Roth, Dane Witherspoon, David Dunard, Holly Fields, Bernard Kates, Anne Betancourt, Sonny Carl Davis; *D:* Peter Manoogian; *W:* Jackson Barr; *M:* Boby Mithoff. **VHS, Beta $19.95** PAR 🐾🐾½

Seeds of Evil Warhol alumnus Dallesandro is a strange gardener who grows flowers that can kill. He can also turn himself into a tree and figures to seduce rich and bored housewife Houghton (niece of Katherine Hepburn) after he finishes tending her garden. Strange, quirky horror flick. *AKA:* The Gardener.
1976 (R) 97m/C Katherine Houghton, Joe Dallesandro, Rita Gam; *D:* James H. Kay. **VHS, Beta $29.95** UNI 🐾🐾

The Seekers The story of the Kent family continues, as Abraham Kent, his wife and young son are forced to leave the safety of Boston for the rugged, untamed Pacific Northwest. TV movie based on the novel by John Jakes; preceded by "The Bastard" and "The Rebels."
1979 200m/C Randolph Mantooth, Edie Adams, Neville Brand, Delta Burke, John Carradine, George DeLoy, Julie Gregg, Roosevelt Grier, George Hamilton, Alex Hyde-White, Brian Keith, Ross Martin, Gary Merrill, Martin Milner, Vic Morrow, Timothy Patrick Murphy, Hugh O'Brian, Robert Reed, Allen Rich, Barbara Rush, Sarah Rush, Stuart Whitman, Ed Harris, Jeremy Licht, Eric Stoltz; *D:* Sidney Hayers. **VHS $29.98** MCA 🐾🐾

Seems Like Old Times A sweet lawyer (Hawn) finds herself helping her ex-husband (Chase) when two robbers force him to hold up a bank. Grodin is the new spouse threatened by Chase's appearance and by the heavies he's trying to escape. Better-than-average script, with funny and appealing characters.
1980 (PG) 102m/C Goldie Hawn, Chevy Chase, Charles Grodin, Robert Guillaume, Harold Gould, George Grizzard, T.K. Carter; *D:* Jay Sandrich; *W:* Neil Simon; *M:* Marvin Hamlisch. **VHS, Beta $19.95** COL 🐾🐾½

Seize the Day A man approaching middle age (Williams) feels that he is a failure. Brilliant performances by all, plus a number of equally fine actors in small roles. Based on the short novel by Saul Bellow.
1986 93m/C Robin Williams, Joseph Wiseman, Jerry Stiller, Glenne Headly, Tony Roberts; *D:* Fielder Cook. **VHS, Beta** NO 🐾🐾🐾

Seizure Three demonic creatures from a writer's dreams come to life and terrorize him and his houseguests at a weekend party. Slick but disjointed. Stone's directorial debut. Interesting cast includes Tattoo from "Fantasy Island."
1974 (PG) 93m/C Jonathan Frid, Herve Villechaize, Christina Pickles; *D:* Oliver Stone; *W:* Oliver Stone. **VHS, Beta $9.99** PSM 🐾🐾

Seizure: The Story of Kathy Morris The real-life anguish and struggle of a young music student who must have brain surgery and comes out of it unable to read or count. Workaday dramatization.
1982 104m/C Leonard Nimoy, Penelope Milford; *D:* Gerald I. Isenberg. **VHS, Beta** TLF 🐾🐾

Self-Defense When a city's police force goes on strike, the citizens band together into vigilante troops.
1988 (R) 85m/C Tom Nardini, Brenda Bazinet. **VHS, Beta $79.95** MED 🐾½

Sell Out A former spy living in Jerusalem is called out of retirement; his protege, who defected to the Soviets, now wants out.

1976 (PG) 102m/C Richard Widmark, Oliver Reed, Gayle Hunnicutt, Sam Wanamaker; *D:* Peter Collinson. **VHS, Beta $59.95** MED 🐾🐾½

Semaforo en Rojo Five men who are planning a robbery run into trouble from some ex-lovers.
1947 95m/B Jose Galvez, Enrique Ponton, Jaime Velasquez, German Robles. **VHS, Beta $44.95** MAD 🐾🐾½

Semi-Tough Likeable, still current social satire involving a couple of pro-football buddies and their mutual interest in their team owner's daughter. Romantic comedy, satire of the sports world, zany highjinks—it's all here, though not enough of any of these. Pleasant and enjoyable. Based on the novel by Dan Jenkins.
1977 (R) 107m/C Burt Reynolds, Kris Kristofferson, Jill Clayburgh, Lotte Lenya, Robert Preston, Bert Convy, Richard Masur, Carl Weathers, Brian Dennehy, John Matuszak, Ron Silver; *D:* Michael Ritchie. **VHS, Beta $14.95** MGM, FOX 🐾🐾½

The Senator was Indiscreet A farcical comedy concerning a slightly loony senator with presidential aspirations. He thinks he can win the nomination because he keeps a diary that would prove embarrassing to numerous colleagues. The diary then falls into the hands of a journalist. Powell is wonderful as the daffy politician. Playwright Kaufman's only directorial effort. *AKA:* Mr. Ashton was Indiscreet.
1947 75m/B William Powell, Ella Raines, Hans Conried; *D:* George S. Kaufman. **VHS $19.98** REP 🐾🐾🐾

Send Me No Flowers Vintage Hudson-Day comedy. Hudson plays a hypochondriac who thinks his death is imminent. He decides to provide for his family's future by finding his wife a rich husband. She thinks he's feeling guilty for having an affair.
1964 100m/C Rock Hudson, Doris Day, Tony Randall, Paul Lynde; *D:* Norman Jewison; *W:* Julius J. Epstein, Philip C. Epstein. **VHS, Beta $14.95** MCA, CCB 🐾🐾🐾

The Sender An amnesiac young man is studied by a psychiatrist. She discovers that her patient is a "sender," who can transmit his nightmares to other patients at a hospital.
1982 (R) 92m/C Kathryn Harrold, Zeljko Ivanek, Shirley Knight, Paul Freeman, Sean Hewitt; *D:* Roger Christian; *M:* Trevor Jones. **VHS, Beta $19.95** PAR 🐾🐾

Senior Trip New York City will never be the same after a bunch of rowdy Midwestern high school seniors tear up the town on their graduation trip. Made for television.
1981 96m/C Scott Baio, Mickey Rooney, Faye Grant, Vincent Spano, Jane Hoffman; *D:* Kenneth Johnson. **VHS, Beta $39.95** WOV 🐾

Senior Week A batch of girl-hungry teens have a wacky time on their Florida vacation just before graduation.
1988 97m/C Michael St. Gerard, Devon Skye, Leesa Bryte; *D:* Stuart Goldman. **VHS, Beta $29.98** LIV, VES Woof!

The Seniors A group of college students decide to open a phony sex clinic, but the joke is on them when the clinic becomes a success. Better than it sounds. Pretty good acting and much harmless goofiness.
1978 (R) 87m/C Dennis Quaid, Priscilla Barnes, Jeffrey Byron, Gary Imhoff; *D:* Rod Amateau. **VHS, Beta $29.98** VES 🐾🐾

Senora Tentacion Musical melodrama about a composer who fights to leave his mother, sister, and girlfriend in order to flee with Hortensia, a famous singer. In Spanish with English subtitles.

1949 82m/B David Silva, Susana Guizar, Ninon Sevilla. VHS, Beta $24.95 *VYY, APD, ING* ✍✍

Sensations A woman and a man who aren't exceptionally fond of one another share a lottery ticket and win. Vincent is best known as a former director of porno flicks, and he manages to work in sexual overtones.
1987 (R) 91m/C Rebecca Lynn, Blake Bahner, Jennifer Delora, Rick Savage, Loretta Palma, Frank Stewart; *D:* Chuck Vincent. VHS, Beta $29.95 *ACA* ✍✍

Sensations of 1945 A press agent turns his firm over to one of his clients, a dancer with some wild promotional ideas. Brings together numerous variety and musical acts. W. C. Fields has a cameo in his last film role. Mostly unremarkable, occasionally fun musical. *AKA:* Sensations.
1944 86m/B Eleanor Powell, Dennis O'Keefe, Sir C. Aubrey Smith, Eugene Pallette, Cab Calloway, Sophie Tucker, Woody Herman, Lyle Talbot, Marie Blake; *Cameos:* W.C. Fields; *D:* Andrew L. Stone. VHS, Beta $19.95 *VDM* ✍✍½

Sense & Sensibility BBC miniseries adaptation of Jane Austen's first novel concerning two sisters striving for happiness in their well-ordered lives.
1985 174m/C Irene Richard, Tracey Childs; *D:* Rodney Benett. VHS, Beta $29.98 *FOX, TVC, HMV* ✍✍

A Sense of Freedom A hopeless racketeering criminal is thrust from institution to institution until the Scottish authorities decide on an innovative style of reform. Based on Jimmy Boyle's autobiographical book. Excellent and disturbing.
1978 (R) 81m/C David Hayman, Alex Norton, Jake D'Arcy, Sean Scanlan, Fulton Mackay; *D:* John MacKenzie. VHS, Beta *NO* ✍✍✍

Senso Tragic story of romance and rebellion as Italian patriots battle the Austro-Hungarian empire for independence in 1866. An Italian noblewoman betrays her marriage, and almost her country, to be with a cynical Austrian soldier in this visually stunning piece of cinematography. In Italian with English subtitles or dubbed. *AKA:* The Wanton Contessa.
1954 125m/C Alida Valli, Massimo Girotti, Heinz Moog, Farley Granger; *D:* Luchino Visconti. VHS $59.95 *VCD, APD* ✍✍✍

The Sensual Man Hot-blooded Italian falls in love and gets married only to find out that his wife cannot consummate their marriage. Exploitative, misogynistic, and unfunny.
1974 (R) 90m/C Giancarlo Giannini, Rossana Podesta, Lionel Stander; *D:* Marco Vicario. VHS, Beta $59.95 *COL* ✍½

Sensual Partners Young actresses are lured to Tangier by a fake movie producer and sold as sex slaves. Emphasis on soft-focus, soft-core flesh.
1987 87m/C Gina Jansen, Eric Falk. VHS, Beta $29.95 *MED Woof!*

The Sensuous Nurse Italian comedy about a beautiful nurse hired by the greedy, treacherous relatives of a weak-hearted count in hopes that her voluptuousness will give him a heart attack. It doesn't, and she falls in love. Mindless, but fun and sexy. Dubbed in English.
1976 (R) 79m/C Ursula Andress, Mario Pisu, Dulio Del Prete, Jack Palance; *D:* Nello Rosatti. VHS, Beta $59.98 *FOX* ✍✍

Sensuous Summer When Bobby returns home to the town of Elk Lake he finds the family business, run by his brother Nick, is in deep trouble. It seems Alex, an unscrupulous banker, wants to foreclose. But busi-

ness comes second to pleasure when Bobby is reunited with old flame Jill and Nick takes up again with ex-girlfriend Cindy.
1993 (R) 80m/C Tom Case, Christina Campbell, Brittany McGrea, Gina Jorand. VHS $79.95 *CEL* ✍½

The Sensuous Teenager Overwhelmingly erotic and uncontrollably seductive, a teenage girl aims to please by releasing all the sensuality within her. *AKA:* Libido; Forbidden Passions.
1970 (R) 80m/C Sandra Jullien, Janine Reynaud, Michel Lemoine; *D:* Max Pecas. VHS *SUN Woof!*

The Sentinel A model, who has moved into a New York City brownstone, encounters an aging priest and some unusual neighbors. When she investigates strange noises she finds out that the apartment building houses the doorway to hell - and that she's intended to be the next doorkeeper. Modest suspense film with a good cast and enough shock and special effects to keep the viewer interested.
1976 (R) 92m/C Chris Sarandon, Christina Raines, Ava Gardner, Jose Ferrer, Sylvia Miles, John Carradine, Burgess Meredith, Tom Berenger, Beverly D'Angelo, Jeff Goldblum; *D:* Michael Winner; *W:* Michael Winner. VHS, Beta $14.98 *MCA* ✍✍

Separate But Equal One of TV's greatest history lessons, a powerful dramatization of the 1954 Brown vs. The Board of Education case that wrung a landmark civil rights decision from the Supreme Court. Great care is taken to humanize all the participants, from the humblest schoolchild to NAACP lawyer Thurgood Marshall (Poitier). On two cassettes.
1991 (PG) 194m/C Sidney Poitier, Burt Lancaster, Richard Kiley, Cleavon Little, John McMartin, Graham Beckel, Lynne Thigpen, Albert Hall; *D:* George Stevens; *W:* George Stevens. VHS $19.98 *REP, FCT, PTB* ✍✍✍½

A Separate Peace Two young men in a New England prep school during WWII come to grips with the war, coming of age, and a tragic accident. Cheap rendition of a not-so-great novel by John Knowles.
1973 (PG) 104m/C John Heyl, Parker Stevenson, William Roerick; *D:* Larry Peerce; *M:* Charles Fox. VHS, Beta $45.95 *PAR, HMV* ✍✍

Separate Tables Adaptation of the Terence Rattigan play about a varied cast of characters living out their personal dramas in a British seaside hotel. Guests include a matriarch and her shy daughter, a divorced couple, a spinster, and a presumed war hero. Their secrets and loves are examined in grand style. Fine acting all around.
1958 98m/B Burt Lancaster, David Niven, Rita Hayworth, Deborah Kerr, Wendy Hiller, Rod Taylor, Gladys Cooper, Felix Aylmer, Cathleen Nesbitt; *D:* Delbert Mann; *W:* John Gay. Academy Awards '58: Best Actor (Niven), Best Supporting Actress (Hiller); Nominations: Best Actress (Kerr), Best Adapted Screenplay, Best Black and White Cinematography, Best Picture, Best Original Score; National Board of Review Awards '58: 10 Best Films of the Year; New York Film Critics Awards '58: Best Actor (Niven). VHS, Beta $19.98 *MGM, FOX, FCT* ✍✍✍½

Separate Tables A remake of the 1958 film adapted from Terence Rattigan's play. Separated into two parts, "Table by the Window" and "Table Number Seven." The lives of the lonely inhabitants of a hotel are dramatized through wonderful acting by Christie and Bates. Made for cable television.
1983 (PG) 50m/C Julie Christie, Alan Bates, Claire Bloom, Irene Worth; *D:* John Schlesinger. VHS, Beta $59.95 *MGM* ✍✍½

Separate Vacations A married man leaves his wife and kids to take a separate vacation, hoping he'll find exciting sex. Wife and kids end up at a ski resort, where romance comes her way. A lightweight, old story.
1986 (R) 91m/C David Naughton, Jennifer Dale, Mark Keyloun; *D:* Michael Anderson Sr. VHS, Beta $79.98 *LIV* ✍½

Separate Ways Unhappily married couple involved in various affairs split up in order to deal with themselves and their marriage. Good cast; bad script wandering down Maudlin Lane.
1982 (R) 92m/C Karen Black, Tony LoBianco, David Naughton, Sybil Danning; *D:* Howard (Hikmet) Avedis. VHS, Beta $79.95 *VES* ✍½

Sepia Cinderella A songwriter, who finds himself with a hit, abandons his current life and love to try high society. He finds out it's not what he wants after all.
1947 67m/B Sheila Guyse, Rubel Blakely, Freddie Bartholomew, Sid Catlett, Deke Wilson. VHS, Beta $29.95 *NOS, DVT, FCT* ✍✍

September Woody does Bergman again with a shuttered, claustrophobic drama about six unhappy people trying to verbalize their feelings in a dark summer house in Vermont. Well-acted throughout and interesting at first, but the whining and angst attacks eventually give way to boredom. Of course, the Woodman went on to "Crimes and Misdemeanors," blending his dark and comedic sides masterfully, so the best way to look at this is as a training film.
1988 (PG-13) 82m/C Mia Farrow, Dianne Wiest, Denholm Elliott, Sam Waterston, Elaine Stritch, Jack Warden; *D:* Woody Allen; *W:* Woody Allen; *M:* Art Tatum. VHS, Beta $89.98 *ORI* ✍✍½

September Affair A married engineer and a classical pianist miss their plane from Naples. When the plane crashes, they're presumed dead, and they find themselves free to continue their illicit love affair. They find they cannot hide forever and must make peace with their pasts. Features the hit "September Song," recorded by Walter Huston.
1950 104m/B Joseph Cotten, Joan Fontaine, Francoise Rosay, Jessica Tandy, Robert Arthur; *D:* William Dieterle. VHS $14.95 *PAR* ✍✍½

September Gun A nun hires an aging gunfighter to escort her and a group of Apache children to a church school two hundred miles away. Preston is excellent as the ornery varmint in this enjoyable, pleasant western comedy. Made for television.
1983 94m/C Robert Preston, Patty Duke, Christopher Lloyd, Geoffrey Lewis, Sally Kellerman; *D:* Don Taylor. VHS, Beta $39.95 *WOV* ✍✍½

September 30, 1955 A college undergrad (Thomas) in a small Arkansas town is devastated when he learns of the death of his idol, James Dean. (The title refers to the day Dean died.) Jimmy gathers a group of friends together for a vigil which turns into a drinking-binge, resulting in police chases and, finally, tragedy. Film debut of Quaid. Also known as "9/30/55."
1977 (PG) 107m/C Richard Thomas, Lisa Blount, Deborah Benson, Tom Hulce, Dennis Christopher, Dennis Quaid, Susan Tyrrell; *D:* James Bridges; *W:* James Bridges. VHS *MCA* ✍✍½

Sergeant Matlovich vs. the U.S. Air Force A serviceman fights to remain in the Air Force after admitting his homosexuality. Compelling theme (from a true story) and good lead performance from Dourif are not

enough to carry a rather flat made for TV script.
1978 100m/C Brad Dourif, Marc Singer, Frank Converse, William Daniels, Stephen Elliott, David Spielberg, Rue McClanahan, Mitchell Ryan, David Ogden Stiers; **D:** Paul Leaf. **VHS $59.95** *LIV* ♫♫½

Sgt. Pepper's Lonely Hearts Club Band "Rip-off" would be putting it kindly. A classic album by one of the greatest rock bands of all time deserves the respect of not having a star-studded extravaganza "filmization" made of it. Gratuitous, weird casting, bad acting give it a surreal feel. And the Bee Gees? Please. A nadir of seventies popular entertainment. ♫Sgt. Pepper's Lonely Hearts Club Band; With a Little Help From My Friends; Fixing a Hole; Getting Better; Here Comes the Sun; I Want You (She's So Heavy); Good Morning, Good Morning; Nowhere Man; Polythene Pam.
1978 (PG) 113m/C Peter Frampton, The Bee Gees, Steve Martin, Aerosmith, Earth Wind & Fire, George Burns, Donald Pleasence; **D:** Michael A. Schultz. **VHS, Beta $19.98** *MCA* ♫½

Sergeant Rutledge The story of a court-martial, told in flashback, about a black calvary officer on trial for rape and murder. A detailed look at overt and covert racism handled by master director Ford. It is always apparent Strode (as Rutledge) is a heroic, yet human, figure who refuses to be beaten down by circumstances. The courtroom setting is deliberately oppressive but does make the film somewhat static. Based on the novel "Captain Buffalo" by James Warner Bellah.
1960 112m/C Woody Strode, Jeffrey Hunter, Constance Towers, Billie Burke, Juano Hernandez, Carleton Young, Charles Seel, Jan Styne, Mae Marsh; **D:** John Ford; **W:** Willis Goldbeck, James Warner Bellah; **M:** Howard Jackson. **VHS $19.98** *WAR* ♫♫♫

Sergeant Ryker Confident lead acting from Marvin as a U.S. serviceman accused of treason during the Korean War carries this otherwise blah army/courtroom drama. Remake of 1963 TV film "The Case Against Sergeant Ryker." Dillman is good as Marvin's energetic lawyer.
1968 85m/C Lee Marvin, Bradford Dillman, Vera Miles, Peter Graves, Lloyd Nolan, Murray Hamilton; **D:** Buzz Kulik; **M:** John Williams. **VHS** *NO* ♫♫½

Sergeant York Timely and enduring war movie based on the true story of Alvin York, the country boy from Tennessee drafted during WWI. At first a pacifist, Sergeant York (Cooper, well cast in an Oscar-winning role) finds justification for fighting and becomes one of the war's greatest heros. Gentle scenes of rural life contrast with horrific battlegrounds. York served as a consultant.
1941 134m/B Gary Cooper, Joan Leslie, Walter Brennan, Dickie Moore, Ward Bond, George Tobias, Noah Beery Jr., June Lockhart, Stanley Ridges, Margaret Wycherly; **D:** Howard Hawks; **W:** Abe Finkel, Harry Chandler, Howard Koch, John Huston; **M:** Max Steiner. Academy Awards '41: Best Actor (Cooper), Best Film Editing; Nominations: Best Black and White Cinematography, Best Director (Hawks), Best Interior Decoration, Best Original Screenplay, Best Picture, Best Sound, Best Supporting Actor (Brennan), Best Supporting Actress (Wycherly), Best Original Score. **VHS, Beta $19.98** *MGM, FOX, BTV* ♫♫♫♫

Serial Fun spoof of hyper-trendiness— open marriage, health foods, fad religions, navel-gazing—in Marin County, the really cool place to live across the Golden Gate from San Francisco. Mull in his first lead is the oddly normal guy surrounded by fruits and nuts. Based on Cyra McFadden's novel.

1980 (R) 90m/C Martin Mull, Sally Kellerman, Tuesday Weld, Tom Smothers, Bill Macy, Peter Bonerz, Barbara Rhoades, Christopher Lee; **D:** Bill Persky. **VHS, Beta $49.95** *PAR* ♫♫♫

Serial Mom June Cleaver-like housewife Turner is nearly perfect, except when someone disrupts her orderly life. Didn't rewind your videotape? Chose the white shoes after Labor Day? Uh oh. Stardom reigns after she's caught and the murderer-as-celebrity phenomenon is exploited to the fullest. Darkly funny Waters satire tends toward the mainstream and isn't as perverse as earlier efforts, but still maintains a shocking edge (vital organs are good for an appearance or two). Turner's chameleonic performance as the perfect mom/crazed killer is right on target, recalling "The War of the Roses." Waterston, Lake, and Lillard are terrific as her generic suburban family.
1994 (R) 93m/C Kathleen Turner, Ricki Lake, Sam Waterston, Matthew Lillard, Mink Stole, Traci Lords; *Cameos:* Suzanne Somers, Joan Rivers, Patty Hearst; **D:** John Waters; **W:** John Waters; **M:** Basil Poledouris. **VHS** *NYR* ♫♫♫

The Serpent and the Rainbow A good, interesting book (by Harvard ethnobotanist Wade Davis) offering serious speculation on the possible existence and origin of zombies in Haiti was hacked and slashed into a cheap Wes Craven-ized screen semblance of itself. And a shame it is: the result is racist, disrespectful, exploitative, and superficial. From the director of "Nightmare on Elm Street."
1987 (R) 98m/C Bill Pullman, Cathy Tyson, Zakes Mokae, Paul Winfield, Conrad Roberts, Badja Djola, Theresa Merritt; **D:** Wes Craven; **W:** Richard Maxwell; **M:** Brad Fiedel. **VHS, Beta $19.95** *MCA* Woof!

Serpent Island Two seamen fight over a Caribbean woman amid voodoo rituals, sea monsters and buried treasure.
1954 63m/C Sonny Tufts. **VHS, Beta $59.95** *MED* ♫½

The Serpent of Death An archaeologist uncovers a statue and a curse which changes his life. Horror and adventure rolled into one.
1990 (R) 90m/C **VHS, Beta $79.95** *PAR* ♫♫

The Serpent's Egg Big disappointment from the great Bergman in his second film in English. Ullman is not sultry and Carradine is horrible. Big budget matched by big Bergman ego, making a big, bad parody of himself. The plot concerns a pair of Jewish trapeze artists surviving in Berlin during Hitler's rise to power by working in a grisly and mysterious medical clinic. *AKA:* Das Schlangenei.
1978 (R) 119m/C David Carradine, Liv Ullmann, Gert Frobe, James Whitmore; **D:** Ingmar Bergman; **W:** Ingmar Bergman. **VHS, Beta $79.98** *LIV, ING* ♫½

Serpico Based on Peter Maas's book about the true-life exploits of Frank Serpico, a New York undercover policeman who exposed corruption in the police department. Known as much for his nonconformism as for his honesty, the real Serpico eventually retired from the force and moved to Europe. South Bronx-raised Pacino gives the character reality and strength. Excellent New York location photography.
1973 (R) 130m/C Al Pacino, John Randolph, Jack Kehoe, Barbara Eda-Young, Cornelia Sharpe, F. Murray Abraham, Tony Roberts; **D:** Sidney Lumet. Academy Awards '73: Nominations: Best Actor (Pacino), Best Adapted Screenplay; Golden Globe Awards '74: Best Actor—Drama (Pacino). **VHS, Beta $14.95** *PAR* ♫♫♫

The Servant A dark, intriguing examination of British class hypocrisy and the master-servant relationship. A rich, bored playboy is ruined by his socially inferior but crafty and ambitious manservant. Playwright Harold Pinter wrote the adaptation of Robin Maugham's novel in his first collaboration with director Losey. The best kind of British societal navel-gazing.
1963 112m/B Dirk Bogarde, James Fox, Sarah Miles, Wendy Craig; **D:** Joseph Losey; **W:** Harold Pinter. **VHS, Beta** *NO* ♫♫♫½

Servants of Twilight Religious zealots target a small boy for assassination because their cult leader says he's the anti-Christ. Adaptation of the Dean R. Koontz novel. Packed with action, its spell on the viewer hinges on a cruel shock ending that undercuts what came before. Made for cable television.
1991 (R) 95m/C Bruce Greenwood, Belinda Bauer, Grace Zabriskie, Richard Bradford, Jarrett Lennon, Carel Struycken, Jack Kehoe, Kelli Maroney; **D:** Jeffrey Obrow. **VHS $89.98** *VMK* ♫♫

Sesame Street Presents: Follow That Bird Television's Big Bird suffers an identity crisis, and leaves Sesame Street to join a family of real birds. He soon misses his home, and returns, in a danger-filled journey. *AKA:* Follow That Bird.
1985 (G) 92m/C Sandra Bernhard, John Candy, Chevy Chase, Joe Flaherty, Dave Thomas, Waylon Jennings, Jim Henson's Muppets; **D:** Ken Kwapis. **VHS, Beta $14.95** *WAR* ♫♫

A Session with the Committee Collection of skits performed by a Los Angeles comedy troupe.
1969 90m/C Peter Bonerz, Barbara Bosson, Garry Goodrow, Carl Gottlieb, Jessica Myerson, Christopher Ross, Melvin Stewart, Melvin Sturdy; **D:** Jack Del. **VHS** *NO* ♫♫

Sessions Mentally exhausted by her roles as sister, single parent, lover, exercise enthusiast, and high-priced prostitute, Leigh Churchill (Hamel) seeks professional counselling. Hamel's first role after "Hill Street Blues" is only average in this made for TV drama.
1983 96m/C Veronica Hamel, Jeffrey DeMunn, Jill Eikenberry, David Marshall Grant, George Coe, Henderson Forsythe, Deborah Hedwall; **D:** Richard Pearce. **VHS, Beta** *NO* ♫♫

The Set-Up Excellent, original if somewhat overwrought morality tale about integrity set in the world of boxing. Filmed as a continuous narrative covering only 72 minutes in the life of an aging fighter (Ryan). Told to throw a fight, he must battle gangsters when he refuses. Powerful, with fine performances, especially from Ryan in the lead. Inspired by Joseph Moncure March's narrative poem.
1949 72m/B Robert Ryan, Audrey Totter, George Tobias, Alan Baxter, James Edwards, Wallace Ford; **D:** Robert Wise. **VHS, Beta $19.95** *CCB, MED* ♫♫♫♫

Seven Freelance desperado Smith takes $7 million of your tax dollars at work from the feds to get rid of Hawaiian gangsters. Might be tongue in cheek, though sometimes it's hard to tell. Fun action pic unfortunately characterized by bad camera work and overearnest direction. Features the original of a gag made famous in "Raiders of the Lost Ark."
1979 (R) 100m/C William Smith, Barbara Leigh, Guich Koock, Art Metrano, Martin Kove, Richard Le Pore, Susan Kiger; **D:** Andy Sidaris. **VHS, Beta $59.95** *LIV* ♫♫½

Seven Alone Family adventure tale (based on Monroe Morrow's book "On to Oregon," based in turn on a true story) about seven siblings who undertake a treacherous 2000-mile journey from Missouri to Oregon, after their parents die along the way. Inspiring and all that; good family movie. **AKA:** House Without Windows.
1975 (G) 85m/C Dewey Martin, Aldo Ray, Anne Collins, Dean Smith, Stewart Peterson; **D:** Earl Bellamy. **VHS, Beta** NO ♂♂½

Seven Beauties Very dark war comedy about a small-time Italian crook in Naples with seven ugly sisters to support. He survives a German prison camp and much else; unforgettably, he seduces the ugly commandant of his camp to save his own life. Good acting and tight direction. **AKA:** Pasqualino Settebellezze; Pasqualino: Seven Beauties.
1976 116m/C Giancarlo Giannini, Fernando Rey, Shirley Stoler, Elena Fiore, Enzo Vitale; **D:** Lina Wertmuller; **W:** Lina Wertmuller. **VHS, Beta** $59.95 COL, APD ♂♂♂♂

Seven Blows of the Dragon The Chinese novel, "All Men Are Brothers," is the basis for this spectacular martial arts epic.
1973 (R) 81m/C David Chiang. **VHS, Beta** WAR ♂♂½

Seven Brides for Seven Brothers The eldest of seven fur-trapping brothers in the Oregon Territory brings home a wife. She begins to civilize the other six, who realize the merits of women and begin to look for romances of their own. Thrilling choreography by Michael Kidd - don't miss "The Barn Raising." Charming performances by Powell and Keel, both in lovely voice. Based on Stephen Vincent Benet's story. Thrills, chills, singin', dancin'—a classic Hollywood good time. ♫When You're In Love; Spring, Spring, Spring; Sobbin' Women; Bless Your Beautiful Hide; Goin' Co'tin; Wonderful, Wonderful Day; June Bride; Lonesome Polecat Lament.
1954 103m/C Howard Keel, Jane Powell, Russ Tamblyn, Julie Newmar, Jeff Richards, Tommy Rall, Virginia Gibson; **D:** Stanley Donen. Academy Awards '54: Best Score; Nominations: Best Color Cinematography, Best Film Editing, Best Picture, Best Screenplay; National Board of Review Awards '54: 10 Best Films of the Year. **VHS, Beta, 8mm** $19.98 MGM, HMV ♂♂♂½

The 7 Brothers Meet Dracula Seven siblings meet guy with dental anomaly. **AKA:** Legend of the Seven Golden Vampires.
1973 110m/C Peter Cushing, David Chang, Robin Stewart, Julie Ege; **D:** Roy Ward Baker. **VHS** NO ♂½

Seven Chances Silent classic that Keaton almost didn't make, believing instead that it should go to Harold Lloyd. Lawyer Keaton finds that he can inherit $7 million if he marries by 7:00 p.m. After his girlfriend turns down his botched proposal, chaos breaks loose when he advertises for someone—anyone—to marry him and make him rich. Suddenly he finds what seems to be hundreds of women willing to make the sacrifice, setting up one of the great film pursuits. Memorable boulder sequence was added after preview audience indicated climax was lacking that certain something.
1925 60m/B Buster Keaton, T. Roy Barnes, Snitz Edwards, Ruth Dwyer, Frankie Raymond; **D:** Buster Keaton. **VHS** NO ♂♂♂½

Seven Cities of Gold An expedition of Spanish conquistadors and missionaries descend on 18th-century California, looking for secret Indian caches of gold. Semi-lavish costume epic.

1955 103m/C Anthony Quinn, Michael Rennie, Richard Egan, Rita Moreno, Jeffrey Hunter, Eduardo Noriega, John Doucette; **D:** Robert D. Webb. **VHS, Beta** $19.98 FOX ♂♂

Seven Days Ashore/Hurry, Charlie, Hurry A comedy double feature. In "Seven Days Ashore," three merchant marines on leave in San Francisco become romantically involved with three women. In "Hurry, Charlie, Hurry," a henpecked husband finds himself in a lot of trouble.
1944 141m/B Gordon Oliver, Virginia Mayo, Dooley Wilson, Margaret Dumont, Leon Errol, Mildred Coles. **VHS, Beta** $34.95 RKO, TTC ♂♂

Seven Days in May Topical but still gripping Cold War nuclear-peril thriller. An American general plans a military takeover because he considers the president's pacifism traitorous. Highly suspenseful, with a breathtaking climax. Houseman's film debut in a small role.
1964 117m/B Burt Lancaster, Kirk Douglas, Edmond O'Brien, Fredric March, Ava Gardner, John Houseman; **D:** John Frankenheimer; **W:** Rod Serling; **M:** Jerry Goldsmith. Academy Awards '64 Nominations: Best Art Direction/Set Decoration (B & W), Best Supporting Actor (O'Brien); Golden Globe Awards '65: Best Supporting Actor (O'Brien). **VHS, Beta** $19.98 WAR ♂♂♂½

Seven Days' Leave Radio star-crammed musical comedy about a soldier who must marry a certain already betrothed gal (Ball) within a week so he can inherit a fortune. Songs include "Can't Get Out of this Mood," "A Touch of Texas," and "Baby, You Speak My Language." Following the completion of the film, Mature joined the Coast Guard. Lively but not memorable.
1942 87m/B Victor Mature, Lucille Ball, Harold Peary, Mary Cortes, Ginny Simms, Marcy McGuire, Peter Lind Hayes, Walter Reed, Wallace Ford, Arnold Stang, Buddy Clark, Charles Victor; **D:** Tim Whelan. **VHS, Beta** $19.98 TTC ♂♂

Seven Deadly Sins A collection of tales concerning destructive emotions and the downfalls they cause. Contains shorts from some of Europe's finest directors (five French and two Italian). Stories and their directors are "Avarice and Anger" (de Filippo), "Sloth" (Dreville), "Lust" (Allegret), "Envy" (Rossellini), "Gluttony" (Rim), "Pride" (Autant-Lara) and "The Eighth Sin" (Lacombe).
1953 127m/B Eduardo de Filippo, Isa Miranda, Jacqueline Plessis, Louis de Funes, Paolo Stoppa, Frank Villard, Jean Richard, Francoise Rosay, Jean Debucourt, Louis Seigner; **D:** Eduardo de Filippo, Jean Dreville, Yves Allegret, Roberto Rossellini, Carlo Rim, Claude Autant-Lara, Georges Lacombe. **VHS** IVY ♂♂♂

Seven Deaths in the Cat's Eye A ravenous beast slaughters people in a small Scottish village. This flick reveals a little-known fact about felines.
1972 90m/C Anton Diffring, Jane Birkin; **D:** Anthony M. (Antonio Margheriti) Dawson. **VHS, Beta** $79.95 PSM ♂♂

Seven Doors of Death A young woman inherits a possessed hotel. Meanwhile, hellish zombies try to check out. Chilling Italian horror flick. **AKA:** The Beyond.
1982 (R) 80m/C Katherine MacColl, David Warbeck, Farah Keller, Tony St. John; **D:** Louis Fuller. **VHS, Beta** $39.95 LIV ♂♂

Seven Doors to Death Young architect tries to solve a crime to avoid being placed under suspicion. The suspects are six shop owners in this low-budget attempt at a murder mystery.

1944 70m/B Chick Chandler, June Clyde, George Meeker, Gregory Gay, Edgar Dearing; **D:** Elmer Clifton. **VHS, Beta** $14.95 VCI, MRV, SNC ♂

Seven Faces of Dr. Lao Dr. Lao is the proprietor of a magical circus that changes the lives of the residents of a small western town. Marvelous special effects and makeup (Randall plays seven characters) highlight this charming family film in the Pal tradition. Charles Finney adapted from his novel.
1963 101m/C Tony Randall, Barbara Eden, Arthur O'Connell, Lee Patrick, Noah Beery Jr., John Qualen; **D:** George Pal. **VHS, Beta** $59.95 MGM ♂♂♂

The Seven Hills of Rome Quiet story of a television star (Lanza) who follows his girlfriend (Castle) to Rome after a lovers' quarrel, and there falls in love with Alassio. Fantastic music makes up for a weak plot. Based on a story by Giuseppi Amato. ♫Arrivederci Roma; Seven Hills of Rome; Never Till Now; Earthbound; Come Dance With Me; Lolita; There's Gonna Be a Party Tonight; Italian Calypso; Questa o Quella.
1958 107m/C Mario Lanza, Peggy Castle, Renato Rascel, Marisa Allasio, Clelia Matania, Rosella Como; **D:** Roy Rowland; **W:** Giorgio Prosperi, Art Cohn; **M:** Georgie Stoll. **VHS** $19.98 MGM ♂♂½

Seven Hours to Judgment When the punks who murdered his wife go free, a psychotic man (Liebman) decides to take justice into his own hands. He kidnaps the wife of the judge in charge (Bridges, who also directed) and leads him on a wild goose chase. Liebman steals the film as the psycho. Ex-Springsteen spouse Phillips plays the judge's wife. Ambitious but credulity-stretching revenge/crime drama. Screenplay written by de Souza under the pseudonym Elliot Stephens.
1988 (R) 90m/C Beau Bridges, Ron Leibman, Julianne Phillips, Al Freeman Jr., Reggie Johnson; **D:** Beau Bridges; **W:** Steven E. de Souza; **M:** John Debney. **VHS, Beta** $19.95 MED, VTR ♂♂

Seven Indignant A group of elite fighters is China's only hope against the invading Japanese.
19?? ?m/C Kong Hoi. **VHS, Beta** OCE ♂

The Seven Little Foys Enjoyable musical biography of Eddie Foy (played ebulliantly by Hope) and his famed vaudevillian troupe. Cagney's appearance as George M. Cohan is brief, but long enough for a memorable dance duet with Hope. ♫Mary's a Grand Old Name; I'm a Yankee Doodle Dandy; I'm the Greatest Father of Them All; Nobody; Comedy Ballet; I'm Tired; Chinatown, My Chinatown.
1955 95m/C Bob Hope, Milly Vitale, George Tobias, Angela Clark, James Cagney; **D:** Melville Shavelson; **W:** Jack Rose, Melville Shavelson. **VHS, Beta** $14.95 COL ♂♂♂

Seven Magnificent Gladiators Seven gladiators team up to save a peaceful Roman village from total annihilation. Dismal effort at a remake of "The Seven Samurai"—see the original instead, please. Ferrigno was "The Incredible Hulk" on TV.
1984 (PG) 86m/C Lou Ferrigno, Sybil Danning, Brad Harris, Dan Vadis, Carla Ferrigno; **D:** Bruno Mattei. **VHS, Beta** $59.95 MGM ♂

Seven Miles from Alcatraz/Flight from Glory Dramatic double feature: Two escaped convicts discover a hideout for Nazi spies in "Seven Miles From Alcatraz," and an evil man tries to recruit pilots to fly planes over the Andes Mountains in "Flight From Glory."

1943 127m/B James Craig, Bonita Granville, Chester Morris, Van Heflin, Onslow Stevens; *D:* Edward Dmytryk. **VHS, Beta $34.95** *RKO, TTC ♂♂*

Seven Minutes in Heaven Sensitive love story about a 15-year-old girl who invites her platonic male friend to live in her house, and finds it disturbs her boyfriend, as these things will. Ever so tasteful (unlike most other teen comedies), with gentle comedy—but forgettable.
1986 (PG) 90m/C Jennifer Connelly, Byron Thames, Maddie Corman; *D:* Linda Feferman. **VHS, Beta $19.98** *WAR ♂♂*

The Seven Percent Solution Dr. Watson persuades Sherlock Holmes to meet with Sigmund Freud to cure his cocaine addiction. Holmes and Freud then find themselves teaming up to solve a supposed kidnapping. Adapted by Nicholas Meyer from his own novel. One of the most charming Holmes films; well-cast, intriguing blend of mystery, drama, and fun.
1976 (PG) 113m/C Alan Arkin, Nicol Williamson, Laurence Olivier, Robert Duvall, Vanessa Redgrave, Joel Grey, Samantha Eggar, Jeremy Kemp, Charles Gray, Regine; *D:* Herbert Ross; *W:* Nicholas Meyer; *M:* John Addison. Academy Awards '76 Nominations: Best Adapted Screenplay; National Board of Review Awards '76: 10 Best Films of the Year. **VHS, Beta $34.98** *MCA ♂♂♂*

Seven Samurai Kurosawa's masterpiece, set in 16th-century Japan. A small farming village, beset by marauding bandits, hires seven professional soldiers to rid itself of the scourge. Wanna watch a samurai movie? This is the one. Sweeping, complex human drama with all the ingredients: action, suspense, comedy. Available in several versions of varying length, all long—and all too short. Splendid acting. In Japanese with English subtitles. *AKA:* Shichinin No Samurai; The Magnificent Seven.
1954 204m/B Toshiro Mifune, Takashi Shimura, Yoshio Inaba, Kuninori Kodo, Ko Kimura, Seiji Miyaguchi, Minoru Chiaki; *D:* Akira Kurosawa; *W:* Akira Kurosawa; *M:* Fumio Hayasaka. Academy Awards '56 Nominations: Best Art Direction/Set Decoration (B & W), Best Costume Design (B & W); Venice Film Festival '54: Silver Prize. **VHS, Beta $34.95** *HMV, SUE, HHT ♂♂♂♂*

Seven Sinners A South Seas cabaret singer (Dietrich) attracts sailors like flies, resulting in bar brawls, romance, and intrigue. Manly sailor Wayne falls for her. A good-natured, standard Hollywood adventure. Well cast; performed and directed with gusto. *AKA:* Cafe of the Seven Sinners.
1940 83m/B Marlene Dietrich, John Wayne, Albert Dekker, Broderick Crawford, Mischa Auer, Billy Gilbert, Oscar Homolka; *D:* Tay Garnett. **VHS, Beta $16.95** *SNC, NOS, BAR ♂♂♂*

Seven Sixgunners A western classic from the book by Nelson Nye.
1987 60m/C *D:* George Potter; *W:* Nelson Nye. **VHS** *NO ♂♂*

Seven Thieves Charming performances and nice direction make this tale of the perfect crime especially watchable. Robinson, getting on in years, wants one last big heist. With the help of Collins and Steiger, he gets his chance. From the Max Catto novel "Lions at the Kill." Surprisingly witty and light-hearted on this subject matter, and good still comes out ahead of evil.
1960 102m/C Joan Collins, Edward G. Robinson, Eli Wallach, Rod Steiger; *D:* Henry Hathaway. **VHS $39.98** *FOX, FCT ♂♂♂*

The Seven-Ups An elite group of New York City detectives seeks to avenge the killing of a colleague and to bust crooks whose felonies are punishable by jail terms of seven years or more. Unoriginal premise portends ill; plotless cop action flick full of car chases. Scheider tries hard. Directed by the producer of "The French Connection."
1973 (PG) 109m/C Roy Scheider, Tony LoBianco, Larry Haines, Jerry Leon; *D:* Phil D'Antoni. **VHS, Beta $59.98** *FOX ♂♂½*

The Seven Year Itch Classic, sexy Monroe comedy. Stunning blonde model (who else?) moves upstairs just as happily married guy Ewell's wife leaves for a long vacation. Understandably, he gets itchy. Monroe's famous blown skirt scene is here, as well as funny situations and appealing performances.
1955 105m/C Marilyn Monroe, Tom Ewell, Evelyn Keyes, Sonny Tufts, Victor Moore, Doro Merande, Robert Strauss, Oscar Homolka, Carolyn Jones; *D:* Billy Wilder; *W:* George Axelrod, Billy Wilder. **VHS, Beta $14.98** *FOX, FUS, GVV ♂♂♂*

Seven Years Bad Luck French comic Linder has the proverbial seven years' bad luck all in one day (!) after he breaks a mirror. Original and quite funny; full of fetching sophisticated sight gags. Silent with music score.
1920 67m/B Max Linder. **VHS, Beta $16.95** *GPV, VYY ♂♂♂*

1776 A musical comedy about America's first Continental Congress. The delegates battle the English and each other trying to establish a set of laws and the Declaration of Independence. Adapted from the Broadway hit with many members of the original cast. Available in widescreen format on laserdisc. ♫The Lees of Old Virginia; He Plays the Violin; But, Mr. Adams; Sit Down John; Till Then; Piddle, Twiddle and Resolve; Yours, Yours, Yours; Mama, Look Sharp; The Egg.
1972 (G) 141m/C William Daniels, Howard da Silva, Ken Howard, Donald Madden, Blythe Danner, Ronald Holgate, Virginia Vestoff, Stephen Nathan, Ralston Hill; *D:* Peter Hunt. Academy Awards '72 Nominations: Best Cinematography; National Board of Review Awards '72: 10 Best Films of the Year. **VHS, Beta $19.95** *COL, FCT ♂♂♂*

The Seventeenth Bride Set in a Czechoslovakian town; a strong-willed young woman is slowly destroyed by the insanity of war and racism.
1984 92m/C Lisa Hartman, Rosemary Leach; *D:* Israeli Nadav Levitan. **VHS** *NO ♂♂*

Seventh Cavalry A somewhat different look at Custer's defeat at the Little Big Horn. A soldier who was branded a coward for not taking part in the festivities tries to assuage his guilt by heading up the burial detail. The muddled ending tries to tell us that the Indians were afraid of Custer's horse.
1956 75m/C Randolph Scott, Barbara Hale, Jay C. Flippen, Jeanette Nolan, Frank Faylen, Leo Gordon, Denver Pyle, Harry Carey Jr., Michael Pate, Donald Curtis, Frank Wilcox, Pat Hogan, Russell Hicks; *D:* Joseph H. Lewis. **VHS $19.95** *NOS ♂♂½*

The Seventh Coin The legendary King Herod minted seven coins bearing his image which have become coin collector Emil Saber's (O'Toole) obsession. (He's a homicidal lunatic who thinks he's the reincarnation of Herod anyway.) Saber has found six of the coins but the seventh has fallen into the unsuspecting hands of Salim (Chowdhry), a pickpocket who has actually snatched it from the equally unsuspecting Ronnnie (Powers), an American teenager visiting Jerusalem

(good local color). The two become allies when Saber comes after them. They're an appealing couple; O'Toole camps it up shamelessly; and the movie is easygoing escapism.
1992 (PG-13) 92m/C Alexandra Powers, Navin Chowdhry, Peter O'Toole, John Rhys-Davies, Ally Walker; *D:* Dror Soref; *W:* Michael Lewis, Dror Soref. **VHS $92.95** *HMD ♂♂½*

The 7th Commandment Unlikely melodrama about a man afflicted with amnesia following an auto accident. He becomes a successful evangelist only to be blackmailed by an old girlfriend. Don't you just hate when that happens?
1961 82m/B Jonathan Kidd, Lynn Statten; *D:* Irvin Berwick. **VHS $15.95** *NOS, LOO ♂♂½*

The Seventh Cross Tracy stars as one of seven men who escape from a German concentration camp. When it is discovered they're gone, the commandant nails seven crosses to seven trees, intending them for the seven escapees. Watch for Tandy ("Driving Miss Daisy") in her first screen appearance. Effective war-time drama. From the novel by Anna Seghers.
1944 110m/B Spencer Tracy, Signe Hasso, Hume Cronyn, Jessica Tandy, Agnes Moorehead, Herbert Rudley, Felix Bressart, Ray Collins, Alexander Granach, George Macready, Steve Geray, Karen Verne, George Zucco; *D:* Fred Zinneman. **VHS $19.98** *MGM ♂♂♂*

The Seventh Seal As the plague sweeps through Europe a weary knight convinces "death" to play one game of chess with him. If the knight wins, he and his wife will be spared. The game leads to a discussion of religion and the existence of God. Considered by some Bergman's masterpiece. Von Sydow is stunning as the knight. In Swedish with English subtitles. Also available on laserdisc with a filmography of Bergman's work and commentary by film historian Peter Cowie. *AKA:* Det Sjunde Inseglet.
1956 96m/B Gunnar Bjornstrand, Max von Sydow, Bibi Andersson, Bengt Ekerot, Nils Poppe, Gunnel Lindblom; *D:* Ingmar Bergman; *W:* Ingmar Bergman; *M:* Erik Nordgren. **VHS, Beta, 8mm $19.95** *VDM, SUE, VYG ♂♂♂♂*

The Seventh Sign A pregnant woman realizes that the mysterious stranger boarding in her house and the bizarre events that accompany him are connected to Biblical prophesy and her unborn child. Tries hard, but it's difficult to get involved in the supernatural goings-on.
1988 (R) 105m/C Demi Moore, Juergen Prochnow, Michael Biehn, John Heard, Peter Friedman, Manny Jacobs, John Taylor, Lee Garlington, Akosua Busia; *D:* Carl Schultz; *M:* Jack Nitzsche. **VHS, Beta $14.95** *COL ♂♂*

The Seventh Veil A concert pianist loses the use of her hands in a fire, and with it her desire to live. Through the help of her friends and a hypnotizing doctor, she regains her love for life. Superb, dark psycho-drama. Todd as the pianist and Mason as her guardian are both unforgettable. Wonderful music and staging.
1946 91m/B James Mason, Ann Todd, Herbert Lom, Hugh McDermott, Albert Lieven; *D:* Compton Bennett. **VHS, Beta** *NO ♂♂♂½*

The Seventh Victim Another Val Lewton-produced low-budget exercise in shadowy suggestion, dealing with a woman searching for her lost sister, who'd gotten involved with Satanists. The Hays Office's squeamishness regarding subject matter makes the film's action a bit cloudy but it remains truly eerie.

1943 71m/B Kim Hunter, Tom Conway, Jean Brooks, Hugh Beaumont, Erford Gage, Isabel Jewell, Evelyn Brent; **D:** Mark Robson. **VHS, Beta** $14.95 *RKO, TTC* 🎬🎬🎬

The Seventh Voyage of Sinbad
Sinbad seeks to restore his fiancee from the midget size to which an evil magician (Thatcher) has reduced her. Ray Harryhausen works his animation magic around a well-developed plot and engaging performances by the real actors. Great score and fun, fast-moving plot.
1958 (G) 94m/C Kerwin Mathews, Kathryn Grant, Torin Thatcher, Richard Eyer; **D:** Nathan Juran; **W:** Kenneth Kolb; **M:** Bernard Herrmann. **VHS, Beta** $14.95 *COL, MLB, CCB* 🎬🎬🎬

Severance
An ex-pilot attempts to save his daughter from the world of drugs and violence.
1988 93m/C Lou Liotta, Lisa Nicole Wolpe, Linda Christian-Jones; **D:** David Max Steinberg. **VHS, Beta** $79.95 *MNC* 🎬

The Severed Arm
Trapped in a cave, five men are compelled to cut off the arm of a companion in order to ward off starvation. Then as luck would have it, they're rescued. Years later, one-by-one they meet a bloody demise. Is it the one-armed man?
1973 (R) 89m/C Deborah Walley, Marvin Kaplan, Paul Carr, John Crawford, David Cannon; **D:** Thomas Alderman. **VHS, Beta** $14.95 *CNG, MRV, GEM Woof!*

Severed Ties
Brilliant genetic scientist experiments with human limb regeneration in order to re-grow his accidentally severed arm. His strange mixture of lizard and serial-killer genes results in a repulsive reptilian limb with a nasty habit of slithering out of his shoulder. His mother discovers his experiments and tries to sell his discovery to the Nazis but her son escapes into a bizarre subterranean society and vows revenge. So bad it's just bad.
1992 (R) 95m/C Billy Morrissette, Elke Sommer, Oliver Reed, Garrett Morris; **D:** Damon Santostefano. **VHS** $89.95 *COL* 🎬½

Sex
Interesting dated relic. Morality play about a Broadway star who uses her charms to destroy a marriage only to dump her lover for richer prospects. The businessman she lands then shamelessly betrays her. What a title, especially for its time!
1920 87m/B Adrienne Renault, Louise Glaum, Irving Cummings, Peggy Pearce, Myrtle Stedman; **D:** Fred Niblo. **VHS, Beta** $19.98 *CCB, GPV, GVV* 🎬🎬½

Sex Adventures of the Three Musketeers
Soft-core spoof of the Dumas classic. Dubbed.
198? 79m/C Inga Steeger, Achim Hammer, Peter Graf, Jurg Coray. **VHS, Beta** $29.95 *MED Woof!*

Sex and Buttered Popcorn
Stylish and entertaining documentary of the Hollywood sexploitation moguls, and their films, from the 1920s through the 1950s. These films shamelessly catered to audience's prurient interests, but typically delivered saccharin-coated morality messages and stock footage of routine baby births or the horrible effects of sexually transmitted diseases. Hosted by Ned Beatty, and featuring clips from the actual films, plus an interview with the widow of Kroger Babb, the most notorious of the exploiteers. A real hoot.
1991 (R) 70m/C David Friedman; **D:** Sam Harrison. **VHS** $29.95 *CPM, FCT Woof!*

Sex and the College Girl
Folks talk about their relationship problems while vacationing in Puerto Rico. Tame talkfest providing Grodin with his first role. Included as part of Joe Bob Brigg's ''Sleaziest Movies in the History of the World'' series, probably just for the title.
1964 ?m/C Charles Grodin, Richard Arlen, Luana Anders; **D:** Joseph Adler. **VHS** *SVI* 🎬

Sex and the Single Girl
Curtis is a reporter for a trashy magazine who intends to write an expose on ''The International Institute of Advanced Marital and Pre-Marital Studies,'' an organization run by Wood. Curtis poses as a man having marital trouble, using his neighbor's name and marital problems, in order to get close to Wood. Things get sticky when Wood wants to meet Curtis' wife and three women show up claiming to be her. This confusing but amusing tale twists and turns until it reaches a happy ending. Loosely based on the book by Helen Gurley Brown.
1964 114m/C Tony Curtis, Natalie Wood, Henry Fonda, Lauren Bacall, Mel Ferrer, Fran Jeffries, Leslie Parrish, Edward Everett Horton, Larry Storch; **D:** Richard Quine; **M:** Count Basie. **VHS** $19.98 *WAR* 🎬🎬½

Sex and the Single Parent
St. James and Farrell, both divorced, both with kids, have a relationship. Complications set in—just how does one be a single parent and have a fulfilling sex life in this day and age? Some of these made for TV efforts are so formulaic!
1982 98m/C Susan St. James, Mike Farrell, Dori Brenner, Warren Berlinger, Julie Sommars, Barbara Rhoades; **D:** Jackie Cooper. **VHS, Beta** *TLF* 🎬½

Sex Crimes
A tough female judge is brutally raped and she keeps the attack a secret. However, she does ask a friendly police detective to teach her how to use a gun. He's suspicious of her reasons and decides to trail her as she sets out for revenge on her attacker. Predictable actioner.
1992 90m/C Jeffery Osterhage, Maria Richwine, Fernando Garzon, Craig Alan, Grace Morley; **D:** David Garcia. **VHS** $89.95 *ATV* 🎬🎬

Sex, Drugs, and Rock-n-Roll
Several girls frequent a rock club looking for all the action they can get their hands on.
1984 90m/C Jeanne Silver, Sharon Kane, Tish Ambrose, Josey Duval. **VHS, Beta** *NO Woof!*

Sex, Drugs, Rock & Roll: Eric Bogosian
Bogosian's 1990 concert performance, taped live at the Wilur Theate in Boston, exhibits the electricity and finely nuanced characters for which he is justly famous. The characters share a depressingly negative side, however, which keeps this film from being strictly belly-laugh territory.
1991 (R) 96m/C Eric Bogosian; **D:** John McNaughton; **W:** Eric Bogosian. **VHS** *MPI Woof!*

Sex is Crazy
A melange from Italian horror director Franco containing some epic, some horror, some sex, some sitcom, and some documentary. Little green aliens touch down and impregnate earth women in one skit. In another, a gambler's girlfriend demands two thugs ravage her for the sheer sexual thrill. And in a third, a severed hand commands a heroine to martyr herself to the great god Cucufat. Spanish with English subtitles.
1979 81m/C Lina Romay, Anthony Mayans, Tony Skios; **D:** Jess (Jesus) Franco. **VHS** $27.90 *VSM* 🎬

sex, lies and videotape
Acclaimed, popular independent film by first-timer Soderbergh, detailing the complex relations among a childless married couple, the wife's adulterous sister, and a mysterious college friend of the husband's obsessed with videotaping women as they talk about their sex lives. Heavily awarded, including first prize at Cannes. Confidently uses much (too much?) dialogue and slow (too slow?) pace. Available on laserdisc with a deleted scene and interviews with the director; also includes two theatrical trailers and a short film by Soderbergh.
1989 (R) 101m/C James Spader, Andie MacDowell, Peter Gallagher, Laura San Giacomo, Ron Vawter, Steven Brill; **D:** Steven Soderberg; **W:** Steven Soderberg; **M:** Cliff Martinez. Academy Awards '89 Nominations: Best Original Screenplay; Cannes Film Festival '89: Best Actor (Spader), Best Film; Independent Spirit Awards '90: Best Actress (MacDowell), Best Director (Soderberg), Best Film, Best Supporting Actress (San Giacomo). **VHS, Beta, 8mm** $19.95 *COL, VYG* 🎬🎬🎬

Sex, Love and Cold Hard Cash
Sarah (Williams) is a high-priced hooker whose life savings ($20 million in stocks and bonds) have just been stolen. She hires an ex-con (Denison) to help recover the money and the two partners find themselves on the wrong side of some Mob trouble as well. Enough twists to keep a viewer interested as well as the prerequisite amount of shootings and chase scenes.
1993 (PG-13) 86m/C JoBeth Williams, Anthony John Denison; **D:** Harry S. Longstreet; **W:** Harry S. Longstreet. **VHS** $89.98 *MCA* 🎬🎬½

The Sex Machine
In the year 2037, a scientist finds two of the world's greatest lovers and unites them so he can transform their reciprocating motion into electricity. It worked on paper.
1976 (R) 80m/C Agostina Belli. **VHS, Beta** $19.95 *MED Woof!*

Sex on the Run
Love-starved wife of an oil-rich sheik, stimulated by the idea of having Casanova for her lover, teases her master into delivering him, but Casanova finds peace in the arms of three convent lovelies. Disgusting, amateurish, and offensive. **AKA:** Cassanova and Co.; Some Like it Cool.
1978 91m/C Tony Curtis, Marisa Berenson, Britt Ekland; **D:** Francois Legrand. **VHS, Beta** $69.95 *VES Woof!*

Sex Through a Window
TV reporter becomes an obsessive voyeur after filing a report on high tech surveillance equipment. Flimsy premise is a yucky, lame excuse to show skin. **AKA:** Extreme Close-Up.
1972 (R) 81m/C James McMullan, James A. Watson Jr., Kate Woodville, Bara Byrnes, Al Checco, Antony Carbone; **D:** Jeannot Szwarc; **W:** Michael Crichton. **VHS, Beta** $69.98 *LIV, VES* 🎬

Sex with a Smile
Five slapstick episodes by five different directors with lots of sexual satire pointed at religion and politics in Italy. Don't know much about Italy? Then you'll be left out of the joke here. And really, only one episode is funny anyway (the one with Feldman of ''Young Frankenstein'' fame).
1976 (R) 100m/C Marty Feldman, Edwige Fenech, Alex Marino, Enrico Monterrano, Giovanna Ralli; **D:** Sergio Martino. **VHS, Beta** $59.95 *GEM* 🎬

Sexo Y Crimen
Two lovers find themselves inextricably tangled in a violent situation.
1987 90m/C Enrique Lizalde, Emily Cranz, Enrique Rambal, Yoland Ciani. **VHS, Beta** $54.95 *MAD* 🎬🎬

Sexpot
A voluptuous woman's rich husbands mysteriously keep dying, but not before they leave their fortunes to her.

1988 (R) 95m/C Ruth Collins, Troy Donahue, Joyce Lyons, Gregory Patrick, Frank Stewart, Jack Carter; *D:* Chuck Vincent. **VHS, Beta** $29.95 *ACA* 🎬

Sextette Lavish film about an elderly star who is constantly interrupted by former spouses and well-wishers while on a honeymoon with her sixth husband. West unwisely came out of retirement for this last film role, based on her own play. Exquisitely embarrassing to watch. Interesting cast.
1978 (PG) 91m/C Mae West, Timothy Dalton, Ringo Starr, George Hamilton, Dom DeLuise, Tony Curtis, Alice Cooper, Keith Moon, George Raft, Rona Barrett, Walter Pidgeon; *D:* Ken Hughes. **VHS, Beta** $9.95 *MED, MLB* Woof!

Sexton Blake and the Hooded Terror Sexton Blake a British private detective a la Holmes, is after "The Snake," a master criminal, and his gang The Hooded Terror. One of a series of melodramatic adventures interesting chiefly for Slaughter's performance as the gangleader.
1938 70m/B Tod Slaughter, Greta Gynt, George Culzon, George King. **VHS, Beta** $24.95 *VYY, SNC, MRV* 🎬

Sexual Intent Based on the true storm of pathological liar John Walsome, known as "the Sweetheart Scammer," who seduced and robbed more than 40 women. This con artist transformed himself into whatever kind of Mr. Right his victim needed—until he picked on the wrong woman.
1994 (R) 88m/C Gary Hudson, Michele Brin, Sarah Hill; *D:* Kurt MacCarley; *W:* Kurt MacCarley. **VHS** *COL* 🎬

Sexual Malice Another erotic thriller finds a bored wife involved in an obsessive affair with a mystery man who has murder on his mind. Also available in an unrated version.
1993 (R) 96m/C Diana Barton, John Laughlin, Chad McQueen, Edward Albert, Don Swayze, Kathy Shower, Samantha Phillips; *D:* Jag Mundhra; *W:* Carl Austin. **VHS** $92.95 *APX* 🎬🎬

Sexual Response Eve, a radio talk show "sexologist," is ironically unhappy in her marriage but scoffs at her producer's suggestion of an affair. That is until she meets a brash sculptor and they begin a torrid, and increasingly obsessive, romance. Her lover suggests that her husband have an "accident" with his hunting rifle, but Eve refuses and throws him out. The sculptor, however, breaks into the husband's loft to steal the rifle and finds some news clippings about the man's past that could ruin the lives of many. Little more than an excuse for torrid love scenes. Also available in an unrated version.
1992 (R) 87m/C Shannon Tweed, Catherine Oxenberg, Vernon Wells, Emile Levisetti; *D:* Yaky Yosha. **VHS** $19.95 *COL* 🎬🎬

S.F.W. Another look at Generation X—a suburban teen unwillingly becomes a media sensation during a terrorist hostage crisis at a convenience store. Dorff is perfectly cast as Cliff Spab, the phrasemaking teen whose words are adopted by his peers. An intelligent commentary on fame in contemporary society. Title acronym stands for "So F***ing What." Based on the novel by Andrew Wellman.
1994 ?m/C Stephen Dorff, Reese Witherspoon, Jake Busey, Joey Adams, Pamela Gidley, David Barry Gray, Jack Noseworthy, Richard Portnow; *D:* Jefery Levy; *W:* Jefery Levy, James Foley. **VHS** 🎬🎬½

Shack Out on 101 A waitress (Moore) in an isolated cafe on a busy highway notices suspicious doings among her customers. What could they be up to? Communist subversion, of course. Of-its-era anti-pinko propaganda, but with a twist: Moore uncovers commie plots, pleases her customers, and fends off unwelcome lecherous advances all in 80 minutes, on a single set!
1955 80m/B Lee Marvin, Terry Moore, Keenan Wynn, Frank Lovejoy, Whit Bissell; *D:* Edward Dein. **VHS** $29.95 *REP* 🎬🎬

Shadey The premise for this oddball comedy came to someone in the wee hours: I've got it! Mild-mannered mechanic can film people's thoughts; wants to use his gift only for good, but needs money for a sex-change operation. Assorted bad guys want to use him for evil purposes. Strange, but not bad; Helmond's character is memorable.
1987 (PG-13) 90m/C Anthony Sher, Billie Whitelaw, Patrick Macnee, Katherine Helmond, Leslie Ash, Larry Lamb, Bernard Hepton; *D:* Philip Saville; *W:* Snoo Wilson; *M:* Colin Towns. **VHS, Beta** $79.98 *FOX* 🎬🎬½

The Shadow Scotland Yard pulls out all the stops to track down a murderous extortionist, enlisting the aid of a novelist in their efforts. Long on talk and short on action.
1936 63m/B Henry Kendall, Elizabeth Allan, Jeanne Stuart, Felix Aylmer, Cyril Raymond; *D:* George Cooper. **VHS, Beta** $16.95 *NOS, SNC* 🎬½

The Shadow Who knows what evil lurks in the hearts of men? Why "The Shadow" of course, as is shown in this highly-stylized big screen version of the '30s radio show that once starred Orson Welles. Billionaire playboy Lamont Cranston (Baldwin) is a master of illusion and defender of justice thanks to his alter ego. Aided by companion Margo Lane (Miller), da Shadow battles super-criminal Shiwan Khan (Lone), the deadliest descendant of Genghis Khan. Numerous and elaborate special effects provide icing on the cake for those in the mood for a journey back to the radio past or a quick superhero fix.
1994 (PG-13) ?m/C Alec Baldwin, John Lone, Penelope Ann Miller, Peter Boyle, Ian McKellan, Tim Curry, Jonathan Winters; *D:* Russell Mulcahy; *W:* David Koepp. **VHS** *NYR* 🎬🎬½

The Shadow Box Three terminally ill people at a California hospice confront their destinies. Pulitzer Prize-winning play by Michael Cristofer is actually improved by director Newman and a superb, well-chosen cast. Powerful.
1980 96m/C Joanne Woodward, Christopher Plummer, Robert Urich, Valerie Harper, Sylvia Sidney, Melinda Dillon, Ben Masters, John Considine, James Broderick; *D:* Paul Newman; *M:* Henry Mancini. **VHS, Beta** *KAR* 🎬🎬🎬

Shadow Dancing The proprietor of the auspicious Beaumont Theater of Dance is haunted by one of his former dancers who died unexpectedly during a performance of "Medusa." Now, over fifty years later, Jessica, the pick for the lead in a new production, begins to take on her predecessor's mannerisms and spirit as she faces her impending doom. Surprisingly believable and suspenseful—and scary!
1988 (PG) 100m/C Nadine Van Der Velde, James Kee, John Colicos, Shirley Douglas, Christopher Plummer; *D:* John Furey; *M:* Jay Gruska. **VHS, Beta** *NO* 🎬🎬🎬

Shadow Force Homicide detective Rick Kelly is investigating the murders of a district attorney and a police sergeant. With the help of Mary, the usual beautiful female journalist, he uncovers a plot to assassinate key law enforcement officers.
1992 ?m/C Dirk Benedict, Lance LeGault, Lise Cutter, Jack Elam, Glenn Corbett, Bob Hastings; *D:* Darrell Davenport. **VHS** $89.95 *IMP* 🎬½

Shadow Killers There's no time to fear your own shadow, for there is a far more terrifying darkness stalking the city.
1980 90m/C Chen Ching, Chang Wu Lang, Chen Chiang. **VHS, Beta** *NO* 🎬½

The Shadow Man A casino operator in London (Romero) is accused of killing a former girlfriend and works to clear himself. Family conventional action mystery: nothing to write home about. *AKA:* Street of Shadows.
1953 76m/B Cesar Romero, Simone Silva, Kay Kendall, John Penrose, Edward Underdown; *D:* Richard Vernon. **VHS, Beta** *NO* 🎬

Shadow Man A mysterious thief, a master of disguise, sets out to steal the Treasure of the Knights Templar and nothing will stand in his way.
1975 (PG) 89m/C Josephine Chaplin, Gert Frobe, Gayle Hunnicutt. **VHS, Beta** $59.95 *MED* 🎬🎬

Shadow of a Doubt Uncle Charlie has come to visit his relatives in Santa Rosa. Although he is handsome and charming, his young niece slowly comes to realize he is a wanted mass murderer - and he comes to recognize her suspicions. Hitchcock's personal favorite movie; a quietly creepy venture into Middle American menace. Good performances, especially by Cronyn. From the story by Gordon McConnell.
1943 108m/B Teresa Wright, Joseph Cotten, Hume Cronyn, MacDonald Carey, Henry Travers, Wallace Ford; *D:* Alfred Hitchcock; *W:* Thorton Wilder; *M:* Dimitri Tiomkin. **VHS, Beta** $19.95 *MCA* 🎬🎬🎬½

Shadow of Chikara A Confederate Army Captain and an orphan girl encounter unexpected adventures as they search for a fortune in diamonds hidden in a river in northern Arkansas. *AKA:* Thunder Mountain; The Curse of Demon Mountain.
1977 (PG) 96m/C Joe Don Baker, Sondra Locke, Ted Neeley, Slim Pickens. **VHS, Beta** $19.95 *STE, NWV* 🎬

Shadow of China A young man struggles for power and love in Hong Kong, while an English beauty and an Oriental activist hold the keys to his future and a past which could destroy him. Excellent acting, stunning location photography. Exotic and intense. Based on the Japanese best-seller "Snakehead."
1991 (PG-13) 100m/C John Lone, Sammi Davis-Voss, Vivian Wu; *D:* Mitsuo Yanagimachi; *W:* Mitsuo Yanagimachi, Richard Maxwell. **VHS** $89.98 *COL, NLC* 🎬🎬🎬

Shadow of Chinatown Mad scientist creates wave of murder and terror in Chinatown. Edited version of a 15-chapter serial.
1936 70m/B Bela Lugosi, Bruce (Herman Brix) Bennett, Joan Barclay. **VHS, Beta** $27.95 *NOS, SNC, VCN* 🎬½

Shadow of the Eagle Former wartime flying ace Wayne is accused of being a criminal known as "The Eagle." He's using his flying skills (which include skywriting) to threaten a corporation which has stolen plans for a new invention. But can Wayne really be our villain? 12-chapter serial.
1932 226m/B John Wayne, Dorothy Gulliver, Walter Miller; *D:* Ford Beebe. **VHS, Beta** $24.95 *GPV, VYY, VCN* 🎬🎬½

Shadow of the Thin Man In the fourth "Thin Man" film, following "Another Thin Man," Nick and Nora stumble onto a murder at the racetrack. The rapport between Powell and Loy is still going strong, providing us with some wonderful entertainment. Followed by "The Thin Man Goes Home."

1941 97m/B William Powell, Myrna Loy, Barry Nelson, Donna Reed, Sam Levene, Alan Baxter, Dickie Hall, Loring Smith, Joseph Anthony, Henry O'Neill; **D:** Woodbridge S. Van Dyke. **VHS, Beta** $19.98 MGM ⅟⅟⅟

Shadow of the Wolf

Phillips is as Agaguk, the son of the village leader, in this epic saga of survival set against the wilderness of the Arctic. Agaguk decides he cannot accept the white man's intrusion, so he sets out on his own. His father believes his departure to be the ultimate betrayal and casts upon him the "curse of the white wolf." Now Agaguk and his companion (Tilly) must face the harsh tundra alone and struggle to stay alive in the Great White North. Based on the novel "Agaguk" by Yves Theriault.
1992 (PG-13) 108m/C Lou Diamond Phillips, Donald Sutherland, Jennifer Tilly, Toshiro Mifune; **D:** Jacques Dorfman; **W:** Rudy Wurlitzer, Evan Jones. **VHS** $14.95 COL ⅟⅟

Shadow on the Sun

The life of Beryl Markham, pioneer female aviator and adventurer of the 1930s. Way too long and boring made for TV answer to "Out of Africa." On two cassettes.
1988 192m/C Stefanie Powers, Claire Bloom, Frederic Forrest, James Fox, John Rubinstein, Jack Thompson; **D:** Tony Richardson. **VHS** $29.95 STE, NWV ⅟ ½

Shadow Play

A successful female playwright is haunted by visions of a past lover. Her life slowly falls apart, but not before this film does.
1986 (R) 98m/C Dee Wallace Stone, Cloris Leachman; **D:** Susan Shadburne; **W:** Susan Shadburne. **VHS, Beta** $19.95 STE, NWV ⅟ ½

The Shadow Riders

Two brothers who fought on opposite sides during the Civil War return home to find their brother's fiancee kidnapped by a renegade Confederate officer who plans to use her as ransom in a prisoner exchange, and they set out to rescue the woman. Preceded by "The Sacketts" and based on the works of Louis L'Amour. Made for television. **AKA:** Louis L'Amour's "The Shadow Riders".
1982 (PG) 96m/C Tom Selleck, Sam Elliott, Ben Johnson, Katharine Ross, Jeffery Osterhage, Gene Evans, R.G. Armstrong, Marshall Teague, Dominique Dunne, Jeanetta Arnetta; **D:** Andrew V. McLaglen. **VHS** $79.98 VMK ⅟⅟

The Shadow Strikes

Adaptation of the radio serial. The sleuth pursues a killer and a gangster. Meanwhile, the police try to pin a robbery on the "Shadow." Who did it? The Shadow knows!
1937 61m/B Rod La Rocque, Lynn Anders. **VHS, Beta** $12.95 GPV, NOS, CAB ⅟ ½

Shadowhunter

Glenn stars as a burned-out big city detective who is sent to a Navajo reservation in Arizona to bring a murder suspect back to Los Angeles. When the alleged killer escapes custody Glenn must track him across forbidding desert territory and face his suspect's unusual mystical powers.
1993 (R) 98m/C Scott Glenn. **VHS** $89.98 REP ⅟⅟

Shadowlands

A look at the later life of bachelor-scholar C.S. Lewis (also the author of the "Chronicles of Narnia"). A devout proponent of Christianity, the middle-aged Lewis fell in love and married Joy Gresham, a divorced American poet with two young sons. Joy was diagnosed with cancer and her illness provided Lewis with the clearest test of his faith. Wonderful performances by both Ackland and Bloom. **AKA:** C.S. Lewis Through the Shadowlands.

1985 90m/C Joss Ackland, Claire Bloom, Rupert Baderman; **D:** Norman Stone. **VHS** $29.95 FRV, VGD, KAR ⅟⅟⅟

Shadowlands

Touching, tragic story of the late-in-life romance between celebrated author and Christian theologian C.S. Lewis (Hopkins) and brash New York divorcee Joy Gresham (Winger). Attenborough's direction is rather stately and sweeping and Winger is really too young for her role but Hopkins is excellent as (another) repressed man who finds more emotions than he can handle. Critically acclaimed adaptation of Nicholson's play will require lots of kleenex.
1993 (PG) 130m/C Anthony Hopkins, Debra Winger, Edward Hardwicke, Joseph Mazzello, Michael Denison, John Wood, Peter Firth, Peter Howell; **D:** Richard Attenborough; **W:** William Nicholson; **M:** George Fenton. Academy Awards '93 Nominations: Best Actress (Winger), Best Adapted Screenplay; British Academy Awards '94: Best Actor (Hopkins), Best Actress (Winger), Best Adapted Screenplay, Best Director (Attenborough); British Academy Awards '94: Best Film; Los Angeles Film Critics Association Awards '93: Best Actor (Hopkins); National Board of Review Awards '93: Best Actor (Hopkins). **VHS** HBO ⅟⅟⅟

Shadows

A Chinese laundryman (Chaney) lives with a group of his countrymen in a New England seacoast village. All is peaceful until the local minister decides to convert the "heathen" Chinese. Ludicrous but worth seeing for Chaney's fun performance. Silent with music score.
1922 70m/B Lon Chaney Sr., Harrison Ford; **D:** Tom Forman. **VHS, Beta, 8mm** $16.95 SNC, NOS, CCB ⅟⅟

Shadows and Fog

Offbeat, unpredictable Allen film that is little more than an exercise in expressionistic visual stylings. The action centers around a haunted, alienated clerk (Allen) who is awakened in the middle of the night to join a vigilante group searching the streets for a killer. Although reminiscent of a silent film, Carlo Di Palma's black and white cinematography is stunning. Several stars appear briefly throughout this extremely unfocused comedy.
1992 (PG-13) 85m/B Woody Allen, Kathy Bates, John Cusack, Mia Farrow, Jodie Foster, Fred Gwynne, Julie Kavner, Madonna, John Malkovich, Kenneth Mars, Kate Nelligan, Donald Pleasence, Lily Tomlin, Philip Bosco, Robert Joy, Wallace Shawn, Kurtwood Smith, Josef Sommer, David Ogden, Michael Kirby, Anne Lange; **D:** Woody Allen; **W:** Woody Allen. **VHS** $67.40 ORI ⅟⅟

Shadows in the Storm

A librarian/poet retreats to a secluded forest after losing his job. There he meets an exotically beautiful young woman who becomes his lover. With her love, she brings blackmail, murder, and mystery.
1988 (R) 90m/C Ned Beatty, Mia Sara, Michael Madsen; **D:** Terrell Tannen. **VHS** VMK ⅟⅟

Shadows of Death

Crabbe is the hero who must track down a gang of outlaws who kill to grab the land along the path of a new railroad. One of the "Billy Carson" series.
1945 60m/B Buster Crabbe, Al "Fuzzy" St. John. **VHS, Beta** $27.95 VCN, VCI ⅟ ½

Shadows of Forgotten Ancestors

Set in rural Russia in the early 20th century. Brings to expressive life the story of a man whose entire life has been overtaken by tragedy. Folk drama about a peasant who falls in with the daughter of his father's killer, then marries another woman. Strange, resonant and powerful with distinctive camera work. In Ukrainian with English subtitles. **AKA:** Tini Zabutykh Predkiv; Shadows of Our Ancestors; Shadows of Our Forgotten Ancestors; Wild Horses of Fire.

1964 99m/C Ivan Micholaichuk, Larisa Kadochnikova; **D:** Sergei Paradjanov. **VHS, Beta** $29.95 CVC, ING, AUD ⅟⅟

Shadows of the Orient

Two detectives are out to smash a Chinese smuggling ring.
1937 70m/B Regis Toomey, Esther Ralston. **VHS** $16.95 SNC, NOS, DVT ⅟⅟⅟

Shadows on the Stairs

A creepy boarding house is the scene of a number of mystery-drenched murders. A bizarre assortment of suspects make things even crazier.
1941 63m/B Frieda Inescort, Paul Cavanagh, Heather Angel, Bruce Lester, Miles Mander, Lumsden Hare, Turhan Bey; **D:** David Ross Lederman. **VHS, Beta** $16.95 SNC ⅟⅟

Shadows Over Shanghai

This adventure relic was set during the Japanese invasion of China prior to WWII and uses much newsreel footage of that infamy. As for the plot, it's a groaner about good guys and bad skulking around the eponymous port in search of a treasure.
1938 66m/B James Dunn, Ralph Morgan, Linda Gray, Robert Barratt, Paul Sutton, Edward Woods; **D:** Charles Lamont. **VHS** $19.95 NOS, LOO ⅟ ½

Shadows Run Black

A police detective must save a college coed from the clutches of a maniac wielding a meat cleaver. Ordinary slash-em-up. Bet Costner's embarrassed now about this early role - like Stallone's porno role in "The Italian Stallion."
1984 89m/C William J. Kulzer, Elizabeth Trosper, Kevin Costner; **D:** Howard Heard. **VHS, Beta** NO ⅟⅟

Shadowzone

As a result of NASA experiments in dream travel, an interdimensional monster invades our world in search of victims. Begins well, with slightly interesting premise, but degenerates into typical monster flick. Good special effects.
1990 (R) 88m/C Louise Fletcher, David Beecroft, James Hong, Shawn Weatherly, Lu Leonard; **D:** J.S. Cardone. **VHS, Beta** $19.95 PAR ⅟⅟

Shaft

A black private eye is hired to find a Harlem gangster's kidnapped daughter. Lotsa sex and violence; suspenseful and well directed. Great ending. Academy Award winning theme song by Isaac Hayes, the first music award from the Academy to an African American. Adapted from the novel by Ernest Tidyman. Followed by "Shaft's Big Score" and "Shaft in Africa."
1971 (R) 98m/C Richard Roundtree, Moses Gunn, Charles Cioffi; **D:** Gordon Parks. Academy Awards '71: Best Song ("Theme from Shaft"); Nominations: Best Original Score; Golden Globe Awards '72: Best Score. **VHS, Beta** $19.95 MGM ⅟⅟⅟

Shaft's Big Score

This first sequel to the extremely sucessful "Shaft" has Roundtree's detective trying to mediate between several mobsters while investigating a friend's murder. Lots of action and an exciting Brooklyn chase scene involving cars, helicopters, and boats but still routine when compared to the original. Followed by "Shaft in Africa."
1972 (R) 105m/C Richard Roundtree, Moses Gunn, Joseph Macolo, Drew Bundi Brown, Wally Taylor, Kathy Imrie, Julius W. Harris, Rosalind Miles, Joe Santos; **D:** Gordon Parks; **W:** Ernest Tidyman; **M:** Gordon Parks. **VHS** $19.98 MGM ⅟⅟½

Shag: The Movie

The time is 1963, the setting Myrtle Beach, South Carolina, the latest craze shaggin' when four friends hit the beach for one last weekend together. Carson (Cates) is getting ready to marry staid Harley (Power); Melaina (Fonda) wants to be discovered in Hollywood; and Pudge

(Gish) and Luanne (Hannah) are off to college. They encounter lots of music, boys, and dancing in this delightful film. Not to be confused with other "teen" movies, this one boasts a good script and an above average cast.
1989 (PG) 96m/C Phoebe Cates, Annabeth Gish, Bridget Fonda, Page Hannah, Scott Coffey, Robert Rusler, Tyrone Power Jr., Jeff Yagher, Carrie Hamilton, Shirley Anne Field, Leilani Sarelle Ferrer; **D:** Zelda Barron; **W:** Robin Swicord, Lanier Laney, Terry Sweeney. **VHS, Beta** $89.99 *HBO* 🎬🎬🎬

The Shaggy D.A. Wilby Daniels is getting a little worried about his canine alter ego as he is about to run for District Attorney. Fun sequel to "The Shaggy Dog."
1976 (G) 90m/C Dean Jones, Tim Conway, Suzanne Pleshette, Keenan Wynn; **D:** Robert Stevenson; **M:** Buddy Baker. **VHS, Beta** *DIS, OM* 🎬🎬

The Shaggy Dog When young Wilby Daniels utters some magical words from the inscription of an ancient ring he turns into a shaggy dog, causing havoc for family and neighbors. Disney slapstick is on target at times, though it drags in places. Followed by "The Shaggy D.A." and "Return of the Shaggy Dog."
1959 (G) 101m/B Fred MacMurray, Jean Hagen, Tommy Kirk, Annette Funicello, Tim Considine, Kevin Corcoran; **D:** Charles T. Barton. **VHS, Beta** $19.99 *DIS, BTV* 🎬🎬½

Shaka Zulu British miniseries depicting the career of Shaka, king of the Zulus (Cele). Set in the early 19th century during British ascendency in Africa. Good, absorbing cross-cultural action drama would have been better with more inspired directing by Faure.
1983 300m/C Edward Fox, Robert Powell, Trevor Howard, Christopher Lee, Fiona Fullerton, Henry Cele; **D:** William C. Faure. **VHS, Beta** $14.99 *STE, PSM, FCT* 🎬🎬🎬

Shake Hands with Murder Three people spend their time bailing criminals out of jail for profit. One is murdered, and the other two become implicated in comedy.
1944 63m/B Iris Adrian, Frank Jenks, Douglas Fowley, Jack Raymond, Claire Rochelle, Herbert Rawlinson, Forrest Taylor; **D:** Albert Herman. **VHS, Beta** $16.95 *SNC* 🎬🎬

Shake Hands with the Devil It's the Irish Republican Army against the British Black and Tans as Ireland fights for independence in 1921. Cagney is a teaching surgeon who is secretly a militant, obsessed with the idea of gaining Irish freedom. He urges his students to join with him, which Irish-American Murray does. When Murray learns that Cagney is out to sabotage a peace treaty, he must decide whether to betray Cagney in order to stop further violence. Cagney is excellent as the hard-bitten revolutionary who can't see beyond his own ideals. Filmed on location in Dublin, which further heightens the film's tension.
1959 110m/B James Cagney, Don Murray, Dana Wynter, Glynis Johns, Michael Redgrave, Sybil Thorndike, Harry Brogan, Robert Brown; **D:** Michael Anderson Sr.; **W:** Ivan Goff. **VHS** $19.98 *MGM, FCT* 🎬🎬🎬

Shake, Rattle and Rock A deejay wants to open a teen music club playing rock 'n' roll, which has all the conservative parents up in arms. A court case follows (which the kids win). Incidental plot to the great music by Fats Domino, Joe Turner, Annita Ray, and Tommy Charles. Songs include "Ain't It a Shame," "Honey Chile," "I'm in Love Again," "Feelin' Happy," and "Sweet Love on My Mind."

1957 76m/C Mike Connors, Lisa Gaye, Sterling Holloway, Margaret Dumont, Raymond Hatton, Douglass Dumbrille; **D:** Edward L. Cahn; **W:** Lou Rusoff. **VHS** $9.95 *COL, MOV, MVD* 🎬🎬½

Shakedown Power-packed action film. An overworked attorney and an undercover cop work together to stop corruption in the N.Y.P.D. Although lacking greatly in logic or plot, the sensational stunts make this an otherwise entertaining action flick.
1988 (R) 96m/C Sam Elliott, Peter Weller, Patricia Charbonneau, Antonio Fargas, Blanche Baker, Richard Brooks, Jude Ciccolella, George Loros, Tom Waits, Shirley Stoler, Rockets Redglare, Kathryn Rossetter; **D:** James Glickenhaus; **W:** James Glickenhaus; **M:** Jonathan Elias. **VHS, Beta** $19.98 *MCA* 🎬🎬½

Shaker Run A stunt car driver and his mechanic transport a mysterious package. They don't know what to do—they're carrying a deadly virus that every terrorist wants! Car chases galore, and not much else. However, if you like chase scenes...
1985 91m/C Leif Garrett, Cliff Robertson, Lisa Harrow; **D:** Bruce Morrison. **VHS, Beta** $19.98 *SUE, NLC* 🎬½

Shakes the Clown Chronicles the rise and fall of Shakes, an alcoholic clown wandering through the all-clown town of Palukaville. Framed for the murder of his boss by his archrival, Binky, Shakes takes it on the lam in order to prove his innocence, aided by his waitress girlfriend Judy, who dreams of becoming a professional bowler. Meant as a satire of substance-abuse recovery programs and the supposed tragedies of a performer's life, the film is sometimes zany, but more often merely unpleasant and unamusing. Williams has an uncredited role as a mime.
1992 (R) 83m/C Bob(cat) Goldthwait, Julie Brown, Blake Clark, Adam Sandler, Tom Kenny, Sydney Lassick, Paul Dooley, Tim Kazurinsky, Florence Henderson, LaWanda Page; *Cameos:* Robin Williams; **D:** Bob(cat) Goldthwait; **W:** Bob(cat) Goldthwait. **VHS** *COL* 🎬

Shakespeare Wallah Tender, plausible drama of romance and postcolonial relations in India. A troupe of traveling Shakespeareans quixotically tours India trying to make enough money to return to England. Wonderfully acted and exquisitely and sensitively directed by Ivory.
1965 120m/B Laura Liddell, Geoffrey Kendal, Felicity Kendal, Shashi Kapoor, Madhur Jaffrey; **D:** James Ivory; **W:** Ruth Prawer Jhabvala, James Ivory. **VHS, Beta** $19.95 *SUE, ING, NLC* 🎬🎬🎬

The Shakiest Gun in the West Don Knotts isn't Bob Hope, but he's pretty funny in the same bumbling way. Remake of Hope's "Paleface" has Philadelphia dentist Knotts unwittingly taking on bad guys and sultry Rhoades.
1968 101m/C Don Knotts, Barbara Rhoades, Jackie Coogan, Donald (Don "Red") Barry, Ruth McDevitt; **D:** Alan Rafkin. **VHS** *MCA* 🎬🎬½

Shaking the Tree Group of four high school buddies are still in quest of self-fulfillment ten years after high school as they grapple with problems in the real world of adulthood, seeking distraction in adventure, romance, friendship, and sex.
1992 (PG-13) 97m/C Arye Gross, Gale Hansen, Doug Savant, Steven Wilde, Courteney Cox, Christina Haag, Michael Arabian, Nathan Davis; **D:** Duane Clark; **W:** Duane Clark; **M:** David E. Russo. **VHS** $19.95 *ACA* 🎬🎬½

Shakma A group of medical researchers involved with experiments on animal and human tendencies toward aggression take a night off to play a quiet game of "Dungeons

and Dragons." The horror begins when their main experimental subject comes along and turns things nasty!
1989 101m/C Roddy McDowall, Christopher Atkins, Amanda Wyss, Ari Meyers; **D:** Hugh Parks. **VHS** $29.95 *HHE* 🎬½

Shalako Connery/Bardot pairing promises something special, but fails to deliver. European aristocrats on a hunting trip in New Mexico, circa 1880, are menaced by Apaches. U.S. Army scout tries to save captured countess Bardot. Strange British attempt at a Euro-western. Poorly directed and pointless. Based on a Louis L'Amour story.
1968 113m/C Brigitte Bardot, Sean Connery, Stephen Boyd, Honor Blackman, Woody Strode, Alexander Knox; **D:** Edward Dmytryk. **VHS, Beta** $19.98 *FOX* 🎬½

Shall We Dance And shall we ever! Seventh Astaire-Rogers pairing has a famous ballet dancer and a musical-comedy star embark on a promotional romance and marriage, to boost their careers, only to find themselves truly falling in love. Score by the Gershwins includes memorable songs. Thin, lame plot—but that's okay. For fans of good singing and dancing, and especially of this immortal pair. ♫Slap That Bass; Beginner's Luck; Let's Call the Whole Thing Off; Walking the Dog; They All Laughed; They Can't Take That Away From Me; Shall We Dance.
1937 116m/B Fred Astaire, Ginger Rogers, Edward Everett Horton, Eric Blore; **D:** Mark Sandrich; **M:** George Gershwin, Ira Gershwin. **VHS, Beta** $14.98 *TTC, RKO, CCB* 🎬🎬🎬

Shallow Grave Four coeds en route to Florida witness a murder in rural Georgia and then are pursued relentlessly by the killer, a local sheriff. Decent premise and talented cast could have offered something better, given a meatier script.
1987 (R) 90m/C Tony March, Lisa Stahl, Tom Law, Carol Cadby; **D:** Richard Styles. **VHS, Beta** $14.95 *PSM, PAR* 🎬½

The Shaman Members of a family succumb to the hypnotic spell of the Shaman as he searches for the perfect one to inherit his powers.
1987 (R) 88m/C Michael Conforti, Elvind Harum, James Farkas, Lynn Weaver; **D:** Michael Yakub. **VHS, Beta** $79.95 *IMP* 🎬½

Shame Strangely unsuccessful low-budget Corman effort, starring pre-"Star Trek" Shatner as a freelance bigot who travels around Missouri stirring up opposition to desegregation. Moralistic and topical but still powerful. Adapted from the equally excellent novel by Charles Beaumont. Uses location filming superbly to render a sense of everydayness and authenticity. *AKA:* The Intruder; I Hate Your Guts; The Stranger.
1961 84m/B William Shatner, Frank Maxwell, Jeanne Cooper, Robert Emhardt, Leo Gordon; **D:** Roger Corman. **VHS, Beta** $19.95 *NOS, DVT, FCT* 🎬🎬🎬

The Shame A Bergman masterpiece focusing on the struggle for dignity in the midst of war. Married concert musicians Ullmann and von Sydow flee a bloody civil war for a small island off their country's coast. Inevitably, the carnage reaches them and their lives become a struggle to endure and retain a small measure of civilized behavior as chaos overtakes them. Deeply despairing and brilliantly acted. In Swedish with English subtitles.
1968 (R) 103m/C Max von Sydow, Liv Ullmann, Gunnar Bjornstrand, Sigge Furst, Birgitta Valberg, Hans Alfredson, Ingvar Kjellson; **D:** Ingmar Bergman; **W:** Ingmar Bergman. **VHS** $19.98 *MGM, BTV* 🎬🎬🎬½

Shame Strange Australian revenge drama about a female lawyer/biker who rides into a small town and finds herself avenging the rape of a 16-year-old girl. Is it a genuinely feminist movie about justice and a strong woman taking charge? Or is it exploitative trash using a politically correct theme and "message" as a peg for much - very much - gratuitous violence? Hard to tell. Cultish for sure; made on a B budget.
1987 (R) 95m/C Deborra-Lee Furness, Tony Barry, Simone Buchanan, Gillian Jones; **D:** Steve Jodrell. **VHS $89.99** *REP* 🎬🎬

Shame In a small logging town a group of violent high school thugs get away with rape because the women are too terrified to go to the cops. Then lawyer Diana Cadell (Donohoe) is stuck in town when her motorcycle breaks down. When she finds out what's been happening, she urges one victim (Balk) to speak out and suddenly they become the targets of both the vicious attackers and a town which would like to hush the entire mess up. Very strong performances by Donohoe and Balk. Made for cable U.S. version of the same-titled 1987 Australian movie.
1992 91m/C Amanda Donohoe, Fairuza Balk, Dean Stockwell, Dan Gauthier; **D:** Dan Lerner; **W:** Rebecca Soladay. **VHS $79.95** *PSM* 🎬🎬

Shame of the Jungle Animated spoof on Tarzan featuring the voices of John Belushi, Bill Murray, and Johnny Weissmuller, Jr.
1990 (R) 73m/C D: Boris Szulzinger, Picha; **V:** Johnny Weissmuller Jr., John Belushi, Bill Murray, Brian Doyle-Murray, Christopher Guest, Andrew Duncan. **VHS $79.95** *JEF* 🎬🎬

Shame, Shame on the Bixby Boys Somewhere in the Old West, outside a small town, lives a band of misfits who persist in rustling cattle. The Bixby Boys and their Pa have made a bad habit into a family tradition.
1982 90m/C Monte Markham, Sammy Jackson; **D:** Anthony Bowers. **VHS, Beta** *TLF* 🎬½

The Shaming Puritanical schoolteacher is raped by a janitor, then develops a voracious sexual appetite. Horrible script, offensive premise can't be saved by good cast. Based on a novel by William Inge. **AKA:** The Sin; Good Luck, Miss Wyckoff.
1971 (R) 90m/C Anne Heywood, Donald Pleasence, Robert Vaughn, Carolyn Jones; **D:** Marvin J. Chomsky. **VHS, Beta** *NO* 🎬½

Shampoo A satire of morals (and lack thereof) set in Southern California, concerning a successful hairdresser (Beatty) and the many women in his life. A notable scene with Julie Christie is set at a 1968 presidential election-night gathering. Fisher's screen debut, only one year before "Star Wars" made her famous. Has a healthy glow in places and a perky bounce, but too many split ends.
1975 (R) 112m/C Warren Beatty, Julie Christie, Goldie Hawn, Jack Warden, Lee Grant, Tony Bill, Carrie Fisher, William Castle, Howard Hesseman; **D:** Hal Ashby; **W:** Warren Beatty, Robert Towne; **M:** John Barry. Academy Awards '75: Best Supporting Actress (Grant); Nominations: Best Art Direction/Set Decoration, Best Original Screenplay, Best Supporting Actor (Warden). **VHS, Beta $14.95** *COL, VYG, CRC* 🎬🎬½

Shamus Private dick Reynolds investigates a smuggling ring, beds a sultry woman, gets in lotsa fights. Classic Burt vehicle meant as a send-up. Unoriginal but fun.
1973 (PG) 91m/C Burt Reynolds, Dyan Cannon, John P. Ryan; **D:** Buzz Kulik; **M:** Jerry Goldsmith. **VHS, Beta $9.95** *GKK* 🎬🎬

Shane A retired gunfighter, now a drifter, comes to the aid of a homestead family threatened by a land baron and his hired gun. Ladd is the mystery man who becomes the idol of the family's young son. Classic, flawless western. Pulitzer prize-winning western novelist A.B. Guthrie, Jr. adapted from the novel by Jack Schaefer. Long and stately; worth savoring.
1953 117m/C Alan Ladd, Jean Arthur, Van Heflin, Brandon de Wilde, Jack Palance, Ben Johnson, Elisha Cook Jr., Edgar Buchanan, Emile Meyer; **D:** George Stevens; **W:** Jack Sher; **M:** Victor Young. Academy Awards '53: Best Color Cinematography; Nominations: Best Director (Stevens), Best Picture, Best Screenplay, Best Supporting Actor (de Wilde, Palance); National Board of Review Awards '53: 10 Best Films of the Year, Best Director (Stevens). **VHS, Beta $14.95** *PAR, TLF* 🎬🎬🎬🎬

The Shanghai Cobra Below-average mystery has Chan hired by the government to investigate several supposed cobra bite murders. All motives lead to stealing a supply of radium.
1945 64m/B Sidney Toler, Benson Fong, Mantan Moreland, Walter Fenner, James B. Cardwell, Joan Barclay, James Flavin; **D:** Phil Karlson. **VHS $19.98** *MGM* 🎬½

Shanghai Express Dietrich is at her most alluring in this mystical and exotic story that made legends out of both star and director. Dietrich plays Shanghai Lily, a woman of objectionable reputation, who has a reunion of sorts with ex-lover Brooks aboard a slow-moving train through China. Remade as "Peking Express." Based on a story by Harry Hervey.
1932 80m/B Marlene Dietrich, Clive Brook, Anna May Wong, Warner Oland, Eugene Pallette, Lawrence Grant, Louise Closser Hale; **D:** Josef von Sternberg; **W:** Jules Furthman. **VHS $14.98** *MCA, FCT* 🎬🎬🎬½

The Shanghai Gesture A wildly baroque, subversive melodrama. An English financier tries to close a gambling den, only to be blackmailed by the female proprietor—who tells him not only is the man's daughter heavily indebted to her, but that she is the wife he abandoned long ago. Based on a notorious Broadway play. Von Sternberg had to make numerous changes to the script in order to get it past the Hays censors; the director's final Hollywood work, and worthy of his oeuvre, but oddly unsatisfying.
1942 97m/B Walter Huston, Gene Tierney, Victor Mature, Ona Munson, Albert Basserman, Eric Blore, Maria Ouspenskaya, Phyllis Brooks, Mike Mazurki; **D:** Josef von Sternberg. **VHS, Beta $29.95** *MFV* 🎬🎬½

Shanghai Surprise Tie salesman Penn and missionary Madonna (yeah, right) are better than you'd think, and the story (of opium smuggling in China in the '30s) is intrepid and wildly fun, but indifferently directed and unsure of itself. Executive producer George Harrison wrote the songs and has a cameo.
1986 (PG-13) 90m/C Sean Penn, Madonna, Paul Freeman, Richard Griffiths; **Cameos:** George Harrison; **D:** Jim Goddard; **M:** George Harrison, Michael Kamen. **VHS, Beta $79.98** *LIV, VES* 🎬½

Shanty Tramp Small-town tramp puts the moves on an evangelist, a motorcycle gang, and a young black man, who risks his life trying to save her from her loose morals. Another cheesy flick made for the drive-in crowd.
1967 72m/B Lee Holland, Bill Rogers, Lawrence Tobin; **D:** Joseph Prieto. **VHS $16.95** *SNC, TPV* 🎬

Shaolin Disciple Kung Fu action-adventure featuring real monks.
19?? 90m/C Ku Feng. **VHS $49.95** *OCE* 🎬

Shaolin Ex-Monk Renegade Shaolin Monk is pursued by a Kung Fu master and his disciple.
1982 94m/C John Liu, Ko Shou Liang, Huang Hsing Shaw. **VHS, Beta** *WVE* 🎬

Shaolin Executioner Several generations of Shaolin defend the Shaolin Temple against all high-kicking odds.
198? 104m/C Chen Kuan-Tai, Lo Lieh; **D:** Lu Chia-Liang. **Beta** *NO* 🎬

Shaolin Kids Shaolin warriors discover a conspiracy and kick it to death.
1977 91m/C VHS, Beta $29.95 *UNI* 🎬

Shaolin Kung Fu Mystagogue In this action-packed chop-fest, the mysterious "Floating in Blood" weapon enlivens the battle between the Ching Dynasty and Ming rebels.
1984 90m/C D: Chang Peng-I. **VHS, Beta** *NO* 🎬

Shaolin Temple Strikes Back The protective inhabitants of the Shaolin temple defend themselves against invading Manchu Barbarians.
1972 90m/C Chen Chien Chang, Sho Kosugi, Chang Shan, Lung Fei; **D:** Joseph Kuo. **VHS, Beta $29.95** *TWE* 🎬

Shaolin Thief A traitor gives the invading Japanese a priceless treasure and the loyal Chinese troops must fight to get it back.
19?? 90m/C VHS $29.95 *OCE* 🎬

Shaolin Traitor Exotic weapons and dazzling martial-arts action are featured in this exciting tale of intrigue and mystery.
1982 (R) 99m/C Carter Wong, Shangkuan Ling-Feng, Lung Chun-Eng, Chang Yi, Lung Fei. **VHS, Beta $59.95** *GEM* 🎬½

Shaolin Vengence Framed for murder and deceived into accepting guilt for the crime, a man does penance in a Shaolin temple. When he learns of the deception, he uses his newly learned Shaolin boxing skills to relentlessly pound the creeps who set him up.
1982 ?m/C Chen Sing. **VHS $24.50** *OCE* 🎬½

Shaolin Warrior A young man must battle an evil Tartar warlord who massacred his family.
19?? 90m/C Kam Kong, Chan Wai, Chen Sing. **VHS, Beta $29.95** *OCE* 🎬

Shark! American gun smuggler Reynolds, stranded in a tiny seaport in Africa, joins the crew of a marine biologist's boat. He soon discovers the boat's owner and his wife are trying to retrieve gold bullion that lies deep in shark-infested waters. Typical Reynoldsian action-infested dumbness. Like "Twilight Zone: The Movie", earned notoriety because of on-location tragedy: a stunt diver really was killed by a shark. Edited without the consent of Fuller, who disowned it. **AKA:** Man-Eater; Un Arma de Dos Filos.
1968 (PG) 92m/C Burt Reynolds, Barry Sullivan, Arthur Kennedy; **D:** Samuel Fuller; **W:** Samuel Fuller. **VHS, Beta $24.95** *REP, MRV* 🎬½

Shark Hunter Shark hunter gets ensnared in the mob's net off the Mexican coast as they race for a cache of sunken millions. The usual garden-variety B-grade adventure.
1984 (PG) 95m/C Franco Nero, Jorge Luke, Mike Forrest. **VHS, Beta $49.95** *PSM, MRV* 🎬

Shark River A man attempts to get his brother, a Civil War veteran accused of murder, through the Everglades and send him to safety in Cuba. Good photography of the great swamp; disappointing story.
1953 80m/C Steve Cochran, Carole Mathews, Warren Stevens; **D:** John Rawlins. **VHS, Beta** *NO* 🎬½

Shark's Paradise A madman threatens to set sharks loose on a popular Australian surf coast if his demands are not met. **1986 93m/C** VHS, Beta **$59.95** *WOV* 🎞️

Sharks' Treasure A band of escaped convicts commandeer a boat filled with gold. Old fashioned sunken-treasure tale unexceptional except as a virtual one man show by writer/actor/director/producer/fitness nut Wilde. **1975 (PG) 96m/C** Cornel Wilde, Yaphet Kotto, John Nellson, Cliff Osmond, David Canary, David Gilliam; **D:** Cornel Wilde. **VHS, Beta $59.95** *MGM* 🎞️½

Sharky's Machine A tough undercover cop (Reynolds) is hot on the trail of a crooked crime czar. Meanwhile he falls for a high-priced hooker. Well done but overdone action, with much violence. Based on the William Diehl novel. **1981 (R) 119m/C** Burt Reynolds, Rachel Ward, Vittorio Gassman, Brian Keith, Charles Durning, Bernie Casey, Richard Libertini, Henry Silva, John Fiedler, Earl Holliman; **D:** Burt Reynolds. **VHS, Beta $14.95** *WAR* 🎞️🎞️½

Sharma & Beyond A teenage would-be science fiction writer falls in love with the daughter of a famous sci-fi author. **1984 85m/C** Suzanne Burden, Robert Urquhart, Michael Maloney; **D:** Brian Gilbert. **VHS, Beta $59.95** *MGM* 🎞️

Sharp Fists in Kung Fu The cruel son of a gentle man returns to terrorize his hometown. Strictly for fans of the genre. **19?? 90m/C** VHS, Beta **$49.95** *OCE* Woof!

Shattered Key film in Germany's kammerspiel (chamber play) movement, which emphasized naturalism with a minimum number of characters. A railway worker's daughter is seduced by her father's supervisor. When the man abandons her, the girl's father takes revenge. **AKA:** Scherben. **1921 62m/B** Werner Krauss, Edith Posca, Paul Otto; **D:** Lupu Pick; **W:** Carl Mayer. **VHS $39.95** *FCT* 🎞️🎞️🎞️

Shattered Finch plays Harry, a man blamed for a failed marriage, held hostage in his home by his own paranoia, and driven to bouts of drinking. Slowly his tenuous grip on sanity slips and at any moment his fragile and crumbling life may be shattered. Tired, over-wrought domestic drama. **AKA:** Something to Hide. **1972 (R) 100m/C** Peter Finch, Shelley Winters, Colin Blakely; **D:** Alastair Reid. **VHS, Beta $24.95** *MED* 🎞️½

Shattered An architect recovering from a serious automobile accident tries to regain the memory that he has lost. As he begins to put together the pieces of his life, some parts of the puzzle don't quite fit. For example, he recalls his now loving wife's affair as well as his own. He remembers that he hired a private detective to follow his wife and shockingly, he remembers that he once believed his wife had planned to kill him. Are these memories the real thing, or are they all part of some mad, recuperative nightmare? Who knows. **1991 (R) 98m/C** Tom Berenger, Bob Hoskins, Greta Scacchi, Joanne Whalley-Kilmer, Corbin Bernsen, Theodore Bikel; **D:** Wolfgang Petersen; **W:** Wolfgang Petersen. **VHS, Beta, 8mm $19.98** *MGM* 🎞️🎞️

Shattered Silence A woman is tormented by phone calls that seem to be coming from her dead son as her life is torn apart by divorce. Leaves unanswered the question: Will there be any suspense? Made for TV. Worthless and dumb. **AKA:** When Michael Calls.

1971 73m/C Elizabeth Ashley, Ben Gazzara, Michael Douglas, Karen Pearson; **D:** Philip Leacock. **VHS $9.99** *CCB* 🎞️½

Shattered Spirits Quiet family man cracks and goes on a rampage through his normally peaceful suburban neighborhood. Been done before and better. **1991 (PG-13) 93m/C** Martin Sheen, Melinda Dillon, Matthew Laborteaux, Roxana Zal, Lukas Haas. **VHS $89.98** *VMK* 🎞️½

Shattered Vows A young nun struggles with her love for a priest and her desire for a child. Bertinelli is convincing as the confused teen in otherwise ordinary TV drama. Adapted from the true story of Dr. Mary Gilligan Wong as told in her book, "Nun: A Memoir." **1984 95m/C** Valerie Bertinelli, David Morse, Caroline McWilliams, Patricia Neal, Millie Perkins, Leslie Ackerman, Lisa Jane Persky; **D:** Jack Bender. **VHS, Beta $14.95** *FRH* 🎞️🎞️

She H. Rider Haggard's famous story about the ageless Queen Ayesha, (Blythe), who renews her life force periodically by walking through a pillar of cold flame. Story and titles by Haggard. Blythe is a stirringly mean queen, and the story remains fresh and fun. Silent film with music score. **1921 69m/B** Betty Blythe, Carlyle Blackwell, Mary Odette. **VHS, Beta $19.95** *NOS, VYY, DVT* 🎞️🎞️½

S*H*E A flashy made for TV spy thriller. The female agent S*H*E (Securities Hazards Expert) must save the world's oil; good locations, nifty plot and looker Sharpe as the she-Bond add up to a reasonably fun time. Scripted by "Bond"-writer Maibaum. **1979 100m/C** Cornelia Sharpe, Robert Lansing, William Taylor, Isabella Rye, Anita Ekberg; *Cameos:* Omar Sharif; **D:** Robert Lewis; **W:** Richard Maibaum; **M:** Michael Kamen. **VHS, Beta $59.95** *PSM* 🎞️🎞️

She A beautiful female warrior rules over the men in a post-holocaust world. She is kidnapped by a wealthy merchant who uses her to fight evil mutants. Utter rubbish vaguely based on the Haggard novel. **1983 90m/C** Sandahl Bergman, Harrison Muller, Quin Kessler, David Goss; **D:** Avi Nesher. **VHS, Beta $29.98** *LIV* 🎞️

She and He Hani's look at the oppression of women, marital and spiritual discontent, and class divisions. Naoko is a bored housewife, living in a sterile high-rise apartment with her equally dissatisfied husband, and yearning for something to express her inner feelings. She accidentally meets an old classmate of her husband's who has become a poor ragpicker and tries to aid him. But all her efforts only lead to further tragedies. In Japanese with English subtitles. **1963 110m/C** Sachiko Hidari, Eiji Okada, Kikuji Yamashita; **D:** Susumu Hani. **VHS $39.95** *FCT* 🎞️🎞️½

The She-Beast Burned at the stake in 18th-century Transylvania, a witch returns in the body of a beautiful young English woman on her honeymoon (in Transylvania?!), and once again wreaks death and destruction. Caution, Barbara Steele fans: she appears for all of fifteen minutes. Sporadically funny. **AKA:** Il Lago di Satana; The Revenge of the Blood Beast. **1965 74m/C** Barbara Steele, Ian Ogilvy, Mel Welles, Lucretia Love; **D:** Michael Reeves. **VHS, Beta $59.95** *SNC, MPI* 🎞️½

She Came on the Bus Young thugs break into a well-kept suburban home and terrorize the housewife through rape and torture. Then they kidnap a bus and pose as the drivers until they can find more victims. Contains scenes of graphic violence which

would be considered offensive even by today's standards. **1969 58m/C** **D:** Harry Vincent. **VHS $23.00** *SMW, TPV* Woof!

She Came to the Valley A tough pioneer woman becomes embroiled in political intrigue during the Spanish-American War. Based on Cleo Dawson's book. **AKA:** Texas in Flames. **1977 (PG) 90m/C** Ronee Blakley, Dean Stockwell, Scott Glenn, Freddy Fender. **VHS, Beta $69.95** *MED, QVD* 🎞️

She Couldn't Say No A wealthy oil heiress (Simmons) with good intentions plans to give her money away to those friends who had helped her when she was struggling. Things don't go quite as planned; her philanthropy leads to unexpected mayhem in her Arkansas hometown. Passable, but not memorable comedy. Mitchum as a small-town doctor? **AKA:** Beautiful But Dangerous. **1952 88m/B** Robert Mitchum, Jean Simmons, Arthur Hunnicutt, Edgar Buchanan, Wallace Ford; **D:** Lloyd Bacon. **VHS, Beta** *CCB* 🎞️🎞️

She Demons Pleasure craft loaded with babes crashes into a remote island controlled by a mad ex-Nazi scientist who transforms pretty girls into rubber-faced Frankensteins. Incomprehensible, to say the least. **1958 68m/B** Irish McCalla, Tod Griffin, Victor Sen Yung; **D:** Richard Cunha. **VHS, Beta $9.95** *RHI, SNC, MWP* Woof!

She-Devil A comic book version of the acidic Fay Weldon novel "The Life and Loves of a She-Devil"; a fat, dowdy suburban wife (Arnold) becomes a vengeful beast when a smarmy romance novelist steals her husband. Uneven comedic reworking of a distinctly unforgiving feminist fiction. Arnold is given too much to handle (her role requires an actual range of emotions); Streep's role is too slight, though she does great things with it. **1989 (PG-13) 100m/C** Meryl Streep, Roseanne (Barr) Arnold, Ed Begley Jr., Linda Hunt, Elizabeth Peters, Bryan Larkin, A. Martinez, Sylvia Miles; **D:** Susan Seidelman; **W:** Mark Burns, Barry Strugatz; **M:** Howard Shore. **VHS, Beta $9.98** *ORI* 🎞️🎞️½

She Devils in Chains A group of traveling female athletes are kidnapped by a groups of sadists who torture and beat them. In the end, however, the girls get their revenge, and it's bloody. **19?? (R) 82m/C** Colleen Camp, Rosanne Katon, Sylvia Anderson, Ken Washington, Leo Martinez; **D:** Cirio H. Santiago. **VHS $9.95** *SIM* 🎞️🎞️

She-Devils on Wheels Havoc erupts as an outlaw female motorcycle gang, known as "Maneaters on Motorbikes," terrorizes a town—especially the men. Really, really bad biker flick finely honed by Lewis. **1968 83m/C** Betty Connell, Christie Wagner, Pat Poston, Nancy Lee Noble, Ruby Tuesday; **D:** Herschell Gordon Lewis. **VHS, Beta $19.95** *SVI* Woof!

She Done Him Wrong West stars as Lil, an 1890s saloon singer in the screen version of her Broadway hit "Diamond Lily," and imparts on the negligible plot her usual share of double entendres and racy comments. Grant is likeable as the hapless sap she beds. ♫Silver Threads Among the Gold; Masie, My Pretty Daisy; Easy Rider; I Like a Guy What Takes His Time; Frankie and Johnny. **1933 65m/B** Mae West, Cary Grant, Owen Moore, Noah Beery Sr., Gilbert Roland, Louise Beavers; **D:** Lowell Sherman. Academy Awards '33 Nominations: Best Picture; National Board of Review Awards '33: 10 Best Films of the Year. **VHS, Beta $14.98** *MCA, MLB, BTV* 🎞️🎞️🎞️

She-Freak Remake of Tod Brownings' "Freaks." A cynical waitress burns everyone in a circus and gets mauled by the resident freaks. Pales beside its unacknowledged, classic original. *AKA:* Alley of Nightmares.
1967 87m/C Claire Brennan, Lynn Courtney, Bill McKinney, Lee Raymond, Madame Lee; *D:* Byron Mabe. **VHS, Beta** *NO ✗*

She Gods of Shark Reef Typical no-budget Corman exploitation tale of two brothers shipwrecked on an island inhabited by beautiful pearl-diving women. Filmed in Hawaii. *AKA:* Shark Reef.
1956 63m/C Bill Cord, Don Durant, Lisa Montell, Carol Lindsay, Jeanne Gerson; *D:* Roger Corman. **VHS $16.95** *SNC, MRV, HEG ✗*

She Goes to War King's first part-sound effort that takes place in the milieu of WWI. Boardman plays a spoiled rich girl who grows up fast when confronted with the horrors of the frontline while working in a canteen.
1929 50m/B Eleanor Boardman, Alma Rubens, Al "Fuzzy" St. John; *D:* Henry King. **VHS, Beta, 8mm $19.95** *NOS, GVV, DVT ✗*

She Likes You, Charlie Brown Romantic travails for Charlie Brown and the gang. Animated.
1986 41m/C VHS, Beta $14.95 *BAR, WTA ✗✗*

She Shall Have Music A magnate hires a dance band to broadcast from a cruise ship. Features music by Jack Hylton and his band, one of Britain's most popular orchestras of the 1930s.
1936 76m/B Jack Hylton, June Clyde, Claude Dampier, Bryan Lawrence, Gwen Farrar. **VHS, Beta** *MWP ✗✗ 1/2*

She Waits When a newlywed couple moves into an old house, the bride becomes possessed by the spirit of her husband's first wife. Unoriginal and mediocre horror. Made for television.
1971 74m/C Dorothy McGuire, Patty Duke, David McCallum; *D:* Delbert Mann. **VHS, Beta $59.95** *PSM ✗✗*

She Wore a Yellow Ribbon An undermanned cavalry outpost makes a desperate attempt to repel invading Indians. Wayne shines as an officer who shuns retirement in order to help his comrades. Excellent color photography by Winston C. Hoch. Still fun and compelling. The second chapter in director Ford's noted cavalry trilogy, preceded by "Fort Apache" and followed by "Rio Grande."
1949 93m/C John Wayne, Joanne Dru, John Agar, Ben Johnson, Harry Carey Jr., Victor McLaglen, Mildred Natwick, George O'Brien; *D:* John Ford. **VHS, Beta $14.95** *TTC, RKO, TLF ✗✗✗ 1/2*

Sheba, Baby A female dick (Grier) heads to Louisville where someone is trying to threaten her rich father and his loan company. Oddly non-violent for action-flick vet Grier; poorly written and directed.
1975 (PG) 90m/C Pam Grier, Rudy Challenger, Austin Stoker, D'Urville Martin, Charles Kissinger; *D:* William Girdler. **VHS, Beta $59.98** *ORI, FCT ✗✗*

Sheena Television sportscaster aids a jungle queen in defending her kingdom from being overthrown by an evil prince. Horrid bubble-gum "action" fantasy.
1984 (PG) 117m/C Tanya Roberts, Ted Wass, Donovan Scott, Elizabeth Toro; *D:* John Guillermin; *W:* David Newman. **VHS, Beta $12.95** *GKK Woof!*

The Sheep Has Five Legs Quintuplet brothers return from around the world for a reunion in their small French village. Fernandel plays the father and all five sons;

otherwise, comedy is only average-to-good. In French with English subtitles.
1954 96m/B Fernandel, Edouard Delmont, Louis de Funes, Paulette Dubost; *D:* Henri Verneuil. **VHS, Beta, 8mm $24.95** *NOS, DVT, VYY ✗✗ 1/2*

Sheer Madness Focuses on the intense friendship between a college professor and a troubled artist, both women. Engrossing and subtle exposition of a relationship. Ambiguous ending underscores film's general excellence. Subtitled.
1984 105m/C Hanna Schygulla, Angela Winkler; *D:* Margarethe von Trotta; *W:* Margarethe von Trotta. **VHS, Beta** *MGM ✗✗✗*

The Sheik High camp Valentino has English woman fall hopelessly under the romantic spell of Arab sheik who flares his nostrils. Followed by "Son of the Sheik."
1921 80m/B Agnes Ayres, Rudolph Valentino, Adolphe Menjou, Walter Long, Lucien Littlefield, George Waggner, Patsy Ruth Miller; *D:* George Melford. **VHS, Beta $19.95** *PAR, GPV ✗✗✗*

She'll Be Wearing Pink Pajamas Eight women volunteer for a rugged survival course to test their mettle. The intense shared experience gives them all food for thought. Well acted from a pretty thin story.
1984 90m/C Julie Walters, Anthony Higgins; *D:* John Goldschmidt; *M:* John Du Prez. **VHS, Beta $59.95** *LHV ✗✗*

The Shell Seekers The widowed Penelope Keeling (Lansbury) is recovering from a heart attack and her three grown children want her to take things easy. But the scare has convinced Penelope to revisit her past and the happiness she once knew. So she returns to her childhood home in Cornwall to see what she can discover. Fine cast in a heart-tugger (with some lovely scenery from Cornwall, England and the island of Ibiza). Adapted from the novel by Rosamunde Pilcher. A Hallmark Hall of Fame presentation.
1989 (PG) 94m/C Angela Lansbury, Sam Wanamaker, Anna Carteret, Michael Gough, Christopher Bowen, Patricia Hodge, Denis Quilley, Sophie Ward, Irene Worth; *D:* Waris Hussein; *W:* John Pielmeier. **VHS $89.98** *REP ✗✗ 1/2*

Shell Shock Four GI's fight off the Germans and the longings for home during WWII.
198? 90m/C *D:* John Hayes. **VHS, Beta** *NO ✗ 1/2*

Shelley Duvall's Bedtime Stories A series of stories based on popular children's books, narrated by celebrities. Each tape is available individually and contains at least two stories. Nominated for cable's ACE award and an Emmy award. Originally produced for cable television.
1992 25m/C VHS $12.98 *MCA ✗ 1/2*

The Sheltering Sky American couple Winger and Malkovich flee the plasticity of their native land for a trip to the Sahara desert where they hope to renew their spirits and rekindle love. Accompanied by socialite acquaintance Scott with whom Winger soon has an affair, their personalities and belief systems deteriorate as they move through the grave poverty of North Africa in breathtaking heat. Based on the existential novel by American expatriate Paul Bowles who narrates and appears briefly in a bar scene. Overlong but visually stunning, with cinematography by Vittorio Storaro.
1990 (R) 139m/C Debra Winger, John Malkovich, Campbell Scott, Jill Bennett, Timothy Spall, Eric Vu-An, Sotigui Koyate, Amina Annabi, Paul Bowles; *D:* Bernardo Bertolucci; *W:* Mark Peploe, Bernardo Bertolucci; *M:* Ryuichi Sakamoto, Richard Horowitz. **VHS, Beta $19.98** *WAR, FCT, CCB ✗✗✗*

Shenandoah A Virginia farmer (Stewart, in a top-notch performance) who has raised six sons and a daughter, tries to remain neutral during the Civil War. War takes its toll as the daughter marries a Confederate soldier and his sons become involved in the fighting. Screen debut for Ross.
1965 105m/C James Stewart, Doug McClure, Glenn Corbett, Patrick Wayne, Rosemary Forsyth, Katharine Ross, George Kennedy; *D:* Andrew V. McLaglen. **VHS, Beta $19.95** *MCA ✗✗✗*

Shep Comes Home Shep the wonder canine accompanies an orphan through the Midwest where he nabs a band of bankrobbers. Sequel to "My Dog Shep."
1949 62m/B Robert Lowery, Sheldon Leonard, Flame. **VHS, Beta** *NO ✗*

Sheriff of Tombstone Trouble begins when a "judge" takes a sharpshooter in a poker game.
1941 60m/B Roy Rogers. **VHS, Beta $19.95** *NOS, DVT, RXM ✗ 1/2*

Sherlock Holmes and the Deadly Necklace Once again, Holmes and Watson are up against their old nemesis Moriarty. This time, Moriarty wants to get his hands on a necklace stolen from Cleopatra's tomb. Not only does Scotland Yard not consider him a suspect, they seek his advice. Enter Holmes and Watson, and the game's afoot. The offbeat casting and direction help make this one of the odder versions of Conan Doyle's work. *AKA:* Sherlock Holmes Und Das Halsband des Todes; Valley of Fear.
1962 84m/B Christopher Lee, Senta Berger, Hans Sohnker, Hans Nielsen, Ivan Desny, Leon Askin, Thorley Walters; *D:* Terence Fisher. **VHS $19.95** *NOS, SNC ✗✗ 1/2*

Sherlock Holmes and the Incident at Victoria Falls A substandard Holmes excursion brings the Baker Street sleuth out of retirement to transport the world's largest diamond from Africa to London. The resulting mystery involves Teddy Roosevelt, the inventor of radio, and poor plotting. *AKA:* Incident at Victoria Falls.
1991 120m/C Christopher Lee, Patrick Macnee, Jenny Seagrove; *D:* Bill Corcoran. **VHS $89.98** *VES ✗ 1/2*

Sherlock Holmes and the Secret Weapon Based on "The Dancing Men" by Sir Arthur Conan Doyle. Holmes battles the evil Moriarty in an effort to save the British war effort. Good Holmes mystery with gripping wartime setting. Hoey is fun as bumbling Inspector Lestrade. Available colorized. *AKA:* Secret Weapon.
1942 68m/B Basil Rathbone, Nigel Bruce, Karen Verne, William Post Jr., Dennis Hoey, Holmes Herbert, Mary Gordon, Henry Victor, Philip Van Zandt, George Eldridge, Leslie Denison, James Craven, Paul Fix, Hugh Herbert, Lionel Atwill; *D:* Roy William Neill. **VHS $14.98** *REP, MED, AOV ✗✗✗*

Sherlock Holmes Faces Death Dead bodies are accumulating in a mansion where the detecting duo are staying. Underground tunnels, life-size dress boards, and unanswered mysteries... Top-notch Holmes. Peter Lawford appears briefly as a sailor. Also available with "Hound of the Baskervilles" on Laser Disc.
1943 68m/B Basil Rathbone, Nigel Bruce, Hillary Brooke, Milburn Stone, Halliwell Hobbes, Arthur Margetson, Gavin Muir; *D:* Roy William Neill. **VHS, Beta $14.98** *FOX ✗✗✗*

Sherlock Holmes in Washington
A top-secret agent is murdered; seems it's those blasted Nazis again! Holmes and Watson rush off to Washington, D.C. to solve the crime and to save some vitally important microfilm. Heavily flag-waving Rathbone-Bruce episode. Dr. Watson is dumbfounded by bubble gum.
1943 71m/B Basil Rathbone, Nigel Bruce, Henry Daniell, George Zucco, Marjorie Lord, John Archer; **D:** Roy William Neill. **VHS, Beta $14.98** FOX *ZZ*½

Sherlock Holmes: The Master Blackmailer
Brett returns as the supersleuth, along with sidekick Dr. Watson, in a tale which has the detective working against the evil scheming of London's most cunning and ruthless blackmailer. When Holmes disguises himself to enter the blackmailer's lair he even finds himself attracting the romantic attentions of a young lady. Based on the story "The Adventure of Charles Augustus Milverton" by Arthur Conan Doyle. Made for television.
1992 120m/C Jeremy Brett, Edward Hardwicke. **VHS $24.98** MPI, SIG *ZZZ*½

Sherlock Holmes: The Sign of Four
Sherlock Holmes must find the man who murdered Bartholomew Sholto with a poison dart in the neck.
1984 48m/C *V:* Peter O'Toole. **VHS, Beta $14.95** WTA, PMS, PAR *ZZ*

Sherlock Holmes: The Silver Blaze
Sherlock Holmes mystery about the theft of a racehorse known as "The Silver Blaze." Remade in 1977.
1941 70m/B Arthur Wontner, Ian Fleming, Lyn Harding. **VHS, Beta $19.95** NOS, BAR, MWP *Z*½

Sherlock Holmes: The Silver Blaze
Sherlock Holmes, with Dr. Watson, in one of the legendary detective's most famous adventures involving the theft of a racehorse and the mysterious murder of his trainer. Remake of a 1941 film.
1977 31m/C Christopher Plummer, Thorley Walters; **D:** John Davies. **VHS, Beta $24.98** LCA *ZZ*

Sherlock Holmes: The Voice of Terror
Holmes and Watson try to decode German radio messages during WWII. First Rathbone-as-Holmes effort for Universal, and first in which we are asked to believe the Victorian sleuth and his hairdo could have lived in this century. Patriotic and all that—and lots of fun.
1942 65m/B Basil Rathbone, Nigel Bruce, Hillary Brooke, Reginald Denny, Evelyn Ankers, Montagu Love; **D:** John Rawlins. **VHS, Beta $14.98** FOX *ZZ*½

Sherlock Hound: Tales of Mystery
Sherlock, Watson and Moriarty are all dogs in this animated children's adaptation of the popular Arthur Conan Doyle stories. Well worth a howl.
1990 115m/C VHS, Beta JFK *ZZ*½

Sherlock's Rivals & Where's My Wife
Double feature includes a detective movie in which two used car dealers become amateur sleuths and a comedy in which a man has a hard time enjoying his weekend at a seashore resort.
1927 53m/B Milburn Morante, Monty Banks. **VHS, Beta $19.98** VYY *Z*½

Sherman's March: An Improbable Search for Love
McElwee's "epic" which was originally planned as a historical documentary about General Sherman's catastrophic march through the South, ends up being about the filmmaker himself, and his disastrous quest for love. When his girlfriend dumps him, he puts Sherman's story aside and films his own battle for romance, which includes help from his meddling family. The melodramatic women he meets and the neurotic energy of McElwee make this a very funny, uncensored film.
1986 155m/C *D:* Ross McElwee; *W:* Ross McElwee. **VHS $59.95** ICA, FRV, ING *ZZ*½

She's a Good Skate, Charlie Brown
Snoopy becomes Peppermint Patty's ice-skating coach, and he helps her train for the local competition.
1980 30m/C *D:* Phil Roman. **VHS, Beta $14.95** VTR, HSE, WTA *Z*½

She's Back
Murderee Fisher pesters hubby Joy from beyond the grave to avenge her death at the hands of a motorcycle gang. Uneven, but occasionally funny.
1988 (R) 89m/C Carrie Fisher, Robert Joy; **D:** Tim Kincaid. **VHS, Beta $79.98** VES, LIV *Z*½

She's Dressed to Kill
Beautiful models are turning up dead during a famous designer's comeback attempt at a mountain retreat. Who could be behind these grisly deeds? Suspenseful in a made for TV kind of way, but not memorable. *AKA:* Someone's Killing the World's Greatest Models.
1979 100m/C Eleanor Parker, Jessica Walter, John Rubinstein, Connie Sellecca; **D:** Gus Trikonis. **VHS $29.95** LIV *ZZ*

She's Gotta Have It
Lee wrote, directed, edited, produced and starred in this romantic comedy about an independent-minded black girl in Brooklyn and the three men and one woman who compete for her attention. Full of rough edges, but vigorous, confident, and hip. Filmed entirely in black and white except for one memorable scene. Put Lee on the film-making map.
1986 (R) 84m/B Spike Lee, Tommy Redmond Hicks, Raye Dowell; **D:** Spike Lee. **VHS, Beta $19.95** FOX, FCT *ZZZ*

She's Having a Baby
Newlyweds Bacon and McGovern tread the marital waters with some difficulty, when news of an impending baby further complicates their lives. Told from Bacon's viewpoint as the tortured young writer/husband, who wonders if the yuppie life they lead is trapping him. Hughes' first venture into the adult world isn't as satisfying as his teen angst flicks, although the charming leads help. Major drawbacks are the arguably sexist premise and dull resolution. Great soundtrack; observant viewers will notice the beemer's license plate is the title's acronym: "SHAB."
1988 (PG-13) 106m/C Kevin Bacon, Elizabeth McGovern, William Windom, Paul Gleason, Alec Baldwin, Cathryn Damon, Holland Taylor, James Ray, Isabel Lorca, Dennis Dugan, Edie McClurg, John Ashton; **D:** John Hughes; **W:** John Hughes; **M:** Stewart Copeland. **VHS, Beta, 8mm $19.95** PAR *ZZ*½

She's in the Army Now
Farce about military life. Two bubble-headed females undergo basic training. Made for TV "Private Benjamin" ripoff was meant as a series pilot.
1981 97m/C Jamie Lee Curtis, Kathleen Quinlan, Melanie Griffith, Susan Blanchard, Julie Carmen, Janet MacLachlan; **D:** Hy Averback. **VHS, Beta $9.98** SUE, NLC *Z*

She's Out of Control
Dad Danza goes nuts when teen daughter Dolenz (real-life daughter of Monkee Mickey Dolenz) takes the advice of Dad's girlfriend on how to attract boys. Formulaic plot could almost be an episode of "Who's the Boss?" Danza is appealing, but not enough to keep this one afloat.
1989 95m/C Tony Danza, Catherine Hicks, Wallace Shawn, Dick O'Neill; **D:** Stan Dragoti. **VHS, Beta, 8mm $19.95** COL *Z*½

Shifting Sands
Compelling film tells the tale of a young girl looking to be a successful artist. Her landlord makes constant overtures towards her. She refuses, so he has her thrown in jail for prostitution as an act of revenge. She fears her past may prevent her from obtaining true love.
1918 52m/B Gloria Swanson, Joe King, Lillian Langdon. **VHS, Beta, 8mm $14.95** GPV, VYY, GVV *Z*½

Shin Heike Monogatari
Mizoguchi's second to last film, in which a deposed Japanese emperor in 1137 endeavors to win back the throne from the current despot, who cannot handle the feudal lawlessness. Acclaimed; his second film in color. In Japanese with English subtitles. Also called "New Tales of the Taira Clan."
1955 106m/C Raizo Ichikawa, Ichijiro Oya, Michiyo Kogure, Eijiro Yanagi, Tatsuya Ishiguro, Yoshiko Kuga; **D:** Kenji Mizoguchi. **VHS, Beta $29.95** FCT *ZZZZ*

Shinbone Alley
Animated musical about Archy, a free-verse poet reincarnated as a cockroach, and Mehitabel, the alley cat with a zest for life. Based on the short stories by Don Marquis.
1970 (G) 83m/C *D:* John D. Wilson; *V:* Carol Channing, Eddie Bracken, John Carradine, Alan Reed. **VHS, Beta $14.95** SIM, GEM, KAR *ZZZ*

Shine on, Harvest Moon
Rogers brings a band of outlaws to justice and clears an old man suspected of being their accomplice. Title bears no relation to storyline.
1938 60m/B Roy Rogers, Lynn (Mary Hart) Roberts, Stanley Andrews; **D:** Joseph Kane. **VHS, Beta $19.95** NOS, VYY, VDM *ZZ*

The Shining
Very loose adaptation of the Stephen King horror novel about a writer and his family, snowbound in a huge hotel, who experience various hauntings caused by either the hotel itself or the writer's dementia. Technically stunning, and pretty dang scary, but too long, pretentious and implausible. Nicholson is excellent as the failed writer gone off the deep end.
1980 (R) 143m/C Jack Nicholson, Shelley Duvall, Scatman Crothers, Danny Lloyd, Joe Turkel, Barry Nelson; **D:** Stanley Kubrick. **VHS, Beta $19.98** WAR *ZZZ*

The Shining Hour
A compelling melodrama in which Crawford portrays a New York night club dancer who is pursued by the rather conservative Douglas. His brother tries to persuade him from marrying Crawford, but then he soon finds himself attracted to her. A devastating fire wipes out all problems of family dissension in this intelligent soap opera.
1938 76m/B Joan Crawford, Margaret Sullavan, Melvyn Douglas, Robert Young, Fay Bainter, Allyn Joslyn; **D:** Frank Borzage; **W:** Ogden Nash, Jane Murfin. **VHS $19.98** MGM *ZZ*½

A Shining Season
Tearjerker about a potential-packed long-distance runner, John Baker, stricken with cancer. He spends his last year training a girls' track team to a championship. Earnest, well-performed and involving. Based on a true story. Made for TV.
1979 100m/C Timothy Bottoms, Rip Torn, Allyn Ann McLerie, Ed Begley Jr., Benjamin Bottoms, Mason Adams, Constance Forslund, Ellen Geer; **D:** Stuart Margolin. **VHS, Beta $59.95** BTV *ZZZ*

Shining Star A recording company is run by the mob. Potentially interesting film is hampered by quality of sound and photography and general lack of purpose or direction. *AKA:* That's the Way of the World.
1975 (PG) 100m/C Harvey Keitel, Ed Nelson, Cynthia Bostick, Bert Parks; *D:* Sig Shore; *M:* Earth Wind & Fire. **VHS $39.95** *LIV* ✗½

Shining Through Baby-voiced Griffith as a spy sent behind enemy lines without training? Douglas as a spy sent behind enemy lines without speaking German? Old-fashioned blend of romance, espionage, and derring-do where noble hero saves spunky heroine from nasty Nazis in WWII Germany works despite thin plot. Series of flash-forwards to an aged Griffith is annoying and tends to stop action cold, but everyone tries hard and period flavor is authentic. Adapted from best-selling Susan Isaacs novel, but bears little resemblance to book.
1992 (R) 133m/C Michael Douglas, Melanie Griffith, Liam Neeson, Joely Richardson, John Gielgud, Francis Guinan, Patrick Winczewski, Sylvia Syms; *D:* David Seltzer; *W:* David Seltzer; *M:* Michael Kamen. **VHS $19.98** *FXV* ✗✗½

Shinobi Ninja Last-surviving member of Koga ninja clan returns to Japan from U.S. to save his homeland from enemy ninja clan. Mediocre pseudo ninja antics. Badly dubbed.
1984 103m/C Tadashi Yamashita, Eric Lee, Karen Lee Sheperd. **VHS, Beta $24.95** *AHV* ✗

Shiokari Pass A man has a divine revelation at the pass. In Japanese with English subtitles.
1977 60m/C *D:* Novuru Nakamuru. **VHS $29.95** *REP, VBL* ✗✗

Ship Ahoy Songs, comedy, a spy spoof, and some patriotism thrown in for good measure. Powell plays a dancer who works with Tommy Dorsey and his orchestra. They're on their way to Puerto Rico, via ocean liner, along with her pulp fiction writer boyfriend (Skelton). Emery, posing as an FBI man, convinces Powell to smuggle a package for him but he's really a spy and the whole thing's a con which turns out to be based on one of Skelton's potboiler plots. An uncredited Frank Sinatra is the singer with the Dorsey band, along with drummer Buddy Rich and trumpeter Ziggy Elman who provide some great musical solos. ♫Last Call For Love; Poor You; On Moonlight Bay; Tampico; I'll Take Tallulah; Cape Dance; Ship Ahoy.
1942 95m/B Eleanor Powell, Red Skelton, Bert Lahr, Virginia O'Brien, John Emery, William Post Jr.; *D:* Edward Buzzell; *W:* Harry Kurnitz, Harry Clork, Irving Brecher. **VHS $19.98** *MGM* ✗✗½

Ship of Fools A group of passengers sailing to Germany in the '30s find mutual needs and concerns, struggle with early evidence of Nazi racism, and discover love on their voyage. Twisted story and fine acting maintain interest. Appropriate tunes written by Ernest Gold. Based on the Katherine Ann Porter novel. Leigh's last film role; she died two years later. Kramer grapples with civil rights issues in much of his work.
1965 149m/B Vivien Leigh, Simone Signoret, Jose Ferrer, Lee Marvin, Oskar Werner, Michael Dunn, Elizabeth Ashley, George Segal, Jose Greco, Charles Korvin, Heinz Ruehmann; *D:* Stanley Kramer; *W:* Abby Mann; *M:* Ernest Gold. Academy Awards '65: Best Art Direction/Set Decoration (B & W), Best Black and White Cinematography; Nominations: Best Actor (Werner), Best Actress (Signoret), Best Adapted Screenplay, Best Costume Design (B & W), Best Picture, Best Supporting Actor (Dunn); National Board of Review Awards '65: 10 Best Films of the Year, Best Actor (Marvin). **VHS, Beta $19.95** *COL, SWC* ✗✗✗

Ships in the Night Logan is the plucky heroine who is searching for her missing brother who has been captured by pirates. She is aided in her search by handsome hero Mower.
1928 86m/B Frank Moran, Jacqueline Logan, Jack Mower, Andy Clyde. **VHS, Beta** *GVV, FCT, GPV* ✗✗

Shipwreck Island Eight boys are ship-wrecked on a deserted island, then make their way to another island where they must survive against wild animals and the elements for two years.
1961 93m/C VHS $19.95 *HTV, FCT* ✗✗

Shipwrecked Kiddie swashbuckler based on the 1873 popular novel "Haakon Haakonsen." A cabin boy is marooned on an island where he defends the hidden pirate treasure he finds by boobytrapping the island. *AKA:* Haakon Haakonsen.
1990 (PG) 93m/C Gabriel Byrne, Stian Smestad, Louisa Haigh, Trond Munch, Bjorn Sundquist, Eva Von Hanno, Kjell Stormoen; *D:* Nils Gaup; *W:* Nick Thiel, Nils Gaup; *M:* Patrick Doyle. **VHS $19.99** *BVV* ✗✗½

Shirley Temple Festival A collection of four Shirley Temple short subjects from the 30s: "Dora's Dunkin Doughnuts," "Pardon My Pups," "War Babies" and "Kid N' Africa."
1933 55m/B Shirley Temple, Andy Clyde. **VHS, Beta $19.95** *MRV* ✗✗½

Shirley Valentine A lively middle-aged English housewife gets a new lease on life when she travels to Greece without her husband. Collins reprises her London and Broadway stage triumph. The character frequently addresses the audience directly to explain her thoughts and feelings; her energy and spunk carry the day. Good script by Russell from his play. From the people who brought us "Educating Rita."
1989 108m/C Pauline Collins, Tom Conti, Alison Steadman, Julia McKenzie, Joanna Lumley, Bernard Hill, Sylvia Syms; *D:* Lewis Gilbert; *W:* George Hadjinassios, Willy Russell; *M:* Willy Russell. Academy Awards '89 Nominations: Best Actress (Collins), Best Song ("The Girl Who Used to Be Me"); British Academy Awards '89: Best Actress (Collins). **VHS, 8mm $14.95** *PAR, TVC, HMV* ✗✗✗

The Shock Crippled low-life Chaney becomes restored spiritually by a small-town girl and rebels against his Chinese boss. This causes an unfortunate string of melodramatic tragedies, including the San Francisco earthquake of 1906. Silent. Odd, desultory tale with bad special effects is worth seeing for Chaney's good acting.
1923 96m/B Lon Chaney Sr., Virginia Valli; *D:* Lambert Hillyer. **VHS, Beta $16.95** *SNC, NOS, HEG* ✗✗½

Shock! A psychiatrist is called on to treat a woman on the edge of a nervous breakdown. He then discovers she saw him murder his wife, and tries to keep her from remembering it. Interesting premise handled in trite B style. Price's first starring role.
1946 70m/B Vincent Price, Lynn Bari, Frank Latimore, Anabel Shaw; *D:* Alfred Werker. **VHS, Beta $16.95** *SNC, NOS, BAR* ✗✗

Shock Corridor A reporter, dreaming of a Pulitzer Prize, fakes mental illness and gets admitted to an asylum, where he hopes to investigate a murder. He is subjected to disturbing experiences, including shock therapy, but does manage to solve the murder. However, he suffers a mental breakdown in the process and is admitted for real. Disturbing and lurid.

1963 101m/B Peter Breck, Constance Towers, Gene Evans, Hari Rhodes, James Best, Philip Ahn; *D:* Samuel Fuller; *W:* Samuel Fuller. **VHS $59.95** *HMV, VYG, CRC* ✗✗½

Shock 'Em Dead A devil worshipper trades his life to Lucifer for a chance at rock and roll fame and beautiful Miss Lords. Sexy thriller, with a good share of violence and tension. Ironically, ex porn great Lords is one of the few starlets who doesn't disrobe in the film.
1990 (R) 94m/C Traci Lords, Aldo Ray, Troy Donahue, Stephen Quadros; *D:* Mark Freed. **VHS $19.95** *ACA* ✗✗

Shock! Shock! Shock! Another low-budget slasher flick, with a homicidal lunatic wielding a butcher knife. Space alien jewel thieves add an element, for what it's worth. Makes one ponder the cosmic question: What's the diff between a bad slasher flick and a spoof of a bad slasher flick? Whichever this one is, it's really bad!
1987 60m/B Brad Issac, Cyndy McCrossen, Allen Rickman, Brian Fuorry; *D:* Todd Rutt, Arn McConnell. **VHS, Beta $29.95** *RHI, MWF* ✗

A Shock to the System Business exec. Caine is passed over for a long-deserved promotion in favor of a younger man. When he accidentally pushes a panhandler in front of a subway in a fit of rage, he realizes how easy murder is and thinks it may be the answer to all his problems. Tries to be a satire take on corporate greed, etc., but somehow loses steam. Excellent cast makes the difference; Caine adds class. Based on the novel by Simon Brett.
1990 (R) 88m/C Michael Caine, Elizabeth McGovern, Peter Riegert, Swoosie Kurtz, Will Patton, Jenny Wright, John McMartin, Barbara Baxley; *D:* Jan Egleson; *W:* Andrew Klavan; *M:* Gary Chang. **VHS, Beta $89.99** *HBO* ✗✗✗

Shock Treatment Seldom-seen mediocre semi-sequel to the cult classic, "The Rocky Horror Picture Show" (1975). Brad and Janet, now married and portrayed by different leads, find themselves trapped on a TV gameshow full of weirdos. Same writers, same director, and several original cast members do make an appearance. *AKA:* Traitement de Choc.
1981 (PG) 94m/C Richard O'Brien, Jessica Harper, Cliff DeYoung, Patricia Quinn, Charles Gray, Ruby Wax; *D:* Jim Sharman. **VHS, Beta $14.98** *FOX* ✗½

Shock Waves Group of mutant-under-water-zombie-Nazi-soldiers terrorizes stranded tourists staying at a deserted motel on a small island. Cushing is the mad scientist intent on recreating the Nazi glory days with the seaweed-attired zombies. Odd B-grade, more or less standard horror flick somehow rises (slightly) above badness. Halpin's name was erroneously listed as Halprin—even on the original movie poster! *AKA:* Death Corps; Almost Human.
1977 (PG) 90m/C Peter Cushing, Brooke Adams, John Carradine, Luke Halpin; *D:* Ken Wiederhorn; *M:* Richard Einhorn. **VHS, Beta $9.99** *PSM* ✗✗

Shocker Another Craven gore-fest. A condemned serial killer is transformed into a menacing electrical force after being fried in the chair. Practically a remake of Craven's original "Nightmare on Elm Street." Great special effects, a few enjoyable weird and sick moments. What's Dr. Timothy Leary doing here?
1989 (R) 111m/C Michael Murphy, Peter Berg, Cami Cooper, Mitch Pileggi, Richard Price, Timothy Leary, Heather Langenkamp, Theodore Raimi, Richard Brooks, Sam Scarber; *D:* Wes

Craven; **W:** Wes Craven; **M:** William Goldstein. **VHS, Beta** $19.98 MCA 🎬🎬½

Shocking Asia For the eye-covering delight of Western audiences, Mr. Fox compiles gruesome Asian oddities.
1975 94m/C D: Emerson Fox. **VHS, Beta** HHE 🎬½

The Shoes of the Fisherman Morris West's interesting, speculative best seller about Russian Pope brought to the big screen at much expense, but with little care or thought. Siberian prison-camp vet Quinn, elected Pope, tries to arrest nuclear war. Director Anderson wasted the prodigious talents of Olivier, Gielgud, et al. Sloppy use of good cast and promising plot.
1968 (G) 160m/C Anthony Quinn, Leo McKern, Laurence Olivier, John Gielgud, Vittorio De Sica, Oskar Werner, David Janssen; **D:** Michael Anderson Sr. Academy Awards '68 Nominations: Best Art Direction/Set Decoration, Best Original Score; Golden Globe Awards '69: Best Score. **VHS, Beta** $29.99 MGM, FCT 🎬½

Shoeshine Two shoeshine boys struggling to survive in post-war Italy become involved in the black market and are eventually caught and imprisoned. Prison scenes detail the sense of abandonment and tragedy that destroys their friendship. A rich, sad achievement in neo-realistic drama. In Italian with English subtitles.
1947 90m/B Franco Interlenghi, Rinaldo Smordoni, Anniello Mele, Bruno Ortensi, Pacifico Astrologo; **D:** Vittorio De Sica; **W:** Cesare Zavattini, Sergio Amidei, Adolfe Franci, C.G. Viola. Academy Awards '47 Nominations: Best Original Screenplay; National Board of Review Awards '47: 10 Best Films of the Year. **VHS, Beta** FCT 🎬🎬🎬🎬

Shogun Television miniseries chronicling the saga of a shipwrecked English navigator who becomes the first Shogun, or Samurai warrior chief, from the Western world. Colorfully adapted from the James Clavell bestseller. Also released in a two-hour version, but this full-length version is infinitely better. **AKA:** James Clavell's Shogun.
1980 550m/C Richard Chamberlain, Toshiro Mifune, Yoko Shimada, John Rhys-Davies, Damien Thomas; **D:** Jerry London; **M:** Maurice Jarre. **VHS, Beta** $249.95 ING, PAR 🎬🎬🎬½

Shogun Assassin Story of a proud samurai named Lone Wolf who served his Shogun master well as the Official Decapitator, until the fateful day when the aging Shogun turned against him. Extremely violent, with record-breaking body counts. Edited from two other movies in a Japanese series called "Sword of Vengeance"; a tour de force of the cutting room. The samurai pushes his son's stroller through much of the film-sets it aside to hack and slash.
1980 (R) 89m/C Tomisaburo Wakayama; **D:** Kenji Misumi, Robert Houston. **VHS, Beta** MCA, OM 🎬🎬½

Shogun's Ninja In 16th-century Japan, an age-old rivalry between two ninja clans sparks a search for a dagger which will lead to one clan's hidden gold. Martial arts performed and directed by Sonny Chiba. In Japanese with usual poor English dubbing.
1983 115m/C Henry Sanada, Sue Shiomi, Sonny Chiba; **D:** Noribumi Suzuki. **VHS, Beta** $49.95 MED 🎬½

Shoot Five hunting buddies fall prey to a group of crazed killers after one man is shot by accident. What's the message: Anti-gun? Anti-hunting? Silly, unbelievable, irresponsibly moralistic, and gratuitously violent.
1985 (R) 98m/C Ernest Borgnine, Cliff Robertson, Henry Silva, Helen Shaver; **D:** Harvey Hart. **VHS, Beta** $59.98 SUE 🎬

Shoot Photographer Katie Tracy goes undercover to expose an illegal gambling ring fronted by an exotic nightclub. The latest gambling stakes involve the Emperor's pearls, offered in a private auction which could turn deadly, especially when Katie gets involved with the group's handsome ringleader.
1992 (R) 90m/C Dedee Pfeiffer, Miles O'Keeffe, Christopher Atkins; **D:** Hugh Parks. **VHS** $89.95 TRI 🎬🎬

Shoot It Black, Shoot It Blue Rogue cop shoots a black purse snatcher and thinks he has gotten away with it. Unknown to him, a witness has filmed the incident and turns the evidence over to a lawyer.
1974 93m/C Michael Moriarty. **VHS, Beta** NO 🎬½

Shoot Loud, Louder, I Don't Understand! A sculptor who has a hard time separating reality from dreams thinks he witnessed a murder. Shenanigans follow. Meant to be a black comedy, but when not dull, it is confusing. Welch looks good, as usual, but doesn't show acting talent here. In Italian with English subtitles. **AKA:** Spara Forte, Piu Forte...Non Capisco.
1966 101m/C Marcello Mastroianni, Raquel Welch; **D:** Eduardo de Filippo. **VHS, Beta** $59.95 NLC 🎬½

Shoot the Living, Pray for the Dead While travelling through Mexico, the leader of a band of killers promises his guide half of a share in stolen gold if he can lead them to it.
1973 90m/C Klaus Kinski. **VHS, Beta** $19.95 CNG 🎬🎬

Shoot the Moon A successful writer, married and with four children, finds his life unrewarding and leaves his family to take up with a younger woman. The wife must learn to deal with her resentment, the fears of her children, and her own attempt at a new love. Fine acting but a worn-out story.
1982 (R) 124m/C Diane Keaton, Albert Finney, Karen Allen, Peter Weller, Dana Hill, Viveka Davis, Tracey Gold, Tina Yothers; **D:** Alan Parker; **W:** Bo Goldman. **VHS, Beta** $19.99 MGM 🎬🎬½

Shoot the Piano Player Former concert pianist (Aznavour, spendidly cast) changes his name and plays piano at a low-class Paris cafe. A convoluted plot ensues; he becomes involved with gangsters, though his girlfriend wants him to try a comeback. Lots of atmosphere, character development, humor, and romance. A Truffaut masterpiece. In French with English subtitles. **AKA:** Tirez sur le Pianiste; Shoot the Pianist.
1962 92m/B Charles Aznavour, Marie DuBois, Nicole Berger, Michele Mercier, Albert Remy; **D:** Francois Truffaut; **W:** Marcel Moussey, Francois Truffaut; **M:** Georges Delerue. **VHS, Beta** $39.95 HMV, HHT, WFV 🎬🎬🎬

Shoot the Sun Down Four offbeat characters united in a search for gold turn against each other. "Gilligan's Island"-style assortment of characters (Indian; gunfighter; girl; sea captain) are cast away in a pointless plot from which they never escape. Too bad: talented cast could have done better.
1981 (PG) 102m/C Christopher Walken, Margot Kidder, Geoffrey Lewis, Bo Brundin, Sacheen Little Feather; **D:** David Leeds. **VHS, Beta** NO 🎬½

Shoot to Kill B-grade noir-esque mystery about a crooked D.A. and a gangster who bite the dust. Suspenseful, dark, street-level crime drama uncovered by ambitious journalist Ward.

1947 64m/B Russell Wade, Susan Walters, Nestor Paiva, Edmund MacDonald, Vince Barnett; **D:** William Berke. **VHS, Beta** $19.99 SNC, VYY 🎬½

Shoot to Kill A city cop (Poitier, better than ever after 10 years off the screen) and a mountain guide (Berenger) reluctantly join forces to capture a killer who is part of a hunting party traversing the Pacific Northwest and which is being led by the guide's unsuspecting girlfriend (Alley). Poitier may be a bit old for the role, but he carries the implausible plot on the strength of his performance. Good action.
1988 (R) 110m/C Sidney Poitier, Tom Berenger, Kirstie Alley, Clancy Brown, Richard Masur, Andrew (Andy) Robinson, Frederick Coffin, Andrew (Andy) Robinson, Kevin Scannell; **D:** Roger Spottiswoode; **W:** Michael Burton, Harv Zimmel, Dan Petrie Jr.; **M:** John Scott. **VHS** $19.99 TOU 🎬🎬🎬

Shooters A wacky platoon of misfits is paired off against a group of vicious killers in a "war game" training session. Not completely unfunny or worthless.
1989 84m/C Ben Schick, Robin Sims, Aldo Ray. **VHS, Beta** $9.95 AIP 🎬½

Shootfighter: Fight to the Death Two boys become experts in the martial arts and constant rivals. Now grown-up they take their rivalry to a deadly level in a "shootfight," a game which has no rules and is so brutal it's banned as a sport. Not that this stops them. An unrated version is also available.
1993 (R) 94m/C Bolo Yeung, Martin Kove, William Zabka, Michael Bernardo, Maryam D'Abo, Edward Albert; **D:** Patrick Allen; **W:** Judd B. Lynn, Larry Feliz Jr., Peter Shaner. **VHS** $19.95 COL 🎬½

The Shooting A mysterious woman, bent on revenge, persuades a former bounty hunter and his partner to escort her across the desert, with tragic results. Offbeat, small film filled strong by performances of Nicholson and Oates. Filmed concurrently with "Ride in the Whirlwind," with the same cast and director. Bang-up surprise ending.
1966 82m/C Warren Oates, Millie Perkins, Jack Nicholson, Will Hutchins; **D:** Monte Hellman. **VHS, Beta** MED, DVT, HHT 🎬🎬🎬

Shooting Three boys run away when they think they have killed a man in a hunting accident.
1982 60m/C Lynn Redgrave, Lance Kerwin, Barry Primus. **VHS, Beta** NO 🎬

Shooting Elizabeth A fed-up husband decides to shut his loudmouthed wife up—permanently. Only before he can kill her, she disappears. The police don't buy it and want to charge him with murder. Can he find his wife before things really get serious?
1992 (PG-13) 96m/C Jeff Goldblum, Mimi Rogers. **VHS** LIV 🎬½

The Shooting Party Told in flashbacks, a story of a crime of passion, an innocent man, and guilty secrets. A magistrate cannot admit his love for a woodsman's daughter so she falls into a loveless marriage and a decadent affair. In a fit of passion, the magistrate kills her and then decides to prosecute her innocent husband for the crime. Based on a story by Chekhov. In Russian with English subtitles.
1977 105m/C Oleg Yankovsky, Galina Belyayeva; **D:** Emil Loteanu. **VHS** $79.95 CVC, FCT 🎬🎬½

The Shooting Party A group of English aristocrats assemble at a nobleman's house for a last bird shoot on the eve of WWI. Splendid cast crowned Mason, in his last role. Fascinating crucible class anxieties, rich

wit social scheming, personality conflicts, and things left unsaid. Adapted from Isabel Colegate's novel.
1985 97m/C James Mason, Dorothy Tutin, Edward Fox, John Gielgud, Robert Hardy, Cheryl Campbell, Judi Bowker; **D:** Alan Bridges; **W:** Julian Bond. **VHS, Beta** NO *ⱵⱵⱵ* ½

Shooting Stars Two actors who play private eyes on television are pushed out of their jobs by a jealous co-star. They take to the streets as "real" crime-fighting dicks. Interesting premise goes nowhere. Made for TV.
1985 96m/C Billy Dee Williams, Parker Stevenson, Efrem Zimbalist Jr., Edie Adams; **D:** Richard Lang. **VHS, Beta** $24.95 AHV *Ɫ*

The Shootist Wayne, in a supporting last role, plays a legendary gunslinger afflicted with cancer who seeks peace and solace in his final days. Town bad guys Boone and O'Brian aren't about to let him rest and are determined to gun him down to avenge past deeds. One of Wayne's best and most dignified performances about living up to a personal code of honor. Stewart and Bacall head excellent supporting cast. Based on Glendon Swarthout's novel.
1976 (PG) 100m/C John Wayne, Lauren Bacall, Ron Howard, James Stewart, Richard Boone, Hugh O'Brian, Bill McKinney, Harry Morgan, John Carradine, Sheree North, Scatman Crothers; **D:** Don Siegel; **M:** Elmer Bernstein. Academy Awards '76 Nominations: Best Art Direction/Set Decoration; National Board of Review Awards '76: 10 Best Films of the Year. **VHS, Beta** $14.95 PAR, TLF *ⱵⱵⱵ* ½

Shop Angel A department store dress designer encounters romance and scandal in this low-budget drama of intrigue and romance. She falls in love with the fiance of her boss's daughter, and schemes to blackmail him (the boss). Competently rendered if unexceptional tale.
1932 66m/B Marion Shilling, Holmes Herbert, Creighton Hale; **D:** Mason Hopper. **VHS, Beta, 8mm** $24.95 VYY *ⱵⱵ*

The Shop Around the Corner A low-key romantic classic in which Stewart and Sullavan are feuding clerks in a small Budapest shop, who unknowingly fall in love via a lonely hearts club. Charming portrayal of ordinary people in ordinary situations. Adapted from the Nikolaus Laszlo's play "Parfumerie." Later made into a musical called "In the Good Old Summertime" and, on Broadway, "She Loves Me."
1940 99m/B Margaret Sullavan, James Stewart, Frank Morgan, Joseph Schildkraut, Sara Haden, Felix Bressart, Charles Halton; **D:** Ernst Lubitsch. **VHS** $19.98 MGM *ⱵⱵⱵ* ½

The Shop on Main Street During WWII, a Slovak takes a job as an "Aryan comptroller" for a Jewish-owned button shop. The owner is an old deaf woman; they slowly build a friendship. Tragedy ensues when all of the town's Jews are to be deported. Sensitive and subtle. Surely among the most gutwrenching portrayals of human tragedy ever on screen. Exquisite plotting and direction. In Czechoslovakian with English subtitles. **AKA:** The Shop on High Street; Obch Od Na Korze.
1965 111m/B Ida Kaminska, Josef Kroner, Hana Slivkoua, Frantisek Holly, Martin Gregor; **D:** Jan Kadar, Elmar Klos. Academy Awards '65: Best Foreign Language Film; Nominations: Best Actress (Kaminska); New York Film Critics Awards '66: Best Foreign Film. **VHS, Beta** $19.98 COL, ING, SWC *ⱵⱵⱵⱵ*

Shopworn Angel Weepy melodrama about a sophisticated actress who leads on a naive Texas soldier who's in New York prior to being shipped out for WWI duty. Later,

just before she goes on stage, she learns he's been killed at the front. She rallys to sing "Pack Up your Troubles in Your Old Kit Bag and Smile, Smile, Smile." Lots of tears. Adapted from the story "Private Pettigrew's Girl" by Dana Burnet. This remake of the same-titled 1929 film considerably softened the characters. Remade again in 1959 as "That Kind of Woman."
1938 85m/B Margaret Sullavan, James Stewart, Walter Pidgeon, Nat Pendleton, Alan Curtis, Sam Levene, Hattie McDaniel, Charley Grapewin, Charles D. Brown; **D:** H.C. Potter; **W:** Waldo Salt. **VHS** $29.98 MGM, MOV *ⱵⱵⱵ*

Shore Leave Dressmaker Mackaill isn't getting any younger. Tough-guy sailor Bilge Smith (Barthelmess, in top form) meets her on shore leave; little does he realize her plans for him! She owns a dry-docked ship, you see, and it (and she) will be ready for him when he comes ashore next. Lovely, fun (if rather plodding) romantic comedy. Later made into musicals twice, as "Hit the Deck" and "Follow the Fleet."
1925 74m/B Richard Barthelmess, Dorothy Mackaill; **D:** John S. Robertson. **VHS** $19.95 GPV, GVV, VYY *ⱵⱵⱵ*

Short Circuit A newly-developed robot designed for the military is hit by lightning and begins to think it's alive. Sheedy and Guttenberg help it hide from the mean people at the weapons lab who want to take it home. Followed two years later, save Sheedy and Guttenberg, by the lame "Short Circuit 2."
1986 (PG) 98m/C Steve Guttenberg, Ally Sheedy, Austin Pendleton, Fisher Stevens, Brian McNamara; **D:** John Badham; **W:** S.S. Wilson, Brent Maddock. **VHS, Beta** $19.98 FOX *ⱵⱵ*

Short Circuit 2 A sequel to the first adorable-robot-outwits-bad-guys tale. The robot, Number Five, makes his way through numerous plot turns without much human assistance or much purpose. Harmless (unless you have to spend time watching it), but pointless and juvenile. Very occasional genuinely funny moments.
1988 (PG) 95m/C Fisher Stevens, Cynthia Gibb, Michael McKean, Jack Weston, David Hemblen; **D:** Kenneth Johnson; **W:** S.S. Wilson, Brent Maddock; **M:** Charles Fox. **VHS, Beta** $19.95 COL *Ɫ* ½

Short Cuts Multi-storied, fish-eyed look at American culture with some 22 characters intersecting—profoundly or fleetingly—through each other's lives. Running the emotional gamut from disturbing to humorous, Altman's portrait of the contemporary human condition is nevertheless fascinating. Based on nine stories and a prose poem by Raymond Carver. Available on laser disc in a movie-only edition or a special edition.
1993 (R) 189m/C Annie Ross, Lori Singer, Jennifer Jason Leigh, Tim Robbins, Madeleine Stowe, Frances McDormand, Peter Gallagher, Lily Tomlin, Tom Waits, Bruce Davison, Andie MacDowell, Jack Lemmon, Lyle Lovett, Fred Ward, Buck Henry, Huey Lewis, Matthew Modine, Anne Archer, Julianne Moore, Lili Taylor, Christopher Penn, Robert Downey Jr., Jarrett Lennon, Zane Cassidy; **D:** Robert Altman; **W:** Frank Barhydt, Robert Altman; **M:** Mark Isham. Academy Awards '93 Nominations: Best Director (Altman); Golden Globe Awards '94: Best Screenplay; Independent Spirit Awards '94: Best Supporting Actress (Moore); Independent Spirit Awards '94: Best Director (Altman), Best Film, Best Screenplay; National Society of Film Critics Awards '93: Best Supporting Actress (Stowe); Venice Film Festival '93: Best Film. **VHS** NLC *ⱵⱵⱵ* ½

Short Eyes When a child molester (Davison) enters prison, the inmates act out their own form of revenge against him. Filmed on location at New York City's Men's House of Detention, nicknamed "The Tombs." Script by Manuel Pinero from his excellent play; he also acts in the film. Top-notch performances and respectful direction from Young bring unsparingly realistic prison drama to the screen. Title is prison jargon for child molester. **AKA:** The Slammer.
1979 (R) 100m/C Bruce Davison, Miguel Pinero, Nathan George, Donald Blakely, Curtis Mayfield, Jose Perez, Shawn Elliott; **D:** Robert M. Young. **VHS, Beta** $69.98 LIV *ⱵⱵⱵ* ½

Short Films of D.W. Griffith, Vol. 1 Three early shorts by the great silent-film director. "The Battle" is a lavish Civil War drama. "The Female of the Species" stars pickford McDowell and Bernard as pioneers struggling to survive hardship and each other's company in the desert. "The New York Hat" is a comedy (written by Anita Loos, aged 14!) starring Pickford as a girl who endures the malice of her peers when she is given a nice hat. Landmark early films from a master director.
1912 59m/B Mary Pickford, Charles West, Blanche Sweet, Claire McDowell; **D:** D.W. Griffith. **VHS, Beta** $19.95 VYY, DVT, HEG *ⱵⱵⱵ* ½

Short Films of D.W. Griffith, Vol. 2 Five early silent shorts by Griffith, with original organ music and some familiar faces in the casts: "A Corner in Wheat," "The Revenue Man and his Girl," "The Musketeers of Pig Alley," "A Girl and her Trust" and "The Battle of Elderbush Gulch."
1909 112m/B Lillian Gish, Bobby Harron, Mae Marsh, Lionel Barrymore, Dorothy Gish, Henry B. Walthall, Kate Bruce, James Kirkwood, Harry Carey Sr. **VHS, Beta, 8mm** VYY, DVT, HEG *ⱵⱵⱵ* ½

Short Fuse A Washington, D.C. reporter uncovers the truth behind the rape and murder of a nurse. Interesting "go-go" music from the Washington D.C. ghetto aids an otherwise uninteresting film. **AKA:** Good to Go.
1988 (R) 91m/C Art Garfunkel, Robert DoQui, Harris Yulin, Richard Brooks, Reginald Daughtry; **D:** Blaine Novak. **VHS, Beta** $79.95 VMK *Ɫ* ½

Short Time Somewhere between "Tango & Cash" and "Airplane" is where you'll find "Short Time." Non-stop action/comedy stars Dabney Coleman and Teri Garr as partners in crime and humor. Coleman is a cop days from retirement; wrongly told he is dying, he tries hard to get killed so his family will be provided for. Coleman is wonderful. Garr, no longer the long-suffering wife of "Oh, God" and "Close Encounters," is appealing here as the indulgent sidekick.
1990 (PG-13) 100m/C Dabney Coleman, Teri Garr, Matt Frewer, Barry Corbin, Joe Pantoliano, Xander Berkeley, Rob Roy, Jak-Erik Eriksen; **D:** Gregg Champion; **W:** John Blumenthal, Michael Berry; **M:** Ira Newborn. **VHS** $14.95 IME, LIV *ⱵⱵⱵ*

A Shot in the Dark A minister suspects murder when a despised miser is thought to have committed suicide. He takes it on himself to investigate in this routine mystery.
1933 53m/B Dorothy Boyd, O.B. Clarence, Jack Hawkins, Russell Thorndike, Michael Shepley; **D:** George Pearson. **VHS, Beta** $16.95 SNC *Ɫ* ½

A Shot in the Dark When his son is murdered at a New England college, a distraught dad takes it on himself to investigate. Movie cowboy Starrett plays the sleuthing pop in this undistinguished mystery.

1935 69m/B Charles Starrett, Robert Warwick, Edward Van Sloan, Marion Shilling, Doris Lloyd, Helen Jerome Eddy, James Bush; *D:* Charles Lamont. **VHS, Beta** $16.95 *NOS, SNC* 𝕀𝕀

A Shot in the Dark Second and possibly the best in the classic ''Inspector Clouseau-Pink Panther'' series of comedies. The bumbling Inspector Clouseau (Sellers, of course) investigates the case of a parlor maid (Sommer) accused of murdering her lover. Clouseau's libido convinces him she's innocent,even though all the clues point to her. Classic gags, wonderful music. After this film, Sellers as Clouseau disappears until 1975's ''Return of the Pink Panther'' (Alan Arkin played him in ''Inspector Clouseau,'' made in 1968 by different folks).
1964 101m/C Peter Sellers, Elke Sommer, Herbert Lom, George Sanders, Bryan Forbes; *D:* Blake Edwards; *W:* William Peter Blatty, Blake Edwards; *M:* Henry Mancini. **VHS, Beta** $19.98 *FOX, FCT* 𝕀𝕀𝕀½

Shotgun A sheriff on the trail of a killer is accompanied by a girl he's saved from Indians. Average western cowritten by western actor Rory Calhoun, who had hoped to star in the film, but was turned down by the studio.
1955 81m/C Sterling Hayden, Zachary Scott, Yvonne De Carlo; *D:* Lesley Selander. **VHS** $29.95 *PAR* 𝕀𝕀½

The Shout From a strange Robert Graves story, an even stranger film. A lunatic befriends a young couple, moves in with them, and gradually takes over their lives. The movie's title refers to the man's ability to kill by shouting, a power he learned from his Australian aboriginal past.
1978 (R) 88m/C Alan Bates, Susannah York, John Hurt, Tim Curry; *D:* Jerzy Skolimowski. **VHS, Beta** $39.98 *COL* 𝕀𝕀𝕀

Shout Romance and rebellion set in a sleepy Texas town during the 1950s. Jesse Tucker's (Walters) rebellious ways land him in the Benedict Home for Boys and he seems lost until Jack Cabe (Travolta) enters town. Jack introduces Jesse and the gang to the exciting new sounds of rock 'n' roll. Been done better and better.
1991 (PG-13) 93m/C John Travolta, James Walters, Heather Graham, Richard Jordan, Linda Fiorentino, Scott Coffey; *D:* Jeffrey Hornaday; *M:* Randy Edelman. **VHS, Beta** $19.98 *MCA* 𝕀𝕀

Shout at the Devil English officer Moore and Irish-American adventurer Marvin seek to blow up a German battleship out for repairs in East Africa before the outbreak of WWI. There's also some intrigue about ivory smuggling. From the novel by Wilbur Smith and based on an actual incident, but that doesn't make the comedy adventure any more palatable. Marvin's hamming is ludicrous, Moore is unusually wooden, and the big budget permits any number of fairly pointless action-oriented excursions and explosions.
1976 (PG) 128m/C Lee Marvin, Roger Moore, Barbara Parkins, Ian Holm; *D:* Peter Hunt; *M:* Maurice Jarre. **VHS, Beta** $29.98 *LIV, VES* 𝕀𝕀½

Show Boat The second of three film versions of the Jerome Kern/Oscar Hammerstein musical, filmed previously in 1929, about a Mississippi showboat and the life and loves of its denizens. Wonderful romance, unforgettable music. Director Whale also brought the world ''Frankenstein.'' The laser edition includes a historical audio essay by Miles Kreuger, excerpts from the 1929 version, Ziegfeld's 1932 stage revival, ''Life Aboard a Real Showboat'' (a vintage short), radio broadcasts, and a 300-photo essay tracing the history of showboats. Remade 15

years later. ♫Ol' Man River; Ah Still Suits Me; Bill; Can't Help Lovin' Dat Man; Only Make Believe; I Have the Room Above Her; You Are Love; Gallivantin' Around; Cotton Blossom.
1936 110m/B Irene Dunne, Allan Jones, Paul Robeson, Helen Morgan, Hattie McDaniel, Charles Winninger, Donald Cook, Bobby Watson; *D:* James Whale; *W:* Oscar Hammerstein; *M:* Oscar Hammerstein, Jerome Kern. **VHS, Beta** $19.98 *MGM, CRC, MLB* 𝕀𝕀𝕀𝕀

Show Boat Third movie version of the 1927 musical about the life and loves of a Mississippi riverboat theater troupe. Terrific musical numbers, with fun dance routines from Champion, who went on to great fame as a choreographer. Grayson is somewhat vapid, but lovely to look at and hear. Gardner didn't want to do the part of Julie, although she eventually received fabulous reviews—her singing was dubbed by Annette Warren. The 171-foot ''Cotton Blossom'' boat was built on the Tarzan lake on the MGM back lot at an astounding cost of $126,468.00. Warfield's film debut—his ''Ole Man River''—was recorded in one take. Laserdisc version features the original motion picture trailer, excerpts from ''Broadway,'' ''Silent Film,'' and radio Version of ''Show Boat,'' a documentary featuring life on a real show boat, and a commentary on the performers, the film, and the history of show boats. ♫Make Believe; Can't Help Lovin' Dat Man; I Might Fall Back On You; Ol' Man River; You Are Love; Why Do I Love You?; Bill; Life Upon the Wicked Stage; After the Ball.
1951 107m/C Kathryn Grayson, Howard Keel, Ava Gardner, William Warfield, Joe E. Brown, Agnes Moorehead, Gower Champion; *D:* George Sidney; *M:* Jerome Kern, Oscar Hammerstein. **VHS, Beta** $19.98 *MGM, VYG, TLF* 𝕀𝕀½

Show Business Historically valuable film record of classic vaudeville acts, especially Cantor and Davis. A number of vaudevillians recreate their old acts for director Marin—unforgettable slapstick and songs. All this pegged on a plot that follows Cantor's rise to fame with the Ziegfeld Follies. ♫Alabamy Bound; I Want a Girl (Just Like the Girl Who Married Dear Old Dad); It Had to Be You; Makin' Whoopee; Why Am I Blue; They're Wearing 'Em Higher in Hawaii; The Curse of an Aching Heart; While Strolling in the Park One Day; You May Not Remember.
1944 92m/B Eddie Cantor, Joan Davis, George Murphy; *D:* Edwin L. Marin. **VHS, Beta** $19.98 *CCB, TTC* 𝕀𝕀𝕀

A Show of Force Reporter Irving investigates the coverup of a murder with political ramifications. Brazilian director Barreto cast (surprise!) his girlfriend in the lead; she doesn't exactly carry the day. Phillips is good, but you'll end up feeling cheated if you expect to see much of highly-billed Duvall or Garcia. Based on a real incident of 1978, but hardly believable as political realism or even moralism.
1990 (R) 93m/C Erik Estrada, Amy Irving, Andy Garcia, Robert Duvall, Lou Diamond Phillips; *D:* Bruno Barreto; *W:* Evan Jones; *M:* Georges Delerue. **VHS, Beta** $14.95 *PAR* 𝕀𝕀

The Show-Off Aubrey Piper (Skelton) has big dreams which far out weigh his modest talents. He tells outlandish tales to impress girlfriend Amy (Maxwell) and schemes to make them come true. Dated material which even gifted comedian Skelton can't rescue. Adapted from a play by George Kelly and previously filmed in 1926, 1929, and 1934.

1946 83m/B Red Skelton, Marilyn Maxwell, Marjorie Main, Virginia O'Brien, Eddie Anderson, George Cleveland, Leon Ames, Marshall Thompson, Jacqueline White, Lila Leeds, Emory Parnell; *D:* Harry Beaumont; *W:* George Wells. **VHS, Beta** $19.98 *MGM, FCT* 𝕀𝕀½

Show People A pretty girl from the boonies tries to make it big in Tinseltown. But as a slapstick star?! She wanted to be a leading lady! Enjoyable, fun silent comedy shows Davies's true talents. Interesting star cameos, including director Vidor at the end.
1928 82m/B Marion Davies, William Haines, Dell Henderson, Paul Ralli, William S. Hart, Rod La Rocque; *Cameos:* King Vidor; *D:* King Vidor. **VHS** $29.95 *MGM* 𝕀𝕀𝕀

Show Them No Mercy A couple and their baby out for a drive unwittingly stumble into a kidnapping that doesn't go as planned. Tense gangster drama reincarnated as the Western ''Rawhide.'' *AKA:* Tainted Money.
1935 76m/B Rochelle Hudson, Cesar Romero, Bruce Cabot, Edward Norris, Edward Brophy, Warren Hymer, Herbert Rawlinson; *D:* George Marshall. **VHS** $19.98 *FOX, FCT* 𝕀𝕀𝕀

The Showdown The title actually refers to a tricky poker game, the highlight of yet another Hopalong Cassidy versus hoss thieves quickie epic. Kermit Maynard is the brother of cowboy hero Ken Maynard.
1940 65m/B William Boyd, Russell Hayden, Britt Wood, Morris Ankrum, Jan Clayton, Roy Barcroft, Kermit Maynard; *D:* Howard Bretherton. **VHS** $19.95 *NOS* 𝕀𝕀

The Showdown Elliott plays trail boss Shad Jones who knows one of his fellow cowhands has murdered his brother. Jones is determined to find out who it is and even the score. Brennan is cast against type as a greedy cattle baron. Elliott's last film for Republic.
1950 86m/B Wild Bill Elliott, Walter Brennan, Marie Windsor, Henry Morgan, Rhys Williams, Jim Davis, Leif Erickson, Yakima Canutt; *D:* Stuart E. McGowan, Dorrell McGowan; *W:* Stuart E. McGowan, Dorrell McGowan. **VHS** $9.98 *REP* 𝕀𝕀½

Showdown Billy Massey (Martin) and Chuck Garvis (Hudson) had been friends since childhood, until they fell out over the attentions of the pretty Kate (Clark), whom Chuck married. Chuck became the honest town sheriff while Billy took to train robbing. Now it's up to Chuck to bring Billy to justice. Director Seaton's final film.
1973 (PG) 99m/C Dean Martin, Rock Hudson, Susan Clark, Donald Moffatt, John McLiam, Ed Begley Jr.; *D:* George Seaton; *W:* Theodore Taylor. **VHS** $14.98 *MCA, FCT* 𝕀𝕀½

Showdown A small southern town is taken over by a motorcycle gang whose leader, Kincade, decides to set up his fencing and drug operations there. But the local law enforcement has other ideas, calling in a martial arts expert who wants revenge against Kincade for the death of his partner.
1993 (R) 92m/C Leo Fong, Werner Hoetzinger, Richard Lynch, Michelle McCormick, Frank Marth, Tom MacDowell, Troy Donahue; *D:* Leo Fong; *W:* Leo Fong. **VHS** $89.95 *AIP* 𝕀½

Showdown Ken, the new kid in a particularly nasty high school, gets picked on by the martial-arts expert school bully. After getting beaten up a lot Ken finds out the school janitor can help turn him into a high-kicking fighter. Lots of fast-paced fight scenes which is all the genre demands. An edited PG-13 version is also available.
1993 (R) 90m/C Ken Scott, Billy Blanks, Patrick Kilpatrick, Kenneth McLeod; *D:* Robert Radler. **VHS** $94.95 *IMP* 𝕀½

Showdown at Boot Hill A U.S. Marshal (Bronson) kills a wanted murderer but cannot collect the reward because the townspeople will not identify the victim.
1958 76m/B Charles Bronson, Robert Hutton, John Carradine; **D:** Gene Fowler. **VHS $19.98** REP ✗✗

Showdown at the Equator Chinese cops are trained to kill criminals with their feet, and they do.
1983 (R) 95m/C Lo Lieh, Bruce Liang, Nora Miao, Lee Kan Kwun. **VHS, Beta $24.95** GEM ✗

Showdown at Williams Creek A graphic Canadian Western set in the old Montana territory, where an outcast settler goes on trial for killing an old man. Testimony recounts a shocking history of greed and betrayal. The dark side of the Gold Rush, generally well-acted. Inspired by an actual incident. **AKA:** Kootenai Brown.
1991 (R) 97m/C Tom Burlinson, Donnelly Rhodes, Raymond Burr, Michael Thrush, John Pyper Ferguson, Alex Bruhanski; **D:** Allen Kroeker; **W:** John Gray; **M:** Michael Conway Baker. **VHS $89.98** REP ✗✗½

Showdown in Little Tokyo Lundgren stars as a martial arts master/L.A. cop who was raised in Japan, and has all the respect in the world for his "ancestors" and heritage. Brandon Lee (son of Bruce) is Lundgren's partner, and he's a bona fide American-made, pop-culture, mall junkie. Together, they go after a crack-smuggling gang of "yakuza" (Japanese thugs). Lots of high-kicking action and the unique angle on stereotypes make this a fun martial arts film.
1991 (R) 78m/C Dolph Lundgren, Brandon Lee, Tia Carrere, Cary-Hiroyuki Tagawa; **D:** Mark L. Lester. **VHS, Beta, 8mm $19.98** WAR ✗✗

Shredder Orpheus Rock star Orpheus skateboards through hell to stop deadly television transmissions and rescue his wife.
1989 93m/C Jesse Bernstein, Robert McGinley, Vera McCaughan, Megan Murphy, Carlo Scandiuzzi; **D:** Robert McGinley. **VHS, Beta $79.95** AIP ✗

Shriek in the Night Two rival reporters (Rogers and Talbot, previously paired in "The Thirteenth Guest") turn detective to solve a string of apartment murders. Made on a proverbial shoestring, but not bad.
1933 66m/B Ginger Rogers, Lyle Talbot, Harvey Clark; **D:** Albert Ray. **VHS, Beta $12.95** SNC, NOS, BAR ✗✗½

Shriek of the Mutilated An anthropological expedition on a deserted island turns into a night of horror as a savage beast kills the members of the group one by one.
1974 (R) 85m/C Alan Brock, Jennifer Stock, Michael Harris; **D:** Michael Findlay. **VHS, Beta $59.98** LIV, SNC Woof!

The Shrieking Black magic women hang out with biker types in Nebraska in 1919. **AKA:** Hex.
1973 (PG) 93m/C Keith Carradine, Christina Raines, Gary Busey, Robert Walker Jr., Dan Haggerty, John Carradine, Scott Glenn; **D:** Leo Garen; **M:** Charles Bernstein. **VHS, Beta $29.95** PSM, IME ✗

The Shrimp on the Barbie When daddy refuses to bless her marriage to dim bulb boyfriend, Australian Samms hires L.A. low life Marin to pose as new beau. Another pseudonymous Smithee effort.
1990 (R) 86m/C Richard "Cheech" Marin, Emma Samms, Vernon Wells, Bruce Spence, Carole Davis; **D:** Alan Smithee. **VHS, Beta $89.98** MED, VTR ✗½

Shy People An urbanized New York journalist and her spoiled daughter journey to the Louisiana bayou to visit long-lost relatives in order to produce an article for "Cosmopolitan." They find ignorance, madness, and ancestral secrets and are forced to examine their motives, their relationships and issues brought to light in the watery, murky, fantastic land of the bayous. Well-acted melodrama with an outstanding performance by Hershey as the cajun matriarch. Music by Tangerine Dream; cinematography by Chris Menges.
1987 (R) 119m/C Jill Clayburgh, Barbara Hershey, Martha Plimpton, Mare Winningham, Merritt Butrick, John Philbin, Don Swayze, Pruitt Taylor Vince; **D:** Andrei Konchalovsky; **W:** Gerard Brach, Marjorie David; **M:** Tangerine Dream. **VHS, Beta $19.98** WAR ✗

The Sibling Two sisters become involved in the accidental murder of a man who was a husband to one woman and lover to the other. Of course, one sister has just been released from the mental rehabilitation clinic. **AKA:** Psycho Sisters; So Evil, My Sister.
1972 (PG) 85m/C Susan Strasberg, Faith Domergue, Sydney Chaplin, Steve Mitchell; **D:** Reginald LeBorg. **VHS, Beta $9.95** SIM, PSM, HHE ✗

Sibling Rivalry Repressed doctor's wife (redundant) Alley rolls in hay with soon to be stiff stranger upon advice of footloose sister. Stranger expires from heart attack in hay and Alley discovers that the corpse is her long-lost brother-in-law. Slapstick cover-up ensues.
1990 (PG-13) 88m/C Kirstie Alley, Bill Pullman, Carrie Fisher, Sam Elliott, Jami Gertz, Ed O'Neill, Scott Bakula, Frances Sternhagen, Bill Macy; **D:** Carl Reiner. **VHS, Beta, 8mm $19.95** COL, SUE, NLC ✗✗

The Sicilian Adapted from the Mario Puzo novel and based on the life of Salvatore Giuliano. Chronicles the exploits of the men who took on the government, the Catholic Church, and the Mafia in an effort to make Sicily secede from Italy and become its own nation in the 1940s. Pretentious, overdone, and confused. This long, uncut version was unseen in America, but hailed by European critics; the 115-minute, R-rated American release is also available, but isn't as good. See "Salvatore Giuliano" (Francesco Rosi, 1962) instead of either version.
1987 146m/C Christopher Lambert, John Turturro, Terence Stamp, Joss Ackland, Barbara Sukowa; **D:** Michael Cimino. **VHS, Beta $14.98** LIV, VES ✗½

Sicilian Connection A narcotics agent poses as a nightclub manager to bust a drug-smuggling organization.
1974 100m/C Ben Gazzara, Silvia Monti, Fausto Tozzi. **VHS, Beta $79.95** VCD ✗½

The Sicilian Connection Two brothers in the mob serve out vendettas and generally create havoc wherever they go. **AKA:** The Pizza Connection.
1985 (R) 117m/C Michele Placido, Mark Switzer, Simona Cavallari. **VHS, Beta $79.95** MGM ✗

Sid & Nancy The tragic, brutal, true love story of The Sex Pistols' Sid Vicious and American groupie Nancy Spungen, from the director of "Repo Man." Remarkable lead performances in a very dark story that manages to be funny at times. Depressing but engrossing; no appreciation of punk music or sympathy for the self-destructive way of life is required. Oldman and Webb are superb. Music by Joe Strummer, the Pogues, and Pray for Rain.

1986 (R) 111m/C Gary Oldman, Chloe Webb, Debbie Bishop, David Hayman; **D:** Alex Cox. **VHS, Beta $14.95** MVD, SUE, NLC ✗✗✗

Side By Side In the same vein as "Cocoon," three senior citizens who aren't ready to retire decide to start their own business and launch a sportswear company designed for seniors. A witty portrayal of graceful aging that is uneven at times.
1988 100m/C Milton Berle, Sid Caesar, Danny Thomas; **D:** Jack Bender. **VHS, Beta $79.95** TRI ✗✗

Side Out The first major film about volleyball!? What a claim! What a bore. Midwestern college guy spends summer in Southern Cal. working for slumlord uncle; instead enters "the ultimate" beach volleyball touring. Bogus. Don't see it, dude.
1990 (PG-13) 100m/C C. Thomas Howell, Peter Horton, Kathy Ireland, Sinjin Smith, Randy Stoklos, Courtney Thorne-Smith, Harley Jane Kozak, Christopher Rydell; **D:** Peter Israelson. **VHS, Beta $89.95** COL ✗½

Side Show A runaway teen joins the circus, witnesses a murder, and must use his wits to stay out of reach of the killer. Forced "suspense" and "drama" of the bad made for TV ilk.
1984 98m/C Lance Kerwin, Red Buttons, Anthony (Tony) Franciosa, Connie Stevens; **D:** William Conrad; **M:** Ralph Burns. **VHS, Beta $19.98** TWE ✗

Sideburns The Pushkin Club, a group of reactionaries who try to remove the western influence from Russia, attack first a rock band, then innocent civilians as they act as a social cleaning service. Uses humor to try and warn people against the rising fascism in Russia because of the battle between conservative and reformist forces. In Russian with English subtitles.
1991 110m/C **D:** Yurii Mamin. **VHS $59.95** FCT ✗✗

Sidekicks Cutesy ego vehicle for executive producer Norris. (Brandis) is bullied by the kids at school and doesn't find much support at home from his well-meaning but ineffectual dad. He has a severe case of hero-worship for Norris, who appears as himself in a series of daydream karate sequences, saving the good guy and maiming the bad. Director Norris is actor Norris' brother. Predictable and sappy.
1993 (PG) 100m/C Chuck Norris, Jonathan Brandis, Beau Bridges, Mako, Julia Nickson-Soul, Danica McKellar, Richard Moll, Joe Piscopo; **D:** Aaron Norris; **W:** Donald W. Thompson, Lou Illar; **M:** Alan Silvestri. **VHS, 8mm $19.95** COL ✗✗

Sidewalks of London Laughton's a sidewalk entertainer who takes in homeless waif Leigh and puts her in his act and in his heart. Harrison steals her away and before long she's a star in the music halls. Meanwhile, Laughton has fallen on hard times. Memorable performances. **AKA:** St. Martin's Lane.
1940 86m/B Charles Laughton, Vivien Leigh, Rex Harrison; **D:** Tim Whelan. **VHS, Beta $19.95** NOS, HHT, CAB ✗✗✗

Sidewalks of New York A hapless New York millionaire (Keaton) falls for tenement gal Page and tries to win her heart by saving her street urchin brother from joining the local gang of toughs. Keaton was a silent screen classic as a comedian but his talkie career was disappointing as he lost creative control and battled alcohol problems.
1931 74m/B Buster Keaton, Anita Page, Cliff Edwards, Frank LaRue, Frank Rowan, Norman Phillips Jr.; **D:** Jules White, Zion Myers. **VHS, Beta $19.98** MGM, FCT ✗✗½

Sidewinder One Motocross racing is the setting for a romance between a racer and an heiress. Good racing footage, but where's the plot? If you like cars a whole lot . . .
1977 (PG) 97m/C Michael Parks, Marjoe Gortner, Susan Howard, Alex Cord, Charlotte Rae; **D:** Earl Bellamy. **VHS, Beta** $59.98 NLC *I*

Sidney Sheldon's Bloodline Wealthy businesswoman Hepburn finds she is marked for death by persons unknown. Exquisitely bad trash from another Sheldon bestseller. **AKA:** Bloodline.
1979 (R) 116m/C Audrey Hepburn, Ben Gazzara, James Mason, Michelle Phillips, Omar Sharif, Irene Papas, Romy Schneider, Gert Frobe, Maurice Ronet, Beatrice Straight; **D:** Terence Young; **M:** Ennio Morricone. **VHS, Beta** $14.95 PAR Woof!

The Siege of Firebase Gloria Story of the Marines who risked their lives defending an outpost against overwhelming odds during the 1968 Tet offensive in Vietnam. Purportedly patriotic war drama made by an Australian director; lead Hauser is a disgusting sadist, and plot is hopelessly hackneyed.
1989 95m/C Wings Hauser, R. Lee Ermey; **D:** Brian Trenchard-Smith. **VHS, Beta** $29.95 FRH *I½*

Siegfried Half of Lang's epic masterpiece "Der Niebelungen," based on German mythology. Title hero bathes in the blood of a dragon he has slain. He marries a princess, but wicked Queen Brumhilde has him killed. Part two, in which Siegfried's widow marries Attila the Hun, is titled "Kriemheld's Revenge." These dark, brooding, archetypal tours de force were patriotic tributes, and were loved by Hitler. Silent with music score. **AKA:** Siegfrieds Tod; Siegfried's Death.
1924 100m/B Paul Richter, Margareta Schoen; **D:** Fritz Lang. **VHS** $16.95 SNC, NOS, GPV *IIII*

Siempre Hay una Primera Vez The different loves of two women are contrasted.
1987 94m/C Ana Martin, Ana Louisa Peluffo, Helena Rojo. **VHS, Beta** $47.95 MAD *I*

Siesta Barkin is a professional stunt woman who leaves her current lover/manager, played by Sheen, and returns to visit her former lover and trainer, Byrne, on the eve of his marriage to another woman. Her trip, marked by flashbacks and flights of seemingly paranoid fantasy, leads to the discovery of murder, but she cannot remember who, when, why, or where. The film distorts time, reality, and perception in a sometimes fascinating, sometimes frustrating psychological mystery. Attractively filmed by video director Lambert. Barkin and Byrne were married in real life a year after the film's release.
1987 (R) 97m/C Ellen Barkin, Gabriel Byrne, Jodie Foster, Julian Sands, Isabella Rossellini, Martin Sheen, Grace Jones, Alexei Sayle; **D:** Mary Lambert; **W:** Patricia Louisiana Knop; **M:** Miles Davis, Marcus Miller. **VHS, Beta** $19.98 LHV, WAR *II½*

Sifted Evidence Woman archeologist who becomes involved with a man promises to show him an obscure archeological site in Mexico.
1983 42m/C NO *I*

The Sign of Four Sherlock Holmes and the ever-faithful Watson are hired by a young woman who has been anonymously sent an enormous diamond. An inept production which looks good but that's all.
1983 97m/C Ian Richardson, David Healy, Thorley Walters, Cherie Lunghi; **D:** Desmond Davis. **VHS, Beta** $59.95 PAR *I½*

Sign of the Wolf Features ten chapters of the rare, early talking serial.
1930 ?m/B Rex Lease, Virginia Brown Faire. **VHS** $16.95 SNC *I½*

The Sign of Zorro Adventures of the masked swordsman as he champions the cause of the oppressed in early California. Full-length version of the popular late-50s Disney television series.
1960 89m/C Guy Williams, Henry Calvin, Gene Sheldon, Romney Brent, Britt Lomond, George Lewis, Lisa Gaye; **D:** Norman Foster, Lewis R. Foster. **VHS, Beta** $69.95 DIS *II*

Signal 7 An improvised, neo-verite document of a night in the lives of two San Francisco taxi drivers. Nilsson's first major release and a notable example of his unique scriptless, tape-to-film narrative technique.
1983 89m/C Bill Ackridge, Dan Leegant; **D:** Rob Nilsson; **W:** Rob Nilsson. **VHS, Beta** $39.98 WAR *II*

Signals Through the Flames A film by Sheldon Rochlin and Maxine Harris outlining the tumultuous history of the famous experimental group, The Living Theatre.
1983 97m/C Julian Beck, Judith Malina, Maxine Harris, Living Theatre Company; **D:** Sheldon Rochlin. **VHS, Beta** $29.95 MFV, TPV *III*

Signs of Life A boat-building company in Maine closes its doors after centuries in business; the employees and families whose lives have been defined by it for generations learn to cope. Wonderful performances compensate only partly for a weak script. An episode on PBS's "American Playhouse." **AKA:** One for Sorrow, Two for Joy.
1989 (PG-13) 95m/C Beau Bridges, Arthur Kennedy, Vincent D'Onofrio, Kevin J. O'Connor, Will Patton, Kate Reid, Michael Lewis, Kathy Bates, Mary-Louise Parker, Georgia Engel; **D:** John David Coles; **W:** Mark malone; **M:** Howard Stone. **VHS, Beta** $89.95 LIV *II½*

Silas Marner Superb made for British television adaptation of the 1861 George Eliot classic about an itinerant weaver subjected to criminal accusation, poverty, and exile. Wonderful detail and splendid acting. Shot on location in the Cotswold district of England.
1985 92m/C Ben Kingsley, Jenny Agutter, Patrick Ryecart, Patsy Kensit; **D:** Giles Foster; **M:** Carl Davis. **VHS, Beta** $29.98 FOX, TVC, HMV *III*

The Silence A brutal, enigmatic allegory about two sisters, one a nymphomaniac, the other a violently frustrated lesbian, traveling with the former's young son to an unnamed country beset by war. Fascinating and memorable but frustrating and unsatisfying: What is it about? What is it an allegory of? Where is the narrative? The third in Bergman's crisis-of-faith trilogy following "Through a Glass Darkly" and "Winter Light." In Swedish with English subtitles or dubbed. **AKA:** Tystnaden.
1963 95m/B Ingrid Thulin, Gunnel Lindstrom, Birger Malmsten; **D:** Ingmar Bergman; **W:** Ingmar Bergman. **VHS, Beta** $24.95 HMV, ING, NLC *III*

Silence An autistic boy gets lost in the wilderness and faces an array of difficulties while his foster parents search for him. **AKA:** Crazy Jack and the Boy.
1973 (G) 82m/C Will Geer, Ellen Geer, Richard Kelton, Ian Geer Flanders, Craig Kelly; **D:** John Korty. **VHS, Beta** NO *II*

Silence Like Glass Diagnosed with life-threatening illness, two young women struggle to overcome their anger at their fate. They find friendship and together, search for reasons to live. Fine performances, with pacing that keeps the melodrama to a minimum.
1990 (R) 102m/C Jami Gertz, Martha Plimpton, George Peppard, Rip Torn, James Remar; **D:** Carl Schenkel; **M:** Anne Dudley. **VHS, Beta** $89.98 MED, VTR *II½*

Silence of the Heart Mother copes with aftermath of suicide of teenage son following her recent divorce. Hartley is captivating in this gripping drama.
1984 100m/C Mariette Hartley, Dana Hill, Howard Hesseman, Chad Lowe, Charlie Sheen; **D:** Richard Michaels; **W:** Phil Penningroth; **M:** Georges Delerue. **VHS** $29.95 PMH, HHE, VTR *III*

The Silence of the Lambs Foster is FBI cadet Clarice Starling, a woman with ambition, a cum laude degree in psychology, and a traumatic childhood. When a serial killer begins his ugly rounds, the FBI wants psychological profiles from other serial killers and she's sent to collect a profile from one who's exceptionally clever—psychiatrist Hannibal Lector, a vicious killer prone to dining on his victims. Brilliant performances from Foster and Hopkins, finely detailed supporting characterizations, and elegant pacing from Demme. Some brutal visual effects. Excellent portrayals of women who refuse to be victims. Based on the Thomas Harris novel.
1991 (R) 118m/C Jodie Foster, Anthony Hopkins, Scott Glenn, Ted Levine, Brooke Smith, Charles Napier, Roger Corman, Anthony Heald, Diane Baker, Chris Isaak; **D:** Jonathan Demme; **W:** Ted Tally. Academy Awards '91: Best Actor (Hopkins), Best Actress (Foster), Best Adapted Screenplay, Best Director (Demme), Best Picture; Nominations: Best Film Editing, Best Sound; British Academy Awards '92: Best Actor (Hopkins), Best Actress (Foster); Directors Guild of America Awards '91: Best Director (Demme); Golden Globe Awards '92: Best Actress—Drama (Foster); National Board of Review Awards '91: 10 Best Films of the Year, 10 Best Films of the Year, Best Director (Demme); People's Choice Awards '92: Best Film—Drama. **VHS, Beta** $19.98 ORI, FCT, IME *III½*

Silence of the North A widow (Burstyn) with three children struggles to survive under rugged pioneer conditions on the Canadian frontier. The scenery is, not surprisingly, stunning. Based on a true but generic story.
1981 (PG) 94m/C Ellen Burstyn, Tom Skerritt; **D:** Allan Winton King; **M:** Michael Conway Baker. **VHS, Beta** $59.95 MCA *II½*

The Silencer Walden stars as Harley-riding Angel who is out to stop a slavery and prostitution ring that abuses young runaways. Video-arcades hold the clues, and Angel must learn to kill without a conscience. Every time she kills, Angel seeks comfort in the arms of anonymous lovers. However, what she doesn't know is that her demented ex-boyfriend is watching.
1992 (R) 85m/C Lynette Walden, Chris Mulkey, Paul Ganus, Morton Downey Jr.; **D:** Amy Goldstein; **W:** Amy Goldstein, Scott Kraft. **VHS** $89.95 ACA *I*

Silent Assassins Fists and bullets fly when a scientist is kidnapped in order to gain secrets to biological warfare. Chong and Rhee, real-life owners of a martial arts studio, produced and choreographed the film. Blair is here, but doesn't figure much. A notch up from most similar martial arts pics.
1988 92m/C Sam Jones, Linda Blair, Jun Chong, Phillip Rhee; **D:** Scott Thomas, Lee Dooyong. **VHS** $79.98 MCG, VTR *II*

Silent Code A Mountie is framed for the murder of a young miner.
1935 55m/B Tom Tyler. **VHS, Beta** NO *I*

The Silent Enemy The true-life exploits of British frogmen battling Italian foes during WWII. Suspenseful and engrossing; good performances and good rendering of underwater action. Video release snips twenty minutes from the original and adds color.
1958 91m/C Laurence Harvey, John Clements, Michael Craig, Dawn Addams, Sidney James, Alec McCowen, Nigel Stock; *D:* William Fairchild. **VHS, Beta $7.00** VTR 🐾🐾½

Silent Killers A scientist is responsible for the deaths of many people because of his research in germ warfare. He's haunted by the ghosts of his victims. Is he losing his mind or is it a sinister plot?
19?? 90m/C Stephen Soul, Daniel Garfield. **VHS** MOV 🐾½

Silent Laugh Makers, No. 1 Four hilarious short movies from the silent era: "Looking for Sally," about an immigrant in search of his best girlfriend; "Lucky Dog," with the young Laurel and Hardy; "His Yum Out," about a wild evening with Charlie Chaplin and Ben Turpin; and "Hop-a-Long." Non-stop side-splitting fun.
1915 50m/B Charley Chase, Stan Laurel, Oliver Hardy, Charlie Chaplin, Ben Turpin, Arthur Lake. **VHS, Beta $24.95** VYY 🐾🐾🐾

Silent Laugh Makers, No. 2 Several short funny films of the silent picture era: "Fluttering Hearts," "Long Live the King," about a king who just can't get along with his nobles, starring Chase and Hardy; and "A Sea Dog Tale." All are unremittingly hilarious.
1917 50m/B Charley Chase, Oliver Hardy, Billy Bevan. **VHS, Beta $24.95** VYY 🐾🐾🐾

Silent Laugh Makers, No. 3 Four comedy shorts: "Picking Peaches" (1924), directed by Frank Capra, Langdon's first for Mack Sennett; "All Tied Up" (1925), featuring "A Ton of Fun"-four rotund comedians; "Don't Shove" (1919), featuring Harold Lloyd wooing Bebe Daniels; and "Some Baby" (1922), with Snub Pollard.
1919 55m/B Harry Langdon, Harold Lloyd, Bebe Daniels, Snub Pollard. **VHS, Beta $24.95** VYY 🐾🐾🐾

Silent Madness A psychiatrist must stop a deranged killer, escaped from an asylum, from slaughtering helpless college coeds in a sorority house. Meanwhile, hospital execs send orderlies to kill the patient, to conceal their mistake. Ludicrous.
1984 (R) 93m/C Belinda J. Montgomery, Viveca Lindfors, Sydney Lassick; *D:* Simon Nuchtern. **VHS, Beta $59.95** MED 🐾

The Silent Mr. Sherlock Holmes These two silent shorts are a rare treat for Holmes fans. "The Copper Beeches" was produced with the "personal supervision of Arthur Conan Doyle." In "The Man with the Twisted Lip," Holmes is hired to find out whether a banker was murdered.
1912 68m/B Ellie Norwood. **VHS $24.95** VYY 🐾🐾

Silent Motive Laura is a Hollywood screenwriter who's shocked to discover that a killer is using her recent script as an outline for a series of film-industry murders. She's even more unnerved when a detective makes Laura her number one suspect.
1991 90m/C Patricia Wettig, Mike Farrell, Ed Asner, Rick Springfield, David Packer; *D:* Lee Philips. **VHS $89.95** WOV 🐾🐾

Silent Movie A has-been movie director (Brooks) is determined to make a comeback and save his studio from being taken over by a conglomerate. Hilarious at times but uneven. An original idea; not as successful as it could have been. Has music and sound

effects, but only one word of spoken dialogue by famous mime Marceau.
1976 (PG) 88m/C Mel Brooks, Marty Feldman, Dom DeLuise, Burt Reynolds, Anne Bancroft, James Caan, Liza Minnelli, Paul Newman, Sid Caesar, Bernadette Peters, Harry Ritz, Marcel Marceau; *D:* Mel Brooks; *W:* Mel Brooks, Ron Clark, Rudy DeLuca, Barry Levinson. **VHS, Beta $14.98** FOX 🐾🐾½

Silent Movies...Just For the Fun of It! Three short silent films: "The Iron Mule" (1925), "For Sadie's Sake" (1926), and "Hazel from Hollywood" (1918).
1926 56m/B Jimmie Adams, Dorothy Devore, Al "Fuzzy" St. John. **VHS, Beta, 8mm $19.95** VYY 🐾🐾½

Silent Night, Bloody Night An escaped lunatic terrorizes a small New England town, particularly a mansion that was once an insane asylum. Not great, but well done by director Gershuny, with some nail-biting suspense and slick scene changes. *AKA:* Night of the Dark Full Moon; Death House.
1973 (R) 83m/C Patrick O'Neal, John Carradine, Walter Abel, Mary Woronov, Astrid Heeren, Candy Darling; *D:* Theodore Gershuny. **VHS** NO 🐾🐾

Silent Night, Deadly Night A psycho ax-murders people while dressed as jolly old St. Nick. Violent and disturbing, to say the least. Caused quite a controversy when it was released to theaters. Santa gimmick sold some tickets at the time, but resist the urge to rent it: it's completely devoid of worth, whatever the killer's outfit. As if one were not enough, we've been blessed with four sequels.
1984 (R) 92m/C Lilyan Chauvin, Gilmer McCormick, Toni Nero; *D:* Charles E. Sellier. **VHS, Beta $14.95** LIV, IME 🐾

Silent Night, Deadly Night 2 The psychotic little brother of the psychotic, Santa Claus-dressed killer from the first film exacts revenge, covering the same bloody ground as before. Almost half this sequel consists of scenes lifted whole from the original.
1987 (R) 88m/C Eric Freeman, James Newman, Elizabeth Cayton, Jean Miller; *D:* Lee Harry. **VHS, Beta $14.95** LIV 🐾

Silent Night, Deadly Night 3: Better Watch Out! The now grown-up psycho goes up against a young blind woman. Santa is no longer the bad guy, thank goodness. The least bad of the lot, with black humor—though not enough to make it worth seeing.
1989 (R) 90m/C Richard Beymer, Bill Moseley, Samantha Scully, Eric Dare, Laura Herring, Robert Culp; *D:* Monte Hellman. **VHS, Beta $14.95** LIV 🐾½

Silent Night, Deadly Night 4: Initiation A secret L.A. cult of she-demons use the slasher Ricky for their own ends—making for more mayhem and horror. Has virtually nothing to do with its three "sequels"—which is not to say it's very good.
1990 (R) 90m/C Maud Adams, Allyce Beasley, Clint Howard, Reggie Bannister; *D:* Brian Yuzna. **VHS $14.95** MOV 🐾

Silent Night, Deadly Night 5: The Toymaker A young boy's Christmas is overrun by murderous Santas and viscious stuffed animals. Definitely for fans of the genre only.
1991 (R) 90m/C Mickey Rooney, William Thorne, Jane Higginson. **VHS $89.95** LIV 🐾🐾

Silent Night, Lonely Night Two lonely middle-aged people (Bridges and Jones) begin an affair at Christmas to stem the pain of their separately disintegrating

marriages. Poignant but not successfully credible. Based on the play by Robert Anderson. Made for television.
1969 98m/C Lloyd Bridges, Shirley Jones, Jeff Bridges, Cloris Leachman, Carrie Snodgress, Lynn Carlin; *D:* Daniel Petrie; *M:* Billy Goldenberg. **VHS, Beta $39.95** MCA 🐾🐾

The Silent One Featuring underwater photography by Ron and Valerie Taylor, this is the odd story of a mysterious Polynesian boy who has a nautical relationship with a sea turtle.
1986 96m/C Telo Malese, George Henare; *D:* Yvonne Mackay. **VHS, Beta** NO 🐾½

The Silent Partner A bank teller (Gould) foils a robbery, but manages to take some money for himself. The unbalanced robber (Plummer) knows it and wants the money. Good script and well directed, with emphasis on suspense and detail. Unexpectedly violent at times. Early, non-comedic role for big guy Candy.
1978 103m/C Elliott Gould, Christopher Plummer, Susannah York, John Candy; *D:* Daryl Duke; *W:* Curtis Hanson. **VHS, Beta $29.98** VES 🐾🐾🐾

The Silent Passenger Amateur sleuth Lord Peter Wimsey makes cinematic debut investigating murder and blackmail on the British railway. Dorothy Sayer's character later inspired BBC mystery series.
1935 75m/B John Loder, Peter Haddon, Mary Newland, Austin Trevor, Donald Wolfit, Leslie Perrins, Aubrey Mather, Ralph Truman; *D:* Reginald Denham. **VHS, Beta $16.95** NOS, SNC 🐾🐾½

Silent Rage Sheriff Norris of a small Texas town must destroy killer Libby who has been made indestructible through genetic engineering. Chuck Norris meets Frankenstein, sort of. Nice try, but still thoroughly stupid and boring.
1982 (R) 100m/C Chuck Norris, Ron Silver, Steven Keats, Toni Kalem, Brian Libby; *D:* Michael Miller; *M:* Peter Bernstein. **VHS, Beta, 8mm $9.95** COL 🐾

Silent Raiders A commando unit is sent to France in 1943 to knock out a Nazi communications center.
1954 72m/B Richard Bartlett, Earle Lyon, Jeanette Bordeau; *M:* Elmer Bernstein. **VHS, Beta** NO 🐾

Silent Rebellion A Greek immigrant (Savalas) and his son return to Greece, where they reunite with mother and brother and re-discover their heritage and each other. Cross-cultural misunderstandings abound; could have been interesting, but the story is just too generic and uninspired.
1982 90m/C Telly Savalas, Keith Gordon, Michael Constantine, Yula Gavala. **VHS, Beta** NO 🐾½

Silent Running Members of a space station orbiting Saturn care for the last vegetation of a nuclear-devastated earth. When orders come to destroy the vegetation, Dern takes matters into his own hands. Speculative sci-fi at its best. Trumbull's directorial debut; he created special effects for "2001" and "Close Encounters." Strange music enhances the alien atmosphere.
1971 (G) 90m/C Bruce Dern, Cliff Potts, Ron Rifkin; *D:* Douglas Trumbull; *W:* Michael Cimino, Deric Washburn, Steven Bochco; *M:* Prof. Peter Schickele. **VHS, Beta $14.98** MCA 🐾🐾🐾

Silent Scream College kids take up residence with the owners of an eerie mansion complete with obligatory murders. Obvious to the point of being gratuitous—and just plain uninteresting.

1980 (R) 87m/C Rebecca Balding, Cameron Mitchell, Avery Schreiber, Barbara Steele, Steve Doubet, Brad Reardon, Yvonne De Carlo; **D:** Denny Harris. **VHS, Beta** $29.95 MED 🎞½

Silent Scream A former Nazi concentration camp commandant collects unusual animals and humans as a hobby.
1984 60m/C Peter Cushing, Brian Cox, Elaine Donnelly; **D:** Alan Gibson. **VHS, Beta** $29.95 LIV 🎞

Silent Tongue Weird western finds the crazed Talbot Roe (Phoenix) alone in the wilderness, guarding the tree that is the burial place of his half-breed wife Awbonnie (Tousey). Roe's father (Harris) bought his son's bride from her greedy and abusive father McCree (Bates). In an effort to return Talbot to some semblance of normality, Roe offers to buy McCree's other daughter (Arredondo) for his son. But Talbot is haunted by his wife's angry ghost, who wants her spirit set free by ritual burning, and McCree himself fears the vengeance of his one-time Indian tribe Silent Tongue (Cardinal). Messy, over-the-top plot with some poignant performances, especially Phoenix's.
1992 (PG-13) 101m/C River Phoenix, Sheila Tousey, Richard Harris, Alan Bates, Jeri Arrendondo, Dermot Mulroney, Tantoo Cardinal; **Cameos:** Bill Irwin, David Shiner; **D:** Sam Shepard; **W:** Sam Shepard; **M:** Patrick O'Hearn. **VHS** $94.99 VMK 🎞🎞

Silent Valley Adventure of the Old West with American cowboy star Tom Tyler.
1935 60m/B Tom Tyler. **VHS, Beta** $19.95 NOS, VCN, DVT 🎞

Silent Victim Greene stars as Bonnie Jackson, a Georgia housewife whose marriage has not only gone wrong but turned violent. She takes a drug overdose in a suicide attempt but it results only in a miscarriage. Her furious husband sues her for the murder of their unborn child while an ambitious district attorney petitions the state to charge Bonnie with committing an illegal abortion. Bonnie's torment soon becomes a media circus as she goes on trial. Based on a true story.
1992 (R) 116m/C Michelle Greene, Kyle Secor, Ely Pouget, Alex Hyde-White, Dori Brenner, Leann Hunley; **D:** Menahem Golan; **W:** Nelly Adnil, Jonathan Platnick; **M:** William T. Stromberg. **VHS** $89.95 COL 🎞½

Silent Victory: The Kitty O'Neil Story Genuinely stirring real-life-overcoming-adversity story of the deaf woman who became a top stunt woman in Hollywood and holder of the land speed record for women. Channing is very good as O'Neil. Made for television.
1979 96m/C Stockard Channing, Brian Dennehy, Colleen Dewhurst, Edward Albert, James Farentino; **D:** Lou Antonio. **VHS** NO 🎞🎞

Silent Witness A woman (Bertinelli) witnesses her brother-in-law and his friend rape a young woman. She must decide whether to testify against them or keep the family secret. Exploitative and weakly plotted. Rip-off of the much-discussed Massachusetts barroom rape case. Made for television.
1985 (R) 97m/C Valerie Bertinelli, John Savage, Chris Nash, Melissa Leo, Pat Corley, Steven Williams, Jacqueline Brookes, Alex McArthur, Katie McCombs; **D:** Michael Miller. **VHS, Beta** $79.95 ACA 🎞

Silhouette Detained in a small Texas town, a woman witnesses the murder of a local girl—but in silhouette, so the killer's identity takes a feature-length running time to resolve. A fair but contrived made for cable TV thriller that the leading lady co-produced.

1991 (R) 89m/C Faye Dunaway, David Rasche, John Terry, Carlos Gomez, Ron Campbell, Margaret Blye, Talisa Soto, Ritch Brinkley; **D:** Carl Schenkel. **VHS** $79.95 MCA 🎞🎞

Silk A beautiful and bloodthirsty detective cuts a swath through local heroin rings.
1986 (R) 84m/C Cec Verrell, Bill McLaughlin, Fred Bailey; **D:** Cirio H. Santiago. **VHS, Beta** $79.95 MGM 🎞

Silk 2 A foreign-made sequel, in which a beautiful cop stops crime in Honolulu. Ludicrous plot, bad acting, lots of skin and violence—what more could you want? Dreadful.
1989 (R) 85m/C Monique Gabrielle, Peter Nelson, Jan Merlin, Maria Clair; **D:** Cirio H. Santiago. **VHS, Beta** $44.98 MGM 🎞

The Silk Road In 11th-century China the ancient trading route leads to Dun Huang, a desert city that is the last Chinese outpost on the road. Zhao, a young scholar, travels in a caravan which is attacked by Chinese mercenaries. His life is spared and when his new home is attacked by a neighboring nation, he hides the city's treasures in nearby caves. Adapted from the novel by Yashushi Inoue, which was based on the Thousand Buddha Caves, where a treasure of Buddhist icons and scrolls were discovered in 1900. Billed as an epic, there's lots of pageantry and some impressive battle scenes but is too stately and overdone to be more than merely interesting. In Japanese with English subtitles.
1992 (PG-13) 99m/C Koichi Sato, Toshiyuki Nishida, Anna Nakagawa, Tsunehiko Watase, Daijiro Harada, Takahiro Tamura; **D:** Junya Sato; **M:** Masaru Sato. **VHS** $89.90 VMK, ING 🎞🎞½

Silk Stockings Splendid musical comedy adaptation of "Ninotchka," with Astaire as a charming American movie man, and Charisse as the cold Soviet official whose commie heart he melts. Music and lyrics by Cole Porter highlight this film adapted from George S. Kaufman's hit Broadway play. Director Mamoulian's last film. 🎵Too Bad; Paris Loves Lovers; Fated to Be Mated; The Ritz Roll 'n Rock; Silk Stockings; Red Blues; All of You; Stereophonic Sound; Josephine.
1957 117m/C Fred Astaire, Cyd Charisse, Janis Paige, Peter Lorre, George Tobias; **D:** Rouben Mamoulian. **VHS, Beta** $29.95 MGM, TTC 🎞🎞🎞

Silkwood The story of Karen Silkwood, who died in a 1974 car crash under suspicious circumstances. She was a nuclear plant worker and activist who was investigating shoddy practices at the plant. Streep acts up a storm, disappearing completely into her character. Cher surprises with her fine portrayal of a lesbian co-worker, and Russell is also good. Nichols has a tough time since we already know the ending, but he brings topnotch performances from his excellent cast.
1983 (R) 131m/C Meryl Streep, Kurt Russell, Cher, Diana Scarwid, Bruce McGill, Fred Ward, David Strathairn, Ron Silver, Josef Sommer, Craig T. Nelson; **D:** Mike Nichols; **W:** Nora Ephron, Alice Arlen; **M:** Georges Delerue. Academy Awards '83 Nominations: Best Actress (Streep), Best Director (Nichols), Best Film Editing, Best Original Screenplay, Best Supporting Actress (Cher); Golden Globe Awards '84: Best Supporting Actress (Cher). **VHS, Beta** $9.98 SUE 🎞🎞🎞

Silver Bandit A bookkeeper is sent to investigate a mine theft. Along the way he sings country and western songs.
1947 54m/B Spade Cooley. **VHS, Beta** $19.95 NOS 🎞

Silver Bears Caine is an unlikely mobster in this comedy. He's sent to Switzerland to buy a bank for laundering purposes and ends up being swindled himself. So-so entry adapted from the novel by Paul Erdman.
1978 (PG) 114m/C Michael Caine, Cybill Shepherd, Louis Jourdan, Stephane Audran, David Warner, Tom Smothers, Martin Balsam, Jay Leno, Charles Gray, Joss Ackland; **D:** Ivan Passer; **M:** Claude Bolling. **VHS, Beta** NO 🎞🎞

Silver Bullet Adapted from Stephen King's "Cycle of the Werewolf," about a town whose inhabitants are being brutally murdered. It finally dawns on them the culprit is a werewolf. Action moves along at a good clip and the film has its share of suspense. **AKA:** Stephen King's Silver Bullet.
1985 (R) 95m/C Corey Haim, Gary Busey, Megan Follows, Everett McGill; **D:** Daniel Attias; **W:** Stephen King. **VHS** $14.95 PAR 🎞🎞

The Silver Chalice Newman's career somehow survived his movie debut in this bloated, turgid Biblical epic about the momentous events that befall a young Greek sculptor who fashions the cup that will be used at the Last Supper. Newman later took out an ad in Variety to apologize for the film, in which Greene also made his debut. Based on the novel by Thomas Costain.
1954 135m/C Paul Newman, Virginia Mayo, Pier Angeli, Jack Palance, Natalie Wood, Joseph Wiseman, Lorne Greene, E.G. Marshall; **D:** Victor Saville; **M:** Franz Waxman. **VHS, Beta** $19.98 WAR 🎞

Silver City A saga depicting the plight of Polish refugees in Australia in 1949. A pair of lovers find each other in a crowded refugee camp. He's married to her friend. Too-complex, slow but earnest effort.
1984 (PG) 110m/C Gosia Dobrowolska, Ivar Kants; **D:** Sophia Turkiewicz. **VHS, Beta** $59.95 LHV 🎞🎞

Silver City Bonanza Lots of action in this outrageous oater that includes a haunted ranch and an undersea battle as plot devices. Singing cowboy Allen and sidekick Ebsen use a seeing-eye dog to track down the killer of a blind man. Since Roy Rogers and Republic parted company the year of this film's release, singing star Allen was groomed to become the new "King of the Cowboys." However, by this time, the singing-cowboy craze was almost old hat.
1951 67m/B Rex Allen, Buddy Ebsen, Mary Ellen Kay, Billy Kimbley, Alix Ebsen, Bill Kennedy, Gregg Barton, Clem Bevans; **D:** George Blair; **W:** Bob Williams. **VHS** $19.99 MOV 🎞🎞½

Silver City Kid A foreman for a silver mine exposes a corrupt local banker as a thief.
1945 56m/B Allan "Rocky" Lane. **VHS, Beta** $24.95 DVT 🎞

Silver Dream Racer An English grease monkey wants to win the World Motorcycle Championship title away from an American biker. He's also after someone else's girlfriend. Boring, stilted, unoriginal "Big Race" flick.
1983 (PG) 103m/C Beau Bridges, David Essex, Christina Raines, Diane Keen, Harry H. Corbett; **D:** David Wickes; **M:** David Essex. **VHS, Beta** $69.98 LIV, VES 🎞½

Silver Lode A man accused of murder on his wedding day attempts to clear his name while the law launches an intensive manhunt for him. Ordinary story improved by good, energetic cast.
1954 92m/C John Payne, Dan Duryea, Lizabeth Scott, Stuart Whitman; **D:** Allan Dwan. **VHS, Beta** NO 🎞🎞½

Silver Queen A woman finds out her father has gambled away a silver mine and left her with debts. She opens a saloon, only to have her fiance use the money to hunt for more silver.
1942 81m/B Priscilla Lane, George Brent, Bruce Cabot, Eugene Pallette; **D:** Lloyd Bacon. **VHS, Beta** NO ♯♯

Silver River Average western that marked the final collaboration between director Walsh and star Flynn. It never even comes close to their previous works. Flynn plays a no-good, power-hungry cad who will stop at nothing to get what he wants. He happens to want Sheridan, who is married to Bennett, so Flynn schemes to get rid of him. Overall, Flynn acts as though he really isn't interested in the material and had to make a pact with Walsh that he would stay sober until five in the afternoon while filming. Based on an unpublished novel by Stephen Longstreet.
1948 108m/B Errol Flynn, Ann Sheridan, Thomas Mitchell, Bruce (Herman Brix) Bennett, Tom D'Andrea, Barton MacLane, Monte Blue, Jonathan Hale; **D:** Raoul Walsh; **W:** Stephen Longstreet, Harriet Frank Jr. **VHS $19.98** MGM ♯♯½

Silver Spurs Villain tries to get some oil-rich property by murdering the ranch's owner. Ranch foreman Rogers saves the day.
1943 60m/B Roy Rogers, Jerome Cowan, John Carradine, Phyllis Brooks, Smiley Burnette, Joyce Compton; **D:** Joseph Kane. **VHS, Beta $19.95** NOS, VCN, DVT ♯♯½

Silver Stallion Thunder the Wonder Horse plays the title character, who fights rattlesnakes, wild dogs and hoss thieves. Too bad he doesn't give acting lessons to the humans in the this frail family western with nice scenery and action scenes.
1941 59m/C David Sharpe, Carol Hughes, Leroy Mason, Walter Long; **D:** Edward Finney. **VHS, Beta $19.95** VYY, GPV ♯½

The Silver Stallion: King of the Wild Brumbies The adolescent Indi is enthralled as her writer-mother relates each new chapter in the saga of Thara, the amazing silver stallion. And she images each adventure as the horse triumphs over evil men, other horses, and the elements to become leader of the herd. Based on the Australian children's novel "The Silver Brumby" by Elyne Mitchell.
1994 (G) 93m/C Caroline Goodall, Ami Daemion, Russell Crowe; **D:** John Tatoulis; **W:** John Tatoulis, Jon Stephens; **M:** Tassos Ioannides. **VHS, Beta** PAR ♯♯½

Silver Star Man elected sheriff of a western town turns down the job because he is a pacifist. He changes his mind when his defeated opponent hires a trio of killers to come after him.
1955 73m/B Jimmy Wakely, Edgar Buchanan, Marie Windsor. **VHS, Beta** NO ♯♯

The Silver Streak The sickly son of a diesel train designer needs an iron lung—pronto. A rival's super-fast locomotive is the only hope for the boy. Murders, runaway engines, and a crew that would rather walk enliven this race against time.
1934 72m/B Sally Blane, Charles Starrett, Arthur Lake, Edgar Kennedy, William Farnum; **D:** Thomas Atkins. **VHS, Beta $17.95** CCB ♯♯

The Silver Streak Pooped exec Wilder rides a train from L.A. to Chicago, planning to enjoy a leisurely, relaxing trip. Instead he becomes involved with murder, intrigue, and a beautiful woman. Energetic Hitchcock parody features successful first pairing of Wilder and Pryor.

1976 (PG) 113m/C Gene Wilder, Richard Pryor, Jill Clayburgh, Patrick McGoohan, Ned Beatty, Ray Walston, Richard Kiel, Scatman Crothers; **D:** Arthur Hiller; **W:** Colin Higgins; **M:** Henry Mancini. **VHS, Beta $14.98** FOX ♯♯♯

Silverado Affectionate pastiche of western cliches has everything a viewer could ask for—except Indians. Straightforward plot has four virtuous cowboys rise up against a crooked lawman in a blaze of six guns. No subtlety from the first big Western in quite a while, but plenty of fun and laughs. Laserdisc edition features a wide screen film-to-tape transfer monitored by the photography director, set photos, release trailers, and other publicity hoohah as well as a special time-lapse sequence of the set construction, and interviews with the stars and director Kasdan. Letterboxed laserdisc version is available with dolby surround sound.
1985 (PG-13) 132m/C Kevin Kline, Scott Glenn, Kevin Costner, Danny Glover, Brian Dennehy, Linda Hunt, John Cleese, Jeff Goldblum, Rosanna Arquette, Jeff Fahey; **D:** Lawrence Kasdan; **W:** Lawrence Kasdan; **M:** Bruce Broughton. **VHS, Beta $14.95** COL, VYG, CRC ♯♯♯

Simba A young Englishman arrives at his brother's Kenyan farm to find him murdered in a local skirmish between the Mau Maus and white settlers. Well made, thoughtful look at colonialism, racial animosity, and violence.
1955 98m/C Dirk Bogarde, Donald Sinden, Virginia McKenna, Orlando Martins; **D:** Brian Desmond Hurst. **VHS, Beta** NO ♯♯♯

Simon A group of bored demented scientists brainwash a college professor into believing he is an alien from a distant galaxy, whereupon he begins trying to correct the evil in America. Screwball comedy, or semi-serious satire of some kind? Hard to tell. Some terrific set pieces but the movie as a whole doesn't quite hold together. Directorial debut of Brickman, who previously worked as a scriptwriter with Woody Allen ("Sleeper," etc.).
1980 (PG) 97m/C Alan Arkin, Madeline Kahn, Fred Gwynne, Adolph Green, Wallace Shawn, Austin Pendleton; **D:** Marshall Brickman; **W:** Marshall Brickman. **VHS, Beta $19.98** WAR ♯♯½

Simon Blanco A hero of the Mexican Revolution is tricked by men who want to kill him and steal his wife.
1987 145m/C Antonio Aguilar, Jacqueline Andere, Mario Almada, Valentin Trujillo. **VHS, Beta $59.95** MAD ♯♯

Simon Bolivar The title character leads the Venezuelan revolution in 1817.
1969 110m/C Maximilian Schell, Rosanna Schiaffino. **VHS, Beta $49.95** UNI ♯♯½

Simon, King of the Witches An L.A. warlock who lives in a sewer drain finds himself the center of attention when his spells actually work. This interesting hippie/witchcraft entry bogs down now and then but Prine's performance is droll and lively.
1971 (R) 90m/C Andrew Prine, Brenda Scott, George Paulsin, Norman Burton, Ultra Violet; **D:** Bruce Kessler. **VHS, Beta $59.95** UNI ♯♯½

Simon of the Desert Not Bunuel's very best, but worthy of the master satirist. An ascetic stands on a pillar in the desert for several decades—closer to God, farther from temptation. Pinal is a gorgeous devil that tempts Simon. Hilarious, irreverent, sophisticated. What's with the weird ending, though? In Spanish with English subtitles.
1966 43m/B D: Luis Bunuel. **VHS, Beta $68.00** NOS, HHT, DVT ♯♯♯½

Simple Justice Mindless, justice-in-own-hands anti-liberal hogwash. Overwrought, smug, and violent story of a young couple beaten by robbers who remain at large.
1989 (R) 91m/C Cesar Romero, John Spencer, Doris Roberts, Candy McClain; **D:** Deborah Del Prete. **VHS $59.95** JTC ♯½

Simple Men Odd-ball brothers Bill (a petty criminal) and Dennis (a shy college student) decide to track down their missing father in this fractured comedy. Dad, a former big-league baseball player who bombed the Pentagon in the '60s, is a long-time fugitive hiding out somewhere in the wilds of Long Island. Their search leads them to two equally opposite women, the wary Kate, whom Bill immediately falls for, and the sexy Elina, who turns out to know dear old dad quite well. Deliberately deadpan and cliched, Hartley's quirky style can either irritate or illuminate via the weird turnings of his characters' lives.
1992 (R) 105m/C Robert Burke, William Sage, Karen Sillas, Elina Lowensohn, Martin Donovan, Mark Bailey, John MacKay; **D:** Hal Hartley; **W:** Hal Hartley; **M:** Hal Hartley. **VHS** COL, IME, NLC ♯♯♯

A Simple Story A woman faces her 40th birthday with increasing uneasiness, though her life seems perfect from the outside. She evaluates her chances at love, child-bearing, and friendship, after having an abortion and breaking up with her lover. Schneider's performance is brilliant in this gentle, quiet drama. In French with English subtitles. **AKA:** Une Histoire Simple.
1979 110m/C Romy Schneider, Bruno Cremer, Claude Brasseur; **D:** Claude Sautet. **VHS, Beta $59.95** COL, ING ♯♯♯

The Simple Truth A woman's romance novel is dramatized, dealing with a receptionist who has a fling with the company president.
1985 90m/C Beta $14.95 PSM Woof!

A Simple Twist of Fate Comedy drama gives Martin chance to flex serious muscles with this update of George Eliot's "Silas Marner." Adoptive father Michael McMann wants to keep his daughter Mathilda (played by the prerequisite adorable twins) in the face of demands from her biological father (Byrne), who happens to be a local politician. Then revelations brought out at the custody hearing threaten the politician's career. Cuddly dad is hardly Martin's image (in spite of "Parenthood"), though strong cast limits the sugar.
1994 ?m/C Steve Martin, Gabriel Byrne, Catherine O'Hara, Stephen Baldwin, Alana Austin, Alyssa Austin, Laura Linney, Anne Heche, Michael Des Barres, Byron Jennings; **D:** Gilles Mackinnon; **W:** Steve Martin. **VHS** NYR ♯♯½

Sin of Adam & Eve The story of Adam and Eve in the Garden of Eden and their fall from grace. Voice-over narrator is only sound in this strange dialogue-less story of the Adam and Eve, how they got kicked out of the Garden of Eden, and how they lose and then find each other outside. Ancient plot, to say the least.
1972 (R) 72m/C Candy Wilson, Jorge Rivero; **D:** Michael Zachary. **VHS, Beta $19.95** VDM, VCI ♯

The Sin of Harold Diddlebock A man gets fired from his job, stumbles around drunk, and wins a fortune gambling. He then buys a circus and uses a lion to frighten investors into backing him. Inventive comedy, but missing the spark and timing of "The Freshman" (1925), of which it is a sequel.

The final feature film for Lloyd (who did all his own stunts), made at the urging of director Sturges. **AKA:** Mad Wednesday.
1947 89m/B Harold Lloyd, Margaret Hamilton, Frances Ramsden, Edgar Kennedy, Lionel Stander, Rudy Vallee, Franklin Pangborn; **D:** Preston Sturges. **VHS, Beta $14.95** NOS, BAR, AOV 🎬🎬½

The Sin of Madelon Claudet
Hayes plays common thief who works her way into upper crust of Parisian society only to tumble back into the street, all in the name of making a better life for her illegitimate son. Very sudsy stuff, with an outstanding performance by Hayes. **AKA:** The Lullaby.
1931 74m/B Helen Hayes, Lewis Stone, Neil Hamilton, Robert Young, Cliff Edwards, Jean Hersholt, Marie Prevost, Karen Morley, Charles Winninger, Alan Hale; **D:** Edgar Selwyn. **VHS $19.98** MGM, FCT 🎬🎬🎬

Sin Salida
A man is chased through Mexico City by the Mafia.
1987 97m/C Jorge Rivero, Nadia Milton, Mario Almada, Daniela Rosen. **VHS, Beta $58.95** MAD 🎬

Sin Takes a Holiday
A woman marries her boss to save him from his girl friend. On a trip to Paris, she is wooed by a refined European gentleman, but finds that she really does love her husband. By today's standards, it doesn't sound like much, but in the '30s, it was pretty sophisticated stuff.
1930 81m/B Constance Bennett, Kenneth MacKenna, Basil Rathbone, Rita La Roy, ZaSu Pitts, Fred Walton, Richard Carle, Helen Johnson; **D:** Paul Stein. **VHS $19.95** NOS, HEG 🎬🎬½

Sin You Sinners
Aging stripper gets ahold of an amulet that allows her to look youthful and manipulate the lives of others. When she loses the amulet, however, bad things happen. Twisted ending.
1963 73m/B June Colbourne, Dian Lloyd, Derek Murcott, Beverly Nazarow, Charles Clements; **D:** Anthony Farrar. **VHS $16.95** SNC 🎬

Sinai Commandos
The story of a group of commandos in the Israeli Six-Day War in 1967 who are assigned to destroy important Arab radar installations. Includes actual combat footage. **AKA:** Sinai Commandos: The Story of the Six Day War; Ha'Matarah Tiran.
1968 99m/C Robert Fuller; **D:** Raphael Nussbaum. **VHS $29.95** ATL, FCT 🎬🎬½

Sinatra
Made for television biopic chronicles the stormy life of crooner Frank Sinatra. Begins with his childhood in Hoboken, New Jersey and works its way through his big band tours, bobby soxer days, career skids, and triumphant comeback with his Oscar-winning performance in "From Here to Eternity," as well as his three marriages, "Rat Pack" friends, and mob connections. Executive Producer Tina Sinatra, Frank's daughter, doesn't gloss over her father's less savory character points and Casnoff does well with his leading role. Songs are lip-synched to classic Sinatra tunes with a few early recordings redone by actor Tom Burlinson and Frank Sinatra, Jr.
1992 245m/C Philip Casnoff, Olympia Dukakis, Joe Santos, Gina Gershon, Nina Siemaszko, Marcia Gay Harden, Rod Steiger, Bob Gunton, David Raynr, James F. Kelly, Matthew Posey, Jay Robinson, Robin Gammell, Todd Waring, Joris Stuyck, Danny Gans, Jeff Corey; **D:** James Sadwith; **W:** William Mastrosimone. **VHS, Beta $29.98** WAR 🎬🎬½

Sinbad
A sardonic portrait of an aging hedonist as he tries to hold onto the pleasures of drink, sex and gluttony. In Magyar (Hungarian), with English subtitles.

1971 98m/C **D:** Zoltan Huszarik. **VHS, Beta $69.95** KIV, FCT 🎬🎬

Sinbad and the Eye of the Tiger
The swashbuckling adventures of Sinbad the Sailor as he encounters the creations of Ray Harryhausen's special effects magic. Don't see this one for the plot, which almost doesn't exist. Otherwise, mildly fun.
1977 (G) 113m/C Patrick Wayne, Jane Seymour, Taryn Power, Margaret Whiting; **D:** Sam Wanamaker; **W:** Beverly Cross. **VHS, Beta $14.95** COL, CCB 🎬🎬

Sinbad of the Seven Seas
Italian muscle epic based on the ancient legends. Ferrigno isn't green, but he's still a hulk, and he still can't act. It's poorly dubbed, which makes little difference; it would be stupid regardless.
1989 90m/C Lou Ferrigno, John Steiner, Leo Gullotta, Teagan Clive; **D:** Enzo G. Castellari. **VHS, Beta $89.95** WAR, OM 🎬½

Sinbad the Sailor
Fairbanks fits well in his luminent father's swashbuckling shoes, as he searches for the treasure of Alexander the Great. Self-mocking but hamhanded, and confusing if you seek the hidden plot. Still, it's all in fun, and it is fun.
1947 117m/C Douglas Fairbanks Jr., Maureen O'Hara, Anthony Quinn, Walter Slezak, George Tobias, Jane Greer, Mike Mazurki, Sheldon Leonard; **D:** Richard Wallace. **VHS, Beta $24.95** RKO, MED, TTC 🎬🎬🎬

Since You Went Away
An American family copes with the tragedy, heartache and shortages of wartime in classic mega-tribute to the home front. Be warned: very long and bring your hankies. Colbert is superb, as is the photography. John Derek unobtrusively made his film debut, as an extra.
1944 172m/B Claudette Colbert, Jennifer Jones, Shirley Temple, Joseph Cotten, Agnes Moorehead, Monty Woolley, Guy Madison, Lionel Barrymore, Robert Walker, Hattie McDaniel, Keenan Wynn, Craig Stevens, Albert Basserman, Alla Nazimova, Lloyd Corrigan, Terry Moore, Florence Bates, Ruth Roman, Andrew V. McLaglen, Dorothy Dandridge, Rhonda Fleming; **D:** John Cromwell; **W:** David O. Selznick; **M:** Max Steiner. Academy Awards '44: Best Score; Nominations: Academy Awards '44: Best Supporting Actress (Jones); Academy Awards '44: Best Actress (Colbert), Best Black and White Cinematography, Best Film Editing, Best Interior Decoration, Best Picture, Best Supporting Actor (Woolley). **VHS, Beta $39.98** FOX 🎬🎬🎬½

Sincerely Charlotte
Huppert directs her sister in this film about a beautiful singer framed for her boyfriend's murder. She enlists an old lover to help her flee across the countryside. Love story/thriller is pleasingly odd and absorbing. In French with English subtitles. **AKA:** Signe Charlotte.
1986 92m/C Isabelle Huppert, Niels Arestrup, Christine Pascal; **D:** Caroline Huppert. **VHS, Beta $79.95** COL, ING 🎬🎬🎬

Sincerely Yours
Liberace wisely stayed away from acting after inauspiciously debuting in this horrible, maudlin remake of "The Man Who Played God." He plays a pianist who loses his hearing and decides to become a philanthropist to help those less fortunate than himself. Laughably cheesy. Thirty-one musical numbers, including Liberace's inimitable arrangement of "Chopsticks."
1956 116m/C Liberace, Joanne Dru, Dorothy Malone, William Demarest; **D:** Gordon Douglas; **W:** Irving Wallace. **VHS, Beta $19.98** WAR Woof!

Sinful Life
A strained, offbeat, B-grade comedy about an odd, infantile mother fighting to keep her unusual child from being taken away. Definitely not a must-see; can be irritating and obnoxious, depending on

viewer and mood. Morris is at her oddball comedic best as the mother and former show dancer. Adult Tefkin plays her little girl. Based on the play "Just Like the Pom Pom Girls."
1989 (R) 112m/C Anita Morris, Rick Overton, Dennis Christopher, Blair Tefkin, Mark Rolston, Cynthia Szigeti; **D:** William Schreiner. **VHS, Beta $89.95** COL 🎬🎬

Sing
The students in the real-life Brooklyn public school "Sing" program endure the trials of adolescence while putting together a musical revue. Hurtles over the edge into cheesiness from the start, with way too much (cheesy) music. From the creator of "Fame" and "Footloose."
1989 (PG-13) 111m/C Lorraine Bracco, Peter Dobson, Jessica Steen, Louise Lasser, George DiCenzo, Patti LaBelle; **D:** Richard Baskin; **M:** Jay Gruska. **VHS, Beta $89.95** COL 🎬½

Sing, Cowboy, Sing
Decent adventure story about a wagon train heading west that runs into a band of outlaws doing outlaw stuff and must somehow get through.
1937 60m/B Tex Ritter. **VHS, Beta $19.95** NOS, DVT 🎬🎬

Sing Sing Nights
A world-famous journalist is killed with three bullets. Three men have confessed, but only one could have actually done it. A professor sets out to solve the case. **AKA:** Reprieved.
1935 60m/B Conway Tearle, Mary Doran, Hardie Albright, Patricia "Boots" Mallory, Ferdinand Gottschalk, Berton Churchill, Jameson Thomas; **D:** Lewis Collins. **VHS $16.95** SNC 🎬½

Sing Your Worries Away
Songwriter Ebsen inherits 3 million dollars and finds the money causes him nothing but trouble. Band of crooks cause the requisite wacky complications. Fun, harmless musical comedy. 🎵It Just Happened to Happen; Sally, My Dear Sally; Sing Your Worries Away; Cindy Lou McWilliams; How Do You Fall in Love.
1942 71m/B Buddy Ebsen, Bert Lahr, June Havoc, Patsy Kelly, Margaret Dumont; **D:** Edward Sutherland. **VHS, Beta** CCB 🎬🎬

Singin' in the Rain
One of the all-time great movie musicals—an affectionate spoof of the turmoil that afflicted the motion picture industry in the late 1920s during the changeover from silent films to sound. Co-director Kelly and Hagen lead a glorious cast. Music and lyrics by Arthur Freed and Nacio Herb Brown. Served as basis of story by Betty Comden and Adolph Green. Also available on laserdisc with the original trailer, outtakes, behind the scenes footage, and commentary by film historian Ronald Haver. Later a Broadway musical. 🎵All I Do is Dream of You; Should I?; Singin' in the Rain; Wedding of the Painted Doll; Broadway Melody; Would You; I've Got a Feelin' You're Foolin'; You Are My Lucky Star; Broadway Rhythm.
1952 103m/C Gene Kelly, Donald O'Connor, Jean Hagen, Debbie Reynolds, Rita Moreno, King Donovan, Millard Mitchell, Cyd Charisse, Douglas Fowley, Madge Blake, Joi Lansing; **D:** Gene Kelly, Stanley Donen; **W:** Adolph Green, Betty Comden. Academy Awards '52: Nominations: Best Supporting Actress (Hagen), Best Original Score; Golden Globe Awards '53: Best Actor—Musical/Comedy (O'Connor); National Board of Review Awards '52: 10 Best Films of the Year. **VHS, Beta $19.98** MGM, VYG, TLF 🎬🎬🎬🎬

The Singing Blacksmith
A relic of American Yiddish cinema, adapting popular 1909 play by David Pinski. A married blacksmith is wooed by another woman and falls victim to alcoholism. Overlong, but Oysher and his rich baritone voice still shine. In Yiddish with English subtitles.

1938 95m/B Miriam Riselle, Florence Weiss, Moishe Oysher; *D:* Edgar G. Ulmer. **VHS** $79.95 ERG, ING *〽〽½*

Singing Buckaroo Dastardly bandits try to pilfer money from pretty blonde damsel and have to battle with yodelin' cowboy. B-level western good guy Scott belts out a few numbers and saves the day. Innocuously pleasant.
1937 58m/B Fred Scott, Victoria Vinton, Cliff Nazarro; *D:* Tom Gibson. **VHS, Beta** $19.95 NOS, VYY *〽〽*

The Singing Nun The true story of a Belgian nun who takes a liking to a motherless little boy. She writes a song for him, and a kind-hearted priest talks to a record producer to see about getting the song to go somewhere. The song soon becomes an international hit, and the nun ends up on the "Ed Sullivan Show." Sentimental and sugary sweet, but a big box-office hit.
1966 98m/C Debbie Reynolds, Ricardo Montalban, Greer Garson, Agnes Moorehead, Chad Everett, Katharine Ross, Juanita Moore, Ricky Cordell, Michael Pate, Tom Drake; *D:* Henry Koster. **VHS** $19.98 MGM *〽〽*

Singing the Blues in Red Dark, pessimistic character study of a protest singer/songwriter who leaves his native East Germany to escape repression and finds his loyalties divided. A moving personal story, as well as insightful, subtle social commentary. In English and German with subtitles. Cinematography by Chris Menges.
1987 110m/C Gerulf Pannach, Fabienne Babe, Cristine Rose, Trevor Griffiths; *D:* Ken Loach; *W:* Trevor Griffiths. **VHS, Beta** NO *〽〽〽*

Single Bars, Single Women Utterly formulaic made for TV comedy-drama based on Dolly Parton's song is not entirely without merit. Lonely people gather in a local pickup joint and share their miseries and hopes.
1984 96m/C Shelley Hack, Christine Lahti, Tony Danza, Mare Winningham, Keith Gordon, Paul Michael Glaser; *D:* Harry Winer. **VHS, Beta** $79.95 PSM, PAR, VTR *〽½*

Single Room Furnished The fall of a buxom blonde from uncorrupted innocence through pregnancies to desperate prostitution. Fails to demonstrate any range of talent in Mansfield, who died before it was completed. Exploitative and pathetic.
1968 93m/C Jayne Mansfield, Dorothy Keller; *D:* Matt Cimber, Matteo Ottaviano. **VHS, Beta** $29.95 VCI, HEG *〽½*

The Single Standard San Francisco deb Garbo flings with artsy Asther and finds out the Hayes Code is just around the corner.
1929 93m/B Greta Garbo, Nils Asther, Johnny Mack Brown, Dorothy Sebastian, Lane Chandler, Zeffie Tilbury; *D:* John S. Robertson. **VHS** $29.99 MGM, FCT *〽〽*

Single White Female Psycho thriller casts Fonda as chic Manhattan computer consultant Allison Jones, who advertises for a roommate after a falling out with her boyfriend. Leigh is the frumpy, shy, bookstore clerk Hedra who answers the ad and moves into Allie's great Upper West Side apartment. They hit it off, that is until Allie notices Hedra's beginning to look and sound very familiar. Hmm... Derivative, though bonus points for creative murder implements and interesting performances throughout, including Friedman as Allie's gay upstairs neighbor. Based on the novel "SWF Seeks Same" by John Lutz.
1992 (R) 107m/C Bridget Fonda, Jennifer Jason Leigh, Steven Weber, Peter Friedman, Stephen Tobolowsky, Francis Bay, Renee Estevez, Kenneth Tobey; *D:* Barbet Schroeder; *W:* Don

Roos; *M:* Howard Shore. **VHS, Beta, 8mm** $19.95 COL, BTV *〽〽½*

Singles Seattle's music scene is the background for this lighthearted look at single twentysomethings in the '90s. Hits dead on thanks to Crowe's tight script and a talented cast, and speaks straight to its intended audience—the "Generation X" crowd. Real life band Pearl Jam plays alternative band Citizen Dick and sets the tone for a great soundtrack featuring the hot Seattle sounds of Alice in Chains, Soundgarden, and Mudhoney. The video contains six extra minutes of footage after the credits that was thankfully edited out of the final cut. Look for Horton, Stoltz (as a mime), Skerritt, and Burton in cameos.
1992 (PG-13) 100m/C Matt Dillon, Bridget Fonda, Campbell Scott, Kyra Sedgwick, Sheila Kelley, Jim True, Bill Pullman, James LeGros, Ally Walker, Devon Raymond, Camillo Gallardo, Jeremy Piven; *Cameos:* Tom Skerritt, Peter Horton, Eric Stoltz, Tim Burton; *D:* Cameron Crowe; *W:* Cameron Crowe; *M:* Paul Westerberg. **VHS, Beta** $19.98 WAR, PMS *〽〽〽*

Singleton's Pluck Touching British comedy about a determined farmer who must walk his 500 geese 100 miles to market because of a strike. He becomes a celebrity when the TV stations start covering his odyssey. *AKA:* Laughterhouse.
1984 89m/C Ian Holm, Penelope Wilton, Bill Owen, Richard Hope; *D:* Richard Eyre. **VHS, Beta** $19.95 STE, NWV *〽〽〽*

The Sinister Invasion A turn-of-the-century scientist (Karloff) discovers a death ray. Aliens, who would like a closer peek at what makes it work, use a sex-fiend's body to do so. One of Karloff's last four films, made simultaneously in Mexico. The great horror master's final offering. Excruciating. *AKA:* Alien Terror; The Incredible Invasion.
1968 95m/C Boris Karloff, Enrique Guzman, Jack Hill; *D:* Juan Ibanez. **VHS, Beta** $49.95 SNC *〽*

The Sinister Urge Vice cops Duncan and Moore search for the murderer of three women. Seems the disturbed slayer is unbalanced because he's been looking at pictures of naked ladies. Was this meant to be taken seriously at the time? The last film by camp director Wood, maker of the infamous "Plan 9 From Outer Space." A must see for Wood fans. *AKA:* The Young and the Immortal; Hellborn.
1960 82m/B Kenne Duncan, Duke Moore, Jean Fontaine; *D:* Edward D. Wood Jr. **VHS, Beta** $59.98 AOV, SNC Woof!

Sink the Bismarck British navy sets out to locate and sink infamous German battleship during WWII. Good special effects with battle sequences in this drama based on real incidents. One of the better of the plethora of WWII movies, with stirring naval battles and stylish documentary-style direction.
1960 97m/B Kenneth More, Dana Wynter, Karel Stepanek, Carl Mohner, Laurence Naismith, Geoffrey Keen, Michael Hordern, Maurice Denham, Esmond Knight; *D:* Lewis Gilbert. **VHS, Beta** $19.98 FOX, HMV *〽〽〽*

Sinners Outrageous portrait of an Italian family in the Big Apple trying to come to terms with the violence that surrounds their neighborhood.
1989 90m/C Joey Travolta, Robert Gallo, Joe Palese, Lou Calvelli, Angie Daglas, Sabrina Ferrand; *D:* Charles Kanganis. **VHS, Beta** $29.95 PMH *〽*

Sinner's Blood Bikers terrorize and torture a small town.

1970 (R) 81m/C Stephen Jacques, Crusty Beal, Nancy Sheldon, Parriott Herriott, Julie Connors; *D:* Neil Douglas. **VHS, Beta** $24.95 GHV Woof!

Sinners in Paradise An assortment of trouble-plagued characters alternately hide and face up to their mysterious pasts when their plane crashes on a deserted island. Interesting "crucible" premise runs out of steam, but plucky, resourceful cast and competent direction keep it going.
1938 64m/B Madge Evans, John Boles, Bruce Cabot, Marion Martin, Gene Lockhart, Dwight Frye, Charlotte Wynters, Nana Bryant, Milburn Stone, Donald (Don "Red") Barry, Morgan Conway; *D:* James Whale. **VHS, Beta** $16.95 SNC, MLB *〽〽*

Sins On her way up the ladder of success in the fashion industry, Helene has stepped on a few toes. Those rivals and her ever-increasing acquisition of power and money make this film an exciting drama.
1985 336m/C Joan Collins, Timothy Dalton, Catherine Mary Stewart, Gene Kelly, James Farentino; *D:* Douglas Hickox. **VHS, Beta** $29.95 STE, NWV, HHE *〽〽*

Sins of Desire Highly erotic thriller with Roberts going undercover as a nurse in a sex therapy clinic. It seems her sister was a former patient at the clinic and has since died a mysterious death. Linking up with private eye Cassavetes, Roberts sets out to investigate the doctors who treated her sister, searching for clues to her untimely death.
1992 90m/C Tanya Roberts, Jay Richardson, Delia Sheppard, Nick Cassavetes, Jan-Michael Vincent; *D:* Jim Wynorski; *W:* Mark McGee, Peter Paul Liapis. **VHS** $89.95 COL, VMK, PMS *〽〽*

The Sins of Dorian Gray A modernized adaptation of "The Portrait of Dorian Grey" by Oscar Wilde, with Dorian as a beautiful woman who remains young for 30 years, while a video screen test ages, like the original character's mirror image. Might have been intriguing and stylish; instead, only disappointing and incompetent. Made for television.
1982 (PG) 95m/C Belinda Bauer, Joseph Bottoms, Anthony Perkins; *D:* Tony Maylam. **VHS, Beta** $59.98 FOX *〽*

Sins of Jezebel Biblical epic about Jezebel, who worships an evil god. She marries the king of Israel and brings the kingdom nothing but trouble.
1954 74m/C Paulette Goddard, George Nader, John Hoyt, Eduard Franz; *D:* Reginald LeBorg. **VHS, Beta** NO *〽*

Sins of Rome Spartacus risks it all in a bold attempt to free his fellow slaves. Not nearly the equal of Kirk Douglas's "Spartacus," but much better than later Italian adventure epics.
1954 75m/B Ludmila Tcherina, Massimo Girotti, Giana Maria Canale, Yves Vincent; *D:* Riccardo (Robert Hampton) Freda. **VHS** $16.95 SNC *〽〽*

Sins of the Night An ex-con insurance investigator is hired to find a sultry exotic dancer. Also available in an unrated version.
1993 (R) 82m/C Nick Cassavetes, Deborah Shelton. **VHS** ACA *〽*

Sinthia: The Devil's Doll A little girl is thought to be possessed by a demon after she has horrible dreams about killing her father.
1970 ?m/C Shula Roan, Diane Webber; *D:* Ray Dennis Steckler. **VHS** $16.95 SNC, TPV *〽〽*

Sioux City Sue Talent scouts looking to cast a western musical find Autry, then trick him into being the voice of a singing donkey in an animated production. But, the yodelin' cowboy belts out a number or two, and the

poobahs give him the lead. Singin' and fancy ridin' abound in Autry's first post-WWII role.
1946 69m/B Gene Autry, Lynn (Mary Hart) Roberts, Sterling Holloway. **VHS, Beta** NO 🎬🎬

Sirens Staid minister takes Australian artist Norman Lindsay to task for submitting scandalous works to public exhibitions. Noted by one reviewer as ''Enchanted April with nipples,'' comedy of manners is witty and sly but lacks plot and looks remarkably like a centerfold layout. Ample displays of nudity as the models (including supermodel MacPherson in her acting debut) frolic in the buff. Grant is terrific as the seemingly enlightened but easily shocked minister, but Neill's Lindsay is thinly written and too often takes a back seat to the vamping models. Fictionalized account of a true incident from the 1930s; Lindsay's home and some of his artworks were used. Check out writer/director Duigan as a pompous village minister.
1994 (R) 96m/C Hugh Grant, Tara Fitzgerald, Sam Neill, Elle Macpherson, Kate Fischer, Portia de Rossi, Pamela Rabe, Ben Mendelsohn, John Polson, Mark Gerber, Julia Stone, Ellie MacCarthy, Vincent Ball; *Cameos:* John Duigan; *D:* John Duigan; *W:* John Duigan; *M:* Rachel Portman. **VHS** NYR 🎬🎬

Sirocco An American gun-runner (Bogart) stuck in Syria in 1925 matches wits with a French intelligence officer amid civil war and intrigue. About the underbelly of human affair.
1951 111m/B Humphrey Bogart, Lee J. Cobb, Zero Mostel, Everett Sloane, Gerald Mohr; *D:* Curtis Bernhardt. **VHS, Beta $9.95** COL 🎬🎬½

Sister Act Surprising box office hit casts Goldberg as a Reno lounge singer and inadvertent witness to a mob murder who hides out in a convent—where she's as comfortable in a habit as a fish is out of water. Much to the dismay of poker-faced Mother Superior Smith, she takes over the rag-tag choir and molds them into a swinging, religious version of a '60s girls group. Stock characters and situations are deflected by some genuinely funny moments and good performances, especially by Najimy and Makkena. Coached by the very clever Shaiman, Whoopie handles her singing bits with gusto, highlight of which is ''My God,'' sung to the tune of ''My Guy.''
1992 (PG) 100m/C Whoopi Goldberg, Dame Maggie Smith, Harvey Keitel, Bill Nunn, Kathy Najimy, Wendy Makkena, Mary Wickes, Robert Miranda, Richard Portnow, Joseph Maher; *D:* Emile Ardolino; *W:* Joseph Howard; *M:* Marc Shaiman. **VHS, Beta $19.99** TOU, PMS 🎬🎬½

Sister Act 2: Back in the Habit Mediocre retread finds Goldberg once again donning her nun's habit and getting a choir rocking. Deloris has established her singing career in Vegas, but she's persuaded by her nun friends to whip the incorrigible music students at a troubled inner-city high school into shape for an all-state choral competition. The musical numbers and singing are catchy and well-done but Goldberg seems to have phoned her work in; given her reported 7 million bucks salary a little more life is expected. She's still sharp with the one-liners but it's all familiar ground. Geared directly towards young viewers.
1993 (PG) 107m/C Whoopi Goldberg, Kathy Najimy, James Coburn, Dame Maggie Smith, Wendy Makkena, Barnard Hughes, Mary Wickes, Sheryl Lee Ralph, Michael Jeter, Robert Pastorelli, Thomas Gottschalk, Lauryn Hill, Brad Sullivan; *D:* Bill Duke; *W:* James Orr, Jim Cruickshank, Judi Ann Mason; *M:* Miles Goodman. **VHS** BVV 🎬🎬

Sister Dora An idealistic young woman joins a nursing sisterhood in 19th century England but she questions her vocation when she falls in love. Adapted from a popular romance novel.
1977 147m/C Dorothy Tutin, James Grout, Peter Cellier; *D:* Mark Miller. **VHS** NO 🎬🎬½

The Sister-in-Law Shady dealings, seduction, and adultery run rampant. Savage (who also wrote and sings the folk score) reluctantly agrees to deliver a package across the Canadian border for his brother. Intriguing.
1974 (R) 80m/C John Savage, Anne Saxon, W.G. McMillan, Meredith Baer; *D:* Joseph Rubin. **VHS, Beta $79.95** PSM 🎬🎬

Sister Kenny Follows the story of a legendary Australian nurse crusading for the treatment of infantile paralysis. Stirring, well-made screen biography. Based on Elizabeth Kenny's memoir, ''And They Shall Walk.''
1946 116m/B Rosalind Russell, Dean Jagger, Alexander Knox, Philip Merivale, Beulah Bondi, Charles Halton; *D:* Dudley Nichols. Academy Awards '46 Nominations: Best Actress (Russell); Golden Globe Awards '47: Best Actress—Drama (Russell). **VHS, Beta $19.98** NOS, CCB, TTC 🎬🎬🎬

Sister, Sister A Congressional aide on vacation in Louisiana takes a room in an old mansion. He gradually discovers the secret of the house and its resident sisters. Dark Southern gothicism, full of plot surprises, with a twisted ending.
1987 (R) 91m/C Eric Stoltz, Judith Ivey, Jennifer Jason Leigh, Dennis Lipscomb, Anne Pitoniak, Natalija Nogulich; *D:* Bill Condon; *W:* Joel Cohen; *M:* Richard Einhorn. **VHS, Beta $19.95** STE, NWV 🎬🎬

The Sisterhood A pair of amazons fight for women's rights in a post-nuclear future. Cheap feminist theme laid over warmed-over sci-fi plot.
1988 (R) 75m/C Rebecca Holden, Chuck Wagner, Lynn-Holly Johnson, Barbara Hooper; *D:* Cirio H. Santiago. **VHS, Beta $79.95** MED 🎬

The Sisters Lavish film of three sisters and their marital problems in turn of the century San Francisco. Davis gives a great performance as the oldest sister with the most trouble—notably in the form of unreliable sports reporter Flynn. Look for Susan Hayward in a bit role, as well as Bogart's wife, Mayo Methot. Based on the bestselling novel by Myron Brinig.
1938 98m/B Bette Davis, Errol Flynn, Anita Louise, Jane Bryan, Ian Hunter, Henry Travers, Beulah Bondi, Donald Crisp, Dick Foran, Patric Knowles; *D:* Anatole Litvak. **VHS $19.98** MGM 🎬🎬🎬

Sisters Siamese twins are separated surgically, but one doesn't survive the operation. The remaining sister is scarred physically and mentally with her personality split into bad and good. The bad side commits a murder, witnessed (or was it?) by an investigative reporter. And then things really get crazy. DePalma's first ode to Hitchcock, with great music by Hitchcock's favorite composer, Bernard Herrmann. Scary and suspenseful.
1973 (R) 93m/C Margot Kidder, Charles Durning, Barnard Hughes; *D:* Brian DePalma; *W:* Brian DePalma, Brian DePalma; *M:* Bernard Herrmann. **VHS, Beta $29.98** WAR, OM 🎬🎬🎬

Sisters of Death Five members of a sorority gather together for a reunion in a remote California town. Little do they know, a psychopath is stalking them, one by one. Could it have something to do with the terrible secret they each keep? Good, cheap thrills and some Bicentennial fashions to boot.

1976 (PG) 87m/C Arthur Franz, Claudia Jennings, Cheri Howell, Sherry Boucher, Paul Carr; *D:* Joseph Mazzuca. **VHS, Beta $29.95** VCI 🎬

Sisters of Gion Mizoguchi's most famous and arguably best pre-war film. Two geisha sisters in Tokyo's red-light district reflect the tension in Japanese culture by waging a quiet battle of tradition vs. progressiveness. Highly acclaimed. In Japanese with English subtitles.
1936 69m/B Isuzu Yamada, Yoko Umemura; *D:* Kenji Mizoguchi. **VHS, Beta** FCT 🎬🎬🎬½

Sisters of Satan The nuns of the infamous convent St. Archangelo choose to survive by trading God for the devil.
1975 (R) 91m/C Claudio Brook, David Silva, Tina Romero, Susana Kamini; *D:* Juan Monteczuma. **VHS, Beta $19.95** ACA, MPI 🎬🎬

Sitting Ducks Mild-mannered accountant and lecherous pal rip off and then attempt to outrun the mob—all while swapping songs and confessions. Emil and Norman make it up as they go along; their hilarious repartee is largely improvised. They pick up a gorgeous lady (Townsend) and go about their way.
1980 (R) 88m/C Michael Emil, Zack Norman, Patrice Townsend, Richard Romanus, Irene Forrest, Henry Jaglom; *D:* Henry Jaglom; *W:* Henry Jaglom. **VHS, Beta $19.95** MED 🎬🎬🎬

The Situation Two years of life and death in El Salvador's civil war. Also the tale of an American film crew who spent the time with a Salvadoran family covering the events. Many events in the movie ''Salvador'' were inspired by incidents portrayed here.
1987 91m/C Richard Boyle; *M:* Bob Dylan, Peter, Paul & Mary, Paul & Mary. **Beta** VDE 🎬🎬🎬

Six Degrees of Separation Some believe that any two people, anywhere in the world, are connected by links to only six other people, hence the six degrees of separation. For the upper crust New Yorker Kittredges, Ouisa (Channing) and Flan (Sutherland), this becomes an issue when they encounter a charming young man (Smith) who claims to be Sidney Poitier's son and a friend of their children. The story unfolds as they realize they've been hustled—and don't understand why. Guare adapted his hit play, but what worked well there is almost too talky here. Channing, reprising her stage role, is very good as the stuffy Ouisa, with Sutherland delivering another interesting performance. Incredibly, the play was based on a true story.
1993 (R) 112m/C Stockard Channing, Will Smith, Donald Sutherland, Mary Beth Hurt, Bruce Davison, Ian McKellan, Richard Masur, Anthony Michael Hall, Heather Graham, Eric Thal, Anthony Rapp, Osgood Perkins, Kitty Carlisle Hart, Catherine Kellner; *D:* Fred Schepisi; *W:* John Guare; *M:* Jerry Goldsmith. **VHS $34.98** MGM 🎬🎬½

Six Fois Deux/Sur et Sous la Communication A six-part experimental series made for French television, in which Godard and Mieville analyze modern culture and socioeconomics via a free-form essay format, combining interviews, screened text, self-referential devices and news footage. In French with English voice-over.
1976 100m/C *D:* Jean-Luc Godard, Anne-Marie Mieville. **VHS, Beta** EAI 🎬🎬🎬

Six Gun Gospel Hatton masquerades as a preacher to investigate some shady dealings. Laughs come when the women of the congregation prevail upon him to sing, and he croons a ballad about Jesse James!

1943 59m/B Johnny Mack Brown, Raymond Hatton, Inna Gest, Eddie Dew, Roy Barcroft, Kenneth MacDonald, Bud Osborne; **D:** Lambert Hillyer. **VHS $19.95** *DVT, HEG* 🎞🎞

Six Gun Rhythm Novelty western plot has football player traveling to Texas to avenge his father's murder.
1939 59m/B Tex Fletcher. **VHS, Beta $19.95** *NOS, VDM, HEG* 🎞½

633 Squadron A skilled R.A.F. pilot attempts to lead his squadron on a mission deep into the fjords of Norway in search of a Nazi fuel plant. Robertson tries hard, as always, but is really not British officer material. Well-made war flick, based on a true story.
1964 102m/C Cliff Robertson, George Chakiris, Maria Perschy, Harry Andrews; **D:** Walter Grauman; **W:** James Clavell. **VHS, Beta $19.98** *MGM* 🎞🎞½

Six in Paris Six short films by acclaimed French New Wave directors, each depicting a different Parisian neighborhood. "Saint-Germain-des-Pres" finds an American girl disillusioned by two French boys. "Gare du Nord" has a woman meeting a handsome stranger who announces he's going to kill himself. A shy dishwasher brings a prostitute to his room in the "Rue Saint-Denis." When a salesman is accosted by a derelict in the "Place de l'Etoile" he hits him with his umbrella and then thinks he's killed the man. "Montparnasse-Levallois" has a woman thinking she's mixed-up her meetings with her two lovers. "La Muette" finds a small boy buying earplugs to shut out the noise of his parents constant arguing. In French with English subtitles. **AKA:** Paris vu Par.
1968 93m/C Barbara Wilkin, Jean-Francois Chappey, Jean-Pierre Andreani, Nadine Ballot, Barbet Schroeder, Gilles Queant, Micheline Dax, Claude Melki, Jean-Michel Rouziere, Marcel Gallon, Joanna Shimkus, Philippe Hiquilly, Serge Davri, Stephane Audran, Gilles Chusseau, Dinah Saril, Claude Chabrol; **D:** Jean Douchet, Jean Rouch, Jean-Daniel Pollet, Eric Rohmer, Jean-Luc Godard, Claude Chabrol; **W:** Jean Douchet, George Keller, Jean Rouch, Jean-Daniel Pollet, Eric Rohmer, Jean-Luc Godard, Claude Chabrol. **VHS $69.95** *NYF, FCT* 🎞🎞½

Six Pack The Gambler goes auto racing. Rogers, in his theatrical debut, stars as Brewster Baker, a former stock car driver. He returns to the racing circuit with the help of six larcenous orphans (the six-pack, get it?) adept at stripping cars. Kinda cute if you're in the mood for sugar-powered race car story.
1982 (PG) 108m/C Kenny Rogers, Diane Lane, Erin Gray, Barry Corbin, Anthony Michael Hall; **D:** Daniel Petrie; **M:** Charles Fox. **VHS, Beta $14.98** *FOX* 🎞½

Six Shootin' Sheriff A cowboy framed for bank robbery is released and seeks to rid his town of all evil. And he gets the girl!
1938 59m/B Ken Maynard, Marjorie Reynolds, Walter Long; **D:** Harry Fraser. **VHS, Beta $19.95** *VYY, VCI, VCN* 🎞🎞

Six Weeks A young girl dying of leukemia brings together her work-driven mother and an aspiring married politician. Manipulative hanky-wringer has good acting from both Moores but oddly little substance.
1982 (PG) 107m/C Dudley Moore, Mary Tyler Moore, Katherine Healy; **D:** Tony Bill. **VHS, Beta $12.95** *COL* 🎞🎞

Six Wives of Henry VIII Michell has been called the definitive Henry VIII, and this BBC Classic Television Series (shown as part of "Masterpiece Theatre" on PBS) is perhaps the most praised series on British TV. Henry's wives were: Catherine of Ara-

gon, Anne Boleyn, Jane Seymour, Anne of Cleves, Catherine Howard, and Catherine Parr. Each episode tells of their, sometimes tragic, fates as pawns in Henry's quest for an heir, and his changes from an eager young man to aged, bitter monarch. The 90-minute videos are available individually or as a boxed set.
197? 540m/C Keith Michell, Annette Crosbie, Dorothy Tutin, Anne Stallybrass, Elvi Hale, Angela Pleasence, Rosalie Crutchley. **VHS $129.95** *SIG, FCT, BFS* 🎞🎞🎞

Sixteen A naive country lass is attracted to the glitter and hum of the outside world. Her determination and optimism help her triumph. **AKA:** Like a Crow on a June Bug.
1972 (R) 84m/C Mercedes McCambridge, Parley Baer, Ford Rainey, Beverly Powers, John Lozier, Simone Griffeth, Maddie Norman; **D:** Lawrence Dobkin. **VHS, Beta $19.95** *NWV* 🎞🎞

Sixteen Candles Hughes gathers his stable of young stars again for one of his best films. Every girl's sixteenth birthday is supposed to be special, but in the rush of her sister's wedding nobody remembers Ringwald's. After that, everything seems to go downhill in hilarious fashion. Ringwald and Hall are especially charming in this humorous look at teenage traumas. Title song performed by The Stray Cats.
1984 (PG) 93m/C Molly Ringwald, Justin Henry, Michael Schoeffling, Haviland Morris, Gedde Watanabe, Anthony Michael Hall, Paul Dooley, Carlin Glynn, Blanche Baker, Edward Andrews, Carole Cook, Max Showalter, Liane Curtis, John Cusack, Joan Cusack, Brian Doyle-Murray, Jami Gertz, Cinnamon Idles, Zelda Rubinstein; **D:** John Hughes; **W:** John Hughes. **VHS, Beta $19.95** *MCA* 🎞🎞🎞

Sixteen Fathoms Deep A sponge fisherman risks it all, including his love, when a mean businessman threatens his operation. Good underwater photography, but otherwise undistinguished.
1934 57m/B Lon Chaney Jr., Sally O'Neil, George Regas, Maurice Black, Russell Simpson; **D:** Armand Schaefer. **VHS $14.95** *VYY, NOS, DVT* 🎞

'68 A Hungarian family struggles with the generation gap in 1968 America.
1987 (R) 99m/C Eric Larson, Terra Vandergaw, Neil Young; **D:** Steven Kovacks. **VHS, Beta $19.95** *STE, NWV* 🎞

Sizzle When her boyfriend is murdered by the mob, nightclub singer Anderson, newly arrived from Hicksville in Roaring '20s Chicago, stops at nothing to get revenge. Bad-guy gangster Forsythe falls for her charms. Fun but unsophisticated. Made for TV.
1981 100m/C Loni Anderson, John Forsythe, Leslie Uggams, Roy Thinnes, Richard Lynch, Michael Goodwin; **D:** Don Medford. **VHS, Beta $59.95** *PSM* 🎞🎞

Sizzle Beach U.S.A. Three young women who want a shot at becoming famous travel to Los Angeles and play on the beach with little budget and no particular purpose. Also available in an unrated version. Although released in 1986, this was made in 1974. Kevin Costner's film debut.
1986 90m/C Terry Congie, Leslie Brander, Roselyn Royce, Kevin Costner; **D:** Richard Brander. **VHS, Beta $19.95** *STE, VMK* 🎞

Skag Disabled following a stroke, a Pittsburgh steel worker confronts a change in family roles and long-ignored family problems during his convalescence. Malden is exceptional and believable as a Joe Lunchbucket in this well-written, well-cast TV outing, pilot for the NBC series.

1979 145m/C Karl Malden, Piper Laurie, Craig Wasson, Leslie Ackerman, Peter Gallagher, Kathryn Holcomb, Powers Boothe; **D:** Frank Perry. **VHS, Beta** *NO* 🎞🎞🎞

Skateboard A down-and-out Hollywood agent creates a pro skateboarding team and enters them in a race worth $20,000. Quickie premise executed lamely.
1977 (PG) 97m/C Allen (Gooritz) Garfield, Kathleen Lloyd, Chad McQueen, Leif Garrett, Richard Van Der Wyk, Tony Alva, Antony Carbone; **W:** Dick Wolf. **VHS, Beta** *NO* 🎞

The Skateboard Kid When an outsider finds a magical talking skateboard, he suddenly becomes the envy of the in-group of skateboarding thrashers.
1993 (PG) 90m/C Bess Armstrong, Timothy Busfield; **D:** Larry Swerdlove; **W:** Roger Corman; **V:** Dom DeLuise. **VHS $89.98** *NHO* 🎞

Skeeter Yes, it's the attack of the killer mosquito! Not just any mosquito of course, but a new gigantic species bred on toxic waste. They're invading the quiet desert town of Mesquite—and they're out for blood!
1993 (R) 95m/C Tracy Griffith, Jim Youngs, Charles Napier, Michael J. Pollard; **D:** Clark Brandon; **W:** Clark Brandon, Lanny Horn; **M:** David Lawrence. **VHS** *COL* 🎞½

Skeezer A dog becomes a key factor in a sympathetic doctor's efforts to communicate with emotionally unstable children. Based on reality, and a good cast makes it believable and moving. Quality family fare.
1982 100m/C Karen Valentine, Dee Wallace Stone, Tom Atkins, Mariclare Costello, Leighton Greer, Justine Lord; **D:** Peter Hunt. **VHS $39.95** *LIV* 🎞½

Skeleton Coast Borgnine plays a retired U.S. Marine colonel who organizes a Magnificent Seven-like group of tough mercenaries to go into eastern Africa to save hostages held by Angolan terrorists. Cliches abound, including a token large-breasted woman, Mulford, getting her t-shirt ripped open. No plot and a bad script. Also called "Fair Trade."
1989 (R) 94m/C Ernest Borgnine, Robert Vaughn, Oliver Reed, Herbert Lom, Daniel Greene, Nancy Mulford, Leon Isaac Kennedy; **D:** John Cardos. **VHS $19.98** *SUE, NLC* 🎞

Sketch Artist Jack Whitfield is a police sketch artist whose latest rendering of a murder suspect looks suspiciously like his wife. Jack decides to keep this information to himself while he does some quiet investigating but he may not have any time. The police have a new murder suspect in mind—Jack! Made for cable television.
1992 (R) 89m/C Jeff Fahey, Sean Young, Drew Barrymore, Frank McRae, Tcheky Karyo, James Tolkan, Charlotte Lewis; **D:** Phedon Papamichael. **VHS, Beta $89.98** *FXV, VTR* 🎞🎞

Sketches of a Strangler A psychotic art student sketches, then murders prostitutes. Interesting lead character but hardly chilling—just horrible to watch. Made for TV.
1978 91m/C Allen (Gooritz) Garfield, Meredith MacRae; **D:** Paul Leder. **VHS, Beta $59.95** *MED* 🎞½

Ski Bum A ski bum discovers corruption and violence at a Colorado Rockies resort. Eminently forgettable trash. Scantily based on a novel by Romain Gary.
1975 (R) 94m/C Charlotte Rampling, Zalman King, Dimitra Arliss, Anna Karina; **D:** Bruce Clark. **VHS, Beta $59.98** *NLC* 🎞

Ski Patrol Wacky ski groupies try to stop an evil developer. Good ski action in a surprisingly plotful effort from the crazy crew that brought the world "Police Academy."

1989 (PG) 85m/C Roger Rose, Yvette Nipar, T.K. Carter, Leslie Jordan, Ray Walston, Martin Mull; **D:** Richard Correll. **VHS, Beta $19.95** COL 🐾

Ski School Rival ski instructors compete for jobs and babes. Brow lowering.
1991 (R) 89m/C Ava Fabian, Dean Cameron, Tom Breznahan, Stuart Fratkin; **D:** Damian Lee. **VHS $19.98** HBO 🐾

Ski Troop Attack During WWII, an American ski patrol is sent behind Nazi lines to blow up a German railway bridge. Unexceptional low-budget Corman outing; not among the greatest of war movies.
1960 61m/B Michael Forest, Frank Wolff, Sheila Carol. **VHS, Beta $16.95** SNC, NOS, DVT 🐾🐾

Skier's Dream This spectacular action-packed film focuses on a young executive in search of the ultimate run. Shot on the most exotic ski locations in the world; covers freestyle skiing, powder skiing, snowboarding, extreme skiing, cliff jumping, paragliding, and wave riding.
1988 75m/C John Eaves, Ian Boyd; **M:** Jimi Hendrix, Tom Cochrane. **VHS $14.95** COL, RAP 🐾🐾

Skin Art Very offbeat character study focusing on Will, a tormented tattoo artist who specializes in decorating the backs of the young Asian prostitutes who work in a nearby brothel. Haunted by his memories as a Vietnam POW, Will decides to exorcise some demons in his latest female canvas.
1993 (R) 90m/C Kirk Baltz, Jake Weber, Nora Ariffin; **D:** W. Blake Herron; **W:** W. Blake Herron. **VHS** FXV 🐾½

Skin Deep A boyish Don Juan tries everything to win back his ex-wife. Ritter whines about his mid-life crisis and seduces women; this substitutes for plot. A few funny slapstick scenes still don't make this worth watching.
1989 (R) 102m/C John Ritter, Vincent Gardenia, Julianne Phillips, Alyson Reed, Nina Foch, Chelsea Field, Denise Crosby; **D:** Blake Edwards; **W:** Blake Edwards. **VHS, Beta $9.99** CCB, MED, VTR 🐾🐾½

Skin Game Two British families feud over land rights. Not thrilling; not characteristic of working with Hitchcock. Way too much talking in excruciating, drawn-out scenes. Adapted from the play of the same name.
1931 87m/B Phyllis Konstam, Edmund Gwenn, Frank Lawton, C.V. France, Jill Esmond, Helen Hayes; **D:** Alfred Hitchcock; **W:** Alfred Hitchcock. **VHS, Beta $9.98** REP, NOS, MLB 🐾½

Skin Game A fast talking con-artist (Garner) and his black partner (Gossett) travel throughout the antebellum South setting up scams—Gossett is sold to a new owner by Garner, who helps him escape. Garner and Gossett make a splendid comedy team in this different kind of buddy flick. All is well until Asner turns the tables on them. Finely acted comedy-drama.
1971 (PG) 102m/C James Garner, Louis Gossett Jr., Susan Clark, Ed Asner, Andrew Duggan; **D:** Paul Bogart. **VHS, Beta $19.98** WAR 🐾🐾🐾

Skinheads: The Second Coming of Hate Neo-fascists run rampant. Exploitative effort from schlock-doyen Clark.
1988 (R) 93m/C Chuck Connors, Barbara Bain, Brian Brophy, Jason Culp, Elizabeth Sagal; **D:** Greydon Clark. **VHS** NO 🐾

Skinned Alive A woman and her children travel cross-country to sell leather goods. When a detective discovers where the leather comes from he's hot on their trail.
1989 90m/C Mary Jackson, Scott Spiegel; **D:** Jon Killough; **W:** Jon Killough. **VHS, Beta** NO Woof!

Skinner's Dress Suit Meek, henpecked office clerk tells domineering wife he got a raise so she'll get off his back. She quickly insinuates them into upper crusty social circle, where the fib pays off big. Remake of the 1917 version based on Henry Irving Dodge's novel.
1926 79m/B Reginald Denny, Laura La Plante, Arthur Lake, Hedda Hopper; **D:** William A. Seiter. **VHS, Beta $19.95** GPV 🐾🐾½

Skirts Ahoy! Williams, Evans, and Blaine are three WAVES who have their eyes set on three handsome men. To get them, of course, they must sing and dance a lot, and Williams must perform one of her famous water ballets. 🎵Oh By Jingo; Hold Me Close to You; What Makes a WAVE?; What Good is a Gal Without a Guy?; Skirts Ahoy!; Glad to Have You Aboard; The Navy Waltz; I Get a Funny Feeling; We Will Fight.
1952 109m/C Esther Williams, Joan Evans, Vivian Blaine, Barry Sullivan, Keefe Brasselle, Billy Eckstine, Debbie Reynolds; **D:** Sidney Lanfield. **VHS $19.98** MGM 🐾🐾

The Skull Horror abounds when Cushing gets his hands on the skull of the Marquis de Sade that has mysterious, murderous powers. Based on a story by Robert Bloch.
1965 83m/C Peter Cushing, Patrick Wymark, Christopher Lee, Nigel Green, Jill Bennett, Michael Gough, George Coulouris, Patrick Magee; **D:** Freddie Francis. **VHS** PAR 🐾🐾

Skull: A Night of Terror A cop vows not to use guns after a tragic accident, then single-handed and unarmed, takes on terrorists who kidnap his family.
1988 (R) 80m/C Nadia Capone, Robert Bideman, Robbie Fox, Paul Sanders; **D:** Robert Bergman; **W:** Robert Bergman, Gerard Ciccoritti. **VHS, Beta $79.95** ACA 🐾🐾

Skull & Crown Rin Tin Tin, Jr. helps the hero break up a group of smugglers. A favorite of Tin fans everywhere.
1938 58m/B Rin Tin Tin Jr, Regis Toomey, Jack Mulhall, James Murray. **VHS, Beta $19.95** VYY, DVT, HEG 🐾🐾

Skullduggery When a peaceful race of blond ape-people are discovered in New Guinea, a courtroom battle ensues to prevent their slaughter at the hands of developers. Interesting premise sadly flops.
1970 (PG) 105m/C Burt Reynolds, Susan Clark, Roger C. Carmel, Chips Rafferty, Edward Fox, Wilfrid Hyde-White, Rhys Williams; **D:** Gordon Douglas. **VHS, Beta** MED 🐾½

Skullduggery Costume-store minion Haverstock carries a curse that makes him kill and mutilate. The usual unspeakable horror ensues for a group of medieval-game players. **AKA:** Warlock.
1979 (PG) 95m/C Thom Haverstock, Wendy Crewson, David Calderisi; **D:** Ota Richter. **VHS, Beta $59.95** MED Woof!

The Sky Above, the Mud Below An acclaimed documentary following a band of explorers transversing New Guinea in 1959, and their confrontations with native rituals, heretofore unknown cannibal tribes and physical calamities. French title: "Le Ciel et la Boue." In HiFi.
1961 90m/C **D:** Pierre-Dominique Gaisseau. **VHS, Beta** LHV, WAR, FCT Woof!

Sky Bandits Mounties uncover the mystery of a disappearing plane carrying gold from a Yukon mine. Last of the "Renfrew of the Mounties" pictures.
1940 56m/B James Newill, Dave O'Brien, Louise Stanley. **VHS, Beta, 8mm $14.95** NOS, SNC, VCN 🐾½

Sky Hei$t Criminals plan robbery of police helicopter carrying fortune in gold bullion. Made for television.
1975 96m/C Stefanie Powers, Joseph Campanella, Don Meredith, Larry Wilcox, Frank Gorshin, Shelley Fabares, Ken Swofford, Ray Vitte, Nancy Belle Fuller, Suzanne Somers; **D:** Lee H. Katzin. **VHS $29.95** UNI 🐾🐾

Sky High Mix is an immigration agent after a gang smuggling Chinese laborers across the Mexican border. Thrills involve an airplane and mountaintop battles as well as some terrific location footage from the Grand Canyon.
1922 58m/B Tom Mix, Eva Novak, J. Farrell MacDonald, Sid Jordan; **D:** Lynn F. Reynolds; **W:** Lynn F. Reynolds. **VHS $19.95** GPV, GVV 🐾🐾½

Sky High A spy at an Air Force base is trying to get hold of the plans to a secret plane. A GI is recruited to catch him.
1951 60m/B Sid Melton, Mara Lynn, Douglas Evans. **VHS, Beta** NO 🐾

Sky High Three college students become immersed in international intrigue when the C.I.A. and the K.G.B. pursue them through Greece looking for a secret Soviet tape.
1984 103m/C Daniel Hirsch, Clayton Norcross, Frank Schultz, Lauren Taylor; **D:** Nico Mastorakis. **VHS, Beta $79.98** LIV 🐾

The Sky is Gray A young black Louisiana boy journeys with his mother to the dentist, and on the way is confronted with prejudice and poverty. Set in the 1940s. Based on a story by Ernest Gaines. Made for television, with an introdution by Henry Fonda.
1980 46m/C Olivia Cole, James Bond III, Margaret Avery, Cleavon Little; **D:** Stan Lathan. **VHS, Beta $24.95** MON, KAR, FCT 🐾🐾🐾

Sky Liner An FBI agent is trailing a spy who has taken secret documents aboard a west-bound flight..
1949 62m/B Richard Travis, Pamela Blake. **VHS, Beta** NO 🐾

The Sky Pilot Young clergyman sets up a parish on North Pacific coast and finds he must prove himself to the cowboys. He saves young woman from stampede, but her father blames him for her maimed legs and sets the preacher's church on fire, providing girl with excuse to overcome handicap.
1921 63m/M John Bowers, Colleen Moore, David Butler, Donald Ian Macdonald; **D:** King Vidor. **VHS, Beta $29.95** GPV, FCT, GVV 🐾🐾½

Sky Pirates Space epic deals about pieces of ancient stone left by prehistoric extraterrestrials, now lost in a time warp. Bad stunts, bad script and notably bad acting make it a woofer in any era.
1987 88m/C John Hargreaves, Max Phipps, Meredith Phillips; **D:** Colin Eggleston. **VHS, Beta $79.98** FOX Woof!

Sky Riders Hang-gliders risk it all to take on a group of political kidnappers. Fine hang-gliding footage and glorious Greek locations make up for garden-variety plot.
1976 (PG) 93m/C James Coburn, Susannah York, Robert Culp, Charles Aznavour, Harry Andrews, John Beck; **D:** Douglas Hickox; **W:** Jack DeWitt, Garry Michael White, Jack DeWitt. **VHS** FOX 🐾🐾

Skylark In a sequel to Hallmark Hall of Fame's hugely successful "Sarah, Plain and Tall," the whole Kansas crew shows up for more of their little-farm-on-the-prairie life. After two years in America's squarest state, mail-order bride Sarah (Close) loves Jacob (Walken), but not the scenery and still yearns for the lush greenery of Maine. When drought and fire threaten the farm, Jacob

fears for the family's health and safety, and sends them back East for a visit. Close's "tough Yankee" expression grows a bit tiresome in a plot that is a tad predictable, yet the simplistic charm and nostalgia are unresistable and work to propel this quality Hallmark production.
1993 (G) 98m/C Glenn Close, Christopher Walken, Lexi Randall, Christopher Bell, Tresa Hughes, Lois Smith, Lee Richardson, Elizabeth Wilson, Margaret Sophie Stein, Jon DeVries, James Rebhorn, Woody Watson, Lois Smith; *D:* Joseph Sargent; *W:* Patricia MacLachlan. **VHS** $14.98 REP, BTV ⬛⬛½

Skyline A Spanish photographer comes to New York City to work for a magazine and tries to adjust to his cultural dislocation. Quietly funny, with a startling ending. Partly in Spanish with English subtitles. *AKA:* La Linea Del Cielo.
1984 (R) 84m/C Antonio Resines, Beatriz Perez-Porro, Jaime Nos, Roy Hoffman; *D:* Fernando Colombo. **VHS, Beta** $29.95 KIV, FCT, TPV ⬛⬛⬛

The Sky's the Limit Astaire spends his leave in Manhattan and falls in love with fetching journalist Leslie. He's in civvies, so little does she know he's a war hero. Nothing-special semi-musical, with Fred-Ginger spark missing. ♫One For My Baby; My Shining Hour; I've Got a Lot in Common With You.
1943 89m/B Fred Astaire, Joan Leslie, Robert Benchley, Robert Ryan, Elizabeth Patterson; *D:* Edward H. Griffith. **VHS, Beta** $14.98 TTC, VYY, RKO ⬛⬛½

Skyscraper Souls William stars as David Dwight, a ruthless businessman who manipulates stock prices and double-crosses lovers in order to have complete control of a 100-story office building. He sacrifices everything and everyone in this story of big business. Based on the novel "Skyscraper" by Faith Baldwin.
1932 98m/B Warren William, Maureen O'Sullivan, Gregory Ratoff, Anita Page, Verree Teasdale, Norman Foster, Jean Hersholt, Wallace Ford; *D:* Edgar Selwyn. **VHS** $19.98 MGM ⬛⬛⬛

Slacker Defines a new generation: Overwhelmed by the world and it's demands, "Slackers" react by retreating into lives of minimal expectations. Filmed as a series of improvisational stories about people living on the fringes of the working world and their reactions (or lack thereof) to the life swirling around them. First feature for writer/director Linklater on a budget of $23,000; filmed on location in Austin, Texas with a cast of primarily non-professional actors.
1991 (R) 97m/C Richard Linklater; *D:* Richard Linklater; *W:* Richard Linklater. **VHS** $79.95 ING, ORI ⬛⬛⬛

Slamdance A struggling cartoonist is framed for the murder of a beautiful young woman while being victimized by the real killer. A complicated murder mystery with a punk beat and visual flash. But the tale is unoriginal - and where's the slamdancing?
1987 (R) 99m/C Tom Hulce, Virginia Madsen, Mary Elizabeth Mastrantonio, Harry Dean Stanton, Adam Ant, John Doe; *D:* Wayne Wang. **VHS, Beta** $19.98 FOX ⬛½

Slammer Girls In this sex-drenched, unfunny spoof on women's prison films, the inmates of Loch Ness Penitentiary try to break out using their sexual wiles. The actresses are pseudonymous porn stars.
1987 (R) 82m/C Tally Brittany, Jane Hamilton, Jeff Eagle, Devon Jenkin; *D:* Chuck Vincent. **VHS, Beta** $19.98 LIV ⬛

The Slap French teens learn about love the French way. *AKA:* La Gifle.

1976 (PG) 103m/C Isabelle Adjani, Lino Ventura; *D:* Claude Pinoteau; *M:* Georges Delerue. **VHS** SUE ⬛

Slap Shot A profane satire of the world of professional hockey. Over-the-hill player-coach Newman gathers an odd-ball mixture of has-beens and young players and reluctantly initiates them, using violence on the ice to make his team win. The strip-tease on ice needs to be seen to be believed. Charming in its own bone-crunching way.
1977 (R) 123m/C Paul Newman, Michael Ontkean, Jennifer Warren, Lindsay Crouse, Jerry Houser, Melinda Dillon, Strother Martin; *D:* George Roy Hill; *M:* Elmer Bernstein. **VHS, Beta** $14.98 MCA ⬛⬛⬛

Slapstick An anthology of great moments from Mack Sennett comedy shorts, featuring many great stars in some of their earliest film appearances.
193? 76m/B Charlie Chaplin, Harold Lloyd, Charley Chase, Buster Keaton, Ben Turpin, Stan Laurel. **VHS, Beta** $39.95 REP ⬛⬛⬛

Slapstick of Another Kind Lewis and Kahn play dual roles as an alien brother and sister and their adoptive Earth parents, who are being pursued by U.S. agents. Rather miserable rendition of a Kurt Vonnegut novel.
1984 (PG) 85m/C Jerry Lewis, Madeline Kahn, Marty Feldman, Jim Backus, Noriyuki "Pat" Morita, Samuel Fuller, Orson Welles; *D:* Steven Paul. **VHS, Beta** $79.98 LIV, VES ⬛½

Slash Each of four people caught in a political takeover harbors a secret that could harm one of the others. Extremely violent.
1987 90m/C Romano Kristoff, Michael Monty, Gwen Hung; *D:* John Gale. **VHS, Beta** NO ⬛½

Slashdance A really pathetic thriller follows a lady cop undercover in a chorus line to find out who's been murdering the dancers. The acting is on the level of pro wrestling. Don't be fooled by the naked babes on the cassette box - there's no nudity.
1989 83m/C Cindy Maranne, James Carroll Jordan, Queen Kong, Joel von Ornsteiner, Jay Richardson; *D:* James Shyman; *W:* James Shyman. **VHS, Beta** $9.95 SIM Woof!

Slashed Dreams Hippie couple travels to California wilderness in search of a friend. A pair of woodsmen assault them and rape the woman, which really messes with their heads. Retitled and packaged as slasher movie. *AKA:* Sunburst.
1974 (R) 74m/C Peter Hooten, Katherine Baumann, Ric Carrott, Anne Lockhart, Robert Englund, Rudy Vallee, James Keach, David Pritchard, Peter Brown; *D:* James Polakof; *W:* James Keach, David Pritchard. **VHS** $19.95 ACA ⬛⬛

The Slasher A policeman must find the madman who has been killing off unfaithful married women. Miserably gory, pointless slasher (hence the title) interesting only as an early example of its kind.
1974 88m/C Farley Granger, Sylva Koscina, Susan Scott. **VHS, Beta** $59.95 MON Woof!

Slate, Wyn & Me Two bank-robbing, kidnapping brothers flee cross-country from the law, and fall in love with the girl they've snatched. Pointless, and pointlessly violent and vulgar.
1987 (R) 90m/C Sigrid Thornton, Simon Burke, Martin Sacks; *D:* Don McLennan. **VHS, Beta** $19.98 SUE, NLC ⬛

Slaughter After his parents are murdered, a former Green Beret goes after their killers. Plenty of brutality. Followed by "Slaughter's Big Ripoff."

1972 (R) 92m/C Jim Brown, Stella Stevens, Rip Torn, Cameron Mitchell, Don Gordon, Marlene Clark; *D:* Jack Starrett. **VHS, Beta** $59.98 FOX ⬛

Slaughter High A high school nerd is accidentally disfigured by a back-firing prank. Five years later, he returns to exact bloody revenge. Available in an unrated version.
1986 (R) 90m/C Caroline Munro, Simon Scuddamore, Kelly Baker; *D:* George Dugdale. **VHS, Beta** $79.98 LIV, VES ⬛

Slaughter Hotel An asylum already inhabited by extremely bizarre characters is plagued by a series of gruesome murders. Lots of skin and lots of blood; Neri shines as a nymphomaniacal lesbian nurse. *AKA:* Asylum Erotica; La Bestia Uccide a Sangue Freddo.
1971 72m/C Klaus Kinski, Rosalba (Sara Bay) Neri, Margaret Lee, John Ely; *D:* Fernando Di Leo. **VHS, Beta** MPI, GRG ⬛

Slaughter in San Francisco A Chinese-American cop leads a one-man fight against corruption in the department in Daly City, near San Francisco. Norris is the bad guy; made in 1973 but not released until he had an established following. Plenty of kicking and karate chops. *AKA:* Chuck Norris vs. the Karate Cop.
1981 (R) 92m/C Chuck Norris, Don Wong; *D:* William Lowe. **VHS, Beta** $9.95 SUE, RHI ⬛

Slaughter of the Innocents FBI agent Broderick (Glenn) is sent to Salt Lake City to investigate the murders of two children which are found to be connected to a series of bizarre killings that have occurred around Monument Valley. Unbeknownst to his associates, Broderick often uses his 11-year-old whiz-kid son Jesse's (Cameron-Glickenhaus) computer skills to aid his research. Only this time, his inquisitive son gets too close to a serial killer and unless Dad can figure things out on his own, Jesse will be the next victim.
1993 (R) 104m/C Scott Glenn, Jesse Cameron-Glickenhaus, Sheila Tousey, Darlanne Fluegel, Zitto Kazann; *D:* James Glickenhaus; *W:* James Glickenhaus. **VHS** MCA ⬛

The Slaughter of the Vampires Newlyweds meet a bloodthirsty vampire in a Viennese chalet. Real, real bad horror flick, poorly dubbed. *AKA:* Curse of the Blood-Ghouls; Curses of the Ghouls.
1962 81m/C Walter Brandi, Dieter Eppler, Graziella Granta; *D:* Robert Mauri; *W:* Robert Mauri. **VHS, Beta** $39.95 SNC Woof!

Slaughter Trail Rancher-turned-stage robber Young shoots two Indians and cavalry colonel Donlevy has to deal with the fallout. Peace returns when Young dies. Ordinary western with balladeer device helping the plot along, or trying to.
1951 78m/C Brian Donlevy, Gig Young, Virginia Grey, Andy Devine, Robert Hutton; *D:* Irving Allen. **VHS, Beta** $19.98 TTC ⬛⬛

Slaughterday An innocent woman is caught in the middle of an ex-con's elaborate scheme to commit the largest heist of his life.
1977 (R) 87m/C Rita Tushingham, William Berger, Frederick Jaeger, Michael Hauserman, Gordon Mitchell; *D:* Peter Patzak. **VHS, Beta** GHV ⬛½

Slaughterhouse A rotund, pig-loving country boy kills, maims, and eats numerous victims. Features the requisite dumb teens and plenty of blood.
1987 (R) 87m/C Joe Barton, Sherry Bendorf, Don Barrett; *D:* Rick Roessler. **VHS, Beta** $14.98 NLC Woof!

Slaughterhouse Five A suburban optometrist becomes "unstuck" in time and flits randomly through the experiences of his life, from the Dresden bombing to an extraterrestrial zoo. Noticed at Cannes but not at theatres; ambitious failure to adapt Kurt Vonnegut's odd novel.
1972 (R) 104m/C Michael Sacks, Valerie Perrine, Ron Leibman, Eugene Roche, Perry King; **D:** George Roy Hill. **VHS, Beta** $19.95 MCA 🎬🎬🎬

Slaughterhouse Rock The ghost of a sexy rock star draws a young man into a confrontation with a sadistic spirit that rules a deserted prison. There's also some cannibalism involved. Music group Devo did the score for this flick.
1988 (R) 90m/C Nicholas Celozzi, Donna Denton, Toni Basil, Hope Marie Carlton; **D:** Dimitri Logothetis; **M:** Devo. **VHS, Beta** NO Woof!

Slaughter's Big Ripoff Slaughter is back battling the Mob with guns, planes and martial arts. This undistinguished sequel features McMahon as a mob boss.
1973 (R) 92m/C Jim Brown, Brock Peters, Don Stroud, Ed McMahon, Art Metrano, Gloria Hendry; **D:** Gordon Douglas. **VHS, Beta** $59.98 FOX 🎬½

Slave Girls from Beyond Infinity In this B-movie spoof, two beautiful intergalactic slave girls escape their penal colony, land on a mysterious planet, and meet a cannibalistic despot. Fun spoof of '50s "B" sci-fi movies.
1987 80m/C Elizabeth Cayton, Cindy Beal, Brinke Stevens; **D:** Ken Dixon. **VHS, Beta** NO 🎬🎬

A Slave of Love Poignant love story set in the Crimea as the Bolshevik Revolution rages around a film crew attempting to complete a project. Interesting as ideological cinema but also enjoyable romantic drama. In Russian with English subtitles.
1978 94m/C Elena Solovei, Rodion Nakhapetov, Alexander Kalyagin; **D:** Nikita Mikhalkov; **M:** Eduard Artemyev. **VHS, Beta** $29.95 COL, AUD, ING 🎬🎬🎬

Slave of the Cannibal God Beautiful Andress is captured by "native" cannibals; Keach must save her. **AKA:** Il Montagna di Dio Cannibale; Mountain of Cannibal Gods.
1979 (R) 86m/C Stacy Keach, Ursula Andress, Claudio Cassinelli; **D:** Sergio Martino. **VHS, Beta** $49.95 VES Woof!

Slave Trade in the World Today Slavery practices in the modern world are shown, including actual scenes of a sheik's harem, slave auctions, and the kidnapping and selling of young women.
1964 87m/C **D:** Roberto Malenotti. **VHS, Beta** $19.95 VDC, TPV 🎬

Slavers Detailed depiction of the 19th century African slave trade with a little romance thrown in.
1977 (R) 102m/C Trevor Howard, Britt Ekland, Ron Ely, Cameron Mitchell, Ray Milland; **D:** Jurgen Goslar. **VHS, Beta** $69.95 VCD 🎬🎬

Slaves in Bondage Young, country girls are lured into the big city and initiated into a life of ill repute in this exploitation classic. A must for camp fans of the 30's.
1937 ?m/C Lona Andre, Wheeler Oakman. **VHS** $16.95 SNC 🎬

Slaves of New York Greenwich Village artists worry about life and love in the '80s and being artistic enough for New York. Adapted from the stories of Tama Janowitz, who also wrote the screenplay and appears as Abby. Disastrous adaptation of a popular novel.

1989 (R) 115m/C Bernadette Peters, Chris Sarandon, Mary Beth Hurt, Madeleine Potter, Adam Coleman Howard, Nick Corri, Mercedes Ruehl, Joe Leeway, Charles McCaughan, John Harkins, Anna Katarina, Tama Janowitz; **D:** James Ivory; **W:** Tama Janowitz. **VHS, Beta** $89.95 COL 🎬½

The Slayer It's movies like this that give getting back to nature a bad name. That horrible monster is after those nice young people again! This time it's on an island off the coast of Georgia. **AKA:** Nightmare Island.
1982 (R) 95m/C **D:** J.S. Cardone; **W:** J.S. Cardone; **M:** Robert Folk. **VHS, Beta** NO Woof!

The Slayer/The Scalps Double feature. "Scalps" is a slasher set in a Native American burial ground. "The Slayer" is about vacationing couples who run into more than they bargained for on their island retreat.
1982 (R) 150m/C **D:** J.S. Cardone. **VHS, Beta** NO 🎬

Slayground Man, distraught at the accidental death of his daughter, hires a hitman to exact revenge. Excruciating adaptation of the novel by Richard Stark (Donald E. Westlake).
1984 (R) 85m/C Peter Coyote, Mel Smith, Billie Whitelaw, Philip Sayer, Kelli Maroney; **D:** Terry Bedford. **VHS, Beta** $9.98 REP 🎬½

Sleazemania Compilation of trailers 'n bits reviews some of the sleazier, sicker, and sexier selections of celluloid from the past 50 years.
1985 60m/C **VHS, Beta** $19.95 RHI 🎬½

Sleazemania III: The Good, the Bad & the Sleazy Another compilation of the cheapest, funniest and scurviest moments, from grade-Z horror films, including "Mondo Psycho" and "Smut Peddler Meets Emmanuel."
1986 90m/B **VHS, Beta** $39.95 RHI 🎬½

The Sleazy Uncle A successful but bored businessman is energized by an encounter with his vice-ridden uncle, a mooching, womanizing beatnik poet who knows how to enjoy life. An energetic but rather formulaic comedy. In Italian with English subtitles. **AKA:** Lo Zio Indegno.
1989 104m/C Giancarlo Giannini, Vittorio Gassman, Andrea Ferreol, Stefania Sandrelli; **D:** Franco Brusati. **VHS, Beta** $89.95 ING, TRI 🎬🎬

Sledgehammer A madman is wreaking havoc on a small town, annihilating young women with a sledgehammer.
1983 87m/C Ted Prior, Doug Matley, Steven Wright. **VHS, Beta** NO Woof!

Sleep of Death Young Englishman's pursuit of a blue-blooded woman seems to set off a series of bizarre and mysterious murders. A gothic thriller based on Sheridan Le Fanu's short story.
1979 90m/C Brendan Price, Marilu Tolo, Patrick Magee, Curt Jurgens, Per Oscarsson; **D:** Calvin Floyd. **VHS, Beta** $59.95 PSM 🎬½

Sleepaway Camp Crazed killer hacks away at the inhabitants of a peaceful summer camp in this run-of-the-mill slasher.
1983 (R) 88m/C Mike Kellin, Jonathan Tiersten, Felissa Rose, Christopher Collet. **VHS, Beta** $9.95 MED 🎬

Sleepaway Camp 2: Unhappy Campers A beautiful camp counselor is actually a blood-thirsty, murdering madwoman. Sequel to the 1983 slasher, "Sleepaway Camp."
1988 (R) 82m/C Pamela Springsteen, Renee Estevez, Walter Gotell, Brian Patrick Clark; **D:** Michael A. Simpson. **VHS, Beta** $14.98 SUE, NLC 🎬½

Sleepaway Camp 3: Teenage Wasteland This second sequel is as bad as the first two movies. Another disturbed camper hacks up another bevy of teenagers. Better luck at the Motel Six.
1989 (R) 80m/C Pamela Springsteen, Tracy Griffith, Michael J. Pollard; **D:** Michael A. Simpson. **VHS, Beta** $19.98 SUE, NLC Woof!

Sleeper Hapless nerd Allen is revived two hundred years after an operation gone bad. Keaton portrays Allen's love interest in a futuristic land of robots and giant vegetables. He learns of the hitherto unknown health benefits of hot fudge sundaes; discovers the truth about the nation's dictator, known as The Leader; and gets involved with revolutionaries seeking to overthrow the government. Hilarious, fast-moving comedy, full of slapstick and satire. Don't miss the "orgasmatron."
1973 (PG) 88m/C Woody Allen, Diane Keaton, John Beck, Howard Cosell; **D:** Woody Allen; **W:** Woody Allen, Marshall Brickman; **M:** Woody Allen. **VHS, Beta** $14.95 MGM, FOX, FUS 🎬🎬🎬½

Sleeping Beauty Classic Walt Disney version of the famous fairy tale is set to the music of Tchaikovsky's ballet. Lavishly produced. With the voices of Mary Copsta, Bill Shirley, and Vera Vague.
1959 (G) 75m/C **D:** Clyde Geronomi, Eric Larson, Wolfgang Reitherman, Les Clark. **VHS, Beta** DIS, OM 🎬🎬🎬

Sleeping Beauty Peters is the princess put to sleep by evil queen Kellerman. Handsome prince Reeve comes to the rescue in this classy retelling of the Sleeping Beauty legend. Combines live action and animation. From Shelley Duvall's "Faerie Tale Theatre."
1983 60m/C Christopher Reeve, Bernadette Peters, Beverly D'Angelo. **VHS, Beta** $14.95 FOX, FCT, WKV 🎬🎬🎬

Sleeping Beauty Live action version of the beloved fairy tale, with Welch in the title role.
1989 92m/C Tahnee Welch, Morgan Fairchild, Nicholas Clay, Sylvia Miles. **VHS** $14.95 MGM, PSM, CVC 🎬🎬

The Sleeping Car A vindictive ghost haunts a group of people living in an old railway car. Fairly fun, fairly competent horror.
1990 87m/C David Naughton, Judie Aronson, Kevin McCarthy, Jeff Conaway, Dani Minnick, John Carl Buechler; **D:** Douglas Curtis. **VHS** $89.95 VMK 🎬🎬

Sleeping Car to Trieste Conspirators in the theft of a diplomat's diary ride the Orient Express, as a wily detective on board tries to piece together murder clues. Based on the story "Rome Express" by Clifford Grey.
1945 95m/B Jean Kent, Albert Lieven, David Tomlinson, Finlay Currie; **D:** John Paddy Carstairs. **VHS, Beta** LCA 🎬🎬

Sleeping Dogs A man in near-future New Zealand finds it hard to remain neutral when he is caught between a repressive government and a violent resistance movement. The first New Zealand film ever to open in the U.S., and a fine debut for director Donaldson.
1982 107m/C Sam Neill, Ian Mune, Nevan Rowe, Dona Akersten, Warren Oates; **D:** Roger Donaldson. **VHS, Beta** NO 🎬🎬½

The Sleeping Tiger A thief breaks into the home of a psychiatrist, who captures him. In exchange for his freedom, the thief agrees to become a guinea pig for the doctor's rehabilitation theories with ultimately tragic results. Director Losey was originally compelled to release the film under a pseud-

onym, "Victor Hanbury," because he had been blacklisted by Hollywood during the 1950s red scare. First pairing of Losey and Bogarde, who collaborated on several later films, including "Modesty Blaise" (1966) and "Accident" (1967).
1954 89m/B Alexis Smith, Alexander Knox, Dirk Bogarde, Hugh Griffith; **D:** Joseph Losey; **M:** Malcolm Arnold. VHS $16.95 *NOS, SNC ♫♫ ½*

Sleeping with the Enemy Roberts escapes from abusive husband by faking death, flees to Iowa, falls for drama professor, and, gasp, is found by psycho husband. Occasionally chilling but oft predictable thriller based on novel by Nancy Price.
1991 (R) 99m/C Julia Roberts, Kevin Anderson, Patrick Bergin, Elizabeth Lawrence, Kyle Secor, Claudette Nevins; **D:** Joseph Ruben; **W:** Ronald Bass; **M:** Jerry Goldsmith. VHS, Beta $19.98 *FXV, IME, FCT ♫♫ ½*

Sleepless in Seattle Witty, sweet romantic comedy explores the differences between men and women when it comes to love and romance. When widower Hanks talks about his wife on a national talk show, recently engaged Ryan responds. Writer/director Ephron's humorous screenplay is brought to life by a perfectly cast ensemble; it also breathed new life into the classic weepie "An Affair to Remember," comparing it to "The Dirty Dozen" in an unforgettable scene. A movie full of fine detail, from Sven Nykvist's camera work to the graphic layout of the opening credits to the great score. Captured millions at the box office, coming in as the fourth highest grossing movie of 1993.
1993 (PG) 105m/C Tom Hanks, Meg Ryan, Bill Pullman, Ross Malinger, Rosie O'Donnell, Gaby Hoffman, Victor Garber, Rita Wilson, Barbara Garrick, Carey Lowell, Rob Reiner, Sarah Trigger; **D:** Nora Ephron; **W:** Jeffrey Arch, Larry Atlas, David S. Ward, Nora Ephron; **M:** Marc Shaiman. VHS, 8mm $99.95 *COL, BTV, FCT ♫♫♫ ½*

Sleepwalk Odd independent effort about a bored New York desk worker who is given an ancient text of Chinese fairy tales to translate, and finds they're manifesting themselves in dangerous ways in real life. Cinematography by Jim Jarmusch and Franz Prinzi.
1988 (R) 78m/C Suzanne Fletcher, Ann Magnuson; **D:** Sara Driver. VHS, Beta $19.98 *SUE, NLC, ICA ♫♫*

Sleepwalkers When Mary and her son Charles arrive in the small town of Travis, Indiana, ugly things begin to happen. And no wonder, it seems the deadly duo are sleepwalkers—fiendish, cat-like vampire creatures who can only survive by sucking the life force out of unsuspecting virgins. Gory but not without some humor, particularly in Krige's portrayal of the sexy and too-loving mother. Not nearly as good as some of King's other horror classics. *AKA:* Stephen King's Sleepwalkers.
1992 (R) 91m/C Brian Krause, Madchen Amick, Alice Krige, Jim Haynie, Cindy Pickett, Lyman Ward, Ron Perlman; *Cameos:* Dan Martin, Glenn Shadix, Joe Dante, John Landis, Clive Barker, Tobe Hooper, Stephen King, Mark Hamill; **D:** Mick Garris; **W:** Stephen King. VHS $19.95 *COL ♫ ½*

The Slender Thread Based on a true story, Poitier plays a college student who volunteers at a crisis center and must keep would-be suicide Bancroft on the phone until the police can find her. Filmed on location in Seattle. First film for director Pollack.
1965 98m/C Sidney Poitier, Anne Bancroft, Telly Savalas, Steven Hill; **D:** Sydney Pollack; **W:** Sterling Silliphant; **M:** Quincy Jones. VHS $14.95 *PAR ♫♫♫*

Sleuth A mystery novelist and his wife's lover face off in ever shifting, elaborate, and diabolical plots against each other, complete with red herrings, traps, and tricks. Playful, cerebral mystery thriller from top director Mankiewicz. Schaeffer also scripted "Frenzy" for Hitchcock, from his play.
1972 (PG) 138m/C Laurence Olivier, Michael Caine; **D:** Joseph L. Mankiewicz; **W:** Anthony Shaffer; **M:** John Addison. Academy Awards '72 Nominations: Best Actor (Caine), Best Actor (Olivier), Best Director (Mankiewicz), Best Original Score; Edgar Allan Poe Awards '72: Best Screenplay. VHS, Beta $19.95 *MED, HMV, VTR ♫♫♫ ½*

Slightly Honorable A lawyer gets involved in political scandals and becomes a murder suspect. Snappy comedy-drama with good performances but too many subplots. Based on the novel "Send Another Coffin" by F. G. Presnell.
1940 75m/B Pat O'Brien, Broderick Crawford, Edward Arnold, Eve Arden, Evelyn Keyes, Phyllis Brooks; **D:** Tay Garnett. VHS, Beta $19.95 *NOS, VYY, BAR ♫♫ ½*

A Slightly Pregnant Man Comic complications abound as a construction worker becomes the world's first pregnant man. Surprise ending saves this simple and not very exciting film.
1979 (PG) 92m/C Catherine Deneuve, Marcello Mastroianni; **D:** Jacques Demy. VHS, Beta *NO ♫♫*

Slightly Scarlet Small-time hood Payne carries out an assignment from boss DeCorsia to smear a law-and-order politico running for mayor. He falls in love with the candidate's secretary, tries to go straight, and ends up running the mob when DeCorsia flees town. A spiffy, low-budget noir crime drama.
1956 99m/C Rhonda Fleming, Arlene Dahl, John Payne, Kent Taylor, Ted de Corsia; **D:** Allan Dwan. VHS, Beta *NO ♫♫ ½*

Slime City The widow of an alchemist poisons her tenants so they will join her husband in the hereafter. Very low-budget; occasionally funny.
1989 90m/C Robert C. Sabin, Mary Huner, T.J. Merrick, Dick Biel; **D:** Gregory Lamberson. VHS, Beta *NO ♫*

The Slime People Huge prehistoric monsters are awakened from long hibernation by atomic testing in Los Angeles. They take over the city, creating the fog they need to live. Thank goodness for scientist Burton, who saves the day. Filmed in a butcher shop in Los Angeles.
1963 76m/B Robert Hutton, Robert Burton, Susan Hart, William Boyce, Les Tremayne; **D:** Robert Hutton. VHS, Beta $19.95 *NOS, GEM, RHI Woof!*

Slipping into Darkness Three spoiled, rich college girls are held responsible for a retarded local boy's death. Honest and overwrought.
1988 (R) 86m/C Belle Mitchell, Laslo Papas, Rigg Kennedy, Beverly Ross, T.J. McFadden, Michelle Johnson, John DiAquino; **D:** Eleanor Gaver. VHS, Beta $24.95 *GHV, HHE ♫ ½*

Slipstream "Turgid" and "gloomy" are the words for this romantic drama set in remote Alberta. The minor plot concerns a young woman who teaches a lonely disc jockey a lesson about life and love. This film feels like a long Canadian winter.
1972 93m/C Julie Askew, Patti Oatman, Eli Rill. VHS, Beta $19.95 *TWE ♫♫*

Slipstream A sci-fi adventure set on a damaged Earthscape where people seek to escape a giant jetstream. While tracking down a bounty hunter gone bad, a futuristic cop follows his quarry into the dangerous river of wind. Ambitious "Blade Runner" clone with big names (Hamill is good) was never released theatrically in the US.
1989 (PG-13) 92m/C Mark Hamill, Bill Paxton, Bob Peck, Eleanor David, Kitty Aldridge, Robbie Coltrane, Ben Kingsley, F. Murray Abraham; **D:** Steven Lisberger; **M:** Elmer Bernstein. VHS, Beta *VTR ♫♫*

Slither Caan and Boyle become wrapped up in a scheme to recover $300,000 in cash, stolen seven years previously. Along the way they pick up speed freak Kellerman, who assists them in a variety of loony ways. Frantic chase scenes are the highlight.
1973 (PG) 97m/C James Caan, Peter Boyle, Sally Kellerman, Louise Lasser, Allen (Gooritz) Garfield, Richard B. Shull, Alex Rocco; **D:** Howard Zieff; **W:** W.D. Richter. VHS, Beta $19.98 *MGM ♫♫*

Slithis Slithis, the nuclear-waste creature, is the menace of Venice, California. Keep your pets (and yourself) indoors!
1978 (PG) 86m/C Alan Blanchard, Judy Motulsky; **D:** Stephen Traxler; **W:** Stephen Traxler. VHS, Beta $19.95 *MED Woof!*

Sliver Another voyeuristic thriller starring Stone. She's Carly Norris, a lonely book editor who moves into one of Manhattan's toothpick thin buildings (the "sliver" of the title). She meets pulp novelist Jack (Berenger), whose libido is as overheated as his prose, but gets involved in a steamy affair with handsome neighbor Zeke (Baldwin), a computer whiz who also owns the building. Oh, by the way, he's installed video cameras in every unit that reveal many intimate secrets. Lots of sex and murders. Murky and underdeveloped and the ending, which was reshot, still leaves much to be desired. Lots of hype, little to recommend.
1993 (R) 106m/C Sharon Stone, William Baldwin, Tom Berenger, Martin Landau, Polly Walker, Colleen Camp, CCH Pounder, Nina Foch, Keene Curtis; **D:** Phillip Noyce; **W:** Joe Eszterhas; **M:** Howard Shore. MTV Movie Awards ' Nominations: 4: Most Desirable Female (Stone), Best Song ("I Can't Help Falling in Love"); MTV Movie Awards '94: Most Desirable Male (Baldwin). VHS, Beta, CDV *PAR ♫ ½*

Sloane Typical sleazy sex and violence flick. For the record: organized crime baddies kidnap good guy Resnick's girlfriend and he seeks revenge.
1984 95m/C Robert Resnick, Debra Blee, Paul Aragon; **D:** Dan Rosenthal. VHS, Beta $69.98 *LIV, VES Woof!*

Slow Burn An ex-reporter tries some detective work in the seamy side of Palm Springs, and becomes embroiled in the standard drug, kidnapping, murder routine. Based on the novel "Castles Burning" by Arthur Lyons. Made for cable television.
1986 92m/C Eric Roberts, Beverly D'Angelo, Dan Hedaya, Dennis Lipscomb; **D:** Matthew Chapman; **W:** Matthew Chapman; **M:** Loek Dikker. VHS, Beta $59.95 *MCA ♫♫*

Slow Burn The Mafia and Chinese Triads are having troubles and a tired cop attempts to reach a peaceful solution.
1990 (R) 90m/C William Smith, Anthony James, Ivan Rogers. VHS $79.95 *XVC, PHX ♫*

Slow Moves Slow story of slow people who meet slowly, have sluggish affair, and find tragedy eventually.
1984 93m/C Roxanne Rogers; **D:** Jon Jost. VHS, Beta $69.95 *FCT ♫ ½*

The Slugger's Wife The marriage between an Atlanta Braves outfielder and a rock singer suddenly turns sour when their individual careers force them to make some tough choices. *AKA:* Neil Simon's The Slugger's Wife.
1985 (PG-13) 105m/C Michael O'Keefe, Rebecca DeMornay, Martin Ritt, Randy Quaid, Loudon Wainwright III, Rene Lefevre, Lynn Whitfield; *D:* Hal Ashby; *W:* Neil Simon. **VHS, Beta $19.95** COL *⫔½*

Slugs A health inspector discovers that spilled toxic waste is being helpfully cleaned up by the slug population, saving Uncle Sam countless dollars. But wait! The slugs are mutating into blood-thirsty man-eaters. Is this the answer to military cut-backs?
1987 (R) 90m/C Michael Garfield, Kim Terry, Philip Machale; *D:* J.P. Simon. **VHS, Beta $19.95** STE, NWV Woof!

Slumber Party '57 At a slumber party, six girls get together and exchange stories of how they lost their virginity. Lots of great music by the Platters, Big Bopper, Jerry Lee Lewis, the Crewcuts, and Paul and Paula but complete schlock otherwise.
1976 (R) 89m/C Noelle North, Bridget Hollman, Debra Winger, Mary Ann Appleseth, Cheryl "Rainbeaux" Smith, Janet Wood, R.L. Armstrong, Rafael Campos, Larry Gelman, Will Hutchins, Joyce Jillson, Victor Rogers, Joe E. Ross, Bill Thurman; *D:* William A. Levey; *M:* Miles Goodman. **VHS, Beta $14.95** MGM, VES *⫔½*

The Slumber Party Massacre A psychotic killer with a power drill terrorizes a high school girls' slumber party. Contrived and forced, but not always unfunny.
1982 (R) 84m/C Michele Michaels, Robin Stille, Andre Honore, Michael Villela, Debra Deliso, Gina Mari, Brinke Stevens; *D:* Amy Jones, Aaron Lipstadt; *W:* Rita Mae Brown. **VHS, Beta $14.98** SUE *⫔½*

Slumber Party Massacre 2 Drowsy babes in lingerie are drilled to death by a perverse madman. Another disappointing sequel.
1987 75m/C Crystal Bernard, Kimberly McArthur, Juliette Cummins, Patrick Lowe; *D:* Deborah Brock; *W:* Deborah Brock. **VHS, Beta $14.98** SUE, NLC Woof!

Slumber Party Massacre 3 Parents: Don't let your daughters have any slumber parties! Yes, it's a drill—for the third time.
1990 (R) 76m/C Keely Christian, Brittain Frye, M.K. Harris, David Greenle, Hope Marie Carlton, Maria Ford; *D:* Sally Mattison. **VHS, Beta $79.98** MGM Woof!

The Small Back Room A crippled WWII munitions expert leads a tormented existence and laments government bureaucracy. Powerfully presented adult storyline. *AKA:* Hour of Glory.
1949 106m/B Emeric Pressburger, David Farrar, Jack Hawkins, Cyril Cusack, Kathleen Byron, Anthony Bushell, Michael Gough, Robert Morley; *D:* Michael Powell. **VHS $24.95** VYY, LOO, FCT *⫔⫔⫔*

Small Change Pudgy, timid Desmouceaux and scruffy, neglected Goldman lead a whole pack of heartwarming tykes. A realistically and tenderly portrayed testament to the great director's belief in childhood as a "state of grace." Criticized for sentimentality, "Small Change" followed Truffaut's gloomy "The Story of Adele H." Steven Spielberg suggested the English translation of "L'Argent de Poche." In French with English subtitles.
1976 (PG) 104m/C Geory Desmouceaux, Philippe Goldman, Jean-Francois Stevenin, Chantal Mercier, Claudio Deluca, Frank Deluca, Richard Golfier, Laurent Devlaeminck, Francis Devlaeminck; *D:* Francois Truffaut; *W:* Suzanne Schiffman. **VHS, Beta $19.99** MGM, FCT, ING *⫔⫔⫔*

A Small Circle of Friends Three Harvard students struggle through their shifting relationships during their college years in the 1960s.
1980 (R) 112m/C Brad Davis, Jameson Parker, Karen Allen, Shelley Long; *D:* Rob Cohen. **VHS, Beta $59.98** FOX *⫔½*

Small Hotel After discovering that he is to be replaced as headwaiter by a young woman, Harker plots to save his job through espionage, blackmail and cajolery. Average comedy, adapted from a popular British stage play as a star vehicle for Harker.
1957 59m/B Gordon Harker, Marie Lohr, John Loder, Irene Handl, Janet Munro, Billie Whitelaw, Francis Matthews, Dora Bryan; *D:* David MacDonald. **VHS $19.95** NOS *⫔*

Small Kill Burghoff leaves his lovable MASH character far behind, testing his acting skills as a psycho who disguises himself as a female fortune teller to rob his victims of their life savings so he can become head druglord of his town (what a goal). Two cops try to stop him/her.
1993 (R) 86m/C Gary Burghoff, Rebecca Ferratti, Donnie Kehr, Jason Miller, Fred Carpenter; *D:* Robert M. Fresco; *W:* James McTernan. **VHS $59.95** VCI *⫔½*

A Small Killing An undercover cop and a college professor pose as a wino and a bag lady, when trying to put the tabs on a druglord. Made for TV mystery/romance based on "The Rag Bag Clan" by Richard Barth.
1981 100m/C Ed Asner, Jean Simmons, Sylvia Sidney, Andrew Prine, J. Pat O'Malley, Anne Ramsey; *D:* Steven Hilliard Stern. **VHS, Beta $59.95** LIV *⫔⫔*

Small Sacrifices The true story of Diane Downs, an Oregon woman who may have murdered her own three children in 1983. Fine performance from Fawcett, who seems to like made for TV tales of true-life domestic violence as an antidote to her earlier ditzy persona as a Charlie's Angel. Gripping, with a superb script.
1989 159m/C Farrah Fawcett, Ryan O'Neal, John Shea, Emily Perkins, Gordon Clapp; *D:* David Greene; *W:* Joyce Eliason. **VHS, Beta $19.95** FRH *⫔⫔½*

Small Time Chronicles the downfall of a young, samll-time Harlem thief. Vince knows nothing but the streets and peer pressure, indifference, and police abuse lead to a fatal crime. Near documentary style only heightens the tensions.
1991 88m/B Richard Barboza, Carolyn Hinebrew, Keith Allen, Scott Ferguson, Jane Williams; *D:* Norman Loftis; *W:* Norman Loftis; *M:* Arnold Bieber. **VHS $69.95** XVC *⫔⫔*

Small Town Boy The cast does what they can with the brief, hackneyed story of a guy whose personality changes for the worse when he finds a "fortune" (one thousand pre-inflationary dollars).
1937 61m/B Stuart Erwin, Joyce Compton, Jed Prouty, Clara Blandick, James "Doc" Blakely; *D:* Glenn Tryon; *W:* Glenn Tryon. **VHS $19.95** NOS, LOO, VYY *⫔⫔*

Small Town Girl Typical romantic musical of the era, as a city slicker picked up for speeding in a hick town is pursued by the sheriff's daughter. Several Busby Berkeley blockbuster musical numbers are shoehorned incongruously into the rural doings.

♪Take Me To Broadway; I've Got To Hear That Beat; My Flaming Heart; Fine, Fine, Fine; The Fellow I'd Follow; Lullaby of the Lord; Small Towns Are Smile Town; My Gaucho. *AKA:* One Horse Town.
1953 93m/C Jane Powell, Farley Granger, Bobby Van, Ann Miller, Billie Burke, Robert Keith, S.Z. Sakall, Fay Wray, Nat King Cole, Chill Wills; *D:* Leslie Kardos. **VHS, Beta $19.98** MGM *⫔½*

A Small Town in Texas An ex-con returns home looking for the sheriff who framed him on a drug charge, and who has stolen his woman. Not-too-violent, predictable revenge flick.
1976 (PG) 96m/C Timothy Bottoms, Susan George, Bo Hopkins; *D:* Jack Starrett; *W:* William W. Norton Sr.; *M:* Charles Bernstein. **VHS, Beta $69.98** VES, LIV *⫔⫔*

The Smallest Show on Earth A couple inherit not only an old movie house, but the three people who work there as well. Very funny and charming, with a wonderful cast. Sellers is delightful as the soused projectionist. *AKA:* Big Time Operators.
1957 80m/B Bill Travers, Virginia McKenna, Margaret Rutherford, Peter Sellers, Bernard Miles, Leslie Phillips; *D:* Basil Dearden. **VHS $19.95** NOS, FCT, VEC *⫔⫔⫔*

Smart-Aleck Kill An episode of the cable television-produced Phillip Marlowe series involving the drug-related murder of a Hollywood actor in the 20s.
1985 53m/C Powers Boothe, Michael J. Shannon, Liza Ross; *D:* Peter Hunt. **VHS, Beta $39.98** FOX *⫔⫔⫔*

Smart Alecks The Bowery Boys get involved with gangsters when Jordan helps capture a crook. The usual wise-cracking from Hall and Gorcey helps keep things moving.
1942 88m/B Leo Gorcey, Huntz Hall, Gabriel Dell, Gale Storm, Roger Pryor Jr., Walter Woolf King, Herbert Rawlinson, Joe Kirk, Marie Windsor; *D:* Wallace Fox. **VHS $19.95** NOS *⫔½*

Smart Money A wrongly-jailed man enlists the help of his oddball pals to get revenge on the real thief who committed the computer fraud that put him behind bars. They get even while padding their pockets.
1988 88m/C Spencer Leigh, Alexandra Pigg, Ken Campbell. **VHS** NO *⫔⫔½*

Smash Palace A compelling drama of a marriage jeopardized by his obsession with building a race car and her need for love and affection. Melodramatic, but worth watching. Robson as their young daughter is wonderful.
1982 100m/C Bruno Lawrence, Anna Jemison, Greer Robson, Keith Aberdein; *D:* Roger Donaldson; *W:* Bruno Lawrence. **VHS, Beta $69.98** LIV, VES *⫔⫔½*

Smash-Up: The Story of a Woman A famous nightclub singer gives up her career for marriage and a family, only to become depressed when her husband's career soars. She turns to alcohol and her life falls apart. When her husband sues for divorce and custody of their child, she fights to recover from alcoholism. Hayward's first major role. *AKA:* A Woman Destroyed.
1947 103m/B Susan Hayward, Lee Bowman, Marsha Hunt, Eddie Albert; *D:* Stuart Heisler; *W:* John Howard Lawson. **VHS, Beta $19.95** NOS, PSM, DVT *⫔⫔⫔*

Smile Barbed, merciless send-up of small-town America focusing on a group of naive California girls who compete for the "Young American Miss" crown amid rampant commercialism, exploitation and pure middle-class idiocy. Hilarious neglected '70s-style satire. Early role for Griffith.

1975 (PG) 113m/C Bruce Dern, Barbara Feldon, Michael Kidd, Nicholas Pryor, Geoffrey Lewis, Colleen Camp, Joan Prather, Annette O'Toole, Melanie Griffith, Denise Nickerson; *D:* Michael Ritchie; *W:* Jerry Belson. **VHS, Beta $19.95** *MGM 🐾🐾🐾*

Smile, Jenny, You're Dead Janssen discovers that close friend's son-in-law has been murdered, and falls in love with the daughter, the main suspect. Pilot for Janssen's "Harry-O" detective series.
1974 100m/C David Janssen, John Anderson, Howard da Silva, Martin Gabel, Clu Gulager, Zalman King, Jodie Foster, Barbara Leigh; *D:* Jerry Thorpe. **VHS $59.95** *UNI 🐾🐾*

Smiles of a Summer Night The best known of Bergman's rare comedies; sharp satire about eight Swedish aristocrats who become romantically and comically intertwined over a single weekend. Inspired Sondheim's successful Broadway musical "A Little Night Music," and Woody Allen's "A Midsummer Night's Sex Comedy." In Swedish with English subtitles. *AKA:* Sommarnattens Leende.
1955 110m/B Gunnar Bjornstrand, Harriet Andersson, Ulla Jacobsson, Eva Dahlbeck, Jarl Kulle, Margit Carlquist; *D:* Ingmar Bergman; *W:* Ingmar Bergman. **VHS, Beta $29.95** *HMV, VYG, DVT 🐾🐾🐾½*

Smilin' Through First sound version of this melodrama/romance which Franklin had directed as a silent in 1922. Shearer is set to marry Howard when jealous rival March shows up armed at the wedding and accidentally kills the bride. March escapes and Howard spends his years as a recluse until his young niece, the image of his dead fiance (naturally, since she's also played by Shearer) arrives to live with him. She meets a young man who turns out to be March's son (played again by March) and they fall in love. Pure sentiment done with high gloss. Remade in 1941.
1932 97m/B Norma Shearer, Fredric March, Leslie Howard, O.P. Heggie, Ralph Forbes, Beryl Mercer, Margaret Seddon; *D:* Sidney Franklin. **VHS $19.98** *FCT 🐾🐾🐾*

Smilin' Through Third filming, second with sound, first in color, of a popular melodrama. An embittered man whose wife was murdered on their wedding day raises an orphaned niece, only to have her fall in love with the son of her aunt's murderer. Made MacDonald into a singing star. Songs include title tune and "A Little Love, a Little Kiss."
1941 101m/C Jeanette MacDonald, Brian Aherne, Gene Raymond, Ian Hunter, Frances Robinson; *D:* Frank Borzage. **VHS, Beta $19.98** *MGM 🐾🐾½*

Smiling Madame Beudet/The Seashell and the Clergyman Two famous shorts by Dulac; the second scripted by Artaud. Both are pioneering examples of surrealistic film. Silent.
1928 62m/B Alix Allin; *D:* Germaine Dulac; *W:* Antonin Artaud. **VHS, Beta $19.95** *FCT 🐾🐾🐾½*

Smith! Naive but well intentioned look at present-day treatment of Native Americans. Rancher Ford becomes embroiled in the trial of murder suspect Ramirez. Based on Paul St. Pierre's novel "Breaking Smith's Quarter Horse."
1969 101m/C Glenn Ford, Frank Ramirez, Keenan Wynn; *D:* Michael O'Herlihy. **VHS, Beta $69.95** *DIS 🐾🐾½*

Smithereens Working-class girl leaves home for New York's music scene. Rugged, hip character study. Director Seidelman's first feature.

1982 (R) 90m/C Susan Berman, Brad Rinn, Richard Hell; *D:* Susan Seidelman; *W:* Ron Nyswaner. **VHS, Beta $59.95** *MED, TPV, FCT 🐾🐾½*

Smoke A young boy nurses a lost German sheperd back to health with the help of his new stepfather, whom he learns to trust. Then he runs away with the dog when the original owners show up. Made for television Disney fare starring Opie/Richie (and later successful director) Howard.
1970 89m/C Earl Holliman, Ron Howard, Andy Devine; *D:* Vincent McEveety. **VHS, Beta $69.95** *DIS 🐾🐾½*

Smoke Three days in the life of Michael, as he travels between fantasy and reality, past and present, searching for love with the perfect older man.
1993 90m/C *D:* Mark D'Aruia. **VHS $39.95** *WBF 🐾🐾*

Smoke in the Wind Subpar western about men accused of complicity with the Union in postbellum Arkansas. Minor role for Brennan was his last; also director Kane's last film.
1975 (PG) 93m/C John Ashley, Walter Brennan, John Russell, Myron Healey; *D:* Joseph Kane. **VHS, Beta $49.95** *PSM 🐾½*

Smokescreen A young ad exec meets the girl of his dreams, and finds himself working for her gangster boyfriend. Competently made and acted, but phoney ending wrecks it.
1990 (R) 91m/C Kim Cattrall, Dean Stockwell, Matt Craven, Kim Coates, Brian George, Michael Hogan; *D:* Martin Lavut. **VHS $89.95** *COL 🐾🐾½*

Smokey and the Bandit If you don't know how to end a movie, you call for a car chase. The first and best of the horrible series about bootlegger Reynolds is one long car chase. Reynolds makes a wager that he can have a truck load of Coors beer—once unavailable east of Texas—delivered to Atlanta from Texas in 28 hours. Gleason is the "smokey" who tries to stop him. Field is the hitchhiker Reynolds picks up along the way. Great stunts; director Needham was a top stunt man.
1977 (PG) 96m/C Burt Reynolds, Sally Field, Jackie Gleason, Jerry Reed, Mike Henry, Paul Williams, Pat McCormick; *D:* Hal Needham; *W:* Charles Shyer. **VHS, Beta $14.98** *MCA 🐾🐾🐾*

Smokey and the Bandit, Part 2 Pathetic sequel to "Smokey and the Bandit" proved a box-office winner, grossing $40 million. The Bandit is hired to transport a pregnant elephant from Miami to the Republican convention in Dallas. Sheriff Buford T. Justice and family are in hot pursuit. *AKA:* Smokey and the Bandit Ride Again.
1980 (PG) 101m/C Burt Reynolds, Sally Field, Jackie Gleason, Jerry Reed, Mike Henry, Dom DeLuise, Pat McCormick, Paul Williams; *D:* Hal Needham; *W:* Jerry Belson, Michael Kane. **VHS, Beta $14.98** *MCA 🐾*

Smokey and the Bandit, Part 3 You thought the second one was bad? Another mega car chase, this time sans Reynolds and director Needham.
1983 (PG) 88m/C Burt Reynolds, Jackie Gleason, Jerry Reed, Paul Williams, Pat McCormick, Mike Henry, Colleen Camp; *D:* Dick Lowry. **VHS, Beta $14.98** *MCA 🐾*

Smokey & the Hotwire Gang A convoy of truckers try to track down a beautiful woman driving a stolen car.
1979 85m/C James Keach, Stanley Livingston, Tony Lorea, Alvy Moore, George Barris. **VHS, Beta** *NO 🐾½*

Smokey & the Judge Police officer has his hands full with a trio of lovely ladies.

1980 (PG) 90m/C Gene Price, Wayde Preston, Juanita Curiel. **VHS** *SUN 🐾*

Smokey Bites the Dust Car-smashing gag-fest about a sheriff's daughter kidnapped by her smitten beau. Near-plotless and literally unoriginal: lifted footage from several other Corman-produced flicks, a technique that can aptly be called garbage picking.
1981 (PG) 87m/C Janet Julian, Jimmy McNichol, Patrick Campbell, Kari Lizer, John Blythe Barrymore Jr.; *D:* Charles B. Griffith; *W:* Max Apple. **VHS, Beta $19.98** *NLC 🐾*

Smokey Smith Ubiquitous Hayes and steely Steele hunt down the slayers of an elderly couple. Ordinary oater directed by Steele's father, Bradbury.
1936 59m/B Bob Steele, George "Gabby" Hayes; *D:* Robert North Bradbury. **VHS, Beta $27.95** *VCN 🐾*

A Smoky Mountain Christmas Dolly gets away from it all in a secluded cabin that has been appropriated by a gang of orphans, and sings a half dozen songs. Innocuous seasonal country fun. Winkler's TV directing debut.
1986 94m/C Dolly Parton, Bo Hopkins, Dan Hedaya, Gennie James, David Ackroyd, Rene Auberjonois, John Ritter, Anita Morris, Lee Majors; *D:* Henry Winkler; *W:* Dolly Parton. **VHS, Beta $79.98** *FOX 🐾🐾*

Smooth Talk An innocent, flirtatious teenager catches the eye of a shady character, played by Williams. Disturbing and thought-provoking film that caused some controversy when it opened. Dern gives a brilliant performance as the shy, sheltered girl. Based on the Joyce Carol Oates story of the same name. Made for PBS' "American Playhouse" series.
1985 (PG-13) 92m/C Laura Dern, Treat Williams, Mary Kay Place, Levon Helm; *D:* Joyce Chopra. **VHS, Beta $29.98** *LIV, VES 🐾🐾🐾*

Smooth Talker A serial killer stalks the women of a 976 party line. Bad acting, bad dialog, not a scare to be found.
1990 (R) 89m/C Joe Guzaldo, Peter Crombie, Stuart Whitman, Burt Ward, Sydney Lassick, Blair Weickgenant; *D:* Tom Milo. **VHS $89.95** *ACA Woof!*

Smouldering Fires A tough businesswoman falls in love with an ambitious young employee, who is fifteen years her junior. After they marry, problems arise in the form of the wife's attractive younger sister. Surprisingly subtle melodrama, if that's not an oxymoron.
1925 100m/B Pauline Frederick, Laura La Plante, Tully Marshall, Malcolm McGregor, Wanda Hawley, Helen Lynch, George Cooper, Bert Roach; *D:* Clarence Brown. **VHS, Beta $24.95** *VYY, GPV 🐾🐾½*

Smugglers Opportunistic smugglers take advantage of the Russian Revolution to sack the land and make a bundle. *AKA:* Lover of the Great Bear.
1975 110m/C Senta Berger, Giuliano Gemma; *D:* Valentino Orsini. **VHS, Beta $59.95** *VCD 🐾*

Smugglers' Cove Gorcey wrongly believes he has inherited a mansion. He and the Bowery Boys move in, only to stumble across a smuggling ring. Plenty of slapstick; the boys at their best.
1948 66m/B Leo Gorcey, Huntz Hall, Gabriel Dell; *D:* William Beaudine. **VHS** *NO 🐾🐾🐾*

Smuggler's Cove A young boy doggedly pursues a mysterious trawler captain despite warnings from his parents.
1983 75m/C **VHS, Beta** *NO 🐾½*

Snake Dancer Softcore epic concerning the gyrations of a particular dancer.
19?? 87m/C Glenda Kemp, Peter Elliott, Christine Basson; *D:* Dirk DeVilliers. **VHS $29.95** *ACA* 🐾

The Snake Hunter Strangler A young girl is rescued after fifteen years from an evil cult of snake people.
1966 65m/C Guy Madison, Ivan Desny; *D:* Luigi Capuano. **VHS, Beta** *NO* 🐾

Snake in the Eagle's Shadow 2 Three champions of self-defense mount a major offensive and win battle after battle.
1983 89m/C Wang Tao, Chen Shing, Lung Fei; *D:* Chang Shinn I. **VHS, Beta $39.95** *TWE* 🐾

The Snake People A police captain investigates a small island littered with LSD-experimenting scientists, snake-worshippers, and voodoo. One of the infamous quartet of Karloff's final films, all made in Mexico. *AKA:* Isle of the Snake People; Cult of the Dead; La Muerte Viviente; Isle of the Living Dead.
1968 90m/C Boris Karloff, Julissa, Carlos East; *D:* Enrique Vergara. **VHS, Beta $49.95** *SNC, MPI, HEG* 🐾

The Snake Pit One of the first films to compassionately explore mental illness and its treatment. Following an emotional collapse de Havilland is placed in a mental institution by her husband. The severity of her depression causes her sympathetic doctor to try such treatments as electric shock, hydrotherapy, and drugs, along with the psychoanalysis which gradually allows her to accept her fears and make her recovery. Tour-de-force performance by de Havilland. Based on the novel by Mary Jane Ward.
1948 108m/B Olivia de Havilland, Mark Stevens, Leo Genn, Celeste Holm, Glenn Langan, Helen Craig, Leif Erickson, Beulah Bondi; *D:* Anatole Litvak; *W:* Frank Partos, Millen Brand; *M:* Alfred Newman. Academy Awards '48: Best Sound; Nominations: Best Actress (de Havilland), Best Picture; Academy Awards '48: Best Director (Litvak), Best Screenplay, Best Original Score. **VHS $19.99** *FXV, MOV, BTV* 🐾🐾🐾½

The Snake Woman A herpetologist working in a small English village during the 1890s is conducting strange experiments to try to cure his wife's madness. He tries injecting his pregnant wife with snake venom and she gives birth to a cold-blooded daughter, who, when she grows up, has the ability to change herself into a deadly snake. She promptly begins killing the local male populace until Scotland Yard is called in to investigate. The curvy Travers is appropriately snakey but this movie is dull.
1961 68m/C John P. McCarthy, Susan Travers, Arnold Marle; *D:* Sidney J. Furie. **VHS** *CNM* 🐾

SnakeEater Loner cop tracks down swine who killed his parents and kidnapped his sister. "Rambo" rip-off with little plot, but lots of action. Followed by two sequels.
1989 (R) 89m/C Lorenzo Lamas, Larry Csonka, Ron Palillo; *D:* George Erschbamer. **VHS, Beta $89.95** *MED, VTR* 🐾

SnakeEater 2: The Drug Buster A cop goes nuts and kills four drug dealers. As a result he is committed to an institution. Iron bars don't make a prison for this guy though, and he's soon back on the streets fighting crime with his pal "Speedboat." Silly sequel is quite bad; followed by yet another.
1989 (R) 93m/C Lorenzo Lamas, Larry B. Scott, Michelle Scarabelli, Harvey Atkin, Jack Blum, Kathleen Kinmont; *D:* George Erschbamer. **Beta $14.95** *PAR* 🐾

SnakeEater 3: His Law Tough cop Jack Kelly (Lamas), aka SnakeEater, is out to avenge a woman's beating by a gang of thug bikers. Lots of action and violence, not much plot; based on W. Glenn Duncan's novel "Rafferty's Rules."
1992 (R) 109m/C Lorenzo Lamas, Minor Mustain, Tracy Cook, Holly Chester, Scott "Bam Bam" Bigelow; *D:* George Erschbamer; *W:* John Dunning. **VHS, Beta $14.95** *PAR* 🐾

Snapdragon Police psychologist is led astray by his libido while investigating a luscious amnesiac. His sensible vice cop girlfriend then discovers the sexpot is actually a psycho serial killer calling herself the Snapdragon but will her boyfriend even care?
1993 (R) 96m/C Steven Bauer, Pamela Anderson, Chelsea Field; *D:* Worth Keeter; *W:* Gene Church. **VHS, Beta $92.95** *PSM* 🐾🐾

The Snapper Originally made for BBC television, Frears creates a small comic gem based on the second novel of Doyle's Barrytown trilogy. Set in Dublin, 20-year-old Sharon Curley (Kelleher) finds herself unexpectedly pregnant and refuses to name the father. Family and friends are understanding—until they discover the man's identity. Affecting performances, particularly from Meany as Sharon's dad who takes a much greater interest in the birth of his grandchild than he ever did with his own children. Cheerful semi-sequel to "The Commitments" serves up domestic upheavals graced with humor and a strong sense of family loyalty.
1993 (R) 90m/C Tina Kellegher, Colm Meaney, Ruth McCabe, Colm O'Byrne, Pat Laffan, Eanna MacLiam, Ciara Duffy; *D:* Stephen Frears; *W:* Roddy Doyle. **VHS** *NYR* 🐾🐾🐾½

Snapshot Typical grade Z sex comedy; a free-lance photographer ogles lots of variously dishabilled young women through his lens.
1977 (R) 84m/C Jim Henshaw, Susan Petrie. **VHS, Beta $19.95** *VCI* 🐾

Snatched The wives of three wealthy men are held for ransom, but one man doesn't want to pay, while one of the victims needs insulin. Standard made for television fare.
1972 73m/C Howard Duff, Leslie Nielsen, Sheree North, Barbara Parkins, Robert Reed, John Saxon, Tisha Sterling; *D:* Sutton Roley; *M:* Randy Edelman. **VHS $79.95** *REP* 🐾🐾

Sneakers Competent thriller about five computer hackers with questionable pasts and an equally questionable government job. Of course, nothing is as it seems. Rather slow-going considering the talents and suspense involved but includes enough turns to keep a viewer's interest.
1992 (PG-13) 125m/C Robert Redford, Sidney Poitier, River Phoenix, Dan Aykroyd, Ben Kingsley, David Strathairn, Mary McDonnell, Timothy Busfield, George Hearn, Eddie Jones, James Earl Jones, Stephen Tobolowsky; *D:* Phil Alden Robinson; *W:* Lawrence Lasker, Walter F. Parkes, Phil Alden Robinson; *M:* James Horner, Branford Marsalis. **VHS, Beta $19.98** *MCA, PMS* 🐾🐾½

Sniper Suspenseful television drama based on true story of Charles Whitman, who shot at University of Texas students from Texas Tower on a summer day in 1966. Disney alumnus Russell breaks type as mass killer, with fine support by Yniguez as a police officer on the scene and Beatty as the passerby who lends a hand. Finely crafted recreation of disturbing, true event. *AKA:* The Deadly Tower.
1975 85m/C Kurt Russell, Richard Yniguez, John Forsythe, Ned Beatty, Pernell Roberts, Clifton James, Paul Carr, Alan Vint, Pepe Serna; *D:* Jerry Jameson. **VHS $39.95** *XVC* 🐾🐾🐾

The Sniper A law-abiding citizen becomes a vigilante killer after witnessing a violent crime.
1987 90m/C Claudia Cardinale. **VHS, Beta** *NO* 🐾½

Sniper Less than compelling shoot-'em-up set in Panama. Lead characters include Sgt. Beckett (Berenger), a seasoned assassin who gets a rush from killing. Also assigned to the case is Richard Miller (Zane), a newcomer who knows his guns but not his jungles. Together they go in search of their target, a politician planning a coup with the help of a druglord. Action is poorly choreographed and plot is cursory at best. The laserdisc version is available letterboxed.
1992 (R) 99m/C Tom Berenger, Billy Zane, J.T. Walsh, Aden Young, Ken Radley, Reinaldo Arenas, Carolos Alvarez, Roy Edmonds; *D:* Luis Llosa; *W:* Michael Frost Beckner, Crash Leyland; *M:* Gary Chang. **VHS, 8mm $19.95** *COL* 🐾½

Sno-Line A New York gangster moves to Texas and begins to wipe out the competition on his way to building his drug and gambling dynasty. Bo-ring excuse for entertainment. No hope, no redemption, no titillation: just ultra-"realistic" depiction of organized crime, poorly acted.
1985 (R) 89m/C Vince Edwards, Paul Smith, June Wilkinson; *D:* Douglas F. Oneans. **VHS, Beta $69.98** *LIV* 🐾

Snoopy, Come Home Snoopy leaves Charlie Brown to visit his former owner Lila in the hospital and returns with her to her apartment house. From Charles Schultz's popular comic strip "Peanuts."
1972 (G) 80m/C *D:* Bill Melendez; *W:* Charles M. Schulz. **VHS, Beta $14.98** *FOX* 🐾🐾🐾

Snoopy's Getting Married, Charlie Brown An animated Peanuts adventure wherein Snoopy prepares to get married.
1985 30m/C VHS, Beta $14.95 *BAR* 🐾🐾🐾

Snow Country Romantic drama of an unsuccessful, married artist from Tokyo who travels to a mountain resort to find himself. He requests a Geisha for the evening and, when none are available, the beautiful adopted daughter of the local music teacher is sent to him instead. Based on the novel by Nobel Prize winner Yasunari Kawabata. In Japanese with English subtitles. Remade in 1965.
1957 104m/B Ryo Ikebe, Keiko Kishi, Akira Kubo, Kaoru Yachigusa, Hisaya Morishige, Mineko Yorozuyo, Etsuko Ichihara, Noriko Sengoku, Kumeko Urabe, Eiko Miyoshi, Akira Tan, Chieko Naniwa, Daisuke Kato, Haruo Tanaka; *D:* Shiro Toyoda. **VHS, Beta $29.95** *CVC, ING* 🐾🐾½

The Snow Creature Stupid troop of explorers bring back a snow creature from the Himalayas. Critter escapes in L.A. and terrorizes all in its path before blending in with club crowd. Very bad monster epic (the first about a snow monster) that strains credibility frame by frame. Occasionally, depending upon camera angle, light, and viewer mood, monster appears to be something other than guy in bad suit sweating. Directed by Billy Wilder's brother and another argument against genetic consistency.
1954 72m/B Paul Langton, Leslie Denison; *D:* W. Lee Wilder. **VHS, Beta $19.95** *NOS, SNC, VCI* Woof!

Snow Kill Five city-dwellers travel into the mountains for a fun survival training weekend, but the fun turns deadly when they accidentally come across a murderous drug gang. Pseudo - '30s suspense adventure fails to thrill or surprise. Made for cable.
1990 90m/C Terence Knox, Patti D'Arbanville, David Dukes; **D:** Thomas J. Wright; **W:** Harv Zimmel. **VHS, Beta $29.95** PAR, TTC *ℤ* ½

The Snow Queen From "Fairie Tale Theatre" comes this adaptation of the Hans Christian Andersen tale. A boy and girl who grow up together are separated by evil when the boy is held captive in the icy palace of the Snow Queen. The girl sets out to rescue him.
1983 60m/C Lauren Hutton, Linda Manz, David Hemmings, Melissa Gilbert, Lee Remick, Lance Kerwin; **D:** Peter Medak. **VHS, Beta $14.98** KUI, FOX, FCT *ℤ* ½

Snow: The Movie Rates creative zero for title, though there is snow, as well as skiing, growing up, romance, and good times among the young people involved. Filmed in Australia.
1983 83m/C David Argue, Lance Curtis; **D:** Robert Gibson. **VHS, Beta $59.95** VCD *ℤ*

Snow Treasure With the help of an underground agent, Norwegian children smuggle gold out of the country right under the noses of the Nazis. Based on the novel by Marie McSwigan.
1967 (G) 96m/C James Franciscus, Paul Anstad; **D:** Irving Jacoby. **VHS, Beta $29.95** LIV *ℤ*

Snow White and the Seven Dwarfs Classic adaptation of the Grimm Brothers fairy tale about the fairest of them all. Beautiful animation, memorable characters, and wonderful songs mark this as the definitive "Snow White." Set the stage for other animated features after Walt Disney took an unprecedented gamble by attempting the first animated feature-length film, a project which took over two years to create and $1.5 million to make, and made believers out of those who laughed at the concept. Lifelike animation was based on real stars; Margery Belcher (later Champion) posed for Snow, Louis Hightower was the Prince, and Lucille LaVerne gave the Queen her nasty look. ♫Some Day My Prince Will Come; One Song; With a Smile and a Song; Whistle While You Work; Bluddle-Uddle-Um-Dum; The Dwarfs' Yodel Song; Heigh Ho; I'm Wishing; Isn't This a Silly Song?.
1937 (G) 83m/C **D:** David Hand; **W:** Ted Sears, Otto Englander, Earl Hurd, Dorothy Blank, Richard Creedon, Dick Richard, Merrill De Maris, Webb Smith; **M:** Frank Churchill, Paul Smith, Larry Morey, Leigh Harline; **V:** Adriana Caselotti, Harry Stockwell, Lucille LaVerne, Moroni Olsen, Billy Gilbert, Pinto Colvig, Otis Harlan, Scotty Matraw, Roy Atwell, Stuart Buchanan, Marion Darlington, Jim Macdonald. **VHS $26.99** DIS *ℤℤℤℤ*

Snow White and the Seven Dwarfs From cable television's "Faerie Tale Theatre" comes the story of a princess who befriends seven little men to protect her from the jealous evil queen.
1983 60m/C Elizabeth McGovern, Rex Smith, Vincent Price, Vanessa Redgrave; **D:** Peter Medak. **VHS, Beta $14.98** KUI, FOX, FCT *ℤℤℤℤ*

Snow White and the Three Stooges The Stooges fill in for the Seven Dwarfs when they go off prospecting in King Solomon's mines. Alas, see any Stooge movie but this one. **AKA:** Snow White and the Three Clowns.
1961 107m/C Moe Howard, Curly Howard, Larry Fine, Carol Heiss, Patricia Medina; **D:** Walter Lang. **VHS, Beta $14.98** FOX, FCT *ℤ*

Snowball Express When a New York City accountant inherits a hotel in the Rocky Mountains, he decides to move his family west to attempt to make a go of the defunct ski resort, only to find that the place is falling apart. Run-of-the-mill Disney comedy, based on the novel "Chateau Bon Vivant" by Frankie and John O'Rear.
1972 (G) 120m/C Dean Jones, Nancy Olson, Harry Morgan, Keenan Wynn; **D:** Norman Tokar. **VHS, Beta $69.95** DIS *ℤ*

Snowballin' A ski instructor gives private lessons to a bunch of snow bunnies.
1985 90m/C Seline Lomez, Daniel Pilon. **VHS, Beta $59.95** JEF *ℤ*

Snowballing Part of the polluted wave of teen-sex flicks of the 1980s, this is very mild for the genre but still no prize. Lusty high schoolers at a skiing competition look for action on and off the slopes, end up exposing a resort fraud.
1985 (PG) 96m/C Mary McDonough, Bob Hastings. **VHS, Beta $79.95** PSM *ℤ*

Snowbeast The residents of a ski resort are being terrorized by a half-human, half-animal beast leaving a path of dead bodies in its wake. "Jaws" hits the slopes. Not scary or even funny. Made for TV.
1977 96m/C Bo Svenson, Yvette Mimieux, Sylvia Sidney, Clint Walker, Robert F. Logan; **D:** Herb Wallerstein. **VHS, Beta $9.95** WOV *ℤ* ½

Snowblind Two ski gondolas derail, placing the passengers in jeopardy. Among the passengers is a mobster being pursued by an assassin. **AKA:** Ski Lift to Death.
1978 98m/C Deborah Raffin, Charles Frank, Howard Duff, Don Galloway, Gail Strickland, Don Johnson, Veronica Hamel, Clu Gulager, Lisa Reeves, Suzy Chaffee; **D:** William Wiard. **VHS $9.95** SIM *ℤ*

The Snows of Kilimanjaro Called by Hemingway "The Snows of Zanuck," in reference to the great producer, this film is actually an artful pastiche of several Hemingway short stories and novels. The main story, "The Snows of Kilimanjaro," acts as a framing device, in which the life of a successful writer is seen through his fevered flashbacks as he and his rich wife, while on safari, await a doctor to save his gangrenous leg.
1952 117m/C Gregory Peck, Susan Hayward, Ava Gardner, Hildegarde Neff, Leo G. Carroll, Torin Thatcher, Ava Norring, Helene Stanley, Marcel Dalio, Vincente Gomez, Richard Allen, Leonard Carey; **D:** Henry King; **W:** Casey Robinson. **Beta $7.50** NOS, GKK, VEC *ℤℤℤ*

Snuff-Bottle Connection Russian envoy is spying for the government while delivering a gift to a Ching dynasty emperor.
1982 96m/C Hwang Jang Lee, John Liu, Roy Horan. **VHS, Beta** WVE *ℤ*

Snuffy Smith, Yard Bird The pint-sized moonshiner finds himself in the Army, clashing with his sergeant. Followed by "Hillbilly Blitzkrieg" later the same year. Duncan is perfect for the part, and Kennedy is right on as his foil. **AKA:** Private Snuffy Smith; Snuffy Smith.
1942 67m/B Bud Duncan, Edgar Kennedy, Sarah Padden, Doris Linden, J. Farrell MacDonald, Frank Austin, Jimmie Dodd; **D:** Eddie Cline. **VHS $19.95** NOS, VYY *ℤ* ½

So Dear to My Heart A farm boy and his misfit black sheep wreak havoc at the county fair. Several sequences combine live action with animation. Heartwarming and charming; straightforward and likeable but never sentimental. Wonderful, vintage Disney. ♫Sourwood Mountain; Billy Boy; So Dear To My Heart; County Fair; Stick-To-It-

ivity; Ol' Dan Patch; It's Whatcha Do With Watcha Got; Lavender Blue (Dilly Dilly).
1949 82m/C Bobby Driscoll, Burl Ives, Beulah Bondi, Harry Carey Sr., Luanna Patten; **D:** Harold Schuster. **VHS, Beta $69.95** DIS, WTA *ℤℤℤ* ½

So Ends Our Night German scorns Nazi ideology, flees Austria, and meets young Jewish couple seeking asylum. Fine adaptation of Erich Maria Remarque's novel "Flotsam," with splendid performances from Sullavan (on loan from Universal) and young Ford.
1941 117m/B Fredric March, Margaret Sullavan, Frances Dee, Glenn Ford, Anna Sten, Erich von Stroheim; **D:** John Cromwell. **VHS** IVY *ℤℤℤ*

So Fine Absent-minded English professor O'Neal tries to rescue his father's clothing business from going bottom-up. He accidentally invents peek-a-boo bottomed jeans, which become an immediate hit and make him rich. Comedy smorgasbord, setting outing from sometime novelist Bergman, hits and misses. O'Neal is memorable, as is the ubiquitous Warden and his sidekick.
1981 (R) 91m/C Ryan O'Neal, Jack Warden, Mariangela Melato, Richard Kiel; **D:** Andrew Bergman; **W:** Andrew Bergman; **M:** Ennio Morricone. **VHS, Beta $19.98** WAR *ℤℤ* ½

So I Married an Axe Murderer Combination comedy/romance/thriller. Charlie is a hip bookstore owner with a commitment problem. When he finally falls in love with a butcher, he comes to suspect she's a serial killer and he's in line as her next victim. "Saturday Night Live" star Myers has a dual role: as Charlie and as Scottish dad Stuart, allowing him to be fanatically Scottish as Stuart and somewhat more restrained as the angst-ridden Charlie. One-gag movie counted on Myers' "Wayne's World" popularity, which didn't pan out at the box office. Best appreciated by Myers' fans, this one is better on the small screen.
1993 (PG-13) 92m/C Mike Myers, Nancy Travis, Anthony LaPaglia, Amanda Plummer, Brenda Fricker, Matt Doherty, Charles Grodin; **Cameos:** Phil Hartman, Steven Wright, Alan Arkin; **D:** Thomas Schlamme; **W:** Mike Myers, Robbie Fox; **M:** Bruce Broughton. **VHS, 8mm** COL *ℤℤ* ½

So This is Paris Roguish pre-Hayes Code dancing duo seeks spice through alternative lovemates. Classic sophisticated Lubitsch, with outstanding camerawork and a bit of jazz.
1926 68m/B Monte Blue, Patsy Ruth Miller, Lilyan Tashman, Andre de Beranger, Myrna Loy; **D:** Ernst Lubitsch. **VHS, Beta $24.95** GPV, FCT *ℤℤℤ*

So This is Washington The comedy team go to Washington with wacky inventions to help the war effort. Turns out there's too entirely too much nonsense going around, and the boys give 'em a piece of their mind. Fun, featherweight wartime comedy.
1943 70m/B Lum & Abner, Alan Mowbray. **VHS, Beta $24.95** NOS, DVT, HEG *ℤℤ* ½

Soapdish The back stage lives of a daytime soap opera, "The Sun Also Sets," and its cast. When the soap's ratings fall, a character written out of series via decapitation is brought back to give things a lift. While the writer struggles to make the reincarnation believable, the cast juggles old and new romances, and professional jealousies abound. Some genuinely funny moments as film actors spoof the genre that gave many of them a start.

1991 (PG-13) 97m/C Sally Field, Kevin Kline, Robert Downey Jr., Cathy Moriarty, Whoopi Goldberg, Elisabeth Shue, Carrie Fisher, Garry Marshall, Teri Hatcher, Paul Johansson, Costas Mandylor, Stephen Nichols, Kathy Najimy, Sheila Kelley; *Cameos:* Leeza Gibbons, John Tesh, Finola Hughes; *D:* Michael Hoffman; *W:* Andrew Bergman, Robert Harling; *M:* Alan Silvestri. **VHS, Beta, 8mm $14.95** PAR 🐾🐾🐾

S.O.B. Blake Edwards' bitter farce about Hollywood and the film industry wheelers and dealers who inhabit it. When a multi-million dollar picture bombs at the box office, the director turns suicidal, until he envisions re-shooting it with a steamy, X-rated scene starring his wife, a star with a goody-two-shoes image. Edwards used his real-life wife, Julie ("Mary Poppins") Andrews, for the scene in which she bared her breasts. Oft-inspired, but oft-terrible. Zestfully vengeful. William Holden's last film. **1981** (R) 121m/C William Holden, Robert Preston, Richard Mulligan, Julie Andrews, Robert Webber, Shelley Winters, Robert Vaughn, Larry Hagman, Stuart Margolin, Loretta Swit, Craig Stevens, Larry Storch, Jennifer Edwards, Robert Loggia, Rosanna Arquette, Marisa Berenson; *D:* Blake Edwards; *W:* Blake Edwards. **VHS, Beta $19.98** FOX, WAR 🐾🐾½

Social Error An heiress mistakes her guards for a group of kidnappers. **1935** 60m/B Gertrude Messinger, David Sharpe. **VHS, Beta $19.95** NOS, HEG 🐾🐾

The Social Secretary Driven from the rat race by lecherous men, Talmadge gets new job as rich woman's secretary, where she down-dresses to avoid further lewd encounters. She falls for her boss's son, but isn't considered marriage material until she proves herself. **1916** 56m/B Norma Talmadge, Kate Lester, Helen Weir, Gladden James, Herbert Frank; *D:* John Emerson. **VHS, Beta $19.95** GPV, FCT 🐾🐾½

Society A teenager wonders if his visions are real or hallucinations when he believes his family, and everyone else around him, are flesh-eating predators. The puzzle isn't much but wait for the special-effects ladened ending to get your fill of gore. **1992** (R) 99m/C Billy Warlock, Devin Devasquez, Evan Richards; *D:* Brian Yuzna. **VHS $89.98** REP 🐾

Sodom and Gomorrah The Italian-made, internationally produced epic about Lot, the Hebrews and the destruction of the two sinful biblical cities. Moderately entertaining—but ponderous, to say the least, and very long. *AKA:* Sodome et Gomorrhe; The Last Days of Sodom and Gomorrah. **1962** 154m/C Stewart Granger, Stanley Baker, Pier Angeli, Anouk Aimee, Rossana Podesta; *D:* Robert Aldrich. **VHS, Beta $19.98** FOX, IME 🐾🐾

Sofie Sweet family melodrama about a late 19th century Jewish family in Denmark. Sofie (Mynster) is the unmarried 28-year-old daughter of loving, protective parents. She has fallen in love with a gentile artist (Christensen) but gives him up to marry within her faith. Unsuited, Sofie and Jonas (Zeller) lead melancholy lives, which Sofie redeems through her joy in her son. Self-effacing drama is Ullmann's directorial debut. Adapted from the novel "Mendel Philipsen & Son" by Henri Nathansen. In Swedish with English subtitles. **1992** 145m/C Karen-Lise Mynster, Ghita Norby, Erland Josephson, Jesper Christensen, Henning Moritzen, Torben Zeller, Stig Hoffmeyer, Kirsten Rolffes, Lotte Herman; *D:* Liv Ullmann; *W:* Liv Ullmann, Peter Poulsen. **VHS $79.95** FCT, ING 🐾🐾½

Soft and Hard Made for English television, this video by Godard and Mieville intends to address the role of media and television in everyday life via a seemingly informal look at the couple's daily existence and the propensity for image production in it. In French with English subtitles. **1985** 48m/C *D:* Anne-Marie Mieville, Jean-Luc Godard. **VHS, Beta** EAI 🐾🐾½

The Soft Skin A classic portrayal of marital infidelity by the master director. A writer and lecturer has an affair with a stewardess. After the affair ends, his wife confronts him, with tragic results. Cliche plot is forgivable; acted and directed to perfection. Frequent Truffaut star Jean-Pierre Leaud served here as an apprentice director. In French with English subtitles. *AKA:* Le Peau Douce; Silken Skin. **1964** 120m/B Jean Desailly, Nelly Benedetti, Francoise Dorleac; *D:* Francois Truffaut; *M:* Georges Delerue. **VHS, Beta $39.95** HMV, FOX 🐾🐾🐾

Soggy Bottom U.S.A. A sheriff has his hands full trying to keep the law enforced in a small Southern town. Quite-good cast keeps the plot from disappearing altogether. **1984** (PG) 90m/C Don Johnson, Ben Johnson, Dub Taylor, Ann Wedgeworth, Lois Nettleton, Anthony Zerbe; *D:* Theodore J. Flicker. **VHS, Beta $9.99** PSM, HHE 🐾🐾

Sois Belle et Tais-Toi A police detective tracks jewel thieves and falls in love with a young waif. Several interesting and later famous actors have small parts. Light-hearted adventure. Subtitled in English. **1958** 110m/B Henri Vidal, Mylene Demongeot, Jean-Paul Belmondo, Alain Delon; *D:* Marc Allegret. **VHS, Beta $19.95** BAR 🐾🐾½

Solar Crisis Eye-popping special effects highlight this Earth-on-the-edge-of-destruction sci-fier. In 2050 the sun has gone on self-destruct and begins throwing off giant solar flares which turn the Earth extra-crispy. A space team is sent to divert the flares but the mission may become a victim of sabotage. **1992** (PG-13) 111m/C Tim Matheson, Charlton Heston, Peter Boyle, Annabel Schofield, Jack Palance, Corin "Corky" Nemec; *M:* Maurice Jarre. **VHS $92.95** VMK 🐾🐾½

Solarbabies Rollerskating youths in a drought-stricken future vie for a mysterious power that will replenish the Earth's water. Shades of every sci-fi movie you've ever seen, from "Mad Max" to "Ice Pirates." Pathetic. **1986** (PG-13) 95m/C Richard Jordan, Sarah Douglas, Charles Durning, Lukas Haas, Jami Gertz, Jason Patric; *D:* Alan Johnson; *W:* Walon Green; *M:* Maurice Jarre. **VHS, Beta $14.95** MGM 🐾

Solaris With this the USSR tried to eclipse "2001: A Space Odyssey" in terms of cerebral science-fiction. Some critics thought they succeeded. You may disagree now that the lumbering effort is available on tape. Adapted from a Stanislaw Lem novel, it depicts a dilapidated space lab orbiting the planet Solaris, whose ocean, a vast fluid "brain," materializes the stir-crazy cosmonauts' obsessions—usually morose ex-girlfriends. Talk, talk, talk, minimal special effects. In Russian with English subtitles. In a two-cassette package, with a letterbox format preserving Tarkovsky's widescreen compositions. **1972** 167m/C Donatas Banionis, Natalya Bondarchuk; *D:* Andrei Tarkovsky; *M:* Eduard Artemyev. **VHS $79.95** FXL, FCT, ING 🐾🐾

Soldat Duroc...Ca Va Etre Ta Fete! Days after the 1944 liberation of Paris, a French soldier crosses back over the French lines to see his lover, and is caught as a German sympathizer by American troops. *AKA:* Soldier Duroc. **1967** 105m/C Pierre Tornade, Robert Webber, Michel Galabru, Roger Carel. **VHS, Beta** NO 🐾🐾

The Soldier The Russians are holding the world at ransom with a pile of stolen plutonium, and a soldier finds himself in the position to carry out an unauthorized and dangerous plan to preserve the balance of world power. Wildly implausible, gratuitously violent spy trash. *AKA:* Codename: The Soldier. **1982** (R) 90m/C Ken Wahl, Klaus Kinski; *D:* James Glickenhaus. **VHS, Beta $14.95** COL, SUE 🐾

Soldier Blue Two survivors of an Indian attack make their way back to an army outpost. The cavalry then seeks revenge on the Cheyenne tribe accused of the attack. Gratuitously violent Vietnam-era western hits hard on racial themes. Based on the novel "Arrow in the Sun" by Theodore V. Olsen on the Sand Creek Indian massacre. **1970** (R) 109m/C Candice Bergen, Peter Strauss, Donald Pleasence, Dana Elcar, Jorge Rivero; *D:* Ralph Nelson; *W:* John Gay. **VHS, Beta $14.95** COL, SUE 🐾🐾

Soldier in Love Teleplay from "George Schaefer's Showcase Theatre" is based on the life of John Churchill, first Duke of Marlborough, and his wife Sarah. The ambitious young couple held the favor of Queen Anne for a time, until political intrigue brought about their downfall. **1967** 76m/C Jean Simmons, Claire Bloom, Keith Michell; *D:* George Schaefer. **VHS, Beta** FHS 🐾🐾

Soldier in the Rain An unusual friendship develops between career sergeant Gleason and wheeler-dealer McQueen. Gleason is in good form, but McQueen is listless, and the story (set in a Southern army camp) is unsatisfying. Weld is the comely teen who makes for an intriguing love triangle. From the novel by William Goldman. **1963** 88m/B Steve McQueen, Jackie Gleason, Tuesday Weld, Tony Bill, Tom Poston, Ed Nelson; *D:* Ralph Nelson; *W:* Blake Edwards; *M:* Henry Mancini. **VHS, Beta $59.98** FOX 🐾🐾½

Soldier of Fortune A woman (Hayward) enlists mercenaries to help find her lost husband in Red China. Late Gable vehicle with the formula beginning to feel the post-war strain and the star looking a trifle long in the tooth. Still, a fun adventure from a top star. Hayward had been among the myriad starlets vying for the Scarlett O'Hara roles nearly two decades earlier. **1955** 96m/C Clark Gable, Susan Hayward, Gene Barry, Alexander D'Arcy, Michael Rennie, Tom Tully, Anna Sten, Russell Collins, Leo Gordon, Jack Kruschen, Robert Quarry; *D:* Edward Dmytryk. **VHS, Beta $39.98** FOX 🐾🐾½

Soldier of Orange The lives of six Dutch students are forever changed by the WWII invasion of Holland by the Nazis. Based on the true-life exploits of Dutch resistance leader Erik Hazelhoff. Exciting and suspenseful; cerebral; carefully made and well acted. Made Rutger Hauer an international star. **1978** 144m/C Rutger Hauer, Jeroen Krabbe, Edward Fox, Susan Penhaligon; *D:* Paul Verhoeven; *W:* Paul Verhoeven. **VHS, Beta $59.95** MED 🐾🐾🐾

Soldier of the Night Toy-store worker by day, vigilante killer by night. Israeli thriller set in Tel Aviv lacks vim and is badly dubbed.

1984 89m/C **D:** Dan Wolman. **VHS, Beta** $59.95 MGM &#x1f; 1/2

Soldier's Fortune A traveling gun for hire leaves the combat of Central America for the jungles of Los Angeles, only to find out that his daughter had been taken hostage. That's the last thing these kidnappers will ever do when they are found by this tough guy looking for his child.
1991 (R) 96m/C Gil Gerard, Charles Napier, Dan Haggerty, P.J. Soles, Barbara Bingham, Janus Blythe; **D:** Arthur N. Mele. **VHS** $89.98 REP &#x1f; 1/2

Soldier's Revenge A Vietnam vet has a hard time adjusting to life at home.
197? 92m/C John Savage. **VHS, Beta** $19.98 TWE &#x1f;&#x1f;

A Soldier's Story A black army attorney is sent to a Southern base to investigate the murder of an unpopular sergeant. Features WWII, Louisiana, jazz and blues, and racism in and outside the corps. From the Pulitzer-prize winning play by Charles Fuller, with most of the Broadway cast. Fine performances from Washington and Caesar.
1984 (PG) 101m/C Howard E. Rollins Jr., Adolph Caesar, Denzel Washington, Patti LaBelle, Robert Townsend, Scott Paulin, Wings Hauser, Art Evans, Larry Riley, David Alan Grier; **D:** Norman Jewison; **M:** Herbie Hancock. Academy Awards '84 Nominations: Best Adapted Screenplay, Best Picture, Best Supporting Actor (Caesar); Edgar Allan Poe Awards '84: Best Screenplay. **VHS, Beta** $14.95 COL, FCT &#x1f;&#x1f;&#x1f;

A Soldier's Tale During WWII, a menage-a-trois develops that can only lead to tragedy, yet the participants find themselves unable to resist.
1991 (R) 96m/C Gabriel Byrne, Marianne Basler, Judge Reinhold, Paul Wyett; **D:** Larry Parr; **M:** John Charles. **VHS** $89.98 REP &#x1f;&#x1f;

Sole Survivor A group of zombies are searching for a beautiful advertising executive who was the sole survivor of a plane crash.
1984 (R) 85m/C Anita Skinner, Kurt Johnson, Caren Larkey; **D:** Thom Eberhardt. **VHS, Beta** $79.98 LIV, VES &#x1f; 1/2

The Solitary Man Glum look at a family breakup, from the husband's point of view. Holliman is good, but the exercise at large is regularly blues-inducing, and not especially inspiring or artful. Made for TV.
1982 96m/C Earl Holliman, Carrie Snodgress, Lara Parker, Lane Smith, Nicholas Coster, Michelle Pfeiffer; **D:** John Llewellyn Moxey. **VHS, Beta** TLF &#x1f;&#x1f;

Solo Young hitchhiker Peers enters the lives of fire patrol pilot Gil and his teenage son. A plotless friendship develops, headed nowhere—like this movie. Great New Zealand scenery might be worth the price of rental.
1977 (PG) 90m/C Vincent Gil, Perry Armstrong, Martyn Sanderson, Lisa Peers; **D:** Tony Williams. **VHS, Beta** $29.95 BPG, VES, HHE &#x1f;&#x1f;

Solo Voyage: The Revenge A Russian "Rambo" goes on a murderous rampage, the likes of which humanity has not yet seen.
1990 91m/C Mikhail Nojkine, Alexandre Fatiouchine; **D:** Mikhail Toumanichulli. **VHS** NO &#x1f;&#x1f;

Solomon and Sheba King Solomon's brother and the Egyptian Pharaoh send the Queen of Sheba to Israel to seduce King Solomon so they may gain his throne. Tyrone Power had filmed most of the lead role in this silly, overwrought epic when he died of a heart attack. The role was reshot, with Brynner (with a full head of hair) replacing him. Director Vidor's unfortunate last film. Shot on location in Spain.
1959 139m/C Yul Brynner, Gina Lollobrigida, Marisa Pavan, George Sanders, Alejandro Rey; **D:** King Vidor; **M:** Malcolm Arnold. **VHS, Beta** $19.98 MGM, FOX &#x1f;&#x1f;

The Sombrero Kid The Kid unwittingly gets involved in a murder and is nearly hanged before his friends help him discover the real culprits. Plenty of action in this straight forward, fun western.
1942 54m/B Donald (Don "Red") Barry, Lynn Merrick, Rand Brooks; **D:** George Sherman. **VHS, Beta** $19.95 VDM &#x1f;&#x1f;

Some Call It Loving Bad, pretentious modern version of Sleeping Beauty, set in L.A. King buys the sleeping girl (Farrow) from a carnival show, but she doesn't live up to his ideal.
1973 (R) 103m/C Zalman King, Carol White, Tisa Farrow, Richard Pryor, Pat Priest; **D:** James B. Harris. **VHS** NO &#x1f;

Some Came Running James Jones's follow-up novel to "From Here to Eternity" does not translate nearly as well to the screen. Overlong and with little plot, the action centers around a would-be writer, his floozy girl friend, and the holier-than-thou characters which populate the town in which he grew up and to which he has now returned. Strong performances by all.
1958 136m/C Frank Sinatra, Dean Martin, Shirley MacLaine, Martha Hyer, Arthur Kennedy, Nancy Gates; **D:** Vincente Minnelli; **M:** Elmer Bernstein. **VHS, Beta** $19.98 MGM &#x1f;&#x1f;&#x1f;

Some Girls A man goes to Quebec to see his college girlfriend who informs him that she is not in love with him anymore. But she has two sisters ready to comfort him! Strange black comedy; Gregory as the girl's father elevates the so-so story. **AKA:** Sisters.
1988 (R) 104m/C Patrick Dempsey, Andre Gregory, Lila Kedrova, Florinda Bolkan, Jennifer Connelly, Sheila Kelly; **D:** Michael Hoffman; **M:** James Newton Howard. **VHS, Beta** $89.95 MGM &#x1f;&#x1f; 1/2

Some Kind of Hero A Vietnam prisoner-of war returns home to a changed world. Pryor tries hard, but can't get above this poorly written, unevenly directed film.
1982 (R) 97m/C Richard Pryor, Margot Kidder, Ray Sharkey, Ronny Cox, Lynne Moody, Olivia Cole; **D:** Michael Pressman. **VHS, Beta** $14.95 PAR &#x1f;&#x1f;

Some Kind of Wonderful A high-school tomboy has a crush on a guy who also happens to be her best friend. Her feelings go unrequited as he falls for a rich girl with snobbish friends. In the end, true love wins out. Deutch also directed (and John Hughes also produced) the teen flick "Pretty in Pink," which had much the same plot, with the rich/outcast characters reversed by gender. OK, but completely predictable.
1987 (PG-13) 93m/C Eric Stoltz, Lea Thompson, Mary Stuart Masterson, Craig Sheffer, John Ashton, Elias Koteas, Molly Hagan; **D:** Howard Deutch; **W:** John Hughes. **VHS** $19.95 PAR &#x1f;&#x1f;

Some Like It Hot Two unemployed musicians witness the St. Valentine's Day massacre in Chicago. They disguise themselves as women and join an all-girl band headed for Miami to escape the gangsters' retaliation. Flawless cast includes a fetching Monroe at her best; hilarious script. Curtis does his Cary Grant impression. Classic scenes between Lemmon in drag and Joe E. Brown as a smitten suitor. Brown also has the film's famous closing punchline. Monroe sings "I Wanna Be Loved By You," "Running Wild," and "I'm Through With Love." One of the very funniest movies of all time.
1959 120m/B Marilyn Monroe, Tony Curtis, Jack Lemmon, George Raft, Pat O'Brien, Nehemiah Persoff, Edward G. Robinson, Joe E. Brown, Joan Shawlee, Mike Mazurki; **D:** Billy Wilder; **W:** Billy Wilder; **M:** Adolph Deutsch. Academy Awards '59: Best Costume Design (B & W); Nominations: Best Actor (Lemmon), Best Adapted Screenplay, Best Art Direction/Set Decoration (B & W), Best Black and White Cinematography, Best Director (Wilder); British Academy Awards '59: Best Actor (Lemmon); Golden Globe Awards '60: Best Actor—Musical/Comedy (Lemmon), Best Actress—Musical/Comedy (Monroe), Best Film—Musical/Comedy; National Board of Review Awards '59: 10 Best Films of the Year. **VHS, Beta** $19.95 MGM, FOX, VYG &#x1f;&#x1f;&#x1f;

Somebody Has to Shoot the Picture Photographer Scheider is hired by a convicted man to take a picture of his execution. Hours before the event, Scheider uncovers evidence that leads him to believe the man is innocent. He then embarks in a race against time to save him. Adapted by Doug Magee from his book "Slow Coming Dark." Unpretentious, tough drama. Made for cable.
1990 (R) 104m/C Roy Scheider, Bonnie Bedelia, Robert Carradine, Andre Braugher, Arliss Howard; **D:** Frank Pierson; **W:** Doug Magee. **VHS, Beta** $79.98 MCA &#x1f;&#x1f;&#x1f;

Somebody Up There Likes Me Story of Rocky Graziano's gritty battle from his poor, street-wise childhood to his prison term and his eventual success as the middle-weight boxing champion of the world. Adapted from Graziano's autobiography. Superior performance by Newman (in his third screen role, after the miserable "The Silver Chalice" and forgettable "The Rack"); screen debuts for McQueen and Loggia.
1956 113m/B Paul Newman, Pier Angeli, Everett Sloane, Eileen Heckart, Sal Mineo, Robert Loggia, Steve McQueen; **D:** Robert Wise; **W:** Ernest Lehman. Academy Awards '56: Best Art Direction/Set Decoration (B & W), Best Black and White Cinematography; Nominations: Best Film Editing. **VHS, Beta** $19.98 MGM &#x1f;&#x1f;&#x1f;

Someday You'll Find Her, Charlie Brown Charlie Brown tries to find a beautiful girl he saw on tv.
1981 24m/C **VHS** $14.95 WTA &#x1f;&#x1f;

Someone at the Door Reporter Medwin arranges to be suspected of killing his sister, thus providing him with a good story and advancing his career. His plan almost backfires, when he is almost executed. Remake of a 1936 film of the same name.
1950 65m/B Michael Medwin, Garry Marsh, Yvonne Owen, Hugh Latimer; **D:** Francis Searle. **VHS, Beta** $16.95 SNC &#x1f;&#x1f;

Someone Behind the Door Evil brain surgeon Perkins implants murderous suggestions into psychopathic amnesia victim Bronson's mind, then instructs him to kill his (the surgeon's) wife and her lover. **AKA:** Two Minds for Murder; Quelqu' Un Derriere la Porte.
1971 (PG) 97m/C Charles Bronson, Anthony Perkins, Jill Ireland, Henri Garcin; **D:** Nicolas Gessner. **VHS, Beta** $39.95 UNI, VTR &#x1f; 1/2

Someone I Touched Way-overdone melodrama starring Leachman as a finally-pregnant woman who learns her husband and a teenager he slept with have venereal disease.
1975 74m/C Cloris Leachman, James Olson, Glynnis O'Connor, Andrew (Andy) Robinson, Allyn Ann McLerie; **D:** Lou Antonio. **VHS, Beta** $34.95 WOV &#x1f; 1/2

Someone to Love Rootless filmmaker gathers all his single friends together and interviews them about their failed love lives. Welles's last film as an actor. Wildly uneven, interesting experiment.
1987 (R) 110m/C Henry Jaglom, Orson Welles, Sally Kellerman, Andrea Marcovicci, Michael Emil, Oja Kodar, Stephen Bishop, Ronee Blakley, Kathryn Harrold, Monte Hellman; **D:** Henry Jaglom; **W:** Henry Jaglom. VHS, Beta $79.95 PAR ♪♪

Someone to Watch Over Me After witnessing the murder of a close friend, a beautiful and very wealthy woman must be protected from the killer. The working-class New York detective assigned the duty is more than taken with her, despite the fact that he has both a wife and son at home. A highly watchable, stylish romantic crime thriller.
1987 (R) 106m/C Tom Berenger, Mimi Rogers, Lorraine Bracco, Jerry Orbach, Andreas Katsulas, Tony DiBenedetto, James Moriarty, John Rubinstein; **D:** Ridley Scott; **W:** Howard Franklin; **M:** Michael Kamen. VHS, Beta $19.95 COL ♪♪♪

Something for Everyone A corrupt footman uses sex and murder in an attempt to take over the estate of an aristocratic Bavarian family in post-WWII Germany. He nearly succeeds in marrying the countess (Lansbury), but someone has been keeping tabs on him. Funny, ambitious black comedy. From the novel "The Code" by Harry Kressing. **AKA:** The Rook; Black Flowers for the Bride.
1970 (R) 112m/C Angela Lansbury, Michael York, Anthony Corlan, Heidelinde Weis; **D:** Harold Prince. VHS, Beta $59.98 FOX ♪♪½

Something in Common A woman discovers her 22-year-old son is having an affair with a woman her own age. Nicely done comedy; Burstyn and Weld both make good use of a solid script. Made for TV.
1986 94m/C Ellen Burstyn, Tuesday Weld, Don Murray, Patrick Cassidy, Eli Wallach; **D:** Glenn Jordan; **W:** Susan Rice; **M:** John Addison. VHS, Beta $19.95 STE, NWV ♪♪½

Something of Value Good ensemble performances in a serious colonial story about the Mau Mau rebellion in Kenya. Hudson and Poitier are torn between their friendship and their opposing loyalties. Drama solidly grounded in fact from the book by Robert Ruark.
1957 113m/B Rock Hudson, Sidney Poitier, Wendy Hiller, Dana Wynter, Juano Hernandez; **D:** Richard Brooks; **W:** Richard Brooks. VHS, Beta $24.95 MGM ♪♪♪

Something Short of Paradise The owner of a Manhattan movie theater has an on again/off again romance with a magazine writer. Would-be Allenesque romantic comedy is too talky and pretentious.
1979 (PG) 87m/C David Steinberg, Susan Sarandon, Jean-Pierre Aumont, Marilyn Sokol; **D:** David Helpern. VHS, Beta $29.98 LIV, VES ♪½

Something Special A fourteen-year-old girl has her wish come true when she is turned into a boy. Charming, original fantasy-comedy is fun for young and old. **AKA:** Willy Milly; I Was a Teenage Boy.
1986 (PG-13) 93m/C Pamela Segall, Patty Duke, Eric Gurry, John Glover, Seth Green; **D:** Paul Schneider. VHS NO ♪♪½

Something to Sing About Musical melodrama about a New York bandleader's attempt to make it big in Hollywood. Allows Cagney the opportunity to demonstrate his dancing talents; he also sings. Rereleased in 1947. Also available colorized. Frawley was Fred on "I Love Lucy." ♫Any Old Love; Right or Wrong; Loving You; Out of the Blue;

Something to Sing About. **AKA:** Battling Hoofer.
1936 84m/B James Cagney, William Frawley, Evelyn Daw, Gene Lockhart; **D:** Victor Schertzinger. VHS, Beta $19.95 NOS, VHE, CAB ♪♪

Something Weird McCabe is disfigured horribly in an electrical accident. A seemingly beautiful witch fixes his face, on condition that he be her lover. The accident also gave him ESP—and it gets cheesier from there.
1968 80m/C Tony McCabe, Elizabeth Lee; **D:** Herschell Gordon Lewis. VHS, Beta $29.95 VMK, VDM, TWE Woof!

Something Wicked This Way Comes Two young boys discover the evil secret of a mysterious traveling carnival that visits their town. Bradbury wrote the screenplay for this much-anticipated, expensive adaptation of his own novel. Good special effects, but disappointing.
1983 (PG) 94m/C Jason Robards Jr., Jonathan Pryce, Diane Ladd, Pam Grier, Richard Davalos, James Stacy; **D:** Jack Clayton; **W:** Ray Bradbury; **M:** James Horner. VHS, Beta $14.99 DIS ♪♪

Something Wild Mild-mannered business exec Daniels is picked up by an impossibly free-living vamp with a Louise Brooks hairdo, and taken for the ride of his up-till-then staid life, eventually leading to explosive violence. A sharp-edged comedy with numerous changes of pace. Too-happy ending wrecks it, but it's great until then. Look for cameos from filmmakers John Waters and John Sayles.
1986 (R) 113m/C Jeff Daniels, Melanie Griffith, Ray Liotta, Margaret Colin, Tracy Walter, Dana Peru, Jack Gilpin, Su Tissue, Kenneth Utt, Sister Carol East; **Cameos:** John Sayles, John Waters; **D:** Jonathan Demme; **W:** E. Max Frye; **M:** Rosemary Paul, John Cale. VHS, Beta $19.99 HBO ♪♪½

Sometimes a Great Notion Trouble erupts in a small Oregon town when a family of loggers decide to honor a contract when the other loggers go on strike. Newman's second stint in the director's chair; Fonda's first role as an old man. Based on the novel by Ken Kesey. **AKA:** Never Give an Inch.
1971 (PG) 115m/C Paul Newman, Henry Fonda, Lee Remick, Richard Jaeckel, Michael Sarrazin; **D:** Paul Newman; **W:** John Gay; **M:** Henry Mancini. VHS, Beta $14.98 MCA ♪♪♪

Sometimes Aunt Martha Does Dreadful Things Another deranged-slasher movie, this one featuring a female psychopath.
1988 95m/C VHS, Beta NO ♪

Sometimes It Works, Sometimes It Doesn't A film in two parts, the first being interviews with Merce Cunningham and John Case about their work together, the second being the filmdance "Channels/Inserts," in its entirety.
1983 63m/C VHS, Beta NO ♪♪½

Sometimes They Come Back Another Stephen King tale of terror. Matheson plays a man haunted by the tragedy in his past. A witness to his brother's death, he also witnesses the fiery crash of his brother's killers. Only now the killers have returned from the dead, to take their revenge on him. Made for television.
1991 (R) 97m/C Tim Matheson, Brooke Adams, Robert Rusler. VHS $89.95 VMK ♪♪

Somewhere I'll Find You Clark and Turner heat up the screen as correspondents running all over the war-torn world in their second film together. ("Honky Tonk" was their first.) Notable mainly because Gable's

beloved wife, Carole Lombard, was killed in a plane crash only three days into production. Gable forced himself to finish the film and it became one of the studio's biggest hits. Although critics applauded his determination to complete the film, many felt his performance was subdued and strained. Film debut of Wynn. Based on a story by Charles Hoffman.
1942 108m/B Clark Gable, Lana Turner, Robert Sterling, Reginald Owen, Lee Patrick, Charles Dingle, Tamara Shayne, Leonid Kinskey, Diana Lewis, Molly Lamont, Patricia Dane, Sara Haden, Keenan Wynn; **D:** Wesley Ruggles; **W:** Walter Reisch, Marguerite Roberts. VHS $19.98 MGM ♪♪♪

Somewhere in Sonora Early Wayne Western set in Old Mexico. Wayne plays a rodeo performer who joins an outlaw gang to save a friend and a silver mine. Like most of the other films of the series, this was a remake of a Ken Maynard silent. Based on a story and the novel "Somewhere South in Sonora" by Wsll Levington Comfort.
1933 59m/B John Wayne, Henry B. Walthall, Shirley Palmer, J.P. McGowan, Frank Rice, Billy Franey, Paul Fix, Ralph Lewis; **D:** Mack V. Wright; **W:** Joe Roach. VHS $19.98 MGM ♪♪

Somewhere in Time Playwright Reeve (in his first post-Clark Kent role) falls in love with a beautiful woman in an old portrait. Through self-hypnosis he goes back in time to 1912 to discover what their relationship might have been. The film made a star of the Grand Hotel, located on Mackinac Island in Michigan, where it was shot. Drippy rip-off of the brilliant novel "Time and Again" by Jack Finney. Reeve is horrible; Seymour is underused. All in all, rather wretched.
1980 (PG) 103m/C Christopher Reeve, Jane Seymour, Christopher Plummer, Teresa Wright; **D:** Jeannot Szwarc; **W:** Richard Matheson; **M:** John Barry. VHS, Beta $19.95 MCA ♪♪½

Somewhere Tomorrow A lonely, fatherless teenage girl is befriended by the ghost of a young man killed in a plane crash. Charming and moving, if not perfect.
1985 (PG) 91m/C Sarah Jessica Parker, Nancy Addison, Tom Shea; **D:** Robert Wiemer. VHS, Beta $59.95 MED ♪♪½

Sommersby A too-good-to-be-true period romance based on the film "The Return of Martin Guerre." A Civil War veteran (Gere) returns to his wife's (Foster) less-than-open arms. She soon warms up to his kind, sensitive and caring manner, but can't quite believe the change that the war has wrought. Neither can the neighbors, especially the one (Pullman) who had his own eye on Laurel Sommersby. So is he really Jack Sommersby or an all too clever imposter? Lots of hankies needed for the tender-hearted. Strong performance by Foster. Filmed in Virginia (passing for the state of Tennessee.) The laserdisc version is available in letterbox format.
1993 (PG-13) 114m/C Richard Gere, Jodie Foster, Bill Pullman, James Earl Jones, William Windom, Brett Kelley, Richard Hamilton, Maury Chaykin, Lanny Flaherty, Frankie Faison, Wendell Wellman, Clarice Taylor, R. Lee Ermey; **D:** Jon Amiel; **W:** Nicholas Meyer, Sarah Kernochan; **M:** Danny Elfman. VHS, Beta, 8mm $19.98 WAR, FCT ♪♪½

Somos Novios Publicity agent and his friend, along with a salesclerk in a record store, find themselves at the top of the music charts. In Spanish. **AKA:** In Love and Engaged.
1968 100m/C Angelica Maria, Armando Manzanero, Palito Ortega, Olga Zubarry, Raul Ross; **D:** Enrique Carreras. VHS, Beta $69.95 MAD ♪

Son-in-Law Surfer-dude comic Shore's a laconic fish out of water as a city-boy rock 'n' roller who falls in love with a country beauty, marries her, and visits the family farm to meet the new in-laws. Once there, he weirds out family and neighbors before showing everyone how to live, Pauly style. Silly entertainment best appreciated by Shore fans.
1993 (PG-13) 95m/C Pauly Shore, Carla Gugino, Lane Smith, Cindy Pickett, Mason Adams, Patrick Renna, Dennis Burkley, Dan Gauthier, Tiffani-Amber Thiessen; *D:* Steve Rash; *W:* Shawn Schepps, Fax Bahr, Adam Small; *M:* Richard Gibbs. **VHS, Beta $96.03** HPH ✍️½

Son of a Gun A loveable but ornery cowboy gets banished from the county for disturbing the peace. However, he wins the favor of the townspeople when he stands up to a gang of gambling swindlers. Silent.
1919 68m/B Billy Anderson. **VHS, Beta $19.95** NOS, DVT, RXM ✍️½

Son of Ali Baba Kashma Baba, son of Ali Baba, enters the military academy to learn to withstand adversity. He has other ideas however, until he must suddenly fill his father's shoes and fight the evil Caliph. He fights bravely with the help of his childhood friend, a beautiful princess, in this swashbuckler.
1952 85m/C Tony Curtis, Piper Laurie, Susan Cabot, Victor Jory, Hugh O'Brian, William Reynolds, Gerald Mohr; *D:* Ross Hunter. **VHS $14.98** MCA, FCT ✍️✍️

Son of Blob A scientist brings home a piece of frozen blob from the North Pole; his wife accidentally revives the dormant gray mass. It begins a rampage of terror by digesting nearly everyone within its reach. A host of recognizable faces make for fun viewing. Post-Jeannie, pre-Dallas Hagman directed this exercise in zaniness. *AKA:* Beware! The Blob.
1972 (PG) 87m/C Robert Walker Jr., Godfrey Cambridge, Carol Lynley, Shelley Berman, Larry Hagman, Burgess Meredith, Gerrit Graham, Dick Van Patten; *D:* Larry Hagman. **VHS, Beta $19.95** GEM ✍️✍️

Son of Captain Blood The son of the famous pirate meets up with his father's enemies on the high seas. The son of the famous actor Errol Flynn—Sean—plays the son of the character the elder Flynn played in "Captain Blood." Let's just say the gimmick didn't work. *AKA:* Il Figlio del Capitano Blood.
1962 (G) 90m/C Sean Flynn, Ann Todd; *D:* Tulio Demicheli. **VHS, Beta $59.95** PSM, MLB ✍️½

Son of Dracula In this late-coming sequel to the Universal classic, a stranger named Alucard is invited to America by a Southern belle obsessed with eternal life. It is actually Dracula himself, not his son, who wreaks havoc in this spine-tingling chiller. *AKA:* Young Dracula.
1943 80m/B Lon Chaney Jr., Evelyn Ankers, Frank Craven, Robert Paige, Louise Allbritton, J. Edward Bromberg, Samuel S. Hinds; *D:* Robert Siodmak. **VHS, Beta $14.95** MCA ✍️✍️✍️

Son of Flubber Sequel to "The Absent Minded Professor" finds Fred MacMurray still toying with his prodigious invention, Flubber, now in the form of Flubbergas, which causes those who inhale it to float away. Disney's first-ever sequel is high family wackiness.
1963 96m/C Fred MacMurray, Nancy Olson, Tommy Kirk, Leon Ames, Joanna Moore, Keenan Wynn, Charlie Ruggles, Paul Lynde; *D:* Robert Stevenson. **VHS, Beta** DIS ✍️✍️½

Son of Frankenstein The second sequel (after "The Bride of Frankenstein") to the 1931 version of the horror classic. The good doctor's skeptical son returns to the family manse and becomes obsessed with his father's work and with reviving the creature. Full of memorable characters and brooding ambience. Karloff's last appearance as the monster.
1939 99m/C Basil Rathbone, Bela Lugosi, Boris Karloff, Lionel Atwill, Josephine Hutchinson, Donnie Dunagan, Emma Dunn, Edgar Norton, Lawrence Grant; *D:* Rowland V. Lee. **VHS, Beta $14.98** MCA ✍️✍️✍️

Son of Fury Dashing Ben Blake (Power) is left penniless when his sinister uncle (Sanders) wrongfully takes the family fortune. Ben escapes to sea and then to an island paradise—all the while plotting his revenge. But he still finds time to fall for the beautous Tierney. Fine 18th-century costumer done in grand style. Based on the novel "Benjamin Blake" by Edison Marshall.
1942 98m/C Tyrone Power, Gene Tierney, George Sanders, Frances Farmer, Roddy McDowall, John Carradine, Elsa Lanchester, Harry Davenport, Kay Johnson, Dudley Digges, Halliwell Hobbes, Marten Lamont, Arthur Hohl, Pedro de Cordoba, Dennis Hoey, Heather Thatcher; *D:* John Cromwell; *W:* Philip Dunne; *M:* Alfred Newman. **VHS $19.99** FXV ✍️✍️✍️

Son of God's Country Utterly hackneyed, near-comic attempt at a western. Good-guy U.S. Marshall poses as a crook to get the lowdown on the varmints.
1948 60m/B Monte Hale, Pamela Blake, Adrian Booth. **VHS, Beta $29.95** DVT ✍️½

Son of Godzilla Dad and junior protect beauty Maeda from giant spiders on a remote island ruled by a mad scientist. Fun monster flick with decent special effects. *AKA:* Gojira no Musuko.
1966 86m/C Tadao Takashima, Akira Kubo; *D:* Jun Fukuda. **VHS, Beta $19.95** PSM, HHT, DVT ✍️✍️

Son of Hercules vs. Venus Mortals battle the gods in this low budget action-adventure.
19?? 93m/C VHS, Beta $19.99 BFV ✍️

Son of Ingagi Lonely ape-man kidnaps woman in search of romance. Early all-black horror film stars Williams of "Amos 'n' Andy."
1940 70m/B Zack Williams, Laura Bowman, Alfred Grant, Spencer Williams Jr.; *D:* Richard C. Kahn; *W:* Spencer Williams Jr. **VHS $19.98** NOS, SNC, MLB ✍️½

Son of Kong King Kong's descendant is discovered on an island amid prehistoric creatures in this often humorous sequel to RKO's immensely popular "King Kong." Hoping to capitalize on the enormous success of its predecessor, director Schoedsack quickly threw this together. As a result, its success at the box office did not match the original's, and didn't deserve to, but it's fun. Nifty special effects from Willie O'Brien, the man who brought them to us the first time!
1933 70m/B Robert Armstrong, Helen Mack; *D:* Ernest B. Schoedsack. **VHS, Beta $19.98** NOS, MED, FCT ✍️✍️½

Son of Lassie It seems that Lassie's son Laddie just isn't quite as smart as his mother. After the dog sneaks onto his master's plane during WWII, the plane gets shot down, and Lawford parachutes out with Laddie in his arms. The dog goes to get help because Lawford is hurt, but he brings back two Nazis! A sequel to "Lassie Come Home."
1945 (G) 102m/C Peter Lawford, Donald Crisp, June Lockhart, Nigel Bruce, William Severn, Leon Ames, Donald Curtis, Nils Asther, Robert Lewis; *D:* Sylvan Simon. **VHS $14.95** MGM ✍️✍️½

The Son of Monte Cristo Illegitimate offspring of the great swashbuckler with Robert Donat proves they made pathetic, pointless sequels even back then.
1941 102m/B Louis Hayward, Joan Bennett, George Sanders, Florence Bates, Montagu Love, Ralph Byrd, Clayton Moore; *D:* Rowland V. Lee. **VHS, Beta $19.95** DVT, BAR, CAB ✍️✍️½

Son of Paleface Hilarious sequel to the original Hope gag-fest, with the Harvard-educated son of the original character (again played by Hope) heading west to claim an inheritance. Hope runs away with every cowboy cliche and even manages to wind up with the girl. Songs include "Buttons and Bows" (reprised from the original), "There's a Cloud in My Valley of Sunshine," and "Four-legged Friend."
1952 95m/C Bob Hope, Jane Russell, Roy Rogers, Douglass Dumbrille, Iron Eyes Cody, Bill Williams, Harry von Zell; *D:* Frank Tashlin. **VHS, Beta $14.95** COL ✍️✍️✍️½

Son of Samson Man with large pectoral muscles puts an end to the evil Queen of Egypt's reign of terror *AKA:* Le Geant de la Vallee Das Rois.
1962 89m/C Mark Forest, Chelo Alonso, Angelo Zanolli, Vira Silenti, Frederica Ranchi; *D:* Carlo Campogalliani. **VHS $19.98** SNC ✍️½

Son of Sinbad Sinbad, captured by the Khalif of Baghdad, must bring him the secret of Greek fire to gain his freedom and free the city from the forces of mighty Tamerlane. About three dozen nubile young women wear very little and gambol with our hero herein; much-anticipated skinfest caused a scandal, nurtured by Howard Hughes for profit. *AKA:* Nights in a Harem.
1955 88m/C Dale Robertson, Sally Forrest, Vincent Price, Lili St. Cyr, Mari Blanchard, Joi Lansing; *D:* Ted Tetzlaff. **VHS, Beta $15.95** VCI ✍️✍️

Son of the Morning Star Lavish made for TV retelling of Custer's famed-butt kicking. Complex characterizations and unusual points of view, based on the book by Evan S. Connell.
1991 (PG-13) 186m/C Gary Cole, Rosanna Arquette, Dean Stockwell, Rodney Grant, Terry O'Quinn, David Strathairn, Stanley Anderson, George American Horse; *D:* Mike Robe. **VHS $19.98** REP, FCT ✍️✍️✍️

Son of the Pink Panther Lame leftover from the formerly popular comedy series. Director Edwards has chosen not to resurrect Inspector Clouseau, instead opting for his son (Benigni), who turns out to be just as much of a bumbling idiot as his father. Commissioner Dreyfus (Lom), the twitching, mouth-foaming former supervisor of the original Clouseau is looking for a kidnapped princess (Farentino) along with Clouseau, Jr., who himself does not know he is the illegitimate son of his partner's dead nemesis. Many of the sketches have been recycled from previous series entrants. Rather than being funny, they seem used and shopworn like a threadbare rug. *AKA:* Blake Edwards' Son of the Pink Panther.
1993 (PG) 115m/C Roberto Benigni, Herbert Lom, Robert Davi, Debrah Farentino, Claudia Cardinale, Burt Kwouk, Shabana Azmi; *D:* Blake Edwards; *W:* Blake Edwards; *M:* Henry Mancini. **VHS** MGM ✍️½

Son of the Sheik A desert sheik abducts an unfaithful dancing girl. Valentino's well-done, slightly self-mocking last film. Silent. Sequel to "The Sheik" (1921).

1926 62m/B Rudolph Valentino, Vilma Banky, Agnes Ayres; *D:* George Fitzmaurice. **VHS, Beta** $19.95 *NOS, CCB, VCN* ♪♪♪

Son of Zorro Zorro takes the law into his own hands to protect ranchers from bandits. A serial in thirteen chapters.
1947 164m/B George Turner, Peggy Stewart, Roy Barcroft, Edward Cassidy. **VHS** $27.95 *REP, VCN, MLB* ♪♪♪

A Song is Born A group of music professors try to trace the history of music. Kaye is in charge of a U.S. music foundation whose research has led him up to ragtime. He is soon, however, thrust into the sometimes seedy world of jazz joints and night spots, all in the name of research. Enter love interest Mayo, a woman on the run from her gangster boyfriend who hides out at the foundation. Not one of Kaye's funniest or best, but if you enjoy big band music, you'll love this. Includes music by Louis Armstrong and his orchestra, Tommy Dorsey and his orchestra, and Charlie Barnet and his orchestra. This was Kaye's last film for Goldwyn. ♪A Song is Born; Bach Boogie; Anitra's Dance; I'm Getting Sentimental Over You; Blind Barnabas; Mockin' Bird; Redskin Rhumba; The Goldwyn Stomp; Daddy-O.
1948 113m/B Danny Kaye, Virginia Mayo, Benny Goodman, Hugh Herbert, Steve Cochran, J. Edward Bromberg, Felix Bressart; *D:* Howard Hawks. **VHS** *HBO, GVV* ♪♪♪

Song O' My Heart An early musical starring popular Irish tenor McCormack as a singer forced to abandon his career when he marries a woman he does not love. A tour de force for the lead in his movie debut. ♪Little Boy Blue; Paddy Me Lad; I Hear You Calling Me; A Fair Story by the Fireside; Just For a Day; Kitty My Love; The Rose of Tralee; A Pair of Blue Eyes; I Feel You Near Me.
1929 91m/B John McCormack, Maureen O'Sullivan, John Garrick, J.M. Kerrigan, Tommy Clifford, Alice Joyce; *D:* Frank Borzage. **VHS, Beta** $39.95 *VAI, FCT, TVC* ♪♪♪

Song of Arizona Rogers and the Sons of the Pioneers arrive to aid their pal Hayes against a gang of bank robbers in this modern-day oater. Eight songs perpetually punctuate the perfunctory plot, particularly "Will Ya Be My Darling," "Half-a-Chance Ranch," and the title tune.
1946 54m/B Roy Rogers, Dale Evans, George "Gabby" Hayes, Lyle Talbot, Bob Nolan, The Pioneers; *D:* Frank McDonald. **VHS, Beta** $19.95 *NOS, VCN, HEG* ♪♪

The Song of Bernadette Depicts the true story of a peasant girl who sees a vision of the Virgin Mary in a grotto at Lourdes in 1858. The girl is directed to dig at the grotto for water that will heal those who believe in its powers, much to the astonishment and concern of the townspeople. Based on Franz Werfel's novel. Directed with tenderness and carefully cast, and appealing to religious and sentimental susceptibilities, it was a box-office smash.
1943 156m/B Charles Bickford, Lee J. Cobb, Jennifer Jones, Vincent Price, Anne Revere, Gladys Cooper; *D:* Henry King; *M:* Alfred Newman. Academy Awards '43: Best Actress (Jones), Best Black and White Cinematography, Best Interior Decoration, Best Interior Decoration, Best Score; Nominations: Best Director (King), Best Film Editing, Best Picture, Best Screenplay, Best Sound, Best Supporting Actor (Bickford), Best Supporting Actress (Cooper); Golden Globe Awards '44: Best Actress—Drama (Jones), Best Director (King), Best Film—Drama. **VHS, Beta** $19.98 *FOX, KEP, IGP* ♪♪♪

Song of Freedom The story of a black dockworker whose gift of voice is discovered by an opera impresario. After realizing a career as a concert performer, Robeson ventures to Africa to investigate his ancestry and finds he has royal roots. Robeson turns in a fine performance in what is otherwise an average film.
1938 70m/B Paul Robeson, Elizabeth Welch, George Mozart; *D:* J. Elder Wills. **VHS, Beta** $24.95 *VYY, HHT, NOS* ♪♪½

Song of Nevada Rogers woos the high-society daughter (Evans, of course) of a rancher (Hall). Quintessential Roy-n-Dale. ♪It's Love, Love, Love; New Moon Over Nevada; Hi Ho Little Dogies; The Harum Scarum Baron of the Harmonium; What Are We Going to Do?; A Cowboy Has to Yodel in the Morning.
1944 60m/B Roy Rogers, Dale Evans, Mary Lee; *D:* Joseph Kane. **VHS, Beta** $9.95 *NOS, HHT, DVT* ♪♪½

Song of Norway A dramatization of the early life of the beloved Norwegian Romantic composer Edvard Grieg. Filmed against the beautiful mountains, waterfalls, and forests of Norway and based on the popular '40s stage production. The scenery is the best thing because Grieg's life was dull—even with cinematic liberties taken. ♪Strange Music; The Song of Norway; The Little House; Be a Boy Again; Three There Were; A Rhyme and a Reason; Wrong to Dream; I Love You; The Solitary Wanderer.
1970 (G) 143m/C Toralv Maurstad, Florence Henderson, Edward G. Robinson, Christina Schollin, Frank Porretta, Oscar Homolka, Robert Morley, Harry Secombe; *D:* Andrew L. Stone. **VHS, Beta** $59.98 *FOX* ♪♪

Song of Old Wyoming Three of those songs are presented in the course of an ordinary western about a spunky widow driving badmen out of Wyoming territory. La Rue plays the villainous Cheyanne Kid; this was before he got his own series as the heroic "Lash" La Rue.
1945 65m/C Eddie Dean, Sarah Padden, Lash LaRue, Jennifer Holt, Emmett Lynn, John Carpenter, Ian Keith, Bob Barron; *D:* Robert Tansey. **VHS** $19.95 *NOS, HEG* ♪½

Song of Texas When a young woman journeys west to visit her father at "his" ranch, Roy and his pals must keep the father's secret that he is just another hired hand. Whenever possible, everyone breaks into song.
1943 54m/B Roy Rogers, Harry Shannon, Pat Brady, Barton MacLane, Arline Judge; *D:* Joseph Kane. **VHS, Beta** $19.95 *NOS, VYY, VCN* ♪½

Song of the Exile A Chinese/Japanese student living in London in the early 1970s faces racial discrimination and decides to return to her native Hong Kong. But on the home front, she and her family clash emotionally until daughter and mother come to a gradual understanding of how the past affects the present. In Cantonese and Japanese with English subtitles.
1990 100m/C Maggie Cheung, Shwu-Fen Chang; *D:* Ann Hui. **VHS** $79.95 *KIV, FCT, ING* ♪♪½

Song of the Gringo Tex Ritter stars in his first singing western as a sheriff going after a gang of claim jumpers. *AKA:* The Old Corral.
1936 57m/B Tex Ritter, Monte Blue, Joan Woodbury, Fuzzy Knight, Richard Adams, Warner Richmond; *D:* John P. McCarthy. **VHS, Beta** $19.95 *NOS, VCI, VCN* ♪♪

Song of the Islands Landing families in Hawaii feud over a beach, while the son of one (Mature) and the daughter of the other (Grable) fall in love. Plenty of songs, and dancing to display Grable's legs. Of course happiness and concord reign at the end. Songs include "O'Brien Has Gone Hawaiian," "Sing Me a Song of the Islands," and "What's Buzzin', Cousin?"
1942 75m/C Betty Grable, Victor Mature, Jack Oakie, Thomas Mitchell, Billy Gilbert; *D:* Walter Lang. **VHS, Beta** $19.98 *FOX, MLB* ♪♪½

Song of the Thin Man The sixth and final "Thin Man" mystery. This time Nick and Nora Charles (Powell and Loy) investigate the murder of a bandleader. Somewhat more sophisticated than its predecessor, due in part to its setting in the jazz music world. Sequel to "The Thin Man Goes Home."
1947 86m/B William Powell, Myrna Loy, Keenan Wynn, Dean Stockwell, Philip Reed, Patricia Morison, Gloria Grahame, Jayne Meadows, Don Taylor, Leon Ames, Ralph Morgan, Warner Anderson; *D:* Edward Buzzell. **VHS, Beta** $19.98 *MGM* ♪♪½

Song of the Trail Our hero saves an old man hornswoggled at cards.
1936 65m/B Kermit Maynard, George "Gabby" Hayes, Fuzzy Knight, Wheeler Oakman, Evelyn Brent, Andrea Leeds; *D:* Russell Hopton. **VHS, Beta** $19.95 *NOS, VDM, VCN* ♪½

A Song to Remember With music performed by Jose Iturbi, this film depicts the last years of the great pianist and composer Frederic Chopin, including his affair with famous author George Sand, the most renowned French woman of her day. Typically mangled film biography. ♪Valse in D Flat (Minute Waltz); Mazurka In B Flat, Opus 7, No. 1; Fantasie Impromptu, Opus 66; Etude In A Flat, Opus 25, No. 1 (partial); Polonaise In A Flat, Opus 53 (partial); Scherzo In B Flat Minor; Etude In C Minor, Opus 10, No. 12; Nocturne In C Minor, Opus 48, No. 1; Nocturn In E Flat, Opus 9, No. 2.
1945 112m/C Cornel Wilde, Paul Muni, Merle Oberon, Nina Foch, George Coulouris; *D:* Charles Vidor; *M:* Miklos Rozsa. **VHS, Beta** $19.95 *COL, RDG, TVC* ♪♪♪

Song Without End This musical biography of 19th century Hungarian pianist/composer Franz Liszt is given the Hollywood treatment. The lavish production emphasizes Liszt's scandalous exploits with married women and his life among the royal courts of Europe rather than his musical talents. Features music from several composers including Handel, Beethoven, Bach and Schumann. This film marked the debut of Capucine. Director Vidor died during filming and Cukor stepped in, so there is a noticeable change in style. Although there is much to criticize in the story, the music is beautiful. ♪Mephisto Waltz; Spozalizio; Sonata In B Minor; Un Sospiro; Fantasy on Themes From "Rigoletto"; Consolation in D Flat; Liebestraum; Les Preludes; Piano Concerto No. 1.
1960 130m/C Dirk Bogarde, Capucine, Genevieve Page, Patricia Morison, Ivan Desny, Martita Hunt, Lou Jacobi; *D:* Charles Vidor, George Cukor; *M:* Morris Stoloff, Harry Sukman. **VHS** $19.95 *COL, TVC* ♪♪½

Songs and Bullets Simple zen-like title sums it up. The songs total five in number, the bullets somewhat more as hero cowboys battle rustlers in routine fashion. One of a handful of films (westerns and comedies) produced by funnyman Stan Laurel.
1938 57m/B Fred Scott, Al "Fuzzy" St. John, Alice Ardell, Charles "Blackie" King, Karl Hackett, Frank LaRue, Budd Buster; *D:* Sam Newfield. **VHS** $19.95 *NOS, HEG* ♪½

Songwriter A high-falutin' look at the lives and music of two popular country singers with, aptly, plenty of country tunes written and performed by the stars. Singer-businessman Nelson needs Kristofferson's help keeping a greedy investor at bay. Never mind the plot; plenty of good music. ♫How Do You Feel About Foolin' Around?; Songwriter; Who'll Buy My Memories; Write Your Own Songs; Nobody Said It Was Going To Be Easy; Good Times; Eye of the Storm; Crossing the Border; Down to Her Socks.
1984 (R) 94m/C Willie Nelson, Kris Kristofferson, Rip Torn, Melinda Dillon, Lesley Ann Warren; **D:** Alan Rudolph. **VHS, Beta** $12.95 COL 🐾🐾½

Sonny and Jed An escaped convict and a free-spirited woman travel across Mexico pillaging freely, followed determinedly by shiny-headed lawman Savalas. Lame rip-off of the Bonnie and Clyde legend. **AKA:** La Banda J.&S.; Cronaca Criminale del Far West.
1973 (R) 85m/C Tomas Milian, Telly Savalas, Susan George, Rosanna Janni, Laura Betti; **D:** Sergio Corbucci; **M:** Ennio Morricone. **VHS, Beta** NO 🐾

Sonny Boy A transvestite and a psychopath adopt a young boy, training him to do their bidding, which includes murder.
1987 (R) 96m/C David Carradine, Paul Smith, Brad Dourif, Conrad Janis, Sydney Lassick, Savina Gersak, Alexandra Powers, Steve Carlisle, Michael Griffin; **D:** Robert Martin Carroll; **W:** Graeme Whifler. **VHS, Beta** $89.98 TWE, MED Woof!

Sonora Stagecoach Okay sagebrush saga with an interesting lineup; two cowboys, a heroic Indian and a tough gal pilot escort a murder suspect in the title conveyance and manage to clear him when the real bad guys attack.
1944 61m/B Hoot Gibson, Bob Steele, Chief Thundercloud, Rocky Camron, Betty Miles, Glenn Strange, George Eldridge, Karl Hackett; **D:** Robert Tansey. **VHS** $19.95 NOS, HEG 🐾🐾

Sons A Vietnam veteran's son joins the military, causing strains within the family.
1991 ?m/C **D:** Alexandre Rockwell; **W:** Alexandre Rockwell, Brandon Cole. **VHS** $79.95 LRP 🐾🐾

Sons of Hercules in the Land of Darkness Hercules' sons kill dragons, fight titans, and generally flex up a storm.
1955 74m/B Dan Vadis. **VHS, Beta** $24.95 VYY 🐾

Sons of Katie Elder After their mother's death, four brothers are reunited. Wayne is a gunman; Anderson is a college graduate; silent Holliman is a killer; and Martin is a gambler. When they learn that her death might have been murder, they come together to devise a way to seek revenge on the killer. The town bullies complicate matters; the sheriff tells them to lay off. Especially strong screen presence by Wayne, in his first role following cancer surgery. One of the Duke's most popular movies of the '60s.
1965 122m/C John Wayne, Dean Martin, Earl Holliman, Michael Anderson Jr., Martha Hyer; **D:** Henry Hathaway; **M:** Elmer Bernstein. **VHS, Beta** $14.95 PAR, TLF 🐾🐾½

Sons of Steel Two brothers, owners of a steel mill, lead vastly different lives. They raise their sons in their own images, causing problems.
1935 65m/B Charles Starrett, Polly Ann Young, William "Billy" Bakewell, Walter Walker, Aileen Pringle, Holmes Herbert, Florence Roberts, Adolf Millar, Lloyd Ingraham; **D:** Charles Lamont. **VHS** $19.95 NOS 🐾🐾

Sons of the Desert Laurel and Hardy in their best-written film. The boys try to fool their wives by pretending to go to Hawaii to cure Ollie of a bad cold when in fact, they are attending their lodge convention in Chicago. Also includes a 1935 Thelma Todd/Patsy Kelly short, "Top Flat." **AKA:** Sons of the Legion; Convention City; Fraternally Yours.
1933 73m/B Stan Laurel, Oliver Hardy, Mae Busch, Charley Chase, Dorothy Christy; **D:** William A. Seiter. **VHS, Beta** $19.95 MED, MLB, FFF 🐾🐾🐾

Sons of the Pioneers Small town sheriff Hayes hires cowboy Roy to rid town of outlaws.
1942 61m/B Roy Rogers, George "Gabby" Hayes, Maris Wrixon, Forrest Taylor; **D:** Joseph Kane. **VHS** $12.98 REP 🐾🐾

Sooner or Later 13-year-old girl passes herself off as 16 with a local rock idol and must decide whether to go all the way.
1978 100m/C Rex Smith, Judd Hirsch, Denise Miller, Morey Amsterdam, Lynn Redgrave; **D:** Bruce Hart. **VHS** STE, NWV 🐾½

Sophia Loren: Her Own Story Bio of Sophia Loren, watching her grow from a spindly child in working-class Naples to a world-renowned movie star, beauty queen, and mother. Loren plays herself and her mother in this tedious account. Based on the biography by A.E. Hotchner. Made for TV.
1980 150m/C Sophia Loren, Armand Assante, Ed Flanders, John Gavin; **D:** Mel Stuart; **W:** Joanna Crawford. **VHS, Beta** $69.95 HBO 🐾🐾

Sophie's Choice A haunting modern tragedy about Sophie Zawistowska, a beautiful Polish Auschwitz survivor settled in Brooklyn after WWII. She has intense relationships with a schizophrenic genius and an aspiring Southern writer. An artful, immaculately performed and resonant drama, with an astonishing, commanding performance by the versatile Streep; a chilling portrayal of the banality of evil. From the best-selling, autobiographical novel by William Styron.
1982 (R) 157m/C Meryl Streep, Kevin Kline, Peter MacNicol, Rita Karin, Stephen D. Newman, Josh Mostel; **D:** Alan J. Pakula; **W:** Alan J. Pakula; **M:** Marvin Hamlisch. Academy Awards '82: Best Actress (Streep); Nominations: Best Adapted Screenplay, Best Cinematography, Best Costume Design, Best Original Score; Golden Globe Awards '83: Best Actress—Drama (Streep); Los Angeles Film Critics Association Awards '82: Best Actress (Streep); National Board of Review Awards '82: Best Actress (Streep); New York Film Critics Awards '82: Best Actress (Streep); National Society of Film Critics Awards '82: Best Actress (Streep). **VHS, Beta** $19.98 FOX, SWC 🐾🐾🐾½

Sophisticated Gents Nine boyhood friends, members of a black athletic club, reunite after 25 years to honor their old coach and see how each of their lives has been affected by being black men in American society. Based on the novel "The Junior Bachelor Society" by John A. Williams. Originally made for television.
1981 200m/C Paul Winfield, Roosevelt Grier, Bernie Casey, Raymond St. Jacques, Thalmus Rasulala, Dick Anthony Williams, Ron O'Neal, Rosalind Cash, Denise Nicholas, Alfre Woodard, Melvin Van Peebles; **D:** Harry Falk; **W:** Melvin Van Peebles. **VHS** $89.95 XVC 🐾🐾🐾

Sorcerer To put out an oil fire, four men on the run in South America agree to try to buy their freedom by driving trucks loaded with nitroglycerin over dangerous terrain—with many natural and man-made obstacles to get in their way. Remake of "The Wages of Fear" is nowhere as good as the classic original, but has exciting moments. Puzzlingly retitled, which may have contributed to the box-office failure, and the near demise of Friedlein's directing career. **AKA:** Wages of Fear.
1977 (PG) 121m/C Roy Scheider, Bruno Cremer, Francesco Rabal, Soudad Amidou, Ramon Bieri; **D:** William Friedkin; **W:** Walon Green. **VHS** $19.98 MCA, FCT 🐾🐾½

Sorceress The Harris girls are sisters who use their powers of sorcery and fighting skills to battle demons, dragons, and evil. Yeah, sure. Really, they're just a pair of babes parading for the camera.
1982 (R) 83m/C Leigh Anne Harris, Lynette Harris, Bob Nelson, David Milbern, Bruno Rey, Anna De Sade; **D:** Brian Stuart; **W:** Jim Wynorski. **VHS, Beta** NO Woof!

Sorceress A friar in medieval Europe feels insecure in his religious beliefs after encountering a woman who heals through ancient practices. Historically authentic and interestingly moody. Written, produced, and directed by two women: an art history professor and a collaborator of Francois Truffaut's. In French with English subtitles or dubbed.
1988 98m/C Tcheky Karyo, Christine Boisson, Jean Carmet; **D:** Suzanne Schiffman; **W:** Pamela Berger, Suzanne Schiffman. **VHS** $29.95 MFV, ING 🐾🐾🐾

Sorority Babes in the Slimeball Bowl-A-Rama An ancient gremlin-type creature is released from a bowling alley, and the great-looking sorority babes have to battle it at the mall, with the help of a wacky crew of nerds. Horrible horror spoof shows plenty of skin.
1987 (R) 80m/C Linnea Quigley, Brinke Stevens, Andras Jones, John Wildman; **D:** David DeCoteau. **Beta** NO 🐾

Sorority Girl Camp classic in which beautiful co-ed Cabot is presented as a malicious rich kid involved in everything from petty fights to blackmail. Cheap production from the Corman factory.
1957 60m/B Susan Cabot, Dick Miller, Barbara Crane, June Kennedy, Fay Baker, Jeane Wood; **D:** Roger Corman. **VHS** $9.95 NLC 🐾½

Sorority House Massacre A knife-wielding maniac stalks a sorority girl while her more elite sisters are away for the weekend. Yawn—haven't we seen this one before? Unfortunately for us we'll see it again because this one's followed by a sequel.
1986 (R) 74m/C Angela O'Neill, Wendy Martel, Pamela Ross, Nicole Rio; **D:** Carol Frank. **VHS, Beta** $79.95 WAR Woof!

Sorority House Massacre 2: Nighty Nightmare Another no-brainer with a different cast and director. This time around three lingerie-clad lovelies are subjected to the terrors of a killer their first night in their new sorority house. College just keeps getting tougher all the time.
1992 80m/C Melissa Moore, Robin Harris, Stacia Zhivago, Dana Bentley; **D:** Jim Wynorski. **VHS** $89.98 NHO Woof!

Sorority House Party A famous rock guitarist is held against his will at the sexiest sorority house on campus. He definitely has mixed feelings about the experience considering the inhabitants saunter around in bikinis and "force" him to party with them. Anders and Attila are transplants from the modeling circuit.
1992 (R) 95m/C Attila, April Lerman, Kim Little, Avalon Anders, Joe Mundi, Rachel Latt, Mark Stulce, Michael Xavier; **D:** David Michael Latt; **W:** John Murdy, Steve Taylor. **VHS** $92.95 APX 🐾

The Sorrow and the Pity A classic documentary depicting the life of a small French town and its resistance during the Nazi occupation. Lengthy, but totally compelling. A great documentary that brings home the atrocities of war. In French with English narration.
1971 265m/B *D:* Marcel Ophuls. **VHS, Beta** COL, OM *ÆÆÆ* ½

Sorrowful Jones A "Little Miss Marker" remake, in which bookie Hope inherits a little girl as collateral for an unpaid bet. Good for a few yuks, but the original is much better.
1949 88m/B Bob Hope, Lucille Ball, William Demarest, Bruce Cabot, Thomas Gomez, Mary Jane Saunders; *D:* Sidney Lanfield; *W:* Jack Rose, Melville Shavelson. **VHS, Beta** $14.98 MCA *ÆÆ*

Sorrows of Gin Eight-year-old girl searches for a sense of family amid her parents' lives. Her efforts to deal with alienation and emotional isolation lead her to run away from home. From a short story by John Cheever.
1979 60m/C Edward Herrmann, Sigourney Weaver, Mara Hobel, Eileen Heckart, Rachel Roberts. **VHS, Beta** FLI *ÆÆ* ½

The Sorrows of Satan Dempster and Cortez star as writers in love with each other, but Cortez can't take his poverty and the rejection of publishers. As he is about to end it all, the devil appears to him in disguise and makes an offer he can hardly refuse. He is introduced to London society and winds up marrying a fortune hunter. When he discovers this he goes back to Dempster, who still loves him, and vows to give up everything for her. Menjou then reveals himself to be the devil but Dempster's faith is so strong that the evil is vanquished.
1926 111m/B Adolphe Menjou, Carol Dempster, Ricardo Cortez, Lya de Putti; *D:* D.W. Griffith. **VHS, Beta** $24.95 GPV *ÆÆÆ*

Sorry, Wrong Number A wealthy, bedridden wife overhears two men plotting a murder on a crossed telephone line, and begins to suspect that one of the voices is her husband's. A classic tale of paranoia and suspense. Based on a radio drama by Louise Fletcher, who also wrote the screenplay. Remade for television in 1989.
1948 89m/B Barbara Stanwyck, Burt Lancaster, Ann Richards, Wendell Corey, Harold Vermilyea, Ed Begley Sr.; *D:* Anatole Litvak. **VHS, Beta** $19.95 PAR *ÆÆÆ* ½

Sorry, Wrong Number Cable remake of the 1948 Barbara Stanwyck thriller about a bed-ridden woman trying to get help after she realizes she's being stalked by a killer. Offers a new twist (drug dealing), but doesn't even approach the Stanwyck original. From the story by Lucille Fletcher.
1989 90m/C Loni Anderson, Hal Holbrook, Patrick Macnee, Miguel Fernandez, Carl Weintraub; *D:* Tony Wharmby; *W:* Ann Louise Bardach; *M:* Bruce Broughton. **VHS, Beta** $79.95 PAR *Æ* ½

S.O.S. Coast Guard A fiendish scientist creates a disintegrating gas and the U.S. Coast Guard must stop him from turning it over to unfriendly foreigners. Loads of action in this 12-part serial.
1937 224m/B Ralph Byrd, Bela Lugosi, Maxine Doyle. **VHS** $29.98 NOS, SNC, REP *ÆÆ* ½

S.O.S. Pacific A seaplane crashes on a nuclear-test island and the survivors find that they have only five hours before they get nuked. Even though there is plenty of the usual action one would expect from such a film, the story really revolves around the

characters. The British and U.S. versions have different endings.
1960 91m/B Eddie Constantine, Pier Angeli, Richard Attenborough, John Gregson, Eva Bartok; *D:* Guy Green. **VHS** $19.95 NOS *ÆÆ*

S.O.S. Titanic The story of the Titanic disaster, recounted in flashback, in docudrama style. James Costigan's teleplay of the familiar story focuses on the courage that accompanied the horror and tragedy. Thoroughly professional, absorbing made-for-TV drama.
1979 98m/C David Janssen, Cloris Leachman, Susan St. James, David Warner, Ian Holm, Helen Mirren, Harry Andrews; *D:* Billy Hale; *M:* Howard Blake. **VHS, Beta** NO *ÆÆ* ½

Sotto, Sotto A minor Wertmuller comedy about an Italian businessman who is constantly suspicious of his wife's fidelity. As it happens, she's attracted to another woman (de Santis). Massimo Wertmuller is Lina's nephew. Entertaining. In Italian with English subtitles.
1985 (R) 104m/C Enrico Montesano, Veronica Lario, Massimo Wertmuller, Luisa de Santis; *D:* Lina Wertmuller; *W:* Lina Wertmuller. **VHS, Beta** $69.95 COL, APD, ING *ÆÆ* ½

Soul-Fire South Pacific high seas induce Cupid's arrow. Silent.
1925 100m/B Richard Barthelmess, Bessie Love, Walter Long, Arthur Metcalfe; *D:* John S. Robertson. **VHS, Beta** $24.95 GPV, FCT, GVV *ÆÆ*

Soul Hustler A con man becomes rich and famous as a tent-show evangelist. Pathetic drivel.
1976 (PG) 81m/C Fabian, Casey Kasem, Larry Bishop, Nai Bonet; *D:* Burt Topper. **VHS, Beta** $39.95 LIV, MON Woof!

Soul Man Denied the funds he expected for his Harvard tuition, a young white student (Howell) masquerades as a black in order to get a minority scholarship. As a black student at Harvard, Howell learns about racism and bigotry. Pleasant lightweight comedy with romance thrown in (Chong is the black girl he falls for), and with pretensions to social satire that it never achieves.
1986 (PG-13) 101m/C C. Thomas Howell, Rae Dawn Chong, James Earl Jones, Leslie Nielsen, Arye Gross; *D:* Steve Miner. **VHS, Beta** $9.95 NWV, STE *ÆÆ*

Soul of Samurai Duo searches for the essence of kung fu but finds terror instead.
19?? 90m/C Kong Pun. **VHS, Beta** $29.95 OCE *Æ*

Soul of the Beast An elephant repeatedly saves Bellamy from the villainous Beery. Silent with original organ score.
1923 77m/B Madge Bellamy, Cullen Landis, Noah Beery Sr. **VHS, Beta, 8mm** $16.95 GPV, VYY *Æ* ½

Soul Patrol Black newspaper reporter clashes with the all-white police department in a racist city.
1980 (R) 90m/C Nigel Davenport, Ken Gampu, Peter Dyneley; *D:* Christopher Rowley. **VHS, Beta** SUN *Æ*

Soul Vengeance Black man is jailed and brutalized for crime he didn't commit and wants revenge when he's released. Many afros and platform shoes. Vintage blaxploitation. *AKA:* Welcome Home Brother Charles.
1975 91m/C Mario Monte, Reatha Grey, Stan Kamber, Tiffany Peters, Ven Bigelow, Jake Carter; *D:* Jamaa Fanaka; *W:* Jamaa Fanaka. **VHS** $39.95 XVC *Æ*

Soultaker The title spirit is after a young couple's souls, and they have just an hour to reunite with their bodies after a car crash. Meanwhile, they're in limbo (literally) between

heaven and earth. The ending's OK, if you can make it that far.
1990 (R) 94m/C Joe Estevez, Vivian Schilling, Gregg Thomsen, David Shark, Jean Reiner, Chuck Williams, Robert Z'Dar; *D:* Michael Rissi; *W:* Vivian Schilling. **VHS** $89.95 AIP *Æ* ½

The Sound and the Silence Bio of inventor Alexander Graham Bell (Bach). The Scottish Bell's father was a speech specialist and his beloved mother Eliza (Fricker) was severely hearing impaired. Bell himself trained to work with the deaf in Boston and experimented with transmitting speech electronically—a project which only grew when Bell married the deaf Mable Hubbard (Quinn). Bell's lifelong devotion lead to his development of the telephone as well as numerous other inventions (and his founding of "National Geographic" magazine). Bell was hardly a lively character but this made for television drama is lavishly done. In two parts.
1993 93m/C John Bach, Elizabeth Quinn, Brenda Fricker, Ian Bannen; *D:* John Kent Harrison; *W:* John Kent Harrison, Tony Foster, William Schmidt. **VHS** TTC *ÆÆ* ½

Sound of Horror The Hound usually admires creative efforts to keep budgets down, but this is too much (or too little). A dinosaur egg hatches, and out lashes an invisible predator. Yes, you'll have to use your imagination as archaeologists are slashed to bits by the no-show terror. *AKA:* El Sonido de la Muerte; Sound From a Million Years Ago; The Prehistoric Sound.
1964 85m/B James Philbrook, Arturo Fernandez, Soledad Miranda, Ingrid Pitt; *D:* Jose Antonio Nieves-Conde. **VHS** $15.95 NOS, LOO *Æ* ½

Sound of Love The mutual attraction between a deaf female hustler and a deaf race car driver leads to a deep relationship where they both learn about their own fears and desires.
1977 74m/C Celia de Burgh, John Jarratt. **VHS, Beta** $49.98 SUE *Æ*

Sound of Murder A successful children's book writer wants to exact revenge on his adulterous wife, but is himself murdered before he can "execute" his plan.
1982 114m/C Michael Moriarty, Joanna Miles. **VHS, Beta** $59.95 LIV *Æ*

The Sound of Music The classic film version of the Rodgers and Hammerstein musical based on the true story of the singing von Trapp family of Austria and their escape from the Nazis under WWII. Beautiful Salzburg, Austria location photography and an excellent cast. Andrews, fresh from her Oscar for "Mary Poppins," is effervescent, in beautiful voice, but occasionally too good to be, true. Not Rodgers & Hammerstein's most innovative score, but lovely to hear and see. Plummer's singing was dubbed by Bill Lee. Marni Nixon, behind-the-scenes songstress for "West Side Story" and "My Fair Lady," makes her on-screen debut as one of the nuns. ♫I Have Confidence In Me; Something Good; The Sound of Music; Preludium; Morning Hymn; Alleluia; How Do You Solve A Problem Like Maria?; Sixteen, Going on Seventeen; My Favorite Things.
1965 174m/C Julie Andrews, Christopher Plummer, Eleanor Parker, Peggy Wood, Charmian Carr, Heather Menzies, Marni Nixon, Richard Haydn, Anna Lee, Norma Varden, Nicholas Hammond, Angela Cartwright, Portia Nelson, Duane Chase, Debbie Turner, Kym Karath; *D:* Robert Wise; *W:* Ernest Lehman; *M:* Richard Rodgers, Oscar Hammerstein. Academy Awards '65: Best Adapted Score, Best Director (Wise), Best Film Editing, Best Picture, Best Sound; Nominations: Best Actress (Andrews), Best Art Direction/Set Decoration (Color), Best

Color Cinematography, Best Costume Design (Color), Best Supporting Actress (Wood); Directors Guild of America Awards '65: Best Director (Wise); Golden Globe Awards '66: Best Actress—Musical/Comedy (Andrews), Best Film—Musical/Comedy; National Board of Review Awards '65: 10 Best Films of the Year. **VHS, Beta** $24.98 *FOX, BTV, RDG* 🎬🎬🎬🎬

Sounder The struggles of a family of black sharecroppers in rural Louisiana during the Depression. When the father is sentenced to jail for stealing in order to feed his family, they must pull together even more, and one son finds education to be his way out of poverty. Tyson brings strength and style to her role, with fine help from Winfield. Moving and well made, with little sentimentality and superb acting from a great cast. Adapted from the novel by William Armstrong. **1972 (G) 105m/C** Paul Winfield, Cicely Tyson, Kevin Hooks, Taj Mahal, Carmin Mathews, James Best, Janet MacLachlan; **D:** Martin Ritt; **M:** Taj Mahal. Academy Awards '72 Nominations: Best Actor (Winfield), Best Actress (Tyson), Best Adapted Screenplay, Best Picture; National Board of Review Awards '72: 10 Best Films of the Year; National Society of Film Critics Awards '72: Best Actress (Tyson). **VHS, Beta** $14.95 *KUI, PAR, PTB* 🎬🎬🎬🎬

Sounds of Silence A young deaf boy fears that a killer arsonist may be at large—but can he prove it? One of a number of obscure oddities featuring former youth idol Donahue. **1991 108m/C** Troy Donahue, Peter Nelson. **VHS, Beta** *NO* 🎬🎬

Soup for One Writer-director Kaufer's first film is a solid entry in the Woody Allen-esque Manhattanite's angst genre. Young Jewish guy Rubinek pines for the woman of his dreams, finds her, is rejected, persists, gets her, wonders if she's what he wants after all. If you like Woody Allen, this is worth seeing. **1982 (R) 84m/C** Saul Rubinek, Marcia Strassman, Gerrit Graham, Richard Libertini, Andrea Martin; **D:** Jonathan Kaufer. **VHS, Beta** $19.98 *WAR* 🎬🎬½

Sourdough Fur trapper Perry escapes the hustle and bustle of modern life by fleeing to the Alaskan wilderness. Near-plotless travel-og depends heavily on scenery—and there's plenty of that, for sure. **1977 94m/C** Gil Perry, Charles Brock, Slim Carlson, Carl Clark; **D:** Martin J. Spinelli. **VHS, Beta** $89.95 *IMP* 🎬🎬

South Beach Two ex-football players turned private eyes are living the good life and partying it up in Miami Beach. However, their leisurely lifestyles are soon disrupted when they accept a mysterious challenge from the beautiful Vanity. **1992 (R) 93m/C** Fred Williamson, Gary Busey, Vanity, Peter Fonda; **D:** Fred Williamson; **W:** Mark Montgomery; **M:** Joe Renzetti. **VHS** $89.95 *PSM* 🎬🎬

South Bronx Heroes A police officer helps two children when they discover their foster home is the headquarters for a pornography ring. **AKA:** The Runaways; Revenge of the Innocents. **1985 (R) 105m/C** Brendan Ward, Mario Van Peebles, Megan Van Peebles, Melissa Esposito, Martin Zurla, Jordan Abeles; **D:** William Szarka. **VHS, Beta** *NO* 🎬½

South Central A low-budget urban drama set in a gang-infested L.A. neighborhood. Bobby is a young black man, and former gang leader, who has spent ten years in prison for murder. His wife has become a drug addict and his young son Jimmie has begun running with his dad's old gang. Now paroled, Bobby hopes to re-establish the

bond with his son—enough to protect him from following in his nowhere-to-go-but-down footsteps. Worthy effort with an emotional ending. Feature debut of director Anderson. Based on the novel "Crips" by Donald Bakeer. **1992 (R) 99m/C** Glenn Plummer, Carl Lumbly, Christian Coleman, LaRita Shelby, Byron Keith Minns; **D:** Steve Anderson; **W:** Steve Anderson. **VHS, Beta** $92.99 *WAR, PMS* 🎬🎬

South of Hell Mountain On the run from a gold mine robbery where they left 20 dead, the McHenry brothers meet a mother-daughter team that slows them down. **1970 (R) 87m/C** Ann Stewart, Sam Hall, Nicol Britton; **D:** William Sachs, Louis Leahman. **VHS, Beta** $59.95 *MGM* 🎬½

South of Monterey Western adventure with the Cisco kid. **1947 63m/B** Gilbert Roland, Martin Garralaga, Frank Yaconelli, Marjorie Riordan; **D:** William Nigh. **VHS, Beta** $29.95 *VCN* 🎬½

South of Pago Pago The unsuspecting natives of a tropical isle are exploited by a gang of pirates searching for a seabed of rare pearls. A notch up from most similar adventure outings, with great violent action and excellent cinematography. Leading lady Farmer was thought to be a rising star, but retired at 29 in 1942 because of alcoholism and spent some time in mental institutions. "Frances" (1982), with Jessica Lange, is based on her life. **1940 98m/B** Victor McLaglen, Jon Hall, Frances Farmer, Gene Lockhart; **D:** Alfred E. Green. **VHS, Beta** *NO* 🎬🎬½

South of Reno A man living a secluded life in the desert dreams of moving to Reno and learns his wife is cheating on him. Odd, minimal plot. Impressive first feature for Polish diretor Rezyka, who cut his teeth on music videos. **1987 (R) 98m/C** Jeffery Osterhage, Lisa Blount, Joe Phelan, Lewis Van Bergen, Julia Montgomery, Brandis Kemp, Danitza Kingsley, Mary Grace Canfield, Bert Remsen; **D:** Mark Rezyka; **M:** Nigel Holton. **VHS** $79.98 *REP* 🎬🎬

South of St. Louis A peaceful cattle rancher turns renegade gunrunner during the Civil War when his stock is destroyed by Union guerrillas. Overplotted but exciting and action-packed western, with Smith dazzling in a plethora of costumes. **1948 88m/C** Joel McCrea, Zachary Scott, Victor Jory, Douglas Kennedy, Alexis Smith, Alan Hale, Dorothy Malone; **D:** Ray Enright. **VHS** $14.95 *REP* 🎬🎬½

South of Santa Fe Mexican rebels give the hero a hard time in this standard Western. **1932 60m/B** Bob Steele, Janis Elliott, Chris-Pin Martin, Jack Clifford, Eddie Dunn, Robert Burns, Hank Bell, Allan Garcia; **D:** Bert Glennon. **VHS** $19.95 *NOS* 🎬🎬

South of Santa Fe Rogers and friends take on the mob—yes, the mob, armed with machine guns and airplanes—after they are falsely implicated in a crime. In lulls between the rootin' tootin' gunfights, Rogers belts out "We're Headin' for the Home Corral," "Down the Trail," and "Open Range Ahead." **1942 60m/B** Roy Rogers, George "Gabby" Hayes, Linda Hayes, Paul Fix, Judy Clark; **D:** Joseph Kane. **VHS, Beta** $19.95 *NOS, DVT, CAB* 🎬🎬

South of the Border Autry and Burnette are government agents sent to Mexico to investigate a possible revolution instigated by foreign agents. Propaganda-heavy singing western appeared just before the U.S. en-

tered WWII; did well at the box office and boosted Autry's career. **1939 70m/B** Gene Autry, Smiley Burnette. **VHS, Beta** $19.88 *CCB, VCN* 🎬

South of the Rio Grande The Cisco Kid rides again as he comes to the aid of a rancher whose horses were stolen. Garden-variety law-and-order western. **1945 60m/B** Duncan Renaldo; **D:** Lambert Hillyer. **VHS, Beta** $12.95 *VCI* 🎬½

South Pacific A young American Navy nurse and a Frenchman fall in love during WWII. Expensive production included much location shooting in Hawaii. Based on Rodgers and Hammerstein's musical; not as good as the play, but pretty darn good still. The play in turn was based on James Michener's novel "Tales of the South Pacific." 🎵My Girl Back Home; Dites-Moi; Bali Ha'i; Happy Talk; A Cockeyed Optimist; Soliloquies; Some Enchanted Evening; Bloody Mary; I'm Gonna Wash That Man Right Out of My Hair. **1958 167m/C** Mitzi Gaynor, Rossano Brazzi, Ray Walston, France Nuyen, John Kerr, Juanita Hall, Tom Laughlin; **D:** Joshua Logan; **M:** Richard Rodgers, Oscar Hammerstein; **V:** Giorgio Tozzi. Academy Awards '58: Best Sound; Nominations: Best Color Cinematography; Academy Awards '58: Best Original Score. **VHS, Beta** $19.98 *FOX, RDG, HMV* 🎬½

South Seas Massacre A cop and a prisoner, shackled together, try to survive modern-day pirates, natives, and each other. They may make it through, but viewers may wish they didn't. **19?? 60m/C** Troy Donahue; **D:** Pablo Santiago. **VHS, Beta** $59.95 *PSM* Woof!

Southern Comfort A group of National Guardsmen are on weekend maneuvers in the swamps of Louisiana. They run afoul of some of the local Cajuns, and are marked for death in this exciting and disturbing thriller. Booth is excellent in a rare exploration of a little-understood way of life. Lots of blood. If you belong to the National Guard, this could make you queasy. **1981 (R) 106m/C** Powers Boothe, Keith Carradine, Fred Ward, Franklyn Seales, Brion James, T.K. Carter, Peter Coyote; **D:** Walter Hill; **W:** Walter Hill, David Giler, Michael Kane; **M:** Ry Cooder. **VHS, Beta** $29.95 *SUE, HHE* 🎬🎬🎬

A Southern Yankee Skelton plays a bumbling bellboy who ends up as a Union spy during the Civil War. Enjoyable comedy, thanks largely to the off-screen input of Buster Keaton. **AKA:** My Hero. **1948 90m/B** Red Skelton, Brian Donlevy, Arlene Dahl, George Coulouris, Lloyd Gough, John Ireland, Minor Watson, Charles Dingle, Art Baker, Reed Hadley, Arthur Space, Addison Richards, Joyce Compton, Paul Harvey, Jeff Corey; **D:** Edward Sedgwick. **VHS, Beta** $19.98 *MGM* 🎬🎬½

The Southerner A man used to working for others is given some land by an uncle and decides to pack up his family and try farming for himself. They find hardships as they struggle to support themselves. A superb, naturalistic celebration of a family's fight to survive amid all the elements. From the story "Hold Autumn in Your Hand," by George Sessions Perry. Novelist Faulkner had an uncredited hand in the script. He thought Renoir the best contemporary director, and later said "The Southerner" gave him more pleasure than any of his other Hollywood work (though this is faint praise; Faulkner is said to have hated Hollywood). **1945 91m/B** Zachary Scott, Betty Field, Beulah Bondi, Norman Lloyd, Bunny Sunshine, Jay Gilpin, Estelle Taylor, Blanche Yurka, Percy Kilbride, J. Carroll Naish; **D:** Jean Renoir; **W:** Hugo Butler, William Faulkner, Jean Renoir. Academy Awards '45 Nominations: Best Director

(Renoir), Best Sound, Best Original Score; National Board of Review Awards '45: Best Director (Renoir); Venice Film Festival '46: Best Film. **VHS, Beta, 8mm** $19.95 *NOS, PSM, VYY* 🎦🎦🎦🎦

Southward Ho! In the first western to team Rogers with sidekick Gabby Hayes, they portray ranchers investigating bloodshed in their valley, Roy meanwhile yodelin' four tunes. Fun outing.
1939 56m/B Roy Rogers, George "Gabby" Hayes. **VHS, Beta** $19.95 *NOS, VCN, CAB* 🎦🎦

Souvenir A German soldier returns to France after WWII to find the woman he left behind and the daughter he never saw. Might have been good, but too melodramatic and overwrought, with lukewarm acting.
1988 (R) 93m/C Christopher Plummer, Catherine Hicks, Christopher Cazenove, Michael Lonsdale; *D:* Geoffrey Reeve. **VHS, Beta** *PAR* 🎦🎦

Soviet Spy A French docu-drama written by Hans Otto Meissner, Chief of Protocol at the German Embassy in Tokyo during WWII, about the journalist Richard Sorge, a German hanged in 1944 for supplying information to the Soviets. In French with subtitles.
1961 130m/B **VHS, Beta** $19.95 *FCT* 🎦🎦

Soy un Golfo A lazy bum is inspired to do something with his life by a pretty girl who he later finds out is his brother's fiancee.
1965 90m/C Adalberto "Resortes" Martinez, Luz Maria Aguilar, Che Reyes. **VHS, Beta** $39.95 *MAD* 🎦🎦

Soylent Green In the 21st Century, hard-boiled police detective Heston investigates a murder and discovers what soylent green—the people's principal food—is made of. Robinson's final film is a disappointing end to a great career. Its view of the future and of human nature is relentlessly dark. Don't watch it with kids.
1973 (PG) 95m/C Charlton Heston, Leigh Taylor-Young, Chuck Connors, Joseph Cotten, Edward G. Robinson, Brock Peters; *D:* Richard Fleischer. **VHS, Beta** $19.98 *MGM* 🎦🎦½

Space Monster Really bad, low-budget flick with a rubber monster and a climactic crash into a "sea of monsters" which is really a fish tank full of crabs. Ultra cheap production with handed down cast and props. *AKA:* First Woman Into Space; Voyage Beyond the Sun.
1964 ?m/B **VHS** $20 *SMW Woof!*

Space Mutiny Spaceship falls under the attack of the mutinous Kalgan. To keep everyone from being sold into slavery, a small band of loyal passengers strike back. Will they be successful in thwarting the attack? Who cares?
1988 (PG) 93m/C Reb Brown, James Ryan, John Phillip Law, Cameron Mitchell; *D:* David Winters. **VHS, Beta** $79.95 *AIP* 🎦

Space: 1999 Landau and Bain star as the leaders of Moonbase Alpha, a scientific outpost which is hurled out of orbit by a nuclear explosion. In "Voyager's Return" the crew of Moonbase Alpha discover the original Voyager probe and excitedly prepare to extract its vast knowledge of the universe. To their horror, they discover that it has somehow been transformed into a planet-destroying monster. Bitter aliens are coming to exact their revenge on the machine and the crew is caught in the middle! Additional episodes available.
1975 52m/C Martin Landau, Barbara Bain, Barry Morse, Nick Tate, Jeremy Kemp, Barry Stokes, Alex Scott, Lawrence Trimble; *D:* Bob Kellett. **VHS** $14.99 *MOV* 🎦

Space: 1999—Alien Attack After an explosion on the moon, Moonbase Alpha loses contact with Earth forever. Pilot episode of the popular British sci-fi series.
1979 109m/C Martin Landau, Barbara Bain, Barry Morse, Nick Tate, Roy Dotrice, Philip Madoc, Lou Satton, Eric Carte; *D:* Lee H. Katzin. **VHS, Beta** $39.95 *LIV* 🎦🎦🎦

Space Ninja: Sword of the Space Ark A young fighter pilot returns home to find his planet under siege and his family dead. He vows to seek revenge and sets out to destroy the evil emperor who is wreaking such havoc.
1981 75m/C *D:* Bunker Jenkins. **VHS, Beta** $39.95 *LIV* 🎦½

Space Patrol Buzz Corey, Commander-in-Chief of the Space Patrol, tries to maintain interplanetary peace and protect the people of Earth's neighboring planets. These episodes television series include previews of coming attractions from classic science fiction films. Additional episodes are available.
1950 120m/B Edward Kemmer, Lyn Osborn. **VHS, Beta** $19.95 *RHI, MED, MOV* 🎦½

Space Rage A criminal sentenced to life on a prison planet leads a revolt of the inmates. Lame, formula western set in outer space.
1986 (R) 78m/C Michael Pare, Richard Farnsworth, John Laughlin, Lee Purcell; *D:* Conrad Palmisano. **VHS, Beta** $19.98 *LIV* 🎦

Space Raiders A plucky 10-year-old blasts off into a futuristic world of intergalactic desperados, crafty alien mercenaries, starship battles and cliff-hanging dangers. Recycled special effects (from producer Corman's movie factory) and plot (lifted near-whole from "Star Wars"). *AKA:* Star Child.
1983 (PG) 84m/C Vince Edwards, David Mendenhall; *D:* Howard R. Cohen. **VHS, Beta** $19.98 *WAR* 🎦🎦

Space Riders Action-adventure about the world's championship motorcycle race, with a rock soundtrack featuring Duran Duran, Simple Minds and Melba Moore.
1983 (PG) 93m/C Barry Sheene, Gavan O'Herlihy, Toshiya Ito, Stephanie McLean, Sayo Inaba; *D:* Joe Massot. **VHS, Beta** *NO Woof!*

Space Soldiers Conquer the Universe Edited version of the Flash Gordon serial "Flash Gordon Conquers the Universe." The evil Emperor Ming introduces a horrible plague from outer space called "The Purple Death." Dr. Zarkov, Dale, and Flash Gordon travel from the frozen wastes of Frigia to the palaces of Mongo and must take risk after risk. Twelve chapters at 20 minutes each.
1940 240m/B Buster Crabbe, Charles Middleton, Carol Hughes. **VHS, Beta** $49.95 *NOS, CAB* 🎦🎦

Spaceballs A humorous Brooks parody of recent science fiction pictures, mostly notably "Star Wars," with references to "Alien," the "Star Trek series," and "The Planet of the Apes." Disappointingly tame and tentative, but chuckle-laden enough for Brooks fans. The great man himself appears in two roles, including puny wise man/wise guy Yogurt.
1987 (PG) 96m/C Mel Brooks, Rick Moranis, John Candy, Bill Pullman, Daphne Zuniga, Dick Van Patten, John Hurt, George Wyner, Joan Rivers, Lorene Yarnell, Sal Viscuso, Stephen Tobolowsky, Dom DeLuise, Michael Winslow; *D:* Mel Brooks; *W:* Mel Brooks, Ronny Graham, Thomas Meehan; *M:* John Morris. **VHS, Beta** $14.95 *MGM* 🎦🎦½

SpaceCamp Gang o'teens and their instructor at the US Space Camp are accidentally launched on a space shuttle, and then must find a way to return to Earth. Hokey plot, subpar special effects; why bother? Well, it is "inspirational".
1986 (PG) 115m/C Kate Capshaw, Tate Donovan, Leaf (Joaquin Rafael) Phoenix, Kelly Preston, Larry B. Scott, Tom Skerritt, Lea Thompson, Terry O'Quinn; *D:* Harry Winer; *M:* John Williams. **VHS, Beta** $29.98 *LIV, VES, IME* 🎦🎦

Spaced Invaders Five ultra-cool aliens crash-land in a small midwestern town at Halloween. Local denizens mistake them for trick-or-treaters. Poorly made and a waste of time.
1990 (PG) 102m/C Douglas Barr, Royal Dano, Ariana Richards, Kevin Thompson, Jimmy Briscoe, Tony Cox, Debbie Lee Carrington, Tommy Madden; *D:* Patrick Read Johnson. **VHS, Beta** $14.99 *TOU, BVV* 🎦🎦

Spaced Out Naughty sci-fi sex comedy that parodies everything from "Star Wars" to "2001," though not very well. The sultry female aliens are visually pleasing, though. Watch this one with the sound turned off. *AKA:* Outer Reach.
1980 (R) 85m/C Barry Stokes, Glory Annen; *D:* Norman J. Warren. **VHS, Beta** *NO Woof!*

Spacehunter: Adventures in the Forbidden Zone Galactic bounty hunter agrees to rescue three damsels held captive by a cyborg. Strauss ain't no Harrison Ford. Filmed in 3-D, but who cares?
1983 (PG) 90m/C Peter Strauss, Molly Ringwald, Michael Ironside, Ernie Hudson, Andrea Marcovicci; *D:* Lamont Johnson; *W:* Len Blum; *M:* Elmer Bernstein. **VHS, Beta** $12.95 *COL* 🎦½

Spaceship Misguided attempt to spoof creature-features. Mad scientist tries to protect kindly monster from crazed crew. Not very funny, with the exception of the song-and-dance routine by the monster. *AKA:* The Creature Wasn't Nice; Naked Space.
1981 (PG) 88m/C Cindy Williams, Bruce Kimmel, Leslie Nielsen, Gerrit Graham, Patrick Macnee, Ron Kurowski; *D:* Bruce Kimmel. **VHS** $69.98 *LIV* 🎦½

Spaceways Scientist Duff is beset by all sorts of troubles: his experimental rockets explode, his wife has an affair with an ambitious scientist, and when they disappear together, he's accused of killing them and placing their bodies in the exploded rocket. All in all, a pretty bad (and long) day for our hero. Why should we suffer through it with him?
1953 76m/B Howard Duff, Eva Bartok, Cecile Cheyreau, Andrew Osborn; *D:* Terence Fisher. **VHS, Beta** *MLB* 🎦½

Spaghetti House A handful of waiters are held hostage by ruthless killers in this innocuous but worthless Italian comedy. Dubbed.
1982 103m/C Nino Manfredi, Rita Tushingham; *D:* Giullo Paradisi. **VHS, Beta** $29.95 *ING* 🎦½

Spaghetti Western A farmer and a publisher take on the vile oil baron who is taking over the town. A parody-or is it?—of Eastwoodian B-grade spaghetti westerns. No director credited.
1969 90m/C Franco Nero, Martin Balsam, Sterling Hayden. **VHS, Beta** $19.98 *VDC* 🎦½

Spalding Gray: Terrors of Pleasure The ultra-cool Gray tells the story of one man's dream to own land in his own inimitable way. HBO comedy special.
1988 60m/C Spalding Gray; *D:* Thomas Schlamme. **VHS, Beta** $39.99 *HBO* 🎦½

Spangles Silent circus drama.

1926 58m/B Marion Nixon, Hobart Bosworth, Pat O'Malley, Gladys Brockwell; *D:* Frank O'Connor. **VHS, Beta** $14.95 *GPV ℐ*

The Spaniard's Curse When a man is convicted for a murder he did not commit, he puts a curse on the judge and jury responsible. Mysteriously, the marked people begin dying. Is he responsible? Then he dies and the mystery thickens. Intriguing but sloppy murder mystery.
1958 80m/B Tony Wright, Lee Patterson, Michael Hordern, Ralph Truman, Henry Oscar; *D:* Ralph Kemplen. **VHS, Beta** $16.95 *SNC ℐℐ½*

The Spanish Gardener A boy in a prominent family spends more time with the gentle gardner than with the domineering father, so dad arranges for his rival to be framed and sent to prison. An affecting British adaptation of the A.J. Cronin novel, turned into a showcase for Bogarde in the title role.
1957 95m/C Dirk Bogarde, Jon Whiteley, Michael Hordern, Cyril Cusack, Maureen Swanson, Lyndon Brook, Josephine Griffin, Bernard Lee; *D:* Philip Leacock. **VHS** $19.95 *NOS, VEC ℐℐℐ*

The Spanish Main Typical, gusto-laden swashbuckler, RKO's first in Technicolor. Evil Spanish governor Slezak captures Dutch crew led by Henreid. They escape and kidnap his fiancee (O'Hara) off a ship coming from Mexico. Henreid forces her to marry him, but his crew uses the might of the armada and returns O'Hara to Slezak behind Henreid's back. Wow!
1945 100m/C Paul Henreid, Maureen O'Hara, Walter Slezak, Binnie Barnes, John Emery, Barton MacLane; *D:* Frank Borzage. $39.95 *IME ℐℐ½*

Spare Parts Guests at a remote hotel discover that it is run by black marketeers who kill guests and sell the body parts. Of course, they don't bother signing out.
1985 108m/C Judith Speidel, Wolf Roth. **VHS, Beta** $69.95 *VMK Woof!*

Sparkle The saga of three singing sisters struggling to rise to the top of the charts in the 1950s. Sound familiar? Well done but cliched fictional version of the Supremes' career. McKee shines. Alcohol, drugs, and mobsters get in the way. Excellent musical score.
1976 (PG) 98m/C Irene Cara, Lonette McKee, Dwan Smith, Philip Michael Thomas, Mary Alice, Dorian Harewood, Tony King; *D:* Sam O'Steen; *W:* Joel Schumacher; *M:* Curtis Mayfield. **VHS, Beta** $39.98 *WAR ℐℐ½*

Sparrows A woman cares for nine orphan children on an impoverished farm, warding off starvation and kidnappers. Silent melodrama features notable performance by Pickford, and a musical score.
1926 81m/B Mary Pickford, Roy Stewart, Gustav von Seyffertitz; *D:* William Beaudine; *M:* William Perry. **VHS, Beta** $19.95 *NOS, CCB, DVT ℐℐℐ*

Spartacus The true story of a gladiator who leads other slaves in a rebellion against the power of Rome in 73 B.C. The rebellion is put down and the rebels are crucified. Douglas, whose political leanings are amply on display herein, also served as executive producer, surrounding himself with the best talent available. Magnificent climactic battle scene features 8,000 real, live Spanish soldiers to stunning effect. A version featuring Kubrick's "director's cut" is also available, featuring a restored, controversial homoerotic bath scene with Olivier and Curtis. Anthony Mann is uncredited as co-director. A box-office triumph that gave Kubrick much-desired financial independence.

1960 (PG-13) 196m/C Kirk Douglas, Laurence Olivier, Jean Simmons, Tony Curtis, Charles Laughton, Herbert Lom, Nina Foch, Woody Strode, Peter Ustinov, John Gavin, John Ireland, Charles McGraw, Joanna Barnes; *D:* Stanley Kubrick; *W:* Dalton Trumbo; *M:* Alex North. Academy Awards '60: Best Art Direction/Set Decoration (Color), Best Color Cinematography, Best Costume Design (Color), Best Supporting Actor (Ustinov); Nominations: Best Film Editing. **VHS, Beta** $14.95 *MCA, APD, BTV ℐℐℐℐ*

Spasms Reed is the unfortunate big game hunter who encounters The Demon Serpent, known as N'Gana Simbu, the deadliest snake in the world. Lame-brained horror fantasy; the producers should have released the nifty Tangerine Dream soundtrack and chucked the movie. *AKA:* Death Bite.
1982 (R) 92m/C Peter Fonda, Oliver Reed; *D:* William Fruet. **VHS, Beta** *NO Woof!*

The Spawning The sequel to "Piranha." At Club Elysium the main course is the vacationers themselves.
1982 (R) 88m/C Steve Marachuk; *D:* James Cameron. **VHS, Beta** *NO ℐ*

Speak Easily Keaton is bored with his dull life as a college professor. Durante tries to spice things up with a phony inheritance letter, and Keaton decides to spend his supposed money backing a stage show. Keaton is the star, but Durante steals the show. Great supporting cast.
1932 82m/B Buster Keaton, Jimmy Durante, Ruth Selwyn, Thelma Todd, Hedda Hopper, Sidney Toler, Lawrence Grant, Henry Armetta, Edward Brophy; *D:* Edward Sedgwick. **VHS** $19.95 *MGM, GPV, NOS ℐℐ½*

Speak of the Devil A New Orleans evangelist who seduces his followers moves to Los Angeles and strikes a bargain with Satan. Exploitative, unthinking spoof of Swaggart/Bakker scandals of recent years.
1990 99m/C Robert Elarton, Jean Miller, Bernice Tamara Goor, Louise Sherill, Walter Kay, Shawn Patrick Greenfield. **VHS** $79.95 *AIP ℐ*

Speaking Parts VCR-obsessed laundry worker and another woman battle for the attention of bit-part actor McManus who works in ritzy hotel. A telling picture of the inextricable nature of modern technology.
1989 92m/C Michael McManus, Arsinee Khanjian, David Hemblen, Gabrielle Rose, Tony Nardi, Patricia Collins, Gerard Parkes; *D:* Atom Egoyan; *W:* Atom Egoyan; *M:* Mychael Danna. **VHS** $79.95 *FXL, FCT, ING ℐℐℐ*

Special Bulletin A pacifistic terrorist threatens to blow up Charleston, South Carolina with a nuclear warhead. Done quite well in docu-drama style as a TV news bulletin. Interesting examination of the media's treatment of dramatic events. Top-notch made-for-TV fare.
1983 105m/C Ed Flanders, Christopher Allport, Kathryn Walker, Roxanne Hart; *D:* Edward Zwick; *W:* Marshall Herskovitz, Edward Zwick. **VHS, Beta** $59.95 *BAR, LHV, WAR ℐℐℐ*

A Special Day The day of a huge rally celebrating Hitler's visit to Rome in 1939 serves as the backdrop for an affair between weary housewife Loren and lonely, unhappy homosexual radio announcer Mastroianni. Good performances from two thorough pros make a depressing film well worth watching. In Italian with English subtitles or dubbed. *AKA:* Una Giornata Speciale; The Great Day.
1977 105m/C Sophia Loren, Marcello Mastroianni; *D:* Ettore Scola; *W:* Ettore Scola. Academy Awards '77 Nominations: Best Actor (Mastroianni), Best Foreign Language Film; Golden Globe Awards '78: Best Foreign Film; National Board of Review Awards '77: 5 Best Foreign Films of the Year. **VHS, Beta** $59.95 *COL, APD, ING ℐℐℐ*

Special Delivery Three unemployed Vietnam veterans decide to rob a bank but their getaway plans go awry. Svenson, the only robber who escapes, stashes the cash in a mailbox only to have it discovered by nutty artist, Shepherd, and crooked barkeep Gwynne.
1976 (PG) 99m/C Bo Svenson, Cybill Shepherd, Vic Tayback, Michael C. Gwynne, Tom Atkins, Sorrell Booke, Deidre Hall, Gerrit Graham, Jeff Goldblum; *D:* Paul Wendkos. **VHS, Beta** $69.98 *LIV, VES ℐℐ½*

Special Effects A desperate movie director murders a young actress, then makes a movie about her death. Solid, creepy premise sinks in the mire of flawed execution; a good film about Hollywood ego trips and obsession is lurking inside overdone script.
1985 (R) 103m/C Zoe Tamerlis, Eric Bogosian, Brad Rijn, Bill Oland, Richard Greene; *D:* Larry Cohen; *W:* Larry Cohen. **VHS, Beta** $24.98 *SUE, NLC ℐℐ*

Special Forces Eight specially trained soldiers drop behind enemy lines to rescue prisoners of war in WWII. *AKA:* Hell in Normandy.
1968 90m/C Peter Lee Lawrence, Guy Madison, Erika Blanc, Tony Norton. **VHS, Beta** *NO ℐ*

Special Investigator Dix is a criminal attorney who specializes in getting his mob clients freed. Then his FBI brother gets killed by the same criminals he's been defending. So Dix becomes a special agent and sets out to get the mob boss responsible for his brother's murder. Climax is the big shootout at the gang's hideaway. Based on the novel by Earle Stanley Gardner.
1936 60m/B Richard Dix, J. Carroll Naish, Margaret Callahan, Erik Rhodes, Owen Davis Jr., Ray Mayer, Joseph Sawyer; *D:* Louis King. **VHS** $16.95 *GPV ℐℐ½*

Special Olympics A father attempts to care for his three sons, one of whom is mentally retarded, following the death of his wife. Made for television.
1978 104m/C Charles Durning, Philip Brown, George Parry, Irene Tedrow, Mare Winningham, Herb Edelman, Debra Winger, Constance McCashin; *D:* Lee Philips. **VHS, Beta** $59.95 *GEM ℐℐ½*

Special Police Police inspector protecting old friend's murder-witnessing sister learns that important politicians are involved with a seedy underground political movement. French thriller also available dubbed.
1985 92m/C Richard Berry, Carol Bouquet, Fanny Cottencon; *D:* Michael Vianey; *W:* Michael Vianey. **VHS** $79.95 *FRA, FCT ℐℐ½*

The Specialist Lawyer West thinks he has seduced stunning Capri, but she has lured him into her clutches—she's been hired to kill him. Campy crud. It's old home week for '60s TV alums: West was Batman; bailiff Moore was Mr. Kimbell on Green Acres.
1975 (R) 93m/C Adam West, John Anderson, Anna Capri, Alvy Moore; *D:* Hikmet Avedis. **VHS, Beta** *NO ℐ½*

The Speckled Band Set in 1930, this early talkie is a Sherlock Holmes adventure wherein the great detective must solve the mysterious death of a young woman. Massey makes his screen debut as Holmes, making the sleuth cynical, unhappy and pessimistic. Interesting prototypical Holmes case, faithful to the like-titled Conan Doyle story.
1931 84m/B Raymond Massey, Lyn Harding, Athole Stewart, Angela Baddeley, Nancy Price; *D:* Jack Raymond. **VHS, Beta, 8mm** $16.95 *SNC, NOS, VYY ℐℐℐ*

Specters Archaeologists excavating the Roman catacombs break open the gates of hell. Hellishly confused plot is unoriginal, to boot; decent production values hardly compensate. *AKA:* Spettri.
1987 95m/C Donald Pleasence, John Pepper, Erna Schurer; *D:* Marcello Avallone. **VHS, Beta** $79.95 *IMP* 🎞

The Spectre of Edgar Allen Poe The horridly fictionalized writer of horror fiction visits the asylum where his love Lenore is being held, and discovers murder and torture. Based very loosely on Poe's own torments. Dorky, rip-off horror.
1973 87m/C Cesar Romero, Robert Walker Jr., Tom Drake; *D:* Mohy Quandour. **VHS, Beta** $49.95 *UNI* 🎞½

Spectre of the Rose Strange film set in the world of ballet. An impressario contends with an over-the-hill ballerina and a young male dancer with a deadly affinity for knives.
1946 90m/B Judith Anderson, Michael Chekhov, Ivan Kirov, Viola Essen, Lionel Stander; *D:* Ben Hecht; *W:* Ben Hecht. **VHS** $19.98 *REP* 🎞🎞½

Speed Excellent dude Reeves has grown up (and bulked up) as Los Angeles SWAT cop Jack Traven, up against bomb expert Howard Payne (Hopper, more maniacal than usual), who's after major ransom money. First it's a rigged elevator in a very tall building. Then it's a rigged bus—slow up and it will blow up, bad enough any day, but a nightmare in LA traffic. And that's still not the end. Terrific directorial debut for cinematographer De Bont, who certainly knows how to keep the adrenaline pumping. Fine support work by Daniels, Bullock, and Morton and enough wit in Yost's script to keep you chuckling. Great nonstop actioner from the "Die Hard" school.
1994 (R) 115m/C Keanu Reeves, Dennis Hopper, Sandra Bullock, Joe Morton, Jeff Daniels, Alan Ruck, Glenn Plummer, Richard Lineback, Beth Grant, Hawthorne James, David Kriegel, Carlos Carrasco, Natsuko Ohama, Daniel Villarreal; *D:* Jan De Bont; *W:* Graham Yost; *M:* Mark Mancina. **VHS** *NYR* 🎞🎞🎞½

The Speed Lovers Stock car driver Lorenzen plays himself as an inspiration to a young man to join the auto racing circuit. More of a pat on the industry's back than a serious drama. Features footage from a number of race tracks around the country although shot principally in Atlanta. 🎵Speed Lovers.
1968 102m/C Fred Lorenzen, William F. McGaha, Peggy O'Hara, David Marcus, Carol Street, Glenda Brunson; *D:* William F. McGaha; *W:* William F. McGaha, Elaine Wilkerson, Fred Tuch. **VHS** $23.00 *SMW, TPV* 🎞

Speed Reporter Talmadge is the intrepid reporter investigating a phony reform movement that's really a front for a gang of criminals. Mediocre drama with Talmadge's thick German accent a hindrance.
1936 56m/B Richard Talmadge, Luana Walters, Richard Cramer; *D:* Bernard B. Ray. **VHS** $14.95 *GPV* 🎞

The Speed Spook Silent ghost races car and steals documents.
1924 85m/B Johnny Hines, Warner Richmond; *D:* Charles Hines. **VHS, Beta** $19.95 *GPV* 🎞

Speed Zone Comic celebrities take over a high speed auto race when a redneck cop locks up the real drivers. Unfunny sequel to "Cannonball Run."
1988 (PG) 96m/C Melody Anderson, Peter Boyle, Tim Matheson, Donna Dixon, John Candy, Eugene Levy, Joe Flaherty, Matt Frewer, Shari Belafonte-Harper, Tom Smothers, Dick Smothers, Brooke Shields, Lee Van Cleef, Jamie Farr, John

Schneider, Michael Spinks; *D:* Jim Drake. **VHS, Beta** $89.95 *MED, VTR* 🎞

Speeding Up Time An angry man wants to ice the dudes who torched his mother's tenement.
1971 (R) 90m/C Winston Thrash, Pamela Donegan. **VHS, Beta** *NO* 🎞

Speedtrap Typical chase scenes and cross-gender sparring characterize this tale of a private detective and a police officer pursuing car thieves. Good cast and fun chemistry between the leads; weak, typical script.
1978 (PG) 101m/C Joe Don Baker, Tyne Daly, Richard Jaeckel, Robert Loggia, Morgan Woodward, Timothy Carey; *D:* Earl Bellamy. **VHS, Beta** $69.95 *MED* 🎞🎞

Speedway Elvis the stock car driver finds himself being chased by Nancy the IRS agent during an important race. Will Sinatra keep to the business at hand? Or will the King melt her heart? Some cameos by real-life auto racers. Watch for a young Garr. Movie number 27 for Elvis. 🎵Speedway; He's Your Uncle, Not Your Dad; There Ain't Nothing Like a Song.
1968 (G) 90m/C Elvis Presley, Nancy Sinatra, Bill Bixby, Gale Gordon, William Schallert, Carl Ballantine, Ross Hagen; *Cameos:* Richard Petty, Cale Yarborough, Teri Garr; *D:* Norman Taurog. **VHS, Beta** $14.95 *MGM* 🎞🎞

Speedy Lloyd comes to the rescue when the last horse car in New York City, operated by his fiance's grandfather, is stolen by a gang. Thoroughly phony, fun pursuit/action comedy shot on location. Look for a brief appearance by Babe Ruth.
1928 72m/B Harold Lloyd, Bert Woodruff, Ann Christy; *D:* Ted Wilde. **VHS, Beta** *TLF* 🎞🎞🎞

The Spell An obese fifteen-year-old girl has the power to inflict illness and death on the people she hates. Necessarily mean-spirited, if we're being asked to sympathize with the main character. Therein lies the rub. Made for TV.
1977 86m/C Lee Grant, James Olson, Susan Myers, Barbara Bostock, Lelia Goldoni, Helen Hunt; *D:* Lee Philips. **VHS, Beta** $14.99 *GKK, WOV* 🎞🎞

The Spellbinder L.A. lawyer Daly falls in love with a woman he saves from an attacker, then discovers she's a fugitive from a satanic cult that wants her back. Unoriginal, but slickly made.
1988 (R) 96m/C Timothy Daly, Kelly Preston, Rick Rossovich, Audra Lindley; *D:* Janet Greek; *W:* Tracy Torme. **VHS, Beta** $19.98 *FOX* 🎞½

Spellbound Broken-hearted over dead girlfriend, young college student attempts to contact her through spiritualism, succeeds, and suffers nervous breakdown. *AKA:* The Spell of Amy Nugent.
1941 75m/B Derek Farr, Vera Lindsay, Frederick Leister, Hay Petrie, Felix Aylmer; *D:* John Harlow. **VHS** $19.98 *SNC* 🎞🎞

Spellbound Peck plays an amnesia victim accused of murder. Bergman plays the psychiatrist who uncovers his past through Freudian analysis and ends up falling in love with him. One of Hitchcock's finest films of the 1940s, with a riveting dream sequence designed by Salvador Dali. Full of classic Hitchcock plot twists and Freudian imagery. Based on Francis Bleeding's novel "The House of Dr. Edwardes."
1945 111m/B Ingrid Bergman, Gregory Peck, Leo G. Carroll, Michael Chekhov, Wallace Ford, Rhonda Fleming, Regis Toomey; *D:* Alfred Hitchcock; *M:* Miklos Rozsa. Academy Awards '45: Best Score; Nominations: Best Actor (Chekhov), Best Black and White

Cinematography, Best Director (Hitchcock), Best Picture. **VHS, Beta** $19.98 *FOX, IME, TLF* 🎞🎞🎞½

Spellcaster An evil wizard invites a DJ and a band of rock 'n roll fanatics to his thousand-year-old Italian castle for an evil and bloodcurdling treasure hunt.
1991 (R) 83m/C Richard Blade, Gail O'Grady, Harold Pruett, Bunty Bailey, Rafal Zeilinski, Adam Ant; *D:* Rafal Zeilinski. **VHS** $79.95 *COL* 🎞

Spencer's Mountain Fonda plays the larger-then-life patriarch of 9 (with O'Hara as his wife), who's inherited the Wyoming mountain land claimed by his father. Fonda's dream is to build a new house large enough to contain his brood but something always gets in his way. This time it's eldest son MacArthur's dream of a college education. Sentimental family fare based on a novel by Earl Hamner, Jr., which also became the basis for the television series "The Waltons."
1963 118m/C Henry Fonda, Maureen O'Hara, James MacArthur, Donald Crisp, Wally Cox, Mimsy Farmer, Virginia Gregg, Lillian Bronson, Whit Bissell, Hayden Rorke, Dub Taylor, Victor French, Veronica Cartwright; *D:* Delmer Daves; *W:* Delmer Daves; *M:* Max Steiner. **VHS** $29.98 *WAR* 🎞🎞½

Spetters Four Dutch teenagers follow the motorcycle racing circuit and motocross champ Hauer. Misdirected youth film with a spicy performance from Soutendijk. Plenty of violence, sex, and gripping photography. Verhoeven went on to direct "Robocop" and "Total Recall."
1980 (R) 108m/C Rutger Hauer, Renee Soutendijk; *D:* Paul Verhoeven. **VHS, Beta** $29.98 *SUE* 🎞🎞½

The Sphinx A murderer causes havoc for his deaf-mute twin (Atwill, good in a dual role) when he frames him for his own crimes. Remade as "The Phantom Killer."
1933 63m/B Lionel Atwill, Theodore Newton, Sheila Terry, Paul Hurst, Luis Alberni, George "Gabby" Hayes; *D:* Phil Rosen. **VHS** $16.95 *SNC, VYY* 🎞🎞½

Sphinx Woman archaeologist searches for hidden riches in the tomb of an Egyptian king. The scenery is impressive, but otherwise, don't bother. Based on the novel by Robin Cook.
1981 (PG) 117m/C Lesley-Anne Down, Frank Langella, John Gielgud, Maurice Ronet, John Rhys-Davies; *D:* Franklin J. Schaffner; *W:* John Byrum. **VHS, Beta** $19.98 *WAR* Woof!

Spices Poor woman Sonbai revolts against the sexist mores of rural colonial India in the 1940s. Features actress Patil in her final role. In Hindi with English subtitles.
1986 98m/C Smita Patil; *D:* Ketan Mehta. **VHS** $29.95 *MFV, FCT, ING* 🎞🎞

Spider Baby A tasteless horror-comedy about a chauffeur who takes care of a psychotic family. Theme song sung by Lon Chaney. *AKA:* The Liver Eaters; Spider Baby, or the Maddest Story Ever Told; Cannibal Orgy, or the Maddest Story Ever Told.
1964 86m/B Lon Chaney Jr., Mantan Moreland, Carol Ohmart, Sid Haig; *D:* Jack Hill. **VHS, Beta** $19.98 *VEC, SNC, AOV* 🎞

Spider Woman A modernized Holmes and Watson adventure as the duo track down a woman responsible for a series of murders. His adversary uses poisonous spiders to do her work. Zestful, superior Holmes. *AKA:* Sherlock Holmes and the Spider Woman.
1944 62m/B Basil Rathbone, Nigel Bruce, Gale Sondergaard, Dennis Hoey; *D:* Roy William Neill. **VHS, Beta** $14.98 *FOX* 🎞🎞🎞

Spiderman: The Deadly Dust A live-action episode of Spider-Man, as he attempts to prevent a city-destroying plutonium accident.
1978 93m/C Nicholas Hammond, Robert F. Simon, Chip Fields; **D:** Ron Satlof. **VHS, Beta** FOX *♫♫♫*

Spiders One of the earliest surviving films by director Lang, and predates Indiana Jones by almost 60 years. In these first two chapters ("The Golden Lake" and "The Diamond Ship") of an unfinished 4-part thriller, Carl deVogt battles with the evil Spider cult for a mystically powerful Incan diamond. Restored version has original color-tinted scenes. Silent with organ score.
1918 137m/B Lil Dagover; **D:** Fritz Lang; **M:** Gaylord Carter. **VHS, Beta $29.95** KIV, IME, GLV *♫♫♫*

The Spider's Stratagem Thirty years after his father's murder by the facists, a young man returns to a small Italian town to learn why his father was killed. The locals resist his efforts, and he is trapped in a mysterious web where history and lies exert a stranglehold on the truth. Intriguing, high literate thriller; outrageously lovely color photography. Based on a short story by Jorge Luis Borges. In Italian with English subtitles.
1970 97m/C Giulio Brogi, Alida Valli; **D:** Bernardo Bertolucci; **W:** Bernardo Bertolucci. **VHS $59.95** NYF, FCT, APD *♫♫♫*

Spies A sly criminal poses as a famous banker to steal government information and create chaos in the world in this silent Lang masterpiece. Excellent entertainment, tight plotting and pacing, fine performances. Absolutely relentless intrigue and tension. **AKA:** Spione.
1928 88m/B Rudolf Klein-Rogge, Lupu Pick, Fritz Rasp, Gerda Maurus, Willy Fritsch; **D:** Fritz Lang. **VHS, Beta $19.95** GPV, NOS, VYY *♫♫♫½*

Spies, Lies and Naked Thighs A pair of crackpot CIA agents find themselves in a whirlpool of comedic madness when they are assigned to track down a deadly assassin. The problem? The assassin happens to be the ex-wife of one of the guys. Can he go another round with her and this time come out on top? Who cares?
1991 90m/C Harry Anderson, Ed Begley Jr., Rachel Ticotin, Linda Purl, Wendy Crewson; **D:** James Frawley. **VHS $19.95** COL, NLC *♫½*

Spies Like Us Chase and Aykroyd meet while taking the CIA entry exam. Caught cheating on the test, they seem the perfect pair for a special mission. Pursued by the Soviet government, they nearly start WWIII. Silly, fun homage to the Bing Crosby-Bob Hope "Road" movies that doesn't capture those classics' quota of guffaws, but comes moderately close. Look for several cameos by film directors.
1985 (PG) 103m/C Chevy Chase, Dan Aykroyd, Steve Forrest, Bruce Davison, William Prince, Bernie Casey, Tom Hatton, Donna Dixon, Frank Oz; **Cameos:** Michael Apted, Constantin Costa-Gavras, Terry Gilliam, Ray Harryhausen, Joel Coen, Martin Brest, Bob Swaim; **D:** John Landis; **W:** Dan Aykroyd, Lowell Ganz, Babaloo Mandel; **M:** Elmer Bernstein. **VHS, Beta $19.98** WAR *♫♫½*

Spike of Bensonhurst A Brooklyn street kid dreams of becoming a championship boxer. He tries to gain the mob's help by courting the local Don's daughter. Hip-but-stereotyped Morrissey effort is helped by great cast.
1988 (R) 101m/C Sasha Mitchell, Ernest Borgnine, Maria Pitillo, Talisa Soto, Sylvia Miles, Anne DeSalvo, Geraldine Smith, Rick Aviles, Antonia Rey; **D:** Paul Morrissey; **W:** Alan Bowne;

Paul Morrissey; **M:** Coati Munde. **VHS, Beta** NO *♫♫½*

Spinout A pouty traveling singer decides to drive an experimental race car in a rally. Usual Elvis fare with the King being pursued by an assortment of beauties. ♫Adam and Eve; Stop, Look, Listen; All That I Am; Am I Ready; Smorgasbord; Never Say Yes; Beach Shack; I'll Be Back; Spinout. **AKA:** California Holiday.
1966 93m/C Elvis Presley, Shelley Fabares, Carl Betz, Diane McBain, Cecil Kellaway, Jack Mullaney, Deborah Walley, Una Merkel, Warren Berlinger, Will Hutchins, Dodie Marshall; **D:** Norman Taurog. **VHS, Beta $14.95** MGM *♫♫*

The Spiral Staircase A mute servant, working in a creepy Gothic mansion, may be the next victim of a murderer preying on women afflicted with deformities, especially when the next murder occurs in the mansion itself. Great performance by McGuire as the terrified victim. Remade for television in 1975.
1946 83m/B Dorothy McGuire, George Brent, Ethel Barrymore, Kent Smith, Rhonda Fleming, Gordon Oliver, Elsa Lanchester, Sara Allgood; **D:** Robert Siodmak. **VHS $39.95** FOX *♫♫♫*

Spiral Staircase Mild TV remake of the 1946 classic about a mute servant who is menaced by a psychopathic killer. Why didn't they just show the original?
1975 99m/C Jacqueline Bisset, Christopher Plummer, John Phillip Law, Mildred Dunnock, Sam Wanamaker, Gayle Hunnicutt; **D:** Peter Collinson; **W:** Allan Scott. **VHS, Beta $59.95** WAR *♫½*

Spirit of St. Louis A lavish Hollywood biography of famous aviator Charles Lindbergh and his historic transatlantic flight from New York to Paris in 1927, based on his autobiography. Intelligent; Stewart shines as the intrepid airman. Inexplicably, it flopped at the box office.
1957 137m/C James Stewart, Patricia Smith, Murray Hamilton, Marc Connelly; **D:** Billy Wilder; **W:** Billy Wilder, Wendell Mayes; **M:** Franz Waxman. **VHS, Beta $19.98** WAR, HMV *♫♫♫*

Spirit of '76 In the 22nd century, the Earth faces certain disaster as a magnetic storm wipes out all of American culture. Now time travellers must return to 1776 to reacquire the Constitution to fix things up. But when their computer goes on the blink, the do-gooders land, not in 1776, but in 1976 at the beginning of disco fever!
1991 (PG-13) 82m/C David Cassidy, Olivia D'Abo, Leif Garrett, Geoff Hoyle, Jeff McDonald, Steve McDonald, Liam O'Brien, Barbara Bain, Julie Brown, Thomas Chong, Devo, Iron Eyes Cody, Kipper Kids, Don Novello, Carl Reiner, Rob Reiner, Moon Zappa; **D:** Lucas Reiner; **W:** Lucas Reiner. **VHS** NO *♫½*

Spirit of the Beehive An acclaimed and haunting film about a young Spanish girl enthralled by the 1931 "Frankenstein," embarking on a journey to find the creature in the Spanish countryside. One of the best films about children's inner life; in Spanish with subtitles. **AKA:** El Espiritu de la Colmena.
1973 95m/C Fernando Gomez, Teresa Gimpera, Ana Torrent; **D:** Victor Erice. **VHS, Beta $29.95** HMV, ING, CVC *♫♫♫*

Spirit of the Eagle Man and young son wander in mountains and make friends with feathered creature. Then boy is kidnapped, creating problems for dad. Somnolent family fare.
1990 (PG) 93m/C Dan Haggerty, Bill Smith, Don Shanks, Jeri Arrendondo, Trever Yarrish; **D:** Boon Collins; **W:** Boon Collins. **VHS** SGE, IME *♫♫*

Spirit of the West Rodeo star Gibson and his ranch foreman brother work together to save a fair damsel's land from a gang of rustlers. Routine western of its era.
1932 61m/B Hoot Gibson, Hooper Atchley; **D:** Otto Brower. **VHS, Beta $19.95** NOS, DVT, VCI *♫½*

The Spirit of West Point The true story of West Point's two All-American football greats, Doc Blanchard and Glenn Davis (who play themselves), while on leave after graduation from the title school.
1947 77m/B Felix "Doc" Blanchard, Glenn Davis, Tom Harmon, Alan Hale Jr., Anne Nagel, Robert Shayne; **D:** Ralph Murphy. **VHS, Beta $19.95** STE, NWV *♫½*

The Spirit of Youth Joe Louis supports his family with menial jobs until he shows his knack as a fighter. When he's knocked down, his gal appears at ringside to inspire him, and does.
1937 70m/B Joe Louis, Mantan Moreland. **VHS, Beta $24.95** VYY, NOS, VCN *♫♫*

Spirit Rider Jesse Threebears is a sullen 16-year-old Ojibway who has been shuttled from foster homes since the age of six. Repatriated to his family's Canadian reservation, he's left in the care of his grandfather, Joe Moon. The entire community works to make Jesse's return successful but there are Jesse's resentments and some family tragedies to be overcome first. Based on the novel "Winners" by Mary-Ellen Lang Collura.
1993 120m/C Herbie Barnes, Adam Beach, Graham Greene, Tantoo Cardinal, Gordon Tootoosis, Tom Jackson, Michelle St. John. **VHS $29.95** PME, BTV *♫♫♫*

Spiritism Mother uses one of her three wishes to bring back her dead son. Adapted from the "Monkey's Paw." **AKA:** Espiritismo.
1961 85m/B Nora Veyran, Jose Luis Jimenez, Jorge Mondragon, Rene Cardona Jr.; **D:** Benito Alazraki. **VHS $19.98** SNC *♫♫*

Spirits A priest tormented by his lust-filled dreams breaks his vows of chastity with a woman who turns out to be a murderer. Bad luck.
1990 (R) 88m/C Erik Estrada, Carol Lynley, Robert Quarry, Brinke Stevens, Oliver Darrow, Kathrin Lautner; **D:** Fred Olen Ray. **VHS $89.98** VMK *♫½*

Spirits of the Dead Three Edgar Allan Poe stories adapted for the screen and directed by three of Europe's finest. "Metzengerstein," directed by Roger Vadim stars the Fonda siblings in a tale of incestuous lust. "William Wilson" finds Louis Malle directing Delon and Bardot in the story of a vicious Austrian army officer haunted by a murder victim. Finally, Fellini directs "Never Bet the Devil Your Head" or "Toby Dammit" in which Stamp plays a drunken British film star who has a gruesome date with destiny. Although Fellini's segment is generally considered the best (and was released on its own) all three provide an interesting, atmospheric vision of Poe. **AKA:** Histoires Extraordinaires.
1968 (R) 117m/C Jane Fonda, Peter Fonda, Carla Marlier, Francoise Prevost, James Robertson Justice, Brigitte Bardot, Alain Delon, Katia Christine, Terence Stamp, Salvo Randone; **D:** Roger Vadim, Louis Malle, Federico Fellini. **VHS $18.00** FRG, MLB *♫♫♫*

Spite Marriage When Sebastian's lover dumps her like yesterday's garbage, she marries Keaton out of spite. Much postnuptual levity follows. Keaton's final silent.
1929 82m/B Buster Keaton, Dorothy Sebastian, Edward Earle, Leila Hyams, William Bechtel, Hank Mann; **D:** Edward Sedgwick. **VHS, Beta $29.99** MGM, FCT *♫♫♫*

Spitfire Sentimental comedy drama starring Hepburn as a hillbilly faith healer from the Ozarks who falls into a love triangle. One in a string of early box-office flops for Hepburn. She wanted to play a role other than patrician Eastern Seaboard, and did, but audiences didn't buy it.
1934 90m/B Katharine Hepburn, Robert Young, Ralph Bellamy, Sidney Toler; *D:* John Cromwell. VHS, 8mm $44.95 NO ⅃⅃⅃

Spitfire True story of Reginald J. Mitchell, who designed "The Spitfire" fighter plane, which greatly assisted the Allies during WWII. Howard's last film. Heavily propagandist but enjoyable and uncomplicated biography, with a splendid score. *AKA:* The First of the Few.
1942 88m/B Leslie Howard, David Niven, Rosamund John, George King, Jon Stafford, Adrian Brunel, Patricia Medina; *D:* Leslie Howard; *M:* William Walton. VHS, Beta $9.95 CNG, NOS, HHT ⅃⅃⅃

Spittin' Image After falling from her mean-spirited father's wagon, a young girl befriends a kind mountain man. She learns the ways of the wilderness and tobacco spitting.
1983 92m/C Sunshine Parker, Trudi Cooper, Sharon Barr, Karen Barr; *D:* Russell Kern. VHS, Beta $59.95 PSM ⅃

Splash A beautiful mermaid ventures into New York City in search of a man she's rescued twice when he's fallen overboard. Now it's her turn to fall—in love. Charming performances by Hanks and Hannah. Well-paced direction from Howard, with just enough slapstick. Don't miss the lobster scene.
1984 (PG) 109m/C Tom Hanks, Daryl Hannah, Eugene Levy, John Candy, Dody Goodman, Shecky Greene, Richard B. Shull, Bobby DiCicco, Howard Morris; *D:* Ron Howard; *W:* Babaloo Mandel, Lowell Ganz. VHS, Beta, 8mm $79.95 TOU, BVV ⅃⅃½

Splatter University A deranged killer escapes from an asylum and begins to slaughter and mutilate comely coeds at a local college. Abysmally motiveless killing and gratuitous sex. Also available in a 78-minute "R" rated version.
1984 79m/C Francine Forbes, Dick Biel, Cathy Lacommaro, Ric Randing, Dan Eaton; *D:* Richard W. Haines. VHS, Beta $69.98 LIV, VES Woof!

Splendor in the Grass A drama set in rural Kansas in 1925, concerning a teenage couple who try to keep their love on a strictly intellectual plane and the sexual and family pressures that tear them apart. After suffering a mental breakdown and being institutionalized, the girl returns years later in order to settle her life. Film debuts of Beatty, Dennis, and Diller. Inge wrote the screenplay specifically with Beatty in mind, after the actor appeared in one of Inge's stage plays. Filmed not in Kansas, but on Staten Island and in upstate New York.
1961 124m/C Natalie Wood, Warren Beatty, Audrey Christie, Barbara Loden, Zohra Lampert, Phyllis Diller, Sandy Dennis; *D:* Elia Kazan; *W:* William Inge; *M:* David Amram. Academy Awards '61: Best Story & Screenplay; Nominations: Best Actress (Wood). VHS, Beta $19.98 WAR ⅃⅃⅃

Split Humanoids from another dimension manipulate earth activity.
1990 85m/C John Flynn, Timothy Dwight, Chris Shaw, Joan Bechtel; *D:* Chris Shaw. VHS $79.95 AIP ⅃

Split Decisions An Irish family of boxers, dad and his two sons, slug it out emotionally and physically, as they come to terms with career choices and each other. Good scenes in the ring but the drama leans toward melodrama. Decent family drama, but somewhat of a "Rocky" rip-off.
1988 (R) 95m/C Gene Hackman, Craig Sheffer, Jeff Fahey, Jennifer Beals, John McLiam, Eddie Velez, Carmine Caridi, James Tolkan; *D:* David Drury; *W:* David Fallon. VHS, 8mm $19.95 WAR ⅃⅃⅃

Split Image An all-American boy comes under the spell of a cult. His parents then hire a deprogrammer to bring the boy back to reality. Exceptional performances by Dennehy and Woods. This is a worthwhile film that spent far too little time in theatres.
1982 (R) 113m/C Michael O'Keefe, Karen Allen, Peter Fonda, Brian Dennehy, James Woods; *D:* Ted Kotcheff; *W:* Robert Mark Kamen; *M:* Bill Conti. VHS, Beta $24.98 SUE ⅃⅃⅃

Split Second An escaped prisoner holds hostages in a Nevada atomic bomb testing area. McNally's excellent performance as the kidnapper, in addition to strong supporting performances, enhance a solid plot. Powell's directorial debut.
1953 85m/B Paul Kelly, Richard Egan, Jan Sterling, Alexis Smith, Stephen McNally; *D:* Dick Powell; *W:* William Bowers, Irving Wallace. VHS, Beta $39.95 RKO, TTC ⅃⅃½

Split Second Hauer is a futuristic cop tracking down a vicious alien serial killer in London in the year 2008. The monster rips out the hearts of his victims and then eats them in what appears to be a satanic ritual in this blood-soaked thriller wanna-be. Hauer gives a listless performance and overall, the action is quite dull. The music soundtrack also manages to annoy with the Moody Blues song "Nights in White Satin" playing at the most inappropriate times. A British/American co-production.
1992 (R) 91m/C Rutger Hauer, Kim Cattrall, Neil Duncan, Michael J. Pollard, Alun Armstrong, Peter Postlethwaite, Ian Dury, Roberta Eaton; *D:* Tony Maylam. VHS $92.99 HBO ⅃½

Splitting Heirs Idle stars as the offspring of titled parents who is accidentally abandoned in a restaurant as an infant and raised by poor Pakistanis. (His mother winds up claiming the wrong abandoned baby.) When he discovers he's actually the 15th Duke of Bournemouth he plots, ineffectually, to kill off the present unknowing imposter, a nitwit American (Moranis). Cleese pops in as a shabby lawyer hired by Idle to help him claim the title with Hershey as Idle's real mother, the addle-brained and sex-starved Duchess. Convoluted plot, bland comedy.
1993 (PG-13) 87m/C Eric Idle, Rick Moranis, Barbara Hershey, John Cleese, Catherine Zeta Jones, Sadie Frost, Stratford Johns, Brenda Bruce, William Franklyn, Jeremy Clyde; *D:* Robert M. Young; *W:* Eric Idle; *M:* Michael Kamen. VHS $19.98 MCA ⅃½

Splitz An all-girl rock band agrees to help out a sorority house by participating in a series of sporting events.
1984 (PG-13) 89m/C Robin Johnson, Patti Lee, Shirley Stoler, Raymond Serra; *D:* Domonic Paris. VHS, Beta $79.98 LIV, VES Woof!

Spoiled Children A famous film director (Piccoli) tries to work on his new script at home but is too distracted by his family life. So he rents a high-rise apartment for peace and quiet but winds up involved in a tenant/landlord dispute and with a girl half his age. In French with English subtitles. *AKA:* Des Enfants Gates.
1977 113m/C Michel Piccoli, Christine Pascal, Michel Aumont, Gerard Jugnot, Arlette Bonnard; *D:* Bertrand Tavernier; *W:* Christine Pascal, Charlotte Dubreuil, Bertrand Tavernier; *M:* Philippe Sarde. VHS $79.95 FCT, CVC ⅃⅃½

The Spoilers Virtually unstaged account of gold hunting in the Alaskan wilderness enhanced by gritty film quality. Was a gold mine when released.
1914 110m/B William Farnum, Thomas Santschi, Kathlyn Williams, Bessie Eyton, Frank Clark, Wheeler Oakman; *D:* Colin Campbell. VHS, Beta $19.95 GPV ⅃⅃½

The Spoilers Two adventurers in the Yukon are swindled out of their gold mine and set out to even the score. A trademark scene of all versions of the movie (and there are many) is the climactic fistfight, in this case between hero Wayne and bad-guy Scott. One of the better films adapted from the novel by Rex Beach. William Farnum, who starred in both the 1914 and the 1930 versions, has a small part.
1942 88m/B John Wayne, Randolph Scott, Marlene Dietrich, Margaret Lindsay, Harry Carey Sr., Richard Barthelmess, Charles Halton; *D:* Ray Enright. VHS, Beta $14.98 MCA, MLB, FCT ⅃⅃⅃

Spontaneous Combustion A grisly horror film detailing the travails of a hapless guy who has the power to inflict the title phenomenon on other people.
1989 (R) 97m/C Brad Dourif, Jon Cypher, Melinda Dillon, Cynthia Bain, William Prince; *D:* Tobe Hooper; *M:* Graeme Revell. VHS, Beta $89.98 LIV, VTR ⅃⅃

Spook Busters The Bowery Boys take jobs as exterminators, only to find themselves assigned the unenviable task of ridding a haunted house of ghosts. To make matters worse, the resident mad scientist wants to transplant Sach's brain into a gorilla. Essential viewing for anyone who thought "Ghostbusters" was an original story.
1946 68m/B Leo Gorcey, Huntz Hall, Douglass Dumbrille, Bobby Jordan, Gabriel Dell, Billy Benedict, David Gorcey, Bernard Gorcey, Tanis Chandler, Maurice Cass, Charles Middleton; *D:* William Beaudine. VHS $14.98 WAR, GPV ⅃⅃½

The Spook Who Sat By the Door A black CIA agent organizes an army of inner-city youths and launches a revolution. Based on the novel by Sam Greenlee.
1973 (PG) 95m/C Lawrence Cook, Paula Kelly, J.A. Preston; *D:* Ivan Dixon; *M:* Herbie Hancock. VHS, Beta $69.95 VCD ⅃½

Spookies An old master sorcerer who lives in a run-down haunted house sacrifices humans to give eternal life to his unconscious bride. He needs only a few more vitims when a group of teenagers come along to explore the house.
1985 85m/C Felix Ward, Dan Scott, Maria Pechukas, Brendan Faulkner, Eugine Joseph; *D:* Thomas Doran. VHS, Beta NO Woof!

Spooks Run Wild The East Side Kids seek refuge in a spooky mansion owned by the eerie Lugosi. A fun horror-comedy with the Kids' antics playing off Lugosi's scariness quite well. Co-scripter Carl Foreman later co-wrote "High-Noon," "The Bridge on the River Kwai," and "The Guns of Navarone." Not the same movie as "Ghosts on the Loose" which followed in '43 and also featured Lugosi and the Kids.
1941 64m/B Huntz Hall, Leo Gorcey, Bobby Jordan, Sammy Morrison, Dave O'Brien, Dennis Moore, Bela Lugosi; *D:* Phil Rosen; *W:* Carl Foreman. VHS, Beta $19.95 NOS, SNC, VYY ⅃⅃½

The Sporting Club A semi-gothic melodrama about a strict all men's club which, during a 100th anniversary party, reverts to savagery and primitive rites.

1972 (R) 104m/C Robert Fields, Margaret Blye, Nicholas Coster, Ralph Waite, Jack Warden, Linda Blair; **D:** Larry Peerce. **VHS, Beta** $24.98 *NLC Woof!*

Spotlight Scandals A barber and a vaudevillian team up and endure the ups and downs of showbiz life in this low-budget musical from prolific B-movie director Beaudine. ♫The Restless Age; Goodnight Now; The Lilac Tree; Tempo of the Trail; Oh Johnny.
1943 79m/B Billy Gilbert, Frank Fay, Bonnie Baker; **D:** William Beaudine. **VHS** $19.95 *NOS, LOO ♫♫*

Spraggue A Boston professor and his eccentric aunt put the moves on a doctor who may have committed murder. Served as a TV pilot for a series that never materialized.
1984 78m/C Michael Nouri, Glynis Johns, James Cromwell, Mark Herrier, Patrick O'Neal, Andrea Marcovicci; **D:** Larry Elikann. **VHS** $59.95 *LIV ♫♫*

The Spring Two archaeologists search Florida for the fountain of youth after they find new clues to its whereabouts. However, a greedy industrialist and an evil priest are both on their trail, fighting to keep the secret for themselves at any cost.
1989 110m/C Dack Rambo, Gedde Watanabe, Shari Shattuck, Steven Keats; **D:** John D. Patterson. **VHS** *NO ♫½*

Spring Break Four college students go to Fort Lauderdale on their spring vacation and have a wilder time that they bargained for, though viewer is deprived of excitement.
1983 (R) 101m/C Perry Lang, David Knell, Steve Bassett, Paul Land, Jayne Modean, Corinne Alphen; **D:** Sean S. Cunningham. **VHS, Beta** $14.95 *COL ♫*

Spring Fever Heartaches of the junior tennis circuit are brought to the screen in this sports comedy. Previews promised a lot more than this film could ever hope to deliver. Even tennis fans will be disappointed.
1981 93m/C Susan Anton; **D:** Joseph L. Scanlan. **VHS, Beta** $69.98 *LIV, VES ♫½*

Spring Symphony A moody, fairy-tale biography of composer Robert Schumann, concentrating on his rhapsodic love affair with pianist Claire Weick. Kinski is very good as the rebellious daughter, while the music is even better. Reasonably accurate in terms of history; dubbed. *AKA:* Fruhlingssinfonie.
1986 (PG-13) 102m/C Nastassia Kinski, Rolf Hoppe, Herbert Gronemeyer; **D:** Peter Schamoni. **VHS, Beta** $79.98 *LIV ♫♫½*

Springfield Rifle Based on the real-life story of Major Les Kearney, who joined forces with outlaws to catch the thief stealing government weapons. Average.
1952 93m/C Gary Cooper, Phyllis Thaxter, David Brian, Lon Chaney Jr., Paul Kelly, Phil Carey, Guinn Williams; **D:** Andre de Toth. **VHS** $29.99 *WAR ♫♫½*

Springhill The true story of a mining disaster in which seven miners fought to survive the elements while buried 13,000 feet underground.
197? 90m/C **VHS, Beta** $49.95 *TWE ♫½*

Springtime in the Rockies Autry is a cattle-ranch foreman whose employer decides to try raising sheep. This doesn't set well with the other ranchers, but Autry manages to save the day and sing a little too.
1937 60m/B Gene Autry, Polly Rowles, Smiley Burnette; **D:** Joseph Kane. **VHS, Beta** $19.98 *NOS, VCN, DVT ♫♫*

Springtime in the Rockies A Broadway duo just can't get along despite being in love with each other. Top-notch musical, with a touch of romantic tension and comedy.

Beautifully filmed in the Canadian Rockies. ♫I Had the Craziest Dream; Run Little Rainrop Run; A Poem Set to Music; Pan American Jubilee; I Like to Be Love by You; Chattanooga Choo Choo; Tic Tac Do Meu Coracao.
1942 91m/C Betty Grable, John Payne, Carmen Miranda, Cesar Romero, Charlotte Greenwood, Edward Everett Horton, Jackie Gleason; **D:** Irving Cummings. **VHS** $19.95 *FOX, MLB ♫♫½*

Springtime in the Sierras Rogers and Devine band together to fight a gang of poachers who prey on the wildlife of a game preserve. Features a number of songs by Rogers and The Sons of the Pioneers. *AKA:* Song of the Sierra.
1947 54m/B Roy Rogers, Andy Devine, Jane Frazee, Stephanie Bachelor; **D:** William Whitney. **VHS, Beta** $19.95 *NOS, CAB, DVT ♫♫½*

The Sprinter A young homosexual, while trying to submerge his confusion in professional track and field, gets to know a homely shot-putter and is seduced by her. In German with English subtitles.
1984 90m/C **VHS, Beta** $39.95 *VCD, GLV ♫♫½*

Spurs A rodeo star takes on a whole gang of rustlers and their imposing machine gun. This transitional western was made both with and without sound.
1930 60m/B Hoot Gibson, Robert E. Homans; **D:** Hoot Gibson. **VHS** $19.95 *NOS, DVT, HEG ♫♫*

Sputnik A Frenchman, amnesiac after a car crash, comes up against Russian scientists, space-bound dogs, and weightlessness. Pleasant and charming family fun though clearly dated. Another fine performance from Auer. Dubbed. *AKA:* A Dog, a Mouse, and a Sputnik.
1961 80m/B Noelia Noel, Mischa Auer, Denise Grey; **D:** Jean Dreville. **VHS, Beta** $39.95 *ING ♫♫*

Spy A former spy who knows too much becomes the target of a renegade agency. Made for television.
1989 88m/C Ned Beatty, Tim Choate, Bruce Greenwood, Catherine Hicks, Jameson Parker, Michael Tucker; **D:** Philip Frank Messina. **VHS, Beta** $79.95 *PAR ♫♫*

Spy in Black A German submarine captain returns from duty at sea during WWI and is assigned to infiltrate one of the Orkney Islands and obtain confidential British information. Known in the U.S. as "U-Boat 29," this film is based on a J. Storer Clouston novel. This was the first teaming of director Powell and writer Pressburger, who followed with "Contraband" in 1940.
1939 82m/B Conrad Veidt, Valerie Hobson, Sebastian Shaw, Marius Goring, June Duprez, Helen Hayes, Cyril Raymond, Hay Petrie; **D:** Michael Powell; **M:** Miklos Rozsa. **VHS, Beta** $19.95 *NOS, VYY, DVT ♫♫♫*

Spy of Napoleon A French aristocrat agrees to marry the illegitimate daughter of Emperor Napoleon III and finds himself working to uncover traitors to the throne. Based on Baroness Orczy's novel.
1936 77m/B Richard Barthelmess, Dolly Hass, Francis L. Sullivan. **VHS, Beta** $24.95 *VYY ♫♫*

Spy Smasher Returns The exciting 12-part serial "Spy Smasher" was cut and edited into feature length and released under this title. The masked marvel and his twin brother battle enemy agents during WWII. This new version is just as exciting as the original cliffhanger.
1942 185m/B Kane Richmond, Marguerite Chapman, Sam Flint, Hans Schumm, Tristram Coffin; **D:** William Witney. **VHS** $29.98 *REP, MLB ♫♫*

Spy Story A Cold War conflict, counterintelligence, conspiracy, and a nuclear sub chase highlight this tale by Len Deighton.
1986 105m/C **VHS, Beta** $69.95 *VCD, MOV ♫♫*

Spy Trap Four junior-high school friends concoct bogus military plans using futuristic toys for blueprints. The "secret" plans get sold to the Russians and the kids find themselves chased by the unhappy KGB and the CIA. Family adventure.
1992 96m/C Elya Baskin, Danielle Du Clos, Jason Kristofer, Cameron Johann, Devin Ratray, Kimble Joyner; **D:** Arthur Sherman. **VHS** $89.95 *HMD ♫♫½*

The Spy Who Came in from the Cold The acclaimed adaptation of the John Le Carre novel about an aging British spy who attempts to infiltrate the East German agency. Prototypical Cold War thriller, with emphasis on de-glamorizing espionage. Gritty and superbly realistic with a documentary style which hampered it at the box office.
1965 110m/B Richard Burton, Oskar Werner, Claire Bloom, Sam Wanamaker, Peter Van Eyck, Cyril Cusack, Rupert Davies, Michael Hordern; **D:** Martin Ritt. Academy Awards '65 Nominations: Best Actor (Burton); British Academy Awards '66: Best Film; Edgar Allan Poe Awards '65: Best Screenplay; Golden Globe Awards '66: Best Supporting Actor (Werner). **VHS, Beta** $19.95 *PAR ♫♫♫½*

The Spy Who Loved Me James Bond teams up with female Russian Agent XXX to squash a villain's plan to use captured American and Russian atomic submarines in a plot to destroy the world. The villain's henchman, 7'2" Kiel, is the steel-toothed Jaws. Carly Simon sings the memorable, Marvin Hamlisch theme song, "Nobody Does It Better."
1977 (PG) 136m/C Roger Moore, Barbara Bach, Curt Jurgens, Richard Kiel, Caroline Munro, Walter Gotell, Geoffrey Keen, Valerie Leon, Bernard Lee, Lois Maxwell, Desmond Llewelyn; **D:** Lewis Gilbert; **M:** Marvin Hamlisch. **VHS, Beta** $19.98 *MGM, FOX, TLF ♫♫♫*

Spy with a Cold Nose A sporadically funny spy spoof about a bugged dog passed between British and Soviet intelligence. Hard-working cast keeps it from collapsing.
1966 93m/C Laurence Harvey, Daliah Lavi, Lionel Jeffries; **D:** Daniel Petrie. **VHS, Beta** $59.95 *NLC ♫♫*

Spymaker: The Secret Life of Ian Fleming Fictionalized account of the creator of the ultimate spy, James Bond, and his early days in the British Secret Service. Fans of the Bond movies will appreciate the numerous inside jokes. Connery is the son of Sean. Made for British television. *AKA:* Spymaker.
1990 96m/C Jason Connery, Kristin Scott Thomas, Joss Ackland, Patricia Hodge, David Warner, Fiona Fullerton, Richard Johnson; **D:** Ferdinand Fairfax. **VHS** *TTC ♫♫½*

S*P*Y*S An attempt to cash in on the success of "M*A*S*H," this unfunny spy spoof details the adventures of two bumbling CIA men who botch a Russian defection, and get both sides after them. Usually competent director Kershner had a bad day.
1974 (PG) 87m/C Donald Sutherland, Elliott Gould, Joss Ackland, Zouzou, Shane Rimmer, Vladek Sheybal, Nigel Hawthorne; **D:** Irvin Kershner; **W:** Malcolm Marmorstein; **M:** Jerry Goldsmith. **VHS, Beta** $59.98 *FOX ♫*

Square Dance A Texas teenager leaves the farm where she's been raised by her grandfather to live in the city with her promiscuous mother (Alexander, cast against type) where she befriends a retarded young man (yes, it's Lowe, also cast against type). Too

slow, but helped by good acting. **AKA:** Home is Where the Heart Is.
1987 (PG-13) 118m/C Jane Alexander, Jason Robards Jr., Rob Lowe, Winona Ryder, Deborah Richter, Guich Koock, Elbert Lewis; **D:** Daniel Petrie; **W:** Alan Hines; **M:** Bruce Broughton. **VHS, Beta** *NO* ♫♫½

Square Dance Jubilee Television scouts hit Prairie City in search of cowboy stars, and stumble onto cattle rustlers. Twenty-one C & W tunes support a near-invisible plot, suitable for fridge runs.
1951 78m/B Mary Beth Hughes, Donald (Don ''Red'') Barry, Wally Vernon, John Eldridge; **D:** Paul Landres. **VHS, Beta** *NO* ♫½

Square Shoulders Adventures of young military school student with geometric anatomy (Coghlan).
1929 58m/B Frank ''Junior'' Coghlan, Louis Wolheim, Anita Louise, Montague Shaw; **D:** E. Mason Hopper. **VHS, Beta** *$19.95* GPV, FCT ♫½

The Squeaker Good Edgar Wallace mystery about a disgraced inspector trying to clear his name. **AKA:** Murder on Diamond Row.
1937 ?m/C Edmund Lowe, Sebastian Shaw; **M:** Miklos Rozsa. **VHS** *$16.95* SNC ♫♫½

The Squeaker Complicated but interesting thriller about the underworld goings-on after a big-time diamond heist. German remake of an early (1930) British talkie, also done in 1937, based on the Edgar Wallace novel.
1965 95m/B Heinz Drache, Eddi Arent, Klaus Kinski, Barbara Rutting; **D:** Alfred Vohrer. **VHS** SNC ♫♫½

The Squeeze Scotland Yard detective Keach, fired for drunkeness, gets a chance to reinstate himself when his ex-wife is caught up in a brutal kidnapping scheme. Slim script gives good cast uphill work. Ordinary thriller. Available with Spanish subtitles.
1977 (R) 106m/C Stacy Keach, Carol White, David Hemmings, Edward Fox, Stephen Boyd; **D:** Michael Apted. **VHS, Beta** *$19.98* WAR ♫♫

The Squeeze An aging safecracker is hired for a final job, but learns that his cohorts plan to kill him when the heist is finished. Blah revenge thriller. Dawson is a pseudonym for Antonio Margheriti.
1980 93m/C Lee Van Cleef, Karen Black, Edward Albert, Lionel Stander, Robert Alda; **D:** Anthony M. (Antonio Margheriti) Dawson. **VHS, Beta** *NO* ♫½

The Squeeze Keaton is wasted in this attempt at a comedy about a small-time con artist who discovers a Mafia plan to fix a lottery electromagnetically.
1987 (PG-13) 101m/C Michael Keaton, Rae Dawn Chong, John Davidson, Ric Abernathy, Bobby Bass, Joe Pantoliano, Meatloaf, Paul Herman; **D:** Roger Young; **M:** Miles Goodman. **VHS, Beta** *$14.99* HBO Woof!

Squeeze Play Group of young women start a softball team and challenge the boyfriends to a game. Standard battle of the sexes takes places, with a wet T-shirt contest thrown in for good measure. Cheap, plotless, offensive trash from Troma.
1979 92m/C Al Corley, Jenni Hetrick, Jim Metzler; **D:** Lloyd Samuel Weil Kaufman. **VHS, Beta** *NO* Woof!

Squirm Storm disrupts a highly charged power cable, electrifying a host of garden-variety worms. The worms then turn them into giant monsters that terrorize a small town in Georgia. The opening credits claim it's based on an actual 1975 incident. Yeah, right. Okay entry in the giant worm genre.

1976 (R) 92m/C Don Scardino, Patricia Pearcy, Jean Sullivan; **D:** Jeff Lieberman; **W:** Jeff Lieberman. **VHS, Beta** *$59.98* LIV, VES ♫½

Squizzy Taylor The rise and fall of real-life Australian mob boss Squizzy Taylor in the 1920s. Colorful period gangster drama loses steam about halfway through.
1984 82m/C Jacki Weaver, Alan Cassell, David Atkins; **D:** Kevin Dobson. **VHS, Beta** *NO* ♫♫

S.S. Experiment Camp 2 Hitler's elite corps of sadists get their kicks torturing and maiming prisoners during the dark days of WWII.
1986 90m/C John Braun, Macha Magal. **VHS, Beta** *NO* ♫

SS Girls After the assassination attempt of July 1944, Hitler does not trust the Wermacht and extends the power of the SS over Germany. General Berger entrusts Hans Schillemberg to recruit a specially chosen group of prostitutes who must test the fighting spirit and loyalty of the generals. Seedy exploitation.
1978 82m/C Gabriele Carrara, Marina Daunia, Vassili Karis, Macha Magal, Thomas Rudy, Lucic Bogoljub Benny, Ivano Staccioli. **VHS, Beta** MED Woof!

S.S. Love Camp No. 27 A beautiful young girl's life is torn to shreds when she is imprisoned in a Nazi brothel.
197? 90m/C **VHS, Beta** VCD Woof!

Stacey Ex-Playmate Randall stars as Stacey Hansen, a beautiful, implausibly talented private detective. Hyper-convoluted plot, too much sex and violence detract from a potentially not-wretched whodunit. **AKA:** Stacey and Her Gangbusters.
1973 (R) 87m/C Anne Randall, Marjorie Bennett, Anitra Ford, Alan Landers, James Westmoreland, Christina Raines; **D:** Andy Sidaris. **VHS, Beta** *$59.95* GEM ♫½

Stacking In the 1950s, a Montana family is threatened with losing their farm. Typical, boring '80s farmland tragedy with coming of age tale. **AKA:** Season of Dreams.
1987 (PG) 111m/C Christine Lahti, Megan Follows, Frederic Forrest, Peter Coyote, Jason Gedrick; **D:** Martin Rosen; **M:** Patrick Gleeson. **VHS, Beta** *$14.95* NLC ♫♫

Stacy's Knights A seemingly shy girl happens to have an uncanny knack for blackjack. With the odds against her and an unlikely group of ''knights'' to aid her, she sets up an implausible ''sting'' operation. Blah TV fodder for the big screen. **AKA:** Double Down.
1983 (PG) 95m/C Kevin Costner, Andra Millian; **D:** Jim Wilson; **W:** Michael Blake. **VHS, Beta** *$29.98* LIV, VES ♫½

Stage Door An energetic ensemble peek at the women of the theater. A boarding house for potential actresses houses a wide variety of talents and dreams. Patrician Hepburn and wisecracking Rogers make a good team in a talent-packed ensemble. Realistic look at the sub-world of Broadway aspirations includes dialogue taken from idle chat among the actresses between takes. Based on the play by Edna Ferber and George S. Kaufman, who suggested in jest a title change to ''Screen Door,'' since so much had been changed. Watch for young stars-to-be like Ball, Arden and Miller.
1937 92m/B Katharine Hepburn, Ginger Rogers, Lucille Ball, Eve Arden, Andrea Leeds, Jack Carson, Adolphe Menjou, Gail Patrick; **D:** Gregory La Cava. Academy Awards '37 Nominations: Best Director (La Cava), Best Picture, Best Screenplay, Best Supporting Actress (Leeds); National Board of Review Awards '37: 10 Best Films of the Year. **VHS, Beta** *$19.98* TTC, CCB, MED ♫♫♫½

Stage Door Canteen The Stage Door Canteens were operated by the American Theatre Wing during WWII for servicemen on leave. They were staffed by some of the biggest stars of the day, 65 of whom are featured here. The slight, hokey plot concerns three soldiers who fall for canteen workers while on furlough in New York City. Many musical numbers, cameos, and walk-ons by a plethora of stars. ♫We Mustn't Say Goodbye; Bombshell From Brooklyn; The Machine Gun Song; Sleep, Baby, Sleep in Your Jeep; Quick Sands; You're Pretty Terrific Yourself; Don't Worry Island; We Meet in the Funniest Places; A Rookie and His Rhythm.
1943 135m/B Cheryl Walker, William Terry, Marjorie Riordan, Lon McCallister, Sunset Carson, Tallulah Bankhead, Merle Oberon, Katharine Hepburn, Paul Muni, Ethel Waters, Judith Anderson, Ray Bolger; **Cameos:** Helen Hayes, Harpo Marx, Gertrude Lawrence, Ethel Merman, Edgar Bergen, George Raft, Benny Goodman, Peggy Lee, Count Basie, Kay Kyser, Guy Lombardo, Xavier Cugat, Johnny Weissmuller; **D:** Frank Borzage. **VHS, Beta** *$9.95* CNG, NOS, PSM ♫♫½

Stage Fright Wyman will stop at nothing to clear her old boyfriend, who has been accused of murdering the husband of his mistress, an actress (Dietrich). Disguised as a maid, she falls in love with the investigating detective, and discovers her friend's guilt. Dietrich sings ''The Laziest Gal in Town.'' The Master's last film made in England until ''Frenzy'' (1971).
1950 110m/B Jane Wyman, Marlene Dietrich, Alastair Sim, Sybil Thorndike, Michael Wilding, Kay Walsh; **D:** Alfred Hitchcock. **VHS, Beta** *$19.98* WAR, MLB ♫♫♫

Stage Fright Bashful actress is transformed into a homicidal killer after a latent psychosis in her becomes active.
1983 82m/C Jenny Neumann, Gary Sweet. **VHS, Beta** *NO* ♫

Stage Struck Strasberg reprises the role made famous by Katharine Hepburn as a determined, would-be actress in this mediocre remake of ''Morning Glory'' (1933). Christopher Plummer's screen debut shows little of his later talent.
1957 95m/B Henry Fonda, Susan Strasberg, Christopher Plummer, Herbert Marshall, Joan Greenwood; **D:** Sidney Lumet. **VHS, Beta** *$29.95* VCI, IME ♫♫½

Stage to Mesa City Marshall LaRue must find out who is behind the pesky attacks on the stage line to Mesa City. Cheseboro, as usual, is a good bad guy. A few chuckles between fist fights and shoot-em-ups.
1948 52m/B Lash LaRue, Al ''Fuzzy'' St. John, George Cheseboro, Jennifer Holt, Russell Arms; **D:** Ray Taylor. **VHS, Beta** *$12.95* COL, GPV ♫♫

Stagecoach Varied group of characters with nothing in common are stuck together inside a coach besieged by bandits and Indians. Considered structurally perfect, with excellent direction by Ford, it's the film that made Wayne a star as the Ringo Kid, an outlaw looking to avenge the murder of his brother and father. The first pairing of Ford and Wayne changed the course of the modern western. Stunning photography by Bert Glennon and Ray Binger captured the mythical air of Monument Valley, a site that Ford was often to revisit. Based on the story ''Stage to Lordsburg'' by Ernest Haycox. Remade miserably with in 1966 and again— why?—as a TV movie in 1986.

1939 100m/B John Wayne, Claire Trevor, Thomas Mitchell, George Bancroft, John Carradine, Andy Devine, Donald Meek, Louise Platt, Berton Churchill, Tim Holt, Tom Tyler, Chris-Pin Martin, Francis Ford, Jack Pennick; **D:** John Ford. Academy Awards '39: Best Supporting Actor (Mitchell), Best Score; Nominations: Best Black and White Cinematography, Best Director (Ford), Best Film Editing, Best Interior Decoration, Best Picture; National Board of Review Awards '39: 10 Best Films of the Year; New York Film Critics Awards '39: Best Director (Ford). **VHS, Beta** $19.98 *WAR, VES, TLF* 🎞🎞🎞🎞

Stagecoach A forgettable made-for-television remake of the classic 1939 western about a motley crew of characters in a cross-country coach beset by thieves and Indians. 1986 95m/C Willie Nelson, Waylon Jennings, Johnny Cash, Kris Kristofferson, John Schneider, Elizabeth Ashley, Mary Crosby, Anthony Newley, Anthony (Tony) Franciosa; **D:** Ted Post. **VHS, Beta** $19.95 *STE, VMK* 🎞

Stagecoach to Denver Lane as Red Ryder investigates a stagecoach wreck and uncovers a land-grabbing plot led by-who else?—the pillar of the community (Barcroft). Well-directed "Red Ryder" episode. 1946 53m/B Allan "Rocky" Lane, Roy Barcroft, Robert (Bobby) Blake, Peggy Stewart, Martha Wentworth; **D:** R.G. Springsteen. **VHS, Beta** $19.95 *NOS, CAB, VCN* 🎞🎞

Stagefright A maniacal serial killer tries to cover his trail by joining the cast of a play about mass murder. The other actors soon have more to worry about than remembering their lines. Typical low-grade horror. 1987 95m/C David Brandon, Barbara Cupisti, Robert Gligorov; **D:** Michele (Michael) Soavi. **VHS, Beta** $79.95 *IMP* 🎞

Stakeout An ex-con tries to start life anew, but every time he finds a good job, his past catches up with him. A return to the life of crime looks tempting. Predictable and familiar plot, but performances are sincere. 1962 81m/B Bing Russell, Billy Hughes, Bill Hale, Jack Harris; **D:** James Landis; **W:** James Landis. **VHS** $16.95 *SNC* 🎞🎞

Stakeout A sometimes violent comedy-thriller about a pair of detectives who stake out a beautiful woman's apartment, hoping for a clue to the whereabouts of her psycho boyfriend who has broken out of prison. One of them (Dreyfuss) then begins to fall in love with her. Natural charm among Estevez, Dreyfuss, and Stowe that adds to the proceedings, which are palpably implausible and silly. Slapstick sequel "Another Stakeout" followed in 1993. 1987 (R) 117m/C Richard Dreyfuss, Emilio Estevez, Madeleine Stowe, Aidan Quinn, Forest Whitaker, Dan Lauria, Earl Billings; **D:** John Badham; **W:** Jim Kouf; **M:** Arthur B. Rubinstein. **VHS, Beta, 8mm** $89.95 *TOU* 🎞🎞½

Stalag 17 A group of American G.I.s in a German POW camp during WWII suspects the opportunistic Holden of being the spy in their midst. One of the very best American movies of the 1950's, adapted from the play by Donald Bevan and Edmund Trzcinski. Wilder, so good at comedy, proved himself equally adept at drama, and brought a top-drawer performance out of Holden. Features superb photography from Ernest Laszlo, and a wonderful score. 1953 120m/B William Holden, Don Taylor, Peter Graves, Otto Preminger, Harvey Lembeck, Robert Strauss, Sig Rumann, Richard Erdman, Neville Brand, A. Dedinstev; **D:** Billy Wilder; **W:** Billy Wilder; **M:** Franz Waxman. Academy Awards '53: Best Actor (Holden); Nominations: Best Director (Wilder), Best Supporting Actor (Strauss); National Board of Review Awards '53:

10 Best Films of the Year. **VHS, Beta** $14.95 *PAR, TLF, BTV* 🎞🎞🎞🎞

Stalin The story of the leader of the Soviet Union who ruled with an iron fist from 1924-1953. One of the most feared men of the 20th century, he wrenched the largest country in the world singlehandedly from a backward, pastoral farmland to an industrial landscape. He was also responsible for the feared purges of the late 1930s where more than a million people were executed. Also explored is the dictator's relationships with his family, including how marriage to a cunning, sadistic, paranoid tyrant affected his wife. Filmed at actual historical locations in Russia. Made for cable television. 1992 173m/C Robert Duvall, Julia Ormond, Jeroen Krabbe, Joan Plowright, Maximilian Schell, Frank Finlay, Roshan Seth, Daniel Massey, Miriam Margolyes, Jim Carter, Joanna Roth, Andras Balint; **D:** Ivan Passer; **W:** Paul Monash. **VHS** $19.98 *MGM, BTV* 🎞🎞½

Stalk the Wild Child Well-intentioned but unconvincing American remake of Truffaut's "The Wild Child," about a child psychologist's efforts to rehabilitate a boy raised by wolves. TV pilot inspired "Lucan," a short-lived series. 1976 78m/C David Janssen, Trish Van Devere, Benjamin Bottoms, Joseph Bottoms; **D:** William Hale. **VHS** *WOV* 🎞½

Stalker A meteorite, crashing to Earth, has caused a wasteland area known as the Zone. The Zone is forbidden to anyone except special guides called Stalkers. Three Stalkers enter the region searching for its center, which contains a room that supposedly reveals fantasies. From the Soviet team that made "Solaris." Filmed with both color and black-and-white sequences. Suspenseful atmosphere due to the director's use of long takes, movement, and color. In Russian with English subtitles. 1979 160m/C Alexander Kaidanovsky, Nikolai Grinko, Anatoli Solonitzin, Alice Freindlikh; **D:** Andrei Tarkovsky; **M:** Eduard Artemyev. **VHS** $89.95 *FXL, FCT* 🎞🎞🎞

Stalking Danger A secret government group must terminate an assassination plot by a terrorist organization. **AKA:** C.A.T. Squad. 1986 (PG) 97m/C Joe Cortese, Steve James, Patricia Charbonneau, Jack Youngblood; **D:** William Friedkin; **M:** Ennio Morricone. **VHS, Beta** $19.95 *STE, VMK* 🎞½

The Stalking Moon Indian scout Peck, ready to retire, meets a woman and her half-breed son who have been captives of the Apaches for 10 years. He agrees to help them escape but learns that the woman's Indian husband is hunting them down. Skeletal plot with little meat on it; great scenery but you wouldn't know it. 1969 (G) 109m/C Gregory Peck, Eva Marie Saint, Robert Forster, Noland Clay; **D:** Robert Mulligan; **W:** Alvin Sargent. **VHS** *ACE, WAR* 🎞½

Stallion A city slicker brings his reputation as a womanizer to a small town. 1988 90m/C Alberto Rojas, Fernando Lujan, Leticia Perdigon, Charly Valentino, Luis Aguilar, Hilda Aguirre. **VHS, Beta** $79.95 *MED* 🎞

Stamp Day for Superman Based on the "Superman" television series, this program was made to promote defense savings stamps for kids. A "Superman" cartoon is also included. 1953 25m/B George Reeves, Jack Larson, Robert Shayne. **VHS, Beta** $19.95 *VDM* 🎞🎞

Stamp of a Killer A tough cop tries to decipher the pattern of a rampaging serial killer. Made for television.

1987 (PG) 95m/C Jimmy Smits, Judith Light, Audra Lindley, Michael Parks, Billy Sullivan, Rhea Perlman; **D:** Larry Elikann. **VHS** $19.95 *STE, NWV* 🎞

Stan Without Ollie, Vol. 1 Three silent comedy shorts featuring Laurel on his own, years before teaming with Ollie: "Kill or Cure," "Oranges & Lemons," and "The Noon Whistle." 1923 53m/B Stan Laurel. **VHS, Beta** $19.95 *VYY* 🎞

Stan Without Ollie, Vol. 2 Three silent shorts from Laurel before he met the big guy. 1923 55m/B Stan Laurel. **VHS, Beta** $19.95 *VYY* 🎞

Stan Without Ollie, Vol. 3 Three early Laurel shorts: "White Wings," "Man About Town," and "Smithy." 1923 51m/B Stan Laurel, James Finlayson. **VHS, Beta** $19.95 *VYY* 🎞

Stan Without Ollie, Vol. 4 Three classic pre-Hardy shorts featuring Laurel: "Half a Man," "Yes, Yes, Nanette," and "Save the Ship." 1925 64m/B Stan Laurel, Blanche Payson, James Finlayson. **VHS, Beta, 8mm** $24.95 *VYY* 🎞

Stand Alone WWII vet Durning battles local dope dealers in his New York neighborhood. Self-serious anti-drug flick miscasts Durning (overweight and looking silly in fight scenes) and Grier. 1985 (R) 94m/C Charles Durning, Pam Grier, James Keach; **D:** Alan Beattie; **W:** Roy Carlson. **VHS, Beta** $19.95 *NWV, STE* 🎞

Stand and Deliver War vet joins Greek ranks for the smell of gunpowder in the morning and meets woman of his dreams. Kidnapped by infamous outlaws, he pledges allegiance to them before turning them over to the authorities, and he's free to live happily ever after with heartthrob. 1928 57m/B Rod La Rocque, Lupe Velez, Warner Oland, James Dime, Frank Lanning, Donald Crisp; **D:** Donald Crisp. **VHS, Beta** $14.95 *GPV* 🎞

Stand and Deliver A tough teacher inspires students in an East L.A. barrio to take the Advanced Placement Test in calculus. A superb, inspirational true story, with a wonderful performance from Olmos. 1988 (PG) 105m/C Edward James Olmos, Lou Diamond Phillips, Rosana De Soto, Andy Garcia, Will Gotay, Ingrid Oliu, Virginia Paris, Mark Eliot; **D:** Ramon Menendez; **W:** Tom Musca, Ramon Menendez; **M:** Craig Safan. Academy Awards '88 Nominations: Best Actor (Olmos); Independent Spirit Awards '89: Best Actor (Olmos), Best Director (Menendez), Best Film, Best Screenplay, Best Supporting Actor (Phillips), Best Supporting Actress (De Soto). **VHS, 8mm** $19.98 *WAR, HMV* 🎞🎞🎞

Stand By Me A sentimental, observant adaptation of the Stephen King novella "The Body." Four 12-year-olds trek into the Oregon wilderness to find the body of a missing boy, learning about death and personal courage. Told as a reminiscence by narrator "author" Dreyfuss with solid performances from all four child actors. Too much gratuitous obscenity, but a very good, gratifying film from can't-miss director Reiner. Based on the novella "The Body" by Stephen King. 1986 (R) 87m/C River Phoenix, Wil Wheaton, Jerry O'Connell, Corey Feldman, Kiefer Sutherland, Richard Dreyfuss, Casey Siemaszko, John Cusack; **D:** Rob Reiner; **W:** Raynold Gideon; **M:** Jack Nitzsche. **VHS, Beta, 8mm** $14.95 *COL* 🎞🎞🎞

Stand-In When a Hollywood studio is threatened with bankruptcy, the bank sends in timid efficiency expert Howard to save it. Satire of studio executives and big-budget movie making. Bogart is interestingly cast and effective in his first comedy role, playing a drunken producer in love with star Shelton.
1937 91m/B Humphrey Bogart, Joan Blondell, Leslie Howard, Alan Mowbray, Jack Carson; *D:* Tay Garnett. **VHS, Beta** NO ♩♩♩

Stand-In A strange comedy-action film that takes a behind-the-scenes look at sleaze films and organized crime.
1985 87m/C Danny Glover; *D:* Robert Zagone. **VHS, Beta** NO ♩

Stand Off Two young hoodlums with guns take eighteen girls hostage in a dormitory. In Hungarian with English subtitles.
1989 97m/C Ary Beri, Gabor Svidrony, Zbigniew Zapassiewicz, Istvan Szabo; *D:* Gyula Gazdag. **VHS** $79.95 EVD, FCT, ING ♩1/2

Stand Up and Cheer The new federal Secretary of Entertainment organizes a huge show to raise the country's depressed spirits. Near-invisible plot, fantastic premise are an excuse for lots of imagery, dancing, and comedy, including four-year-old Temple singing "Baby Take a Bow." Also available colorized. ♫I'm Laughing; We're Out of the Red; Broadway's Gone Hillbilly; Baby Take a Bow; This Is Our Last Night Together; She's Way Up Thar; Stand Up and Cheer.
1934 80m/B Shirley Temple, Warner Baxter, Madge Evans, Nigel Bruce, Stepin Fetchit, Frank Melton, Lila Lee, James Dunn, John Boles, Scotty Beckett; *D:* Hamilton MacFadden; *W:* Will Rogers, Ralph Spence. **VHS, Beta** $19.98 FOX ♩♩1/2

Standing Tall A small-time cattle rancher takes on a high-class land baron in this average, made-for-TV western set during the Depression. Playing a "half-breed," Forster carries an otherwise mediocre effort.
1978 100m/C Robert Forster, Linda Evans, Will Sampson, L.Q. Jones; *D:* Harvey Hart. **VHS** $14.98 WOV ♩♩

Stanley Seminole Vietnam veteran Robinson uses rattlesnakes as his personal weapon of revenge against most of mankind. Thoroughly wretched effort in the gross-pets vein of "Willard" and "Ben."
1972 (PG) 108m/C Chris Robinson, Alex Rocco, Susan Carroll; *D:* William Grefe. **VHS, Beta** NO ♩1/2

Stanley and Iris Blue collar recent widow Fonda meets co-worker De Niro, whose illiteracy she helps remedy. Romance follows, inevitably but excruciatingly. Leads' strong presence helps along a very slow, underdeveloped plot.
1990 (PG-13) 107m/C Jane Fonda, Robert De Niro, Swoosie Kurtz, Martha Plimpton, Harley Cross, Jamey Sheridan, Feodor Chaliapin, Zohra Lampert, Loretta Devine, Julie Garfield; *D:* Martin Ritt; *W:* Harriet Frank Jr., Irving Ravetch; *M:* John Williams. **VHS, Beta** $14.95 MGM, FCT ♩♩1/2

Stanley and Livingstone The classic Hollywood kitsch version of the Victorian legend-based-on-fact. American journalist Tracy sets out into darkest Africa to locate a long lost Brisith explorer. Lavish, dramatically solid fictionalized history. (The real Stanley did not become a missionary—but hey, this is the movies). Tracy is excellent, as usual, and low-key.
1939 101m/B Spencer Tracy, Cedric Hardwicke, Nancy Kelly, Walter Brennan, Richard Greene, Charles Coburn, Henry Hull, Henry Travers, Miles Mander, Holmes Herbert, Paul Stanton, Brandon Hurst, Joseph Crehan, Russell Simpson; *D:* Henry

King; *M:* Alfred Newman. **VHS, Beta** $39.98 FOX ♩♩♩

Star! Campy showbiz extravaganza based on the life of famed musical comedy performer Gertrude Lawrence (Andrews), star of the London and Broadway stage. Film follows Lawrence's adventures from the British music halls to her fateful meeting with Noel Coward (Massey), who would not only become her dearest friend but perform with and write for her as well. A tumultuous private life is also on display. 17 lavishly staged musical numbers helped boost the cost of the film to $14 million—big bucks in '68. Movie was a colossal flop on opening and was recut, deleting 50 minutes, but still didn't recoup its losses. Has gained a cult following. ♫Down at the Old Bull and Bush; Piccadilly; Star!; Oh, It's a Lovely War; In My Garden of Joy; Forbidden Fruit; Parisian Pierrot; Someday I'll Find You; Has Anybody Seen Our Ship?.
AKA: Those Were the Happy Times.
1968 172m/C Julie Andrews, Daniel Massey, Richard Crenna, Michael Craig, Robert Reed, Bruce Forsyth, Beryl Reid, John Collin, Alan Oppenheimer, Anthony Eisley, Jenny Agutter, J. Pat O'Malley, Richard Karlan, Lynley Laurence, Harvey Jason, Elizabeth St. Clair; *D:* Robert Wise; *W:* William Fairchild. **VHS** $89.98 FXV, BTV, FCT ♩♩

The Star Chamber A conscientious judge (Douglas) sees criminals freed on legal technicalities and wonders if he should take justice into his own hands. He finds a secret society that administers justice extra-legally. Implausible yet predictable.
1983 (R) 109m/C Michael Douglas, Hal Holbrook, Yaphet Kotto, Sharon Gless, James B. Sikking; *D:* Peter Hyams; *W:* Peter Hyams, Roderick Taylor. **VHS, Beta** $19.98 FOX ♩♩

Star Crash Trio of adventurers (woman, man, and robot) sent by emperor Plummer square off against interstellar evil (Spinnell) by using their wits and technological wizardry. Semi-funny and cheesy sci-fi, done with style beyond its limited budget. *AKA:* Stella Star.
1978 (PG) 92m/C Caroline Munro, Marjoe Gortner, Christopher Plummer, David Hasselhoff, Robert Tessier, Joe Spinell, Nadia Cassini, Judd Hamilton; *D:* Lewis (Luigi Cozzi) Coates; *M:* John Barry. **VHS, Beta** $19.98 NLC ♩♩1/2

Star Crystal Aboard a spaceship, an indestructible alien hunts down the human crew. Cheap imitation of "Alien."
1985 (R) 93m/C C. Jutson Campbell, Faye Bolt, John W. Smith; *D:* Lance Lindsay. **VHS, Beta** $14.95 NWV, STE, HHE ♩

Star 80 Based on the true-life tragedy of Playmate of the Year Dorothy Stratten and her manager-husband Paul Snider as they battle for control of her body, her mind, and her money, with gruesome results. Roberts is overpowering as the vile Snider, but the movie is generally unpleasant. Fosse's last film.
1983 (R) 104m/C Mariel Hemingway, Eric Roberts, Cliff Robertson, David Clennon, Josh Mostel, Roger Rees, Carroll Baker; *D:* Bob Fosse; *M:* Ralph Burns. **VHS, Beta** $79.95 WAR ♩♩1/2

A Star is Born A movie star declining in popularity marries a shy girl and helps her become a star. Her fame eclipses his and tragic consequences follow. Shows Hollywood-behind-the-scenes machinations. Stunning ending is based on the real-life tragedy of silent film star Wallace Reid, who died of a morphine overdose in 1923 at age 31. Remade twice, in 1954 and 1976.

1937 111m/C Janet Gaynor, Fredric March, Adolphe Menjou, May Robson, Andy Devine, Lionel Stander, Franklin Pangborn; *D:* William A. Wellman; *W:* William A. Wellman, David O. Selznick, Dorothy Parker. Academy Awards '37: Best Story; Nominations: Best Actor (March), Best Actress (Gaynor), Best Director (Wellman), Best Picture, Best Screenplay; National Board of Review Awards '37: 10 Best Films of the Year. **VHS, Beta** $9.95 CNG, NOS, VYY ♩♩♩1/2

A Star is Born Aging actor helps a young actress to fame. She becomes his wife, but alcoholism and failure are too much for him. She honors his memory. Remake of the 1937 classic was Garland's triumph, a superb and varied performance. Newly restored version reinstates over 20 minutes of long-missing footage, including three Garland musical numbers. ♫I'll Get By; You Took Advantage of me; Black Bottom; Peanut Vendor; My Melancholy Baby; Swanee; It's A New World; Gotta Have Me Go With You; Somewhere There's Someone.
1954 (PG) 175m/C Judy Garland, James Mason, Jack Carson, Tommy Noonan, Charles Bickford, Emerson Tracy, Charles Halton; *D:* George Cukor. Academy Awards '54 Nominations: Best Actor (Mason), Best Actress (Garland), Best Art Direction/Set Decoration (Color), Best Costume Design (Color), Best Song ("The Man That Got Away"), Best Original Score; Golden Globe Awards '55: Best Actor—Musical/Comedy (Mason), Best Actress—Musical/Comedy (Garland). **VHS, Beta** $19.95 WAR ♩♩♩1/2

A Star is Born Miserable update of the 1937 and 1954 classics permitting Ms. Streisand to showcase her hit song "Evergreen." The tragic story of one rock star (the relentlessly un-hip Streisand) on her way to the top and another (good old boy Kristofferson) whose career is in decline. Kristofferson is miscast, Streisand eventually numbing, but film may interest those looking into big-budget, big-star misfires. ♫Watch Closely Now; Spanish Lies; Hellacious Acres; With One More Look At You; Woman in the Moon; Queen Bee; Everything; Crippled Cow; I Believe in Love.
1976 (R) 140m/C Barbra Streisand, Kris Kristofferson, Paul Mazursky, Gary Busey, Sally Kirkland, Oliver Clark, Marta Heflin, Robert Englund; *D:* Frank Pierson; *W:* Frank Pierson, Joan Didion, Gregory Dunne. Academy Awards '76: Best Song ("Evergreen"); Nominations: Best Cinematography, Best Sound, Best Original Score; Golden Globe Awards '77: Best Actor—Musical/Comedy (Kristofferson), Best Actress—Musical/Comedy (Streisand), Best Film—Musical/Comedy, Best Song ("Evergreen"), Best Score. **VHS, Beta** $19.98 WAR ♩♩

Star of Midnight A lawyer/detective becomes involved in the disappearance of the leading lady in a Broadway show and the murder of a columnist. Powell and Rogers take on characters similar to Nick and Nora Charles, but the pizazz of the "Thin Man" series is missing.
1935 90m/B Ginger Rogers, William Powell, Paul Kelly; *D:* Stephen Roberts. **VHS, Beta** $39.95 RKO, TTC ♩♩

The Star Packer Wayne puts on a marshal's badge, straightens out a gang of crooks, and still finds time for romance. Implausible and kind of dull early Wayne vehicle.
1934 53m/B John Wayne, George "Gabby" Hayes, Earl Dwire, Yakima Canutt; *D:* Robert North Bradbury. **VHS, Beta** $9.98 REP, COL, NOS ♩♩

Star Quest A genetically engineered woman fights for freedom from her corporate creators. Mediocre effects and some pointless action; done much better by Ridley

Scott in "Blade Runner." *AKA:* Beyond the Rising Moon; Space 2074.
1989 90m/C Tracy Davis, Hans Bachman, Michael Mack; *D:* Phillip Cook. **VHS, Beta** NO ✗

Star Reporter A son takes over his father's newspaper when dad is killed by gangsters. The son uses the paper in an attempt to destroy the underworld, but stumbles on some startling personal information that could drastically backfire on him. Generally interesting plot, but has some implausibility and too-broad characterization.
1939 62m/B Warren Hull, Marsha Hunt, Morgan Wallace, Clay Clement, Wallis Clark, Virginia Howell, Paul Fix, Joseph Crehan; *D:* Howard Bretherton. **VHS, Beta $16.95** SNC ✗½

Star Slammer A beautiful woman is unjustly sentenced to a brutal intergalactic prison ship. She leads the convicts to escape amid zany situations. Unevenly funny sci-fi comedy.
1987 (R) 85m/C Ross Hagen, John Carradine, Sandy Brooke, Aldo Ray; *D:* Fred Olen Ray. **VHS, Beta $79.95** VMK ✗½

Star Spangled Girl One of Neil Simon's lesser plays, one of his least movies. A pert, patriotic young lady captures the hearts of two left-wing alternative-newspaperguys next door; their political conflicts never rise above bland sitcom level.
1971 (G) 94m/C Sandy Duncan, Tony Roberts, Todd Susman, Elizabeth Allan; *D:* Jerry Paris; *W:* Neil Simon; *M:* Charles Fox. **VHS $14.95** PAR ✗½

Star Time Henry is a mentally ill loser who wants to be as happy and famous as his favorite TV stars. Deciding to kill himself, Henry is stopped by the mysterious Sam Bones, who offers him TV stardom—at a steep price. Henry achieves his 15 minutes of fame as a serial killer and his only link to reality is a female social worker.
1992 85m/C Michael St. Gerard, John P. Ryan, Maureen Teefy; *D:* Alexander Cassini; *W:* Alexander Cassini. **VHS $89.95** MNC ✗½

Star Trek: The Motion Picture The Enterprise fights a strange alien force that threatens Earth in this first film adaptation of the famous television series. Very slow moving; followed by numerous sequels. Twelve additional minutes of previously unseen footage have been added to this home video version of the theatrical feature. The laserdisc edition offers the film in widescreen format.
1980 (G) 143m/C William Shatner, Leonard Nimoy, DeForest Kelley, James Doohan, Stephen Collins, Persis Khambatta, Nichelle Nichols, Walter Koenig, George Takei; *D:* Robert Wise; *M:* Jerry Goldsmith. **VHS, Beta $14.95** PAR ✗✗½

Star Trek 2: The Wrath of Khan Picking up from the 1967 Star Trek episode "Space Seed," Admiral James T. Kirk and the crew of the Enterprise must battle Khan, an old foe out for revenge. Warm and comradly in the nostalgic mode of its successors. Introduced Kirk's former lover and unknown son to the series plot, as well as Mr. Spock's "death," which led to the next sequel (1984's "The Search for Spock"). Can be seen in widescreen format on laserdisc.
1982 (PG) 113m/C William Shatner, Leonard Nimoy, Ricardo Montalban, DeForest Kelley, Nichelle Nichols, James Doohan, George Takei, Walter Koenig, Kirstie Alley, Merritt Butrick, Paul Winfield; *D:* Nicholas Meyer; *M:* James Horner. **VHS, Beta, 8mm $14.95** PAR ✗✗✗

Star Trek 3: The Search for Spock Captain Kirk hijacks the USS Enterprise and commands the aging crew to go on a mission to the Genesis Planet to discover whether Mr. Spock still lives (supposedly he died in the last movie). Klingons threaten, as usual. Somewhat slow and humorless, but intriguing. Third in the series of six (so far) Star Trek movies. The laserdisc edition carries the film in widescreen format.
1984 (PG) 105m/C William Shatner, Leonard Nimoy, DeForest Kelley, James Doohan, George Takei, Walter Koenig, Mark Lenard, Robin Curtis, Merritt Butrick, Christopher Lloyd, Judith Anderson, John Larroquette, James B. Sikking, Nichelle Nichols, Cathie Shirriff, Miguel Ferrer, Grace Lee Whitney; *D:* Leonard Nimoy; *M:* James Horner. **VHS, Beta, 8mm $14.95** PAR ✗✗½

Star Trek 4: The Voyage Home Kirk and the gang go back in time (to the 1980s, conveniently) to save the Earth of the future from destruction. Filled with hilarious moments and exhilarating action; great special effects enhance the timely conservation theme. Watch for the stunning going-back-in-time sequence. Spock is particularly funny as he tries to fit in and learn the 80s lingo! Can be seen in widescreen format on laserdisc. Also available as part of Paramount's "director's series," in which Nimoy discusses various special effects aspects in the making of the film. The best in the six-part (so far) series.
1986 (PG) 119m/C William Shatner, DeForest Kelley, Catherine Hicks, James Doohan, Nichelle Nichols, George Takei, Walter Koenig, Mark Lenard, Leonard Nimoy; *D:* Leonard Nimoy; *W:* Nicholas Meyer. **VHS, Beta, 8mm $14.95** PAR ✗✗✗

Star Trek 5: The Final Frontier A renegade Vulcan kidnaps the Enterprise and takes it on a journey to the mythic center of the universe. Shatner's big-action directorial debut (he also co-wrote the script) is a poor follow-up to the Nimoy-directed fourth entry in the series. Heavy-handed and pretentiously pseudo-theological. Available in widescreen format on laserdisc.
1989 (PG) 107m/C William Shatner, Leonard Nimoy, DeForest Kelley, James Doohan, Laurence Luckinbill, Walter Koenig, George Takei, Nichelle Nichols, David Warner; *D:* William Shatner; *W:* William Shatner; *M:* Jerry Goldsmith. **VHS, Beta, 8mm $14.95** PAR ✗½

Star Trek 6: The Undiscovered Country The final chapter in the long running Star Trek series is finally here. The Federation and the Klingon Empire are preparing a much-needed peace summit but Captain Kirk has his doubts about the true intentions of the Federation's longtime enemies. When a Klingon ship is attacked, Kirk and the crew of the Enterprise, who are accused of the misdeed, must try to find the real perpetrator. Has an exciting, climactic ending. As is typical of the series, the film highlights current events—glasnost—in its plotlines. Meyer also directed Star Trek movies 2 ("The Wrath of Khan") and 4 ("The Voyage Home").
1991 (PG) 110m/C William Shatner, Leonard Nimoy, DeForest Kelley, James Doohan, George Takei, Walter Koenig, Nichelle Nichols, Christopher Plummer, Kim Cattrall, Iman, David Warner, Mark Lenard, Grace Lee Whitney, Brock Peters, Kurtwood Smith, Rosana De Soto, John Schuck, Michael Dorn; *D:* Nicholas Meyer; *W:* Nicholas Meyer, Denny Martin; *M:* Cliff Eidelman. **VHS, Beta, CDV $14.95** PAR ✗✗½

Star Trek Bloopers The television cast of "Star Trek" appears in these flubs and goofs that were edited out of the actual episodes. The blooper reels from all three seasons are included on this tape.
1969 25m/C William Shatner, Leonard Nimoy, DeForest Kelley, Nichelle Nichols, James Doohan, George Takei, Walter Koenig, Frank Gorshin. **VHS, Beta $24.95** MOV ✗✗½

Star Trek: The Cage This cult series only ran from 1966-1969 but it's impact has been lasting. Join Captain Kirk and the crew of the starship Enterprise on its voyages of discovery. Additional episodes available. In this original pilot episode for the series Captain Chris Pike of the Enterprise faces the challenge of his life when he is captured by the telepathic aliens of Talos IV. Never telecast in its original form and later edited to form the flashback sequences of the two-part episode "Menagerie." Some portions are in black and white. Version was long believed to be lost, but was reconstituted from original color footage.
1965 73m/C Jeffrey Hunter, Leonard Nimoy, Susan Oliver, Majel Barrett, Meg Wyllie, John Hoyt, Gene Roddenberry; *D:* Robert Butler. **VHS, Beta $12.95** PAR, MOV ✗✗½

Star Trek the Next Generation: Encounter at Farpoint Roddenberry, the creator of the original "Star Trek" television series, spearheaded this episodic reincarnation for network syndication. Set 80 or so years beyond the original, with an entirely new crew and a modernized vessel, it places less emphasis on violent solutions to conflicts than the original TV series. In this first installment, a powerful life force named "Q" threatens the lives of Captain Picard and his crew as they attempt to figure out what's going on at Farpoint Station. Look for a cameo by Kelly, "Bones" from the original series, as a very old man waxing nostalgic about the old U.S.S. Enterprise. Excellent production values, including fine special effects. Additional episodes available.
1987 96m/C Patrick Stewart, Michael Dorn, Jonathon Frakes, Gates McFadden, Marina Sirtis, Denise Crosby, Brent Spiner, Wil Wheaton, LeVar Burton; *Cameos:* DeForest Kelley; *W:* Gene Roddenberry. **VHS $19.95** PAR, MOV ✗✗½

Star Trek 25th Anniversary Special Shatner and Nimoy are joined by other members of the original series as well as cast from "Star Trek: The Next Generation" in this tribute to the enduring popularity of the television/film series. Includes commentary by "Star Trek" creator Gene Roddenberry, highlights from the films and both television series, bloopers, and a behind-the-scenes look at "Star Trek VI: The Undiscovered Country."
1991 100m/C Gene Roddenberry. **VHS, Beta $14.95** PAR ✗✗½

Star Wars First entry Lucas's "Star Wars" trilogy proved to be one of the biggest box-office hits of all time. A young hero, a captured princess, a hot-shot pilot, cute robots, a vile villain, and a heroic and mysterious Jedi knight blend together with marvelous special effects in a fantasy tale about rebel forces engaged in a life or death struggle with the tyrant leaders of the Galactic Empire. Set a new cinematic standard for realistic special effects, making many pre-"Star Wars" effects seem almost laughable in retrospect. Followed by "The Empire Strikes Back" (1980) and "Return of the Jedi" (1983).

1977 (PG) 121m/C Mark Hamill, Carrie Fisher, Harrison Ford, Alec Guinness, Peter Cushing, Kenny Baker, James Earl Jones, David Prowse, Anthony Daniels; **D:** George Lucas; **W:** George Lucas; **M:** John Williams. Academy Awards '77: Best Art Direction/Set Decoration, Best Costume Design, Best Film Editing, Best Sound, Best Visual Effects, Best Original Score; Nominations: Best Director (Lucas), Best Original Screenplay, Best Picture, Best Supporting Actor (Guinness); Golden Globe Awards '78: Best Score; Los Angeles Film Critics Association Awards '77: Best Film; National Board of Review Awards '77: 10 Best Films of the Year; People's Choice Awards '78: Best Film. **VHS, Beta $19.98** *FOX, RDG, HMV* 🎬🎬🎬🎬

Starbird and Sweet William On a solo plane flight, a young Native American crashes in the wilderness. He must fight for survival in the harsh woods with his only friend, a bear cub. Good family fare.
1973 (G) 95m/C A. Martinez, Louise Fitch, Dan Haggerty, Skip Homeier; **D:** Jack B. Hively. **VHS $79.95** *VCI* 🎬🎬

Starchaser: The Legend of Orin Animated fantasy about a boy who must save the world of the future from malevolent hordes.
1985 (PG) 107m/C **D:** Steven Hahn. **VHS, Beta $14.95** *PAR* 🎬🎬½

Stardust Memories Allen's "8 1/2." A comic filmmaker is plagued with creative blocks, relationships, modern fears and fanatical fans. The last film in Allen's varying self-analysis, with explicit references to Fellini and Antonioni.
1980 (PG) 88m/B Woody Allen, Charlotte Rampling, Jessica Harper, Marie-Christine Barrault, Tony Roberts, Helen Hanft, Cynthia Gibb, Amy Wright, Daniel Stern; **D:** Woody Allen; **W:** Woody Allen. **VHS, Beta $14.95** *MGM, FOX* 🎬🎬½

The Starfighters Air Force Lieutenant Dornan must prove his courage to his disapproving war hero Congressman father. Dornan flies his F-104 through a dangerous storm, thereby earning his father's respect, which leads them to form a bond.
1963 84m/C Robert Dornan, Richard Jordahl, Shirley Olmstead. **VHS, Beta** *NO* 🎬½

Starflight One A space shuttle is called on to save the world's first hypersonic airliner trapped in an orbit above earth. Also called "Starflight: The Plane That Couldn't Land." The film features good special effects, but also a predictable "rescue-mission" plot.
1983 155m/C Ray Milland, Lee Majors, Hal Linden, Lauren Hutton, Robert Webber, Terry Kiser; **D:** Jerry Jameson. **VHS, Beta $69.98** *LIV, VES* 🎬🎬

Starhops A trio of buxom young women attract business to their drive-in restaurant by wearing skimpy outfits. Surprisingly inoffensive for an "R" rating.
1978 (R) 92m/C Dorothy Buhrman, Sterling Frazier, Jillian Kesner, Peter Paul Liapis, Paul Ryan, Anthony Mannino, Dick Miller; **D:** Barbara Peeters; **W:** Stephanie Rothman. **VHS** *NO* 🎬½

Stark Wichita detective journeys to Las Vegas in an effort to locate his missing sister. During his search, he finds himself taking on the mob. A television pilot for a series that never happened, and Tidyman's last screenplay. A sequel "Stark: Mirror Image," was made in 1986.
1985 94m/C Nicolas Surovy, Dennis Hopper, Marilu Henner, Seth Jaffe; **D:** Rod Holcomb; **W:** Ernest Tidyman. **VHS, Beta $59.98** *FOX* 🎬½

Starlight Hotel An unhappy teenage girl sets off to find her father, with the help of a shellshocked veteran wrongly accused of a crime. Set in New Zealand during the De-

pression. Lovely scenery and good acting highlight nice story of odd friendship.
1990 (PG) 90m/C Greer Robson, Peter Phelps, Marshall Napier, Wizzard, Pat Smythe, Alice Fraser; **D:** Sam Pillsbury. **VHS $79.95** *REP* 🎬🎬½

Starman An alien from an advanced civilization lands in Wisconsin. He hides beneath the guise of a grieving young widow's recently deceased husband. He then makes her drive him across country to rendezvous with his spacecraft so he can return home. Well-acted, interesting twist on the "Stranger in a Strange Land" theme. Bridges is fun as the likeable starman; Allen is lovely and earthy in her worthy follow-up to "Raiders of the Lost Ark." Available in widescreen format on laserdisc.
1984 (PG) 115m/C Jeff Bridges, Karen Allen, Charles Martin Smith, Richard Jaeckel; **D:** John Carpenter; **W:** Bruce A. Evans, Raynold Gideon; **M:** Jack Nitzsche. **VHS, Beta $12.95** *COL* 🎬🎬🎬

Starring Bugs Bunny! Bug Bunny teams up with Yosemite Sam and others in some of these great hits. Friz Freleng's "Buccaneer Bunny" and "Hare Force," as well as Chuck Jones' "Hare Tonic."
1948 54m/C **D:** Friz Freleng, Chuck Jones, Robert McKimson. **VHS $14.95** *MGM, WTA* 🎬🎬🎬

Stars and Bars O'Connor misfire strands Day-Lewis in the midst of hillbillies. A stuffy English art expert travels from New York to Georgia to price a Renoir, and happens on a bizarre backwoods family marginally run by Stanton. Stereotypical pursuit of humor teeters precariously on the edge of black comedy without actually being funny. Stinky script dooms fine cast to just acting weird in a "Deliverance" sort of way. Based on the novel by William Boyd.
1988 (R) 95m/C Daniel Day-Lewis, Harry Dean Stanton, John Cusack, Joan Cusack, Spalding Gray, Will Patton, Martha Plimpton, Glenne Headly, Laurie Metcalf, Maury Chaykin; **D:** Pat O'Connor; **W:** William Boyd. **VHS, Beta $19.95** *COL* 🎬🎬

Stars and Stripes Forever Sumptious, Hollywoodized bio of composer John Phillip Sousa, based on his memoir "Marching Along," but more concerned with the romantic endeavors of young protege Wagner. Accuracy aside, it's solid entertainment even if you're not mad about march music. 🎵Stars and Stripes Forever; El Capitan; Washington Post; King Cotton; The Battle Hymn of the Republic; Dixie; Light Cavalry; Turkey in the Straw; Hail to the Chief. *AKA:* Marching Along.
1952 89m/C Clifton Webb, Debra Paget, Robert Wagner, Ruth Hussey, Finlay Currie; **D:** Henry Koster. **VHS $19.98** *FXV, FCT* 🎬🎬🎬

Stars in My Crown McCrea provides a moving performance as the pistol-wielding preacher who helps the residents of a 19th-century small town battle a typhoid epidemic and KKK terrorism. Adapted from the novel by Joe David Brown.
1950 89m/B Joel McCrea, Ellen Drew, Dean Stockwell, Alan Hale, Lewis Stone, Amanda Blake, Juano Hernandez, Charles Kemper, Connie Gilchrist, Ed Begley Sr., James Arness, Jack Lambert, Arthur Hunnicutt; **D:** Jacques Tourneur; **W:** Margaret Fitts; **M:** Adolph Deutsch. **VHS $19.98** *MGM* 🎬🎬🎬

The Stars Look Down A mine owner forces miners to work in unsafe conditions in a Welsh town and disaster strikes. Redgrave is a miner's son running for office, hoping to improve conditions, and to escape the hard life. Forceful, well-directed effort suffered at the box office, in competition with John Ford's similar classic "How Green Was My Valley." From the novel by A.J. Cronin.

1939 96m/B Michael Redgrave, Margaret Lockwood, Emlyn Williams, Cecil Parker; **D:** Carol Reed. **VHS, Beta $19.95** *NOS, HHT, CAB* 🎬🎬🎬

Starship British sci-fi seems to be an oxymoron. To wit, this lame "Star Wars" ripoff is about human slaves on a planet run by evil robots.
1987 (PG) 91m/C John Tarrant, Cassandra Webb, Donough Rees, Deep Roy, Ralph Cotterill; **D:** Roger Christian. **VHS, Beta** *HHE* 🎬

Starship Invasions Lee leads a group of bad aliens seeking to take over the Earth. He's thwarted by UFO expert Vaughn, who is aided by a group of good aliens. Cheesy special effects have this one looking like a bad sci-fi serial from the '40s.
1977 (PG) 89m/C Christopher Lee, Robert Vaughn, Daniel Pilon, Helen Shaver, Henry Ramer, Victoria (Vicki) Johnson; **D:** Edward Hunt; **W:** Edward Hunt. **VHS $19.98** *WAR* 🎬

Starstruck Fun-loving folly about a teen who tries to help his talented cousin make it as a singer. Playfully tweeks Hollywood musicals. Enjoyable and fun.
1982 (PG) 95m/C Jo Kennedy, Ross O'Donovan, Pat Evison; **D:** Gillian Armstrong. **VHS $69.98** *SUE* 🎬🎬

Start the Revolution Without Me Hilarious, Moliere-esque farce about two sets of identical twins (Wilder and Sutherland) separated at birth, who meet 30 years later, just before the French Revolution. About as hammy as they come; Wilder is unforgettable. Neglected when released, but now deservedly a cult favorite.
1970 (PG) 91m/C Gene Wilder, Donald Sutherland, Orson Welles, Hugh Griffith, Jack MacGowran, Billie Whitelaw, Victor Spinetti, Ewa Aulin; **D:** Bud Yorkin; **M:** John Addison. **VHS, Beta $19.98** *WAR* 🎬🎬🎬

Starting Over His life racked by divorce, Phil Potter learns what it's like to be single, self-sufficient, and lonely once again. When a blind date grows into a serious affair, the romance is temporarily halted by his hang-up for his ex-wife. Enjoyable love-triangle comedy loses direction after a while, but Reynolds is subtle and charming, and Bergen good as his ex, a very bad songwriter. Based on a novel by Dan Wakefield.
1979 (R) 106m/C Burt Reynolds, Jill Clayburgh, Candice Bergen, Frances Sternhagen, Austin Pendleton, Mary Kay Place, Kevin Bacon, Daniel Stern; **D:** Alan J. Pakula; **W:** James L. Brooks; **M:** Marvin Hamlisch. **VHS, Beta $14.95** *PAR* 🎬🎬🎬

Starvengers Animated adventures with action and excitement meeting futuristic technology, resulting in the high-powered super-intelligence of the robot Starvenger.
1982 105m/C **VHS, Beta $19.98** *FUS, WTA, FHE* 🎬🎬🎬

State Department File 649 Insipid spy drama set in northern China. Mongolian rebels hold U.S. agent Lundigan captive; he hopes to capture a Chinese warlord.
1949 87m/C Virginia Bruce, William Lundigan; **D:** Peter Stewart. **VHS, Beta $16.95** *SNC, NOS, DVT* 🎬½

State Fair The second version of the glossy slice of Americana about a family at the Iowa State Fair, featuring plenty of great songs by Rodgers and Hammerstein. Adapted from the 1933 screen version of Phil Strong's novel. Remade again in 1962. 🎵It Might as Well Be Spring; It's a Grand Night for Singing; That's For Me; Isn't It Kinda Fun?; All I Owe Iowa; Our State Fair. *AKA:* It Happened One Summer.

1945 100m/C Charles Winninger, Jeanne Crain, Dana Andrews, Vivian Blaine, Dick Haymes, Fay Bainter, Frank McHugh, Percy Kilbride, Donald Meek, William Marshall, Harry Morgan; **D:** Walter Lang; **W:** Oscar Hammerstein; **M:** Richard Rodgers, Oscar Hammerstein. Academy Awards '45: Best Song ("It Might as Well Be Spring"); Nominations: Best Original Score. **VHS, Beta** $19.98 *FOX* 🎞🎞🎞

State Fair The third film version of the story of a farm family who travel to their yearly state fair and experience life. The original songs are still there, but otherwise this is a letdown. Texas setting required dropping the song "All I Owe Iowa." 🎵 Our State Fair; It's a Grand Night for Singing; That's for Me; It Might as Well Be Spring; Isn't It Kinda Fun?; More Than Just a Friend; It's the Little Things in Texas; Willing and Eager; This Isn't Heaven.
1962 118m/C Pat Boone, Ann-Margret, Bobby Darin, Tom Ewell, Alice Faye, Pamela Tiffin, Wally Cox; **D:** Jose Ferrer. **VHS, Beta** $19.98 *FOX* 🎞🎞

State of Emergency John Novelli (Mantegna) is a cynical, overworked emergency-room doctor for an over-crowded, underequipped big-city hospital. His latest casualty is a head trauma case the hospital is ill-prepared to handle and as the patient's condition worsens both doctor and hospital are put at risk. Made for television.
1994 (R) 97m/C Joe Mantegna, Lynn Whitfield, Paul Dooley; **D:** Lesli Linka Glatter; **W:** Susan Black, Dr. Lance Gentile. **VHS** *HBO* 🎞🎞½

State of Grace Irish hood Penn returns to old NYC neighborhood as undercover cop and becomes involved with an Irish Westies mob in a fight for survival as urban renewal encroaches on their Hell's Kitchen turf. Shrinking client base for shakedown schemes and protection rackets forces them to become contract killers for the Italian mafia. Fine performances, with Penn tense but restrained, gang honcho Harris intense, and Oldham chewing up gritty urban scenery as psycho brother of Harris, but the story is long and meandering. Well-choreographed violence.
1990 (R) 134m/C Sean Penn, Ed Harris, Gary Oldman, Robin Wright, John Turturro, Burgess Meredith, John Reilly; **D:** Phil Joanou; **W:** Dennis McIntyre; **M:** Ennio Morricone. **VHS** $9.98 *ORI* 🎞🎞🎞

State of Siege Third pairing of Montand and Costa-Gavras, about the real-life death of USAID employee Daniel Mitrione, suspected to be involved in torture and murder in Uruguay in the '60s. Quietly suspenseful, with snazzy editing; conspiracy-theory premise is similar to Stone's "JFK," and similarly disturbing, whether you believe it or not. Dubbed. **AKA:** Etat de Siege.
1973 119m/C Yves Montand, Renato Salvatori, O.E. Hasse, Jacques Perrin; **D:** Constantin Costa-Gavras. **VHS, Beta** $59.95 *COL, ING* 🎞🎞🎞

State of the Union Liberal multimillionaire Tracy is seeking the Republican presidential nomination. His estranged wife (Hepburn) is asked to return so they can masquerade as a loving couple for the sake of his political career. Hepburn tries to help Tracy, as the backstage political machinations erode his personal convictions. Adapted from a highly successful, topical Broadway play; the writers changed dialogue constantly to reflect the news. Capra and his partners at Liberty Pictures originally hoped to cast Gary Cooper and Claudette Colbert. Hepburn and Menjou were at odds politically (over communist witch hunts in Hollywood) but are fine together onscreen. **AKA:** The World and His Wife.

1948 124m/B Spencer Tracy, Katharine Hepburn, Angela Lansbury, Van Johnson, Adolphe Menjou, Lewis Stone, Howard Smith; **D:** Frank Capra. **VHS, Beta** $19.98 *MCA* 🎞🎞🎞½

State of Things Ostensibly a mystery involving a film crew trying to remake a B-movie, "The Most Dangerous Man On Earth," but also an in-depth look at the process of filmmaking, a scathing look at nuclear warfare and an homage to Roger Corman and Hollywood at large. An enigmatic, complex film from Wenders prior to his American years. In German with English subtitles; some dialogue in English.
1982 120m/B Patrick Bauchau, Allen (Gooritz) Garfield, Isabelle Weingarten, Viva, Samuel Fuller, Paul Getty III, Roger Corman; **D:** Wim Wenders. **VHS, Beta** $59.95 *GLV, ING* 🎞🎞🎞

Stateline Motel Cheap Italian ripoff of "The Postman Always Rings Twice," with a surprise ending but little of great interest. **AKA:** Last Chance For a Born Loser.
1975 (R) 86m/C Eli Wallach, Ursula Andress, Fabio Testi, Barbara Bach; **D:** Maurizio Lucidi. **VHS, Beta** *NO* 🎞½

State's Attorney A burned-out attorney finds himself falling in love with the least likely person, a prostitute he is defending. Contrived, improbable story succumbs to star-quality lead acting from Barrymore. Remade in 1937 with Lee Tracy as "Criminal Lawyer." **AKA:** Cardigan's Last Case.
1931 79m/B John Barrymore, Jill Esmond, William Boyd, Helen Twelvetrees; **D:** George Archainbaud. **VHS, Beta** $19.98 *TTC* 🎞🎞½

Static A strange, disquieting independent film about an eccentric youth who claims to have built a machine through which one can see heaven. Uneven, with some dull stretches.
1987 (PG-13) 89m/C Keith Gordon, Amanda Plummer, Bob Gunton, Jane Hoffman, Barton Heyman, Lily Knight; **D:** Mark Romanek; **W:** Keith Gordon, Mark Romanek. **VHS, Beta** $19.98 *MCG* 🎞🎞½

Station A Japanese detective's love affair is corrupted by his ruthless search for a bloodthirsty cop killer. With English subtitles.
1981 130m/C Ken Takakura, Chieko Baisho; **D:** Yasuo Furuhata. **VHS, Beta** *NO* 🎞🎞½

The Station A sophisticated woman, who has just abandoned her fiancee, waits in a tiny station for an early train. The only person around is the young and ordinary stationmaster. Gradually the two are drawn together in a number of charming and comic romantic fantasies. In Italian with English subtitles.
1992 92m/C Margherita Buy, Ennio Fantastichini; **D:** Sergio Rubini; **W:** Sergio Rubini. **VHS** $89.95 *FXL* 🎞🎞

Station West A disguised Army officer is sent to uncover a mystery of hijackers and murderers. Along the way, he meets up with and falls for a beautiful woman who may be involved in the treachery. Good, solid western with a fine cast and plenty of fun action shot against the requisite beautiful western landscapes. Based on the Luke Short story. Also available colorized.
1948 92m/B Dick Powell, Jane Greer, Agnes Moorehead, Burl Ives, Tom Powers, Raymond Burr; **D:** Sidney Lanfield. **VHS, Beta** $19.95 *RKO, CCB, TTC* 🎞🎞🎞

The Stationmaster's Wife In Germay's Weimar Republic a provincial stationmaster's wife expresses her boredom with her pleasant ineffectual husband by having numerous meaningless affairs. Meant to invoke postwar German dread and the fake bourgeois morality which covered political and social resentments. Originally shown as

a 200-minute miniseries for German television. In German with English subtitles.
1977 111m/C Elisabeth Trissenaar, Kurt Raab, Gustal Bayrhammer, Bernard Helfrich, Udo Kier, Volker Spengler; **D:** Rainer Werner Fassbinder; **W:** Rainer Werner Fassbinder; **M:** Peer Raben. **VHS** $79.95 *NYF, FCT* 🎞🎞½

The Statue Famed sculptress unveils a nude rendering of her Nobel Prize-winning husband. Much hilarity in the British vein is meant to ensue, but doesn't. Niven is OK, but this empty, plotless farce should have been much shorter.
1971 (R) 84m/C David Niven, Virna Lisi, Robert Vaughn, Ann Bell, John Cleese; **D:** Rod Amateau. **VHS, Beta** $59.95 *PSM* 🎞

Stavisky Sumptuously lensed story of Serge Stavisky, a con-artist and bon-vivant whose machinations almost brought down the French government when his corruption was exposed in 1934. Belmondo makes as charismatic an antihero as you could find. Excellent score complements the visuals. In French with English subtitles.
1974 117m/C Jean-Paul Belmondo, Anny Duperey, Charles Boyer, Francois Perier, Gerard Depardieu; **D:** Alain Resnais; **M:** Stephen Sondheim. **VHS** $59.95 *ING, INT* 🎞🎞🎞

Stay As You Are Aging French architect Mastroianni has designs on a teenager who may be his illegitimate daughter from an earlier affair.
1978 95m/C Marcello Mastroianni, Nastassia Kinski, Francesco Rabal; **D:** Alberto Lattuada. **VHS, Beta** $19.98 *WAR, OM* 🎞½

Stay Awake A demon stalks, haunts and tortures eight young girls sleeping together at a secluded Catholic school. Title might be addressed to the viewer, who will be tempted to snooze.
1987 (R) 90m/C Shirley Jane Harris, Tanya Gordon, Jayne Hutton, Heath Porter; **D:** John Bernard. **VHS, Beta** $19.98 *SUE, NLC* 🎞

Stay Away, Joe The King is a singing half-breed rodeo star who returns to his reservation where he finds love and trouble. Utterly cliche, embarrassing, and stupid even by Elvis-movie standards.
1968 (PG) 98m/C Elvis Presley, Burgess Meredith, Joan Blondell, Thomas Gomez, L.Q. Jones, Katy Jurado, Henry Jones; **D:** Peter Tewkesbury. **VHS, Beta** $14.95 *MGM* 🎞

Stay Hungry A wealthy southerner (Bridges) is involved in a real estate deal which depends on the sale of a gym where a number of body builders hang out. He becomes immersed in their world and finds himself in love with the working-class Field. Big Arnold's first speaking role in his own inimitable accent (his first role in "Hercules in New York" was dubbed.) Offbeat and occasionally uneven comedy-drama based on a novel by Charles Gaines is a sleeper.
1976 (R) 102m/C Jeff Bridges, Sally Field, Arnold Schwarzenegger, Robert Englund, Scatman Crothers; **D:** Bob Rafelson; **W:** Bob Rafelson. **VHS, Beta** $14.95 *MGM, FOX* 🎞🎞🎞

Stay Tuned Suburban yuppie couple buys a large-screen TV and satellite dish from Hellvision salesman; are sucked into their dish, and wind up starring in hellish TV shows such as "Wayne's Underworld," "Northern Overexposure," "Sadistic Home Videos," and "My Three Sons of Bitches." If they can survive for 24 hours, they'll be able to return to their normal lives. Clever idea for a film is wasted as this one never really gets off the ground; viewers may not want to stay tuned to the low comedy and frantic yucks.

1992 (PG-13) 90m/C John Ritter, Pam Dawber, Jeffrey Jones, Eugene Levy, David Tom, Heather McComb; **D:** Peter Hyams; **W:** Tom S. Parker; **M:** Bruce Broughton. **VHS $19.98** *WAR* ⅡⅡ

Stay Tuned for Murder A sexy news reporter gets caught in a web of financial wrongdoings and corruption. The financiers, lawyers, and other sinister types she's investigating decide to give her a story she will never forget—if she ever gets the chance to tell it!
1988 92m/C Terry Reeves Wolf, Christopher Ginnaven; **D:** Gary Jones. **VHS, Beta $79.95** *IME* Ⅱ½

Staying Alive "Saturday Night Fever" was the ultimate cheesy 70's musical, hence likeable in a dorky way. This pathetic sequel (directed by Stallone from a Rocky-esque script about beating the odds, etc.) is utterly predictable and forgettable. Music mostly by Frank Stallone, the great heir to Rogers and Hammerstein. ♫The Woman In You; I Love You Too Much; Breakout; Someone Belonging to Someone; Life Goes On; Far From Over; Devils and Seducers; (We Dance) So Close to the Fire; Hope We Never Change.
1983 (PG) 96m/C John Travolta, Cynthia Rhodes, Finola Hughes; **D:** Sylvester Stallone; **W:** Sylvester Stallone; **M:** Frank Stallone. **VHS, Beta $19.95** *PAR* Ⅱ½

Staying On Based on the Paul Scott novel, this English drama follows the life of a post-colonial British colonel and his wife who chose to remain in India.
1980 87m/C Trevor Howard, Celia Johnson; **D:** Irene Shubik. **VHS, Beta $19.95** *MTI* ⅡⅡ½

Staying Together Three midwestern brothers go into a panic when their father decides to sell the restaurant they've worked at all their adult lives. Somehow they manage the transition and learn about life. Sloppy comedy-drama with way too many unresolved subplots.
1989 (R) 91m/C Dermot Mulroney, Tim Quill, Sean Astin, Stockard Channing, Melinda Dillon, Daphne Zuniga; **D:** Lee Grant; **W:** Miles Goodman. **VHS, Beta $89.99** *HBO* Ⅱ½

The Steagle The threat of the Cuban missile crisis lets a fantasizing professor loose to enact his wildest dreams. Odd Mitty-esque fantasy comedy might have worked, but ends up confusing and frustrating.
1971 (R) 101m/C Richard Benjamin, Cloris Leachman; **D:** Paul Sylbert. **VHS, Beta $9.98** *NLC* Ⅱ

Steal the Sky Israeli agent Hemingway seduces Iraqi pilot Cross and persuades him to steal a Soviet MIG jet and defect to Israel. Unlikely plot but swell flying scenes. Hemingway is poorly cast, as she often is. Made for cable television.
1988 110m/C Mariel Hemingway, Ben Cross, Etta Ankri; **D:** John Hancock. **VHS, Beta $89.99** *HBO* ⅡⅡ

Stealing Heaven Based on the lives of Abelard and Heloise. In 12th-century Paris, a theologian and teacher falls in love with a beautiful young woman, and the two must defend their bond from all comers, including her righteous uncle. Steamy; trimmed to 108 minutes after threatened X rating. Attractive and cerebral. Available in a 115 minute-uncut, unrated version.
1988 (R) 108m/C Derek De Lint, Kim Thomson, Denholm Elliott, Mark Jax, Bernard Hepton, Kenneth Cranham, Angela Pleasence, Rachel Kempson; **D:** Clive Donner; **W:** Chris Bryant; **M:** Nick Bicat. **VHS, Beta** *NO* ⅡⅡ½

Stealing Home A washed-up baseball player learns his former babysitter (who was also his first love and inspiration), has committed suicide. Their bittersweet relationship is told through flashbacks. Foster's superb performance steals the show in this quiet sleeper.
1988 (PG-13) 98m/C Mark Harmon, Jodie Foster, William McNamara, Blair Brown, Harold Ramis, Jonathan Silverman, John Shea, Helen Hunt, Richard Jenkins, Ted Ross, Thatcher Goodwin, Yvette Croskey; **D:** Steven Kampmann, Will Aldis; **W:** Steven Kampmann, Will Aldis; **M:** David Foster. **VHS $19.98** *WAR* ⅡⅡ½

Steamboat Bill, Jr. City-educated student returns to his small home-town and his father's Mississippi river boat, where he's an embarrassment to dad. But bond they do, to ward off the owner of a rival riverboat, whose daughter Keaton falls for. Engaging look at small-town life and the usual wonderful Keaton antics, including braving the big tornado.
1928 75m/B Buster Keaton, Ernest Torrence, Marion Byron, Tom Lewis; **D:** Charles Riesner. **VHS, Beta $19.95** *NOS, CCB, DVT* ⅡⅡⅡ½

Steaming Six women get together in a London bathhouse and review their various troubles with men. Unfortunate adaptation of the good play by Nell Dunn. Where are the laughs—and what happened to the dramatic tension? The last film of Dors and director Losey.
1986 (R) 102m/C Vanessa Redgrave, Sarah Miles, Diana Dors; **D:** Joseph Losey. **VHS, Beta $19.95** *STE, NWV* ⅡⅡ

Steel Construction workers on a mammoth skyscraper face insurmountable odds and strong opposition. Will they finish their building? Worth watching, if you don't have anything else to do. *AKA:* Look Down and Die; Men of Steel.
1980 (R) 100m/C Lee Majors, Jennifer O'Neill, Art Carney, George Kennedy, Harris Yulin, Terry Kiser, Richard Lynch, Roger E. Mosley, Albert Salmi, R.G. Armstrong; **D:** Steve Carver; **M:** Michel Colombier. **VHS, Beta $69.95** *VES* ⅡⅡ

Steel and Lace Davison is the scientist brother of a classical pianist who commits suicide after being raped. He revives her as a cyborg, which promptly sets out to enact its revenge. Depressing, morbid sci-fi.
1990 (R) 92m/C Bruce Davison, Clare Wren, Stacy Haiduk, David Naughton, David Lander; **D:** Ernest Farino; **W:** Joseph Dougherty, Dave Edison. **VHS, Beta $89.95** *FRH* Ⅱ½

Steel Arena Several real life stunt-car drivers appear in this action-packed film, crammed with spins, jumps, explosions and world-record-breaking, life risking stunts.
1972 (PG) 99m/C Dusty Russell, Gene Drew, Buddy Love; **D:** Mark L. Lester. **VHS, Beta $69.98** *LIV, VES* Ⅱ

The Steel Claw One-handed ex-Marine Montgomery organizes guerilla forces against the Japanese in the Philippines in WWII. Good location shooting and plenty of action.
1961 95m/C George Montgomery, Charito Luna, Mario Barri; **D:** George Montgomery. **VHS, Beta** *NO* ⅡⅡ

Steel Cowboy With his marriage, sanity, and livelihood on the line, an independent trucker agrees to haul a hot herd of stolen steers. Passable made-for-TV macho adventure.
1978 100m/C James Brolin, Rip Torn, Jennifer Warren, Strother Martin, Melanie Griffith, Lou Frizzell; **D:** Harvey Laidman; **M:** Charles Bernstein. **VHS, Beta** *NO* ⅡⅡ

Steel Dawn Another "Mad Max" clone: A leather-clad warrior wields his sword over lots of presumably post-apocalyptic desert terrain. Swayze stars with his real-life wife Niemi in unfortunate follow-up to "Dirty Dancing."
1987 (R) 90m/C Patrick Swayze, Lisa Niemi, Christopher Neame, Brett Hool, Brion James, Anthony Zerbe; **D:** Lance Hool. **VHS, Beta $14.98** *LIV, VES* Ⅱ½

Steel Fisted Dragon Son seeks revenge on the gang who murdered his mother and burned her house to the ground.
1982 (R) 85m/C Stephen Lee, Johnny Kong Kong, Peter Chan. **VHS, Beta** *NO* Ⅱ

The Steel Helmet Hurriedly made Korean War drama stands as a top-notch war film. Brooding and dark, GIs don't save the world for democracy or rescue POWs; they simply do their best to survive a horrifying situation. Pointless death, confused loyalties and cynicism abound in writer-director Fuller's scathing comment on the madness of war.
1951 84m/B Gene Evans, Robert Hutton, Steve Brodie, William Chun, James Edwards, Richard Loo, Sid Melton; **D:** Samuel Fuller; **W:** Samuel Fuller. **VHS, Beta $14.95** *RXM* ⅡⅡⅡ½

Steel Magnolias Julia Roberts plays a young woman stricken with severe diabetes who chooses to live her life to the fullest despite her bad health. Much of the action centers around a Louisiana beauty shop where the women get together to discuss the goings-on of their lives. Screenplay by R. Harling, based on his partially autobiographical play. Sweet, poignant, and often hilarious, yet just as often overwrought. MacLaine is funny as a bitter divorcee; Parton is sexy and fun as the hairdresser. But Field and Roberts go off the deep end and make it all entirely too weepy.
1989 (PG) 118m/C Sally Field, Dolly Parton, Shirley MacLaine, Daryl Hannah, Olympia Dukakis, Julia Roberts, Tom Skerritt, Sam Shepard, Dylan McDermott, Kevin J. O'Connor, Bil McCurcheon, Ann Wedgeworth, Janine Turner; **D:** Herbert Ross; **W:** Robert Harling; **M:** Georges Delerue. Academy Awards '89 Nominations: Best Supporting Actress (Wiest); Golden Globe Awards '90: Best Supporting Actress (Roberts); People's Choice Awards '90: Best Film—Drama. **VHS, Beta, 8mm $19.95** *COL* ⅡⅡⅡ

Steele Justice A tough 'Nam vet takes on the whole Vietnamese Mafia in Southern California after his friend is murdered. One of those head-scratchers: Should I laugh, or be offended?
1987 (R) 96m/C Martin Kove, Sela Ward, Ronny Cox, Bernie Casey, Joseph Campanella, Sarah Douglas; **D:** Robert Boris. **VHS, Beta $19.95** *PAR* Ⅱ

Steele's Law A loner cop is forced to take the law into his own hands in order to track down an insane international assassin.
1991 (R) 90m/C Fred Williamson, Bo Svenson, Doran Inghram, Phyllis Cicero; **D:** Fred Williamson. **VHS $89.95** *ACA* ⅡⅡ

Steelyard Blues A motley-crew comedy about a wacky gang that tries to steal an abandoned WW II airplane. Zany pranks abound. Technically flawed direction from Myerson mars a potentially hilarious story. *AKA:* The Final Crash.
1973 (PG) 93m/C Jane Fonda, Donald Sutherland, Peter Boyle, Howard Hesseman, John Savage; **D:** Alan Myerson; **W:** David S. Ward. **VHS, Beta $19.98** *WAR* ⅡⅡ½

Stella Mercouri's film debut has her as a free-spirited bar singer who gets involved in a tragic romantic triangle with a middle-class writer and a local football hero. Melodramatic but Mercouri's earthy joie de vivre is already apparent. In Greek with English subtitles.
1955 94m/B Melina Mercouri, Yiorgo Fountas, Aiekos Alexandrikis, Sophia Vembo; **D:** Michael Cacoyannis; **M:** Manos Hadjidakis. VHS $59.95 FCT *II* ½

Stella Anachronistic remake update of "Stella Dallas" casts Midler as a single mother who sacrifices everything to give her daughter a better life. Barbara Stanwyck did it much better in 1937. Based on Olive Higgins Prouty's novel.
1989 (PG-13) 109m/C Bette Midler, John Goodman, Stephen Collins, Eileen Brennan, Ben Stiller, Trini Alvarado, Marsha Mason; **D:** John Erman; **W:** Robert Getchell. VHS, Beta $12.95 TOU *II* ½

Stella Dallas An uneducated woman lets go of the daughter she loves when she realizes her ex-husband can give the girl more advantages. What could be sentimental turns out believable and worthwhile under Vidor's steady hand. Stanwyck never makes a wrong step. From a novel by Olive Higgins Prouty. Remade in 1989 as "Stella," starring Bette Midler.
1937 106m/B Barbara Stanwyck, Anne Shirley, John Boles, Alan Hale, Marjorie Main; **D:** King Vidor. VHS, Beta $14.98 SUE *III*

Stella Maris Pickford plays tattered waif who's a slave to an alcoholic who's married to the man she loves. But he's in love with Pickford playing a sheltered rich invalid. Brimming with the tragic consequences of love.
1918 70m/B Mary Pickford, Conway Tearle, Camille Ankewich, Ida Waterman; **D:** Marshall Neilan. VHS, Beta $24.95 GPV, FCT *III*

Step Lively A young playwright tries to recover the money he lent to a fast-talking Broadway producer and is forced to take the leading role in his play. Lively musical remake of "Room Service" (1938) was Sinatra's first starring role. Look for Dorothy Malone as a brunette switchboard operator. ♫Some Other Time; As Long As There's Music; Where Does Love Begin?; Come Out, Come Out, Wherever You Are; Why Must There Be an Opening Song?; And Then You Kissed Me; Ask the Madame.
1944 88m/B Frank Sinatra, Gloria De Haven, George Murphy, Walter Slezak, Adolphe Menjou, Anne Jeffreys; **D:** Tim Whelan. VHS, Beta $19.98 RKO, CCB *II* ½

The Stepfather Creepy thriller about a seemingly ordinary stepfather who is actually a homicidal maniac searching for the "perfect family." An independently produced sleeper tightly directed and well written. Followed by two inferior sequels.
1987 (R) 89m/C Terry O'Quinn, Shelley Hack, Jill Schoelen, Stephen Shellan, Charles Lanyer; **D:** Joseph Ruben; **W:** Donald E. Westlake; **M:** Patrick Moraz. VHS, Beta $14.95 COL, SUE *III*

Stepfather 2: Make Room for Daddy A poor sequel to the suspenseful sleeper, wherein the psychotic family man escapes from an asylum and woos another suburban family, murdering anyone who may suspect his true identity. Followed by yet another sequel.
1989 (R) 93m/C Terry O'Quinn, Meg Foster, Caroline Williams, Jonathan Brandis; **D:** Jeff Burr. VHS, Beta NO *I* ½

Stepfather 3: Father's Day The father from Hell is back! Escaping from the loony bin with a surgically altered face, the stepfather settles in a small town and gets a job at a nursery (the plant kind, not the children kind). His favorite gardening tool fast becomes the mulch machine, and soon locals are fertilizing the garden. Well below the original, but it may please fans of this genre.
1992 (R) 110m/C Robert Wightman, Priscilla Barnes, Season Hubley; **D:** Guy Magar. VHS $92.95 VMK *I*

Stephen King's Golden Years Stephen King creates a chilling vision of scientific progress gone awry in this shocking techno-thriller. After being accidentally exposed to exotic chemicals in a lab explosion, an aging janitor undergoes an extraordinary transformation and the government will sacrifice anything to learn more about it. Originally a made-for-television miniseries.
1991 232m/C Keith Szarabajka, Frances Sternhagen, Ed Lauter, R.D. Call. VHS $89.95 WOV *I* ½

Stephen King's It A group of small town children, who were terrorized by an evil force in their youth, are traumatized again some thirty years later, when they learn a new series of child murders occurred in their Eastern home town. The adults, who now all have successful and diverse careers, must come to terms with the terrible secret they share, as "IT" has returned to wreak havoc in their New England home town. Based on horror master King's bestselling novel of the same name.
1990 193m/C Tim Reid, Richard Thomas, John Ritter, Annette O'Toole, Richard Masur, Dennis Christopher, Harry Anderson, Olivia Hussey, Tim Curry; **D:** Tommy Lee Wallace; **W:** Stephen King. VHS, Beta $79.99 WAR *II* ½

Stephen King's The Stand Ghoulish made for TV adaptation of the King novel about a superflu/plague that decimates the U.S. population. The few survivors are soon divided into two camps—those dreaming of a godly old black woman known as Mother Abigail and others of the satanic Randall Flagg, the Walkin' Dude. Boulder, Colorado (where King was living when he wrote the novel) serves as headquarters for Abigail's brood while Las Vegas (where else) is Flagg territory. It all comes down to a battle of good vs. evil, with the future of mankind at stake. Religious allegory can get tedious but it's a varied cast with some scenes not for those with queasy stomachs. On four cassettes. **AKA:** The Stand.
1994 360m/C Jamey Sheridan, Ruby Dee, Gary Sinise, Molly Ringwald, Miguel Ferrer, Laura San Giacomo, Rob Lowe, Adam Storke, Matt Frewer, Corin "Corky" Nemec, Ray Walston, Bill Fagerbakke, Ossie Davis, Shawnee Smith, Rick Aviles; **Cameos:** Ed Harris, Kathy Bates, Kareem Abdul-Jabbar, Stephen King; **D:** Mick Garris; **W:** Stephen King. VHS REP *II* ½

Stephen King's The Tommyknockers Another of King's creepy tales, adapted for TV. Bobbi (Helgenberger) and Gard (Smits) live in the small town of Haven, Maine (actually filmed on New Zealand's North Island). She's an aspiring writer; he's a fading poet with a drinking problem and a metal plate in his head (this is important). Walking in the woods, Bobbi stumbles over a long-buried spaceship which begins to take possession of the townspeople—their eyes shine green, their teeth fall out, and they act out their (often violent) fantasies—all but Gard. The whole thing's more silly than scary. The title comes from an old children's rhyme. **AKA:** The Tommyknockers.
1993 (R) 120m/C Jimmy Smits, Marg Helgenberger, Joanna Cassidy, E.G. Marshall, Traci Lords, John Ashton, Allyce Beasley, Cliff DeYoung, Robert Carradine, Leon Woods, Paul McIver; **D:** John Power; **W:** Lawrence D. Cohen. VHS $92.95 VMK *II* ½

Stepmonster A boy tries to convince his father that his new stepmother is a monster—literally. Doesn't work any better that "My Stepmother Is an Alien."
1992 (PG-13) ?m/C Alan Thicke, Robin Riker, Corey Feldman, John Astin, Ami Dolenz, George Gaynes. VHS $89.98 NHO *I* ½

The Stepmother Yet another Hitchcock ripoff story involving an evil stepmother. Rey is passable, but there's not much else to recommend this dredge.
1971 100m/C Alejandro Rey, John Anderson, Katherine Justice, John David Garfield, Marlene Schmidt, Claudia Jennings, Larry Linville; **D:** Hikmet Avedis. VHS $19.95 ACA *I* ½

Steppenwolf Static, enigmatic film version of the famous Herman Hesse novel about a brooding writer searching for meaning and self-worth. Interesting to watch, but the offbeat novel doesn't translate to the screen; leaves you flat.
1974 (PG) 105m/C Max von Sydow, Dominique Sanda; **D:** Fred Haines. VHS, Beta $59.95 VMK, GLV *II* ½

Stepping Out Minnelli stars as a would-be Broadway dancer who gives tap dancing lessons in an old church to an assortment of offbeat and interesting characters. When the troupe is asked to perform for a local charity, they make the most of their opportunity. A warm and touching ensemble piece that avoids over-sentimentalizing and utilizes its cast to best advantage.
1991 (PG) 113m/C Liza Minnelli, Shelley Winters, Bill Irwin, Ellen Greene, Julie Walters, Robyn Stevan, Jane Krakowski, Sheila McCarthy, Andrea Martin, Carol Woods, Nora Dunn; **D:** Lewis Gilbert; **W:** Richard Harris; **M:** Peter Matz. VHS, Beta $14.95 PAR *III*

Steps from Hell Vald Tempest is an evil immortal in control of a cult of zombie women. He's stolen a sacred map that will lead to a gateway which, when opened, will unleash a supreme evil on the world. Unless the heroic John Clark can find a way to prevent it, of course.
1992 90m/C Bernardo Rosa, Rocky Tucker, Ron Odell, Philip Cable, Liz Stoeckel, Steve Quimby, Lisa Lund; **D:** James Tucker; **W:** James Tucker. VHS $29.95 CTC *I*

Stepsisters Murderous double-crosses occur among a pilot, his wife, and her sister.
1985 75m/C Hal Fletcher, Sharyn Talbert, Bond Gideon. VHS, Beta NO Woof!

The Sterile Cuckoo An aggressive co-ed pursues a shy freshman who seems to embody her romantic ideal. Minnelli's performance is outstanding; Burton as the naive young man is also fine. Pakula's splendid first directing job. **AKA:** Pookie.
1969 (PG) 108m/C Liza Minnelli, Wendell Burton, Tim McIntire; **D:** Alan J. Pakula; **W:** Alvin Sargent. VHS, Beta $49.95 PAR *III*

Steve Martin Live Martin shows veteran comedians his famous Universal Amphitheatre performance and his short "The Absent-Minded Waiter."
1985 58m/C Steve Martin, Teri Garr, Buck Henry, David Letterman, Paul Simon. VHS, Beta $14.98 LIV, VES *II* ½

Stevie Jackson brings her flawless skill to the role of British poet Stevie Smith. Excellent performance from Washbourne as Stevie's spinster aunt. Wooden, lifeless screen rendition for the Hugh Whitemore stage play is helped greatly by good performances, but is too talky and, frankly, rather dull and self-absorbed.
1978 102m/C Glenda Jackson, Mona Washbourne, Alec McCowen, Trevor Howard; **D:** Robert Enders. VHS **$29.95** *UAV, SUE* ♂♂

Stewardess School Airline spoof aims at wackiness, but misses the runway. Generic title betrays probable badness which turns out to be all too real. An utter woofer.
1986 (R) 84m/C Sandahl Bergman, Wendie Jo Sperber, Judy Landers, Julia Montgomery, Corinne Bohrer; **D:** Ken Blancato; **M:** Robert Folk. VHS, Beta *NO Woof!*

Stick Ex-con Stick (Reynolds, directing himself) wants to start a new life for himself in Miami. Lots of drug dealers and guns don't help the interest level in this dull underworld tale. Based upon the Elmore Leonard novel.
1985 (R) 109m/C Burt Reynolds, Candice Bergen, George Segal, Charles Durning, Dar Robinson; **D:** Burt Reynolds; **W:** Elmore Leonard; **M:** Stephen Dorff. VHS, Beta **$14.98** *MCA* ♂½

The Stick-Up In 1935, a young American traveling in Great Britain is introduced to some native illegal fun. Rather sorry attempt at romance/comedy/adventure. **AKA:** Mud.
1977 101m/C David Soul, Pamela McMyler; **D:** Jeffrey Bloom; **W:** Jeffrey Bloom. VHS, Beta *HHE* ♂

Stickfighter The oppressive reign of an evil Spanish ruler of the Philippines is challenged by the world's best stickfighter.
1989 (PG) 102m/C Dean Stockwell, Nancy Kwan, Alejandro Rey, Roland Dantes; **D:** Luis Nepomuceno. VHS **$59.95** *PSM* ♂

Sticky Fingers Two female musicians, asked to watch nearly a million bucks in drug money, go on a mega shopping spree. Completely incredible, unlikeable and mean-spirited attempt at zany comedy.
1988 (PG-13) 89m/C Melanie Mayron, Helen Slater, Eileen Brennan, Carol Kane, Christopher Guest, Danitra Vance, Gwen Welles, Stephen McHattie; **D:** Catlin Adams; **W:** Melanie Mayron, Catlin Adams; **M:** Gary Chang. VHS, Beta **$19.95** *MED* ♂

Stigma "Miami Vice" star Thomas (then 23; later to restore his middle name, Michael) is a young doctor who treats a syphilis epidemic in a small town. He's indistinguishable, but better than anything else here. Ever seen close-ups of advanced syphilis? Here's your chance—but it's not pretty.
1973 93m/C Philip Michael Thomas, Harlan Cary Poe; **D:** David E. Durston. Beta *NO* ♂½

Stiletto Good cast is wasted in this mediocre depiction of the trouble encountered by a contract Mafia assassin when he decides to change careers. Based on the usual pulp cheese by Harold Robbins.
1969 101m/C Alex Cord, Britt Ekland, Patrick O'Neal, Joseph Wiseman, Barbara McNair, Roy Scheider, M. Emmet Walsh; **Cameos:** Raul Julia; **D:** Bernard L. Kowalski. VHS, Beta **$59.98** *SUE* ♂½

Still Life The press has dubbed him "the Art Killer," a serial murderer who makes sculptures out of his victims. He's a sensation—and not ready to stop. This sicko's next "Still Life" may just be a struggling young musician.
1992 (PG-13) 83m/C Jason Gedrick, Jessica Steen, Stephen Shellan; **D:** Graeme Campbell; **M:** Mychael Danna. VHS **$79.95** *PSM* ♂♂

Still Not Quite Human Teenage android Chip must do battle with unscrupulous industrialists and their robot weapon Spartacus to rescue his inventor father from their deadly clutches.
1992 84m/C Alan Thicke, Christopher Neame, Betsy Palmer, Adam Philipson, Rosa Nevin, Ken Pogue, Jay Underwood; **D:** Eric Luke; **W:** Eric Luke. VHS, Beta **$39.99** *DIS* ♂♂

Still of the Night A Hitchcock-style thriller about a psychiatrist infatuated with a mysterious woman who may or may not be a killer.
1982 (PG) 91m/C Meryl Streep, Roy Scheider, Jessica Tandy, Joe Grifasi, Sara Botsford, Josef Sommer; **D:** Robert Benton; **W:** David Newman. VHS, Beta **$14.95** *MGM* ♂♂

The Stilts From modern Spanish cinema's preeminent director, this is a study of sexual dynamics revolving around a doomed love triangle. Aging professor Gomez wants young Del Sol to commit to him, but she won't; she has another, younger lover. Overwrought at times, but well acted. In Spanish with English subtitles.
1984 95m/C Laura Del Sol, Francesco Rabal, Fernando Gomez; **D:** Carlos Savrat. VHS, Beta **$24.95** *XVC, MED, ING* ♂♂♂

The Sting Newman and Redford together again in this sparkling story of a pair of con artists in 1930s Chicago. They set out to fleece a big-time racketeer, pitting brain against brawn and pistol. Very inventive, excellent acting, and Scott Joplin's wonderful ragtime music adapted by Marvin Hamlisch. The same directorial and acting team from "Butch Cassidy and the Sundance Kid" triumphs again.
1973 (PG) 129m/C Paul Newman, Robert Redford, Robert Shaw, Charles Durning, Eileen Brennan, Harold Gould, Ray Walston; **D:** George Roy Hill; **W:** David S. Ward; **M:** Marvin Hamlisch. Academy Awards '73: Best Adapted Score, Best Art Direction/Set Decoration, Best Costume Design, Best Director (Hill), Best Film Editing, Best Picture, Best Story & Screenplay; Nominations: Best Actor (Redford), Best Cinematography, Best Sound; Directors Guild of America Awards '73: Best Director (Hill); People's Choice Awards '75: Best Film. VHS, Beta **$14.95** *MCA, BTV* ♂♂♂½

The Sting 2 Complicated comic plot concludes with the final con game, involving a fixed boxing match where the stakes top a million dollars and the payoff could be murder. Lame sequel to "The Sting" (1973).
1983 (PG) 102m/C Jackie Gleason, Mac Davis, Teri Garr, Karl Malden, Oliver Reed; **D:** Jeremy Paul Kagan; **W:** David S. Ward. VHS, Beta **$19.98** *MCA* ♂½

Sting of the Dragon Masters Martial arts adventure featuring Bruce Lee's female Kung-Fu counterpart, Angela Mao.
1974 (R) 96m/C Angela Mao, Thoon Rhee, Carter Huang; **D:** Huang Feng. VHS, Beta **$19.95** *VCI* ♂

Sting of the West Journeyman con artist swindles his way across the Wild West.
1976 (PG) 90m/C Jack Palance, Timothy Brent, Lionel Stander. VHS, Beta **$59.95** *MPI* ♂

Stingray Two guys buy a Corvette, not knowing it's loaded with stolen heroin. Gangsters with an interest in the dope come after them, and the chase is on. Very violent and not all that funny.
1978 (PG) 105m/C Chris Mitchum, Sherry Jackson, Les Lannom; **D:** Richard Taylor. VHS, Beta **$14.95** *COL, SUE* ♂½

Stir Crazy Two down-on-their luck losers find themselves convicted of a robbery they didn't commit and sentenced to 120 years behind bars with a mean assortment of inmates.
1980 (R) 111m/C Richard Pryor, Gene Wilder, Nicholas Coster, Lee Purcell, Craig T. Nelson, JoBeth Williams; **D:** Sidney Poitier. VHS, Beta **$14.95** *COL* ♂♂½

Stitches Adolescent comedy about med students playing practical jokes on the dean using laboratory specimens. So bad the director (actually Rod Holcomb) allegedly did not want his name associated with it.
1985 (R) 92m/C Eddie Albert, Parker Stevenson, Geoffrey Lewis, Brian Tochi; **D:** Alan Smithee. VHS, Beta **$19.95** *MED* ♂

Stocks and Blondes The world of industrial finance is used as a background for some raunchy sex humor.
1985 (R) 79m/C VHS, Beta **$69.98** *LIV, VES* Woof!

A Stolen Face Creepy, implausible drama of a plastic surgeon, spurned by a beautiful concert pianist, who transforms a female convict to look just like her. The convict runs away, but perhaps there's hope in the future with the pianist.
1952 71m/B Paul Henreid, Lizabeth Scott, Andre Morell, Susan Stephen, John Wood; **D:** Terence Fisher; **M:** Malcolm Arnold. VHS, Beta *MLB* ♂♂

Stolen Hours Inferior remake of Bette Davis' "Dark Victory" casts Hayward as an oil-rich heiress who learns she has a fatal illness. Bring the tissues for this tearjerker. Based on the play "Dark Victory" by George Emerson Brewer, Jr. and Bertram Block.
1963 100m/C Susan Hayward, Michael Craig, Diane Baker, Edward Judd, Paul Rogers; **D:** Daniel Petrie; **W:** Jessamyn West, Joseph Hayes. VHS **$19.98** *MGM, FCT* ♂♂½

Stolen Identity A Viennese cabbie sees his American dream dashed for lack of the proper papers. When an American businessman is murdered in his cab he is quick to seize the moment...and the dead man's identity. In no time at all he finds himself involved with the widow, entangled with the murderer and under suspicion for the killing. Predictable and sluggish, the story inches its way to the foregone conclusion.
1953 81m/B Francis Lederer, Donald Buka, Joan Camden, Adrienne Gessner; **D:** Gunther Fritsch. VHS, Beta **$16.95** *SNC* ♂½

Stolen Kisses Sequel to "The 400 Blows," the story of Antoine Doinel: his unsuccessful career prospects as a detective in Paris, and his initially awkward but finally successful adventures with women. Made during Truffaut's involvement in a political crisis involving the sack of Cinematique Francais director Henri Langlois. Truffaut dedicated the film to Langlois and the Cinematique, but it is a thoroughly apolitical, small-scale, charming (some say too charming) romantic comedy, Truffaut-style. Followed by "Bed and Board." **AKA:** Baisers Voles.
1968 90m/C Jean-Pierre Leaud, Delphine Seyrig; **D:** Francois Truffaut; **M:** Antoine Duhamel. Academy Awards '68 Nominations: Best Foreign Language Film; National Board of Review Awards '69: 5 Best Foreign Films of the Year; National Society of Film Critics Awards '69: Best Director (Truffaut). VHS, Beta **$59.95** *COL* ♂♂♂½

A Stolen Life Remake of 1939 film of the same title starring Elizabeth Berguer. Oddly, Davis chose this as her first and last producing effort. Implausible tale of an evil twin (Davis) who takes her sister's (Davis) place so she can have the man they both love. Davis pulls it off as both twins; Ford is good as the hapless hubby. **1946 107m/B** Bette Davis, Glenn Ford, Dane Clark, Walter Brennan, Charlie Ruggles, Bruce (Herman Brix) Bennett, Esther Dale, Peggy Knudsen; **D:** Curtis Bernhardt. **VHS, Beta $19.95** *MGM ♫♫*

Stolen Painting A man's wife is kidnapped by an evil gang while having her portrait painted. Her husband rescues her, and they, in turn, are chased by the kidnappers. **1979 11m/C VHS, Beta** *BFA ♫ ½*

The Stone Boy A boy accidentally kills his older brother on their family's Montana farm. The family is torn apart by sadness and guilt. Sensitive look at variety of reactions during a crisis, with an excellent cast led by Duvall's crystal-clear performance. **1984 (PG) 93m/C** Glenn Close, Robert Duvall, Jason Presson, Frederic Forrest, Wilford Brimley, Linda Hamilton; **D:** Christopher Cain; **M:** James Horner. **VHS, Beta $59.98** *FOX ♫♫♫ ½*

Stone Cold Flamboyant footballer Bosworth made his acting debut in this sensitive human document, playing the usual musclebound, one-punk-army terminator cop, out to infiltrate a sadistic band of fascist biker barbarians engaged in drug running and priest shooting. Profane, lewd, gory, self-deifying; a crash course (accent on crashes) in everything despicable about modern action pics. **1991 (R) 91m/C** Brian Bosworth, Lance Henriksen, William Forsythe, Arabella Holzbog, Sam McMurray; **D:** Craig R. Baxley. **VHS, Beta, 8mm $64.99** *COL Woof!*

Stone Cold Dead Rugged cop Crenna battles crime lord Williams (Paul Williams? Yeah, sure) over a prostitution ring. Meanwhile, a sniper starts killing hookers. Unoriginal and thoroughly dull would-be thriller. **1980 (R) 100m/C** Richard Crenna, Paul Williams, Linda Sorensen, Belinda J. Montgomery; **D:** George Mendeluk. **VHS, Beta $59.95** *MED ♫ ½*

Stone Fox Heartwarming family drama in which a young man must win a dogsled race to save the family farm. Based on John Reynolds Gardiner's popular children's book. **1987 96m/C** Buddy Ebsen, Joey Cramer, Belinda J. Montgomery, Gordon Tootoosis; **D:** Harvey Hart. **VHS $14.98** *WOV ♫♫*

The Stone Killer Bronson stars as a tough plainclothes cop in this action-packed drama about a Mafia plot to use Vietnam vets in a mass killing. Violent but tense and action-packed revenge adventure set in the underworlds of New York and Los Angeles. **1973 (R) 95m/C** Charles Bronson, Martin Balsam, Norman Fell, Ralph Waite, John Ritter; **D:** Michael Winner. **VHS, Beta $59.95** *COL ♫♫ ½*

Stones of Death An aboriginal curse is invoked when a subdivision is built too close to an ancient burial site. Teenagers begin having all-too-real nightmares about death. **1988 (R) 90m/C** Tom Jennings, Natalie McCurray, Zoe Carides, Eric Oldfield; **D:** James Bagle. **VHS, Beta** *NO ♫*

The Stooge Singer Bill Miller (Martin) asks the antic Ted Rogers (Lewis) to join him in his vaudeville act, where Rogers' clowning has them on the road to success. But then Miller decides he wants to go solo. Sounds more than a little autobiographical. ♫A Girl Named Mary and a Boy Named Bill; Who's Your Little Whozis?; Just One More Chance; With My Eyes Wide Open I'm Dreaming; Louise; I'm Yours.

1951 100m/B Dean Martin, Jerry Lewis, Polly Bergen, Marion Marshall, Eddie Mayehoff, Richard Erdman, Francis Bavier; **D:** Norman Taurog; **W:** Martin Rackin, Fred Finklehoff, Elwood Ullman. **VHS $14.95** *PAR ♫♫ ½*

Stoogemania A nerd becomes so obsessed with the Three Stooges that they begin to take over his life and ruin it. Harmless except as a waste of time. Includes actual Stooge footage including some colorized—but see an old Stooges movie instead. **1985 95m/C** Josh Mostel, Melanie Chartoff, Sid Caesar; **D:** Chuck Workman. **VHS, Beta $19.95** *PAR ♫*

The Stoogephile Trivia Movie A program of trivia points, quizzes and clips about Larry, Moe, Curly and Shemp for Stooges fanatics. **1986 55m/C VHS, Beta $19.95** *MPI ♫*

Stooges Shorts Festival This collection of shorts includes "Disorder in the Court" (1936), "Sing a Song of Six Pants" (1947), and "Malice in the Palace" (1949). **194? 55m/B VHS, Beta $34.95** *HHT ♫*

The Stooges Story "The Stooges Anthology" presents a history of the comedy team, from their vaudevillian beginnings to their television resurgence in the 60s. "Disorder in the Court" finds the trio making a mockery of the United States justice system, and in "Brideless Groom," Shemp must find a bride within forty-eight hours in order to collect an inheritance. **1990 90m/B** Moe Howard, Larry Fine, Curly Howard, Shemp Howard. **VHS $9.95** *SIM ♫♫♫*

Stop Making Sense The Talking Heads perform eighteen of their best songs in this concert filmed in Los Angeles. Considered by many to be the best concert movie ever made. The band plays with incredible energy and imagination, and Demme's direction and camera work is appropriately frenzied and original. Features such Talking Heads songs as "Burning Down the House," "Psycho Killer," and "Once in a Lifetime." Band member Tina Weymouth's Tom Tom Club also performs for the audience. **1984 99m/C D:** Jonathan Demme; **Performed by:** David Byrne, Tina Weymouth, Chris Franz, Jerry Harrison. **VHS, Beta $19.95** *MVD, COL ♫♫♫ ½*

Stop! or My Mom Will Shoot Getty is an overbearing mother paying a visit to her cop son (Stallone) in Los Angeles. When mom witnesses a crime she has to stay in town longer than intended, which gives her time to meddle in her son's work and romantic lives. If Stallone wants to change his image this so-called comedy isn't the way to do it—because the joke is only on him. Viewers who rent this may find the joke is on them. **1992 (PG-13) 87m/C** Sylvester Stallone, Estelle Getty, JoBeth Williams, Roger Rees, Martin Ferrero, Gailard Sartain, Dennis Burkley; **D:** Roger Spottiswoode; **W:** William Osborne. **VHS, Beta $19.98** *MCA ♫*

Stop That Cab Sloppy crooks accidentally leave precious jewels in the back seat of a taxi, and pursue and torture the cabby who found and hid them. Rather mean-spirited, uninteresting comedy. **1951 56m/B** Sid Melton, Iris Adrian, Tom Neal. **VHS, Beta** *NO ♫ ½*

Stopover Tokyo An American intelligence agent uncovers a plot to assassinate the American ambassador while on leave in Japan. Nice location shooting and scenery; limp story and characters. Based on a novel by John P. Marquand.

1957 100m/C Robert Wagner, Joan Collins, Edmond O'Brien, Ken Scott; **D:** Richard L. Breen. **VHS, Beta $59.98** *FOX ♫♫*

The Stork Club A little song, a little dance, will Betty Hutton find romance? The actors manage to rise above the script in this silly, overdone fable. Hutton stars as the poor but spunky hatcheck girl who unwittingly saves the life of a cynical billionaire. His expressions of gratitude are less than appreciated by her G.I. beau. Done mainly as a vehicle for Hutton's promotion, so Betty's die-hard fans may find it to their liking. ♫Doctor, Lawyer, Indian Chief; Baltimore Oriole; I'm a Square in the Social Circle; If I Had a Dozen Hearts; Love Me; China Boy; In the Shade of the Old Apple Tree. **1945 98m/B** Betty Hutton, Barry Fitzgerald, Don DeFore, Robert Benchley, Bill Goodwin, Iris Adrian, Noel Neill, Andy Russell; **D:** Hal Walker. **VHS $19.95** *NOS ♫♫*

Storm Uneven thriller finds college students on a camping trip who must fight for their lives when they are confronted by killer thieves. Somewhat contrived, but interesting ending to this low-budget outing. **1987 (PG-13) 99m/C** David Palfy, Stan Kane, Harry Freedman, Lawrence Elion, Tom Schioler; **D:** David Winning. **VHS $17.95** *WAR ♫ ½*

Storm and Sorrow Molly Higgins is known as the "Spiderwoman of the Rockies" for her legendary mountain climbing abilities. Then she joins a team looking to scale the 24,000-foot peaks of Russia's Pamir Mountains. The group meets deadly hazards—both natural and those caused by the ego-driven rivalries of the group's members. A fact-based drama based on the novel by Richard Craig. **1990 96m/C** Lori Singer, Todd Allen, Steve Anderson, Jay Baker. **VHS $89.98** *WOV ♫♫*

Storm in a Teacup A reporter starts a campaign to save a sheepdog that the town magistrate has ordered killed because the owner, an old woman, is unable to pay the license tax. As the dog's fate hangs in the balance, this often humorous film provides an interesting look at British society of the 1930s. **1937 80m/B** Vivien Leigh, Rex Harrison, Cecil Parker, Sara Allgood; **D:** Victor Saville. **VHS, Beta $19.95** *NOS, BAR, DVT ♫♫ ½*

Storm Over Asia A Mongolian trapper is discovered to be descended from Genghis Khan and is made puppet emperor of a Soviet province. Beautiful and evocative. Silent masterpiece. **AKA:** The Heir to Genghis Khan. **1928 70m/B** I. Inkizhinov, Valeri Inkizhinov, A. Christiakov, A. Dedinstev, V. Tzoppi, Paulina Belinskaya; **D:** Vsevolod Pudovkin. **VHS, Beta $35.95** *IHF, FST, ING ♫♫♫♫*

Storm Over Wyoming The old sheep-and-cattle battle again; Holt and Martin find themselves haplessly embroiled in a Wyoming range war. Action-packed but thin, ordinary western. **1950 60m/B** Tim Holt, Richard Martin. **VHS, Beta $39.95** *RKO ♫♫*

Storm Rider A gunman hired to protect a group of ranchers from a powerful rancher falls in love with a local widow. After his job is done, however, he leaves her behind. Typical western fare. **1957 70m/B** Scott Brady, Mala Powers, Bill Williams, Olin Howland, William Fawcett, John Goddard; **D:** Edward L. Bernds; **W:** Edward L. Bernds; **M:** Les Baxter. **VHS** *NO ♫♫*

Stormquest Deep in the jungle, a band of women warriors live without men. When it is discovered that one of the group has a male lover, she is sentenced to death. Her man tries to rescue her, and it turns into a war of the sexes—literally. In Spanish with subtitles.
1987 90m/C Kai Baker, Brent Huff; **D:** Alex Sessa. **VHS $79.95** *MED Woof!*

Stormy Monday An American developer conspires to strike it rich in Newcastle, England real estate by resorting to violence and political manipulations. Sting plays the jazz club owner who opposes him. Slow plot, but acted and directed well; interesting photography.
1988 (R) 108m/C Melanie Griffith, Tommy Lee Jones, Sting, Sean Bean, James Cosmo, Mark Long, Brian Lewis; **D:** Mike Figgis; **W:** Mike Figgis; **M:** Mike Figgis. **VHS, Beta, 8mm** *PAR, OM* �✶½

Stormy Trails Bell battles bellicose bad guys who are after his property. At least all the gunfights should keep a viewer awake!
1936 59m/B Rex Bell. **VHS, Beta $27.95** *VCN* ✶

Stormy Waters A romantic French drama about a sea captain falling in love with a woman he rescues from a storm. He goes back to his wife, however, when she becomes critically ill. Director Gremillon insisted on realistic footage of storms at sea; production was delayed because of the difficulties of the German occupation. Dubbed. **AKA:** Remorques.
1941 75m/B Jean Gabin, Michele Morgan, Madeleine Renaud; **D:** Jean Gremillon. **VHS, Beta $24.95** *VYY, ING* ✶✶½

Stormy Weather In this cavalcade of black entertainment the plot takes a back seat to the nearly non-stop array of musical numbers, showcasing this stellar cast at their performing peak. ♫There's No Two Ways About Love; Stormy Weather; Ain't Misbehavin'; Rhythm Cocktail; Rang Tang Tang; Dat, Dot, Dah; That Ain't Right; I Can't Give You Anything But Love, Baby; Digga Digga Doo.
1943 77m/B Lena Horne, Bill Robinson, Fats Waller, Dooley Wilson, Cab Calloway, Nicholas Brothers, Katherine Dunham & Her Dance Troupe; **D:** Andrew L. Stone. **VHS, Beta $19.98** *FOX, PTB, FCT* ✶✶½

The Story Lady A retiree uses her story-telling abilities as a hostess on a public-access children's program. She becomes so popular that two network execs want to exploit her as a spokesperson for a toy company. Only a young girl can help her find a way to resist going commercial.
1993 (G) 93m/C Jessica Tandy, Lisa Jakub, Ed Begley Jr., Charles Durning, Stephanie Zimbalist; **D:** Larry Elikann. **VHS $89.95** *UNT* ✶✶½

Story of a Cowboy Angel On the Christmas Mountain Ranch, a cowboy angel descends to Earth to bestow various beneficences.
1981 90m/C Slim Pickens. **VHS, Beta $69.98** *LIV, VES* ✶

The Story of a Love Story Bates plays a writer whose imagination gets the better of him when he attempts an extramarital affair. Was he with her or not? Unusual concept doesn't stand up in the long run. Fine cast is under-utilized. **AKA:** Impossible Object.
1973 110m/C Alan Bates, Dominique Sanda, Evans Evans, Lea Massari, Michel Auclair, Laurence De Monaghan; **D:** John Frankenheimer; **W:** Alan Bates. **VHS** *NO* ✶✶½

The Story of a Three Day Pass A black American GI falls in love with a French girl he meets in peacetime Paris. With English subtitles. Made on a low budget and flawed, but poignant and impressive. **AKA:** La Permission.
1968 87m/B Harry Baird, Nicole Berger, Pierre Doris; **D:** Melvin Van Peebles; **W:** Melvin Van Peebles. **VHS, Beta $24.95** *DVT, FCT, HEG* ✶✶½

Story of Adele H. The story of Adele Hugo, daughter of Victor Hugo, whose love for an English soldier leads to obsession and finally to madness after he rejects her. Sensitive and gentle unfolding of characters and story. Beautiful photography. In French with English subtitles. **AKA:** L'Histoire d'Adele H.
1975 (PG) 97m/C Isabelle Adjani, Bruce Robinson; **D:** Francois Truffaut; **W:** Suzanne Schiffman, Jean Gruault. Academy Awards '75 Nominations: Best Actress (Adjani); National Board of Review Awards '75: 5 Best Foreign Films of the Year, Best Actress (Adjani); National Society of Film Critics Awards '75: Best Actress (Adjani). **VHS, Beta $19.98** *MGM, FCT, ING* ✶✶✶

The Story of Boys & Girls Two very different families come together for the wedding feast of their children, during which family secrets are revealed and we come to know and care for everyone present. A twenty-course meal rivals the food scenes in "Babette's Feast" and is guaranteed to make your mouth water. Fine ensemble of actors, well directed, with a vivid evocation of 1930s Italy. In Italian with English subtitles. **AKA:** Storia di Ragazzi e di Ragazze.
1991 92m/C Lucrezia Lante della Rovere, Massimo Bonetti, Davide Bechini, Enrica Maria Modugno, Valeria Bruni Tadeschi, Lina Bernardi, Anna Bonaiuto, Alessandro Haber; **D:** Pupi Avati; **W:** Pupi Avati; **M:** Riz Ortolani. **VHS $89.95** *FXL, ING* ✶✶✶

The Story of David Well-done Old Testament Bible drama about the shepherd boy who slew Goliath, overcame the Philistines, and united Israel. Then, as King David, he winds up involved in an illicit love affair with Bathsheba that threatens to destroy his kingdom. Fine acting and a literate script highlight this made for television production. On two cassettes.
1976 (PG) 192m/C Timothy Bottoms, Anthony Quayle, Jane Seymour, Keith Michell, Susan Hampshire; **D:** Alex Segal; **W:** Ernest Kinoy. **VHS $29.95** *COL* ✶✶✶

The Story of Drunken Master A drunken kung fu master? That's the premise for this film.
19?? 90m/C Yang Pan Pan, Chi Hsiao Fu. **VHS $49.95** *OCE* ✶

The Story of Fausta An unhappily married cleaning woman in the slums of Rio entices all the money and gifts she can out of an elderly widower. Decidedly grim comedy-drama, well-done but unsparing in its depiction of overwhelming greed. In Portuguese with English subtitles. **AKA:** Romance da Empregada.
1988 (R) 90m/C Betty Faria, Daniel Filho, Brandao Filho; **D:** Bruno Barreto; **M:** Ruben Blades. **VHS $79.95** *FXL, ING* ✶✶½

The Story of Jacob & Joseph Fine Biblical drama finds brothers Jacob and Esau fighting over their birthright, tearing apart their family for twenty years. When the brothers finally reconcile it's only to cast an envious eye on youngest brother Joseph, whom they sell into slavery. Taken to Egypt Joseph uses his talents to become the Pharoah's chief advisor but he can never forget his family or what was done to him. All-around good acting, directing and writing. Made for television.

1974 (R) 96m/C Keith Michell, Tony LoBianco, Julian Glover, Colleen Dewhurst, Herschel Bernardi, Harry Andrews; **D:** Michael Cacoyannis; **W:** Ernest Kinoy. **VHS $19.95** *COL* ✶✶✶

The Story of Louis Pasteur Formulaic Hollywood biopic raised a notch or two by Muni's superb portrayal of the famous scientist and his career leading up to his most famous discoveries. Acclaimed in its time; excellent despite low budget.
1936 85m/B Paul Muni, Josephine Hutchinson, Anita Louise, Fritz Leiber, Donald Woods, Porter Hall, Akim Tamiroff, Walter Kingsford; **D:** William Dieterle. Academy Awards '36: Best Actor (Muni), Best Story & Screenplay; Nominations: Best Picture; National Board of Review Awards '36: 10 Best Films of the Year. **VHS, Beta $19.98** *MGM, BTV* ✶✶✶

The Story of O A young woman's love for one man moves her to surrender herself to many men, in order to please him. Softcore porn with bondage and S&M beautified by camera work. Based on the classic Freudian-erotic novel by Pauline Reage.
1975 97m/C Corinne Clery, Anthony Steel; **D:** Just Jaeckin. **VHS, Beta $39.95** *HHE* ✶✶

The Story of O, Part 2 A sort-of sequel to the erotic classic, in which the somewhat soiled vixen takes over an American conglomerate by seducing everyone in it.
1987 107m/C Sandra Wey, Carole James. **Beta $69.98** *LIV, VES, HHE* ✶

The Story of Qui Ju A simple story, beautifully directed and acted, about a peasant woman's search for justice. The pregnant Qui Ju's husband is assaulted and injured by the head of their village. Outraged, Qui Ju slowly climbs the Chinese administrative ladder from official to higher official as she insistently seeks redress. Presents a close observance of daily life and customs with a strong female lead. Adapted from the novel "The Wan Family's Lawsuit" by Chen Yuan Bin. In Mandarin Chinese with English subtitles.
1991 (PG) 100m/C Gong Li, Lei Lao Sheng, Liu Pei Qu, Ge Zhi Jun, Ye Jun, Yang Liu Xia; **D:** Zhang Yimou; **W:** Liu Heng. Independent Spirit Aw Nominations: rds '94: Best Foreign Film; National Society of Film Critics Awards '93: Best Foreign Language Film; Venice Film Festival '92: Best Actress (Li), Best Film. **VHS** *COL* ✶✶✶

The Story of Robin Hood & His Merrie Men Well-made swashbuckler based on the English legend as Disney's second live action feature. Almost, but not quite, as memorable as the 1938 Micheal Curtiz "Adventures of Robin Hood." Curtiz's version had Errol Flynn, after all. **AKA:** The Story of Robin Hood.
1952 83m/C Richard Todd, Joan Rice, Peter Finch, Martita Hunt; **D:** Ken Annakin. **VHS, Beta $19.99** *DIS* ✶✶✶

The Story of Ruth Biblical saga of adventures of Ruth as she denounces her pagan gods and flees to Israel. Typically "epic" with overwrought performances. Alternately not too bad to downright boring.
1960 132m/C Elana Eden, Viveca Lindfors, Peggy Wood, Tom Tryon, Stuart Whitman, Jeff Morrow, Thayer David, Eduard Franz; **D:** Henry Koster. **VHS, Beta $19.98** *FOX, IGP* ✶✶

The Story of Seabiscuit The famous racing winner Seabiscuit is featured in a fluffy story of a racetrack romance. Temple is in love with a jockey (McCallister) but wants him to give up racing. Her uncle (Fitzgerald), who is Seabiscuit's trainer, has other other things in mind. **AKA:** Pride of Kentucky.
1949 93m/C Shirley Temple, Barry Fitzgerald, Lon McCallister, Rosemary DeCamp; **D:** David Butler. **VHS $19.98** *MGM, BTV* ✶✶½

Story of the Dragon How Bruce Lee developed the martial arts technique of Jeet Kune Do.
1982 93m/C Bruce Li, Hwang Jang Lee, Carter Wong, Roy Horan. **VHS, Beta** *WVE* 🐾🐾

The Story of the Late Chrysanthemum Classic drama about the son of a Kabuki actor who falls in love with a servant girl against his father's wishes. Their doomed affair is the center of the plot. Acclaimed and sensitive drama, in Japanese with English subtitles.
1939 115m/B Shotaro Hanayagi, Kakuo Mori, Kokichi Takada, Gonjuro Kawarazaki, Yoko Umemura; *D:* Kenji Mizoguchi. **VHS, Beta** $79.95 *FCT* 🐾🐾🐾½

Story of the Silent Serials Girls in Danger These two selections capture the best of more than fourteen silent serials. Featured are Swanson tied to the railroad tracks by Beery, Marsh threatened with death (or worse) in caveman times, and other classic cliffhanger situations. Narration and musical score.
197? 54m/B Gloria Swanson, Mae Marsh, Wallace Beery. **VHS, Beta** $29.98 *CCB* 🐾🐾🐾½

The Story of Vernon and Irene Castle In this, their last film together for RKO, Astaire and Rogers portray the internationally successful ballroom dancers who achieved popularity in the early 1900s. Irene Castle served as technical advisor for the film and exasperated everyone on the set by insisting that Rogers be a brunette. Still fun, vintage Fred and Ginger. 🎵Only When You're In My Arms; Missouri Waltz; Oh, You Beautiful Doll; Nights of Gladness; By the Beautiful Sea; Glow, Little Glow Worm; Destiny Waltz; Row, Row, Row; The Yama Yama Man.
1939 93m/B Fred Astaire, Ginger Rogers, Edna May Oliver, Lew Fields, Jack Perrin, Walter Brennan; *D:* H.C. Potter. **VHS, Beta** $14.98 *TTC, MED* 🐾🐾🐾

Story of William S. Hart/Sad Clowns Features William S. Hart as a cowboy in "Hell's Hinges" and "Tumbleweeds" (1925). From "The History of the Motion Picture" series.
192? 50m/B William S. Hart, Buster Keaton, Harry Langdon. **VHS, Beta** $29.98 *CCB* 🐾🐾🐾

The Story of Women Riveting factual account of a woman (Huppert) who was guillotined for performing abortions in Nazi-occupied France. In French with English subtitles. *AKA:* Une Affaire de Femmes.
1988 110m/C Isabelle Huppert, Francois Cluzet, Marie Trintignant, Nils Tavernier, Louis Ducreux; *D:* Claude Chabrol; *W:* Claude Chabrol, Colo Tavernier O'Hagan; *M:* Matthieu Chabrol. **VHS** $79.95 *NYF, ING* 🐾🐾

Storytime Classics A collection of popular fairy tales narrated by Katharine Hepburn.
1983 78m/C **VHS, Beta** *VES* 🐾🐾🐾

Storyville Love and music overcome prostitution and poverty in this turn-of-the-century New Orleans jazz drama, but tragedy prevails.
1974 (PG) 96m/C Tim Rooney, Jeannie Wilson, Butch Benit, Wayne Mack, Bond Gideon, Oley Sassone; *D:* Jack Weis. **VHS, Beta** *NO* 🐾½

Storyville Southern Gothic tale set in New Orleans about a feckless young lawyer running for a local congressional seat. Neither Cray nor his family are strong candidates for the family values vote. Cray is separated from his wife and willingly indulges in an affair with a beautiful and mysterious young woman. This leads to a blackmail plot when

he finds out his lover has been videotaping their antics. There's also a murder investigation and a host of family skeletons rattling around. Robards is fine as the crafty uncle but Spader's low-key attitude works against the story. Directorial debut of Frost.
1992 (R) 112m/C James Spader, Joanne Whalley-Kilmer, Jason Robards Jr., Charlotte Lewis, Michael Warren, Piper Laurie, Michael Parks, Chuck McCann, Woody Strode, Charles Haid; *D:* Mark Frost; *W:* Mark Frost; *M:* Carter Burwell. **VHS** $19.95 *COL* 🐾🐾

Stowaway After her missionary parents are killed in a Chinese revolution, Shirley stows away on a San Francisco-bound liner and plays cupid to a bickering couple who adopt her. 🎵Good Night, My Love; One Never Knows, Does One; You Gotta S-M-I-L-E to Be H-A-P-P-Y; I Wanna Go To the Zoo; That's What I Want For Christmas.
1936 86m/B Shirley Temple, Robert Young, Alice Faye, Eugene Pallette, Helen Westley, Arthur Treacher, Astrid Allwyn; *D:* William A. Seiter. **VHS, Beta** $19.98 *FOX* 🐾🐾🐾

Straight for the Heart Photojournalist Pierre returns to Montreal after a harrowing assignment in Nicaragua. His homecoming is less than happy when he discovers both his lovers, David and Sarah, have deserted him. Pierre takes to wandering the Montreal streets, taking pictures, hoping they will help him make some sense of his life and help him re-establish a connection with beauty and humanity. In French with English subtitles. *AKA:* A Corps Perdu.
1988 92m/C Matthias Habich, Johanne-Marie Tremblay; *D:* Lea Pool. **VHS** $79.95 *WBF* 🐾🐾

Straight Line T.S. Turner is a private investigator who goes after street gangs in order to prevent further violence in this action-packed story.
1988 95m/C Mr. T, Sean Roberge, Ron Ryan. **VHS** $49.95 *CAF, MOV* 🐾🐾

Straight Out of Brooklyn A bleak, nearly hopeless look at a struggling black family in a Brooklyn housing project. The son seeks escape through crime, his father in booze. An up-close and raw look at part of society seldom shown in mainstream film, its undeniable power is sapped by ragged production values and a loose narrative prone to melodrama. Rich (seen in a supporting role) was only 19 years old when he completed this, funded partly by PBS-TV's "American Playhouse."
1991 (R) 91m/C George T. Odis, Ann D. Sanders, Lawrence Gilliard, Mark Malone Jr., Reana E. Drummond, Barbara Sanon; *D:* Matty Rich; *W:* Matty Rich. **VHS** $14.95 *HBO, FCT, WAR* 🐾🐾

Straight Shooter An early sagebrush programmer.
1940 60m/B Tim McCoy. **VHS, Beta** $19.95 *NOS, DVT* 🐾

Straight Shootin' Ford's first major effort launched both Carey and Gibson to national fame. Prototypical western; great action, great scenery. Silent.
1917 53m/B Harry Carey Sr., Hoot Gibson, Mollie Malone; *D:* John Ford. **VHS, Beta** $16.95 *GPV, VCN, DVT* 🐾🐾½

Straight Talk Shirlee (Parton), a down-home gal from Arkansas, heads for Chicago to start life anew. She finds a job as a receptionist at WNDY radio, but is mistaken for the new radio psychologist. Her homespun advice ("Get off the cross. Somebody needs the wood.") becomes hugely popular and soon "Dr." Shirlee is the toast of the town. Parton's advice is the funniest part of this flimsy movie, but she is helped immense-

ly by Dunne and Orbach. Woods, however, is not in his element in a romantic comedy, and holds the movie down.
1992 (PG) 91m/C Dolly Parton, James Woods, Griffin Dunne, Michael Madsen, Deidre O'Connell, John Sayles, Teri Hatcher, Spalding Gray, Jerry Orbach, Philip Bosco, Charles Fleischer, Jay Thomas; *D:* Barnet Kellman; *W:* Craig Bolotin, Patricia Resnick; *M:* Brad Fiedel. **VHS, Beta** $19.99 *HPH* 🐾🐾½

Straight Time Ex-con Hoffman hits the streets for the first time in six years and finds himself again falling into a life of crime. Well-told, sobering story flopped at the box office and has never received the recognition it deserved. Convincing, realistic portrayal of a criminal. Hoffman was the original director, but gave the reins to Grosbard. Based on the novel "No Beast So Fierce" by Edward Bunker.
1978 (R) 114m/C Dustin Hoffman, Harry Dean Stanton, Gary Busey, Theresa Russell, M. Emmet Walsh, Kathy Bates; *D:* Ulu Grosbard; *W:* Jeffrey Boam, Alvin Sargent. **VHS, Beta** $19.98 *WAR* 🐾🐾🐾

Straight to Hell A wildly senseless, anachronistic western spoof about a motley, inept gang of frontier thieves. An overplayed, indiscriminating punk spaghetti oat-opera.
1987 (R) 86m/C Dennis Hopper, Joe Strummer, Elvis Costello, Grace Jones, Jim Jarmusch, Dick Rude, Courtney Love, Sy Richardson; *D:* Alex Cox. **VHS, Beta** *FOX, OM* 🐾½

Straight Up A musical f/x-ridden attempts to warn MTV-era children about drugs, but visual gimmicks often overwhelm the message. Gossett sings nicely as a cosmic sage of abstinence, who cautions a boy against substance abuse. The smartest segment lambasts cigarette and alcohol ads.
1990 75m/C Chad Allen, Louis Gossett Jr. **VHS, Beta** *RHI* 🐾½

Strait-Jacket After Crawford is released from an insane asylum where she was sent 20 years for axing her husband and his mistress, mysterious axe murders begin to occur in the neighborhood. Coincidence? Aging axist Crawford is the prime suspect, and even she cannot say for sure who's doing it. Daughter Baker is there to help her adjust. Moderately creepy grade B+ slasher is lifted somewhat by Crawford. Written by Robert Bloch ("Psycho"). Never one to miss a gimmick, director Castle arranged for the distribution of cardboard "bloody axes" to all theater patrons attending the movie.
1964 89m/B Joan Crawford, Leif Erickson, Diane Baker, George Kennedy; *D:* William Castle; *W:* Robert Bloch. **VHS, Beta** $59.95 *COL* 🐾🐾½

Stranded A group of aliens escaping interplanetary persecution land on Earth and enlist the aid of an Earth family. Solid characters make it more than sci-fi; sort of a parable of intolerance, human (and alien) goodness, etc.
1987 (PG-13) 80m/C Maureen O'Sullivan, Ione Skye, Cameron Dye; *D:* Tex Fuller. **VHS, Beta** $79.95 *COL* 🐾🐾

The Strange Affair of Uncle Harry Small-town gothic with fine acting by Sanders, an aging bachelor who plots murder when his romance is threatened by a jealous sister. A title card asks you not to reveal the 'surprise' ending—a hackneyed twist that appeased the censors but made producer Joan Harris resign in protest. Based on a play by Robert Job. Tape suffers from poor film-video transfer. *AKA:* Uncle Harry.

1945 80m/B George Sanders, Geraldine Fitzgerald, Ella Raines, Sara Allgood, Moyna MacGill, Samuel S. Hinds, Harry von Zell; *D:* Robert Siodmak. VHS **$19.98** REP, FCT ♂♂½

A Strange and Deadly Occurence Strange things start to happen to a family when they move to a house in a remote area. Made-for-television.
1974 74m/C Robert Stack, Vera Miles, L.Q. Jones, Herb Edelman; *D:* John Llewellyn Moxey. VHS, Beta **$34.95** WOV ♂♂½

Strange Awakening Traveling in France while recuperating from amnesia, Barker is trapped in a plot of fraud and theft. Confused and contrived.
1958 75m/B Lex Barker, Carole Mathews, Nora Swinburne, Richard Molinos, Peter Dyneley; *D:* Montgomery Tully. VHS **$16.95** SNC ♂

Strange Behavior In a small Midwestern town, the police chief follows the clues from a series of murders to the experimental lab of the local college. Seems there's a mad scientist involved... Grisly and creepy, but unduly ballyhooed when it appeared. Shot on location in New Zealand. *AKA:* Dead Kids; Small Town Massacre.
1981 (R) 105m/C Michael Murphy, Louise Fletcher, Dan Shor, Fiona Lewis, Arthur Dignam, Marc McClure, Scott Brady; *D:* Michael Laughlin. Beta **$59.95** COL, RHI ♂♂

Strange Brew The screen debut of the SCTV alumni's characters Doug & Bob MacKenzie, the Great White North duo. They do battle with a powerful, megalomaniacal brew master over - what else? - a case of beer. Dumb, but what did you expect? Watch it, or be a hoser.
1983 (PG) 91m/C Rick Moranis, Dave Thomas, Max von Sydow, Paul Dooley; *D:* Rick Moranis, Dave Thomas; *W:* Rick Moranis, Dave Thomas, Steve DeJarnatt; *M:* Charles Fox. VHS, Beta **$19.98** MGM ♂♂½

Strange Cargo Convicts escaping from Devil's Island are mystically entranced by a Christ-like fugitive en route to freedom. An odd, pretentious Hollywood fable waiting for a cult following. Gable and Crawford's eighth and final pairing. Adapted by Anita Loos from the book "Not Too Narrow...Not Too Deep" by Richard Sale.
1940 105m/B Clark Gable, Joan Crawford, Ian Hunter, Peter Lorre, Paul Lukas, Albert Dekker, J. Edward Bromberg, Eduardo Ciannelli, Frederick Worlock; *D:* Frank Borzage. VHS, Beta **$19.98** MGM ♂♂½

Strange Case of Dr. Jekyll & Mr. Hyde An adaptation of the classic Robert Louis Stevenson book about a scientist who conducts experiments on himself to separate good from evil. Palance is oddly but appealingly cast; Jarrott's bad direction wrecks it. Made for TV.
1968 128m/C Jack Palance, Leo Genn, Oscar Homolka, Billie Whitelaw, Denholm Elliott; *D:* Charles Jarrott. VHS, Beta **$49.95** LIV, MPI ♂♂

Strange Case of Dr. Jekyll & Mr. Hyde The Robert Louis Stevenson classic, with Hyde portrayed as an icy, well-dressed sociopath. In Shelley Duvall's "Nightmare Classics" series. More psychological than special effect-y. Made for cable.
1989 60m/C Anthony Andrews, Laura Dern, George Murdock, Nicholas Guest; *D:* Michael Lindsay-Hogg. VHS, Beta **$59.95** WAR, OM ♂♂½

The Strange Case of the End of Civilization as We Know It Cleese stars as the detective grandson of Sherlock Holmes, who also has a reputation for making a mockery of police investigations. Nevertheless, the police commissioner summons him to capture that diabolical criminal Professor Moriarty.
1993 55m/C John Cleese, Stratford Johns, Connie Booth, Arthur Lowe. VHS **$19.95** KUL, FCT, SIG ♂♂½

The Strange Countess A girl is almost murdered and no apparent motive can be found until a 20-year old murder is uncovered in this Edgar Wallace story.
1961 96m/C Joachim Fuchsberger, Lil Dagover, Marianne Hoppe, Brigitte Grothum; *D:* Josef von Baky. VHS **$16.95** SNC ♂♂

Strange Fruit Based on Lillian Smith's novel, this program tells the story of a black painter in Georgia, 1948, who faces racism. At first avoiding voter registration, he becomes involved and is killed. His death serves as an inspiration to his community.
1979 33m/C VHS, Beta LCA ♂♂

Strange Illusion Unbalanced teen Lydon believes his mother, about to remarry, was responsible for his father's death. He feigns insanity in a plan to catch her, but is sent to an asylum, where he nearly goes insane for real. Slow and implausible, but creepy enough to hold your interest. *AKA:* Out of the Night.
1945 87m/B Jimmy Lydon, Warren William, Sally Eilers, Regis Toomey, Charles Arnt, George Reed; *D:* Edgar G. Ulmer. VHS, Beta **$16.95** SNC ♂♂½

Strange Interlude Shearer is at her best in screen adaptation of talky Eugene O'Neill play in which she portrays a young wife who wants a child, but discovers that insanity runs in her husband's family. Doing the only sensible thing, she decides to have a child by another man (Gable). Interesting because the characters' thoughts are revealed to the audience through voice-overs. *AKA:* Strange Interval.
1932 110m/B Norma Shearer, Clark Gable, May Robson, Ralph Morgan, Robert Young, Mary Alden, Maureen O'Sullivan, Henry B. Walthall; *D:* Robert Z. Leonard. VHS **$19.98** MGM ♂♂½

Strange Interlude Slow PBS production of Eugene O'Neill's famous drama covering two decades of the lives and loves of an upper-class family. Excellent performances help to make up for talkiness. On two cassettes.
1990 190m/C Glenda Jackson, Jose Ferrer, David Dukes, Ken Howard, Edward Petherbridge; *D:* Herbert Wise. VHS **$29.95** FRH, TVC ♂♂½

Strange Invaders Body-snatchers-from-space sci-fi with an attitude—fun spoof of '50s alien flicks. Space folks had taken over a midwestern town in the '50s, assuming the locals' appearance and attire before returning to their ship. Seems one of them married an earthling—but divorced and moved with her half-breed daughter to New York City. So the hicksters from space arrive in Gotham wearing overalls...
1983 (PG) 94m/C Paul LeMat, Nancy Allen, Diana Scarwid, Michael Lerner, Louise Fletcher, Wallace Shawn, Fiona Lewis, Kenneth Tobey, June Lockhart, Charles Lane, Dey Young, Mark Goddard; *D:* Michael Laughlin. VHS, Beta **$79.95** VES ♂♂♂

The Strange Love of Martha Ivers Douglas is good in his screen debut as the wimpy spouse of unscrupulous Stanwyck. Stanwyck shines as the woman who must stay with Douglas because of a crime she committed long ago... Tough, dark melodrama; classic film noir.
1946 117m/B Barbara Stanwyck, Van Heflin, Kirk Douglas, Lizabeth Scott, Judith Anderson; *D:* Lewis Milestone; *M:* Miklos Rozsa. VHS, Beta **$19.95** NOS, BAR, DVT ♂♂♂

The Strange Love of Molly Louvain Unwed mother Dvorak finds herself in hiding after her criminal beau fatally shoots a police officer. She falls in love with the unsuspecting newsman (Tracy) hot on her trail. Good performance from Dvorak but the film in general lacks sparkle. Adapted from the play "Tinsel Girl" by Maurine Watkins. *AKA:* Molly Louvain.
1932 70m/B Ann Dvorak, Lee Tracy, Richard Cromwell, Guy Kibbee, Leslie Fenton, Frank McHugh, Evelyn Knapp, Charles Middleton, Mary Doran, C. Henry Gordon; *D:* Michael Curtiz; *W:* Edwin Gelsey, Brown Holmes. VHS **$19.98** MGM ♂½

Strange New World Three astronauts awake from 188 years in the fridge to find cloning has arrived. Made for TV as a pilot for a hoped-for series that might have been even worse.
1975 100m/C John Saxon, Kathleen Miller, Keene Curtis, Martine Beswick, James Olson, Catherine Bach, Richard Farnsworth, Ford Rainey; *D:* Robert Butler. VHS **$59.95** UNI ♂½

Strange Shadows in an Empty Room Sleuth Whitman wants answers about the murder of his kid sis. He beats lots of people up, and the viewer leaves the empty living room to look at the inside of the fridge, which is more interesting. *AKA:* Blazing Magnums; Shadows in an Empty Room.
1976 (R) 97m/C Stuart Whitman, John Saxon, Martin Landau, Tisa Farrow, Carole Laure, Gayle Hunnicutt; *D:* Martin Herbert. VHS, Beta **$69.95** VES ♂

Strange Tales A collection of fantasy shorts, including "Twilight Journey," "The Crystal Quest" and "The Visitant."
198? 60m/C VHS, Beta VDC ♂

Strange Tales/Ray Bradbury Theatre An anthology of thrillers based on Bradbury stories: "Banshee," "The Screaming Woman," and "The Town Where No One Got Off."
1986 (R) 86m/C Jeff Goldblum, Peter O'Toole, Drew Barrymore, Charles Martin Smith. VHS, Beta **$14.95** CNG, HBO ♂♂½

The Strange Woman Uneventful Hollywood costume drama. Lamarr stalks man after man, but never creates much excitement in spite of Ulmer's fancy camera work and intense pace.
1946 100m/B Hedy Lamarr, George Sanders, Louis Hayward, Gene Lockhart, Hillary Brooke, June Storey; *D:* Edgar G. Ulmer. VHS **$29.95** NOS, FCT ♂♂

Strange World of Coffin Joe A collection of three shocking horror episodes about a truly disgusting dollmaker who becomes tempted by his human-like creations, a balloon seller's repulsive necrophiliac impulses, and a doctor (the disguised Coffin Joe) with a sadistic gift for excruciating torture. In Spanish with English subtitles.
1968 ?m/C Jose Mojica Marins; *D:* Jose Mojica Marins. VHS **$23.00** SMW, FCT, TPV ♂

The Strangeness Miners in search of gold release a "strange" creature from far beneath the earth—eek! Made on a negative budget.
1985 90m/C Dan Lunham, Terri Berland; *D:* David Michael Hillman. VHS, Beta **$49.95** TWE Woof!

The Stranger Notably conventional for Welles, but swell entertainment nonetheless. War crimes tribunal sets Nazi thug Shayne free hoping he'll lead them to his superior, Welles. Robinson trails Shayne through Europe and South America to a small town in Connecticut. Tight suspense made on a tight budget saved Welles's directorial career.

1946 95m/B Edward G. Robinson, Loretta Young, Martha Wentworth, Konstantin Shayne, Richard Long, Orson Welles; D: Orson Welles. VHS, Beta $9.95 CNG, NOS, PSM 🎬🎬🎬½

The Stranger Corbett crash-lands on a planet an awful lot like Earth - and must stay on the run. Uneven fugitive thriller in sci-fi drag. Made for TV.
1973 100m/C Cameron Mitchell, Glenn Corbett, Sharon Acker, Lew Ayres, George Coulouris, Dean Jagger; D: Lee H. Katzin. VHS NO 🎬½

The Stranger Amnesiac car-wreck victim Bedelia begins regaining her memory, and realizes she witnessed several grisly murders. Is her shrink (Riegert) helping her remember, or keeping something from her? Good, neglected thriller.
1987 (R) 93m/C Bonnie Bedelia, Peter Riegert, Barry Primus, David Spielberg, Julio de Grazia, Celia Roth, Marcus Woinski; D: Adolfo Aristarain; W: Dan Gurskis; M: Craig Safan. VHS, Beta, 8mm $79.95 COL 🎬🎬🎬

A Stranger Among Us A missing jeweler turns up dead and more than $1 million in diamonds has disappeared. NYPD Detective Emily Eden (Griffith) is called in to solve the case, and she decides she must go undercover in a community of Hasidic Jews to find the perpetrator. She not only finds the criminal, but she also falls in love with one of the group's most devout residents. Griffith is out of her element as a tough cop with her baby voice and cutesy style, but other actors, including Thal (in his movie debut) and Sara, perform splendidly, even though they are held back by a cumbersome script that is similar in many respects to "Witness."
1992 (PG-13) 109m/C Melanie Griffith, Eric Thal, John Pankow, Tracy Pollan, Lee Richardson, Mia Sara, Jamey Sheridan; D: Sidney Lumet; W: Robert J. Avereen. VHS, Beta $94.95 HPH 🎬🎬

The Stranger and the Gunfighter The baddest spaghetti western of all time - or is it a kung fu movie? Alcoholic cowpoke Van Cleef and kung fu master Lieh pair up to find hidden treasure. There is a map, but parts are printed on the assorted fannies of various women.
1976 106m/C Patty Shepard, Lee Van Cleef, Lo Lieh; D: Anthony M. (Antonio Margheriti) Dawson. VHS, Beta $59.95 COL 🎬🎬

The Stranger from Pecos Brown fights a cheater who swindles people at poker and then uses the money to buy their mortgages. Meanwhile, his pal Hatton finds a novel way to help a robbery victim buy back his property.
1945 55m/B Johnny Mack Brown, Raymond Hatton, Kirby Grant, Christine McIntyre, Steve Clark, Kermit Maynard; D: Lambert Hillyer. VHS $19.95 DVT, HEG 🎬🎬

The Stranger from Venus "The Day the Earth Stood Still" warmed over. Venusian Dantine tells earth lady Neal he's worried about the future of her planet. Real low budget. Includes previews of coming attractions from classic sci-fi. AKA: Immediate Disaster; The Venusian.
1954 78m/C Patricia Neal, Helmut Dantine, Derek Bond. VHS, Beta $19.95 MED, MLB Woof!

Stranger in Paso Bravo A distraught drifter returns to a strange Italian town to avenge the murders of his wife and daughter years before. Dubbed.
1973 92m/C Anthony Steffen, Giulia Rubini, Eduardo Fajardo, Andriana Ambesi. VHS, Beta $57.95 UNI 🎬

Stranger in Town A young journalist looks into the murder of an American composer in a sleepy English village. He discovers blackmail and intrigue. So-so thriller.

Based on the novel "The Uninvited" by Frank Chittenden.
1957 73m/B Alex Nicol, Ann Page, Mary Laura Wood, Mona Washbourne, Charles Lloyd Pack; D: George Pollock. VHS, Beta $16.95 SNC 🎬🎬

A Stranger is Watching Rapist-murderer Torn holds his victim's 10-year-old daughter hostage, along with a New York television anchorwoman. Complicated and distasteful. Made for TV.
1982 (R) 92m/C Rip Torn, Kate Mulgrew, James Naughton; D: Sean S. Cunningham. VHS, Beta $19.98 MGM 🎬½

Stranger on the Third Floor Reporter McGuire's testimony helped convict cabbie Cook of murder, but he begins to have doubts. Odd, shadowy psycho-thriller considered by some the first film noir. The reporter comes to be suspected of the crime...and his fiancee pounds the pavement to prove him innocent. Average acting, but great camera work gives the whole a deliciously menacing feel.
1940 64m/B Peter Lorre, John McGuire, Elisha Cook Jr., Margaret Tallichet, Charles Halton; D: Boris Ingster. VHS, Beta $19.95 CCB, MED 🎬🎬🎬

Stranger than Paradise Regular guy, nerdy sidekick and Hungarian girl cousin traipse around America being bored and having fun and adventure. New York, then -- to Cleveland! The thinking person's mindless flick. Inventive, independent comedy made on quite a low budget was acclaimed at Cannes.
1984 (R) 90m/B Richard Edson, Eszter Balint, John Lurie; D: Jim Jarmusch; W: Jim Jarmusch; M: John Lurie. VHS, Beta $79.98 FOX 🎬🎬🎬

The Stranger Who Looks Like Me Adoptees Baxter and Bridges set out to find their real parents. Not-bad TV fare. Blake is Baxter's real-life mom. Look for a young Patrick Duffy.
1974 74m/C Meredith Baxter Birney, Beau Bridges, Whitney Blake; D: Larry Peerce. VHS, Beta $29.95 WOV 🎬🎬

The Stranger Within Made-for-TV "Rosemary's Baby" rip-off. Eden is in a family way, though hubby Grizzard is impotent. The stranger within begins commanding her to do its bidding, just as if she were a genie.
1974 74m/C Barbara Eden, George Grizzard, Joyce Van Patten, Nehemiah Persoff; D: Lee Philips; M: Charles Fox. VHS, Beta $49.95 LIV 🎬½

The Stranger Wore a Gun Hoping to remove a black mark against his name, Jeff Travis (Scott) goes to Arizona and ends up helping a stagecoach robbery. Features a great action sequence in a burning saloon. Originally shot in 3-D, this is based on the novel "Yankee Gold" by John M. Cunningham.
1953 83m/C Randolph Scott, Claire Trevor, Joan Weldon, George Macready, Alfonso Bedoya, Lee Marvin, Ernest Borgnine, Pierre Watkin, Joseph Vitale; D: Andre de Toth. VHS $19.95 COL 🎬🎬

Strangers Australian horror film revolves around a man in a troubled marriage who fools around with another woman, only to realize she is dead set on mating for life. When he hesitates, she vows to murder his wife. Very similar to the smash hit "Fatal Attraction."
1990 83m/C James Healey, Anne Looby; D: Craig Lahiff. VHS NO 🎬🎬

Strangers Features three provocative vignettes that take place far from home. Fiorentino, Chen, and Hutton each star in an erotic story played out in a foreign land.

1991 (R) 85m/C Linda Fiorentino, Joan Chen, Timothy Hutton; D: Joan Tewkesbury. VHS $89.98 PSM 🎬🎬

Stranger's Gold A mysterious gunslinger eliminates corruption in a western mining town.
1971 90m/C John Garko, Antonio Vilar, Daniela Giordano. VHS, Beta $19.95 GEM 🎬

Strangers in Good Company A loving metaphor to growing older. Director Scott uses non-actors for every role in this quiet little film about a bus-load of elderly women lost in the Canadian wilderness. They wait for rescue without hystrionics, using the opportunity instead to get to know each other and nature. Beautifully made, intelligent, uncommon and worthwhile. AKA: The Company of Strangers.
1991 (PG) 101m/C Alice Diabo, Mary Meigs, Cissy Meddings, Beth Webber, Winifred Holden, Constance Garneau, Catherine Roche, Michelle Sweeney; D: Cynthia Scott; W: Cynthia Scott, David Wilson, Gloria Demers, Sally Bochner; M: Marie Bernard. VHS, Beta $94.95 TOU 🎬🎬🎬

Strangers in Paradise A scientist who had cryogenically frozen himself to escape the Nazis is thawed out in the present, and his powers are used by a delinquent-obsessed sociopath.
1986 81m/C D: Ulli Lommel; W: Ulli Lommel. VHS, Beta $69.98 LIV, VES 🎬½

Strangers in the City Puerto Ricans newly arrived in New York try to make their way. Serious but slightly overwrought immigrant-family melodrama.
1962 80m/B Robert Gentile, Camilo Delgado, Rosita De Triana; D: Rick Carrier. VHS, Beta $59.98 NLC 🎬🎬

Strangers Kiss Circa 1955: Hollywood director encourages his two leads to have an off-screen romance to bring reality to his film. Conflict arises when the leading lady's boyfriend, the film's financier, gets wind of the scheme. Intriguing, fun, slightly off-center. Based on Stanley Kubrick's film "Killer Kiss."
1983 (R) 93m/C Peter Coyote, Victoria Tennant, Blaine Novak, Dan Shor, Richard Romanus, Linda Kerridge, Carlos Palomino; D: Matthew Chapman; W: Blaine Novak, Matthew Chapman. VHS, Beta $69.99 CNG 🎬🎬½

Strangers of the Evening In its day this dark comedy/mystery caught flak for its gruesomeness. There's been a mixup at the undertaker's, and the wrong body was buried— possibly alive. Good photography and acting make the humor work, intentionally or not. Based on the novel "The Illustrious Corpse," by Tiffany Thayer.
1932 70m/B ZaSu Pitts, Eugene Pallette, Lucien Littlefield, Tully Marshall, Miriam Seegar, Theodore von Eltz; D: H. Bruce Humberstone. VHS $12.95 SNC, NOS 🎬🎬

Strangers on a Train Long before there was "Throw Momma from the Train," there was this Hitchcock super-thriller about two passengers who accidentally meet and plan to "trade" murders. Amoral Walker wants the exchange and the money he'll inherit by his father's death; Granger would love to end his stifling marriage and wed Roman, a senator's daughter, but finds the idea ultimately sickening. What happens is pure Hitchcock. Screenplay co-written by murder-mystery great Raymond Chandler. Patricia Hitchcock, the director's only child, plays Roman's sister. The concluding "carousel" scene is a masterpiece. From the novel by Patricia Highsmith.
1951 101m/B Farley Granger, Robert Walker, Ruth Roman, Leo G. Carroll, Patricia Hitchcock, Marion Lorne; D: Alfred Hitchcock; W: Raymond Chandler; M: Dimitri Tiomkin. Academy Awards

'51 Nominations: Best Black and White Cinematography; National Board of Review Awards '51: 10 Best Films of the Year. **VHS, Beta $19.98** WAR, MLB ✂✂✂

Strangers: The Story of a Mother and Daughter Rowlands is the long-estranged daughter of Davis, who won an Emmy for her portrayal of the embittered widow. The great actress truly is at her recent best in this made-for-TV tearjerker, and Rowlands keeps pace.
1979 88m/C Bette Davis, Gena Rowlands, Ford Rainey, Donald Moffatt; **D:** Milton Katselas. **VHS, Beta $69.95** TLF ✂✂✂

Strangers When We Meet A married architect and his equally married neighbor begin an affair. Their lives become a series of deceptions. Lavish but uninvolving soaper. Written by Evan Hunter and based on his novel.
1960 117m/B Kirk Douglas, Kim Novak, Ernie Kovacs, Walter Matthau, Barbara Rush, Virginia Bruce, Kent Smith; **D:** Richard Quine. **VHS, Beta $19.95** COL ✂✂ ½

The Strangler A confused, mother-fixated psychopath strangles young women. Made at the time the Boston Strangler was terrorizing Beantown. The film slayer strangles ten lasses before his love of dolls gives him away.
1964 89m/B Victor Buono, David McLean, Diane Sayer, Ellen Corby, Jeanne Bates, James B. Sikking; **D:** Burt Topper. **VHS, Beta $14.98** FXV, FOX, FCT ✂ ½

Strangler of Blackmoor Castle Someone is murdering people at an old English castle and Scotland Yard sends an investigator to track down the killer.
1963 ?m/C Karin Dor, Ingmar Zeisberg. **VHS $16.95** SNC ✂✂

Strangler of the Swamp The ghost of an innocent man wrongly hanged for murder returns to terrorize the village where he was lynched. Decidedly B-grade horror features an out-of-focus ghost and Edwards—on the other side of the camera—as one of his would-be victims.
1946 60m/B Rosemary La Planche, Blake Edwards, Charles Middleton, Robert Barratt; **D:** Frank Wisbar. **VHS, Beta $14.95** COL ✂ ½

Strangler of the Tower Edgar Wallace thriller made in Germany.
1964 ?m/C VHS NO ✂ ½

Strapless Just-turned-40 American doctor Brown lives and works in London. She has just ended a long-term romance, and takes up with suave foreigner Ganz. Her young sister Fonda arrives for a visit. Good, interesting if sometimes plodding story of adult relationships.
1990 (R) 99m/C Blair Brown, Bridget Fonda, Bruno Ganz, Alan Howard, Michael Gough, Hugh Laurie, Suzanne Burden, Camille Coduri, Alexandra Pigg, Billy Roch, Gary O'Brien; **D:** David Hare; **W:** David Hare; **M:** Nick Bicat. **VHS, Beta $79.95** COL ✂✂ ½

Strapped Earnest urban drama about a young man who needs quick cash and turns to selling guns to get it. ("Strapped" in street lingo means both carrying a gun and needing money.) Diquan's (Woodbine) pregnant girlfriend is in jail for selling crack and he doesn't have the bail money. So he and a partner begin selling guns but it turns out Diquan has also cut a deal with the cops and the deal doesn't stay a secret for long. Whitaker's directorial debut. Made for cable television.
1993 102m/C Bokeem Woodbine, Kia Joy Goodwin, Fred "Fredro" Scruggs, Michael Biehn, Craig Wasson; **D:** Forest Whitaker; **W:** Dena Kleiman. **VHS** HBO ✂✂ ½

Strategic Air Command A classic post-WWII chunk of Air Force patriotism. Veteran third baseman Stewart is recalled to flight duty at the hint of a nuclear war. He's already put in his time in the Big One and thinks he's being singled out now, but he answers his Uncle Sam's call. Allyson plays Stewart's wife for the third time.
1955 114m/C James Stewart, June Allyson, Frank Lovejoy, Barry Sullivan; **D:** Anthony Mann. **VHS, Beta $14.95** PAR ✂✂ ½

The Stratton Story Stewart and Allyson teamed up for the first of the three pictures they'd make together in this true story of Monty Stratton, the Chicago White Sox pitcher. A baseball phenom, Stratton suffers a devastating hunting accident which leads to the amputation of one leg. Learning to walk with an artificial limb, Stratton also struggles to resume his baseball career. Stewart's fine as always, with Allyson lending noble support as the loving wife. Chisox manager Jimmy Dykes played himself as did pitcher Gene Bearden, lending further authenticity to an excellent production.
1949 106m/B James Stewart, June Allyson, Frank Morgan, Agnes Moorehead, Bill Williams, Bruce Cowling; **D:** Sam Wood; **W:** Guy Trosper, Douglas Morrow. **VHS, Beta $19.98** MGM, FCT, BTV ✂✂✂

Straw Dogs An American mathematician, disturbed by the predominance of violence in American society, moves with his wife to an isolated Cornish village. He finds that primitive savagery exists beneath the most peaceful surface. After his wife is raped, Hoffman's character seeks revenge. Hoffman is good, a little too wimpy at times. A violent, frightening film reaction to the violence of the 1960s.
1972 (R) 118m/C Dustin Hoffman, Susan George, Peter Vaughan, T.P. McKenna, David Warner; **D:** Sam Peckinpah; **W:** David Zelag Goodman. **VHS, Beta $59.98** FOX ✂✂✂

Strawberry Blonde A romantic comedy set in the 1890s, with Cagney as a would-be dentist infatuated with money-grubbing Hayworth (the strawberry blonde of the title), who wonders years later whether he married the right woman (chestnut brunette de Havilland). Attractive period piece remade from 1933's "One Sunday Afternoon," and revived yet again in 1948 by Raoul Walsh.
1941 100m/B James Cagney, Olivia de Havilland, Rita Hayworth, Alan Hale, George Tobias, Jack Carson, Una O'Connor, George Reeves; **D:** Raoul Walsh; **W:** Julius J. Epstein, Philip C. Epstein. **VHS, Beta $19.98** MGM ✂✂✂

Strawberry Roan Maynard plays a stubborn rodeo cowboy, out to prove he ain't whipped yet. One of Maynard's most popular films. Gene Autry bought the story to help him out in later years; the 1948 Autry "remake" uses only the title.
1933 59m/B Ken Maynard, Ruth Hall; **D:** Ken Maynard. **VHS $19.95** NOS, DVT, HEG ✂✂

The Strawberry Statement Dated message film about a campus radical who persuades a college student to take part in the student strikes on campus during the '60s. Ambitious anti-violence message is lost in too many subplots. Soundtrack features songs by Crosby, Stills, Nash and Young and John Lennon.
1970 (R) 109m/C Kim Darby, Bruce Davison, Bud Cort, James Coco, Kristina Holland, Bob Balaban, David Dukes, Jeannie Berlin; **D:** Stuart Hagmann; **W:** Israel Horovitz. **VHS, Beta $69.95** MGM ✂✂

Stray Dog A tense, early genre piece by Kurosawa, about a police detective who has his revolver picked from his pocket on a bus, and realizes soon after it's being used in a

series of murders. Technically somewhat flawed, but tense and intense. Mifune's pursuit of the criminal with his gun becomes metaphorically compelling. In Japanese with English subtitles.
1949 122m/B Toshiro Mifune, Takashi Shimura, Isao Kimura; **D:** Akira Kurosawa. **VHS, Beta $24.95** ING, COL ✂✂✂

Strays Here kitty kitty! A young couple move into their dream home, convinced it is the perfect place to raise their daughter. What they don't know is that the area is populated by a pack of wild cats. Before they can get rid of the kitties, one has marked their bedroom as his territory and they find themselves battling a swarm of mean kitties during a bad storm.
1991 (R) 83m/C Kathleen Quinlan, Timothy Busfield, Claudia Christian; **D:** John McPherson; **W:** Shaun Cassidy. **VHS $79.98** MCA ✂✂

Streamers Six young soldiers in a claustrophobic army barracks tensely await the orders that will send them to Vietnam. Written by Rabe from his play. Well acted but downbeat and drawn out.
1983 118m/C Matthew Modine, Michael Wright, Mitchell Lichtenstein, George Dzundza; **D:** Robert Altman; **W:** David Rabe. **VHS, Beta $69.95** MED, IME, FCT ✂✂

The Street A dark classic of German Kammerspiel film, notable for its expressionist treatment of Paris street life. A middle-aged man decides to abandon his wife and job to see what excitement he can find. He is duped by a prostitute, accused of murder, imprisoned, and nearly commits suicide before being rescued. Silent.
1923 87m/B D: Karl Grune; **W:** Karl Grune. **VHS, Beta $24.95** VYY, ING ✂✂ ½

Street Asylum Real-life Watergate spook Liddy is pathetically bad as an evil genius who cooks up a scheme to rid the streets of deadbeats and scumbags by implanting cops with a gizmo that makes them kill. Also available in a 94-minute unrated version.
1990 (R) 94m/C Wings Hauser, Alex Cord, Roberta Vasquez, G. Gordon Liddy, Marie Chambers, Sy Richardson, Jesse Doran, Jesse Aragon, Brion James; **D:** Gregory Brown. **VHS, Beta** NO ✂

Street Crimes A street-wise cop convinces gang members to put down their weapons and settle their grudges in the boxing ring. But when a gang leader starts shooting down the police and civilians, the cop and his young partner must work together to keep the neighborhood safe.
1992 (R) ?m/C Dennis Farina, Max Gail, Mike Worth; **D:** Stephen Smoke; **W:** Stephen Smoke; **M:** John Gonzalez. **VHS $89.95** PMH ✂✂

The Street Fighter's Last Revenge The theft of a formula for synthetic heroin brings martial artist Sonny Chiba to the rescue. Lots of action, not much acting.
1979 (R) 80m/C Sonny Chiba, Sue Shiomi; **D:** Sakae Ozawa. **VHS $49.98** VCI ✂

Street Girls A father enters the world of urban drugs and prostitution to find his runaway daughter.
1975 (R) 77m/C Carol Case, Christine Souder, Paul Pompian; **D:** Michael Miller. **VHS, Beta $59.98** NLC ✂

Street Hawk A government agent operates an experimental, crime-fighting motorcycle in battling against a high-powered drug smuggling ring.
1984 60m/C Rex Smith, Jayne Modean, Richard Venture, Christopher Lloyd. **VHS, Beta $39.95** MCA ✂

Street Hero A young thug is torn between familial common sense and Mafia connections.
1984 102m/C Vince Colosimo, Sigrid Thornton, Sandy Gore. VHS, Beta $69.98 LIV, VES Woof!

Street Hitz Two brothers in the South Bronx find their family loyalties tested. Joey wants to finish college and get away from the violence in the streets while his brother Junior turns to the gangs to survive.
1992 92m/C Angelo Lopez, Melvin Muza, Lyota Ramirez; D: Joseph P. Vasquez. VHS $89.95 AIP ℤ½

Street Hunter Former cop turned freelance fighter quit the force when his integrity was questioned, but he still helps out now and then. Scumbag drug dealers line up a thug to waste him; epic kung fu battle ensues.
1990 (R) 120m/C Steve James, Reb Brown, John Leguizamo, Valarie Pettiford, Frank Vincent, Richie Havens; D: John A. Gallagher. VHS $79.95 COL Woof!

Street Justice Over-complex tale of a CIA agent on the lam. Returning from years of Russian imprisonment, Ontkean finds his wife remarried, his daughter grown and both battling the corrupt town government. Good performances can't help the confusion of too many characters too flatly developed.
1989 94m/C Michael Ontkean, Joanna Kerns, Catherine Bach, J.D. Cannon, Jeanette Nolan, Richard Cox, William Windom; D: Richard Sarafian. VHS, Beta $19.98 WAR ℤ½

Street Knight Gang warfare in L.A. in a routine actioner. Jake is an ex-cop who gets drawn into a battle between two rival gangs when their truce is broken by mysterious murders on both sides. Seems there's an unsuspected third party involved—a paramilitary band of professional killers that want the gang violence to divert police interest from their own nefarious operations.
1993 (R) 88m/C Jeff Speakman, Christopher Neame, Lewis Van Bergen, Bernie Casey, Jennifer Gatti, Richard Coca; D: Albert Magnoli. VHS, Beta $89.95 WAR, CAN ℤℤ

Street Law Vivid and violent study of one man's frustrated war on crime.
1979 (R) 77m/C Franco Nero, Barbara Bach, Reno Palmer. VHS, Beta NO ℤ

Street Music The elderly people living in an old hotel join forces with a young couple to organize a protest that may save their building. Well-directed urban comedy-drama; good location shooting in San Francisco's Tenderloin.
1981 88m/C Larry Breeding, Elizabeth Daily, Ned Glass; D: Jenny Bowen. VHS, Beta $69.98 LIV, VES ℤℤ½

Street of Forgotten Women Hollywood, in one of its periodic morality binges, came up with this purported expose on prostitution. An innocent girl is seduced and brutalized by a theatrical agent and eventually finds herself walking the pavement for less than moral purposes. Lots of shots of scantily clad showgirls and our heroine in her undies.
1925 55m/B VHS $16.95 SNC, VYY ℤ

Street of Shame A portrayal of the abused lives of six Tokyo prostitutes. Typically sensitive to the roles and needs of women and critical of the society that exploits them, Mizoguchi creates a quiet, inclusive coda to his life's work in world cinema. Kyo is splendid as a hardened hooker and has a memorable scene with her father. Kogure is also good. The great director's last finished work was instrumental in the outlaw-

ing of prostitution in Japan. In Japanese with English subtitles.
1956 88m/B Machiko Kyo, Aiko Mimasu; D: Kenji Mizoguchi. VHS, Beta $29.98 SUE, ING, NLC ℤℤℤ½

Street People Gratuitous car chases and violence do not a movie make, as in this case in point. Utter woofer has Brit Moore cast as a mafiosa. Yeah, right.
1976 (R) 92m/C Roger Moore, Stacy Keach, Ivo Garrani, Ettore Manni; D: Maurizio Lucidi. VHS, Beta $29.98 LIV, VES Woof!

Street Scene Life in a grimy New York tenement district, circa 1930. Audiences nationwide ate it up when Elmer Rice adapted his own Pulitzer Prize-winning play and top helmsman Vidor gave it direction.
1931 80m/B Sylvia Sidney, William Collier Jr., Estelle Taylor, Beulah Bondi, David Landau; D: King Vidor; M: Alfred Newman. VHS, Beta, 8mm $19.95 NOS, HHT, CAB ℤℤℤ

Street Smart Reeve was blah as Superman (let's be frank), and he's blah here as a desperate New York freelance writer who fakes a dramatic story about prostitution. When his deception returns to haunt him, he's in trouble with pimps and murderers, as well as the D.A. Freeman and Baker are both superb. Based on screenwriter David Freeman's own experience with "New York" magazine.
1987 (R) 97m/C Christopher Reeve, Morgan Freeman, Kathy Baker, Mimi Rogers, Andre Gregory, Jay Patterson, Anna Maria Horsford; D: Jerry Schatzberg; W: David Freeman; M: Miles Davis. Academy Awards '87 Nominations: Best Supporting Actor (Freeman); Independent Spirit Awards '88: Best Supporting Actor (Freeman). VHS, Beta $19.95 MED, IME ℤℤ½

Street Soldiers Martial artists are out to take back the streets from the punks and scum who now rule them.
1991 (R) 98m/C Jun Chong, Jeff Rector, David Homb, Jonathan Gorman, Joon Kim, Katherine Armstrong, Joel Weiss; D: Lee Harry. VHS, Beta $19.95 ACA ℤ½

Street Trash In Brooklyn, a strange poisonous liquor is being sold cheap to bums, making them melt and explode. A gross, cheap, tongue-in-cheek shocker from the makers of "The Toxic Avenger."
1987 91m/C R.L. Ryan, Vic Noto, Miriam Zucker, Bill Chepil, Mike Lackey; D: Jim Muro. VHS, Beta $79.98 LIV Woof!

Street War A cop pursues the Mob in the name of revenge as well as duty.
197? 90m/C James Mason, Cyril Cusack, Raymond Pellegrin. VHS, Beta NO ℤ

Street Warriors Ostensibly "serious" look at juvenile crime. Actually miserable, exploitative, offensive junk.
1987 105m/C Christa Leem, Nadia Windell, Victor Petit, Francisco (Frank) Brana; D: Jose Antonio De La Loma. VHS, Beta NO Woof!

Street Warriors, Part 2 Even worse than its predecessor, and that's saying something. Horrible dubbing from Spanish would be laughable, if the rapes weren't so graphic.
1987 105m/C Angel Fernandez, Paul Ramirez, Teresa Giminez, Veronica Miriel, Conrad Tortosa; D: Jose Antonio De La Loma. VHS, Beta NO Woof!

The Street with No Name In followup to "Kiss of Death," Widmark confirms rep as one disturbed guy playing psychotic career criminal whose life is grisly trail of murder and brutality.
1948 93m/B Mark Stevens, Richard Widmark, Lloyd Nolan, Barbara Lawrence, Ed Begley Sr., Donald Buka, Joseph Pevney; D: William Keighley. VHS $19.98 FOX, FCT ℤℤℤ

A Streetcar Named Desire Powerful film version of Tennessee Williams' play about a neurotic southern belle with a hidden past who comes to visit her sister and is abused and driven mad by her brutal brother-in-law. Grim New Orleans setting for terrific performances by all, with Malden, Leigh, and Hunter winning Oscars, and Brando making highest impact on audiences. Brando disliked the role, despite the great impact it had on his career. Remade for television in 1984.
1951 (PG) 122m/B Vivien Leigh, Marlon Brando, Kim Hunter, Karl Malden; D: Elia Kazan; W: Tennessee Williams; M: Alex North. Academy Awards '51: Best Actress (Leigh), Best Art Direction/Set Decoration (B & W), Best Supporting Actor (Malden), Best Supporting Actress (Hunter); Nominations: Best Actor (Brando), Best Director (Kazan), Best Picture; Academy Awards '51: Best Black and White Cinematography, Best Costume Design (B & W), Best Screenplay, Best Sound, Best Original Score; Golden Globe Awards '52: Best Supporting Actress (Hunter); National Board of Review Awards '51: 10 Best Films of the Year; New York Film Critics Awards '51: Best Actress (Leigh), Best Director (Kazan), Best Film. VHS, Beta $19.98 FOX, WAR, BTV ℤℤℤℤ

A Streetcar Named Desire Excellent made for television adaptation of the Tennessee Williams drama about fading southern belle Blanche du Bois (Ann-Margret in a terrific performance). D'Angelo is her plain sister Stella who lives with brutish husband Stanley (Williams) in the seamy French Quarter of New Orleans. Can't surpass the original but this version does have the advantage of not having to soft-pedal the drama for the fifties censors.
1984 94m/C Ann-Margret, Beverly D'Angelo, Treat Williams, Randy Quaid, Rafael Campos, Erica Yohn; D: John Erman; M: Marvin Hamlisch. VHS $9.98 FCT ℤℤℤ

Streetfight Semi-animated racist exploitation from the creator of "Fritz the Cat." Features some superb animation. AKA: Coonskin.
1975 (R) 89m/C Philip Michael Thomas, Scatman Crothers; D: Ralph Bakshi. VHS, Beta $29.95 ACA, WTA ℤ½

Streets Applegate (of Fox TV's "Married...With Children") is believable as an illiterate runaway teen. Good drama set in Venice, California about life on the streets is flawed by near-gratuitous pairing with story of a crazy prostitute-killing cop.
1990 (R) 90m/C Christina Applegate, David Mendenhall, Eb Lottimer; D: Katt Shea Ruben, Andy Ruben; W: Andy Ruben. VHS, Beta $89.99 MGM ℤℤ

Streets of Fire A soldier of fortune rescues his ex-girlfriend, now a famous rock singer, after she's been kidnapped by a malicious motorcycle gang. Violently energetic in its insistent barrage of imagery. Director Hill's never-never land establishes a retro-futuristic feel and is beautifully photographed, however vacuous the ending may be.
1984 93m/C Michael Pare, Diane Lane, Rick Moranis, Amy Madigan, Willem Dafoe, Deborah Van Valkenburgh, Richard Lawson, Rick Rossovich, Bill Paxton, Lee Ving, Stoney Jackson, Robert Townsend, Grand Bush, Mykel T. Williamson, Elizabeth Daily, Lynne Thigpen, Marine Jahan, Ed Begley Jr., John Dennis Johnston, Olivia Brown; D: Walter Hill; W: Walter Hill, Larry Gross; M: Ry Cooder. VHS, Beta $14.98 MCA ℤℤ½

Streets of Gold Brandauer is good as a Soviet boxer who defected and now washes dishes in Brooklyn. He trains a pair of street youngsters in the hope of beating his old coach in the Olympics. "Rocky"-like in the boxing, and in the rags-to-riches optimism. **1986 (R) 94m/C** Klaus Maria Brandauer, Adrian Pasdar, Wesley Snipes; **D:** Joe Roth; **W:** Richard Price, Heywood Gould; **M:** Jack Nitzsche. **VHS, Beta** $79.98 LIV, VES 🎬🎬½

The Streets of L.A. A frustrated middle-aged woman teaches some punks from an L.A. barrio a thing or two about pride and motivation when she demands reimbursement for the tires they slashed. Without thoroughly professional Woodward to carry it, there would not be much of a movie. Woodward's character is resourceful, and so is the actress. Made for TV. **1979 94m/C** Joanne Woodward, Robert Webber, Michael C. Gwynne; **D:** Jerrold Freedman. **VHS, Beta** NO 🎬🎬½

The Streets of San Francisco The pilot that spawned the popular TV series. A streetwise old cop and his young college-boy partner (who else but Malden and Douglas as Stone and Keller) investigate the murder of a young woman. Adapted from "Poor, Poor Ophelia" by Carolyn Weston. **1972 120m/C** Karl Malden, Robert Wagner, Michael Douglas, Andrew Duggan, Tom Bosley, Kim Darby, Mako; **D:** Walter Grauman. **VHS, Beta** $14.99 GKK 🎬🎬🎬

Streets of Sin Written and produced by movie star Lupino, this morality play tells the story of a naive girl's tribulations when she becomes infatuated with a musician and allows herself to become pregnant by him. Shunned by the musician, she enters a home for unwed mothers to sort out her life and feelings for a crippled veteran who wants to marry her. **AKA:** Not Wanted. **1949 91m/B** Sally Forrest, Keefe Brasselle, Leonard Penn, Dorothy Adams, Rita Lupino; **D:** Elmer Clifton; **W:** Ida Lupino. **VHS** $19.95 NOS 🎬🎬½

Streetwalkin' Life in the Big Apple isn't always rosy for a brother and sister who must contend with prostitutes, drug dealers, and tough cops. She turns to prostitution to get by. Miserable, exploitative trash. **1985 (R) 86m/C** Melissa Leo, Dale Midkiff, Leon Robinson, Julie Newmar, Randall Batinkoff, Annie Golden, Antonio Fargas; **D:** Joan Freeman. **VHS, Beta** $79.98 LIV, VES 🎬

Streetwise Eye-opening and candid documentary inspired by a "Life" magazine article. Frank and honest look at homeless children making a living on the streets. Seattle provides the backdrop to the story as the filmmakers hang around with the kids, earning their trust, and receive the truth from them. Cruel, funny, enraging, but always sobering look into a population of homeless in America. A deservedly acclaimed, terrifying vision of urban America. **1985 92m/C D:** Martin Bell; **M:** Tom Waits. **VHS, Beta** $19.95 NWV 🎬🎬🎬½

Strictly Ballroom Offbeat, cheerfully tacky dance/romance amusingly turns every movie cliche slightly askew. Scott (Mercurio) has been in training for the Pan-Pacific ballroom championships since the age of six. While talented, he also refuses to follow convention and scandalizes the stuffy dance establishment with his new steps. When his longtime partner leaves him, Scott takes up with a love-struck beginner (Morice), with some surprises of her own. Ballet dancer Mercurio (in his film debut) is appropriately arrogant yet vulnerable, with Morice as the plain Jane turned steel butterfly. Wonderful supporting cast; great debut for director Luhrmann.

1992 (PG) 94m/C Paul Mercurio, Tara Morice, Bill Hunter, Pat Thomsen, Barry Otto, Gia Carides, Peter Whitford, John Hannan, Sonia Kruger-Tayler, Kris McQuade, Pip Mushin, Leonie Page, Antonio Vargas, Armonia Benedito; **D:** Baz Luhrmann; **W:** Craig Pearce, Baz Luhrmann; **M:** David Hershfelder. Golden Globe Awards Nominations: s 94: Best Film—Musical/Comedy; Australian Film Institute '92: Best Costume Design, Best Director (Luhrmann), Best Film, Best Supporting Actor (Otto), Best Supporting Actress (Thomsen), Best Writing. **VHS** $96.03 MAX, TOU, BTV 🎬🎬🎬½

Strictly Business An upwardly mobile black broker has his career aspirations in order until he meets a beautiful club promoter who finds him square and boring. Wanting to impress her he asks the advice of a young man who works in the mail room for the proper way to dress and talk. A low-rent Pygmalion story. **1991 (PG-13) 83m/C** Halle Berry, Tommy Davidson, Joseph C. Phillips; **D:** Kevin Hooks; **M:** Michel Colombier. **VHS** $94.99 WAR, FCT 🎬🎬½

Strictly G.I. A collection of war-time patriotic shorts, including "All Star Bond Rally." The support and perception of WWII is historically intriguing. **1944 45m/B** Bing Crosby, Frank Sinatra, Betty Grable, Judy Garland, Harpo Marx, Harry James, Bob Hope, Jerry Colonna. **VHS, Beta** $19.95 NOS, DVT, HEG 🎬½

Strike Eisenstein's debut, and a silent classic. Stirring look at a 1912 clash between striking factory workers and Czarist troops. **1924 78m/B D:** Sergei Eisenstein. **VHS, Beta** $24.95 NOS, KIV, IHF 🎬🎬🎬½

Strike a Pose Erotic thriller finds international model-turned-fashion photographer Miranda Cross, her boyfriend LAPD detective Nick Carter, and Miranda's model friends stalked by a revenge-minded killer. Also available in an unrated version. **1993 (R) ?m/C** Margie Peterson, Robert Eastwick, Michelle LaMothe; **D:** Dean Hamilton. **VHS** $89.95 PMH 🎬½

Strike Back A convict escapes from prison to find the girl he loves, and is hounded by the police and the mob. **1980 89m/C** Dave Balko, Brigette Wollner; **D:** Carl Schenkel. **VHS, Beta** $69.98 LIV, VES 🎬🎬

Strike Commando Cheap, exploitative ripoff of the expensive, exploitative megaaction thriller "Rambo." Sleepwalking actors; horrible, overwrought script. **1987 (R) 92m/C** Reb Brown, Christopher Connelly, Locs Kamme; **D:** Vincent Dawn. **VHS, Beta** NO Woof!

Strike Force A New York City cop, a Federal agent and a state trooper work together to battle a large drug ring. Failed made-for-TV pilot. Early Gere appearance; not related to later Robert Stack film with the same title. **AKA:** Crack. **1975 74m/C** Cliff Gorman, Richard Gere, Donald Blakely; **D:** Barry Shear. **VHS, Beta** $24.95 VMK 🎬

Strike Force The jurors on an embezzlement case turn up bloody and headless around town, so a special criminal strike force is brought in to solve the murders. Why do the murders happen only on Tuesdays? Made for TV. **1981 90m/C** Robert Stack, Dorian Harewood, Herb Edelman; **D:** Richard Lang. **VHS, Beta** $24.95 AHV 🎬🎬

Strike It Rich A honeymooning couple find themselves resorting to the Monte Carlo gambling tables in order to raise money for the ride home. Lightweight fluff unfortunately adapted from Graham Greene's short novel

"Loser Takes All." Only for hard-core Gielgudites. **AKA:** Loser Take All. **1990 (PG) 86m/C** Molly Ringwald, Robert Lindsay, John Gielgud, Max Wall, Simon de la Brosse; **D:** James Scott; **M:** Cliff Eidelman. **VHS, Beta** $89.99 HBO 🎬½

Strike Up the Band A high school band turns to hot swing music and enters a national radio contest. Rooney and Garland display their usual charm in this high-energy stroll down memory lane. ♫Over the Waves; The Light Cavalry Overture; Walkin Down Broadway; Five Foot Two, Eyes of Blue; After the Ball; Nobody; Strike Up the Band. **1940 120m/B** Judy Garland, Mickey Rooney, Paul Whiteman, William Tracy, June Preisser; **D:** Busby Berkeley. Academy Awards '40: Best Sound; Nominations: Best Song ("Our Love Affair"), Best Score. **VHS, Beta** $19.98 MGM 🎬🎬½

Strikeback A young boy comes painfully of age in West Berlin. **1984 88m/C** VHS, Beta $69.98 VES 🎬🎬

Striker Mercenary John "Striker" Slade is sent to Nicaragua to free a captured American journalist, not knowing his superiors have betrayed him to the Contras and the Sandinistas. He battles it out with both groups while seeking revenge on the businessmen who set him up. **1988 (R) 90m/C** Frank Zagarino, Melanie Rogers, Paul Werner; **D:** Stephen M. Andrews. **VHS, Beta** $39.95 AIP 🎬🎬

Striker's Mountain Story of a sports enthusiast who creates heliskiing and builds it into a business. Great ski scenes, but skip the rest. **1987 99m/C** Bruce Greenwood, Mimi Kuzyk, Leslie Nielsen, August Schellenberg; **D:** Allen Simmonds. **VHS** $9.95 SIM, VTR 🎬½

Striking Distance Tom Hardy (Willis) is a hard-nosed fifth-generation Pittsburgh homicide cop whose police detective father (Mahoney) is killed, apparently by a serial killer. Hardy insists the perp was really a fellow cop and winds up on the River Rescue squad (at least his partner is the fetching Parker). When the serial killer starts striking at women with some connection to Hardy, he finds scant support from his fellow cops. High action quotient but the killer's identity won't be any surprise. **1993 (R) 101m/C** Bruce Willis, Sarah Jessica Parker, Dennis Farina, Tom Sizemore, Brion James, Robert Pastorelli, Timothy Busfield, John Mahoney, Andre Braugher; **D:** Rowdy Herrington; **W:** Marty Kaplan, Rowdy Herrington; **M:** Brad Fiedel. **VHS, 8mm** COL 🎬🎬½

Stripes Feeling like losers and looking to straighten out their lives, two friends enlist in the Army under the mistaken impression that military life is something like a summer camp for grownups. A box-office success (despite a poorly written and directed script) due in large part to Murray's charm and his verbal and sometimes physical sparring with Oates, who is good as the gruff-tempered platoon sergeant. Features humorous stints from various "Second City" players, including Candy, whom Murray turns into a "lean, mean fighting machine." **1981 (R) 105m/C** Bill Murray, Harold Ramis, P.J. Soles, Warren Oates, John Candy, John Larroquette, Judge Reinhold, Sean Young, Dave Thomas, Joe Flaherty; **D:** Ivan Reitman; **W:** Len Blum, Harold Ramis; **M:** Elmer Bernstein. **VHS, Beta** $29.95 COL 🎬🎬½

Stripped to Kill A female cop goes undercover to lure a psycho killing strippers. Not-bad entry from Corman and cohorts. Followed by—you guessed it—"Stripped to Kill II."

1987 (R) 88m/C Kay Lenz, Greg Evigan, Norman Fell; D: Katt Shea Ruben; W: Katt Shea Ruben, Andy Ruben. VHS, Beta $79.95 MGM ♂♂

Stripped to Kill II: Live Girls A young woman with extra-sensory powers dreams of murders which she discovers are all too real. A weak sequel, despite the interesting premise.
1989 83m/C Maria Ford, Eb Lottimer, Karen Mayo Chandler, Marjean Holden, Birke Tan, Debra Lamb; W: Katt Shea Ruben. VHS, Beta $79.95 MGM ♂♂

The Stripper A middle-aged stripper in a traveling show returns to the small Kansas town of her youth. Left stranded, she moves in with an old friend whose teenage son promptly falls in love with her. Based on the play "A Loss of Roses" by William Inge. *AKA:* Woman of Summer.
1963 95m/B Joanne Woodward, Richard Beymer, Claire Trevor, Carol Lynley, Robert Webber, Gypsy Rose Lee; D: Franklin J. Schaffner; M: Jerry Goldsmith. VHS, Beta $39.95 FOX ♂♂½

Stripper A good under-the-covers glimpse of the life and work of several real-life strippers, culminating in the First Annual Stripper's Convention in 1984.
1986 (R) 90m/C Janette Boyd, Sara Costa, Kimberly Holcomb; D: Jerome Gary; M: Jack Nitzsche. VHS, Beta $79.98 FOX ♂♂½

Striptease A slew of slowly-declothing women do their thing.
198? 60m/C VHS, Beta $59.95 JEF ♂

Stroke of Midnight Souped-up Cinderella with Lowe as egotistic high fashion designer, Grey as struggling shoe designer and a pumpkin-colored VW Bug.
1990 (PG) 102m/C Rob Lowe, Jennifer Grey, Andrea Ferreol; D: Tom Clegg. VHS, Beta $89.98 MED, VTR ♂½

Stroker Ace Flamboyant stock car driver tries to break an iron-clad promotional contract signed with a greedy fried-chicken magnate. Off duty, he ogles blondes as dopey as he is. One of the worst from Reynolds—and that's saying something.
1983 (PG) 96m/C Burt Reynolds, Ned Beatty, Jim Nabors, Parker Stevenson, Loni Anderson, Bubba Smith; D: Hal Needham; W: Hal Needham, Hugh Wilson. VHS, Beta $19.98 WAR Woof!

Stromboli Bergman is a Czech refugee who marries an Italian fisherman in order to escape from her displaced persons camp. He brings her to his home island of Stromboli where she finds the life bleak and isolated and her marriage a trial. In Italian with English subtitles. The melodrama was even greater off-screen than on; this is the movie which introduced Bergman and Rossellini and began their (then) scandalous affair.
1950 81m/B Ingrid Bergman, Mario Vitale, Renzo Cesana; D: Roberto Rossellini. VHS, Beta $19.95 VCI, ING ♂♂½

Strong Man A WWI veteran, passing himself off as an unlikely circus strongman, searches an American city for the girl whose letters gave her hope during the war. Perhaps Langdon's best full-length film. With a new score by Davis.
1926 78m/B Harry Langdon, Gertrude Astor, Tay Garnett; D: Frank Capra. VHS, Beta $39.99 HBO, IME, GPV ♂♂♂

Strong Medicine Strange, avant-garde film about a strange, off-written young woman. Cleverly directed experiment that's not for everyone.

1984 84m/C Carol Kane, Raul Julia, Wallace Shawn, Kate Manheim, David Warrilow; D: Guy Green. VHS, Beta NO ♂♂½

Stroszek Three German misfits—a singer, a prostitute and an old man—tour the U.S. in search of their dreams. Touching, hilarious comedy-drama with a difference and an attitude. One of Herzog's easiest and also best films. In English and German with English subtitles.
1977 108m/C Eva Mattes, Bruno S, Clemens Scheitz; D: Werner Herzog. VHS $79.95 NYF, FCT, ING ♂♂♂

The Structure of Crystals A member of the scientific elite meets with an old friend who has moved to a remote meteorological station and tries to persuade him to return to the city and resume his work. Zanussi's cerebral first feature was also the first of a series of films to explore the scientific community. In Polish with English subtitles. *AKA:* Struktura Krysztalu.
1969 76m/B Andrzej Zarnecki, Jan Myslowicz, Barbara Wrzesinska, Wladyslaw Jarema, Daniel Olbrychski; D: Krzysztof Zanussi; W: Edward Zebrowski, Krzysztof Zanussi. VHS $59.95 FCT ♂♂½

Stryker The ever-lovin' nuclear holocaust has occurred, and good guys and bad guys battle it out for scarce water. If you liked "Mad Max," go see it again; don't watch this miserable effort.
1983 (R) 86m/C Steve Sandor, Andria Fabio; D: Cirio H. Santiago. VHS, Beta $19.98 SUE, STE Woof!

Stuck on You Couple engaged in a palimony suit takes their case to a judge to work out their differences. Wing-clipped angel Gabriel (Corey) comes to earth to help them patch it up. Never mind.
1984 (R) 90m/C Prof. Irwin Corey, Virginia Penta, Mark Mikulski; D: Lloyd Samuel Weil Kaufman, Michael Herz. VHS, Beta $9.98 SUE ♂

Stuckey's Last Stand A group of camp counselors prepare to take 22 children on a nature hike they will never forget. Mindless teen fodder.
1978 (PG) 95m/C Whit Reichert, Tom Murray, Rich Casentino. VHS, Beta NO ♂

The Stud Owner of a fashionable "after hours" dance spot hires a young, handsome stud to manage the club and attend to her personal needs. Low-budget look and seemingly scriptless. Faithfully adapted by sister Jackie Collins from her novel.
1978 (R) 90m/C Joan Collins, Oliver Tobias; D: Quentin Masters; W: Jackie Collins. VHS, Beta $19.99 HBO Woof!

Student Affairs A bunch of highschool misfits vie for roles in a movie about a bunch of high school misfits.
1988 (R) 92m/C Louie Bonanno, Jim Abele, Alan Fisler, Deborah Blaisdell; D: Chuck Vincent. VHS, Beta $79.98 LIV, VES Woof!

Student Bodies A "Halloween"-style spoof of high-school horror films, except it's not funny. And what's so funny about bloody murder anyway? When the on-the-set problems and strife arose (which they did), why didn't everyone just cut their losses and go home?
1981 (R) 86m/C Kristen Riter, Matthew Goldsby, Richard Brando, Joe Flood; D: Mickey Rose. VHS, Beta $72.95 PAR Woof!

Student Confidential A Troma-produced spoof of seedy high school youth movies, new and old, involving four students who are led into the world of adult vices by a mysterious millionaire. Badly made and dull. Douglas and Jackson both have brothers named Michael.

1987 (R) 99m/C Eric Douglas, Marlon Jackson, Susan Scott, Ronee Blakley, Elizabeth Singer; D: Richard Horian. VHS, Beta $79.95 MED ♂

The Student Nurses The adventures, amourous and otherwise, of four last-year nursing students. Followed by four sequels: "Private Duty Nurses," "Night Call Nurses," "The Young Nurses," and "Candy Stripe Nurses." Better than average exploitation fare. First release from Roger Corman's New World studios; it goes down hill from there.
1970 (R) 89m/C Elaine Giftos, Karen Carlson, Brioni Farrell, Barbara Leigh, Reni Santoni, Richard Rust, Lawrence Casey, Darrell Larson, Paul Camen, Richard Stahl, Scottie MacGregor, Pepe Serna; D: Stephanie Rothman. VHS, Beta $59.98 NLC ♂♂

Student of Prague Early silent classic based on the German Faust legend: a student makes a pact with the devil to win a beautiful woman. Poor fellow. With either German or English title cards. Music track.
1913 60m/B Lothar Koemer, Grete Berger, Paul Wegener; D: Paul Wegener, Stellan Rye. VHS, Beta $19.95 DVT, GLV, GVV ♂♂♂

The Student Prince Delightful rendition of Sigmund Romberg's famous operetta in which Purdom stars as the Prince of Heidelberg who falls for barmaid Blyth. Lanza recorded the soundtrack, but could not star in this film because of his weight problem. Previously filmed in 1919 and 1927 without music. ♫Golden Days; Serenade; Deep in My Heart; To the Inn We're Marching; Drink, Drink, Drink; Come Boys, Let's All Be Gay, Boys; Summertime in Heidelberg; Beloved; I Walk With God.
1954 107m/C Ann Blyth, Edmund Purdom, John Ericson, Louis Calhern, Edmund Gwenn, S.Z. Sakall, Betta St. John; D: Richard Thorpe. VHS $19.98 MGM ♂♂

The Student Prince in Old Heidelberg Prince Karl Heinrich silently falls in love with lowly barmaid. *AKA:* Old Heidelberg.
1927 102m/B Ramon Novarro, Norma Shearer; D: Ernst Lubitsch. VHS $29.98 MGM, FCT ♂♂½

The Student Teachers Yet another soft-core Corman product. Three student teachers sleep around, on screen.
1973 79m/C Susan Damante Shaw, Brooke Mills, Bob Harris, John Cramer, Chuck Norris; D: Jonathan Kaplan. VHS, Beta $59.98 SUE ♂½

Studs Lonigan Drifting, too artsy rendering a James T. Farrell's trilogy about an Irish drifter growing up in Chicago in the twenties. Good period detail, but oddly off-kilter and implausible as history.
1960 96m/B Christopher Knight, Frank Gorshin, Jack Nicholson; D: Irving Lerner; W: Philip Yordan; M: Jerry Goldsmith. VHS, Beta $24.95 MGM ♂♂

A Study in Scarlet Owen played Watson the previous year in "Sherlock Holmes;" here he's miscast as Holmes, and the plot differs from the Doyle story of the same title.
1933 77m/B Reginald Owen, Alan Mowbray, Anna May Wong, June Clyde, Alan Dinehart; D: Edwin L. Marin; W: Reginald Owen. VHS, Beta $16.95 SNC, NOS, CAB ♂♂

A Study in Terror A well-appointed Sherlock Holmes thriller. The second Holmes film in color. Premise has a young, athletic Holmes in pursuit of a well-educated Jack the Ripper in the atmosphere of London in the 1880s. *AKA:* Sherlock Holmes Grosster Fall; Fog.
1966 94m/C John Neville, Donald Houston, Judi Dench, Anthony Quayle, Robert Morley, Frank Finlay, Cecil Parker; D: James Hill. VHS, Beta $69.95 COL ♂♂♂

The Stuff Surreal horror semi-spoof about an ice cream mogul and a hamburger king who discover that the new, fast-selling confection in town zombifies its partakers. Forced, lame satire from producer/director/writer Cohen.
1985 (R) 93m/C Michael Moriarty, Andrea Marcovicci, Garrett Morris, Paul Sorvino, Danny Aiello, Brooke Adams; *D:* Larry Cohen; *W:* Larry Cohen. **VHS, Beta** $9.95 NWV, STE *ℐℐ*

Stuff Stephanie in the Incinerator A Troma gagfest about wealthy cretins who torture and kill young women. "Funny" title betrays utter, exploitive mindlessness.
1989 (PG-13) 97m/C Catherine Dee, William Dame, M.R. Murphy, Dennis Cunningham; *D:* Don Nardo. **VHS, Beta** $79.95 LIV *ℐ*

The Stunt Man A marvelous and unique exercise in meta-cinematic manipulation. O'Toole, in one of his very best roles, is a power-crazed movie director; Railsback is a fugitive sheltered by him from sherrif Rocco. When a stunt man is killed in an accident, O'Toole prevails on Railsback to replace him, leading Railsback to wonder if O'Toole wants him dead. A labor of love for director-producer Rush, who spent nine years working on it, and waited two years to see it released, by Fox. Based on the novel by Paul Brodeur.
1980 (R) 129m/C Peter O'Toole, Steve Railsback, Barbara Hershey, Chuck Bail, Alex Rocco, Allen (Gooritz) Garfield, Adam Roarke, Sharon Farrell, Philip Bruns; *D:* Richard Rush; *W:* Richard Rush, Lawrence B. Marcus; *M:* Leo Shuken, Charles Bradshaw. Academy Awards '80 Nominations: Best Actor (O'Toole), Best Adapted Screenplay, Best Director (Rush); Golden Globe Awards '81: Best Score; Montreal World Film Festival '80: Best Film; National Board of Review Awards '80: 10 Best Films of the Year; National Society of Film Critics Awards '80: Best Actor (O'Toole). **VHS, Beta** $19.98 FOX *ℐℐℐℐ*

Stunt Pilot A young man takes a job at a film studio as a stunt pilot and finds mayhem and romance on and off the ground. One in the "Tailspin Tommy" series. Well-paced and fun to watch.
1939 61m/C John Trent, Marjorie Reynolds, Milburn Stone, Jason Robards Sr., Pat O'Malley; *D:* George Waggner. **VHS** $19.95 NOS, MOV *ℐℐ*

Stunt Rock A feature film combining rock music, magic, and some of the most incredible stunts ever attempted.
1980 (PG) 90m/C **VHS, Beta** NO *ℐℐ*

Stunts See "The Stunt Man" instead. OK script hides near-invisible plot; stunt man engages in derring-do. *AKA:* Who is Killing the Stuntman.
1977 (PG) 90m/C Robert Forster, Fiona Lewis, Joanna Cassidy, Darrell Fetty, Bruce Glover, James Luisi; *D:* Mark L. Lester; *M:* Michael Kamen. **VHS, Beta** NO *ℐℐ*

Stuntwoman Welch plays a stuntwoman whose death-defying job interferes with her love life. What ever shall she do?
1981 95m/C Raquel Welch, Jean-Paul Belmondo; *D:* Claude Zidi. **VHS** $14.95 LPC *ℐ½*

Submarine Seahawk When a group of Japanese warships mysteriously disappear, allied intelligence suspect a big battle is brewing. An inexperienced commander who has been tracking the movement of the Japanese ships is put in charge of the submarine Seahawk, even though the crew lacks faith in his command abilities. His own men may prove a bigger obstacle than any of the Japanese. Lots of action and stock WWII footage.
1959 83m/B John Bentley, Brett Halsey, Wayne Heffley, Steve Mitchell, Henry McCann, Frank Gerstle; *D:* Spencer Gordon Bennet. **VHS** $9.95 COL *ℐℐ*

Submission A pharmacist's sensuality is reawakened when she has a provocative affair with a clerk in her shop.
1977 (R) 107m/C Franco Nero, Lisa Gastoni; *D:* Salvatore Samperi. **VHS, Beta** $59.95 PSM *ℐ½*

Subspecies New improved vampire demons descend on earth. The first full-length feature film shot on location in Transylvania. For horror buffs only.
1991 (R) 90m/C Laura Tate, Michael Watson, Anders Hove, Michelle McBride, Irina Movila, Angus Scrimm; *D:* Ted Nicolaou. **VHS, 8mm** $19.95 PAR, BTV *ℐℐ½*

The Substitute Donohue plays a sexy high-school substitute teacher who turns out to have homicidal tendencies, which she decides to take out on her students. Film debut for rapper/underwear model Mark.
1993 (R) 86m/C Amanda Donohoe, Dalton James, Natasha Gregson Wagner, Eugene Glazer, "Marky" Mark Wahlberg; *D:* Martin Donovan; *W:* Cynthia Verlaine; *M:* Gerald Gouriet. **VHS, Beta** PAR *ℐℐ*

Subterfuge When a special American security agent goes to England for a "vacation," his presence causes speculation and poses several serious questions for both British Intelligence and the underworld. Nothing special, with the occasional suspenseful moment.
1968 89m/C Joan Collins, Gene Barry, Richard Todd; *D:* Peter Graham Scott. **VHS, Beta** REP *ℐℐ*

Suburban Commando A goofy, muscular alien mistakenly lands on Earth while on vacation. He does his best to remain inconspicuous, resulting in numerous hilarious situations. Eventually he is forced to confront his arch, interstellar nemesis in order to defend the family who befriended him. A harmless, sometimes cute vehicle for wrestler Hogan, which will certainly entertain his younger fans.
1991 (PG) 88m/C Hulk Hogan, Christopher Lloyd, Shelley Duvall, Larry Miller, William Ball, JoAnn Dearing, Jack Elam, Roy Dotrice, Christopher Neame, Tony Longo; *D:* Burt Kennedy. **VHS** $14.95 COL, NLC *ℐℐ*

Suburban Roulette "Adults only" feature from splattermaster Lewis caters to the prurient. Groovy themes like wife swapping and other very daring subjects. Totally sixties. Presented as part of Joe Bob Brigg's "Sleaziest Movies in the History of the World" series.
1967 91m/C *D:* Herschell Gordon Lewis. **VHS** $19.98 SVI *ℐ*

Suburbia When a group of punk rockers move into a condemned suburban development, they become the targets of a vigilante group. Low budget, needless violent remake of anyone of many '50s rebellion flicks that tries to have a "message." *AKA:* The Wild Side.
1983 (R) 99m/C Chris Pederson, Bill Coyne, Jennifer Clay, Timothy Eric O'Brien, Andrew Pece, Don Allen; *D:* Penelope Spheeris. **VHS, Beta** $29.98 LIV, VES *ℐ*

Subway Surreal, MTV-esque vision of French fringe life from the director of "Le Dernier Combat." A spike-haired renegade escapes the law by plunging into the Parisian subway system. Once there, he encounters a bizarre subculture living under the city. Plenty of angry-youth attitude, but where's the point? And frankly, too much bad New Wave music.
1985 (R) 103m/C Christopher Lambert, Isabelle Adjani; *D:* Luc Besson; *W:* Luc Besson. **VHS, Beta** $79.98 FOX *ℐ½*

Subway to the Stars Young saxophonist Fontes searches the back streets of Rio for his missing girlfriend. Realistic and sometimes depressing, if aimless at times. Overall, an intriguing "underworld" flick from Brazil. *AKA:* Un Trem Para as Estrelas.
1987 103m/C Guilherme Fontes, Milton Goncalves, Taumaturgo Ferreira, Ze Trindade, Ana Beatriz Wiltgen; *D:* Carlos Diegues. **VHS** $19.95 STE, NWV *ℐℐ½*

Success is the Best Revenge A Polish film director living in London struggles with his rebellious teenage son. Both struggle with questions of exile and identity. Uneven but worthwhile and based on Skolimowski's own experiences. His better earlier film is "Moonlighting."
1984 95m/C Michael York, Michel Piccoli, Anouk Aimee, John Hurt, Jane Asher, Joanna Szerbic, Michael Lyndon, George Skolimowski; *D:* Jerzy Skolimowski. **VHS** IME *ℐℐ½*

Sucker Money Newspaper reporter works to expose phony spiritualist. Good title; little else. Boring. *AKA:* Victims of the Beyond.
1934 59m/C Mischa Auer, Phyliss Barrington, Earl McCarthy, Ralph Lewis, Mae Busch; *D:* Dorothy Davenport Reid. **VHS, Beta** $16.95 NOS, SNC, VYY *ℐℐ½*

Sudden Death Shamrock and Lucky are back as cowboys posing as hired gunmen in order to foil a wealthy, homesteader-hating land baron.
1950 55m/B James Ellison, Russell Hayden, Stanley Price, Raymond Hatton, Betty Adams. **VHS, Beta** NO *ℐ*

Sudden Death Two professional violence merchants put themselves up for hire.
1977 (R) 84m/C Robert Conrad, Felton Perry, Don Stroud, Bill Raymond, Ron Vawter, Harry Roskolenko; *D:* Richard Foreman. **VHS, Beta** $49.95 MED *ℐ*

Sudden Death A beautiful businesswoman decides to kill every rapist she can find after she herself has been attacked. Exploitative in its own fashion; fueled and felled by rage.
1985 95m/C Denise Coward, Frank Runyeon, Jamie Tirelli; *D:* Sig Shore. **VHS, Beta** $29.98 LIV, VES *ℐ*

Sudden Impact Eastwood directs himself in this formula thriller, the fourth "Dirty Harry" entry. This time "Dirty Harry" Callahan tracks down a revenge-obsessed murderess and finds he has more in common with her than he expected. Meanwhile, local mobsters come gunning for him. This is the one where he says, "Go ahead. Make my day." Followed by "The Dead Pool."
1983 (R) 117m/C Clint Eastwood, Sondra Locke, Pat Hingle, Bradford Dillman; *D:* Clint Eastwood; *W:* Charles B. Pierce. **VHS, Beta, 8mm** $19.98 WAR, TLF *ℐℐ½*

Sudden Terror The murder of an African dignitary is witnessed by a young boy who has trouble convincing his parents and the police about the incident. Suspenseful but less than original. Shot on location in Malta. *AKA:* Eyewitness.
1970 (PG) 95m/C Mark Lester, Lionel Jeffries, Susan George, Tony Bonner; *D:* John Hough. **VHS, Beta** FOX *ℐℐ*

Suddenly Crazed gunman Sinatra holds a family hostage in the hick town of Suddenly, California, as part of a plot to kill the president, who's passing through town. Tense thriller is a good display for Sinatra's acting talent. Unfortunately hard to find because

Sinatra forced United Artists to take it out of distribution after hearing that Kennedy assassin Lee Harvey Oswald had watched ''Suddenly'' only days before November 22, 1963. Really, Ol' Blue Eyes should have stuck with making top-notch thrillers like this one, instead of degenerating into the world's greatest lounge singer.
1954 75m/B Frank Sinatra, Sterling Hayden, James Gleason, Nancy Gates, Paul Frees; **D:** Lewis Allen. **VHS, Beta $16.95** *SNC, NOS, VEC* 🎬🎬½

Suddenly, Last Summer Brain surgeon is summoned to the mansion of a rich New Orleans matron who wishes him to perform a lobotomy on her niece, supposedly suffering from a mental breakdown. Based on the play by Tennessee Williams. Softened for the censors, though the themes of homosexuality, insanity, and murder, characterizations of evil, and unusual settings presage many movies of the next two decades. Extremely fine performances from Hepburn and Taylor. Clift never completely recovered from his auto accident two years before and does not come across with the strength of purpose really necessary in his character. Still, fine viewing.
1959 114m/B Elizabeth Taylor, Katharine Hepburn, Montgomery Clift, Mercedes McCambridge, Albert Dekker; **D:** Joseph L. Mankiewicz; **W:** Gore Vidal; **M:** Malcolm Arnold. Academy Awards '59 Nominations: Best Actress (Hepburn), Best Actress (Taylor), Best Art Direction/Set Decoration (B & W); Golden Globe Awards '60: Best Actress—Drama (Taylor); National Board of Review Awards '59: 10 Best Films of the Year. **VHS, Beta $19.95** *COL* 🎬🎬🎬½

Sudie & Simpson Heart-tugging tale of friendship set in rural 1940s Georgia. Twelve-year-old white Sudie's forbidden friendship with the adult black Simpson provides a lot of talk in their small town. Racial barriers finally cause Simpson to be accused of child molestation and the odds of his survival, despite his innocence, don't seem great. Based on Sara Flanigan Carter's autobiographical novel. Made for cable television.
1990 95m/C Sara Gilbert, Louis Gossett Jr., Frances Fisher, John M. Jackson, Paige Danahy, Ken Strong; **D:** Joan Tewkesbury; **W:** Sara Flanigan Carter, Ken Koser. **VHS $89.95** *WOV* 🎬🎬🎬

Suds Pickford is tragic laundress with major crush on a guy who left his shirt at the laundry.
1920 75m/B Mary Pickford, William Austin, Harold Goodwin, Rose Dione, Theodore Roberts; **D:** Jack Dillon. **VHS, Beta $19.95** *GPV* 🎬🎬½

Suffering Bastards Buddy and Al have never worked a day in their lives—Mom's nightclub always gave them something to do and a regular paycheck. But when Mom's swindled out of the family business, they decide it's time to take charge. Soon they're caught between bullets, babes, and belly laughs in this action-filled comedy.
1990 95m/C Eric Bogosian, John C. McGinley, David Warshofsky. **VHS $89.95** *AIP* 🎬🎬½

Sugar Cane Alley After the loss of his parents, an 11-year-old orphan boy goes to work with his grandmother on a sugar plantation. She realizes that her young ward's only hope is an education. Set in Martinique in the 1930s among black workers. Poignant and memorable. **AKA:** Rue Cases Negres.
1983 (PG) 106m/C Garry Cadenat, Darling Legitimus, Douta Seck; **D:** Euzhan Palcy; **W:** Euzhan Palcy. **VHS, Beta $29.95** *MED, FCT* 🎬🎬🎬

Sugar Cookies Erotic horror story in which young women are the pawns as a satanic satyr and an impassioned lesbian play out a bizarre game of vengeance, love, and death.
1977 (R) 89m/C Mary Woronov, Lynn Lowry, Monique Van Vooren; **D:** Michael Herz. **VHS, Beta** *NO Woof!*

Sugar Hill Two brothers (Wright & Snipes) are heroin dealers who have built their own crime empire in the Sugar Hill section of Harlem. Snipes is moved to reconsider his career options when he falls for an aspiring actress (Randle). A recap of the seminal event in the brothers' upbringing (in a jarring editing sequence) serves to explain how the wide-eyed boys became cold-blooded pushers. Good performances by all but formulaic plot will leave viewers asking themselves if they haven't seen it before. Junkie dad Williams was Linc on ''The Mod Squad'' on television in the late 1960's.
1994 (R) 123m/C Wesley Snipes, Michael Wright, Theresa Randle, Clarence Williams III, Abe Vigoda, Ernie Hudson, Larry Joshua, Leslie Uggams, Khandi Alexander, Raymond Serra, Joe Dallesandro, Vondie Curtis-Hall; **D:** Leon Ichaso; **W:** Barry Michael Cooper; **M:** Terence Blanchard. **VHS** *FXV* 🎬🎬🎬

Sugarbaby An acclaimed German film about a fat mortuary attendant living in Munich who transforms herself (but doesn't lose weight) in order to seduce a young, handsome subway conductor. Touching and warm film that introduced Sagebrecht to American audiences. A bit too cutting-edge cinematographically. In German with English subtitles. Remade as ''Babycakes.'' Sagebrecht and director Adlon team up again for ''Bagdad Cafe'' and ''Rosalie Goes Shopping.'' **AKA:** Zuckerbaby.
1985 (R) 103m/C Marianne Sagebrecht, Eisi Gulp, Toni Berger, Will Spendler, Manuela Denz; **D:** Percy Adlon; **W:** Percy Adlon. **VHS, Beta $29.95** *LHV, GLV, APD* 🎬🎬🎬

The Sugarland Express To save her son from adoption, a young woman helps her husband break out of prison. In their flight to freedom, they hijack a police car, holding the policeman hostage. Speilberg's first feature film is a moving portrait of a couple's desperation. Based on a true story, adapted by Hal Barwood and Matthew Robbins.
1974 (PG) 109m/C Goldie Hawn, Ben Johnson, Michael Sacks, William Atherton; **D:** Steven Spielberg; **W:** Steven Spielberg, Matthew Robbins; **M:** John Williams. **VHS, Beta $59.95** *MCA* 🎬🎬🎬

Suicide Battalion/Hell Squad A war movie double feature. In ''Suicide Battalion,'' American troops must sneak through enemy territory to destroy a captured American command outpost in the Philippines during WWII. Five American soldiers are lost in the North African desert in ''Hell Squad.'' After a series of fights with various enemies, one soldier survives, only to nearly be doublecrossed by a Nazi he meets in the desert.
1958 150m/B Mike Connors, John Ashley, Russ Bender, Jewell Lain, Bing Russell, Wally Campo, Brandon Carroll, Frederic Galvin; **D:** Edward L. Cahn, Burt Topper; **W:** Burt Topper. **VHS $14.95** *COL* 🎬🎬

The Suicide Club A wealthy, depressed young woman joins a club filled with affluent people who play mysterious games. She finds that winning their games means more than she bargained for. Hemingway looks great in her off-kilter way, but really, there's no point, and the on-screen decadence gets tiresome.

1988 (R) 92m/C Mariel Hemingway, Robert Joy, Lenny Henry, Madeleine Potter, Michael O'Donoghue, Anne Carlisle; **D:** James Bruce. **VHS, Beta $29.95** *ACA* 🎬½

Suicide Cult A CIA employee predicts the second coming of Christ, and a battle ensues between the forces of good and evil for possession of the child.
1977 82m/C **VHS, Beta** *NO Woof!*

Suicide Patrol A small band of saboteurs patrols a German-controlled Mediterranean island during WWII.
1977? 90m/C Gordon Mitchell, Pierre Richard, Max Dean. **VHS, Beta $57.95** *UNI, MOV* 🎬

The Suitors When a group of Iranians decide to sacrifice a lamb in their apartment, the New York police send in SWAT team assuming they're terrorists. First time effort by Ebrahimian, in Farsi with English subtitles.
1988 106m/C **D:** Ghasem Ebrahimian. **VHS $59.95** *FCT, ING* 🎬

Sullivan's Travels Sturges' masterpiece is a sardonic, whip-quick romp about a Hollywood director tired of making comedies who decides to make a serious, socially responsible film and hits the road masquerading as a hobo in order to know hardship and poverty. Beautifully sustained, inspired satire that mercilessly mocked the ambitions of Depression-era social cinema. Gets a little over-dark near the end before the happy ending; Sturges insisted on 20-year-old Lake as The Girl; her pregnancy forced him to rewrite scenes and design new costumes for her. As ever, she is stunning.
1941 90m/B Joel McCrea, Veronica Lake, William Demarest, Robert Warwick, Franklin Pangborn, Porter Hall, Eric Blore, Byron Foulger, Robert Greig, Torben Meyer, Jimmy Conlin, Margaret Hayes, Chester Conklin, Alan Bridge; **D:** Preston Sturges; **W:** Preston Sturges. **VHS, Beta $14.98** *MCA* 🎬🎬🎬🎬

Summer The fifth and among the best of Rhomer's ''Comedies and Proverbs'' series. A romantic but glum young French girl finds herself stuck in Paris during the tourist season searching for true romantic love. Takes time and patience to seize the viewer; moving ending makes it all worthwile. In French with English subtitles. **AKA:** Le Rayon Vert; The Green Ray.
1986 (R) 90m/C Marie Riviere, Lisa Heredia, Beatrice Romand, Eric Hamm, Rosette, Isabelle Riviere; **D:** Eric Rohmer; **W:** Eric Rohmer. **VHS, Beta $29.95** *FCT, ING, TPV* 🎬🎬🎬½

Summer Affair Two young lovers run away from their bickering parents and get shipwrecked on a desert island.
1979 90m/C Ornella Muti, Les Rannow; **D:** George S. Casorati. **VHS, Beta** *NO* 🎬½

Summer and Smoke Repressed, unhappy Page falls for handsome doctor Harvey. A tour de force for Page, but that's all; adapted clumsily from the overwrought Tennessee Williams play.
1961 118m/C Laurence Harvey, Geraldine Page, Rita Moreno, Una Merkel, John McIntire, Thomas Gomez, Pamela Tiffin, Lee Patrick, Casey Adams, Earl Holliman, Harry Shannon, Pattee Chapman; **D:** Peter Glenville; **M:** Elmer Bernstein. Academy Awards '61 Nominations: Best Actress (Page), Best Art Direction/Set Decoration (Color), Best Supporting Actress (Merkel), Best Original Score; Golden Globe Awards '62: Best Actress—Drama (Page). **VHS, Beta $19.95** *PAR, FCT* 🎬🎬½

Summer Camp Nightmare See ''Lord of the Flies'' instead. A young fascist incites children at two summer camps to overthrow and imprison the adults. Barbarism rears its ugly head. Self-serious and anticlimatic. Based on the novel ''The Butterfly Revolution" by William Butler. *AKA:* The Butterfly Revolution.

1986 (PG-13) 89m/C Chuck Connors, Charles Stratton, Harold Pruett, Tom Fridley, Adam Carl; *D:* Bert L. Dragin. **VHS, Beta $19.95** SUE, NLC ✰✰½

Summer City Fun-and-sun surfing movie complete with romance, hot rods, murder and great shots of the sea features Gibson in his debut. Ever wonder what Australian surf bums do on weekends? The same as their California counterparts—except they talk funny. *AKA:* Coast of Terror.

1977 83m/C Mel Gibson, Phillip Avalon, John Jarratt, Christopher Fraser. **VHS, Beta $59.95** VCD, VTR ✰✰½

Summer Fantasy Mindless TV surf saga about a curvy teen who would rather watch the beach hunks then go to medical school.

1984 96m/C Julianne Phillips, Ted Shackleford, Michael Gross, Dorothy Lyman; *D:* Noel Nosseck; *M:* Peter Bernstein. **VHS, Beta** NO ✰

Summer Heat In rural, mid-Depression North Carolina, a young, lonely wife and mother is seduced by a drifter and together they plot murder. Her husband neglects her, and you should neglect to see this utter yawner. Based on a Louise Shivers novel.

1987 (R) 80m/C Lori Singer, Anthony Edwards, Bruce Abbott, Kathy Bates; *D:* Michie Gleason. **VHS, Beta $19.95** PAR ✰½

Summer Holiday Rooney comes of age with a vengeance during summer vacation in musical rendition of "Ah, Wilderness." Undistinguished musical numbers, inferior to the original, but jazzy Technicolor cinematography. Ended up in the red by over $1.5 million, lotsa money back then. ♫It's Our Home Town; Afraid to Fall in Love; All Hail, Danville High; The Stanley Steamer; It's Independence Day; I Think You're the Sweetest Kid I've Ever Known; Weary Blues.

1948 92m/C Mickey Rooney, Gloria De Haven, Walter Huston, Frank Morgan, Jackie "Butch" Jenkins, Marilyn Maxwell, Agnes Moorehead, Selena Royle, Anne Francis; *D:* Rouben Mamoulian. **VHS $19.98** MGM, TTC, FCT ✰✰½

Summer Interlude A ballerina recalls a romantic summer spent with an innocent boy, who was later tragically killed. Contains many earmarks and visual ideas of later Bergman masterpieces. In Swedish with English subtitles. *AKA:* Illicit Interlude; Summerplay; Sommarlek.

1950 95m/B Maj-Britt Nilsson, Birger Malmsten, Alf Kjellin; *D:* Ingmar Bergman; *W:* Ingmar Bergman. **VHS, Beta $19.98** SUE, ING, NLC ✰✰✰½

Summer Lovers Summer vacation finds young couple traveling to the exotic Greek island of Santorini. They meet up with a fun-loving woman and discover three-way sexual tension, but little in the way of plot, dialogue, or acting. From the director of "Grease" and "Blue Lagoon" and best watched late at night while half conscious.

1982 (R) 98m/C Peter Gallagher, Daryl Hannah, Valerie Quennessen; *D:* Randal Kleiser. **VHS, Beta $9.95** COL, SUE ✰

Summer Magic An impecunious recent widow is forced to leave Boston and settle her family in a small town in Maine. Typical, forgettable Disney drama; early Mills vehicle. A remake of "Mother Carey's Chickens."

1963 116m/C Hayley Mills, Burl Ives, Dorothy McGuire, Deborah Walley, Una Merkel, Eddie Hodges; *D:* James Neilson; *M:* Buddy Baker. **VHS, Beta $69.95** DIS ✰✰

Summer Night A female tycoon who is concerned for the environment decides to strike out at the terrorists who are destroying it. This caper turns into one big comedy. In Italian with English subtitles.

1987 (R) 94m/C Mariangela Melato, Michele Placido, Roberto Herlitzka, Massimo Wertmuller; *D:* Lina Wertmuller. **VHS, Beta $79.95** LIV ✰✰

Summer Night with Greek Profile, Almond Eyes & Scent of Basil A wealthy woman tycoon hires an ex-CIA man to kidnap a high-priced, professional terrorist and hold him for ransom. An ironic battle of the sexes follows. In Italian with English subtitles.

1987 (R) 94m/C Mariangela Melato, Michele Placido, Roberto Herlitzka; *D:* Lina Wertmuller; *W:* Lina Wertmuller. **VHS, Beta $19.95** TPV, ING ✰✰

Summer of Fear A happy young woman must overcome evil forces when her cousin comes to live with her family. Based on a novel by Lois Duncan. Pretty scary if ordinary, dumb made-for-TV horror from later-famous Craven. *AKA:* Stranger in Our House.

1978 94m/C Linda Blair; *D:* Wes Craven. **VHS, Beta** NO ✰✰

Summer of '42 Touching if sentimental story about a 15-year-old boy's sexual coming of age during his summer vacation on an island off New England. While his friends are fumbling with girls their own age, he falls in love with a beautiful 22-year-old woman whose husband is off fighting in the war.

1971 (R) 102m/C Jennifer O'Neill, Gary Grimes, Jerry Houser, Oliver Conant; *D:* Robert Mulligan. Academy Awards '71: Best Original Score; Nominations: Best Cinematography, Best Film Editing, Best Story & Screenplay. **VHS, Beta $19.98** WAR ✰✰✰

The Summer of Miss Forbes A governess rules over two young boys with an iron hand by day and cavorts nude and drunk by night. The boys fantasize about her murder, but fate has different plans. In Spanish with English subtitles. *AKA:* El Verano de la Senora Forbes.

1988 85m/C Hanna Schygulla, Alexis Castanares, Victor Cesar Villalobos, Guadalupe Sandoval, Fernando Balzaretti, Yuriria Munguia; *D:* Jaime Humberto Hermosillo. **VHS $79.95** FXL, FCT, ING ✰✰

The Summer of My German Soldier A young Jewish girl befriends an escaped German prisoner of war in a small town in Georgia during WWII. Occasionally sentimental but more often genuinely moving made for TV drama. Rolle won a deserved Emmy as the housekeeper. Adapted from Bette Green's novel.

1978 98m/C Kristy McNichol, Esther Rolle, Bruce Davison; *D:* Michael Tuchner. **VHS, Beta $14.95** MTI ✰✰✰

Summer of Secrets Young couple get more than they bargained for when they make love in a demented doctor's beach house.

1976 (PG) 100m/C **VHS, Beta** NO ✰

A Summer Place Melodrama about summer liaisons amid the young and middle-aged rich on an island off the coast of Maine. Too slick; romantic drama is little more than skin-deep, and dialogue is excruciating. Donahue's first starring role. Based on the novel by Sloan Wilson. Featuring "Theme from a Summer Place," which was a number-one hit in 1959.

1959 130m/C Troy Donahue, Richard Egan, Sandra Dee, Dorothy McGuire, Arthur Kennedy, Constance Ford, Beulah Bondi; *D:* Delmer Daves; *M:* Max Steiner. **VHS, Beta $19.98** WAR ✰✰

Summer Rental That John Candy just can't win, can he? Here, as a hopeless, harried air traffic controller, he tries to have a few days to relax in sunny Florida. Enter mean rich guy Crenna. Candy can add something hefty to the limpest of plots, and does so here. Watch the first hour for yuks, then rewind.

1985 (PG) 87m/C John Candy, Rip Torn, Richard Crenna, Karen Austin, Kerri Green, John Larroquette, Pierrino Mascarino; *D:* Carl Reiner. **VHS, Beta, 8mm $14.95** PAR ✰✰

Summer School A teenaged boy's girlfriend will stop at nothing to prevent him from going out with the pretty new girl in town.

1977 (R) 80m/C John McLaughlin, Steve Rose, Phoebe Schmidt. **VHS, Beta $19.95** AHV ✰

Summer School A high-school teacher's vacation plans are ruined when he gets stuck teaching remedial English in summer school. It seems all these students are interested in is re-enacting scenes from "The Texas Chainsaw Massacre." Actually, one of the better films of this genre.

1987 (PG-13) 98m/C Mark Harmon, Kirstie Alley, Nels Van Patten, Courtney Thorne-Smith, Lucy Lee Flippin, Shawnee Smith, Robin Thomas, Dean Cameron; *D:* Carl Reiner; *W:* Jeff Franklin; *M:* Danny Elfman. **VHS, Beta $14.95** PAR ✰✰½

Summer School Teachers Three sultry femmes bounce about Los Angeles high school and make the collective student body happy. Typical Corman doings; sequel to "The Students Teachers."

1975 (R) 87m/C Candice Rialson, Pat Anderson, Rhonda Leigh Hopkins, Christopher Wales; *D:* Barbara Peeters. **VHS, Beta $59.95** NLC Woof!

Summer Solstice Fonda and Loy are splendid as a couple married half a century who revisit the beach where they first met. Fonda especially shines, as a crusty old artist. Yes, it is an awful lot like "On Golden Pond." Made for TV.

1981 75m/C Henry Fonda, Myrna Loy, Lindsay Crouse, Stephen Collins; *D:* Ralph Rosenblum. **VHS, Beta $59.99** MTT ✰✰½

Summer Stock Garland plays a farm owner whose sister arrives with a summer stock troupe, led by Kelly, to rehearse a show in the family barn. Garland agrees, if the troupe will help her with the farm's harvest. When her sister decamps for New York, leaving the leading lady role open, guess who steps into the breach. Slim plot papered over with many fun song-and-dance numbers. Also features Garland's first MGM short, "Every Sunday," made in 1936 with Deanna Durbin. ♫Friendly Star; Mem'ry Island; Dig-Dig-Dig For Your Dinner; If You Feel Like Singing, Sing; Howdy Neighbor; Blue Jean Polka; Portland Fancy; You, Wonderful You; Get Happy. *AKA:* If You Feel Like Singing.

1950 109m/C Judy Garland, Gene Kelly, Gloria De Haven, Carleton Carpenter, Eddie Bracken, Phil Silvers, Hans Conried, Marjorie Main, Ray Collins, Deanna Durbin; *D:* Charles Walters. **VHS, Beta $19.98** MGM, TTC ✰✰✰

A Summer Story Superbly acted, typically British period drama about beautiful farm girl Stubbs and city lawyer Wilby, who fall in love. But can they overcome difference of social class? From the story "The Apple Tree" by John Galsworthy.

1988 (PG-13) 97m/C James Wilby, Imogen Stubbs, Susannah York, Sophie Ward, Kenneth Colley, Jerome Flynn; **D:** Piers Haggard; **W:** Penelope Mortimer; **M:** Georges Delerue. VHS, Beta $79.98 MED ✱✱✱

A Summer to Remember A five-year-old boy spends a summer with his stepfather on a Soviet collective farm. The two become deeply attached. Scenes of collective life will be of more interest to Westerners than the near-sentimental story. Star Bondarchuk later directed the epic, award-winning "War and Peace." **AKA:** Seryozha.
1961 80m/B Borya Barkhazov, Sergei Bondarchuk, Irana Skobtseva. VHS, Beta NO ✱✱✱

A Summer to Remember A deaf boy (played by Gerlis, himself deaf since birth) develops a friendship with an orangutan through sign language. Bad guys abduct the friendly ape - but all is right in the end. Nice, innocuous family viewing. Based on a story by Scott Swanton and Robert Lloyd Lewis.
1984 (PG) 93m/C Tess Harper, James Farentino, Burt Young, Louise Fletcher, Sean Gerlis, Bridgette Anderson; **D:** Robert Lewis; **M:** Charles Fox. VHS, Beta $14.98 MCA ✱✱½

Summer Vacation: 1999 Four boys are left behind at boarding school during their summer vacation. They experience all the early pangs of adolescence from love to jealousy. Their summer is then disturbed by the arrival of another boy who appears to be the reincarnation of a dead friend. Romantic look at youth caught between innocence and awareness. In Japanese with English subtitles. **AKA:** 1999—Nen No Natsu Yasumi.
1988 90m/C Eri Miyagima, Miyuki Nakano, Tomoko Otakra, Rie Mizuhara; **D:** Shusuke Kaneko. VHS, Beta $69.95 NYF, FCT, ING ✱✱

Summer Wishes, Winter Dreams Woodward and Balsam are a materially prosperous middle-aged couple with little but tedium in their lives—a tedium accurately replicated, in what feels like real life, in this slow, dull film. The two leads and Sidney—in her first screen role in 17 years—are all excellent, but the story of regret and present unhappiness wears the viewer down.
1973 (PG) 95m/C Joanne Woodward, Martin Balsam, Sylvia Sidney, Dori Brenner, Ron Richards; **D:** Gilbert Cates; **W:** Stewart Stern. Academy Awards '73 Nominations: Best Actress (Woodward), Best Supporting Actress (Sidney); British Academy Awards '74: Best Actress (Woodward); National Board of Review Awards '73: Best Supporting Actress (Sidney); New York Film Critics Awards '73: Best Actress (Woodward). VHS, Beta $59.95 COL ✱✱

Summerdog Harmless family tale about vacationers who rescue a cheerful, lovable mutt named Hobo. And a good thing they found him: He saves them from many perils. Thanks, Hobo!
1978 (G) 90m/C James Congdon, Elizabeth Eisenman, Oliver Zabriskie, Tavia Zabriskie; **D:** John Clayton. VHS, Beta $29.95 GEM ✱

Summer's Children Man who suffers from amnesia as a result of a car crash becomes the target of a mysterious killer. Forget about it.
1984 90m/C Tom Haoff, Paully Jardine, Kate Lynch. VHS, Beta $49.95 TWE ✱

Summer's Games Buxom girls cavort on the beach, competing in various games designed specifically to expose as much flesh as possible—mud wrestling, bikini boxing, wet T-shirting and more.
1987 60m/C VHS, Beta $24.95 CEL ✱½

Summertime Spinster Hepburn vacations in Venice and falls in love with Brazzi. She is hurt when inadvertently she learns he is married, but her life has been so bleak she is not about to end her one great romance. Moving, funny, richly photographed in a beautiful Old World city. From Arthur Laurents' play "The Time of the Cuckoo." **AKA:** Summer Madness.
1955 98m/C Katharine Hepburn, Rossano Brazzi; **D:** David Lean. Academy Awards '55 Nominations: Best Actress (Hepburn), Best Director (Lean); National Board of Review Awards '55: 10 Best Films of the Year; New York Film Critics Awards '55: Best Director (Lean). VHS, Beta $14.98 SUE, VYG, CRC ✱✱✱½

Summertree Douglas stars as a young musician in the 1960s trying to avoid the draft and the wrath of his parents. Contrived and heavy-handed. Produced by Douglas pere, Kirk. Adapted from the play by Ron Cower.
1971 (PG) 88m/C Michael Douglas, Jack Warden, Brenda Vaccaro, Barbara Bel Geddes, Kirk Calloway, Bill Vint; **D:** Anthony Newley. VHS, Beta WAR, OM ✱✱

The Sun Comes Up MacDonald, in her last screen appearance, plays a bitter widow whose life is changed by an orphan's love for a collie. Songbird MacDonald manages to sing a number of songs, some of them backed by a chorus of "orphans." Based on short stories by Marjorie Kinnan Rawlings.
1949 93m/C Jeanette MacDonald, Lloyd Nolan, Claude Jarman Jr., Lewis Stone, Dwayne Hickman; **D:** Richard Thorpe; **W:** William Ludwig; **M:** Andre Previn. VHS $14.95 MGM, FCT ✱✱

Sun Ra & His Intergalactic Solar Arkestra: Space is the Place Space age flick starring most appropriately Sun Ra, space-age prophet/jazz musician. Sun Ra returns from a space odyssey and embarks on saving black youth from the world's oppressive control by bringing them back into space with him. The shaman's philosophy on film. ♫Watusi; Outer Spaceways Inc.; The Satellites are Spinning.
1974 63m/C **D:** John Coney; **W:** Joshua Smith. VHS $24.95 RHP ✱✱

The Sun Shines Bright Heavily stereotyped, contrived tale of a Southern judge with a heart of gold who does so many good deeds (defending a black man accused of rape; helping a desperate prostitute) that he jeopardizes his re-election. Set during Reconstruction. An unfortunate remake of Ford's own 1934 "Judge Priest," starring Will Rogers.
1953 92m/B Charles Winninger, Arleen Whelan, John Russell, Stepin Fetchit, Milburn Stone, Russell Simpson; **D:** John Ford. VHS $19.98 REP ✱✱

Sun Valley Serenade Wartime musical fluff about a band that adopts a Norwegian refugee waif as a publicity stunt. She turns out to be a full-grown man-chaser who stirs up things at a ski resort. Fun, but it ends abruptly—because, they say, Henie fell during the huge skating finale, and Darryl Zanuck wouldn't greenlight a reshoot. One of only two feature appearances by Glenn Miller and his Orchestra (the other was "Orchestra Wives"), on video with a soundtrack restored from original dual-track recordings. ♫Chattanooga Choo Choo; I Know Why and So Do You; It Happened In Sun Valley; The Kiss Polka; In the Mood.
1941 86m/C Sonja Henie, John Payne, Glenn Miller, Milton Berle, Lynn Bari, Joan Davis, Dorothy Dandridge; **D:** H. Bruce Humberstone. VHS $19.98 FXV, FCT, MLB ✱✱½

Sunburn Insurance investigator Grodin hires model Fawcett to pretend to be his wife to get the scoop on a suicide/murder case of a rich guy in Acapulco. Made-for-TV drivel.
1979 (PG) 110m/C Farrah Fawcett, Charles Grodin, Joan Collins, Art Carney, William Daniels; **D:** Richard Sarafian; **W:** James Booth. VHS, Beta $49.95 PAR ✱✱½

Sundance Surf dudes get together on the beaches of Hawaii and California for some romance and, of course, plenty of wave riding.
1972 87m/C VHS, Beta NO ✱

Sundance and the Kid Two brothers try to collect an inheritance against all odds. Originally known as "Sundance Cassidy and Butch the Kid."
1976 (PG) 84m/C John Wade, Karen Blake; **D:** Arthur Pitt. VHS, Beta NO ✱

Sunday, Bloody Sunday Adult drama centers around the intertwined love affairs of the homosexual Finch, the heterosexual Jackson, and self-centered bisexual artist Head, desired by both. Fully-drawn characters brought to life by excellent acting make this difficult story well worth watching—though Head's central character is sadly rather dull. Day-Lewis makes his first (brief) screen appearance as a car vandalizing teenager. Powerful, sincere and sensitive.
1971 (R) 110m/C Glenda Jackson, Peter Finch, Murray Head, Daniel Day-Lewis; **D:** John Schlesinger. Academy Awards '71 Nominations: Best Actor (Finch), Best Actress (Jackson), Best Director (Schlesinger), Best Story & Screenplay; British Academy Awards '71: Best Actor (Finch), Best Actress (Jackson), Best Director (Schlesinger), Best Film; Golden Globe Awards '72: Best Foreign Film; National Society of Film Critics Awards '71: Best Actor (Finch). VHS $59.98 FOX ✱✱✱

Sunday Daughters A teenage girl kept in a detention home constantly tries to escape and find some kind of familial love. Stronge performances with keen direction. In Hungarian with English subtitles.
1980 100m/C Julianna Nyako; **D:** Janosz Rozsa. VHS, Beta $59.95 FCT ✱✱✱

A Sunday in the Country A lush, distinctively French affirmation of nature and family life. This character study with a minimal plot takes place during a single summer day in 1910 France. An elderly impressionist painter-patriarch is visited at his country home by his family. Highly acclaimed, though the pace may be too slow for some. Beautiful location photography. In French with English subtitles. **AKA:** Un Dimanche a la Campagne.
1984 (G) 94m/C Louis Ducreux, Sabine Azema, Michel Aumont; **D:** Bertrand Tavernier; **W:** Bertrand Tavernier, Colo Tavierniev O'Hagan. VHS, Beta $19.98 MGM ✱✱✱½

Sunday in the Park with George Taped theatrical performance of the Tony, Grammy, and Pulitzer Prize-winning musical play, which is based upon impressionist Georges Seurat's painting "A Sunday Afternoon on the Island of Grande Jatte." Features a celebrated music score by Sondheim.
1986 120m/C Mandy Patinkin, Bernadette Peters, Barbara Byrne, Charles Kimbrough; **D:** James Lapine; **M:** Stephen Sondheim. VHS, Beta $19.98 LHV, WAR, STS ✱✱✱

Sunday Too Far Away The rivalries between Australian sheep shearers and graziers leads to an ugly strike at a remote outback area in 1955. An uncomplicated story and a joy to watch.
1974 100m/C Jack Thompson; **D:** Ken Hannam. VHS, Beta $59.98 SUE ✱✱✱

Sundays & Cybele A ragged war veteran and an orphaned girl develop a strong emotional relationship, which is frowned upon by the townspeople. Warm and touching. In French with English subtitles. Also available in a letterboxed edition. *AKA:* Les Dimanches de Ville d'Arvay; Cybele.
1962 110m/B Hardy Kruger, Nicole Courcel; *D:* Serge Bourguignon; *M:* Maurice Jarre. **VHS, Beta $24.95** *NOS, HHT, DVT* 🎜🎜🎜½

Sundown In Africa at the beginning of WWII, a local girl aids the British against a German plot to run guns to the natives and start a rebellion. Engaging performances and efficient direction keep it above the usual cliches. Also available in a colorized version.
1941 91m/B Gene Tierney, Bruce Cabot, George Sanders, Harry Carey Sr., Cedric Hardwicke, Joseph Calleia, Dorothy Dandridge, Reginald Gardiner; *D:* Henry Hathaway; *M:* Miklos Rozsa. **VHS, Beta $19.95** *NOS, VYY, DVT* 🎜🎜½

Sundown An ambitious shot at a vampire western fails because it drains almost all vampire lore and winds up resembling a standard oater. Carradine plays a reformed vampire king (guess who) running a desert clinic that weans bloodsuckers away from preying on humans. But undead renegades attack using sixguns and wooden bullets. The climax may outrage horror purists.
1991 (R) 104m/C David Carradine, Bruce Campbell, Deborah Foreman, Maxwell Caulfield, Morgan Brittany; *D:* Anthony Hickox. **VHS $89.98** *VES* 🎜½

Sundown Fury Young cowboy fights against a group of bandits to hold a telegraph office.
1942 56m/B Donald (Don "Red") Barry. **VHS, Beta $27.95** *VCN* 🎜

Sundown Kid A Pinkerton agent goes undercover to break up a counterfeiting operation. Routine western.
1943 55m/B Donald (Don "Red") Barry. **VHS, Beta** *DVT* 🎜½

Sundown Riders Cowhands are victimized by noose-happy outlaws. Filmed in just over a week on a $30,000 budget and originally shot on 16mm to make it accessible to hospitals and schools with basic viewing equipment. The lesson here: it takes time and money to make a good western.
1948 56m/B Russell Wade, Andy Clyde, Jay Kirby; *D:* Lambert Hillyer. **VHS, Beta** *NO* 🎜

Sundown Saunders A standard oater about a cowboy whose prize for winning a horse race is a ranch. Trouble is, an outlaw wants the homestead as well.
1936 64m/B Bob Steele; *D:* Robert North Bradbury. **VHS, Beta $19.95** *NOS, VYY, HEG* 🎜

The Sundowners Slow, beautiful, and often moving epic drama about a family of Irish sheepherders in Australia during the 1920s who must continually uproot themselves and migrate. They struggle to save enough money to buy their own farm and wind up training a horse they hope will be a money-winner in racing. Well-acted by all, with Johns and Ustinov providing some humorous moments. Adapted from the novel by Jon Cleary. Filmed in Australia and London studios.
1960 133m/C Deborah Kerr, Robert Mitchum, Peter Ustinov, Glynis Johns, Dina Merrill, Chips Rafferty, Michael Anderson Jr., Lola Brooks, Wylie Watson; *D:* Fred Zinneman; *M:* Dimitri Tiomkin. Academy Awards '60 Nominations: Best Actress (Kerr), Best Adapted Screenplay, Best Director (Zinneman), Best Picture, Best Supporting Actress (Johns); National Board of Review Awards '60: 10 Best Films of the Year, Best Actor (Mitchum). **VHS, Beta $19.98** *WAR, VTR, CCB* 🎜🎜🎜½

Sunny Another glossed-over, love-conquers-all musical with Neagle as a circus star who falls for a wealthy car maker's son. Dad and crew disapprove, putting a damper on the romance. In spite of the weak storyline and flat direction, Kerns' music and Bolger's dancing make it enjoyable. 🎜Who?; D'ya Love Me?; Sunny; Two Little Bluebirds.
1941 98m/B Anna Neagle, Ray Bolger, John Carroll, Edward Everett Horton, Frieda Inescort, Helen Westley, Benny Rubin, Richard Lane, Martha Tilton; *D:* Herbert Wilcox. **VHS $19.95** *NOS* 🎜🎜

Sunny Side Up As stress of pickle factory work takes toll on woman's friend, she makes heroic effort to help her to the country to recover.
1928 66m/B Vera Reynolds, ZaSu Pitts, Edmund Burns, Sally Rand; *D:* Donald Crisp. **VHS, Beta $16.95** *GPV* 🎜🎜½

Sunny Skies Bargain-basement retread has Lease donating a pint of blood. 🎜Sunny Days; I Must Have You; Wanna Find a Boy; Must Be Love.
1930 75m/B Benny Rubin, Marceline Day, Rex Lease, Marjorie Kane, Wesley Barry; *D:* Norman Taurog. **VHS $19.95** *NOS* 🎜

Sunnyside Travolta plays a street kid trying to bring an end to the local gang warfare so he can move to Manhattan. Features a host of pop tunes in an attempt to ride the coattails of brother John's successful "Saturday Night Fever." Laughably bad.
1979 (R) 100m/C Joey Travolta, John Lansing, Stacey Pickren, Andrew Rubin, Michael Tucci, Talia Balsam, Joan Darling; *D:* Timothy Galfas. **VHS $19.98** *AIP, FOX Woof!*

Sunrise Magnificent silent story of a simple country boy who, prodded by an alluring city woman, tries to murder his wife. Production values wear their age well. Gaynor won an Oscar for her stunning performance. Remade in Germany as "The Journey to Tilsit." Based on a story by Hermann Suderman. *AKA:* Sunrise—A Song of Two Humans.
1927 110m/B George O'Brien, Janet Gaynor, Bodil Rosing, Margaret Livingston, J. Farrell MacDonald, Carl Mayer; *D:* F.W. Murnau. Academy Awards '28: Best Actress (Gaynor), Best Cinematography; Nominations: Best Interior Decoration. **VHS** *VTR, GPV* 🎜🎜🎜🎜

Sunrise at Campobello A successful adaptation (with Bellamy and Donehue repeating their roles) of the Tony award-winning play that chronicles Franklin D. Roosevelt's battle to conquer polio and ultimately receive the Democratic presidential nomination in 1924. Garson gives an excellent performance as Eleanor Roosevelt. Screenplay by Schary, who adapted his own play, and also produced.
1960 143m/C Ralph Bellamy, Greer Garson, Hume Cronyn, Jean Hagen, Jack Perrin, Lyle Talbot; *D:* Vincent J. Donehue; *W:* Dore Schary. Academy Awards '60 Nominations: Best Actress (Garson), Best Art Direction/Set Decoration (Color), Best Costume Design (Color), Best Sound; Golden Globe Awards '61: Best Actress—Drama (Garson); National Board of Review Awards '60: 10 Best Films of the Year, Best Actress (Garson). **VHS, Beta $59.95** *WAR* 🎜🎜🎜

Sunrise Trail Lots of action with Steele working undercover for the sheriff, trying to stop a rustler. He also finds the time to fall for barmaid Mehaffey.
1931 65m/B Bob Steele, Blanche Mehaffey, Jack Clifford, Eddie Dunn; *D:* John P. McCarthy. **VHS $11.95** *GPV* 🎜🎜½

The Sun's Burial Oshima's stylized and violent drama depicts life in Osaka's worst slum—a teeming underworld populated by teen gangs, prostitutes, and criminals. All want control of the area's most profitable business, an illegal blood-selling operation. In Japanese with English subtitles.
1960 87m/C Kayoko Honoo, Koji Nakahara, Masahiko Tsugawa, Fumio Watanabe; *D:* Nagisa Oshima. **VHS $79.95** *NYF* 🎜🎜🎜

Sunset Edwards wanders the range in this soft-centered farce about a couple of Western legends out to solve a mystery. On the backlots of Hollywood, silent screen star Tom Mix (Willis) meets aging marshall Wyatt Earp (Garner) and participates in a time-warp western circa 1927. They encounter a series of misadventures while trying to finger a murderer. Garner ambles enjoyably, lifting him a level above the rest of the cast.
1988 (R) 101m/C Bruce Willis, James Garner, Mariel Hemingway, Darren McGavin, Jennifer Edwards, Malcolm McDowell, Kathleen Quinlan, M. Emmet Walsh, Patricia Hodge, Richard Bradford, Joe Dallesandro, Dermot Mulroney; *D:* Blake Edwards; *W:* Blake Edwards. **VHS, Beta $14.95** *COL* 🎜🎜

Sunset Boulevard Famed tale of Norma Desmond (Swanson), aging silent film queen, who refuses to accept that stardom has ended for her and hires a young down-on-his-luck screenwriter (Holden) to help engineer her movie comeback. The screenwriter, who becomes the 'actress' kept man, assumes he can manipulate her, but finds out otherwise. Reality was almost too close for comfort, as Swanson, von Stroheim (as her major domo), and others very nearly play themselves. A darkly humorous look at the legacy and loss of fame with witty dialog, stellar performances, and some now-classic scenes. Based on the story "A Can of Beans" by Brackett and Wilder.
1950 100m/B Gloria Swanson, William Holden, Erich von Stroheim, Nancy Olson, Buster Keaton, Jack Webb, Cecil B. DeMille, Fred Clark; *D:* Billy Wilder; *W:* Billy Wilder, Charles Brackett, D. M. Marshman Jr. Academy Awards '50: Best Art Direction/Set Decoration (B & W), Best Story & Screenplay, Best Score; Nominations: Best Actor (Holden), Best Actress (Swanson), Best Black and White Cinematography, Best Director (Wilder), Best Film Editing, Best Picture, Best Supporting Actor (von Stroheim), Best Supporting Actress (Olson); Golden Globe Awards '51: Best Actress—Drama (Swanson), Best Director (Wilder), Best Film—Drama, Best Score. **VHS, Beta $14.95** *PAR, HMV* 🎜🎜🎜½

Sunset Grill While investigating his wife's murder, detective Ryder Hart (Weller) discovers a pattern of grisly killings. Sexy singer Loren Duquesne (Singer) leads him south of the border to her boss and his bloody money-making scheme. Unrated version also available.
1992 (R) 103m/C Peter Weller, Lori Singer, Alexandra Paul, John Rhys-Davies, Michael Anderson Jr., Stacy Keach; *D:* Kevin Connor. **VHS $89.95** *NLC, PMS* 🎜🎜

Sunset Heat Former drug dealer (Pare) returns to his home in Los Angeles with a legit job as a photojournalist. He stays with an old friend who turns out to be involved with the obsessed drug czar that Pare used to work for. Trouble comes along when the drug lord is robbed and blames Pare for the crime. Action-packed, with some good plot twists. An unrated version contains two additional minutes of footage. *AKA:* Midnight Heat.
1992 (R) 94m/C Michael Pare, Dennis Hopper, Adam Ant, Daphne Ashbrook, Charlie Schlatter; *D:* John Nicolella. **VHS $89.95** *NLC* 🎜🎜

Sunset in El Dorado Roy and Dale thwart a villainous scheme to defraud farmers of their land.
1945 56m/B Roy Rogers, Dale Evans, George "Gabby" Hayes, Hardie Albright, Roy Barcroft, Tom London, Edmund Cobb; **D:** Frank McDonald. **VHS, Beta $10.95** GPV, VCN ✶ ½

Sunset Limousine An out-of-work stand-up comic gets thrown out by his girlfriend, then takes a job as a chauffeur. Standard vehicle with occasional bursts of speed.
1983 92m/C John Ritter, Martin Short, Susan Dey, Paul Reiser, Audrie Neehan, Lainie Kazan; **D:** Terry Hughes. **VHS, Beta $59.95** LIV ✶✶ ½

Sunset on the Desert Rogers gets to wear a white hat and a black hat as both the leader of a gang of outlaws and the hero who brings them to justice. A poor man's Western omelette.
1942 53m/B Roy Rogers, George "Gabby" Hayes, Lynne Carver, Frank M. Thomas Sr., Bob Nolan, Beryl Wallace, Glenn Strange, Douglas Fowley, Roy Barcroft, Pat Brady; **D:** Joseph Kane. **VHS, Beta $19.95** YYY ✶ ½

Sunset Range The "World's All-Around Champion Cowboy" of 1912 stars in this chaps-slappin', bit-chompin', dust-raisin' saga of the plains.
1935 59m/B Hoot Gibson. **VHS, Beta $19.95** NOS, VCN, VCI ✶ ½

Sunset Serenade Roy and Gabby outwit murderous duo who plan to eliminate the new heir to a ranch.
1942 60m/B Roy Rogers, George "Gabby" Hayes, Helen Parrish; **D:** Joseph Kane. **VHS, Beta $19.95** NOS, MED, HEG ✶✶

Sunset Strip A photographer investigates a friend's murder, and enters the seamy world of drugs and rock and roll in L.A.
1985 83m/C Tom Elpin, Cheri Cameron Newell, John Mayall. **VHS, Beta $69.98** LIV, VES ✶

Sunset Strip A young dancer finds a job in a strip club and competes against the other women there to find the man of her dreams. The women take their jobs very seriously—even attending ballet classes to improve their performances. However, the viewer probably won't take this movie very seriously since it is just another excuse to show women in as little clothing as possible.
1991 (R) 95m/C Jeff Conaway, Michelle Foreman, Shelley Michelle; **D:** Paul G. Volk; **M:** John Gonzalez. **VHS $29.95** PMH Woof!

Sunset Trail Routine Maynard sagebrush saga with the hero protecting a woman rancher from outlaws.
1932 60m/B Ken Maynard. **VHS, Beta $19.95** NOS, VCI, DVT ✶

The Sunshine Boys Two veteran vaudeville partners, who have shared a love-hate relationship for decades, reunite for a television special. Adapted by Neil Simon from his play. Matthau was a replacement for Jack Benny, who died before the start of filming. Burns, for his first starring role since "Honolulu" in 1939, won an Oscar.
1975 (PG) 111m/C George Burns, Walter Matthau, Richard Benjamin, Lee Meredith, F. Murray Abraham, Carol Arthur, Howard Hesseman; **D:** Herbert Ross; **W:** Neil Simon. Academy Awards '75: Best Supporting Actor (Burns); Nominations: Best Actor (Matthau), Best Adapted Screenplay, Best Art Direction/Set Decoration; Golden Globe Awards '76: Best Actor—Musical/Comedy (Matthau), Best Film—Musical/Comedy, Best Supporting Actor (Benjamin). **VHS, Beta $14.95** MGM, BTV ✶✶✶

Sunshine Run Two escaped slaves and a young widow search for Spanish treasure in the Everglades. Also on video as "Black Rage."
1979 (PG) 102m/C Chris Robinson, Ted Cassidy, David Legge, Phyllis Robinson; **D:** Chris Robinson. **VHS, Beta** NO ✶

Sunstroke Seymour plays a desperate mother searching for her kidnapped child through the Arizona desert. Framed for murder, she cannot contact the police but must track the kidnappers herself, until she meets a drifter with secrets of his own.
1992 (R) 91m/C Jane Seymour, Stephen Meadows, Steve Railsback, Ray Wise, Don Ameche; **D:** James Keach; **W:** Duane Poole. **VHS, Beta** PAR ✶✶

The Super Pesci stars as a slumlord who faces a prison sentence thanks to his terminal neglect. The option given to him is to live in his own rat hole until he provides reasonable living conditions. This he does, and predictably learns a thing or two about his own greed and the people who suffer as a result of it. Pesci as always gives an animated performance but poor scripting laden with stereotypes and cliches successfully restricts effort.
1991 (R) 86m/C Joe Pesci, Vincent Gardenia, Madolyn Smith, Ruben Blades; **D:** Rod Daniel. **VHS $19.98** FXV, CCB ✶ ½

Super Bitch Nasty, cold, and uncaring woman uses men to keep up her expensive habits, then ruthlessly tosses them aside when she is done. She purposely entangles them in her drug trade and thinks nothing of their deaths. Proving once again that you get what you pay for. **AKA:** Mafia Junction.
1989 90m/C Stephanie Beacham, Patricia Hayes, Gareth Thomas; **D:** Massimo Dallamano. **VHS $79.95** ATL ✶ ½

Super Brother The feared and respected leader of an oppressed people is imprisoned, much to everyone's regret.
1990 (R) 90m/C Woody Strode. **VHS, Beta** ELE ✶

Super Force When astronaut Zach Stone (Olandt) returns from an assignment on Mars he finds his policeman brother has been murdered. He quits NASA and joins the force to get revenge, battling evil crime boss Tao Satori (Liddy). Stone also moonlights as a vigilante, complete with motorcycle and high-tech armoured suit. It's dumb but there's lots of action.
1990 92m/C Ken Olandt, G. Gordon Liddy, Larry B. Scott, Lisa Niemi, Marshall Teague; **Cameos:** Patrick Macnee; **D:** Richard Compton. **VHS $89.98** MCA ✶✶

Super Fuzz Rookie policeman develops super powers after being accidentally exposed to radiation. Somewhat ineptly, he uses his abilities to combat crime. Somewhat ineptly acted, written, and directed as well. **AKA:** Supersnooper.
1981 (PG) 97m/C Terence Hill, Joanne Dru, Ernest Borgnine; **D:** Sergio Corbucci. **VHS, Beta $69.98** SUE ✶ ½

Super Kung Fu Kid A kung fu hero is pursued by countless villains out to murder him but no one knows why.
19?? 90m/C Nan Kung Fan, Chung Lick, Yeung Si, Kong Yeh. **VHS $29.95** OCE ✶ ½

Super Mario Bros. $42 million adventure fantasy based on the popular Nintendo video game. The brothers are in hot pursuit of the Princess Daisy who's been kidnapped by evil slimebucket Hopper and taken to Dinohattan, a fungi-infested, garbage-strewn, rat-hole version of Manhattan. Hopper will amuse the adults, doing a gleeful reptilian version of Frank Booth from "Blue Velvet." Hoskins and Leguizamo act gamely in broad Nintendo style, enthusiastically partaking in high-tech wizardry and the many gags. Hits bullseye of target audience—elementary and junior high kids—with frenetic pace, gaudy special effects, oversized sets, and animatronic monsters.
1993 (PG) 104m/C Bob Hoskins, John Leguizamo, Samantha Mathis, Fisher Stevens, Richard Edson, Dana Kaminsky, Dennis Hopper, Fiona Shaw, Mojo Nixon, Lance Henriksen; **D:** Rocky Morton, Annabel Jankel; **W:** Edward Solomon, Parker Bennett, Terry Runte; **M:** Alan Silvestri. **VHS, Beta $96.03** HPH, BTV, TOU ✶✶ ½

Super Ninja A modern day ninja must battle modern-day bad guys.
19?? 90m/C Yu Jin Boa, Yi Dao Dao, Alexander Lou, Lou Mei, Wang Qiang, Yang Song, Yau Jin Tomas. **VHS $59.95** OCE ✶

Super Ninjas A ninja battles evil hordes of like-trained ninja warriors, and wins over and over again.
198? 104m/C Cheng Tien Chi, Lung Tien Hsiang, Chen Pei Hsi. **VHS, Beta** NO ✶

Super Seal An injured seal pup disrupts a family's normal existence after the young daughter adopts him.
1977 (G) 95m/C Foster Brooks, Sterling Holloway, Sarah Brown; **D:** Michael Dugan. **VHS, Beta $39.95** VCI ✶

Super Soul Brother A lazy no-goodnik accidentally ingests a strange potion which turns him into a master thief.
198? 80m/C Wildman Steve. **VHS $39.95** XVC ✶

Superargo A wrestler becomes a superhero with psychic powers and a bulletproof leotard. He fights against a madman who is turning athletes into robots. Successful Italian hero who wouldn't last two minutes in the ring with Batman. **AKA:** Il Re Dei Criminali; Superargo the Giant; The King of Criminals.
1967 95m/C Guy Madison, Ken Wood, Liz Barrett, Diana Loris; **D:** Paul Maxwell. **VHS, Beta $19.98** SNC, MAD ✶✶

Superbug Super Agent Dodo, the wonder car puts the brakes on crime in this silly action-adventure tale. A lemon in a lot full of Herbies.
1976 90m/C Robert Mark, Heidi Hansen, George Goodman. **VHS, Beta $59.95** JEF ✶ ½

Superchick Mild-mannered stewardess by day, sexy blonde with karate blackbelt by night. In addition to stopping a skyjacking she regularly makes love to men around the world. A superbomb that never gets off the ground.
1971 (R) 94m/C Joyce Jillson, Louis Quinn, Thomas Reardon; **D:** Ed Forsyth. **VHS, Beta $19.95** PSM Woof!

Superdad A middle-aged parent is determined to bridge the generation gap by trying his hand at various teenage activities. Disney family fare that's about as complicated as a television commercial. The adolescents are two-dimensional throwbacks to the fun-loving fifties.
1973 (G) 94m/C Bob Crane, Kurt Russell, Joe Flynn, Barbara Rush, Kathleen Cody, Dick Van Patten; **D:** Vincent McEveety; **M:** Buddy Baker. **VHS, Beta** DIS ✶

Superfly Controversial upon release, pioneering blaxploitation has Harlem dope dealer finding trouble with gangs and police as he attempts to establish retirement fund from one last deal. Excellent period tunes by Curtis Mayfield. Two lesser sequels.
1972 (R) 98m/C Ron O'Neal, Carl Lee, Sheila Frazier, Julius W. Harris; **D:** Gordon Parks Jr.; **M:** Curtis Mayfield. **VHS, Beta $19.98** WAR ✶✶ ½

Superfly T.N.T. This confusing sequel to ''Superfly'' finds O'Neal returning as Young-blood Priest. The now ex-drug dealer has retired with his girlfriend to Rome where he is approached by an African gun-runner (Browne) for help in a revolution against an oppressive government. Cheap exploitation. *AKA:* Super Fly T.N.T.
1973 (R) 87m/C Ron O'Neal, Roscoe Lee Browne, Sheila Frazier, Robert Guillaume, Jacques Sernas, William Berger; *D:* Ron O'Neal; *W:* Alex Haley. **VHS $14.95** *PAR* Woof!

Supergirl Big-budget bomb in which Slater made her debut and nearly killed her career, with the help of Kryptonite. Unexciting and unsophisticated story of a young woman, cousin to Superman, with super powers, based on the comic book series. She's in pursuit of a magic paperweight, but an evil sorceress wants it too. Dunaway is a terrifi-cally vile villainess with awesome black mag-ic powers. Slater is great to look at, but is much better in almost any other film.
1984 (PG) 114m/C Faye Dunaway, Helen Slater, Peter O'Toole, Mia Farrow, Brenda Vaccaro, Marc McClure, Simon Ward, Hart Bochner, Maureen Teefy, David Healy, Matt Frewer; *D:* Jeannot Szwarc; *M:* Jerry Goldsmith. **VHS, Beta $19.95** *LIV ℤ½*

Supergrass A low-brow British farce about a nebbish who poses as a drug smuggler to impress his girlfriend, and is then mistaken for a real one by the authorities.
1987 (R) 105m/C Adrian Edmondson, Peter Richardson, Nigel Planer, Jennifer Saunders, Ronald Allen, Dawn French; *D:* Peter Richardson. **VHS, Beta $19.98** *NLC ℤℤ*

Superman: The Movie The DC Com-ics legend comes alive in this wonderfully entertaining saga of Superman's life from a baby on the doomed planet Krypton to Earth's own Man of Steel. Hackman and Beatty pair marvelously as super criminal Lex Luthor and his bumbling sidekick. Award-winning special effects and a script that doesn't take itself too seriously make this great fun. Followed by three sequels.
1978 (PG) 144m/C Christopher Reeve, Margot Kidder, Marlon Brando, Gene Hackman, Glenn Ford, Susannah York, Ned Beatty, Valerie Perrine, Jackie Cooper, Marc McClure, Trevor Howard, Sarah Douglas, Terence Stamp, Jack O'Halloran, Phyllis Thaxter; *D:* Richard Donner; *W:* Mario Puzo, Robert Benton, David Newman; *M:* John Williams. Academy Awards '78: Best Visual Effects; Nominations: Best Film Editing, Best Sound, Best Original Score; National Board of Review Awards '78: 10 Best Films of the Year. **VHS, Beta $19.98** *WAR ℤℤℤ½*

Superman 2 The sequel to ''the movie'' about the Man of Steel. This time, he has his hands full with three super-powered villains from his home planet of Krypton. The ro-mance between reporter Lois Lane and our superhero is made believable and the story-line has more pace to it than the original. A sequel that often equals the first film—leave it to Superman to pull off the impossible.
1980 (PG) 127m/C Christopher Reeve, Margot Kidder, Gene Hackman, Ned Beatty, Jackie Cooper, Sarah Douglas, Jack O'Halloran, Susannah York, Marc McClure, Terence Stamp, Valerie Perrine, E.G. Marshall; *D:* Richard Lester; *W:* Mario Puzo, David Newman; *M:* John Williams. **VHS, Beta $19.98** *WAR ℤℤℤ*

Superman 3 Villainous businessman Vaughn tries to conquer Superman via the expertise of bumbling computer expert Pryor and the judicious use of and artifical form of Kryptonite. Superman explores his darker side after undergoing transformation into sleaze ball. Promising satiric start ultimately defeated by uneven story and direction and

boring physical comedy. Notable is the ab-sence of Lois Lane as a main character. Followed by ''Superman 4.''
1983 (PG) 123m/C Christopher Reeve, Richard Pryor, Annette O'Toole, Jackie Cooper, Margot Kidder, Marc McClure, Annie Ross, Robert Vaughn; *D:* Richard Lester; *W:* David Newman; *M:* John Williams. **VHS, Beta $19.98** *WAR ℤℤ*

Superman 4: The Quest for Peace The third sequel, in which the Man of Steel endeavors to rid the world of nuclear weapons, thereby pitting himself against nuclear-entrepreneur Lex Luthor and his su-perpowered creation, Nuclear Man. Special effects are dime-store quality and it appears that someone may have walked off with parts of the plot. Reeve deserves credit for remaining true to character through four films.
1987 (PG) 90m/C Christopher Reeve, Gene Hackman, Jon Cryer, Marc McClure, Margot Kidder, Mariel Hemingway, Sam Wanamaker; *D:* Sidney J. Furie; *W:* Mark Rosenthal; *M:* John Williams; *V:* Susannah York. **VHS, Beta $19.98** *WAR, APD ℤℤ*

Superman & the Mole Men The cast of the popular 1950s' television show made this rarely seen feature as a ''pilot'' for the series. Superman faces the danger threatened by the invasion of radioactive mole-men who make their way to the surface world from the bowels of the earth through an oil-well shaft. Simple fun. *AKA:* Superman and the Strange People.
1951 58m/C George Reeves, Phyllis Coates, Phyllis Coates, Jeff Corey; *D:* Lee Sholem. **VHS, Beta $19.98** *WAR ℤℤ½*

Superman: The Serial, Vol. 1 Su-perman was first seen in live action in this 15-part theatrical serial that has been rarely shown since its original release.
1948 248m/B Kirk Alyn, Noel Neill, Pierre Watkin, Tommy ''Butch'' Bond, Thomas Carr; *D:* Spencer Gordon Bennet. **VHS, Beta $29.95** *WAR ℤℤ½*

The Supernaturals Confederate Civil War-era ghosts, bent on avenging their deaths, haunt a wooded area in which mo-dern Yankee army maneuvers are practiced. Antebellum boredom.
1986 (R) 85m/C Maxwell Caulfield, LeVar Burton, Nichelle Nichols; *D:* Armand Mastroianni. **VHS, Beta $19.98** *SUE, NLC ℤ½*

Supersonic Man Incoherent shoestring-budget Superman spoof with a masked hero fighting to save the world from the evil intentions of a mad scientist.
1978 (PG) 85m/C Michael Coby, Cameron Mitchell, Diana Polakov; *D:* Piquer Simon. **VHS, Beta $59.95** *VCI* Woof!

Superstar: The Life and Times of Andy Warhol Even if you didn't grok Andy's 'pop' artwork and self-created celeb-rity persona, this ironic, kinetic, oft-rollicking documentary paints a vivid picture of the wild era he inspired and exploited. Interviewees range from Warhol cohorts like Dennis Hop-per to proud executives at the Campbell Soup plant. One highlight: a Warhol guest shot on ''The Love Boat.''
1990 87m/C Tom Wolfe, Sylvia Miles, David Hockney, Taylor Mead, Dennis Hopper; *D:* Chuck Workman. **VHS $89.98** *VES ℤℤℤ*

Superstition A reverend and his family move into a vacant house despite warnings about a curse from the townsfolk. Some people never learn. *AKA:* The Witch.
1982 85m/C James Houghton, Albert Salmi, Lynn Carlin; *D:* James Robertson Justice. **VHS, Beta $79.98** *LIV ℤ½*

Supervixens True to Meyer's low-rent exploitation film canon, this wild tale is filled with characteristic Amazons, sex and vio-lence. A gas station attendant is framed for the grisly murder of his girlfriend and hustles out of town, meeting a succession of well-endowed women during his travels. As if it needed further problems, it's hampered by a tasteless storyline and incoherent writing.
1975 105m/C Shari Eubank, Charles Napier; *D:* Russ Meyer. **VHS $59.99** *RMF ℤℤ*

Support Your Local Gunfighter Garner plays a western con man with his tongue firmly in his cheek. He comes to the small town of Purgatory and is thought to be a notorious gunfighter. He decides to go with the mistaken identity and use it to his profitable advantage. Elam is his bumbling sidekick and Pleshette the love interest. A delightful, deliberately cliche-filled western. A follow-up, not a sequel, to ''Support Your Local Sheriff'' (1969).
1971 (G) 92m/C James Garner, Jack Elam, Suzanne Pleshette, Harry Morgan, Dub Taylor, John Dehner, Joan Blondell, Ellen Corby, Henry Jones; *D:* Burt Kennedy. **VHS $19.98** *MGM ℤℤ*

Support Your Local Sheriff Ami-able, irreverent western spoof with more than its fair share of laughs. When a stranger stumbles into a gold rush town, he winds up becoming sheriff. Garner is perfect as the deadpan sheriff, particularly in the scene where he convinces Dern to remain in jail, in spite of the lack of bars. Neatly subverts every western cliche it encounters, yet keeps respect for formula western. Followed by ''Support Your Local Gunfighter.''
1969 (G) 92m/C James Garner, Joan Hackett, Walter Brennan, Bruce Dern, Jack Elam, Harry Morgan; *D:* Burt Kennedy; *W:* William Bowers. **VHS, Beta $19.98** *FOX, MGM ℤℤℤ½*

Suppose They Gave a War and Nobody Came? A small Southern town battles with a local army base in this enter-taining but wandering satire. The different acting styles used as the producers wavered on making this a comedy or drama were more at war with one another than the characters involved. *AKA:* War Games.
1970 (G) 113m/C Tony Curtis, Brian Keith, Ernest Borgnine, Suzanne Pleshette, Ivan Dixon, Bradford Dillman, Don Ameche; *D:* Hy Averback; *W:* Don McGuire. **VHS $59.98** *FOX ℤℤ½*

Surabaya Conspiracy Mystery and intrigue surround a quest for gold in Africa.
1975 90m/C Michael Rennie, Richard Jaeckel, Barbara Bouchet, Mike Preston; *D:* Roy Davis. **VHS, Beta** *NO ℤ½*

Sure Fire Wes (Blair) is a mercurial entre-preneur who thinks he has found the financial ticket to paradise with his vacation home scheme. Much to the chagrin of his wife Ellen (Dezina), he refuses to let anything stand in the way of his sure-fire fortune, even his family. Wes develops a little self-control as he realizes he's beginning to flake out, but it may be too late. Director Jost has put together a surprisingly unpretentious film with a virtually no-name cast, its plot speak-ing volumes on the American condition while unfolding in the bleak Utah desert.
1990 86m/C Tom Blair, Kristi Hager, Robert Ernst, Kate Dezina, Phillip R. Brown; *D:* Jon Jost; *W:* Jon Jost. **VHS $89.98** *WAC ℤℤ*

The Sure Thing College students who don't like each other end up travelling to California together, and of course, falling in love. Charming performances make up for predictability. Can't-miss director (and ex-Meathead) Reiner's second direct hit at the box office.

1985 (PG-13) 94m/C John Cusack, Daphne Zuniga, Anthony Edwards, Boyd Gaines, Lisa Jane Persky, Viveca Lindfors, Nicolette Sheridan, Tim Robbins; *D:* Rob Reiner; *W:* Jonathan Roberts. VHS, Beta, 8mm $14.95 COL, SUE *🐾🐾🐾*

Surf Nazis Must Die A piece of deliberate camp in the Troma mold, about a group of psychotic neo-Nazi surfers taking over the beaches of California in the wake of a devastating earthquake. Tongue-in-cheek, tasteless and cheap, but intentionally so. **1987** 83m/C Barry Brenner, Gail Neely, Michael Sonye, Dawn Wildsmith, Tom Shell, Bobbie Bresee; *D:* Peter George. VHS, Beta $19.98 MED, VTR *🐾*

Surf Ninjas Action comedy for the kiddies finds two young surfer dudes who are actually the long-lost crown princes of the obscure nation of Patu San. The country's incompetent (what a surprise, it's Nielsen) warlord wants the boys to stay lost. Lame jokes and tame martial arts sequences. *AKA:* Surf Warriors. **1993** (PG) 87m/C Ernie Reyes Jr., Nick Cowen, Rob Schneider, Leslie Nielsen, Tone Loc, John Karlen, Ernie Reyes Sr.; *D:* Neal Israel; *W:* Dan Gordon; *M:* David Kitay. VHS COL, NLC, IME *🐾🐾1/2*

Surf Party Romance among the sands of Malibu with Vinton as the owner of a surf shop. Risque in 1964; utterly campy today. *🎵*If I was an Artist; That's What Love Is; Pearly Shells. **1964** 68m/C Bobby Vinton, Jackie De Shannon, Patricia Morrow, Kenny Miller; *D:* Maury Dexter. VHS $39.95 MOV *🐾*

Surf 2 A most excellent group of surfers get sick from drinking tainted Buzz Cola concocted by demented chemist Deezen in most heinous effort to obliterate surfer population from Southern California. Bogus, dude. No, you didn't miss "Surf 1" (there's not one), the title is the sort of in-joke this exercise in mental meltdown perpetuates as comedy. Ha. *AKA:* Surf 2: The End of the Trilogy. **1984** (R) 91m/C Morgan Paull, Cleavon Little, Lyle Waggoner, Ruth Buzzi, Linda Kerridge, Carol Wayne, Eddie Deezen, Eric Stoltz, Brandis Kemp, Terry Kiser; *D:* Randall Badat; *W:* Randall Badat; *M:* Peter Bernstein. VHS, Beta $59.95 MVD, MED Woof!

Surfacing A girl braves the hostile northern wilderness to search for her missing father. This pseudo-psychological, sex-driven suspense flick makes little sense. **1984** 90m/C Joseph Bottoms, Kathleen Beller, R.H. Thomson, Margaret Dragu; *D:* Claude Jutra. VHS, Beta NO Woof!

Surprise Attack The Spanish Civil War forms the backdrop for this action opus. **197?** 124m/C Simon Andrew, Danny Martin, Patty Shepard; *D:* Joseph Loman. VHS, Beta $19.95 CNG *🐾*

Surrender A struggling woman artist and a divorced author fall in love but won't admit it for fear of being hurt again. Jumbled plot, unfortunate casting. Available in a Spanish-subtitled version. **1987** (PG) 95m/C Michael Caine, Sally Field, Steve Guttenberg, Peter Boyle, Jackie Cooper, Julie Kavner, Louise Lasser, Iman; *D:* Jerry Belson; *W:* Jerry Belson; *M:* Michel Colombier. VHS, Beta $19.98 WAR, GVV *🐾1/2*

Surrogate A young couple fights to keep their marriage afloat by turning to a sex surrogate. Strong cast helps carry odd, confusing script, with plenty of (you guessed it) sex, and a mystery to solve.

1988 100m/C Art Hindle, Shannon Tweed, Carole Laure, Michael Ironside, Marilyn Lightstone; *D:* Don Carmody. VHS, Beta MED *🐾*

Survival Earth After civilization collapses, humans begin reverting back to a primitive way of life. A young couple and a soldier of fortune fight against it, hoping for a better existence. **197?** 90m/C VHS NO *🐾*

Survival Game A young combat expert (Chuck Norris's son) gets involved with some ex-hippies in search of a $2 million cache. High-kickin' action. **1987** 91m/C Mike Norris, Deborah Goodrich, Seymour Cassel; *D:* Herb Freed. VHS, Beta $79.95 MED *🐾*

Survival of a Dragon A medieval Chinese warrior is transported into the future, where he goes on a kicking rampage. **197?** 88m/C Squall Hung, Jaguar Lee. VHS, Beta NO *🐾*

Survival of Spaceship Earth Man, his world and the protection of its ecology are discussed in this beautiful and fascinating film. Winner of numerous international awards due to the strength of its production values and writing. Nominated for 10 Emmy awards, winner of 2 Emmys. **1990** 63m/C Rue McClanahan; *D:* Dirk Summers; *W:* Dirk Summers. VHS $24.95 CPM, FCT, CRY *🐾*

Survival Quest Students in a Rocky Mountain survival course cross paths with a band of bloodthirsty mercenaries-in-training. A battle to the death ensues; you'll wish they'd all put each other out of their misery a lot sooner. **1989** (R) 90m/C Lance Henriksen, Dermot Mulroney, Mark Rolston, Steve Antin, Paul Provenza, Ben Hammer, Traci Lin, Catherine Keener, Reggie Bannister; *D:* Don A. Coscarelli. VHS, Beta $89.98 FOX *🐾1/2*

Survival Run Six California teenagers become stranded in the Mexican desert, where they witness Graves and Millard making a shady deal. The chase is on, the story is lame, the gory parts aren't gory—so why bother? **1980** (R) 90m/C Peter Graves, Ray Milland, Vincent Van Patten; *D:* Larry Spiegel. VHS, Beta $54.95 MED *🐾*

Survival Zone Nuclear holocaust survivors battle a violent band of marauding motorcyclists on the barren ranches of the 21st century. Advice to director Rubens and cohorts: Next time, find a plot that's not growing mold. **1984** (R) 90m/C Gary Lockwood, Morgan Stevens, Camilla Sparv; *D:* Percival Rubens. VHS, Beta $9.99 PSM Woof!

The Survivalist An arms-ready survivalist nut defends his family and supplies against a panicked society awaiting nuclear war. Poorly acted, little tension, and ineffective plotting make boredom seem a more critical issue than survival. **1987** (R) 96m/C Steve Railsback, Susan Blakely, Marjoe Gortner, David Wayne, Cliff DeYoung; *D:* Sig Shore; *W:* Robert Dillon. VHS, Beta $79.98 VES *🐾*

Surviving Desire Donovan plays Jude, a neurotic, romantic English professor who falls madly in love with an independently-minded student, Sophie. Unfortunately, Sophie is more interested in how the seduction will advance her writing than how it will affect her life. The lovers explore their brief affair by analyzing every emotion and motive in a series of quirky conversations. Intelligent, amusing, and stylized film from director Hartley. The tape also includes two Hartley

shorts: "Theory of Achievement" and "Ambition." **1991** 86m/C Martin Donovan, Mary B. Ward, Matt Malloy, Rebecca Nelson; *D:* Hal Hartley. VHS $89.95 FXL, ING *🐾🐾🐾*

Surviving the Game Poorly made hunt-the-human story. Homeless Ice-T is hired by a group of men to assist them on their annual hunt. But wait, he's the prey. Unbelievable premise pits the streetwise, down and out Ice-T against the savvy and weapons rich group—and he beats them at their own game. Few high-impact action sequences. The violence, although there isn't as much as might be expected, is graphic. **1994** (R) 94m/C Rutger Hauer, Ice-T, F. Murray Abraham, Gary Busey, Charles S. Dutton, John C. McGinley, William McNamara, Jeff Corey; *D:* Ernest R. Dickerson; *W:* Eric Bernt; *M:* Stewart Copeland. VHS NYR *🐾*

Survivor A jetliner crashes, leaving but one survivor, the pilot, who is then plagued by visions, tragedies, and ghosts of dead passengers. Viewers also suffer. **1980** 91m/C Robert Powell, Jenny Agutter, Joseph Cotten, Angela Punch McGregor; *D:* David Hemmings; *W:* David Ambrose. VHS, Beta $19.95 LHV, WAR *🐾*

Survivor A lone warrior on a post-nuclear holocaust wasteland battles a megalomaniac ruler. Moll as the evil villian is watchable, but overall the film is a wasteland, too. **1987** 92m/C Chip Mayer, Richard Moll, Sue Kiel; *D:* Michael Shackleton. VHS, Beta $19.98 LIV, VES *🐾🐾*

Survivors Two unemployed men find themselves the target of hit man, whom they have identified in a robbery attempt. One of the men goes gun-crazy protecting himself. Uneven comedy with wild Williams and laid-back Matthau. **1983** (R) 102m/C Robin Williams, Walter Matthau, Jerry Reed, John Goodman; *D:* Michael Ritchie; *W:* Michael Leeson. VHS, Beta $12.95 COL *🐾🐾*

Susan and God A selfish socialite returns from Europe and starts practicing a new religion, much to the dismay of her friends and family. Despite her preaching, her own domestic life is falling apart and she realizes that her preoccupation and selfish ways have caused a strain on her marriage and her relationship with her daughter. An excellent script and a fine performance from Crawford make this a highly satisfying film. *AKA:* The Gay Mrs. Trexel. **1940** 115m/B Joan Crawford, Fredric March, Ruth Hussey, John Carroll, Rita Hayworth, Nigel Bruce, Bruce Cabot, Rose Hobart, Rita Quigley, Marjorie Main, Gloria De Haven; *D:* George Cukor; *W:* Anita Loos. VHS $19.98 MGM *🐾🐾🐾*

Susan Lenox: Her Fall and Rise Garbo, the daughter of an abusive farmer, falls into the arms of the handsome Gable to escape an arranged marriage. Both stars are miscast, but the well-paced direction keeps the melodrama moving. *AKA:* The Rise of Helga; Rising to Fame. **1931** 84m/B Greta Garbo, Clark Gable, Jean Hersholt, John Miljan, Alan Hale, Hale Hamilton; *D:* Robert Z. Leonard. VHS, Beta $19.98 MGM, FCT *🐾🐾1/2*

Susan Slept Here While researching a movie on juvenile delinquents, a Hollywood script writer (Powell) is given custody of a spunky 18-year-old delinquent girl (Reynolds) during the Christmas holidays. Cute sex comedy. Based on the play "Susan," by Alex Gottlieb and Steve Fisher. **1954** 98m/C Dick Powell, Debbie Reynolds, Anne Francis; *D:* Frank Tashlin. VHS, Beta $15.95 VCI *🐾🐾1/2*

Susana Minor though still interesting Bunuel, in which a sexy delinquent young girl is rescued from vagrancy by a Spanish family, and how she subsequently undermines the family's structure through sexual allurement and intimidation. In Spanish with English subtitles.
1951 87m/B Rosita Quintana, Fernando Soler, Victor Manuel Mendoza, Matilde Palou; **D:** Luis Bunuel. **VHS, Beta $24.95** XVC, ING, APD 𝄢𝄢𝄢

Susanna Pass Oil deposits underneath a fish hatchery attract bad guys. They set off explosions to destroy the fishery, but game warden Rogers investigates. Minor outing for Roy.
1949 67m/C Roy Rogers, Dale Evans, Estelita Rodriguez, Martin Garralaga, Robert Emmett Keane, Lucien Littlefield, Douglas Fowley; **D:** William Witney. **VHS $12.98** REP 𝄢𝄢

Susannah of the Mounties An adorable young girl is left orphaned after a wagon train massacre and is adopted by a Mountie. An Indian squabble gives Shirley a chance to play little peacemaker and teach Scott how to tap dance, too. Could she be any cuter? Available colorized.
1939 78m/B Shirley Temple, Randolph Scott, Margaret Lockwood, J. Farrell MacDonald, Moroni Olsen, Victor Jory; **D:** William A. Seiter. **VHS, Beta $19.98** FOX 𝄢𝄢½

Suspect An overworked Washington, DC, public defender (Cher) is assigned to a controversial murder case in which her client is a deaf-mute, skid-row bum. A cynical lobbyist on the jury illegally researches the case himself. They work together to uncover a far-reaching conspiracy. Unrealistic plot, helped along by good performances and tight direction.
1987 (R) 101m/C Dennis Quaid, Cher, Liam Neeson, E. Katherine Kerr, Joe Mantegna, John Mahoney, Philip Bosco; **D:** Peter Yates; **W:** Eric Roth; **M:** Michael Kamen. **VHS, Beta, 8mm $14.95** COL 𝄢𝄢½

Suspended Alibi British crime-drama about an adulterous man unjustly accused when his alibi is murdered. Overlook the convenient coincidence. **AKA:** Suspected Alibi.
1956 64m/B Patrick Holt, Honor Blackman, Andrew Keir, Valentine Dyall; **D:** Alfred Shaughnessy. **VHS $16.95** NOS, SNC 𝄢½

Suspicion Alfred Hitchcock's suspense thriller about a woman who gradually realizes she is married to a killer and may be next on his list. An excellent production unravels at the end due to RKO's insistence that Grant retain his "attractive" image. This forced the writers to leave his guilt or innocence undetermined. Available colorized.
1941 99m/B Cary Grant, Joan Fontaine, Cedric Hardwicke, Nigel Bruce, May Whitty, Leo G. Carroll, Heather Angel; **D:** Alfred Hitchcock. Academy Awards '41: Best Actress (Fontaine); Nominations: Best Picture. **VHS, Beta $19.98** RKO, MED, MLB 𝄢𝄢𝄢½

Suspicion Remake of the chilling Hitchcock tale. Newlywed bride is consumed with fears about her wealthy new husband. The suspense builds as she comes to suspect that she is married to a cold-blooded killer. Curtin in way over her head.
1987 97m/C Jane Curtin, Anthony Andrews; **D:** Andrew Grieve. **VHS, Beta $79.95** MED 𝄢𝄢

Suspiria An American dancer enters a weird European ballet academy and finds they teach more than movement as bodies begin piling up. Sometimes weak plot is aided by great-but-gory special effects, fine photography, good music, and a chilling opening sequence. Also available in unrated version.

1977 (R) 92m/C Jessica Harper, Joan Bennett, Alida Valli, Udo Kier; **D:** Dario Argento; **W:** Dario Argento. **VHS, Beta** HHE, QVD 𝄢𝄢𝄢

Suzanne Set in 1950s Quebec, the story of a good woman whose criminal boyfriend leaves her pregnant when he is sent to prison. Ten years later, he returns, threatening her happy marriage. Confused script can't be saved by valiant cast.
1980 (R) 90m/C Sondra Locke, Richard Dreyfuss, Gene Barry. **VHS, Beta $69.98** VES 𝄢½

Suzy Harlow's fourth film and her only one with Grant is a mixture of romance, action, and comedy set during WWI. Grant plays a French flier who falls in love with Harlow, although she is married to Tone. Excellent air footage and some good funny scenes keep this film moving right along. Even has Grant singing hit song, "Did I Remember?"
1926 99m/B Jean Harlow, Franchot Tone, Cary Grant, Benita Hume, Lewis Stone, Inez Courtney; **D:** George Fitzmaurice. **VHS $19.98** MGM 𝄢𝄢½

Svengali A music teacher uses his hypnotic abilities to manipulate one of his singing students and make her a star. Soon the young woman is singing for sell-out crowds, but only if her teacher is present. Barrymore in a hypnotic performance. Adapted from "Trilby" by George Du Maurier. Remade in 1955 and 1983.
1931 76m/B John Barrymore, Marian Marsh, Donald Crisp; **D:** Archie Mayo. **VHS, Beta $19.95** NOS, GPV, SNC 𝄢𝄢𝄢

Svengali Limp remake of the 1931 film about Trilby, an artist's model, falling under the mesmerizing spell of the title character, who is determined to make her into a famous singer. Chiefly notable for its visuals which were based on the illustrations from the original novel "Trilby" by George du Maurier.
1955 82m/C Hildegarde Neff, Donald Wolfit, Terence Morgan, Derek Bond, Paul Rogers, David Kossoff; **D:** Noel Langley; **W:** Noel Langley. **VHS** NO 𝄢𝄢½

Svengali Flamboyant but faded music star O'Toole mentors Foster, a young pop singer looking for stardom. Boring, made for television remake of the Barrymore classic.
1983 96m/C Peter O'Toole, Jodie Foster, Elizabeth Ashley, Larry Joshua, Pamela Blair, Barbara Byrne, Holly Hunter; **D:** Anthony Harvey; **M:** John Barry. **VHS** NO 𝄢𝄢½

Swamp Fire Mississippi river-boat captain Weismuller, wrestles aligators and battles with Crabbe for the woman he loves in this turgid drama. Look for Janssen in an early screen performance.
1946 69m/B Johnny Weissmuller, Virginia Grey, Buster Crabbe, Carol Thurston, Edwin Maxwell, Pedro de Cordoba, Pierre Watkin, David Janssen; **D:** William H. Pine. **VHS, Beta $19.95** NOS, SNC 𝄢½

Swamp of the Lost Monster An incredible Mexican horror/western/musical that features a mouse-like monster that'll scare the cheese out of you.
1965 88m/B Gaston Santos, Sarah Cabrera, Manuel Donde; **D:** Rafael Baledon. **VHS, Beta $24.95** NOS, SNC, GHV 𝄢

Swamp Thing Overlooked camp drama about scientist accidentally turned into tragic half-vegetable, half-man swamp creature, with government agent Barbeau caught in the middle, occasionally while topless. A vegetarian nightmare or ecology propaganda? You be the judge. Adapted from the comic book by Craven.
1982 (PG) 91m/C Adrienne Barbeau, Louis Jourdan, Ray Wise; **D:** Wes Craven; **W:** Wes Craven. **VHS, Beta $14.95** COL, SUE 𝄢𝄢½

Swamp Women Four escaped women convicts, known as the "Nardo Gang," chase after a stash of diamonds in this super cheap, super bad action adventure from cult director Corman. **AKA:** Swamp Diamonds; Cruel Swamp.
1955 73m/C Mike Connors, Marie Windsor, Beverly Garland, Carole Mathews, Susan Cummings; **D:** Roger Corman. **VHS $16.95** SNC 𝄢

The Swan Princess' arranged marriage with a prince is complicated by a poor man also in love with her. Classic romantic comedy of the silent era. Remade in 1956. Based on a play by Ferenc Molnar.
1925 50m/B Adolphe Menjou, Ricardo Cortez, Frances Howard; **D:** Dimitri Buchowetzki. **VHS, Beta $19.95** NOS, DVT 𝄢𝄢½

The Swan A twist on the Cinderella story with Kelly (in her last film before her marriage) as the charming beauty waiting for her prince. Both Guinness, as the crown prince, and Jourdan, as her poor tutor, want her hand (and the rest of her). Attractive cast, but story gets slow from time to time. Remake of a 1925 silent film. The laser disc version also includes "Wedding in Monaco," the news short showing Kelly's wedding to Prince Rainier.
1956 112m/C Grace Kelly, Louis Jourdan, Alec Guinness, Jessie Royce Landis, Brian Aherne, Estelle Winwood; **D:** Charles Vidor. **VHS $19.98** MGM 𝄢𝄢𝄢

Swann in Love A handsome, wealthy French aristocrat makes a fool of himself over a beautiful courtesan who cares nothing for him. Elegant production lacks spark. Based upon a section of Marcel Proust's "Remembrance of Things Past." In French with English subtitles or an English language version. **AKA:** Un Amour De Swann.
1984 (R) 110m/C Jeremy Irons, Ornella Muti, Alain Delon, Fanny Ardant, Marie-Christine Barrault; **D:** Volker Schlondorff; **W:** Peter Brook, Jean-Claude Carriere. **VHS, Beta $24.95** XVC, MED, ING 𝄢𝄢½

The Swap Ex-con searches for his brother's killer. Muddled story uses clips from early De Niro film "Sam's Song."
1971 (R) 120m/C Robert De Niro, Jered Mickey, Jennifer Warren, Terrayne Crawford, Martin Kelley; **D:** Jordan Leondopolous. **VHS $14.95** MGM, CAN 𝄢½

Swap Meet Wacky teen sex comedy about shenanigans at a small town swap meet. Strictly bargain basement.
1979 86m/C Ruth Cox, Deborah Richter, Danny Goldman, Cheryl Rixon, Jonathan Gries; **D:** Brice Mack. **VHS** VCI 𝄢

The Swarm Low-brow insect contest as scientist Caine fends off a swarm of killer bees when they attack metro Houston. The bees are really just black spots painted on the film. And the acting is terrible. "B" movie on bees, but it's still better than "The Bees."
1978 (PG) 116m/C Michael Caine, Katharine Ross, Richard Widmark, Lee Grant, Richard Chamberlain, Olivia de Havilland, Henry Fonda, Fred MacMurray, Patty Duke, Ben Johnson, Jose Ferrer, Slim Pickens, Bradford Dillman, Cameron Mitchell; **D:** Irwin Allen; **W:** Sterling Silliphant; **M:** Jerry Goldsmith, John Williams. **VHS, Beta $19.98** WAR 𝄢

Swashbuckler Jaunty pirate returns from sea to find his friends held captive by dastardly dictator for their political views. He rescues them, and helps them overthrow the erstwhile despot. **AKA:** Scarlet Buccaneer.

S

1976 (PG) 101m/C Robert Shaw, James Earl Jones, Peter Boyle, Genevieve Bujold, Beau Bridges, Geoffrey Holder; **D:** James Goldstone; **W:** Jeffrey Bloom; **M:** John Addison. **VHS** $79.95 *MCA* 🎬

Swashbuckler Eighteenth-century pirate fracas that can't compete with Errol Flynn. *AKA:* The Scarlet Buccaneer.
1984 100m/C Jean-Paul Belmondo, Marlene Jobert, Laura Antonelli, Michel Auclair, Julien Guiomar; **D:** Jean-Paul Rappeneau. **VHS** *MCA* 🎬½

Sweater Girls Sex comedy about two girls starting their own club called the "Sweater Girls." Terrible teen exploitaiton film.
1978 (R) 90m/C Charlene Tilton, Harry Moses, Meegan King, Noelle North, Kate Sarchet, Carol Seflinger, Tamara Barkley, Julie Parsons; **D:** Donald M. Jones. **VHS, Beta** *NO Woof!*

Swedenhielms A poor Swedish scientist struggles to support his family while hoping to win a Nobel prize, while his two sons get involved in a moneylending scandal. Bergman is the rich fiance of one son, to whom poverty is a puzzlement. Fine performances by Ekman and the 20-year-old Bergman (in her third film). In Swedish with English subtitles.
1935 92m/B Gosta Ekman, Karin Swanstrom, Bjorn Berglund, Hakan Westergren, Tutta Rolf, Ingrid Bergman, Sigurd Wallen; **D:** Gustaf Molander. **VHS, Beta** $29.95 *WAC, LUM, ING* 🎬🎬½

Sweeney Todd: The Demon Barber of Fleet Street A filmed performance of Sondheim's Tony-winning Broadway musical. Creepy thriller about a demon barber, his razor, and his wife's meatpies.
1984 139m/C Angela Lansbury, George Hearn; **D:** Harold Prince; **M:** Stephen Sondheim. **VHS, Beta** $39.95 *MVD, RKO, STS* 🎬🎬½

Sweet Adeline Smalltime hayseed makes it big in the music business while brother steals his girl back home. Not easily put off, young songster perseveres.
1926 60m/B Charles Ray, Gertrude Olmsted, Jack Clifford, Ida Lewis; **D:** Jerome Storm. **VHS, Beta** $19.95 *GPV, FCT* 🎬🎬

Sweet Adeline Dunne attracts all the men in her father's Hoboken beer garden but Woods plays the songwriter with whom she finds real love. Wonderful score. 🎵Play Us a Polka, Dot; Here Am I; We Were So Young; Why Was I Born?; Mollie O'Donahue; Lonely Feet; 'Twas Not So Long Ago; Don't Ever Leave Me.
1935 87m/B Irene Dunne, Donald Woods, Hugh Herbert, Ned Sparks, Joseph Cawthorn, Louis Calhern; **D:** Mervyn LeRoy; **M:** Jerome Kern, Oscar Hammerstein. **VHS** $19.98 *MGM* 🎬🎬½

Sweet Beat A young woman gets a chance to become a singer when she reaches the finals of a British beauty contest. Pedestrian story enlivened by music from popular British bands of the time. *AKA:* The Amorous Sex.
1962 66m/B Julie Amber, Sheldon Lawrence, Irv Bauer, Billy Myles. **VHS, Beta** $19.95 *NOS, INC, TPV* 🎬

Sweet Bird of Youth An acclaimed adaptation of the Tennessee Williams play about Chance Wayne, a handsome drifter who travels with an aging movie queen to his small Florida hometown, hoping she'll get him started in a movie career. However, coming home turns into a big mistake, as the town boss wants revenge on Chance for seducing his daughter, Heavenly. Williams' original stage ending was cleaned up, provid-

ing a conventional "happy" movie ending for the censors. Remade for television in 1989 with Elizabeth Taylor and Mark Harmon in the lead roles.
1962 120m/C Paul Newman, Geraldine Page, Ed Begley Sr., Mildred Dunnock, Rip Torn, Shirley Knight, Madeline Sherwood; **D:** Richard Brooks; **W:** Richard Brooks. Academy Awards '62: Best Supporting Actor (Begley); Nominations: Best Actress (Page), Best Supporting Actress (Knight); Golden Globe Awards '63: Best Actress—Drama (Page). **VHS, Beta** $19.95 *MGM, BTV, TRI* 🎬🎬🎬

Sweet Bird of Youth Made for television remake of the Tennessee Williams play, which was filmed for the big screen in 1962, with Harmon and Taylor having the unenviable task of following in the roles played by Paul Newman and Geraldine Page. She is an egotistical, has-been movie star and he is her ambitious gigolo who wants a movie career of his own. Unfortunately, the trouble that drove him from his Florida hometown is still there when he reappears, actress in tow. Things don't bode well. The television production uses Williams' original ending, which was cleaned up for a "happier" version in the '62 film.
1989 (R) 95m/C Elizabeth Taylor, Mark Harmon, Rip Torn, Valerie Perrine, Ruta Lee, Seymour Cassel, Kevin Geer, Michael Wilding Jr.; **D:** Nicolas Roeg; **W:** Gavin Lambert; **M:** Ralph Burns. **VHS** $89.95 *TRI* 🎬🎬

Sweet Charity An ever-optimistic dime-a-dance girl has a hard time finding a classy guy to marry. MacLaine is appealing in this big-budget version of the popular Broadway musical by Neil Simon (derived from Fellini's "Notti di Cabiria"). Fosse's debut as film director. Watch for Cort as a flower child. 🎵My Personal Property; It's a Nice Face; Hey, Big Spender; Rich Man's Frug; If My Friends Could See Me Now; There's Gotta Be Something Better Than This; Rhythm of Life; Sweet Charity; I'm a Brass Band.
1969 148m/C Shirley MacLaine, Chita Rivera, John McMartin, Paula Kelly, Sammy Davis Jr., Ricardo Montalban, Bud Cort; **D:** Bob Fosse; **M:** Cy Coleman. **VHS, Beta** $14.98 *MCA* 🎬🎬🎬

Sweet Country During the overthrow of the Allende government in Chile, the lives of a Chilean family and an American couple intertwine. Heavy-going propaganda is a cross between tragedy and unintentional comedy. Made by the director of "Zorba the Greek."
1987 (R) 147m/C Jane Alexander, John Cullum, Carole Laure, Franco Nero, Joanna Pettet, Randy Quaid, Irene Papas, Jean-Pierre Aumont, Pierre Vaneck, Katia Dandoulaki; **D:** Michael Cacoyannis. **VHS, Beta** *NO* 🎬½

Sweet Country Road A rock singer journeys to Nashville to try to cross over into country music.
1981 95m/C Buddy Knox, Kary Lynn, Gordy Trapp, Johnny Paycheck, Jeanne Pruett. **VHS, Beta** $19.95 *NWV* 🎬½

Sweet Creek County War Retired sheriff must leave his quiet ranch to battle a greedy businessman.
1982 90m/C Richard Egan, Albert Salmi, Nita Talbot, Slim Pickens. **VHS, Beta** *NO* 🎬

Sweet Dreams Biography of country singer Patsy Cline, focusing mostly on her turbulent marriage. Her quick rise to stardom ended in an early death. Fine performances throughout. Cline's original recordings are used. 🎵Walking After Midnight; Crazy; Sweet Dreams; San Antonio Rose; Blue Moon of Kentucky; Lovesick Blues; Seven Lonely Days; Foolin' Around; Your Cheatin' Heart.

1985 (PG-13) 115m/C Jessica Lange, Ed Harris, Ann Wedgeworth, David Clennon; **D:** Karel Reisz; **W:** Robert Getchell. **VHS, Beta** *NO* 🎬🎬½

Sweet Ecstasy Wealthy shenanigans on the French Riviera. Pezy is the upright young man who can't sleep with anyone unless he's in love, much to Sommer's dismay. *AKA:* Douce Violence; Sweet Violence.
1962 75m/B Elke Sommer, Pierre Brice, Christian Pezy, Claire Maurier; **D:** Max Pecas. **VHS** $29.95 *NO* 🎬½

Sweet 15 A young Hispanic girl learns that there is more to growing up than parties when she learns her father is an illegal alien. Originally aired on PBS as part of the "Wonderworks" family movie series.
1990 120m/C Karla Montana, Panchito Gomez, Tony Plana, Jenny Gago, Susan Ruttan; **D:** Victoria Hochberg. **VHS** $29.95 *PME, HMV, FCT* 🎬🎬

Sweet Georgia Soft-core star Jordan is a lusty wife whose husband is an alcoholic, so she has a roll in the hay with almost every other cast member. Lots of action, too, including a pitchfork fight. Ride 'em cowboy.
1972 80m/C Marsha Jordan. **VHS** $19.95 *VDM* 🎬

Sweet Hearts Dance Parallel love stories follow two long-time friends, one just falling in love, the other struggling to keep his marriage together. Charming performances from all, but a slow pace undermines the film.
1988 (R) 95m/C Don Johnson, Jeff Daniels, Susan Sarandon, Elizabeth Perkins, Justin Henry, Holly Marie Combs; **D:** Robert Greenwald; **W:** Ernest Thompson; **M:** Richard Gibbs. **VHS, Beta** $89.95 *COL* 🎬🎬

Sweet Hostage Escaped mental patient kidnaps uneducated farm girl and holds her captive in a remote cabin. Blair and Sheen turn in good performances. Adaptation of Nathaniel Benchley's "Welcome to Xanadu." Made-for-television.
1975 93m/C Linda Blair, Martin Sheen, Jeanne Cooper, Lee DeBroux, Dehl Berti, Bert Remsen; **D:** Lee Philips. **VHS** *IMP* 🎬🎬½

Sweet Justice This time its the women who get to be commandos, have all the adventures, and get revenge on various scum. The nominal plotline has Sunny Justice (Carter) and her group of gal-warriors avenging the sadistic murder of a friend. Martial arts, weapons, and action galore.
1992 (R) 92m/C Finn Carter, Kathleen Kinmont, Marc Singer, Frank Gorshin; **Cameos:** Mickey Rooney; **D:** Allen Plone; **W:** Allen Plone, Jim Tabilio. **VHS** $89.95 *TRI* 🎬½

Sweet Killing A banker murders his shrewish wife to be with another woman. He thinks he has the perfect alibi, but then his fictitious excuse comes to life when a mysterious stranger begins stalking him. Based on the novel "Qualthrough" by Agnes Hall.
1993 (R) 87m/C Anthony Higgins, F. Murray Abraham, Leslie Hope, Michael Ironside, Andrea Ferreol; **D:** Eddy Matalon; **W:** Eddy Matalon. **VHS, Beta** *PAR* 🎬🎬

Sweet Liberty Alda's hometown is overwhelmed by Hollywood chaos during the filming of a movie version of his novel about the American Revolution. Pleasant but predictable.
1986 (PG) 107m/C Alan Alda, Michael Caine, Michelle Pfeiffer, Bob Hoskins, Lillian Gish; **D:** Alan Alda; **W:** Alan Alda; **M:** Bruce Broughton. **VHS, Beta** $19.95 *MCA* 🎬🎬

Sweet Lies An insurance investigator tracking a scam artist in Paris is preyed upon by a group of single women betting one another that any man can be seduced. Slow comedy.

1988 (R) 86m/C Treat Williams, Joanna Pacula, Julianne Phillips, Laura Manszky, Norbert Weisser, Marilyn Dodd-Frank; **D:** Nathalie Delon; **M:** Trevor Jones. VHS, Beta $79.98 FOX 🎬½

Sweet Light in a Dark Room A student in Prague during the Nazi Occupation hides a Jewish girl. He falls in love with her but becomes the suspect in the murder of a Nazi officer. Directed by the great Czech filmmaker Weiss who was himself forced to leave his country during Nazi occupation. In Czech with English subtitles. *AKA:* Romeo, Julia a Tma; Romeo, Juliet and Darkness. 1960 93m/B Ivan Mistrik, Dana Smutna; **D:** Jiri Weiss. VHS $29.95 FCT, DVT, HEG 🎬🎬

Sweet Lorraine A bittersweet, nostalgic comedy about the staff and clientele of a deteriorating Catskills hotel on the eve of its closing. 1987 (PG-13) 91m/C Maureen Stapleton, Lee Richardson, Trini Alvarado, Freddie Roman, John Bedford Lloyd, Giancarlo Esposito, Edie Falco, Todd Graff, Evan Handler; **D:** Steve Gomer; **W:** Michael Zettler, Shelly Altman; **M:** Richard Robbins. VHS, Beta $79.98 PAR 🎬🎬🎬

Sweet Love, Bitter The downfall of a black jazz saxophonist in the 1950's. The character is loosely based on the life of legendary musician Charlie "Bird" Parker. Alto sax man McPherson dubs Gregory's solos. Adapted from the novel "Night Song" by John A. Williams. *AKA:* It Won't Rub Off, Baby; Black Love, White Love. 1967 92m/C Dick Gregory, Don Murray, Diane Varsi, Robert Hooks; **D:** Herbert Danska; **W:** Lewis Jacobs, Herbert Danska; **M:** Mal Waldron. VHS $59.95 RHP, MVD, FCT 🎬🎬½

Sweet Movie A provocative cult classic concerning a South African tycoon who purchases a virgin bride and then exploits her sexually. In English and French with subtitles. 1975 120m/C Carole Laure, Pierre Clementi, Sami Frey; **D:** Dusan Makavejev; **W:** Dusan Makavejev; **M:** Manos Hadjidakis. VHS, Beta $79.95 FCT, MOV 🎬🎬

Sweet Perfection Jackson plans a big promotion for her beauty contest. Who will be voted the "Perfect Woman?" Tired premise, but it has its moments. 1990 (R) 90m/C Stoney Jackson, Anthony Norman McKay, Catero Colbert, Liza Crusat, Reggie Theus, Tatiana Tumbtzen. VHS $59.95 XVC, HHE 🎬🎬

Sweet Poison Bobby Stiles is a ruthless criminal who has just broken out of prison. He wants to get home and settle the score with his brother, who actually committed the crime Bobby was imprisoned for. Henry and Charlene Odell are traveling cross-country when Bobby crosses their path and forces them to drive him home. Bobby's not too busy eluding the police to notice that his captives marriage is a little shaky—and that Charlene is attractive and sexy. As Bobby and Charlene get closer husband Henry just becomes another problem. 1991 (R) 101m/C Steven Bauer, Patricia Healy, Edward Herrmann; **D:** Brian Grant. VHS $79.98 MCA 🎬🎬

Sweet Revenge TV journalist kidnapped by a white slavery ring in the Asian jungles. After escaping, she returns for vengeance. Meek drama. 1987 (R) 79m/C Ted Shackleford, Nancy Allen, Martin Landau; **D:** Mark Sobel. VHS, Beta $79.95 MED 🎬🎬

Sweet Revenge When a judge tells a divorced couple that the woman must pay the man alimony, she hires an actress to marry her ex. The tables are turned in this way-out marriage flick, reminiscent of the screwball comedies of the 1940s. 1990 89m/C Rosanna Arquette, Carrie Fisher, John Sessions; **D:** Charlotte Brandstrom; **W:** Janet Brownell. VHS, Beta $79.98 TTC 🎬🎬

Sweet Rosie O'Grady Musical-comedy star Grable has returned to New York after success in England, where she caught the eye of nobleman Gardiner. Ex-boyfriend Young is a tabloid reporter who's expected by editor Menjou to get the scoop on her past. Seems she used to perform in Bowery saloons although that's not what Grable's been telling everyone. Slight story, charming performers, and lots of songs. Remade in 1948 as "That Wonderful Urge." 🎵My Heart Tells Me; My Sam; Oh Where is the Groom?; The Wishing Waltz; Going to the Country Fair; Get Your Police Gazette; Battle Cry; Sweet Rosie O'Grady; Two Little Girls in Blue. 1943 74m/C Betty Grable, Robert Young, Adolphe Menjou, Reginald Gardiner, Virginia Grey, Phil Regan, Sig Rumann, Alan Dinehart; **D:** Irving Cummings. VHS RXM 🎬🎬½

Sweet 16 Serial killings in Texas town begin to set off muffled alarms in big head of sheriff Hopkins. Sixteen-year-old Melissa has recently moved into town. She's beautiful, mysterious, and promiscuous, and she has a big problem—all her boyfriends end up dead. No real puzzle. 1981 (R) 90m/C Susan Strasberg, Bo Hopkins, Don Stroud, Dana Kimmell, Patrick Macnee, Larry Storch; **D:** Jim Sotos. VHS, Beta $69.95 VES 🎬🎬

Sweet Smell of Success Evil New York City gossip columnist J.J. Hunsecker (Lancaster) and sleazy press agent (Curtis) cook up smear campaign to ruin career of jazz musician in love with J.J.'s sister. Engrossing performances, great dialogue. 1957 96m/C Burt Lancaster, Tony Curtis, Martin Milner, Barbara Nichols, Sam Levene; **D:** Alexander MacKendrick; **W:** Ernest Lehman, Clifford Odets; **M:** Elmer Bernstein. VHS $19.98 MGM 🎬🎬🎬½

Sweet Spirits Soft-sell European fluff about a modern mannequin having a raucous affair with an artist. 198? 87m/C Erika Blanc, Farley Granger. VHS, Beta $29.95 MED Woof!

Sweet Sugar Slave girls try to escape from a Costa Rican sugar cane plantation and its cruel owner. Needless to say, vulgar exploitation runs hither and yon in this film. *AKA:* Chaingang Girls; Captive Women 3: Sweet Sugar. 1972 (R) 90m/C Phyllis E. Davis, Ella Edwards, Pamela Collins, Cliff Osmond, Timothy Brown; **D:** Michel Levesque. VHS NO 🎬½

Sweet Sweetback's Baadasssss Song A black pimp kills two policemen who beat up a black militant. He uses his streetwise survival skills to elude his pursuers and escape to Mexico. A thriller, but racist, sexist, and violent. 1971 97m/C Melvin Van Peebles, Simon Chuckster, John Amos; **D:** Melvin Van Peebles; **W:** Melvin Van Peebles. VHS, Beta $59.98 SUN 🎬🎬🎬

Sweet Talker Following his release from prison, a charming con man shows up in a small coastal village, thinking the townsfolk will be ripe for the picking. What he doesn't know is they can do some sweet talking of their own, and he soon finds himself caring for a pretty widow and her son. Enjoyable light comedy works thanks to likable leads. 1991 (PG) 91m/C Bryan Brown, Karen Allen, Chris Haywood, Bill Kerr, Bruce Spence, Bruce Myles, Paul Chubb, Peter Hehir, Justin Rosniak; **D:** Michael Jenkins; **W:** Tony Morphett; **M:** Richard Thompson. VHS $89.98 LIV 🎬🎬

Sweet Trash A vice cop, having an affair with a 17-year-old prostitute, is blackmailed by an underworld figure. Lives up to its name. 1989 (R) 80m/C Sebastian Gregory, Sharon Matt, Luke Perry, Bonnie Clark, Gene Blackey; **D:** John Hayes. VHS NO Woof!

Sweet William A philandering and seemingly irresistible young man finds that one sensitive woman hasn't the patience or time for his escapades. Adult comedy concerned with sex without displaying any on the screen. 1979 (R) 88m/C Sam Waterston, Jenny Agutter, Anna Massey, Arthur Lowe; **D:** Claude Whatham. VHS, Beta $59.95 PSM 🎬🎬🎬

Sweet Young Thing Young students at a French girls' school receive all sorts of attention from the male staff. 19?? 83m/C Jean Tolzac, Bernard Musson. VHS, Beta MED 🎬🎬🎬

Sweetheart! Biography of Hal Banks, convicted for strong-arming shipping unions in an effort to destroy them. 19?? 115m/C Maury Chaykin. VHS NO 🎬½

Sweetheart of the Navy Sailors help a cafe singer out of a jam, with one of them almost giving up his career for her. Standard fare, but Parker is well worth listening to. 1937 63m/B Eric Linden, Cecilia Parker, Roger Imhof, Bernadene Hayes, Jason Robards Sr., Don Barclay; **D:** Duncan Mansfield. VHS $19.95 NOS 🎬½

Sweethearts MacDonald and Eddy star as married stage actors trying to get some time off from their hectic schedule in this show-within-a-show. Trouble ensues when their conniving producer begs, pleads and tricks them into staying. Lots of well-staged musical numbers. 🎵Wooden Shoes; Every Lover Must Meet His Fate; Sweethearts; Pretty as a Picture; Summer Serenade; On Parade. 1938 114m/C Jeanette MacDonald, Nelson Eddy, Frank Morgan, Florence Rice, Ray Bolger, Mischa Auer; **D:** Woodbridge S. Van Dyke. VHS $19.98 MGM 🎬🎬

Sweetie Bizarre, expressive Australian tragicomedy about a pair of sisters—one a withdrawn, paranoid Plain Jane, the other a dangerously extroverted, overweight sociopath who re-enters her family's life and turns it upside down. Campion's first feature. 1989 (R) 97m/C Genevieve Lemon, Karen Colston, Tom Lycos, Jon Darling, Dorothy Barry, Michael Lake, Andre Pataczek; **D:** Jane Campion; **W:** Gerard Lee, Jane Campion; **M:** Martin Armiger. VHS, Beta $89.95 LIV 🎬🎬🎬

Sweetwater An independent woman and a feisty young orphan find each other amid society's rejections. 1984 30m/C VHS, Beta LCA 🎬🎬

Swept Away... A rich and beautiful Milanese woman is shipwrecked on a desolate island with a swarthy Sicilian deck hand, who also happens to be a dedicated communist. Isolated, the two switch roles, with the wealthy woman dominated by the crude proletarian. Sexy and provocative. *AKA:* Swept Away...By an Unusual Destiny in the Blue Sea of August. 1975 (R) 116m/C Giancarlo Giannini, Mariangela Melato; **D:** Lina Wertmuller; **W:** Lina Wertmuller. VHS, Beta $59.95 COL, APD 🎬🎬🎬

Swift Justice Mayor of a small town thinks he's gotten away with murder after leaving a young girl for dead in a junk yard. However, the mayor and his violent pals are soon hunted by an ex-Green Beret with a penchant for justice.
1988 90m/C Jon Greene, Sindi Rome, Cameron Mitchell, Aldo Ray, Chuck "Porky" Mitchell, Wilson Dunster, Ted Leplat; **D:** Harry Hope. VHS, Beta $79.95 TWE ⨂

Swifty A cowpoke is accused of murder but escapes to track down the real culprit and win the hand of the girl he loves.
1936 60m/B Hoot Gibson. VHS, Beta $27.95 VCN ⨂½

Swim Team New coach for a terminally inept school swimming team whips them into shape. Doesn't hold much water.
1979 81m/C Stephen Furst, James Daughton, Jenny Neumann, Kim Day, Buster Crabbe; **D:** James Polakof. VHS, Beta $9.99 STE, PSM ⨂

Swimmer A lonely suburbanite swims an existential swath through the pools of his neighborhood landscape in an effort at self-discovery. A surreal, strangely compelling work based on a story by John Cheever.
1968 (PG) 94m/C Burt Lancaster, Janice Rule, Janet Landgard, Marge Champion, Kim Hunter, Rose Gregorio, John David Garfield; **D:** Frank Perry; **M:** Marvin Hamlisch. VHS, Beta $9.95 GKK ⨂½

Swimming Pool Two men and two women spend a weekend in a villa on the French Riviera, manipulating each other, playing sexual games, and changing partners. Their escapades end in murder. Romantic melodrama is sensuous if slow-moving. French film dubbed in English.
1970 (PG) 85m/C Romy Schneider, Alain Delon, Maurice Ronet, Jane Birkin; **D:** Jacques Deray. VHS, Beta $59.95 NLC ⨂⨂½

Swimming to Cambodia Gray tells the story of his bit part in "The Killing Fields," filmed in Cambodia, and makes ironic observations about modern life. It works.
1987 87m/C Spalding Gray; **D:** Jonathan Demme; **M:** Laurie Anderson. VHS, Beta $19.98 LHV, WAR ⨂⨂⨂

Swimsuit: The Movie A young ad executive decides to revitalize a swimsuit company's failing business by sponsoring a contest for the perfect swimsuit model. Made-for-television fluff.
1989 100m/C William Katt, Catherine Oxenberg, Cyd Charisse, Nia Peeples, Tom Villard, Cheryl Pollak, Billy Warlock, Jack Wagner; **D:** Chris Thomson; **W:** Robert Schiff; **M:** John D'Andrea. VHS $79.95 AIP ⨂½

The Swindle Three Italian conmen pull capers in Rome trying to make a better life for themselves. Dark overtones permeate one of Fellini's lesser efforts. Good cast can't bring up the level of this film. In Italian with English subtitles. **AKA:** Il Bidone.
1955 92m/C Broderick Crawford, Giulietta Masina, Richard Basehart, Franco Fabrizi; **D:** Federico Fellini; **W:** Federico Fellini, Tullio Pinelli, Ennio Flaino. VHS $69.95 ING, IME, CVC ⨂⨂

Swindle Two life-long friends set up scam after scam in their quest for sex and money. Their latest con involves a phony marriage broker business, which provides the opportunity to meet a lot of lovely ladies. Only it turns out the hustlers may be the ones getting hustled.
1992 85m/C Robby West, Britt Houston, Elaina Dunn, Samantha Fong, Bobby Tess, Donna Thomas; **D:** Jason Holt. VHS $79.95 CEL ⨂

Swing An all-black musical revue.
1947 80m/B VHS, Beta $29.95 NOS, DVT ⨂

Swing High, Swing Low A trumpet player fights the bottle and the dice to become a hit in the jazz world and marry the woman he loves. Solid drama. From the stage play "Burlesque." Made first as "The Dance of Life," then as "When My Baby Smiles At Me."
1937 95m/B Carole Lombard, Fred MacMurray, Charles Butterworth, Dorothy Lamour; **D:** Mitchell Leisen. VHS, Beta $19.95 NOS, HHT, DVT ⨂⨂½

Swing It, Professor A stodgy music professor refuses to recognize jazz as a valid musical form and subsequently loses his job. During his unemployment, he wanders into a nightclub and discovers jazz isn't so bad after all. Nice camera work. ♫I'm Sorta Kinda Glad I Met You; An Old-Fashioned Melody; Richer Than A Millionaire. **AKA:** Swing it Buddy.
1937 62m/B Pinky Tomlin, Paula Stone, Mary Kornman, Milburn Stone, Pat Gleason; **D:** Maurice Conn. VHS $24.95 NOS, DVT, HEG ⨂⨂½

Swing It, Sailor! Two footloose sailors go after the same woman while on shore leave. Decent screwball comedy.
1937 61m/B Wallace Ford, Ray Mayer, Isabel Jewell, Mary Treen; **D:** Raymond Connon. VHS, Beta $19.95 VYY, NOS ⨂⨂

Swing Kids In 1939 in Germany, big band or "swing" music is the instrument used by a group of young people to rebel against the conformity demanded by Hitler. Highlights the politics of the era, but concentrates mainly on three teenagers and the strains that Nazi power put on their friendship. Although the premise is based in historic fact, there is still something disturbingly silly about the entire production. Dance sequences are lively and well-choreographed. Branagh (in an uncredited role) plays a smooth-talking Gestapo chief. Filmed on location in Prague, Czechoslovakia (as a substitute for Hamburg, Germany).
1993 (PG-13) 114m/C Robert Sean Leonard, Christian Bale, Frank Whaley, Barbara Hershey, Tushka Bergen, David Tom, Kenneth Branagh; **D:** Thomas Carter; **W:** Jonathan Marc Feldman; **M:** James Horner. VHS, Beta $19.99 HPH ⨂⨂

Swing Parade of 1946 One of the multitude of 1940s musicals. Young songwriter falls in love with club owner. Highlights include an appearance by the Three Stooges. ♫Stormy Weather; Just a Little Fond Affection; Don't Worry About the Mule; A Tender Word Will Mend It All; On the Sunny Side of the Street; Oh, Brother; After All This Time; Caledonia.
1946 74m/B Gale Storm, Phil Regan, Moe Howard, Edward Brophy, Connee Boswell; **D:** Phil Karlson. VHS NO ⨂½

Swing Shift When Hawn takes a job at an aircraft plant after her husband goes off to war, she learns more than riveting. Lahti steals the film as her friend and co-worker. A detailed reminiscence of the American home front during WWII that never seems to gel. Produced by Hawn.
1984 (PG) 100m/C Goldie Hawn, Kurt Russell, Ed Harris, Christine Lahti, Holly Hunter, Chris Lemmon, Belinda Carlisle, Fred Ward, Roger Corman, Lisa Pelikan; **D:** Jonathan Demme; **W:** Ron Nyswaner, Bo Goldman. VHS, Beta $19.98 WAR ⨂⨂½

Swing Time Astaire, a dancer who can't resist gambling, is engaged to marry another woman, until he meets Ginger. One of the team's best efforts. Laserdisc version includes: production photos and stills, commentary on Fred Astaire and musical films, and excerpts from "Hooray for Love" featuring Bill "Bojangles" Robinson and Fats Waller. ♫The Way You Look Tonight; Waltz in

Swing Time; Never Gonna Dance; Pick Yourself Up; A Fine Romance; Bojangles of Harlem.
1936 103m/B Fred Astaire, Ginger Rogers, Helen Broderick, Betty Furness, Eric Blore, Victor Moore; **D:** George Stevens; **M:** Jerome Kern, Dorothy Fields. VHS, Beta $14.98 TTC, RKO, MED ⨂⨂⨂

A Swingin' Summer A bunch of groovy guys and gals go-go to the beach for a vacation of fun and sun and end up starting a rock 'n' roll concert series. Everybody gets part of the action...even the bespectacled Welch, who gets a chance to sing. Performances from the Righteous Brothers and rock semi-legends Donnie Brooks, Gary Lewis and the Playboys, and the Rip Chords. ♫Red Hot Roadster; Justine; Penny the Poo; Out to Lunch; Nitro; Ready to Groove.
1965 81m/C James Stacy, William Wellman Jr., Quinn O'Hara, Martin West, Mary Mitchell, Allan Jones, Raquel Welch; **D:** Robert Sparr. VHS NO ⨂½

The Swinging Cheerleaders A group of amorous cheerleaders turn on the entire campus in this typical sexploiter.
1974 (PG) 90m/C Cheryl "Rainbeaux" Smith, Colleen Camp, Jo Johnston; **D:** Jack Hill. VHS, Beta $29.95 MON ⨂½

Swinging Wives Ribald humor for the discriminating viewer.
1979 (R) 84m/C Gale Mayberrie, Ron James. VHS, Beta NO ⨂½

Swiss Conspiracy Against the opulent background of the world's richest financial capital and playground of the wealthy, one man battles to stop a daring and sophisticated blackmailer preying on the secret bank account set. Fast-paced, if sometimes confusing.
1977 (PG) 92m/C David Janssen, Senta Berger; **D:** Jack Arnold. VHS, Beta $49.95 VCI ⨂⨂

The Swiss Family Robinson A family, seeking to escape Napoleon's war in Europe, sets sail for New Guinea, but shipwrecks on a deserted tropical island. There they build an idyllic life, only to be confronted by a band of pirates. Lots of adventure for family viewing. Filmed on location on the island of Tobago. Based on the novel by Johann Wyss.
1960 126m/C John Mills, Dorothy McGuire, James MacArthur, Tommy Kirk, Janet Munro, Sessue Hayakawa; **D:** Ken Annakin. VHS, Beta $19.99 DIS, IGP ⨂⨂⨂

Swiss Miss Stan and Ollie are mousetrap salesmen on the job in Switzerland. Highlights include Stan's tuba serenade and the gorilla-on-the-bridge episode. Also included on this tape is a 1935 Thelma Todd/Patsy Kelly short, "Hot Money."
1938 97m/B Stan Laurel, Oliver Hardy, Della Lind, Walter Woolf King, Eric Blore, Thelma Todd, Patsy Kelly; **D:** John Blystone. VHS, Beta $14.98 CCB, MED, FCT ⨂⨂½

The Switch An escaped convict takes the place of a talented conman and chaos ensues.
1989 (R) ?m/C Anthony Quinn, Adriano Celentano, Capucine, Corinne Clery. VHS NO ⨂⨂

Switch A chauvinist louse, slain by the girlfriends he misused, is sent back to Earth as an alluring female to learn the other side's point of view. The plot may lack urgency, but this is a sparkling adult comedy that scores as it pursues the gimmicky concept to a logical, outrageous and touching conclusion. Barkin's act as swaggering male stuck in a woman's body is a masterwork of physical humor.

1991 (R) 104m/C Ellen Barkin, Jimmy Smits, JoBeth Williams, Lorraine Bracco, Perry King, Bruce Martyn Payne, Tony Roberts; **D:** Blake Edwards; **M:** Henry Mancini. **VHS** $92.99 HBO, WAR

Switchblade Sisters Crime gang of female ex-cons wreaks pseudo-feminist havoc. Bruce is Lenny Bruce's daughter. **AKA:** The Jezebels; Playgirl Gang.
1975 90m/C Robbie Lee, Joanne Nail, Monica Gayle, Kitty Bruce; **D:** Jack Hill; **M:** Les Baxter. **VHS, Beta** $59.95 MON, HHE *Woof!*

Switched at Birth A fact-based made for television drama about two girls, switched in a hospital nursery at birth. Only when one girl dies, a decade later, do her parents discover that she could not have been their biological child. Their search for their daughter leads to an emotional conflict between the girl, the man that raised her, and the biological parents who seek to claim her. Beware of the sappy Hollywood ending, five years later the story of Kimberly Mays is still going through the U.S. judicial system.
1991 (PG) 200m/C Bonnie Bedelia, Brian Kerwin, Ed Asner, Caroline McWilliams, John M. Jackson, Lois Smith, Eve Gordon, Judith Hoag, Ariana Richards; **D:** Waris Hussein. **VHS** COL, PMS ⅃⅃½

Switching Channels A modernized remake of "His Girl Friday," and therefore the fourth version of "The Front Page." Beautiful television anchorwoman (Turner) wants to marry handsome tycoon (Reeve), but her scheming ex-husband (Reynolds) gets in the way. Weak performances from everyone but Beatty and lackluster direction render this off-told story less funny than usual.
1988 (PG) 108m/C Burt Reynolds, Kathleen Turner, Christopher Reeve, Ned Beatty, Henry Gibson, George Newbern, Al Waxman, Ken James, Joe Silver, Charles Kimbrough, Tony Rosato; **D:** Ted Kotcheff; **W:** Jonathan Reynolds; **M:** Michel Legrand. **VHS, Beta** $14.95 COL ⅃⅃½

Swoon Kalin's directorial debut is a stylish rendering of the sensational 1924 kidnapping and murder of Bobby Franks by Richard Loeb and Nathan Leopold Jr. and their subsequent trial and imprisonment. Core elements of the case remain but Kalin imposes contemporary styles and morals on the past, particularly his protest against the homophobic attitudes influencing the trial while acknowledging the jaded and dispassionate behavior of the two young men. Previous cinematic versions of the murder case include "Rope" and "Compulsion" but Kalin graphically portrays the characters homosexuality, which was only hinted at in the earlier films.
1991 95m/B Daniel Schlachet, Craig Chester, Ron Vawter, Michael Kirby, Michael Stumm, Valda Z. Drabla, Natalie Stanford; **D:** Tom Kalin; **W:** Tom Kalin; **M:** James Bennett. **VHS** NLC, IME ⅃⅃⅃

The Sword and the Cross A grade-B adventure about the life of Mary Magdalene.
1958 93m/B Yvonne De Carlo, George Mistral; **D:** Carlo L. Bragaglia. **VHS, Beta** NO ⅃½

Sword & the Dragon A young warrior must battle any number of giant mythical creatures. **AKA:** Ilya Mourometz.
1956 81m/C Boris Andreyer, Andrei Abrikosov; **D:** Alexander Ptushko. **VHS, Beta** $59.95 VCI, SNC ⅃⅃

The Sword & the Rose Mary Tudor, sister of King Henry VIII, shuns the advances of a nobleman for the love of a commoner; Justice, a fine king. Based on the book "When Knighthood

Was in Flower." **AKA:** When Knighthood Was in Flower.
1953 91m/C Richard Todd, Glynis Johns, Michael Gough, Jane Barrett, James Robertson Justice; **D:** Ken Annakin. **VHS, Beta** $19.99 DIS, HHE, BTV ⅃⅃½

Sword & the Sorcerer Young prince strives to regain control of his kingdom, now ruled by an evil knight and a powerful magician. Mediocre script and acting is enhanced by decent special effects.
1982 (R) 100m/C Lee Horsely, Kathleen Beller, George Maharis, Simon MacCorkindale, Richard Lynch, Richard Moll, Robert Tessier, Anna Van Pallandt, Anna Bjorn, Jeff Corey; **D:** Albert Pyun; **W:** Albert Pyun. **VHS, Beta** $24.95 MCA ⅃½

The Sword in the Stone The Disney version of the first volume of T.H. White's "The Once and Future King" wherein King Arthur, as a boy, is instructed in the ways of the world by Merlin and Archimedes the owl. Although not in the Disney masterpiece fold, boasts the usual superior animation and a gripping mythological tale.
1963 (G) 79m/C **D:** Wolfgang Reitherman, Wolfgang Reitherman; **V:** Ricky Sorenson, Sebastian Cabot, Karl Swenson, Junius Matthews, Alan Napier, Norman Alden, Martha Wentworth, Barbara Jo Allen. **VHS, Beta** $24.99 DIS, KUI, HMV ⅃⅃⅃

Sword of Doom A rousing samurai epic detailing the training of an impulsive, bloodlusting warrior by an elder expert. In Japanese with English subtitles. **AKA:** Daibosatsu Toge.
1967 120m/B Tatsuya Nakadai, Toshiro Mifune; **D:** Kihachi Okamoto. **VHS, Beta** $29.98 SUE, ING, NLC ⅃⅃⅃

The Sword of El Cid Not much dash and very little daring-do in this poorly plotted, overly dramatic saga of good vs. evil, Spanish style. Rightful heir to the crown threatens, challenges and enevitably crosses swords with the pretender to his throne. Costume mavens may find something to hold their interest. **AKA:** La Spada del Cid.
1962 86m/C Roland Carey, Sandro Moretti, Chantal Deberg, Iliana Grimaldi, Jose Luis Pellicena, Daniela Bianchi; **D:** Miguel Iglesias. **VHS, Beta** $16.95 SNC ⅃½

Sword of Fury II The sequel. Two samurai fight to the death to determine who will become the premier swordsman of all Japan. With English subtitles.
1973 77m/C Hideki Takahashi, Jiro Tamiya. **VHS, Beta** NO ⅃½

Sword of Gideon An action packed and suspenseful made for television film about an elite commando group who set out to avenge the Munich Olympic killings of 1972. Adapted from "Vengeance" by George Jonas.
1986 148m/C Steven Bauer, Michael York, Rod Steiger, Colleen Dewhurst, Robert Joy, Laurent Malet, Lino Ventura, Leslie Hope; **D:** Michael Anderson Sr.; **W:** Chris Bryant; **M:** Georges Delerue. **VHS** $79.99 HBO ⅃⅃½

Sword of Lancelot A costume version of the Arthur-Lancelot-Guinevere triangle, with plenty of swordplay and a sincere respect for the old legend. **AKA:** Lancelot and Guinevere.
1963 115m/C Cornel Wilde, Jean Wallace, Brian Aherne, George Baker; **D:** Cornel Wilde. **VHS, Beta** $59.95 MCA ⅃⅃½

Sword of Monte Cristo Masked female avenger, seeking the liberty of the French people, discovers a valuable sword that holds the key to a vast fortune. But the sword is also desired by an evil government minister.

1951 80m/C George Montgomery, Paula Corday; **D:** Maurice Geraghty. **VHS, Beta** $29.95 VHE ⅃½

Sword of Sherwood Forest The Earl of Newark plots the murder of the Archbishop of Canterbury in yet another rendition of the Robin Hood legend. Cushing is truly evil as the villain.
1960 80m/C Richard Greene, Peter Cushing, Niall MacGinnis, Richard Pasco, Jack Gwillim, Sarah Branch, Nigel Green, Oliver Reed; **D:** Terence Fisher. **VHS** COL, MLB ⅃⅃½

Sword of the Valiant The Green Knight arrives in Camelot to challenge Gawain. Remake of "Gawain And The Green Knight." Connery adds zest to a minor epic.
1983 (PG) 102m/C Sean Connery, Miles O'Keeffe, Cyrielle Claire, Leigh Lawson, Trevor Howard, Peter Cushing, Wilfrid Brambell, Lila Kedrova, John Rhys-Davies; **D:** Stephen Weeks. **VHS, Beta** $69.95 MGM ⅃⅃

Sword of Venus Uninspired production finds the son of the Count of Monte Cristo the victim in a scheme to deprive him of his wealth. **AKA:** Island of Monte Cristo.
1953 73m/B Robert Clarke, Catherine McLeod, Dan O'Herlihy, William Schallert; **D:** Harold Daniels. **VHS** $29.95 FCT ⅃

Swords of Death Final film by Uchida, released posthumously, deals with the adventurous period exploits of the irrepressible Miyamoto Musashi. With English subtitles.
1971 76m/C Kinnosuke Nakamura, Rentaro Mikuni; **D:** Tomu Uchida. **VHS, Beta** VDA ⅃⅃

The Swordsman The quest to return the stolen sword of the legendary Alexander the Great to a museum is muscular detective Lamas' assignment. Turns out the detective and his evil millionaire antagonist have been chasing each other through time in their endless quest for revenge and power.
1992 (R) 98m/C Lorenzo Lamas, Claire Stansfield, Michael Champion; **D:** Michael Kennedy; **W:** Michael Kennedy. **VHS** $9.98 REP ⅃⅃½

Sybil Fact-based story of a woman who developed 16 distinct personalities, and the supportive psychiatrist who helped her put the pieces of her ego together. Excellent made-for-television production with Field's Emmy-winning performance.
1976 122m/C Sally Field, Joanne Woodward, Brad Davis, Martine Bartlett, Jane Hoffman; **D:** Daniel Petrie. **VHS, Beta** $19.98 FOX ⅃⅃⅃

Sylvester A 16-year-old girl and a cranky stockyard boss team up to train a battered horse named Sylvester for the National Equestrian trials. Nice riding sequences and good performances can't overcome familiar plot, but the kids will enjoy this one.
1985 (PG) 104m/C Melissa Gilbert, Richard Farnsworth, Michael Schoeffling, Constance Towers; **D:** Tim Hunter. **VHS, Beta** $79.95 COL ⅃⅃

Sylvia Biography of author/educator Sylvia Ashton-Warner, and her efforts to teach Maori children in New Zealand to read via unorthodox methods. David is a marvel. Based on Ashton-Warner's books "Teacher" and "I Passed This Way."
1986 (PG) 99m/C Eleanor David, Tom Wilkinson, Nigel Terry, Mary Regan; **D:** Michael Firth. **VHS, Beta** $79.98 FOX ⅃⅃½

Sylvia and the Phantom A charming French comedy about a lonely young girl who is befriended by the ghost of a man killed decades earlier in a duel over the girl's grandmother. Based on the play by Alfred Adam. In French with English subtitles. **AKA:** Sylvia and the Ghost.

1945 97m/B Odette Joyeux, Jacques Tati, Francois Perier; **D:** Claude Autant-Lara. **VHS, Beta** $29.98 *SUE, ING, NLC* ✁✁✁

Sylvia Scarlett An odd British comedy about a woman who masquerades as a boy while on the run with her father, who causes all kinds of instinctive confusion in the men she meets.
1935 94m/B Katharine Hepburn, Cary Grant, Brian Aherne, Edmund Gwenn, Natalie Paley, Dennis Moore, Lennox Pawle, Daisy Belmore, Nola Luxford; **D:** George Cukor. **VHS, Beta** $19.95 *RKO, FCT, TTC* ✁✁ 1/2

Sympathy for the Devil Rolling Stones provide music for confused, revolutionary documentary. Episodic jumble is odd, sometimes fascinating. **AKA:** One Plus One.
1970 110m/C Mick Jagger, Rolling Stones; **D:** Jean-Luc Godard. **VHS, Beta** *FOX, OM* ✁✁

Symphony in the Mountains An early German sound romance, where an Austrian singing teacher falls in love with the sister of one of his student's. Featuring choral work by the Vienna Boys' Choir. In German with English subtitles.
1935 75m/B **V:** The Vienna Boys' Choir. **VHS, Beta** $35.95 *FCT, IHF, GLV* ✁✁ 1/2

Symphony of Living Intended heartwarmer about a man's bitter betrayal by his family and the hardship and tragedy he experiences.
1935 73m/B **VHS, Beta** $29.95 *VYY* ✁ 1/2

Syngenor Syngenor stands for Synthesized Genetic Organism, to differentiate it from all other organisms. Created by science, it escapes, and a crack team of scientists and gung-ho military types are mobilized to track it down.
1990 (R) 98m/C Starr Andreeff, Michael Laurence, David Gale, Charles Lucia, Riva Spier, Jeff Doucette, Bill Gratton, Lewis Arquette, Jon Korkes, Melanie Shatner; **D:** George Elanjian Jr.; **M:** Tom Chase, Steve Rucker. **VHS** $14.95 *HMD* ✁ 1/2

T-Bird Gang A high school student goes undercover to infiltrate a teen gang. When his cover is blown, things get hairy. Laughable sleazebag production.
1959 75m/B Ed Nelson, John Brinkley, Pat George, Beach Dickerson, Tony Miller; **D:** Richard Harbinger; **M:** Shelley Manne. **VHS** $19.98 *SNC* ✁ 1/2

T Bone N Weasel Hines and Lloyd play not-so-ex-cons who steal a car and try to lead a life of ease. Crime doesn't pay. Made for cable television.
199? (PG-13) 94m/C Gregory Hines, Christopher Lloyd. **VHS** $89.98 *TTC* ✁✁

T-Men Two agents of the Treasury Department infiltrate a counterfeiting gang. Filmed in semi-documentary style, exciting tale serves also as an effective commentary on the similarities between the agents and those they pursue. Mann and cinematographer John Alton do especially fine work here.
1947 96m/B Alfred Ryder, Dennis O'Keefe, June Lockhart, Mary Meade, Wallace Ford, Charles McGraw; **D:** Anthony Mann. **VHS, Beta** $29.95 *MED* ✁✁✁

Table for Five A divorced father takes his children on a Mediterranean cruise and while sailing, he learns that his ex-wife has died. The father and his ex-wife's husband struggle over who should raise the children. Sentimental and well-acted.
1983 (PG) 120m/C Jon Voight, Millie Perkins, Richard Crenna, Robbie Kiger, Roxana Zal, Son Hoang Bui, Marie-Christine Barrault, Kevin Costner; **D:** Robert Lieberman; **W:** David Seltzer; **M:** Miles Goodman. **VHS, Beta** $14.98 *FOX* ✁✁ 1/2

Table Settings A taped performance of James Lapines' comedy about the lives of three generations of a Jewish family.
1984 90m/C Robert Klein, Stockard Channing, Dinah Manoff, Eileen Heckart. **VHS, Beta** $39.95 *RKO* ✁✁

Tabloid! Unorthodox woman prints and sells racy trash for enquiring minds.
1988 99m/C Scott Davis, Glen Cobum; **D:** Bret McCormick, Matt Shaffen. **VHS** *HHE* ✁ 1/2

Tabu: A Story of the South Seas Fascinating docudrama about a young pearl diver's ill-fated romance. The gods have declared the young woman he desires "taboo" to all men. Filmed on location in Tahiti. Authored and produced by Murnau and Flaherty. Flaherty left in mid-production due to artistic differences with Murnau, who was later killed in an auto accident one week before the premiere of film. Oscar-winning cinematography by Floyd Crosby.
1931 81m/B **D:** Robert Flaherty, F.W. Murnau. **VHS, Beta** $39.95 *MIL, GVV, LUM* ✁✁✁ 1/2

Tacos al Carbon A singer falls in love with a beautiful woman.
1987 103m/C Vicente Fernandez, Nadia Milton, Sonia Amelio, Ana Martin, Sergio Ramos. **VHS, Beta** $59.95 *MAD* ✁✁

Taffin An Irish bill collector battles a group of corrupt businessmen who want to replace the local soccer field with a hazardous chemical plant. Pretty dull fare, overall, with Brosnan much less charismatic than usual.
1988 (R) 96m/C Pierce Brosnan, Ray McAnally, Alison Doody, Patrick Bergin; **D:** Francis Megahy; **W:** David Ambrose. **VHS, Beta** $14.95 *MGM* ✁ 1/2

Tag: The Assassination Game An exciting new game has been discovered by a group of university students. Players act as spies and assassins, "killing" each other to make points. But a school newspaper sportswriter finds the game has become more real than make-believe. Timely topic in the early '80s when Dungeons and Dragons and other "war" games were popular on college campuses across the nation.
1982 (PG) 92m/C Robert Carradine, Linda Hamilton, Michael Winslow, Kristine DeBell, Perry Lang; **D:** Nick Castle. **VHS, Beta** $59.98 *SUE* ✁ 1/2

Tagget A former CIA operative who has erased his nightmarish stint in Vietnam gradually begins to recall his past. When pieces of the puzzle begin to come together, he remembers a few things that the government would prefer he forget. Soon, CIA men are on his trail and their mission is to see that he forgets his past—permanently. Made for cable television.
1990 (PG-13) 89m/C Daniel J. Travanti, William Sadler, Roxanne Hart, Stephen Tobolowsky, Peter Michael Goetz, Sarah Douglas, Noel Harrison; **D:** Richard T. Heffron. **VHS** $79.95 *MCA* ✁

Tai-Pan A 19th century Scottish trader and his beautiful Chinese mistress are the main characters in this confusing attempt to dramatize the story of Hong Kong's development into a thriving trading port. Too many subplots and characters are introduced in a short time to do justice to James Clavell's novel of the same name, the basis for the movie. The first American production completely filmed in China.
1986 (R) 130m/C Bryan Brown, Joan Chen, John Stanton, Kyra Sedgwick, Tim Guinee, Russell Wong, Bert Remsen; **D:** Daryl Duke; **W:** John Briley; **M:** Maurice Jarre. **VHS, Beta** $79.98 *VES* ✁ 1/2

Tailspin: Behind the Korean Airline Tragedy Made-for-TV docudrama on the 1983 downing of Korean Aire flight 007 in Soviet airspace. Purports to show the U.S. government's reaction to what became a major international incident.
1989 82m/C Michael Moriarty, Michael Murphy, Chris Sarandon, Harris Yulin, Gavan O'Herlihy, Ed O'Ross; **D:** David Darlow; **M:** David Ferguson. **VHS, Beta** *PSM, PAR* ✁✁

Tailspin Tommy Features twelve chapters of the great action serial.
1934 ?m/B Maurice Murphy, Noah Beery Jr., Walter Miller, Patricia Farr, Grant Withers, John Davidson, William Desmond, Charles A. Browne; **D:** Louis Friedlander. **VHS** $24.95 *GPV* ✁✁

Tainted Small-town woman tries to endure after being raped. Both her husband and the attacker are killed, and she is forced to conceal their deaths. Poorly scripted.
1988 90m/C Shari Shattuck, Park Overall, Gene Tootle, Magilla Schaus, Blaque Fowler; **D:** Orestes Matacena. **VHS, Beta** $14.95 *HMD* ✁ 1/2

Tainted Blood Welch stars as an investigative reporter whose latest story has her attempting to find the teenage twin of a psychotic killer.
1993 (R) 86m/C Raquel Welch, Alley Mills, Kerri Green, Natasha Gregson Wagner, Joan VanArk; **D:** Matthew Patrick; **W:** Kathleen Rowell. **VHS, Beta** *PAR* ✁✁

Tainted Image Artist woman starts to lose sanity with help of boyfriend, psycho neighbor and rash of bizarre deaths. She turns to canvas for solace and decides she needs secret ingredient that can't be found in art supply store to complete masterpiece.
1991 95m/C Tom Saunders, Sandra Frances, Annetta Arpin, Ken La Mothe, Heidi Emerich, Steve Kornacki. **VHS** $79.95 *HHT, PHX* ✁✁

The Take Recovering alcoholic cop faces wrath of drug lord and marriage on the rocks.
1990 (R) 91m/C Ray Sharkey, R. Lee Ermey, Lisa Hartman, Larry Manetti, Joe Lala; **D:** Leon Ichaso; **W:** Edward Anhalt, Handel Glassberg. **VHS** $79.95 *MCA* ✁✁

Take a Hard Ride Dull spaghetti western about a cowboy transporting money to Mexico, evading bandits and bounty hunters.
1975 (R) 103m/C Jim Brown, Lee Van Cleef, Fred Williamson, Jim Kelly, Barry Sullivan; **D:** Anthony M. (Antonio Marghereti) Dawson; **M:** Jerry Goldsmith. **VHS, Beta** $19.98 *FOX* ✁ 1/2

Take Down Hermann is charming as a high school English teacher turned reluctant wrestling coach.
1979 96m/C Lorenzo Lamas, Kathleen Lloyd, Maureen McCormick, Edward Herrmann; **D:** Keith Merrill. **VHS, Beta** $29.95 *UNI* ✁✁

Take It Big Uninspired B-musical starring the Tin Man from the "Wizard of Oz." Haley is an impoverished actor who inherits a ranch and saves it by—surprise—putting on a show. ♫Sunday, Monday, and Always; Love and Learn; Life Can Be Beautiful; Take It Big; I'm a Big Success with You.
1944 75m/B Jack Haley, Harriet Hilliard Nelson, Mary Beth Hughes, Arline Judge, Nils T. Granlund, Fuzzy Knight, Ozzie Nelson; **D:** Frank McDonald. **VHS, Beta** $19.95 *NOS, VYY, DVT* ✁ 1/2

Take Me Back to Oklahoma Musical western with comedy.
1940 64m/B Tex Ritter, Terry Walker, Karl Hackett, George Eldridge; **D:** Al Herman. **VHS, Beta** $19.95 *NOS, VCN, VYY* ✁

Take Me Out to the Ball Game Williams manages a baseball team, locks horns with players Sinatra and Kelly, and wins them over with song. Naturally, there's a water ballet scene. Contrived and forced, but enjoyable. ♫Take Me Out to the Ball

Game; The Hat My Father Wore on St. Patrick's Day; O'Brien to Ryan to Goldberg; The Right Girl for Me; It's Fate, Baby, It's Fate; Yes, Indeedy; Strictly U.S.A. *AKA:* Everybody's Cheering.
1949 93m/C Frank Sinatra, Gene Kelly, Esther Williams, Jules Munshin, Betty Garrett, Edward Arnold, Tom Dugan, Richard Lane; *D:* Busby Berkeley. **VHS, Beta** $19.98 *MGM* &&½

Take the Money and Run Allen's directing debut; he also co-wrote and starred. "Documentary" follows a timid, would-be bank robber who can't get his career off the ground and keeps landing in jail. Little plot, but who cares? Nonstop one-liners and slapstick.
1969 (PG) 85m/C Woody Allen, Janet Margolin, Marcel Hillaire, Louise Lasser; *D:* Woody Allen; *W:* Woody Allen; *M:* Marvin Hamlisch. **VHS, Beta** $19.98 *FOX* &&&

Take This Job & Shove It The Johnny Paycheck song inspired this story of a hot-shot efficiency expert who returns to his hometown to streamline the local brewery. Encounters with old pals inspire self-questioning. Alternately inspired and hackneyed. Cameos by Paycheck and other country stars.
1981 (PG) 100m/C Robert Hays, Art Carney, Barbara Hershey, David Keith, Martin Mull, Eddie Albert, Penelope Milford; *Cameos:* Johnny Paycheck, David Allen Coe, Charlie Rich, Lacy J. Dalton; *D:* Gus Trikonis; *W:* Barry Schneider. **VHS, Beta** $14.95 *COL, SUE* &&

Take Two A woman has an affair with her husband's twin brother. Interesting metaphysically: Are you my husband or my lover? But is an adultery/murder drama with Frank Stallone worth 101 minutes of your time?
1987 (R) 101m/C Grant Goodeve, Robin Mattson, Frank Stallone, Warren Berlinger, Darwyn Swalve, Nita Talbot; *D:* Peter Rowe. **VHS, Beta** $14.95 *ACA* &

Take Your Best Shot Standard TV fare about an out-of-work actor struggling with his low self-esteem and his failing marriage. Made-for-television comedy.
1982 96m/C Robert Urich, Meredith Baxter Birney, Jeffrey Tambor, Jack Bannon, Claudette Nevins; *D:* David Greene. **VHS, Beta** $39.95 *LIV* &½

Taken Away Struggling young divorcee Stephanie Monroe waits tables during the day and studies to be a computer at night in order to provide her 8-year-old daughter Abby with a better life. Unable to afford child care, Stephanie leaves Abby alone in the afternoon until she can get home from work. But when the welfare system finds out Stephanie is accused of child neglect and must fight a bureaucratic nightmare in order to get her child back. Made for television.
1989 94m/C Valerie Bertinelli, Kevin Dunn, Joshua Maurer, Anna Maria Horsford, Juliet Sorcey, Nada Despotovich, Matthew Faison, James Arone; *D:* John D. Patterson; *W:* Robert Freedman, Selma Thomson. **VHS** $89.98 *MCA* &&½

Takin' It All Off In this sequel to "Takin' It Off," Kitten does it again with unbelievable bumps and grinds.
1987 90m/C Francesca "Kitten" Natavidad; *D:* Ed Hansen. **VHS** $69.98 *LIV, VES* &&½

Taking Care of Business Too familiar tale of switched identity has crazed Cubs fan Belushi find Grodin's Filofax, allowing him to pose as businessman. Old jokes and a story full of holes. *AKA:* Filofax.
1990 (R) 108m/C James Belushi, Charles Grodin, Anne DeSalvo, Loryn Locklin, Veronica Hamel, Hector Elizondo, Mako, Gates McFadden, Stephen Elliott; *D:* Arthur Hiller; *W:* Jeffrey Abrams. **VHS, Beta** $19.99 *HPH* &½

Taking it to the Street It's an all-out high-stakes battle between good and evil.
19?? 90m/C **VHS** *NO* &½

Taking My Turn A taped performance of the off Broadway musical revue about growing old gracefully.
1984 87m/C **VHS, Beta** *NO* &½

The Taking of Beverly Hills Deranged billionaire Bat Masterson designs a bogus toxic spill that leaves the wealth of Beverly Hills his for the taking. Football hero Boomer Hayes teams up with renegade cop Ed Kelvin to try and stop Masterson and save the city of Beverly Hills.
1991 (R) 96m/C Ken Wahl, Matt Frewer, Robert Davi, Harley Jane Kozak, Lee James, Branscombe Richmond, Lyman Ward, Michael Bowen, William Prince, Ken Swofford, George Wyner; *D:* Sidney J. Furie; *W:* Sidney J. Furie. **VHS** $19.95 *COL, NLC* &½

The Taking of Flight 847: The Uli Derickson Story Wagner plays the stewardess who acted as a go-between for the passengers during a 1985 terrorist hijacking, saving all but one life. True-story drama is suspenseful and entertaining, nominated for several Emmys. Made-for-television drama. *AKA:* The Flight.
1988 100m/C Laurie Walters, Sandy McPeak, Ray Wise, Leslie Easterbrook, Lindsay Wagner, Eli Danker, Joseph Naser; *D:* Paul Wendkos; *W:* Norman Merrill. **VHS** *IME* &&&

The Taking of Pelham One Two Three A hijack team, lead by the ruthless Shaw, seizes a New York City subway car and holds the 17 passengers for one million dollars ransom. Fine pacing keeps things on the edge. New cinematic techniques used by cameraman Owen Roizman defines shadowy areas like never before.
1974 (R) 105m/C Robert Shaw, Walter Matthau, Martin Balsam, Hector Elizondo, James Broderick, Earl Hindman, Dick O'Neill, Jerry Stiller, Tony Roberts, Doris Roberts, Kenneth McMillan, Julius W. Harris, Sal Viscuso; *D:* Joseph Sargent. **VHS, Beta** $14.95 *MGM, FOX* &&&

Taking the Heat When mobster Arkin kills a sporting-goods dealer with a golf club the murder is witnessed by yuppie Goldwyn. Whitfield is the ambitious cop who wants Goldwyn to testify against the gangster—if she can keep him alive long enough to get him to court. One long chase scene. Made for cable television.
1993 (R) 91m/C Lynn Whitfield, Tony Goldwyn, Alan Arkin, George Segal, Peter Boyle; *D:* Tom Mankiewicz; *W:* Dan Gordon. **VHS** *FXV* &&½

Tale of a Vampire In present day London, ageless vampire Alex (Sands) still mourns his long-lost vampiric love, Virginia, when he meets Anne (Hamilton) (who resembles Virginia). Alex doesn't know he's being stalked by Virginia's husband, Edgar (Cranham), also a vampire. Edgar decides to use Anne (with whom Alex has fallen in love) as bait, in a revenge plot. A tiny budget and slow pacing mar the film's fine visual style and good work by the two male leads. Film debut for director Sato.
1992 (R) 93m/C Julian Sands, Kenneth Cranham, Suzanna Hamilton; *D:* Shimako Sato; *W:* Jane Corbett, Shimako Sato; *M:* Julian Joseph. **VHS** $92.95 *VMK* &&½

The Tale of Ruby Rose Living in the mountains of Tasmania, Ruby Rose, her husband Henry, and their adopted son Gem, struggle to survive the '30s depression by hunting and trapping. Having spent all her life in the mountains, Ruby Rose has a very superstitious view of life and a terror of nightfall. But after an argument with her husband, Ruby Rose sets out on a cross-country journey to find her grandmother and discover the secrets of her past.
1987 (PG) 101m/C Melita Jurisic, Chris Haywood; *D:* Roger Sholes; *W:* Roger Sholes; *M:* Paul Schutze. **VHS** *NO* &&&

A Tale of Springtime Comedy-romance is the first film in Rohmer's planned new series, the "Tales of the Four Seasons," not to be confused with his "Six Moral Tales" or his "Comedies and Proverbs." Centers around Jeanne, a high school philosophy teacher; Natacha, a young student; and Igor, Natacha's father. As characteristic of Rohmer films, texture and character largely overshadow linear plots and social messages. However, the efficiency and directness of his camerawork make it a pleasure to watch.
1992 (PG) 107m/C Anne Teyssedre, Hugues Quester, Florence Darel, Eloise Bennett, Sophie Robin; *D:* Eric Rohmer; *W:* Eric Rohmer. **VHS** $19.98 *ORI* &&½

The Tale of the Frog Prince Superb edition of Shelley Duvall's "Faerie Tale Theatre" finds Williams the victim of an angry fairy godmother's spell. Garr to the rescue as the self-centered princess who saves him with a kiss. Directed and written by Idle of Monty Python fame.
1983 60m/C Robin Williams, Teri Garr; *D:* Eric Idle; *W:* Eric Idle. **VHS, Beta** $14.98 *FOX* &&&½

A Tale of Two Cities Lavish production of the Dickens' classic set during the French Revolution, about two men who bear a remarkable resemblance to each other, both in love with the same girl. Carefree lawyer Sydney Carton (Colman) roused to responsibility, makes the ultimate sacrifice. A memorable Madame DeFarge from stage star Yurka in her film debut, with assistance from other Dickens' film stars Rathbone, Oliver and Walthall.
1935 128m/B Ronald Colman, Elizabeth Allan, Edna May Oliver, Reginald Owen, Isabel Jewell, Walter Catlett, H.B. Warner, Donald Woods, Basil Rathbone, Blanche Yurka, Henry B. Walthall; *D:* Jack Conway; *W:* W.P. Lipscomb, S.N. Behrman; *M:* Herbert Stothart. **VHS, Beta** $24.95 *MGM, KUI, IGP* &&&&

A Tale of Two Cities A well-done British version of the Dickens' classic about a lawyer who sacrifices himself to save another man from the guillotine during the French Reign of Terror. The sixth remake of the tale.
1958 117m/B Dirk Bogarde, Dorothy Tutin, Christopher Lee, Donald Pleasence, Ian Bannen, Cecil Parker; *D:* Ralph Thomas. **VHS, Beta** $19.98 *SUE, LCA, FHS* &&&

A Tale of Two Cities Impressive looking but bloodless adaptation of the Dickens novel set in the French Revolution. Saradon takes on the dual role of sacrificing English lawyer Carton and French nobleman Darnay, with Krige as the lovely woman caught between the two. Made for television.
1980 156m/C Chris Sarandon, Alice Krige, Peter Cushing, Kenneth Morse, Barry Morse, Flora Robson, Billie Whitelaw; *D:* Jim Goddard; *W:* John Gay. **VHS** $19.98 *LIV, FUS* &&½

A Tale of Two Cities Masterpiece Theatre production of the classic Dickens tale. The French revolution was a time of revenge and brutality, but also provided the

proving ground for a love greater than life. Terrific cast and perfectly detailed production. On two cassettes.
1991 240m/C James Wilby, Serena Gordon, John Mills, Jean-Pierre Aumont, Anna Massey. **VHS $39.95** *PBS, TVC* 𝄞𝄞𝄞

Tale of Two Cities/In the Switch Tower A package of two medium-length silent films, the latter featuring a rare acting appearance by director Borzage.
1915 70m/B Walter Edwards, Maurice Costello, Florence Turner, Frank Borzage, Norma Talmadge, Leo Delaney. **VHS, Beta, 8mm $24.95** *VYY* 𝄞½

Tale of Two Sisters Sheen narrates sensual drama about two beautiful, ambitious sisters.
1989 90m/C Valerie Breiman, Claudia Christian, Sydney Lassick, Jeff Conaway. **VHS** *NO* 𝄞𝄞½

Talent for the Game A slight but handsomely produced baseball pleasantry about a talent scout who recruits a phenomenonal young pitcher, then sees the kid exploited by the team owner. More like an anecdote than a story, with an ending that aims a little too hard to please. Good for sports fans and family audiences.
1991 (PG) 91m/C Edward James Olmos, Lorraine Bracco, Jeff Corbett, Jamey Sheridan, Terry Kinney; **D:** Robert M. Young; **W:** David Himmelstein, Tom Donnelly, Larry Ferguson; **M:** David Newman. **VHS, Beta $14.95** *PAR* 𝄞𝄞½

Tales from Avonlea, Vol. 1: The Journey Begins From the producer of the popular "Anne of Green Gables" movie and its sequel comes this weekly TV series, a collaboration of the Disney channel and CBC Television. In "The Journey Begins," Sara meets her stuffy Aunt Hetty and cousins Felix and Felicity. Unhappy with her life, she decides whether to stay or run away. "The Proof of the Pudding" finds the grownups away and Felicity in charge of her siblings and Sara for the weekend. The same attention to detail, particularly in scenic views of lovely Prince Edward Island and the costumes, is shown in the series. Based on the writings of Lucy Maud Montgomery. **AKA:** Road to Avonlea.
1990 106m/C Sarah Polley. **VHS, Beta $19.99** *DIS, BTV* 𝄞𝄞𝄞½

Tales from the Crypt A collection of five scary stories from the classic EC comics that bear the movie's title. Richardson tells the future to each of five people gathered in a cave, each tale involving misfortune and, of course, gore.
1972 (PG) 92m/C Ralph Richardson, Joan Collins, Peter Cushing, Richard Greene, Ian Hendry; **D:** Freddie Francis. **VHS, Beta $59.95** *PSM* 𝄞𝄞𝄞

Tales from the Crypt Three contemporary tales of the macabre, "The Man Who Was Death," "'Twas the Night Before," and "Dig That Cat...He's Real Gone," linked together by a special-effects host. Ry Cooder provides the musical score for the second episode. Based on stories published by William M. Gaines in EC Comics; made-for-cable-television.
1989 81m/C William Sadler, Mary Ellen Trainor, Larry Drake, Joe Pantoliano, Robert Wuhl, Gustav Vintas; **D:** Walter Hill, Robert Zemeckis, Richard Donner; **M:** Ry Cooder. **VHS, Beta $89.99** *HBO* 𝄞𝄞𝄞

Tales from the Crypt, Vol. 3 Three more tales of terror from the made-for-cable-television series. "Dead Right" has Moore as a golddigger who takes a fortuneteller's advice and marries a penniless slob. "Cutting Cards" has Tighe and Hendricksen involved

in a very high stakes game. "The Switch" features Hickey as a wealthy old man bartering for a new body to woo the beautiful Preston.
1990 80m/C Demi Moore, William Hickey, Kelly Preston, Jeffrey Tambor, Rick Rossovich, Lance Henriksen, Kevin Tighe; **D:** Arnold Schwarzenegger, Walter Hill, Howard Deutch. **VHS, Beta $19.98** *WAR, MOV* 𝄞𝄞𝄞

Tales from the Darkside Each episode of this series features several short Twilight Zone-esque stories of fantasy and suspense. Additional tapes available.
1985 70m/C VHS, Beta $29.95 *LIV, MOV* 𝄞𝄞𝄞

Tales from the Darkside: The Movie Three short stories in the tradition of the ghoulish TV show are brought to the big screen, with mixed results. The plot centers around a boy who is being held captive by a cannibal. In order to prolong his life, he tells her horror stories. The tales were written by Sir Arthur Conan Doyle, Stephen King, and Michael McDowell.
1990 (R) 93m/C Deborah Harry, Christian Slater, David Johansen, William Hickey, James Remar, Rae Dawn Chong, Julianne Moore, Robert Klein; **D:** John Harrison; **W:** Stephen King, Michael McDowell, Sir Arthur Conan Doyle. **VHS, Beta $14.95** *PAR* 𝄞𝄞𝄞

Tales from the Gimli Hospital A smallpox outbreak at the turn of the century finds Einar and Gunnar sharing a hospital room. They begin telling each other increasingly bizarre personal secrets and develop a serious rivalry. Sharp dialogue with some equally grotesque imagery. Director Maddin first feature film.
1988 72m/B Kyle McCulloch, Michael Gottli; **D:** Guy Maddin. **VHS $79.95** *KIV, FCT* 𝄞𝄞

Tales from the Snow Zone "Tales from the Snow Zone" is the latest feature length ski film from RAP producers Jon Long and James Angrove. Filmed entirely in the 1991 ski season, this film captures the essence of the sport and lifestyle. "Tales" covers true extreme skiing, radical free skiing, moguls, downhill ski racing, telemarking, snowboarding, and monoskiing. Filmed in Europe and North America, "Tales" features skiers from the United States, Canada, France, Sweden, and Australia.
1991 70m/C VHS *RAP* 𝄞𝄞

Tales of Beatrix Potter The Royal Ballet Company of England performs in this adaptation of the adventures of Beatrix Potter's colorful and memorable creatures. Beautifully done. **AKA:** Peter Rabbit and Tales of Beatrix Potter.
1971 (G) 90m/C D: Reginald Mills. **VHS $14.98** *REP, HMV* 𝄞𝄞½

The Tales of Hoffmann A ballet-opera consisting of three stories by Jacques Offenbach covering romance, magic and mystery arising out of a poet's misadventures in love. Lavishly designed and highly stylized.
1951 138m/C Robert Rounseville, Robert Helpmann, Moira Shearer; **D:** Michael Powell, Emeric Pressburger; **M:** Royal Philharmonic Orchestra. **VHS $39.95** *HMV, PME* 𝄞𝄞½

Tales of Ordinary Madness Gazzara as a poet who drinks and sleeps with assorted women. Based on the stories of Charles Bukowski. Pretentious and dull.
1983 107m/C Ben Gazzara, Ornella Muti, Susan Tyrrell, Tanya Lopert, Roy Brocksmith, Katya Berger; **D:** Marco Ferreri. **VHS, Beta $69.98** *LIV, VES* 𝄞

Tales of Robin Hood A low-budget depiction of the Robin Hood legend.

1952 59m/B Robert Clarke, Mary Hatcher; **D:** James Tinling. **VHS, Beta** *NO* 𝄞½

Tales of Terror Three tales of terror based on stories by Edgar Allan Poe: "Morella," "The Black Cat," and the "The Case of M. Valdemar." Price stars in all three segments and is excellent as the bitter and resentful husband in "Morella." **AKA:** Poe's Tales of Terror.
1962 90m/C Vincent Price, Peter Lorre, Basil Rathbone, Debra Paget, Joyce Jameson; **D:** Roger Corman; **W:** Richard Matheson; **M:** Les Baxter. **VHS, Beta** *MLB, ORI* 𝄞𝄞

Tales of the Klondike: In a Far Country An adaptation of Jack London's story exploring the fears, dangers, and joys experienced by prospectors in the harsh wilderness of northwest Canadian gold country.
1987 60m/C Robert Carradine, Scott Hylands; **D:** Janine Manatis. **VHS, Beta $19.95** *AHV* 𝄞𝄞

Tales of the Klondike: Race for Number One Two men compete in a highly contested dog-sled race—the goal of which is to be the first to reach a tract of gold-laden land. Adapted from a story by Jack London.
1987 60m/C David Ferry, John Ireland; **D:** David Cobham. **VHS, Beta $19.95** *AHV* 𝄞𝄞

Tales of the Klondike: The Scorn of Women An available man is enthusiastically courted by every single woman in Dawson City, Alaska. From a story by Jack London.
1987 60m/C Tom Butler, Eva Gabor; **D:** Claude Fournier. **VHS, Beta $19.95** *AHV* 𝄞𝄞

Tales of the Klondike: The Unexpected Five gold prospectors grow rich, but lose all that is most valuable through overwhelming greed. Adapted from a story by Jack London.
1987 60m/C John Candy, Cherie Lunghi; **D:** Peter Pearson. **VHS, Beta $19.95** *AHV* 𝄞𝄞

Tales of the Unexpected Four tales designed to startle the senses and provoke the imagination. Episodes include "People Don't Do Such Things," about a marriage gone awry, "Youth from Vienna," about a weird fountain of youth, "Skeleton in the Cupboard," which tells of a man desperately trying to hide some strange secret and finally, "Bird of Prey," in which a pet parrot leaves its owners an enormous egg before dying.
1991 101m/C Arthur Hill, Samantha Eggar, Don Johnson, Dick Smothers, Sharon Gless, James Carroll Jordan, Charles Dance, Zoe Wanamaker, Sondra Locke, Frank Converse; **D:** Gordon Hessler, Norman Lloyd, Paul Annett, Ray Danton. **VHS, Beta $19.95** *PSM, IME* 𝄞𝄞½

Tales That Witness Madness An asylum is the setting for four tales of horror, as a doctor tells a visitor how four patients ended up in his clinic. Stories are "Mr. Tiger," "Penny Farthing," "Mel" and "Luau." At the time this was Novak's first film appearance in four years.
1973 (R) 90m/C Jack Hawkins, Donald Pleasence, Suzy Kendall, Joan Collins, Kim Novak, Mary Tamm, Georgia Brown, Donald Houston, David Wood, Peter McEnery; **D:** Freddie Francis. **VHS $14.95** *PAR* 𝄞𝄞½

Talion A western revenge movie that features two disabled men, a rancher and a bounty hunter, who team up to find the gang that slaughtered the rancher's family. **AKA:** An Eye for an Eye.
1966 (PG) 92m/C Robert Lansing, Slim Pickens, Patrick Wayne; **D:** Michael Moore. **VHS, Beta $9.95** *COL, NLC, QVD* 𝄞𝄞

Talk of the Town A brilliantly cast, strange mixture of screwball comedy and lynch-mob melodramatics. An accused arsonist, a Supreme Court judge and the girl they both love try to clear the former's name and evade the cops.
1942 118m/B Ronald Colman, Cary Grant, Jean Arthur, Edgar Buchanan, Glenda Farrell, Rex Ingram, Emma Dunn; **D:** George Stevens. **VHS, Beta $19.95** COL ♂♂♂

Talk Radio Riveting Stone adaptation of Bogosian's one-man play. An acidic talk radio host confronts America's evil side and his own past over the airwaves. The main character is loosely based on the life of Alan Berg, a Denver talk show host who was murdered by white supremacists.
1988 (R) 110m/C Eric Bogosian, Alec Baldwin, Ellen Greene, John Pankow, John C. McGinley, Michael Wincott, Leslie Hope; **D:** Oliver Stone; **W:** Eric Bogosian, Oliver Stone; **M:** Stewart Copeland. **VHS, Beta $19.95** MCA ♂♂♂

Talk to Me A successful New York accountant checks into the Hollins Communication Institute to cure his stuttering. While there, he meets and falls in love with a squirrel-hunting stuttering woman from Arkansas.
1982 90m/C Austin Pendleton, Michael Murphy, Louise Fletcher, Brian Backer, Clifton James. **VHS, Beta $59.98** FOX ♂½

Talkin' Dirty After Dark Sexy comedy starring Lawrence as a suave comedian who will do anything to get a late-night spot at Dukie's comedy club.
1991 (R) 89m/C Martin Lawrence, Jedda Jones, Phyllis Stickney, Darryl Sivad; **D:** Topper Carew; **W:** Topper Carew. **VHS $14.95** NLC, FCT ♂♂

Talking Walls A college sociology student uses high-tech surveillance equipment to spy on the clients of a seedy motel, in order to complete his thesis on human sexuality. **AKA:** Motel Vacancy.
1985 85m/C Stephen Shellan, Marie Laurin, Barry Primus, Sally Kirkland; **D:** Stephen Verona. **VHS, Beta $19.95** STE, NWV ♂½

The Tall Blond Man with One Black Shoe A violinist is completely unaware that rival spies mistakenly think he is also a spy, and that he is the center of a plot to booby-trap an overly ambitious agent at the French Secret Service. A sequel followed called "Return of the Tall Blond Man with One Black Shoe" which was followed by a disappointing American remake, "The Man with One Red Shoe." In French with English subtitles or dubbed. **AKA:** Le Grand Blond Avec Une Chaussure Noire.
1972 (PG) 90m/C Pierre Richard, Bernard Blier, Jean Rochefort, Mireille Darc, Jean Carmet; **D:** Yves Robert; **W:** Francis Veber; **M:** Vladimir Cosma. **VHS, Beta, 8mm $24.95** CVC, COL, VYY ♂♂♂

The Tall Guy Goldblum is a too-tall actor who tries the scene in London and lands the lead in a musical version of 'The Elephant Man,' becoming an overnight success. Not consistently funny, but good British comedy, including an interesting sex scene.
1989 (R) 92m/C Jeff Goldblum, Emma Thompson, Rowan Atkinson, Geraldine James, Kim Thomson, Anna Massey; **D:** Mel Smith; **W:** Richard Curtis; **M:** Peter Brewis. **VHS $89.95** COL, FCT ♂♂

Tall in the Saddle A misogynist foreman (Wayne) finds himself accused of murder. Meanwhile, he falls in love with his female boss's niece. An inoffensive and memorable western.

1944 79m/B John Wayne, Ella Raines, George "Gabby" Hayes, Ward Bond; **D:** Edwin L. Marin. **VHS, Beta $19.95** MED, TTC ♂♂½

Tall Lie A student quits a fraternity hazing exercise. He's pursued by a psychotic bunch of his fraternity brothers and is killed in a smash-up. A local doctor goes onto an anti-hazing campaign in the aftermath. **AKA:** For Men Only.
1953 93m/B Paul Henreid, Robert Sherman; **D:** Paul Henreid. **VHS, Beta** NO ♂♂

The Tall Men Standard western features frontier macho on a rough cattle drive confronting Indians, outlaws, and the wilderness while vying with each other for the love of Russell.
1955 122m/C Clark Gable, Jane Russell, Robert Ryan, Cameron Mitchell, Mae Marsh; **D:** Raoul Walsh. **VHS, Beta $19.95** FOX ♂♂

Tall Story Perkins is a star basketball player who must pass a crucial test in order to continue to play the game. In addition to the pressure of the exam, he is being pressured by gamblers to throw a game against the Russians. Fonda makes her screen debut as a cheerleader who is so awe-struck by Perkins that she takes the same classes just to be close to him. Based on the play by Howard Lindsay and Russel Crouse, and the novel "The Homecoming Game" by Howard Nemerov.
1960 91m/C Anthony Perkins, Jane Fonda, Ray Walston, Marc Connelly, Anne Jackson, Tom Laughlin; **D:** Joshua Logan; **W:** Julius J. Epstein, Philip C. Epstein. **VHS $19.98** WEA ♂♂

The Tall T A veteran rancher (Pat) stumbles onto big trouble when by chance he catches a stage coach that is eventually overrun by an evil band of cut-throats. After killing everyone on the coach except Pat and the daughter of a wealthy copper mine owner (Doretta), the renegades decide to leave the scene with the unfortunate two as hostages. Pat and Doretta, although in dire straights, find time to fall in love and devise an intricate plan for their escape. Regarded in certain western-lover circles as a cult classic.
1957 77m/B Randolph Scott, Richard Boone, Maureen O'Sullivan, Arthur Hunnicutt, Skip Homeier, Henry Silva, Robert Burton, Robert Anderson; **D:** Budd Boetticher; **W:** Burt Kennedy. **VHS** GKK ♂♂

Tall, Tan and Terrific Things really go crazy when the owner of a nightclub in Harlem is accused of murder.
1946 40m/C Mantan Moreland, Monte Hawley, Francine Everett, Dots Johnson; **D:** Bud Pollard. **VHS, Beta $24.95** NOS ♂♂

Tall Texan A motley crew seeks gold in an Indian burial ground in the desert. Flawed but interesting and suspenseful. Greed, lust, Indians and desert heat.
1953 82m/B Lloyd Bridges, Lee J. Cobb, Marie Windsor, George Steele; **D:** Elmo Williams. **VHS, Beta** RXM ♂♂

Talons of the Eagle Martial arts adventure centers around three undercover agents who go up against crimelord Mr. Li (Hong). To impress Li, martial arts champion Tyler Wilson (Blanks) and vice detective Michael Reeds (Merhi) enter a deadly martial arts tournament. They later hook up with beautiful agent Cassandra Hubbard (Barnes), who has already investigated Li's drug, gambling, and prostitution rings. Features the most advanced fighting techniques ever filmed.
1992 (R) 96m/C Billy Blanks, Jalal Merhi, James Hong, Priscilla Barnes, Matthias Hues; **D:** Michael Kennedy; **W:** J. Stephen Maunder. **VHS $19.98** MCA, SGE ♂♂

Tamango A confusing drama set on a slave ship travelling from Africa to Cuba in 1830. Jurgens is the ship's captain who takes the black Dandridge as his mistress. Meanwhile, the slaves are plotting a revolt, with Dandridge as a conspirator. Will Jurgens quell the rebellion and still keep his mistress? The interracial romance does takes a secondary role to the racial conflicts. The title refers to the leader of the slave revolt, played by Cressan. Filmed in both English- and French-language versions.
1959 98m/C Curt Jurgens, Dorothy Dandridge, Jean Servais, Alex Cressan; **D:** John Berry. **VHS $29.95** IVY ♂½

The Tamarind Seed Andrews and Sharif are star-crossed lovers kept apart by Cold War espionage. Dated, dull and desultory.
1974 123m/C Julie Andrews, Omar Sharif, Anthony Quayle, Dan O'Herlihy, Sylvia Syms; **D:** Blake Edwards; **W:** Blake Edwards; **M:** John Barry. **VHS, Beta $24.98** SUE ♂½

The Taming of the Shrew Historically interesting early talkie featuring sole (if perhaps unfortunate) pairing of Pickford and Fairbanks. Features the legendary credit line "By William Shakespeare, with additional dialogue by Sam Taylor." Re-edited in 1966; 1967 Zeffirelli remake featured Taylor and Burton.
1929 66m/B Mary Pickford, Douglas Fairbanks Sr., Edwin Maxwell, Joseph Cawthorn; **D:** Sam Taylor. **VHS, Beta $19.95** NOS, CCB ♂♂½

The Taming of the Shrew A lavish screen version of the classic Shakespearean comedy. Burton and Taylor are violently physical and perfectly cast as the battling Katherine and Petruchio. At the time the film was made, Burton and Taylor were having their own marital problems, which not only added an inner fire to their performances, but sent the interested moviegoers to the theatres in droves.
1967 122m/C Elizabeth Taylor, Richard Burton, Michael York, Michael Hordern, Cyril Cusack; **D:** Franco Zeffirelli; **W:** Franco Zeffirelli. Academy Awards '67 Nominations: Best Art Direction/Set Decoration, Best Costume Design; National Board of Review Awards '67: 10 Best Films of the Year. **VHS, Beta $19.95** COL, TVC, PBS ♂♂♂½

The Taming of the Shrew The classic Shakespearean comedy about the battle of the sexes where Petruchio attempts to tame his fiery, free-spirited wife, Kate.
1981 152m/C D: Peter Dews. **VHS, Beta $59.95** SUE ♂♂

Tammy and the Bachelor A backwoods Southern girl becomes involved with a romantic pilot and his snobbish family. They don't quite know what to make of her but she wins them over with her down-home philosophy. Features the hit tune, "Tammy." Charming performance by Reynolds.
1957 89m/C Debbie Reynolds, Leslie Nielsen, Walter Brennan, Fay Wray, Sidney Blackmer, Mildred Natwick, Louise Beavers; **D:** Joseph Pevney, Oscar Brodney. **VHS, Beta $14.98** MCA ♂♂½

Tammy and the Doctor Sandra Dee reprises Debbie Reynolds's backwoods gal ("Tammy and the Bachelor"). Dee becomes a nurse's aide and is wooed by doctor Fonda, in his film debut.
1963 88m/C Sandra Dee, Peter Fonda, MacDonald Carey; **D:** Harry Keller; **W:** Oscar Brodney. **VHS, Beta $14.98** MCA ♂♂

Tampopo A hilarious, episodic Japanese comedy. A widowed noodle shop owner is coached by a ten-gallon-hatted stranger in how to make the perfect noodle. Popular,

free-form hit that established Itami in the West. In Japanese with English subtitles.
1986 114m/C Ken Watanabe, Tsutomu Yamazaki, Nobuko Miyamoto, Koji Yakusho, Rikiya Yasuoka, Kinzo Sakura, Shoji Otake; *D:* Juzo Itami. **VHS $79.95** *REP, ING* 🎬🎬🎬

Tangiers The disappearance of a British intelligence agent in Gibraltar sets off a chain-reaction of violent incidents.
1983 82m/C Ronny Cox. **VHS** *WAR* 🎬

Tangled Destinies Old dark house thriller involving a deserted mansion, murder, and faux diamonds. Good acting and a decent storyline make it one of the few successful independently made films of its time.
1932 64m/B Lloyd Whitlock, Glenn Tryon, Vera Reynolds, Doris Hill, Sidney Bracy; *D:* Frank Strayer; *W:* Edward T. Lowe. **VHS $12.95** *SNC* 🎬🎬½

Tango An early melodrama follows the ups and down of a chorus girl and the guy who sticks with her through thick and thin and poorly-filmed dance routines. Based on a novel by Vida Hurst.
1936 66m/B Marion Nixon, Chick Chandler, Matty Kemp, Marie Prevost, Warren Hymer, Herman Bing, Franklin Pangborn, George Meeker; *D:* Phil Rosen. **VHS $15.95** *NOS, LOO* 🎬½

Tango and Cash Stallone and Russell are L.A. cops with something in common: they both think they are the best in the city. Forced to work together to beat drug lord Palance, they flex their muscles a lot. Directing completed by Albert Magnoli, after Andrei Konchalovsky left in a huff.
1989 (R) 104m/C Sylvester Stallone, Kurt Russell, Jack Palance, Brion James, Teri Hatcher, Michael J. Pollard, James Hong, Marc Alaimo, Robert Z'Dar; *D:* Andrei Konchalovsky; *W:* Randy Feldman; *M:* Harold Faltermeyer. **VHS, Beta, 8mm $19.98** *WAR* 🎬🎬

Tango Bar A romantic triangle between a tango dancer who leaves Argentina during a time of political unrest, his former partner, and his wife, who both stay behind. They are reunited after years of separation. Gives the viewer a detailed vision of the historical and cultural significance of the tango. Charming, interesting and very watchable. In Spanish with English subtitles.
1988 90m/C Raul Julia, Valeria Lynch, Ruben Juarez; *D:* Marcos Zurinaga. **VHS, Beta $79.95** *WAR, ING* 🎬🎬½

Tank Retired Army officer Garner's son is thrown into jail on a trumped-up charge by a small town sheriff. Dad comes to the rescue with his restored Sherman tank. Trite and unrealistic portrayal of good versus bad made palatable by Garner's performance.
1983 (PG) 113m/C James Garner, Shirley Jones, C. Thomas Howell, Mark Herrier, Sandy Ward, Jenilee Harrison, Dorian Harewood, G.D. Spradlin; *D:* Marvin J. Chomsky. **VHS, Beta $19.95** *MCA* 🎬½

Tank Commando Mediocre WWII actioner, set in Italy, about a demolition squad of battle-hardened Americans trying to locate a secret German crossing point. It turns out to be an underwater bridge and an Italian orphan is the only one, besides the Germans, to know its location. Can the Americans persuade the kid to talk?
1959 79m/B Robert Barron, Wally Campo, Maggie Lawrence, Donato Farretta, Leo V. Metranga, Jack Sowards, Anthony Rich, Larry Hudson; *D:* Burt Topper; *W:* Burt Topper. **VHS $9.95** *COL* 🎬½

Tanks a Million Despite the title, tanks aren't even mentioned in this. Tracy stars as a wacky genius who gets drafted. His excellent memory keeps getting him into one predicament after another. Though he gets promoted quickly, he shows himself no leader. Lots of time-worn gags, but they still work.
1941 50m/B William Tracy, James Gleason, Noah Beery Jr., Joseph Sawyer, Elyse Knox, Douglas Fowley, Frank Faylen, Dick Wessel, Frank Melton, Harold Goodwin, William Gould, Norman Kerry; *D:* Fred Guiol. **VHS $19.95** *NOS* 🎬🎬

Tanner '88 Murphy is excellent as a longshot politician on the trail of the Democratic presidential nomination. Story by Gary Trudeau of Doonesbury fame. A precise political satire made for cable. *AKA:* Tanner: A Political Fable.
1988 120m/C Michael Murphy, Pamela Reed, Cynthia Nixon; *D:* Robert Altman. **VHS $79.99** *ING, PBS, BTV* 🎬🎬

Tanya's Island Abused girlfriend fantasizes about life on deserted island and romance with an ape. Vanity billed as D.D. Winters.
1981 (R) 100m/C Vanity, Richard Sargent, Mariette Levesque, Don McCleod; *D:* Alfred Sole. **VHS, Beta** *NO* 🎬🎬½

Taoism Drunkard It's alcoholism at its funniest as a juice-guzzling martial artist goes nuts.
19?? 100m/C Yuen Tat Chor, Yuen Cheung Yan, Chu Hai Ling. **VHS, Beta $49.95** *OCE* 🎬🎬½

Tap The son of a famous tap dancer, a dancer himself, decides to try to get away from his former life of crime by helping an aging hoofer revitalize the art of tap dancing. Fun to watch for the wonderful dancing scenes. Davis' last big screen appearance. Hines is sincere in this old-fashioned story, and dances up a storm. Captures some never-before filmed old hoofers.
1989 (PG-13) 106m/C Gregory Hines, Sammy Davis Jr., Suzanne Douglas, Joe Morton, Terrance McNally, Steve Condos, Jimmy Slyde, Harold Nicholas, Etta James, Savion Glover, Dick Anthony Williams, Sandman Sims, Bunny Briggs, Pat Rico, Arthur Duncan; *D:* Nick Castle; *W:* Nick Castle; *M:* James Newton Howard. **VHS, Beta $14.95** *COL, MVD* 🎬🎬½

Tapeheads Silly, sophomonic, sexy comedy starring Cusack and Robbins as young wannabe rock-video producers who strike it big. Many big-name cameos; good soundtrack; laughs.
1989 (R) 93m/C John Cusack, Tim Robbins, Mary Crosby, Connie Stevens, Susan Tyrrell, Lyle Alzado, Don Cornelius, Katy Boyer, Doug McClure, Clu Gulager, Jessica Walter; *Cameos:* Stiv Bators, Sam Moore, Junior Walker, Martha Quinn, Ted Nugent, Weird Al Yankovic; *D:* Bill Fishman. **VHS, Beta** *NO* 🎬🎬½

Taps Military academy students led by Hutton are so true to their school they lay siege to it to keep it from being closed. An antiwar morality play about excesses of zeal and patriotism. Predictable but impressive.
1981 (PG) 126m/C Timothy Hutton, George C. Scott, Ronny Cox, Sean Penn, Tom Cruise; *D:* Harold Becker; *W:* Darryl Ponicsan, Robert Mark Kamen; *M:* Maurice Jarre. **VHS, Beta $19.98** *FOX* 🎬🎬½

Tarantula If you're into gigantic killer insect movies this is one of the best with nifty special effects and some good action. Carroll plays a scientist who's testing on a growth formula which he's testing on a spider when it accidentally gets loose. This eight-legged horror grows to 100 feet high and causes havoc in the Arizona desert until the Air Force napalms the sucker. Look for Eastwood in the final sequence as an Air Force pilot.
1955 81m/B Leo G. Carroll, John Agar, Mara Corday, Nestor Paiva, Ross Elliott, Clint Eastwood; *D:* Jack Arnold; *W:* Robert M. Fresco, Martin Berkeley. **VHS $14.98** *MCA* 🎬🎬🎬

Tarantulas: The Deadly Cargo Eek! Hairy spiders terrizing our sleepy town and destroying our orange crop! Made-for-TV cheapie not creepy; will make you sleepy.
1977 100m/C Claude Akins, Charles Frank, Deborah Winters, Pat Hingle, Sandy McPeak, Bert Remsen, Howard Hesseman, Tom Atkins, Charles Siebert; *D:* Stuart Hagmann. **VHS $49.95** *LIV* 🎬

Taras Bulba Well-photographed costume epic on the 16th century Polish revolution. Brynner as the fabled Cossack; Curtis plays his vengeful son. Good score. Shot on location in Argentina. Based on the novel by Nikolai Gogol.
1962 122m/C Tony Curtis, Yul Brynner, Christine Kaufmann, Sam Wanamaker, George Macready, Vladimir Sokoloff, Perry Lopez; *D:* J. Lee Thompson. **VHS $19.98** *MGM* 🎬🎬½

Target Normal dad/hubby Hackman slips into a figurative phone booth and emerges as former CIA when his better half is kidnapped in Paris. Good action scenes, but poorly scripted and too long.
1985 (R) 117m/C Gene Hackman, Matt Dillon, Gayle Hunnicutt, Josef Sommer; *D:* Arthur Penn. **VHS, Beta $19.98** *FOX* 🎬🎬

Target Eagle Spanish police chief von Sydow hires mercenary Rivero to infiltrate drug ring. Good performances; ho-hum story.
1984 99m/C Max von Sydow, George Peppard, Maud Adams, Chuck Connors, George Rivero, Susana Dosamantes; *D:* J. Anthony Loma. **VHS, Beta** *NO* 🎬

Target: Favorite Son An attractive, ammunition-laden woman sharp-shoots her way to power in this made-for-TV movie.
1987 (R) 115m/C Linda Kozlowski, Harry Hamlin, Robert Loggia, Ronny Cox, James Whitmore. **VHS $89.95** *VMK* 🎬🎬

Target for Killing Mediocre thriller about a secret agent who must protect a young heiress from a Lebanese syndicate that's out to kill her.
1966 93m/C Stewart Granger, Curt Jurgens, Molly Peters, Adolfo Celi, Klaus Kinski; *D:* Rupert Davies. **VHS $16.95** *SNC* 🎬🎬

Targets Bogdanovich's suspenseful directorial debut. An aging horror film star plans his retirement, convinced that real life is too scary for his films to have an audience. A mad sniper at a drive-in movie seems to prove he's right. Some prints still have anti-gun prologue, which was added after Robert Kennedy's assassination.
1969 (PG) 90m/C Boris Karloff, James Brown, Tim O'Kelly; *D:* Peter Bogdanovich. **VHS, Beta $44.95** *PAR* 🎬🎬

Tarka the Otter The story of Tarka the Otter who encounters many dangers as he pursues his favorite eel meals.
198? 91m/C **VHS, Beta $39.95** *TWE* 🎬🎬🎬

Tartuffe Popular French leading man Depardieu makes directorial debut with Moliere classic about religious hypocrisy and an imposter taking advantage of a wealthy merchant and his family. In French with English subtitles.
1984 140m/C Gerard Depardieu, Francois Perier, Elisabeth Depardieu; *D:* Gerard Depardieu. **VHS $79.95** *CVC, FCT, APD* 🎬🎬½

Tartuffe Moliere's famous comedy has Tartuffe posing as a holy man who has attracted the incredulous merchant Orgon. Orgon is willing to give Tartuffe anything—money, social position, even his daughter—and Tartuffe is more than happy to accept.
1990 110m/C Anthony Sher, Nigel Hawthorne, Alison Steadman; **D:** Bill Alexander. **VHS, Beta** $39.95 TTC, ING ✍✍½

Tarzan and His Mate Second entry in the lavishly produced MGM Tarzan series. Weissmuller and O'Sullivan cohabit in unmarried bliss before the Hays Code moved them to a tree house with twin beds. Many angry elephants, nasty white hunters, and hungry lions. Laserdisc includes the original trailer.
1934 93m/B Johnny Weissmuller, Maureen O'Sullivan, Neil Hamilton, Paul Cavanagh; **D:** Jack Conway. **VHS** $19.98 MGM, FCT ✍✍✍

Tarzan and the Green Goddess Tarzan searches for a statue that could prove dangerous if in the wrong hands. **AKA:** New Adventures of Tarzan.
1938 72m/B Bruce (Herman Brix) Bennett, Ula Holt, Frank Baker; **D:** Edward Kull. **VHS, Beta** $19.95 HHT, SNC, VYY ✍½

Tarzan and the Trappers Bad-guy trappers and would-be treasure-seekers wish they hadn't messed with the ape man.
1958 74m/B Gordon Scott, Eve Brent, Ricky Sorenson, Maurice Marsac, Cheetah; **D:** H. Bruce Humberstone. **VHS, Beta** $16.95 SNC, NOS, VYY ✍½

Tarzan Escapes Jane is tricked by evil hunters into abandoning her fairy tale life with Tarzan, so the Ape Man sets out to reunite with his one true love. The third entry in MGM's Weissmuller/O'Sullivan series is still among the better Tarzan movies thanks to the leads, but the Hays Office made sure Jane was wearing a lot more clothes this time around.
1936 95m/B Johnny Weissmuller, Maureen O'Sullivan, John Buckler, Benita Hume, William Henry; **D:** Richard Thorpe. **VHS** $19.98 FOX, FCT ✍✍✍

Tarzan Finds a Son Weissmuller and O'Sullivan returned to their roles after three years with the addition of the five-year-old Sheffield as Boy. He's an orphan whose awful relatives hope he stays lost so they can collect an inheritance. Jane and Tarzan fight to adopt the tyke and when the new family are captured by a wicked tribe only an elephant stampede can save them!
1939 90m/B Johnny Weissmuller, Maureen O'Sullivan, Johnny Sheffield, Ian Hunter, Henry Stephenson, Frieda Inescort, Henry Wilcoxon; **D:** Richard Thorpe. **VHS** $19.98 MGM ✍✍✍

Tarzan of the Apes Brawny Lincoln is the original screen Tarzan. Silent film well done and more faithful to the book than later versions.
1917 63m/B Elmo Lincoln, Enid Markey; **D:** Scott Sidney. **VHS, Beta** $16.95 GPV, VYY, WFV ✍✍

Tarzan, the Ape Man The definitive Tarzan movie; the first Tarzan talkie; the original of the long series starring Weissmuller. Dubiously faithful to the Edgar Rice Burroughs story, but recent attempts to remake, update or improve it (notably the pretentious 1984 Greystoke) have failed to near the original's entertainment value or even its technical quality. O'Sullivan as Jane and Weissmuller bring style and wit to their classic roles.
1932 99m/B Johnny Weissmuller, Maureen O'Sullivan, Neil Hamilton; **D:** Woodbridge S. Van Dyke. **VHS, Beta** $19.98 MGM, FCT ✍✍✍

Tarzan, the Ape Man Plodding, perverted excuse to see Derek cavort nude in jungle. So bad not even hard-core Tarzan fans should bother.
1981 (R) 112m/C Bo Derek, Richard Harris, John Phillip Law, Miles O'Keeffe; **D:** John Derek. **VHS, Beta** $79.95 MGM Woof!

Tarzan the Fearless Tarzan (Crabbe) helps a young girl find her missing father.
1933 84m/B Buster Crabbe, Jacqueline Wells, E. Allen Warren, Edward Woods, Philo McCullough, Matthew Betz; **D:** Robert F. Hill. **VHS, Beta** $16.95 SNC, NOS, CAB ✍½

Tarzan the Tiger Series of 15 chapters is loosely based on the Edgar Rice Burroughs novel entitled "Tarzan and the Jewels of Opar." These chapters were filmed as silent pieces, and were later released with a musical score and synchronized sound effects. Here Merrill is the first to sound the cry of the bull ape, Tarzan's trademark.
1929 ?m/B Frank Merrill, Natalie Kingston, Lilian Worth, Al Ferguson; **D:** Henry MacRae. **VHS** $49.95 NOS, FCT, MOV ✍½

Tarzana, the Wild Girl Jungle cheapie about an expedition that finds a beautiful, scantily clad girl living wildly in the jungle.
1972 87m/C Kenneth Clark, Franca Polesello, Frank Ressel, Andrew Ray, James Reed; **W:** Philip Shaw. **VHS** $16.95 SNC ✍

Tarzan's New York Adventure O'Sullivan's final appearance as Jane is a so-so adventure with some humorous moments when Tarzan meets the big city. When Boy is kidnapped by an evil circus owner, Tarzan, Jane, and Cheta head out to rescue him. Tarzan shows off his jungle prowess by climbing skyscrapers and diving off the Brooklyn Bridge into the Hudson River. Lincoln, the screen's first Tarzan, has a cameo.
1942 70m/B Johnny Weissmuller, Maureen O'Sullivan, Johnny Sheffield, Virginia Grey, Charles Bickford, Paul Kelly, Chill Wills, Russell Hicks, Cy Kendall; **Cameos:** Elmo Lincoln; **D:** Richard Thorpe. **VHS** $19.98 MGM ✍✍½

Tarzan's Revenge Morris is a better Olympic runner than actor; Holm is horrible. Only for serious Tarzan fans.
1938 70m/B Glenn Morris, Eleanor Holm, Hedda Hopper; **D:** David Ross Lederman. **VHS, Beta** $16.95 SNC, NOS, VYY ✍

Tarzan's Secret Treasure Tarzan saves an expedition from a savage tribe only to be repaid by having the greedy hunters hold Jane and Boy hostage. They want Tarzan's help in finding a secret cache of gold. But Tarzan doesn't take kindly to threats to his family and teaches those evildoers a lesson!
1941 81m/B Johnny Weissmuller, Maureen O'Sullivan, Johnny Sheffield, Reginald Owen, Barry Fitzgerald, Tom Conway, Philip Dorn; **D:** Richard Thorpe. **VHS** $19.98 MGM ✍✍½

Task Force History of naval aviation and the development of the aircraft carrier highlighted by actual WWII combat footage (in color). Cooper and his naval buddies try to convince the brass that planes can be landed on the decks of ships. Slowly the Navy goes ahead and when Pearl Harbor is attacked, Cooper is given command of his own aircraft carrier. The use of the carriers proved very effective in Pacific battles and Cooper is finally vindicated.
1949 116m/B Gary Cooper, Jane Wyatt, Wayne Morris, Walter Brennan, Julie London, Bruce (Herman Brix) Bennett, Jack Holt, Stanley Ridges, John Ridgely, Richard Rober, Art Baker, Moroni Olsen; **D:** Delmer Daves; **W:** Delmer Daves. **VHS, Beta** $19.98 MGM, FCT ✍✍½

A Taste for Flesh and Blood A monster from outer space comes to earth and is delighted with the easy pickings for his insatiable appetite. A brave boy and girl, and a NASA commander must join forces to take the alien out. This one is billed as a campy salute to '50s B movies.
1990 (R) 84m/C Rubin Santiago, Lori Karz, Tim Ferrante. **VHS** NO ✍✍½

A Taste for Killing Two boys, both from well-to-do families, decide to take summer jobs on an offshore Texas oil rig. The best friends think a summer of adventure awaits them; however, their lives are made miserable by their blue-collar boss, who is resentful of their high society background. Then they meet Bo Landry, who befriends them and helps them survive. Unfortunately, Bo turns out to be anything but a friend as he reveals himself as a deadly con-artist in this intense psychological thriller.
1992 (R) 87m/C Jason Bateman, Henry Thomas, Michael Biehn, Blue Deckert, Helen Cates; **D:** Lou Antonio; **W:** Dan Bronson. **VHS** $89.98 MCA ✍✍

Taste of Death A youth discovers his courage within when he stands up to the bandits invading his village.
1977 90m/C John Ireland. **VHS, Beta** NO ✍

A Taste of Hell Two American soldiers fight a guerilla outfit in the Pacific during WWII. A low-budget film with few redeeming characteristics.
1973 (PG) 90m/C William Smith, John Garwood. **VHS, Beta** $19.95 NWV, STE ✍

A Taste of Honey A plain working-class girl falls in love with a black sailor. When she becomes pregnant, a homosexual friend helps her out. A moving film with strong, powerful performances. Based on the London and Broadway hit play by Shelagh Delaney.
1961 100m/B Rita Tushingham, Robert Stephens, Dora Bryan, Murray Melvin, Paul Danquah; **D:** Tony Richardson; **W:** Tony Richardson, Shelagh Delaney; **M:** John Addison. **VHS** NO ✍✍✍

Taste the Blood of Dracula Lee's Dracula only makes a brief appearance in this Hammer horror film which has three children taking over from the bloodsucker. Three Victorian dandies have killed the wizard who revived Dracula and he seeks their deaths by using their own children as the means of his revenge. Not enough Lee but still creepy. Preceded by "Dracula Has Risen from the Grave" and followed by "Scars of Dracula."
1970 (PG) 91m/C Christopher Lee, Ralph Bates, Geoffrey Keen, Gwen Watford, Linda Hayden, John Carson, Peter Sallis, Isla Blair, Martin Jarvis, Roy Kinnear; **D:** Peter Sasdy. **VHS** $19.98 WAR ✍✍½

Tatie Danielle Pitch-black comedy from the director of "Life Is a Long Quiet River" sees a bitter, elderly widow moving in with her young nephew and making his life a hell. In French with yellow English subtitles.
1991 114m/C Tsilla Chelton, Catherine Jacob, Isabelle Nanty, Neige Dolsky, Eric Prat, Laurence Fevrier; **D:** Etienne Chatiliez; **W:** Etienne Chatiliez. **VHS** $19.98 LIV, ING ✍✍✍

The Tattered Web A police sergeant confronts and accidently kills the woman with whom his son-in-law has been cheating. He's then assigned the case. When he tries to frame a wino for the murder, things get more and more messy. Fine performances aid this made-for-television story.
1971 74m/C Lloyd Bridges, Frank Converse, Broderick Crawford, Murray Hamilton, Sallie Shockley; **D:** Paul Wendkos. **VHS, Beta** $59.95 LHV ✍✍

Tattoo A model becomes the object of obsession for a crazy tattoo artist. He relentlessly pursues her, leaving behind all his other more illustrated clients. Starts out fine, but deteriorates rapidly. Controversial love scene between Dern and Adams.
1981 (R) 103m/C Bruce Dern, Maud Adams, Leonard Frey, Rikke Borge, John Getz; **D:** Bob Brooks. **VHS, Beta** $19.98 *FOX* 🎬🎬

Tattoo Connection A gang of lethal Oriental diamond thieves is pursued with whip-snapping flamboyance by a taciturn kung-fu investigator.
1978 (R) 95m/C Jim Kelly; **D:** Luk Pak Sang. **VHS, Beta** $9.98 *SUE, ORI* 🎬

Tattooed Hit Man Japanese gangster violence in a revenge-doesn't-pay action story.
1976 81m/C Mayumi Nagisa, Bunta Sugawara, Tsunehiko Watase. **VHS, Beta** $59.95 *MED* 🎬

Tax Season A small-time businessman buys a Hollywood tax service sight-unseen, and finds it employing a hooker, a bookie and a variety of other unconventional types.
1990 (PG-13) 93m/C Fritz Bronner, James Hong, Jana Grant, Toru Tanaka, Dorie Krum, Kathryn Knotts, Arte Johnson, Rob Slyker; **D:** Tom Law. **VHS, Beta** $29.95 *PAR* 🎬🎬

Taxi Blues A political allegory with the two protagonists representing the new and old Soviet Union. A hard-working, narrow-minded cabdriver keeps the saxophone of a westernized, Jewish, jazz-loving musician who doesn't have his fare. The two strike up a wary friendship as each tries to explain his view of life to the other. Good look at the street life of Moscow populated by drunks, punks, and black marketeers. Directorial debut of Lounguine. In Russian with English subtitles.
1990 110m/C Piotr Mamonov, Piotr Zaitchenko, Natalia Koliakanova, Vladimir Kachpour; **D:** Pavel Lounguine; **W:** Pavel Lounguine. **VHS** $89.95 *NYF, ING* 🎬🎬½

Taxi Dancers Smalltown Billie arrives in Hollywood with dreams of becoming an actress. Naturally, her dreams turn to despair and she resorts to "dancing" at the Shark Club where she becomes involved with a gambler who owes money to the wrong people.
1993 97m/C Sonny Landham, Robert Miano, Brittany McCrena, Tina Fite, Mirage Micheaux, Michele Hess, Randall Irwin; **D:** Norman Thaddeus Vane; **W:** Norman Thaddeus Vane. **VHS** $89.95 *AIP* 🎬½

Taxi Driver A psychotic New York City taxi driver tries to save a child prostitute and becomes infatuated with an educated political campaigner. He goes on a violent rampage when his dreams don't work out. Repellant, frightening vision of alienation and urban catharsis. On-target performances from Foster and De Niro. The laserdisc version is slightly longer, with commentary by Scorsese and screenwriter Paul Schrader, storyboards, complete screenplay, and Scorsese's production photos.
1976 (R) 112m/C Robert De Niro, Jodie Foster, Harvey Keitel, Cybill Shepherd, Peter Boyle, Albert Brooks; **D:** Martin Scorsese; **W:** Paul Schrader. Academy Awards '76 Nominations: Best Actor (De Niro), Best Picture, Best Supporting Actress (Foster), Best Original Score; British Academy Awards '76: Best Supporting Actress (Foster); Cannes Film Festival '76: Best Film; Los Angeles Film Critics Association Awards '76: Best Actor (De Niro); New York Film Critics Awards '76: Best Actor (De Niro); National Society of Film Critics Awards '76: Best Actor (De Niro), Best Director (Scorsese), Best Supporting Actress (Foster). **VHS, Beta, 8mm** $14.95 *COL, VYG* 🎬🎬🎬

The Taxi Mystery Guy saves Broadway starlet from band of ne'er-do-wells thanks to deserted taxi, then tries to figure out who she is, unaware that her sinister understudy plans to do her in.
1926 50m/B Edith Roberts, Robert Agnew, Virginia Pearson, Phillips Smalley; **D:** Fred Windermere. **VHS, Beta** $16.95 *GPV* 🎬

Taxi zum Klo An autobiographical semi-documentary about the filmmaker's aimless existence and attempts at homosexual affairs after being fired from his job as a teacher. Explicit. In German with English subtitles. Sordid sexual situations.
1981 98m/C Bernd Broaderup, Frank Ripploh; **D:** Frank Ripploh. **VHS, Beta** $79.95 *FCT, GLV, CCN* 🎬🎬🎬

A Taxing Woman Satiric Japanese comedy about a woman tax collector in pursuit of a crafty millionaire tax cheater. Followed by the equally hilarious "A Taxing Woman's Return." In Japanese with English subtitles. **AKA:** Marusa No Onna.
1987 127m/C Nobuko Miyamoto, Tsutomu Yamazaki; **D:** Juzo Itami; **W:** Juzo Itami. **VHS, Beta** $79.95 *FXL, ING, LUM* 🎬🎬🎬½

A Taxing Woman's Return Funny, sophisticated, action-packed. Miyamoto returns as the dedicated tax investigator to fight industrialists, politicians, and other big swindlers, who have contrived to inflate Tokyo's real estate values. Sequel to "A Taxing Woman." In Japanese with English subtitles. **AKA:** Marusa No Onna II.
1988 127m/C Nobuko Miyamoto, Rentaro Mikuni, Masahiko Tsugawa, Tetsuro Tamba, Toru Masuoka, Takeya Nakamura, Hosei Komatsu, Mihoko Shibata; **D:** Juzo Itami; **W:** Juzo Itami. **VHS** $79.95 *NYF, ING* 🎬🎬🎬

TC 2000 Jason Storm and Zoey Kinsella are cops working for The Controller, who has the unenviable task of protecting the community from roving gangs of vicious punks. When Zoey is killed, The Controller converts her into a super-cybernetic killing machine unleashed on the gangs. Meanwhile Jason is considered a liability and must battle the gangs, The Controller, and cyber-Zoey to save himself. Oh, there's also something about saving the Earth's atmosphere from nuclear destruction. Lots of action.
1993 (R) 92m/C Billy Blanks, Bobbie Philips, Jalal Merhi, Bolo Yeung, Matthias Hues; **D:** T.J. Scott; **W:** T.J. Scott. **VHS** *MCA, SGE* 🎬🎬

Tchaikovsky The glorious music is all that saves this pedestrian biography of the 19th century Russian composer, which ignores his homosexuality and glosses over the dissolution of his marriage. Lead performance by Smoktunovsky does manage to rise above the moribund script. Originally released at 191 minutes. In Russian with English subtitles.
1971 153m/C Innokenti Smoktunovsky, Antonina Shuranova, Yevgeny Leonov, Maya Plisetskaya, Vladislav Strzeltchik, Alla Demidova, Kirill Lavrov; **D:** Igor Talankin. **VHS** $59.95 *KIV, FCT* 🎬🎬½

Tchao Pantin An acclaimed French film noir about an ex-cop being drawn into drug smuggling underground via a young Arab. English version. Finely drawn characters skillfully portrayed make this a winner.
1984 100m/C Coluche, Richard Anconina, Agnes Soral; **D:** Claude Berri. **VHS, Beta** $29.98 *SUE* 🎬🎬🎬

Tea and Sympathy A young prep school student, confused about his sexuality, has an affair with an older woman, his teacher's wife. The three leads recreate their Broadway roles in this tame adaption of the Robert Anderson play which dealt more openly with the story's homosexual elements.
1956 122m/C Deborah Kerr, John Kerr, Leif Erickson, Edward Andrews, Darryl Hickman, Norma Crane, Dean Jones; **D:** Vincente Minnelli; **W:** Robert Anderson. **VHS** $19.98 *MGM, FCT* 🎬🎬🎬

Tea For Three Sexual trio develops and seeks therapy after a fledgling doctor has been having sexual relationships with two women, and the females finally meet.
1984 (R) 89m/C Iris Berben, Mascha Gonska, Heinz Marecek; **D:** Gerhard Janda. **VHS, Beta** *MED* 🎬🎬

Tea for Two This take-off on the Broadway play "No, No, Nanette" features Day as an actress who takes a bet that she can answer "no" to every question for twenty-four hours (life was less complex back then). If she can, she gets to finance and star in her own Broadway musical. 🎵I Know That You Know; Crazy Rhythm; Charleston; I Only Have Eyes For You; Tea For Two; I Want to be Happy; Oh Me, Oh My; The Call of the Sea; Do Do Do.
1950 98m/C Doris Day, Gordon MacRae, Gene Nelson, Patrice Wymore, Eve Arden, Billy DeWolfe, S.Z. Sakall, Bill Goodwin, Bill Gibson, Virginia Gibson, Crauford Kent, Harry Harvey; **D:** David Butler. **VHS** $19.98 *WAR, CCB, MVD* 🎬🎬🎬

The Teacher TV's "Dennis the Menace" (North) has an affair with his high school teacher; the pair is menaced by a deranged killer. Cheap but enjoyable. **AKA:** The Seductress.
1974 (R) 97m/C Angel Tompkins, Jay North, Anthony James; **D:** Hikmet Avedis. **VHS, Beta** *NO* 🎬🎬

Teachers A lawsuit is brought against a high school for awarding a diploma to an illiterate student. Comedy-drama starts slowly and seems to condemn the school system, never picking up strength or resolving any issues, though Nolte is fairly intense. Shot in Columbus, Ohio.
1984 106m/C Nick Nolte, JoBeth Williams, Lee Grant, Judd Hirsch, Ralph Macchio, Richard Mulligan, Royal Dano, Morgan Freeman, Laura Dern, Crispin Glover, Madeline Sherwood, Zohra Lampert; **D:** Arthur Hiller. **VHS, Beta** $14.95 *MGM, FOX* 🎬🎬

Teacher's Pet This charming comedy features a cynical newspaper editor who enrolls in a night college journalism course, believing that it won't teach anything of substance. He later becomes enamored of his instructor. Well written script and superb performance by Young as Gable's rival for Day.
1958 120m/B Clark Gable, Doris Day, Mamie Van Doren, Gig Young, Nick Adams; **D:** George Seaton; **W:** Fay Kanin, Michael Kanin. **VHS, Beta** $14.95 *PAR, BAR* 🎬🎬🎬

The Teahouse of the August Moon An adaptation of the John Patrick play. Post-war American troops are assigned to bring civilization to a small village in Okinawa and instead fall for Okinawan culture and romance. Lively cast keeps it generally working, but assessments of Brando's comedic performance vary widely.
1956 123m/C Glenn Ford, Marlon Brando, Eddie Albert, Paul Ford, Machiko Kyo, Henry Morgan; **D:** Daniel Mann. **VHS, Beta** $19.98 *MGM* 🎬🎬½

Teamster Boss: The Jackie Presser Story A well-done made-for-cable-television movie powered by a riveting performance by Dennehy. Presser followed Jimmy Hoffa as president of the Teamsters and was equally caught between the mob and the government as he tried to do what he considered best for the union.

1992 (R) 111m/C Brian Dennehy, Jeff Daniels, Maria Conchita Alonso, Eli Wallach, Robert Prosky, Donald Moffatt, Tony LoBianco, Kate Reid, Henderson Forsythe, Al Waxman; *D:* Alastair Reid. VHS $89.99 *HBO, PMS* ✯✯✯

Tearaway Australian story of a street punk with an alcoholic father. Story has potential, but ends up going nowhere.
1987 (R) 100m/C Matthew Hunter, Mark Pilisi, Peter Bland, Kim Willoughby, Rebecca Saunders; *D:* Bruce Morrison. VHS, Beta $79.95 *LHV, WAR* ✯✯½

Tears in the Rain Casey Cantrell (Stone) travels to London to deliver a deathbed letter from her mother to Lord Richard Bredon. While in England, she is pursued by two men, an heir to the Bredon fortune, and his wealthy friend. After she finds a love which is forbidden, she makes a bizarre discovery that changes her life forever. Made for British television.
1988 100m/C Sharon Stone, Christopher Cazenove, Leigh Lawson, Paul Daneman; *D:* Don Sharp. VHS $89.98 *BFS* ✯✯

Ted & Venus Cort plays Ted, an oddball cult beat in love with Linda, a beach beauty who finds him repulsive. The more she rejects him, the more obsessed about her Ted gets, especially when his equally oddball friends offer him romantic advice.
1993 (R) 100m/C Bud Cort, Kim Adams, Rhea Perlman, James Brolin, Carol Kane; *Cameos:* Gena Rowlands, Martin Mull, Woody Harrelson, Andrea Martin, Timothy Leary, Cassandra Peterson; *D:* Bud Cort; *W:* Bud Cort, Paul Ciotti. VHS $89.95 *COL* ✯✯½

Teddy at the Throttle Teddy, the Great Dane, must rescue Gloria Swanson from a villain who has tied up her boyfriend. Silent.
1916 20m/B Bobby Vernon, Gloria Swanson, Wallace Beery; *D:* Clarence Badger. VHS, Beta *CCB* ✯✯

Teddy at the Throttle/Speeding Along A silent comedy about stealing fortunes from innocent heroines and another about racing cars in a farm area.
1917 54m/B Gloria Swanson, Wallace Beery, Bobby Vernon. VHS, Beta $24.95 *VYY* ✯✯

Teen Alien On Halloween, a young boy and his friends run into a hostile alien. It could happen.
1988 (PG) 88m/C Vern Adix, Michael Dunn. VHS, Beta $79.95 *PSM* ✯

Teen Mothers Bittersweet story of two unwed teenagers forced to take their child and leave home for the tenements of New York. *AKA:* Seed of Innocence.
1980 (R) 91m/C VHS, Beta *NO* ✯✯

Teen Vamp Dorky high schooler is bitten by a prostitute; becomes a cool vampire. Mindless "comedy."
1988 87m/C Clu Gulager, Karen Carlson, Angela Brown; *D:* Samuel Bradford. VHS, Beta $19.95 *STE, NWV* ✯

Teen Witch A demure high schooler uses black magic to woo the most popular guy in school.
1989 (PG-13) 94m/C Robin Lively, Zelda Rubinstein, Dan Gauthier, Joshua Miller, Dick Sargent; *D:* Dorian Walker. VHS, Beta $89.95 *MED, VTR* ✯✯

Teen Wolf A nice, average teenage basketball player begins to show werewolf tendencies which suddenly make him popular at school when he leads the team to victory. The underlying message is to be yourself, regardless of how much hair you have on your body. Lighthearted comedy carried by the Fox charm; followed by subpar "Teen Wolf Too."
1985 (PG) 92m/C Michael J. Fox, James Hampton, Scott Paulin, Susan Ursitti; *D:* Rod Daniel; *M:* Miles Goodman. VHS, Beta, 8mm $14.95 *PAR* ✯✯½

Teen Wolf Too The sequel to "Teen Wolf" in which the Teen Wolf's cousin goes to college on a boxing scholarship. More evidence that the sequel is rarely as good as the original.
1987 (PG) 95m/C Jason Bateman, Kim Darby, John Astin, Paul Sand; *D:* Christopher Leitch. VHS, Beta $14.95 *PAR* ✯✯

Teenage Low budget juvenile schlock film that tries to figure out what's wrong with modern youth. Pure camp.
1944 ?m/C Herbert Heyes, Wheeler Oakman. VHS $16.95 *SNC* ✯

Teenage Bad Girl A woman who edits a magazine for teenagers can't control her own daughter. The kid does time in the pen after staying out all night and generally running around with the wrong crowd. Syms first lead performance is memorable in an otherwise routine teensploitation flick. *AKA:* Bad Girl; My Teenage Daughter.
1959 100m/B Anna Neagle, Sylvia Syms, Norman Wooland, Wilfrid Hyde-White, Kenneth Haigh, Julia Lockwood; *D:* Herbert Wilcox. VHS, Beta $16.95 *SNC* ✯✯½

Teenage Bonnie & Klepto Clyde Like their 30s namesakes Clyde Barrow and Bonnie Parker are just two high-spirited kids who let their need for excitement get in the way of their better judgement (ha!). Bonnie and Clyde meet in a fast-food joint, become shoplifting buddies, fall in love, graduate to armed robbery, try to run for the border, and die.
1993 (R) 90m/C Maureen Flannigan, Scott Wolf; *Cameos:* Don Novello. VHS $92.95 *VMK* ✯½

Teenage Caveman A teenage boy living in a post-apocalypse yet prehistoric world journeys across the river, even though he was warned against it, and finds an old man who owns a book about past civilizations in the 20th Century. Schlocky, and one of the better bad films around. The dinosaur shots were picked up from the film "One Million B.C." *AKA:* Out of the Darkness; Prehistoric World.
1958 66m/B Robert Vaughn, Darrah Marshall, Leslie Bradley, Frank De Kova; *D:* Roger Corman. VHS $9.95 *COL* ✯✯

Teenage Crime Wave Route 66 provides thrills for a couple of teen punks, but things get out of hand when they blow a sheriff's head off. They scoop up a couple of babes and hightail it with the police close behind, ultimately confronting their destiny at a mountain top observatory.
1955 77m/B Tommy Cook, Mollie McCart, Sue England, Frank Griffin, James Bell, Kay Riehl; *D:* Fred F. Sears. VHS, Beta $16.95 *SNC, AOV* ✯

Teenage Devil Dolls A cheap exploitation teenage flick wherein an innocent girl is turned on to reefer and goofballs, and eventually ends up on the street.
1953 70m/C Barbara Marks, Bramlel L. Price Jr.; *D:* B. Lawrence Price. VHS, Beta $9.95 *RHI* ✯

Teenage Exorcist Tired horror spoof finds the prim Diane (Stevens) renting a creepy house from an equally creepy real estate agent (Berryman). After she moves in, Diane begins having horrible nightmares and calls her family for help. When they arrive Diane has turned into a chainsaw-wielding seductress. The family is so distressed that they misdial the phone and wind up with a pizza delivery geek (Deezen) instead of the exorcist they need.
1993 90m/C Brinke Stevens, Eddie Deezen, Michael Berryman, Robert Quarry, Jay Richardson, Tom Shell, Elena Sahagun; *D:* Grant Austin Waldman; *W:* Brinke Stevens. VHS $89.95 *AIP* ✯

Teenage Frankenstein A descendent of Dr. Frankenstein makes his own scramble-faced monster out of a teenage boy. Lurid '50s drive-in fare (companion to "I Was a Teenage Werewolf") is campy fun in small doses only.
1958 72m/B Whit Bissell, Phyllis Coates, Robert Burton, Gary Conway, George Lynn, John Cliff; *D:* Herbert L. Strock. VHS $29.95 *COL* ✯½

Teenage Gang Debs These chicks throw a sleazy coming out party the likes of which defy description. Simply the most important social function of 1966.
1966 77m/B Diana Conti, Linda Gale, Eileen Scott, Sandra Kane, Robin Nolan, Linda Cambi, Sue McManus, Geri Tyler, Joey Naudic, John Batis, Tom Yourk, Thomas Andrisano, George Winship, Doug Mitchell, Tom Eldred, Frank Spinella, Alec Primrose, Gene Marrin, Lyn Kennedy, Janet Banzet; *D:* Sande Johnsen; *W:* Hy Cahl. VHS $23.00 *SMW, TPV* ✯

Teenage Mother A Swedish sex education teacher comes to town and poisons the minds of the local high school kids. Naturally one becomes pregnant and has to try to trick the father into marrying her. More awful stuff from the director of "Girl on a Chain Gang."
1967 78m/C Arlene Sue Farber, Frederick Riccio, Julie Ange, Howard Le May, George Peters; *D:* Jerry Gross. VHS, Beta $16.95 *SNC, TPV* Woof!

Teenage Mutant Ninja Turtles: The Movie Four sewer-dwelling turtles that have turned into warrior ninja mutants due to radiation exposure take it upon themselves to rid the city of crime and pizza. Aided by a television reporter and their ninja master, Splinter the Rat, the turtles encounter several obstacles, including the evil warlord Shredder. A most excellent live-action version of the popular comic book characters which will hold the kids' interest. Much head-kicking and rib-crunching action as Leonardo, Donatello, Raphael, and Michelangelo fight for the rights of pre-adolescents everywhere. Combines real actors with Jim Henson creatures.
1990 (PG) 95m/C Judith Hoag, Elias Koteas; *D:* Steven Barron; *W:* Todd W. Langen; *M:* John Du Prez; *V:* Robbie Rist, Corey Feldman, Brian Tochi, Kevin Clash, David McCharen. VHS, Beta, 8mm $24.99 *FHE, LIV, WTA* ✯✯½

Teenage Mutant Ninja Turtles 2: The Secret of the Ooze Amphibious pizza-devouring mutants search for the toxic waste that turned them into marketable martial artist ecologically correct kid idols. Same formula as the first go-round with some new characters tossed in. Animatronic characters from the laboratory of Jim Henson, first screen appearance by rapper Vanilla Ice. Marked end of pre-teen turtle craze.
1991 (PG) 88m/C Francois Chau, David Warner, Paige Turco, Ernie Reyes Jr., Vanilla Ice; *D:* Michael Pressman. VHS, Beta $22.98 *COL, NLC* ✯✯

Teenage Mutant Ninja Turtles 3 Check it out dudes, the Teenage Mutant Ninja Turtles hit 17th century Japan to rescue loyal friend, reporter April O'Neil. Plenty of smoothly executed, blood-free martial arts moves keep the pace rolling, while the turtles battle an evil lord and English pirates. Seeing the TMNT's use a little more of their reptilian grey matter, and snarf a little less pizza should contribute to a relatively high adult tolerance level (considering the genre), and loads of good clean fun for the kiddies.

1993 (PG) 95m/C Elias Koteas, Paige Turco, Stuart Wilson, Sab Shimono, Vivian Wu; **D:** Stuart Gillard; **W:** Stuart Gillard; **M:** John Du Prez; **V:** Randi Mayem Singer, Matt Hill, Jim Raposa, David Fraser. **VHS** NLC, COL, IME &&

Teenage Strangler
A homicidal teen terrorizes his school. Cheap film features drag races, rumbles, dances, babes, rock 'n' roll and more. One for the "bad enough to be fun" category.
1964 61m/C Bill A. Bloom, Jo Canterbury, John Ensign; **D:** Bill Posner. **VHS, Beta** $16.95 SNC, SMW Woof!

Teenage Wolfpack
Boring film about German juvenile delinquents, robbery, violence, and murder.
1957 90m/C Horst Buchholz, Karin Baal, Christian Doermer; **D:** Georg Tressier. **VHS** $16.95 SNC & 1/2

Teenage Zombies
Mad scientist on remote island kidnaps teenagers and uses her secret chemical formula to turn them into zombies as part of her plan to enslave the world. Not as good as it sounds.
1958 71m/B Don Sullivan, Katherine Victor, Chuck Niles; **D:** Jerry Warren; **W:** Jacques LeCotier. **VHS, Beta** $19.95 NOS, SNC, VYY Woof!

Teenager
Three desperate, reckless individuals, all caught up in making a low budget movie, interact and eventually self-destruct.
1974 (R) 91m/C Andrea Cagan, Reid Smith, Susan Bernard; **D:** Gerald Seth Sindell. **VHS, Beta** $19.95 NWV &

Teenagers from Outer Space
Low-budget sci-fi effort finds extraterrestrial youngsters visiting earth to conquer it and find food for their "monstrous pets" (they're really lobster shadows.) So cheaply made and melodramatic that it just may be good for a laugh. **AKA:** The Gargon Terror.
1959 86m/B Tom Graeff, Dawn Anderson, Harvey B. Dunn, Bryant Grant, Tom Lockyear; **D:** Tom Graeff. **VHS** $16.95 SNC Woof!

Telefon
Suspenseful, slick spy tale. Soviet agents battle a lunatic comrade who tries to use hypnotized Americans to commit sabotage. Daly, later of TV's "Cagney and Lacey," is memorable.
1977 (PG) 102m/C Charles Bronson, Lee Remick, Donald Pleasence, Tyne Daly, Patrick Magee, Sheree North; **D:** Don Siegel; **W:** Sterling Silliphant, Peter Hyams. **VHS, Beta** $19.95 MGM &&

Telegraph Trail
Weak Wayne entry about an Army scout who helps some workers complete the first transcontinental wire line. Of course, Wayne ends up getting tough with some Indians. Cheaply made, with most of the action footage lifted from the 1926 silent, "The Red Raiders."
1933 60m/B John Wayne, Marceline Day, Frank McHugh, Otis Harlan, Yakima Canutt, Lafe McKee; **D:** Tenny Wright; **W:** Kurt Kempler. **VHS** $19.98 MGM & 1/2

The Telephone
A neurotic out-of-work actress begins a comedic chain of events via a few prank phone calls. Goldberg has managed to salvage some bad material with the strength of her comedic performances, but not so here. In fact, she sued to prevent this version from ever seeing the light of day. Too bad she didn't have a better lawyer. Torn's directorial debut.
1987 (R) 96m/C Whoopi Goldberg, Elliott Gould, John Heard, Amy Wright; **D:** Rip Torn; **W:** Terry Southern. **VHS, Beta** $19.95 STE, NWV Woof!

Tell It to the Judge
Russell plays the exuberant ex-wife of lawyer Cummings. They repeatedly try reconciling but ditzy blonde McDonald always manages to catch

Cummings eye. Fed up Russell takes off for a holiday in the mountains where she meets Young. When her ex-hubby follows her, she decides to try and make him jealous using Young as the bait.
1949 87m/B Rosalind Russell, Robert Cummings, Gig Young, Marie McDonald, Harry Davenport, Louise Beavers; **D:** Norman Foster. **VHS** $19.95 FCT & 1/2

Tell Me a Riddle
A dying woman attempts to reconcile with her family in this poignant drama about an elderly couple rediscovering their mutual love after 47 years of marriage. Fine acting; Grant's directorial debut.
1980 (PG) 94m/C Melvyn Douglas, Lila Kedrova, Brooke Adams, Peter Coyote; **D:** Lee Grant; **W:** Joyce Eliason. **VHS, Beta** $19.95 MED && 1/2

Tell Me That You Love Me
A tear-jerking portrait of a disintegrating modern marriage.
1984 (R) 88m/C Nick Mancuso, Barbara Williams, Belinda J. Montgomery; **D:** Tzipi Trope. **VHS, Beta** $59.98 LIV, VES & 1/2

Tell Me Where It Hurts
A middle-aged housewife changes her life when she forms a women's consciousness-raising group with her friends. The script won an Emmy. Stapleton's performance is redeeming in this otherwise slow movie.
1974 78m/C Maureen Stapleton, Paul Sorvino; **D:** Paul Bogart. **VHS, Beta** LCA &&

The Tell-Tale Heart
Daydreaming author fantasizes about falling for major babe and killing his best friend for her. Adapted Poe tale. **AKA:** The Hidden Room of 1,000 Horrors.
1962 78m/B Laurence Payne, Adrienne Corri, Dermot Walsh, Selma Vaz Dias, John Scott, John Martin, Annette Carell, David Lander; **D:** Ernest Morris; **W:** Brian Clemens. **VHS** $19.98 NOS, SNC, LOO && 1/2

Tell Them Willie Boy Is Here
Western drama set in 1909 California about a Paiute Indian named Willie Boy and his white bride. They become the objects of a manhunt (led by the reluctant local sheriff, Redford) after Willie kills his wife's father in self-defense. This was once-blacklisted Polonsky's first film in 21 years.
1969 (PG) 98m/C Robert Redford, Katharine Ross, Robert (Bobby) Blake, Susan Clark, Barry Sullivan, John Vernon, Charles McGraw; **D:** Abraham Polonsky; **W:** Abraham Polonsky; **M:** Dave Grusin. **VHS, Beta** $39.95 MCA &&&

The Temp
Unbelievably bad attempt at office horror. Beautiful, mysterious Kris temps for Hutton, a junior exec at the Mrs. Appleby baked goods company. She's almost too good to be true with unbelievable organizational skills and her dead serious ambition to climb the corporate ladder. Pyscho-drama has psycho, but lacks drama, direction, plot development, intelligent dialogue, and anything resembling motive. While Hutton is tolerable, we nominate ex-Twin Peaker Boyle for the bad acting hall of shame as the conniving psycho.
1993 (R) 99m/C Timothy Hutton, Lara Flynn Boyle, Faye Dunaway, Dwight Schultz, Oliver Platt, Steven Weber, Scott Coffey, Colleen Flynn, Dakin Matthews, Maura Tierney; **D:** Tom Holland; **W:** Kevin Falls. **VHS, Beta** $19.95 PAR Woof!

The Tempest
A Russian peasant soldier rises through the ranks to become an officer, only to be undone by his love for the daughter of his commanding officer. Silent with musical score.

1928 105m/B John Barrymore, Louis Wolheim; **D:** Sam Taylor. Academy Awards '28: Best Interior Decoration; Nominations: Best Cinematography. **VHS, Beta** $9.95 NOS, CCB, VYY &&&

The Tempest
Shakespeare's classic tale of the fantasy world of spirits, sorcerers, maidens, monsters, and scheming noblemen is brought to life in George Schaefer's ethereal production.
1963 76m/C Maurice Evans, Richard Burton, Roddy McDowall, Lee Remick, Tom Poston; **D:** George Schaefer. **VHS, Beta** $34.95 TVC, FHS && 1/2

The Tempest
A New York architect, fed up with city living, chucks it all and brings his daughter to live with him on a barren Greek island. Based on Shakespeare's play of the same name. Well-written, thoughtfully acted, and beautifully filmed.
1982 (PG) 140m/C John Cassavetes, Gena Rowlands, Susan Sarandon, Vittorio Gassman, Molly Ringwald, Paul Stewart, Sam Robards, Raul Julia; **D:** Paul Mazursky; **W:** Paul Mazursky, Leon Capetanos. **VHS, Beta** COL &&&

The Tempest/The Eagle
A Russian soldier during the Revolution is betrayed and humiliated by the woman he loves in "The Tempest." In "The Eagle," an outcast guardsman becomes the Russian version of Robin Hood.
1927 56m/B John Barrymore, Camilla Horn, Rudolph Valentino, Louise Dresser; **D:** Sam Taylor, Clarence Brown. **VHS, Beta** $29.98 CCB &&&

Temporada Salvaje
Three criminals try to steal a fortune in platinum. Also known as Savage Season. **AKA:** Savage Season.
1987 90m/C Armando Silvestre, Isela Vega, Ron Harper, Diane McBain. **VHS, Beta** $77.95 MAD && 1/2

The Tempter
Mirrors the gruesomeness of "The Exorcist," with story following an invalid's adventures with witchcraft, bestiality, and Satanism. **AKA:** L'Anticristo; The Antichrist.
1974 (R) 96m/C Mel Ferrer, Carla Gravina, Arthur Kennedy, Alida Valli, Anita Strindberg, George Coulouris; **D:** Alberto De Martino; **M:** Ennio Morricone. **VHS, Beta** $24.98 SUE &

The Temptress
A doctor attempting to find a cure for polio is coerced by an irresistible woman into murder and blackmail. Well-told story, if somewhat grim.
1949 85m/B Joan Maude, Arnold Bell, Don Stannard, Shirley Quentin, John Stuart, Ferdinand "Ferdy" Mayne; **D:** Oswald Mitchell. **VHS, Beta** $16.95 SNC && 1/2

10
A successful songwriter who has everything finds his life is incomplete without the woman of his dreams, the 10 on his girl-watching scale. His pursuit brings surprising results. Also popularizes Ravel's "Bolero."
1979 (R) 121m/C Dudley Moore, Julie Andrews, Bo Derek, Dee Wallace Stone, Brian Dennehy, Robert Webber; **D:** Blake Edwards; **W:** Blake Edwards; **M:** Henry Mancini. **VHS, Beta** $19.98 WAR, FCT && 1/2

Ten Brothers of Shao-lin
Martial arts adventure from the days of warlords and warriors, when men were fierce and strong and struggles to the death occurred several times a day.
198? 90m/C Chia Ling, Wang Tao, Chang Yi. **VHS, Beta** NO &

The Ten Commandments
The silent epic that established DeMille as a popular directorial force and which he remade 35 years later as an even bigger epic with sound. Follows Moses' adventures in Egypt, plus a modern story of brotherly love and

T

corruption. Features a new musical score by Gaylord Carter. Remade in 1956.
1923 146m/B Theodore Roberts, Richard Dix, Rod La Rocque, Edythe Chapman, Nita Naldi; *D:* Cecil B. DeMille; *M:* Gaylord Carter. **VHS, Beta** $19.95 *PAR* ♫♫½

The Ten Commandments DeMille's remake of his 1923 silent classic (and his last film) is a lavish Biblical epic that tells the life story of Moses, who turned his back on a privileged life to lead his people to freedom outside of Egypt. Exceptional cast, with Fraser Heston (son of Charlton) as the baby Moses. Parting of Red Sea rivals any modern special effects. Available in widescreen on laserdisc. A 35th Anniversary Collector's Edition is available uncut at 245 minutes, in widescreen format and Dolby Surround stereo, and 1,000 copies of an Autographed Limited Edition that includes an engraved bronze plaque and an imprinted card written and personally signed by Charlton Heston are also available.
1956 (G) 219m/C Charlton Heston, Yul Brynner, Anne Baxter, Yvonne De Carlo, Nina Foch, John Derek, H.B. Warner, Henry Wilcoxon, Judith Anderson, John Carradine, Douglass Dumbrille, Cedric Hardwicke, Martha Scott, Vincent Price, Debra Paget; *D:* Cecil B. DeMille; *M:* Elmer Bernstein. Academy Awards '56: Best Special Effects; Nominations: Best Art Direction/Set Decoration (Color), Best Color Cinematography, Best Costume Design (Color), Best Film Editing, Best Picture, Best Sound. **VHS, Beta** $35.00 *PAR, FUS, IGP* ♫♫♫

Ten Days That Shook the World Silent masterpiece based on American author John Reed's book of the same name. Eisenstein, commissioned by the Soviet government, spared no expense to chronicle the Bolshevik Revolution of 1917 (in a flattering Communist light, of course). He was later forced to cut his portrayal of Leon Trotsky, who was then an enemy of the state. Includes rare footage of the Czar's Winter Palace in Leningrad. Haunting score, combined with some of Eisenstein's most striking work. See Warren Beatty's "Reds" for a fictional look at Reed and the Russian Revolution. *AKA:* October.
1927 104m/B Nikandrov, N. Popov, Boris Livanov; *D:* Grigori Alexandrov, Sergei Eisenstein; *M:* Dimitri Shostakovich. **VHS, Beta** $24.95 *VYY, IHF, WFV* ♫♫♫½

Ten Days Wonder Mystery/drama focuses on the patriarch of a wealthy family (Welles), his young wife, and his adopted son (Perkins), who is having an affair with his stepmother. It also turns out that Perkins is certifiable and is trying to break all of the Ten Commandments, which he succeeds in doing before killing himself (gruesomely). Based on the mystery novel by Ellery Queen.
1972 (PG) 101m/C Orson Welles, Anthony Perkins, Marlene Jobert, Michel Piccoli, Guido Alberti; *D:* Claude Chabrol. **VHS** $39.95 *ING, MOV, CVC* ♫♫½

Ten Little Indians Ten people are gathered in an isolated inn under mysterious circumstances. One by one they are murdered, each according to a verse from a children's nursery rhyme. British adaptation of the novel and stage play by Agatha Christie. *AKA:* And Then There Were None.
1975 (PG) 98m/C Herbert Lom, Richard Attenborough, Oliver Reed, Elke Sommer, Charles Aznavour, Stephane Audran, Gert Frobe, Adolfo Celi, Orson Welles; *D:* Peter Collinson. **VHS, Beta** $59.98 *NLC* ♫♫½

Ten Little Indians A group of prize-winning vacationers find themselves embarking on an African adventure. They all wind up at the same camp, and realize that they are

being murdered one by one. Based on the work of Agatha Christie. *AKA:* Agatha Christie's Ten Little Indians.
1989 (PG) 100m/C Donald Pleasence, Brenda Vaccaro, Frank Stallone, Herbert Lom, Sarah Maur-Thorp; *D:* Alan Birkinshaw. **VHS, Beta** $89.95 *CAN* ♫♫

The Ten Million Dollar Getaway True story of the 1978 Lufthansa robbery at Kennedy Airport in which the criminals were forced to leave ten of their twenty-million-dollar heist behind when a pick-up van didn't show. Standard made-for-cable fare produced to cash in on the same scenario played out in "Goodfellas."
1991 (PG-13) 93m/C John Mahoney, Karen Young, Tony LoBianco, Gerry Bamman, Joseph Carberry, Terrence Mann, Kenneth John McGregor, Christopher Murney; *D:* James A. Contner. **VHS, Beta** *PAR* ♫♫

Ten Nights in a Bar Room The evils of alcohol are dramatized when they ruin a man's life. One of many propaganda films about alcohol and the problems that it caused that were made during the prohibition era. Silent, with a musical score. Remade in 1931.
1913 68m/B Robert Lawrence, Marie Trado. **VHS, Beta** $29.95 *VCN* ♫♫

Ten Nights in a Bar-Room A turn-of-the-century mill owner succumbs to alcoholism and ruins his life and family. Later, he sees the error of his ways and gives up drinking. This was one of many films made during this era that chronicled the evils of alcohol and fanned the flames of the prohibition debate. Remake of the 1913 silent film.
1931 60m/B William Farnum, Thomas Santschi, John Darrow, Robert Frazer; *D:* William O'Connor. **VHS, Beta** $19.95 *VYY, GPV* ♫♫

Ten North Frederick A shrewish wife (Fitzgerald) forces her gentle lawyer husband (Cooper) into cut-throat politics. He consoles himself in the arms of a much younger woman. Good performances, hokey script, based on the John O'Hara novel.
1958 102m/B Gary Cooper, Diane Varsi, Suzy Parker, Geraldine Fitzgerald, Tom Tully, Stuart Whitman; *D:* Philip Dunne; *W:* Philip Dunne. **VHS** *TCF* ♫♫½

10 Rillington Place A grimy, upsetting British film about the famed serial killer John Christie and the man wrongly hanged for his crimes, the incident that led to the end of capital punishment in England. Impeccably acted. One of Hurt's earliest films.
1971 (PG) 111m/C Richard Attenborough, John Hurt, Judy Geeson, Gabrielle Daye, Andre Morell; *D:* Richard Fleischer. **VHS, Beta** $59.99 *MOV* ♫♫♫

Ten Speed Two advertising executives compete in a 400-mile bicycle race from San Francisco to Malibu.
1976 89m/C William Woodbridge, Patricia Hume, David Clover. **VHS, Beta** $69.98 *LIV* ♫♫

Ten to Midnight Vigilante Bronson is on the prowl again, this time as a police officer after a kinky serial murderer. The psychotic killer stalks his daughter and Dad's gonna stop him at any cost.
1983 (R) 101m/C Charles Bronson, Wilford Brimley, Lisa Eilbacher, Andrew Stevens; *D:* J. Lee Thompson; *W:* William Roberts. **VHS, Beta** $14.95 *MGM* ♫♫

10 Violent Women Ten women who take part in a million dollar jewelry heist are tossed into a women's prison where brutal lesbian guards subject them to degradation and brutality.

1979 (R) 97m/C Sherri Vernon, Dixie Lauren, Sally Gamble; *D:* Ted V. Mikels. **VHS, Beta** NO Woof!

Ten Wanted Men A successful cattle baron is confronted by a pistol-wielding land-owner determined to ruin him. Standard fare, with better than average performances from Scott and Boone.
1954 80m/C Randolph Scott, Jocelyn Brando, Richard Boone, Skip Homeier, Leo Gordon, Jack Perrin, Donna Martell; *D:* H. Bruce Humberstone; *W:* Harriet Frank Jr., Irving Ravetch. **VHS, Beta** $69.95 *COL* ♫♫

Ten Who Dared Ten Civil War heroes brave the Colorado River in an effort to chart its course. Although it's based on an actual historic event, the film is poorly paced and lacks suspense.
1960 92m/C Brian Keith, John Beal, James Drury; *D:* William Beaudine. **VHS, Beta** $69.95 *DIS* ♫♫

The Tenant Disturbing story of a hapless office worker who moves into a spooky Paris apartment house. Once lodged inside its walls, he becomes obsessed with the previous occupant, who committed suicide, and the belief that his neighbors are trying to kill him. Based on a novel by Roland Topor. *AKA:* Le Locataire.
1976 (R) 126m/C Roman Polanski, Isabelle Adjani, Melvyn Douglas, Jo Van Fleet, Bernard Fresson, Shelley Winters; *D:* Roman Polanski; *W:* Roman Polanski, Gerard Brach. **VHS, Beta** $49.95 *PAR* ♫♫♫½

The Tender Age Troubled 18-year-old girl gets out of a detention home and is put on probation. She captivates her idealistic probation officer, whose interest may extend beyond professional concern. Fine idea, but under-played. *AKA:* The Little Sister.
1984 103m/C John Savage, Tracy Pollan, Roxanne Hart, Richard Jenkins; *D:* Jan Egleson; *W:* Jan Egleson. **VHS, Beta** $79.98 *LIV* ♫♫

Tender Comrade Flag-waving violin-accompanied tearjerker about five women who live together to make ends meet while their men do manly things during WWII. Intended to puff your heart up with patriotic gusto. Ironically, thanks to the girls' communal living arrangement, director Dmytryk was later accused of un-American activities.
1943 101m/B Ginger Rogers, Robert Ryan, Ruth Hussey, Patricia Collinge, Mady Christians, Kim Hunter, Jane Darwell, Mary Forbes, Richard Martin; *D:* Edward Dmytryk. **VHS** $19.98 *TTC, FCT* ♫♫

Tender Is the Night A television-special adaptation of the F. Scott Fitzgerald classic, set in the roaring '20s, in which a psychiatrist marries one of his patients and then heads down the road to ruin, driven by his marriage and the times in which he lives. An entry from the "Front Row Center" series.
1955 60m/B Mercedes McCambridge, James Daly. **VHS, Beta** $24.95 *NOS, DVT* ♫♫½

Tender Loving Care Three nurses dispense hefty doses of T.L.C. in their hospital, and the patients aren't the only ones on the receiving end.
1973 72m/C Donna Desmond, Leah Simon, Anita King; *D:* Don Edmunds. **VHS, Beta** $39.98 *SUE* ♫

Tender Mercies A down-and-out country western singer finds his life redeemed by the love of a good woman. Aided by Horton Foote's script, Duvall, Harper and Barkin keep this from being simplistic and sentimental. Duvall wrote as well as performed the songs in his Oscar-winning performance. Wonderful, life-affirming flick.

1983 (PG) 88m/C Robert Duvall, Tess Harper, Betty Buckley, Ellen Barkin, Wilford Brimley; *D:* Bruce Beresford; *W:* Horton Foote Jr.; *M:* George Dreyfus. Academy Awards '83: Best Actor (Duvall), Best Original Screenplay; Nominations: Best Director (Beresford), Best Picture, Best Song ("Over You"); Golden Globe Awards '83: Best Actor—Drama (Duvall). **VHS, Beta $14.98** *REP, BTV, HMV* ☆☆☆

The Tender Trap Charlie Reader (Sinatra) is a bachelor not content with the many women in his life. He meets the innocent Julie Gillis (Reynolds) and falls head over heels for her. He then torments himself over a marriage proposal, unwilling to let go of his freedom.
1955 111m/C Frank Sinatra, Debbie Reynolds, Celeste Holm, David Wayne, Carolyn Jones, Lola Albright, Tom Helmore, Howard St. John, Willard Sage, James Drury, Benny Rubin, Frank Sully, David White; *D:* Charles Walters; *W:* Julius J. Epstein. **VHS $19.98** *MGM, MOV* ☆☆½

The Tender Warrior A beautifully photographed animal adventure with Haggerty as the woodsman.
1971 (G) 85m/C Dan Haggerty, Charles Lee, Liston Elkins; *D:* Stewart Raffill. **VHS, Beta $59.95** *VCD* ☆

The Tender Years Sentimental drama of a minister trying to outlaw dog fighting, spurred on by his son's fondness for a particular dog.
1947 81m/B Joe E. Brown, Richard Lyon, Noreen Nash, Charles Drake, Josephine Hutchinson; *D:* Harold Schuster. **VHS, Beta $12.95** *TCF* ☆☆

Tenement Unspeakably violent story of urban low-lifes, frightened slum-dwellers, and revenge. *AKA:* Game of Survival.
1985 94m/C **VHS, Beta** *NO* ☆

Tennessee Stallion A low-class horse-trainer breaks into the world of aristocratic thoroughbred racing.
1978 87m/C Audrey Landers, Judy Landers, James Van Patten. **VHS, Beta $69.98** *LIV, VES* ☆

Tennessee's Partner Enjoyable, unexceptional buddy Western. Reagan intervenes in an argument and becomes Payne's pal. Adapted from a story by Bret Harte.
1955 87m/C Ronald Reagan, Rhonda Fleming, John Payne; *D:* Allan Dwan. **VHS, Beta** *NO* ☆☆

Tension at Table Rock Accused of cowardice, a lone gunman must prove he killed in self-defense. Well-cast serious Western.
1956 93m/C Richard Egan, Dorothy Malone, Cameron Mitchell; *D:* Charles Marquis. **VHS, Beta** *VCI* ☆☆

Tentacles Cheesy Italian version of "Jaws" lacking only the suspense and cogent storytelling. Huston slums as the investigator charged with finding the octopus gone mad, while Fonda collects check and makes a quick exit. Hopkins is in charge of the killer whales that save the day. You'll cheer when Winters is devoured by sea beast. From the director of an "Exorcist" rip-off, "Beyond the Door" (that's not a recommendation).
1977 (PG) 90m/C John Huston, Shelley Winters, Bo Hopkins, Henry Fonda, Cesare Danova; *D:* Oliver Hellman. **VHS, Beta $59.98** *LIV, VES* Woof!

Tentacles of the North Two ships are trapped in the ice of the Arctic with the only survivor of one ship being a fearful young girl. Tinted print.
1926 54m/B Gaston Glass, Alice Calhoun, Al Ferguson, Joseph Girard; *D:* Louis Chaudet. **VHS $14.95** *GPV* ☆☆½

The Tenth Man Hopkins stars as a wealthy French lawyer, captured by the Nazis and sentenced to death. He discovers a fellow prisoner who is willing to take his place in exchange for Hopkins' wealth going to support the man's family. After his release, Hopkins returns to his old home, now occupied by the dead man's family, but doesn't reveal his true identity. When an imposter appears, claiming to be Hopkins, another twist is added. Slow-going but the usual excellent performances by Hopkins and Jacobi. Based on a novella by Graham Greene. Made for television.
1988 99m/C Anthony Hopkins, Kristin Scott Thomas, Derek Jacobi, Cyril Cusack, Brenda Bruce, Paul Rogers; *D:* Jack Gold. **VHS $19.98** *MGM* ☆☆½

Tenth Month Carol Burnett plays a divorced, middle-aged woman who becomes pregnant by a married man. She refuses help, choosing instead to live alone and keep an ever hopeful vigil for the birth of her child. Sappy but touching made-for-TV drama.
1979 123m/C Carol Burnett, Keith Mitchell, Dina Merrill; *D:* Joan Tewkesbury. **VHS, Beta $59.95** *TLF* ☆☆

10th Victim Sci-fi cult film set in the 21st century has Mastroianni and Andress pursuing one another in a futuristic society where legalized murder is used as the means of population control. Intriguing movie where Andress kills with a double-barreled bra, the characters hang out at the Club Masoch, and comic books are considered literature. Based on "The Seventh Victim" by Robert Sheckley. *AKA:* La Decima Vittima; La Dixieme Victime.
1965 92m/C Ursula Andress, Marcello Mastroianni, Elsa Martinelli, Salvo Randone, Massimo Serato; *D:* Elio Petri; *W:* Tonino Guerra. **VHS, Beta $14.95** *SUE, NLC* ☆☆☆

Teorema Scathing condemnation of bourgeois complacency. Stamp, either a devil or a god, mysteriously appears and enters into the life of a well-to-do Milanese family and raises each member's spirituality by sleeping with them. Ultimately, the experience leads to tragedy. In Italian with English subtitles.
1968 98m/C Terence Stamp, Silvana Mangano, Massimo Girotti, Anna Wiazemsky, Laura Betti, Andres Jose Cruz; *D:* Pier Paolo Pasolini; *M:* Ennio Morricone. **VHS $39.95** *TPV, ING, CVC* ☆☆

Tequila Sunrise Towne's twisting film about two lifelong friends and a beautiful woman. Gibson is a (supposedly) retired drug dealer afraid of losing custody of his son to his nagging ex-wife. Russell is the cop and old friend who's trying to get the lowdown on a drug shipment coming in from Mexico. Pfeiffer runs the poshest restaurant on the coast and is actively pursued by both men. Questions cloud the plot and confuse the viewer; loaded with double-crosses, intrigue and surprises around every corner, still the photogenic leads are pleasant to watch. Steamy love scene between Pfeiffer and Gibson.
1988 (R) 116m/C Mel Gibson, Kurt Russell, Michelle Pfeiffer, Raul Julia, Arliss Howard, Arye Gross, J.T. Walsh, Ann Magnuson; *D:* Robert Towne; *W:* Robert Towne; *M:* Dave Grusin. **VHS, Beta, 8mm $14.95** *WAR* ☆☆½

Teresa Venerdi An unusual Italian comedy about a man and his financial difficulties. His mistress, his fiance and a young girl make his troubles more confusing. Unusually sweet and humorous DeSica.
1941 90m/B *D:* Vittorio De Sica. **VHS, Beta $49.95** *CIG* ☆☆☆

Tereza In politically chaotic Czechoslovakia, a female police detective tries to solve an intricate murder mystery. In Czech with English subtitles.
1961 91m/B Jirina Svorcova; *D:* Pavel Blumenfeld. **VHS, Beta $39.95** *FCT, IHF* ☆☆☆

Terminal Bliss Teen heartthrob Perry stars as a spoiled rich druggie in this "Less Than Zero" knock-off. Perry and childhood pal Owen grow up sharing everything—lacrosse, girlfriends, and drugs. However, their friendship is really put to the test when a beautiful new girl (Chandler) moves to town just before graduation. Release was delayed, but obviously wants to capitalize on Perry's popularity.
1991 (R) 94m/C Luke Perry, Timothy Owen, Estee Chandler; *D:* Jordan Allen; *W:* Jordan Allen; *M:* Frank Becker. **VHS $19.98** *WAR, CAN* ☆½

Terminal Choice Staff at a hospital conduct a betting pool on patients' life expectancies. Someone decides he should win more often and uses a computer to help hedge his bets. Wasted cast on this unsuspenseful and bloody film.
1985 (R) 98m/C Joe Spano, Diane Venora, David McCallum, Ellen Barkin; *D:* Sheldon Larry. **VHS, Beta $79.95** *VES* ☆½

Terminal Entry Teen computer geeks accidentally find a terrorist online network, and inadvertently begin transmitting instructions to destroy U.S. targets. The premise is intriguing but poorly done.
1987 (R) 95m/C Edward Albert, Yaphet Kotto, Kabir Bedi; *D:* John Kincade. **VHS, Beta $79.95** *CEL* ☆½

Terminal Exposure Predictable but likeable comedy-mystery. A pair of Venice, CA, beach denizens capture a murder on film and try to solve it.
1989 (R) 105m/C Steve Donmyer, John Vernon, Ted Lange, Joe Phelan, Hope Marie Carlton, Mark Hennessy, Scott King; *D:* Nico Mastorakis. **VHS, Beta $79.98** *LIV, VES* ☆

Terminal Force Stupid, poorly executed story of kidnapping and the mob. So bad it never saw the inside of a theater; went straight to video.
1988 (R) 83m/C Troy Donahue, Richard Harrison, Dawn Wildsmith; *D:* Fred Olen Ray. **VHS $19.95** *STE, NWV* ☆

Terminal Island Tough southern California penal colony is crowded with inmates from death row. When prison becomes coed, violence breaks out. Exploitative and unappealing.
1973 (R) 88m/C Phyllis E. Davis, Tom Selleck, Don Marshall, Ena Hartman, Marta Kristen; *D:* Stephanie Rothman. **VHS, Beta $29.95** *VCI* ☆½

The Terminal Man A slick, visually compelling adaptation of the Michael Crichton novel. A scientist plagued by violent mental disorders has a computer-controlled regulator implanted in his brain. The computer malfunctions and he starts a murdering spree. Futuristic vision of man-machine symbiosis gone awry. Well acted, but still falls short of the novel.
1974 (R) 107m/C George Segal, Joan Hackett, Jill Clayburgh, Richard Dysart, James B. Sikking, Norman Burton; *D:* Mike Hodges; *W:* Mike Hodges. **VHS, Beta $19.98** *WAR* ☆☆½

Terminal Velocity Skydiving instructor Sheen thinks he sees student Kinski plummet to her death. Only it turns out she's maybe not dead and certainly not a beginner. Upon further investigation, he finds the usual web of international intrigue descending upon him, and that the KGB definitely want him to mind his own business. Still, he

pushes on. Another no-brainer actioner with few surprises.
1994 ?m/C Charlie Sheen, Nastassia Kinski, James Gandolfini, Christopher MacDonald; **D:** Deran Sarafian; **W:** David N. Twohy. **VHS** *NYR* 🐾🐾

The Terminator Futuristic cyborg is sent to present-day Earth. His job: kill the woman who will conceive the child destined to become the great liberator and arch-enemy of the Earth's future rulers. The cyborg is also pursued by another futuristic visitor, who falls in love with the intended victim. Cameron's pacing is just right in this exhilarating, explosive thriller which displays Arnie as one-blooded villain who utters a now famous line: "I'll be back." Followed by "Terminator 2: Judgment Day."
1984 (R) 108m/C Arnold Schwarzenegger, Michael Biehn, Linda Hamilton, Paul Winfield, Lance Henriksen, Bill Paxton, Rick Rossovich, Dick Miller; **D:** James Cameron; **M:** Brad Fiedel. **VHS, Beta** *NO* 🐾🐾🐾

Terminator 2: Judgment Day He said he'd be back and he is, programmed to protect the boy who will be mankind's post-nuke resistance leader. But the T-1000, a shape-changing, ultimate killing machine, is also on the boy's trail. Twice the mayhem, five times the special effects, ten times the budget of the first, but without Arnold it'd be half the movie. The word hasn't been invented to describe the special effects, particularly THE scariest nuclear holocaust scene yet. Worldwide megahit, but the $100 million budget nearly ruined the studio; Arnold accepted his $12 million in the form of a jet. Laserdisc features include pan and scan, widescreen and a "Making of T-2" short.
1991 (R) 139m/C Arnold Schwarzenegger, Linda Hamilton, Edward Furlong, Robert Patrick, Earl Boen, Joe Morton; **D:** James Cameron; **M:** Brad Fiedel. Academy Awards '91: Best Makeup, Best Sound, Best Sound Effects Editing, Best Visual Effects; Nominations: Best Cinematography, Best Sound; MTV Movie Awards '92: Best Actor (Schwarzenegger), Best Actress (Hamilton), Best Film, Breakthrough Performance (Furlong), Most Desirable Female (Hamilton), Best Action Sequence; People's Choice Awards '92: Best Film. **VHS, 8mm $29.98** *LIV* 🐾🐾🐾½

Termini Station Dewhurst gives an excellent performance as the alcoholic matriarch of a small-town Canadian family. She drinks all day and dreams of traveling to Italy, while her children work and believe there is something more to life than their mundane existence. When they finally do leave, they discover an intriguing new world. Dewhurst and Follows also appear together in "Anne of Green Gables" and "Anne of Avonlea."
1989 105m/C Colleen Dewhurst, Megan Follows, Gordon Clapp, Hannah Lee, Leon Pownall, Debra McGrath, Elliott Smith, Norma Dell'Agnese; **D:** Allen King; **M:** Mychael Danna. **VHS $79.95** *MNC, FCT* 🐾🐾½

Terms of Endearment A weeper following the changing relationship between a young woman and her mother, over a thirty-year period. Beginning as a comedy, turning serious as the years go by, this was Brooks' debut as screenwriter and director. Superb supporting cast headed by Nicholson's slyly charming neighbor/astronaut, with stunning performances by Winger and MacLaine as the two women who often know and love each other too well. Adapted from Larry McMurtry's novel.
1983 (PG) 132m/C Shirley MacLaine, Jack Nicholson, Debra Winger, John Lithgow, Jeff Daniels, Danny DeVito; **D:** James L. Brooks; **W:** James L. Brooks; **M:** Michael Gore. Academy Awards '83: Best Actress (MacLaine), Best Adapted Screenplay, Best Director (Brooks), Best

Picture, Best Supporting Actor (Nicholson); Nominations: Best Actress (Winger), Best Art Direction/Set Decoration, Best Film Editing, Best Sound, Best Supporting Actor (Lithgow), Best Original Score; Golden Globe Awards '84: Best Actress—Drama (MacLaine), Best Film—Drama, Best Screenplay, Best Supporting Actor (Nicholson). **VHS, Beta $19.95** *PAR, BTV, HMV* 🐾🐾🐾

Terraces TV series pilot about high-rise tenants whose balconies are their only common ground. Good performances.
1977 90m/C Lloyd Bochner, Eliza Garrett, Julie Newmar, Tim Thomerson; **D:** Lila Garrett. **VHS, Beta** *WOV* 🐾🐾½

Terronauts When man begins space exploration, Earth is attacked by aliens. The defenders are taken to an out-dated fortress where they learn that their forebears were similarly attacked. Juvenile, lackluster, contrived, and really dumb.
1967 77m/C Simon Oates, Zena Marshall, Charles Hawtrey, Stanley Meadows; **D:** Montgomery Tully. **VHS, Beta $59.98** *NLC Woof!*

The Terror A hostelry is the scene of a number of brutal murders. Remake of a 1928 film and based on a play by Edgar Wallace. Good story, but weak version of it.
1938 63m/B Wilfred Lawson, Bernard Lee, Arthur Wontner, Linden Travers, Henry Oscar, Alastair Sim; **D:** Richard Bird. **VHS, Beta $16.95** *SNC* 🐾🐾

The Terror A lieutenant in Napoleon's army chases a lovely maiden and finds himself trapped in a creepy castle by a mad baron. Movie legend has it Corman directed the movie in 3 days as the sets (from his previous movie "The Raven") were being torn down around them. **AKA:** Lady of the Shadows.
1963 81m/C Boris Karloff, Jack Nicholson, Sandra Knight; **D:** Roger Corman. **VHS, Beta $19.95** *NOS, SNC, PSM* 🐾🐾

The Terror After 100 years, a man reveals in a film that his family killed a witch. Friends who see the film are attacked by supernatural forces. Originally double-billed with "Dracula's Dog."
1979 (R) 86m/C John Nolan, Carolyn Courage, James Aubrey; **D:** Norman J. Warren. **VHS, Beta $19.95** *VCI, VCD, HHE Woof!*

Terror at London Bridge London Bridge is transported brick by brick to Arizona. It carries its history with it, including the havoc-wreaking spirit of Jack the Ripper. Campy made-for-TV effort. **AKA:** Bridge Across Time; Arizona Ripper.
1985 96m/C David Hasselhoff, Stephanie Kramer, Adrienne Barbeau, Randolph Mantooth; **D:** E.W. Swackhamer. **VHS, Beta $29.95** *FRH* 🐾🐾

Terror at Red Wolf Inn Young woman wins a vacation; finds she's been invited for dinner, so to speak. Not campy enough to overcome stupidity. **AKA:** Club Dead; Terror House; The Folks at Red Wolf Inn.
1972 (R) 90m/C Linda Gillin, Arthur Space, John Neilson, Mary Jackson, Janet Wood, Margaret Avery; **D:** Bud Townsend. **VHS, Beta $29.95** *ACA* 🐾🐾

Terror at Tenkiller Two girls vacationing in the mountains are seemingly surrounded by a rash of mysterious murders. Made for video.
1986 87m/C Mike Wiles, Stacey Logan. **VHS, Beta $19.95** *VCI* 🐾

Terror at the Opera A bizarre staging of Verdi's "Macbeth" is plagued by depraved gore murders. But the show must go on, as one character chirps in badly-dubbed English. Italian horrormeister Argento's ever-

fluid camera achieves spectacular shots, but the lurid, ludicrous script make this one for connoisseurs only. The operatic scenes employ the voice of Maria Callas. Available in an edited "R" rated version.
1988 (R) 107m/C Christina Marsillach, Ian Charleson, Urbano Barberini, William McNamara, Antonella Vitale, Barbara Cupisti, Coralina Cataldi Tassoni, Daria Nicolodi; **D:** Dario Argento; **W:** Dario Argento. **VHS $89.98** *FCT* 🐾🐾½

Terror Beach A doctor and his bride move to a coastal village, only to find it enmeshed in witchcraft and devil worship.
1987? 90m/C Victor Petit, Julie James, Mary Costi, Sandra Mozar. **VHS, Beta** *NO* 🐾

Terror Beneath the Sea A mad scientist wants to rule the world with his cyborgs. American and Japanese scientists unite to fight him. Fine special effects, especially the transformation from human to monster. **AKA:** Kaitei Daisenso; Water Cyborgs.
1966 85m/C Sonny Chiba, Peggy Neal, Franz Gruber, Gunther Braun, Andrew Hughes, Mike Daneen; **D:** Hajime Sato. **VHS, Beta $39.95** *DVT* 🐾🐾½

Terror by Night Holmes and Watson attempt to solve the murder of the owner of a gigantic, beautiful jewel. Their investigation must be completed before their train arrives at its destination, where the murderer can escape.
1946 60m/B Basil Rathbone, Nigel Bruce; **D:** Roy William Neill. **VHS $14.95** *CNG, REP, FOX* 🐾🐾½

Terror by Night/Meeting at Midnight In "Terror by Night" (1946), Sherlock Holmes and Dr. Watson board a train to protect a fabulous diamond. In "Meeting at Midnight" (1944), Charlie Chan becomes involved in magic and murder.
1946 122m/B Basil Rathbone, Nigel Bruce, Sidney Toler; **D:** Roy William Neill. **VHS, Beta** *MED* 🐾🐾

Terror Creatures from the Grave Husband summons medieval plague victims to rise from the grave to drop in on his unfaithful wife. Should've been better.
1966 85m/C Barbara Steele, Riccardo Garrone, Walter Brandi; **D:** Ralph Zucker. **VHS $19.98** *SNC* 🐾

Terror Eyes Spoof-thriller revolves around an "agent from Hell," sent to Earth to recruit writers for a horror film.
1987 (PG-13) 90m/C Daniel Roebuck, Vivian Schilling, Dan Bell, Lance August. **VHS, Beta $39.95** *AIP* 🐾½

Terror in Beverly Hills When the President's daughter is kidnapped, it's up to an ex-marine to save her. The trouble is, the head terrorist hates the marine's guts as he blames him for the deaths of his wife and children. So incredibly bad it's campy and fun.
1990 88m/C Frank Stallone, Cameron Mitchell, William Smith; **D:** John Myhers; **W:** John Myhers. **VHS, Beta $14.95** *AIP Woof!*

Terror in Paradise Jason and Vickie think they're going to have a romantic holiday on a beautiful island paradise. But they've picked the wrong spot to vacation. It seems the island harbors a terrorist group and when they see more than they should the lovers become the next targets.
19?? (R) ?m/C Joanna Pettet, Gary Lockwood, David Anthony Smith, Leslie Ryan; **D:** Peer J. Oppenheimer. **VHS $89.98** *NHO* 🐾½

Terror in the Haunted House Newlyweds move into an old house. The bride remembers it from her nightmares. First release featured the first use of Psychorama,

a technique in which scary words or advertising messages were flashed on the screen for a fraction of a second—just long enough to cause subliminal response. The technique was banned later in the year.
1958 90m/C Gerald Mohr, Cathy O'Donnell, William Ching; **D:** Harold Daniels. **VHS, Beta** $9.95 *RHI, MLB, CCB* 🐾🐾½

Terror in the Jungle Plane crashes in Peruvian wilds and young boy survivor meets Jivaro Indians who think he's a god. Much struggling to survive and battling with horrible script.
1968 (PG) 95m/C Jimmy Angle, Robert Burns, Fawn Silver; **D:** Tom De Simone; **M:** Les Baxter. **VHS** $19.95 *ACA* 🐾

Terror in the Swamp When not hanging out in the local murky waters, a swamp creature terrorizes the residents of a small town.
1985 (PG) 89m/C Billy Holliday; **D:** Joe Catalanotto. **VHS, Beta** $9.95 *NWV, STE* 🐾

Terror in the Wax Museum The owner of a wax museum is killed while mulling over the sale of the museum. The new owner has little better luck as the bodies continue to pile up. Production uses every out-of-work horror film actor of the time. The most suspenseful part of this low-budget flick is waiting to see how long the "wax dummies" can hold their breath.
1973 (PG) 94m/C Ray Milland, Broderick Crawford, Elsa Lanchester, Louis Hayward, Maurice Evans, John Carradine; **D:** Georg Fenady; **M:** George Duning. **VHS, Beta** $69.98 *LIV* Woof!

Terror in Toyland Once again a knife-wielding lunatic dresses as Santa Claus to strike terror and death into the hearts of children. **AKA:** Christmas Evil; You Better Watch Out.
1985 90m/C Brandon Maggart, Jeffrey DeMunn; **D:** Lewis Jackson. **VHS, Beta** $19.95 *ACA* 🐾½

Terror is a Man A mad scientist attempts to turn a panther into a man on a secluded island. Early Filipino horror attempt inspired by H.G. Wells' "The Island of Doctor Moreau." **AKA:** Blood Creature.
1959 89m/B Francis Lederer, Greta Thyssen, Richard Derr, Oscar Keesee; **D:** Gerardo (Gerry) De Leon. **VHS** $16.95 *SNC* 🐾🐾

Terror of Mechagodzilla It's monster vs. machine in the heavyweight battle of the universe as a huge mechanical Godzilla built by aliens is pitted against the real thing. The last Godzilla movie made until "Godzilla 1985." **AKA:** Monsters from the Unknown Planet; The Escape of Megagodzilla; Mekagojira No Gyakushu.
1978 (G) 79m/C Katsuhiko Sasakai, Tomoko AI. **VHS, Beta** $19.95 *PAR* 🐾½

Terror of Rome Against the Son of Hercules Muscle-bound gladiators battle it out in this low-budget Italian action flick. Dubbed.
1964 100m/C Mark Forest, Marilu Tolo; **D:** Mario Ciano. **VHS, Beta** $16.95 *SNC, NLC* 🐾

Terror of the Bloodhunters A French author is sentenced to Devil's Island for a crime he didn't commit. The warden's daughter takes a liking to him and arranges for him and a friend to escape, but numerous perils await them in the jungle.
1962 60m/B Robert Clarke, Steve Conte, Dorothy Haney; **D:** Jerry Warren; **W:** Jerry Warren. **VHS, Beta** $16.95 *SNC* 🐾

Terror of the Steppes Yet another sword and sandal extravaganza in which a musclebound hero conquers all.

1964 ?m/C Kirk Morris. **VHS, Beta** $16.95 *SNC* 🐾

Terror of Tiny Town Main characteristic of this musical/western is its entire midget cast, all members of Jed Buell's Midgets. Otherwise the plot is fairly average and features a bad guy and the good guy who finally teaches him a lesson. Newfield plays up the cast's short stature—they walk under saloon doors and ride Shetland ponies.
1938 65m/B Bill Curtis, Yvonne Moray; **D:** Sam Newfield. **VHS, Beta** $16.95 *SNC, NOS, DVT* 🐾🐾

Terror on Alcatraz The only prisoner to successfully escape from Alcatraz Island returns to retrieve the safety deposit box key he needs to get his stolen loot. And anyone who gets in his way is in for trouble.
1986 96m/C Veronica Porsche Ali, Sandy Brooke, Aldo Ray, Scott Ryder; **D:** Philip Marcus. **VHS** $79.95 *TWE, HHE* 🐾

Terror on the 40th Floor Seven people make an attempt to escape from the 40th floor of a modern skyscraper. Poorly done re-hash of "Towering Inferno." Uninspired.
1974 98m/C John Forsythe, Anjanette Comer, Don Meredith, Joseph Campanella; **D:** Jerry Jameson. **VHS, Beta** $49.95 *PSM* 🐾

Terror on Tour The Clowns, a rock group on their way up, center their stage performance around sadistic, mutilating theatrics. When real murders begin, they become prime suspects. Exploitive, bloody, disgusting.
1983 90m/C Dave Galluzzo, Richard Styles, Rick Pemberton; **D:** Don Edmunds. **VHS, Beta** $54.95 *MED* Woof!

Terror Out of the Sky A scientist must disguise himself as one of the insects to divert the attention of a horde of killing bees from a busload of elementary children. Sub-par sequel to "The Savage Bees."
1978 95m/C Efrem Zimbalist Jr., Dan Haggerty; **D:** Lee H. Katzin; **M:** William Goldstein. **VHS, Beta** $49.95 *LIV* 🐾½

Terror Ship Three people find an abandoned yacht which they believe was used for smuggling. While searching it, they find that it was used to transport stolen uranium. Before the police can arrive, the thieves show up. Not a very good handling of what was actually an interesting idea. Released as "Dangerous Voyage" in Great Britain.
1954 72m/B William Lundigan, Naomi Chance, Vincent Ball, Jean Lodge, Richard Stewart; **D:** Vernon Sewell. **VHS** $19.95 *NOS* 🐾🐾

Terror Squad An unsuspecting high school population is put under siege by Libyan terrorists. The students get a hands-on lesson in revolution and guerrilla war tactics.
1987 95m/C Kerry Brennan, Bill Calvert, Chuck Connors, Greer Brodie; **D:** Peter Maris. **VHS** $79.98 *MCG, VTR* 🐾🐾

Terror Stalks the Class Reunion Kay (Nelligan) is a teacher who disappears at a class reunion. Police dismiss the case as a runaway wife, except for Virignia, a young detective (Beals) who doesn't accept that theory. And she's right—Kay is held hostage in a remote cabin by an obsessed former student (Davies). Kay needs all her wits to fend off her deranged and possibly deadly suitor while Virginia races to find her. Based on the novel by Mary Higgins Clark.
1993 (PG-13) 95m/C Kate Nelligan, Jennifer Beals, Geraint Wyn Davies. **VHS** $89.98 *REP* 🐾🐾½

Terror Street An Air Force pilot's wife is murdered. He has 36 hours to clear his name and find the killer.
1954 84m/B Dan Duryea, Elsy Albiin, Ann Gudrun, Eric Pohlmann. **VHS, Beta** NO 🐾

Terror Trail As usual, Mix uses guns and fists to bring bad guys to justice, and gets the girl in the bargain.
1933 62m/B Tom Mix, Naomi Judge, Arthur Rankin, Raymond Hatton, Francis McDonald, Robert F. (Bob) Kortman, John St. Polis, Lafe McKee, Buffalo Bill Jr.; **D:** Armand Schaefer. **VHS** $11.95 *GPV, HEG, DVT* 🐾½

Terror Train A masquerade party is held on a chartered train. But someone has more than mask-wearing in mind as a series of dead bodies begin to appear. Copperfield provides magic, Curtis provides screams in this semi-scary slasher movie. **AKA:** Train of Terror.
1980 (R) 97m/C Jamie Lee Curtis, Ben Johnson, Hart Bochner, David Copperfield, Vanity; **D:** Roger Spottiswoode. **VHS, Beta** $14.98 *FOX* 🐾🐾

The Terror Within Reptilian mutants hit the streets searching for human women to breed with. Have the Teenage Mutant Ninja Turtles grown up?
1988 (R) 90m/C George Kennedy, Andrew Stevens, Starr Andreeff, Terri Treas; **D:** Thierry Notz; **W:** Thomas McKelvey Cleaver; **M:** Rick Conrad. **VHS, Beta** $14.95 *MGM* 🐾

The Terror Within 2 In a world destroyed by biological warfare, a warrior and the woman he rescued traverse the badlands occupied by hideous mutants. What they don't know is that the real terror comes from within. How can they possibly survive? Not without decent dialogue, that's for sure.
1991 (R) 90m/C Andrew Stevens, Stella Stevens, Chick Vennera, R. Lee Ermey; **D:** Andrew Stevens. **VHS** $14.98 *VES, LIV* 🐾½

Terrorgram Not a very special delivery. An offscreen James Earl Jones introduces three lesser tales of terror. Best seg: a sleazy filmmaker gets trapped in the world of his own exploitation scripts. The other two are bloody but negligible revenge-from-the-grave yarns. All start off with the receipt of a sinister package, hence a postal motif.
1990 (R) 88m/C Michael Hartson, J.T. Wallace. **VHS** $29.95 *MNC* 🐾

The Terrorists Just as later he was a Scottish Lithuanian sub-commander in "The Hunt for Red October" (1990), here Connery is a Scottish Norwegian security chief. Good cinematography and premise are wasted; generic title betrays sloppy execution.
1974 (PG) 89m/C Sean Connery, Ian McShane, John Quentin; **D:** Caspar Wrede; **M:** Jerry Goldsmith. **VHS, Beta** $59.98 *FOX* 🐾½

Terrorists An Army investigator discovers a plot to assassinate the President. It's up to him to move quickly enough to stop it. Brutal action.
1983 61m/C Marland Proctor, Irmgard Millard. **VHS, Beta** NO 🐾

The Terrornauts Astronomer inadvertently contacts alien race and his entire building is transported across the galaxy. Supposed nuclear precautionary.
1967 75m/C Simon Oates, Zena Marshall, Charles Hawtrey, Patricia Hayes; **D:** Montgomery Tully. **VHS** *NLC* 🐾½

Terrorvision OUR TV GAVE BIRTH TO SPACE ALIENS! It's amazing what modern technology can do: Suburban family buys a fancy satellite dish; bad black comedy and gory special effects result.

1986 (R) 84m/C Gerrit Graham, Mary Woronov, Diane Franklin, Bert Remsen, Alejandro Rey; **D:** Ted Nicolaou; **W:** Ted Nicolaou; **M:** Richard Band. **VHS, Beta $79.98** *LIV Woof!*

The Terry Fox Story
In the spring of 1980, a young man who had lost his right leg to cancer dipped his artificial limb into the Atlantic Ocean and set off on a fund-raising "Marathon of Hope" across Canada, drawing national attention. Inspiring made-for-TV true story is well-scripted and avoids corniness. Good acting from real-life amputee Fryer and, as usual, from Duvall.
1983 96m/C Eric Fryer, Robert Duvall, Chris Makepeace, Michael Zelniker, Rosalind Chao; **D:** Ralph L. Thomas; **M:** Bill Conti. **VHS, Beta $69.95** *VES ♪♪♪*

Tess
Sumptuous adaptation of the Thomas Hardy novel "Tess of the D'Ubervilles." Kinski is wonderful as an innocent farm girl who is seduced by the young aristocrat she works for and then finds marriage to a man of her own class only brings more grief. Polanski's direction is faithful and artful. Nearly three hours long, but worth every minute.
1980 (PG) 170m/C Nastassia Kinski, Peter Firth, Leigh Lawson, John Collin; **D:** Roman Polanski; **W:** Roman Polanski. Academy Awards '80: Best Art Direction/Set Decoration, Best Cinematography, Best Costume Design; Nominations: Best Director (Polanski), Best Picture, Best Original Score; Cesar Awards '80: Best Director (Polanski), Best Film; Golden Globe Awards '81: Best Foreign Film; Los Angeles Film Critics Association Awards '80: Best Director (Polanski); National Board of Review Awards '80: 10 Best Films of the Year. **VHS, Beta $14.95** *COL ♪♪♪*

Test of Donald Norton
Good early Western. A young man raised by Indians finds work with the Hudson's Bay Company and does well, but is haunted by suspicions that he is a half-breed.
1926 68m/B George Walsh, Tyrone Power Sr., Eugenia Gilbert, Robert Graves, Virginia True Boardman; **D:** B. Reeves Eason. **VHS, Beta, 8mm $16.95** *GPV, VYY ♪♪ ½*

A Test of Love
Incorrectly diagnosed as retarded, a young woman with cerebral palsy struggles to adjust to life outside an institution. Predictable but touching and well-acted. *AKA:* Annie's Coming Out.
1984 (PG) 93m/C Angela Punch McGregor, Drew Forsythe, Tina Arhondis; **D:** Gil Brealey. **VHS, Beta $69.95** *MCA ♪♪*

Test Pilot
Gable and Spencer star as daring test pilot and devoted mechanic respectively. When Gable has to land his experimental craft in a Kansas cornfield, he meets and falls in love with farm girl Loy. The two marry and raise a family, all the while she worries over his dangerous profession. When the Air Force asks him to test their new B-17 bomber, she refuses to watch, thinking the test will end in tragedy. Superb aviation drama featuring excellent cast.
1938 118m/B Clark Gable, Myrna Loy, Spencer Tracy, Lionel Barrymore, Samuel S. Hinds; **D:** Victor Fleming. **VHS, Beta $19.98** *MGM, TLF, CCB ♪♪♪ ½*

Test Tube Babies
A married couple's morals begin to deteriorate as they mourn the fact that they can't have a child. The day is saved, however, when they learn about the new artificial insemination process. Amusing, campy propaganda in the vein of "Reefer Madness." Rereleased in 1967 as "The Pill" with extra scenes featuring Monica Davis and John Maitland.
1948 83m/B Dorothy Dube, Timothy Farrell, William Thompson; **D:** W. Merle Connell. **VHS, Beta $19.95** *GVV, SNC Woof!*

Test Tube Teens from the Year 2000
When sex is banned in the year 2000, horny teenagers are left with no choice but to travel through time for some action. *AKA:* Virgin Hunters.
1993 (R) 74m/C Morgan Fairchild, Ian Abercrombie, Brian Bremer, Christopher Wolf, Michelle Matheson, Sara Suzanne Brown, Don Dowe; **D:** Ellen Cabot; **W:** Kenneth J. Hall; **M:** Reg Powell. **VHS, Beta** *PAR ♪*

Testament
Well-made and thought-provoking story of the residents of a small California town struggling to survive after a nuclear bombing. Focuses on one family who tries to accept the reality of post-holocaust life. We see the devastation but it never sinks into sensationalism. An exceptional performance from Alexander.
1983 (PG) 90m/C Jane Alexander, William Devane, Ross Harris, Roxana Zal, Kevin Costner, Rebecca DeMornay; **D:** Lynne Littman; **W:** John Sacret Young; **M:** James Horner. **VHS, Beta $14.95** *PAR ♪♪♪*

The Testament of Dr. Cordelier
A strange, experimental fantasy about a Jekyll and Hyde-type lunatic stalking the streets and alleys of Paris. Originally conceived as a television play, Renoir attempted to create a new mise-en-scene, using multiple cameras covering the sequences as they were performed whole. In French with English subtitles.
1959 95m/C Jean-Louis Barrault; **D:** Jean Renoir. **VHS, Beta $29.95** *FCT ♪♪♪*

Testament of Dr. Mabuse
The director of an asylum is controlled by the evil genius, Dr. Mabuse, who hypnotizes him in this well-done remake of Lang's 1933 classic. *AKA:* The Crimes of Dr. Mabuse; The Last Will of Dr. Mabuse.
1962 ?m/C Gert Frobe, Wolfgang Preiss, Senta Berger. **VHS $16.95** *SNC, LSV ♪♪ ½*

The Testament of Orpheus
Superb, personal surrealism; writer-director Cocteau's last film. Hallucinogenic, autobiographical dream-journey through time. Difficult to follow, but rewarding final installment in a trilogy including "The Blood of the Poet" and "Orpheus." In French with English subtitles.
1959 80m/B Jean Cocteau, Edouard Dermithe, Maria Casares, Francois Perier, Yul Brynner, Jean-Pierre Leaud, Daniel Gelin, Jean Marais, Pablo Picasso, Charles Aznavour; **D:** Jean Cocteau. **VHS, Beta $29.95** *HMV, FCT, ING ♪♪♪ ½*

Tetsuo: The Iron Man
A weird live-action science-fiction cartoon about a white-collar Japanese worker who finds himself being gradually transformed into a walking metal collection of cables, drills, wires, and gears. The newly-formed metal creature then faces off with an equally bizarre metals fetishist (played by the director). In Japanese with English subtitles.
1992 67m/B Tomoroh Taguchi, Kei Fujiwara, Shinya Tsukamoto; **D:** Shinya Tsukamoto; **W:** Shinya Tsukamoto. **VHS $79.95** *FXL ♪♪*

Tevye
Sholom Aleichem's story of Jewish family life, intermarriage, and turmoil in Poland. When Khave, the daughter of Tevye the dairyman, seeks to marry a Ukrainian peasant, Tevye must come to terms with his love for his daughter and his faith and loyalty to tradition. Also the basis for the musical "Fiddler on the Roof." In Yiddish with English subtitles. *AKA:* Tevye der Milkhiker.
1939 96m/B Maurice Schwartz, Miriam Riselle; **D:** Maurice Schwartz. **VHS, Beta $89.95** *ERG, NCJ, ING ♪♪ ½*

Tex
Fatherless brothers in Oklahoma come of age. Dillon is excellent. Based on the novel by S.E. Hinton.
1982 (PG) 103m/C Matt Dillon, Jim Metzler, Meg Tilly, Bill McKinney, Frances Lee McCain, Ben Johnson, Emilio Estevez; **D:** Tim Hunter; **M:** Pino Donaggio. **VHS, Beta** *DIS, OM ♪♪♪*

Tex Rides with the Boy Scouts
Scouts aid Ritter in capturing gold bandits with a little bit of singing thrown in for good measure.
1937 60m/B Tex Ritter. **VHS, Beta $19.95** *NOS, DVT ♪½*

Texas
Two friends wander through the West after the Civil War getting into scrapes with the law and eventually drifting apart. Ford takes a job on a cattle ranch run by Trevor and discovers Holden has joined a gang of rustlers aiming to steal her herd. The two men vie for Trevor's affections. Although friends, a professional rivalry also existed between the two leading actors and they competed against each other, doing their own stunts during filming. Well-acted, funny, and enthusiastic Western.
1941 94m/B William Holden, Glenn Ford, Claire Trevor, Edgar Buchanan, George Bancroft; **D:** George Marshall. **VHS, Beta $9.95** *COL ♪♪♪*

Texas Across the River
Sam Hollis (Martin) is a wise-cracking gun runner who, along with Indian sidekick Kronk (Bishop), is recruiting men to help him ship guns through hostile Comanche territory. Don Andrea, a Spanish nobleman (played by Frenchman Delon) wrongly accused of murder, joins up and much comic misadventure ensues.
1966 101m/C Dean Martin, Alain Delon, Joey Bishop, Rosemary Forsyth, Tina Aumont, Peter Graves, Michael Ansara, Linden Chiles, Andrew Prine, Richard Farnsworth; **D:** Michael Gordon; **W:** Ben Starr, Wells Root, Harold Greene. **VHS $14.98** *MCA, BTV, FCT ♪♪ ½*

Texas Bad Man
Sheriff Mix goes undercover to get in with Kohler's gang of outlaws and bring them to justice.
1932 60m/B Tom Mix, Fred Kohler Sr., Lucille Powers, Ed LeSaint, Richard Alexander; **D:** Edward Laemmle. **VHS $12.95** *GPV ♪½*

Texas Buddies
Steele plays a former military pilot who uses his trusty monoplane to round up outlaws. Interesting twist on standard oater, but suffers from poor execution.
1932 57m/B Bob Steele, Nancy Drexel, George "Gabby" Hayes, Francis McDonald, Harry Semels; **D:** Robert North Bradbury; **W:** Robert North Bradbury. **VHS $19.99** *MOV, GPV ♪½*

Texas Carnival
Williams and Skelton star as carnival performers who operate the dunk tank. When Skelton is mistaken for an oil tycoon, he lives high on the hog until the mistake is discovered. Believe it or not, this musical has only one water ballet sequence. Songs include "It's Dynamite," "Whoa! Emma," and "Young Folks Should Get Married."
1951 77m/C Esther Williams, Red Skelton, Howard Keel, Ann Miller, Paula Raymond, Keenan Wynn, Tom Tully; **D:** Charles Walters. **VHS $19.98** *MGM ♪♪*

The Texas Chainsaw Massacre
The movie that put the "power" in power tools. An idyllic summer afternoon drive becomes a nightmare for a group of young people pursued by a chainsaw-wielding maniac. Made with tongue firmly in cheek, this is nevertheless a mesmerizing saga of gore, flesh, mayhem, and violence.

1974 (R) 86m/C Marilyn Burns, Allen Danzinger, Paul A. Partain, William Vail, Teri McMinn, Edwin Neal, Jim Siedow, Gunnar Hansen, John Dugan, Jerry Lorenz; *D:* Tobe Hooper; *W:* Tobe Hooper, Kim Henkel. **VHS $19.98** MPI *ℐℐ½*

Texas Chainsaw Massacre, Part 2 A tasteless, magnified sequel to the notorious blood-bucket extravaganza, about a certain family in southern Texas who kill and eat passing travelers. Followed by ''Leatherface: Texas Chainsaw Massacre III.''
1986 (R) 90m/C Dennis Hopper, Caroline Williams, Bill Johnson, Jim Siedow; *D:* Tobe Hooper. **VHS, Beta $19.95** MED, VTR *Woof!*

Texas Cyclone A stranger rides into a town that turns out to be incredibly friendly. Later he realizes the entire town thinks he is a prominent citizen who disappeared years ago.
1932 58m/B Tim McCoy, Wheeler Oakman, Shirley Grey, Walter Brennan, John Wayne, Wallace MacDonald, Vernon Dent, Mary Gordon; *D:* Irving Briskin. **VHS $14.95** COL, DVT, NOS *ℐℐ*

Texas Detour On a trip across country, a trio of young Californians have their van stolen. They decide to take the law into their own hands when the redneck sheriff gives them no help. Dull, undistinguished ''action'' flick.
1977 90m/C Cameron Mitchell, Priscilla Barnes, Patrick Wayne, Mitch Vogel, Lindsay Bloom, R.G. Armstrong; *D:* Hikmet Avedis. **VHS, Beta $59.95** PSM *ℐ*

Texas Gunfighter Your basic western from the Maynard series, with everything a western could have.
1932 60m/B Ken Maynard. **VHS, Beta $19.95** NOS, VCI, DVT *ℐℐ*

Texas Guns A gritty western about an old-time gunman (Nelson) and his quest for one last robbery, killing those who stand in his way and some just for fun. Also watch for Cassidy's comeback. *AKA:* Once Upon a Texas Train.
1990 (PG) 96m/C Willie Nelson, Richard Widmark, Shaun Cassidy, Angie Dickinson, Kevin McCarthy, Royal Dano, Chuck Connors, Ken Curtis, Dub Taylor. **VHS $89.95** VMK *ℐℐ*

Texas Jack The head of a medicine show tries to trace the disappearance of his sister.
1935 55m/B Jack Perrin, Jayne Regan, Nelson McDowell, Budd Buster, Lew Meehan; *D:* Bernard B. Ray. **VHS $11.95** GPV *ℐ½*

Texas John Slaughter: Geronimo's Revenge An Indian-loving rancher frets and fights when Geronimo attacks innocent settlers. Compiled fom Walt Disney television episodes.
1960 77m/C Tom Tryon, Darryl Hickman, Betty Lynn; *D:* Harry Keller. **VHS, Beta $69.95** DIS *ℐℐ*

Texas John Slaughter: Stampede at Bitter Creek Good guy Texas John Slaughter meets a variety of threatening obstacles when he tries to move his cattle herd into New Mexico. Originally from the ''Walt Disney Presents'' television series.
1962 90m/C Tom Tryon; *D:* Harry Keller. **VHS, Beta $69.95** DIS *ℐℐ*

Texas Justice The ''Lone Rider'' cavorts around in the desert, dispensing justice in the guise of a monk.
1942 60m/B George Houston, Al ''Fuzzy'' St. John, Dennis Moore, Wanda McKay, Claire Rochelle; *D:* Sam Newfield. **VHS, Beta $19.95** NOS, DVT *ℐℐ½*

Texas Kid A typical western. Hero helps a vengeance-minded kid catch the robbergang who robbed and killed his father. Yee-Haw.
1943 53m/B Johnny Mack Brown, Kermit Maynard, Raymond Hatton, Shirley Patterson, Edmund Cobb, Charles ''Blackie'' King; *D:* Lambert Hillyer. **VHS, Beta $19.95** VDM, GPV *ℐ½*

Texas Lady When a woman wins $50,000 gambling, she buys a Texas newspaper on the stipulation that she can edit it in this standard fare western. Good vehicle for Colbert to look beautiful, but the plot and script are average and uninspired.
1956 86m/C Claudette Colbert, Barry Sullivan, Gregory Walcott; *D:* Tim Whelan. **VHS $19.98** REP *ℐℐ*

Texas Layover Impossible-to-describe western/exploitation entry from trashmeister Adamson involving multiple stewardesses and the remnants of the Ritz Brothers.
1975 88m/C Yvonne De Carlo, Bob Livingston, Donald (Don ''Red'') Barry, Connie Hoffman, Regina Carrol, Jimmy Ritz, Harry Ritz; *D:* Al Adamson. **VHS** NO *Woof!*

Texas Legionnaires Roy comes back to his home town and gets caught between feuding cattle and sheep herders. *AKA:* Man from Music Mountain.
1943 71m/B Roy Rogers, Ruth Terry, Paul Kelly, Anne Gillis, George Cleveland, Pat Brady; *D:* Joseph Kane. **VHS $19.95** NOS, DVT *ℐℐ*

Texas Lightning Innocuous B-grade touching movie about a father and son and their family woes.
1981 (R) 93m/C Cameron Mitchell, Channing Mitchell, Maureen McCormick, Peter Jason. **VHS, Beta $49.95** MED *ℐ½*

Texas Masquerade Standard good cowboys versus land-grabbers action filler. William Boyd plays Hopalong Cassidy. Andy Clyde plays California Carson. Jimmy Rogers plays...Jimmy Rogers.
1944 59m/B William Boyd, Andy Clyde, Jimmy Rogers, Mady Correll, Don Costello, Russell Simpson, Nelson Leigh, Francis McDonald, J. Farrell MacDonald; *D:* George Archainbaud. **VHS $19.95** NOS, RXM *ℐℐ*

Texas Pioneers A frontier scout is sent to an outpost town besieged by crooks. *AKA:* The Blood Brother.
1932 54m/B Bill Cody. **VHS, Beta $19.95** VDM *ℐ½*

The Texas Rangers A prisoner is given the opportunity to capture the notorious Sam Bass gang in exchange for freedom. Good B Western; lotsa shootin'.
1951 68m/C George Montgomery, Gale Storm, Jerome Courtland, Noah Beery Jr.; *D:* Phil Karlson. **VHS, Beta** GKK *ℐℐ*

Texas Terror Young Wayne resigns his badge when he mistakenly believes he has shot and killed his friend. He later rescues his friend's sister, learns the truth, and (naturally) finds true love.
1935 50m/B John Wayne, George ''Gabby'' Hayes, Lucille Browne. **VHS $9.98** REP, CNG, NOS *ℐℐ*

Texas to Bataan The Range Busters ship horses to the Philippines and encounter enemy spies. Part of the ''Range Busters'' series.
1942 56m/B John ''Dusty'' King, David Sharpe, Max Terhune; *D:* Robert Tansey. **VHS, Beta $19.95** VYY *ℐ½*

Texas Trouble Standard matinee fare with cowboy Bob Steele.
193? 0m/B Bob Steele. **VHS, Beta $27.95** VCN *ℐ½*

Texas Wildcats A cowboy helps make sure that sinister adversaries are brought to justice on the American Frontier.
1939 60m/B Tim McCoy. **VHS, Beta $19.95** NOS, DVT, MOV *ℐ½*

Texasville Sequel to ''The Last Picture Show'' finds the characters still struggling after 30 years, with financial woes from the energy crisis, mental illness inspired by the Korean War, and various personal tragedies. Lacks the melancholy sensitivity of its predecessor, but has some of the wit and wisdom that comes with age. Based again on a Larry McMurtry novel. Not well received during its theatrical release.
1990 (R) 120m/C Timothy Bottoms, Jeff Bridges, Annie Potts, Cloris Leachman, Eileen Brennan, Randy Quaid, Cybill Shepherd, William McNamara; *D:* Peter Bogdanovich; *W:* Peter Bogdanovich. **VHS $19.95** COL, VMK *ℐℐ½*

Thank God It's Friday Episodic and desultory disco-dancing vehicle which won the Best Song Oscar for Donna Summer's rendition. Life is irony. Co-produced by Motown. ♫Last Dance; After Dark; Find My Way; It's Serious; Let's Make A Deal; Romeo and Juliet; You're the Reason I Feel Like Dancing; From Here to Eternity; Dance All Night.
1978 (PG) 100m/C Valerie Landsburg, Teri Nunn, Chick Vennera, Jeff Goldblum, Debra Winger; *D:* Robert Klane. **VHS, Beta $12.95** COL *ℐ½*

Thank You & Good Night Director Oxenberg gathers members of her own family around a purple armchair of grandma's to talk about life, love, and family memories, including grandma's illness and recent death.
1991 81m/C *D:* Jan Oxenberg; *W:* Jan Oxenberg. **VHS $79.95** FXL, BTV *ℐ½*

Thank Your Lucky Stars A lavish, slap-dash wartime musical that emptied out the Warner's lot for an array of uncharacteristic celebrity turns. Features Shore in her movie debut. ♫They're Either Too Young or Too Old; Blues in the Night; Hotcha Cornia; Ridin' For A Fall; We're Staying Home Tonight; Goin' North; Love Isn't Born, It's Made; No You, No Me; Ice Cold Katie.
1943 127m/B Eddie Cantor, Dinah Shore, Joan Leslie, Errol Flynn, Bette Davis, Edward Everett Horton, Humphrey Bogart, John Garfield, Alan Hale, Ann Sheridan, Ida Lupino, Jack Carson, Dennis (Stanley Morner) Morgan, Olivia de Havilland; *D:* David Butler; *W:* Norman Panama. **VHS, Beta $29.95** MGM *ℐℐℐ*

Thanksgiving Story When John-Boy's college career is jeopardized by a freak accident, the Walton family gathers together for comfort. Very sentimental family-fare, originally shown as a holiday special from the popular television series ''The Waltons.''
1973 95m/C Richard Thomas, Ralph Waite, Michael Learned, Ellen Corby, Will Geer; *D:* Philip Leacock. **VHS, Beta $14.98** LHV, WAR, TVC *ℐℐ½*

Tharus Son of Attila A couple of sword-wielding barbarians battle each other and an evil emperor.
1987 89m/C Jerome Courtland, Rik von Nutter, Lisa Gastoni; *D:* Robert Montero. **VHS, Beta $59.95** TWE *ℐ*

That Brennan Girl A maudlin soap opera about how a girl's upbringing by an inconsiderate mother makes her a devious little wench. Fortunately her second husband had a better mom, and redemption is at hand.

1946 95m/B James Dunn, Mona Freeman, William Marshall, June Duprez, Frank Jenks, Charles Arnt; *D:* Alfred Santell. **VHS $19.95** *NOS* ♫♫½

That Certain Thing Very early silent Capra comedy about a bachelor with a silver spoon in his mouth who loses his inheritance when he marries for love. It's got that certain Capra screwball feeling.
1928 65m/B Viola Dana, Ralph Graves, Burr McIntosh, Aggie Herring, Syd Crossley; *D:* Frank Capra. **VHS, Beta $18.95** *GPV* ♫♫½

That Certain Woman Sentimental drama with Davis portraying a gangster's widow who wants to make a new life for herself. Fonda plays the rich playboy with whom she falls in love. Because of Davis' star power, she demanded that Fonda play opposite her. It seems Davis had a real life crush on him when they were both players in a stock company several years earlier. Remake of Goulding's "The Trespasser" which starred Gloria Swanson.
1937 91m/B Bette Davis, Henry Fonda, Ian Hunter, Anita Louise, Donald Crisp, Katherine Alexander, Minor Watson; *D:* Edmund Goulding; *W:* Edmund Goulding. **VHS $19.98** *MGM* ♫♫½

That Championship Season Long-dormant animosities surface at the reunion of a championship basketball team. Unfortunate remake of Miller's Pulitzer-prize winning play, with none of the fire which made it a Broadway hit.
1982 (R) 110m/C Martin Sheen, Bruce Dern, Stacy Keach, Robert Mitchum, Paul Sorvino, Jason Miller; *D:* Jason Miller; *M:* Bill Conti. **VHS, Beta $24.95** *MGM* ♫♫

That Cold Day in the Park Early Altman. An unhappy woman takes in a homeless young man from the park near her home. The woman (Dennis) is obsessive and odd; so is the film. Dennis is excellent. Reminiscent of "The Collector."
1969 (R) 91m/C Sandy Dennis, Michael Burns, Suzanne Benton, Michael Murphy, John David Garfield; *D:* Robert Altman. **VHS, Beta $14.98** *REP, FCT* ♫♫½

That Darn Cat Vintage Disney comedy about a Siamese cat that helps FBI Agent Jones thwart kidnappers. Could be shorter, but suspenseful and funny with characteristic Disney slapstick. Based on the book "Undercover Cat" by The Gordons.
1965 (G) 115m/C Hayley Mills, Dean Jones, Dorothy Provine, Neville Brand, Elsa Lanchester, Frank Gorshin, Roddy McDowall; *D:* Robert Stevenson. **VHS, Beta $19.99** *DIS* ♫♫½

That Darn Sorceress A child witch has grown up, and so has her power. To keep her disciples, she must perform increasingly horrible feats.
1988 89m/C Pauline Adams, Betty Page; *D:* Whitney Bain. **VHS, Beta** *NO* ♫

That Forsyte Woman Based on the novel "A Man of Property" by John Galsworthy, a married Victorian woman falls for an architect engaged to be wed. Remade later, and better for BBC-television as "The Forsythe Saga." *AKA:* The Forsyte Saga.
1950 112m/C Errol Flynn, Greer Garson, Walter Pidgeon, Robert Young, Janet Leigh, Harry Davenport, Stanley Logan, Lumsden Hare, Aubrey Mather, Matt Moore; *D:* Compton Bennett. **VHS $19.98** *MGM, CCB* ♫♫

That Gang of Mine "East Side Kids" episode about gang member Mugg's ambition to be a jockey. Good racing scenes.
1940 62m/B Bobby Jordan, Leo Gorcey, Clarence Muse, Dave O'Brien; *D:* Joseph H. Lewis. **VHS, Beta $24.95** *NOS, DVT, HEG* ♫♫

That Girl from Paris An opera singer from Paris stows away on an ocean liner to be near the swing bandleader she has fallen in love with. An entertaining film with many songs; remade as "Four Jacks and a Jill." ♫Una Voce Poco Fa; The Blue Danube; Love and Learn; The Call to Arms; Seal It With A Kiss; My Nephew From Nice; Moon Face; Tarantella.
1936 105m/B Lily Pons, Gene Raymond, Jack Oakie, Herman Bing, Lucille Ball, Mischa Auer, Frank Jenks; *D:* Leigh Jason. **VHS, Beta $19.98** *TTC* ♫♫½

That Hamilton Woman Screen biography of the tragic 18th-century love affair between British naval hero Lord Nelson and Lady Hamilton. Korda exaggerated the film's historical distortions in order to pass the censor's production code about adultery. Winston Churchill's favorite film which paralleled Britain's heroic struggles in WWII. *AKA:* Lady Hamilton.
1941 125m/B Laurence Olivier, Vivien Leigh, Gladys Cooper, Alan Mowbray, Sara Allgood, Henry Wilcoxon; *D:* Alexander Korda; *M:* Miklos Rozsa. Academy Awards '41: Best Sound; Nominations: Best Black and White Cinematography, Best Interior Decoration. **VHS, Beta $19.98** *HBO, SUE* ♫♫♫

That Long Night in '43 A gripping story of fascist terror during WWII.
1960 110m/B *D:* Florestano Vancini. **VHS, Beta** *CIG* ♫♫½

That Lucky Touch York is a reporter covering NATO games; Moore is Bond warmed over as an arms dealer. Sexual and professional tension becomes unlikely romance. Slight and dull. Cobb's last film.
1975 92m/C Roger Moore, Susannah York, Shelley Winters, Lee J. Cobb, Jean-Pierre Cassel, Raf Vallone, Sydne Rome; *D:* Christopher Miles; *W:* John Briley. **VHS, Beta $69.95** *TWE* ♫♫

That Man from Rio Engaging adventure spoof with Belmondo as a pilot whose girlfriend (Dorleac) has just been kidnapped. Her father led an expedition to South America in search of an Amazon treasure and the kidnappers think she knows how to find it. So of course Belmondo does some international adventuring in order to rescue her. In French with English subtitles. *AKA:* L'Homme de Rio; L'Uomo di Rio.
1964 114m/C Jean-Paul Belmondo, Francoise Dorleac, Jean Servais, Simone Renant; *D:* Philippe de Broca; *M:* Jean-Paul Rappeneau; *M:* Georges Delerue. **VHS $19.99** *MGM* ♫♫½

That Man Is Pregnant NYPD detective gets the incredible news that he is pregnant. Viewers can't believe it, either.
1980 (PG) 80m/C **VHS, Beta** *NO* ♫

That Midnight Kiss Glossy production of a musical romance featuring Lanza in his film debut. Thin plot has Lanza starring as a singing truck driver who is discovered by opera diva Grayson. ♫They Didn't Believe Me; I Know, I Know, I Know; Three O'Clock in the Morning; Santa Lucia; Down Among the Sheltering Palms; Revolutionary Etude; Cara Nome; Celeste Aida; Una Furtiva Lacrima.
1949 96m/C Kathryn Grayson, Jose Iturbi, Ethel Barrymore, Mario Lanza, Keenan Wynn, J. Carroll Naish, Jules Munshin; *D:* Norman Taurog. **VHS $19.98** *MGM* ♫♫

That Naughty Girl The bored daughter of a nightclub owner decides to experience all life has to offer.
1958 77m/C Brigitte Bardot, Jean Bretonniere, Francoise Fabian; *D:* Michel Boisrond. **VHS, Beta $69.95** *JEF* ♫♫

That Night A view of romance through the eyes of a young girl, circa 1961. Ten-year-old Alice (Dushku) is the confidant of rebellious 17-year-old neighbor Cheryl (Lewis), who enlists the young girl's aid as a go-between with her wrong-side-of-the-tracks boyfriend Rick (Howell). 21 soundtrack oldies are featured. Directorial debut for screenwriter Bolotin. Based on a novel by Alice McDermott.
1993 (PG-13) 89m/C C. Thomas Howell, Juliette Lewis, Eliza Dushku, Helen Shaver, John Dossett; *D:* Craig Bolotin; *W:* Craig Bolotin. **VHS, Beta** *WAR* ♫♫

That Obscure Object of Desire Bunuel's last film, a comic nightmare of sexual frustration. A rich Spaniard obtains a beautiful girlfriend who, while changing physical identities, refuses to sleep with him. Based on a novel by Pierre Louys, which has been used as the premise for several other films, including "The Devil is a Woman," "La Femme et le Pantin," and "The Female." Available with subtitles or dubbed. *AKA:* Cet Obscur Objet Du Desir.
1977 (R) 100m/C Fernando Rey, Carol Bouquet, Angela Molina; *D:* Luis Bunuel; *W:* Luis Bunuel, Jean-Claude Carriere. Academy Awards '77 Nominations: Best Adapted Screenplay, Best Foreign Language Film; Los Angeles Film Critics Association Awards '77: Best Foreign Film; National Board of Review Awards '77: 5 Best Foreign Films of the Year, Best Director (Bunuel). **VHS, Beta $19.95** *COL, VYG, APD* ♫♫♫½

That Sinking Feeling A group of bored Scot teenagers decide to steal 90 sinks from a plumber's warehouse. Well received early film from Forsythe is genuinely funny as the boys try to get rid of the sinks and turn a profit.
1979 (PG) 82m/C Robert Buchanan, John Hughes, Billy Greenlees, Alan Love; *D:* Bill Forsyth; *W:* Bill Forsyth. **VHS, Beta $59.98** *SUE* ♫♫♫

That Summer of White Roses Compelling action drama about a lifeguard working at a resort in Nazi-occupied Yugoslavia and his love for a woman resistance fighter and her child.
1990 (R) 98m/C Tom Conti, Susan George, Rod Steiger; *D:* Rajko Grlic. **VHS, Beta $89.98** *MED, IME, VTR* ♫♫½

That Touch of Mink In New York City, an unemployed secretary finds herself involved with a business tycoon. On a trip to Bermuda, both parties get an education as they play their game of "cat and mouse." Enjoyable romantic comedy.
1962 99m/C Cary Grant, Doris Day, Gig Young, Audrey Meadows, John Astin, Dick Sargent; *D:* Delbert Mann. Academy Awards '62 Nominations: Best Art Direction/Set Decoration (Color), Best Sound, Best Story & Screenplay; Golden Globe Awards '63: Best Film—Musical/Comedy. **VHS $19.98** *REP, MLB* ♫♫½

That Uncertain Feeling Light comedy about a couple's marital problems increasing when she develops the hiccups and a friendship with a flaky piano player. A remake of the earlier Lubitsch silent film, "Kiss Me Again." Available colorized.
1941 86m/B Merle Oberon, Melvyn Douglas, Burgess Meredith, Alan Mowbray, Eve Arden, Sig Rumann, Harry Davenport; *D:* Ernst Lubitsch. **VHS, Beta $14.95** *NOS, VYY, DVT* ♫♫½

That Was Then...This Is Now Lame adaptation of S.E. Hinton teen novel about a surly kid who is attached to his adoptive brother and becomes jealous when the brother gets a girlfriend.

1985 (R) 102m/C Emilio Estevez, Craig Sheffer, Kim Delaney, Jill Schoelen, Barbara Babcock, Frank Howard, Larry B. Scott, Morgan Freeman; *D:* Christopher Cain; *W:* Emilio Estevez. **VHS, Beta** $79.95 *PAR ♂♂*

That'll Be the Day The early rock 'n' roll of the 1950s is the only outlet for a frustrated young working-class Brit. Prequel to "Stardust." Good, meticulous realism; engrossing story.
1973 (PG) 86m/C Ringo Starr, Keith Moon, David Essex, Rosemary Leach; *D:* Claude Whatham. **VHS, Beta** $14.98 *REP, CNG ♂♂½*

That's Adequate Mock documentary about a fictional film studio. Lampoons just about every movie made in the last 60 years. Premise might have been adequate for a sketch, but hardly for a feature-length film. Zaniness gets old quickly.
1990 (R) 82m/C Tony Randall, Robert Downey, Rocky Aoki, Bruce Willis, Robert Townsend, James Coco, Jerry Stiller, Peter Riegert, Susan Dey, Richard Lewis, Robert Vaughn, Renee Taylor, Stuart Pankin, Brother Theodore, Anne Bloom, Chuck McCann, Anne Meara; *D:* Harry Hurwitz; *W:* Harry Hurwitz. **VHS** $14.95 *HMD ♂♂*

That's Dancing! This anthology features some of film's finest moments in dance from classical ballet to break-dancing.
1985 (G) 104m/C Fred Astaire, Ginger Rogers, Ruby Keeler, Cyd Charisse, Gene Kelly, Shirley MacLaine, Liza Minnelli, Sammy Davis Jr., Mikhail Baryshnikov, Ray Bolger, Jennifer Beals, Dean Martin; *D:* Jack Haley Jr. **VHS, Beta** $19.98 *MGM ♂♂*

That's Entertainment A compilation of scenes from the classic MGM musicals beginning with "The Broadway Melody" (1929) and ending with "Gigi" (1958). Great fun, especially for movie buffs.
1974 (G) 132m/C Judy Garland, Fred Astaire, Frank Sinatra, Gene Kelly, Esther Williams, Bing Crosby; *D:* Jack Haley Jr.; *M:* Henry Mancini. **VHS, Beta** $19.98 *MGM ♂♂*

That's Entertainment, Part 2 A cavalcade of great musical and comedy sequences from MGM movies of the past. Also stars Jeanette MacDonald, Nelson Eddy, the Marx Brothers, Laurel and Hardy, Jack Buchanan, Ann Miller, Mickey Rooney, Louis Armstrong, Oscar Levant, Cyd Charisse, Elizabeth Taylor, Maurice Chevalier, Bing Crosby, Jimmy Durante, Clark Gable, and the Barrymores. Not as unified as its predecessor, but priceless nonetheless.
1976 (G) 133m/C Fred Astaire, Gene Kelly. **VHS, Beta** $19.98 *MGM ♂♂*

That's Entertainment, Part 3 Third volume contains 62 MGM musical numbers from over 100 films, hosted by nine of the original stars, and is based on outtakes and unfinished numbers from studio archives. One new technique used here is a split-screen showing both the actual film with a behind-the-scenes shot that includes cameramen, set designers, and dancers scurrying around. Although it has its moments, TE3 doesn't generate the same reverence for Hollywood's Golden Age that its predecessors managed to do. That 18-year gap between sequels may say something about what the studio execs thought of their film vault's remainders.
1993 (G) 113m/C *D:* Bud Friedgen, Michael J. Sheridan; *W:* Bud Friedgen, Michael J. Sheridan; *M:* Marc Shaiman. **VHS** *♂♂*

That's Life! A lackluster semi-home movie starring Edwards' family and friends. A single weekend in the lives of a writer who's turning sixty, his singer wife who has been diagnosed with cancer, and their family.

1986 (PG-13) 102m/C Jack Lemmon, Julie Andrews, Sally Kellerman, Chris Lemmon, Emma Walton, Rob Knepper, Robert Loggia, Jennifer Edwards; *D:* Blake Edwards; *W:* Blake Edwards. **VHS, Beta** $14.98 *CCB, LIV, VES ♂♂*

That's My Baby! A man wants his girlfriend to have their baby, but the only thing she wants is a career. War between the sexes poorly done.
1988 (PG-13) 97m/C Sonja Smits, Timothy Webber; *D:* Edie Yolles, John Bradshaw. **VHS, Beta** $79.98 *TWE ♂*

That's Singing: The Best of Broadway A tribute to the American musical theatre featuring performances of memorable songs from twenty Broadway shows.
1984 111m/C **VHS, Beta** $19.98 *LHV, WAR ♂*

Theatre of Blood Critics are unkind to Shakespearian ham Price, and he eliminates them by various Bard-inspired methods with the assistance of his lovely daughter. Top drawer comedy noir.
1973 (R) 104m/C Vincent Price, Diana Rigg, Ian Hendry, Robert Morley, Dennis Price, Diana Dors, Milo O'Shea; *D:* Douglas Hickox **VHS** $14.95 *MGM ♂♂♂*

Theatre of Death Horror master Lee is back, this time as a theatre director in Paris. Meanwhile, police are baffled by a series of mysterious murders, each bearing a trace of vampirism. Well-plotted suspense. A racy voodoo dance sequence, often cut, is available on some video versions. *AKA:* Blood Fiend.
1967 90m/C Christopher Lee, Lelia Goldoni, Julian Glover, Evelyn Laye, Jenny Till, Ivor Dean; *D:* Samuel Gallu. **VHS, Beta** $54.95 *VCI, SNC ♂♂½*

Thelma & Louise Hailed as the first "feminist-buddy" movie, Sarandon and Davis bust out as best friends who head directly into one of the better movies of the year. Davis is the ditzy Thelma, a housewife rebelling against her dominating, unfaithful, abusive husband (who, rather than being disturbing, provides some of the best comic relief in the film). Sarandon is Louise, a hardened and world-weary waitress in the midst of an unsatisfactory relationship. They hit the road for a respite from their mundane lives, only to find violence and a part of themselves they never knew existed. Outstanding performances from Davis and especially Sarandon, with Pitt notable as the stud who gets Davis' motor revved. Director Scott has a fine eye for set details.
1991 (R) 130m/C Susan Sarandon, Geena Davis, Harvey Keitel, Christopher McDonald, Michael Madsen, Brad Pitt, Timothy Carhart, Stephen Tobolowsky, Lucinda Jenney; *D:* Ridley Scott; *W:* Callie Khouri; *M:* Hans Zimmer. Academy Awards '91: Best Original Screenplay; Nominations: Best Actress (Davis), Best Actress (Sarandon), Best Cinematography, Best Director (Scott), Best Film Editing; National Board of Review Awards '91: 10 Best Films of the Year, Best Actress (Sarandon, Davis). **VHS, Beta, 8mm** $19.98 *MGM ♂♂♂*

Them! A group of mutated giant ants wreak havoc on a southwestern town. The first of the big-bug movies, and far surpassing the rest, this is a classic fun flick. See how many names you can spot among the supporting cast.
1954 93m/B James Whitmore, Edmund Gwenn, Fess Parker, James Arness, Onslow Stevens, Jack Perrin; *D:* Gordon Douglas. **VHS, Beta** $19.98 *WAR ♂♂♂*

The Theme Esenin is a mediocre middle-aged playwright who knows his success comes from kow-towing to the party line. Trying to find inspiration he visits his native

village where he meets the young Sasa, an artist who has refused to compromise. Although Esenin falls for her, Sasa has only contempt for his lack of principles and stays with her poet/lover, who is reduced to digging graves and has decided to emigrate to Israel. The film went unreleased for 8 years because of its themes of artistic freedom and emigration. In Russian with English subtitles. *AKA:* Tema.
1979 100m/C Mikhail Ulyanov, Inna Churikova, Stanislav Lyubshin, Evgeny Vesnik, Sergei Nikonenko, Natalya Selezneva; *D:* Gleb Panfilov. **VHS** $59.95 *KIV, FCT ♂♂♂*

There Goes Barder Constantine plays a con-man who's hired by a crooked ship owner to be a security agent.
1964 ?m/C Eddie Constantine, May Britt. **VHS** $16.95 *SNC, VYY ♂♂*

There Goes Kelly Moran and Miller are page boys at a radio station who try to get the station receptionist a singing job. When the vocalist on a popular show is murdered, the duo not only get their protege a break but get themselves a mystery to solve as well.
1945 62m/B Jackie Moran, Sidney Miller, Wanda McKay, Ralph Sanford, Jan Wiley, Anthony Warde; *D:* Phil Karlson. **VHS** $12.95 *GPV ♂½*

There Goes the Neighborhood A dying convict tells prison psychiatrist Daniels where he has buried 8.5 million dollars—under the home of neighbor O'Hara. Daniels and O'Hara try to discreetly dig up the fortune but when the neighborhood finds out everyone wants a chance at the cash.
1992 (PG-13) 88m/C Chazz Palminteri, Mary Gross, Jeff Daniels, Catherine O'Hara, Dabney Coleman, Hector Elizondo, Judith Ivey, Rhea Perlman, Harris Yulin, Jonathan Banks; *D:* Bill Phillips. **VHS, Beta** *PAR ♂♂½*

There was a Crooked Man An Arizona town gets some new ideas about law and order when an incorruptible and innovative warden takes over the town's prison. The warden finds he's got his hands full with one inmate determined to escape. Offbeat western black comedy supported by an excellent and entertaining production, with fine acting all around.
1970 (R) 123m/C Kirk Douglas, Henry Fonda, Warren Oates, Hume Cronyn, Burgess Meredith, John Randolph, Arthur O'Connell, Alan Hale Jr., Lee Grant; *D:* Joseph L. Mankiewicz; *W:* Robert Benton, David Newman. **VHS, Beta** $19.98 *WAR ♂♂♂½*

There's a Girl in My Soup Sellers is a gourmet who moonlights as a self-styled Casanova. Early post "Laugh-In" Hawn is the young girl who takes refuge at his London love nest when her boyfriend dumps her. Lust ensues. Has its funny parts, but not a highlight of anyone's career. Based on the hit play.
1970 (R) 95m/C Peter Sellers, Goldie Hawn, Diana Dors; *D:* Roy Boulting. **VHS, Beta** $9.95 *GKK ♂♂*

There's No Business Like Show Business A top husband and wife vaudevillian act make it a family affair. Filmed in CinemaScope, allowing for full and lavish musical numbers. Good performances and Berlin's music make this an enjoyable ride. ♫When the Midnight Choo-Choo Leaves for Alabam; Let's Have Another Cup of Coffee; Play a Simple Melody; After You Get What You Want You Don't Want It; You'd Be Surprised; A Sailor's Not a Sailor; A Pretty Girl is Like a Melody; If You Believe Me; A Man Chases a Girl Until She Catches Him.

1954 117m/C Ethel Merman, Donald O'Connor, Marilyn Monroe, Dan Dailey, Johnny Ray, Mitzi Gaynor, Frank McHugh, Hugh O'Brian; *D:* Walter Lang. **VHS, Beta $19.98** *FOX, FCT* ぴぴぴ

There's No Time for Love, Charlie Brown An animated adventure with the Peanuts gang as they travel to a museum on a class trip.
1987 30m/C VHS, Beta $14.95 *BAR* ぴぴぴ

There's Nothing Out There A group of seven teenagers spends Spring Break at a secluded mountain cabin. It sounds wonderful, but one of the boys (who claims to have seen every horror movie on video) knows the signs of a horror movie just waiting to happen.
1990 91m/C Craig Peck, Wendy Bednarz, Mark Collver, Bonnie Bowers, John Carhart III, Claudia Flores, Jeff Dachis; *D:* Rolfe Kanefsky; *W:* Rolfe Kanefsky. **VHS, Beta $49.95** *PSM* ぴぴ

Therese Stylish biography of a young French nun and her devotion to Christ bordering on romantic love. Explores convent life. Real-life Therese died of TB and was made a saint. A directorial tour de force for Cavalier. In French with English subtitles.
1986 90m/C Catherine Mouchet, Aurore Prieto, Sylvie Habault, Ghislaine Mona; *D:* Alain Cavalier; *W:* Alain Cavalier. **VHS, Beta $39.95** *ING, APD, MED* ぴぴぴ

Therese & Isabelle Story of growing love and physical attraction between two French schoolgirls. On holiday together, they confront their mutual desires. Richly photographed soft porn. Not vulgar, but certainly for adults. *AKA:* Therese Und Isabell.
1968 102m/C Essy Persson, Anna Gael, Barbara Laage, Anne Vernon; *D:* Radley Metzger. **VHS, Beta** *NO* ぴぴ½

These Girls Won't Talk Three female stars of early silent pictures are featured separately in: "Her Bridal Nightmare," "Campus Carmen," and "As Luck Would Have It."
192? 50m/B Colleen Moore, Carole Lombard, Betty Compson. **VHS, Beta $24.95** *VYY* ぴぴ½

These Three A teenaged girl ruins the lives of two teachers by telling a malicious lie. Excellent cast. Script by Lillian Hellman, based on her play "The Children's Hour." Remade by the same director as "The Children's Hour" in 1961.
1936 92m/B Miriam Hopkins, Merle Oberon, Joel McCrea, Bonita Granville, Marcia Mae Jones, Walter Brennan, Margaret Hamilton; *D:* William Wyler. **VHS, Beta $19.98** *SUE* ぴぴぴ½

They Beings from beneath the earth's crust take their first trip to the surface.
198? 88m/C Paul Dentzer, Debbie Pick, Nick Holt. **VHS, Beta** *NO* ぴ

They All Laughed Three detectives become romantically involved with the women they were hired to investigate. Essentially light-hearted fluff with little or no script. Further undermined by the real-life murder of Stratten before the film's release.
1981 (PG) 115m/C Ben Gazzara, John Ritter, Audrey Hepburn, Colleen Camp, Patti Hansen, Dorothy Stratten, Elizabeth Pena; *D:* Peter Bogdanovich; *W:* Peter Bogdanovich. **VHS, Beta $19.98** *VES* ぴぴ

They Call It Sin Often told story of a young country girl heading to the Big Apple in search of her big break and "Mr. Right." Young is a chorus line girl romantically involved with her married producer (Calhern) while faithful admirer Brent waits nearby. Predictable plot adapted from the novel by Alberta Stedman Eagan. *AKA:* The Way of Life.

1932 68m/B Loretta Young, George Brent, David Manners, Louis Calhern, Una Merkel, Joseph Cawthorn, Helen Vinson; *D:* Thornton Freeland; *W:* Lillie Hayward, Howard J. Green. **VHS $19.98** *MGM* ぴぴ

They Call Me Bruce? A bumbling Bruce Lee look-alike meets a karate-chopping Mafia moll in this farce. Silly premise creates lots of laughs. Followed by a sequel, "They Still Call Me Bruce." *AKA:* A Fist Full of Chopsticks.
1982 (PG) 88m/C Johnny Yune, Margaux Hemingway; *D:* Elliot Hong. **VHS, Beta $29.98** *VES* ぴ

They Call Me Mr. Tibbs! Lieutenant Virgil Tibbs (Poitier) investigates the murder of a prostitute. The prime suspect is his friend, the Reverend Logan Sharpe (Landau). He is torn between his duty as a policeman, his concern for the reverend, and the turmoil of his domestic life. Less tense, less compelling sequel to "In the Heat of the Night."
1970 (R) 108m/C Sidney Poitier, Barbara McNair, Martin Landau, Juano Hernandez, Anthony Zerbe, Ed Asner, Norma Crane, Jeff Corey; *D:* Gordon Douglas; *W:* Alan R. Trustman; *M:* Quincy Jones. **VHS, Beta $14.95** *MGM, FOX* ぴぴ

They Call Me Trinity Lazy drifter-gunslinger and his outlaw brother join forces with Mormon farmers to rout bullying outlaws. Spoofs every western cliche with relentless comedy, parodying "The Magnificent Seven" and gibing the spaghetti western. Followed by "Trinity is Still My Name." Dubbed. *AKA:* Lo Chiamavano Trinita.
1972 (G) 110m/C Terence Hill, Bud Spencer, Farley Granger, Steffen Zacharias; *D:* E.B. Clucher. **VHS, Beta $14.95** *CCB, SUE, HHE* ぴぴ½

They Came from Beyond Space Aliens invade the earth and possess the brains of humans. They only want a few slaves to help them repair their ship which crashed on the moon. The only person able to stop them is a scientist with a steel plate in his head. Silly and forgettable.
1967 86m/C Robert Hutton, Michael Gough; *D:* Freddie Francis. **VHS, Beta $59.98** *SUE* ぴ

They Came from Within The occupants of a high-rise building go on a sex and violence spree when stricken by an aphrodisiac parasite. Queasy, sleazy and weird. First major film by Cronenberg. *AKA:* Shivers; The Parasite Murders.
1975 (R) 87m/C Paul Hampton, Joe Silver, Lynn Lowry, Barbara Steele; *D:* David Cronenberg; *W:* David Cronenberg. **VHS, Beta $69.98** *LIV, VES* ぴぴ½

They Came to Cordura Mexico, 1916: a woman and six American soldiers—five heroes and one who has been branded a coward—begin a journey to the military headquarters in Cordura. Slow journey brings out personalities. Look for "Bewitched" hubby Dick York. Based on Glendon Swarthout's best-seller.
1959 123m/C Gary Cooper, Rita Hayworth, Van Heflin, Tab Hunter, Dick York, Richard Conte; *D:* Robert Rossen. **VHS, Beta $14.95** *COL* ぴぴ½

They Died with Their Boots On The Battle of Little Big Horn is recreated Hollywood style. Takes liberties with historical fact, but still an exciting portrayal of General Custer's last stand. The movie also marks the last time de Havilland worked with Flynn. Also available colorized.
1941 141m/B Errol Flynn, Sydney Greenstreet, Anthony Quinn, Hattie McDaniel, Arthur Kennedy, Gene Lockhart, Regis Toomey, Olivia de Havilland, Charley Grapewin; *D:* Raoul Walsh. **VHS, Beta $19.98** *MGM, MLB, FOX* ぴぴぴ

They Drive by Night Two truck-driving brothers break away from a large company and begin independent operations. After an accident to Bogart, Raft is forced to go back to the company where Lupino, the boss's wife, becomes obsessed with him and kills her husband to gain the company and win Raft. When he rejects her, she accuses him of the murder. Well-plotted film with great dialogue. Excellent cast gives it their all. *AKA:* Road to Frisco.
1940 97m/B Humphrey Bogart, Ann Sheridan, George Raft, Ida Lupino, Alan Hale, Gale Page, Roscoe Karns, Charles Halton; *D:* Raoul Walsh. **VHS, Beta $19.98** *FOX, FCT* ぴぴぴ½

They Got Me Covered Two WWII-era journalists get involved in a comic web of murder, kidnapping and romance. Hope is very funny and carries the rest of the cast. Look for Doris Day in a bit part and listen for Bing Crosby singing whenever Hope opens his cigarette case.
1943 95m/B Bob Hope, Dorothy Lamour, Otto Preminger, Eduardo Ciannelli, Donald Meek, Walter Catlett; *D:* David Butler. **VHS, Beta $19.98** *SUE* ぴぴ

They Knew What They Wanted A lonely San Francisco waitress begins a correspondence romance with a grape grower and agrees to marry him after he sends her a photo which shows him as being young and handsome. She arrives to discover Laughton had sent her a picture of another man. An accident, an affair, and a pregnancy provide further complications before a satisfactory ending is suggested. Flawed adaptation of Sidney Howard's play still has strong performances from Lombard and Laughton.
1940 96m/B Charles Laughton, Carole Lombard, Harry Carey Sr., Karl Malden, William Gargan; *D:* Garson Kanin. **VHS, Beta $34.95** *RKO* ぴぴぴ

They Live A semi-serious science-fiction spoof about a drifter who discovers an alien conspiracy. They're taking over the country under the guise of Reaganism, capitalism and yuppiedom. Screenplay written by Carpenter under a pseudonym. Starts out fun, deteriorates into cliches and bad special effects makeup.
1988 (R) 88m/C Roddy Piper, Keith David, Meg Foster, George Flower, Peter Jason, Raymond St. Jacques, John Lawrence, Sy Richardson, Jason Robards III, Larry Franco; *D:* John Carpenter; *W:* John Carpenter; *M:* Alan Howarth, John Carpenter. **VHS, Beta $19.95** *MCA* ぴぴ½

They Live by Night A young fugitive sinks deeper into a life of crime thanks to his association with two hardened criminals. Classic film noir was Ray's first attempt at directing. Based on Edward Anderson's novel "Thieves Like Us," under which title it was remade in 1974. Compelling and suspenseful. *AKA:* The Twisted Road; Your Red Wagon.
1949 95m/B Cathy O'Donnell, Farley Granger, Howard da Silva, Jay C. Flippen, Helen Craig; *D:* Nicholas Ray. **VHS, Beta $59.95** *HHT* ぴぴぴ½

They Made Me a Criminal A champion prizefighter, believing he murdered a man in a drunken brawl, runs away. He finds refuge in the West with the Dead End Kids. Remake of "The Life of Jimmy Dolan." Berkeley was best-known for directing and choreographing musicals and surprisingly did very well with this movie. *AKA:* I Became a Criminal; They Made Me a Fugitive.
1939 92m/B John Garfield, Ann Sheridan, Claude Rains, Leo Gorcey; *D:* Busby Berkeley. **VHS, Beta $9.95** *CNG, NOS, PSM* ぴぴ½

They Meet Again The final segment of the Dr. Christian series. The country doctor sets out to prove the innocence of a man who has been wrongly accused of stealing money. Slow moving and not particularly exciting.
1941 68m/B Jean Hersholt, Dorothy Lovett; *D:* Erle C. Kenton. **VHS, Beta, 8mm** $19.95 NOS, VYY, VYY ♟♟

They Met in Bombay Two jewel thieves team up in this romantic action-comedy, complete with exotic locations and two big box-office stars. A Japanese invasion makes Russell reconsider her life of crime and gives Gable a chance to play hero. Look for Alan Ladd in a bit part in his pre-"This Gun for Hire" days. Based on a story by John Kafka.
1941 86m/B Clark Gable, Rosalind Russell, Peter Lorre, Jessie Ralph, Reginald Owen, Eduardo Ciannelli, Alan Ladd; *D:* Clarence Brown; *W:* Anita Loos, Edwin Justus Mayer, Leon Gordon. **VHS** $19.98 MGM ♟♟½

They Might Be Giants Woodward is a woman shrink named Watson who treats retired judge Scott for delusions that he is Sherlock Holmes. Scott's brother wants him committed so the family loot will come to him. Very funny in places; Woodward and Scott highlight a solid cast.
1971 (G) 98m/C George C. Scott, Joanne Woodward, Jack Gilford, Eugene Roche, Kitty Winn, F. Murray Abraham, M. Emmet Walsh; *D:* Anthony Harvey; *M:* John Barry. **VHS, Beta** $12.95 MCA ♟♟♟

They Never Come Back A boxer is thrown in jail and then stages a comeback.
1932 62m/B Regis Toomey, Dorothy Sebastian. **VHS, Beta** $16.95 SNC ♟½

They Only Kill Their Masters Garner plays a California police chief investigating the death of a wild beach town resident, supposedly killed by her doberman pinscher. He discovers the woman was actually drowned and there are any number of secrets to uncover. Mild whodunit.
1972 (PG) 98m/C James Garner, Katharine Ross, June Allyson, Hal Holbrook, Harry Guardino, Christopher Connelly, Tom Ewell, Peter Lawford, Edmond O'Brien, Arthur O'Connell, Ann Rutherford, Art Metrano; *D:* James Goldstone. **VHS** $19.98 MGM ♟♟½

They Paid with Bullets: Chicago 1929 The story of one man's rise to power, and eventual downfall as a Mafia consigliatore.
197? 88m/C Peter Lee Lawrence, Ingrid Schoeller. **VHS, Beta** $19.95 CNG ♟½

They Saved Hitler's Brain Fanatical survivors of the Nazi holocaust gave eternal life to the brain of their leader in the last hours of the war. Now it's on a Caribbean island giving orders again. One of the truly great "bad" movies. Shot in pieces in the U.S., the Philippines, and elsewhere, with chunks of other films stuck in to hold the "story" together. *AKA:* Madmen of Mandoras; The Return of Mr. H.
1964 91m/B Walter Stocker, Audrey Caire; *D:* David Bradley. **VHS, Beta, 8mm** $24.95 VYY, VCI Woof!

They Shall Have Music A poverty-stricken child hears a concert by violinist Heifetz and decides to become a musician. He joins Brennan's nearly bankrupt music school and persuades Heifetz to play at a benefit concert. Hokey but enjoyable Goldwyn effort to bring classical music to the big screen. ♪Rondo Capriccioso; Hora Staccato; Estrellita; Melody; Concerto in E Minor for Violin and Orchestra; Waltz in D Flat,

Opus 64, No. 1; Cara Nome; Casta Diva. *AKA:* Melody of Youth; Ragged Angels.
1939 101m/B Walter Brennan, Joel McCrea, Gene Reynolds, Jascha Heifetz, Marjorie Main, Porter Hall, Andrea Leeds, Terence Kilburn; *D:* Archie Mayo. **VHS, Beta** $19.98 SUE, HBO ♟♟

They Shoot Horses, Don't They? Powerful period piece depicting the desperation of the Depression Era. Contestants enter a dance marathon in the hopes of winning a cash prize, not realizing that they will be driven to exhaustion. Fascinating and tragic.
1969 (R) 121m/C Jane Fonda, Michael Sarrazin, Susannah York, Gig Young, Red Buttons, Bonnie Bedelia, Bruce Dern, Allyn Ann McLerie, Chaing I; *D:* Sydney Pollack. Academy Awards '69: Best Supporting Actor (Young); Nominations: Best Actress (Fonda), Best Adapted Screenplay, Best Art Direction/Set Decoration, Best Costume Design, Best Director (Pollack), Best Film Editing, Best Supporting Actress (York), Best Original Score; British Academy Awards '70: Best Supporting Actress (York); Golden Globe Awards '70: Best Supporting Actor (Young). **VHS** ABC, TCF, FOX ♟♟♟½

They Still Call Me Bruce A Korean searches for the American who saved his life when he was young and instead becomes big brother to an orphan. Supposedly a sequel to "They Call Me Bruce," but has little in common with it. Poorly done and not particularly entertaining.
1986 (PG) 91m/C Johnny Yune, Robert Guillaume, Pat Paulsen; *D:* Johnny Yune. **VHS, Beta** $14.95 NWV, STE ♟

They Watch Workaholic Bergin neglects his family and suffers the consequences when his young daughter dies in an auto accident. In fact, he's so distressed that he relies on blind psychic Redgrave to get in touch with his little girl's spirit. Based on the story "They" by Rudyard Kipling. Made for television.
1993 (PG-13) 100m/C Patrick Bergin, Vanessa Redgrave, Valerie Mahaffey; *D:* John Korty; *W:* Edithe Swensen; *M:* Gerald Gouriet. **VHS** COL ♟♟½

They Went That-a-Way & That-a-Way Two bumbling deputies pose as convicts in this madcap prison caper. Terrible rehash of Laurel-and-Hardy has nothing going for it.
1978 (PG) 96m/C Tim Conway, Richard Kiel; *D:* Edward Montagne; *W:* Tim Conway. **VHS, Beta** $69.98 SUE Woof!

They Were Expendable Two American captains pit their PT boats against the Japanese fleet. Based on the true story of a PT boat squadron based in the Philippines during the early days of WWII. One of the best (and most underrated) WWII films. Also available in a colorized version.
1945 135m/B Robert Montgomery, John Wayne, Donna Reed, Jack Holt, Ward Bond, Cameron Mitchell, Leon Ames, Marshall Thompson; *D:* John Ford. **VHS, Beta** $19.95 MGM ♟♟♟½

They Were So Young European models become the pawns of wealthy Brazilian magnates when they are sent to South America. They are threatened with death if they do not cooperate. The scenes were shot in Italy and Berlin. Well acted and believable, although rather grim story.
1955 78m/B Scott Brady, Johanna Matz, Raymond Burr; *D:* Kurt Neumann. **VHS, Beta** NO ♟♟½

They Were Ten Ten Soviet Jews make Palestine their home in the 1800s despite Arab and Turkish persecution and pressures among themselves. In Hebrew with English subtitles.

1961 105m/B Ninette, Oded Teomi, Leo Filer, Yosef Safra; *D:* Baruch Dienar. **VHS, Beta** $79.95 ERG, FCT, ING ♟½

They Won't Believe Me A man plots to kill his wife, but before he does, she commits suicide. He ends up on trial for her "murder." Interesting acting by Young and Hayward against type. Surprising, ironic ending.
1947 95m/B Robert Young, Susan Hayward, Rita Johnson, Jane Greer; *D:* Irving Pichel. **VHS, Beta** $19.98 MED, TTC ♟♟♟

They Won't Forget When a young girl is murdered in a southern town, personal interests take precedence over justice. Turner is excellent in her first billed role, as are the other actors. Superb script, and expert direction by LeRoy pulls it all together. Based on Ward Greene's "Death in the Deep South."
1937 95m/B Claude Rains, Otto Kruger, Lana Turner, Allyn Joslyn, Elisha Cook Jr., Edward Norris; *D:* Mervyn LeRoy; *W:* Robert Rossen, Aben Kandel. **VHS** WAR, OM ♟♟♟½

They're Playing with Fire An English teacher seduces a student and gets him involved in a murder plot to gain an inheritance. Turns out someone else is beating them to the punch. Sleazy semi-pornographic slasher.
1984 (R) 96m/C Sybil Danning, Eric Brown, Andrew Prine, Paul Clemens, K.T. Stevens, Alvy Moore; *D:* Howard (Hikmet) Avedis. **VHS, Beta** $19.95 STE Woof!

The Thief An American commits treason and is overcome by guilt. Novel because there is not one word of dialogue, though the gimmick can't sustain the ordinary story. A product of the Communist scare of the 1950s, it tends to be pretentious and melodramatic.
1952 84m/C Ray Milland, Rita Gam, Martin Gabel, Harry Bronson, John McKutcheon; *D:* Russel Rouse. **VHS, Beta** $19.95 VCI ♟♟

Thief A successful businessman (Crenna) attempts to put his criminal past behind him. He's trapped when looking for a quick way to get some money to pay off a gambling debt. Made for television drama that's well-written and directed with tepid acting.
1971 74m/C Richard Crenna, Angie Dickinson, Cameron Mitchell, Hurd Hatfield, Robert Webber; *D:* William A. Graham. **VHS, Beta** $59.95 LHV ♟♟

Thief A big-time professional thief likes working solo, but decides to sign up with the mob in order to make one more big score and retire. He finds out it's not that easy. Taut and atmospheric thriller is director Mann's feature film debut. *AKA:* Violent Streets.
1981 (R) 126m/C James Caan, Tuesday Weld, Willie Nelson, James Belushi, Elizabeth Pena, Robert Prosky; *D:* Michael Mann; *W:* Michael Mann. **VHS, Beta** $19.95 MGM, FOX ♟♟♟

The Thief of Baghdad The classic silent crowd-pleaser, about a roguish thief who uses a genie's magic to outwit Baghdad's evil Caliph. With famous special effects in a newly struck print, and a new score by Davis based on Rimsky-Korsakov's "Scheherezade." Remade many times.
1924 153m/B Douglas Fairbanks Sr., Snitz Edwards, Charles Belcher, Anna May Wong, Etta Lee, Brandon Hurst, Sojin, Julanne Johnston; *D:* Raoul Walsh; *M:* Carl Davis. **VHS, Beta** $19.98 HBO, SNC, NOS ♟♟♟

Thief of Baghdad A wily young thief enlists the aid of a powerful genie to outwit the Grand Vizier of Baghdad. An Arabian Nights spectacular with lush photography, fine special effects, and striking score. Out-

standing performance by Ingram as the genie.
1940 106m/C Sabu, Conrad Veidt, June Duprez, Rex Ingram, Tim Whelan, Michael Powell; **D:** Ludwig Berger; **M:** Miklos Rozsa. **VHS, Beta** $14.98 *SUE, MLB, FUS 𝄞𝄞𝄞½*

Thief of Baghdad An Arabian Nights fantasy about a thief in love with a Sultan's daughter who has been poisoned. He seeks out the magical blue rose which is the antidote. Not as lavish as the previous two productions by this title, nor as much fun. **AKA:** Il Ladro Di Bagdad; Le Voleur De Bagdad.
1961 89m/C Georgia Moll, Steve Reeves; **D:** Arthur Lubin. **VHS, Beta** $59.98 *SUE 𝄞𝄞*

The Thief of Baghdad A fantasy-adventure about a genie, a prince, beautiful maidens, a happy-go-lucky thief, and magic. Easy to take, but not an extraordinary version of this oft-told tale. Ustinov is fun as he tries to marry off his daughter. Made for television.
1978 (G) 101m/C Peter Ustinov, Roddy McDowall, Terence Stamp, Frank Finlay, Ian Holm; **D:** Clive Donner. **VHS, Beta** $29.95 *GEM 𝄞𝄞½*

Thief of Hearts A thief steals a woman's diary when he's ransacking her house. He then pursues the woman, using his secret knowledge. Slick, but too creepy. Re-edited with soft porn scenes in some video versions. Stewart's first film.
1984 (R) 101m/C Steven Bauer, Barbara Williams, John Getz, Christine Ebersole, George Wendt; **D:** Douglas Day Stewart; **M:** Harold Faltermeyer. **VHS, Beta** $14.95 *PAR 𝄞𝄞*

The Thief Who Came to Dinner A computer analyst and a wealthy socialite team up to become jewel thieves and turn the tables on Houston's high society set. Comedy plot gets complex, though O'Neal and Bissett are likeable. Early Clayburgh role as O'Neal's ex. Based on a novel by Terence Lore Smith.
1973 (PG) 103m/C Ryan O'Neal, Jacqueline Bisset, Warren Oates, Jill Clayburgh, Ned Beatty, Gregory Sierra, Michael Murphy, Austin Pendleton, John Hillerman, Charles Cioffi; **D:** Bud Yorkin; **W:** Walter Hill; **M:** Henry Mancini. **VHS, Beta** $19.98 *WAR 𝄞𝄞*

Thieves Like Us Story of doomed lovers during the Depression is thoughtfully told by Altman. Older criminals Remsen and Schuck escape from jail with young killer Carradine. They only know one way to make a living—robbing banks—and it isn't long before they're once more working at their trade. They get a lot of press but they have a distinct problem. They're not really very good at what they do. Cops on their trail, the gang tries, unsuccessfully, to survive. Fletcher's film debut as Remsen's sister-in-law. Good period atmosphere and strong characters. Based on the novel by Edward Anderson and previously filmed as "They Live by Night."
1974 (R) 123m/C Keith Carradine, Shelley Duvall, Bert Remsen, John Schuck, Louise Fletcher, Anne Latham, Tom Skerritt; **D:** Robert Altman; **W:** Joan Tewkesbury, Calder Willingham, Robert Altman. **VHS** $19.98 *MGM 𝄞𝄞𝄞½*

Thieves of Fortune Former Miss Universe stars as a contestant in a high stakes fortune hunt that spans half the globe. She meets with more than her share of action-packed encounters among the ruffians who compete for the $28 million purse. Implausible; horrible script; cliched.
1989 (R) 100m/C Michael Nouri, Lee Van Cleef, Shawn Weatherly. **VHS, Beta** $29.95 *ACA Woof!*

The Thin Blue Line The acclaimed docudrama about the 1977 shooting of a cop in Dallas County, and the incorrect conviction of Randall Adams for the crime. A riveting, spellbinding experience. Due to the film's impact and continued lobbying by Morris, Adams is now free.
1988 101m/C D: Errol Morris; **M:** Philip Glass. **VHS, Beta** $19.95 *HBO, CCB 𝄞𝄞𝄞½*

Thin Ice Successful musical romance featuring European prince Power falling for commoner Henie. A fine score, solid script, and Henie's excellent ice skating routines make this her best film. Based on the play "Der Komet" by Attila Obok. 𝄞I'm Olga from the Volga; My Swiss Hillbilly; My Secret Love Affair; Over Night.
1937 78m/B Sonja Henie, Tyrone Power, Arthur Treacher, Raymond Walburn, Joan Davis, Alan Hale, Sig Rumann, Melville Cooper, Maurice Cass, George Givot, Torben Meyer; **D:** Sidney Lanfield; **W:** Boris Ingster, Milton Sperling. **VHS** $19.98 *FXV 𝄞𝄞𝄞*

The Thin Man Married sleuths Nick and Nora Charles investigate the mysterious disappearance of a wealthy inventor. Charming and sophisticated, this was the model for all husband-and-wife detective teams that followed. Don't miss Asta, their wire-hair terrier. Based on the novel by Dashiell Hammett. Its enormous popularity triggered five sequels, starting with "After the Thin Man."
1934 90m/B William Powell, Myrna Loy, Maureen O'Sullivan, Cesar Romero, Porter Hall, Nat Pendleton, Minna Gombell, Natalie Moorhead, Edward Ellis; **D:** Woodbridge S. Van Dyke. **VHS, Beta** $19.95 *MGM, HMV 𝄞𝄞𝄞½*

The Thin Man Goes Home Married sleuths Nick and Nora Charles solve a mystery with Nick's disapproving parents looking on in the fifth film from the "Thin Man" series. Despite a three-year gap and slightly less chemistry between Powell and Loy, audiences welcomed the skinny guy. Sequel to "Shadow of the Thin Man;" followed by "Song of the Thin Man."
1944 100m/B William Powell, Myrna Loy, Lucile Watson, Gloria De Haven, Anne Revere, Harry Davenport, Helen Vinson, Lloyd Corrigan, Donald Meek, Edward Brophy, Charles Halton; **D:** Richard Thorpe. **VHS, Beta** $19.98 *MGM 𝄞𝄞½*

The Thing One of the best of the Cold War allegories and a potent lesson to those who won't eat their vegetables. Sci fi classic about an alien craft and creature (Arness in monster drag), discovered by an Arctic research team. The critter is accidentally thawed and then wreaks havoc, sucking the blood from sled dog and scientist alike. It's a giant seed-dispersing vegetable run amuck, unaffected by missing body parts, bullets, or cold. In other words, Big Trouble. Excellent direction, assisted substantially by producer Hawks, and supported by strong performances. Available colorized; remade in 1982. Loosely based on "Who Goes There?" by John Campbell. **AKA:** The Thing From Another World.
1951 87m/B James Arness, Kenneth Tobey, Margaret Sheridan, Dewey Martin; **D:** Christian Nyby; **W:** Charles Lederer; **M:** Dimitri Tiomkin. **VHS, Beta** $14.98 *MED, TTC, MLB 𝄞𝄞𝄞½*

The Thing A team of scientists at a remote Antarctic outpost discover a buried spaceship with an unwelcome alien survivor still alive. Bombastic special effects overwhelm the suspense and the solid cast. Less a remake of the 1951 science fiction classic than a more faithful version of John Campbell's short story "Who Goes There?," since the seeds/spores take on human shapes.

1982 (R) 127m/C Kurt Russell, Wilford Brimley, T.K. Carter, Richard Masur, Keith David, Richard Dysart, David Clennon, Donald Moffatt, Thomas G. Waites, Charles Hallahan; **D:** John Carpenter; **M:** Ennio Morricone. **VHS, Beta** $19.95 *MCA 𝄞𝄞½*

The Thing Called Love Take last year's surprise hit "Singles" and replace grunge rock and Seattle with Country/Western and Nashville for this unsentimental tale of four twentysomething singles trying to make their mark in the world of country music. The idea for the plot comes from the real-life Bluebird Cafe—the place where all aspiring singers and songwriters want to perform. Phoenix, Mathis, Mulroney, and Bullock did their own singing; look for Oslin as the Cafe owner. Phoenix's last completed film role.
1993 (PG-13) 116m/C River Phoenix, Samantha Mathis, Sandra Bullock, Dermot Mulroney, K.T. Oslin, Anthony Clark, Webb Wilder; **Cameos:** Trisha Yearwood; **D:** Peter Bogdanovich; **W:** Allan Moyle, Carol Heikkinen. **VHS, Beta** *PAR 𝄞𝄞½*

Things A man creates a monster during his freakish experiments with artificial insemination. The monster returns to his house seeking revenge, and the man's visiting brother and a friend disappear, probably a clever move given their lackluster circumstances.
198? 90m/C Barry Gillis, Amber Lynn, Doug Bunston, Bruce Roach; **D:** Andrew Jordan. **VHS, Beta** *NO 𝄞*

Things Change An old Italian shoeshine guy agrees, for a fee, to be a fall guy for the Mafia. A lower-echelon mob hood, assigned to watch over him, decides to give the old guy a weekend of fun in Vegas before going to jail. Director Mamet co-wrote the screenplay with Silverstein, best-known for his children's books ("Where the Sidewalk Ends," "The Giving Tree"). Combines charm and menace with terrific performances, especially from Ameche and Mantegna.
1988 (PG) 114m/C Joe Mantegna, Don Ameche, Robert Prosky, J.J. Johnston, Ricky Jay, Mike Nussbaum, Jack Wallace, Dan Conway, J.T. Walsh; **D:** David Mamet; **W:** Shel Silverstein, David Mamet; **M:** Alaric Jans. **VHS, Beta** $14.95 *COL 𝄞𝄞𝄞*

Things Happen at Night Scientist and insurance investigator determine that friendly ghost has possessed a family's youngest daughter. Not much happens.
1948 79m/B Gordon Harker, Alfred Drayton, Robertson Hare, Olga Lindo, Wylie Watson; **D:** Francis Searle. **VHS, Beta** $16.95 *NOS, SNC 𝄞*

Things in Their Season Made for TV melodrama about the imminent death of the mother of a Wisconsin farm family who makes those around her realize the value of happiness. Neal is excellent, rest of cast better than average in a well-told and sincere film.
1974 79m/C Patricia Neal, Ed Flanders, Marc Singer, Meg Foster; **D:** James Goldstone. **VHS, Beta** *LCA 𝄞𝄞½*

The Things of Life A car crash makes a man re-evaluate his life, goals, and loves. In the end he must choose the course of his future and decide between his wife and mistress. In French with English subtitles. **AKA:** Les Choses De La Vie.
1970 90m/C Romy Schneider, Michel Piccoli, Lea Massari; **D:** Claude Sautet. **VHS, Beta** $79.95 *CVC, ING 𝄞𝄞𝄞*

Things to Come Using technology, scientists aim to rebuild the world after a lengthy war, followed by a plague and other unfortunate events. Massey and Scott each

play two roles, in different generations. Startling picture of the world to come, with fine sets and good acting. Based on an H.G. Wells story, "The Shape of Things to Come."
1936 92m/B Raymond Massey, Ralph Richardson, Cedric Hardwicke, Derrick DeMarney; **D:** William Cameron Menzies. **VHS, Beta $19.95** NOS, PSM, SNC *ℐℐℐ*½

Think Big Former professional wrestlers, the Pauls are truck drivers in this silly, enjoyable comedy. They pick up a brilliant teenager running from bad guys. Mayhem ensues.
1990 (PG-13) 86m/C Peter Paul, David Paul, Martin Mull, Ari Meyers, Richard Kiel, David Carradine, Richard Moll, Peter Lupus; **W:** Jim Wynorski, R.J. Robertson. **VHS, Beta $89.98** LIV, VTR *ℐℐ*½

Think Dirty Lascivious comedy about advertising executive Feldman's attempt to develop a series of sexy commercials to sell cereal. At the same time his wife forms a "clean up television" group. Not very interesting or funny. **AKA:** Every Home Should Have One.
1970 (R) 93m/C Marty Feldman, Judy Cornwell, Shelley Berman; **D:** Jim Clark. **VHS, Beta $59.95** COL *ℐℐ*

Thinkin' Big Guys and gals cavort on the Texas coast, except for one lonely fat guy who tries to increase his sexual prowess. The usual teen sex frenzy.
1987 (R) 96m/C Bruce Anderson, Kenny Sargent, Randy Jandt, Nancy Buechler, Darla Ralston; **D:** S.F. Brownrigg. **VHS, Beta $9.99** STE, PSM *ℐ*

Third Degree Burn A made-for-cable-television mystery about a small-time detective hired by a businessman to follow a woman, only to become a suspect when the woman's real husband is killed.
1989 97m/C Treat Williams, Virginia Madsen, Richard Masur; **D:** Roger Spottiswoode. **VHS, Beta $14.95** PAR *ℐℐ*

The Third Key A solid British crime drama follows a dogged detective as he probes serial safe-crackings, with a climax set in London's Festival Hall. Based on the book by Robert Barr, who co-scripted. **AKA:** The Long Arm.
1957 96m/B Jack Hawkins, Dorothy Allison, Geoffrey Keen, Richard Leech, Ian Bannen; **D:** Charles Frend. **VHS $19.95** NOS *ℐℐ*½

The Third Man An American writer of pulp westerns (Cotten) arrives in post-war Vienna to take a job with an old friend, but discovers he has been murdered. Or has he? Based on Graham Greene's mystery, this classic film noir thriller plays on national loyalties during the Cold War. Welles is top-notch as the manipulative Harry Lime, black-market drugdealer extraordinare. The underground sewer sequence is not to be missed. With a haunting (sometimes irritating) theme by Anton Karas on unaccompanied zither. Special edition features trailer.
1949 104m/B Joseph Cotten, Orson Welles, Alida Valli, Trevor Howard, Bernard Lee, Wilfrid Hyde-White; **D:** Carol Reed; **W:** Graham Greene. Academy Awards '50: Best Black and White Cinematography; Nominations: Best Director (Reed), Best Film Editing; British Academy Awards '49: Best Film; Cannes Film Festival '49: Best Film; Directors Guild of America Awards '49: Best Director (Reed); National Board of Review Awards '50: 5 Best Foreign Films of the Year. **VHS, Beta, 8mm $16.95** SNC, REP, MED *ℐℐℐℐ*

Third Man on the Mountain A family epic about mountain climbing, shot in Switzerland and based on James Ramsey Ullman's "Banner in the Sky." A young man is determined to climb the "Citadel" as his ancestors have. He finds there's more to climbing than he imagined. Look for Helen Hayes (MacArthur's mother) in a cameo. Standard Disney adventure drama. **AKA:** Banner in the Sky.
1959 (G) 106m/C James MacArthur, Michael Rennie, Janet Munro, James Donald, Herbert Lom, Laurence Naismith; **Cameos:** Helen Hayes; **D:** Ken Annakin. **VHS, Beta $69.95** DIS *ℐℐ*½

The Third Sex One of the first films to deal with homosexuality in which parents try to "straighten out" their gay son.
1959 ?m/C Paul Dahlke, Paula Wesley. **VHS $16.95** SNC *ℐ*

Third Solution An Italian-made film about the discovery of a secret pact made between the Kremlin and the Vatican that may start WWIII. Well-cast, but poorly conceived spook drama, with music by Vangelis. **AKA:** Russicum.
1989 (R) 93m/C Treat Williams, F. Murray Abraham, Danny Aiello, Nigel Court, Rita Rusic, Rossano Brazzi; **D:** Pasquale Squitieri; **M:** Vangelis. **VHS, Beta $79.95** COL *ℐℐ*

Third Walker A desperate woman sacrifices her marriage to immerse herself in efforts to reunite her twin sons, who were inadvertently separated at birth. An original and intriguing directorial debut by McLuhan.
1979 85m/C William Shatner, Colleen Dewhurst; **D:** Marshall McLuhan. **VHS, Beta NO** *ℐℐℐ*

Thirst A girl is abducted by a secret society that wants her to become their new leader. There is just one catch: she has to learn to like the taste of human blood. Chilling but weakly plotted.
1987 (R) 96m/C David Hemmings, Henry Silva, Chantal Contouri; **D:** Rod Hardy. **VHS, Beta $79.95** MED *ℐℐ*

The Thirsty Dead Maybe they could learn to like Gatorade. An eternally young jungle king is looking for a wife. She can be young forever too, if she's not above vampirism and sacrificing virgins. In spite of the jungle vampire slant, this Filipino-made movie is a woofer. Also released on video, as "Blood Hunt." **AKA:** The Blood Cult of Shangri-La.
1974 (PG) 90m/C John Considine, Jennifer Billingsley, Judith McConnell, Fredricka Meyers, Tani Phelps Guthrie; **D:** Terry Becker. **VHS, Beta NO** *Woof!*

13 Ghosts A dozen ghosts need another member to round out their ranks. They have four likely candidates to choose from when a family moves into the house inhabited by the ghoulish group. Originally viewed with "Illusion-O," a technology much like 3-D, which allowed the viewing of the ghosts only through a special pair of glasses.
1960 88m/C Charles Herbert, Jo Morrow, Martin Milner, Rosemary DeCamp, Donald Woods, Margaret Hamilton; **D:** William Castle. **VHS, Beta $9.95** GKK *ℐℐ*½

13 Rue Madeleine Cagney plays a WWII spy who infiltrates Gestapo headquarters in Paris in order to find the location of a German missile site. Actual OSS footage is used in this fast-paced early postwar espionage propaganda piece. Rex Harrison rejected the part taken by Cagney.
1946 95m/B James Cagney, Annabella, Richard Conte, Frank Latimore, Walter Abel, Sam Jaffe, Melville Cooper, E.G. Marshall, Karl Malden, Red Buttons; **D:** Henry Hathaway. **VHS, Beta $19.98** FOX, FCT *ℐℐℐ*

Thirteenth Day of Christmas A made-for-British-television yarn about a psychotic boy left alone by his parents on Christmas night.
1985 60m/C Patrick Allen, Elizabeth Spiggs. **VHS, Beta $59.95** PSM *ℐℐℐ*

The 13th Floor A young girl fuses with the spirit of a young boy her father ruthlessly killed years before, and together they wreak havoc.
1988 (R) 86m/C Lisa Hensley, Tim McKenzie, Miranda Otto; **D:** Chris Roach. **VHS, Beta $19.95** PAR *ℐ*½

13th Guest Two people try to solve a murder that occurred at a dinner party. An incredibly creaky early talkie melodrama that created some of the cliches of the genre. **AKA:** Lady Beware.
1932 70m/B Ginger Rogers, Lyle Talbot, J. Farrell MacDonald, Paul Hurst; **D:** Albert Ray. **VHS, Beta $12.95** SNC, NOS, VYY *ℐℐ*

The Thirteenth Man When a journalist investigating the murder of a district attorney is also killed, the paper's gossip columnist takes the case. Entertaining, fast-paced mystery.
1937 70m/B Weldon Heyburn, Inez Courtney, Selmer Jackson, Milburn Stone, Matty Fain; **D:** William Nigh. **VHS, Beta $16.95** NOS, SNC, MLB *ℐℐ*½

The 13th Mission A low-budget overseas combat adventure, no better than the first twelve.
1991 95m/C Robert Marius, Jeff Griffith, Michael Monty, David Morisson, Paul Home, John Falch, Albert Bronski, Chantal Manz; **D:** Antonio Perez. **VHS** VTR, KBE *ℐ*½

Thirteenth Reunion A newspaperwoman uncovers a bizarre secret society when she does a routine story on a health spa.
1981 60m/C Julia Foster, Dinah Sheridan, Richard Pearson; **D:** Peter Sasdy. **VHS, Beta $29.95** LIV *ℐ*

30-Foot Bride of Candy Rock A junk dealer invents a robot, catapults into space and causes his girlfriend to grow to 30 feet in height. Lightweight, whimsical fantasy was Costello's only solo starring film, and his last before his untimely death.
1959 73m/B Lou Costello, Dorothy Provine, Gale Gordon; **D:** Sidney Miller. **VHS, Beta $9.95** GKK *ℐ*

30 Is a Dangerous Age, Cynthia Dudley Moore stars as a nightclub pianist who spends a lot of his time daydreaming about being rich, famous and married to a beautiful woman. Moore determines to attain all these dreams before his thirtieth birthday, which is only six weeks away.
1968 85m/C Dudley Moore, Suzy Kendall, Eddie Foy Jr.; **D:** Joseph McGrath; **W:** Dudley Moore; **M:** Dudley Moore. **VHS, Beta NO** *ℐℐ*½

The Thirty-Nine Steps Hitchcock remake is a visually interesting, but mostly uninvolving, mystery. Powell is the man suspected of stealing plans to begin WWI. Above average, but not by much.
1979 98m/C Robert Powell, David Warner, Eric Porter, Karen Dotrice, John Mills, Andrew Keir; **D:** Don Sharp. **VHS, Beta $14.95** MED, VYY, CNG *ℐℐ*½

Thirty Seconds Over Tokyo Dated but still interesting classic wartime flagwaver details the conception and execution of the first bombing raids on Tokyo by Lt. Col. James Doolittle and his men. Look for Blake Edwards, as well as Steve Brodie in his first screen appearance. Based on a true story.

1944 138m/B Spencer Tracy, Van Johnson, Robert Walker, Robert Mitchum, Phyllis Thaxter, Scott McKay, Stephen McNally, Louis Jean Heydt, Leon Ames, Paul Langton; **D:** Mervyn LeRoy; **W:** Dalton Trumbo. Academy Awards '44: Best Special Effects; Nominations: Best Black and White Cinematography. **VHS, Beta** $19.98 *MGM, FCT, TLF* ♫♫♫

32 Short Films About Glenn Gould
Perceptive docudrama about the iconoclastic Canadian classical pianist who secluded himself in the studio, forsaking live performances for much of his career. A combination of dramatic recreation, archival material, and interviews depict the biographical details of the driven artist who died at the age of 50. Feore is memorable in the title role, especially since he's never actually shown playing the piano. Title and film structure refer to Bach's "Goldberg" Variations, a recording which made Gould's reputation.
1993 93m/C Colm Feore, Gale Garnett, David Hughes; **D:** Francois Girard; **W:** Don McKellar, Francois Girard. **VHS** *NYR* ♫♫♫

36 Fillete
Lili, an intellectually precocious 14-year old French girl who's literally bursting out of her children's dress size 36 fillete, discovers her sexuality. So while on vacation with her family she becomes determined to see if she can seduce a middle-aged playboy. In French with English subtitles.
1988 88m/C Delphine Zentout, Etienne Chicot, Oliver Parniere, Jean-Pierre Leaud; **D:** Catherine Breillat. **VHS** $79.95 *FXL, ING* ♫♫♫

Thirty-Six Hours of Hell
A troop of Marines battle Japanese forces in the South Pacific during WWII. Dubbed.
1977 95m/C Richard Harrison, Pamela Tudor; **D:** Roberto Marrtero. **VHS, Beta** $59.95 *UNI* ♫½

'38: Vienna Before the Fall
Wartime Vienna explodes with love and politics. Academy Award Nominee for best foreign language film. In German with English subtitles.
1988 97m/C Tobias Engel, Sunnyi Melles; **D:** Wolfgang Gluck. **VHS** $34.95 *LUM* ♫♫½

The 39 Steps
The classic Hitchcock mistaken-man-caught-in-intrigue thriller, featuring some of his most often copied set-pieces and the surest visual flair of his pre-war British period. The laserdisc version includes a twenty-minute documentary tracing the director's British period. Remade twice, in 1959 and 1979.
1935 81m/B Robert Donat, Madeleine Carroll, Godfrey Tearle, Lucie Mannheim, Peggy Ashcroft, John Laurie, Wylie Watson; **D:** Alfred Hitchcock; **W:** Charles Bennett, Alma Reville; **M:** Louis Levy. **VHS, Beta, 8mm** $8.95 *CNG, NOS, SUE* ♫♫♫♫

This Boy's Life
Carolyn and her teenage son are in search of a new life, far from her abusive ex-boyfriend. In the town of Concrete, just outside Seattle, she meets ex-military man Dwight (De Niro), a slick but none too suave mechanic who might be the answer to her dreams, but then again, he might not. Nicely crafted performances from all, but keep your eye on DiCaprio (great in his first major role) as the confused and abused teen divided between dreams of prep school and the allure of the going-nowhere crowd. Based on the memoirs of Tobias Wolff; director Caton-Jones sensitively illustrates the skewed understanding of masculinity in the 1950s. Vintage soundtrack takes you back.
1993 (R) 115m/C Robert De Niro, Ellen Barkin, Leonardo DiCaprio, Jonah Blechman, Eliza Dushku, Chris Cooper, Carla Gugino, Zachary Ansley, Tracey Ellis, Kathy Kinney, Gerrit Graham; **D:** Michael Caton-Jones; **W:** Robert

Getchell; **M:** Carter Burwell. **VHS, Beta** $95.99 *WAR, FCT, BTV* ♫♫♫

This Could Be the Night
Rocco and Tony are two small-fry gangsters who run a nightclub. Anne is a prim schoolteacher who takes a part-time job as their secretary. She falls for the handsome Tony much to the dismay of Rocco who knows his partner's less-than-sterling character. Sweet but minor comedy. Franciosa's first film. ♫This Could Be The Night; Hustlin' News Gal; I Got It Bad; I'm Gonna Live Till I Die; Taking a Chance on Love; Trumpet Boogie; Mamba Combo; Blue Moon; Dream Dancing.
1957 105m/B Jean Simmons, Paul Douglas, Anthony (Tony) Franciosa, Joan Blondell, Julie Wilson, Neile Adams, J. Carroll Naish, Rafael Campos, ZaSu Pitts, Tom Helmore; **D:** Robert Wise. **VHS** $19.98 *MGM, MOV* ♫♫½

This Gun for Hire
In his first major film role, Ladd plays a hired gun seeking retribution from a client who betrays him. Preston is the cop pursuing him and hostage Lake. Ladd's performance as the cold-blooded killer with a soft spot for cats is stunning; his train-yard scene is an emotional powerhouse. Based on Graham Greene's novel "A Gun for Sale." Remade as "Short Cut to Hell." The first of several films using the Ladd-Lake team, but the only one in which Ladd played a villain.
1942 81m/B Alan Ladd, Veronica Lake, Robert Preston, Laird Cregar; **D:** Frank Tuttle; **W:** Albert Maltz, W.R. Burnett. **VHS, Beta** $14.98 *MCA, FCT* ♫♫♫½

This Gun for Hire
A professional assassin finds that he has been duped into killing a powerful political figure, whom he was told was a New Orleans mobster. Now on the run, he takes a nightclub performer hostage, unaware that she is the fiance of the FBI agent who is after him. All odds are against him, but the special relationship he forms with the woman may just be his ticket out. Adapted from novel by Graham Greene.
1990 (R) 89m/C Robert Wagner, Nancy Everhard, Frederic Lehne, John Harkins; **D:** Lou Antonio. **VHS** $14.95 *MCA* ♫♫

This Happy Breed
A celebrated film version of Noel Coward's classic play depicts the changing fortunes of a large family in England between the world wars. Happiness, hardships, triumph and tragedy mix a series of memorable episodes, including some of the most cherished moments in popular British cinema, though its appeal is universal. Narrated by Laurence Olivier.
1947 114m/C Robert Newton, Celia Johnson, John Mills, Kay Walsh, Stanley Holloway; **D:** David Lean; **W:** David Lean. **VHS** $39.95 *HMV, FCT* ♫♫♫½

This Happy Feeling
Reynolds is a young woman who is romantically attracted to both Jurgens, a sophisticated retired actor, and Saxon, a younger suitor who is Jurgens' neighbor. Good acting all around. Charming telling of old tale.
1958 83m/C Curt Jurgens, Debbie Reynolds, John Saxon, Alexis Smith, Mary Astor, Estelle Winwood; **D:** Blake Edwards; **W:** Blake Edwards. **VHS, Beta** $14.95 *BAR, FCT* ♫♫½

This is a Hijack
Gambler hijacks the plane carrying his wealthy boss to help pay his debts. What it lacks in suspense, it lacks in performance and direction as well.
1975 (PG) 90m/C Adam Roarke, Neville Brand, Jay Robinson, Lynn Borden, Dub Taylor. **VHS, Beta** *NO* ♫

This is Elvis
The life of Elvis, combining documentary footage with dramatizations of events in his life. Includes more than three dozen songs. Generally seen as an attempt

to cash in on the myth, but was well-received by his fans.
1981 (PG) 144m/C Elvis Presley; **D:** Malcolm Leo, Andrew Solt; **W:** Malcolm Leo, Andrew Solt. **VHS, Beta** $19.95 *MVD, WAR* ♫♫

This is My Life
The story of a working mother torn between her skyrocketing career as a stand-up comic and her two daughters. Kavner plays the divorced mom who is determined to chuck her cosmetic sales job for comic success. Her career starts to really take off; she hires an agent and makes appearances on talk shows. As offers pour in, she eventually realizes that her girls are suffering as a result of her success. Good performances highlight an otherwise average drama.
1992 (PG-13) 105m/C Julie Kavner, Samantha Mathis, Carrie Fisher, Dan Aykroyd, Gaby Hoffman; **D:** Nora Ephron; **W:** Nora Ephron, Delia Ephron. **VHS** $19.98 *FXV* ♫♫½

This is Not a Test
When news comes of an impending nuclear attack, a state trooper at a roadblock offers sanctuary to passing travellers. The effectiveness of the film's social commentary is hindered by its small budget.
1962 72m/B Seamon Glass, Mary Morlass, Thayer Roberts, Aubrey Martin; **D:** Frederic Gadette. **VHS, Beta** $16.95 *SNC* ♫♫

This is Spinal Tap
Pseudo-rockumentary about heavy-metal band Spinal Tap, profiling their career from "England's loudest band" to an entry in the "where are they now file." Hilarious satire, featuring music performed by Guest, McKean, Shearer, and others. Included are Spinal Tap's music video "Hell Hole," and an ad for their greatest hits album, "Heavy Metal Memories." Features great cameos, particularly David Letterman's Paul Schaefer as a record promoter and Billy Crystal as a surly mime. First feature for Reiner (Meathead on "All in the Family"). Followed by "The Return of Spinal Tap." **AKA:** Spinal Tap.
1984 (R) 82m/C Michael McKean, Christopher Guest, Harry Shearer, Tony Hendra, Bruno Kirby, Rob Reiner, June Chadwick, Howard Hesseman, Dana Carvey, Ed Begley Jr., Patrick Macnee, Anjelica Huston; **Cameos:** Billy Crystal, Paul Shaffer; **D:** Rob Reiner; **W:** Christopher Guest. **VHS, Beta, 8mm** $14.95 *MVD, SUE, NLC* ♫♫♫½

This is the Army
A robust tribute to the American soldier of WWII based on the hit play by Irving Berlin. Murphy, who later was a senator from California, played Reagan's father. ♫Your Country and My Country; My Sweetie; Poor Little Me, I'm on K.P.; We're On Our Way to France; What Does He Look Like?; This is the Army, Mr. Jones; I'm Gettin' Tired So I Can Sleep; Mandy; Ladies of the Chorus.
1943 105m/C George Murphy, Joan Leslie, Ronald Reagan, Alan Hale, Kate Smith, George Tobias, Irving Berlin, Joe Louis; **D:** Michael Curtiz. Academy Awards '43: Best Score; Nominations: Best Interior Decoration, Best Sound. **VHS, Beta** $19.95 *NOS, DVT, CAB* ♫♫½

This Island Earth
The planet Metaluna is in desperate need of uranium to power its defense against enemy invaders. A nuclear scientist and a nuclear fission expert from Earth are kidnapped to help out. The first serious movie about interplanetary escapades. Bud Westmore created pulsating cranium special effects make-up.
1955 86m/C Jeff Morrow, Faith Domergue, Rex Reason, Russell Johnson; **D:** Joseph M. Newman; **M:** Henry Mancini. **VHS, Beta** $14.98 *MCA, MLB* ♫♫½

This Land is Mine A timid French schoolteacher gathers enough courage to defy the Nazis when they attempt to occupy his town. Laughton's characterization is effective as the meek fellow who discovers the hero within himself in this patriotic wartime flick.
1943 103m/B Charles Laughton, Maureen O'Hara, George Sanders, Walter Slezak, George Coulouris, Una O'Connor; **D:** Jean Renoir. **VHS, Beta** $19.98 *RKO, TTC* 🎬🎬🎬

This Lightning Always Strikes Twice An elegant murder mystery made for British television.
1985 60m/C Claire Bloom, Trevor Howard, Charles Dance. **VHS, Beta** $59.95 *PSM* 🎬🎬🎬

This Man Must Die A man searches relentlessly for the driver who killed his young son in a hit-and-run. When found, the driver engages him in a complex cat-and-mouse chase. Another stunning crime and punishment tale from Chabrol. **AKA:** Que La Bete Meure; Uccidero Un Uomo.
1970 (PG) 112m/C Michael Duchaussoy, Caroline Cellier, Jean Yanne; **D:** Claude Chabrol. **VHS, Beta** $59.95 *FOX* 🎬🎬🎬½

This Nude World A campy "expose" of the secret world of nudist colonies, including a look at volleyball players in Camp Olympia, New York.
1932 55m/B **VHS, Beta** $24.95 *NOS, VDM, MLB* 🎬🎬

This Property is Condemned It's a hot time down south once again in this adaptation of the Tennessee Williams play. Wood is the overly-flirtatious southern charmer who takes a shine to the latest tenant of her loathsome mama's boardinghouse. And since it's Redford, who can blame her. Things steam up when he returns her interest but there's trouble a'brewin'. Both leads are lovely but the film itself is overly southern-fried. Williams was reportedly unhappy with the script and wanted his name removed from the film.
1966 109m/C Robert Redford, Natalie Wood, Charles Bronson, Kate Reid, Mary Badham, Jon Provost, Robert (Bobby) Blake, John Harding; **D:** Sydney Pollack; **W:** Francis Ford Coppola, Edith Sommer, Fred Coe. **VHS, Beta** $19.95 *PAR* 🎬🎬

This Special Friendship Powerful, if overdone French drama about an emotionally sensitive young man at a Catholic boarding school. His sexual relationship with another boy leads to tragedy. Based on the novel by Roger Peyrefitte. **AKA:** Les Amities Particulieres.
1967 99m/B Francis Lacombrade, Didier Haudepin, Lucien Nat, Louis Seigner, Michel Bouquet, Francois Leccia; **D:** Jean Delannoy. **VHS, Beta** *FCT* 🎬🎬½

This Sporting Life A gritty, depressing portrait of a former coal miner who breaks into the violent world of professional rugby, and whose inability to handle social differences causes problems. He begins an affair with the widow from whom he rents a room but finds they are capable of only a physical attachment. One of the best of the British early '60s working-class angry young man melodramas.
1963 134m/B Richard Harris, Rachel Roberts, Alan Badel, William Hartnell, Colin Blakely, Vanda Godsell, Arthur Lowe; **D:** Lindsay Anderson; **W:** David Storey. Academy Awards '63 Nominations: Best Actor (Harris), Best Actress (Roberts); British Academy Awards '63: Best Actress (Roberts); Cannes Film Festival '63: Best Actor (Harris); National Board of Review Awards '63: 10 Best Films of the Year. **VHS, Beta** $19.95 *PAR* 🎬🎬🎬

This Stuff'll Kill Ya! A backwoods preacher who believes in free love and moonshining runs into trouble with the locals when a series of gruesome religious murders are committed. Southern drive-in material from one of the genre's masters. Holt's last film.
1971 (PG) 100m/C Jeffrey Allen, Tim Holt, Gloria King, Ray Sager, Eric Bradly, Terence McCarthy; **D:** Herschell Gordon Lewis; **W:** Herschell Gordon Lewis. **VHS** $29.95 *TWE, FRG, TPV* Woof!

This Sweet Sickness Destructive passion and sexual delusion is explored in this adaptation of the Patricia Highsmith novel. David seems to be a hardworking loner who is loved by the sweet Juliette. Rejected by him, Juliette then discovers that David has built a remote mountain chalet for the woman he does love, Lise, who's married and unaware of David's obsessional devotions. Extravagant emotions lead to tragedy. In French with English subtitles. **AKA:** Dites-Lui Que Je L'Aime.
1977 107m/C Gerard Depardieu, Miou-Miou, Dominique Laffin, Claude Pieplu, Christian Clavier; **D:** Claude Miller; **W:** Luc Beraud, Claude Miller. **VHS** $79.95 *WAC, FCT* 🎬🎬🎬

This Time I'll Make You Rich Two American hoodlums work out a drug-ring heist in the Far East.
1975 (PG) 97m/C Tony Sabato, Robin McDavid; **D:** Frank Kramer. **VHS, Beta** $59.98 *NLC* 🎬

Thomas Crown Affair A multi-millionaire (McQueen) decides to plot and execute the perfect theft, a daring daylight robbery of a bank. Dunaway is the gorgeous and efficient insurance investigator determined to nab him. One of the best visual scenes is the chess match between the two as they begin to fall in love. Strong production with Oscar-winning theme "Windmills of Your Mind." **AKA:** Thomas Crown and Company; The Crown Caper.
1968 (R) 102m/C Steve McQueen, Faye Dunaway, Jack Weston, Yaphet Kotto; **D:** Norman Jewison; **W:** Alan R. Trustman. **VHS, Beta** $19.98 *MGM, FCT, FOX* 🎬🎬🎬

Thomas Graal's Best Film The famous comical adventures of a film scriptwriter wooing his secretary, followed by "Thomas Graal's First Child." Silent.
1917 70m/B Victor Sjostrom, Karin Molander; **D:** Mauritz Stiller. **VHS, Beta** $49.95 *FCT, GPV* 🎬🎬🎬

Thomas Graal's First Child The sequel to "Thomas Graal's Best Film." The comical screenwriter and actress couple attempt to raise a baby. Silent.
1918 70m/B Victor Sjostrom, Karin Molander; **D:** Mauritz Stiller. **VHS, Beta** $49.95 *FCT* 🎬🎬🎬

Thompson's Last Run Boyhood friends grow up on either side of the law. They come face-to-face, though, when one is assigned to transport the other to prison. Made for television.
1990 95m/C Robert Mitchum, Wilford Brimley, Kathleen York, Susan Tyrrell; **D:** Jerrold Freedman; **M:** Miles Goodman. **VHS, Beta** *NO* 🎬🎬

Thor and the Amazon Women The mighty Thor leads his enslaved men on an attack against the evil Queen Nera and her female-dominated Amazon society.
1960 85m/C Joe Robinson, Susy Anderson. **VHS** $39.95 *AIP* 🎬

Thor el Conquistador The mighty Thor risks it all in a savage prehistoric land to avenge the slaying of his parents.
1986 90m/C Maria Romano, Malisa Lang, Ralf Falcone, Christopher Holm. **VHS, Beta** $59.95 *MED* 🎬

Thorn The Virgin Mary and Joseph try to raise Jesus Christ in the modern world.
1973 (R) 90m/C Bette Midler, John Bassberger. **VHS, Beta** *NO* 🎬🎬½

The Thorn Birds Pioneers find danger and romance in the Australian outback as they struggle to begin a dynasty. Charismatic priest sometimes hurts, sometimes helps them. One of Stanwyck's last performances; Ward's American television debut. Originally a ten-hour television epic based on Colleen McCullough novel. Emmy nominations for Actor Chamberlain, Supporting Actor(s) Brown and Plummer, Supporting Actress Laurie, direction, photography, music, costume design, and editing. On four cassettes.
1983 486m/C Rachel Ward, Richard Chamberlain, Jean Simmons, Ken Howard, Mare Winningham, Richard Kiley, Piper Laurie, Bryan Brown, Christopher Plummer, Barbara Stanwyck; **D:** Daryl Duke. **VHS, Beta** $199.92 *WAR, MOV, TVC* 🎬🎬🎬

Thoroughbreds Don't Cry Rooney plays a jockey who throws a race so his no-good father can win enough money to pay for his supposed medical problems. The owner of the horse then drops dead from a heart attack. Rooney feels guilty, so he asks his father to loan the owner's grandson $1,000 to run in another race. His father says no, so Rooney steals the money from him, and when the father finds out he tells the track officials that Rooney threw the race. Garland is Rooney's best friend and moral support, and she sings a few songs too! A fairly good horse racing story.
1937 80m/B Judy Garland, Mickey Rooney, Sophie Tucker, Sir C. Aubrey Smith, Ronald Sinclair, Forrester Harvey; **D:** Alfred E. Green. **VHS** $19.98 *MGM, MVD* 🎬🎬½

Thoroughly Modern Millie Andrews is a young woman who comes to New York in the early 1920s where she meets another newcomer, the innocent Moore. Andrews decides to upgrade her image to that of a "modern" woman, a flapper, and sets out to realize her ambition, to become a stenographer and marry the boss. Meanwhile, Moore has become an object of interest to Lillie, who just happens to run a white-slavery ring. Lots of frantic moments and big production numbers in this campy film. Channing and Lillie are exceptional fun. ♫Thoroughly Modern Millie; The Tapioca; Jimmy; The Jewish Wedding Song; Baby Face; Do It Again; Poor Butterfly; Rose of Washington Square; I Can't Believe That You're In Love With Me.
1967 (G) 138m/C Julie Andrews, Carol Channing, Mary Tyler Moore, John Gavin, Beatrice Lillie, James Fox, Noriyuki "Pat" Morita; **D:** George Roy Hill; **M:** Elmer Bernstein. Academy Awards '67: Best Original Score; Nominations: Best Art Direction/Set Decoration, Best Costume Design, Best Song ("Thoroughly Modern Millie"), Best Supporting Actress (Channing), Best Original Score; Golden Globe Awards '68: Best Supporting Actress (Channing). **VHS, Beta** $19.95 *MCA* 🎬🎬½

Those Calloways A small town family attempts to establish a sanctuary for the flocks of wild geese who fly over the woods of Swiftwater, Maine. Fine Disney family fare, with good cast. Based on Paul Annixter's novel "Swiftwater."
1965 (PG) 131m/C Brian Keith, Vera Miles, Brandon de Wilde, Walter Brennan, Ed Wynn, Joan Qualen, Linda Evans; **D:** Norman Tokar. **VHS, Beta** $69.95 *DIS* 🎬🎬

Those Daring Young Men in Their Jaunty Jalopies Daring young men in noisy slow cars trek 1500 miles across country in the 1920s and call it a race. **AKA:** Monte Carlo or Bust; Quei Temerari

Sulle Loro Pazze, Scatenate, Scalcinate Carriole.
1969 (G) 125m/C Tony Curtis, Susan Hampshire, Terry-Thomas, Eric Sykes, Gert Frobe, Peter Cook, Dudley Moore, Jack Hawkins; **D:** Ken Annakin. **VHS $39.95** PAR, FCT ♫♫

Those Endearing Young Charms Romance develops between a young Air Corps mechanic and a salesgirl. Complications arise when another man enters the scene. Light romantic comedy. Based on the play by Edward Chodorov.
1945 82m/B Robert Young, Laraine Day, Anne Jeffreys, Lawrence Tierney; **D:** Lewis Allen. **VHS, Beta** CCB ♫♫

Those Fantastic Flying Fools A mad race to be the first on the moon brings hilarious results. Loosely based on a Jules Verne story. **AKA:** Blast-Off; Jules Verne's Rocket to the Moon.
1967 95m/C Burl Ives, Troy Donahue, Gert Frobe, Terry-Thomas, Hermione Gingold, Daliah Lavi, Lionel Jeffries; **D:** Don Sharp. **VHS** NO ♫♫½

Those Glory, Glory Days An English woman, secure in her position as an outstanding sports journalist, reminisces about the days when she and her friends idolized the boys on the soccer team. Nothing extraordinary, but nicely made.
1983 92m/C Zoe Nathenson, Liz Campion, Cathy Murphy; **D:** Philip Saville; **M:** Trevor Jones. **VHS, Beta $59.95** MGM ♫½

Those Lips, Those Eyes A pre-med student takes a job as a prop boy in a summer stock company and winds up falling in love with the company's lead dancer. Subplot about aging actor is more interesting, better played by Langella. O'Conner is appropriately lovely. Nicely made, charming sleeper of a film.
1980 (R) 106m/C Frank Langella, Tom Hulce, Glynnis O'Connor, Jerry Stiller, Kevin McCarthy; **D:** Michael Pressman. **VHS, Beta $59.95** MGM ♫½

Those Magnificent Men in Their Flying Machines In 1910, a wealthy British newspaper publisher is persuaded to sponsor an air race from London to Paris. Contestants come from all over the world and shenanigans, hijinks, double-crosses, and romance are found along the route. Skelton has fun in prologue, while Terry-Thomas is great as the villain. Fun from start to finish.
1965 138m/C Stuart Whitman, Sarah Miles, Robert Morley, Alberto Sordi, James Fox, Gert Frobe, Jean-Pierre Cassel, Flora Robson, Sam Wanamaker, Terry-Thomas, Irina Demick, Benny Hill, Gordon Jackson, Millicent Martin, Red Skelton; **D:** Ken Annakin. **VHS, Beta $14.98** FOX ♫♫♫

Thou Shalt Not Kill...Except A Vietnam vet seeks revenge on the violent cult who kidnapped his girlfriend.
1987 84m/C Brian Schulz, Robert Rickman, John Manfredi, Tim Quill, Cheryl Hansen, Sam Raimi. **VHS, Beta $9.99** PSM ♫

Thoughts are Free A young soldier, wounded in WWII, escapes from the train that is transporting him and his comrades to a Soviet labor camp and rejoins his family. Under the repressive communist regime, he plots his family's escape to the West but his plans are thwarted when the Berlin Wall is erected, leaving him in the West and his wife and daughter in the East. As the years go by, they can get together only by outwitting the bureaucrats. The film's title is taken from an old German folk song "Die Gedanken sind frei," sung here by Heino.

1984 (PG) 93m/C Herbert Ludwig, Kathrin Kratzer; **D:** Josef Sommer. **VHS, Beta** NO ♫♫♫½

A Thousand Clowns A nonconformist has resigned from his job as chief writer for an obnoxious kiddie show in order to enjoy life. But his independence comes under fire when he becomes guardian for his young nephew and social workers take a dim view of his lifestyle. Balsam won an Oscar for his role as Robard's agent brother. Adapted from Herb Gardner's Broadway comedy.
1965 118m/B Jason Robards Jr., Barry Gordon, William Daniels, Barbara Harris, Gene Saks, Martin Balsam; **D:** Fred Coe; **W:** Herb Gardner. Academy Awards '65: Best Supporting Actor (Balsam); Nominations: Best Adapted Screenplay, Best Picture, Best Original Score; National Board of Review Awards '65: 10 Best Films of the Year. **VHS, Beta $19.98** MGM, FOX, BTV ♫♫♫

The Thousand Eyes of Dr. Mabuse Lang's last film is a return to his pre-war German character, the evil Dr. Mabuse. A series of strange murders occur in a Berlin hotel and police believe the killer thinks he's a reincarnation of the doctor. Disorienting chiller. **AKA:** The Secret of Dr. Mabuse; The Diabolical Dr. Mabuse; The Shadow Versus the Thousand Eyes of Dr. Mabuse.
1960 103m/B Dawn Addams, Peter Van Eyck, Gert Frobe, Wolfgang Preiss; **D:** Fritz Lang. **VHS $39.95** FCT, GPV ♫♫½

A Thousand Heroes Based on the true story of United Airlines Flight 232 which took off on a flight from Denver to Chicago and then suffered engine explosions over Iowa. The jumbo jet crashed in a fiery explosion but some 200 people survived.
1994 (PG) 95m/C Richard Thomas, Charlton Heston, James Coburn. **VHS** NHO ♫♫½

Thousand Mile Escort Chinese peasants struggle to survive amid poverty and power-mad warlords. Dubbed.
19?? 86m/C Pak Ying. **VHS, Beta** NO ♫

Thousand Pieces of Gold A young Chinese woman is sold by her father to a marriage broker, but instead of a respectable marriage she is shipped to America and expected to work as a prostitute in an Idaho mining town. Instead she works taking in laundry as she tries to make her way in a man's world, finding a sweet romance of opposites along the way. Based on a true story. Excellent performances by Chao and Cooper.
1991 (PG-13) 105m/C Rosalind Chao, Dennis Dun, Michael Paul Chan, Chris Cooper, Jimmie F. Skaggs, William Oldham, David Hayward, Beth Broderick; **D:** Nancy Kelly; **W:** Anne Makepeace; **M:** Gary Remal Malkin. **VHS $9.95** HMD, ING ♫♫♫

Thousands Cheer A flag-waving wartime musical about a tap-dancing Army private who falls in love with the colonel's daughter, culminating with an all-star (MGM) USO show. Songs include "Honeysuckle Rose," sung by Horne, and "The Joint Is Really Jumping Down at Carnegie Hall," sung by Garland.
1943 126m/C Gene Kelly, Kathryn Grayson, Judy Garland, Mickey Rooney, Mary Astor, John Boles, Lucille Ball, Eleanor Powell, Virginia O'Brien, Margaret O'Brien, Red Skelton, Lionel Barrymore, June Allyson, Frank Morgan, Kay Kyser, Bob Crosby, Lena Horne, Donna Reed; **D:** George Sidney. **VHS, Beta $19.98** MGM ♫♫½

Thrashin' A new-to-L.A. teen must prove himself to a tough gang on skateboards by skateboarding a certain treacherous race. For skateboarding fans only.

1986 (PG-13) 93m/C Josh Brolin, Pamela Gidley, Robert Rusler, Chuck McCann; **D:** David Winters; **M:** Barry Goldberg. **VHS, Beta** NO ♫

Threads The famed dramatic recreation of the effects of nuclear war on a British city and two of its families. A disturbing, uncompromising, and somewhat plausible drama. Made for British television.
1985 110m/C Karen Meagher, Rita May, David Brierly, Reece Dinsdale, Harry Beety; **D:** Mick Jackson. **VHS, Beta** NO ♫♫♫

Threat A killer escapes from jail and returns to settle the score with those who convicted him. Tense, fast-moving thriller.
1949 66m/B Michael O'Shea, Virginia Grey, Charles McGraw; **D:** Felix Feist. **VHS, Beta $34.95** RKO ♫♫½

Three Ages A parody of D.W. Griffith's 1916 film "Intolerance." Keaton's first feature film casts him in prehistoric days, ancient Rome, and in modern times. Silent with musical score.
1923 59m/B Wallace Beery, Oliver Hardy, Buster Keaton; **D:** Buster Keaton, Eddie Cline. **VHS, Beta $19.95** NOS, VDM, DVT ♫♫♫

Three Amigos Three out-of-work silent screen stars are asked to defend a Mexican town from bandits; they think it's a public appearance stint. Spoof of Three Stooges and Mexican bandito movies that at times falls short, given the enormous amount of comedic talent involved. Generally enjoyable with some very funny scenes. Co-written by former "Saturday Night Live" producer Michaels. Short's first major film appearance.
1986 (PG) 105m/C Chevy Chase, Steve Martin, Martin Short, Joe Mantegna, Patrice Martinez, Jon Lovitz, Alfonso Arau, Randy Newman; **D:** John Landis; **W:** Steve Martin, Randy Newman, Lorne Michaels; **M:** Elmer Bernstein. **VHS, Beta $14.99** HBO ♫♫

Three Broadway Girls Three golddiggers go husband-hunting. Well-paced, very funny telling of this old story. Remade many times, including "How to Marry a Millionaire," "Three Blind Mice," "Moon Over Miami," and "Three Little Girls in Blue." **AKA:** The Greeks Had a Word for Them.
1932 78m/B Joan Blondell, Ina Claire, Madge Evans, David Manners, Lowell Sherman; **D:** Lowell Sherman. **VHS, Beta $19.95** NOS, CAB, BAR ♫♫♫

Three Brothers An acclaimed Italian film by veteran Rosi about three brothers summoned to their small Italian village by a telegram saying their mother is dead. Sensitive and compassionate. In Italian with English subtitles. Adapted from Platonov's story "The Third Son."
1980 (PG) 113m/C Philippe Noiret, Charles Vanel, Michele Placido, Vittorio Mezzogiorno, Andrea Ferreol; **D:** Francesco Rosi; **W:** Francesco Rosi. **VHS, Beta $29.98** SUE, APD ♫♫♫

Three Bullets for a Long Gun Two prairie renegades battle bandits as they search for an inherited gold mine.
1973 (PG) 89m/C Keith Van Der Wat, Beau Brummel, Patrick Munhardt; **D:** Peter Henkel; **W:** Keith Van Der Wat. **VHS, Beta $14.95** COL, NLC, SIM ♫½

Three by Hitchcock Condensed versions of three of Hitchcock's early films (1927-28). Consists of "The Ring," "Champagne," and "The Manxman," his last silent film.
1928 90m/B **D:** Alfred Hitchcock. **VHS, Beta $60.50** GVV ♫♫

The Three Caballeros Donald Duck stars in this journey through Latin America. Full of music, variety, and live-action/animation segments. Stories include "Pablo the Penguin," "Little Gauchito," and adventures with Joe Carioca, who was first introduced in Disney's "Saludos Amigos." Today this film stands as one of the very best pieces of animation ever created. Great family fare. ♫The Three Caballeros; Baia.
1945 71m/C V: Sterling Holloway, Aurora Miranda. **VHS, Beta $24.99** DIS, APD, WTA ♫♫ ½

Three Came Home Colbert is an American married to a British administrator in the Far East during WWII. Conquering Japanese throw the whole family into a brutal POW concentration camp, and their confinement is recounted in harrowing and unsparing detail. Superior drama, also laudable for a fairly even-handed portrayal of the enemy captors. Based on an autobiographical book by Agnes Newton-Keith.
1950 106m/B Claudette Colbert, Patric Knowles, Sessue Hayakawa; **D:** Jean Negulesco. **VHS $19.95** NOS, HEG ♫♫♫

Three Charlies and One Phoney! Three of Charlie Chaplin's best comedy shorts, plus one featuring his best-known imitator—Billy West. Included are "Recreation" ("Fun is Fun") ("Spring Fever"), "His Musical Career" ("The Piano Movers") ("Musical Tramps"), "The Bond" (featuring Charlie in a Liberty Bond appeal) and "His Day Out" with Billy West imitating Chaplin. All but "His Day Out" were written and directed by Chaplin.
1918 69m/B Charlie Chaplin, Mack Swain, Charley Chase, Edna Purviance, Sydney Chaplin, Albert Austin; **D:** Charlie Chaplin; **W:** Charlie Chaplin. **VHS, Beta, 8mm $24.95** YYY ♫♫♫

Three Coins in the Fountain Three women throw money into fountain and get romantically involved with Italian men. Outstanding CinemaScope photography captures beauty of Italian setting. Sammy Cahn theme song sung by Frank Sinatra.
1954 102m/C Clifton Webb, Dorothy McGuire, Jean Peters, Louis Jourdan, Maggie McNamara, Rossano Brazzi; **D:** Jean Negulesco. **VHS, Beta $59.98** FOX ♫♫½

Three Comrades Taylor, Tone, and Young are three friends, reunited in bleak, post-WWI Germany, who meet and befriend Sullavan, a tubercular beauty. Reluctant to marry because of her health, she's finally persuaded to wed Taylor, amidst the country's increasing unrest. Tragedy strikes Sullavan and the politicized Young and the two remaining comrades face an uncertain future. Bleak but forceful and passionate drama. Sullavan's performance is superb. Based on the novel by Erich Maria Remarque. Fitzgerald's script was heavily re-written because both Sullavan and producer Mankiewicz found his approach too literary with unspeakable dialogue.
1938 99m/B Robert Taylor, Margaret Sullavan, Robert Young, Franchot Tone, Lionel Atwill, Guy Kibbee, Henry Hull, George Zucco, Monty Woolley, Charley Grapewin, Spencer Charters, Sarah Padden; **D:** Frank Borzage; **W:** F. Scott Fitzgerald, Edward Paramore; **M:** Franz Waxman. **VHS $19.98** MGM, MOV, BTV ♫♫♫

Three Daring Daughters When her husband leaves her and she almost misses her daughter's graduation due to a fainting spell, MacDonald takes hiatus on a cruise ship where she meets and marries pianist Iturbi. Unknowning, the three daughters at home conspire to get Dad back in the family. Enraged when Mom returns with newfound hubby, the threesome do all in their power to

make the newlyweds as miserable as possible. Happily-ended musical-comedy is chock full of memorable tunes. Based on the play "The Bees and the Flowers" by Kohner and Albert Manning. ♫Route 66; The Dickey Bird Song; Alma Mater; Fleurette; Passepied; Where There's Love; Ritual Fire Dance; You Made Me Love You; Happy Birthday.
1948 115m/C Jeanette MacDonald, Jose Iturbi, Jane Powell, Edward Arnold, Harry Davenport, Moyna MacGill, Elinor Donahue, Ann Todd; **D:** Fred M. Wilcox; **W:** Sonya Levien, John Meehan, Albert Mannheimer, Frederick Kohner. **VHS $19.98** MGM ♫♫½

Three Days in Beirut A soldier of fortune and a beautiful interpreter join forces against a backdrop of Middle Eastern politics, espionage, and violence.
1983 (PG) 94m/C Diana Sands, Calvin Lockhart; **D:** Michael A. Schultz. **VHS, Beta $59.95** PSM ♫

Three Days of the Condor CIA researcher Redford finds himself on the run from unknown killers when he is left the only survivor of the mass murder of his office staff. Good performance by Dunaway as the photographer who shelters him. Excellent suspense tale. Based on "Six Days of the Condor" by James Grady.
1975 (R) 118m/C Robert Redford, Faye Dunaway, Cliff Robertson, Max von Sydow, John Houseman; **D:** Sydney Pollack; **W:** David Rayfiel; **M:** Dave Grusin. Academy Awards '75 Nominations: Best Film Editing; Edgar Allan Poe Awards '75: Best Screenplay. **VHS, Beta $24.95** PAR ♫♫♫

Three Days to a Kill Calvin Sims is a mercenary hired to rescue a kidnapped ambassador—by any means necessary.
1991 (R) 90m/C Fred Williamson, Bo Svenson, Henry Silva, Chuck Connors, Van Johnson, Sonny Landham; **D:** Fred Williamson. **VHS $89.99** HBO ♫♫

Three Desperate Men Three brothers accused of murder become outlaws. Not innovative, but satisfactory tale of the Old West.
1950 71m/B Preston Foster, Virginia Grey, Jim Davis; **D:** Sam Newfield. **VHS, Beta** NO ♫

The Three Faces of Eve An emotionally disturbed woman seeks the help of a psychiatrist, who discovers she has three distinct personalities. Powerful performances highlight this fascinating study based on a true story.
1957 91m/B Joanne Woodward, David Wayne, Lee J. Cobb, Nancy Kulp, Vince Edwards; **D:** Nunnally Johnson. **VHS $19.98** FXV, BTV ♫♫♫½

Three Faces West A dust bowl community is helped by a Viennese doctor who left Europe to avoid Nazi capture. He's aided by the Duke in this odd combination of Western frontier saga and anti-Nazi propaganda. Works only part of the time. **AKA:** The Refugee.
1940 79m/B John Wayne, Charles Coburn, Sigrid Gurie, Sonny Bupp, Russell Simpson; **D:** Bernard Vorhaus. **VHS $14.98** REP ♫♫

3:15—The Moment of Truth A vicious high school gang is confronted by an angry ex-member in this so-so teen delinquent film.
1986 (R) 86m/C Adam Baldwin, Deborah Foreman, Rene Auberjonois, Danny De La Paz; **D:** Larry Gross; **M:** Gary Chang. **VHS, Beta $19.95** MED ♫

Three for Bedroom C A movie star and a scientist make romance on a train bound for Los Angeles. Swanson's follow-up to "Sunset Boulevard."
1952 74m/C Gloria Swanson, Fred Clark, Steve Brodie, Hans Conried, Margaret Dumont; **D:** Milton Bren. **VHS, Beta $12.95** LIV ♫♫

Three for the Road A young aspiring political aide and his roommate must escort a Senator's ill-mannered and spoiled daughter to a reform institution. On the road, they run into more than a few obstacles. Good performances elevate a bland script. Sheen made this movie before his riveting performance as a young GI in "Platoon."
1987 (PG) 98m/C Charlie Sheen, Kerri Green, Alan Ruck, Sally Kellerman; **D:** B.W.L. Norton; **W:** Tim Metcalfe; **M:** Barry Goldberg. **Beta** NO ♫♫

Three Fugitives An ex-con holdup man determined to go straight is taken hostage by a bungling first-time bank robber, who is only attempting the holdup in order to support his withdrawn young daughter. Ex-con Nolte winds up on the lam with the would-be robber and his daughter. The comedy is fun, the sentimental moments too sweet and slow. Remake of French "Les Fugitifs."
1989 (PG-13) 96m/C Nick Nolte, Martin Short, James Earl Jones, Kenneth McMillan, Sarah Rowland Doroff, Alan Ruck; **D:** Francis Veber; **W:** Francis Veber. **VHS, Beta $19.99** TOU ♫♫

Three Godfathers A sweet and sentimental western has three half-hearted outlaws on the run, taking with them an infant they find in the desert. Dedicated to western star and Ford alumni Harry Carey, Sr. (whose son is one of the outlaws in the film), who died of cancer the year before. Ford had first filmed the tale with Carey Sr. as "Marked Men" in 1919.
1948 82m/C John Wayne, Pedro Armendariz Sr., Harry Carey Jr., Ward Bond, Mae Marsh, Jane Darwell, Ben Johnson, Mildred Natwick, Guy Kibbee; **D:** John Ford. **VHS, Beta $19.98** MGM ♫♫♫

Three Guys Named Mike Wyman plays an overly enthusiastic airline stewardess who finds herself the object of affection from three guys named Mike, including an airline pilot, an advertising man, and a scientist. A cute comedy.
1951 89m/B Jane Wyman, Van Johnson, Barry Sullivan, Howard Keel, Phyllis Kirk, Jeff Donnell; **D:** Charles Walters; **W:** Sidney Sheldon. **VHS $19.95** VDM ♫♫

The 317th Platoon An emotionally gripping war drama of the French-Vietnamese War in which the 317th Platoon of the French Army, consisting of 4 French commanders and 41 Laotians, is ordered to retreat to camp Dien Bien Phu. The men begin their march and slowly succomb to the elements and ambushes. Days later, when what is left of the platoon finally reaches Dien Bien Phu, the camp is in enemy hands and the remnants of the 317th Platoon are killed in cold blood. Director Shoendoerffer portrays this struggle, conflict, and the quiet haunting tension of war with great skill. In French with English subtitles.
1965 100m/B Jacques Perrin, Bruno Cremer, Pierre Fabre, Manuel Zarzo; **D:** Pierre Schoendoerffer; **W:** Pierre Schoendoerffer. **VHS $49.95** INT, IME, FCT ♫♫♫

357 Magnum Jonathan Hightower, the CIA's special investigator in the Far East, speaks softly and carries a very big gun.
1977 71m/C Marland T. Stewart, James Whitworth, Kathryn Hayes. **VHS, Beta** NO ♫

Three Husbands A deceased playboy leaves letters for the title characters incriminating their wives in extramarital affairs. The men's reactions are pure farce—even though this same concept was played straight with a sex change in the earlier "A Letter to Three Wives."

1950 79m/B Eve Arden, Ruth Warrick, Vanessa Brown, Howard da Silva, Sheppard Strudwick, Jane Darwell; *D:* Irving Reis. **VHS $19.95** *NOS, VDM* 🎬🎬½

Three in the Attic A college student juggles three girlfriends at the same time. When the girls find out they are being two-timed, they lock their boyfriend in an attic and exhaust him with forced sexual escapades. Then they talk. Limited trashy and foolish appeal.
1968 (R) 92m/C Christopher Jones, Yvette Mimieux, John Beck; *D:* Richard Wilson. **VHS, Beta $9.98** *SUE, MLB* 🎬½

Three in the Cellar A disgruntled college student seeks revenge on the school president by seducing his wife, daughter and mistress. Good screenplay helps carry it off. *AKA:* Up in the Cellar.
1970 (R) 92m/C Wes Stern, Joan Collins, Larry Hagman, Judy Pace; *D:* Theodore J. Flicker. **VHS $79.95** *HBO* 🎬🎬

Three in the Saddle Ritter and the Texas Rangers fight for law and order.
1945 61m/B Tex Ritter, Dave O'Brien, Charles "Blackie" King; *D:* Harry Fraser. **VHS, Beta $19.95** *NOS, VCN* 🎬½

Three Kinds of Heat Three Interpol agents track down a warring Oriental crime lord. Alternately tongue-in-cheek and silly. Never released in theaters, it found a home on video. Stevens created "The Outer Limits" for television.
1987 (R) 88m/C Robert Ginty, Victoria Barrett, Shakti; *D:* Leslie Stevens. **VHS, Beta $19.98** *WAR* 🎬

Three Legionnaires Three soldiers cavort in a post-WWI Siberian tank town. *AKA:* Three Crazy Legionnaires.
1937 67m/B Robert Armstrong, Lyle Talbot, Fifi d'Orsay, Anne Nagel, Donald Meek. **VHS, Beta $24.95** *VYY* 🎬🎬½

The Three Little Pigs From "Faerie Tale Theatre" comes the story of three little pigs, the houses they lived in and the wolf that tried to do them in.
1984 60m/C Billy Crystal, Jeff Goldblum, Valerie Perrine; *D:* Howard Storm. **VHS, Beta $14.98** *KUI, FOX, FCT* 🎬🎬½

Three Little Words A musical biography of songwriting team Harry Ruby and Bert Kalmar, filled with Kalmar-Ruby numbers. Helen Kane (famous for her boop-boop-de-boops) dubbed "I Wanna Be Loved By You" for Reynolds. A musical in the best MGM tradition. 🎵I Wanna Be Loved By You; Who's Sorry Now?; Three Little Words; I Love You So Much; She's Mine, All Mine; So-Long, Oo-Long; Hooray for Captain Spaulding; Up In the Clouds; All Alone Monday.
1950 102m/C Fred Astaire, Red Skelton, Vera-Ellen, Arlene Dahl, Keenan Wynn, Gloria De Haven, Debbie Reynolds, Gale Robbins; *D:* Richard Thorpe. Academy Awards '50 Nominations: Best Original Score; Golden Globe Awards '51: Best Actor—Musical/Comedy (Astaire). **VHS, Beta $19.98** *MGM* 🎬🎬½

The Three Lives of Thomasina In turn-of-the-century Scotland, a veterinarian orders his daughter's beloved cat destroyed when the pet is diagnosed with tetanus. After the cat's death (with scenes of kitty heaven), a beautiful and mysterious healer from the woods is able to bring the animal back to life and restore the animal to the little girl. Lovely Disney fairy tale with good performances by all.
1963 (PG) 95m/C Patrick McGoohan, Susan Hampshire, Karen Dotrice, Matthew Garber; *D:* Don Chaffey. **VHS, Beta $19.99** *DIS, TVC* 🎬🎬🎬

Three Men and a Baby The arrival of a young baby forever changes the lives of three sworn bachelors living in New York. Well-paced, charming and fun, with good acting from all. A remake of the French movie "Three Men and a Cradle."
1987 (PG) 102m/C Tom Selleck, Steve Guttenberg, Ted Danson, Margaret Colin, Nancy Travis, Philip Bosco, Celeste Holm, Derek De Lint, Cynthia Harris, Lisa Blair, Michelle Blair; *D:* Leonard Nimoy; *W:* James Orr, Jim Cruickshank; *M:* Marvin Hamlisch. **VHS, Beta, 8mm $19.99** *TOU, BVV* 🎬🎬🎬

Three Men and a Cradle Remade in the U.S. in 1987 as "Three Men and a Baby," this French film is about three bachelors living together who suddenly find themselves the guardians of a baby girl. After the initial shock of learning how to take care of a child, they fall in love with her and won't let her go. Fans of the American version may find themselves liking the original even more. In French with English subtitles. *AKA:* Trois Hommes et un Couffin.
1985 (PG-13) 100m/C Roland Giraud, Michel Boujenah, Andre Dussollier; *D:* Coline Serreau; *W:* Coline Serreau. Academy Awards '85 Nominations: Best Foreign Language Film; Cesar Awards '86: Best Film, Best Supporting Actor (Boujenah). **VHS $19.98** *LIV, MGM, ING* 🎬🎬🎬½

Three Men and a Little Lady In this sequel to "Three Men and a Baby," the mother of the once abandoned infant decides that her child needs a father. Although she wants Selleck, he doesn't get the message and so she chooses a snooty British director. The rest of the movie features various semi-comic attempts to rectify the situation.
1990 (PG) 100m/C Tom Selleck, Steve Guttenberg, Ted Danson, Nancy Travis, Robin Weisman, Christopher Cazenove, Fiona Shaw, Sheila Hancock, John Boswall, Jonathan Lynn, Sydney Walsh; *D:* Emile Ardolino; *W:* Charlie Peters, Sara Parriott, Josann McGibbon; *M:* James Newton Howard. **VHS, Beta $19.99** *TOU* 🎬🎬½

Three Men on a Horse Comedy classic about mild-mannered McHugh's ability to predict horse races and the bettors that try to take advantage of him. Blondell is great as the Brooklynese girlfriend of one of the bettors. Lots of laughs, but don't watch for the horse-racing scenes, because there aren't many.
1936 88m/B Frank McHugh, Joan Blondell, Carol Hughes, Allen Jenkins, Guy Kibbee, Sam Levene; *D:* Mervyn LeRoy. **VHS $19.98** *MGM* 🎬🎬🎬

The Three Musketeers One of the many movie adaptation of Alexandre Dumas' adventure, but this one comes from the hand of famed movie pioneer Ince. D'Artagnan joins the title characters in saving France's Queen Anne from a nefarious plot. Silent with the original organ score. *AKA:* D'Artagnan.
1916 74m/B Orin Johnson, Dorothy Dalton, Louise Glaum, Walt Whitman; *D:* Thomas Ince. **VHS, Beta, 8mm $24.95** *VYY, GPV, DVT* 🎬🎬

The Three Musketeers D'Artagnan swashbuckles silently amid stylish sets, scores of extras and exquisite costumes. Relatively faithful adaptation of Alexandre Dumas novel, slightly altered in favor of D'Artagnan's lover. Classic Fairbanks, who also produced.
1921 120m/B Douglas Fairbanks Sr., Leon Barry, George Siegmann, Eugene Pallette, Boyd Irwin, Thomas Holding, Sidney Franklin, Charles Stevens, Nigel de Brulier, Willis Robards; *D:* Fred Niblo. **VHS, Beta $29.95** *GPV, FCT* 🎬🎬🎬½

The Three Musketeers Modern adaptation of the classic tale by Alexander Dumas depicts the three friends as members of the Foreign Legion. Weakest of Wayne serials, in 12 parts.
1933 215m/B John Wayne, Raymond Hatton, Lon Chaney Jr. **VHS, Beta $24.95** *NOS, VCN, VDM* 🎬½

The Three Musketeers Three swordsmen, loyal to each other, must battle the corrupt Cardinal Richelieu. Generally regarded as the least exciting adaptation of Alexander Dumas' classic tale. The first talking version.
1935 95m/B Walter Abel, Paul Lukas, Moroni Olsen, Ian Keith, Margot Grahame, Heather Angel, Onslow Stevens, Miles Mander; *D:* Rowland V. Lee. **VHS, Beta $29.95** *RKO, IME, TTC* 🎬🎬

The Three Musketeers Musical-comedy version of the famed Alexandre Dumas swashbuckling saga. Ameche is a singing D'Artagnan and the three Ritz brothers are the inept and cowardly Musketeers (who turn out to be phonies, after all). Silly fun. 🎵My Lady; Song of the Musketeers; Voila; Chicken Soup. *AKA:* The Singing Musketeer.
1939 73m/B Don Ameche, The Ritz Brothers, Binnie Barnes, Lionel Atwill, Miles Mander, Gloria Stuart, Pauline Moore, Joseph Schildkraut, John Carradine, Douglass Dumbrille; *D:* Allan Dwan; *W:* M.M. Musselman, William A. Drake, Sam Hellman. **VHS $19.98** *FXV* 🎬🎬½

The Three Musketeers The three musketeers who are "all for one and one for all" join forces with D'Artagnan to battle the evil Cardinal Richelieu in this rambunctious adaptation of the classic tale by Alexander Dumas. Good performances by the cast, who combined drama and comedy well. Turner's first color film.
1948 126m/C Lana Turner, Gene Kelly, June Allyson, Gig Young, Angela Lansbury, Van Heflin, Keenan Wynn, Robert Coote, Reginald Owen, Frank Morgan, Vincent Price, Patricia Medina; *D:* George Sidney. **VHS, Beta $19.98** *MGM, CCB* 🎬🎬½

The Three Musketeers Extravagant and funny version of the Dumas classic. Three swashbucklers and their country cohort, who wishes to join the Musketeers, set out to save the honor of the French Queen. To do so they must oppose the evil cardinal who has his eyes on the power behind the throne. A strong cast leads this winning combination of slapstick and high adventure. Followed by "The Four Musketeers" and "The Return of the Musketeers."
1974 (PG) 105m/C Richard Chamberlain, Oliver Reed, Michael York, Raquel Welch, Frank Finlay, Christopher Lee, Faye Dunaway, Charlton Heston, Geraldine Chaplin, Simon Ward, Jean-Pierre Cassel; *D:* Richard Lester. **VHS, Beta** *COL* 🎬🎬🎬½

The Three Musketeers Yet another version of the classic swashbuckler with Porthos, Athos, Aramis, and the innocent D'Artagnan banding together against the evil Cardinal Richelieu and the tempting Milady DeWinter to save France. Cute stars, a little swordplay, a few jokes, and cartoon bad guys. Okay for the younger crowd.
1993 (PG) 105m/C Kiefer Sutherland, Charlie Sheen, Chris O'Donnell, Oliver Platt, Rebecca DeMornay, Tim Curry, Gabrielle Anwar, Julie Delpy, Michael Wincott; *D:* Stephen Herek; *W:* David Loughery; *M:* Michael Kamen. **VHS** *DIS* 🎬🎬½

3 Ninjas Lively kid's actioner about three brothers who are trained as ninjas by their grandpa. When a group of bad guys tries to kidnap the boys, they're in for trouble. Sort of a cross between "The Karate Kid" and

"Home Alone" that is suitable for family viewing. Followed by "3 Ninjas Kick Back."

1992 (PG) 84m/C Victor Wong, Michael Treanor, Max Elliott Slade, Chad Power, Rand Kingsley, Alan McRae, Margarita Franco, Toru Tanaka, Patrick Laborteaux; **D:** Jon Turteltaub; **W:** Edward Emanuel; **M:** Rick Marvin. VHS, Beta $19.99 *TOU, ☆☆☆½*

3 Ninjas Kick Back Sequel to the popular "3 Ninjas." Three brothers help their grandfather protect a ceremonial knife won in a ninja tournament in Japan 50 years earlier. Gramps' ancient adversary in that tournament, now an evil tycoon, wants the sword back and he's willing to enlist the aid of his three American grandchildren, members of garage band Teenage Vomit, to get it. The showdown eventually heads to Japan, where "Kick Back," unlike predecessors, dispenses with the Japan-bashing. High-spirited action fare that kids will enjoy.

1994 (PG) 95m/C Victor Wong, Max Elliott Slade, Sean Fox, Evan Bonifant, Sab Shimono, Dustin Nguyen, Jason Schomberg, Caroline Junko King, Angelo Tiffe; **D:** Charles Kanganis; **W:** Mark Saltzman; **M:** Rick Marvin. VHS *NYR ☆☆☆*

Three Nuts in Search of a Bolt Three neurotics send a surrogate to a comely psychiatrist for help, but the shrink thinks the surrogate's a three-way multiple personality. Raunchy monkey-shines ensue. Includes Van Doren's infamous beer bath scene.

1964 (R) 78m/C Mamie Van Doren, Tommy Noonan, Paul Gilbert, Alvy Moore; **D:** Tommy Noonan. VHS, Beta *NO ☆½*

Three O'Clock High A nerdy high school journalist is assigned a profile of the new kid in school, who turns out to be the biggest bully, too. He approaches his task with great unease. Silly teen-age farce is given souped-up direction by Spielberg protege Joanou. Features decent work by the young cast.

1987 (PG) 97m/C Casey Siemaszko, Anne Ryan, Stacey Glick, Jonathan Wise, Richard Tyson, Jeffrey Tambor, Philip Baker Hall, John P. Ryan; **D:** Phil Joanou; **W:** Richard Christian Matheson; **M:** Thomas Szollosi; **M:** Tangerine Dream. VHS, Beta $79.95 *MCA ☆☆½*

Three of a Kind A compilation of the best skits and satires from the British comedy series.

198? 84m/C Tracey Ullman, David Copperfield, Lenny Henry. VHS, Beta $14.98 *FOX ☆☆½*

Three of Hearts Slick look at love in contemporary downtown New York. The triangle consists of Connie (Lynch), just dumped by bisexual girlfriend Ellen (Fenn), who is in turn seduced by hired escort Joe (Baldwin), who will break her heart, causing her to turn back to the sympathetic Connie. But guess what happens. Hiply superficial plot is transparent although the three leads are likeable, especially Lynch as the lanky lovelorn Connie. Don't read further if you don't want to know what happens since the film was shot with two endings. The U.S. release pairs Joe and Ellen for a typically American happy ending; the European release doesn't.

1993 (R) 102m/C Kelly Lynch, William Baldwin, Sherilyn Fenn, Joe Pantoliano, Gail Strickland, Cec Verrell, Claire Callaway, Tony Amendola; **D:** Yurek Bogayevicz; **W:** Philip C. Epstein, Adam Greenman; **M:** Richard Gibbs. VHS $19.95 *NLC, IME, FCT ☆½*

Three on a Match An actress, a stenographer and a society woman get together for a tenth year reunion. They become embroiled in a world of crime when Blondell's gangster boyfriend takes a liking to Dvorak. She leaves her husband and takes up with

the crook. The results are tragic. Bogart's first gangster role.

1932 64m/B Joan Blondell, Warren William, Ann Dvorak, Bette Davis, Lyle Talbot, Humphrey Bogart, Patricia Ellis, Grant Mitchell; **D:** Mervyn LeRoy. VHS, Beta $19.98 *MGM, FCT ☆☆☆*

Three on a Meathook When a young man and his father living on an isolated farm receive female visitors, bloodshed is quick to follow. Essentially a remake of "Psycho," and very loosely based on the crimes of Ed Gein. Filmed in Louisville, Kentucky.

1972 85m/C Charles Kissinger, James Pickett, Sherry Steiner, Carolyn Thompson; **D:** William Girdler; **W:** William Girdler. VHS, Beta *NO Woof!*

The Three Penny Opera Mack the Knife presides over an exciting world of thieves, murderers, beggars, prostitutes and corrupt officials in a seedy section of London. Based on the opera by Kurt Weill and Bertold Brecht, which was based on "The Beggar's Opera" by John Gay. Remake of "The Threepenny Opera" (1931). **AKA:** Die Dreigroschenoper.

1962 124m/C Curt Jurgens, Hildegarde Neff, Gert Frobe, June Ritchie, Lino Ventura, Sammy Davis Jr. VHS, Beta $29.98 *MVD, VYG, FCT ☆☆☆*

Three Secrets A plane crashes and the only survivor is a five-year-old boy. Three women, each with a secret, seek to claim him as the child each gave up for adoption five years before. Tearjerker with good cast.

1950 98m/B Eleanor Parker, Patricia Neal, Ruth Roman, Frank Lovejoy, Leif Erickson; **D:** Robert Wise. VHS $19.98 *REP ☆☆½*

Three Sovereigns for Sarah Witch-hunters tortured and toasted Sarah's two sisters for practicing witchcraft in the past. Now, accused of witchery herself, she struggles to prove the family's innocence. Excellent, made-for-PBS. Fine performances from all, especially Redgrave.

1985 152m/C Vanessa Redgrave, Phyllis Thaxter, Patrick McGoohan; **D:** Philip Leacock. VHS, Beta $79.95 *PSM, PBS ☆☆½*

Three Stooges Comedy Capers: Vol. 1 Compilation includes: "Disorder in the Court" (1936), "Malice in the Palace" (1949), "Sing a Song of Six Pants" (1947), and "The Brideless Groom" (1947).

194? 80m/B Moe Howard, Larry Fine, Curly Howard, Shemp Howard. VHS, Beta $9.95 *NOS, MED ☆☆½*

Three Stooges Comedy Classics The antics of the Stooges are featured in this collection of five original shorts, along with an early Ted Healy comedy that features all four Stooges: "Hollywood on Parade," "Disorder in the Court," "Malice in the Palace," "Brideless Groom," and "Sing a Song of Six Pants."

1949 79m/B Moe Howard, Larry Fine, Curly Howard, Shemp Howard, Ted Healy. VHS $19.95 *REP ☆☆½*

Three Stooges: Cookoo Cavaliers and Other Nyuks The boys star in "Cookoo Cavaliers," "Busy Buddies," and "Booby Dupes."

1940 55m/B Moe Howard, Curly Howard, Larry Fine. VHS $14.95 *COL ☆☆½*

Three Stooges Festival Three original shorts by the comedy trio, including: "Disorder in the Court" (1936-Curly), "Sing a Song of Six Pants" (1949-Shemp) and "Malice in the Palace" (1949-Shemp).

1949 60m/B Moe Howard, Larry Fine, Shemp Howard, Curly Howard. VHS, Beta $29.95 *AOV, VYY ☆☆½*

Three Stooges: From Nurse to Worse and Other Nyuks The irrepressible Stooges star in "From Nurse to Worse," "Crash Goes the Hash," and "G.I. Wanna Go Home."

1945 55m/B Moe Howard, Larry Fine, Curly Howard. VHS $14.95 *COL ☆☆½*

The Three Stooges: Half-Wit's Holiday and Other Nyuks Includes, "Half-Wit's Holiday," "Horse Collars," and "How High Is Up?"

1935 55m/B Moe Howard, Curly Howard, Larry Fine. VHS $14.95 *COL ☆☆½*

The Three Stooges: Idiots Deluxe and Other Nyuks Curly, Larry and Moe star in, "Idiots Deluxe," "I Can Hardly Wait," and "Idle Roomers."

1940 55m/B Moe Howard, Curly Howard, Larry Fine. VHS $14.95 *COL ☆☆½*

The Three Stooges Meet Hercules The Three Stooges are transported back to ancient Ithaca by a time machine with a young scientist and his girlfriend. When the girl is captured, they enlist the help of Hercules to rescue her.

1961 80m/B Moe Howard, Larry Fine, Joe DeRita, Vicki Trickett, Quinn Redeker; **D:** Edward L. Bernds. VHS, Beta $9.95 *GKK ☆☆½*

The Three Stooges: Nutty but Nice and Other Nyuks The boys star in "Nutty but Nice," "The Sitter-Downers," and "Slippery Silks."

1936 55m/B Moe Howard, Curly Howard, Larry Fine. VHS $14.95 *COL ☆☆½*

The Three Stooges: They Stooge to Conga and Other Nyuks WWII madness from the Stooges in "They Stooge to Conga," "You Natzy Spy!" and "I'll Never Heil Again."

1940 55m/B Moe Howard, Curly Howard, Larry Fine. VHS $14.95 *COL ☆☆½*

Three Stops to Murder An FBI agent investigates the murder of a beautiful model in this early, unspectacular Hammer production.

1953 76m/B Tom Conway, Mila Parely, Naomi Chance, Eric Pohlmann, Andrew Osborn, Richard Wattis, Eileen Way, Delphi Lawrence; **D:** Terence Fisher. VHS, Beta $16.95 *SNC, MLB ☆*

Three Strange Loves Men and women struggle with loneliness, old age, and sterility. Sometimes disjointed, but for the most part, well-made. Finely acted. In Swedish with English subtitles. **AKA:** Thirst.

1949 88m/B Eva Henning, Brigit Tengroth, Birger Malmsten; **D:** Ingmar Bergman. VHS, Beta $29.98 *NOS, HHT, SUE ☆☆☆*

3:10 to Yuma In order to collect $200 he desperately needs, a poor farmer has to hold a dangerous killer at bay while waiting to turn the outlaw over to the authorities arriving on the 3:10 train to Yuma. Stuck in a hotel room with the outlaw's gang gathering outside, the question arises as to who is the prisoner. Farmer Heflin is continually worked on by the outlaw Ford, in a movie with more than its share of great dialogue. Suspenseful, well-made action western adapted from an Elmore Leonard story.

1957 92m/B Glenn Ford, Van Heflin, Felicia Farr, Richard Jaeckel; **D:** Delmer Daves; **M:** Frankie Laine. VHS, Beta $9.95 *GKK ☆☆☆½*

Three Texas Steers A circus owner inherits some land that the government wants for a water project and her manager tries to get it for himself. Enter the terrific trio to set things right. Last of the series for Terhune. The scenes of the circus fire were

taken from "Circus Girl" (1937). *AKA:* Danger Rides the Range.
1939 59m/B John Wayne, Ray Corrigan, Max Terhune, Carole Landis, Ralph Graves, Roscoe Ates; *D:* George Sherman. VHS $19.95 NOS *♫♫½*

Three the Hard Way An insane white supremacist has a plan to eliminate blacks by contaminating water supplies. A big blaxploitation money maker and the first to team Brown, Williamson, and Kelly, who would go on to make several more pictures together.
1974 (R) 93m/C Jim Brown, Fred Williamson, Jim Kelly, Sheila Frazier, Jay Robinson, Alex Rocco; *D:* Gordon Parks. VHS $39.95 XVC *♫♫½*

Three Violent People Family feud set in post-Civil War Old West features Heston and Baxter impulsively marrying and returning to run the family ranch. Heston's brother (Tryon) wants to sell the ranch in order to get his share of the inheritance and then Heston finds out Baxter was once a prostitute. In this case family squabbles don't make for an exciting film.
1957 100m/C Charlton Heston, Anne Baxter, Gilbert Roland, Tom Tryon, Forrest Tucker, Elaine Stritch, Bruce (Herman Brix) Bennett, Barton MacLane; *D:* Rudolph Mate; *W:* James Edward Grant; *M:* Walter Scharf. VHS $14.95 PAR *♫♫*

Three Warriors Young Native American boy is forced to leave the city and return to the reservation, where his contempt for the traditions of his ancestors slowly turns to appreciation and love.
1977 100m/C Charles White Eagle, Lois Red Elk, McKee "Kiko" Red Wing, Christopher Lloyd, Randy Quaid. VHS, Beta NO *♫½*

Three Way Weekend Two young girls set off on a back-packing trip through the mountains of Southern California to enjoy camping and romance.
1981 (R) 78m/C Dan Diego, Jody Lee Olhava, Richard Blye, Blake Parrish; *D:* Emmett Alston. VHS, Beta $19.95 ACA *♫*

The Three Weird Sisters The three weird sisters from "Macbeth" strive to maintain their life of luxury by plotting to kill their half-brother for the inheritance. Not a bad effort for Birt's first time out as director; script co-written by his wife, Louise and poet Thomas.
1948 82m/B Nancy Price, Mary Clare; *D:* Daniel Birt; *W:* Dylan Thomas, Louise Birt. VHS $19.95 VDM, SNC, VMK *♫♫*

Three Word Brand Hart plays three roles in this film, a homesteader who is killed by Indians and his twin sons, who are separated after their father's death and reunited many years later. Silent with musical score.
1921 75m/B William S. Hart, Jayne Navak, S.J. Bingham; *D:* Lambert Hillyer. VHS, Beta $18.95 GPV, VYY *♫♫*

The Three Worlds of Gulliver A colorful family version of the Jonathan Swift classic about an Englishman who discovers a fantasy land of small and giant people. Visual effects by Ray Harryhausen. *AKA:* The Worlds of Gulliver.
1959 100m/C Kerwin Mathews, Jo Morrow, Basil Sydney, Mary Ellis; *D:* Jack Sher; *W:* Arthur Ross, Jack Sher; *M:* Bernard Herrmann. VHS, Beta $14.95 COL, MLB, CCB *♫♫½*

The Threepenny Opera A musical about the exploits of gangster Mack the Knife. Adapted from Bertolt Brecht's play and John Gay's "The Beggar's Opera." In German with English subtitles. *AKA:* Die Dreigroschenoper; L'Opera De Quat'Sous; Beggars' Opera.
1931 107m/B Rudolph Forster, Lotte Lenya, Carola Neher, Reinhold Schunzel, Fritz Rasp, Valeska Gert; *D:* G.W. Pabst. VHS $14.95 VDM, AUD, ING *♫♫*

Three's Trouble A middle-class family erupts when a young male babysitter enters to care for its three mischievous sons.
1985 93m/C John Waters, Jacki Weaver, Steven Vidler; *D:* Chris Thomson. VHS, Beta $19.95 STE, NWV *♫*

Threesome Another Generation X movie that tries hard to be hip, but fails miserably. Due to a college administrative error, Alex (Boyle) winds up sharing a suite with two male roommates, Eddy (Charles) and Stuart (Baldwin). Despite having completely different personalities, they soon become best friends and form one cozy little group, with cozy being the key word. Sexual tension abounds—Alex wants Eddy who wants Stuart who wants Alex. Filled with pathetic dialogue (most of it relating to bodily functions and body parts) and shallow, obnoxious characters, this menage a trois film is a flop.
1994 (R) 93m/C Lara Flynn Boyle, Stephen Baldwin, Josh Charles, Alexis Arquette, Mark Arnold, Martha Gehman, Michelle Matheson; *D:* Andrew Fleming; *W:* Andrew Fleming; *M:* Thomas Newman. VHS NYR Woof!

Threshold An internationally-acclaimed research biologist is frustrated by his inability to save a dying 20-year-old woman born with a defective heart. She becomes the recipient of the first artificial heart. Solid performances.
1983 (PG) 97m/C Donald Sutherland, Jeff Goldblum, John Marley, Mare Winningham; *D:* Richard Pearce. VHS, Beta $59.98 FOX *♫♫½*

The Thrill Killers Young murderous thugs rampage through Los Angeles suburbs, killing indiscriminately. Pretentious and exploitative. Sometimes shown with Hallucinogenic Hypo-Vision—a prologue announcing the special effect would be shown before the film, and on cue, hooded ushers would run through the theatre with cardboard axes. Weird. *AKA:* The Monsters Are Loose; The Maniacs Are Loose.
1965 82m/C Cash Flagg, Liz Renay, Brick Bardo, Carolyn Brandt, Atlas King; *D:* Ray Dennis Steckler. VHS, Beta NO Woof!

Thrill of a Romance Johnson, an Army hero, meets Williams, a swimming instructor of all things, at a resort in the Sierra Nevadas. The only problem is that she's married. Typical swim-romance vehicle. ♫Please Don't Say No, Say Maybe; I Should Care; Lonely Night; Vive L'Amour; Schubert's Serenade; The Thrill of a Romance.
1945 105m/C Esther Williams, Van Johnson, Frances Gifford, Henry Travers, Spring Byington, Lauritz Melchior; *D:* Richard Thorpe. VHS $19.98 MGM *♫♫*

The Thrill of It All! An average housewife becomes a star of television commercials, to the dismay of her chauvinist husband, a gynecologist. Fast and funny, with numerous acidic jokes about television sponsors and programs.
1963 108m/C James Garner, Doris Day, Arlene Francis, Edward Andrews, Carl Reiner, Elliott Reid, Reginald Owen, ZaSu Pitts; *D:* Norman Jewison; *W:* Carl Reiner. VHS, Beta $14.98 MCA *♫♫½*

Thrilled to Death An utterly naive husband and wife get caught in the middle of a lethal game when they befriend a scheming couple.
1988 (R) 90m/C Blake Bahner, Rebecca Lynn, Richard Maris, Christine Moore; *D:* Chuck Vincent. VHS $79.98 REP *♫½*

Thrillkill A young girl is enmeshed in a multi-million-dollar burglary scheme after her computer-whiz/embezzler sister disappears.
1984 88m/C Robin Ward, Gina Massey, Anthony Kramroither; *D:* Anthony D'Andrea. VHS, Beta $9.95 MED *♫*

Throne of Blood Kurosawa's masterful adaptation of "Macbeth" transports the story to medieval Japan and the world of the samurai. Mifune and Chiaki are warriors who have put down a rebellion and are to be rewarded by their overlord. On their way to his castle they meet a mysterious old woman who prophesizes that Mifune will soon rule—but his reign will be short. She is dismissed as crazy but her prophesies come to pass. So steeped in Japanese style that it bears little resemblance to the Shakespearean original, this film is an incredibly detailed vision in its own right. In Japanese with English subtitles. *AKA:* Kumonosujo, Kumonosu-djo; Cobweb Castle; The Castle of the Spider's Web.
1957 105m/B Toshiro Mifune, Isuzu Yamada, Takashi Shimura, Minoru Chiaki, Akira Kubo; *D:* Akira Kurosawa; *W:* Hideo Oguni, Shinobu Hashimoto, Riyuzo Kikushima, Akira Kurosawa; *M:* Masaru Sato. VHS, Beta $39.95 HMV, ING, VYG *♫♫♫♫*

Throne of Fire A mighty hero battles the forces of evil to gain control of the powerful Throne of Fire. Dubbed.
1982 91m/C Peter McCoy, Sabrina Siani; *D:* Franco Prosperi. VHS, Beta $59.95 MGM Woof!

Through a Glass Darkly Oppressive interactions within a family sharing a holiday on a secluded island: a woman recovering from schizophrenia, her husband, younger brother, and her psychologist father. One of Bergman's most mysterious, upsetting and powerful films. In Swedish with English subtitles. Part of Bergman's Silence-of-God trilogy followed by "Winter Light" and "The Silence."
1961 91m/B Harriet Andersson, Max von Sydow, Gunnar Bjornstrand, Lars Passgard; *D:* Ingmar Bergman; *W:* Ingmar Bergman. Academy Awards '61: Best Foreign Language Film; Nominations: Best Story & Screenplay; National Board of Review Awards '62: 5 Best Foreign Films of the Year. VHS, Beta $24.95 NOS, SUE, ING *♫♫♫*

Through Naked Eyes Made-for-television thriller about two people who spy on each other. They witness a murder and realize that someone else is watching them. What a coincidence.
1987 91m/C David Soul, Pam Dawber; *D:* John Llewellyn Moxey. VHS, Beta $79.95 MED *♫♫½*

Through the Breakers Heartbroken woman suffers silently on South Pacific isle.
1928 55m/B Margaret Livingston, Holmes Herbert, Clyde Cook, Natalie Joyce. VHS, Beta $19.95 GPV, FCT *♫½*

Throw Momma from the Train DeVito plays a man, henpecked by his horrific mother, who tries to persuade his writing professor (Crystal) to exchange murders. DeVito will kill Crystal's ex-wife and Crystal will kill DeVito's mother. Only mama isn't going to be that easy to get rid of. Fast-paced and entertaining black comedy. Ramsey steals the film. Inspired by Hitchcock's "Strangers on a Train."
1987 (PG-13) 88m/C Danny DeVito, Billy Crystal, Anne Ramsey, Kate Mulgrew, Kim Greist, Branford Marsalis, Rob Reiner, Bruce Kirby; *D:* Danny DeVito; *W:* Stu Silver; *M:* David Newman. VHS, Beta $9.98 ORI *♫♫♫*

The Throwback When Jones was a lad the townspeople accused his father of cattle rustling. When he returns as an adult he sets out to clear his father's name.

1935 61m/B Buck Jones, Muriel Evans, Eddie Phillips, George "Gabby" Hayes, Bryant Washburn, Paul Fix, Frank LaRue; **D:** Ray Taylor. **VHS** $12.95 GPV ♂♂½

Thumb Tripping A dated sixties/hippie film. Two flower children hitchhike and encounter all kinds of other strange people in their travels on the far-out roads.
1972 (R) 94m/C Meg Foster, Michael Burns, Bruce Dern, Marianna Hill, Michael Conrad, Joyce Van Patten; **D:** Quentin Masters. **VHS, Beta** $59.98 NLC ♂♂

Thumbelina From "Faerie Tale Theatre" comes the story of a tiny girl who gets kidnapped by a toad and a mole, but meets the man of her dreams in the nick of time. Adapted from the classic tale by Hans Christian Andersen. Made for television.
1982 60m/C Carrie Fisher, William Katt, Burgess Meredith; **D:** Michael Lindsay-Hogg. **VHS, Beta** $14.98 KUI, FOX, FCT ♂♂♂

Thumbelina Ornery little girl named Mia gets magically sucked into the pages of the "Thumbelina" storybook she's reading and finds all sorts of adventures. Loose adaptation of Hans Christian Andersen fairy tale from Bluth is lackluster, with acceptable songs. Not up to the level of recent Disney animated features, but pleasant enough for the kids. **AKA:** Hans Christian Andersen's Thumbelina.
1994 (G) 86m/C **D:** Don Bluth, Gary Goldman; **W:** William Ross, Barry Manilow, Barry Manilow, Jack Feldman, Bruce Sussman; **V:** Jodi Benson, Gary Imhoff, Charo, Gilbert Gottfried, Carol Channing, John Hurt, Will Ryan, June Foray, Kenneth Mars. **VHS, Beta** $24.95 WAR ♂♂½

Thunder Alley In middle America, two friends and their rock group struggle for success. One of the friends dies after an accidental overdose and the other's grief propels him to stardom. ♫Can't Look Back; Just Another Pretty Boy; Sometimes in the Night; Heart to Heart; Can You Feel My Heart Beat; Do You Feel Alright?; Danger, Danger; Surrender; Gimme Back My Heart.
1985 102m/C Roger Wilson, Leif Garrett, Jill Schoelen; **D:** J.S. Cardone; **W:** J.S. Cardone. **VHS, Beta** $79.95 MGM ♂½

Thunder and Lightning A mismatched young couple chase a truckload of poisoned moonshine. Action-packed chases ensue. Nice chemistry between Carradine and Jackson.
1977 (PG) 94m/C David Carradine, Kate Jackson, Roger C. Carmel, Sterling Holloway, Eddie Barth; **D:** Corey Allen. **VHS, Beta** $59.98 FOX ♂♂

Thunder & Mud Female mud wrestlers battle over their favorite rock band. Hahn's attempt to cash in on her notoriety after the Bakker scandal.
1989 90m/C Jessica Hahn; **D:** Penelope Spheeris. **VHS, Beta** $59.95 COL ♂♂

Thunder Bay Stewart and Duryea are a pair of Louisiana wildcat oil drillers who believe there is oil at the bottom of the Gulf of Mexico off the coast of the town of Port Felicity. They decide to construct an oil platform which the shrimp fisherman of the town believe will interfere with their livelihoods. Tensions rise between the two groups and violence seems likely. Action packed, with timely storyline as modern oil drillers fight to drill in waters that have historically been off-limits.
1953 82m/C James Stewart, Joanne Dru, Dan Duryea, Gilbert Roland, Marcia Henderson; **D:** Anthony Mann; **W:** John Michael Hayes. **VHS, Beta** $19.95 MCA ♂♂♂

Thunder County Federal agents and drug runners are after a group of four convicts who have just escaped from prison.
1974 78m/C Mickey Rooney, Ted Cassidy, Chris Robinson. **VHS, Beta** $49.95 PSM ♂½

Thunder in God's Country A dishonest gambler eyes a peaceful western town as the next Vegas-like gambling capital. Before this occurs he is exposed as a cheat.
1951 67m/B Rex Allen, Mary Ellen Kay. **VHS, Beta** $24.95 DVT ♂

Thunder in Paradise R.J. Hurricane Spencer (Hogan) is a soldier of fortune who heads into Cuba to help a woman and child escape political imprisonment, using his high-tech, weapon-filled speedboat. He has to fight off a small army and manages to find a buried treasure as well. Simple-minded.
1993 (PG-13) ?m/C Hulk Hogan, Robin Weisman, Chris Lemmon, Carol Alt. **VHS** $92.95 VMK ♂♂½

Thunder in the City Robinson is an intense American promoter in the sales game who is sent to London by his employers to learn a more subdued way of doing business. Instead, he meets a pair of down-on-their-luck aristocrats whose only asset is an apparently worthless Rhodesian mine. Robinson, however, comes up with a way to promote the mine and get enough capital together to make it profitable. Good satire with Robinson well cast. Robinson wasn't taken with the script in its original form and persuaded his friend, playwright Robert Sherwood, to re-write it.
1937 85m/B Edward G. Robinson, Nigel Bruce, Ralph Richardson, Constance Collier; **D:** Marion Gering; **M:** Miklos Rozsa. **VHS, Beta** $19.95 NOS, DVT, BAR ♂♂♂

Thunder in the Desert A cowhand joins an outlaw gang in order to catch his uncle's killer.
1938 56m/C Bob Steele, Louise Stanley, Don Barclay, Charles "Blackie" King, Lew Meehan, Budd Buster; **D:** Sam Newfield. **VHS, Beta** $19.95 NOS, DVT, GPV ♂

Thunder in the Pines Two lumber-jack buddies send for the same French girl to marry, unbeknownst to each other. When she arrives, the dismayed men agree to a contest to see who will marry her. Meanwhile the French girl falls for the local saloon owner and his jilted girlfriend vows to get even. She does, with the help of the lumberjacks.
1949 61m/B Denise Darcel, George Reeves, Ralph Byrd, Lyle Talbot, Michael Whalen, Roscoe Ates, Vince Barnett; **D:** Robert Edwards. **VHS, Beta** NO ♂

Thunder Mountain Zane Grey's novel about two prospectors who are bush-whacked on their way to file a claim comes to life on the screen.
1935 56m/B George O'Brien. **VHS, Beta** $24.95 DVT, HHE, MLB ♂½

Thunder Over Texas The cowboy hero gets embroiled in a railroad scandal that involves a kidnapping. Directed by Edgar G. Ulmer, who used the alias John Warner because he was moonlighting. His first western; previously he was best known for "The Black Cat."
1934 52m/B Marion Shilling, Helen Westcott, Victor Potel, Tiny Skelton; **D:** Edgar G. Ulmer. **VHS, Beta** $19.95 VDM ♂

Thunder Pass Gold and greed are the motives for murder as two young brothers become separated when their wagon train is attacked and their family is slaughtered. One brother searches for the other and finds him several years later. Based on the novel

"Arizona Ames" by Zane Grey. Also released as "Thunder Trail."
1937 58m/B Charles Bickford, Marsha Hunt, Gilbert Roland, Monte Blue; **D:** Charles T. Barton. **VHS** $14.95 NOS, VDM, DVT ♂♂

Thunder Pass Routine story about a wagon train threatened by hostile Indians and the Army officer who leads them to safety. Based on a story by George Van Marter.
1954 76m/B Dane Clark, Dorothy Patrick, Andy Devine, Raymond Burr, John Carradine, Mary Ellen Kay; **D:** Frank McDonald; **W:** Tom Hubbard, Fred Eggers. **VHS** $14.99 MOV ♂♂

Thunder River Feud The Rangebusters help two ranchers avoid a range war. Part of "The Rangebusters" series.
1942 58m/B Ray Corrigan, John "Dusty" King, Max Terhune. **VHS, Beta** $19.95 NOS, VCN, DVT ♂♂

Thunder Road Mitchum comes home to Tennessee from Korea and takes over the family moonshine business, fighting both mobsters and federal agents. An exciting chase between Mitchum and the feds ends the movie with the appropriate bang. Robert Mitchum not only produced, wrote and starred in this best of the moonshine-running films, but also wrote the theme song "Whippoorwill" (which later became a radio hit). Mitchum's son, James, made his film debut, and later starred in a similar movie "Moonrunners." A cult favorite, still shown in many drive-ins around the country.
1958 (PG) 92m/B Robert Mitchum, Jacques Aubuchon, Gene Barry, Keely Smith, Trevor Bardette, Sandra Knight, Jim Mitchum, Betsy Holt, Frances Koon; **D:** Arthur Ripley; **W:** Robert Mitchum. **VHS, Beta** $19.98 MGM ♂♂♂

Thunder Run When a load of uranium needs to be transferred across Nevada, a retired trucker takes on the job. The trip is made more difficult since terrorists are trying to hijack the shipment to use for a bomb.
1986 (PG-13) 84m/C Forrest Tucker, John Ireland, John Shepherd, Jill Whitlow, Wally Ward, Cheryl Lynn; **D:** Gary Hudson. **VHS, Beta** $79.95 MED ♂

Thunder Warrior A young Indian turns into a one-man army determined to punish the local authorities who are abusing his fellow tribe members. **AKA:** Thunder.
1985 (R) 84m/C Raymond Harmstorf, Bo Svenson, Mark Gregory; **D:** Larry Ludman. **VHS, Beta** $79.95 TWE ♂

Thunder Warrior 2 A tough Native American is provoked to violence by small-town prejudice.
1985 (PG-13) 114m/C Mark Gregory, Karen Reel, Bo Svenson; **D:** Larry Ludman. **VHS, Beta** $79.95 TWE ♂

Thunder Warrior 3 The Indian Thunder has vowed to live in peace, but forswears the oath when his wife is kidnapped and family is terrorized. Revenge is the top priority as he torments the bad guys.
1988 90m/C Mark Gregory, John Phillip Law, Ingrid Lawrence, Werner Pochat, Horts Schon; **D:** Larry Ludman. **VHS** $79.95 IMP ♂

Thunderball The fourth installment in Ian Fleming's James Bond series finds 007 on a mission to thwart SPECTRE, which has threatened to blow up Miami by atomic bomb if 100 million pounds in ransom is not paid. One of the more tedious Bond entries but a big box-office success. Tom Jones sang the title song. Remade as "Never Say Never Again" in 1983 with Connery reprising his role as Bond after a 12-year absence.

1965 (PG) 125m/C Sean Connery, Claudine Auger, Adolfo Celi, Lucianna Paluzzi, Rik von Nutter, Martine Beswick, Molly Peters, Guy Doleman, Bernard Lee, Lois Maxwell, Desmond Llewelyn; **D:** Terence Young; **W:** John Hopkins, Richard Maibaum; **M:** John Barry. **VHS, Beta** $19.98 MGM, TLF *ℐℐ* ½

Thunderbolt & Lightfoot Eastwood is an ex-thief on the run from his former partners (Kennedy and Lewis) who believe he's made off with the loot from their last job, the robbery of a government vault. He joins up with drifter Bridges, who helps him to escape. Later, Eastwood manages to convince Kennedy he doesn't know where the money is. Bridges then persuades the men that they should plan the same heist and rob the same government vault all over again, which they do. But their getaway doesn't go exactly as planned. All-around fine acting; notable is Bridges' scene dressed in drag. First film for director Cimino. **1974 (R) 115m/C** Clint Eastwood, Jeff Bridges, George Kennedy, Geoffrey Lewis, Gary Busey; **D:** Michael Cimino; **W:** Michael Cimino. **VHS, Beta** $19.98 MGM *ℐℐℐ*

Thunderground A beautiful con artist teams with a fighter and together they travel to New Orleans to arrange a bout with the king of bare-knuckled fighting. **1989 (R) 92m/C** Paul Coufos, Margaret Langrick, Jesse Ventura, M. Emmet Walsh; **D:** David Mitchell. **VHS** IME *ℐℐ*

Thunderheart Young FBI agent Kilmer is sent to an Oglala Sioux reservation to investigate a murder. He is himself part Sioux, but resents being chosen for the assignment because of it. Aided by a veteran partner (Shepard), Ray learns, professionally and personally, from a shrewd tribal police officer (well played by Greene). Set in the late 70's the film is loosely based on actual events plaguing the violence-torn Native American community at that time. Great cinematography by Roger Deakins. Filmed on the Pine Ridge Reservation in South Dakota. Director Apted deals with the actual incidents this film is based on in his documentary about Leonard Peltier, "Incident at Oglala." **1992 (R) 118m/C** Val Kilmer, Sam Shepard, Graham Greene, Fred Ward, Fred Dalton Thompson, Sheila Tousey, Chief Ted Thin Elk, John Trudell, Dennis Banks, David Crosby; **D:** Michael Apted; **W:** John Fusco; **M:** James Horner. **VHS** $19.95 COL, FCT, BTV *ℐℐℐ*

Thundering Forest Australian actioneer pitting loggers against saboteurs. **1941 ?m/C** Frank Leighton. **VHS** $15.95 LOO *ℐℐ*

Thundering Gunslingers A group of gunmen terrorizing townspeople finally meet their match in this Western. **1940 61m/B** Buster Crabbe. **VHS, Beta** $19.95 NOS, DVT *ℐ*

Thundering Ninja Three secret agents fight off an army of ninjas. Plenty of heel-to-head antics. **198? 89m/C** Bernard Geurts, Joe Redner, Klaus Mutter, Ken Kerr, Jimmy Wang Yu; **D:** Joseph Kong. **VHS, Beta** $59.95 TWE *ℐ* ½

Thundering Trail Two cowboys encounter plenty of trouble before they take the President's newly appointed territorial governor to his office. **AKA:** Thunder on the Trail. **1951 55m/B** Lash LaRue, Al "Fuzzy" St. John, Sally Anglim, Archie Twitchell, Ray Bennett. **VHS, Beta** $19.95 NOS, DVT *ℐ*

Thundersquad Mercenaries help a South American rebel leader rescue his kidnapped son. **1985 90m/C** Sal Borgese, Julia Fursich, Antonio Sabato. **VHS, Beta** NO *ℐ*

Thursday's Child A child's success in films causes trouble for her family. Melodramatic and sappy, but Howes, as the kid, is excellent. One of Granger's early supporting roles. **1943 95m/B** Stewart Granger, Sally Ann Howes; **D:** Rodney Ackland. **VHS, Beta** $24.95 NOS, DVT, HEG *ℐℐ*

Thursday's Game Two crisis-besieged businessmen meet every Thursday, using poker as a ruse to work on their business and marital problems. Wonderful cast; intelligently written. Made for television. **1974 (PG) 99m/C** Gene Wilder, Ellen Burstyn, Bob Newhart, Cloris Leachman, Nancy Walker, Valerie Harper, Rob Reiner; **D:** James L. Brooks; **W:** James L. Brooks. **VHS, Beta** $69.95 VMK *ℐℐℐ*

THX 1138 In the dehumanized world of the future, people live in underground cities run by computer, are force-fed drugs to keep them passive, and no longer have names—just letter/number combinations (Duvall is THX 1138). Emotion is also outlawed and when the computer-matched couple THX 1138 and LUH 3417 discover love, they must battle the computer system to escape. George Lucas' first film, which was inspired by a student film he did at USC. The laserdisc format carries the film in widescreen. **1971 (PG) 88m/C** Robert Duvall, Donald Pleasence, Maggie McOmie; **D:** George Lucas; **W:** George Lucas. **VHS, Beta** $19.98 WAR, FUS *ℐℐℐ*

Tiara Tahiti Intrigue, double-cross, romance, and violence ensue when two old army acquaintances clash in Tahiti. Very fine performances from the two leading men. **1962 100m/C** James Mason, John Mills, Claude Dauphin, Rosenda Monteros, Herbert Lom; **D:** Ted Kotcheff. **VHS, Beta** $59.98 SUE *ℐℐ*

Ticket of Leave Man London's most dangerous killer fronts a charitable organization designed to help reform criminals. It actually steers them into a crime syndicate that cheats philanthropists out of their fortunes. **1937 71m/B** Tod Slaughter, John Warwick, Marjorie Taylor. **VHS, Beta** $24.95 VYY, SNC *ℐℐ*

Ticket to Heaven A young man, trying to deal with the painful breakup of a love affair, falls under the spell of a quasi-religious order. His friends and family, worried about the cult's influence, have him kidnapped in order for him to be de-programmed. Mancuso is excellent, as are his supporting players Rubinek and Thomson. **1981 (PG) 109m/C** Nick Mancuso, Meg Foster, Kim Cattrall, Saul Rubinek, R.H. Thomson; **D:** Ralph L. Thomas. **VHS, Beta** $79.95 MGM *ℐℐℐ*

Ticket to Tomahawk A gunslinger is hired by a stagecoach company to sabotage a railroad. Look for Marilyn Monroe as a chorus girl in a musical number. **1950 90m/C** Anne Baxter, Rory Calhoun, Walter Brennan, Charles Kemper, Connie Gilchrist, Arthur Hunnicutt, Victor Sen Yung; **D:** Richard Sale. **VHS** TCF *ℐℐ* ½

Tickle Me An unemployed rodeo star finds work at an all-girl health spa and dude ranch. He falls in love with a young lady who has a treasure map and keeps her safe from the evil men who want her fortune. For die-hard Elvis fans only. ♫(It's a) Long, Lonely Highway; Night Rider; It Feels So Right; Dirty, Dirty Feeling; (Such an) Easy Question; Put the Blame on Me; I'm Yours; I Feel That I'v Known You Forever; Slowly but Surely. **1965 90m/C** Elvis Presley, Julie Adams, Jack Mullaney; **D:** Norman Taurog. **VHS, Beta** $14.98 FOX, MVD *ℐ* ½

Ticks Mammoth mutant killer insects terrorize a Northern California campground! The predatory woodticks are the victims of steroids dumped in the water supply and a group of unwary teen campers fall prey to their deadly venom! And if that's not bad enough, a forest fire breaks out, trapping the teens! **1993 (R) 85m/C** Ami Dolenz, Rosalind Allen, Alfonso Ribeiro, Peter Scolari; **D:** Tony Randel. **VHS** REP *ℐ* ½

Tidal Wave Scientists discover that Japan is slowly sinking and order the island to be evacuated. Originally a popular Japanese production, the American version is a poorly dubbed, re-edited mess. **AKA:** Nippon Chiubotsu; The Submersion of Japan; Japan Sinks. **1975 (PG) 82m/C** Lorne Greene, Keiju Kobayashi, Rhonda Leigh Hopkins, Hiroshi Fujioka, Shiro Moriana; **D:** Andrew Meyer. **VHS** NWV *ℐ* ½

Tides of War In the twilight of the second world war, a German officer begins to question his role in a proposed missile attack on Washington in light of the S.S. brutality he witnesses. **1990 90m/C** Yvette Heyden, Rodrigo Obregon, David Soul, Bo Svenson; **D:** Neil Rossati. **VHS** NO *ℐ* ½

Tidy Endings A man who died from AIDS leaves behind his male lover and his ex-wife. The two form a friendship as they both try to cope with the man's death. Based on the play by Fierstein. **1988 54m/C** Harvey Fierstein, Stockard Channing; **D:** Gavin Millar; **W:** Harvey Fierstein. **VHS, Beta** $79.95 PSM *ℐ* ½

Tie Me Up! Tie Me Down! A young psychiatric patient kidnaps a former porno actress he has always had a crush on, and holds her captive, certain that he can convince her to love him. Black comedy features a fine cast and is well directed. At least one fairly explicit sex scene and the bondage theme caused the film to be X-rated, although it was originally released unrated by the distributor. In Spanish with English subtitles. **1990 (NC-17) 105m/C** Victoria Abril, Antonio Banderas, Loles Leon, Francesco Rabal, Julieta Serrano, Maria Barranco, Rossy de Palma; **D:** Pedro Almodovar; **W:** Pedro Almodovar; **M:** Ennio Morricone. **VHS** $19.95 COL, ING *ℐℐ* ½

Tiefland Melodrama based on the libretto for D'Abert's opera about a gypsy dancer and her loves. Unreleased until 1954, this film is the last of Riefenstahl's career; she subsequently turned to still photography. In German with English subtitles. **1944 98m/B** Leni Riefenstahl, Franz Eichberger, Bernard Minetti, Maria Koppenhofer, Luise Rainer; **D:** Leni Riefenstahl. **VHS, Beta** $24.95 NOS, FCT, GLV *ℐℐ* ½

Tiffany Jones Tiffany Jones is a secret agent who has information that presidents and revolutionaries are willing to kill for. **1975 (R) 90m/C** Anouska Hempel, Ray Brooks, Eric Pohlmann, Martin Benson, Susan Sneers; **D:** Pete Walker. **VHS, Beta** $39.95 MON *ℐ*

Tiger and the Pussycat A successful Italian businessman's infatuation with an attractive American art student leads him to marital and financial woes. **AKA:** Il Tigre. **1967 (R) 110m/C** Ann-Margret, Vittorio Gassman, Eleanor Parker; **D:** Dino Risi. **VHS, Beta** $59.98 SUE, HHE *ℐ*

Tiger Bay A young Polish sailor, on leave in Cardiff, murders his unfaithful girlfriend. Lonely ten-year-old Gillie sees the crime and takes the murder weapon, thinking it will

make her more popular with her peers. Confronted by a police detective, she convincingly lies but eventually the sailor finds Gillie and kidnaps her, hoping to keep her quiet until he can get aboard his ship. A delicate relationship evolves between the child and the killer as she tries to help him escape and the police close in. Marks Hayley Mills' first major role and one of her finest performances.
1959 107m/B John Mills, Horst Buchholz, Hayley Mills, Yvonne Mitchell; **D:** J. Lee Thompson. **VHS, Beta $19.95** PAR *♫♫♫*

Tiger Claws The pretty, petite Rothrock has been called the female Bruce Lee. Perhaps, but at least he got a good script every once in a while. This time Rothrock's a kung-fu cop investigating the strange ritual-murders of martial-arts champions.
1991 (R) 93m/C Cynthia Rothrock, Bolo Yeung, Jalal Merhi; **D:** Kelly Markin. **VHS, Beta $19.98** MCA *♫♫*

Tiger Fangs When Nazis threaten the Far East rubber production with man-eating tigers, real-life big game hunter Frank Buck comes to the rescue.
1943 57m/B Frank Buck, June Duprez, Duncan Renaldo; **D:** Jack Schwartz. **VHS $16.95** SNC, NOS, DVT *♫♫*

Tiger Joe There's trouble in Southeast Asia, and the U.S. military confuses things even more.
1985 96m/C Alan Collins, David Warbeck; **D:** Anthony M. (Antonio Margheriti) Dawson. **VHS $69.98** LIV *♫*

Tiger of the Seven Seas A female pirate takes over her father's command and embarks on adventures on the high seas. Generous portions of action, intrigue, and romance. Sequel to "Queen of the Pirates."
1962 90m/C Giana Maria Canale, Anthony Steel, Grazia Maria Spina, Ernesto Calindri; **D:** Luigi Capuano. **VHS** *♫♫*

Tiger Town A baseball player, ending an illustrious career with the Detroit Tigers, sees his chance of winning a pennant slipping away. A young fan, however, proves helpful in chasing that elusive championship. Made for the Disney cable station.
1983 (G) 76m/C Roy Scheider, Justin Henry, Ron McLarty, Bethany Carpenter, Noah Moazezi; **D:** Alan Shapiro. **VHS, Beta $69.95** DIS *♫♫½*

A Tiger Walks A savage tiger escapes from a circus and local children start a nationwide campaign to save its life. Notable for its unflattering portrayal of America's heartland and small town dynamics. Radical departure from most Disney films of the period.
1964 88m/C Sabu, Pamela Franklin, Brian Keith, Vera Miles, Kevin Corcoran, Peter Brown, Una Merkel, Frank McHugh, Edward Andrews; **D:** Norman Tokar; **M:** Buddy Baker. **VHS, Beta $69.95** DIS *♫♫½*

Tiger Warsaw A young man returns to the town where he once lived, before he shot his father. He hopes to sort out his life and repair family problems. Muddled and sappy. **AKA:** The Tiger.
1987 (R) 92m/C Patrick Swayze, Barbara Williams, Piper Laurie, Bobby DiCicco, Kaye Ballard, Lee Richardson, Mary McDonnell; **D:** Amin Q. Chaudhri. **VHS, Beta $14.95** COL *♫½*

Tigers in Lipstick Seven short vignettes featuring the beautiful actresses as aggressive women and the men that they influence. **AKA:** Wild Beds.
1980 (R) 88m/C Laura Antonelli, Monica Vitti, Ursula Andress, Sylvia Kristel; **D:** Luigi Zampa. **VHS, Beta $39.95** MON *♫½*

A Tiger's Tale A middle-aged divorced nurse begins an affair with her daughters's ex-boyfriend.
1987 (R) 97m/C Ann-Margret, C. Thomas Howell, Charles Durning, Kelly Preston, Ann Wedgeworth, Tim Thomerson, Steven Kampmann, Traci Lin, Angel Tompkins; **D:** Peter Douglas. **VHS, Beta** NO *♫½*

Tigershark A martial arts expert goes to Southeast Asia to rescue his girlfriend, who has been kidnapped by communist forces and held captive for arms and ammunition. Strictly for fans of the martial arts.
1987 (R) 97m/C Mike Stone, John Quade, Pamela Bryant; **D:** Emmett Alston; **W:** Ivan Rogers. **VHS, Beta** NO *♫*

Tightrope Police inspector Wes Block pursues a killer of prostitutes in New Orleans' French Quarter. The film is notable both as a thriller and as a fascinating vehicle for Eastwood, who experiments with a disturbing portrait of a cop with some peculiarities of his own.
1984 (R) 115m/C Clint Eastwood, Genevieve Bujold, Dan Hedaya, Jennifer Beck, Alison Eastwood, Randi Brooks, Regina Richardson, Jamie Rose; **D:** Richard Tuggle. **VHS, Beta $19.98** WAR, TLF *♫♫♫*

The Tigress In 1920s Berlin two con artists set out to scam a rich American using sex as a lure. Things don't go as planned. Also available in an unrated version.
1993 (R) 89m/C Valentina Vargas, James Remar, George Peppard. **VHS $92.95** VMK *♫½*

Till Death Do Us Part Three married couples spend a weekend at a counseling retreat, unaware that the proprietor is a murderous maniac.
1972 (PG) 77m/C James Keach, Claude Jutra, Matt Craven; **D:** Timothy Brand. **VHS, Beta $69.95** VES *♫*

Till Death Do Us Part An ex-cop turns into an evil killer who seduces unsuspecting women and murders them for their insurance money. Contains footage not seen in the TV movie. Based on a true story and the book by Vincent Bugliosi.
1992 (R) 93m/C Treat Williams, Arliss Howard, Rebecca Jenkins; **D:** Yves Simoneau. **VHS, Beta $89.95** TRI *♫♫*

Till Marriage Do Us Part An innocent couple discover on their wedding night that they are really brother and sister. Since they can't in good conscience get a divorce or consummate their marriage, they must seek sexual gratification elsewhere. Antonelli is deliciously tantalizing in this silly satire. In Italian with English subtitles. **AKA:** Dio Mio, Come Sono Caduta in Basso; How Long Can You Fall?
1974 (R) 97m/C Laura Antonelli, Alberto Lionello, Jean Rochefort, Michele Placido, Karin Schubert; **D:** Luigi Comencini. **VHS, Beta $59.95** VES, TPV, ING *♫♫½*

Till the Clouds Roll By An all-star, high-gloss musical biography of songwriter Jerome Kern, that, in typical Hollywood fashion, bears little resemblance to the composer's life. Filled with wonderful songs from his Broadway hit. ♫Showboat Medley; Till the Clouds Roll By; Howja Like to Spoon with Me?; The Last Time I Saw Paris; They Didn't Believe Me; I Won't Dance; Why Was I Born?; Who?; Sunny.
1946 137m/C Robert Walker, Van Heflin, Judy Garland, Frank Sinatra, Lucille Bremer, Kathryn Grayson, June Allyson, Dinah Shore, Lena Horne, Virginia O'Brien, Tony Martin; **D:** Richard Whorf. **VHS, Beta $19.98** CNG, NOS, MGM *♫♫½*

Till the Clouds Roll By/A Star Is Born Ostensibly concerns the life and career of songwriter Jerome Kern. Highlighted by stellar performances from a number of musical stars of the day. Maudlin and unconcerned with factual accuracy, the film nonetheless is an exuberant celebration of Kern's talent.
1946 249m/C Judy Garland, Frank Sinatra, Robert Walker, Fredric March, Janet Gaynor, Andy Devine, Lionel Stander, Franklin Pangborn, Van Heflin, Lucille Bremer, Kathryn Grayson, Lena Horne, Tony Martin, Angela Lansbury, Dinah Shore, Virginia O'Brien, Cyd Charisse, Adolphe Menjou; **D:** William A. Wellman, Richard Whorf. **VHS, Beta $29.95** DVT *♫♫♫*

Till the End of Time Three GIs have trouble adjusting to civilian life in their home town after WWII. Fine performances and excellent pacing. Popular title song. Adapted from "They Dream of Home" by Niven Busch.
1946 105m/C Robert Mitchum, Guy Madison, Bill Williams, Dorothy McGuire, William Gargan, Tom Tully; **D:** Edward Dmytryk. **VHS, Beta $19.98** RKO, TTC *♫♫½*

Till There was You A struggling musician travels to a faraway tropical isle to solve the mystery of his brother's death.
1991 (PG-13) 94m/C Mark Harmon, Deborah Unger, Jeroen Krabbe, Shane Briant; **D:** John Seale; **M:** Graeme Revell. **VHS $19.98** MCA *♫*

Tillie Wakes Up Third in the Tillie series, following "Tillie's Punctured Romance" and "Tillie's Tomato Surprise." Tillie (Dressler) decides she needs a little fun in her life so she asks her hen-pecked nieghbor Mr. Pipkin (Hines) to spend the day with her on Coney Island.
1917 48m/B Marie Dressler, Johnny Hines, Frank Beamish, Ruby de Remer; **D:** Harry Davenport; **W:** Francis Marion. **VHS $16.95** GPV *♫♫½*

Tillie's Punctured Romance The silent comedy which established Chaplin and Dressler as comedians. Chaplin, out of his Tramp character, is the city slicker trying to put one over on farm girl Dressler, who pursues revenge. First feature length comedy film. Followed by "Tillie's Tomato Surprise" and "Tillie Wakes Up," which starred Dressler but not Chaplin.
1914 73m/B Charlie Chaplin, Marie Dressler, Mabel Normand, Mack Swain, Chester Conklin; **D:** Mack Sennett. **VHS, Beta $12.95** NOS, CCB, HHT *♫♫*

Tilt Flimsy storyline concerns a young runaway's adventures with an aspiring rock star. Shields' pinball expertise eventually leads her to a match against pinball champ Durning.
1978 (PG) 111m/C Charles Durning, Ken Marshall, Brooke Shields, Geoffrey Lewis; **D:** Rudy Durand; **W:** Rudy Durand, Donald Cammell. **VHS** NO *♫*

Tim Follows the relationship between a handsome, mentally retarded young man and an attractive older businesswoman. Sappy storyline is redeemed by Gibson's fine debut performance. Based on Colleen McCullough's first novel.
1979 94m/C Mel Gibson, Piper Laurie, Peter Gwynne, Alwyn Kurts, Pat Evison; **D:** Michael Pate. **VHS, Beta** MED, OM *♫♫½*

Tim Tyler's Luck Lost but not forgotten serial in its twelve-chapter entirety. The fearless Tim Tyler uses whatever he can to do battle with the sinister Spider Web gang.
1937 235m/B Frankie Thomas Jr., Frances Robinson, Al Shear, Norman Willis, Earl Douglas, Jack Mulhall, Frank Mayo, Pat O'Brien; **D:** Ford Beebe, Wyndham Gittens. **VHS $29.95** NOS, GPV, FCT *♫♫½*

Timber Queen A WWII flier comes home and aids his best friend's widow, who must make a quota of timber or lose her sawmill to gangsters. Old-fashioned.
1944 66m/B Richard Arlen, Mary Beth Hughes, June Havoc, Sheldon Leonard, George E. Stone, Dick Purcell; **D:** Frank McDonald. **VHS $19.95** *NOS, LOO ✍✍*

Timber Terrors A Mountie investigates his partner's murder. **AKA:** Morton of the Mounted.
1935 50m/B VHS, Beta *NO ✍*

Time After Time In Victorian London, circa 1893, H.G. Wells is experimenting with his time machine. He discovers the machine has been used by an associate, who turns out to be Jack the Ripper, to travel to San Francisco in 1979. Wells follows to stop any further murders and the ensuing battle of wits is both entertaining and imaginative. McDowell is charming as Wells and Steenburgen is equally fine as Well's modern American love interest.
1979 (PG) 112m/C Malcolm McDowell, David Warner, Mary Steenburgen, Patti D'Arbanville, Charles Cioffi; **D:** Nicholas Meyer; **W:** Nicholas Meyer; **M:** Miklos Rozsa. **VHS, Beta $19.98** *WAR ✍✍✍*

Time Bandits A group of dwarves help a young boy to travel through time and space with the likes of Robin Hood, Napoleon, Agamemnon, and other time-warp playmates. Epic fantasy from Monty Python alumni.
1981 (PG) 110m/C John Cleese, Sean Connery, Shelley Duvall, Katherine Helmond, Ian Holm, Michael Palin, Ralph Richardson, Kenny Baker, Peter Vaughan, David Warner; **D:** Terry Gilliam; **W:** Michael Palin, Terry Gilliam. **VHS, Beta $19.95** *PAR ✍✍½*

Time Burst: The Final Alliance A man fights for his soul to protect the secret of immortality at any cost.
1989 93m/C VHS, Beta $9.95 *AIP ✍✍½*

Time Fighters A time machine has the ability to travel at the speed of light from prehistoric times to the distant future. This is a great help to the Time fighters.
1985 60m/C VHS, Beta *SUE ✍½*

Time Flies When You're Alive A made-for-cable-television presentation of actor Linke's performance monologue detailing the traumas and experiences he and his family underwent as his wife Francesca slowly died of cancer.
1989 79m/C Paul Linke; **D:** Roger Spottiswoode. VHS, Beta $79.99 *HBO ✍½*

A Time for Miracles Dramatic biography of the first native-born American saint, Elizabeth Bayley Seton, who was canonized in 1975. Made for television.
1980 97m/C Kate Mulgrew, Lorne Greene, Rossano Brazzi, John Forsythe, Jean-Pierre Aumont, Milo O'Shea; **D:** Michael O'Herlihy. VHS, Beta $9.98 *NLC ✍½*

Time for Murder A series of British dramatizations of famous murder mystery stories. Made for television.
1987? 60m/C Beta *PSM ✍½*

Time for Revenge A demolitions worker attempts to blackmail his corrupt employer by claiming a workplace explosion made him speechless. He finds himself in a contest of silence and wits. In Spanish with English subtitles.
1982 112m/C Federico Luppi, Haydee Padilla, Julio de Grazia, Ulises Dumont; **D:** Adolfo Aristarain. VHS, Beta $24.95 *XVC, MED, AUD ✍✍½*

The Time Guardian Time-travelers of the future arrive in the Australian desert in 1988, intent on warning the local populace of the impending arrival of killer cyborgs from the 40th century. Muddled and confusing.
1987 (PG) 89m/C Tom Burlinson, Carrie Fisher, Dean Stockwell, Nikki Coghill; **D:** Brian Hannant; **W:** Brian Hannant, John Baxter. **VHS, Beta, 8mm $14.95** *COL, SUE, NLC ✍½*

Time Indefinite Cinema verite effort once again follows filmmaker McElwee who returns to his Southern roots to confront personal tragedy by recording every moment on film. It is an emotional journey in which he discovers that his camera may not be enough to protect him from his own feelings. Moving, with occasional lapses into self-absorption. Companion film to McElwee's "Sherman's March."
1993 117m/C D: Ross McElwee; **W:** Ross McElwee. VHS $79.95 *ICA ✍✍*

Time is Running Out A man races against the clock in this taut thriller.
1952 ?m/C Dave Clark, Mike Smith, Lenny Davidson. VHS $16.95 *SNC ✍*

Time Lock An expert safecracker races against time to save a child who is trapped inside a bank's pre-set time-locked vault. Canada is the setting, although the film was actually made in England. Based on a play by Arthur Hailey.
1957 73m/B Sean Connery, Robert Beatty, Lee Patterson, Betty McDowall, Vincent Winter; **D:** Gerald Thomas. VHS, Beta $39.95 *MON ✍✍*

The Time Machine English scientist living near the end of the 19th century invents time travel machine and uses it to travel into various periods of the future. Rollicking version of H.G. Wells' classic cautionary tale boasts Oscar-winning special effects. Remade in 1978.
1960 103m/C Rod Taylor, Yvette Mimieux, Whit Bissell, Sebastian Cabot, Alan Young; **D:** George Pal. VHS, Beta $19.95 *MGM, MLB ✍✍✍*

Time Machine Yet another adaptation of H.G. Wells' classic novel about a scientist who invents a machine that enables him to travel through time. Inferior remake of the 1960 version.
1978 (G) 99m/C John Beck, Priscilla Barnes, Andrew Duggan; **D:** Henning Schellerup. VHS, Beta $19.95 *VCI ✍½*

A Time of Destiny During WWII, an American soldier vows to kill his brother-in-law, who he believes caused his father's death. Meanwhile, the two men have become good friends in the army, never realizing their connection. A strange, overblown family saga from the director of "El Norte." Beautiful photography, terrific editing.
1988 (PG-13) 118m/C William Hurt, Timothy Hutton, Melissa Leo, Stockard Channing, Megan Follows, Francesco Rabal; **D:** Gregory Nava; **W:** Gregory Nava, Anna Thomas; **M:** Ennio Morricone. VHS, Beta, 8mm $14.95 *COL, SUE ✍✍*

Time of Indifference Based on the novel by Alberto Moravia. Tale of the disintegration of values in 1920s Italy is unable to take full advantage of its fine cast or potentially thought-provoking themes. **AKA:** Gli Indifferenti; Les Deux Rivales.
1964 84m/B Rod Steiger, Shelley Winters, Claudia Cardinale, Paulette Goddard, Tomas Milian; **D:** Francesco Maselli. VHS *GKK ✍✍*

Time of Tears A young boy, grieving after his grandfather's death, meets a lonely old man and they fill each other's emotional needs.
1987 (PG) 95m/C VHS, Beta $19.95 *STE, NWV ✍½*

Time of the Apes A Japanese-made horror film about a woman and two kids thrust into an underground world ruled by intelligent gorillas.
1987 98m/C VHS, Beta $39.95 *CEL ✍*

Time of the Gypsies Acclaimed Yugoslavian saga about a homely, unlucky Gypsy boy who sets out to steal his way to a dowry large enough to marry the girl of his dreams. Beautifully filmed, magical, and very long. In the Gypsy language, Romany, it's the first feature film made in the Gypsy tongue. **AKA:** Dom Za Vesanje.
1990 (R) 136m/C Davor Dujmovic, Sinolicka Trpkova, Ljubica Adzovic, Hunsija Hasimovic, Bora Todorovic; **D:** Emir Kusturica. VHS, Beta $79.95 *COL, ING ✍✍✍*

The Time of Their Lives A pair of Revolutionary War-era ghosts haunt a modern country estate. One of the best A & C comedies. **AKA:** The Ghost Steps Out.
1946 82m/B Bud Abbott, Lou Costello, Marjorie Reynolds, Binnie Barnes, Gale Sondergaard, John Shelton; **D:** Charles T. Barton. VHS, Beta $14.95 *MCA ✍✍½*

The Time of Your Life The only Cagney film that ever lost money. A simple but engaging story of people trying to live their dreams. Cagney is delightful as a barroom philosopher who controls the world around him from his seat in the tavern. Although it was not very popular with audiences at the time, the critics hailed it as an artistic achievement. Based on William Saroyan's play.
1948 109m/B James Cagney, William Bendix, Jeanne Cagney, Broderick Crawford, Ward Bond, James Barton, Paul Draper, Natalie Schafer; **D:** H.C. Potter. VHS $19.95 *NOS, VEC, HEG ✍✍✍½*

Time Out for Love An American girl travels to Paris in search of romance, but discovers more than she bargained for. In French with English subtitles. **AKA:** Les Grandes Personnes; The Five Day Lover.
1961 91m/B Jean Seberg, Micheline Presle, Maurice Ronet, Francoise Prevost, Annabelle Ninchi, Fernando Bruno; **D:** Jean Valere; **M:** Georges Delerue. VHS $29.95 *DVT, HEG ✍✍½*

Time Runner It's 2022 and the Earth is being used as target practice by alien invaders. Space captain Hamill manages to find a hole in time and slip back to 1992 where he can battle the first of the alien infiltrators and maybe change Earth's destiny. The time-travel theme (including Hamill watching his own birth) is fun and the special effects are well done.
1992 (R) 90m/C Mark Hamill, Brion James, Rae Dawn Chong; **D:** Michael Mazo. VHS $19.95 *NLC, COL ✍✍*

Time Stands Still Two brothers experience troubled youth in Budapest. Artful, somberly executed, with American pop soundtrack. Subtitled in English.
1982 99m/C Istvan Znamenak, Henrik Pauer, Aniko Ivan, Sander Soth, Peter Galfy; **D:** Peter Gothar. VHS, Beta $59.95 *COL ✍✍✍*

Time to Die WWII victim of heinous war crimes, obsessed with revenge, stalks his prey for a final confrontation, while eluding U.S. intelligence. Disappointing despite good cast working with Mario Puzo story. **AKA:** Seven Graves for Rogan.
1983 (R) 89m/C Edward Albert, Rex Harrison, Rod Taylor, Raf Vallone; **D:** Matt Cimber; **M:** Ennio Morricone. VHS, Beta $59.95 *MED ✍½*

A Time to Die Lords plays a police photographer who, well, photographs the police. But her camera catches one in the act of murder. Routine crime thriller.

1991 (R) 93m/C Traci Lords, Jeff Conaway, Richard Roundtree, Bradford Bancroft, Nitchie Barrett; **D:** Charles Kanganis; **W:** Charles Kanganis; **M:** Ennio Morricone. **VHS** $89.95 PMH ✂✂½

Time to Kill A young soldier in Africa wanders away from his camp and meets a woman whom he rapes and kills. But when he returns to his outfit he finds he can't escape his tormenting conscience. *AKA:* Tempo di Uccidere.
1989 (R) 110m/C Nicolas Cage, Giancarlo Giannini, Robert Liensol; **D:** Guiliano Montaldo; **W:** Furio Scarpelli; **M:** Ennio Morricone. **VHS** $19.98 REP ✂✂½

A Time to Live Made-for-television adaptation of Mary Lou Weisman's ''Intensive Care'' about a family's adjustment to a young boy's fight with Muscular Dystrophy. Minnelli's first appearance in a television movie.
1985 97m/C Liza Minnelli, Jeffrey DeMunn, Swoosie Kurtz, Corey Haim, Scott Schwartz; **D:** Rick Wallace; **M:** Georges Delerue. **Beta** NO ✂✂½

A Time to Love & a Time to Die Lush adaptation of Erich Maria Remarque novel about WWII German soldier who falls in love with a young girl during furlough. The two are married, only to be separated when he is forced to return to the Russian front. Sympathetic treatment of Germans opposed to Hitler's policies.
1958 133m/C John Gavin, Lilo (Liselotte) Pulver, Jock Mahoney, Keenan Wynn, Klaus Kinski, Jim Hutton, Dana J. Hutton; **D:** Douglas Sirk. **VHS, Beta** $14.95 BAR ✂✂½

A Time to Remember Sticky with sentiment, this family film tells of a boy with a gift for singing, encouraged by a priest, discouraged by his father. At one point the kid loses his voice—he probably choked on the pathos.
1990 90m/C Donald O'Connor, Morgana King. **VHS** $29.95 IGP ✂✂½

Time Trackers A Roger Corman cheapie about a race through time, from present-day New York to medieval England, to recover a time machine before it alters the course of history.
1988 (PG) 87m/C Kathleen Beller, Ned Beatty, Will Shriner; **D:** Howard R. Cohen. **VHS, Beta** $14.95 MGM ✂✂

The Time Travelers Scientists discover and pass through a porthole leading to earth's post-armageddon future where they encounter unfriendly mutants. Frightened, they make a serious effort to return to the past. Remade as ''Journey to the Center of Time.'' *AKA:* Time Trap.
1964 82m/C Preston Foster, Phil Carey, Merry Anders, John Hoyt, Joan Woodbury, Dolores Wells, Dennis Patrick; **D:** Ib Melchior. **VHS, Beta** NO ✂✂

Time Troopers In another post-nuke society, special police must execute anyone who has misused their allotted ''energy clips'' for illicit behavior. Dime-store budget sci-fi. *AKA:* Morgen Grauen; Morning Terror.
1989 (R) 90m/C Albert Fortell, Hannelore Elsner; **D:** L.E. Neiman. **VHS, Beta** $59.95 PSM ✂

Time Walker An archaeologist unearths King Tut's coffin in California. An alien living inside is unleashed and terrorizes the public.
1982 (PG) 86m/C Ben Murphy; **D:** Tom Kennedy; **M:** Richard Band. **VHS, Beta** $19.98 NLC ✂

Timebomb When someone attempts to kill Biehn, he turns to a beautiful psychiatrist for help. She triggers flashbacks that send her hunted patient on a dangerous, perhaps deadly, journey into his past.

1991 (R) 96m/C Michael Biehn, Patsy Kensit, Tracy Scoggins, Robert Culp, Richard Jordan, Raymond St. Jacques, Jim Maniaci, Billy Blanks, Ray ''Boom Boom'' Mancini, Steven J. Oliver; **D:** Avi Nesher; **W:** Avi Nesher; **M:** Patrick Leonard. **VHS, Beta** $14.95 MGM ✂✂½

Timecop ''Terminator'' rip-off is fodder for Van Damme followers, but holds little appeal for fans of actors with talent. Van Damme is a policeman who must travel back in time to prevent a politician from altering history for personal gain. Futuristic thriller based on a Dark Horse comic.
1994 ?m/C Jean-Claude Van Damme, Ron Silver, Mia Sara, Bruce McGill, Scott Lawrence, Kenneth Welsh, Gabrielle Rose, Duncan Fraser, Ian Tracey, Gloria Reuben, Scott Bellis, Jason Schombing, Kevin McNulty, Sean O'Byrne, Malcolm Stewart, Alfonso Quijada, Glen Roald, Theodore Thomas; **D:** Peter Hyams; **W:** Mark Verheiden, Gary De Vore. **VHS** NYR ✂✂½

Timepiece This tape features one of Jim Henson's earlier films about an overworked, young executive.
1965 10m/C Jim Henson. **VHS, Beta** FLL ✂✂

Timerider Motorcyclist riding through the California desert is accidentally thrown back in time to 1877, the result of a scientific experiment that went awry. There he finds no gas stations and lots of cowboys. Co-written and co-produced by Michael Nesmith, best known for his days with the rock group ''The Monkees.'' *AKA:* The Adventure of Lyle Swan.
1983 (PG) 93m/C Fred Ward, Belinda Bauer, Peter Coyote, Richard Masur, Ed Lauter, L.Q. Jones, Tracy Walter; **D:** William Dear. **VHS, Beta** NO ✂✂½

Times of Harvey Milk A powerful and moving documentary about the life and career of San Francisco supervisor and gay activist Harvey Milk. The film documents the assassination of Milk and Mayor George Moscone by Milk's fellow supervisor, Dan White. Highly acclaimed by both critics and audiences, the film gives an honest and direct look at the murder and people's reactions. News footage of the murders and White's trial is included.
1983 90m/C **D:** Robert Epstein. **VHS, Beta** $59.95 TPV ✂½

Times Square A 13-year-old girl learns about life on her own when she teams up with a defiant, anti-social child of the streets. Unappealing and unrealistic, the film features a New Wave music score.
1980 (R) 111m/C Tim Curry, Trini Alvarado, Robin Johnson, Peter Coffield, Elizabeth Pena, Anna Maria Horsford; **D:** Allan Moyle; **W:** Jacob Brackman. **VHS, Beta** NO ✂½

Times to Come Taut thriller reminiscent of bleak futuristic movies like ''Clockwork Orange.'' Three people try to survive in a desolate, aggressive, and unstable future. In Spanish with English subtitles. *AKA:* Lo Que Vendra.
1981 98m/C Hugo Soto, Juan Leyrado, Charly Garcia; **D:** Gustavo Mosquera. **VHS** $79.95 CCN, FCT, ING ✂✂✂

Timestalkers A college professor's infatuation with a young woman is complicated by their pursuit of a criminal from the 26th century into the past. Mildly entertaining adventure. Tucker's last film. Made for television.
1987 100m/C William Devane, Lauren Hutton, Klaus Kinski, John Ratzenberger, Forrest Tucker, Gail Youngs; **D:** Michael A. Schultz. **VHS** $29.95 FRH ✂✂½

Timothy and the Angel A young man with a deep desire to be a ranger must pass up the rival temptations of a baseball scholarship and a life of speed and drugs offered by a motorcyclist.
1979 29m/C **VHS, Beta** LCA ✂½

The Tin Drum German child in the 1920s wills himself to stop growing in response to the increasing Nazi presence in Germany. He communicates his anger and fear by pounding on a tin drum. Memorable scenes, excellent cast. In German with English subtitles. Adapted from the novel by Gunter Grass. *AKA:* Die Blechtrommel.
1979 (R) 141m/C David Bennent, Mario Adorf, Angela Winkler, Daniel Olbrychski, Katharina Thalbach, Heinz Bennent, Andrea Ferreol, Charles Aznavour; **D:** Rainer Werner Fassbinder, Volker Schlondorff; **W:** Jean-Claude Carriere, Volker Schlondorff; **M:** Maurice Jarre. **VHS, Beta** $59.95 WAR, APD, GLV ✂✂✂✂

Tin Man Garage mechanic born totally deaf designs and builds a computer that can both hear and speak for him. His world is complicated, however, when a young speech therapist introduces him to new and wonderful sounds and unscrupulous and exploitative computer salesmen. Interesting premise and nice performances.
1983 95m/C Timothy Bottoms, Deana Jurgens, Troy Donahue; **D:** John G. Thomas. **VHS, Beta** $59.95 MED ✂✂½

Tin Men Set in Baltimore in the 1960s, this bitter comedy begins with two aluminum-siding salesmen colliding in a minor car accident. They play increasingly savage pranks on each other until one seduces the wife of the other, ruining his marriage. Like ''Diner,'' the movie is full of Levinson's idiosyncratic local Baltimore color.
1987 (R) 112m/C Richard Dreyfuss, Danny DeVito, Barbara Hershey, John Mahoney, Jackie Gayle, Stan Brock, Seymour Cassel, Bruno Kirby, J.T. Walsh, Michael Tucker; **D:** Barry Levinson; **W:** Barry Levinson; **M:** David Steele. **VHS, Beta** $19.95 TOU ✂✂½

Tin Pan Alley Tin Pan Alley songwriters Oakie and Payne meet singing sisters Faye and Grable, who agree to plug their material. At first their music business thrives but when the women head off to sing in a hit London show, the business goes downhill. Since WWI has been declared, the boys enlist and wind up in England, where they get a second chance to see their gals. The first teaming of Faye and Payne, who would star together in three more films. Remade as ''I'll Get By.'' ♫The Sheik of Araby; You Say the Sweetest Things, Baby; America I Love You; Goodbye Broadway, Hello France; K-K-K-Katy; Moonlight Bay; Honeysuckle Rose; Moonlight and Roses.
1940 92m/B Alice Faye, John Payne, Betty Grable, Jack Oakie, Allen Jenkins, Esther Ralston, John Loder, Elisha Cook Jr., Fred Keating, Billy Gilbert; **D:** Walter Lang; **W:** Robert Ellis, Helen Logan; **M:** Alfred Newman. **VHS** $19.98 FXV ✂✂½

The Tin Star Perkins is the young sheriff who persuades veteran bounty hunter Fonda to help him rid the town of outlaws. Excellent Mann western balances humor and suspense.
1957 93m/B Henry Fonda, Anthony Perkins, Betsy Palmer, Neville Brand, Lee Van Cleef, John McIntire, Michel Ray; **D:** Anthony Mann; **M:** Elmer Bernstein. **VHS, Beta** $14.95 PAR, BAR ✂✂✂

Tintorera...Tiger Shark Three shark hunters attempt to discover why buxom swimmers are disappearing. Phony takeoff of ''Jaws.'' *AKA:* Tintorera; Tintorera...Bloody Waters.
1978 (R) 91m/C Susan George, Fiona Lewis, Jennifer Ashley; *D:* Rene Cardona Jr. **VHS, Beta $54.95** *MED Woof!*

Tiny Toon Adventures: How I Spent My Vacation How the tiny toons of Acme Acres spend their summer vacation in this animated adventure that spoofs several popular films and amusements. Plucky Duck and Hampton Pig journey to ''Happy World Land'' (a takeoff on Walt Disney World), Babs and Buster Bunny's water adventure parodies ''Deliverance,'' there's a spoof of ''The Little Mermaid,'' and the Road Runner even makes a cameo appearance. Parents will be equally entertained by the level of humor and the fast-paced action. Based on the Steven Spielberg TV cartoon series, this is the first made-for-home-video animated feature ever released in the United States.
1991 80m/C VHS, Beta, 8mm $19.95 *WAR ♫♫♫*

The Tioga Kid Dean takes on two roles here, that of a Texas Ranger and an outlaw who goes by the name of ''The Tioga Kid.'' Andy Parker and the Plainsmen provide the cowboy tunes.
1948 54m/B Eddie Dean, Roscoe Ates, Jennifer Holt, Dennis Moore, Bill Fawcett; *D:* Ray Taylor; *W:* Ed Earl Repp. **VHS $19.99** *MOV ♫1/2*

The Tip-Off Lovable boxer (Armstrong) and vivacious girlfriend (Rogers) save less-than-bright friend from getting involved with mean mobster's girlfriend. Major chemistry between Rogers and Armstrong.
1931 75m/B Eddie Quillan, Robert Armstrong, Ginger Rogers, Joan Peers, Ernie Adams; *D:* Albert Rogell. **VHS $19.98** *TTC, FCT ♫♫1/2*

'Tis a Pity She's a Whore A brother and sister engage in an incestuous affair. She becomes pregnant and is married off. Her husband, however, becomes infuriated when he learns of his wife's pregnancy. Photography is by Vittorio Storaro in this highly stylized drama set in Renaissance Italy. *AKA:* Addio, Fratello, Crudele.
1973 (R) 102m/C Charlotte Rampling, Oliver Tobias, Fabio Testi, Antonio Falsi, Rick Battaglia, Angela Luce, Rino Imperio; *D:* Giuseppe Patroni Griffi; *M:* Ennio Morricone. **VHS, Beta $14.95** *ACA ♫♫1/2*

Title Shot A crafty manager convinces a millionaire to bet heavily on the guaranteed loss of his heavyweight contender in an upcoming fight. He doesn't realize the boxer is too stupid to throw the fight.
1981 (R) 88m/C Tony Curtis, Richard Gabourie, Susan Hogan, Robert Delbert; *D:* Les Rose. **VHS, Beta $69.98** *LIV ♫*

Tito and Me Ten-year-old Zoran lives in 1954 Belgrade and is fascinated by Yugoslavian leader Marshall Tito. Crowded into a flat with his extended family, Zoran learns about volatility firsthand. Then there's romance—he has a crush on a classmate who breaks up with him when she is chosen as one of Tito's Young Pioneers, which means a two-week trip to the country. Political indoctrination means nothing but love—ahh. Debut role for the young Vojnov, who carries the weight of the movie with perfect aplomb. In Serbo-Croation with English subtitles.
1992 104m/C Dimitrie Vojnov, Laza Ristovski, Anica Dobra, Predrag Manojlovic, Olivera Markovic; *D:* Goran Markovic; *W:* Goran Markovic. **VHS $89.98** *FXL, FCT ♫♫♫*

TNT Jackson A kung fu mama searches for her brother while everyone in Hong Kong tries to kick her out of town.
1975 (R) 73m/C Jeanne Bell; *D:* Cirio H. Santiago. **VHS, Beta $19.95** *NLC Woof!*

To All a Goodnight Five young girls and their boyfriends are planning an exciting Christmas holiday until a mad Santa Claus puts a damper on things. Total gorefest, with few, if any, redeeming virtues.
1980 90m/C Jennifer Runyon, Forrest Swanson, Linda Gentile, William Lover; *D:* David Hess. **VHS, Beta $59.95** *MED Woof!*

To All My Friends on Shore A made-for-television story about a father dealing with his young son's sickle cell anemia. Fine performances, realistic script make this an excellent outing.
1971 74m/C Bill Cosby, Gloria Foster, Dennis Hines; *D:* Gilbert Cates. **VHS, Beta** *NO ♫♫♫*

To Be or Not to Be Sophisticated black comedy set in wartime Poland. Lombard and Benny are Maria and Josef Tura, the Barrymores of the Polish stage, who use the talents of their acting troupe against the invading Nazis. The opening sequence is regarded as a cinema classic. One of Benny's finest film performances, the movie marks Lombard's final screen appearance. Classic Lubitsch. Remade in 1983.
1942 102m/B Carole Lombard, Jack Benny, Robert Stack, Sig Rumann, Lionel Atwill, Felix Bressart, Helmut Dantine, Tom Dugan, Charles Halton; *D:* Ernst Lubitsch. **VHS, Beta $59.95** *VES, WAR ♫♫♫1/2*

To Be or Not to Be In this remake of the 1942 film, Bancroft and Brooks are actors in Poland during WWII. They accidently become involved with the Polish Resistance and work to thwart the Nazis. Lots of laughs, although at times there's a little too much slapstick.
1983 (PG) 108m/C Mel Brooks, Anne Bancroft, Charles Durning, Jose Ferrer, Tim Matheson, Christopher Lloyd; *D:* Alan Johnson; *W:* Ronny Graham. **VHS, Beta $14.98** *FOX ♫♫1/2*

To Be the Best Eric, a member of the U.S. Kickboxing Team, lets his love for the beautiful Cheryl and his hot temper get the best of him. When a ruthless gambler threatens to kill Cheryl if Eric doesn't throw his big match, he joins with his family, fellow teammates, and most feared opponent, to set things right.
1993 (R) 99m/C Mike Worth, Martin Kove, Phillip Troy, Brittney Powell, Alex Cord, Steven Leigh; *D:* Joseph Merhi; *W:* Michael January. **VHS $89.95** *PMH ♫1/2*

To Catch a Killer A chilling performance by Dennehy highlights this true-crime tale of a detective's relentless pursuit of serial killer John Wayne Gacy, who preyed on young men and hid the bodies in his home. Made for television.
1992 95m/C Brian Dennehy, Michael Riley, Margot Kidder, Meg Foster; *D:* Eric Till. **VHS $89.95** *WOV ♫♫1/2*

To Catch a King Garr is a singer working in Wagner's nightclub in 1940s' Lisbon. The pair becomes involved in trying to foil the Nazi plot to kidnap the vacationing Duke and Duchess of Windsor. Average made-for-cable fare.
1984 120m/C Robert Wagner, Teri Garr, Horst Janson, Barbara Parkins, John Standing; *D:* Clive Donner; *M:* Nick Bicat. **VHS, Beta $49.95** *PSM ♫♫*

To Catch a Thief On the French Riviera, a reformed jewel thief falls for a wealthy American woman, who suspects he's up to his old tricks when a rash of jewel

thefts occur. Oscar-winning photography by Robert Burks, a notable fireworks scene, and snappy dialogue. A change of pace for Hitchcock, this charming comedy-thriller proved to be as popular as his other efforts. Kelly met future husband Prince Ranier during shooting in Monaco. Based on the novel by David Dodge.
1955 103m/C Cary Grant, Grace Kelly, Jessie Royce Landis, John Williams, Charles Vanel, Brigitte Auber; *D:* Alfred Hitchcock; *W:* John Michael Hayes. Academy Awards '55: Best Color Cinematography; Nominations: Best Art Direction/Set Decoration (Color), Best Costume Design (Color). **VHS, Beta $19.95** *PAR, MLB, HMV ♫♫♫*

To Dance with the White Dog Robert Samuel Peek (Cronyn) is a pecan-tree grower from rural Georgia who has been married to Cora (Tandy) for 57 years. Then she dies and their fussing daughters (Baranski and Wright) wonder how their father will survive. But Sam's increasing loneliness is checked when he befriends a stray white dog that it seems no one else can see. Based on the novel by Terry Kay. Made for television.
1993 (PG) 98m/C Hume Cronyn, Jessica Tandy, Christine Baranski, Amy Wright, Esther Rolle, Harley Cross, Frank Whaley, Terry Beaver, Dan Albright, David Dwyer; *D:* Glenn Jordan; *W:* Susan Cooper. **VHS** *REP ♫♫♫*

To Die for A vampire stalks, woos, and snacks on a young real estate woman.
1989 (R) 99m/C Brendan Hughes, Scott Jacoby, Duane Jones, Steve Bond, Sydney Walsh, Amanda Wyss, Ava Fabian; *D:* Deran Sarafian; *M:* Cliff Eidelman. **VHS, Beta $14.95** *ACA ♫1/2*

To Die for 2 This far outclasses part one in terms of acting and production values, but the plot still isn't back from the grave. Strange, because all the vampires are; despite their fiery deaths last time they flock around the adoptive mother of a baby secretly sired by a bloodsucker.
1991 (R) 95m/C Rosalind Allen, Steve Bond, Scott Jacoby, Michael Praed, Jay Underwood, Amanda Wyss, Remy O'Neill; *D:* David F. Price. **VHS $89.95** *VMK ♫1/2*

To Die Standing Two mavericks team up to do what the D.E.A. and cops simply cannot... capture a dangerous international drug lord. High action.
1991 (R) 87m/C Cliff DeYoung, Robert Beltran, Jamie Rose, Gerald Anthony, Orlando Sacha, Michael Ford; *D:* Louis Morneau; *W:* Ross Bell, Daryl Haney. **VHS $89.95** *COL ♫1/2*

To Forget Venice Portrays the sensitive relationships among four homosexuals, and their shared fears of growing older. Dubbed in English.
1979 90m/C Erland Josephson, Mariangela Melato, David Pontremoli, Elenora Giorgi; *D:* Franco Brusati. **VHS, Beta $59.95** *COL ♫♫1/2*

To Have & Have Not Martinique charter boat operator gets mixed up with beautiful woman and French resistance fighters during WWII. Top-notch production in every respect. Classic dialogue and fiery romantic bouts between Bogart and Bacall. Bacall's first film. Based on a story by Ernest Hemingway. Remade in 1950 as ''The Breaking Point'' and in 1958 as ''The Gun Runners.''
1944 100m/B Humphrey Bogart, Lauren Bacall, Walter Brennan, Hoagy Carmichael, Marcel Dalio, Dolores Moran, Sheldon Leonard, Dan Seymour; *D:* Howard Hawks. **VHS, Beta $19.95** *MGM ♫♫♫1/2*

To Heal a Nation The story of veteran Jan Scruggs, who spearheaded the movement to build the Vietnam Veterans memorial. The then little-known Ross Perot provided

major financial support for Scruggs' dream. Made for television.
1988 100m/C Eric Roberts, Conrad Bachmann, Glynnis O'Connor, Marshall Colt, Scott Paulin, Lee Purcell, Laurence Luckinbill, Linden Chiles, Brock Peters; **D:** Michael Pressman; **W:** Lionel Chetwynd. **VHS $89.98** TTC ♫♫½

To Hell and Back Adaptation of Audie Murphy's autobiography. Murphy plays himself, from his upbringing to WWII, where he was the most-decorated American soldier. Features realistic battle sequences punctuated with grand heroics.
1955 106m/C Audie Murphy, Marshall Thompson, Jack Kelly; **D:** Jesse Hibbs. **VHS, Beta $19.95** MCA, TLF ♫♫½

To Joy The rocky marriage of a violinist and his wife illuminate the problems of the young in Swedish society. Early Bergman. In Swedish with English subtitles or dubbed.
1950 90m/B D: Ingmar Bergman. **VHS, Beta $29.98** SUE, ING ♫♫♫

To Kill a Clown Painter and his wife working to save their marriage are trapped on an isolated island and terrorized by a crazed Vietnam veteran. This helps pull them together. Some holes in the plot, but generally effective.
1972 (R) 82m/C Alan Alda, Blythe Danner, Heath Lamberts; **D:** George Bloomfield. **VHS, Beta $9.95** MED ♫♫

To Kill a Mockingbird Faithful adaptation of powerful Harper Lee novel, both an evocative portrayal of childhood innocence and a denunciation of bigotry. Peck's performance as southern lawyer defending a black man accused of raping a white woman is flawless. Duvall debuted as the dim-witted Boo Radley. Lee based her characterization of "Dill" on Truman Capote, a childhood friend.
1962 129m/B Gregory Peck, Brock Peters, Phillip Alford, Mary Badham, Robert Duvall, Rosemary Murphy, William Windom, Alice Ghostley, John Megna, Frank Overton, Paul Fix, Collin Wilcox; **D:** Robert Mulligan; **W:** Horton Foote; **M:** Elmer Bernstein. Academy Awards '62: Best Actor (Peck), Best Adapted Screenplay, Best Art Direction/Set Decoration (B & W); Nominations: Best Black and White Cinematography, Best Director (Mulligan), Best Picture, Best Supporting Actress (Badham), Best Original Score; Golden Globe Awards '63: Best Actor—Drama (Peck), Best Score. **VHS, Beta $14.95** KUI, MCA, BTV ♫♫♫♫

To Kill a Priest Based on the true story of Father Jerzy Popieluszko, a young priest in 1984 Poland who defies his church and speaks out publicly on Solidarity. He is killed by the government as a result. Harris is good as the menacing police official.
1989 (R) 110m/C Christopher Lambert, Ed Harris, David Suchet, Tim Roth, Joanne Whalley-Kilmer, Peter Postlethwaite, Cherie Lunghi, Joss Ackland; **D:** Agnieszka Holland; **W:** Agnieszka Holland; **M:** Georges Delerue. **VHS, Beta $89.95** COL ♫♫

To Kill a Stranger A beautiful pop singer is stranded in a storm, and then victimized by a mad rapist/murderer.
197? 100m/C Donald Pleasence, Dean Stockwell, Angelica Maria, Aldo Ray, Sergio Aragones. **VHS, Beta** NO ♫♫

To Live and Die in Hong Kong Two sailors arrive in Hong Kong for a little R & R, until they are mistaken for spies by both the Hong Kong police and the Chinese mob. Action-packed tale.
1989 98m/C Rowena Cortes, Lawrence Jan, Mike Kelly, Laurens C. Postma; **D:** Lau Shing Hon. **VHS** ELV ♫½

To Live & Die in L.A. Fast-paced, morally ambivalent tale of cops and counterfeiters in L.A. After his partner is killed shortly before his retirement, a secret service agent sets out to track down his ruthless killer. Lots of violence; some nudity. Notable both for a riveting car chase and its dearth of sympathetic characters.
1985 (R) 114m/C William L. Petersen, Willem Dafoe, John Pankow, Dean Stockwell, Debra Feuer, John Turturro, Darlanne Fluegel, Robert Downey Jr.; **D:** William Friedkin; **W:** William Friedkin. **VHS, Beta $9.99** LIV, VES ♫♫

To Love Again A middle-aged love story about a reclusive college professor and the campus handyman.
1980 96m/C Lynn Redgrave, Brian Dennehy, Conchata Ferrell; **D:** Joseph Hardy. **VHS, Beta $9.98** NLC ♫½

To Paris with Love A British man and his son fall in love with a shop girl and her boss while on vacation in Paris. Charming and humorous, with a witty performance from Guinness.
1955 75m/C Alec Guinness, Odile Versois, Vernon Gray; **D:** Robert Hamer. **VHS, Beta** NO ♫♫½

To Play or To Die The introverted Kees attends an all-boy school where powerful bullies and sadomasochistic games are the rule. Kees is fascinated by the handsome Charel, the bullies leader. He invites Charel to his home, intending to turn the tables on his tormentor, but nothing goes as planned. Intense and controversial look at gay teens. Directorial debut of Krom. In Dutch with English subtitles.
1991 150m/C Geert Hunaerts, Tjebbo Gerritsma; **D:** Frank Krom; **W:** Anne Van De Putte, Frank Krom. **VHS $39.95** WBF ♫♫

To Please a Lady Romantic comedy-drama about race car driver Gable and reporter Stanwyck. Although leads do their best with the script, they're unable to generate any sparks. However, race track scenes are excellent. Filmed at the Indianapolis Speedway, the spectacular racing footage makes up for overall average film. **AKA:** Red Hot Wheels.
1950 91m/C Clark Gable, Barbara Stanwyck, Adolphe Menjou, Will Geer, Roland Winters; **D:** Clarence Brown; **W:** Barre Lyndon, Marge Decker. **VHS $19.98** MGM ♫♫½

To Protect and Serve When crooked cops start getting killed, two young cops are assigned to investigate. Suspicion points to a rookie (Howell), who just may have decided to clean things up his own way.
1992 (R) 93m/C C. Thomas Howell, Leslie Deane, Richard Romanus, Joe Cortese; **D:** Eric Weston. **VHS $49.98** LIV ♫♫

To Race the Wind Blind man wants to be treated like a normal person as he struggles through Harvard Law School. Based upon Harold Krents' autobiography "Butterflies Are Free." Made for television.
1980 97m/C Steve Guttenberg, Lisa Eilbacher, Randy Quaid, Barbara Barrie; **D:** Walter Grauman. **VHS, Beta $39.95** UNI ♫♫

To See Such Fun Hilarious excerpts from 80 years of the greatest British movie comedies.
1981 90m/C Peter Sellers, Marty Feldman, Benny Hill, Eric Idle, Alec Guinness, Margaret Rutherford, Dirk Bogarde, Spike Milligan. **VHS, Beta** NO ♫♫

To Sir, with Love Teacher in London's tough East End tosses books in the wastebasket and proceeds to teach his class about life. Skillful and warm performance by Poitier as idealistic teacher; supporting cast also

performs nicely. Based on the novel by E.R. Braithwaite. LuLu's title song was a big hit in 1967-68.
1967 105m/C Sidney Poitier, Lulu, Judy Geeson, Christian Roberts, Suzy Kendall, Faith Brook; **D:** James Clavell; **W:** James Clavell. **VHS, Beta $14.95** COL ♫♫½

To Sleep with a Vampire A Los Angeles bloodsucker is tired of his violent existence and craves the one thing he can't have—daylight. As he stalks his latest victim, a stripper, he decides to take her home and have her tell him about living in daytime. When she realizes what's going on, the intended victim decides to fight for her life. Action and eroticism raises this one above the norm. Remake of "Dance of the Damned."
1992 (R) 90m/C Scott Valentine, Charlie Spradling, Richard Zobel, Ingrid Vold, Stephanie Hardy; **D:** Adam Friedman. **VHS $89.98** NHO ♫♫

To Sleep with Anger At first a comic, introspective look at a black middle-class family going about their business in the heart of Los Angeles. Sly charmer Glover shows up and enthralls the entire family with his slightly sinister storytelling and a gnawing doom gradually permeates the household. Insightful look into the conflicting values of Black America. Glover's best performance.
1990 (PG) 105m/C Danny Glover, Mary Alice, Paul Butler, Richard Brooks, Carl Lumbly, Vonetta McGee, Sheryl Lee Ralph; **D:** Charles Burnett; **W:** Charles Burnett. **VHS, Beta $19.95** COL, FCT, IME ♫♫♫½

To Subdue the Evil In a tale of brutality and betrayal, twin brothers oppose each other after being separated at birth.
19?? 90m/C Lung Chunem, Chen Hung Lieh, Tien Pang. **VHS $49.95** OCE ♫

To the Camp & Back A romantic novel transposed to tape, with equal amounts of unfettered sentiment, fantasy, and style.
1985 60m/C Jan Niklas. **Beta $11.95** PSM ♫½

To the Death A kickboxer wants to retire from the boxing tournaments but the corrupt promoters refuse to let him go unless he manages to kill his rivals in the ring.
1993 (R) 90m/C John Barrett, Michael Quissi; **D:** Darrell Roodt. **VHS** CAN ♫½

To the Devil, A Daughter A nun is put under a spell by a priest who has been possessed by Satan. She is to bear his child. A writer on the occult intervenes. Based on the novel by Dennis Wheatley. One of Kinski's early films. **AKA:** Child of Satan.
1976 (R) 93m/C Richard Widmark, Christopher Lee, Nastassia Kinski, Honor Blackman, Denholm Elliott, Michael Goodliffe; **D:** Peter Sykes. **VHS, Beta $19.95** MLB ♫♫

To the Last Man An early Scott sagebrush epic, about two feuding families. Temple is seen in a small role. Based on Zane Grey's novel of the same name.
1933 70m/B Randolph Scott, Esther Ralston, Jack LaRue, Noah Beery Sr., Buster Crabbe, Gail Patrick, Barton MacLane, Fuzzy Knight, John Carradine, Jay Ward, Shirley Temple; **D:** Henry Hathaway. **VHS, Beta $9.95** NOS, DVT, MLB ♫

To the Lighthouse A proper British holiday turns into a summer of disillusionment in this adaptation of the Virginia Woolf novel.
1983 115m/C Rosemary Harris, Michael Clough, Suzanne Bertish, Lynsey Baxter. **VHS, Beta** NO ♫♫

To the Shores of Hell Leaving his sweetheart behind, Major Greg Donahue attacks Da Nang and plots to rescue his brother from the Viet Cong.
1965 82m/C Marshall Thompson, Kiva Lawrence, Richard Jordahl. **VHS, Beta** NO 🎬🎬

To the Shores of Tripoli Wartime propaganda in the guise of drama, in which a smarmy playboy is transformed into a Marine in boot camp.
1942 82m/C John Payne, Maureen O'Hara, Randolph Scott, Nancy Kelly, Henry Morgan, Maxie "Slapsie" Rosenbloom, William Tracy, Minor Watson, Alan Hale, Hugh Beaumont, Hillary Brooke; **D:** H. Bruce Humberstone. **VHS, Beta $14.98** FOX, MLB 🎬

The Toast of New Orleans A poor fisherman rises to stardom as an opera singer. Likable, though fluffy production features a plethora of musical numbers. 🎵Be My Love; Tina Lina; I'll Never Love You; The Toast of New Orleans; Song of the Bayou; Boom Biddy Boom Boom.
1950 97m/C Kathryn Grayson, Mario Lanza, David Niven, Rita Moreno, J. Carroll Naish; **D:** Norman Taurog. **VHS, Beta $19.98** MGM 🎬🎬½

Toast of New York Arnold plays Jim Fisk, a New England peddler who rises to become one of the first Wall Street giants of industry. Atypical Grant performance.
1937 109m/B Edward Arnold, Cary Grant, Frances Farmer, Jack Oakie, Donald Meek, Billy Gilbert; **D:** Rowland V. Lee. **VHS, Beta $19.98** RKO, TTC 🎬🎬🎬

Tobor the Great Sentimental and poorly executed, this film tells the tale of a boy, his grandfather, and Tobor the robot. Villainous communists attempt to make evil use of Tobor, only to be thwarted in the end.
1954 77m/B Charles Drake, Billy Chapin, Karin Booth, Taylor Holmes, Joan Gerber, Steve Geray; **D:** Lee Sholem. **VHS $19.98** REP 🎬½

Tobruk American GI's endeavor to knock out the guns of Tobruk, to clear the way for a bombing attack on German fuel supply depots of North Africa in this WWII actioner.
1966 110m/C Rock Hudson, George Peppard, Guy Stockwell, Nigel Green; **D:** Arthur Hiller. **VHS, Beta $19.95** MCA 🎬🎬

Toby McTeague A story about an Alaskan family that breeds Siberian Huskies. When his father is injured, the youngest son tries to replace him in the regional dog-sled race.
1987 (PG) 94m/C Winston Rekert, Wannick Bisson, Timothy Webber; **D:** Jean-Claude Lord. **VHS, Beta $14.95** COL, NLC 🎬🎬

Toby Tyler A boy runs off to join the circus, and teams up with a chimpanzee. A timeless and enjoyable Disney film that still appeals to youngsters. Good family-fare.
1959 (G) 93m/C Kevin Corcoran, Henry Calvin, Gene Sheldon, Bob Sweeney, Mr. Stubbs; **D:** Charles T. Barton. **VHS, Beta $69.95** DIS 🎬🎬🎬

Today I Hang A man is framed for murder and sentenced to hang. His buddies on the outside do their best to prove his innocence. Meanwhile, in prison, the accused encounters any number of interesting characters.
1942 67m/B Walter Woolf King, Mona Barrie, William Farnum, Harry Woods, James Craven; **D:** Oliver Drake. **VHS, Beta $16.95** SNC 🎬🎬

Today We Kill, Tomorrow We Die A rancher is unjustly sent to prison; when his sentence is over he hires a gang to relentlessly track down the culprit who framed him.

1971 (PG) 95m/C Montgomery Ford, Bud Spencer, William Berger, Tatsuya Nakadai, Wayde Preston; **D:** Tonino Cervi. **VHS, Beta $59.95** PSM 🎬

Today We Live Triangle love story set in WWI. Crawford is a hedonistic Brit having a fling with her naval brother's (Tone) friend (Young). When American flyer Cooper appears she sets his sights on him but soon he's off to combat in France where he's reported killed. Crawford returns to Young but, naturally, reports of Cooper's death have been greatly exaggerated and the two eventually reunite. Faulkner co-scripted from his story "Turn About" which had no female character and concerned the rivalry between naval officers and fly boys.
1933 113m/B Gary Cooper, Joan Crawford, Franchot Tone, Robert Young, Roscoe Karns, Louise Closser Hale; **D:** Howard Hawks; **W:** Dwight Taylor, William Faulkner, Edith Fitzgerald. **VHS, Beta $19.98** MGM, FCT 🎬🎬½

The Todd Killings A psychotic young man commits a series of murders involving young women. Sleazy, forgettable picture wastes a talented cast. AKA: A Dangerous Friend; Skipper.
1971 (R) 93m/C Robert F. Lyons, Richard Thomas, Barbara Bel Geddes, Ed Asner, Sherry Miles, Gloria Grahame, Belinda J. Montgomery; **D:** Barry Shear; **W:** Joel Oliansky. **VHS $59.95** WAR 🎬½

Toga Party Fraternity house throws a wild toga party in this raunchy low-rent depiction of college life.
1979 (R) 82m/C Bobby H. Charles, Mary Mitchell. **VHS, Beta $59.95** MON 🎬

Together? Divorced woman and a male chauvinist test the limits of their sexual liberation as well as viewer patience.
1979 (R) 91m/C Maximilian Schell, Jacqueline Bisset, Terence Stamp, Monica Guerritore; **D:** Armenia Balducci; **M:** Burt Bacharach. **VHS, Beta $24.98** SUE 🎬½

Togetherness Two wealthy, good-for-nothing playboys chase after the same blonde, a Communist, in Greece.
1970 101m/C George Hamilton, Peter Lawford, Olinka Berova, John Banner, Jesse White; **D:** Arthur Marks. **VHS, Beta** NO 🎬½

Tokyo Decadence Ai is a high-paid prostitute working in Tokyo for an agency that specializes in sado-masochism. Film follows her various sexual escapades in humiliating detail as well as her drug-addled search for a client Ai thinks she's in love with. Since Ai remains a cipher, the film also remains unfocused except for its creepy and explicit sex scenes. Adaptation of director Murakami's novel "Topaz." In Japanese with English subtitles or dubbed.
1991 (NC-17) 92m/C Miho Nikaido, Tenmei Kano, Yayoi Kusama, Sayoko Amano; **D:** Ryu Murakami; **W:** Ryu Murakami; **M:** Ryuichi Sakamoto. **VHS $89.95** TRI, FCT 🎬½

Tokyo-Ga Impelled by his love for the films of Yasujiro Ozu, Wenders traveled to Tokyo and fashioned a caring document of both the city and of Ozu's career, using images that recall and comment on Ozu's visual motifs.
1985 92m/C **D:** Wim Wenders; **W:** Wim Wenders. **VHS, Beta $59.95** ING, TPV 🎬🎬🎬½

Tokyo Joe A war hero/nightclub owner returns to Tokyo and becomes ensnared in blackmail and smuggling while searching for his missing wife and child. Slow-moving tale has never been considered one of Bogart's better movies.
1949 88m/B Humphrey Bogart, Florence Marly, Alexander Knox, Sessue Hayakawa, Jerome Courtland, Lore Lee Michel; **D:** Stuart Heisler. **VHS, Beta $69.95** COL 🎬½

Tokyo Olympiad A monumental sports documentary about the 1964 Olympic Games in its entirety. Never before available for home viewing. Letterboxed with digital sound. In Japanese with English subtitles.
1966 170m/C **D:** Kon Ichikawa. **VHS, Beta $99.95** TPV, WFV, CRC 🎬½

Tokyo Pop A punk rocker travels to Japan to find stardom and experiences a series of misadventures. Enjoyable in its own lightweight way. Hamilton is the daughter of Carol Burnett.
1988 (R) 99m/C Carrie Hamilton, Yutaka Tadokoro, Tetsuro Tamba, Taiji Tonoyama, Masumi Harukawa; **D:** Fran Rubel Kazui; **W:** Lynn Grossman, Fran Rubel Kazui; **M:** Alan Brewer. **VHS $19.95** WAR 🎬🎬½

Tokyo Story Poignant story of elderly couple's journey to Tokyo where they receive little time and less respect from their grown children. Masterful cinematography, and sensitive treatment of universally appealing story. In Japanese with English subtitles.
1953 134m/B Chishu Ryu, Chieko Higashiyama, So Yamamura, Haruko Sugimura, Setsuko Hara; **D:** Yasujiro Ozu; **W:** Yasujiro Ozu. **VHS $69.95** NYF, FCT, ING 🎬🎬🎬🎬

Tol'able David A simple tale of mountain folk, done in the tradition of Mark Twain stories. A family of hillbillies is embroiled in a feud with a clan of outlaws. When the community's mail is stolen by the troublesome ruffians, the family's youngest member, who harbors dreams of becoming a mail driver, comes to the rescue. Silent film.
1921 79m/B Richard Barthelmess, Gladys Hulette, Ernest Torrence; **D:** Henry King. **VHS, Beta $19.95** NOS, VYY, CCB 🎬🎬

Toll Gate Quick on the draw outlaw Hart risks capture to rescue drowning child, and consequently gets involved with the boy's mother. Silent classic.
1920 55m/B William S. Hart, Anna Q. Nilsson, Jack Richardson, Joseph Singleton; **D:** Lambert Hillyer. **VHS, Beta $19.95** GPV, VCN 🎬🎬½

Toll of the Desert A lawman learns that his father is a ruthless, back-stabbing renegade. Now he must try and catch him.
1935 58m/B Roger Williams, Ted Adams, Edward Cassidy, Tom London, John Elliott, Earl Dwire, Betty Mack, Fred Kohler Jr.; **D:** William Berke. **VHS, Beta $19.95** NOS, DVT 🎬

Tom and Jerry: The Movie Everybody's favorite animated cat/mouse duo (who began life in a 1940 MGM short "Puss Gets the Boot") hit the big screen, this time talking (unlike their animated shorts). Rather than cartoon mayhem our two protagonists are goody-two-shoes (with songs yet!) but still retain their charm. Kids will like it, but true "Tom and Jerry" fans should probably stick to the original cartoons.
1993 (G) 84m/C **D:** Phil Roman; **W:** Dennis Marks; **M:** Henry Mancini, Leslie Bricusse; **V:** Richard Kind, Dana Hill, Charlotte Rae, Henry Gibson, Rip Taylor, Howard Morris, Edmund Gilbert, David Lander. **VHS $24.98** FHE, WTA 🎬🎬

Tom Brown's School Days Depicts life among the boys in an English school during the Victorian era. Based on the classic novel by Thomas Hughes. Remade in 1951. AKA: Adventures at Rugby.
1940 86m/B Cedric Hardwicke, Jimmy Lydon, Freddie Bartholomew; **D:** Robert Stevenson. **VHS, Beta $19.95** NOS, HHT, PSM 🎬🎬½

Tom Brown's School Days Tom enrolls at Rugby and is beset by bullies in classic tale of English school life. British remake of the 1940 version. Based on the novel by Thomas Hughes.

1951 93m/B Robert Newton, John Howard Davies, James Hayter; *D:* Gordon Parry. **VHS, Beta** $19.95 *VCI 𝄆𝄆𝄆*

Tom, Dick, and Harry Dreamy girl is engaged to three men and unable to decide which to marry. It all depends on a kiss. Remade as "The Girl Most Likely."
1941 86m/B Ginger Rogers, George Murphy, Burgess Meredith, Alan Marshal, Phil Silvers; *D:* Garson Kanin. Academy Awards '41 Nominations: Best Story; National Board of Review Awards '41: 10 Best Films of the Year. **VHS, Beta** $19.98 *CCB, TTC, FCT 𝄆𝄆½*

Tom Edison: The Boy Who Lit Up the World This is the story of Tom Edison's life and how he changed the world.
1978 49m/C David Huffman, Adam Arkin, Michael Callan; *D:* Henning Schellerup. **VHS, Beta** *NO 𝄆𝄆*

Tom Horn The final days of one of the Old West's legends. Gunman Tom Horn, hired by Wyoming ranchers to stop cattle rustlers, goes about his job with a zeal that soon proves embarrassing to his employers. Beautifully photographed and authentic in its attention to details of the period, the film nonetheless takes liberties with the facts of Horn's life and is lacking in other aspects of production.
1980 (R) 98m/C Steve McQueen, Linda Evans, Richard Farnsworth, Billy Green Bush, Slim Pickens; *D:* William Wiard; *W:* Thomas McGuane; *M:* Ernest Gold. **VHS, Beta** $19.98 *WAR 𝄆𝄆*

Tom Jones Bawdy comedy based on Henry Fielding's novel about a rustic playboy's wild life in 18th century England. Hilarious and clever with a grand performance by Finney. One of the sexiest eating scenes ever. Redgrave's debut. Theatrically released at 129 minutes, the film was recut by the director, who decided it needed tightening before its 1992 re-release on video.
1963 121m/C Albert Finney, Susannah York, Hugh Griffith, Edith Evans, Joan Greenwood, Diane Cilento, George Devine, David Tomlinson, Joyce Redman, Lynn Redgrave, Julian Glover, Peter Bull, David Warner; *D:* Tony Richardson; *W:* John Osborne; *M:* John Addison. Academy Awards '63: Best Adapted Screenplay, Best Director (Richardson), Best Picture, Best Original Score; Nominations: Best Actor (Finney), Best Art Direction/Set Decoration (Color), Best Supporting Actor (Griffith), Best Supporting Actress (Cilento, Evans, Redman); British Academy Awards '63: Best Film; Directors Guild of America Awards '63: Best Director (Richardson); Golden Globe Awards '64: Best Film—Musical/Comedy, Best Foreign Film. **VHS, Beta** $19.98 *HBO, FOX, BTV 𝄆𝄆𝄆𝄆*

Tom Mix Compilation 1 This compilation of six "Great American Cowboy" films from Tom Mix's early period includes: "Jimmy Hayes and Muriel," "The Stagecoach Driver and the Girl," "Sagebrush Tom," "An Arizona Wooing," "Roping a Bride" and "Local Color."
1916 60m/B Tom Mix. **VHS, Beta** *GVV 𝄆𝄆𝄆𝄆*

Tom Mix Compilation 2 Five films from Tom Mix's early period include "Never Again," "An Angelic Attitude," "A Western Masquerade," "A $5,000 Elopement," and "Local Color."
1916 60m/B Tom Mix. **VHS, Beta** *GVV 𝄆𝄆𝄆𝄆*

Tom Sawyer Winning adaptation of Mark Twain's oft told tale of boyhood in Hannibal, Missouri. Cast reprised their roles the following year in "Huckleberry Finn."
1930 86m/B Jackie Coogan, Mitzie Green, Lucien Littlefield, Tully Marshall; *D:* John Cromwell. **VHS, Beta** $19.98 *MGM 𝄆𝄆𝄆*

Tom Sawyer Musical version of the Mark Twain tale of the boisterous Tom, his friend Becky Thatcher, and various adventures, including the fence whitewashing. Amusing kid fare shot on location in Missouri. ♫River Song; Gratification; Tom Sawyer; Freebootin'; Aunt Polly's Soliloquy; If'n I Was God; A Man's; Gotta Be What He's Born To Be; How Come?; Hannibal, Mo.
1973 (G) 104m/C Johnny Whitaker, Jodie Foster, Celeste Holm, Warren Oates, Jeff East; *D:* Don Taylor; *M:* John Williams. **VHS** $19.98 *MGM 𝄆𝄆½*

Tom Thumb Diminutive boy saves village treasury from bad guys. Adapted from classic Grimm fairy tale. Special effects combine live actors, animation, and puppets.
1958 92m/C Russ Tamblyn, Peter Sellers, Terry-Thomas; *D:* George Pal. **VHS, Beta** $39.95 *MGM 𝄆𝄆𝄆*

Tomb Fortune seekers disturb the slumber of a magical, sadistic princess much to their everlasting regret. Adapted from a Bram Stoker novel.
1986 106m/C Cameron Mitchell, John Carradine, Sybil Danning, Richard Hench, Michelle (McClellan) Bauer; *D:* Fred Olen Ray. **VHS, Beta** $19.98 *TWE 𝄆𝄆*

Tomb of Ligeia The ghost of a man's first wife expresses her displeasure when groom and new little missus return to manor. One of the better Corman adaptations of Poe. Also available with "The Conqueror Worm" on Laser Disc. *AKA:* Tomb of the Cat.
1964 82m/C Vincent Price, Elizabeth Shepherd, John Westbrook, Oliver Johnston, Richard Johnson; *D:* Roger Corman; *W:* Robert Towne. **VHS, Beta** $59.99 *HBO, MLB 𝄆𝄆𝄆*

Tomb of the Undead The sadistic guards of a prison camp are rudely awakened by the prisoners they tortured to death when they return as flesh-eating zombies looking to settle the score.
1972 60m/C Duncan McLeod, Lee Frost, John Dennis; *D:* John Hayes. **VHS, Beta** $19.95 *NOS, INC 𝄆½*

Tomb of Torture Murdered countess is reincarnated in the body of a newspaperman's mistress. Together they investigate monster reports in a murder-ridden castle. The butler may have something to do with it. Filmed in Sepiatone and dubbed. *AKA:* Metempsycose.
1965 88m/B Annie Albert, Thony Maky, Mark Marian, Queen Elizabeth; *D:* William Grace. **VHS, Beta** $39.99 *MSP Woof!*

The Tomboy A young woman behaves boyishly in Colonial America.
1924 64m/B Dorothy Devore, Lotta Williams, Herbert Rawlinson, Harry Gibbon, Lee Moran; *D:* David Kirkland. **VHS, Beta** $19.95 *GPV, FCT 𝄆½*

Tomboy Shy country boy and a not-so-shy city girl meet, fall in love, and overcome obstacles that stand in their path.
1940 70m/B Jackie Moran, Marcia Mae Jones. **VHS, Beta** $24.95 *VYY 𝄆*

Tomboy A pretty auto mechanic is determined to win not only the race but the love and respect of a superstar auto racer.
1985 (R) 91m/C Betsy Russell, Eric Douglas, Jerry Dinome, Kristi Somers, Richard Erdman, Toby Iland; *D:* Herb Freed. **VHS, Beta** $79.98 *LIV, VES Woof!*

Tomboy & the Champ Despite many obstacles, a music-loving calf becomes a prize winner with the help of its loving owner. Kids will love it, but adults will find this one a little sugary.

1958 82m/C Candy Moore, Ben Johnson, Jesse White; *D:* Francis D. Lyon. **VHS, Beta** $29.95 *VCI 𝄆𝄆*

Tombs of the Blind Dead Blinded by crows for using human sacrifice in the thirteenth century, zombies rise from the grave to wreak havoc upon 20th-century Spaniards. Atmospheric chiller was extremely popular in Europe and spawned three sequels. Originally titled "The Blind Dead." The sequels, also on video, are "Return of the Evil Dead" and "Horror of the Zombies." *AKA:* The Blind Dead; La Noche dell Terror Ciego.
1972 (PG) 86m/C Caesar Burner, Lone Fleming, Helen Harp; *D:* Armando de Ossorio. **VHS, Beta** *NO 𝄆𝄆½*

Tombstone Saga of Wyatt Earp and his band of law-abiding large moustaches beat the Kasdan/Costner vehicle to the big screen by several months. Legendary lawman Wyatt (Russell) moves to Tombstone, AZ aiming to start a new life with his brothers, but alas, that's not to be. The infamous gunfight at the OK Corral is here, and so is best buddy Doc Holliday, gunslinger and philosopher, a role designed for scenery chewing (Kilmer excels). Romance is supplied by actress Josephine, though Delany lacks the necessary romantic spark. Russell spends a lot of time looking troubled by the violence while adding to the body count. Too self-conscious, suffers from '90s western revisionism, but blessed with a high energy level thanks to despicable villains Lang, Biehn, and Booth.
1993 (R) 130m/C Kurt Russell, Val Kilmer, Michael Biehn, Sam Elliott, Dana Delany, Bill Paxton, Powers Boothe, Stephen Lang, Jason Priestly, Dana Wheeler-Nicholson, Billy Zane, Thomas Haden Church, Joanna Pacula, Michael Rooker, Harry Carey Jr., Billy Bob Thornton, Charlton Heston, Robert Burke, John Corbett, Buck Taylor, Terry O'Quinn, Pedro Armendariz Jr., Chris Mitchum, Jon Tenney; *D:* George P. Cosmatos; *W:* Kevin Jarre; *M:* Bruce Broughton. **VHS** *HPH 𝄆𝄆𝄆*

Tombstone Canyon Death rides the range until Maynard and his horse Tarzan put a halt to it.
1935 60m/B Ken Maynard, Sheldon Lewis, Cecilia Parker. **VHS, Beta** $12.95 *SNC, NOS, RXM 𝄆½*

Tombstone Terror A cowboy is beleaguered by a case of mistaken identity.
1934 55m/B Bob Steele. **VHS, Beta** *NO 𝄆*

Tomcat: Dangerous Desires Tom (Grieco) suffers from a rare degenerative condition and agrees to become a guinea pig in a secret, genetic imprinting experiment that has him injected with feline RNA. Tom's health is restored but the side effects give him the predatory instincts of a cat and the need to kill to stay alive.
1993 (R) 96m/C Richard Grieco, Maryam D'Abo, Natalie Radford. **VHS** $89.98 *REP 𝄆𝄆*

Tommy Peter Townsend's rock opera as visualized in the usual hyper-Russell style about the deaf, dumb, and blind boy who becomes a celebrity due to his amazing skill at the pinball machines. A parade of rock musicians perform throughout the affair, with varying degrees of success. Despite some good moments, the film ultimately falls prey to ill-conceived production concepts and miscasting. ♫Underture; Captain Walker Didn't Come Home; It's A Boy; '51 is Going to Be A Good Year; What About the Boy?; The Amazing Journey; Christmas; See Me, Feel Me; Eyesight to the Blind.

1975 (PG) 108m/C Ann-Margret, Elton John, Oliver Reed, Tina Turner, Roger Daltrey, Eric Clapton, Keith Moon, Pete Townshend, Jack Nicholson, Robert Powell; *D:* Ken Russell; *W:* Ken Russell. Academy Awards '75 Nominations: Best Actress (Ann-Margret), Best Original Score; Golden Globe Awards '76: Best Actress— Musical/Comedy (Ann-Margret). **VHS, Beta** $14.95 *COL, MVD, WME* 🎟🎟

Tomorrow Powerful tale of the love of two lonely people. Outstanding performance by Duvall as lumber mill worker who falls for a pregnant woman. Based on the neglected Faulkner story.
1983 (PG) 102m/B Robert Duvall, Olga Bellin, Sudie Bond; *D:* Joseph Anthony; *W:* Horton Foote Jr. **VHS, Beta** $24.95 *MON* 🎟🎟🎟

Tomorrow at Seven A mystery writer is determined to discover the identity of the Ace of Spades, a killer who always warns his intended victim, then leaves an ace of spades on the corpse as his calling card.
1933 62m/B Chester Morris, Vivienne Osborne, Frank McHugh, Allen Jenkins, Henry Stephenson; *D:* Ray Enright. **VHS, Beta** $12.95 *SNC, NOS, VYY* 🎟🎟½

Tomorrow is Forever Welles and Colbert marry shortly before he goes off to fight in WWI. Badly wounded and disfigured, he decides to stay in Europe while Colbert, believing Welles dead, eventually marries Brent. Fast forward to WWII when Brent, a chemical manufacturer, hires a new scientist to work for him in the war effort (guess who). This slow-moving melodrama wastes a good cast. Six-year-old Wood debuts as Colbert's daughter.
1946 105m/B Claudette Colbert, Orson Welles, George Brent, Lucile Watson, Richard Long, Natalie Wood; *D:* Irving Pichel. **VHS** $19.98 *MGM* 🎟🎟½

Tomorrow Never Comes When he discovers his girlfriend has been unfaithful, a guy goes berserk and eventually finds himself in a stand-off with the police. Violent.
1977 109m/C Oliver Reed, Susan George, Raymond Burr, John Ireland, Stephen McHattie, Donald Pleasence; *D:* Peter Collinson. **VHS, Beta** $79.95 *UNI, HHE* 🎟½

Tomorrow's Child Made-for-television drama about in vitro fertilization (test-tube babies) and surrogate motherhood.
1982 100m/C Stephanie Zimbalist, William Atherton, Bruce Davison, Ed Flanders, Salome Jens, James Shigeta, Susan Oliver, Arthur Hill; *D:* Joseph Sargent. **VHS, Beta** $59.98 *FOX* 🎟🎟

Tomorrow's Children An alarmist melodrama warning against the threat of government-induced female sterilization asks the question: if a woman's family is weird, should her tubes be tied?
1934 55m/B Sterling Holloway, Diana Sinclair, Sarah Padden, Don Douglas; *D:* Crane Wilbur. **VHS, Beta** $16.95 *SNC, NOS, VYY* 🎟

The Tong Man Robbins owes the tong money and Hayakawa, as the tong's executioner, is sent to kill him when he won't pay up. Only it turns out Hayakawa is in love with Eddy, Robbins daughter, and refuses. Then the tong decide to kill him for disobeying their orders.
1919 58m/B Sessue Hayakawa, Helen Jerome Eddy, Marc Robbins, Toyo Fujita; *D:* William Worthington. **VHS** $16.95 *GPV* 🎟

The Tongfather The Tongfather is a ruthless crime boss who leads a Chinese opium ring. An undercover agent sets out to bring him down.
1978 (R) 92m/C VHS *NO* 🎟

Tongs: An American Nightmare Chinese-American street gangs in Chinatown battle over turf and drug shipments.
1988 (R) 80m/C Ian Anthony Leung, Christopher O'Conner, Simon Yam; *D:* Philip Chan. **VHS, Beta** $29.95 *ACA* 🎟

Toni An Italian worker falls for his landlady and they make plans to marry. A grim turn of events, however, brings tragic consequences. Based on the lives of several townsfolk in the village of Les Martiques, the film was shot in the town and members of the local populace were used as characters. In French with English subtitles.
1934 90m/B Charles Blavette, Jenny Helia, Edouard Delmont, Celia Montalvan; *D:* Jean Renoir. **VHS, Beta** $24.95 *DVT* 🎟🎟½

Tonight and Every Night Cabaret singer and RAF pilot fall in love during WWII. Her music hall post puts her in the midst of Nazi bombing, and her dedication to her song and dance career puts a strain on the romance. Imaginative production numbers outweigh pedestrian storyline. 🎵Cry and You Cry Alone; What Does an English Girl Think of a Yank; Anywhere; The Boy I Left Behind; You Excite Me; Tonight and Every Night.
1945 92m/C Rita Hayworth, Lee Bowman, Janet Blair, Marc Platt, Leslie Brooks; *D:* Victor Saville. **VHS, Beta** $19.95 *COL* 🎟🎟½

Tonight for Sure Coppola made this nudie, his first film, as a student at UCLA. Two men, one who spies on women and the other who imagines nude women everywhere, plan an escapade.
1961 66m/C *D:* Francis Ford Coppola; *W:* Francis Ford Coppola; *M:* Carmine Coppola. **VHS, Beta** $29.95 *VYY, TPV* 🎟½

Tonio Kroger A young writer travels through Europe in search of intellectual and sensual relationships and a home that will suit him. He must balance freedom and responsibility. Works best if one is familiar with the Thomas Mann novel on which film is based. In German with English subtitles.
1965 92m/B Jean-Claude Brialy, Nadja Tiller, Gert Frobe; *D:* Rolf Thiele. **VHS, Beta** $24.95 *VYY, APD, GLV* 🎟🎟

Tonka A children's story about a wild horse tamed by a young Indian, only to have it recruited for the Battle of Little Bighorn. Mineo is fine as the Indian brave determined to be reunited with his steed. The film also makes a laudable effort to portray the Indians as a dignified race. The movie, however, stumbles at its conclusion and is contrived throughout. *AKA:* A Horse Named Comanche.
1958 97m/C Sal Mineo, Phil Carey, Jerome Courtland; *D:* Lewis R. Foster. **VHS, Beta** $69.95 *DIS* 🎟🎟½

Tonto Basin Outlaws The Range Busters team up with Teddy Roosevelt's Rough Riders in order to stop a gang of cattle rustlers. Standard oater material. Based on the story by Earle Snell.
1941 60m/B Ray Corrigan, John "Dusty" King, Max Terhune, Jan Wiley, Tristram Coffin, Edmund Cobb; *D:* S. Roy Luby; *W:* John Vlahos. **VHS** $19.99 *MOV* 🎟

The Tonto Kid Action-packed western featuring Rex Bell.
1935 56m/B Rex Bell, Ruth Mix, Buzz Barton, Joseph Girard, Jack Rockwell, Murdock McQuarrie; *D:* Harry Fraser. **VHS, Beta** $19.95 *NOS, DVT, VDM* 🎟

Tony Draws a Horse An eight-year old draws an anatomically correct horse on the door of his father's office, leading to a rift between the parents as they argue how to

handle the heartbreak of precociousness. Somewhat uneven but engaging comedy, based on a play by Lesley Storm.
1951 90m/B Cecil Parker, Anne Crawford, Derek Bond, Barbara Murray, Mervyn Johns, Barbara Everest, David Hurst; *D:* John Paddy Carstairs. **VHS** $19.95 *NOS* 🎟🎟½

Tony Rome The Marvin H. Albert private eye agency investigates a millionaire's daughter's disappearance and her involvement in organized crime. Entertaining and complex plot, although the cast is a numbingly large one.
1967 110m/C Frank Sinatra, Jill St. John, Simon Oakland, Gena Rowlands, Richard Conte, Lloyd Bochner, Jeffrey Lynn, Sue Lyon; *D:* Gordon Douglas. **VHS, Beta** $59.95 *FOX* 🎟🎟½

Too Beautiful for You A successful car salesman, married for years to an extraordinarily beautiful woman, finds himself head over heels for his frumpy secretary. Depardieu plays the regular guy who finds he's never believed in the love and fidelity of a woman he thinks is too beautiful for him. In French with English subtitles. *AKA:* Trop Belle Pour Toi.
1988 (R) 91m/C Gerard Depardieu, Josiane Balasko, Carol Bouquet, Roland Blanche; *D:* Bertrand Blier; *W:* Bertrand Blier. **VHS** $79.95 *ORI, FXL, FCT* 🎟🎟

Too Hot to Handle Two rival photographers searching for a beautiful lady-pilot's missing brother wind up in Brazil, where they encounter a dangerous tribe of voodoo types. Amusing, if exaggerated, picture of the lengths to which reporters will go to for a story. Classic Gable.
1938 105m/B Clark Gable, Myrna Loy, Walter Pidgeon, Walter Connolly, Leo Carrillo, Virginia Weidler; *D:* Jack Conway. **VHS** $19.98 *MGM, FCT* 🎟🎟🎟

Too Hot to Handle Voluptuous lady contract killer fights against the mob with all the weapons at her disposal. Filmed on location in Manila.
1976 88m/C Cheri Caffaro, Aharon Ipale, Vic Diaz, Corinne Calvet; *D:* Don Schain. **VHS, Beta** $39.98 *WAR* 🎟

Too Late for Tears An honest husband and his not so honest wife stumble on a load of mob-stolen cash and become entangled in a web of deceit and murder as the wife resorts to increasingly desperate measures to keep her newfound fortune. Atmospheric and entertaining film noir albeit sometimes confusing. *AKA:* Killer Bait.
1949 99m/C Lizabeth Scott, Don DeFore, Dan Duryea, Arthur Kennedy, Kristine Miller, Barry Kelley, Denver Pyle; *D:* Byron Haskin. **VHS, Beta** $16.95 *SNC, VDM, NOS* 🎟🎟

Too Late the Hero Unlikely band of allied soldiers battle Japanese force entrenched in the Pacific during WWII. Rousing adventure, fine cast. *AKA:* Suicide Run.
1970 (PG) 133m/C Michael Caine, Cliff Robertson, Henry Fonda, Ian Bannen, Harry Andrews, Denholm Elliott; *D:* Robert Aldrich. **VHS, Beta** $14.98 *FOX* 🎟🎟🎟

Too Many Crooks A British spoof of crime syndicate films. Crooks try to extort, but bungle the job. Terry-Thomas is fun, as always.
1959 85m/B Terry-Thomas, Brenda de Banzie, George Cole; *D:* Mario Zampi. **VHS, Beta** *NO* 🎟🎟

Too Many Girls Beautiful heiress goes to a small New Mexico college to escape from a cadre of gold-digging suitors. Passable adaptation of the successful Rodgers and Hart Broadway show, with many original cast members and the original stage director. Lucy and Desi met while making this film,

and married shortly after. ♫Spic and Spanish; Heroes in the Fall; Pottawatomie; 'Cause We All Got Cake; Love Never Went to College; Look Out; I Didn't Know What Time It Was; The Conga; You're Nearer.
1940 85m/B Lucille Ball, Richard Carlson, Eddie Bracken, Ann Miller, Desi Arnaz Sr., Hal LeRoy, Libby Bennett, Frances Langford, Van Johnson; **D:** George Abbott; **M:** Richard Rodgers, Lorenz Hart. **VHS, Beta $14.98** RKO, TTC ⅊⅊½

Too Much Sun A dying man can prevent his fortune from falling into the hands of a corrupt priest simply by having one of his two children produce an heir. The problem is, they're both gay!
1990 (R) 97m/C Robert Downey Jr., Ralph Macchio, Eric Idle, Andrea Martin, Laura Ernst, Jim Haynie; **D:** Robert Downey. **VHS $89.95** COL ⅊½

Too Pretty to Be Honest Four women sharing an apartment witness a robbery and begin to suspect that their neighbor is the culprit. So they decide to steal the money from him. In French with subtitles. **AKA:** Trop Jolie pour Etre Honette.
1972 95m/C Jane Birkin, Bernadette LaFont, Serge Gainsbourg; **D:** Richard Balducci; **M:** Serge Gainsbourg. **VHS, Beta $39.95** FCT ⅊⅊

Too Scared to Scream Policeman and an undercover agent team up to solve a bizarre series of murders at a Manhattan apartment house.
1985 (R) 104m/C Mike Connors, Anne Archer, Leon Isaac Kennedy, John Heard, Ian McShane, Maureen O'Sullivan, Murray Hamilton; **D:** Tony LoBianco. **VHS, Beta $79.98** LIV, VES ⅊½

Too Shy to Try A incredibly shy man meets his dream girl, and enrolls in a psychology course to overcome his ineptitude. A ribald, slapstick French comedy.
1982 (PG) 89m/C Pierre Richard, Aldo Maccione; **D:** Pierre Richard. **VHS, Beta $29.98** SUE ⅊⅊

Too Wise Wives A story of would-be marital infidelity and misunderstandings. Silent.
1921 90m/C Louis Calhern, Claire Windsor; **D:** Lois Weber. **VHS, Beta $57.95** GVV ⅊⅊

The Toolbox Murders Unknown psychotic murderer brutally claims victims one at a time, leaving police mystified and townsfolk terrified. Sick and exploitative, with predictably poor production values.
1978 (R) 93m/C Cameron Mitchell, Pamelyn Ferdin, Wesley Eure, Nicholas Beauvy, Aneta Corseaut, Tim Donnelly, Evelyn Guerrero; **D:** Dennis Donnelly. **VHS, Beta $19.95** VCI, VTR ⅊

Tootsie A stubborn, unemployed actor disguises himself as a woman to secure a part on a soap opera. As his popularity on television mounts, his love life becomes increasingly soap operatic. Hoffman is delightful, as is the rest of the stellar cast. Debut of Davis; Murray's performance unbilled. Laserdisc version features audio commentary by director Sidney Pollack, behind the scenes footage and photographs, and complete coverage of Tootsie's production.
1982 (PG) 110m/C Dustin Hoffman, Jessica Lange, Teri Garr, Dabney Coleman, Bill Murray, Charles Durning, Geena Davis, George Gaynes, Estelle Getty, Christine Ebersole, Sydney Pollack; **D:** Sydney Pollack; **W:** Larry Gelbart, Murray Schisgal, Don McGuire; **M:** Dave Grusin. Academy Awards '82: Best Supporting Actress (Lange); Nominations: Best Actor (Hoffman), Best Cinematography, Best Director (Pollack), Best Film Editing, Best Original Screenplay, Best Picture, Best Song ("It Might Be You"), Best Sound, Best Supporting Actress (Garr); British Academy Awards '83: Best Actor (Hoffman); Golden Globe Awards '83: Best Actor—Musical/Comedy (Hoffman), Best Film—Musical/Comedy,

Best Supporting Actress (Lange). **VHS, Beta $29.95.** COL, VYG, CRC ⅊⅊⅊

Top Gun Young Navy pilots compete against one another on the ground and in the air at the elite Fighter Weapons School. Cruise isn't bad as a maverick who comes of age in Ray Bans, but Edwards shines as his buddy. Awesome aerial photography and high-cal beefcake divert from the contrived plot and stock characters. The Navy subsequently noticed an increased interest in fighter pilots. Features Berlin's Oscar-winning song "Take My Breath Away."
1986 (PG) 109m/C Tom Cruise, Kelly McGillis, Val Kilmer, Tom Skerritt, Anthony Edwards, Meg Ryan, Rick Rossovich, Michael Ironside, Barry Tubb, Whip Hubley, John Stockwell, Tim Robbins, Adrian Pasdar; **D:** Tony Scott; **W:** Jim Cash, Jack Epps Jr.; **M:** Harold Faltermeyer. Academy Awards '86: Best Song ("Take My Breath Away"); Nominations: Best Film Editing, Best Sound; Golden Globe Awards '87: Best Song ("Take My Breath Away"); People's Choice Awards '87: Best Film. **VHS, Beta, 8mm, CDV $14.95** PAR ⅊⅊½

Top Hat Ginger isn't impressed by Fred's amorous attentions since she's mistaken him for a friend's other half. Many believe it to be the duo's best film together. Choreography by Astaire and score by Berlin makes this one a classic Hollywood musical. Look for a young Lucille Ball as a clerk in a flower shop. ♫Cheek to Cheek; Top Hat, White Tie and Tails; Isn't This A Lovely Day; The Piccolino; No Strings.
1935 97m/B Fred Astaire, Ginger Rogers, Erik Rhodes, Helen Broderick, Edward Everett Horton, Eric Blore, Lucille Ball; **D:** Mark Sandrich; **W:** Dwight Taylor, Allan Scott; **M:** Irving Berlin. **VHS, Beta, 8mm $14.98** TTC, RKO, HMV ⅊⅊⅊⅊

Top of the Heap A cop is denied a promotion and gets angry. Deciding to chuck the laws of due process, he goes on a criminal-killing rampage.
1972 (R) 91m/C Christopher St. John, Paula Kelly, Patrick McVey; **D:** Christopher St. John. **VHS, Beta** NO ⅊

Top Secret! Unlikely musical farce parodies spy movies and Elvis Presley films. Young American rock Nick Rivers star goes to Europe on goodwill tour and becomes involved with Nazis, the French Resistance, an American refugee, and more. Sophisticated it isn't. From the creators of "Airplane!"
1984 (PG) 90m/C Val Kilmer, Lucy Gutteridge, Christopher Villiers, Omar Sharif, Peter Cushing, Jeremy Kemp, Michael Gough; **D:** Jim Abrahams, Jerry Zucker, David Zucker; **W:** Jim Abrahams, Jerry Zucker, David Zucker; **M:** Maurice Jarre. **VHS, Beta $14.95** PAR ⅊⅊⅊

Topaz American CIA agent and French intelligence agent combine forces to find information about Russian espionage in Cuba. Cerebral and intriguing, but not classic Hitchcock. Based on the novel by Leon Uris. Laser disc video release includes two alternate endings.
1969 (PG) 126m/C John Forsythe, Frederick Stafford, Philippe Noiret, Karin Dor, Michel Piccoli; **D:** Alfred Hitchcock; **M:** Maurice Jarre. **VHS, Beta $19.95** MCA ⅊⅊⅊

Topaze A shy, depressed teacher is fired from his job at a private school and takes a new job, unaware that his boss is being him in a business scam. From the French play by Marcel Pagnol. An American version was also filmed in 1933; Pagnol produced his own version in '51. In French with English subtitles.
1933 92m/B Louis Jouvet, Edwige Feuillere, Marcel Vallee; **D:** Louis Gasnier; **W:** Marcel Pagnol. **VHS, Beta $59.95** INT, FOX, ING ⅊⅊⅊

Topaze American adaptation of the Marcel Pagnol play, about an innocent, doltish schoolmaster who becomes the unknowing front for a baron's illegal business scam. Remade in two French versions, in 1933, and in 1951 by Pagnol.
1933 127m/B John Barrymore, Myrna Loy, Jobyna Howland, Jackie Searl; **D:** Harry D'Abbadie D'Arrast. **VHS, Beta $39.98** FOX ⅊⅊⅊

Topaze After losing his job, a pathetic school teacher gets involved with the mob and winds up a powerful businessman. Remake of two earlier versions, one French and one American. Based on the play by director Pagnol. In French with English subtitles.
1951 95m/B Fernandel, Helen Perdriere, Pierre Larquey; **D:** Marcel Pagnol. **VHS, Beta $29.95** DVT, APD, ING ⅊⅊⅊½

The Topeka Terror Lane stars as a federal agent who joins forces with a frontier lawyer to stop greedy land-grabber Barcroft from ripping off a group of homesteaders. Based on a story by Patricia Harper.
1945 55m/B Allan "Rocky" Lane, Linda Stirling, Roy Barcroft, Earle Hodgins, Bud Geary; **D:** Howard Bretherton; **W:** Patricia Harper, Norman S. Hall. **VHS $19.99** MOV ⅊⅊

Topkapi An international bevy of thieves can't resist the treasures of the famed Topkapi Palace Museum, an impregnable fortress filled with wealth and splendor. Comic thriller based on Erie Ambler's "The Light of Day."
1964 122m/C Melina Mercouri, Maximilian Schell, Peter Ustinov, Robert Morley, Akim Tamiroff; **D:** Jules Dassin; **M:** Manos Hadjidakis. **VHS, Beta $59.98** FOX ⅊⅊⅊

Topper George and Marion Kerby return as ghosts after a fatal car accident, determined to assist their pal Cosmo Topper. Immensely popular at the box office, followed by "Topper Takes a Trip" and "Topper Returns." The series uses trick photography and special effects to complement the comedic scripts. Inspired a television series and remade in 1979 as television movie. Also available colorized.
1937 97m/B Cary Grant, Roland Young, Constance Bennett, Billie Burke, Eugene Pallette, Hoagy Carmichael; **D:** Norman Z. McLeod. **VHS, Beta $9.95** MED, CCB, VTR ⅊⅊⅊½

Topper Returns Cosmo Topper helps ghost find the man who mistakenly murdered her and warns her friend, the intended victim. Humorous conclusion to the trilogy preceded by "Topper" and "Topper Takes a Trip." Followed by a television series. Also available colorized.
1941 87m/B Roland Young, Joan Blondell, Dennis O'Keefe, Carole Landis, Eddie Anderson, H.B. Warner, Billie Burke; **D:** Roy Del Ruth. **VHS, Beta $16.95** SNC, NOS, CAB ⅊⅊⅊

Topper Takes a Trip Cosmo Topper and his wife have a falling out and ghosts Kerby help them get back together. The special effects sequences are especially funny. Followed by "Topper Returns." Also available colorized.
1939 85m/B Constance Bennett, Roland Young, Billie Burke, Franklin Pangborn, Alan Mowbray; **D:** Norman Z. McLeod. **VHS, Beta $14.95** MED, VTR ⅊⅊⅊

Topsy Turvy A comedy about reckless romance and not much else.
1984 (R) 90m/C Lisbet Dahl, Ebbe Rode; **D:** Edward Fleming. **VHS, Beta $69.98** LIV, VES ⅊½

Tor Medieval barbarian endeavors to free an enslaved village from a band of murderous hoodlums.

1964 94m/C Joe Robinson, Bella Cortez, Harry Baird; *D:* Antonio Leonuiola. VHS, Beta $59.95 TWE 🎬½

Tora! Tora! Tora! The story of events leading up to December 7, 1941, is retold by three directors from both Japanese and American viewpoints in this tense, large-scale production. Well-documented and realistic treatment of the Japanese attack on Pearl Harbor that brought the US into WWII; notable for its good photography but lacks a storyline equal to its epic intentions. **1970** (G) 144m/C Martin Balsam, Soh Yomamura, Joseph Cotten, E.G. Marshall, Tatsuya Mihashi, Wesley Addy, Jason Robards Jr., James Whitmore, Leon Ames, George Macready; *D:* Richard Fleischer, Toshio Masuda, Kinji Fukasaku; *M:* Jerry Goldsmith. Academy Awards '70: Best Visual Effects; Nominations: Best Art Direction/Set Decoration, Best Cinematography, Best Film Editing; National Board of Review Awards '70: 10 Best Films of the Year. VHS, Beta $14.98 FOX, TLF, HMV 🎬🎬

Torch Song In this muddled melodrama, a tough, demanding Broadway actress meets her match when she is offered true love by a blind pianist. Contains a couple of notoriously inept musical numbers. Made to show off Crawford's figure at age 50. Crawford's singing in the movie is dubbed. **1953** 90m/C Joan Crawford, Michael Wilding, Marjorie Rambeau, Gig Young, Harry Morgan, Dorothy Patrick, Benny Rubin, Nancy Gates; *D:* Charles Walters. VHS $19.98 MGM 🎬🎬

Torch Song Trilogy Adapted from Fierstein's hit Broadway play about a gay man who "just wants to be loved." Still effective, but the rewritten material loses something in the translation to the screen. Bancroft heads a strong cast with a finely shaded performance as Fierstein's mother. **1988** (R) 126m/C Anne Bancroft, Matthew Broderick, Harvey Fierstein, Brian Kerwin, Karen Young, Charles Pierce; *D:* Paul Bogart; *W:* Harvey Fierstein; *M:* Peter Matz. VHS, Beta COL 🎬🎬½

Torchlight A young couple's life begins to crumble when a wealthy art dealer teaches them how to free base cocaine. Heavy-handed treatment of a subject that's been tackled with more skill elsewhere. **1985** (R) 90m/C Pamela Sue Martin, Steve Railsback, Ian McShane, Al Corley, Rita Taggart; *D:* Thomas J. Wright. VHS, Beta $19.98 SUE 🎬

Torero A young man becomes a bullfighter to overcome his fear of bulls. *AKA:* Bullfighter. **1956** 89m/B Luis Procuna, Manolete, Dolores Del Rio, Carlos Arruza; *D:* Carlos Velo. VHS, Beta $44.95 MAD 🎬

Torment Tragic triangle has young woman in love with fellow student and murdered by sadistic teacher. Atmospheric tale hailed by many as Sjoberg's finest film. Ingmar Bergman's first filmed script. In Swedish with English subtitles. *AKA:* Hets; Frenzy. **1944** 90m/B *D:* Alf Sjoberg; *W:* Ingmar Bergman. VHS, Beta $69.95 SUE, ING, NLC 🎬🎬🎬

Torment A mild-mannered fellow is secretly a mass murderer specializing in young lovers. He struggles to hide his secret as his daughter approaches dating age and a relentless detective gets closer to the truth. A low-budget slasher. **1985** (R) 85m/C Taylor Gilbert, William Witt, Eve Brenner; *D:* Samson Aslanian, John Hopkins; *W:* Samson Aslanian, John Hopkins. VHS, Beta $19.95 STE, NWV 🎬

Tormented Man pushes his mistress out of a lighthouse, killing her. Her ethereal body parts return to haunt him.

1960 75m/B Richard Carlson, Susan Gordon, Juli Reding; *D:* Bert I. Gordon. VHS $16.95 SNC 🎬½

The Tormentors Vaguely neo-Nazi gangs rape and murder a man's family, and he kills them all in revenge. **198?** (R) 78m/C James Craig, Anthony Eisley, Chris Nole; *D:* Boris Eagle. VHS, Beta NO Woof!

Torn Allegiance An Australian anti-war epic set in the Boer War about the effects of war on one family and their fight for survival on the veldt. **1984** 102m/C VHS, Beta $79.95 PSM, FCT 🎬

Torn Apart Traditional Middle East hatreds undermine the love affair between two young people. Excellent performances from the principals highlight this drama. Adapted from the Chayin Zeldis novel "A Forbidden Love." **1989** (R) 95m/C Adrian Pasdar, Cecilia Peck, Machram Huri, Arnon Zadok, Barry Primus; *D:* Jack Fisher. VHS, Beta $89.95 WAR, BTV 🎬

Torn Between Two Lovers A beautiful married woman has an affair with an architect while on a trip. Remick is enjoyable to watch, but it's a fairly predictable yarn. Made for television. **1979** 100m/C Lee Remick, Joseph Bologna, George Peppard, Giorgio Tozzi; *D:* Delbert Mann. VHS $59.95 LIV 🎬

Torn Curtain American scientist poses as a defector to East Germany in order to uncover details of the Soviet missile program. He and his fiancee, who follows him behind the Iron Curtain, attempt to escape to freedom. Derivative and uninvolving. **1966** 125m/C Paul Newman, Julie Andrews, Lila Kedrova, David Opatoshu; *D:* Alfred Hitchcock; *W:* Brian Moore; *M:* John Addison. VHS, Beta $19.95 MCA 🎬🎬

Tornado An army sergeant revolts against his superiors and the enemy when his captain leaves him stranded in Vietnam. **1983** 90m/C Timothy Brent, Tony Marsina, Alan Collins; *D:* Anthony M. (Antonio Margheriti) Dawson. VHS, Beta $69.98 LIV 🎬

Torpedo Alley A guilt-ridden WWII Navy pilot feels responsible for the deaths of his crew. After the war, he joins a submarine crew and gradually learns to deal with his guilt. Average drama with plenty of submarine footage. **1953** 84m/B Dorothy Malone, Mark Stevens, Charles Winninger, Bill Williams; *D:* Lew Landers. VHS $19.98 REP 🎬🎬

Torpedo Attack Greek sailors, in an outdated submarine, bravely but hopelessly attack Mussolini's Italy during WWII. **1972** 88m/C John Ferris, Sidney Kazan; *D:* George Law. VHS, Beta $39.95 LIV 🎬

Torpedo Run Standard submarine melodramatics, about a U.S. sub that must torpedo a Japanese aircraft carrier which holds some of the crew's family members. Sometimes slow, generally worthwhile. **1958** 98m/C Glenn Ford, Ernest Borgnine, Dean Jones, Diane Brewster, L.Q. Jones; *D:* Joseph Pevney. VHS, Beta $19.98 MGM 🎬🎬

Torrents of Spring Based on an Ivan Turgenev story, this lavishly filmed and costumed drama concerns a young Russian aristocrat circa 1840 who is torn between two women. Predictably, one is a good-hearted innocent, the other a scheming seductress. **1990** (PG-13) 102m/C Timothy Hutton, Nastassia Kinski, Valeria Golino, William Forsythe, Urbano Barberini, Francesca De Sapio, Jacques Herlin; *D:* Jerzy Skolimowski. VHS, Beta NO 🎬🎬

Torso Crazed psychosexual killer stalks beautiful women and dismembers them. Fairly bloodless and uninteresting, in spite of lovely Kendall. Italian title translates: The Bodies Showed Signs of Carnal Violence—quite an understatement for people missing arms and legs. *AKA:* I Corpi Presentano Tracce Di Violenza Carnale. **1973** (R) 91m/C Suzy Kendall, Tina Aumont, John Richardson; *D:* Sergio Martino; *W:* Ernesto Gastaldi, Sergio Martino. VHS, Beta $79.95 MPI, PSM Woof!

Tortilla Flat Based on the John Steinbeck novel of the same name, two buddies, Tracy and Garfield, struggle to make their way on the wrong side of the tracks in California. Garfield gets a break by inheriting a couple of houses, Tracy schemes to rip-off a rich, but eccentric, dog owner. In the meantime, both fall for the same girl, Lamarr, in perhaps the finest role of her career. Great performances from all, especially Morgan. **1942** 105m/B Spencer Tracy, Hedy Lamarr, John Garfield, Frank Morgan, Akim Tamiroff, Sheldon Leonard, John Qualen, Donald Meek, Connie Gilchrist; *D:* Victor Fleming. VHS $19.98 MGM, CCB 🎬🎬🎬

Torture Chamber of Baron Blood Baron with gorgeous thirst for the red stuff is reanimated and lots of innocent bystanders meet a grisly fate in this spaghetti gorefest. Familiar story has that certain Bava feel. *AKA:* Baron Blood. **1972** (PG) 90m/C Joseph Cotten, Elke Sommer, Massimo Girotti, Rada Rassimov; *D:* Mario Bava; *M:* Les Baxter. VHS, Beta $19.99 HBO 🎬🎬½

The Torture Chamber of Dr. Sadism Decapitated and drawn and quartered for sacrificing twelve virgins, the evil Count Regula is pieced together forty years later to continue his wicked ways. Great fun, terrific art direction. Very loosely based on Poe's "The Pit and the Pendulum." Beware of the heavily edited video version. *AKA:* Blood Demon; Castle of the Walking Dead; Die Schlangengrube und das Pendel. **1969** 120m/C Christopher Lee, Karin Dor, Lex Barker, Carl Lange, Vladimir Medar, Christiane Rucker, Dieter Eppler; *D:* Harald Reinl. VHS, Beta NO 🎬🎬½

Torture Dungeon Director Milligan tortures audience with more mindless medieval pain infliction from Staten Island. **1970** (R) 80m/C Jeremy Brooks, Susan Cassidy; *D:* Andy Milligan. VHS NO 🎬

Torture Garden A sinister man presides over an unusual sideshow where people can see what is in store if they allow the evil side of their personalities to take over. Written by Bloch ("Psycho") and based on four of his short stories. **1967** 93m/C Jack Palance, Burgess Meredith, Peter Cushing, Beverly Adams; *D:* Freddie Francis; *W:* Robert Bloch. VHS, Beta $59.95 COL 🎬🎬

The Torture of Silence A simple little drama about a doctor's neglected wife seeking out the doctor's best friend for love, remade by Gance again in 1932; both originally titled "Mater Dolorosa." Silent. *AKA:* Master Dolorosa. **1917** 55m/B *D:* Abel Gance. VHS, Beta $44.95 FCT 🎬🎬½

Torture Ship Director Halperin, who earlier made the minor horror classic "White Zombie," was all at sea in this becalmed thriller about a mad doctor who uses convicts for glandular experiment in his shipboard laboratory. Based on the short story "A Thousand Deaths" by Jack London.

1939 57m/B Lyle Talbot, Irving Pichel, Jacqueline Wells, Sheila Bromley; **D:** Victor Halperin. **VHS** $15.95 *NOS, LOO* ⅋ ½

Torture Train Mayhem, murder and knife-wielding psychosis occurs on board a train.
1983 (R) 78m/C Patty Edwards, Kay Beal. **VHS, Beta** $59.95 *JEF* ⅋ ½

Total Exposure Total idiocy involving unclad babes and hormonally imbalanced men in blackmail and murder. 1990 Playboy Playmate Deborah Driggs proves there is life of sorts after playmatedom.
1991 (R) 96m/C Michael Nouri, Season Hubley, Christian Bocher, Robert Prentiss, Deborah Driggs, Jeff Conaway; **D:** John Quinn. **VHS** $89.95 *REP* ⅋

Total Recall Mind-bending sci-fi movie set in the 21st century. Construction worker Quaid (Schwarzenegger) dreams every night about the colonization of Mars, so he decides to visit a travel service that specializes in implanting vacation memories into its clients' brains and buy a memory trip to the planet. Only during the implant, Quaid discovers his memories have been artificially altered and he must find out just what's real and what's not. Intriguing plot and spectacular special effects. Laced with graphic violence. Based on Phillip K. Dick's "We Can Remember It For You Wholesale."
1990 (R) 113m/C Arnold Schwarzenegger, Rachel Ticotin, Sharon Stone, Michael Ironside, Ronny Cox, Roy Brocksmith, Marshall Bell, Mel Johnson Jr.; **D:** Paul Verhoeven; **W:** Gary Goldman, Dan O'Bannon; **M:** Jerry Goldsmith. Academy Awards '90: Best Visual Effects; Nominations: Best Sound. **VHS, Beta, 8mm** $19.95 *IME, FUS, LIV* ⅋⅋⅋

Toto le Heros Bitter old man, who as a child fantasized that he was a secret agent named Toto, harbors deep resentment over not living the life he's convinced he should have had. He maintains a childhood fantasy that he and his rich neighbor were switched at birth in the confusion of a fire at the hospital. Series of flashbacks and fast-forwards show glimpses of his life, not necessarily as it was, but how he perceived it. Sounds complex, but it's actually very clear and fluid. Mix of comedy and tragedy, with lots of ironic twists, and precise visuals. In French with English subtitles. **AKA:** Toto the Hero.
1991 (PG-13) 90m/C Michel Bouquet, Jo De Backer, Thomas Godet, Mireille Perrier, Sandrine Blancke, Didier Ferney, Hugo Harold Harrisson, Gisela Uhlen, Peter Bohlke; **D:** Jaco Van Dormael; **W:** Jaco Van Dormael. **VHS, Beta** $89.95 *PAR, BTV* ⅋⅋⅋

The Touch Straightforward story of a woman who is satisfied with her husband until the arrival of a stranger. The stranger soon has her yearning for a life she has never known. Bergman's first English film lacks the sophistication of his earlier work. **AKA:** Be Roringen.
1971 113m/C Bibi Andersson, Elliott Gould, Max von Sydow; **D:** Ingmar Bergman; **W:** Ingmar Bergman. **VHS, Beta** *FOX* ⅋ ½

Touch & Go Three beautiful women commit grand larceny in order to raise funds for underprivileged children.
1980 (PG) 92m/C Wendy Hughes; **D:** Peter Maxwell; **W:** Alan Ormsby. **VHS, Beta** *NO* ⅋⅋

Touch and Go Sentimental drama about a self-interested hockey pro who learns about love and giving through a young delinquent and his attractive mother.

1986 (R) 101m/C Michael Keaton, Maria Conchita Alonso, Ajay Naidu, Maria Tucci, Max Wright; **D:** Robert Mandel. **VHS, Beta** $14.99 *HBO* ⅋ ½

Touch Me Not A neurotic secretary is used by an industrial spy to gain information on her boss. Weak thriller. **AKA:** The Hunted.
1974 (PG) 84m/C Lee Remick, Michael Hinz, Ivan Desny, Ingrid Garbo; **D:** Douglas Fifthian. **VHS** *NO* ⅋⅋

A Touch of Class Married American insurance adjustor working in London plans quick and uncommitted affair but finds his heart doesn't obey the rules. Jackson and Segal create sparkling record of a growing relationship.
1973 (PG) 105m/C George Segal, Glenda Jackson, Paul Sorvino, Hildegarde Neil, K. Callan, Mary Barclay, Cec Linder; **D:** Melvin Frank; **W:** Jack Rose. Academy Awards '73: Best Actress (Jackson); Nominations: Best Picture, Best Song ("All That Love Went to Waste"), Best Story & Screenplay, Best Original Score; Golden Globe Awards '74: Best Actor—Musical/Comedy (Segal), Best Actress—Musical/Comedy (Jackson). **VHS, Beta** $9.99 *MED* ⅋⅋⅋

Touch of Evil Stark, perverse story of murder, kidnapping and police corruption in Mexican border town. Welles portrays a police chief who invents evidence to convict the guilty. Filled with innovative photography reminiscent of "Citizen Kane," as filmed by Russell Metty.
1958 108m/B Charlton Heston, Orson Welles, Janet Leigh, Joseph Calleia, Akim Tamiroff, Marlene Dietrich, Valentin de Vargas, Dennis Weaver, Zsa Zsa Gabor, Mort Mills, Victor Milian, Joanna Moore, Joi Lansing; **Cameos:** Ray Collins, Mercedes McCambridge, Joseph Cotten; **D:** Orson Welles; **W:** Orson Welles; **M:** Henry Mancini. **VHS, Beta** $29.95 *MCA* ⅋⅋⅋⅋

The Touch of Satan Lost on the road, a young man meets a lovely young woman and is persuaded to stay at her nearby farmhouse. Things there are not as they seem, including the young woman—who turns out to be a very old witch. **AKA:** The Touch of Melissa; Night of the Demon; Curse of Melissa.
1970 (PG) 90m/C Michael Berry, Emby Mallay, Lee Amber, Yvonne Wilson, Jeanne Gerson; **D:** Don Henderson. **VHS, Beta** *NO* ⅋

Touched Two young people struggle with the outside world after their escape from a mental institution. Although melodramatic and poorly scripted, the film is saved by fine performances by Hays and Beller.
1982 (R) 89m/C Robert Hays, Kathleen Beller, Ned Beatty, Gilbert Lewis; **D:** John Flynn. **VHS, Beta** $59.95 *MED* ⅋⅋

Touched by Love The true story of a handicapped child who begins to communicate when her teacher suggests she write to Elvis Presley. Sincere and well performed. **AKA:** To Elvis, With Love.
1980 (PG) 95m/C Deborah Raffin, Diane Lane, Christina Raines, Clu Gulager, John Amos; **D:** Gus Trikonis; **W:** Hesper Anderson; **M:** John Barry. **VHS, Beta** $59.95 *COL* ⅋⅋ ½

Tough Assignment A reporter in the West discovers and infiltrates a gang of organized rustlers who are forcing butchers to buy inferior meat.
1949 64m/B Donald (Don "Red") Barry, Marjorie Steele, Steve Brodie. **VHS, Beta** *NO* ⅋

Tough Enough A country-western singer and songwriter decides to finance his fledgling singing career by entering amateur boxing matches. Insipid and predictable, with fine cast wasted.

1983 (PG) 107m/C Dennis Quaid, Charlene Watkins, Warren Oates, Pam Grier, Stan Shaw, Bruce McGill, Wilford Brimley, Bob Watson; **D:** Richard Fleischer. **VHS, Beta** $59.98 *FOX* ⅋⅋

Tough Guy Based on the play by Bruce Walker, a London hood carouses, mugs, breaks hearts and personifies his generation's anxiety.
1953 73m/B James Kenney, Hermione Gingold, Joan Collins; **D:** Lewis Gilbert. **VHS, Beta** $19.95 *UNI* ⅋

Tough Guy Two undercover policemen battle local gangsters in a bid to smash their crime ring.
197? 90m/C Chen Ying, Charlie Chiang; **D:** Chieng Hung. **VHS, Beta** *NO* ⅋

Tough Guys Two aging ex-cons, who staged America's last train robbery in 1961, try to come to terms with modern life after many years in prison. Amazed and hurt by the treatment of the elderly in the 1980s, frustrated with their inability to find something worthwhile to do, they begin to plan one last heist. Tailor-made for Lancaster and Douglas, who are wonderful. Script becomes cliched at end.
1986 (PG) 103m/C Burt Lancaster, Kirk Douglas, Charles Durning, Eli Wallach, Lyle Alzado, Dana Carvey, Alexis Smith, Darlanne Fluegel, Billy Barty, Monty Ash; **D:** Jeff Kanew; **W:** James Orr, Jim Cruickshank; **M:** James Newton Howard. **VHS, Beta** $19.95 *TOU* ⅋⅋ ½

Tough Guys Don't Dance Mailer directed this self-satiric mystery thriller from his own novel. A writer may have committed murder—but he can't remember. So he searches for the truth among various friends, enemies, lovers, and cohorts.
1987 (R) 110m/C Ryan O'Neal, Isabella Rossellini, Wings Hauser, Debra Sandlund, John Bedford Lloyd, Lawrence Tierney, Clarence Williams III, Penn Jillette, Frances Fisher; **D:** Norman Mailer; **W:** Norman Mailer; **M:** Angelo Badalamenti. **VHS, Beta** $19.95 *MED, CVS, VTR* ⅋⅋ ½

Tough Kid A bad kid with gang connections attempts to shield his boxer brother from corruption at the hands of the same gang. Poor production all around.
1939 61m/B Frankie Darro, Dick Purcell, Judith Allen, Lillian Elliot; **D:** Howard Bretherton. **VHS, Beta** $16.95 *SNC* ⅋

Tough to Handle ...And no picnic to watch, either. A reporter cracks a criminal racket that rips off lottery sweepstakes winners. A laughably inept production.
1937 58m/B Frankie Darro, Kane Richmond, Phyllis Fraser, Harry Worth; **D:** S. Roy Luby. **VHS** $15.95 *NOS, LOO* ⅋ ½

Tougher than Leather The rap triumvirate battles criminals, vigilante-style, in their home neighborhood. Poorly executed and exploitative fare.
1988 (R) 92m/C Run DMC, The Beastie Boys, Slick Rick, Richard Edson, Jenny Lumet; **D:** Rick Rubin. **VHS, Beta** $89.95 *COL* ⅋

Toughlove The parents of a juvenile delinquent organize a tough parental philosophy and a support group for other parents having a difficult time with their teens. Made for television.
1985 100m/C Lee Remick, Bruce Dern, Piper Laurie, Louise Latham, Dana Elcar, Jason Patric, Eric Schiff, Dedee Pfeiffer; **D:** Glenn Jordan. **VHS, Beta** $39.95 *FRH* ⅋

Tour of Duty Follows the trials that the members of an American platoon face daily during the Vietnam war. The pilot movie for a television series.
1987 93m/C Terence Knox, Stephen Caffrey, Joshua Maurer, Ramon Franco; **D:** Bill L. Norton. **VHS, Beta** $59.95 *NWV, HHE* ⅋⅋ ½

Tourist Trap While traveling through the desert, a couple's car has a flat. A woman's voice lures the man into an abandoned gas station, where he discovers that the voice belongs to a mannequin. Or is it? Not very interesting or suspenseful.
1979 (PG) 90m/C Tanya Roberts, Chuck Connors, Robin Sherwood; **D:** David Schmoeller; **W:** David Schmoeller; **M:** Pino Donaggio. **VHS, Beta $79.95** *PAR* ♫

Tournament Renoir's second-to-last silent film, in which Protestants and Catholics joust out their differences in era of Catherine de Medici. French title: ''Le Tournoi dans la Cite.''
1929 90m/B Aldo Nadi; **D:** Jean Renoir. **VHS, Beta $29.95** *FCT* ♫♫½

Tous les Matins du Monde Haunting tale of two 17th century French baroque composers and their relationship with each other and their music. Gerard Depardieu plays Marin Marais who eventually becomes a court composer at Versailles. As a young man, he studies under Sainte Colombe, a private and soulful musician, about whom little is known even today. Depardieu's son Guillaume (in his film debut) plays the young Marais, who startles the quiet Sainte Colombe home and has an affair with one of his daughters (Brochet). Filmmaker Corneau lends a quiet austere tone which parallels the life and music of Sainte Colombe. In French with English subtitles. *AKA:* All the Mornings of the World.
1992 114m/C Gerard Depardieu, Guillaume Depardieu, Jean-Pierre Marielle, Anne Brochet, Caroline Sihol, Carole Richert, Violaine Lacroix, Nadege Teron, Miriam Boyer, Michel Bouquet; **D:** Alain Corneau; **W:** Pascal Quignard, Alain Corneau; **M:** Jordi Savall. **VHS $96.98** *TOU* ♫♫♫

Toute Une Nuit Assorted people stumble melodramatically in and out of one another's lives on steamy summer night in Brussels. Fine combination of avant-garde technique and narrative. In French with English subtitles. *AKA:* All Night Long.
1982 90m/C Aurore Clement, Tcheky Karyo, Veronique Silver, Angelo Abazoglou, Natalia Ackerman; **D:** Chantal Akerman; **W:** Andra Akers. **VHS $29.95** *WAC, FCT, ING* ♫♫♫

Toward the Terra In the distant future mankind is forced to evacuate Earth and settles on the planet Atarakusha. Society ruthlessly suppresses anything which could destabalize it in an effort to prevent the mistakes which destroyed the Earth. The most destabilizing presence is the MU, a new race with incredible mental powers, who are ruthlessly hunted and eliminated. But the leader of the MU reaches out to a human with his own inexplicable powers to aid in establishing a new world. In Japanese with subtitles.
1980 112m/C VHS $29.95 *CPM* ♫♫

Tower of Evil Anthropologists and treasure hunters unite in search of Phoenician hoard on Snape Island. Suddenly, inanimate bodies materialize. Seems the island's single inhabitant liked it quiet. Cult favorite despite uneven performances. So bad it's not bad. *AKA:* Horror on Snape Island; Beyond the Fog.
1972 (R) 86m/C Bryant Halliday, Jill Haworth, Jack Watson, Mark Edwards, George Coulouris; **D:** James O'Connolly. **VHS, Beta $59.95** *MPI* Woof!

The Tower of London Tells the story of Richard III (Rathbone), the English monarch who brutally executed the people who tried to get in his way of the throne. This melodrama was considered extremely graph-ic for its time, and some of the torture scenes had to be cut before it was released.
1939 93m/B Basil Rathbone, Boris Karloff, Barbara O'Neil, Ian Hunter, Vincent Price, Nan Grey, John Sutton, Leo G. Carroll, Miles Mander; **D:** Rowland V. Lee. **VHS $14.98** *MCA* ♫♫½

Tower of London A deranged lord (Price) murdering his way to the throne of England is eventually crowned Richard III. Sophisticated and well-made Poe-like thriller. More interesting as historic melodrama than as horror film. A remake of the 1939 version starring Basil Rathbone, in which Price played a supporting role.
1962 79m/B Vincent Price, Michael Pate, Joan Freeman, Robert Brown; **D:** Roger Corman. **VHS, Beta $14.95** *MGM, FCT* ♫♫

Tower of Screaming Virgins The Queen of France maintains a tower in which she has her lovers killed—after she makes love to them. An extremely loose adaptation of a Dumas novel; with English subtitles.
1968 89m/C Terry Torday, Jean Piat. **VHS, Beta, 8mm $14.95** *VYY, VDM, SNC* ♫

Tower of Terror Woman escapes from a German concentration camp and takes refuge in a lighthouse. The proprietor sees in her an uncanny resemblance to his late wife, whom he killed, and soon plots to do away with her. Story hampered by poor acting.
1942 (NC-17) 62m/B Wilfred Lawson, Movita, Michael Rennie, Morland Graham, John Longden, George Woodbridge; **D:** Lawrence Huntington. **VHS, Beta $16.95** *NOS, SNC* ♫½

The Towering Inferno Raging blaze engulfs the world's tallest skyscraper on the night of its glamorous dedication ceremonies. Allen had invented the disaster du jour genre two years earlier with ''The Poseidon Adventure.'' Features a new but equally noteworthy cast.
1974 (PG) 165m/C Steve McQueen, Paul Newman, William Holden, Faye Dunaway, Fred Astaire, Jennifer Jones, Richard Chamberlain, Susan Blakely, O.J. Simpson, Robert Vaughn, Robert Wagner; **D:** John Guillermin, Irwin Allen; **W:** Sterling Silliphant; **M:** John Williams. Academy Awards '74: Best Cinematography, Best Film Editing, Best Song (''We May Never Love Like This Again''); Nominations: Best Art Direction/Set Decoration, Best Picture, Best Sound, Best Supporting Actor (Astaire), Best Original Score; Golden Globe Awards '75: Best Supporting Actor (Astaire). **VHS, Beta $19.98** *FOX* ♫♫

A Town Called Hell Two men hold an entire town hostage while looking for ''Aguila,'' the Mexican revolutionary. Greed, evil, and violence take over. Shot in Spain. Whatever you call it, just stay out of it. *AKA:* A Town Called Bastard.
1972 (R) 95m/C Robert Shaw, Stella Stevens, Martin Landau, Telly Savalas, Fernando Rey; **D:** Robert Parrish. **VHS, Beta $24.95** *GEM* ♫

A Town Like Alice An Australian miniseries based on a novel by Nevil Shute. The story follows women prisoners of war during WWII. Jean Paget is a British prisoner in the camps of Malaya when she meets and falls in love with a fellow prisoner, the rugged Australian, Joe. Separated by their captors, they reunite years later and try to see if their love has survived. Remake of a 1951 film of the same name that is also known as ''Rape of Malaya.''
1985 301m/C Bryan Brown, Helen Morse, Gordon Jackson; **D:** David Stevens. **VHS, Beta $29.95** *SIG, NWV, IME* ♫♫½

Town that Dreaded Sundown A mad killer is on the loose in a small Arkansas town. Based on a true story, this famous 1946 murder spree remains an unsolved mystery.
1976 (R) 90m/C Ben Johnson, Andrew Prine, Dawn Wells; **D:** Charles B. Pierce. **VHS, Beta $19.98** *WAR, OM* ♫♫½

The Toxic Avenger Tongue-in-cheek, cult fave has 98-pound weakling fall in barrel of toxic waste to emerge as a lumbering, bloodthirsty hulk of sludge and mire. He falls for a blind babe and sets out to do good (and get revenge). Billed as ''The first Super-Hero from New Jersey.'' Two sequels followed: ''Toxic Avenger Part II'' and ''Toxic Avenger Part III: The Last Temptation of Toxie.''
1986 (R) 90m/C Mitchell Cohen, Andree Maranda, Jennifer Baptist, Robert Prichard, Cindy Manion; **D:** Michael Herz, Lloyd Samuel Weil Kaufman; **W:** Joe Ritter. **VHS, Beta $29.98** *VES, LIV* ♫½

The Toxic Avenger, Part 2 Sequel to ''Toxic Avenger.'' Hulky slimer targets Japanese corporations that built toxic chemical dump in Tromaville. Followed by ''Toxic Avenger Part III: The Last Temptation of Toxie.''
1989 (R) 90m/C Ron Fazio, Phoebe Legere, Rick Collins, John Altamura; **D:** Michael Herz, Lloyd Samuel Weil Kaufman; **W:** Lloyd Samuel Weil Kaufman, Gay Partington Terry. **VHS, Beta $14.95** *WAR* ♫

The Toxic Avenger, Part 3: The Last Temptation of Toxie Unemployed superhero is tempted to sell out to greedy capitalists when his cutie Claire needs an eye operation. Also available in an unrated version.
1989 (R) 102m/C Ron Fazio, Phoebe Legere, John Altamura, Rick Collins, Lisa Gaye, Jessica Dublin; **D:** Michael Herz, Lloyd Samuel Weil Kaufman; **W:** Lloyd Samuel Weil Kaufman, Gay Partington Terry. **VHS $14.98** *VES, LIV* ♫½

Toxic Zombies Pot farmers become crazy cannibals when the marijuana is sprayed with an untested chemical.
1989 90m/C VHS, Beta $99.97 *MON* ♫

The Toy Penniless reporter finds himself the new ''toy'' of the spoiled son of a multimillionaire oil man. Unfortunate casting of Pryor as the toy owned by Gleason, with heavy-handed lecturing about earning friends. Slow and terrible remake of the Pierre Richard comedy ''Le Jouet.''
1982 (PG) 99m/C Richard Pryor, Jackie Gleason, Ned Beatty, Wilfrid Hyde-White; **D:** Richard Donner. **VHS, Beta, 8mm $9.95** *COL* ♫½

Toy Soldiers A group of college students are held for ransom in a war-torn Central American country. When they escape, they join forces with a seasoned mercenary who leads them as a vigilante force.
1984 (R) 85m/C Cleavon Little, Jason Miller, Tim Robbins, Tracy Scoggins; **D:** David Fisher. **VHS, Beta $9.95** *NWV, STE* ♫½

Toy Soldiers This unlikely action tale stops short of being laughable but still has a fair share of silliness. South American narco-terrorists seize an exclusive boys' school. The mischievous students turn their talent for practical jokes to resistance-fighting. Orbach has an uncredited cameo. Based on a novel by William P. Kennedy.
1991 (R) 104m/C Sean Astin, Wil Wheaton, Keith Coogan, Andrew Divoff, Denholm Elliott, Louis Gossett Jr.; **Cameos:** Jerry Orbach; **D:** Dan Petrie Jr.; **W:** Dan Petrie Jr.; **M:** Robert Folk. **VHS, Beta, 8mm $92.95** *COL* ♫♫

Toys Diappointingly earnest comedy about Leslie (Williams), the whimsical son of a toy manufacturer who must fight to keep the playful spirit of the factory alive after it passes into the hands of his deranged uncle (Gambon). This uncle is a general who attempts to transform the factory into an armaments plant. Leslie receives assistance in this battle from his sister Alsatia (Cusack) and his cousin Patrick (L.L. Cool J). Flat characters; generally falls short by trying too hard to send a message to viewers about the folly of war. Does have extremely vivid and intriguing visuals and special effects.
1992 (PG-13) 121m/C Robin Williams, Joan Cusack, Michael Gambon, L.L. Cool J., Robin Wright; *Cameos:* Donald O'Connor; *D:* Barry Levinson; *W:* Valerie Curtin, Barry Levinson. **VHS** $19.98 FXV *⫶½*

Toys in the Attic A man returns to his home in New Orleans with his child bride, where they will live with his two impoverished, spinster sisters. Toned-down version of the Lillian Hellman play.
1963 88m/B Dean Martin, Geraldine Page, Yvette Mimieux, Wendy Hiller, Gene Tierney, Nan Martin, Larry Gates, Frank Silvera; *D:* George Roy Hill; *W:* James Poe. **VHS** $19.98 MGM *⫶⫶½*

Traces of Red Set in affluent Palm Beach, and filled with dead bodies, colorful suspects, and red herrings. The complex plot, often so serious it's funny, leads viewers through a convoluted series of events. Cop Jack Dobson (Belushi) is found dead in the opening scene; in homage to "Sunset Boulevard," his corpse acts as the narrator, a vehicle which unfortunately doesn't work as well here. He promises to recount the events leading up to his death which circle around a series of murders, and the people in his life who are possible suspects. Although Belushi's performance is average, Goldwyn, as Dobson's partner, shows off the talent he displayed in "Ghost."
1992 (R) 105m/C James Belushi, Lorraine Bracco, Tony Goldwyn, William Russ, Michelle Joyner, Joe Lisi, Jim Piddock; *D:* Andy Wolk; *M:* Graeme Revell. **VHS** $92.99 HBO *⫶⫶*

Track of the Moonbeast An American Indian uses mythology to capture the Moonbeast, a lizard-like creature that is roaming the deserts of New Mexico.
1976 90m/C Chase Cordell, Donna Leigh Drake; *D:* Richard Ashe. **VHS, Beta** $49.95 PSM *⫶⫶*

Track of the Vampire Half an hour of leftover footage from a Yugoslavian vampire movie stuck into the story of a California painter who kills his models. Gripping and atmospheric, but disjointed. *AKA:* Blood Bath.
1966 80m/B William Campbell, Jonathan Haze, Sid Haig, Marissa Mathes, Lori Saunders, Sandra Knight; *D:* Stephanie Rothman; Jack Hill. **VHS** SNC, GNS *⫶½*

Track 29 A confusing black comedy about a lonely woman, her husband who has a model train fetish, and a stranger who claims to be her son. Filmed in North Carolina.
1988 (R) 90m/C Theresa Russell, Gary Oldman, Christopher Lloyd, Colleen Camp, Sandra Bernhard, Seymour Cassel, Leon Rippy, Vance Colvig; *D:* Nicolas Roeg; *W:* Dennis Potter. **VHS** $14.95 MGM, CAN *⫶½*

The Tracker HBO western about a retired gunman/tracker who must again take up arms. His college-educated son joins him as he searches for a murdering religious fanatic. Fairly decent for the genre. Made for cable television. *AKA:* Dead or Alive.

1988 102m/C Kris Kristofferson, Scott Wilson, Mark Moses, David Huddleston, John Quade, Don Swayze, Brynn Thayer; *D:* John Guillermin. **VHS, Beta** $14.95 HBO, WAR *⫶⫶½*

The Trackers A frontier man searches for the people who kidnapped his daughter and killed his son. He is joined by a cocky black tracker. Borgnine brings strength to his character as the rancher seeking revenge. Made for television.
1971 73m/C Sammy Davis Jr., Ernest Borgnine, Julie Adams, Connie Kreski, Jim Davis; *D:* Earl Bellamy. **VHS, Beta** $19.98 FOX *⫶½*

Tracks Vietnam veteran accompanies the body of a buddy on a long train ride home. He starts suffering flashbacks from the war and begins to think some of the passengers are out to get him.
1976 (R) 90m/C Dennis Hopper, Dean Stockwell, Taryn Power; *D:* Henry Jaglom; *W:* Henry Jaglom. **VHS, Beta** $39.95 PAR *⫶½*

Trade Secrets Special investigator Jerry Morrison is assigned to probe the mysterious death of an heiress to a wine fortune. His investigation leads to the secrets and private fantasies of the woman's family and friends.
199? 91m/C Sam Waterston, Marisa Berenson, Lauren Hutton, Arielle Dombasle; *D:* Claude Feraldo; *W:* Claude Feraldo. **VHS** $89.95 TRI *⫶⫶*

Trader Horn Early talkie was the first Hollywood picture to be filmed in Africa. Carey and Renaldo are traders who tangle with a native tribe while searching for the long-lost daughter of a missionary, who turns out to be a tribal goddess. Based on a novel by Alfred Aloysius Horn and Ethelreda Lewis. Boring remake in 1973.
1931 105m/B Harry Carey Sr., Duncan Renaldo, Edwina Booth, Sir C. Aubrey Smith, Mutia Omoolu, Olive Golden Carey; *D:* Woodbridge S. Van Dyke; *W:* Cyril Hume, Richard Schayer, Dale Van Every, John Thomas Neville. **VHS** $19.98 MGM *⫶⫶½*

Trader Tom of the China Seas A young island trader and a shipwrecked beauty get involved in espionage while helping the UN to safeguard the Asian corridor. A 12-part serial on two cassettes.
1954 167m/B Harry Lauter, Aline Towne, Lyle Talbot, Fred Graham. **VHS** $29.98 REP *⫶½*

Trading Hearts Over-the-hill baseball player falls for an unsuccessful singer and single mom at a Florida training camp set in the 1950s.
1987 (PG) 88m/C Beverly D'Angelo, Raul Julia, Jerry Lewis, Parris Buckner, Robert Gwaltney; *D:* Neil Leifer; *W:* Frank Deford. **VHS, Beta** $14.95 LIV *⫶⫶*

Trading Places Two elderly businessmen wager whether environment is more important than heredity in creating a successful life, using a rich nephew and an unemployed street hustler as guinea pigs. Curtis is winning as a hooker-with-a-heart-of-gold who helps the hapless Aykroyd. Oft-told tale succeeds thanks to strong cast. Murphy's second screen appearance.
1983 (R) 118m/C Eddie Murphy, Dan Aykroyd, Jamie Lee Curtis, Ralph Bellamy, Don Ameche, Denholm Elliott, Paul Gleason, James Belushi; *D:* John Landis; *W:* Herschel Weingrod, Timothy Harris; *M:* Elmer Bernstein. Academy Awards '83 Nominations: Best Original Score; British Academy Awards '83: Best Supporting Actor (Elliott), Best Supporting Actress (Curtis). **VHS, Beta, 8mm** $14.95 PAR *⫶⫶½*

Traenen in Florenz A woman involved in a car accident winds up falling in love with the man who injured her, only to discover later that they are actually brother and sister, long separated. In German with English subtitles. *AKA:* Tears in Florence.

1984 90m/C *D:* Marianne Schafer. **VHS, Beta** $39.95 VCD, APD, GLV *⫶*

Traffic in Souls A silent melodrama dealing with white slavery. Immigrants and gullible country girls are lured into brothels where they are trapped with no hope of escape until, in a hail of bullets, the police raid the dens of vice and rescue them.
1913 74m/B Matt Moore, Jane Gail, William Welsh; *D:* George Tucker. **VHS, Beta** $24.95 GPV *⫶⫶⫶*

Traffik A tense, unnerving look at the international world of heroin smuggling. The British drama follows the lives of three men involved in the drug trade: a farmer in the poppy fields of Pakistan, a drug smuggler in Hamburg, and a Tory cabinet minister who heads his government's anti-drug cabinet and then comes to realize his own daughter is an addict. On three cassettes. Made for British television.
1990 360m/C Lindsay Duncan, Bill Paterson, Jamal Shah, Talat Hussain, Fritz Muller-Scherz; *D:* Alastair Reid. **VHS** $99.95 SIG, TVC, PBS *⫶⫶⫶*

The Tragedy of a Ridiculous Man The missing son of an Italian cheese manufacturer may or may not have been kidnapped by terrorists. Lesser Bertolucci effort may or may not have a point. In Italian with English subtitles. *AKA:* La Tragedia di un Uomo Ridicolo.
1981 (PG) 116m/C Ugo Tognazzi, Anouk Aimee, Victor Cavallo, Ricardo Tognazzi, Laura Morante; *D:* Bernardo Bertolucci; *W:* Bernardo Bertolucci; *M:* Ennio Morricone. Cannes Film Festival Nominations: cs 81: Best Film; Cannes Film Festival '81: Best Actor (Tognazzi). **VHS** $59.99 WAR, FCT, ING *⫶⫶*

Tragedy of Flight 103: The Inside Story Dramatization of the events surrounding the destruction of Pan Am flight 103 over Lockerbie, Scotland, due to a terrorist-planted bomb.
1991 (PG) 89m/C Ned Beatty, Peter Boyle, Vincent Gardenia, Timothy West, Michael Wincott, Harry Ditson, Aharon Ipale, John Shrapnel; *D:* Leslie Woodhead. **VHS** $89.95 MGM *⫶⫶⫶*

The Tragedy of King Richard II Shakespeare's tale of the fight for the English crown between the current king, Richard II, and the usurper, Henry Bolingbroke, who seizes the throne. Made for television.
1982 180m/C David Birney, Paul Shenar. **VHS, Beta** NO *⫶⫶*

Trail Beyond A cowboy and his sidekick go on the trek to the northwest to find a girl and a gold mine.
1934 57m/B John Wayne, Noah Beery Sr., Verna Hillie; *D:* Robert North Bradbury. **VHS** $19.95 COL, REP, NOS *⫶½*

Trail Drive Adventures of a cowboy during a big cattle drive.
1935 63m/B Ken Maynard. **VHS, Beta** $19.95 NOS, VCN, CAB *⫶*

Trail of Robin Hood Rogers sees to it that poor families get Christmas trees, in spite of the fact that a big business wants to raise the prices. Features a number of western stars, including Holt playing himself.
1950 67m/C Roy Rogers, Penny Edwards, Gordon Jones, Jack Holt, Emory Parnell, Rex Allen, Allan "Rocky" Lane, Clifton Young, Monte Hale, Kermit Maynard, Tom Keene, Ray Corrigan, William Farnum; *D:* William Witney. **VHS** $12.98 REP *⫶⫶½*

Trail of Terror G-Man poses as an escaped convict to get the goods on a gang.

1935 60m/B Bob Steele, Beth Marion, Forrest Taylor, Charles "Blackie" King, Lloyd Ingraham, Charles French; **D:** Robert North Bradbury. **VHS, Beta** $11.95 *GPV ♪*

Trail of the Hawk Saga of frontier justice and love on the plains.
1937 50m/B Yancey Lane, Betty Jordan, Dick Jones; **D:** Edward Dmytryk. **VHS, Beta** $19.95 *NOS, DVT, RXM ♪*

Trail of the Mounties A Mountie gallops smack into a murdering slew of fur thieves.
1947 41m/B Donald (Don "Red") Barry, Robert Lowery, Tom Neal, Russell Hayden. **VHS, Beta** *NO ♪*

Trail of the Pink Panther The sixth in Sellers' "Pink Panther" series. Inspector Clouseau disappears while he is searching for the diamond known as the Pink Panther. Notable because it was released after Sellers' death, using clips from previous movies to fill in gaps. Followed by "Curse of the Pink Panther."
1982 (PG) 97m/C Peter Sellers, David Niven, Herbert Lom, Capucine, Burt Kwouk, Robert Wagner, Robert Loggia; **D:** Blake Edwards; **W:** Blake Edwards, Frank Waldman. **VHS, Beta** $14.95 *MGM ♪♪*

Trail of the Silver Spurs A lone man remaining in a ghost town discovers gold and becomes rich. Part of the "Range Busters" series.
1941 57m/B Ray Corrigan, John "Dusty" King, Max Terhune, I. Stanford Jolley, Dorothy Short; **D:** S. Roy Luby. **VHS** $19.95 *NOS, DVT ♪♪*

Trail Riders The Range Busters set a trap to capture a gang of outlaws who killed the son of the town marshal during a bank robbery. Part of the "Range Busters" series.
1942 55m/B John "Dusty" King, David Sharpe, Max Terhune, Evelyn Finley, Forrest Taylor, Charles "Blackie" King. **VHS, Beta** $19.95 *NOS, VYY, DVT ♪½*

Trail Street Scott is Bat Masterson, the western hero. He aids the struggle of Kansans as they conquer the land and local ranchers.
1947 84m/B Randolph Scott, Robert Ryan, Anne Jeffreys, George "Gabby" Hayes, Madge Meredith, Jason Robards Sr.; **D:** Ray Enright. **VHS, Beta** $34.95 *CCB, MED ♪½*

Trailin' Mix stars as a cowboy in search of his parentage. Based on the Max Brand story.
1921 58m/B Tom Mix, Eva Novak, James Gordon; **D:** Lynn F. Reynolds. **VHS** $19.95 *GPV ♪♪½*

Trailing Double Trouble A corrupt attorney murders a rancher to pursue a business scheme. Three ranch hands kidnap the rancher's orphaned baby to keep her safe from the attorney. The second entry in the "Range Busters" series.
1940 56m/B Ray Corrigan, John "Dusty" King, Max Terhune. **VHS, Beta** $19.95 *NOS, VDM, VYY ♪½*

Trailing Trouble Gibson is a cowpoke who gets robbed of the money he received for a cattle sale. When he rescues a Chinese girl from danger he helps him recover the money. He also has to battle a rival for his girlfriend's affections. He should have battled for a better script.
1930 58m/B Hoot Gibson, Margaret Quimby, Peter Morrison, Olive Young, William McCall; **D:** Arthur Rosson. **VHS** $11.95 *GPV, VYY, DVT ♪½*

Trails West Western adventure starring Steele.
194? 7m/B Bob Steele. **VHS, Beta** $27.95 *VCN ♪*

The Train During the German occupation of Paris in 1944, a German general (Scofield) is ordered to ransack the city of its art treasures and put them on a train bound for Germany. Word gets to the French Resistance who then persuade the train inspector (Lancaster) to sabotage the train. A battle of wills ensues between Scofield and Lancaster as each becomes increasingly obsessed in outwitting the other—though the cost to all turns out to be as irreplaceable as the art itself. Filmed on location in France. Frankenheimer used real locomotives, rather than models, throughout the film, even in the spectacular crash sequences. **AKA:** Le Train; Il Treno.
1965 133m/C Burt Lancaster, Paul Scofield, Jeanne Moreau, Michel Simon, Suzanne Flon, Wolfgang Preiss, Albert Remy; **D:** John Frankenheimer; **W:** Frank Davis, Walter Bernstein; **M:** Maurice Jarre. **VHS** $19.98 *MGM ♪♪♪♪*

The Train Killer A mad Hungarian is bent on destroying the Orient Express.
1983 90m/C Michael Sarrazin; **D:** Sandor Simo. **VHS, Beta** $69.98 *VES ♪*

Train of Events An interesting look at lives affected by a train wreck just outside London, taking the form of four short episodes. Three are frankly somber, depressing tales of the ill-fated train driver, a murderer and an escaped prisoner-of-war. The fourth segment is a refreshingly lighthearted piece about romantic jealousies in a traveling orchestra. A precursor to the later swarm of crass disaster movies, except here emphasis is on character over special effects.
1949 89m/B Jack Warner, Gladys Henson, Susan Shaw, Patric Doonan, Miles Malleson, Leslie Phillips, Joan Dowling, Laurence Payne, Valerie Hobson, John Clements, Peter Finch, Mary Morris, Laurence Naismith, Michael Hordern; **D:** Sidney Cole, Basil Dearden, Charles Crichton. **VHS** $29.95 *NOS, FCT ♪♪½*

Train Robbers A widow employs the services of three cowboys to help her recover some stolen gold in order to clear her late husband's name. At least that's what she says.
1973 (PG) 92m/C John Wayne, Ann-Margret, Rod Taylor, Ben Johnson, Christopher George, Ricardo Montalban, Bobby Vinton, Jerry Gatlin; **D:** Burt Kennedy; **W:** Burt Kennedy. **VHS, Beta** $19.98 *WAR ♪♪*

Train Station Pickups Trashy film about young girls who hook at a local train depot, until something goes wrong.
197? 96m/C Marco Knoger, Katja Carrol, Ingeborg Steinbach, Benjamin Carwath; **D:** Walter Boos. **VHS** $29.95 *ACN ♪*

Train to Hollywood Marilyn Monroe-obsessed young Polish girl daydreams incessantly as she works on dining car. Funny and surreal. Polish dialogue with English subtitles.
1986 96m/C **D:** Radoslaw Piwowarski. **VHS** $49.98 *FCT ♪♪♪*

Train to Tombstone A train running from Albuquerque to Tombstone carries a motley mob of the usual characters.
1950 60m/B Donald (Don "Red") Barry, Judith Allen, Robert Lowery, Tom Neal; **D:** Charles F. Reisner. **VHS, Beta** *NO ♪*

Trained to Kill, U.S.A. Vietnam veteran relives his war experiences when a gang of terrorists threaten his hometown.
1983 (R) 88m/C Stephen Sander, Heidi Vaughn, Rockne Tarkington. **VHS, Beta** *NO ♪½*

The Traitor Undercover man joins a gang of bandits.

1936 57m/B Tim McCoy; **D:** Sam Newfield. **VHS, Beta** $19.95 *NOS, VCI, VCN ♪½*

Tramp & a Woman Two shorts made for the Essanay Company in 1915 which offer the Little Tramp wooing Purviance in typical Chaplin fashion. Silent with musical score.
1915 45m/B Charlie Chaplin, Edna Purviance. **VHS, Beta** $19.95 *VYY ♪♪*

Tramp at the Door Delightful drama about a wandering, magical man who enters the lives of an embittered family. He helps them sort the skeletons in their closets, and works wonders on their relationships.
1987 81m/C Ed McNamara, August Schellenberg, Monique Mercure, Eric Peterson; **D:** Allen Kroeker. **VHS, Beta** *NO ♪♪½*

Tramplers A rebel father and son split over the hanging of a Yankee during the Civil War. Italian made spaghetti western without much plot and lots of gratuitous gunplay.
1966 103m/C Joseph Cotten, Gordon Scott; **D:** Albert Band, Mario Sequi. **VHS, Beta** $9.95 *COL, SUE, HHE ♪*

Trancers A time-traveling cult from the future goes back in time to 1985 to meddle with fate. Only Jack Deth, defender of justice, can save mankind. Low-budget "Blade Runner." Followed by two sequels. **AKA:** Future Cop.
1985 (PG-13) 76m/C Tim Thomerson, Michael Stefoni, Helen Hunt, Art LaFleur, Telma Hopkins; **D:** Charles Band; **W:** Danny Bilson. **VHS, Beta** $19.98 *LIV, VES ♪♪*

Trancers 2: The Return of Jack Deth Retro cop is back from the future again, but seems to have lost his wit and nerve in between sequels. Ward is miscast and the pacing undermines whatever suspense that might have been.
1991 (R) 85m/C Tim Thomerson, Helen Hunt, Megan Ward, Biff Manard, Martine Beswick, Jeffrey Combs, Barbara Crampton, Richard Lynch; **D:** Charles Band. **VHS, Beta** $19.95 *PAR ♪*

Trancers 3: Deth Lives In the third film of the "Trancers" series, time-traveling cop Jack Deth fights the deadliest form of government-sponsored Trancer yet—it has a brain.
1992 (R) 83m/C Tim Thomerson, Melanie Smith, Andrew (Andy) Robinson, Tony Pierce, Dawn Ann Billings, Helen Hunt, Megan Ward, Stephen Macht, Telma Hopkins; **D:** C. Courtney Joyner; **W:** C. Courtney Joyner; **M:** Richard Band. **VHS, Beta** *PAR ♪½*

Trancers 4: Jack of Swords Time-traveling cop Jack Deth finds himself in a mystical new dimension where the blook-sucking Trancers have enslaved the local population as feeders. If Jack expects to conquer he'll first need to survive an ancient wizard's prophecy of death. Filmed on location in Romania.
1993 (R) 74m/C Tim Thomerson, Stacie Randall, Ty Miller, Terri Ivens, Mark Arnold, Clare Hartley, Alan Oppenheimer, Stephen Macht, David Nutter; **W:** Peter David; **M:** Gary Fry. **VHS, Beta** *PAR ♪♪½*

Transatlantic Merry-Go-Round An early semi-musical mystery about an eclectic assortment of passengers aboard a luxury liner. ♫ It Was Sweet of You; Rock and Roll; Moon Over Monte Carlo; Oh Leo, It's Love; If I Had a Million Dollars.
1934 90m/B Jack Benny, Gene Raymond, Nancy Carroll, Boswell Sisters, Ralph Morgan, Sidney Blackmer; **D:** Ben Stoloff. **VHS, Beta** *NO ♪♪*

Transatlantic Tunnel An undersea tunnel from England to America is attempted, despite financial trickery and undersea disasters. Made with futuristic sets which were advanced for their time. **AKA:** The Tunnel. **1935 94m/B** Richard Dix, Leslie Banks, Madge Evans, Helen Vinson, Sir C. Aubrey Smith, George Arliss, Walter Huston; **D:** Maurice Elvey. **VHS, Beta $24.95** VYY, SNC, HHT ✰✰½

Transformations An interplanetary pilot battles a deadly virus that threatens life throughout the universe. Obscure space jetsam. **1988 (R) 84m/C** Rex Smith, Patrick Macnee. **VHS $19.95** STE ✰½

Transformers: The Movie A full-length animated film featuring the universe-defending robots fighting the powers of evil. These robots began life as real toys, so there's some marketing going on. **1986 (G) 85m/C D:** Nelson Shin; **V:** Orson Welles, Eric Idle, Judd Nelson, Leonard Nimoy, Robert Stack. **VHS, Beta $19.95** FHE ✰

Transmutations Mad scientist Elliott develops a mind-altering drug which is tested by a group of young people. They find out too late that the drug causes horrible facial disfigurement, as well as leaving them hopelessly addicted, and they hide out underground, plotting their revenge. Cowper, a young hooker in the group, turns out to be immune to the side effects and works with her ex-mobster boss to get help. Confusing. Barker co-scripted from one of his stories but later disowned the film. **AKA:** Underworld. **1985 (R) 103m/C** Denholm Elliott, Steven Berkoff, Miranda Richardson, Nicola Cowper, Larry Lamb, Art Malik, Ingrid Pitt, Irina Brook, Paul Brown; **D:** George Pavlou; **W:** James Caplin, Clive Barker. **VHS, Beta $79.95** LIV, VES ✰

Transport from Paradise Follows the story of Jewish life in the Terezin ghetto before the inhabitants are imprisoned and shipped off to Auschwitz as part of Hitler's final solution. Based on a novel by Arnold Lustig. In Czech with English subtitles. **AKA:** Transport Z Raje. **1965 93m/B D:** Zbynek Brynych. **VHS, Beta $59.95** FCT ✰✰½

Transylvania 6-5000 Agreeably stupid horror spoof about two klutzy reporters who stumble into modern-day Transylvania and encounter an array of comedic creatures. Shot in Yugoslavia. **1985 (PG) 93m/C** Jeff Goldblum, Joseph Bologna, Ed Begley Jr., Carol Kane, John Byner, Geena Davis, Jeffrey Jones, Norman Fell; **D:** Rudy DeLuca; **W:** Rudy DeLuca. **VHS, Beta $19.95** STE, NWV ✰

Transylvania Twist Moronic comedy about vampires, teenage vampire hunters and half-naked babes. **1989 (PG-13) 90m/C** Robert Vaughn, Teri Copley, Steve Altman, Ace Mask, Angus Scrimm, Jay Robinson, Brinke Stevens; **D:** Jim Wynorski; **W:** R.J. Robertson. **VHS, Beta $14.95** MGM ✰½

The Trap Chaney kidnaps the son of a man he's sent to prison on false charges. Rather than give up the kid when the man is released, he plans a trap. **1922 ?m/C** Lon Chaney Sr., Alan Hale, Irene Rich. **VHS $16.95** SNC, GVV ✰✰

The Trap In trying to escape justice, a ruthless crime syndicate boss holds a small desert town in a grip of fear. **AKA:** The Baited Trap. **1959 84m/C** Richard Widmark, Tina Louise, Lee J. Cobb, Earl Holliman, Lorne Greene, Carl Benton Reid; **D:** Norman Panama; **W:** Norman Panama. **VHS, Beta $19.95** BAR ✰✰½

Trap A trapper buys a mute girl as his wife. Together they try to make a life for themselves in the Canadian wilderness. Fine telling of interesting western tale. Unusual and realistic. **AKA:** L'Aventure Sauvage. **1966 106m/C** Rita Tushingham, Oliver Reed, Rex Sevenoaks; **D:** Sidney Hayers. **VHS, Beta** NO ✰✰

Trap on Cougar Mountain A young boy begins a crusade to save his animal friends from the traps and bullets of hunters. **1972 (G) 97m/C** Erik Larsen, Keith Larsen, Karen Steele; **D:** Keith Larsen. **VHS, Beta $9.95** NWV, STE ✰

Trap Them & Kill Them American group traveling through the Amazon jungle encounter a terrifying aborigine tribe. Point of trip undergoes considerable reexamination. **1984 90m/C** Gabriele Tinti, Susan Scott, Donald O'Brien. **VHS, Beta $59.95** TWE ✰

Trapeze Lancaster is a former trapeze artist, now lame from a triple somersault accident. Curtis, the son of an old friend, wants Lancaster to teach him the routine. Lollobrigida, an aerial acrobat, is interested in both men. Exquisite European locations, fine camera work. The actors perform their own stunts. **1956 105m/C** Burt Lancaster, Tony Curtis, Gina Lollobrigida, Katy Jurado, Thomas Gomez; **D:** Carol Reed; **M:** Malcolm Arnold. **VHS, Beta $19.98** MGM, FOX ✰✰✰

Trapped Semi-documentary crime drama shows in semi-documentary style how the feds hunt down a gang of counterfeiters by springing one of their comrades from prison. Well-paced, suspenseful and believable. **1949 78m/B** Lloyd Bridges, Barbara Payton, John Hoyt, James Todd; **D:** Richard Fleischer. **VHS $19.95** NOS, DVT, HEG ✰✰½

Trapped A woman working late in her high-rise office is stalked by a killer and must rely on her ingenuity to outwit him. Made-for-cable-television movie. **1989 (R) 93m/C** Kathleen Quinlan, Bruce Abbott, Katy Boyer, Ben Loggins; **D:** Fred Walton; **W:** Fred Walton. **VHS, Beta $79.95** MCA ✰½

Trapped Alive Robin and Monica are abducted by three escaped convicts who want their car as a getaway vehicle. Trying to avoid a police roadblock the car crashes through the cover of a long-abandoned mine. When the group try to find their way out of the maze of tunnels they realize they're not down there alone. **1993 92m/C** Alex Kubik, Elizabeth Kent, Michael Nash, Randolph Powell, Mark Witsken, Sullivan Hester, Laura Kallison, Cameron Mitchell; **D:** Leszek Burzynski; **W:** Leszek Burzynski. **VHS $89.95** AIP ✰½

Trapped by the Mormons Mormons seduce innocent young girls to add to their harems. An interesting piece of paranoid propaganda. Silent with original organ music. **AKA:** The Mormon Peril. **1922 97m/B** Evelyn Brent, Lewis Willoughby. **VHS, Beta, 8mm $18.95** GPV, VYY, NOS ✰✰

Trapped in Silence Young Sutherland, abused since childhood, stops speaking to protect himself mentally and physically. Psychologist Mason is determined to break down the walls to help him confront his pain. Interesting cameo by Silver as a gay counselor forced out of his job when his sexual preference is discovered. Mildly melodramatic made-for-TV message drama. **1986 94m/C** Marsha Mason, Kiefer Sutherland, John Mahoney, Amy Wright; **Cameos:** Ron Silver; **D:** Michael Tuchner. **VHS $59.98** TTC ✰✰

Trapper County War A city boy and a Vietnam vet band together to rescue a young woman held captive by a backwoods clan. **1989 (R) 98m/C** Robert Estes, Bo Hopkins, Ernie Hudson, Betsy Russell, Don Swayze; **D:** Worth Keeter. **VHS $9.98** REP ✰

Trash Andy Warhol's profile of a depraved couple (Warhol-veteran Dallesandro and female impersonater Woodlawn) living in a lower east side basement and scouting the streets for food and drugs. Not for those easily offended by nymphomaniacs, junkies, lice, and the like; a must for fans of underground film and the cinema verite style. **1970 110m/C** Joe Dallesandro, Holly Woodlawn, Jane Forth, Micael Sklar, Geri Miller, Bruce Pecheur; **D:** Paul Morrissey. **VHS, Beta** PAR ✰✰

Trauma A girl suffers amnesia after the trauma of witnessing her aunt's murder. She returns to the mansion years later to piece together what happened. A sometimes tedious psychological thriller. **1962 93m/C** John Conte, Lynn Bari, Lorrie Richards, David Garner, Warren Kemmerling, William Bissell, Bond Blackman, William Justine; **D:** Robert M. Young. **VHS, Beta** ✰✰½

Traveling Man A made-for-cable-television drama about a veteran traveling salesman who's assigned an eager young apprentice when his sales go down. Lithgow gives a great performance as the burnt-out traveling salesman. **1989 105m/C** John Lithgow, Jonathan Silverman, Margaret Colin, John Glover; **D:** Irvin Kershner; **M:** Miles Goodman. **VHS, Beta $89.99** HBO ✰✰

Travelling North A belligerent retiree falls in love with a divorcee and they move together to a rustic retreat. They have an idyllic existence until the man discovers he has a serious heart condition. Adaptation of David Williamson's play has fine performances. **1987 (PG-13) 97m/C** Leo McKern, Julia Blake; **D:** Carl Schultz; **W:** David Williamson. **VHS, Beta** NO ✰✰

Travels with My Aunt A banker leading a mundane life is taken on a wild, whirlwind tour of Europe by an eccentric woman claiming to be his aunt. Based on Graham Greene's best-selling novel. **1972 (PG) 109m/C** Dame Maggie Smith, Alec McCowen, Louis Gossett Jr., Robert Stephens, Cindy Williams; **D:** George Cukor; **W:** Jay Presson Allen. Academy Awards '72: Best Costume Design; Nominations: Best Actress (Smith), Best Art Direction/Set Decoration, Best Cinematography. **VHS** MGM ✰✰½

Traxx Satire about an ex-cop soldier of fortune. Not surprisingly, Stevens doesn't do much with this lame script. **1987 (R) 84m/C** Shadoe Stevens, Priscilla Barnes, William E. Pugh, John Hancock, Robert Davi, Rick Overton; **D:** Jerome Gary; **W:** Gary De Vore; **M:** Jay Gruska. **VHS, Beta $79.99** HBO ✰

Treacherous Crossing When her husband disappears on their honeymoon cruise heiress Wagner tries to get the ship's crew to help her. They think she's crazy, but aided by new friend Dickinson, Wagner intends to find out just what's going on. Based on the radio play "Cabin B-13" by John Dickson Carr. **1992 (PG) 88m/C** Lindsay Wagner, Angie Dickinson, Grant Show, Joseph Bottoms, Karen Medak, Charles Napier, Jeffrey DeMunn; **D:** Tony Wharmby. **VHS, Beta** PAR, PMS ✰✰

Treasure Island Fleming's adaptation of Robert Louis Stevenson's eighteenth century English pirate tale of Long John Silver is a classic. Beery is great as the pirate; Cooper has trouble playing the boy. Also available colorized. Multitudinous remakes.

1934 102m/B Wallace Beery, Jackie Cooper, Lionel Barrymore, Lewis Stone, Otto Kruger, Douglass Dumbrille, Chic Sale, Nigel Bruce; *D:* Victor Fleming. **VHS, Beta $19.98** *MGM, TLF, HMV* ♪♪♪½

Treasure Island Spine-tingling Robert Louis Stevenson tale of pirates and buried treasure, in which young cabin boy Jim Hawkins matches wits with Long John Silver. Some editions excise extra violence. Stevenson's ending is revised. Full Disney treatment, excellent casting.
1950 (PG) 96m/C Bobby Driscoll, Robert Newton, Basil Sydney, Walter Fitzgerald, Denis O'Dea, Ralph Truman, Finlay Currie; *D:* Byron Haskin. **VHS, Beta $19.99** *DIS, IGP* ♪♪♪½

Treasure Island Unexceptional British reheat of familiar pirate tale. Welles' interpretation of Long John Silver may be truer to Stevenson, but it's one heckuva blustering binge. *AKA:* La Isla Del Tersoro.
1972 (G) 94m/C Orson Welles, Kim Burfield, Walter Slezak, Lionel Stander; *D:* John Hough; *W:* Orson Welles. **VHS $79.95** *BTV* ♪♪

Treasure Island Excellent made for cable version of the classic Robert Louis Stevenson pirate tale with Heston as Long John Silver. Written, produced and directed by Fraser Heston, son of Charlton.
1989 131m/C Charlton Heston, Christian Bale, Julian Glover, Richard Johnson, Oliver Reed, Christopher Lee, Clive Wood, Nicholas Amer, Michael Halsey; *D:* Fraser Heston; *W:* Fraser Heston. **VHS $79.98** *TTC* ♪♪½

Treasure of Arne A 16th century Scottish mercenary kills and loots the estate of rich, well-to-do property owner Sir Arne. Famous early Swedish silent that established Stiller as a director.
1919 78m/B *D:* Mauritz Stiller. **VHS, Beta $49.95** *FCT* ♪♪½

The Treasure of Bengal Sabu attempts to stop his chief from trading the village's precious gem (the largest ruby in the world) for firearms.
1953 72m/C Sabu. **VHS** *NO* ♪½

Treasure of Fear A bungling newspaper reporter gets involved with four jade chessmen once owned by Kubla Khan. A few laughs in this contrived haunted house story. *AKA:* Scared Stiff.
1945 66m/B Jack Haley, Barton MacLane, Ann Savage, Veda Ann Borg; *D:* Frank McDonald. **VHS, Beta $16.95** *SNC, NOS, FCT* ♪½

The Treasure of Jamaica Reef Adventurers battle sharks and other nasty fish as they seek a sunken Spanish galleon and its cache of golden treasure.
1974 (PG) 96m/C Cheryl Ladd, Stephen Boyd, Roosevelt Grier, David Ladd, Darby Hinton; *D:* Virginia Lively Stone. **VHS, Beta** *NO* ♪½

The Treasure of Matecumbe A motley crew of adventurers led by a young boy search for buried treasure as they are pursued by Indians and other foes. Filmed in the Florida Key Islands.
1976 (G) 107m/C Billy Attmore, Robert Foxforth, Joan Hackett, Peter Ustinov, Vic Morrow; *D:* Vincent McEveety; *M:* Buddy Baker. **VHS, Beta $69.95** *DIS* ♪♪

Treasure of Monte Cristo A woman marries a seaman said to be an ancestor of the Count for his inheritance. Instead, she finds love and mystery.
1950 78m/B Adele Jergens, Steve Brodie, Glenn Langan; *D:* William Berke. **VHS, Beta** *NO* ♪♪

Treasure of Pancho Villa An American adventurer plots a gold heist to help Villa's revolution. He encounters every obstacle in the West while on his way to help the Mexican rebel.

1955 96m/C Rory Calhoun, Shelley Winters, Gilbert Roland; *D:* George Sherman. **VHS, Beta $15.95** *VCI* ♪½

The Treasure of the Amazon Three fortune hunters embark on a perilous search for wealth in the South American jungles. Silly and unnecessarily violent. *AKA:* El Tesoro del Amazones.
1984 105m/C Stuart Whitman, Donald Pleasence, Ann Sydney, Bradford Dillman, John Ireland; *D:* Rene Cardona Jr. **VHS, Beta $69.98** *LIV, VES* ♪½

Treasure of the Four Crowns Aging history professor hires a team of tough commandos to recover four legendary crowns containing the source of mystical powers. The crowns are being held under heavy guard by a crazed cult leader.
1982 (PG) 97m/C Tony Anthony, Anna Obregon, Gene Quintano; *D:* Ferdinando Baldi; *M:* Ennio Morricone. **VHS, Beta $59.95** *MGM* ♪

Treasure of the Golden Condor A swashbuckler heads to the jungles of 18th-century Guatemala in search of ancient treasure. Contains interesting footage of Mayan ruins, but otherwise ordinary. A remake of "Son of Fury."
1953 93m/C Cornel Wilde, Connie Smith, Fay Wray, Anne Bancroft, Leo G. Carroll, Robert (Bobby) Blake; *D:* Delmer Daves. **VHS** *TCF* ♪♪½

Treasure of the Lost Desert A Green Beret crushes a terrorist operation in the Middle East.
1983 93m/C Bruce Miller, Susan West, Larry Finch; *D:* Tony Zarindast. **VHS, Beta $69.98** *LIV* ♪½

Treasure of the Moon Goddess A dizzy nightclub singer is mistaken by Central American pirates and natives for the earthly manifestation of their Moon Goddess.
1988 (R) 90m/C Don Calfa, Joann Ayres, Asher Brauner; *D:* Joseph Louis Agraz. **VHS, Beta $79.95** *VMK* Woof!

Treasure of the Sierra Madre Three prospectors in search of gold in Mexico find suspicion, treachery and greed. Bogart is superbly believable as the paranoid, and ultimately homicidal, Fred C. Dobbs. Huston directed his father and wrote the screenplay, based on a B. Traven story.
1948 126m/B Humphrey Bogart, Walter Huston, Tim Holt, Bruce (Herman Brix) Bennett, Barton MacLane, Robert (Bobby) Blake, Alfonso Bedoya; *D:* John Huston; *W:* John Huston; *M:* Max Steiner. Academy Awards '48: Best Director (Huston), Best Screenplay, Best Supporting Actor (Huston); Nominations: Best Picture; National Board of Review Awards '48: 10 Best Films of the Year, Best Actor (Huston). **VHS, Beta $19.98** *MGM, FOX, TLF* ♪♪♪♪

Treasure of the Yankee Zephyr Trio join in the quest for a plane that has been missing for 40 years...with a cargo of $50 million. They have competition in the form of Peppard and cronies. Decent cast muddles through the predictable plotting. *AKA:* Race for the Yankee Zephyr.
1983 (PG) 108m/C Ken Wahl, George Peppard, Donald Pleasence, Lesley Ann Warren, Bruno Lawrence, Grant Tilly; *D:* David Hemmings. **VHS, Beta $69.98** *LIV, VES, SIM* ♪♪

The Treasure Seekers Four rival divers set off on a perilous Caribbean expedition in search of the legendary treasure of Morgan the Pirate.
1979 88m/C Rod Taylor, Stuart Whitman, Elke Sommer, Keenan Wynn, Jeremy Kemp. **VHS, Beta $59.95** *MGM* ♪

A Tree Grows in Brooklyn Sensitive young Irish lass growing up in turn-of-the-century Brooklyn tries to rise above her tenement existence. Based on the novel by Betty Smith. Kazan's directorial debut.
1945 128m/B Peggy Ann Garner, James Dunn, Dorothy McGuire, Joan Blondell, Lloyd Nolan, Ted Donaldson, James Gleason, John Alexander, Charles Halton; *D:* Elia Kazan; *M:* Jerry Goldsmith. Academy Awards '45: Best Supporting Actor (Dunn); Nominations: Best Screenplay; National Board of Review Awards '45: 10 Best Films of the Year. **VHS, Beta $14.98** *KUI, FOX, BTV* ♪♪♪½

The Tree of Wooden Clogs Epic view of the lives of four peasant families working on an estate in turn of the century Northern Italy. The title comes from the shoes the peasants wear. When a young boy breaks a shoe, his father risks punishment by cutting down one of his landlord's trees to make a new pair of clogs. Slow moving and beautiful, from former industrial filmmaker Olmi. In Italian with English subtitles. *AKA:* L'Albero Degli Zoccoli.
1978 185m/C Luigi Ornaghi, Francesca Moriggi, Omar Brignoll, Antonio Ferrari; *D:* Ermanno Olmi; *W:* Ermanno Olmi. **VHS, Beta $79.95** *FXL, APD, ING* ♪♪♪½

Tremors A tiny desert town is attacked by giant man-eating worm-creatures. Bacon and Ward are the handymen trying to save the town. Amusing, with good special effects.
1989 (PG-13) 96m/C Kevin Bacon, Fred Ward, Finn Carter, Michael Gross, Reba McEntire, Bibi Besch, Bobby Jacoby, Charlotte Stewart, Victor Wong, Tony Genaros; *D:* Ron Underwood; *W:* S.S. Wilson, Brent Maddocki. **VHS, Beta $19.95** *MCA* ♪♪½

Trenchcoat Aspiring mystery writer travels to Malta to research her new novel and is drawn into a real-life conspiracy. Silly and contrived spoof of the detective genre.
1983 95m/C Margot Kidder, Robert Hays; *D:* Michael Tuchner; *W:* Jeffrey Price, Peter S. Seaman; *M:* Charles Fox. **VHS, Beta** *DIS, OM* ♪½

Trespass Violent crime tale set in East St. Louis, Illinois. Two redneck firemen learn about stolen gold artifacts supposedly hidden in an abandoned building and go on a treasure hunt. When they witness a murder they also get involved in a battle between two crime lords—who want these interlopers dead. What follows is a deadly game of cat-and-mouse. Lots of action but it's all fairly routine. Original release date of summer 1992 was delayed until the winter because of unfortunate similarities to the L.A. riots. *AKA:* Looters.
1992 (R) 104m/C Ice Cube, Ice-T, William Sadler, Bill Paxton, Art Evans; *D:* Walter Hill; *W:* Robert Zemeckis, Bob Gale; *M:* Ry Cooder. **VHS, Beta $19.98** *MCA* ♪♪

Trespasser A painter has an affair with a young woman. He comes to regret destroying his family and their life together. Based on a D.H. Lawrence novel.
1985 90m/C Alan Bates, Dinah Stabb, Pauline Morgan, Margaret Whiting. **VHS, Beta** *NO* ♪♪

Trespasses A rape victim and a cattleman get involved and become the target of her husband's revenge. Murder and lust in a small Texas town in this tedious film.
1986 (R) 90m/C Lou Diamond Phillips, Robert Kuhn, Ben Johnson, Adam Roarke, Mary Pillot, Van Brooks; *D:* Lauren Bivens. **VHS, Beta $29.95** *ACA, MTX, VTR* ♪

The Trial Expressionistic Welles adaptation of classic Kafka novella about an innocent man accused, tried, and convicted of an unknown crime in an unnnamed exaggerat-

edly bureaucratic country. Another Welles project that met with constant disaster in production, with many lapses in continuity. *AKA:* Le Procès; Der Prozess; Il Processo.
1963 118m/B Anthony Perkins, Jeanne Moreau, Orson Welles, Romy Schneider, Akim Tamiroff, Elsa Martinelli; *D:* Orson Welles. **VHS, Beta $39.95** *CVC, NOS, HHT* 🐾🐾🐾

The Trial Spare adaptation of Franz Kafka's novel finds Prague bank clerk Joseph K (MacLachlan) arrested on unknown charges. His increasing guilt and paranoia fit well into a world where the most illogical things happen in the most matter of fact way. Good visuals.
1993 120m/C Kyle MacLachlan, Anthony Hopkins, Jason Robards Jr., Polly Walker, Juliet Stevenson, Alfred Molina; *D:* David Jones; *W:* Harold Pinter. **VHS $89.98** *ORI* 🐾🐾

Trial and Error Peter Hudson (Matheson) is an overly-zealous prosecutor who successfully convicts a small time criminal of murder, sending him to death row. This launches Hudson's political career and five years later he's about to be nominated for Lieutenant Governor, just as the felon's execution draws near. Suddenly, new evidence points to the man's innocence, but if Hudson investigates it could ruin his political future. But he's got a bigger problem—the real killer decides to make Hudson's wife his next victim.
1992 91m/C Tim Matheson, Helen Shaver, Sean McCann, Eugene C. Clark; *D:* Mark Sobel. **VHS, Beta $89.98** *MCA* 🐾🐾½

Trial of Bernhard Goetz A re-enactment of the celebrated vigilante's trial, taken from the actual court transcripts.
1988 135m/C VHS, Beta $59.95 *ALL* 🐾🐾

The Trial of Billy Jack Billy Jack takes on the feds and beats the hell out of a lot of people to prove that the world can live in peace. Awful, pretentious film.
1974 (PG) 175m/C Tom Laughlin, Delores Taylor, Victor Izay, Terasa Laughlin, William Wellman Jr.; *D:* Frank Laughlin; *M:* Elmer Bernstein. **VHS** *NO Woof!*

The Trial of Lee Harvey Oswald What would've happened if Jack Ruby had not shot Oswald. Oswald's trial and its likely results are painstakingly created. In 2 volumes. Made for television.
1977 192m/C Ben Gazzara, Lorne Greene, John Pleshette, Lawrence Pressman; *D:* Gordon Davidson. **VHS, Beta $69.95** *WOV* 🐾🐾

Trial of the Catonsville Nine Riveting political drama that focuses on the trial of nine anti-war activists, including Father Daniel Berrigan, during the Vietnam War days of the late 1960s. Imperfect, but involving.
1972 (PG) 85m/C Ed Flanders, Douglas Watson, William Schallert, Peter Strauss, Richard Jordan; *D:* Gordon Davidson. **VHS, Beta $59.95** *COL* 🐾🐾½

The Trial of the Incredible Hulk The Hulk returns to battle organized crime and is aided by his blind superhero/lawyer friend Daredevil. Followed by ''The Death of the Incredible Hulk.'' Made for television.
1989 96m/C Bill Bixby, Lou Ferrigno, Rex Smith, John Rhys-Davies, Marta DuBois, Nancy Everhard, Nicholas Hormann; *D:* Bill Bixby. **VHS $19.95** *STE* 🐾🐾

The Triangle Factory Fire Scandal Based on the true-life Triangle factory fire at the turn of the century. The fire killed 145 garment workers and drastically changed industrial fire and safety codes. Made for television.

1979 100m/C Tom Bosley, David Dukes, Tovah Feldshuh, Janet Margolin, Stephanie Zimbalist, Lauren Front, Stacey Nelkin, Ted Wass, Charlotte Rae, Milton Selzer, Valerie Landsburg; *D:* Mel Stuart. **VHS $59.95** *LIV* 🐾🐾

Tribes A made-for-television movie about a hippie drafted into the Marines. Despite the furious efforts of his drill sergeant, he refuses to conform to military life. Soon his boot-camp mates are trying his methods of defiance and survival. Well-made mix of comedy and social commentary. *AKA:* The Soldier Who Declared Peace.
1970 90m/C Jan-Michael Vincent, Darren McGavin, Earl Holliman; *D:* Joseph Sargent. **VHS, Beta $59.98** *MGM, FOX* 🐾🐾½

Tribute A dying man is determined to achieve a reconciliation with his estranged son. Adapted by Bernard Slade from his play.
1980 (PG) 125m/C Jack Lemmon, Robby Benson, Lee Remick, Kim Cattrall; *D:* Bob (Benjamin) Clark. **VHS, Beta $19.98** *VES, FCT* 🐾🐾

Tribute to a Bad Man Hard-nosed rancher Cagney will stop at nothing to retain his worldly possessions in this 1870's Colorado territory western. His ruthless behavior drives girlfriend Papas into the arms of hired hand Dubbins. Spencer Tracy and Grace Kelly were originally cast for the roles of Jeremy Rodock and Jocasta Constantine, but Kelly backed out and Tracy was fired due to differences with director Wise. Based on the short story by Jack Schaefer.
1956 95m/C James Cagney, Don Dubbins, Stephen McNally, Irene Papas, Vic Morrow, Royal Dano, Lee Van Cleef, James Griffith, Onslow Stevens, James Bell, Jeanette Nolan, Bud Osborne, Tom London, Dennis Moore, Buddy Roosevelt, Carl Pitti; *D:* Robert Wise; *W:* Michael Blankfort. **VHS $19.98** *MGM* 🐾🐾

A Tribute to the Boys An all-star salute to the comedy of Laurel & Hardy featuring clips from more than 30 of their comedies, including scenes from their silent film days. Guests include Johnny Carson, Steve Allen, Walter Matthau, Rich Little, Henny Youngman, Robert Klein, Bronson Pinchot, and The Smothers Brothers.
1992 85m/C VHS $59.95 *CAF* 🐾🐾🐾

Tricheurs Scam artists hit largest casino in the world and look forward to golden years of retirement. From the director of ''Reversal of Fortune.'' In French with English subtitles. *AKA:* Cheaters.
1984 95m/C Jacques Dutronc, Bulle Ogier, Kurt Raab, Virgilio Teixeira, Steve Baes; *D:* Barbet Schroeder. **VHS, Beta $59.99** *WAR, BTV, FCT* 🐾🐾

Trick or Treat A high school student is helped to exact violent revenge against his bullying contemporaries. His helper is the spirit of a violent heavy metal rock star who he raises from the dead. Sometimes clever, not terribly scary.
1986 (R) 97m/C Tony Fields, Marc Price, Ozzy Osbourne, Gene Simmons; *D:* Charles Martin Smith. **VHS, Beta $19.98** *LHV, WAR* 🐾½

Trick or Treats Young boy's pranks on his terrified babysitter backfire on Halloween night. His deranged father, escaped from an asylum, shows up to help him ''scare'' her. Giroux doesn't look very frightened in this extremely tedious film from Welles' best camera man.
1982 (R) 90m/C Carrie Snodgress, David Carradine, Jackie Giroux, Steve Railsback; *D:* Gary Graver. **VHS, Beta $69.98** *LIV, VES Woof!*

Tricks of the Trade Goody-two-shoe housewife and hooker accomplice search for husband's murderer. Racy made-for-television fodder.

1988 (R) 100m/C Cindy Williams, Markie Post, Chris Mulkey, James Whitmore Jr., Scott Paulin, John Ritter, Apollonia; *D:* Jack Bender. **VHS $19.95** *ACA* 🐾🐾

Trident Force International counter-terrorism team is ordered to destroy the Palestinian Revolutionary Legion by any means possible.
1988 90m/C Anthony Alonzo, Mark Gil, Nanna Anderson, Steve Rogers, Eddie M. Gaerlan; *D:* Richard Smith. **VHS, Beta** *NO* 🐾

Trifles Five people enter a farmhouse kitchen in the bleak Midwest plains where a man was murdered upstairs. Whodunit? The solution lies in piecing together certain ''trifles'' that seem even more trivial later.
1979 21m/C VHS, Beta *BFA* 🐾½

Trigger, Jr. Rogers and Evans team up to battle an extortion ring and a murderous stallion.
1950 68m/C Roy Rogers, Dale Evans, Pat Brady, Gordon Jones, Grant Withers; *D:* William Witney. **VHS $12.98** *REP* 🐾🐾

Trigger Men Steele, Young, and St. John find a dying U.S. marshal who has been ambushed by the villainous Peil. Seems Peil and his gang have taken over a small border town in order to set up a smuggling operation with Mexico. So the trio avenge the marshal by putting a stop to the nefarious doings. Newfield directed under the pseudonym Sherman Scott. *AKA:* Billy the Kid's Fighting Pals.
1941 59m/B Bob Steele, Al ''Fuzzy'' St. John, Carleton Young, Edward Peil Sr., Phyllis Adair, Charles ''Blackie'' King, Curly Dresden, Hal Price, George Chesebro, Forrest Taylor, Budd Buster; *D:* Sam Newfield. **VHS $11.95** *GPV* 🐾½

Trigger Pals Jarrett stars in this basic oater about bringing a gang of rustlers to justice. Besides the usual gunplay, he also attempts to sing a few songs.
1939 58m/B Art Jarrett, Lee Powell, Al ''Fuzzy'' St. John, Dorothy Fay, Charles ''Blackie'' King, Frank LaRue; *D:* Sam Newfield. **VHS $11.95** *GPV, VCN* 🐾½

Trigger Tricks Gibson's brother becomes the victim of a vicious cattleman and Hoot is out for revenge.
1930 60m/B Hoot Gibson, Sally Eilers, Neal Hart, Monte Montague, Peter Morrison, Robert E. Homans, Jack Richardson; *D:* B. Reeves Eason. **VHS $11.95** *GPV* 🐾½

The Trigger Trio Rancher with diseased cattle kills a ranch inspector. The Three Mesquiteers are called in to crack the case.
1937 54m/B Ray Corrigan, Max Terhune, Ralph Byrd, Robert Warwick, Cornelius Keefe, Wally Wales; *D:* William Witney. **VHS, Beta $19.95** *VCN, DVT, GPV* 🐾½

Trilby Original screen production of Du Maurier's classic tale of Svengali.
1917 59m/B Clara Kimball Young, Wilton Lackaye, Chester Barnett; *D:* Maurice Tourneur. **VHS, Beta $16.95** *GPV, FCT* 🐾🐾🐾

Trilogy of Terror Black shows her versatility as she plays a tempting seductress, a mousy schoolteacher and the terrified victim of an African Zuni fetish doll in three horror shorts. Made for television.
1975 78m/C Karen Black, Robert Burton, John Karlen, Gregory Harrison; *D:* Dan Curtis; *W:* Richard Matheson. **VHS, Beta $59.95** *MPI* 🐾🐾½

Trinity is Still My Name Sequel to ''They Call Me Trinity.'' Insouciant bumbling brothers Trinity and Bambino, oblivious to danger and hopeless odds, endure mishaps and adventures as they try to right wrongs. A funny parody of Western cliches that never

becomes stale. *AKA:* Continuavamo A Chiamarlo Trinita.
1975 (G) 117m/C Bud Spencer, Terence Hill, Harry Carey Jr.; *D:* E.B. Clucher. **VHS, Beta** $9.99 *CCB, SUE, HHE* 🎬🎬½

Trio Sequel to "Quartet," featuring the W. Somerset Maugham stories "The Verger," "Mr. Knowall" and "Sanatorium Acclaimed." Cinematography by Geoffrey Unsworth and Reg Wyer.
1950 88m/B Jean Simmons, Michael Rennie, Bill Travers, James Hayter, Kathleen Harrison, Felix Aylmer, Nigel Patrick, Finlay Currie, John Laurie; *D:* Ken Annakin, Harold French. **VHS, Beta** *NO* 🎬🎬🎬

The Trip A psychedelic journey to the world of inner consciousness, via drugs. A television director, unsure where his life is going, decides to try a "trip" to expand his understanding. Hopper is the drug salesman, Dern, the tour guide for Fonda's trip through sex, witches, torture chambers and more. Great period music.
1967 85m/C Peter Fonda, Dennis Hopper, Susan Strasberg, Dick Miller, Peter Bogdanovich, Bruce Dern; *D:* Roger Corman; *W:* Jack Nicholson; *M:* Barry Goldberg. **VHS, Beta** $29.98 *LIV, VES* 🎬🎬

The Trip to Bountiful An elderly widow, unhappy living in her son's fancy modern home, makes a pilgrimage back to her childhood home in Bountiful, Texas. Based on the Horton Foote play. Fine acting with Oscar-winning performance from Page.
1985 (PG) 102m/C Geraldine Page, Rebecca DeMornay, John Heard, Carlin Glynn, Richard Bradford; *D:* Peter Masterson; *W:* Horton Foote. Academy Awards '85: Best Actress (Page); Nominations: Best Adapted Screenplay; Independent Spirit Awards '86: Best Actress (Page), Best Screenplay; National Media Owl Awards '87: First Prize. **VHS, Beta, 8mm** $14.95 *COL, BTV, SUE* 🎬🎬🎬

Triple Cross Plummer is a British safecracker imprisoned on the channel islands at the outbreak of WWII. When the Germans move in, he offers to work for them if they set him free. The Germans buy his story and send him to England, but once there he offers his services to the British as a double agent. Based on the exploits of Eddie Chapman, adapted from his book, "The Eddie Chapman Story."
1967 91m/C Christopher Plummer, Romy Schneider, Trevor Howard, Gert Frobe, Yul Brynner, Claudine Auger, Georges Lycan, Jess Hahn, Howard Vernon; *D:* Terence Young. **VHS, Beta** $39.99 *ACE, MOV, HHE* 🎬🎬🎬

Triple Echo A young woman falls for an army deserter who is hiding from the military police by dressing as a woman. Mistrust and deception get the best of some of the involved parties. *AKA:* Soldier in Skirts.
1977 (R) 90m/C Glenda Jackson, Oliver Reed, Brian Deacon; *D:* Michael Apted. **VHS, Beta** *NO* 🎬🎬½

Triple Impact Hall, Cook, and Riley are three martial-arts experts who join forces against illegal gambling syndicates who are staging full-contact bloodmatches. Their alliance leads them to Asia where the prize is death—or a fortune in gold.
1992 97m/C Dale "Apollo" Cook, Ron Hall, Bridgett "Baby Doll" Riley, Robert Marius, Steve Rogers, Nick Nicholson, Ned Hourani, Mike "Cobra" Cole; *D:* David Hunt; *W:* Steve Rogers. **VHS** $89.95 *AIP* 🎬

Triple Trouble/Easy Street Two of Chaplin's classic two-reel silent comedy shorts are shown on video.
1918 60m/B Charlie Chaplin, Edna Purviance, Eric Campbell. **VHS, Beta, 8mm** $19.95 *VYY* 🎬

TripleCross Three former cops strike it rich and although they love the money, they miss the game, so they get involved in a murder case. These wealthy detectives encounter high-level gangsters, a baseball scandal, and a hit man in their race to solve the perfect crime.
1985 97m/C Ted Wass, Markie Post, Gary Swanson; *D:* David Greene. **VHS, Beta** $79.95 *PSM* 🎬½

Tripods: The White Mountains Sci-fi thriller about the takeover of earth by alien tripods. The conquerors start controlling human minds, but not until after they are sixteen years old. Two boys seek to end the terror.
1984 150m/C John Shackley, Jim Baker, Cari Seel; *D:* Groham Theakston. **VHS, Beta** $79.95 *IME* 🎬½

Tripwire A vengeance-crazed government agent tracks down the terrorist who murdered his wife.
1989 (R) 120m/C Terence Knox, David Warner, Charlotte Lewis, Isabella Hoffman, Yaphet Kotto, Thomas Chong, Meg Foster; *D:* James Lemmo. **VHS, Beta** $89.95 *COL* 🎬½

Tristana Allegorical tale of a beautiful girl (Deneuve) who moves in with a hypocritical benefactor following the death of her mother. She is quickly exploited and seduced by the one who would protect her, but runs away with an artist in pursuit of love. Searing in its commentary on Catholicism, death, lust, and the woebegone place of humanity in the world, the movie is also widely seen as a depiction of fascist Spain's attempt to find its place in the twentieth century. Based on the novel by Benito Perez Galdos. In Spanish with English subtitles.
1970 (PG) 98m/C Catherine Deneuve, Fernando Rey, Franco Nero, Lola Gaos, Antonio Casas, Jesus Fernandez, Vincent Solder; *D:* Luis Bunuel; *W:* Luis Bunuel. **VHS** $59.95 *HTV, ING* 🎬🎬🎬

The Triumph of Sherlock Holmes Wontner and Fleming teamed for an early series of Holmesian romps. In one of their best outings, Sherlock Holmes comes out of retirement as a series of bizarre murders of Pennsylvania coal miners lure him back into action. From "The Valley of Fear" by Sir Arthur Conan Doyle.
1935 84m/B Arthur Wontner, Ian Fleming; *D:* Leslie Hiscott. **VHS, Beta** $16.95 *SNC, NOS, CAB* 🎬🎬½

Triumph of the Son of Hercules All other victories pale when compared to this, the Son of Hercules' greatest!
1963 ?m/C Kirk Morris, Cathia Caro. **VHS, Beta** $16.95 *SNC* 🎬🎬

Triumph of the Spirit Gritty account of boxer Salamo Arouch's experiences in Auschwitz. The boxer became champion in matches between prisoners conducted for the amusement of Nazi officers. Filmed on location in Auschwitz.
1989 (R) 115m/C Willem Dafoe, Robert Loggia, Edward James Olmos, Wendy Gazelle, Kelly Wolf, Costas Mandylor, Kario Salem; *D:* Robert M. Young; *W:* Andrzej Krakowski, Laurence Heath, Arthur Coburn, Millard Lampell, Robert M. Young; *M:* Cliff Eidelman. **VHS, Beta** $89.95 *COL* 🎬🎬🎬

Triumph of the Will Director Riefenstahl's formidable, stunning film, documenting Hitler and the Sixth Nazi Party Congress in 1934 in Nuernberg, Germany. The greatest and most artful propaganda piece ever produced. German dialogue. Includes English translation of the speeches.
1934 115m/B *D:* Leni Riefenstahl. **VHS, Beta** $24.95 *NOS, SUE, VYY* 🎬🎬🎬

Triumphs of a Man Called Horse An Indian must save his people from prospectors in order to keep his title as Peace, Chief of the Yellow Hand Sioux. Inadequate sequel to two previous films: "A Man Called Horse" and "The Return of a Man Called Horse."
1983 (R) 91m/C Richard Harris; *D:* John Hough; *W:* Carlos Aured, Jack DeWitt. **VHS, Beta** *NO* 🎬🎬

Trois Couleurs: Blanc Bittersweet comedic rags-to-riches tale spiced with revenge and lasting love. "White" focuses on equality and begins when a bewildered Polish hairdresser is divorced by his disdainful French wife, who takes him for everything he has. Returning to his family in Poland, Karol doggedly works his way into wealth. Then he decides to fake his death and leave his fortune to the ex he still loves. In Polish and French with English subtitles. Part 2 of Kieslowski's trilogy following "Trois Couleurs: Bleu" and followed by "Trois Couleurs: Rouge." *AKA:* White; Three Colors: White.
1994 (R) 89m/C Zbigniew Zamachowski, Julie Delpy, Janusz Gajos, Jerzy Stuhr; *Cameos:* Juliette Binoche, Florence Pernel; *D:* Krzysztof Kieslowski; *W:* Krzysztof Piesiewicz. **VHS** *NYR* 🎬🎬🎬

Trois Couleurs: Bleu First installment of director Kieslowski's trilogy inspired by the French tricolor flag. "Blue" stands for liberty—here freedom is based on tragedy as Julie (Binoche) reshapes her life after surviving an accident which killed her famous composer husband and their young daughter. Excellent performance by Binoche, which relies on the internalized grief and brief emotion which flits across her face rather than overwhelming displays for expression. In French with English subtitles. *AKA:* Three Colors: Blue; Blue.
1993 (R) 98m/C Juliette Binoche, Benoit Regent, Florence Pernel, Charlotte Very; *Cameos:* Emmanuelle Riva; *D:* Krzysztof Kieslovski; *W:* Krzysztof Piesiewicz, Krzysztof Kieslowski. Golden Globe Awards Nominations: s 94: Best Actress—Drama (Binoche), Best Foreign Language Film, Best Original Score; Cesar Awards '94: Best Actress (Binoche); Venice Film Festival '93: Best Actress (Binoche), Best Film. **VHS** *TOU* 🎬🎬🎬

Trois Couleurs: Rouge "Red" is for fraternity in the French tricolor flag and, in director Kieslowski's last film in his trilogy, emotional connections are made between unlikely couples. There's law student Auguste and his girlfriend Karin, young fashion model Valentine, and a nameless retired judge, brought together by circumstance and destined to change each other's lives. Subtle details make for careful viewing but it's a rewarding watch. Binoche and Delphy, who starred in the earlier films, also make an appearance. In French with English subtitles. *AKA:* Three Colors: Red; Red.
1994 99m/C Irene Jacob, Jean-Louis Trintignant, Frederique Feder, Jean-Pierre Lorit; *Cameos:* Juliette Binoche, Julie Delpy, Benoit Regent, Zbigniew Zamachowski; *D:* Krzysztof Kieslowski; *W:* Krzysztof Kieslowski, Krzysztof Piesiewicz; *M:* Zbigniew Preisner. **VHS** *NYR* 🎬🎬🎬

Trojan Women Euripides' tragedy on the fate of the women of Troy after the Greeks storm the famous city. The play does not translate well to the screen, in spite of tour-de-force acting.
1971 (G) 105m/C Katharine Hepburn, Vanessa Redgrave, Irene Papas, Genevieve Bujold, Brian Blessed, Patrick Magee; *D:* Michael Cacoyannis. **VHS, Beta** $39.95 *FHS* 🎬🎬

Troll A malevolent troll haunts an apartment building and possesses a young girl in hopes of turning all humans into trolls. Sometimes imaginative, sometimes embarrassing. Followed by a sequel.
1985 (PG-13) 86m/C Noah Hathaway, Gary Sandy, Anne Lockhart, Sonny Bono, Shelley Hack, June Lockhart, Michael Moriarty; *D:* John Carl Buechler; *M:* Richard Band. **VHS, Beta** $79.98 LIV, VES ♫½

Troll 2 A young boy can only rely on his faith in himself when no one believes his warnings about an evil coming to destroy his family. Entering into a nightmare world, Joshua must battle witches' spells and the evil trolls who carry out their bidding.
1992 (PG-13) 95m/C Michael Stephenson, Connie McFarland; *D:* Drago Floyd; *W:* Clyde Anderson. **VHS** $79.95 COL ♫½

A Troll in Central Park Animated fantasy about a troll who is cast out of his kingdom and winds up in New York's Central Park, where he brings happiness to a little girl and her skeptical brother. Strictly average family fare.
1994 (G) ?m/C *D:* Don Bluth, Gary Goldman; *W:* Stu Krieger; *M:* Robert Folk; *V:* Dom DeLuise, Cloris Leachman, Jonathan Pryce, Hayley Mills, Charles Nelson Reilly, Phillip Glasser, Robert Morley, Sy Goraleb, Tawney Sunshine Glover, Jordan Metzner. **VHS** NYR ♫♫½

Troma's War The survivors of an air crash find themselves amid a tropical terrorist-run civil war. Also available in a 105-minute, unrated version. Devotees of trash films shouldn't miss this one.
1988 (R) 90m/C Ara Romanoff, Michael Ryder, Carolyn Beauchamp, Sean Bowen; *D:* Michael Herz, Lloyd Samuel Weil Kaufman. **VHS, Beta** $19.98 MED Woof!

Tromba, the Tiger Man A circus tiger tamer uses a special drug that hypnotizes the critters into obeying his every whim. When he tries the same drug on women, things get out of hand. *AKA:* Tromba.
1952 62m/B Rene Deltgen, Angelika Hauff, Gustav Knuth, Hilde Weissner, Grethe Weiser, Gardy Granass, Adrian Hoven; *D:* Helmut Weiss. **VHS, Beta** $16.95 SNC ♫½

Tron A video game designer enters into his computer, where he battles the computer games he created and seeks revenge on other designers who have stolen his creations. Sounds better than it plays. Terrific special effects, with lots of computer-created graphics.
1982 (PG) 96m/C Jeff Bridges, Bruce Boxleitner, David Warner, Cindy Morgan, Barnard Hughes, Dan Shor; *D:* Steven Lisberger. **VHS, Beta** $19.99 DIS ♫♫

Troop Beverly Hills When spoiled housewife Long is chosen to lead her daughter's Girl Scout troop from posh Beverly Hills, everyone gets lessons deviating from the standard fare. From "camp-outs" at exclusive hotels to minks in the rain, the troop of unwilling, uncooperative little brats must eventually learn to work together to survive the wilderness and come out on top. Silly, light fun.
1989 (PG) 105m/C Shelley Long, Craig T. Nelson, Betty Thomas, Mary Gross, Stephanie Beacham, Audra Lindley, Edd Byrnes, Ami Foster, Jenny Lewis, Kellie Martin; *D:* Jeff Kanew; *W:* Pamela Norris, Margaret Grieco Oberman; *M:* Randy Edelman. **VHS, Beta, 8mm** $14.95 COL ♫♫½

Tropic of Cancer Based on Henry Miller's once-banned, now classic novel, this film portrays the sexual escapades of the expatriate author living in 1920's Paris. Torn stars as the carefree, loose-living writer and Burstyn plays his disgusted wife.
1970 (NC-17) 87m/C Rip Torn, James Callahan, Ellen Burstyn, David Bauer, Phil Brown; *D:* Joseph Strick. **VHS** $19.95 PAR, FCT ♫♫♫

Tropical Heat When the Maharajah is killed on safari, his grieving widow (D'Abo) files a five-million-dollar insurance claim before returning to India. She's followed by an investigator (Rossovich) who becomes infatuated with the lovely D'Abo. Through palaces, primitive villages, and ancient jungle temples, they are drawn into a mystery involving blackmail and murder. Based on a story by Jag Mundhra, Michael W. Potts, and Simon Levy.
1993 (R) 86m/C Rick Rossovich, Maryam D'Abo, Lee Ann Beaman, Asha Siewkumar; *D:* Jag Mundhra; *W:* Michael W. Potts; *M:* Del Casher. **VHS** $89.95 PSM ♫♫

Tropical Snow A pair of lovers living poorly in Colombia decide to enter the drug trade in exchange for passage to the U.S. offered to them by drug kingpin Carradine. Unfortunately, they get more than they bargained for. Shot on location.
1988 (R) 87m/C David Carradine, Madeleine Stowe, Nick Corri, Argermiro Catiblanco; *D:* Ciro Duran. **VHS, Beta** $34.95 PAR ♫

Trouble Along the Way Wayne is a once big-time college football coach who takes a coaching job at a small, financially strapped Catholic college in an effort to retain custody of his young daughter. His underhanded recruiting methods result in his firing—and the probable loss of his daughter. Unusual and sentimental role for Wayne proves he can handle comedy as well as action.
1953 110m/B John Wayne, Donna Reed, Charles Coburn, Tom Tully, Sherry Jackson, Marie Windsor, Tom Helmore, Dabbs Greer, Leif Erickson, Douglas Spencer; *D:* Michael Curtiz; *W:* Jack Rose, Melville Shavelson. **VHS** $19.98 WAR ♫♫½

Trouble Bound Madsen is Harry, a guy just out of prison, on his way to Nevada with trouble dogging him every step. He's got a dead body in the car trunk, drug dealers after him, and when he offers a lift to a pretty cocktail waitress (Arquette) his luck only gets worse. She plans to kill a Mob boss and it's no secret. Chases and violence.
1992 (R) 90m/C Michael Madsen, Patricia Arquette, Florence Stanley, Seymour Cassel, Sal Jenco; *D:* Jeff Reiner; *W:* Darrell Fetty, Francis Delia; *M:* Vinnie Golia. **VHS** $89.98 FXV ♫♫

Trouble Busters Troubled locals worry about who to call when oil is discovered in their town, bringing evil profiteers with it. The Trouble Busters come into town to set things straight.
1933 51m/B Jack Hoxie, Lane Chandler; *D:* Lewis Collins. **VHS, Beta** $19.95 NOS, DVT ♫

Trouble in Mind Stylized romance is set in the near future in a rundown diner. Kristofferson is an ex-cop who gets involved in the lives of a young couple looking for a better life. Look for Divine in one of her/his rare appearances outside of John Waters' works.
1986 (R) 111m/C Kris Kristofferson, Keith Carradine, Genevieve Bujold, Lori Singer, Divine, Joe Morton, George Kirby, John Considine; *D:* Alan Rudolph; *W:* Alan Rudolph. **VHS, Beta, 8mm** $14.95 COL, NLC ♫♫♫

Trouble in Paradise Welch stars as a widow stranded in a tropical island paradise with an Australian sailor. The two must struggle as they are stalked by a gang of drug smugglers, hence the title. Made for television.
1988 92m/C Raquel Welch, Jack Thompson, Nicholas Hammond, John Gregg; *D:* Di Drew. **VHS** CAF ♫♫

Trouble in Store A bumbling department store employee stumbles on a gangster's plot. Fun gags and a good cast.
1953 85m/B Margaret Rutherford, Norman Wisdom, Moira Lister, Megs Jenkins; *D:* John Paddy Carstairs. **VHS** REP ♫♫½

Trouble in Texas Outlaws go to a rodeo and try to steal the prize money. Tex wants to find out who killed his brother and in his spare time, sings and tries to stop the crooks. Notable because it is the last film Hayworth made under her original stage name (Rita Cansino).
1937 65m/B Tex Ritter, Rita Hayworth, Earl Dwire, Yakima Canutt; *D:* Robert North Bradbury. **VHS, Beta** $19.95 NOS, DVT, VCI ♫♫

Trouble in the Glen A Scottish-American soldier returns to his ancestral home and becomes involved in a dispute between the town residents and a lord over a closed road. Uneven script undermines comic idea.
1954 91m/C Orson Welles, Victor McLaglen, Forrest Tucker, Margaret Lockwood; *D:* Herbert Wilcox. **VHS** $19.98 REP ♫♫½

The Trouble with Angels Two young girls turn a convent upside down with their endless practical jokes. Russell is everything a Mother Superior should be: understanding, wise, and beautiful.
1966 112m/C Hayley Mills, June Harding, Rosalind Russell, Gypsy Rose Lee, Binnie Barnes; *D:* Ida Lupino; *M:* Jerry Goldsmith. **VHS, Beta** $14.95 COL ♫♫½

The Trouble with Dick An ambitious young science fiction writer's personal troubles begin to appear in his writing. Although the box cover displays a "Festival Winner" announcement, don't be fooled! Story becomes tedious after first five minutes.
1988 (R) 86m/C Tom Villard, Susan Dey; *D:* Gary Walkow; *M:* Roger Bourland. **VHS, Beta** $14.95 ACA ♫

The Trouble with Father Erwin starred in the classic comedy series about a bumbling father which aired from 1950-1955. Two episodes per tape. On this tape: "Yvette," a 1954 episode in which Stu tries to surprise June with a lifelike female mannequin as an anniversary gift and the 1952 episode "What Paper Do you Read" when June enrolls in Stu's evening government classes. *AKA:* The Stu Erwin Show.
1950 50m/B Stuart Erwin, June Collyer Erwin, Sheila James, Ann Todd, Martin Milner, Willie Best. **VHS, Beta** $19.95 NOS, MOV, DVT ♫

The Trouble with Girls (and How To Get Into It) A 1920s traveling show manager tries to solve a local murder. Not as much singing as his earlier films, but good attention is paid to details. This is definitely one of the better Elvis vehicles. ♫Almost; Clean Up Your Own Back Yard. *AKA:* The Chautauqua.
1969 (G) 99m/C Elvis Presley, Marlyn Mason, Nicole Jaffe, Sheree North, Edward Andrews, John Carradine, Vincent Price, Joyce Van Patten, Dabney Coleman, John Rubinstein, Anthony Teague; *D:* Peter Tewkesbury. **VHS, Beta** $14.95 MGM ♫♫

The Trouble with Harry When a little boy finds a dead body in a Vermont town, it causes all kinds of problems for the community. No one is sure who killed Harry and what to do with the body. MacLaine's film debut and Herrmann's first musical score for Hitchcock.

1955 (PG) 90m/C John Forsythe, Shirley MacLaine, Edmund Gwenn, Jerry Mathers, Mildred Dunnock, Mildred Natwick, Royal Dano; *D:* Alfred Hitchcock; *W:* John Michael Hayes; *M:* Bernard Herrmann. **VHS, Beta $19.98** *MCA, HMV* ✨✨✨

The Trouble with Spies A bumbling British spy goes to Ibizia to locate a Russian agent, makes a million mistakes and wins anyway. A loser of a film, wasted a fine cast. Made in 1984; no one bothered to release it for 3 years.
1987 (PG-13) 91m/C Donald Sutherland, Malcolm Morley, Lucy Gutteridge, Ruth Gordon, Ned Beatty, Michael Hordern, Robert Morley; *D:* Burt Kennedy; *W:* Burt Kennedy. **VHS, Beta $79.99** *HBO* ✨

Truck Stop This truck stop has all a trucker needs—including the owner, voluptuous Pamela.
19?? 80m/C Nikki Gentile, Elizabeth Turner; *D:* Jean Marie Pallardy. **VHS** *MED* ✨

Truck Stop Women Female truckers become involved in smuggling and prostitution at a truck stop. The mob wants a cut of the business and will do anything to get their way. Better than it sounds.
1974 (R) 88m/C Claudia Jennings, Lieux Dressler, John Martino, Dennis Fimple, Dolores Dorn, Gene Drew, Paul Carr, Jennifer Burton; *D:* Mark L. Lester. **VHS, Beta $59.95** *VES* ✨✨

Truck Turner He's a bounty hunter, he's black and he's up against a threadbare plot. Hayes methodically eliminates everyone involved with his partner's murder while providing groovy soundtrack. Quintessential blaxploitation.
1974 (R) 91m/C Isaac Hayes, Yaphet Kotto, Annazette Chase, Nichelle Nichols, Scatman Crothers, Dick Miller; *D:* Jonathan Kaplan; *M:* Isaac Hayes. **VHS $59.95** *ORI, FCT* ✨½

Trucker's Woman Man takes a job driving an 18-wheel truck in order to find the murderers of his father.
1983 (R) 90m/C Michael Hawkins, Mary Cannon; *D:* Will Zens. **VHS, Beta** *NO* ✨

True Believer Cynical lawyer, once a '60s radical, now defends rich drug dealers. Spurred on by a young protege, he takes on the hopeless case of imprisoned Asian-American accused of gang-slaying. Tense thriller with good cast.
1989 (R) 103m/C James Woods, Robert Downey Jr., Yuji Okumoto, Margaret Colin, Kurtwood Smith, Tom Bower, Miguel Fernandez, Charles Hallahan; *D:* Joseph Ruben; *W:* Wesley Strick; *M:* Brad Fiedel. **VHS, Beta $14.95** *COL* ✨✨½

True Blood A man returns to his home turf to save his brother from the same ruthless gang who set him up for a cop's murder.
1989 (R) 100m/C Chad Lowe, Jeff Fahey, Sherilyn Fenn; *D:* Peter Maris. **VHS, Beta $29.95** *FRH, IME* ✨✨

True Colors A woman fights for her homeland of France in order to save the country from being taken over by Hitler.
1987 (PG-13) 160m/C Noni Hazlehurst, John Waters, Patrick Ryecart, Shane Briant, Alan Andrews; *D:* Pina Amenta. **VHS, Beta $29.95** *ACA* ✨✨½

True Colors Law school buddies take divergent paths in post grad real world. Straight and narrow Spader works for Justice Department while dropout Cusack manipulates friends and acquaintances to further his position as Senator's aid. Typecast, predictable and moralizing.
1991 (R) 111m/C John Cusack, James Spader, Imogen Stubbs, Mandy Patinkin, Richard Widmark; *D:* Herbert Ross. **VHS $19.95** *PAR* ✨✨

True Confessions Tale of corruption pits two brothers, one a priest and the other a detective, against each other. Nice 1940s period look, with excellent performances from De Niro and Duvall. Based on a true case from the Gregory Dunne novel.
1981 (R) 110m/C Robert De Niro, Robert Duvall, Kenneth McMillan, Charles Durning, Cyril Cusack, Ed Flanders, Burgess Meredith, Louisa Moritz; *D:* Ulu Grosbard; *W:* Gregory Dunne, Joan Didion; *M:* Georges Delerue. **VHS, Beta $19.98** *MGM* ✨✨✨

The True Game of Death A story of the circumstances behind the death of superstar Bruce Lee.
197? 90m/C Shou Lung. **VHS, Beta** *NO* ✨✨✨

True Grit Hard-drinking U.S. Marshal Rooster Cogburn (Wayne) is hired by a young girl (Darby) to find her father's killer. Won Wayne his only Oscar. Based on the Charles Portis novel. Prompted sequel, "Rooster Cogburn."
1969 (G) 128m/C John Wayne, Glen Campbell, Kim Darby, Robert Duvall; *D:* Henry Hathaway; *M:* Elmer Bernstein. Academy Awards '69: Best Actor (Wayne); Nominations: Best Song ("True Grit"); Golden Globe Awards '70: Best Actor—Drama (Wayne); National Board of Review Awards '69: 10 Best Films of the Year. **VHS, Beta $14.95** *PAR, HHE, TLF* ✨✨✨

True Heart Susie A simple, moving story about a girl who is in love with a man who marries another girl from the city. Silent.
1919 87m/B Lillian Gish, Robert Harring; *D:* D.W. Griffith. **VHS, Beta $19.95** *NOS, VYY, DVT* ✨✨½

True Identity Henry, a comic superstar in England, stars as an innocent black man marked for death by the Mafia. He hides by disguising himself as white and gets a taste of life on the other side of the color line. The interesting premise was based on a classic Eddie Murphy sketch on "Saturday Night Live," but isn't treated with sufficient imagination or humor here.
1991 (R) 94m/C Lenny Henry, Frank Langella, Anne-Marie Johnson; *D:* Charles Lane. **VHS, Beta $94.95** *TOU, FCT* ✨✨

True Lies Schwarzenegger and director Cameron reunite again for their annual blockbuster, an action comedy very loosely adapted from the 1991 French comedy "La Total." A counter-terrorism agent has kept his undercover work a secret from his wife, making her one very suspicious lady. Meanwhile, a sly romeo falsifies his resume to hit on Curtis during one of Schwarzenegger's frequent absences, telling her HE's a spy. Ah-nuld fights to save his marriage and the world from nuclear destruction. Humongous effects and a host of locales keep the Cameron-Schwarzenegger express rolling.
1994 ?m/C Arnold Schwarzenegger, Jamie Lee Curtis, Tom Arnold, Bill Paxton, Tia Carrere, Art Malik, Eliza Dushku, Charlton Heston, Grant Heslov; *D:* James Cameron; *W:* James Cameron. **VHS** *NYR* ✨✨✨

True Love Low-budget, savagely observed comedy follows the family and community events leading up to a Bronx Italian wedding. Authentic slice-of-life about two young people with very different ideas about what marriage and commitment mean. Acclaimed script and performances.
1989 (R) 104m/C Annabella Sciorra, Ron Eldard, Aida Turturro, Roger Rignack, Michael J. Wolfe, Star Jasper, Kelly Cinnante, Rick Shapiro, Suzanne Costallos, Vinny Pastore; *D:* Nancy Savoca; *W:* Nancy Savoca, Richard Guay. **VHS, Beta $89.95** *MGM* ✨✨✨

True Romance Geeky Clarence (Slater) and wide-eyed whore Alabama (Arquette) meet and fall instantly in love (and marriage). The inept duo skips town after an accidental murder and hit the road to L.A. with the mob in pursuit. Gem performances in small roles include Walken's debonair mafioso who's not adverse to torture; Clarence's dad (Hopper), an ex-cop who runs afoul of Walken; Pitt's space-case druggie; and the ghost of Elvis (Kilmer), whom Clarence talks to in times of stress. Horrific violence mixed with very black humor (courtesy of a script by pre "Reservoir Dogs" Tarantino and "Last Boy Scout" director Scott). An unrated version is also available.
1993 (R) 116m/C Christian Slater, Patricia Arquette, Gary Oldman, Brad Pitt, Val Kilmer, Dennis Hopper, Christopher Walken, Samuel L. Jackson, Christopher Penn, Bronson Pinchot, Michael Rappaport, Saul Rubinek, Conchata Ferrell, James Gandolfini; *D:* Tony Scott; *W:* Quentin Tarantino; *M:* Hans Zimmer. **VHS, Beta** *WAR, BTV* ✨✨½

True Stories Quirky, amusing look at the eccentric denizens of a fictional, off-center Texas town celebrating its 150th anniversary. Notable are Kurtz as the Laziest Woman in America and Goodman as a blushing suitor. Directorial debut of Byrne. Worth a look.
1986 (PG) 89m/C David Byrne, John Goodman, Swoosie Kurtz, Spalding Gray, Annie McEnroe, Pops Staples, Tito Larriva; *D:* David Byrne; *W:* David Byrne, Beth Henley; *M:* David Byrne. **VHS, Beta $19.98** *MVD, WAR* ✨✨✨½

True West Filmed performance of the acclaimed Sam Shepard play about two mismatched brothers. Made for Television.
1986 110m/C John Malkovich, Gary Sinise; *D:* Allan Goldstein. **VHS, Beta $59.95** *ACA* ✨✨✨

Truly, Madly, Deeply The recent death of her lover drives a young woman into despair and anger, until he turns up at her apartment one day. Tender and well written tale of love and the supernatural, with believable characters and plot-line. Playwright Minghella's directorial debut.
1991 (PG) 107m/C Juliet Stevenson, Alan Rickman, Bill Paterson, Michael Maloney, Christopher Rozycki, Keith Bartlett, David Ryall, Stella Maris; *D:* Anthony Minghella; *W:* Anthony Minghella. **VHS** *TOU* ✨✨✨

The Trumpet and I An eight-year-old boy inherits magical powers when he plays a "silver sounding" trumpet.
1985 53m/C VHS, Beta $29.95 *GEM* ✨✨½

Trumps Startling relationship between man and woman has dire consequences. *AKA:* Enormous Changes at the Last Minute.
1988 (R) 90m/C Ellen Barkin, Kevin Bacon, Maria Tucci, Ron McLarty, Zvee Scooler. **VHS $29.95** *HHE* ✨✨

Trust An obnoxious girl, tossed out by her family after becoming pregnant, forms a loving bond with a strange, possibly deranged guy from an abusive household. Similar in style and theme to Hartley's "The Unbelievable Truth" - a peculiar sardonic comedy/drama not for every taste.
1991 (R) 107m/C Adrienne Shelly, Martin Donovan, Merritt Nelson, Edie Falco, John MacKay; *D:* Hal Hartley; *W:* Hal Hartley. **VHS $19.98** *REP* ✨✨

Trust Me A cynical L.A. art dealer decides to promote a young artist's work and then kill him off to increase the value of his paintings. Satirical view of the Los Angeles art crowd.
1989 (R) 94m/C Adam Ant, Talia Balsam, David Packer, Barbara Bain, Joyce Van Patten, William DeAcutis; *D:* Bobby Houston. **VHS, Beta** *NO* ✨✨

Truth About Women An old aristocrat recounts his youthful adventures to his son-in-law. A pale British comedy of manners.
1958 107m/C Laurence Harvey, Julie Harris, Mai Zetterling, Eva Gabor, Wilfrid Hyde-White, Derek Farr; **D:** Muriel Box. **VHS, Beta $19.95** NOS &&

Truth or Dare? The childhood game of truth or dare turns deadly in this violent thriller.
1986 87m/C John Brace, Mary Fanaro, Geoffrey Lewis Miller; **D:** Yale Wilson. **VHS, Beta $49.95** HHE &

Truth or Dare A quasi-concert-documentary—here is music superstar Madonna tarted up in fact, fiction, and fantasy—exhibitionism to the nth power. Tacky, self-conscious and ultimately, if you are a Madonna fan, moving. On camera Madonna stings ex-boyfriend Warren Beatty, disses admirer Kevin Costner, quarrels with her father, reminisces, and does sexy things with a bottle. Oh yes, she occasionally sings and dances. Both those who worship and dislike the Material Girl will find much to pick apart here. Available in Widescreen format on laserdisc. **AKA:** In Bed with Madonna; Madonna Truth or Dare.
1991 (R) 118m/C Madonna; **D:** Alek Keshishian. **VHS $92.95** LIV, FCT && ½

Truth or Die This trite, cliched TV movie chronicles the life of convict Jerry Rosenberg, the first prisoner to earn a law degree from his cell. Still, an uncharacteristic role for sitcom guy Danza. Based on Rosenberg's book "Doing Life." **AKA:** Doing Life.
1986 (PG-13) 96m/C Tony Danza, Jon DeVries, Lisa Langlois, Rocco Sisto; **D:** Gene Reynolds. **VHS** VMK &&

Try and Get Me A small town is incited into a manhunt for kidnappers who murdered their victim. Suspenseful melodrama analyzes mob rule and the criminal mind. **AKA:** Sound of Fury.
1950 91m/B Lloyd Bridges, Kathleen Ryan, Richard Carlson, Frank Lovejoy, Katherine Locke; **D:** Cy Endfield. **VHS $19.95** REP &&

The Tsar's Bride A lovely young woman is chosen to be the bride of the horrible Tsar Glebov but when the Tsar's bodyguard falls for her, romantic difficulties ensue. A hybrid of the 1899 Rimsky-Korsakov opera and an 1849 play. **AKA:** Tsarskaya Nevesta.
1966 95m/B Raisa Nedashkovskaya, Natalya Rudnaya, Otar Koberidze; **D:** Vladimir Gorikker. **VHS $49.95** KUL, MVD, PME &&&

Tucker and the Horse Thief A girl dresses and lives like a boy for safety's sake during the California Gold Rush.
1985 45m/C **VHS, Beta** NO &&

Tucker: The Man and His Dream Portrait of Preston Tucker, entrepreneur and industrial idealist, who in 1946 tried to build the car of the future and was effectively run out of business by the powers-that-were. Ravishing, ultra-nostalgic lullaby to the American Dream. Watch for Jeff's dad, Lloyd, in a bit role.
1988 (PG) 111m/C Jeff Bridges, Martin Landau, Dean Stockwell, Frederic Forrest, Mako, Joan Allen, Christian Slater, Lloyd Bridges, Elias Koteas, Nina Siemaszko, Corin "Corky" Nemec, Marshall Bell, Don Novello, Peter Donat, Dean Goodman, Patti Austin; **D:** Francis Ford Coppola; **W:** Arnold Schulman, David Seidler; **M:** Joe Jackson, Carmine Coppola. Academy Awards '88 Nominations: Best Art Direction/Set Decoration, Best Costume Design, Best Supporting Actor (Landau); Golden Globe Awards '89: Best Supporting Actor (Landau). **VHS, Beta, 8mm $14.95** PAR &&&

Tuff Turf The new kid in town must adjust to a different social lifestyle and a new set of rules when his family is forced to move to a low-class section of Los Angeles. He makes enemies immediately when he courts the girlfriend of one of the local toughs. Fast-paced with a bright young cast. Music by Jim Carroll, Lene Lovich, and Southside Johnny.
1985 (R) 113m/C James Spader, Kim Richards, Paul Mones, Matt Clark, Olivia Barash, Robert Downey Jr., Catya Sassoon; **D:** Fritz Kiersch; **M:** Jonathan Elias. **VHS, Beta $9.95** NWV, STE &&

Tulips Would-be suicide takes a contract out on himself, and then meets a woman who makes life worth living again. Together they attempt to evade the gangland hit man. Limp comedy.
1981 (PG) 91m/C Gabe Kaplan, Bernadette Peters, Henry Gibson; **D:** Stan Ferris. **VHS, Beta $19.95** SUE & ½

Tulsa High-spirited rancher's daughter begins crusade to save her father's oil empire when he's killed. Having become ruthless and determined to succeed at any cost, she eventually sees the error of her ways. Classic Hayward.
1949 96m/C Susan Hayward, Robert Preston, Chill Wills, Ed Begley Sr., Pedro Armendariz Sr.; **D:** Stuart Heisler. **VHS, Beta $19.95** NOS, BPG, MED &&&

Tumbledown Ranch in Arizona After a rodeo accident, an unconscious college student dreams of adventure out west. Part of the "Range Busters" series.
1941 60m/B Ray Corrigan, John "Dusty" King, Max Terhune, Sheila Darcy, Marian Kerby; **D:** S. Roy Luby. **VHS $19.95** NOS, DVT &

Tumbleweed Trail Action-packed thundering western.
1942 57m/B William Boyd, Art Davis, Lee Powell, Jack Rockwell; **D:** Sam Newfield. **VHS, Beta $27.95** VCN & ½

Tumbleweeds William S. Hart's last western. Portrays the last great land rush in America, the opening of the Cherokee Strip in the Oklahoma Territory to homesteaders. Preceded by a sound prologue, made in 1939, in which Hart speaks for the only time on screen, to introduce the story. Silent, with musical score.
1925 114m/B William S. Hart, Lucien Littlefield, Barbara Bedford; **D:** King Baggott. **VHS, Beta $19.95** GPV, CCB, VYY &&&

Tundra Quasi adventure-drama/documentary set in the Alaskan tundra. A young man, known only as the "Flying Doctor," tends to the sick in small villages throughout the wilderness. But his own survival is at stake when his small plane crashes. Filmed on location. **AKA:** The Mighty Thunder.
1936 72m/B Del Cambre; **D:** Norman Dawn. **VHS $24.95** VYY && ½

The Tune 30,000 ink and watercolor drawings make up this animated gem which tells the story of Del (Neiden), a failed songwriter who gets a fresh start when he makes a wrong turn on the freeway and winds up in Flooby Nooby. The strange inhabitants of this town teach Del to throw out his rhyming dictionary and write about his experiences. Plympton's first full-length animated feature. Also includes "The Making of The Tune" and the animated short "Draw."
1992 80m/C **D:** Bill Plympton; **W:** Maureen McElheron, Bill Plympton; **V:** Daniel Neiden, Maureen McElheron, Marty Nelson, Emily Bindiger, Chris Hoffman. **VHS $59.95** TRI, WTA &&

Tune in Tomorrow Lovesick young Martin (Reeves) wants to woo divorced older babe aunt-by-marriage Julia (Hershey) and is romantically counseled by wacky soap opera writer Pedro (Falk). Seems even soap operas draw on real life, and Martin's story is immortalized on the airwaves, circa 1951 New Orleans. The story-within-a-story also features Pedro's radio characters coming to hammy life. Sometimes funny, sometimes not (the Albanian jokes are tiresome). Adapted from the novel "Aunt Julia and the Scriptwriter" by Mario Vargas Llosa.
1990 (PG-13) 90m/C Barbara Hershey, Keanu Reeves, Peter Falk, Bill McCutcheon, Patricia Clarkson, Peter Gallagher, Dan Hedaya, Buck Henry, Hope Lange, John Larroquette, Elizabeth McGovern, Robert Sedgwick, Henry Gibson; **D:** Jon Amiel; **W:** William Boyd; **M:** Wynton Marsalis. **VHS $19.98** HBO &&

Tunes of Glory Guinness and Mills are wonderful in this well made film about a brutal, sometimes lazy colonel and a disciplined and educated man moving up through the ranks of the British military. York's film debut. From the novel by James Kennaway, who adapted it for the screen. Laserdisc version contains interview with director Neame.
1960 107m/C Alec Guinness, John Mills, Dennis Price, Kay Walsh, Susannah York; **D:** Ronald Neame; **M:** Malcolm Arnold. **VHS, Beta $19.98** SUE, VYG, NLC &&& ½

Tunes of Glory/Horse's Mouth Guinness double feature. First, "Tunes of Glory" looks at the relationship between good and bad soldiers vying for the same rank. "Horse's Mouth" takes a much lighter tone. Guinness plays a truly obsessed painter who creates his work on public property. Wildly humorous.
1960 305m/C Alec Guinness, Kay Walsh, Renee Houston, John Mills, Robert Coote; **D:** James Kennaway, Ronald Neame. **VHS, Beta $69.95** CRC &&& ½

The Tunnel Obsessive romance film with a trace of suspense. Artist sees the woman of his dreams at a showing of his work. Her marriage, and her trepidation, don't keep his obsession from consuming him.
1989 (R) 99m/C Jane Seymour, Peter Weller, Fernando Rey; **D:** Antonio Drove. **VHS, Beta $79.98** VES, IME && ½

The Tunnel of Love Day and Widmark are a married couple who find themselves over their heads in red tape when they try to adopt a baby. A beautiful, disapproving adoption investigator also causes more problems for the couple when she believes Widmark is less than ideal father material. Widmark is not in his element at comedy but Day and Young (as their next-door neighbor) are fine in this lightweight adaptation of the Joseph Fields-Peter DeVries play.
1958 98m/B Doris Day, Richard Widmark, Gig Young, Gia Scala, Elisabeth Fraser, Elizabeth Wilson; **D:** Gene Kelly. **VHS $19.98** MGM, MOV && ½

Tunnelvision A spoof of television comprised of irreverent sketches. Fun to watch because of the appearances of several now-popular stars.
1976 (R) 70m/C Chevy Chase, John Candy, Laraine Newman, Joe Flaherty, Howard Hesseman, Gerrit Graham, Al Franken, Tom Davis, Ron Silver; **D:** Neal Israel. **VHS, Beta** NO && ½

Turf Boy Desperate for cash, a boy and his uncle try to get an old horse into prime condition for racing. A minor equine melodrama, just the right length for an old-time matinee double-feature. **AKA:** Mr. Celebrity.

1942 68m/B Robert "Buzzy" Henry, James Seay, Doris Day, William Halligan, Gavin Gordon; *D:* William Beaudine. VHS $15.95 *NOS, LOO* 🐾🐾

Turk 182! The angry brother of a disabled fireman takes on City Hall in order to win back the pension that he deserves. He attacks through his graffiti art. Hutton is too heavy for the over-all comic feel of this mostly silly film.
1985 (PG-13) 96m/C Timothy Hutton, Robert Culp, Robert Urich, Kim Cattrall, Peter Boyle, Darren McGavin, Paul Sorvino; *D:* Bob (Benjamin) Clark. VHS, Beta $79.98 *FOX* 🐾🐾

Turkish Delights Free spirit sculptor falls in love with free spirit gal from bourgeois family and artsy soft porn ensues. That is until a brain tumor puts an end to their fun, and he's left to wallow in flashbacks and more artsy soft porn. Dubbed. Verhoeven later became big box office in the U.S. with "Total Recall."
1973 100m/C Monique Van De Ven, Rutger Hauer, Tonny Huurdeman, Wim Van Den Brink; *D:* Paul Verhoeven. VHS *NO* 🐾🐾½

The Turn of the Screw Supernatural powers vie with a young governess for control of the souls of the two children in her charge. Redgrave does well in this chilling film adapted from the Henry James story. Remade in 1989.
1974 120m/C Lynn Redgrave, Jasper Jacobs, Eva Griffith; *D:* Dan Curtis. VHS, Beta $29.95 *LIV* 🐾🐾

The Turn of the Screw The young charges of an English nanny are sought for their souls by a dark, unimaginable evil in the mansion. Another version of the Henry James classic.
1989 (R) 60m/C Amy Irving, David Hemmings; *D:* Graeme Clifford. VHS, Beta $59.95 *CAN* 🐾🐾

The Turn of the Screw Yet another version of the Henry James classic as a young governess struggles with sexual obsession and the two children in her care who are possessed by evil.
1992 (R) 95m/C Julian Sands, Patsy Kensit, Stephane Audran, Marianne Faithfull. VHS $89.94 *LIV* 🐾🐾

Turnaround Unusual action/suspense film set in a small town. Relentless gang rampages the citizens. Finally, a man decides he's had enough, and turns on the heathens with his knowledge of magic.
1987 (R) 97m/C Doug McKeon, Tim Maier, Eddie Albert, Gayle Hunnicutt; *D:* Ola Solum. VHS, Beta *NO* 🐾🐾

Turner and Hooch A dog witnesses a murder, and a fussy cop is partnered with the drooling mutt and a weak script in his search for the culprit. Drool as a joke will only go so far, but Hanks is his usual entertaining self.
1989 (PG) 99m/C Tom Hanks, Mare Winningham, Craig T. Nelson, Scott Paulin, J.C. Quinn; *D:* Roger Spottiswoode; *W:* Jim Cash, Jack Epps Jr., Michael Blodgett. VHS, Beta $19.99 *TOU* 🐾🐾

The Turning Point A woman who gave up ballet for motherhood must come to terms as her daughter launches a ballet career and falls for the lead male dancer. The mother finds herself threatened by her daughter's affection toward an old friend who sacrificed a family life for the life of a ballerina. Baryshnikov's film debut. Melodramatic ending and problems due to ballet sequences.
1977 (PG) 119m/C Shirley MacLaine, Anne Bancroft, Tom Skerritt, Leslie Browne, Martha Scott, Marshall Thompson, Mikhail Baryshnikov; *D:* Herbert Ross; *W:* Arthur Laurents. Academy Awards '77 Nominations: Best Actress (Bancroft), Best Actress (MacLaine), Best Art Direction/Set Decoration, Best Cinematography,

Best Director (Ross), Best Film Editing, Best Original Screenplay, Best Picture, Best Sound, Best Supporting Actor (Baryshnikov), Best Supporting Actress (Browne); Golden Globe Awards '78: Best Director (Ross), Best Film—Drama; Los Angeles Film Critics Association Awards '77: Best Director (Ross); National Board of Review Awards '77: 10 Best Films of the Year, Best Actress (Bancroft), Best Supporting Actor (Skerritt). VHS, Beta $19.98 *FOX* 🐾🐾½

Turtle Diary Two lonely Londoners collaborate to free giant turtles from the city aquarium with the aid of a zoo-keeper, and the turtles' freedom somehow frees them as well. Jackson and Kingsley are stunning. Adapted by Harold Pinter from the Russell Hoban book.
1986 (PG) 90m/C Ben Kingsley, Glenda Jackson, Richard Johnson, Michael Gambon, Rosemary Leach, Jeroen Krabbe, Eleanor Bron; *D:* John Irvin; *W:* Harold Pinter. VHS, Beta $79.98 *LIV, VES* 🐾🐾🐾

Turumba A quiet satire about a family of papier-mache animal makers in a Philippine village who get a gargantuan order in time for the Turumba holiday, and desperately try to fill it. In Tagalog with English subtitles.
1984 94m/C *D:* Kidlat Tahimik. VHS, Beta $59.95 *FFM, FCT* 🐾🐾🐾

Tusks A ruthless hunter tries to kill elephants. *AKA:* Fire in Eden.
1989 (R) 99m/C Andrew Stevens, John Rhys-Davies, Lucy Gutteridge, Julian Glover; *D:* Tara Hawkins Moore. VHS, Beta *NO* 🐾½

Tut & Tuttle Young dabbler in magic is transported to ancient Egypt where he is able to demonstrate courage and wits against the evil Horemheb, who has kidnapped Prince Tut.
1982 97m/C Christopher Barnes, Eric Greene, Hans Conried, Vic Tayback. VHS, Beta *TLF* 🐾½

The Tuttles of Tahiti The Tuttles lead a life of leisure in the South Seas. Laughton's child becomes enamoured of his rival's offspring, causing problems between the two families. More interesting than it sounds.
1942 91m/C Charles Laughton, Jon Hall, Peggy Drake, Victor Francen, Gene Reynolds, Florence Bates, Mala, Alma Ross, Curt Bois; *D:* Charles Vidor. VHS, Beta $19.95 *HHT* 🐾🐾🐾

Tuxedo Warrior Set in South Africa, this film involves the adventures of a well-dressed mercenary who is caught between the police, diamond thieves, and an old girlfriend's bank robbing.
1982 93m/C John Wyman, Carol Royle, Holly Palance; *D:* Andrew Sinclair. VHS, Beta $19.95 *STE, NWV* 🐾½

TV's Best Adventures of Superman This first package of episodes from the original television series, which ran from 1951-1957, contains "Superman on Earth," the black & white series pilot about the Man of Steel's childhood on Krypton and Earth, and "All That Glitters," the series' final episode, wherein Lois Lane and Jimmy Olsen acquire super powers. Also includes the 1941 animated cartoon "Superman," the first-ever screen appearance of the superhero. Additional episodes available.
1951 62m/C George Reeves, Phyllis Coates, Noel Neill, Jack Larson, John Hamilton, Robert Shayne. VHS, Beta $19.98 *WAR, MOV* 🐾½

Twelve Angry Men Fonda sounds the voice of reason as a jury inclines toward a quick-and-dirty verdict against a boy on trial. Excellent ensemble work. Lumet's feature film debut, based on a television play by Reginald Rose.

1957 95m/B Henry Fonda, Martin Balsam, Lee J. Cobb, E.G. Marshall, Jack Klugman, Robert Webber, Ed Begley Sr., John Fiedler, Jack Warden, George Voskovec, Edward Binns, Joseph Sweeney; *D:* Sidney Lumet; *W:* Reginald Rose. Academy Awards '57 Nominations: Best Adapted Screenplay, Best Director (Lumet), Best Picture; Berlin International Film Festival '57: Golden Berlin Bear; British Academy Awards '57: Best Actor (Fonda); Edgar Allan Poe Awards '57: Best Screenplay; National Board of Review Awards '57: 10 Best Films of the Year. VHS, Beta $19.98 *MGM, FOX, VYG* 🐾🐾🐾🐾

Twelve Chairs Take-off on Russian folk-tale first filmed in Yugoslavia in 1927. A rich matron admits on her deathbed that she has hidden her jewels in the upholstery of one of twelve chairs that are no longer in her home. A Brooksian treasure hunt ensues.
1970 94m/C Mel Brooks, Dom DeLuise, Frank Langella, Ron Moody, Bridget Brice; *D:* Mel Brooks; *W:* Mel Brooks. VHS, Beta $59.95 *MED* 🐾🐾🐾

Twelve O'Clock High Epic drama about the heroic 8th Air Force, with Peck as bomber-group commander sent to shape up a hard-luck group, forced to drive himself and his men to the breaking point. Compelling dramatization of the strain of military command. Includes impressive footage of actual WWII battles. Best-ever flying fortress movie.
1949 132m/B Gregory Peck, Hugh Marlowe, Gary Merrill, Millard Mitchell, Dean Jagger, Paul Stewart; *D:* Henry King. Academy Awards '49: Best Sound, Best Supporting Actor (Jagger); Nominations: Best Actor (Peck), Best Picture. VHS, Beta $14.98 *FXV, FCT, BTV* 🐾🐾🐾½

12:01 It's the "Groundhog Day" premise played for thrills. Barry Thompson (Silverman) is an employee at a scientific research firm who finds himself reliving the same twenty-four hour period over and over again. And what a day it is—he discovers a secret project is causing the mysterious time warp, falls in love with beauteous scientist Lisa (Slater) and watches as she gets murdered. Can Barry figure out how to stop what's going on and change things enough to save her? Adaptation of the short story "12:01" by Richard Lupoff, which was previously made into a short film. Made for television.
1993 (PG-13) 92m/C Jonathan Silverman, Helen Slater, Martin Landau, Nicolas Surovy, Jeremy Piven; *D:* Jack Sholder. VHS $89.95 *COL, NLC, IME* 🐾🐾½

12 Plus 1 A man sells 13 chairs left to him by his aunt, only to find that one of them contained a hidden fortune. He chases across Europe in search of each of them. Some good cameos help move this re-make of a Russian folk-tale along, but it remains lightweight. Tate's last movie, before her death at the hands of Manson and his "family." *AKA:* The Thirteen Chairs.
1970 (R) 94m/C Sharon Tate, Orson Welles, Vittorio Gassman, Mylene Demongeot, Terry-Thomas, Tim Brooke; *Cameos:* Vittorio De Sica; *D:* Nicolas Gessner. VHS, Beta *NO* 🐾🐾🐾

Twentieth Century Maniacal Broadway director Barrymore transforms shop girl Lombard into a smashing success adored by public and press. Tired of Barrymore's manic-excessive ways, she heads for the Hollywood hills, pursued by the Profile in fine form.
1934 91m/B Carole Lombard, John Barrymore, Walter Connolly, Roscoe Karns, Edgar Kennedy, Ralph Forbes, Charles Lane, Etienne Girardot, Snow Flake; *D:* Howard Hawks; *W:* Charles MacArthur, Ben Hecht. Beta $19.95 *COL* 🐾🐾🐾🐾

Twenty Bucks Whimsical film follows a $20 dollar bill from its ''birth'' at a cash machine to its ''death'' as it is returned to the bank, tattered and torn, for shredding. The bill is passed from owner to owner, sometimes simply and briefly, sometimes altering fate. The original screenplay is nearly 60 years old: Endre Boehm originally drafted it in 1935, and his son revised and updated it. Clever transitions allow the various stories and characters to blend almost seamlessly. The strongest character is Shue's, a young waitress and aspiring writer. Rosenfeld's directorial debut is worth a look. Filmed in Minneapolis.
1993 (R) 91m/C Linda Hunt, David Rasche, George Morfogen, Brendan Fraser, Gladys Knight, Elisabeth Shue, Steve Buscemi, Christopher Lloyd, Sam Jenkins, Kamal Holloway, Melora Walters, William H. Macy, Diane Baker, Spalding Gray, Matt Frewer; *D:* Keva Rosenfeld; *W:* Leslie Boehm, Endre Boehm; *M:* David Robbins. VHS COL 𝄞𝄞𝄞

Twenty Dollar Star Steamy thriller about an prominent actress who leads a double life as a cheap hooker, and consequent occupational hazards. The title may as well refer to the budget.
1991 (R) 92m/C Rebecca Holden, Bernie White, Eddie Barth, Marilyn Hassett, Dick Sargent; *D:* Paul Leder. VHS PAR 𝄞 ½

20 Million Miles to Earth A spaceship returning from an expedition to Venus crashes on Earth, releasing a fast-growing reptilian beast that rampages throughout Athens. Another entertaining example of stop-motion animation master Ray Harryhausen's work, offering a classic battle between the monster and an elephant.
1957 82m/B William Hopper, Joan Taylor, Frank Puglia, Joan Zaremba; *D:* Nathan Juran. NO 𝄞𝄞 ½

20,000 Leagues Under the Sea Outstanding silent adaptation of Jules Verne's ''20,000 Leagues Under the Sea'' and ''The Mysterious Island'' filmed with a then revolutionary underwater camera. Much octopus fighting. Look for newly mastered edition.
1916 105m/B Matt Moore, Allen Holubar, June Gail, William Welsh, Chris Benton, Dan Hamlion; *D:* Stuart Paton; *W:* Stuart Paton. VHS, Beta $19.98 KIV, GPV, DVT 𝄞𝄞𝄞

20,000 Leagues Under the Sea From a futuristic submarine, Captain Nemo wages war on the surface world. A shipwrecked scientist and sailor do their best to thwart Nemo's dastardly schemes. Buoyant Disney version of the Jules Verne fantasy.
1954 127m/C Kirk Douglas, James Mason, Peter Lorre, Paul Lukas, Robert J. Wilke, Carleton Young; *D:* Richard Fleischer. Academy Awards '54: Best Art Direction/Set Decoration (Color), Best Special Effects; Nominations: Best Film Editing; National Board of Review Awards '54: 10 Best Films of the Year. VHS, Beta $19.99 DIS 𝄞𝄞𝄞 ½

Twenty-One Modern morality tale of a young English woman who moves to the U.S. to make a new start, but falls into the same old habits. Kensit is frank and charming, in spite of difficulties with her drug addict boyfriend and the illegal alien she marries. Director Boyd leaves it to the viewer to decide between right and wrong and where Kensit fits.
1991 (R) 92m/C Patsy Kensit, Jack Shepherd, Patrick Ryecart, Maynard Eziashi, Rufus Sewell, Sophie Thompson, Susan Wooldridge, Julia Goodman; *D:* Don Boyd; *W:* Don Boyd; *M:* Michael Berkeley. VHS NO 𝄞𝄞 ½

21 Days Dull film somewhat redeemed by its stars. Leigh is a married woman carrying on with Olivier. When her husband confronts them, Olivier accidentally kills him in a fight. They keep quiet but then a mentally deranged man is taken into custody for the crime. Since he will be held 21 days before coming to trial, the lovers decide to spend the time together before Olivier confesses. Based on the play ''The First and the Last'' by John Galsworthy. *AKA:* Twenty-One Days Together; The First and the Last.
1937 75m/C Vivien Leigh, Laurence Olivier, Leslie Banks, Francis L. Sullivan, Hay Petrie, Esme Percy, Robert Newton; *D:* Basil Dean; *W:* Graham Greene, Basil Dean. VHS $29.95 FCT 𝄞𝄞 ½

21 Hours at Munich Made-for-TV treatment of the massacre of Israeli athletes by Arab terrorists at the 1972 Olympics. Well-done. The film was produced using the actual Munich locations.
1976 100m/C William Holden, Shirley Knight, William Knight, Franco Nero, Anthony Quayle, Noel Willman; *D:* William A. Graham. VHS MOV 𝄞𝄞𝄞

23 1/2 Hours Leave Amusing WWI service comedy as a barracks wiseacre bets that by the following morning he'll be breakfasting with a general. It's a song-filled remake of a 1919 film, whose star Douglas MacClean later produced this.
1937 73m/B James Ellison, Terry Walker, Morgan Hill, Arthur Lake, Paul Harvey; *D:* John Blystone. VHS $15.95 NOS, LOO 𝄞𝄞

Twenty-Four Eyes Miss Oishi (Takamine), a teacher on a remote Japanese island in the 1920's, attempts to transmit peaceful values to her 12 pupils amidst the clamor of a nation gearing up for war. As she watches them grow up, many of them doomed to an early death, she remains a pillar of quiet strength. In Japanese with English subtitles. *AKA:* Nijushi No Hitomi.
1954 158m/B Hideko Takamine, Chishu Ryu, Toshiko Kobayashi; *D:* Keisuke Kinoshita. VHS, Beta $59.95 JPN, ING 𝄞𝄞

24 Hours in a Woman's Life A girl in love with an irresponsible guy hears a cautionary tale from grandma Bergman, who once had a whirlwind romance with a young gambler and naively thought she could reform him. A static TV adaptation of an oft-filmed Stefan Zweig novel, unusually lavish for its time but on the dull side.
1961 90m/C Ingrid Bergman, Rip Torn, John Williams, Lili Darvas, Jerry Orbach; *D:* Silvio Narizzano; *W:* John Mortimer. VHS $29.95 FCT 𝄞𝄞

24 Hours to Midnight A widow uses her ninja skills to wipe out the crime bosses and henchmen who killed her husband.
1992 91m/C Cynthia Rothrock, Stack Pierce; *D:* Leo Fong. VHS $89.95 AIP 𝄞 ½

25 Fireman's Street An evocative drama about the residents of an old house in Hungary which is about to be torn down, and their evening of remembrances of life before, during and after WWII. In Hungarian with English subtitles.
1973 97m/C Rita Bekes, Peter Muller, Lucyna Winnicka; *D:* Istvan Szabo. VHS, Beta $69.95 KIV, ING 𝄞𝄞𝄞

The 27 Day Temperate cold war allegory has aliens deliver five mysterious capsules to five Earthlings from different countries. Each capsule, if opened, is capable of decimating the population of the entire planet, but is rendered ineffective after 27 days or upon the death of the holder. Wild ending. Based on John Mantley novel.

1957 75m/B Gene Barry, Valerie French, George Voskovec, Arnold Moss, Stefan Schnabel, Ralph Clanton, Friedrich Ledebur, Mari Tsien. VHS $14.98 MOV, MLB 𝄞𝄞 ½

29th Street Compelling comedy-drama based on the true story of Frank Pesce, a New York actor who won six million dollars in that state's first lottery. Great performance from Aiello, as usual, but the direction falters in the dramatic sequences. Based on the book by Frank Pesce and James Franciscus.
1991 (R) 101m/C Danny Aiello, Anthony LaPaglia, Lainie Kazan, Frank Pesce, Donna Magnani, Rick Aiello, Vic Manni, Ron Karabatsos, Robert Forster, Joe Franklin, Pete Antico; *D:* George Gallo; *W:* George Gallo; *M:* William Olvis. VHS $19.98 FXV, CCB 𝄞𝄞 ½

Twice a Judas An amnesiac is swindled and has his family killed by a ruthless renegade. He wants to get even, even though he can't remember who anyone is.
196? 90m/C Klaus Kinski. VHS, Beta $49.95 UNI, MOV 𝄞

Twice a Woman Man and woman divorce, and then both fall in love with the same provocative young woman. It's complicated.
1979 90m/C Bibi Andersson, Anthony Perkins, Sandra Dumas. VHS, Beta $59.95 PSM 𝄞

Twice Dead A family moves into a ramshackle mansion haunted by a stage actor's angry ghost. The ghost helps them battle some attacking delinquent boys. Uninteresting story, poorly done. Never released in theaters.
1988 94m/C Tom Breznahan, Jill Whitlow, Sam Melville, Brooke Bundy, Todd Bridges, Jonathan Chapin, Christopher Burgard; *D:* Bert L. Dragin. VHS, Beta $19.98 SUE, NLC Woof!

Twice in a Lifetime Middle-aged man takes stock of his life when he's attracted to Ann-Margret. Realizing he's married in name only; he moves in with his new love while his former wife and children struggle with shock, disbelief, and anger. Well-acted, realistic, and unsentimental.
1985 (R) 117m/C Gene Hackman, Ellen Burstyn, Amy Madigan, Ann-Margret, Brian Dennehy, Ally Sheedy; *D:* Bud Yorkin; *W:* Colin Welland. VHS, Beta $79.98 LIV, VES 𝄞𝄞𝄞

Twice-Told Tales Horror trilogy based loosely on three Nathaniel Hawthorne tales, ''Dr. Heidegger's Experiment,'' ''Rappaccini's Daughter,'' and ''The House of Seven Gables.'' Price is great in all three of these well-told tales. *AKA:* Nathaniel Hawthorne's ''Twice Told Tales''.
1963 120m/C Vincent Price, Sebastian Cabot, Brett Halsey; *D:* Sidney Salkow. VHS, Beta $14.95 MGM, MLB 𝄞𝄞𝄞

Twigs Taped performance of George Furthis' Tony Award-winning drama about a mother and her three daughters who meet the day before Thanksgiving.
1984 138m/C Cloris Leachman. VHS, Beta $39.95 RKO 𝄞 ½

Twilight in the Sierras Lots of heroics and music in this action-packed western. An ex-outlaw gone straight is kidnapped for his notorious criminal finesse. Rogers must come to rescue.
1950 67m/B Roy Rogers, Dale Evans, Estelita Rodriguez, Pat Brady, Russ Vincent, George Meeker; *D:* William Witney. VHS $12.98 REP 𝄞𝄞 ½

Twilight of the Cockroaches Mr. Saito is a slovenly bachelor who winds up leaving the remains of his meals for the anthropomorphic cockroaches that infest his apartment. The cockroaches have had it so good for so long that they don't know about

insecticides and fearing humans. That is, until Mr. Saito's fastidious new girlfriend makes her appearance and declares war on the vermin. A lifelessly animated tale too dumb for both children and adults and with decidedly unpleasant subject matter, despite the singing, dancing insects. In Japanese with English subtitles. *AKA:* Gokiburi.
1990 105m/C *D:* Hiroaki Yoshida; *V:* Kaoru Kobayashi, Setsuko Karamsumaru. **VHS $34.95** *FCT, STP, LUM* ♪♪1/2

Twilight on the Rio Grande Autry runs into a female knife thrower and some jewel smugglers in this far-fetched western.
1941 54m/B Gene Autry, Sterling Holloway, Adele Mara, Bob Steele; *D:* Frank McDonald. **VHS, Beta $27.95** *VCN* ♪

Twilight on the Trail Cattle rustlers disappear and Hopalong Cassidy and his sidekicks become "dude" detectives to solve the crime.
1941 54m/B William Boyd, Brad King, Andy Clyde, Jack Rockwell, Wanda McKay, Howard Bretherton; *D:* GVV ♪♪

Twilight People When a mad scientist's creations turn on him for revenge, he runs for his life. Boring, gory, with bad make-up and even poorer acting. This one should fade away into the night. *AKA:* Beasts.
1972 (PG) 84m/C John Ashley, Pat Woodell, Jan Merlin, Pam Grier; *D:* Eddie Romero. **VHS, Beta $29.95** *VCI* Woof!

The Twilight Zone Travel through another dimension in Rod Serling's classic science fiction series. Two episodes per tape. On this tape: "The Invaders," written by Richard Matheson, sees a farm house inhabited by a mute woman become the destination of strange, miniature space travelers. In "Nothing in the Dark," written by George Clayton Johnson, an elderly woman is given an interesting lesson regarding her fear of death.
1961 50m/B Agnes Moorehead, Douglas Heyes, Gladys Cooper, Robert Redford, R.G. Armstrong; *D:* Lamont Johnson; *W:* Richard Matheson, George Clayton Johnson. **VHS, Beta $14.98** *FXV, FOX, MOV* Woof!

Twilight Zone: The Movie Four short horrific tales are anthologized in this film as a tribute to Rod Sterling and his popular television series. Three of the episodes, "Kick the Can," "It's a Good Life" and "Nightmare at 20,000 Feet," are based on original "Twilight Zone" scripts. Morrow was killed in a helicopter crash during filming.
1983 (PG) 101m/C Dan Aykroyd, Albert Brooks, Vic Morrow, Kathleen Quinlan, John Lithgow, Billy Mumy, Scatman Crothers, Kevin McCarthy, Bill Quinn, Selma Diamond, Abbe Lane, John Larroquette, Jeremy Licht, Patricia Barry, William Schallert, Burgess Meredith, Cherie Currie; *D:* John Landis, Steven Spielberg, George Miller, Joe Dante; *W:* John Landis; *M:* Jerry Goldsmith. **VHS, Beta $19.98** *WAR* ♪♪1/2

Twilight's Last Gleaming A maverick general takes a SAC missile base hostage, threatening to start WWIII if the U.S. government doesn't confess to its Vietnam policies and crimes. Gripping film, with good performances. Based on a novel by Walter Wager, "Viper Three."
1977 (R) 144m/C Burt Lancaster, Charles Durning, Richard Widmark, Melvyn Douglas, Joseph Cotten, Paul Winfield, Burt Young, Roscoe Lee Browne, Richard Jaeckel, William Marshall, Vera Miles, Leif Erickson, Charles McGraw, William Smith, John Ratzenberger; *D:* Robert Aldrich; *M:* Jerry Goldsmith. **VHS, Beta $59.98** *FOX* ♪♪1/2

Twin Peaks Sketchy home video distillation of the eccentric TV series. It preserves much of the setup episode (the murder of teen-queen Laura Palmer and nest of small-town weirdness it reveals), then rushes piecemeal through the rest of the season. There's an altered quasi-solution to the enigma and a bizarre backward sequence not broadcast in the US. In this compressed form it's best for initiates of the TP cult; others won't be converted.
1990 113m/C Kyle MacLachlan, Michael Ontkean, Sherilyn Fenn, Lara Flynn Boyle, Joan Chen, Peggy Lipton, Piper Laurie, Michael Horse, Russ Tamblyn, Richard Beymer, Madchen Amick, Catherine Coulson, Warren Frost, Everett McGill, Jack Nance, Ray Wise, Eric Da Re, Harry Goaz, Sheryl Lee; *D:* David Lynch; *M:* Angelo Badalamenti. **VHS $79.99** *WAR, FCT* ♪♪

Twin Peaks Premiere episode of David Lynch's bizarre TV drama. In this episode, Agent Cooper and Sheriff Truman begin the investigation into the death of prom queen, Laura Palmer. All seven episodes are available in a boxed set.
1990 50m/C Michael Ontkean, Kyle MacLachlan, Joan Chen, Piper Laurie, Sherilyn Fenn, Peggy Lipton, Madchen Amick, Lara Flynn Boyle, Michael Horse, Russ Tamblyn, Richard Beymer, Dana Ashbrook, Warren Frost, Everett McGill, Jack Nance, Ray Wise, Eric Da Re, Catherine Coulson, Harry Goaz, Sheryl Lee; *D:* David Lynch; *M:* Angelo Badalamenti. **VHS $14.99** *WOV, MOV* ♪♪

Twin Peaks: Fire Walk with Me Prequel to the cult TV series is weird and frustrating, chronicling the week before Laura Palmer's death. Suspense is lacking since we know the outcome, but Lynch manages to intrigue with dream-like sequences and interestingly offbeat characters. On the other hand, it's exploitative and violent enough to alienate series fans. Includes extremely brief and baffling cameos by Bowie as an FBI agent and Stanton as the manager of a trailer park. Several of the show's regulars are missing, and others appear and disappear very quickly. On the plus side are the strains of Badalamenti's famous theme music and Isaak as an FBI agent with amazingly acute powers of observation.
1992 (R) 135m/C Kyle MacLachlan, Sheryl Lee, Moira Kelly, Chris Isaak, Ray Wise, Kiefer Sutherland, Peggy Lipton, Dana Ashbrook, James Marshall, David Lynch; *Cameos:* David Bowie, Harry Dean Stanton; *D:* David Lynch; *W:* David Lynch; *M:* Angelo Badalamenti. Cannes Film Festival Nominations: cs 92: Best Film; Independent Spirit Awards '93: Best Score. **VHS $19.95** *NLC, COL* ♪♪

Twins A genetics experiment gone awry produces twins rather than a single child. One is a genetically-engineered superman, the other a short, lecherous petty criminal. Schwarzenegger learns he has a brother, and becomes determined to find him, despite their having been raised separately. The two meet and are immediately involved in a contraband scandal. Amusing pairing of Schwarzenegger and DeVito.
1988 (PG) 107m/C Arnold Schwarzenegger, Danny DeVito, Kelly Preston, Hugh O'Brian, Chloe Webb, Bonnie Bartlett, Marshall Bell, Trey Wilson, Nehemiah Persoff; *D:* Ivan Reitman; *W:* William Davies, William Osborne, Timothy Harris, Herschel Weingrod; *M:* Georges Delerue, Randy Edelman. **VHS, Beta $19.95** *MCA* ♪♪

Twins of Evil Beautiful female twins fall victim to the local vampire, and their God-fearing uncle is out to save/destroy them. Hammer sex and blood-sucking epic starring the Collinsons, who were featured in the October 1970 issue of Playboy as the first twin Playmates.

1971 86m/C Madeleine Collinson, Mary Collinson, Peter Cushing, Kathleen Byron, Dennis Price, Damien Thomas, David Warbeck, Katya Wyeth, Maggie Wright, Luan Peters, Kristen Lindholm, Judy Matheson; *D:* John Hough. **VHS, Beta $14.98** *MLB* ♪♪1/2

Twinsanity Evil twins are charged with the murder of a man who attempted to blackmail them. *AKA:* Goodbye Gemini.
1970 (R) 91m/C Judy Geeson, Martin Potter, Alexis Kanner, Michael Redgrave, Freddie Jones, Peter Jeffrey; *D:* Alan Gibson; *W:* Edmund Ward; *M:* Christopher Gunning. **VHS, Beta $59.95** *PSM* ♪

Twirl Satirical look at the cutthroat world of baton twirling. Parents apply relentless pressure on their daughters to win a contest. Decent made-for-TV movie.
1981 100m/C Stella Stevens, Charles Haid, Lisa Whelchel, Erin Moran, Edd Byrnes, Sharon Spelman, Matthew Tobin, Donna McKechnie, Rosalind Chao, Heather Locklear, Deborah Richter, Jamie Rose, Tracy Scoggins; *D:* Gus Trikonis. **VHS, Beta $39.95** *LIV* ♪♪

Twist A tepid French drama chronicling the infidelities of various wealthy aristocrats. The aristocrats are boring, as is the film. In French with English subtitles or dubbed. *AKA:* Folies Bourgeoises.
1976 105m/C Bruce Dern, Stephane Audran, Ann-Margret, Sydne Rome, Jean-Pierre Cassel, Curt Jurgens, Maria Schell, Charles Aznavour; *D:* Claude Chabrol; *M:* Manuel De Sica. **VHS, Beta $49.95** *LIV* ♪♪1/2

Twist & Shout Sequel to the popular Danish import "Zappa," in which two teen-age lovers discover sex and rock and roll. Transcends the teens discovering sex genre. Danish with English subtitles. Profanity, nudity, and sex. *AKA:* Hab Og Karlighed.
1984 (R) 107m/C Lars Simonsen, Adam Tonsberg, Ulrikke Juul Bondo, Camilla Soeberg; *D:* Bille August; *W:* Bille August. **VHS, Beta $79.99** *HBO* ♪♪♪

Twisted This curio from Slater's early career came out on tape to take advantage of his rising stardom. He's properly creepy as a brilliant but evil teen using electronics, psychology, and swordplay to terrorize victims. The suspense isn't too bad when direction doesn't go overboard, which unfortunately is half the time. Based on the play "Children! Children!" by Jack Horrigan
1986 (R) 87m/C Lois Smith, Christian Slater, Tandy Cronyn, Brooke Tracy, Dina Merrill, Dan Ziskie, Karl Taylor, Noelle Parker, John Cunningham, J.C. Quinn; *D:* Adam Holender. **VHS** *NO* ♪♪

Twisted Brain An honor student develops a serum that makes him half man and half beast. Now he can exact revenge on all the jocks and cheerleaders who have humiliated him in the past. Cardi is okay, the rest of the cast is awful. Silly, horrific teen monster epic. *AKA:* Horror High.
1974 (R) 89m/C Pat Cardi, Austin Stoker, Rosie Holotik, John Niland, Joyce Hash, Jeff Alexander, Joe "Mean Joe" Greene; *D:* Larry N. Stouffer. **VHS, Beta $29.95** *VCI* ♪

Twisted Justice Set in 2020, Heavener is a cop determined to stop a ruthless killer. Matters become complicated, however, when his gun is taken away. Now he's forced to rely on his cunning to outwit his sadistic opponent.
1989 90m/C David Heavener, Erik Estrada, Jim Brown, Shannon Tweed, James Van Patten, Don Stroud, Karen Black, Lori Warren; *D:* David Heavener; *W:* David Heavener. **VHS** *NO* ♪1/2

Twisted Nightmare The people responsible for a young retarded boy's death are hunted by a strange figure lurking in the shadows.
1987 (R) 95m/C Rhonda Gray, Cleve Hall, Brad Bartrum, Robert Padilla; *D:* Paul Hunt. **Beta** TWE *Ⅱ*

Twisted Obsession A man becomes passionately obsessed with a woman, and it leads to murder.
1990 (R) 109m/C Jeff Goldblum, Miranda Richardson, Anemone, Dexter Fletcher, Daniel Ceccaldi, Liza Walker, Jerome Natali, Arielle Dombasle; *D:* Fernando Trueba; *M:* Antoine Duhamel. **VHS, Beta** $89.95 *LIV* *Ⅱ*

Twister An intriguing independent feature about a bizarre midwestern family, its feverish eccentricities and eventual collapse. Awaiting a cult following.
1989 (PG-13) 93m/C Dylan McDermott, Crispin Glover, Harry Dean Stanton, Suzy Amis, Jenny Wright, Lindsay Christman, Lois Chiles; *D:* Michael Almereyda. **VHS, Beta** $89.98 *LIV,* *VES* *ⅡⅡ*

Twister Kicker When the woman he loves is in jeopardy, an invincible man battles the best of fighters from three continents. Despite all this action, it's pretty ho-hum.
1985 93m/C Wang Hoi, Yeung Oi Wa, Po Pei. **VHS** *NO* *Ⅱ*

Twitch of the Death Nerve Four vacationers are relentlessly pursued by a homicidal maniac armed with a sickle, bent on decapitation. Supposedly the inspiration for the "Friday the 13th" series. *AKA:* Bay of Blood; Last House on the Left, Part 2; Carnage.
1971 (R) 87m/C Claudine Auger, Chris Avran, Isa Miranda, Claudio Volonte, Luigi Pistilli; *D:* Mario Bava. **VHS, Beta** $79.95 *MPI* *Ⅱ*

Two Assassins in the Dark Martial arts adventure about a pair of kung-fu killers who fight in the dark.
198? 90m/C Wang Tao, Chang Yi, Lung Chun-Eng. **VHS, Beta** *NO* *Ⅱ*

Two by Forsyth Two short films based on stories by Frederick Forsyth, one dealing with a dying millionaire's clever efforts to prevent his fortune from being inherited by greedy relatives, the other about a mild-mannered stamp dealer who avenges himself on a nasty gossip columnist.
1986 60m/C Dan O'Herlihy, Cyril Cusack, Milo O'Shea, Shirley Anne Field. **VHS, Beta** $59.95 *PSM* *ⅡⅡ*

Two Can Play This is a taped production of Trevor Rhone's play about political upheaval in Jamaica in the 1970's.
1983 105m/C **VHS, Beta** *KET* *ⅡⅡ*

Two Daughters Director Ray wrote the scripts for two stories based on the writings of Nobel Prize winner Rabindranath Tagore, one about the relationship between an orphan and a postman, the other about a young man who declines to marry the girl arranged to be his intended. In Hindi with English subtitles. *AKA:* Teen Kanya.
1961 114m/B *D:* Satyajit Ray; *W:* Satyajit Ray. **VHS, Beta** $29.98 *SUE, ING, NLC* *ⅡⅡⅡ*

Two Dragons Fight Against the Tiger Kung fu equals survival in this martial arts adventure. Several men strike a gold vein in a Chinese mine. They wind up fighting against corruption and greed.
19?? 90m/C Kao Tien Chu, Wang Luan Hsiung, Tse Lan, Huang I Lung. **VHS** $49.95 *OCE* *Ⅱ*

Two English Girls A pre-WWI French lad, with a possessive mother, loves two English sisters, one an impassioned, reckless artist, the other a repressed spinster. Ten-derly delineates the triangle's interrelating love and friendship over seven years. Based on the novel "Les Deux Anglaises et le Continent" by Henri-Pierre Roche. In French with English subtitles. *AKA:* Les Deux Anglaises et le Continent.
1972 (R) 108m/C Jean-Pierre Leaud, Kika Markham, Stacey Tendeter, Sylvia Marriott, Marie Mansert, Philippe Leotard; *D:* Francois Truffaut; *M:* Georges Delerue. **VHS, Beta** $39.95 *HMV, FOX, APD* *ⅡⅡ½*

Two Evil Eyes Horror kings Romero and Argento each direct an Edgar Allan Poe tale in this release, hence the title. Barbeau, the scheming younger wife of a millionaire, hypnotizes her husband with the help of a her lover in "The Facts in the Case of M. Valdemar." When hubby dies too soon to validate changes made in his will, the lovers decide to freeze him for two weeks in order that death can be recorded at the correct time. In "Black Cat" a crime photographer used to photographing gore adopts a feline friend and starts getting sick on the job. *AKA:* Due Occhi Diabolici.
1990 (R) 121m/C Adrienne Barbeau, Ramy Zada, Harvey Keitel, Madeleine Potter; *D:* George A. Romero, Dario Argento; *M:* Pino Donaggio. **VHS, Beta** $92.98 *FXV, VTR* *ⅡⅡ*

Two-Faced Woman Garbo, in her last film, attempts a ruse when she finds her husband may be interested in an old flame. Pretending to be her twin sister in an attempt to lure Douglas away from the other woman, she's fooled a little herself. Romantic comedy unfortunately miscasts Garbo as an Americanized ski bunny.
1941 90m/B Greta Garbo, Melvyn Douglas, Constance Bennett, Roland Young, Ruth Gordon, Robert Sterling, George Cleveland, Frances Carson; *D:* George Cukor. **VHS, Beta** $19.98 *MGM* *ⅡⅡⅡ*

The Two Faces of Evil A family's vacation turns into a night of unbearable terror when they pick up a sinister hitchhiker.
1982 60m/C Anna Calder-Marshall, Gary Raymond, Denholm Elliott, Pauline Delany, Philip Latham; *D:* Peter Sasdy, Alan Gibson. **VHS, Beta** $29.95 *LIV* *Ⅱ*

Two Fathers' Justice Two dads, one tough and one a wimp, seek revenge on the men who killed their kids. Made for television.
1985 100m/C Robert Conrad, George Hamilton, Brooke Bundy, Catherine Corkill, Whitney Kershaw, Greg Terrell; *D:* Rod Holcomb. **VHS** $19.98 *MCG* *Ⅱ*

Two Fisted Justice A cowboy protects a town against a daring and deadly Indian attack.
1931 45m/B Tom Tyler. **VHS, Beta** $19.95 *VDM* *Ⅱ*

Two-Fisted Justice The Range Busters do their part to maintain law and order in the old West.
1943 57m/B John "Dusty" King, David Sharpe, Max Terhune. **VHS, Beta** $19.95 *NOS, DVT* *Ⅱ*

Two-Fisted Law McCoy plays a rancher who borrows big bucks from the corrupt Oakman, who's actually a land grabber. McCoy then teams up with a posse to bring the evildoer to justice. Early (and small) screen roles for Wayne and Brennan.
1932 58m/B Tim McCoy, Tully Marshall, Wheeler Oakman, Alice Day, Wallace MacDonald, John Wayne, Walter Brennan; *D:* David Ross Lederman. **VHS** $14.95 *COL* *Ⅱ½*

Two for the Road After over a decade of marriage, Finney and Hepburn look back and find only fragments of their relationship. Mancini score adds poignancy to the cou-ple's reflections on their stormy life. Touching and well-acted.
1967 112m/C Audrey Hepburn, Albert Finney, Eleanor Bron, William Daniels, Claude Dauphin, Nadia Gray, Jacqueline Bisset; *D:* Stanley Donen; *W:* Frederic Raphael; *M:* Henry Mancini. **VHS** $19.98 *FXV, BTV, FUS* *ⅡⅡⅡ½*

Two for the Seesaw Mitchum stars as a Nebraska attorney who comes to New York and gets involved with MacLaine. Humorous and touching comedy-drama worked better on stage, because the large screen magnified the talkiness of Gibson's play. Unusual casting of Mitchum as a Midwest lawyer and MacLaine as a New York Jewish bohemian.
1962 119m/B Robert Mitchum, Shirley MacLaine, Edmond Ryan, Elisabeth Fraser, Eddie Firestone, Billy Gray, Vic Lundin; *D:* Robert Wise; *W:* Isobel Lennart. **VHS** $19.98 *MGM* *ⅡⅡⅡ*

Two Girls and a Sailor Wartime musical revue loosely structured around a love triangle involving a sailor on leave. Vintage hokum with lots of songs. ♫Paper Doll; The Young Man with a Horn; Concerto for Index Finger; Take it Easy; Ritual Fire Dance; Inka Dinka Doo; My Mother Told Me; A Love Like Ours; In A Moment of Madness.
1944 124m/B June Allyson, Gloria De Haven, Van Johnson, Xavier Cugat, Jimmy Durante, Tom Drake, Lena Horne, Harry James, Gracie Allen, Virginia O'Brien, Jose Iturbi, Carlos Ramirez, Donald Meek, Ben Blue; *Cameos:* Buster Keaton; *D:* Richard Thorpe. **VHS, Beta** $19.98 *MGM* *ⅡⅡⅡ*

Two Graves to Kung-Fu Young kung-fu student is framed for murder. When the real murderers kill his teacher, he escapes from prison to seek revenge.
1982 (R) 95m/C Liu Chia-Yung, Shek Kin, Chen Hung-Lieh. **VHS, Beta** $59.95 *GEM* *Ⅱ*

The Two Great Cavaliers A Ming warrior has a hard time with the Manchurian army, fending it off as he must with only his bare instep, heel, and wrist.
1973 95m/C Chen Shing, Mao Ying; *D:* Yeung Ching Chen. **VHS, Beta** $39.95 *UNI* *Ⅱ*

Two Gun Man America's first singing cowboy, Ken Maynard, performs hair-raising stunts in this old oater. One of the first "talkies!"
1931 60m/B Ken Maynard, Lafe McKee, Charles "Blackie" King, Tom London, Lucille Powers; *D:* Phil Rosen. **VHS, Beta** $12.95 *GPV, VCN, DVT* *Ⅱ½*

Two-Gun Man from Harlem Big city guy travels to the wild West in search of a little truth.
1938 60m/B Herbert Jeffries, Marguerite Whitten, Mantan Moreland, Matthew "Stymie" Beard; *D:* Richard C. Kahn. **VHS** $24.95 *NOS, TPV* *Ⅱ½*

Two-Gun Troubador A masked singing cowboy struggles to uncovers his father's murderer. *AKA:* The Lone Troubador.
1937 59m/B Fred Scott, Claire Rochelle, John Merton. **VHS, Beta** $19.95 *NOS, BAR, HEG* *Ⅱ*

200 Motels Rambling, non-narrative self-indulgent video album by and about Frank Zappa and the Mothers of Invention, as they document a long and especially grueling road tour. For fans only.
1971 (R) 99m/C Frank Zappa, Ringo Starr, The Mothers of Invention; *D:* Frank Zappa. **VHS, Beta** $19.95 *MVD, MGM* *Ⅱ½*

The Two Jakes Ten years have passed and Jake Gittes is still a private investigator in this sequel to 1974's "Chinatown." When a murder occurs while he's digging up dirt on an affair between the wife of a real estate executive and the executive's partner, Jake must return to Chinatown to uncover the

killer and face the painful memories buried there. Despite solid dialogue and effective performances, it's unreasonably difficult to follow if you haven't seen "Chinatown." Outstanding photography by Vilmos Zsigmond.
1990 (R) 137m/C Jack Nicholson, Harvey Keitel, Meg Tilly, Madeleine Stowe, Eli Wallach, Ruben Blades, Frederic Forrest, David Keith, Richard Farnsworth, Tracy Walter; **D:** Jack Nicholson, Vilmos Zsigmond; **W:** Robert Towne; **M:** Van Dyke Parks. **VHS, Beta $19.95** *PAR, FCT* ✍✍

Two Kinds of Love Adapted from Peggy Mann's novel "There Are Two Kinds of Terrible" this is the story of a young boy who learns to love his distant, workaholic father after his protective mother suddenly dies. Made for television.
1985 94m/C Rick Schroder, Lindsay Wagner, Peter Weller; **D:** Jack Bender. **VHS, Beta $59.98** *FOX* ✍✍

Two Lost Worlds A young hero battles monstrous dinosaurs, pirates, and more in this cheapy when he and his shipmates are shipwrecked on an uncharted island. Don't miss the footage from "Captain Fury," "One Billion B.C." , and "Captain Caution" and Arness long before his Sheriff Dillon fame, and his "big" role in "The Thing."
1950 63m/B James Arness, Laura Elliott, Bill Kennedy; **D:** Norman Dawn. **VHS, Beta** *NO Woof!*

Two Men & a Wardrobe Polanski's project while a student at the Polish Film Institute. Consideration of modern man's lack of privacy and made without dialogue. Two men emerge from the sea carrying nothing but a large piece of furniture. Absurd and funny.
1958 19m/B **D:** Roman Polanski. **VHS, Beta** *IHF, GVV Woof!*

Two Minute Warning A sniper plans to take out the president of the United States at an NFL playoff game in this boring, pointless, disaster film that goes on forever. Features all the ready-made characters inherent in the genre, but, until its too late, precious little of the mayhem. To get caught watching the TV version, which features more characters and an additional subplot, would be truly disastrous.
1976 (R) 116m/C Charlton Heston, John Cassavetes, Martin Balsam, Beau Bridges, Marilyn Hassett, David Janssen, Jack Klugman, Walter Pidgeon, Gena Rowlands; **D:** Larry Peerce; **M:** Charles Fox. **VHS $89.95** *MCA* ✍

The Two Mrs. Carrolls Bogart is a psycho-killer/artist who paints portraits of his wives as the Angel of Death—and then kills them. The married Bogart falls for Stanwyck, poisons his current wife, and the two marry. After a few years, Bogart falls for Smith and decides to rid himself of Stanwyck in the same manner as his first killing. Stanwyck, however, becomes increasingly suspicious and calls on an old beau for help. Melodrama cast Bogart against type (not always successfully). Filmed in 1945, but was unreleased until 1947.
1947 99m/B Humphrey Bogart, Barbara Stanwyck, Alexis Smith, Nigel Bruce, Pat O'Moore, Ann Carter; **D:** Peter Godfrey. **VHS $19.98** *MGM* ✍✍

Two Moon Junction A soon-to-be-wed Southern debutante enters into a wild love affair with a rough-edged carnival worker. Poorly acted, wildly directed, with many unintentional laughs.
1988 (R) 104m/C Sherilyn Fenn, Richard Tyson, Louise Fletcher, Burl Ives, Kristy McNichol, Millie Perkins, Don Galloway, Herve Villechaize, Dabbs Greer, Jay Hawkins; **D:** Zalman King; **W:** Zalman

King; **M:** Jonathan Elias. **VHS, Beta $14.95** *COL* ✍ ½

Two Mules for Sister Sara American mercenary in 19th century Mexico gets mixed up with a cigar-smoking nun and the two make plans to capture a French garrison. MacLaine and Eastwood are great together. Based on a Boetticher story.
1970 (PG) 105m/C Clint Eastwood, Shirley MacLaine; **D:** Don Siegel; **W:** Albert Maltz; **M:** Ennio Morricone. **VHS, Beta $19.95** *MCA* ✍✍✍

Two Nights with Cleopatra A piece of Italian pizza involving Cleopatra's double (also played by Loren) falling in love with one of the guards. Notable only for the 19-year-old Sophia's brief nudity. **AKA:** Due Notti Con Cleopatra.
1954 77m/C Sophia Loren, Ettore Manni, Alberto Sordi, Paul Muller, Alberto Talegalli, Rolf Tasna, Gianni Cavalieri, Fernando Bruno, Riccardo Garrone, Carlo Dale; **D:** Mario Mattoli; **W:** Nino Maccari, Ettore Scola. **VHS, Beta $29.95** *VDM* ✍ ½

Two of a Kind In his television movie debut, Burns plays an elderly man whose mentally handicapped grandson helps him put the starch back in his shirt. Sensitively produced and performed.
1982 102m/C George Burns, Robby Benson, Cliff Robertson, Barbara Barrie, Frances Lee McCain, Geri Jewell, Ronny Cox; **D:** Roger Young. **VHS, Beta $49.95** *FOX* ✍✍ ½

Two of a Kind Angels make a bet with God—two selfish people will redeem themselves or God can blow up the Earth. Bad acting, awful direction, and the script needs divine intervention.
1983 (PG) 88m/C John Travolta, Olivia Newton-John, Charles Durning, Beatrice Straight, Scatman Crothers, Oliver Reed; **D:** John Herzfeld. **VHS, Beta $19.98** *FOX* ✍

The Two of Us Young Jewish boy flees Nazi-occupied Paris to live in the country with an irritable, bigoted guardian. Sensitive, eloquent movie about racial prejudice and anti-Semitism. In French with English subtitles. **AKA:** Le Vieil Homme Et L'Enfant; Claude; The Old Man and the Boy.
1968 86m/B Michel Simon, Alain Cohen, Luce Fabiole, Roger Carel, Paul Preboist, Charles Denner; **D:** Claude Berri; **M:** Georges Delerue. **VHS** *NO* ✍✍✍ ½

Two Reelers: Comedy Classics
1 Includes a 1944 Edgar Kennedy short, "Feather Your Nest" (RKO), and two 1933 films, "How Comedies Are Born" and "Dog Blight."
1933 54m/B Edgar Kennedy, Harry Gribbon, Harry Sweet, Jack Norton, Maxine Jennings, Willie Best. **VHS, Beta $19.95** *VYY* ✍✍✍ ½

Two Reelers: Comedy Classics
2 Three vintage shorts: "Chicken Feed" (1939) with Billy Gilbert, "Twin Husbands" (1946) with Leon Errol, and Edgar Kennedy in "False Roomers" (1938).
1946 53m/B Leon Errol, Dorothy Granger, Billy Gilbert, Edgar Kennedy. **VHS, Beta $19.95** *VYY* ✍✍✍ ½

Two Reelers: Comedy Classics
3 More laughs, with two Edgar Kennedy shorts, "A Merchant of Menace" (1933), and "Social Terrors" (1946). Also, Jed Prouty is featured in "Coat Tales" (193).
1933 52m/B Edgar Kennedy, Jed Prouty. **VHS, Beta $19.95** *VYY* ✍✍✍ ½

Two Reelers: Comedy Classics
4 "Bridal Bail" (1934), "No More West" (Educational-1934) with Bert Lahr singing and clowning, and "Bad Medicine" (1936) with crooner Gene Austin comprise this comedy package.

1936 56m/B Bert Lahr, Gene Austin, June Brewster, Carol Tevis, Grady Sutton. **VHS, Beta $19.95** *VYY* ✍✍✍ ½

Two Reelers: Comedy Classics
5 A compilation of three vintage comedy shorts by popular stars of the 1930's: "Dear Deer" (1942) with Leon Errol, "Hotel Anchovy" (1934) with the Ritz Brothers and "Love Your Neighbor" (1930) with Charlotte Greenwood.
1938 55m/B Leon Errol, The Ritz Brothers, Charlotte Greenwood. **VHS, Beta $19.95** *VYY* ✍✍✍ ½

Two Reelers: Comedy Classics
6 Three vintage comedy shorts: "LePutt, The Specialist," "Dumb Luck," and "Our Gang Follies of 1938."
1935 59m/B Charles Sale, Goodman Ace. **VHS, Beta $19.95** *VYY* ✍✍✍ ½

Two Reelers: Comedy Classics
7 Three more comedy shorts from the '30s: "Dumb Dicks," "Love and Onions," and "Julius Sizzler."
1938 56m/B Benny Rubin, Harry Gribbon, Johnny Johnson, Pat Rooney Jr. **VHS, Beta $19.95** *VYY* ✍✍✍ ½

Two Reelers: Comedy Classics
8 Three comedy shorts from the zany 30's.
1933 57m/B Billy Bevan, Tom Patricola, Charles Judels, Dorothy Sebastian, William Farnum, Mack Swain. **VHS, Beta $19.95** *VYY* ✍✍✍ ½

Two Reelers: Comedy Classics
9 Three early comedy shorts featuring several stars-to-be. Includes "A Slip at the Switch" (directed by Mark Sandrich), "No Sleep on the Deep," and "Going Spanish."
1934 57m/B Bob Hope, Leah Ray, Betty Compson, Robert Warwick, Chic Sale, George Hay. **VHS, Beta, 8mm $19.95** *VYY* ✍✍✍ ½

Two Reelers: Comedy Classics
10 Three shorts: "The Stolen Jools" stars more than 40 name performers and was produced by the Masquers Club of Hollywood. The plot has Shearer's jewels being stolen after a party and each of her illustrious guests is a suspect. "Easy on the Eyes" features Pangborn as a millionaire who has a romantic rival for his pretty fiance. "Knight Duty" portrays Langdon as a simpleton vagrant in constant trouble with a brawny cop.
1931 59m/B Norma Shearer, Franklin Pangborn, Harry Langdon, Vernon Dent. **VHS $19.95** *VYY* ✍✍✍ ½

Two Rode Together A Texas marshal and an army lieutenant negotiate with the Comanches for the return of captives, but complications ensue.
1961 109m/C James Stewart, Richard Widmark, Shirley Jones, Linda Cristal, Andy Devine, John McIntire; **D:** John Ford. **VHS, Beta $14.95** *COL* ✍✍ ½

The Two Sisters Goldstein, in her only film role, plays an older sister who sacrifices everything for the younger. The younger thanks her by stealing her fiance. In Yiddish with English subtitles.
1937 70m/B Jenney Goldstein, Michael Rosenberg. **VHS $89.95** *ALD* ✍✍ ½

2000 Maniacs One of cult director Lewis' most enjoyably watchable films. A literal Civil War "ghost town" takes its revenge 100 years after being slaughtered by renegade Union soldiers by luring unwitting "yankee" tourists to their centennial festival. The hapless Notherners are then chopped, crushed, ripped apart etc. while the ghostly rebels party. Quite fun in a cartoonishly gruesome sort of way. Filmed in St. Cloud, FL.

1964 75m/C Thomas Wood, Connie Mason, Jeffrey Allen, Ben Moore, Gary Bakeman, Jerome Eden, Shelby Livingston, Michael Korb, Yvonne Gilbert, Mark Douglas, Linda Cochran, Vincent Santo, Andy Wilson; **D:** Herschell Gordon Lewis; **W:** Herschell Gordon Lewis. **VHS, Beta** $29.95 RHI ⅛⅛½

2001: A Space Odyssey
Space voyage to Jupiter turns chaotic when a computer, HAL 9000, takes over. Seen by some as a mirror of man's historical use of machinery and by others as a grim vision of the future, the special effects and music are still stunning. Critically acclaimed and well accepted by the some, simply confusing to others. Martin Balsam originally recorded the voice of HAL, but was replaced by Rain. From Arthur C. Clarke's novel "The Sentinel." Followed by a sequel "2010: The Year We Make Contact." Laserdisc edition is presented in letterbox format and features a special supplementary section on the making of "2001," a montage of images from the film, production documents, memos and photos. Also included on the disc is a NASA film entitled "Art and Reality," which offers footage from the Voyager I and II flybys of Jupiter.
1968 139m/C Keir Dullea, Gary Lockwood, William Sylvester, Dan Richter; **D:** Stanley Kubrick; **W:** Arthur C. Clarke, Stanley Kubrick; **V:** Douglas Raines. Academy Awards '68: Best Visual Effects; Nominations: Best Art Direction/ Set Decoration, Best Director (Kubrick), Best Story & Screenplay; National Board of Review Awards '68: 10 Best Films of the Year. **VHS, Beta** $19.98 MGM, VYG, CRC ⅛⅛⅛⅛

2010: The Year We Make Contact
The film version of Arthur C. Clarke's novel "The Sentinel" continues in this sequel to "2001: A Space Odyssey." Americans and Russians unite to investigate the abandoned starship Discovery's decaying orbit around Jupiter and try to determine why the HAL 9000 computer sabotaged its mission years before, while signs of cosmic change are detected on and around the giant planet.
1984 (PG) 116m/C Roy Scheider, John Lithgow, Helen Mirren, Bob Balaban, Keir Dullea, Madolyn Smith, Mary Jo Deschanel; **D:** Peter Hyams; **W:** Peter Hyams; **V:** Douglas Raines. **VHS, Beta** $19.95 MGM ⅛⅛⅛

2020 Texas Gladiators
In the post-nuclear holocaust world, two groups, one good, one evil, battle for supremacy.
1985 (R) 91m/C Harrison Muller, Al Cliver, Daniel Stephen, Peter Hooten, Al Yamanouchi, Sabrina Santi; **D:** Kevin Mancuso. **VHS, Beta** $59.95 MED Woof!

2069: A Sex Odyssey
Team of beautiful, sensuous astronauts are sent to Earth to obtain male sperm which they must bring back to Venus. Tongue-in-cheek soft core sci-fi spoof.
1978 (R) 73m/C Alena Penz, Nina Fredric, Gerti Sneider, Raul Retzer, Catherine Conti, Heidi Hammer, Michael Mein, Herb Heesel; **D:** George Keil. **VHS, Beta** $19.95 ACA, HHE ⅛½

Two Tickets to Broadway
A small-town singer and a crooner arrange a hoax to get themselves on Bob Crosby's television show. Appealing but lightweight. ♫ Let the Worry Bird Worry For You; Pagliacci; There's No Tomorrow; Manhattan; Big Chief Hole in the Ground; The Closer You Are; Baby, You'll Never Be Sorry; Pelican Falls High; It Began In Yucatan.
1951 106m/C Tony Martin, Janet Leigh, Gloria De Haven, Joi Lansing; **D:** James V. Kern; **M:** Leo Robin, Jule Stein; **Performed by:** Smith & Dale. **VHS, Beta** TTC ⅛⅛½

Two to Tango
A hired assassin goes to Buenos Aires to kill a crime boss, and falls in love with his tango-dancing mistress. Based on the novel by J.P. Feinman.
1988 (R) 87m/C Don Stroud, Adrienne Sachs; **D:** Hector Olivera. **VHS, Beta** NO ⅛½

Two Top Bananas
A Las Vegas-style burlesque show, featuring song, dance, sketch comedy, and impersonations.
1987 45m/C Don Rickles, Don Adams, Carol Wayne, Sandy O'Hara, Murray Langston, Dorit Stevens. **VHS, Beta** $11.95 PSM ⅛⅛

Two-Way Stretch
Three prison inmates in a progressive jail plan to break out, pull a diamond heist, and break back in, all in the same night. Fast-paced slapstick farce.
1960 84m/B Peter Sellers, Wilfrid Hyde-White, Liz Fraser, David Lodge; **D:** Robert Day. **VHS, Beta** NO ⅛⅛½

Two Weeks in Another Town
Douglas and Robinson are a couple of Hollywood has-beens who set out to make a comeback picture but meet with adversity at every turn. Extremely sappy melodrama is based on Irwin Shaw's trashy novel and represents one of director Minelli's poorer efforts. Laserdisc features a letterboxed screen and the original movie trailer.
1962 107m/C Kirk Douglas, Edward G. Robinson, Cyd Charisse, George Hamilton, Daliah Lavi, Claire Trevor, James Gregory, Rosanna Schiaffino, George Macready, Stefan Schnabel, Vito Scotti, Leslie Uggams; **D:** Vincente Minnelli. **VHS** MGM ⅛

Two Weeks to Live
The comedy team inherits a railroad line, only to find it's a pile of junk.
1943 60m/B Lum & Abner, Franklin Pangborn. **VHS, Beta** $24.95 NOS, DVT, HEG ⅛½

Two Weeks with Love
Reynolds and family wear funny bathing suits in the Catskills in the early 1900s while the Debster sings songs and blushes into young adulthood. ♫ Aba Daba Honeymoon; The Oceana Roll; A Heart That's Free; By the Light of the Silvery Moon; My Hero; Row, Row, Row; That's How I Need You; Beautiful Lady.
1950 92m/C Debbie Reynolds, Jane Powell, Ricardo Montalban, Louis Calhern, Ann Harding, Phyllis Kirk, Carleton Carpenter, Clinton Sundberg, Gary Gray; **D:** Roy Rowland. **VHS** $19.98 MGM, FCT ⅛

Two Women
A mother and her 13-year-old daughter travel war-torn Italy during WWII and must survive lack of food, crazed monks and brutal soldiers. Tragic, moving, well-directed. Loren received well-deserved Oscar. In Italian with English subtitles or dubbed. **AKA:** La Ciociara.
1961 99m/B Sophia Loren, Raf Vallone, Eleonora Brown, Jean-Paul Belmondo; **D:** Vittorio De Sica; **W:** Cesare Zavattini, Vittorio De Sica; **M:** Armando Trovajoli. **VHS, Beta** $19.95 COL, APD, BTV ⅛⅛⅛⅛

Two Wondrous Tigers
Awesome Kung-fu gang terrorizes a small town until a local dares to out-chop the bullies.
1979 87m/C John Chang; **D:** Wilson Tong. **VHS, Beta** $39.95 TWE ⅛

The Two Worlds of Jenny Logan
A woman travels back and forth in time whenever she dons a 19th century dress she finds in her old house. She is also able to fall in love twice, in different centuries. Made for television and adapted from "Second Sight," a novel by David Williams. Stylish and well made.
1979 97m/C Lindsay Wagner, Marc Singer, Alan Feinstein, Linda Gray, Constance McCashin, Henry Wilcoxon, Irene Tedrow, Joan Darling, Allen Williams, Pat Corley, Gloria Stuart; **D:**

Frank de Felitta. **VHS, Beta** $14.95 FRH, LIV ⅛⅛½

Two Wrongs Make a Right
A quiet nightclub owner beats and clubs his way through his tough neighborhood to protect himself and his woman.
1989 85m/C Ivan Rogers, Ron Blackstone, Rich Komenich; **D:** Robert Brown. **VHS, Beta** $79.95 UNI ⅛

Tycoon
Wayne goes to Latin America to build a road for an American industrialist. When the industrialist insists on a shorter but more dangerous route, Wayne must satisfy his own sense of honor. Meanwhile, he's found romance with the industrialist's half-Spanish daughter. Long, but well-acted.
1947 129m/C John Wayne, Laraine Day, Cedric Hardwicke, Judith Anderson, James Gleason, Anthony Quinn; **D:** Richard Wallace. **VHS, Beta** $19.95 CCB, RKO, TTC ⅛⅛½

Typhoon Treasure
Whilst recovering his sunken treasure, the hero battles bad guys, savage natives and a crocodile, all of whom could probably have made a more sophisticated film.
1939 68m/B Campbell Copelin, Gwen Munro, Joe Valli, Douglas Herald; **D:** Noel Monkman. **VHS** $15.95 NOS, LOO ⅛

Tyrant of Lydia Against the Son of Hercules
Hercules' son takes on a wicked king in this startling adventure.
1963 ?m/C Gordon Scott, Massimo Serato. **VHS, Beta** $16.95 SNC ⅛

U-Boat Prisoner
Bennett is an American sailor who's captured by a Nazi U-boat. He promptly defeats the crew, leaving the U-boat to the mercy of a U.S. destroyer. Silly, silly, silly.
1944 65m/B Bruce (Herman Brix) Bennett, John Abbott, Robert Williams, Kenneth MacDonald, Erik Rolf, John Wengraf; **D:** Lew Landers. **VHS** $12.95 GPV ⅛

UFO: Target Earth
Scientist attempts to fish flying saucer out of lake and costs studio $70,000.
1974 (G) 80m/C Nick Plakias, Cynthia Cline, Phil Erickson; **D:** Michael de Gaetano. **VHS** $14.98 MOV ⅛

Uforia
Two rival evangelists meet up with a UFO-infatuated girl. Under her guidance, they wait for UFO encounters they intend to use to milk their revivalist audiences. Sometimes clumsy, but more often fun.
1981 92m/C Cindy Williams, Harry Dean Stanton, Fred Ward; **D:** John Binder; **M:** Richard Baskin. **VHS, Beta** $59.95 MCA ⅛

Ugetsu
The classic film that established Mizoguchi's reputation outside of Japan. Two 16th century Japanese peasants venture from their homes in pursuit of dreams, and encounter little more than their own hapless folly and a bit of the supernatural. A wonderful mix of comedy and action with nifty camera movement. Based on the stories of Akinara Ueda. In Japanese with English subtitles. **AKA:** Ugetsu Monogatari.
1953 96m/B Machiko Kyo, Masayuki Mori, Kinuyo Tanaka, Sakae Ozawa; **D:** Kenji Mizoguchi. Academy Awards '55 Nominations: Best Costume Design (B & W); Venice Film Festival '53: Silver Prize. **VHS, Beta, 8mm** $24.95 HMV, SUE, WFV ⅛⅛½

The Ugly American
A naive American ambassador to a small, civil-war-torn Asian country fights a miniature Cold War against northern communist influence. Too preachy, and the "Red Menace" aspects are now very dated, but Brando's performance is worth watching. Based on the William J. Lederer novel.

1963 120m/C Marlon Brando, Sandra Church, Eiji Okada, Pat Hingle, Arthur Hill; *D:* George Englund; *W:* Stewart Stern. VHS, Beta $19.95 MCA 🎬🎬½

The Ugly Dachshund Jones and Pleshette are married dog lovers who raise Dachshunds. When Ruggles convinces them to take a Great Dane puppy, the fun begins! The Great Dane thinks he is a Dachshund because he has been raised with them—just imagine what happens when such a large dog acts as if he is small! Kids will love this wacky Disney film.
1965 93m/C Dean Jones, Suzanne Pleshette, Charlie Ruggles, Kelly Thordsen, Parley Baer; *D:* Norman Tokar. VHS, Beta DIS, OM 🎬🎬½

Ugly Little Boy Nurse is placed in charge of a child brought back through time from the Neanderthal age. Problems occur when the scientists involved ignore the fact that he is human.
1977 26m/C Kate Reid; *D:* Barry Morse, Don Thompson. VHS, Beta LCA 🎬½

UHF A loser is appointed manager of a bargain-basement UHF television station. He turns it around via bizarre programming ideas. Some fun parodies of TV enhance this minimal story. Developed solely as a vehicle for Yankovic.
1989 (PG-13) 97m/C Weird Al Yankovic, Kevin McCarthy, Victoria Jackson, Michael Richards, David Bowie, Anthony Geary; *D:* Jay Levey; *M:* John Du Prez. VHS, Beta $19.98 ORI 🎬🎬

Ulterior Motives P.I. Jack Blaylock agrees to protect a pretty reporter from Japanese gangsters. He finds himself caught up in deception and betrayal and uses all his considerable, and violent, skills to make certain he does his job.
1992 (R) ?m/C Thomas Ian Griffith, Mary Page Keller, Joe Yamanaka, Ellen Crawford, Ken Howard, Tyra Ferrell; *D:* James Becket. VHS $89.95 IMP 🎬½

Ultimate Desires When a high class hooker is brutally killed, beautiful Scoggins puts on what there is of the victim's clothes in order to solve the mystery. But trouble lies in wait as she actually begins to enjoy her funky new double life. Can she solve the crime before becoming lost in her own hot fantasy world?
1991 (R) 93m/C Tracy Scoggins, Brion James, Marc Singer, Marc Baur, Marc Bennett, Suzy Joachim, Jason Scott, Frank Wilson; *D:* Lloyd A. Simandl. VHS, Beta $29.95 PSM 🎬🎬

The Ultimate Imposter A secret agent acquires voluminous knowledge through a computer brain linkup, but can only retain the knowledge for 72 hours. In that timespan he has to rescue a defecting Russian from hordes of assassins. Made for television.
1979 97m/C Keith Andes, Erin Gray, Joseph Hacker, Macon McCalman; *D:* Paul Stanley. VHS, Beta $39.95 MCA 🎬

The Ultimate Thrill Businessman's paranoia about his wife's affairs leads him to follow her to Colorado on a ski holiday and stalk her lovers. Well-filmed skiing scenes and not much else. Also known as "The Ultimate Chase." *AKA:* The Ultimate Chase.
1974 (PG) 84m/C Britt Ekland, Barry Brown, Michael Blodgett, John Davis Chandler, Eric (Hans Gudegast) Braeden; *D:* Robert Butler. VHS, Beta $19.95 GEM, CNG 🎬½

The Ultimate Warrior Yul Brynner must defend the plants and seeds of a pioneer scientist to help replenish the world's food supply in this thriller set in 2012.

1975 (R) 92m/C Yul Brynner, Max von Sydow, Joanna Miles, Richard Kelton, Lane Bradbury, William Smith; *D:* Robert Clouse. VHS, Beta $59.95 WAR 🎬🎬½

Ultra Flash A fantasy that is performed to some of today's hottest dance music. In stereo
1983 60m/C VHS, Beta $39.98 LIV, VES 🎬🎬½

Ultra Warrior A basic post-apocalyptic adventure tale of a radioactive earth, mutants, and various battles by the good guys to save the planet.
1999? (R) 80m/C Dack Rambo, Meshach Taylor, Clare Beresford. VHS $89.98 NHO 🎬½

Ulysses An Italian made version of the epic poem by Homer, as the warrior returns to his homeland and the ever-faithful Penelope after the Trojan war. Ambitious effort provides for the ultimate mixed review. Douglas is good in the role and his stops along the ten-year way are well visualized. Sometimes sluggish with poor dubbing. Seven writers helped bring Homer to the big screen. *AKA:* Ulisse.
1955 104m/C Kirk Douglas, Silvana Mangano, Anthony Quinn, Rossana Podesta; *D:* Mario Camerini. VHS, Beta $39.98 WAR, OM 🎬🎬½

Ulysses James Joyce's probably unfilmable novel was given a noble effort in this flawed film covering a day in the life of Leopold Bloom as he wanders through Dublin. Shot in Ireland with a primarily Irish cast.
1967 140m/B Milo O'Shea, Maurice Roeves, T.P. McKenna, Martin Dempsey, Sheila O'Sullivan, Barbara Jefford; *D:* Joseph Strick. VHS $29.95 MFV 🎬🎬½

Ulzana's Raid An aging scout and an idealistic Cavalry lieutenant lock horns on their way to battling a vicious Apache chieftain. A violent, gritty western that enjoyed critical re-evaluation years after its first release.
1972 (R) 103m/C Burt Lancaster, Bruce Davison, Richard Jaeckel, Lloyd Bochner, Jorge Luke; *D:* Robert Aldrich. VHS, Beta $14.98 MCA 🎬🎬🎬

Umberto D A government pensioner, living alone with his beloved dog, struggles to keep up a semblance of dignity on his inadequate pension. De Sica considered this his masterpiece. A sincere, tender treatment of the struggles involved with the inevitability of aging. In Italian with English subtitles. Laser edition features letterboxed print.
1955 89m/B Carlo Battista, Maria Pia Casilio, Lina Gennari; *D:* Vittorio De Sica; *W:* Cesare Zavattini, Vittorio De Sica. Academy Awards '56 Nominations: Best Story; New York Film Critics Awards '55: Best Foreign Film. VHS, Beta, 8mm $29.98 NOS, SUE, HHT 🎬🎬🎬🎬

Umbrellas of Cherbourg A bittersweet film operetta with no spoken dialog. Deneuve is the teenaged daughter of a widow who owns an umbrella shop. She and her equally young boyfriend are separated by his military duty in Algeria. Finding she is pregnant, the girl marries a wealthy man, and when her former lover returns, he too marries someone else. But when they meet once again will their love be rekindled? Lovely photography and an evocative score enhance the story. In French with subtitles; also available dubbed in English (not with the same effectiveness). Oscar nominee for cinematography and story. *AKA:* Les Parapluies De Cherbourg; Die Regenschirme Von Cherbourg.
1964 90m/C Catherine Deneuve, Nino Castelnuovo, Anne Vernon, Ellen Farner, Marc Michel, Mireille Perrey, Jean Champion, Alfred Wolff, Dorothee Blanck; *D:* Jacques Demy; *W:* Jacques Demy; *M:* Michel Legrand. Academy

Awards '65 Nominations: Best Foreign Language Film, Best Song ("I Will Wait for You"), Best Story & Screenplay, Best Original Score; Cannes Film Festival '64: Best Film. VHS, Beta $39.95 LIV, APD 🎬🎬🎬

Un Chien Andalou Masterful surrealist short features a host of classic sequences, including a razor across an eye, a severed hand lying in the street, ants crawling from a hole in a man's hand, priests, dead horses, and a piano dragged across a room. A classic. Score features both Wagner and tango.
1928 20m/B Pierre Batcheff, Simone Marevil, Jaime Miravilles; *D:* Luis Bunuel, Salvador Dali. VHS, Beta $34.95 HHT, GVV, APD 🎬🎬🎬🎬

Un Coeur en Hiver An anti-romance romantic drama where passion is frozen and real emotion is reserved for the inanimate. Serious Stephane (Auteuil) is a master craftsman at repairing violins; his partner Maxime (Dussollier) runs the business side and deals with the musicians, including beautiful violinist Camille (Beart) with whom he has fallen in love. Camille is single-mindedly fixated on her career and she recognizes a kindred spirit in Stephane but their calculated emotional seduction causes problems for all. Can be frustrating since the smooth surface of the characters is rarely cracked. In French with English titles. *AKA:* A Heart in Winter.
1993 100m/C Emmanuelle Beart, Daniel Auteuil, Andre Dussollier, Elisabeth Bourgine, Brigitte Catillon, Maurice Garrel, Miriam Boyer; *D:* Claude Sautet; *W:* Yves Ulmann, Jacques Fieschi, Jerome Tonnerre. British Academy Award Nominations: '93; Best Foreign Language Film; Cesar Awards '93: Best Director (Sautet), Best Supporting Actor (Dussollier). VHS $92.98 REP 🎬🎬½

Un Singe en Hiver A young wanderer (Belmondo) befriends a crusty old alcoholic (Gabin) who has kept his vow to abstain since his village survived the German bombing of WWII. Moving tale of regret and the passage of time. In French with English subtitles. *AKA:* A Monkey in Winter; It's Hot in Hell.
1962 105m/B Jean-Paul Belmondo, Jean Gabin, Suzanne Flon, Paul Frankeur; *D:* Henri Verneuil. VHS, Beta $19.95 BAR, ING 🎬🎬

Una Vez en la Vida A young farm girl travels to the big city, where she becomes a nightclub dancer and gets involved with a shady character. In Spanish.
1949 75m/B Libertad Lamarque, Luis Aldas, Raimundo Pastore. VHS, Beta $24.95 VYY, APD 🎬

The Unapproachable A rendition of the Polish director's two one-act plays concerning a reclusive aging stage star being manipulated by her hangers-on.
1982 92m/C Leslie Caron, Daniel Webb, Leslie Malton; *D:* Krzysztof Zanussi. VHS, Beta $59.95 MGM 🎬

The Unbearable Lightness of Being Tomas (Day Lewis), a young Czech doctor in the late 1960s, leads a sexually and emotionally carefree existence with a number of women, including provocative artist Olin. When he meets the fragile Binoche, he may be falling in love for the first time. On the eve of the 1968 Russian invasion of Czechoslovakia the two flee to Switzerland, but Binoche can't reconcile herself to exile and returns, followed by the reluctant Tomas who has lost his position because of his newfound political idealism. They lead an increasingly simple life, drawn ever closer together. The haunting ending caps off superb performances. Based on the novel by Milan Kundera.

1988 (R) 172m/C Daniel Day-Lewis, Juliette Binoche, Lena Olin, Derek De Lint, Erland Josephson, Pavel Landovsky, Donald Moffatt, Daniel Olbrychski, Stellan Skarsgard; **D:** Philip Kaufman; **W:** Jean-Claude Carriere, Philip Kaufman. Academy Awards '88 Nominations: Best Adapted Screenplay, Best Cinematography; Independent Spirit Awards '89: Best Cinematography; National Society of Film Critics Awards '88: Best Director (Kaufman), Best Film. **VHS, Beta** $19.98 ORI, ING ♫♫½

The Unbeaten 28 A group of kung fu masters is forced to fight for their lives against evil criminals.
198? 90m/C Lisa Chang, Meng Fei, Lung Sikar; **D:** Joseph Kuo. **VHS, Beta** $39.95 MPI ♫

The Unbelievable Truth Ex-con Robocop-to-be Burke meets armageddon-obsessed model and sparks fly until bizarre murder occurs. Quirky black comedy shot in less than two weeks.
1990 (R) 100m/C Adrienne Shelly, Robert Burke, Christopher Cooke, Julia Mueller, Julia McNeal, Mark Bailey, Gary Sauer, Kathrine Mayfield; **D:** Hal Hartley; **W:** Hal Hartley; **M:** Jim Coleman. **VHS** $89.95 VMK ♫♫½

The Unborn An infertile wife gets inseminated at unorthodox clinic. But once pregnant she suspects that her unborn baby is a monstrous being. Tasteless B-movie with an A-performance from Adams; if the rest had been up to her standard this could have been another "Stepford Wives." Instead it cops out with cheap gore.
1991 (R) 85m/C Brooke Adams, Jeff Hayenga, James Karen, K. Callan, Jane Cameron; **D:** Rodman Flender. **VHS** $89.95 COL ♫½

The Unborn 2 Greene's blood-craving baby finds nothing of feasting off the babysitter until a gun-wielding avenger comes to the rescue. Some notably gross scenes.
1994 (R) ?m/C Michelle Greene, Scott Valentine, Robin Curtis. **VHS** $91.50 NHO ♫

The Unbreakable Alibi A wealthy young man asks Tommy and Tuppence Beresford to help him prove that one of two alibis an Australian journalist created is false. Based on the mysteries by Agatha Christie. Made for television.
1983 51m/C Francesca Annis, James Warwick. **VHS, Beta** $14.95 TPV ♫♫

Uncaged Five beautiful young prostitutes hit Sunset Strip, each of them dreaming of a better life. When a crazy pimp brutally murders one of their friends, they set out to avenge that girl, and her broken dreams. **AKA:** Angel in Red.
1991 (R) 78m/C Leslie Bega, Jeffrey Dean Morgan, Pamella O'Pella, Gregory Millar, Henry Brown, Jason Oliver, Elena Sahagun; **D:** William Duprey. **VHS** $79.95 COL, CCV ♫

The Uncanny Horror anthology of three tales concerned with feline attempts to control the world. Waste of good cast and cats on silly stories. Not released in the U.S.
1978 85m/C Peter Cushing, Ray Milland, Samantha Eggar, Donald Pleasence; **D:** Denis Heroux. **VHS, Beta** $49.95 MED Woof!

Uncensored This fast-paced comedy special features dozens of hilarious skits and sketches.
1985 60m/C Murray Langston, Cassandra Peterson, John Paragon, Ben Powers. **VHS, Beta** NO ♫½

The Unchastened Woman A married couple is torn apart by infidelity despite their impending parenthood, and wife Bara heads overseas to run wild and have the baby. She returns with a foreign flame, whom she dumps when erstwhile husband

finds fatherly feelings in his heart. One of Bara's last films.
1925 52m/B Theda Bara, Wyndham Standing, Dale Fuller, John Miljan; **D:** James Young. **VHS, Beta** $19.95 GPV, FCT ♫♫

Uncle Buck When Mom and Dad have to go away suddenly, the only babysitter they can find is good ol' Uncle Buck, a lovable lout who spends much of his time smoking cigars, trying to make up with his girlfriend, and enforcing the teenage daughter's chastity. More intelligent than the average slob/teen comedy with a heart, due in large part to Candy's dandy performance. Memorable pancake scene.
1989 (PG) 100m/C John Candy, Amy Madigan, Jean Kelly, Macaulay Culkin, Jay Underwood, Gaby Hoffman, Laurie Metcalf, Elaine Bromka, Garrett M. Brown; **D:** John Hughes; **W:** John Hughes; **M:** Ira Newborn. **VHS, Beta** $19.95 MCA ♫♫♫

Uncle Moses The clash of old-world values and new-world culture in a story of East European Jewish immigrants transplanted to turn of the century New York's Lower East Side. Patriarch Uncle Moses struggles to keep traditional family values as romantic difficulties and labor union struggles intrude. Based on the novel by Sholem Asch. In Yiddish with English subtitles.
1932 87m/B Maurice Schwartz, Rubin Goldberg, Judith Abarbanel, Zvee Scooler; **D:** Sidney Goldin, Aubrey Scotto. **VHS** $59.95 ERG, NCJ ♫♫½

Uncle Tom's Cabin Satisfying version of Harriet Beecher Stowe's tale from the view of a founder of the underground railroad. Lucas was the first black actor to garner a lead role.
1914 54m/C Mary Eline, Irving Cummings, Sam Lucas; **D:** William Robert Daly. **VHS, Beta** $14.95 GPV, FCT, DVT ♫♫

Uncle Tom's Cabin Ambitious adaptation of Harriet Beecher Stowe's stirring book about the Southern slavery and the famous underground railroad devised to aid those most determined to reach freedom. The film has the habit of drifting away from the facts. Though set in Kentucky, the picture was filmed in Yugoslavia with an international cast. **AKA:** Onkel Toms Hutte; La Case de L'Oncle Tom; Cento Dollari D'Odio; Cica Tomina Koliba.
1969 (G) 120m/C Herbert Lom, John Kitzmiller, O.W. Fischer, Eleanora Rossi-Drago, Mylene Demongeot, Juliette Greco; **D:** Geza von Radvanyi; **V:** Ella Fitzgerald. **VHS, Beta** $19.95 XVC, AFR ♫½

Uncle Tom's Cabin The first American sound version of this film. Excellent cast and interestingly adapted script are perfect for a message that is still socially relevant today. Based on the novel by Harriet Beecher Stowe. Made for television.
1987 110m/C Avery Brooks, Kate Burton, Bruce Dern, Paula Kelly, Phylicia Rashad, Kathryn Walker, Edward Woodward, Frank Converse, George Coe, Albert Hall; **D:** Stan Lathan. **VHS** $9.98 FCT, WOV ♫♫½

Uncle Was a Vampire Lee stars as Count Dracula in this vampire story.
1959 ?m/C Christopher Lee, Kay Fisher. **VHS** $16.95 SNC ♫♫

Uncommon Valor After useless appeals to the government for information on his son listed as "missing in action" in Vietnam, Colonel Rhodes takes matters into his own hands. Hackman is solid and believable as always, surrounded with good cast in generally well-paced film.

1983 (R) 105m/C Gene Hackman, Fred Ward, Reb Brown, Randall "Tex" Cobb, Robert Stack, Patrick Swayze, Harold Sylvester, Tim Thomerson; **D:** Ted Kotcheff; **M:** James Horner. **VHS, Beta, 8mm** $14.95 PAR ♫♫½

The Undead A prostitute is accidentally sent back to the Middle Ages as the result of a scientific experiment and finds herself condemned to die for witchcraft. Early Corman script filled with violence and heaving bosoms.
1957 75m/B Pamela Duncan, Richard Garland, Allison Hayes, Mel Welles; **D:** Roger Corman. **VHS** $19.95 NOS, AIP, MLB ♫♫♫

Undeclared War Suspenseful espionage thriller that takes you behind the scenes of an international terrorist plot, which has been cleverly disguised as a bloody global revolution. Intense action heightened by conflicts between worldwide intelligence networks, the news media and terrorist organizations.
1991 (R) 103m/C Vernon Wells, David Hedison, Olivia Hussey, Peter Lapis; **D:** Ringo Lam. **VHS** $89.95 IMP ♫♫

The Undefeated A Confederate and Yankee find they must team up on the Rio Grande. They attempt to build new lives in the Spanish held Mexico territory, but are caught in the battle for Mexican independence. Standard fare made palatable only by Wayne and Hudson.
1969 (G) 119m/C John Wayne, Rock Hudson, Lee Meriwether, Merlin Olsen, Bruce Cabot, Ben Johnson, Jan-Michael Vincent, Harry Carey Jr., Antonio Aguilar, Roman Gabriel; **D:** Andrew V. McLaglen. **VHS, Beta** $19.98 FOX ♫♫

Under California Stars Shady gang making a living rounding up wild horses decides they can make more money by capturing Rogers' horse, Trigger. **AKA:** Under California Skies.
1948 71m/C Roy Rogers, Andy Devine, Jane Frazee, The Pioneers; **D:** William Witney. **VHS, Beta** $19.95 NOS, VYY, DVT ♫♫

Under Capricorn Bergman is an Irish lass who follows her convict husband Cotten out to 1830s Australia where he makes a fortune. She turns to drink, perhaps because of his neglect, and has her position usurped by a housekeeper with designs on her husband. When Bergman's cousin (Wilding) arrives, Cotten may have cause for his violent jealousy. There's a plot twist involving old family skeletons, but this is definitely lesser Hitchcock. Adapted from the Helen Simpson novel. Remade in 1982.
1949 117m/C Ingrid Bergman, Joseph Cotten, Michael Wilding, Margaret Leighton, Jack Watling, Cecil Parker, Denis O'Dea; **D:** Alfred Hitchcock. **VHS, Beta** $14.98 VES ♫♫½

Under Capricorn An Australian remake of the 1949 Hitchcock film about family secrets, an unhappy marriage, and violence set in 1830's Australia.
1982 120m/C Lisa Harrow, John Hallam, Peter Cousens, Julia Blake, Catherine Lynch; **D:** Rod Hardy. **VHS, Beta** $59.95 PSM ♫♫

Under Fire Three foreign correspondents, old friends from the past working together, find themselves in Managua, witnessing the 1979 Nicaraguan revolution. In a job requiring objectivity, but a situation requiring taking sides, they battle with their ethics to do their job right. Fine performances, including Camp as a mercenary. Interesting view of American media and its political necessities.
1983 (R) 128m/C Gene Hackman, Nick Nolte, Joanna Cassidy, Ed Harris, Richard Masur, Hamilton Camp, Jean-Louis Trintignant; **D:** Roger Spottiswoode; **W:** Ron Shelton, Clayton

Frohman; **M:** Jerry Goldsmith. **VHS, Beta $19.98**
VES ♂♂♂½

Under Investigation Burned out cop Hamlin is after a crazed killer. His cool lover Pacula turns out to be the prime suspect. Who's deceiving who?
1993 (R) 94m/C Harry Hamlin, Joanna Pacula, Ed Lauter, Richard Beymer, Lydie Denier; **D:** Kevin Meyer; **W:** Kevin Meyer. **VHS $19.95** *COL* ♂♂½

Under Milk Wood An adaptation of the Dylan Thomas play about the lives of the residents of a village in Wales. Burton and O'Toole are wonderful in this uneven, but sometimes engrossing film.
1973 (PG) 90m/C Richard Burton, Elizabeth Taylor, Peter O'Toole, Glynis Johns, Vivien Merchant; **D:** Andrew Sinclair. **VHS, Beta $59.98** *FOX* ♂♂½

Under Montana Skies An early talkie western features music and comedy in abundance, relegating the action to second place. A singing cowboy protects a travelling burlesque show from evildoers.
1930 55m/B Kenneth Harlan, Dorothy Gulliver, Lafe McKee, Ethel Wales, Slim Summerville; **D:** Dave Thorpe. **VHS, Beta** *GPV* ♂

Under Nevada Skies Fairly good matinee-era western centers on a missing map to a uranium deposit, climaxing with Rogers heading a posse of Indian allies to the rescue. The Sons of the Pioneers contribute songs.
1946 69m/B Roy Rogers, George "Gabby" Hayes, Dale Evans, Douglass Dumbrille, Tristram Coffin, Rudolph Anders, Iron Eyes Cody; **D:** Frank McDonald. **VHS $19.95** *NOS, HEG* ♂♂½

Under Satan's Sun A rural priest is tortured by what he sees as his sins and failings to his parishioners. He is further tempted from the straight path by a beautiful murderess, a worldly priest, and, perhaps by Satan in disguise. Stylized film is not easily accessible, but Depardieu's performance is worth the effort. Based on the Georges Bernanos book "Diary of a Country Priest." In French with English subtitles. **AKA:** Under the Sun of Satan; Sous le Soleil de Satan.
1987 97m/C Gerard Depardieu, Sandrine Bonnaire, Yann Dedet, Alain Artur, Maurice Pialat; **D:** Maurice Pialat; **W:** Maurice Pialat. **VHS $79.95** *ING, FCT, CVC* ♂♂♂

Under Siege The USS Missouri becomes the battleground for good-guy-with-a-secret-past Seagal. He's up against the deranged Jones, as an ex-Special Forces leader, and Busey, a corrupt naval officer looking to steal the battleship's nuclear arsenal. May be predictable (especially the graphic violence) but the action is fast, the villains swaggering, and Seagal efficient at dispatching the enemy. Work for "Die Hard 3" was reportedly scrapped after Warner announced this film because DH's John McClane was supposed to save the passengers of a boat from terrorists. Sound familiar?
1992 (R) 100m/C Steven Seagal, Tommy Lee Jones, Gary Busey, Patrick O'Neal, Erika Eleniak; **W:** J.F. Lawton; **M:** Gary Chang. **VHS, Beta, 8mm $19.98** *WAR* ♂♂

Under Suspicion Christmas 1959 in Brighton finds seedy private eye Tony Aaron and his wife faking adultery cases for those desperate to get around England's strict divorce laws. Sordid tale takes a turn when Tony bursts in to snap incriminating photos and finds both his wife and their client, a famous artist, murdered. Dark who-dunnit has some interesting twists that could have made this exceptional rather than the conventional melodrama it turned out to be. Neeson is very good as the charmingly sleazy Tony

but nobody else stands out, except the unfortunately miscast San Giacomo. Theatrical feature debut for director Moore.
1992 (R) 99m/C Liam Neeson, Laura San Giacomo, Alphonsia Emmanuel, Kenneth Cranham, Maggie O'Neill, Martin Grace, Stephen Moore; **D:** Simon Moore; **W:** Simon Moore; **M:** Christopher Gunning. **VHS** *COL* ♂♂½

Under the Biltmore Clock F. Scott Fitzgerald's story, "Myra Meets His Family," is the basis for this American Playhouse installment for PBS television. It is outwit or be outwitted in this tale of a fortune-hunting '20s flapper who is outsmarted by the man she has set her sights on when he hires actors to play his eccentric "family."
1985 70m/C Sean Young, Lenny Von Dohlen, Barnard Hughes; **D:** Neal Miller. **VHS, Beta, 8mm $19.98** *SUE, NLC* ♂

Under the Boardwalk A pair of star-crossed teenage lovers struggle through familial and societal differences in 1980s California. This is, like, bogus, ya know.
1989 (R) 102m/C Keith Coogan, Danielle von Zerneack, Richard Joseph Paul, Hunter von Leer, Tracy Walter, Roxana Zal, Dick Miller, Sonny Bono, Corky Carroll; **D:** Fritz Kiersch. **VHS, Beta $19.95** *STE, NWV* ♂½

Under the Cherry Moon Prince portrays a fictional musician of the 1940s who travels to the French Riviera, seeking love and money. Songs include "Under the Cherry Moon," "Kiss," "Anotherloverholeinyohead," "Sometimes It Snows in April," and "Mountains." A vanity flick down to its being filmed in black and white.
1986 (PG-13) 100m/B Prince, Jerome Benton, Francesca Annis, Kristin Scott Thomas; **D:** Prince. **VHS, Beta $14.95** *MVD, WAR, FCT* ♂½

Under the Earth An Argentine-Czech co-production, depicting the plight of a family of Polish Jews forced to live underground for two years to avoid the Nazis. Harrowing and critically well-received. In Spanish with subtitles. **AKA:** Debajo del Mundo.
1986 (R) 100m/C Victor Laplace; **D:** Beda Ocampo Feijoo, Juan Bautista Stagnaro. **VHS, Beta $19.95** *NWV, SWC* ♂♂♂

Under the Gun A cop recruits a lawyer to help him find the man who murdered his brother. Action drives this formulaic plot along.
1988 (R) 89m/C Sam Jones, Vanessa Williams, John Russell, Michael Halsey; **D:** James Sbardellati. **VHS $79.89** *IME* ♂♂

Under the Rainbow Comic situations encountered by a talent scout and a secret service agent in a hotel filled with Munchkins during filming of "The Wizard of Oz." Features midgets, spies, and a prevailing lack of taste. International intrigue adds to the strange attempt at humor.
1981 (PG) 97m/C Chevy Chase, Carrie Fisher, Eve Arden, Joseph Maher, Robert Donner, Mako, Pat McCormick, Billy Barty, Zelda Rubinstein; **D:** Steve Rash; **W:** Pat McCormick, Martin Smith, Harry Hurwitz. **VHS, Beta $19.98** *WAR* Woof!

Under the Red Robe A French soldier of fortune is trapped into aiding Cardinal Richelieu in his persecution of the Huguenots and winds up falling in love with the sister of his intended victim. Good costume adventure-drama. Sjostrom's last film as a director.
1936 82m/B Raymond Massey, Conrad Veidt, Annabella, Romney Brent; **D:** Victor Sjostrom. **VHS, Beta $19.95** *NOS, HHT, WFV* ♂♂½

Under the Roofs of Paris An early French sound film about the lives of young Parisian lovers. A gentle, highly acclaimed melodrama. In French with English subtitles. **AKA:** Sous les Toits de Paris.

1929 95m/B Albert Prejean, Pola Illery, Gaston Modot; **D:** Rene Clair. **VHS, Beta $24.95** *VYY, NOS, CAB* ♂♂♂½

Under the Volcano An alcoholic British ex-consul finds his life further deteriorating during the Mexican Day of the Dead in 1939. His half-brother and ex-wife try to save him from himself, but their affair sends him ever-deeper into his personal hell. Finney's performance is pathetic and haunting. Adapted from the novel by Malcolm Lowry.
1984 112m/C Albert Finney, Jacqueline Bisset, Anthony Andrews, Katy Jurado; **D:** John Huston. **VHS, Beta $79.95** *MCA* ♂♂♂

Under Western Stars Roy's first starring vehicle. A newly elected congressman goes to Washington and fights battles for his constituents, caught in the middle of the Dust Bowl and drought.
1945 83m/B Roy Rogers, Trigger, Smiley Burnette; **D:** Jean Yarborough. **VHS, Beta $19.95** *NOS, DVT, VCN* ♂

The Underachievers A night school is the scene for typical libido-oriented gags, but this time instead of teenagers it's adult education providing the plot. Only a few real laughs in this one.
1988 (R) 90m/C Barbara Carrera, Edward Albert, Michael Pataki, Vic Tayback, Garrett Morris, Susan Tyrrell; **D:** Jackie Kong. **VHS, Beta $79.98** *LIV, VES* ♂

Undercover Routine cop action film in which an eastern detective finds himself undercover in a southern high school in search of a cop-murdering drug ring. Plagued with cliches. Director Stockwell is appropriately better known for his role as "Cougar" in "Top Gun."
1987 (R) 92m/C David Neidorf, Jennifer Jason Leigh, Barry Corbin, David Harris, Kathleen Wilhoite; **D:** John Stockwell. **VHS $79.98** *WAR* ♂½

Undercover Blues Comedy-thriller starring Turner and Quaid as married spies Jane and Jeff Blue, on parental leave from the espionage biz, who are on vacation with their 11-month-old daughter in New Orleans. But the holiday is interrupted when they're recruited by their boss to stop an old adversary from selling stolen weapons. The leads play cute together and the baby is adorable but this is strictly routine escapism. Stick with "The Thin Man" instead.
1993 (PG-13) 90m/C Kathleen Turner, Dennis Quaid, Fiona Shaw, Stanley Tucci, Larry Miller, Obba Babatunde, Park Overall, Tom Arnold, Saul Rubinek, Michelle Schuelke; **D:** Herbert Ross; **W:** Ian Abrams; **M:** David Newman. **VHS** *MGM* ♂♂½

Undercover Cop True story of Sergeant George Aguilar and the high-speed chase that left one dead and the police dealing their revenge on all the offenders.
1994 90m/C Danny Trejo, Kevin Anthony Cole; **D:** Martin Greene; **W:** Glenn A. Bruce; **M:** Randall Kent Heddon. **VHS $89.95** *AIP* ♂♂

Undercover Man A Wells Fargo agent goes undercover to expose a crooked sheriff.
1936 57m/B Johnny Mack Brown, Suzanne Kaaren, Ted Adams, Lloyd Ingraham, Horace Murphy; **D:** Albert Ray. **VHS $19.95** *NOS, DVT, RXM* ♂½

The Underdog After the bank forecloses, a farm family must move to the city. The family's young son has only his loyal dog to turn to for friendship, but the gallant animal proves his mettle by rounding up a gang of spies plotting some WWII sabotage. Believe it if you dare.
1943 65m/B Barton MacLane, Bobby Larson, Jan Wiley; **D:** William Nigh. **VHS, Beta, 8mm $24.95** *VYY* ♂½

Undergrads A bright generational Disney comedy with Carney, estranged from his stick-in-the-mud son, deciding to attend college with his free-thinking grandson. Made for television.
1985 102m/C Art Carney, Chris Makepeace, Jackie Burroughs, Len Birman; **D:** Steven Hilliard Stern. VHS, Beta $59.95 DIS ♫♫♫

Underground Aces A group of parking lot attendants transforms a sheik into an attendant in order to help him meet the girl of his dreams. A bad "Car Wash" spinoff.
1980 (PG) 93m/C Dirk Benedict, Melanie Griffith, Frank Gorshin, Jerry Orbach, Robert Hegyes, Audrey Landers; **D:** Robert Butler; **W:** Jim Carabatsos. VHS, Beta $69.98 LIV, VES Woof!

Underground Rustlers The Range Busters are commissioned by the government to stop unscrupulous gold-marketeers.
1941 58m/B Ray Corrigan, Max Terhune, John "Dusty" King; **D:** S. Roy Luby. VHS, Beta $19.95 VDM ♫

Underground Terror A gang of murderers, organized by a psychopath, rampages through the New York City subway system. One cop enthusiastically tries to snuff out each one.
1988 91m/C Doc Dougherty, Lenny Y. Loftin; **D:** James McCalmont. VHS NO ♫

Underground U.S.A. Street hustler picks up a has-been underground movie star at the chic New York new wave disco, The Mudd Club.
1984 85m/C Patti Astor, Eric Mitchell; **D:** Eric Mitchell. VHS, Beta NO ♫

Undersea Kingdom Adventure beneath the ocean floor. In twelve chapters of thirteen minutes each; the first chapter runs twenty minutes. Later re-edited into one film, "Sharad of Atlantis."
1936 226m/B Ray Corrigan, Lon Chaney Jr.; **D:** B. Reeves Eason. VHS $29.98 NOS, SNC, VCN ♫

Understudy: The Graveyard Shift 2 Vampire survives poorly directed cliche-riddled original to be cast as a vampire cast as a vampire in a horror movie within a horrible sequel.
1988 (R) 88m/C Wendy Gazelle, Mark Soper, Silvio Oliviero; **D:** Gerard Ciccoritti. VHS, Beta NO ♫ ½

The Undertaker and His Pals Undertaker teams up with diner owners in murder scheme to improve mortician's business and expand restaurateurs' menu. Pretty violent stuff, with some good laughs and a campy flare, but not for every one's palate.
1967 70m/C Ray Dannis, Brad Fulton, Larrene Ott, Robert Lowery, Sally Frei; **D:** David C. Graham. VHS MTH ♫♫

Underwater A team of skin divers faces danger when they try to retrieve treasure from a Spanish galleon. The second film after "The Outlaw" masterminded by Howard Hughes, primarily to show off Russell's figure.
1955 99m/C Jane Russell, Richard Egan, Gilbert Roland, Jayne Mansfield; **D:** John Sturges. VHS, Beta $19.98 MED, TTC ♫♫

Underworld Scandal An editor attempts to break up a ring of basketball game fixers.
1947 ?m/C Philip Reed, Hillary Brooke. VHS $16.95 SNC ♫♫

The Underworld Story Big city journalist at large moves to smalltown New England after losing job for unethical reporting and uncovers scheme to frame innocent man for murder. Solid performances.
1950 90m/B Dan Duryea, Herbert Marshall, Gale Storm, Howard da Silva, Michael O'Shea, Mary Anderson, Gar Moore, Melville Cooper, Frieda Inescort, Art Baker, Harry Shannon, Alan Hale Jr., Steve Dunne, Roland Winters; **D:** Cy Endfield. VHS $19.98 FOX, FCT ♫♫ ½

Underworld, U.S.A. A man infiltrates a tough crime syndicate to avenge his father's murder, which winds up with him caught between the mob and the feds. A well-acted and directed look at the criminal underworld.
1960 99m/B Cliff Robertson, Dolores Dorn, Beatrice Kay, Robert Emhardt, Larry Gates, Paul Dubov; **D:** Samuel Fuller; **W:** Samuel Fuller. VHS, Beta $69.95 COL ♫♫♫

The Undying Monster Upper crusty Brit is werewolf with insatiable appetite. Familiar story with lots of atmosphere and style. Photography by Lucien Ballard. **AKA:** The Hammond Mystery.
1942 63m/B James Ellison, Heather Angel, John Howard, Bramwell Fletcher, Heather Thatcher, Aubrey Mather, Halliwell Hobbes, Heather Wilde; **D:** John Brahm. VHS $19.98 MOV ♫♫ ½

Une Jeunesse A middle-aged French couple reminisce about their meeting and courtship. In French with English subtitles.
1983 100m/C VHS, Beta $29.95 FCT ♫♫♫

The Unearthing An unwanted pregnancy seems to find a happy solution when a woman decides to marry the heir to a wealthy estate and pass off her child as his. Only the family has some very strange tastes, including a taste for the blood of the unborn. Based on a Filipino vampire legend (!)
1993 (R) 83m/C Norman Moses, Tina Ona Paukstelis; **D:** Wyre Martin, Barry Poltermann; **W:** Wyre Martin, Barry Poltermann. VHS PSM ♫

The Unearthly A mad scientist is trying to achieve immortality through his strange experiments, but all he winds up with is a basement full of mutants. When his two latest about-to-be victims fall in love, the doctor's mutant assistant decides enough is enough and things come to an unpleasant end. Carradine is typecast. Absurd, but fun.
1957 76m/B John Carradine, Tor Johnson, Allison Hayes, Myron Healey; **D:** Brooke L. Peters. VHS, Beta $9.95 RHI, SNC, DVT ♫ ½

The Unearthly Stranger Earth scientist marries woman and decides she's from another planet. Not a nineties style gender drama; seems she's part of an invading alien force, but really does love her earth man. Surprisingly good low-budget sci-fi.
1964 75m/B John Neville, Gabriella Licudi, Philip Stone, Patrick Newell, Jean Marsh, Warren Mitchell; **D:** John Krish. VHS $19.95 MOV ♫♫ ½

Uneasy Terms Rennie is a detective investigating the murder of one of his own clients. Evidence points to stepchildren and inheritance money but things may not be as they seem. Written for the screen by Peter Cheyney, adapted from his own novel.
1948 91m/B Michael Rennie, Moira Lister, Faith Brook, Joy Shelton, Patricia Goddard, Barry Jones; **D:** Vernon Sewell. VHS, Beta $16.95 SNC ♫

Unexplained Laughter A cynical journalist vacations in Wales with her timid vegetarian friend and stumbles across a mystery in this darkly comic British TV-movie.
1989 85m/C Diana Rigg, Elaine Page, Jon Finch. VHS $49.95 FCT ♫♫

Unfaithfully Yours A conductor suspects his wife is cheating on him and considers his course of action. He imagines punishment scenarios while directing three classical works. Well-acted by all, but particularly by Harrison as the egotistical and jealous husband. Another of Sturges' comedic gems. Remade in 1984.
1948 105m/B Rex Harrison, Linda Darnell, Kurt Kreuger, Rudy Vallee, Lionel Stander, Edgar Kennedy; **D:** Preston Sturges. VHS, Beta $59.98 FOX ♫♫♫

Unfaithfully Yours A symphony conductor suspects his wife of fooling around with a musician; in retaliation, he plots an elaborate scheme to murder her with comic results. No match for the 1948 Preston Sturges film it's based on.
1984 (PG) 96m/C Dudley Moore, Nastassia Kinski, Armand Assante, Albert Brooks, Cassie Yates, Richard Libertini, Richard B. Shull; **D:** Howard Zieff; **W:** Valerie Curtin, Barry Levinson, Robert Klane; **M:** Bill Conti. VHS, Beta $79.98 FOX ♫♫

Unfinished Business A 17 year-old girl leads a troubled adolescent life with her divorced parents. She decides running away will ease her problems—not a smart move. Sequel to "Nobody Waved Goodbye."
1989 88m/C Isabelle Mejias, Peter Kastner, Leslie Toth, Peter Spence, Chuck Shamata, Julie Biggs; **D:** Don Owen. VHS, Beta $79.95 JEF ♫♫ ½

An Unfinished Piece for a Player Piano A general's widow invites family and friends to a weekend house party in 1910 Russia. Romantic and familial entanglements begin to intrude in a lyrical adaptation of Chekov's play "Platonov." In Russian with English subtitles.
1977 100m/C Alexander Kalyagin, Elena Solovei, Antonina Shuranova, Oleg Tabakov, Yuri Bogatyrev, Nikita Mikhalkov; **D:** Nikita Mikhalkov. VHS, Beta $69.95 FCT, ING, CVC ♫♫♫ ½

The Unforgiven A western family is torn asunder when it is suspected that the eldest daughter is of Indian birth. Film takes place in 1850s' Texas. One of Huston's weakest ventures, but viewed in terms of 1950s' prejudices it has more resonance. Fine acting from all the cast, especially Gish. Watch for the stunning Indian attack scene.
1960 123m/C Burt Lancaster, Audrey Hepburn, Lillian Gish, Audie Murphy, John Saxon, Charles Bickford, Doug McClure, Joseph Wiseman, Albert Salmi; **D:** John Huston. VHS, Beta $19.98 MGM, BTV ♫♫♫

Unforgiven Will Munny (Eastwood) lives a quiet life with his stepchildren on his failing pig farm, but his desperado past catches up with him when the Schofield Kid invites him to a bounty hunt. Munny reluctantly agrees, mistakenly believing that once the killing is through he can take up his peaceful ways again. Enter sadistic sheriff Little Bill Daggett (Hackman), who doesn't want any gunmen messing up his town. Eastwood uses his own status as a screen legend to full advantage as the aging gunman who realizes too late that his past can never be forgotten. Director Eastwood is also in top form with his well-seasoned cast and myth-defying Old West realism. Surprising critical and box office hit. The laserdisc version is available in letterbox format.
1992 (R) 131m/C Clint Eastwood, Gene Hackman, Morgan Freeman, Richard Harris, Jaimz Woolvett, Saul Rubinek, Frances Fisher, Anna Thomson, David Mucci, Rob Campbell, Anthony James; **D:** Clint Eastwood; **W:** David Peoples. Academy Awards '92: Best Director (Eastwood), Best Film Editing, Best Picture, Best Supporting Actor (Hackman); Nominations: Best Actor (Eastwood), Best Art Direction/Set Decoration, Best Cinematography, Best Original Screenplay, Best Sound; Directors Guild of America Awards '92: Best Director (Eastwood); Golden Globe Awards '93: Best Director (Eastwood), Best Supporting Actor (Hackman);

New York Film Critics Awards '92: Best Supporting Actor (Hackman); National Society of Film Critics Awards '92: Best Director (Eastwood), Best Film, Best Supporting Actor (Hackman). **VHS, Beta, 8mm $19.98** *WAR, MOV, BTV* 𝄢𝄢𝄢 ½

Unforgotten Crime A small town murder mystery.
1941 ?m/C George E. Stone, Dennis O'Keefe. **VHS $16.95** *SNC* 𝄢𝄢

The Unholy A New Orleans priest battles a demon that's killing innocent parishioners. Confusing and heavy-handed.
1988 (R) 100m/C Ben Cross, Hal Holbrook, Trevor Howard, Ned Beatty, William Russ, Jim Carroll; *D:* Camilo Vila; *W:* Philip Yordan. **VHS, Beta $19.98** *LIV, VES, HHE* 𝄢 ½

Unholy Four An amnesiac returns home after three years to attempt to find out which of his three fishing buddies left him for dead. Confusing at times, but has some suspenseful moments. British title was "A Stranger Came Home."
1954 80m/B Paulette Goddard, Paul Carpenter, William Sylvester, Patrick Holt, Russell Napier; *D:* Terence Fisher. **VHS, Beta** *NO* 𝄢 ½

Unholy Rollers Jennings stars as a factory worker who makes it big as a tough, violent roller derby star. Typical "Babes-on-Wheels" film that promises nothing and delivers even less. *AKA:* Leader of the Pack.
1972 (R) 88m/C Claudia Jennings, Louis Quinn, Betty A. Rees, Roberta Collins, Alan Vint, Candice Roman; *D:* Vernon Zimmerman. **VHS $79.95** *HBO* 𝄢

The Unholy Three Ventriloquist Chaney, working with other carnival cohorts, uses his talent to gain entrance to homes which he later robs. Things go awry when two of the gang strike out on their own and the victim is killed. When the wrong man is accused, his girl, one of Chaney's gang, begs Chaney to get him free, which he does by using his vocal talents. Chaney decides being a criminal is just too hard and goes back to his ventriloquism.
1925 70m/B Lon Chaney Sr., Harry Earles, Victor McLaglen, Mae Busch, Matt Moore, Matthew Betz, William Humphreys; *D:* Tod Browning. **VHS** *NO* 𝄢𝄢𝄢 ½

The Unholy Three Chaney remade his silent hit of 1925 for his first and only talking picture (he died before the film was released). The story is essentially the same. Chaney is a ventriloquist who, with his circus friends, work as scam artists and thieves. When an innocent man is accused of their crimes Chaney tries his ventriloquist tricks to come to his aid, only in this version Chaney is exposed as a fraud and is sent to prison. Rumors that Chaney was a mute had him agreeing to appear in a "talkie" and he actually used five different voices for his various roles.
1930 75m/B Lon Chaney Sr., Lila Lee, Elliott Nugent, Harry Earles, John Miljan; *D:* Jack Conway. **VHS $29.95** *FCT* 𝄢𝄢𝄢

Unholy Wife A young woman plans to murder her wealthy husband, but her plan goes awry when she accidentally kills someone else. Muddled and heavy-handed, with Steiger chewing scenery.
1957 94m/C Rod Steiger, Diana Dors, Tom Tryon, Marie Windsor, Beulah Bondi; *D:* John Farrow. **VHS, Beta $15.95** *VCI, HHE* 𝄢 ½

Unicorn A small boy hears the legend that if one rubs the horn of a Unicorn his wishes will come true. Mistakenly he buys a one-horned goat and sets out to fulfill his dreams.
1983 29m/C Diana Dors, David Kossoff, Celia Johnson; *D:* Carol Reed. **VHS, Beta $24.98** *SUE, NLC* 𝄢𝄢

Unidentified Flying Oddball An astronaut and his robotic buddy find their spaceship turning into a time machine that throws them back into Arthurian times and at the mercy of Merlin the magician. Futuristic version of Twain's "A Connecticut Yankee at King Arthur's Court."
1979 (G) 92m/C Dennis Dugan, Jim Dale, Ron Moody, Kenneth More, Rodney Bewes; *D:* Russ Mayberry. **VHS, Beta $69.95** *DIS* 𝄢𝄢 ½

The Uninvited A brother and sister buy a house in England, only to find it is haunted. Doors open and close by themselves, strange scents fill the air, and they hear sobbing during the night. Soon they are visited by a woman with an odd link to the house—her mother is the spirit who haunts the house. Chilling and unforgettable, this is one of the first films to deal seriously with ghosts.
1944 99m/B Ray Milland, Ruth Hussey, Donald Crisp, Cornelia Otis Skinner, Gail Russell; *D:* Lewis Allen. **VHS $14.98** *MCA* 𝄢𝄢𝄢

The Uninvited A mutant cat goes berserk onboard a luxury yacht, killing the passengers one by one with big, nasty, pointy teeth.
1988 89m/C George Kennedy, Alex Cord, Clu Gulager, Toni Hudson, Eric Larson, Shari Shattuck, Austin Stoker; *D:* Greydon Clark. **VHS, Beta** *NO* Woof!

Uninvited Grady is a mysterious old man who leads eight misfits to the top of a sacred mountain with the promise of finding gold. But the fortune hunters have trespassed in a sacred Indian burial ground and find their nightmares becoming a violent reality.
1993 (R) ?m/C Jack Elam, Christopher Boyer, Erin Noble, Bari Buckner, Jerry Rector, Zane Paolo, Dennis Gibbs, Ted Haler, Eno Brutto; *D:* Michael Derek Bohusz; *W:* Michael Derek Bohusz. **VHS $92.95** *IMP, IME* 𝄢𝄢 ½

Union City Deborah "Blondie" Harry's husband gets a little edgy when someone steals the milk. Murder ensues, and they're on the run from the law. Intended as a film noir spoof, and not without some good moments.
1981 (R) 82m/C Deborah Harry, Everett McGill, Dennis Lipscomb, Pat Benatar; *D:* Mark Reichart. **VHS, Beta $59.95** *COL* 𝄢𝄢

Union Station Holden plays the chief of the railway police for Chicago's Union Station. He learns the station is to be used as a ransom drop in a kidnapping; but for all his security, the main thug gets away with the money, and the hunt is on. Good acting raises this film above the ordinary.
1950 80m/B William Holden, Barry Fitzgerald, Nancy Olson, Jan Sterling, Lee Marvin, Allene Roberts, Lyle Bettger; *D:* Rudolph Mate. **VHS, Beta $19.95** *BAR* 𝄢𝄢

Universal Soldier A reporter discovers a secret government project to design perfect robo-soldiers by using the bodies of dead GIs, including tough guys Lundgren and Van Damme who were killed in Vietnam. But the knowledge is going to get her killed until Van Damme has flashbacks of his past (the soldier's memories have supposedly been erased) and agrees to help her. Lundgren doesn't have the same compassion and goes after them both. Big-budget thriller with some good action sequences and a lot of violence.
1992 (R) 98m/C Jean-Claude Van Damme, Dolph Lundgren, Ally Walker, Ed O'Ross, Jerry Orbach; *D:* Roland Emmerich. **VHS $94.98** *LIV, PMS* 𝄢𝄢

The Unkissed Bride A young newlywed couple are driven to distraction by the husband's inexplicable fainting spells and his strange obsession with Mother Goose. *AKA:* Mother Goose A Go-Go.
1966 87m/C Tommy Kirk, Anne Helm, Danica D'Hondt, Henny Youngman; *D:* Jack H. Harris. **VHS, Beta $19.95** *NWV* 𝄢

The Unknown Typically morbid Chaney fare has him working as a circus freak while trying to win the heart of his assistant. After drastic romancing he's still rejected by her, so he plots to kill the object of her intentions. Ghoulish as it is, the picture is really top-notch.
1927 60m/B Lon Chaney Sr., Norman Kerry, Joan Crawford, Nick De Ruiz, Frank Lanning, John St. Polis; *D:* Tod Browning. **VHS $24.95** *FCT* 𝄢𝄢𝄢 ½

Unknown Island Scientists travel to a legendary island where dinosaurs supposedly still exist. Bogus dinosaurs and cliche script.
1948 76m/C Virginia Grey, Philip Reed, Richard Denning, Barton MacLane; *D:* Jack Bernhard. **VHS $19.95** *NOS, MOV, HEG* Woof!

Unknown Powers Science and drama are combined to examine ESP and magic. Are they gifts or curses, and how are peoples' lives affected by them? Members of the cast introduce various sections of this totally inept film.
1980 (PG) 97m/C Samantha Eggar, Jack Palance, Will Geer, Roscoe Lee Browne; *D:* Don Como. **VHS, Beta $39.95** *GEM* Woof!

The Unknown Ranger Allen's first cowboy role has him foiling a gang of rustlers. The real highlight turns out to be the battle between his horse and a wild stallion. Eat your heart out, Trigger!
1936 57m/B Robert Allen, Harry Woods, Martha Tibbetts, Hal Taliaferro, Robert "Buzzy" Henry; *D:* Spencer Gordon Bennet. **VHS $11.95** *GPV* 𝄢 ½

Unknown World A group of scientists tunnel to the center of the Earth to find a refuge from the dangers of the atomic world. Big start winds down fast. Director Terry Morse sometimes credited as Terrell O. Morse.
1951 73m/B Bruce Kellogg, Marilyn Nash, Victor Kilian, Jim Bannon; *D:* Terry Morse; *M:* Ernest Gold. **VHS, Beta $19.95** *NOS, PSM, SNC* 𝄢

Unlawful Entry After a break-in, Karen and Michael Carr naturally call the cops. Handsome, polite policeman Pete Davis responds to the call and agrees to help burglar-proof their home. But Pete has some definite quirks—he falls for the beauteous Karen and begins stalking the couple, deciding to get rid of Michael in order to have his wife. A lurid combination of the worst moments of "Internal Affairs" and "Fatal Attraction" undermines this usually-talented cast.
1992 (R) 107m/C Kurt Russell, Ray Liotta, Madeleine Stowe, Roger E. Mosley, Ken Lerner, Deborah Offner, Carmen Argenziano, Andy Romano, Barry W. Blaustein, Dick Miller; *D:* Jonathan Kaplan; *M:* James Horner. **VHS $19.98** *FXV* 𝄢𝄢

Unmarried Mothers A number of young ladies engage in sex before marriage and must suffer the consequences.
1955 ?m/C **VHS $16.95** *SNC* 𝄢

An Unmarried Woman Suddenly divorced by her husband of 17 years, a woman deals with change. She enters the singles scene, copes with her daughter's growing sexuality, and encounters a new self-awareness. Mazursky puts real people on screen from start to finish.

1978 (R) 124m/C Jill Clayburgh, Alan Bates, Cliff Gorman, Michael Murphy; **D:** Paul Mazursky; **W:** Paul Mazursky; **M:** Bill Conti. Academy Awards '78 Nominations: Best Actress (Clayburgh), Best Original Screenplay, Best Picture; Cannes Film Festival '78: Best Film; Cannes Film Festival '78: Best Actress (Clayburgh); National Board of Review Awards '78: 10 Best Films of the Year. **VHS, Beta** $69.98 *FOX* 🎬🎬🎬

Unmasked Part 25 A second-generation serial killer takes up where dad left off. This one is intended to be a parody of slasher films, but it's still very bloody.
1988 85m/C Gregory Cox, Fiona Evans, Edward Brayshaw, Debbie Lee London; **D:** Anders Palm. **VHS, Beta** $79.95 *ACA* 🎬½

Unmasking the Idol A suave hero with tongue firmly in check battles Ninja warlords. Sequel to "Order of the Black Eagle."
1986 90m/C Ian Hunter, William T. Hicks, Charles K. Bibby; **D:** Worth Keeter. **VHS, Beta** $19.95 *CEL* 🎬

The Unnamable The adaptation of the H.P. Lovecraft story about a particular New England ancestral home haunted by a typically Lovecraftian bloodthirsty demon borne of a woman hundreds of years before. College students, between trysts, investigate the myths about it. Uncut version, unseen in theaters, available only on video good for a few giggles and thrills.
1988 87m/C Mark Kinsey Stephenson, Alexandra Durrell; **D:** Jean-Paul Ouellette. **VHS, Beta** $9.99 *STE, VMK* 🎬

The Unnamable 2: The Statement of Randolph Carter Randolph Carter is investigating a series of murders at Miskatonic University. Evidence leads Carter back to a 17th-century warlock who had the misfortune to summon an evil creature known as Alyda. The half-demon, half-woman now wants to permanently return to the mortal plane and every new victim just helps her evil purpose along. Based on a story by H.P. Lovecraft.
1992 (R) 104m/C Mark Kinsey Stephenson, John Rhys-Davies, David Warner, Julie Strain, Maria Ford; **D:** Jean-Paul Ouellette. **VHS** $89.95 *PSM* 🎬½

Unnatural A mad scientist creates a souless child from the genes of a murderer and a prostitute. The child grows up to be the beautiful Neff, who makes a habit of seducing and destroying men. Dark, arresting film from a very popular German story.
1952 90m/B Hildegarde Neff, Erich von Stroheim, Karl-Heinz Boehm, Harry Meyen, Harry Helm, Denise Vernanc, Julia Koschka; **D:** Arthur Maria Rabenalt. **VHS** $19.98 *SNC* 🎬🎬½

Unnatural Causes A dying Vietnam vet believes that his illness is the result of exposure to Agent Orange. With the help a VA counselor, they lobby for national programs to assist other veterans who have been exposed to the chemical and together bring publicity to the issue. A made-for-television drama that is exceptionally well-acted.
1986 96m/C John Ritter, Patti LaBelle, Alfre Woodard, John Sayles, Sean McCann, John Vargas, Gwen E. Davis; **D:** Lamont Johnson; **W:** John Sayles; **M:** Charles Fox. **VHS, Beta** *NO* 🎬🎬🎬

An Unremarkable Life Two aging sisters live symbiotically together, until one views the other's romantic attachment to a charming widower as destructive to her own life.

1989 (PG) 97m/C Shelley Winters, Patricia Neal, Mako, Rochelle Oliver, Charles S. Dutton, Lily Knight; **D:** Amin Q. Chaudhri. **VHS, Beta** $14.95 *IME, COL* 🎬🎬

Unsane A mystery novelist realizes that a series of bizarre murders strangely resembles the plot of his latest book. Bloody fun from Argento. **AKA:** Tenebrae.
1982 91m/C Anthony (Tony) Franciosa, John Saxon, Daria Nicolodi, Giuliano Gemma, Christian Borromeo, Mirella D'Angelo, Veronica Lario; **D:** Dario Argento; **W:** Dario Argento. **VHS** $9.95 *MED* 🎬🎬½

The Unseen Three young women from a television station are covering a story in a remote area of California. Before nightfall, two are horribly killed, leaving the third to come face to face with the terror.
1980 91m/C Barbara Bach, Sydney Lassick, Stephen Furst; **D:** Peter Foleg. **VHS, Beta** *NO* 🎬½

Unsettled Land Young Israeli settlers try to survive the elements and Bedouin attackers in Palestine during the 1920s.
1988 (PG) 109m/C Kelly McGillis, John Shea, Arnon Zadok, Christine Boisson; **D:** Uri Barbash. **VHS, Beta, 8mm** $19.98 *SUE, NLC* 🎬

The Unsinkable Molly Brown A spunky backwoods girl is determined to break into the upper crust of Denver's high society and along the way survives the sinking of the Titanic. This energetic version of the Broadway musical contains many Meredith Wilson (Music Man) songs and lots of hokey, good-natured fun. ♫Colorado Is My Home; Leadville Johnny Brown (Soliloquy); I Ain't Down Yet; Belly Up to the Bar, Boys; He's My Friend; I've Already Started; The Beautiful People of Denver; I May Never Fall in Love with You; Up Where the People Are.
1964 128m/C Debbie Reynolds, Harve Presnell, Ed Begley Sr., Martita Hunt, Hermione Baddeley; **D:** Charles Walters; **M:** Meredith Wilson. **VHS, Beta** $19.98 *MGM* 🎬🎬🎬

The Unstoppable Man The son of an American businessman is kidnapped while they are in London. No pushover he, dad develops his own plan to destroy the criminals, eventually pursuing them with a flame thrower.
1959 68m/B Cameron Mitchell, Marius Goring, Harry H. Corbett, Lois Maxwell, Denis Gilmore; **D:** Terry Bishop. **VHS, Beta** $16.95 *NOS, SNC* 🎬½

Unsuitable Job for a Woman Independent Cordelia Gray, following the death of her boss, takes over his detective agency and gets involved with murder. Based on the novel by P.D. James.
1982 94m/C Pippa Guard, Paul Freeman, Billie Whitelaw; **D:** Christopher Petit. **VHS, Beta** *NO* 🎬🎬

The Untamable Unusual silent about volatile woman suffering from schizophrenia.
1923 65m/B Gladys Walton, Malcolm McGregor, John St. Polis, Etta Lee; **D:** Herbert Blache. **VHS, Beta** $16.95 *GPV, FCT* 🎬

Untamed Heart Adam (Slater), the painfully shy busboy with a heart condition, loves Caroline (Tomei), the bubbly waitress, from afar. She doesn't notice him until he saves her from some would-be rapists and their love blooms in the coffee shop where they both work. Tomei and Slater are both strong in the leads and Perez, as Caroline's best buddy Cindy, hurls comic barbs with ease. Charmingly familiar surroundings help set this formulaic romance apart. Filmed on location in Minneapolis. Laserdisc version is in letterbox format.

1993 (PG-13) 102m/C Christian Slater, Marisa Tomei, Rosie Perez, Kyle Secor, Willie Garson; **D:** Harold Ramis; **W:** Tom Sierchio; **M:** Cliff Eidelman. **VHS, Beta** $19.98 *MGM* 🎬🎬½

Until September An American tourist becomes stranded in Paris. She meets and falls in love with a married banker while she is stuck in her hotel. Routine romance.
1984 (R) 96m/C Karen Allen, Thierry Lhermitte, Christopher Cazenove, Johanna Pavlis; **D:** Richard Marquand; **M:** John Barry. **VHS, Beta** $14.95 *MGM* 🎬🎬

Until The End of The World Convoluted road movie set in 1999 follows the travails of Sam Farber (Hurt) through 15 cities in 8 countries on 4 continents as he is chased by Dommartin, her lover (Neill), a bounty hunter, a private detective, and bank robbers, until all wind up in the Australian outback. And this is only the first half of the movie. For true cinematic satisfaction, don't expect logic—just go with the flow. Visually stunning, unexpectedly humorous, with excellent performances from an international cast. Footage created with high definition (HDTV) video technology is a technological first. The soundtrack features Lou Reed, David Byrne, U2, and others.
1991 (R) 158m/C William Hurt, Solveig Dommartin, Sam Neill, Max von Sydow, Ruediger Vogler, Ernie Dingo, Jeanne Moreau; **D:** Wim Wenders; **W:** Wim Wenders, Peter Carey; **M:** Graeme Revell. **VHS, Beta** $92.99 *WAR* 🎬🎬🎬½

Until They Get Me Northern Mountie rides horse in silence as he tracks criminal to the edge of the earth.
1918 58m/B Pauline Starke, Joe King. **VHS, Beta** $24.95 *GPV, FCT* 🎬½

Until They Sail Soap opera set in New Zealand during WWII. Plot centers around the lives of four sisters involved in love and murder. Dee's film debut. Based on a story by James Michener.
1957 95m/B Jean Simmons, Joan Fontaine, Paul Newman, Piper Laurie, Charles Drake, Sandra Dee, Wally Cassell, Alan Napier; **D:** Robert Wise; **W:** Robert Anderson. **VHS** $19.98 *MGM* 🎬🎬½

The Untouchables Big-budget, fast-paced and exciting re-evaluation of the popular TV series about the real-life battle between Treasury officer Eliot Ness and crime boss Al Capone in 1920s' Chicago. History sometimes takes a back seat to Hollywood's imagination in the screenplay, but it doesn't really matter since there are splendid performances by De Niro as Capone and Connery as Ness' mentor to help it look realistic. Costner does a fine job showing the change in Ness from naive idealism to steely conviction. Beautifully filmed with excellent special effects.
1987 (R) 119m/C Kevin Costner, Sean Connery, Robert De Niro, Andy Garcia, Charles Martin Smith, Billy Drago, Richard Bradford, Jack Kehoe; **D:** Brian DePalma; **W:** David Mamet; **M:** Ennio Morricone. Academy Awards '87: Best Supporting Actor (Connery); Nominations: Best Art Direction/Set Decoration, Best Costume Design, Best Original Score; Golden Globe Awards '88: Best Supporting Actor (Connery); National Board of Review Awards '87: 10 Best Films of the Year, Best Supporting Actor (Connery). **VHS, Beta, 8mm** $14.95 *PAR, BTV* 🎬🎬🎬½

Up Against the Wall A black kid from the Chicago projects attends school in the affluent suburbs, but there too he must resist temptation, crime and violence. A well-intentioned but didactic cautionary drama, adapted from the book by African-American author/commentator Dr. Jawanza Kunjufu.

1991 (PG-13) 103m/C Marla Gibbs, Stoney Jackson, Catero Colbert, Ron O'Neal, Salli Richardson; **D:** Ron O'Neal. VHS $79.98 BMG ✂✂

Up from the Depths Something from beneath the ocean is turning the paradise of Hawaii into a nightmare. Prehistoric fish are returning to the surface with one thing on their minds—lunch. "Jaws" rip-off played for humor.
1979 (R) 85m/C Sam Bottoms, Suzanne Reed, Virgil Frye; **D:** Charles B. Griffith; **W:** Alfred Sweeny; **M:** James Horner. VHS, Beta $59.98 LIV, VES ✂½

Up in Arms Danny Kaye's first film presents a typical Kaye scenario: he plays a twitching hypochondriac who is drafted into the Army and sneaks his girlfriend aboard the troopship bound for the Pacific. Features an appearance by the Goldwyn Girls. Remake of the film "The Nervous Wreck." ♫ Theatre Lobby Number; Now I Know; All Out for Freedom; Tess's Torch Song; Melody in 4-F.
1944 105m/C Danny Kaye, Dinah Shore, Constance Dowling, Dana Andrews, Margaret Dumont, Goldwyn Girls, Lyle Talbot, Louis Calhern, Charles Halton; **D:** Elliott Nugent. VHS, Beta $19.98 SUE ✂✂

Up in the Air Darro and Moreland have ambitions as radio comedians, and their friend Reynolds wants to be a singer. Their break comes when other performers are murdered on the air. First, though, they must solve the killings.
1940 62m/B Frankie Darro, Marjorie Reynolds, Mantan Moreland, Gordon Jones, Tristram Coffin, John Holland, Carleton Young; **D:** Howard Bretherton. VHS $19.95 NOS ✂✂

Up Periscope Garner is a demolitions expert unwillingly assigned to a submarine commanded by O'Brien. His mission: to sneak onto a Japanese-held island and steal a top-secret code book. Trouble is, O'Brien may not wait for Garner to complete his mission before taking the sub back underwater. A routine submarine film.
1959 111m/C James Garner, Edmond O'Brien, Andra Martin, Alan Hale Jr., Carleton Carpenter, Frank Gifford, Richard Bakalayan; **D:** Gordon Douglas. VHS WAR ✂✂½

Up River Wealthy land baron rapes and murders the wife of a simple pioneer, who is beaten and whose homestead is burned by the baron as well. The pioneer lives to seek terrible vengeance.
1979 90m/C Jeff Corey, Morgan Stevens, Debbie AuLuce; **D:** Carl Kitt. VHS NO ✂

Up the Academy Four teenaged delinquents are sent to an academy for wayward boys where they encounter a sadistic headmaster and a gay dance instructor. Sometimes inventive, often tasteless fare from "Mad" magazine. **AKA:** Mad Magazine's Up the Academy; The Brave Young Men of Weinberg.
1980 (R) 88m/C Ron Leibman, Ralph Macchio, Barbara Bach, Tom Poston, Stacey Nelkin, Wendell Brown, Tom Citera; **D:** Robert Downey. VHS, Beta $19.98 WAR ✂

Up the Creek Crazy antics abound in this tale of an old British destroyer, a black-market scheme run by the crew, and the new skipper whose hobby is rocket building. Followed by "Further Up the River."
1958 83m/B David Tomlinson, Wilfrid Hyde-White, Peter Sellers, Vera Day, Michael Goodliffe, Lionel Jeffries; **D:** Val Guest. VHS, Beta $39.95 MON ✂✂

Up the Creek Four college losers enter a whitewater raft race to gain some respect for their school. The soundtrack features songs by Heart, Cheap Trick and The Beach Boys. Routine.
1984 (R) 95m/C Tim Matheson, Jennifer Runyon, Stephen Furst, John Hillerman, James B. Sikking, Julia Montgomery, Jeana Tomasina; **D:** Robert Butler; **W:** William Goldstein. VHS, Beta $29.98 LIV, VES ✂½

Up the Down Staircase A naive, newly trained New York public school teacher is determined to teach the finer points of English literature to a group of poor students. She almost gives up until one student actually begins to learn. Good production and acting. Based on Bel Kaufman's novel.
1967 124m/C Sandy Dennis, Patrick Bedford, Eileen Heckart, Ruth White, Jean Stapleton, Sorrell Booke; **D:** Robert Mulligan. VHS WAR, OM ✂✂✂

Up the Sandbox A bored housewife fantasizes about her life in order to avoid facing her mundane existence. Fine acting from Streisand, with real problems of young mothers accurately shown.
1972 (R) 98m/C Barbra Streisand, David Selby, Jane Hoffman, Barbara Rhoades; **D:** Irvin Kershner; **M:** Billy Goldenberg. VHS, Beta $19.98 WAR ✂✂

Up Your Alley A female reporter, pursuing a story on homelessness, and a skidrow bum find romance. Langston, who produced and co-wrote the film, is better known as "The Unknown Comic."
1989 (R) 90m/C Linda Blair, Murray Langston, Ruth Buzzi, Johnny Dark, Bob Zany, Yakov Smirnoff; **D:** Bob Logan. VHS, Beta $89.95 LIV ✂✂

Uphill All the Way A couple of card-cheatin' good old boys are pursued by posses and cavalry alike, and end up killing real outlaws. Made for television.
1985 91m/C Roy Clark, Mel Tillis, Glen Campbell, Trish Van Devere, Burl Ives, Burt Reynolds; **D:** Frank Q. Dobbs. VHS, Beta $19.95 NWV, STE ✂✂

Upper Crust Boring tale of corruption and greed that takes place at the highest levels of American business and government.
1988 95m/C Frank Gorshin, Broderick Crawford, Nigel Davenport. VHS, Beta NO ✂½

The Uprising A Nicaraguan drama filmed just months after the 1979 Sandinista revolution, wherein a young guard of Somoza retains his job for the money, while his father is active in the revolutionary forces. In Spanish with English subtitles.
1981 96m/C **D:** Peter Lilienthal. VHS, Beta $69.95 KIV, ING ✂✂✂

Uptown Angel A young woman is determined to work her way out of her home on the wrong side of town. Black cast brings new life to old premise.
1990 (R) 90m/C Caron Tate, Cliff McMullen, Gloria Davis Hill, Tracy Hill; **D:** Joy Shannon; **W:** Joy Shannon. VHS $59.95 XVC ✂✂

Uptown New York A young man pressured by his family marries a rich girl instead of the woman he loves, who in turn marries a man she does not love. Routine melodrama.
1932 81m/B Jack Oakie, Shirley Green, Leon Waycoff, Shirley Grey, George Cooper, Raymond Hatton; **D:** Victor Schertzinger. VHS, Beta $19.95 NOS, FCT, DVT ✂✂

Uptown Saturday Night Two working men attempt to recover a stolen lottery ticket from the black underworld after being ripped off at an illegal gambling place. Good fun, with nice performances from both leads and from Belafonte doing a black "Godfa-ther" parody of Brando. Followed by "Let's Do It Again."
1974 (PG) 104m/C Sidney Poitier, Bill Cosby, Harry Belafonte, Flip Wilson, Richard Pryor, Calvin Lockhart; **D:** Sidney Poitier; **W:** Richard Wesley. VHS, Beta $19.98 WAR ✂✂½

The Uranium Conspiracy A secret agent and a mercenary soldier try to stop a shipment of uranium out of Zaire from falling into enemy hands. It won't be easy.
1978 (PG) 100m/C Fabio Testi, Janet Agren, Assaf Dayan. VHS, Beta NO ✂½

Uranus After WWII a French provincial town has been liberated from Nazi invaders—but not its own suspicions, as citizens try to rebuild knowing some of them collaborated with the enemy. An important subject is heavily talked over in static fashion, with a robust Depardieu either a standout or a ham as the earthy saloon-keeper. Based on a novel by Marcel Ayme, himself accused of pro-Vichy leanings during the era. In French with English subtitles.
1991 (R) 100m/C Gerard Depardieu, Michel Blanc, Jean-Pierre Marielle, Philippe Noiret, Gerard Desarthe, Michel Galabru, Fabrice Luchini, Daniel Prevost; **D:** Claude Berri; **W:** Claude Berri; **M:** Jean-Claude Petit. VHS $89.99 HBO, ING ✂✂✂

Urban Cowboy A young Texas farmer comes to Houston to work in a refinery. After work he hangs out at Gilley's, a roadhouse bar. Here he and his friends, dressed in their cowboy gear, drink, fight, and prove their manhood by riding a mechanical bull. Film made Winger a star, was an up in Travolta's roller coaster career, and began the craze for country western apparel and dance and them there mechanical bulls. Ride 'em, cowboy!
1980 (PG) 135m/C John Travolta, Debra Winger, Scott Glenn, Madolyn Smith, Barry Corbin; **D:** James Bridges; **W:** James Bridges, Aaron Latham; **M:** Ralph Burns. VHS, Beta PAR ✂✂½

Urban Warriors Savage barbarians roam and pillage a post-nuclear war Earth, but one invincible warrior ushers them out.
1975 90m/C Karl Landgren, Alex Vitale, Deborah Keith; **D:** Joseph Warren. VHS, Beta $59.95 CAN ✂

Urge to Kill A man returning from a mental hospital after pleading temporary insanity to the murder of his girlfriend returns to her town and tries to uncover the truth, with the help of her younger sister. Made for television.
1984 (PG) 96m/C Karl Malden, Holly Hunter, William Devane, Alex McArthur; **D:** Mike Robe. VHS, Beta $59.98 FOX, VTR ✂

Urotsukidoji 1: Legend of the Overfiend Legend has it that the world is made up of Humans, Man-Beasts, and Monster-Demons. Every 3000 years superfiend Chojin is supposed to unite the three into a single Land of Eternity. However, the heroic Amano discovers this land will be a nightmare world and unless he can successfully battle Chojin humanity may not survive. Ultra-violent and sexually explicit. Animated; dubbed into English. **AKA:** The Wandering Kid.
1993 (NC-17) 108m/C VHS $39.95 CPM, MOV ✂✂

Urotsukidoji 2: Legend of the Demon Womb The fiendish Dr. Munhihausen's life work has been to render the dimensional boundaries between the World of Man-Beasts and the World of Monster Demons and to conjure the dreaded Overfiend. Years later, his son seeks to find a way to conquer the Overfiend and his cohorts from Hell and assume its powers for himself. Munhihausen's efforts may soon be reward-

ed when his hapless cousin, who accidentally received the demon's blood, begins developing monstrous powers. Animated; dubbed from Japanese.
1993 88m/C VHS $34.95 CPM, MOV �️🎬🎬

Ursus in the Valley of the Lions Ursus attempts to rescue love from druids but is dismayed to find that she has taken up homicide in her free time. *AKA:* The Mighty Ursus; Ursus.
1962 92m/C Ed Fury, Luis Prendes, Moira Orfei, Cristina Gajoni, Maria Luisa Merlo; *D:* Carlo Campogalliani. **VHS $19.98** SNC ✍️½

Urusei Yatsura Movie 1: Only You Lum is a Princess of the Oni, an alien race who have come to repossess Earth. The planet's one chance is for an earthling to beat Lum in the Oni's national sport—tag. When unlucky teenager Ataru Moroboshi is chosen he actually beats Lum. Which means he has to marry her. In Japanese with English subtitles.
198? 100m/C VHS $39.95 ANI ✍️½

Urusei Yatsura Movie 2: Beautiful Dreamer Unlucky teenager Ataru Moroboshi and his classmates at Tomobiki High School find themselves reliving the day before the School Festival over and over again. Funny and dreamlike. In Japanese with English subtitles.
1992 90m/C *D:* Oshii Mamoru. **VHS $39.95** CPM, ING, ANI ✍️½

Urusei Yatsura Movie 3: Remember My Love A magician family friend of Princess Lum put a curse on her at birth when she wasn't invited to Lum's christening (shades of "Sleeping Beauty")—that Lum would never be happy with her true love. But Ataru is the real victim. When the magician happens upon him in the new amusement park she turns him into a pink hippotamus to spite Lum. In Japanese with English subtitles.
1985 93m/C VHS $39.95 ANI ✍️½

Urusei Yatsura Movie 4: Lum the Forever When a great cherry tree is cut down near where Lum and friends are making a movie she mysteriously loses her horns, and with them her powers. In Japanese with English subtitles.
1986 94m/C VHS $39.95 ANI, WTA, ING ✍️½

Urusei Yatsura Movie 6: Always My Darling Space princess Lupica abducts Aturu in order to get the greatest love potion in the galaxy. Lum wants him back. In Japanese with English subtitles.
1991 77m/C VHS $39.95 ANI, ING ✍️½

Used Cars A car dealer is desperate to put his jalopy shop competitors out of business. The owners go to great lengths to stay afloat. Sometimes too obnoxious, but often funny.
1980 (R) 113m/C Kurt Russell, Jack Warden, Deborah Harmon, Gerrit Graham, Joe Flaherty, Michael McKean; *D:* Robert Zemeckis; *W:* Robert Zemeckis. **VHS, Beta, 8mm $12.95** COL ✍️✍️✍️

Used People A study in ethnicity and characterization, three Oscar-winning actresses lead a talented cast playing a Jewish family living in Queens in 1969. When the father dies, Joe (Mastroianni), an old friend with an old torch for the widow, Pearl (MacLaine), shows up at the funeral and manages to charm her into a date for coffee. Pearl's new relationship with her Italian suitor affects each' of the somewhat off-balance family members and washes the whole clan with a sense of hope and renewal. Adpated from screenwriter Graff's play "The Grandma

Plays" that was based on memories of his grandmother. Director Kidron's American debut.
1992 (PG-13) 116m/C Shirley MacLaine, Marcello Mastroianni, Kathy Bates, Marcia Gay Harden, Jessica Tandy, Sylvia Sidney, Bob Dishy, Joe Pantoliano, Matthew Branton, Louis Guff, Charles Cioffi, Doris Roberts, Helen Hanft; *D:* Beeban Kidron; *W:* Todd Graff; *M:* Rachel Portman. **VHS $19.98** FXV ✍️✍️½

Users Small-town girl who worked as a prostitute meets a faded film star and becomes involved in the movie business. Ode to decadent Hollywood. Based on the Joyce Haber novel. Made for television.
1978 125m/C Jaclyn Smith, Tony Curtis, John Forsythe, Red Buttons, George Hamilton; *D:* Joseph Hardy; *M:* Maurice Jarre. **VHS, Beta $49.95** PSM ✍️✍️

Utah A musical comedy star who inherits a ranch wishes to sell it to finance one of her shows. She is persuaded not to by Rogers, the ranch foreman.
1945 54m/B Roy Rogers, Dale Evans, George "Gabby" Hayes; *D:* John English. **VHS, Beta $19.95** NOS, VDM, VCN ✍️½

Utah Trail Lawman Ritter is hired to stop a gang of cattle rustlers. Cheapie oater made for Grand National, which went bankrupt soon after.
1938 57m/B Tex Ritter; *D:* Al Herman. **VHS, Beta $19.95** NOS, VCN, DVT ✍️

Utamaro and His Five Women Utamaro is a legendary 19th-century Edo artist who gained inspiration from Tokyo's "floating world," of courtesans, brothels, drinking parties, and violent passions. His gorgeous portraits worship women but he dislikes the complications that flesh-and-blood females bring. Heavily stylized look at the artistic impulse. In Japanese with English subtitles. *AKA:* Five Women Around Utamaro; Utamaro O Meguru Gonin No Onna.
1946 89m/B Minnosuke Bando, Kinuyo Tanaka, Kotaro Bando, Hisato Osawa, Tamezo Mochizuki, Hiroko Kawasaki; *D:* Kenji Mizoguchi; *W:* Yoshikata Yoda. **VHS $69.95** NYF, FCT ✍️✍️½

Utilities A frustrated social worker enlists the help of his friends in his efforts to impress an attractive policewoman by taking on a large corporate utility. *AKA:* Getting Even.
1983 (PG) 94m/C Robert Hays, Brooke Adams, John Marley, Ben Gordon, Helen Burns; *D:* Harvey Hart. **VHS, Beta $79.98** LIV, VES ✍️½

Utopia Laurel and Hardy inherit a paradisaical island, but their peace is disturbed when uranium is discovered. Final screen appearance of the team is diminished by poor direction and script. *AKA:* Atoll K; Robinson Crusoeland; Escapade.
1951 82m/B Stan Laurel, Oliver Hardy, Suzy Delair, Max Elloy; *D:* Leo Joannon. **VHS, Beta $9.95** CNG, MRV, VYY ✍️✍️

Utu A Maori tribesman serving with the colonizing British army in 1870 explodes into ritual revenge when his home village is slaughtered. Filmed in New Zealand.
1983 (R) 104m/C Anzac Wallace, Kelly Johnson, Tim Elliot, Bruno Lawrence; *D:* Geoff Murphy. **VHS, Beta $79.98** FOX ✍️✍️✍️

Utz The Baron von Utz (Mueller-Stahl) collects both women and priceless porcelain figures. When his friend, art dealer Marius Fischer (Riegert), travels to Prague for a visit he finds that both Utz's housekeeper (Fricker), who has suffered from unrequited love, and the porcelain have disappeared. So Marius teams up with the Baron's old friend Dr. Orlick (Scofield) to find out what's going on. Based on the novel by Bruce Chatwin.

1993 95m/C Armin Mueller-Stahl, Peter Riegert, Brenda Fricker, Paul Scofield; *D:* George Sluizer. **VHS $79.95** FRV, BTV, FCT ✍️✍️

The Vagabond The Little Tramp is a pathetic fiddler making a scanty living who rescues a damsel in distress. Silent with musical. soundtrack added.
1916 20m/B Charlie Chaplin, Edna Purviance, Eric Campbell, Albert Austin; *D:* Charlie Chaplin. **VHS, Beta** CAB, GVV, VYY ✍️✍️

Vagabond Bleak, emotionally shattering, powerful and compelling, this film traces the peripatetic life of an amoral and selfish young French woman who has no regard for social rules and tremendous fear of responsibility in her drifting yet inexorable journey into death. Told via flashbacks from the moment when she is found dead, alone, and unaccounted for by the roadside, this film will not leave you unscathed. Written by New Wave director Varda. In French with English subtitles. *AKA:* Sans Toit Ni Loi.
1985 105m/C Sandrine Bonnaire, Macha Meril, Stephane Freiss, Elaine Cortadellas, Marthe Jarnias, Yolanda Moreau; *D:* Agnes Varda; *W:* Agnes Varda. **VHS, Beta $29.95** ING, TPV ✍️✍️✍️½

Vagabond Lover The amusing tale of the loves, hopes, and dreams of an aspiring saxophone player. Rudy croons through his megaphone in his movie debut. Appealing, with Dressler sparkling in the role of the wealthy aunt. 🎵If You Were the Only Girl in the World; A Little Kiss Each Morning; Heigh Ho Everybody; Piccolo Pete; I Love You; I'll Be Reminded of You; I'm Just a Vagabond Lover.
1929 66m/B Rudy Vallee, Sally Blane, Marie Dressler; *D:* Marshall Neilan. **VHS, Beta $24.95** VYY, RXM ✍️✍️½

The Vagrant Run-of-the-mill creeper with a mind-game playing derelict inhabiting the home of a young exec. A series of murders has this wimp yuppie wondering how to get rid of his unwelcome intruder.
1992 (R) 91m/C Bill Paxton, Michael Ironside, Marshall Bell, Stuart Pankin; *D:* Chris Walas. **VHS $14.95** MGM ✍️

Valdez is Coming Though not a world-class western, this filmed-in-Spain saga does feature a probing script (based on an Elmore Leonard novel) on the nature of race relations. Fine performance by Lancaster as a Mexican-American who ignites the passions of a town, and ultimately confronts the local land baron.
1971 (PG) 90m/C Burt Lancaster, Susan Clark, Jon Cypher, Barton Heyman, Richard Jordan, Frank Silvera, Hector Elizondo; *D:* Edwin Sherin; *W:* David Rayfiel. **VHS $19.98** MGM ✍️✍️½

Valentino Another one of director Russell's flamboyantly excessive screen biographies, this time of silent screen idol Rudolph Valentino (Nureyev). The details hardly matter but the movie is told in flashback from Valentino's funeral to his beginnings as a dance instructor and his eventually success as a screen lover. Nureyev is noticeably stiff in his screen debut but at least he possesses some charisma.
1977 (R) 127m/C Rudolf Nureyev, Leslie Caron, Michelle Phillips, Carol Kane, Felicity Kendal, Seymour Cassel, Peter Vaughan, William Hootkins, Huntz Hall, David DeKeyser, Alfred Marks, Anton Diffring; *D:* Ken Russell; *W:* Mardik Martin, Ken Russell. **VHS $19.98** MGM ✍️✍️

Valentino Returns A kid in 1955 California buys a pink Cadillac he nicknames "Valentino Returns," thinking it will help him meet girls, as his parents undergo a stormy divorce. Weak script fades fast from fine premise, good start. Nice period feel.

1988 (R) 97m/C Frederic Forrest, Veronica Cartwright, Jenny Wright, Barry Tubb; *D:* Peter Hoffman. **VHS, Beta $29.95** *VMK* 𝟚𝟙

Valley Girl Slight but surprisingly likeable teen romantic-comedy inspired by Frank Zappa novelty tune. Title stereotype falls for a leather-jacketed rebel. Really. It may look like a music video, but the story is straight from "Romeo and Juliet" via Southern California. Helped launch Cage's career. Music by Men at Work, Culture Club, and others.
1983 (R) 95m/C Nicolas Cage, Deborah Foreman, Colleen Camp, Frederic Forrest; *D:* Martha Coolidge. **VHS, Beta $29.98** *VES* 𝟚𝟙½

The Valley Obscured by the Clouds A group of dropouts and seekers search for the valley of the gods in the wilds of New Guinea, and experience a sexual and spiritual metamorphosis. In French with English subtitles.
1972 106m/C *D:* Barbet Schroeder; *M:* Pink Floyd. **VHS $59.99** *FCT, WAR, BTV* 𝟚𝟙

The Valley of Decision Entertaining poor-girl-meets-rich-boy story with Peck as a wealthy mill owner who falls in love with beautiful housemaid Garson (the Queen of MGM at the time). Set in 1870 Pittsburgh; based on Marcia Davenport's novel.
1945 111m/B Gregory Peck, Greer Garson, Donald Crisp, Lionel Barrymore, Preston Foster, Gladys Cooper, Marsha Hunt, Reginald Owen, Dan Duryea, Jessica Tandy, Barbara Everest; *D:* Tay Garnett; *W:* John Meehan, Sonya Levien. **VHS $19.98** *MGM* 𝟚𝟙𝟙

Valley of Fire Autry is the mayor of a boom town that suffers from a lack of women. He decides to import a caravan of brides for the men in town but villains attempt to kidnap the women.
1951 63m/B Gene Autry, Gail Davis, Pat Buttram; *D:* John English. **VHS, Beta $29.98** *CCB* 𝟚𝟙

The Valley of Gwangi One of the best prehistoric-monster-westerns out there. Cowboys discover a lost valley of dinosaurs and try to capture a vicious, carnivorous allosaurus. Bad move, kemosabe! The creatures move via the stop-motion model animation by f/x maestro Ray Harryhausen, here at his finest.
1969 (G) 95m/C James Franciscus, Gila Golan, Richard Carlson, Laurence Naismith, Freda Jackson; *D:* James O'Connolly. **VHS, Beta $19.98** *WAR* 𝟚𝟙𝟙

Valley of Terror Maynard is framed for cattle rustling. Can he prove his innocence?
1938 59m/B Kermit Maynard, Rocky the Horse, Harley Wood, John Merton, Jack Ingram, Dick Curtis, Roger Williams; *D:* Al Herman. **VHS, Beta $19.98** *NOS, CCB, DVT* 𝟚𝟙

Valley of the Dolls Camp/trash classic was rated as a bomb by many critics but is really of the so-bad-it's-good variety. Three beauties, Tate, Duke, and Parkins, dream of Hollywood stardom but fall victim to Hollywood excess, including drug dependency (the "dolls" of the title). There's unhappy love affairs, porno parts, health risks, and hysterics of various kinds—all designed to have you dropping your jaw in disbelief. The bathroom scene between Duke and Hayward involving a wig is not to be missed. Based on the novel by Jacqueline Susann who has a bit part as a reporter. Remade for television as "Jacqueline Susann's Valley of the Dolls" in 1981.
1967 (PG) 123m/C Barbara Parkins, Patty Duke, Sharon Tate, Paul Burke, Tony Scotti, Martin Milner, Susan Hayward, Charles Drake, Lee Grant, Alex Davion, Robert Harris, Robert Viharo, Joey Bishop, George Jessel; *Cameos:* Jacqueline Susann; *D:* Mark Robson; *W:* Dorothy

Kingsley, Helen Deutch; *M:* John Williams. **VHS $19.98** *FXV, BTV* 𝟚𝟙

Valley of the Eagles When his wife and partner take off into the Lapland wilderness with his new invention, a scientist leads the police across the tundra in pursuit. Setting is at least a plus.
1951 83m/B Jack Warner, Nadia Gray, John McCallum, Martin Boddeg, Christopher Lee; *D:* Terence Young. **VHS, Beta $39.95** *MSP* 𝟚𝟙½

Valley of the Lawless A cowboy rides into trouble aplenty while out searching for treasure. A routine western for Brown fans only.
1936 59m/B Johnny Mack Brown; *D:* Robert North Bradbury; *W:* Robert North Bradbury. **VHS, Beta** *NO* 𝟙

Valley of the Sun A government agent tracks a crooked Indian liaison to prevent an Indian uprising in Arizona. Ball, well before her "Lucy" days, plays the restaurant owner both men romance. Better than average, with good cast, some laughs, and lots of excitement.
1942 84m/B Lucille Ball, James Craig, Cedric Hardwicke, Dean Jagger, Peter Whitney, Billy Gilbert, Tom Tyler, Antonio Moreno, George Cleveland, Hank Bell; *D:* George Marshall. **VHS, Beta** *RKO, TTC* 𝟚𝟙𝟙

Valley of Wanted Men Three cons escape during a jailbreak and one uses his wits and nerve to prove another was framed.
1935 56m/B Frankie Darro. **VHS, Beta, 8mm $19.95** *VYY* 𝟚𝟙½

Valmont Another adaptation of the Choderlos de Laclos novel "Les Liaisons Dangereuses." Various members of the French aristocracy in 1782 mercilessly play each other for fools in a complex game of lust and deception. Firth and Bening are at first playfully sensual, then the stakes get too high. They share an interesting bathtub scene. Well-acted, the 1988 Frears version, "Dangerous Liaisons," is edgier. Seeing the two films together makes for interesting comparisons of characters and styles.
1989 (R) 137m/C Colin Firth, Meg Tilly, Annette Bening, Fairuza Balk, Sian Phillips, Jeffrey Jones, Fabia Drake, Henry Thomas, Vincent Schiavelli, T.P. McKenna, Ian McNeice; *D:* Milos Forman; *W:* Jean-Claude Carriere; *M:* Christopher Palmer. **VHS, Beta $89.98** *ORI, ING* 𝟚𝟙𝟙

The Vals The glibly hip lethargy which is characteristic of four southern California teenaged girls turns to socially conscious resolve when a local orphanage is threatened. Like, for sure.
1985 (R) 100m/C Jill Carroll, Elana Stratheros, Gina Calabrese, Michelle Laurita, Chuck Connors, Sonny Bono, John Carradine, Michael Leon; *D:* James Polakof. **VHS, Beta $69.98** *LIV, VES* 𝟙½

Vamp Two college freshmen encounter a slew of weird, semi-vampiric people in a seamy red-light district nightclub. Starts cute but goes kinky. Jones is great as the stripping vampire.
1986 (R) 93m/C Grace Jones, Chris Makepeace, Robert Rusler, Gedde Watanabe; *D:* Richard Wenk; *M:* Jonathan Elias. **VHS, Beta $19.95** *NWV, STE* 𝟙½

Vamping Struggling musician plans to burglarize a wealthy widow's home. Once inside, he finds himself attracted to his proposed victim. Tedious going.
1984 (PG) 110m/C Patrick Duffy, Catherine Hyland, Rod Arrants, Fred A. Keller; *D:* Frederick King Keller. **VHS, Beta $59.98** *FOX* 𝟙½

The Vampire Pale man with big teeth attempts to swindle a beautiful babe out of fortune. Followed by "The Vampire's Coffin." *AKA:* Mark of the Vampire.

1957 95m/B Abel Salazar, Ariadne Welter, German Robles, Carmen Montejo, Jose Luis Jimenez; *D:* Fernando Mendez. **VHS $19.90** *SNC* 𝟚𝟙

Vampire at Midnight Fairly stupid homicide detective stalks a rampaging vampire in Los Angeles. Occasional moments of gratitious sex thrown in for good measure.
1988 93m/C Jason Williams, Gustav Vintas, Jeanie Moore, Christina Whitaker, Leslie Milne; *D:* Gregory McClatchy. **VHS, Beta $79.98** *FOX* 𝟙½

The Vampire Bat A mad scientist and a vampire bat and its supernatural demands set the stage for murders in a small town. Sets and actors borrowed from Universal Studios in this low-budget flick that looks and plays better than it should. Weird and very exploitative for 1932, now seems dated.
1932 69m/B Lionel Atwill, Fay Wray, Melvyn Douglas, Dwight Frye, Maude Eburne, George E. Stone; *D:* Frank Strayer. **VHS, Beta $14.95** *VYY, SNC, WFV* 𝟚𝟙½

Vampire Circus A circus appears in an isolated Serbian village in the 19th century but instead of bringing joy and happiness, this circus brings only death, mutilation and misery. It seems all the members are vampires who have the unique ability to transform themselves into animals. They intend to take revenge on the small town, whose inhabitants killed their evil ancestor 100 years previously. Excellent Hammer production.
1971 (R) 84m/C Adrienne Corri, Laurence Payne, Thorley Walters, John Moulder-Brown, Lynne Frederick, Elizabeth Seal, Anthony Corlan, Richard Owens, Domini Blythe, David Prowse; *D:* Robert Young. **VHS $18.00** *FRG, MLB* 𝟚𝟙½

Vampire Cop A vampire cop (not to be confused with zombie, maniac, midnight, psycho, future or Robo) teams up with a beautiful reporter to 'collar' a drug kingpin.
1990 (R) 89m/C Melissa Moore, Ed Cannon, Terence Jenkins. **VHS $79.95** *ATL* 𝟙½

The Vampire Happening An actress discovers to her chagrin that her ancestors were vampires and so is she.
1971 (R) 90m/C Ferdinand "Ferdy" Mayne; *D:* Freddie Francis. **VHS, Beta $24.95** *CNG* 𝟙½

The Vampire Hookers Man in make-up recruits bevy of beautiful bloodsuckers to lure warm blooded victims to his castle. High ham performance by Carradine. Alternate titles: "Cemetery Girls," "Sensuous Vampires," "Night of the Bloodsuckers." *AKA:* Cemetary Girls; Sensuous Vampires; Night of the Bloodsuckers; Twice Bitten.
1978 (R) 82m/C John Carradine, Bruce Fairbairn, Trey Wilson, Karen Stride, Lenka Novak, Katie Dolan, Lex Winter; *D:* Cirio H. Santiago. **VHS, Beta** *NO* 𝟙

The Vampire Lovers An angry father goes after a lesbian vampire who has ravished his daughter and other young girls in a peaceful European village. Innovative story was soon used in countless other vampire vehicles. Hammer Studio's first horror film with nudity, another addition to the genre which spread rapidly. Based on the story "Carmilla" by Sheridan Le Fanu. Followed by, "Lust for a Vampire."
1970 (R) 91m/C Ingrid Pitt, Pippa Steele, Madeleine Smith, Peter Cushing, George Cole, Dawn Addams, Kate O'Mara, Ferdinand "Ferdy" Mayne; *D:* Roy Ward Baker. **VHS, Beta $9.98** *ORI, MLB, SUE* 𝟚𝟙½

The Vampire People A dwarf-assisted vampire attempts to save the life of his true love by transplanting her sister's heart. Typical Filipino vampire movie. In color and sepia-tone. *AKA:* The Blood Drinkers.
1966 (PG) 79m/C Ronald Remy, Amalia Fuentes, Eddie Fernandez, Eva Montez; *D:* Gerardo (Gerry) De Leon. **VHS, Beta $16.95** *SNC* ⅟½

Vampire Raiders—Ninja Queen The white ninjas versus the black ninjas. The evil black ninjas are plotting to infiltrate the hotel industry. The white ninjas come to the rescue.
1989 90m/C Agnes Chan, Chris Petersen; *D:* Bruce Lambert. **VHS $59.95** *TWE* Woof!

The Vampire's Coffin Count Lavud is relieved when faithful servant removes stake implanted in his heart. *AKA:* El Ataud Del Vampiro; El Ataud Del Coffin.
1958 86m/B Abel Salazar, Ariadne Welter, German Robles; *D:* Fernando Mendez. **VHS $19.98** *SNC* ⅟½

The Vampire's Ghost A 400-hundred-year-old vampire/zombie, doomed to walk the earth forever, heads the African underworld. He can't be killed and can even go out during the day if he wears sunglasses. His future's so bright he's just gotta wear shades.
1945 59m/B John Abbott, Peggy Stewart; *D:* Lesley Selander. **VHS $24.95** *NOS, DVT, HEG* ⅟

Vampire's Kiss Cage makes this one worthwhile; his twisted transformation from pretentious post-val dude to psychotic yuppie from hell is inspired. If his demented torment of his secretary (Alonso) doesn't give you the creeps, his scene with the cockroach will. Cage fans will enjoy his facial aerobics; Beals fans will appreciate her extensive sucking scenes (she's the vamp of his dreams). More for psych majors than horror buffs.
1988 (R) 103m/C Nicolas Cage, Elizabeth Ashley, Jennifer Beals, Maria Conchita Alonso, Kasi Lemmons, Bob Lujan, Jennifer Lundy; *D:* Robert Bierman. **VHS, Beta $89.99** *HBO* ⅟⅟⅟

Vampyr Dreyer's classic portrays a hazy, dreamlike world full of chilling visions from the point of view of a young man who believes himself surrounded by vampires and who dreams of his own burial in a most disturbing way. Evil lurks around every corner as camera angles, light and shadow sometimes overwhelm plot. A high point in horror films based on a collection of horror stories by Sheridan le Fanu. In German with English subtitles. *AKA:* Vampyr, Ou L'Etrange Aventure De David Gray; Vampyr, Der Traum Des David Gray; Not Against the Flesh; Castle of Doom; The Strange Adventure of David Gray; The Vampire.
1931 75m/C Julien West, Sybille Schmitz, Harriet Gerard, Maurice Schutz; *D:* Carl Theodor Dreyer; *W:* Carl Theodor Dreyer; *M:* Wolfgang Zeller. **VHS, Beta $24.95** *VYY, NOS, SNC* ⅟⅟⅟⅟

The Vampyr Uncut version of the BBC musical production about a lustful vampire. Text sets present-day lyrics to the 1827 opera by Heinrich Marschner. Vampire Ripley (Ebrahim) has just been set free in London after having been trapped in an underground tomb for 200 years. Unless he puts the bite on three lovely ladies within three days he will be condemned to eternal damnation. Everyone gets to sing in the nude. Surreally amusing.
1992 115m/C Omar Ebrahim, Willemijn Van Gent, Fiona O'Neill, Sally-Ann Shepherdson. **VHS $89.98** *FOX* ⅟⅟

Vampyres Alluring female vampires coerce unsuspecting motorists to their castle for a good time, which ends in death. Anulka was the centerfold girl in Playboy's May 1973 issue. Originally titled "Vampyres, Daughters of Dracula." *AKA:* Vampyres, Daughters of Dracula; Blood Hunger; Satan's Daughters.
1974 (R) 90m/C Marianne Morris, Anulka, Murray Brown, Brian Deacon, Sally Faulkner; *D:* Joseph Larraz. **VHS, Beta** *NO* ⅟⅟½

The Van A recent high school graduate passes on the college scene so he can spend more time picking up girls in his van. A lame sex (and sexist) comedy. *AKA:* Chevy Van.
1977 (R) 92m/C Stuart Getz, Deborah White, Danny DeVito, Harry Moses, Maurice Barkin; *D:* Sam Grossman. **VHS, Beta** *NO* ⅟

Van Gogh "One doesn't produce 100 masterpieces in a state of depression—Van Gogh died from having had a glimpse of happiness." This is the way director Pialat sums up his approach to the last 67 days in the life of Vincent Van Gogh. Dutronc is skillful in portraying Van Gogh as a man with no excuses, and even a sense of humor. Not a psychological portrait and offers no answers—it's simply one artist's view of another. In French with English subtitles.
1992 (R) 155m/C Jacques Dutronc, Alexandra London, Gerard Sety, Bernard LeCoq, Corinne Bourdon; *D:* Maurice Pialat; *W:* Maurice Pialat; *M:* Edith Vesperini. **VHS $94.95** *COL, FCT* ⅟⅟⅟

Van Nuys Blvd. The popular boulevard is the scene where the cool southern California guys converge for cruising and girl watching, so naturally it's where a country hick comes to test his drag racing skills and check out the action.
1979 (R) 93m/C Bill Adler, Cynthia Wood, Dennis Bowen, Melissa Prophet; *D:* William Sachs. **VHS, Beta $9.99** *STE, VCI* ⅟½

Vanina Vanini An acclaimed Rossellini historical drama about the daughter of an Italian aristocrat in 1824 who nurses and falls in love with a wounded patriot hiding in her house. Based on a Stendhal short story. In Italian with English subtitles.
1961 113m/B Sandra Milo, Laurent Terzieff; *D:* Roberto Rossellini. **VHS, Beta $59.95** *FCT, ING* ⅟⅟⅟½

The Vanishing When his wife suddenly disappears, a young husband finds himself becoming increasingly obsessed with finding her. Three years down the road, his world has become one big, mad nightmare. Then, just as suddenly, the answer confronts him, but the reality of it may be too horrible to face. Well-made dark thriller based on "The Golden Egg" by Time Krabbe. In French and Dutch with English subtitles. Remade by Sluizer in 1992. *AKA:* Spoorloos.
1988 107m/C Barnard Pierre Donnadieu, Johanna Ter Steege, Gene Bervoets; *D:* George Sluizer. **VHS $89.95** *FXL, ING* ⅟⅟⅟

The Vanishing Director Sluizer remakes his own 1988 Dutch film "Spoorloos" to lesser effect. Tense thriller about the disappearance of a woman (Bullock) at a highway rest stop. Her boyfriend (Sutherland) becomes obsessed with locating her, searching for some three years as he is haunted by her memory. Unlike the Dutch original, the remake resorts to a clumsy ending designed for feel-good appeal. Based on the novel "The Golden Egg" by Tim Krabbe.
1993 (R) 110m/C Jeff Bridges, Kiefer Sutherland, Nancy Travis, Sandra Bullock, Park Overall, Lisa Eichhorn, George Hearn, Maggie Linderman, Lynn Hamilton; *D:* George Sluizer; *W:* Todd Graff; *M:* Jerry Goldsmith. **VHS $19.98** *FXV* ⅟⅟½

Vanishing Act While on his honeymoon, Harry Kenyon reports his wife missing to the local police. Within a short period of time his wife is found, but Harry says the woman is an impostor. This thriller follows Harry's desperate attempt to get to the truth. Made for television.
1988 (PG) 94m/C Mike Farrell, Margot Kidder, Elliott Gould, Fred Gwynne, Graham Jarvis; *D:* David Greene; *W:* Richard Levinson, William Link. **VHS, Beta $89.95** *VMK* ⅟⅟½

Vanishing American The mistreatment of the American Indian is depicted in this sweeping Western epic. Musical score.
1926 114m/B Richard Dix, Noah Beery Sr.; *D:* George B. Seitz. **VHS, Beta $19.95** *GPV, VYY* ⅟⅟

Vanishing Legion Western serial with outdoor action and gunplay. Twelve chapters, 13 minutes each.
1931 156m/B Frankie Darro, Harry Carey Sr.; *D:* B. Reeves Eason. **VHS, Beta $24.95** *GPV, NOS, VCN* ⅟⅟

Vanishing Point An ex-racer makes a bet to deliver a souped-up car from Denver to San Francisco in 15 hours. Taking pep pills along the way, he eludes police, meets up with a number of characters, and finally crashes into a roadblock. Rock score helps attract this film's cult following.
1971 (PG) 98m/C Barry Newman, Cleavon Little, Gilda Texler, Dean Jagger, Paul Koslo, Robert Donner, Severn Darden, Victoria Medlin; *D:* Richard Sarafian. **VHS, Beta $59.98** *FOX* ⅟⅟

Vanishing Prairie This documentary examines the wonders of nature that abound in the American prairie. From the "True-Life Adventures" series.
1954 60m/C *D:* James Algar. **VHS, Beta $69.95** *DIS* ⅟⅟⅟

The Vanishing Westerner A cowboy, falsely accused of murder, works to vindicate himself and uncovers a series of robberies. This one has enough plot twists to take it out of the routine.
1950 60m/B Monte Hale, Arthur Space, Aline Towne, Paul Hurst, Roy Barcroft, Richard Anderson, William Phipps, Rand Brooks; *D:* Philip Ford. **VHS, Beta $24.95** *DVT* ⅟⅟

Vanishing Wilderness This documentary looks at the wild animals roaming across North America.
1973 (G) 90m/C *D:* Arthur Dubs. **VHS, Beta $9.98** *MED, VTR* ⅟⅟

Vanity Fair Loy stars in this tale of a wily and manipulative woman looking for the perfect marriage. This was the 58th film for the 27-year-old Loy, but even she couldn't save it. Of course, none of the three films based on the story by Thackeray have done it justice.
1932 67m/B Myrna Loy, Conway Tearle, Barbara Kent, Walter Byron, Anthony Bushell, Billy Bevan, Montagu Love, Mary Forbes; *D:* Chester M. Franklin. **VHS $19.95** *NOS, HEG* ⅟⅟

Varan the Unbelievable A chemical experiment near a small island in the Japanese archipelago disturbs a prehistoric monster beneath the water. The awakened monster spreads terror on the island. Most difficult part of this movie is deciding what the rubber monster model is supposed to represent. *AKA:* Daikaiju Baran; The Monster Baran.
1961 70m/B Myron Healey, Tsuruko Kobayashi; *D:* Inoshiro Honda. **VHS, Beta $19.95** *NOS, VCI* ⅟

Varieties on Parade A vaudeville show on film, featuring an array of second-rate comics and musical personalities. Sad to watch its demise.

1952 55m/B Jackie Coogan, Eddie Garr, Tom Neal, Iris Adrian. **VHS, Beta** NO 🐾

Variety Simple and tragic tale of a scheming young girl and the two men of whom she takes advantage. The European circus in all its beautiful sadness is the setting. Extraordinary cast and superb cinematography. Silent.
1925 104m/B Emil Jannings, Lya de Putti, Warwick Ward, Werner Krauss; **D:** E.A. Dupont. **VHS, Beta** $24.95 VYY, NOS, DVT 🐾🐾🐾

Variety A girl takes a job selling tickets in a Times Square porn theater. Her initial loathing for the genre gives way to a fascination with its clients, one of whom is a gangster, and she becomes drawn to the seamy world inside. An independently made feature.
1983 101m/C Sandy McLeod, Will Patton, Richard Davidson; **D:** Bette Gordon. **VHS, Beta** $69.95 MED 🐾🐾½

Variety Lights Fellini's first (albeit joint) directorial effort, wherein a young girl runs away with a travelling vaudeville troupe and soon becomes its main attraction as a dancer. Filled with Fellini's now-familiar delight in the bizarre and sawdust/tinsel entertainment. In Italian with English subtitles. **AKA:** Luci Del Varieta; Lights of Variety.
1951 93m/B Giulietta Masina, Peppino de Filippo, Carla Del Poggio, Folco Lulli; **D:** Federico Fellini, Alberto Lattuada; **W:** Federico Fellini, Tullio Pinelli, Ennio Flaino, Alberto Lattuada. **VHS, Beta** $29.95 CVC, ING, APD 🐾🐾½

Vasectomy: A Delicate Matter A mother of eight issues a final decree to her husband about their sex life. He must get a vasectomy or there won't be any. As good as it sounds. **AKA:** Vasectomy.
1986 (PG-13) 92m/C Paul Sorvino, Abe Vigoda, Cassandra Edwards, Lorne Greene, Ina Balin, June Wilkinson, William Marshall; **D:** Robert Burge. **VHS, Beta** WOV Woof!

Vatican Conspiracy The members of the Vatican's College of Cardinals do everything in their power to discredit a newly-appointed radical pontiff.
1981 90m/C Terence Stamp; **D:** Marcello Aliprandi. **VHS, Beta** NO 🐾½

Vault of Horror A collection of five terrifying tales based on original stories from the E.C. comic books of the 1950s. Stories include, "Midnight Mess," "Bargain in Death," "This Trick'll Kill You," "The Neat Job" and "Drawn and Quartered." **AKA:** Tales from the Crypt II.
1973 (R) 86m/C Terry-Thomas, Curt Jurgens, Glynis Johns, Dawn Addams, Daniel Massey, Tom Baker, Michael Craig, Anna Massey, Denholm Elliott; **D:** Roy Ward Baker; **W:** Milton Subotsky. **VHS, Beta** MED 🐾🐾½

Vegas A private detective, with Las Vegas beauties as assistants and pursuers, solves the murder of a teenage runaway girl. Pilot for television series. Scriptwriter Mann went on to do "Miami Vice."
1978 74m/C Robert Urich, June Allyson, Tony Curtis, Will Sampson, Greg Morris; **D:** Richard Lang; **W:** Michael Mann. **VHS, Beta** $49.95 PSM 🐾

The Vegas Strip Wars Rival casino owners battle it out in the land of lady luck. Unmemorable except for Jones's Don King impersonation and the fact that it was Hudson's last TV movie. **AKA:** Las Vegas Strip War.
1984 100m/C Rock Hudson, James Earl Jones, Noriyuki "Pat" Morita, Sharon Stone, Robert Costanzo; **D:** George Englund. **VHS, Beta** $69.98 LIV 🐾🐾

Velnio Nuotaka A popular Lithuanian musical based on the play "Baltargio Malunas" by K. Boruta. English subtitles. **AKA:** The Devil's Bride.
1975 78m/C VHS, Beta IHF 🐾🐾½

Velvet Smooth A protection agency's sultry boss, Velvet Smooth, gets involved solving the problems of a numbers racket.
1976 (R) 89m/C Johnnie Hill; **D:** Janace Fink. **VHS** NO 🐾

Velvet Touch Well-engineered thriller about an actress who craftily murders her producer. A theater-loving police detective winds up accusing the wrong woman—sending the overwrought murderess into a moral tailspin. Things don't work out as you may expect. Fine acting.
1948 97m/B Rosalind Russell, Leo Genn, Claire Trevor, Sydney Greenstreet, Leon Ames, Frank McHugh, Walter Kingsford, Dan Tobin, Lex Barker, Nydia Westman; **D:** John Gage; **W:** Leo Rosten. **VHS, Beta** RKO, TTC 🐾🐾🐾

The Velvet Vampire Yarnall is a sexy, sun-loving, dune buggy-riding vampiress who seduces a young, sexy, swinging, Southern California couple in her desert home. Lots of atmosphere to go along with the blood and nudity. **AKA:** Cemetary Girls; Through the Looking Glass.
1971 (R) 82m/C Michael Blodgett, Sherry Miles, Celeste Yarnall, Gene Shane, Jerry Daniels, Sandy Ward, Paul Prokop, Chris Woodley, Robert Tessier; **D:** Stephanie Rothman. **VHS, Beta** $9.95 SIM, SUE 🐾🐾

Vendetta A woman gets herself arrested and sent to the penitentiary in order to exact revenge there for her sister's death. Acting and pacing make this better than the average sexploitation flick.
1985 89m/C Karen Chase, Sandy Martin, Durga McBroom, Kin Shriner; **D:** Bruce Logan. **VHS, Beta** $79.98 LIV, VES 🐾½

Vendetta for the Saint A feature-length episode of the television series "The Saint," in which Simon Templar pursues a Sicilian mobster on a personal vendetta.
1968 98m/C Roger Moore; **D:** James O'Connolly. **VHS, Beta** $59.98 FOX 🐾

Vengeance A police officer resigns in shame after failing to thwart a holdup. He attempts to redeem himself by working on his own to infiltrate the same gang.
1937 61m/B Lyle Talbot, Wendy Barrie, Wally Albright, Marc Lawrence; **D:** Del Lord. **VHS** $19.95 VYY, MOV 🐾

Vengeance Four burglars take hostages after their robbery is bungled, but they won't get away—especially after the hostages die.
1980 92m/C Sally Lockett, Nicholas Jacquez, Bob Elliott; **D:** Bob Blizz. **VHS, Beta** NO 🐾

Vengeance A low-budget film about rebels fighting off an authoritarian government.
1986 114m/C Jason Miller, Lea Massari; **D:** Antonio Isasi. **VHS, Beta** $69.95 TWE 🐾

Vengeance A bereaved young man strikes out against the injustice of his parents' murder. His revenge against the killers takes him several steps beyond the law, and he's not so sure it was the right idea. Made for television. **AKA:** Vengeance: The Story of Tony Cimo.
1989 (R) 90m/C Brad Davis, Roxanne Hart, Brad Dourif, William Conrad; **D:** Marc Daniels. **VHS** $39.95 IME 🐾🐾

Vengeance Is Mine Told in flashbacks, the film focuses on the life of a habitual criminal whose life of deprivation leads to murder. Contains violence and nudity. Based on a true story. In Japanese with English subtitles.

1979 129m/C Ken Ogata; **D:** Shohei Imamura. **VHS** $59.95 FCT, ING 🐾🐾½

Vengeance Is Mine A demented farmer captures three criminals and tortures them in horrifyingly sadistic ways. Gratuitously grisly.
1984 (R) 90m/C Ernest Borgnine, Michael J. Pollard, Hollis McLaren; **D:** John Trent. **VHS, Beta** $9.99 VTR, GEM, VYG Woof!

Vengeance of the Snowmaid Some Kung Fu creepies raped her mom. Now nobody can get a sword in edgewise on the Snow Maid as she seeks revenge.
197? 82m/C Mo Ka Kei, Chen Chen. **VHS, Beta** NO 🐾½

Vengeance of the Zombies A madman seeks revenge by setting an army of walking corpses to stalk the streets of London.
1972 90m/C Paul Naschy; **D:** Leon Klimovsky. **VHS, Beta** $19.95 SNC 🐾½

Vengeance Valley Lancaster and Walker are foster brothers with Walker being an envious weasel who always expects Lancaster to get him out of scrapes. Lancaster is even accused of a crime committed by Walker and must work to clear himself. Good cast is let down by uneven direction.
1951 83m/C Burt Lancaster, Joanne Dru, Robert Walker, Sally Forrest, John Ireland, Hugh O'Brian; **D:** Richard Thorpe. **VHS, Beta** $14.95 NOS, DVT, CAB 🐾🐾

Venom Deadly black mamba is loose in an elegant townhouse, terrorizing big-name cast. The snake continually terrorizes an evil kidnapper, his accomplices and his kidnapped victim. Participants walk through tired cliches with that far-away look in their eyes—like they wish they were anywhere else. Original director Tobe Hooper was replaced.
1982 (R) 92m/C Sterling Hayden, Klaus Kinski, Sarah Miles, Nicol Williamson, Cornelia Sharpe, Susan George, Michael Gough, Oliver Reed; **D:** Piers Haggard; **M:** Michael Kamen. **VHS, Beta** $59.95 VES Woof!

Venus Against the Son of Hercules Our hero must use all his genetically procured musculature in his battle against the lovely but deadly Venus.
1962 ?m/C Roger Brown, Jackie Lane. **VHS, Beta** $16.95 SNC Woof!

Venus in Furs Jazz musician working in Rio de Janeiro becomes obsessed with a mysterious woman; she resembles a murder victim whose body he discovered months earlier. Weird mix of horror, sadism, black magic, and soft porn. **AKA:** Paroxismus; Puo Una Morta Rivivere Per Amore?; Venus in Peltz.
1970 (R) 90m/C James Darren, Klaus Kinski, Barbara McNair, Dennis Price, Maria Rohm; **D:** Jess (Jesus) Franco. **VHS, Beta** $39.98 REP, TPV 🐾½

Venus the Ninja A comely female Ninja battles an evil warlord.
198? 90m/C Pearl Cheung, Meng Fei; **D:** Sze Ma Peng. **VHS, Beta** $39.95 TWE 🐾

Vera Cruz Two soldiers of fortune become involved in the Mexican Revolution of 1866, a stolen shipment of gold, divided loyalties, and gun battles. Less than innovative plot is made into an exciting action flick.
1953 94m/C Gary Cooper, Burt Lancaster, Denise Darcel, Cesar Romero, George Macready, Ernest Borgnine, Charles Bronson; **D:** Robert Aldrich. **VHS, Beta** $19.98 MGM, FOX, FCT 🐾🐾½

Verboten! In post-war occupied Berlin, an American G.I. falls in love with a German girl. Good direction maintains a steady pace.

1959 93m/B James Best, Susan Cummings, Tom Pittman, Paul Dubov; **D:** Samuel Fuller. VHS *IME* 🐾🐾½

Verdi The story of the Italian operatic composer and the loves of his life. Dubbed in English.
1953 80m/C Pierre Cressoy. **VHS $29.95** FCT 🐾🐾

The Verdict Newman plays an alcoholic failed attorney reduced to ambulance chasing. A friend gives him a supposedly easy malpractice case which turns out to be a last chance at redeeming himself and his career. Adapted from the novel by Barry Reed. One of Newman's finest performances.
1982 (R) 122m/C Paul Newman, James Mason, Charlotte Rampling, Jack Warden, Milo O'Shea, Lindsay Crouse; **D:** Sidney Lumet; **W:** David Mamet. VHS, Beta **$19.98** FOX 🐾🐾🐾

Verne Miller A film of the true story of Verne Miller, Al Capone's hit man. After rescuing a friend from the Feds, Miller is hunted down by both the cops and the mob.
1988 (R) 95m/C Scott Glenn, Barbara Stock, Thomas G. Waites, Lucinda Jenney, Sonny Carl Davis; **D:** Rob Hewitt. VHS, Beta **$19.98** SUE, NLC 🐾🐾

Vernon, Florida A quixotic, eccentric documentary by Morris dealing simply with the backwater inhabitants of the small Florida town of the title, each speaking openly about his or her slightly strange lifestyle, dreams and life experiences.
1982 72m/C Beta **$79.95** COL 🐾🐾🐾

The Vernonia Incident Urban guerillas invade a small town, killing the police chief. The townspeople gather up their shotguns and fight back. That's entertainment.
1989 95m/C David Jackson, Shawn Stevens, Floyd Ragner, Ed Justice, Robert Louis Jakson; **D:** Ray Etheridge; **W:** Ray Etheridge. VHS, Beta NO 🐾½

Veronico Cruz Despite its sincerity, Pereira's feature debut offers muddled response to the human waste incurred by the Falklands War. Set in a tiny remote village in the Argentinean mountains, the film's narrative is derived from the growing friendship between a shepherd boy and a teacher from the city. Well-meaning anti-war movie. In Spanish with English subtitles. **AKA:** La Dueda Interna; The Debt.
1987 96m/C Juan Jose Camero, Gonzalo Morales, Rene Olaguivel, Guillermo Delgado; **D:** Miguel Pereira. VHS **$79.95** CCN, TPV 🐾🐾½

Veronika Voss Highlights the real life of fallen film star Sybille Schmitz who finally took her own life out of despair. Played by Zech, Voss is exploited by her physician to turn over all of her personal belongings for morphine. A lover discovers the corruption and reveals it to the authorities. This causes great upheaval resulting in Voss' suicide. Highly metaphoric and experimental in its treatment of its subject. In German with English subtitles. **AKA:** Die Sehns Ucht Der Veronika Voss.
1982 (R) 105m/C Rosel Zech, Hilmar Thate, Conny Froboess, Anna Marie Duringer, Volker Spengler; **D:** Rainer Werner Fassbinder; **M:** Peer Raben. VHS **$48.00** APD, FCT, ING 🐾🐾🐾

Vertigo Hitchcock's romantic story of obsession, manipulation and fear. Stewart plays a detective forced to retire after his fear of heights causes the death of a fellow policeman and, perhaps, the death of a woman he'd been hired to follow. The appearance of her double (Novak), whom he compulsively transforms into the dead girl's image, leads to a mesmerizing cycle of

madness and lies. Features Herrmann's haunting music.
1958 (PG) 126m/C James Stewart, Kim Novak, Barbara Bel Geddes, Tom Helmore, Ellen Corby, Henry Jones, Raymond Bailey, Lee Patrick; **D:** Alfred Hitchcock; **W:** Sam Taylor; **M:** Bernard Herrmann. VHS, Beta **$19.95** MCA, TLF 🐾🐾🐾🐾

A Very Brady Christmas Many of the original Bradys returned for this yuletide special. After Mike and Carol's vacation plans go awry, they decide to invite the whole bunch home for a family reunion. This was the highest rated television movie in 1989. Spawned yet another unsuccessful "Brady" series sequel.
1988 94m/C Florence Henderson, Robert Reed, Ann B. Davis, Maureen McCormick, Eve Plumb, Jennifer Runyon, Barry Williams, Christopher Knight, Michael Lookinland, Jerry Houser, Caryn Richman; **D:** Peter Baldwin. VHS **$14.95** PAR 🐾🐾

A Very British Coup McAnally plays Harry Perkins, a former steelworker who gets involved in British politics. Although a left-wing radical, the charismatic Perkins is actually elected Prime Minister. However, his radical policies cause the entrenched government officials to conspire to bring him down. And you thought American politics were dirty! Made for British television.
199? 180m/C Ray McAnally. VHS **$59.95** SIG, TVC, FUS 🐾🐾🐾

Very Close Quarters Thirty people face many trials and tribulations as they share an apartment in Moscow. Interesting cast is wasted in this mostly un-funny flick.
1984 97m/C Shelley Winters, Paul Sorvino, Theodore Bikel, Farley Granger; **D:** Vladmir Rif. VHS, Beta **$69.98** LIV, VES 🐾

A Very Curious Girl A peasant girl realizes she is being used by the male population of her village, and decides to charge them for sex, creating havoc. In French with English subtitles. **AKA:** La Fiancee du Pirate; Dirty Mary; Pirate's Fiancee.
1969 (R) 105m/C Bernadette LaFont, Georges Geret; **D:** Nelly Kaplan. VHS, Beta SUE, OM 🐾🐾½

The Very Edge A pregnant woman suffers a miscarriage after being brutally attacked. The repercussions nearly destroy her marriage until her attacker is caught. A disturbing psycho-drama.
1963 90m/C Anne Heywood, Richard Todd, Jeremy Brett; **D:** Cyril Frankel. VHS, Beta NO 🐾🐾½

A Very Old Man with Enormous Wings An angel, battered during a hurricane, seeks refuge on a tiny Caribbean island. There, two men keep him and charge an increasingly curious world admission to view the creature. A colorful, musical expose of human failings based on a story by Gabriel Garcia Marquez. In Spanish with English subtitles. **AKA:** Un Senor Muy Viejo Con Unas Alas Enormes.
1988 90m/C Daisy Granados, Asdrubal Melendez, Luis Alberto Ramirez, Fernando Birri; **D:** Fernando Birri. VHS **$79.95** FXL, FCT, ING 🐾🐾

A Very Private Affair A movie star finds that she has no privacy from the hordes of fans and paparazzi who flock to her side. The glare of publicity helps to destroy their relationship with a married director, and to fuel her desire for privacy, a desire that ends tragically. An appealing, better-than-average Bardot vehicle, it is nonetheless below-average (early) Malle. In French with English subtitles. **AKA:** La Vie Privee; Vita Privata.
1962 95m/C Marcello Mastroianni, Brigitte Bardot; **D:** Louis Malle. VHS, Beta **$19.98** MGM 🐾🐾½

V.I. Warshawski The filmmakers seem to think they can slum with the oldest cliches in detective shows just as long as the tough gumshoe is a woman. They're wrong. Turner is terrific as the leggy shamus of the title (from a popular series of books by Sara Paretsky), but the plot is nothing special, featuring stock characters in the killing of a pro athlete and a real-estate deal.
1991 (R) 89m/C Kathleen Turner, Jay O. Sanders, Angela Goethals, Charles Durning; **D:** Jeff Kanew; **W:** Nick Thiel; **M:** Randy Edelman. VHS, Beta **$19.99** HPH 🐾🐾

Via Appia Fictional documentary about Frank, a German airline steward who brings a film crew with him when travels back to Rio de Janeiro in search of the street hustler who gave him AIDS. Grim guided tour of the city's gay subculture along the "Via Appia," the Rio district where the male prostitutes hang out. Film is firmly unapologetic for its sexual explicitness and lack of moralizing. In German and Portuguese with English subtitles.
1992 90m/C Peter Senner, Guilherme de Padua, Yves Jansen, Margarita Schmidt, Luiz Kleber; **D:** Jochen Hick; **W:** Jochen Hick. VHS **$49.99** MOV, FCT 🐾🐾

Vibes Two screwball psychics are sent on a wild goose chase through the Ecuadorean Andes in search of cosmic power and, of course, fall in love. Flat offering from the usually successful team of writers, Lowell Ganz and Babaloo Mandel ("Splash" and "Night Shift"). Lauper's first starring role (and so far, her last).
1988 (PG) 99m/C Jeff Goldblum, Cyndi Lauper, Julian Sands, Googy Gress, Peter Falk, Elizabeth Pena; **D:** Ken Kwapis; **W:** Babaloo Mandel, Lowell Ganz; **M:** James Horner. VHS, Beta **$89.95** COL 🐾

Vice Academy Two females join the Hollywood vice squad. Allen was a former porn queen.
1988 (R) 90m/C Linnea Quigley, Ginger Lynn Allen, Karen Russell, Jayne Hamil, Ken Abraham, Stephen Steward, Jeannie Carol; **D:** Rick Sloane. VHS, Beta **$79.95** PSM 🐾½

Vice Academy 2 Two vice cop babes try to stop a female crime boss from dumping aphrodisiacs in the city's water supply.
1990 (R) 90m/C Linnea Quigley, Ginger Lynn Allen, Jayne Hamil, Scott Layne, Jay Richardson, Joe Brewer, Marina Benvenga, Teagan Clive; **D:** Rick Sloane. VHS, Beta **$29.95** PSM 🐾

Vice Academy 3 The worst of the series, and not just because cult actress Linnea Quigley is absent. Wit, pacing and even sets are nonexistent as the girls battle a toxic villainess called Malathion.
1991 (R) 88m/C Ginger Lynn Allen, Elizabeth Kaitan, Julia Parton, Jay Richardson, Johanna Grika, Steve Mateo; **D:** Rick Sloane; **W:** Rick Sloane. VHS, Beta **$79.95** PSM Woof!

Vice Squad Lukas is forced to turn police informer to save his own neck, which almost ruins him. Just when he thinks he's free of the cops they come back threatening the woman he loves unless he plays stoolie again. Rather flat, but the different cop/criminal angle makes for some unusual twists.
1931 80m/B Paul Lukas, Kay Francis, Helen Johnson, William B. Davidson, Esther Howard; **D:** John Cromwell. VHS, Beta **$19.98** SUE 🐾🐾

Vice Squad Violent and twisted killer-pimp goes on a murderous rampage, and a hooker helps a vice squad plainclothesman trap him. Sleazy and disturbing, with little to recommend it.
1982 (R) 97m/C Wings Hauser, Season Hubley, Gary Swanson, Cheryl "Rainbeaux" Smith; **D:** Gary Sherman; **W:** Robert Vincent O'Neil. VHS, Beta **$19.98** SUE, NLC Woof!

Vice Versa Another 80s comedy about a workaholic father and his 11-year-old son who switch bodies, with predictable slapstick results. Reinhold and Savage carry this, appearing to have a great time in spite of over-done story.
1988 (PG) 97m/C Judge Reinhold, Fred Savage, Swoosie Kurtz, David Proval, Corinne Bohrer, Jane Kaczmarek, William Prince, Gloria Gifford; **D:** Brian Gilbert; **W:** Dick Clement, Ian LaFrenais; **M:** David Shire. VHS, Beta $14.95 COL 𝕚𝕚𝕚

Vicious A bored young woman falls in with people your mother warned you about and soon their high school hi-jinks turn into murder. Graphic violence.
1988 88m/C Tamblyn Lord, Craig Pearce, Tiffany Dowe; **D:** Karl Zwicky. VHS NO 𝕚

The Vicious Circle A prominent London physician becomes involved in murder and an international crime ring when he agrees to perform an errand for a friend. Good performances and tight pacing. *AKA:* The Circle.
1957 84m/B John Mills, Wilfrid Hyde-White, Rene Ray, Lionel Jeffries, Noelle Middleton; **D:** Gerald Thomas. VHS, Beta NO 𝕚𝕚½

Victim A successful married English barrister (Bogarde) with a hidden history of homosexuality is threatened by blackmail after the death of his ex-lover. When the blackmailers, who are responsible for his lover's suicide, are caught, Bogarde decides to prosecute them himself, even though it means revealing his hidden past. One of the first films to deal straightforwardly with homosexuality. Fine performances.
1962 100m/C Dirk Bogarde, Sylvia Syms, Dennis Price, Peter McEnery; **D:** Basil Dearden. VHS, Beta $19.95 SUE 𝕚𝕚𝕚½

The Victim Chan Wing meets up with Master Leung and decides to become his follower. Intent on impressing the master, Chan proves an inept chopsocker.
19?? 90m/C Samo Hung. VHS, Beta $24.50 OCE 𝕚𝕚

Victim of Beauty A small-town girl comes to the big city and becomes a successful model. However, she then becomes the victim of a fatal attraction killer as all her would-be suitors get killed off one by one. Made for cable television.
1991 90m/C Jennifer Rubin, Sally Kellerman, Stephen Shellan, Peter Outerbridge; *Cameos:* Michael Ironside; **D:** Paul Lynch. VHS $89.95 WOV, PMS 𝕚𝕚

Victim of Love A therapist doesn't know whom to believe when she finds out she and one of her more neurotic patients are sharing the same boyfriend. Only the patient claims the man murdered his wife to be with his lover. Who will be the next victim? Made for television.
1991 (PG-13) 92m/C Pierce Brosnan, JoBeth Williams, Virginia Madsen, Georgia Brown; **D:** Jerry London. VHS, Beta $19.95 ACA 𝕚𝕚

Victimless Crimes The seemingly victimless crime of robbing art galleries turns deadly when betrayal and murder enter the picture.
1990 (R) 85m/C Debra Sandlund, Craig Bierko, Larry Brandenburg, Peggy Dunne, Richard Redlin, Cheryl Lynn Bruce; **D:** Peter Hawley. VHS NO 𝕚

Victims Four young women head out for a weekend in the country not realizing that a host of freaks await them.
19?? 85m/C VHS NO 𝕚½

Victor/Victoria An unsuccessful actress in Depression-era Paris impersonates a man impersonating a woman and becomes a star. Luscious music and sets. Warren as femme fatale and Preston as Andrews' gay mentor are right on target; Garner is charming as the gangster who falls for the woman he thinks she is. ♫You and Me; The Shady Dame from Seville; Le Jazz Hot; Crazy World; Chicago Illinois; Gay Peree.
1982 (PG) 133m/C Julie Andrews, James Garner, Robert Preston, Lesley Ann Warren, Alex Karras, John Rhys-Davies; **D:** Blake Edwards; **W:** Blake Edwards; **M:** Henry Mancini. Academy Awards '82: Best Score; Nominations: Best Actress (Andrews), Best Adapted Screenplay, Best Art Direction/Set Decoration, Best Costume Design, Best Supporting Actor (Preston), Best Supporting Actress (Warren); Cesar Awards '83: Best Foreign Film; Golden Globe Awards '83: Best Actress—Musical/Comedy (Andrews). VHS, Beta $19.95 MGM 𝕚𝕚𝕚

Victoria Regina In a succession of vignettes, the life of Queen Victoria is viewed, from her ascension to the throne of England in 1837 through the celebration of her Diamond Jubilee. A presentation from "George Schaefer's Showcase Theatre." Made for television.
1961 76m/C Julie Harris, James Donald, Felix Aylmer, Pamela Brown, Basil Rathbone; **D:** George Schaefer. VHS, Beta FHS 𝕚𝕚

Victory Soccer match between WWII American prisoners of war and a German team is set up so that the players can escape through the sewer tunnels of Paris. Of course they want to finish the game first. Not particularly believable as either a soccer flick (even with Pele and other soccer stars) or a great escape, but watchable.
1981 (PG) 116m/C Sylvester Stallone, Michael Caine, Max von Sydow, Pele, Carole Laure, Bobby Moore, Daniel Massey; **D:** John Huston; **W:** Jeff Maguire, Djordje Milicevic; **M:** Bill Conti. VHS, Beta $19.98 FOX, WAR 𝕚𝕚½

The Victory In 1967 Montreal, an American college exchange student falls in love with a French-Canadian co-ed. Can love survive their different cultures?
1988 (PG) 95m/C Vincent Van Patten, Cloris Leachman, Eddie Albert, Claire Pimpare, Nicholas Campbell, Jack Wetherall, Jacques Godin, Marthe Mercure; **D:** Larry Kent. VHS, Beta $9.99 PSM 𝕚𝕚

Video Americana A collection of seven video shorts by various avant-garde artists depicting the absurdities of modern life.
1985 60m/C VHS, Beta NO 𝕚𝕚

Video Baby The joys and frustrations of parenting a video child can be yours without the mess, expense or longterm responsibility. Watch baby laugh, cry and sleep on command.
1989 13m/C VHS, Beta $9.98 LIV 𝕚

The Video Dead Gore-farce in which murderous zombies emerge from a possessed television and wreak havoc.
1987 (R) 90m/C Roxanna Augesen, Rocky Duvall, Michael St. Michaels; **D:** Robert Scott. VHS, Beta $19.98 SUE, NLC Woof!

Video Murders A police detective tracks down a rapist/murderer who tapes all his own crimes.
1987 90m/C Eric Brown, Virginia Loridans, John Ferita. VHS, Beta $19.98 TWE 𝕚

Video Violence A gory spoof about a video store owner who discovers that his customers have grown bored with the usual Hollywood horror movies and decide to shoot some flicks of their own. Followed by a sequel.
1987 90m/C Art Neill, Jackie Neill, William Toddie, Bart Sumner; **D:** Gary P. Cohen. VHS, Beta NO 𝕚

Video Violence Part 2...The Exploitation! Two sickos named Howard and Eli run a cable television network where talk show guests are spindled and mutilated.
1987 90m/C Uke, Bart Sumner, Lee Miller; **D:** Gary P. Cohen. VHS, Beta NO 𝕚

Video Wars Video games explode randomly. A wicked computer whiz is behind it all in a blackmail scheme.
1984 90m/C George Diamond. VHS $19.99 BFV Woof!

Videodrome Woods is a cable TV programmer with a secret yen for sex and violence, which he satisfies by watching a pirated TV show. "Videodrome" appears to show actual torture and murder, and also seems to control the thoughts of its viewers—turning them into human VCRs. Cronenberg's usual sick fantasies are definitely love 'em or leave 'em. Special effects by Rick Baker.
1983 87m/C James Woods, Deborah Harry, Sonja Smits, Peter Dvorsky; **D:** David Cronenberg; **W:** David Cronenberg. VHS, Beta $19.95 MCA 𝕚𝕚

Vietnam: Chronicle of a War Drawing upon the resources of the CBS News archives, this CBS News Collectors Series program presents a retrospective portrait of American military involvement as witnessed by on-the-scene correspondents and camera crews. Some portions are in black-and-white.
1981 88m/C VHS, Beta $49.98 FOX, KUI 𝕚𝕚

Vietnam, Texas Vietnam vet leaves his past to become a priest. But he returns to violence when he discovers that his Vietnamese daughter is in the hands of Houston's most relentless gangster.
1990 (R) 101m/C Robert Ginty, Haing S. Ngor, Tamlyn Tomita, Tim Thomerson; **D:** Robert Ginty; **W:** C. Courtney Joyner. VHS, Beta $89.95 COL 𝕚

Vietnam War Story 1 Three hard-hitting Vietnam War stories on tape. "The Mine," "Home," and "The Pass." Each is an intimate account straight from the men who lived them. Poignant and action-packed. Made for television.
1988 87m/C Eriq La Salle, Nicholas Cascone, David Harris, Tom Fridley. VHS NO 𝕚

Vietnam War Story 2 Three short, made-for-television war stories set in Vietnam: "An Old Ghost Walks the Earth," "R & R," and "The Fragging."
1988 90m/C Tim Guinee, Tate Donovan, Cynthia Bain, Wesley Snipes, David Niedorf. VHS, Beta NO 𝕚

Vietnam War Story 3 Three episodes of the television series: "Separated," "Dusk to Dawn" and "The Promise."
1989 90m/C Tom Hodges, Todd Graff, Gregory Cooke, Francois Chau, Stacy Edwards, Laura Harrington, Raymond Cruz. VHS, Beta NO 𝕚

A View to a Kill This James Bond mission takes him to the United States, where he must stop the evil Max Zorin from destroying California's Silicon Valley. Feeble and unexciting plot with unscary villain. Duran Duran performs the catchy title tune. Moore's last appearance as 007.
1985 (PG) 131m/C Roger Moore, Christopher Walken, Tanya Roberts, Grace Jones, Patrick Macnee, Lois Maxwell, Desmond Llewelyn; **D:** John Glen; **W:** Michael G. Wilson; **M:** John Barry. VHS, Beta $19.98 FOX, TLF 𝕚𝕚

Vigil A stark, dreamy parable about a young girl, living on a primitive farm in a remote New Zealand valley, who watches her family collapse after a stranger enters their territory. Visually ravishing and grim; Ward's first American import. Predecessor to "The Navigator."
1984 90m/C Penelope Stewart, Bill Kerr, Fiona Kay, Gordon Shields, Frank Whitten; *D:* Vincent Ward; *W:* Vincent Ward. **VHS, Beta** $79.95 *PSM* 🎬🎬🎬

Vigilante Frustrated ex-cop, tired of seeing criminals returned to the street, joins a vigilante squad dedicated to law and order. Often ridiculous and heavy handed. *AKA:* Street Gang.
1983 (R) 91m/C Carol Lynley, Robert Forster, Rutanya Alda; *D:* William Lustig. **VHS, Beta** $79.98 *LIV, VES* **Woof!**

The Vigilantes are Coming "The Eagle" sets out to avenge his family and upsets a would-be dictator's plot to establish an empire in California. In twelve chapters; the first is 32 minutes, and additional chapters are 18 minutes each.
1936 230m/B Bob Livingston, Kay Hughes, Guinn Williams, Raymond Hatton, William Farnum; *D:* Mack V. Wright, Ray Taylor. **VHS, Beta** $49.95 *NOS, VCN, MED* 🎬🎬

Vigilantes of Boom Town A championship prize fight is the cover for a bank robbery which must be foiled by Red Ryder.
1946 54m/B Allan "Rocky" Lane, Robert (Bobby) Blake, Peggy Stewart, Martha Wentworth, Roscoe Karns, Roy Barcroft, George Turner, John Dehner; *D:* R.G. Springsteen. **VHS, Beta** $9.99 *NOS, VCN, MED* 🎬½

Viking Massacre Brutal ax-bearing Vikings ruin the days of hundreds in this primitive story of courage and desperation. John Hold is the pseudonym for director Mario Bava. *AKA:* Knives of the Avenger; I Coltelli Del Vendicatore.
197? 90m/C Cameron Mitchell; *D:* John Hold. **VHS, Beta** *NO* 🎬½

The Vikings A Viking king and his son kidnap a Welsh princess and hold her for ransom. Depicts the Vikings' invasion of England. Great location footage of both Norway and Brittany. Basic costume epic with good action scenes. Narrated by Welles.
1958 116m/C Kirk Douglas, Ernest Borgnine, Janet Leigh, Tony Curtis, James Donald, Alexander Knox; *D:* Richard Fleischer; *W:* Calder Willingham. **VHS, Beta** $19.98 *MGM* 🎬🎬½

Villa Rides A flying gun-runner aids Francisco "Pancho" Villa's revolutionary Mexican campaign. Considering the talent involved, this one is a disappointment. Check out Brynner's hair.
1968 125m/C Yul Brynner, Robert Mitchum, Charles Bronson, Herbert Lom, Jill Ireland, Robert Towne; *D:* Buzz Kulik; *W:* Robert Towne, Sam Peckinpah; *M:* Maurice Jarre. **VHS, Beta** $19.95 *BAR* 🎬🎬

Village of the Damned A group of unusual children are born in a small English village. They avoid their fathers and other men, except for the one who is their teacher. He discovers they are the vanguard of an alien invasion and leads the counter-attack. Exciting and bone-chilling low-budget thriller. From the novel, "The Midwich Cuckoos," by John Wyndham. The sequel, "The Children of the Damned" (1964) is even better.
1960 78m/B George Sanders, Barbara Shelley, Martin Stephens, Laurence Naismith, Michael C. Goetz; *D:* Wolf Rilla; *W:* Sterling Silliphant. **VHS, Beta** $14.95 *MGM, MLB* 🎬🎬🎬

Village of the Giants A group of beer-guzzling teenagers become giants after eating a mysterious substance invented by a twelve-year-old genius. Fun to pick out all the soon-to-be stars. Totally silly premise with bad special effects and minimal plot follow-through. Based on an H.G. Wells story.
1965 82m/C Ron Howard, Johnny Crawford, Tommy Kirk, Beau Bridges, Freddy Cannon, Beau Brummel; *D:* Bert I. Gordon; *M:* Jack Nitzsche. **VHS, Beta** $19.95 *NLC, MLB, SUE* 🎬

The Villain An unfunny spoof of "B" westerns that is almost like a live-action "Roadrunner" cartoon. Douglas plays Cactus Jack, a highwayman who keeps trying to kidnap fair damsel Ann-Margret. Hero Schwarzenegger keeps rescuing her. Lynde is amusing as the uptight Indian chief Nervous Elk. *AKA:* Cactus Jack.
1979 (PG) 93m/C Kirk Douglas, Ann-Margret, Arnold Schwarzenegger, Paul Lynde, Foster Brooks, Ruth Buzzi, Jack Elam, Strother Martin, Robert Tessier, Mel Tillis; *D:* Hal Needham. **VHS** $14.95 *COL* 🎬½

The Villain Still Pursued Her A poor hero and rich villain vie for the sweet heroine in this satire of old-fashioned temperance melodrama. Keaton manages to shine as the hero's sidekick.
1941 67m/B Anita Louise, Alan Mowbray, Buster Keaton, Hugh Herbert; *D:* Eddie Cline. **VHS, Beta** $19.95 *NOS, VYY, DVT* 🎬🎬

Vincent & Theo The story of Impressionist painter Vincent van Gogh, and his brother Theo, a gallery owner who loved his brother's work, yet could not get the public to buy it. Increasing despair and mental illness traps both men, as each struggles to create beauty in a world where it has no value. Altman has created a stunning portrait of "the artist" and his needs. The exquisite cinematography will make you feel as if you stepped into van Gogh's work.
1990 (PG-13) 138m/C Tim Roth, Paul Rhys, Johanna Ter Steege, Wladimir Yordanoff; *D:* Robert Altman. **VHS, Beta** $19.95 *ING, TVC* 🎬🎬🎬½

Vincent, Francois, Paul and the Others Three middle-aged Frenchmen rely on their friendships to endure a host of mid-life crises. In French with English subtitles.
1976 113m/C Yves Montand, Gerard Depardieu, Michel Piccoli, Stephane Audran; *D:* Claude Sautet. **VHS, Beta** $79.95 *FCT, ING, CVC* 🎬🎬🎬

Vincent: The Life and Death of Vincent van Gogh Van Gogh's work and creativity is examined in a documentary manner through his life and his letters. Thoughtful and intriguing production. Narrated by John Hurt as van Gogh.
1987 99m/C *D:* Paul Cox; *W:* Paul Cox; *M:* Norman Kaye; *V:* John Hurt. **VHS** $89.95 *FCT, SIG, TVC* 🎬🎬🎬

The Vindicator A scientist killed in a lab accident is transformed into a cyborg who runs amok and murders indiscriminately. A modernized Frankenstein, with interesting special effects and well drawn characters. *AKA:* Frankenstein '88.
1985 (R) 92m/C Terri Austin, Richard Cox, David McIlwraith, Pam Grier; *D:* Jean-Claude Lord. **VHS, Beta** $79.98 *FOX* 🎬

The Vineyard Hapless victims are lured to a Japanese madman's island, where he drinks their blood and maintains a questionable immortality.
1989 (R) 95m/C James Hong, Karen Witter, Michael Wong; *D:* James Hong, Bill Rice. **VHS, Beta** $19.95 *STE, NWV* 🎬

Violated Pathetic production about New York police attempting to track down a sex-maniac murderer who slays his victims and then gives them a haircut. Unbelievably bad.
1953 78m/B Wim Holland, Lili Dawn, Mitchell Kowal, Vicki Carlson, William Martel; *D:* Walter Strate. **VHS** $16.95 *SNC* 🎬

Violated A detective endeavors to implicate a local businessman in the rapes of two beautiful women. Exploitative and dreary.
1984 88m/C John Heard, J.C. Quinn, April Daisy White, Samantha Fox; *D:* Richard Cannistraro. **VHS, Beta** $69.98 *LIV, VES* **Woof!**

Violence at Noon Highly disturbing film in which two women protect a brutal sex murderer from the law. Living among a quiet community of intellectuals, this conspiracy ends in a shocking finale in Oshima's stylized masterpiece. In Japanese with English subtitles.
1966 99m/B Saeda Kawaguchi, Akiko Koyama; *D:* Nagisa Oshima. **VHS** $79.95 *KIV, ING* 🎬🎬🎬

Violent Blood Bath Justice takes on a terrifying new meaning. A grisly death romp occurs after one judge becomes a bit too interested by his own most despicable cases. He sheds his robe to try a life of crime on for size.
19?? 91m/C Fernando Rey. **VHS** *NO* 🎬🎬🎬

Violent Breed A CIA operative is sent on a mission to put a black marketeer out of business.
1983 91m/C Henry Silva, Harrison Muller, Woody Strode; *D:* Fernando Di Leo. **VHS, Beta** $59.95 *MGM* 🎬

The Violent Men Big-time land baron Robinson is trying to push out all other landowners in the valley, including Ford. At first Ford refuses to fight back, but after one of Robinson's henchmen kills one of his hired hands, he starts an all-out war against Robinson to save his land. Stanwyck as Robinson's wife and Keith as his brother are wicked as the two urging him on and having an affair behind his back. Based on the novel "Rough Company" by Donald Hamilton. *AKA:* Rough Company.
1955 95m/C Glenn Ford, Barbara Stanwyck, Edward G. Robinson, Dianne Foster, Brian Keith, May Wynn; *D:* Rudolph Mate. **VHS** $19.95 *COL* 🎬🎬½

Violent Ones Three men who are suspected of raping a young girl are threatened with lynching by an angry mob of townspeople. Badly acted, poorly directed, uneven and feeble.
1968 96m/C Fernando Lamas, David Carradine; *D:* Fernando Lamas. **VHS, Beta** *REP* **Woof!**

Violent Professionals Suspended cop runs into resistance inside and outside the force when he infiltrates the mob to get the goods on a crime boss.
1982 100m/C Richard Conte, Luc Merenda; *D:* Sergio Martino. **VHS, Beta** *NO* 🎬½

Violent Women Five female convicts escape and embark on a bloody journey through the countryside, pursued by the authorities. Shows women can be just as brutal as any man.
1959 61m/C Jennifer Slater, Jo Ann Kelly, Sandy Lyn, Eleanor Blair, Pati Magee; *D:* Barry Mahon. **VHS, Beta** $29.95 *VMK* 🎬

The Violent Years Spoiled high-school debutantes form a vicious all-girl gang and embark on a spree that includes murder, robbery, and male rape. Justice wins out in the end. Exploitive trash written by Wood, who directed the infamous "Plan 9 from Outer Space." *AKA:* Female.

1956 60m/B Jean Moorehead, Barbara Weeks, Glenn Corbett; **D:** Edward D. Wood Jr., Franz Eichorn; **W:** Edward D. Wood Jr. **VHS, Beta** $16.95 SNC, RHI, AOV Woof!

Violent Zone Mercenaries go on a supposed rescue mission in the wilderness. 1989 92m/C John Douglas, Chad Hayward, Christopher Weeks; **D:** John Garwood; **W:** David Pritchard. **VHS** $14.95 HMD ⅃

Violets Are Blue Two high-school sweethearts are reunited in their hometown years later and try to rekindle their romance—even though the man is married. 1986 (PG-13) 86m/C Kevin Kline, Sissy Spacek, Bonnie Bedelia, John Kellogg, Augusta Dabney, Jim Standford; **D:** Jack Fisk; **W:** Naomi Foner; **M:** Patrick Williams. **VHS, Beta** $79.95 COL ⅃⅃½

Violette Fascinating true-life account of a nineteen-year-old French girl in the 1930s who, bored with her life and wanting to be with her lover, decides to poison her parents so she can receive her inheritance. Her mother survives but her father dies, and the girl is sent to prison for murder. Extraordinary performance by Huppert and the film is visually stunning. **AKA:** Violette Noziere. 1978 (R) 122m/C Isabelle Huppert, Stephane Audran, Jean Carmet, Jean Francoise, Bernadette LaFont; **D:** Claude Chabrol. Cannes Film Festival Nominations: cs 78: Best Film; Cannes Film Festival '78: Best Actress (Huppert); Cesar Awards '79: Best Supporting Actress (Audran). **VHS** NYF ⅃⅃⅃

Vip, My Brother Superman The Vips are modern-day descendants of superbeings about to become legends in their own times. SuperVip is broad of chest and pure in spirit while his brother MiniVip possesses only limited powers. From the creator of "Allegro Non Troppo" comes this enticing, amusing piece of animation. 1990 90m/C **D:** Bruno Bozzetto. **VHS** $59.95 EXP, TPV ⅃⅃⅃

Viper A woman battles a cryptic anti-terrorist band to avenge the murder of her husband. 1988 96m/C Linda Purl, Chris Robinson, James Tolkan; **D:** Peter Maris. **VHS** $29.95 FRH ⅃

The V.I.P.'s Slick, sophisticated drama set in the V.I.P. lounge of a British airport. Trapped by fog, several of the passengers get acquainted and are forced to face their problems as they spend the night in the airport lounge. Taylor stars as Frances Andros, a wealthy young woman leaving her husband (Burton) for life in the U.S. with her lover, Jourdan. A movie tycoon, an Australian entrepreneur, his secretary, and a duchess are among the other passengers grounded by the fog. Both Rutherford and Smith give excellent performances and it was a tossup as to which actress would be nominated for the Oscar. 1963 119m/C Elizabeth Taylor, Richard Burton, Louis Jourdan, Elsa Martinelli, Margaret Rutherford, Dame Maggie Smith, Rod Taylor, Orson Welles, Linda Christian, Dennis Price; **D:** Anthony Asquith; **W:** Terence Rattigan. **VHS** $19.98 MGM ⅃⅃⅃

Virgin Among the Living Dead Young woman travels to remote castle when she hears of relative's death. Once there, she finds the residents a tad weird and has bad dreams in which zombies chase her. Bizarre even for Franco, who seems to have been going through a "Pasolini" phase while making this one. 1971 (R) 90m/C Christina von Blanc, Britt Nichols, Howard Vernon, Anne Libert, Rose Kiekenis, Paul Muller; **D:** Jess (Jesus) Franco. **VHS, Beta** NO ⅃

The Virgin and the Gypsy An English girl brought up in a repressive household in 1920s England falls in love with a gypsy. Based on the novel by D.H. Lawrence. Directorial debut of Miles. 1970 (R) 92m/C Joanna Shimkus, Franco Nero, Honor Blackman, Mark Burns; **D:** Christopher Miles; **W:** Alan Plater. **VHS** NO ⅃⅃½

Virgin High Three young men sneak into an all-girls Catholic boarding school with hilarious consequences. Ward (TV's Robin, from "Batman") makes a special appearance in bondage in this sex farce. 1990 (R) 90m/C Burt Ward, Linnea Quigley, Tracy Dali, Richard Gabai, Catherine McGuiness, Chris Dempsey; **D:** Richard Gabai; **W:** Richard Gabai, Jeff Neal. **VHS** $79.95 COL ⅃

The Virgin of Nuremberg A young woman enters her new husband's ancestral castle and is stalked by the specter of a legendary sadist. **AKA:** Horror Castle; Terror Castle; Castle of Terror; La Vergine de Norimberga. 1965 82m/C Rossana Podesta, George Riviere, Christopher Lee, Jim Dolen; **D:** Anthony M. (Antonio Margheriti) Dawson. **VHS, Beta** MOV ⅃½

The Virgin Queen Davis stars in this historical drama, which focuses on the stormy relationship between the aging Queen and Sir Walter Raleigh. Collins is the lady-in-waiting who is the secret object of Raleigh's true affections. Previously, Davis played Queen Elizabeth I in "Elizabeth and Essex." Davis holds things together. 1955 92m/C Bette Davis, Richard Todd, Joan Collins, Herbert Marshall, Dan O'Herlihy, Jay Robinson, Romney Brent; **D:** Henry Koster. **VHS, Beta** $19.98 FOX ⅃⅃⅃

Virgin Queen of St. Francis High Two high school foes make a bet that one of them can take the "virgin" title away from gorgeous Christensen by summer's end. She has to fight off their advances, but grows to like Straface. 1988 (PG) 89m/C Joseph R. Straface, Stacy Christensen, J.T. Wotton; **D:** Francesco Lucente. **VHS, Beta** $79.95 MED ⅃

Virgin Sacrifice A great white hunter looking for zoo-bound jaguars confronts the virgin-sacrificing, Tiger God-revering natives of Guatemala. 1959 67m/C David Dalie, Antonio Gutierrez, Angelica Morales, Fernando Wagner; **D:** Fernando Wagner. **VHS, Beta** NO ⅃

The Virgin Soldiers A British comedy about greenhorn military recruits stationed in Singapore, innocent of women as well as battle, and their struggles to overcome both situations. A good cast raises this above the usual low-brow sex farce. Based on the novel by Leslie Thomas. Followed by "Stand Up Virgin Soldiers." 1969 (R) 96m/C Hywel Bennett, Nigel Davenport, Lynn Redgrave, Nigel Patrick, Rachel Kempson, Jack Shepherd, Tsai Chin; **D:** John Dexter; **W:** John Hopkins. **VHS, Beta** $69.95 COL ⅃⅃½

The Virgin Spring Based on a medieval ballad and set in 14th-century Sweden. The rape and murder of a young innocent spurs her father to vengeance and he kills her attackers. Over the girl's dead body, the father questions how God could have let any of it happen, but he comes to find solace and forgiveness. Stunning Bergman compositions. In Swedish with English subtitles; also available in dubbed version. **AKA:** Jungfrukallan. 1959 88m/B Max von Sydow, Brigitta Valberg, Gunnel Lindblom, Brigitta Pattersson, Axel Duborg; **D:** Ingmar Bergman. Academy Awards '60: Best Foreign Language Film; Nominations: Best Costume Design (B & W); Golden Globe Awards '61: Best Foreign Film. **VHS, Beta** $29.98 SUE, ING ⅃⅃⅃½

The Virgin Witch Two beautiful sisters are sent to the British countryside, ostensibly for a modeling job. They soon find themselves in the midst of a witches' coven however, and discover one of them is to be sacrificed. The Michelles were "Playboy" magazine's first sister centerfolds. **AKA:** Lesbian Twins. 1970 (R) 89m/C Anne Michelle, Vicki Michelle, Patricia Haines, Keith Buckley, James Chase, Neil Hallett; **D:** Ray Austin. **VHS, Beta** $59.95 PSM ⅃½

Virginia City Action-packed western drama set during the Civil War. Flynn is a Union soldier who escapes from a Confederate prison run by Scott, after learning of a gold shipment being sent by Southern sympathizers to aid the Confederacy. He ends up in Virginia City (where the gold-laden wagon train is to leave from) and falls for a dance-hall girl (Hopkins) who turns out to be a Southern spy working for Scott but who falls for Flynn anyway. Bogart is miscast as a half-breed outlaw who aids Scott but wants the gold for himself. Considered a follow-up to "Dodge City." 1940 121m/C Errol Flynn, Miriam Hopkins, Randolph Scott, Humphrey Bogart, Frank McHugh, Alan Hale, Guinn Williams, Douglass Dumbrille, Charles Halton; **D:** Michael Curtiz. **VHS** $19.98 MGM ⅃⅃⅃

The Virginia Hill Story Fictionalized biography of mobster Bugsy Siegel's girlfriend who, in the mid-fifties, was subpoenaed to appear before the Kefauver investigation on crime in the U.S. As the examining lawyer presents questions regarding her background and connections with the underworld, we see the story of her life. Made for television. 1976 90m/C Dyan Cannon, Harvey Keitel, Robby Benson, Allen (Gooritz) Garfield, John Vernon; **D:** Joel Schumacher. **VHS, Beta** NO ⅃⅃

The Virginian The second silent version of Owen Wister's classic western novel, inferior to both the 1914 Cecil B. DeMille silent and the 1929 Victor Fleming talkie. Harlan plays the title role as the cowpoke who leads a posse against cattle rustlers and falls in love with a schoolteacher. 1923 79m/B Kenneth Harlan, Florence Vidor, Russell Simpson, Pat O'Malley, Raymond Hatton; **D:** Tom Forman. **VHS** GPV ⅃⅃½

The Virginian A classic early-talkie western about a ranch-hand defeating the local bad guys. One line of dialogue has become, with modification, a standard western cliche: "If you want to call me that, smile." Based on the novel by Owen Wister. With this starring role, Cooper broke away from the juvenile lovers he had been playing to the laconic, rugged male leads he would be known for. Huston is perfectly cast as the outlaw leader. 1929 95m/B Gary Cooper, Walter Huston, Richard Arlen, Chester Conklin, Eugene Pallette; **D:** Victor Fleming. **VHS, Beta** $14.95 BAR ⅃⅃⅃

Viridiana Innocent girl, with strong ideas about goodness, visits her worldly uncle's home before she takes her vows as a nun. He has developed a sick obsession for her, but after drugging the girl he finds he cannot violate her purity. He tells her, however, she is no longer chaste so she will not join the church. After her uncle's suicide, Viridiana

learns she and his illegitimate son Jorge have inherited her uncle's rundown estate. Viridiana opens the house to all sorts of beggars, who take shameless advantage, while Jorge works slowly to restore the estate and improve the lives of those around him. Considered to be one of Bunuel's masterpieces and a bitter allegory of Spanish idealism versus pragmatism and the state of the world. In Spanish with English subtitles.
1961 90m/B Silvia Pinal, Francesco Rabal, Fernando Rey, Margarita Lozano, Victoria Zinny; **D:** Luis Bunuel; **W:** Luis Bunuel. VHS, Beta $68.00 NOS, HHT, DVT 𝄞𝄞𝄞𝄞

Virtue's Revolt A small-town girl is corrupted by the sleazy world of showbiz. Silent.
1924 51m/B Edith Thornton, Crauford Kent. VHS, Beta $19.95 NO 𝄞½

Virus After nuclear war and plague destroy civilization, a small group of people gather in Antarctica and struggle with determination to carry on life. A look at man's genius for self-destruction and his endless hope. **AKA:** Fukkatsu no Hi.
1982 (PG) 102m/C George Kennedy, Sonny Chiba, Glenn Ford, Robert Vaughn, Stuart Gillard, Stephanie Faulkner, Ken Ogata, Bo Svenson, Olivia Hussey, Chuck Connors, Edward James Olmos; **D:** Kinji Fukasaku. VHS, Beta $19.95 STE, MED 𝄞𝄞

The Vision Suspenseful British production about televangelists who attempt to control their viewers' minds through worldwide satellite broadcasting.
1987 103m/C Lee Remick, Dirk Bogarde, Helena Bonham Carter, Eileen Atkins; **D:** Norman Stone. VHS, Beta NO 𝄞𝄞

Vision Quest A high school student wants to win the Washington State wrestling championship and the affections of a beautiful older artist. He gives it his all as he trains for the meet and goes after his "visionquest." A winning performance by Modine raises this above the usual teen coming-of-age movie. Madonna sings "Crazy for You" in a nightclub. Based on novel by Terry Davis. **AKA:** Crazy for You.
1985 (R) 107m/C Matthew Modine, Linda Fiorentino, Ronny Cox, Roberts Blossom, Daphne Zuniga, Charles Hallahan, Michael Schoeffling; **D:** Harold Becker; **W:** Darryl Ponicsan; **Performed by:** Madonna. VHS, Beta $19.98 WAR 𝄞𝄞½

Visions A man's ability to "see" murders before they happen leads police to suspect him of committing them, and he must clear himself.
1990 90m/C Joe Balogh, Alice Villarreal, Tom Taylor, A.R. Newman, J.R. Pella; **D:** Stephen E. Miller. VHS $79.95 MNC 𝄞½

Visions of Evil A young woman, recently released from a mental institution, is plagued by a series of terrifying visions when she moves into a house where a brutal axe murder took place.
1973 85m/C Lori Sanders, Dean Jagger. VHS, Beta $49.95 PSM 𝄞

Visions of Light: The Art of Cinematography Excellent documentary on the way films look and how the art of photographing movies can contribute as much, if not more, than cast, director, and script. Scenes from 125 films, from "Birth of a Nation" to "Goodfellas" are shown, with commentary from a number of cinematographers, including Gordon Willis, William A. Fraker, Conrad Hall, Ernest Dickerson, Vilmos Zsigmond, and Michael Chapman, on how they achieved certain effects and their collaborations with the director of the film.

1993 95m/C D: Arnold Glassman, Stuart Samuels, Todd McCarthy; **W:** Todd McCarthy. VHS $96.98 FXV 𝄞𝄞𝄞

Visitants Aliens descend irreverently on a small town in the 1950s, with unexpected comedic results.
1987 93m/C Marcus Vaughter, Johanna Grika, Joel Hile, Nicole Rio; **D:** Rick Sloane. VHS, Beta $69.95 TWE 𝄞

Visiting Hours Psycho-killer slashes his female victims and photographs his handiwork. Grant is one of his victims who doesn't die, so the killer decides to visit the hospital and finish the job. Fairly graphic and generally unpleasant. **AKA:** The Fright; Get Well Soon.
1982 (R) 101m/C Lee Grant, William Shatner, Linda Purl, Michael Ironside; **D:** Jean-Claude Lord; **W:** Brian Taggert. VHS, Beta $59.98 FOX 𝄞

The Visitor Affluent handsome doctor and mate conspire with grisly devil worshippers to conceive devil child.
1980 (R) 90m/C Mel Ferrer, Glenn Ford, Lance Henriksen, John Huston, Shelley Winters, Joanne Nail, Sam Peckinpah; **D:** Giullo Paradisi. VHS $29.95 UAV, HHE 𝄞½

Visitor from the Grave When an American heiress and her boyfriend dispose of a dead man's body, his spirit comes back to haunt them. This annoys them.
1981 60m/C Simon MacCorkindale, Kathryn Leigh Scott, Gareth Thomas, Mia Nadasi. VHS, Beta $29.95 LIV 𝄞

The Visitors Ghosts come to stay at a young family's dream house in Sweden. Not exactly a novel treatment or a novel premise.
1989 (R) 102m/C Keith Berkeley, Lena Endre, John Force, John Olsen, Joanna Berg, Brent Landiss, Patrick Ersgard; **D:** Joakim Ersgard. VHS, Beta $79.95 VMK 𝄞½

Vital Signs Hackneyed drama about six medical students enduring the tribulations of their profession.
1990 (R) 102m/C Adrian Pasdar, Diane Lane, Jack Gwaltney, Laura San Giacomo, Jane Adams, Tim Ransom, Bradley Whitford, Lisa Jane Persky, William Devane, Norma Aleandro, Jimmy Smits, James Karen, Telma Hopkins; **D:** Marisa Silver; **W:** Jeb Stuart; **M:** Miles Goodman. VHS, Beta $19.98 FOX 𝄞

Viva Chihuahua (Long Live Chihuahua) Supposed to be one of the greatest achievements of Tin Tan.
1947 95m/B German Valdes, Miguel Aceves Mejia, Norma Mora, Marcelo Chavez. VHS, Beta $44.95 MAD 𝄞𝄞½

Viva Knievel Crooks plan to sabotage Knievel's daredevil jump in Mexico and then smuggle cocaine back into the States in his coffin. Unintentionally campy. **AKA:** Seconds to Live.
1977 (PG) 106m/C Evel Knievel, Gene Kelly, Lauren Hutton, Red Buttons, Leslie Nielsen, Cameron Mitchell, Marjoe Gortner, Albert Salmi, Dabney Coleman; **D:** Gordon Douglas; **M:** Charles Bernstein. VHS, Beta $59.95 WAR Woof!

Viva Las Vegas Race care driver Elvis needs money to compete against rival Danova in the upcoming Las Vegas Grand Prix. He takes a job in a casino and romances fellow employee Ann-Margaret, who turns out to be his rival for the grand prize in the local talent competition. Good pairing between the two leads, and the King does particularly well with the title song. ♫The Lady Loves Me; Viva Las Vegas; What'd I Say; I Need Somebody to Lean On; Come On, Everybody; Today, Tomorrow and Forever; If You Think I Don't Need You; Appreciation; My Rival. **AKA:** Love in Las Vegas.

1963 85m/C Elvis Presley, Ann-Margret, William Demarest, Jack Carter, Cesare Danova, Nicky Blair, Larry Kent; **D:** George Sidney. VHS, Beta $14.95 MGM 𝄞𝄞½

Viva Maria! Tongue-in-cheek comedy with Bardot and Moreau as two dancers (both named Maria) in a show traveling through Mexico. The two become incensed by the poverty of the peasants and decide to turn revolutionary (especially after Moreau has an affair with revolutionary leader Hamilton, who promptly gets killed). The two French sex symbols are a fine match.
1965 (R) 119m/C Jeanne Moreau, Brigitte Bardot, George Hamilton, Paulette Dubost, Claudio Brook; **D:** Louis Malle; **W:** Louis Malle, Jean-Claude Carriere; **M:** Georges Delerue. VHS $19.98 MGM 𝄞𝄞½

Viva Max A blundering modern-day Mexican general and his men recapture the Alamo, and an equally inept American force, headed by Winters, is sent to rout them out. Mostly works, with some very funny scenes. Ustinov is great.
1969 93m/C Peter Ustinov, Jonathan Winters, John Astin, Pamela Tiffin, Keenan Wynn; **D:** Jerry Paris. VHS $14.98 REP 𝄞𝄞½

Viva Villa! Exciting action biography of Mexican revolutionary Pancho Villa, well-portrayed by the exuberant Beery. The film follows the early Robin Hood-like exploits of Villa and his men who soon join Walthall and his peasant army in overthrowing the government. But Villa's bandito instincts and ego cause problems and a power struggle ensues. Director Howard Hawks went uncredited for his work on the film, being fired by the studio after an incident while on location in Mexico.
1934 115m/B Wallace Beery, Fay Wray, Stuart Erwin, Leo Carrillo, Donald Cook, George E. Stone, Joseph Schildkraut, Henry B. Walthall, Katherine DeMille, David Durand, Frank Puglia; **D:** Jack Conway; **W:** Ben Hecht. VHS $19.98 MGM, MOV, BTV 𝄞𝄞𝄞

Viva Zapata! Chronicles the life of Mexican revolutionary Emiliano Zapata. Brando is powerful as he leads the peasant revolt in the early 1900s, only to be corrupted by power and greed. Quinn well deserved his Best Supporting Actor Oscar for his performance as Zapata's brother. Based on the novel "Zapata the Unconquered" by Edgcumb Pinchon.
1952 112m/B Marlon Brando, Anthony Quinn, Jean Peters, Margo, Arnold Moss, Joseph Wiseman, Mildred Dunnock; **D:** Elia Kazan; **W:** John Steinbeck; **M:** Alex North. Academy Awards '52: Best Supporting Actor (Quinn); Nominations: Best Actor (Brando), Best Art Direction/Set Decoration (B & W), Best Story & Screenplay, Best Original Score; British Academy Awards '52: Best Actor (Brando); Cannes Film Festival '52: Best Actor (Brando). VHS, Beta $19.98 FOX, BTV 𝄞𝄞𝄞𝄞

Vivacious Lady Romantic comedy about a mild-mannered college professor who marries a chorus girl. Problems arise when he must let his conservative family and his former fiancee in on the marriage news. Good performances. Appealing.
1938 90m/B Ginger Rogers, James Stewart, James Ellison, Beulah Bondi, Charles Coburn, Jack Carson, Franklin Pangborn; **D:** George Stevens. VHS, Beta $39.95 CCB, MED 𝄞𝄞𝄞

Vivo o Muerto Action and adventure abound in this shoot 'em up Spanish-language film.
1987 100m/B Manuel Capetillo, Flor Silvestre, Aldo Monti, Wolf Ruvinskis. VHS, Beta $44.95 MAD 𝄞

Vogues of 1938 As a lark, a rich girl takes a job as a fashion model and incurs the displeasure of Baxter, the owner of the chic fashion house where she works. An early Technicolor fashion extravaganza. ♫That Old Feeling; Lovely One; Turn On the Red Hot Heat (Burn the Blues Away); King of Jam. *AKA:* All This and Glamour Too; Vogues.
1937 110m/C Joan Bennett, Warner Baxter, Helen Vinson, Mischa Auer, Hedda Hopper, Penny Singleton, Alan Mowbray; *D:* Irving Cummings. VHS, Beta NO 𝄢𝄢

Voice of Hollywood Some of Hollywood's great stars are caught off guard in this collection of short subjects.
1929 60m/B Buster Keaton, Ken Maynard, Johnny Mack Brown. VHS, Beta $19.95 VDM, DVT, GVV 𝄢½

Volere Volare Shy sound engineer Nichetti shares a studio with his brother. The brother employs a bevy of beauties to dub sound effects onto soft-core porn films while Nichetti works on dubbing classic cartoons. He becomes so involved in his work he actually turns into a cartoon figure, which does nothing for his love life. Then he meets Martina, who's strangely attracted to this cartoon figure. Quirky comedy mixes animation and live action with too many gimmicks and not enough heart. In Italian with English subtitles.
1992 (R) 92m/C Maurizio Nichetti, Angela Finocchiaro, Mariella Valentini, Patrizio Roversi, Remo Remotti, Renato Scarpa; *D:* Maurizio Nichetti, Guido Manuli; *W:* Maurizio Nichetti, Guido Manuli. VHS $94.95 COL, WTA, FCT 𝄢𝄢½

Volpone A classic adaptation of Ben Jonson's famous tale. A greedy merchant pretends he is dying, leaving a fortune behind, in order see what his family will do to become his heir. In French with English subtitles.
1939 95m/B Harry Baur, Louis Jouvet, Fernand Ledoux; *D:* Maurice Tourneur. VHS, Beta $24.95 NOS, HHT, APD 𝄢𝄢½

Volunteers Ivy League playboy joins the newly formed Peace Corps to escape gambling debts and finds himself on a bridge-building mission in Thailand. Has its comedic moments, especially with Candy.
1985 (R) 107m/C Tom Hanks, John Candy, Rita Wilson, Tim Thomerson, Gedde Watanabe, George Plimpton, Ernest Harada; *D:* Nicholas Meyer; *M:* James Horner. VHS, Beta NO 𝄢𝄢

Volver, Volver, Volver! A beautiful woman is abused by the brother of her dead husband.
1987 90m/C Antonio Aguilar, Jorge Rivero, Claudia Islas, Consuelo Frank, Bruno Rey. VHS, Beta $59.95 MAD 𝄢

Von Ryan's Express An American Air Force colonel leads a group of prisoners-of-war in taking control of a freight train in order to make their exciting escape from a WWII P.O.W. camp in Italy. Strong cast.
1965 117m/C Frank Sinatra, Trevor Howard, Brad Dexter, Raffaella Carra, Sergio Fantoni, John Leyton, Vito Scotti, Edward Mulhare, Adolfo Celi, James Brolin, James B. Sikking; *D:* Mark Robson; *W:* Wendell Mayes; *M:* Jerry Goldsmith. VHS, Beta $19.98 FOX, FCT 𝄢𝄢𝄢

Voodoo Black Exorcist Some 3000 years ago, a black prince was buried alive for messin' with another man's woman. Now he's back...and he's mad—real mad. He's prepared to kill just about everyone. Can he be stopped before all in the modern world are dead??
1989 ?m/C Aldo Sambrel, Tenyeka Stadle, Fernando Sancho. VHS $19.95 HHE 𝄢

Voodoo Dawn Two New Yorkers travel to the Deep South to visit a friend who, it turns out, is the latest victim in a series of really gross voodoo murders. A beautiful girl is written into the plot, and the New York guys have an excuse to stay in voodooville, even though bimbolina's southern accent comes and goes for no discernable reason. Filmed near Charleston, South Carolina and co-written by Russo of "Night of the Living Dead" fame.
1989 (R) 83m/C Raymond St. Jacques, Theresa Merritt, Gina Gershon, Kirk Baily, Billy "Sly" Williams, J. Grant Albrecht, Tony Todd; *D:* Steven Fierberg; *W:* John Russo, Jeffrey Delman. VHS $19.95 ACA 𝄢𝄢

Voodoo Woman An innocent girl is lured into the jungle by an evil scientist who is trying to create the perfect woman to commit murders. He turns the girl into an ugly monster in an attempt to get her to obey his telepathic commands. A campy classic that's as bad as it sounds.
1957 77m/B Marla English, Tom Conway, Mike Connors, Lance Fuller; *D:* Edward L. Cahn. VHS $9.95 COL, PAR 𝄢

Vortex Punk/film noir style in which a female private eye becomes immersed in corporate paranoia and political corruption.
1981 87m/C Lydia Lunch, James Russo, Bill Rice; *D:* Scott B, Beth B; *W:* Scott B, Beth B. VHS ICA 𝄢½

Voulez-Vous Danser Avec Moi? A young bride endeavors to clear her husband of murder charges and find the real killer. In French with English subtitles. *AKA:* Come Dance with Me; Do You Want to Dance with Me?.
1959 90m/C Brigitte Bardot, Henri Vidal; *D:* Michel Boisrond. VHS, Beta $19.95 BAR, ING 𝄢𝄢

Voyage Boring rip-off of "Dead Calm" and other couple-in-peril-from-psycho-on-boat films. Hauer and Allen are having marital problems and decide to sail away from their troubles with new-found friends Roberts and Nielson. Only their guests are sociopaths. Hauer takes a breather from his psycho roles for a turn as the good guy while Roberts could do his patented crazy act in his sleep. Made for cable television.
1993 (R) ?m/C Rutger Hauer, Karen Allen, Eric Roberts, Connie Nielson; *D:* John MacKenzie. VHS $89.98 ITC 𝄢½

Voyage en Balloon This is the delightful story of a young boy (played by the star of "The Red Balloon") who stows away on his grandfather's hot air balloon for an adventurous trip across France.
1959 82m/C Pascal Lamorisse, Andre Gille, Maurice Baquet; *D:* Albert Lamorisse; *W:* Albert Lamorisse. VHS, Beta $14.95 COL, ING, SUE 𝄢𝄢½

The Voyage of Tanai A young Polynesian battles nature's snarls on his quest to save his village.
1975 (G) 90m/C *D:* John Latos. VHS, Beta NO 𝄢

Voyage of Terror: The Achille Lauro Affair Recounting of the 1985 Italian cruise-ship hijacking by four Palestinians. Lancaster is the wheelchair-bound Leon Klinghoffer and Saint is wife Marilyn. Shot on the actual ship and route where the tragedy occurred. Originally a made-for-television miniseries.
1990 120m/C Burt Lancaster, Eva Marie Saint, Robert Culp, Brian Bloom, Dominique Sanda, Rebecca Schaeffer, Joseph Nasser, Gabriel Ferzetti, Renzo Nontagnani; *D:* Alberto Negrin. VHS $79.95 PSM 𝄢𝄢½

Voyage of the Damned The story of one of the most tragic incidents of WWII. In 1939, 1,937 German-Jewish refugees fleeing Nazi Germany are bound for Cuba aboard the Hamburg-America liner S.S. St. Louis. They are refused permission to land in Cuba (and everywhere else) and must sail back to Germany and certain death. Based on the novel by Gordon Thomas and Max Morgan-Witts.
1976 (G) 134m/C Faye Dunaway, Max von Sydow, Oskar Werner, Malcolm McDowell, Orson Welles, James Mason, Lee Grant, Katharine Ross, Ben Gazzara, Lynne Frederick, Wendy Hiller, Jose Ferrer, Luther Adler, Sam Wanamaker, Denholm Elliott, Nehemiah Persoff, Julie Harris, Maria Schell, Janet Suzman; *D:* Stuart Rosenberg. Academy Awards '76 Nominations: Best Adapted Screenplay, Best Supporting Actress (Grant), Best Original Score; Golden Globe Awards '77: Best Supporting Actress (Ross). VHS, Beta $79.98 FOX 𝄢𝄢𝄢

Voyage of the Heart An aging fisherman meets up with a sexy college girl and the passion begins.
1990 88m/C Bill Aldrij, Dunja Djordjenic. VHS $79.95 AIP 𝄢𝄢

Voyage of the Rock Aliens A quasi-satiric space farce about competing alien rock stars.
1987 97m/C Pia Zadora, Tom Nolan, Craig Sheffer, Rhema, Ruth Gordon, Michael Berryman, Jermaine Jackson; *D:* James Fargo. VHS, Beta $79.95 PSM 𝄢

The Voyage of the Yes Two teenagers, one white and one black, in a small sailboat hit rough weather and battle the elements while learning about themselves. Average made-for-television movie.
1972 (PG) 100m/C Desi Arnaz Jr., Mike Evans, Beverly Garland, Skip Homeier, Della Reese, Scoey Mitchell; *D:* Lee H. Katzin. VHS NO 𝄢𝄢

A Voyage' Round My Father John Mortimer's adaptation of his semi-autobiographical stage play. Olivier is the eccentric, opinionated blind barrister-father and Bates the exasperated son as both try to come to terms with their stormy family relationship. Well-acted and directed. Made for television.
1989 85m/C Laurence Olivier, Alan Bates, Jane Asher, Elizabeth Sellars; *D:* Alvin Rakoff. VHS, Beta $89.99 HBO 𝄢𝄢𝄢

Voyage-Suprise A slapstick comedy about a crazy old man who runs a mystery tour from a dilapidated bus as he takes an unknowing mob of tourists on a cross-country escapade through a brothel, a wedding, criminals, police, terrorists and the Haute-Provence. In French with English subtitles.
1946 108m/B Martine Carol, Sioel; *D:* Pierre Prevert. VHS, Beta $59.95 FCT, FST 𝄢𝄢𝄢

Voyage to Italy An unhappy couple, on the verge of divorce, inherit a house in Italy and make a trip to see it. In Italy, they dally with other people but realize their attachment to each other demands they attempt to salvage their marriage. Not the best of the Rossellini-Bergman collaborations. Poor editing and directing undermine weak script. Sanders and Bergman do their best.
1953 87m/B Ingrid Bergman, George Sanders; *D:* Roberto Rossellini. VHS, Beta $29.95 NOS, FCT 𝄢𝄢½

Voyage to the Bottom of the Sea The crew of an atomic submarine must destroy a deadly radiation belt which has set the polar ice cap ablaze. Fun stuff, with good special effects and photography. Later became a television show.

1961 106m/C Walter Pidgeon, Joan Fontaine, Barbara Eden, Peter Lorre, Robert Sterling, Michael Ansara, Frankie Avalon; *D:* Irwin Allen; *W:* Irwin Allen, Charles Bennett. **VHS, Beta** $14.98 *FOX, FCT ♂♂♂*

Voyage to the Planet of Prehistoric Women Astronauts journey to Venus, where they discover a race of gorgeous, sea-shell clad women led by Van Doren, as well as a few monsters. Incomprehensible but fun. The third film incorporating the Russian "Planeta Burg" footage. Directed (and narrated) by Bogdanovich under the pseudonym Derek Thomas. *AKA:* Gill Woman; Gill Women of Venus.
1968 78m/C Mamie Van Doren, Mary Mark, Paige Lee; *D:* Peter Bogdanovich. **VHS** $16.95 *SNC Woof!*

Voyage to the Prehistoric Planet In the year 2020, an expedition to Venus is forced to deal with dinosaurs and other perils. In the making of this movie, Roger Corman edited in special effects and additional footage from a recently acquired Russian film, "Planeta Burg," and his own "Queen of Blood." *AKA:* Voyage to a Prehistoric Planet.
1965 80m/C Basil Rathbone, Faith Domergue, Marc Shannon, Christopher Brand; *D:* John Sebastian. **VHS** $16.95 *NOS, SNC ♂ ½*

Voyager Restless, middle-aged engineer Walter Faber (Shepherd) tells his life story in a series of flashbacks. Twenty years before (the film starts in 1957) he abandons his pregnant girlfriend who promises to get an abortion. He laters hears she married, had a child, and divorced. While sailing to New York from France Walter falls in love with a young student and accompanies her to Greece to visit her mother. Only then does he realize her true identity, leading to a tragic conclusion. Shepherd's is a glum, repressed performance (in keeping with the character) while Delpy personifies youthful sweetness. Based on the novel "Homo Faber" by Max Frisch.
1991 (PG-13) 110m/C Sam Shepard, Julie Delpy, Barbara Sukowa, Dieter Kirchlechner, Traci Lin, Deborra-Lee Furness, August Zirner, Thomas Heinze; *D:* Volker Schlondorff; *W:* Volker Schlondorff, Rudy Wurlitzer. **VHS** $89.95 *ACA, ING ♂♂♂*

Vulcan God of Fire A foreign film featuring various Steve Reeves style musclemen portraying the gods of Olympus.
19?? 76m/C Rob Flash, Gordon Mitchell, Bella Cortez. **VHS, Beta** $59.95 *TWE Woof!*

Vulture In an attempt to carry out a curse on the descendants of the man who killed his forefather, a scientist tries an atomic transmutation experiment and winds up combining himself with a bird.
1967 91m/C Robert Hutton, Akim Tamiroff, Broderick Crawford, Diane Clare, Philip Friend, Patrick Holt, Annette Carell; *D:* Lawrence Huntington. **VHS, Beta** $14.95 *CNG ♂*

Vultures A dying patriarch summons his predatory family to his home in order to straighten out the distribution of inheritance. One by one, they fall victim to a mysterious murderer.
1984 101m/C Yvonne De Carlo, Stuart Whitman, Jim Bailey, Meredith MacRae, Aldo Ray; *D:* Paul Leder. **VHS, Beta** $79.95 *PSM ♂*

W A woman and her husband are terrorized and must find out why. A single letter "W" is found at the scene of the crimes. Notable only as model Twiggy's first film. *AKA:* I Want Her Dead.
1974 (PG) 95m/C Twiggy, Dirk Benedict, John Vernon, Eugene Roche; *D:* Richard Quine. **VHS, Beta** $69.98 *LIV, VES ♂ ½*

W Hour A tragic story of young Polish soldiers participating in the Warsaw uprisings of 1944.
19?? 85m/C **VHS** $39.99 *FCT ♂♂ ½*

Wackiest Ship in the Army A completely undisciplined warship crew must smuggle an Australian spy through Japanese waters during WWII. Odd, enjoyable mixture of action and laughs. Became a TV series. In the middle of the war effort, Nelson straps on a guitar and sings "Do You Know What It Means to Miss New Orleans."
1961 99m/C Jack Lemmon, Ricky Nelson, Chips Rafferty, John Lund, Mike Kellin, Patricia Driscoll; *D:* Richard Murphy. **VHS, Beta** $14.95 *COL ♂♂ ½*

Wackiest Wagon Train in the West Hapless wagon master is saddled with a dummy assistant as they guide a party of five characters across the West. Based on the minor TV sitcom "Dusty's Trail." Produced by the same folks who delivered the similarly premised TV series "Gilligan's Island" and "The Brady Bunch."
1977 (G) 86m/C Bob Denver, Forrest Tucker, Jeannine Riley. **VHS, Beta** $19.95 *MED ♂*

Wacko Group of nymphettes and tough guys get caught up in a wild Halloween-pumpkin-lawnmower murder. This spoof of the "Halloween" series works too hard for as few laughs as it can.
1983 (PG) 84m/C Stella Stevens, George Kennedy, Joe Don Baker, Andrew Dice Clay; *D:* Greydon Clark. **VHS, Beta** *VES Woof!*

The Wacky World of Wills & Burke Comedy based on the adventures of Wills and Burke, the two 19th-century explorers who led the first unsuccessful expedition across the outback—the Lewis and Clark of Australia, if you will. In real life they died during the adventure, a less than wacky finale. "Burke and Wills," out the same year, was a serious treatment of the same story.
1985 102m/C Garry McDonald, Kim Gyngell, Peter Collingwood, Jonathon Hardy, Mark Little; *D:* Bob Weis. **VHS, Beta** $79.95 *MNC ♂♂*

Wager of Love While vacationing on their annual pleasure cruise, four women bet on their individual power of seduction. They find themselves competing for passion as each woman's erotic adventure unravels in this exciting and sensual tale.
1990 75m/C Steve Landers, Shelly Johnson, Elliot Silverman, Lisa Cook; *D:* Jason Holt. **VHS** $49.95 *CEL ♂♂*

Wages of Fear American oil company controls a desolate Central American town whose citizens desperately want out—so desperately that four are willing to try a suicide mission to deliver nitroglycerine to put out a well-fire raging 300 miles away. The company's cynical head has offered $2,000 to each man, enough to finance escape from the hell-hole they live in. Complex, multidimensional drama concentrates on character development for the first half—crucial to the film's greatness. This is the restored version. Remade by William Friedkin as "Sorcerer" in 1977. Based on a novel by Georges Arnaud. In French with English subtitles. *AKA:* Le Salaire De La Peur.
1955 138m/B Yves Montand, Charles Vanel, Peter Van Eyck, Vera Clouzot, Folco Lulli, William Tubbs; *D:* Henri-Georges Clouzot; *W:* Henri-Georges Clouzot; *M:* Georges Auric. **VHS, Beta** $24.95 *HHT, SNC, VYY ♂♂♂♂*

Wagner: The Complete Epic The unedited version of the epic made-for-television miniseries dramatizing the life of German composer Richard Wagner. The excellent photography does justice to the elabo-

rate production, shot on some 200 different locations. The actors cringe in the presence of the subject's grandeur; Burton, a shell of his former cinematic self, is painful to watch in his last released film. Frankly, this is way too long.
1985 540m/C Richard Burton, Vanessa Redgrave, Ralph Richardson, John Gielgud, Laurence Olivier; *D:* Tony Palmer; *M:* George Solti. **VHS, Beta** $124.95 *MVD, KUL ♂*

Wagner: The Movie Slightly half it's original length, the world's biggest biopic is still huge, sweeping, and long. Incoherent and over-acted. Wagner's music is conducted by Sir Georg Solti. Made for television.
1985 300m/C Richard Burton, Vanessa Redgrave, John Gielgud, Franco Nero, Laurence Olivier; *D:* Tony Palmer. **VHS, Beta** $29.95 *MVD, SUE, GLV ♂ ½*

Wagon Master Two cowboys are persuaded to guide a group of Mormons, led by Bond, in their trek across the western frontier. They run into a variety of troubles, including a band of killers who joins the wagon train to escape a posse. Sensitively directed, realistic and worthwhile. Inspired the TV series "Wagon Train." Also available colorized.
1950 85m/B Ben Johnson, Joanne Dru, Harry Carey Jr., Ward Bond, Jane Darwell, James Arness; *D:* John Ford. **VHS, Beta** $19.95 *MED, TTC ♂♂♂*

Wagon Tracks Hart searches for the man responsible for his brother's death.
1919 64m/B William S. Hart, Jane Novak, Robert McKim, Lloyd Bacon; *D:* Lambert Hillyer. **VHS** $17.95 *GPV ♂♂ ½*

Wagon Trail The sheriff's son is blackmailed into helping a gang of robbers, with terrible consequences for himself and his father (Carey), who is fired from his job after the son breaks jail. The new sheriff is secretly chief of the outlaw band. Carey rides back into town and eventually virtue triumphs. Good, tense—but not too tense—western.
1935 59m/B Harry Carey Sr.; *D:* Harry Fraser. **VHS, Beta** $27.95 *VCN ♂♂ ½*

Wagon Wheels Recycling was in vogue in '34, when unused footage from "Fighting Caravans" (1931) with Gary Cooper was used to remake the very same plot. The result is biodegradable. Settlers heading to Oregon are ambushed by bad guy Blue, employed by fur traders. Blue sics Injuns on them too, but don't worry, they make it. Adapted from Zane Grey's novel "Fighting Caravans." *AKA:* Caravans West.
1934 54m/B Randolph Scott, Gail Patrick, Billy Lee; *D:* Charles T. Barton. **VHS, Beta** $9.95 *NOS, DVT ♂♂*

Wagons East Pioneers head west and then change their minds. Candy (who died during filming) plays the drunken former wagonmaster hired to get them back home. Hard to watch Candy's performance (it's good) knowing this is his last role.
1994 ?m/C John Candy, Richard Lewis, Ellen Greene, John C. McGinley, Robert Picardo, William Sanderson, Thomas F. Duffy, Russell Means, Rodney Grant, Michael Horse, Gailard Sartain, Lochlynm Munro, Stuart Proud Eagle Grant; *D:* Peter Markle; *W:* Matthew Carlson. **VHS** *NYR ♂ ½*

Waikiki Two private eyes set out to prove that their friend is not the "cane field murderer" who is terrorizing the Hawaiian island of Oahu. Harmless but pointless TV pilot.
1980 96m/C Dack Rambo, Steve Marachuk, Donna Mills, Cal Bellini, Darren McGavin; *D:* Ron Satlof. **VHS, Beta** $59.95 *LHV ♂ ½*

Wait Till Your Mother Gets
Home "Mr. Mom"-like zaniness abounds as a football coach cares for the kids and does chores while his wife takes her first job in 15 years. Almost too darn cute, but well written. Made for television.
1983 97m/C Paul Michael Glaser, Dee Wallace Stone, Peggy McKay, David Doyle, Raymond Buktenica, James Gregory, Joey Lawrence, Lynne Moody; **D:** Bill Persky. **VHS, Beta $9.99** PSM *ℐℐ*

Wait Until Dark
A photographer unwittingly smuggles a drug-filled doll into New York, and his blind wife, alone in their apartment, is terrorized by murderous crooks in search of it. A compelling thriller based on the Broadway hit by Frederick Knott, who also wrote "Dial M for Murder." The individual actors' performances were universally acclaimed in this spinetingler.
1967 105m/C Audrey Hepburn, Alan Arkin, Richard Crenna, Efrem Zimbalist Jr., Jack Weston; **D:** Terence Young; **M:** Henry Mancini. **VHS, Beta $59.95** WAR *ℐℐℐ*

Wait Until Spring, Bandini
A flavorful immigrant tale about a transplanted Italian family weathering the winter in 1925 Colorado, as seen through the eyes of a young son. Alternately funny and moving, with one of Dunaway's scenery-chewing performances as a local temptation for the father. Based on the autobiographical novel by John Fante, co-produced by Francis Ford Coppola.
1990 (PG-13) 104m/C Joe Mantegna, Faye Dunaway, Burt Young, Ornella Muti, Alex Vincent, Renato Vanni, Michael Bacall, Daniel Wilson; **D:** Dominique Deruddere; **M:** Angelo Badalamenti. **VHS $19.98** WAR *ℐℐ½*

Waiting for the Light
When a woman takes over a small-town diner, she gets the surprise of her life. Seems an angel has made his home there and now the townsfolk are flocking to see him. MacLaine is wonderful and Garr is fetching and likeable. Set during the Cuban missile crisis. Enjoyable, tame comedy.
1990 (PG) 94m/C Shirley MacLaine, Teri Garr, Vincent Schiavelli, John Bedford Lloyd; **D:** Christopher Monger; **W:** Christopher Monger. **VHS, 8mm $19.95** COL *ℐℐ½*

Waiting for the Moon
Hunt as Alice B. Toklas is a relative treat in this ponderous, frustrating biopic about Toklas and Gertrude Stein, her lover. Made for "American Playhouse" on PBS.
1987 (PG) 88m/C Linda Hunt, Linda Bassett, Andrew McCarthy; **D:** Jill Godmilow. **VHS, Beta $79.98** FOX *ℐ½*

Waitress
Three beautiful girls are waitresses in a crazy restaurant where the chef gets drunk, the kitchen explodes, and the customers riot. Awful premise, worse production. **AKA:** Soup to Nuts.
1981 (R) 85m/C Jim Harris, Carol Drake, Carol Bever; **D:** Lloyd Samuel Weil Kaufman. **VHS, Beta** No Woof!

Wake Island
After Pearl Harbor, a small group of Marines face the onslaught of the Japanese fleet on a small Pacific Island. Although doomed, they hold their ground for 16 days. Exciting, realistic, and moving. The first film to capitalize on early "last stands" of WWII; also among the most popular war movies. Shown to soldiers in training camps with great morale-raising success.
1942 88m/B Robert Preston, Brian Donlevy, William Bendix, William Bendix, MacDonald Carey, Albert Dekker, Walter Abel, Rod Cameron, Barbara Britton; **D:** John Farrow. Academy Awards '42 Nominations: Best Director (Farrow), Best Original Screenplay, Best Picture, Best Supporting Actor (Bendix); New York Film Critics Awards '42: Best Director (Farrow). **VHS, Beta $19.95** MCA, TLF *ℐℐℐ*

Wake of the Red Witch
Wayne captains the ship of the title and battles shipping tycoon Adler for a fortune in pearls and the love of a beautiful woman (Russell). Wayne shows impressive range in a non-gun-totin' role.
1949 106m/B John Wayne, Gail Russell, Gig Young, Luther Adler, Henry Daniell; **D:** Edward Ludwig. **VHS, Beta $9.98** REP *ℐℐ½*

Walk, Don't Run
Romantic comedy involving a British businessman (Grant) unable to find a hotel room in Tokyo due to the crowds staying for the 1964 summer Olympic Games. He winds up renting a room from an Embassy secretary (Eggar) and then meets and invites Hutton, a member of the U.S. Olympic walking team, also without a place to stay, to share it with him. Grant then proceeds to play matchmaker, despite the fact that Eggar has a fiance. Grant's last film. Innocuous, unnecessary remake of "The More the Merrier."
1966 114m/C Cary Grant, Samantha Eggar, Jim Hutton, John Standing, Miiko Taka; **D:** Charles Walters; **M:** Quincy Jones. **VHS, Beta $69.95** COL *ℐℐ½*

Walk in the Spring Rain
The bored wife of a college professor follows him to rural Tennessee when he goes on sabbatical, where she meets the married Quinn and the two begin an affair. When Quinn's disturbed son learns of the affair, he attacks the woman, with tragic results. Fine cast should have had better effect on low-key script.
1970 (PG) 98m/C Ingrid Bergman, Anthony Quinn, Fritz Weaver, Katherine Crawford, Tom Fielding, Virginia Gregg; **D:** Guy Green; **W:** Sterling Silliphant; **M:** Elmer Bernstein. **VHS, Beta** NO *ℐℐ½*

A Walk in the Sun
The trials of a group of infantrymen in WWII from the time they land in Italy to the time they capture their objective, a farmhouse occupied by the Germans. Excellent ensemble acting shows well the variety of civilians who make up any fighting force and explores their fears, motivations, and weaknesses. Producer and director Milestone also made "All Quiet on the Western Front" and the Korean War masterpiece "Pork Chop Hill." Released in the final days of the war, almost concurrently with two other WWII films of the first echelon, "The Story of G.I. Joe" and "They Were Expendable." **AKA:** Salerno Beachhead.
1946 117m/B Dana Andrews, Richard Conte, John Ireland, Lloyd Bridges, Sterling Holloway; **D:** Lewis Milestone; **W:** Robert Rossen. **VHS, Beta, 8mm $19.95** LUM, NOS, DVT *ℐℐℐ½*

Walk into Hell
A mining engineer and his assistant searching for oil meet the primitive natives of New Guinea. Tedious at times and dated, but pleasant enough.
1957 91m/C Chips Rafferty, Francoise Christophe, Reg Lye; **D:** Lee Robinson. **VHS, Beta $24.95** VYY, NLC *ℐℐ*

Walk Like a Man
In a take-off of Tarzan movies, Mandel plays a man raised by wolves. Comic problems arise when he is found by his mother and the family attempts to civilize him. Juvenile script wastes fine cast.
1987 (PG) 86m/C Howie Mandel, Christopher Lloyd, Cloris Leachman, Colleen Camp, Amy Steel, George DiCenzo; **D:** Melvin Frank. **VHS, Beta $79.95** MGM *ℐ½*

Walk on the Wild Side
In 1930s New Orleans, a man searches for his long-lost love, finds her working in a whorehouse and fights to save her from the lesbian madame Stanwyck. Melodrama, based only loosely on the Nelson Algren novel and adapted by cult novelist John Fante, with Edmund Morris. Much-troubled on the set, and it shows.
1962 114m/B Jane Fonda, Laurence Harvey, Barbara Stanwyck, Capucine, Anne Baxter; **D:** Edward Dmytryk; **M:** Elmer Bernstein. **VHS, Beta $69.95** COL

Walk Softly, Stranger
Two-bit crook is reformed by the love of an innocent peasant girl. If you can stand the cliche masquerading as a plot, the performances are good.
1950 81m/B Alida Valli, Joseph Cotten, Spring Byington, Paul Stewart, Jack Paar, Jeff Donnell, John McIntire; **D:** Robert Stevenson. **VHS, Beta $19.98** TTC *ℐℐ*

Walker
Slapdash, tongue-in-cheek historical pastiche about the real-life American William Walker (played previously in "Burn!" by Marlon Brando), and how he led a revolution in Nicaragua in 1855 and became its self-declared president. A bitter, revisionist farce never for a moment attempting to be accurate. Matlin's unfortunate, though fortunately brief, follow-up to her Oscar-winning performance.
1987 (R) 95m/C Ed Harris, Richard Masur, Peter Boyle, Rene Auberjonois, Marlee Matlin, Miguel Sandoval; **D:** Alex Cox; **W:** Rudy Wurlitzer; **M:** Joe Strummer. **VHS, Beta $79.95** MCA *ℐℐ*

Walker: Texas Ranger: One Riot,
One Ranger Norris sticks with the action-adventure mode with this tv pilot movie about Cordell Walker, a good guy with a code and some martial arts skills, who teams up with an ex-gridiron star and a female district attorney to go after lawbreakers. This time its bank robbers and three hoods after a teenaged girl.
1993 (PG-13) 96m/C Chuck Norris, Sheree J. Wilson, Clarence Gilyard Jr., Gailard Sartain, Floyd "Red Crow" Westerman, James Drury; **D:** Virgil W. Vogel; **W:** Louise McCarn. **VHS $89.99** CAN, MOV *ℐℐ½*

Walking Back
Troubled teens go for joyride and bash mirthmobile to smithereens. The body shop agrees to give them a different car, but they find themselves in the middle of a heist at a plant belonging to the father of one of the boys.
1926 53m/B Sue Carol, Richard Walling, Ivan Lebedeff, Robert Edeson, Florence Turner, Arthur Rankin; **D:** Rupert Julian. **VHS, Beta $16.95** GPV, FCT *ℐℐ*

Walking on Air
Ray Bradbury's story comes to life as a handicapped boy dreams of completing a real space walk. Originally aired on PBS as part of the "Wonderworks" series.
1987 60m/C Lynn Redgrave, Jordan Marder, James Treuer, Katheryn Trainor; **D:** Ed Kaplan. **VHS $14.95** PME, FCT, BTV *ℐℐ*

Walking Tall
A Tennessee sheriff takes a stand against syndicate-run gambling and his wife is murdered in response. Ultra-violent crime saga wowed the movie going public and spawned several sequels and a TV series. Based on the true story of folk-hero Buford Pusser, admirably rendered by Baker.
1973 (R) 126m/C Joe Don Baker, Elizabeth Hartman, Noah Beery Jr., Gene Evans, Rosemary Murphy, Felton Perry; **D:** Phil Karlson. **VHS, Beta $29.98** LIV *ℐℐ½*

Walking Tall: Part 2
Club-wielding Tennessee sheriff Buford Pusser, this time played less memorably by Svenson, attempts to find the man who killed his wife. Even more violent than the original.

1975 (PG) 109m/C Bo Svenson, Noah Beery Jr., Angel Tompkins, Richard Jaeckel; **D:** Earl Bellamy. **VHS, Beta** $29.98 *LIV, VES 💾💾*

Walking Tall: The Final Chapter
The final months in the life of Tennessee sheriff Buford Pusser and the mystery surrounding his death. It wasn't the final chapter. Still to come: a TV flick and series.
1977 (PG) 112m/C Bo Svenson, Forrest Tucker, Leif Garrett, Morgan Woodward; **D:** Jack Starrett. **VHS, Beta** $29.98 *LIV 💾½*

Walking the Edge
A widow hires a taxi driver to help her seek vengeance against the men who killed her husband and her son. Forster does what he can with the lousy story and script.
1983 (R) 94m/C Robert Forster, Nancy Kwan, Joe Spinell, Aarika Wells; **D:** Norbert Meisel. **VHS, Beta** $79.98 *LIV 💾½*

Walking Through the Fire
A young woman's real-life struggle with Hodgkin's disease. Her fight for her own and her unborn baby's survival is a stirring testament to the power of faith. Absorbing made-for-television drama.
1980 143m/C Bess Armstrong, Tom Mason, Bonnie Bedelia, Richard Masur, Swoosie Kurtz, J.D. Cannon, June Lockhart; **D:** Robert Day. **VHS, Beta** *TLF 💾💾½*

The Wall
The last film by Guney, author of "Yol," about orphaned boys in prison in the Turkish capitol of Ankara trying to escape and/or rebel after ceaseless rapings, beatings and injustice. An acclaimed, disturbing film made from Guney's own experience. He died in 1984, three years after escaping from prison. Brutal and horrifying. In Turkish with English subtitles. *AKA:* Guney's The Wall; Le Mur; Duvar.
1983 117m/C Ayse Emel Mesci, Saban, Sisko; **D:** Yilmaz Guney; **W:** Yilmaz Guney. **VHS, Beta** $69.95 *KIV, ING 💾💾💾½*

Wall Street
Stone's energetic, high-minded big business treatise in which naive, neophyte stockbroker Sheen is seduced into insider trading by sleek entrepreneur Douglas, much to his blue-collar father's chagrin. A fast-moving drama of 80's-style materialism with a mesmerizing, award-winning performance by Douglas as greed personified. Expert direction by Stone, who co-wrote the not-very-subtle script. His father, to whom this film is dedicated, was a broker. Look for Stone in a cameo.
1987 (R) 126m/C Michael Douglas, Charlie Sheen, Martin Sheen, Daryl Hannah, Sean Young, James Spader, Hal Holbrook, Terence Stamp, Richard Dysart, John C. McGinley, Saul Rubinek, James Karen, Josh Mostel, Millie Perkins, Cecilia Peck, Grant Shaud, Franklin Cover; *Cameos:* Oliver Stone; **D:** Oliver Stone; **W:** Oliver Stone, Stanley Weiser; **M:** Stewart Copeland. **VHS, Beta** $19.98 *FOX, BTV 💾💾💾*

Wall Street Cowboy
When his land is threatened, a cowboy fights big business in the big city.
1939 54m/B Roy Rogers. **VHS, Beta** $9.99 *NOS, DVT, TIM 💾*

Wallaby Jim of the Islands
The singing captain of a pearl fishing boat must protect his treasure from marauding pirates. Pleasant enough musical adventure.
1937 61m/B George Houston, Douglas Walton; **D:** Bud Barsky. **VHS** $24.95 *NOS, DVT, HEG 💾💾*

The Walloping Kid
A B-western with photography done in Monument Valley. Silent with original organ music.
1926 67m/B Kit Carson; **D:** Pauline Curley. **VHS, Beta, 8mm** $24.95 *VYY 💾½*

Walls of Glass
An aging New York cabby tries to make it as an actor. Effective performances by all override the thin plot. Slow and uneven, but involving. Also called "Flanagan."
1985 (R) 85m/C Geraldine Page, Philip Bosco, William Hickey, Olympia Dukakis, Brian Bloom, Linda Thorson; **D:** Scott Goldstein. **VHS, Beta** $79.95 *MED 💾💾½*

Walpurgis Night
Soapy Swedish drama about abortion was racy for its time. Office gal Bergman secretly loves her boss (Hanson). His wife refuses to have children and goes through an abortion. An unscrupulous fellow blackmails her with this knowledge. Bergman bides her time. Stay tuned... Interesting document on the mores of another time. In Swedish with English subtitles. *AKA:* Valborgmassoafton.
1941 82m/B Lars Hanson, Karin Carlsson, Victor Sjostrom, Ingrid Bergman, Erik Berglund, Sture Lagerwall, Georg Rydeberg, Georg Blickingberg; **D:** Gustaf Edgren. **VHS, Beta** $29.95 *WAC, ING 💾💾💾*

The Waltons: A Thanksgiving Story
As the Walton family anticipates the Thanksgiving holiday, John-Boy prepares for college entrance exams and Jenny Pendleton's visit. John-Boy suffers a head injury and is faced with a risky operation that may either help him or leave him permanently disabled. A holiday special from the television series.
1973 100m/C Richard Thomas, Ralph Waite, Michael Learned, Will Geer, Ellen Corby, Judy Norton-Taylor, Kami Cotler, Jon Walmsley, Mary McDonough, Eric Scott, David W. Harper; **D:** Philip Leacock. **VHS** $19.95 *IGP 💾💾💾*

Waltz Across Texas
Young oil man Jastrow and good-lookin' rock scientist Archer at first don't take to each other, but there's something in the air, and romance blossoms. Not great, but enjoyable.
1983 100m/C Terry Jastrow, Anne Archer, Mary Kay Place, Richard Farnsworth; **D:** Ernest Day; **M:** Stephen Dorff. **VHS, Beta** $69.95 *VES 💾💾½*

Waltz King
Typically hokey Disney biography of the young composer Johann Strauss during his Old Viennese heyday. Fine music, pretty German locations. Well-made family fare.
1963 94m/C Kerwin Mathews, Senta Berger, Brian Aherne; **D:** Steve Previn. **VHS, Beta** $69.95 *DIS 💾💾*

Waltz of the Toreadors
Retired general Sellers doesn't care for his wealthy, shrewish wife and tries to re-kindle a 17-year-old romance with a French woman. It doesn't work out (seems his illegitimate son also has a soft spot for the lady), but the general decides to keep his eyes open for other possibilities. Interestingly cast adaptation of Jean Anouilh's play. Sellers is hilarious, as usual. *AKA:* The Amorous General.
1962 105m/C Peter Sellers, Dany Robin, Margaret Leighton, Cyril Cusack; **D:** John Guillermin. **VHS, Beta** *NO 💾💾💾*

A Waltz Through the Hills
Two orphans head into the Australian outback and experience many adventures en route to the coast where they can set sail for England and their grandparents. Aired on PBS as part of the "Wonderworks" series.
1988 116m/C Tina Kemp, Andre Jansen, Ernie Dingo, Dan O'Herlihy; **D:** Frank Arnold. **VHS** $29.95 *PME, HMV, FCT 💾💾💾*

Wanda Nevada
Gambler Fonda wins nubile young Shields in a poker game, so he drags her with him to the Grand Canyon to look for gold. Director/star Fonda sure picked a lemon for his only screen appear-

ance with dad Henry (a grizzled old varmint appearing briefly). Shields is in her usual form—stellar for a shampoo commercial.
1979 (PG) 105m/C Peter Fonda, Brooke Shields, Henry Fonda, Fiona Lewis, Luke Askew, Ted Markland, Severn Darden, Paul Fix; **D:** Peter Fonda. **VHS, Beta** *NO 💾½*

Wanda, The Sadistic Hypnotist
A comely vixen hypnotizes an innocent pedestrian, ties him up and whips him to indulge her whims. Despite the "victim's" protests, she unleashes a gang of sexually playful women on him, and he is subjected to a multitude of "tortures."
1967 70m/C Katharine Shubeck, Janice Sweet, Dick Dangerfield, Daryl Cobinot; **D:** Gregory Corarito. **VHS** $23.00 *SMW, TPV 💾*

The Wanderer
Two friends fall in love— Frantz with Valentine and his friend Augustin with Frantz's sister, Yvonne. When the two women disappear on Frantz's wedding day, the two men begin a search to find both the women and the reasons for their disappearance. In French with English subtitles. *AKA:* Le Grand Meaulnes.
1967 108m/C Brigitte Fossey, Jean Blaise, Alain Noury, Juliette Villard; **D:** Jean-Gabriel Albicocco. **VHS** $79.95 *ING, CVC 💾💾*

Wanderers
Richard Price's acclaimed novel about youth gangs coming of age in the Bronx in 1963. The "Wanderers," named after the Dion song, are a gang of Italian-American teenagers about to graduate high school, who prowl the Bronx with the feeling that something is slipping away from them. Fascinating, funny and touching. Manz is unforgettable as a scrappy gal. A wonderful 60s soundtrack (Dion, the Four Seasons) colors this "coming of age the hard way" film.
1979 (R) 113m/C Ken Wahl, John Friedrich, Karen Allen, Linda Manz; *Cameos:* Richard Price; **D:** Philip Kaufman; **W:** Philip Kaufman. **VHS, Beta** $19.98 *WAR 💾💾💾½*

Wandering Jew
An excellent print of the rare Austrian film version of the classic legend, one of at least three silent versions. A Jew is condemned to wander the earth for eternity.
1920 65m/B Rudolf Schildkraut, Joseph Schildkraut. **VHS, Beta** *GVV 💾💾½*

The Wannsee Conference
A startling, important film depicting, in real time, the conference held at the Wannsee on January 20, 1942, during which 14 members of the Nazi hierarchy decided in 85 minutes the means and logistics of effecting the Final Solution. Recreated from the original secretary's notes. Horrifying and chilling. Along with "Shoah," a must-see for understanding the Holocaust and the psychology of genocide. In German with English subtitles. *AKA:* Wannseekonferenz.
1984 87m/C Dietrich Mattausch, Gerd Brockmann, Friedrich Beckhaus; **D:** Heinz Schirk. **VHS, Beta** $19.95 *HMV, APD, GLV 💾💾💾½*

Wanted: Babysitter
A young student accidentally becomes involved by her roommate in a plot to kidnap the child she is babysitting. Schneider is truly awful; Italian comic Pozzetto is at sea in a bad role as her boyfriend. Also released as "The Babysitter."
1975 90m/C Robert Vaughn, Vic Morrow, Maria Schneider, Renato Pozzetto, Nadja Tiller, Carl Mohner, Sydne Rome; **D:** Rene Clement. **VHS, Beta** $24.95 *AHV Woof!*

Wanted: Dead or Alive
This western series, which ran from 1958-1961, launched the career of McQueen who starred as bounty hunter Josh Randall. In this episode,

"Reunion for Revenge," Randall must protect the man in his custody from escaped criminals with vengeance on their mind. Also available colorized. Additional episodes available.
1959 22m/B Steve McQueen, Wright King, Jane Burns, James Coburn, Cloris Leachman, John Baer, Ralph Meeker; *D:* Thomas Carr, Richard Donner. **VHS, Beta** $9.98 *MOV* Woof!

Wanted Dead or Alive Ex-CIA agent Hauer is now a high-tech bounty hunter assigned to bring in an international terrorist. When the terrorist kills Hauer's friend and girlfriend, he forgets the $50,000 bonus for bringing him in alive. Official "sequel" to the Steve McQueen television series with Hauer as the McQueen character's great-grandson. The link is meaningless, and the plot is a thin excuse for much violence and anti-terrorist flag-waving.
1986 (R) 104m/C Rutger Hauer, Gene Simmons, Robert Guillaume, William Russ, Jerry Hardin, Mel Harris; *D:* Gary Sherman; *W:* Brian Taggert. **VHS, Beta** $14.95 *NWV, STE* 𝘐𝘐½

Wanted: The Perfect Guy Danny and Melanie try to find Mister Right for their divorced Mom (Kahn). An Emmy Award winner about single parents and their children.
1990 45m/C Madeline Kahn, Melanie Mayron. **VHS** $99.95 *AIM* 𝘐𝘐𝘐½

War & Love Two Jewish teenagers in Warsaw are torn apart by WWII and Nazi persecution. After the war they search for each other. Sincere, but not adequately developed, drama based on the book "The Survivors" by film's producer Jack Eisner.
1984 (PG-13) 112m/C Sebastian Keneas, Kyra Sedgwick; *D:* Moshe Mizrahi. **VHS, Beta** $79.95 *MGM, SWC* 𝘐𝘐

War and Peace Lengthy adaptation of Tolstoy's great (and likewise lengthy) novel about three families caught up in Russia's Napoleonic Wars from 1805 to 1812; filmed in Rome. Bad casting and confused script (by six writers) are somewhat overcome by awesome battle scenes and Hepburn. Remade in 1968.
1956 208m/C Audrey Hepburn, Mel Ferrer, Henry Fonda, Anita Ekberg, Vittorio Gassman, John Mills, Oscar Homolka, Herbert Lom, Helmut Dantine; *D:* King Vidor; *M:* Nino Rota. Academy Awards '56 Nominations: Best Color Cinematography, Best Costume Design (Color), Best Director (Vidor); Golden Globe Awards '57: Best Foreign Film; National Board of Review Awards '56: 5 Best Foreign Films of the Year. **VHS, Beta** $14.95 *PAR* 𝘐𝘐𝘐½

War and Peace The massive Russian production of Leo Tolstoy's masterpiece, adapting the classic tome practically scene by scene. All of the production took place in the Soviet Union. So painstaking that it took more than five years to finish, no other adaptation can touch it. Hugely expensive ($100 million, claimed the Russians), wildly uneven production. Great scenes of battle and aristocratic life. Though this version is far from perfect, one asks: Is it humanly possible to do screen justice to such a novel? In Russian with English subtitles. On four tapes. (Beware the two-part, poorly dubbed version that was also released.)
1968 373m/C Lyudmila Savelyeva, Sergei Bondarchuk, Vyacheslav Tihonov, Hira Ivanov-Golarko, Irina Gubanova, Antonina Shuranova; *D:* Sergei Bondarchuk. Academy Awards '68: Best Foreign Language Film; Nominations: Best Art Direction/Set Decoration; Golden Globe Awards '69: Best Foreign Film; National Board of Review Awards '68: 5 Best Foreign Films of the Year; New York Film Critics Awards '68: Best Foreign Film. **VHS, Beta** $99.95 *KUL, ING, TVC* 𝘐𝘐𝘐

War & Remembrance, Part 1 Tedious sequel to the epic television mini-series "The Winds of War," based on the novel by Herman Wouk. Historical fiction is created around the events of WWII, including Nazi persecution and naval battles in the Pacific. Seven cassette series. Followed by "War and Remembrance: The Final Chapter."
1988 120m/C Robert Mitchum, Jane Seymour, Hart Bochner, Victoria Tennant, Barry Bostwick, Polly Bergen, David Dukes, Michael Woods, Sharon Stone, Robert Morley, Sami Frey, Chaim Topol, John Rhys-Davies, Ian McShane, William Schallert, Jeremy Kemp, Steven Berkoff, Robert Hardy, Ralph Bellamy, John Gielgud; *D:* Dan Curtis. **VHS, Beta** $139.98 *MPI, MOV* 𝘐𝘐½

War & Remembrance, Part 2 The final installments of the excruciatingly boring and long mini-series. Herman Wouk's historical fiction concerning the last years of WWII. Six cassettes, in Hi-Fi stereo.
1989 120m/C Robert Mitchum, Jane Seymour, Hart Bochner, Ralph Bellamy, Victoria Tennant, Barry Bostwick, John Gielgud, Polly Bergen, David Dukes, Michael Woods; *D:* Dan Curtis. **VHS, Beta** *MPI* 𝘐𝘐½

War & Remembrance, Part 3 A brief glimmer of hope appears in this volume involving the lovers' reunion in Hawaii and the military power's changing of hands due to command of the Americans following the infamous Midway battle.
1988 120m/C Robert Mitchum, Jane Seymour, Hart Bochner, Victoria Tennant, Polly Bergen, David Dukes, Michael Woods; *D:* Dan Curtis. **VHS, Beta** *MPI* 𝘐𝘐½

War & Remembrance, Part 4 The middle part of 1942 sees its way through the American infiltration of Guadacanal, the treacherous stranglehold of Nazi Germany on Europe and other parts of the world, and the defiance toward defeat of the Russian Army.
1988 120m/C Robert Mitchum, Jane Seymour, Hart Bochner, Victoria Tennant, Polly Bergen, David Dukes, Michael Woods; *D:* Dan Curtis. **VHS, Beta** *MPI* 𝘐𝘐½

War & Remembrance, Part 5 As 1942 draws to a close, Wouk's well-known character, Pug, finds himself heading for a new assignment. North Africa welcomes the Allies in lieu of the Nazis. Stalingrad is mortified by an ever-strong Nazi invasion.
1988 120m/C Robert Mitchum, Jane Seymour, Hart Bochner, Victoria Tennant, Polly Bergen, David Dukes, Michael Woods; *D:* Dan Curtis. **VHS, Beta** *MPI* 𝘐𝘐½

War & Remembrance, Part 6 After leaving his dear cruiser behind, Pug says hello to Russia. The Ally leaders meet with much to discuss. Hitler is getting stronger and shrewder.
1988 120m/C Robert Mitchum, Jane Seymour, Hart Bochner, Victoria Tennant, Polly Bergen, David Dukes, Michael Woods; *D:* Dan Curtis. **VHS, Beta** *MPI* 𝘐𝘐½

War & Remembrance, Part 7 The Sicilian win by Patton brings about the devestation of Mussolini. Hitler's henchman are getting nervous and tired of battle. Germany succumbs to Allied troops in North Africa.
1988 120m/C Robert Mitchum, Jane Seymour, Hart Bochner, Victoria Tennant, Polly Bergen, David Dukes, Michael Woods; *D:* Dan Curtis. **VHS, Beta** *MPI* 𝘐𝘐½

War & Remembrance: The Final Chapter, Part 8 The final episodes of Herman Wouk's sweeping saga, following "The Winds of War" and "War and Remembrance," deal with the struggle of a Jewish family in war-torn Europe. Natalie and her

son, Louis, are trapped in a ghetto under the reign of a vicious Nazi, who considers a bribe for the sake of the mother and son. On 5 cassettes.
1989 120m/C Robert Mitchum, Jane Seymour, Hart Bochner, Victoria Tennant, Polly Bergen, David Dukes, Michael Woods, Sharon Stone, Robert Morley, Sami Frey, Chaim Topol, John Rhys-Davies, Ian McShane, William Schallert, Jeremy Kemp, Steven Berkoff, Robert Hardy, Ralph Bellamy, John Gielgud; *D:* Dan Curtis. **VHS, Beta** $99.98 *MPI, MOV* 𝘐𝘐½

War & Remembrance: The Final Chapter, Part 9 Both D-Day and an assassination of Hitler are in the works. Natalie and Louis are still in a desperate situation with the tyrannical Nazi endangering them constantly.
1989 120m/C Robert Mitchum, Jane Seymour, Hart Bochner, Victoria Tennant, Polly Bergen, David Dukes, Michael Woods; *D:* Dan Curtis. **VHS, Beta** *MPI* 𝘐𝘐½

War & Remembrance: The Final Chapter, Part 10 Though Louis becomes gravely ill, Natalie and Aaron are shipped to Auschwitz. Hitler lives in spite of the botched assasination threat, but the allies are closing in rapidly.
1989 120m/C Robert Mitchum, Jane Seymour, Hart Bochner, Victoria Tennant, Polly Bergen, David Dukes, Michael Woods; *D:* Dan Curtis. **VHS, Beta** *MPI* 𝘐𝘐½

War & Remembrance: The Final Chapter, Part 11 The infamous Battle of the Bulge takes place. Louis is taken away in the Nazi retreat. Natalie and Aaron continue to defy death in Auschwitz.
1989 120m/C Robert Mitchum, Jane Seymour, Hart Bochner, Victoria Tennant, Polly Bergen, David Dukes, Michael Woods; *D:* Dan Curtis. **VHS, Beta** *MPI* 𝘐𝘐½

War & Remembrance: The Final Chapter, Part 12 The climax culminates into the death of both FDR and Hitler, whose suicide shocked and relieved an entire world. The Nazi reign of terror crumbles, and the allies are victorious. But this series ends on the note of displacement and the effort of rebuilding what has so quickly and deftly been destroyed.
1989 120m/C Robert Mitchum, Jane Seymour, Hart Bochner, Victoria Tennant, Polly Bergen, David Dukes, Michael Woods; *D:* Dan Curtis. **VHS, Beta** *MPI* 𝘐𝘐½

War Between the Tates A college professor's affair with a female student is the basis for a tension filled stand-off with his wife. Mediocre made for television adaptation of the Allison Lurie novel, somewhat redeemed by Ashley's performance.
1976 90m/C Richard Crenna, Elizabeth Ashley, Granville Van Dusen; *D:* Lee Philips; *M:* John Barry. **VHS, Beta** *TLF* 𝘐𝘐

The War Boy Difficulties encountered by a young Canadian boy as he grows up in Central Europe during WWII. Not to be compared with "Empire of the Sun" or "Hope and Glory," both of which were released later; successful in its modest ambitions. Beautiful performance from 12-year-old star Hopely.
1985 (R) 86m/C Helen Shaver, Kenneth Welsh, Jason Hopely; *D:* Allan Eastman. **VHS** $79.98 *HHE* 𝘐𝘐½

War Brides Civil War brides confront life after the war. Low-budget drama.
198? 100m/C Elizabeth Richardson, Sharry Fleet, Sonja Smits. **VHS, Beta** $49.95 *TWE* 𝘐

War Bus Commando A fully loaded bus is the only way out when soldiers are caught behind enemy lines in Afghanistan. A case of the spoof coming first: The plot is almost exactly the same as "Stripes"—only this one isn't funny. In Hi-Fi.
1989 90m/C Savina Gersak, Mark Gregory, John Vernon; **D:** Frank Valenti. **VHS** NO *🎞*

War in Space Powerful U.N. Space Bureau Starships and UFOs band together to battle alien invaders among the volcanoes and deserts of Venus.
1977 91m/C Kensaku Marita, Yuko Asano, Ryo Ikebe. **VHS, Beta** VDA *🎞*

War in the Sky Director William Wyler's documentary account of the Army Air Corps in action. Extraordinary footage of the Thunderbolt, the P47 Fighter, and the B17 Bomber.
1982 90m/C **D:** William Wyler. **VHS, Beta** $59.95 GEM *🎞🎞🎞*

The War Lord Set in the 11th century, Heston stars as Chrysagon, a Norman knight and war lord who commands a peasant village. While battling his enemies, he becomes enamored of a peasant girl named Bronwyn (Forsyth), who is unfortunately engaged to someone else. Pulling rank, Chrysagon uses an ancient law that allows noblemen the first night with a bride and the two fall in love. The two vow to never part, but that sets the stage for even more bloody battles. Fine acting and great production values make this a well-adapted version of the play "The Lovers" by Leslie Stevens.
1965 121m/C Charlton Heston, Richard Boone, Rosemary Forsyth, Guy Stockwell, Niall MacGinnis, Henry Wilcoxon, James Farentino, Maurice Evans, Michael Conrad; **D:** Franklin J. Schaffner; **W:** John Collier, Millard Kaufman. **VHS, Beta** $19.98 MCA *🎞🎞🎞*

War Lover An American daredevil flying captain and his co-pilot find themselves vying for the affections of a woman during WWII in England. Seeks human frailty beneath surface heroism. McQueen is impressive, no thanks to mediocre script. Excellent aerial photography, and featuring one of a very few serviceable WWII B-17s then remaining. Based on John Hersey's novel.
1962 105m/B Steve McQueen, Robert Wagner, Shirley Anne Field, Bill Edwards, Gary Cockrell; **D:** Philip Leacock; **W:** Howard Koch. **VHS, Beta** $9.95 GKK *🎞🎞½*

The War of the Colossal Beast This sequel to "The Amazing Colossal Man" finds the seventy-foot Colonel Manning even angrier at the attempts to kill him than he was in the first film. So he wreaks more havoc until scolded by his sister into committing suicide for being such a troublemaker. Cheesy special effects but good for a laugh. **AKA:** The Terror Strikes.
1958 68m/B Dean Parkin, Sally Fraser, Russ Bender, Roger Pace, Charles Stewart; **D:** Bert I. Gordon. **VHS** $9.95 COL *🎞½*

War of the Gargantuas Tokyo is once again the boxing ring for giant monsters. This time it's a good gargantua (half human, half monster) against a bad gargantua. This is a strange one. **AKA:** Furankenshutain No Kaijusanda Tai Gailah; Sanda Tai Gailah; Duel of the Gargantuas.
1970 (G) 92m/C Russ Tamblyn, Kimi Mizuno, Kipp Hamilton, Yu Fujiki. **VHS** PAR *🎞*

War of the Robots A dying alien civilization kidnaps two brilliant Earth scientists in the hope that they'll help it survive.
1978 99m/C Antonio Sabato, Melissa Long, James R. Stuart. **VHS, Beta** $59.95 VCI *🎞*

The War of the Roses Acidic black comedy about a well-to-do suburban couple who can't agree on a property settlement in their divorce so they wage unreserved and ever-escalating combat on each other, using their palatial home as a battleground. Expertly and lovingly (if that's the word) directed by DeVito, who plays the lawyer. Turner and Douglas are splendid. Adapted from the novel by Warren Adler. Laserdisc version includes previously deleted scenes and commentary from DeVito.
1989 (R) 116m/C Michael Douglas, Kathleen Turner, Danny DeVito, Marianne Sagebrecht, Sean Astin, G.D. Spradlin, Peter Donat, Heather Fairfield, Dan Castellaneta, Danitra Vance; **D:** Danny DeVito; **W:** Michael Leeson; **M:** David Newman. **VHS, Beta** $12.00 FOX, IME *🎞🎞🎞*

War of the Wildcats Fast-moving western with Wayne as a tough cowboy battling a powerful land baron. They fight over land, oil and a woman. Unusual because Wayne's character acts on behalf of the Indians to drill and transport oil. **AKA:** In Old Oklahoma.
1943 102m/B John Wayne, Martha Scott, Albert Dekker, George "Gabby" Hayes, Sidney Blackmer; **D:** Albert Rogell. **VHS** $14.98 REP *🎞🎞½*

War of the Wizards Low-budget sci-fi thriller about an alien woman with supernatural powers who comes to take over the Earth. But, lucky for all earthlings, she's challenged by a hero-type just in the nick of time. **AKA:** The Phoenix.
1981 (PG) 90m/C Richard Kiel; **D:** Richard Caan. **VHS, Beta** NO *🎞½*

The War of the Worlds H.G. Wells's classic novel of the invasion of Earth by Martians, updated to 1950s California, with spectacular special effects of destruction caused by the Martian war machines. Pretty scary and tense; based more on Orson Welles's radio broadcast than on the book. Still very popular; hit the top 20 in sales when released on video. Classic thriller later made into a TV series. Produced by George Pal, who brought the world much sci-fi, including "The Time Machine," "Destination Moon," and "When Worlds Collide," and who appears here as a street person.
1953 85m/C Gene Barry, Ann Robinson, Les Tremayne, Lewis Martin, Robert Cornthwaite, Sandro Giglio; **D:** Byron Haskin. Academy Awards '53: Best Special Effects; Nominations: Best Film Editing, Best Sound. **VHS, Beta** $14.95 PAR *🎞🎞🎞½*

War Party During a 100-year commemoration of an Indian massacre in the Midwest, a murder occurs and a lynch mob chases a pack of young Blackfeet into the mountains before the inevitable showdown. A feeble attempt at portraying the unfair treatment of Native Americans. Un-subtle, Hollywood style, this time in favor of the Indians, and therefore un-serious. Too bad; the premise had potential.
1989 (R) 99m/C Kevin Dillon, Billy Wirth, Tim Sampson, M. Emmet Walsh; **D:** Franc Roddam. **VHS, Beta** $89.99 HBO *🎞🎞*

The War Room Eye opening, sometimes disturbing documentary presents a behind the scenes peek at what really goes on during a Presidential campaign. When filming began in June '92 Bill Clinton was an unknown political quantity and advisors George Stephanopoulous and James Carville were masterminding his campaign. The "War Room" refers to the building in Little Rock where they struggled to organize a small army of volunteers into a winning team. Highlights include the Democratic National Convention, the North Carolina leg of Clinton's campaign bus tour, three Presidential debates, and the week leading up to election night.
1993 (PG) 93m/C **D:** Chris Hegedus, D.A. Pennebaker. Academy Awards '93 Nominations: Best Feature Documentary; National Board of Review Awards '93: Best Documentary. **VHS** $94.95 VMK *🎞🎞🎞*

War Victims Drama about Japanese POW prisons in WWII.
1985 90m/C **VHS, Beta** $59.95 VCD *🎞½*

The War Wagon The Duke plans revenge on Cabot, the greedy mine owner who stole his gold claim and framed him for murder for which he spent years in prison. He assembles a gang to aid him, including a wise-cracking Indian (Keel) and the man sent by Cabot to kill him (Douglas). Wayne's plan is to steal the gold being shipped in Cabot's armor-plated stagecoach, the "war wagon." Well-written, good performances, lots of action. Based on the book "Badman" by Clair Huffaker. The laserdisc version is available in letterbox format.
1967 101m/C John Wayne, Kirk Douglas, Howard Keel, Robert Walker Jr., Keenan Wynn, Bruce Dern, Bruce Cabot, Joanna Barnes; **D:** Burt Kennedy. **VHS, Beta** $19.98 MCA *🎞🎞🎞*

Warbirds American pilots are off to quell a revolution in a Middle East country. Too little action fails to support mediocre plot and characters.
1988 (R) 88m/C Jim Eldert, Cully Holland, Bill Brinsfield; **D:** Ulli Lommel; **W:** Ulli Lommel. **VHS, Beta** $19.95 STE, VMK *🎞🎞*

Warbus Marines lead a school bus load of Americans through war-torn Vietnam to safety. Decent action and surprisingly enjoyable characters. Otherwise mediocre.
1985 (R) 90m/C Daniel Stephen, Romano Kristoff, Urs Althaus; **D:** Ted Kaplan. **VHS, Beta** $19.98 SUE, NLC *🎞🎞*

WarCat The daughter of a green beret fights for her life against a blood-thirsty gang. **AKA:** Angel of Vengeance.
1988 78m/C Macka Foley, Jannina Poynter, David O'Hara, Carl Erwin; **D:** Ted V. Mikels. **VHS** $79.95 TWE *🎞*

Ward Six An insane asylum is the setting for various analogies regarding the perception of reality as defined by societal values. When it is felt that the residing physician is no more sane than his patients, he is placed among them, in Ward Six. Adapted from a story by Anton Chekhov. In Serbian with English subtitles.
19?? 93m/C **D:** Lucian Pintilie. **VHS, Beta** $59.95 FCT *🎞🎞*

Wardogs A man tries to rescue his brother from becoming one of an elite, brainwashed group of ex-Vietnam vets trained by the government as professional assassins. Might not have been quite so bad; promising inversion of many 'Nam cliches wrecked by unnecessary violence and bad acting. **AKA:** The Assassination Team.
1987 95m/C Tim Earle, Bill Redvers, Daniel Hubenbecker; **D:** Daniel Hubenbecker. **Beta** NO *🎞½*

WarGames A young computer whiz, thinking that he's sneaking an advance look at a new line of video games, breaks into the country's NORAD missile-defense system and challenges it to a game of Global Thermonuclear Warfare. The game might just turn out to be the real thing. Slick look at the possibilities of an accidental start to WWIII. Entertaining and engrossing, but with a B-grade ending.

1983 (PG) 110m/C Matthew Broderick, Dabney Coleman, John Wood, Ally Sheedy; **D:** John Badham; **W:** Walter F. Parkes, Lawrence Lasker. **VHS, Beta** $19.98 FOX ♫♫½

Warkill WWII action set in the jungles of the Philippines. Journalist who idolizes violent, hard-edged colonel, loses his illusions, but gains a more genuine respect for his men. Not-bad war flick.
1965 99m/C George Montgomery, Tom Drake, Eddie Infante; **D:** Ferde Grofe Jr.; **W:** Ferde Grofe Jr. **VHS, Beta** $19.95 AHV ♫♫½

Warlock Claustrophic, resonant townbound tale of a marshal (Fonda) and his adoring sidekick (Quinn) who clean up a town which then turns against him. Unusual story, fine performances carry this well beyond the run-of-the-mill cow flick. Fonda re-established himself at the box office as a western star, after "Stage Struck" and "Twelve Angry Men." From the novel by Oakley Hall. Look for "Bones" McCoy from "Star Treck" in a bit part.
1959 122m/C Henry Fonda, Anthony Quinn, Richard Widmark, Dorothy Malone, Wallace Ford, Richard Arlen, Regis Toomey, DeForest Kelley; **D:** Edward Dmytryk; **W:** Robert Arthur. **VHS, Beta** $9.99 STE, FOX ♫♫♫

Warlock It's 1691 and the most powerful warlock (Sands) in the New World is only hours away from execution. Luckily, his pal, Satan, whisks him (and witchhunter Grant, by mistake) three hundred years in the future to present-day Los Angeles, where he crashlands in Singer's house. Surprisingly witty dialogue and neat plot twists outshine occasionally cheesy special effects.
1991 (R) 103m/C Richard E. Grant, Julian Sands, Lori Singer, Mary Woronov, Richard Kuss, Kevin O'Brien, Anna Levine, Allan Miller, David Carpenter; **D:** Steve Miner; **W:** David N. Twohy; **M:** Jerry Goldsmith. **VHS** $92.95 VMK ♫♫½

Warlock Moon Young woman is lured to a secluded spa and falls prey to a coven of witches.
1973 75m/C Laurie Walters, Joe Spano; **D:** Bill Herbert. **VHS, Beta** $49.95 UNI ♫½

Warlock: The Armageddon Sequel finds Sands back again as the sinister Warlock. This time he's out to gather six Druidic rune stones which have the power to summon Satan's emissary (in the wrong hands) or to stop his nefarious activities (in the right ones). A sect in a small California town serves as the keeper of the stones, only their designated champions are two unprepared teenagers. Sands has all the fun, gleefully dispatching his would-be opponents with some good special effects.
1993 (R) 93m/C Julian Sands, Chris Young, Paula Marshall, Steve Kahan, Charles Hallahan, R.G. Armstrong, Bruce Glover, Zach Galligan, Dawn Ann Billings, Joanna Pacula; **D:** Anthony Hickox; **W:** Kevin Rock, Sam Bernard. **VHS** $94.95 VMK ♫♫½

Warlords Lone soldier Carradine battles mutant hordes in a post-apocalyptic desert. Amateurish futuristic drivel.
1988 (R) 87m/C David Carradine, Sid Haig, Ross Hagen, Fox Harris, Robert Quarry, Victoria Sellers, Brinke Stevens, Dawn Wildsmith; **D:** Fred Olen Ray. **VHS, Beta** $79.95 VMK ♫½

Warlords from Hell Two young men motorcycling through Mexico are captured by a bloodthirsty gang and forced to do hard labor in the marijuana fields. We can only hope that they just learn to say no.
1987 (R) 76m/C Brad Henson, Jeffrey Rice; **D:** Clark Henderson. **VHS, Beta** WAR Woof!

Warlords of the 21st Century Bandit gang speed around the galaxy in an indestructible battle cruiser. Then the boys are challenged by a space lawman. Gratuitously violent action pic lacking real action. Filmed on planet New Zealand. **AKA:** Battletruck.
1982 91m/C Michael Beck, Annie McEnroe, James Wainwright; **D:** Harley Cokliss. **VHS, Beta** $19.98 SUE ♫½

Warlords 3000 In the future, Earth is a barren wasteland ravaged by raging electrical storms. Deadly cancers are rampant and the few people who have survived take their comfort in a hallucinogenic drug that provides a temporary pleasure and a permanent madness. Drug lords control the planet but one man is out to eliminate the scum and save the future.
1993 (R) 92m/C Jay Roberts Jr., Denise Marie Duff, Steve Blanchard, Wayne Duvall; **D:** Faruque Ahmed; **W:** Ron Herbst, Faruque Ahmed. **VHS** $89.95 COL ♫½

Warm Nights on a Slow-Moving Train A hot-blooded schoolteacher turns tricks for cash to support her brother on the Sunday-night train to Melbourne, until she meets a stranger who has a deadly masquerade of his own. Interestingly different; much sex, as you can imagine. Australian-made.
1987 (R) 90m/C Wendy Hughes, Colin Friels, Norman Kaye, John Clayton, Peter Whitford; **D:** Bob Ellis; **W:** Bob Ellis, Denny Lawrence. **VHS, Beta** $79.95 PSM, PAR ♫♫

Warm Summer Rain A young couple meet under unusual circumstances and develop a relationship in a desert cabin as they reflect on their unfulfilled pasts. Lust, self-doubt and longing for something to hold onto draw them together as the days pass. Thoroughly self-indulgent romantic comedy that's oddly self-pitying and poorly directed.
1989 (R) 85m/C Kelly Lynch, Barry Tubb; **D:** Joe Gayton. **VHS, Beta** $19.95 COL ♫½

The Warning A pair of proverbial honest cops investigate ties between the mob and the police department. Hard to follow.
1980 101m/C Martin Balsam, Giuliano Gemma, Giancarlo Zanetti; **D:** Damiano Damiani. **VHS, Beta** $49.95 MED ♫

Warning from Space Aliens visit Earth to warn of impending cosmic doom. When it becomes apparent that the one-eyed starfish look is off-putting, they assume human form. Japanese sci fi. **AKA:** The Mysterious Satellite; The Cosmic Man Appears in Tokyo; Space Men Appear in Tokyo; Unknown Satellite Over Tokyo; Uchujin Tokyo Ni Arawaru.
1956 87m/B Toyomi Karita, Keizo Kawasaki, Isao Yamagata, Shozo Nanbu, Buntaro Miake, Mieko Nagai, Kiyoko Hirai; **D:** Koji Shima. **VHS** $19.98 NOS, SMW, SNC ♫½

Warning Shadows Classic example of interior German Expressionism. Brilliantly portrays a jealous husband's emotions and obsessions through shadows. Innocent events seem to reek of sin. A seldom-seen study of the oft-precarious distinction between love and obsession; directly influenced by the classic "The Cabinet of Dr. Caligari." Silent with German and English titles.
1923 93m/B Fritz Kortner; **D:** Arthur Robinson. **VHS, Beta, 8mm** $19.95 GPV, FCT, VPR ♫♫♫

Warning Sign A high-tech thriller in which a small town is terrorized by the accidental release of an experimental virus at a research facility. Shades of "The Andromeda Strain" and "The China Syndrome," though less originality and quality.

1985 (R) 99m/C Sam Waterston, Kathleen Quinlan, Yaphet Kotto, Richard Dysart, Rick Rossovich; **D:** Hal Barwood; **W:** Matthew Robbins. **VHS, Beta** $79.98 FOX ♫½

The Warrior A young warrior is trapped in a corrupt ring of competitive boxing and karate.
19?? 50m/C Dennis Brown, Cheng Tien Chi. **VHS, Beta** $49.95 OCE ♫

The Warrior & the Sorceress Mercenary Carradine offers his services to rival factions fighting for control of a water well in an impoverished desert village located on a planet with two suns. He attempts to aggravate the conflicts between the factions, playing the shifty go-between. The sorceress is topless throughout. "A Fistful of Dollars" goes to outer space. Inoffensive, except that better judgment is expected of Carradine.
1984 81m/C David Carradine, Luke Askew, Maria Socas, Harry Townes; **D:** John Broderick. **VHS, Beta** $29.98 LIV, VES ♫½

Warrior of the Lost World A warrior must destroy the evil Omega Force who tyrannically rules the world in the distant future, etcetera, etcetera. One-size-fits-all premise; horrible special effects; miserably directed. Only for really hard-core Pleasance fans.
1984 90m/C Robert Ginty, Persis Khambatta, Donald Pleasence; **D:** David Worth. **VHS, Beta** $69.99 HBO Woof!

Warrior Queen Long ago in ancient Rome, overly histrionic mayor Pleasence married porn queen with a wandering eye Fox, and much gratuitous sex and erupting volcanoes resulted. Even the score blows. Also available in an "Unrated" version. Brit pop star Fox is billed as Stasia Micula.
1987 (R) 69m/C Sybil Danning, Donald Pleasence, Richard Hill, Josephine Jacqueline Jones, Tally Chanel, Samantha Fox. **VHS** $79.98 LIV, VES ♫

Warrior Within Eight Kung Fu greats pay tribute to the memory of Bruce Lee by kicking and jumping about.
1980 85m/C Chuck Norris, Dan Inosanto, Mike Stone, Fumio Demura, Ron Taganashi. **VHS, Beta** VTR ♫

The Warriors Swashbuckling adventure about Prince Edward's valiant rescue of Lady Joan and her children from the clutches of the evil Count De Ville. Flynn looks old and pudgy, but buckles his way gallantly through intrepid adventure. Also the last Flynn to see: fun, but more or less completely derivative and familiar. Filmed in England. **AKA:** The Dark Avenger.
1955 85m/C Errol Flynn, Peter Finch, Joanne Dru, Yvonne Furneaux, Noel Willman, Michael Hordern; **D:** Henry Levin. **VHS, Beta** $59.98 FOX, MLB ♫♫½

The Warriors Action story about a turf battle between New York City street gangs that rages from Coney Island to the Bronx. Silly plot works because of fine performances and direction, excellent use of action and color, and nonstop pace. Fight scenes are very carefully, even obviously, choreographed.
1979 (R) 94m/C Michael Beck, James Remar, Deborah Van Valkenburgh, Thomas G. Waites, David Patrick Kelly; **D:** Walter Hill; **W:** Walter Hill. **VHS, Beta** $14.95 PAR ♫♫½

Warriors from Hell Western forces in a small African country battle rebel fighters who threaten the hapless native villagers.
1990 (R) 90m/C Deon Stewardson, Shayne Leith, Adrienne Pierce, Glen Gabela, Hector Manthanda, Ivan Dean, Connie Chume; **D:** Ronnie Isaacs; **W:** Ronnie Isaacs. **VHS** $89.95 COL ♫½

Warriors of the Apocalypse After a nuclear holocaust, heavily sworded and loin-clothed men search for the secret of eternal life and instead find an Amazon realm in the jungle. A terrible waste of post-apocalyptic scenery. *AKA:* Searchers of the Voodoo Mountain; Time Raiders.
1985 (R) 96m/C Michael James, Debrah Moore, Ken Metcalfe, Franco Guerrero; *D:* Bobby Suarez. **VHS, Beta $19.98** *LIV* Woof!

Warriors of the Sung Dynasty Warriors given amnesty by the Emperor are tricked into a bloody confrontation. Adaption of a classic Chinese tale.
19?? 90m/C Mu Huan Hu. **VHS $34.95** *OCE 🐾*

Warriors of the Wasteland It's the year 2019, and the world has been devastated by a nuclear war. The few survivors try to reach a distant land which emits radio signals indicating the presence of human life. They are hindered by attacks from the fierce homosexual Templars, led by a self-proclaimed priest called One. Mindless rip-off of "Road Warrior" and obviously made on the proverbial shoestring budget. Dubbed. *AKA:* The New Barbarians; I Nuovi Barbari.
1983 (R) 92m/C Fred Williamson, Timothy Brent, Anna Kanakis; *D:* Enzo G. Castellari. **VHS, Beta** NO Woof!

The Wash Quiet domestic drama about a couple who drift apart after 40 years of marriage. Set interestingly among Japanese-Americans in California; treats social and cultural factors with intelligence. Superb cast takes it a notch higher.
1988 94m/C Mako, Nobu McCarthy, Sab Shimono; *D:* Michael Toshiyuki Uno. **VHS, Beta $79.95** *ACA 🐾🐾🐾*

Washington Affair A tale of intrigue in the nation's capital. Sullivan is a businessman who uses women and blackmail to capture government contracts. Selleck is the hapless bureaucrat he preys on. Remake of Soloff's own "Intimacy" was not released until "Magnum P.I." became a hit.
1977 (PG) 90m/C Tom Selleck, Carol Lynley, Barry Sullivan; *D:* Victor Stoloff. **VHS, Beta $69.98** *SUE 🐾🐾*

Washington Mistress Eminently ordinary made-for-TV grist about Capitol Hill aide Arnaz, politician Jordan, and their affair. Listless performances.
1981 96m/C Lucie Arnaz, Richard Jordan, Tony Bill; *D:* Peter Levin. **VHS** NO 🐾 1/2

The Wasp Woman In her quest for eternal beauty, a woman uses a potion made from wasp enzymes. Naturally, she turns into a wasp monster at night. Good fun, courtesy of Corman.
1959 84m/B Susan Cabot, Anthony Eisley, Barboura Morris, Michael Marks, William Roerick, Frank Gerstle, Bruno Ve Sota, Frank Wolf; *D:* Roger Corman. **VHS $9.95** *NOS, RHI, SNC* 🐾 1/2

Watch It Four self-absorbed twenty-something guys share a house in Chicago for the summer. They pursue a post-adolescent game, consisting of increasingly complicated practical jokes, where the unsuspecting victim is set up for a "watch it" gag. The rivalry escalates, and turns increasingly unpleasant, when cousins John and Michael vie for the affections of Anne, who's wary of involvement because of male selfishness. A first-rate cast with recognizable situations and emotions.
1993 (R) 102m/C Jon Tenney, Peter Gallagher, Suzy Amis, John C. McGinley, Tom Sizemore, Lili Taylor, Cynthia Stevenson, Terri Hawkes, Jordanna Capra; *D:* Tom Flynn; *W:* Tom Flynn; *M:* Stanley Clarke. **VHS** *PAR* 🐾🐾🐾

Watch Me When I Kill We'd rather not. A young nightclub dancer stops by a drugstore seconds after the owner was killed. She doesn't see the killer's face, but his rasping voice remains to torment her and the viewer. Dubbed.
1981 (R) 95m/C Richard Stewart, Sylvia Kramer, Anthony Bido. **VHS, Beta** NO 🐾

Watch on the Rhine Couple involved with the anti-Nazi underground has escaped the country, but is pursued and harassed by Nazi agents. Adapted by Hammett and Hellman from her play. Performed on stage before the U.S. entered the war, it was the first American play and movie to portray the ugliness of fascism as an ideology, as opposed to the more devious evil of its practical side. The Production Code at the time required that a killer always be punished; the murderer (whose screen motives had been noble) refused to film the offending scene, which explains the tacked-on ending. Superb drama from a pair of highly gifted writers and a great cast. Shumlin also directed the play.
1943 114m/B Bette Davis, Paul Lukas, Donald Woods, Beulah Bondi, Geraldine Fitzgerald, George Coulouris, Henry Daniell, Helmut Dantine; *D:* Herman Shumlin; *W:* Lillian Hellman, Dashiell Hammett. Academy Awards '43: Best Actor (Lukas); Nominations: Best Picture, Best Screenplay, Best Supporting Actress (Watson); Golden Globe Awards '44: Best Actor—Drama (Lukas); National Board of Review Awards '43: 10 Best Films of the Year; New York Film Critics Awards '43: Best Actor (Lukas), Best Film. **VHS, Beta $19.98** *FOX, MGM, FCT* 🐾🐾🐾 1/2

Watch the Birdie It's Skelton three times over as cameraman, father, and grandfather! First, he accidentally films a scam that would send the lovely Miss Dahl filing for bankruptcy. Later a crazy chase scene unfolds, that will have viewers rolling, as Skelton the cameraman nabs the bad guys and turns them over to the cops. Light fun that will charm Skelton fans.
1950 70m/B Red Skelton, Arlene Dahl, Ann Miller, Leon Ames; *D:* Jack Donohue. **VHS, Beta $19.98** *MGM* 🐾🐾 1/2

Watched A former U.S. attorney, gone underground, has a nervous breakdown and kills the narcotics agent who has him under surveillance. Self-important, too serious social/political conspiracy drama of the Watergate era. Keach and Yulin are good, but not good enough to save it.
1973 95m/C Stacy Keach, Harris Yulin, Bridgit Polk; *D:* John Parsons; *M:* Weather Report. **VHS, Beta $69.98** *LIV, VES, SIM* 🐾🐾

The Watcher in the Woods When an American family rents an English country house, the children are haunted by the spirit of a long-missing young girl. A very bland attempt at a ghost story.
1981 (PG) 83m/C Bette Davis, Carroll Baker, David McCallum, Ian Bannen, Lynn-Holly Johnson; *D:* John Hough; *W:* Brian Clemens. **VHS, Beta $14.99** *DIS* 🐾🐾

Watchers From the suspense novel by Dean R. Koontz, a secret experiment goes wrong, creating half-human monsters. A boy and his extremely intelligent dog are soon pursued. Low-budget, Corman-influenced production is tacky but effective.
1988 (R) 99m/C Barbara Williams, Michael Ironside, Corey Haim; *D:* Jon Hess; *M:* Joel Goldsmith. **VHS, Beta $14.95** *LIV* 🐾🐾

Watchers 2 Sequel to "Watchers" follows the further adventures of a super-intelligent golden retriever who leads a Marine to an animal psychologist and then attempts to warn them both of a mutant killer. The dog

says woof, but this movie doesn't quite. Fun for lovers of hounds or horror flicks.
1990 (R) 101m/C Marc Singer, Tracy Scoggins; *D:* Thierry Notz; *M:* Rick Conrad. **VHS, Beta $14.95** *LIV* 🐾🐾

Water The resident governor of a Caribbean British colony juggles various predatory interests when a valuable mineral water resource is found. The good cast is wasted in this all-too-silly effort.
1985 (PG-13) 89m/C Michael Caine, Brenda Vaccaro, Leonard Rossiter, Valerie Perrine, Jimmie Walker; *Cameos:* Eric Clapton, George Harrison, Fred Gwynne, Ringo Starr; *D:* Dick Clement; *W:* Dick Clement, Ian LaFrenais, Bill Persky. **VHS, Beta $29.95** *PAR* 🐾

Water Babies When a chimney sweep's 12-year-old apprentice is wrongly accused of stealing silver, the boy and his dog fall into a pond and eventually rescue some of the characters they find there. Combination of live-action and animated fairy-tale story set in nineteenth-century London. Boring, unless you're a young child with equivalent standards. Based on the book by Charles Kingsley. *AKA:* Slip Slide Adventures.
1979 93m/C James Mason, Billie Whitelaw, David Tomlinson, Paul Luty, Sammantha Coates; *D:* Lionel Jeffries. **VHS, Beta $29.98** *SUE* 🐾🐾

Water Rustlers Unscrupulous land baron builds a dam on his side of the creek with the intention of drying out the cattle pastures. Heroine Page, whose pop has been rubbed out by varmints, and good guy/lover O'Brien save her property and avenge her father. Second of three Page westerns.
1939 55m/B Dorothy Page, Dave O'Brien; *D:* Samuel Diege. **VHS, Beta $27.95** *VCN, VDM* 🐾 1/2

The Waterdance Autobiographical film based on the experiences of writer/co-director Jimenez. When writer Joel Garcia (Stolz) is paralyzed in a hiking accident he finds himself dealing with not only the rehab process itself but his feelings, the feelings of his married lover, and those of his fellow patients. Deals unsentimentally with all the physical adjustments, including the sexual ones. Resolutions may be predictable but the performances rise above any script weaknesses. The title refers to Hill's dream of dancing on water—and the fear of drowning if he stops.
1991 (R) 106m/C Eric Stoltz, Wesley Snipes, William Forsythe, Helen Hunt, Elizabeth Pena, Grace Zabriskie; *D:* Neal Jimenez, Michael Steinberg; *W:* Neal Jimenez; *M:* Michael Convertino. **VHS $19.95** *COL, PMS, BTV* 🐾🐾🐾

Waterfront Dreary dockside melodrama, with drinking and brawling longshoreman Jim (Morgan) avenging his brother's death. Based on the play "Blindspot" by Kenyon Nicholson.
1939 59m/B Dennis (Stanley Morner) Morgan, Gloria Dickson, Marie Wilson, Larry Williams, Sheila Bromley, Ward Bond, Frank Faylen; *D:* Terry Morse; *W:* Arthur Ripley, Lee Katz. **VHS $12.95** *GPV* 🐾 1/2

Waterfront Nazis coerce German-Americans into helping them in WWII-era San Francisco. Credulity defying spy doings, but that's okay. Fairly entertaining wartime drama about paranoia on the home front.
1944 68m/B John Carradine, J. Carroll Naish, Terry Frost, Maris Wrixon, Edwin Maxwell; *D:* Steve Sekely. **VHS, Beta $16.95** *SNC, VCI* 🐾🐾

Waterfront Effective romantic drama set in Melbourne, Australia. Australian workers strike after taking forced pay cuts. As a result, Italian immigrants are hired as scabs to keep the docks going. Despite the tension, an Italian woman and an Australian man fall

deeply in love, only to find that they must struggle to keep that love alive.
1983 294m/C Jack Thompson, Greta Scacchi, Frank Gallacher, Tony Rickards, Mark Little, Jay Mannering, Ray Barrett, Chris Haywood, Warren Mitchell, Noni Hazlehurst, John Karlsen, Elin Jenkins; *D:* Chris Thomson. **VHS, Beta $79.95** PSM, PAR ♫♫½

Waterhole #3 Three Confederate army buddies steal a fortune in gold bullion from the Union Army and hide it in a waterhole in the desert. One of the funnier entries in the Western comedy genre.
1967 (PG) 95m/C James Coburn, Carroll O'Connor, Margaret Blye, Claude Akins, Bruce Dern, Joan Blondell, James Whitmore; *D:* William A. Graham; *M:* Dave Grusin. **VHS $14.95** PAR ♫♫½

Waterland Meandering drama about a history teacher who tries to solve a personal crisis by using his class as a sounding board to describe his troubled past in England. Dark secrets abound, including incest, madness, murder, and the terrifying love between the teacher and his childhood bride. Melancholy, overwrought but partially redeemed by the lead performances of Irons and his (real-life and cinematic) wife, Cusack. The film's setting has been unfortunately moved from London to Pittsburgh, destroying story links. Based on the novel by Graham Swift.
1992 (R) 95m/C Jeremy Irons, Ethan Hawke, Sinead Cusack, John Heard, Grant Warnock, Lena Headey, Peter Postlethwaite, Cara Buono; *D:* Stephen Gyllenhaal; *W:* Peter Prince; *M:* Carter Burwell. **VHS $19.95** NLC, COL ♫♫

Waterloo Massive chronicle of Napoleon's European conquests and eventual defeat at the hands of Wellington. Filmed on location in Italy and the Ukraine, it bombed due largely to Steiger's bizarre rendition of Napoleon.
1971 (G) 122m/C Rod Steiger, Orson Welles, Virginia McKenna, Michael Wilding, Donal Donnelly, Christopher Plummer, Jack Hawkins, Dan O'Herlihy, Terence Alexander, Rupert Davies, Ivo Garrani, Gianno Garko; *D:* Sergei Bondarchuk. **VHS $14.95** PAR, FCT, FUS ♫♫

Waterloo Bridge In London during WWI, a soldier from an aristocratic family and a ballet dancer begin a tragic romance when they meet by chance on the foggy Waterloo Bridge. When he's listed as dead, her despair turns her to prostitution. But then he returns from POW camp, they once again meet by accident on Waterloo Bridge, and their romance resumes. Four-hanky drama with fine performances by Leigh (her first after "Gone with the Wind") and Taylor.
1940 109m/B Vivien Leigh, Robert Taylor, Lucile Watson, Sir C. Aubrey Smith, Maria Ouspenskaya, Virginia Field; *D:* Mervyn LeRoy. **VHS, Beta $19.98** MGM ♫♫♫

Watermelon Man The tables are turned for a bigoted white guy when he wakes up one morning to discover he has become a black man. Broad comedy with not much place to go is still engaging. Cambridge takes on both roles, appearing in unconvincing white makeup.
1970 (R) 97m/C Godfrey Cambridge, Erin Moran, Estelle Parsons, Howard Caine; *D:* Melvin Van Peebles. **VHS, Beta $59.95** COL, FCT ♫♫

Watership Down Wonderfully animated story based on Richard Adams's allegorical novel about how a group of rabbits escape fear and overcome oppression while searching for a new and better home. It's really an adult theme with sufficient violence to the poor wittle wabbits to scare the kiddies.
1978 (PG) 92m/C *D:* Martin Rosen; *W:* Martin Rosen; *V:* Ralph Richardson, Zero Mostel, John Hurt, Denholm Elliott, Harry Andrews, Michael Hordern, Joss Ackland. **VHS, Beta, 8mm $14.95** WAR, TVC, WTA ♫♫½

Wavelength A rock star living in the Hollywood Hills with his girlfriend stumbles on an ultra-secret government project involving friendly aliens from outer space recovered from a recent UFO crash site. Fun, enthusiastically unoriginal cheap sci-fi. Soundtrack by Tangerine Dream.
1983 (PG) 87m/C Robert Carradine, Cherie Currie, Keenan Wynn; *D:* Mike Gray; *W:* Mike Gray. **VHS, Beta $9.98** SUE, STE ♫♫½

Wax, or the Discovery of Television Among the Bees Intricate and eccentric fable dealing with alternate realities and perceptions. Jacob Maker (Blair) keeps a hive of very unusual bees, a family legacy passed down from his grandfather. Jacob begins experiencing a eerie communication with his bees and suffering mysterious blackouts, which cause him to perceive the world through blurred bee vision. New Mexico desert setting provides a surreal and desolate landscape.
1993 85m/C David Blair, Meg Savlov, Florence Ormezzano, William S. Burroughs; *D:* David Blair; *W:* David Blair; *M:* Beo Morales, Brooks Williams. **VHS** ICA ♫♫

Waxwork A wax museum opens up, and it is soon evident that the dummies are not what they seem. Garbled nonthriller. Available in a 100-minute unrated version.
1988 (R) 97m/C Zach Galligan, Deborah Foreman, Michelle Johnson, Dana Ashbrook, Miles O'Keeffe, Patrick Macnee, David Warner; *D:* Anthony Hickox. **VHS, Beta $14.98** LIV, VES ♫½

Waxwork 2: Lost in Time A young couple (Galligan and Schnarre) barely escape with their lives when the infamous waxworks museum burns down. A severed hand also gets loose and follows Schnarre home and murders her stepfather, leaving her to take the blame. In order to prove her innocence, the couple must travel through a bizarre time machine. Extraordinary special effects, strange plot twists, and recreations of scenes from past horror movies make this a highly entertaining sequel.
1991 (R) 104m/C Zach Galligan, Alexander Godunov, Bruce Campbell, Michael Des Barres, Monika Schnarre; *D:* Anthony Hickox. **VHS $14.98** LIV ♫♫½

Waxworks A major achievement in German Expressionism, in which a poet imagines scenarios in a wax museum fairground that involve Jack the Ripper, Ivan the Terrible and Haroun al-Rashid. Influential and considered ahead of its time. Silent.
1924 63m/B William Dieterle, Emil Jannings, Conrad Veidt, Werner Krauss, John Gottowt, Olga Belajeff; *D:* Paul Leni; *W:* Henrik Galeen. **VHS, Beta $16.95** SNC, NOS, LIV ♫♫♫

Way Back Home Man wants to adopt a boy to release him from the clutches of his cruel guardian. Minor role for the then unknown Davis. *AKA:* Old Greatheart; Other People's Business.
1932 81m/B Phillips Lord, Frank Albertson, Bette Davis; *D:* William A. Seiter. **VHS, Beta $19.98** TTC, FCT ♫♫

Way Down East Melodramatic silent drama of a country girl who is tricked into a fake marriage by a scheming playboy. The famous final scene of Gish adrift on the ice floes is in color. One of Griffith's last critical and popular successes. This tape includes the original Griffith-approved musical score. Remade in 1935 with Henry Fonda.

1920 107m/B Lillian Gish, Richard Barthelmess, Lowell Sherman, Creighton Hale; *D:* D.W. Griffith. **VHS, Beta $19.95** NOS, BAR, VYY ♫♫♫

Way Down South The orphan son of a plantation owner tries to take over his father's estate, only to find out that the place has been run into the ground by a corrupt lawyer and a cruel slave driver. Black poet Hughes and actor Muse collaborated on the screenplay. German-born director Vorhaus was in his second year in Hollywood, after making his mark in Britain directing talkies. ♫Good Ground; Louisiana; Nobody Know De Trouble I See; Sometimes I Feel Like a Motherless Child; Lord I You Can't Come Send One Angel Down.
1939 62m/B Bobby Breen, Alan Mowbray, Ralph Morgan, Clarence Muse, Steffi Duna, Sally Blane, Edwin Maxwell; *D:* Bernard Vorhaus; *W:* Clarence Muse, Langston Hughes. **VHS $24.95** NOS ♫½

Way He Was A satirical re-enactment of the events that led up to the Watergate burglary and the coverup that followed.
1976 (R) 87m/C Steve Friedman, Al Lewis, Merrie Lynn Ross, Doodles Weaver. **VHS, Beta $54.95** VCI ♫♫

Way of the Black Dragon When slave-trading drug traffickers threaten the moral fiber of our nation, two commandoes join forces to halt their operation.
1981 88m/C Ron Van Cliff, Carter Wang, Charles Bonet; *D:* Chan Wui Ngai. **VHS, Beta $39.95** TWE ♫

Way of the West Them durn pesky sheepherders are up to it again! Okay, so the cow/sheep thing is a classic western plot, but here it's offered perfunctorily.
1935 52m/B Wally Wales, William Desmond, Art Mix, Jim Sheridan, Bobby Nelson; *D:* Robert Emmett. **VHS, Beta $19.95** NOS, DVT, RXM ♫½

The Way Out Average crime drama starring Nelson as a fugitive accused of killing a bookie. *AKA:* Dial 999.
1956 90m/C Gene Nelson, Mona Freeman, John Bentley, Michael Goodliffe, Sydney Tafler; *D:* Montgomery Tully. **VHS $16.95** SNC ♫♫

Way Out West The classic twosome journey way out west to deliver the deed to a gold mine to the daughter of their late prospector pal. The obligatory romance is missing, but you'll be laughing so hard you won't notice. One of Stan and Ollie's best. Score includes the song "Trail of the Lonesome Pine." Also included on this tape is a 1932 Todd and Pitts short, "Red Noses." Available colorized.
1937 86m/B Stan Laurel, Oliver Hardy, Rosina Lawrence, James Finlayson, Sharon Lynne, ZaSu Pitts, Thelma Todd, William Haines; *D:* James W. Horne. **VHS, Beta $19.95** CCB, MED, MLB ♫♫♫

The Way We Were Big box-office hit follows a love story between opposites from the 1930s to the 1950s. Streisand is a Jewish political radical who meets the handsome WASP Redford at college. They're immediately attracted to one another, but it takes years before they act on it and eventually marry. They move to Hollywood where Redford is a screenwriter and left-wing Streisand becomes involved in the Red scare and the blacklist, much to Redford's dismay. Though always in love, their differences are too great to keep them together. An old-fashioned and sweet romance, with much gloss. Hit title song sung by Streisand. Adapted by Arthur Laurents from his novel.
1973 (PG) 118m/C Barbra Streisand, Robert Redford, Bradford Dillman, Viveca Lindfors, Herb Edelman, Murray Hamilton, Patrick O'Neal, James Woods, Sally Kirkland; *D:* Sydney Pollack; *W:* Arthur Laurents; *M:* Marvin Hamlisch.

Academy Awards '73: Best Song ("The Way We Were"), Best Original Score; Nominations: Best Actress (Streisand), Best Art Direction/Set Decoration, Best Cinematography; Academy Awards '76: Best Costume Design; Golden Globe Awards '74: Best Song ("The Way We Were"); National Board of Review Awards '73: 10 Best Films of the Year. **VHS, Beta, 8mm $19.95** COL *♪♪♪*

The Way West A wagon train heads to Oregon. A poor and muddled attempt at recreating the style of a John Ford western. What really galls is that it's based on the Pulitzer-winning novel by A.B. Guthrie, Jr. Boy, is the book better than the movie. Field's first film.
1967 122m/C Kirk Douglas, Robert Mitchum, Richard Widmark, Lola Albright, Michael Witney, Stubby Kaye, Sally Field, Jack Elam; **D:** Andrew V. McLaglen. **VHS $14.95** MGM *♪ ½*

Wayne Murder Case A fast-moving, cleverly constructed murder mystery. A rich old man dies just as he is about to sign a new will. Though no one was standing near him, a knife is found stuck in his back. **AKA:** Strange Adventure.
1938 61m/B June Clyde, Regis Toomey, Jason Robards Sr. **VHS, Beta $12.95** SNC, VYY *♪♪♪*

Wayne's World Destined to become one of the top movies of all time—Not! This "Saturday Night Live" skit proved to be so popular that it got its own movie, not unlike the plot, which has slimy producer Lowe take the public access "Wayne's World" into the world of commercial television. The zany duo of Wayne and Garth are as much fun on the big screen as they are on SNL and there are many funny moments, several of which are destined to become comedy classics. A huge box office hit that spawned a sequel.
1992 (PG-13) 93m/C Mike Myers, Dana Carvey, Rob Lowe, Tia Carrere, Brian Doyle-Murray, Lara Flynn Boyle, Kurt Fuller, Colleen Camp, Donna Dixon, Ed O'Neill; **Cameos:** Alice Cooper, Meatloaf; **D:** Penelope Spheeris; **W:** Mike Myers, Bonnie Turner, Terry Turner; **M:** J. Peter Robinson. **VHS $24.95** PAR, FCT *♪♪♪*

Wayne's World 2 Good-natured rerun of the original has plenty of sophomoric gags, but feels tired. Wayne and Garth are on their own, planning a major concert, Waynestock. "If you book them they will come," Jim Morrison says in a dream. Meanwhile, Wayne's girlfriend (Carrere) is falling for slimeball record promoter Walken. Offers a few brilliantly funny segments. If you liked the "Bohemian Rhapsody" spot in the original, get ready for the Village People here. Heston has a funny cameo, and Walken and Basinger push the limits without going over the top. Feature film debut for director Surjik.
1993 (PG-13) 94m/C Mike Myers, Dana Carvey, Tia Carrere, Christopher Walken, Ralph Brown, Kim Basinger, James Hong, Chris Farley, Ed O'Neill, Olivia D'Abo, Kevin Pollak, Drew Barrymore; **Cameos:** Charlton Heston, Rip Taylor, Aerosmith; **D:** Stephen Surjik; **W:** Mike Myers, Bonnie Turner, Terry Turner; **M:** Carter Burwell. **VHS, Beta** PAR *♪♪*

W.C. Fields Comedy Bag Compilation of three classic Fields shorts: "The Golf Specialist" (1930), "The Dentist" (1932) and "The Fatal Glass of Beer" (1933).
1933 56m/B W.C. Fields, Babe Kane, Dorothy Granger, George Chandler. **VHS, Beta $19.95** BAR *♪♪*

W.C. Fields: Flask of Fields Three classic Fields shorts: "The Golf Specialist" (1930), in which J. Effington Bellweather finds himself teaching a lovely young lady how to play the game; "The Fatal Glass of Beer" (1933); and "The Dentist" (1932), in

which Fields tackles a room filled with patients.
1930 61m/B W.C. Fields, Babe Kane, Elise Cavanna, Bud Jamison, Rosemary Theby. **VHS, Beta, 8mm $24.95** VYY *♪♪*

We All Loved Each Other So Much Sensitive comedy follows three friends over 30 years, beginning at the end of WWII. All three have loved the same woman, an actress. Homage to friendship and to postwar Italian cinema. Includes a full-scale recreation of the fountain scene in "La Dolce Vita." In Italian with English subtitles.
1977 124m/C Vittorio Gassman, Nino Manfredi, Stefano Satta Flores, Stefania Sandrelli, Marcello Mastroianni, Federico Fellini; **D:** Ettore Scola. **VHS, Beta $59.95** COL, APD, ING *♪♪♪ ½*

We are the Children Cynical reporter covering the famine in Ethiopia meets an idealistic nurse who's been living there for years. Romance blossoms among the starving in made-for-TV drama co-produced by Danson.
1987 92m/C Ally Sheedy, Ted Danson, Judith Ivey, Zia Mohyeddi; **D:** Robert M. Young. **VHS, Beta $79.95** PSM *♪♪*

We Dive at Dawn Interesting, tense British submarine drama. The "Sea Tiger" attempts to sink the German battleship "Brandenburg" off Denmark. Good cast. Mills prepared for the role by riding an actual submarine, turning "a pale shade of pea-green" when it crash-dived.
1943 98m/B Eric Portman, John Mills; **D:** Anthony Asquith. **VHS, Beta $19.95** NOS, DVT, MED *♪♪♪*

We of the Never Never In turn-of-the-century Australia a city-bred woman marries a cattle rancher and moves from civilized Melbourne to the barren outback of the Northern Territory. Based on the autobiographical story written by Jeannie Gunn, the first white woman to travel in the aboriginal wilderness. She finds herself fighting for her own rights as well as for those of the aborigines in this sincere, well-done film.
1982 (G) 136m/C Angela Punch McGregor, Arthur Dignam, Tony Barry; **D:** Igor Auzins. **VHS, Beta $59.95** COL *♪♪*

We the Living The torpid long-lost and restored Italian version of Ayn Rand's unique political tome. Deals with a young Soviet woman in revolutionary Petrograd who is slowly ruined by the system and her affair with a romantic counter-revolutionary. Made under the Fascists' nose during WWII. A fascinating dialectic between utopian melodrama and Rand dogma. In Italian with subtitles.
1942 174m/B Alida Valli, Rossano Brazzi, Fosco Giachetti; **D:** Goffredo Alessandrini. **VHS, Beta $49.95** LUM *♪♪ ½*

We Think the World of You When bisexual Oldman goes to prison, his lover Bates, whose feelings are unresolved and complex, finds friendship with Oldman's dog. Odd, oft-bitter comedy-drama of love and loyalty characterized by excellent acting and respectful, gentle direction. From the novel by Joseph R. Ackerly.
1988 (PG) 94m/C Alan Bates, Gary Oldman, Frances Barber, Liz Smith, Max Wall, Kerry Wise; **D:** Colin Gregg. **VHS, Beta $19.98** SUE, NLC *♪♪♪*

We Will Not Enter the Forest Moral dilemmas afflict a group of French Resistance fighters during WWII when they must decide what to do with four German deserters they've captured. In French with subtitles.

1979 88m/C Marie-France Pisier; **D:** Georges Dumoulin. **VHS, Beta $39.95** FCT *♪♪♪*

Weapons of Death Kung Fu expert Lee splatters his enemies all over San Francisco's Chinatown.
1983 90m/C Eric Lee, Bob Ramos, Ralph Catellanos. **VHS, Beta** NO *♪*

Weather in the Streets A young woman enters into an ill-fated love affair after spending a few moments with an aristocratic married man. Cliched drama set in England between the two world wars.
1984 (PG) 108m/C Michael York, Joanna Lumley, Lisa Eichhorn, Isabel Dean, Norman Pitt; **M:** Carl Davis. **VHS, Beta** NO *♪ ½*

Web of Deceit Defense lawyer Purl returns to her Southern hometown to defend an unjustly accused teenager. She falls in love with the prosecutor, but could he be the killer? Shades of "Jagged Edge." Good, suspenseful made-for-TV movie.
1990 (PG-13) 93m/C Linda Purl, James Read, Paul DeSouza, Larry Black, Len Birman, Barbara Rush; **D:** Sandor Stern; **W:** Sandor Stern. **VHS, Beta** PAR *♪♪ ½*

Web of Deception A jewel thief disappears with five million dollars worth of jewels. When the case turns to murder, a private detective becomes the prime suspect.
1971 (R) 90m/C Thomas Hunter, Aelina Nathaniel, Gabriele Tinti, Marilia Branco. **VHS, Beta** NO *♪*

Web of the Spider Kinski as Poe is really the only good thing about this run-of-the-mill horror outing. A man stays the night in a spooky house to prove it's not haunted. Remake of "Castle of Blood." **AKA:** Nella Stretta M Orsa Del Ragno; In the Grip of the Spider; Dracula in the Castle of Blood; And Comes the Dawn...But Colored Red.
1970 94m/C Anthony (Tony) Franciosa, Klaus Kinski, Michele Mercier, Peter Carsten, Karin Field; **D:** Anthony M. (Antonio Margheriti) Dawson. **VHS $16.95** SNC *♪♪*

A Wedding The occasion of a wedding leads to complications galore for the relatives and guests on the happy day. Silent film legend Gish's 100th screen role. Miserable, self-indulgent outing for Altman, who went through quite a dry spell after "Nashville."
1978 (PG) 125m/C Mia Farrow, Carol Burnett, Lillian Gish, Lauren Hutton, Viveca Lindfors, Geraldine Chaplin, Paul Dooley, Howard Duff, Dennis Christopher, Peggy Ann Garner, John Considine, Nina Van Pallandt, Dina Merrill, Pat McCormick, Vittorio Gassman, Desi Arnaz Jr.; **D:** Robert Altman; **W:** John Considine, Allan Nicholls, Patricia Resnick, Robert Altman. **VHS, Beta $59.98** FOX *♪ ½*

Wedding Band Episodic comedy about a rock 'n roll band that plays all sorts of weddings. Thin and lame but inoffensive.
1989 95m/C William Katt, Joyce Hyser, Tino Insana, Fran Drescher, David Rasche, Joe Flaherty, Tim Kazurinsky, James Belushi; **D:** Daniel Raskov. **VHS, Beta $89.95** COL *♪♪*

The Wedding Banquet Charming story about a clash of customs and secrets. Naturalized American Wai Tung (Chao, in his debut) lives comfortably with his lover Simon (Lichtenstein) while hiding the fact that he's gay from his Chinese parents. To appease his parents and get his "wife" a green card, he marries for convenience and watches as the deception snowballs. Comedy of errors was shot on a small budget ($750,000) and examines small details with as much care as the larger ones. A fine effort from director Lee that's solidly humorous, but also poignant. In English and Chinese with English subtitles. **AKA:** Xiyan.

1993 (R) 111m/C Winston Chao, May Chin, Mitchell Lichtenstein, Sihung Lung, Ah-Leh Gua; D: Ang Lee; W: Ang Lee, Neil Peng, James Schamus. VHS NYR ℣℣℣

Wedding in Blood Two French lovers plot to kill their respective spouses, and proceed to do so amid calamity and much table-turning. Sharp social satire and suspenseful mystery. Based on a true story. In French with English subtitles.
1974 (PG) 98m/C Claude Pieplu, Stephane Audran, Michel Piccoli; D: Claude Chabrol. VHS, Beta $69.95 COL ℣℣℣

A Wedding in Galilee The elder of a Palestinian village is given permission to have a traditional wedding ceremony for his son if Israeli military officers can attend as the guests of honor. As the event approaches, conflicts arise among the villagers, the family, and the Israelis. Long but fascinating treatment of traditional culture in the modern world amidst political tension. In Arabic and Hebrew, with English subtitles. AKA: Noce In Galilee.
1987 113m/C Ali M. El Aleili, Nazih Akleh, Anna Achdian; D: Michel Khleifi. VHS $79.95 KIV, ING ℣℣℣

Wedding in White A rape and out-of-wedlock pregnancy trouble a poor British clan living in Canada during WWII. Sad, glum way to spend an evening. Kane is good in a non-comic role. Her screen father cares more for her honor than he does for her.
1972 (R) 103m/C Donald Pleasence, Carol Kane, Leo Phillips; D: William Fruet. VHS, Beta $39.95 SUE ℣℣

The Wedding March Von Stroheim's famous silent film about romantic couplings in pre-WWI Vienna. The director also stars as a prince preparing to marry for money, who falls in love with a beautiful, but poor woman. Romance and irony, with a memorable finale. Like many of his other great films, it was taken from him and re-edited. Initially the first of two halves; the second, "The Honeymoon," has been lost. Next to "Greed," his most successful film.
1928 113m/B Erich von Stroheim, Fay Wray, ZaSu Pitts, George Fawcett, Maude George, Matthew Betz, George Nicholls, Cesare Gravina; D: Erich von Stroheim; M: Gaylord Carter. VHS, Beta $29.95 PAR ℣℣℣℣

The Wedding Party Apprehensive groom is overwhelmed by his too-eager bride and her inquisitive relatives at a prenuptial celebration. Hokey, dull, would-be comedy. First screen appearances of both Clayburgh and De Niro (spelled DeNero in the credits).
1969 90m/C Jill Clayburgh, Robert De Niro, William Finley; D: Brian DePalma, Cynthia Munroe, Wilford Leach; W: Brian DePalma. VHS, Beta NO ℣½

Wedding Rehearsal A young nobleman thwarts his grandmother's plans to marry him off by finding suitors for all the young ladies offered to him until he finally succumbs to the charms of his mother's secretary. Enjoyable, fun comedy. First featured roles for actresses Oberon, Barrie, and Gardner.
1932 84m/B Merle Oberon, Roland Young, John Loder, Wendy Barrie, Maurice Evans, Joan Gardner; D: Alexander Korda. VHS, Beta SUE ℣℣½

Wee Willie Winkie A precocious little girl is taken in by a British regiment in India. Sugar-coated. If you're a cinematic diabetic, be warned. If you're a Temple fan, you've probably already seen it. If not, you're in for a treat. Inspired by the Rudyard Kipling story.

1937 99m/B Shirley Temple, Victor McLaglen, Sir C. Aubrey Smith, June Lang, Michael Whalen, Cesar Romero, Constance Collier; D: John Ford. VHS, Beta $19.98 FOX ℣℣℣

Weeds A highly fictionalized account of the career of Rick Cluchey, who, as a lifer in San Quentin federal prison, wrote a play. He was eventually paroled and went on to form a theater group made up of ex-cons. Original and often enjoyable with a tight ensemble performance. Filmed on location at Stateville Correctional Center in Illinois, with inmates serving as extras.
1987 (R) 115m/C Nick Nolte, Rita Taggart, William Forsythe, Lane Smith, Joe Mantegna, Ernie Hudson, John Toles-Bey, Mark Rolston, Anne Ramsey, Charlie Rich; D: John Hancock; W: John Hancock, Dorothy Tristan; M: Angelo Badalamenti. VHS, Beta $19.99 HBO ℣℣℣

Week-End In Havana Set in pre-revolution Cuba, this frothy musical finds salesgirl Faye on a long-awaited cruise when her ship gets stranded in Havana. She's escorted around town by shipping-official Payne and catches the eye of gambler-lothario Romero, who has a jealous girlfriend in Miranda. Fun fluff. ♫Romance and Rhumba; Tropical Magic; The Nango; A Weekend in Havana; When I Love, I Love; Maria Inez; Rebola a Bola.
1941 80m/C Alice Faye, John Payne, Cesar Romero, Carmen Miranda, Cobina Wright Jr., George Barbier, Sheldon Leonard, Billy Gilbert; D: Walter Lang; W: Karl Tunberg; M: Alfred Newman. VHS $19.98 FXV ℣℣½

Weekend A Parisian couple embark on a drive to the country. On the way they witness and are involved in horrifying highway wrecks. Leaving the road they find a different, equally grotesque kind of carnage. Godard's brilliant, surreal, hyper-paranoiac view of modern life was greatly influenced by the fact that his mother was killed in an auto accident in 1954 (he himself suffered a serious motorcycle mishap in 1975). In French with English subtitles.
1967 105m/C Mireille Darc, Jean Yanne, Jean-Pierre Kalfon, Valerie Lagrange, Jean-Pierre Leaud, Yves Beneyton; D: Jean-Luc Godard; W: Jean-Luc Godard; M: Antoine Duhamel. VHS $79.95 NYF, FCT, ING ℣℣℣

Weekend at Bernie's Two computer nerds discover embezzlement at their workplace after being invited to their boss's beach house for a weekend party. They find their host murdered. They endeavor to keep up appearances by (you guessed it) dressing and strategically posing the corpse during the party. Kiser as the dead man is memorable, and the two losers gamely keep the silliness flowing. Lots of fun. AKA: Hot and Cold.
1989 (PG-13) 101m/C Andrew McCarthy, Jonathan Silverman, Catherine Mary Stewart, Terry Kiser, Don Calfa, Louis Giambalvo; D: Ted Kotcheff; W: Robert Klane; M: Andy Summers. VHS, VHS, Beta $14.95 LIV ℣℣½

Weekend at Bernie's 2 Unlikely but routine sequel to the original's cavorting cadaver slapstick, except now McCarthy and Silverman are frantically hunting for Bernie's (Kiser) cash stash, a quest that takes them and poor dead Bernie to the Caribbean. See Bernie get stuffed in a suitcase, see Bernie hang glide, see Bernie tango, see Bernie attract the opposite sex. Thin script with one-joke premise done to death but fun for those in the mood for the postmortem antics of a comedic stiff. Plenty of well-executed gags involving the well-preserved corpse (particularly one that's been dead for two films now) should lure back fans of the 1989 original.

1993 (PG) 89m/C Andrew McCarthy, Jonathan Silverman, Terry Kiser, Tom Wright, Steve James, Troy Beyer, Barry Bostwick; D: Robert Klane; W: Robert Klane; M: Peter Wolf. VHS COL ℣½

Weekend at the Waldorf Glossy, americanized remake of "Grand Hotel" set at the famous Park Avenue hotel, the Waldorf-Astoria, in New York City. Turner and Rogers star in the roles originated by Joan Crawford and Greta Garbo. Johnson and Pidgeon play their love interests. Combining drawing room comedy with slapstick and a touch of romance proved to be a hit, as this film was one of the top grossers of 1945 and was just what war-weary moviegoers wanted to see. Based on the play "Grand Hotel" by Vicki Baum.
1945 130m/B Ginger Rogers, Walter Pidgeon, Van Johnson, Lana Turner, Robert Benchley, Edward Arnold, Leon Ames, Warner Anderson, Phyllis Thaxter, Keenan Wynn, Porter Hall, Samuel S. Hinds; D: Robert Z. Leonard; W: Samuel Spewack, Bella Spewack, Guy Bolton. VHS $19.98 MGM ℣℣℣

Weekend of Shadows Confident, moralistic murder drama about a posse after an innocent immigrant they believe has killed a woman. Police sergeant Roberts is interested only in his reputation, not in justice. Posse member Waters begins to sympathize with the hunted man and defends his innocence. Intelligent, well-conceived, and professionally directed.
1977 94m/C John Waters, Melissa Jaffer, Graeme Blundell, Wyn Roberts, Barbara West, Graham Rouse; D: Tom Jeffrey. VHS, Beta $49.98 SUE ℣℣℣

Weekend Pass Moronic rookie sailors who have just completed basic training are out on a weekend pass, determined to forget everything they have learned. They find this surprisingly easy to do.
1984 (R) 92m/C D.W. Brown, Peter Ellenstein, Phil Hartman, Patrick Hauser, Chip McAllister; D: Lawrence Bassoff. VHS, Beta $79.98 LIV, VES ℣

Weekend War A group of National Guardsmen are sent to the Honduras for their annual tour of duty. But when a guerilla war between Honduras and Nicaragua breaks out, the Guardsmen are forced to fight for their lives. The "Bridge on the River Kwai" finale features the dilemma over a bridge linking the two countries. Made for television.
1988 (PG-13) 96m/C Daniel Stern, Stephen Collins, Charles Haid, Evan Mirand, Michael Beach, Scott Paulin, James Tolkan; D: Steven Hilliard Stern; M: Brad Fiedel. VHS $59.95 COL ℣℣½

Weekend Warriors Young film-studio employees evade the draft in 1961 by enlisting for National Guard weekend duty. Grade "C" dumb comedy from professional celebrity and first-time director Convy.
1986 (R) 88m/C Chris Lemmon, Lloyd Bridges, Daniel Greene, Tom Villard, Vic Tayback; D: Bert Convy. VHS, Beta $79.98 LIV ℣½

Weekend with the Babysitter Sordid teen drama about a weekend babysitter who goes to a film director's house and babysits everyone but the kids, running into a heroin-smuggling ring along the way. Casting-couch story with a twist. AKA: Weekend Babysitter.
1970 (R) 93m/C Susan Roman, George E. Carey, James Almanzar, Luanne Roberts; D: Don Henderson. VHS, Beta $59.95 PSM Woof!

Weep No More My Lady Suspense-filled whodunit about a wealthy businessman who comes between two sisters and a sibling rivalry that turns into a deadly game of

murder. Based on the best-selling book by Mary Higgins Clark.
1993 (PG-13) 92m/C Daniel J. Travanti, Shelley Winters, Kristin Scott Thomas. **VHS** $89.98 *REP* ♫♫

Weird Science Hall is appealing, and Hughes can write dialogue for teens with the best of them. However, many of the jokes are in poor taste, and the movie seems to go on forever. Hall and his nerdy cohort Mitchell-Smith use a very special kind of software to create the ideal woman who wreaks zany havoc in their lives from the outset.
1985 (PG-13) 94m/C Kelly Le Brock, Anthony Michael Hall, Ilan Mitchell-Smith, Robert Downey Jr., Bill Paxton; *D:* John Hughes; *W:* John Hughes. **VHS, Beta** $19.95 *MCA* ♫♫

Weird World of LSD Cheap exploitation film featuring the evil effects of LSD.
1967 ?m/C Terry Tessem, Ann Lindsay, Yolanda Morino. **VHS** $16.95 *SNC, TPV* ♫½

The Weirdo "The Jerk" meets Freddie Krueger. This film is absolutely wretched, even by horror movie standards.
1989 91m/C Steve Burlington, Jessica Straus; *D:* Andy Milligan. **VHS, Beta** *NO* ♫

Welcome Back Mr. Fox An award-winning science fiction short wherein an obnoxious movie producer cheats death by being cryogenically frozen, and then wakes up years later no wiser for the experience. Suitably, he receives his comeuppance.
1983 21m/C E.D. Phillips, Gustav Vintas; *D:* Walter W. Pitt III. **VHS, Beta** *NO* ♫

Welcome Home A missing-in-action Vietnam vet (Kristofferson) leaves his wife and children in Cambodia to return to America more than 15 years after he was reported dead. He finds his first wife remarried and discovers a teen-aged son he unknowingly fathered. This plotless, sporadically-moving film was Schaffner's last. Made for cable television.
1989 (R) 92m/C Kris Kristofferson, JoBeth Williams, Sam Waterston, Brian Keith, Trey Wilson, Thomas Wilson Brown; *D:* Franklin J. Schaffner. **VHS, Beta** $89.98 *VES, LIV* ♫♫

Welcome Home, Roxy Carmichael Ryder, as a young misfit, is the bright spot in this deadpan, would-be satire. Hollywood star Roxy Charmichael returns to her small Ohio hometown and begins fantasizing that she is really her mother. It is obvious why this deadpan, hard-to-follow movie was a box-office flop.
1990 (PG-13) 98m/C Winona Ryder, Jeff Daniels, Laila Robins, Dinah Manoff, Ava Fabian, Robbie Kiger, Sachi Parker; *D:* Jim Abrahams. **VHS, Beta, 8mm** $14.95 *PAR* ♫♫

Welcome to Blood City An anonymous totalitarian organization kidnaps a man and transports him electronically to a fantasy western town where the person who murders the most people becomes the town's "kill master." Amateurish and low-budget.
1977 96m/C Jack Palance, Keir Dullea, Samantha Eggar, Barry Morse. **VHS, Beta** $69.98 *LIV* ♫½

Welcome to 18 Three girls, just out of high school, take summer jobs at a dude ranch, work a local casino, flirt, tease and get in trouble. The movie isn't funny in the least, and is filled with utter nonsense. Hargitay is the daughter of actress Jayne Mansfield.
1987 (PG-13) 91m/C Courtney Thorne-Smith, Mariska Hargitay, Jo Ann Willette, Christine Kaufmann; *D:* Terry Carr. **VHS, Beta** $19.95 *LIV* ♫

Welcome to L.A. Rudolph's ambitious directorial debut focuses on the sexual escapades of a group of Southern Californians. Based on the music suite "City of the One Night Stands" by Baskin, which also (unfortunately) serves as the soundtrack. Rudolph improved greatly after this initial effort.
1977 (R) 106m/C Sissy Spacek, Sally Kellerman, Keith Carradine, Geraldine Chaplin, Lauren Hutton, Viveca Lindfors, Harvey Keitel, John Considine; *D:* Alan Rudolph; *W:* Alan Rudolph; *M:* Richard Baskin. **VHS, Beta** *FOX* ♫♫♫

Welcome to Spring Break College co-eds are stalked by a killer on the beaches of Florida.
1988 (R) 92m/C John Saxon, Michael Parks. **VHS, Beta** *NO* ♫½

The Well A young black girl disappears and a white man (Morgan) is accused of kidnapping her. When it is discovered that the girl is trapped in a deep well, Morgan's expertise is needed to help free her.
1951 85m/B Richard Rober, Harry Morgan, Barry Kelley, Christine Larson; *D:* Leo Popkin, Russel Rouse. **VHS, Beta** *VCI* ♫♫

Well-Digger's Daughter As her lover goes off to war, a well-digger's daughter discovers that she is pregnant causing both sets of parents to feud over who's to blame. This is the first film made in France after the end of WWII and marks the return of the French film industry. In French with English subtitles. *AKA:* La Fille Du Puisatier.
1946 142m/B Raimu, Josette Day, Fernandel, Charpin; *D:* Marcel Pagnol. **VHS, Beta** $29.95 *NOS, DVT, APD* ♫♫♫

Wellington: The Duel Scandal A look at how the man who was Britain's greatest hero managed to garner the hatred of his countrymen in eighteen months.
19?? 60m/C **VHS** *NO* ♫♫♫

We're Back! A Dinosaur's Story Animated adventures of a pack of revived dinosaurs who return to their old stomping grounds—which are now modern-day New York City. Smart-mouth human boy Louie and his girlfriend Cecilia take the dinos under their wing (so to speak), wise them up to modern life, and try to prevent their capture by the evil Professor Screweyes. Slow-moving with some violence. Adapted from the book by Hudson Talbott.
1993 (G) 78m/C *D:* Dick Zondag, Ralph Zondag, Phil Nibbelink, Simon Wells; *W:* John Patrick Shanley; *V:* John Goodman, Felicity Kendal, Walter Cronkite, Joey Shea, Jay Leno, Julia Child, Kenneth Mars, Martin Short, Rhea Perlman, Rene LeVant, Blaze Berdahl, Charles Fleischer, Yeardley Smith. **VHS** $24.98 *MCA* ♫♫½

We're in the Legion Now Denny and Barnett star as a couple of American gangsters who join the French Foreign Legion to escape rival hoods from back home.
1937 56m/B Reginald Denny, Vince Barnett, Esther Ralston. **VHS, Beta, 8mm** $19.95 *VYY* ♫½

We're in the Navy Now The famed comedy duo is back again with another armed forces farce. A mild successor to "Behind the Front."
1927 60m/B Wallace Beery, Raymond Hatton. **VHS, Beta** $19.95 *GPV, FCT* ♫½

We're No Angels Three escapees from Devil's Island hide out with the family of a kindly French storekeeper. One of Bogart's few comedies. From the French stage play of the same name. Claustrophobic and talky. Later remade with De Niro and Penn.
1955 103m/C Humphrey Bogart, Aldo Ray, Joan Bennett, Peter Ustinov, Basil Rathbone, Leo G. Carroll; *D:* Michael Curtiz. **VHS, Beta** $14.95 *PAR* ♫♫½

We're No Angels Two escaped cons disguise themselves as priests and get in the appropriate series of jams. De Niro and Penn play off each other well, turning in fine comic performances. Distantly related to the 1955 film of the same name and the David Mamet play.
1989 (R) 110m/C Robert De Niro, Sean Penn, Demi Moore, Hoyt Axton, Bruno Kirby, James Russo, John Reilly, Ray McAnally, Wallace Shawn; *D:* Neil Jordan; *W:* David Mamet; *M:* George Fenton. **VHS, Beta** $19.95 *PAR* ♫♫½

We're Not Married Five couples learn that they are not legally married when a judge realizes his license expired before he performed the ceremonies. The story revolves around this quintet of couples who now must cope with whether or not they really do want to be married. Although the episodes vary in quality, the Allen-Rogers sequence is excellent. Overall, the cast performs well in this lightweight comedy.
1952 85m/B Ginger Rogers, Fred Allen, Victor Moore, Marilyn Monroe, Paul Douglas, David Wayne, Eve Arden, Louis Calhern, Zsa Zsa Gabor, James Gleason, Jane Darwell, Eddie Bracken, Mitzi Gaynor; *D:* Edmund Goulding; *W:* Nunnally Johnson, Dwight Taylor. **VHS** $14.98 *FXV* ♫♫♫

We're Talkin' Serious Money Sal and Charlie are a couple of loser scam-artists always after the elusive big score. They borrow $10,000 from the mob for another get-rich-quick scheme and wind up over their heads with both the mob and the FBI out to get them.
1992 (PG-13) 92m/C Dennis Farina, Leo Rossi, Fran Drescher, John Lamotta; *D:* James Lemmo; *W:* Leo Rossi, James Lemmo; *M:* Scott Grusin. **VHS** $89.95 *COL* ♫♫½

Werewolf in a Girl's Dormitory Girls' school headmaster undergoes dental transformation at night. Atrocious dubbing, with equally atrocious theme song "The Ghoul in School." *AKA:* Lycanthropus; The Ghoul in School.
1961 82m/B Barbara Lass, Carl Schell, Curt Lowens, Maurice Marsac; *D:* Richard Benson. **VHS** $19.98 *SMW, SNC* ♫

Werewolf of London A scientist searching for a rare Tibetan flower is attacked by a werewolf. He scoffs at the legend, but once he's back in London, he goes on a murderous rampage every time the moon is full. Dated but worth watching as the first werewolf movie made.
1935 75m/B Henry Hull, Warner Oland, Valerie Hobson, Lester Matthews, Spring Byington; *D:* Stuart Walker. **VHS** $14.98 *MCA* ♫♫½

Werewolf of Washington Stockwell is a White House press secretary with a problem—he turns into a werewolf. And bites the President, among others. Sub-plot involves a short mad scientist who operates a secret monster-making lab in a White House bathroom. Occasionally engaging horror spoof and political satire made during Watergate era.
1973 (PG) 90m/C Dean Stockwell, Biff Maguire, Clifton James; *D:* Milton Moses Ginseberg. **VHS, Beta** *NO* ♫♫

The Werewolf vs. the Vampire Woman Hirsute Spanish wolfman teams with two female students in search of witch's tomb. One is possessed by the witch, and eponymous title results. *AKA:* Blood Moon.

1970 (R) 82m/C Paul Naschy, Gaby Fuchs, Barbara Capell, Patty Shepard, Valerie Samarine, Julio Pena, Andres Resino; **D:** Leon Klimovsky. **VHS $19.98** *SNC, HEG* 𝄞 ½

Werewolves on Wheels
A group of bikers are turned into werewolves due to a Satanic spell. A serious attempt at a biker/werewolf movie, however, too violent and grim, not at all funny, and painful to sit through. McGuire had a hit with "Eve of Destruction."
1971 (R) 85m/C Stephen Oliver, Severn Darden, Donna Anderson, Duece Barry, Billy Gray, Barry McGuire; **D:** Michel Levesque. **VHS, Beta $59.95** *UNI* Woof!

West-Bound Limited
A Romantic adventurer rescues a girl from certain death as a train is about to hit her, and the two fall in love. Lucky for him, she happens to be the boss' daughter. This film is a good example of classic early silent melodrama with music score.
1923 70m/B John Harron, Ella Hall, Claire McDowell. **VHS, Beta $24.95** *VYY* 𝄞𝄞 ½

West of Nevada
A rare film, featuring the former Lieutenant Governor of Nevada (and Clara Bow's husband) in a fast-moving adventure about a band of Indians who must protect their gold from thieves. Bell is the good guy who aids the Indians.
1936 59m/B Rex Bell, Joan Barclay, Al "Fuzzy" St. John, Steve Clark. **VHS, Beta $52.95** *GVV* 𝄞𝄞

West of Pinto Basin
The Range Busters are riding around checking the territory for badmen in this tale of the old west. The music score includes "That Little Prairie Gal of Mine," "Rhythm of the Saddle," and "Ridin' the Trail Tonight."
1940 60m/B Ray Corrigan, Max Terhune, John "Dusty" King, Jack Perrin. **VHS, Beta $19.95** *NOS, DVT* 𝄞𝄞

West of the Divide
A young cowboy (Wayne) impersonates an outlaw in order to hunt down his father's killer and find his missing younger brother. He saves a proud rancher and his feisty daughter along the way. A remake of "Partners of the Trail," and a solid early Wayne oater.
1934 53m/B John Wayne, George "Gabby" Hayes, Lloyd Whitlock, Yakima Canutt; **D:** Robert North Bradbury. **VHS, Beta $19.95** *COL, REP, NOS* 𝄞𝄞 ½

West of the Law
A group of ranchers turn to lawmen for protection from a band of outlaws. Part of the Rough Riders series.
1942 60m/B Buck Jones, Tim McCoy, Raymond Hatton; **D:** Howard Bretherton. **VHS, Beta $19.95** *NOS, VCN, DVT* 𝄞𝄞

West of the Pecos
Rill (Hale) is a society gal on her way to the family ranch in Texas. She's disguised as a boy for safety, which turns out to be a smart idea when outlaws attack the stagecoach. Fortunately, Pecos Smith (Mitchum) is also around to lend a hand. Based on the novel by Zane Grey; first filmed in 1935.
1945 66m/B Robert Mitchum, Barbara Hale, Richard Martin, Thurston Hall, Rita Corday, Russell Hopton, Harry Woods; **D:** Edward Killy. **VHS $12.95** *GPV* 𝄞𝄞 ½

West of Zanzibar
Chaney plays an ivory trader, ruling a jungle kingdom, who lives for revenge on the man who left him a cripple. He decides to ruin the man's daughter and turn her into a prostitute but his plan backfires. Chaney and director Browning offer a steamy atmosphere amidst a number of script flaws.
1928 63m/B Lon Chaney Sr., Lionel Barrymore, Warner Baxter, Mary Nolan; **D:** Tod Browning. **VHS $29.95** *FCT* 𝄞𝄞 ½

The West Point Story
Cagney stars as an on-the-skids Broadway director offered a job staging a show at West Point. Seems cadet MacRae has written a musical and his uncle happens to be a producer. Cagney, with girlfriend Mayo, finds all the rules and regulations getting the better of his temper, so much so that he's told unless he can conform to academy standards the show won't go on! Day is the showgirl MacRae falls for. Cagney's energy and charm carry the too-long film but it's not one of his better musical efforts. ♫ Ten Thousand Sheep; You Love Me; By the Kissing Rock; Long Before I Knew You; Brooklyn; It Could Only Happen in Brooklyn; Military Polka. *AKA:* Fine and Dandy.
1950 107m/B James Cagney, Virginia Mayo, Gordon MacRae, Doris Day, Roland Winters, Gene Nelson, Alan Hale Jr., Wilton Graff, Jerome Cowan; **D:** Roy Del Ruth; **W:** John Monks Jr., Charles Hoffman, Irving Wallace; **M:** Sammy Cahn, Jules Styne. **VHS $19.98** *WAR, MVD* 𝄞𝄞

West Side Story
Gang rivalry and ethnic tension on New York's West Side erupts in a ground-breaking musical. Loosely based on Shakespeare's "Romeo and Juliet," the story follows the Jets and the Sharks as they fight for their turf while Tony and Maria fight for love. Features frenetic and brilliant choreography by co-director Robbins, who also directed the original Broadway show, and a high-caliber score by Bernstein and Sondheim. Wood's voice was dubbed by Marni Nixon and Jimmy Bryant dubbed Beymer's. The laserdisc version includes the complete storyboards, production sketches, re-issue trailer, and an interview with Wise in a letterbox format with digital stereo surround sound. ♫ Prologue; Jet Song; Something's Coming; Dance at the Gym; Maria; America; Tonight; One Hand, One Heart; Gee, Officer Krupke.
1961 151m/C Natalie Wood, Richard Beymer, Russ Tamblyn, Rita Moreno, George Chakiris, Simon Oakland, Ned Glass; **D:** Robert Wise, Jerome Robbins; **W:** Ernest Lehman; **M:** Leonard Bernstein, Stephen Sondheim. Academy Awards '61: Best Art Direction/Set Decoration (Color), Best Color Cinematography, Best Costume Design (Color), Best Director (Wise), Best Film Editing, Best Picture, Best Sound, Best Supporting Actor (Chakiris), Best Supporting Actress (Moreno), Best Score; Nominations: Best Adapted Screenplay; Directors Guild of America Awards '61: Best Director (Wise), Best Director (Robbins). **VHS, Beta $19.98** *MGM, KUI, FOX* 𝄞𝄞𝄞 ½

West to Glory
Glory isn't necessarily exciting, as the hero helps a Mexican rancher save his gold and jewels from evildoers in this slow-paced oater.
1947 61m/B Eddie Dean, Roscoe Ates, Dolores Castle, Gregg Barton, Alex Montoya, Harry Vejar; **D:** Ray Taylor. **VHS, Beta $19.95** *NOS* 𝄞 ½

Western Double Feature 1
In "Utah" (1945, 55 minutes), Rogers foils a land swindle and helps a lady ranch owner; in "Man from Music Mountain" (1938, 60 minutes), Autry foils a worthless gold mining stock swindle.
1938 115m/B Roy Rogers, Dale Evans, George "Gabby" Hayes, Gene Autry, Smiley Burnette; **D:** Joseph Kane. **VHS, Beta $59.95** *HHT* 𝄞 ½

Western Double Feature 1: Wild Bill & Sunset Carson
Double feature: in "Calling Wild Bill Elliot" (1943), Wild Bill comes to the aid of homesteaders; in "Santa Fe Saddlemates" (1945), Carson breaks up a diamond smuggling ring.
194? 120m/B Wild Bill Elliott, Sunset Carson; **D:** Spencer Gordon Bennet. **VHS, Beta** *MED* 𝄞 ½

Western Double Feature 2
Wayne and Hayes are teamed together in two hour-long B-westerns: "Star Packer" (1934) and "West of the Divide" (1933).
1933 120m/B John Wayne, George "Gabby" Hayes; **D:** Robert North Bradbury. **VHS, Beta $59.95** *HHT* 𝄞 ½

Western Double Feature 2: Wayne & Hale
Double feature; in "Night Riders" (1939), Wayne battles injustice; in "Home on the Range" (1946, color), Hale protects a wild animal refuge. *AKA:* Nightriders; Home on the Range.
198? 120m/B John Wayne, Monte Hale; **D:** George Sherman. **VHS, Beta** *MED* 𝄞 ½

Western Double Feature 3
Two Wayne westerns are on this tape: "Helltown" (1938, 59 minutes), in which Wayne catches a cattle rustler, and "Winds of the Wasteland" (1936, 54 minutes), where he plays an out-of-work Pony Express rider.
1936 113m/B John Wayne, Johnny Mack Brown, Marsha Hunt, Phyllis Fraser; **D:** Charles T. Barton, Mack V. Wright. **VHS, Beta $59.95** *HHT* 𝄞 ½

Western Double Feature 3: Rogers & Allen
Double feature. In "Twilight in the Sierras" (1950), Rogers catches a gang of crooks; in "Under Mexicali Stars" (1950), Allen is a cowboy who uncovers a counterfeiting ring.
1950 134m/C Roy Rogers, Dale Evans, Rex Allen; **D:** William Witney. **VHS, Beta** *MED* 𝄞 ½

Western Double Feature 4
Rogers plays a dual role in a case of mistaken identity in "Billy the Kid Returns" (1938, 56 minutes); in "Round Up Time in Texas" (1937, 56 minutes), Autry is framed on a charge of diamond smuggling.
1937 112m/B Roy Rogers, Gene Autry, Smiley Burnette; **D:** Joseph Kane. **VHS, Beta $59.95** *HHT* 𝄞 ½

Western Double Feature 4: Rogers & Evans
In "Don't Fence Me In" (1945), Rogers helps out a woman reporter; in "Sheriff of Wichita" (1948), a frontier investigator solves a crime. *AKA:* Don't Fence Me In; Sheriff of Wichita.
194? 120m/B Roy Rogers, Dale Evans, George "Gabby" Hayes, Allan "Rocky" Lane. **VHS, Beta** *MED* 𝄞 ½

Western Double Feature 5
Wayne stars in both halves of this double feature: in "Desert Trail" (1935, 54 minutes), he plays a rodeo star; in "Man from Utah" (1934, 55 minutes), he brings a gang of murderers to justice.
1935 109m/B John Wayne, Polly Ann Young; **D:** Robert North Bradbury. **VHS, Beta $59.95** *HHT* 𝄞 ½

Western Double Feature 5: Rogers & Autry
"The Big Show" (1937) features songs, action, and horses; in "Home in Oklahoma" (1946), Roger tracks down a murderer.
1937 108m/B Gene Autry, Roy Rogers, Smiley Burnette, The Pioneers; **D:** Max Wright. **VHS, Beta** *MED* 𝄞 ½

Western Double Feature 6: Rogers & Trigger
"Trigger Jr." (1950) is the story of Trigger's colt; "Gangs of Sonora" (1941, black and white) deals with a fight to save a small frontier newspaper. *AKA:* Trigger, Jr.; Gangs of Sonora.
1950 120m/C Roy Rogers, Dale Evans, Trigger, Bob Livingston, Bob Steele; **D:** William Witney. **VHS, Beta** *MED* 𝄞 ½

Western Double Feature 7: Wild Bill & Crabbe "Phantom of the Plains" deals with a plan to save a woman from a gigolo; "Prairie Rustlers" tells of the problems of a man who is the identical double of Billy the Kid. *AKA:* Phantom of the Plains; Prairie Rustlers.
1945 120m/B Wild Bill Elliott, Buster Crabbe. VHS, Beta MED 🎬½

Western Double Feature 8: Hale & Carradine In "Silver Spurs" (1943), ranchers wanting to get the right-of-way through oil land run into an ambitious resort owner; in "Out California Way" (1946), Hale is a young cowboy looking for work in Hollywood.
194? 121m/B Roy Rogers, Monte Hale, John Carradine. VHS, Beta MED 🎬½

Western Double Feature 9: LaRue & Beery In "Cheyenne Takes Over" (1947), LaRue battles outlaws; in "Tulsa Kid" (1940), a young man must face a gunfighter.
194? 120m/B Lash LaRue, Donald (Don "Red") Barry, Noah Beery Sr. VHS, Beta MED 🎬½

Western Double Feature 10: Roy, Dale, & Trigger In "Bells of Coronado" (1950), Rogers must solve a murder and uranium ore theft; in "King of the Cowboys" (1943, black and white), Roy investigates a band of saboteurs.
198? 120m/C Roy Rogers, Dale Evans, Trigger; *D:* William Witney. VHS, Beta MED 🎬½

Western Double Feature 11 Roy and Trigger act as modern day Robin Hoods to end crooked dealing in the West; Roy hides behind a smile and a song to capture murderers of a deputy and a ranch owner.
1950 121m/B Roy Rogers, Penny Edwards, Gordon Jones, Purple Sage, George "Gabby" Hayes. VHS, Beta MED 🎬½

Western Double Feature 12 Red Ryder learns of a plot to scare ranchers into selling out before an oil strike is discovered; the Three Musketeers are sent to the Caribbean as U.S. envoys to sell Army horses.
1944 108m/B Bob Livingston, Wild Bill Elliott, Duncan Renaldo, Robert (Bobby) Blake. VHS, Beta MED 🎬½

Western Double Feature 13 Red Ryder foils outlaws trying to swindle the Duchess' stage line in a small isolated town in "Wagon Wheels Westward" (1945). "Rocky Mountain Rangers" (1940), features the Three Mesquiteers pursuing the deadly Barton Gang.
194? 108m/B Red Ryder, Bob Livingston, Robert (Bobby) Blake. VHS, Beta MED 🎬½

Western Double Feature 14 Outlaws, good guys, and romance on the old frontier. Amateur Robin Hoods steal back money wrongfully taken.
1952 123m/B Tim Holt, Jack Holt, Nan Leslie, Noreen Nash. VHS, Beta MED 🎬½

Western Double Feature 15 Rogers breaks up a cattle rustling ring; the good guys try to bring law and order to a vast Wyoming territory plagued by a crooked political boss.
1950 122m/B Roy Rogers, Trigger, Penny Edwards, Donald (Don "Red") Barry, Lynn Merrick. VHS, Beta MED 🎬½

Western Double Feature 16 Autry is sent to quell a revolution in Mexico; Rogers's horse Lady and Hayes's horse Golden Sovereign are the focal points of the second part of this double feature.
1946 108m/B Gene Autry, Smiley Burnette, Roy Rogers, George "Gabby" Hayes. VHS, Beta MED 🎬½

Western Double Feature 17 Rogers stars in "The Golden Stallion" (1949). Roy battles diamond smugglers who use wild horses to transport the goods. "The Cherokee Flash" (1945), starring Carson, deals with a respectable citizen's outlaw past catching up to him.
194? 121m/C Roy Rogers, Sunset Carson; *D:* William Witney. VHS, Beta MED 🎬½

Western Double Feature 18 A Rogers double feature: in "Eyes of Texas" (1948), a westerner turns his ranch into a camp for war-orphaned boys; in "Helldorado" (1946), Roy travels to Las Vegas.
194? 108m/B Roy Rogers, Andy Devine, Dale Evans; *D:* William Witney. VHS, Beta MED 🎬½

Western Double Feature 19 Rogers helps a young woman foil a plot by crooks to swindle her inheritance. Roy appears in his first starring role (1938) and fights an outlaw gang.
1945 108m/B Roy Rogers, Dale Evans, Pat Brady, Trigger. VHS, Beta MED 🎬½

Western Double Feature 20 "Night Time in Nevada" (1948), has Roy bringing a ruthless murderer to justice. "The Old Corral" (1937) features a clash between gangsters in limousines and deputies on horseback.
19?? 108m/B Roy Rogers, Gene Autry; *D:* Joseph Kane. VHS, Beta MED 🎬½

Western Double Feature 21 Roy battles crooks in "Susanna Pass" (1949). In "Sheriff of Las Vegas" (1944), Red must find the murderer of Judge Blackwell.
194? 121m/C Roy Rogers, Red Ryder, Dale Evans, Robert (Bobby) Blake; *D:* William Witney. VHS, Beta MED 🎬½

Western Double Feature 22 A Rogers double feature: "Under California Stars" (1948), Roy rounds up a gang of wild horse rustlers; "San Fernando Valley" (1944), Roy brings law and order to the valley.
194? 108m/B Roy Rogers; *D:* William Witney. VHS, Beta MED 🎬½

Western Double Feature 23 In "Spoilers of the Plains" (1951), Roy finds cattle rustlers and sets out to capture the spoilers. "Lights of Old Santa Fe" (1947) features Roy as a cowboy who rescues a beautiful rodeo owner from bankruptcy.
19?? 122m/B Roy Rogers, Dale Evans. VHS, Beta MED 🎬½

Western Double Feature 24 In "Cowboy and the Senorita" (1944), Roy solves the mystery of a missing girl. "Colorado Serenade" (1946) is a musical western in Cinecolor starring Dean.
194? 122m/C Roy Rogers, Dale Evans, Eddie Dean. VHS, Beta MED 🎬½

Western Double Feature 25 In "Pals of the Golden West" (1951), Roy discovers how valuable Trigger is. "Springtime in the Sierras" (1947) features Roy raising and selling thoroughbreds.
19?? 122m/B Roy Rogers, Dale Evans, Andy Devine, The Pioneers; *D:* William Witney. VHS, Beta MED 🎬½

Western Frontier Ordinary cowpoke Maynard is called on to lead the fight against a band of outlaws led by the Indian-raised sister he never knew he had. Action-packed, fast, and fun. Maynard's first outing for Columbia.
1935 56m/B Ken Maynard, Lucille Browne, Nora Lane, Robert "Buzzy" Henry, Frank Yaconelli; *D:* Al Herman. VHS, Beta $19.95 NOS, DVT 🎬🎬

Western Justice Good Guy Steele brings western-style justice to a lawless town. Ordinary oater with horses, etc., and a few chuckles on the side.
1935 56m/B Bob Steele; *D:* Robert North Bradbury. VHS, Beta $6.99 VTR, NOS 🎬🎬

Western Mail Yet another western in which the hero goes undercover so he can bring the bad guys to justice. Yaconelli plays a guitar tune, accompanied by his monkey.
1942 54m/B Tom Keene, Frank Yaconelli, Leroy Mason, Jean Trent, Fred Kohler Jr.; *D:* Robert Tansey. VHS $19.95 NOS, DVT, HEG 🎬🎬

Western Pacific Agent A Western Pacific agent chases an outlaw who has committed robbery and murder. The agent falls in love with the victim's sister and, of course, prevails. Rather violent.
1951 62m/B Kent Taylor, Sheila Ryan, Mickey Knox, Robert Lowery; *D:* Sam Newfield. VHS, Beta NO 🎬🎬

Western Trails Forgettable western about the clean-up of a Wild West town terrorized by outlaws. Thin script, bad acting, and a little singin' and funnin' around.
1938 59m/B Bob Baker, Marjorie Reynolds, Robert Burns; *D:* George Waggner. VHS, Beta $19.95 NOS, DVT, HEG 🎬

Western Union A lavish, vintage epic romantically detailing the political machinations, Indian warfare and frontier adventure that accompanied the construction of the Western Union telegraph line from Omaha, Nebraska, to Salt Lake City, Utah, during the Civil War. A thoroughly entertaining film in rich Technicolor. This was Lang's second western, following his personal favorite, "The Return of Frank James." Writer Carson utilized the title, but not the storyline, of a Zane Grey book. The German Lang showed himself a master of the most American of genres, yet made only one more western, "Rancho Notorious" (1952), another masterpiece.
1941 94m/C Randolph Scott, Robert Young, Dean Jagger, Slim Summerville, Virginia Gilmore, John Carradine, Chill Wills, Barton MacLane, Minor Watson, Charles Middleton, Irving Bacon; *D:* Fritz Lang. VHS, Beta $39.98 FOX, MLB 🎬🎬🎬½

The Westerner A sly, soft-spoken drifter champions Texas border homesteaders in a land war with the legendary Judge Roy Bean. "The Law West of the Pecos" sentences drifter Cooper to hang, but Cooper breaks out of jail. He falls for damsel Davenport and stays in the area, advocating the rights of homesteaders to Brennan. Brennan's Bean is unforgettable and steals the show from Cooper. Film debuts of actors Tucker and Andrews. Amazing cinematography; Brennan's Oscar was his third, making him the first performer to pull a hat trick.
1940 100m/B Gary Cooper, Walter Brennan, Doris Davenport, Dana Andrews, Forrest Tucker, Charles Halton; *D:* William Wyler. Academy Awards '40: Best Supporting Actor (Brennan); Nominations: Best Interior Decoration, Best Story. VHS, Beta $19.98 HBO, SUE, BTV 🎬🎬🎬½

Westfront 1918 A dogmatic anti-war film by the German master (his first talkie), about German and French soldiers on the fields of WWI, dying together without victory. Stunning in its portrayal of war's futility, with excellent photography that achieves a palpable realism. In German with English subtitles.
1930 90m/B Gustav Diesl, Fritz Kampers, Claus Clausen, Hans Joachim Moebis; *D:* G.W. Pabst. VHS, Beta $29.98 SUE, GLV, ING 🎬🎬🎬

Westward Ho Wayne is determined to bring to justice his parents' slayer. Haven't we seen this one before? Seems the bad guys have corrupted his brother. Wayne's group of vigilantes is called "The Singing Riders," so naturally he sings—or is made to appear to. He looks and sounds ridiculous.
1935 55m/B John Wayne, Sheila Manners; **D:** Robert North Bradbury. **VHS $9.98** REP, VCN, NOS 🎞️½

Westward Ho, the Wagons! The promised land lies in the west, but to get there these pioneers must pass unfriendly savages, thieves, villains, and scoundrels galore. Suitable for family viewing, but why bother? Well, the cast does include four Mouseketeers.
1956 94m/B Fess Parker, Kathleen Crowley, Jeff York, Sebastian Cabot, George Reeves; **D:** William Beaudine. **VHS, Beta $69.95** DIS 🎞️½

Westward the Women Taylor is Buck Wyatt, a scout hired to wagon-train 150 mail-order brides from Chicago to California. When his lustful hired hands turn out to be all hands, Taylor and the ladies must fight off attacking Indians on their own. Notable film allowing women to be as tough as men is not your typical western. Based on the Frank Capra story.
1951 116m/C Robert Taylor, Denise Darcel, Hope Emerson, John McIntire, Beverly Dennis, Lenore Lonergan, Marilyn Erskine, Julie Bishop, Renato Vanni, Frankie Darro, George Chandler; **D:** William A. Wellman; **W:** Charles Schnee; **M:** Jeff Alexander. **VHS $19.98** MGM 🎞️🎞️🎞️

Westworld Crichton wrote and directed this story of an adult vacation resort of the future which offers the opportunity to live in various fantasy worlds serviced by lifelike robots. Brolin and Benjamin are businessmen who choose a western fantasy world. When an electrical malfunction occurs, the robots begin to go berserk. Brynner is perfect as a western gunslinging robot whose skills are all too real.
1973 (PG) 90m/C Yul Brynner, Richard Benjamin, James Brolin, Dick Van Patten, Majel Barrett; **D:** Michael Crichton; **W:** Michael Crichton. **VHS, Beta $19.98** MGM 🎞️🎞️🎞️

Wet Gold A beautiful young woman and three men journey to retrieve a sunken treasure. Nice scenery. Proves that it is possible to make "The Treasure of the Sierra Madre" without making a classic. John Huston, where are you? Made for television.
1984 90m/C Brooke Shields, Brian Kerwin, Burgess Meredith, Tom Byrd; **D:** Dick Lowry. **VHS, Beta** NO 🎞️

Wetherby Playwright David Hare's first directorial effort, which he also wrote, about a Yorkshire schoolteacher whose life is shattered when a young, brooding stranger comes uninvited to a dinner party, and then shoots himself in her living room. Compelling but oh, so dark. Richardson, who plays a young Redgrave, is actually Redgrave's daughter.
1985 (R) 97m/C Vanessa Redgrave, Ian Holm, Judi Dench, Joely Richardson, Tim McInnery, Suzanna Hamilton; **D:** David Hare; **W:** David Hare; **M:** Nick Bicat. **VHS, Beta $19.98** MGM 🎞️🎞️🎞️

Whale for the Killing An ecologist stranded in a remote Alaskan fishing village battles to save a beached humpbacked whale from a malicious Russian fisherman. Platitudinous and self-congratulatory, if well-meaning. Made for television from a book by Farley Mowat.

1981 145m/C Richard Widmark, Peter Strauss, Dee Wallace Stone, Bruce McGill, Kathryn Walker; **D:** Richard T. Heffron. **VHS, Beta $59.98** FOX 🎞️🎞️½

Whale of a Tale A young boy trains a killer whale to appear in the big show in the main tank at "Marineland."
1976 (G) 90m/C William Shatner, Marty Allen, Abby Dalton, Andy Devine, Nancy O'Conner; **D:** Ewing Miles Brown. **VHS, Beta $39.95** VCI, WTA 🎞️

The Whales of August Based on the David Berry play, the story of two elderly sisters—one caring, the other cantankerous, blind, and possibly senile—who decide during a summer in Maine whether or not they should give up their ancestral house and enter a nursing home. Gish and Davis are exquisite to watch, and the all-star supporting cast is superb—especially Price as a suave Russian. Lovingly directed by Anderson in his first US outing.
1987 91m/C Lillian Gish, Bette Davis, Vincent Price, Ann Sothern, Mary Steenburgen, Harry Carey Jr.; **D:** Lindsay Anderson. Academy Awards '87 Nominations: Best Supporting Actress (Sothern); National Board of Review Awards '87: Best Actress (Gish); National Media Owl Awards '88: First Prize. **VHS, Beta, 8mm $14.98** SUE, NLC 🎞️🎞️½

What a Carve-Up! A group of relatives gather in an old, spooky mansion to hear the reading of a will. Tries too hard. Remake of "The Ghoul." **AKA:** No Place Like Homicide.
1962 87m/B Kenneth Connor, Sidney James, Shirley Eaton, Donald Pleasence, Dennis Price, Michael Gough; **D:** Pat Jackson. **VHS $16.95** SNC 🎞️🎞️

What a Way to Die An evil assassin plots dispatching with a difference.
1970 (R) 87m/C William Berger, Anthony Baker, Helga Anders, Georgia Moll; **D:** Helmut Foernbacher. **VHS, Beta** NO 🎞️½

What About Bob? Bob, a ridiculously neurotic patient, follows his psychiatrist on vacation, turning his life upside down. The psychiatrist's family find Bob entertaining and endearing. Murray is at his comedic best; Dreyfuss's overly excitable characterization occasionally wears thin.
1991 99m/C Richard Dreyfuss, Bill Murray, Julie Hagerty, Charlie Korsmo, Tom Aldredge, Roger Bowen, Fran Brill, Kathryn Erbe, Doris Belack, Susan Willis; **D:** Frank Oz; **W:** Tom Schulman, Alvin Sargent; **M:** Miles Goodman. **VHS, Beta $19.99** BVV 🎞️🎞️🎞️

What Comes Around A good-ole-boy drama about a doped-up country singer who is kidnapped by his brother for his own good. The singer's evil manager sends his stooges out to find him. Might have been funny, but isn't. But is it meant to be? Good Reed songs; mildly interesting plot.
1985 (PG) 92m/C Jerry Reed, Bo Hopkins, Arte Johnson, Barry Corbin; **D:** Jerry Reed. **VHS, Beta $19.98** NLC 🎞️🎞️

What Did You Do in the War, Daddy? Unfunny comedy set in WWII about a group of weary American soldiers trying to get a small town in Sicily to surrender. Things don't go smoothly thanks to a combination soccer game/wine festival, not to mention the Germans deciding to attack. Director Edwards comedic verve deserted him.
1966 119m/C Dick Shawn, James Coburn, Sergio Fantoni, Giovanna Ralli, Aldo Ray, Harry Morgan, Carroll O'Connor, Jay Novello, Vito Scotti; **D:** Blake Edwards; **W:** William Peter Blatty, Blake Edwards; **M:** Henry Mancini. **VHS $14.95** MGM 🎞️½

What Do You Say to a Naked Lady? Funt takes his Candid Camera to the streets to find out how people react when confronted by nude members of the opposite sex. Sporadically hilarious.
1970 92m/C D: Allen Funt. **VHS, Beta** FOX 🎞️🎞️½

What Ever Happened to Baby Jane? Davis and Crawford portray aging sisters and former child stars living together in a decaying mansion. When the demented Jane (Davis) learns of her now-crippled sister's (Crawford) plan to institutionalize her, she tortures the wheelchair-bound sis. Davis plays her part to the hilt, unafraid of Aldrich's unsympathetic camera, and the viciousness of her character. She received her tenth Oscar nomination for the role.
1962 132m/B Bette Davis, Joan Crawford, Victor Buono, Anna Lee, B.D. Merrill; **D:** Robert Aldrich. **VHS, Beta $19.98** WAR 🎞️🎞️🎞️½

What Happened to Rosa? This early Goldwyn release, a whimsical Cinderella story, casts Normand as an endearing shop girl duped by a gypsy's bogus predictions. Believing herself to be the reincarnation of a Castillian noblewoman she dons a fancy gown, attends a fancy shipboard ball and captures the heart of the fancy doctor of her dreams. But fearing his rejection of her true identity she slips away during the chaos of a brawl, leading the good doctor to believe that she is dead. A comedy of errors unfolds before they meet again and live happily ever after. No doubt it jerked a few tears in its day.
1921 42m/B Mabel Normand, Hugh Thompson, Doris Pawn, Tully Marshall, Eugenie Besserer, Buster Trow; **D:** Victor Schertzinger. **VHS $19.95** NOS, FHV 🎞️🎞️🎞️

What Have I Done to Deserve This? A savage parody on Spanish mores, about a speed-addicted housewife who ends up selling her son and killing her husband with a ham bone. Black, black comedy, perverse and funny as only Almodovar can be. In Spanish with subtitles. Nudity and profanity. **AKA:** Que He Hecho Yo Para Merecer Estol?
1985 100m/C Carmen Maura, Chus Lampreave; **D:** Pedro Almodovar; **W:** Pedro Almodovar. **VHS, Beta $79.95** ING, CCN, TPV 🎞️🎞️🎞️

What! No Beer? Two dim-bulb friends decide to put their money into a defunct brewery hoping for the end of Prohibition. They start up operations too soon and wind up attracting the unwelcome attentions of gangster bootleggers and the cops. Mediocre comedy and Keaton's last starring role as his own problems with alcohol affected his work.
1933 66m/B Buster Keaton, Jimmy Durante, Phyllis Barry, Roscoe Ates, John Miljan, Henry Armetta, Edward Brophy; **D:** Edward Sedgwick. **VHS $19.98** MGM 🎞️🎞️

What Price Glory? Remake of the 1926 silent classic about a pair of comradely rivals for the affections of women in WWI France. Strange to have Ford directing an offbeat comedy, but it works: masterful direction, good acting. Demarest broke both legs in a motorcycle accident during shooting.
1952 111m/C James Cagney, Dan Dailey, Corinne Calvet, William Demarest, James Gleason, Robert Wagner, Casey Adams, Craig Hill, Marisa Pavan; **D:** John Ford. **VHS, Beta $19.98** FOX, FCT 🎞️🎞️🎞️

What Price Hollywood? Aspiring young starlet decides to crash film world by using an alcoholic director as her stepping stone. Bennett is lovely; Sherman is superb as an aging, dissolute man who watches his potential slip away. From a story by Adela Rogers St. John. Remade three times as "A Star is Born."
1932 88m/B Constance Bennett, Lowell Sherman, Neil Hamilton; **D:** George Cukor. **VHS, Beta $19.98** *CCB, TTC, FCT* 🎬🎬🎬

What the Moon Saw When a young boy is confronted by a less than friendly theater owner, he uses favorite scenes from "Sinbad" to deal with the aggressor.
1990 86m/C VHS $39.98 *FHE, BTV* 🎬🎬½

What the Peeper Saw The wife of a wealthy author finds her comfortable life turning into a terrifying nightmare when her young stepson starts acting funny. Juicy and terrifying. **AKA:** Night Hair Child; Child of the Night.
1972 97m/C Britt Ekland, Mark Lester, Hardy Kruger, Lilli Palmer. **VHS, Beta $29.95** *VCI* 🎬🎬

What Waits Below A scientific expedition encounters a lost race living in caves in South America. Good cast, bad acting, and lousy script. Might have been better.
1983 (PG) 88m/C Timothy Bottoms, Robert Powell, Lisa Blount; **D:** Don Sharp. **VHS, Beta $69.98** *LIV* 🎬½

Whatever Happened to Aunt Alice? After murdering her husband to inherit his estate, a poor, eccentric widow develops an awful habit: she hires maids, only to murder them and steal their savings. The only evidence is a growing number of trees by the drive. Sleuth Ruth Gordon (of "Harold and Maude" fame, acting here just as odd) takes the job in hopes of solving the mystery. Thoroughly amusing.
1969 (PG) 101m/C Geraldine Page, Ruth Gordon, Rosemary Forsyth, Robert Fuller, Mildred Dunnock; **D:** Lee H. Katzin. **VHS, Beta $59.98** *FOX, MLB* 🎬🎬🎬

Whatever Happened to Susan Jane? A bored housewife searches for an off-beat college friend, and enters into the seamy, strange world of San Francisco's lunatic fringe. Music by Tuxedo Moon, Indoor Life and other punk groups.
1984 90m/C VHS, Beta $39.95 *MPI* 🎬1½

What's Eating Gilbert Grape Offbeat is mildly descriptive. Depp stars as Gilbert Grape, the titular head of a very dysfunctional family living in a big house in a small Iowa town. His Momma (Cates) weighs more than 500 pounds and hasn't left the house in 7 years, he has two squabbling teenage sisters, and 17-year-old brother Arnie (DiCaprio) is mentally retarded and requires constant supervision. What's a good-hearted grocery clerk to do? Well, when free-spirited Becky (Lewis) is momentarily marooned in town, Gilbert may have found a true soulmate. Performances, especially DiCaprio's, save this from the oddball/cute factor although flick would have benefitted from streamlining, particularly the scenes involving Depp and bad-haircut Lewis. Based on the novel by Hedges. **AKA:** Gilbert Grape.
1993 (PG-13) 118m/C Johnny Depp, Leonardo DiCaprio, Juliette Lewis, Mary Steenburgen, Darlene Cates, Laura Harrington, Mary Kate Schellhardt, Kevin Tighe, John Reilly, Crispin Glover, Penelope Branning; **D:** Lasse Hallstrom; **W:** Peter Hedges; **M:** Alan Parker, Bjorn Isfalt. Academy Awards '93 Nominations: Best Supporting Actor (DiCaprio); Golden Globe Awards '94: Best Supporting Actor (DiCaprio); National Board of Review Awards '93: Best Supporting Actor (DiCaprio). **VHS, Beta** *PAR* 🎬🎬🎬

What's Good for the Goose Stuffy, married financial institution executive's life-style receives a major overhaul when he attends a banking conference and meets a beautiful and free-spirited young woman whom he takes as a lover. Unfortunately, he perpetually finds her in bed with other men, and then his wife gets in on the act, too. Classic British humor.
1993 ?m/C Norman Wisdom, Sally Geeson, Sarah Atkinson, Sally Bazely; **D:** Menahem Golan; **W:** Norman Wisdom, Menahem Golan; **M:** Reg Tilsley. **VHS $79.95** *NMD* 🎬🎬½

What's Love Got to Do With It? Energetic biopic of powerhouse songstress Tina Turner. Short sequences cover her early life before moving into her abusive relationship with Ike and solo comeback success. Bassett may not look like Tina, but her exceptionally strong performance leaves no question as to who she's supposed to be, even during on-stage Tina sequences. Some credibility is lost when Turner is shown in the final concert sequence—Gibson would have been wise to let Bassett finish what she started. Fishburne is a sympathetic but still chilling Ike, rising to the challenge of showing both Ike's initial charm and longtime cruelty. Based on "I, Tina" by Turner and Kurt Loder.
1993 (R) 118m/C Angela Bassett, Laurence "Larry" Fishburne, Vanessa Bell Calloway, Jenifer Lewis, Phyllis Stickney, Khandi Alexander, Pamela Tyson, Penny Johnson, Rae'ven Kelly, Robert Miranda, Chi; **D:** Brian Gibson; **W:** Kate Lanier; **M:** Stanley Clarke. Academy Awards '93 Nominations: Best Actor (Fishburne), Best Actress (Bassett); Golden Globe Awards '94: Best Actress—Musical/Comedy (Bassett). **VHS** *BVV* 🎬🎬½

What's New Pussycat? A young engaged man, reluctant to give up the girls who love him, seeks the aid of a married psychiatrist who turns out to have problems of his own. Allen's first feature as both actor and screenwriter. Oscar-nominated title song sung by Tom Jones. **AKA:** Quoi De Neuf, Pussycat?.
1965 108m/C Peter Sellers, Peter O'Toole, Romy Schneider, Paula Prentiss, Woody Allen, Ursula Andress, Capucine; **D:** Clive Donner; **W:** Woody Allen; **M:** Burt Bacharach, Hal David. **VHS, Beta $19.98** *FOX, FCT* 🎬🎬🎬

What's the Matter with Helen? Two women, the mothers of murderous sons, move to Hollywood to escape their past and start a new life. They open a school for talented children, and seem to be adjusting to their new lives until strange things start happening. It is soon revealed that one of the mothers is a psychotic killer, and the other mother becomes part of an eerie finale. A fine starring vehicle for two aging actresses. Great score.
1971 (PG) 101m/C Debbie Reynolds, Shelley Winters, Dennis Weaver, Agnes Moorehead, Michael MacLiammoir; **D:** Curtis Harrington. **VHS $14.95** *MGM* 🎬🎬½

What's Up, Doc? A shy musicologist from Iowa (Ryan) travels to San Francisco with his fiance (Kahn) for a convention. He meets the eccentric Streisand at his hotel and becomes involved in a chase to recover four identical flight bags containing top secret documents, a wealthy woman's jewels, the professor's musical rocks, and Streisand's clothing. Bogdanovich's homage to the screwball comedies of the '30s. Kahn's feature film debut.
1972 (G) 94m/C Barbra Streisand, Ryan O'Neal, Kenneth Mars, Austin Pendleton, Randy Quaid; **D:** Peter Bogdanovich; **W:** David Newman, Buck Henry. **VHS, Beta $14.95** *WAR* 🎬🎬🎬

What's Up Front Occasionally funny '60s gag-fest about an ogle-eyed bra salesman who decides to sell door-to-door in order to save a failing brassiere company. Filmed in "Girl-O-Rama" by the young Vilmos Zsigmond. Dated and weird, with camp value. No nudity. Costumes were done by Frederick's of Hollywood. **AKA:** The Fall Guy; A Fourth for Marriage.
1963 90m/C Tommy Holden, Marilyn Manning, Carolyn Walker, William Watters; **D:** Bob Whealing. **VHS, Beta $59.95** *RHI* 🎬½

What's Up, Tiger Lily? This legitimate Japanese spy movie—"Kagi No Kag" (Key of Keys), a 1964 Bond imitation—was re-edited by Woody Allen, who added a new dialogue track, with hysterical results. Characters Terri and Suki Yaki are involved in an international plot to secure egg salad recipe; Allen's brand of Hollywood parody and clever wit sustain the joke. Music by the Lovin' Spoonful, who make a brief appearance.
1966 90m/C Woody Allen, Tatsuya Mihashi, Mie Hama, Akiko Wakabayashi; **D:** Woody Allen, Senkichi Taniguhi; **M:** The Lovin' Spoonful. **VHS, Beta $29.98** *VES, CAB* 🎬🎬🎬

Wheel of Fortune A shrewd small-town lawyer, working on a case in the big city, is forced to expose his girlfriend's father as a crooked politician. Strange to see the Duke here in the lead, but what the hey. Not great, but interesting. **AKA:** A Man Betrayed; Citadel of Crime.
1941 83m/B John Wayne, Frances Dee, Edward Ellis; **D:** John H. Auer. **VHS $14.98** *REP* 🎬🎬

The Wheeler Dealers Garner plays a supposedly penniless investor (actually a Texas millionaire) who comes to New York stock analyst Remick for investment advice. Her shyster boss (Backus) tells her to sell the aw-shucks cowboy worthless stock which turns out to be worth a fortune. Zany spoof of Wall Street ethics. **AKA:** Separate Beds.
1963 100m/C James Garner, Lee Remick, Jim Backus, Phil Harris, Shelley Berman, Chill Wills, John Astin, Louis Nye; **D:** Arthur Hiller. **VHS $19.98** *MGM* 🎬🎬🎬

Wheels of Fire The earth is a wasteland controlled by sadistic highway hoodlums. When they kidnap the hero's sister, he fights back in a flame-throwing car. Horrible "Road Warrior" rip-off. **AKA:** Vindicator.
1984 (R) 81m/C Gary Watkins, Lynda Wiesmeier; **D:** Cirio H. Santiago. **VHS, Beta $79.98** *LIV, VES* 🎬

Wheels of Terror Possessed black car stalks children in isolated village. Bus driver Cassidy gets behind the wheel of V-8 supercharged school bus to initiate most interminable chase scene in screen history.
1990 (R) 86m/C Joanna Cassidy, Marcie Leeds, Carlos Cervantes, Arlen Dean Snyder; **D:** Christopher Cain; **M:** Jay Gruska. **VHS, Beta $79.95** *PAR* 🎬

When a Man Loves a Woman Time to get suspicious when song titles become film titles. Alice Green (Ryan) is the mother in a perfect little family, with a loving husband (Garcia), two little girls, and a satisfying career. She's also a closet alcoholic. Less about her alcoholism than the effect on her family and her hubby in particular, shown as a '90s sort of guy who allows Alice to keep her secret. Ryan's detox treatments and struggle back to sobriety are fertile ground for psycho-babble and 12-step cliches, but solid performances save this picture from drying out. **AKA:** To Have and to Hold; Significant Other.

1994 (R) 124m/C Meg Ryan, Andy Garcia, Lauren Tom, Philip S. Hoffman, Tina Majorino, Mae Whitman, Ellen Burstyn, Eugene Roche, Latanya Richardson; **D:** Luis Mandoki; **W:** Ronald Bass, Al Franken; **M:** Zbigniew Preisner. VHS NYR ♪♪½

When a Man Rides Alone Tyler relieves trains of their gold shipments in order to reimburse swindled investors. Lovely Lacey frowns on his initiative, so he kidnaps her to keep her quiet. The two fall in love, and the man who rides alone works beside his beloved.
1933 60m/B Tom Tyler, Adele Lacey, Alan Bridge, Bob Burns, Frank Ball, Alma Chester, Bud Osborne; **D:** J.P. McGowan. VHS $19.99 NOS, GPV ♪♪

When a Man Sees Red Jones is a ranch foreman whose new boss is Campbell (she inherited the property). The two argue constantly but then come to realize all the fighting is just hiding true love.
1934 60m/B Buck Jones, Peggy Campbell, Dorothy Revier, Syd Saylor, Leroy Mason, Charles French, Robert F. (Bob) Kortman; **D:** Alan James. VHS $12.95 GPV ♪½

When a Stranger Calls Babysitter is terrorized by threatening phone calls and soon realizes that the calls are coming from within the house. Story was expanded from director Walton's short film "The Sitter." Distasteful and unlikely, though the first half or so is tight and terrifying.
1979 (R) 97m/C Carol Kane, Charles Durning, Colleen Dewhurst, Rachel Roberts; **D:** Fred Walton. VHS, Beta $64.95 COL ♪½

When a Stranger Calls Back Sequel to "When a Stranger Calls" finds college student Julia Jenz (Schoelen) still trying to put her life together five years after a terrifying ordeal with a stalker. She turns to her advisor Jill (Kane), who went through a similar fate, but once Jill becomes involved she again becomes the pawn of a psychopath. It's up to retired detective John Clifford (Durning), who saved Jill before, to do his heroics once again. Scary opening sequence but suspense peters out toward the end. Made for cable television.
1993 (R) 94m/C Carol Kane, Charles Durning, Jill Schoelen, Gene Lythgow, Karen Austin; **D:** Fred Walton; **W:** Fred Walton. MCA ♪♪½

When a Woman Ascends the Stairs A young widow with an elderly mother and a useless brother supports them all by working as a Ginza bar hostess. As she approaches the perilous professional age of 30, Keiko must decide whether to open her own bar or marry once again. In Japanese with English subtitles. **AKA:** Onna Ga Kaidan O Agaru Toki.
1960 110m/B Hideko Takamine, Tatsuya Nakadai, Masayuki Mori; **D:** Mikio Naruse. VHS $79.95 WAC, ING ♪♪

When Angels Fly In this emotional tale of love and murder, a young woman sets out to find the exact circumstances surrounding the mysterious death of her sister.
1982 96m/C Jennifer Dale, Robin Ward. VHS, Beta $49.95 UNI, MOV ♪

When Comedy was King A compilation of the greatest silent screen comedians, including Keaton, Chaplin, Langdon, and Turpin.
1959 81m/C Buster Keaton, Charlie Chaplin, Harry Langdon, Ben Turpin; **D:** Robert Youngson. VHS, Beta NO ♪

When Dinosaurs Ruled the Earth When "One Million Years B.C." ruled the box office the Brits cranked out a few more lively prehistoric fantasies. A sexy cavegirl, exiled because of her blond hair, acquires a cavebeau and a dinosaur guardian. Stop-motion animation from Jim Danforth, story by J.G. Ballard. Under the name Angela Dorian, Vetri was Playmate of the Year in 1968 (A.D.).
1970 (G) 96m/C Victoria Vetri, Robin Hawdon, Patrick Allen, Drewe Henley, Sean Caffrey, Magda Konopka, Imogen Hassall, Patrick Holt, Jan Rossini; **D:** Val Guest; **W:** Val Guest. VHS, Beta $19.95 WAR, FCT, MLB ♪♪

When Every Day was the Fourth of July A nine-year-old girl asks her father, a lawyer, to defend a mute handyman accused of murder, knowing this will bring on him the contempt of the community. Well handled, but see "To Kill a Mockingbird" first. Based on producer/director Curtis's childhood. Sequel: "The Long Days of Summer." Made for television.
1978 100m/C Katy Kurtzman, Dean Jones, Louise Sorel, Harris Yulin, Chris Petersen, Geoffrey Lewis, Scott Brady, Henry Wilcoxon, Michael Pataki; **D:** Dan Curtis. VHS, Beta $49.95 LIV ♪♪½

When Father was Away on Business Set in 1950s Yugoslavia. A family must take care of itself when the father is sent to jail for philandering with a woman desired by a Communist Party official. The moving story of the family's day-to-day survival is seen largely through the eyes of the father's six-year-old son, who believes dad is "away on business." In Yugoslavian with English subtitles.
1985 (R) 144m/C Moreno D'E Bartolli, Miki Manojlovic, Mirjana Karanovic; **D:** Emir Kusturica. Academy Awards '85 Nominations: Best Foreign Language Film; Cannes Film Festival '85: Best Film. VHS $89.95 FXL, ING ♪♪♪½

When Gangland Strikes A country lawyer, blackmailed by the mob, tries to protect his family without caving in. Unexceptional remake of "Main Street Lawyer."
1956 70m/B Raymond Greenleaf, Marjie Millar, Anthony Caruso, Jack Perrin, John Hudson; **D:** R.G. Springsteen. VHS $14.98 REP ♪♪

When Harry Met Sally Romantic comedy follows the long relationship between two adults who try throughout the changes in their lives (and their mates) to remain platonic friends—and what happens when they don't. Wry and enjoyable script is enhanced by wonderful performances. Another directional direct hit for "Meathead" Reiner, and a tour de force of comic screenwriting for Ephron, with improvisational help from Crystal. Great songs by Sinatra soundalike Connick.
1989 (R) 96m/C Billy Crystal, Meg Ryan, Carrie Fisher, Bruno Kirby, Steven Ford, Lisa Jane Persky, Michelle Nicastro, Harley Jane Kozak; **D:** Rob Reiner; **W:** Nora Ephron; **M:** Harry Connick Jr., Marc Shaiman. VHS, Beta, 8mm $14.95 NLC, SUE, SUP ♪♪♪

When Hell Broke Loose Routine WWII actioner about a small-time crook (Bronson) who joins the Army, changes his ways because of the love of a good woman, and gets a chance to be a hero when he stumbles upon a Nazi assassination plot against General Eisenhower.
1958 78m/B Charles Bronson, Violet Rensing, Richard Jaeckel, Arvid Nelson, Robert Easton; **D:** Kenneth Crane; **W:** Oscar Brodney. VHS $14.95 PAR ♪½

When Hell Was in Session In more than seven years as a prisoner of the Viet Cong, Holbrook is subjected to torture, starvation, and psychological warfare to break his will. Based on the true story of Navy Commander Jeremiah Denton. Painful and violent. Made for TV.
1982 98m/C Hal Holbrook, Eva Marie Saint, Ronny Cox; **D:** Paul Krasny. VHS, Beta TLF ♪♪♪

When He's Not a Stranger Date rape is the subject of this made-for-television drama. Lyn is a college freshman who goes to a campus party hosted by the football team. When Ron, the star quarterback, invites Lyn to his dorm room, the situation gets out of hand. Only Lyn calls it rape and Ron calls her a liar. Intense performances are a highlight of this well-done story.
1989 100m/C Annabeth Gish, John Terlesky, Kevin Dillon, Paul Dooley, Kim Meyers; **D:** John Gray. VHS $89.95 TRI ♪♪♪

When Knights were Bold An English nobleman living in India inherits a castle in his native land. Returning home, he is knocked unconscious by a falling suit of armor while trying to impress a young lady and dreams himself back to medieval days. Enjoyable comedy about that ubiquitous British class hierarchy.
1936 55m/B Fay Wray, Jack Buchanan, Martita Hunt. VHS, Beta $19.95 VYY ♪♪½

When Ladies Meet Entertaining story of a love quadrangle that features several of MGM's top stars of the '40s. In this remake of the 1933 film, Crawford plays a novelist and an early proponent of the women's liberation movement. She falls in love with her publisher (Marshall), who just happens to be married to Garson. Meanwhile, Taylor, who is in love with Crawford, attempts to show her that he isa more suitable match for her than Marshall, but Crawford has yet to catch on. The lengthy dialogue on women's rights is badly dated, but the real-life rivalry between Crawford and Garson adds a certain bite to their witty exchanges. Also known as "Strange Skirts."
1941 105m/B Joan Crawford, Robert Taylor, Greer Garson, Herbert Marshall, Spring Byington; **D:** Robert Z. Leonard, Anita Loos, S.K. Lauren; **W:** Anita Loos, S.K. Lauren. VHS $19.98 MGM ♪♪½

When Lightning Strikes Lightning the Wonder Dog prevents the owner of a rival lumber company from stealing his master's land. He gets to use his talents of running, swimming, barking, and smoking cigars. Proves that real woofers were made way back when, even though in 1934 they didn't feature scantily clad babes. Part of Video Yesteryear's Golden Turkey series.
1934 51m/B Francis X. Bushman, Lightning the Wonder Dog. VHS, Beta $19.95 VYY Woof!

When Nature Calls A city family "gets back to nature" in this collection of mostly ineffective gags and poor satirical ideas. Probably your first and last chance to see Liddy and Mays on screen together.
1985 (R) 76m/C Davie Orange, Barbara Marineau, Nicky Beim, Tina Marie Staiano, Willie Mays, G. Gordon Liddy; **D:** Charles Kaufman. VHS, Beta $59.95 MED Woof!

When Taekwondo Strikes One brave Taekwondo master leads the Korean freedom fighters against the occupying army of WWII Japan.
1983 (R) 95m/C Jhoon Rhee, Ann Winton, Angela Mao, Huang Ing Sik; **D:** Raymond Chow. VHS, Beta $9.98 SUE ♪

When the Bough Breaks A psychologist helps the police with the case of a murder-suicide witnessed by a child. He finds one sick secret society at work in this unkinder, ungentler TV thriller, based on the novel by Jonathan Kellerman. Danson co-produced.

1986 100m/C Ted Danson, Richard Masur, Rachel Ticotin, David Huddleston, James Noble, Kim Miyori, Merritt Butrick; *D:* Waris Hussein. **VHS** *WOV* 🐾🐾

When the Clouds Roll By
Psycho-satire pits demented doctor against Fairbanks in experiment to make him suicidal basket case. Fairbanks seems to contract ferocious nightmares, passionate superstitions, a spurning lover, and a warrant for his arrest, none of which suppresses his penchant for acrobatics.
1919 77m/B Douglas Fairbanks Sr., Herbert Grimwood, Kathleen Clifford, Frank Campeau, Ralph Lewis, Daisy Robinson, Albert MacQuarrie; *D:* Victor Fleming. **VHS, Beta $24.95** *GPV, FCT* 🐾🐾🐾½

When the Legends Die
A Ute Indian strives to preserve his heritage in an often harsh modern world. Recorded in hi-fi.
1972 (PG) 105m/C Richard Widmark, Frederic Forrest; *D:* Stuart Millar. **VHS, Beta $19.98** *FOX* 🐾🐾🐾

When the Line Goes Through
A drifter arrives in a small West Virginia town and changes the lives of two pretty sisters.
1971 90m/C Martin Sheen, Davey Davidson, Beverly Washburn. **VHS, Beta $39.95** *CNG* 🐾

When the North Wind Blows
An old, lone trapper hunts for and later befriends the majestic snow tiger of Siberia in the Alaskan wilderness. A good family film.
1974 (G) 113m/C Henry Brandon, Herbert Nelson, Dan Haggerty; *D:* Stewart Raffill. **VHS, Beta $54.95** *VCI* 🐾🐾

When the Screaming Stops
A hunter is hired to find out who has been cutting the hearts out of young women who reside in a small village near the Rhine River. Turns out it's a she-monster who rules a kingdom beneath the river. Bad effects; gory gore; outlandish plot. All the ingredients, in other words, of a classic dog.
1973 (R) 86m/C Tony Kendall, Helga Line, Sylvia Tortosa; *D:* Armando de Ossorio. **VHS, Beta $59.98** *LIV* 🐾

When the Time Comes
A woman dying of cancer wants to take her own life, but when her husband refuses, she seeks the help of a male friend. Excellent acting doesn't provide the needed depth. Less a disease-of-the-week TV movie, more of an ethical-dilemma-of-the-week, and just as trivial.
1991 (PG-13) 94m/C Bonnie Bedelia, Brad Davis, Terry O'Quinn, Karen Austin, Donald Moffatt, Wendy Schaal; *D:* John Erman; *M:* Marvin Hamlisch. **VHS $79.98** *REP* 🐾🐾

When the West Was Young
An outdoor adventure about rounding up horses in the Old West. Based on a novel by Zane Grey; also titled "Wild Horse Mesa."
1932 58m/B Randolph Scott, Sally Blane, Guinn Williams; *D:* Henry Hathaway. **VHS, Beta $19.95** *NOS, DVT, VYY* 🐾½

When the Whales Came
A conservationist fable about two children and a grizzled old codger living on a remote British isle during WWI. They try to avert disaster as mysterious narwhal whales descend on the island. Moralistic and uninvolving; poorly acted; slumber-inducing. Adapted from the novel by Morpugo.
1989 (PG) 100m/C Paul Scofield, Helen Mirren, David Threlfall, David Suchet, Jeremy Kemp, Max Rennie, Helen Pearce, Barbara Jefford; *D:* Clive Rees; *W:* Michael Morpugo; *M:* Christopher Gunning, Ruth Rennie. **VHS, Beta $14.98** *FOX* 🐾🐾½

When the Wind Blows
An animated feature about a retired British couple when their peaceful—and naive—life in the country is destroyed by nuclear war. Poignant, sad, and thought-provoking, and just a little scary. Features the voices of Ashcroft and Mills; Roger Waters, David Bowie, Squeeze, Genesis, Hugh Cornell, and Paul Hardcastle all contribute to the soundtrack. Based on the novel by Raymond Briggs.
1986 80m/C *D:* Jimmy T. Murakami; *V:* Peggy Ashcroft, John Mills. **VHS, Beta $79.95** *LIV* 🐾🐾🐾

When Thief Meets Thief
A cat burglar finds his world turned upside down when he begins to fall in love with one of his victims. Not much happening except a few nice stunts by Fairbanks.
1937 85m/B Douglas Fairbanks Jr., Valerie Hobson, Alan Hale, Jack Melford, Leo Genn, Ian Fleming; *D:* Raoul Walsh. **VHS, Beta $16.95** *NOS, SNC* 🐾½

When Time Ran Out
A volcano erupts on a remote Polynesian island covered with expensive hotels and tourists with no way to escape. Contains scenes not seen in the theatrically released print of the film. A very good cast is wasted in this compilation of disaster film cliches.
1980 (PG) 144m/C Paul Newman, Jacqueline Bisset, William Holden, Ernest Borgnine, Edward Albert, Barbara Carrera, Valentina Cortese, Burgess Meredith, Noriyuki "Pat" Morita, Red Buttons; *D:* James Goldstone; *W:* Sterling Silliphant. **VHS, Beta $19.98** *WAR* 🐾

When Wolves Cry
Tearjerker about an estranged father and young son reunited on a Corsican vacation. Their newfound joy sours when the lad is diagnosed with a fatal illness. Hardly one of Holden's best films. *AKA:* The Christmas Tree.
1969 (G) 108m/C William Holden, Virna Lisi, Brook Fuller, Andre Bourvil; *D:* Terence Young. **VHS, Beta $24.95** *GEM, VCI* 🐾½

When Women Had Tails
A primitive comedy about prehistoric man's discovery of sex. And boy, did they ever discover it. Harmless (more or less), though not exactly cerebral. Followed by "When Women Lost Their Tails." *AKA:* Quando De Donne Avevando La Coda.
1970 (R) 99m/C Senta Berger, Frank Wolff; *D:* Pasquale Festa Campanile; *M:* Ennio Morricone. **VHS, Beta $16.95** *SNC* 🐾½

When Women Lost Their Tails
Ostensible sequel to "When Women Had Tails" about prehistoric cavemen and their sexual habits.
1975 (R) 94m/C Senta Berger; *D:* Pasquale Festa Campanile; *M:* Ennio Morricone. **VHS, Beta** *NO* 🐾

When Worlds Collide
Another planet is found to be rushing inevitably towards earth, but a select group of people attempt to escape in a spaceship; others try to maneuver their way on board. Oscar-quality special effects and plot make up for cheesy acting and bad writing.
1951 81m/C Richard Derr, Barbara Rush, Larry Keating, Peter Hanson; *D:* Rudolph Mate. Academy Awards '51: Best Special Effects; Nominations: Best Color Cinematography. **VHS, Beta $49.95** *PAR* 🐾🐾½

When Your Lover Leaves
Alleged comedy about a woman, dumped by her married boyfriend, who gets involved in a short-lived relationship with a neighbor. When that also doesn't work out, she decides she must first do something to please herself. Here endeth the lesson. Produced by Fonzie and Richie of "Happy Days." Made for television.

1983 100m/C Valerie Perrine, Betty Thomas, David Ackroyd, Ed O'Neill, Dwight Schultz, Shannon Wilcox; *D:* Jeff Bleckner; *M:* Randy Edelman. **VHS $9.99** *NWV, STE* 🐾

When's Your Birthday?
Brown stars in this comedy about a prize-fighter who is working his way through astrology school with his fighting skills. The stars, in turn, tell him when to fight. Lame zaniness (what other kind is there?) meant as a vehicle for Brown, though Kennedy is funnier. The opening sequence, an animated cartoon showing the influence of the moon over the planets, was filmed in Technicolor.
1937 77m/B Joe E. Brown, Marian Marsh, Edgar Kennedy; *D:* Harry Beaumont. **VHS, Beta $19.95** *NOS, VYY, JEF* 🐾🐾

Where Angels Fear to Tread
Another turn-of-the-century tale of the English in Italy from the pen of E.M. Forster. Widowed, fortyish Lilia (Mirren) is urged by her stuffy in-laws to spend some time in Italy. Much to everyone's dismay she impulsively marries a 21-year-old Italian—with disastrous consequences. Based on Forster's first novel, the characters are more stereotypical and the story less defined than his later works and the movies made from them. Impressive performances and beautiful settings make up for a somewhat lackluster direction that isn't up to the standards set by the team of Merchant Ivory, responsible for the Forster films "A Room with a View" and "Howard's End."
1991 (PG) 112m/C Rupert Graves, Helena Bonham Carter, Judy Davis, Helen Mirren, Giovanni Guidelli, Barbara Jefford, Thomas Wheatley, Sophie Kullman; *D:* Charles Sturridge. **VHS $19.95** *NLC, ING* 🐾🐾🐾

Where Angels Go, Trouble Follows
Follow-up to "The Trouble with Angels," with Russell reprising her role as the wise Mother Superior challenged by her mischief loving students. Younger, modern nun Stevens tries to convince Russell to update her old-fashioned ways and persuades her to take the convent students on a bus trip to a California peace rally. A very young Saint James is one of the convent's irrepressible troublemakers. Very dated but still mildly amusing.
1968 94m/C Rosalind Russell, Stella Stevens, Binnie Barnes, Mary Wickes, Susan St. James, Dolores Sutton, Alice Rawlings; *Cameos:* Milton Berle, Arthur Godfrey, Van Johnson, Robert Taylor; *D:* James Neilson; *W:* Blanche Hanalis. **VHS $14.95** *COL* 🐾🐾½

Where Are the Children?
Based on Mary Higgins Clark's bestseller. A woman who was cleared of murdering the children from her first marriage remarries. Then the children from her second marriage are kidnapped. Sustains suspense completely, until it falls apart.
1985 (R) 92m/C Jill Clayburgh, Max Gail, Barnard Hughes, Clifton James, Harley Cross, Elisabeth Harnois, Elizabeth Wilson, Frederic Forrest; *D:* Bruce Malmuth. **VHS, Beta $79.95** *COL* 🐾½

Where Eagles Dare
During WWII, a small group of Allied commandos must rescue an American general held by the Nazis in a castle in the Bavarian Alps. Relentless plot twists and action keep you breathless. Well-made suspense/adventure. Alistair MacLean adapted his original screenplay into a successful novel.
1968 (PG) 158m/C Clint Eastwood, Richard Burton, Mary Ure, Michael Hordern, Anton Diffring, Ingrid Pitt, Patrick Wymark, Robert Beatty; *D:* Brian G. Hutton. **VHS, Beta $19.98** *MGM, TLF* 🐾🐾🐾

W

VIDEOHOUND'S GOLDEN MOVIE RETRIEVER • 988 ▲

Where East is East In Indochina a badly scarred trapper (Chaney) lives with his daughter (Velez) and sells wild animals to circuses. Velez falls in love with a circus owner's son but finds out her own mother, seeking revenge on her ex-husband, trying to seduce the young man. A gorilla figures in the plot as well. Chaney's makeup, which contributed to his "Man of a Thousand Faces" nickname, highlights a contrived movie.
1929 140m/B Lon Chaney Sr., Lupe Velez, Estelle Taylor, Lloyd Hughes. **VHS** $29.95 FCT ♂♂½

Where Have All the People Gone? Solar explosion turns most of Earth's inhabitants to dust while the Anders family vacations in a cave. The family tries to return home amid the devastation. Bad timing, bad acting, bad script. Made for television.
1974 74m/C Peter Graves, Kathleen Quinlan, Michael-James Wixted, George O'Hanlon Jr., Verna Bloom; **D:** John Llewellyn Moxey. **VHS, Beta** $59.95 LHV ♂

Where is My Child? Immigration to the New World brings only misfortune and betrayal in this tale of Jews in Eastern Europe between 1911 and 1937, as many experience the loss of family ties and religion. In Yiddish with English subtitles.
1937 92m/B Celia Adler, Anna Lillian, Morris Strassberg; **D:** Abraham Leff, Harry Lynn. **VHS** $54.00 NCJ ♂♂½

Where Love Has Gone A soaper about a teenage daughter who kills her nympho mother's current boyfriend. Her divorced parents end up dragging the ordeal out in a murder trial/custody battle and a lot of family skeletons come out of their closets. Davis is the manipulative grand dame grandmother. Based on the novel by Harold Robbins.
1964 114m/C Bette Davis, Susan Hayward, Joey Heatherton, Jane Greer, George Macready; **D:** Edward Dmytryk; **W:** John Michael Hayes. **VHS** $14.95 PAR, FCT ♂♂½

Where Sleeping Dogs Lie A struggling writer moves into an abandoned California home five years after a wealthy family was murdered there. While doing research for his novel on their brutal killings, he revives their ghosts as well as the very real presence of their killer.
1991 (R) 92m/C Dylan McDermott, Tom Sizemore, Sharon Stone; **D:** Charles Finch. **VHS** $19.95 COL ♂♂

Where the Boys Are Four college girls go to Fort Lauderdale to have fun and meet boys during their Easter vacation. Features the film debuts of Francis, who had a hit single with the film's title song, and Prentiss. Head and shoulders above the ludicrous '84 remake.
1960 99m/C George Hamilton, Jim Hutton, Yvette Mimieux, Connie Francis, Paula Prentiss, Dolores Hart; **D:** Henry Levin. **VHS, Beta** $19.98 MGM ♂♂½

Where the Boys Are '84 Horrible remake of the 1960 comedy still features girls searching for boys during spring break in Fort Lauderdale. Telling about its era: charm gives way to prurience.
1984 (R) 95m/C Lisa Hartman, Wendy Schaal, Lorna Luft, Lynn-Holly Johnson; **D:** Hy Averback. **VHS, Beta** $79.98 FOX Woof!

Where the Buffalo Roam Early starring role for Murray as the legendary "gonzo" journalist Hunter S. Thompson. Meandering satire based on Thompson's books "Fear and Loathing in Las Vegas" and "Fear and Loathing on the Campaign Trail '72." Either confusing or offensively sloppy, depending on whether you've read Thompson. Music by Neil Young, thank goodness, or this might be a woof.
1980 (R) 98m/C Bill Murray, Peter Boyle, Susan Kellerman; **D:** Art Linson; **M:** Neil Young. **VHS, Beta** $19.95 MCA ♂½

Where the Bullets Fly Fast-paced Bond spoof. A British spy takes on the intelligence forces of several governments in his search for a new fuel elixir. Fun, if not scintillating.
1966 88m/C Tom Adams, Dawn Addams, Michael Ripper, Tim Barrett; **D:** John Gilling. **VHS** FOX ♂♂

Where the Day Takes You Runaways on Hollywood Boulevard are depicted in an unfortunately heavy-handed drama. King (Mulroney) is the slightly older leader of a group of street kids who tries to discourage his friends from getting involved in the violence and drugs they see all around them. He falls in love with new runaway Heather (Boyle) but their love is blighted by the relentless bleakness of their lives. Among the other members of King's "family" are Astin, as a young druggie in thrall to his older dealer (MacLachlan) and Getty, as a young hustler drawn to violence. The story's predictability undercuts some convincing acting.
1992 (R) 105m/C Dermot Mulroney, Lara Flynn Boyle, Balthazar Getty, Sean Astin, James LeGros, Ricki Lake, Kyle MacLachlan, Rob Knepper, Peter Dobson, Stephen Tobolowsky, Will Smith, Adam Baldwin, Christian Slater, Nancy McKeon, Alyssa Milano, David Arquette, Leo Rossi, Rachel Ticotin; **D:** Marc Rocco; **W:** Michael Hitchcock, Kurt Voss, Marc Rocco; **M:** Mark Morgan; **V:** Laura San Giacomo. **VHS** $19.95 COL ♂♂½

Where the Eagle Flies Ersatz sixties rock'n'roll road movie shuffles together free spirited college coed, hobo with heart of gold, and rock and roller who's making a lane change out of the fast track. **AKA:** Pickup on 101.
1972 (PG) 93m/C Jack Albertson, Lesley Ann Warren, Martin Sheen, Michael Ontkean; **D:** John Florea. **VHS** NO ♂♂

Where the Green Ants Dream A mining excavation in the Outback is halted by Aborigines who declare ownership of the sacred place where the mythical green ants are buried. A minor entry in the Herzog vision of modern-versus-primal civilization. Too obvious and somehow unsure of itself artistically. **AKA:** Wo Die Grunen Ameisen Traumen.
1984 99m/C Bruce Spence, Wandjuk Marika, Roy Marika, Ray Barrett, Norman Kaye, Colleen Clifford; **D:** Werner Herzog. **VHS, Beta** $24.95 XVC, MED, ING ♂♂½

Where the Heart Is Wealthy dad Coleman kicks his spoiled kids out on the streets to teach them the value of money. Meant as farce with a message. Flops in a big way; one senses it should have been much better.
1990 (R) 111m/C Dabney Coleman, Uma Thurman, Joanna Cassidy, Suzy Amis, Crispin Glover, Christopher Plummer; **D:** John Boorman. **VHS** $89.95 TOU ♂♂

Where the Hot Wind Blows The sexual scene in Sicily is sadly not succinctly summarized in this so-so cinematic soap. Cross-generational and cross-class couplings are constant. Think of it as "The Last Picture Show" in a similarly sorry setting, except boring. **AKA:** La Legge; La Loi; The Law.
1959 120m/C Gina Lollobrigida, Marcello Mastroianni, Yves Montand, Melina Mercouri, Paolo Stoppa; **D:** Jules Dassin; **W:** Jules Dassin. **VHS, Beta** $24.95 VYY, NOS, FCT ♂♂

Where the Lilies Bloom The touching story of four backwoods children who are left orphans when their father dies. They don't report his death to authorities, because they are afraid the family will be separated and sent to an orphanage. Stanton is great as the crusty landlord the children gradually accept as a friend. Based on the book by Vera and Bill Cleaver.
1974 (G) 96m/C Julie Gholson, Jan Smithers, Matthew Burrill, Helen Harmon, Harry Dean Stanton, Rance Howard, Sudie Bond, Tom Spratley, Helen Bragdon, Alice Beardsley; **D:** William A. Graham. **VHS** $14.95 MGM ♂♂♂

Where the North Begins A Mountie ransacks the Canadian countryside in search of crime.
1947 41m/B Russell Hayden, Jennifer Holt. **VHS, Beta** NO ♂

Where the Red Fern Grows A young boy in Dust Bowl-era Oklahoma learns maturity from his love and responsibility for two Redbone hounds. Well produced, but tends to be hokey; good family fare. Followed by a sequel nearly twenty years later.
1974 (G) 97m/C James Whitmore, Beverly Garland, Jack Ging, Loni Chapman, Stewart Peterson; **D:** Norman Tokar. **VHS, Beta** $14.98 FHE, VES, HHE ♂♂½

Where the Red Fern Grows: Part 2 Sequel to one of the most popular family movies of all time starring Brimley as Grandpa Coleman. Set deep in the Louisiana woods, this magical coming of age tale will touch the hearts of young and old viewers alike.
1992 (G) 105m/C Wilford Brimley, Doug McKeon, Lisa Whelchel, Chad McQueen; **D:** Jim McCullough. **VHS** $14.95 VCI ♂♂½

Where the River Runs Black An orphaned Indian child is raised in the Brazilian jungles by river dolphins. He is eventually befriended by a kindly priest who brings him into the modern world of violence and corruption. Slow pace is okay until the boy arrives at the orphanage, at which point the dolphin premise sadly falls by the wayside.
1986 (PG) 96m/C Charles Durning, Peter Horton, Ajay Naidu, Conchata Ferrell, Alessandro Rabelo, Castulo Guerra; **D:** Christopher Cain; **M:** James Horner. **VHS, Beta** $79.98 FOX ♂♂

Where the Sky Begins From the director of "Black Orpheus," this is a seven-part recreated history of turn-of-the-century aviation.
1984 420m/C D: Marcel Camus. **VHS, Beta** $19.00 VCD ♂♂

Where the Spirit Lives Native children kidnapped by Canadian government agents are forced to live in dreadful boarding schools where they are abused emotionally and physically. St. John is a new arrival who refuses to put up with it and tries to escape. Engrossing and moving.
1989 (PG) 97m/C Michelle St. John; **D:** Bruce Pittman. **VHS** $79.95 BTV, HHE, UWA ♂♂½

Where Time Began The discovery of a strange manuscript of a scientist's journey to the center of the earth leads to the decision to recreate the dangerous mission. Based on Jules Verne's classic novel "Journey to the Center of the Earth," but not anywhere near as fun or stirring.
1977 (G) 87m/C Kenneth More, Pep Munne, Jack Taylor; **D:** J.P. Simon. **VHS, Beta** $69.98 SUE ♂♂

Where Trails Divide Keene is a U.S. Marshal who poses as a lawyer to bring a gang of thieves to justice. Lacks action.
1937 54m/B Tom Keene, Eleanor Stewart, Warner Richmond, David Sharpe, Charles French, Hal Price, Bud Osborne; **D:** Robert North Bradbury. **VHS $11.95** GPV ✓½

Where Trails End Novel sci-fi western set during WWII with just about everything, including phosphorescent-clothed good guys, Nazis, scoundrels, literate horses, and Gallic sidekicks. Interestingly different.
1942 54m/B Tom Keene, Joan Curtis, Charles "Blackie" King; **D:** Robert Tansey. **VHS, Beta $12.95** VDM, VYY ✓✓

Where Were You When the Lights Went Out? A complicated, unsuccessful farce about a retiring Broadway actress, her jealous, possibly philandering husband, her greedy agent, an embezzler, and a citywide blackout. Film was actually not based on the 1965 New York City blackout but on a French play, "Monsieur Masure" by Claude Magnier, which was written nine years before.
1968 (PG) 94m/C Doris Day, Patrick O'Neal, Robert Morse, Terry-Thomas, Lola Albright, Steve Allen, Jim Backus, Ben Blue, Pat Paulsen; **D:** Hy Averback. **VHS $19.98** MGM, MOV ✓½

Where's Piccone A woman attempts, with the assistance of a two-bit hustler, to locate her missing husband, only to discover that he has led a double life in the Neapolitan underworld. Giannini as the sleazy hubby is perfectly cast. On-target social and political satire. In Italian with English subtitles.
1984 110m/C Giancarlo Giannini, Lina Sastri, Aldo Guiffre, Clelia Rondinelli; **D:** Nanni Loy. **VHS, Beta $29.95** ING, FCT, WBF ✓✓✓

Where's Poppa? A Jewish lawyer's senile mother constantly ruins his love life, and he considers various means of getting rid of her, including dressing up as an ape to scare her to death. Filled with outlandish and often tasteless humor, befitting its reign as a black comedy cult classic. Adapted by Robert Klane from his novel. **AKA:** Going Ape.
1970 84m/C George Segal, Ruth Gordon, Ron Leibman, Vincent Gardenia, Rob Reiner, Trish Van Devere; **D:** Carl Reiner. **VHS, Beta $19.95** FOX ✓✓✓

Where's Willie? Willie is a very bright boy; perhaps a little too bright. When he reveals his latest invention to the folks in his small town, everyone is out to get him.
1977 (G) 91m/C Guy Madison, Henry Darrow, Kate Woodville, Marc Gilpin; **D:** John Florea. **VHS, Beta** NO ✓✓✓

Which Way Home A Red Cross nurse attempts to flee Cambodia with four young orphans. An Australian smuggler befriends and helps her. Way too long and wandering, though like many a TV movie, it means well.
1990 141m/C Cybill Shepherd, John Waters, Peta Toppano, John Ewart, Ruben Santiago-Hudson, Marc Gray; **D:** Carl Schultz; **W:** Michael Laurence. **VHS, Beta $79.98** TTC ✓✓

Which Way Is Up? Pryor plays three roles in this story of an orange picker who accidentally becomes a union hero. He leaves his wife and family at home while he seeks work in Los Angeles. There he finds himself a new woman, starts a new family, and sells out to the capitalists. American version of the Italian comedy "The Seduction of Mimi" tries with mixed success for laughs. Pryor as a dirty old man is the high point.
1977 (R) 94m/C Richard Pryor, Lonette McKee, Margaret Avery, Morgan Woodward, Marilyn Coleman; **D:** Michael A. Schultz; **W:** Carl Gottlieb. **VHS, Beta $79.95** MCA ✓✓½

Which Way to the Front? Assorted Army rejects form a guerilla band and wage their own small-scale war during WWII.
1970 (G) 96m/C Jerry Lewis, Jan Murray, John Wood, Steve Franken; **D:** Jerry Lewis. **VHS, Beta $19.98** WAR ✓½

Whiffs A gullible man plays guinea pig in an Army experiment on germ warfare which leaves him with the intellect of a chimpanzee. Naturally, he then devises a plan to use the volatile gas in a chain of bank robberies. The title is appropriate—this movie is a stinker.
1975 (PG) 91m/C Elliott Gould, Eddie Albert, Harry Guardino, Godfrey Cambridge, Jennifer O'Neill, Alan Manson; **D:** Ted Post; **W:** Malcolm Marmorstein. **VHS $79.95** MED ✓✓

While I Live Woman meets female pianist with uncanny resemblance to sister who's been dead 25 years and rethinks her position on reincarnation.
1947 85m/B Tom Walls, Clifford Evans, Carole Raye, Patricia Burke, Sonia Dresdel, John Warwick; **D:** John Harlow. **VHS, Beta $16.95** SNC ✓½

While the City Sleeps Three newspaper reporters vie to crack the case of a sex murderer known as "The Lipstick Killer" with the editorship of their paper the prize. Good thriller-plus with the emphasis on the reporters' ruthless methods of gaining information rather than on the killer's motivations. Lang's last big success. Based on "The Bloody Spur" by Charles Einstein.
1956 100m/B Dana Andrews, Rhonda Fleming, George Sanders, Howard Duff, Thomas Mitchell, Ida Lupino, Vincent Price, Mae Marsh; **D:** Fritz Lang. **VHS, Beta $15.95** VCI ✓✓✓

Whirlwind Horseman Substandard horse opera. Maynard's search for a gold prospector friend leads him to a rancher and his pretty daughter. He beats up some bad guys, etcetera.
1938 60m/B Ken Maynard, Joan Barclay, Bill Griffith; **D:** Bob Hill. **VHS, Beta $19.95** NOS, DVT, VCN ✓

Whiskey Galore During WWII, a whiskey-less Scottish island gets a lift when a ship, carrying 50,000 cases of spirits, wrecks off the coast. A full-scale rescue operation and the evasion of both local and British government authorities ensue. The classic Ealing studio comedy is based on the actual wreck of a cargo ship off the Isle of Eriskay in 1941. **AKA:** Tight Little Island.
1948 81m/B Basil Radford, Joan Greenwood, Gordon Jackson, James Robertson Justice; **D:** Alexander MacKendrick. **VHS, Beta $59.99** HMV ✓✓✓½

Whiskey Mountain Two couples go on a treasure hunt to Whiskey Mountain but instead find terror.
1977 (PG) 95m/C Christopher George, Preston Pierce, Linda Borgeson, Roberta Collins, Robert Leslie; **D:** William Grefe. **VHS, Beta $19.99** BFV ✓

A Whisper to a Scream An actress, in researching a film part, takes a job at a telephone sex service, creating different personas as she talks to keep herself interested. Soon, women resembling the personas are being murdered. Great premise fails to deliver fully, though there is some suspense.
1988 (R) 96m/C Nadia Capone, Yaphet Kotto, Lawrence Bayne, Silvio Oliviero; **D:** Robert Bergman; **W:** Robert Bergman, Gerard Ciccoritti. **VHS, Beta** NO ✓✓

Whispering City A female reporter receives an inside tip incriminating a prominent attorney in a murder committed several years earlier. She tries to get the evidence she needs before she becomes his latest victim.

Highly suspenseful, thanks to competent scripting and directing.
1947 89m/B Helmut Dantine, Mary Anderson, Paul Lukas; **D:** Fedor Ozep. **VHS, Beta $16.95** NOS, SNC ✓✓✓

Whispering Shadow Serial starring the master criminal known as the "faceless whisperer." Twelve chapters, 13 minutes each.
1933 156m/B Bela Lugosi, Robert Warwick; **D:** Al Herman, Colbert Clark. **VHS, Beta $39.95** NOS, SNC, VCN ✓✓✓

Whispers Psycho Le Clerc repeatedly bothers writer Tennant even though she seems to have killed him. This dismays police guy Sarandon. Based on the novel by Dean R. Koontz.
1989 (R) 96m/C Victoria Tennant, Chris Sarandon, Jean LeClerc; **D:** Douglas Jackson; **W:** Anita Doohan. **VHS $89.95** LIV ✓✓

Whispers in the Dark A psychiatrist counsels two odd patients—one is an ex-con turned painter with a violent streak, the other is a woman who reveals her kinky sexual experiences with a mystery man. Things get interesting when the doctor finds out her new lover is her patient's mystery man, and the patient turns up murdered. Confusing thriller seems forced but the experienced cast is worth watching.
1992 (R) 103m/C Annabella Sciorra, Jamey Sheridan, Anthony LaPaglia, Jill Clayburgh, John Leguizamo, Deborah Unger, Alan Alda, Anthony Heald; **D:** Christopher Crowe; **W:** Christopher Crowe. **VHS, Beta $14.95** PAR, PMS ✓✓

Whispers of White Bridgetown's mayor has been trying for years to put a stop to the drug dealing going on in his fair community. Finally, his new Chief of Police decides to deploy a special task force to clean-up the streets—using whatever methods are necessary (and they're all violent).
1993 (R) 98m/C Nicholette Goulet, Anthony De Sardo, Tony Craig, April Bransome, Ron Gorton Sr.; **D:** Ron Gorton Sr.; **W:** Ron Gorton Sr. **VHS $89.95** AIP ✓½

The Whistle Blower A young government worker in England with a high-security position mysteriously dies. His father, a former intelligence agent, begins investigating his son's death and discovers sinister Soviet-related conspiracies. A lucid, complex British espionage thriller. Adapted from the John Hale novel by Julian Bond.
1987 98m/C Michael Caine, Nigel Havers, John Gielgud, James Fox, Felicity Dean, Gordon Jackson, Barry Foster; **D:** Simon Langton; **W:** Julian Bond; **M:** John Scott. **VHS, Beta $19.98** SUE, NLC ✓✓✓

Whistle Down the Wind Three children of strict religious upbringing find a murderer hiding in their family's barn and believe him to be Jesus Christ. Well done and hardly grim or dull allegory of childhood innocence based on a novel by Mills's mother, Mary Hayley Bell. For a film relying heavily on child characters, it's important to portray childhood well and realistically. That is done here, as in "To Kill a Mockingbird." Mills is perfect. The film is Forbes's directorial debut and Richard Attenborough's second production.
1962 98m/B Hayley Mills, Bernard Lee, Alan Bates; **D:** Bryan Forbes; **M:** Malcolm Arnold. **VHS, Beta $19.98** SUE, NLC ✓✓✓½

Whistle Stop A small-town girl divides her attentions between low-life gambler Raft, and villainous nightclub owner McLaglen, who plans a robbery-murder to get rid of any rivals. A forgettable gangster drama.

1946 85m/B George Raft, Ava Gardner, Victor McLaglen; *D:* Leonide Moguy; *W:* Philip Yordan. VHS, Beta $19.95 *NOS, DVT, FCT* 🎬🎬

Whistlin' Dan Yet another lead cowpoke sets out to avenge the murder of a close relative. Maynard whistles while he walks (and rides) woodenly through this one.
1932 60m/B Ken Maynard, Joyzelle Joyner, Lew Meehan, Georges Renevant, Dan Terry, Harlan E. Knight, Bud McClure, Hank Bell, Iron Eyes Cody, Frank Ellis; *D:* Phil Rosen. VHS, Beta $19.95 *NOS, VCI, GPV* 🎬🎬

Whistling Bullets Action galore in the story of an undercover Texas Ranger infiltrating a gang of thieves. The low budget doesn't detract from an exciting script and tight direction.
1936 58m/B Kermit Maynard, Jack Ingram; *D:* John English. VHS, Beta $19.95 *NOS, DVT, RXM* 🎬🎬½

Whistling in Brooklyn Skelton again plays radio crime-solver Wally Benton in this third and last entry following "Whistling in the Dark" and "Whistling in Dixie." A cop-killer and the Brooklyn Dodgers baseball team figure in the mystery, which finds Skelton a suspect in the crimes.
1943 87m/B Red Skelton, Ann Rutherford, Jean Rogers, Rags Ragland, Ray Collins, Henry O'Neill, William Frawley, Sam Levene; *D:* Sylvan Simon. VHS $19.98 *MGM* 🎬🎬½

Whistling in Dixie The second appearance of Skelton as radio sleuth Wally "The Fox" Benton (following "Whistling in the Dark") finds him traveling to Georgia with girlfriend Carol (Rutherford). She's worried about an ex-sorority sister who knows the secret of a hidden Civil War treasure. When Wally gets involved, humorous trouble follows. Followed by "Whistling in Brooklyn."
1942 73m/B Red Skelton, Ann Rutherford, George Bancroft, Guy Kibbee, Diana Lewis, Peter Whitney, Rags Ragland; *D:* Sylvan Simon; *W:* Nat Perrin. VHS, Beta $19.98 *MGM, FCT* 🎬🎬½

Whistling in the Dark Skelton plays Wally Benton, a radio sleuth nicknamed "The Fox," in the first of a three-film series. Veidt (an always excellent villain) is the leader of a phony religious cult, after the money of one of his followers. He decides to kidnap Skelton and have him come up with a plan for the perfect murder but of course there are all sorts of comic complications. Skelton's first starring role is a clever comic mystery and a remake of the 1933 film. Followed by "Whistling in Dixie" and "Whistling in Brooklyn."
1941 78m/B Red Skelton, Ann Rutherford, Conrad Veidt, Virginia Grey, Rags Ragland, Eve Arden, Don Douglas, Don Costello, Paul Stanton, William Tannen, Reed Hadley; *D:* Sylvan Simon. VHS $19.98 *MGM* 🎬🎬

Whitcomb's War Small town becomes a battleground among a host of comic characters who are unaware who really is in charge.
1988 67m/C Patrick Pankhurst, Leon Charles, Bill Morey, Robert Denison, Garnett Smith; *D:* Russell S. Doughten Jr. VHS *MIV* 🎬½

White Apache Emotionally charged saga of a man barred from both Indian and white societies, focusing on the impact of prejudice toward a white man raised by Apaches.
1988 90m/C VHS, Beta $19.95 *IMP* 🎬🎬

The White Buffalo A strange, semisurreal western parable about the last days of Wild Bill Hickok (Bronson) and his obsession with a mythical white buffalo that represents his fear of mortality. Something of a "Moby Dick" theme set in the Wild West. Clumsy but intriguing. *AKA:* Hunt to Kill.

1977 (PG) 97m/C Charles Bronson, Jack Warden, Will Sampson, Kim Novak, Clint Walker, Stuart Whitman, John Carradine, Slim Pickens, Cara Williams, Douglas Fowley; *D:* J. Lee Thompson; *M:* John Barry. VHS, Beta $14.95 *MGM* 🎬🎬

The White Butterfly Killer A young girl who witnesses her grandfather's murder by a group of ruthless opium dealers gets revenge by using her deadly kung fu.
19?? 90m/C Au Fong, Chee Fong, Wah Hon, Kwok H. Ting. VHS, Beta $49.95 *OCE* 🎬

White Cannibal Queen A young girl is captured by cannibals in the Amazon jungle, and her father spends years tracking her down.
1974 90m/C VHS, Beta $39.95 *VCD* Woof!

White Cargo Lamarr holds the corny story together with one of her best-known roles as sultry native girl Tondelayo. Pidgeon is a cynical African rubber planter who advises new assistant Carlson against Lamarr's sarong-clad charms. But hormones speak louder than warnings and Pidgeon has to take some strong action to save Carlson from this femme fatale. Based on the novel "Hell's Playground" by Ida Vera Simonton and adapted for both stage and screen by Gordon.
1942 90m/B Hedy Lamarr, Walter Pidgeon, Richard Carlson, Frank Morgan, Reginald Owen, Bramwell Fletcher, Henry O'Neill, Clyde Cook, Richard Ainley; *D:* Richard Thorpe; *W:* Leon Gordon; *M:* Bronislau Kaper. VHS $19.98 *MGM* 🎬🎬½

White Christmas Two ex-army buddies become a popular comedy team and play at a financially unstable Vermont inn at Christmas for charity's sake. Many swell Irving Berlin songs rendered with zest. Paramount's first Vista Vision film. Presented in widescreen on laserdisc. ♫The Best Things Happen While You're Dancing; Love, You Didn't Do Right By Me; Choreography; Count Your Blessings Instead of Sheep; What Can You Do With a General; Mandy; The Minstrel Show; Sisters; Heat Wave.
1954 120m/C Bing Crosby, Danny Kaye, Rosemary Clooney, Vera-Ellen, Dean Jagger; *D:* Michael Curtiz; *W:* Norman Panama. VHS, Beta, 8mm, CDV $14.95 *PAR, FUS* 🎬🎬½

The White Cliffs of Dover Prime example of a successful 40s "women's weepie." American Dunne goes to England in 1914, falls in love, and marries the British Marshal. He joins the WWI troops and is killed, without knowing he had a son. Dunne raises the boy in England as a new threat looms with the rise of Hitler. Now grown, he goes off to do his duty and she joins the Red Cross, where she sees him again among the wounded, another victim of the ravages of war. Dunne is fine in her noble, sacrificing role. McDowall is the young son with Taylor (with whom he'd already worked in "Lassie Come Home") as a childhood friend. Based on the poem by Alice Duer Miller. Bring the hankies.
1944 126m/B Irene Dunne, Alan Marshal, Frank Morgan, Peter Lawford, Gladys Cooper, May Whitty, Sir C. Aubrey Smith, Roddy McDowall, Van Johnson, Elizabeth Taylor, June Lockhart, John Warburton, Jill Esmond, Norma Varden, Tom Drake, Arthur Shields; *D:* Clarence Brown. VHS $19.98 *MGM, MOV* 🎬🎬🎬

White Comanche Half-breed twins battle themselves and each other to a rugged climax.
1967 90m/C William Shatner, Joseph Cotten, Perla Cristal, Rossana Yanni; *D:* Gilbert Kay. VHS, Beta $19.95 *NOS, VCI, VTR* 🎬½

The White Dawn Three whalers are stranded in the Arctic in the 1890s and are taken in by an Eskimo village. They teach the villagers about booze, gambling, and other modern amenities. Resentment grows until a clash ensues. All three leads are excellent, especially Oates. Much of the dialogue is in an Eskimo language, subtitled in English, as in "Dances with Wolves."
1975 (PG) 110m/C Warren Oates, Timothy Bottoms, Louis Gossett Jr., Simonie Kopapik, Joanasie Salomonie; *D:* Philip Kaufman; *M:* Henry Mancini. VHS, Beta $19.95 *PAR* 🎬🎬½

White Eagle A white man who believes himself to be an Indian gets a job as a Pony Express rider and gets mixed up with horse rustlers. When he finds out who he really is, he is free to marry the white woman he's had his eye on. Interesting plot twist caused by the narrow-mindedness of the Hays Office.
1932 64m/B Buck Jones, Barbara Weeks, Robert Ellis, Jason Robards Sr., Robert Elliott, Jim Thorpe, Ward Bond; *D:* Lambert Hillyer. VHS $19.95 *DVT, HEG* 🎬🎬

White Fang Boy befriends canine with big teeth and both struggle to survive in third celluloid rendition of Alaska during the Gold Rush. Beautiful cinematography. Fun for the entire family based on Jack London's book. Followed by "White Fang 2: The Myth of the White Wolf."
1991 (PG) 109m/C Klaus Maria Brandauer, Ethan Hawke, Seymour Cassel, James Remar, Susan Hogan; *D:* Randal Kleiser; *W:* Jeanne Rosenberg, Nick Thiel, David Fallon; *M:* Basil Poledouris. VHS $19.99 *BVV, DIS, TVC* 🎬🎬🎬

White Fang 2: The Myth of the White Wolf White boy and his wolf-dog lead starving Native American tribe to caribou during the Alaskan Gold Rush. Simplistic story with obvious heroes and villains, yes, but this is also wholesome (and politically correct) family fare compliments of Disney. Focuses less on the wolf, a flaw, and more on Bairstow and his love interest Craig, a Haida Indian princess, while exploring Native American mythology and dreams in sequences that tend to stop the action cold. Still, kids will love it, and there are plenty of puppies to achieve required awwww factor. Beautiful scenery filmed on location in Colorado and British Columbia.
1994 (PG) 106m/C Scott Bairstow, Alfred Molina, Geoffrey Lewis, Charmaine Craig, Victoria Racimo, Paul Coeur, Anthony Michael Ruivivar, Al Harrington; *Cameos:* Ethan Hawke; *D:* Ken Olin; *W:* David Fallon; *M:* John Debney. VHS *NYR* 🎬🎬

White Fang and the Hunter The adventures of a boy and his dog who survive an attack from wild wolves and then help to solve a murder mystery. Loosely based on the novel by Jack London.
1985 (G) 87m/C Pedro Sanchez, Robert Wood; *D:* Alfonso Brescia. VHS, Beta $19.95 *STE, HHE* 🎬½

White Fire Brady, in search of his lost brother, gets involved in a smuggling ring. Seems the brother is falsely accused of murder and about to hang. Brady and bar singer Castle solve the case. Good photography; bad script. *AKA:* Three Steps to the Gallows.
1953 82m/C Scott Brady, Mary Castle, Ferdinand "Ferdy" Mayne; *D:* John Gilling. VHS, Beta $16.95 *NOS, SNC, VYY* 🎬🎬

White Fire Two jewel thieves will stop at nothing to own White Fire, a two hundred-carat diamond.
1983 90m/C Robert Ginty, Fred Williamson. VHS, Beta $19.98 *TWE* 🎬

White Fury Couples on a campout are victimized by sleazy hoodlums during a snowstorm.
1990 89m/C Deke Anderson, Sean Holton, Douglas Hartier, Christine Shinn, Chastity Hammons; **D:** David A. Prior. VHS $14.95 *AIP* ☺

White Ghost An Intelligence Officer who disappeared in the jungles of Asia 18 years ago is ready to come back to the United States, but not everyone wants to see him again.
1988 (R) 90m/C William Katt, Rosalind Chao, Martin Hewitt, Wayne Crawford, Reb Brown; **D:** B.J. Davis. VHS, Beta $19.98 *TWE* ☺

White Gold Shepherd's son weds Mexican woman and his disgruntled father contrives apparent rendezvous between the wife and a ranch-hand, who's found dead in her bedroom. Seems no one believes the wife's story. Unprecedented, dark, silent drama.
1928 73m/B Jetta Goudal, Kenneth Thomson, George Bancroft, George Nichols, Clyde Cook; **D:** William K. Howard. VHS, Beta $19.95 *GPV* ☺☺☺

White Gorilla A great white hunter sets out to kill a gigantic white gorilla that is terrorizing the black natives. Imperialist trash. On any informed person's list of all-time worst movies.
1947 62m/B Ray Corrigan, Lorraine Miller. VHS, Beta *NO Woof!*

White Heat A classic gangster film with one of Cagney's best roles as a psychopathic robber/killer with a mother complex. The famous finale—perhaps Cagney's best-known scene—has Cagney trapped on top of a burning oil tank shouting "Made it, Ma! Top of the world!" before the tank explodes. Cagney's character is allegedly based on Arthur "Doc" Barker and his "Ma," and his portrayal is breathtaking. Also available colorized.
1949 114m/B James Cagney, Virginia Mayo, Edmond O'Brien, Margaret Wycherly, Steve Cochran; **D:** Raoul Walsh. VHS, Beta $19.95 *MGM, FOX* ☺☺☺½

White Hot A young businessman loses his prestigious Wall Street job, and in order to live the good life, he resorts to selling drugs. Benson stars and directs.
1988 95m/C Robby Benson, Tawny Kitaen, Danny Aiello, Sally Kirkland, Judy Tenuta; **D:** Robby Benson. VHS, Beta $89.95 *ACA* ☺½

White Hot: The Mysterious Murder of Thelma Todd Thelma Todd was a Hollywood starlet found dead under strange circumstances in 1935. Buffs have sought a solution to the maybe-murder ever since; this treatment (based on the book "Hot Toddy" by Andy Edmunds) leaves too many loose ends for purists and isn't sufficiently gripping for the uninitiated.
1991 95m/C Loni Anderson, Robert Davi, Paul Dooley, Lawrence Pressman; **D:** Paul Wendkos. VHS *NO* ☺☺

White Hunter, Black Heart Eastwood casts himself against type as Huston-esque director who is more interested in hunting great tusked creatures than shooting the film he came to Africa to produce. Based on Peter Viertel's 1953 account of his experiences working on James Agee's script for Huston's "African Queen." Eastwood's Huston impression is a highlight, though the story occasionally wanders off with the elephants.
1990 (PG) 112m/C Clint Eastwood, Marisa Berenson, George Dzundza, Jeff Fahey, Timothy Spall, Charlotte Cornwell, Mel Martin, Alun Armstrong, Richard Vanstone; **D:** Clint Eastwood; **W:** Peter Viertel, James Bridges, Burt Kennedy;

M: Richard Vanstone. VHS, Beta, 8mm $19.98 *MGM, FCT, WAR* ☺☺☺

White Huntress Two brothers venturing into the jungle encounter a beautiful young woman, the daughter of a settlement leader. Meanwhile, a killer is on the loose. **AKA:** Golden Ivory.
1957 86m/C Robert Urquhart, John Bentley, Susan Stephen; **D:** George Breakston. VHS, Beta $16.95 *SNC* ☺½

The White Legion Workers and engineers push their way through steaming jungles and reeking swamps while building the Panama Canal. Many fall victim to yellow fever. Physician Keith does some medical sleuthing and saves the day. Plodding, predictable drama.
1936 81m/B Ian Keith, Tala Birell, Snub Pollard; **D:** Karl Brown. VHS, Beta $24.95 *VYY* ☺½

White Lie Len Madison, Jr. (Hines), a press secretary for the mayor of New York, receives an old photo of a lynched black man who he learns is his father, hung for raping a white woman. Madison returns to his Southern hometown to find out the truth behind his father's death, assisted by a white doctor (O'Toole) whose mother was a rape victim. They fall in love, adding to an already complicated situation, and incur the wrath of locals who are trying to keep the truth hidden. Based on the novel "Louisiana Black" by Samuel Charters.
1991 (PG-13) 93m/C Gregory Hines, Annette O'Toole, Bill Nunn; **D:** Bill Condon. VHS $89.98 *MCA* ☺½

White Light "Flatliners" with a flatfoot; after a near-death experience a cop returns with memories of a beautiful woman. He tries to find out who she is/was in plodding fashion. The voyage to the afterlife is represented by a jog through a storm sewer.
1990 (R) 96m/C Martin Kove, Allison Hossack, Martha Henry, Heidi von Palleske, James Purcell, Bruce Boa; **D:** Al Waxman. VHS $19.95 *ACA* ☺☺

White Lightning Good ol' boy Reynolds plays a moonshiner going after the crooked sheriff who murdered his brother. Good stunt-driving chases enliven the formula. The inferior sequel is "Gator." **AKA:** McKlusky.
1973 (PG) 101m/C Burt Reynolds, Ned Beatty, Bo Hopkins, Jennifer Billingsley, Louise Latham; **D:** Joseph Sargent; **W:** William W. Norton Sr.; **M:** Charles Bernstein. VHS, Beta $29.95 *MGM* ☺☺½

White Line Fever A young trucker's search for a happy life with his childhood sweetheart is complicated by a corrupt group in control of the long-haul trucking business. Well-done action film of good triumphing over evil.
1975 (PG) 89m/C Jan-Michael Vincent, Kay Lenz, Slim Pickens, L.Q. Jones, John David Garfield; **D:** Jonathan Kaplan; **W:** Jonathan Kaplan, Ken Friedman. VHS, Beta $59.95 *COL* ☺☺½

White Mama A poor widow (Davis, in a splendid role) takes in a street-wise black kid (Harden) in return for protection from the neighborhood's dangers, and they discover friendship. Poignant drama, capably directed by Cooper, featuring sterling performances all around Made-for-TV drama at its best.
1980 96m/C Bette Davis, Ernest Harden, Eileen Heckart, Virginia Capers, Lurene Tuttle, Anne Ramsey; **D:** Jackie Cooper. VHS, Beta $59.95 *LIV* ☺☺☺

White Mane The poignant, poetic story of a proud and fierce white stallion that continually eludes attempts by ranchers to capture it. In French with English subtitles.

1952 38m/B Alain Emery, Frank Silvera; **D:** Albert Lamorisse. VHS, Beta $14.95 *NLC, SUE, VYG* ☺☺☺

White Men Can't Jump Sometimes they can't act either. Small-time con man Harrelson stands around looking like a big nerd until someone dares him to play basketball and he proves to be more adept than he looks. After he beats Snipes, they become friends and start hustling together. Harrelson lays to rest the rumor that he can't act; here, he proves it. Fast-paced, obscenity-laced dialogue does not cover up for the fact that the story line hovers between dull and dismal, redeemed only by the surreal "Jeopardy" game show sequence and the convincing b-ball action. Snipes manages to rise above the material as well as the rim, while Perez, as wooden Woody's spitfire Hispanic girlfriend, is appropriately energetic.
1992 (R) 115m/C Wesley Snipes, Woody Harrelson, Rosie Perez, Tyra Ferrell, Cylk Cozart, Kadeem Hardison, Ernest Harden Jr., John Jones; **D:** Ron Shelton; **W:** Ron Shelton. VHS $19.98 *FXV* ☺☺

White Mischief An alternately ghastly and hilarious indictment of the English upper class between the World Wars, and the decadence the British colonists perpetrated in Kenya, which came to world attention with the murder of the philandering Earl of Errol in 1941. Exquisitely directed and photographed. Acclaimed and grandly acted, especially by Scacchi; Howard's last appearance.
1988 (R) 108m/C Greta Scacchi, Charles Dance, Joss Ackland, Sarah Miles, John Hurt, Hugh Grant, Geraldine Chaplin, Trevor Howard, Murray Head, Susan Fleetwood, Alan Dobie, Jacqueline Pearce; **D:** Michael Radford; **M:** George Fenton. VHS, Beta, 8mm $14.98 *SUE, SUP, NLC* ☺☺☺

White Nights Based on a love story by Dostoyevski. A young woman pines for the return of her sailor while a mild-mannered clerk is smitten by her. Both of their romantic fantasies are explored the dance-hall cadence is mixed with dreamy, fantastic flashbacks. In Italian with English subtitles. Equally good Soviet version made in 1959.
1957 107m/C Maria Schell, Jean Marais, Marcello Mastroianni; **D:** Luchino Visconti. VHS $59.95 *FCT, ING* ☺☺☺

White Nights A Russian ballet dancer who defected to the U.S. (Baryshnikov) is a passenger on a jet that crashes in the Soviet Union. With the aid of a disillusioned expatriate tap dancer (Hines), he plots to escape again. The excellent dance sequences elevate the rather lame story.
1985 (PG-13) 135m/C Mikhail Baryshnikov, Gregory Hines, Isabella Rossellini, Helen Mirren, Jerzy Skolimowski, Geraldine Page; **D:** Taylor Hackford; **M:** Michel Colombier. Academy Awards '85: Best Song ("Say You, Say Me"); Nominations: Best Song ("Separate Lives (Love Theme from White Nights)"); Golden Globe Awards '86: Best Song ("Say You, Say Me"). VHS, Beta $19.95 *COL* ☺☺½

White of the Eye A murdering lunatic is on the loose in Arizona, and an innocent man must bind him to acquit himself of the murders. A tense, effective thriller; dazzling technique recalls the experimental films of the 1960s.
1988 (R) 111m/C David Keith, Cathy Moriarty, Art Evans, Alan Rosenberg, Michael Greene, Alberta Watson, Marc Hayashi; **D:** Donald Cammell; **W:** China Cammell, Donald Cammell; **M:** Nick Mason, Rick Fenn, George Fenton. VHS, Beta $14.95 *PAR* ☺☺☺

The White Orchid Romantic triangle ventures into the wilds of Mexico in search of Toltec ruins. Exceptional sets.

1954 81m/C William Lundigan, Peggy Castle, Armando Silvestre, Rosenda Monteros; **D:** Reginald LeBorg. **VHS, Beta $16.95** SNC, DVT, HEG ✂✂

White Palace Successful widowed Jewish lawyer Spader is attracted to older, less educated hamburger waitress Sarandon, and ethnic/cultural strife ensues, as does hot sex. Adapted from the Glenn Savan novel, it starts out with promise but fizzles toward the end. **1990 (R)** 103m/C Susan Sarandon, James Spader, Jason Alexander, Eileen Brennan, Griffin Dunne, Kathy Bates, Steven Hill, Rachel Levin, Corey Parker, Spiros Focas, Renee Taylor, Kim Myers; **D:** Luis Mandoki; **W:** Alvin Sargent, Ted Tally; **M:** George Fenton. **VHS $19.95** MCA, FCT, CCB ✂✂½

White Phantom: Enemy of Darkness Ninja warriors in modern day society battling against other evil ninjas. **1987** 89m/C Page Leong, Jay Roberts Jr., Bo Svenson; **D:** Dusty Nelson; **W:** David Hamilton, Chris Gallagher. **VHS, Beta $79.95** VMK ✂

White Pongo A policeman goes undercover with a group of British biologists to capture a mythic white gorilla believed to be the missing link. A camp jungle classic with silly, cheap special effects. **1945** 73m/B Richard Fraser, Maris Wrixon, Lionel Royce; **D:** Sam Newfield. **VHS, Beta $16.95** SNC, NOS, HHT Woof!

The White Rose An aspiring minister travels to see the world he intends to save, and winds up falling from grace. Complicated menage a trois is finally sorted out at the end. Silent. **1923** 120m/B Mae Marsh, Carol Dempster, Ivor Novello, Neil Hamilton, Lucille LaVerne; **D:** D.W. Griffith. **VHS, Beta $19.95** GPV ✂✂✂

The White Rose The true story of a group of dissident students in Munich in 1942, who put their lives in danger by distributing leaflets telling the truth of what was going on in the concentration camps. Hans Scholl was an Army officer who discovered the truth and told the others. In the end, most of the students were captured by the Gestapo and executed. "The White Rose" was the name of the group, but none survived to tell where the name came from. Verhoeven's film telling is engrossing and compelling, with excellent acting from the young cast. In German with English subtitles. **1983** 108m/C Lena Stolze, Wulf Kessler, Oliver Siebert, Ulrich Tucker; **D:** Michael Verhoeven. **VHS, Beta $79.00** MGM, GLV, SWC ✂✂✂

White Sands When a dead man's body is found at a remote Indian reservation clutching a gun and a briefcase filled with $500,000, the local sheriff (Dafoe) takes his identity to see where the money leads. Using a phone number found on a piece of paper in the dead man's stomach, the sheriff follows clues until he finds himself mixed up with a rich woman (Mastrantonio) who sells black market weapons and uses the money to support "worthy" causes, and an FBI man (Jackson) who uses him as bait to lure a CIA turncoat/arms dealer (Rourke). Sound confusing? It is, and despite the strong cast and vivid scenery of the southwest United States, this film just doesn't cut it. **1992 (R)** 101m/C Willem Dafoe, Mary Elizabeth Mastrantonio, Mickey Rourke, Mimi Rogers, Samuel L. Jackson, M. Emmet Walsh, James Rebhorn, Maura Tierney, Beth Grant, Miguel Sandoval, John Lafayette; **Cameos:** Fred Dalton Thompson, John P. Ryan; **D:** Roger Donaldson; **W:** Daniel Pyne; **M:** Patrick O'Hearn. **VHS, Beta $94.99** WAR, FCT ✂✂½

The White Shadow, Vol. 1 After an injury curtails his career with the Chicago Bulls, Ken Reeves (Howard) becomes the basketball coach at Carver High School in Los Angeles, an inner-city school with a team of wisecracking players. The pilot episode finds Reeves trying to adjust to his new life and help his students. **1978** 60m/C Ken Howard, Ed Bernard, Kevin Hooks, Byron Stewart, Thomas Carter, Timothy Van Patten, Ira Angustain, Joan Pringle, Eric Kilpatrick, Nathan Cook, Ken Michelman. **VHS $14.99** MOV, MTM ✂✂½

White Shadows in the South Seas Alcohol, drugs, and prostitution take their toll on the native population of Tahiti in this early talkie. Blue plays a western doctor who marries the daughter of a native chief. However, he finds greed for the island's pearl treasures drawing other unscrupulous westerners to destroy the unspoiled paradise. **1928** 88m/B Monte Blue, Robert Anderson, Raquel Torres; **D:** Woodbridge S. Van Dyke. **VHS $29.95** FCT ✂✂½

The White Sheik Fellini's first solo effort. A newly wed bride meets her idol from the comic pages (made with photos, not cartoons; called fumetti) and runs off with him. She soon finds he's as ordinary as her husband. Brilliant satire in charming garb. Remade as "The World's Greatest Lover." Woody Allen's "The Purple Rose of Caine" is in a similar spirt. In Italian with subtitles. **AKA:** Lo Sceicco Bianco. **1952** 86m/B Alberto Sordi, Giulietta Masina, Brunella Bova, Leopoldo Trieste; **D:** Federico Fellini; **W:** Federico Fellini, Tullio Pinelli, Ennio Flaino. **VHS, Beta $24.95** VYY, CVC, ING ✂✂✂

The White Sin An innocent country girl hires on as maid of a rich woman and is seduced and abandoned by the woman's profligate son, but everything turns out all right by the end of the third handkerchief. Silent with original organ music. **1924** 93m/B Madge Bellamy, John Bowers, Billy Bevan; **D:** William A. Seiter. **VHS, Beta, 8mm $24.95** VYY ✂✂

The White Sister Gish is an Italian aristocrat driven from her home by a conniving sister. When her true love (Colman) is reported killed she decides to become a nun and enters a convent. When her lover does return he tricks her into leaving the convent but before he can persuade her to renounce her vows Vesuvius erupts and he goes off to warn the villagers, dying for his efforts. Gish then re-dedicates herself to her faith. Colman's first leading role, which made him a romantic star. Filmed on location in Italy. **1923** 108m/B Lillian Gish, Ronald Colman, Gail Kane, J. Barney Sherry, Charles Lane; **D:** Henry King. **VHS, Beta $19.98** DVT, HEG ✂✂✂½

White Slave An Englishwoman is captured by bloodthirsty cannibals and, rather than being eaten, is tormented and made a slave. **AKA:** Amazonia: The Catherine Miles Story. **1986 (R)** 90m/C Elvive Avoray, Will Gonzales, Andrew Louis Coppola; **D:** Roy Garrett. **VHS, Beta** NO ✂

White Tiger Three crooks pull off a major heist and hide out in a mountain cabin where their mistrust of each other grows. **1923** 81m/C Priscilla Dean, Matt Moore, Raymond Griffith, Wallace Beery; **D:** Tod Browning. **VHS $19.95** GPV ✂✂½

The White Tower Five men and a woman set out to scale the infamous White Tower in the Alps. Each person's true nature is revealed as he or she scales the peak, which has defied all previous attempts.

Slightly overwrought, but exciting. Filmed in Technicolor on location in the Swiss Alps. **1950** 98m/C Glenn Ford, Claude Rains, Cedric Hardwicke, Oscar Homolka, Lloyd Bridges; **D:** Ted Tetzlaff. **VHS, Beta $19.98** HHT, TTC ✂✂✂

White Water Summer A group of young adventurers trek into the Sierras, and find themselves struggling against nature and each other to survive. Bacon is the rugged outdoorsman (yeah, sure) who shows them what's what. Chances are it was never at a theater near you, and with good reason. **AKA:** Rites of Summer. **1987 (PG)** 90m/C Kevin Bacon, Sean Astin, Jonathan Ward, Matt Adler; **D:** Jeff Bleckner; **M:** Michael Boddicker. **VHS, Beta $29.95** COL ✂½

The White Zombie Lugosi followed his success in "Dracula" with the title role in this low-budget horror classic about the leader of a band of zombies who wants to steal a beautiful young woman from her new husband. Set in Haiti; the first zombie movie. Rich and dark, though ludicrous. Based on the novel "The Magic Island" by William Seabrook. **1932** 73m/B Bela Lugosi, Madge Bellamy, John Harron; **D:** Victor Halperin; **M:** Xavier Cugat. **VHS, Beta $19.95** NOS, PSM, CAB ✂✂✂

WhiteForce A secret agent tracks an enemy. His government tracks him. He runs around with a big machine gun and a couple of hand grenades. He fires the gun and throws the grenades. **1988 (R)** 90m/C Sam Jones, Kimberly Pistone; **D:** Eddie Romero. **Beta** NO ✂

Whitewater Sam Whitewater Sam and his Siberian Husky, Sybar, embark on an exciting trip through the uncharted wilds of the Great Northwest. The likeable, intelligent hound steals the show. Good family adventure. **1978 (G)** 87m/C Keith Larsen; **D:** Keith Larsen; **W:** Keith Larsen. **VHS, Beta** MON ✂✂½

Who Am I This Time? Two shy people can express their love for each other only through their roles in a local theater production of "A Streetcar Named Desire." Good cast responds well to competent direction from Demme; poignant, touching and memorable. Based on a story by Kurt Vonnegut, Jr. Made for television. **1982** 60m/C Susan Sarandon, Christopher Walken, Robert Ridgely; **D:** Jonathan Demme. **VHS, Beta $24.95** MON, BTV ✂✂✂

Who Done It? Average Abbott and Costello comedy about two would-be radio mystery writers, working as soda-jerks, who play detective after the radio station's president is murdered. **1942** 77m/B Bud Abbott, Lou Costello, William Gargan, Patric Knowles, Louise Allbritton, Don Porter, Jerome Cowan, William Bendix, Mary Wickes; **D:** Erle C. Kenton. **VHS, Beta $14.95** MCA ✂✂

Who Framed Roger Rabbit? Technically marvelous, cinematically hilarious, eye-popping combination of cartoon and live action create a Hollywood of the 1940s where cartoon characters are real and a repressed minority working in films. A 'toon-hating detective is hired to uncover the unfaithful wife of 2-D star Roger, and instead uncovers a conspiracy to wipe out all 'toons. Special appearances by many cartoon characters from the past. Coproduced by Touchstone (Disney) and Amblin (Spielberg). Adapted from "Who Censored Roger Rabbit?" by Gary K. Wold.

1988 (PG) 104m/C Bob Hoskins, Christopher Lloyd, Joanna Cassidy, Alan Tilvern, Stubby Kaye; *D:* Robert Zemeckis; *W:* Jeffrey Price, Peter S. Seaman; *V:* Charles Fleischer, Mae Questel, Kathleen Turner, Amy Irving, Mel Blanc, June Foray, Frank Sinatra. Academy Awards '88: Best Film Editing, Best Visual Effects; Nominations: Best Art Direction/Set Decoration, Best Cinematography, Best Sound; National Board of Review Awards '88: 10 Best Films of the Year. **VHS, Beta $19.99** *TOU, WTA* 🎬🎬🎬½

Who Has Seen the Wind? Two boys grow up in Saskatchewan during the Depression. So-so family viewing drama. Ferrer as a bootlegger steals the otherwise small-paced show.
1977 102m/C Jose Ferrer, Brian Painchaud, Charmion King, Helen Shaver. **VHS, Beta** *SUE* 🎬🎬

Who is Killing the Great Chefs of Europe? A fast-paced, lightly handled black comedy. When a gourmand, well-played by Morley, learns he must lose weight to live, a number of Europe's best chefs are murdered according to their cooking specialty. A witty, crisp, international mystery based on Ivan and Nan Lyon's novel. *AKA:* Too Many Chefs; Someone is Killing the Great Chefs of Europe.
1978 (PG) 112m/C George Segal, Jacqueline Bisset, Robert Morley, Jean-Pierre Cassel, Philippe Noiret, Jean Rochefort, Joss Ackland, Nigel Havers; *D:* Ted Kotcheff; *M:* Henry Mancini. **VHS** *WAR* 🎬🎬½

Who Is the Black Dahlia? In L.A. in 1947, a detective tries to find out who murdered a star-struck 22-year-old woman nicknamed "The Black Dahlia" (Arnez). Based on a famous unsolved murder case which was later the basis for "True Confessions." Made for TV.
1975 96m/C Efrem Zimbalist Jr., Lucie Arnaz, Ronny Cox, MacDonald Carey, Linden Chiles; *D:* Joseph Pevney; *W:* Robert W. Lenski. **VHS, Beta $29.95** *WOV* 🎬🎬

Who Killed Baby Azaria? Parents are arrested for infanticide after they claim their baby was stolen by a wild dog while vacationing on a supposedly haunted Australian mountain, or was it an aboriginal spirit that absconded with the tyke? Less compelling than the American remake, "A Cry in the Dark." Made for Australian TV.
1983 96m/C Elaine Hudson, John Hamblin, Peter Carroll; *D:* Judy Rymer. **VHS, Beta $59.95** *PSM* 🎬🎬

Who Killed Doc Robbin? A group of youngsters try to clear their friend, Dan, the town handyman, when the sinister Dr. Robbin is murdered. The follow-up to "The Adventures of Curly and His Gang;" intended as part of a Roach kid-comedy series in the manner of "Our Gang." Fast pace and lots of slapstick give a first impression of spirited juvenile hijinks, but not much is genuinely funny. And the names of the two black kids—"Dis" and "Dat"—aren't funny either. *AKA:* Sinister House; Curley and His Gang in the Haunted Mansion.
1948 50m/C Larry Olsen, Don Castle, Bernard Carr, Virginia Grey. **VHS, Beta $16.95** *SNC, NOS, HHT* 🎬🎬

Who Killed Mary What's 'Er Name? A diabetic ex-fighter tracks a prostitute's killer through Greenwich Village. Illogical, incredible and disjointed attempt at comedy/mystery. Odd, unsatisfying ending, with the boxer going into a coma. Good supporting cast. *AKA:* Death of a Hooker.
1971 (PG) 90m/C Red Buttons, Sylvia Miles, Conrad Bain, Ron Carey, David Doyle, Sam Waterston; *D:* Ernie Pintoff. **VHS, Beta $59.95** *GEM, PSM* 🎬🎬

Who Shot Pat? Funny, nostalgic, coming of age story set in fifties Brooklyn. Knight stars as Bic Bickham, the leader of a clean-living "gang" of seniors at a Brooklyn vocational school. Memorable vintage soundtrack features hits by legendary artists Chuck Berry and Bo Diddly. *AKA:* Who Shot Patakango?
1992 (R) 102m/C David Knight, Sandra Bullock, Kevin Otto, Aaron Ingram, Brad Randall; *D:* Robert Brooks; *W:* Halle Brooks, Robert Brooks. **VHS $89.99** *WAR* 🎬🎬½

Who Slew Auntie Roo? An updated twist on the Hansel and Gretel fairy tale. Features Winters as an odd, reclusive widow mistaken for the fairy tale's children-eating witch by one of the orphans at her annual Christmas party—with dire consequences. *AKA:* Whoever Slew Auntie Roo?; Gingerbread House.
1971 (PG) 90m/C Shelley Winters, Ralph Richardson, Mark Lester, Lionel Jeffries, Hugh Griffith; *D:* Curtis Harrington. **VHS, Beta $69.95** *VES* 🎬🎬½

Whodunit The bad horror flicks always seem to have (usually young) characters murdered one at a time, often on a remote island. This loser is no exception.
1982 (R) 82m/C Rick Bean, Gary Phillips; *D:* Bill Naud; *W:* Anthony Shaffer. **VHS, Beta $69.98** *LIV, VES* 🎬

The Whole Shootin' Match Two thirty something Texas nobodies chase the American Dream via a sure-fire invention called the Kitchen Wizard, after failing in the small-animal biz and polyurethane. Offbeat, very low-budget independent feature shot interestingly in sepia tones. Sympathetic and human.
1979 108m/C Matthew L. Perry, Sonny Carl Davis, Doris Hargrave; *D:* Eagle Pennell. **VHS** *NO* 🎬🎬🎬

Who'll Save Our Children? Two children are abandoned and left on the doorstep of a middle-aged, childless couple. Years later the natural parents, now reformed, attempt to reclaim their children. Well cast and topical. Made for TV.
1982 96m/C Shirley Jones, Len Cariou; *D:* George Schaefer. **VHS** *TLF* 🎬🎬

Who'll Stop the Rain? A temperamental Vietnam vet (Nolte) is enlisted in a smuggling scheme to transport a large amount of heroin into California. An excellent blend of drama, comedy, action, suspense, and tragedy. Based on Robert Stone's novel "Dog Soldiers." Outstanding period soundtrack by Creedence Clearwater Revival, including title song. Violent and compelling tale of late-'60s disillusionment. *AKA:* Dog Soldiers.
1978 (R) 126m/C Nick Nolte, Tuesday Weld, Michael Moriarty, Anthony Zerbe, Richard Masur, Ray Sharkey, David Opatoshu, Charles Haid, Gail Strickland; *D:* Karel Reisz; *W:* Judith Rascoe. **VHS, Beta $14.95** *MGM* 🎬🎬½

Wholly Moses! Set in biblical times, this alleged comedy concerns a phony religious prophet who begins to believe that his mission is to lead the chosen. Horrible ripoff of "Life of Brian," released the previous year. What a cast—what a waste!
1980 (PG) 125m/C Dudley Moore, Laraine Newman, James Coco, Paul Sand, Dom DeLuise, Jack Gilford, John Houseman, Madeline Kahn, Richard Pryor, John Ritter; *D:* Gary Weis. **VHS, Beta $9.95** *COL* Woof!

Whoopee! Cantor stars in his first sound picture as a rich hypochondriac sent out west for his health, where he encounters rugged cowboys and Indians. Filmed in two-color Technicolor and based on Ziegfeld's 1928

Broadway production with the same cast. Dances supervised by Busby Berkeley. ♫The Song of the Setting Sun; Mission Number; Makin' Whoopee; A Girlfriend of a Boyfriend of Mine; My Baby Just Cares for Me; I'll Still Belong to You; Stetson.
1930 93m/C Eddie Cantor, Ethel Shutta, Paul Gregory, Eleanor Hunt, Betty Grable, George Olsen & His Orchestra; *D:* Thornton Freeland. **VHS, Beta $19.98** *SUE, HBO* 🎬🎬

The Whoopee Boys A New York lowlife in Palm Beach tries to reform himself by saving a school for needy children so his rich girlfriend will marry him. Full of unfunny jokes and very bad taste, with no redeeming qualities whatever.
1986 (R) 89m/C Michael O'Keefe, Paul Rodriguez; *D:* John Byrum; *M:* Jack Nitzsche. **VHS, Beta $79.95** *PAR* 🎬

Whoops Apocalypse Satiric account of events leading up to WWIII. Invasion in South America leads British prime minister to suggest nuclear retaliation. Uneven, lacking in the Strangelovian element, but funny in spots. Based on the British hit television series and scripted by series writers Marshall and Renwick.
1983 137m/C John Cleese, John Barron, Richard Griffiths, Peter Jones, Bruce Montague, Barry Morse, Rik Mayall, Ian Richardson, Alexei Sayle, Herbert Lom, Joanne Pearce; *D:* Tom Bussmann; *W:* Andrew Marshall, David Renwick. **VHS, Beta** *NO* 🎬🎬½

Whoops Apocalypse America's first female president Swit, recently ensconced after the untimely death of the ex-circus clown previous president, is forced to contend with hotheaded superpowers who want to kick off WWIII with a bang. Uneven black comedic satire of holocaust genre. Based on the BBC TV series.
1988 (R) 93m/C Loretta Swit, Peter Cook, Michael Richards. **VHS, Beta $14.95** *MGM* 🎬🎬

Whore Ken Russell's gritty night in the life of cynical prostitute Theresa Russell is strong medicine, a powerful antidote to sappy Hollywood films that glorify streetwalking. Also available in the 92-minute original uncut version, an 85-minute NC-17 version, and an alternate R-Rated version. *AKA:* If You Can't Say It, Just See It.
1991 (R) 80m/C Theresa Russell, Antonio Vargas; *D:* Ken Russell; *W:* Ken Russell. **VHS $9.98** *VMK* 🎬🎬

Who's Afraid of Virginia Woolf? Nichols debuts as a director in this biting Edward Albee play. A teacher and his wife (Segal and Dennis) are invited to the home of a burned-out professor and his foul-mouthed, bitter, yet seductive wife (Burton and Taylor). The guests get more than dinner, as the evening deteriorates into brutal verbal battles between the hosts. Taylor and Dennis won Oscars; Burton's Oscar-nominated portrait of the tortured husband is magnificent. Richard and Liz's best film together.
1966 127m/B Richard Burton, Elizabeth Taylor, George Segal, Sandy Dennis; *D:* Mike Nichols; *W:* Ernest Lehman; *M:* Alex North. Academy Awards '66: Best Actress (Taylor), Best Art Direction/Set Decoration (B & W), Best Black and White Cinematography, Best Costume Design (B & W), Best Supporting Actress (Dennis); Nominations: Best Actor (Burton), Best Adapted Screenplay, Best Director (Nichols), Best Film Editing, Best Picture, Best Sound, Best Supporting Actor (Segal), Best Original Score; National Board of Review Awards '66: 10 Best Films of the Year, Best Actress (Taylor). **VHS, Beta $19.98** *WAR, BTV* 🎬🎬🎬🎬

Who's Got the Action? Martin and Turner are a husband and wife divided by his love of playing the ponies. In order to keep his gambling under control Turner schemes to become his new bookie. But when Martin suddenly goes on a winning streak, the new bookie is in trouble with her former competition, who just happen to be the Mob. Strained, flat comedy with Turner especially miscast.
1963 93m/C Lana Turner, Dean Martin, Walter Matthau, Eddie Albert, Nita Talbot, Margo, Paul Ford, John McGiver, Jack Albertson; *D:* Daniel Mann; *W:* Jack Rose. **VHS** $14.95 *PAR* ♫♫½

Who's Harry Crumb? Bumbling detective Candy can't even investigate a routine kidnapping! His incompetence is catching: the viewer can't detect a single genuinely funny moment. Candy is the only likeable thing in this all-around bad, mindless farce.
1989 (PG-13) 95m/C John Candy, Jeffrey Jones, Annie Potts, Tim Thomerson, Barry Corbin, Shawnee Smith, Valri Bromfield, Renee Coleman, Joe Flaherty, Lyle Alzado, James Belushi, Stephen Young; *D:* Paul Flaherty; *M:* Michel Colombier. **VHS, Beta** $14.95 *COL* ♫½

Who's Minding the Mint? A money checker at the U.S. Mint must replace $50,000 he accidentally destroyed. He enlists a retired money printer and an inept gang to infiltrate the mint and replace the lost cash, with predictable chaos resulting. Nonstop zaniness in this wonderful comedy that never got its due when released. Thieves who befriend Hutton include Denver of "Gilligan's Island" and Farr, later of "M*A*S*H."
1967 97m/C Jim Hutton, Dorothy Provine, Milton Berle, Joey Bishop, Bob Denver, Walter Brennan, Jamie Farr; *D:* Howard Morris. **VHS, Beta** $9.95 *GKK* ♫♫♫

Who's That Girl? A flighty, wrongly-convicted parolee kidnaps her uptight lawyer and they have wacky adventures as she goes in search of the crumb that landed her in the pokey. Plenty of Madonna tunes, if that's what you like; they briefly keep you from wondering why you're not laughing. Kind of a remake (a bad one) of "Bringing Up Baby" (1938).
1987 (PG) 94m/C Madonna, Griffin Dunne, John Mills, Haviland Morris; *D:* James Foley. **VHS, Beta, 8mm** $19.98 *WAR* ♫

Who's That Knocking at My Door? Interesting debut for Scorsese, in which he exercises many of the themes and techniques that he polished for later films. An autobiographical drama about an Italian-American youth growing up in New York City, focusing on street life, Catholicism and adolescent bonding. Begun as a student film called "I Call First"; later developed into a feature. Keitel's film debut. *AKA:* J.R.; I Call First.
1968 90m/B Harvey Keitel, Zena Bethune; *D:* Martin Scorsese. **VHS, Beta** $59.99 *DCL, FCT, WAR* ♫♫♫

Who's the Man? Two clowning companions who work in a barbershop in Harlem get recruited onto the police force to investigate a murder. Doctor Dre and Ed Lover (themselves) make use of their hip-hop music connections and full-throttle slapstick humor to enliven the search. Salt of "Salt 'n' Pepa," is the female lead and Ice-T plays a gangster. First-time director Demme works his star duo for both foolish and vulgar humor. Filming done mostly on location in Harlem. Includes a lengthy list of cameo appearances by several hip-hop performers. For fans; based on a story by Dre, Lover, and Seth Greenland.

1993 (R) 124m/C Dr. Dre, Ed Lover, Cheryl "Salt" James, Ice-T, Jim Moody, Colin Quinn, Kim Chan, Rozwill Young, Badja Djola, Richard Bright, Denis Leary, Andre B. Blake, Bill Bellamy; *D:* Ted Demme; *W:* Seth Greenland; *M:* Andre Harrell. **VHS** *NLC, IME, COL* ♫♫

Who's Who In a satire on climbing the British social ladder, workers in a London brokerage firm struggle with class issues and find the higher you climb, the more you find greed, pettiness, and stupidity.
1978 75m/C Bridget Kane, Simon Chandler, Adam Norton, Philip Davis, Joolia Cappleman; *D:* Mike Leigh; *W:* Mike Leigh. **VHS** $79.95 *WBF, BTV, FCT* ♫♫

Whose Child Am I? A woman so desperately wants a child of her own that she doesn't mind who the father is. Ludicrous and vulgar.
1975 (R) 90m/C Kate O'Mara, Paul Freeman, Edward Judd, Felicity Devonshire; *D:* Lawrence Britten. **VHS** $59.95 *ATL* ♫

Whose Life Is It Anyway? Black humor abounds. Sculptor Dreyfuss is paralyzed from the neck down in an auto accident. What follows is his struggle to persuade the hospital authorities to let him die. Excellent cast headed impressively by Dreyfuss; Lahti as his doctor and hospital head Cassavetes also are superb. From Brian Clark's successful Broadway play.
1981 (R) 118m/C Richard Dreyfuss, John Cassavetes, Christine Lahti, Bob Balaban, Kenneth McMillan, Kaki Hunter, Thomas Carter; *D:* John Badham; *W:* Reginald Rose, Brian Clark, Reginald Rose. **VHS, Beta** $79.95 *MGM* ♫♫♫½

Why Does Herr R. Run Amok? Notorious Fassbinder black comedy about a middle-class man, unable to cope with the increasing problems of modern life, who suddenly murders his family. The characters are called by the actors' names to heighten the sense of reality. Film is based on a case history. In German with English subtitles. *AKA:* Warum Lauft Herr R Amok?.
1969 88m/C Kurt Raab, Lilith Ungerer, Amadeus Fengler, Hanna Schygulla, Franz Maron; *D:* Rainer Werner Fassbinder, Michael Fengler; *W:* Rainer Werner Fassbinder, Michael Fengler. **VHS** $79.95 *NYF, FCT, ING* ♫♫

Why Me? Two jewel thieves unknowingly steal an enormously valuable ruby ring and are in over their heads trying to evade the cops and everyone else. In the same vein as the much-funnier "Nuns on the Run," this caper is done in by bad acting and too much ill-conceived slapstick. Adapted by Donald E. Westlake from his own novel.
1990 (R) 96m/C Christopher Lambert, Christopher Lloyd, Kim Greist, J.T. Walsh, Michael J. Pollard, Tony Plana, John Hancock, Lawrence Tierney; *D:* Gene Quintano; *W:* Donald E. Westlake. **VHS** $89.95 *COL* ♫♫

Why Shoot the Teacher A young teacher sent to a one-room schoolhouse in a small prairie town in Saskatchewan during the Depression gets a cold reception on the cold prairie. One of the more popular films at the Canadian box office. Cort was Harold in "Harold and Maude." Based on the novel by Max Braithwaite.
1979 101m/C Bud Cort, Samantha Eggar, Chris Wiggins; *D:* Silvio Narizzano. **VHS, Beta** $69.98 *SUE* ♫♫♫

The Wicked Though packaged as serious horror, this is a cheap, tacky spoof with folks stranded at the country residence of a vampire family. Sole point of interest: these Transylvanian cliches take place in the Australian outback. Kids might actually like this

(gore isn't severe), if they can surmount the thick Down Under accents.
1989 87m/C Brett Cumo, Richard Morgan, Angela Kennedy, Maggie Blinco, John Doyle; *D:* Colin Eggleston. **VHS** $14.95 *HMD* ♫

The Wicked Lady Posh but lame costume drama about a bored 17th century noblewoman who takes to highway robbery to spice up her life. Credulity-stretcher extraordinaire. Based on "The Life and Death of Wicked Lady Skelton" by Magdalen King-Hall. Mason is cheeky as a fellow highwayman. Remade in 1983 with Faye Dunaway.
1945 103m/B James Mason, Margaret Lockwood, Patricia Roc, Michael Rennie, Felix Aylmer, Enid Stamp-Taylor, Griffith Jones; *D:* Louis Levy. **VHS, Beta** *NO* ♫♫

The Wicked Lady Remake of the 1945 costumer about a 17th-century noblewoman trying her hand at highway robbery. More noted for its low-cut costumes and racy humor than any talent involved.
1983 (R) 99m/C Faye Dunaway, John Gielgud, Denholm Elliott, Alan Bates, Glynis Barber, Oliver Tobias, Prunella Scales; *D:* Michael Winner; *W:* Michael Winner. **VHS, Beta** $14.95 *MGM* ♫♫½

Wicked Stepmother A family discovers that an aged stepmother is actually a witch. Davis walked off the film shortly before she died, and was replaced by Carrera. Davis's move was wise; the result is dismal, and would have been had she stayed. As it is the newer wonders: How come the stepmother isn't Davis anymore? Davis's unfortunate last role.
1989 (PG-13) 90m/C Bette Davis, Barbara Carrera, Colleen Camp, Lionel Stander, David Rasche, Tom Bosley, Seymour Cassel, Evelyn Keyes, Richard Moll, Laurene Landon; *D:* Larry Cohen; *W:* Larry Cohen; *M:* Robert Folk. **VHS, Beta** $14.95 *MGM* ♫

The Wicker Man The disappearance of a young girl leads a devoutly religious Scottish policeman to an island whose denizens practice bizarre pagan sexual rituals. An example of occult horror that achieves its mounting terror without gratuitous gore. The first original screenplay by playwright Shaffer. Beware shortened versions that may still lurk out there; the 103-minute restored director's cut is definitive.
1975 103m/C Edward Woodward, Christopher Lee, Britt Ekland, Diane Cilento, Ingrid Pitt; *D:* Robin Hardy; *W:* Anthony Shaffer. **VHS, Beta** $19.95 *MED* ♫♫♫½

Wide Open Faces Every crook in town is looking for some missing stolen loot. Soda jerk Brown outwits them all in his own inimitable way. The story may be predictable, but Brown's physical humor keeps things interesting.
1938 67m/B Joe E. Brown, Jane Wyman, Alison Skipworth, Alan Baxter, Lucien Littlefield, Sidney Toler, Berton Churchill, Barbara Pepper, Stanley Fields, Horace Murphy; *D:* Kurt Neumann. **VHS** $19.95 *NOS* ♫♫

Wide Sargasso Sea Jamaica in the 1840's is a seething, mysterious paradise—a former British slave colony with a mix of powerful voodoo culture, beauty, and eroticism providing a very potent brew, a perfect setting for this soaper. Based on the novel by Jean Rhys, which is something of a prequel to Charlotte Bronte's "Jane Eyre." Properly English Edward Rochester meets and marries the tragic Antoinette—the same mad wife locked in the attic in the Bronte novel. Explicit nudity and sex earn the NC-17, but the film is tragic without being sensationalized. Also available in an edited R-rated and unrated versions.

1992 (NC-17) 98m/C Karina Lombard, Nathaniel Parker, Rachel Ward, Michael York, Martine Beswick, Claudia Robinson, Rowena King, Huw Christie Williams; *D:* John Duigan; *W:* Jan Sharp, Carole Angier, John Duigan; *M:* Stewart Copeland. VHS NLC, IME, BTV 🐾🐾

The Widow A story about a woman slowly learning to deal with her own grief, her children's traumas and monetary worries after the death of her husband. Straightforward, passable made for TV domestic drama based on Lynn Caine's best-selling novel. 1976 99m/C Michael Learned, Farley Granger, Bradford Dillman, Robert Lansing; *D:* J. Lee Thompson. VHS, Beta TLF 🐾🐾

Widow Couderc A provincial widow unknowingly includes an escaped murderer among her liaisons. Based on a novel by Georges Simenon. In French with English subtitles. 1974 92m/C Simone Signoret, Alain Delon; *D:* Pierre Granier-Deferre. VHS, Beta $59.00 FCT 🐾🐾🐾

Widow's Nest Three widowed sisters live in a bizarre fantasy world when they lock themselves in a dingy mansion in Cuba of the 1930s. Filmed in Spain. 1977 90m/C Patricia Neal, Susan Oliver, Lila Kedrova, Valentina Cortese; *D:* Tony Navarro. VHS, Beta NO 🐾🐾

Widow's Peak 1920's Irish community is run by a dictatorship of well-to-do widows with Mrs. Doyle-Counihan (Plowright) at the helm. Troubles begin for the town non-widow (Farrow) upon the arrival of recently widowed Broome (Richardson), who attracts Dunbar, the nitwit son of Plowright. Entertaining performances (Farrow shows that success is possible after the Wood-man) and beautiful scenery help boost a script that seems torn between whimsical comedy and dark drama. 1994 (PG) 101m/C Mia Farrow, Joan Plowright, Natasha Richardson, Adrian Dunbar, Jim Broadbent, John Kavanagh, Gerard McSorley, Anne Kent, Rynagh O'Grady, Michael James Ford, Garrett Keogh; *D:* John Irvin; *W:* Hugh Leonard; *M:* Carl Davis. VHS NYR 🐾🐾½

Wife Versus Secretary Excellent acting against type creates a near-perfect picture of romantic relationships. Harlow and Gable play a secretary and her boss who have a wonderful professional relationship, but Loy worries something else is afoot. Could have been a heavy-handed soap opera, but the witty dialogue and Brown's fine pacing make it much more. Stewart later claimed that he purposely messed up his romantic scenes with Harlow in order to spend more time in her arms. 1936 89m/B Clark Gable, Jean Harlow, Myrna Loy, May Robson, Hobart Cavanaugh, James Stewart, George Barbier, Gilbert Emery; *D:* Clarence Brown. VHS $19.98 MGM 🐾🐾🐾½

Wifemistress In the early 1900s, an invalid wife resents her neglectful husband. When he goes into hiding because of a murder he didn't commit, she begins to drift into a world of sexual fantasies. Fine performances. Italian dialogue with English subtitles. *AKA:* Mogliamante; Lover, Wife. 1979 (R) 101m/C Marcello Mastroianni, Laura Antonelli; *D:* Marco Vicario. VHS, Beta $59.95 COL 🐾🐾½

The Wilby Conspiracy A political activist and an Englishman on the wrong side of the law team up to escape the clutches of a prejudiced cop in apartheid Africa. The focus of the film is on the chase, not the political uprising taking place around it. Well-done chase film with fine performances throughout. 1975 (PG) 101m/C Sidney Poitier, Michael Caine, Nicol Williamson, Prunella Gee, Persis Khambatta, Saeed Jaffrey, Rutger Hauer, Helmut Dantine; *D:* Ralph Nelson. VHS $14.95 MGM, FCT 🐾🐾🐾

The Wild Aces A relentless action flick with real documentary footage of the aerial war above Vietnam. 1985 58m/C VHS, Beta $24.95 BMV, FGF 🐾½

The Wild and the Free Light-hearted comedy about research chimps. The lab-raised bunch become the instruments for radioactive experimenting. Scheming scientists return the chimps to their home to save them from their demise. Made for TV. 1980 100m/C Granville Van Dusen, Linda Gray, Bill Gribble; *D:* James Hill. VHS, Beta $39.95 LIV 🐾🐾

Wild & Wooly In 1903, a tough cowgirl and her friends must prevent the assassination of the President. Made for television. 1978 120m/C Chris DeLisle, Susan Bigelow, Elyssa Davalos, Jessica Walter, Doug McClure, David Doyle, Ross Martin, Vic Morrow, Charles Seibert, Sherry Bain, Paul Burke; *D:* Philip Leacock; *M:* Charles Bernstein. VHS, Beta $59.95 PSM 🐾½

The Wild Angels Excessively violent film but B-movie classic about an outlaw biker gang and the local townspeople. Typical Corman fodder was one of AIP's most successful productions. 1966 (PG) 124m/C Peter Fonda, Nancy Sinatra, Bruce Dern, Diane Ladd, Michael J. Pollard, Gayle Hunnicutt; *D:* Roger Corman; *W:* Charles B. Griffith, Peter Bogdanovich. VHS, Beta $9.98 SUE 🐾🐾½

Wild at Heart Dern and Cage are on the lam, going across country to escape her mother, his parole officer, and life. Humorous and frightening, sensual and evocative as only Lynch can be. Sweet love story of Sailor and Lula is juxtaposed with the violent and bizarre, obsessive brand of love of the people they encounter. Unmistakable Wizard of Oz imagery sprinkled throughout, as are some scenes of graphic violence. Ladd is unnerving as Dern's on-screen mother (she also has the role off-screen). 1990 (R) 125m/C Nicolas Cage, Laura Dern, Diane Ladd, Willem Dafoe, Isabella Rossellini, Harry Dean Stanton, Crispin Glover, Grace Zabriskie, J.E. Freeman, Freddie Jones, Sherilyn Fenn, Sheryl Lee; *D:* David Lynch; *W:* David Lynch; *M:* Angelo Badalamenti. Academy Awards '90 Nominations: Best Supporting Actress (Ladd); Cannes Film Festival '90: Best Film; Independent Spirit Awards '91: Best Cinematography. VHS, Beta $19.98 CCB, MED, IME 🐾🐾🐾½

The Wild Beasts Children and animals clash violently after drinking water tainted with PCP. Disgusting premise; unredeemably violent. *AKA:* Savage Beasts. 1985 92m/C John Aldrich, Lorraine De Selle; *D:* Franco Prosperi. VHS, Beta $59.98 LIV Woof!

The Wild Bunch Acclaimed western about a group of aging outlaws on their final rampage, realizing time is passing them by. Highly influential in dialogue, editing style, and lyrical slow-motion photography of violence; Peckinpah's main claim to posterity. Holden and Ryan create especially memorable characters. Arguably the greatest western and one of the greatest American films of all times. Beware of shortened versions; after a pre-release showing to the East Coast critics, producer Feldman cut key scenes without Peckinpah's knowledge or consent. 1969 (R) 145m/C William Holden, Ernest Borgnine, Robert Ryan, Warren Oates, Strother Martin, L.Q. Jones, Albert Dekker, Bo Hopkins, Edmond O'Brien, Ben Johnson, Jaime Sanchez, Emilio Fernandez, Dub Taylor; *D:* Sam Peckinpah; *W:* Walon Green, Sam Peckinpah. VHS, Beta $19.98 WAR 🐾🐾🐾🐾

Wild Cactus Philip and Alexandra Marcus decide to take a romantic vacation at a desert resort where they meet up with a homicidal ex-con and his seductive girlfriend. The two couples find themselves entangled in some violent and kinky games. An unrated version is also available. 1992 (R) 92m/C David Naughton, India Allen, Gary Hudson, Michelle Moffett, Kathy Shower, Robert Z'Dar, Paul Gleason, Anna Karin, David Wells; *D:* Jag Mundhra; *W:* Carl Austin. VHS $89.95 IMP 🐾½

The Wild Child The brilliant film based on the journal of a 19th century physician who attempts to educate and civilize a young boy who has been found living in the wilderness, without any comprehension of human life. Tenderly told coming of age tale, with surprising sensitivity for its subject. In French with English subtitles. *AKA:* L'Enfant Sauvage. 1970 (G) 85m/B *D:* Francois Truffaut; *W:* Jean Gruault; *M:* Antoine Duhamel. VHS $19.99 MGM, ING, FCT 🐾🐾🐾½

Wild Country Tame western. A U.S. Marshall races to stop the bad guy from killing the late sheriff's daughter and snatching her ranch. 1947 57m/B Eddie Dean, Roscoe Ates, Peggy Wynn, Douglas Fowley, I. Stanford Jolley, Bill Fawcett; *D:* Ray Taylor. VHS $19.95 NOS, HEG 🐾½

The Wild Country Children's fare detailing the trials and tribulations of a Pittsburgh family moving into an inhospitable Wyoming ranch in the 1880s. Based on the novel "Little Britches" by Ralph Moody. *AKA:* The Newcomers. 1971 (G) 92m/C Steve Forrest, Ron Howard, Clint Howard, Rance Howard; *D:* Robert Totten. VHS, Beta $69.96 DIS 🐾🐾½

The Wild Duck A father discovers that his beloved daughter is illegitimate and turns against her. To regain his love, she plans to sacrifice her most prized possession. Irons overacts; Ullman almost disappears into the woodwork. Child star Jones is insufferable, and the whole family squeaks with "literary" pomposity. A horrid adaptation of the classic Ibsen play. 1984 (PG) 96m/C Jeremy Irons, Liv Ullmann, Lucinda Jones, Arthur Dignam; *D:* Henri Safran. VHS, Beta $79.98 LIV, VES 🐾½

Wild Engine/Mistaken Orders The early screen daredevil Holmes stars in two railroad-and-betrayal epics. 1923 48m/B Helen Holmes, Jack Hoxie, Hoot Gibson. VHS, Beta $19.98 CCB 🐾🐾

Wild Frontier A rugged old lawman and his sons team up to rid a town of outlaws. Lane, playing a character with his own name for first time, takes over from his murdered father and roots out the evildoer (Holt, a pillar, as a bad guy for once). Decent, enjoyable, good-guys-win western. 1948 59m/B Allan "Rocky" Lane, Tim Holt. VHS, Beta $29.95 DVT 🐾½

Wild Geese The adventure begins when a veteran band of mercenaries land deep inside Africa to rescue the imprisoned leader of an emerging African nation, in the interest of protecting British commercial interest. Their mission meets an unexpected turn when they are betrayed by their financial backers. Too much training in the early part; too long; too much dialogue. Where's the action?

1978 (R) 132m/C Richard Burton, Roger Moore, Richard Harris, Hardy Kruger, Stewart Granger, Frank Finlay, Jeff Corey; **D:** Andrew V. McLaglen; **W:** Reginald Rose. VHS, Beta $59.98 FOX 🎞🎞

Wild Geese 2 Lame sequel to the flamed and overlong "Wild Geese," which depended on its name stars. More of the same, this time Sams Burton, Harris and Moore. Sure, it's got Olivier, but it still stinks. 1985 (R) 124m/C Laurence Olivier, Edward Fox, Scott Glenn, Barbara Carrera, Robert Webber; **D:** Peter Hunt; **W:** Reginald Rose. VHS, Beta $14.95 MGM 🎞½

Wild Guitar A swinging youth cycles into Hollywood and, improbably, becomes an instant teenidol. Considered a top contender for "Worst Picture of All Time" honors. 1962 92m/B Arch Hall Jr.; **D:** Ray Dennis Steckler. VHS, Beta $24.95 RHI Woof!

Wild Gypsies A band of gypsies seek revenge against a renegade member who returned to rape and pillage. Without merit except for the good photography of Steven Burum, who has become respected doing cinematographically intriguing films like "Rumblefish." 1969 85m/C Todd Grange, Gayle Clark, Laurel Welcome. VHS, Beta $19.95 STE, NWV 🎞

Wild Hearts Can't Be Broken Depicts the true-life story of Sonora Webster, a small town Georgia girl who runs away from a foster home to join a carnival in the early 1930s, hoping to become a stunt rider. She becomes a horse-diver (a Depression-era sideshow phenomena) and is blinded in a diving accident, but returns to find romance and ride again. Storyline has little screen tension, but it doesn't detract from this fresh family film with a feisty heroine, a sweet romance, and horses. Nice U.S. screen debut for British actress Anwar. 1991 (G) 89m/C Gabrielle Anwar, Cliff Robertson, Dylan Kussman, Michael Schoeffling, Kathleen York, Frank Renzulli; **D:** Steve Miner; **W:** Oley Sassone; **M:** Mason Daring. VHS, Beta $19.99 DIS 🎞🎞🎞

Wild Horse Gibson is the lead (in his favorite talking role), but his magnificent mount Mut commands most of the attention. Interesting historically as an example of stars' (Gibson's in this case) difficulty adjusting to talking pictures. **AKA:** Silver Devil. 1931 68m/B Hoot Gibson, Stepin Fetchit, Edmund Cobb, Alberta Vaughn; **D:** Richard Thorpe, Sidney Algier. VHS, Beta $19.95 NOS, GPV, VYY 🎞½

Wild Horse Canyon Yakima Canutt, the man credited with creating the profession of stunt man, stars in this tale about a lady rancher who requires saving from her evil foreman. The climactic stampede scene gives Yakima a chance to demonstrate a high dive off a cliff and a somersault onto his horse. Silent, with musical score. 1925 68m/B Yakima Canutt, Edward Cecil, Helene Rosson, Jay Talbet. VHS, Beta $19.95 NOS, GPV, VYY 🎞🎞

Wild Horse Canyon One of those westerns designed to run as half of a double-feature, this one's shorter than most, but hardly notable. The hero goes after a rustler who shot his brother. 1939 57m/B Jack Randall, Dorothy Short, Frank Yaconelli, Dennis Moore, Warner Richmond, Charles "Blackie" King, Sherry Tansey; **D:** Robert F. Hill. VHS $19.95 NOS, GPV 🎞½

Wild Horse Hank A young woman risks everything to save a herd of wild mustangs from being slaughtered for use as dog food. Creena is good; otherwise, it's sentimental

family fare. Based on the novel "The Wild Horse Killers" by Mel Ellis. 1979 94m/C Linda Blair, Richard Crenna, Michael Wincott, Al Waxman; **D:** Eric Till. VHS, Beta $69.98 LIV, VES 🎞🎞

Wild Horse Phantom A Wild West banker plans to fake a robbery in a diabolical deception to part honest ranchers from their lands. Surely this man's not a member of the F.D.I.C. Okay sagebrush saga. 1944 56m/B Buster Crabbe, Al "Fuzzy" St. John, Charles "Blackie" King, John Merton, Lane Chandler, Edward Cassidy, Bud Osborne; **D:** Sam Newfield. VHS, Beta GPV 🎞🎞

Wild Horse Rodeo When a gunman appears at a rodeo, trouble starts. Part of "The Three Mesquiteers" series. Ordinary action-packed western, the good guys win. Actor Dick Weston, who sings, later gained fame as singing cowboy Roy Rogers. 1937 53m/B Ray Corrigan. VHS, Beta $9.95 NOS, DVT 🎞½

Wild Horses A man attempts to make a living by capturing and selling wild horses. Adventure fans will love this film which deals with the common theme of man against nature. 1982 88m/C Keith Aberdein, John Bach, Robyn Gibbes; **D:** Derek Morton. VHS, Beta $29.98 VES 🎞🎞

Wild Horses Ex-rodeo champ Rogers is hankering to escape his dull life. He joins a roundup of wild horses and with Dawber's help exposes a bureaucrat's scheme for them. Rogers is likable and sings, but the supporting cast carries this one. Made for TV. 1984 90m/C Kenny Rogers, Pam Dawber, Ben Johnson, Richard Masur, David Andrews, Karen Carlson; **D:** Dick Lowry. VHS, Beta NO 🎞🎞

Wild in the Country Backwoods delinquent Presley is aided in his literary aspirations by woman psychiatrist Lange. Okay, so that's fairly novel. Strange plot lines but in general Elvis is going to college and reading and writing and singing and playing his guitar. Meanwhile Weld wanders around seductively to provide that hint of Tennessee Williams ambience as interpreted by Odet but hey, who cares? Interesting if convoluted Elvis dramatic turn. 🎵Wild in the Country; In My Way; I Slipped, I Stumbled, I Fell; Lonely Man. 1961 114m/C Elvis Presley, Hope Lange, Tuesday Weld, Millie Perkins, John Ireland, Gary Lockwood, Alan Napier; **D:** Philip Dunne; **W:** Clifford Odets. VHS, Beta $14.98 FOX, MVD 🎞🎞½

Wild in the Streets Satire set in the future, where a malcontent rock star becomes president after the voting age is lowered to 14. Adults over 30 are imprisoned and fed a daily dose of LSD. The president gets his comeuppance when challenged by even younger youths. Very groovy, very political in its own way, very funny. 1968 97m/C Shelley Winters, Christopher Jones, Hal Holbrook, Richard Pryor, Diane Varsi, Millie Perkins, Ed Begley Sr.; **D:** Barry Shear; **M:** Les Baxter. VHS, Beta $19.99 HBO 🎞🎞½

The Wild Life A recent high school graduate takes on a wild and crazy wrestler as his roommate in a swinging singles apartment complex. The same writer and producer as "Fast Times at Ridgemont High" but that film's commercial success. Just as adolescent, though. 1984 (R) 96m/C Christopher Penn, Randy Quaid, Rick Moranis, Hart Bochner, Eric Stoltz, Jenny Wright, Lea Thompson, Sherilyn Fenn, Lee Ving, Ashley St. John, Francesca "Kitten" Natavidad;

D: Art Linson; **W:** Cameron Crowe. VHS, Beta $79.98 MCA 🎞

Wild Man A Las Vegas gambling magnate with supernatural powers decides to avenge the murder of his friend and sets out on an adventure to find the killer. Crummy acting in yet another "ex-agent called back for one more mission" yarn. 1989 106m/C Ginger Lynn Allen, Michelle (McClellan) Bauer, Don Scribner, Kathleen Middleton; **D:** Fred J. Lincoln. VHS, Beta CEL 🎞

Wild Mustang Sheriff's son (Gordon) joins some outlaws to help father (Carey) spring a trap. The plan is sidetracked, and Gordon is captured and nearly branded by the baddies. Don't worry, though; everything turns out all right. Good western. 1935 62m/B Harry Carey Sr.; **D:** Harry Fraser. VHS, Beta $19.95 NOS, VCN, DVT 🎞🎞½

The Wild One The original biker flick: two motorcycle gangs descend upon a quiet midwestern town and each other. Brando is the leader of one, struggling against social prejudices and his own gang's lawlessness to find love and a normal life. The classic tribute to 1950s rebelliousness. Based vaguely on a real incident in California. Quaint after nearly 40 years, but still the touchstone for much that has come since, and still a central role in Brando's now-long career. Brando himself believes it failed to explore Motivations for youth gangs and violence, only depicting them. Banked in Britain until 1967. 1954 79m/B Marlon Brando, Lee Marvin, Mary Murphy, Robert Keith, Jerry Paris, Alvy Moore, Jay C. Flippen; **D:** Laslo Benedek. VHS, Beta $19.95 COL 🎞🎞🎞½

Wild Ones on Wheels A gang of teenage hot-rod punks meet an ex-con in the Mojave desert who is searching for the half-a-million bucks he buried three years earlier. Before they find out where the money is, they kill him. In an attempt to find the stash, they kidnap the dead con's wife, hoping she'll sing like a bird. Plenty of unintended laughter. **AKA:** Drivers to Hell. 1962 92m/B Francine York, Edmund Tontini, Robert Blair; **D:** Rudolph Cusumano. VHS, Beta $16.95 SNC Woof!

Wild Orchid One of the most controversial theatrical releases of 1990. Rourke is a mystery millionaire involved with two beautiful women in lovely Rio de Janeiro. Bisset is strange as an international real estate developer with unusual sexual mores. Very explicit sex scenes, but otherwise mostly boring and unbelievable. Rourke allegedly took his method-acting technique to the limit in the last love scene with Otis. Available in an unrated version as well. From the producers of "9 1/2 Weeks." Followed by an unrelated sequel. 1990 (R) 107m/C Mickey Rourke, Jacqueline Bisset, Carre Otis, Assumpta Serna, Bruce Greenwood; **D:** Zalman King; **W:** Zalman King. VHS, Beta $19.95 COL, FCT 🎞

Wild Orchid 2: Two Shades of Blue Blue's jazz-musician, heroin-addict dad dies after a bad fix and she's sold into prostitution, until she runs away to find her true love and live a "normal" life. Effort from soft-core expert King has nothing to do with the first "Wild Orchid" (which was directed by Adrian Lyne) and is almost laughably bad. Siemaszko is whiny, the plot is unbelievable, and the dialogue is unintentionally funny. Yes, you get sex, lots of it, but rather than passionate, it merely looks staged. Also available in an unrated version at 111 minutes.

1992 (R) 105m/C Nina Siemaszko, Wendy Hughes, Brent Fraser, Robert Davi, Tom Skerritt, Joe Dallesandro, Christopher McDonald, Liane Curtis; *D:* Zalman King; *W:* Zalman King. **VHS** $19.95 *COL Woof!*

Wild Orchids A husband suspects his wife of infidelity while they take a business cruise to Java. One of Garbo's earliest silent films. Garbo is lushly surrounded with great scenery, costumes and sets, making the best of her as she makes the best of a cheery tale.
1928 119m/B Greta Garbo, Lewis Stone, Nils Asther; *D:* Sidney Franklin. **VHS, Beta** $29.99 *MGM, FCT* 𝄢𝄢½

The Wild Pair Two cops track down a cocaine smuggling ring and uncover a private army planning to conquer the United States. Lloyd Bridges is memorable as a rabid right-winger, and the wild pairing of Bubba and Beau inspires head-scratching. Otherwise, what we have here is a typical action pic, complete with car chases. Beau Bridges' inauspicious feature directing debut. *AKA:* Hollow Point; Devil's Odds.
1987 (R) 89m/C Beau Bridges, Bubba Smith, Lloyd Bridges, Gary Lockwood, Raymond St. Jacques; *D:* Beau Bridges; *M:* John Debney. **VHS, Beta** $19.95 *MED, VTR* 𝄢½

Wild Palms In 2007 Los Angeles, Harry (Belushi) takes a job at a TV station that offers virtual reality programming to viewers, only this isn't benign technology. Delany is stuck in a thankless role as his wife, Cattrall is his former lover, but Dickinson has the most fun as Harry's power-mad mother-in-law who's also a sadistic co-conspirator of a nasty senator (Loggia). Lesson in weird style over substance really doesn't make much sense, but unlike "Twin Peaks" (to which this TV miniseries was heavily compared) it at least has an ending. Executive producer Stone has a cameo which concerns the JFK conspiracy. Based on the comic strip by Wagner. In two parts.
1993 300m/C James Belushi, Robert Loggia, Dana Delany, Kim Cattrall, Angie Dickinson, Ernie Hudson, Bebe Neuwirth, Nick Mancuso, Charles Hallahan, Robert Morse, David Warner, Ben Savage, Bob Gunton, Brad Dourif, Charles Rocket; *Cameos:* Oliver Stone; *D:* Phil Joanou, Kathryn Bigelow, Keith Gordon, Pete Hewitt; *W:* Bruce Wagner; *M:* Ryuichi Sakamoto. **VHS** $99.98 *ABC, FCT* 𝄢𝄢½

Wild Party It's 1929, a year of much frivolity in Hollywood. Drinking, dancing, maneuvering and almost every sort of romance are the rule of the night at silent film comic Jolly Grimm's sumptuous, star-studded party that climaxes with, among other things, a murder. Well performed but somehow hollow; ambitious Ivory effort unfortunately falls short. Based on Joseph Moncure March's poem, and loosely on the Fatty Arbuckle scandal.
1974 (R) 90m/C Raquel Welch, James Coco, Perry King, David Dukes, Royal Dano, Tiffany Bolling; *D:* James Ivory. **VHS, Beta** $9.98 *SUE* 𝄢𝄢½

Wild Pony A young boy spurns his new stepfather, preferring to live with his pony instead. Reversal of the evil-stepmother-and-girl-loves-horse theme.
1983 87m/C Marilyn Lightstone, Art Hindle, Josh Byrne; *D:* Kevin Sullivan; *M:* Hagood Hardy. **VHS, Beta** $14.98 *FHE, VES, LIV* 𝄢

Wild Rapture The hunting and dissecting of an elephant and gorilla, a look at a tribe that practices lip-splitting, and other gruesome events abound in this shock-fest. Banned for 18 years.
1950 68m/B **VHS, Beta** $24.95 *NOS, HEG* 𝄢

Wild Rebels A two-faced member of a ruthless motorcycle gang informs the police of the gang's plans to rob a bank. Lots of bullet-flying action. Dumb, ordinary biker flick; star Pastrano was a former boxing champ in real life.
1971 (R) 90m/C Steve Alaimo, Willie Pastrano, John Vella, Bobbie Byers; *D:* William Grefe. **VHS, Beta** $59.95 *ACA* 𝄢

The Wild Ride Nicholson, in an early starring role, portrays a rebellious punk of the Beat generation who hotrods his way into trouble and tragedy. He kidnaps now-straight ex-buddy Bean's squeeze (Carter); kills a few cops; then is killed. Interesting only if you're interested in Nicholson.
1960 59m/B Jack Nicholson, Georgianna Carter, Robert Bean; *D:* Harvey Berman. **VHS, Beta** $16.95 *SNC, NOS, VYY* 𝄢𝄢

Wild Ride Ruthless bandits on horseback rape and pillage their way through a series of pioneer towns.
19?? 86m/C **VHS** *NO* 𝄢𝄢

Wild Riders Two ruthless, amoral bikers molest, kidnap, rape, and beat two beautiful, naive young society ladies. Despicable story, with deplorable acting, but the ending, in which a husband slays a biker with a cello, surely is unique. *AKA:* Angels for Kicks.
1971 (R) 91m/C Alex Rocco, Elizabeth Knowles, Sherry Bain, Arell Blanton; *D:* Richard Kanter. **VHS, Beta** $19.95 *ACA Woof!*

Wild Rovers An aging cowboy and his younger colleague turn to bank robbing and are pursued by a posse in a wacky comedy-adventure from director Edwards. Uneven script and too much referential baggage (faint shades of "Butch Cassidy") doom this valiant effort, with the two stars hanging right in there all the way.
1971 (PG) 138m/C William Holden, Ryan O'Neal, Karl Malden, Lynn Carlin, Tom Skerritt, Joe Don Baker, Rachel Roberts, Moses Gunn; *D:* Blake Edwards; *W:* Blake Edwards; *M:* Jerry Goldsmith. **VHS, Beta** $19.98 *MGM* 𝄢𝄢

Wild Strawberries Bergman's landmark film of fantasy, dreams and nightmares. An aging professor, on the road to accept an award, must come to terms with his anxieties and guilt. Brilliant performance by Sjostrom, Sweden's first film director and star. Excellent use of flashbacks and film editing. An intellectual and emotional masterpiece. In Swedish with English subtitles. *AKA:* Smultron-Stallet.
1957 90m/B Victor Sjostrom, Bibi Andersson, Max von Sydow, Ingrid Thulin, Gunnar Bjornstrand, Folke Sundquist, Bjorn Bjelvenstam; *D:* Ingmar Bergman; *W:* Ingmar Bergman. Academy Awards '59 Nominations: Best Story & Screenplay; Golden Globe Awards '60: Best Foreign Film; National Board of Review Awards '59: 5 Best Foreign Films of the Year. **VHS, Beta, 8mm** $24.95 *VYY, HMV, FOX* 𝄢𝄢𝄢𝄢

Wild Style Zoro, a mild-mannered Bronx teenager, spends his evenings spray-painting subway cars. Intended as a depiction of urban street life, including graffiti, breakdancing and rap music. Mildly interesting social comment, but uncommincing as cinema. Too "realistic," with too little vision.
1983 82m/C Lee George Quinones, Fredrick Braithwaite, Dondi White; *D:* Charlie Ahearn. **VHS, Beta** $49.95 *FCT* 𝄢𝄢

Wild Thing A modern variation on the Wild Child/Tarzan myth, as a feral kid stalks a crime-ridden ghetto. Sayles, a usually imaginative writer and director, really takes a dive here. And of course, the Troggs' overplayed title hit is abused as the theme.

1987 (PG-13) 92m/C Kathleen Quinlan, Rob Knepper, Robert Davi, Betty Buckley, Maury Chaykin; *D:* Max Reid, Ken Cameron; *W:* John Sayles; *M:* George S. Clinton. **VHS, Beta** *NO* 𝄢½

Wild Times Too long but pleasant rendition of the life of High Candill, early Wild West showman. Based on the novel by Brian Garfield. Made for TV, originally in two parts.
1979 200m/C Sam Elliott, Trish Stewart, Ben Johnson, Dennis Hopper, Pat Hingle; *D:* Richard Compton. **VHS, Beta** $69.95 *PSM* 𝄢𝄢

Wild Weed Funny smelling cigarettes ruin the lives of all who inhale. Viewers' advice: just say no. Leed's actual drug bust with Robert Mitchum got her the lead. *AKA:* The Devil's Weed; She Shoulda Said No; Marijuana the Devil's Weed.
1949 70m/B Lila Leeds, Alan Baxter, Lyle Talbot, Jack Elam, David Gorcey; *D:* Sam Newfield. **VHS** $16.95 *SNC, AOV, TPV* 𝄢

Wild West The hero and loyal companions (with names like Skinny, Stormy and Soapy) tackle desperadoes trying to stop telegraph line construction. More mild than wild, it was later trimmed and released under its alternate title, but here you're getting the original. *AKA:* Prairie Outlaws.
1946 73m/C Eddie Dean, Roscoe Ates, Lash LaRue, Robert "Buzzy" Henry, Sarah Padden, Louise Currie, Warner Richmond, Chief Yowlachie, Bud Osborne; *D:* Robert Tansey. **VHS** $19.95 *NOS, HEG* 𝄢

Wild West A compilation of scenes from dozens of western films.
1987 90m/C John Wayne, Clint Eastwood, Steve McQueen, Charles Bronson. **VHS, Beta** *NO* 𝄢

Wild Wheels A group of dune-buggy enthusiasts seek revenge against a gang of motorcyclists who have ravaged a small California beach town.
1975 (PG) 81m/C Casey Kasem, Dovie Beams, Terry Stafford, Robert Dix. **VHS, Beta** $59.95 *GEM Woof!*

Wild, Wild Planet Alien beings from a distant planet are miniaturizing Earth's leaders in a bid to destroy our planet, and a dubbed, wooden hero comes to the rescue. A rarely seen Italian SF entry, great fun for genre fans. A must for "robot girls in skin tight leather outfits" completists.
1965 93m/C Tony Russell, Lisa Gastoni, Massimo Serato, Franco Nero; *D:* Anthony M. (Antonio Marghereti) Dawson. **VHS** $20.00 *SMW* 𝄢½

Wild, Wild West Revisited A feature-length reprise of the tongue-in-cheek western series. Irreverent and fun, in the spirit of its admirable predecessor-though it's probably just as well the proposed new series didn't see fruition. Made for television.
1979 95m/C Robert Conrad, Ross Martin, Harry Morgan, Rene Auberjonois; *D:* Burt Kennedy. **VHS, Beta** $59.98 *FOX* 𝄢𝄢

Wild, Wild World of Jayne Mansfield The life and times of Mansfield are explored in this unique documentary, which was unfinished at the time of her death. Jayne takes the viewer on a worldwide examination of sexual mores, from prostitution, nudist colonies, and the racy strip clubs of Europe, to the transvestite and topless bars of America. Perverse (but did you expect otherwise?), footage of her fatal car crash was included.
1968 89m/C Jayne Mansfield. **VHS, Beta** $19.99 *VDM, DVT, TPV* 𝄢½

Wild Women Extremely hilarious schlocker about a safari of white men captured by a savage tribe of jungle women. Total camp.

W

1953 ?m/C Lewis Wilson, Frances Dubay, Dana Wilson. **VHS** $16.95 *SNC, HEG* 🐾

Wild Women Five female convicts are released during the Texas/Mexico dispute to help smuggle arms to American forces. Innocuous western, original in a made-for-TV kind of way.
1970 90m/C Hugh O'Brian, Anne Francis, Marilyn Maxwell, Marie Windsor; *D:* Don Taylor. **VHS, Beta** $19.98 *FOX* 🐾½

Wild Women of Wongo The denizens of a primitive isle, essentially beautiful women and ugly men, meet the natives of a neighboring island, handsome men and ugly women. Not quite bad enough to be true camp fun, but stupidly silly in a low-budget way.
1959 73m/C Pat Crowley, Ed Fury, Adrienne Bourbeau, Jean Hawkshaw, Johnny Walsh; *D:* James L. Wolcott. **VHS, Beta** $19.98 *DVT, MED, HEG* 🐾½

The Wild World of Batwoman A campy cult film in which Batwoman and a bevy of Bat Girls are pitted against an evil doctor in order to find the prototype of an atomic hearing aid/nuclear bomb. Also released theatrically as "She Was a Hippy Vampire."
1966 70m/C Katherine Victor, George Andre, Steve Brodie, Lloyd Nelson; *D:* Jerry Warren. **VHS, Beta** $9.95 *RHI, SNC, DVT* 🐾

Wild Zone An American ex-soldier combats mercenaries in Africa in order to rescue his kidnapped father.
1989 (R) 100m/C Edward Albert, Philip Brown, Carla Herd; *D:* Percival Rubens. **VHS, Beta** $79.95 *COL* 🐾

Wildcard When a veteran pilot is killed in a helicopter crash, a friend suspects foul play. He calls in Preacher, a special forces veteran, to investigate and what he discovers is murder, greed, and corruption.
1992 (PG-13) 86m/C Powers Boothe, Cindy Pickett, Rene Auberjonois, Terry O'Quinn, M. Emmet Walsh, John Lacy; *D:* Mel Damski; *W:* Scobie Richardson. **VHS** *MCA* 🐾½

Wildcat Crabbe, famous as the serials' Flash Gordon, is a villain in this petrochemical adventure. The hero overextends his credit when he buys an oil well and must produce a gusher or else.
1942 73m/B Richard Arlen, Arline Judge, Buster Crabbe, William Frawley, Arthur Hunnicutt, Elisha Cook Jr., Billy Benedict; *D:* Frank McDonald. **VHS** $19.95 *NOS* 🐾🐾

Wildcats A naive female phys-ed teacher (Hawn) is saddled with the job of coach for a completely undisciplined, inner city, high school football team. Formulaic, connect-the-dots comedy; moderately funny, and of course Hawn triumphs in adversity, but at nearly two hours a very long sitcom episode.
1986 (R) 106m/C Goldie Hawn, James Keach, Swoosie Kurtz, Bruce McGill, M. Emmet Walsh, Woody Harrelson, Wesley Snipes, Tab Thacker; *D:* Michael Ritchie; *M:* James Newton Howard. **VHS, Beta** $19.98 *WAR* 🐾🐾

Wilder Napalm Lame comedy about two at-odds brothers, the woman they both love, and their dangerous pyrokinetic abilities. Wilder (Howard) and Wallace (Quaid) Foudroyant have been feuding for years—and not just over the fact that Wallace is in love with Wilder's wife Vida (Winger). Wallace wants to use their family "gift" to become rich and famous but Wilder doesn't want them to exploit their fiery powers. They finally decide on an incendiary showdown to settle the score once and for all. Good actors lost in witless characters and a incoherent plot.

1993 (PG-13) 109m/C Dennis Quaid, Arliss Howard, Debra Winger, M. Emmet Walsh, Jim Varney, Mimi Lieber, Marvin J. McIntyre; *D:* Glenn Gordon Caron; *W:* Vince Gilligan; *M:* Michael Kamen. **VHS** *COL* 🐾½

Wildest Dreams Released from its bottle by a lovely nebbish, a genie puts a love spell on one beautiful girl after another in order to find him the right one, resulting in a bevy of women clamoring for our hero's attention. *AKA:* Bikini Genie.
1990 (R) 84m/C James Davies, Heidi Paine, Deborah Blaisdell, Ruth Collins, Jane Hamilton, Jill Johnson; *D:* Chuck Vincent. **VHS, Beta** $79.98 *LIV, VES* 🐾½

The Wildest Office Party A sex-filled tape for and about wild, rowdy office parties.
1987 60m/C **VHS, Beta** $59.98 *LIV, VES* Woof!

Wildfire Two horse traders come to the aid of ranchers beset by horse thieves. Early color outing for Steele. Harmless, ordinary oater.
1945 60m/C Bob Steele, Sterling Holloway; *D:* Robert Tansey. **VHS, Beta** $19.95 *NOS, VDM, HEG* 🐾½

Wildfire As teenagers, Frank and Kay run away to get married but Frank is sent to prison for robbing a bank and Kay winds up making a new life for herself. Released from prison after eight years, Frank discovers Kay is married with two children and doesn't want anything further to do with him. But when Frank violates his parole, Kay discovers she can't leave him again and the two go on the run together.
1988 (PG) 98m/C Steven Bauer, Linda Fiorentino, Will Patton, Marshall Bell; *D:* Zalman King; *W:* Zalman King; *M:* Maurice Jarre. **VHS** *MCA* 🐾🐾

Wildflower Set in the Depression-era South, Alice is a 17 year-old partially deaf girl who also suffers from epilepsy. Her stepfather believes she's possessed and confines her to a shed. Growing up ignorant and abused Alice is befriended by a neighboring brother and sister who decide to rescue her. A three-hankie family picture with moving performances and inspirational themes. Based on the novel "Alice" by Sara Flanigan. Made for television.
1991 94m/C Patricia Arquette, Beau Bridges, Susan Blakely, William McNamara, Reese Witherspoon, Collin Wilcox Paxton; *D:* Diane Keaton. **VHS** $89.98 *WOV* 🐾🐾½

Wilding A pair of cops are on the trail of a gang of kids who go "wilding," which involves sprees of killing, raping and looting. Exploitive fare based on horrible, recent events in New York. The filmmakers skirt controversy by making the criminals rich suburban kids.
1990 92m/C Wings Hauser, Joey Travolta, Karen Russell, Steven Cooke; *D:* Eric Louzil. **VHS, Beta** $14.95 *AIP* 🐾½

Wildrose Eichhorn is memorable as a recent divorcee who must assert herself among her otherwise all-male co-workers at a Minnesota strip mine. She finds a new love, and tries to put her life back together. Filmed on location.
1985 96m/C Lisa Eichhorn, Tom Bower, James Cada; *D:* John Hanson; *W:* John Hanson, Eugene Corr. **VHS, Beta** $69.98 *LIV* 🐾🐾🐾

Will: G. Gordon Liddy The life of the Watergate conspirator, based on his autobiography. Made for TV. Producer/star Conrad reportedly objected strongly to cuts from the original three-hour length, apparently with cause: the first half is superficial pap. The

portrayal of Liddy's time in prison, though, is fascinating, and Conrad is excellent.
1982 100m/C Robert Conrad, Kathy Cannon, Gary Bayer, Peter Ratray, James Rebhorn, Red West, Maurice Woods, Danny Lloyd; *D:* Robert Lieberman. **VHS** $39.95 *LIV* 🐾🐾

Will Penny Just back from a cattle drive, a range-wandering loner looks for work in the wrong place and offends a family of outlaws who come after him. His escape from them leads to another kind of trap—one set by a love-hungry woman (Hackett, in a strong performance). Heston considers this film his personal best, and he's probably right. Superbly directed western, with excellent cinematography and professional, realistic portrayals, flopped in theaters, moviegoers preferring simultaneous Heston outing "Planet of the Apes." Photography by Lucien Ballard.
1967 109m/C Charlton Heston, Joan Hackett, Donald Pleasence, Lee Majors, Bruce Dern, Anthony Zerbe, Ben Johnson, Clifton James; *D:* Tom Gries; *M:* Elmer Bernstein. **VHS, Beta** $14.95 *PAR* 🐾🐾🐾½

Willa Raffin, a hash-joint waitress with two kids and one in the pipeline, is deserted by her husband and determines to get ahead by becoming a trucker. Okay made-for-TV drama.
1979 95m/C Cloris Leachman, Deborah Raffin, Clu Gulager, John Amos, Diane Ladd; *D:* Claudio Guzman, Joan Darling; *M:* John Barry. **VHS, Beta** $39.95 *PSM* 🐾🐾

Willard Willard is a lonely, psychotic youngster who trains a group of rats, his only friends, to attack his enemies. Not as disgusting as it might have been (rated PG), but pretty weird and not redeemed by any sense of style or humor. Popular at the box office; followed by inferior "Ben." Based on Stephen Gilbert's novel "Ratman's Notebooks."
1971 (PG) 95m/C Bruce Davison, Ernest Borgnine, Elsa Lanchester, Sondra Locke; *D:* Daniel Mann. **VHS, Beta** $59.95 *PSM, PAR* 🐾🐾

Willie & Phil At the start of the '70s, two buddies (Ontkean and Sharkey) fall for the same girl (Kidder). They become a threesome and are entangled in each other's lives for the rest of the decade. Insightful comedy-drama.
1980 (R) 111m/C Michael Ontkean, Margot Kidder, Ray Sharkey, Jan Miner, Julie Bovasso, Natalie Wood, Laurence "Larry" Fishburne, Louis Guss, Kaki Hunter, Kristine DeBell; *D:* Paul Mazursky; *W:* Paul Mazursky; *M:* Claude Bolling. **VHS** $59.98 *FXV* 🐾🐾½

The Willies Three youngsters gross each other out with juvenile tales of horror and scariness while camping out in the backyard. Pointless but not without a few yuks (in both senses of the term).
1990 (PG-13) 120m/C James Karen, Sean Astin, Kathleen Freeman, Jeremy Miller; *D:* Brian Peck. **VHS** $19.95 *PSM* 🐾🐾

Willow Blockbuster fantasy epic combines the story of Moses with "Snow White," dwarves and all. Willow is the little Nelwyn who finds the lost baby Daikini and is assigned the task of returning her safely to her people. Willow discovers that the girl is actually a sacred infant who is destined to overthrow the evil queen Bavmorda and rule the land. As you might expect from executive producer George Lucas, there is much action and plenty of clever, high-quality special effects. But the "Star Wars"-esque story (by Lucas) is strangely predictable, and a bit too action-packed. Not really for children.

1988 (PG) 118m/C Warwick Davis, Val Kilmer, Jean Marsh, Joanne Whalley-Kilmer, Billy Barty, Pat Roach, Ruth Greenfield, Patricia Hayes, Gavan O'Herlihy, Kevin Pollak; *D:* Ron Howard; *W:* Bob Dolman; *M:* James Horner. **VHS, Beta, 8mm $14.95** COL ♫♫½

Willy Wonka & the Chocolate Factory When the last of five coveted "golden tickets" falls into the hands of sweet but very poor Charlie, he and his Grandpa Joe get a tour of the most wonderfully strange chocolate factory in the world. The owner is the most curious hermit ever to hit the big screen. He leads the five young "winners" on a thrilling and often dangerous tour of his fabulous factory. Adapted from Roald Dahl's "Charlie and the Chocolate Factory." Without a doubt one of the best "kid's" movies ever made; a family classic worth watching again and again. ♫Willy Wonka, the Candy Man; Cheer Up, Charlie; I've Got a Golden Ticket; Oompa-Loompa-Doompa-Dee-Doo; Pure Imagination. **1971** (G) 100m/C Gene Wilder, Jack Albertson, Denise Nickerson, Peter Ostrum, Roy Kinnear, Aubrey Woods, Michael Bollner, Ursula Reit, Leonard Stone, Dodo Denney; *D:* Mel Stuart; *M:* Leslie Bricusse. **VHS, Beta $14.95** WAR, APD, HMV ♫♫♫½

Wilma Based on the true story of Wilma Rudolph, a young black woman who overcame childhood illness to win three gold medals at the 1960 Olympics. Plodding made-for-TV biography suffers from sub-par script and acting. **1977** 100m/C Joe Seneca, Cicely Tyson, Shirley Jo Finney; *D:* Bud Greenspan. **VHS, Beta $14.95** COL, FCT ♫♫

Wilson Biography of Woodrow Wilson from his days as the head of Princeton University, to the governorship of New York, and as U.S. President during WWI. After the war, Wilson conceives of the League of Nations but is unable to sell it to a U.S. public bent on isolationism. This lavish film won critical plaudits but was a major money-loser. **1944** 154m/C Alexander Knox, Charles Coburn, Geraldine Fitzgerald, Thomas Mitchell, Ruth Nelson, Cedric Hardwicke, Vincent Price, William Eythe, Sidney Blackmer, Stanley Ridges, Eddie Foy Jr., Charles Halton; *D:* Henry King; *W:* Lamar Trotti; *M:* Alfred Newman. Academy Awards '44: Best Color Cinematography, Best Film Editing, Best Interior Decoration, Best Original Screenplay, Best Sound; Nominations: Best Actor (Knox), Best Director (King), Best Picture, Best Original Score; Golden Globe Awards '45: Best Actor—Drama (Knox). **VHS $19.99** FXV, MOV, BTV ♫♫♫

Wimps A collegiate wimp is subjected to a brutal fraternity initiation, but eventually gets the girl. Cheap ripoff of Cyrano de Bergerac, turned into a teen sex flick. **1987** (R) 94m/C Louie Bonanno, Jim Abele, Deborah Blaisdell; *D:* Chuck Vincent. **VHS, Beta $79.98** LIV ♫

Win, Place, or Steal Lame comedy set at the racetrack about three grown men and their adolescent schemes to win big. Better you should scratch. *AKA:* The Big Payoff; Three For the Money; Just Another Day at the Races. **1972** (PG) 88m/C McLean Stevenson, Alex Karras, Dean Stockwell; *D:* Richard Bailey. **VHS, Beta $69.98** LIV, VES ♫½

Winchester '73 Superb acting and photography characterize this classic, landmark western. Simple plot—cowboy Stewart pursues his stolen state-of-the-art rifle as it changes hands—speeds along and carries the viewer with it, ending with an engrossing and unforgettable shoot-out. Almost single-handedly breathed new life into the whole

genre. Laser videodisc version contains a special narration track provided by Stewart. Mann's and Stewart's first teaming. **1950** 82m/C James Stewart, Shelley Winters, Stephen McNally, Dan Duryea, Millard Mitchell, John McIntire, Will Geer, Jay C. Flippen, Rock Hudson, Tony Curtis, Charles Drake; *D:* Anthony Mann. **VHS, Beta $19.95** MCA ♫♫♫½

The Wind One of the last great silents still stands as a magnificent entertainment. Gish, in possibly her best role, is an innocent Easterner who finds herself married to a rough cowpoke and raped by a married man in a bleak frontier town. Director Sjostrom has a splendid feel for landscape, and the drama—climaxing with a tumultuous desert storm—is intense yet fully believable. Based on the novel by Dorothy Scarborough. **1928** 74m/B Lillian Gish, Lars Hanson, Montagu Love, Dorothy Cumming, Edward Earle, William Orlamond; *D:* Victor Sjostrom; *W:* Francis Marion. **VHS, Beta $29.95** MGM ♫♫♫♫

The Wind Foster is terrorized by Hauser while attempting to write her next thriller in Greece. Let's hope her book is more exciting than this movie. Shot on location in Greece. **1987** 92m/C Meg Foster, Wings Hauser, Steve Railsback, David McCallum, Robert Morley; *D:* Nico Mastorakis. **VHS, Beta $79.98** LIV ♫

Wind Sailor Will Parker (Modine) chooses the opportunity to be on the America's Cup team over girlfriend Grey and, then has the dubious honor of making a technical error that causes their loss. Undaunted, he locates Grey and her new engineer boyfriend (Skarsgard) and convinces them to design the ultimate boat for the next set of races. ESPN carried extensive coverage of the America's Cup races for the first time in the summer of '92 and viewers discovered that a little goes a long way. The same holds true for "Wind" which has stunning race footage, but little else. The script lacks substance and was written as filming progressed, and it shows. **1992** (PG-13) 123m/C Matthew Modine, Jennifer Grey, Cliff Robertson, Jack Thompson, Stellan Skarsgard, Rebecca Miller, Ned Vaughn; *D:* Carroll Ballard; *W:* Rudy Wurlitzer, Mac Gudgeon; *M:* Basil Poledouris. **VHS, 8mm** COL ♫♫½

The Wind and the Lion In turn-of-the-century Morocco, a sheik (Connery) kidnaps a feisty American woman (Bergen) and her children and holds her as a political hostage. President Teddy Roosevelt (Keith) sends in the Marines to free the captives, who are eventually released by their captor. Directed with venue and style by Milius. Highly entertaining, if heavily fictionalized. Based very loosely on a historical incident. **1975** (PG) 120m/C Sean Connery, Candice Bergen, Brian Keith, John Huston, Geoffrey Lewis; *D:* John Milius; *W:* John Milius; *M:* Jerry Goldsmith. **VHS, Beta $59.95** MGM ♫♫♫

A Wind Named Amnesia A strange amnesia wind sweeps away all of mankind's knowledge and human civilization vanishes. Then a mysterious young man is miraculously re-educated and searches for those who destroyed man's memories. In Japanese with English subtitles. **1993** 80m/C **VHS $29.95** CPM ♫♫♫

The Wind That Walks Two girls trek into the New Jersey wilds after an unknown animal called by the Indians "the wind that walks." **1985** 30m/C Beta NJN ♫♫♫

Windjammer Western star O'Brien took a break from the lone prairie to make this seafaring rescue drama. He is a deputy state's attorney who signs up for a yacht

race in order to serve a subpoena. Bad guys arrive on the scene, and the initially moody yacht denizens rely on our trusty hero to save them. Decent adventure. **1931** 75m/B George O'Brien, Constance Worth; *D:* Ewing Scott. **VHS $24.95** NOS, DVT, HEG ♫♫

Windmills of the Gods Glamor, romance, intrigue, and politics all mixed together in eastern Europe. Smith is named ambassador to Romania, finds the suave Wagner in residence, and becomes the target of assassins. Based on the novel by Sidney Sheldon. Made for television. *AKA:* Sidney Sheldon's Windmills of the Gods. **1988** 95m/C Jaclyn Smith, Robert Wagner, Franco Nero, Christopher Cazenove, David Ackroyd, Jean-Pierre Aumont, Ruby Dee, Jeffrey DeMunn, Michael Moriarty, Ian McKellan, Susan Tyrrell; *D:* Lee Philips; *W:* John Gay. **VHS $79.98** LIV ♫♫½

Windom's Way Finch, in a strong role in this intriguing political drama, is an idealistic doctor in a remote village in Malaysia. He juggles a failing marriage and a budding romance, then finds himself caught in a local labor dispute. He works for a peaceful solution, but is captured by an insurgent army. Disillusioned, he plans to leave the country, but his wife persuades him to stay and tend the wounded. Based on a novel by James Ramsey Ullman. **1957** 90m/B Peter Finch, Mary Ure; *D:* Ronald Neame. **VHS, Beta NO** ♫♫♫

The Window A little boy (Disney star Driscoll, intriguingly cast by director, Tetzlaff) has a reputation for telling lies, so no one believes him when he says he witnessed a murder...except the killers. Almost unbearably tense, claustrophobic thriller about the helplessness of childhood. Tetzlaff clearly learned more than a thing or two from the master, Hitchcock, for whom he photographed "Notorious." Based on "The Boy Who Cried Murder" by Cornell Woolrich, on whose writing "Rear Window" was also based. Driscoll was awarded a special miniature Oscar as Outstanding Juvenile for his performance. **1949** 73m/B Bobby Driscoll, Barbara Hale, Arthur Kennedy, Ruth Roman; *D:* Ted Tetzlaff. Academy Awards '49 Nominations: Best Film Editing; Edgar Allan Poe Awards '49: Best Screenplay. **VHS, Beta $19.95** MED ♫♫♫½

Window Shopping Multiple, confusing romances occur at the "Toison d' Or" shopping mall in Paris. A modern, French homage to the classic Hollywood musical. In French with English subtitles. **1986** 96m/C Delphine Seyrig, Charles Denner, Fanny Cottencon, Miriam Boyer, Lio, Pascale Salkin, Jean-Francois Balmer; *D:* Chantal Akerman; *W:* Chantal Akerman. **VHS $29.95** WAC, FCT, ING ♫♫½

Windows A lonely lesbian (Ashley) becomes obsessed with her quiet neighbor (Shire) and concocts a plot to get close to her. Director Willis is known for his unbeatable cinematography, most notably for Woody Allen in "Manhattan." His debut in the chair is a miserable, offensive flop. **1980** (R) 93m/C Talia Shire, Joe Cortese, Elizabeth Ashley, Kay Medford, Linda Gillin; *D:* Gordon Willis; *M:* Ennio Morricone. **VHS NO** ♫

Windrider Simple love story made in Australia. A wind surfer and a rock star become lovers. Self-indulgent overwrought garbage with rare moments of promise. **1986** 83m/C Tom Burlinson, Nicole Kidman, Charles Tingwell, Jill Perryman, Simon Chilvers; *D:* Vincent Monton. **VHS $79.95** MGM ♫½

The Winds of Jarrah English woman runs from broken heart to Australia to become nanny for misogynist, and Harlequin code prevails. Based on a Harlequin romance novel.
1983 78m/C Terence Donovan, Susan Lyons; **D:** Mark Egerton. **VHS, Beta** NO ⅂⅂½

The Winds of Kitty Hawk Visually interesting but talky account of the Wright brothers attempt to beat their rival Glenn Curtiss and his backer, phone man Alexander Graham Bell. Rule of thumb: Fast-forward through the parts when they are on the ground, or see Stacy Keach's public-TV version instead.
1978 96m/C Michael Moriarty, David Huffman, Kathryn Walker, Eugene Roche, John Randolph, Scott Hylands; **D:** E.W. Swackhamer; **M:** Charles Bernstein. **VHS, Beta** $14.95 FRH ⅂⅂

Winds of the Wasteland Would-be Pony Express contractors, Wayne and Chandler, race rivals to land government work. Competent western that put Wayne on the Hollywood map.
1936 54m/B John Wayne, Phyllis Fraser, Lane Chandler, Yakima Canutt; **D:** Mack V. Wright. **VHS** $19.95 REP, NOS, VCN ⅂⅂½

The Winds of War On seven tapes, the excruciatingly long and dull television mini-series based on Herman Wouk's bestseller about WWII. The book was much better; Mitchum appears to be fighting sleep unsuccessfully for much of the show. Two follow-ups were produced: "War and Remembrance" and "War and Remembrance: The Final Chapter."
1983 900m/C Robert Mitchum, Ali MacGraw, Ralph Bellamy, Polly Bergen, Jan-Michael Vincent, David Dukes, John Houseman, Victoria Tennant, Peter Graves, Chaim Topol, Ben Murphy, Jeremy Kemp, Anton Diffring, Lawrence Pressman, Andrew Duggan, Barbara Steele; **D:** Dan Curtis. **VHS, Beta** $139.95 PAR, MOV ⅂⅂

Windwalker Howard, the only cast member who is not a Native American, is an aged chief who shares the memories of his life with his grandchildren. Filmed in the Crow and Cheyenne Indian languages and subtitled in English throughout. A beautifully photographed, intelligent independent project.
1981 108m/C Trevor Howard, James Remar, Dusty Iron Wing McCrea; **D:** Keith Merrill. **VHS, Beta** $59.98 FOX ⅂⅂⅂

Windy City A group of seven childhood friends must come to terms with the harsh realities of their failed ambitions when they meet for a weekend in Chicago. Told from the point of view of one of the group, recounting the sorts of memories we all prefer to forget. Typical and overwrought '80s yuppie reunion/regret drama. Aren't these people too young to be unhappy?
1984 (R) 103m/C John Shea, Kate Capshaw, Josh Mostel, Jeffrey DeMunn, Lewis J. Stadlen, James Sutorius; **D:** Armyan Bernstein; **M:** Jack Nitzsche. **VHS, Beta** $79.92 FOX ⅂⅂

A Wing and a Prayer Better-than-average WWII Air Force action flick. Battles rage throughout the Pacific theater and the men aboard the aircraft carrier struggle to do their part to save the world for freedom. Fine cast receives Hathaway's excellent unsentimental direction.
1944 97m/B Don Ameche, Dana Andrews, William Eythe, Charles Bickford, Cedric Hardwicke, Kevin O'Shea, Richard Jaeckel, Harry Morgan; **D:** Henry Hathaway. **VHS** $14.98 FXV ⅂⅂⅂

Wings The silent classic about friends, Rogers and Arlen, their adventures in the Air Corps during WWI, and their rivalry for the hand of a woman. Contains actual footage of combat flying from the Great War. Won the very first Best Picture Oscar. Too-thin plot hangs on (barely) to the stirring, intrepid dogfight scenes.
1927 139m/B Clara Bow, Charles "Buddy" Rogers, Richard Arlen, Gary Cooper; **D:** William A. Wellman. **VHS, Beta** $14.95 BTV, PAR ⅂⅂½

Wings of Danger A pilot tries to save his friend from blackmailing gold smugglers.
AKA: Dead on Course.
1952 72m/B Zachary Scott, Kay Kendall, Robert Beatty, Naomi Chance; **M:** Malcolm Arnold. **VHS, Beta** MLB, RXM ⅂

Wings of Desire An ethereal, haunting modern fable about one of many angels observing human life in and above the broken existence of Berlin, and how he begins to long to experience life as humans do. A moving, unequivocable masterpiece, with as many beautiful things to say about spiritual need as about the schizophrenic emptiness of contemporary Germany; Wenders' magnum opus. In German with English subtitles, and with black-and-white sequences. Magnificent cinematography by Henri Alekan.
AKA: Der Himmel Uber Berlin.
1988 (PG-13) 130m/C Bruno Ganz, Peter Falk, Solveig Dommartin, Otto Sander, Curt Bois; **D:** Wim Wenders; **W:** Wim Wenders, Peter Handke. **VHS, Beta** $19.98 ORI, GLV, ING ⅂⅂⅂½

Wings of Eagles Hollywood biography of Frank 'Spig' Wead, a famous WWI aviation pioneer turned screenwriter. Veers wildly from comedy to stolid drama, though Bond's lampoon of Ford as "John Dodge" is justly famous.
1957 110m/C John Wayne, Ward Bond, Maureen O'Hara, Dan Dailey, Edmund Lowe, Ken Curtis, Kenneth Tobey, Sig Rumann, Veda Ann Borg; **D:** John Ford. **VHS, Beta** $19.98 MGM ⅂⅂½

Wings of Fame Comic afterlife fantasy skewering celebrity status. Recently departed celebs check into a posh hotel, but as their fame on earth declines so do their afterlife accomodations, until they reach the state of oblivion. The latest hotel arrivals are a renowned, arrogant actor (O'Toole) and the frustrated writer (Firth) whose claim to fame has come from murdering him.
1993 (R) 109m/C Peter O'Toole, Peter Firth; **D:** Otakar Votocek; **W:** Herman Koch, Otakar Votocek. **VHS, Beta** PAR ⅂⅂½

Wings Over the Pacific Love and his daughter Cooper are living quietly on a Pacific island when a pair of pilots, American Norris and the Nazi Guttman, crash-land after a dogfight. The island is strategic because of its oil supply but Norris manages to prevent the Nazis from taking control and wins Cooper's love in the process. Veteran actor Love died shortly before the film's release.
1943 60m/B Montagu Love, Inez Cooper, Edward Norris, Henry Guttman; **D:** Phil Rosen; **W:** George Wallace Sayre. **VHS** $12.95 GPV ⅂½

A Winner Never Quits A true story based on the life of 1940s baseball player Pete Gray. As a boy Gray lost his right arm above the elbow in an accident. He's determined to prove himself as a baseball player and during WWII is given a tryout, although his teammates consider him a sideshow freak. A Memphis sportswriter takes an interest in Pete's career and Gray's success on the field leads to a career with the St. Louis Browns. Along the way he becomes the inspiration to a young fan, who's also lost an arm. Made for television.

1986 (PG) 96m/C Keith Carradine, Mare Winningham, Huckleberry Fox, Dennis Weaver, Dana Delany, G.W. Bailey, Charles Hallahan, Fionnula Flanagan, Jack Kehoe; **D:** Mel Damski; **W:** Burt Prelutsky. **VHS** $59.95 COL ⅂⅂½

Winner Takes All A young college student during the Vietnam War comes to grips with maturity and growing pains.
1986 (R) 94m/C Jason Connery, Diane Cilento. **VHS, Beta** $59.95 ACA ⅂⅂

Winners of the West A landowner schemes to prevent a railroad from running through his property. The railroad's chief engineer leads the good guys in an attempt to prevent sabotage. A fun serial in thirteen chapters, full of shooting, blown-up bridges, locomotives afire, etc.; and of course, the requisite damsel in distress.
1940 250m/B Anne Nagel, Dick Foran, James Craig, Harry Woods; **D:** Ray Taylor, Ford Beebe. **VHS** $24.95 GPV, VCN, NOS ⅂⅂½

Winners Take All A handful of friends compete in Supercross races. Spirited but thoroughly cliche sports flick.
1987 (PG-13) 103m/C Don Michael Paul, Kathleen York, Robert Krantz; **D:** Fritz Kiersch. **VHS, Beta** $19.98 SUE, NLC ⅂⅂

Winning A race car driver (Newman) will let nothing, including his new wife (Woodward), keep him from winning the Indianapolis 500. Newman does his own driving. Thomas' film debut.
1969 (PG) 123m/C Paul Newman, Joanne Woodward, Robert Wagner, Richard Thomas, Clu Gulager; **D:** James Goldstone; **M:** Dave Grusin. **VHS, Beta** $14.98 MCA ⅂⅂⅂

Winning of the West Yodelin' ranger Autry vows to protect a crusading publisher from unscrupulous crooks, including his own dog-gone brothers. The brothers see the lights, and the two corral the varmints. Autry tunes include "Cowboy Blues," "Cowpoke Poking Along," and "Find Me My 45."
1953 57m/B Gene Autry, Smiley Burnette, Gail Davis, Richard Crane; **D:** George Archainbaud. **VHS, Beta** $24.95 CCB ⅂⅂

The Winning Team Reagan stars in this biography of baseball legend Grover Cleveland Alexander and Day plays his dedicated wife. Some controversial issues were glossed over in the film, such as Alexander's real-life drinking problem and the fact that he had epilepsy. Although this was one of Reagan's favorite roles, he was upset by the studio's avoidance of all-too-human problems. Nonetheless, it's an entertaining enough movie about a very talented ballplayer.
1952 98m/B Doris Day, Ronald Reagan, Frank Lovejoy, Eve Miller, James Millican, Russ Tamblyn; **D:** Lewis Seiler. **VHS** $19.98 WAR ⅂⅂½

The Winslow Boy A cadet at the Royal Naval College is wrongly accused of theft and expelled. Donat as the boy's lawyer leads a splendid cast. Despite consequences for his family, the boy's father (Hardwicke) sues the government and fights his son's battle, as the case makes the papers and he approaches bankruptcy. Plot would seem far-fetched if it weren't based on fact. Absorbing. Based on a play by Rattigan, who co-wrote the script.
1948 112m/B Robert Donat, Cedric Hardwicke, Margaret Leighton, Frank Lawton, Kathleen Harrison, Basil Radford; **D:** Anthony Asquith; **W:** Terence Rattigan. **VHS, Beta** $59.95 HEG ⅂⅂⅂½

Winter Flight A small, gentle British drama about an RAF recruit and a barmaid who quickly become lovers, and then are confronted with her pregnancy.

1984 105m/C Reece Dinsdale, Nicola Cowper, Gary Olsen; D: Roy Battersby. VHS, Beta $59.95 MGM ♂♂

Winter Kills

Distinctive political black comedy suffers a hilariously paranoid version of American public life. Bridges, the younger brother of a U.S. president assassinated 15 years earlier, uncovers the plot. Huston is delightful as Bridges' horny old father. Uneven, but well worth seeing; flopped at the box office, but was re-released in 1983. Taylor was not billed.
1979 (R) 97m/C Jeff Bridges, John Huston, Anthony Perkins, Richard Boone, Sterling Hayden, Eli Wallach, Ralph Meeker, Belinda Bauer, Dorothy Malone, Toshiro Mifune, Elizabeth Taylor, Donald Moffatt, Tisa Farrow, Brad Dexter, Joe Spinell; D: William Richert; M: Maurice Jarre. VHS, Beta $14.95 COL, SUE ♂♂♂

The Winter Light

The second film in Bergman's famous trilogy on the silence of God, preceded by "Through a Glass Darkly" and followed by "The Silence." Bleak and disturbing view of a tortured priest who searches for the faith and guidance he is unable to give his congregation. Hard to swallow for neophyte Bergmanites, but challenging, deeply serious and rewarding for those accustomed to the Swede's angst. Polished and personal. In Swedish with English subtitles. AKA: Nattvardsgaesterna.
1962 80m/B Gunnar Bjornstrand, Ingrid Thulin, Max von Sydow; D: Ingmar Bergman; W: Ingmar Bergman. VHS, Beta $29.98 SUE, ING, NLC ♂♂♂½

Winter Meeting

Overwrought drama with Bette Davis starring as a spinster poetess who falls in love with a war hero who wants to be a priest. Very talky script, of interest only as the sole romantic lead for James Davis, whose claim to fame was westerns and the TV series "Dallas."
1948 104m/B Bette Davis, Janis Paige, James Davis, John Hoyt, Florence Bates, Walter Baldwin, Ransom Sherman; D: Bretaigne Windust. VHS $19.98 MGM ♂♂

The Winter of Our Dreams

Down Under slice of seamy life as a heroin-addicted prostitute becomes involved with an unhappy bookshop owner. Davis shines in otherwise slow and confusing drama.
1982 89m/C Judy Davis, Bryan Brown, Cathy Downes, Baz Luhrmann, Peter Mochrie, Mervyn Drak, Margie McCrae, Marcie Deane-Johns; D: John Duigan. VHS, Beta $59.95 LIV ♂♂½

Winter People

A clock-making widower and a woman living alone with her illegitimate son experience tough times together with feuding families in a Depression-era Appalachian community. Silly, rehashed premise doesn't deter McGillis, who gamely gives a fine performance. Based on the novel by John Ehle.
1989 (PG-13) 109m/C Kurt Russell, Kelly McGillis, Lloyd Bridges, Mitchell Ryan, Jeffrey Meek, Eileen Ryan, Amelia Burnette; D: Ted Kotcheff; W: Carol Sobieski; M: John Scott. VHS, Beta, 8mm $19.98 SUE, NLC ♂♂½

Winterbeast

Winter resort community dwellers begin mysteriously disappearing until somebody remembers that the resort was built over a sacred Indian burial ground. Sgt. Bill Whitman, the valiant park ranger and his Barney Fife-like assistant Stillman, question the town's wise old sage, Sheldon, who's sitting on a secret that could threaten the entire community.
1992 77m/C Tim R. Morgan, Mike Magri. VHS $30.00 TEM, MOV ♂

Winterset

A son seeks to clear his father's name of a falsely accused crime 15 years after his electrocution. Powerful at the time, though time has lessened its impact. Loosely based on the trial of Sacco and Vanzetti and adapted from Maxwell Anderson's Broadway play, with stars in the same roles. Meredith's film debut.
1936 85m/B Burgess Meredith, Margo, John Carradine; D: Alfred Santell. VHS, Beta $19.95 NOS, HHT, CAB ♂♂½

Wintertime

Forgettable and mindless Henie musical. Plot revolves around Henie travelling in Canada with her wealthy uncle, and saving an old, run-down hotel. An appearance by Woody Herman and his Orchestra give the film a much-needed boost. Based on a story by Arthur Kober.
1943 82m/B Sonja Henie, Jack Oakie, Cesar Romero, Carole Landis, S.Z. Sakall, Cornel Wilde, Woody Herman; D: John Brahm; W: E. Edwin Moran, Jack Jevne, Lynn Starling. VHS $19.98 FXV ♂½

Wired

A justly lambasted, unintentionally hilarious biography of comic genius and overdose victim John Belushi, very loosely based on Bob Woodward's bestselling muckraking book. The chronicle of addiction and tragedy is tried here as a weird sort of comedy; was it meant as a tribute to its off-kilter subject? If so, it misses by a mile. And, we're sorry, but Chiklis doesn't cut is as Belushi—who would?!
1989 (R) 112m/C Michael Chiklis, Ray Sharkey, Patti D'Arbanville, J.T. Walsh, Gary Groomes, Lucinda Jenney, Alex Rocco, Jere Burns, Billy Preston; D: Larry Peerce. VHS, Beta $89.95 LIV ♂

Wired to Kill

In a futuristic world, two teenagers seek justice for their parents' murder by building a remote-controlled erector set programmed for revenge. Laughably porous plot drops any pretence of credibility. Dizzyingly bad.
1986 (R) 96m/C Merritt Butrick, Emily Longstreth, Devin Hoelscher, Frank Collison; D: Franky Schaeffer. VHS, Beta $79.98 LIV Woof!

Wisdom

Unemployed young guy (Estevez) becomes a bank robber with Robin Hood aspirations, coming to the aid of American farmers by destroying mortgage records. Estevez became the youngest person to star in, write, and direct a major motion picture. And, my goodness, it shows.
1987 (R) 109m/C Emilio Estevez, Demi Moore, Tom Skerritt, Veronica Cartwright; D: Emilio Estevez; M: Danny Elfman. VHS, Beta $19.98 WAR ♂½

Wise Blood

Gothic drama about a drifter who searches for sin and becomes a preacher for a new religion, The Church Without Christ. Excellent cast in achingly realistic portrayal of ersatz religion, southern style. Many laughs are more painful than funny. Superb, very dark comedy from Huston. Adapted from the Flannery O'Connor novel.
1979 (PG) 106m/C Brad Dourif, John Huston, Ned Beatty, Amy Wright, Harry Dean Stanton; D: John Huston. VHS, Beta $59.95 MCA ♂♂♂½

Wise Guys

Two small-time hoods decide to rip off the mob. When their boss figures out their plan he decides to set them up instead. Lame black comedy that has too few moments.
1986 (R) 100m/C Joe Piscopo, Danny DeVito, Ray Sharkey, Captain Lou Albano, Dan Hedaya, Julie Bovasso, Patti LuPone; D: Brian DePalma. VHS, Beta $19.99 FOX, FCT ♂½

Wisecracks

Women comics perform and talk about their work in this documentary directed by Gail Singer. The comics featured have, in some cases, little more in common

than their work, but all share interesting perspectives on what they do. Interesting mix of performance clips and interviews sometimes includes banal comments about the nature of comedy, but is more often insightful, especially remarks by seasoned vet Phyllis Diller. Although there exists here the potential for an angry feminist diatribe on gender-based humor, the focus is more towards talented women who are just plain funny.
1993 93m/C D: Gail Singer; Performed by: Whoopi Goldberg, Paula Poundstone, Ellen DeGeneres, Kim Wayans, Pam Stone, Joy Behar, Maxine Lapidus, Phyllis Diller, Jenny Jones. VHS $49.95 MNC ♂♂♂

Wish You Were Here

Poignant yet funny slice of British postwar life roughly based on the childhood memoirs of famous madame, Cynthia Payne. A troubled and freedom-loving teenager expresses her rebellion in sexual experimentation. Mum is dead and Dad just doesn't understand, so what's a girl to do, but get the boys excited? Lloyd, in her first film, plays the main character with exceptional strength and feistiness. Payne's later life was dramatized in the Leland-scripted "Personal Services."
1987 92m/C Emily Lloyd, Tom Bell, Clare Clifford, Barbara Durkin, Geoffrey Hutchings, Charlotte Barker, Chloe Leland, Trudy Cavanagh, Jesse Birdsall, Geoffrey Durham, Pat Heywood; D: David Leland; W: David Leland; M: Stanley Myers. VHS, Beta $19.95 FRH, TVC ♂♂♂

Wishful Thinking

A lovelorn screenwriter rescues a peculiar man from mysterious assassins and receives a magical writing pad for his efforts. It seems that whatever Michael writes on the paper will come true, so he decides to write himself into the life of the luscious Diane.
1992 94m/C Murray Langston, Michelle Johnson, Ruth Buzzi, Billy Barty, Johnny Dark, Ray "Boom Boom" Mancini, Vic Dunlop, Kip Addotta; D: Murray Langston. VHS $89.95 HMD ♂♂

The Wishing Ring

Light and charming romance, beautifully filmed by Tourneur, based on Owen Davis' play. The son of an earl in Old England is expelled from college and told by his father he must earn half a crown on his own before the family will take him back. With the help of a minister's daughter, he sets things right.
1914 50m/B Vivian Martin, Alec B. Francis, Chester Barnett, Simeon Wiltsie, Walter Morton; D: Maurice Tourneur; W: Maurice Tourneur. VHS, Beta $18.95 GPV ♂♂♂

The Wishmaker

A young man squanders the three wishes granted to him for helping a strange old woman and her timid daughter.
1985 54m/C VHS, Beta $29.95 GEM ♂♂♂

Wishman

Hollywood hustler Basie Banks (Le Mat) meets Hitch (Lewis), a two million year old genie whose magic bottle has been stolen. In exchange for Banks' help in recovering his home, Hitch agrees to help Banks get the girl of his dreams.
1993 89m/C Paul LeMat, Geoffrey Lewis, Paul Gleason, Quin Kessler, Nancy Parsons, Gailard Sartain, Brion James; D: Mike Marvin; W: Mike Marvin. VHS $89.95 MNC ♂♂½

The Wistful Widow of Wagon Gap

Lou, a traveling salesman, accidentally kills a man, and according to the law of the west he has to take care of the dead man's widow and children—all seven of them. Because the family is so unsavory, Lou knows that no other man will kill him, so he allows himself to be appointed sheriff and clears the town of lowlifes. Usual Abbott &

Costello fare is highlighted with their zany antics. *AKA:* The Wistful Widow.
1947 78m/B Bud Abbott, Lou Costello, Marjorie Main, George Cleveland, Gordon Jones, William Ching, Peter Thompson, Glenn Strange, Olin Howland; *D:* Charles T. Barton. **VHS $14.98** MCA *♬♬*

The Witch Historian hired by family to assemble the late father's works falls in love with beautiful daughter. Seems she's no angel. *AKA:* La Strega in Amore; Aura.
1966 103m/B Rosanna Schiaffino, Richard Johnson, Sarah Ferrati, Gian Marie Volonte, Margherita Guzzinati; *D:* Damiano Damiani. **VHS $19.98** SNC *♬ ½*

Witch Who Came from the Sea Witch terrorizes all the ships at sea, but doesn't exactly haunt the viewer.
1976 (R) 98m/C Millie Perkins, Loni Chapman, Vanessa Brown, Peggy Feury, Rick Jason; *D:* Matt Cimber. **VHS, Beta $49.95** UNI *♬ ½*

A Witch Without a Broom Shoestring time travel fantasy. When an American professor catches the eye of a 15th century apprentice witch, the trip begins. Since the witch is only learning the ropes, they end up visiting a number of periods other than their own before the professor gets home. *AKA:* Una Bruja Sin Escoba.
1968 78m/C Jeffrey Hunter, Maria Perschy, Perla Cristal, Gustavo Rojo; *D:* Joe Lacy. **VHS** NO *♬ ½*

Witchboard During a college party, a group of friends bring out the Ouija board and play with it for laughs. One of the girls discovers she can use the board to communicate with a small boy who died years before. In her effort to talk with him she unwittingly releases the evil spirit of an ax murderer who haunts and murders members of the group. An entertaining, relatively inoffensive member of its genre that displays some attention to characterization and plot.
1987 (R) 98m/C Todd Allen, Tawny Kitaen, Stephen Nichols, Kathleen Wilhoite, Burke Byrnes, Rose Marie, James W. Quinn, Judy Tatum, Gloria Hayes, J.P. Luebsen, Susan Nickerson; *D:* Kevin S. Tenney; *W:* Kevin S. Tenney; *M:* Dennis Michael Tenney. **VHS, Beta** HHE *♬♬ ½*

Witchboard 2: The Devil's Doorway There seem to be a lot of doorways to hell because someone is always finding a new one (and making a movie about it). This time it's the innocent Paige Benedict (Dolenz), who moves into an artist's loft and finds an old Ouija board in a closet. Through the board, Paige is contacted by a former tenant who claims to be a murder victim. Soon her fellow tenants are dying in violent and mysterious ways and Paige's dreams are haunted by evil. What hath she wrought—and can she get it back in the closet where it belongs.
1993 (R) 98m/C Ami Dolenz, Laraine Newman, Timothy Gibbs, John Gatins; *D:* Kevin S. Tenney; *W:* Kevin S. Tenney; *M:* Dennis Michael Tenney. **VHS $34.98** REP *♬♬ ½*

Witchcraft A young mother meets a couple killed three centuries ago for performing witchcraft. They want her baby, of course, to be the son of the devil. "Rosemary's Baby" rip-off, that is thoroughly predictable.
1988 (R) 90m/C Anat "Topol" Barzilai, Gary Sloan, Lee Kisman, Deborah Scott; *D:* Robert Spera. **VHS, Beta $29.95** ACA Woof!

Witchcraft 2: The Temptress A sensuous woman seduces an innocent young man into the rituals of witchcraft and the occult. Sequel to "Witchcraft" does not succeed where original failed, but does have a fair share of sex and violence.

1990 (R) 88m/C Charles Solomon, Mia Ruiz, Delia Sheppard; *D:* Mark Woods. **VHS, Beta $29.95** ACA *♬*

Witchcraft 3: The Kiss of Death Once a master of the occult, William Spanner now seeks only to live a normal life. His plans are changed, however, when a sensual creature from Hell is sent to seduce him. More sex and violence, with an emphasis on sex. The best of the "Witchcraft" trio, for those trying to plan a festive evening.
1990 (R) 85m/C Charles Solomon, Lisa Toothman, William L. Baker, Lena Hall; *D:* R.L. Tillmanns. **VHS $19.95** ACA *♬♬*

Witchcraft 4: Virgin Heart Supernatural horror continues as attorney Will Spanner sinks even deeper into his enemy's satanic trap in this shocking sequel to the popular series. His only hope is to use his own black magic powers and to enlist the help of a seductive stripper (Penthouse Pet Strain).
1992 92m/C Charles Solomon, Julie Strain, Clive Pearson, Jason O'Gulihar, Lisa Jay Harrington, Barbara Dow; *D:* James Merendino. **VHS $89.95** ACA *♬*

Witchcraft 5: Dance with the Devil This undistinguished horror series continues with several successful people finding the unpleasant loopholes in their satanic contracts. A demon named Cain is behind all the trouble. The horror special effects are cheap but there are several softcore sex scenes (pointless to the plot) which provide a minimal interest. An unrated version is also available.
1992 (R) 94m/C Marklen Kennedy, Carolyn Taye-Loren, Nicole Sassaman, Aysha Hauer; *D:* Talun Hsu. **VHS $89.95** ACA *♬*

Witchcraft 6 Police detectives Lutz and Garner's new case involves young women turning up naked and dead. Turns out satanic disciple Savanti is expected to impress the boss with a virgin sacrifice before an impending eclipse. But since virgins are scarce, he's having a real tough time. Practically no gore but lots of skin, along with hit-or-miss humor.
1994 (R) ?m/C Kurt Alan, John E. Holiday, Bryan Nutter, Jerry Spicer, Shannon Lead. **VHS $92.95** AEV *♬*

Witchcraft Through the Ages The demonic Swedish masterpiece in which witches and victims suffer against various historical backgrounds. Nightmarish and profane, especially the appearance of the Devil as played under much make-up by Christiansen himself. Silent. *AKA:* Haxan.
1922 74m/B Maren Pedersen, Clara Pontoppidan; *D:* Benjamin Christiansen. **VHS, Beta $29.98** GPV, MPI, WFV *♬♬♬*

Witchery A photographer and his girlfriend vacation at a New England hotel where they discover a horrifying, satanic secret. One by one (as always, in this kind of bad flick, in the interest of "suspense"), people are killed off. Seems it's a witch, bent on revenge. Forget room service and bar the door.
1988 96m/C David Hasselhoff, Linda Blair, Catherine Hickland, Hildegarde Knef, Leslie Cumming, Bob Champagne, Richard Farnsworth, Michael Manches; *D:* Fabrizio Laurenti. **VHS, Beta $79.95** VMK *♬*

The Witches Nine-year-old boy on vacation finds himself in the midst of a witch convention, and grand high witch Huston plans to turn all children into furry little creatures. The boy, with the help of his good witch grandmother, attempts to prevent the mass transmutation of children into mice. Top-notch fantasy probably too spooky for the training wheel set. Wonderful special

effects; the final project of executive producer Jim Henson. Based on Roald Dahl's story.
1990 (PG) 92m/C Anjelica Huston, Mai Zetterling, Jasen Fisher, Rowan Atkinson, Charlie Potter, Bill Paterson, Brenda Blethyn, Jane Horrocks; *D:* Nicolas Roeg; *W:* Allan Scott; *M:* Stanley Myers. **VHS, Beta, 8mm $14.95** WAR, FCT, LHV *♬♬♬ ½*

Witches' Brew Three young women try to use their undeveloped skills in witchcraft and black magic to help Garr's husband get a prestigious position at a university, with calamitous results. Oft-funny spoof is silly and oft-predictable. Turner's role is small as an older, experienced witch.
1979 (PG) 98m/C Teri Garr, Richard Benjamin, Lana Turner, Kathryn Leigh Scott; *D:* Richard Shorr, Herbert L. Strock. **VHS, Beta $59.98** SUE *♬♬*

Witches' Mountain A troubled couple is captured by a coven of witches in the Pyrenees. Dull and pointless.
1971 98m/C Patty Shepard, John Caffari, Monica Randall; *D:* Raul Artigot. **VHS, Beta $49.95** UNI, HEG *♬*

The Witches of Eastwick "Mad Max" director Miller meets Hollywood in this unrestrained, vomit-filled treatment of John Updike's novel about three lonely small-town New England women and their sexual liberation. A strange, rich, overweight and balding, but nonetheless charming man knows their deepest desires and makes them come true with decadent excess. Raunchy fun, with Nicholson over-acting wildly as the Mephisto. Miller lends a bombastic violent edge to the effort, sometimes at the expense of the story. Filmed on location in Cohasset, Massachusetts.
1987 (R) 118m/C Jack Nicholson, Cher, Susan Sarandon, Michelle Pfeiffer, Veronica Cartwright, Richard Jenkins, Keith Joakum, Carel Struycken; *D:* George Miller; *W:* Michael Cristofer; *M:* John Williams. Academy Awards '87 Nominations: Best Sound, Best Original Score; Los Angeles Film Critics Association Awards '87: Best Actor (Nicholson); New York Film Critics Awards '87: Best Actor (Nicholson). **VHS, Beta, 8mm $14.95** WAR *♬♬ ½*

Witchfire After their pyschiatrist dies in an automobile accident, three maniacal women escape from an asylum and hide out in the woods. Winters then holds seances to contact the dead doctor, but instead captures a young, very much alive hunter. For dedicated fans of Winters.
1986 (R) 92m/C Shelley Winters, Gary Swanson, David Mendenhall, Corinne Chateau; *D:* Vincent J. Privitera; *W:* Vincent J. Privitera. **VHS, Beta $79.98** LIV *♬*

The Witching Poorly made story of man's continuing quest for supernatural power. Welles slums as the high priest out to get victim Franklin. *AKA:* Necromancy.
1972 90m/C Orson Welles, Pamela Franklin, Michael Ontkean, Lee Purcell; *D:* Bert I. Gordon. **VHS, Beta** NO Woof!

Witching Time Elvira presents this film, in which a young composer is visited by a horny 17th-century witch while his wife is away from home. When the wife returns, both women fight to possess him.
1984 60m/C Jon Finch, Prunella Gee, Patricia Quinn, Ian McCulloch; *D:* Don Leaver. **VHS, Beta $29.95** LIV *♬ ½*

The Witchmaker Remote, crocodile-infested bayou in Louisiana is the scene of witchcraft and the occult as young girls are murdered in order for a group of witches to become youthful again. *AKA:* Legend of Witch Hollow; Witchkill.

1969 101m/C John Lodge, Alvy Moore, Thordis Brandt, Anthony Eisley, Shelby Grant, Robyn Millan; *D:* William O. Brown; *W:* William O. Brown. VHS, Beta *NO ⫿*

The Witch's Mirror A sorceress plots to destroy the murderer of her god-daughter. The murderer, a surgeon, begins a project to restore the disfigured face and hands of his burned second wife, and he doesn't care how he gets the materials. For true fans of good bad horror flicks. Badly dubbed (which adds to the charm); dark (of course); and offbeat (naturally).
1960 75m/B Rosita Arenas, Armando Calvo, Isabela Corona, Dina De Marco; *D:* Chano Urueto. VHS, Beta $59.95 *SNC, HHT ⫿⫿*

WitchTrap Lame sequel to "Witchboard." A mansion's new owner hires psychics to exorcise the disturbed ghost of his predecessor.
1989 (R) 87m/C James W. Quinn, Kathleen Bailey, Linnea Quigley; *D:* Kevin S. Tenney. VHS, Beta *IME ⫿*

With Honors Pesci is a bum who finds desperate Harvard student Fraser's Honors thesis, and, like any quick-witted bum with a yen for literature, holds it for ransom. Desperate to salvage his future gold card, Fraser and his roommates agree to fix Joe's homeless state. Self-involved students learn something about love and life while Madonna drones in the background. Fraser is believable as the ambitious student about to endure Pesci's enlightenment. Pesci is Pesci, doing his best to overcome numerous script difficulties.
1994 (PG-13) 100m/C Joe Pesci, Brendan Fraser, Moira Kelly, Patrick Dempsey, Josh Hamilton, Gore Vidal; *D:* Alek Keshishian; *W:* William Mastrosimone; *M:* Patrick Leonard. VHS *⫿⫿½*

With Kit Carson Over the Great Divide A large-scale silent western about a doctor's family gone asunder and then reunited during the Fremont expeditions out of St. Louis in the 1840s. Snow's final screen appearance. Recently refound. Fun cinematic history (in two senses of the phrase). Beautiful landscape.
1925 72m/B Roy Stewart, Henry B. Walthall, Marguerite Snow, Sheldon Lewis, Earl Metcalfe; *D:* Frank S. Mattison. VHS, Beta, 8mm $24.95 *VYY ⫿⫿½*

With Six You Get Eggroll A widow with three sons and a widower with a daughter elope and then must deal with the antagonism of their children and even their dogs. Brady Bunch-esque family comedy means well, but doesn't cut it. Hershey's debut. Jamie Farr, William Christopher, and Vic Tayback have small parts. To date, Day's last big-screen appearance. *AKA:* A Man in Mommy's Bed.
1968 (G) 95m/C Doris Day, Brian Keith, Pat Carroll, Alice Ghostley, Vic Tayback, Jamie Farr, William Christopher, Barbara Hershey; *D:* Howard Morris. VHS, Beta $59.98 *FOX ⫿⫿*

Withnail and I A biting and original black comedy about a pair of unemployed, nearly starving English actors during the late 1960s. They decide to retreat to a country house owned by Withnail's uncle, for a vacation and are beset by comic misadventures, particularly when the uncle, who is gay, starts to hit on his nephew's friend. Robinson, who scripted "The Killing Fields," makes his successful directorial debut, in addition to drafting the screenplay from his own novel. Co-produced by George Harrison and Richard Starkey (Ringo Starr).

1987 (R) 108m/C Richard E. Grant, Paul McGann, Richard Griffiths; *D:* Bruce Robinson; *W:* Bruce Robinson; *M:* David Dundas. VHS, Beta $79.95 *MED ⫿⫿⫿½*

Without a Clue Spoof of the Sherlock Holmes legend, in which Holmes is actually portrayed by a bumbling, skirt-chasing actor, and Watson is the sole crime-solving mastermind, hiring the actor to impersonate the character made famous by the doctor's published exploits. The leads have some fun and so do we; but laughs are widely spaced.
1988 (PG) 107m/C Michael Caine, Ben Kingsley, Jeffrey Jones, Lysette Anthony, Paul Freeman, Nigel Davenport, Peter Cook, Pat Keen; *D:* Thom Eberhardt; *W:* Gary Murphy, Larry Strawther; *M:* Henry Mancini. VHS, Beta $19.98 *ORI ⫿⫿½*

Without a Trace One morning, a six-year-old boy is sent off to school by his loving mother, never to return. The story of the mother's relentless search for her son. Cardboard characters, wildly unrealistic ending that is different from the real-life incident on which it's based. Scripted by Gutcheon from her book "Still Missing." Jaffe's directorial debut.
1983 (PG) 119m/C Kate Nelligan, Judd Hirsch, Stockard Channing, David Dukes; *D:* Stanley R. Jaffe; *M:* Jack Nitzsche. VHS, Beta $59.98 *FOX ⫿⫿*

Without Honors A man seeks to restore the reputation of his dead brother, accused of murder and theft. He joins the Texas Rangers and brings the real criminals to justice. Excellent location shooting lifts ordinary early western.
1932 62m/B Harry Carey Sr., Mae Busch, Gibson Gowland, George "Gabby" Hayes; *D:* William Nigh. VHS, Beta *NO ⫿⫿*

Without Love Tracy is a scientist, Hepburn, a woman with an empty basement for his laboratory. Since the neighbors would be scandalized by the idea of unmarried people living together, however platonically, they decide to get married, although each has sworn off romance. Snappy dialogue, expertly rendered by the Tracy/Hepburn team. Terrific supporting cast keeps this minimally plotted outing afloat. Adapted from the play of the same name by Philip Barry.
1945 113m/B Spencer Tracy, Katharine Hepburn, Lucille Ball, Keenan Wynn, Carl Esmond, Patricia Morison, Felix Bressart; *D:* Harold Bucquet; *W:* Donald Ogden Stewart. VHS, Beta $19.98 *MGM ⫿⫿½*

Without Love Ambitious young journalist experiences resentment from her peers because of her aggressive methods, and they decide to teach her a lesson by drawing her into a situation destined for disaster. In Polish with English subtitles.
1980 104m/C *D:* Barbara Sass. VHS $49.95 *FCT ⫿⫿*

Without Reservations Hollywood-bound novelist Colbert encounters Marine flyer Wayne and his pal (DeFore) aboard a train. She decides he would be perfect for her newest movie. They both dislike her famous book and don't realize they're traveling with the renowned author. Misadventures and misunderstandings abound as this trio make their way to Tinseltown. Of course, Colbert and Wayne fall in love. Box-office success with a tired script and too few real laughs. The Duke is interesting but miscast. Based on the novel "Thanks, God, I'll Take It From Here" by Jane Allen.

1946 101m/B Claudette Colbert, John Wayne, Don DeFore, Phil Brown, Frank Puglia; *Cameos:* Louella Parsons, Cary Grant, Jack Benny; *D:* Mervyn LeRoy. VHS, Beta $19.98 *VCI, VCN, TTC ⫿⫿½*

Without Warning Inexperienced director and actors pull out a minor success in this fairly ordinary murder mystery, about a serial killer of beautiful blondes. *AKA:* The Story Without A Name.
1952 75m/C Maurice Ronet, Adam Williams, Gloria Franklin, Edward Binns; *D:* Arnold Laven. VHS *NO ⫿⫿½*

Without Warning: The James Brady Story White House Press Secretary Brady took a bullet in the brain during the 1981 shooting of President Reagan, and made a slow, grueling recovery. This fine made for cable TV film spares none of it, concentrating on the stricken man and his family, and opting out of disease-of-the-week cliches (though the pic's politics won't please the gun-adorers). Based on Mollie Dickinson's biography "Thumbs Up."
1991 (R) 120m/C Beau Bridges, Joan Allen, David Strathairn, Christopher Bell, Bryan Clark, Steve Flynn, Christine Healy, Susan Brown; *D:* Michael Toshiyuki Uno; *W:* Robert Bolt. VHS $89.98 *HBO ⫿⫿⫿*

Witness A young Amish boy traveling from his father's funeral witnesses a murder in a Philadelphia bus station. The investigating detective (Ford, in one of his best roles) soon discovers the killing is part of a conspiracy involving corruption in his department. He follows the child and his young widowed mother to their home in the country. A thriller with a difference, about the encounter of alien worlds, with a poignant love story. McGillis, in her first major role, is luminous as the Amish mother, while Ford is believable as both a cop and a sensitive man. An artfully crafted drama, richly focusing on the often misunderstood Amish lifestyle.
1985 (R) 112m/C Harrison Ford, Kelly McGillis, Alexander Godunov, Lukas Haas, Josef Sommer, Danny Glover, Patti LuPone; *D:* Peter Weir; *M:* Maurice Jarre. Academy Awards '85: Best Film Editing, Best Original Screenplay; Nominations: Best Actor (Ford), Best Art Direction/Set Decoration, Best Cinematography, Best Director (Weir), Best Picture, Best Original Score; Edgar Allan Poe Awards '85: Best Screenplay. VHS, Beta $14.95 *PAR, HMV ⫿⫿⫿*

Witness for the Prosecution An unemployed man is accused of murdering a wealthy widow whom he befriended. Ailing defense attorney Laughton can't resist taking an intriguing murder case, and a straitforward court case becomes increasingly complicated in this energetic adaptation of an Agatha Christie story and stage play. Outstanding performances by Laughton, with excellent support by real life wife, Lanchester, as his patient nurse. Power, as the alleged killer, and Dietrich as a tragic woman are top-notch (see if you can detect Dietrich in an unbilled second role).
1957 116m/B Charles Laughton, Tyrone Power, Marlene Dietrich, Elsa Lanchester, John Williams, Henry Daniell, Una O'Connor; *D:* Billy Wilder; *W:* Harry Kurnitz, Billy Wilder. Academy Awards '57 Nominations: Best Actor (Laughton), Best Director (Wilder), Best Film Editing, Best Picture, Best Sound, Best Supporting Actress (Lanchester); Golden Globe Awards '58: Best Supporting Actress (Lanchester). VHS, Beta $19.98 *MGM, FOX, MLB ⫿⫿⫿½*

Wives Under Suspicion While prosecuting a man who murdered his wife out of jealousy, a district attorney finds his own home life filled with similar tension. Director Whale's unnecessary remake of his own earlier film, "The Kiss Before the Mirror." He is best known for "Frankenstein."

1938 75m/B Warren William, Gail Patrick, Constance Moore, William Lundigan; **D:** James Whale. **VHS, Beta $24.95** NOS, DVT, HEG ✍✍½

The Wiz Black version of the long-time favorite "The Wizard of Oz," based on the Broadway musical. Ross plays a Harlem schoolteacher who is whisked away to a fantasy version of New York City in a search for her identity. Some good character performances and musical numbers, but generally an overblown and garish effort with Ross too old for her role. Pryor is poorly cast, but Jackson is memorable as the Scarecrow. High-budget ($24 million) production with a ton of name stars, lost $11 million, and cooled studios on black films. Horne's number as the good witch is the best reason to sit through this one. ♫The Feeling That We HAve; Can I Go On Not Knowing; Glinda's Theme; He's the Wizard; Soon as I Get Home; You Can't Win; Ease on Down the Road; What Would I Do If I Could Feel?; Slide Some Oil to Me.

1978 (G) 133m/C Diana Ross, Michael Jackson, Nipsey Russell, Ted Ross, Mabel King, Thelma Carpenter, Richard Pryor, Lena Horne; **D:** Sidney Lumet; **W:** Joel Schumacher; **M:** Quincy Jones. **VHS, Beta $19.98** MCA, FCT ✍✍

The Wizard Facing the dissolution of his dysfunctional family, a youngster decides to take his autistic, video game-playing little brother across the country to a national video competition. Way too much plot in pretentious, blatantly commercial feature-length Nintendo ad, featuring the kid from "The Wonder Years." For teen video addicts only.

1989 (PG) 99m/C Fred Savage, Beau Bridges, Christian Slater, Luke Edwards, Jenny Lewis; **D:** Todd Holland; **W:** David Chisholm. **VHS, Beta $19.95** MCA ✍½

The Wizard of Gore The prototypical Lewis splatter party, about a magician whose on-stage mutilations turn out to be messily real. High camp and barrels of bright movie blood.

1970 (R) 96m/C Ray Sager, Judy Cler, Wayne Ratay, Phil Lauenson, Jim Rau, John Elliott, Don Alexander, Monika Blackwell, Corinne Kirkin; **D:** Herschell Gordon Lewis. **VHS, Beta** RHI ✍

The Wizard of Loneliness A disturbed young boy goes to live with his grandparents during WWII, and slowly discovers family secrets centering on his aunt. Excellent performances barely save an aimless plot with an overdone denouement. Based on the novel by John Nichols.

1988 (PG-13) 110m/C Lukas Haas, Lea Thompson, John Randolph, Lance Guest, Anne Pitoniak, Jeremiah Warner, Dylan Baker; **D:** Jenny Bowen; **W:** Nancy Larson; **M:** Michel Colombier. **VHS, Beta** NO ✍✍

The Wizard of Oz An early silent version of the L. Frank Baum fantasy, with notable plot departures from the book and later 1939 adaptation, starring long-forgotten comedian Semon as the Scarecrow, supported by a pre-Laurel Hardy as the Tin Woodman. With music score.

1925 93m/B Larry Semon, Dorothy Dwan, Bryant Washburn, Charles Murray, Oliver Hardy, Josef Swickard, Virginia Pearson; **D:** Larry Semon. **VHS, Beta, 8mm $19.95** NOS, VYY, MLB ✍✍½

The Wizard of Oz From the book by L. Frank Baum. Fantasy about a Kansas farm girl (Garland, in her immortal role) who rides a tornado to a brightly colored world over the rainbow, full of talking scarecrows, munchkins and a wizard who bears a strange resemblance to a Kansas fortune-teller. She

must outwit the Wicked Witch if she is ever to go home. Delightful performances from Lahr, Bolger, and Hamilton; King Vidor is uncredited as co-director. Director Fleming originally wanted Deanna Durbin or Shirley Temple for the role of Dorothy, but settled for Garland who made the song "Somewhere Over the Rainbow" her own. She received a special Academy Award for her performance. For the 50th anniversary of its release, "The Wizard of Oz" was restored and includes rare film clips of Bolger's "Scarecrow Dance" and the cut "Jitterbug" number, and shots by Buddy Ebsen as the Tin Man before he became ill and left the production. Laserdisc edition includes digital sound, commentary by film historian Ronald Haver, and test footage, trailers and stills, as well as Jerry Maren talking about his experiences as a Munchkin. Yet another special release of the film, "The Ultimate Oz," contains a documentary on the making of the film, a reproduction of the original script, still photos, and liner notes. ♫Munchkinland; Ding Dong the Witch is Dead; Follow the Yellow Brick Road; If I Only Had a Brain/a Heart/the Nerve; If I Were the King of the Forest; The Merry Old Land of Oz; Threatening Witch; Into the Forest of the Wild Beast; The City Gates are Open.

1939 101m/C Judy Garland, Margaret Hamilton, Ray Bolger, Jack Haley, Bert Lahr, Frank Morgan, Charley Grapewin, Clara Blandick, Mitchell Lewis, Billie Burke; **D:** Victor Fleming; **W:** Noel Langley; **M:** Herbert Stothart. Academy Awards '39: Best Song ("Over the Rainbow"), Best Original Score; Nominations: Best Color Cinematography, Best Interior Decoration, Best Picture, Best Special Effects. **VHS, Beta $19.98** MGM, VYG, APD ✍✍✍✍

The Wizard of Speed and Time A special-effects wizard gets the break of his life when he's hired by a movie studio, but there's more to this particular studio than he realizes. Jittlov, a real special-effects expert, plays himself in this personally financed production. Although brimming with inside jokes and references, this self-indulgence succeeds with its enthusiasm and ambition, despite being rather obviously self-produced. Unique special effects make it memorable.

1988 (PG) 95m/C Mike Jittlov, Richard Kaye, Page Moore, David Conrad, Steve Brodie, John Massari, Frank Laloggia, Philip Michael Thomas, Angelique Pettyjohn, Arnetia Walker, Paulette Breen; **D:** Mike Jittlov; **W:** Mike Jittlov, Richard Kaye, Deven Chierighino; **M:** John Massari. **VHS** WTA ✍✍½

Wizards A good, bumbling sorcerer battles for the sake of a magic kingdom and its princess against his evil brother who uses Nazi propaganda films to inspire his army of mutants. Profane, crude, & typically Bakshian fantasy with great graphics. Animated.

1977 (PG) 81m/C **D:** Ralph Bakshi. **VHS, Beta $19.98** FOX, WTA ✍✍½

Wizards of the Lost Kingdom A boy magician, aided by various ogres and swordster Svenson battles an all-powerful wizard for control of his kingdom. Family fare a bit too clean and harmless.

1985 (PG) 76m/C Bo Svenson, Vidal Peterson, Thom Christopher; **D:** Hector Olivera. **VHS, Beta $19.95** MED ✍½

Wizards of the Lost Kingdom 2 A boy wizard is charged with vanquishing the evil tyrants from three kingdoms. Barely a sequel; no plot continuation or cast from earlier kiddie sword epic.

1989 (PG) 80m/C David Carradine, Bobby Jacoby, Lana Clarkson, Mel Welles, Susan Lee Hoffman, Sid Haig; **D:** Charles B. Griffith. **VHS, Beta $79.95** MED ✍

WKRP in Cincinnati, Vol. 1 In the pilot episode for the TV sitcom, WKRP is a failing radio station with the cautious Arthur Carlson as the station manager (the station is owned by his mother). Andy Travis is hired as the new program director to turn things around and promptly turns WKRP towards rock and roll. Other regulars included newsman Les Nesman, sales manager Herb Tarlek, DJs Dr. Johnny Fever and Venus Flytrap, as well as ever-efficient secretary Jennifer Marlowe.

1978 50m/C Gary Sandy, Gordon Jump, Loni Anderson, Richard Sanders, Frank Bonner, Jan Smithers, Howard Hesseman, Tim Reid. **VHS** MTM ✍

Wolf To everyone's lasting regret, an ex-Vietnam POW strives to rescue an American ambassador kidnapped by Central American rebels.

1986 95m/C J. Antonio Carreon, Ron Marchini; **D:** Charlie Ordonez. **VHS, Beta $79.95** TWE ✍

Wolf Harrison's original script is massaged by Nichols into an upscale new age men's movement horror spectacle lacking a suitable climax. Stressed out Manhattan book editor Will Randall's (Nicholson) car hits a wolf on a country road and he's bitten when he tries to help the animal. Normally a wishy-washy guy, he notices some distinctly hairy changes to both his body and personality, leading him to make some drastic changes at work by knocking off his firm's greedy honchos and taking over. Talk about being ruthless in business. Boss' daughter Pfeiffer takes a shine to Randall's new animal magnetism, but is just visual candy. Walks a fine line between black comedy, camp, romance, and horror, though Jack baying at the moon seems sort of campy.

1994 (R) 125m/C Jack Nicholson, Michelle Pfeiffer, James Spader, Kate Nelligan, Christopher Plummer, Richard Jenkins, Eileen Atkins, David Hyde Pierce, Om Puri, Ron Rifkin, Prunella Scales; **D:** Mike Nichols; **W:** Wesley Strick, Jim Harrison; **M:** Ennio Morricone. **VHS** NYR ✍✍½

The Wolf at the Door A well-appointed, sincere biography of impressionist Paul Gauguin in the middle period of life, during his transition from the petty demands of his Parisian life to the freedom of Tahiti. Not definitive or compelling, but serves the purpose of a biography—arousing interest in the subject's life and art.

1987 (R) 90m/C Donald Sutherland, Jean Yanne, Sofie Graboel, Ghita Norby, Max von Sydow, Merete Voldstedlund, Fanny Bastien, Valerie Morea; **D:** Henning Carlsen; **W:** Christopher Hampton; **M:** Roger Bourland. **VHS, Beta $79.98** FOX, ING ✍✍½

Wolf Blood When Dick (Chesebro) is hurt in an accident, Dr. Horton uses wolf's blood for a transfusion. Soon there are unexplained deaths and Dick fears he's becoming a man-beast. Early precursor to the wolfman films.

1925 68m/B George Cheseboro, Marguerite Clayton, Ray Hanford, Roy Watson, Milburn Morante; **D:** George Cheseboro, George Mitchell. **VHS $17.95** GPV ✍✍½

Wolf Call Carroll plays the son of a miner who travels with his devoted hound to see his father's old mine and start it working again. Gangsters and a beautiful Indian maiden get in his way. Master and pooch both find romance, and both sing. From the Jack London novel.

1939 62m/B John Carroll, Movita, Wheeler Oakman, Peter George Lynn; **D:** George Waggner. **VHS, Beta, 8mm $19.95** VYY, FCT ✍✍½

Wolf Dog A boy and his dog. Outdoor action and adventure. Twelve chapters, 13 minutes each.
1933 156m/B Rin Tin Tin Jr, Frankie Darro, Patricia "Boots" Mallory; *D:* Harry Fraser, Colbert Clark. **VHS, Beta $26.95** *SNC, VCN, MLB* 🐾½

Wolf Lake WWII veteran, whose son was killed in Vietnam, and a Vietnam army deserter clash with tragic consequences during their stay at a Canadian hunting lodge. Steiger gives it a go, but overwrought revenge pic resists quality upgrade.
1979 90m/C Rod Steiger, David Hoffman, Robin Mattson, Jerry Hardin, Richard Herd, Paul Mantu; *D:* Burt Kennedy. **VHS, Beta $9.99** *PSM* 🐾½

The Wolf Man Fun, absorbing classic horror with Chaney as a man bitten by werewolf Lugosi. His dad thinks he's gone nuts, his screaming gal pal just doesn't understand, and plants on the Universal lot have no roots. Ouspenskaya's finest hour as the prophetic gypsy woman. Ow-ooo! Chilling and thrilling.
1941 70m/B Lon Chaney Jr., Claude Rains, Maria Ouspenskaya, Ralph Bellamy, Bela Lugosi, Warren William, Patric Knowles, Evelyn Ankers; *D:* George Waggner. **VHS, Beta $14.95** *MCA* 🐾🐾🐾½

Wolfen Surrealistic menace darkens this original and underrated tale of super-intelligent wolf creatures terrorizing New York City. Police detective Finney tries to track down the beasts before they kill again. Notable special effects in this thriller, which covers environmental and Native American concerns while maintaining the tension. Feature film debuts of Hines and Venora. Based on the novel by Whitley Strieber. Available in widescreen on laserdisc.
1981 (R) 115m/C Albert Finney, Gregory Hines, Tommy Noonan, Diane Venora, Edward James Olmos; *D:* Michael Wadleigh; *M:* James Horner. **VHS, Beta $14.95** *WAR* 🐾🐾🐾

Wolfen Ninja A girl is raised by wolves and is taught by them the secrets of Ninja fighting.
198? 92m/C **VHS, Beta $59.95** *TWE* 🐾

Wolfheart's Revenge An honest cowboy, helped by Wolfheart the Wonder Dog, steps in when a sheep rancher is murdered. Silent film with original organ score.
1925 64m/B Guinn Williams. **VHS, Beta, 8mm $24.95** *VYY, GPV* 🐾

The Wolfman In 1910, a young man learns that his family is heir to the curse of the Werewolf. Same old stuff.
1982 91m/C Earl Owensby, Kristina Reynolds; *D:* Worth Keeter. **VHS, Beta** *NO* 🐾

The Wolves Gosha shows the world of the yakuza (gangster) during the 1920s. Reminiscent of the samurai, the movie combines ancient Japanese culture with the rapidly changing world of 20th Century Japan. In Japanese with English subtitles.
1982 131m/C Tatsuya Nakadai; *D:* Hideo Gosha. **VHS $79.95** *ING* 🐾🐾🐾

A Woman and a Woman Covers a ten-year period in the friendship of Barbara and Irena and how it survives their professional and personal conflicts. In Polish with English subtitles.
1980 99m/C Halina Labonarska, Anna Romantowska; *D:* Richard Bugajski. **VHS $49.95** *FCT* 🐾🐾

A Woman Called Golda Political drama following the life and career of Golda Meir, the Israeli Prime Minister and one of the most powerful political figures of the 20th century. Davis portrays the young Golda,

Bergman taking over as she ages. Superior made-for-television bio-epic.
1982 192m/C Ingrid Bergman, Leonard Nimoy, Anne Jackson, Ned Beatty, Robert Loggia, Judy Davis; *D:* Alan Gibson; *W:* Steven Gethers, Howard Gast. **VHS, Beta $69.95** *PAR* 🐾🐾🐾

A Woman Called Moses The story of Harriet Ross Tubman, who bought her freedom from slavery, founded the underground railroad, and helped lead hundreds of slaves to freedom before the Civil War. Wonderful performance by Tyson but the made-for-television film is bogged down by a so-so script. Based on the novel by Marcy Heldish.
1978 200m/C Cicely Tyson, Dick Anthony Williams, Will Geer, Robert Hooks, Hari Rhodes, James Wainwright; *D:* Paul Wendkos. **VHS $89.95** *XVC, FCT, CAM* 🐾🐾½

Woman Condemned A reporter tries to clear a woman's name of murder.
1933 58m/B Mischa Auer, Lola Lane, Claudia Dell, Richard Hemingway. **VHS, Beta** *NO* 🐾½

The Woman He Loved The infamous romance of Edward VIII, who gave up the throne of England for American divorcee, Wallis Warfield Simpson. Seymour and Andrews are fine in their roles but the made-for-television drama is slow-going.
1988 100m/C Anthony Andrews, Jane Seymour, Olivia de Havilland, Lucy Gutteridge, Julie Harris, Robert Hardy, Phyllis Calvert; *D:* Charles Jarrott. **VHS** *STE* 🐾½

A Woman, Her Men and Her Futon A beautiful woman tries to find her identity by having a number of lovers but none can satisfy her every need.
1992 (R) 90m/C Jennifer Rubin, Lance Edwards, Grant Show, Michael Ceveris, Delaune Michel, Robert Lipton; *D:* Mussef Sibay; *W:* Mussef Sibay; *M:* Joel Goldsmith. **VHS $89.98** *REP* 🐾🐾

Woman Hunt Men kidnap women, then hunt them in the jungle for fun. So deeply offensive, we would give it negative bones if we could. "Hee Haw" bimbo Todd plays a sadistic lesbian. *AKA:* The Highest Bidder.
1972 (R) 81m/C John Ashley, Lisa Todd, Eddie Garcia, Laurie Rose; *D:* Eddie Romero. **VHS, Beta $59.98** *NLC Woof!*

The Woman Hunter A wealthy woman recovering from a traffic accident in Mexico believes someone is after her for her jewels and possibly her life. Eden dressed well, if nothing else; suspense builds ploddingly to a "Yeah, sure" climax. Made for television.
1972 73m/C Barbara Eden, Robert Vaughn, Stuart Whitman, Sydney Chaplin, Larry Storch, Enrique Lucero; *D:* Bernard L. Kowalski. **VHS, Beta** *NO* 🐾½

Woman in Black Chilling ghost story set in Victorian times and adapted from the novel by Susan Hill. Soliciter Arthur Kidd is sent to a remote house to settle the estate of a client. He's haunted by the mysterious figure of a woman in black, who according to the locals, has put a curse on the village. Arthur's driven close to the edge of sanity by the ghostly figure and the tragedy that haunts the past. Made for television.
1993 100m/C Adrian Rawlins; *D:* Herbert Wise. **VHS $29.98** *BFS, FCT* 🐾🐾½

Woman in Brown It's Hungary, 1882, and five Jewish men are on trial for the murder of a man who actually committed suicide. Despite the prejudice and hatred from the locals, their lawyer believes in and fights for their innocence. *AKA:* The Vicious Circle; The Circle.

1948 77m/B Conrad Nagel, Fritz Kortner, Reinhold Schunzel, Philip Van Zandt, Eddie LeRoy, Edwin Maxwell; *D:* W. Lee Wilder. **Beta $16.95** *SNC* 🐾🐾½

A Woman in Flames A bored middle-class housewife leaves her overbearing husband and becomes a high-priced prostitute. She has a passionless affair with an aging bisexual gigolo. Dark and dreary tale of human relationships and the role of sex in people's lives. Interesting but depressing. *AKA:* Die Flambierte Frau.
1984 (R) 106m/C Gudrun Landgrebe, Robert Van Ackeren, Matthieu Carriere, Gabriele Lafari, Hanns Zischler; *D:* Robert Van Ackeren. **VHS, Beta $39.98** *GLV* 🐾🐾

The Woman in Green Murder victims are found with missing index fingers, and it's up to Holmes and Watson to try to solve this apparently motiveless crime. Available colorized. *AKA:* Sherlock Holmes and the Woman in Green.
1945 68m/B Basil Rathbone, Nigel Bruce, Hillary Brooke, Henry Daniell, Paul Cavanagh, Frederick Worlock, Mary Gordon, Billy Bevan; *D:* Roy William Neill. **VHS $14.98** *SNC, REP, VYY* 🐾🐾

Woman in Grey A man and a woman battle wits when they attempt to locate and unravel the Army Code while staying one step ahead of J. Haviland Hunter, a suave villain after the same fortune. Silent.
1919 205m/B Arline Pretty, Henry Sell. **VHS, Beta $49.98** *NOS, CCB, MLB* 🐾🐾

The Woman in Red Executive Wilder's life unravels when he falls hard for stunning Le Brock. Inferior Hollywood-ized remake of the ebulliant "Pardon Mon Affaire." Somehow the French seem to do the sexual force thing with more verve, but this one has its moments, and Wilder is likeable. Music by Stevie Wonder.
1984 (PG-13) 87m/C Gene Wilder, Charles Grodin, Kelly Le Brock, Gilda Radner, Judith Ivey, Joseph Bologna; *D:* Gene Wilder; *W:* Gene Wilder; *M:* Stevie Wonder. **VHS, Beta $79.98** *LIV, VES* 🐾🐾½

Woman in the Dunes Splendid, resonant allegorical drama. A scientist studying insects in the Japanese sand dunes finds himself trapped with a woman in a hut at the bottom of a pit. Superbly directed and photographed (by Hiroshi Segawa). Scripted by Kobo Abe from his acclaimed novel. In Japanese with English subtitles. *AKA:* Suna No Onna; Woman of the Dunes.
1964 123m/B Eiji Okada, Kyoko Kishida, Koji Mitsui, Hiroko Ito, Sen Yano; *D:* Hiroshi Teshigahara; *M:* Toru Takemitsu. **VHS, Beta $29.95** *CVC, NOS, VDM* 🐾🐾🐾🐾

Woman in the Moon Assorted people embark on a trip to the moon and discover water, and an atmosphere, as well as gold. Lang's last silent outing is nothing next to "Metropolis," with a rather lame plot (greedy trip bashers seek gold), but interesting as a vision of the future. Lang's predictions about space travel often hit the mark. Silent with music. *AKA:* By Rocket to the Moon; Girl in the Moon.
1929 115m/B Klaus Pohl, Willy Fritsch, Gustav von Wagenheim, Gerda Maurus; *D:* Fritz Lang. **VHS, Beta $39.95** *VYY, IHF, LSV* 🐾🐾½

Woman in the Shadows A ex-con retreats to the woods for serenity and peace, but is assaulted by mysterious women, jealous lovers, and gun-slinging drunks, until he explodes. A man can only take so much. From a Dashiell Hammett story.
1934 70m/B Fay Wray, Ralph Bellamy, Melvyn Douglas, Roscoe Ates, Joe King. **VHS, Beta $24.95** *VYY* 🐾🐾

The Woman Inside Low-budget gender-bender depicts the troubled life of a Vietnam veteran who decides on a sex-change operation to satisfy his inner yearnings. Blondell's unfortunate last role as his/her aunt. Cheesy like Limburger; almost too weird and boring even for camp buffs.
1983 (R) 94m/C Gloria Manon, Dave Clark, Joan Blondell; **D:** Joseph Van Winkle. **VHS, Beta** *NO* *⌀½*

A Woman is a Woman Godard's affectionate sendup of Hollywood musicals is a hilarious comedy about a nightclub dancer (Karina) who desperately wants a baby. When boyfriend Belmondo balks, she asks his best friend Brialy. Much ado is had, with the three leads all splendid. Godard's first film shot in color and cinemascope, with great music. In French with English subtitles. **AKA:** Une Femme Est Une Femme; La Donna E Donna.
1960 88m/C Jean-Claude Brialy, Jean-Paul Belmondo, Anna Karina, Marie DuBois; **D:** Jean-Luc Godard; **M:** Michel Legrand. **VHS $59.95** *INT, ING* *⌀⌀⌀*

A Woman Named Jackie Three-part TV miniseries covering the life of Jacqueline Bouvier Kennedy Onassis. Downey offers a pretty picture as the enigmatic and beleaguered heroine but this version is simplistic at best. Based on the book by C. David Heymann. On three cassettes.
1991 246m/C Roma Downey, Stephen Collins, William Devane, Joss Ackland, Rosemary Murphy, Wendy Hughes, Josef Sommer; **D:** Larry Peerce; **W:** Roger O. Hirson. **VHS $99.98** *NHO, IME* *⌀⌀½*

The Woman Next Door One of Truffaut's last films before his sudden death in 1984. The domestic drama involves a suburban husband who resumes an affair with a tempestuous now-married woman after she moves next door, with domestic complications all around. An insightful, humanistic paean to passion and fidelity by the great artist, though one of his lesser works. Supported by strong outings from the two leads. In French with English subtitles. **AKA:** La Femme d'a Cote.
1981 (R) 106m/C Gerard Depardieu, Fanny Ardant, Michele Baumgartner, Veronique Silver, Roger Van Hool; **D:** Francois Truffaut; **W:** Suzanne Schiffman; **M:** Georges Delerue. **VHS, Beta $39.95** *HMV, FOX* *⌀⌀⌀*

A Woman Obsessed Pathetic, overcooked drama about a woman obsessed with her long-lost son. "Ruth Raymond" is really porn-flick vet Georgina Spelvin. Soon-to-be camp classic takes itself with utter seriousness.
1988 (R) 105m/C Ruth Raymond, Gregory Patrick, Troy Donahue, Linda Blair; **D:** Chuck Vincent. **VHS, VHS, Beta $29.95** *ACA* *⌀*

A Woman of Affairs Garbo, who can't have the guy she really loves (Gilbert), marries scoundrel. When she finds out husband's true profession, he kills himself and Gilbert comes back. In order to preclude happy ending, she decides the affair wasn't meant to be and expires. Tragically. Silent.
1928 90m/B Greta Garbo, John Gilbert, Lewis Stone, Johnny Mack Brown, Douglas Fairbanks Jr., Hobart Bosworth, Dorothy Sebastian; **D:** Clarence Brown. **VHS $29.98** *MGM, FCT* *⌀⌀*

Woman of Desire Christina Ford (Derek) is a femme fatale who is yachting with rich boyfriend Ted when there is a terrible storm. Christina, Ted, and yacht captain Jack are washed overboard and Jack is found washed ashore with no memory. When Christina turns up she claims Jack killed Ted. So Jack gets a lawyer, Walter J. Hill (played

by the redoubtable Mitchum) but is he wily enough to discredit the deceitful Christina? Bo's body is once again on display. Also available in an unrated version.
1993 (R) 97m/C Bo Derek, Jeff Fahey, Steven Bauer, Robert Mitchum. **VHS $92.95** *VMK* *⌀*

A Woman of Distinction Slapstick comedy with potential to be ordinary is taken over the top by a good, vivacious cast. Russell, the stuffy Dean of a women's college, is driven to distraction by a reporter linking her romantically to Milland, a visiting professor.
1950 85m/C Ray Milland, Rosalind Russell, Edmund Gwenn, Francis Lederer; **Cameos:** Lucille Ball; **D:** Edward Buzzell. **VHS, Beta $69.95** *COL* *⌀⌀*

Woman of Paris/Sunnyside This double feature highlights the talents of Charlie Chaplin. "A Woman of Paris" is the tragic story of a French country girl who winds up a kept woman. Chaplin's only dramatic directional outing; he makes only a cameo appearance. Straightforward but hip story of sex and society. In "Sunnyside," an example of high Chaplin highjinks, the comic plays a hotel handyman who can't win.
1923 111m/B Adolphe Menjou, Edna Purviance, Carl Miller, Lydia Knott; **Cameos:** Charlie Chaplin; **D:** Charlie Chaplin. **VHS, Beta $19.98** *FOX* *⌀⌀⌀½*

A Woman of Rome Standard Italian star vehicle, with Lollobrigida portraying a successful prostitute in Rome who decides to change her life. Dubbed. **AKA:** La Romana.
1956 93m/B Gina Lollobrigida, Daniel Gelin, Franco Fabrizi, Raymond Pellegrin; **D:** Luigi Zampa. **VHS, Beta $24.95** *NOS, FCT* *⌀⌀*

A Woman of Substance, Episode 1: Nest of Vipers The woman of the title, Emma Harte, rises from poverty to wealth and power through self-discipline. First episode of three. Made for TV saga has our heroine working as a servant for the snooty Fairley family.
1984 100m/C Jenny Seagrove, Barry Bostwick, Deborah Kerr; **D:** Don Sharp. **VHS, Beta $69.98** *LIV* *⌀⌀½*

A Woman of Substance, Episode 2: The Secret is Revealed Emma Harte struggles to rise from a life of poverty to wealth and social acceptance. Second miniseries episode has Emma fighting to get by in the big city. Fun TV drama.
1984 100m/C Jenny Seagrove, Barry Bostwick, Deborah Kerr; **D:** Don Sharp. **VHS, Beta $69.98** *LIV* *⌀⌀½*

A Woman of Substance, Episode 3: Fighting for the Dream Third installment is pretty good romantic TV saga. Rags-to-riches Emma finds love and happiness—at last!
1984 100m/C Jenny Seagrove, Barry Bostwick, Deborah Kerr; **D:** Don Sharp. **VHS, Beta $69.98** *LIV* *⌀⌀½*

The Woman of the Town Frontier marshall and newspaperman Bat Masterson is portrayed convincingly by Dekker as a very human hero who seeks justice when the woman he loves, a dance hall girl who works in the town for social causes, is killed by an unscrupulous rancher. Fictionalized but realistic western shows "heroes" as good, ordinary people.
1944 90m/B Claire Trevor, Albert Dekker, Barry Sullivan, Henry Hull, Porter Hall, Percy Kilbride; **D:** George Archainbaud; **M:** Miklos Rozsa. **VHS, Beta $19.95** *NOS, HEG, FCT* *⌀⌀½*

Woman of the Year First classic Tracy/Hepburn pairing concerns the rocky marriage of a renowned political columnist and a lowly sportswriter. Baseball scene with Hepburn at her first game is delightful. Hilarious, rich entertainment that tries to answer the question "What really matters in life?" Tracy and Hepburn began a close friendship that paralleled their quarter-century celluloid partnership. Hepburn shepherded Kamin and Lardner's Oscar-winning script past studio chief Louis B. Mayer, wearing four-inch heels to press her demands. Mayer caved in, Tracy was freed from making "The Yearling," and the rest is history.
1942 114m/B Spencer Tracy, Katharine Hepburn, Fay Bainter, Dan Tobin, Reginald Owen, Roscoe Karns, William Bendix, Minor Watson; **D:** George Stevens; **W:** Ring Lardner Jr., Michael Kanin; **M:** Franz Waxman. Academy Awards '42: Best Original Screenplay; Nominations: Best Actress (Hepburn). **VHS, Beta $19.95** *MGM* *⌀⌀⌀⌀*

A Woman Rebels A young Victorian woman challenges Victorian society by fighting for women's rights. Excellent performance from Hepburn lifts what might have been a forgettable drama. Screen debut of Van Heflin. Based on Netta Syrett's "Portrait of a Rebel."
1936 88m/B Katharine Hepburn, Herbert Marshall, Elizabeth Allan, Donald Crisp, Van Heflin; **D:** Mark Sandrich. **VHS, Beta $34.98** *CCB* *⌀⌀½*

Woman Times Seven Italian sexual comedy: seven sketches, each starring MacLaine with a different leading man. Stellar cast and good director should have delivered more, but what they have provided has its comedic moments. **AKA:** Sept Fois Femme; Sette Volte Donna.
1967 (PG) 99m/C Shirley MacLaine, Peter Sellers, Rossano Brazzi, Vittorio Gassman, Lex Barker, Elsa Martinelli, Robert Morley, Alan Arkin, Michael Caine, Patrick Wymark, Anita Ekberg, Philippe Noiret; **D:** Vittorio De Sica. **VHS, Beta $14.95** *COL, SUE, NLC* *⌀⌀½*

A Woman Under the Influence Strong performances highlight this overlong drama about a family's disintegration. Rowlands is the lonely, middle-aged housewife who's having a breakdown and Falk is her blue-collar husband who can't handle what's going on.
1974 (R) 147m/C Gena Rowlands, Peter Falk, Matthew Cassel, Matthew Laborteaux, Christina Grisanti; **D:** John Cassavetes; **W:** John Cassavetes. Academy Awards '74 Nominations: Best Actress (Rowlands), Best Director (Cassavetes); Golden Globe Awards '75: Best Actress—Drama (Rowlands). **VHS, Beta $94.95** *TOU, FCT* *⌀⌀⌀*

The Woman Who Came Back A young woman who believes she suffers from a witch's curse returns to her small hometown with unhappy results. Good cast; bad script. Indifference inducing.
1945 69m/B Nancy Kelly, Otto Kruger, John Loder, Ruth Ford, Jeanne Gail; **D:** Walter Colmes. **VHS, Beta $14.95** *COL* *⌀⌀*

The Woman Who Willed a Miracle Made-for-television drama has a devoted mother encouraging her mentally retarded son to pursue his interest in the piano.
1983 72m/C Cloris Leachman, James Noble; **D:** Sharron Miller. **VHS, Beta** *NO* *⌀⌀*

A Woman Without Love A rarely seen film from Bunuel's Mexican period based on a classic Guy de Maupassant tale about a forbidden romance. Family tragedy results later when the husband "misbequeaths" his fortune. Minor but fascinating bug-the-bourgeoisie Bunuel. In Spanish with English subtitles.

1951 91m/C Rosario Granados, Julio Villareal, Tito Junco; **D:** Luis Bunuel. **VHS, Beta $24.95** *XVC, MED, ING* 🎬🎬🎬

A Woman's Face An unpleasant, bitter woman with a hideous scar on her face blackmails illicit lovers as a form of revenge for a happiness she doesn't know. She even plots to murder a child for his inheritance. But after plastic surgery, she becomes a nicer person and doubts her plan. Lean, tight suspense with a bang-up finale. In Swedish with English subtitles. Remade in Hollywood in 1941. *AKA:* En Kvinnas Ansikte.

1938 100m/B Ingrid Bergman, Anders Henrikson, Karin Carlsson, Georg Rydeberg, Goran Bernhard, Tore Svennberg; **D:** Gustaf Molander. **VHS, Beta $29.95** *WAC, ING* 🎬🎬

A Woman's Face A physically and emotionally scarred woman becomes part of a blackmail ring. Plastic surgery restores her looks and her attitude. Begins with a murder trial and told in flashbacks; tight, suspenseful remake of the 1938 Swedish Ingrid Bergman vehicle. Climax will knock you out of your chair.

1941 107m/B Joan Crawford, Conrad Veidt, Melvyn Douglas, Osa Massen, Reginald Owen, Albert Basserman, Marjorie Main, Donald Meek, Charles Quigley, Henry Daniell, George Zucco, Robert Warwick; **D:** George Cukor. **VHS, Beta $19.98** *MGM* 🎬🎬🎬

A Woman's Secret O'Hara admits to murder she didn't commit. Why? It's as indiscernible as why the plot should be muddled by flashbacks. RKO lost big bucks on this one.

1949 85m/B Maureen O'Hara, Melvyn Douglas, Gloria Grahame, Bill Williams, Victor Jory, Jay C. Flippen; **D:** Nicholas Ray; **W:** Herman J. Mankiewicz. **VHS, Beta $19.98** *TTC, FCT* 🎬🎬

A Woman's Tale The superlative performance of Florence highlights this look at aging and death. Martha, 78, has been diagnosed with terminal lung cancer. She is looked after by a much-younger nurse and in turn looks after the older friends who share her apartment house. This gentle story quietly depicts the feisty, joyous Martha's last days and the simple pleasures she derives from her remaining time. Florence herself died from cancer not long after completing the film.

1992 (PG-13) 94m/C Sheila Florence, Gosia Dobrowolska, Norman Kaye, Chris Haywood, Myrtle Woods, Ernest Gray, Monica Maughan, Bruce Myles, Alex Menglet; **D:** Paul Cox; **W:** Paul Cox. **VHS** *ORI, BTV* 🎬🎬

Wombling Free An English girl makes friends with a race of tiny, litter-hating furry creatures called Wombles. The creatures are visible only to the little girl because she is the only one who believes. Together they try to clean up a dirty world. British society is less cutting-edge about social roles, etc. than our enlightened one; be prepared for retrograde characterizations. Fun scene with Kelly/Astaire-style dance number.

1977 86m/C Bonnie Langford, David Tomlinson; **D:** Lionel Jeffries. **VHS, Beta $39.95** *COL* 🎬🎬

The Women A brilliant adaptation of the Clare Boothe Luce stage comedy about a group of women who destroy their best friends' reputations at various social gatherings. Crawford's portrayal of the nasty husband-stealer is classic, and the fashion-show scene in Technicolor is one not to miss. Hilarious bitchiness all around. Remade semi-musically as "The Opposite Sex." Another in that long list of stellar 1939 pics.

1939 133m/B Norma Shearer, Joan Crawford, Rosalind Russell, Joan Fontaine, Mary Boland, Lucile Watson, Margaret Dumont, Paulette Goddard, Ruth Hussey, Marjorie Main; **D:** George Cukor; **W:** Anita Loos. **VHS, Beta $19.98** *MGM* 🎬🎬🎬½

The Women Sexy secretary seduces a world-weary writer. *AKA:* Les Femmes; The Vixen.

1969 86m/C Brigitte Bardot, Maurice Ronet. **VHS, Beta $59.95** *UNI* 🎬🎬½

Women & Men: In Love There Are No Rules Made for cable extravaganza chronicling the relationships of three couples, each adapted from the short story of a renowned author. Irwin Shaw's "Return to Kansas City" tells of a young boxer who is prematurely pushed into a match by his ambitious wife. In Carson McCullers' "A Domestic Dilemma," a marriage begins to crumble thanks to an alcoholic wife. Finally, Henry Miller's "Mara" has an aging man and a young Parisian prostitute spending a revealing evening together.

1991 (R) 90m/C Matt Dillon, Kyra Sedgwick, Ray Liotta, Andie MacDowell, Scott Glenn, Juliette Binoche, Jerry Stiller; **D:** Kristi Zea, Walter Bernstein, Mike Figgis. **VHS $89.99** *HBO* 🎬🎬½

Women & Men: Stories of Seduction Three famous short stories are brought to the screen in this made for TV collection. Mary McCarthy's "The Man in the Brooks Brothers Shirt," Dorothy Parker's "Dusk Before Fireworks," and Hemingway's "Hills Like White Elephants" between them cover every aspect of male-female relationships. Since there are three casts and three directors, there is little to join the stories in style, calling attention to some flaws in pacing and acting ability; still, worth watching.

1990 90m/C James Woods, Melanie Griffith, Peter Weller, Elizabeth McGovern, Beau Bridges, Molly Ringwald; **D:** Ken Russell, Tony Richardson, Frederic Raphael. **VHS $89.99** *HBO, FCT* 🎬🎬½

Women in Cell Block 7 Exploitative skinfest about women in prison suffering abuse from their jailers and each other. Seems that one of the prisoners knows the location of massive heroin stash. Badly dubbed. *AKA:* Diario Segreto Di Un Carcere Femminele.

1977 (R) 100m/C Anita Strindberg, Eve Czemeys, Olga Bisera, Jane Avril, Valeria Fabrizi, Jenny Tamburi; **D:** Rino Di Silvestro. **VHS, Beta** *NO* Woof!

Women in Fury A woman is sentenced to imprisonment in a mostly lesbian Brazilian jail, and subsequently leads a breakout.

1984 94m/C Suzanne Carvalno, Gloria Cristal, Zeni Pereira, Leonardo Jose. **VHS, Beta $19.98** *LIV* Woof!

Women in Love Drama of two steamy affairs, based on D.H. Lawrence's classic novel. Deservedly Oscar-winning performance by Jackson; controversial nude wrestling scene with Bates and Reed is hard to forget. Plot is dumped on in favor of atmosphere. Followed nearly two decades later (1989) by a "prequel": "The Rainbow," also from Lawrence, also directed by Russell and starring Jackson.

1970 (R) 129m/C Glenda Jackson, Jennie Linden, Alan Bates, Oliver Reed, Michael Gough, Eleanor Bron; **D:** Ken Russell; **M:** Georges Delerue. Academy Awards '70: Best Actress (Jackson); Nominations: Best Adapted Screenplay, Best Cinematography, Best Director (Russell); Golden Globe Awards '71: Best Foreign Film; National Board of Review Awards '70: 10 Best Films of the Year, Best Actress

(Jackson); National Society of Film Critics Awards '70: Best Actress (Jackson). **VHS, Beta $19.98** *MGM, FOX, BTV* 🎬🎬🎬

The Women of Brewster Place Seven black women living in a tenement fight to gain control of their lives. (Men in general don't come out too well.) Excellent, complex script gives each actress in a fine ensemble headed by Winfrey (in her TV dramatic debut) time in the limelight. Pilot for the series "Brewster Place." Based on the novel by Gloria Naylor. Winfrey was executive producer.

1989 180m/C Oprah Winfrey, Mary Alice, Olivia Cole, Robin Givens, Moses Gunn, Jackee, Paula Kelly, Lonette McKee, Paul Winfield, Cicely Tyson; **D:** Donna Deitch; **W:** Karen Hall. **VHS, Beta $79.95** *JTC, FCT* 🎬🎬🎬

Women of the Prehistoric Planet On a strange planet, the members of a space rescue mission face deadly perils. Typical bad sci-fi of its era, with horrid special effects, including "giant" lizards. Get this: there's one woman, and she's not of the planet in question. See if you can last long enough to catch the amazing plot twist at the end.

1966 87m/C Wendell Corey, Irene Tsu, Robert Ito, Stuart Margolin, Lyle Waggoner, Adam Roarke, Merry Anders; **D:** Arthur C. Pierce. **VHS, Beta** *NO* Woof!

Women of Valor During WWII, a band of American nurses stationed in the Philippines are captured by the Japanese and struggle to survive in a brutal POW camp. TV feature was made 40 years too late, adding up to a surreal experience.

1986 95m/C Susan Sarandon, Kristy McNichol, Alberta Watson, Valerie Mahaffey, Suzanne Lederer, Pat Bishop, Terry O'Quinn, Neva Patterson; **D:** Buzz Kulik; **M:** Georges Delerue. **VHS, Beta $9.99** *STE, PSM* 🎬½

Women on the Verge of a Nervous Breakdown Surreal and hilarious romp through the lives of film dubber Maura, her ex-lover, his crazed ex-mistress, his new lover, his son, and his son's girlfriend. There's also Maura's friend Barranco, who inadvertantly lent her apartment to Shiite terrorists and now believes the police are after her as an accomplice in an airline hijacking. They meet in a comedy of errors, missed phone calls, and rental notices, while discovering the truth and necessity of love. Fast-paced and full of black humor, with loaded gazpacho serving as a key element. Introduced Almodovar to American audiences. In Spanish with English subtitles. *AKA:* Mujeres al Borde de un Ataque de Nervios.

1988 (R) 88m/C Carmen Maura, Fernando Guillen, Julieta Serrano, Maria Barranco, Rossy de Palma, Antonio Banderas; **D:** Pedro Almodovar; **W:** Pedro Almodovar; **M:** Bernardo Bonazzi. Academy Awards '88 Nominations: Best Foreign Language Film; National Board of Review Awards '88: 5 Best Foreign Films of the Year; New York Film Critics Awards '88: Best Foreign Film. **VHS, Beta $79.98** *ORI, ING* 🎬🎬🎬½

Women Unchained Five women escape from a maximum security prison and make a run for the Mexican border, shunning civilized behavior along the way. Much less-than-honorable entry in desperate women genre.

1977 (R) 82m/C Carolyn Judd, Teri Guzman, Darlene Mattingly, Angel Colbert, Bonita Kalem; **D:** Kent Osborne; **W:** Kent Osborne. **VHS, Beta $59.95** *GEM* Woof!

Women's Club Table-turning sex comedy about a wealthy matron who patronizes a talented (?) young movie writer, but really wants—you know what. She begins lending

his services to friends—and does he ever get worn out! This excuse may be intended to be uproarious, but it's hard to tell. And all that sex gets very perfunctory after awhile.
1987 (R) 89m/C Michael Pare, Maud Adams, Eddie Velez; **D:** Sandra Weintraub. **VHS, Beta** $79.98 LIV, VES ⅔½

Women's Prison Escape Four tough broads blow the pen and are forced to hightail it through the Everglades. They can't decide which is worse, the snakes and 'gators, or the corrupt and sleazy life they left behind. Only cinematic pairing of Rooney and Lurch. **AKA:** Cell Block Girls.
19?? 90m/C Ted Cassidy, Chris Robinson, Mickey Rooney; **D:** Chris Robinson. **VHS** $9.99 QVD ⅔½

Women's Prison Massacre Four male convicts temporarily detained at a woman's prison (why?) violently take hostages and generally make trouble for the authorities and the women. Horribly dubbed.
1985 89m/C Laura Gemser, Lorraine De Selle, Francoise Perrot, Ursula Flores, Gabriele Truti; **D:** Gilbert Roussel. **VHS, Beta** $19.98 LIV, VES Woof!

Wonder Man When a brash nightclub entertainer (Kaye) is killed by gangsters, his mild-mannered twin brother (Kaye) takes his place to smoke out the killers. One of Kaye's better early films. The film debuts of Vera-Ellen and Cochran. Look for Mrs. Howell of "Gilligan's Island." ♫So In Love; Bali Boogie; Ortchi Chornya; Opera Number.
1945 98m/C Danny Kaye, Virginia Mayo, Vera-Ellen, Steve Cochran, S.Z. Sakall, Otto Kruger; **D:** H. Bruce Humberstone. Academy Awards '45: Best Special Effects; Nominations: Best Song ("So in Love"), Best Sound, Best Original Score. **VHS, Beta** $19.98 HBO, SUE ⅔⅔½

The Wonderful World of the Brothers Grimm Big-budget fantasy based very loosely on the Grimm Brothers' lives and three of their stories: "The Dancing Princesses," "The Cobbler and the Elves," and "The Singing Bone." Good, fun Puppetoon scenes, but leaves much else to be desired. A megawatt cast and the ubiquitous hand of producer-director Pal are not enough to cover the flaws. The biographical parts are hokey, and the tales used are the wrong ones. Disappointing but historically interesting. The second-ever story film done in Cinerama. ♫The Theme From the Wonderful World of the Brothers Grimm; Gypsy Rhapsody; Christmas Land; Ah-Oom; Above the Stars; Dee-Are-A-Gee-O-En (Dragon).
1962 134m/C Laurence Harvey, Karl-Heinz Boehm, Claire Bloom, Buddy Hackett, Terry-Thomas, Russ Tamblyn, Yvette Mimieux, Oscar Homolka, Walter Slezak, Beulah Bondi, Martita Hunt, Otto Kruger, Barbara Eden, Jim Backus, Arnold Stang; **D:** Henry Levin, George Pal; **W:** William Roberts. Academy Awards '62: Best Costume Design (Color); Nominations: Best Art Direction/Set Decoration (Color), Best Color Cinematography, Best Original Score. **VHS, Beta** $19.98 MGM ⅔⅔½

Wonderland Campy thriller follows two young gay boys in England, inadvertent witnesses to a murder, who find themselves on the run. Fast paced, dreamy atmosphere makes up for the sometimes confusing plot. Often overlooked British import. **AKA:** The Fruit Machine.
1988 103m/C Emile Charles, Tony Forsyth, Robert Stephens, Clare Higgins, Bruce Payne, Robbie Coltrane; **D:** Philip Saville. **VHS** $79.98 LIV, VES ⅔⅔⅔

Wonderland Cove Seafaring adventurer adopts five orphan children and embarks on journeys to exotic locales.

1975 78m/C Clu Gulager; **D:** Jerry Thorpe. **Beta** $59.95 PSM ⅔

The Wonders of Aladdin Slapstick comedy based on the ancient rubbed-lamp-and-genie chestnut. Kids'll love it; adults will yawn. **AKA:** Les Mille Et Une Nuits; Le Meraviglie Di Aladino.
1961 93m/C Donald O'Connor, Vittorio De Sica; **D:** Henry Levin, Mario Bava. **VHS, Beta** $59.95 NLC ⅔½

Wonderwall: The Movie Bizarre characters trip over themselves in love while groovy music plays in background.
1969 82m/C Jack MacGowran, Jane Birkin, Irene Handl; **D:** Joe Massot; **M:** George Harrison, Eric Clapton, Ravi Shankar. **VHS, Beta** $79.95 FCT, MVD ⅔½

Wonsan Operation U.N. soldiers plunge into the muddy depths of enemy territory in search of secret information that would end the Korean War. Dubbed.
1978 100m/C Lew Montania, Frederick Hill; **D:** Terrence Sul. **VHS, Beta** VDA ⅔

Woodchipper Massacre Aunt Tess is frozen in the freezer, waiting to be turned into whatever the fleshy equivalent of woodchips is by her three unloving relations, and her totally evil son has just broken out of prison looking to retrieve his inheritance. You think you have problems? You'll have one less if you leave this one on the shelf.
1989 90m/C Jon McBride, Patricia McBride; **D:** Jon McBride. **VHS, Beta** DMP Woof!

The Wooden Gun Conflicts arise between two teenage factions in 1950's Tel Aviv: native Israelis, and the children of Jews arrived from Europe since WWII. In Hebrew with English subtitles.
1979 91m/C D: Han Moshenson. **VHS, Beta** $79.95 ERG, FCT, ING ⅔⅔½

Wooden Horse Lean thriller of British POWs escaping a Nazi camp through a tunnel beneath their exercise horse. Based on a true incident in 1943 and on "The Tunnel Escape" by Eric Williams; set the tone for all British prison-camp movies to follow: stiff upper lip and all that, and adolescent-style trickery reminiscent of English boarding schools.
1950 98m/C Anthony Steel, Leo Genn, David Tomlinson, Bryan Forbes, Peter Finch; **D:** Jack Lee. **VHS, Beta** NO ⅔⅔

Woodstock Step into the way-back machine and return to the times of luv, peace, and understanding. Powerful chronicle of the great 1969 Woodstock rock concert celebrates the music and lifestyle of the late '60s. More than 400,000 spectators withstood lack of privacy, bathrooms, parking, and food while wallowing in the mud for four days to catch classic performances by a number of popular performers and groups. Martin Scorcese helped edit the documentary, trailblazing in its use of split-screen montage.
1970 (R) 180m/C Canned Heat, Richie Havens, Roger Daltrey, Pete Townshend, Keith Moon, Joan Baez, Country Joe & the Fish, Jimi Hendrix, Carlos Santana, David Crosby, Stephen Stills, The Jefferson Airplane, Joe Cocker, Sly & the Family Stone, John Sebastian, Arlo Guthrie, Ten Years After; **D:** Michael Wadleigh. Academy Awards '70: Best Feature Documentary; Nominations: Best Film Editing, Best Sound. **VHS, Beta** $29.95 MVD, WAR ⅔⅔⅔⅔

Woof! Follows the misadventures of a boy who metamorphosed into a dog.
1990 82m/C VHS $39.98 FHE, UND, BTV ⅔⅔½

The Word Intriguing premise has an archeologist finding a perviously unknown text purporting to be written by the younger brother of Jesus. If authentic and publicized,

it would wreak theological havoc. Janssen is off to Italy to check up; he finds murder and skullduggery. Well-acted, interesting story.
1978 300m/C David Janssen, James Whitmore, Florinda Bolkan, Eddie Albert, Geraldine Chaplin, Hurd Hatfield, John Huston, Kate Mulgrew, Janice Rule, Nicol Williamson; **D:** Richard Long. **VHS, Beta** $24.95 FRH ⅔⅔½

Words and Music Plot based on the careers of Rodgers and Hart is little more than a peg on which to hang lots of classic songs, sung by a parade of MGM stars. Also includes Kelly's dance recreation of "Slaughter on Tenth Avenue." Good advice: if no one's singing or dancing, fast forward.
1948 122m/C Mickey Rooney, Tom Drake, Judy Garland, Gene Kelly, Lena Horne, Mel Torme, Cyd Charisse, Marshall Thompson, Janet Leigh, Betty Garrett, June Allyson, Perry Como, Vera-Ellen, Ann Sothern; **D:** Norman Taurog; **M:** Richard Rodgers, Lorenz Hart. **VHS, Beta** $29.95 MGM ⅔⅔½

Words by Heart An African American family in turn of the century Missouri faces issues of discrimination and prejudice. Twelve-year-old Lena wins a speech contest and begins to question their place in the community and their aspirations for a better life. Based on a book by Ouida Sebestyen. Aired by PBS as part of the "Wonderworks" family movie series.
1984 116m/C Charlotte Rae, Robert Hooks, Alfre Woodard; **D:** Robert Thompson. **VHS** $29.95 PME, FCT, HMV ⅔⅔½

Work/Police Two Chaplin two-reelers. In "Work (The Paper Hanger)" (1915), a family hires Charlie and cohorts Armstrong and Purviance to re-paper a house. Little did they know! In "Police" (1916), Charlie plays an ex-con released into the cruel world. Unremittingly hilarious. Silent with music score.
1916 54m/B Charlie Chaplin, Billy Armstrong, Charles Insley, Marta Golden, Edna Purviance; **D:** Charlie Chaplin. **VHS, Beta** $39.95 VYY ⅔⅔⅔½

Workin' for Peanuts A young man who sells beer at a baseball stadium falls in love with the stadium owner's daughter.
1985 52m/C Carl Marotte, Jessica Steer. **VHS, Beta** NO ⅔⅔⅔

Working Girl Romantic comedy set in the Big Apple has secretary Griffith working her way to the top in spite of her manipulative boss (Weaver in a powerful parody). Griffith gets her chance to shine when Weaver breaks a leg. She meets Ford for business that turns to romance. A 1980s Cinderella story that's sexy, funny, and sharply written and directed. Nice work by Ford, but this is definitely Griffith's movie. And keep an eye on gal pal Cusack.
1988 (R) 115m/C Melanie Griffith, Harrison Ford, Sigourney Weaver, Joan Cusack, Alec Baldwin, Philip Bosco, Ricki Lake, Nora Dunn, Olympia Dukakis, Oliver Platt, James Lally, Kevin Spacey, Robert Easton; **D:** Mike Nichols; **W:** Kevin Wade; **M:** Carly Simon, Rob Mounsey. Academy Awards '88: Best Song ("Let the River Run"); Nominations: Best Actress (Griffith), Best Director (Nichols), Best Picture, Best Supporting Actress (Cusack, Weaver); Golden Globe Awards '89: Best Actress—Musical/Comedy (Griffith), Best Film—Musical/Comedy, Best Song ("Let the River Run"), Best Supporting Actress (Weaver). **VHS, Beta** $19.98 FOX ⅔⅔⅔

Working Girls Three girls who share an apartment in Los Angeles are willing to do anything for money. And they do. For lack of anything else to recommend, watch for the striptease by Peterson, better known as Elvira on TV.
1975 (R) 80m/C Sarah Kennedy, Laurie Rose, Mark Thomas, Cassandra Peterson; **D:** Stephanie Rothman. **VHS, Beta** $19.98 VCI ⅔

Working Girls An acclaimed, controversial look by independent filmmaker Borden into lives of modern brothel prostitutes over the period of one day. The sex is realistically candid and perfunctory; the docudrama centers on a prostitute who is a Yale graduate and aspiring photographer living with a female lover. Compelling, touching, and lasting, with sexually candid language and scenery.
1987 93m/C Amanda Goodwin, Louise Smith, Ellen McElduff, Maurisia Zach, Janne Peters, Helen Nicholas; *D:* Lizzie Borden; *W:* Sandra Kay; *M:* David Van Tiegham. VHS, Beta $14.95 *COL, NLC, HHE* 🐾🐾🐾

Working Winnie/Oh So Simple Two rare, second-echelon short silent comedies.
1922 61m/B Ethlyn Gibson, Bobby Ray. VHS, Beta, 8mm $19.95 *VYY* 🐾🐾🐾

The World According to Garp Comedy turns to tragedy in this relatively faithful version of John Irving's popular (and highly symbolic) novel, adapted by Steve Tesich. Chronicles the life of T.S. Garp, a struggling everyman beset by the destructive forces of modern society. Nevertheless, Garp maintains his optimism even as his life unravels around him. At the core of the film is a subplot involving a group of extreme feminists inspired in part by Garp's mother, the author of "A Sexual Suspect." Close and Lithgow (as a giant transsexual) are spectacular, while Williams is low-key and tender as the beleagured Garp. Ultimately pointless, perhaps, but effectively and intelligently so.
1982 (R) 136m/C Robin Williams, Mary Beth Hurt, John Lithgow, Glenn Close, Hume Cronyn, Jessica Tandy, Swoosie Kurtz, Amanda Plummer, Warren Berlinger, Brandon Maggart; *Cameos:* George Roy Hill; *D:* George Roy Hill; *W:* Steve Tesich. VHS, Beta $19.98 *WAR* 🐾🐾🐾

The World Accuses A woman takes a job in a nursery, unaware that one child is her own, put up for adoption after her wealthy husband died. Then, her ex-lover shows up in her attic after escaping from prison and takes her hostage. Whew! Everything works out, except that the viewer is left confused and incredulous.
1935 62m/B Vivian Tobin, Dickie Moore, Russell Hopton, Cora Sue Collins, Mary Carr; *D:* Charles Lamont. VHS $24.95 *NOS, DVT* 🐾🐾 1/2

A World Apart Cinematographer Menges' first directoral effort is a blistering, insightful drama told from the point of view of a 13-year-old white girl living in South Africa, oblivious to apartheid until her crusading journalist mother is arrested under the 90-Day Detention Act, under which she might remain in prison permanently. Political morality tale is also a look at the family-vs-cause choices activists must make. Heavily lauded, with good reason; the autobiographical script is based on Slovo's parents, persecuted South African journalists Joe Slovo and Ruth First.
1988 (PG) 114m/C Barbara Hershey, Jodhi May, Linda Mvusi, David Suchet, Jeroen Krabbe, Paul Freeman, Tim Roth; *D:* Chris Menges; *W:* Shawn Slovo. VHS, Beta $9.98 *MED* 🐾🐾🐾 1/2

The World Gone Mad During Prohibition, a tough reporter discovers the district attorney is the intended victim of a murder plot involving crooked Wall Street types. Full circle: this interesting drama of white-collar crime is again topical, though dialogue heavy and desultory. *AKA:* The Public Be Hanged; Public Be Damned.
1933 70m/B Pat O'Brien, Louis Calhern, J. Carroll Naish; *D:* Christy Cabanne. VHS, Beta $19.95 *NOS, CAB, DVT* 🐾🐾 1/2

World Gone Wild Action yarn about a post-apocalyptic world of the future where an evil cult leader brainwashes his disciples. Together they battle a small band of eccentrics for the world's last water source. Stale rehash (with ineffective satiric elements) of the Mad Max genre, served with Ant for campy appeal.
1988 (R) 95m/C Bruce Dern, Michael Pare, Adam Ant, Catherine Mary Stewart, Rick Podell; *D:* Lee H. Katzin. VHS, Beta $89.95 *MED, VTR* 🐾 1/2

The World is Full of Married Men A philandering ad exec gets involved with a reckless model, inspiring his fed-up wife also to look for extramarital sex. Promiscuously raunchy melodrama was written by the queen of sleaze, Jackie Collins, based on her novel.
1980 (R) 106m/C Anthony (Tony) Franciosa, Carroll Baker, Sherrie Croon, Gareth Hunt, Paul Nicholas; *D:* Robert Young; *W:* Jackie Collins. VHS, Beta $59.98 *FOX Woof!*

The World of Apu Finale of director Ray's acclaimed Apu trilogy (following "Pather Panchali" and "Aparajito"). Aspiring writer Apu drops out of the university for want of money and takes up with an old chum. An odd circumstance leads him to marry his friend's cousin, whom he comes to love. She dies in childbirth (though her baby boy lives); Apu is deeply distraught, destroys the novel he was working on, and becomes a wanderer. His friend finds him five years later and helps him begin again with his young son. Wonderfully human, hopeful story told by a world-class director. From the novel "Aparajito" by B. Bandopadhaya. In Bengali with English subtitles. *AKA:* Apu Sansat; Apur Sansar.
1959 103m/B Soumitra Chatterjee, Sharmila Tagore, Alok Charkravarty, Swapan Makerji; *D:* Satyajit Ray; *W:* Satyajit Ray; *M:* Ravi Shankar. VHS, Beta $24.95 *HHT, VYY, DVT* 🐾🐾🐾🐾

The World of Henry Orient Charming, eccentric comedy about two 15-year-old girls who, madly in love with an egotistical concert pianist, pursue him all around New York City. Sellers is hilarious, Walker and Spaeth are adorable as his teen groupies; Bosley and Lansbury are great as Walker's indulgent parents. For anyone who has ever been uncontrollably infatuated. Screenplay by the father/daughter team, Nora and Nunnally Johnson, based on Nora Johnson's novel.
1964 106m/C Peter Sellers, Tippy Walker, Merrie Spaeth, Tom Bosley, Angela Lansbury, Paula Prentiss; *D:* George Roy Hill; *W:* Nunnally Johnson, Nora Johnson; *M:* Elmer Bernstein. VHS, Beta $19.98 *MGM, FCT* 🐾🐾🐾 1/2

A World of Strangers A harsh look at apartheid through the eyes of an Englishman who has traveled to South Africa to manage a publishing house. Filmed in strict secrecy in Johannesburg due to the film's aggressive condemnation of the practice. Based on a novel by Nadine Gordimer.
1962 89m/B Ivan Jackson, Zakes Mokae; *D:* Henning Carlsen. VHS $59.95 *CVC, ING* 🐾🐾🐾

The World of Suzie Wong Asian prostitute Kwan plays cat-and-mouse with American painter Holden. She lies to him about her profession, her family, and herself. His association with her ruins relationships in his life. Why, then, does he not get a clue? Good question, not answered by this soap opera that would be a serious drama. Offensively sanitized picture of the world of prostitution in an Asian metropolis. On the other hand, it's all nicely shot, much of it on location in Hong Kong. Based on Paul Os-

born's play which was taken from Richard Mason's novel.
1960 129m/C William Holden, Nancy Kwan, Sylvia Syms, Michael Wilding, Laurence Naismith, Jackie Chan; *D:* Richard Quine. VHS, Beta $19.95 *PAR* 🐾🐾

World of the Depraved Tango (Storm) runs an exercise club for young lovelies that are systematically being stalked by the mysterious full moon sex killer. Enter police detectives Riley and Hamilton (Decker, Reed), joking types who peep on their charges through keyholes, etc. When the plot finally gets around to the issue of the killer, the point of the movie has already been made clear. Silly, trivial, sophomoric humor lacking a trace of sincerity. Volume 6 of Frank Henenlotter's Sexy Shockers series.
1967 73m/C Tempest Storm, Johnnie Decker, Larry Reed; *D:* Herbert Jeffries; *W:* Herbert Jeffries. VHS $23.00 *SMW* 🐾

World of the Vampires Evil count commands his vampire legions to wreak vengeance upon the family whose ancestors condemned him. Fairly miserable Mexican horror entry. Spanish title: "El Mundo de los Vampiros."
1960 75m/B Mauricio Garces, Erna Martha Bauman, Silvia Fournier, Guillermo Murray; *D:* Alfonso Corona Blake. VHS, Beta $54.95 *SNC, HHT, MAD Woof!*

The World Owes Me a Living Melodrama about pilot Farrar losing his memory in a plane crash and Campbell trying to spark his recollection of the past.
1947 91m/B David Farrar, Judy Campbell, Jack Livesey, John Laurie; *D:* Vernon Sewell; *W:* Vernon Sewell. VHS $15.95 *LOO* 🐾🐾

World War II: When Lions Roared The "Lions" are Franklin Delano Roosevelt, Winston Churchill, and Joseph Stalin. The three Allied leaders formed an uneasy alliance to crush Hitler and Mussolini, all against much internal treachery. Uses lots of WWII newsreel footage. Made for television; on two cassettes.
1994 186m/C John Lithgow, Bob Hoskins, Michael Caine, Ed Begley Jr., Jan Tiska; *D:* Joseph Sargent; *W:* David Rintel. VHS $39.98 *MPI* 🐾🐾 1/2

World War III How's that for a title? A Russian plot is afoot to seize and destroy the Alaskan pipeline. When the plot is discovered, negotiation is needed to prevent world war. Executive branch showdown ensues between U.S. prez Hudson and Soviet chief Keith. Director Boris Sagal was killed on location, whereupon Greene took over, and shooting was moved indoors with dramatic tension lost in the transition. Made for TV.
1986 186m/C Brian Keith, David Soul, Rock Hudson, Cathy Lee Crosby, Katherine Helmond, Robert Prosky, James Hampton, Richard Yniguez, Herbert Jefferson Jr.; *D:* David Greene; *W:* Robert L. Joseph. VHS, Beta $79.98 *FOX* 🐾🐾 1/2

The Worldly Madonna Young plays two roles as Janet, a convent novitiate, and her cabaret dancer sister, Lucy. Lucy thinks she's killed a man and Janet agrees to change places with her.
1922 47m/B Clara Kimball Young, Richard Tucker, George Hackathorne, William P. Carleton, Jean De Limur, William Marion, Milla Davenport; *D:* Harry Garson. VHS $14.95 *GPV* 🐾🐾 1/2

The World's Greatest Athlete Lame Disney comedy about a Tarzan-like jungle-man (Vincent) recruited by an unsuccessful American college coach (Amos) and his bumbling assistant (Conway). Fun special effects, weak script add up to mediocre

family fare. Cameo by Howard Cosell as—who else?—himself.
1973 (G) 89m/C Jan-Michael Vincent, Tim Conway, John Amos, Roscoe Lee Browne, Dayle Haddon; *Cameos:* Howard Cosell; *D:* Robert Scheerer; *M:* Marvin Hamlisch. **VHS, Beta** DIS, OM 🐾🐾

World's Greatest Lover Milwaukee baker Rudi Valentine, played oft-hilariously by Wilder, tries to make it big in 1920s Hollywood. He has a screen test as a Hollywood movie sheik, but his wife (Kane) leaves him for the real McCoy. Episodic and uneven, it's alternately uproarious, touching and downright raunchy.
1977 (PG) 89m/C Gene Wilder, Carol Kane, Dom DeLuise, Fritz Feld, Carl Ballantine, Michael Huddleston, Matt Collins, Ronny Graham; *D:* Gene Wilder; *W:* Gene Wilder. **VHS $59.98** FOX 🐾🐾½

The World's Oldest Living Bridesmaid Hokey romantic comedy about a successful woman attorney who just can't find Mr. Right. Brenda feels even worse when she attends yet another friend's wedding. However, when she hires a younger, male secretary (former model Wimmer) the romantic sparks fly. An appealing and attractive cast helps this made-for-television fare.
1992 100m/C Donna Mills, Brian Wimmer, Beverly Garland, Winston Reckert, Art Hindle, Laura Press; *D:* Joseph L. Scanlan. **VHS $89.95** AIP 🐾🐾

The Worm Eaters Mean developers want to take over a reclusive worm farmer's land. He unleashes his livestock on them. The bad guys turn into—eeck!—"worm people." A truck runs over our hero nearly 75 minutes too late to save the viewer.
1977 (PG) 75m/C Herb Robins, Barry Hostetler, Lindsay Armstrong Black; *D:* Herb Robins; *W:* Herb Robins. **VHS, Beta** NO *Woof!*

The Worst of Faces of Death Grisly deaths recorded on film by sick Dr. Flellis. Absolutely gruesome.
1990 60m/C VHS, Beta $39.98 GRG *Woof!*

The Worst of Hollywood: Vol. 1 Two really bad movies for your viewing displeasure. "Maniac" is a mad-scientist fest and "Protect Your Daughter" warns of the perils of the Flapper era.
1990 115m/B Bill Woods, Horace Carpenter, Phyllis Diller; *D:* Dwain Esper. **VHS, Beta $29.95** INC *Woof!*

The Worst of Hollywood: Vol. 2 A von Stroheim-fest of mediocrity. In "Fugitive Road" Erich plays an Austrian officer of the First World War. "The Crime of Dr. Crespi" has him portray a mad scientist.
1990 131m/B Erich von Stroheim, Dwight Frye; *D:* Erich von Stroheim. **VHS, Beta $29.95** INC *Woof!*

The Worst of Hollywood: Vol. 3 Two more awful, exploitive docudramas. "Nation Aflame" features many silent screen stars who teach the virtues of living in racial harmony. "Probation" boasts the first screen appearance of Grable, as a promiscuous woman who ends up in prison.
1990 140m/B Betty Grable. **VHS, Beta $29.95** INC *Woof!*

The Worst Witch Fantasy about a school for young witches where the educational lessons never go quite as planned. Adapted from the children's book "The Worst Witch" by Jill Murphy.
1986 (G) 70m/C Diana Rigg, Charlotte Rae, Tim Curry, Fairuza Balk; *D:* Robert Young. **VHS, Beta $79.95** PSM 🐾🐾½

Worth Winning A notoriously eligible Philadelphia bachelor takes a bet to become engaged to three women within three months, and finds himself in hot water. A critically dead-in-the-water chucklefest.
1989 (PG-13) 103m/C Mark Harmon, Lesley Ann Warren, Madeleine Stowe, Maria Holvoe, Mark Blum, Andrea Martin, Alan Blumenfeld, Brad Hall, Tony Longo; *D:* Will MacKenzie; *W:* Sara Parriott, Josann McGibbon. **VHS, Beta $89.98** FOX 🐾½

The Would-Be Gentleman The Comedie Francaise troupe performs Moliere's famous farce-comedy. Valuable as a record of the famous troupe on stage. When they're long gone, our grandkids can enjoy this. We can too (if we can't afford the trip to France), though it's less a film than a filming of a play. In French with English subtitles.
1958 93m/C Louis Seigner, Jean Meyer, Jean Piat. **VHS, Beta $24.95** DVT, ING 🐾🐾½

Woyzeck Chilling portrayal of a man plunging into insanity. Mired in the ranks of the German Army, Woyzeck is harassed by his superiors and tortured in scientific experiments, gradually devolving into homicidal maniac. Based on Georg Buchner play. In German with English subtitles.
1978 82m/C Klaus Kinski, Eva Mattes, Wolfgang Reichmann, Josef Bierbichler; *D:* Werner Herzog; *W:* Werner Herzog. **VHS $59.95** NYF, ING 🐾🐾🐾

Woza Albert! An international hit play makes tries to transfer its appeal to film, not an easy feat. Set in South Africa and performed by black South Africans, (using their townships as a backdrop) it explores in stylized fashion events resulting from the second coming of Christ to a hypocritical nation.
1982 55m/C VHS $195.00 CAL, FLI 🐾🐾½

WR: Mysteries of the Organism Makavejev's breakthrough film, a surreal, essayist exploration of the conflict/union between sexuality and politics—namely, Wilheim Reich and Stalin. A raunchy, bitterly satiric non-narrative that established the rule-breaking Yugoslav internationally. In Serbian with English subtitles.
1971 84m/C Milena Dravic, Jagoda Kaloper, Tuli Kupferberg, Jackie Curtis; *D:* Dusan Makavejev; *W:* Dusan Makavejev. **VHS, Beta $79.95** FCT 🐾🐾🐾

The Wraith Drag-racing Arizona teens find themselves challenged by a mysterious, otherworldly stranger. Hot cars; cool music; little else to recommend it. Lousy script; ludicrous excuse for a premise. Most of the stars herein are related to somebody famous.
1987 (PG-13) 92m/C Charlie Sheen, Nick Cassavetes, Sherilyn Fenn, Randy Quaid, Matthew Barry, Clint Howard, Griffin O'Neal; *D:* Mike Marvin. **VHS, Beta $14.98** LIV 🐾½

Wrangler When an Australian rancher dies his daughter tries to hang on to the family ranch from a ruthless creditor. She also has to deal with the attentions of two men—one a businessman and the other a cattleman, both equally dashing and handsome. Beautiful scenery of the Australian Outback as well as romance and adventure.
1988 93m/C Jeff Fahey, Tushka Bergen, Steven Vidler, Richard Moir, Shane Briant, Drew Forsythe, Cornelia Frances, Sandy Gore, Frederick Parslow; *D:* Ian Barry; *W:* John Sexton; *M:* Mario Millo. **VHS** NO 🐾🐾½

The Wreck of the Mary Deare Slow-moving adventure drama focusing on the wreck of the freighter called the Mary Deare. Heston plays a ship salvager who comes upon a seemingly empty ship one

night and Cooper is the only crew member on board. Special effects are the main attraction in this interesting sea drama. Film originally was to be directed by Hitchcock, but he turned down the offer to do "North by Northwest."
1959 105m/C Gary Cooper, Charlton Heston, Michael Redgrave, Emlyn Williams, Cecil Parker, Alexander Knox, Virginia McKenna, Richard Harris; *D:* Michael Anderson Sr. **VHS $19.98** MGM 🐾🐾½

The Wrestler All-star wrestling, which is fictional anyway, gets said treatment in the appropriate way. Honest promoter (yeah, sure) bumps heads with bad-guy crooks who want in on the action. Made-for-TV opportunity for Asner to slum.
1973 103m/C Ed Asner, Elaine Giftos, Verne Gagne, Harold Sakata. **VHS, Beta $19.95** NWV, STE 🐾

Wrestling Ernest Hemingway A shy barber and a rollicking sea captain, both 75 and retired, form an unlikely companionship in a Florida retirement mecca. Duvall is the persnickety introvert who quietly follows routine and Harris is the would-be ladies' man whose endless tall tales include having tangled with Papa Hemingway in his youth. They share walks in the park, little league baseball from the bleachers, and coffee klatches that reveal the emptiness of their lives. Director Haines' focus on the principals' emotional baggage considerably dampens the proceedings. Depression in the elderly may be a topic that is not quite ready to come out of Hollywood's closet.
1993 (PG-13) 123m/C Robert Duvall, Richard Harris, Piper Laurie, Shirley MacLaine, Sandra Bullock; *D:* Randa Haines; *W:* Steve Conrad; *M:* Michael Convertino. **VHS** WAR 🐾🐾

Wrestling Racket Girls An alleged white slavery expose, replete with seamy material that is only slightly laughable by modern terms, reducing overall camp appeal and increasing rating on boredom meter.
1939 72m/B VHS, Beta $24.95 TPV *Woof!*

Wrestling Women vs. the Aztec Ape An unclassifiable epic wherein female wrestlers battle a mad doctor and his Aztec robot gorilla. Dubbed badly, of course. Much anticipated follow-up to "Wrestling Women vs. the Aztec Mummy." *AKA:* Doctor of Doom.
1962 75m/C Elizabeth Campbell, Lorena Velasquez, Armando Silvestre, Roberto Canedo; *D:* Rene Cardona Sr. **VHS, Beta $19.95** RHI, HHT, SNC *Woof!*

Wrestling Women vs. the Aztec Mummy Women, broad of shoulder, wrestle an ancient Aztec wrestler who comes to life. Furnished with a new rock soundtrack.
1959 88m/C Lorena Velasquez, Armando Silvestre; *D:* Rene Cardona Sr. **VHS, Beta $54.95** SNC, RHI, HHT *Woof!*

Write to Kill A young mystery writer seeks revenge when his brother is murdered by a ring of counterfeiters.
1991 (R) 120m/C Scott Valentine, Chris Mulkey, Joan Severance, G.W. Bailey, Ray Wise; *D:* Ruben Preuss. **VHS** COL 🐾½

Writer's Block Fairchild is a successful thriller writer whose latest books feature a serial killer. She decides to kill the character off and is soon stalked by a psycho who is using her plots for some copy-cat killings. Tepid made for cable television movie with San Diego locations the only highlight.
1991 (R) 90m/C Morgan Fairchild, Joe Regalbuto, Michael Praed, Cheryl Anderson, Mary Ann Pascal, Douglas Rowe, Ned Bellamy; *D:* Charles Correll; *W:* Elisa Bell. **VHS, Beta** PAR 🐾🐾

Written on the Wind Sirk's frenzied, melodrama-as-high-art dissection of both the American Dream and American movies follows a Texas oil family's self-destruction through wealth, greed and unbridled lust. Exaggerated depiction of and comment on American ambition and pretension, adapted from Robert Wilder's novel.
1956 99m/C Lauren Bacall, Rock Hudson, Dorothy Malone, Robert Stack, Robert Keith, Grant Williams, Edward Platt, Harry Shannon; **D:** Douglas Sirk; **W:** George Zuckerman. Academy Awards '56: Best Supporting Actress (Malone); Nominations: Best Song ("Written on the Wind"), Best Supporting Actor (Stack). **VHS, Beta** $14.95 MCA, BTV ✍✍✍½

The Wrong Arm of the Law Loopy gangster yarn about a trio of Aussie gangsters who arrive in London and upset the local crime balance when they dress up as cops and confiscate loot from apprehended robbers. General confusion erupts among the police, the local crooks, and the imposters. Riotous and hilarious, with Sellers leading a host of familiar faces.
1963 94m/B Peter Sellers, Lionel Jeffries, Nanette Newman, Bernard Cribbins, Dennis Price; **D:** Cliff Owen; **M:** Richard Rodney Bennett. **VHS, Beta** $39.95 MON ✍✍✍

The Wrong Box Two elderly Victorian brothers try to kill each other so that one of them may collect the large inheritance left to them. Based on a Robert Louis Stevenson novel. Well-cast black comedy replete with sight gags, many of which flop.
1966 105m/C Peter Sellers, Dudley Moore, Peter Cook, Michael Caine, Ralph Richardson, John Mills; **D:** Bryan Forbes; **W:** Larry Gelbart; **M:** John Barry. **VHS, Beta** $59.95 COL ✍✍✍

The Wrong Guys Five giants of stand-up comedy star as a group of men who reunite their old boy scout pack and go camping. A crazed convict mistakes them for FBI agents. It's supposed to get zany after that, but succeeds only in being clumsy and embarassing.
1988 (PG) 86m/C Richard Lewis, Richard Belzer, Louie Anderson, Tim Thomerson, Franklin Ajaye, John Goodman, Ernie Hudson, Timothy Van Patten; **D:** Danny Bilson; **W:** Danny Bilson, Paul DeMeo. **VHS, Beta** $19.95 STE, NWV ✍

Wrong is Right A black action comedy about international terrorism, news reporting and the CIA. Connery is terrific, as usual, as a TV reporter in a head-scratching attempt at satire of our TV-influenced society. **AKA:** The Man With The Deadly Lens.
1982 (R) 117m/C Sean Connery, Katharine Ross, Robert Conrad, George Grizzard, Henry Silva, G.D. Spradlin, John Saxon, Leslie Nielsen, Robert Webber, Rosalind Cash, Hardy Kruger, Dean Stockwell, Ron Moody, Jennifer Jason Leigh; **D:** Richard Brooks; **W:** Richard Brooks. **VHS, Beta** $79.95 COL ✍✍

The Wrong Man Nightclub musician Fonda is falsely accused of a robbery and his life is destroyed. Taken almost entirely from the real-life case of mild-mannered bass player "Manny" Balestrero; probes his anguish at being wrongly accused; and showcases Miles (later to appear in "Psycho") and her character's agony. Harrowing, especially following more lighthearted Hitchcock fare such as "The Trouble with Harry." Part of the "A Night at the Movies" series, this tape simulates a 1956 movie evening with a color Bugs Bunny cartoon, "A Star Is Bored," a newsreel and coming attractions for "Toward the Unknown."
1956 126m/B Henry Fonda, Vera Miles, Anthony Quayle, Nehemiah Persoff; **D:** Alfred Hitchcock. **VHS, Beta** $19.98 WAR, MLB ✍✍✍½

The Wrong Man American sailor Alex Walker (Anderson) is framed for the murder of a Mexican smuggler. He eludes the police and winds up hitching a ride from wacko couple Phillip (Lithgow) and Missy Mills (Arquette). Missy does topless table dancing and is very interested in their fugitive passenger. Alex may be better off with the police. Made for cable television.
1993 (R) 98m/C Kevin Anderson, John Lithgow, Rosanna Arquette, Robert Harper; **D:** Jim McBride. **VHS** $92.98 REP ✍✍½

The Wrong Move A loose adaptation of Goethe's "Sorrows of Young Werther" by screenwriter Peter Handke. Justly acclaimed and engrossing, though slow. Kinski's first film. A young poet, searching for life's meaning, wanders aimlessly through Germany. In German with English subtitles.
1978 103m/C Nastassia Kinski, Hanna Schygulla, Ruediger Vogler, Hans-Christian Blech; **D:** Wim Wenders. **VHS, Beta** $59.95 FCT, GLV, ING ✍✍½

The Wrong Road A young couple embark on a robbery spree, and subsequently end up in prison. On their release, they search for the loot they had previously hidden, but find the man who was holding it for them has died. Will they ever recover their ill-gotten stash?
1937 62m/B Richard Cromwell, Helen Mack, Lionel Atwill, Horace McMahon, Russ Powell, Billy Bevan, Marjorie Main, Rex Evans; **D:** James Cruze. **VHS, Beta** $16.95 SNC ✍½

Wuthering Heights The first screen adaptation of Emily Bronte's romantic novel about the doomed love between Heathcliff and Cathy on the Yorkshire moors. This film dynamically captures the madness and ferocity of the classic novel, remaining possibly the greatest romance ever filmed. Excellent performances by Wyler's sure direction, particularly Olivier's, which made him a star, and Oberon in her finest hour as the exquisite but selfish Cathy. Remade twice, in 1953 (by Luis Bunuel) and in 1970.
1939 104m/B Laurence Olivier, Merle Oberon, David Niven, Geraldine Fitzgerald, Flora Robson, Donald Crisp, Cecil Kellaway, Leo G. Carroll, Miles Mander, Hugh Williams; **D:** William Wyler; **W:** Ben Hecht, Charles MacArthur; **M:** Alfred Newman. Academy Awards '39: Best Black and White Cinematography; Nominations: Best Actor (Olivier), Best Director (Wyler), Best Interior Decoration, Best Picture, Best Screenplay, Best Supporting Actress (Fitzgerald), Best Original Score; National Board of Review Awards '39: 10 Best Films of the Year; New York Film Critics Awards '39: Best Film. **VHS, Beta** $19.98 HBO, SUE, HMV ✍✍✍✍

Wuthering Heights Bunuel tackles the Bronte classic during his Mexican period, and comes up with a film containing little passion, but much of the customary Bunuel manic cynicism. The 1939 version is far superior, but fans of Bunuel will probably enjoy this one. Loosely adapted; in Spanish with English subtitles. Remade in another English-language version in 1970. **AKA:** Abismos de Pasion.
1953 90m/B Irasema Dilian, Jorge Mistral, Lilia Prado, Ernesto Alonso; **D:** Luis Bunuel. **VHS, Beta** $24.95 XVC, MED, APD ✍✍½

Wuthering Heights The third screening of the classic Emily Bronte romance about two doomed lovers. Fuest's version features excellent photography, and Calder-Marshall and Dalton's performances are effective, but fail even to approach the intensity and pathos of the 1939 film original (or of the book). Filmed on location in Yorkshire, England.

1970 (G) 105m/C Anna Calder-Marshall, Timothy Dalton, Harry Andrews, Pamela Brown, Judy Cornwell, James Cossins, Rosalie Crutchley, Hilary Dwyer, Hugh Griffith, Ian Ogilvy; **D:** Robert Fuest. **VHS, Beta** $14.95 CNG, KAR, TVC ✍✍½

Wyatt Earp Revisionist epic follows "Tombstone" in telling the story of tarnished badge Earp (Costner), his brothers, and tubercular friend Doc Holliday (Quaid). Costner is barely believable as a twentysomething lad, but fares better as he ages. 40 pounds lighter, Quaid is unrecognizable but terrific, hacking his way to supporting Oscar territory. Huge cast is great, though most roles are fleeting. Kasdan not only likes ensemble pieces ("Big Chill," anyone?) but also enjoys tweaking his western lore (see "Silverado"). Originally envisioned as a TV miniseries till sheriff Costner took a hankering to bring tall tale to the big screen. Visually appealing but 40 minutes too long, due to prolonged intro to early Wyatt life. Filmed on location in Sante Fe, New Mexico. For the full Earp effect, see it with "Tombstone" and relive the legend.
1994 (PG-13) 189m/C Kevin Costner, Dennis Quaid, Gene Hackman, Jeff Fahey, Mark Harmon, Michael Madsen, Catherine O'Hara, Bill Pullman, Isabella Rossellini, Tom Sizemore, JoBeth Williams, Mare Winningham, Betty Buckley, Adam Baldwin, Rex Linn, Todd Allen, David Andrews, Linden Ashby, Annabeth Gish, Joanna Going, Martin Kove, Tea Leoni, James Caviezel, Karen Grassle; **D:** Lawrence Kasdan; **W:** Dan Gordon, Lawrence Kasdan; **M:** James Newton Howard. **VHS** NYR ✍

Wyoming Outlaw Based on an actual incident, the story revolves around a small-town man who kills an outlaw. Barry, in the role that made him a western star, is forced into crime after a corrupt politician extorts money from him in exchange for a job. Lincoln, the screen's first Tarzan, appears in a supporting role.
1939 62m/B John Wayne, Ray Corrigan, Raymond Hatton, Donald (Don "Red") Barry, Adele Pearce, Leroy Mason, Charles Middleton, Elmo Lincoln, Jack Ingram, Yakima Canutt, Curly Dresden; **D:** George Sherman. **VHS** $19.95 NOS, MLB ✍✍

X from Outer Space A space voyage to Mars brings back a giant rampaging creature. Badly dubbed.
1967 (PG) 85m/C Eiji Okada, Peggy Neal, Toshiya Wazaki, Itoko Harada, Shinichi Yanagisawa, Franz Gruber, Keisuke Sonoi, Mike Daning, Torahiko Hamada; **D:** Nazui Nihonmatsu. **VHS, Beta** $19.98 ORI ✍

X Marks the Spot When a police sergeant is killed, his detective son investigates his murder. He's drawn into a crime ring which smuggles rubber (a scarce commodity during WWII). Quick pacing enlivens standard cliches.
1942 55m/B Damian O'Flynn, Helen Parrish, Dick Purcell, Jack LaRue, Neil Hamilton, Robert E. Homans, Anne Jeffreys, Dick Wessel, Vince Barnett; **D:** George Sherman. **VHS, Beta** $16.95 SNC ✍✍

X: The Man with X-Ray Eyes First-rate Corman has Milland gain power to see through solid materials. Predates Little Caesars campaign. **AKA:** The Man With the X-Ray Eyes; X.
1963 79m/C Ray Milland, Diana Van Der Vlis, Harold J. Stone, John Hoyt, Don Rickles, Dick Miller, Jonathan Haze; **D:** Roger Corman; **W:** Ray Russell, Robert Dillon; **M:** Les Baxter. **VHS, Beta** $59.95 WAR ✍✍✍

X, Y & Zee A brassy, harsh version of the menage a trois theme, wherein the vicious wife (Taylor) of a philanderer (Caine) decides to avenge herself by seducing his

mistress. An embarrassment for everyone involved. *AKA:* Zee & Co.
1972 (R) 110m/C Michael Caine, Elizabeth Taylor, Susannah York, Margaret Leighton; **D:** Brian G. Hutton; **W:** Edna O'Brien. **VHS, Beta** $69.95 COL 🎬½

Xanadu Dorky star-vehicle remake (of 1947's "Down to Earth") eminently of its era, which is now better forgotten. Newton-John is a muse who descends to Earth to help two friends open a roller disco. In the process she proves that as an actor, she's a singer. Kelly attempts to soft shoe some grace into the proceedings, though he seems mystified as anyone as to why he's in the movie. Don Bluth adds an animated sequence. 🎵I'm Alive; The Fall; Don't Walk Away; All Over the World; Xanadu; Magic; Suddenly; Dancing; Suspended in Time.
1980 (PG) 96m/C Olivia Newton-John, Michael Beck, Gene Kelly, Sandahl Bergman; **D:** Robert Greenwald. **VHS, Beta** $14.98 MCA, MLB Woof!

Xica A diamond rush in 18th century Brazil transformed that country's interior into a place of undreamed wealth and excess. Black slave Xica uses her sexual allure to rise out of poverty and capture the attentions of Joao, the governor of the diamond-mining town. She gleefully wields her increasing wealth and power, becoming the unofficial Empress of Brazil. Reportedly based on a real-life character. In Portuguese with English subtitles.
1976 109m/C Zeze Motta, Walmor Chagas, Altair Lima, Jose Wilker, Marcus Vinicius, Elke Maravilha; **D:** Carlos Diegues; **W:** Joao Felicio. **VHS** $79.95 NYF, BTV, FCT 🎬🎬🎬

Xtro An Englishman, abducted by aliens three years before, returns to his family with a deadly, transforming disease. Slime-bucket splatter flick notable for the scene where a woman gives birth to a full-grown man, and various sex slashings.
1983 (R) 80m/C Philip Sayer, Bernice Stegers, Danny Brainin, Simon Nash, Maryam D'Abo, David Cardy, Anna Wing, Peter Mandell, Robert Fyfe; **D:** Harry Bromley Davenport. **VHS, Beta** $19.95 NLC Woof!

Xtro 2: The Second Encounter Research facility conducts an experiment to transfer people to a parallel dimension. Out of the three researchers sent to the other side, only one returns, unconscious. Turns out that he is playing host to a biohazardous creature brought over from the other dimension who escapes into the air shafts and threatens to kill everyone in the building. One more problem: if the creature isn't killed, the computer system will fill the building with radiation. Sound familiar? It should, because this is a low-budget remake of "Alien." Good photography, adequate acting, but Vincent just isn't credible as a brillian scientist. A sequel to "Xtro" in name only.
1991 (R) 92m/C Jan-Michael Vincent, Paul Koslo, Tara Buckman, Jano Frandsen, Nicholas Lea, W.F. Wadden, Rolf Reynolds, Nic Amoroso, Tracy Westerholm; **D:** Harry Bromley Davenport. **VHS** $19.95 NLC 🎬🎬

Y Donde Esta el Muerto? (And... Where Is the Dead) This mystery/comedy centers around a weird gathering of people who are trying to find out if a man is really dead.
1987 73m/C Yvonne Fraissinet, Ricardo Fernandez, Nilda Munoz. **VHS, Beta** $69.95 MAD 🎬🎬½

The Yakuza An ex-G.I. (Mitchum) returns to Japan to help an old army buddy find his kidnapped daughter. He learns the daughter has been kidnapped by the Japanese version of the Mafia (the Yakuza) and he must call on

old acquaintances to help free her. A westernized oriental gangster drama with a nice blend of buddy moments, action, ancient ritual, and modern Japanese locations. *AKA:* Brotherhood of the Yakuza.
1975 (R) 112m/C Robert Mitchum, Richard Jordan, Ken Takakura, Brian Keith, Herb Edelman; **D:** Sydney Pollack; **W:** Paul Schrader, Leonard Schrader, Robert Towne; **M:** Dave Grusin. **VHS, Beta** $14.95 WAR, HBO 🎬🎬½

Yanco A young Mexican boy makes visits to an island where he plays his homemade violin. Unfortunately, no one can understand or tolerate his love for music, save for an elderly violinist, who gives him lessons on an instrument known as "Yanco." No dialogue. Not exactly riveting, but sensitively played.
1964 95m/B Ricardo Ancona, Jesus Medina, Maria Bustamante. **VHS, Beta** $19.95 WFV, DVT, ING 🎬🎬

A Yank in Australia Australian farce/war mystery/romance/documentary tells the story of two WWII newspaper reporters whose ship gets torpedoed, stranding them in the Australian outback, where they manage to foil a Japanese invasion.
1943 56m/B VHS, Beta, 8mm $19.95 VYY 🎬🎬

Yank in Libya No, not the American bombing raid of Khadafy, rather a low-budget WWII adventure pitting an American man and an English girl against Libyan Arabs and Nazis.
1942 65m/B Walter Woolf King, John Woodbury, H.B. Warner, Parkyakarkus. **VHS, Beta** VCI 🎬½

A Yank in the R.A.F. Power's enthusiastic performance as a brash American pilot boosts this dated WWII adventure. He and his British allies seem more concerned over who gets showgirl Betty Grable than in the Nazis, but climactic air attacks retain excitement. Produced by Darryl F. Zanuck to drum up American support for embattled Britain and France.
1941 98m/B Tyrone Power, Betty Grable, John Sutton, Reginald Gardiner; **D:** Henry King. **VHS, Beta** $19.98 FOX, FCT 🎬🎬½

Yankee Clipper Deceit, treachery, and romance are combined in this depiction of a fierce race from China to New England between the American ship Yankee Clipper, and the English ship Lord of the Isles. Silent.
1927 68m/B William Boyd, Elinor Fair, Frank "Junior" Coghlan, John Miljan, Walter Long; **D:** Rupert Julian. **VHS, Beta** $19.95 GPV, VYY, CCB 🎬🎬½

Yankee Doodle Dandy Nostalgic view of the Golden Era of show business and the man who made it glitter—George M. Cohan. His early days, triumphs, songs, musicals and romances are brought to life by the inexhaustible Cagney in a rare and wonderful song-and-dance performance. Told in flashback, covering the Irishman's struggling days as a young song writer and performer to his salad days as the toast of Broadway. Cagney, never more charismatic, dances up a storm, reportedly inventing most of the steps on ths spot. 🎵Give My Regards to Broadway; Yankee Doodle Dandy; You're a Grand Old Flag; Over There; I Was Born in Virginia; Off the Record; You're a Wonderful Girl; Blue Skies, Grey Skies; Oh You Wonderful Girl.
1942 126m/B James Cagney, Joan Leslie, Walter Huston, Richard Whorf, Irene Manning, Rosemary DeCamp, Jeanne Cagney, S.Z. Sakall, Walter Catlett, Frances Langford, Eddie Foy Jr., George Tobias, Michael Curtiz; **D:** Michael Curtiz; **W:** Robert Buckner. Academy Awards '42: Best Actor (Cagney), Best Sound, Best Score; Nominations: Best Director (Curtiz), Best Picture,

Best Story, Best Supporting Actor (Huston). **VHS, Beta** $29.98 MGM, FOX, FCT 🎬🎬🎬

Yankee Doodle in Berlin A spoof of WWI dramas, with the hero dressing up as a woman and seducing the Kaiser into giving up his war plans. Typical Sennett slapstick with a music and effects score added to the silent film.
1919 60m/B Ford Sterling, Ben Turpin, Marie Prevost, Bothwell Browne. **VHS, Beta** $14.95 GPV, CCB 🎬🎬½

Yanks An epic-scale but uneventful drama depicts the legions of American soldiers billeted in England during WWII, and their impact—mostly sexual—on the staid Britons. No big story, no big deal, despite a meticulous recreation of the era.
1979 139m/C Richard Gere, Vanessa Redgrave, William Devane, Lisa Eichhorn, Rachel Roberts, Chick Vennera, Arlen Dean Snyder, Annie Ross; **D:** John Schlesinger; **W:** Colin Welland, Walter Bernstein; **M:** Richard Rodney Bennett. **VHS** $14.98 MCA 🎬🎬

A Year in Provence Retired London executive Peter Mayle and his wife Annie decide to leave England to live in the south of France. They buy a 200-year-old farmhouse and experience all the trials and amusements of forging a new life in a different country, complete with different language and customs. They hoped for tranquility and what they got were eccentric neighbors, endless renovations, lots of company, and a taste for good food and drink. Based on Mayle's autobiographical novels "A Year in Provence" and "Tonjours Provence" and filmed on location. Made for British television. On four cassettes, each depicting one season of the year.
1989 360m/C John Thaw, Lindsay Duncan, Bernard Spiegel, Jean-Pierre Delage, Maryse Kuster, Louis Lyonnet; **D:** David Tucker; **W:** Michael Sadler. **VHS** $79.95 AAE, SIG, BTV 🎬🎬🎬

The Year My Voice Broke Above average adolescent drama: a girl breaks a boy's heart by getting pregnant by a tougher, older boy; then leaves town. Blues-inducing, explicit, and not pleasant; but good acting from newcomers carries the day. Followed by "Flirting."
1987 (PG-13) 103m/C Noah Taylor, Loene Carmen, Ben Mendelsohn, Graeme Blundell, Lynette Curran, Malcolm Robertson, Judi Farr; **D:** John Duigan; **W:** John Duigan; **M:** Christine Woodruff. **VHS, Beta** $89.95 LIV 🎬🎬🎬

The Year of Living Dangerously Political thriller features Gibson as an Australian journalist covering a political story in Indonesia, circa 1965. During the coup against President Sukarno, he becomes involved with a British attache (Weaver) at the height of the bloody fighting and rioting in Jakarta. Hunt is excellent as male photographer Billy Swan, central to the action as the moral center. Rumored to be based on the activities of CNN's Peter Arnett, although the original source is a novel by C.J. Koch, who reportedly collaborated/battled with Weir on the screenplay. Fascinating, suspenseful film, set up brilliantly by Weir. Shot on location in the Philippines (then moved to Sydney after cast and crew were threatened). First Australian movie financed by a U.S. studio.
1982 (PG) 114m/C Mel Gibson, Sigourney Weaver, Linda Hunt, Michael Murphy; **D:** Peter Weir; **W:** Peter Weir, David Williamson; **M:** Maurice Jarre. Academy Awards '83: Best Supporting Actress (Hunt); Nominations: s 83: Best Film. **VHS, Beta** $19.98 MGM, BTV 🎬🎬🎬½

Year of the Comet Amusing adventure/romantic comedy throws straightlaced Maggie (Miller) together with carefree Oliver (Daly) in a quest for a rare bottle of wine. Fine wine is Maggie's passion, and snagging this particular bottle will boost her status in the family business. Oliver is a pretzels and beer kind of guy, but his boss wants this bottle and will pay a lot to get it. Wants to be another ''Romancing the Stone,'' but plot and characters are too thin. Nice chemistry between Miller and Daly sort of saves this one despite a disappointing script. Beautiful location shots of Scotland.
1992 (PG-13) 135m/C Penelope Ann Miller, Timothy Daly, Louis Jourdan, Art Malik, Ian Richardson, Ian McNeice, Timothy Bentinck, Julia McCarthy, Jacques Mathou; **D:** Peter Yates; **W:** William Goldman; **M:** Hummie Mann. **VHS $19.95** NLC ♫♫

Year of the Dragon Polish police Captain Stanley White of the NYPD vows to neutralize the crime lords running New York's Chinatown. Brilliant cinematography, well-done action scenes with maximum violence, a racist hero you don't want to root for, murky script, and semi-effective direction are the highlights of this tour through the black market's underbelly and hierarchy. Based on Robert Daley's novel.
1985 (R) 136m/C Mickey Rourke, John Lone, Ariane, Leonard Termo, Raymond J. Barry; **D:** Michael Cimino; **W:** Oliver Stone, Michael Cimino. **VHS, Beta $14.95** MGM ♫♫½

Year of the Gun McCarthy is an American journalist in Rome who begins a novel based on the political instability around him, using the names of real people in his first draft. Soon, ambitious photojournalist Stone wants to collaborate with him, and the Red Brigade terrorist group wants to ''remove'' anyone associated with the book. Although failing on occassion to balance the thin line it establishes between reality and perception, ''Gun'' aspires to powerful drama, offering a realistic look at the lives and priorities of political terrorists. Love scenes between Stone and McCarthy are torrid.
1991 (R) 111m/C Andrew McCarthy, Sharon Stone, Valeria Golino, John Pankow, Mattia Sbragia, George Murcell; **D:** John Frankenheimer; **W:** David Ambrose, Jay Presson Allen; **M:** Bill Conti. **VHS, 8mm $19.95** COL ♫♫½

Year of the Quiet Sun A poignant, acclaimed love story about a Polish widow and an American soldier who find each other in the war-torn landscape of 1946 Europe. Beautifully rendered, with a confident sense of time and place, making this much more than a simple love story. In Polish with English subtitles.
1984 (PG) 106m/C Scott Wilson, Maja Komorowska; **D:** Krzysztof Zanussi. **VHS, Beta $29.98** BAR, WAR, ING ♫♫♫½

The Yearling This family classic is a tearjerking adaptation of the Marjorie Kinnan Rawlings novel about a young boy's love for a yearling fawn during the post civil-war era. His father's encouragement and his mother's bitterness play against the story of unqualified love amid poverty and the boy's coming of age. Wonderful footage of Florida. Jarman was awarded a special Oscar as outstanding child actor.
1946 128m/C Gregory Peck, Jane Wyman, Claude Jarman Jr., Chill Wills, Henry Travers, Jeff York, Forrest Tucker, June Lockhart, Margaret Wycherly; **D:** Clarence Brown. Academy Awards '46: Best Color Cinematography, Best Interior Decoration; Nominations: Best Actor (Peck), Best Actress (Wyman), Best Director (Brown), Best Film Editing, Best Picture; Golden

Globe Awards '47: Best Actor—Drama (Peck). **VHS, Beta $19.98** KUI, MGM, TLF ♫♫♫½

The Yellow Cab Man Skelton plays a cab driver who is also an inventor of safety gadgets. When he invents unbreakable elastic glass he finds various crooks after him for the formula. Skelton's wacky inventions are amusing and the movie culminates in a breakneck chase through a home show exposition.
1950 85m/B Red Skelton, Gloria De Haven, Walter Slezak, Edward Arnold, James Gleason, Jay C. Flippen, Paul Harvey; **D:** Jack Donohue. **VHS $19.98** MGM ♫♫½

Yellow Cargo Ingenious ''B'' movie about a pair of undercover agents who blow the lid off a smuggling scam. It seems that the smugglers have been masquerading as a movie crew, and use disguised Chinese ''extras'' to transport their goods. The agents pose as actors to infiltrate the gang.
1936 70m/B Conrad Nagel, Eleanor Hunt, Vince Barnett, Jack LaRue, Claudia Dell; **D:** Crane Wilbur; **W:** Crane Wilbur. **VHS, Beta $16.95** SNC ♫

Yellow Dust Dull story of a gold miner (Dix) who hits a big strike but before he can make good on it he's accused of a series of stagecoach robberies. So he goes undercover to clear his name. Based on the play ''Mother Lode'' by Dan Totheroh and George O'Neil.
1936 68m/B Richard Dix, Leila Hyams, Andy Clyde, Onslow Stevens, Moroni Olsen, Jessie Ralph; **D:** Wallace Fox. **VHS $19.95** GPV ♫½

Yellow Earth In 1939 a soldier arrives in a small Chinese village to research folk songs. He becomes involved in the lives of a local peasant family, including a 14-year-old girl who wishes to escape from a pre-arranged marriage. Mixture of poetry, dance, music, and drama set against the barren landscape of the title. In Mandarin Chinese with English subtitles. **AKA:** Huang Tudi.
1989 89m/C Xue Bai, Wang Xueqi, Tan Tuo, Liu Qiang; **D:** Chen Kaige; **W:** Zhang Ziliang. **VHS $79.95** FXL, FCT, BTV ♫♫½

Yellow Hair & the Fortress of Gold Princess who's part Indian and her sidekick fight bad guys and seek gold. Well-meaning, self-conscious parody. **AKA:** Yellow Hair and the Pecos Kid.
1984 (R) 102m/C Laurene Landon, Ken Robertson; **D:** Matt Cimber. **VHS, Beta $79.98** LIV ♫½

The Yellow Rose of Texas Rogers works as an undercover insurance agent (he's singing on a river boat) to clear the name of an old man falsely accused of a stagecoach robbery. The usual melodious Rogers lead.
1944 55m/B Roy Rogers, Dale Evans, Grant Withers, Harry Shannon; **D:** Joseph Kane. **VHS, Beta $19.95** NOS, VCN, CAB ♫½

Yellow Submarine The acclaimed animated fantasy based on a plethora of mid-career Beatles songs, sees the Fab Four battle the Blue Meanies for the sake of Sgt. Pepper, the Nowhere Man, Strawberry Fields, and Pepperland. The first full-length British animated feature in 14 years features a host of talented cartoonists. Fascinating LSD-esque animation and imagery. Speaking voices provided by John Clive (John), Geoff Hughes (Paul), Peter Batten (George), and Paul Angelis (Ringo). The Beatles themselves do appear in a short scene at the end of the film. Martin fills in as music director, and Segal of ''Love Story'' fame co-scripts. ♫Yellow Submarine; All You Need Is Love; Hey, Bulldog; When I'm Sixty Four; Nowhere

Man; Lucy in the Sky With Diamonds; Sgt. Pepper's Lonely Hearts Club Band; A Day in the Life; All Together Now.
1968 (G) 87m/C **D:** George Dunning, Dick Emery; **W:** Erich Segal; **M:** George Martin. **VHS, Beta $19.95** MVD, MGM, WTA ♫♫♫½

Yellowbeard An alleged comedy with a great cast who wander about with little direction. Follows the efforts of an infamous pirate (Chapman) to locate a buried treasure using the map tattooed on the back of his son's head. Final role for Feldman, who died during production.
1983 (PG) 97m/C Graham Chapman, Peter Boyle, Richard ''Cheech'' Marin, Thomas Chong, Peter Cook, Marty Feldman, Martin Hewitt, Michael Hordern, Eric Idle, Madeline Kahn, James Mason, John Cleese, Susannah York, David Bowie; **D:** Mel Damski; **W:** Graham Chapman, Peter Cook, Bernard McKenna. **VHS, Beta $14.95** VES ♫♫

Yellowneck A handful of Confederate Army soldiers desert, hoping to cross the Florida Everglades and eventually reach Cuba. The swamp takes its toll, however, and one by one the men fall by the wayside. A sole survivor reaches the coast. Will the escape boat be waiting for him?
1955 83m/C Lin McCarthy, Stephen Courtleigh, Berry Kroeger, Harold Gordon, Bill Mason; **D:** R. John Hugh. **VHS $29.95** FCT ♫½

Yellowstone An ex-con is murdered at Yellowstone National Park, at the site of a hidden cache of money, of which assorted folks are in search. Uncomplicated, well-meaning mystery.
1936 65m/B Andy Devine, Ralph Morgan, Judith Barrett; **D:** Arthur Lubin. **VHS, Beta, 8mm $14.95** NOS, DVT, VYY ♫♫

Yentl The famous Barbra adaptation of Isaac Bashevis Singer's story set in 1900s Eastern Europe about a Jewish girl who masquerades as a boy in order to study the Talmud, and who becomes enmeshed in romantic miscues. Lushly photographed, with a repetitive score that nevertheless won an Oscar. Singer was reportedly appalled by the results of Streisand's hyper-controlled project. ♫A Piece of Sky; No Matter What Happens; This Is One of Those Moments; Tomorrow Night; Where Is It Written; No Wonder; The Way He Makes Me Feel; Papa, Can You Hear Me; Will Someone Ever Look at Me That Way?.
1983 (PG) 134m/C Barbra Streisand, Mandy Patinkin, Amy Irving, Nehemiah Persoff, Steven Hill, Allan Corduner, Ruth Goring, David DeKeyser, Bernard Spear; **D:** Barbra Streisand; **M:** Michel Legrand, Alan Bergman, Marilyn Bergman. Academy Awards '83: Best Original Score; Nominations: Best Art Direction/Set Decoration, Best Song (''Papa, Can You Hear Me?'', ''The Way He Makes Me Feel''), Best Supporting Actress (Irving); Golden Globe Awards '84: Best Director (Streisand), Best Film—Musical/Comedy. **VHS, Beta $39.98** MGM, IME ♫♫♫½

Yes, Giorgio Opera singer Pavarotti in his big-screen debut. He has an advantage over other non-actors in trapped in similar situations (e.g., Hulk Hogan): He can sing (but of course, not wrestle). Lame plot (famous opera star falls for lady doctor) is the merest excuse for the maestro to belt out ''If We Were in Love,'' ''I Left My Heart in San Francisco,'' and arias by Verdi, Donizetti, and Puccini.
1982 (PG) 111m/C Luciano Pavarotti, Kathryn Harrold, Eddie Albert, James Hong; **D:** Franklin J. Schaffner; **W:** Norman Steinberg; **M:** John Williams. **VHS, Beta $19.98** MGM ♫♫

Yes, Sir, Mr. Bones Entertaining but dated musical about a boy who wanders into a rest home and inspires the old folks there to reminisce about their days as riverboat minstrels. ♫I Want to Be a Minstrel Man; Stay Out of the Kitchen; Is Your Rent Paid Up in Heaven?; Flying Saucers; Memphis Bill; Southland.
1951 60m/B Pete Daily, Jimmy O'Brien, Sally Anglim, Cotton Watts, Chick Watts, Chet Davis, F.E. Miller, Scatman Crothers; *D:* Ron Ormond; *W:* Ron Ormond. **VHS, Beta** NO ♫½

The Yesterday Machine Camp sci-fi: A mad doctor tries to bring back Hitler. Don't worry, though: the good guys win. Predictable, dumb drivel.
1963 85m/B Tim Holt, James Britton, Jack Herman; *D:* Russ Marker. **VHS, Beta** $19.95 SNC, VCD Woof!

Yesterday, Today and Tomorrow Trilogy of comic sexual vignettes featuring Loren and her many charms. She plays a black marketeer, a wealthy matron, and a prostitute. Funny, and still rather racy. Loren at her best, in all senses; includes her famous striptease for Mastroianni. *AKA:* Ieri, Oggi E Domani; She Got What She Asked For.
1964 119m/C Sophia Loren, Marcello Mastroianni, Tony Pica, Giovanni Ridolfi; *D:* Vittorio De Sica. **VHS** $29.95 JEF, HHE, ING ♫♫♫½

Yesterday's Hero A fading soccer star finds his career and love-life on the upswing. Poor production with equally lame pop music score.
1979 95m/C Ian McShane, Suzanne Somers, Adam Faith, Paul Nicholas, Glynis Barber, Sandy Ratcliff; *D:* Neil Leifer; *W:* Jackie Collins. **VHS, Beta** HHE ♫½

Yidl Mitn Fidl Disguised as a man, a young woman travels about the countryside with a group of musicians, revealing her female identity only after falling for a man. One of Picon's finest roles and Green's biggest successes. Vaudevillian fare in Yiddish with English subtitles. ♫Yiddle With His Fiddle; Arye With His Bass. *AKA:* Yiddle with a Fiddle; Castle in the Sky.
1936 92m/B Molly Picon, Simche Fostel, Max Bozyk, Leon Liebgold; *D:* Joseph Green. **VHS, Beta** $89.95 ERG, DVT, ING ♫♫

Yin & Yang of Mr. Go A CIA operative must retrieve the stolen plans of an awesome weapons system. Set in Hong Kong, features a strong cast in a tangled tale of no particular merit. Unworthy spoof of Oriental intrigue flicks.
1971 (R) 89m/C Jeff Bridges, James Mason, Broderick Crawford, Burgess Meredith; *D:* Burgess Meredith; *W:* Burgess Meredith. **VHS, Beta** NO ♫

Yodelin' Kid From Pine Ridge Autry tries to stop a war between cattlemen and woodsmen in Georgia. Standard horse opera notable for its location. *AKA:* The Hero of Pine Ridge.
1937 59m/B Gene Autry, Smiley Burnette, Betty Bronson, Charles Middleton, Art Mix; *D:* Joseph Kane. **VHS, Beta** $19.95 NOS, VCN, DVT ♫½

Yog, Monster from Space When a spaceship crashes somewhere near Japan, the aliens in it create monsters out of ordinary critters in order to destroy all the cities. A promoter gets a gleam in his eye and sees the potential for a vacation spot featuring the viscious creatures. Standard Japanese monster flick utilizing the usual out-of-synch dub machine. Dubbed. *AKA:* The Space Amoeba.
1971 (G) 105m/C Akira Kubo, Yoshio Tsuchiya; *D:* Inoshiro Honda. **VHS, Beta** $49.95 SNC ♫

Yojimbo Two clans vying for political power bid on the services of a samurai (Mifune) who comes to town. The samurai sells his services to both parties, with devastating results for all. In Japanese with English subtitles or dubbed. Re-made by Sergio Leone as the western "A Fist Full of Dollars."
1961 110m/B Toshiro Mifune, Eijiro Tono, Suuzu Yamda, Seizaburo Kawazu, Isuzu Yamada; *D:* Akira Kurosawa; *W:* Hideo Oguni, Shinobu Hashimoto, Akira Kurosawa; *M:* Masaru Sato. **VHS, Beta, 8mm** $24.95 VYY, SUE, HHT ♫♫♫♫

Yol Five Turkish prisoners are granted temporary leave to visit their families. An acclaimed, heartfelt film, written by Guney while he himself was in prison. A potent protest against totalitarianism. In Turkish with English subtitles.
1982 (PG) 126m/C Tarik Akan, Serif Sezer; *D:* Serif Goren; *W:* Yilmaz Guney. **VHS, Beta** $19.98 COL, AUD, ING ♫♫♫½

Yolanda and the Thief A charming, forgotten effort from the Arthur Freed unit about a con man who convinces a virginal South American heiress that he is her guardian angel. Songs include a lengthy Dali-esque ballet built around "Will You Marry Me?" ♫This is the Day for Love; Angel; Yolanda; Coffee Time; Will You Marry Me.
1945 109m/C Fred Astaire, Lucille Bremer, Leon Ames, Mildred Natwick; *D:* Vincente Minnelli; *M:* Arthur Freed, Harry Warren. **VHS, Beta** $19.98 MGM ♫♫½

Yongkari Monster of the Deep A giant burrowing creature is causing earthquakes and generally ruining scores of Japanese models. Dubbed. *AKA:* Dai Koesu Yongkari; Monster Yongkari; Great Monster Yongkari.
1967 (PG) 79m/C Oh Young Il, Nam Chung-Im; *D:* Kim Ki-dak. **VHS, Beta** $19.98 ORI ♫

Yor, the Hunter from the Future Lost in a time warp where the past and the future mysteriously collide, Yor sets out on a search for his real identity, with his only clue a golden medallion around his neck. *AKA:* Il Mondo Di Yor; The World of Yor.
1983 (PG) 88m/C Reb Brown, Corinne Clery, John Steiner; *D:* Anthony M. (Antonio Margheriti) Dawson; *W:* Anthony M. (Antonio Margheriti) Dawson. **VHS, Beta** $79.95 COL ♫

You Are Not Alone Boys in a small parochial school grow up and try to draw a defining line between friendship and love. In Danish with English subtitles.
1982 90m/C **VHS, Beta** FCT ♫♫

You are Not I After a multi-car accident a young woman escapes from psychiatric confinement and goes to her sister's house.
1984 50m/B **VHS, Beta** NO ♫♫

You Can't Cheat an Honest Man The owner of a misfit circus suffers a variety of headaches including the wisecracks of Charlie McCarthy. Contains Field's classic ping-pong battle and some of his other best work.
1939 79m/B W.C. Fields, Edgar Bergen, Constance Moore, Eddie Anderson, Mary Forbes, Thurston Hall; *D:* George Marshall. **VHS, Beta** $14.95 BAR ♫♫♫

You Can't Fool Your Wife Ball in two roles gives zip to this otherwise ordinary marital comedy. Previously blah hubby has a fling; previously blah better half wins him back with glamour.
1940 69m/C Lucille Ball, James Ellison, Robert Coote, Emma Dunn, Nita Naldi; *D:* Ray McCarey. **VHS, Beta** $19.98 RKO, TTC ♫♫

You Can't Hurry Love A jilted-at-the-altar Ohio bachelor moves to Los Angeles and flounders in the city's fast-moving fast lane. A dull film with Fonda, daughter of "Easy Rider" Peter, playing a minor role.
1988 (R) 92m/C David Leisure, Scott McGinnis, Sally Kellerman, Kristy McNichol, Charles Grodin, Anthony Geary, Bridget Fonda, David Packer, Frank Bonner; *D:* Richard Martini. **VHS, Beta** $79.98 LIV, VES ♫

You Can't Take It with You The Capra version of the Kaufman-Hart play about an eccentric New York family and their non-conformist houseguests. Alice Sycamore (Arthur), the stable family member of an offbeat clan of free spirits, falls for Tony Kirby (Stewart), the down-to-earth son of a snooty, wealthy and not always quite honest family. Amidst the confusion over this love affair, the two families rediscover the simple joys of life.
1938 127m/B James Stewart, Jean Arthur, Lionel Barrymore, Spring Byington, Edward Arnold, Mischa Auer, Donald Meek, Samuel S. Hinds, Ann Miller, H.B. Warner, Halliwell Hobbes, Dub Taylor, Mary Forbes, Eddie Anderson, Harry Davenport, Lillian Yarbo; *D:* Frank Capra; *W:* Robert Riskin. Academy Awards '38: Best Director (Capra), Best Picture; Nominations: Best Cinematography, Best Film Editing, Best Screenplay, Best Sound, Best Supporting Actress (Byington). **VHS, Beta** $19.95 COL, BTV ♫♫♫

You Can't Take It with You Taped performance of the Kaufman and Hart comedy about the strange pastimes of the Sycamore family who must behave themselves to impress their daughter's boyfriend's stuffy family.
1984 116m/C Colleen Dewhurst, James Coco, Jason Robards Jr., Elizabeth Wilson, George Rose; *D:* Ellis Raab. **VHS, Beta** $19.95 COL, VES, LIV ♫♫♫

You Light Up My Life Sappy sentimental story of a young singer trying to break into the music business. Premise of the movie was loosely taken from Debbie Boone's title song, which was a radio smash that drove many people over the edge.
1977 (PG) 91m/C Didi Conn, Michael Zaslow, Melanie Mayron; *D:* Joseph Brooks; *W:* Joseph Brooks; *M:* Joseph Brooks. **VHS, Beta** $14.95 COL Woof!

You Must Remember This When Uncle Buddy (Guillaume) receives a mysterious trunk, Ella's curiosity gets the best of her. She opens the trunk to discover a number of old movies made by W.B. Jackson—Uncle Buddy. Ella takes the films to a movie archive to find out about her uncle's past as an independent black filmmaker. After researching the history of black cinema, Ella convinces her uncle to be proud of his contribution to the film world. Includes a viewers' guide. Part of the "Wonderworks" series.
199? 110m/C Robert Guillaume, Tim Reid, Daphne Maxwell Reid, Vonetta McGee. **VHS** $29.95 PME, HMV, BTV Woof!

You Only Live Once Ex-con Fonda wants to mend his ways and tries to cross into Canada with his girlfriend in tow. Impressively scripted, but a glum and dated Depression-era tale.
1937 86m/B Henry Fonda, Sylvia Sidney, Ward Bond, William Gargan, Barton MacLane, Margaret Hamilton; *D:* Fritz Lang. **VHS, Beta** NO ♫♫½

You Only Live Twice 007 travels to Japan to take on arch-nemesis Blofeld, who has been capturing Russian and American spacecraft in an attempt to start WWIII. Great location photography; theme sung by

VIDEOHOUND'S GOLDEN MOVIE RETRIEVER

Nancy Sinatra. Implausible plot, however, is a handicap, even though this is Bond. **1967 (PG) 125m/C** Sean Connery, Mie Hama, Akiko Wakabayashi, Tetsuro Tamba, Karin Dor, Charles Gray, Donald Pleasence, Tsai Chin, Bernard Lee, Lois Maxwell, Desmond Llewelyn; **D:** Lewis Gilbert; **M:** John Barry. **VHS, Beta $19.98** *MGM, TLF* 🎬🎬½

You So Crazy Scandalous star of television show "Martin" and host of HBO's "Def Comedy Jam" follows in the footsteps of raunchy humorists Richard Pryor and Eddie Murphy. Threatened with an NC-17 rating, Lawrence refused to edit and Miramax, the original distributor, dropped it. It was picked up by Samuel Goldwyn, who released the original version, uncut and unrated. Filmed live at the Brooklyn Academy of Music, Lawrence displays too little of his considerable talent, and too much vulgarity and poor taste. **1994 89m/C** Martin Lawrence; **D:** Thomas Schlamme. **VHS** *NYR* 🎬½

You Talkin' to Me? Fledgling actor who idolizes De Niro moves to the West Coast for his big break. He fails, so he dyes his hair blond and digs the California lifestyle. Embarrassingly bad. **1987 (R) 97m/C** Chris Winkler, Jim Youngs, Faith Ford; **D:** Charles Winkler; **W:** Charles Winkler. **VHS, Beta $79.95** *MGM* 🎬

You Were Never Lovelier Charming tale of a father who creates a phony Romeo to try to interest his daughter in marriage. Astaire appears and woos Hayworth in the flesh. The dancing, of course, is superb, and Hayworth is stunning. 🎵Dearly Beloved; I'm Old Fashioned; Shorty George; Wedding in the Spring; You Were Never Lovelier. **1942 98m/B** Fred Astaire, Rita Hayworth, Leslie Brooks, Xavier Cugat, Adolphe Menjou, Larry Parks; **D:** William A. Seiter; **M:** Jerome Kern, Johnny Mercer. **VHS, Beta $19.95** *COL* 🎬🎬🎬½

You'll Find Out A comic mix of music and mystery as Kay Kyser and his Band, along with a debutante in distress, are terrorized by Lugosi, Karloff, and Lorre. 🎵The Bad Humor; Id' Know You Anywhere; You've Got Me This Way; Like the Fella Once Said; I've Got a One-Track Mind; Don't Think it Ain't Been Charming. **1940 97m/B** Peter Lorre, Kay Kyser, Boris Karloff, Bela Lugosi, Dennis O'Keefe, Helen Parrish; **D:** David Butler. **VHS, Beta $59.95** *HHT, MLB* 🎬🎬

You'll Never Get Rich A Broadway dance director is drafted into the Army, where his romantic troubles cause him to wind up in the guardhouse more than once. He of course gets the girl. Exquisitely funny. 🎵Since I Kissed My Baby Goodbye; The A-stairable Rag; Shootin' the Works for Uncle Sam; Wedding Cake Walk; Dream Dancing; Boogie Barcarolle; So Near and Yet So Far. **1941 88m/B** Fred Astaire, Rita Hayworth, Robert Benchley; **D:** Sidney Lanfield. **VHS, Beta $19.95** *COL* 🎬🎬🎬

Young & Free Following the death of his parents, a young man must learn to face the perils of an unchartered wilderness alone. Ultimately he must choose between returning to civilization, or remain with his beloved wife and life in the wild. **1978 87m/C** Erik Larsen; **D:** Keith Larsen. **VHS, Beta $59.95** *MON* 🎬½

Young and Innocent Somewhat uneven thriller about a police constable's daughter who helps a fugitive prove he didn't strangle a film star. **AKA:** The Girl Was Young.

1937 80m/B Derrick DeMarney, Nova Pilbeam, Percy Marmont; **D:** Alfred Hitchcock. **VHS, Beta $16.95** *SNC, NOS, VDM* 🎬🎬

The Young and the Guilty Two star-crossed teenagers are frustrated in their romance when their parents find one of their love letters and hit the ceiling. Told not to see each other again, the two take to sneaking around, which adds an edge to their relationship. Moving performances by the two young leads. **1958 65m/B** Phyllis Calvert, Andrew Ray, Edward Chapman, Janet Munro, Campbell Singer; **D:** Peter Cotes. **VHS $19.95** *NOS* 🎬🎬

Young & Willing A group of struggling actors gets hold of a terrific play and tries various schemes to get it produced. Based on the Broadway Play "Out of the Frying Pan" by Francis Swann. Unexceptional but enjoyable comedy. **1942 83m/B** William Holden, Susan Hayward, Eddie Bracken, Robert Benchley, Martha O'Driscoll, Barbara Britton; **D:** Edward H. Griffith; **W:** Mordecai Richler. **VHS, Beta** *NO* 🎬🎬½

Young Aphrodites Two young teenagers of a primitive Greek tribe discover sexuality. An acclaimed film retelling the myth of Daphnis and Chloe. Narrated in English. **AKA:** Mikres Aphrodites. **1963 87m/B** *D:* Nikos Koundouros. **VHS, Beta $29.98** *SUE, NLC* 🎬🎬½

Young at Heart Fanny Hurst's lighthearted tale of a cynical hard-luck musician who finds happiness when he falls for a small town girl. A remake of the 1938 "Four Daughters." 🎵Young at Heart; Someone to Watch Over Me; One for My Baby; Hold Me in Your Arms; Ready, Willing and Able; Till My Love Comes Back to Me; There's a Rising Moon For Every Falling Star; You, My Love. **1954 117m/C** Frank Sinatra, Doris Day, Gig Young, Ethel Barrymore, Dorothy Malone, Robert Keith, Elisabeth Fraser, Alan Hale Jr.; **D:** Gordon Douglas; **W:** Julius J. Epstein, Lenore Coffee. **VHS $19.98** *REP* 🎬🎬½

Young Bess Simmons and real-life husband Granger star in this splashy costume drama about 16th century England's young Queen. Features outstanding performances by Simmons as Elizabeth I and Laughton (repeating his most famous role) as Henry VIII. Based on the novel by Margaret Irwin. **1953 112m/C** Jean Simmons, Stewart Granger, Deborah Kerr, Charles Laughton, Kay Walsh, Guy Rolfe, Kathleen Byron, Cecil Kellaway, Rex Thompson; **D:** George Sidney; **W:** Jan Lustig, Arthur Wimperis; **M:** Miklos Rozsa. **VHS $19.98** *MGM* 🎬🎬🎬½

Young Bill Hickok A Rogers vehicle in the form of a very fictionalized biography of the famous gunfighter. **1940 54m/B** Roy Rogers, George "Gabby" Hayes. **VHS, Beta $9.99** *NOS, DVT, TIM* 🎬🎬

Young Blood A cowboy robs from the rich to help the poor. He's also interested in a foreign actress having trouble bonding with the townfolk. Lots of old fashioned western violence. **1933 61m/B** Bob Steele, Charles "Blackie" King, Helen Foster; **D:** Phil Rosen. **VHS, Beta $19.95** *NOS, DVT* 🎬🎬

The Young Bruce Lee Bruce learns and uses the deadly skills that made him famous while only knee-high to a grasshopper. **19?? 90m/C** Han Kwok Choi. **VHS, Beta $19.95** *OCE* 🎬🎬

Young Buffalo Bill Buffalo Bill battles the Spanish land-grant patrons.

1940 54m/B Roy Rogers, George "Gabby" Hayes, Pauline Moore; **D:** Joseph Kane. **VHS, Beta $19.95** *NOS, DVT* 🎬

Young Caruso Dramatic biography of legendary tenor Enrico Caruso, following his life from childhood poverty in Naples to the beginning of his rise to fame. Dubbed in English. **1951 78m/B** Gina Lollobrigida, Ermanno Randi, Mario del Monaco. **VHS, Beta $24.95** *VYY, NOS, MVD* 🎬🎬

Young Catherine Made-for-TV account of Russia's strongest female ruler, the girl who would be Catherine the Great. Star-studded cast and excellent production values. Script and strong cast make Ormond look like a lightweight. Filmed in Leningrad. Also available in 186-minute version. **1991 150m/C** Vanessa Redgrave, Christopher Plummer, Marthe Keller, Franco Nero, Julia Ormond, Maximilian Schell, Reece Dinsdale, Mark Frankel; **D:** Michael Anderson Sr.; **W:** Chris Bryant. **VHS, Beta $89.98** *TTC* 🎬🎬🎬

Young Charlie Chaplin A British-made TV biography of the legendary silent screen comic. **1988 160m/C** Ian McShane, Twiggy. **VHS, Beta $39.99** *HBO* 🎬🎬

The Young Detectives on Wheels Brother and sister team find a $3 million stolen treasure in their backyard, which authorities believe was planted there by the duo's father. The siblings solve the crime and clear their father's name. **1987 107m/C VHS $39.98** *VMK, FHE, BTV* 🎬🎬½

Young Doctors in Love Spoof of medical soap operas features a chaotic scenario at City Hospital, where the young men and women on the staff have better things to do than attend to their patients. Good cast keeps this one alive, though many laughs are forced. Includes cameos by real soap star, including then General Hospital star Moore. Director Marshall is from "Laverne and Shirley" fame. **1982 (R) 95m/C** Dabney Coleman, Sean Young, Michael McKean, Harry Dean Stanton, Hector Elizondo, Patrick Macnee, Pamela Reed, Saul Rubinek; **Cameos:** Demi Moore, Janine Turner; **D:** Garry Marshall; **M:** Maurice Jarre. **VHS, Beta $29.98** *VES* 🎬🎬

Young Dragon The Young Dragon's girlfriend is kidnapped by the underworld society, and he sets out to rescue her single-handedly. **1977 90m/C** Yang Sze, Lo Lai, Yuen Man Chi, Wong Ching, Nora Miao. **VHS $54.95** *SUN* 🎬½

Young Eagles Serial with 12 chapters, 13 minutes each. **1934 156m/B** Bobby Cox, Jim Vance, Carter Dixon. **VHS, Beta $39.95** *VYY, VCN, MLB* 🎬½

Young Einstein A goofy, irreverent Australian farce starring, directed, co-scripted and co-produced by Serious, depicting Einstein as a young Outback clod who splits beer atoms and invents rock and roll. Winner of several Aussie awards. Fun for the kids. **1989 (PG) 91m/C** Yahoo Serious, Odile Le Clezio, John Howard, Pee Wee Wilson, Su Cruickshank; **D:** Yahoo Serious; **W:** Yahoo Serious. **VHS, Beta $19.95** *WAR* 🎬🎬

Young Frankenstein Young Dr. Frankenstein (Wilder), a brain surgeon, inherits the family castle back in Transylvania. He's skittish about the family business, but when he learns his grandfather's secrets, he becomes obsessed with making his own monster. Wilder and monster Boyle make a memorable song-and-dance team to Irving Berlin's "Puttin' on the Ritz," and Hackman's cameo

as a blind man is inspired. Garr ("What knockers!" "Oh, sank you!") is adorable as a fraulein, and Leachman ("He's vass my—boyfriend!") is wonderfully scary. Wilder saves the creature with a switcheroo, in which the doctor ends up with a certain monster-sized body part. Hilarious parody.
1974 (PG) 108m/B Peter Boyle, Gene Wilder, Marty Feldman, Madeline Kahn, Cloris Leachman, Teri Garr, Kenneth Mars, Richard Haydn; *Cameos:* Gene Hackman; *D:* Mel Brooks; *W:* Gene Wilder, Mel Brooks; *M:* John Morris. **VHS, Beta $14.98** FOX, HMV ✶✶✶

The Young Graduates Hormonally imbalanced teens come of age in spite of meandering plot. Features "Breaking Away" star Christopher in big screen debut.
1971 (PG) 99m/C Patricia Wymer, Steven Stewart, Gary Rist, Bruce Kirby, Jennifer Ritt, Dennis Christopher; *D:* Robert Anderson. **VHS $19.95** ACA ✶

Young Guns A sophomoric Wild Bunch look-alike that ends up resembling a western version of the Bowery Boys. Provides a portrait of Billy the Kid and his gang as they move from prairie trash to demi-legends. Features several fine performances by a popular group of today's young stars.
1988 (R) 107m/C Emilio Estevez, Kiefer Sutherland, Lou Diamond Phillips, Charlie Sheen, Casey Siemaszko, Dermot Mulroney, Terence Stamp, Terry O'Quinn, Jack Palance, Brian Keith, Patrick Wayne, Sharon Thomas; *D:* Christopher Cain; *W:* John Fusco; *M:* Anthony Marinelli, Brian Backus. **VHS, Beta $14.98** LIV, VES ✶✶½

Young Guns 2 Brat Pack vehicle neo-Western sequel about Billy the Kid (Estevez) and his gang. This time they're making a run for the border with the law on their trail.
1990 (PG-13) 105m/C Emilio Estevez, Kiefer Sutherland, Lou Diamond Phillips, Christian Slater, William L. Petersen, Alan Ruck, R.D. Call, James Coburn, Balthazar Getty, Jack Kehoe, Rob Knepper, Jenny Wright, Tracy Walter, Ginger Lynn Allen, Jon Bon Jovi; *D:* Geoff Murphy; *W:* John Fusco. Academy Awards '90 Nominations: Best Song ("Blaze of Glory"); Golden Globe Awards '91: Best Song ("Blaze of Glory"). **VHS $14.98** FXV, BTV, CCB ✶✶

Young Hero of Shaolin When facing the fury of a thousand violent monks, one is forced to use the infamous "swastika" formation if one is to achieve victory.
19?? 90m/C Guo Liang, Shih Bao Hwa. **VHS $49.95** OCE ✶

The Young in Heart A lonely, old woman allows a family of con-artists into her life for companionship. Impressed by her sweet nature, the parasitic brood reforms. The cute comedy was a real crowd-pleaser in its day, especially after the bittersweet ending was replaced with a happier variety. Based on the novel "The Gay Banditti" by I.A.R. Wylie.
1938 90m/C Janet Gaynor, Douglas Fairbanks Jr., Paulette Goddard, Roland Young, Billie Burke, Minnie Dupree, Richard Carlson, Charles Halton; *D:* Richard Wallace. **VHS $9.99** VTR ✶✶✶

Young Lady Chatterly 2 A poor sequel to the popular MacBride film, with only the name of the Lawrence classic. Chatterly inherits the family mansion and fools around with the servants and any one else who comes along. Unrated version with 13 minutes of deleted footage is also available.
1985 87m/C Sybil Danning, Adam West, Harlee MacBride; *D:* Alan Roberts. **VHS, Beta $79.98** LIV ✶½

The Young Lions A cynical WWII epic following the experiences of a young American officer and a disillusioned Nazi in the war's last days. Martin does fine in his first dramatic role. As the Nazi, Brando sensitively considers the belief that the Hitler would save Germany. A realistic anti-war film.
1958 167m/B Marlon Brando, Montgomery Clift, Dean Martin, Hope Lange, Barbara Rush, Lee Van Cleef, Maximilian Schell; *D:* Edward Dmytryk; *W:* Edward Anhalt. **VHS, Beta $19.98** FOX ✶✶✶

Young Love, First Love A made-for-television movie about a young woman who must decide whether to have sex with her boyfriend. Sound familiar? Pretty blah, earnest story, though well cast.
1979 100m/C Valerie Bertinelli, Leslie Ackerman, Timothy Hutton, Arlen Dean Snyder, Fionnula Flanagan; *D:* Steven Hilliard Stern. **VHS, Beta $59.95** LIV ✶½

Young Love—Lemon Popsicle 7 Three hunks stalk the beaches in search of babes.
1987 (R) 91m/C Yftach Katzur, Zachi Noy, Jonathan Segall, Sonja Martin; *D:* Walter Bennett. **VHS, Beta $79.95** WAR ✶

Young Man with a Horn Dorothy Baker's novel, which was loosely based on the life of jazz immortal Bix Beiderbecke, was even more loosely adapted for this film, featuring Kirk as an angst-ridden trumpeter who can't seem to hit that mystical "high note." ♫ The Very Thought of You; I May be Wrong; The Man I Love; Too Marvelous for Words; With a Song in My Heart; Pretty Baby; I Only Have Eyes for You; Limehouse Blues; Melancholy Rhapsody.
1950 112m/B Kirk Douglas, Doris Day, Lauren Bacall, Hoagy Carmichael; *D:* Michael Curtiz. **VHS, Beta $19.98** WAR ✶✶✶

Young Mr. Lincoln A classy Hollywood biography of Lincoln in his younger years from log-cabin country boy to idealistic Springfield lawyer. A splendid drama, and one endlessly explicated as an American masterpiece by the French auteur critics in "Cahiers du Cinema."
1939 100m/B Henry Fonda, Alice Brady, Marjorie Weaver, Arleen Whelan, Eddie Collins, Ward Bond, Donald Meek, Richard Cromwell, Eddie Quillan, Charles Halton; *D:* John Ford; *W:* Lamar Trotti. Academy Awards '39 Nominations: Best Story; National Board of Review Awards '39: 10 Best Films of the Year. **VHS, Beta $19.98** FOX ✶✶✶½

The Young Nurses The fourth entry in the Roger Corman produced "nurses" series. Three sexy nurses uncover a drug ring run from their hospital, headed by none other than director Fuller. Also present is Moreland, in his last role. Preceded by "The Student Nurses," "Private Duty Nurses," "Night Call Nurses," followed by "Candy Stripe Nurses." Also on video as "Young L.A. Nurses 3." **AKA:** Nightingale.
1973 (R) 77m/C Jean Manson, Ashley Porter, Angela Gibbs, Zack Taylor, Dick Miller, Jack LaRue, William Joyce, Sally Kirkland, Allan Arbus, Mary Doyle, Don Keefer, Nan Martin, Mantan Moreland, Samuel Fuller; *D:* Clinton Kimbrough. **VHS, Beta $59.98** NLC ✶

Young Nurses in Love Low-budget sex farce in which a foreign spy poses as a nurse to steal sperm from a sperm bank donated by world leaders, celebrities and geniuses.
1989 (R) 82m/C Jeanne Marie, Alan Fisher, Barbra Robb, James Davies; *D:* Chuck Vincent. **VHS, Beta $79.98** LIV, VES ✶

The Young One Traver (Hamilton) is a black jazz musician who escapes from his southern town when he's wrongly accused of raping a white woman. He hides out on a small island which is used as a private hunting ground for rich sportsmen, overseen by Miller (Scott), the game keeper. Hamilton gets work as the new handyman and becomes close to the young Evalyn (Meersman). When Miller rapes Evalyn, it's Traver who's once again accused until things can be put right. Racist elements are heavy-handed; one of Bunuel's lesser efforts. Based on the story "Travelin' Man" by Peter Matthiessen. **AKA:** La Joven.
1961 94m/C Bernie Hamilton, Zachary Scott, Kay Meersman, Claudio Brook, Crahan Denton; *D:* Luis Bunuel; *W:* Luis Bunuel. **VHS $59.95** CVC, FCT ✶✶½

The Young Ones Three episodes from the hilarious, offbeat British television sitcom about four violently eccentric college roommates. Episodes included are "Oil," "Boring," and "Flood."
1988 96m/C Rik Mayall, Ade Edmondson, Nigel Planer, Christopher Ryan, Alexei Sayle; *D:* Geoffrey Posner. **VHS, Beta $14.98** FOX ✶✶½

The Young Philadelphians Ambitious young lawyer Newman works hard at making an impression on the snobbish Philadelphia upper crust. As he schemes and scrambles, he woos debutante Rush and defends buddy Vaughn on a murder charge. Long, but worth it. Part of the "A Night at the Movies" series, this package simulates a 1959 movie evening with a Bugs Bunny cartoon, "People Are Bunny," a newsreel and coming attractions for "The Nun's Story" and "The Hanging Tree." **AKA:** The City Jungle.
1959 136m/B Paul Newman, Barbara Rush, Alexis Smith, Billie Burke, Brian Keith, John Williams, Otto Kruger, Robert Vaughn; *D:* Vincent Sherman; *M:* Ernest Gold. **VHS, Beta $69.95** WAR ✶✶✶

Young Sherlock Holmes Holmes and Watson meet as schoolboys. They work together on their first case, solving a series of bizarre murders gripping London. Watch through the credits for an interesting plot twist. Promising "what if" sleuth tale crashes and burns, becoming a typical high-tech Spielberg film. Second half bears too strong a resemblance to "Indiana Jones and the Temple of Doom."
1985 (PG-13) 109m/C Nicholas Rowe, Alan Cox, Sophie Ward, Freddie Jones, Michael Hordern; *D:* Barry Levinson; *W:* Chris Columbus; *M:* Bruce Broughton. **VHS, Beta, 8mm $14.95** PAR ✶✶

The Young Taoism Fighter The kung-fu film that tells it like it is—or was. Wacky shenanigans and zany pranks are the order of the day in a Taoist temple. Confucianism was never like this.
19?? 90m/C Yuen Tat Chor, Kwan Chung, Liu Hao Yi. **VHS, Beta $49.95** OCE ✶✶

The Young Teacher A novice teacher finds out that trying to apply her college education to a real life elementary school environment isn't as easy as it sounds.
1985 90m/C **VHS, Beta $29.95** GEM ✶½

Young Tiger First a ninety-minute movie never before seen in the U.S. featuring an expert in martial arts who is accused of murder. Next a twelve-minute documentary featuring Jackie Chan, kung-fu sensation, demonstrating his skills. What an evening.
1980 (R) 102m/C Jackie Chan. **VHS, Beta $24.95** GEM ✶✶

Young Tom Edison Two teenaged years in the life of Thomas Alva Edison, as he drives his family crazy with his endless experiments on his way to becoming the famed inventor. Rooney manages to be enthusiastic without being overwhelming. Followed by "Edison the Man," with Spencer Tracy in the adult role.
1940 82m/B Mickey Rooney, Fay Bainter, George Bancroft, Virginia Weidler, Eugene Pallette, Victor Kilian, Bobby Jordan, Lloyd Corrigan; **D:** Norman Taurog; **W:** Dore Schary, Bradbury Foote, Hugo Butler. **VHS, Beta $19.98** MGM, FCT, BTV ᵴᵴ½

Young Warlord Arthur roams western England in 500 AD, leading a band of guerrilla cavalrymen. When the Saxons invade, Arthur unites the tribe, holds off the attack and becomes king.
1975 97m/C Oliver Tobias, Michael Gothard, Jack Watson, Brian Blessed; **D:** Peter Sasdy. **VHS, Beta** NO ᵴᵴ

Young Warriors Frat boys turn vigilante to avenge a street gang murder. Weird mix of teen sex comedy, insufferable self-righteous preachiness, and violence.
1983 (R) 104m/C Ernest Borgnine, James Van Patten, Richard Roundtree, Lynda Day George, Dick Shawn; **D:** Lawrence Foldes; **W:** Richard Matheson. **VHS, Beta $59.95** MGM ᵴ½

Young Winston Based on Sir Winston Churchill's autobiography "My Early Life: A Roving Commission." Follows him through his school days, journalistic career in Africa, early military career, and his election to Parliament at the age of 26. Ward is tremendous as the prime minister-to-be.
1972 (PG) 145m/C Simon Ward, Robert Shaw, Anne Bancroft, John Mills, Jack Hawkins, Ian Holm, Anthony Hopkins, Patrick Magee, Edward Woodward, Jane Seymour; **D:** Richard Attenborough. Academy Awards '72 Nominations: Best Art Direction/Set Decoration, Best Costume Design, Best Story & Screenplay; Golden Globe Awards '73: Best Foreign Film. **VHS, Beta $19.95** COL, TVC ᵴᵴᵴ

Youngblood An underdog beats the seemingly insurmountable odds and becomes a hockey champion. Some enjoyable hockey scenes although the success storyline is predictable.
1986 (R) 111m/C Rob Lowe, Patrick Swayze, Cynthia Gibb, Ed Lauter, George Finn, Fionnula Flanagan, Keanu Reeves; **D:** Peter Markle. **VHS, Beta $14.98** MGM ᵴᵴ

Your Place or Mine Self-indulgent made-for-television yuppie pap about middle-aged singles trying to find the right mate.
1983 100m/C Bonnie Franklin, Robert Klein, Peter Bonerz, Tyne Daly, Penny Fuller; **D:** Robert Day. **VHS, Beta $39.95** LIV ᵴ½

Your Show of Shows The legendary variety program was a Saturday night fixture from 1950-1954 and featured the comedic talents of Sid Caesar, Imogene Coca, Carl Reiner, Howard Morris, and a bevy of guest stars. Additional episodes available.
1950 30m/B VHS, Beta $19.99 MOV, RDG, VYY ᵴ½

Your Ticket Is No Longer Valid Prurient excuse for a serious drama. Impotent failed businessman has disturbing erotic dreams about his girlfriend. Adapted from a novel by Romain Gary.
1984 (R) 96m/C Richard Harris, George Peppard, Jeanne Moreau; **D:** George Kaczender. **VHS, Beta $69.95** VES ᵴ

Your Turn Darling French espionage thriller with Constantine once again playing Lemmy Caution, a U.S. secret agent involved with a gang of spies. **AKA:** A Toi De Faire; Mignonne.

1963 93m/C Eddie Constantine, Gaia Germani, Elga Andersen; **D:** Bernard Borderie. **VHS $16.95** SNC ᵴᵴ

You're a Big Boy Now Kastner, a virginal young man working in the New York Public Library, is told by his father to move out of his house and grow up. On his own, he soon becomes involved with man-hating actress Hartman and a discotheque dancer. A wild and weird comedy. Coppola's commercial directorial debut.
1966 96m/C Elizabeth Hartman, Geraldine Page, Peter Kastner, Julie Harris, Rip Torn, Michael Dunn, Tony Bill, Karen Black; **D:** Francis Ford Coppola; **W:** Francis Ford Coppola. **VHS, Beta $19.98** WAR ᵴᵴᵴ

You're a Good Man, Charlie Brown A filmed version of Charles Schulz's Broadway musical, based on his famous characters.
1987 60m/C VHS, Beta $14.95 BAR, KAR, WTA ᵴᵴᵴ

You're in Love, Charlie Brown The animated Peanuts gang in a new adventure about Charlie Brown and the proverbial little red-haired girl.
1967 30m/C VHS, Beta $14.95 BAR ᵴᵴᵴ

You're Jinxed, Friend, You've Met Sacramento The tongue-in-cheek adventures of a cool-headed cowboy as he passes from town to colorful town. Great title, too.
1970 99m/C Ty Hardin, Christian Hay, Jenny Atkins; **D:** George Cristallini. **VHS, Beta $57.95** UNI ᵴᵴ

Yours, Mine & Ours Bigger, better, big screen version of "The Brady Bunch." It's the story of a lovely lady (Ball) with eight kids who marries a a widower (Fonda) who has ten. Imagine the zany shenanigans! Family comedy manages to be both wholesome and funny. Based on a true story.
1968 114m/C Lucille Ball, Henry Fonda, Van Johnson, Tim Matheson, Tom Bosley, Tracy Nelson; **D:** Melville Shavelson; **W:** Melville Shavelson. **VHS, Beta $14.95** MGM ᵴᵴ½

Youth Aflame Trash film that tells the tale of two sisters—one good, one bad. Poor dialogue and weak performances do, however, make for some great camp. Based on a story by Helen Kiedy. **AKA:** Hoodlum Girls.
1959 61m/B Joy Reese, Warren Burr, Kay Morley, Michael Owen, Rod Rogers; **D:** Elmer Clifton; **W:** Elmer Clifton. **VHS $16.95** SNC Woof!

Youth on Parole Same old story: Boy gets paroled. Girl gets paroled. Parolee meets parolette and romance blossoms as they beat a further rap.
1937 60m/B Marian Marsh, Gordon Oliver. **VHS** LOO, VYY ᵴ½

You've Got to Have Heart A young bridegroom's life gets complicated after he does not sexually satisfy his bride on their wedding night.
1977 (R) 98m/C Carroll Baker, Edwige French. **VHS, Beta $49.95** PSM ᵴ

You've Ruined Me, Eddie A spoiled rich girl gets knocked up and her boyfriend will never know peace again. Meanwhile, their once quiet town is outraged.
1958 m/B VHS $23.00 SMW, TPV ᵴ

Yukon Flight A Renfrew of the Mounties adventure. The hero finds illegal gold mining operations and murder in the Yukon.
1940 57m/B James Newill, Dave O'Brien. **VHS, Beta $19.95** NOS, VCN ᵴᵴ

The Yum-Yum Girls Pair of innocent girls arrive in New York City to pursue their dreams. Gives an inside looks as the fashion industry. Not as funny or as cute as it wants to be.
1978 (R) 89m/C Judy Landers, Tanya Roberts, Barbara Tully, Michelle Daw; **D:** Barry Rosen. **VHS, Beta** MCA ᵴ½

Yuma An old-style made-for-television Western about a sheriff (Walker) who rides into town, cleans it up, and saves his own reputation from a plot to discredit him. Dull in places, but action-packed ending saves the day.
1970 73m/C Clint Walker, Barry Sullivan, Edgar Buchanan; **D:** Ted Post; **M:** George Duning. **VHS, Beta $19.98** FOX, VTR ᵴᵴ

Yuri Nosenko, KGB Fact-based account of a KGB defector and the CIA agent who must determine if he's on the up-and-up. Made for British television.
1986 85m/C Tommy Lee Jones, Oleg Rudnik, Josef Sommer, Ed Lauter, George Morfogen, Stephen D. Newman; **D:** Mick Jackson. **VHS $19.99** HBO, CNG ᵴᵴ½

Z The assassination of a Greek nationalist in the 1960s and its aftermath are portrayed by the notorious political director as a gripping detective thriller. Excellent performances, adequate cinematic techniques, and important politics in this highly acclaimed film.
1969 128m/C Yves Montand, Jean-Louis Trintignant, Irene Papas, Charles Denner, Georges Geret, Jacques Perrin, Francois Perier, Marcel Bozzuffi; **D:** Constantin Costa-Gavras; **W:** Constantin Costa-Gavras. Academy Awards '69: Best Film Editing, Best Foreign Language Film; Nominations: Best Adapted Screenplay, Best Director (Costa-Gavras), Best Picture; Cannes Film Festival '69: Best Film; Cannes Film Festival '69: Best Actor (Trintignant); Edgar Allan Poe Awards '69: Best Screenplay; Golden Globe Awards '70: Best Foreign Film; New York Film Critics Awards '69: Best Director (Costa-Gavras), Best Film; National Society of Film Critics Awards '69: Best Film. **VHS, Beta $64.95** COL ᵴᵴᵴᵴ

Zabriskie Point Antonioni's first U.S. feature. A desultory, surreal examination of the American way of life. Worthy but difficult. Climaxes with a stylized orgy in Death Valley.
1970 (R) 112m/C Mark Frechette, Daria Halprin, Paul Fix, Rod Taylor, Harrison Ford, G.D. Spradlin; **D:** Michelangelo Antonioni; **W:** Michelangelo Antonioni, Sam Shepard, Fred Gardner, Tonino Guerra, Clare Peploe. **VHS, Beta $59.95** MGM, MLB ᵴᵴᵴ

Zachariah A semi-spoof '60s rock western, wherein two gunfighters given to pursuing wealth-laden bands of outlaws separate and experience quixotic journeys through the cliched landscape. Scripted by members of The Firesign Theater and featuring appearances by Country Joe and The Fish, The New York Rock Ensemble and The James Gang.
1970 (PG) 93m/C Don Johnson, John Rubinstein, Pat Quinn, Dick Van Patten, Country Joe & the Fish; **D:** George Englund. **VHS, Beta $19.98** FOX ᵴᵴ½

Zalmen or the Madness of God Elie Wiesel's mystical story about a rabbi's struggle against religious persecution in post-Stalin Russia.
1975 120m/C Joseph Wiseman, The Arena Stage Company. **VHS, Beta** WNE ᵴᵴ½

Zandalee The sexual adventures of a bored sexy young woman who has a fling with her husband's friend. Bad script, graphic sex. Also available in an unrated version.

1991 (R) 100m/C Nicolas Cage, Judge Reinhold, Erika Anderson, Viveca Lindfors, Aaron Neville, Joe Pantoliano, Ian Abercrombie, Marisa Tomei, Zach Galligan; **D:** Sam Pillsbury; **W:** Mari Kornhauser. VHS **$89.95** LIV *Woof!*

Zandy's Bride Basic story about a rancher who sents for a mail-order bride. She's shocked by his ill-treatment of her and stands up to his bullying, thus winning his respect and love. Beautiful scenery, courtesy of Big Sur, California, but predictable all-around and essentially a waste of an experienced cast. Based on the novel "The Stranger" by Lillian Bos Ross.
1974 (PG) 97m/C Gene Hackman, Liv Ullmann, Eileen Heckart, Harry Dean Stanton, Joe Santos, Sam Bottoms, Susan Tyrrell, Frank Cady; **D:** Jan Troell; **W:** Marc Norman; **M:** Michael Franks. VHS **$19.98** WAR ✍½

The Zany Adventures of Robin Hood Hackneyed spoof of the Robin Hood legend. Medieval man robs from the rich to help the poor. Not nearly as funny as. Mel Brooks' TV series that spoofed "Robin Hood."
1984 95m/C George Segal, Morgan Fairchild, Roddy McDowall, Roy Kinnear, Janet Suzman, Tom Baker; **D:** Ray Austin. VHS, Beta **$79.95** MED ✍

Zapped! Teen genius discovers he possesses telekinetic powers. He does the natural thing, using his talent to remove clothing from nearby females. A teen boy's dream come true.
1982 (R) 98m/C Scott Baio, Willie Aames, Robert Mandan, Felice Schachter, Scatman Crothers, Roger Bowen, Marya Small, Greg Bradford, Hilary Beane, Sue Ane Langdon, Heather Thomas, Merritt Butrick, LaWanda Page, Rosanne Katon; **D:** Robert J. Rosenthal; **M:** Charles Fox. VHS, Beta **$14.98** SUE, NLC ✍

Zapped Again The lame-brained sequel to 1982's "Zapped" about a high schooler who has telekinetic powers and lust on his mind.
1989 (R) 93m/C Todd Eric Andrews, Kelli Williams, Reed Rudy, Linda Blair, Karen Black, Lyle Alzado; **D:** Douglas Campbell. VHS, Beta, 8mm **$14.95** COL, SUE ✍

Zardoz A surreal parable of the far future, when Earth society is broken into strict classes: a society of intellectuals, a society of savages, and an elite unit of killers who keep the order. Connery is the man who destroys the old order of things. Visually interesting but pretentious.
1973 105m/C Sean Connery, Charlotte Rampling, John Alderton, Sara Kestelman; **D:** John Boorman. VHS, Beta **$19.98** FOX ✍✍

Zatoichi: Master Ichi and a Chest of Gold A violent thriller about a blind gambler and former samurai who tries to clear his name after being framed for a gold robbery. Adapted from a novel by Kazuo Miyagawa. In Japanese with English subtitles.
1964 83m/C Shintaro Katsu; **D:** Kazuo Ikehiro. VHS **$59.95** FCT ✍✍

Zatoichi: The Blind Swordsman and the Chess Expert Zatoichi, the blind gambler and former samurai, befriends a master chess player and gets involved with Japanese gangsters. In Japanese with English subtitles.
1965 87m/C Shintaro Katsu; **D:** Kenji Misumi. VHS **$59.95** FCT ✍✍

Zatoichi: The Blind Swordsman and the Fugitives This time Zatoichi, the blind masseur and master swordsman, is pitted against a band of outlaws. When the local bandits brutalize the countryside Zatoi-

chi steps in to defend the weak and faces a showdown with outlaw leader Genpachiro. In Japanese with English subtitles.
1968 82m/C Shintaro Katsu, Yumiko Nogawa, Kayo Mikimoto, Kyosuke Machida; **D:** Kimiyoshi Yasuda. VHS **$59.95** FCT ✍✍

Zatoichi: The Blind Swordsman's Vengeance Zatoichi defends a dying man against a group of gangsters who have taken over an isolated village. In Japanese with English subtitles.
1966 83m/C Shintaro Katsu, Shigeru Amachi, Kei Sato, Mayumi Ogawa; **D:** Tokuzo Tanaka. VHS **$59.95** FCT ✍✍

Zatoichi: The Life and Opinion of Masseur Ichi The first film in the action series about the Zen-like blind masseur, gambler, and swordsman. Zatoichi is drawn into a revenge match between two ruthless gangs. When one gang tries to hire him the other hires a savage killer. This sets in motion a war between the yakuza gangs and mercenary samurai. In Japanese with English subtitles.
1962 96m/C Shintaro Katsu, Masayo Mari, Ryuzo Shimada, Gen Mitamura, Shigeru Amachi; **D:** Kenji Misumi. VHS **$59.95** FCT ✍✍

Zatoichi vs. Yojimbo The legendary blind warrior-samurai, Zatoichi, wants to retire, but his village is being held captive by outlaws. He is forced to fight Yojimbo, the crude wandering samurai without a master, and the sparks really fly! This was a comic send-up of Akira Kurosawa's "Yojimbo" with Mifune recreating his role here and playing it for laughs. Subtitled. *AKA:* Zatoichi Meets Yojimbo; Zato Ichi To Yojimbo.
1970 90m/C Toshiro Mifune, Shintaro Katsu, Osamu Takizawa; **D:** Kihachi Okamoto. VHS VDA ✍✍½

Zatoichi: Zatoichi's Flashing Sword Blind swordsman Zatoichi gets caught up in a feud between two competing yakuza bosses. When Zatoichi declares his alliegence to Tsumugi, the unhappy Yasu tries to get his revenge. In Japanese with English subtitles.
1964 82m/C Shintaro Katsu, Mayumi Nagisa, Naoko Kubo, Ryutaro Gami, Yutaka Nakamura; **D:** Kazuo Ikehiro. VHS **$59.95** FCT ✍✍

Zazie dans le Metro One of Malle's early movies, this is one of the best of the French New Wave comedies. A young girl, wise beyond her years, visits her drag queen uncle in Paris. She wants to ride the subway, but the ensuing hilarious adventures keep her from her goal. In French with English subtitles. *AKA:* Zazie in the Underground; Zazie in the Subway.
1961 92m/C Catherine Demonget, Philippe Noiret, Carla Marlier; **W:** Louis Malle. VHS **$69.95** NYF, ING ✍✍✍½

Zebra Force Group of army veterans embark on a personal battle against organized crime, using their military training with deadly precision. Non-distinguished substandard action-adventure.
1976 (R) 81m/C Mike Lane, Richard X. Slattery, Rockne Tarkington, Glenn Wilder, Anthony Caruso; **D:** Joe Tornatore. VHS, Beta **$69.95** MED ✍

Zebra in the Kitchen A 12-year-old boy living in a small town is upset when he sees the run-down condition of the local zoo. So he decides to set all the animals free, which causes pandemonium in the town. Pleasant family fare.
1965 92m/C Jay North, Martin Milner, Andy Devine, Joyce Meadows, Jim Davis; **D:** Ivan Tors. VHS **$19.98** MGM, BTV ✍✍½

Zebrahead Zack and Nikki are two high schoolers in love—which would be okay except Zack's white and Nikki's black. Will their romance succumb to the pressures of society, family, and friends? Writer/director Drazan's expressive debut features one of last appearances by Sharkey as Zack's dad. Outstanding performances by the young and largely unknown cast, particularly Rappaport and Wright, and a great musical score enrich the action. Filmed on location in Detroit, with plenty of authentic Motown scenery to chew on, including Cody High School and a shoot-out at the eastside Skateland. Developed with assistance by the Sundance Institute.
1992 (R) 102m/C Michael Rappaport, N'Bushe Wright, Ray Sharkey, DeShonn Castle, Ron Johnson, Marsha Florence, Paul Butler, Abdul Hassan Sharif, Dan Ziskie, Candy Ann Brown, Helen Shaver, Luke Reilly, Martin Priest; **D:** Tony Drazan; **W:** Tony Drazan; **M:** Taj Mahal. VHS, 8mm **$29.95** COL ✍✍✍

A Zed & Two Noughts A serio-comic essay by the acclaimed British filmmaker. Twin zoologists, after their wives are killed in an accident, explore their notions of death by, among other things, filming the decay of animal bodies absconded from the zoo. Heavily textured and experimental; Greenaway's second feature film.
1988 115m/C Eric Deacon, Brian Deacon, Joss Ackland, Andrea Ferreol, Frances Barber; **D:** Peter Greenaway; **W:** Peter Greenaway. VHS, Beta **$29.95** TPV ✍✍✍

Zelig Documentary spoof stars Allen as Leonard Zelig, the famous "Chameleon Man" of the 1920s, whose personality was so vague he would assume the characteristics of those with whom he came into contact, and who had a habit of showing up among celebrities and at historic events. Filmed in black-and-white; intersperses bits of newsreel and photographs with live action. Allen-style clever filmmaking at its best.
1983 (PG) 79m/B Woody Allen, Mia Farrow, Susan Sontag, Saul Bellow, Irving Howe; **D:** Woody Allen; **W:** Woody Allen. VHS, Beta, 8mm **$19.98** WAR ✍✍✍½

Zelly & Me A strange little drama about a young orphan living with her maniacally possessive grandmother, who forces the child into her own interior life through humiliation and isolation from anyone she cares for. Well-acted and interesting film that suffers from an overly introspective plot and confusing gaps in the narrative. Look for director Lynch on the other side of the camera. *AKA:* Phoebe.
1988 (PG) 87m/C Isabella Rossellini, Alexandra Johnes, David Lynch, Glynis Johns, Kaiulani Lee, Joe Morton; **D:** Tina Rathborne; **W:** Tina Rathborne; **M:** Pino Donaggio. VHS, Beta **$79.95** COL ✍✍

Zentropa Clever cinematic allusions and visuals aside, this is essentially a conventional thriller. German-American pacifist Leopold travels to Germany in 1945 to help in the postwar rebuilding. He finds work as a sleeping-car conductor for a giant railway system called Zentropa and finds himself romancing the mysterious Katharina, who draws the hapless Leopold into an intrigue involving Nazi sympathizers. Director von Trier uses the voice of Von Sydow as an omniscient narrator to address the audience and move the story along. Filmed primarily in black-and-white with bursts of color denoting dramatic moments. In English and German with English subtitles.
1992 (R) 112m/C Jean-Marc Barr, Barbara Sukowa, Udo Kier, Eddie Constantine; **D:** Lars von Trier; **W:** Niels Vorsel, Lars von Trier. VHS, Beta **$94.95** TOU ✍✍

Zeppelin During WWI, the British enlist the aid of York as a double agent. His mission is to steal Germany's plans for a super-dirigible. Accompanying the Germans on the craft's maiden voyage, York discovers they are actually on a mission to steal British treasures. Although the script is poor, the battle scenes and the blimp itself are very impressive.
1971 (G) 102m/C Michael York, Elke Sommer, Peter Carsten, Marius Goring, Anton Diffring, Andrew Keir, Rupert Davies, Alexandra Stewart; **D:** Etienne Perier. **VHS, Beta** $19.98 WAR, FCT ⅛⅛½

Zeram Zeram is a giant renegade space alien lured to earth by a female bounty hunter. How does she expect to capture it? Why with a warp machine, space bazooka, electric shield, and a computer named Bob, of course. Dubbed.
1991 92m/C Yuko Moriyama, Yukihiro Hotaru, Kunihiko Ida; **D:** Keita Amemiya; **W:** Hajime Matsumoto. **VHS** $89.95 FXL, FCT ⅛⅛

Zero WWII story about the building of the zero fighter that was used to devastating effect in the invasion of Pearl Harbor.
1984 128m/C Yuzo Kayama, Tetsuro Tamba; **D:** Toshio Masuda. **VHS, Beta** NO ⅛⅛

Zero Boys Teenage survivalists in the Californian wilderness are stalked by a murderous lunatic. Exploitative and mean-spirited.
1986 (R) 89m/C Daniel Hirsch, Kelli Maroney, Nicole Rio, Joe Phelan; **D:** Nico Mastorakis. **VHS, Beta** $19.98 LIV Woof!

Zero for Conduct Vigo's classic French fantasy about an outrageous rebellion of schoolboys against bureaucratic adults. More of a visual poem than a drama, it inspired Lindsay Anderson's "If...." One of only four films created by Vigo before his early death. Banned across Europe at release. In French with English subtitles. **AKA:** Zero de Conduit.
1933 49m/B Jean Daste, Robert Le Flon, Louis Lef'evre, Constantin Kelber, Gerard de Bedarieux; **D:** Jean Vigo; **W:** Jean Vigo. **VHS, Beta** $19.95 VYY, NOS, HHT ⅛⅛⅛⅛

Zero for Conduct/Taris/A Propos de Nice Three short films by the famed Jean Vigo. "Zero for Conduct" is a fascinating and fluid surrealist film about rebellion in a boy's prep school. "Taris" consists of underwater footage of the swimmer Jean Taris, and "A Propos de Nice" is a documentary that focuses on the great economic schism of the rich and the poor in the popular French vacation spot, Nice.
1991 75m/B Jean Renoir. **VHS** NO ⅛⅛⅛⅛

Zero Pilot A Japanese film about the heroic fighter pilots of WWII.
1984 90m/C VHS, Beta VCD Woof!

Zero Population Growth In the 21st century the government has decreed that no babies may be born for a 30-year span in order to control the population. But Chaplin and Reed secretly have a child and when they are discovered are sent to be executed. Can they escape? Maudlin and simplistic. **AKA:** Z.P.G.
1972 95m/C Oliver Reed, Geraldine Chaplin, Diane Cilento, Don Gordon; **D:** Michael Campus; **W:** Frank de Felitta, Max Ehrlich. **VHS** $14.95 PAR ⅛½

Zero to Sixty Newly divorced man finds his car has been repossessed for nonpayment. Seeking out the manager of the finance company, he gets a job as a repo man with a sassy 16-year-old girl as his assistant. Repartee develops, stuff happens, and the movie ends.

1978 (PG) 96m/C Darren McGavin, Sylvia Miles, Denise Nickerson, Joan Collins; **D:** Don Weis. **VHS, Beta** $69.98 SUE ⅛

Zertigo Diamond Caper Utilizing his heightened senses, a blind boy solves a diamond caper and proves his mother's innocence.
1982 50m/C Adam Rich, David Groh, Jane Elliot. **VHS, Beta** $29.95 GEM ⅛

Ziegfeld Follies A lavish revue of musical numbers and comedy sketches featuring many MGM stars of the WWII era. Highlights include Astaire and Kelly's only duet and a Astaire-Bremer ballet number. ♫Bring on Those Wonderful Men; Bring on Those Beautiful Girls; The Drinking Song; La Traviata; This Heart is Mine; Love; When Television Comes; There's Beauty Everywhere; The Babbitt and the Bromide.
1946 109m/C Fred Astaire, Judy Garland, Gene Kelly, Red Skelton, Fanny Brice, William Powell, Jimmy Durante, Edward Arnold, Lucille Bremer, Hume Cronyn, Victor Moore, Lena Horne, Lucille Ball, Esther Williams; **D:** Vincente Minnelli. **VHS, Beta** $19.98 MGM, MLB ⅛⅛½

Ziegfeld Girl Three star-struck girls are chosen for the Ziegfeld follies and move on to success and heartbreak. Lavish costumes and production numbers in the MGM style. ♫You Stepped Out of a Dream; I'm Always Chasing Rainbows; Minnie from Trinidad; Mr. Gallagher & Mr. Shean; You Never Looked So Beautiful.
1941 131m/B James Stewart, Judy Garland, Hedy Lamarr, Lana Turner, Tony Martin, Jackie Cooper, Ian Hunter, Charles Winninger, Al Shear, Edward Everett Horton, Philip Dorn, Paul Kelly, Eve Arden, Dan Dailey, Fay Holden, Felix Bressart, Mae Busch, Reed Hadley; **D:** Robert Z. Leonard. **VHS, Beta** $19.98 MGM ⅛⅛⅛

Zipperface A Palm Beach serial killer is making mincemeat of the local prostitutes. In order to capture the scum, the prerequisite beautiful police detective goes undercover only to find herself the killer's biggest thrill.
1992 90m/C Dona Adams, David Clover, John Dagnen; **D:** Mansour Pourmand. **VHS** $89.95 AIP ⅛

Zis Boom Bah Musical-comedy star buys a cafe for her college son. He and his friends transform the place into a restaurant-theater with predictable results. ♫Annabella; It Makes No Difference When You're In the Army; Put Your Trust in the Moon; Zis Boom Bah; Good News Tomorrow; I've Learned to Smile Again.
1942 61m/B Peter Lind Hayes, Mary Healy, Grace Hayes, Huntz Hall, Benny Rubin. **VHS, Beta** $19.95 NOS, HEG, DVT ⅛½

The Zodiac Killer Based on a true story, this tells the violent tale of the San Francisco murders that occurred in the late 1960s. Doesn't have the suspense it should.
1971 (R) 87m/C Tom Pittman, Hal Reed, Bob Jones, Ray Lynch; **D:** Tom Hanson. **VHS, Beta** $59.95 ACA ⅛½

Zoltan...Hound of Dracula The vampire and his bloodthirsty dog go to Los Angeles to find the last of Count Dracula's living descendants. Campy and just original enough to make it almost worth watching. **AKA:** Dracula's Dog.
1977 85m/C Michael Pataki, Reggie Nalder, Jose Ferrer; **D:** Albert Band; **W:** Frank Ray Perilli. **VHS, Beta** $9.98 REP, VCI, FCT ⅛½

Zombie Italian-made white-men-in-the-Caribbean-with-flesh-eating-zombies cheapie. **AKA:** Zombie Flesh Eaters.
1980 91m/C Tisa Farrow, Ian McCulloch, Richard Johnson, Al Cliver, Arnette Gay, Olga Karlatos, Stefania D'Amario; **D:** Lucio Fulci. **VHS, Beta** VES ⅛

The Zombie Army Tough drill sergeant tries to whip a bunch of raw female recruits up to muster for a special mission. Toward that end, the government has conveniently bought a defunct lunatic asylum as a training ground. Only problem is that a few of the former inmates have been left behind and are able to menace the troops with their penchant for psychotic weirdness.
1993 80m/C Eileen Saddow. **VHS** $20.00 TEM, MOV ⅛

Zombie High Students at a secluded academy are being lobotomized by the school president. Mindless, in two senses of the word. **AKA:** The School That Ate My Brain.
1987 (R) 91m/C Virginia Madsen, Richard Cox, Kay E. Kuter, James Wilder, Sherilyn Fenn, Paul Williams, Scott Coffey; **D:** Ron Link. **VHS, Beta** $9.95 VTR ⅛

Zombie Island Massacre In this trying film, tourists travel to see a voodoo ritual, and then are systematically butchered by the rite-inspired zombies. Featuring former congressional wife and Playboy Magazine model Jenrette.
1984 89m/C Rita Jenrette, David Broadnax; **D:** John N. Carter. **VHS, Beta** $79.95 MED ⅛

Zombie Lake Killed in an ambush by villagers during WWII, a group of Nazi soldiers turned zombies reside in the town's lake, preying on unsuspecting swimmers, especially dog paddling nude young women. Laughable FX, almost bad enough to be good. From the team that produced "Oasis of the Zombies."
1984 90m/C Howard Vernon, Pierre Escourrou, Anouchka, Anthony Mayans, Nadine Pascale, Jean Rollin; **D:** J.A. Laser. **VHS** $59.95 VCI ⅛

Zombie Nightmare A murdered teenager is revived by a voodoo queen and slaughters his punk-teen assailants. Cheap and stupid just about sums this one up. Music by Motorhead, Death Mask, Girlschool and Thor.
1986 (R) 89m/C Adam West, Jon Mikl Thor, Tia Carrere, Frank Dietz, Linda Singer, Mandn E. Turbride, Hamibh McEwen; **D:** John Bravman. **VHS, Beta** $19.95 NWV, STE Woof!

Zombies of Moratau A diver and his girlfriend seek to retrieve an undersea treasure of diamonds protected by zombies. So boring you'll want to die.
1957 70m/B Gregg Palmer, Allison Hayes, Jeff Clark, Autumn Russel, Joel Ashley; **D:** Edward L. Cahn. **VHS, Beta** $59.95 COL, MLB Woof!

Zombies of the Stratosphere A serial in twelve chapters in which a cosmic policeman fights Zombies attempting to blow the Earth out of orbit. Also available in a 93 minute, colorized version. **AKA:** Satan's Satellites.
1952 152m/B Judd Holdren, Aline Towne, Leonard Nimoy, John Crawford, Ray Boyle; **D:** Fred Brannon. **VHS, Beta** $14.98 REP, VCN, MLB Woof!

Zombies on Broadway Two press agents travel to the Caribbean in search of new talent, but find Lugosi performing experiments on people and turning them into sequel material. RKO hoped this would be equally successful follow-up to "I Walked with a Zombie." **AKA:** Loonies On Broadway.
1944 68m/B Wally Brown, Alan Carney, Bela Lugosi, Anne Jeffreys, Sheldon Leonard, Frank Jenks, Russell Hopton, Joseph Vitale, Ian Wolfe, Louis Jean Heydt, Darby Jones, Sir Lancelot; **D:** Gordon Douglas. **VHS** $29.95 TTC, FCT, IME ⅛⅛½

Zombiethon A campy compilation of clips from cheapo zombie films, such as "Space Zombies," "Zombie Lake," and "The Invisible Dead."
1986 90m/C Dominique Singleton, Janelle Lewis, Tracy Burton. **VHS, Beta** NO ♫½

Zone of the Dead A mortician is using his morgue for other than embalming—and it isn't pretty!
1978 81m/C John Ericson, Ivor Francis, Charles Aidman, Bernard Fox. **VHS, Beta $79.95** MNC ♫

Zone Troopers Five American G.I.'s in WWII-ravaged Europe stumble upon a wrecked alien spacecraft and enlist the extraterrestrial's help in fending off the Nazis.
1985 (PG) 86m/C Timothy Van Patten, Tim Thomerson, Art LaFleur, Biff Manard; **D:** Danny Bilson; **W:** Danny Bilson, Paul DeMeo; **M:** Richard Band. **VHS, Beta $19.98** LIV ♫½

Zontar, the Thing from Venus Scientist is taken over by alien batlike thing from Venus, and attempts to take over the Earth. A parody of itself.
1966 68m/C John Agar, Anthony Huston; **D:** Larry Buchanan. **VHS $19.98** SNC, VDM ♫

The Zoo Gang A group of teens want to open a nightclub. Will they bring their dream to fruition, or will the mean rival gang foil their plans?
1985 (PG-13) 96m/C Jackie Earle Haley, Tiffany Helm, Ben Vereen, Jason Gedrick, Eric Gurry; **D:** John Watson, Pen Densham; **W:** John Watson, Pen Densham; **M:** Patrick Gleeson. **VHS, Beta $9.99** NWV, STE ♫½

Zoo Radio Run by a wacky assortment of characters, a zany underground radio station embarks on a battle against bureaucracy.
1990 (R) 90m/C VHS $89.95 WAX ♫½

Zoot Suit Based on Luis Valdez' play, this murder mystery/musical is rooted in the historical Sleepy Lagoon murder in the 1940s. Valdez plays a Mexican-American accused of the crime. His friends (and defense lawyers) rally around him to fight this travesty of justice. Lots o'music and dancing.
1981 (R) 104m/C Edward James Olmos, Daniel Valdez, Tyne Daly, Charles Aidman, John Anderson; **D:** Luis Valdez; **W:** Luis Valdez. **VHS $14.98** MCA, FCT ♫♫♫

Zora Is My Name! The funny, moving story of Zora Neal Hurston, a Black writer known for her stories and folklore of the rural South of the '30s and '40s. From PBS's American Playhouse.
1990 90m/C Ruby Dee, Louis Gossett Jr. **VHS $19.95** PBS, KAR, FCT ♫♫½

Zorba the Greek A young British writer (Bates) comes to Crete to find himself by working his father's mine. He meets Zorba, an itinerant Greek laborer (Quinn), and they take lodgings together with an aging courtesan, who Zorba soon romances. The writer, on the other hand, is attracted to a lovely young widow. When she responds to him, the townsmen jealously attack her. Zorba teaches the young man the necessary response to life and its tragedies. Based on a novel by Nicolai Kazantzakis. Masterpiece performance from Quinn. Beautifully photographed, somewhat overlong. Film later written for stage production. *AKA:* Zormba.
1964 142m/B Anthony Quinn, Alan Bates, Irene Papas, Lila Kedrova; **D:** Michael Cacoyannis. Academy Awards '64: Best Art Direction/Set Decoration (B & W), Best Black and White Cinematography, Best Supporting Actress (Kedrova); Nominations: Best Actor (Quinn), Best Adapted Screenplay, Best Director (Cacoyannis), Best Picture. **VHS, Beta $19.98** FXV, BTV, FUS ♫♫♫½

Zorro Rides Again Zorro risks his life to outwit enemy agents endeavoring to secure ancestor's property. In twelve chapters, the first runs 30 minutes, the rest 17.
1937 217m/B John Carroll, Helen Christian, Noah Beery Sr., Duncan Renaldo; **D:** William Witney, John English. **VHS, Beta $27.95** NOS, VCN, MED ♫♫½

Zorro, the Gay Blade Tongue-in-cheek sword play with Hamilton portraying the swashbuckling crusader and his long-lost brother, Bunny Wigglesworth, in this spoof of the Zorro legend. The fashion-conscious hero looks his best in plum. Leibman is fun to watch.
1981 (PG) 96m/C George Hamilton, Lauren Hutton, Brenda Vaccaro, Ron Leibman; **D:** Peter Medak. **VHS, Beta $59.98** FOX ♫♫½

Zorro's Black Whip A young girl dons the mask of her murdered brother (Zorro) to fight outlaws in the old West. Serial in twelve episodes.
1944 182m/B George Lewis, Linda Stirling, Lucien Littlefield, Francis McDonald, Tom London; **D:** Spencer Gordon Bennet; **W:** Wallace Grissell. **VHS $29.98** NOS, GPV, MED ♫♫½

Zorro's Fighting Legion Zorro forms a legion to help the president of Mexico fight a band of outlaws endeavoring to steal gold shipments. A serial in 12 chapters.
1939 215m/B Reed Hadley, Sheila Darcy; **D:** William Witney, John English. **VHS $29.98** NOS, VCN, VDM ♫♫

Zotz! The holder of a magic coin can will people dead by uttering "zotz"; spies pursue the mild-mannered professor who possesses the talisman. Adapted from a Walter Karig novel. Typical William Castle fare; his gimic in the theatrical release of the movie was to distribute plastic "zotz" coins to the theatre patrons.
1962 87m/B Tom Poston, Julia Meade, Jim Backus, Fred Clark, Cecil Kellaway; **D:** Ray Russell; **W:** Ray Russell. **VHS, Beta $59.95** COL ♫♫

Zou Zou Lavish backstage musical/drama of a laundress who fills in for the leading lady on opening night and becomes a hit. Baker's talking picture debut. In French with English subtitles.
1934 92m/B Josephine Baker, Jean Gabin; **D:** Marc Allegret. **VHS $29.95** MVD, KIV, APD ♫♫½

Zulu In 1879, a small group of British soldiers try to defend their African outpost from attack by thousands of Zulu warriors. Amazingly, the British win. Dated colonial epic based on an actual incident; battle scenes are magnificent. Prequel "Zulu Dawn" (1979) depicts British mishandling of the situation that led to the battle.
1964 139m/C Michael Caine, Jack Hawkins, Stanley Baker, Nigel Green; **D:** Cy Endfield; **M:** John Barry. **VHS, Beta $19.98** NLC, VYG ♫♫½

Zulu Dawn An historical epic about British troops fighting the Zulus at Ulandi in 1878. Shows the increasing tensions between the British colonial government and the Zulus. Stunning landscapes unfortunately don't translate to the small screen. Good but unoriginal colonial-style battle drama.
1979 (PG) 117m/C Burt Lancaster, Peter O'Toole, Denholm Elliott, Nigel Davenport, John Mills, Simon Ward, Bob Hoskins, Freddie Jones; **D:** Douglas Hickox; **M:** Elmer Bernstein. **VHS, Beta $19.98** TWE ♫♫♫

Zvenigora Dovzhenko's first major film, and a lyrical revelation in the face of Soviet formality: a passionate, funny fantasy tableaux of 1,000 years of Ukrainian history, encompassing wild folk myths, poetic drama, propaganda and social satire. Silent.
1928 73m/B Mikola Nademsy, Alexander Podorozhny, Semyon Svashenko; **D:** Alexander Dovzhenko. **VHS, Beta $39.95** FCT, ING ♫♫♫

CATEGORY LIST

The **CATEGORY INDEX** contains 500 genre, sub-genre, thematic, or significant scene classifications, ranging from the very general (such as drama) to the fairly particular (such as phone terror). The terms are defined (more or less) below. While we've done our best to provide serious subject references, we've also had a bit of fun in the making of the various lists. No one list is inclusive; we're continually reclassifying, adding, and subtracting movies. Some 100 or so of the categories are new to this edition, and in some cases represent only a beginning. We're also trying to pare down some of the larger lists, like **Romance**, by creating more targeted categories (such as **Lovers on the Lam, Romantic Triangles**). *VideoHound* invites readers to join in this sometimes fascinating pastime by sending in new titles for existing categories, as well as suggestions on new categories. With your suggestion, please list at least five movies that could be classified under the new category.

Action-Adventure: Adrenaline testers for those weary of the conventions of plot–think Stallone, think Snipes, and quit thinking

Adoption & Orphans: Cute kids lacking permanent authority figures, ranging from Annie to Wild Hearts Can't Be Broken

Adventure Drama: Action with more attention to dramatic content–Apocalypse Now to Robin Hood, Prince of Thieves

Advertising: Corporate shenanigans at the agency–How to Get Ahead in Advertising to The Horse in the Gray Flannel Suit

Africa: Banana Republic franchise; Out of Africa to Zulu Dawn

African America: Dominant African American themes

AIDS: Someone usually dies; An Early Frost to Longtime Companion

Airborne: Contraptions up in the sky

Air Disasters: Contraptions up in the sky, but not for long

Alien Beings–Benign: Friendly space visitors, including Howard the Duck and little buddy E.T.

Alien Beings–Vicious: Not-so-friendly space visitors, notably the multi-jawed Alien continually harassing Sigourney Weaver

American South: Theatrics amid much brow mopping and drawling; A Streetcar Named Desire rattling down Flamingo Road

Amnesia: Phone call for Anastasia

*****Amusement Parks:** Cotton candy, ferris wheels, Coney Island, Godzilla on Monster Island, Rollercoaster

Angels: Benevolent winged visitors from above: Wings of Desire

*****Animated Musicals:** Boys, girls, dogs, ducks, birds, mice, and monkeys croon; many of Disney vintage, including Aladdin and Sleeping Beauty

Animation & Cartoons: Antics of Daffy, Donald, Bugs, Mickey, Chip, Dale, Tom, Jerry, Fred, Wilma, Charlie, and the rest of the gang

Anthology: More than one story to a cassette

*****Anti-Heroes:** From Billy Jack to Dirty Harry to Thelma & Louise

Anti-War War Movies: All Quiet on the Western Front to Glory to *M*A*S*H

Apartheid: Afrikaans term for racial segregation in South Africa

Art & Artists: They paint, pause, propagate with equal passion

Asia: China White, Red Dust, Sand Pebbles

*****Asian America:** Asian experience in the US–The Joy Luck Club, Come See the Paradise

Assassinations: Lincoln, JFK, La Femme Nikita, Times of Harvey Milk, and more

At the Movies: The movie within the movie or movies about watching the movies, from Purple Rose of Cairo to Last Action Hero to Matinee

Avant-garde: Ahead of its time or completely bewildering to most in the audience

Babysitting: Supervision of small-fry pranksters not your own; Uncle Buck to Hand that Rocks the Cradle

*****Bad Dads:** Daddy-Os with unpredictable mean streak: The Shining, Kiss Daddy Goodbye

Ballet: On your toes–The Turning Point

Ballooning: Up, up and away, or Around the World in 80 Days

Baseball: Action on the diamond, ranging from Bull Durham to A League of Their Own to Rookie of the Year

Basketball: Roundball thrillers, including the memorable The Fish that Saved Pittsburgh and White Men Can't Jump

Beach Blanket Bingo: Annette, Frankie, sand, surf, bikinis

Behind the Scenes: Peek behind show business curtain, from A Chorus Line to Truth or Dare

Bicycling: Two wheels, no motor, much leg action and sweating

Big Battles: Big-budget (or at least illusion of such) clash of large, opposing military forces, from Cromwell to Ran

Big Budget Stinkers: Millions spent for no apparent reason

Big Daddies: Usually troublesome, with Freudian overtones

Big Digs: Anthropology and archaeology, from Indiana Jones to various mummy on-the-loose stories

Big Ideas: Philosophy, ideology and other semi-mental pursuits somehow translated to film

*****Bigfoot/Yeti:** Large, hairy, seldom-seen beast with really big feet

Bikers: Usually with a mean streak and traveling in leather-bound packs

Birds: Beaks, feathers, talons, bird #%!*; The Birds, Beaks: The Movie, Howard the Duck

Bisexuality: Going both ways–Basic Instinct, Three of Hearts

Black Comedy: Funny in a biting or despairing sort of way, from The Addams Family to The Hospital

Black Gold: That's oil; aka Oklahoma Crude

*****Blaxploitation:** '70s remakes of horror classics with black casts: Blacula, Blackenstein, Dr. Black, Mr. Hyde

Blindness: Can't see or sight impaired: Afraid of the Dark

Bloody Mayhem: Expanded scenes of arterial explosions, including Blood Bride, Blood Cult, Blood Diner, Blood Feast, Blood Lake, Blood Legacy, Blood Mania, and Bloodbath in Psycho Town

Bodyguards: Costner looks after Whitney's personal business

*****Books:** As a major plot device: La Lectrice to Crossing Delancey

*****Boomer Reunions:** thirtysomethings gather and reminisce: The Big Chill

*****Bowling:** Heavy round ball is thrown down waxed alley toward club- like pins; all fall down

Boxing: Yo, Adrian!

Bringing Up Baby: Look Who's Talking to Raising Arizona, plus infants with that little something different–Alien 3, Enemy Mine,

Basket Case 3: The Progeny

Buddies: Butch and Sundance, Bill and Ted, Rubin and Ed, Thelma and Louise

Buddy Cops: Couple of police hanging together, usually practicing limited repartee at donut shop; Lethal Weapon, Tango and Cash

*****Buses:** Large truck like passenger vehicles–Speed, The Big Bus, The Trip to Bountiful

*****Camelot (New):** The exploits of JFK, Jackie, and various relatives and hangers-on

*****Camelot (Old):** The exploits of King Arthur and his Knights of the Round Table

Campus Capers: What really goes on at college–Assault of the Party Nerds

Canada: Renfrew the Mountie plus lots of wildness and the occasional hockey puck

Cannibalism: People who eat people are the luckiest people; Alive, Rabid Grannies, Cannibal Women in the Avocado Jungle of Death, The Cook, the Thief, His Wife & Her Lover

*****Capitol Capers:** Hollywood versions of hijinks in Washington–Dave, Mr. Smith Goes to Washington, All the President's Men

Carnivals & Circuses: Big top, little top, domes: Shakes the Clown to Rollercoaster, plus Big Top Pee Wee, State Fair, and metaphoric circuses: Brewster McCloud, La Strada

Cats: Lesser vertebrate nonetheless much beloved by Hollywood

*****Cave People:** From the most primitive (The Clan of the Cave Bear) to the fairly modernized (The Flintstones)

Central America: Mostly Latin warfare, with at least three sides to every conflict

Chases: Who are those guys? Someone's after someone else, usually at high-speed with transportation ranging from horses to autos to bikes to trains to trucks

*****Cheerleaders:** Give me an A! The Positively True Adventures of the Alleged Texas Cheerleader-Murdering Mom meets Revenge of the Cheerleaders

Child Abuse: Not very funny at all–Mommie Dearest, Fallen Angel

Childhood Visions: Stories dominated by the kid point of view, or by an adult flashbacking to childhood; Au Revoir Les Enfants, Home Alone

China: Last Emperor to Red Sorghum to The World of Suzie Wong

Christmas: Reindeer, Santa, children make appearance amid much sentimentality

*****Cinderella Stories:** Gal down on her luck meets fairy godmother (or father) and finds true love–Pretty Woman, Flashdance, Cinderella

City Lights: Various urban sprawls used to good advantage; L.A. Story; Last Tango in Paris; The Blues Brothers (Chicago)

1023 ▲ CATEGORY LIST

Civil Rights: Fighting for equality–Autobiography of Miss Jane Pittman, Mississippi Burning

Civil War: The Blue and the Gray

Classic Horror: Boris Karloff, Vincent Price, piercing screams

*Clowns: Big red noses, huge feet, painted smiles frighten many

Cold Spots: Set in a frostbitten locale with lots of shivering; Ice Station Zebra, Never Cry Wolf, Quest for Fire

Comedy: Yuck fests not listed in other comedy categories–Fletch, I Wanna Hold Your Hand, Tampopo

Comedy Anthologies: More than one yuck fest on a cassette

Comedy Drama: Drama with a comedic touch or comedy underwired with drama–Avalon, The Big Chill, Fried Green Tomatoes, One Flew Over the Cuckoo's Nest, Tootsie

Comic Adventure: Adventurous romps liberally laced with humor: Romancing the Stone to Bird on a Wire to Crocodile Dundee

Coming of Age: Hard-fought adolescent battle for adulthood, led by American Graffiti, The Apprenticeship of Duddy Kravitz, Karate Kid

Computers: Bits and bytes play major role

*Concert Films: Rock or comedy concerts–from Woodstock to Divine Madness to Eddie Murphy: Raw

Contemporary Musicals: Thematically modern and made during last 20 years; All That Jazz

Cops: Police and pseudo-police work, including Action Jackson, Blue Steel, The Choirboys, RoboCop, Lethal Weapon, National Lampoon's Loaded Weapon 1

Corporate Shenanigans: Big Business runs amuck–Barbarians at the Gate, Wall Street

*Creepy Houses: Scary dwellings–Amityville Horror 1 through 33

Crime & Criminals: Bad guys and gals, including the Avenging Disco Godfather, The Grifters, In Cold Blood

Crime Sprees: Boy meets girl and together begin life of crime and other tales of obsessional criminal activity, including Bonnie & Clyde, The Boys Next Door

Crimes of Passion: Love, sex, and death

Crop Dusters: Down on the farm: Bitter Harvest, Pelle the Conqueror, Jean de Florette, The River

Cult Items: Recognized for that something different by a relatively small group of people (at least initially); Basket Case, Blood Simple, Harold and Maude, Mad Max, and the greatest cult of them all–The Rocky Horror Picture Show

Cults: Something like a gang but more intense and usually governed by a state of mind similar to irrationality–Helter Skelter

Dance Fever: Whole lotta foot-tapping going on, including An American in Paris, Daddy Long Legs, and Dirty Dancing

Deafness: Can't hear or hearing impaired; Bridge to Silence, The Miracle Worker

Death & The Afterlife: Could be ghosts, could be voices from the beyond, could be any number of post-dead things–Beetlejuice, Carnival of Souls, Flatliners, Poltergeist, Weekend at Bernie's

*Dedicated Teachers: The Dead Poet's Society to Blackboard Jungle to The Miracle Worker

Deep Blue: The sea around us, including ffolkes and Splash

Demons & Wizards: Swords, sorcery and wrinkled old men with wands–The Alchemist, The Hobbit, Sword & the Sorcerer

Dental Mayhem: Tooth-pickin' uproars; Marathon Man, The Dentist

Detective Spoofs: Putting together clues in humorous fashion–Adventures of Sherlock Holmes Smarter Brother, Naked Gun

Detectives: Clue happy but often grizzled and cynical–The Drowning Pool, V.I. Warshawski

*Devils: Some may meet on Judgment Day

Dinosaurs: Jurassic Park and other less animated thundering lizards

Disaster Flicks: Natural and man-made, including 47 'Airport' sequels

Disease of the Week: Bulimia, anorexia, polio, cancer, and so on

*Disco Musicals: '70s tackiness reigns supreme, from Saturday Night Fever to Xanadu

Disorganized Crime: Stupid crime, including Amos and Andrew, Dog Day Afternoon, Home Alone, Quick Change

Divorce: Breaking up is hard to do; Accidental Tourist, Heartburn, Kramer vs. Kramer

Doctors & Nurses: Men and women in white concerned about health of complete strangers for profit, often to the dismay of the patient–Autopsy, Candy Stripe Nurses, Dead Ringers

Docudrama: Thin Blue Line between documentaries and drama

Documentary: Real life manipulated on film–A Brief History of Time, The Last Waltz, Paris is Burning, Roger and Me

Down Under: Australian, New Zealand settings–Rescuers Down Under, Gallipoli, Man from Snowy River, The Thorn Birds

Drama: Conflict, tension, climax, resolution

Dream Girls: Product of mid-life male crisis; Battling Amazons, Cycle Vixens, The Doll Squad, The Woman in Red

Earthquakes: Common occurrence in California

*Eco-Vengeance!: Nature wreaks havoc on man–watch out for Alligators, Frogs and Piranhas

Edibles: Something's cooking–Babette's Feast, Like Water for Chocolate

Erotic Thrillers: Hot sex and murder, including Basic Instinct, Body of Evidence

Ethics & Morals: Examination of values (or lack of)–Crimes & Misdemeanors, Judgment at Nuremberg

Etiquette: Usually comedy of manners: Educating Rita, My Fair Lady

*Evil Doctors: Don't go to these guys for a checkup–Malice, Dead Ringers, and Doctor X

Exploitation: Rigged to take advantage of viewer, including historic treats like Reefer Madness and more recent ventures such as Sleazamania

Explorers: Going boldly where no man or woman has regularly gone before

*Extraordinary Pairings: Jesse James Meets Frankenstein's Daughter

*Eyeballs!: Unnerving scenes involving pupils, irises, lids, and occasionally, lashes

Fairs & Expositions: Short term amusement parks: State Fair

Family Ties: Blood runs deep–Back to the Future, Five Easy Pieces, The Godfather, Homeward Bound, Lorenzo's Oil, The Mosquito Coast, Rocket Gibraltar

Fantasy: Tales of the imagination, including Alice and her looking glass, E.T., Ladyhawke, My Stepmother is an Alien

Fast Cars: Eat My Dust; racing in the street or on the track; The Last American Hero

Feds: Men and women of the Bureau, the Agency, or any national police organization with a dress code

Femme Fatale: She done him and him and him wrong

Fencing: En garde, dude

Film & Film History: America at the Movies; includes movies important to film history

Film Noir: Dark and moody or tributes to dark and moody–Farewell, My Lovely, The Postman Always Ring Twice, The Third Man, Who Framed Roger Rabbit?

Film Stars: Movies or bios about cinema celebs, real or make-believe–Bogie, Chaplin, Sinatra

Filmmaking: The making of a film within a film: The Player

Firemen: Backdraft, Fahrenheit 451, and other tales of brave people with hoses

Fires: Frankenstein, Quest for Fire, Pyrates

Flower Children: The sixties are still alive at Alice's Restaurant–reflect on The Big Chill, The Doors, and Woodstock; we all live on a Yellow Submarine

Folklore & Mythology: Age-old adult tales covering Atlantis, little people, Hercules, Ulysses

Football: Everything from terrorist attacks on the Superbowl (Black Sunday) to prison competition (The Longest Yard) plus Diner

Foreign Intrigue: Overseas mystery, with emphasis on accent and location

Frame-ups: Someone's set up to take the rap: My Cousin Vinny to Consenting Adults

France: Dirty Rotten Scoundrels to The Moderns to Gigi to The Last Metro to Killer Tomatoes Eat France

Front Page: Citizen Kane, All the President's Men, The Philadelphia Story, and other journalistic stories

Fugitives: Running from the law: Breathless, Nowhere to Hide, Posse

*Funerals: The final good-bye–Four Weddings and a Funeral, Gardens of Stone, The Big Chill

Gambling: Aces and Eights, The Color of Money, Eight Men Out, Honeymoon in Vegas

Game Shows: The Running Man and Queen for a Day

Gangs: Criminally enterprising teens and adults running in packs: State of Grace, Miller's Crossing, Public Enemy, Wanderers

Gender Bending: Crying Game, La Cage aux Folles, Her Life as a Man and other instances of boys becoming girls and vice versa

*Generation X: Slacking in the '90s–Reality Bites, Singles

Genetics: Fooling with the double helix–see The Fly

Genies: Aladdin finds magic lamp filled with compressed Robin Williams

*Genre Spoofs: Wacky takes on serious films, starting with the granddaddy of them all: Airplane!

Germany: The Blue Angel, The Sound of Music, Wings of Desire

Ghosts, Ghouls, & Goblins: Ghostbusters, Topper, Poltergeist

Giants: The Amazing Colossal Man visits Village of the Giants

*Gifted Children: Kids show amazing talents that astound adults, from Rookie of the Year to Little Man Tate

*Gigolos: Men try the oldest profession in the world, working around biological limitations

Go Fish: Casting a line in the river that runs through it; Man of Aran, A Fish Called Wanda, Captains Courageous

*Going Native: Outsiders try to blend in: Dances with Wolves, The Swiss Family Robinson

Golf: Slow boring game best experienced on screen ('Be the ball, Danny')

Good Earth: Ecology, environment, nature, sod

Grand Hotel: Checkout time is noon; Blame it on the Bellboy

Great Britain: Thwarted royals (Charles & Diana: A Palace Divided, Edward and Mrs. Simpson), kings (King Ralph), queens (The Naked Civil Servant), class distinctions (The Ruling Class), vanished empires (Cromwell, A Man for All Seasons), criminals (The Krays, The Long Good Friday) plus multiple stiff upper lips, the Brontes, and Dickens

Great Death Scenes: Signing off with style or elaboration: Buffy the Vampire Killer, Bonnie and Clyde, Breaker Morant

Great Depression: The era, not the state of mind–Bound for Glory, Of Mice and Men, The Grapes of Wrath, Rambling Rose

Great Escapes: Seizing the day for freedom–The Big Doll House, Escape from Alcatraz, Papillon

Growing Older: On Golden Pond, *batteries not included, *Cocoon, Driving Miss Daisy, The Shootist, The Wild Bunch

*Gymnastics: Human pretzels like Nadia

*Happy Hookers: Prostitution with a rosy glow; The Happy Hooker Goes to Hollywood and meets Pretty Woman

Hard Knock Life: Poverty and bad luck: City of Joy, The Match Factory Girl

Heaven Sent: Visits or returns from the place where good souls and all dogs go–Field of Dreams to Made in Heaven to Oh God!

Heists: The big lift

Hell High School: Place where adolescents gather against their will; also known as Rock 'n' Roll High School

*Hispanic America: Dominant Hispanic American themes (Salsa, Mi Vida Loca)

Historical Drama: Usually at least loosely based on a real incident or personality

Hit Men: Boys and girls armed with silencers; Prizzi's Honor, Romeo is Bleeding

Hockey: Slap Shot and other icy tales of passing the puck

Holidays: Easter, Thanksgiving, New Year's, Halloween, but generally not Christmas

Holocaust: Playing for Time

*Home Alone: Kids find themselves without adult supervision– Adventures in Babysitting to Young Sherlock Holmes

Homeless: Street people with no homes

Homosexuality: Gay and lesbian themes–Kiss of the Spider Woman, The Hunger, Cruising, Lianna, My Own Private Idaho

*Horrible Holidays: Holidays with a ghoulish twist–Bloody New Year, Halloween, My Bloody Valentine, Silent Night, Bloody Night

Horror: Modern cut 'em up scare theater

Horror Anthologies: More than one scarefest on a cassette

Horror Comedy: Tongue-in-bloody cheek–The Fearless Vampire Killers, Piranha, Sorority Babes in the Slimeball Bowl-A-Rama

Horses: Can you say Black Beauty?

Hospitals & Medicine: Dysfunctional institutional health care– Article 99, The Hospital, One Flew Over the Cuckoo's Nest, Young Doctors in Love

Hostage!: People held against their will for bargaining purposes

*Hunted!: Humans tracking humans for trophy purposes

Hunting: Where's dat wascally wabbit? Caddyshack, The Bear, White Hunter, Black Heart

Identity: Who am I? Who are you? Who are we? Why do you ask so many questions?

Immigration: Melting pot stories–Avalon, Far and Away, Living on Tokyo Time

India: On the road to Bombay

Interviews: When asked questions, people talk

Inventors & Inventions: Those wacky folks and their newfangled machines; Chitty Chitty Bang Bang

Ireland: Aye, make that a pint for take away: The Field, Cal, The Playboys

Islam: Religious themes

Island Fare: Thin, isolated stretch of land surrounded by water notorious for encouraging natural appetites in men and women

Israel: Cast a Giant Shadow, Exodus

Italy: Passion, vino, lust, vino, Sophia Loren

Japan: Land of the Rising Sun, Godzilla, Hiroshima, Mon Amour

*Japanimation: Animated cartoons from Japan with cult following

Judaism: Fiddler on the Roof meets Funny Girl

Jungle Stories: Tarzan, tribes, trees, treasure, temperature, temptresses, tigers

*Justice Prevails?: The verdict's in, but is it fair? And Justice for All, In the Name of the Father, Presumed Innocent

Kidnapped!: Held for ransom or just for the heck of it–A Perfect World, Raising Arizona

Killer Apes: King Kong lives on The Planet of the Apes

Killer Appliances: Defrosted refrigerator goes on killing binge

Killer Beasts: Cloned dinosaurs run amuck in backyard, destroying patio

*Killer Brains: Literally has a mind of its own, i.e., The Brain That Wouldn't Die

Killer Bugs: Giant and/or miserably mean spiders, ants, bees, worms, flies, slugs, tarantulas, wasps, and other creepy things

*Killer Cars: You should have changed Christine's oil

*Killer Dogs: Fido takes a walk on the wild side–Cujo, baby

*Killer Dreams: More like nightmares on elm street

*Killer Kats: Kitties with a killer instinct

*Killer Pigs: Evil swine

Killer Plants: Too much fertilizer produces killer tomatoes (stewed)

*Killer Rodents: Nasty mice, rats, bats, and shrews

Killer Toys: Demented play things develop homicidal urges; why hello, Chucky

Kindness of Strangers: Baffling altruistic behavior

King of Beasts (Dogs): Need we say more?

Korean War: M*A*S*H and friends

Labor & Unions: Hoffa and other working stiffs

Late Bloomin' Love: Better late than not blooming at all

Law & Lawyers: Tom Cruise joins The Firm and other realistic legal adventures

Loner Cops: Dirty Harry Syndrome

*Lost Worlds: From Brigadoon to The People That Time Forgot

*Lovers on the Lam: Couple commits crimes and find themselves on the run–Badlands, Natural Born Killers, True Romance

Macho Men: Ah-nuld, The Duke, Van Damme, Stallone, Burt, Clint, Norris, Seagal, and many more cases of excessive testosterone

Mad Scientists: The Brain That Wouldn't Die spends an evening with Frankenhooker

Magic: Hocus pocus, often with evil intent

Magic Carpet Rides: Aladdin joins Sinbad the Sailor for the Golden Voyage of Sinbad

Marriage: Wedding bells, honeymoons, affairs, divorce, and growing old together, as well as the occasional unfortunate marital union with a blood-sucking vampire or knife-wielding satanist

Martial Arts: Fists of Aluminum Foil; much head-kicking, rib-crunching, chop-socky action

Martyred Pop Icons: For us, they gave their all: Buddy Holly, Elvis, Marilyn, James Dean, Stardust Memories

Mass Media: From Network to Broadcast News to My Favorite Year

*The Meaning of Life: The search for the elusive answer–My Life, The Remains of the Day, Shadowlands

Medieval Romps: Dirty peasants, deodorized and glorified kings and queens, splendid knights in shining armor, and one for all and all for one

Meltdown: Or how I learned to stop worrying and love the bomb; also bad wiring at local nuclear plants

Men: What is man? Is he neither fish nor fowl? Or perhaps linoleum?

Men in Prison: Working on a chain gang; what we have here is a failure to communicate

Mental Retardation: Bill, Charly, Dominick, Lenny, Raymond (definitely)

*Metamorphosis: Ch-ch-ch-changes.... From The Fly to Wolf

Mexico: South of Sante Fe and Against All Odds

Middle East: Desert fare and camel close-ups ranging from Ishtar to Lawrence of Arabia to The Jewel of the Nile

Military Comedy: Marching to a different drummer, including Stripes, M*A*S*H, and No Time for Sergeants

Miners & Mining: Helmets with the little flashlights are nifty; Matewan and McCabe & Mrs. Miller

Missing Persons: People who disappear for a variety of reasons, sometimes because other people have taken them away

Missionaries: On a mission from God to save native populations

Misspelled Titles: Not proper Anglish

Mistaken Identity: You mean to say you're not the King of France?

*Modern Cowboys: Fun-lovin' rascals adept at riding horses through busy city streets or with a yen to experience mid-life crisis by doing a rodeo

*Monster Moms: Loving on the outside, evil on the inside–Mommie Dearest, Serial Mom

Monsters, General: Not killer beasts, bugs, plants, appliances, aliens, toys, giants, vampires, werewolves, or politicians

Motor Vehicle Dept.: Chitty Chitty Bang Bang at the Car Wash, plus Tucker, Herbie, and the Repo Man

Mountaineering: Cliffhangers

Movie & TV Trailers: Snippets of stuff

*Mummies: Dead guys with leather-like skin, often wrapped in sheets

Music: Amadeus meets the Fabulous Baker Boys and The Commitments by way of Mo' Better Blues at The Cotton Club

Musical Comedy: Laughter, singing, and dancing

Musical Drama: Singing and dancing, less laughter, more tension

Musical Fantasy: Chitty Chitty Bang Bang; The Wizard of Oz

Musicals: High-energy singing and dancing, often for no particular reason

*Musician Biopics: Real-life musicians get the Hollywood treatment

Mystery & Suspense: Edge-of-the-couch thrillers and whodunits

Nashville Narratives: Honkytonk Man elopes with the Coal Miner's Daughter

Native America: Dancing with the wolves on Pow Wow Highway

Nazis & Other Paramilitary Slugs: Boys from Brazil and The Dirty Dozen plus SS she-wolf Ilsa and modern David Duke adaptations

Negative Utopia: Things seemed so perfect until...

New Black Cinema: Spike is Godfather

Nifty '50s: Grease, La Bamba, The Man in the Moon, Peggy Sue Got Married, School Ties and 60 more from the Eisenhower era

Nightclubs: Casablanca, of course

*No-Exit Motel: Sleazy motels with extremely lenient late-checkout policies

Nuns & Priests: Collars and habits: Agnes of God, The Cardinal, Going My Way, Nuns on the Run, Sister Act

*Nursploitation!: Night Call Nurses offer Tender Loving Care in The Hospital of Terror

Occult: Witches, warlocks, devil worshippers, spell makers, spell breakers, haunted houses, and so on

Oldest Profession: It's not accounting

*The Olympics: Chariots of Fire and other tales of athletic displine

On the Rocks: Alcoholism, alcohol, barflies, moonshining, Prohibition–Arthur, Days of Wine and Roses, Papa's Delicate Condition, My Favorite Year

Only the Lonely: 50 ways to play solitaire–The Cemetery Club, The Heart is a Lonely Hunter, Sleepless in Seattle

Opera: Shouting in a melodic way while in costume

Order in the Court: Courtroom tales, including The Accused, And Justice for All, A Few Good Men, Witness for the Prosecution

Organized Crime: Gangsters with Franklin Planners

*Ostracism: Odd man out

Outtakes & Bloopers: Inadvertent laugh riots

*Overlooked Gems: No box office to speak of, but worth a rent

Pacific Islands: Hawaii, Tahiti, Philippines, etc.

Parades & Festivals: Animal House and Ferris Bueller's Day Off

Parenthood: Moms, dads, substitutes–Dutch, Ma Barker's Killer Brood, Father of the Bride, Three Men and a Baby, Yours, Mine, and Ours, Raising Arizona

*Party Hell: Psycho Girls have fun at a sleepover until Monsters Crash the Pajama Party and it becomes The Slumber Party Massacre

Patriotism & Paranoia: Run the flag up the pole and salute it–Rambo, Patton, Norris, etc.

Peace: Friendly Persuasion, Gandhi

Period Piece: Costume epics or evocative of a certain time and place–Bugsy, Cleopatra, Doctor Zhivago, The French Lieutenant's Woman, Swing Kids

Persian Gulf War: Smart bombs away

*Phobias!: Eeeeeeeeeeeeeeeeek!

Phone Terror: Don't Answer the Phone

Physical Problems: My Left Foot, Coming Home, The Elephant Man, The Other Side of the Mountain, Untamed Heart, The Waterdance

Pill Poppin': Life with a drugstore cowboy; consumption of drugs, mostly illegal or in extra-large dosages

Poetry: Not exactly a booming category, but think of Poetic Justice

Poisons: Arsenic and Old Lace and D.O.A.

Politics: Bob Roberts, Mandela, Whoops Apocalypse

Pool: The Hustler

Pornography: Hardcore, Body Double

Post Apocalypse: No more convenience stores

Postwar: After effects of war, generally WWI or WWII but sometimes the Civil War, the War of 1812, the Revolutionary War, and the Ohio Automobile Dealers War

POW/MIA: Captured by the enemy

Presidency: Mr. Lincoln, JFK, LBJ, FDR, and, of course, Dave

Price of Fame: What goes up...

Propaganda: Deliberately stretching the truth in order to persuade

Psycho-Thriller: It's all in your mind–Bad Influence, House of Games, The Silence of the Lambs

Psychotics/Sociopaths: Killer Inside Me, Reservoir Dogs, The Stepfather

Puppets: Usually with strings, but also muppets

Pure Ego Vehicles: Big stars doing their big star thing–Hudson Hawk, Harlem Nights, Yes, Giorgio

Race Against Time: China Syndrome, Lorenzo's Oil

Radio: Choose Me, The Fisher King, Radio Days, Sleepless in Seattle

Rags to Riches: Grit, determination, and hustling (or just pure dumb luck) lead to fortune–Trading Places, Working Girls

Rape: Victims and often their revenge

Rebel With a Cause: Bucking the establishment for a reason

Rebel Without a Cause: Bucking the establishment just because it's the establishment

Red Scare: Cold War and Communism–The Commies are Coming, The Commies are Coming, Reds

Religion: Witness, The Last Temptation of Christ

Religious Epics: Charlton Heston parting the Red Sea–religion on a really big scale

Renegade Body Parts: Hands, fingers, eyes, brains with a life of their own

*Repressed Men: Often British (see Anthony Hopkins or Hugh Grant), always with plenty of stiffness in upper lip and little elsewhere

*Rescue Missions: I'll save you–The Searcher, Free Willy

*Rescue Missions Involving Time Travel: I'll save you in another dimension–Back to the Future

Revenge: A key motivating factor–Cape Fear, Death Wish, Hamlet

Revolutionary War: Fought over tea

Road Trip: Escapism courtesy of two- and four-wheel vehicles–Easy Rider, Coupe de Ville, Pee Wee's Big Adventure, Wild at Heart

*Roaring '20s: Flappers, prohibition, bobbed hair

Robots/Androids: Mechanical but fascinating; Blade Runner and The Terminator

Rock Stars on Film: But can they act? Prince (Symbol), Sting, Elvis, Lennon, The Monkees, Whitney, and so on

Rodeos: Rope tricks with steers

Role Reversal: Vice versa; empathy test–Freaky Friday, My Fair Lady, Switch, Soul Man

Romantic Adventures: The African Queen, Romancing the Stone

Romantic Comedy: Falling in love has its hilarious moments–Benny and Joon, Crossing Delancey, Modern Romance, Much Ado About Nothing

Romantic Drama: Love thing leads to tension and anxiety–Cyrano de Bergerac, Far and Away, Sommersby, Tender Mercies

*Romantic Triangles: Three where there's only room for two–The Age of Innocence, Casablanca, Three of Hearts

Roommates from Hell: Single White Female

Royalty: Emperors, kings, queens, princes, princesses, crowns, scepters

Running: Jogging, panting, collapsing

Russia: Back in what used to be the U.S.S.R.

Sail Away: Vessels on the water–Mutiny on the Bounty, Erik the Viking, Mister Roberts

*Saints: Bernadette, Saint Joan, A Time for Miracles

Sanity Check: Inmates running the asylum; also deviant mental states

Satanism: Speak of the Devil

Satire & Parody: Biting social comment or genre spoofs, including Being There, Airplane, Down and Out in Beverly Hills, I'm Gonna Git You Sucka, Monty Python's The Meaning of Life, The Player

Savants: Half-minded geniuses: Rain Man, Forrest Gump

Scams, Stings & Cons: The hustle–Billionaire Boys Club, The Color of Money, A Fish Called Wanda, The Grifters, The Sting

Schmaltz: Extra cloying with sugar on top

School Daze: Education, school, and teachers–Lean on Me, Dead Poet's Society, To Sir, with Love, Teachers

Sci Fi: Imagination fueled by science and a vision of the future

Science & Scientists: Altered States, Darkman, Them, They, Son of Flubber, The Story of Louis Pasteur

Scotland: Brigadoon, Local Hero, Whiskey Galore

Screwball Comedy: Snappy repartee between sexes dueling in impossible situation

Scuba: Wet suits, including The Abyss, Navy Seals

Sea Critter Attack: Monsters from the deep (and not so deep)

surface and surprise: Jaws, Orca, Moby Dick

Sea Disasters: We've sprung a leak–The Poseiden Adventure

Serial Killers: Henry: Portrait of a Serial Killer, The Rosary Murders

Serials: Heyday was in the 1930s; includes Adventures of Red Ryder, Little Rascals, Flash Gordon

Sex & Sexuality: Focus is on lust, for better or worse–Alfie, Barbarella, Emmanuelle, Looking for Mr. Goodbar, Rambling Rose, She's Gotta Have It

Sexploitation: Softcore epics usually lacking in plot but not skin–The Erotic Adventures of Pinocchio

Sexual Abuse: Victims and their stories–Twin Peaks, Fire Walk with Me

*Showbiz Comedies: Laughter behind the scenes in Hollywood or on Broadway

*Showbiz Dramas: Tension behind the scenes in Hollywood or on Broadway

*Showbiz Thrillers: Screaming behind the scenes in Hollywood or on Broadway

Shower & Bath Scenes: Encompassing bathtubs, hottubs, showers, sinks and toilets, including Psycho, Fatal Attraction and that poor fellow in Jurassic Park

Shrinks: Psychiatry or equivalent, with The Prince of Tides, One Flew Over the Cuckoo's Nest

Shutterbugs: Photographers and their pictures–Public Eye, Eyes of Laura Mars, Peeping Tom

Silent Films: No small talk/no big talk/no talk talk

*Silent Horror/Fantasy Classics: Silent screams, expressions of terror

Singles: Not always swinging but still solidly single–About Last Night, Singles, When Harry Met Sally

Skateboarding: Teens on wheels–Gleaming the Cube

Skating: Roller and ice, including The Cutting Edge, Xanadu

Skiing: Downhill Racer, Swinging Ski Girls

Slapstick Comedy: Humor of the physical sort, including Abbott and Costello, Marx Brothers, sports comedies, Ernest, Pink Panther, Home Alone, Three Stooges

Slavery: Roots, Spartacus

Slice of Life: Charming small stories of life the way it might be– The Bicycle Thief, Fried Green Tomatoes, Marty

Soccer: Victory, Ladybugs

South America: Aguirre, the Wrath of God, The Mission

Southern Belles: Blaze, Driving Miss Daisy, Steel Magnolias

Space Operas: Going where no spam has gone before–Alien, Star Trek, 2001: A Space Odyssey

Spaghetti Western: Clint with a squint, A Fistful of Dollars, My Name is Nobody, Once Upon a Time in the West

Spain: Siesta

Speculation: In search of...

Spies & Espionage: Trench coats, dark glasses, Bond, North by Northwest

*Sports Comedies: The Angels in the Outfield formed A League of Their Own and it was the Day the Bookies Wept

*Sports Dramas: Intense athletic tales, often based on a true story

Spousal Abuse: Burning Bed, What's Love Got to Do With It?

Star Gazing: Not Hollywood stars, astrology/astronomy type stars

Stepparents: New spouse hiding either alien origins or sociopathic tendencies greets existing clan

Stewardesses: Three Guys Named Mike go to Stewardess School and meet Blazing Stewardesses

Storytelling: Amazing Stories, Grim Prairie Tales

Strained Suburbia: Neighborhood is not what it seems–Dennis the Menace, Neighbors, Edward Scissorhands

*Struggling Musicians: Talented, but still reaching for the top

Submarines: Deep sea diving; Das Boot, Up Periscope, Run Silent, Run Deep, Hunt for Red October

*Subways: A train for shorter trips–Speed, The Taking of Pelham One Two Three

Suicide: Premature ends–The Big Chill, Scent of a Woman, Romeo and Juliet

Summer Camp: Where children go to misbehave, including Meatballs and Sleepaway Camp

*Super Heroes: Men and women of extraordinary strength and abilities wearing silly looking costumes

*Supernatural Comedies: Beetlejuice marries She-Devil and they take The Ghost Train to their Haunted Honeymoon

*Supernatural Cop Thrillers: Angel Heart, Maniac Cop, Wolfen

Supernatural Horror: Forces from beyond terrorize those who are here

*Supernatural Martial Arts: Kung Fu From Beyond the Grave

*Supernatural Westerns: Jesse James Meets Frankenstein's Daughter

Surfing: Awesome wave, dude! Mad Wax, The Surf Movie, Surf Nazis Must Die, Endless Summer

Survival: Alive, The Bridge of the River Kwai, Testament

Swashbucklers: Crossed swords, rope swinging including Robin Hood, Zorro, various Musketeers, Captain Blood, Three Amigos

Swimming: Ranging from Gremlins to Jaws to The Swimmer to Cocoon

*Swingers: Bob & Carol & Ted & Alice try Group Marriage and Carol and Alice become Swinging Wives

Sword & Sandal: See Arnold Schwarzenegger's early career

*Team Efforts: Working together pays off–Hoosiers, The Memphis Belle, Renaissance Man

Tearjerkers: Crying fests–Love Story, Steel Magnolias, Old Yeller

Technology–Rampant: Machines that wreak havoc–Metropolis, Death Ray 2000, Blade Runner

Teenage Angst: Adolescent anxieties, including Baby It's You and almost everything produced or directed by John Hughes

Tennis: Anyone?

Terror in Tall Buildings: Sometimes in elevators: From Die Hard to Speed to The Towering Inferno

Terrorism: Love affairs with hidden bombs

This Is Your Life: Biography and autobiography, including The Babe Ruth Story, Amazing Howard Hughes, Amadeus, Catherine the Great, Great Balls of Fire, Raging Bull, What's Love Got to Do With It?

3-D Flicks: Bring your special glasses

Time Travel: Fast forward or reverse with Bill and Ted, Dr. Who, Back to the Future, and Peggy Sue Got Married

Torrid Love Scenes: Steamy and/or sticky–Angel Heart, Bull Durham, From Here to Eternity, Risky Business, The Unbearable Lightness of Being

Toys: Babes in Toyland, The Toy, Toys

Tragedy: The fate of humankind, magnified–King Lear, Madame Bovary, Tess, The World According to Garp

Trains: Rhythm of the clackity clack–Romance on the Orient Express, Throw Momma from the Train, Running Scared, The Silver Streak

*Trapped with a Killer!: And there's no escape–Dead Calm, Misery, The Shining

Treasure Hunt: Looking for hidden riches–Klondike Fever, Treasure of Sierra Madre, Romancing the Stone

Trees & Forests: Can't see one for the other, that wilderness paradox–includes Mr. Sycamore and The Wizard of Oz

True Crime: Based on fact, including The Boston Strangler, The Executioner's Song, Helter Skelter

True Stories: Approximations of real-life events often significantly fictionalized for the screen, including All The President's Men, Chariot's of Fire, Cry Freedom, Heart Like a Wheel, The Killing Fields, Silkwood

TV Movies: First shown on broadcast, cable, or foreign television (BBC, etc.)–Adam, Autobiography of Miss Jane Pittman, Barbarians at the Gate, I, Claudius, Longtime Companion, The Day After

TV Pilot Movies: Some became series; some did not

TV Series: Collections, anthologies, and individual episodes of memorable shows–I Love Lucy, Star Trek, The Fugitive

*Twins: Double Trouble, Double Vision, Mirror Images

*Unexplained Phenomena: No apparent reason for an event

Urban Drama: American Me to Boyz N the Hood to Grand Canyon to Zebrahead

*Vacations: From City Slickers to Deliverance to Fraternity Vacation

*Vampire Babes: Blood sucking dames–The Brides of Dracula

Vampire Spoof: Comedic blood suckers, including Buffy, Andy Warhol's Dracula, Dracula Sucks

Vampires: More serious vein of blood sucking varmint, including Dracula in his many manifestations

Variety: Little bit of everything

Veterans: Alamo Bay to Who'll Stop the Rain

Vietnam War: Platoon, Hamburger Hill, Apocalypse Now, Good Morning, Vietnam

Vigilantes: Individuals taking the law into their own hands–Death Wish, The Outlaw Josie Wales

Viva Las Vegas!: Honeymoon in Vegas, Sister Act

Volcanoes: Mountain blowing off steam, including Joe Versus the Volcano

Volleyball: Side Out is the only one

*Voodoo: From Angel Heart to How to Stuff a Wild Bikini to Weekend at Bernie's 2

*Waitresses: Alice Doesn't Live Here Anymore, she went to Atlantic City to get some Mystic Pizza

War Between the Sexes: Men and women battle for supremacy–It Happened One Night, The King and I, He Said, She Said, Romancing the Stone, When Harry Met Sally, The War of the Roses, Thelma & Louise

War, General: Generally any conflict that defies other classification–The Alamo, Gunga Din, The Last of the Mohicans

*Wedding Bells: Memorable weddings: Father of the Bride, Four Weddings and a Funeral, Sixteen Candles, The Wedding

*Wedding Hell: Horror-filled or anxiety-ridden weddings: The Blood Spattered Bride, The Brides Wore Blood, The Graduate, Wedding Banquet

Werewolves: Full moon
   wonders, like Wolf
Western Comedy: Gags and
   horses–Ballad of Cable
   Hogue, Blazing Saddles,
   Rancho Deluxe, Support
   Your Local Sheriff
Westerns: Cowboys, cowgirls,
   horses and jingle jangling
   spurs on the frontier
Wild Kingdom: Animals on their
   own and interacting with
   confused humans, including
   The Bear, Dumbo, Born
   Free, Free Willy, Never Cry
   Wolf
Wilderness: More trees than a
   forest, plus wild critters–Life
   and Times of Grizzly Adams
Witchcraft: From Hocus Pocus
   to Three Sovereigns for
   Sarah to The Wizard of Oz
Women: Impressive women,
   less than impressive women,
   and issues concerning
   women–Crimes of the Heart,
   My Brilliant Career, Passion
   Fish, Working Girls
Women Cops: Female officers
   of the law
Women in Prison: The things
   that go on in the big doll
   house
Wonder Women: Attack of the
   50-Foot Woman, Ripley, La
   Femme Nikita, Supergirl
World War I: African Queen,
   Gallipoli, Grand Illusion
World War II: The Last Big One,
   including A Bridge Too Far,
   Guadalcanal Diary, The
   Guns of Navarone, Hope
   and Glory, Memphis Belle,
   Tora! Tora! Tora!
Wrestling: Choreographed
   sports involving men and
   women–No Holds Barred, All
   the Marbles, Wrestling
   Women vs. the Aztec Ape
Wrong Side of the Tracks:
   Often involves relationship
   with someone on the right
   side–Cannery Row, The
   Flamingo Kid, Pretty in Pink,
   White Palace
*You Lose, You Die: Sports
   gone nuts–only the winner
   survives; Arena, Rollerball,
   Tron
Yuppie Nightmares: Young
   adults find best-laid plans for
   attaining wealth and
   privilege going astray–Baby
   Boom, Desperately Seeking
   Susan, The Mighty Ducks,
   Pacific Heights, Something
   Wild, Wall Street
*Zombie Soldiers: Recently
   undead in the army–They
   Saved Hitler's Brain
Zombies: Recently undead
   everywhere–I Walked with a
   Zombie, Night of the Living
   Dead

CATEGORY INDEX

The **CATEGORY INDEX** includes nearly 400 terms ranging from the orthodox to the slightly eccentric, allowing you to search for genres (Comedy), themes (Baseball), places (Great Britain), events (World War II), things (Killer Appliances), people (Doctors & Nurses), and more. Category definitions and cross-references precede the index; category terms are listed alphabetically.

Action Adventure

see also Adventure Drama; Comic Adventure; Disaster Flicks; Macho Men; Martial Arts; Romantic Adventures; Swashbucklers

The Abductors
Above and Beyond▶
Above the Law
The Abyss▶
Aces: Iron Eagle 3
Across the Great Divide
Act of Vengeance
Action in Arabia
Action Jackson
Action U.S.A.
Adventure of the Action Hunters
The Adventurers
Adventures of Captain Fabian
The Adventures of Captain Marvel
Adventures of Don Juan▶
The Adventures of Ford Fairlane
The Adventures of Frank and Jesse James
The Adventures of Huckleberry Finn
The Adventures of Marco Polo
Adventures of Red Ryder
The Adventures of Rex & Rinty
The Adventures of Rin Tin Tin
Adventures of Smilin' Jack
The Adventures of Tartu
The Adventures of Tarzan
The Adventures of the Masked Phantom
The Adventures of Tom Sawyer
After the Fall of Saigon
Against All Flags▶
Ain't No Way Back
Alamut Ambush
Ali Baba and the 40 Thieves▶
Alice to Nowhere
Alien Private Eye
All the Brothers Were Valiant
The Amateur
The Amazing Spider-Man
The Amazing Transparent Man
Amazon Jail
Amazons
American Autobahn
American Born

American Commandos
American Eagle
American Justice
American Ninja 3: Blood Hunt
Americano
The Amsterdam Kill
And Then You Die▶
Android
Angel 3: The Final Chapter
Angel of Death
Angel of Destruction
Angel's Brigade
Angels Die Hard
Angels from Hell
Angels One Five
Angels' Wild Women
The Annihilators
Antarctica
Appointment in Honduras
Archer: The Fugitive from the Empire
Ark of the Sun God
Armed for Action
Armed Response
Around the World Under the Sea
Aroused
Arrest Bulldog Drummond
Ashanti, Land of No Mercy
Assassin
Assault on a Queen
Assault on Agathon
Assault with a Deadly Weapon
Assignment Skybolt
At Gunpoint
At Sword's Point
Atlantis, the Lost Continent
Ator the Fighting Eagle
Attack Force Z
Avenged
The Avenger
Avenging Force
Baby Cart 4: Heart of a Parent...Heart of a Child
Back in Action
Back to Back
Back to Bataan
Background to Danger▶
Bad Attitude
Bad Guys
Badge 373
Bail Out
Balkan Express
Ballbuster
Band of the Hand
The Banker
Banzai Runner
Barbarian Queen

Barbarian Queen 2: The Empress Strikes Back
The Barbarians
The Barbary Coast
Bare Knuckles
Bat 21
Batman
Batman▶
Batman Returns
Battle of Neretva
Battle of the Commandos
Battle of Valiant
The Beast
Beasts
Bedford Incident
Behind the Mask
Bells of Coronado
The Belstone Fox
Beretta's Island
Berlin Tunnel 21
Best Revenge
A Better Tomorrow
A Better Tomorrow, Part 2
Beyond Fear
Beyond Justice
Beyond the Call of Duty
Beyond the Carribean
Big Bad John
The Big Bust Out
Big Chase
The Big Doll House
The Big House▶
Big Jim McLain
Big Steal▶
The Big Sweat
The Big Wheel
Billy the Kid in Texas
Bimini Code
Birds of Prey
Black Brigade
Black Caesar
The Black Cobra
Black Cobra 2
Black Cobra 3: The Manila Connection
The Black Coin
The Black Devils of Kali
Black Eliminator
Black Force
Black Force 2
Black Gestapo
Black Magic
Black Market Rustlers
Black Oak Conspiracy
The Black Pirate▶
The Black Pirate
The Black Raven
Black Shampoo
The Black Six

The Black Stallion▶
The Black Stallion Returns
Black Sunday
Black Terrorist
Black Water Gold
The Black Widow
Blackbeard the Pirate
Blackjack
Blade
Blade in Hong Kong
Blade Master
Blink of an Eye
Blonde in Black Leather
Blonde Savage
Blood Alley
Blood & Concrete: A Love Story
Blood and Guns
Blood and Steel
Blood Brothers
Blood Money
Blood Money: The Story of Clinton and Nadine
Blood on the Badge
Blood Ties
Bloodfist
Bloodfist 2
The Bloody Tattoo
Blown Away▶
Blue Blazes Rawden
Blue Jeans and Dynamite
The Blue Lightning
Blue Tornado
BMX Bandits
Bobbie Jo and the Outlaw
The Bold Caballero
Boomerang
Border Radio
Borderline
Born American
Born Killer
Born to Be Wild
Born to Race
Born to Ride
Bounty Hunters
Boxcar Blues
Boy of Two Worlds
Braddock: Missing in Action 3
Brady's Escape
Brannigan
The Brave Bunch
Breaking Loose
Breakout
Breathing Fire
A Breed Apart
The Bridge at Remagen
Bridge to Hell
The Bridge to Nowhere
The Bridges at Toko-Ri▶

Bring Me the Head of Alfredo Garcia
The Brotherhood of the Rose
Brothers Lionheart
The Buccaneer
Buffalo Stampede
Bulldog Drummond
Bulldog Drummond Escapes
Bulldog Drummond's Peril
Bulldog Drummond's Secret Police
The Bulldozer Brigade
Bulletproof
Bummer
Bunco
Burn 'Em Up Barnes
The Bushbaby
The Bushwackers
The C-Man
The Cage
Caged Fear
Caged Fury
Caged Heat
Caged Terror
Call Him Mr. Shatter
Call of the Wild
Camorra: The Naples Connection
Canadian Mounties Vs. Atomic Invaders
Candleshoe
Cannonball
The Canon Operation
Canvas: The Fine Art of Crime
Captain America
Captain America 2: Death Too Soon
Captain Blood▶
Captain Kidd
Captain Scarlett
Captain Sinbad
Captive Rage
The Capture of Bigfoot
Captured in Chinatown
Car Crash
Carolina Skeletons
Cartel
The Cary Grant Collection
Casey Jones and Fury (Brave Stallion)
Catch Me...If You Can
Ceiling Zero▶
Chain Gang Killings
Chained Heat
Chained Heat 2
Chains
The Challenge
Challenge To Be Free
Challenge to White Fang

Chance
Chandu on the Magic Island
Chandu the Magician
Charlie and the Great Balloon
　Chase
Charlie Bravo
Charlie Grant's War
Charlie, the Lonesome Cougar
The Chase
Chasers
The Cheaters
Cheetah
Child of Glass
China O'Brien
China Seas▶
China White
Chinatown Connection
The Chinatown Murders: Man
　Against the Mob
Chinese Boxes
Chinese Web
Choke Canyon
Chrome and Hot Leather
Chrome Hearts
C.I.A.: Code Name Alexa
C.I.A. 2: Target Alexa
Circle Man
Circle of Fear
Class of Fear
The Claw
Clayton County Line
Cliffhanger▶
Cloak & Dagger
Cloud Waltzing
Cobra
Cobra Woman
Code Name: Dancer
Code Name: Zebra
Code of Silence
Codename Kyril
Codename: Terminate
Codename: Vengeance
Codename: Wildgeese
Cold Steel
Cold Steel for Tortuga
Cold Sweat
Cold War Killers
Coldfire
The Colditz Story
Cole Justice
The Colombian Connection
Colossus and the Amazon
　Queen
Colossus of the Arena
Combat Killers
Combat Shock
Commando▶
Commando Invasion
Commando Squad
Commandos
Commandos Strike at Dawn
Comrades in Arms
Conan the Barbarian▶
Conan the Destroyer
Conexion Mexico
Confidential
Conflict of Interest
The Conqueror
Conqueror & the Empress
Conquest of the Normans
Contra Company
Contraband
Convoy
Cool As Ice
Cop in Blue Jeans
Corleone
Coroner Creek
The Corrupt Ones
The Corsican Brothers
Could It Happen Here?
Counter Measures
Counterforce
Cover Girl Models
Cover-Up
Covert Action
Crack House
Crash Dive
Crazed Cop
Crazy Streets
Crime Killer
Crime Lords
Crime Zone

Crimson Pirate▶
Cross Mission
Cross of Iron
Crossfire
Crossing the Line
Crusoe
A Cry in the Wild▶
Cry of Battle
Cry of the Black Wolves
Cry of the Innocent▶
Crystalstone
Cuba▶
Curiosity Kills
Curse of the Crystal Eye
The Cut Throats
Cyborg Cop
Cycle Vixens
Cyclone
Cyclone Cavalier
Cyclotrode ''X''
Damn the Defiant▶
Dance with Death
Danger: Diabolik
Danger Zone
Danger Zone 2
Danger Zone 3: Steel Horse
　War
Dangerous Charter
Dangerous Orphans
Darby's Rangers
Daredevils of the Red Circle
Daring Dobermans
Dark Age
Dark Justice
Dark of the Sun
Dark Rider
Darkest Africa
Daughter of Don Q
DaVinci's War
Davy Crockett and the River
　Pirates
Davy Crockett, King of the
　Wild Frontier▶
Dawn of the Pirates
Day of Atonement
Day of the Assassin
Day of the Cobra
The Day of the Dolphin
Days of Hell
Dayton's Devils
Dead Aim
Dead Bang
Dead Easy
Dead End City
The Dead Pool
Dead Wrong
Deadline Auto Theft
Deadly Alliance
The Deadly and the Beautiful
Deadly Bet
Deadly Breed
Deadly Commando
Deadly Conspiracy
Deadly Diamonds
Deadly Encounter▶
Deadly Mission
Deadly Prey
Deadly Reactor
Deadly Revenge
Deadly Stranger
Deadly Surveillance
Deadly Thief
Deadly Vengeance
Deadly Weapon
Deadly Weapons
Death Before Dishonor
Death Chase
Death Feud
Death House
Death Hunt
Death Journey
Death of the Incredible Hulk
Death Race 2000
Death Ray
Death Ring
Death Shot
The Death Squad
Death Target
Death Wish
Death Wish 2
Death Wish 3

Death Wish 4: The
　Crackdown
Death Wish 5: The Face of
　Death
Deathstalker 4: Clash of the
　Titans
Deep Cover
Defenders of the Law
Defiant
Delos Adventure
Delta Force
Delta Force 2: Operation
　Stranglehold
Delta Force 3: The Killing
　Game
Delta Force Commando
Delta Force Commando 2
Delta Fox
Delta Heat
Demolition
Demolition Man
Demon with a Glass Hand
Dersu Uzala▶
Desert Commandos
Desert of the Lost
The Desert of the Tartars
Desperate Cargo
Desperate Crimes
Desperate Journey
Desperate Target
Destroyer▶
The Destructors
Detonator
Detroit 9000
Devastator
Devil Dogs of the Air
Devil Monster
Devil of the Desert Against the
　Son of Hercules
Devil Wears White
Devil's Angels
The Devil's Brigade
Devil's Crude
Diamond Fleece
Diamond Ninja Force
Diamonds are Forever▶
Diary of a Hitman
Diary of a Rebel
Dick Tracy, Detective
Dick Tracy Double Feature #1
Dick Tracy Double Feature #2
Dick Tracy Meets Gruesome
Dick Tracy Returns
Dick Tracy: The Original
　Serial, Vol. 1▶
Dick Tracy: The Original
　Serial, Vol. 2▶
Dick Tracy: The Spider Strikes
Dick Tracy vs. Crime Inc.
Dick Tracy vs. Cueball
Dick Tracy's Dilemma
The Dirty Dozen▶
The Dirty Dozen: The Deadly
　Mission
The Dirty Dozen: The Fatal
　Mission
The Dirty Dozen: The Next
　Mission
Dirty Games
Dirty Heroes
Dirty Mary Crazy Larry▶
Dirty Work
Disaster at Silo 7
The Divine Enforcer
Divine Nymph
Dixie Dynamite
Do or Die
The Doberman Gang
Doc Savage
Dr. No▶
Dr. Syn
Dr. Syn, Alias the Scarecrow
Dog Eat Dog
The Dogs of War
The Doll Squad
Dollman
The Don is Dead
Don Juan▶
Don Q., Son of Zorro
Don Quixote▶
Don Winslow of the Coast
　Guard

Don Winslow of the Navy
Don't Change My World
Door to Door Maniac
Double Revenge
The Dove
Down Twisted
Dragon Force
Dragon Princess
The Dragon Returns
Dragon vs. Needles of Death
Dragonard
Dragonfight
Dragon's Claw
The Dragon's Showdown
Dreadnaught Rivals
Driven to Kill
The Driver
Driving Force
Drums
Drums of Fu Manchu▶
Dual Flying Kicks
Dudes
Duel of Champions
Dune Warriors
Dynamite
Dynasty
The Eagle▶
Eagles Attack at Dawn
East L.A. Warriors
East of Kilimanjaro
Easy Kill
800 Leagues Down the
　Amazon
Eighteen Jade Arhats
El Barbaro
El Cid▶
El Hombre Contra el Mundo
El Mariachi▶
El Rey
El Zorro Blanco
Electra Glide in Blue▶
Elephant Boy▶
Emerald of Artama
Emil and the Detective
Emilio Varela vs. Camelia La
　Texana
Emperor of the Bronx
Empire State
The Enchanted Forest
Enemy Gold
Enemy Unseen
The Enforcer
Enforcer from Death Row
Enigma
Enter the Dragon▶
Enter the Panther
Erik
Erik, the Viking
Erotic Touch of Hot Skin
Escapade in Japan
Escape from Alcatraz▶
Escape from Cell Block 3
Escape from Death Row
Escape from DS-3
Escape from El Diablo
Escape from New York
Escape from Safehaven
Escape from the Bronx
Escape from the KGB
Escape to Athena
Escape to Burma
Escape to the Sun
The Evil Below
The Evil That Men Do
Ex-Cop
Excessive Force
Executioner of Venice
Exiled in America
Exterminator
Exterminator 2
Extreme Prejudice
Extreme Vengeance
An Eye for an Eye
Eye of the Eagle
Eye of the Eagle 2
Eye of the Eagle 3
Eye of the Stranger
Eye of the Tiger
F/X 2: The Deadly Art of
　Illusion
Fabiola▶

Fabulous Adventures of
　Baron Munchausen
Fair Game
Falcon
The Family
Famous Five Get Into Trouble
Far East
Fass Black
Fast Kill
Fast Money
Faster Pussycat! Kill! Kill!
Fatal Beauty
Fatal Chase
Fatal Error
Fatal Justice
Fatal Mission
Fatal Skies
A Father's Revenge
Fear in the City
Federal Agents vs.
　Underworld, Inc.▶
Federal Operator 99
The Female Bunch
Fever
ffolkes
Field of Fire
Fight for Us
Fighting Devil Dogs
Fighting Mad
Fighting Marines
The Fighting Rookie
Fighting Seabees
The Fighting 69th▶
The Final Alliance
The Final Countdown▶
Final Justice
Final Mission
Final Round
Final Sanction
The Finest Hour
Fire Birds
Fire, Ice and Dynamite
The Fire in the Stone
Fire Monsters Against the Son
　of Hercules
Fireback
Firecracker
Firefall
Firefight
Firefox
Firehawk
Firehead
Firepower
Firewalker
The Firing Line
First Blood
First Yank into Tokyo
Fish Hawk
F.I.S.T.
Fist
Fist Fighter
Fist of Fear, Touch of Death
Fist of Honor
Fists of Blood
Fit to Kill
Five Came Back
Five Fingers▶
Five for Hell
Five Golden Dragons
Five Miles to Midnight
Five Weeks in a Balloon
The Fix
The Flame & the Arrow▶
Flaming Signal
Flash & Firecat
Flashpoint Africa
Flat Top
Flatbed Annie and Sweetiepie:
　Lady Truckers
Flesh and Blood
Fleshburn
The Flight
Flight from Glory
Flight from Singapore
Flight of Black Angel
Flight of Dragons
Flight of the Eagle
Flight of the Intruder
The Flight of the Phoenix▶
Flight to Fury
Flight to Nowhere
Flipper's New Adventure▶

Flipper's Odyssey
The Florida Connection
Florida Straits
Flying Discman from Mars
Follow That Car
For Your Eyes Only▶
Force: Five
Force of One
Force 10 from Navarone
Forced to Kill
Forced Vengeance
The Forgotten
Fortune Dane
48 Hours to Live
The Four Hands of Death:
    Wily Match
Four Robbers
Foxtrap
Foxy Brown
Frame Up
Framed
The French Connection▶
French Connection 2▶
French Quarter Undercover
Friday Foster
From Hell to Borneo
From Russia with Love▶
Frontera Sin Ley
Full Metal Ninja
Further Adventures of the
    Wilderness Family, Part 2
Fury
The Fury of Hercules
Fury on Wheels
Future Cop
Future Force
Future Hunters
Future Kill
Futurekick
G-Men Never Forget
G-Men vs. the Black Dragon
Gallagher's Travels
The Galloping Ghost
Galyon
The Gamble
The Gambling Samurai
Game of Death
Game of Survival
Gang Justice
Gang Wars
Gangsters
Gator
Gator Bait
Gator Bait 2: Cajun Justice
The Gauntlet
The General Died at Dawn▶
Gentle Giant
Get Christie Love!
The Getaway
Getting Even
Ghetto Blaster
The Ghost of Fletcher Ridge
Ghostwarrior
G.I. Executioner
The Giant of Marathon
The Giant of Metropolis
The Gift Horse
Ginger
Girls Are for Loving
Girls Riot
The Gladiator
The Glass Jungle
Gloria
Glory Boys
The Glory Stompers
The Glove
Go for Broke
Go Kill and Come Back
Go Tell the Spartans▶
God's Bloody Acre
Goetz von Berlichingen
Goin' Coconuts
Gold Raiders
Golden Lady
The Golden Salamander
Golden Sun
The Golden Triangle
Golden Voyage of Sinbad
Goldfinger▶
Goliath Against the Giants
Goliath and the Barbarians
Goliath and the Dragon

Goliath and the Sins of
    Babylon
Goliathon
Gone in 60 Seconds
Good Guys Wear Black
Goodbye Pork Pie
The Goonies
Gordon's War
Government Agents vs.
    Phantom Legion
Grand Canyon Trail
Grand Larceny
Grand Theft Auto
Great K & A Train Robbery
The Great Los Angeles
    Earthquake
Great Movie Stunts & the
    Making of Raiders of the
    Lost Ark
Great Ride
The Great Skycopter Rescue
Great Smokey Roadblock
The Great Texas Dynamite
    Chase
The Great Waldo Pepper▶
The Green Berets
The Green Hornet
Green Inferno
Greenstone
Ground Zero
Ground Zero
The Groundstar Conspiracy▶
Gung Ho!
Guns
Guns Don't Argue
The Guns of Navarone▶
The Guy from Harlem
Gypsy
Gypsy Angels
H-Bomb
Hangmen
Hard-Boiled
Hard Drivin'
Hard Hunted
Hard Knocks
Hard Target
Hard Ticket to Hawaii
Hard Vice
Hardcase and Fist
Hardware
Harley Davidson and the
    Marlboro Man
Harry Black and the Tiger
Hatari!
Haunted Harbor
Hawk of the Wilderness
Hawk the Slayer
Hawkeye
Heartbreak Ridge▶
Heartbreaker
Hearts & Armour
Heat
Heat of the Flame
Heat Street
Heated Vengeance
The Heist
Hell Hounds of Alaska
Hell Hunters
Hell is for Heroes▶
Hell on the Battleground
Hell on Wheels
Hell Raiders
Hell Ship Mutiny
Hell Up in Harlem
Hellbenders
Hellbent
Hellcats
The Hellfire Club
Hellriders
Hell's Angels Forever
Hell's Angels '69
Hell's Headquarters
Hercules
Hercules 2
Hercules Against the Moon
    Men
Hercules and the Captive
    Women
Hercules in New York
Hercules in the Haunted World
Hercules, Prisoner of Evil
Hercules Unchained

Hero Bunker
Hero of Rome
Heroes in Hell
Heroes Stand Alone
Hi-Riders
The Hidden Fortress▶
High Ballin'
High Crime
High Ice
High Risk
High Rolling in a Hot Corvette
High Velocity
Highlander▶
Highlander 3: The Sorcerer
Highlander: The Gathering
Hired to Kill
His Majesty O'Keefe
His Majesty, the American
Hit Men
Hit Woman: The Double Edge
Hitler: Dead or Alive
The Hitman
The Hitter
Hollywood Cop
Holt of the Secret Service
Homeboy
Honeybaby
Hong Kong Nights
Honor Among Thieves
Honor and Glory
The Hooked Generation
Hornet's Nest
Horsemen
Hostage
The Hostage Tower
Hostile Takeover
Hot Blood
Hot Box
Hot Pursuit
Hot Rod
Hot Rod Girl
Hour of the Assassin
Hula
The Human Shield
Hundra
The Hunt for Red October▶
Hunted
The Hunted Lady
Hunter
The Hunter
Hunter's Blood
Hunters of the Golden Cobra
Hurricane Express
I Spit on Your Corpse
Ice
The Ice Runner
Ice Station Zebra
The Idol Dancer
If Looks Could Kill
Illegal Entry: Formula for Fear
In Deadly Heat
In Gold We Trust
In Hot Pursuit
In Search of the Castaways▶
In Your Face
The Incredible Hulk
The Incredible Hulk Returns
The Incredible Journey
Indiana Jones and the Last
    Crusade▶
Indiana Jones and the Temple
    of Doom▶
Indio
Indio 2: The Revolt
Inside Edge
Inside Information
The Inside Man
Inside Out
Instant Justice
Interceptor
The Invaders
Invaders from Mars
Invasion Force
Invasion U.S.A.
Invincible Barbarian
Invincible Gladiators
The Invincible Six
The Invisible Monster
Iron Angel
The Iron Crown
Iron Eagle
Iron Eagle 2

Iron Horsemen
Iron Thunder
Iron Will
Ironheart
Ironmaster
The Island
The Island at the Top of the
    World
Island of the Lost
Istanbul
Jacare
Jack the Giant Killer▶
Jail Bait
Jailbait
Jailbreakin'
Jakarta
Jaws of Death
Jericho
Jericho Fever
Jessie's Girls
The Jesus Trip
Jet Attack/Paratroop
    Command
Jive Turkey
Johnny Handsome▶
Johnny Shiloh
Jornada de Muerte
Journey
Journey of Honor
Journey to the Lost City
Judgment Night
Jungle Assault
The Jungle Book
Jungle Bride
Jungle Drums of Africa
Jungle Heat
Jungle Hell
Jungle Holocaust
Jungle Inferno
Jungle Master
Jungle Raiders
Jungle Siren
Jungle Warriors
Junior G-Men
Junior G-Men of the Air
The Junkman
K-9000
Kagemusha▶
The Karate Kid▶
The Karate Kid: Part 2
The Karate Kid: Part 3
Karate Warriors
Keep Talking Baby
Kelly's Heroes
Kentucky Blue Streak
The Key to Rebecca
Key to Vengeance
Kickboxer the Champion
Kicks
Kid and the Killers
The Kill
Kill Alex Kill
Kill Line
Kill or Be Killed
Kill Slade
Killcrazy
Killer Commandos
Killer Force
Killers
The Killer's Edge
Killing at Hell's Gate
The Killing Device
The Killing Edge
The Killing Game
Killing in the Sun
Killing Streets
The Killing Zone
Killzone
Kilma, Queen of the Amazons
Kim▶
King Arthur, the Young
    Warlord
King Boxers
King Dinosaur
King Kong▶
King Kong
King Kong Lives
King Kong Versus Godzilla
King of the Congo
King of the Damned
King of the Forest Rangers
King of the Kongo

King of the Mountain
King of the Rocketmen
King Solomon's Mines▶
King's Ransom
The King's Thief
Kinjite: Forbidden Subjects
Knightriders
Knock Outs
Koroshi
Kowloon Assignment
L.A. Bounty
La Choca
La Corona de un Campeon
La Fuga del Rojo
L.A. Gangs Rising
L.A. Heat
La Montana del Diablo
L.A. Vice
L.A. Wars
Lady of the Lake
Lady Street Fighter
Lady Terminator
Lafayette Escadrille
Land of the Pharaohs
Laser Mission
Laserblast
Lassie, Come Home
The Last Boy Scout
The Last Contract
The Last Flight of Noah's Ark
Last Flight to Hell
The Last Hit
The Last Hour
Last Mercenary
The Last of the Mohicans▶
The Last of the Redmen
Last Plane Out
The Last Reunion
The Last Valley
The Last Warrior
Last Witness
Laughing at Danger
Law of the Jungle
Law of the Sea
Law of the Wild
The Lawless Land
Le Mans▶
The Leatherneck
The Left Hand of God▶
The Legend of Hillbilly John
Legend of the Lost
Legend of the Northwest
Legion of Iron
Legion of Missing Men
Let 'Em Have It
Lethal Games
Lethal Weapon▶
Lethal Weapon 2▶
Lethal Weapon 3
Lethal Woman
Let's Get Harry
Liberty & Bash
License to Kill▶
The Lifetaker
Light at the Edge of the World
The Light in the Forest
Lightblast
Lightning Bolt
Lion Man
Lion of Africa
The Lion's Share
Little Caesar▶
Little Laura & Big John
Little Marines
Little Ninjas
Little Treasure
The Littlest Horse Thieves
Live and Let Die
Live Wire
The Lives of a Bengal
    Lancer▶
The Living Daylights▶
The Lone Runner
Long John Silver
Loophole
Lords of Magick
Los Caciques
Los Caifanes
The Lost City
Lost City of the Jungle
The Lost Command
The Lost Continent

The Lost Empire
The Lost Idol/Shock Troop
The Lost Patrol▶
Lost Squadron
The Lost Tribe
The Lost World
Love and Bullets
The Loves of Hercules
The Lucifer Complex
Mad Dog
Mad Max▶
Mad Max: Beyond Thunderdome
Mad Wax: The Surf Movie
Madman
The Magic Sword
The Magic Voyage of Sinbad
Magnum Force
Malaya
Malibu Express
Malone
Mama's Dirty Girls
A Man, a Woman and a Killer
Man from Cairo
Man from Deep River
The Man from U.N.C.L.E.
The Man in the Iron Mask▶
The Man Inside
Man on a String
The Man Who Would Be King▶
Manfish
Manhunt
Manhunt in the African Jungle
Mankillers
Marauder
March or Die
Mark of the Beast
Mark of Zorro▶
The Mark of Zorro▶
Marked for Death
Marked for Murder
Marked Money
Martial Law
Martial Law 2: Undercover
Mask of the Dragon
The Masked Marvel
Massive Retaliation
Master Blaster
Master Key
Master Ninja
Master of Dragonard Hill
Maximum Breakout
Maximum Force
Maya
McBain
McQ
Mean Frank and Crazy Tony
Mean Johnny Barrows
Mean Machine
The Mechanic
Melvin Purvis: G-Man
Men of Sherwood Forest
Men of the Fighting Lady▶
Menace on the Mountain
The Mercenaries
Mercenary Fighters
Merchants of War
Merlin
Merrill's Marauders
Messalina vs. the Son of Hercules
The Messenger
Miami Cops
Miami Vendetta
Midnight Warrior
Midnite Spares
Mighty Jungle
Mind Trap
Mines of Kilimanjaro
Ministry of Vengeance
Mision Suicida
Missing in Action
Missing in Action 2: The Beginning
Missing Link
Mission Batangas
Mission Corbari
Mission in Morocco
Mission Inferno
Mission Manila
Mission to Kill

Mr. Majestyk
Mister Mean
Mistress of the Apes
Mob War
Model by Day
Mole Men Against the Son of Hercules
Molly and Gina
Mona Lisa▶
Money to Burn
The Mongols
Mooncussers
Moonfleet
Moonraker
Moonshine County Express
Morgan the Pirate
Mother Lode
Motor Psycho
Mountain Charlie
Mountain Fury
Mountains of the Moon▶
Murder on Flight 502
Murder One
Mutiny
Mutiny on the Bounty▶
Mutiny on the Bounty
My New Partner
Mysterious Island of Beautiful Women
Mystery Island
Mystery of the Million Dollar Hockey Puck
Mystery Squadron
Nabonga
Nails
The Naked and the Dead
The Naked Angels
The Naked Prey▶
Naked Warriors
Namu, the Killer Whale
Napoleon and Samantha▶
Nasty Hero
Nate and Hayes
The Navigator▶
Navy SEALS
Neptune Factor
Neutron and the Black Mask
Neutron vs. the Amazing Dr. Caronte
Neutron vs. the Death Robots
Neutron vs. the Maniac
Never Let Me Go
Never Pick Up a Stranger
Never Say Never Again
Never So Few
Never Too Young to Die
The New Adventures of Tarzan
Next of Kin
Nick Knight
Night Ambush
Night Children
Night Flight from Moscow
Night of the Fox
Night of the Juggler
Night of the Sharks
The Night Patrol
Nightforce
Nightmare at Noon
Nikki, the Wild Dog of the North
9 1/2 Ninjas
1990: The Bronx Warriors
Ninja 3: The Domination
Ninja Connection
Ninja, the Violent Sorcerer
No Dead Heroes
No Escape
No Escape, No Return
No Holds Barred
No Man's Land
No Mercy
No Safe Haven
No Way Back
Nomad Riders
Northeast of Seoul
Northville Cemetery Massacre
Nowhere to Run
Nukie
Number 1 of the Secret Service
Nyoka and the Tigermen

Octopussy
The Odyssey of the Pacific
Off Limits
O.H.M.S.
Old Ironsides▶
Omoo Omoo, the Shark God
On Deadly Ground
On Her Majesty's Secret Service▶
On the Run
Once a Hero
One Down, Two to Go!
One-Eyed Soldiers
One Man Out
One Step to Hell
Operation C.I.A.
Orca
Order of the Black Eagle
Order of the Eagle
Order to Kill
The Original Flash Gordon Collection
Orphans of the North
Osa
Out of Control
The Outfit
The Outlaw Bikers—Gang Wars
Outpost in Morocco
Overkill
Overthrow
Overture
Pacific Inferno
Panther Squad
Paper Tiger
Paradise Canyon
Pay or Die
Payback
Peacemaker
Pepper
Perfect Crime
The Perfect Weapon
The Perils of Pauline
Perils of the Darkest Jungle
The Persuaders
Phantom Express
The Phantom Flyer
Phantom of the Air
Phoenix
P.I. Private Investigations
Picasso Trigger
Pink Cadillac
Pirate Warrior
Pirates of the Coast
Pirates of the Seven Seas
Platoon the Warriors
Platypus Cove
Point Break
Point of Impact
The Polar Bear King
The Port of Missing Girls
The P.O.W. Escape
Powder Keg
Pray for Death
Prayer of the Rollerboys
The President's Plane is Missing
President's Target
Presumed Guilty
Prettykill
Prey for the Hunter
Primary Target
Prime Risk
Prince Valiant
Prison Planet
Prisoner of Zenda▶
Prisoner of Zenda
Private Life of Don Juan
Private Road: No Trespassing
Private War
Private Wars
Professionals
Project: Eliminator
Project: Shadowchaser
Protector
Provoked
Psychopath
Pucker Up and Bark Like a Dog
Punch the Clock
The Punisher
Python Wolf

Q & A
Queen of Diamonds
Queen of the Amazons
Queen of the Jungle
Queen of the Road
The Quest
Quest for Fire▶
Quest of the Delta Knights
Quick
Quiet Cool
Quiet Fire
Quiet Thunder
Quo Vadis
The Racers
Radar Secret Service
Rage of Honor
Rage to Kill
Raid on Entebbe▶
Raid on Rommel
Raiders of Atlantis
Raiders of Ghost City
Raiders of the Sun
Rainbow Drive
The Rainbow Gang
Rambo: First Blood, Part 2
Rambo 3
Ransom Money
Ranson's Folly
The Rape of the Sabines
Rapid Fire
Raw Deal
Raw Justice
Raw Power
Real Bullets
The Real McCoy
Reason to Die
Rebel Storm
Red Dawn
Red Dust▶
The Red Fury
Red Heat
Red Scorpion
Red Signals
Red Snow
Red Tent▶
Relentless 2: Dead On
Rent-A-Cop
Repo Jake
Rescue Force
Retrievers
Return Fire
The Return of Casey Jones
Return of Chandu
The Return of Eliot Ness
The Return of Grey Wolf
Return of Superfly
Return of the Dinosaurs
Return of the Dragon
Return of the Man from U.N.C.L.E.
Return of the Tiger
Return to Africa
Return to Fantasy Island
Return to Macon County
Return to the Lost World
Revenge of the Barbarians
Revenge of the Ninja
The Revenger
Revolt of the Barbarians
Revolt of the Dragon
Revolver
Ricco
The Riddle of the Sands
Riding High
Riding the Edge
Ring of Steel
Rip-Off
The Rip Off
Rip Roarin' Buckaroo
River of Death
River of Diamonds
River of Evil
Road House
The Road Warrior▶
Roadkill
Robbers of the Sacred Mountain
Robby
Robin Hood▶
Robin Hood...The Legend: Herne's Son

Robin Hood...The Legend: Robin Hood and the Sorcerer
Robin Hood...The Legend: The Swords of Wayland
Robin Hood...The Legend: The Time of the Wolf
Robinson Crusoe
Robinson Crusoe & the Tiger
Robinson Crusoe of Clipper Island
Robinson Crusoe of Mystery Island
RoboCop 2
RoboCop 3
Rock House
The Rocketeer▶
Rocketship X-M
Rogue Lion
Roller Blade Warriors: Taken By Force
Rollercoaster
Rolling Vengeance
The Rookie
Rosebud
R.O.T.O.R.
Rough Cut
Roughnecks
The Rousters
Ruckus
Rulers of the City
Run
Run, Angel, Run!
Run, Rebecca, Run
Runaway
The Runaway Barge
Runaway Island, Part 1
Runaway Island, Part 2
Runaway Island, Part 3
Runaway Island, Part 4
Runaway Nightmare
Running Blind
Running Cool
Running Hot
The Running Man
Running Scared
Rush
The Russian Terminator
The Rutanga Tapes
Safari 3000
Saga of the Vagabond
Sahara▶
Sahara
Saigon Commandos
Salty
Salvador▶
Samar
Samson Against the Sheik
Samurai 1: Musashi Miyamoto▶
Samurai 2: Duel at Ichijoji Temple▶
Samurai 3: Duel at Ganryu Island▶
Sands of Sacrifice
Sanjuro▶
S.A.S. San Salvador
The Satan Killer
Satan's Sadists
Savage!
Savage Beach
Savage Dawn
Savage Drums
Savage Fury
The Savage Girl
Savage Instinct
Savage Island
Scarface▶
The Scarlet & the Black
Sea Devils
Sea Hound
Sea Prince and the Fire Child
The Sea Wolf▶
The Sea Wolf
Search and Destroy
Second Chance
Secret Agent Super Dragon
The Secret Code
The Secret of El Zorro
Secret of the Ice Cave
Serpent Island

Sesame Street Presents: Follow That Bird
Seven Blows of the Dragon
Seven Magnificent Gladiators
Seven Sinners▶
The Seven-Ups
The Seventh Coin
The Seventh Voyage of Sinbad▶
Sex, Love and Cold Hard Cash
Shadow Man
Shadow of Chikara
Shadow of the Eagle
Shadow of the Wolf
Shadowhunter
Shaft's Big Score
Shakedown
Shaker Run
Shamus
Shaolin Ex-Monk
Shaolin Vengence
Shark Hunter
Shark River
Sharks' Treasure
Sharky's Machine
S*H*E
She Devils in Chains
Sheba, Baby
Sheena
The Sheik▶
Shep Comes Home
Ships in the Night
Shipwrecked
Shogun's Ninja
Shoot
Shoot the Sun Down
Showdown at the Equator
Sidekicks
Sidewinder One
Sign of the Wolf
The Sign of Zorro
Silk 2
The Silver Stallion: King of the Wild Brumbies
Sinbad and the Eye of the Tiger
Sinbad of the Seven Seas
Sinbad the Sailor▶
633 Squadron
Sixteen Fathoms Deep
The Skateboard Kid
Skeleton Coast
Ski Bum
Ski Troop Attack
Skull: A Night of Terror
Skull & Crown
Sky Hei$t
Sky High
Sky Pirates
Slate, Wyn & Me
Slaughter
Slaughter's Big Ripoff
Slave of the Cannibal God
Sloane
Slow Burn
Smokey & the Hotwire Gang
Smuggler's Cove
SnakeEater
SnakeEater 2: The Drug Buster
SnakeEater 3: His Law
Soldier's Fortune
Solo Voyage: The Revenge
Son of Captain Blood
Son of Fury▶
Son of Hercules vs. Venus
Son of Kong
The Son of Monte Cristo
Son of Samson
Son of Sinbad
Son of Zorro
S.O.S. Coast Guard
Sourdough
South Beach
South of Pago Pago
South Seas Massacre
Southern Comfort▶
Space Mutiny
Space Raiders
Space Riders
SpaceCamp

Spacehunter: Adventures in the Forbidden Zone
The Spanish Main
Spartacus▶
Special Investigator
Speeding Up Time
Speedtrap
Spiderman: The Deadly Dust
Spiders▶
The Spirit of Youth
The Spoilers
Spy
Spy in Black▶
Spy Smasher Returns
The Spy Who Loved Me
Stalking Danger
Stamp Day for Superman
Stand and Deliver
Star Quest
Starbird and Sweet William
Starchaser: The Legend of Orin
Starflight One
Steel Arena
Steel Dawn
Stone Cold
Storm and Sorrow
Stormquest
The Story of Robin Hood & His Merrie Men▶
Straight Line
Street Asylum
Street Hawk
Street Knight
Street Soldiers
Strike Back
Strike Commando
Stunt Pilot
Stunt Rock
Stunts
Subway
Sudden Death
Sudden Impact
Suicide Battalion/Hell Squad
Suicide Patrol
Summerdog
Sunshine Run
Super Mario Bros.
Superargo
Superbug Super Agent
Superchick
Superfly T.N.T.
Supergirl
Superman: The Movie▶
Superman 2▶
Superman 3
Superman 4: The Quest for Peace
Superman & the Mole Men
Supersonic Man
Supervixens
Surprise Attack
Survival Quest
Surviving the Game
Swamp Fire
Swamp Thing
Swamp Women
Swashbuckler
Sweet Justice
Sweet Revenge
Sweet Sugar
Sweet Trash
Swift Justice
The Switch
Switchblade Sisters
The Sword & the Rose
The Sword of El Cid
Sword of Gideon
Sword of Lancelot
Sword of Monte Cristo
Sword of Sherwood Forest
Sword of Venus
The Swordsman
Taffin
Tailspin Tommy
The Take
Taking it to the Street
The Taking of Beverly Hills
Tales of Robin Hood
Tales of the Klondike: In a Far Country

Tales of the Klondike: Race for Number One
Tales of the Klondike: The Unexpected
Tangiers
Tango and Cash
Tank Commando
Target Eagle
Target: Favorite Son
Target for Killing
Tarka the Otter
Tarzan and His Mate▶
Tarzan and the Green Goddess
Tarzan and the Trappers
Tarzan Finds a Son▶
Tarzan of the Apes
Tarzan, the Ape Man▶
Tarzan, the Ape Man
Tarzan the Fearless
Tarzan the Tiger
Tarzana, the Wild Girl
Tarzan's New York Adventure
Tarzan's Revenge
Tarzan's Secret Treasure
A Taste of Hell
Tattooed Hit Man
Taxi Dancers
TC 2000
Teenage Bonnie & Klepto Clyde
Temporada Salvaje
Ten to Midnight
10 Violent Women
Ten Who Dared
The Tender Warrior
Terminal Island
Terminal Velocity
The Terminator▶
Terminator 2: Judgment Day▶
Terror in Beverly Hills
Terror in Paradise
Terror in the Jungle
Terror of Rome Against the Son of Hercules
Terror of the Bloodhunters
Terror on Alcatraz
Terror on the 40th Floor
Terror Ship
Terror Squad
The Terrorists
Texas Detour
Tharus Son of Attila
Thieves of Fortune
Third Man on the Mountain
13 Rue Madeleine▶
The 13th Mission
This Gun for Hire
This is a Hijack
Thoughts are Free▶
Thrashin'
Three Days in Beirut
Three Days to a Kill
357 Magnum
Three Legionnaires
The Three Musketeers
Throne of Fire
Thumb Tripping
Thunder Bay▶
Thunder County
Thunder in Paradise
Thunder Road▶
Thunder Run
Thunder Warrior
Thunder Warrior 2
Thunderball
Thunderbolt & Lightfoot▶
Thundering Forest
Thundersquad
Tiara Tahiti
Tiffany Jones
Tiger Joe
Tiger of the Seven Seas
Tilt
Time Machine
Time to Die
The Time Travelers
Time Walker
Timebomb
Tintorera...Tiger Shark
To Die Standing
To Live and Die in Hong Kong

To Live & Die in L.A.
To Protect and Serve
To the Shores of Hell
Tobruk
Toby McTeague
Tokyo Joe
Tomorrow Never Comes
Tongs: An American Nightmare
Tonka
Top of the Heap
Tor
Tora! Tora! Tora!
Torero
The Tormentors
Total Exposure
Touch & Go
Tough Guy
Tougher than Leather
A Town Called Hell
Toy Soldiers
Trader Horn
Trader Tom of the China Seas
Trap
Trap on Cougar Mountain
Trapper County War
Treasure Island▶
Treasure Island
The Treasure of Bengal
The Treasure of Jamaica Reef
The Treasure of Matecumbe
Treasure of Monte Cristo
The Treasure of the Amazon
Treasure of the Four Crowns
Treasure of the Golden Condor
Treasure of the Sierra Madre▶
Treasure of the Yankee Zephyr
The Treasure Seekers
Trespass
The Trial of the Incredible Hulk
Trident Force
Triple Impact
Tripwire
Troma's War
Tropical Snow
Trouble Bound
Truck Stop Women
Truck Turner
Try and Get Me
Tucker and the Horse Thief
Tundra
Tusks
Tut & Tuttle
20,000 Leagues Under the Sea▶
Twilight's Last Gleaming
2020 Texas Gladiators
Two to Tango
Two Wrongs Make a Right
Typhoon Treasure
U-Boat Prisoner
Ulterior Motives
Ultra Warrior
Ulysses
Undeclared War
Under Siege
Under the Gun
Under the Red Robe
Undercover
Underground Terror
Underwater
Unholy Rollers
Universal Soldier
Unknown Island
Unmasking the Idol
Until They Get Me
The Uranium Conspiracy
Urban Warriors
Utu▶
Valley of the Eagles
Vengeance
Vera Cruz
The Vernonia Incident
V.I. Warshawski
Vice Squad
Vietnam, Texas
A View to a Kill
The Vigilantes are Coming
The Vikings
Violent Professionals

Violent Zone
Viper
Virgin Sacrifice
Viva Knievel
Viva Villa!▶
Vivo o Muerto
Voyage en Balloon
The Voyage of Tanai
The Voyage of the Yes
Wake of the Red Witch
Walk into Hell
Walker: Texas Ranger: One Riot, One Ranger
Wanted Dead or Alive
War & Remembrance, Part 1
War & Remembrance, Part 2
War & Remembrance: The Final Chapter, Part 8
War & Remembrance: The Final Chapter, Part 9
War Bus Commando
War Party
Warbirds
Warbus
WarCat
Wardogs
Warlords from Hell
Warlords 3000
The Warriors
Warriors from Hell
Warriors of the Apocalypse
Warriors of the Wasteland
Web of Deception
Wet Gold
Wheels of Fire
When Hell Broke Loose
When Lightning Strikes
When the North Wind Blows
Where Eagles Dare▶
Where the River Runs Black
Whispers of White
White Cannibal Queen
The White Dawn
White Fang▶
White Fang 2: The Myth of the White Wolf
White Fang and the Hunter
White Ghost
White Gorilla
White Huntress
White Lightning
White Line Fever
The White Orchid
White Pongo
White Slave
White Water Summer
WhiteForce
Whitewater Sam
Who Killed Mary What's 'Er Name?
The Wild Angels
Wild Geese
Wild Gypsies
Wild Horses
Wild Man
Wild Rebels
Wild Ride
Wild Women
The Wild World of Batwoman
Wild Zone
Wilding
Willow
The Wind That Walks
Windjammer
Wings of Danger
Wings Over the Pacific
Winners Take All
Wisdom
Wolf
Wolf Dog
Woman in Grey
Women in Fury
Women's Prison Escape
Women's Prison Massacre
Wonderland Cove
The Wreck of the Mary Deare
Write to Kill
The Yakuza
Yank in Libya
Yankee Clipper
Yellowstone
Yojimbo▶

Yor, the Hunter from the Future
You Only Live Twice
Young Eagles
Zatoichi: Master Ichi and a Chest of Gold
Zatoichi: The Blind Swordsman and the Chess Expert
Zatoichi: The Blind Swordsman and the Fugitives
Zatoichi: The Blind Swordsman's Vengeance
Zatoichi: The Life and Opinion of Masseur Ichi
Zatoichi: Zatoichi's Flashing Sword
Zebra Force
Zero
Zipperface

Adolescence

see Coming of Age; Hell High School; Summer Camp; Teen Angst

Adoption & Orphans

see also Hard Knock Life; Only the Lonely
Across the Great Divide
Adoption▶
Aladdin▶
All Mine to Give
Angel in a Taxi
Anne of Green Gables▶
Annie
Babes on Broadway
Bachelor Mother▶
The Beniker Gang
Big Red
Blossoms in the Dust
Born Free▶
Born in America
The Boy with the Green Hair▶
The Children of An Lac
Christmas Lilies of the Field
City Boy▶
A Cry from the Streets
Crystalstone
Daddy Long Legs▶
Dangerous Orphans
D.A.R.Y.L.
David Copperfield▶
David Copperfield
Deadly Sanctuary
Defiant
Dick Tracy▶
Don't Cry, It's Only Thunder
Duelo en el Dorado
Eagle's Shadow
Earthling
Escape to Witch Mountain▶
A Far Off Place
The Father Clements Story
Fighting Father Dunne
Free Willy
Goldy: The Last of the Golden Bears
Goldy 2: The Saga of the Golden Bear
Great Expectations▶
Great Expectations
Great Expectations▶
Great Expectations: The Untold Story
Heaven on Earth
Hector's Bunyip
Home at Last
A Home of Our Own
Hoodoo Ann
Immediate Family
The Jack Knife Man▶
Jane Eyre
Jane Eyre▶
The Kid
The Kid/Idle Class▶
The Kid Who Loved Christmas
King, Queen, Knave▶
Korczak▶
La Passante▶

Lady from Yesterday
The Lady is Willing
The Land Before Time▶
Little Orphan Annie
The Little Princess
A Long Way Home
Love Without Fear
The Loves of Edgar Allen Poe
Mad Max: Beyond Thunderdome
The Magic Christian▶
Man, Woman & Child
Manny's Orphans
Mighty Joe Young
Min & Bill
My Dog Shep
Mystery of the Million Dollar Hockey Puck
Napoleon and Samantha▶
Nice Girl Like Me
Nothing But the Night
The Odyssey of the Pacific
The Official Story▶
Oliver!▶
Oliver Twist▶
Oliver Twist
Oliver Twist▶
Oliver Twist
On the Right Track
One Good Cop
The Orphan
Orphan Train▶
Orphans▶
Orphans of the Storm▶
Paper Moon▶
Peck's Bad Boy
Penny Serenade▶
Pixote▶
Pollyanna
Pollyanna▶
The Poor Little Rich Girl
The Prince of Central Park▶
Problem Child
Queen Kelly▶
Rags to Riches
Rebecca of Sunnybrook Farm
The Revolt of Job▶
Rikisha-Man▶
Sally of the Sawdust
Samantha
Scout's Honor
The Sea Serpent
Shep Comes Home
Sidewalks of London▶
A Simple Twist of Fate
Snow White and the Seven Dwarfs▶
Sois Belle et Tais-Toi
Sparrows▶
The Stranger Who Looks Like Me
Streetwise▶
Sugar Cane Alley▶
The Sugarland Express▶
Sundays & Cybele▶
Superman: The Movie▶
Susannah of the Mounties
Sweetwater
Tarzan Finds a Son▶
They Still Call Me Bruce
Three Secrets
The Tunnel of Love
Way Back Home
Where the River Runs Black
Which Way Home
Who'll Save Our Children?▶
Wild Hearts Can't Be Broken▶
The World Accuses
Young & Free

Adventure Drama

see also Action Adventure; Drama
Ace of Aces
Act of Piracy
Action in the North Atlantic
The Adventures of Frontier Fremont
The Adventures of Huck Finn▶
The Adventures of Huckleberry Finn▶

The Adventures of Huckleberry Finn
The Adventures of Milo & Otis▶
The Adventures of Robin Hood▶
The Adventures of the Wilderness Family
The Adventures of Tom Sawyer▶
Air Force▶
Al Capone▶
The Alaska Wilderness Adventure
Alexander Nevsky▶
Ali Baba and the Forty Thieves
All the Rivers Run
Allan Quartermain and the Lost City of Gold
Alligator Alley
Aloha, Bobby and Rose
Amazon
The Amazons
American Empire
American Roulette
The American Scream
American Tiger
And I Alone Survived
Angels of the City
Anzacs: The War Down Under▶
Apocalypse Now▶
Appointment with Crime
The Arab Conspiracy
Archer's Adventure
Arizona Heat
Around the World in 80 Days▶
Assassination
Assault on Precinct 13▶
The Association
The Aviator
Back in the USSR
Backdraft
Backlash
Barbary Coast▶
The Baron
Bataan
Battle Hell
The Battle of El Alamein
Battle of the Eagles
The Battle of the Japan Sea
Battleforce
Bear Island
Beau Geste▶
The Beloved Rogue▶
Beneath the 12-Mile Reef
Benji the Hunted
The Berlin Conspiracy
Between Heaven and Hell▶
Big Bad Mama
The Big Push
The Big Scam
Billy Budd▶
Black Arrow▶
The Black Arrow
The Black Arrow
Black Bikers from Hell
Black Moon Rising
Black Rain
Blackout
Blood and Sand▶
Blood Debts
Bloody Che Contra
Blowing Wild
The Blue and the Gray
Blue Fin
The Blue Lamp▶
Blue Thunder
Boiling Point
Bomb at 10:10
Bombardier
Botany Bay
The Bounty▶
Brighty of the Grand Canyon
Brotherhood of Death
A Bullet Is Waiting
Burke & Wills
Cadence
California Gold Rush
Call of the Wild
Camel Boy
Casablanca Express

The Castilian
Casualties of War▶
The Cat
Chain Reaction
Chains of Gold
The Challenge▶
Challenge of a Lifetime
The Charge of the Light Brigade▶
Children of the Wild
Children's Island
China Gate▶
Chrome Soldiers
Clarence, the Cross-eyed Lion▶
Claws
Clear and Present Danger▶
The Climb
The Coast Patrol
Code Name: Emerald
Cold Heat
Cold Justice
Command Decision
Commando Attack
Con Man
Coogan's Bluff▶
The Cop & the Girl
Cop-Out
Corsair
The Count of Monte Cristo
The Count of Monte Cristo▶
The Count of Monte Cristo
Courage Mountain
Courage of Black Beauty
Courage of Rin Tin Tin
Crimebusters
Crimson Romance
Dam Busters▶
Dangerous Moonlight▶
Dangerous Passage
Daring Game
Dark Before Dawn
Dark Mountain
Dark Tide
The Darkside
The Dawson Patrol
The Day Will Dawn▶
Days of Thunder
Deadlock
Deadly Sanctuary
The Death Merchant
Death Stalk
The Deceivers
Deliverance▶
Desert Warrior
Destination Tokyo
Dick Tracy▶
Dick Turpin
Die Hard▶
Die Hard 2: Die Harder▶
Dillinger▶
Dillinger
Dinosaur Island
Diplomatic Immunity
Dive Bomber▶
Down to the Sea in Ships
Dragonfly Squadron
Dust▶
Each Dawn I Die
The Eagle Has Landed▶
East of Borneo
Edge of Honor
84 Charlie Mopic▶
The Elusive Pimpernel
The Emerald Forest▶
Enchanted Island
Enemy Below▶
The Enforcer
Escape to Witch Mountain▶
Evel Knievel
The Expendables
Eye of the Octopus
Fangs of the Wild
Fantastic Balloon Voyage
Fantastic Seven
A Far Off Place
Farewell to the King
Ferry to Hong Kong
55 Days at Peking▶
The Fighting Prince of Donegal
Fire Alarm

Fire in the Night
Firepower
Flame Over India▶
The Flash
The Flash 2: Revenge of the Trickster
Flight of the Grey Wolf
Flipper▶
Flying Leathernecks▶
Flying Tigers
Follow Me
Forty Thousand Horsemen
The Four Feathers▶
The Four Feathers
F.P. 1
F.P. 1 Doesn't Answer
Free Grass
The Fugitive▶
Full Eclipse
Fury to Freedom: The Life Story of Raul Ries
Future Zone
Game for Vultures
Gente Violenta
God's Country
Goliath Awaits
Great Adventure
The Great Escape▶
The Great Escape 2: The Untold Story
The Great Locomotive Chase
The Great Train Robbery▶
The Green Glove
Greystoke: The Legend of Tarzan, Lord of the Apes
Grizzly Mountain
Guadalcanal Diary
Gun Cargo
Gunblast
Gunga Din▶
The Gunrunner
The Halls of Montezuma
Hamlet▶
Hangfire
Hard Knocks
Hard Rain-The Tet 1968
Harley
Hawk and Castile
Hell Commandos
Hell in the Pacific▶
Hell River
Hell Squad
Hell to Eternity
Hellcats of the Navy
Hellfighters
Hell's Angels▶
Hell's Brigade: The Final Assault
Here Come the Littles: The Movie
The Heroes of Desert Storm
Heroes Three
High Country Calling
Himatsuri▶
Hired to Kill
Hiroshima: Out of the Ashes▶
Hit!
Homeward Bound: The Incredible Journey▶
Huck and the King of Hearts
Hurricane Smith
Hustler Squad
Immortal Sergeant
Imperial Navy
In Harm's Way
In Love and War
In Search of a Golden Sky
In Which We Serve▶
Inferno in Paradise
The Iron Mask
Island of Adventure
Island of the Blue Dolphins
Island Trader
Islands
Isle of Forgotten Sins
Istanbul
It Rained All Night the Day I Left
Jaguar
Jamaica Inn
Jaws of Justice
Jenny's War

Jet Pilot
The Journey of Natty Gann▶
Journey to the Center of the Earth
Joy Ride to Nowhere
Juggernaut▶
Jungle
Jungle Goddess
Jurassic Park▶
Kamikaze
Kamikaze '89▶
Karate Polish Style
Kashmiri Run
Kavik the Wolf Dog
Keeper of the City
Keeping Track
Kid Colter
Kidnap Syndicate
Kidnapped
The Killer▶
The Killer Elite
Killer Instinct
King of New York▶
King Solomon's Mines▶
King Solomon's Mines
King Solomon's Treasure
Kingfisher Caper
Kiss and Kill
Klondike Fever
Kojiro▶
K2: The Ultimate High
La Chamuscada
La Isla Encantada
Lady Avenger
Lady Cocoa
Lady Scarface/The Threat
Landslide
Lassie: Adventures of Neeka
Lassie: Well of Love
Lassiter
The Last Hunter
Last Man Standing
The Last of the Finest
The Last of the Mohicans
The Last Riders
The Last Season
Legend of Billie Jean
Legend of Lobo
The Legend of Sea Wolf
The Legend of the Sea Wolf
The Legend of Wolf Mountain
Lethal Pursuit
Liana, Jungle Goddess
Life & Times of Grizzly Adams
The Lion Man
Lion of the Desert▶
The Lion of Venice
The Live Wire
Loaded Guns
Lockdown
Lost
Lost Zeppelin
Macao▶
The Mad Bomber
Made for Love
Magnificent Adventurer
The Man from Beyond
The Man in the Iron Mask▶
Man of Legend
Manhunt for Claude Dallas
Massacre in Dinosaur Valley
The Master of Ballantrae
The McConnell Story
Memphis Belle▶
Men in War
Men of Steel
Merlin and the Sword
Miami Vice
Miami Vice 2: The Prodigal Son
Midnight Crossing
Midway
Milo & Otis
Ms. 45▶
Mission Phantom
Mission to Death
Mr. Kingstreet's War
Mobsters
Moby Dick▶
Money Movers
The Moon-Spinners
Moran of the Lady Letty

Mountain Family Robinson
Moving Target
The Mutiny of the Elsinore
My Dog Shep
Naked Jungle▶
The Navy Comes Through
Night Crossing
The Night Train to Kathmandu
Nightstick
No Greater Love
No Time to Die
Noon Sunday
Norseman
The North Star▶
Northern Pursuit
Northwest Passage▶
Number One with a Bullet
Objective, Burma!▶
Obsessed
Oceans of Fire
Omega Syndrome
On Wings of Eagles
One Armed Executioner
One Man Force
One Minute to Zero
One of Our Aircraft Is Missing▶
One That Got Away▶
Operation Cross Eagles
Operation Haylift
Operation Inchon
Operation Julie
Operation 'Nam
Operation Thunderbolt
Operation War Zone
Opposing Force
Oubliette
Outlaw Blues
Outlaw Force
The Package
Paco
Palais Royale
The Palermo Connection
Papillon▶
Party Line
Passenger 57
Pathfinder▶
Patriot
Patriot Games▶
Payoff
Penitentiary
Penitentiary 2
Penitentiary 3
The Perils of Gwendoline
Permission To Kill
Pharaoh
Pirates of the High Seas
Place in Hell
Platoon▶
Platoon Leader
Plunder Road
Plunge Into Darkness
Policewomen
Pork Chop Hill▶
Portrait of a Hitman
Pray for the Wildcats
The Presidio
Prime Target
Prisoner in the Middle
Private Investigations
PT 109
Pursuit of the Graf Spee
Radio Patrol
Raiders in Action
Raiders of the Lost Ark▶
Ran▶
Raw Courage
The Real Glory▶
Reap the Wild Wind
Red Barry
Red Flag: The Ultimate Game
Renegades
Report to the Commissioner▶
Requiem for a Heavyweight▶
The Rescue
Retreat, Hell!
Revenge
Riot in Cell Block 11▶
The Roaring Twenties▶
Robbery
Robin Hood: Prince of Thieves
RoboCop▶

Runaway Train▶
The St. Valentine's Day Massacre
San Demetrio, London
The Sand Pebbles▶
Sands of Iwo Jima▶
Sardinia Kidnapped
Savage Hunger
Savage Justice
Savage Sam
Savage Streets
Scaramouche▶
Scarface▶
The Scarlet Car
Scarlet Spear
Scorchy
Scott of the Antarctic
Sea Chase
Sea Devils
Sea Gypsies
The Sea Hawk▶
The Sea Shall Not Have Them
Sea Wolves
Search and Destroy
Secret Weapon
Self-Defense
Sell Out
Sergeant York▶
Seven Alone
Seven Indignant
Sex Crimes
The Shadow
Shadow Force
Shame
Shark!
She Came to the Valley
Shell Shock
Shipwreck Island
Shogun Assassin
Shoot to Kill▶
Shooting Stars
Shout at the Devil
The Siege of Firebase Gloria
The Silent Enemy
Silent Raiders
Silk
Simon Blanco
Sinai Commandos
The Sinister Urge
Sink the Bismarck▶
Sins of Rome
Six Pack
Sky Riders
Slow Moves
Smugglers
The Sniper
Sniper
Sno-Line
Sodom and Gomorrah
Soldier of Fortune
Sonny Boy
Sorcerer
Soul Vengeance
South of Hell Mountain
Special Forces
Speed▶
Spirit of the Eagle
The Spring
Stanley and Livingstone▶
The Starfighters
State of Grace▶
The Steel Claw
The Steel Helmet▶
Steele Justice
Steele's Law
The Sting▶
The Stone Killer
Street Crimes
Street War
Streets of Fire
Strike Force
Striker
Striker's Mountain
Submarine Seahawk
Sundown
Sunset Grill
Sunset Heat
Surabaya Conspiracy
Surfacing
Survival Run
The Swiss Family Robinson▶

The Taking of Pelham One Two Three▶
Tank
Taps
The Ten Million Dollar Getaway
Tenement
Thelma & Louise▶
They Were Expendable▶
Thirty-Six Hours of Hell
Thomas Crown Affair▶
Those Calloways
The 317th Platoon▶
The Three Musketeers
The Three Musketeers▶
Three the Hard Way
Thunderground
Tides of War
Tiger Fangs
A Tiger Walks
Tim Tyler's Luck
Tom Sawyer
Top Gun
Tour of Duty
Toy Soldiers
Triple Cross▶
Trouble in Paradise
True Blood
Truth or Die
Turnaround
Twisted Justice
The Untouchables▶
Up Periscope
Valley of Wanted Men
Viking Massacre
Violent Breed
Von Ryan's Express▶
Wake Island▶
A Walk in the Sun▶
Walking Back
A Waltz Through the Hills
War & Remembrance, Part 3
War & Remembrance, Part 4
War & Remembrance, Part 5
War & Remembrance, Part 6
War & Remembrance, Part 7
War & Remembrance: The Final Chapter, Part 10
War & Remembrance: The Final Chapter, Part 11
War & Remembrance: The Final Chapter, Part 12
The War Boy
Warkill
We Dive at Dawn▶
Weekend War
What a Way to Die
Wheel of Fortune
Where the Spirit Lives
White Fire
White Fury
White Hot
The White Tower▶
The Wicked Lady
The Wild Pair
Wild Riders
Wild Thing
A Wing and a Prayer▶
Winning▶
Wooden Horse▶
World War III
The Year of Living Dangerously▶
Yellowneck
Young & Free
Young Warlord
Young Warriors
Zeppelin
Zero Pilot
Zulu
Zulu Dawn▶

Advertising

see also Front Page; Mass Media
The Agency
Beer
Bliss▶
C.O.D.
Crazy People

A Few Moments with Buster Keaton and Laurel and Hardy▶
The Girl Can't Help It
Her Husband's Affairs
The Horse in the Gray Flannel Suit
How to Get Ahead in Advertising▶
The Hucksters▶
I Married a Woman
Image of Passion
Kramer vs. Kramer▶
Lost in America▶
Lover Come Back
The Man in the Gray Flannel Suit
Mr. Blandings Builds His Dream House▶
Nothing in Common
Pray for the Wildcats
Renaissance Man
Ten Speed
Think Dirty
The Thrill of It All!
Thunder in the City▶
Transformers: The Movie

Africa

see also Apartheid
Abdulla the Great
The Adventurers
Africa Screams
An African Dream
African Journey
The African Queen▶
African Rage
The Air Up There
Albino
Algiers▶
Allan Quartermain and the Lost City of Gold
Amin: The Rise and Fall
Black Force
Black Terrorist
Black Vampire
Bopha!▶
The Bushbaby
Call Me Bwana
Cheetah
Chocolat▶
City of Blood
The Claw
Cleopatra
Come Back, Africa▶
Coming to America▶
Country Lovers, City Lovers
Curse 3: Blood Sacrifice
Dark of the Sun
Darkest Africa
The Desert Fox▶
The Desert Tigers
Dingaka
The Dogs of War
A Dry White Season▶
East of Kilimanjaro
The Egyptian
A Far Off Place
Five Weeks in a Balloon
The Flame Trees of Thika▶
The Garden of Allah▶
The Gods Must Be Crazy▶
The Gods Must Be Crazy 2
The Golden Salamander
Guns at Batasi
Hatari!▶
In Desert and Wilderness
In the Army Now
In the Shadow of Kilimanjaro
It Rained All Night the Day I Left
Ivory Hunters
Jaguar
Jericho
The Jewel of the Nile
Jungle Drums of Africa
Jungle Master
The Key to Rebecca
Killers
King Kong▶
King Solomon's Mines▶
King Solomon's Mines

The Kitchen Toto▶
The Last Safari
Les Aventuriers
The Light in the Jungle
Lion of Africa
The Lost Patrol▶
The Lost World
Made for Love
Mandela▶
Manhattan Baby
Manhunt in the African Jungle
March or Die
The Mark of the Hawk▶
Master Harold and the Boys▶
Men of Two Worlds
Mercenary Fighters
Mighty Joe Young
Mines of Kilimanjaro
Mister Johnson▶
Mr. Kingstreet's War
Mogambo▶
Monster from Green Hell
Mountains of the Moon▶
My African Adventure
Nairobi Affair
The Naked Prey▶
Night of the Sorcerers
Notes for an African Orestes
Oddball Hall
One Step to Hell
Options
Out of Africa▶
Over Indulgence
Overseas: Three Women with
    Man Trouble▶
The Passenger▶
Pepe Le Moko▶
Place of Weeping
Red Scorpion
Return to Africa
Rhodes
Rogue Lion
Sanders of the River▶
Sarafina!▶
Satan's Harvest
Secret Obsession
Shaka Zulu▶
The Sheltering Sky▶
Simba▶
Skeleton Coast
The Snows of Kilimanjaro▶
Something of Value▶
Song of Freedom
Sundown
Time to Kill
Tobruk
Trader Horn
The Treasure of Bengal
Tuxedo Warrior
Warriors from Hell
We are the Children
White Cargo
White Hunter, Black Heart▶
White Mischief▶
Wild Geese
A World Apart▶
Zulu
Zulu Dawn▶

African America

see also New Black
    Cinema
Above the Rim
Across 110th Street
Almos' a Man
Ashes and Embers
Assault at West Point: The
    Court-Martial of Johnson
    Whittaker
The Autobiography of Miss
    Jane Pittman▶
Avenging Disco Godfather
Bebe's Kids
Beware
Bingo Long Traveling All-Stars
    & Motor Kings▶
Black Brigade
The Black King
Black Like Me
Black Vampire
Blood of Jesus
Boardinghouse Blues

Body and Soul
Bopha!▶
Bronze Buckaroo
Bush Mama
Charlotte Forten's Mission:
    Experiment in Freedom▶
Christmas Lilies of the Field
Chuck Berry: Hail! Hail! Rock
    'n' Roll▶
Come Back, Africa▶
Crooklyn▶
The Devil's Daughter
Do the Right Thing▶
Double Deal
A Dream for Christmas▶
Drums O'Voodoo
Dutchman▶
The Ernest Green Story
The Five Heartbeats▶
For Us, the Living▶
Gang War
The George McKenna Story
Girl from Chicago
Glory▶
Go Down Death
The Great White Hope
Green Pastures▶
Guess Who's Coming to
    Dinner▶
Half Slave, Half Free
Hallelujah!▶
Harlem on the Prairie
A Hero Ain't Nothin' But a
    Sandwich
Hollywood Shuffle
Home Feeling
House Party▶
House Party 2: The Pajama
    Jam
House Party 3
How U Like Me Now?▶
I Know Why the Caged Bird
    Sings▶
Identity Crisis
I'm Gonna Git You Sucka▶
Imitation of Life▶
In the Heat of the Night▶
The Inkwell
The Jackie Robinson Story▶
J.D.'s Revenge
Jericho
The Jesse Owens Story▶
The Joe Louis Story
Joe's Bed-Stuy Barbershop:
    We Cut Heads
Juice
Just Another Girl on the I.R.T.
Keep Punching
Killing Floor
King▶
Laurel Avenue
Livin' Large
Look Out Sister▶
Love Your Mama
Lying Lips
Malcolm X▶
Mandela▶
Menace II Society▶
The Meteor Man
Miracle in Harlem
Monkey Hustle
Moon Over Harlem
Murder on Lenox Avenue
New Faces of 1952
New Jack City
No Fear, No Die
Nothing But a Man
Paris is Burning▶
Perfume
Piece of the Action
Poetic Justice
Putney Swope▶
A Raisin in the Sun▶
The Respectful Prostitute
Return of Superfly
The River Niger
Rockwell: A Legend of the
    Wild West
Roots▶
Roots: The Gift
Roots: The Next Generation▶
Sarafina!▶

Scar of Shame
Sergeant Rutledge▶
Shaft▶
Shaft's Big Score
Shanty Tramp
Small Time
Sophisticated Gents▶
Sounder▶
South Central
Strapped
Sugar Hill▶
Sun Ra & His Intergalactic
    Solar Arkestra: Space is
    the Place
Superfly
Superfly T.N.T.
Sweet Love, Bitter
Sweet Sweetback's
    Baadasssss Song▶
Truck Turner
Uncle Tom's Cabin
Way Down South
Words by Heart
A World of Strangers▶
Xica▶
You Must Remember This
You So Crazy
Zebrahead▶

AIDS

see also Disease of the
    Week; Homosexuality
And the Band Played On▶
As Is
Blue
Common Threads: Stories
    from the Quilt
An Early Frost▶
Intimate Contact▶
Joey Breaker▶
Les Nuits Fauves▶
Longtime Companion▶
Love Without Fear
Men in Love
Parting Glances▶
Peter's Friends
Philadelphia▶
Via Appia

Air Disasters

see also Airborne; Disaster
    Flicks; Sea Disasters
Airport▶
Airport '75
Airport '77
Alive
The Buddy Holly Story▶
The Concorde: Airport '79
The Crash of Flight 401
Die Hard 2: Die Harder▶
Fearless▶
Fire and Rain
Flight to Fury
Hero▶
The Hindenburg
Jet Over the Atlantic
Madam Satan
Sole Survivor
Survivor
Tailspin: Behind the Korean
    Airline Tragedy
A Thousand Heroes
Tragedy of Flight 103: The
    Inside Story▶

Airborne

see also Air Disasters
Above and Beyond▶
Ace Drummond
Ace of Aces
Aces: Iron Eagle 3
Adventures of Smilin' Jack
The Adventures of the Flying
    Cadets
Afterburn▶
Air America
Air Force▶
Air Hawk
Airplane!▶
Airplane 2: The Sequel
Airport▶

Airport '75
Airport '77
Always
And I Alone Survived
Angels One Five
Attack Squadron
The Aviator
Bail Out at 43,000
Battle of Britain
Battle of the Eagles
Beyond the Time Barrier
Biggles
Birds of Prey
Black Box Affair
The Blue Max
Blue Thunder
Blue Tornado
Boeing Boeing
Bombardier
Brewster McCloud▶
Bulldog Drummond at Bay
By Dawn's Early Light
Captains of the Clouds
Ceiling Zero▶
Chain Lightning
Christopher Strong
The Concorde: Airport '79
The Crash of Flight 401
Crimson Romance
Danger in the Skies
Dangerous Moonlight▶
Dawn Patrol▶
Deadly Encounter▶
Delta Force
Devil Dogs of the Air
Die Hard 2: Die Harder▶
Dive Bomber▶
The Doomsday Flight
Dragonfly Squadron
Dumbo▶
Enola Gay: The Men, the
    Mission, the Atomic Bomb
Fighter Attack
Fighting Pilot
Final Approach
Fire Birds
Firefox
Five Came Back
Five Weeks in a Balloon
Flaming Signal
Flat Top
Flight from Glory
Flight from Singapore
Flight of Black Angel
Flight of the Intruder
The Flight of the Phoenix▶
Flight to Fury
Flying Blind
The Flying Deuces▶
Flying Down to Rio
Flying Leathernecks▶
Flying Tigers
The Great Skycopter Rescue
The Great Waldo Pepper▶
A Guy Named Joe
Gypsy Angels
Hell's Angels▶
High Road to China
Hostage
Hot Shots!▶
The Hunters
Interceptor
Into the Sun
Iron Eagle
Iron Eagle 2
The Island at the Top of the
    World
It Happened at the World's
    Fair
Jet Over the Atlantic
Jet Pilot
Kamikaze
Keep 'Em Flying
La Bamba▶
La Grande Vadrouille▶
Lafayette Escadrille
L'Anne Sainte
The Left Hand of God▶
The Lion Has Wings
Look Who's Talking Now
Lost Squadron
Malta Story

The Man with the Golden Gun
The McConnell Story
The Medal of Honor
Memphis Belle▶
Memphis Belle: A Story of a
    Flying Fortress
Men of Steel
Men of the Fighting Lady▶
Millenium
Moon Pilot
Murder on Flight 502
Mystery Squadron
One of Our Aircraft Is
    Missing▶
Only Angels Have Wings▶
Out of Control
Pancho Barnes
Party Plane
Passenger 57
Phantom of the Air
Phone Call from a Stranger
Piece of Cake
The Pursuit of D.B. Cooper
Reach for the Sky
Red Flag: The Ultimate Game
Return to Earth
Revenge of the Red Baron
The Right Stuff▶
Robot Pilot
Sabre Jet
Savage Hunger
Seven Miles from Alcatraz/
    Flight from Glory
Shadow of the Eagle
Shadow on the Sun
633 Squadron
Sky Hei$t
Sky Liner
Sky Riders
Spirit of St. Louis▶
Spitfire▶
The Starfighters
Starflight One
Steal the Sky
Strategic Air Command
Stunt Pilot
Survivor
Tailspin: Behind the Korean
    Airline Tragedy
The Taking of Flight 847: The
    Uli Derickson Story▶
Task Force
Terminal Velocity
Test Pilot▶
Texas Buddies
Those Endearing Young
    Charms
Those Magnificent Men in
    Their Flying Machines▶
Today We Live
Top Gun
Tragedy of Flight 103: The
    Inside Story▶
Twelve O'Clock High▶
War in the Sky▶
War Lover
Warbirds
Where the Sky Begins
The Wild Aces
Winds of Kitty Hawk
A Wing and a Prayer▶
Wings
Wings of Danger
Wings of Eagles
The World Owes Me a Living
Zeppelin
Zero
Zero Pilot

Airplanes

see Air Disasters;
    Airborne

Alcoholism

see On the Rocks

Alien Beings—
Benign

see also Alien Beings—
    Vicious; Space Operas
The Abyss▶

Aftershock
Alien from L.A.
Alien Nation
Alien Private Eye
Alien Women
The Aurora Encounter
*batteries not included
Big Meat Eater
The Brother from Another
 Planet▶
The Cat from Outer Space
Close Encounters of the Third
 Kind▶
Cocoon▶
Cocoon: The Return
Communion
Coneheads
The Cosmic Eye▶
The Cosmic Man
The Day the Earth Stood
 Still▶
Doin' Time on Planet Earth
Earth Girls are Easy
Earth vs. the Flying Saucers
The Empire Strikes Back▶
Enemy Mine
Escape to Witch Mountain▶
E.T.: The Extra-Terrestrial▶
The Ewok Adventure
The Ewoks: Battle for Endor
Fire in the Sky
Flight of the Navigator
Gremlins▶
Gremlins 2: The New Batch▶
The Hidden▶
Howard the Duck
Hyper-Sapien: People from
 Another Star
Intruders
It Came From Outer Space▶
Labyrinth▶
The Last Starfighter
Mac and Me
Man Facing Southeast▶
The Man from Atlantis
The Man Who Fell to Earth▶
Martians Go Home!
Masters of Venus
Missile to the Moon
Morons from Outer Space
Munchie
My Stepmother Is an Alien
Mysterious Planet
Mysterious Two
Nukie
Official Denial
Pajama Party
The Phantom Planet
Project: Genesis
Purple People Eater
Real Men
Repo Man▶
Return of the Jedi▶
Search for the Gods
Simon
Spaced Invaders
Star Trek 3: The Search for
 Spock
Star Trek 4: The Voyage
 Home▶
Star Wars▶
Stardust Memories
Starman▶
Starship Invasions
Suburban Commando
Super Mario Bros.
Supergirl
Superman: The Movie▶
Superman 2▶
Superman 3
Superman 4: The Quest for
 Peace
Teenage Mutant Ninja Turtles
 2: The Secret of the Ooze
Terronauts
The 27 Day
The Twilight Zone
UFO: Target Earth
Voyage of the Rock Aliens
War of the Robots
Warning from Space
Wavelength

Alien Beings— Vicious

see also Alien Beings— Benign; Space Operas

The Adventures of Buckaroo
 Banzai Across the Eighth
 Dimension▶
Alien▶
Alien 3
Alien Contamination
Alien Dead
The Alien Factor
Alien Massacre
Alien Predators
Alien Prey
Alien Seed
Alien Space Avenger
Alienator
Aliens▶
Aliens Are Coming
The Alpha Incident
The Ambushers
The Angry Red Planet
The Astounding She-Monster
The Astro-Zombies
Atomic Submarine
Bad Taste▶
The Bamboo Saucer
Battle Beyond the Stars
Battle of the Worlds
Battlestar Galactica
The Blob
The Blob▶
Bloodsuckers from Outer
 Space
Blue Monkey
Body Snatchers
The Borrower
The Brain
The Brain Eaters
The Brain from Planet Arous
Cat Women of the Moon
The Cosmic Monsters
Creature
Creeping Terror
The Cremators
Critters
Critters 2: The Main Course
Critters 3
Critters 4
The Curse
D-Day on Mars
The Dark
Dark Star▶
Dark Universe
Day the World Ended
Day Time Ended
Dead Space
Deceit
Deep Space
Destroy All Monsters
Destroy All Planets
Devil Girl from Mars
Dr. Alien
Doctor Who: An Unearthly
 Child
Doctor Who and the Daleks
Doctor Who: Cybermen—The
 Early Years
Doctor Who: Daleks Invasion
 of Earth 2150 A.D.
Doctor Who: Day of the
 Daleks
Doctor Who: Death to the
 Daleks
Doctor Who: Earthshock
Doctor Who: Mawdryn
 Undead
Doctor Who: Pyramids of
 Mars
Doctor Who: Revenge of the
 Cybermen
Doctor Who: Robots of Death
Doctor Who: Spearhead from
 Space
Doctor Who: Terror of the
 Zygons
Doctor Who: The Ark in Space
Doctor Who: The Brain of
 Morbius

Doctor Who: The Curse of
 Fenric
Doctor Who: The Deadly
 Assassin
Doctor Who: The Five Doctors
Doctor Who: The Hartnell
 Years
Doctor Who: The Keeper of
 Traken
Doctor Who: The Mind
 Robber
Doctor Who: The Seeds of
 Death
Doctor Who: The Sontaran
 Experiment/The Genesis of
 the Daleks
Doctor Who: The Talons of
 Weng-Chiang
Doctor Who: The Three
 Doctors
Doctor Who: The Time
 Warrior
Doctor Who: The Troughton
 Years
Doctor Who: The Twin
 Dilemma
Doctor Who: The War Games
Doctor Who: Tomb of the
 Cyberman
Dollman
Dracula vs. Frankenstein
Earth vs. the Flying Saucers
Eat and Run
The Empire Strikes Back▶
Encounter at Raven's Gate
End of the World
Escape from Galaxy Three
Escapes
Evils of the Night
The Eye Creatures
Eyes Behind the Stars
The Fear Chamber
First Man into Space
Flight to Mars
Flying Discman from Mars
Forbidden World
From Beyond▶
Fugitive Alien
Galaxy Invader
Galaxy of Terror
Gamera vs. Guiron
Gamera vs. Zigra
Ghidrah the Three Headed
 Monster
The Giant Claw
The Giant Spider Invasion
God Told Me To
Godzilla vs. the Cosmic
 Monster
Grampa's Sci-Fi Hits
Grand Tour: Disaster in Time
The Green Slime
Gremlins▶
Gremlins 2: The New Batch▶
The Guyver
Hands of Steel
The Hidden▶
The Hidden 2
High Desert Kill
Horror of the Blood Monsters
Horror Planet
The Human Duplicators
I Come in Peace
I Married a Monster from
 Outer Space
Interzone
Invader
The Invaders
Invaders from Mars
Invasion
Invasion Earth: The Aliens Are
 Here!
Invasion of the Animal People
Invasion of the Bee Girls▶
Invasion of the Body
 Snatchers▶
Invasion of the Body Stealers
Invasion of the Girl Snatchers
Invasion of the Saucer Men
Invasion of the Space
 Preachers
Invisible Adversaries

Island of the Burning Doomed
It Came From Outer Space▶
It Conquered the World
It! The Terror from Beyond
 Space
J-Men Forever!▶
Killer Klowns from Outer
 Space
Killers from Space
Killings at Outpost Zeta
Kronos
Laboratory
Leviathan
Liquid Sky▶
Lords of the Deep
Mars Needs Women
The Martian Chronicles: Part 3
Masters of Venus
Metallica
Midnight Movie Massacre
Mindwarp
Mission Mars
Mom and Dad Save the World
Monolith
The Monolith Monsters
Monster
Monster a Go-Go!
Monster High
Moontrap
Munchies
The Mysterians
Night Beast
Night Caller from Outer Space
Night of the Blood Beast
Night of the Creeps
No Survivors, Please
The Outer Limits: Galaxy
 Being
Peacemaker
Phantom from Space
The Phantom Planet
The Pink Chiquitas
Plan 9 from Outer Space
Planet of Blood
Planets Against Us
Predator
Predator 2
Quatermass 2▶
The Quatermass Experiment▶
Radar Men from the Moon
Reactor
Remote Control
The Return
Return of the Aliens: The
 Deadly Spawn
Return of the Jedi▶
Revenge of the Teenage
 Vixens from Outer Space
Robot Monster
Rock 'n' Roll Nightmare
Scared to Death
The Sinister Invasion
Slapstick of Another Kind
Son of Blob
Split
Split Second
Star Crystal
Star Trek: The Motion Picture
Star Trek 3: The Search for
 Spock
Star Trek: The Cage
Star Wars▶
Starship Invasions
Stephen King's The
 Tommyknockers
Strange Invaders▶
The Stranger from Venus
Super Mario Bros.
Superman: The Movie▶
A Taste for Flesh and Blood
Teen Alien
Teenagers from Outer Space
Terror of Mechagodzilla
They
They Came from Beyond
 Space
They Live
The Thing▶
The Thing
This Island Earth
Time Runner
Time Walker

Tripods: The White Mountains
20 Million Miles to Earth
The Twilight Zone
The Unearthly Stranger
Village of the Damned▶
War in Space
War of the Wizards
The War of the Worlds▶
Wild, Wild Planet
Women of the Prehistoric
 Planet
X from Outer Space
Xtro
Xtro 2: The Second Encounter
Zeram
Zombies of the Stratosphere
Zontar, the Thing from Venus

American Indians

see Native America

American South

see also Nashville Narratives; Southern Belles

Ain't No Way Back
Alligator Alley
Angel Baby
Angel City
As Summers Die
The Autobiography of Miss
 Jane Pittman▶
Baby Doll▶
Bad Georgia Road
The Ballad of the Sad Cafe
The Beguiled▶
Belizaire the Cajun
Between Heaven and Hell▶
Beulah Land
The Big Easy▶
Black Like Me
Blind Vengeance
Boxcar Bertha
Bucktown
Cape Fear▶
Cat on a Hot Tin Roof▶
Cat on a Hot Tin Roof
Chiefs
Cold Sassy Tree▶
The Color Purple▶
Dead Right
Delta Heat
The Displaced Person▶
Dixiana
Driving Miss Daisy▶
The Drowning Pool
Drum
Final Cut
Fire in the Night
Flamingo Road▶
Fletch Lives
Follow That Car
Foxfire▶
Fried Green Tomatoes▶
The Fugitive Kind
Gettysburg▶
The Ghost of Fletcher Ridge
The Girl from Tobacco Row
The Glass Menagerie▶
God's Little Acre▶
Gone with the Wind▶
The Great Santini▶
Hard Drivin'
Home from the Hill▶
Hooch
Hootch Country Boys
Hot Spell
Hunter's Blood
Hush, Hush, Sweet
 Charlotte▶
I Know Why the Caged Bird
 Sings▶
In a Shallow Grave
In the Heat of the Night▶
Intruder in the Dust▶
Invitation to a Gunfighter
Jezebel▶
Judge Horton and the
 Scottsboro Boys
Judge Priest▶
Kentucky Kernels

The Klansman
Lady for a Night
Lady from Louisiana
The Lash of the Penitents
The Life and Assassination of the Kingfish
A Lion is in the Streets
The Lords of Discipline
Louisiana
Louisiana Story▶
Macon County Line
Mandingo
Miss Firecracker▶
Mississippi Burning▶
Mississippi Masala▶
Moonshine Mountain
Morning Glory
Murder in Coweta County
The Murder of Mary Phagan▶
Murder on the Bayou▶
My Cousin Vinny▶
My Sweet Charlie
Mystery of the Riverboat
Netherworld
Norma Rae▶
North and South Book 1▶
North and South Book 2▶
Nothing But a Man
On the Run
On Valentine's Day
One False Move▶
Orpheus Descending
Outside Chance
Paradise▶
Paris Trout
Passion Fish▶
Perfect Harmony
Poor Pretty Eddie
Poor White Trash
Poor White Trash 2
The Prince of Tides▶
Psycho from Texas
Rambling Rose▶
A Real American Hero
Reflections in a Golden Eye
Return to Mayberry
Return to Two Moon Junction
Rich in Love
Riverbend
Road to Nashville
Roll of Thunder, Hear My Cry
Rooster: Spurs of Death!
Roots▶
Roots: The Next Generation▶
The Rose Tattoo▶
Ruby Gentry
Running Mates▶
Scorchers
Shag: The Movie▶
Shanty Tramp
Shy People▶
Sister, Sister
Sixteen
Smokey Bites the Dust
Snuffy Smith, Yard Bird
Sounder▶
Southern Comfort▶
The Southerner▶
Storyville
A Streetcar Named Desire▶
Summer and Smoke
The Supernaturals
Swamp Fire
Sweet Bird of Youth▶
Sweet Bird of Youth
Sweet Country Road
Tammy and the Bachelor
Tammy and the Doctor
Tank
Texasville
They Won't Forget▶
This Stuff'll Kill Ya!
A Tiger's Tale
To Kill a Mockingbird▶
The Trip to Bountiful▶
2000 Maniacs
Uncle Tom's Cabin
Uphill All the Way
Voodoo Dawn
Walk in the Spring Rain
Walking Tall
Walking Tall: Part 2

Walking Tall: The Final Chapter
What Comes Around
Where the Lilies Bloom▶
White Lie
The White Rose▶
Wildflower▶
Wise Blood▶
A Woman Called Moses

Amnesia

see also Identity
Anastasia▶
Anastasia: The Mystery of Anna
As You Desire Me▶
Blackout
The Bourne Identity▶
Clean Slate
Crack-Up
Dead Again▶
Diabolically Yours
Final Approach
The Great Dictator▶
Hellhole
I Love You Again▶
Jane Doe
Landslide
Lost Honeymoon
Memories of Murder
Mirage▶
Murder by Night
Overboard
Palombella Rossa
Regarding Henry▶
Return of the Soldier▶
Second Woman
The Sender
Shattered
Siesta
Someone Behind the Door
Spellbound▶
Strange Awakening
The Stranger▶
Summer's Children
Twice a Judas
Unholy Four

Amusement Parks

see also Carnivals & Circuses; Fairs & Expositions
The Beast from 20,000 Fathoms
Bebe's Kids
Beverly Hills Cop 3
Fatal Attraction▶
Funland
Godzilla on Monster Island
KISS Meets the Phantom of the Park
The Lady from Shanghai▶
Luv
My Life
National Lampoon's Vacation▶
Rollercoaster
Strangers on a Train▶
The Third Man▶

Angels

see also Heaven Sent
Always
Angels in the Outfield▶
Angels in the Outfield
The Bishop's Wife▶
Clarence
Date with an Angel
Defending Your Life▶
Faraway, So Close!
Fear No Evil
Field of Dreams▶
For Heaven's Sake
Forever Darling
Green Pastures▶
A Guy Named Joe
Heart and Souls
Heaven Can Wait▶
The Heavenly Kid
Here Comes Mr. Jordan▶
The Horn Blows at Midnight▶

I Married an Angel
It Came Upon a Midnight Clear
It's a Wonderful Life▶
The Kid with the Broken Halo
La Merveilleuse Visite
The Littlest Angel
Made in Heaven
One Magic Christmas
Two of a Kind
Waiting for the Light
Wings of Desire▶

Animals

see Birds; Cats; Horses; King of Beasts (Dogs); Wild Kingdom

Animated Musicals

see also Animation & Cartoons
Aladdin▶
All Dogs Go to Heaven
An American Tail
An American Tail: Fievel Goes West
Beauty and the Beast▶
Charlotte's Web
Cinderella▶
Gay Purr-ee
Jack & the Beanstalk
The Jungle Book▶
Lady and the Tramp▶
The Lion King▶
The Little Mermaid▶
The Magic Voyage
Pink Floyd: The Wall
Pinocchio▶
Robin Hood▶
Rock-a-Doodle
Rub a Dub Dub—There's a Zoo in This Tub!, Vol. 2
Shinbone Alley
Sleeping Beauty▶
Snow White and the Seven Dwarfs▶
Thumbelina
The Tune
Water Babies
Yellow Submarine▶
You're a Good Man, Charlie Brown

Animation & Cartoons

see also Animated Musicals
The Adventures of Ichabod and Mr. Toad▶
The Adventures of Mark Twain▶
Alakazam the Great!
Alice in Wonderland
Alice in Wonderland
Allegro Non Troppo▶
Animal Farm
Babar: The Movie
Baby Snakes: The Complete Version
Bambi▶
Batman: Mask of the Phantasm
Be My Valentine, Charlie Brown
Bebe's Kids
Best of Bugs Bunny & Friends
Bon Voyage, Charlie Brown▶
A Boy Named Charlie Brown▶
Bugs & Daffy: The Wartime Cartoons
Bugs Bunny: Hollywood Legend
The Bugs Bunny/Road Runner Movie
Bugs Bunny Superstar
Bugs Bunny's Comedy Classics
Bugs Bunny's 3rd Movie: 1,001 Rabbit Tales
Butterfly Ball

The Care Bears Movie
The Care Bears Movie 2: A New Generation
The Castle of Cagliostro
A Charlie Brown Celebration
A Charlie Brown Christmas
A Charlie Brown Thanksgiving
Charlie Brown's All-Stars
The Chipmunk Adventure
Chuck Amuck: The Movie
Cool World
The Cosmic Eye▶
Daffy Duck's Movie: Fantastic Island
Daffy Duck's Quackbusters
Disney's Storybook Classics
DuckTales the Movie: Treasure of the Lost Lamp
Dumbo▶
Evil Toons
Family Dog: Complete Series
Fantasia▶
Fantastic Planet▶
Felix the Cat: The Movie
Ferngully: The Last Rain Forest
Fire and Ice
Flight of Dragons
The Flintstones
The Fox and the Hound▶
Freddie as F.R.O.7
Fritz the Cat▶
Fun & Fancy Free
Good Grief, Charlie Brown
The Good, the Bad, and Huckleberry Hound
Grave of the Fireflies▶
The Great Mouse Detective▶
Grendel, Grendel, Grendel
Gulliver's Travels
Happily Ever After
Happy New Year, Charlie Brown
Harmagedon
Heavy Traffic▶
Here Come the Littles: The Movie
He's Your Dog, Charlie Brown!
Hey Good Lookin'
Hey There, It's Yogi Bear
The Hobbit▶
Hoppity Goes to Town
How the Grinch Stole Christmas▶
Huckleberry Finn
Hugo the Hippo
Is This Goodbye, Charlie Brown?
It Was a Short Summer, Charlie Brown
It's a Mystery, Charlie Brown
It's an Adventure, Charlie Brown!
It's Arbor Day, Charlie Brown
It's Flashbeagle, Charlie Brown/She's a Good Skate, Charlie Brown
It's Magic, Charlie Brown/Charlie Brown's All Star
It's the Great Pumpkin, Charlie Brown
It's Three Strikes, Charlie Brown
It's Your First Kiss, Charlie Brown/Someday You'll Find Her, Charlie Brown
The Jetsons Meet the Flintstones
Jetsons: The Movie
Journey Back to Oz
Journey to the Center of the Earth
The Land Before Time▶
The Land Before Time: The Great Valley Adventure
The Last Unicorn
The Legend of Sleepy Hollow
Lensman
Life is a Circus, Charlie Brown/You're the Greatest, Charlie Brown

Light Years
The Little Mermaid
Little Nemo: Adventures in Slumberland
Looney Looney Looney Bugs Bunny Movie▶
The Lord of the Rings
Lucky Luke: Daisy Town
Lucky Luke: The Ballad of the Daltons
Mad Monster Party
Man from Button Willow
Marco Polo, Jr.
Mickey's Christmas Carol▶
Mouse and His Child
My Little Pony: The Movie
The Nightmare Before Christmas▶
Nine Lives of Fritz the Cat
The Nutcracker Prince
The Old Curiosity Shop
Once Upon a Forest
Once Upon a Time
101 Dalmations▶
1001 Arabian Nights
Peter Pan▶
Pete's Dragon
Phantom Tollbooth▶
The Plague Dogs
Play It Again, Charlie Brown
Pogo for President: "I Go Pogo"
The Point
Pound Puppies and the Legend of Big Paw
The Princess and the Goblin
Project A-ko
Race for Your Life, Charlie Brown
Raggedy Ann and Andy: A Musical Adventure
The Reluctant Dragon
The Rescuers▶
The Rescuers Down Under
The Return of Jafar
Return of the Dinosaurs
The Return of the King
Rock & Rule
Rover Dangerfield
Rudolph & Frosty's Christmas in July
Rudolph the Red-Nosed Reindeer
Santa Claus is Coming to Town
Scruffy
Sea Prince and the Fire Child
The Secret of NIMH▶
Shame of the Jungle
She Likes You, Charlie Brown
Shelley Duvall's Bedtime Stories
Sherlock Hound: Tales of Mystery
She's a Good Skate, Charlie Brown
Sinbad and the Eye of the Tiger
Snoopy, Come Home▶
Snoopy's Getting Married, Charlie Brown
Someday You'll Find Her, Charlie Brown
Starchaser: The Legend of Orin
Starvengers
Streetfight
The Sword in the Stone▶
There's No Time for Love, Charlie Brown
The Three Caballeros
Tiny Toon Adventures: How I Spent My Vacation▶
Tom and Jerry: The Movie
Tom Thumb
Transformers: The Movie
A Troll in Central Park
Twilight of the Cockroaches
Urotsukidoji 1: Legend of the Overfiend

Urotsukidoji 2: Legend of the Demon Womb
Vip, My Brother Superman
Watership Down
We're Back! A Dinosaur's Story
When the Wind Blows▶
A Wind Named Amnesia
Wizards
You're in Love, Charlie Brown

Anthology

see also Comedy Anthologies; Horror Anthologies; Serials
Actors and Sin
Akermania, Vol. 1▶
America at the Movies
American Tickler
Amore▶
Bad Girls in the Movies
The Best of Bogart▶
The Best of the Kids in the Hall
Bim/Dream of the Wild Horses
Black Sabbath▶
The Brighton Strangler/Before Dawn
The Busby Berkeley Disc
Buster Keaton Festival, Vol. 1
Buster Keaton Festival, Vol. 2
Camp Classics #1
Cannon Ball/Eyes Have It
The Cary Grant Collection
Cat's Eye
The Chaplin Revue
Charade
The Charlie Chan Collection
Charlie Chaplin Centennial Collection
Charlie Chaplin Festival
Charlie Chaplin's Keystone Comedies #5
Chasing Those Depression Blues
Comedy Classics
Comedy Classics of Mack Sennett and Hal Roach
Cord & Dischords/Naughty Nurse
Country Lovers, City Lovers
Dark Eyes▶
Dawn Rider/Frontier Horizon
The Deadliest Art: The Best of the Martial Arts Films
Deadtime Stories
The Decameron▶
Decameron Nights
The Devil Thumbs a Ride/ Having Wonderful Crime
Dr. Terror's House of Horrors
Duke: The Films of John Wayne
Early Cinema Vol. 1
Early Russian Cinema, Vol. 1: Beginnings
Early Russian Cinema, Vol. 2: Folklore & Legend
Early Russian Cinema, Vol. 3: Starewicz's Fantasies
Early Russian Cinema, Vol. 4: Provincial Variations
Early Russian Cinema, Vol. 5: Chardynin's Pushkin
Early Russian Cinema, Vol. 6: Class Distinctions
Early Russian Cinema, Vol. 7: Evgenii Bauer
Early Russian Cinema, Vol. 8: Iakov Protazanov
Early Russian Cinema, Vol. 9: High Society
Early Russian Cinema, Vol. 10: The End of an Era
Early Sound Films
Escapes
Eyes of Turpin Are Upon You!
Fallen Angels 1▶
Fallen Angels 2▶
Film House Fever
The First Movie Cowboy
Frightshow

From Beyond the Grave
Gene Autry Matinee Double Feature #1
Gene Autry Matinee Double Feature #2
Gene Autry Matinee Double Feature #3
The Great Train Robbery: Cinema Begins
Grit of the Girl Telegrapher/In the Switch Tower
Gun Smugglers/Hot Lead
Hitchcock Collection
Hotel Room
John Wayne Anthology: Star Packer/Lawless Range
Kaos▶
The Kid/Idle Class▶
Kino Pravda/Enthusiasm
Kurt Vonnegut's Monkey House
Kwaidan▶
Le Plaisir
Letters from My Windmill▶
Little Rascals, Book 4
The Little Theatre of Jean Renoir▶
Love in the City▶
Mack Sennett Comedies: Vol. 1
Mack Sennett Comedies: Vol. 2
Mania
Masque of the Red Death/ Premature Burial
Max
Mickey the Great
Monty Python Meets Beyond the Fringe
More American Graffiti
Mutant Video
Mystery of the Leaping Fish/ Chess Fever
Mystery Train▶
Night Gallery▶
Night on Earth▶
Nightmares
Once Upon a Midnight Scary
One Step Beyond
Paisan▶
Prison Stories: Women on the Inside▶
Pulp Fiction▶
Range Rider
Red Balloon/Occurrence at Owl Creek Bridge▶
Red Shoe Diaries 3: Another Woman's Lipstick
Red Shoe Diaries 4: Auto Erotica
Renegade Ranger/Scarlet River
Renoir Shorts▶
Riders of the Range/Storm Over Wyoming
Seven Deadly Sins▶
Sherlock's Rivals & Where's My Wife
Short Cuts▶
The Silent Mr. Sherlock Holmes
Six in Paris
Slacker▶
Sleazemania III: The Good, the Bad & the Sleazy
Smiling Madame Beudet/The Seashell and the Clergyman▶
Strange Tales
Strange Tales/Ray Bradbury Theatre
Strictly G.I.
Tales from the Crypt▶
Tales from the Crypt
Tales from the Darkside
Tales of the Unexpected
Tales That Witness Madness
Terrorgram
That's Dancing!
That's Entertainment
That's Entertainment, Part 2
That's Entertainment 3

Time for Murder
Tom Mix Compilation 1
Tom Mix Compilation 2
Tunes of Glory/Horse's Mouth
Twice-Told Tales▶
Twilight Zone: The Movie
The Unapproachable
The Uncanny
Vanishing Legion
Video Americana
Vietnam War Story 1
Vietnam War Story 2
Vietnam War Story 3
Western Double Feature 1: Wild Bill & Sunset Carson
Western Double Feature 3: Rogers & Allen
Western Double Feature 3: Rogers & Allen
Western Double Feature 4: Rogers & Evans
Western Double Feature 5: Rogers & Autry
Western Double Feature 5: Rogers & Trigger
Western Double Feature 6: Rogers & Trigger
Western Double Feature 7: Wild Bill & Crabbe
Western Double Feature 8: Hale & Carradine
Western Double Feature 9: LaRue & Beery
Western Double Feature 10: Roy, Dale, & Trigger
Western Double Feature 11
Western Double Feature 12
Western Double Feature 13
Western Double Feature 14
Western Double Feature 15
Western Double Feature 16
Western Double Feature 17
Western Double Feature 18
Western Double Feature 19
Western Double Feature 20
Western Double Feature 21
Western Double Feature 22
Western Double Feature 23
Western Double Feature 24
Western Double Feature 25
Woman of Paris/Sunnyside▶
Women & Men: In Love There Are No Rules
Women & Men: Stories of Seduction
Zero for Conduct/Taris/A Propos de Nice

Anti-Heroes

The Adventures of Robin Hood▶
Billy Jack
Bonnie & Clyde▶
Born Losers
Butch Cassidy and the Sundance Kid▶
The Dead Pool
Dirty Harry▶
Easy Rider▶
The Enforcer
Hero▶
In a Lonely Place▶
Magnum Force
Rebel Without a Cause▶
Robin Hood: Prince of Thieves
Sudden Impact
Thelma & Louise▶
The Trial of Billy Jack
Wisdom

Anti-War War Movies

see also Satire & Parody
All Quiet on the Western Front▶
All Quiet on the Western Front
Amazing Grace & Chuck
The Big Parade
Born on the Fourth of July▶
The Bridges at Toko-Ri▶
The Burmese Harp▶
Catch-22▶

Civilization▶
Come and See▶
Coming Home▶
Cup Final
Dr. Strangelove, or: How I Learned to Stop Worrying and Love the Bomb▶
Field of Honor
Fires on the Plain▶
Forbidden Games▶
The Four Horsemen of the Apocalypse▶
The Four Horsemen of the Apocalypse
Gallipoli▶
Glory▶
Grand Illusion▶
Hamburger Hill
Hell in the Pacific▶
Henry V▶
J'Accuse▶
Jud
The King of Hearts▶
Latino
Les Carabiniers▶
The Line
M*A*S*H▶
M*A*S*H: Goodbye, Farewell & Amen▶
Master of the World
Nurse Edith Cavell▶
Paths of Glory▶
Platoon▶
The Red Badge of Courage▶
San Demetrio, London
She Goes to War
The Steel Helmet▶
A Time to Love & a Time to Die
The Tin Drum▶
Torn Allegiance
Twilight's Last Gleaming
Veronico Cruz
Wackiest Ship in the Army
Westfront 1918▶
What Price Glory?▶
The Young Lions▶

Apartheid

see also Africa; Civil Rights
An African Dream
Bopha!▶
City of Blood
Come Back, Africa▶
Cry Freedom
Cry, the Beloved Country▶
A Dry White Season▶
Funeral for an Assassin
Mandela▶
Master Harold and the Boys▶
Place of Weeping
The Power of One
Sarafina!▶
The Wilby Conspiracy▶
A World Apart▶
A World of Strangers▶
Woza Albert!

Archaeology

see Big Digs

Art & Artists

The Adventures of Picasso
The Agony and the Ecstasy
All the Vermeers in New York▶
An American in Paris▶
Andrei Rublev▶
Artists and Models
Back in the USSR
Backbeat▶
The Belly of an Architect▶
Bergonzi Hand
Black Magic Woman
The Blue Light▶
Bluebeard
A Bucket of Blood▶
Camille Claudel▶
Canvas: The Fine Art of Crime
Caravaggio▶

Cauldron of Blood
Circle of Two
Color Me Blood Red
The Competition▶
Crucible of Terror
Dante's Inferno: Life of Dante Gabriel Rossetti
Death in Venice▶
Dishonored Lady
Driller Killer
Ebony Tower
Echoes
Edie in Ciao! Manhattan
Edvard Munch
Empty Canvas
Entre-Nous▶
Escapade in Florence
Et La Tenoresse?...Bordel!
Femme Fatale
Fleshtone
Framed
Frida
Gothic▶
Guitarras Lloren Guitarras
Haunted Summer
Headless Eyes
The Hideaways
The Horse's Mouth▶
Hot Touch
Hour of the Wolf▶
House of Horrors
House of Wax▶
Hullabaloo Over Georgie & Bonnie's Pictures
Hunger
The Hypothesis of the Stolen Painting
In the Land of the Owl Turds
I've Heard the Mermaids Singing▶
A Kink in the Picasso
La Belle Noiseuse▶
La Vie de Boheme▶
The Life of Emile Zola▶
Little Noises
Lust for Life▶
Mahler▶
Men...▶
Milo Milo
Mistral's Daughter
The Moderns▶
Modigliani
The Moon and Sixpence▶
Morgan!
Moulin Rouge▶
Murder by Numbers
The Naked Maja
New York Stories▶
The Object of Beauty▶
Paint It Black
Portrait in Terror
Portrait of Grandpa Doc
Portrait of Jennie▶
Prick Up Your Ears▶
Pucker Up and Bark Like a Dog
A Question of Attribution
Rembrandt▶
Rembrandt—1669
Retribution
Salut l'Artiste▶
The Sandpiper
Savage Messiah▶
Scenario du Film Passion▶
Scream, Baby, Scream
The Seventh Veil▶
Sheer Madness▶
Shifting Sands
The Silver Chalice
Sirens▶
Slaves of New York
Stars and Bars
Still Life
Strange Fruit
A Sunday in the Country▶
Sunday in the Park with George▶
Superstar: The Life and Times of Andy Warhol▶
Tainted Image
The Testament of Orpheus▶
Track of the Vampire

Trespasser
Trust Me
Tunes of Glory/Horse's Mouth
The Two Mrs. Carrolls
Utamaro and His Five Women
Utz
Van Gogh▶
Victimless Crimes
Video Americana
Vincent & Theo▶
Vincent: The Life and Death of Vincent van Gogh▶
The Wolf at the Door
The World of Suzie Wong

Asia

see also China
China White
Emmanuelle
Emmanuelle in Bangkok
Emmanuelle, the Joys of a Woman
Escape to Burma
Far East
Flight from Singapore
Flower Drum Song
The Golden Triangle
Inn of Temptation
Jakarta
The Kill
The Killing Beach
Little Buddha
Lost Horizon▶
Love is a Many-Splendored Thing
Malaya
The Man with the Golden Gun
The Mongols
Red Dust▶
The Sand Pebbles▶
The Scent of Green Papaya▶
Shadow of China▶
Shanghai Surprise
Shocking Asia
The 13th Mission
Tigershark
The Two Great Cavaliers
The Ugly American
White Ghost

Asian America

Chan is Missing▶
Combination Platter
Come See the Paradise▶
Dim Sum: A Little Bit of Heart▶
Eat a Bowl of Tea▶
Golden Gate
The Joy Luck Club▶
The Wedding Banquet▶

Assassinations

see also Camelot (New); Foreign Intrigue; Hit Men; Spies & Espionage
Abraham Lincoln
Ace of Hearts
Act of Vengeance
An Affair in Mind
African Rage
The American Friend▶
The American Soldier
Antonio Das Mortes
The Arab Conspiracy
Ashes and Diamonds▶
Assassination
The Assassination Bureau▶
The Assignment
Belfast Assassin
Black Sunday
Brass Target
Brother Orchid▶
The Brotherhood of the Rose
Cal▶
Center of the Web
The Clockmaker▶
Cold Front
Coming Out Alive
Dagger Eyes
Dangerous Pursuit
The Day of the Dolphin

The Day of the Jackal▶
The Day that Shook the World
Deadly Exposure
Death Force
The Destructors
Diamond Run
The Dirty Dozen: The Next Mission
Disappearance
The Domino Principle
The Eagle Has Landed▶
Emmanuelle, the Queen
Enigma
Equalizer 2000
The Evil That Men Do
Executive Action
F/X▶
Fatal Justice
Flirting with Fate▶
Foul Play▶
Friday Foster
From Russia with Love▶
Funeral for an Assassin
Godson▶
Hard Way
Harum Scarum
Hit Lady
I Spit on Your Corpse
In the Line of Fire▶
Invitation to a Gunfighter
JFK▶
John F. Kennedy
Judgment Night
Kill Castro
The Killer Elite
Killer Likes Candy
The Killing Device
King Richard and the Crusaders
Kung Fu Terminator
La Femme Nikita▶
La Passante▶
Love and Anarchy▶
Love Kills
Loves & Times of Scaramouche
Malcolm X▶
The Man Who Knew Too Much▶
The Man Who Knew Too Much
The Man with the Golden Gun
The Manchurian Candidate▶
Maniac
Mark of the Beast
The Mercenaries
Murder of a Moderate Man
Night of the Assassin
Ninja Death Squad
Nowhere to Hide
The Odd Job
Omar Khayyam
One Man Out
Operation C.I.A.
The Ordeal of Dr. Mudd▶
Parallax View▶
Paris Belongs to Us
Point of No Return
Programmed to Kill
PT 109
Quicker Than the Eye
Quiet Thunder
Red King, White Knight
Red Scorpion
Revenge of the Pink Panther
Ruby
Running Against Time
Russian Roulette
Scorpio
Stalking Danger
State of Siege▶
Steele's Law
Target: Favorite Son
The Terminator▶
This Gun for Hire
Times of Harvey Milk
Two Minute Warning
Wardogs
What a Way to Die
When Hell Broke Loose
Windmills of the Gods
Winter Kills▶

Without Warning: The James Brady Story▶
Yojimbo▶
Z▶

Astronomy & Astrology

see Star Gazing

At the Movies

see also Behind the Scenes
Anguish
Cinema Paradiso▶
Come See the Paradise▶
Dangerous Game
Dead End Drive-In
Demons
Last Action Hero
The Long Day Closes▶
Matinee
Midnight Movie Massacre
The Movie House Massacre
One Summer Love
The Player▶
Popcorn
The Projectionist▶
The Purple Rose of Cairo▶
Rorret▶
Something Short of Paradise
The Stunt Man▶
Sullivan's Travels▶

Australia

see Down Under

Automobiles

see Fast Cars; Motor Vehicle Dept.

Avant-Garde

All Screwed Up▶
Angel City
Anita, Dances of Vice
Aria
Band of Outsiders
Bell Diamond
Bim/Dream of the Wild Horses
Blonde Cobra/The Doctor's Dream
The Blood of a Poet
The Boxer and Death▶
Boy Meets Girl▶
Breathless▶
Caligari's Cure▶
Careful
Cave Girls
Chameleon
Complex
Corrida Interdite
The Cosmic Eye▶
David Holzman's Diary▶
Death of the Rat
Diamonds of the Night▶
Dr. Caligari
Dog Star Man▶
Dreamwood▶
Empty Suitcases
Entr'acte
Eraserhead▶
False Note
Fat and the Lean▶
Films by Peter Thompson
The Foreigner
France/Tour/Detour/Deux/Enfants▶
Godard/Truffaut Shorts
Hiroshima, Mon Amour▶
The Hypothesis of the Stolen Painting
Italianamerican/The Big Shave
Journeys from Berlin/1971
The Joy of Knowledge
Koyaanisqatsi▶
The Last Movie
The Last of England▶
Les Carabiniers▶
Liquid Sky▶
Lola▶

A Man, a Woman and a Killer
The Man Who Envied Women
Mere Jeevan Saathi
Mixed Blood
My Neighborhood
News from Home
Notes for an African Orestes
Numero Deux
An Occurrence at Owl Creek Bridge▶
Offnight
Paul Bartel's The Secret Cinema
Peril
Periphery
Permanent Vacation
Phantom of Liberty▶
Powaqqatsi: Life in Transformation▶
Renoir Shorts▶
The Report on the Party and the Guests▶
Repulsion▶
Rome '78
Sans Soleil▶
Santa Sangre▶
Scenario du Film Passion▶
Scherzo
Seduction of Mimi▶
Sherman's March: An Improbable Search for Love
Shoot Loud, Louder, I Don't Understand!
Signals Through the Flames▶
Six Fois Deux/Sur et Sous la Communication▶
Smiling Madame Beudet/The Seashell and the Clergyman▶
Soft and Hard
Sometimes It Works, Sometimes It Doesn't
Strong Medicine
The Testament of Dr. Cordelier▶
The Testament of Orpheus▶
The Thrill Killers
Time Indefinite
Two Men & a Wardrobe
Un Chien Andalou
Underground U.S.A.
Veronika Voss▶
Video Americana
Wild at Heart▶
WR: Mysteries of the Organism▶
You are Not I
A Zed & Two Noughts▶

Babysitting

see also Bringing Up Baby; Parenthood
Addams Family Values
Adventures in Babysitting
Are You in the House Alone?
The Babysitter
Battling for Baby
Bebe's Kids
Don't Bother to Knock
Fright
A Global Affair
The Guardian
The Hand that Rocks the Cradle
Laurel & Hardy: Brats
Look Who's Talking▶
Midnight's Child
Mr. Nanny
My Daughter's Keeper
Perfect Family
Three's Trouble
Uncle Buck▶
Wanted: Babysitter
Weekend with the Babysitter
When a Stranger Calls
When a Stranger Calls Back

Bad Dads

see also Monster Moms; Parenthood
The Attic

Beatrice▶
First Born
Flesh and Bone▶
The Great Santini▶
Kiss Daddy Goodbye
Kiss Daddy Goodnight
Parents▶
The Shining
The Stepfather▶
Stepfather 2: Make Room for Daddy
Stepfather 3: Father's Day

Ballet

see also Dance Fever
The Bacchantes
Black Tights
Body Beat
Brain Donors
Carmen▶
The Children of Theatre Street▶
Cowboy & the Ballerina
Dance
Dancers
George Balanchine's The Nutcracker
Le Bourgeois Gentilhomme
Limelight▶
Little Ballerina
Mirrors
Never Let Me Go
Nijinsky
Nutcracker Sweet
Nutcracker: The Motion Picture
The Red Shoes▶
Shadow Dancing▶
Shall We Dance▶
Spectre of the Rose
Suspiria▶
Tales of Beatrix Potter▶
The Tales of Hoffmann
The Turning Point
Waterloo Bridge▶

Ballooning

Around the World in 80 Days▶
The Balloonatic/One Week
Charlie and the Great Balloon Chase
Fantastic Balloon Voyage
Five Weeks in a Balloon
Flight of the Eagle
Frankenstein Island
Lost Zeppelin
Mysterious Island▶
Night Crossing
Olly Olly Oxen Free
The Red Balloon▶
Voyage en Balloon

Baseball

Amazing Grace & Chuck
Angels in the Outfield▶
Angels in the Outfield
The Babe
Babe Ruth Story
The Bad News Bears▶
The Bad News Bears Go to Japan
The Bad News Bears in Breaking Training
Bang the Drum Slowly
Bang the Drum Slowly▶
Battling Orioles
Big Mo
Bingo Long Traveling All-Stars & Motor Kings▶
Blood Games
Blue Skies Again
Brewster's Millions
Bull Durham▶
The Busher
Casey at the Bat
Charlie Brown's All-Stars
Chasing Dreams
Chu Chu & the Philly Flash
Comeback Kid
The Comrades of Summer
Cooperstown

Damn Yankees▶
Don't Look Back: The Story of Leroy "Satchel" Paige
Eight Men Out▶
Fear Strikes Out▶
Field of Dreams▶
Heading Home
Ironweed▶
It Happens Every Spring▶
It's Arbor Day, Charlie Brown
It's Good to Be Alive
It's My Turn
The Jackie Robinson Story▶
Jim Thorpe: All American
The Kid from Left Field
A League of Their Own▶
Little Big League
Long Gone
Love Affair: The Eleanor & Lou Gehrig Story▶
Major League
Major League 2
Mr. Baseball
Mr. Destiny
The Natural▶
Night Game
One in a Million: The Ron LaFlore Story
Pastime▶
Pride of St. Louis
The Pride of the Yankees▶
Rookie of the Year
The Sandlot▶
The Scout▶
The Slugger's Wife
Squeeze Play
Stealing Home
The Stratton Story▶
Take Me Out to the Ball Game
Taking Care of Business
Talent for the Game
Tiger Town
Timothy and the Angel
Trading Hearts
Wait Until Spring, Bandini
Whistling in Brooklyn
A Winner Never Quits
The Winning Team
Woman of the Year▶
Workin' for Peanuts

Basketball
Above the Rim
The Absent-Minded Professor▶
The Air Up There
Blue Chips
Coach
Cornbread, Earl & Me
Fast Break
Final Shot: The Hank Gathers Story
The Fish that Saved Pittsburgh
For Heaven's Sake
Heaven is a Playground
Hoosiers▶
Inside Moves
One on One
Pistol: The Birth of a Legend
Tall Story
Teen Wolf
That Championship Season
White Men Can't Jump
The White Shadow, Vol. 1

Beach Blanket Bingo
see also Surfing; Swimming
Back to the Beach
Beach Blanket Bingo▶
Beach Girls
The Beach Girls and the Monster
Beach House
Beach Party
Bikini Beach
Bikini Summer
Body Waves
California Dreaming
Computer Beach Party

Horror of Party Beach
How to Stuff a Wild Bikini
Malibu Beach
Muscle Beach Party
Pajama Party
Ride the Wild Surf
Seaside Swingers
Shag: The Movie▶
Surf Party
A Swingin' Summer
Where the Boys Are

Behind Bars
see Great Escapes; Men in Prison; Women in Prison

Behind the Scenes
see also At the Movies; Film & Film History
Actors and Sin
The Affairs of Annabel
Bela Lugosi Scrapbook
Bellissimo: Images of the Italian Cinema
Best Friends
The Big Knife▶
Big Show
Body Chemistry 3: Point of Seduction
The Bodyguard
Bombay Talkie
Boy Meets Girl▶
Broadway Rhythm
Bugs Bunny Superstar
Buster Keaton Rides Again/ The Railrodder
Carny▶
Chaplin▶
The Chaplin Revue
A Chorus Line
A Chorus of Disapproval
Chuck Berry: Hail! Hail! Rock 'n' Roll▶
Contempt▶
Crossover Dreams
Dames▶
Dance of Life
Dancing Lady
Dangerous Game
The Death Kiss
Delirious
Double Threat
Dracula: A Cinematic Scrapbook
The Dresser▶
Elvis on Tour
Epic That Never Was
Face the Music
Fangoria's Weekend of Horrors
Footlight Parade▶
Frankenstein: A Cinematic Scrapbook
Free and Easy
The Freeway Maniac
The French Lieutenant's Woman▶
The Ghost Walks
Give a Girl a Break
Going Hollywood▶
The Goldwyn Follies
Goodbye, Norma Jean
Goodnight, Sweet Marilyn
Grunt! The Wrestling Movie
The Hard Way▶
He Said, She Said
The Hearst and Davies Affair
Hearts of Darkness: A Filmmaker's Apocalypse▶
Help!▶
Hollywood Boulevard
Hollywood Man
Hollywood Mystery
Hollywood Scandals and Tragedies
Hollywood Shuffle
Hooper
The Horror of It All
In a Moment of Passion
In the Soup

Inside Daisy Clover
Into the Sun
The Jayne Mansfield Story
Joey Breaker▶
The Killing of Sister George
La Dolce Vita▶
L.A. Goddess
Last Action Hero
Legs
The Lonely Lady
Make a Wish
The Making of "A Brief History of Time"
The Making of a Legend: "Gone With the Wind"
A Man in Love▶
Man of a Thousand Faces▶
Matinee
Miss All-American Beauty
Mistress
The Mozart Brothers▶
The Muppets Take Manhattan▶
Naked in New York
New Faces of 1952
A Night for Crime
Night of the Living Dead, 25th Anniversary Documentary
Noises Off
On an Island with You
Opening Night
Pastime▶
Pick a Star
The Pickle
The Player▶
The Purple Rose of Cairo▶
Roadie
Rorret▶
Sex is Crazy
Silent Motive
Sioux City Sue
S.O.B.
Stage Door▶
Stand-In
Star Trek 25th Anniversary Special
State of Things▶
Steve Martin Live
The Stunt Man▶
Stunts
Sullivan's Travels▶
Summer Stock▶
Sunset
Sunset Boulevard▶
Sweet Liberty
Sweet Perfection
Teenager
Tootsie▶
Truth or Dare
Under the Rainbow
Users
Valley of the Dolls
Velvet Touch▶
A Very Private Affair
The West Point Story
What Price Hollywood?▶
Whodunit
Zou Zou

Bicycling
American Flyers
BMX Bandits
Breaking Away▶
Off the Mark
Pee Wee's Big Adventure▶
Quicksilver
Rad
Rush It
Ten Speed

Big Battles
see also Civil War; Korean War; Korean War; Persian Gulf War; Revolutionary War; Vietnam War; World War I; World War II
The Alamo▶
Alexander Nevsky▶
Alexander the Great
Aliens▶

Anzio
Apocalypse Now▶
Arena
Back to Bataan
Barry Lyndon▶
Battle Beyond the Sun
Battle of Britain
The Battle of El Alamein
Battle of the Bulge
The Battle of the Japan Sea
Battle of the Worlds
Battleground▶
The Battleship Potemkin▶
Ben-Hur▶
The Big Parade▶
The Big Red One▶
The Birth of a Nation▶
A Bridge Too Far
Captain Caution
The Castilian
Cromwell
Cross of Iron
Das Boot▶
Diamonds are Forever▶
Dragonslayer▶
El Cid▶
The Empire Strikes Back▶
Enemy Below▶
Excalibur▶
The Fall of the Roman Empire▶
The Fighting Sullivans▶
Gallipoli▶
Gettysburg▶
The Giant of Marathon
Giants of Rome
Gladiators 7
Glory▶
Godzilla vs. the Smog Monster
Goldfinger▶
The Guns of Navarone▶
Heaven & Earth▶
Henry V▶
Highlander▶
John Paul Jones
The King of the Kickboxers
The Last Command
The Lighthorsemen▶
The Long Riders▶
The Longest Day▶
The Man Who Would Be King▶
Memphis Belle▶
Midway
The Mongols
Monty Python and the Holy Grail▶
Moonraker
Motel Hell
Naked Warriors
A Nightmare on Elm Street
Patton▶
Raiders of the Lost Ark▶
Ran▶
Rawhide▶
Red Dawn
Return of the Jedi▶
Revolution
Ring of Fire
Robot Jox
Samson and His Mighty Challenge
The Sand Pebbles▶
Sands of Iwo Jima▶
The Siege of Firebase Gloria
The Silk Road
Son of the Morning Star▶
Star Crash
Star Wars▶
Street Hunter
Ten Days That Shook the World▶
They Died with Their Boots On▶
Thunderball
To Hell and Back
Tora! Tora! Tora!
Twelve O'Clock High▶
War and Peace
War and Peace▶
The War Lord▶

The Wild Bunch▶
Zulu
Zulu Dawn▶

Big Budget Stinkers
see also Pure Ego Vehicles
The Adventurers
Alexander the Great
American Anthem
Annie
Christopher Columbus: The Discovery
Cleopatra
The Conqueror
The Cotton Club▶
Dune
Harlem Nights
Heaven's Gate
Howard the Duck
Hudson Hawk
I'll Do Anything
Ishtar
Last Action Hero
Midway
Moon in the Gutter
1941
One from the Heart
Pirates
Rambo 3
Santa Claus: The Movie
The Shoes of the Fisherman
The Silver Chalice
Summer Holiday
Supergirl
Tora! Tora! Tora!
Two Minute Warning
Two of a Kind
Waterloo

Big Daddies
see also American South
All the King's Men▶
Big Country
Cat on a Hot Tin Roof▶
Cat on a Hot Tin Roof
Fire in the Night
The Great Santini▶
The Learning Tree
The Long, Hot Summer▶
Man of Evil
Other People's Money
Papa's Delicate Condition▶
The Paper Chase▶
A Piece of Pleasure▶
Running Mates▶
Smokey Bites the Dust
Sons of Hercules in the Land of Darkness
Stay As You Are
Sweet Bird of Youth▶
This Property is Condemned
Touch of Evil▶
Vultures
Where the Heart Is

Big Digs
The Curse of King Tut's Tomb
Deadly Intent
The Golden Salamander
Indiana Jones and the Last Crusade▶
Indiana Jones and the Temple of Doom▶
King of the Forest Rangers
March or Die
The Mask
The Mole People
The Mummy▶
The Mummy's Hand
Pimpernel Smith
Raiders of the Lost Ark▶
Search for the Gods
The Serpent of Death
Sound of Horror
Specters
Tomb
The Word

Big Ideas

see also Ethics & Morals

Barefoot in Athens
Being Human
Blaise Pascal▶
Blue
Faraway, So Close!
The Incredible Shrinking
 Man▶
Jonathan Livingston Seagull
Judgment at Nuremberg▶
Meetings with Remarkable
 Men
The Messiah▶
Metropolitan▶
Mr. North
My Dinner with Andre▶
1900▶
The Occult Experience
The Razor's Edge▶
The Razor's Edge
Return to Eden
Samurai 3: Duel at Ganryu
 Island▶
Sans Soleil▶
The Seventh Seal▶
Sorceress▶
The Wrong Move
Zabriskie Point▶

Bigfoot/Yeti

Big Foot
The Capture of Bigfoot
Half Human
Harry and the Hendersons
Legend of Big Foot
Legend of Boggy Creek
Man Beast
Night of the Demon
Night of the Howling Beast
Return to Boggy Creek
Sasquatch
The Snow Creature
Snowbeast

Bikers

The Acid Eaters
Adventures Beyond Belief
Angels Die Hard
Angels from Hell
Angels Hard as They Come
Angels' Wild Women
Beach Party
Black Bikers from Hell
Blonde in Black Leather
Born Losers
Born to Ride
Breaking Loose
Bury Me an Angel
Chopper Chicks in
 Zombietown
Chrome and Hot Leather
Chrome Hearts
Chrome Soldiers
City Limits
Cleopatra Jones
Club Life
Crossing the Line
Cycle Psycho
Cycle Vixens
Cyclone
Danger Zone
Danger Zone 2
Danger Zone 3: Steel Horse
 War
Dark Rider
Darktown Strutters
Deadly Reactor
Devil's Angels
Dirt Bike Kid
Dirt Gang
Easy Rider▶
Easy Wheels
Easyriders Video Magazine
Eat the Peach
Electra Glide in Blue▶
Evel Knievel
Every Which Way But Loose
Eye of the Tiger
The Final Alliance
The Girl on a Motorcycle

The Glory Stompers
Go for Broke
The Great Escape▶
Great Ride
The Great Skycopter Rescue
Greedy Terror
Harley
Harley Davidson and the
 Marlboro Man
Hellcats
Hellriders
Hell's Angels Forever
Hell's Angels on Wheels
Hell's Angels '69
Hog Wild
Hollywood Chaos
In Your Face
Iron Horsemen
The Jesus Trip
Knightriders
Loners
The Losers
Loveless
Mad Max▶
Mask▶
The Masters of Menace
Master's Revenge
Motor Psycho
Motorcycle Gang
The Naked Angels
Nam Angels
Nomad Riders
Northville Cemetery Massacre
The Only Way Home
The Outlaw Bikers—Gang
 Wars
Outlaw Riders
Peacekillers
Pray for the Wildcats
Psychomania
Punk Vacation
Race for Glory
Raising Arizona▶
Raw Courage
Rebel Rousers
Return of the Rebels
Riding High
Riding the Edge
Roadside Prophets
Run, Angel, Run!
Running Cool
Satan's Sadists
Savage Dawn
The Savage Seven
Savages from Hell
Shame
She-Devils on Wheels
The Shrieking
Sidewinder One
Silver Dream Racer
Sinner's Blood
Space Riders
Spetters
Stone Cold
Street Hawk
Streets of Fire
Survival Zone
Timerider
Timothy and the Angel
Viva Knievel
Warlords from Hell
Werewolves on Wheels
The Wild Angels
Wild Guitar
The Wild One▶
Wild Rebels
Wild Riders
Wild Wheels
Winners Take All

Biography

see This is Your Life

Birds

Beaks: The Movie
Bill and Coo
Birdman of Alcatraz▶
The Birds▶
Blade Master
A Breed Apart
Brewster McCloud▶

Cockfighter▶
Continental Divide
El Gallo de Oro
The Giant Claw
The Goodbye Bird
High Anxiety
Howard the Duck
Mating Season
Million Dollar Duck
No Fear, No Die
Rooster: Spurs of Death!
Sesame Street Presents:
 Follow That Bird
Spirit of the Eagle
Vulture

Bisexuality

see also Homosexuality

Basic Instinct
California Suite▶
The Crying Game▶
Dog Day Afternoon▶
Dona Herlinda & Her Son
Happily Ever After
Les Biches▶
Liquid Sky▶
Mary, Mary, Bloody Mary
Three of Hearts
Threesome
A Woman in Flames▶

Black Comedy

*see also Comedy; Comedy
 Drama; Satire & Parody*

Abigail's Party
The Addams Family
Addams Family Values
After Hours▶
Age Isn't Everything
Alberto Express
Alice▶
All Over Town
Alone in the T-Shirt Zone
The Americanization of
 Emily▶
America's Deadliest Home
 Video
Angels Over Broadway▶
The Applegates
Ariel▶
Army Brats
Arnold
Arrivederci, Baby!
Arsenic and Old Lace▶
The Assassination Bureau▶
The Atomic Kid
Baby Face Morgan
Baby Love
Bad Charleston Charlie
Bare Hunt
Barjo
Barton Fink▶
Battle of the Bullies
Beat the Devil▶
Bizarre Bizarre▶
Bliss▶
Brazil▶
Brewster McCloud▶
Buddy Buddy
Buffet Froid▶
Canadian Bacon
Careful
The Cars That Ate Paris▶
Catch-22▶
Checking Out
Choice of Weapons
The Choirboys
The Comic▶
Consuming Passions
The Cook, the Thief, His Wife
 & Her Lover▶
Coup de Torchon▶
Crimes of the Heart
The Criminal Life of
 Archibaldo de la Cruz▶
The Dark Backward
A Day in the Death of Joe
 Egg▶
Death Becomes Her▶
Delicatessen▶

Divine
Don's Party▶
Eat the Rich
Eating Raoul▶
El: This Strange Passion▶
Ellie
The End▶
Enid is Sleeping
Entertaining Mr. Sloane
Exquisite Corpses
The Exterminating Angel▶
Female Trouble
A Fine Madness▶
The Firemen's Ball▶
A Fish Called Wanda▶
Four Bags Full
The 4th Man▶
Freaked
The Funeral▶
Funny, Dirty Little War
The Garden of Delights▶
Gas-s-s-s!
The Gazebo▶
Ghost Chase
The Gift
Goodbye Cruel World
Grace Quigley
The Great Madcap
Greetings!
Guilty as Charged
Harold and Maude▶
Hawks
Heart Condition
Heathers▶
Hexed
Hi, Mom!▶
High Heels
High Heels▶
Highway 61
Hold Me, Thrill Me, Kiss Me
Homebodies
The Honey Pot
The Hospital▶
The Hot Rock▶
How to Get Ahead in
 Advertising▶
The Hudsucker Proxy▶
Husbands, Wives, Money, and
 Murder
I Love You to Death
I Ought to Be in Pictures
Infernal Trio
Into the Night
The Killing of Sister George
Kind Hearts and Coronets▶
King of Comedy▶
King, Queen, Knave▶
Ladykillers▶
Leolo
Life is Sweet▶
Little Murders▶
Loot...Give Me Money, Honey!
The Loved One▶
Lucky Stiff
L'Udienza
Mad Dog and Glory▶
Man Bites Dog▶
Matador
A Matter of WHO
Max, Mon Amour
Miracle Mile▶
Mixed Blood
Mondo Balardo
Monsieur Verdoux▶
Montenegro▶
Mortuary Academy
Mother, Jugs and Speed
Murphy's Fault
My New Gun
Mystery Train▶
No Problem
No Surrender▶
Nuts in May
O Lucky Man!▶
The Oak
The Odd Job
Oh Dad, Poor Dad (Momma's
 Hung You in the Closet &
 I'm Feeling So Sad)
Out Cold
Pain in the A——▶
Parents▶

Passed Away
Paul Bartel's The Secret
 Cinema
Penn and Teller Get Killed
The Pornographers▶
Private Parts
Pulp Fiction▶
Raising Arizona▶
Red Earth
The Ref▶
Repo Man▶
Reuben, Reuben▶
Riff Raff▶
Rubin & Ed
Salvation!
The Scent of a Woman
Serial Mom▶
Seven Beauties▶
Shadey
Shakes the Clown
She-Devil
Shoot Loud, Louder, I Don't
 Understand!
Sinful Life
So I Married an Axe Murderer
Some Girls
Something for Everyone
Something Wild
Stars and Bars
The Steagle
Sticky Fingers
The Story of Fausta
Sweet Movie
Tatie Danielle▶
That Obscure Object of
 Desire▶
There was a Crooked Man▶
Throw Momma from the
 Train▶
Tie Me Up! Tie Me Down!
To Be or Not to Be▶
Toto le Heros▶
Transylvania Twist
Trois Couleurs: Blanc▶
The Unbelievable Truth
Unexplained Laughter
Vampire's Kiss▶
The War of the Roses▶
What Have I Done to Deserve
 This?▶
Where's Piccone▶
Where's Poppa?▶
Who is Killing the Great Chefs
 of Europe?▶
Why Does Herr R. Run
 Amok?
Wilder Napalm
Wise Guys
The Witches of Eastwick▶
Withnail and I▶
Women on the Verge of a
 Nervous Breakdown▶
World of the Depraved
The Wrong Box▶

Black Gold

The Abyss▶
Black Gold
Blowing Wild
Boom Town
Comes a Horseman
Country Gentlemen
Dead Ahead: The Exxon
 Valdez Disaster▶
Devil's Crude
The Dive
Double Deal
Fighting Texans
Five Easy Pieces▶
The Formula
Gas Pump Girls
Giant▶
The Guns and the Fury
Hellfighters
Intruder Within
Legend of Frenchie King
Local Hero▶
Louisiana Story▶
The Madwoman of Chaillot
Mission in Morocco
Naked Gun 2 1/2: The Smell
 of Fear

'Neath the Arizona Skies
Oceans of Fire
Oklahoma Crude
On Deadly Ground
Red Rock West▶
Roughnecks
Thunder Bay▶
Tulsa▶
Waltz Across Texas
War of the Wildcats
Wildcat
Written on the Wind▶

Blaxploitation

see also African America;
New Black Cinema
Black Vampire
Black Werewolf
Blackenstein
Blacula
Dr. Black, Mr. Hyde
The House on Skull Mountain
No Way Back
Scream Blacula Scream

Blindness

see also Physical
Problems
Afraid of the Dark
Against the Drunken Cat
  Paws
Alligator Eyes
Amy
Ballad in Blue
Blackout
Blind Fear
Blind Man's Bluff
Blind Witness
Blink
Butterflies Are Free▶
Cactus
Can You Feel Me Dancing?
City for Conquest▶
City Lights▶
Don't Look Now▶
Eight Witnesses
Eighteen Jade Arhats
Elmer
Eye on the Sparrow
The Human Monster
Ice Castles
If You Could See What I Hear
Jennifer 8
The Killer▶
La Symphonie Pastorale▶
Last Game
Life on a String
Love at First Sight
Love Leads the Way
Marianela
Minnesota Clay
The Miracle Worker▶
Night Gallery▶
Night Is My Future
Octavia
On Dangerous Ground▶
Ordinary Heroes
A Patch of Blue
People Who Own the Dark
Places in the Heart▶
Proof▶
Return of the Evil Dead
The Scent of a Woman
Scent of a Woman▶
See No Evil▶
See No Evil, Hear No Evil
They Watch
To Race the Wind
Until The End of The World▶
Wait Until Dark▶
The Whales of August▶
Zertigo Diamond Caper

Bloody Mayhem

see also Horror
Alien▶
Alien 3
Anguish
Army of Darkness▶
Aroused
The Art of Dying▶

At Midnight, I'll Take Your
  Soul
The Avenger
The Awful Dr. Orlof
Baby Cart 4: Heart of a
  Parent...Heart of a Child
Bad Blood
Bad Dreams
Ballbuster
The Banker
Barn of the Naked Dead
Basket Case▶
Basket Case 2
Basket Case 3: The Progeny
Beast of the Yellow Night
Between God, the Devil & a
  Winchester
Big Meat Eater
Bits and Pieces
Black Christmas
Black Shampoo
Blade of the Ripper
Blood and Black Lace
Blood Bride
Blood Cult
Blood Diner
Blood Feast
Blood Lake
Blood Legacy
Blood Mania
Blood of Ghastly Horror
Blood Orgy of the She-Devils
Blood Screams
Blood Sisters
Blood Tide
Blood Tracks
Bloodbath in Psycho Town
Bloodshed
Bloodstalkers
Bloody Birthday
Bloody Mama
The Bloody Tattoo
Body Count
Body Parts
The Body Shop
The Borrower
The Boys Next Door
The Brainiac
The Brides of Dracula
Bring Me the Head of Alfredo
  Garcia
Brothers in Arms
Brujo Luna
Burial Ground
Buried Alive
Cannibal Campout
Cardiac Arrest
Carnage
Carnival of Blood
The Carpathian Eagle
Carrie▶
Castle of the Creeping Flesh
Cataclysm
Challenge
The Channeler
Cheerleader Camp
Children of the Corn 2: The
  Final Sacrifice
Child's Play
Child's Play 2
Child's Play 3
Chopping Mall
C.H.U.D.
The Church▶
Circus of Horrors
City of the Walking Dead
Cocaine Wars
Color Me Blood Red
The Corpse Vanishes
Crawlspace
Craze
Crazed
The Crazies
Cujo
Curfew
Curse of the Alpha Stone
Curse of the Screaming Dead
Cutting Class
Dangerous Game
The Dark Half
Dawn of the Dead▶
Day of Judgment

Day of the Dead
Dead Alive
Dead Girls
The Dead Next Door
Deadly Blessing
Deadly Dreams
Deadly Neighbor
Dear Dead Delilah
Death Magic
Death Promise
Death Screams
Death Spa
Deep Red: Hatchet Murders
Delirium
Dementia 13
The Demon
Demon Possessed
Demonic Toys
Demons
Demons 2
Deranged
Destroy All Monsters
Devastator
The Devil
Devil Rider
Dirty Harry▶
Doctor Butcher M.D.
Dr. Hackenstein
Dr. Jekyll's Dungeon of Death
Dogs of Hell
Dollman vs Demonic Toys
Dolls
Don't Go in the Woods
Doom Asylum
Dorm That Dripped Blood
Dracula vs. Frankenstein
Driller Killer
Drive-In Massacre
Eat and Run
Edge of the Axe
El Cuarto Chino
Encounter at Raven's Gate
Epitaph
The Evictors
Evil Clutch
Evil Dead
Evil Dead 2: Dead by Dawn
Evil Laugh
Evils of the Night
The Executioner
Exquisite Corpses
The Eye Creatures
Eyes of a Stranger
The Fan
Fatal Games
Fatal Pulse
The Fiend
Fiend Without a Face
Final Exam
The Final Terror
First Blood
The First Power
Flesh and Blood Show
Forbidden World
Forced Entry
The Forest
Forever Evil
Frankenstein '80
Freddy's Dead: The Final
  Nightmare
The Freeway Maniac
Friday the 13th
Friday the 13th, Part 2
Friday the 13th, Part 3
Friday the 13th, Part 4: The
  Final Chapter
Friday the 13th, Part 5: A New
  Beginning
Friday the 13th, Part 6: Jason
  Lives
Friday the 13th, Part 7: The
  New Blood
Friday the 13th, Part 8: Jason
  Takes Manhattan
Frightmare
Frozen Terror
The Funhouse
Gates of Hell
The Ghastly Ones
Ghoulies
Girly
Goblin

The Godfather, Part 3▶
The Gore-Gore Girls
Gore-Met Zombie Chef From
  Hell
Graduation Day
The Graveyard
Greedy Terror
Grim Reaper
Grotesque
Gruesome Twosome
Hack O'Lantern
Halloween▶
Halloween 2: The Nightmare
  Isn't Over!
Halloween 3: Season of the
  Witch
Halloween 4: The Return of
  Michael Myers
Halloween 5: The Revenge of
  Michael Myers
Hamburger Hill
He Knows You're Alone
Headless Eyes
Heartstopper
Hellcats
Hellmaster
Hello Mary Lou: Prom Night 2
Hellraiser 3: Hell on Earth
Helter Skelter
The Hidden▶
The Hidden 2
Hide and Go Shriek
Hitcher
Hollywood Chainsaw Hookers
The Hollywood Strangler
  Meets the Skid Row
  Slasher
The Horror Show
Hospital Massacre
Hospital of Terror
The House by the Cemetery
House of Death
House of Psychotic Women
House of Whipcord
House on the Edge of the
  Park
The House on Tombstone Hill
The House that Bled to Death
Howling 4: The Original
  Nightmare
Howling 5: The Rebirth
Howling 6: The Freaks
Humanoids from the Deep
Humongous
I, Claudius, Vol. 2: Waiting in
  the Wings/What Shall We
  Do With Claudius?
I, Claudius, Vol. 4: Queen of
  Heaven/Reign of Terror
I, Claudius, Vol. 5: Zeus, By
  Jove!/Hail Who?
I Come in Peace
I Drink Your Blood
I Eat Your Skin
I, Madman
I Spit on Your Grave
Icebox Murders
The Initiation
Innocent Blood
Intruder
Invasion of the Blood Farmers
Island of Blood
Jason Goes to Hell: The Final
  Friday
Junior
Keep My Grave Open
Kid
Killcrazy
The Killer Elite
Killer Workout
The Killing Game
L.A. Gangs Rising
The Last Horror Film
Last House on the Left
The Lawnmower Man
Leatherface: The Texas
  Chainsaw Massacre 3
The Legend of Blood Castle
Leprechaun
Leprechaun 2
Looker
Love Butcher

Lunatic
The Mad Butcher
The Mad Executioners
Madhouse
Madman
The Majorettes
Maniac
Maniac Cop 2
Maniac Cop 3
Maniac Warriors
Mardi Gras Massacre
Marked for Death
Martin▶
Masque of the Red Death
The Meateater
Midnight
Militant Eagle
Monster
Motel Hell
The Movie House Massacre
Murder-in-Law
Mutator
The Mutilator
My Bloody Valentine
Nail Gun Massacre
Naked Massacre
Neon Maniacs
Never Pick Up a Stranger
New York Ripper
Next of Kin
The Night Brings Charlie
Night of a Thousand Cats
Night of Bloody Horror
Night of the Bloody Apes
Night of the Bloody Transplant
Night of the Demons
Night of the Demons 2
Night of the Living Dead▶
Night of the Living Dead
Night of the Strangler
Night of the Zombies
Night Ripper
Night School
Night Screams
Night Warning
Nightmare
A Nightmare on Elm Street
A Nightmare on Elm Street 2:
  Freddy's Revenge
A Nightmare on Elm Street 3:
  Dream Warriors
A Nightmare on Elm Street 4:
  Dream Master
A Nightmare on Elm Street 5:
  Dream Child
Nightstalker
Noon Sunday
Offerings
The Offspring
Out Cold
Out of the Body
The Outing
Overexposed
Phantom of the Mall: Eric's
  Revenge
Pieces
Platoon Leader
Play Dead
Popcorn
Possession
Predator 2
The Prey
Prime Evil
Prom Night 4: Deliver Us From
  Evil
Psycho 3
Psycho from Texas
Psychopath
Pumpkinhead
Puppet Master 3: Toulon's
  Revenge
Puppet Master 4
The Pyx▶
Quiet Fire
Rabid Grannies
Rambo 3
Ran▶
The Rats are Coming! The
  Werewolves are Here!
The Re-Animator▶
Redneck Zombies
Rest In Pieces

Bloody

Return of the Aliens: The Deadly Spawn
Return of the Family Man
Return to Horror High
Revenge
The Ripper
Road Games
RoboCop 2
Rocktober Blood
Ruby
The Rue Morgue Massacres
The Samurai
Samurai Blood, Samurai Guts
Samurai Death Bells
Samurai Sword of Justice
S.A.S. San Salvador
Satan's Blade
Savage!
Scalpel
Scanners
Scanners 2: The New Order
Scanners 3: The Takeover
Scream, Baby, Scream
Scream Bloody Murder
Scream of the Demon Lover
Screamers
The Screaming Dead
Secret of Tai Chi
Seven Doors of Death
The Severed Arm
Shadowzone
Shakma
She Came on the Bus
Shock! Shock! Shock!
Shocker
The Silence of the Lambs▶
Silent Night, Deadly Night
Silent Night, Deadly Night 2
Silent Night, Deadly Night 3: Better Watch Out!
Silent Night, Deadly Night 4: Initiation
Silent Rage
Silk
The Slasher
Slaughter High
Slaughter Hotel
Slaughterhouse
The Slayer
The Slayer/The Scalps
Sleepaway Camp
Sleepaway Camp 2: Unhappy Campers
Sleepaway Camp 3: Teenage Wasteland
Slumber Party Massacre 2
Snow Kill
Society
Sometimes Aunt Martha Does Dreadful Things
Sorority House Massacre
Sorority House Massacre 2: Nighty Nightmare
Spare Parts
Splatter University
Split Second
Stagefright
Star Time
Steps from Hell
Stone Cold
Strait-Jacket
The Strangler
Stripped to Kill II: Live Girls
Stuff Stephanie in the Incinerator
Swamp of the Lost Monster
TC 2000
Tenement
Terminal Choice
Terror at Tenkiller
Terror on Tour
Terror Train
The Texas Chainsaw Massacre
Texas Chainsaw Massacre, Part 2
They're Playing with Fire
Thirst
Three on a Meathook
The Thrill Killers
The Toolbox Murders
Top of the Heap

Torment
Torture Chamber of Baron Blood
Torture Train
The Tower of London
Town that Dreaded Sundown
The Toxic Avenger
The Toxic Avenger, Part 2
Twin Peaks: Fire Walk with Me
Twisted Brain
Twitch of the Death Nerve
The Two Faces of Evil
2000 Maniacs
Underground Terror
Unmasked Part 25
The Unnamable
Unsane
The Unseen
Vengeance Is Mine
Vicious
The Video Dead
Video Violence
Video Violence Part 2...The Exploitation!
The Vineyard
Violent Blood Bath
Violent Women
Visiting Hours
The Visitor
Voodoo Black Exorcist
Walking Tall
Walking Tall: Part 2
Waxwork 2: Lost in Time
Welcome to Blood City
Welcome to Spring Break
When the Screaming Stops
The Wicked
The Wild Bunch▶
Witchboard
The Wizard of Gore
Woodchipper Massacre
Zero Boys
Zombie
Zombie Island Massacre
Zone of the Dead

Boating

see Sail Away

Bodyguards

Assassination
The Bodyguard
The Chase
Fatal Beauty
Genuine Risk
Guarding Tess
Half a Loaf of Kung Fu
Heat
In the Line of Fire▶
Man on Fire
Mr. Nanny
My Bodyguard▶
Pushed to the Limit
The Tsar's Bride▶

Books

Cross Creek
Crossing Delancey▶
84 Charing Cross Road▶
Falling in Love
I, Madman
The Joy Luck Club▶
La Lectrice
The NeverEnding Story▶
A Night to Remember▶
The Paper Chase▶
Priest of Love
Providence▶
QB VII▶
The Seven Year Itch▶

Boomer Reunions

see also Flower Children
The Big Chill▶
Indian Summer
Peter's Friends
Return of the Secaucus 7▶

Bowling

Dreamer
Grease 2
Mr. Wonderful

Boxing

Abbott & Costello Meet the Invisible Man▶
Any Which Way You Can
Arena
Back Roads
Battling Bunyon
Battling Butler
Belle of the Nineties
Best of the Best
The Big Man: Crossing the Line▶
Billyboy
Blue Ribbon Babes
Body and Soul▶
Body & Soul
Bowery Blitzkrieg
Boxcar Blues
The Boxer and Death▶
Breakdown
Brutal Glory
The Cage
The Champ▶
The Champ
Champion▶
Circle Man
City for Conquest▶
Confessions of Tom Harris
Counter Punch
Dempsey
Diggstown
Dynamite Dan
Fallen Champ: The Untold Story of Mike Tyson▶
Far and Away
Fat City▶
Fight for the Title
The Fighter▶
Fighting Champ
Firepower
Fist Fighter
Gentleman Jim▶
Gladiator
Golden Boy▶
Great Guy
The Great White Hope
The Greatest
Hard Times▶
The Harder They Fall▶
Heart
Heart of a Champion: The Ray Mancini Story
Here Comes Mr. Jordan▶
The Hitter
Hollywood Stadium Mystery
Homeboy
Honeyboy
The Joe Louis Story
Keep Punching
Kelly the Second
Kid Dynamite
Kid from Brooklyn
Kid Galahad▶
Kid Galahad
Killer's Kiss
La Corona de un Campeon
The Last Fight
Last Man Standing
The Main Event
Marciano
Matilda
Meatballs 2
Milky Way
Miracle Kid
Movie, Movie
Navy Way
Night and the City▶
Off Limits
On the Waterfront▶
One-Punch O'Day
The Opponent
Palooka
Penitentiary
Penitentiary 2
Penitentiary 3
The Power of One

Pride of the Bowery
Prison Shadows
Prize Fighter
The Prizefighter and the Lady▶
Pulp Fiction▶
The Quiet Man▶
Raging Bull▶
Requiem for a Heavyweight▶
Ricky 1
The Ring
Ringside
Rip Roarin' Buckaroo
Roaring City
Rocky▶
Rocky 2
Rocky 3
Rocky 4
Rocky 5
The Set-Up▶
Shaolin Vengence
Somebody Up There Likes Me▶
Spike of Bensonhurst
The Spirit of Youth
Split Decisions
The Sting 2
Street Crimes
Streets of Gold
Teen Wolf Too
They Made Me a Criminal
They Never Come Back
Thunderground
Title Shot
Tough Enough
Tough Kid
Triumph of the Spirit▶
Vigilantes of Boom Town
The Warrior
When's Your Birthday?

Bringing Up Baby

see also Parenthood
Addams Family Values
Alien 3
Almost Pregnant
Alternative
And Baby Makes Six
Angie
The Baby
The Baby and the Battleship
Baby Boom
The Baby Maker
Baby's Day Out
Bachelor Mother▶
Basket Case 3: The Progeny
Billy: Portrait of a Street Kid
Brand New Life
Brink of Life
The Brood
Bundle of Joy
By Design
Celia: Child Of Terror
Child of Darkness, Child of Light
Desde el Abismo
Donde Duermen Dos...Duermen Tres
Enemy Mine
Eraserhead▶
Eye on the Sparrow
Fanny▶
Father's Little Dividend▶
For Keeps
Four Days in July
Fran
From Here to Maternity
Funny Girl▶
Generation
The Girls of Huntington House
Grave of the Vampire
The Great Lie▶
Growing Pains
Hell Comes to Frogtown
Help Wanted: Male
A Hole in the Head
I Don't Want to Be Born
Immediate Family
In Search of a Golden Sky
It's Alive▶
It's Alive 2: It Lives Again
It's Alive 3: Island of the Alive

A Kind of Loving▶
Le Cas du Dr. Laurent▶
Let's Get Married
The Lightning Incident
Little Man Tate▶
Look Who's Talking▶
Look Who's Talking, Too
Love Child
Mamele
The Match Factory Girl▶
Micki & Maude
The Miracle▶
Mom & Dad
Monika
My Life
Nickel Mountain
Night Cries
Parenthood▶
Paternity
Penny Serenade▶
Problem Child 2
Promises! Promises!
Psycho 4: The Beginning
Rabbit Test
Raising Arizona▶
Rosemary's Baby▶
Rumpelstiltskin
The Saga of the Draculas
Scarred
She's Having a Baby
The Snapper▶
Son of Godzilla
The Stranger Within
The Sugarland Express▶
Table for Five
A Taste of Honey▶
The Tender Years
Tenth Month
The Terminator▶
Test Tube Babies
That Man Is Pregnant
That's My Baby!
The 13th Floor
Thomas Graal's First Child▶
Three Men and a Baby▶
Three Men and a Cradle▶
Tomorrow▶
Tomorrow's Child
Tomorrow's Children
The Unborn
The Unborn 2
Unnatural
The Very Edge
Video Baby
Willa
Winter Flight
A Woman is a Woman▶

Buddies

Abbott and Costello Meet Frankenstein▶
Adios Amigo
The Adventures of Huck Finn▶
The Adventures of Huckleberry Finn
The Adventures of Milo & Otis▶
African Journey
Ain't No Way Back
The Alamo▶
Alan & Naomi
Amongst Friends
Angie
Another 48 Hrs.
Another You
Antonia and Jane▶
Anzacs: The War Down Under▶
Armistead Maupin's Tales of the City
Bachelor Party
Back to Hannibal: The Return of Tom Sawyer and Huckleberry Finn
Backbeat▶
Bad Company▶
Bad Girls
Baker's Hawk
The Battle of Blood Island
Beaches▶

The Bear▶
Becket▶
Behind Prison Walls
Best of the Best 2
Betrayal of the Dove
A Better Tomorrow
A Better Tomorrow, Part 2
Between Friends
Between Heaven and Hell▶
Beverly Hills 90210: The
    Graduation
The Big Chill▶
Big Deadly Game
Big Mo
Big Shots
The Big Slice
Bill & Ted's Bogus Journey
Birdy▶
Black Beauty
Blonde in Black Leather
Blue De Ville
The Blue Lamp▶
Boot Hill
Boots Malone
Born to Be Wild
A Boy and His Dog
The Boy Who Could Fly▶
The Boys in the Band
The Bramble Bush
Branded Men
Breaking the Rules
Bride of Killer Nerd
Broadway Melody of 1940
The Broken Chain
The Buddy System
Bundle of Joy
But Where Is Daniel Wax?
Butch Cassidy and the
    Sundance Kid▶
The Caddy
Cafe Romeo
Calendar Girl
Camilla▶
The Campus Corpse
Campus Man
Captain Scarlett
Captive Hearts
Carny▶
The Cat
Cat's Play
Celebrity
Celeste▶
The Cemetery Club
Chantilly Lace
Cheap Shots
Circle of Two
The Cisco Kid
City Heat
City Slickers▶
City Slickers 2: The Legend of
    Curly's Gold
Class Act
Clayton County Line
Close to Eden
Clown Murders
The Color Purple▶
Colorado Serenade
Come Back to the Five &
    Dime Jimmy Dean, Jimmy
    Dean▶
Common Bonds
Company Business
The Concrete Cowboys
Cooperstown
Cops and Robbers
Corleone
Country Gentlemen
Courage of Black Beauty
The Cowboy Way
Crime Busters
Crime Lords
Cross My Heart
Crossfire
Crossing the Bridge
Crush
Cry Freedom
The Crying Game▶
Cycle Vixens
Daniel and the Towers
Dazed and Confused▶
Dead Reckoning▶
Deadlock

Deadly Surveillance
December
Decoration Day▶
The Deer Hunter▶
Defenseless
The Defiant Ones▶
Dennis the Menace: Dinosaur
    Hunter
Departamento Compartido
Dersu Uzala▶
Devil's Party
Diner▶
Dogfight▶
Dominick & Eugene▶
Donovan's Reef▶
Double Obsession
Down Under
Downtown
Drachenfutter▶
Dragonworld
The Dresser▶
Driving Miss Daisy▶
Drop Dead Fred
Drums in the Deep South
Easy Rider▶
Eat the Peach
Eating
El Dorado▶
Elmer
Emanon
Enchanted April
Enemy Mine
Entre-Nous▶
E.T.: The Extra-Terrestrial▶
Every Which Way But Loose
Extreme Prejudice
Eye Witness
F/X 2: The Deadly Art of
    Illusion
The Falcon and the
    Snowman▶
Fandango
Farewell My Concubine
The Favor
The Fifth Seal
The Finest Hour
Finishing School
Fire Down Below
Fish Hawk
The Five Heartbeats▶
The Flesh and the Devil▶
The Flintstones
Forsaking All Others
48 Hrs.▶
Four Adventures of Reinette
    and Mirabelle▶
Four Friends▶
The Four Seasons
Four Weddings and a
    Funeral▶
Francis in the Navy
Freaks▶
Free Willy
Freeze-Die-Come to Life▶
Fried Green Tomatoes▶
Friends
Friends Forever▶
A Friendship in Vienna
The Frisco Kid
From Hell to Victory
Frontier Fugitives
Gallipoli▶
Gambler's Choice
George Washington
Getting Even
Giant Steps
Gladiator
Going Back
Goodfellas▶
Grand Canyon▶
Grand Illusion▶
Grandes Amigos
The Great Lie
Great Love Experiment
Grizzly Mountain
Grumpy Old Men▶
Guarding Tess
Gunga Din▶
Gunmen
Half a Lifetime
Hangin' with the Homeboys▶
The Hanging Tree▶

A Happy New Year!
Harley Davidson and the
    Marlboro Man
The Hasty Heart
Hats Off
Hawaii Calls
Heartaches▶
Heartbreakers▶
The Highest Honor
Hired Hand
Hollywood or Bust
Home Free All
Home Remedy
Hong Kong Nights
How Many Miles to Babylon?
How U Like Me Now?▶
Howard's End▶
Huck and the King of Hearts
The Hunt▶
The Hunters
Husbands and Wives▶
I Killed Rasputin
The In-Laws▶
In the Navy
Indian Summer
Inn of Temptation
Inside Monkey Zetterland
Ishtar
Jersey Girl
Jimmy Hollywood
Johnny Come Lately
Jonah Who Will Be 25 in the
    Year 2000▶
Journey to Spirit Island
Joy Ride to Nowhere
Judgment Night
Juice
Jules and Jim▶
Julia▶
Just Between Friends
K-9000
The Kansas Terrors
The Karate Kid▶
The Karate Kid: Part 2
The Karate Kid: Part 3
The Killing Fields▶
King of the Mountain
Kings of the Road—In the
    Course of Time▶
K2: The Ultimate High
Ladies on the Rocks
Last American Virgin
The Last Boy Scout
Last Summer
Le Beau Serge▶
Le Crabe Tambour▶
Le Doulos▶
Leaving Normal
The Lemon Sisters
Les Comperes▶
Less Than Zero
Let 'er Go Gallegher
Lethal Weapon▶
Lethal Weapon 2▶
Lethal Weapon 3
Let's Do It Again
A Letter to Three Wives▶
Little Heroes
Little Rascals, Book 1
Little Rascals, Book 2
Little Rascals, Book 3
Little Rascals, Book 4
Little Rascals, Book 6
Little Rascals, Book 7
Little Rascals, Book 8
Little Rascals, Book 9
Little Rascals, Book 10
Little Rascals, Book 11
Little Rascals, Book 12
Little Rascals, Book 13
Little Rascals, Book 14
Little Rascals, Book 15
Little Rascals, Book 17
Little Rascals, Book 18
Little Rascals: Choo Choo/
    Fishy Tales
Little Rascals Christmas
    Special
Little Rascals Collector's
    Edition, Vol. 1-6

Little Rascals Comedy
    Classics, Vol. 2
Little Rascals: Fish Hooky/
    Spooky Hooky
Little Rascals: Honkey
    Donkey/Sprucin' Up
Little Rascals: Little Sinner/
    Two Too Young
Little Rascals: Mush and Milk/
    Three Men in a Tub
Little Rascals on Parade
Little Rascals: Pups is Pups/
    Three Smart Boys
Little Rascals: Readin' and
    Writin'/Mail and Female
Little Rascals: Reunion in
    Rhythm/Mike Fright
Little Rascals: Spanky/Feed
    'Em and Weep
Little Rascals: The Pinch
    Singer/Framing Youth
Little Rascals Two Reelers,
    Vol. 1
Little Rascals Two Reelers,
    Vol. 2
Little Rascals Two Reelers,
    Vol. 3
Little Rascals Two Reelers,
    Vol. 4
Little Rascals Two Reelers,
    Vol. 5
Little Rascals Two Reelers,
    Vol. 6
Little Rascals, Vol. 1
Little Rascals, Vol. 2
Little Vegas
The Littlest Outlaw
Lockdown
The Long Voyage Home▶
Looking for Miracles
The Lords of Flatbush
Los Cacos
Lost in Alaska
Lost in the Barrens
Love Field
Love Film
Loyalties
Macaroni
Mad Dog and Glory▶
Mame
The Man Upstairs
The Man Who Would Be
    King▶
Manhattan Melodrama▶
March or Die
Mark Twain and Me
Maya
Me and Him
Mean Frank and Crazy Tony
Meet Danny Wilson
The Meeting: Eddie Finds a
    Home
The Men's Club
Metropolitan▶
Mi Vida Loca
Midnight Cowboy▶
Midnight Run▶
The Mighty Quinn
Mikey & Nicky
Milo & Otis
The Miracle
The Mission▶
Mr. Deeds Goes to Town▶
Misunderstood
Molly and Gina
Money to Burn
Moon Over Miami▶
Mortal Thoughts
A Movie Star's Daughter
Much Ado About Nothing▶
My Beautiful Laundrette▶
My Best Friend's Girl
My Dinner with Andre▶
My Girl
Mystic Pizza▶
Nabonga
Naked Youth
The Naughty Nineties
Navy Blue and Gold
Night Beat
Nightforce
The Nightingale

North and South Book 1▶
North and South Book 2▶
Ocean's 11
Odd Birds
The Odd Couple▶
Of Mice and Men▶
Okoge
Old Enough
Old Explorers
On the Nickel
On the Right Track
Once Upon a Time in
    America▶
One Crazy Summer
One Flew Over the Cuckoo's
    Nest▶
One Little Indian
One Sings, the Other Doesn't
The Opposite Sex and How to
    Live With Them
Ordinary Magic
Our Gang
Our Gang Comedies
Our Gang Comedy Festival 2
Our Time
Pals
Papillon▶
Paradise▶
Passion Fish▶
Peck's Bad Boy with the
    Circus
The Penitent
Perfect Harmony
Perfectly Normal
Perfume
Peter's Friends
The Phantom of 42nd Street
Piece of Cake
P.K. and the Kid
Platoon▶
Playmates
A Pleasure Doing Business
Plunder Road
Portrait of a Showgirl
Princes in Exile
Proof▶
Psycho Cop 2
Racing with the Moon▶
Rafferty & the Gold Dust
    Twins
Rape
Reality Bites
The Red Balloon▶
The Reivers▶
Reno and the Doc
Requiem for Dominic▶
The Return of Grey Wolf
The Return of the Musketeers
Return of the Secaucus 7▶
Reunion▶
Revenge of the Nerds
Revenge of the Nerds 2:
    Nerds in Paradise
Revolt of the Dragon
Rich and Famous
Ride the High Country▶
Rio Conchos
The Road to Hong Kong
The Road to Morocco▶
Roadside Prophets
Robby
Robert et Robert▶
Rubin & Ed
The Runaways
Running Scared
Russkies
St. Elmo's Fire
St. Helen's, Killer Volcano
The Saint of Fort Washington
Salut l'Artiste▶
The Sandlot▶
Scared Stiff
Scent of a Woman▶
Secret Places
September 30, 1955
The Seventh Veil▶
Shag: The Movie▶
Shaking the Tree
She Gods of Shark Reef
Shoeshine▶
Showdown
Showdown in Little Tokyo

Buddies

Side By Side
Silence Like Glass
Slumber Party '57
Snoopy's Getting Married,
    Charlie Brown
Snow White and the Seven
    Dwarfs
So This is Washington
Solo
Some Like It Hot▶
Something of Value▶
Songwriter
Sophisticated Gents▶
Spies Like Us
Spirit Rider▶
Spittin' Image
Spotlight Scandals
Stand By Me▶
Star Trek 4: The Voyage
    Home▶
Starbird and Sweet William
Stealing Home
Steaming
The Steel Helmet▶
The Structure of Crystals
Stuckey's Last Stand
Sudden Death
Sudie & Simpson▶
Summer City
Sundays & Cybele▶
Sunny Side Up
Sunny Skies
The Sunshine Boys▶
Swing Kids
A Taste for Killing
Taxi Blues▶
Ten Who Dared
Tequila Sunrise
Terminal Bliss
That Brennan Girl
That Sinking Feeling▶
Thelma & Louise▶
There's No Time for Love,
    Charlie Brown
Three Amigos
Three Comrades▶
Three Legionnaires
Three Men and a Baby▶
Three Men and a Cradle▶
The Three Musketeers
The Three Musketeers
The Three Musketeers
Thunder in the Pines
Thunderbolt & Lightfoot▶
Thursday's Game▶
Tiger Bay▶
To Forget Venice
Tobor the Great
Tombstone▶
Top Gun
Topper▶
Tough Guys
Tour of Duty
Trois Couleurs: Rouge▶
Troop Beverly Hills
True Colors
The Turning Point
Two of a Kind
Two Weeks to Live
Ugetsu▶
The Undefeated
Unholy Four
The Valley Obscured by the
    Clouds
Veronico Cruz
The Victim
Vincent, Francois, Paul and
    the Others▶
Watchers 2
Wayne's World▶
Wayne's World 2
We're in the Legion Now
What Price Glory?▶
Whatever Happened to Susan
    Jane?
When Harry Met Sally▶
Where the River Runs Black
White Christmas▶
White Mama▶
White Men Can't Jump
White Nights
Who Shot Pat?

Who's the Man?
Why Me?
The Wild Life
Wild Rovers
Wildflower▶
Willie & Phil
Windy City
Winners Take All
Withnail and I▶
A Woman and a Woman
Wrestling Ernest Hemingway
The Wrong Guys
The Wrong Road
The Yakuza
You Are Not Alone
Young Guns 2
You're in Love, Charlie Brown

Buddy Cops

**see also Cops; Women
Cops**
Another 48 Hrs.
Another Stakeout
Arizona Heat
Car 54, Where Are You?
City Heat
Collision Course
48 Hrs.▶
The Hard Way▶
La Chevre▶
Lethal Weapon▶
Lethal Weapon 2▶
Lethal Weapon 3
Liberty & Bash
National Lampoon's Loaded
    Weapon 1
Night Children
Nighthawks
The Presidio
Red Heat
Renegades
The Rookie
Shakedown
Shoot to Kill▶
Speed▶
Stakeout
Tango and Cash

Buses

Big Bus
Bull Durham▶
The Fugitive▶
A League of Their Own▶
Magical Mystery Tour
Mexican Bus Ride
Planes, Trains & Automobiles
The Runaway Bus
Speed▶
The Trip to Bountiful▶
Where Angels Go, Trouble
    Follows

Camelot (New)

**see also Assassinations;
Presidency**
Jacqueline Bouvier Kennedy
JFK▶
The JFK Conspiracy
JFK: Reckless Youth
JFK Remembered
Kennedy
The Kennedys Don't Cry
Prince Jack
PT 109
Robert Kennedy and His
    Times
Ruby

Camelot (Old)

**see also Medieval Romps;
Swashbucklers**
Camelot
A Connecticut Yankee▶
A Connecticut Yankee in King
    Arthur's Court
Excalibur▶
King Arthur, the Young
    Warlord
Knights of the Round Table
Merlin and the Sword

Monty Python and the Holy
    Grail▶
The Sword in the Stone▶
Sword of Lancelot
Sword of the Valiant

Campus Capers

**see also Hell High
School; School Daze**
Accident
Adventures in Spying
The Affairs of Dobie Gillis
All-American Murder
American Tiger
Animal Behavior
Assault of the Party Nerds
Attack of the Killer
    Refrigerator
Baby Love
Bachelor of Hearts
Back to School
Beware
Beyond Dream's Door
Black Christmas
Black Tower
Blood Cult
Blood Sisters
Blue Chips
Bride of Killer Nerd
The Campus Corpse
Campus Knights
Campus Man
Carnal Knowledge▶
Catch Me...If You Can
The Cheerleaders
A Chump at Oxford
Class
Class of '44
College▶
College Swing
Computer Beach Party
The Computer Wore Tennis
    Shoes
The Cousins▶
Curse of the Alpha Stone
Deadly Obsession
Deadly Possession
Death Screams
Didn't You Hear?
Doctor in the House▶
Dorm That Dripped Blood
Ernest Rides Again
Escapade in Florence
Final Exam
First Affair
First Love
First Time
Fraternity Vacation
The Freshman▶
The Freshman
Fright Night 2
Ghoulies 3: Ghoulies Go to
    College
Girl Crazy▶
Girls Night Out
The Gladiator▶
Good News
Gotcha!
Gross Anatomy
Hamburger...The Motion
    Picture
Harmon of Michigan
Harrad Experiment
Harrad Summer
HauntedWeen
The Heart of Dixie
Hell Night
Higher Education
Horse Feathers▶
H.O.T.S.
The House on Sorority Row
House Party 2: The Pajama
    Jam
How I Got into College
I Don't Buy Kisses Anymore
The Initiation
Initiation of Sarah
Jock Petersen
The Kid with the 200 I.Q.
A Killer in Every Corner
Killer Party
Knock Outs

Let's Go Collegiate
Little Sister
Lucky Jim
Making the Grade
Malice
A Matter of Degrees
Mazes and Monsters
Midnight Madness
The Misadventures of Merlin
    Jones
Monkey's Uncle
Monster on the Campus
Mortuary Academy
Mugsy's Girls
Murder on the Campus
My Lucky Star
The Naked Witch
National Lampoon's Animal
    House▶
Navy Blue and Gold
A Night in the Life of Jimmy
    Reardon
Night of the Creeps
Nightwish
Odd Jobs
The Paper Chase▶
Party Animal
P.C.U.
Pieces
Pledge Night
Preppies
The Program
Return Engagement
Revenge of the Nerds
Revenge of the Nerds 2:
    Nerds in Paradise
Revenge of the Nerds 3: The
    Next Generation
Ring of Terror
Roommate
Rosalie
R.P.M.* (*Revolutions Per
    Minute)
Rudy
Rush Week
Scent of a Woman▶
School Daze▶
School Spirit
The Seniors
Shallow Grave
Silent Madness
Silent Scream
Sky High
Slipping into Darkness
A Small Circle of Friends
Sniper▶
Sorority Babes in the Slimeball
    Bowl-A-Rama
Sorority Girl
Sorority House Massacre
Sorority House Massacre 2:
    Nighty Nightmare
Sorority House Party
Soul Man
Spellbound
The Spirit of West Point
Splatter University
Splitz
Spring Break
Star Spangled Girl
Stitches
The Sure Thing▶
Surviving Desire▶
Sweet Young Thing
Tag: The Assassination Game
Talking Walls
Tall Lie
Tall Story
Teen Wolf Too
Three in the Attic
Three in the Cellar
Threesome
Toga Party
Undergrads▶
The Unnamable
Up the Creek
The Victory
War Between the Tates
When He's Not a Stranger▶
The Wild Life
Witchboard
Witches' Brew

With Honors
Zero for Conduct▶
Zis Boom Bah

Canada

**see also Cold Spots;
Hockey**
Abducted
The Adjuster
The Agency
American Boyfriends
The Amityville Curse
And Then You Die▶
Angel Square
Angela
Anne of Avonlea▶
Anne of Green Gables▶
The Apprenticeship of Duddy
    Kravitz▶
Atlantic City▶
The Bay Boy
Beautiful Dreamers
The Best of the Monsters
The Big Crimewave
Big Meat Eater
Big Red
Black Christmas
Black Robe▶
Blades of Courage
Blood Clan
Blood Relations
The Bloody Brood
Boy in Blue
Breaking All the Rules
The Brood
Buffalo Jump▶
Bullies
Busted Up
By Design
Bye Bye Blues
Cafe Romeo
Canadian Bacon
Candy Mountain
The Cariboo Trail
Cathy's Curse
The Changeling
Christina
Circle of Two
City on Fire
Class of 1984
Clearcut
Close to Home
Cold Comfort
Concrete Angels
Confidential
Cordelia
Covergirl
Cross Country
A Cry in the Wild▶
Curtains
Dan Candy's Law
Dancing in the Dark
Danger Ahead
Daughter of Death
The Dawson Patrol
Dead Ringers▶
Death Ship
Death Weekend
Deathdream
The Decline of the American
    Empire▶
Deranged▶
The Deserters
Dirty Tricks
Disappearance
Distant Thunder
Dog Pound Shuffle▶
The Dog Who Stopped the
    War
A Doll's House▶
The Double Negative
Drying Up the Streets
Eddie and the Cruisers 2:
    Eddie Lives!
Explosion
Fighting Mad
Going Home
Heaven on Earth
House of the Living Dead
The Incredible Journey
Intersection
Jaws of Justice

Ladies of the Lotus
Lassie's Great Adventure
Maria Chapdelaine
Men of Steel
Murder on the Yukon
My American Cousin▶
Mystery Trooper
A Name for Evil
'Neath Canadian Skies
90 Days▶
Nomads of the North
Northern Extremes
Obsessed
Phantom Patrol
Renfrew of the Royal
   Mounted
Renfrew on the Great White
   Trail
The Return of Grey Wolf
Riel
Rose Marie▶
Silent Code
Slipstream
Some Girls
Spirit Rider▶
Strangers in Good Company▶
Tales from Avonlea, Vol. 1:
   The Journey Begins▶
Tales of the Klondike: In a Far
   Country
Tales of the Klondike: Race
   for Number One
Tales of the Klondike: The
   Unexpected
Termini Station
Timber Terrors
Time Lock
Trail of the Mounties
Wedding in White
Where the North Begins
Who Has Seen the Wind?
Yukon Flight

Cannibalism

see also Edibles; Horror
Adventures of Eliza Fraser
Alién Prey
Alive
Auntie Lee's Meat Pies
Back from Eternity
Beast of the Yellow Night
Black Werewolf
Blood Clan
Blood Diner
Blood Hook
Blood Sisters
Blood Tracks
Bloodsucking Freaks
Bloodsucking Pharoahs of
   Pittsburgh
Body Count
A Boy and His Dog
Brujo Luna
The 'Burbs
Buried Alive
Cannibal Campout
Cannibal Women in the
   Avocado Jungle of Death
The Chilling
C.H.U.D.
C.H.U.D. 2: Bud the Chud
Consuming Passions
The Cook, the Thief, His Wife
   & Her Lover▶
The Corpse Grinders
Crazy Fat Ethel II
Criminally Insane
Curse of the Living Dead
Dawn of the Dead▶
Dawn of the Mummy
Delicatessen▶
Demon Barber of Fleet Street
Deranged▶
Donner Pass: The Road to
   Survival
Eat the Rich
Eating Raoul▶
Emerald Jungle
Enchanted Island
Fiend
Flesh Eating Mothers
The Forest

Frightmare
The Further Adventures of
   Tennessee Buck
Gore-Met Zombie Chef From
   Hell
Grim Reaper
Gruesome Twosome
The Hills Have Eyes
Human Beasts
I Drink Your Blood
I Eat Your Skin
Igor & the Lunatics
Incredible Melting Man
Invasion of Flesh Hunters
Jungle Holocaust
Leatherface: The Texas
   Chainsaw Massacre 3
The Mad Butcher
A Man Called Rage
Mom
The Monster Club
Motel Hell
Murderer's Keep
Night of the Living Dead▶
Night of the Living Dead
Night of the Zombies
Nightstalker
The Offspring
Parents▶
The Perverse Countess
Porcile
Rabid Grannies
Raw Force
Redneck Zombies
The Severed Arm
The Silence of the Lambs▶
Slaughterhouse
Slaughterhouse Rock
Slave Girls from Beyond
   Infinity
Slave of the Cannibal God
Society
Soylent Green
Suddenly, Last Summer▶
Terror at Red Wolf Inn
The Texas Chainsaw
   Massacre
Texas Chainsaw Massacre,
   Part 2
Three on a Meathook
Toxic Zombies
The Undertaker and His Pals
Warlock Moon
White Cannibal Queen
Zombie
Zombie Island Massacre
Zombie Lake
Zombiethon

Capitol Capers

see also City Lights
Abraham Lincoln
All the President's Men▶
Born Yesterday▶
Born Yesterday
Dave▶
Image of Death
In the Line of Fire▶
J. Edgar Hoover
Mack Sennett Comedies: Vol.
   2
Mr. Smith Goes to
   Washington▶
1776▶
Three Days of the Condor▶
Washington Affair
Washington Mistress
Without Love

Carnivals & Circuses

**see also Amusement
Parks; Clowns; Fairs &
Expositions**
Arizona Mahoney
At the Circus
Bad Man of Deadwood
Barnum
Bells of Rosarita
Berserk!▶
Betrayal from the East
Big Top Pee Wee

Billy Rose's Jumbo▶
Black Orpheus▶
Brewster McCloud▶
The Cabinet of Dr. Caligari▶
Captive Wild Woman
Carnival Lady
Carnival Story
Carny▶
Carousel▶
Castle of the Living Dead
The Circus▶
Circus of Fear
Circus of Horrors
Circus World
Cloud Dancer
Clowning Around
Clowning Around 2
The Clowns▶
Court Jester▶
Dixiana
Dual Alibi
Dumbo▶
Elvira Madigan▶
Encore▶
Flamingo Road▶
Fox and His Friends▶
Freaked
Freaks▶
The Funhouse
Glass Tomb
Goldy: The Last of the Golden
   Bears
The Great Wallendas
The Greatest Show on Earth▶
He Who Gets Slapped▶
Incredibly Strange Creatures
   Who Stopped Living and
   Became Mixed-Up Zombies
Julia Misbehaves▶
Killer Klowns from Outer
   Space
La Strada▶
Life is a Circus, Charlie
   Brown/You're the Greatest,
   Charlie Brown
Lili▶
Lola Montes▶
Luther the Geek
Make-Up
The Man Who Laughs▶
Moscow on the Hudson▶
Multiple Maniacs
One Arabian Night▶
Parade▶
Peck's Bad Boy with the
   Circus
The Road to Zanzibar▶
Roustabout
The Rousters
Sally of the Sawdust
Santa Sangre▶
Sawdust & Tinsel▶
The Serpent's Egg
Seven Faces of Dr. Lao▶
Shakes the Clown
She-Freak
Side Show
So Dear to My Heart▶
Something Wicked This Way
   Comes
Spangles
State Fair
Strong Man▶
Texas Carnival
Three Texas Steers
Tillie Wakes Up
Toby Tyler▶
Trapeze▶
Tromba, the Tiger Man
Two Moon Junction
The Unholy Three▶
The Unknown▶
Vampire Circus
Variety▶
Variety Lights▶
Where East is East
Wild Hearts Can't Be Broken▶
You Can't Cheat an Honest
   Man▶

Cats

see also Killer Kats
The Adventures of Milo &
   Otis▶
After the Revolution
Batman Returns
The Big Cat
The Black Cat▶
The Black Cat
Black Cat
The Cat
The Cat from Outer Space
Cat Girl
Cat People
Cat's Eye
The Corpse Grinders
Felix the Cat: The Movie
Fritz the Cat▶
Gay Purr-ee
Homeward Bound: The
   Incredible Journey▶
The Incredible Journey
The Late Show▶
Le Chat▶
Milo & Otis
Night of a Thousand Cats
Pet Sematary
Puss 'n Boots
Return of Chandu
Rubin & Ed
Seven Deaths in the Cat's Eye
That Darn Cat
The Three Lives of
   Thomasina▶
Tom and Jerry: The Movie
Two Evil Eyes
The Uncanny
The Uninvited

Cave People

Being Human
Cave Girl
Caveman
The Clan of the Cave Bear
Creatures the World Forgot
Encino Man
The Flintstones
One Million B.C.
Prehistoric Women
Quest for Fire
Teenage Caveman
When Dinosaurs Ruled the
   Earth
When Women Had Tails
When Women Lost Their Tails

Central America

**see also Mexico; South
America**
Appointment in Honduras
Cyclone Cavalier
Delta Force Commando
Devil Wears White
El Norte▶
The Evil That Men Do
Exiled in America
The Firing Line
Last Plane Out
The Last Supper▶
Latino
Marie Galante▶
The Mosquito Coast
Panama Menace
Panama Patrol
Romero
The Situation
Toy Soldiers
Under Fire▶
Virgin Sacrifice
Wages of Fear▶

Chases

see also Road Trip
Abbott and Costello Meet the
   Keystone Kops
Abroad with Two Yanks
Action U.S.A.
The Adventures of Ichabod
   and Mr. Toad▶
Against All Odds

Albino
Alfie▶
American Autobahn
American Graffiti▶
At the Circus
Baby on Board
The Bank Dick▶
Beverly Hills Cop
Beverly Hills Cop 3
The Big Sweat
Bird on a Wire
Black Ice
Black Rain
Blue Jeans and Dynamite
The Blue Lamp▶
The Blues Brothers
Boiling Point
Border Radio
Breathless▶
Buck Privates Come Home▶
Bullitt▶
Butch Cassidy and the
   Sundance Kid▶
Charlie and the Great Balloon
   Chase
The Chase
Christine
Comrade X
Corvette Summer
The Cowboy Way
Danger Ahead!
Dead Easy
Deadlock
The Death Merchant
Deja Vu
Desperate
Devil & Leroy Basset
Diamonds are Forever▶
Dick Tracy▶
Dirty Mary Crazy Larry▶
Dr. No▶
Dr. Terror's House of Horrors
Dog Day
The Driver
Duel▶
Eat My Dust
Eddie Macon's Run
Enemy Below▶
Entr'acte
E.T.: The Extra-Terrestrial▶
Every Girl Should Have One
Exiled in America
Fifty/Fifty
Follow That Car
For the Love of It
For Your Eyes Only▶
48 Hrs.▶
Foul Play▶
The Fourth Protocol▶
Freebie & the Bean
The French Connection▶
From Russia with Love▶
The Fugitive▶
The Fugitive: Premiere
   Episode
Gator
The Gauntlet
The Getaway
The Ghost and the Guest
Girl Shy▶
The Golden Child
Goldfinger▶
Gone in 60 Seconds
Goodbye Pork Pie
Grand Theft Auto
Great Chase
The Great Escape▶
Great Smokey Roadblock
The Great Texas Dynamite
   Chase
The Hearse
Honeymoon in Vegas
Hootch Country Boys
Hopscotch▶
Horror of the Zombies
Hot Pursuit
The Hunt for Red October▶
Hunted
Indiana Jones and the Temple
   of Doom▶
Into the Night
The Italian Job

Chases

It's a Mad, Mad, Mad, Mad World
Jackson County Jail
Jericho Fever
The Jewel of the Nile
Judgment Night
The Junkman
Jurassic Park▶
King of the Rodeo
A Kink in the Picasso
The Lavender Hill Mob▶
Les Miserables▶
Lethal Weapon▶
Lethal Weapon 2▶
Lethal Weapon 3
License to Drive
Live and Let Die
Mackintosh Man
Mad Max▶
The Man from Snowy River
A Man with a Maid
The Man with the Golden Gun
Manhunt for Claude Dallas
Memoirs of an Invisible Man
Midnight Run▶
Mr. Billion
Mr. Majestyk
Money to Burn
Monkey Trouble
The Most Dangerous Game▶
My Favorite Blonde▶
Never Give a Sucker an Even Break▶
No Way Out▶
North by Northwest▶
No. 17▶
Nuns on the Run
Octopussy
On Her Majesty's Secret Service▶
One Down, Two to Go!
One Man Jury
Out of Bounds
Outrageous Fortune
Paris Holiday
Paths to Paradise▶
Pee Wee's Big Adventure▶
The Pelican Brief
A Perfect World
The Perverse Countess
Planet Busters
Planet of the Apes▶
Point Break
The Presidio
Profile
Pursuit
Race with the Devil
Raiders of the Lost Ark▶
Raising Arizona▶
Return of the Jedi▶
Return to Macon County
The Road Warrior▶
Romancing the Stone▶
Round Trip to Heaven
Run
Running Scared▶
Seven Chances▶
Sex, Love and Cold Hard Cash
Shaft's Big Score
The Shining
Slither▶
Smokey and the Bandit
Smokey and the Bandit, Part 2
Smokey and the Bandit, Part 3
Smokey & the Hotwire Gang
Smokey Bites the Dust
Son of Lassie
The Spy Who Loved Me
Stagecoach▶
Star Wars▶
Stephen King's Golden Years
The Sting▶
Stray Dog▶
The Sugarland Express▶
Sweet Sweetback's Baadasssss Song▶
Tagget
Taking the Heat
Teenage Crime Wave

Tell Them Willie Boy Is Here▶
The Terminator▶
Terror of the Bloodhunters
Thelma & Louise▶
The Third Man▶
This Man Must Die▶
Thunder and Lightning
Thunder Road▶
Thunderball
Thunderbolt & Lightfoot▶
Time After Time▶
To Live and Die in Hong Kong
To Live & Die in L.A.
Tom and Jerry: The Movie
Top Gun
Trouble Bound
True Lies▶
12 Plus 1▶
Until The End of The World▶
Valley of the Eagles
Vanishing Point
Watch the Birdie
What's Up, Doc?▶
White Lightning
Who Framed Roger Rabbit?▶
Who Killed Mary What's 'Er Name?
The Wilby Conspiracy▶
Wolfen▶
Year of the Comet
You Only Live Twice

Cheerleaders

see also Campus Capers; Hell High School
Buffy the Vampire Slayer▶
Cheering Section
Cheerleader Camp
The Cheerleaders
Cheerleaders' Wild Weekend
Gimme an F
The Majorettes
National Lampoon's Animal House▶
The Positively True Adventures of the Alleged Texas Cheerleader-Murdering Mom▶
Revenge of the Cheerleaders
Satan's Cheerleaders
The Swinging Cheerleaders

Child Abuse

Blind Fools
Close to Home
Fallen Angel
Fatal Confinement
Father Hood
Hush Little Baby, Don't You Cry
Impulse
Johnny Belinda
Judgment▶
Mommie Dearest
The Offence▶
Psychopath
A Question of Guilt
Radio Flyer
Raising Cain
Short Eyes▶
South Bronx Heroes
This Boy's Life▶
Where the Spirit Lives
Who Killed Baby Azaria?
Wildflower▶

Childhood Visions

see also Home Alone
Afraid of the Dark
All I Want for Christmas
Alsino and the Condor▶
American Heart▶
And Now Miguel
Angels in the Outfield
Army Brats
Au Revoir Les Enfants▶
Beethoven Lives Upstairs
The Beniker Gang
Big▶
The Black Stallion▶
Blankman

Born to Run
But Where Is Daniel Wax?
Cameron's Closet
Camp Nowhere
Captain January
Careful, He Might Hear You▶
Casey's Shadow
The Cat
The Cellar
Chapter in Her Life
Child in the Night
The Children Are Watching Us▶
Children of Divorce
Child's Play
China, My Sorrow
Chocolat▶
A Christmas Story▶
Cinema Paradiso▶
Cria▶
Crooklyn▶
David Copperfield▶
Days of Heaven▶
Demons in the Garden▶
Desert Bloom▶
Deutschland im Jahre Null▶
The Diary of Anne Frank▶
Diva▶
Emma's Shadow▶
Empire of the Sun▶
Escapade▶
E.T.: The Extra-Terrestrial▶
The Fallen Idol▶
Fanny and Alexander▶
Far Away and Long Ago▶
Father▶
The Flame Trees of Thika▶
Flight of the Grey Wolf
Flight of the Innocent
Forbidden Games▶
Girl from Hunan▶
A Girl of the Limberlost
The Golden Seal
Grazuole
Heidi
Heidi▶
Heidi
Heidi▶
Home Alone▶
Home for Christmas
Hook
Hope and Glory▶
Hue and Cry▶
Into the West▶
Invaders from Mars
Jacquot
Josh and S.A.M.
Journey for Margaret▶
The Kid from Left Field
The Kid with the Broken Halo
King of the Hill▶
The Kitchen Toto▶
The Lady in White▶
Lassie's Great Adventure
Last Action Hero
Le Grand Chemin▶
Leolo
Les Violons du Bal
Lies My Father Told Me▶
Little Buddha
Little Man Tate▶
Little Monsters
The Little Princess▶
The Little Rascals▶
The Littlest Horse Thieves
The Long Days of Summer
Look Who's Talking▶
Look Who's Talking, Too
Lord of the Flies▶
Lord of the Flies
Lost in Yonkers
Louisiana Story▶
Love Film
Magic of Lassie
Merlin of the Crystal Cave
The Mirror▶
Misty
Mommie Dearest
Mosby's Marauders
My Childhood▶
My Friend Flicka▶
My Life as a Dog▶

My Mother's Castle▶
My Name is Ivan▶
National Velvet▶
New York Stories▶
The Night of the Shooting Stars▶
Old Swimmin' Hole
Oliver!▶
An Orphan Boy of Vienna
Orphans▶
Our Gang
Parents▶
Peck's Bad Boy
Pelle the Conqueror▶
Pixote▶
Pollyanna▶
Poltergeist▶
Poltergeist 2: The Other Side
A Poor Little Rich Girl▶
The Poor Little Rich Girl
Psycho 4: The Beginning
Radio Flyer
Railway Children▶
Real Genius▶
The Red Balloon▶
The Red Pony▶
The Reflecting Skin
Return from Witch Mountain
Rock-a-Doodle
Roll of Thunder, Hear My Cry
Salaam Bombay!▶
Savage Sam
Searching for Bobby Fischer▶
The Secret Garden▶
The Secret Garden
The Secret Garden▶
The Secret Garden
Sidekicks
The Silence of the Lambs▶
Small Change▶
Sounds of Silence
Spirit of the Beehive▶
Square Shoulders
Stealing Home
Sudden Terror
Sudie & Simpson▶
A Summer to Remember▶
Sunday Daughters▶
Taps
The Tin Drum▶
Tito and Me▶
To Kill a Mockingbird▶
Toto le Heros▶
Train to Hollywood▶
Treasure Island▶
Turf Boy
Unicorn
Wait Until Spring, Bandini
The War Boy
What the Moon Saw
When Father was Away on Business▶
Where's Willie?
Whistle Down the Wind▶
White Fang▶
The Wild Country
The Wizard of Loneliness
Wombling Free
A World Apart▶
The Yearling▶
Yes, Sir, Mr. Bones
Zazie dans le Metro▶
Zero for Conduct▶

Children

see Animated Musicals; Animation & Cartoons; Childhood Visions; Storytelling

China

see also Asia
Adventures of Smilin' Jack
Battle of China
Bethune
Beyond the Next Mountain
The Bitter Tea of General Yen▶
China Cry
China, My Sorrow
Dragon Seed

Empire of the Sun▶
Farewell My Concubine
Fight to the Death
A Fist Full of Talons
The General Died at Dawn▶
Girl from Hunan▶
The Good Earth▶
A Great Wall▶
The Horse Thief▶
The Inn of the Sixth Happiness▶
Iron & Silk
The Joy Luck Club▶
Ju Dou▶
Kashmiri Run
The Keys of the Kingdom▶
The Killer▶
Lai Shi: China's Last Eunuch
The Last Emperor▶
The Leatherneck
M. Butterfly
The Mountain Road
Princess Yang Kwei Fei▶
Raise the Red Lantern▶
The Rebellious Reign
Red Sorghum▶
The Reincarnation of Golden Lotus▶
The Sand Pebbles▶
Seven Indignant
Shadows of the Orient
Shadows Over Shanghai
Shanghai Express▶
The Silk Road
Soldier of Fortune
Song of the Exile
The Story of Qiu Ju▶
Tai-Pan
The Tongfather
The World of Suzie Wong

Christmas

see also Holidays; Horrible Holidays
ABC Stage 67: Truman Capote's A Christmas Memory
All I Want for Christmas
An American Christmas Carol
Babes in Toyland
Benji's Very Own Christmas Story
Bernard and the Genie
The Best Christmas Pageant Ever
The Bishop's Wife▶
Black Christmas
Bloodbeat
A Charlie Brown Christmas
Children's Carol
Child's Christmas in Wales
A Christmas Carol▶
A Christmas Carol
The Christmas Coal Mine Miracle
Christmas Comes to Willow Creek
Christmas in Connecticut▶
Christmas in Connecticut
Christmas Lilies of the Field
A Christmas Story▶
The Christmas That Almost Wasn't
A Christmas to Remember
The Christmas Wife
A Christmas Without Snow
Don't Open Till Christmas
Dorm That Dripped Blood
Elves
Ernest Saves Christmas
The Gathering
The Gathering: Part 2
George Balanchine's The Nutcracker
The Gift of Love
Gremlins▶
Here Comes Santa Claus
Hobo's Christmas
Holiday Affair
Holiday Inn▶
Home Alone▶

Home Alone 2: Lost in New York
Home for Christmas
Homecoming: A Christmas Story
A House Without a Christmas Tree
How the Grinch Stole Christmas▶
It Came Upon a Midnight Clear
It's a Bundyful Life
It's a Wonderful Life▶
The Kid Who Loved Christmas
La Pastorela
The Lion in Winter▶
The Little Match Girl
Little Rascals Christmas Special
The Man in the Santa Claus Suit
The Man Upstairs
March of the Wooden Soldiers▶
A Matter of Principle
Mickey's Christmas Carol▶
Miracle Down Under
Miracle in the Wilderness
Miracle on 34th Street▶
Mr. Corbett's Ghost
The Muppet Christmas Carol
National Lampoon's Christmas Vacation
Nativity
The Night They Saved Christmas
The Nightmare Before Christmas▶
Nutcracker, A Fantasy on Ice
The Nutcracker Prince
Nutcracker: The Motion Picture
One Magic Christmas
Pee Wee's Playhouse Christmas Special
Planes, Trains & Automobiles
Prancer
Railway Children▶
The Ref▶
Roots: The Gift
Rudolph & Frosty's Christmas in July
Rudolph the Red-Nosed Reindeer
Santa Claus
Santa Claus Conquers the Martians
Santa Claus is Coming to Town
Santa Claus: The Movie
Scrooge▶
Scrooge
Scrooged
Silent Night, Deadly Night
Silent Night, Deadly Night 2
Silent Night, Deadly Night 3: Better Watch Out!
Silent Night, Deadly Night 5: The Toymaker
Silent Night, Lonely Night
A Smoky Mountain Christmas
Susan Slept Here
Terror in Toyland
Thirteenth Day of Christmas
Three Godfathers▶
A Time to Remember
To All a Goodnight
Trail of Robin Hood
A Very Brady Christmas
White Christmas▶
Who Slew Auntie Roo?

CIA
see Feds; Spies & Espionage

Cinderella Stories
Arthur▶
Born Yesterday
Born Yesterday
Cinderella▶

Flashdance
Hero▶
The Little Mermaid▶
Milk Money
My Fair Lady▶
Once Around
Pretty Woman▶
Pygmalion▶
Splash
A Star is Born
Stroke of Midnight
Working Girl▶
The World of Suzie Wong

Circuses
see Carnivals & Circuses; Clowns

Cities
see City Lights; Urban Drama

City Lights
see also Capitol Capers; Urban Drama
Abbott and Costello in Hollywood
Across 110th Street
Adventures in Babysitting
The Adversary
An Affair to Remember
After Hours▶
Against All Odds
All the Lovin' Kinfolk
All the Vermeers in New York▶
Alone in the Neon Jungle
Armistead Maupin's Tales of the City
Assault on Precinct 13▶
Berlin Alexanderplatz▶
Beverly Hills Cop
Beverly Hills Cop 2
Beverly Hills Cop 3
The Big Easy▶
Big Town
Black Orpheus▶
Black Rain
Blown Away▶
The Blues Brothers
The Bramble Bush
Breakfast at Tiffany's▶
Breathless▶
Carolina Skeletons
Cass Timberlane
City of Hope▶
City That Never Sleeps
Cool Blue
The Cotton Club▶
The Cowboy Way
Delightfully Dangerous
Desperate Characters▶
Dodes 'ka-den▶
Don't Look Now▶
Down and Out in Beverly Hills
The Dream Team
Eye of the Stranger
Fear, Anxiety and Depression
Ferris Bueller's Day Off▶
Fleshpot on 42nd Street
For Love or Money
The Foreigner
Fort Apache, the Bronx▶
Foul Play▶
Foxstyle
Frame Up
Freeway
French Quarter
French Quarter Undercover
Go West, Young Man
Gorky Park▶
Hangin' with the Homeboys▶
Hard Target
Hello, Frisco, Hello
Home Alone 2: Lost in New York
Hometown Boy Makes Good
Jersey Girl
Jimmy Hollywood
The Knack▶
La Boum

La Merveilleuse Visite
L.A. Story▶
The Last Metro▶
Last Tango in Paris▶
Laws of Gravity▶
Let Freedom Ring
A Life of Her Own
Light Sleeper
A Little Sex
Lonely in America
The Long Island Four
Love Affair▶
Love is Better Than Ever
Ma and Pa Kettle Go to Town
Manhattan▶
Manhattan Murder Mystery▶
Moscow on the Hudson▶
My Sister Eileen▶
Naked▶
Naked in New York
Nashville▶
The Neighbor
A New Kind of Love
New Orleans After Dark
New York, New York▶
New York Stories▶
News from Home
Next Stop, Greenwich Village▶
Night and the City▶
The Night the City Screamed
1918
Once in Paris...
One More Saturday Night
Our Vines Have Tender Grapes▶
The Out-of-Towners▶
Outrageous!▶
Peppermint Soda▶
The Pope of Greenwich Village
The Public Eye▶
A Rage in Harlem▶
The Rat Race▶
Rich, Young and Pretty
Risky Business▶
Ruby in Paradise▶
Running Scared
Scrooged
Showdown
Singles▶
Six Degrees of Separation
Slaves of New York
Sleepless in Seattle▶
Speed▶
Stephen King's The Tommyknockers
Straight for the Heart
Super Mario Bros.
Tampopo▶
Tarzan's New York Adventure
They Call It Sin
Time Out for Love
Times Square
To Live & Die in L.A.
Tokyo Pop
Tootsie▶
A Troll in Central Park
Urban Cowboy
Vernon, Florida▶
V.I. Warshawski
Viva Las Vegas
Wall Street▶
We're Back! A Dinosaur's Story
Where Were You When the Lights Went Out?
Whispers of White
Wolf

Civil Rights
see also Apartheid; Slavery
An African Dream
Alamo Bay
Ali: Fear Eats the Soul▶
Alien Nation
All God's Children
All the Young Men▶
Aloha Summer
The Ambush Murders
American Dream▶

Amos and Andrew
And the Children Shall Lead
As Summers Die
Assault at West Point: The Court-Martial of Johnson Whittaker
The Autobiography of Miss Jane Pittman▶
Backlash
Bad Bunch
The Bears & I
Belizaire the Cajun
Betrayed
Between Heaven and Hell▶
Bhowani Junction
The Big Dis
Billy Jack
Bingo Long Traveling All-Stars & Motor Kings▶
The Bitter Tea of General Yen▶
Black Bikers from Hell
The Black Klansman
Black Like Me
The Black Maid
Black Sister's Revenge
The Blum Affair
The Bonfire of the Vanities
The Border▶
Boyz N the Hood▶
Brother John▶
Bucktown
The Bus Is Coming
Carbon Copy
Charlotte Forten's Mission: Experiment in Freedom▶
China O'Brien
Chinatown After Dark
Chocolat▶
The Color Purple▶
Colors▶
Come Back, Africa▶
The Conversation▶
Cornbread, Earl & Me
Country Lovers, City Lovers
Crazy from the Heart▶
Criminal Justice▶
Crisis at Central High▶
Crossfire▶
Crusoe
The Defiant Ones▶
Dingaka
Do the Right Thing▶
Don't Look Back: The Story of Leroy "Satchel" Paige
D.P.
Dragon: The Bruce Lee Story▶
Driving Miss Daisy▶
Drum
A Dry White Season▶
Duel at Diablo▶
Dutchman▶
The Ernest Green Story
A Fight for Jenny
Fight for Your Life
Fighting Back
Final Comedown
Finian's Rainbow▶
Firehouse
The Five Heartbeats▶
Flaming Signal
Flaming Star▶
Flirting▶
For Love of Ivy
For Us, the Living▶
Free, White, and 21
Freedom Road
The Fringe Dwellers
Game for Vultures
Gang Justice
Georgia, Georgia
Getting Over
The Great Santini▶
The Great White Hope
Guess Who's Coming to Dinner▶
Guilty of Innocence
Hairspray▶
Half Slave, Half Free
Hawaii▶
Hawmps!

Heart Condition
The Heart of Dixie
Heat Wave
Hidden Agenda
Hollywood Shuffle
Home of the Brave▶
Homicide▶
Honky
I Know Why the Caged Bird Sings▶
Imitation of Life▶
In the Heat of the Night▶
In Your Face
Intolerance▶
Intruder in the Dust▶
Island in the Sun
The Jackie Robinson Story▶
Joe Panther▶
Judge Horton and the Scottsboro Boys
Judge Priest▶
Jungle Fever▶
Killer Commandos
Killing Floor
King▶
King of the Gypsies
Kings Go Forth
The Kitchen Toto▶
The Klansman
Lady Sings the Blues
L'Etat Sauvage▶
Liberation of L.B. Jones
Long Shadows
The Long Walk Home▶
The Lords of Discipline
Love Field
Mack
Made in America
Man & Boy
Man Friday
Mandela▶
Map of the Human Heart
Master Harold and the Boys▶
The McMasters
Menace II Society▶
Mississippi Burning▶
Mississippi Masala▶
Missourians
Mister Johnson▶
Murder on the Bayou▶
My Beautiful Laundrette▶
My Sweet Charlie
A Nation Aflame
Native Son
Night of the Strangler
Norman, Is That You?
Nothing But a Man
One False Move▶
Paris Trout
A Passage to India▶
A Patch of Blue
Perfect Harmony
Pinky▶
A Place Called Today
Places in the Heart▶
Posse▶
The Power of One
Powwow Highway▶
Prayer of the Rollerboys
Pressure Point▶
Prime Suspect 2▶
Purlie Victorious
Ragtime▶
A Raisin in the Sun▶
The Red Fury
The Ring
Riverbend
Robby
Roll of Thunder, Hear My Cry
Romper Stomper
Samurai Cowboy
Sapphire▶
Sarafina!▶
Sayonara▶
Scandal Man
Separate But Equal▶
Sergeant Rutledge▶
Shadow of China▶
Shadows
Shame▶
Ship of Fools▶
Simba▶

The Sky is Gray▶
Smith!
A Soldier's Story▶
Soul Man
Soul Patrol
Straight Out of Brooklyn
Strange Fruit
Streetfight
Sudie & Simpson▶
Sylvia
Tamango
Tell Them Willie Boy Is Here▶
Test of Donald Norton
Three the Hard Way
To Kill a Mockingbird▶
True Identity
Two of Us▶
Uncle Tom's Cabin
Utu▶
Valdez is Coming
The Voyage of the Yes
Walk into Hell
Watermelon Man
We of the Never Never▶
The Well▶
White Lie
The Wind and the Lion▶
Words by Heart
A World Apart▶
The Young One
Zebrahead▶
Zulu Dawn▶

Civil War

see also American South; Southern Belles
Abraham Lincoln
Alvarez Kelly
The Andersonville Trial▶
Bad Company▶
Band of Angels
The Beguiled▶
The Birth of a Nation▶
Blood at Sundown
Bloody Trail
The Blue and the Gray
The Bushwackers
Cavalry
Cavalry Charge
Charlotte Forten's Mission: Experiment in Freedom▶
Civil War Diary
The Civil War, Episode 1: The Cause—1861▶
The Civil War, Episode 2: A Very Bloody Affair—1862▶
The Civil War, Episode 3: Forever Free—1862▶
The Civil War, Episode 4: Simply Murder—1863▶
The Civil War, Episode 5: The Universe of Battle—1863▶
The Civil War, Episode 6: Valley of the Shadow of Death—1864▶
The Civil War, Episode 7: Most Hallowed Ground—1864▶
The Civil War, Episode 8: War is All Hell—1865▶
The Civil War, Episode 9: The Better Angels of Our Nature—1865▶
Colorado
Copper Canyon
Dark Command▶
Drums in the Deep South
Escape from Fort Bravo
Finger on the Trigger
The Fool Killer
Friendly Persuasion▶
Frontier Pony Express
Frontier Scout
The General▶
General Spanky
Gettysburg▶
Glory▶
Gone with the Wind▶
The Good, the Bad and the Ugly▶
Gore Vidal's Lincoln
Great Day in the Morning

The Great Locomotive Chase
Hangman's Knot
Hellbenders
The Horse Soldiers
How the West was Won▶
Ironclads
It Happened in New Orleans
Johnny Shiloh
Kansas Pacific
Little Women▶
Little Women
The Littlest Rebel
Louisiana
Love Me Tender
Love's Savage Fury
Macho Callahan
The McMasters
Menace on the Mountain
Mosby's Marauders
Mysterious Island▶
No Drums, No Bugles
North and South Book 1▶
North and South Book 2▶
Of Human Hearts
The Old Maid▶
The Ordeal of Dr. Mudd▶
The Private History of a Campaign That Failed
Raiders of Ghost City
Raintree County
Rebel Love
Rebel Vixens
The Red Badge of Courage▶
The Rose and the Jackal
Run of the Arrow
The Sacketts
Shadow of Chikara
The Shadow Riders
Shenandoah▶
South of St. Louis
A Southern Yankee
The Supernaturals
Tramplers
The Undefeated
Virginia City▶
War Brides
Way Down South
Yellowneck

Classic Horror

see also Horror
The Abominable Dr. Phibes▶
And Now the Screaming Starts
The Ape
The Ape Man
The Appointment
Asylum
Asylum of Satan
Atom Age Vampire
Attack of the Beast Creatures
Attack of the Mayan Mummy
Attack of the Swamp Creature
Avenging Conscience
Awakening
Barn of the Naked Dead
The Bat▶
The Bat
The Bat People
The Beast from Haunted Cave
Bedlam▶
Before I Hang▶
The Birds▶
The Black Cat▶
The Black Room▶
Black Sabbath▶
The Black Scorpion
Black Sunday▶
Black Werewolf
Blood and Roses
Blood Beast Terror
Blood Island
Blood of Dracula
Blood of Dracula's Castle
Blood of the Vampire
The Bloodsuckers
Bluebeard
The Body Snatcher▶
The Bride
The Bride of Frankenstein▶
Bride of the Gorilla
Bride of the Monster

Bring Me the Vampire
The Brute Man
Burn Witch, Burn!▶
The Cabinet of Dr. Caligari▶
Carnival of Souls▶
Castle of Blood
Castle of Evil
Castle of the Living Dead
Cat Girl
Cat in the Cage
Cat People▶
Cat People
Cauldron of Blood
Cave of the Living Dead
Chamber of Horrors
The Changeling
Circus of Fear
Condemned to Live
The Conqueror Worm▶
Corridors of Blood
Count Dracula
Count Yorga, Vampire
The Crawling Eye
Creature from the Black Lagoon▶
Creature of Destruction
Creature of the Walking Dead
The Creature Walks Among Us
Creature with the Blue Hand
The Creeper
The Creeping Flesh
Creeping Terror
Creepshow
Creepshow 2
The Crime of Dr. Crespi
Crimes at the Dark House▶
Crimes of Dr. Mabuse▶
The Crimes of Stephen Hawke
The Crimson Cult
Crucible of Horror
Cry of the Banshee
Cry of the Werewolf
Crypt of the Living Dead
The Curse of Frankenstein
Curse of the Devil
Curse of the Swamp Creature
Cyclops
Dance of the Damned
Daughters of Darkness▶
Dementia 13
Demon Barber of Fleet Street
Demons of the Mind
The Devil Bat
The Devil Bat's Daughter
Devil Doll▶
Devil Kiss
Dr. Death, Seeker of Souls
Dr. Jekyll and Mr. Hyde▶
Dr. Jekyll and Mr. Hyde
Doctor X
Dolly Dearest
Dorian Gray
Dracula▶
Dracula
Dracula/Garden of Eden
Dracula (Spanish Version)
Dracula vs. Frankenstein
Dracula's Daughter▶
Dracula's Great Love
Dracula's Last Rites
Dracula's Widow
The Evil of Frankenstein
The Exorcist 3
Eye of the Demon
Eyes of Fire
Eyes of the Panther
The Fall of the House of Usher
The Fall of the House of Usher▶
The Fall of the House of Usher
Fangs of the Living Dead
The Fear Chamber
Fear No Evil
The Fog
Frankenstein▶
Frankenstein
Frankenstein and the Monster from Hell
Frankenstein '80
Frankenstein Island

Frankenstein Meets the Wolfman▶
Frankenstein Unbound▶
Frankenstein's Daughter
Fright Night
Fright Night 2
The Fury
The Fury of the Wolfman
Genie of Darkness
The Ghost of Frankenstein
The Ghoul
The Gorgon
Gothic▶
Grampa's Monster Movies
Grave of the Vampire
Graveyard Shift
The Greed of William Hart
Growing Pains
Guardian of the Abyss
Halloween Night
The Hanging Woman
The Haunted
The Haunted Strangler
Haunted Summer
The Haunting▶
Haunting Fear
The Haunting of Morella
The Head
The Horror of Dracula▶
House of Dark Shadows
House of Dracula
House of Frankenstein
House of the Black Death
The House of Usher
House of Wax▶
House on Haunted Hill
The House that Dripped Blood
How to Make a Monster
The Hunchback of Notre Dame▶
The Hunger
I Walked with a Zombie▶
I Was a Teenage Werewolf
Invasion of the Vampires
The Invisible Dr. Mabuse▶
The Invisible Man▶
The Invisible Ray
Island of Dr. Moreau
Island of Lost Souls▶
Isle of the Dead
Jaws▶
Jaws 2
Jaws 3
Jaws: The Revenge
King of the Zombies
La Chute de la Maison Usher▶
Lady Frankenstein
The Lair of the White Worm▶
The Legend of Blood Castle
Legend of the Werewolf
The Legend of the Wolf Woman
Lemora, Lady Dracula
The Living Coffin
The Mad Monster
The Man They Could Not Hang
Mark of the Vampire▶
Martin▶
Masque of the Red Death▶
Masque of the Red Death
Masque of the Red Death/ Premature Burial
Miami Horror
Mirrors
The Mummy▶
Mummy & Curse of the Jackal
The Mummy's Curse
The Mummy's Ghost
The Mummy's Hand
The Mummy's Tomb
Murders in the Rue Morgue
Mystery of the Wax Museum▶
Night of Dark Shadows
Nosferatu▶
Once Upon a Midnight Scary
Orlak, the Hell of Frankenstein
Pandora's Box▶
Phantom of the Opera▶
The Phantom of the Opera
Picture of Dorian Gray▶

The Pit and the Pendulum▶
The Pit & the Pendulum
Psycho 4: The Beginning
The Raven▶
Return of the Vampire
Revenge of the Creature
Revenge of the Zombies
Scared to Death
The Snow Creature
Son of Dracula▶
Son of Frankenstein▶
Teenage Frankenstein
The Undying Monster
The Vampire
The Vampire Bat
The Vampire People
The Vampire's Coffin
The Vampire's Ghost
Vampyr▶
Werewolf of London
The Werewolf vs. the Vampire Woman
The White Zombie▶
Witchcraft Through the Ages▶
The Wolf Man▶

Clowns

see also Carnivals & Circuses
Clown House
Clown Murders
Clowning Around
Clowning Around 2
The Clowns▶
Court Jester▶
The Funhouse
Funland
He Who Gets Slapped▶
Killer Klowns from Outer Space
Make-Up
The Man Who Laughs▶
Poltergeist▶
Quick Change
Shakes the Clown

Cold Spots

The Alaska Wilderness Adventure
Antarctica
Atomic Submarine
The Big Push
Bog
Call of the Wild
Challenge To Be Free
Christmas Comes to Willow Creek
Cool Runnings
The Day the Earth Froze
Dead Ahead: The Exxon Valdez Disaster▶
Doctor Zhivago▶
Ice Palace
The Ice Runner
Ice Station Zebra
Intruder Within
Kavik the Wolf Dog
Klondike Annie
Lost in Alaska
Lost Zeppelin
Map of the Human Heart
Never Cry Wolf▶
Operation Haylift
Pathfinder▶
Pipe Dreams
Quest for Fire▶
Salmonberries
Shadow of the Wolf
The Spoilers▶
Tentacles of the North
Virus
The White Dawn
White Fang 2: The Myth of the White Wolf

Cold War

see *Red Scare*

Comedy

see also *Black Comedy;
Comedy Drama; Comic
Adventure; Horror
Comedy; Military
Comedy; Musical Comedy;
Romantic Comedy; Satire
& Parody; Screwball
Comedy; Slapstick
Comedy; Sports Comedies;
Western Comedy*

The Adventures of a Gnome
   Named Gnorm
Afrita Hanem▶
After the Revolution
Ah, Wilderness!▶
The Air Up There
Airheads
Alfie▶
...All the Marbles
Amazing Grace
Andy Griffith Show
Angels in the Outfield▶
Another You
April Fool
Baby Face Harry Langdon
Baby Love
Baby of the Bride
Backfield in Motion
Based on an Untrue Story
Battling for Baby
Beach Girls
Beach House
Behave Yourself!
Behind Prison Walls
Bellas de Noche
The Bellboy and the Playgirls
Belle of the Nineties
The Belles of St. Trinian's▶
Ben Turpin: An Eye for an Eye
Best Friends
The Best of the Monsters
Better Late Than Never
Better Off Dead
Between the Lines▶
The Beverly Hillbillies
Beverly Hills Brats
Big Business Girl
Big Deal on Madonna Street▶
The Big Dis
The Big Gag
A Big Hand for the Little Lady
Big Man on Campus
Big Shots
Big Top Pee Wee
Big Trouble
The Bikini Car Wash
   Company 2
Bikini Summer
Bikini Summer 2
Billie
The Billion Dollar Hobo
A Billion for Boris
Biloxi Blues
Birthday Boy
The Black Maid
Black Venus
The Blacksmith/The
   Balloonatic
The Blacksmith/The Cops
Blank Check
Blankman
Blazing Stewardesses
Blessed Event▶
Blondie
Blondie Has Trouble
Blondie Hits the Jackpot
Blondie in Society
Blondie Knows Best
Blondie Takes a Vacation
Blondie's Blessed Event
Blue De Ville
Blue Money
Boarding School
The Boatniks
Bombs Away!
Bon Voyage!

Book of Love
Boom in the Moon
The Boss' Wife
Boudu Saved from
   Drowning▶
Bound and Gagged: A Love
   Story
Boy Meets Girl▶
Boy's Night Out▶
Boys of the City
The Brain
Brain Smasher...A Love Story
Breakfast in Hollywood
Breaking In▶
Brewster's Millions
The Bride Walks Out
Broadway Bill▶
Broadway Bound
Broadway Danny Rose▶
Broadway Limited
Bromas S.A.
Broth of a Boy
Brothers in Law
Buffy the Vampire Slayer▶
Buford's Beach Bunnies
Burlesque of Carmen
Buster Keaton Festival, Vol. 1
Buster Keaton Festival, Vol. 2
Buster Keaton Festival, Vol. 3
Buster Keaton: The Golden
   Years
Buster Keaton: The Great
   Stone Face
Bustin' Loose▶
Buy & Cell
By Design
By Hook or Crook
Cabin Boy
Cadillac Man
California Girls
Call Me Bwana
Camp Nowhere
Campus Man
Can I Do It...Till I Need
   Glasses?
Cancel My Reservation
Candy Stripe Nurses
Cannon Ball/Eyes Have It
The Canterville Ghost
Captain Ron
The Captain's Table
Car 54, Where Are You?
Carlton Browne of the F.O.
The Case of the Lucky Legs
Casual Sex?
Catch as Catch Can
Catherine & Co.
Caught in the Draft▶
Cave Girl
Champagne for Breakfast
The Charge of the Model T's
Charley and the Angel
Charley Chase Festival, Vol. 1
Charlie Chase and Ben Turpin
Chasing Those Depression
   Blues
Chattanooga Choo Choo
Chatterbox
Cheap Shots
Check Is in the Mail
Cheech and Chong's Nice
   Dreams
Cheering Section
The Cheerleaders
Cheerleaders' Wild Weekend
Cherry Hill High
Chesty Anderson USN
The Chicken Chronicles
C.H.O.M.P.S.
A Christmas Story▶
Circonstances Attenuantes
Citizens Band▶
Clarence
Class
Class Act
Clean Slate
Cleo/Leo
Clifford
Club Fed
Club Paradise
Clue
Cocoon▶

C.O.D.
Colonel Effingham's Raid
Comedy Classics
Comedy Classics of Mack
   Sennett and Hal Roach
Comedy Festival #2
Comedy Festival #3
Comedy Reel, Vol. 1
Comfort and Joy▶
Comic Cabby
Coming Up Roses
Complex World
Computer Beach Party
Computer Wizard
The Computer Wore Tennis
   Shoes
Comrade X
The Comrades of Summer
Condorman
Coneheads
A Connecticut Yankee▶
Cookie
Cooking Up Trouble
Cool Runnings
Cop and a Half
Cops and Robbers
Cops and Robbersons
Cops/One Week
Corporate Affairs
Cotton Comes to Harlem▶
Cotton Queen
Country Gentlemen
Coupe de Ville
Crazy for Love
Crazy Mama
Crazy People
Crime & Passion
Crime Busters
Critical Condition
The Crooked Circle
Crooks & Coronets
Curley
Daddy's Boys
Daddy's Dyin'...Who's Got the
   Will?
Daffy Duck's Quackbusters
Danger Ahead!
Dangerous Curves
Dave▶
Day the Bookies Wept
The Day the Women Got Even
The Daydreamer
Dazed and Confused▶
D.C. Cab
Dead Solid Perfect
Dear Wife
Deceit
Delinquent School Girls
Delirious
Delivery Boys
Delusions of Grandeur
Dennis the Menace
Dennis the Menace: Dinosaur
   Hunter
Departamento Compartido
Despedida de Casada
Desperate Scoundrel/The
   Pride of Pikeville
Detective Sadie & Son
The Devil & Max Devlin
Diamante, Oro y Amor
Die Laughing
Digby, the Biggest Dog in the
   World
Digging Up Business
Diggstown
Diner▶
Dirty Laundry
Dirty Mind of Young Sally
Dirty Tricks
Disorganized Crime
The Distinguished Gentleman
Divorce—Italian Style▶
Dixie: Changing Habits▶
Dr. Alien
Doctor at Large
Doctor Duck's Super Secret
   All-Purpose Sauce
Dr. Goldfoot and the Bikini
   Machine
Doin' Time
Doin' Time on Planet Earth

Dollars▶
Donovan's Reef▶
Don't Go Near the Water
Don't Tell Mom the
   Babysitter's Dead
Door to Door
Double Dynamite
Double Trouble
Doughnuts & Society
Downtown
Dream a Little Dream
Dream Machine
Dreaming Out Loud
Dressmaker
Drive-In
Driving Me Crazy
Drop Dead Fred
Drop-Out Mother
Dumb Waiter
Dutch
Dutch Girls
Dutch Treat
Early Cinema Vol. 1
Early Days
Earthworm Tractors
East Side Kids
East Side Kids/The Lost City
Echo Park
The Efficiency Expert
18 Again!
El Aviador Fenomeno
El Aviso Inoportuno
El Derecho de Comer
Elvis Stories
Encino Man
Ensign Pulver
Enter Laughing
Ernest Saves Christmas
Erotic Dreams
Escapade▶
Esta Noche Cena Pancho
Et La Tenoresse?...Bordel!
Every Day's a Holiday
Evil Toons
Ex-Mrs. Bradford▶
Experience Preferred... But
   Not Essential
Expertos en Pinchazos
The Experts
Explorers
Eyes of Turpin Are Upon You!
Fabulous Joe
Fall and Rise of Reginald
   Perrin 1▶
Fall and Rise of Reginald
   Perrin 2▶
Falling in Love Again
Family Reunion
Fancy Pants
The Fantastic World of D.C.
   Collins
Fantasy Man
Far Out Man
The Farmer's Wife
Fast Food
Fast Times at Ridgemont
   High▶
Fat Guy Goes Nutzoid
Fatal Instinct
Father of the Bride▶
Father of the Bride
Father's Little Dividend▶
Fatty and Mabel Adrift/Mabel,
   Fatty and the Law
Fatty Finn
Fawlty Towers
Fear, Anxiety and Depression
Feel My Pulse
Felix the Cat: The Movie
Fernandel the Dressmaker
Ferris Bueller's Day Off▶
The Fiendish Plot of Dr. Fu
   Manchu
Find the Lady
Firehouse
Firesign Theatre Presents
   Nick Danger in the Case of
   the Missing Yolks
The First Time
Flashback▶
Fletch▶
Fletch Lives

A Flight of Rainbirds
The Flintstones
Flush
The Flustered Comedy of
   Leon Errol
Flying Karamazov Brothers
   Comedy Hour
Flying Wild
Follow Me, Boys!▶
For Better and For Worse
For Pete's Sake
For Richer, For Poorer
For the Love of It
Foreign Body
Foreplay
Forever, Lulu
Fowl Play
Francis in the Navy
Frasier the Sensuous Lion
Fraternity Vacation
Freaky Friday
Freebie & the Bean
Frog
Frogs!
The Front Page▶
The Front Page
Frozen Assets
Fun with Dick and Jane
The Funny Farm
Gambit
Games Girls Play
The Garbage Pail Kids Movie
Gas Pump Girls
The General▶
General Spanky
Getting Even with Dad
Ghost Crazy
The Gift
Ginger Ale Afternoon
A Girl in a Million
Girl in His Pocket
Girls Just Want to Have Fun
Girls Next Door
The Gladiator▶
Glitch!
A Global Affair
Glory Years
The Go-Getter
Go West, Young Man
Goin' to Town
Going Ape!
Going in Style▶
Going to Town
Going Under
Going Undercover
Gold of the Amazon Women
The Gold Rush▶
Golden Earrings
Gone are the Days
Goodbye Love
Goon Movie
Gotcha!
Grad Night
Gran Valor en la Facultad de
   Medicina
The Grass is Always Greener
   Over the Septic Tank
Greased Lightning
Great Dane Hoax
Great Bikini Off-Road
   Adventure
The Great Impostor
The Great Muppet Caper▶
The Great Outdoors
The Great Rupert▶
The Great St. Trinian's Train
   Robbery
Greedy
Green Grow the Rushes
Green Pastures▶
Group Marriage
Guarding Tess
The Guardsman▶
Guest Wife
A Guide for the Married
   Woman
Gumball Rally
The Gun in Betty Lou's
   Handbag
Gung Ho
Hail Caesar

Comedy

Halloween with the Addams Family
Hamburger...The Motion Picture
Hanging on a Star
The Happiest Days of Your Life▶
Happy Birthday, Gemini
The Happy Hooker
The Happy Hooker Goes Hollywood
The Happy Hooker Goes to Washington
Happy Hour
A Happy New Year!
Happy New Year
Hardbodies
Hardbodies 2
Harper Valley P.T.A.
Harry and the Hendersons
Harry & Walter Go to New York
Harry's War
Hawmps!
Head Office
Heading for Heaven
Headline Woman
Heart and Souls
Heartbreak Hotel
Heaven Help Us
The Heavenly Kid
Heavy Traffic▶
Hello Again
Help Wanted: Male
Her Life as a Man
Herbie Goes Bananas
Herbie Rides Again
Hero at Large
Hi-Di-Hi
Hiding Out
High School USA
Hijazo de Mi Vidaza
Hillbilly Blitzkrieg
His Girl Friday▶
His Picture in the Papers
Hit the Ice
The Hoboken Chicken Emergency
Hocus Pocus
Hog Wild
Hold 'Em Jail
Holiday Hotel
Holiday Rhythm
Hollywood Zap
Home is Where the Hart is
Home Remedy
Homer Comes Home
Hometown Boy Makes Good
Hometown U.S.A.
Homo Eroticus/Man of the Year
Honey, I Blew Up the Kid
Honey, I Shrunk the Kids
The Honeymoon Machine
Honky Tonk Freeway
Hooch
Hootch Country Boys
Hopscotch▶
The Horse in the Gray Flannel Suit
The Horse's Mouth▶
Hot Millions▶
Hot Pursuit
Hot Resort
Hot Stuff
Hot Summer in Barefoot County
Hot T-Shirts
Hot Touch
Hot Under the Collar
Hot Wire
Hotel Paradiso
H.O.T.S.
House of Errors
House Party▶
House Party 2: The Pajama Jam
House Party 3
Housemaster
How Come Nobody's On Our Side?
How Funny Can Sex Be?

How I Won the War
How to Be a Perfect Person in Just Three Days
How to Beat the High Cost of Living
How to Break Up a Happy Divorce
How to Commit Marriage
How to Kill 400 Dupons
How to Make a Doll
How to Murder Your Wife▶
How to Pick Up Girls
How to Seduce a Woman
How to Succeed with Girls
Huckleberry Finn
Hullabaloo Over Georgie & Bonnie's Pictures
Hunk
I Love Lucy
I Wanna Hold Your Hand
I Was a Male War Bride▶
I Was a Teenage TV Terrorist
I Wonder Who's Killing Her Now?
Identity Crisis
If I Were Rich
If It's Tuesday, This Must Be Belgium▶
If You Don't Stop It...You'll Go Blind
Illegally Yours
I'm No Angel▶
The Immigrant▶
Immortal Bachelor
Importance of Being Earnest▶
The Imported Bridegroom
The Impossible Years
Improper Channels
The In-Laws▶
In the Army Now
In the Money
In the Spirit
Inn of Temptation
The Innocents Abroad
Innocents in Paris
Inside the Law
The Inspector General▶
Intervista
Into the Sun
Invasion of the Space Preachers
The Invisible Kid
The Invisible Woman▶
Irish Luck
Irreconcilable Differences
Is This Goodbye, Charlie Brown?
It Could Happen to You
It Happens Every Spring▶
It Runs In the Family▶
It Was a Short Summer, Charlie Brown
The Italian Job
It's A Gift▶
It's a Great Life
It's a Joke, Son!
It's Not the Size That Counts
It's Pat
Izzy & Moe
Jabberwalk
Jack and His Friends
The Jackpot
Jeeves & Wooster: Jeeves' Arrival
Jimmy the Kid
Jinxed
Jocks
Johnny Stecchino▶
Jokes My Folks Never Told Me
Jonah Who Will Be 25 in the Year 2000▶
Josh and S.A.M.
Julia Misbehaves▶
Jumpin' Jack Flash
Just One of the Guys
Just William's Luck
K-9
Keaton's Cop
Kelly the Second
Kid from Brooklyn
Kid Sister

The Kid with the 200 I.Q.
Kidco
Kill My Wife...Please!
Killer Dill
A Kink in the Picasso
Kiss Me, Stupid!
Kisses for My President
Kitty and the Bagman
Klondike Annie
The Knack▶
Konrad
Kung Fu Vampire Buster
La Boum
La Cage aux Folles▶
La Cage aux Folles 2
La Cage aux Folles 3: The Wedding
La Grande Vadrouille▶
Lady Godiva Rides
Lady Killer▶
Lady of the Evening
L'Anne Sainte
Las Vegas Hillbillys
Las Vegas Weekend
Last Night at the Alamo▶
Last of the Red Hot Lovers
The Last Porno Flick
Last Resort
The Lavender Hill Mob▶
Law of Desire▶
Le Bourgeois Gentilhomme
Le Cavaleur
Le Gendarme de Saint-Tropez
Le Gentleman D'Epsom
Le Sex Shop▶
Leader of the Band
The League of Gentlemen▶
Leap Year
The Lemon Drop Kid
Leningrad Cowboys Go America
Leon the Pig Farmer
Les Aventuriers
Les Comperes▶
Les Patterson Saves the World
Lesson in Love
Let It Ride
Let's Do It Again
Let's Get Tough
License to Drive
The Life & Times of the Chocolate Killer
Life Is a Long Quiet River▶
Life with Father▶
Life with Mikey
Like Father, Like Son
Li'l Abner
Listen, Darling
Little Big League
Little Darlings
Little Miss Marker▶
Little Miss Marker
Little Miss Millions
The Little Rascals▶
Little World of Don Camillo▶
Livin' Large
Living on Tokyo Time
Lobster for Breakfast
Lonely Wives
The Longest Yard
Look Who's Laughing
Look Who's Talking Now
Lookin' to Get Out
Loose Cannons
Los Cacos
Lost Diamond
Lost Honeymoon
Lost in America
The Love Boat
Love Nest
Lucky Jim
Luggage of the Gods
Lupo
Luv
Mabel & Fatty
Macaroni
Mack Sennett Comedies: Vol. 1
Mack Sennett Comedies: Vol. 2
Mad About You

Mad Miss Manton
The Magic Christian▶
Maid to Order
Major League
Major League 2
Make a Million
Make Me an Offer
Making the Grade
Malcolm
The Malibu Beach Vampires
Man from Clover Grove
Man from Nowhere
Man in the Silk Hat
Man of Destiny
The Man on the Box
The Mandarin Mystery
Manhattan Murder Mystery▶
The Marquise
Marriage is Alive and Well
Married to It
Martians Go Home!
Master Minds
A Matter of Degrees
Max
Maxie
Me and the Kid
Medicine Man
Meet the Hollowheads
Meet the Mob
Meet the Parents
Melvin and Howard▶
Men at Work
Merton of the Movies
Mexican Spitfire at Sea
Mexican Spitfire/Smartest Girl in Town
Mickey Rooney in the Classic Mickey McGuire Silly Comedies
Mickey the Great
Million Dollar Duck
Million Dollar Mystery
Milo Milo
The Misadventures of Mr. Wilt
Miss Firecracker▶
Miss Grant Takes Richmond
The Missing Corpse
Mrs. Doubtfire
Mistaken Identity
Mr. Baseball
Mr. Blandings Builds His Dream House▶
Mr. Hobbs Takes a Vacation▶
Mr. Mike's Mondo Video
Mr. Nice Guy
Mr. Peek-A-Boo
Mister Roberts▶
Mr. Skitch
Mr. Walkie Talkie
Mr. Wise Guy
Mistress
Modern Problems
Mon Oncle▶
Mon Oncle D'Amerique▶
Monsieur Beaucaire▶
Mother Goose Rock 'n' Rhyme
Motorama
Movie...In Your Face
Movie Maker
Moving
Moving Violations
Musico, Poeta y Loco
Mutant Video
My Blue Heaven
My Cousin Vinny▶
My Father is Coming
My Father the Hero
My Favorite Blonde▶
My Favorite Year▶
My Geisha
My Lady of Whims
My Little Chickadee▶
My Pleasure Is My Business
Mystery of the Leaping Fish/ Chess Fever
The Naked Truth
National Lampoon Goes to the Movies
National Lampoon's Class Reunion
Nature's Playmates

Naughty Knights
Near Misses
Necessary Roughness
The Neighborhood Thief
Neighbors
Never a Dull Moment
Never on Tuesday
Never Wave at a WAC
Never Weaken/Why Worry?▶
New Pastures
New York Stories▶
New York's Finest
Ni Chana Ni Juana
Nickel & Dime
Night After Night
The Night Before
A Night in the Life of Jimmy Reardon
Night of the Comet
Night of the Living Babes
Night Partners
Night Shift
The Night They Raided Minsky's▶
The Night They Robbed Big Bertha's
Nine Ages of Nakedness
Nine Lives of Fritz the Cat
9 to 5
1941
Ninja Academy
Nobody's Perfect
Nobody's Perfekt
Norman Loves Rose
Norman's Awesome Experience
Northern Extremes
Now You See Him, Now You Don't
Nudity Required
Nudo di Donna▶
Nutcase
O.C. and Stiggs
Ocean Drive Weekend
Ocean's 11
The Odd Couple▶
The Odd Squad
Oddballs
Off the Mark
Oh, God!
Oh, God! Book 2
Oh, God! You Devil
Oh, Heavenly Dog!
Oh, Mr. Porter
Oklahoma Bound
Old Enough
Old Spanish Custom
Oldest Profession
On the Air Live with Captain Midnight
On the Right Track
On Top of the Whale
Once Upon a Crime
Once Upon a Honeymoon
Once Upon a Scoundrel
The One and Only
One Body Too Many
One Cooks, the Other Doesn't
One Crazy Summer
One More Saturday Night
One of Our Dinosaurs Is Missing
One-Punch O'Day
One Wish Too Many
Only Two Can Play▶
Open All Hours
Operation Dames
Operation Petticoat▶
Opportunity Knocks
Options
Our Gang
Our Gang Comedies
Our Gang Comedy Festival
Our Gang Comedy Festival 2
Our Hospitality▶
The Out-of-Towners▶
Out on a Limb
Outtakes
Packin' It In
Palombella Rossa
Pals
Panic Button

Papa's Delicate Condition▶
Paper Lion
Paper Moon▶
Para Servir a Usted
Parade▶
Paradise Motel
Paradisio
Pardon Mon Affaire, Too!
The Parent Trap
Parlor, Bedroom and Bath
Party Animal
Party Camp
Party Favors
Party Incorporated
Party! Party!
Party Plane
Passionate Thief
Passport to Pimlico
Paternity
Paths to Paradise▶
Pauline at the Beach▶
Peck's Bad Boy
Peck's Bad Boy with the
    Circus
The Pee Wee Herman Show
Pee Wee's Big Adventure▶
Pee Wee's Playhouse
    Christmas Special
Pee Wee's Playhouse Festival
    of Fun
People Are Funny
People's Choice
Pepper and His Wacky Taxi
A Perfect Little Murder
The Perfect Marriage
Personal Exemptions
Petit Con
Pick a Star
Pick-Up Summer
The Pickwick Papers
Piece of the Action
The Pinchcliffe Grand Prix
Pink Motel
Pizza Man
Plain Clothes
Planes, Trains & Automobiles
Playing Away
Playing Dead
Playing for Keeps
Playmates
Plaza Suite▶
Please Don't Eat My Mother
Please Don't Eat the Daisies
A Pleasure Doing Business
The Plot Against Harry▶
Poison Ivy
Poker Alice
A Polish Vampire in Burbank
Pom Pom Girls
Pop Goes the Cork
The Pope Must Diet
Porky's
Porky's 2: The Next Day
Porky's Revenge
Porridge
Portrait of a White Marriage
Pot O' Gold
Pouvoir Intime
Prehistoric Bimbos in
    Armageddon City
Prep School
Preppies
Pretty Smart
The Primitive Lover
Prince of Pennsylvania
Princess Academy
Private Affairs
The Private Eyes
Private Lessons
Private School
The Private Secretary
Prize Fighter
The Projectionist▶
The Promoter▶
Property
Prurient Interest
The Pure Hell of St. Trinian's
Pure Luck
Purlie Victorious
Pyrates
Queen for a Day
Rabbit Test

Race for Your Life, Charlie
    Brown
Radio Days▶
Rascal Dazzle
Ratings Game
Ravishing Idiot
Real Genius▶
Real Life▶
Really Weird Tales
Rebel High
Reg'lar Fellers
Remote
Renaissance Man
Rendez-Moi Ma Peau
Rented Lips
The Return of Our Gang
Return of the Tall Blond Man
    With One Black Shoe
Return to Mayberry
Revenge of the Cheerleaders
Revenge of the Nerds
Revenge of the Nerds 2:
    Nerds in Paradise
Revenge of the Nerds 3: The
    Next Generation
Revenge of the Teenage
    Vixens from Outer Space
Rhinestone
Rich Hall's Vanishing America
Riders of the Storm
Riding on Air
Rikky and Pete
Ring of the Musketeers
Rink/Immigrant
Ripping Yarns
Rising Damp
Risky Business▶
Rita, Sue & Bob Too▶
Road Lawyers and Other
    Briefs
Road Show
Rock & the Money-Hungry
    Party Girls
Rockula
Roller Boogie
Rookie of the Year
Rosebud Beach Hotel
Rosencrantz & Guildenstern
    Are Dead
Ruddigore
The Ruggles of Red Gap▶
The Runaway Bus
The Russians are Coming, the
    Russians are Coming▶
Ryder P.I.
Sailor-Made Man/Grandma's
    Boy▶
St. Benny the Dip
Sally of the Sawdust
Salut l'Artiste▶
Samantha
Sammy, the Way-Out Seal
The Sandlot▶
Santa Claus Conquers the
    Martians
The Saphead
Sawmill/The Dome Doctor
Say Yes!
Scandalous
Scared Stiff▶
Scavenger Hunt
School Daze▶
The Scout▶
Screwball Academy
Second Sight
The Secret Life of Walter
    Mitty▶
The Secret War of Harry Frigg
Senior Trip
The Seniors
Sensations
Seven Chances▶
Sex and Buttered Popcorn
Sex on the Run
Sexpot
Shadow of the Thin Man▶
The Shaggy D.A.
The Shaggy Dog
Shake Hands with Murder
She Couldn't Say No
The Sheep Has Five Legs
She's Out of Control

Shooting Elizabeth
Short Circuit 2
The Show-Off
Side By Side
Silver Bears
Simple Men▶
The Sin of Harold Diddlebock
Singleton's Pluck▶
Sinners
Sirens▶
Sister Act
Sister Act 2: Back in the Habit
Sitting Ducks▶
Skinner's Dress Suit
Skyline▶
The Slap
The Sleazy Uncle
A Slightly Pregnant Man
Slumber Party '57
Small Change▶
Small Hotel
Smart Money
Snapshot
Snowball Express
Snowballing
Snuffy Smith, Yard Bird
So Fine
So This is Washington
Social Error
Soggy Bottom U.S.A.
Son-in-Law
Sorority House Party
Sorrowful Jones
Sotto, Sotto
Speak Easily
Splitting Heirs
Splitz
Squeeze Play
Story of William S. Hart/Sad
    Clowns
The Strange Case of the End
    of Civilization as We Know
    It
Strike It Rich
Summer Rental
Summer School
The Super
Super Seal
The Sure Thing▶
Surf 2
Susan Slept Here
Sweet Liberty
Swimsuit: The Movie
Swindle
A Swingin' Summer
Switch▶
Sylvia and the Phantom▶
Tabloid!
Taking Care of Business
Talkin' Dirty After Dark
Tall Story
Tampopo▶
Tax Season
Teen Wolf
Teen Wolf Too
The Telephone
That Darn Cat
That Gang of Mine
That Man Is Pregnant
That's Entertainment, Part 2
There Goes the Neighborhood
These Girls Won't Talk
Things Happen at Night
Think Dirty
Three Men on a Horse▶
Three Nuts in Search of a Bolt
Three O'Clock High
Three's Trouble
The Thrill of It All!
Tonight for Sure
Too Much Sun
Topper▶
Topper Returns▶
Topper Takes a Trip▶
The Toy
Trading Places
Troop Beverly Hills
The Trouble with Angels
True Identity
The Tunnel of Love
Turner and Hooch
The Tuttles of Tahiti▶

Twelve Chairs▶
Twentieth Century▶
200 Motels
Two Top Bananas
The Ugly Dachshund
Uncle Buck▶
Undercover Blues
Undergrads▶
Unfaithfully Yours▶
Unfaithfully Yours
Unidentified Flying Oddball
Used Cars▶
Varieties on Parade
Vasectomy: A Delicate Matter
A Very Brady Christmas
Virgin High
Visitants
Viva Chihuahua (Long Live
    Chihuahua)
Voice of Hollywood
Volere Volare
Volunteers
The Wacky World of Wills &
    Burke
Water
Wayne's World▶
Wayne's World 2
A Wedding
Wedding Band
Wedding Rehearsal
Weekend Warriors
Weekend with the Babysitter
Weird Science
Welcome to 18
We're in the Legion Now
We're in the Navy Now
We're Talkin' Serious Money
What About Bob?▶
What Did You Do in the War,
    Daddy?
What Do You Say to a Naked
    Lady?
What's Up Front
The Wheeler Dealers▶
When Knights were Bold
When's Your Birthday?
Where Angels Go, Trouble
    Follows
Where's Willie?
Whiffs
Whiskey Galore▶
Whistling in Brooklyn
Whistling in Dixie
Whistling in the Dark▶
Who Framed Roger Rabbit?▶
Wholly Moses!
Who's Got the Action?
Who's Harry Crumb?
Who's Minding the Mint?▶
Who's the Man?
The Wild Life
Win, Place, or Steal
Wings of Fame
Women's Club
Woof!
Working Winnie/Oh So Simple
The Wrong Guys
Y Donde Esta el Muerto?
    (And... Where Is the Dead)
You Can't Hurry Love
You So Crazy
You Talkin' to Me?
Young Einstein
Young Love—Lemon
    Popsicle 7
Zazie dans le Metro▶
Zebra in the Kitchen
Zero to Sixty

Comedy Anthologies
see also Comedy
The Adventures of
    Hairbreadth Harry
All Night Long/Smile Please
Amazon Women on the Moon
And Now for Something
    Completely Different▶
The Best of Chaplin
Best of Eddie Murphy
Best of Ernie Kovacs
The Best of John Candy on
    SCTV

The Best of the Kenny Everett
    Video Show
The Best of the Kids in the
    Hall
The Best of the Two Ronnies
Best of W.C. Fields
Billy Crystal: Don't Get Me
    Started
Boccaccio '70
Charlie Chaplin: The Early
    Years, Vol. 1
Charlie Chaplin: The Early
    Years, Vol. 2
Charlie Chaplin: The Early
    Years, Vol. 3
Charlie Chaplin: The Early
    Years, Vol. 4
Classic Comedy Video
    Sampler
Comedy Festival #1
Comedy Festival #2
Comedy Festival #3
Comedy Festival #4
Daffy Duck's Quackbusters
Desperate Scoundrel/The
    Pride of Pikeville
Early Cinema Vol. 1
Elvis Stories
Everything You Always
    Wanted to Know About
    Sex (But Were Afraid to
    Ask)▶
A Few Moments with Buster
    Keaton and Laurel and
    Hardy▶
The Flintstones
The Floorwalker/By the Sea▶
For Auld Lang Syne: The
    Marx Brothers
Foreplay
Going to Congress/Don't Park
    There
Golden Age of Comedy
Great Chase
The Groove Tube
His Prehistoric Past/The Bank
His Royal Slyness/Haunted
    Spooks
Hollywood Boulevard
Hollywood Clowns
Hot Foot/A Happy Married
    Couple
Hot Water/Safety Last
I'm on My Way/The Non-Stop
    Kid
Kentucky Fried Movie▶
Kid 'n' Hollywood and Polly
    Tix in Washington
Kid's Auto Race/Mabel's
    Married Life
Kings, Queens, Jokers
The Knockout/Dough and
    Dynamite▶
Laugh with Linder!
Laughfest
Laurel & Hardy and the Family
Laurel & Hardy: At Work
Laurel & Hardy Comedy
    Classics, Vol. 1
Laurel & Hardy Comedy
    Classics, Vol. 2
Laurel & Hardy Comedy
    Classics, Vol. 3
Laurel & Hardy Comedy
    Classics, Vol. 4
Laurel & Hardy Comedy
    Classics, Vol. 5
Laurel & Hardy Comedy
    Classics, Vol. 6
Laurel & Hardy Comedy
    Classics, Vol. 7
Laurel & Hardy Comedy
    Classics, Vol. 8
Laurel & Hardy Comedy
    Classics, Vol. 9
Laurel & Hardy On the Lam
Laurel & Hardy Special
Laurel & Hardy Spooktacular
Laurel & Hardy: Stan "Helps"
    Ollie
Little Rascals, Book 1
Little Rascals, Book 2

Comedy

Little Rascals, Book 3
Little Rascals, Book 4
Little Rascals, Book 5
Little Rascals, Book 6
Little Rascals, Book 7
Little Rascals, Book 8
Little Rascals, Book 9
Little Rascals, Book 10
Little Rascals, Book 12
Little Rascals, Book 13
Little Rascals, Book 14
Little Rascals, Book 15
Little Rascals, Book 16
Little Rascals, Book 17
Little Rascals, Book 18
Little Rascals: Choo Choo/
  Fishy Tales
Little Rascals Collector's
  Edition, Vol. 1-6
Little Rascals Comedy
  Classics, Vol. 1
Little Rascals Comedy
  Classics, Vol. 2
Little Rascals: Fish Hooky/
  Spooky Hooky
Little Rascals: Honkey
  Donkey/Sprucin' Up
Little Rascals: Little Sinner/
  Two Too Young
Little Rascals: Mush and Milk/
  Three Men in a Tub
Little Rascals on Parade
Little Rascals: Pups is Pups/
  Three Smart Boys
Little Rascals: Readin' and
  Writin'/Mail and Female
Little Rascals: Reunion in
  Rhythm/Mike Fright
Little Rascals: Spanky/Feed
  'Em and Weep
Little Rascals: The Pinch
  Singer/Framing Youth
Little Rascals Two Reelers,
  Vol. 1
Little Rascals Two Reelers,
  Vol. 2
Little Rascals Two Reelers,
  Vol. 3
Little Rascals Two Reelers,
  Vol. 4
Little Rascals Two Reelers,
  Vol. 5
Little Rascals Two Reelers,
  Vol. 6
Little Rascals, Vol. 1
Little Rascals, Vol. 2
The Lizzies of Mack Sennett
Looney Looney Looney Bugs
  Bunny Movie►
The Lost Stooges
Love Notes
Mack & Carole
The Marx Brothers in a
  Nutshell►
MGM's The Big Parade of
  Comedy
Monty Python's Parrot Sketch
  Not Included
Monty Python's The Meaning
  of Life►
National Lampoon Goes to the
  Movies
Never Weaken/Why Worry?►
New York Stories►
Oldest Profession
Our Gang
Our Gang Comedies
Our Gang Comedy Festival
Our Gang Comedy Festival 2
Outtakes
Parade►
Plaza Suite►
Pop Goes the Cork
Queen for a Day
Rascal Dazzle
Really Weird Tales
The Return of Our Gang
Rink/Immigrant
Ripping Yarns
Road Lawyers and Other
  Briefs

Sailor-Made Man/Grandma's
  Boy►
Sawmill/The Dome Doctor
Sex and Buttered Popcorn
Shirley Temple Festival
Silent Laugh Makers, No. 1►
Silent Laugh Makers, No. 2►
Silent Laugh Makers, No. 3
Silent Movies...Just For the
  Fun of It!
Slapstick
Stan Without Ollie, Vol. 1
Stooges Shorts Festival
The Stooges Story►
Three of a Kind
Three Stooges Comedy
  Capers: Vol. 1
Three Stooges Comedy
  Classics
Three Stooges: Cookoo
  Cavaliers and Other Nyuks
Three Stooges Festival
Three Stooges: From Nurse to
  Worse and Other Nyuks
The Three Stooges: Half-Wit's
  Holiday and Other Nyuks
The Three Stooges: Idiots
  Deluxe and Other Nyuks
The Three Stooges: Nutty but
  Nice and Other Nyuks
The Three Stooges: They
  Stooge to Conga and Other
  Nyuks
Tigers in Lipstick
To See Such Fun
A Tribute to the Boys
Tunnelvision
Two Reelers: Comedy
  Classics 1
Two Reelers: Comedy
  Classics 2
Two Reelers: Comedy
  Classics 3
Two Reelers: Comedy
  Classics 4
Two Reelers: Comedy
  Classics 5
Two Reelers: Comedy
  Classics 6
Two Reelers: Comedy
  Classics 7
Two Reelers: Comedy
  Classics 8
Two Reelers: Comedy
  Classics 9
Uncensored
When Comedy was King
Woman Times Seven
The Young Ones
Yours, Mine & Ours

Comedy Drama

see also Black Comedy;
Comedy
Adventure
Alice Doesn't Live Here
  Anymore
Alice's Restaurant
All I Want for Christmas
All My Good Countrymen
All Screwed Up►
An Almost Perfect Affair
Aloha Summer
Always►
Amarcord►
American Boyfriends
American Graffiti►
And Baby Makes Six
Androcles and the Lion
Andy Hardy Gets Spring Fever
Andy Hardy's Double Life
Andy Hardy's Private
  Secretary
Angel in a Taxi
Angie
The Apprenticeship of Duddy
  Kravitz►
Arabian Nights►
Armistead Maupin's Tales of
  the City
Article 99
Author! Author!

Autumn Marathon
Avalon►
Awakenings►
Ay, Carmela!►
Babette's Feast►
Baby It's You►
Baby, Take a Bow
Back Roads
Bad Behavior
Bail Jumper
The Baker's Wife►
The Ballad of Paul Bunyan
Band of Outsiders
Barcelona►
Bartleby
Baxter
Being Human
Being Two Isn't Easy
The Bells of St. Mary's►
Benji►
The Best Way
Big►
The Big Chill►
Big Girls Don't Cry...They Get
  Even
Big Wednesday
Billy Liar►
The Bishop's Wife►
The Black King
Blat
Blueberry Hill
Blues Busters
Blume in Love►
Born to Win
Borsalino►
The Breakfast Club►
Breaking Away►
Breaking the Rules
Breaking Up Is Hard to Do
The Bretts►
Bright Eyes
Brighton Beach Memoirs►
Broadcast News►
Bud and Lou
The Buddy System
Buddy's Song
Buffalo Bill
Bulldog Drummond's
  Revenge
A Bunny's Tale
Bureau of Missing Persons
Butterflies Are Free►
Caesar and Cleopatra
Cafe Express
Calendar Girl
Camilla►
Candy Mountain
Cannery Row
Captain Newman, M.D.
Carbon Copy
Carnal Knowledge►
Carnival in Flanders►
The Cary Grant Collection
Casey's Shadow
Cesar►
Cesar & Rosalie►
The Challengers
Charles et Lucie►
Charlie and the Great Balloon
  Chase
Cheaper to Keep Her
Chimes at Midnight►
China, My Sorrow
Chips, the War Dog
Chloe in the Afternoon►
Choose Me►
A Chorus of Disapproval
The Christmas Wife
City Lights►
City of Women
Claire's Knee►
Clara's Heart
Class Reunion
Cleo from 5 to 7►
Clipped Wings
Clown
Coast to Coast
Cocoon: The Return
Combination Platter
Comment Ca Va?
Conspiracy of Terror
Cooperstown

Corvette Summer
Coupe de Ville
The Courtship of Eddie's
  Father►
Cousin, Cousine►
Cousins►
Crazy from the Heart►
Crimes & Misdemeanors►
Crooklyn►
Danny Boy
David Holzman's Diary►
Death of the Rat
The Decameron►
The Decline of the American
  Empire►
Der Purimshpler
Desperate Teenage Lovedolls
Details of a Duel: A Question
  of Honor
Detour to Danger
The Devil & Daniel Webster►
Devil on Horseback
The Devil's Eye
Diary of a Chambermaid►
Diary of a Mad Housewife►
Diary of a Young Comic
Diary of Forbidden Dreams►
Dim Sum: A Little Bit of
  Heart►
The Dining Room
Dinner at Eight►
Dinner at Eight
The Discovery Program
Dixie Lanes
Do the Right Thing►
Doctor at Sea
Dr. Christian Meets the
  Women
Dog Eat Dog
Don Quixote►
Don't Drink the Water
Down by Law►
Dream Chasers
The Dream Team
Drugstore Cowboy►
D2: The Mighty Ducks
Eat a Bowl of Tea►
Eat My Dust
Eat the Peach
Eating
Educating Rita►
El Cochecito►
Eli Eli
Elizabeth of Ladymead►
Emanon
End of the Line
Enemies, a Love Story►
Enormous Changes►
Even Cowgirls Get the Blues
Extra Girl
Eyes Right!
The Fabulous Baker Boys►
Family Business
Far North
Fast Talking
Fatso
The Fifth Monkey
First Name: Carmen►
The Fisher King►
Five Corners►
The Five Heartbeats►
The Flamingo Kid►
Flesh►
Flirting►
FM
Follow the Leader
For Keeps
For the Love of Benji
Forrest Gump►
Four Adventures of Reinette
  and Mirabelle►
Four Days in July
Four Deuces
Four Friends►
The Four Musketeers►
The Four Seasons
Fried Green Tomatoes►
From the Hip
Full Moon in Blue Water
Fuzz
Garbo Talks
Generation

George!
Georgy Girl►
Getting Over
Getting Straight
Ghost Chasers
The Gig
Gin Game►
Ginger & Fred►
The Girl with the Hat Box
Girlfriends►
A Girl's Folly
The Gold of Naples►
Gone are the Days
Good Morning, Vietnam►
Good Sam
The Goodbye Bird
Goodbye Columbus►
The Goodbye People
Goodnight, Michelangelo
The Gospel According to Vic
The Graduate►
Grandes Amigos
Grandview U.S.A.
The Great Man Votes►
The Great McGinty►
The Great Moment
A Great Wall►
The Great War
Gregory's Girl►
Gross Anatomy
Grown Ups
Grumpy Old Men►
Guess What We Learned in
  School Today?
Guess Who's Coming to
  Dinner►
Half a Sixpence
Hangin' with the Homeboys►
Hannah and Her Sisters►
Happily Ever After
Happy Since I Met You►
Hard-Boiled Mahoney
Hard Promises
The Hard Way►
Harlem Nights
The Hawks & the Sparrows
Headwinds
The Heartbreak Kid►
Heartburn►
Here Come the Marines
Hero►
Hero of the Year
Hey, Babu Riba
The Hideaways
His Double Life
His First Command
Hold Your Man►
A Hole in the Head
Hollywood Heartbreak
Hollywood Vice Sqaud
Home Free All
Homer and Eddie
Horsemasters
The Hot Line
The Hotel New Hampshire
House of Angels►
Household Saints►
The Householder
Housekeeping►
I Live My Life
I Live with Me Dad
I Vitelloni►
The Ice Flood
If You Could See What I Hear
Il Sorpasso
Immediate Family
Impure Thoughts
In Praise of Older Women►
In the Land of the Owl Turds
In the Mood
In the Soup
Indian Summer
Inside Monkey Zetterland
Insignificance►
It Couldn't Happen Here
It Started in Naples►
It's a Wonderful Life►
Jamon, Jamon
The January Man
Jazzman►
Jimmy Hollywood

Jo Jo Dancer, Your Life is Calling
Joe
Joe's Bed-Stuy Barbershop: We Cut Heads
Johnny Suede
The Jolly Paupers
Joshua Then and Now▶
Judge Priest▶
The Jumper
Junior High School
Just Another Pretty Face
The Kid▶
Kid Dynamite
The Kid from Left Field
The Kid/Idle Class▶
The Killing Game
A King in New York
Knights & Emeralds
Kostas
Kotch▶
La Discrete▶
La Dolce Vita▶
La Ronde▶
Lady by Choice
Lady for a Day▶
The Lady Says No
Larks on a String▶
The Last American Hero▶
The Last Days of Chez Nous
The Last Detail▶
Last Holiday▶
The Last of Mrs. Cheyney▶
Law and Disorder▶
Le Beau Serge▶
Le Petit Amour▶
A League of Their Own▶
Leap of Faith
Leave 'Em Laughing
The Lemon Sisters
Les Grandes Gueules
Letter to Brezhnev▶
Letters from My Windmill▶
Letting Go
Like Water for Chocolate▶
Lily in Love
Little Annie Rooney
Little Red Schoolhouse
A Little Sex
The Little Theatre of Jean Renoir▶
The Little Thief▶
Little Vegas
Local Hero▶
Long Shot
Loose Connections
The Lovable Cheat
Love Finds Andy Hardy▶
Love in the City▶
Lovers and Other Strangers▶
Loves of a Blonde▶
Lucas▶
Mac and Me
Madame Sousatzka▶
Made for Each Other▶
Made in USA
Magic Town
Make Room for Tomorrow
Mama Turns a Hundred▶
The Man That Corrupted Hadleyburg
The Man Upstairs
Manny's Orphans
Mantrap
Marathon
Maria's Child
Marius▶
The Marriage of Maria Braun▶
Marry Me, Marry Me▶
Masala
M*A*S*H▶
M*A*S*H: Goodbye, Farewell & Amen▶
Max Dugan Returns
May Fools▶
Mediterraneo▶
Memories of Me
Men at Work
Men Don't Leave
Mermaids▶
Metropolitan▶
Mexican Bus Ride

Middle Age Crazy
Midnight Auto Supply
The Mighty Ducks
The Mighty Quinn
The Milagro Beanfield War▶
Million Dollar Kid
Min & Bill
Mischief
The Misfit Brigade
Miss Annie Rooney
Mrs. Wiggs of the Cabbage Patch
Mr. Deeds Goes to Town▶
Mr. Mom▶
Mr. North
Mr. Saturday Night
Mr. Winkle Goes to War
M'Lady's Court
Mom, the Wolfman and Me
Money for Nothing
Moon Over Parador
Moonlighting
More American Graffiti
Morgan Stewart's Coming Home
Moscow on the Hudson▶
The Mozart Brothers▶
Murmur of the Heart▶
My Beautiful Laundrette▶
My Bodyguard▶
My Dinner with Andre▶
My Father's Nurse
My Girl
My Life as a Dog▶
My Other Husband
My Therapist
My Twentieth Century▶
My Wonderful Life
Mystic Pizza▶
Nadine
The Nasty Girl▶
Nasty Rabbit
Nea
'Neath Brooklyn Bridge
Never Let Go
A New Life
New Year's Day▶
Next Stop, Greenwich Village▶
Next Summer▶
Night on Earth▶
1969▶
90 Days▶
The Ninth Configuration▶
No Man of Her Own
No Small Affair
Norman, Is That You?
North▶
North Dallas Forty▶
Nothing in Common
Nurse on Call
The Object of Beauty▶
Oblomov▶
Off Your Rocker
Oh, Alfie
Oh, What a Night
Olly Olly Oxen Free
Once Around
One Arabian Night▶
One Flew Over the Cuckoo's Nest▶
Only One Night
Only When I Laugh▶
Orphans▶
Other People's Money
Our Little Girl
Out
Outrageous!▶
Outside Chance of Maximillian Glick
Over the Brooklyn Bridge
Paddy
Padre Nuestro
Palm Springs Weekend
Palooka
The Paper▶
The Paper Chase▶
Parenthood▶
Patti Rocks▶
People Will Talk▶
Peppermint Soda▶
Perfect Timing

Perfumed Nightmare▶
Period of Adjustment▶
Pete 'n' Tillie
Peter's Friends
The Philadelphia Story▶
The Pickle
Pictures
Ping Pong
Pink Cadillac
Pink Nights
P.K. and the Kid
Playboy of the Western World
Pocketful of Miracles▶
The Pointsman
Pollyanna
Pollyanna▶
Popi▶
Portnoy's Complaint
Postcards from the Edge▶
Power
Powwow Highway▶
Preacherman
Pretty in Pink
Pride of the Bowery
The Prime of Miss Jean Brodie▶
Primrose Path
The Princess & the Call Girl
Prisoner of Second Avenue
Prisoners of Inertia
The Private History of a Campaign That Failed
Prizzi's Honor▶
Problem Child
Promised Land▶
Psychedelic Fever
Punchline
Purple People Eater
Quarterback Princess
Queen of Hearts▶
The Rachel Papers▶
Racquet
Rafferty & the Gold Dust Twins
Rags to Riches
The Rascals
Ratboy
The Red Light Sting
Remedy for Riches
Reno and the Doc
Return of the Secaucus 7▶
Rich and Famous
Ride the Wild Surf
Robert et Robert▶
Rocket Gibraltar▶
Romance of a Horsethief
Roommate
The Rules of the Game▶
The Runnin' Kind
Sadie McKee▶
Saving Grace
Say Anything▶
Scenes from a Mall
Scoumoune
Second Thoughts
Secrets of Women▶
Seduced and Abandoned▶
The Seducer
The Seven Percent Solution▶
Seven Thieves
Shadows and Fog
Shag: The Movie▶
Shirley Valentine▶
A Shock to the System▶
Shooters
Short Cuts▶
Side Out
Signs of Life
Simon, King of the Witches
A Simple Twist of Fate
Single Bars, Single Women
Six in Paris
Six Weeks
Sizzle Beach U.S.A.
Skin Game▶
Slap Shot▶
Slaves of New York
Slightly Honorable
The Slugger's Wife
Smart Alecks
Smugglers' Cove▶
The Snapper▶

Snoopy, Come Home▶
Soldier in the Rain
Some Kind of Hero
Some Kind of Wonderful
Something in Common
Something Special
Song of the Thin Man
Soul Man
Spencer's Mountain
Spike of Bensonhurst
Spitfire▶
Splash
Spoiled Children
Spook Busters
The Sprinter
Stage Door▶
Star of Midnight
Star Spangled Girl
Stardust Memories
Starlight Hotel
Starting Over▶
Staying Together
Steamboat Bill, Jr.▶
Stoogemania
Storm in a Teacup
The Story of Seabiscuit
Stranger than Paradise▶
Strawberry Blonde▶
Street Music
Strong Man▶
Stroszek▶
Stuck on You
Student Confidential
Sugarbaby▶
The Sugarland Express▶
Summer Fantasy
The Sunshine Boys▶
Suppose They Gave a War and Nobody Came?
Swedenhielms
Sweet Adeline
Sweet Hearts Dance
Sweet Lorraine▶
Sweet William▶
Sweetie▶
Swept Away...▶
Swing Shift
Sylvia Scarlett
T Bone N Weasel
Table Settings
Take Down
Take This Job & Shove It
Take Your Best Shot
A Tale of Springtime
Talking Walls
Taxi Blues▶
A Taxing Woman▶
Teachers
Teacher's Pet▶
Teddy at the Throttle
Teddy at the Throttle/ Speeding Along
10
Teresa Venerdi▶
Texasville
That's Life!
That's My Baby!
They Might Be Giants▶
The Thin Man Goes Home
Things Change▶
This is My Life
Those Lips, Those Eyes
A Thousand Clowns▶
Three for the Road
Three in the Attic
Three Men and a Baby▶
Three Men and a Cradle▶
Three Men and a Little Lady
Thunder in the City▶
Thursday's Child
Thursday's Game▶
A Tiger's Tale
The Time of Your Life▶
Timepiece
Tin Men
The Tip-Off
Tito and Me▶
To Please a Lady
To Sleep with Anger▶
Toby Tyler▶
Tom Brown's School Days
Tom Brown's School Days▶

Tom Sawyer▶
Tony Draws a Horse
Too Pretty to Be Honest
Tootsie▶
Topaze▶
Torch Song Trilogy
Toys
Trading Hearts
The Tragedy of a Ridiculous Man
Train to Hollywood▶
Travels with My Aunt
Trouble Along the Way
Trouble in the Glen
True Love▶
Truly, Madly, Deeply▶
Trust
Truth About Women
Tunes of Glory/Horse's Mouth
Turk 182!
Turkish Delights
Twenty Bucks▶
Twenty-One
29th Street
Twister
Two for the Road▶
Two for the Seesaw▶
Ugetsu▶
Under the Biltmore Clock
Under the Boardwalk
An Unfinished Piece for a Player Piano▶
Up the Down Staircase▶
Up the Sandbox
Used People
The Vals
Very Close Quarters
The Virgin Soldiers
Volpone▶
Wait Until Spring, Bandini
Walls of Glass
We Think the World of You▶
Weekend at the Waldorf▶
Welcome Home, Roxy Carmichael
We're No Angels
Whatever Happened to Susan Jane?
When Your Lover Leaves
Where the Heart Is
Whitcomb's War
The Whole Shootin' Match▶
Who's Who
Whose Life Is It Anyway?▶
Widow's Peak
Wild in the Streets
Willie & Phil
Wings of Eagles
Winter Kills▶
Wired
Wise Blood▶
Wish You Were Here▶
With Honors
The Wizard
The Women
The World According to Garp▶
World of Henry Orient▶
Woza Albert!
WR: Mysteries of the Organism▶
The Wrong Arm of the Law▶
A Yank in Australia
A Year in Provence▶
The Year My Voice Broke▶
Yesterday, Today and Tomorrow▶
You Are Not Alone
The Young in Heart▶
You're a Big Boy Now▶
A Zed & Two Noughts▶

Comedy Performance

see Concert Films

Comic Adventure

see also Action Adventure; Comedy

The Absent-Minded Professor▶

Comic

Adventures Beyond Belief
Adventures in Babysitting
Adventures in Spying
Adventures of a Private Eye
Adventures of a Taxi Driver
The Adventures of Bullwhip
   Griffin
Air America
Alien from L.A.
All the Lovin' Kinfolk
All the Way, Boys
The Amazing Dobermans
The Ambushers
Amenaza Nuclear
The Americano
Andy and the Airwave
   Rangers
Angel of H.E.A.T.
Angels Hard as They Come
Another 48 Hrs.
Another Stakeout
The Armour of God
Avenging Disco Godfather
Baby on Board
Back Roads
Back to the Future▶
Back to the Future, Part 2
Back to the Future, Part 3▶
Bad Guys
Bagdad Cafe▶
The Balloonatic/One Week
The Baltimore Bullet
Bananas Boat
Behind the Front
Beverly Hills Cop
Beverly Hills Cop 2
Beverly Hills Cop 3
The Big Slice
Big Zapper
Bingo
Bird on a Wire
Bloodstone
Blue Iguana
Body Trouble
Boris and Natasha: The Movie
Brink's Job▶
Brothers O'Toole
Burglar
Butler's Dilemma
California Straight Ahead
Campus Knights
Cannibal Women in the
   Avocado Jungle of Death
Cannonball Run
Cannonball Run 2
The Captain from Koepenick
Captain Swagger
Cartouche▶
Chan is Missing▶
Chu Chu & the Philly Flash
City Heat
Club Med
Collision Course
The Concrete Cowboys
Crocodile Dundee▶
Crocodile Dundee 2
Dirt Bike Kid
Doctor Detroit
Dog Pound Shuffle▶
Dolemite 2: Human Tornado
The Double O Kid
Down to Earth▶
El Profesor Hippie
Every Girl Should Have One
Explosion
Fast Getaway
Feds
The Fifth Musketeer
Fifty/Fifty
The Fighting American
Filthy Harry
Flatfoot
Flirting with Fate▶
Flush It
Forever Young
48 Hrs.▶
Foul Play▶
Free Ride
The Further Adventures of
   Tennessee Buck
Ghostbusters▶
Ghostbusters 2

Go for It
The Golden Child
The Gumshoe Kid
Gunmen
Hambone & Hillie
Having Wonderful Time/
   Carnival Boat
Hawthorne of the USA
Here We Go Again!
High Road to China
High Voltage
Highpoint
Hudson Hawk
Ice Pirates
In Like Flint
In 'n Out
It's in the Bag
Jake Speed
Jane & the Lost City
The Jewel of the Nile
Just Tell Me You Love Me
Kindergarten Cop
King Kung Fu
Kiss My Grits
Kuffs
La Petite Bande
Landlord Blues
Last Action Hero
Leonard Part 6
Low Down Dirty Shame
Lucky Devil
Lunch Wagon
Lust in the Dust▶
Mad About Money
Mademoiselle Striptease
Madigan's Millions
Magic Kid
A Man Called Sarge
The Man in the Raincoat
The Man Who Wasn't There
The Man With One Red Shoe
Master Mind
The Masters of Menace
Memoirs of an Invisible Man
Messalina, Empress of Rome
Miami Supercops
Midnight Madness
Midnight Run▶
Miracles
Mr. Billion
Mr. Nanny
Mr. Robinson Crusoe
Mr. Superinvisible
Mitchell
Mo' Money
Mob Story
Mom and Dad Save the World
The Money
Monkey Hustle
Monkey's Uncle
Mutants In Paradise
My African Adventure
My Breakfast with Blassie
My Dog, the Thief
My Science Project
The Naked Sword of Zorro
No Deposit, No Return
Oddball Hall
Odds and Evens
Our Man Flint
Over the Hill
Pippi Goes on Board
Pippi in the South Seas
Pippi Longstocking
Pippi on the Run
Pirates
Prehysteria
The Prince of Thieves
Red Lion
Reggie Mixes In▶
Rescue Me
The Return of the Musketeers
Return of the Rebels
Riff-Raff
Romancing the Stone▶
Round Trip to Heaven
Running Scared
Russkies
Seven
Sherlock's Rivals & Where's
   My Wife

She's Back
Shoot
Short Time▶
Shredder Orpheus
The Silver Streak▶
Ski Patrol
Sky High
Slither▶
Smokey and the Bandit
Smokey and the Bandit, Part
   2
Smokey and the Bandit, Part
   3
Smokey & the Judge
Smokey Bites the Dust
Spaghetti House
Special Delivery
Speed Zone
Speedy▶
Spies, Lies and Naked Thighs
Spy Trap
Spy with a Cold Nose
S*P*Y*S
The Squeeze
Stakeout
Stand-In
Steelyard Blues
Stepmonster
The Stick-Up
The Sting 2
Stingray
Stop! or My Mom Will Shoot
Stop That Cab
Stuntwoman
Suburban Commando
Suffering Bastards
The Suitors
Summer Night
Summer Night with Greek
   Profile, Almond Eyes &
   Scent of Basil
Sunburn
Super Fuzz
Super Kung Fu Kid
Super Soul Brother
Surf Nazis Must Die
Surf Ninjas
Survivors
Swashbuckler
The Tall Blond Man with One
   Black Shoe▶
Tall, Tan and Terrific
A Taxing Woman's Return▶
Teenage Mutant Ninja Turtles:
   The Movie
Teenage Mutant Ninja Turtles
   2: The Secret of the Ooze
Teenage Mutant Ninja Turtles
   3
Terminal Exposure
That Man from Rio
That Sinking Feeling▶
They Met in Bombay
The Thief Who Came to
   Dinner
Think Big
This Time I'll Make You Rich
Those Daring Young Men in
   Their Jaunty Jalopies
Those Fantastic Flying Fools
Those Magnificent Men in
   Their Flying Machines▶
Three Amigos
Three Fugitives
Three Kinds of Heat
The Three Musketeers▶
3 Ninjas
3 Ninjas Kick Back
Thunder and Lightning
Thunder in the Pines
Title Shot
Toga Party
Too Hot to Handle▶
Topkapi▶
Tough Guys
Treasure of the Moon
   Goddess
Trenchcoat
TripleCross
Trouble in Store
The Trouble with Spies
True Lies▶

12 Plus 1▶
Twins
Under the Rainbow
Up the Creek
Uphill All the Way
Uptown Saturday Night
Van Nuys Blvd.
Vice Academy
Vice Academy 2
Vice Academy 3
The Victim
Viva Maria!
Wackiest Ship in the Army
We're No Angels
When the Clouds Roll By▶
Who Killed Mary What's 'Er
   Name?
The Wild and the Free
Wishman
World Gone Wild
Wrong is Right
Year of the Comet
The Yum-Yum Girls

Coming of Age

see also Teen Angst
The Abe Lincoln of Ninth
   Avenue
Across the Great Divide
The Affairs of Annabel
Ah, Wilderness!▶
Alan & Naomi
All Fall Down
All the Right Moves
Aloha Summer
Alpine Fire
Amarcord▶
American Boyfriends
American Graffiti▶
An American Summer
Among the Cinders
Angele▶
Angelo My Love▶
Anne of Green Gables▶
Anthony Adverse
Aparajito▶
The Apprenticeship of Duddy
   Kravitz▶
Au Revoir Les Enfants▶
Baby It's You▶
Back Door to Heaven▶
Battling Bunyon
Big▶
The Big Bet
The Big Red One▶
Billy Bathgate
Billyboy
The Birch Interval
Blue Fin
Blue Jeans
The Blue Lagoon
Blue Velvet▶
Boss' Son▶
The Boys in Company C
Breaking Away▶
Breaking Home Ties
Brighton Beach Memoirs
A Bronx Tale▶
Buddy's Song
Calendar Girl
Can You Feel Me Dancing?
Can't Buy Me Love
Carnal Knowledge▶
The Chicken Chronicles
China, My Sorrow
City Boy▶
Civil War Diary
Class
Class of '44
The Claw
Closely Watched Trains▶
Clowning Around 2
Cocktail
Cold Sassy Tree▶
The Color of Money▶
Come and See▶
Courage Mountain
Courtship▶
Crazy Moon
Cria▶
The Crossing
Crossing the Bridge

A Cry in the Wild▶
Cry of Battle
Culpepper Cattle Co.
Dakota
David Holzman's Diary▶
Dead Poets Society▶
December
The Deer Hunter▶
Desert Bloom▶
The Devil's Playground▶
Diner▶
Dirty Dancing▶
Dogfight▶
Dragstrip Girl
Dutch Girls
Edward Scissorhands▶
Emanon
Ernesto
Experience Preferred... But
   Not Essential
The Eyes of Youth
Eyes Right!
Family Prayers
Fandango
Fast Times at Ridgemont
   High▶
Father▶
Feelin' Screwy
Fellini Satyricon▶
The Fire in the Stone
First Affair
First Love
The First Time
The Flamingo Kid▶
For Love Alone
Forever
Forever Young
The 400 Blows▶
Foxes
Freedom is Paradise▶
Friends Forever▶
A Friendship in Vienna
Frogs!
Gas Food Lodging▶
A Generation▶
The Getting of Wisdom
Gidget
A Girl of the Limberlost
The Gold & Glory
Goodbye Columbus▶
Goodbye, Miss 4th of July
Goodbye, My Lady
The Graduate▶
The Great Outdoors
The Great Santini▶
Gregory's Girl▶
Grown Ups
Hairspray▶
Hangin' with the Homeboys▶
Happy Birthday, Gemini
Hard Choices▶
Heathers▶
Heaven Help Us
A Hero Ain't Nothin' But a
   Sandwich
Higher Education
Homeboy
Homework
The Horse▶
Horsemen
Hot Moves
The Hour of the Star▶
How I Learned to Love
   Women
Huck and the King of Hearts
The Human Comedy▶
I Know Why the Caged Bird
   Sings▶
I Vitelloni▶
If Looks Could Kill
Il Sorpasso
In Praise of Older Women
In the Custody of Strangers▶
Indian Paint
Inga
The Inheritors
The Islander
Jacob Have I Loved
Joey
Johnny Be Good
Jory
The Journey of Natty Gann▶

Junior High School
The Karate Kid▶
The Karate Kid: Part 2
The Karate Kid: Part 3
King of the Gypsies
King of the Hill▶
Kings Row▶
Kipperbang
The Kitchen Toto▶
La Boum
La Symphonie Pastorale▶
Labyrinth▶
The Last Prostitute
Late Summer Blues
The Lawrenceville Stories
Le Grand Chemin▶
The Learning Tree
Les Mistons▶
L'Homme Blesse▶
The Lion King▶
Little Ballerina
A Little Romance▶
Little Women▶
Little Women
The Long Day Closes▶
The Lords of Flatbush
Lost Legacy: A Girl Called
    Hatter Fox
Love Film
Lucas▶
Maid to Order
The Man from Snowy River
The Man in the Moon▶
A Man of Passion
The Man Without a Face
The Mango Tree
Matinee
Mean Streets▶
The Member of the Wedding▶
Men of Ireland
Metropolitan▶
Mickey
A Midnight Clear▶
Milk Money
Mirrors
Mischief
Monika
More American Graffiti
Mosby's Marauders
Murmur of the Heart▶
My American Cousin▶
My Apprenticeship▶
My Bodyguard▶
My Brilliant Career▶
My Girl
My Girl 2▶
My Life as a Dog▶
My Tutor
My Universities▶
Mystic Pizza▶
Next Stop, Greenwich
    Village▶
Nicholas Nickleby▶
A Night in the Life of Jimmy
    Reardon
1969▶
No Regrets for Our Youth▶
No Secrets
No Time for Sergeants▶
Norman Loves Rose
A Nos Amours▶
Odd Birds
Oddballs
Ode to Billy Joe
Oh, What a Night
Old Enough
One on One
Out of the Blue▶
The Outsiders
Over the Edge▶
Over the Summer
Palm Beach
The Paper Chase▶
Paradise
The Passing of Evil
Pather Panchali▶
Pauline at the Beach▶
P.C.U.
Peck's Bad Boy
Peppermint Soda▶
Peter Lundy and the Medicine
    Hat Stallion

Platoon▶
Portrait of a Lady
The Power of One
The Prodigal
Promised Land▶
Quadrophenia▶
Racing with the Moon▶
Rambling Rose▶
Ramparts of Clay▶
The Rascals
The Razor's Edge▶
The Razor's Edge
The Red Fury
Red Kiss▶
Red Nights
The Reivers▶
Reunion▶
Risky Business▶
The River▶
A River Runs Through It▶
A Room with a View▶
Rumble Fish▶
St. Elmo's Fire
Samurai 1: Musashi
    Miyamoto▶
The Sandlot▶
Sands of Iwo Jima▶
Sarafina!▶
Savage is Loose
Scent of a Woman▶
The Scent of Green Papaya▶
A Secret Space
Secrets
A Separate Peace
Seven Minutes in Heaven
Shaking the Tree
Sharma & Beyond
She's Out of Control
Shipwrecked
Shout
Side Show
Sixteen
Smooth Talk▶
Snow: The Movie
Soldier of Orange▶
Some Kind of Wonderful
Sons of Steel
Sounder▶
SpaceCamp
Spy of Napoleon
Square Dance
Stacking
Star Wars▶
Starlight Hotel
Strikeback
The Stripper
Stuckey's Last Stand
Studs Lonigan
Summer Affair
Summer Fantasy
Summer Holiday
Summer Interlude▶
Summer of '42▶
Summer Vacation: 1999
Sunnyside
Sweet 15
Swing Kids
The Sword in the Stone▶
Teenage Mutant Ninja Turtles
    2: The Secret of the Ooze
Tex
That Brennan Girl
That Naughty Girl
That Night
That Was Then...This Is Now
36 Fillete▶
This Boy's Life▶
Those Glory, Glory Days
Thunder Alley
A Tiger's Tale
Time of the Gypsies▶
Time Stands Still▶
A Time to Remember
Toby Tyler▶
Tomboy & the Champ
Tonio Kroger
Top Gun
A Tree Grows in Brooklyn▶
Twenty-One
Twist & Shout▶
Two Daughters▶
Vision Quest▶

Wanderers▶
What's Eating Gilbert Grape▶
Where the Red Fern Grows:
    Part 2
Who Has Seen the Wind?
Who Shot Pat?
Who's That Knocking at My
    Door?▶
Why Shoot the Teacher▶
The Wild Child▶
Winner Takes All
The Wishing Ring▶
With Honors
The Year My Voice Broke▶
The Yearling▶
The Young and the Guilty
The Young Graduates
Young Guns 2
Young Love, First Love
Young Sherlock Holmes
Young Tom Edison
Youngblood
You're a Big Boy Now▶
Zapped!

Computers

**see also Robots &
Androids; Technology-
Rampant**
The Computer Wore Tennis
    Shoes
Dangerous Game
Demon Seed▶
Desk Set▶
The Double O Kid
Electric Dreams
Evilspeak
Homewrecker
The Honeymoon Machine
The Human Factor
Interface
The Lawnmower Man
Prime Risk
The Scorpio Factor
Superman 3
Tin Man
WarGames

Concert Films

**see also Rock Stars on
Film**
Benny Hill's Crazy World
The Best of Abbott & Costello
    Live
Best of Comic Relief
Best of Comic Relief '90
The Best of the Kids in the
    Hall
Bill Cosby, Himself
Bill Murray Live from the
    Second City
Billy Crystal: A Comic's Line
Billy Crystal: Midnight Train to
    Moscow
Bloodhounds of Broadway
Clark & McCullough
Divine Madness
Eddie Murphy "Delirious"
Eddie Murphy: Raw
An Evening with Robin
    Williams
George Carlin: Doin' It Again
George Carlin: Jammin' in
    New York
Gimme Shelter
Hollywood Goes to War
Jo Jo Dancer, Your Life is
    Calling
John Cleese on How to Irritate
    People
The Last Waltz
Lenny
Lenny Bruce Performance
    Film
Mad Dog and Glory▶
Mr. Mike's Mondo Video
Monster in a Box▶
Monterey Pop▶
Monty Python Live at the
    Hollywood Bowl▶

Monty Python Meets Beyond
    the Fringe
National Lampoon's Class of
    '86
Punchline
Rap Master Ronnie
Scrambled Feet
Search for Signs of Intelligent
    Life in the Universe▶
Second City Insanity
The Secret Policeman's Other
    Ball▶
Secret Policeman's Private
    Parts
A Session with the Committee
Sex, Drugs, Rock & Roll: Eric
    Bogosian
Spalding Gray: Terrors of
    Pleasure
Steve Martin Live
Stop Making Sense▶
Wisecracks▶
Woodstock▶
You Can't Take It with You▶
You So Crazy

Contemporary
Musicals

see also Musicals
All That Jazz▶
The Apple
Blame It on the Night
Body Beat
Breakin'
Breakin' 2: Electric Boogaloo
Breakin' Through
Breaking Glass
A Chorus Line
Fame▶
The Josephine Baker Story▶

Cooking

see Edibles

Cops

**see also Buddy Cops;
Detectives; Loner Cops;
Women Cops**
Abraxas: Guardian of the
    Universe
Across 110th Street
Action Jackson
The Adventures of a Gnome
    Named Gnorm
Alien Nation
Alone in the Neon Jungle
American Justice
The Amsterdam Kill
Animal Instincts
Arizona Heat
Armed and Dangerous
Assault on Precinct 13▶
At Gunpoint
B.A.D. Cats
Bad Lieutenant▶
Badge of the Assassin
Badge 373
Ballbuster
Band of the Hand
Before Morning
Belfast Assassin
Bellamy
Beretta's Island
Best Kept Secrets
Best Seller▶
Beverly Hills Cop
Beverly Hills Cop 2
Beverly Hills Cop 3
Big Chase
Big Combo▶
The Big Easy▶
Big Heat▶
Big Score
The Big Slice
Birds of Prey
Black Dragon
Black Eliminator
The Black Marble▶
Black Rain

Blackmail▶
Blackout
Blade
Blink
Blood on the Badge
Bloody Avenger
Blown Away▶
Blue Desert▶
The Blue Knight
The Blue Lamp▶
Blue Steel
Blue Thunder
Bopha!▶
The Boston Strangler
Brannigan
Brass
Broken Badge▶
Bullets or Ballots▶
Bunco
Busting
Car 54, Where Are You?
Caroline at Midnight
The Carpathian Eagle
A Case of Deadly Force▶
Champion Operation
The Chase
Chiefs
China Moon
Chinatown Connection
The Chinatown Murders: Man
    Against the Mob
Choice of Weapons
The Choirboys
City Heat
City That Never Sleeps
Clayton County Line
Cobra
Code of Silence
Cold Front
Cold Steel
Coldfire
Colors▶
Confessions of a Police
    Captain
Conflict of Interest
Coogan's Bluff▶
Cop
Cop and a Half
The Cop & the Girl
Cop-Out
Cops and Robbersons
Cornbread, Earl & Me
Corrupt▶
Cotton Comes to Harlem▶
Coup de Torchon▶
Crime Busters
The Crow
Danger Ahead
The Dark
Dark Before Dawn
Dead Bang
Dead Heat
Deadly Breed
Deadly Conspiracy
Deadly Diamonds
Deadly Hero▶
Deadly Matrimony
Deadly Surveillance
Death Shot
The Death Squad
Deceptions
Deep Cover
Deep Space
The Delicate Delinquent
Delta Heat
Demolition Man
The Detective▶
Detective Story▶
Detroit 9000
Devil's Angels
The Devil's Undead
Devlin
Die Hard▶
Die Hard 2: Die Harder▶
Dirty Harry▶
Dirty Mind of Young Sally
Diva▶
Do or Die
Dollman
Dollman vs Demonic Toys
Double Trouble
Dragnet

Cops

Drying Up the Streets
El Gendarme Desconocido
Electra Glide in Blue▶
Ex-Cop
Extreme Justice
Extreme Prejudice
Extreme Vengeance
An Eye for an Eye
Eyewitness
Eyewitness to Murder
Fatal Chase
Fatal Error
Fatal Instinct
The Female Jungle
Fever
Final Embrace
Find the Lady
Firepower
The First Deadly Sin
Flashpoint
Flatfoot
Force of One
The Formula
Fort Apache, the Bronx▶
Fortune Dane
48 Hrs.▶
Foul Play
Frame Up
Freebie & the Bean
The French Connection▶
French Connection 2▶
The French Detective▶
French Quarter Undercover
French Silk
Full Eclipse
Full Exposure: The Sex Tape Scandals
Future Cop
Future Force
Fuzz
Gambler's Choice
The Gauntlet
Get Christie Love!
The Glitter Dome
Glitz
Go for It
God Told Me To
Gone are the Days
Gone in 60 Seconds
Gorky Park▶
Hard-Boiled
Hard Vice
The Hard Way▶
Hardcase and Fist
Hawkeye
He Walked by Night▶
Hear No Evil
Heaven's Heroes
Heroes in Blue
The Hidden▶
The Hidden 2
High & Low▶
High Crime
Hill Street Blues, Vol. 1: Hill Street Station
Hollywood Vice Squad
Homicide▶
The Hot Rock▶
Hot Stuff
The Hunted Lady
I Take This Oath
Impulse
In the Heat of the Night▶
Indecent Behavior
The Indian Runner
Innocent Blood
Inside Information
Internal Affairs
It Could Happen to You
Jailbait
The January Man
Jennifer 8
Jigsaw
K-9
K-9000
Kamikaze '89▶
Karate Cop
Keaton's Cop
Keeper of the City
Kidnapped
The Kill Reflex
The Killer's Edge

The Killing Mind
The Killing Time
Kiss of Death▶
The Klansman
Klute▶
Knife in the Head
Kuffs
La Balance▶
L.A. Bounty
L.A. Heat
L.A. Vice
L.A. Wars
Lady Scarface/The Threat
Ladykiller
Laguna Heat
Laser Moon
The Last of the Finest
Laughing Policeman
Law and Disorder▶
Legacy of Lies
Lethal Obsession
Lethal Weapon▶
Lethal Weapon 2▶
Lethal Weapon 3
Lightblast
Lockdown
Lone Star Law Men
Love and Bullets
Love on the Run
Mad Dog and Glory▶
Mad Max▶
Madigan▶
Malarek
The Man Inside
Man on a String
Maniac Cop
Maniac Cop 2
Maniac Cop 3
Mardi Gras for the Devil
Martial Law
Martial Law 2: Undercover
Martial Outlaw
Maximum Force
McQ
Miami Blues
Miami Cops
Miami Vice
Midnight Witness
Mind, Body & Soul
Mind Twister
Mission of Justice
Mr. Inside, Mr. Outside
Mitchell
The Mod Squad
Model by Day
Money to Burn
Monolith
More! Police Squad
Motor Patrol
Moving Violations
My New Partner
Mystery Date
Nails
The Naked City▶
The Naked Gun: From the Files of Police Squad▶
Naked Gun 33 1/3: The Final Insult
Naked Gun 2 1/2: The Smell of Fear
The Narrow Margin▶
National Lampoon's Loaded Weapon 1
The New Centurions
New Jack City
New York Ripper
Next of Kin
Night Children
Night Game
Night of the Cyclone
Night Partners
The Night Patrol
Night Patrol
Night Stalker
Nightstick
Ninja Vengeance
No Escape, No Return
No Man's Land
Northwest Trail
Off the Wall
The Offence▶
One Man Force

One Man Jury
The Onion Field▶
Pair of Aces
Pendulum
P.I. Private Investigations
Piece of the Action
Point of Impact
Police
Police Academy
Police Academy 2: Their First Assignment
Police Academy 3: Back in Training
Police Academy 4: Citizens on Patrol
Police Academy 5: Assignment Miami Beach
Police Academy 6: City Under Siege
Police Squad! Help Wanted!
Policewoman Centerfold
Policewomen
Prime Suspect▶
Prime Suspect 2▶
Prime Target
Prince of the City▶
Private Investigations
Provoked
Prowler
Puppet on a Chain
Q & A
Question of Honor
Rage and Honor 2: Hostile Takeover
Rainbow Drive
Rapid Fire
A Real American Hero
Recruits
Relentless
Relentless 2: Dead On
Renfrew of the Royal Mounted
Rent-A-Cop
Return to Macon County
Return to Mayberry
Ricochet▶
Ring of Death
Rising Sun▶
RoboCop▶
Rock House
Romeo Is Bleeding
The Rookie
Roots of Evil
Rush▶
The Rutherford County Line
Sands of Sacrifice
The Satan Killer
Scanner Cop
Scorchy
Season for Assassins
Self-Defense
Serpico▶
Shadow Force
Shadowhunter
Shakedown
Sharky's Machine
Shoot It Black, Shoot It Blue
Short Time▶
Showdown at the Equator
Silk 2
Sketch Artist
Skull: A Night of Terror
Slipstream
Slow Burn
Small Kill
A Small Killing
Smokey & the Judge
Snapdragon
Soggy Bottom U.S.A.
Son of the Pink Panther
Soul Patrol
South Seas Massacre
Speed▶
Speedtrap
Split Second
Stamp of a Killer
Station
Steele's Law
The Stone Killer
Stop! or My Mom Will Shoot
A Stranger Among Us
Street Crimes

Street War
Strike Force
Striking Distance
Super Force
Super Fuzz
Supervixens
Sweet Trash
The Take
Taking the Heat
Ten to Midnight
Tereza▶
Terror Stalks the Class Reunion
They Call Me Mr. Tibbs!
They Only Kill Their Masters
Tightrope▶
Till Death Do Us Part
A Time to Die
To Protect and Serve
Top of the Heap
Touch of Evil▶
Traces of Red
Trancers
Trancers 2: The Return of Jack Deth
Trancers 3: Deth Lives
Trancers 4: Jack of Swords
True Romance
Turner and Hooch
Twisted Justice
Under Investigation
Undercover
Undercover Cop
Underground Terror
Union Station
Unlawful Entry
Vampire Cop
Vengeance
Vice Academy
Vice Academy 2
Vice Academy 3
Walker: Texas Ranger: One Riot, One Ranger
Walking Tall: The Final Chapter
The Warning
Whispers of White
The Wild Pair
Witchcraft 6
Witness▶
X Marks the Spot
Year of the Dragon
Zipperface

Corporate Shenanigans

see also *Advertising*
The Abduction of Allison Tate
Acceptable Risks
All in a Night's Work
And Nothing But the Truth
Any Wednesday
The Apartment▶
April Fools
As Young As You Feel▶
Ask Any Girl
The Bad Sleep Well▶
Barbarians at the Gate▶
The Battle of the Sexes▶
Beggars in Ermine
Behind Office Doors
Big Business Girl
Big Trees▶
The Bikini Car Wash Company
The Bikini Car Wash Company 2
Blood Red
Body Language
Boom Town
Boomerang
Buy & Cell
The Capture of Bigfoot
The Carpetbaggers
Cash McCall
Catherine & Co.
China White
C.H.O.M.P.S.
Circle of Power
Class of Nuke 'Em High, Part 2: Subhumanoid Meltdown

The Coca-Cola Kid▶
The Colombian Connection
Consuming Passions
Corporate Affairs
Crime of Honor
The Crime of Monsieur Lange▶
Cyborg 2
Dark River: A Father's Revenge
The Daydreamer
Deadly Business▶
Deadly Conspiracy
Dealers
Death Chase
Death Collector
The Devil & Miss Jones▶
Devil's Crude
Dodsworth▶
Dragonfight
Dutch Treat
The Efficiency Expert
The Empty Beach
End of the Line
Eternity
Executive Suite▶
Fatal Confinement
Fatal Skies
Feel the Motion
The Flintstones
FM
For Love or Money
Ford: The Man & the Machine
Freaked
Frozen Assets
Gas
Gas Pump Girls
Glengarry Glen Ross▶
Good Neighbor Sam▶
Goodfellas▶
Gremlins 2: The New Batch▶
Gung Ho
Halloween 3: Season of the Witch
Happy Hour
The Harder They Come
Head Office
Her Husband's Affairs
Herbie Rides Again
His Girl Friday▶
Home Town Story
Hot Chocolate
How to Get Ahead in Advertising▶
How to Succeed in Business without Really Trying▶
The Hucksters▶
The Hudsucker Proxy▶
I Love Trouble
If I Were Rich
Indio 2: The Revolt
Journey to Spirit Island
A Kiss Before Dying
La Truite▶
Land of Promise
The Last Hour
The Lavender Hill Mob▶
Life Stinks
Limit Up
Little Giant
Love or Money?
Major League
Mama, There's a Man in Your Bed▶
The Man in the Gray Flannel Suit
The Man in the White Suit▶
The Man Inside
Married to It
A Matter of WHO
Megaville
Millions
Miss Grant Takes Richmond
Mo' Money
Morals for Women
Naked Gun 2 1/2: The Smell of Fear
Network▶
The Night They Saved Christmas
9 to 5
No Room to Run

No Time to Die
Nowhere to Run
One, Two, Three▶
Other People's Money
The Other Side of Midnight
Pajama Game▶
The Paper▶
Parrish
Patterns▶
The Player▶
Power
Primal Scream
Private Wars
Property
A Public Affair
Putney Swope▶
The Queen of Mean
Quicksand: No Escape
Return Fire
Rising Sun▶
RoboCop 3
Roger & Me▶
Rollover
Scrooged
The Secret of My Success
Sensations of 1945
Shadow of China▶
Shining Star
A Shock to the System▶
The Simple Truth
Sins
Ski Bum
Skyscraper Souls▶
Stand-In▶
Stocks and Blondes
Stormy Monday
The Story of O, Part 2
Strange Brew
Switching Channels
Taffin
Take This Job & Shove It
A Taxing Woman▶
The Temp
They Drive by Night▶
Timepiece
Tin Men
Topaze▶
The Toxic Avenger, Part 3:
    The Last Temptation of
    Toxie
Trading Places
Tucker: The Man and His
    Dream▶
Upper Crust
Utilities
Vortex
Wall Street▶
Wall Street Cowboy
Washington Affair
Weekend at Bernie's
Weekend at Bernie's 2
The Wheeler Dealers▶
Who's Who
The Wildest Office Party
Wolf
Working Girl▶
The World Gone Mad

Courtroom Drama

see Order in the Court

Creepy Houses

see also Horror

Afterward
The Amityville Horror
Amityville 2: The Possession
Amityville 3: The Demon
Amityville 4
The Amityville Curse
Amityville 1992: It's About
    Time
The Bat Whispers
Beyond Darkness
Beyond Evil
Black Cat
Blondie Has Trouble
Blood Island
Blood Legacy
Blue Blood
Burnt Offerings
Candles at Nine

Carnage
Castle in the Desert
Castle of Blood
Castle of the Living Dead
The Cat and the Canary
Cellar Dweller
Contagion
Crazed
Cthulhu Mansion
Demon Wind
Die Sister, Die!
Dolls
Don't Be Afraid of the Dark
Endless Night
The Evictors
The Evil
Evil Laugh
Evil Toons
Fear in the Night▶
Flowers in the Attic
Forever: A Ghost of a Love
    Story
Fright House
Fright Night
The Ghastly Ones
The Ghost Breakers▶
Girls School Screamers
Goblin
House▶
House 2: The Second Story
House 4: Home Deadly Home
House of Mystery
The House of Secrets
House of the Dead
House of the Living Dead
House of the Long Shadows
House on the Rising Sun
House on Haunted Hill
House on Marsh Road
The House on Tombstone Hill
The House that Bled to Death
The House that Dripped Blood
The House that Vanished
House Where Evil Dwells
La Chute de la Maison Usher▶
The Legend of Hell House▶
Malice
The Mephisto Waltz▶
Million Dollar Mystery
Monsters Crash the Pajama
    Party
Mother's Day
Murder Mansion
The Nesting
Next of Kin
Night Nurse
Night of the Demons 2
The Old Dark House▶
The People Under the Stairs
The Perverse Countess
The Phantom
Psycho▶
Psycho 2
Psycho 3
Psycho 4: The Beginning
Rest In Pieces
Revenge in the House of
    Usher
The Rocky Horror Picture
    Show▶
Salem's Lot
The Screaming Skull
The Shining
Silent Scream
Sister, Sister
Spookies
A Strange and Deadly
    Occurence
Superstition
Tangled Destinies
Teenage Exorcist
Terror in the Haunted House
13 Ghosts
Treasure of Fear
The Uninvited▶
Visions of Evil
Web of the Spider
What a Carve-Up!
Who Killed Doc Robbin?

Crime & Criminals

see also Crime Sprees;
Crimes of Passion;
Disorganized Crime;
Fugitives; Organized
Crime; Serial Killers;
Vigilantes

Action Jackson
After Dark, My Sweet▶
Air Hawk
Al Capone▶
Algiers▶
Alien Nation
All Dogs Go to Heaven
Alligator Alley
Almost an Angel
Ambush Trail
American Autobahn
Amongst Friends
Amor Bandido
And Then You Die▶
Angel's Brigade
Angels Hard as They Come
Angels of the City
Angels with Dirty Faces▶
Another 48 Hrs.
Apprentice to Murder
Arrest Bulldog Drummond
Assault
Assault on a Queen
Assault with a Deadly Weapon
At Gunpoint
The Avenging Hand
Baby, the Rain Must Fall
Back Door to Heaven▶
Backlash
Bad Blood
Bad Bunch
Bandits
Batman▶
Batman Returns
The Bay Boy
The Beast from Haunted Cave
Because of the Cats
Behind the Mask
Being at Home with Claude
Bells of San Angelo
Betrayed
Beverly Hills Cop▶
Beverly Hills Cop 2
Beverly Hills Cop 3
Big Bluff
The Big Easy▶
The Big Grab
Big Heat▶
The Big Scam
Billionaire Boys Club
The Black Cobra
Black Hand
Black Sister's Revenge
Blackout
Blastfighter
Blindside
Blonde Blackmailer
Blonde Crazy
Blood Money: The Story of
    Clinton and Nadine
Blood Ties
Bloodstone
Bloody Mama
Blown Away
Blue Canadian Rockies
Blue Iguana
Body Double▶
Bonnie's Kids
Borderline
Borsalino▶
Boss of Big Town
Boys Town▶
Breaking In▶
Breathless▶
Brewster McCloud▶
Brighton Rock▶
Bring Me the Head of Alfredo
    Garcia
Brotherhood of Justice
Bugsy Malone
Bulldog Drummond's
    Revenge
Bulldog Jack▶
Burglar

Burning Vengeance
Busted Up
Buster
Buying Time
The C-Man
Call Northside 777▶
Cape Fear▶
Caper of the Golden Bulls
Capone
Captain Swagger
Captive
Caribe
Carlito's Way▶
Cartel
Cartier Affair
Cast a Dark Shadow▶
The Cat
The Cat o' Nine Tails
Catch the Heat
Catlow
Chance
Charade
Charade▶
Charley Varrick▶
Cheech and Chong: Things
    Are Tough All Over
The China Lake Murders
The Choirboys
The Choppers
C.I.A.: Code Name Alexa
Circle of Fear
Circonstances Attenuantes
The City
City for Conquest▶
City in Fear▶
City in Panic
City of Hope▶
The Clay Pigeon
Cleopatra Jones
Cleopatra Jones & the Casino
    of Gold
Cliffhanger▶
Clown Murders
The Coast Patrol
Cocaine Wars
Codename Kyril
Cold Feet
Cold Sweat
Color Me Dead
Colors▶
Commando Squad
Compromising Positions
The Con Artists
Con Man
Concrete Beat
Conexion Oriental
Confessions of a Hit Man
Confessions of Tom Harris
Confidential
Confidentially Yours▶
The Connection
Contraband
Convicts at Large
Cop
The Cop & the Girl
Cop in Blue Jeans
Cotton Comes to Harlem▶
Couples and Robbers
The Courier
Cover-Up
Covert Action
Crazy Mama
Crime and Punishment▶
Crime of Passion
Crime Story: The Complete
    Saga
Crimes & Misdemeanors▶
Crimewave
Criminal Justice▶
Criminal Law
Criss Cross▶
Crocodile Dundee 2
The Crow
Cruisin' High
The Cursed Mountain Mystery
Daddy's Boys
Dagger Eyes
Dance Fools Dance▶
Dance or Die
Dance with Death
Dance with Me, Henry
Dancing in the Dark

Danger Zone
Dangerous Heart
Dangerous Mission
Dangerous Orphans
Dangerous Pursuit
The Dark Hour
Dark Passage
Dark Side of Midnight
Darktown Strutters
Day of Atonement
Day of the Assassin
Dayton's Devils
Dead Bang
Dead Heat
Dead Heat on a Merry-Go-
    Round▶
Dead in the Water
Dead Men Don't Wear Plaid
The Dead Pool
Dead Wrong
Deadline Assault
Deadly Darling
Deadly Fieldtrip
Deadly Game
Deadly Hero▶
Deadly Illusion
Deadly Matrimony
Deadly Revenge
Deadly Strangers
Deadly Sunday
Deadly Thief
Dear Murderer
Death in the Shadows
Death of a Scoundrel
Death Ring
Death Tide
Death Wish 4: The
    Crackdown
Deathfight
The Defender
Department Store
Desperate Hours▶
Desperate Hours
The Destructors
The Detective▶
Detective Sadie & Son
Detective School Dropouts
Detour to Danger
Detroit 9000
Devil & Leroy Basset
The Devil at 4 O'Clock
Devil Doll▶
The Devil's Brother
The Devil's Commandment
The Devil's Sleep
Devlin Connection
Diamonds
Diamonds on Wheels
Dick Barton, Special Agent
Dick Barton Strikes Back
Dick Tracy
Dick Tracy▶
Dick Tracy, Detective
Dick Tracy, Detective/The
    Corpse Vanishes
Dick Tracy Returns
Dick Tracy: The Original
    Serial, Vol. 1▶
Dick Tracy: The Original
    Serial, Vol. 2▶
Dick Tracy vs. Crime Inc.
Dick Tracy vs. Cueball
Dick Tracy's Dilemma
Dillinger▶
Dirty Hands
Dirty Mary Crazy Larry▶
Dirty Work
Disciple
Disorganized Crime
Disturbance
Diva▶
The Doberman Gang
The Doctor and the Devils
Dr. Death, Seeker of Souls
Dr. Mabuse the Gambler▶
Dr. Mabuse vs. Scotland Yard
Dog Day
Dog Day Afternoon▶
The Doll Squad
Don Amigo/Stage to Chino
The Don is Dead
Doomed to Die

Crime

Door to Door Maniac
Double Identity
Double Indemnity▶
Down & Dirty▶
Down Twisted
Downtown
Dragnet
Dream No Evil
The Dream Team
Dress Gray
Drive-In Massacre
The Driver
Drug Wars 2: The Cocaine Cartel
Dumb Waiter
The Dummy Talks
East Side Kids
Echo Murders
8 Million Ways to Die
El Cristo de los Milagros
El Muerto
The Element of Crime
11 Harrowhouse▶
Emil and the Detective
Emperor Jones/Paul Robeson: Tribute to an Artist
Emperor of the Bronx
Endangered Species
Endplay
The Enforcer
Enforcer from Death Row
The Equalizer: Memories of Manon
Escapade in Florence
Eternal Evil
Every Girl Should Have One
Everybody Wins
Evil Judgement
The Executioner
The Executioner, Part 2: Frozen Scream
Experiment in Terror▶
Experiment Perilous▶
Exquisite Corpses
Extreme Prejudice
An Eye for an Eye
Eye Witness
Eyeball
Eyewitness
The Face at the Window
The Falcon in Hollywood
Family Enforcer
A Family Matter
Family Plot
The Fantasist
Fantastic Seven
The Fast and the Furious
Fast Getaway
Fast Talking
Fatal Beauty
The Fatal Hour
Fatal Vision
FBI Girl
The FBI Story▶
Fear
Fear in the Night▶
Federal Agent
The Female Jungle
Female Trouble
Fever
Fiction Makers
52 Pick-Up
Fight for Your Life
Fighting Back
Filthy Harry
Final Judgement
Final Justice
Final Mission
The Finger Man
Fingers▶
The Fire in the Stone
The First Deadly Sin
First Name: Carmen▶
The First Power
A Fish Called Wanda▶
F.I.S.T.
Fists of Blood
Fit to Kill
Flame of the Islands
A Flash of Green
Flesh and Bone▶

Flight to Nowhere
Flipper's New Adventure▶
Flying Wild
Fog Island
Follow the Leader
Force of Evil▶
Fort Apache, the Bronx▶
Fortune Dane
48 Hrs.▶
Foul Play
Foxy Brown
Frantic▶
Freebie & the Bean
French Connection 2▶
French Quarter Undercover
Frenzy▶
Fresh Kill
Friday Foster
Frontera Sin Ley
Fun with Dick and Jane
Future Force
The Galloping Ghost
Gambler's Choice
Game of Seduction
Gang Bullets
The Gang's All Here
Gangs, Inc.
The Gangster
Gangster Wars
Gangster's Law
Gangway
Gator
The Gauntlet
The Gazebo▶
Genuine Risk
Getting Even
Ginger
Girl from Chicago
The Girl in Lover's Lane
The Girl Said No
The Girl Who Had Everything
The Glass Key▶
Glitz
The Glove
God Told Me To
The Godfather▶
The Godfather 1902-1959: The Complete Epic▶
The Godfather, Part 2▶
Gods of the Plague▶
Godson▶
The Golden Triangle
Gone in 60 Seconds
Gone to Ground
Goodfellas▶
The Goonies
Gordon's War
Government Agents vs. Phantom Legion
Great Flamarion
The Great Lover
The Great Riviera Bank Robbery
The Great Texas Dynamite Chase
Green Ice
The Grey Fox▶
The Grifters▶
The Guardian
Guilty as Charged
Gulliver
A Gun in the House
Gunmen
The Gunrunner
Hallucination
Happy New Year▶
The Hard Way▶
The Harder They Come
The Haunted Strangler
Having Wonderful Crime
He Kills Night After Night After Night
He Walked by Night▶
Heartbeat
Heat Wave
Held for Murder
Hell Harbor
Hell's House
Henry: Portrait of a Serial Killer▶
The Hidden Room▶

Hide-Out
High & Low▶
High Crime
High Sierra▶
Hit Lady
The Hit List
Hollywood Vice Sqaud
Homicide▶
Honeymoon Killers▶
Honor Among Thieves
Honor Thy Father
The Hooded Terror
The Hoodlum
Hoodlum Empire
The Hostage Tower
Hot Blood
Hot Child in the City
Hot Millions▶
Hot Pursuit
The Hot Rock▶
Hot Spot
A House In The Hills
House of Errors
House of Mystery
How Come Nobody's On Our Side?
How to Beat the High Cost of Living
How to Kill 400 Duponts
Hudson Hawk
Hue and Cry▶
The Human Factor
The Hunt for the Night Stalker
Hunt the Man Down
Hunt the Man Down/ Smashing the Rackets
The Hunter
The Hunting
Husbands, Wives, Money, and Murder
Hussy
I Can't Escape
I Hate Blondes
I, Mobster
I Take This Oath
I Wake Up Screaming▶
I'd Give My Life
I'll Get You
Image of Death
In a Stranger's Hand
In Cold Blood▶
In Deadly Heat
In the Heat of the Night▶
In the King of Prussia
The Incident
Infernal Trio
Inn on the River
An Innocent Man
Inside Edge
Instant Justice
Interrupted Journey
The Invincible Six
The Invisible Man Returns▶
The Ipcress File▶
It Takes a Thief
Jack the Ripper
Jack the Ripper▶
Jail Bait
Jamaica Inn
Jesse James▶
Jigsaw▶
Johnnie Gibson F.B.I.
Johnny Apollo
Johnny Dangerously
Johnny Eager▶
Joyride
Kansas
Kansas City Confidential▶
The Kennel Murder Case
Key Largo▶
Kickboxer the Champion
Kid and the Killers
Kidnap Syndicate
Killer Bait
The Killers
Killpoint
King Creole
King of New York▶
Kiss Me Deadly▶
Kiss of Death▶
Knock on Any Door
Kowloon Assignment

L.A. Bounty
L.A. Crackdown
L.A. Crackdown 2
La Grande Bourgeoise
Lady from Nowhere
Lady Ice
Lady in Red
Lady Scarface/The Threat
Lady Street Fighter
The Lady Vanishes
Ladykillers▶
Laguna Heat
L'Argent
Las Vegas Serial Killer
Last House on the Left
The Last Riders
The Last Word
Laughing at Danger
The Lavender Hill Mob▶
Law of the Underworld
Laws of Gravity▶
Le Jour Se Leve▶
Left for Dead
The Leopard Woman
Let 'Em Have It
Let Him Have It▶
Lethal Weapon▶
Lethal Weapon 2▶
Lethal Weapon 3
The Letter▶
Lily was Here
Little Murders▶
Little White Lies
Living to Die
Lock Up
The Lone Rider in Ghost Town
The Long Goodbye▶
Loot...Give Me Money, Honey!
The Lost Capone
Love from a Stranger
Love Thrill Murders
Lure of the Islands
M▶
Ma Barker's Killer Brood
Macao▶
Machine Gun Kelly
Mad Dog
Mademoiselle Striptease
Mafia la Ley Que Non Perdona
Magnificent Obsession
Malarek
Mama's Dirty Girls
Man on Fire
Man on the Run
The Man Outside
The Manhandlers
Manhunter
Mania
Maniac
Mankillers
Marathon Man▶
Marked Woman▶
Marlowe
Maximum Breakout
Meet Sexton Blake
Meet the Mob
Men of Respect
The Meteor Man
Miami Supercops
Miami Vice
Miami Vice 2: The Prodigal Son
Midnight Run▶
Miles from Home
Miller's Crossing▶
Millie
Mision Suicida
Mississippi Burning▶
Mr. Reeder in Room 13
Mitchell
Mixed Blood
Mob War
Mona Lisa▶
Monsieur Verdoux▶
Monte Carlo Nights
Moon in the Gutter
Moonraker
Moonshine Mountain
More! Police Squad
Morning Glory

Motorcycle Squad
Murder at the Vanities
Murder by Phone
Murder or Mercy
Murder Story
Murderous Vision
Nadine
The Naked Gun: From the Files of Police Squad▶
Nashville Beat
National Lampoon's Class Reunion
Native Son
'Neath Brooklyn Bridge
Ned Kelly
The Neon Empire
Neutron vs. the Maniac
Never a Dull Moment
Never Love a Stranger
The New Centurions
New Jack City
New Orleans After Dark
New Year's Evil
Newman's Law
Night and the City▶
Night Beat
Night Birds
Night Children
A Night for Crime
Night Game
Night Nurse▶
The Night of the Following Day
The Night Patrol
Night Screams
Night Shadow
Night Time in Nevada
Nightfall▶
Nightmare at 43 Hillcrest
No Deposit, No Return
No Trace
Norman Conquest
The North Avenue Irregulars
No. 17▶
Nuns on the Run
Oddball Hall
O.H.M.S.
Oliver!▶
Oliver Twist
Oliver Twist▶
On the Edge
One Good Cop
One Man Force
One Shoe Makes It Murder
Open Secret
The Opponent
Ossession▶
Out of Bounds
Out of the Darkness▶
The Outside Man
Outside the Law
Over Indulgence
Parole, Inc.
Party Girl
Passion Flower
Pepe Le Moko▶
A Perfect Little Murder
Perfect Strangers
A Perfect World
Petrified Forest▶
Phantom Killer
Physical Evidence
Pickup on South Street▶
Pierrot le Fou▶
Pigs
Pink Strings and Sealing Wax
Pixote▶
Platypus Cove
Plunder Road
Point Break
Point of Impact
Police Squad! Help Wanted!
The Poppy is also a Flower
Port of New York
Portrait in Terror
Postal Inspector
The Postman Always Rings Twice▶
The Postman Always Rings Twice
Prayer for the Dying
The Preppie Murder

Pretty Poison▶
Prime Cut
The Private Files of J. Edgar Hoover
Probe
Profile
Psycho▶
Public Enemy▶
Pulp Fiction▶
A Question of Guilt
Quicksand
The Racket▶
Rafferty & the Gold Dust Twins
Raiders of Ghost City
The Rain Killer
Rashomon▶
Raw Nerve
The Real McCoy
Rear Window▶
Red Rock West▶
Redneck
Relentless 2: Dead On
Report to the Commissioner▶
The Respectful Prostitute
Return of Captain Invincible
The Return of Dr. Mabuse
Riot Squad
The Rise and Fall of Legs Diamond
River Beat
River's Edge▶
Road House
The Roaring Twenties▶
Rock All Night
Rock, Baby, Rock It
Rogue of the Rio Grande
Rogue's Yarn
Room 43
Room to Let
Ruddigore
Running Hot
Running Scared
Russian Roulette
Ruthless People▶
Ryder P.I.
St. Ives
The St. Valentine's Day Massacre
Savannah Smiles
Scalp Merchant
The Scar
Scarface▶
Scarface Mob
The Scarlet Car
Scene of the Crime
Schnelles Geld
Sea Racketeers
Secret File of Hollywood
The Secrets of Wu Sin
Serpico▶
The Seventh Coin
The 7th Commandment
Sexton Blake and the Hooded Terror
The Shadow
Shadow of a Doubt▶
Shadow of the Eagle
Shaft▶
Shame, Shame on the Bixby Boys
Sherlock Holmes: The Silver Blaze
She's Back
A Shot in the Dark
Show Them No Mercy
The Sicilian Connection
The Silent Partner▶
Sin Salida
Sing Sing Nights
The Sinister Urge
Sinner's Blood
Sizzle
Sleep of Death
Small Time
SnakeEater 2: The Drug Buster
Sois Belle et Tais-Toi
Sonny Boy
South of Hell Mountain
Special Delivery
Special Effects

Special Police
Speed Reporter
Spies▶
Stage Fright▶
Stage Fright
Stakeout
The Star Chamber
Star Reporter
Starlight Hotel
State of Grace▶
Steel Cowboy
Still of the Night
The Stone Killer
Straight Time▶
Strange Awakening
The Strange Love of Molly Louvain
Stranger in Town
Street Hawk
Street Law
The Street with No Name▶
The Streets of San Francisco▶
Strike Force
Summer Heat
The Sun's Burial▶
Sunset Grill
Sunset Strip
Super Force
Superbug Super Agent
Superman 3
Swamp Women
Sweet Sweetback's Baadasssss Song▶
T-Bird Gang
T Bone N Weasel
T-Men▶
The Take
Take the Money and Run▶
Targets▶
Taxi Driver▶
Tchao Pantin▶
Teenage Bonnie & Klepto Clyde
Teenage Crime Wave
The Temptress
Ten Little Indians
The Ten Million Dollar Getaway
10 Rillington Place▶
Tenement
Terminal Entry
Terror Ship
That Darn Cat
That Was Then...This Is Now
They Drive by Night▶
They Live by Night▶
Thief of Hearts
Thieves Like Us▶
This Gun for Hire▶
This Stuff'll Kill Ya!
This Time I'll Make You Rich
Three Fugitives
Three on a Match▶
Three Stops to Murder
Thrillkill
Thunder Road▶
Thunderbolt & Lightfoot▶
Tiger Bay▶
Tightrope▶
Tim Tyler's Luck
Time After Time▶
Time of the Gypsies▶
Timestalkers
The Tong Man
Too Hot to Handle
Too Late for Tears▶
Touch of Evil▶
Tough Guys Don't Dance
Tough to Handle
Traces of Red
The Trap
Trapped
Traxx
Trenchcoat
Truth or Die
21 Days
Two Graves to Kung-Fu
The Ultimate Thrill
Undercover
Undercover Cop
Underworld Scandal

The Underworld Story
Underworld, U.S.A.▶
The Unholy Three▶
Union Station
The Unstoppable Man
Valley of Wanted Men
Vamping
Velvet Touch▶
Vengeance
Vengeance Is Mine▶
V.I. Warshawski
Vice Squad
The Vicious Circle
Victimless Crimes
Video Murders
Vigilante
Violated
Violent Professionals
The Violent Years
Violette▶
Visitor from the Grave
Walking Back
Walking Tall
Walking Tall: Part 2
Warlords of the 21st Century
Watch Me When I Kill
Watch the Birdie
The Way Out
Web of Deception
Wedding in Blood▶
Weekend at Bernie's
We're No Angels
What Have I Done to Deserve This?▶
Whatever Happened to Aunt Alice?▶
When Gangland Strikes
When Thief Meets Thief
Where's Piccone?▶
Where's Poppa?▶
Whispering City▶
White Tiger
Who's That Girl?
The Wicked Lady
Wild Ones on Wheels
The Wild Pair
Wild Weed
Winterset
Wise Guys
Witness▶
The Wolves▶
A Woman's Face▶
A Woman's Secret
The World Accuses
Yellow Cargo

Crime Sprees

see also Fugitives; Lovers on the Lam

America's Deadliest Home Video
Bonnie & Clyde▶
Border Radio
The Boys Next Door
Copkillers
Crackers
Enemy Gold
Explosion
Fatal Bond
Flash & Firecat
Goodnight God Bless
High Rolling in a Hot Corvette
Jessie's Girls
Murder One
Naked Youth
Natural Born Killers
Rampage
She Came on the Bus
Steelyard Blues
Teddy at the Throttle/ Speeding Along
That Sinking Feeling▶
Thieves Like Us▶
Why Does Herr R. Run Amok?
Wild Ride
The Wrong Road

Crimes of Passion

The Amy Fisher Story
Backfire

Being at Home with Claude
Bizarre
Blood Vows: The Story of a Mafia Wife
Born to Kill▶
Casualties of Love: The "Long Island Lolita" Story
China Moon
Crime of Passion
Deadbolt
Deception▶
For Your Love Only
The Girl
Homicidal Impulse
I Love You to Death
Lethal Lolita—Amy Fisher: My Story
Love and Hate: A Marriage Made in Hell
The Love Flower
Make Haste to Live
The Mask of Dijon
Men are not Gods
Murder in New Hampshire: The Pamela Smart Story
Murder Rap
Niagara
The People vs. Jean Harris▶
The Preppie Murder
Roadhouse Girl
Secret Beyond the Door
Sex Crimes
The Shooting Party
Single White Female
Tomorrow Never Comes
Victim of Beauty
The Worldly Madonna

Crop Dusters

Bitter Harvest▶
Bloodsuckers from Outer Space
Boy Takes Girl
Buffalo Jump▶
The Cabin in the Cotton
The Castaway Cowboy
City Girl
Clodhopper
Country▶
The Curse
Dark Before Dawn
Days of Heaven▶
Deadly Stranger
Demon Wind
Desire Under the Elms
The Devil & Daniel Webster▶
The Displaced Person▶
Doc Hollywood
Dog Day
Earth▶
Earthworm Tractors
Egg and I▶
Eli Eli
The Farmer's Other Daughter
The Field▶
The General Line▶
Giant▶
God's Little Acre▶
The Grapes of Wrath▶
The Green Promise
Harvest▶
Jean de Florette▶
Kung Fu Massacre
The Mating Game▶
The Milagro Beanfield War▶
Missouri Traveler▶
Morning Glory
Northern Lights▶
Nowhere to Run
Oklahoma Bound
Our Daily Bread▶
Pelle the Conqueror▶
Places in the Heart▶
The Purchase Price
Rage
The Revolt of Mother▶
The River
Rock-a-Doodle
The Ruggles of Red Gap▶
Skylark
Son-in-Law
Sounder▶

The Southerner▶
Stacking
The Stone Boy▶
Sunday Too Far Away▶
The Sundowners▶
Sunrise▶
Tomboy & the Champ
The Tree of Wooden Clogs▶
Wisdom

Cult Items

The Adventures of Buckaroo Banzai Across the Eighth Dimension▶
The American Friend▶
An American Werewolf in London▶
Android
Andy Warhol's Bad▶
Andy Warhol's Dracula▶
Andy Warhol's Frankenstein
The Angry Red Planet
Annie Hall▶
Apartment Zero▶
Apocalypse Now▶
The Arousers
Attack of the 50 Foot Woman
Attack of the Killer Tomatoes
Bad Girls Go to Hell
Bad Taste▶
Badlands▶
Barbarella
Basket Case▶
Batman
Beat Girl
Bedazzled▶
The Bellboy
Beneath the Valley of the Ultra-Vixens
Beyond the Valley of the Dolls
Billy Jack
Billy the Kid Versus Dracula
Blade Runner▶
Blazing Saddles▶
The Blob
Blood Feast
Blood Simple▶
Bloodsucking Freaks
Blow-Up▶
Blue Velvet▶
Bonnie & Clyde▶
Born to Boogie
Boxing Helena
A Boy and His Dog
The Brain from Planet Arous
Breathless▶
Bride of the Monster
A Bucket of Blood▶
The Cabinet of Dr. Caligari▶
Caged Heat
Caligula
Camp Double Feature
Cannibal Women in the Avocado Jungle of Death
Cannonball
Careful
Carnival of Souls▶
Casablanca▶
Cat People▶
Cat Women of the Moon
Chained Heat
Cheech and Chong's Up in Smoke
Children Shouldn't Play with Dead Things
Chilly Scenes of Winter
Cinema Shrapnel
A Clockwork Orange▶
The Commies are Coming, the Commies are Coming
The Conqueror Worm▶
Contempt▶
Dance, Girl, Dance
Dawn of the Dead▶
Day of the Triffids▶
Demons
Desperate Living
Detour▶
The Devils▶
The Devil's Harvest

Dr. Strangelove, or: How I
    Learned to Stop Worrying
    and Love the Bomb▶
Dog Eat Dog
Driver's Seat
Easy Rider▶
Eaten Alive
Eating Raoul▶
Eraserhead▶
Evil Dead
Faster Pussycat! Kill! Kill!
The Fearless Vampire Killers▶
The Female Jungle
Female Trouble
The First Nudie Musical
Five Easy Pieces▶
The Fly▶
Frankenstein Unbound▶
Freaks▶
Fritz the Cat▶
Geek Maggot Bingo
Glen or Glenda
God Told Me To
The Gods Must Be Crazy▶
Greetings▶
A Hard Day's Night▶
Harold and Maude▶
Hercules Against the Moon
    Men
High School Confidential
Highlander▶
Honeymoon Killers▶
The Horror Chamber of Dr.
    Faustus▶
The Hospital▶
House of Wax▶
The Hunger
I Married a Monster from
    Outer Space
I Walked with a Zombie▶
I Was a Teenage Werewolf
The Incredible Two-Headed
    Transplant
Incredibly Strange Creatures
    Who Stopped Living and
    Became Mixed-Up Zombies
Invasion of the Body
    Snatchers▶
It Conquered the World
It Takes a Thief
It's A Gift▶
Jackson County Jail
Jesse James Meets
    Frankenstein's Daughter
Johnny Guitar▶
Kamikaze Hearts
The King of Hearts▶
Kiss Me Deadly▶
Koyaanisqatsi▶
La Cage aux Folles▶
La Cage aux Folles 2
La Cage aux Folles 3: The
    Wedding
Last Tango in Paris▶
Leningrad Cowboys Go
    America
Liquid Sky▶
Little Shop of Horrors▶
The Lost Stooges
Loveless
The Loves of Hercules
Mad Max▶
The Man Who Fell to Earth▶
Manos, the Hands of Fate
The Manster
Married Too Young
Mars Needs Women
Martin▶
Mill of the Stone Women
Ms. 45▶
Missile to the Moon
Mom & Dad
Mommie Dearest
Mondo Trasho
Monsieur Verdoux▶
Monty Python and the Holy
    Grail▶
Monty Python's Life of Brian▶
Motel Hell
Motor Psycho
Multiple Maniacs
The Mummy▶

The Muppet Movie▶
My Darling Clementine▶
Naked Kiss
Nasty Rabbit
Never Give a Sucker an Even
    Break▶
The Night of the Hunter▶
Night of the Living Dead▶
Oh Dad, Poor Dad (Momma's
    Hung You in the Closet &
    I'm Feeling So Sad)
Orgy of the Dead
Out of the Past▶
The Outlaw
Peeping Tom▶
Performance▶
Petulia
Phantasm
Phantom of the Paradise▶
Pink Flamingos
Plan 9 from Outer Space
Please Don't Eat My Mother
The Plot Against Harry▶
Private Parts
The Producers▶
The Projectionist▶
Psycho▶
Quadrophenia▶
Queen of Outer Space
The Rain People▶
Rancho Deluxe▶
The Re-Animator▶
Rebel Without a Cause▶
Reefer Madness
Repo Man▶
Return of the Killer Tomatoes
Ride the High Country▶
The Road Warrior▶
Roadkill
Robot Monster
Rock 'n' Roll High School▶
The Rocky Horror Picture
    Show▶
Satan's Sadists
Schlock
Sebastiane▶
The Secret Cinema
Sid & Nancy▶
The Slumber Party Massacre
Sorority Babes in the Slimeball
    Bowl-A-Rama
Spider Baby
Start the Revolution Without
    Me▶
Stoogemania
Strange Cargo
Surf Nazis Must Die
Sweet Movie
Tales from the Gimli Hospital
The Tall T
10th Victim▶
Them!▶
There's Nothing Out There
The Thing▶
This is Spinal Tap▶
Thunder Road▶
The Toxic Avenger
The Toxic Avenger, Part 2
Trash
Twin Peaks
Twin Peaks: Fire Walk with
    Me
Twister
2000 Maniacs
2001: A Space Odyssey▶
The Undertaker and His Pals
Vanishing Point
Vortex
Wanderers▶
The Warriors
The Wasp Woman
What Have I Done to Deserve
    This?▶
Where the Boys Are
Where's Poppa?▶
White Heat▶
Wild Rapture
Wild Women of Wongo
The Wild World of Batwoman
Willy Wonka & the Chocolate
    Factory▶
Zachariah

Zardoz
Zontar, the Thing from Venus

Cults

see also Occult; Satanism

Bad Dreams
The Believers
Blinded by the Light
Blood Clan
Bloodbath
Children of the Corn 2: The
    Final Sacrifice
Cobra Woman
Cult of the Cobra
The Dark Secret of Harvest
    Home
Deadly Blessing
Death of an Angel
The Deceivers
Force: Five
Forever Evil
The Guyana Tragedy: The
    Story of Jim Jones
Helter Skelter
In the Line of Duty: Ambush in
    Waco
The Lash of the Penitents
The Lightning Incident
The Mephisto Waltz▶
Mind, Body & Soul
Next One
The Night God Screamed
Night of the Death Cult
Putney Swope▶
The Pyx▶
The Reincarnate
Rest In Pieces
Revenge
Sabaka
Servants of Twilight
Shock 'Em Dead
Shocking Asia
The Snake Hunter Strangler
The Snake People
The Spellbinder
Split Image▶
Steps from Hell
Suicide Cult
Thou Shalt Not Kill...Except
Ticket to Heaven▶
Treasure of the Four Crowns
Withnail and I▶

Dance Fever

see also Ballet; Disco
    Musicals

All That Jazz▶
An American in Paris▶
Anchors Aweigh▶
April In Paris
Babes in Arms
The Bacchantes
The Band Wagon▶
The Barefoot Contessa▶
The Barkleys of Broadway▶
Beat Street
The Belle of New York
Bert Rigby, You're a Fool
The Best of the Kenny Everett
    Video Show
Billy Rose's Jumbo▶
Black Orpheus▶
Blood Wedding▶
Body Moves
Body Rock
Born to Dance
Breakin'
Breakin' 2: Electric Boogaloo
Breakin' Through
Broadway Melody of 1940
Cabin in the Sky▶
Can-Can
Captain January
Carefree▶
Carmen▶
Charleston▶
A Chorus Line
Chu Chu & the Philly Flash
Cover Girl▶
Daddy Long Legs▶
Dames▶

Dance, Girl, Dance
Dance or Die
Dancing Lady
Danzon▶
Deadly Dancer
Delightfully Dangerous
Delivery Boys
Dirty Dancing▶
The Discovery Program
Doll Face
The Eighties
El Amor Brujo▶
Everybody's Dancin'
Faith
Fame▶
Fass Black
Fast Forward
Faster Pussycat! Kill! Kill!
Femmes de Paris
Flashdance
Flower Drum Song
Flying Down to Rio
Follies Girl
Follow the Fleet▶
Footlight Parade▶
Footloose
For Ladies Only
The Forbidden Dance
42nd Street▶
French Can-Can▶
The Gay Divorcee▶
Ginger & Fred▶
Girl in Gold Boots
Girls Just Want to Have Fun
Give a Girl a Break
The Glass Slipper
Gold Diggers of 1933▶
Gold Diggers of 1935▶
Gotta Dance, Gotta Sing
Grease▶
Grease 2
The Harvey Girls▶
Heavenly Bodies
Hit the Deck
Holiday in Havana
Idiot's Delight▶
The In Crowd
Invitation to the Dance
Isadora▶
It Started in Naples▶
Kiss Me Kate▶
Lambada
Last Dance
Le Bal▶
Legs
Les Girls
Let's Dance
Liquid Dreams
Little Ballerina
Mad Youth
Mantis in Lace
Meet Me in Las Vegas
Midnight Dancer
Minsky's Follies
Music in My Heart
Neurotic Cabaret
No Time for Romance
Nutcracker: The Motion
    Picture
Orgy of the Dead
Paris is Burning▶
Party Girl▶
Pennies From Heaven▶
Pilot
The Pirate▶
Portrait of a Showgirl
Portrait of a Stripper
Queen of the Stardust
    Ballroom▶
The Red Shoes
Risky Business▶
Roberta▶
Romance in Manhattan
Rooftops
Roseland▶
Salome, Where She Danced
Salsa
Saturday Night Fever
Scent of a Woman▶
Second Chorus
Seven Brides for Seven
    Brothers▶

Shag: The Movie▶
Shall We Dance▶
Silk Stockings▶
Singin' in the Rain▶
Slashdance
Snake Dancer
So This is Paris▶
Sometimes It Works,
    Sometimes It Doesn't
Spirit of '76
Staying Alive
Stepping Out▶
The Story of Vernon and Irene
    Castle▶
Strictly Ballroom▶
Stripped to Kill II: Live Girls
Summer Stock▶
Sunset Strip
Sweet Charity▶
Swing Kids
Swing Time▶
Take Me Out to the Ball Game
Tango
Tango Bar
Tap
Taxi Dancers
Thank God It's Friday
That's Dancing!
That's Entertainment, Part 2
That's Entertainment 3
They Shoot Horses, Don't
    They?▶
Those Lips, Those Eyes
Top Hat▶
The Turning Point
Ultra Flash
Urban Cowboy
What's the Matter with Helen?
Words and Music
Yankee Doodle Dandy▶
You Were Never Lovelier▶
You'll Never Get Rich▶
Ziegfeld Follies
Ziegfeld Girl▶
Zou Zou

Deafness

see also Physical
    Problems

Amy
Bridge to Silence
Children of a Lesser God▶
Crazy Moon
For the First Time
Hear No Evil
The Heart is a Lonely Hunter▶
Johnny Belinda▶
Johnny Belinda
Mandy▶
The Miracle Worker▶
Murderer's Keep
Psych-Out
Secret of Yolanda
See No Evil, Hear No Evil
Silent Victory: The Kitty O'Neil
    Story▶
Sincerely Yours
The Sound and the Silence
Sound of Love
The Sphinx
A Summer to Remember
Suspect
Tin Man

Death & the Afterlife

see also Angels; Funerals;
    Ghosts, Ghouls, &
    Goblins; Great Death
    Scenes; Heaven Sent;
    Occult; Suicide

The Alchemist
All of Me
All That Jazz▶
Always
The Amityville Horror
Amityville 2: The Possession
Amityville 3: The Demon
Amityville 4
The Amityville Curse
Amityville 1992: It's About
    Time

Angel on My Shoulder▶
Angel on My Shoulder
Another Chance
The Asphyx▶
Audrey Rose
Avanti!
Baby Girl Scott
Backwoods
Beetlejuice▶
Beyond Tomorrow
Bill & Ted's Bogus Journey
Black Force 2
Black Magic
Bliss▶
Blithe Spirit▶
Blood of the Vampire
Bloody New Year
The Bone Yard
Bowery at Midnight
The Bramble Bush
Breaking the Rules
Burnt Offerings
The Canterville Ghost
Carnival of Souls▶
Carousel▶
Carry Me Back
Castle of the Creeping Flesh
The Cat and the Canary▶
Cathy's Curse
The Chair
Chances Are▶
The Changeling
A Christmas Carol▶
A Christmas Carol
Cold Heaven
The Corridor: Death
The Crow
Curse of the Cat People▶
Curse of the Living Corpse
Da
Daddy's Dyin'...Who's Got the Will?
Dark of the Night
Dark Tower
Dark Victory▶
Daughter of Horror
The Day It Came to Earth
Dead Heat
Dead Mate
Death Be Not Proud▶
The Death Curse of Tartu
Death Row Diner
Defending Your Life▶
Deja Vu
The Devil & Max Devlin
Devil Kiss
The Diabolical Dr. Z
Diary of the Dead
Digging Up Business
D.O.A.▶
D.O.A.
Dr. Death, Seeker of Souls
Dr. Hackenstein
Doctor Phibes Rises Again
Dominique is Dead
Dona Flor and Her Two Husbands▶
Donkey Skin▶
Donovan's Brain▶
Don't Go in the House
Doomed Love
The Duellists▶
Dying Young
Early Days
Earthling
Eleni
The Elvis Files
Emerald of Artama
Encounter with the Unknown
The End▶
Enrapture
The Entertainer▶
Epitaph
Estate of Insanity
Evil Spirits
Executive Suite▶
The Eyes, the Mouth
Faces of Death, Part 1
Faces of Death, Part 2
Fearless▶
The Fig Tree
Flatliners

The Forgotten One
Friendly Fire▶
Frightmare
From the Dead of Night▶
The Funeral▶
Funeral Home
Garbo Talks
Gates of Hell
The Ghost
Ghost▶
The Ghost and Mrs. Muir▶
Ghost Writer
Ghosts Can Do It
Ghosts Can't Do It
Ghosts of Berkeley Square
Go Down Death
Gotham▶
Grave Secrets
The Green Room
Griffin and Phoenix: A Love Story
Hawks
Heart and Souls
Heart Condition
Heaven
Heaven Can Wait▶
The Heavenly Kid
Hello Again
Here Comes Mr. Jordan▶
High Spirits
Highway 61
Hocus Pocus
Hold That Ghost▶
Hollow Gate
Homeward Bound
I Bury the Living▶
I Married a Witch▶
I Walked with a Zombie▶
Impure Thoughts
In an Old Manor House
In Between
The Indestructible Man
Into the West▶
It Came Upon a Midnight Clear
It Could Happen to You
It's a Wonderful Life▶
The Kid with the Broken Halo
Kill and Go Hide
Kiss Me Goodbye
La Vie Continue
The Lady in White▶
The Lady's Maid's Bell
Last Light
The Legend of Hell House▶
Lightning Over Water
Liliom▶
Loot...Give Me Money, Honey!
The Loved One▶
Macbeth▶
Macbeth
Made in Heaven
The Man with Two Lives
Mannequin
Mausoleum
Maxie
Medea
The Midnight Hour
The Miracle of the Bells
Mr. Corbett's Ghost
Mister Halpren & Mister Johnson
Mortuary Academy
My Life
Necropolis
The Newlydeads
Night of the Death Cult
Night of the Demons
Night of the Demons 2
Night Shift
The Nightcomers
Nightmare Castle
An Occurrence at Owl Creek Bridge
Oh, Dad, Poor Dad (Momma's Hung You in the Closet & I'm Feeling So Sad)
Oh, Heavenly Dog!
On Borrowed Time▶
One Minute Before Death
The Oracle
Out of the Rain

Passed Away
The Peanut Butter Solution
Pet Sematary
Phantasm
Phantasm II
The Phantom Chariot
Phantom of the Ritz
The Plague
Playroom
Poltergeist▶
Poltergeist 2: The Other Side
Poltergeist 3
Portrait of Jennie▶
The Possessed
Postmark for Danger/ Quicksand
Premonition
The Premonition
Prison
Promises in the Dark
The Psychic
Psychomania
The Reincarnation of Peter Proud
Resurrection of Zachary Wheeler
Retribution
Return
Revenge of the Dead
Riders to the Sea
Rimfire
The Rue Morgue Massacres
Scared Stiff▶
School Spirit
Scrooge▶
Scrooge
Scrooged
The Seventh Seal▶
Shadow Play
She Waits
Shock Waves
Sibling Rivalry
Silence Like Glass
Sole Survivor
Sometimes They Come Back
Somewhere Tomorrow
Soultaker
Stand By Me▶
Star Trek 3: The Search for Spock
Stones of Death
Strangers of the Evening
Tell Me a Riddle
Terror Eyes
They Watch
13 Ghosts
Time Flies When You're Alive
To Dance with the White Dog▶
To Forget Venice
Tomb of Torture
Topper▶
Topper Returns▶
Topper Takes a Trip▶
Trick or Treat
Truly, Madly, Deeply▶
Truth or Dare?
Twice Dead
The Twilight Zone
Two of a Kind
The Unnamable
Unnatural
The Vampire's Ghost
Vengeance
Visitor from the Grave
The Visitors
Weekend at Bernie's
Weekend at Bernie's 2
Welcome Back Mr. Fox
Where the Lilies Bloom▶
Whispers
White Light
The Widow
Wings of Fame
A Woman's Tale▶
The Worst of Faces of Death
A Zed & Two Noughts▶
Zone of the Dead

Dedicated Teachers

see also Hell High School; School Daze
Amy
Blackboard Jungle▶
Born Yesterday▶
Born Yesterday
Burn Witch, Burn!▶
Cheers for Miss Bishop
A Child is Waiting▶
Children of a Lesser God▶
Conrack▶
The Corn is Green▶
Dead Poets Society▶
Educating Rita▶
El Profesor Hippie
Forever Mary▶
Homework
Johnny Tiger
Kindergarten Cop
Lean on Me▶
Lovey: A Circle of Children 2
Madame Sousatzka▶
The Miracle Worker▶
Night Visitor
The Paper Chase▶
Passion for Life
The Prime of Miss Jean Brodie▶
Renaissance Man
Stand and Deliver▶
Teachers
To Sir, with Love
Up the Down Staircase▶

Deep Blue

see also Go Fish; Sail Away; Submarines
Assault on a Queen
ffolkes
Free Willy
Lords of the Deep
Mission of the Shark▶
Namu, the Killer Whale
The Silent Enemy
Splash
The Spy Who Loved Me
Whale of a Tale
Wind

Demons & Wizards

see also Occult
The Alchemist
Archer: The Fugitive from the Empire
Army of Darkness▶
Beyond Darkness
Bloodlust: Subspecies 3
Bloodstone: Subspecies 2
Blue Blood
Born of Fire
The Church▶
Conan the Barbarian▶
Conan the Destroyer
Cthulhu Mansion
Curse 4: The Ultimate Sacrifice
Deathstalker
Deathstalker 3
Deathstalker 4: Clash of the Titans
Demon Rage
Demon Wind
Demon Witch Child
Demonoid, Messenger of Death
The Demons
Demons
Demons of Ludlow
Demonstone
Demonwarp
The Devil
The Devil's Web
El Barbaro
Ernest Scared Stupid
Evil Dead
Evil Dead 2: Dead by Dawn
Evil Toons
Excalibur▶
Fire and Ice

Gate 2
Ghosts That Still Walk
The Giants of Thessaly
Gor
Hellraiser
The Hobbit▶
Krull
Ladyhawke
The Legacy
The Mephisto Waltz▶
Mirror, Mirror
Natas...The Reflection
Outlaw of Gor
Pumpkinhead
Quest for the Mighty Sword
The Raven▶
Rawhead Rex
Red Sonja
The Return of the King
Rock & Rule
Seizure
Silent Night, Deadly Night 4: Initiation
Sinthia: The Devil's Doll
Sorceress
Spellcaster
Stay Awake
Supergirl
Sword & the Sorcerer
The Sword in the Stone▶
Terror Eyes
Trancers 4: Jack of Swords
Troll
Troll 2
The Unholy
The Unnamable 2: The Statement of Randolph Carter
Urotsukidoji 1: Legend of the Overfiend
Urotsukidoji 2: Legend of the Demon Womb
Warlock
Warlock: The Armageddon
Willow
Witchcraft 5: Dance with the Devil
The Witchmaker
Wizards of the Lost Kingdom
Wizards of the Lost Kingdom 2

Dental Mayhem

Bill Cosby, Himself
Brazil▶
Chasing Those Depression Blues
Comedy Reel, Vol. 1
Compromising Positions
The Dentist▶
Don't Raise the Bridge, Lower the River
Eversmile New Jersey
The In-Laws▶
Little Shop of Horrors▶
Marathon Man▶
The Paleface▶
Reuben, Reuben▶
The Shakiest Gun in the West
Strawberry Blonde▶
W.C. Fields: Flask of Fields

Detective Spoofs

see also Detectives
Ace Ventura: Pet Detective
The Adventures of Sherlock Holmes' Smarter Brother▶
Clean Slate
Clue
Cry Uncle
Curse of the Pink Panther
Dead Men Don't Wear Plaid
Dragnet
Fatal Instinct
Gumshoe
Hollywood Harry
The Hound of the Baskervilles
The Man with Bogart's Face
More! Police Squad
Murder by Death

Detective

The Naked Gun: From the
Files of Police Squad▶
Naked Gun 33 1/3: The Final
Insult
Naked Gun 2 1/2: The Smell
of Fear
Night Patrol
One Body Too Many
The Pink Panther▶
The Pink Panther Strikes
Again▶
Police Squad! Help Wanted!
Rentadick
Return of the Pink Panther
Revenge of the Pink Panther
A Shot in the Dark
The Strange Case of the End
of Civilization as We Know
It
Trail of the Pink Panther

Detectives

see also Cops; Detective
Spoofs; Feds
Abbott & Costello Meet the
Invisible Man▶
Abduction of St. Anne
Above the Law
Accomplice
Ace Crawford, Private Eye
Ace Ventura: Pet Detective
Adventures of a Private Eye
The Adventures of Sherlock
Holmes
The Adventures of Sherlock
Holmes: Hound of the
Baskervilles
The Adventures of Sherlock
Holmes' Smarter Brother▶
The Affair of the Pink Pearl
After the Thin Man▶
All-American Murder
The Alphabet Murders
Alphaville▶
Angel City
Angel Heart
Another Stakeout
Appointment with Death
Are You Lonesome Tonight
Arrest Bulldog Drummond
The Art of Crime
The Barbary Coast
Bare Hunt
Behind Locked Doors
Below the Deadline
Beretta's Island
The Big Sleep▶
The Big Sleep
Big Store
Black Bird
Blackmail▶
Blackout
Blade in Hong Kong
Bloody Avenger
The Blue Lightning
The Body in the Library
Bootleg
Bulldog Drummond
Bulldog Drummond Comes
Back
Bulldog Drummond Escapes
Bulldog Drummond in Africa/
Arrest Bulldog Drummond
Bulldog Drummond's Bride
Bulldog Drummond's Peril
Bulldog Drummond's
Revenge
Bulldog Drummond's Secret
Police
Bulldog Jack▶
Bullitt▶
Calling Paul Temple
Carry On Dick
Carry On Screaming
Case of the Baby Sitter
The Case of the Lucky Legs
The Case of the Missing Lady
Cast a Deadly Spell▶
Castle in the Desert
Cat and Mouse▶
Cave of the Living Dead

Charlie Chan and the Curse of
the Dragon Queen
Charlie Chan at the Opera▶
Charlie Chan at the Wax
Museum
The Charlie Chan Collection
Charlie Chan in Paris
Charlie Chan in Rio
Charlie Chan in the Secret
Service
Charlie Chan's Secret
The Cheap Detective▶
Chinatown▶
The Chinese Cat
Clean Slate
The Clergyman's Daughter
Columbo: Murder By the Book
Columbo: Prescription
Murder▶
Conspiracy of Terror
The Crackler
Criminals Within
The Crooked Circle
The Crucifer of Blood
Cry Uncle
Curse of the Pink Panther
The Dain Curse
Dark Corner▶
The Dark Hour
Dark Side of Midnight
Dead Again▶
Dead Connection
Dead Men Don't Wear Plaid
Deadly Force
Deadly Illusion
Deadly Passion
Death from a Distance
Death on the Nile
Death Train
Deathmask
The Detective▶
Detective Sadie & Son
Detective School Dropouts
Detective Story▶
The Devil's Cargo
Devlin Connection
Dick Barton, Special Agent
Dick Barton Strikes Back
Dick Tracy▶
Dick Tracy, Detective
Dick Tracy, Detective/The
Corpse Vanishes
Dick Tracy Double Feature #1
Dick Tracy Double Feature #2
Dick Tracy Meets Gruesome
Dick Tracy Returns
Dick Tracy: The Original
Serial, Vol. 1▶
Dick Tracy: The Original
Serial, Vol. 2▶
Dick Tracy: The Spider Strikes
Dick Tracy vs. Crime Inc.
Dick Tracy vs. Cueball
Dick Tracy's Dilemma
Dirkham Detective Agency
Dragnet
Dressed to Kill
The Drowning Pool
Edge of Darkness
El Aviador Fenomeno
The Element of Crime
Emil and the Detective
The Empty Beach
Endangered Species
The Enforcer
Entangled
Everybody Wins
Evil Under the Sun
Ex-Mrs. Bradford▶
The Falcon in Hollywood
The Falcon in Mexico
Falcon Takes Over/Strange
Bargain
Falcon's Adventure/Armored
Car Robbery
The Falcon's Brother
Falling Down
False Witness
Farewell, My Lovely▶
Fearless
Fiction Makers
Final Notice

Finessing the King
Follow Me Quietly▶
The Foreigner
Fourth Story▶
Freddie as F.R.O.7
The French Detective▶
From Hollywood to Deadwood
Ginger
Girl Hunters
The Glass Key▶
The Gore-Gore Girls
Gotham▶
Great K & A Train Robbery
The Great Mouse Detective▶
Green Eyes
Green for Danger
Gumshoe
The Gumshoe Kid
Hands of a Stranger
Hard-Boiled Mahoney
Hat Box Mystery
Heart Condition
The Hollywood Detective
Hollywood Harry
Hollywood Stadium Mystery
The Hound of the
Baskervilles▶
The Hound of the Baskervilles
Hour of Decision
House of Fear
The House of Lurking Death
House of Mystery
The House of the Arrow▶
How to Kill 400 Duponts
The Human Monster
The Hunt for the Night Stalker
Hustle
I Killed That Man
I, the Jury
Infamous Crimes
The Inner Circle
Inspector Hornleigh
The Invisible Avenger
The Invisible Killer
Irish Luck
The Jade Mask
Jigsaw
Just Another Pretty Face
K-9
The Kennel Murder Case
The Kill
Kill Me Again
Killing 'em Softly
The King Murder Case
Kiss Me Deadly▶
Kojak: The Belarus File
La Rupture
Lady in Cement
Lady in the Lake
The Late Show▶
Laura▶
Little Miss Millions
The Long Goodbye▶
Long Time Gone
Loose Cannons
Love at Large▶
Love Happy
Low Down Dirty Shame
Lure of the Islands
Lying Lips
The Mad Bomber
Magnum Force
The Maltese Falcon▶
Man from Cairo
The Man in the Mist
Man on the Eiffel Tower▶
The Man Who Would Not Die
The Man with Bogart's Face
The Mandarin Mystery
Manhattan Murder Mystery▶
Margin for Murder
Marlowe
Masks of Death
Master Mind
Meet Sexton Blake
Meeting at Midnight
Messenger of Death
Miami Vice 2: The Prodigal
Son
Midnight 2: Sex, Death, and
Videotape
Midnight Limited

Missing Pieces
Mr. Arkadin▶
Mr. Moto's Last Warning▶
Mr. Wong, Detective
Mr. Wong in Chinatown
Moonlighting
More! Police Squad
Mortal Sins
Murder Ahoy
Murder at the Baskervilles
Murder at the Gallop▶
Murder at the Vanities
Murder by Death
Murder by Decree▶
Murder by the Book
Murder in the Doll House
A Murder is Announced
Murder Most Foul▶
Murder, My Sweet▶
Murder on Approval
Murder on the Orient
Express▶
Murder Over New York
Murder She Said
Murderous Vision
My Favorite Brunette
My New Partner
Mystery Island
Mystery Liner
Mystery of Mr. Wong
The Naked Gun: From the
Files of Police Squad▶
Naked Gun 33 1/3: The Final
Insult
Nancy Drew, Reporter
Nature's Playmates
New Orleans After Dark
Newman's Law
Nick Knight
Night Moves▶
Night School
Night Stalker
No Way to Treat a Lady▶
Nocturne
Number One with a Bullet
No. 17▶
On Dangerous Ground▶
One Body Too Many
One Good Cop
One of My Wives Is Missing
One Shoe Makes It Murder
Operation Julie
The Organization▶
Out of the Darkness
Out of the Past▶
The Panther's Claw
The Pearl of Death
Peter Gunn
The Phantom Light
Phantom of Chinatown
The Phantom of Soho
Pier 23
The Pink Chiquitas
The Pink Panther▶
The Pink Panther Strikes
Again▶
Play Nice
Police Squad! Help Wanted!
Postmark for Danger
The Presidio
Prettykill
The Private Eyes
Private Hell 36
The Private Life of Sherlock
Holmes▶
Pursuit to Algiers
Radioactive Dreams
Red Barry
The Red Raven Kiss-Off
Relentless 3
Remington Steele, Vol. 1:
License to Steele
Rentadick
The Return of Boston Blackie
The Return of Dr. Mabuse
Return of Frank Cannon
Return of Superfly
Return of the Pink Panther
Revenge of the Pink Panther
Roaring City
The Rose and the Jackal
Rough Cut

Ryder P.I.
The Saint
Saint in London
The Saint in New York
The Saint Strikes Back
The Saint Takes Over
The Saint's Double Trouble
The Saint's Vacation/The
Narrow Margin
Sapphire▶
Satan Met a Lady
Satan's Harvest
Scalp Merchant
Scarlet Claw▶
The Scarlet Clue
Sea of Love▶
Second Sight
Seven Doors to Death
The Seven Percent Solution▶
The Seven-Ups
Sexton Blake and the Hooded
Terror
Shadow of the Thin Man▶
The Shadow Strikes
Shadows of the Orient
Shaft's Big Score
Shamus
The Shanghai Cobra
Sheba, Baby
Sherlock Holmes and the
Deadly Necklace
Sherlock Holmes and the
Incident at Victoria Falls
Sherlock Holmes and the
Secret Weapon▶
Sherlock Holmes Faces
Death▶
Sherlock Holmes in
Washington
Sherlock Holmes: The Master
Blackmailer
Sherlock Holmes: The Sign of
Four
Sherlock Holmes: The Silver
Blaze
Sherlock Holmes: The Voice
of Terror
Sherlock's Rivals & Where's
My Wife
Shoot to Kill▶
Shooting Stars
A Shot in the Dark
A Shot in the Dark▶
The Sign of Four
The Silent Mr. Sherlock
Holmes
The Silent Passenger
Silk
Slow Burn
Smart-Aleck Kill
Smile, Jenny, You're Dead
Someone to Watch Over Me▶
Song of the Thin Man
South Beach
The Speckled Band▶
Speedtrap
Spider Woman▶
The Squeeze
Stakeout
Star of Midnight
Station
Stolen Kisses▶
The Strange Case of the End
of Civilization as We Know
It
Strange Shadows in an Empty
Room
Stray Dog▶
Strike a Pose
A Study in Scarlet
A Study in Terror▶
Sunset Grill
Sweet Lies
Terror by Night
Terror by Night/Meeting at
Midnight
They All Laughed
They Might Be Giants▶
The Thin Man▶
The Thin Man Goes Home
Third Degree Burn
The Third Key

13th Guest
To Catch a Killer▶
Tomorrow at Seven
Tony Rome
Trail of the Pink Panther
TripleCross
The Triumph of Sherlock Holmes
The Two Jakes
Ulterior Motives
The Unbreakable Alibi
Under Suspicion
Uneasy Terms
Unsuitable Job for a Woman
Vegas▶
Vertigo▶
V.I. Warshawski
Video Murders
Violated
Vortex
Waikiki
Web of Deception
Whistling in Brooklyn
Whistling in Dixie
Whistling in the Dark▶
Who Done It?
Who Framed Roger Rabbit?▶
Who Is the Black Dahlia?▶
Who's Harry Crumb?
Without a Clue
Witness▶
The Woman in Green
World of the Depraved
X Marks the Spot
The Young Detectives on Wheels
Young Sherlock Holmes

Devils

The Devil & Max Devlin
The Devils▶
Faust▶
God, Man and Devil
Guardian of the Abyss
Highway to Hell
Judgment Day
Les Visiteurs du Soir▶
Mr. Frost
Second Time Lucky
The Sorrows of Satan▶
Stephen King's The Stand

Dinosaurs

see also Killer Beasts
Adventures in Dinosaur City
At the Earth's Core
Baby...Secret of the Lost Legend
Carnosaur
Caveman
Clifford
The Crater Lake Monster
Dennis the Menace: Dinosaur Hunter
Dinosaur Island
Dinosaurus!
Ganjasaurus Rex
Jurassic Park▶
King Dinosaur
The Land Before Time▶
The Land Before Time: The Great Valley Adventure
The Land That Time Forgot
The Land Unknown
Legend of the Dinosaurs
The Lost Continent
The Lost World
Massacre in Dinosaur Valley
My Science Project
One Million B.C.
One of Our Dinosaurs Is Missing
The People That Time Forgot
Planet of the Dinosaurs
Prehysteria
Return of the Dinosaurs
Return to the Lost World
Sound of Horror
Super Mario Bros.
Teenage Caveman
Two Lost Worlds

Unknown Island
The Valley of Gwangi
We're Back! A Dinosaur's Story
When Dinosaurs Ruled the Earth

Disaster Flicks

see also Action Adventure; Air Disasters; Meltdown; Sea Disasters
Accident
After the Shock
Airport▶
Airport '75
Airport '77
Alive
Assignment Outer Space
Avalanche
Avalanche Express
Beyond the Poseidon Adventure
Big Bus
The Cassandra Crossing
The China Syndrome▶
City on Fire
The Concorde: Airport '79
The Crash of Flight 401
The Day the Sky Exploded
Dead Ahead: The Exxon Valdez Disaster▶
The Doomsday Flight
Earthquake
Final Warning
Fire
Fire and Rain
Flood!
Gray Lady Down
The Hindenburg
Hurricane
Hurricane
In Old Chicago▶
Last Days of Pompeii
The Last Voyage
The Last Woman on Earth
The Lost Missile
Meteor
A Night to Remember▶
Planet on the Prowl
The Poseidon Adventure
The Rains Came
Raise the Titanic
Red Alert
St. Helen's, Killer Volcano
Snowball
S.O.S. Titanic
Space: 1999—Alien Attack▶
The Survivalist
Survivor
Tailspin: Behind the Korean Airline Tragedy
Terror on the 40th Floor
Tidal Wave
The Towering Inferno
Tragedy of Flight 103: The Inside Story▶
Two Minute Warning
When Time Ran Out

Disco Musicals

see also Musicals
Can't Stop the Music
Car Wash
KISS Meets the Phantom of the Park
Pirate Movie
The Rocky Horror Picture Show▶
Thank God It's Friday
The Wiz
Xanadu

Disease of the Week

see also AIDS
The Affair▶
And the Band Played On▶
The Ann Jillian Story
Bang the Drum Slowly
Beaches▶
The Best Little Girl in the World▶

Between Two Women
Bobby Deerfield
The Boy in the Plastic Bubble
Brian's Song▶
Camille▶
The Carrier
The Cassandra Crossing
Champions
Checking Out
C.H.U.D.
Cleo from 5 to 7▶
Cries and Whispers▶
Crystal Heart
The Curse
Damien: The Leper Priest
Daybreak
Dead Space
Dick Barton, Special Agent
The Doctor
A Dream of Kings▶
Duet for One
Dying Young
An Early Frost▶
East of Kilimanjaro
The End▶
Eric▶
The First Deadly Sin
Fourth Wish
Gaby: A True Story▶
Germicide
Glory Enough for All: The Discovery of Insulin
Griffin and Phoenix: A Love Story
Incredible Melting Man
Interrupted Melody▶
Intimate Contact▶
Isle of the Dead
Jericho Fever
Killer on Board
L.A. Bad
The Last Man on Earth
Lightning Over Water
Lorenzo's Oil▶
Love Affair: The Eleanor & Lou Gehrig Story▶
Love Story▶
Mad Death
A Matter of WHO
Miles to Go
My Father's House
My Life
Nasty Rabbit
On Her Majesty's Secret Service▶
Panic in Echo Park
Parting Glances▶
Philadelphia▶
Pilgrim, Farewell
The Plague
The Plague Dogs
The Pride of the Yankees▶
Princes in Exile
Project: Alien
Promises in the Dark
The Proud Ones
Quarantine
Question of Faith
Rabid
Reborn
Right of Way
The Shadow Box▶
Shadowlands▶
A Shining Season▶
Silence Like Glass
The Silver Streak
Six Weeks
Stephen King's The Stand
Stigma
Terror Creatures from the Grave
Time to Live
Walking Through the Fire
When the Time Comes
When Wolves Cry
The White Legion
Xtro

Disorganized Crime

see also Crime & Criminals; Organized Crime
Ace Crawford, Private Eye
Airheads
Amos and Andrew
The Apple Dumpling Gang
The Apple Dumpling Gang Rides Again
Armed and Dangerous
Baby on Board
Baby's Day Out
Cop and a Half
Crackers
Dr. Otto & the Riddle of the Gloom Beam
Ernest Goes to Jail
Finders Keepers
A Fine Mess
Glitch!
The Gun in Betty Lou's Handbag
Happy New Year
Her Alibi
Herbie Goes Bananas
Home Alone
Home Alone 2: Lost in New York
I Wonder Who's Killing Her Now?
Inside the Law
The Italian Job
The League of Gentlemen▶
Leather Jackets
Lunch Wagon
Mad Dog and Glory▶
A Man, a Woman, and a Bank
Menage▶
Mexican Hayride
Milo Milo
Miss Grant Takes Richmond
Mutant on the Bounty
The Night They Robbed Big Bertha's
Ocean's 11
Once Upon a Crime
Oscar
Out on a Limb
Pouvoir Intime
Quick Change
Ransom Money
Reservoir Dogs▶
Round Trip to Heaven
St. Benny the Dip
See No Evil, Hear No Evil
Shake Hands with Murder
Silver Bears
Sister Act
Sitting Ducks▶
Stop! or My Mom Will Shoot
Stop That Cab
The Super
Super Soul Brother
Survivors
Tall, Tan and Terrific
The Thief Who Came to Dinner
Three Kinds of Heat
Thrilled to Death
Too Many Crooks
We're Talkin' Serious Money
The Wrong Arm of the Law▶
The Young in Heart▶

Divorce

see also Marriage; Singles
The Accidental Tourist▶
All I Want for Christmas
Alpha Beta
The Awful Truth▶
Between Friends
A Bill of Divorcement
Breaking Up
Breaking Up Is Hard to Do
California Suite▶
Can She Bake a Cherry Pie?
Cheaper to Keep Her
Children of Divorce
Clara's Heart
Cold Heat

A Conspiracy of Love
Cross My Heart
Desert Hearts▶
Despedida de Casada
Divorce His, Divorce Hers
Divorce—Italian Style▶
The Divorcee
Early Frost▶
Escapade▶
E.T.: The Extra-Terrestrial▶
Face the Music
Falling Down
Family Pictures▶
Father Figure
Fergie & Andrew: Behind Palace Doors
A Fight for Jenny
Found Alive
The Good Father▶
The Good Mother
Goodbye Love
Hard Promises
Heartburn▶
High Society▶
History is Made at Night▶
How to Break Up a Happy Divorce
How to Commit Marriage
Husbands and Wives▶
Interiors▶
Irreconcilable Differences
Kramer vs. Kramer▶
Let's Make it Legal
Liberation of L.B. Jones
Love and Hate: A Marriage Made in Hell
Love Matters
Marie▶
Melanie
The Misfits▶
Mrs. Doubtfire
Mr. Skeffington▶
Mr. Wonderful
Nadine
Naked Paradise
Necessary Parties
A New Life
Night Life in Reno
Nothing in Common
The Odd Couple▶
The Odd Job
One Cooks, the Other Doesn't
Patti Rocks▶
Peggy Sue Got Married
The Personals
Petulia▶
Pilgrim, Farewell
Play It Again, Sam▶
The Prize Pulitzer
Rich Kids
Riptide▶
Scenes from a Marriage▶
Second Chance
See You in the Morning
Sex and the Single Parent
Shattered Silence
The Solitary Man
Starting Over▶
Sweet Revenge
Table for Five
Tell It to the Judge
Tell Me That You Love Me
Tenth Month
An Unmarried Woman▶
Valentino Returns
Wanted: The Perfect Guy
The War of the Roses▶

Doctors & Nurses

see also AIDS; Disease of the Week; Evil Doctors; Hospitals & Medicine; Nursploitation!; Sanity Check; Shrinks
All Creatures Great and Small▶
Alone in the Dark
And the Band Played On▶
Arrowsmith
Ashanti, Land of No Mercy
The Asphyx▶

Doctors

Autopsy
Awakenings▶
Baby Girl Scott
Bad Medicine
Battle Circus
Bethune
Between Wars
The Black Dragons
Blonde Cobra/The Doctor's Dream
Blood Mania
Bloodlink
Body Parts
Botany Bay
The Bramble Bush
The Broken Mask
Calling Paul Temple
Candy Stripe Nurses
Carry On Doctor▶
Castle of the Creeping Flesh
Caught▶
Children of Rage
China Beach▶
Circus of Horrors
The Citadel▶
City of Joy
The Clonus Horror
Club Havana
Coma▶
Corregidor
Corridors of Blood
Courageous Dr. Christian
Crimes & Misdemeanors▶
Crossover
Dead Ringers▶
Dead Sleep
Death Becomes Her▶
Death by Prescription
Death Nurse
The Devil's Web
Doc Hollywood
The Doctor
Dr. Alien
The Doctor and the Devils
Doctor at Large
Doctor at Sea
Dr. Bethune▶
Dr. Black, Mr. Hyde
Doctor Blood's Coffin
Doctor Butcher M.D.
Dr. Caligari
Dr. Christian Meets the Women
Dr. Cyclops
Dr. Death, Seeker of Souls
Doctor Detroit
Doctor Dolittle
Doctor Faustus
Dr. Frankenstein's Castle of Freaks
Dr. Hackenstein
Dr. Heckyl and Mr. Hype
Doctor in Distress
Doctor in the House▶
Dr. Jack/For Heaven's Sake
Dr. Jekyll and Mr. Hyde
Dr. Kildare's Strange Case
Dr. Mabuse the Gambler▶
Dr. Mabuse vs. Scotland Yard
Doctor Quinn, Medicine Woman
Doctor Satan's Robot
Doctor Takes a Wife▶
Dr. Tarr's Torture Dungeon
Dr. Terror's House of Horrors
Doctor X
Doctors and Nurses
Doctors' Wives
Don't Cry, It's Only Thunder
Don't Look in the Basement
Drunken Angel▶
East of Borneo
The Egyptian
The Elephant Man▶
Emmanuelle in the Country
False Faces
Fantastic Voyage▶
Flatliners
Flesh Feast
Foreign Body
The Fortune Cookie

Glory Enough for All: The Discovery of Insulin
The Great Moment
Gross Anatomy
Guest in the House
Hands Up▶
Healer
High Heels
Holy Terror
The Horrible Dr. Hichcock
The Horror Chamber of Dr. Faustus▶
Horror Hospital
The Hospital▶
Hospital of Terror
House Calls▶
I Love My...Wife
I Never Promised You a Rose Garden▶
The In-Laws▶
The Incredible Journey of Dr. Meg Laurel▶
An Indecent Obsession
The Interns
Invasion
Jesse
Johnny Belinda▶
Johnny Belinda
Kidnapping of Baby John Doe
Korczak▶
The Last Angry Man▶
The Lazarus Syndrome
Le Cas du Dr. Laurent▶
Life Is a Long Quiet River▶
The Light in the Jungle
Love is a Many-Splendored Thing
Mad Love▶
The Mad Monster
Make-Up
Malice
Mania
M*A*S*H▶
M*A*S*H: Goodbye, Farewell & Amen
M*A*S*H: The Collector's Edition
The Mask of Fu Manchu
A Matter of Life and Death
Medic
Meet Dr. Christian
Memories of Me
Men of Ireland
Metamorphosis: The Alien Factor
Mr. North
Monty Python's The Meaning of Life▶
Murder in Texas▶
Murder Once Removed
Murder or Mercy
My Father's Nurse
Night Call Nurses
Night Monster
Night Nurse▶
Night Nurse
Nightbreaker▶
Nomads
Not as a Stranger
Nurse
Nurse Edith Cavell▶
Nurse on Call
Old Swimmin' Hole
One Flew Over the Cuckoo's Nest▶
The Ordeal of Dr. Mudd▶
Panic in Echo Park
Panic in the Streets▶
Paper Mask
People Will Talk▶
Persona▶
Petulia▶
The Plague
Praying Mantis
Private Duty Nurses
Promises in the Dark
Purple Hearts
The Raven▶
Reckless Disregard
Red Beard▶
Riot Squad
Say Goodbye, Maggie Cole

Scalpel
Sister Dora
Sister Kenny▶
Skeezer
Slaughter Hotel
State of Emergency
Stigma
Stitches
The Student Nurses
Teenage Frankenstein
Tender Loving Care
Torture Ship
Tundra
The Unbearable Lightness of Being▶
The Vicious Circle
Vital Signs
We are the Children
Women of Valor
Young Doctors in Love
The Young Nurses

Docudrama

see also Documentary

Above Us the Waves▶
Adam▶
After the Shock
Al Capone▶
All You Need Is Cash▶
The Amy Fisher Story
And the Band Played On▶
The Battle of Algiers▶
Blind Ambition
Bob Roberts▶
The Boston Strangler
Bound for Glory▶
Call Northside 777▶
Casimir the Great
Casualties of Love: The "Long Island Lolita" Story
Christian the Lion
Close to Home
Cocaine: One Man's Seduction
Conspiracy: The Trial of the Chicago Eight▶
Countdown
The Courtesans of Bombay▶
Cruel Sea▶
A Cry in the Dark▶
Edge of the World▶
The Flaming Teen-Age
Free, White, and 21
The General Line▶
Glen or Glenda
Henry: Portrait of a Serial Killer▶
The History of White People in America
The History of White People in America: Vol. 2
Hostages▶
Immortal Battalion▶
In Cold Blood▶
Inside the Third Reich
Iron & Silk
James Dean
The Jayne Mansfield Story
JFK: Reckless Youth
Journey Through Rosebud
Kamikaze Hearts
Kerouac
King▶
The Last Polka▶
Lethal Lolita—Amy Fisher: My Story
The Lion Has Wings
Murder in Texas▶
The Naked City▶
Pickpocket▶
The Poppy is also a Flower
Prince of the City▶
Qui Etes Vous, Mr. Sorge?
Real Life▶
The Red Menace
The Rise of Louis XIV▶
Shaka Zulu▶
S.O.S. Titanic
Soviet Spy
Special Bulletin▶
The Spy Who Came in from the Cold▶

T-Men▶
Tailspin: Behind the Korean Airline Tragedy
Take the Money and Run▶
Teenage Devil Dolls
Ten Days That Shook the World▶
That's Adequate
The Thin Blue Line▶
32 Short Films About Glenn Gould▶
This is Spinal Tap▶
Times of Harvey Milk
Wellington: The Duel Scandal
The Wild Aces
Working Girls▶
Zelig▶

Documentary

see also Docudrama

Alive: 20 Years Later
American Fabulous
The American Gangster
Assassination of Trotsky
The Atomic Cafe▶
Battle of China
The Battle of Russia
The Battle of San Pietro
Beach Boys: An American Band
Born to Boogie
A Brief History of Time▶
Brother's Keeper▶
Bruce Lee: Curse of the Dragon▶
Burden of Dreams▶
Campaign in Poland
Caravaggio▶
The Carnivores
The Children of Theatre Street▶
Chuck Amuck: The Movie
Chuck Berry: Hail! Hail! Rock 'n' Roll▶
Ciao Federico! Fellini Directs Satyricon
The Civil War, Episode 1: The Cause—1861▶
The Civil War, Episode 2: A Very Bloody Affair—1862▶
The Civil War, Episode 3: Forever Free—1862▶
The Civil War, Episode 4: Simply Murder—1863▶
The Civil War, Episode 5: The Universe of Battle—1863▶
The Civil War, Episode 6: Valley of the Shadow of Death—1864▶
The Civil War, Episode 7: Most Hallowed Ground—1864▶
The Civil War, Episode 8: War is All Hell—1865▶
The Civil War, Episode 9: The Better Angels of Our Nature—1865▶
The Clowns▶
Come Back, Africa▶
Common Threads: Stories from the Quilt
Dance Hall Racket
Dear America: Letters Home from Vietnam▶
December 7th: The Movie
Decline of Western Civilization 1▶
Decline of Western Civilization 2: The Metal Years
Derby▶
D.O.A.: A Right of Passage
Don't Look Back▶
The Doors: Soft Parade, a Retrospective
Dracula: A Cinematic Scrapbook
Ebony Dreams
The Elvis Files
Elvis in Hollywood▶
Elvis in the Movies
Elvis Memories
Elvis Presley's Graceland

Elvis: Rare Moments with the King
Elvis: The Echo Will Never Die
Emperor Jones/Paul Robeson: Tribute to an Artist
Empire of the Air: The Men Who Made Radio
Encounter with the Unknown
The Endless Summer▶
The Endless Summer 2▶
Epic That Never Was
Faces of Death, Part 1
Faces of Death, Part 2
Fallen Champ: The Untold Story of Mike Tyson▶
Fangoria's Weekend of Horrors
Flying Saucers Over Hollywood: The Plan 9 Companion
France/Tour/Detour/Deux/Enfants▶
Frankenstein: A Cinematic Scrapbook
Germany in Autumn
Gotta Dance, Gotta Sing
Guilty of Treason
Harlan County, U.S.A.
Hearts of Darkness: A Filmmaker's Apocalypse▶
Hell's Angels Forever
The Hellstrom Chronicle▶
Here's Looking at You, Warner Bros.▶
Hide and Seek
Hollywood Clowns
Hollywood Home Movies
Hollywood Scandals and Tragedies
Hollywood Uncensored
The Horror of It All
Hugh Hefner: Once Upon a Time
Incident at Oglala: The Leonard Peltier Story▶
Indomitable Teddy Roosevelt
Irving Berlin's America
It Happened in the Park
It's All True
James Dean
James Dean Story
James Stewart: A Wonderful Life
The JFK Conspiracy
JFK Remembered
John F..Kennedy
The Kennedys Don't Cry
Kidco
Kino Pravda/Enthusiasm
The Lash of the Penitents
The Last Waltz
LBJ: A Biography
Le Joli Mai
The Legend of Valentino
Let It Be
Let's Get Lost
Lightning Over Water
Long Shadows
Louisiana Story▶
The Love Goddesses
Love Meetings
Love Without Fear
The Making of "A Brief History of Time"
The Making of a Legend: "Gone With the Wind"
Man in the Silk Hat▶
Man of Aran▶
The Man Who Skied Down Everest
The Man with a Movie Camera▶
Many Faces of Sherlock Holmes
Marilyn
Marjoe
Marlon Brando
Mein Kampf
Memphis Belle: A Story of a Flying Fortress
MGM: When the Lion Roars

Minnelli on Minnelli: Liza Remembers Vincente
Moana, a Romance of the Golden Age►
Mondo Cane
Mondo Cane 2
Mondo Magic
Night of the Living Dead, 25th Anniversary Documentary
Oscar's Greatest Moments: 1971-1991
Paris is Burning►
Prelude to War
Pumping Iron
Pumping Iron 2: The Women
Punk Rock Movie
Rascal Dazzle
Rate It X
The Real Buddy Holly Story
Revolution
Rise and Fall of the Third Reich
Roger & Me►
Sasquatch
Sex and Buttered Popcorn
Shocking Asia
Signals Through the Flames►
The Situation
Slave Trade in the World Today
Soft and Hard
The Sorrow and the Pity►
Streetwise►
Stripper
Superstar: The Life and Times of Andy Warhol►
Swimming to Cambodia►
Taxi zum Klo►
Thank You & Good Night
The Thin Blue Line►
Tokyo-Ga►
Tokyo Olympiad
Triumph of the Will
Truth or Dare
Vanishing Prairie►
Vanishing Wilderness
Vernon, Florida►
Vietnam: Chronicle of a War
Visions of Light: The Art of Cinematography►
War in the Sky►
The War Room►
Wild, Wild World of Jayne Mansfield
Wisecracks►

Dogs

see *King of Beasts (Dogs)*

Dolls That Kill

see *Killer Toys*

Down Under

Alvin Purple
Anzacs: The War Down Under►
Around the World in 80 Ways
Between Wars
The Blue Lightning
Born to Run
Botany Bay
Boulevard of Broken Dreams
Burke & Wills
Caddie
The Cars That Ate Paris►
Cass
Cool Change
Dark Age
Dead Easy
Death of a Soldier
The Desert Rats►
Down Under
The Dunera Boys►
Dusty
Eureka Stockade
Fast Talking
Forty Thousand Horsemen
Freedom
The Fringe Dwellers
Gallagher's Travels
Gallipoli►

The Getting of Wisdom
The Good Wife
Great Gold Swindle
Ground Zero►
Hurricane Smith
The Irishman
Kitty and the Bagman
The Lighthorsemen►
Little Boy Lost
The Long Weekend
Mad Dog Morgan
The Man from Snowy River
Miracle Down Under
Money Movers
Monkey Grip►
Moving Out
My Brilliant Career►
The Naked Country
Ned Kelly
Nevil Shute's The Far Country
On the Beach►
Over the Hill
Overlanders►
Palm Beach
Phar Lap
Prince and the Great Race
Prisoners of the Sun►
The Quest
Quigley Down Under
Rebel
The Rescuers Down Under
Return to Snowy River►
Ride a Wild Pony►
The Right Hand Man
Robbery Under Arms
Run, Rebecca, Run
Runaway Island, Part 1
Runaway Island, Part 2
Runaway Island, Part 3
Runaway Island, Part 4
Sara Dane
Savage Attraction
The Shrimp on the Barbie
Silver City
The Silver Stallion: King of the Wild Brumbies
Sirens►
Sister Kenny
Squizzy Taylor
Stones of Death
Strictly Ballroom
The Sundowners►
The Thorn Birds►
Under Capricorn
The Wacky World of Wills & Burke
A Waltz Through the Hills
Waterfront
We of the Never Never►
Where the Green Ants Dream
The Winds of Jarrah
The Winter of Our Dreams

Drama

see *also Adventure Drama; Comedy Drama; Historical Drama; Musical Drama; Romantic Drama; Tearjerkers; Tragedy*
ABC Stage 67: Truman Capote's A Christmas Memory
Abducted
The Abduction of Allison Tate
The Abduction of Kari Swenson
The Abe Lincoln of Ninth Avenue
Above the Rim
Above Us the Waves►
Abraham Lincoln
Absence of Malice
Accatone!►
Acceptable Risks
Accident
The Accused
The Accused►
Across 110th Street
Across the Tracks
Act of Aggression

Act of Passion: The Lost Honor of Kathryn Beck
Act of Vengeance
Action for Slander
Actors and Sin
An Actor's Revenge
Adam►
Adam at 6 A.M.
Adam Had Four Sons
The Adjuster
Adomas Nori Buti Zmogumi
Adoption►
The Adultress
Adventure Island
The Adventures of Mark Twain►
The Adventures of Nellie Bly
The Adventures of the Flying Cadets
The Adventurous Knights
The Adversary
Affair in Trinidad
Africa Texas Style
An African Dream
African Journey
After the Rehearsal►
Afterburn►
Against the Wind
Age Old Friends►
The Agency
Agent on Ice
Agnes of God
Aguirre, the Wrath of God►
Airborne
Akira Kurosawa's Dreams
Alamo Bay
Alan & Naomi
Albino
Alexander: The Other Side of Dawn
Alice in the Cities►
All About Eve►
All Creatures Great and Small►
All God's Children
All My Sons►
All Quiet on the Western Front►
All Quiet on the Western Front
All the King's Men►
All the President's Men►
All the Right Moves
All the Young Men►
Allonsanfan►
Almost Human
Almost Royal Family
Alone in the Neon Jungle
Alpha Beta
Alphabet City
Alpine Fire
Alsino and the Condor►
Alternative
Amazing Grace & Chuck
The Amazing Howard Hughes
Amber Waves
America First
America/The Fall of Babylon►
The American Angels: Baptism of Blood
American Anthem
American Blue Note
An American Christmas Carol
American Dream►
American Flyers
American Heart►
American Me►
American Nightmare
The American Soldier
An American Story
An American Summer
Americana
The Americano/Variety
Amin: The Rise and Fall
Among the Cinders
Amongst Friends
Amor Bandido
Amore►
Amos
Amy
Anatomy of a Murder►
Anatomy of Terror
And God Created Woman

And Hope to Die
And Justice for All
And Nothing But the Truth
And Now Miguel
And the Band Played On►
And the Ship Sails On►
The Andersonville Trial►
Andre
Andy Warhol's Bad►
Angel
An Angel at My Table►
Angel Baby
Angel City
Angel with the Trumpet
Angela
Angele►
Angelo My Love►
Angels with Dirty Faces►
AngKor: Cambodia Express
Angry Harvest►
Angry Joe Bass
Anita de Montemar
The Ann Jillian Story
Anna►
Anna and the King of Siam►
Anne of Green Gables►
Another Country
Another Woman►
Antonia and Jane►
Antonio Das Mortes
Any Number Can Play
Anything for a Thrill
Anzio
Aparajito►
Applause►
Aria
Arizona
Armored Car Robbery
Armored Command
The Arrangement
Arrowsmith
Arthur's Hallowed Ground
Artist's Studio Secrets
As You Desire Me►
Ash Wednesday
Ashes and Diamonds►
Ashes and Embers
Ashik Kerib►
The Asphalt Jungle►
Assassin of Youth
The Assault►
Assault at West Point: The Court-Martial of Johnson Whittaker
Assault of the Rebel Girls
The Assignment
The Assisi Underground
At Gunpoint
At Play in the Fields of the Lord►
Atlantic City►
Atomic Attack
Attack Squadron
Attica►
Au Revoir Les Enfants►
Augustine of Hippo►
Autobiography of a Princess
An Autumn Afternoon►
Autumn Born
Autumn Leaves
Autumn Sonata►
Avenging Angel
Aventure Malgache
Away All Boats
Baba►
Babel!►
The Babe
Babe Ruth Story
Baby Doll►
Baby Girl Scott
The Baby Maker
Baby, the Rain Must Fall
The Babylon Story from ''Intolerance''►
The Bacchantes
The Bachelor►
Back Door to Heaven►
Back Home
Backbeat►
Backstairs
The Bad and the Beautiful►
Bad Blood

Bad Boy
Bad Boys►
Bad Georgia Road
Bad Girls Do Cry
Bad Girls Go to Hell
Bad Girls in the Movies
Bad Lieutenant►
The Bad Sleep Well►
Badge of the Assassin
Badlands►
Bail Out at 43,000
Baker's Hawk
The Balcony►
Ballad of a Soldier►
Ballet Shoes
Baltic Deputy►
Bandits
Bandits of Orgosolo
Barbarians at the Gate►
Bare Knees
The Barefoot Contessa►
Barfly►
Baritone
Barnum
The Baron and the Kid
Barry Lyndon►
Basileus Quartet►
Battle Circus
Battle Cry►
The Battle of Austerlitz
The Battle of Blood Island
Battleground►
Battling Bunyon
Battling Orioles
The Bay Boy
The Bear►
The Bears & I
The Beat
Beat Girl
The Beatniks
Beatrice►
Beau Brummel
Beau Brummell►
Beautiful Dreamers
Beauty for the Asking
Becky Sharp
Becoming Colette
Bed and Sofa►
Beethoven
Beethoven Lives Upstairs
Before the Revolution
Beggars in Ermine
The Beguiled►
Behind Enemy Lines
Behind Office Doors
Behind the Rising Sun
Behold a Pale Horse
Belfast Assassin
Belizaire the Cajun
Bell Diamond
The Bell Jar
Bell Ringer of Antigua
Bellissima►
Bellman and True
The Belly of an Architect►
Below the Belt
Below the Deadline
The Beniker Gang
Benjamin Argumedo
The Benny Goodman Story
Bergonzi Hand
Berlin Alexanderplatz►
Bernadette
The Best Christmas Pageant Ever
Best Enemies
Best Kept Secrets
The Best Little Girl in the World►
The Best Man►
The Best Years of Our Lives►
Bethune
Betrayal
Betrayal from the East
Betrayed►
Betrayed
A Betrayed Man
The Betsy
Between Friends
Between Heaven and Earth
Between Two Women
Between Wars

Drama

Beulah Land
Beverly Hills Madam
Beverly Hills 90210
Beverly Hills 90210: The
   Graduation
Beyond Fear
Beyond Innocence
Beyond Obsession
Beyond Reason
Beyond Reasonable Doubt
Beyond the Forest
Beyond the Limit
Beyond the Next Mountain
Beyond the Time Barrier
Beyond the Walls
The Bible...In the Beginning▶
The Bicycle Thief▶
Big Bad Mama 2
The Big Bird Cage
The Big Blue
Big Boss
Big Combo▶
The Big Hangover
The Big Knife▶
The Big Lift
The Big Man: Crossing the
   Line▶
Big Mo
Big Red
Big Score
Big Town
Big Trees▶
Bilitis
Bill▶
A Bill of Divorcement
Bill: On His Own▶
Billionaire Boys Club
Billy Bathgate
Billy Galvin
Billy Jack
Billy: Portrait of a Street Kid
Billyboy
The Bionic Woman
The Birch Interval
Bird▶
Birdman of Alcatraz▶
Birds of Prey
Birdy▶
The Bitch
Bitter Harvest▶
Bitter Rice▶
Bix
Black Beauty
Black Beauty▶
Black Beauty/Courage of
   Black Beauty
The Black Dragons
Black Eyes
Black Fury▶
Black God & White Devil
Black Godfather
The Black Klansman
Black Lemons
Black Like Me
Black Lizard
Black Narcissus▶
Black Orpheus▶
Black Rain▶
Black Sister's Revenge
Black Starlet
Blackboard Jungle▶
Blackout
Blades of Courage
Blake of Scotland Yard
The Blasphemer
Blast-Off Girls
Blastfighter
Blaze
Bleak House
Bless the Beasts and Children
Blind Ambition
Blind Fools
Blind Spot
Blind Vengeance
Blinded by the Light
Blockhouse
Blood Brothers
Blood Clan
Blood In...Blood Out: Bound
   by Honor
Blood on the Mountain
Blood Red

Blood Ties
Blood Vows: The Story of a
   Mafia Wife
Blood Wedding▶
Bloodbath
Bloodbrothers
The Bloody Brood
Bloody Mama
The Blot
Blown Away
The Blue Angel▶
Blue Chips
Blue Collar
Blue Fire Lady
Blue Heaven
Blue Jeans
The Blue Knight
The Blue Lagoon
The Blue Max
Bluebeard▶
Bluebeard
Bluffing It
The Blum Affair
The Boat is Full▶
Bob le Flambeur▶
Bobby Deerfield
Bodies, Rest & Motion
Body and Soul
Body and Soul▶
Body & Soul
Body of Evidence
Bogie
Bolero
Bon Voyage
Bonnie & Clyde▶
Bonnie's Kids
The Boost
Boots Malone
Bopha!▶
The Border▶
Border Street
Born Again
Born Beautiful
Born Free▶
Born in Flames
Born Innocent
Born Losers
Born on the Fourth of July▶
Born to Run
Boss of Big Town
Boss' Son▶
The Bostonians
Boulevard Nights
Boulevard of Broken Dreams
Bound for Glory▶
Bouquet of Barbed Wire
Boxcar Bertha
The Boxer and Death▶
Boxing Helena
Boy in Blue
The Boy in the Plastic Bubble
Boy Meets Girl▶
The Boy Who Could Fly▶
The Boy with the Green Hair▶
The Boys in Company C
The Boys in the Band
The Boys Next Door
Boy's Reformatory
Boys Town▶
Boyz N the Hood▶
The Bramble Bush
Brand New Life
Brass
The Brave One▶
Braveheart
Break of Hearts
Breakdown
Breaker Morant▶
Breaking Home Ties
Breaking Up
Breakthrough
Breathless
Brenda Starr
The Bride & the Beast
The Bride Is Much Too
   Beautiful
Brideshead Revisited▶
The Bridge of San Luis Rey▶
The Bridge on the River
   Kwai▶
Bridge to Silence
The Brig▶

Bright Angel
Bright Lights, Big City
Brink of Life
A Brivele der Mamen▶
The Broadway Drifter
Broken Angel
Broken Badge▶
Broken Blossoms▶
The Broken Chain
Broken Hearts of Broadway
The Broken Mask
Broken Melody
Broken Mirrors
Broken Strings
A Bronx Tale
The Bronx War
Brother Future
Brother John▶
Brother Orchid▶
The Brotherhood
Brotherhood of Justice
The Brothers Karamazov▶
The Browning Version▶
Brubaker▶
Brussels Transit▶
Brutal Glory
Bucktown
Bugsy▶
Bulldog Edition
Bulldog Jack▶
Bullets or Ballots▶
Bullies
Bullitt▶
Burgess, Philby, and
   MacLean: Spy Scandal of
   the Century
Burglar▶
Buried Alive
The Burmese Harp▶
Burn!▶
The Burning Bed▶
Burning Rage
Burning Vengeance
Bury Me an Angel
The Bus Is Coming
Bush Mama
Business as Usual
Busted Up
Buster
Busting
But Where Is Daniel Wax?
Butterfield 8▶
Butterfly
Butterfly Affair
By the Sword
Bye Bye Brazil
Caches de Oro
Cadillac Girls
The Cage▶
Caged Fury
Caged in Paradiso
Caged Women
The Caine Mutiny▶
The Caine Mutiny Court
   Martial▶
California Dreaming
Caligari's Cure▶
Caligula
Call to Glory
Callie and Son
Camp Double Feature
Can You Hear the Laughter?
   The Story of Freddie Prinze
Cancion en el Alma
Candy Tangerine Man
A Canterbury Tale▶
Capone
Captain Blackjack
Captain Horatio Hornblower▶
Captains Courageous▶
Captains of the Clouds
Captive
Captive Heart▶
The Capture of Grizzly Adams
The Cardinal
Career
Careful, He Might Hear You▶
Carnal Crimes
Carny▶
Caroline?▶
Carrington, V.C.▶
Carry Me Back

Carve Her Name with Pride
A Case of Deadly Force▶
A Case of Libel
Casimir the Great
Cass
Cassie
Cast a Giant Shadow
The Castle▶
Cat on a Hot Tin Roof▶
Cat on a Hot Tin Roof
The Catered Affair▶
Catholic Hour
Catholics▶
Cavalcade▶
Cease Fire
Celebrity
Celeste▶
Celia: Child Of Terror
Certain Fury
Certain Sacrifice
Chain Gang Women
Chained for Life
The Chalk Garden▶
Challenge
Challenge to Lassie
Chameleon
Chameleon Street▶
Champagne
Champion▶
Champions
Change of Habit
Changes
Chantilly Lace
Chapayev▶
Chaplin▶
Chapter in Her Life
Charade
Chariots of Fire▶
Charlotte Forten's Mission:
   Experiment in Freedom▶
The Charmer
The Chase
Chase
Chasing Dreams
Chattahoochee
Cheaters
Cheatin' Hearts
The Checkered Flag
Cheers for Miss Bishop
Chicago Joe & the Showgirl
Chiefs
Child Bride of Short Creek
A Child is Waiting▶
The Children Are Watching
   Us▶
Children in the Crossfire
The Children of An Lac
Children of Divorce
Children of Nature
Children of Rage
Children of Sanchez
The Children of Times Square
Children's Carol
The Children's Hour
China Beach▶
China Cry
China Girl
China Sky
The China Syndrome▶
Chinese Roulette
Chocolat▶
The Chocolate War▶
The Choice
Choices
The Choppers
Christ Stopped at Eboli▶
Christabel
Christiane F.▶
A Christmas Carol▶
The Christmas Coal Mine
   Miracle
Christmas Comes to Willow
   Creek
Christmas Lilies of the Field
A Christmas to Remember
A Christmas Without Snow
Churchill and the Generals
The Cincinnati Kid
Cinema Paradiso▶
Circle of Power
The Citadel▶
Citizen Cohn

Citizen Kane▶
The City
The City and the Dogs▶
City Boy▶
City in Fear▶
City of Hope▶
City of Joy
The City's Edge
Civil War Diary
Civilization▶
Clarence Darrow▶
Class Action▶
The Class of Miss MacMichael
Class of 1984
Class of '63
Claudia
Clean and Sober▶
Clearcut
The Client
The Clockmaker▶
Clodhopper
Close to Eden
The Closer
Closet Land
Cloud Dancer
Clowning Around
Clowning Around 2
The Club▶
Club Life
Coach
Cocaine Cowboys
Cocaine Fiends
Cockfighter▶
Code of Honor
Cody
Coffy
Cold Blood
Cold Days
Cold Front
Cold River
Colonel Redl▶
Colonel Wolodyjowski
The Color of Money▶
The Color of Pomegranates▶
The Color Purple▶
Colors▶
Combat!
Come Along with Me
Come and Get It▶
Come and See▶
Come Back Little Reba
Come Back, Little Sheba▶
Come Back to the Five &
   Dime Jimmy Dean, Jimmy
   Dean▶
Comeback
The Comedians
The Comic
Coming Home▶
Coming Out of the Ice▶
The Commies are Coming, the
   Commies are Coming
Commissar▶
The Commitments▶
Common Bonds
Common Law Wife
Company Business
Company Limited
The Concrete Jungle
Condemned to Hell
Conduct Unbecoming
The Conductor
Confessions of a Police
   Captain
Confessions of a Serial Killer
Confessions of Tom Harris
The Conformist▶
The Connection▶
Conrack▶
Consenting Adult
Conspiracy
Conspiracy of Hearts▶
A Conspiracy of Love
Conspiracy: The Trial of the
   Chicago Eight▶
Conspirator
Contempt▶
Control
Conversation Piece▶
Convicted
Convicted: A Mother's Story
Convoy

Cool Hand Luke▶
The Cool Surface
Cooley High▶
Cop
Copkillers
Cordelia
The Corn is Green▶
Cornbread, Earl & Me
Cornered▶
The Corridor: Death
Corrupt▶
Corruption
Cosh Boy
Cottage to Let
Cotton Candy
The Count of the Old Town
Countdown
Counterblast
The Counterfeit Traitor▶
Country▶
The Country Diary of an
    Edwardian Lady
Country Girl▶
Country Girl
Country Lovers, City Lovers
Countryman
County Fair
Courage▶
Courage of Lassie
Courageous Dr. Christian
The Courier
Courier of Death
The Court Martial of Jackie
    Robinson▶
The Courtesans of Bombay▶
Courtship▶
Covergirl
Coward of the County
Cowboys Don't Cry
The Cracker Factory
Crashout
Cria▶
Cricket on the Hearth
Cries and Whispers▶
Crime and Punishment▶
Crime and Punishment
Crime of Honor
The Crime of Monsieur
    Lange▶
Crime of Passion
Crimes of Passion▶
Criminal Act
Criminal Code
Crisscross
Crooked Hearts
The Cross & the Switchblade
Cross Creek
Cross Examination
Cross My Heart
Crossbar
Crossfire▶
Crossover
Crossroads
The Crowd▶
The Crucified Lovers▶
Cruel Sea▶
The Cruel Story of Youth▶
Cruisin' High
Crush
A Cry for Love
Cry Freedom
Cry from the Mountain
A Cry from the Streets
A Cry in the Dark▶
Cry of a Prostitute: Love Kills
Cry, the Beloved Country▶
Cry Vengeance
The Crying Game▶
Cup Final
The Curse of King Tut's Tomb
Cut and Run
Cyrano de Bergerac
Cyrano de Bergerac▶
D-Day, the Sixth of June▶
Da
Dad
Daddy Nostalgia▶
Daddy-O
Daisy Miller
Dakota
Damien: The Leper Priest▶
The Damned

The Dance Goes On
Dance or Die
Dance with a Stranger▶
Dancing in the Dark
Dancing Man
Dancing Mothers
Dandelions
Danger in the Skies
Danger Lights
Danger UXB
Dangerous
A Dangerous Age
Dangerous Game
Dangerous Holiday
Dangerous Hours
Dangerous Liaisons
Dangerous Life
Dangerous Moves▶
Dangerous Relations
A Dangerous Woman
Dangerously Close
Daniel
Daniel and the Towers
Danny
Danny Boy▶
Dante's Inferno▶
Dante's Inferno: Life of Dante
    Gabriel Rossetti
Danzon▶
Dark Horse
The Dark Hour
Dark Obsession
Dark River: A Father's
    Revenge
The Dark Side of Love
Dark Victory▶
Darling▶
Das Boot▶
Das Testament des Dr.
    Mabuse▶
Date Bait
Daughter of Death
Daughter of the Dragon
Daughter of the Tong
Daughters of the Dust▶
David▶
David and Lisa▶
Dawn!
Dawn Express
Dawn Patrol▶
The Day After▶
The Day and the Hour
Day for Night▶
A Day for Thanks on Walton's
    Mountain
A Day in October
A Day in the Country▶
The Day of the Locust▶
Day of Triumph
Day One▶
Day with Conrad Green
Days of Glory
Days of Heaven▶
Days of Wine and Roses
Days of Wine and Roses▶
The Dead▶
Dead Boyz Can't Fly
Dead End▶
Dead End Street
Dead Man Out▶
Dead Poets Society▶
Dead Right
Dead Silence
Dead Wrong: The John Evans
    Story
Deadline
Deadly Business▶
Deadly Darling
Deadly Encounter
Deadly Game
Deadly Twins
Dealers
Dear Boys
Dear Murderer
Death Be Not Proud▶
Death Blow
Death Driver
Death Drug
Death Force
Death in Deep Water
Death in Venice▶
Death is Called Engelchen▶

Death of a Centerfold
Death of a Salesman▶
Death of a Soldier
The Death of Adolf Hitler
Death of an Angel
The Death of Richie
Death Scream
Death Wish Club
December
Decoration Day▶
Deep End▶
Deep in the Heart
Deep Six
The Deer Hunter▶
The Defender
The Defense Never Rests
Defiance
The Defiant Ones▶
The Defilers
The Deliberate Stranger▶
Delinquent Daughters
Demented
Demons in the Garden▶
Demonstrator
Dempsey
Denial: The Dark Side of
    Passion
Department Store
Desde el Abismo
Desert Bloom▶
The Desert Fox▶
The Desert Rats▶
The Desert Tigers
The Deserters
Desire Under the Elms
Despair▶
Desperate Characters▶
Desperate Lives
Detective Story▶
Detour▶
Deutschland im Jahre Null▶
Devi▶
The Devil at 4 O'Clock
The Devil in Silk
The Devil on Wheels
The Devil's Harvest
The Devil's Playground▶
The Devil's Sleep
Devil's Son-in-Law
D.I.
Diamond Head
Diamonds of the Night▶
Diana: Her True Story
Diane
Diary of a Country Priest▶
Diary of a Lost Girl▶
Diary of a Mad Old Man
Diary of a Teenage Hitchhiker
Diary of a Young Comic
The Diary of Anne Frank▶
Dick Barton, Special Agent
Dick Barton Strikes Back
Didn't You Hear?
Dingaka
Dino
Dirt Gang
Dirty Dancing▶
Dirty Gertie from Harlem
    U.S.A.
The Disappearance of Aimee▶
Discontent
Dishonored
The Displaced Person▶
Disraeli▶
Distant Thunder▶
Distant Thunder
Distant Voices, Still Lives▶
Diving In
Divorce His, Divorce Hers
D.O.A.
Docks of New York▶
The Doctor
Dr. Bethune▶
Doctor Faustus
Dr. Judym
Dr. Kildare's Strange Case
Dr. Strange
Doctors' Wives
Dodes 'ka-den▶
Dodsworth▶
A Dog of Flanders
The Dog Soldier

The Dog Who Stopped the
    War
The Doll
The Dollmaker
A Doll's House
A Doll's House▶
Dominick & Eugene▶
The Domino Principle
Don Segundo Sombra
Don't Cry, It's Only Thunder
Don't Look Back: The Story of
    Leroy "Satchel" Paige
Don't Mess with My Sister!
Doomed Love
The Doors
Double-Crossed
Double Deal
Double Edge
Double Exposure: The Story
    of Margaret Bourke-White
A Double Life▶
The Double Life of Veronique
Double Standard
Double Suicide▶
Downhill Racer
D.P.
Drachenfutter▶
Dragnet
Dragon Seed
Dragon: The Bruce Lee
    Story▶
Dragstrip Girl
The Drake Case
A Dream for Christmas▶
A Dream of Passion
Dream Street
Dream to Believe
Dreamchild▶
Dreamer
Dreaming Lips
Dreams
The Dresser▶
Drifting
Drifting Souls
Drifting Weeds▶
Driving Miss Daisy▶
Drowning by Numbers▶
Drug Wars 2: The Cocaine
    Cartel
Drum
Drums O'Voodoo
Drunken Angel▶
A Dry White Season▶
Drying Up the Streets
Dual Alibi
Dubeat-E-O
The Duellists▶
Duet for One
Duke of the Derby
The Dunera Boys▶
Dusty
Dutchman▶
D.W. Griffith Triple Feature
The Dybbuk▶
Dynamite Dan
An Early Frost▶
Early Summer▶
The Earrings of Madame
    De...▶
Earth Entranced
Earthling
East End Hustle
East of Eden▶
East of Eden
East of Elephant Rock
The Easy Life▶
Easy Living
Easy Rider▶
Ebony Tower
Echoes in the Darkness
Echoes of Paradise
The Eclipse▶
Eddie and the Cruisers
Eddie and the Cruisers 2:
    Eddie Lives!
Eddie Macon's Run
Eden
Eden 2
Eden 3
Eden 4
Edge of Darkness▶
Edge of the World▶

Edie in Ciao! Manhattan
The Education of Sonny
    Carson
Edvard Munch
The Effect of Gamma Rays on
    Man-in-the-Moon
    Marigolds▶
The Egyptian
8 1/2▶
Eight Men Out▶
8 Million Ways to Die
1860
Eijanaika▶
El Bruto
El Callao
El Muerto
El Norte▶
El Super▶
Ele, My Friend
The Elegant Criminal
Eleni
The Elephant Man▶
Elizabeth, the Queen
Elmer
Elmer Gantry
The Elusive Corporal▶
Elvis: The Movie
Emergency▶
The Emigrants▶
Emiliano Zapata
Emily
Eminent Domain
Emmanuelle
Emmanuelle 5
Emmanuelle 6
Emmanuelle & Joanna
Emmanuelle in Bangkok
Emmanuelle in Soho
Emmanuelle in the Country
Emmanuelle on Taboo Island
Emmanuelle, the Joys of a
    Woman
Emmanuelle, the Queen
Emmanuelle's Daughter
Emma's Shadow▶
Emperor Jones
Emperor Jones/Paul
    Robeson: Tribute to an
    Artist
The Empire of Passion▶
Empire of the Sun▶
Employees' Entrance▶
An Empty Bed▶
Empty Suitcases
Encore▶
End of Desire
The End of Innocence
The End of St. Petersburg▶
End of the Road
The Endless Game
Enemy of Women
Enemy Territory
An Englishman Abroad▶
Enigma Secret
Enola Gay: The Men, the
    Mission, the Atomic Bomb
The Entertainer▶
Entre-Nous▶
Equinox
Equinox Flower
Era Notte a Roma▶
Erendira
Eric▶
The Ernest Green Story
Ernesto
Ernie Kovacs: Between the
    Laughter
Erotic Images
Escape
Escape Artist▶
Escape from Hell
Escape from Sobibor▶
Esposa y Amante
Eternally Yours
Eternity
Eureka!
Europa, Europa▶
Europa '51
The Europeans▶
The Everlasting Secret Family
Every Man for Himself & God
    Against All▶

Drama

Everybody's Fine
The Evil Mind
The Execution
The Execution of Private
    Slovik▶
Execution of Raymond
    Graham
The Executioner
The Executioner, Part 2:
    Frozen Scream
The Executioner's Song
Executive Action
Executive Suite▶
Exiled to Shanghai
Exodus▶
Extreme Justice
Extremities
Eye on the Sparrow
Eye Witness
Eyes of Julia Deep
The Eyes of the Amaryllis
F. Scott Fitzgerald in
    Hollywood
The Fabulous Dorseys
A Face in the Crowd▶
Face of Another
Face to Face
Face to Face▶
Faith
Fall from Innocence
Fallen Angel
Fallen Angels 1▶
Fallen Angels 2▶
The Fallen Idol▶
The Fallen Sparrow▶
Falling from Grace
False Arrest
False Note
False Witness
Fame is the Spur
The Family▶
Family Enforcer
Family Life
A Family Matter
Family Prayers
Family Secrets
Family Sins
Family Upside Down▶
Family Viewing▶
Fandango
Fanny and Alexander▶
Fanny Hill
Fanny Hill: Memoirs of a
    Woman of Pleasure
Fantasies
Far Away and Long Ago
Far Cry from Home
Faraway, So Close!
Farewell My Concubine
The Fast and the Furious
Fast Company
Fast Lane Fever
Fast Walking
Fat City▶
Fat Man and Little Boy
Fatal Confinement
Fatal Fix
Fatal Vision
Father▶
Father
The Father Clements Story
Father Figure
Father Hood
Fathers and Sons
Faust▶
The FBI Murders▶
The FBI Story▶
Fear Strikes Out▶
Fearless▶
Federal Agent
Feelin' Up
Fellow Traveler▶
Fever▶
Fever Mounts at El Pao
Fever Pitch
A Few Good Men▶
Fictitious Marriage
The Field▶
Field of Honor
Fifth Day of Peace
The Fifth Seal
The Fig Tree

A Fight for Jenny
Fight for the Title
Fight for Your Life
The Fighter▶
Fighter Attack
Fighting Back
Fighting Father Dunne
Fighting Pilot
The Fighting Sullivans▶
Final Comedown
Final Extra
Final Shot: The Hank Gathers
    Story
Final Warning
Fine Gold
Fine Things
Finish Line
Finishing School
Fiorile▶
The Fire Within▶
Fireball Forward
Firehouse
Fires on the Plain▶
First Born
The First Deadly Sin
First Legion
First Strike
Fitzcarraldo▶
Five Easy Pieces▶
Five Minutes to Love
The Five of Me
The $5.20 an Hour Dream
The Fixer▶
Flambards
Flame of the Islands
Flame to the Phoenix
The Flame Trees of Thika▶
A Flash of Green
Flesh and Blood
Flesh and Bone▶
The Flesh and the Devil▶
Fleshpot on 42nd Street
Flight from Vienna
Flight of the Innocent
Flowers of Reverie
The Flowers of St. Francis▶
Fly with the Hawk
Flying Blind
The Flying Scotsman
A Fool There Was
Foolish Wives▶
Fools of Fortune
For Ladies Only
For the Boys
For Us, the Living▶
For Your Love Only
Forbidden Games▶
Forbidden Passion: The Oscar
    Wilde Movie
Force of Evil▶
Force of Impulse
Forced March
Ford: The Man & the Machine
The Foreigner
The Foreman Went to France
Forest of Little Bear
Forever Amber
Forever Mary▶
Forever Young
Forgotten Prisoners
Fort Apache, the Bronx▶
Fortune and Men's Eyes
Fortunes of War▶
The Forty-Ninth Parallel▶
Foul Play
The Fountainhead▶
The Four Horsemen of the
    Apocalypse▶
The Four Horsemen of the
    Apocalypse
The 400 Blows▶
Four in a Jeep
Four Ways Out
The Fourth War
Fourth Wise Man
Fox and His Friends▶
Foxes
Foxfire▶
Foxstyle
Foxtrot
Fran
Frances▶

Francesco
Francis Gary Powers: The
    True Story of the U-2 Spy
Frauds
Free Amerika Broadcasting
A Free Soul
Free to Love
Free, White, and 21
Freedom
Freedom is Paradise▶
Freeze-Die-Come to Life▶
French Can-Can▶
The French Woman
Frida
Frieda
Friendly Fire▶
Friendly Persuasion▶
Friends
Friends Forever▶
A Friendship in Vienna
The Fringe Dwellers
From Hell to Victory
From Here to Eternity▶
From Here to Eternity
From the Life of the
    Marionettes▶
From the Terrace
Frontera
The Fugitive▶
The Fugitive: Premiere
    Episode
Fugitive Road
The Fugitive: The Final
    Episode
Full Hearts & Empty Pockets
Full Metal Jacket▶
Fun Down There
Fury▶
Fury is a Woman▶
Futz
Fyre
"G" Men▶
Gabriel Over the White
    House▶
Gaby: A True Story▶
The Gallant Hours▶
The Gambler▶
The Gambler & the Lady
Gambler's Choice
The Game is Over
Gandhi▶
Gang Bullets
Gang Busters
Gang War
The Gang's All Here
Gangster Wars
The Garden of Eden▶
Garden of the Finzi-Continis▶
Gardens of Stone
Gas Food Lodging▶
A Gathering of Eagles
A Geisha▶
Gemini Affair
The Gene Krupa Story
Generale Della Rovere▶
A Generation▶
Gentleman Bandit
Gentleman Jim▶
Gentleman's Agreement▶
Genuine Risk
The George McKenna Story
George Washington
George Washington: The
    Forging of a Nation
Germicide
Geronimo▶
Gertrud▶
Gervaise▶
Get Rita
The Getting of Wisdom
Getting Physical
Getting Up and Going Home
Ghetto Revenge
Ghostwriter
Giant▶
Giant Steps
Gideon's Trumpet
Gilda▶
The Gilded Cage
The Girl▶
The Girl
Girl from Hunan▶

The Girl from Tobacco Row
Girl in Gold Boots
A Girl of the Limberlost
Girl on a Chain Gang
The Girl on a Motorcycle
A Girl on Her Own
The Girl Said No
The Girl Who Spelled
    Freedom▶
Girls in Chains
Girls in Prison
The Girls of Huntington House
Girls of the White Orchid
Girls' Town
Git!
Give 'Em Hell, Harry!
Gladiator
The Glass House▶
The Glass Menagerie▶
Gleaming the Cube
Glen or Glenda
Glengarry Glen Ross▶
The Glitter Dome
Glitz
Glory
Glory Enough for All: The
    Discovery of Insulin
Go Down Death
Go for Broke!
Go for the Gold
The Go-Masters▶
The Goalie's Anxiety at the
    Penalty Kick▶
God Bless the Child▶
God, Man and Devil
Godard/Truffaut Shorts
The Goddess▶
The Godfather▶
The Godfather 1902-1959:
    The Complete Epic▶
The Godfather, Part 2▶
The Godfather, Part 3▶
God's Little Acre▶
Gods of the Plague▶
Godson▶
Going Back
Going for the Gold: The Bill
    Johnson Story
Going Home
The Gold & Glory
Golden Boy▶
The Golden Coach▶
The Golden Seal
Goldengirl
Goldenrod
Goldy: The Last of the Golden
    Bears
Goldy 2: The Saga of the
    Golden Bear
The Good Earth▶
Good Evening, Mr.
    Wallenberg
The Good Father▶
The Good Fight
Good Morning, Babylon▶
The Good Mother
The Good Son
The Good Wife
Goodbye Emmanuelle
Goodbye, Miss 4th of July
Goodbye, Norma Jean
Goodfellas▶
Goodnight, Sweet Marilyn
Gore Vidal's Lincoln
Gorilla
Gorillas in the Mist▶
The Gospel According to St.
    Matthew▶
Grain of Sand▶
Grambling's White Tiger
Grand Canyon▶
Grand Hotel▶
Grand Illusion▶
Grand Prix
The Grapes of Wrath▶
Grazuole
The Great Adventure▶
The Great Armored Car
    Swindle
Great Dan Patch
Great Expectations▶
Great Expectations

Great Expectations▶
Great Expectations: The
    Untold Story
Great Flamarion
The Great Gabbo
The Great Gatsby
Great Gold Swindle
Great Guy
Great Leaders of the Bibles
Great Love Experiment
The Great Mike
The Great Santini▶
The Great Wallendas
The Great White Hope
The Greatest
The Greatest Show on Earth▶
Greed▶
The Greek Tycoon
Green Eyes▶
Green Horizon
The Green Promise
The Green Room
The Green Wall▶
Greta▶
The Grey Fox▶
Greyfriars Bobby
The Grifters▶
The Grim Reaper▶
The Grissom Gang▶
Grit of the Girl Telegrapher/In
    the Switch Tower
Grizzly Adams: The Legend
    Continues
The Group
Grown Ups
The Guardian
Guilty of Innocence
Guilty of Treason
Gulag
Gun Girls
A Gun in the House
The Guns and the Fury
Guns at Batasi
Guns of War
The Guyana Tragedy: The
    Story of Jim Jones
Gypsy Blood
Gypsy Colt
The Gypsy Warriors
Hadley's Rebellion
Hail, Hero!
Hail Mary
The Hairy Ape
Half a Lifetime
Half Moon Street
Half of Heaven▶
Half Slave, Half Free
Hallelujah!▶
Hamburger Hill
Hamlet▶
Hamsin▶
A Handful of Dust▶
The Handmaid's Tale
Hands Up▶
Hanna's War
Hanoi Hilton
Hansel and Gretel
Hanussen▶
Happily Ever After
The Happy Ending
Hard Choices▶
Hard Country
Hard Frame
Hard Knox
Hard Part Begins
Hard Times▶
Hard Traveling
Hard Way
Hardcore
The Harder They Fall▶
Harmon of Michigan
Harrad Experiment
Harrad Summer
Harry & Son
Harry and Tonto▶
Harvest▶
The Hasty Heart
The Hatfields & the McCoys
Haunts of the Very Rich
Hawaii▶
Hazel's People
He is My Brother

He Who Gets Slapped▶
He Who Walks Alone
Head of the Family
Heading Home
Healer
Heart
Heart Beat
The Heart is a Lonely Hunter▶
Heart Like a Wheel
Heart of a Champion: The Ray Mancini Story
Heart of a Nation▶
Heart of Darkness
The Heart of Dixie
Heart of Glass▶
Heart of Midnight
Heart of the Stag
Heartbreak House
Heartland
Hearts of Fire
Hearts of the World▶
Heat▶
Heat and Sunlight
Heat of Desire
Heat Wave▶
Heaven & Earth▶
Heaven and Earth
Heaven is a Playground
Heaven on Earth
Heaven Tonight
Heavenly Bodies
Heaven's Heroes
Hedda
Heidi
Heidi▶
Heidi
Heidi▶
Held for Murder
Held Hostage
Hell on Frisco Bay
Hell's Angels on Wheels
Hell's House
Helltrain
Helter Skelter
The Henderson Monster
Hennessy
Henry IV
Henry & June▶
Henry: Portrait of a Serial Killer▶
Here Comes Kelly
The Hero
A Hero Ain't Nothin' But a Sandwich
Herod the Great
Heroes Die Young
Heroes for Sale▶
Heroes in Blue
Hester Street▶
Hidden Enemy
The Hiding Place
High Command
High Country
High School Caesar
High School Confidential
High Tide▶
The Highest Honor
Hill 24 Doesn't Answer▶
The Hills of Home▶
Hiroshima Maiden
Hiroshima, Mon Amour▶
His Kind of Woman▶
The Hit
Hit & Run
The Hit Man
Hit the Dutchman
Hitchhikers
Hitler: The Last Ten Days
Hitler's Children▶
Hitler's Daughter
Hobo's Christmas
Hockey Night
Hoffa▶
Hollywood After Dark
Hollywood Confidential
Hollywood Man
Hollywood Mystery
Holocaust▶
The Holy Innocents▶
Holy Terror
Home Feeling
Home from the Hill▶

A Home of Our Own
Home of the Brave▶
Home to Stay
Home Town Story
Homeboy
Homeboys
Homecoming▶
Homecoming: A Christmas Story
Homeward Bound
Homework
Homicidal Impulse
Honey
Honeyboy
Honeymoon Killers▶
Honkytonk Man
Honor Thy Father and Mother: The True Story of the Menendez Brothers
The Hoodlum Priest▶
Hoosiers▶
Hope and Glory▶
The Horse▶
The Horse of Pride
The Horse Soldiers
The Horse Thief▶
The Hostage
Hostages▶
Hot Money
Hot Spot
Hot Target
Hotel
Hotel du Lac
Hotel Imperial
Houdini
The Hour of the Star▶
Hour of the Wolf▶
House Across the Bay
House of Cards
The House of Dies Drear
The House of Eliott
The House of 1000 Dolls
House of Strangers▶
The House of the Spirits
The House on Chelouche Street
The House on Garibaldi Street
A House Without a Christmas Tree
Housewife
How Green was My Valley▶
How Many Miles to Babylon?
Howard's End▶
The Hucksters▶
Hud▶
Hue and Cry▶
The Human Comedy▶
The Human Condition: A Soldier's Prayer▶
The Human Condition: No Greater Love▶
The Human Condition: Road to Eternity▶
The Human Factor
The Hunchback of Notre Dame▶
Hunger
The Hunt▶
The Hunt for the Night Stalker
Hunted!
The Hunters
Husband Hunting
Husbands and Lovers
Hush Little Baby, Don't You Cry
The Hustler▶
Hustling▶
The Hypothesis of the Stolen Painting
I Accuse My Parents
I Am a Camera▶
I Am a Fugitive from a Chain Gang▶
I Am Curious (Yellow)
I Am the Law▶
I, Claudius, Vol. 1: A Touch of Murder/Family Affairs
I, Claudius, Vol. 2: Waiting in the Wings/What Shall We Do With Claudius?
I, Claudius, Vol. 3: Poison is Queen/Some Justice

I, Claudius, Vol. 4: Queen of Heaven/Reign of Terror
I, Claudius, Vol. 5: Zeus, By Jove!/Hail Who?
I, Claudius, Vol. 6: Fool's Luck/A God in Colchester
I, Claudius, Vol. 7: Old King Log
I Cover the Waterfront
I Died a Thousand Times
I Don't Give a Damn
I Heard the Owl Call My Name
I Killed Rasputin
I Know Why the Caged Bird Sings▶
I Live in Fear▶
I Love You...Goodbye
I Met a Murderer
I Posed for Playboy
I Remember Mama▶
I Take This Oath
I Want to Live!▶
I Want What I Want
Ice House
Ice Palace
Ice Pawn
Icy Breasts▶
Identity Unknown
The Idiot▶
If...▶
If Things Were Different
Ike
Ikiru▶
Il Grido
Illicit
The Illusion Travels by Streetcar▶
Ilsa, She-Wolf of the SS
Ilsa, the Tigress of Siberia
Ilsa, the Wicked Warden
I'm Dancing as Fast as I Can
The Image
Imagemaker
Imitation of Life▶
Immortal Battalion▶
The Imperial Japanese Empire
The Impossible Spy▶
The Imposter
Impulse
In Between
In Celebration▶
In Cold Blood▶
In Country
In Desert and Wilderness
In for Treatment▶
In Memoriam
In Name Only
In the Custody of Strangers▶
In the King of Prussia
In the Line of Duty: Ambush in Waco
In the Name of the Pope-King▶
In the Realm of the Senses▶
In the Region of Ice▶
In the White City▶
In This House of Brede▶
In Trouble
The Incident▶
Incident at Map-Grid 36-80
An Inconvenient Woman
The Incredible Journey of Dr. Meg Laurel
The Incredible Sarah
The Indian Runner
The Indiscreet Mrs. Jarvis
The Informer▶
Inga
Inherit the Wind▶
The Inheritance
The Inheritors
The Inkwell
The Inn of the Sixth Happiness▶
The Inner Circle▶
Innocence Unprotected
The Innocent▶
An Innocent Man
The Insect Woman▶
Inserts
Inside Moves
Inside Out

Inside the Lines
Interiors▶
International Velvet
The Interns
The Interrogation▶
Interrupted Melody▶
Intersection
Intimate Contact▶
Intimate Power
Intimate Story
Intimate Strangers
Into the Homeland
Into the West▶
Into Thin Air▶
Intolerance▶
Intruder in the Dust▶
Invincible Mr. Disraeli
Invitation au Voyage
Iphigenia▶
Iran: Days of Crisis
Irezumi▶
Iris
The Irishman
Iron & Silk
The Iron Major
Iron Maze
The Iron Triangle
Ironweed▶
Is Paris Burning?▶
Isadora▶
The Island▶
Island in the Sun
Island of Lost Girls
The Islander
Islands in the Stream
Isn't Life Wonderful▶
It Came Upon a Midnight Clear
It Could Happen to You
It Happened in New Orleans
Italian
The Italian Stallion
It's a Dog's Life
It's Called Murder, Baby
It's Good to Be Alive
Ivory Hunters
J. Edgar Hoover
J'Accuse▶
Jack Frost
The Jack Knife Man▶
Jack London
Jack the Ripper
Jack the Ripper▶
The Jackie Robinson Story▶
Jackknife▶
Jackson County Jail
The Jacksons: An American Dream
Jacob Have I Loved
Jacqueline Bouvier Kennedy
Jacquot
Jailbait: Betrayed By Innocence
James Dean
James Joyce: A Portrait of the Artist as a Young Man
James Joyce's Women▶
Jane Austen in Manhattan
Java Head▶
The Jayne Mansfield Story
Je Tu Il Elle
Jealousy
Jean de Florette▶
The Jericho Mile
Jesse
The Jesse Owens Story
Jesus
Jesus of Montreal▶
Jesus of Nazareth
Jet Over the Atlantic
The Jeweller's Shop
Jezebel▶
Jigsaw▶
Jigsaw
Jim Thorpe: All American
Joan of Paris▶
The Joe Louis Story
Joe Panther▶
Joey
John and the Missus
John Paul Jones
Johnny Apollo

Johnny Barrows, El Malo
Johnny Come Lately
Johnny Firecloud
Johnny Got His Gun
Johnny Tiger
Johnny We Hardly Knew Ye
Joni
Joseph & His Brethren
Joseph Andrews
Journey of Hope▶
Journey to Spirit Island
Journeys from Berlin/1971
The Joy Luck Club▶
Joyful Laughter
Joyride
Ju Dou▶
Juarez
Jud
Jud Suess▶
Judex
The Judge
The Judge and the Assassin▶
Judgment▶
Judgment at Nuremberg▶
Judgment in Berlin
The Juggler of Notre Dame
Juice▶
Julia▶
July Group
Jumpin' at the Boneyard
June Night
The Jungle Trap
Juno and the Paycock
Just a Gigolo
Just Another Girl on the I.R.T.
Just for the Hell of It
Just Like Weather▶
Justice
Justine
Kalifornia
Kameradschaft▶
Kamikaze Hearts
Kandyland
Kangaroo▶
Kansas
Kansas City Confidential▶
Kansas City Massacre
Kaos▶
Kapo▶
Katherine
Keeping On
Keetje Tippei
Kennedy
Kent State
Kerouac
The Key Man
The Keys of the Kingdom▶
A Kid for Two Farthings
Kid from Not-So-Big
The Kid Who Loved Christmas
Kidnapping of Baby John Doe
Kill Castro
Kill Me Again
The Kill Reflex
Killer
Killer on Board
Killer's Kiss
The Killing▶
The Killing Beach
Killing 'em Softly
The Killing Fields▶
Killing Floor
The Killing of a Chinese Bookie
Killing of Angel Street
Killing of Randy Webster
A Kind of Loving▶
Kindergarten▶
King▶
King of America
King of Kings
The King of Kings▶
The King of Marvin Gardens
King of the Gypsies
King of the Hill▶
The King of the Roaring '20s: The Story of Arnold Rothstein
King of the Wind
King Rat▶
Kings and Desperate Men

Drama

Kings of the Road—In the Course of Time▶
Kings Row▶
Kipps▶
Kismet▶
The Kiss
Kiss of Death▶
Kiss of the Spider Woman▶
Kiss the Night
Kiss Tomorrow Goodbye
The Kissing Place
The Kitchen Toto▶
The Klansman
Knife in the Head
Knock on Any Door
Knute Rockne: All American▶
Kojak: The Belarus File
Korczak▶
Kramer vs. Kramer▶
The Krays▶
Kung Fu
Kurt Vonnegut's Monkey House
L.A. Bad
La Balance▶
La Belle Noiseuse▶
La Boca del Lobo
La Cicada
L.A. Crackdown
L.A. Crackdown 2
La Diosa Arrodillada
La Femme Nikita▶
La Generala
La Hifa Sin Padre
La Hija del General
La Hora 24
La Justicia Tiene Doce Anos
L.A. Law▶
La Merveilleuse Visite
La Notte Brava
La Puritaine
La Signora di Tutti▶
La Symphonie Pastorale▶
La Terra Trema▶
La Trinchera
La Truite▶
La Venganza del Rojo
La Vie Continue
La Virgen de Guadalupe
The Lacemaker▶
L'Addition
The Ladies Club
Ladies of the Lotus
Ladies on the Rocks
Ladies They Talk About
Lady Chatterley's Lover
Lady for a Night
Lady from Nowhere
Lady from Yesterday
Lady Grey
Lady Ice
Lady in Distress
Lady in Red
Lady in the Lake
Lady Mobster
Lady of the House
Lady on the Bus
Lady Windermere's Fan
Lai Shi: China's Last Eunuch
Lake Consequence
Lamp at Midnight
Land of Fury
Land of Promise
Landscape in the Mist▶
Lantern Hill
L'Argent
Larry
Las Vegas Lady
The Las Vegas Story
Lassie
Lassie's Great Adventure
The Last Angry Man▶
The Last Bastion
Last Call
The Last Chance▶
Last Command▶
Last Cry for Help
Last Day of the War
The Last Days of Dolwyn
The Last Days of Patton
Last Exit to Brooklyn▶
The Last Fight

The Last Five Days
Last Flight Out: A True Story
Last Game
Last Hurrah
Last Innocent Man
The Last Laugh▶
Last Light
The Last Metro▶
The Last Mile
The Last Movie
The Last of England▶
The Last of His Tribe
The Last of Mrs. Lincoln
The Last Picture Show▶
The Last Safari
Last Summer
The Last Supper▶
Last Tango in Paris▶
The Last Temptation of Christ▶
The Last Tycoon▶
The Last Wave▶
The Last Winter
The Last Word
Last Year at Marienbad▶
L'Atalante▶
Late Chrysanthemums
Late Extra
Late Spring▶
Late Summer Blues
Latino
Laughing at Life
Laughing Sinners
Laurel Avenue
L'Avventura▶
Law of the Underworld
Lawrence of Arabia▶
The Lawrenceville Stories
Laws of Gravity▶
The Lazarus Syndrome
LBJ: The Early Years▶
Le Bal▶
Le Cas du Dr. Laurent▶
Le Chat▶
Le Crabe Tambour▶
Le Dernier Combat▶
Le Doulos▶
Le Grand Chemin▶
Le Plaisir
Lean on Me▶
The Learning Tree
Leather Boys
Leather Jackets
Leaves from Satan's Book
Leaving Normal
L'Ecole Buisoniere
Legal Tender
The Legend of Sleepy Hollow
Legend of Valentino
Legend of Walks Far Woman
Legs
Lenny▶
Leonor
The Leopard Woman
Lepke
Les Assassins de L'Ordre
Les Biches▶
Les Bons Debarras
Les Carabiniers▶
Les Enfants Terribles▶
Les Miserables▶
Les Miserables
Les Miserables▶
Les Mistons▶
Les Nuits Fauves▶
Les Rendez-vous D'Anna
Les Violons du Bal
Less Than Zero
Let 'er Go Gallegher
Let Him Have It▶
Let It Rock
L'Etat Sauvage▶
Lethal Charm
Lethal Obsession
Let's Get Married
The Letter▶
Letter of Introduction
A Letter to Three Wives▶
Letters to an Unknown Lover
Letting the Birds Go Free
L'Homme Blesse▶
Liar's Moon

Liberation of L.B. Jones
Liberators
License to Kill
Lies My Father Told Me▶
The Life and Assassination of the Kingfish
The Life and Death of Colonel Blimp▶
A Life in the Theater
Life is Beautiful
The Life of Emile Zola▶
Life of Oharu▶
A Life of Sin
Life on a String
Lifeboat▶
The Light Ahead
The Light in the Jungle
The Light of Faith
Light Sleeper
Lightning: The White Stallion
The Lightship
Lilies of the Field▶
Liliom▶
Lillie▶
Limelight▶
The Line
A Lion is in the Streets▶
Lipstick
Lisztomania
Little Ballerina
Little Boy Lost
Little Buddha
Little Church Around the Corner
Little Dorrit, Film 1: Nobody's Fault▶
The Little Foxes▶
Little Girl...Big Tease
Little Gloria...Happy at Last
Little Heroes
Little House on the Prairie
Little Ladies of the Night
Little Lord Fauntleroy▶
Little Lord Fauntleroy
Little Man Tate▶
Little Men
Little Miss Innocence
Little Orphan Annie
The Little Princess
Little Sweetheart
Little Tough Guy
The Little Valentino
Little Vera▶
Little Women▶
Little Women
The Littlest Outlaw
Live! From Death Row
The Living End
Loan Shark
Lock Up
L'Odeur des Fauves
Lois Gibbs and the Love Canal
Lola Montes▶
Lolita▶
London Kills Me
Lone Star Kid
The Loneliest Runner
The Loneliness of the Long Distance Runner▶
The Lonely Lady
The Lonely Passion of Judith Hearne▶
Lonelyhearts
Loners
The Long Dark Hall
The Long Day Closes▶
Long Day's Journey into Night▶
Long Day's Journey into Night
The Long Days of Summer
Long Gone
The Long Good Friday▶
The Long Gray Line▶
The Long Haul
The Long Island Four
Long Journey Back
The Long Voyage Home▶
The Long Walk Home▶
A Long Way Home
The Long Weekend
The Longest Day▶
Longtime Companion▶

Look Back in Anger▶
Look Back in Anger
Look Back in Anger▶
The Lookalike
Looking for Miracles
Looking for Mr. Goodbar
The Looking Glass War
Lord Jim▶
Lord of the Flies▶
Lord of the Flies
The Lords of Discipline
The Lords of Flatbush
Lorenzo's Oil▶
Lorna Doone
Los Dos Hermanos
Los Olvidados▶
The Losers
Lost Angels
The Lost Honor of Katharina Blum▶
Lost Horizon▶
Lost in the Barrens
The Lost Language of Cranes▶
Lost Legacy: A Girl Called Hatter Fox
Lost Moment
The Lost One
The Lost Weekend▶
The Lost World
Love▶
Love Child
Love Field
Love Film
Love for Lydia▶
Love Leads the Way
The Love Machine
Love Matters
Love on the Dole▶
Love Strange Love
Love Under Pressure
Love Your Mama
Loveless
Lovely...But Deadly
The Loves of Edgar Allen Poe
Lovey: A Circle of Children 2
The Lower Depths▶
Loyalties
Loyola, the Soldier Saint
Lucky Luciano
Lucy and Desi: Before the Laughter
Lumiere
Lust for Freedom
Lust for Life▶
Luzia
M. Butterfly
Ma Barker's Killer Brood
Mac▶
Macario
MacArthur
MacArthur's Children▶
Machine Gun Kelly
Mack
Macon County Line
Macumba Love
Mad Death
Mad Dog Morgan
The Mad Whirl
Mad Youth
Madame Bovary▶
Madame Curie▶
Madame Rosa▶
Madame X
M.A.D.D.: Mothers Against Drunk Driving
Made in Argentina
Mademoiselle
Mademoiselle Fifi
The Madwoman of Chaillot
Mae West
Maedchen in Uniform▶
Mafia Princess
Magdalene
Magee and the Lady
The Magic Bubble
The Magic Flute▶
Magic of Lassie
The Magician▶
The Magnificent Ambersons▶
The Magnificent Yankee▶
Mahogany

Maids of Wilko
Maitresse
Major Barbara▶
Make Me an Offer
Make-Up
Making Love
The Makioka Sisters▶
Malarek
Malcolm X▶
Malibu High
Malibu Hot Summer
Malicious
Malou
Malta Story
The Maltese Falcon▶
A Man Called Adam
A Man Called Peter▶
A Man Escaped▶
Man Facing Southeast▶
Man Friday
The Man in the Gray Flannel Suit
Man in the Wilderness
The Man Inside
A Man Like Eva▶
Man of a Thousand Faces▶
Man of Flowers
Man of Iron▶
Man of Marble▶
A Man of Passion
Man of Violence
Man on the Run
The Man Outside
The Man Who Broke 1,000 Chains
The Man Who Laughs▶
The Man Who Never Was▶
Man with a Cross
The Man with the Golden Arm▶
The Man Without a Face
Man, Woman & Child
Mandinga
Mandingo
Mandy▶
The Mango Tree
Manhattan Melodrama▶
Manhunter
Maniac
The Manions of America
Manipulator
Manon of the Spring▶
Mansfield Park
Marat/Sade▶
Marbella
Marcados por el Destino
Marciano
Maria's Day▶
Maria's Lovers
Maricela
Marie▶
Marilyn: The Untold Story▶
Marine Raiders
The Mark of the Hawk▶
Mark Twain and Me
Marked Woman▶
A Married Man
Married People, Single Sex
Married Too Young
A Married Woman▶
Martin's Day
Marvin & Tige
Mary and Joseph: A Story of Faith
Mary White
Masculine Feminine▶
Mask▶
The Mask of Dijon
Mass Appeal
Massacre at Central High
Massacre in Rome
Master Harold and the Boys▶
Master of the House▶
Master Race
Mata Hari▶
The Match Factory Girl▶
Matewan▶
A Matter of Dignity
A Matter of Life and Death
A Matter of Principle
Maurice▶
Max

Max and Helen
Maximum Security
Maybe I'll Be Home in the Spring
Mayflower Madam
Mayhem
McKenzie Break▶
McVicar
Me & Veronica
Mean Dog Blues
Mean Streets▶
Medea
The Mediterranean in Flames
Medium Cool▶
Meet Dr. Christian
Meet John Doe▶
Meet Sexton Blake
Meetings with Remarkable Men
Melanie
Melody for Three
The Member of the Wedding▶
The Member of the Wedding
Memorial Day
Memories of a Marriage▶
Memories of Underdevelopment
Memory of Us
Memphis
The Men▶
Men are not Gods
Men in Love
Men of Boys Town
Men of Ireland
Men of Respect
Men of Two Worlds
The Men Who Tread on the Tiger's Tail
Menace II Society▶
The Men's Club
Mephisto▶
The Merchant of Four Seasons▶
The Merchant of Venice▶
Mere Jeevan Saathi
The Mermaids of Tiburon
Merry Christmas, Mr. Lawrence▶
Mesmerized
The Messiah▶
Mickey
Mid-Channel
Mid Knight Rider
The Midas Touch
A Midnight Clear▶
Midnight Cop
Midnight Cowboy▶
Midnight Dancer
Midnight Express▶
The Mighty Pawns
Mikey & Nicky
Miles from Home
Miles to Go Before I Sleep
Miller's Crossing▶
Millions
Mindwalk: A Film for Passionate Thinkers▶
Mine Own Executioner▶
The Miniver Story
A Minor Miracle
The Miracle▶
The Miracle
Miracle at Moreaux
Miracle Down Under
Miracle in Harlem
Miracle in Rome
Miracle Kid
Miracle of Our Lady of Fatima
The Miracle of the Bells
Miracle of the Heart: A Boys Town Story
The Miracle of the White Stallions
Miracle on Ice
Miracle on 34th Street▶
The Miracle Worker▶
Mirele Efros
The Mirror▶
The Misfits▶
Mishima: A Life in Four Chapters▶
Miss A & Miss M

Miss All-American Beauty
Miss Mary
Miss Melody Jones
Miss Rose White▶
Missing▶
The Mission▶
Mission of the Shark▶
Mission to Glory
Mississippi Burning▶
Missouri Traveler▶
Mrs. Miniver▶
Mrs. Parkington
Mrs. R's Daughter
Mr. Ace
Mr. & Mrs. Bridge▶
Mr. Arkadin▶
Mr. Corbett's Ghost
Mr. Emmanuel
Mister Halpren & Mister Johnson
Mr. Inside, Mr. Outside
Mister Johnson▶
Mr. Klein▶
Mr. Smith Goes to Washington▶
Mistral's Daughter
Mistress▶
Mistress Pamela
Misunderstood
Mo' Better Blues
The Moderns▶
Modigliani
Mohammed: Messenger of God
Molly Maguires
Mommie Dearest
Mon Oncle Antoine▶
Money to Burn
Monika
Monkey Grip▶
Monsieur Beaucaire
Monsieur Vincent▶
Monsignor
Monsignor Quixote
Monte Carlo
Monte Carlo Nights
A Month in the Country▶
The Moon and Sixpence▶
Moon in the Gutter
Moonlighting▶
Moonrise
Moonshine Mountain
Morals for Women
More
Morituri▶
Morning Glory
The Mortal Storm▶
Mortal Thoughts
Moscow Does Not Believe in Tears▶
Moses
The Mosquito Coast
Most Wanted
Mother▶
Mother & Daughter: A Loving War
Mother and Son
Mother Doesn't Always Know Best
Mother Kusters Goes to Heaven▶
Mother of Kings
Motorcycle Gang
Mouchette▶
Moulin Rouge▶
The Mountain
The Mountain Road
A Movie Star's Daughter
Movie Stuntmen
Moving Out
Moving Violation
Mozart: A Childhood Chronicle▶
The Mozart Story
Murder Elite
Murder for Sale
Murder in Coweta County
Murder in New Hampshire: The Pamela Smart Story
Murder in the Old Red Barn
The Murder of Mary Phagan▶
Murder on Lenox Avenue

Murder on the Bayou▶
Murder Ordained
Murderer's Wife
Muriel▶
Murph the Surf
Murphy's War
Murrow
Music Box
The Music of Chance
The Music Teacher
Mussolini & I
The Muthers
Mutiny in the Big House
Mutual Respect
My Apprenticeship▶
My Boy
My Boys are Good Boys
My Brilliant Career▶
My Childhood▶
My Father, My Rival
My Father's Glory▶
My Father's House
My First Wife
My Girl Tisa
My Left Foot▶
My Life
My Life to Live▶
My Little Girl
My Michael▶
My Mother's Castle▶
My Mother's Secret Life
My Name is Ivan▶
My Old Man
My Old Man's Place
My Own Private Idaho▶
My Side of the Mountain
My Sweet Charlie
My Universities▶
My Wicked, Wicked Ways
Mysterious Jane
The Mystery of Alexina
Nadia
Naked Cage
The Naked City▶
The Naked Civil Servant▶
The Naked Country
The Naked Flame
Naked Kiss
Naked Lie
Naked Lunch▶
The Naked Maja
Naked Paradise
Naked Venus
Naked Youth
Nana▶
Nana
Napoleon
The Narcotics Story
Nashville▶
Nashville Beat
Nashville Girl
A Nation Aflame
National Velvet▶
Native Son
The Natural▶
Natural Born Killers
Natural Enemies
Navy Blue and Gold
Navy Way
Nazarin▶
Necessary Parties
Negatives
The Neon Empire
Network▶
Neurotic Cabaret
Never Cry Wolf▶
Never Forget
Never Love a Stranger
Never Too Late to Mend
The New Centurions▶
New Jack City
The New Land▶
New Mafia Boss
New Orleans After Dark
News at Eleven
News from Home
Newsfront▶
The Next Karate Kid
Next of Kin
The Next Voice You Hear
Nice Neighbor▶
Nicholas Nickleby▶

Nickel Mountain
Night and the City▶
Night Beat
Night Call Nurses
Night Friend
Night Gallery▶
Night Game
'night, Mother
Night Nurse▶
Night of Evil
Night of the Generals▶
The Night of the Iguana▶
The Night of the Shooting Stars▶
Night of the Wilding
The Night Porter▶
The Night the City Screamed
The Night the Lights Went Out in Georgia
Night Wars
Night Zoo
Nightbreaker▶
Nightfall▶
Nightmare at 43 Hillcrest
The Nightmare Years
Nights and Days
Nijinsky
9 1/2 Weeks
1900▶
1918
1931: Once Upon a Time in New York
92 in the Shade▶
99 Women
Nitti: The Enforcer
No Big Deal
No Drums, No Bugles
No End
No Fear, No Die
No Love for Johnnie▶
No One Cries Forever
No Place to Run
No Prince for My Cinderella
No Regrets for Our Youth▶
No Room to Run
No Trace
Noa at Seventeen▶
Nobody's Daughter
Nomugi Pass
None But the Brave
None But the Lonely Heart▶
Noon Wine▶
Norma Rae▶
North and South Book 1▶
North and South Book 2▶
Northern Lights▶
Northwest Trail
A Nos Amours▶
Not as a Stranger
Not My Kid
Not Quite Love
Not Tonight Darling
Not Without My Daughter
Notes for an African Orestes
Nothing But a Man
Nous N'Irons Plus au Bois
Novel Desires
Nowhere to Run
Numero Deux
The Nun
The Nun's Story▶
Nurse
Nurse Edith Cavell▶
Nutcracker Sweet
Nuts▶
O Youth and Beauty
An Occurrence at Owl Creek Bridge/Coup de Grace
The Odd Angry Shot
Odd Birds
Odd Man Out▶
Odd Obsession
Ode to Billy Joe
Oedipus Rex▶
Of Human Bondage
Of Human Hearts
Of Mice and Men▶
The Official Story▶
Oh, Bloody Life!
O'Hara's Wife
Oil
Oklahoma Crude

Old Boyfriends
The Old Curiosity Shop
Old Explorers
Old Gun▶
The Old Maid▶
Old Swimmin' Hole
Oldest Living Graduate▶
Oliver Twist▶
Oliver Twist
Oliver Twist▶
Oliver Twist
Olivia
Olivier, Olivier▶
Olongape: The American Dream
On Borrowed Time▶
On Golden Pond▶
On the Beach▶
On the Edge
On the Edge: The Survival of Dana
On the Line
On the Nickel
On the Third Day
On the Waterfront▶
On the Yard
On Valentine's Day
Onassis
Once Before I Die
Once is Not Enough
Once Upon a Time in America▶
Once Upon a Time in Vietnam
One Against the Wind▶
One Away
One Day in the Life of Ivan Denisovich▶
One Deadly Summer▶
One False Move▶
One Good Cop
One in a Million: The Ron LaFlore Story
One Last Run
One Man Jury
One Man's War
One Man's Way
One More Chance
One Night Stand▶
One on One
One Plus One
One Russian Summer
One Sings, the Other Doesn't
One Third of a Nation
Onibaba▶
The Onion Field▶
Only Way
The Only Way Home
Open City▶
Open Doors▶
Opening Night
The Oppermann Family
The Opponent
Ordet▶
Ordinary Heroes
Ordinary Magic
Ordinary People▶
The Organization▶
Oriane
Original Intent
Orlando▶
Orphans▶
Orpheus Descending
Osaka Elegy
The Oscar
Ossessione▶
Othello▶
The Other Side of Midnight
Our Daily Bread▶
Our Family Business
Our Town▶
Our Vines Have Tender Grapes▶
Out of the Blue▶
Out of the Rain
Out on a Limb
The Outcasts▶
The Outlaw and His Wife
Outlaw Riders
Outrage!
Outside Chance
Outside the Law
The Outsiders

Drama

Over the Edge▶
Over the Top
The Overcoat▶
The Overlanders
Overnight Sensation
Overseas: Three Women with Man Trouble▶
Overture to Glory
The Ox
Pace That Kills
Padre Padrone▶
The Painted Hills
The Painted Veil
Paisan▶
Palm Beach
Panama Menace
Panama Patrol
Pancho Barnes
Panic in Echo Park
Panic in Needle Park▶
Panic in the Year Zero!
Paper Man
Paper Mask
Paperback Hero
Paradise▶
Paradise Alley
Parallel Corpse
Paris, Texas▶
Paris Trout
The Park is Mine
Parole, Inc.
Parting Glances▶
Partner▶
Party Girl▶
Party Girls
Pascali's Island▶
A Passage to India▶
Passage to Marseilles▶
The Passenger▶
The Passing of Evil
Passion
Passion Fish▶
Passion for Life
Passion for Power
Pastime▶
Pather Panchali▶
Paths of Glory▶
The Patriots▶
Patterns▶
Patton▶
Patty Hearst
Paul Robeson
Paul's Case
The Pawnbroker▶
Payday
Peacekillers
The Peacock Fan
The Pearl▶
Pearl of the South Pacific
Peck's Bad Boy
Peddlin' in Society
The Pedestrian▶
The Peking Blond
Pelle the Conqueror▶
Penalty Phase
The Penitent
The People Next Door
The People vs. Jean Harris▶
Pepi, Luci, Bom and Other Girls on the Heap
Perfect
Perfect Harmony
Perfect Killer
Perfect Witness
A Perfect World
Perfume
Permanent Record
Permanent Vacation
Permissive
Persona▶
Personal Best▶
Petrified Forest▶
Petulia▶
Peyton Place▶
Phaedra
The Phantom in the House
Phar Lap
Phedre
Philadelphia▶
Phone Call from a Stranger
A Piano for Mrs. Cimino▶
Pickpocket▶

Pickup on South Street▶
Piece of Cake
A Piece of Pleasure▶
Pierrot le Fou▶
Pigeon Feathers
Pilgrim, Farewell
Pilot
Pimpernel Smith
Pink Strings and Sealing Wax
Pinky▶
Pipe Dreams
Pistol: The Birth of a Legend
Pitfall▶
Pixote▶
A Place Called Today
Place of Weeping
Places in the Heart▶
The Plague
Platinum High School
Play Murder for Me
The Player▶
Players
Playing for Time▶
Playing with Fire
Pleasure Palace
Plenty
The Ploughman's Lunch▶
Plutonium Incident
Poco
Poil de Carotte
Point of No Return
Poison▶
Poldark▶
Police
Police Court
Policewoman Centerfold
A Poor Little Rich Girl▶
Poor Little Rich Girl: The Barbara Hutton Story
Poor Pretty Eddie
Poor White Trash 2
Pope John Paul II
The Pope of Greenwich Village
The Poppy is also a Flower
Porcile
Port Arthur
Port of New York
Portfolio
The Portrait▶
Portrait of a Lady
Portrait of a Showgirl
Portrait of a Stripper
Portrait of Grandpa Doc
Portrait of Teresa▶
The Possessed▶
Postal Inspector
The Postman Always Rings Twice▶
The Postman Always Rings Twice
Postmark for Danger
Pot, Parents, and Police
Power
Power, Passion & Murder
Pray TV
A Prayer for Katarina Horovitzova▶
Prayer for the Dying
Premonition
Pressure Point▶
Pretty Baby▶
Prick Up Your Ears▶
Pride and Prejudice
The Pride and the Passion
Pride of Jesse Hallum
Pride of St. Louis
The Pride of the Yankees▶
Priest of Love
Primary Motive
Prime Cut
Prime Suspect
The Prime Time
Primo Baby
Prince and the Great Race
The Prince and the Pauper▶
The Prince and the Pauper
Prince Jack
Prince of Bel Air
The Prince of Central Park▶
The Prince of Tides▶

Princes in Exile
Princess Daisy
The Principal
Prison Break
Prison Stories: Women on the Inside▶
Prison Train
The Prisoner▶
Prisoner Cell Block H
Prisoner of Honor▶
Prisoners of the Sun▶
The Private Affairs of Bel Ami▶
Private Contentment
Private Duty Nurses
The Private Files of J. Edgar Hoover
Private Hell 36
Private Life
A Private Matter▶
Prix de Beaute
The Prize Pulitzer
The Prodigal
The Prodigal Planet
Profile
The Program
Project: Kill!
Promised a Miracle
Promises in the Dark
Proof▶
Proof of the Man
Prospero's Books▶
Protect Your Daughters
Providence▶
Prudential Family Playhouse
Psych-Out
Puberty Blues
A Public Affair
Public Enemy▶
Pudd'nhead Wilson
Pueblo Affair▶
Pulsebeat
Pump Up the Volume
Puppet on a Chain
The Purchase Price
Purgatory
The Purple Heart
The Pursuit of D.B. Cooper
The Pursuit of Happiness
Q Ships
QB VII▶
Quartet▶
Que Viva Mexico▶
Queen Kelly▶
Queen of Diamonds
The Queen of Mean
The Queen of Spades▶
Queenie
Querelle
A Question of Attribution
Question of Faith
Question of Honor
A Question of Love▶
Question of Silence▶
Qui Etes Vous, Mr. Sorge?
Quicksilver
Quiet Day In Belfast▶
Quilombo
Race for Glory
Race for Life
Rachel River
Racing Luck
The Racketeer
Rad
Radio Flyer
Rage▶
A Rage in Harlem▶
Raggedy Man▶
The Raggedy Rawney
Raging Bull▶
Ragtime▶
Railway Children▶
Rain
Rain Man▶
The Rain People▶
The Rainbow▶
Rainbow Bridge
Rainy Day
Raise the Red Lantern▶
A Raisin in the Sun▶
Rambling Rose▶
Ramparts of Clay▶

Rape and Marriage: The Rideout Case
Rape of Love
Rappaccini's Daughter
The Rapture
A Rare Breed
Rashomon▶
The Raven
The Razor's Edge▶
The Razor's Edge
Reach for the Sky
A Real American Hero
Rebel
Rebel Rousers
The Rebel Set
Rebel Vixens
Rebel Without a Cause▶
Reborn
Reckless Disregard
The Reckless Way
The Red and the White▶
The Red Badge of Courage▶
Red Beard▶
The Red Desert▶
The Red Half-Breed
Red Line 7000
The Red Menace
Red Nightmare
Red Nights
The Red Pony▶
Red Shoe Diaries
Red Shoe Diaries 2: Double Dare
Red Shoe Diaries 3: Another Woman's Lipstick
Red Shoe Diaries 4: Auto Erotica
The Red Stallion
Red Surf
Red, White & Busted
Reds▶
Reefer Madness
The Reflecting Skin
Reflections in a Golden Eye
Reform School Girl
Reform School Girls
Regarding Henry▶
The Reincarnation of Golden Lotus▶
The Remains of the Day▶
Rembrandt▶
Rembrandt—1669
Rendez-vous▶
Requiem for Dominic▶
Reservoir Dogs▶
The Respectful Prostitute
Resurrection▶
Return to Earth
Return to Peyton Place
Reunion▶
Revenge of a Kabuki Actor
Reversal of Fortune▶
The Revolt of Job▶
The Revolt of Mother▶
Rhapsody in August
Rhodes
Rich Kids
Rich Man, Poor Man▶
Richard Petty Story
Richard's Things
Riddance▶
Ride a Wild Pony▶
Ride in a Pink Car
Riel
Riff Raff
The Right Hand Man
Right of Way
The Ring
Ring of Bright Water▶
Ringside
Riot
Riot Squad
Riptide▶
Rising Son▶
Risky Business
Rita Hayworth: The Love Goddess
Rivals
The River▶
The River
River Beat
The River Niger

River of Unrest
The River Rat
A River Runs Through It▶
Riverbend
River's Edge▶
Road House
Road Racers
Road to 1984
Roadhouse Girl
Roadhouse 66
Roadside Prophets
Roaring Roads
Roaring Speedboats
Robert Kennedy and His Times
Robot Pilot
Rocco and His Brothers▶
Rock All Night
Rock, Pretty Baby
Rocket to the Moon
The Rocking Horse Winner
Rocky▶
Rocky 2
Rocky 3
Rocky 4
Rocky 5
Rodrigo D.: No Future
Roe vs. Wade▶
Roll of Thunder, Hear My Cry
Rolling Home
Rolling Thunder
Rollover
Rome '78
Romero
The Roof
The Room
Rooster: Spurs of Death!
Rosa Luxemburg
The Rose and the Jackal
The Rose Garden
Roseland▶
Rosie: The Rosemary Clooney Story
Round Midnight▶
The Round Up
R.P.M.* (*Revolutions Per Minute)
Ruby
Ruby Gentry
Ruby in Paradise▶
Ruby's Dream
Rudy
Rumble Fish▶
The Rumor Mill
A Rumor of War▶
Rumpole of the Bailey: Rumpole's Return▶
Run for the Roses
Run Silent, Run Deep▶
Runaway
Runaway Father
The Runaways
The Runner Stumbles
Running Brave
Running Mates▶
Running on Empty▶
Rush▶
The Russia House
The Rutherford County Line
Sabre Jet
The Sacrifice▶
Sacrilege
Sadat
Saigon: Year of the Cat
St. Elmo's Fire
St. Ives
Saint Jack▶
The Saint of Fort Washington
Sakharov▶
Salaam Bombay!▶
Salammbo
Salmonberries
Salo, or the 120 Days of Sodom
Salome
Salome/Queen Elizabeth
Salome, Where She Danced
Salt of the Earth▶
Salute John Citizen▶
Samaritan: The Mitch Snyder Story▶
Sam's Son

Samson and Delilah▶
Samson and Delilah
Sand and Blood
Sandakan No. 8▶
Sanshiro Sugata▶
Sansho the Bailiff▶
Santa Sangre▶
Sara Dane
Satan Met a Lady
Satan's Harvest
Saturday Night Fever
Savage Attraction
Savage is Loose
Savage Run▶
The Savage Seven
The Savage Woman
Savages from Hell
Savannah Smiles
Save the Lady
Save the Tiger▶
Sawdust & Tinsel▶
Say Goodbye, Maggie Cole
Scandal▶
Scandal in a Small Town
The Scar
Scarecrow
Scarface Mob
The Scarlet Letter
The Scarlet Letter▶
The Scarlet Pimpernel▶
Scarred
Scenes from a Marriage▶
Scent of a Woman▶
The Scent of Green Papaya▶
Schindler's List▶
School Ties▶
The Scorpion Woman
Scout's Honor
Scrooge▶
Scrubbers
Scruples
Scum▶
Sea Lion
Sea Racketeers
The Seagull▶
The Search
The Search for Bridey Murphy
Searching for Bobby Fischer▶
Season for Assassins
Sebastian
Second Chance
Second Coming of Suzanne
Second Victory
The Secret
Secret File of Hollywood
The Secret Four
The Secret Garden▶
The Secret Garden
The Secret Garden
The Secret Garden
Secret Honor▶
The Secret of the Loch
Secret Places
A Secret Space
Secret Weapons
Secrets
Secrets of a Soul
The Seducers
The Seduction of Joe Tynan
Seduction: The Cruel Woman
See How She Runs▶
Seize the Day▶
Semaforo en Rojo
A Sense of Freedom▶
Sensual Partners
Sensuous Summer
The Sensuous Teenager
A Separate Peace
Separate Tables▶
Separate Tables
Separate Ways
September
September 30, 1955
Sergeant Matlovich vs. the
  U.S. Air Force
Sergeant Ryker
The Serpent's Egg▶
Serpico▶
The Servant▶
Sessions
The Set-Up▶
Seven Days in May▶

Seven Deadly Sins▶
Seven Miles from Alcatraz/
  Flight from Glory
The Seventeenth Bride
The 7th Commandment
The Seventh Cross▶
The Seventh Seal▶
The Seventh Veil▶
Severance
Sex and the College Girl
Sex, Drugs, and Rock-n-Roll
sex, lies and videotape▶
Sex Through a Window
S.F.W.
Shack Out on 101▶
The Shadow Box▶
Shadow Dancing▶
Shadow on the Sun
Shadowlands▶
Shadows
Shadows of the Orient
Shadows Over Shanghai
Shake Hands with the Devil▶
Shakespeare Wallah▶
Shaking the Tree
Shame▶
The Shame▶
The Shaming
Shanghai Express▶
The Shanghai Gesture
Shanty Tramp
Sharma & Beyond▶
Shattered
Shattered
Shattered Spirits
Shattered Vows
She and He
She-Devils on Wheels▶
Sheer Madness▶
She'll Be Wearing Pink
  Pajamas
The Shell Seekers
The Sheltering Sky▶
Shifting Sands
Shiokari Pass
Ship of Fools▶
Shock Corridor▶
The Shoes of the Fisherman
Shoeshine▶
Shogun▶
Shoot It Black, Shoot It Blue
Shoot the Moon
Shooting
The Shooting Party
The Shooting Party▶
The Shop on Main Street▶
Short Eyes▶
Short Fuse
The Shrieking
Shy People▶
Sicilian Connection
The Sicilian Connection
Sid & Nancy▶
Sidewalks of London▶
Signal 7
Silas Marner▶
The Silence▶
Silence
Silence Like Glass
Silence of the Heart▶
Silence of the North
The Silent One
Silent Rebellion
Silent Victim
Silent Victory: The Kitty O'Neil
  Story▶
Silent Witness
Silkwood▶
The Silver Chalice
Silver Dream Racer
The Silver Streak
Simba▶
Simon Bolivar
Simple Justice
A Simple Story▶
Sin of Adam & Eve
Sin You Sinners
Sinatra
Sinbad
Sing Sing Nights
The Singing Blacksmith
The Singing Nun

Singing the Blues in Red▶
Single Room Furnished
The Single Standard
Sinners in Paradise
Sins
Sins of Jezebel
Sirocco
Sister Kenny▶
The Sisters▶
Sisters of Gion▶
Six Degrees of Separation
Sixteen
'68
Sizzle
Skag▶
Skateboard
Skeezer
Skier's Dream
Skin Art
Skin Game
Skinheads: The Second
  Coming of Hate
Skullduggery
The Sky is Gray▶
The Sky Pilot
Skylark
Skyscraper Souls▶
Slacker▶
Slash
Slashed Dreams
Slaughterday
Slavers
Sleeping Dogs
The Sleeping Tiger
The Slender Thread▶
The Small Back Room▶
A Small Circle of Friends
Small Sacrifices
Small Time
Small Town Boy
A Small Town in Texas
Smash Palace
Smash-Up: The Story of a
  Woman▶
Smith!
Smithereens
Smoke
A Smoky Mountain Christmas
Smooth Talk▶
Smouldering Fires
Snake Dancer
The Snake Pit▶
Sniper▶
Snow Treasure
The Snows of Kilimanjaro▶
So Dear to My Heart▶
So Ends Our Night▶
Sofie
Soldier's Revenge
A Soldier's Story▶
The Solitary Man
Solo
Solomon and Sheba
Some Came Running▶
Somebody Up There Likes
  Me▶
Someone I Touched
Someone to Love
Something of Value▶
Sometimes a Great Notion▶
Son of Lassie
The Song of Bernadette▶
Song of the Exile
Sonny and Jed
Sons
Sons of Steel
Sophia Loren: Her Own Story
Sophie's Choice▶
Sophisticated Gents▶
Sorceress▶
Sorority Girl
Sorrows of Gin
S.O.S. Pacific
Soul Hustler
Soul of the Beast
Soul Patrol
Soultaker
The Sound and the Silence
Sounder▶
South Bronx Heroes
South Central
South of Reno

The Southerner▶
Soviet Spy
Spangles
The Spanish Gardener▶
Speaking Parts▶
Special Bulletin▶
Special Effects
Special Olympics
Speed Reporter
Spellbound▶
Spetters
Spices▶
Spirit of St. Louis▶
Spirit of the Beehive▶
The Spirit of West Point
Spirit Rider▶
Spitfire▶
Spittin' Image
Splendor in the Grass▶
Split Decisions
Split Image▶
Split Second
The Spoilers▶
The Spook Who Sat By the
  Door
The Sporting Club
Spring Symphony
Springhill
Spymaker: The Secret Life of
  Ian Fleming
Square Dance
Square Shoulders
Squizzy Taylor
S.S. Experiment Camp 2
SS Girls
S.S. Love Camp No. 27
Stacking
Stacy's Knights
Stage Struck
Stakeout
Stalag 17▶
Stalin
Stalk the Wild Child
Stand Alone
Stand and Deliver▶
Stand By Me▶
Stand Off
The Star Chamber
Star 80▶
A Star is Born▶
A Star is Born
Star Reporter
Stark
Stars in My Crown▶
The Stars Look Down▶
State of Emergency
State of Siege▶
Stateline Motel
State's Attorney
Static
The Stationmaster's Wife
Stavisky▶
Stay As You Are
Stay Hungry▶
Staying Alive
Staying On
Steal the Sky
Stealing Home
Steaming
Steel
Steel Cowboy
Steppenwolf
Stevie
Stigma
Stiletto
Stolen Identity
A Stolen Life
The Stone Boy▶
Stone Fox
Storm Over Asia▶
The Story Lady
The Story of a Love Story
Story of Adele H.▶
The Story of David▶
The Story of Jacob &
  Joseph▶
The Story of Louis Pasteur▶
The Story of O
The Story of O, Part 2
The Story of Qui Ju▶
The Story of Ruth
The Story of Women▶

Storyville
Straight for the Heart
Straight Out of Brooklyn
Straight Time▶
Straight Up
A Strange and Deadly
  Occurence
Strange Awakening
Strange Cargo
Strange Fruit
Strange Interlude▶
Strange Interlude
The Strange Love of Martha
  Ivers▶
The Strange Woman
The Stranger Who Looks Like
  Me
Strangers in Good Company▶
Strangers in the City
Strategic Air Command
The Stratton Story▶
Straw Dogs▶
The Strawberry Statement
Streamers
The Street
Street Girls
Street Hero
Street Hitz
Street Justice
Street of Shame▶
Street People
Street Smart
Street Warriors
Street Warriors, Part 2
A Streetcar Named Desire▶
Streets
Streets of Gold
The Streets of L.A.
The Streets of San
  Francisco▶
Streets of Sin
Streetwalkin'
Strike▶
Strikeback
The Stripper
Strong Medicine
The Structure of Crystals
The Stud
The Student Nurses
Studs Lonigan
The Stunt Man▶
Submission
Suburban Roulette
Suburbia
Subway to the Stars
Success is the Best Revenge
Sudden Death
Suddenly, Last Summer▶
Sudie & Simpson▶
Sugar Cane Alley▶
Sugar Hill▶
The Suicide Club
Summer City
Summer Interlude▶
Summer Magic
Summer of '42▶
The Summer of Miss Forbes
The Summer of My German
  Soldier▶
Summer Solstice
A Summer to Remember▶
A Summer to Remember
Summer Vacation: 1999
Summer Wishes, Winter
  Dreams
Summertree
The Sun Comes Up
The Sun Shines Bright
Sunday, Bloody Sunday▶
Sunday Daughters▶
A Sunday in the Country▶
Sunday Too Far Away▶
Sundays & Cybele▶
The Sundowners▶
Sunny Side Up
Sunnyside
Sunrise▶
The Sun's Burial▶
Sunset Boulevard▶
Sunset Strip
Super Bitch
Super Brother

Drama

Superfly
Sure Fire
Susan and God▶
Susana▶
Susannah of the Mounties
Suspended Alibi
Suzanne
Swann in Love
The Swap
Sweet Beat
Sweet Bird of Youth▶
Sweet Country
Sweet Country Road
Sweet Creek County War
Sweet 15
Sweet Hostage
Sweet Love, Bitter
Sweet Perfection
Sweet Poison
Sweet Smell of Success▶
Sweet Sweetback's
    Baadasssss Song▶
Sweetheart!
Sweetwater
Swimmer▶
The Swindle
Swing High, Swing Low
Swing Kids
Switched at Birth
The Sword and the Cross
Sybil▶
Sylvester
Sylvia
Symphony of Living
T-Bird Gang
T-Men▶
Table for Five
Tabu: A Story of the South
    Seas▶
Tainted
Taken Away
The Taking of Flight 847: The
    Uli Derickson Story▶
The Tale of Ruby Rose▶
A Tale of Two Cities▶
Tale of Two Sisters
Talent for the Game
Tales from Avonlea, Vol. 1:
    The Journey Begins▶
Tales of Ordinary Madness
Tales of the Klondike: The
    Scorn of Women
Talk Radio▶
Tall Lie
The Tamarind Seed
Taras Bulba
Targets▶
Task Force
A Taste of Honey▶
Taxi Driver▶
Tchaikovsky
Tchao Pantin▶
Tea and Sympathy▶
Tea For Three
Teamster Boss: The Jackie
    Presser Story▶
Tearaway
Teen Mothers
Teenage
Teenage Bad Girl
Teenage Crime Wave
Teenage Mother
Teenage Wolfpack
Teenager
Tell Me a Riddle
Tell Me Where It Hurts
The Tempest▶
The Tempest/The Eagle▶
The Temptress
Ten Nights in a Bar Room
Ten Nights in a Bar-Room
Ten North Frederick
Ten Speed
The Tender Age
Tender Is the Night
Tender Loving Care
The Tender Years
Tennessee Stallion
Tentacles of the North
The Tenth Man
Tenth Month
Teorema

Terminal Bliss
Terminal Force
Termini Station
Terraces
The Terry Fox Story▶
Tess▶
A Test of Love
Testament▶
Tevye
Tex
Texas Lightning
Thanksgiving Story
That Brennan Girl
That Certain Woman
That Championship Season
That Cold Day in the Park
That Forsyte Woman
That Long Night in '43
That Was Then...This Is Now
That'll Be the Day
The Theme▶
Therese & Isabelle
These Three▶
They Came to Cordura
They Knew What They
    Wanted▶
They Live by Night▶
They Made Me a Criminal
They Never Come Back
They Paid with Bullets:
    Chicago 1929
They Shoot Horses, Don't
    They?▶
They Were So Young
They Were Ten
They Won't Forget▶
The Thief
Third Walker▶
Thirteenth Day of Christmas
Thirty Seconds Over Tokyo▶
32 Short Films About Glenn
    Gould▶
This Boy's Life▶
This Happy Breed▶
This Land is Mine▶
This Property is Condemned
This Special Friendship
This Sporting Life▶
Thompson's Last Run
Thoroughbreds Don't Cry
Those Glory, Glory Days
Thou Shalt Not Kill...Except
A Thousand Heroes
Three Brothers▶
Three Came Home▶
The Three Faces of Eve▶
3:15—The Moment of Truth
The Three Lives of
    Thomasina▶
Three on a Match▶
Three Stops to Murder
Three Strange Loves▶
Three Violent People
Three Warriors
The Three Weird Sisters
Threshold
Throne of Blood▶
Through the Breakers
Thunder Warrior 3
Thunderheart▶
Ticket to Heaven▶
Tidy Endings
Tiger Town
Tiger Warsaw
The Tigress
Till the End of Time
Timber Queen
Time Flies When You're Alive
A Time for Miracles
Time Lock
A Time of Destiny
Time of Indifference
Time of Tears
Time Stands Still▶
Time to Kill
A Time to Remember
Times Square
Timothy and the Angel
The Tin Drum▶
Tin Man
'Tis a Pity She's a Whore
To All My Friends on Shore▶

To Catch a Killer▶
To Dance with the White
    Dog▶
To Forget Venice
To Heal a Nation
To Hell and Back
To Joy▶
To Kill a Mockingbird▶
To Kill a Priest▶
To Race the Wind
To Sir, with Love
To the Lighthouse
To the Shores of Tripoli
Toast of New York▶
Today ! Hang
Tokyo Decadence
Tokyo Story▶
Tol'able David
The Tomboy
Tomboy & the Champ
Tomorrow's Child
The Tongfather
Toni▶
Tonio Kroger
Too Hot to Handle
Too Late for Tears▶
Too Late the Hero▶
Too Wise Wives
Torchlight
Torment▶
Torn Allegiance
Tornado
Torpedo Alley
Torpedo Attack
Torpedo Run
Torrents of Spring
Tortilla Flat▶
Torture Ship
Touch and Go
Touched
Touched by Love
Tough Enough
Tough Kid
Tough to Handle
Toughlove
Tournament
Tous les Matins du Monde▶
A Town Like Alice
Toys in the Attic
Tracks
Traenen in Florenz
Traffik▶
The Train▶
Train of Events
Train Station Pickups
Trained to Kill, U.S.A.
Tramp at the Door
Transport from Paradise
Trapped
Trapped in Silence
Traveling Man
Travelling North
Treasure of Arne
Treasure of the Lost Desert
A Tree Grows in Brooklyn▶
The Tree of Wooden Clogs▶
Trespasser
The Trial▶
The Trial
Trial of Bernhard Goetz
The Trial of Billy Jack
The Trial of Lee Harvey
    Oswald
Trial of the Catonsville Nine
Tribes
Tribute
Tricheurs
Trilby▶
Trio▶
The Trip
The Trip to Bountiful▶
Triple Echo
Triumph of the Spirit▶
Trois Couleurs: Bleu▶
Trois Couleurs: Rouge▶
Tromba, the Tiger Man
Tropic of Cancer▶
Trucker's Woman
True Colors
True Confessions▶
True West▶
Trumps

Tucker: The Man and His
    Dream▶
Tuff Turf
Tunes of Glory▶
Turf Boy
The Turning Point
Turtle Diary▶
Tuxedo Warrior
Twelve Angry Men▶
Twelve O'Clock High▶
21 Hours at Munich▶
Twenty-Four Eyes▶
25 Fireman's Street▶
Twice a Woman
Twice in a Lifetime▶
Twigs
Twin Peaks
Twin Peaks: Fire Walk with
    Me
Twirl
Two Can Play
Two Kinds of Love
Two Men & a Wardrobe
Two of a Kind
Two of Us▶
The Two Sisters
Two Weeks in Another Town
Two Women▶
Tycoon
The Ugly American
Ulysses
Umberto D▶
Un Singe en Hiver
The Unapproachable
Uncaged
The Unchastened Woman
Uncle Moses
Uncle Tom's Cabin
Uncommon Valor
Under Fire▶
Under Milk Wood
Under Satan's Sun▶
Under the Earth▶
Under the Volcano▶
Undercover Cop
Underground U.S.A.
Une Jeunesse▶
Unfinished Business
Unicorn
The Unknown▶
Unknown Powers
An Unmarried Woman▶
Unnatural Causes▶
Unsettled Land
The Unstoppable Man
The Untamable
Until They Sail
Up Against the Wall
Upper Crust
The Uprising▶
Uptown Angel
Urban Cowboy
Users
Utamaro and His Five Women
Vagabond▶
Valentino
Valentino Returns
The Valley Obscured by the
    Clouds
Valley of the Dolls
Valmont▶
Van Gogh▶
Vanishing Point
Variety
Variety Lights▶
The Vegas Strip Wars
Velvet Smooth
Vendetta
Vendetta for the Saint
Vengeance
Verdi
Verne Miller
Veronico Cruz
Veronika Voss▶
A Very Old Man with
    Enormous Wings
Via Appia
Vice Squad
Victim▶
Victimless Crimes
Victory
Video Wars

Vietnam War Story 1
Vietnam War Story 2
Vietnam War Story 3
Vigil▶
Vigilante
Vincent & Theo▶
Vincent, Francois, Paul and
    the Others▶
Vincent: The Life and Death of
    Vincent van Gogh▶
Violated
Violence at Noon▶
Violent Ones
Violent Women
The Violent Years
The V.I.P.'s▶
The Virginia Hill Story
Viridiana▶
Virtue's Revolt
Vision Quest
Vital Signs
Volver, Volver, Volver!
Vortex
Voyage of Terror: The Achille
    Lauro Affair
Voyage of the Damned▶
A Voyage' Round My Father▶
Voyage to Italy
W Hour
Wager of Love
Wages of Fear▶
Wagner: The Complete Epic
Wagner: The Movie
Waiting for the Moon
Walking on Air
Walking Tall
Walking Tall: Part 2
Walking Tall: The Final
    Chapter
Walking the Edge
Walking Through the Fire
The Wall▶
Wall Street▶
Wanda, The Sadistic
    Hypnotist
Wanderers▶
Wandering Jew
Wanted: The Perfect Guy
War & Remembrance, Part 1
War & Remembrance, Part 2
War & Remembrance: The
    Final Chapter, Part 8
War & Remembrance: The
    Final Chapter, Part 9
War Between the Tates
War Brides
War Victims
Ward Six
WarGames
The Warning
Warning Shadows▶
The Wash▶
Washington Affair
Watch on the Rhine▶
The Waterdance▶
Waterfront
Waterland
Way Back Home
We are the Children
We of the Never Never▶
We Will Not Enter the Forest▶
A Wedding in Galilee▶
Wedding in White
Wee Willie Winkie▶
Weeds▶
Weekend▶
Weekend of Shadows▶
Welcome to L.A.▶
The Well▶
Well-Digger's Daughter▶
Wellington: The Duel Scandal
Westfront 1918▶
Wetherby▶
Whale for the Killing
Whale of a Tale
The Whales of August▶
What Comes Around
What Price Glory?▶
What Price Hollywood?▶
What the Moon Saw
What's Eating Gilbert Grape▶
When a Man Loves a Woman

When a Woman Ascends the Stairs
When Every Day was the Fourth of July
When Father was Away on Business▶
When Gangland Strikes
When Hell Was in Session▶
When He's Not a Stranger▶
When the Line Goes Through
When the Whales Came
When Wolves Cry
Where Angels Fear to Tread▶
Where Have All the People Gone?
Where is My Child?
Where Love Has Gone
Where the Day Takes You
Where the Eagle Flies
Where the Green Ants Dream
Where the Hot Wind Blows
Where the Lilies Bloom▶
Where the Red Fern Grows: Part 2
While the City Sleeps▶
Whistle Down the Wind▶
White Heat▶
White Hunter, Black Heart▶
The White Legion
White Lie
White Mama▶
White Mane▶
White Nights
White Shadows in the South Seas
The White Sin
White Tiger
Who Shot Pat?
Who'll Save Our Children?▶
Who'll Stop the Rain?▶
Whore
Who's Afraid of Virginia Woolf?▶
Who's That Knocking at My Door?▶
Whose Child Am I?
Why Shoot the Teacher?▶
The Wicked Lady
The Widow
Wifemistress
The Wilby Conspiracy▶
The Wild Child▶
The Wild Duck
Wild Engine/Mistaken Orders
Wild Guitar
Wild Horse Hank
Wild in the Country
The Wild One▶
Wild Ones on Wheels
Wild Orchid
Wild Orchid 2: Two Shades of Blue
Wild Orchids
Wild Party
Wild Pony
The Wild Ride
Wild Strawberries▶
Wild Style
Wild Wheels
Wildcat
Wildflower▶
Wildrose▶
Will: G. Gordon Liddy
Willa
Wilma
Wilson▶
Windom's Way▶
Windows
The Winds of War
Windwalker▶
Windy City
A Winner Never Quits
Winner Takes All
The Winning Team
The Winslow Boy▶
The Winter Light▶
The Winter of Our Dreams
Winterset
Without Love
Without Warning: The James Brady Story▶
Witness▶

Wives Under Suspicion
The Wizard of Loneliness
Wolf Lake
The Wolves▶
A Woman and a Woman
A Woman, Her Men and Her Futon
Woman in Brown
A Woman in Flames▶
Woman in the Dunes▶
Woman in the Shadows
The Woman Inside
A Woman Named Jackie
A Woman Obsessed
A Woman of Rome
A Woman Rebels
A Woman Under the Influence▶
The Woman Who Willed a Miracle
A Woman's Secret
A Woman's Tale▶
Women & Men: In Love There Are No Rules
Women & Men: Stories of Seduction
Women in Cell Block 7
Women in Love▶
The Women of Brewster Place▶
Women of Valor
Women Unchained
Wonsan Operation
The Wooden Gun
Words by Heart
Workin' for Peanuts
Working Girls
A World Apart▶
The World Gone Mad
The World of Apu▶
A World of Strangers▶
World War II: When Lions Roared
The Worldly Madonna
Woyzeck▶
The Wrestler
Wrestling Ernest Hemingway
Wrestling Racket Girls
The Wrong Move
The Wrong Road
X Marks the Spot
Xica▶
Yanco
A Yank in the R.A.F.
Year of the Dragon
Year of the Gun
Yellow Cargo
Yellow Earth
Yol▶
You Must Remember This
You Only Live Once
Young Aphrodites
Young Charlie Chaplin
The Young Graduates
The Young in Heart▶
The Young Lions▶
Young Love, First Love
The Young Nurses
The Young One
The Young Philadelphians▶
The Young Teacher
Young Tom Edison
Young Winston▶
Youngblood
Your Ticket Is No Longer Valid
Youth Aflame
You've Ruined Me, Eddie
Yuri Nosenko, KGB
Zabriskie Point▶
Zalmen or the Madness of God
Zandalee
Zelly & Me▶
The Zoo Gang
Zora Is My Name!
Zorba the Greek▶
Zvenigora▶

Dream Girls

Alien Women
The Barbarians
Beverly Hills Knockouts
The Bikini Car Wash Company
The Bikini Car Wash Company 2
Bikini Island
Bikini Summer
Bluebeard
Bolero
Calendar Girl Murders
California Girls
Cannonball Run
Cannonball Run 2
Cheerleader Camp
City of Women
Cover Girl Models
Creatures the World Forgot
Cycle Vixens
Daddy-O
Deadly Weapons
Desperate Cargo
Desperate Moves
Devil Girl from Mars
The Devil's Hand
Diamonds are Forever▶
Divine Nymph
Do or Die
Dr. Alien
Dr. Goldfoot and the Bikini Machine
Dr. No▶
The Doll
The Doll Squad
The Dolls
Domino
Dream Trap
Easyriders Video Magazine
Emmanuelle
Emmanuelle 4
Emmanuelle & Joanna
Emmanuelle in Bangkok
Emmanuelle in Soho
Emmanuelle in the Country
Emmanuelle on Taboo Island
Emmanuelle, the Joys of a Woman
Emmanuelle, the Queen
Emmanuelle's Daughter
Evil Toons
Fate
Fire Maidens from Outer Space
Fireballs
Forbidden Planet▶
Gamera vs. Guiron
Gator Bait
Ghosts Can't Do It
Girl Shy▶
Gold of the Amazon Women
Great Bikini Off-Road Adventure
Guns
Hard Hunted
Hercules and the Princess of Troy
Hired to Kill
Hollywood Boulevard 2
Hollywood or Bust
How I Learned to Love Women
How to Succeed with Girls
I Married a Centerfold
I Posed for Playboy
It Takes a Thief
Jokes My Folks Never Told Me
Kiss and Kill
Last Dance
Les Girls
Les Mistons▶
The Lion of Thebes▶
The Loves of Hercules
A Man with a Maid
The Mermaids of Tiburon
Mirror Images
Mirror Images 2
Missile to the Moon
Mysterious Island of Beautiful Women
Mystery Date
Naked Warriors
Never Say Never Again
Nine Ages of Nakedness

Obsession: A Taste for Fear
Oxford Blues
Panther Squad
Party Incorporated
Pin-Up Girl
Posed For Murder
Priceless Beauty
Princess Daisy
Private Affairs
Queen of Outer Space
The Reckless Way
Revenge of the Cheerleaders
Round Trip to Heaven
Savage Beach
The Seven Year Itch▶
She Gods of Shark Reef
She's Dressed to Kill
Sidekicks
Sizzle Beach U.S.A.
The Slumber Party Massacre
Some Like It Hot▶
Sorceress
Soup for One
Spinout
The Spring
Star Crash
The Story of a Love Story
Strawberry Blonde▶
The Sure Thing▶
Swimsuit: The Movie
The Swinging Cheerleaders
Tammy and the Doctor
Tanya's Island
Tarzan, the Ape Man
10
Thieves of Fortune
Thunder & Mud
Too Shy to Try
Total Exposure
Underground Aces
Vampire's Kiss▶
Vice Academy 3
Voyage to the Planet of Prehistoric Women
Wayne's World▶
Wayne's World 2
When Dinosaurs Ruled the Earth
Wishful Thinking
The Woman in Red
You Only Live Twice
Young Nurses in Love

Drugs

see Pill Poppin'

Earthquakes

see also Disaster Flicks
After the Shock
Earthquake
The Great Los Angeles Earthquake
Quake
The Rains Came

Eating

see Cannibalism; Edibles

Eco-Vengeance!

Alligator▶
Ants
The Applegates
Arachnophobia
Ben
Body Snatchers
The Crawlers
Day of the Animals
Deadly Harvest
Fangs
The Fire Next Time
Food of the Gods
Frogs
Grizzly
Idaho Transfer
Jaws▶
Jaws 2
Jaws 3
Jaws: The Revenge
Jurassic Park▶
Kingdom of the Spiders

On Deadly Ground
Piranha
Piranha 2: The Spawning
Prophecy
Squirm
The Swarm
Thunder Bay▶
Ticks
The Toxic Avenger
Willard

Edibles

see also Cannibalism
Babette's Feast▶
Blood Diner
Combination Platter
Consuming Passions
The Cook, the Thief, His Wife & Her Lover▶
Eat the Rich
Gabriela
Hamburger...The Motion Picture
Hot Chocolate
Life is Sweet▶
Like Water for Chocolate▶
Of Cooks and Kung-Fu
Tampopo▶
Who is Killing the Great Chefs of Europe?▶

Erotic Thrillers

see also Sex & Sexuality
Basic Instinct
Bitter Harvest
Blindfold: Acts of Obsession
Blown Away
Body Chemistry 3: Point of Seduction
Body of Evidence
Body of Influence
Body Shot
Broken Trust
Caroline at Midnight
Chain of Desire
Cold Sweat
Color of Night
The Crush
Damage▶
Dark Tide
Dead On
Die Watching
Discretion Assured
Double Threat
Entangled
Every Breath
Fatal Bond
Fatal Instinct
Final Judgement
Illicit Behavior
In a Moment of Passion
Indecent Behavior
Invasion of Privacy
Lipstick Camera
Lonely Hearts
Mind Twister
Mirror Images
Mirror Images 2
Night Eyes
Night Eyes 2
Night Eyes 3
The Nightman
Rubdown
Save Me
Scorned
Secret Games
Secret Games 2: The Escort
Sexual Malice
Sins of Desire
Sins of the Night
Sliver
Snapdragon
Strike a Pose
Sunset Grill
Sweet Killing
Under Investigation
Wild Cactus

Ethics & Morals

see also Big Ideas
All the King's Men▶

And Justice for All
Any Man's Death
The Assault▶
Barbarians at the Gate▶
The Best Man▶
Blame It on Rio
Blue Chips
The Border▶
The Boy with the Green Hair▶
Casualties of War▶
Chinese Roulette
Chloe in the Afternoon▶
Circle of Power
The Citadel▶
The Conversation▶
Crimes & Misdemeanors▶
Cutter's Way
A Dangerous Woman
Deep Six
The Defiant Ones▶
The Doctor
The Dog Soldier
Double Identity
El Profesor Hippie
El: This Strange Passion▶
The Elephant Man▶
Elmer Gantry▶
Fifth Day of Peace
The Fifth Seal
Force of Evil▶
The Funeral▶
Fury▶
The Image
It Could Happen to You
Jezebel▶
The Judge and the Assassin▶
Judgment at Nuremberg▶
The Juggler of Notre Dame
Kings Row▶
La Ronde▶
La Truite▶
The Last of England▶
L'Avventura▶
The Lazarus Syndrome
License to Kill
Love with the Proper
   Stranger▶
Malicious
The Man Inside
The Man Who Shot Liberty
   Valance▶
Manhattan Melodrama▶
Marihuana
A Matter of Dignity
Midnight
Mindwalk: A Film for
   Passionate Thinkers▶
Mr. Smith Goes to
   Washington▶
Mom & Dad
Muriel▶
Network▶
News at Eleven
The Next Voice You Hear
No Man's Land
Oedipus Rex
Oedipus Rex▶
One Flew Over the Cuckoo's
   Nest▶
Other People's Money
Overture to Glory
The Ox-Bow Incident▶
Paris Trout
Penalty Phase
A Place in the Sun▶
Platoon▶
The Ploughman's Lunch▶
Prime Suspect
Private Hell 36
Question 7
Ran▶
Reckless Disregard
Riel
The Sacrifice▶
Scandal Man
The Scarlet Letter
The Scarlet Letter▶
Shampoo
The Shootist▶
Silent Witness
Soul Man
S*P*Y*S

SS Girls
The Star Chamber
The Story of Women▶
Strangers When We Meet
Survival of Spaceship Earth
Sweet Smell of Success▶
Test Tube Babies
The Things of Life▶
To Live & Die in L.A.
A Touch of Class▶
The Toy
Tulsa▶
Twelve Angry Men▶
Twenty-One
Tycoon
Under Fire▶
Viridiana▶
Wall Street▶
The Wheeler Dealers▶
With Honors
Zabriskie Point▶

Etiquette

Born Yesterday▶
Educating Rita▶
My Fair Lady▶
Papa's Delicate Condition▶
Phantom of Liberty▶
Pleasure
Pygmalion▶
The Ruling Class▶
True Love▶

Evil Doctors

   see also Doctors &
   Nurses; Mad Scientists
The Abominable Dr. Phibes▶
The Awful Dr. Orlof
Body Melt
The Curious Dr. Humpp
Dead Ringers▶
Dr. Alien
The Doctor and the Devils
Dr. Black, Mr. Hyde
Doctor Blood's Coffin
Doctor Butcher M.D.
Dr. Caligari
Dr. Cyclops
Dr. Death, Seeker of Souls
Dr. Frankenstein's Castle of
   Freaks
Dr. Giggles
Dr. Goldfoot and the Bikini
   Machine
Dr. Hackenstein
Dr. Jekyll and Mr. Hyde▶
Dr. Jekyll and Mr. Hyde
Dr. Jekyll and Sister Hyde
Dr. Jekyll and the Wolfman
Dr. Jekyll's Dungeon of Death
Dr. Mabuse the Gambler▶
Dr. Mabuse vs. Scotland Yard
Dr. No▶
Dr. Otto & the Riddle of the
   Gloom Beam
Doctor Phibes Rises Again
Doctor Satan's Robot
Dr. Tarr's Torture Dungeon
Dr. Terror's House of Horrors
Doctor X
Mad Doctor of Blood Island
Malice
Night of the Bloody Apes
Night of the Bloody Transplant
Slaughter Hotel
Strange World of Coffin Joe

Existentialism

Badlands▶
The Blood of Others
The Castle▶
The Collector▶
End of the Road
The French Lieutenant's
   Woman▶
Funny Face▶
Love and Death▶
The Razor's Edge▶
The Razor's Edge
The Trial
Zabriskie Point▶

Experimental

   see Avant-Garde

Exploitation

   see also Sexploitation
Abduction
Agony of Love
American Nightmare
Angel of H.E.A.T.
Angels of the City
Armed Response
Artist's Studio Secrets
Assassin of Youth
Bachelor Party
Bad Girls from Mars
Barn of the Naked Dead
Basic Training
Beatrice▶
Betrayal
Beyond the Valley of the Dolls
The Black Maid
Black Shampoo
Blackenstein
Blood Games
The Bloody Brood
Blue Movies
Blue Ribbon Babes
Boss
The Cage
Caged Terror
Certain Sacrifice
Chained for Life
Come Back, Africa▶
Common Law Wife
Confessions of a Vice Baron
Cover Girl Models
The Cut Throats
Cycle Psycho
Cycle Vixens
Dance Hall Racket
Dangerous Obsession
The Dark Side of Love
Deadly Sanctuary
Death of a Centerfold
Devil's Wedding Night
Escape from Safehaven
Exterminator 2
Eyes of a Stranger
Faces of Death, Part 1
Faces of Death, Part 2
Film House Fever
Five Minutes to Love
The Flaming Teen-Age
For Ladies Only
Fox and His Friends▶
Foxy Brown
Ghoulies 3: Ghoulies Go to
   College
Girl on a Chain Gang
Gun Girls
Harlow
Heat of the Flame
High School Caesar
Hitler's Children▶
Hollywood After Dark
Hollywood Confidential
The Hollywood Strangler
   Meets the Skid Row
   Slasher
Honky Tonk Girl
House of Whipcord
I Accuse My Parents
In Trouble
Island of Lost Girls
Jock Petersen
Kidnapped
Kinjite: Forbidden Subjects
L.A. Heat
La Nueva Cigarra
L.A. Vice
The Lash of the Penitents
Last Call
Little Girl...Big Tease
Little Miss Innocence
The Lonely Sex
Love Camp
Mack
Malibu Express
Mandinga
M'Lady's Court
My Wonderful Life

The Naked Flame
Naked in the Night
Naked Vengeance
The Narcotics Story
Night Friend
Night of Evil
Nightmare in Red China
Nomugi Pass
One Down, Two to Go!
One Night Only
One Plus One
One Too Many
Overexposed
Paradise Motel
Party Incorporated
Pin Down Girls
Policewoman Centerfold
Poor Pretty Eddie
Protect Your Daughters
Rate It X
Reefer Madness
Revenge of the Zombies
The Road to Ruin
Samurai
Satan's Cheerleaders
Saturday Night Sleazies, Vol.
   1
Savages from Hell
Secrets of Sweet Sixteen
Sensual Partners
Sex Adventures of the Three
   Musketeers
Sin You Sinners
Single Room Furnished
Slaughter
Slaughter's Big Ripoff
Slaves in Bondage
Sleazemania
Sleazemania III: The Good,
   the Bad & the Sleazy
Smile▶
S.O.B.
Something Weird
SS Girls
Star 80
Street of Forgotten Women
Striptease
Student Confidential
Summer School Teachers
Sunset Strip
Swamp Women
Sweet Spirits
Taxi Dancers
The Teacher
Test Tube Babies
Therese & Isabelle
They're Playing with Fire
The Third Sex
This Nude World
Three in the Attic
Thunder & Mud
Tomorrow's Children
Unmarried Mothers
Victims
Violated
Warrior Queen
Weekend with the Babysitter
Weird World of LSD
Wild Rapture
Wild Weed
Wild, Wild World of Jayne
   Mansfield
Woman Hunt
Women's Club
The Worst of Faces of Death
Wrestling Racket Girls
Yesterday's Hero
Young Lady Chatterly 2
Youth Aflame

Explorers

The Adventures of Marco Polo
Cabeza de Vaca▶
Call Me Bwana
Christopher Columbus
Christopher Columbus: The
   Discovery
Conqueror & the Empress
1492: Conquest of Paradise
King Solomon's Mines▶
King Solomon's Mines
The Live Wire

The Lost World
The Magic Voyage
Mountains of the Moon▶
The Sky Above, the Mud
   Below
The Valley Obscured by the
   Clouds
The Wacky World of Wills &
   Burke
Wagon Wheels
Wake of the Red Witch

**Extraordinary
Pairings**

Bela Lugosi Meets a Brooklyn
   Gorilla
Billy the Kid Versus Dracula
Dracula vs. Frankenstein
Frankenstein Meets the Space
   Monster
Frankenstein Meets the
   Wolfman▶
The Hollywood Strangler
   Meets the Skid Row
   Slasher
Jesse James Meets
   Frankenstein's Daughter
King Kong Versus Godzilla
Santa Claus Conquers the
   Martians
Wrestling Women vs. the
   Aztec Ape
Wrestling Women vs. the
   Aztec Mummy

Eyeballs!

Anguish
The Birds▶
A Clockwork Orange▶
The Crawling Eye
Damien: Omen 2
Die Hard 2: Die Harder▶
Evil Dead 2: Dead by Dawn
The Eye Creatures
Eyeball
Eyes of Laura Mars
Friday the 13th, Part 3
The Fury
The Godfather▶
Headless Eyes
Peeping Tom▶
Rocky▶
Scanners
Strange Behavior
X: The Man with X-Ray Eyes▶
Zombie

Fairs & Expositions

   see also Amusement
   Parks; Carnivals &
   Circuses
Howling 6: The Freaks
Ma and Pa Kettle at the Fair
My Girl
State Fair▶
Swap Meet

Family Ties

   see also Parenthood
ABC Stage 67: Truman
   Capote's A Christmas
   Memory
Above the Rim
The Accidental Tourist▶
Adam Had Four Sons
The Addams Family
Addams Family Values
The Adventures of the
   Wilderness Family
An Affair in Mind
Affair in Trinidad
Afraid of the Dark
After Julius
Alberto Express
Alice▶
Alice Doesn't Live Here
   Anymore
All Fall Down
All I Want for Christmas
All Mine to Give

All My Sons▶
All the Brothers Were Valiant
All the Kind Strangers
Alpha Beta
Alpine Fire
An American Christmas Carol
American Dream▶
American Flyers
American Gothic
American Heart▶
American Samurai
And Baby Makes Six
And You Thought Your
    Parents Were Weird!
Andy Hardy Gets Spring Fever
Andy Hardy Meets Debutante
Andy Hardy's Double Life
Andy Hardy's Private
    Secretary
Angel of Destruction
Angela
Angie
Anna Christie▶
Anne of Green Gables▶
Any Number Can Play
Applause▶
The Apprenticeship of Duddy
    Kravitz▶
April Fool
Arabian Nights
Army Brats
The Arrangement
Arsenic and Old Lace▶
Ashanti, Land of No Mercy
Ask Any Girl
At Close Range▶
Atomic Attack
The Attic
Auntie Mame▶
Author! Author!
Autumn Marathon
Autumn Sonata▶
Avalon▶
Avanti!
Baba▶
The Baby
Baby Love
Baby of the Bride
Baby, the Rain Must Fall
Back Home
Back to the Beach
Back to the Future▶
Backdraft
Bad Boy
The Bad Seed
Bandits
Barcelona▶
Bare Knees
Barjo
The Baron and the Kid
Based on an Untrue Story
Basket Case▶
Basket Case 2
Basket Case 3: The Progeny
Battling for Baby
Beast in the Cellar
The Beast Within
Beat Girl
Beau Geste▶
Beau Pere▶
Bed & Breakfast
Beethoven
Beethoven's 2nd
Behind Prison Walls
Being Human
Being Two Isn't Easy
Belle Epoque▶
Bellissima▶
Benefit of the Doubt
Benny & Joon
The Best Christmas Pageant
    Ever
Best Enemies
The Betsy
Betsy's Wedding
Between Men
Between Two Women
Beulah Land
The Beverly Hillbillies
Beverly Hills Brats
Beyond Darkness
Beyond Obsession

Beyond the Door 2
Big Business
Big Country
Big Girls Don't Cry...They Get
    Even
A Bill of Divorcement
Billy Galvin
Billy Liar▶
The Birch Interval
Bittersweet Love
Black Eyes
Black Orchid
The Black Room▶
The Black Windmill
Blind Spot
Blinded by the Light
Blondie Has Trouble
Blondie Takes a Vacation
Blondie's Blessed Event
Blood In...Blood Out: Bound
    by Honor
Blood Mania
Blood Money: The Story of
    Clinton and Nadine
Blood Rage
Blood Red
Blood Relations
Blood Ties
Bloodbrothers
Bloodfist 4: Die Trying
Bloodlink
Bloody Mama
The Blot
Blue City
Blue Fin
The Blue Yonder
Body Count
The Bodyguard
Bolero
Bon Voyage!
Bonanza: The Return
Bonjour Tristesse▶
Bonnie's Kids
Boomerang
Bopha!▶
Border Vengeance
Born to Run
The Borrowers▶
Boss' Son▶
Boulevard of Broken Dreams
Bouquet of Barbed Wire
Branded a Coward
Breaking Home Ties
Breathing Fire
The Bretts▶
Bridge to Silence
Bright Angel
A Brivele der Mamen▶
Broadway Bound
Broadway Melody
Broken Angel
Broken Trust
A Bronx Tale▶
The Brothers Karamazov▶
Brother's Keeper▶
Brussels Transit▶
The Buddy System
Buddy's Song
Butterfly
By the Light of the Silvery
    Moon
Cadillac Girls
Cafe Romeo
Cahill: United States Marshal
Call of the Forest
Call to Glory
Candles at Nine
Candleshoe
The Cantor's Son
Captain Ron
The Captive: The Longest
    Drive 2
The Capture of Grizzly Adams
Carbon Copy
Careful, He Might Hear You▶
Carolina Skeletons
Caroline?▶
Carousel▶
Carry Me Back
Casanova Brown
The Case of the Frightened
    Lady

Casey's Shadow
Cat Girl
Cat on a Hot Tin Roof▶
Cat on a Hot Tin Roof
Cat People▶
Cat People
Cathy's Curse
Cavalcade▶
Cavalcade of the West
Cavalry
Cavalry Charge
The Champ▶
The Champ
Chances Are▶
Charley and the Angel
Cheatin' Hearts
Cheetah
The Children Are Watching
    Us▶
Children of Sanchez
Children's Carol
The Chisholms
Choices
The Christmas Coal Mine
    Miracle
Christmas Comes to Willow
    Creek
A Christmas Story▶
A Christmas to Remember
Cimarron
Cinderella Liberty▶
Circus World
Class Action▶
Clifford
Close to Eden
Close to Home
The Closer
Clown
Cody
Cold Comfort
Cold Heat
Come and Get It▶
Comin' Round the Mountain
Coming Out Alive
Communion
Como Dos Gotas de Agua
Complex World
The Confession
Confessions of a Hit Man
Conflict of Interest
Consenting Adult
A Conspiracy of Love
Cookie
Coquette
The Corsican Brothers
Countdown
Country▶
Country Girl▶
Country Girl
Coupe de Ville
The Courtship of Eddie's
    Father▶
Cousin, Cousine▶
Cousins▶
Crazy in Love
Cries and Whispers▶
Crimes of the Heart
Crooked Hearts
Crooklyn▶
Crossing Delancey▶
Crush
Cry from the Mountain
Cry, the Beloved Country▶
Curly Top
Da
Dad
Daddy Nostalgia▶
Daddy's Boys
Daddy's Dyin'...Who's Got the
    Will?
Damage▶
The Dance Goes On
Dangerous Relations
Daniel
Danielle Steel's "Daddy"
Danielle Steel's Kaleidoscope
The Dark Angel▶
Dark Horse
Dark Mirror▶
D.A.R.Y.L.
Daughter of Don Q
Daughters of the Dust▶

A Day for Thanks on Walton's
    Mountain
Dead Alive
Dead Men Walk
Dead Ringers▶
Deadfall
Deadly Blessing
Deadly Sunday
Dear Dead Delilah
Dear Wife
Death Be Not Proud▶
Death Dreams
Death in the Shadows
Death of a Salesman▶
The Death of Richie
Deathfight
December Flower
Delightfully Dangerous
Demons in the Garden▶
Demons of the Mind
Demonstone
Demonstrator
Demonwarp
Desert Bloom▶
Desire Under the Elms
Desperate Living
Desperate Motives
Detective Sadie & Son
Devi▶
Devil Dog: The Hound of Hell
Devil Woman
The Devil's Daughter
The Devil's Sleep
The Devil's Web
Diamond Head
Diamonds
Diary of a Mad Old Man
Diary of the Dead
Dias de Ilusion
Dick Tracy
Die! Die! My Darling!
Die Screaming, Marianne
Die Sister, Die!
Dim Sum: A Little Bit of
    Heart▶
Dimples
Dirty Hands
Disappearance
Disciple
Discontent
Distant Thunder
Distant Voices, Still Lives▶
Distortions
Divine Nymph
Dixie Dynamite
Dixie Lanes
Dr. Hackenstein
Doctor Phibes Rises Again
Doctor Who and the Daleks
Doin' Time on Planet Earth
The Dollmaker
Dominick & Eugene▶
Dona Herlinda & Her Son
Donde Duermen
    Dos...Duermen Tres
Donkey Skin▶
Donovan's Reef▶
Don't Drink the Water
Don't Go in the House
Don't Go to Sleep
Don't Mess with My Sister!
Down & Dirty▶
A Dream of Kings▶
Dream Street
Drifting Weeds▶
Duel in the Sun▶
Duel of Champions
Dumbo▶
Duplicates
An Early Frost▶
Early Summer▶
East and West▶
East of Eden▶
East of Eden
East Side Kids
Eat a Bowl of Tea▶
Echoes
Ed and His Dead Mother
18 Again!
El Monte de las Brujas
El Norte▶
El Penon de las Animas

El Sabor de la Venganza
Eleni
Eli Eli
Elizabeth of Ladymead▶
Ellie
Embassy
The Emerald Forest▶
Emerald Jungle
The Emigrants▶
Emissary
The Empire Strikes Back▶
Empty Canvas
Encore▶
The End of Innocence
Endless Love
Endplay
Enid is Sleeping
Enter the Panther
The Entertainer▶
Entertaining Mr. Sloane
Epitaph
The Equalizer: Memories of
    Manon
Equinox
Equinox Flower
Erendira
Ernie Kovacs: Between the
    Laughter
Escape
Escape Artist▶
Escape from Safehaven
Eternal Return
The Europeans▶
The Everlasting Secret Family
Everybody's Fine
The Executioner
Experiment in Terror▶
Eye of the Storm
Eyes of a Stranger
The Eyes of the Amaryllis
The Eyes, the Mouth
The Fabulous Baker Boys▶
Face to Face▶
The Fall of the House of
    Usher▶
The Fall of the House of Usher
Falling from Grace
The Family▶
Family Business
Family Pictures▶
Family Prayers
Family Reunion
Family Secrets
Family Sins
Family Viewing▶
Fangs of the Living Dead
Fanny and Alexander▶
Far Away and Long Ago
Far North
A Far Off Place
Fast Talking
Fatal Justice
Father▶
Father
Father Figure
Father Hood
Father of the Bride▶
Father of the Bride
Fathers and Sons
Father's Little Dividend▶
A Father's Revenge
Fear Strikes Out▶
Fearmaker
Feast for the Devil
The Feud
Field of Dreams▶
Fight for Your Life
Fighting Life
The Fighting Sullivans▶
Final Analysis
Final Embrace
Final Mission
Final Verdict
Fingers▶
Finish Line
Finishing School
Fiorile▶
The Fire Next Time
Firesign Theatre Presents
    Nick Danger in the Case of
    the Missing Yolks
First Born

Family

Five Days One Summer
Five Easy Pieces▶
Flambards
The Flame Trees of Thika▶
Flesh and Bone▶
The Flintstones
Flowers in the Attic
The Flying Fool
Follow That Dream
Follow That Rainbow
Fool for Love
For Love or Money
For Richer, For Poorer
Force of Evil▶
Force on Thunder Mountain
Forever and a Day▶
Found Alive
Four Daughters▶
The Four Horsemen of the
  Apocalypse▶
The Four Horsemen of the
  Apocalypse
Fourth Wish
Foxfire Light
Freedom is Paradise▶
Friendly Fire▶
Friendly Persuasion▶
Frightmare
The Fringe Dwellers
From the Terrace
Fulfillment
Full Contact
The Funeral▶
Funny About Love
Further Adventures of the
  Wilderness Family, Part 2
The Fury
Fuzz
The Game is Over
Gang Justice
Garbo Talks
The Garden of Delights▶
Garden of the Finzi-Continis▶
Gas Food Lodging▶
The Gathering
The Gathering: Part 2
Generation
Georgia▶
Gervaise▶
Getting Even with Dad
Ghosts Can't Do It
The Girl▶
A Girl on Her Own
Girly
The Go-Masters▶
The Godfather▶
The Godfather 1902-1959:
  The Complete Epic▶
The Godfather, Part 2▶
Golden Gate
Goldengirl
The Good Earth▶
Good Morning, Babylon▶
Goodbye, Miss 4th of July
Goodnight, Michelangelo
Grand Larceny
The Grapes of Wrath▶
The Grass is Always Greener
  Over the Septic Tank
Grave of the Fireflies▶
Grave of the Vampire
The Graveyard
Great Day
The Great Madcap
The Great Man Votes▶
The Great Outdoors
The Great Santini▶
A Great Wall▶
The Great Wallendas
Greedy
Green Dolphin Street
Green Eyes▶
Green Horizon
The Green Promise
The Green Wall▶
Greenstone
Grown Ups
Guess Who's Coming to
  Dinner▶
Gun Play
Gypsy▶
Gypsy

Gypsy Colt
Halloween with the Addams
  Family
Hamlet▶
The Hand that Rocks the
  Cradle
Hannah and Her Sisters▶
Hard Frame
Hard Promises
Hard Target
Harry & Son
Harry and the Hendersons
The Hatfields & the McCoys
The Haunting of Barney
  Palmer
Head of the Family
Heart of a Nation▶
Heart of the Stag
Heaven Tonight
Heidi
Heidi▶
The Heiress▶
Held for Murder
Hell on Wheels
Hero▶
Hi Diddle Diddle
Hidden Guns▶
Hide in Plain Sight▶
The Hiding Place
High & Low▶
High Command
High Heels▶
High Tide▶
Hijazo de Mi Vidaza
His Private Secretary
The Hit List
Hobo's Christmas
Hobson's Choice▶
Hobson's Choice
A Hole in the Head
Holiday in Mexico
The Holy Innocents▶
Home at Last
Home Feeling
Home for the Holidays
Home from the Hill▶
Home is Where the Hart is
A Home of Our Own
Home to Stay
Homecoming: A Christmas
  Story
Homeward Bound
Homeward Bound: The
  Incredible Journey
Honey, I Blew Up the Kid
Honey, I Shrunk the Kids
Honor Thy Father
Honor Thy Father and Mother:
  The True Story of the
  Menendez Brothers
The Hoodlum
Hope and Glory▶
Horizons West
The Horror Chamber of Dr.
  Faustus▶
The Horse▶
The Horse in the Gray Flannel
  Suit
Horsemen
Hot Lead & Cold Feet
Hot Spell
Hotel Colonial
House of Angels
House of Cards
House of Dreams
The House of Eliott
House of Strangers▶
The House of the Spirits
The House on Chelouche
  Street
The House that Bled to Death
A House Without a Christmas
  Tree
Household Saints▶
Housekeeping▶
How Green was My Valley▶
How the West was Won▶
How to Commit Marriage
The Howards of Virginia
Huck and the King of Hearts
Hud▶
The Human Shield

I Accuse My Parents
I Could Go on Singing
I Live in Fear▶
I Live with My Dad
I Met a Murderer
I Never Sang For My Father▶
I Ought to Be in Pictures
I Sent a Letter to My Love▶
The Ice Flood
I'd Give My Life
If Things Were Different
Il Grido
I'll Do Anything
Immediate Family
The Imported Bridegroom
In Celebration▶
In Country
In Search of a Golden Sky
In Search of the Castaways▶
In the Custody of Strangers▶
In the Name of the Father▶
In This Our Life
The Indian Runner
Indiana Jones and the Last
  Crusade▶
Indochine▶
The Inheritance
The Inkwell
Innocence Unprotected
Inside Monkey Zetterland
Interiors▶
Intermezzo▶
Into the West▶
Into Thin Air▶
Iphigenia▶
The Irishman
Iron Eagle
Ironweed▶
The Island▶
Islands in the Stream
It Could Happen to You
It Runs In the Family▶
It's a Date
It's a Great Life
It's a Wonderful Life▶
It's in the Bag
Jack the Bear
The Jacksons: An American
  Dream
Jacob Have I Loved
Jamon, Jamon
Jason Goes to Hell: The Final
  Friday
Jazz Singer
Jenny's War
JFK: Reckless Youth
Joey
John and the Missus
Johnny Angel▶
Jory
Josh and S.A.M.
Journey of Hope▶
The Joy Luck Club▶
Jumpin' at the Boneyard
Juno and the Paycock
Just for You
Keep the Change
Kid Vengeance
The Kid Who Loved Christmas
Kidnap Syndicate
Kidnapping of Baby John Doe
Kill or Be Killed
Killer with Two Faces
Killing of Randy Webster
Kind Hearts and Coronets▶
The King and Four Queens
King Lear▶
The King of Marvin Gardens
King of the Gypsies
King of the Hill▶
Kingfisher Caper
The Kiss
The Kissing Place
Kotch▶
Kramer vs. Kramer▶
The Krays▶
Kuffs
Kuni Lemel in Tel Aviv
La Bamba▶
La Boum
La Chartreuse de Parme
La Cicada

La Rupture
La Symphonie Pastorale▶
La Terra Trema▶
Labyrinth▶
Ladies of the Chorus
Lady by Choice
Lady Mobster
The Lady Refuses
Lai Shi: China's Last Eunuch
Landscape in the Mist▶
Lantern Hill
The Last Days of Chez Nous
The Last Five Days
The Last Hit
Last Resort
The Last Unicorn
Late Spring▶
Laughing at Life
Laurel Avenue
Law of Desire▶
Legacy of Lies
The Legend of Black Thunder
  Mountain
The Legend of Hillbilly John
Leolo
Leon the Pig Farmer
Les Bons Debarras
Les Comperes▶
Les Enfants Terrible▶
Les Violons du Bal
Lethal Weapon▶
Let's Dance
The Letter▶
Letter of Introduction
Letting the Birds Go Free
Liar's Edge
Liar's Moon
License to Kill
Lies My Father Told Me▶
Life Is a Long Quiet River▶
Life is Sweet▶
Life with Father▶
Light of Day
Like Water for Chocolate▶
The Lion in Winter▶
The Lion King
The List of Adrian
  Messenger▶
Listen, Darling
Little Buddha
Little Dorrit, Film 1: Nobody's
  Fault▶
Little Dorrit, Film 2: Little
  Dorrit's Story▶
Little House on the Prairie▶
Little Nellie Kelly
Little Women▶
Little Women
The Long Day Closes▶
Long Day's Journey into
  Night▶
Long Day's Journey into Night
The Long, Hot Summer▶
The Long Riders▶
A Long Way Home
Look Who's Talking Now
Looking for Miracles
Lorenzo's Oil▶
Lorna Doone
Los Dos Hermanos
The Lost Boys
The Lost Capone
Lost Honeymoon
Lost in Yonkers
The Lost Language of
  Cranes▶
Lots of Luck
Love▶
Love Crazy▶
Love Finds Andy Hardy▶
Love Laughs at Andy Hardy
Love Me Tender
Love on the Dole▶
Love Strange Love
Love Under Pressure
Love Without Fear
Love Your Mama
Lovers and Other Strangers▶
Lucky Stiff
Ma and Pa Kettle
Ma and Pa Kettle at the Fair

Ma and Pa Kettle Back On the
  Farm
Ma and Pa Kettle Go to Town
Ma Barker's Killer Brood
Mac▶
Mad at the Moon
Mad Max▶
Madame X
M.A.D.D.: Mothers Against
  Drunk Driving
Made in America
Madhouse
Mafia Princess
Magic Kid
The Magnificent Ambersons▶
The Maid
Make Room for Tomorrow
The Makioka Sisters▶
Mama Turns a Hundred▶
Mame
A Man About the House
Man & Boy
The Man from Laramie▶
The Man in the Gray Flannel
  Suit
The Man in the Iron Mask▶
The Man in the Moon▶
The Man in the Santa Claus
  Suit
A Man of Passion
Man, Woman & Child
Mandy▶
Maniac
Mansfield Park
Maria Candelaria
Maria's Day▶
The Marshal's Daughter
Martial Outlaw
Masala
Mask▶
The Mating Game▶
A Matter of Principle
Maverick
May Fools▶
Maya
Maybe I'll Be Home in the
  Spring
Me & Veronica
Meet Me in St. Louis▶
Meet the Hollowheads
Meet the Parents
The Member of the Wedding▶
The Member of the Wedding
Memories of Me
Memory of Us
Menace on the Mountain
Merlin
Midnight
Midnight Warning
Mildred Pierce▶
Miles from Home
Milk Money
Min & Bill
Mind Games
The Miniver Story
Miracle Down Under
Miracle on 34th Street▶
Mirele Efros
Miss Rose White▶
Mississippi Masala▶
Missouri Traveler▶
Mrs. Doubtfire
Mrs. Miniver▶
Mrs. Parkington
Mrs. Wiggs of the Cabbage
  Patch
Mr. & Mrs. Bridge▶
Mr. Hobbs Takes a Vacation▶
Mr. Saturday Night
Mr. Skitch
Misunderstood
Mob Boss
Mom & Dad
Mon Oncle▶
Mon Oncle Antoine▶
Monkey Trouble
Monsieur Verdoux▶
Moonstruck▶
The Mortal Storm▶
The Mosquito Coast
Mother▶

Mother & Daughter: A Loving War
Mother and Son
Mother Doesn't Always Know Best
Mother Lode
Mother's Boys
Mouchette▶
Moving
Murder-in-Law
Murder in the Doll House
Murder One
Murmur of the Heart▶
Mussolini & I
Mutual Respect
My Brother's Wife
My Daughter's Keeper
My Father is Coming
My Father the Hero
My Father's Glory▶
My Father's Nurse
My Friend Walter
My Girl 2▶
My Grandpa is a Vampire
My Heroes Have Always Been Cowboys
My Life
My Mother's Castle▶
My Mother's Secret Life
My Old Man
My Old Man's Place
My Other Husband
My Outlaw Brother
My Sister Eileen▶
My Sister, My Love
My Twentieth Century▶
Naked Hills
Naked Paradise
Nancy Goes to Rio
National Lampoon's Christmas Vacation
National Lampoon's European Vacation
Natural Enemies
Never Too Young to Die
The New Land▶
New York Stories▶
Next of Kin
Next Stop, Greenwich Village▶
Next Summer▶
Nicholas Nickleby▶
Night Crossing
'night, Mother
Night Moves▶
Night of Terror
The Night of the Hunter▶
Night Zoo
The Nightman
Nights and Days
Nightstalker
1900▶
No End
No Place to Hide
No Place to Run
Noon Wine
The Norman Conquests, Part 1: Table Manners▶
The Norman Conquests, Part 2: Living Together▶
The Norman Conquests, Part 3: Round and Round the Garden▶
Norman Loves Rose
North▶
Not My Kid
Not Quite Human
Not Quite Human 2
Nothing in Common
Nowhere to Hide
Nowhere to Run
Numero Deux
Of Human Hearts
Oh Dad, Poor Dad (Momma's Hung You in the Closet & I'm Feeling So Sad)
O'Hara's Wife
The Old Dark House▶
The Old Maid▶
Old Yeller▶
Oldest Living Graduate▶
Olivier, Olivier▶

Ollie Hopnoodle's Haven of Bliss
Olly Olly Oxen Free
Omega Syndrome
On Golden Pond▶
On Moonlight Bay
On the Edge
On the Third Day
On the Waterfront▶
On Valentine's Day
Once Around
The One and Only, Genuine, Original Family Band▶
One Cooks, the Other Doesn't
One Good Cop
One More Chance
One Trick Pony
Onibaba▶
Only the Lonely
Only When I Laugh▶
Ordet▶
Ordinary People▶
Orphans▶
Orphans of the Storm▶
The Other▶
Our Little Girl
Our Town▶
Our Vines Have Tender Grapes▶
Out of Sight, Out of Her Mind
Out of the Blue▶
Out on a Limb
Outside Chance of Maximillian Glick
Over the Hill
Over the Top
Overboard
Overture to Glory
The Ox
Ozzie & Harriet
Paco
Padre Nuestro
Padre Padrone▶
Panic in the Year Zero!
Paradise▶
Paradise Alley
The Parent Trap
Parenthood▶
Parents▶
Paris, Texas▶
Parrish
Passed Away
Passion in Paradise
Pathfinder▶
The Peasants
Peeping Tom▶
Peg O' My Heart
Peggy Sue Got Married
Penny Serenade▶
Peppermint Soda▶
Perfect Family
A Perfect Little Murder
The Perils of Gwendoline
Personal Exemptions
Pet Sematary
Pete Townshend: White City
Phaedra
Phantom Brother
Phar Lap
Phedre
Philadelphia▶
Picture Mommy Dead
Pilgrim, Farewell
Ping Pong
The Pit and the Pendulum▶
The Pit & the Pendulum
Pitfall▶
Places in the Heart▶
Platinum High School
Please Don't Eat the Daisies
Poil de Carotte
Poison Ivy
Poldark▶
Pollyanna▶
Pop Always Pays
The Pope of Greenwich Village▶
Popi▶
The Portrait▶
Portrait of a Stripper
Postcards from the Edge▶
Prehysteria

Pride and Prejudice▶
Pride and Prejudice
Prince of Pennsylvania
The Prince of Tides▶
Prizzi's Honor▶
The Prodigal
Promised a Miracle
Proud Men
Psycho Girls
Queen of Hearts▶
A Question of Love▶
The Quiet Man▶
Rachel, Rachel▶
Radio Flyer
Rage of Angels: The Story Continues
Raging Bull▶
Railway Children▶
Rain Man▶
Rainbow's End
A Raisin in the Sun▶
Raising Arizona▶
Ran▶
A Rare Breed
The Real McCoy
Rebecca of Sunnybrook Farm
Reckless Moment▶
The Red Pony▶
Red River▶
The Ref▶
Regarding Henry▶
Regina
Remember Me
Return
Return of Jesse James
Return of the Family Man
Return of Wildfire
Return to Africa
Return to Lonesome Dove
Revenge
Revenge of Doctor X
Revenge of the Barbarians
Revenge of the Red Baron
The Revenger
The Revolt of Job▶
The Revolt of Mother▶
Revolution
Rhapsody in August
Ricco
Rich in Love
Rich Man, Poor Man▶
Rich, Young and Pretty
Riders of the Purple Sage
Riding the Edge
The Right Hand Man
Rikky and Pete
Rivals
The River Niger
The River Rat
A River Runs Through It▶
Road Racers
Road to Salina
Robert Kennedy and His Times
Rocco and His Brothers▶
Rocket Gibralter▶
The Rocking Horse Winner
Roll of Thunder, Hear My Cry
Rolling Home
Romeo and Juliet
Romeo and Juliet▶
Romola
Roses Bloom Twice
The Royal Bed
Rulers of the City
Rumble Fish▶
Runaway Father
Running Mates▶
Running on Empty▶
The Sacketts
Sacred Ground
Sallah▶
Samantha
Santa Sangre▶
The Saphead
Sardinia Kidnapped
Satan in High Heels
Savage is Loose
Scandal in a Small Town
Scent of a Woman▶
Scream for Help
Sea Devils

The Search▶
Searching for Bobby Fischer▶
Season of Fear
The Secret
Secret Ceremony
The Secret Garden▶
The Secret Passion of Robert Clayton
Secrets of Women▶
Seduced and Abandoned▶
The Seducers
See How She Runs▶
See You in the Morning
The Seekers
Sense & Sensibility
Sensuous Summer
Separate Vacations
Separate Ways
Seven Alone
Seven Beauties▶
Seven Faces of Dr. Lao▶
Severance
Sex and the Single Parent
Shadow of a Doubt▶
The Shadow Riders
The Shanghai Gesture
Shark River
Shattered▶
The Sheep Has Five Legs
The Shell Seekers
Shenandoah▶
Sherman's March: An Improbable Search for Love
The Shining Hour
Shoot the Moon
Shy People▶
The Sibling
Sibling Rivalry
The Sicilian Connection
Sidewalks of New York
The Silence▶
Silence
Silent Rebellion
Silent Tongue
Silent Witness
The Silver Stallion: King of the Wild Brumbies
Simple Justice
Simple Men▶
The Sin of Madelon Claudet▶
Since You Went Away▶
Sinful Life
Sinners
The Sisters▶
Sisters▶
Six in Paris
Sixteen Candles▶
'68
Skag▶
Skin Game
Skylark
Slaughter of the Innocents
The Sleazy Uncle
Slightly Scarlet
Small Sacrifices
Smilin' Through▶
Smoke
The Snapper▶
Sofie
The Solitary Man
Sometimes a Great Notion▶
Son-in-Law
Son of Flubber▶
Son of Frankenstein▶
Son of Fury▶
Song of the Exile
Song of the Islands
Sons
Sons of Katie Elder▶
Sons of Steel
Sorrows of Gin
The Sound of Music▶
South Central
South of Hell Mountain
The Southerner▶
Souvenir
The Spanish Gardener▶
Special Olympics
Spencer's Mountain
Spider Baby
Spirit Rider▶
Split Decisions

Split Image▶
Splitting Heirs
State Fair▶
State Fair
Stella
Stella Dallas▶
The Stepfather▶
Stepfather 2: Make Room for Daddy
Stepfather 3: Father's Day
Stepmonster
Stepsisters
Still Not Quite Human
The Stone Boy▶
Stop! or My Mom Will Shoot
The Story of Boys & Girls▶
The Story of Jacob & Joseph▶
Storyville
Strange Interlude▶
Strange Interlude
Strange Shadows in an Empty Room
Strangers in the City
Strangers: The Story of a Mother and Daughter▶
Strapless
Street Girls
Street Hero
Street Hitz
Street Justice
A Streetcar Named Desire▶
Striking Distance
Stuck on You
Suddenly, Last Summer▶
Suffering Bastards
Sugar Cane Alley▶
Sugar Hill▶
Summer Holiday
Summer Magic
Summer of Fear
Summer Wishes, Winter Dreams
A Sunday in the Country▶
The Sundowners▶
Sure Fire
Susan and God▶
Susana▶
Suzanne
Swedenhielms
Sweet Smell of Success▶
Sweetie▶
The Swiss Family Robinson▶
Switched at Birth
Sylvester
Table Settings
The Tale of Ruby Rose▶
Tales from Avonlea, Vol. 1: The Journey Begins▶
Tank
Tatie Danielle▶
Tears in the Rain
Teenage Exorcist
The Tempest▶
Teorema
Termini Station
Terms of Endearment▶
Testament▶
Tevye
Tex
Texas Jack
Texas Lightning
Thank You & Good Night
Thanksgiving Story
That Man Is Pregnant
That Was Then...This Is Now
There's No Business Like Show Business▶
They Watch
Things in Their Season
Third Walker▶
This Boy's Life▶
This Happy Breed▶
This is My Life
This Property is Condemned▶
A Thousand Clowns▶
Threads▶
Three Brothers▶
Three Daring Daughters
The Three Lives of Thomasina▶
Three Men and a Cradle▶

Family

3 Ninjas
3 Ninjas Kick Back
Three Violent People
The Three Weird Sisters
Three's Trouble
Thrillkill
Through a Glass Darkly▶
Thursday's Child
Ticket to Heaven
Tiger Warsaw
Till Marriage Do Us Part
Till There was You
Time Flies When You're Alive
Time Indefinite
A Time of Destiny
Time Stands Still▶
Time to Live
'Tis a Pity She's a Whore
Tito and Me▶
To All My Friends on Shore▶
To Dance with the White
   Dog▶
To Die for 2
To Paris with Love
To Sleep with Anger▶
To Subdue the Evil
Toby McTeague
Tokyo Story▶
Toll of the Desert
Toughlove
Toys
Toys in the Attic
Track 29
Trade Secrets
Traenen in Florenz
Tramp at the Door
Travels with My Aunt
Treacherous Crossing
Treasure of the Sierra Madre▶
The Tree of Wooden Clogs▶
The Trip to Bountiful▶
Trois Couleurs: Blanc▶
Trois Couleurs: Bleu▶
True Blood
True Confessions▶
True Love▶
True West▶
Tucker and the Horse Thief
The Tuttles of Tahiti▶
29th Street
Twice in a Lifetime▶
Twister
Two Kinds of Love
The Two Sisters
The Ugly Dachshund
Uncle Buck▶
Uncle Moses
Uncommon Valor
Under the Boardwalk
Under the Volcano▶
Undergrads▶
Uneasy Terms
The Unforgiven▶
An Unremarkable Life
Until They Sail
Up the Sandbox
The Uprising▶
Used People
Vengeance
Vengeance Valley
A Very Brady Christmas
Vigil▶
Vincent & Theo▶
Violette▶
Viridiana▶
Volver, Volver, Volver!
Voyage en Balloon
A Voyage' Round My Father▶
Voyage to Italy
Voyager▶
Vultures
Wagon Tracks
Wait Till Your Mother Gets
   Home
Walk in the Spring Rain
The Waltons: A Thanksgiving
   Story
War & Remembrance, Part 1
War & Remembrance, Part 2
War & Remembrance: The
   Final Chapter, Part 8

War & Remembrance: The
   Final Chapter, Part 9
Waterfront
The Wedding Banquet▶
Wedding in White
Weep No More My Lady
Welcome Home
The Whales of August▶
What About Bob?▶
What Ever Happened to Baby
   Jane?▶
What the Peeper Saw
What's Eating Gilbert Grape▶
When a Man Loves a Woman
When Nature Calls
When Wolves Cry
Where East is East
Where Have All the People
   Gone?
Where Love Has Gone
Where the Heart Is
Where the Lilies Bloom▶
Where's Poppa?▶
The White Cliffs of Dover▶
White Mane▶
Why Does Herr R. Run
   Amok?
Wicked Stepmother
Wild at Heart▶
The Wild Country
The Wild Duck
Wild Pony
Wild Zone
Wilder Napalm
Wildflower▶
The Winds of War
Winter People
Winterset
The Wistful Widow of Wagon
   Gap
With Six You Get Eggroll
The Wizard
The Wizard of Loneliness
A Woman Under the
   Influence▶
Women on the Verge of a
   Nervous Breakdown▶
Woodchipper Massacre
The World Accuses
A World Apart▶
The World of Apu▶
The Worldly Madonna
Wyatt Earp▶
Yellow Earth
You Can't Take It with You▶
The Young Detectives on
   Wheels
Your Ticket Is No Longer Valid
Yours, Mine & Ours
Zertigo Diamond Caper

Fantasy

*see also Animation &
Cartoons; Musical Fantasy*
A Nous la Liberte▶
The Acid Eaters
Adventures in Dinosaur City
The Adventures of a Gnome
   Named Gnorm
The Adventures of Baron
   Munchausen▶
The Adventures of Mark
   Twain▶
Afrita Hanen▶
Aladdin
Aladdin and His Wonderful
   Lamp
Alice▶
Alice Through the Looking
   Glass
Alice's Adventures in
   Wonderland
Alien from L.A.
...Almost
Alone Against Rome
Amazing Mr. Blunden
The Amazing Spider-Man
Amazing Stories
Amazons
America 3000
Angel on My Shoulder▶
Ashik Kerib▶

Atlantis, the Lost Continent
Atlas
Atlas in the Land of the
   Cyclops
Ator the Fighting Eagle
Baby...Secret of the Lost
   Legend
Barbarella
Barbarian Queen
Baron Munchausen▶
Batman▶
Batman Returns
*batteries not included
Beastmaster
Beastmaster 2: Through the
   Portal of Time
Beauty and the Beast: Once
   Upon a Time in New York
Benji's Very Own Christmas
   Story
Bernard and the Genie
Between Heaven and Earth
Beyond Atlantis
Beyond Tomorrow
Big▶
Big Top Pee Wee
Big Trouble in Little China
Biggles
Bill and Coo
Bill & Ted's Excellent
   Adventure
The Bishop's Wife▶
Bladestorm
Blithe Spirit▶
The Blood of a Poet▶
The Blue Bird▶
Blue Monkey
Blue Paradise
The Borrowers▶
The Boy God
The Boy Who Could Fly▶
The Boy Who Loved Trolls
Bridge to Terabithia
Brothers Lionheart
The Canterville Ghost
The Cat from Outer Space
Cave Girls
The Challenge
Charleston▶
Charley and the Angel
Child's Christmas in Wales
The Christmas That Almost
   Wasn't
The Chronicles of Narnia
Cinderella 2000
Circus Angel▶
The Clan of the Cave Bear
Clarence
Clash of the Titans
Cocoon▶
Cocoon: The Return
The Company of Wolves▶
Conan the Barbarian▶
Conan the Destroyer
A Connecticut Yankee▶
Conquest
Conquest of Mycene
Coriolanus, Man without a
   Country
The Crazy Ray▶
The Crow
Curse of the Cat People▶
Darby O'Gill & the Little
   People▶
The Dark Crystal▶
The Day the Earth Froze
Deathstalker
Deathstalker 2: Duel of the
   Titans
Deathstalker 3
Deathstalker 4: Clash of the
   Titans
Desperate Living
The Devil & Max Devlin
Devil of the Desert Against the
   Son of Hercules
Diary of Forbidden Dreams▶
Dias de Ilusion
Digby, the Biggest Dog in the
   World
Donkey Skin▶

Dos Cruces en Danger Pass▶
Dragonslayer▶
Dragonworld
Dream a Little Dream
Dreamchild▶
Dreamscape
Dreamwood▶
Dungeonmaster
Early Russian Cinema, Vol. 3:
   Starewicz's Fantasies
Edward Scissorhands▶
El Cristo de los Milagros
Elle Voit des Nains Partout
Emmanuelle 4
The Enchanted Cottage▶
The Enchantress
Endgame
Eraserhead▶
Erotic Escape
Erotic Touch of Hot Skin
Escapes
E.T.: The Extra-Terrestrial▶
Eternal Return
The Ewok Adventure
The Ewoks: Battle for Endor
Excalibur▶
Explorers
Falcon
Fantasy Island
Faraway, So Close!
Field of Dreams▶
The Final Programme
Fire and Ice
Firesign Theatre Presents
   Nick Danger in the Case of
   the Missing Yolks
Flight of Dragons
Flight of the Navigator
Francis Goes to the Races
Francis Joins the WACs
Francis the Talking Mule▶
French Quarter
Frogs!
From the Earth to the Moon
George's Island▶
The Ghost and Mrs. Muir▶
Ghost Chase
Ghost Writer
Ghosts Can't Do It
Ghostwarrior
The Giants of Thessaly
Gladiators 7
The Glass Slipper
Gnome-Mobile
Golden Voyage of Sinbad
The Golem▶
Goliath Against the Giants
Goliath and the Barbarians
Goliath and the Dragon
Goliath and the Sins of
   Babylon
Good Time with a Bad Girl
Gor
The Great Land of Small
Greenstone
Grendel, Grendel, Grendel
Gryphon
Gulliver's Travels
A Guy Named Joe
The Hanged Man
Harvey▶
Hawk the Slayer
Heartbreak Hotel
Hearts & Armour
Heaven Can Wait▶
Hector's Bunyip
Herbie Rides Again
Hercules
Hercules and the Captive
   Women
Hercules and the Princess of
   Troy
Hercules in the Haunted World
Hercules, Prisoner of Evil
Here Come the Littles: The
   Movie
Here Comes Mr. Jordan▶
Hey There, It's Yogi Bear
Highlander 2: The Quickening
Highlander 3: The Sorcerer
His Majesty, the Scarecrow of
   Oz/The Magic Cloak of Oz

The Hobbit▶
Hobgoblins
The Holes
Hollywood Erotic Film Festival
Hook
Hoppity Goes to Town
Horrors of the Red Planet
A Hungarian Fairy Tale▶
Hyper-Sapien: People from
   Another Star
I Married a Witch▶
The Incredible Mr. Limpet
Indiana Jones and the Last
   Crusade▶
Inhibition
The Invasion of Carol Enders
The Invincible Gladiator
Invisible Agent
The Invisible Kid
Invisible: The Chronicles of
   Benjamin Knight
Irish Cinderella
The Iron Crown
Iron Warrior
Ironmaster
The Island of Nevawuz
It's a Wonderful Life▶
Jack the Giant Killer▶
Jason and the Argonauts▶
Jimmy, the Boy Wonder
Jonathan Livingston Seagull
Journey Beneath the Desert
Journey to the Center of the
   Earth▶
Journey to the Center of the
   Earth
Journey to the Lost City
Julia and Julia
Julia Has Two Lovers
The Jungle Book
Jungle Hell
A Kid for Two Farthings
King Kong▶
King Kong
Kiss Me Goodbye
Kriemhilde's Revenge▶
Krull
La Merveilleuse Visite
L.A. Story▶
Ladyhawke
Land of Doom
The Land of Faraway
The Last Days of Pompeii
The Last Unicorn
Le Magnifique
Legend
The Legend of Suram
   Fortress
Legend of the Dinosaurs
Legion of Iron
Leprechaun 2
Les Visiteurs du Soir▶
Like Father, Like Son
The Lion of Thebes▶
The Lion of Venice
The Little Mermaid
Little Monsters
Little Nemo: Adventures in
   Slumberland
Little Red Riding Hood▶
Logan's Run
The Lord of the Rings
Lords of Magick
Los Caciques
The Lost Continent
Love Notes
The Loves of Hercules
Maciste in Hell
Made in Heaven
The Magic Fountain
Magic Serpent
The Magic Voyage of Sinbad
Magical Wonderland
The Magician▶
Making Contact
The Man in the Santa Claus
   Suit
The Man Who Could Work
   Miracles▶
The Man Who Wagged His
   Tail
Mannequin 2: On the Move

Marco Polo, Jr.
The Martian Chronicles: Part 1
The Martian Chronicles: Part 2
The Martian Chronicles: Part 3
Master of the World
Masters of the Universe
Max Headroom, the Original Story
Maxie
Mazes and Monsters
Medusa Against the Son of Hercules
Merlin
Merlin and the Sword
Merlin of the Crystal Cave
Messalina vs. the Son of Hercules
A Midsummer Night's Dream▶
Mighty Joe Young
Million Dollar Duck
Miracle Beach
Miracle in Milan▶
Mr. Destiny
Mr. Sycamore
Mole Men Against the Son of Hercules
The Moon Stallion
Mouse and His Child
Munchie
My Friend Walter
My Neighbor Totoro
My Science Project
My Stepmother Is an Alien
The Mysterious Stranger
Mystery Island
Natas...The Reflection
The Navigator▶
Neutron vs. the Amazing Dr. Caronte
Neutron vs. the Death Robots
Neutron vs. the Maniac
The NeverEnding Story▶
The NeverEnding Story 2: Next Chapter
Night Tide
The Nightmare Before Christmas▶
Nine Lives of Fritz the Cat
No Grumps Allowed!
Nutcracker: The Motion Picture
An Occurrence at Owl Creek Bridge▶
Off on a Comet
Once a Hero
Once Upon a Time
One Magic Christmas
1001 Arabian Nights
One Wish Too Many
The Original Fabulous Adventures of Baron Munchausen
Orpheus
Outlaw of Gor
Paperhouse▶
Patchwork Girl of Oz
The Peanut Butter Solution
Peter Pan▶
Pete's Dragon
The Phantom Chariot
Phantom Tollbooth▶
The Plague Dogs
The Point
The Polar Bear King
Prancer
Prehistoric Bimbos in Armageddon City
Prehistoric Women
Prehysteria
Prelude to a Kiss
The Princess and the Swineherd
Private Passions
The Puppetoon Movie
Quest for the Mighty Sword
Quest of the Delta Knights
Radio Flyer
Ratboy
Real Men
The Red Balloon▶
Red Balloon/White Mane▶
Red Sonja

The Reluctant Dragon
Renoir Shorts
The Rescuers Down Under
Return from Witch Mountain
The Return of Jafar
The Return of Peter Grimm
Return of the Fly
The Return of the King
Return to Fantasy Island
Return to Oz
Return to the Lost World
Revolt of the Barbarians
The Rise & Rise of Daniel Rocket
Rock & Rule
Roland the Mighty
Rookie of the Year
Rudolph & Frosty's Christmas in July
Salome's Last Dance
Samson
Samson Against the Sheik
Samson and His Mighty Challenge
Samson and the 7 Miracles of the World
Santa Claus
Santa Claus Conquers the Martians
Santa Claus: The Movie
Saturday Night Serials
Saturday Night Sleazies, Vol. 1
The Scalawag Bunch
Sea of Dreams
The Sea Serpent
Search for the Gods
The Secret of NIMH▶
Serpent Island
Seven Faces of Dr. Lao▶
Seven Magnificent Gladiators
The Seventh Voyage of Sinbad▶
The Shaggy Dog
She
She Gods of Shark Reef
Sherlock Holmes in Washington
Shredder Orpheus
Siegfried▶
Sinbad and the Eye of the Tiger
Sinbad of the Seven Seas
Slave Girls from Beyond Infinity
Sleepwalk
Solarbabies
Some Call It Loving
Something Wicked This Way Comes
Somewhere in Time
Son of Flubber
Son of Kong
Son of Samson
Son of Sinbad
Sons of Hercules in the Land of Darkness
Sorceress
Space Raiders
Space Soldiers Conquer the Universe
Splash
The Spring
Stalker▶
Stand Up and Cheer
The Steagle
Steel Dawn
Story of a Cowboy Angel
Strange Tales
Strange Tales/Ray Bradbury Theatre
Striptease
Student of Prague▶
Super Mario Bros.
Supergirl
Superman: The Movie▶
Superman 2▶
Superman 3
Superman 4: The Quest for Peace
Superman & the Mole Men
Superman: The Serial, Vol. 1

Survival of a Dragon
Sword & the Dragon
Sword & the Sorcerer
The Sword in the Stone▶
Sword of the Valiant
Sylvia and the Phantom▶
Tales of Beatrix Potter▶
Tanya's Island
Teenage Mutant Ninja Turtles: The Movie
The Tempest
Terror of Rome Against the Son of Hercules
Terror of the Steppes
Test Tube Teens from the Year 2000
The Testament of Dr. Cordelier▶
The Testament of Orpheus▶
The Thief of Baghdad▶
Thief of Baghdad
The Thief of Baghdad
Thor and the Amazon Women
Thor el Conquistador
The Three Worlds of Gulliver
Throne of Fire
Thumbelina▶
Time Bandits
Time Burst: The Final Alliance
Time Fighters
The Time of Their Lives
Timestalkers
Tobor the Great
Tom Thumb▶
Train to Hollywood▶
Transformers: The Movie
The Trip
Triumph of the Son of Hercules
A Troll in Central Park
Trouble in Mind▶
The Trumpet and I
The Tune
20,000 Leagues Under the Sea▶
The Twilight Zone
The Two Worlds of Jenny Logan
Tyrant of Lydia Against the Son of Hercules
Ultra Flash
Undersea Kingdom
Unidentified Flying Oddball
Ursus in the Valley of the Lions
The Valley of Gwangi▶
Venus Against the Son of Hercules
A Very Old Man with Enormous Wings
Vibes
Vice Versa▶
Vulcan God of Fire
Walking on Air
The Warrior & the Sorceress
Warrior Queen
Watership Down
Wax, or the Discovery of Television Among the Bees
Waxworks▶
Welcome to Blood City
The White Sheik▶
Wild Women of Wongo
Wildest Dreams
Willow
Wings of Desire▶
Wings of Fame
A Witch Without a Broom
The Wizard of Oz
The Wizard of Speed and Time
Wizards
Wizards of the Lost Kingdom
Wizards of the Lost Kingdom 2
Wombling Free
The Wonderful World of the Brothers Grimm
Woof!
The Worst Witch

Yor, the Hunter from the Future
Zapped!
Zardoz
Zero for Conduct▶
Zone Troopers

Farming
see Crop Dusters

Fast Cars
see also Motor Vehicle Dept.
Baffled
Banzai Runner
The Big Wheel
Bobby Deerfield
Born to Race
Born to Run
Brewster McCloud▶
Bullitt▶
Burn 'Em Up Barnes
Cannonball
Cannonball Run
Cannonball Run 2
Car Crash
Catch Me...If You Can
The Checkered Flag
Daddy-O
Days of Thunder
Death Driver
Death Race 2000
Death Sport
The Devil on Wheels
Diamonds are Forever▶
Dirty Mary Crazy Larry▶
Dorf Goes Auto Racing
Dragstrip Girl
Eat My Dust
The Fast and the Furious
Fast Company
Fast Lane Fever
Faster Pussycat! Kill! Kill!
Fury on Wheels
Genevieve▶
Goldfinger▶
Grand Prix
Grandview U.S.A.
Greased Lightning
Great Race
Gumball Rally
Hard Drivin'
Heart Like a Wheel
The Heavenly Kid
Hell on Wheels
Herbie Goes Bananas
Herbie Goes to Monte Carlo
High Gear
Hot Rod
Hot Rod Girl
King of the Mountain
The Last American Hero▶
Last Chase
Le Mans▶
A Man and a Woman: 20 Years Later
The Pinchcliffe Grand Prix
Private Road: No Trespassing
Race for Life
The Racers
Rebel Without a Cause▶
Red Line 7000
Return to Macon County
Richard Petty Story
Road Racers
Roaring Roads
Safari 3000
Sahara
Shaker Run
Six Pack
Smash Palace
Smokey and the Bandit
Speed Zone
Speedway
Spinout
Stroker Ace
Those Daring Young Men in Their Jaunty Jalopies
To Please a Lady
The Touch of Satan
Van Nuys Blvd.

Vanishing Point
Viva Las Vegas
Winning▶
The Wraith

Feds
see also Detectives; Spies & Espionage
Assassin
Betrayed
Black Widow▶
Bloodfist 5: Human Target
Boiling Point
Burning Vengeance
Capone
Chu Chu & the Philly Flash
C.I.A.: Code Name Alexa
C.I.A. 2: Target Alexa
Class of 1999 2: The Substitute
Clear and Present Danger▶
The Client
Code Name Alpha
Crime Killer
Daughter of the Tong
Deadly Spygames
The Eiger Sanction
Exterminator
FBI Girl
The FBI Murders▶
The FBI Story▶
Federal Agents vs. Underworld, Inc.
Feds
Fifty/Fifty
The Fix
Flashback▶
Flight to Nowhere
Follow That Car
"G" Men▶
G-Men Never Forget
The Glass Jungle
Golden Gate
Government Agents vs. Phantom Legion
Guarding Tess
Gun Grit
Hit Woman: The Double Edge
Honor and Glory
I Was a Zombie for the FBI
I'll Get You
In the Line of Fire▶
J. Edgar Hoover
Johnnie Gibson F.B.I.
Kill Castro
Killer Likes Candy
Let 'Em Have It
Live Wire
Manhunter▶
Mankillers
Married to the Mob▶
Melvin Purvis: G-Man
Memoirs of an Invisible Man
Mississippi Burning▶
No Safe Haven
The Outfit
Patriot Games▶
Point Break
President's Target
The Private Files of J. Edgar Hoover
Raiders of Ghost City
Raw Deal
The Return of Eliot Ness
Revolver
Rosebud
S.A.S. San Salvador
Scam
The Silence of the Lambs▶
Sky High
Slaughter of the Innocents
Special Investigator
The Spook Who Sat By the Door
Street Hawk
Street Justice
Target
That Darn Cat
357 Magnum
Thunderheart▶
To Live & Die in L.A.
The Untouchables▶

Violent Breed
White Ghost
White Sands

Feminism

see Women; Wonder
Women

Femme Fatale

see also Wonder Women
The Accused
Addams Family Values
Algiers▶
All About Eve▶
The Amy Fisher Story
Armored Command
Auntie Lee's Meat Pies
Backstab
Basic Instinct
Beverly Hills Vamp
Bitter Harvest
Black Magic Woman
Black Widow▶
Blood of Dracula
The Blood Spattered Bride
Blown Away
The Blue Angel▶
Body Heat▶
Body of Evidence
Body Trouble
The Cabin in the Cotton
Caesar and Cleopatra
Casualties of Love: The
    "Long Island Lolita" Story
Cat on a Hot Tin Roof
Champagne for Caesar▶
Clash by Night▶
Clean Slate
Cleopatra
Conquest of Mycene
Crime of Passion
Crush
The Crush
Dance Hall
Dangerous Liaisons▶
Daughter of the Tong
Dead Reckoning▶
Death in Deep Water
Deceptions
Detour▶
The Devil's Daughter
Dishonored Lady
Dr. Caligari
Dr. Jekyll and Sister Hyde
Double Indemnity▶
Double Jeopardy
Dream Lover
Drowning by Numbers▶
Emmanuelle, the Queen
Eve of Destruction
Fangs of the Living Dead
Far from the Madding
    Crowd▶
Faster Pussycat! Kill! Kill!
Federal Agents vs.
    Underworld, Inc.
Final Analysis
First Name: Carmen▶
Flame of the Islands
The Flesh and the Devil▶
A Fool There Was
Frankenhooker
The Girl from Tobacco Row
Girl Hunters
Girl in His Pocket
A Girl to Kill for
Girlfriend from Hell
Great Flamarion
Grievous Bodily Harm
Hedda
Hellgate
Human Desire
I Spit on Your Corpse
Illusions
Impact▶
Impulse
Inner Sanctum
Intersection
Into the Fire
Invasion of the Bee Girls▶
The Jayne Mansfield Story

Jezebel▶
Kill Cruise
L'Addition
Lady and the Tramp▶
Lady for a Night
Lady Frankenstein
The Lady from Shanghai▶
The Lair of the White Worm▶
The Legend of the Wolf
    Woman
Lemora, Lady Dracula
The Leopard Woman
Lethal Lolita—Amy Fisher: My
    Story
The Lifetaker
Linda
Mado▶
The Malibu Beach Vampires
Malice
The Maltese Falcon▶
Mantis in Lace
Married to the Mob▶
Mata Hari▶
Mata Hari
Medusa Against the Son of
    Hercules
Mesa of Lost Women
Ms. 45▶
Mountaintop Motel Massacre
Nana▶
Nana
The Natural▶
Night Angel
The Night Evelyn Came Out of
    the Grave
Night of the Cobra Woman
Night Tide
No Way Out▶
Of Human Bondage▶
Of Human Bondage
On Her Majesty's Secret
    Service▶
Out Cold
Out of the Past▶
The Pamela Principle
Party Girls
Pepe Le Moko▶
Planet of Blood
Play Murder for Me
Point of No Return
Poison Ivy
Possession: Until Death Do
    You Part
The Postman Always Rings
    Twice▶
Praying Mantis
Prey of the Chameleon
A Rage in Harlem▶
Ran▶
Range Renegades
Reckless
Ring of Steel
Roadhouse Girl
Salome
Samson and Delilah▶
Samson and Delilah
Satanik
Scandal▶
Scarlet Street▶
Scorned
Sea of Love▶
Secret Weapons
Seven Sinners▶
Sexpot
Shadows in the Storm
Sins of Jezebel
Sleep of Death
Snow White and the Seven
    Dwarfs▶
Some Came Running▶
Something Wild
The Specialist
The Strange Woman
Sunrise▶
Sunset Boulevard▶
The Temp
The Temptress
Third Degree Burn
Tomb
Too Late for Tears▶
Truth or Dare
Under Suspicion

The Untamable
Valmont▶
Vanity Fair
The Velvet Vampire
Venus Against the Son of
    Hercules
Venus in Furs
The Wasp Woman
White Cargo
Who Framed Roger Rabbit?▶
Witchcraft 3: The Kiss of
    Death
Woman of Desire
The Women

Fencing

By the Sword
Ring of Steel

Fifties

see Nifty '50s

Film & Film History

America at the Movies
Assunta Spina
The Bad and the Beautiful▶
Battle of Elderbush Gulch
The Battleship Potemkin▶
Bellissimo: Images of the
    Italian Cinema
The Big Picture
Bombshell▶
Burden of Dreams
The Busby Berkeley Disc
Buster Keaton Rides Again/
    The Railrodder
Buster Keaton: The Great
    Stone Face
Camp Classics #1
Chaplin: A Character Is Born▶
Chaplin: A Character Is Born/
    Keaton: The Great Stone
    Face
Cinema Paradiso▶
Cinema Shrapnel
The Comic▶
Crimes & Misdemeanors▶
Custer's Last Fight
Doctor X
Early Cinema Vol. 1
Early Sound Films
Ed Wood
8 1/2▶
Epic That Never Was
Fangoria's Weekend of
    Horrors
Flying Saucers Over
    Hollywood: The Plan 9
    Companion
Forever James Dean
From "Star Wars" to "Jedi":
    The Making of a Saga
Golden Age of Hollywood
Great Chase
Great Movie Stunts &the
    Making of Raiders of the
    Lost Ark
The Great Train Robbery:
    Cinema Begins
Griffith Biograph Program
Guilty by Suspicion
Happy Anniversary 007: 25
    Years of James Bond
Heavy Petting
Hepburn & Tracy
Here's Looking at You,
    Warner Bros.▶
Hey Abbott!
History of the World: Part 1
Hollywood Boulevard
Hollywood Come Home
Hollywood Crime Wave
Hollywood Home Movies
Hollywood in Trouble
Hollywood My Hometown
Hollywood Outtakes & Rare
    Footage
Hollywood Scandals and
    Tragedies
Hollywood Uncensored
Hollywood without Makeup

Intervista▶
James Dean: The First
    American Teenager
A Kiss for Mary Pickford
Kisses
The Lady Without Camelias
Last Command▶
The Last Tycoon▶
Lies
Lightning Over Water
The Little Theatre of Jean
    Renoir▶
Lobster Man from Mars
Lost Squadron
The Love Goddesses
The Making of a Legend:
    "Gone With the Wind"
Many Faces of Sherlock
    Holmes
Marlon Brando
MGM: When the Lion Roars
Minnelli on Minnelli: Liza
    Remembers Vincente
Modern Romance▶
Movie Maker
The Oscar
Oscar's Greatest Moments:
    1971-1991
Paris When It Sizzles
The Perils of Pauline
Prurient Interest
Rented Lips
Scenario du Film Passion▶
Scherzo
Sex and Buttered Popcorn
sex, lies and videotape▶
Short Films of D.W. Griffith,
    Vol. 1
Short Films of D.W. Griffith,
    Vol. 2
Signals Through the Flames▶
S.O.B.
A Star is Born▶
Stardust Memories
State of Things▶
Story of the Silent Serials Girls
    in Danger
Story of William S. Hart/Sad
    Clowns
Strangers Kiss
The Stunt Man▶
That's Adequate
Thursday's Child
Visions of Light: The Art of
    Cinematography▶
Way Down East▶
When Comedy was King
You Must Remember This

Film Noir

The Accused
After Dark, My Sweet▶
Al Capone
The Asphalt Jungle▶
Beware, My Lovely
Beyond a Reasonable Doubt
Big Combo▶
Big Heat▶
The Big Sleep▶
Black Lizard
Blood Simple▶
Bob le Flambeur▶
Body Heat▶
Born to Kill▶
Chinatown▶
Cornered▶
Crack-Up
Criss Cross▶
Crossfire▶
Dark Corner▶
Dark Mirror▶
Dark Passage▶
Dead Again▶
Dead Silence
Deadline at Dawn
Delusion
Desperate
Detour▶
The Devil Thumbs a Ride▶
The Devil Thumbs a Ride/
    Having Wonderful Crime
D.O.A.▶

D.O.A.
Don't Bother to Knock
Double Indemnity▶
The Element of Crime
The Enforcer
Fallen Angels 1▶
Fallen Angels 2▶
Farewell, My Lovely▶
Force of Evil▶
Frantic▶
Gilda▶
The Glass Key▶
Gotham▶
Gun Crazy▶
High & Low▶
High Sierra▶
The Hitch-Hiker▶
Human Desire
Hustle
In a Lonely Place▶
Jigsaw▶
Johnny Angel▶
Key Largo▶
Killer's Kiss
The Killing▶
King Creole
Kiss Me Deadly▶
Kiss of Death▶
The Lady from Shanghai▶
Lady in the Death House
Lady in the Lake
The Las Vegas Story
Laura▶
Le Doulos▶
Macao▶
The Maltese Falcon▶
Mikey & Nicky
Mildred Pierce▶
Murder, My Sweet▶
The Naked City▶
Naked Kiss
The Narrow Margin▶
Niagara
Night and the City▶
Nightfall▶
Nocturne
On Dangerous Ground▶
Out of the Past▶
Panic in the Streets▶
Pickup on South Street▶
Pitfall▶
Plunder Road
The Postman Always Rings
    Twice▶
The Postman Always Rings
    Twice
Postmark for Danger/
    Quicksand
Prowler
The Public Eye▶
The Red House▶
Red Rock West▶
Rendez-vous▶
Romeo Is Bleeding
Rope▶
The Scar
Scarlet Street▶
The Set-Up▶
Shoot to Kill
Signal 7
Slow Moves
Sorry, Wrong Number▶
Station
Stormy Monday
Strange Illusion
The Strange Love of Martha
    Ivers▶
Sunset Boulevard▶
Sweet Smell of Success▶
Tchao Pantin▶
They Live by Night▶
The Third Man▶
This Gun for Hire▶
Too Late for Tears▶
Touch of Evil▶
Vortex
While the City Sleeps▶
White Heat▶
The Window▶
A Woman's Secret
The Wrong Man▶

Film Stars

see also Price of Fame

Acting on Impulse
Actor: The Paul Muni Story
Bela Lugosi Scrapbook
The Best of Bogart▶
Blonde Cobra/The Doctor's
  Dream
Bogie
Bombshell▶
The Bretts▶
Bruce Lee: Curse of the
  Dragon▶
Bud and Lou
Buster Keaton: The Great
  Stone Face
Calendar Girl
Chaplin▶
Count/Adventurer
Cult People
Dear Brigitte
Death at Love House
Deep in My Heart
Duke: The Films of John
  Wayne
Ed Wood
Emperor Jones/Paul
  Robeson: Tribute to an
  Artist
Frances▶
Go West, Young Man
Hedda Hopper's Hollywood
Hepburn & Tracy
Hollywood Clowns
Hollywood Goes to War
Hollywood Home Movies
The Horror of It All
Hurricane Express
In Person
James Dean
James Stewart: A Wonderful
  Life
The Jayne Mansfield Story
The Josephine Baker Story▶
Judy Garland: The Golden
  Years at MGM
The King of Kings▶
Kisses
L.A. Goddess
Legend of Valentino
The Legend of Valentino
The Love Goddesses
Man of a Thousand Faces▶
Marlon Brando
The Meateater
Merton of the Movies
My Favorite Year▶
My Wicked, Wicked Ways
The Oscar
Oscar's Greatest Moments:
  1971-1991
Overexposed
The Perils of Pauline
Play It Again, Sam▶
The Player▶
Power, Passion & Murder
The Purple Rose of Cairo▶
Queenie
Rainbow
Rascal Dazzle
Rita Hayworth: The Love
  Goddess
Rock Hudson's Home Movies
Sinatra
Sophia Loren: Her Own Story
Superstar: The Life and Times
  of Andy Warhol▶
Targets▶
That's Entertainment
That's Entertainment, Part 2
That's Entertainment 3
Users
Valentino
Veronika Voss▶
W.C. Fields: Flask of Fields
What Ever Happened to Baby
  Jane?▶
White Hot: The Mysterious
  Murder of Thelma Todd
Wild, Wild World of Jayne
  Mansfield

Work/Police▶

Filmmaking

*see also At the Movies;
Behind the Scenes*

Abbott and Costello Meet the
  Keystone Kops
The Adjuster
An Almost Perfect Affair
Barton Fink▶
Big Show
Black Cat
Bloodbath in Psycho Town
Body Chemistry 3: Point of
  Seduction
Bombay Talkie
Cass
Children Shouldn't Play with
  Dead Things
Chuck Amuck: The Movie
Ciao Federico! Fellini Directs
  Satyricon
Comment Ca Va?
Contempt▶
The Cool Surface
Dangerous Game
David Holzman's Diary▶
Day for Night▶
Dead Silence
Dracula: A Cinematic
  Scrapbook
Drifting
Dubeat-E-O
Ed Wood
84 Charlie Mopic▶
Elsa, Elsa
Elvis in Hollywood▶
F/X 2: The Deadly Art of
  Illusion
Final Cut
Finnegan's Wake
Frankenstein: A Cinematic
  Scrapbook
Good Morning, Babylon▶
Hearts of Darkness: A
  Filmmaker's Apocalypse▶
Hi, Mom!▶
Hollywood Chaos
Hollywood Mystery
The Horror of It All
The House of Seven Corpses
How to Make a Monster
I'll Do Anything
In a Moment of Passion
Intervista▶
Invasion Force
Iron Cowboy
Island of Blood
It's All True
Jacquot
Kamikaze Hearts
The King of the Kickboxers
The Last Porno Flick
Les Violons du Bal
The Making of "A Brief
  History of Time"
The Making of a Legend:
  "Gone With the Wind"
A Man, a Woman and a Killer
A Man Like Eva▶
The Mirror Crack'd
Mistress
My Dream is Yours
Nightmare in Blood
Nightmare in Wax
Notes for an African Orestes
Nudity Required
On an Island with You
Once in Paris...
The Pickle
Pictures
The Player▶
The Red Raven Kiss-Off
Secret File of Hollywood
Silent Motive
A Slave of Love▶
Special Effects
Stand-In
The Stunt Man▶
Sullivan's Travels▶
The Swap
Sweet Liberty

Two Weeks in Another Town
Understudy: The Graveyard
  Shift 2
Visions of Light: The Art of
  Cinematography▶
White Hunter, Black Heart▶
The Wizard of Speed and
  Time
You Must Remember This

Firemen

see also Fires

Always
Backdraft
Club Paradise
Fahrenheit 451▶
Fire Alarm
Fireballs
Firehouse
The Fireman
The Firemen's Ball▶
Hellfighters
Inferno in Paradise
Roxanne▶
Trespass
Turk 182!

Fires

*see also Disaster Flicks;
Firemen*

Always
Backdraft
Burning Rage
City on Fire
The Cremators
Dinosaurus!
Don't Go in the House
Endless Love
Erendira
Fire
Fire Alarm
Firehead
The Fireman
Firestarter
The Flaming Urge
Frankenstein▶
In Old Chicago▶
Island of the Burning Doomed
The Michigan Kid
Mighty Joe Young
Nice Girls Don't Explode
Oil
Pretty Poison▶
Pyrates
Quest for Fire▶
Save the Tiger▶
Sounds of Silence
Speeding Up Time
Spontaneous Combustion
Terror on the 40th Floor
Ticks
The Towering Inferno
The Triangle Factory Fire
  Scandal
Wilder Napalm

Flight

see Airborne

Flower Children

see also Boomer Reunions

Adam at 6 A.M.
Alice's Restaurant
American Blue Note
Angels Hard as They Come
Awakenings of the Beast
Best Enemies
Best Revenge
The Big Chill▶
The Big Fix▶
Blast-Off Girls
Bob & Carol & Ted & Alice
Born on the Fourth of July▶
Children Shouldn't Play with
  Dead Things
The Compleat Beatles▶
Conspiracy: The Trial of the
  Chicago Eight▶
The Crimson Cult
Dogfight▶

The Doors
Dreamwood▶
Dynamite Chicken
Easy Rider▶
Even Cowgirls Get the Blues
Flashback▶
Four Friends▶
Free Grass
Fritz the Cat▶
Gimme Shelter
The Glory Stompers
Greetings▶
Hair▶
Head▶
Help Wanted Female
High Hopes▶
I Drink Your Blood
I Love You, Alice B. Toklas
Mantis in Lace
Married to It
The Mod Squad
More
More American Graffiti
Off Limits
Out
Petit Con
Property
Psych-Out
Psychedelic Fever
Rainbow Bridge
The Rebel Set
Revolution
R.P.M.* (*Revolutions Per
  Minute)
Rude Awakening
The Sandpiper
Satan's Sadists
Sea Devils
Second Thoughts
Slashed Dreams
A Small Circle of Friends
The Snake People
The Speed Lovers
The Strawberry Statement
There's a Girl in My Soup
Thumb Tripping
The Trip
Where Angels Go, Trouble
  Follows
Where the Eagle Flies
Who'll Stop the Rain?▶
Wild in the Streets
Woodstock▶
Yellow Submarine▶

Flying Saucers

*see Alien Beings—Benign;
Alien Beings—Vicious;
Space Operas*

Folklore & Mythology

Antonio Das Mortes
Atlantis, the Lost Continent
Atlas in the Land of the
  Cyclops
The Ballad of Paul Bunyan
Black Orpheus▶
Candyman
Clash of the Titans
Colossus and the Amazon
  Queen
Crossroads
Darby O'Gill & the Little
  People▶
Disney's Storybook Classics
Donkey Skin▶
Down to Earth
Dreamwood▶
Early Russian Cinema, Vol. 2:
  Folklore & Legend
Erik the Viking
Faust▶
Field of Dreams▶
The Fool Killer
Force on Thunder Mountain
Freddie as F.R.O.7
The Fury of Hercules
The Giant of Marathon
The Giant of Metropolis
The Giants of Thessaly

Golden Voyage of Sinbad
Goliath Against the Giants
Goliath and the Barbarians
Goliath and the Dragon
Goliath and the Sins of
  Babylon
The Gorgon
Grendel, Grendel, Grendel
Hercules
Hercules 2
Hercules Against the Moon
  Men
Hercules and the Captive
  Women
Hercules in the Haunted World
Hercules Unchained
Into the West▶
Invincible Gladiators
Invitation to the Dance
Iphigenia▶
Jason and the Argonauts▶
Johnny Appleseed
Kismet▶
Kriemhilde's Revenge▶
The Legend of Sleepy Hollow
The Legend of Suram
  Fortress
Leprechaun 2
Life on a String
The Loves of Hercules
Medea
Merlin and the Sword
Messalina vs. the Son of
  Hercules
A Midsummer Night's Dream
Monty Python and the Holy
  Grail▶
My Darlin' Clementine
Pancho Villa Returns
Pathfinder▶
Pecos Bill
Phedre
Phoenix
Rudyard Kipling's Classic
  Stories
The Secret of Navajo Cave
The Secret of the Loch
Siegfried▶
Son of Samson
Sons of Hercules in the Land
  of Darkness
Terror of Rome Against the
  Son of Hercules
Thor and the Amazon Women
Ulysses
Ursus in the Valley of the
  Lions
The Wonderful World of the
  Brothers Grimm
Young Aphrodites
Zvenigora▶

Food

see Edibles

Football

Ace Ventura: Pet Detective
All the Right Moves
Backfield in Motion
The Best of Times
Black Sunday
Brian's Song▶
Cheering Section
Cheerleaders' Wild Weekend
Diner▶
The Dropkick▶
Easy Living
Everybody's All American
First & Ten
First & Ten: The Team Scores
  Again
The Freshman▶
The Galloping Ghost
Good News
Grambling's White Tiger
Gus
Harmon of Michigan
Heaven Can Wait▶
Hold 'Em Jail
Horse Feathers▶
Jim Thorpe: All American

Football

Johnny Be Good
Knute Rockne: All American▶
The Last Boy Scout
Last Game
The Longest Yard
Navy Blue and Gold
Necessary Roughness
North Dallas Forty▶
One Night Only
Paper Lion
The Program
Quarterback Princess
Roberta▶
Rudy
School Ties▶
Semi-Tough
The Spirit of West Point
Trouble Along the Way
Two Minute Warning
Wildcats

Foreign Intrigue
see also Spies & Espionage

Above Suspicion▶
Ambassador Bill
American Roulette
Battle Beneath the Earth
Bulldog Drummond at Bay
Call Him Mr. Shatter
Catch Me a Spy
Chinese Boxes
Chinese Web
Cover-Up
The Day of the Jackal▶
Deadly Alliance
Defense Play
The Destructors
Devil Wears White
Diamonds are Forever▶
Diplomatic Courier▶
Dr. No▶
The Dogs of War
Don't Drink the Water
The Eiger Sanction
An Englishman Abroad▶
Enigma
The Equalizer: Memories of Manon
Erik
Escapade in Florence
Escape from the KGB
Escape to Love
Escape to the Sun
The Executioner
The Experts
Exposed
Exposure
Eye of the Needle
Federal Agent
Foreign Correspondent▶
The Fourth Protocol▶
A Global Affair
Gunpowder
Half Moon Street
The Human Factor
The Hunt for Red October▶
Jaguar Lives
Jumpin' Jack Flash
The Key to Rebecca
La Passante▶
Lady L
License to Kill▶
The Little Drummer Girl▶
Man from Headquarters
The Man Who Knew Too Much▶
The Man Who Knew Too Much
Marathon Man▶
The Odessa File
Overthrow
Panama Hattie
Postmark for Danger
Puzzle
Reilly: Ace of Spies▶
Return of the Man from U.N.C.L.E.
Return of the Tall Blond Man With One Black Shoe
Rollover
The Russia House

Saigon: Year of the Cat
Sebastian
The Spy Who Came in from the Cold▶
Strangers
Sweet Country
They Met in Bombay
The Third Man▶
Tokyo Joe
Topaz▶
Torn Curtain
Undeclared War
Windmills of the Gods

Frame-Ups

Abbott & Costello Meet the Invisible Man▶
Another Pair of Aces: Three of a Kind▶
Backfire
Bedroom Eyes
Below the Deadline
Best Revenge
Big Score
The Big Sweat
The Big Switch
Blind Man's Bluff
The Blum Affair
Breakdown
Buried Alive
Caged Fear
Caught in the Act
Class of Fear
Consenting Adults
Cop-Out
Covered Wagon Days
Cry of the Black Wolves
Cry Vengeance
Dancing Man
Deadline at Dawn
Death Sentence
The Disappearance of Christina
Escape from DS-3
The Fighting Rookie
Fingerprints Don't Lie
Fleshtone
Framed
Free to Love
The Fugitive▶
Get Rita
The Ghost Camera
The Gilded Cage
Girls in Prison
Hi-Jacked
The Inner Circle
An Innocent Man
Kentucky Blue Streak
Killing 'em Softly
The Lady Confesses
Lady in the Death House
Left for Dead
The Life & Times of the Chocolate Killer
The Life of Emile Zola▶
Linda
Louisiana Purchase
Macon County Line
Man Outside
The Manhunt
The Mighty Quinn
Mr. Wise Guy
Murder▶
Murphy's Law
My Cousin Vinny▶
Nasty Hero
Nightmare in Badham County
No Escape, No Return
Now and Forever
The Obsessed
Off the Wall
Prime Suspect
Prison Break
Rubdown
Shakes the Clown
The Sphinx
Stir Crazy
Sunset Heat
Suspended Alibi
Tank
Today I Hang

Voulez-Vous Danser Avec Moi?
White Fire
The Wrong Man

France

The Ambassador's Daughter
An American in Paris▶
And Soon the Darkness
Arch of Triumph
Arch of Triumph
Bedtime Story
Borsalino▶
Breathless▶
Buffet Froid▶
Can-Can
Captain Scarlett
Carnival in Flanders▶
Carve Her Name with Pride
Catherine & Co.
Cesar▶
Charade▶
Cloud Waltzing
Danton▶
Desiree
Diane
Dirty Rotten Scoundrels▶
Dubarry
The Duellists▶
The Elusive Corporal▶
The Fatal Image
The Foreman Went to France
Frantic▶
French Connection 2▶
French Intrigue
The French Lesson
French Postcards
The French Woman
Gentlemen Prefer Blondes▶
Gigi▶
Harvest▶
Heart of a Nation▶
Is Paris Burning?▶
Joan of Paris▶
Killer Tomatoes Eat France
Kings Go Forth
La Marseillaise▶
La Passante▶
La Vie de Boheme▶
The Lacemaker▶
Ladies Man
Lafayette Escadrille
The Last Metro▶
Last Tango in Paris▶
The Last Time I Saw Paris
The Last Train
Le Bal▶
Le Complot▶
Le Corbeau▶
Le Gendarme de Saint-Tropez
Le Joli Mai
Le Million▶
Les Miserables▶
The Life of Emile Zola▶
The Longest Day▶
Lovely to Look At▶
Loves & Times of Scaramouche
Madame Bovary▶
Mademoiselle Fifi
The Man in the Iron Mask▶
Man on the Eiffel Tower▶
Maniac
Manon
Marie Antoinette
Marius▶
May Fools▶
Mr. Klein▶
The Moderns▶
Monkeys, Go Home!
Monsieur Beaucaire
Monsieur Verdoux▶
The Moonraker
Moulin Rouge▶
The Mountain
My Father's Glory▶
Napoleon▶
Napoleon
A New Kind of Love
Paths of Glory▶
Piaf
Prisoner of Honor▶

The Private Affairs of Bel Ami▶
Quality Street
Quatorze Juliet
Reign of Terror
Reunion in France
Round Midnight▶
The Rules of the Game▶
Saint Joan
The Scarlet Pimpernel▶
Silk Stockings▶
Spy of Napoleon
A Tale of Two Cities▶
A Tale of Two Cities
Theatre of Death
This Land is Mine▶
Those Magnificent Men in Their Flying Machines▶
To Catch a Thief▶
Tropic of Cancer▶
True Colors
Until September
Uranus▶
Valmont▶
Waterloo
What Price Glory?▶
A Year in Provence▶

Friendship
see Buddies

Front Page
see also Mass Media; Shutterbugs

Absence of Malice
Act of Passion: The Lost Honor of Kathryn Beck
Action in Arabia
The Adventures of Nellie Bly
Alice in the Cities▶
All Over Town
All the President's Men▶
Ambition
American Autobahn
And Nothing But the Truth
AngKor: Cambodia Express
Another Time, Another Place
Anzio
The Average Woman
The Barcelona Kill
Barton Fink▶
The Beniker Gang
Between the Lines▶
The Big Hurt
Big News
The Big Slice
Big Town
Big Town After Dark
Blankman
Blessed Event▶
Boeing Boeing
Brenda Starr
Broadcast News▶
Broadway Melody of 1936▶
Bulldog Edition
A Bunny's Tale
Call Northside 777▶
Cambio de Cara
Caroline at Midnight
Chill Factor
The China Syndrome▶
Citizen Kane▶
City in Fear
Concrete Beat
Conexion Oriental
Continental Divide
Criminal Act
Cry Freedom
Cut and Run
Dead Connection
Deadline
Deadly Exposure
Defense of the Realm▶
Delirious
Demonstone
The Devil's Commandment
Diamond Trail
Double Cross
Double Edge
Double Exposure

Double Exposure: The Story of Margaret Bourke-White
Eternity
Everything Happens at Night▶
Eyes Behind the Stars
Eyes of a Stranger
A Face in the Fog
Far East
Father Hood
Fever Pitch
Final Extra
Finnegan Begin Again
Fit for a King
A Flash of Green
Fletch
Fletch Lives
Foreign Correspondent▶
Freeze Frame
The Front Page▶
Gentleman's Agreement▶
The Great Muppet Caper▶
Grown Ups
Headline Woman
Heads
Heat Wave▶
Her Life as a Man
Hero▶
His Girl Friday▶
Hit the Ice
Hour of Decision
The Hudsucker Proxy▶
Hue and Cry▶
Hustling▶
I Cover the Waterfront
I Love Trouble
The Image
An Inconvenient Woman
Invasion of Privacy
Istanbul
Johnny Come Lately
Journey for Margaret▶
Just One of the Guys
Keeper of the City
Kid from Not-So-Big
Kill Slade
The Killing Beach
The Killing Device
The Killing Fields▶
Killing Stone
La Dolce Vita▶
Lana in Love
Late Extra
Let 'er Go Gallegher
Lethal Charm
Libeled Lady▶
Lip Service▶
L'Odeur des Fauves
Lonelyhearts
Love is a Many-Splendored Thing
The Love Machine
Malarek
The Man Inside
Man of Iron▶
Mean Season
Meet John Doe▶
Midnight Warrior
Murder on the Campus
Murrow
Mystic Circle Murder
Natas...The Reflection
News at Eleven
Newsfront▶
Newsies
The Nightmare Years
No Time to Die
Not for Publication
Nothing Sacred▶
Novel Desires
The Odessa File
One Man Out
The Paper▶
Paper Lion
Paralyzed
The Payoff
The Pelican Brief
Perfect
The Philadelphia Story▶
Platinum Blonde▶
The Ploughman's Lunch▶
Primary Motive
Private Investigations

Profile
Qui Etes Vous, Mr. Sorge?
Reckless Disregard
Resurrection of Zachary Wheeler
Revenge of the Radioactive Reporter
Riding on Air
Roman Holiday▶
The Rumor Mill
Safari 3000
Salome, Where She Danced
Salvador▶
The Secrets of Wu Sin
Sex and the Single Girl
Sex Through a Window
Shock Corridor▶
Short Fuse
Shriek in the Night
Shy People▶
Somewhere I'll Find You▶
Soul Patrol
Special Bulletin▶
Speed Reporter
Star Reporter
Stavisky▶
Stay Tuned for Murder
Straight Talk
The Strange Love of Molly Louvain
Stranger on the Third Floor▶
Street Smart
Sucker Money
Sweet Rosie O'Grady
Sweet Smell of Success▶
Switching Channels
Tainted Blood
Teacher's Pet▶
That Lucky Touch
They Got Me Covered
The Thirteenth Man
Thirteen Reunion
Those Glory, Glory Days
Three O'Clock High
Tomorrow at Seven
Too Hot to Handle▶
Tough Assignment
Transylvania 6-5000
Under Fire▶
The Underworld Story
Unexplained Laughter
Up Your Alley
Where the Buffalo Roam
While the City Sleeps▶
Whispering City▶
Without Love
Woman Condemned
Woman of the Year▶
A World Apart▶
The World Gone Mad
The Year of Living Dangerously▶

Fugitives

see also Lovers on the Lam
Agent on Ice
Bad Girls
Bail Jumper
Ball of Fire▶
Ballad of Gregorio Cortez▶
Bandits of Orgosolo
Bed & Breakfast
The Big Fix▶
The Bloody Tattoo
Bobbie Jo and the Outlaw
The Boldest Job in the West
Brannigan
Breathless
Butch and Sundance: The Early Days
Butch Cassidy and the Sundance Kid▶
Captured in Chinatown
The Chase
Danger: Diabolik
Dead Easy
The Deserters
Desperate
Eddie Macon's Run
Escape 2000
Father Hood

Free Grass
The Fugitive▶
The Fugitive: Premiere Episode
The Fugitive: The Final Episode
Hard Knocks
Hold Me, Thrill Me, Kiss Me
I Died a Thousand Times
I Met a Murderer
The Jesus Trip
Jungle Inferno
Keeping Track
Kiss of Death
Klondike Annie
Le Doulos▶
Leather Jackets
Liberators
Loners
The Love Flower
The Man Upstairs
Miami Cops
Moving Target
Moving Violation
Northwest Trail
Nowhere to Hide
On the Run
One Away
The Outlaw and His Wife
Outlaw Riders
Paris Express
A Perfect World
Posse▶
The Pursuit of D.B. Cooper
The Red Half-Breed
Rider on the Rain▶
Rough Cut
The Savage Woman
Sea Devils
Shallow Grave
Shoot to Kill▶
Simple Men▶
Slate, Wyn & Me
Sonny and Jed
Stray Dog▶
Strike Back
Teenage Bonnie & Klepto Clyde
Thunder County
Time is Running Out
The Way Out
The Wrong Man

Funerals

see also Death & the Afterlife
The Addams Family
The Big Chill▶
Four Weddings and a Funeral▶
The Funeral▶
Funeral Home
Gardens of Stone
Harold and Maude▶
Heathers▶
Mr. Saturday Night
My Girl
My Girl 2▶
Only the Lonely
Sleepless in Seattle▶
Terms of Endearment▶
What's Eating Gilbert Grape▶

Gambling

see also Viva Las Vegas!
Aces and Eights
Action for Slander
Any Number Can Play
Atlantic City▶
A Big Hand for the Little Lady
Big Town
A Billion for Boris
Birds & the Bees
Bitter Sweet
Bob le Flambeur▶
Casino
Catch Me...If You Can
The Cheaters
The Cincinnati Kid
Cockfighter▶
The Color of Money▶

Dead Lucky
Deadly Impact
Diamonds are Forever▶
Dona Flor and Her Two Husbands▶
Double Dynamite
Draw!
The Duchess and the Dirtwater Fox
Duke of the Derby
Easy Money
Eight Men Out▶
El Gallo de Oro
Family Prayers
Fever Pitch
Firepower
Five Card Stud
Flame of the Barbary Coast
Flame of the Islands
The Flamingo Kid▶
Force of Evil▶
Frankie and Johnny
The Gamble
Gamble on Love
The Gambler▶
The Gambler & the Lady
The Gambler Returns: The Luck of the Draw
Gilda▶
Glory Years
Golden Rendezvous
The Great Mike
Gun Crazy
Guys and Dolls▶
Half a Lifetime
The Harder They Fall▶
Havana
Hell's Angels '69
Here Come the Marines
Honeymoon in Vegas
The Honeymoon Machine
House of Games▶
Household Saints▶
Huck and the King of Hearts
In Like Flint
Indecent Proposal
Inn of Temptation
Inside Out
Jinxed
Kenny Rogers as the Gambler
Kenny Rogers as the Gambler, Part 2: The Adventure Continues
Kenny Rogers as the Gambler, Part 3: The Legend Continues
Lady for a Night
Lady from Louisiana
Las Vegas Hillbillys
Las Vegas Lady
The Las Vegas Story
Las Vegas Weekend
Le Million▶
The Lemon Drop Kid
Let It Ride
Let's Do It Again
Let's Make it Legal
Little Miss Marker▶
Little Miss Marker
Little Vegas
Living to Die
Lookin' to Get Out
Lost in America▶
Manhattan Melodrama▶
The Marrying Man
Maverick
McCabe & Mrs. Miller▶
Meet Me in Las Vegas
Melodie en Sous-Sol
Mr. Lucky▶
Mother and Son
Murderers' Row
The Music of Chance
My Darling Clementine▶
My Little Chickadee▶
Ninja, the Violent Sorcerer
No Man of Her Own
Oklahoma Kid▶
Order to Kill
Our Man Flint
Paradise Island
Pink Cadillac

Pleasure Palace
Poker Alice
The Queen of Spades▶
Quintet
Rain Man▶
Riders of the Range
Rimfire
The Roaring Twenties▶
Robbery
The Rocking Horse Winner
The Ruggles of Red Gap▶
Say Yes!
The Shadow Man
The Shanghai Gesture
Shoot
Silver Queen
Sno-Line
Song of the Thin Man
Sorrowful Jones
The Squeeze
Stacy's Knights
The Sting▶
Strike It Rich
Support Your Local Sheriff▶
Swing Time▶
Tall Story
Talons of the Eagle
Tax Season
Taxi Dancers
Tennessee's Partner
Thief
Things Change▶
This is a Hijack
Thoroughbreds Don't Cry
Three Men on a Horse▶
Trading Places
Uphill All the Way
Uptown Saturday Night
The Vegas Strip Wars
Walking Tall
Wanda Nevada
Welcome to 18
The Westerner▶
Wheel of Fortune
Who's Got the Action?

Game Shows

Champagne for Caesar▶
Deathrow Gameshow
For Love or Money
Prize of Peril
Queen for a Day
The Running Man
Shock Treatment

Gangs

see also Crime & Criminals; Organized Crime
Abduction of St. Anne
Al Capone▶
Alien Private Eye
All Dogs Go to Heaven
Alley Cat
Alvin Rides Again
American Me▶
Angel Town
Angels Die Hard
Apache Woman
Assassin
Assault on Precinct 13▶
Baby Face Morgan
Bad Bunch
Bad Guys
Ballbuster
Behave Yourself!
Bells of Death
A Better Tomorrow
A Better Tomorrow, Part 2
Big Bad Mama
Big Bad Mama 2
The Big Brawl
Black Bikers from Hell
Black Caesar
The Black Cobra
Black Gestapo
Blood In...Blood Out: Bound by Honor
The Bloody Brood
Bloody Mama
Blue

Blues Busters
Bonnie & Clyde▶
Borderline
Borsalino▶
Boss of Big Town
Boulevard Nights
Bowery Blitzkrieg
Boyz N the Hood▶
Breaking Loose
Bring Me the Head of Alfredo Garcia
Broadway Danny Rose▶
The Bronx War
Brother Orchid▶
Buckeye and Blue
Buddy Buddy
Bulldog Drummond's Bride
Bulldog Edition
Bulldog Jack▶
Bullets or Ballots▶
Cartouche▶
Chains
Chains of Gold
The Chase
China Girl
China O'Brien
Chrome and Hot Leather
Chrome Hearts
City Heat
Class of 1984
Class of 1999
Class of 1999 2: The Substitute
Clipped Wings
Code of Silence
Colors▶
Commando Squad
The Concentratin' Kid
Confidential
Contraband
Cookie
Cop on Blue Jeans
Corruption
Corsair
Cosh Boy
The Cross & the Switchblade
Cruisin' High
Cry of a Prostitute: Love Kills
Cry Terror
Danger Zone
Danger Zone 2
Dangerous Mission
Dark Rider
Darktown Strutters
The Day It Came to Earth
Dead End City
Deadly Encounter▶
Deadly Revenge
Defenders of the Law
Defiance
Defiant
Delta Fox
Designing Woman▶
Devil's Angels
Diamante, Oro y Amor
Diamonds on Wheels
Dick Tracy vs. Cueball
Dillinger▶
Dillinger
Dirt Gang
Dirty Laundry
Disorganized Crime
Diva▶
The Divine Enforcer
Dixie Jamboree
The Doberman Gang
The Dog Who Stopped the War
The Don is Dead
Each Dawn I Die
East L.A. Warriors
East Side Kids
The Education of Sonny Carson
El Callao
Emil and the Detective
Enemy Territory
The Enforcer
Escape from the Bronx
Every Which Way But Loose
Exterminator
Eye of the Tiger

Gangs

Fear in the City
The Final Alliance
Force of Evil
Forced Vengeance
Forever, Lulu
Four Deuces
Four Jacks and a Jill
Foxy Brown
Full Eclipse
''G'' Men▶
The Gambler & the Lady
Gambler's Choice
Game of Death
Gang Bullets
Gang Wars
Gangbusters
The Gangster
Gangster Wars
Gangway
The George McKenna Story
Ghetto Blaster
The Ghost and the Guest
Ghost Chasers
Gimme Shelter
Girls of the White Orchid
The Glory Stompers
Golden Lady
The Golden Triangle
Gone are the Days
Goodfellas▶
The Great Mike
The Great Skycopter Rescue
The Grissom Gang▶
The Gumshoe Kid
Gun Girls
The Gunrunner
Guns Don't Argue
Hard-Boiled Mahoney
Harley
Heartbreaker
Heat Street
Hell on Frisco Bay
Hellcats
High Ballin'
High Sierra▶
Hit Men
Hitz
Homeboy
Homeboys
Hoodlum Empire
I Died a Thousand Times
I, Mobster
I'd Give My Life
Impulse
Inside the Law
Jinxed
Johnny Apollo
Johnny Dangerously
Just William's Luck
Kansas City Massacre
Key Largo▶
Killer Dill
King Boxer
The King of the Roaring '20s:
    The Story of Arnold
    Rothstein
Knights of the City
L.A. Bad
La Balance▶
La Choca
L.A. Gangs Rising
Lady from Nowhere
Lady in a Cage▶
Lady in Red
Lady Killer▶
Last Flight to Hell
The Last Ride of the Dalton
    Gang
The Last Riders
Law of the Underworld
Leather Jackets
Lepke
Lethal Games
Lethal Obsession
Little Dragons
Little Laura & Big John
The Longshot
The Lost Capone▶
Love Me or Leave Me▶
Lucky Luciano
Ma Barker's Killer Brood
Machine Gun Kelly

Manhattan Merry-Go-Round
Marked Woman▶
The Masters of Menace
Master's Revenge
Maverick Queen
Meet the Mob
Melvin Purvis: G-Man
Men of Respect
Menace II Society▶
The Meteor Man
Mi Vida Loca
Midnight
Miller's Crossing▶
Million Dollar Kid
Miracle in Harlem
Mr. Majestyk
Mob Boss
Mob Story
Mob War
Mobsters
The Monster and the Stripper
Motorcycle Squad
My Samurai
Mystery Date
The Naked Angels
Nashville Beat
'Neath Brooklyn Bridge
The Neon Empire
Never a Dull Moment
Never Let Go
Never Love a Stranger
The New Kids
99 & 44/100 Dead
Ninja Brothers of Blood
Nitti: The Enforcer
No Trace
The Noose Hangs High▶
The Outsiders
Paco
Paradise in Harlem
Parole, Inc.
Party Girl▶
The Payoff
Peacekillers
Performance▶
Petrified Forest▶
Pickup on South Street▶
Pierrot le Fou▶
Play Murder for Me
Postmark for Danger/
    Quicksand
The Power of the Ninjitsu
Prime Cut
The Prime Time
Prize Fighter
Public Enemy▶
Pulp
Punk Vacation
Quatorze Juliet
The Racket▶
The Racketeer
Rapid Fire
Renegades
Return of the Dragon
Return of the Rebels
Return of the Tiger
Revenge
Revenge of the Ninja
Revolt of the Dragon
Ricco
Riot Squad
The Rise and Fall of Legs
    Diamond
The Ritz▶
The Roaring Twenties▶
Robin and the Seven Hoods
Rooftops
Rumble Fish▶
The St. Valentine's Day
    Massacre
Satan's Sadists
The Savage Seven
Scared Stiff▶
Scarface▶
The Sea Serpent
Second Chance
The Set-Up▶
Sexton Blake and the Hooded
    Terror
Shaft▶
Shark Hunter
She's Back

Shining Star
Shoot the Piano Player▶
Showdown
Showdown in Little Tokyo
Sidewalks of New York
Smart Alecks
SnakeEater 3: His Law
Sno-Line
Some Like It Hot▶
South Central
Speedy▶
Spike of Bensonhurst
Spook Busters
Star Reporter
Stavisky▶
Sticky Fingers
Stingray
Stone Cold
Straight Line
Street Crimes
Street Hitz
Street Knight
Street Soldiers
Street Warriors
Street Warriors, Part 2
The Street with No Name▶
The Streets of L.A.
Sunnyside
The Sun's Burial▶
T-Bird Gang
Tattoo Connection
Tattooed Hit Man
Teenage Gang Debs
Teenage Wolfpack
This Time I'll Make You Rich
Timber Queen
The Tip-Off
Tongs: An American
    Nightmare
Too Late for Tears▶
Topaze▶
Tough Assignment
Tough Kid
Tough to Handle
Tropical Snow
Trouble in Store
Truck Stop Women
True Believer
True Blood
Tuff Turf
Two to Tango
Underground Terror
The Underworld Story
Variety
Vengeance
Verne Miller
Vietnam, Texas
Violent Professionals
The Violent Years
The Virginia Hill Story
Wanderers▶
The Warriors
West Side Story▶
When Gangland Strikes
The Wild One▶
Wilding
The Wolves▶
Wonder Man
Wonderland▶
The Wrong Arm of the Law▶
The Yakuza
Year of the Dragon
Young Warriors

Gender Bending

see also *Homosexuality;*
Role Reversal
Abroad with Two Yanks
At War with the Army
Auntie
Blue Murder at St. Trinian's▶
Boy! What a Girl
The Crying Game▶
The Damned
Desperate Living
Dressed to Kill
Ed Wood
Forever Mary▶
Glen or Glenda
Hairspray▶
Happily Ever After
Her Life as a Man

He's My Girl
I Wanna Be a Beauty Queen
I Want What I Want
I Was a Male War Bride▶
Just One of the Girls
La Cage aux Folles▶
La Cage aux Folles 2
La Cage aux Folles 3: The
    Wedding
Law of Desire▶
Lust in the Dust▶
M. Butterfly
Mascara
Mutant on the Bounty
My Son, the Vampire
Myra Breckinridge
The Mystery of Alexina
The Newlydeads
Nuns on the Run
Old Mother Riley's Ghosts
Outrageous!▶
Paris is Burning▶
Pink Flamingos
Polyester
Psycho▶
The Rocky Horror Picture
    Show▶
Shadey
The Silence of the Lambs▶
Some Like It Hot▶
Sonny Boy
Tootsie▶
Torch Song Trilogy
Trash
Victor/Victoria▶
Wild Party
Wild, Wild World of Jayne
    Mansfield
The Woman Inside
The World According to
    Garp▶

Generation X

Bodies, Rest & Motion
Reality Bites
S.F.W.
Singles▶
Slacker▶

Genetics

see also *Mad Scientists;*
Metamorphosis
The Boys from Brazil
The Fly▶
The Fly 2
Forbidden World
Metamorphosis: The Alien
    Factor
Rats
Tomcat: Dangerous Desires

Genies

Aladdin▶
Aladdin and His Wonderful
    Lamp
Bernard and the Genie
Miracle Beach
The Outing
Priceless Beauty
The Thief of Baghdad▶
Thief of Baghdad▶
The Thief of Baghdad
Wildest Dreams
Wishman
The Wonders of Aladdin

Genre Spoofs

see also *Satire & Parody*
The Adventures of
    Hairbreadth Harry
Airplane!▶
Airplane 2: The Sequel
All Through the Night▶
All You Need Is Cash▶
April Fool's Day
Based on an Untrue Story
Big Bus
The Big Crimewave
Blazing Saddles▶

Bloodbath at the House of
    Death
Bordello
Bugsy Malone
Casino Royale
Closet Cases of the Nerd Kind
Code Name: Chaos
Creature from the Haunted
    Sea
Dead Men Don't Wear Plaid
Dragnet
Drive-In
Fatal Instinct
Ferocious Female Freedom
    Fighters
Flesh Gordon
Frankenstein General Hospital
Frankenstein's Great Aunt
    Tillie
Galactic Gigolo
Galaxina
Ganjasaurus Rex
Get Crazy
Ghoul School
Grunt! The Wrestling Movie
Hell Comes to Frogtown
High Anxiety
The Hollywood Detective
Hollywood Harry
Hot Shots!▶
Hot Shots! Part Deux
The Hound of the Baskervilles
Hysterical
I'm Gonna Git You Sucka▶
J-Men Forever!▶
Jake Speed
Jet Benny Show
Kentucky Fried Movie▶
Last Action Hero
Lust in the Dust▶
The Man with Two Brains▶
Mob Boss
Monster in the Closet
Monty Python and the Holy
    Grail▶
Murder by Death
Mutant on the Bounty
The Naked Gun: From the
    Files of Police Squad▶
Naked Gun 33 1/3: The Final
    Insult
Naked Gun 2 1/2: The Smell
    of Fear
National Lampoon's Loaded
    Weapon 1
99 & 44/100 Dead
Once Bitten
Pandemonium
A Perfect Little Murder
Phantom of the Paradise
The Pink Chiquitas
Repossessed
Return of Captain Invincible
The Return of Spinal Tap
Ricky 1
Robin Hood: Men in Tights
Rustler's Rhapsody
Saturday the 14th
Saturday the 14th Strikes
    Back
Soapdish▶
Spaceballs
Spaceship
Strange Invaders▶
The Stuff
Supersonic Man
Support Your Local
    Gunfighter▶
Support Your Local Sheriff▶
Surf Ninjas
Teenage Exorcist
Terror Eyes
That Man from Rio
They Call Me Bruce?
They Call Me Trinity
They Live
They Still Call Me Bruce
This is Spinal Tap▶
Three Amigos
Too Many Crooks
Top Secret!▶
Transylvania 6-5000

Trinity is Still My Name
2069: A Sex Odyssey
UHF
Union City
Unmasked Part 25
The Video Dead
Video Violence
Video Violence Part 2...The
 Exploitation!
The Villain
Voyage of the Rock Aliens
Wacko
Werewolf of Washington
Who Framed Roger Rabbit?▶
Young Frankenstein▶
The Zany Adventures of
 Robin Hood

Germany

Ali: Fear Eats the Soul▶
Alice in the Cities▶
Backbeat▶
The Battle of Russia
Berlin Alexanderplatz▶
The Blue Angel▶
Carnival Story
The Damned
The Desert Fox▶
Die Grosse Freiheit Nr. 7
Dr. Mabuse the Gambler▶
Faraway, So Close!▶
Geheimakte WB1
G.I. Blues
Hitler: The Last Ten Days
Isn't Life Wonderful▶
Jud Suess▶
Kapo▶
Knife in the Head
The Marriage of Maria Braun▶
Mein Kampf
Mephisto▶
The Merchant of Four
 Seasons▶
Mr. Emmanuel
The Odessa File
Once Upon a Honeymoon
Periphery
Porcile
Prelude to War
The Sound of Music▶
SS Girls
The Stationmaster's Wife
Strikeback
Swing Kids
They Were So Young
Three Comrades▶
Tiefland
Triumph of the Will
Wings of Desire▶
Woyzeck▶

Ghosts, Ghouls, &
Goblins

*see also Death & the
 Afterlife; Demons &
 Wizards; Occult*
Amazing Mr. Blunden
Beetlejuice▶
Beyond Tomorrow
Blondie Has Trouble
The Canterville Ghost
The Changeling
Children Shouldn't Play with
 Dead Things
Cold Sweat
Curse of the Blue Lights
Death Dreams
Death Magic
Dona Flor and Her Two
 Husbands▶
The Empire of Passion▶
Encounter with the Unknown
Feet Foremost
The Fog
Forever: A Ghost of a Love
 Story
The Forgotten One
The Gate
Ghost▶
The Ghost Breakers▶
Ghost Dad

The Ghost Goes West▶
Ghost of Hanley House
The Ghost of Rashmon Hall
Ghost Rider
Ghost Ship
Ghost Story
Ghostbusters▶
Ghostbusters 2
Ghosts of Berkeley Square
The Ghoul
The Green Man▶
The Haunting of Barney
 Palmer
Heart and Souls
High Spirits
Hollywood's New Blood
The House of Dies Drear
House Where Evil Dwells
In the Realm of Passion▶
Kwaidan▶
Last Reunion
Lurking Fear
The Midnight Phantom
The Mummy's Ghost
My Friend Walter
Mystic Circle Murder
No End
O'Hara's Wife
The Phantom
Poltergeist▶
Poltergeist 2: The Other Side
Poltergeist 3
The Princess and the Goblin
Revenge of the Red Baron
Rouge
Shadow Dancing
Silent Tongue
Somewhere Tomorrow
Soultaker
The Speed Spook
The Supernaturals
Sylvia and the Phantom
13 Ghosts
The Time of Their Lives
Topper▶
Topper Returns▶
Topper Takes a Trip▶
Twice Dead
Ugetsu▶
The Uninvited▶
Visitor from the Grave
The Visitors
The Watcher in the Woods
Woman in Black

Giants

*see also Monsters,
 General*
The Amazing Colossal Man
Boggy Creek II
Bride of the Monster
Cyclops
Dr. Cyclops
Giant from the Unknown
Godzilla vs. Megalon
Humongous
Kronos
The Mysterians
The Phantom Planet
The Princess Bride▶
The Spy Who Loved Me
Them!▶
Village of the Giants
The War of the Colossal Beast

Gifted Children

And You Thought Your
 Parents Were Weird!
Dangerous Holiday
Dear Brigitte
Escape to Witch Mountain▶
Little Man Tate▶
On the Right Track
Real Genius▶
Rookie of the Year
Searching for Bobby Fischer▶

Gigolos

*see also Happy Hookers;
 Oldest Profession*
American Gigolo

Midnight Cowboy▶

Go Fish

*see also Deep Blue; Sea
 Critter Attack*
Alamo Bay
Around the World Under the
 Sea
Captains Courageous▶
The Day of the Dolphin
Detour to Danger
Doomwatch
A Fish Called Wanda▶
Free Willy
Grumpy Old Men▶
The Islander
It Came from Beneath the
 Sea▶
It Runs In the Family▶
Jaws▶
Jaws 2
Jaws 3
Jaws: The Revenge
Killer Fish
La Terra Trema▶
Man of Aran▶
Man's Favorite Sport?
Mr. Peabody & the Mermaid
Moby Dick▶
92 in the Shade▶
Northern Extremes
On Golden Pond▶
Orca
Riff Raff
A River Runs Through It▶
Scorpion with Two Tails
Shark Hunter
Sixteen Fathoms Deep
Tabu: A Story of the South
 Seas▶
Thunder Bay▶
The Treasure of Jamaica Reef
Up from the Depths
Wallaby Jim of the Islands
Whale for the Killing
Where the Hot Wind Blows

Going Native

The Blue Lagoon
The Bounty▶
Dances with Wolves▶
The Emerald Forest▶
Farewell to the King
Lord of the Flies▶
Lord of the Flies
A Man Called Horse▶
The Mosquito Coast
Pagan Island
Paradise
The Return of a Man Called
 Horse
Robinson Crusoe
A Stranger Among Us
The Swiss Family Robinson▶

Golf

Babe!▶
Blades
The Caddy
Caddyshack▶
Caddyshack 2
Dead Solid Perfect
Goof Balls
W.C. Fields: Flask of Fields

Good Earth

*see also Trees & Forests;
 Wilderness*
A Cry in the Wild▶
Deadly Harvest
Doctor Dolittle
Don't Change My World
A Flash of Green
Fly with the Hawk
Godzilla vs. the Smog
 Monster
The Great Adventure▶
Green Horizon
Impulse
Jonathan Livingston Seagull

Lassie: Adventures of Neeka
The Legend of Black Thunder
 Mountain
The Long Weekend
Man of Aran▶
Nothing Personal
The Overlanders
Silent Running▶
Slipstream
Spirit of the Eagle
Vanishing Prairie▶
Vanishing Wilderness
Whale for the Killing
When the North Wind Blows

Grand Hotel

see also No-Exit Motel
Ants
The Avenging Hand
Blame It on the Bellboy
Blondie Takes a Vacation
Bloody Wednesday
Bugsy▶
Crawlspace
Dirty Dancing▶
Eden
Eden 2
Eden 3
Eden 4
Fawlty Towers
For Love or Money
Girl in Black Stockings
Grand Hotel▶
The Green Man▶
Holiday Hotel
Holiday Inn▶
Hook, Line and Sinker
Hotel
Hotel du Lac
Hotel Imperial
Hotel Room
It Happened at Nightmare Inn
Mistaken Identity
Murderer in the Hotel
Mystery Train▶
A Night in Casablanca▶
The Night Porter
Nightmare on the 13th Floor
Plaza Suite▶
Psycho▶
Psycho 2
Psycho 3
The Queen of Mean
Roadside Prophets
Room Service
Rosebud Beach Hotel
Secret of the Black Trunk
Separate Tables▶
Separate Tables
The Shining
Snowball Express
Spare Parts
Sweet Lorraine▶
The Terror
Terror at Red Wolf Inn
This Property is Condemned
Weekend at the Waldorf▶
Witchery

Great Britain

see also Ireland; Scotland
Alien Prey
Amazing Mr. Blunden
American Friends
And a Nightingale Sang
Angels One Five
Anne of the Thousand Days▶
Back Home
Barry Lyndon▶
Beau Brummel▶
The Big Scam
Black Panther
The Black Windmill
Blue Jeans
Bonnie Prince Charlie
Brighton Rock▶
Bullshot
Camelot
The Charge of the Light
 Brigade

Charles & Diana: A Palace
 Divided
Chicago Joe & the Showgirl
A Chump at Oxford
The Corn is Green▶
The Courtney Affair
Cromwell
A Cry from the Streets
Danger UXB
Devotion
Diamonds on Wheels
Diana: Her True Story
Dick Turpin
Disraeli▶
Distant Voices, Still Lives▶
The Eagle Has Landed▶
Edge of the World▶
Edward and Mrs. Simpson
Elizabeth of Ladymead▶
Elizabeth, the Queen
Emmanuelle in Soho
Everybody Wins
Excalibur▶
Fame is the Spur
Fergie & Andrew: Behind
 Palace Doors
Flambards
Foreign Affairs▶
Forever and a Day▶
Four Weddings and a
 Funeral▶
Goodbye, Mr. Chips
Great Expectations: The
 Untold Story
The Great Muppet Caper▶
The Green Man▶
The Hellfire Club
High Hopes▶
The House of Eliott
The House of Secrets
How Green was My Valley▶
Invincible Mr. Disraeli
The Iron Duke
Jamaica Inn
King Ralph
The King's Thief
The Krays▶
Lady Jane▶
The Last of England▶
Lillie▶
The Lion in Winter▶
The Long Day Closes▶
The Long Good Friday▶
Lorna Doone
Love for Lydia▶
Made in Heaven
A Man for All Seasons▶
The Man in Grey▶
Mary of Scotland▶
The Mill on the Floss
Mrs. Miniver▶
The Moonraker
Murder Elite
Naked▶
The Naked Civil Servant▶
Nine Days a Queen▶
No Surrender▶
None But the Lonely Heart▶
Passport to Pimlico
Pictures
Pink Strings and Sealing Wax
Plenty
Poldark▶
A Question of Attribution
The Riddle of the Sands
Riff Raff▶
Robbery
Room to Let
Royal Wedding▶
The Ruling Class▶
Saint in London
Say Hello to Yesterday
Scandal▶
The Secret Garden▶
Secret of the Black Trunk
The Servant▶
Shadowlands▶
Silver Dream Racer
Six Wives of Henry VIII▶
Soldier in Love
Split Second
The Stick-Up

Great

That Sinking Feeling▶
Those Magnificent Men in
  Their Flying Machines▶
A Touch of Class▶
Tunes of Glory▶
A Very British Coup▶
Victoria Regina
The Virgin Queen▶
We Think the World of You▶
Wellington: The Duel Scandal
Whiskey Galore▶
The Whistle Blower▶
The White Cliffs of Dover▶
White Mischief▶
The Woman He Loved
Woman in Black
Wuthering Heights▶
Yanks
Year of the Comet▶
Young Bess▶
Young Winston▶

Great Death Scenes
Bonnie & Clyde▶
Breaker Morant▶
Bring Me the Head of Alfredo
  Garcia
Buffy the Vampire Slayer▶
Butch Cassidy and the
  Sundance Kid▶
Camille▶
The Champ
Coquette
Dangerous Liaisons▶
Dark Victory▶
Gallipoli▶
Gettysburg▶
Glory▶
Highlander▶
Highlander: The Gathering
Julius Caesar▶
Jurassic Park▶
Mimi
Monty Python and the Holy
  Grail▶
Pat Garrett & Billy the Kid▶
Public Enemy▶
Shadowlands▶
A Song to Remember▶
Valmont▶
The Wizard of Oz▶

Great Depression
see also Hard Knock Life;
  Homeless
After the Promise
All the King's Men▶
The Ballad of the Sad Cafe
Big Bad Mama
Big Bad Mama 2
Billy Bathgate
Bloody Mama
Bonnie & Clyde▶
Bound for Glory▶
Broadway Melody of 1938
Charley and the Angel
A Christmas to Remember
Dance Fools Dance▶
Dream Chasers
Eleanor & Franklin▶
Fatty Finn
Four Deuces
Fresh Horses
The Grapes of Wrath▶
The Group
Hallelujah, I'm a Bum
Hard Times▶
Hard Traveling
Homecoming: A Christmas
  Story
Honkytonk Man▶
Ironweed▶
It Happened One Night▶
The Journey of Natty Gann▶
Just Around the Corner
Kansas City Massacre
King of the Hill▶
Laurel & Hardy: Below Zero
Love on the Dole▶
Melvin Purvis: G-Man
Modern Times▶

Morning Glory▶
Of Mice and Men▶
Our Daily Bread▶
Paper Moon▶
Pennies From Heaven▶
Places in the Heart▶
Possessed
The Postman Always Rings
  Twice▶
The Postman Always Rings
  Twice
Rambling Rose▶
Reaching for the Moon
Sounder▶
Street Scene▶
Sullivan's Travels▶
The Tale of Ruby Rose▶
They Shoot Horses, Don't
  They?▶
Thieves Like Us▶
Victor/Victoria▶
Who Has Seen the Wind?
Why Shoot the Teacher?▶
Wild Hearts Can't Be Broken▶
Wildflower▶
Winter People
You Only Live Once

Great Escapes
see also Men in Prison;
  POW/MIA; War,
  General; Women in Prison
Assassination
Berlin Tunnel 21
The Big Doll House
Blood on the Mountain
Brady's Escape▶
Breakout
Butch Cassidy and the
  Sundance Kid▶
Caged Fear
The Chase
The Colditz Story
Crashout
A Day in October
Deadly Mission
The Deer Hunter▶
The Desert Tigers
Desperate
Diamonds of the Night▶
Die Hard▶
Dirty Heroes
Down by Law▶
Era Notte a Roma▶
Escape
Escape Artist▶
Escape from Alcatraz▶
Escape from Cell Block 3
Escape from Death Row
Escape from El Diablo
Escape from Fort Bravo
Escape from Galaxy Three
Escape from Hell
Escape from New York▶
Escape from Safehaven
Escape from Sobibor▶
Escape from the KGB
Escape to Love
Escape to Witch Mountain▶
Escapist
Fantastic Voyage▶
Fast Walking
Flame Over India▶
Fortress
Gang Busters
Girls in Prison
The Great Escape▶
The Great Escape 2: The
  Untold Story
The Great Train Robbery▶
Hangfire
Houdini
The Ice Runner
In Hot Pursuit
Inside Out
Iron Eagle
Jailbreakin'
La Nuit de Varennes▶
Ladyhawke▶
Leaving Normal
Les Miserables▶
Les Violons du Bal

Lonely are the Brave▶
The Long Riders▶
Macho Callahan
A Man Escaped▶
The Man Who Broke 1,000
  Chains
The Manhunt
McKenzie Break▶
McVicar
Midnight Express▶
Missing in Action
Mrs. Soffel▶
The Mole People
Murder One
The Muthers
Mysterious Island▶
Naked Youth
Night Crossing
No Escape
North by Northwest▶
Not Without My Daughter
On Wings of Eagles
One That Got Away▶
Operation Thunderbolt
Pacific Inferno
Papillon▶
Passage to Marseilles▶
A Perfect World
Prison Break
The Prize▶
Raiders of the Lost Ark▶
Raising Arizona▶
Romancing the Stone▶
Run
Runaway Train▶
Samar
The Secret War of Harry Frigg
The Seventh Cross▶
The Shining▶
Skin Game▶
The Sound of Music▶
The Spy Who Came in from
  the Cold▶
Stalag 17▶
Strange Cargo▶
Strike Back
The Sugarland Express▶
Sweet Poison
Tequila Sunrise▶
Three Days of the Condor▶
Thunder County
To Catch a Thief▶
Torn Curtain
Victory
Violent Women
Von Ryan's Express▶
Warbus
We're No Angels▶
White Nights
Women Unchained
Wooden Horse▶
Zebra in the Kitchen

Growing Older
see also Death & the
  Afterlife; Late Bloomin'
  Love
After the Rehearsal▶
Age Isn't Everything
Age Old Friends▶
Amos
Anna▶
Around the World in 80 Ways
As Young As You Feel▶
Atlantic City▶
Autumn Leaves
The Ballad of Narayama▶
*batteries not included
The Best of Times
Better Late Than Never
Camilla▶
Captain Kronos: Vampire
  Hunter▶
The Cemetery Club
The Cheyenne Social Club
Children of Nature
Chimes at Midnight▶
Choices
Citizen Kane▶
City Slickers▶
Cocoon▶
Cocoon: The Return

Come Along with Me
The Conductor
Cooperstown
Dad
Daddy Nostalgia▶
Death of a Salesman▶
Dorian Gray
Draw!
Dream a Little Dream
Dream Chasers
Driving Miss Daisy▶
Early Days
Easy Living
Eating
Ebony Tower
An Empty Bed▶
The Enchanted Forest
Family Upside Down▶
Fantasy Man
The Field▶
The Firemen's Ball▶
Folks!
Forty Carats
Foxfire▶
Getting Up and Going Home
Gin Game▶
Ginger & Fred▶
The Godfather, Part 3▶
Going in Style▶
The Golden Honeymoon
The Good Guys and the Bad
  Guys
The Goodbye People
Grace Quigley
Great Smokey Roadblock
Greedy
Grumpy Old Men▶
Hardbodies
Harry and Tonto▶
Home Free All
Home is Where the Hart is
Home to Stay
Homebodies
The Hunger
Hurry Up or I'll Be Thirty
Hush, Hush, Sweet
  Charlotte▶
I, Claudius, Vol. 7: Old King
  Log
Iron Horsemen
Kotch▶
The Last Laugh▶
Late Chrysanthemums
The Leech Woman
Lifeguard
Light Sleeper▶
Lightning Jack
Lip Service▶
The Magic Bubble
Mama Turns a Hundred▶
The Man Upstairs
Marathon
Middle Age Crazy
Miss Firecracker▶
Mister Halpren & Mister
  Johnson
Mr. Saturday Night
Money to Burn
Monte Walsh▶
My Heroes Have Always Been
  Cowboys
Next of Kin
Off Your Rocker
Old Explorers
Oldest Living Graduate▶
On Golden Pond▶
Over the Hill
Pals
Pastime▶
Pelle the Conqueror▶
A Piano for Mrs. Cimino
The Pickle
Picture of Dorian Gray▶
The Portrait▶
The Private Life of Henry VIII▶
Queens Logic
Rabid Grannies
Ran▶
The Rejuvenator
Return of the Rebels
Rhapsody in August▶
Rocket Gibraltar▶

Roses Bloom Twice
The Rounders
Satanik
The Set-Up▶
Seven Thieves
The Shell Seekers
Shirley Valentine▶
A Shock to the System▶
The Shootist▶
Side By Side
Stephen King's Golden Years
Strangers in Good Company▶
Street Music
Summer Solstice
Summer Wishes, Winter
  Dreams
The Sunshine Boys▶
Taking My Turn
Tatie Danielle▶
Tell Me a Riddle
Texas Guns
That's Life!
Things Change▶
30 Is a Dangerous Age,
  Cynthia
Three Strange Loves▶
To Dance with the White
  Dog▶
To Forget Venice
Tokyo Story▶
Toto le Heros▶
Tough Guys
Two for the Road▶
Two of a Kind
Two Weeks in Another Town
Umberto D▶
Unforgiven▶
Voyage of the Heart
The Wasp Woman
The Whales of August▶
When a Woman Ascends the
  Stairs
The Wild Bunch▶
Wild Strawberries▶
A Woman's Tale▶
Wrestling Ernest Hemingway

Gymnastics
American Anthem
Dream to Believe
I Was a Teenage Werewolf
Nadia

Happy Hookers
see also Gigolos; Oldest
  Profession
Arthur▶
Dixie: Changing Habits▶
Doctor Detroit
The Duchess and the
  Dirtwater Fox
For Pete's Sake
The Happy Hooker
The Happy Hooker Goes
  Hollywood
The Happy Hooker Goes to
  Washington
Irma La Douce
The Last Prostitute
McCabe & Mrs. Miller▶
Milk Money
Night Shift
The Owl and the Pussycat▶
Pretty Woman▶
Risky Business▶
Sweet Charity▶
Working Girls

Hard Knock Life
see also Great Depression;
  Homeless
Beggars in Ermine
Black Tower
A Brivele der Mamen▶
Cafe Express
Captain Scarlett
Carrie▶
City of Joy
Crisscross
Elena and Her Men▶
The Good Earth▶

The Grim Reaper▶
A Home of Our Own
Italian
Jude the Obscure
Juno and the Paycock
Laughing Sinners
Les Miserables▶
Lies My Father Told Me▶
Little Heroes
The Match Factory Girl▶
None But the Lonely Heart▶
One Third of a Nation
Pocketful of Miracles▶
The Pope of Greenwich
  Village
Salaam Bombay!▶
The Story of Fausta
Street Scene▶
The Super
Yellow Earth

Hard Knuckle Sandwich

see Boxing

Heaven Sent

see also Angels
All Dogs Go to Heaven
All of Me
Almost an Angel
Always
Angel on My Shoulder▶
Angel on My Shoulder
Angels in the Outfield▶
Angels in the Outfield
The Bishop's Wife▶
Brewster McCloud▶
Brother John▶
Carousel▶
Chances Are▶
Charley and the Angel
Clarence
Date with an Angel
Defending Your Life▶
Field of Dreams▶
Forever Darling
Ghost▶
Ghost Dad
A Guy Named Joe
Heading for Heaven
Heart Condition
Heaven
Heaven Can Wait▶
The Heavenly Kid
Hello Again
Here Comes Mr. Jordan▶
The Horn Blows at Midnight▶
I Married an Angel
It Came Upon a Midnight
  Clear
It's a Wonderful Life▶
Kiss Me Goodbye
Liliom▶
The Littlest Angel
Made in Heaven
Miracle in Milan▶
Mr. Destiny
The Next Voice You Hear
North▶
Oh, God!
Oh, God! Book 2
Oh, God! You Devil
One Magic Christmas
The Return of Peter Grimm
Static
The Three Lives of
  Thomasina▶
Truly, Madly, Deeply▶
Two of a Kind
White Light
Xanadu

Heists

*see also Scams, Stings &
Cons*
Alberto Express
Almost Partners
The Amazing Transparent
  Man
The Anderson Tapes▶

The Apple Dumpling Gang
Armored Car Robbery
The Armour of God
The Asphalt Jungle▶
Assault of the Rebel Girls
At Gunpoint
Back in the USSR
B.A.D. Cats
The Badlanders▶
Bandits
The Bank Dick▶
Bank Shot▶
Bellman and True
Bells of Coronado
Beyond Fear
The Bicycle Thief▶
Big Chase
Big Deal on Madonna Street▶
The Big Scam
The Black Lash
Black Moon Rising
The Boatniks
Bob le Flambeur▶
Bonnie & Clyde▶
The Brain
Breathing Fire
Butch and Sundance: The
  Early Days
Canvas: The Fine Art of Crime
Captain Blackjack
The Catamount Killing
The Cobra Strikes
Colt is My Law
Crooks & Coronets
Daring Dobermans
Deadly Diamonds
Death Tide
The Deputy Drummer
Desperate Cargo
Diamond Fleece
Diamond Trail
The Diamond Trap
Dog Eat Dog
Dollars▶
Double Deal
Double Trouble
11 Harrowhouse▶
Five Golden Dragons
The Florida Connection
Four Ways Out
Free Ride
Gambit
The Getaway
Getting Even with Dad
Going in Style▶
Grand Larceny
Great Bank Hoax
Great Gold Swindle
The Great Train Robbery▶
The Green Glove
Gun Crazy▶
Gun Girls
Guns Don't Argue
Gypsy
Happy New Year
Hard Hunted
Harley Davidson and the
  Marlboro Man
The Heist
High Risk
The Hoodlum
The Horse Without a Head
Hot Money
Hot Target
Hot Touch
I Died a Thousand Times
Ice
Inside Information
Interceptor
The Italian Job
Joy Ride to Nowhere
Kansas City Confidential▶
Killer
Killer Force
The Killing▶
Killing in the Sun
King's Ransom
Lassiter
The Last of Mrs. Cheyney▶
Late Extra
The League of Gentlemen▶
Letting the Birds Go Free

Lightning Jack
The Lion's Share
Loophole
Los Cacos
Mad Mission 3
A Man, a Woman, and a Bank
Man Trouble
Marbella
Marked Money
Master Touch
Melodie en Sous-Sol
Midnight Limited
Million Dollar Haul
Mission Batangas
Money Movers
Money to Burn
Motor Patrol
Motorama
Murph the Surf
My Dog, the Thief
The Neighborhood Thief
No Man's Land
Ocean's 11
Operation Amsterdam
Pardon My Sarong
Passionate Thief
The Pink Panther▶
Professionals
Queen of Diamonds
The Real McCoy
The Rebel Set
Reservoir Dogs▶
The Return of Boston Blackie
Rififi▶
The Rip Off
Robbery
Rough Cut
Scarlet Street▶
Seven Thieves▶
Shadow Man
Slaughterday
Sneakers
The Squeaker
The Squeeze
Super Soul Brother
Temporada Salvaje
They Met in Bombay
Thief▶
The Thief Who Came to
  Dinner
To Catch a Thief▶
Too Many Crooks
Topkapi▶
Tough Guys
Two-Way Stretch
White Fire
White Tiger
Who'll Stop the Rain?▶
The Wrong Arm of the Law▶
The Wrong Road
X Marks the Spot

Hell High School

*see also Campus Capers;
School Daze; Teen Angst*
The Beat
Beverly Hills 90210
Blackboard Jungle▶
Blood of Dracula
Bloodmoon
Born Innocent
Boy's Reformatory
Buffy the Vampire Slayer▶
Carrie▶
Cemetery High
Cheering Section
Cherry Hill High
The Chicken Chronicles
Class Act
Class of Fear
The Class of Miss MacMichael
Class of 1984
Class of 1999
Class of 1999 2: The
  Substitute
Class of Nuke 'Em High
Class of Nuke 'Em High, Part
  2: Subhumanoid Meltdown
Class Reunion Massacre
The Club
Coach
Coneheads

Cooley High▶
Creepers
Crisis at Central High▶
Cry-Baby▶
Cutting Class
Dangerously Close
Dazed and Confused▶
Deadly Fieldtrip
Death Goes to School
Echoes in the Darkness
The Ernest Green Story
Fast Times at Ridgemont
  High▶
Ferris Bueller's Day Off▶
Finishing School
The George McKenna Story
The Girl, the Body and the Pill
Girls in Chains
Grad Night
Graduation Day
Grease 2
Great Love Experiment
The Great St. Trinian's Train
  Robbery
Hadley's Rebellion
Hard Knox
Heathers▶
Hell High
Hide and Go Shriek
Hiding Out
High School Caesar
High School Confidential
High School USA
Hollywood High
Homework
Hoosiers▶
I Was a Teenage Werewolf
I Was a Teenage Zombie
If...▶
The Imposter
The Invisible Kid
The Invisible Maniac
Joy of Sex
Just One of the Girls
The Lawrenceville Stories
Lone Wolf
Loose Screws
Lust for a Vampire
The Majorettes
Massacre at Central High
Maya
Mirror, Mirror
Monster High
My Bodyguard▶
Night Visitor
Nowhere to Run
On the Edge: The Survival of
  Dana
One Night Only
Only the Strong
Pandemonium
Peggy Sue Got Married
Platinum High School
Porky's
Porky's 2: The Next Day
The Positively True
  Adventures of the Alleged
  Texas Cheerleader-
  Murdering Mom▶
Princess Academy
Prom Night
Prom Night 3: The Last Kiss
Prom Night 4: Deliver Us From
  Evil
Pump Up the Volume
Rebel High
Return to Horror High
Rock 'n' Roll High School▶
Rock 'n' Roll High School
  Forever
Rock, Pretty Baby
Satan's Cheerleaders
School Ties▶
Screwballs
Senior Trip
Showdown
Sidekicks
Sister Act 2: Back in the Habit
Slaughter High
Some Kind of Wonderful
Stay Awake
Student Affairs

Student Bodies
The Substitute
Summer School
Teenage Strangler
Terror Squad
3:15—The Moment of Truth
Three O'Clock High
Tom Brown's School Days▶
Trick or Treat
Twisted Brain
Undercover
Urusei Yatsura Movie 2:
  Beautiful Dreamer
Wanderers▶
Werewolf in a Girl's Dormitory
Zombie High

Hispanic America

Hitz
Maricela
Mi Vida Loca
The Ring
Salsa
Sweet 15
Zoot Suit▶

Historical Drama

*see also Medieval Romps;
Period Piece*
Abe Lincoln in Illinois▶
Across the Wide Missouri
The Adventures of Tom
  Sawyer
The Agony and the Ecstasy
The Alamo▶
The Alamo: Thirteen Days to
  Glory
Alexander the Great
Alone Against Rome
Amadeus▶
Anastasia▶
Anastasia: The Mystery of
  Anna
Andrei Rublev▶
Anne of the Thousand Days▶
Antony and Cleopatra
Assassination of Trotsky
Assunta Spina
The Attic: The Hiding of Anne
  Frank
Augustine of Hippo▶
The Autobiography of Miss
  Jane Pittman▶
The Ballad of Narayama▶
Barabbas
Barefoot in Athens
The Bastard
The Battle of Algiers▶
Battle of Britain
Battle of the Bulge
Battle of Valiant
The Battleship Potemkin▶
Beau Brummel▶
Becket▶
Beethoven's Nephew
Ben-Hur▶
Bhowani Junction
The Big Red One▶
The Birth of a Nation▶
Black Robe▶
Blaise Pascal▶
The Blue Yonder
Bonnie Prince Charlie
A Bridge Too Far
Brother Sun, Sister Moon
The Bushido Blade
Cabeza de Vaca▶
Cabiria
Caesar and Cleopatra
Captain Caution
Carthage in Flames
Catherine the Great
The Charge of the Light
  Brigade▶
The Charge of the Light
  Brigade
Children of Paradise▶
Christopher Columbus
Christopher Columbus: The
  Discovery
Cleopatra

Historical

Condemned to Live
A Connecticut Yankee▶
Conquest▶
The Court Martial of Billy Mitchell▶
Crisis at Central High▶
Cromwell
Dances with Wolves▶
A Dangerous Man: Lawrence after Arabia▶
Danton▶
David and Bathsheba▶
David Copperfield▶
David Copperfield
The Day that Shook the World
Demetrius and the Gladiators
Desiree
The Devils▶
The Devil's Disciple▶
Diane
Doctor Zhivago▶
Drums in the Deep South
Dynasty
Edward II
El Cid▶
Eleanor & Franklin▶
Eleanor: First Lady of the World
Elizabeth, the Queen
Erik, the Viking
The Eternal Waltz
Eureka Stockade
Fabiola▶
The Fall of the Roman Empire▶
Fellini Satyricon▶
Fire Over England▶
The First Olympics: Athens 1896
Forever and a Day▶
Forty Days of Musa Dagh
47 Ronin, Part 1▶
47 Ronin, Part 2▶
1492: Conquest of Paradise
Freedom Road
Gallipoli▶
Gate of Hell▶
The Gathering Storm▶
Geheimakte WB1
Geronimo: An American Legend
Gettysburg▶
Giants of Rome
Gladiator of Rome
Glory▶
Gonza the Spearman
The Great Commandment
The Greatest Story Ever Told
Guilty by Suspicion
The Hellfire Club
Henry V▶
Hill Number One
Hitler
The Howards of Virginia
The Hunchback of Notre Dame▶
Hunter in the Dark
I Beheld His Glory
Imperial Venus
In Old Chicago▶
Independence
The Invaders
The Iron Crown
The Iron Duke
Ironclads
Ivan the Terrible, Part 1▶
Ivan the Terrible, Part 2▶
Jesus of Nazareth▶
The Jewel in the Crown
JFK▶
Joan of Arc
Johnny Tremain & the Sons of Liberty
Judith of Bethulia▶
Julius Caesar▶
Justin Morgan Had a Horse
Khartoum
King David
King Richard and the Crusaders
Kolberg
La Marseillaise▶

La Nuit de Varennes▶
Lady Jane▶
Last Days of Pompeii
The Last Emperor▶
Last Four Days
The Last of the Mohicans
The Last Valley
Le Complot▶
The Lighthorsemen▶
The Lindbergh Kidnapping Case▶
The Lion in Winter▶
The Lion of Thebes▶
Lionheart
Little House on the Prairie▶
Long Shadows
Luther
The Magician of Lublin
The Mahabharata
Mahler▶
A Man for All Seasons▶
Mandela▶
Marie Antoinette
Martin Luther
Mary of Scotland▶
Masada▶
Mata Hari
Missiles of October▶
The Mission▶
Mockery
The Moonraker
Mountain Man
Mutiny on the Bounty▶
Napoleon▶
Nefertiti, Queen of the Nile
Nicholas and Alexandra
Nine Days a Queen▶
Norseman
Omar Khayyam
The Ordeal of Dr. Mudd▶
Orphan Train▶
Orphans of the Storm▶
Overlanders▶
The Passion of Joan of Arc▶
The Passover Plot
Peter the First: Part 1
Peter the First: Part 2
Peter the Great▶
Portrait of a Rebel: Margaret Sanger
The Power of One
Pride and Prejudice▶
The Private Life of Henry VIII▶
The Private Lives of Elizabeth & Essex▶
Queen Christina▶
Quo Vadis
Quo Vadis
Quo Vadis
Raintree County
Rasputin
Rasputin and the Empress▶
The Rebels
The Red and the Black▶
Reign of Terror
Revolt of the Barbarians
Revolution
Richard III▶
The Right Stuff▶
Rikyu▶
The Rise of Louis XIV▶
Road to Yesterday/The Yankee Clipper
Roanoak
Rob Roy—The Highland Rogue
The Robe
Robin and Marian
Roots▶
Roots: The Gift
Roots: The Next Generation▶
Saint Joan
Salome
Samurai Reincarnation
Scarlet Empress
The Scarlet Pimpernel▶
Sebastiane▶
The Seekers
Senso▶
Separate But Equal▶
Shaka Zulu▶
Shenandoah▶

Shin Heike Monogatari▶
The Sicilian
The Silk Road
Sins of Rome
Six Wives of Henry VIII▶
Soldier in Love
Soldier of Orange▶
Spartacus▶
Spy of Napoleon
Sunrise at Campobello▶
The Sword of El Cid
Tai-Pan
A Tale of Two Cities▶
Tale of Two Cities/In the Switch Tower
Tamango
The Ten Commandments
The Ten Commandments
Ten Days That Shook the World▶
Ten Who Dared
Tharus Son of Attila
That Hamilton Woman▶
Therese▶
They Died with Their Boots On▶
'38: Vienna Before the Fall
The Thorn Birds▶
Three Sovereigns for Sarah
Tom Edison: The Boy Who Lit Up the World
The Tower of London
Tower of London
Tower of Screaming Virgins
The Tragedy of King Richard II
The Triangle Factory Fire Scandal
Uncle Tom's Cabin
Uranus▶
Vanina Vanini▶
Victoria Regina
The Virgin Queen▶
Viva Zapata!▶
The Wannsee Conference▶
The War Lord▶
The Warriors
Waterloo
Where the Sky Begins
White Mischief▶
The White Rose▶
Who Has Seen the Wind?▶
Winds of Kitty Hawk
The Wolf at the Door
A Woman Called Golda▶
A Woman Called Moses
Young Bess▶
Young Catherine▶
Young Mr. Lincoln▶

Hit Men

see also Assassinations

African Rage
Cold Sweat
Confessions of a Hit Man
DaVinci's War
Deja Vu
Diary of a Hitman
El Mariachi▶
The Family
Fatal Chase
Fatal Justice
Fight to the Death
Final Mission
Firepower
The Hit List
Hit Woman: The Double Edge
Honor and Glory
La Femme Nikita▶
The Last Hit
The Mechanic
Mr. Nice Guy
The Naked City▶
The Outside Man
Paid to Kill
Perfect Killer
Point of No Return
Portrait of a Hitman
The Positively True Adventures of the Alleged Texas Cheerleader-Murdering Mom▶
Prizzi's Honor▶

The Professional: Golgo 13
Project: Kill!
Quick
Red King, White Knight
Red Rock West▶
Season for Assassins
The Specialist
Stiletto
Strangers on a Train▶
Suddenly▶

Hockey

see also Skating

Accident
The Cutting Edge
D2: The Mighty Ducks
Dutch Girls
Hockey Night
The Mighty Ducks
Miracle on Ice
Mystery of the Million Dollar Hockey Puck
Paperback Hero
Slap Shot▶
Touch and Go
Youngblood

Holidays

see also Christmas; Horrible Holidays

Bloody New Year
Carry On Behind
A Charlie Brown Thanksgiving
Clown Murders
A Day for Thanks on Walton's Mountain
Easter Parade▶
Fourth Wise Man
Groundhog Day▶
A Happy New Year!
Happy New Year, Charlie Brown
The Hoboken Chicken Emergency
Hocus Pocus
It's the Great Pumpkin, Charlie Brown
The Legend of Sleepy Hollow
Mrs. Wiggs of the Cabbage Patch
New Year's Evil
Night of the Demons 2
Spaced Invaders
Thanksgiving Story
Turumba▶
Two Weeks with Love
The Waltons: A Thanksgiving Story

Holocaust

see also Germany; Judaism; Nazis & Other Paramilitary Slugs; World War II

Alan & Naomi
The Assault
The Assisi Underground
The Attic: The Hiding of Anne Frank
Au Revoir Les Enfants▶
Border Street
The Boxer and Death▶
Charlie Grant's War
Christabel
Cold Days
David▶
Diamonds of the Night▶
The Diary of Anne Frank
Enemies, a Love Story▶
Era Notte a Roma▶
Europa, Europa▶
The Execution
Forced March
Garden of the Finzi-Continis▶
Good Evening, Mr. Wallenberg
Hanna's War
The Hiding Place
Hitler
The Holcroft Covenant

Holocaust▶
Holocaust Survivors...Remembrance of Love
Hunted!
In a Glass Cage
Kanal▶
Kapo▶
Korczak▶
The Last Metro▶
Les Violons du Bal
Max and Helen
Murderers Among Us: The Simon Wiesenthal Story▶
Never Forget
The Pawnbroker▶
Playing for Time▶
Reunion▶
The Revolt of Job▶
The Rose Garden
Schindler's List▶
The Shop on Main Street▶
Sophie's Choice▶
Transport from Paradise
Triumph of the Spirit▶
The Wannsee Conference▶
War & Love
The White Rose▶

Home Alone

see also Childhood Visions

Adventures in Babysitting
And You Thought Your Parents Were Weird!
Anything for a Thrill
The Apple Dumpling Gang
Baby's Day Out
Blank Check
Bless the Beasts and Children
The Blue Lagoon
Camp Nowhere
Children's Island
Cloak & Dagger
Cohen and Tate
Courage Mountain
Cross My Heart
Dirkham Detective Agency
Dirt Bike Kid
Don't Tell Mom the Babysitter's Dead
Explorers
Famous Five Get Into Trouble
A Far Off Place
Fatal Skies
Gleaming the Cube
The Goonies
He is My Brother
Home Alone▶
Home Alone 2: Lost in New York
Honey, I Shrunk the Kids
Hook
The Horse Without a Head
Invaders from Mars
Island Trader
Just William's Luck
Legend of Billie Jean
The Littlest Horse Thieves
Lord of the Flies▶
Lord of the Flies
Mr. Wise Guy
Monkey Trouble
The Monster Squad
Paradise
The Rescue
Return to the Blue Lagoon
Shipwrecked
Snow Treasure
3 Ninjas
3 Ninjas Kick Back
A Waltz Through the Hills
The Window▶
Young Sherlock Holmes

Homeless

see also Great Depression; Hard Knock Life; Yuppie Nightmares

Accatone!▶
All Mine to Give

The Billion Dollar Hobo
Billy: Portrait of a Street Kid
Bums
Children of Sanchez
City Lights▶
Curly Sue
Distant Thunder▶
Dodes 'ka-den▶
El Derecho de Comer
Emanon
God Bless the Child▶
The Grapes of Wrath▶
Home for Christmas
Into the West▶
Kanal▶
The Kid▶
The Kid/Idle Class▶
Life Stinks
Los Olvidados▶
The Lower Depths▶
Midnight Cowboy▶
None But the Lonely Heart▶
Original Intent
An Orphan Boy of Vienna
Pardon My Trunk
The Saint of Fort Washington
Salaam Bombay!▶
Samaritan: The Mitch Snyder Story▶
Scarecrow
Silas Marner▶
Sounder▶
Streetwise▶
Sullivan's Travels▶
Summer Magic
They Shall Have Music
Times Square
Up Your Alley
The Vagrant
Where the Day Takes You
With Honors

Homosexuality

see also AIDS; Bisexuality; Gender Bending

Alien Prey
American Fabulous
And the Band Played On▶
Another Country
Another Way▶
Arabian Nights▶
Armistead Maupin's Tales of the City
As Is
The Berlin Affair
The Best Way
The Bitter Tears of Petra von Kant
Black Cobra
The Blood Spattered Bride
Blue
The Boys in the Band
Carmilla
The Children's Hour
City in Panic
Claire of the Moon
Colonel Redl▶
The Conformist▶
Consenting Adult
Cruising
The Crying Game▶
Curse of the Queerwolf
Daughters of Darkness▶
Dear Boys
Death in Venice▶
Desert Hearts▶
The Detective▶
Different Story
Double Face
Drifting
An Early Frost▶
Edward II▶
El Diputado▶
An Empty Bed▶
Entertaining Mr. Sloane
Entre-Nous▶
Ernesto
Even Cowgirls Get the Blues
The Everlasting Secret Family
Forbidden Passion: The Oscar Wilde Movie

Fortune and Men's Eyes
Four Weddings and a Funeral▶
Fox and His Friends▶
Fun Down There
Hearing Voices
The Hunger
I've Heard the Mermaids Singing▶
Joey Breaker▶
Kamikaze Hearts
The Killing of Sister George
Kiss of the Spider Woman▶
La Cage aux Folles▶
La Cage aux Folles 2
La Cage aux Folles 3: The Wedding
Law of Desire▶
Les Nuits Fauves▶
L'Homme Blesse▶
Lianna▶
The Living End
Longtime Companion▶
The Lost Language of Cranes▶
Maedchen in Uniform▶
Making Love
Maurice▶
Men in Love
Menage▶
Midnight Cowboy▶
The Music Lovers
My Beautiful Laundrette▶
My Father is Coming
My Own Private Idaho▶
My Sister, My Love
The Naked Civil Servant▶
Naked Lunch▶
Nijinsky
Norman, Is That You?
Okoge
Paris is Burning▶
Parting Glances▶
Partners
Personal Best▶
Philadelphia▶
Prick Up Your Ears▶
Querelle
A Question of Love▶
The Rainbow▶
Reflections in a Golden Eye
The Ritz▶
Rock Hudson's Home Movies
The Rocky Horror Picture Show▶
Rope▶
Sand and Blood
The Scorpion Woman
Seducers
Sergeant Matlovich vs. the U.S. Air Force
The Silence▶
Smoke
The Sprinter
Straight for the Heart
Sugar Cookies
Sunday, Bloody Sunday▶
Swoon▶
Taxi zum Klo▶
Therese & Isabelle
These Three▶
The Third Sex
This Special Friendship
Three of Hearts
Threesome
Tidy Endings
Times of Harvey Milk
To Forget Venice
To Play or To Die
Too Much Sun
Torch Song Trilogy
The Vampire Lovers
Vampyres
Via Appia
Victim▶
Victor/Victoria▶
Walk on the Wild Side
We Think the World of You▶
The Wedding Banquet▶
Windows
Withnail and I▶
Wonderland▶

X, Y & Zee

Horrible Holidays

see also Christmas; Holidays

April Fool's Day
Black Christmas
Bloodbeat
Bloody New Year
Don't Open Till Christmas
Dorm That Dripped Blood
Halloween▶
Halloween 2: The Nightmare Isn't Over!
Halloween 3: Season of the Witch
Halloween 4: The Return of Michael Myers
Halloween 5: The Revenge of Michael Myers
Halloween Night
Happy Birthday to Me
Home for the Holidays
Home Sweet Home
Mother's Day
My Bloody Valentine
New Year's Evil
The Night After Halloween
Night of the Demons
The Ref▶
Silent Night, Bloody Night
Silent Night, Deadly Night
Silent Night, Deadly Night 2
Silent Night, Deadly Night 3: Better Watch Out!
Silent Night, Deadly Night 4: Initiation
Silent Night, Deadly Night 5: The Toymaker
Teen Alien
Trick or Treats
Wacko

Horror

see also Bloody Mayhem; Cannibalism; Classic Horror; Horror Comedy; Killer Appliances; Killer Beasts; Killer Bugs; Killer Plants; Killer Toys; Mad Scientists; Monsters, General; Occult; Phone Terror; Renegade Body Parts; Satanism; Supernatural Horror; Vampire Spoof; Vampires; Werewolves; Zombies

The Abomination
After Midnight
Afterward
Alice Sweet Alice
Alien Dead
Alien Prey
Alien Seed
Alligator▶
Alligator 2: The Mutation
Alone in the Dark
The Amazing Transplant
The Ambulance
American Gothic
An American Werewolf in London▶
An Angel for Satan
Anguish
Ants
A*P*E*
At Midnight, I'll Take Your Soul
Autopsy
The Avenger
Awakenings of the Beast
The Awful Dr. Orlof
The Baby
Backwoods
Bad Girls Dormitory
The Bad Seed
Barracuda
Basket Case▶
Basket Case 2
Basket Case 3: The Progeny

The Beach Girls and the Monster
Beaks: The Movie
Beast in the Cellar
Beast of Morocco
Beast of the Yellow Night
The Beast that Killed Women
The Beast with Five Fingers
The Beast Within
Because of the Cats
The Being
Ben
Berserker
Bestia Nocturna
Beyond Darkness
Beyond Dream's Door
Beyond the Door
Beyond the Door 2
Beyond the Door 3
Big Foot
Bio Hazard
Black Cat
Black Christmas
Black Devil Doll from Hell
Black Magic Terror
Black Pit of Dr. M
The Black Room
Black Roses
Black Vampire
Blackenstein
Blackout
Blacula
A Blade in the Dark
Blade of the Ripper
Blades
Blind Faith
Blood and Black Lace
Blood Bride
Blood Cult
Blood Diner
Blood Feast
Blood Freak
Blood Games
Blood Lake
Blood Legacy
Blood Lust
Blood Mania
Blood of Ghastly Horror
The Blood on Satan's Claw▶
Blood Rage
Blood Salvage
Blood Screams
Blood Sisters
Blood Song
The Blood Spattered Bride
Blood Thirst
Blood Tide
Blood Tracks
Blood Voyage
Bloodbath in Psycho Town
Bloodlink
Bloodlust: Subspecies 3
Bloodmoon
Bloodshed
Bloodspell
Bloodstalkers
Bloodstone: Subspecies 2
Bloodsuckers from Outer Space
Bloodsucking Freaks
Bloodsucking Pharoahs of Pittsburgh
Bloody Birthday
Bloody Moon
Bloody New Year
The Bloody Pit of Horror
The Bloody Vampire
Bloody Wednesday
Blue Blood
Blue Sunshine
Boarding House
The Body Beneath
Body Count
Body Melt
Body Parts
The Body Shop
Body Snatcher from Hell
Boggy Creek II
The Boogey Man
Boogey Man 2
The Borrower
Bowery at Midnight

The Brain
Brain Dead▶
Brain of Blood
The Brain That Wouldn't Die
Brainscan
Bram Stoker's Dracula
Bride of Killer Nerd
The Brides of Dracula
Brides of the Beast
The Brides Wore Blood
The Brood
The Brotherhood of Satan
Brothers in Arms
Brujo Luna
Bulldance
Burial Ground
Buried Alive
The Burning
The Burning Court
Burnt Offerings
Cameron's Closet
The Campus Corpse
Cannibal Campout
Captain Kronos: Vampire Hunter▶
Captive Wild Woman
Carmilla
Carnage
Carnival of Blood
Carnosaur
The Carpathian Eagle
The Carpenter
Carpet of Horror
Carrie▶
The Carrier
Castle of the Creeping Flesh
Cataclysm
Cathy's Curse
Cat's Eye
The Cellar
Cellar Dweller
Cemetery High
The Chair
The Channeler
Cheerleader Camp
Child in the Night
Child of Darkness, Child of Light
The Children
Children of the Corn
Children of the Corn 2: The Final Sacrifice
Children of the Full Moon
Children Shouldn't Play with Dead Things
Child's Play
Child's Play 2
Child's Play 3
Chillers
The Chilling
Chopper Chicks in Zombietown
Chopping Mall
The Chosen
The Church▶
Cinemagic
Circus of Horrors
City of the Walking Dead
Class of Nuke 'Em High
Class Reunion Massacre
Claws
Clown House
The Club
Color Me Blood Red
The Comeback
Commando Squad
Committed
The Confessional
Confidential
Contagion
Copperhead
The Corpse Grinders
Count Dracula's Great Love
The Crater Lake Monster
The Craving
The Crawlers
The Crawling Hand
Crawlspace
Craze
Crazed
Crazy Fat Ethel II
Creature from Black Lake

Horror

Creepers
Creepozoids
The Cremators
Criminally Insane
Crocodile
The Crow
Crucible of Terror
Cthulhu Mansion
Cujo
Cult of the Cobra
Curfew
The Curious Dr. Humpp
The Curse
Curse 2: The Bite
Curse 3: Blood Sacrifice
Curse 4: The Ultimate
  Sacrifice
Curse of the Alpha Stone
The Curse of the Aztec
  Mummy
Curse of the Living Dead
Curse of the Screaming Dead
Curtains
Cutting Class
Dario Argento's Trauma
The Dark
Dark August
The Dark Half
The Dark Power
Dark Sanity
Dawn of the Dead▶
Day of Judgment
Day of the Animals
Day of the Dead
Day the World Ended
Dead Alive
Dead Girls
Dead Mate
Dead Men Walk
The Dead Next Door
Dead of Night▶
Dead of Night
Dead Pit
Dead Ringers▶
Dead Sleep
Deadline
Deadly Blessing
Deadly Dreams
Deadly Eyes
Deadly Friend
Deadly Game
Deadly Intruder
Deadly Neighbor
Deadly Obsession
Deadtime Stories
Death by Dialogue
Death Collector
Death Nurse
Death Promise
Death Row Diner
Death Screams
Death Spa
Death Warmed Up
Delirium
The Demon
Demon Hunter
A Demon in My View
Demon Lust
Demon Possessed
Demon Queen
Demonic Toys
Deranged▶
Devil Rider
Devil Times Five
Devilfish
The Devil's Commandment
Dr. Black, Mr. Hyde
Doctor Blood's Coffin
Dr. Caligari
Dr. Giggles
Dr. Hackenstein
Dr. Jekyll and the Wolfman
Dr. Jekyll vs. the Werewolf
Dr. Jekyll's Dungeon of Death
Dr. Orloff's Invisible Horror
Dr. Orloff's Monster
Dogs of Hell
Dollman vs Demonic Toys
Don't Go in the Woods
Don't Look in the Basement
Don't Open Till Christmas
Doomwatch

Dorm That Dripped Blood
Dracula Has Risen from the
  Grave
Dracula Rising
Driller Killer
Drive-In Massacre
Dungeon of Harrow
Eaten Alive
Edge of Sanity
Edge of the Axe
Eegah!
El Cuarto Chino
Elves
Emerald Jungle
Endplay
The Entity
Epitaph
Eternal Evil
The Evictors
Evil Clutch
Evil Dead
Evil Dead 2: Dead by Dawn
Evil Laugh
Evil Spirits
Evil's Commandment
Evils of the Night
Exorcism's Daughter
Eyeball
Eyes of a Stranger
Fade to Black
Fatal Images
Fatal Pulse
The Fiend
Fiend
Final Exam
The Final Terror
Flesh and Blood Show
Flesh Eating Mothers
Flesh Feast
Food of the Gods
Food of the Gods: Part 2
Forced Entry
The Forest
Forever Evil
Frankenstein
The Freakmaker
Freaks▶
Freddy's Dead: The Final
  Nightmare
The Freeway Maniac
Friday the 13th
Friday the 13th, Part 2
Friday the 13th, Part 3
Friday the 13th, Part 4: The
  Final Chapter
Friday the 13th, Part 5: A New
  Beginning
Friday the 13th, Part 6: Jason
  Lives
Friday the 13th, Part 7: The
  New Blood
Friday the 13th, Part 8: Jason
  Takes Manhattan
Frightmare
Frightshow
Frogs
Frozen Terror
Funeral Home
The Funhouse
Funland
Future Shock
Gates of Hell
Geek Maggot Bingo
Ghost in the Machine
Ghost of Hanley House
The Ghoul
Ghoul School
The Girl in Room 2A
Girlfriend from Hell
Girls Night Out
Girls on the Road
Girls School Screamers
The Godsend
The Gore-Gore Girls
Graduation Day
Grandma's House
The Graveyard
Graveyard of Horror
Graveyard Shift
The Great Alligator
Greedy Terror
Grim Prairie Tales

Grim Reaper
Grizzly
Grotesque
Gruesome Twosome
The Guardian
Hack O'Lantern
Halloween▶
Halloween 2: The Nightmare
  Isn't Over!
Halloween 3: Season of the
  Witch
Halloween 4: The Return of
  Michael Myers
Halloween 5: The Revenge of
  Michael Myers
Hallucinations of a Deranged
  Mind
The Hand▶
Hands of a Stranger
The Hands of Orlac
Hands of the Ripper
Happy Birthday to Me
Hard Rock Zombies
Hatchet for the Honeymoon
Haunted: The Ferryman
HauntedWeen
Haunting of Sarah Hardy
Haunts
He Kills Night After Night After
  Night
He Knows You're Alone
Headhunter
Headless Eyes
Heartstopper
Hell High
Hell Night
Hellgate
Hellhole
Hellmaster
Hello Mary Lou: Prom Night 2
Help Wanted Female
The Hereafter
Hide and Go Shriek
Hider in the House
The Hills Have Eyes
The Hills Have Eyes, Part 2
Hitcher
The Hitchhiker
Hitchhiker 2
Hitchhiker 3
Hitchhiker 4
Hollow Gate
Hollywood Chainsaw Hookers
Hollywood Ghost Stories
The Hollywood Strangler
  Meets the Skid Row
  Slasher
Hollywood's New Blood
Home Sweet Home
Honeymoon Horror
The Horror Chamber of Dr.
  Faustus▶
Horror Hospital
Horror House on Highway 5
Horror of Party Beach
Horror of Spider Island
Horror of the Zombies
The Horror Show
Horrors of Burke & Hare
Horrors of Spider Island
Hospital Massacre
Hospital of Terror
House 4: Home Deadly Home
House of Death
House of Dreams
House of Horrors
House of Psychotic Women
House of Terror
House of the Dead
House of the Living Dead
House of Whipcord
The House on Sorority Row
The House on Straw Hill
House on the Edge of the
  Park
The House on Tombstone Hill
The House that Vanished
Human Experiments
Humanoids from the Deep
Humongous
Hyena of London
I Dismember Mama
I Don't Want to Be Born

I Drink Your Blood
I Eat Your Skin
I Like Bats
I Spit on Your Grave
Icebox Murders
Iced
Igor & the Lunatics
I'm Dangerous Tonight
The Immortalizer
In the Shadow of Kilimanjaro
In the Steps of a Dead Man
The Incredible Two-Headed
  Transplant
Incubus
The Initiation
Inn of the Damned
Innocent Blood
Into the Darkness
Intruder
Invasion of the Flesh Hunters
Invasion of the Saucer Men
The Invisible Dead
The Invisible Man's Revenge
The Invisible Strangler
Island Claw
Island of Blood
It's Alive▶
It's Alive 2: It Lives Again
It's Alive 3: Island of the Alive
The Jar
Jason Goes to Hell: The Final
  Friday
The Jitters
Junior
Just Before Dawn
The Keep
Keep My Grave Open
Keeper
Killer Party
The Killer Shrews
Killer Workout
Killer's Moon
The Kindred
King of Kong Island
Kingdom of the Spiders
Kiss and Be Killed
Kiss of the Tarantula
La Mansion de la Locura
Lady Stay Dead
Las Vegas Serial Killer
The Last Horror Film
Last House on Dead End
  Street
Last House on the Left
The Last Ride
The Last Slumber Party
Leatherface: The Texas
  Chainsaw Massacre 3
The Leech Woman
Legacy of Horror
Legend of Big Foot
Legend of Boggy Creek
The Leopard Man
Leprechaun
Leprechaun 2
Link
Liquid Dreams
The Loch Ness Horror
The Lodger▶
Lone Wolf
The Lost Boys
Lost, Lonely, and Vicious
The Lost Platoon
Love Butcher
Love Me Deadly
Lunatic
Lurking Fear
Luther the Geek
Macabre
The Mad Butcher
Mad Doctor of Blood Island
The Mad Ghoul
Mad Love▶
Madhouse
Madhouse Mansion
Madman
The Majorettes
Man Beast
Man Made Monster
The Man Who Lived Again
Man with Two Heads
The Man with Two Lives

Mania
Maniac
Maniac Cop
Maniac Cop 2
Maniac Cop 3
Man's Best Friend
Mantis in Lace
The Mask
The Mask of Fu Manchu
Mausoleum
Maximum Overdrive
Maximum Thrust
The Meateater
Memorial Valley Massacre
Metamorphosis: The Alien
  Factor
Midnight
Midnight 2: Sex, Death, and
  Videotape
The Midnight Hour
Midnight Kiss
The Midnight Phantom
Mikey
Mill of the Stone Women
The Milpitas Monster
Mongrel
Monkey Shines
The Monster▶
Monster
The Monster and the Girl
The Monster and the Stripper
The Monster Club
Monster Dog
Monster High
The Monster of London City
The Monster Squad
Monsters Crash the Pajama
  Party
Moon of the Wolf
Mortuary
Mother's Day
Mountaintop Motel Massacre
The Movie House Massacre
Multiple Maniacs
Murder-in-Law
Murder Mansion
Murder Motel
Murder on Line One
Murderer's Keep
Mutant
My Bloody Valentine
My Daughter's Keeper
Nail Gun Massacre
The Naked Witch
Needful Things
The New Kids
The Newlydeads
Next of Kin
The Night After Halloween
Night Breed
The Night Brings Charlie
Night Creature
The Night God Screamed
Night Monster
Night of Bloody Horror
Night of Terror
Night of the Bloody Apes
Night of the Bloody Transplant
Night of the Cobra Woman
Night of the Demon
Night of the Howling Beast
Night of the Living Dead▶
Night of the Living Dead
Night of the Strangler
Night of the Zombies
Night Ripper
Night Screams
Night Slasher
Night Terror
Night Train to Terror
Night Warning
Nightmare
Nightmare in Wax
A Nightmare on Elm Street
A Nightmare on Elm Street 2:
  Freddy's Revenge
A Nightmare on Elm Street 3:
  Dream Warriors
A Nightmare on Elm Street 4:
  Dream Master
A Nightmare on Elm Street 5:
  Dream Child

Nightmare on the 13th Floor
Nightmares
976-EVIL
976-EVIL 2: The Astral Factor
Oasis of the Zombies
Offerings
One Dark Night
One Deadly Owner
125 Rooms of Comfort
One Minute Before Death
The Orphan
The Outcast
The Pack
Pagan Island
Pale Blood
Panic
Paralyzed
The Passing
Patrick
Pay Off
The People Under the Stairs
The Perverse Countess
The Phantom
Phantom of Death
Phantom of the Mall: Eric's
    Revenge
Pieces
Pigs
Pin
The Pit
Play Dead
Playroom
Pledge Night
Plutonium Baby
Point of Terror
Popcorn
Possession
Possession: Until Death Do
    You Part
The Power
Premature Burial
The Prey
Primal Rage
Prime Evil
Prince of Darkness
Prison
Project: Nightmare
Prom Night
Prom Night 3: The Last Kiss
Prom Night 4: Deliver Us From
    Evil
Prophecy
The Prowler
The Psychic
Psychic Killer
Psycho Cop
Psycho Cop 2
Psycho from Texas
Psychopath
Puppet Master
Puppet Master 2
Puppet Master 3: Toulon's
    Revenge
Puppet Master 4
The Pyx▶
Rabid
Race with the Devil
Rana: The Legend of Shadow
    Lake
Rape
The Rats are Coming! The
    Werewolves are Here!
Rattlers
The Raven▶
Razorback
Red Blooded American Girl
The Redeemer
The Reincarnate
The Rejuvenator
Rest In Pieces
The Resurrected
Retribution
The Return of Count Yorga
Return of Dracula
Return of the Ape Man
Return of the Evil Dead
Return of the Family Man
Return to Boggy Creek
Return to Horror High
Return to Salem's Lot
Revenge

Revenge in the House of
    Usher
Revenge of Doctor X
Revenge of the Dead
Revenge of the Living
    Zombies
Revenge of the Radioactive
    Reporter
Revenge of the Zombies
Ring of Terror
The Ripper
The Robot vs. the Aztec
    Mummy
Rock 'n' Roll Nightmare
Rocktober Blood
Rodan
Rogue
Rosemary's Baby▶
Ruby
The Rue Morgue Massacres
Run, Stranger, Run
The Runestone
Rush Week
Sabaka
The Sadist
The Saga of the Draculas
Salem's Lot
Samson in the Wax Museum
Samson vs. the Vampire
    Women
Satan in High Heels
The Satanic Rites of Dracula
Satanik
Satan's Black Wedding
Satan's Blade
Satan's Cheerleaders
Satan's Princess
Satan's School for Girls
Satan's Touch
Satanwar
Saturday Night Shockers
Saturday Night Shockers, Vol.
    2
Saturday Night Shockers, Vol.
    3
Saturday Night Shockers, Vol.
    4
The Savage Bees
Savage Intruder
Savage Weekend
Savages
Scalpel
Scanners
Scanners 2: The New Order
Scanners 3: The Takeover
Scared Stiff
Scared to Death
The Scars of Dracula
Schizo
Schizoid
Science Crazed
Scorpion with Two Tails
The Scorpion's Tail
Scream, Baby, Scream
Scream Blacula Scream
Scream Dream
Scream of Fear▶
Scream of the Demon Lover
Screamers
The Screaming Dead
The Screaming Skull
Screams of a Winter Night
Screamtime
Season of the Witch
The Secret Cinema
Seducers
See No Evil▶
Seedpeople
Seeds of Evil
Seizure
The Sender
The Sentinel
The Serpent and the Rainbow
The Serpent of Death
Servants of Twilight
Seven Deaths in the Cat's Eye
Seven Doors of Death
The Seventh Victim▶
The Severed Arm
Severed Ties
Sex is Crazy
Shadow of Chinatown

Shadows Run Black
Shakma
The Shaman
Shark's Paradise
The She-Beast
She Came on the Bus
She Demons
She-Freak
Shock 'Em Dead
Shock! Shock! Shock!
Shock Waves
Shocker
Shriek of the Mutilated
The Sibling
Silent Madness
Silent Night, Bloody Night
Silent Night, Deadly Night
Silent Night, Deadly Night 2
Silent Night, Deadly Night 3:
    Better Watch Out!
Silent Night, Deadly Night 4:
    Initiation
Silent Night, Deadly Night 5:
    The Toymaker
Silent Scream
Silver Bullet
The Sinister Invasion
Sinner's Blood
The Sins of Dorian Gray
Sinthia: The Devil's Doll
Sisters▶
Sisters of Satan
Skinned Alive
The Skull
Skullduggery
Slashdance
The Slasher
Slaughter High
Slaughter Hotel
The Slaughter of the Vampires
Slaughterhouse
Slaughterhouse Rock
The Slayer
The Slayer/The Scalps
Sleazemania III: The Good,
    the Bad & the Sleazy
Sledgehammer
Sleep of Death
Sleepaway Camp
Sleepaway Camp 2: Unhappy
    Campers
Sleepaway Camp 3: Teenage
    Wasteland
Sleepwalkers
Slime City
The Slime People
Slithis
Slugs
The Slumber Party Massacre
Slumber Party Massacre 2
Slumber Party Massacre 3
The Snake Hunter Strangler
The Snake People
The Snake Woman
Snowbeast
Society
Sole Survivor
Something Weird
Sometimes Aunt Martha Does
    Dreadful Things
Sometimes They Come Back
Son of Blob
Sorority House Massacre
Sorority House Massacre 2:
    Nighty Nightmare
Sound of Horror
Sounds of Silence
Spasms
The Spawning
The Spectre of Edgar Allen
    Poe
The Speed Lovers
The Spell
The Spellbinder
Spellcaster
Spiritism
Spirits
Spirits of the Dead▶
Splatter University
Spontaneous Combustion
Spookies
Squirm

Stage Fright
Stagefright
Stanley
Stay Awake
Stephen King's Golden Years
Stephen King's It
Stephen King's The Stand
Stephen King's The
    Tommyknockers
Steps from Hell
Stepsisters
Stones of Death
Strait-Jacket
Strange Behavior
Strange Case of Dr. Jekyll &
    Mr. Hyde
Strange World of Coffin Joe
The Strangeness
Strangers
Strays
Stuff Stephanie in the
    Incinerator
Subspecies
Sugar Cookies
Suicide Cult
Summer of Fear
Summer of Secrets
Sundown
Superstition
Survivor
Suspiria▶
Swamp of the Lost Monster
The Swarm
Sweet 16
Tainted Image
Tales from the Crypt▶
Tales from the Crypt
Tales from the Gimli Hospital
Tales of Terror
Tales That Witness Madness
Tarantulas: The Deadly Cargo
Taste the Blood of Dracula
Teenage Gang Debs
Teenage Strangler
Teenage Zombies
The Tell-Tale Heart
The Tempter
Tentacles
The Terror
Terror at Red Wolf Inn
Terror at Tenkiller
Terror at the Opera
Terror Beach
Terror Eyes
Terror in the Haunted House
Terror in the Swamp
Terror in the Wax Museum
Terror in Toyland
Terror on Tour
Terror Out of the Sky
Terror Train
The Terror Within
Terrorgram
Testament of Dr. Mabuse
The Texas Chainsaw
    Massacre
Texas Chainsaw Massacre,
    Part 2
That Darn Sorceress
Theatre of Death
They Came from Within
They Saved Hitler's Brain
Things
Thirst
The Thirsty Dead
The 13th Floor
Thirteenth Reunion
The Thousand Eyes of Dr.
    Mabuse
Three on a Meathook
Time of the Apes
To All a Goodnight
To Die for
To Die for 2
To Sleep with a Vampire
To the Devil, A Daughter
Tomb
Tomb of Ligeia▶
Tomb of the Undead
Tomb of Torture
Tombs of the Blind Dead
Tomcat: Dangerous Desires

The Toolbox Murders
Tormented
Torso
Torture Chamber of Baron
    Blood
The Torture Chamber of Dr.
    Sadism
Torture Dungeon
Torture Garden
Torture Train
The Touch of Satan
Tower of Evil
Tower of Screaming Virgins
Toxic Zombies
Track of the Moonbeast
Track of the Vampire
Transmutations
Trap Them & Kill Them
Trapped Alive
Trick or Treat
Trick or Treats
Trilogy of Terror
Troll
Troll 2
Truth or Dare?
Twice Dead
Twice-Told Tales▶
Twilight People
Twilight Zone: The Movie
Twins of Evil
Twinsanity
Twisted
Twisted Brain
Twisted Nightmare
Twitch of the Death Nerve
Two Evil Eyes
The Two Faces of Evil
2000 Maniacs
The Unborn
The Unborn 2
The Uncanny
Uncle Was a Vampire
The Undead▶
Understudy: The Graveyard
    Shift 2
The Unearthing
The Unearthly
The Unholy
The Uninvited▶
The Uninvited
Unmasked Part 25
The Unnamable
The Unnamable 2: The
    Statement of Randolph
    Carter
The Unseen
Vampire at Midnight
Vampire Circus
Vampire Cop
The Vampire Hookers
The Vampire Lovers
Vampyres
Varan the Unbelievable
Vault of Horror
The Velvet Vampire
Vengeance Is Mine
Vengeance of the Zombies
Venom
Venus in Furs
Victims
The Video Dead
Video Violence
Video Violence Part 2...The
    Exploitation!
Videodrome
The Vindicator
The Vineyard
Violent Blood Bath
Virgin Among the Living Dead
The Virgin of Nuremberg
The Virgin Witch
Visions of Evil
The Visitor
Visitor from the Grave
Voodoo Black Exorcist
Voodoo Dawn
Voodoo Woman
Vulture
Wacko
Warlock
Warlock Moon
Warlock: The Armageddon

Horror

The Wasp Woman
Watch Me When I Kill
The Watcher in the Woods
Watchers
Watchers 2
Waxwork
Web of the Spider
The Weirdo
Welcome to Spring Break
Werewolf in a Girl's Dormitory
Werewolf of Washington
Werewolves on Wheels
What a Carve-Up!
What Ever Happened to Baby Jane?▶
What the Peeper Saw
What's the Matter with Helen?
Wheels of Terror
When the Screaming Stops
Whiskey Mountain
Whispers
Who Slew Auntie Roo?
The Wicked
The Wicker Man▶
The Wild Beasts
Willard
The Willies
Winterbeast
The Witch
Witch Who Came from the Sea
Witchboard
Witchboard 2: The Devil's Doorway
Witchcraft
Witchcraft 2: The Temptress
Witchcraft 3: The Kiss of Death
Witchcraft 5: Dance with the Devil
Witchcraft 6
Witchery
Witches' Mountain
The Witching
Witching Time
The Witchmaker
The Witch's Mirror
WitchTrap
The Wizard of Gore
Wolf
Wolf Blood
Wolfen▶
The Wolfman
Woodchipper Massacre
World of the Vampires
The Worm Eaters
The Worst of Faces of Death
Wrestling Women vs. the Aztec Ape
Wrestling Women vs. the Aztec Mummy
You are Not I
Zoltan...Hound of Dracula
Zombie
The Zombie Army
Zombie High
Zombie Island Massacre
Zombie Lake
Zombie Nightmare
Zombies of Moratau
Zombiethon
Zone of the Dead

Horror Anthologies

see also Horror Anthologies
Alien Massacre
Asylum
Body Bags
Cinemagic
Creepshow
Creepshow 2
Dead of Night▶
Dead of Night
Deadtime Stories
Dr. Terror's House of Horrors
Escapes
Ghost Stories: Graveyard Thriller
Grim Prairie Tales
The Hitchhiker
Hitchhiker 2

Hitchhiker 3
Hitchhiker 4
The House that Dripped Blood
The Monster Club
Night Gallery▶
Nightmares
The Offspring
Once Upon a Midnight Scary
Screamtime
Spirits of the Dead▶
Tales from the Crypt▶
Tales from the Crypt, Vol. 3
Tales from the Darkside: The Movie
Tales That Witness Madness
Twice-Told Tales▶
Twilight Zone: The Movie
Two Evil Eyes
The Uncanny
Vault of Horror
The Willies

Horror Comedy

Adventures of Eliza Fraser
Andy Warhol's Dracula▶
Andy Warhol's Frankenstein
April Fool's Day
Arachnophobia
Army of Darkness▶
Attack of the Killer Refrigerator
Attack of the Killer Tomatoes
Attack of the Robots
Auntie Lee's Meat Pies
Autopsy of a Ghost
Bad Channels
Bad Taste▶
Beauty on the Beach
Beetlejuice▶
Bela Lugosi Meets a Brooklyn Gorilla
Beverly Hills Bodysnatchers
Big Meat Eater
Billy the Kid Versus Dracula
Black Magic
Blood Beach
Blood Hook
Bloodbath at the House of Death
Body Bags
The Bone Yard
Brain Damage
Bride of Re-Animator
A Bucket of Blood▶
Carry On Screaming
C.H.U.D.
C.H.U.D. 2: Bud the Chud
The Comedy of Terrors▶
Creature from the Haunted Sea
Critters
Critters 2: The Main Course
Critters 3
Curse of the Queerwolf
Cutting Class
Dead Heat
Dr. Jekyll and Sister Hyde
Dolls
Doom Asylum
Dracula & Son
Dracula Blows His Cool
Dracula: Up in Harlem
Eat and Run
Ed and His Dead Mother
Elvira, Mistress of the Dark
Evil Spawn
Face of the Screaming Werewolf
The Fearless Vampire Killers▶
Frankenhooker
Frankenstein's Great Aunt Tillie
From Beyond▶
The Ghost Breakers▶
Ghoulies
Ghoulies 2
Ghoulies 3: Ghoulies Go to College
Goblin
Gore-Met Zombie Chef From Hell

Gremlins▶
Gremlins 2: The New Batch▶
Hard to Die
Highway to Hell
Hillbillies in a Haunted House
The Horror of Frankenstein House▶
House 2: The Second Story
House of the Long Shadows
Human Beasts
Hysterical
I Married a Vampire
I Was a Teenage Zombie
Incredibly Strange Creatures Who Stopped Living and Became Mixed-Up Zombies
The Invisible Maniac
It Came from Hollywood
Killer Klowns from Outer Space
Killer Tomatoes Eat France
Killer Tomatoes Strike Back
Little Shop of Horrors▶
Mama Dracula
A Man with a Maid
The Mask▶
Matinee
Microwave Massacre
Mindkiller
Mom
Monster in the Closet
Motel Hell
Munchies
My Boyfriend's Back
My Demon Lover
My Grandpa is a Vampire
My Mom's a Werewolf
My Son, the Vampire
Near Dark▶
Night of a Thousand Cats
Night of the Creeps
Night of the Laughing Dead
Nightlife
Nocturna
Nothing But Trouble
The Old Dark House▶
Old Mother Riley's Ghosts
Once Bitten
Out of the Dark
Phantom Brother
Phantom Empire
Piranha
Piranha 2: The Spawning
Psycho Girls
Psychos in Love
Q (The Winged Serpent)▶
Rabid Grannies
The Re-Animator▶
Redneck Zombies
The Refrigerator
Return of the Killer Tomatoes
Return of the Living Dead
Return of the Living Dead 2
Return of the Living Dead 3
Revenge of the Red Baron
Saturday the 14th
Saturday the 14th Strikes Back
Schlock
Son of Ingagi
Sorority Babes in the Slimeball Bowl-A-Rama
Speak of the Devil
Spider Man
Spooks Run Wild
Strangers of the Evening
Street Trash
Student Bodies
The Stuff
Teenage Exorcist
Terrorvision
Theatre of Blood▶
There's Nothing Out There
The Thrill Killers
The Toxic Avenger
The Toxic Avenger, Part 2
The Toxic Avenger, Part 3: The Last Temptation of Toxie
Treasure of Fear
Tremors
The Undertaker and His Pals

Vamp
The Vampire Happening
Zombies on Broadway

Horse Racing

see Gambling; Horses

Horses

The Adventures of Gallant Bess
The Appaloosa
Archer's Adventure
The Bashful Bachelor
Bells of San Angelo
Bite the Bullet▶
Black Beauty
Black Beauty▶
Black Beauty/Courage of Black Beauty
The Black Stallion▶
The Black Stallion Returns
Blue Fire Lady
Boots Malone
Born to Run
Broadway Bill▶
Call of the Forest
Casey's Shadow
Champions
Chino
City Slickers 2: The Legend of Curly's Gold
Cold Feet
Come On Tarzan
Courage of Black Beauty
Courage of the North
Danny
Dark Horse
A Day at the Races▶
Day the Bookies Wept
Devil Horse
Devil on Horseback
The Devil's Cargo
Duke of the Derby
Eagle's Wing
The Electric Horseman
Equus
Ex-Mrs. Bradford▶
Far North
The Fighting Stallion▶
A Fine Mess
The Flying Deuces▶
Forbidden Trails
Francis Goes to the Races
A Girl in Every Port
Glory
The Golden Stallion
Great Dan Patch
The Great Mike
Gypsy Colt
Heart of the Rockies
Hell's Hinges
Hit the Saddle
The Horse in the Gray Flannel Suit
Horsemasters
Horsemen
Hot to Trot!
I'm a Fool
Indian Paint
International Velvet
Into the West
Italian Straw Hat▶
It's a Great Life
Justin Morgan Had a Horse
Kentucky Blue Streak
King of the Sierras
King of the Stallions
King of the Wild Horses▶
King of the Wind
Law of the Land
Le Gentleman D'Epsom
The Lemon Drop Kid
The Lighthorsemen▶
Lightning: The White Stallion
The Littlest Horse Thieves
The Littlest Outlaw
The Longshot
Ma and Pa Kettle at the Fair
The Man from Snowy River
Marshal of Cedar Rock

The Miracle of the White Stallions
The Misfits▶
Misty
My Friend Flicka▶
My Old Man
My Pal Trigger
National Lampoon's Animal House▶
National Velvet▶
On the Right Track
Phar Lap
Primo Baby
Prince and the Great Race
The Quiet Man▶
Racing Luck
A Rare Breed
The Red Fury
The Red Pony▶
The Red Stallion
Return of Wildfire
Return to Snowy River▶
Ride a Wild Pony▶
Ride Him, Cowboy▶
Rolling Home
The Rounders
Run for the Roses
Running Wild
Saddle Buster
Saratoga
Silver Stallion
The Silver Stallion: King of the Wild Brumbies
Speedy▶
The Story of Seabiscuit
Sundown Saunders
Sylvester
Tennessee Stallion
Texas to Bataan
Thoroughbreds Don't Cry
Three Men on a Horse▶
Turf Boy
The Undefeated
Western Double Feature 16
When the West Was Young
White Mane▶
Wild Hearts Can't Be Broken▶
Wild Horse Hank
Wild Horses
Wild Pony
Win, Place, or Steal
Winds of the Wasteland

Hospitals & Medicine

see also Disease of the Week; Doctors & Nurses; Sanity Check; Shrinks
Article 99
B.O.R.N.
Britannia Hospital
Carry On Nurse
A Child is Waiting
China Beach▶
City of Joy
The Clonus Horror
Coma▶
Critical Condition
Dead Ringers▶
Disorderlies
Disorderly Orderly
Doctor at Large
Dr. Kildare's Strange Case
Doctors' Wives
East of Kilimanjaro
The Egyptian
Frankenstein General Hospital
Green for Danger
Gross Anatomy
The Hasty Heart
Horror Hospital
The Hospital▶
Hospital Massacre
Hospital of Terror
In for Treatment▶
The Interns
Invasion
Lifespan
Naked Is Better
Nurse
One Flew Over the Cuckoo's Nest▶
State of Emergency

A Stolen Face
Tales from the Gimli Hospital
Tender Loving Care
Threshold
Vital Signs
Whose Life Is It Anyway?▶
Young Doctors in Love

Hostage!

see also Kidnapped!;
Missing Persons
Airheads
Amos and Andrew
Autumn Born
Black Cobra 2
Blackout
Codename: Vengeance
Cold Sweat
Cul de Sac▶
Days of Hell
Death Stalk
Die Hard▶
Die Hard 2: Die Harder▶
Distortions
Door to Door Maniac
Escape from New York
Fatal Mission
Field of Fire
48 Hours to Live
Hostages▶
Housewife
Iron Eagle
The Jesus Trip
The Legend of Wolf Mountain
Live! From Death Row
Midnight Fear
Operation Thunderbolt
A Perfect World
Provoked
Quake
The Ref▶
Rock All Night
S.F.W.
Snatched
Spaghetti House
Split Second
A Stranger is Watching
Suddenly▶
Sweet Hostage
The Taking of Pelham One
Two Three▶
Terror Stalks the Class
Reunion
The Trap
Vengeance

Hunted!

see also Survival
Beyond Fear
The Cursed Mountain Mystery
Cyborg 2
Damned River
Deadly Game
Death Hunt
Deliverance▶
Diary of a Hitman
Ex-Cop
Eyes of the Beholder
Final Round
Fortress
Freejack
The Ghost of Fletcher Ridge
Goetz von Berlichingen
The Good Guys and the Bad
Guys
Hard Target
Hunter's Blood
Illegal Entry: Formula for Fear
Killing at Hell's Gate
Ladykillers
Last Witness
The Most Dangerous Game▶
The Naked Prey▶
Nightmare at Bittercreek
Prey for the Hunter
Shadowhunter
Shoot to Kill▶
Southern Comfort▶
Survival Quest
Surviving the Game
Trial and Error

Hunting

see also Go Fish
The Bear▶
The Belstone Fox
The Bridge to Nowhere
Caddyshack▶
Dan Candy's Law
Deadly Prey
First Blood
Forest of Little Bear
Gaiety
Git!
Harry Black and the Tiger
The Hunt▶
The Last Hunt
The Last Safari
Mogambo▶
The Most Dangerous Game▶
Night of the Grizzly
Shoot
Shooting
Those Calloways
White Hunter, Black Heart▶

Identity

see also Amnesia; Role
Reversal
Brainwaves
The Broken Chain
Changes
The Crimes of Stephen
Hawke
The Dark Half
Dark Passage
Diabolically Yours
Dr. Heckyl and Mr. Hype
Dumbo▶
The Effect of Gamma Rays on
Man-in-the-Moon
Marigolds▶
Far Out Man
The Great Gabbo
High Country
Joe Versus the Volcano
Leon the Pig Farmer
Marnie▶
Middle Age Crazy
Montenegro▶
Moving Out
My Brilliant Career▶
My Dinner with Andre▶
Nevil Shute's The Far Country
Next Year If All Goes Well
The Nutty Professor▶
O Youth and Beauty
Old Boyfriends
Olivier, Olivier▶
Orlando▶
Partner▶
Pocketful of Miracles▶
Point of No Return
The Promise
Rebel Without a Cause▶
Return of the Secaucus 7▶
Ruby in Paradise▶
Sorrows of Gin
Timothy and the Angel
Torment
Vincent, Francois, Paul and
the Others▶
Woof!
The Wrong Move
Zelig▶

Immigration

Arizona
Avalon▶
Blood Red
Borderline
Buck Privates Come Home▶
Combination Platter
The Cowboy Way
The Displaced Person▶
Does This Mean We're
Married?
Drachenfutter▶
Driving Me Crazy
El Super▶
The Emigrants▶
Far and Away

Green Card
Hester Street▶
I Cover the Waterfront
The Immigrant▶
Italian
Journey of Hope▶
A King in New York
Living on Tokyo Time
The Manions of America
Marcados por el Destino
Maricela
Midnight Auto Supply
Monkey Business▶
Moscow on the Hudson▶
My Girl Tisa
My Sweet Victim
The New Land▶
Pelle the Conqueror▶
Sky High
Skyline▶
Wait Until Spring, Bandini
Where is My Child?

India

The Adversary
Aparajito▶
Autobiography of a Princess
Bhowani Junction
The Black Devils of Kali
Black Narcissus▶
City of Joy
Company Limited
Conduct Unbecoming
The Courtesans of Bombay▶
The Deceivers
Distant Thunder▶
Drums
Ele, My Friend
The Far Pavilions
Flame Over India▶
Gandhi▶
Gunga Din▶
Heat and Dust▶
The Home and the World▶
Hullabaloo Over Georgie &
Bonnie's Pictures
The Jewel in the Crown
Journey to the Lost City
Jungle Hell
Kim▶
The Lives of a Bengal
Lancer▶
The Mahabharata
The Man Who Would Be
King▶
Masala
Maya
Octopussy
A Passage to India▶
Pather Panchali▶
The Rains Came
The Razor's Edge▶
The River▶
Sabaka
Shakespeare Wallah▶
Spices▶
Staying On
Two Daughters▶
Wee Willie Winkie▶
The World of Apu▶

Insects

see Killer Bugs

Insects

see Killer Bugs
The Hellstrom Chronicle▶
Twilight of the Cockroaches
Wax, or the Discovery of
Television Among the Bees

Interviews

see also This is Your Life
Bugs Bunny Superstar
Chuck Berry: Hail! Hail! Rock
'n' Roll▶
The Compleat Beatles▶
Cult People
Hearts of Darkness: A
Filmmaker's Apocalypse▶

Hedda Hopper's Hollywood
Hollywood Ghost Stories
James Dean
The JFK Conspiracy
The Making of ''A Brief
History of Time''
The Making of a Legend:
''Gone With the Wind''
Roger & Me▶
Sometimes It Works,
Sometimes It Doesn't
Stripper
Wisecracks▶

Inventors &
Inventions

see also Mad Scientists;
Science & Scientists
Chitty Chitty Bang Bang
C.H.O.M.P.S.
The Demi-Paradise▶
Edison the Man
The Great Moment
Hidden Enemy
Homer Comes Home
Homewrecker
Honey, I Blew Up the Kid
Honey, I Shrunk the Kids
The Man in the White Suit▶
The Man Who Fell to Earth▶
The Mosquito Coast
Mystery Plane
Not Quite Human
Not Quite Human 2
The Pinchcliffe Grand Prix
Roaring Speedboats
Rogue's Gallery
So This is Washington
The Sound and the Silence
Spitfire▶
Still Not Quite Human
Tom Edison: The Boy Who Lit
Up the World
Where's Willie?
The Whole Shootin' Match▶
The Yellow Cab Man
Young Tom Edison

Ireland

see also Great Britain
Belfast Assassin
Beloved Enemy▶
Cal▶
Children in the Crossfire
The Commitments▶
The Crying Game▶
Danny Boy▶
Darby O'Gill & the Little
People▶
The Dawning
The Dead▶
Far and Away
The Field▶
The Fighting Prince of
Donegal
Fools of Fortune
Four Days in July
Hennessy
I See a Dark Stranger▶
In the Name of the Father▶
The Informer▶
Into the West▶
Irish Cinderella
James Joyce: A Portrait of the
Artist as a Young Man
Johnny Nobody
The Lonely Passion of Judith
Hearne▶
Man of Aran▶
The Manions of America
Men of Ireland
Odd Man Out▶
Oh, Mr. Porter
The Playboys▶
Prayer for the Dying
The Purple Taxi
Quiet Day In Belfast▶
The Quiet Man▶
Rawhead Rex
River of Unrest
Ryan's Daughter

Shake Hands with the Devil▶
The Snapper▶
Song O' My Heart▶
Taffin
Ulysses
Widow's Peak

Islam

see also Middle East
Hamsin▶
Mohammed: Messenger of
God
The Suitors

Island Fare

see also Pacific Islands
The Adventures of Sadie
All the Brothers Were Valiant
Atlantis, the Lost Continent
Bare Essentials
Bikini Island
Bird of Paradise
The Blue Lagoon
Blue Paradise
Body Trouble
Cabin Boy
Captain Ron
The Castaway Cowboy
Chandu on the Magic Island
Club Paradise
Conqueror & the Empress
The Cover Girl Murders
Crusoe
Deadly Currents
Dinosaur Island
Echoes of Paradise
Emmanuelle on Taboo Island
Father Goose
F.P. 1
Gilligan's Island: Meet the
Crew
Hawk of the Wilderness
Horrors of Spider Island
Hurricane
The Idol Dancer
The Island
Island in the Sun
Island of Adventure
Island of Lost Souls▶
Island of the Blue Dolphins
Island of the Lost
Joe Versus the Volcano
Jurassic Park▶
King of the Damned
The Lunatic
Magic on Love Island
A Man of Passion
Mediterraneo▶
Melody in Love
My Father the Hero
Mysterious Island of Beautiful
Women
No Escape
Northern Extremes
One Night in the Tropics
Pagan Island
Paradise
Passion in Paradise
The Passion of Anna▶
Pearl of the South Pacific
Pippi in the South Seas
Return to Paradise
Return to the Blue Lagoon
Savage is Loose
The Seducers
Son of Fury▶
Summer Affair
A Swingin' Summer
Terror in Paradise
Trouble in Paradise
The Tuttles of Tahiti▶
Utopia
Week-End In Havana
When Time Ran Out
Wide Sargasso Sea
Wings Over the Pacific

Israel

see also Holocaust;
Judaism
Cast a Giant Shadow

Children of Rage
Cup Final
Diamonds
Double Edge
Eagles Attack at Dawn
Echoes of Conflict
Exodus▶
Hide and Seek
Hill 24 Doesn't Answer▶
Intimate Story
Late Summer Blues
The Little Drummer Girl▶
Operation Thunderbolt
The Seventh Coin
Sinai Commandos
Soldier of the Night

Italy

Accatone!▶
Acqua e Sapone
All Screwed Up▶
Amarcord▶
The Assisi Underground
Assunta Spina
Avanti!
The Bicycle Thief▶
A Blade in the Dark
Blame It on the Bellboy
Blood Feud
The Children
Christ Stopped at Eboli▶
Cinema Paradiso▶
Cobra
The Conformist▶
Cry of a Prostitute: Love Kills
Divorce—Italian Style▶
1860
Enchanted April
Escapade in Florence
Europa '51
Executioner of Venice
Fellini's Roma
Final Justice
Francesco
Garden of the Finzi-Continis▶
The Godfather, Part 3▶
Hornet's Nest
It Started in Naples▶
Kaos▶
La Chartreuse de Parme
La Dolce Vita▶
La Notte Brava
La Terra Trema▶
The Lion of Venice
Lost Moment
Love and Anarchy▶
Love in the City▶
Macaroni
A Man About the House
Massacre in Rome
Mussolini & I
1900▶
Obsession
Only You
Open City▶
Ossessione▶
Paisan▶
Passion of Love▶
A Rare Breed
Roman Spring of Mrs. Stone▶
Rome Adventure
The Scent of a Woman
Season for Assassins
The Seven Hills of Rome
Shoeshine▶
The Sicilian
A Special Day▶
Three Coins in the Fountain
The Tree of Wooden Clogs▶
Von Ryan's Express▶
What Did You Do in the War, Daddy?
Where Angels Fear to Tread▶
Year of the Gun

Jail

see *Great Escapes; Men in Prison; Women in Prison*

Japan

see also *Asia*

Akira
The Ballad of Narayama▶
Barbarian and the Geisha
Battle of China
The Battle of the Japan Sea
Behind the Rising Sun
Black Rain▶
Black Rain
Blood on the Sun
Captive Hearts
The Cruel Story of Youth▶
Destination Tokyo
Dodes 'ka-den▶
Eijanaika▶
Escapade in Japan
47 Ronin, Part 1▶
47 Ronin, Part 2▶
Girls of the White Orchid
Heaven & Earth▶
Hiroshima Maiden
Hiroshima, Mon Amour▶
The Idiot▶
The Imperial Japanese Empire
Imperial Navy
Journey of Honor
King's Ransom
Life of Oharu▶
Love and Faith▶
MacArthur's Children▶
The Makioka Sisters▶
The Men Who Tread on the Tiger's Tail
Midway
Mishima: A Life in Four Chapters▶
Mr. Baseball
Mother▶
Ninja Wars
No Regrets for Our Youth▶
Nomugi Pass
Objective, Burma!▶
Okoge
Osaka Elegy
Prisoners of the Sun▶
Professional Killers 1
Ran▶
Rashomon▶
Red Beard▶
Revenge of a Kabuki Actor
Rikyu▶
Rising Sun▶
Saga of the Vagabond
Samurai Cowboy
Samurai Reincarnation
Sansho the Bailiff▶
Sayonara▶
Seven Indignant
Seven Samurai▶
She and He
Shin Heike Monogatari▶
Shogun▶
Shogun's Ninja
Showdown in Little Tokyo
Snow Country
The Sun's Burial▶
Sword of Fury II
Thirty Seconds Over Tokyo▶
3 Ninjas Kick Back
Tokyo Decadence
Tokyo-Ga▶
Tokyo Pop
Tora! Tora! Tora!
Twenty-Four Eyes▶
Ugetsu▶
Utamaro and His Five Women
Walk, Don't Run
What's Up, Tiger Lily?▶
The Wolves▶
The Yakuza
You Only Live Twice
Zatoichi vs. Yojimbo▶

Japanimation

see also *Animation & Cartoons*

Akira
Alakazam the Great!
Arcadia of My Youth
The Dagger of Kamui
Demon City Shinjuku
GUY: Awakening of the Devil
Lensman
My Neighbor Totoro
Otaku no Video
Planet Busters
The Professional: Golgo 13
Project A-ko
Project A-ko 2: Plot of the Daitokuji Financial Group
Project A-ko 3: Cinderella Rhapsody
Starvengers
Toward the Terra
Urotsukidoji 1: Legend of the Overfiend
Urotsukidoji 2: Legend of the Demon Womb
Urusei Yatsura Movie 1: Only You
Urusei Yatsura Movie 2: Beautiful Dreamer
Urusei Yatsura Movie 3: Remember My Love
Urusei Yatsura Movie 4: Lum the Forever
Urusei Yatsura Movie 6: Always My Darling

Journalism

see *Front Page*

Judaism

see also *Holocaust; Israel*

American Matchmaker
Angry Harvest▶
The Apprenticeship of Duddy Kravitz▶
The Assisi Underground
Atalia
The Attic: The Hiding of Anne Frank
Au Revoir Les Enfants▶
The Blum Affair
Border Street
A Brivele der Mamen▶
Brussels Transit▶
The Cantor's Son
Charlie Grant's War
Commissar▶
Conspiracy of Hearts▶
The Corridor: Death
Crossfire▶
Crossing Delancey▶
David▶
The Diary of Anne Frank▶
Drifting
The Dunera Boys▶
The Dybbuk▶
East and West▶
Eli Eli
Enemies, a Love Story▶
Every Time We Say Goodbye
Exodus▶
Fiddler on the Roof▶
The Fixer▶
A Friendship in Vienna
The Frisco Kid
Funny Girl▶
Garden of the Finzi-Continis▶
Gentleman's Agreement▶
God, Man and Devil
The Golem▶
Good Evening, Mr. Wallenberg
Goodbye, New York
Green Fields
Hamsin▶
Hanna's War
Hester Street▶
Hill 24 Doesn't Answer▶
Holocaust▶
Homicide▶

The House on Chelouche Street
Hunted!
I Love You, Alice B. Toklas
I Love You Rosa
Jazz Singer
Jud Suess▶
King David
Kuni Lemel in Tel Aviv
The Last Metro▶
The Last Winter
Leon the Pig Farmer
Les Violons du Bal
Lies My Father Told Me▶
The Light Ahead
Madman
Masada▶
Miracle at Moreaux
Miss Rose White▶
Mr. Emmanuel
My Michael▶
No Way to Treat a Lady▶
Noa at Seventeen▶
Only Way
Outside Chance of Maximillian Glick
Over the Brooklyn Bridge
The Pawnbroker▶
Power
Radio Days▶
The Revolt of Job▶
Sallah▶
Schindler's List▶
School Ties▶
A Secret Space
The Serpent's Egg
The Shop on Main Street▶
Sofie
The Sorrow and the Pity▶
A Stranger Among Us
The Summer of My German Soldier▶
Table Settings
Tevye
They Were Ten
'38: Vienna Before the Fall
Transport from Paradise
Two of Us▶
Uncle Moses
Under the Earth▶
Unsettled Land
Used People
Voyage of the Damned▶
Wandering Jew
War & Love
Where is My Child?
Where's Poppa?▶
The Wooden Gun
Yentl
Zalmen or the Madness of God

Jungle Stories

see also *Treasure Hunt*

Africa Screams
Aguirre, the Wrath of God▶
All the Way, Boys
Amazon
Amazon Jail
Baby...Secret of the Lost Legend
Back from Eternity
Bat 21
Bela Lugosi Meets a Brooklyn Gorilla
Beyond the Carribean
Black Cobra 3: The Manila Connection
The Black Devils of Kali
Blonde Savage
Bride of the Gorilla
Cannibal Women in the Avocado Jungle of Death
Codename: Terminate
The Colombian Connection
Commando Invasion
Delta Force Commando
Diplomatic Immunity
Dr. Cyclops
East of Borneo
Elephant Boy▶
Elephant Walk

The Emerald Forest▶
Emerald Jungle
Emmanuelle 6
Enemy Unseen
Escape to Burma
Escape 2000
Farewell to the King
Fatal Mission
Field of Fire
Field of Honor
Final Mission
Firehawk
Fitzcarraldo▶
Five Came Back
Flight from Singapore
Found Alive
The Further Adventures of Tennessee Buck
Fury
Gold Raiders
Goliathon
Green Fire
Green Inferno
Green Mansions
Greystoke: The Legend of Tarzan, Lord of the Apes
Harry Black and the Tiger
Heart of Darkness
Hell's Headquarters
Indio
Indio 2: The Revolt
Invincible Barbarian
Jacare
Jane & the Lost City
Jungle
The Jungle Book
The Jungle Book▶
Jungle Bride
Jungle Drums of Africa
Jungle Goddess
Jungle Heat
Jungle Hell
Jungle Inferno
Jungle Master
Jungle Patrol
Jungle Raiders
Jungle Siren
The Jungle Trap
Killers
Killing Heat
King of the Kongo
King Solomon's Treasure
La Choca
The Land Unknown
Law of the Jungle
Liana, Jungle Goddess
The Lion King
The Lion Man
Lion Man
The Lost City
Lost City of the Jungle
The Lost Continent
The Lost Jungle
The Lost Tribe
Medicine Man
Merrill's Marauders
Mighty Jungle
Miracles
Missing in Action
The Mission▶
Mistress of the Apes
Mogambo▶
The Mosquito Coast
The Muthers
Nabonga
Naked Jungle▶
The Naked Prey▶
The New Adventures of Tarzan
Night Creature
Nightforce
Objective, Burma!▶
Omoo Omoo, the Shark God
Options
Perils of the Darkest Jungle
Predator
Queen of the Amazons
Queen of the Jungle
Red Dust▶
Revenge of Doctor X
River of Death
River of Evil

The Road to Zanzibar▶
Robbers of the Sacred
  Mountain
Romancing the Stone▶
Samar
The Savage Girl
Shame of the Jungle
Sheena
Sniper
Son of Kong
Stormquest
Sweet Revenge
Tarzan and His Mate▶
Tarzan and the Green
  Goddess
Tarzan and the Trappers
Tarzan Escapes▶
Tarzan Finds a Son▶
Tarzan of the Apes
Tarzan, the Ape Man▶
Tarzan, the Ape Man
Tarzan the Fearless
Tarzan the Tiger
Tarzan's Revenge
Tarzan's Secret Treasure
Terror in the Jungle
Terror of the Bloodhunters
The Thirsty Dead
Tiger Fangs
Trap Them & Kill Them
The Treasure of the Amazon
Troma's War
Tropical Heat
Typhoon Treasure
Virgin Sacrifice
Volunteers
Voodoo Woman
The Voyage of Tanai
Wages of Fear▶
Warkill
Warriors of the Apocalypse
West of Zanzibar
Where the River Runs Black
White Cannibal Queen
White Ghost
White Gorilla
White Huntress
The White Legion
The White Orchid
White Pongo
Woman Hunt
The World's Greatest Athlete
Zombie Island Massacre

Justice Prevails...?

*see also Order in the
  Court*
Absence of Malice
The Accused▶
All-American Murder
And Justice for All
Assault at West Point: The
  Court-Martial of Johnson
  Whittaker
Beau Geste▶
Beyond Reasonable Doubt
A Case for Murder
Creature with the Blue Hand
Cross Examination
A Cry in the Dark▶
Dark Justice
Dead Right
Dingaka
A Dry White Season▶
Eddie Macon's Run
The Execution of Private
  Slovik▶
False Arrest
Forgotten Prisoners
The Good Fight
Guilty as Charged
Guilty as Sin
A Gun in the House
The Hanging Tree▶
Honor Thy Father and Mother:
  The True Story of the
  Menendez Brothers
In the Name of the Father▶
The Jagged Edge
JFK▶
Lawman▶
Let Him Have It▶

Life & Times of Judge Roy
  Bean
The Magnificent Yankee▶
Music Box
Nuts▶
The Paper▶
Presumed Innocent▶
Prisoners of the Sun▶
Reversal of Fortune▶
Roe vs. Wade▶
Separate But Equal▶
The Shooting Party
Showdown
The Story of Qui Ju▶
Trial and Error
The Verdict▶
Weekend of Shadows▶
White Lie
The Wrong Man▶
The Young One

Kidnapped!

*see also Hostage!;
  Missing Persons*
Abducted
Abduction
The Abduction of Allison Tate
The Abduction of Kari
  Swenson
Ace Ventura: Pet Detective
Act of Piracy
Adam▶
African Rage
Against A Crooked Sky
And Hope to Die
The Armour of God
Ashanti, Land of No Mercy
The Atomic City
Autumn Born
Baby's Day Out
Beach Blanket Bingo▶
Beethoven's 2nd
Benji▶
Best Revenge
Beverly Hills Brats
Beyond Fear
Beyond Justice
Black Samurai
Blood at Sundown
Blown Away
Bound and Gagged: A Love
  Story
The Chase
Cohen and Tate
Cold Blood
Commando▶
The Concentratin' Kid
Crimebusters
The Crying Game▶
Deadly Commando
Doctor Who: The Twin
  Dilemma
Door to Door Maniac
Fire in the Sky
Fireback
The Grissom Gang▶
Guarding Tess
Gun Fury
Hangfire
Harem
Hearts & Armour
Hollywood Cop
In a Stranger's Hand
Island Monster
Jack and His Friends
Jailbait
Kickboxer 3: The Art of War
Kid Colter
Kidnapped
Lake Consequence
The Light in the Forest
The Lightning Incident
The Lindbergh Kidnapping
  Case▶
Lorna Doone
Manipulator
Martin's Day
Memphis
Mr. Nanny
The Money
Moran of the Lady Letty

The Night of the Following
  Day
The Nightmare Before
  Christmas▶
Nightstick
No Deposit, No Return
The Only Way Home
Orphans▶
Outlaw Force
Parker
A Perfect World
Prince of Pennsylvania
Rage of Wind
Raising Arizona▶
Ransom Money
The Real McCoy
Rescue Me
The Revenger
Riders of the Purple Sage
Ring of Fire 2: Blood and Steel
Ring of the Musketeers
Rio Diablo
Rosebud
Runaway Nightmare
Sahara
Savage Abduction
Second Sight
Seven Hours to Judgment
Slate, Wyn & Me
Sloane
SnakeEater
Son of the Pink Panther
The Squeeze
Still Not Quite Human
Sunstroke
Sweet Poison
Tarzan's New York Adventure
Terror Stalks the Class
  Reunion
That Man from Rio
Thou Shalt Not Kill...Except
Three Days to a Kill
3 Ninjas
Tie Me Up! Tie Me Down!
The Trap
Trapped Alive
Try and Get Me
The Vanishing
Whistling in the Dark▶

Killer Apes

The Ape
A*P*E*
The Ape Man
Battle for the Planet of the
  Apes
Beneath the Planet of the
  Apes
Blue Monkey
Conquest of the Planet of the
  Apes
In the Shadow of Kilimanjaro
King Kong▶
King Kong
King Kong Lives
King Kong Versus Godzilla
King of Kong Island
Link
Mighty Joe Young
Monkey Shines
Planet of the Apes▶
Primal Rage
Return of the Ape Man
Son of Ingagi
Son of Kong

Killer Appliances

*see also Technology-
  Rampant*
Attack of the Killer
  Refrigerator
Ghost in the Machine
Microwave Massacre
The Refrigerator

Killer Beasts

*see also Killer Apes;
  Killer Dogs; Killer Kats;
  Killer Pigs; Killer Rodents*
The Abomination
Alligator▶

Alligator 2: The Mutation
The Angry Red Planet
The Ape
A*P*E*
The Ape Man
Attack of the Beast Creatures
Attack of the Giant Leeches
Beaks: The Movie
Ben
Berserker
Big Foot
Bog
The Brain Eaters
The Bride & the Beast
Claws
Copperhead
Creepshow
Crocodile
Dark Age
Day of the Animals
The Devil Bat
The Devil Bat's Daughter
Devil Dog: The Hound of Hell
Devil Monster
Dinosaurus!
Dragonslayer▶
Fangs
Fer-De-Lance
Food of the Gods
Frogs
Gamera, the Invincible
Gamera vs. Barugon
Gamera vs. Gaos
The Giant Gila Monster
Godzilla on Monster Island
Godzilla Raids Again
Godzilla vs. Biollante
Godzilla vs. Megalon
Godzilla vs. the Cosmic
  Monster
Godzilla vs. the Sea Monster
Gorilla
Grizzly
In the Shadow of Kilimanjaro
Island of Terror▶
It Came from Beneath the
  Sea▶
It Conquered the World
Jabberwocky
Jaws of Satan
Jurassic Park▶
The Killer Shrews
King Kong
King Kong
King Kong Lives
Legend of Big Foot
The Leopard Man
Link
Mad Death
Mighty Joe Young
The Mole People
Monkey Shines
The Monster Walks
Monty Python and the Holy
  Grail▶
Mutator
Mysterious Island▶
Night Creature
Night of the Grizzly
Night of the Howling Beast
Nightwing
Pigs
Q (The Winged Serpent)▶
Rana: The Legend of Shadow
  Lake
The Rats are Coming! The
  Werewolves are Here!
Rattlers
Razorback
Return to Boggy Creek
Rodan
Shakma
Shriek of the Mutilated
Sleepwalkers
The Slime People
Slithis
Snowbeast
Son of Kong
Spasms
Stanley
Subspecies
Swamp of the Lost Monster

Tremors
Tromba, the Tiger Man
Venom
Vulture
The Wild Beasts
Winterbeast
Wrestling Women vs. the
  Aztec Ape
X from Outer Space
Yongkari Monster of the Deep

Killer Brains

Blood of Ghastly Horror
The Brain
Brain Damage
The Brain from Planet Arous
Brain of Blood
The Brain That Wouldn't Die
Donovan's Brain▶
Fiend Without a Face
Mindkiller

Killer Bugs

Ants
The Applegates
Arachnophobia
The Bees
Beginning of the End
The Black Scorpion
Blood Beast Terror
Blue Monkey
Bug
The Cosmic Monsters
Creepers
Creepshow
Curse of the Black Widow
The Deadly Mantis
Doctor Who: The Ark in Space
Earth vs. the Spider
Empire of the Ants
Evil Spawn
Food of the Gods
The Giant Spider Invasion
Horrors of Spider Island
Kingdom of the Spiders
Kiss of the Tarantula
The Lair of the White Worm▶
Monster from Green Hell
The Monster that Challenged
  the World
Mothra▶
Naked Jungle▶
The Nest
Parasite
Phase 4
Return of the Fly
The Savage Bees
The Scorpion's Tail
Skeeter
Slugs
Son of Godzilla
Spider Woman▶
Squirm
The Swarm
Tarantula▶
Tarantulas: The Deadly Cargo
Terror Out of the Sky
Them!▶
They Came from Within
Ticks
The Wasp Woman
The Worm Eaters

Killer Cars

The Cars That Ate Paris▶
Christine
Dark of the Night
Death Race 2000
Death Sport
Duel▶
The Hearse
Mad Max▶
Mad Max: Beyond
  Thunderdome
Maximum Overdrive
One Deadly Owner
The Road Warrior▶
Wheels of Terror

Killer

Killer Dogs
see also *King of Beasts (Dogs)*
Cujo
Devil Dog: The Hound of Hell
Dogs of Hell
The Hound of the Baskervilles▶
The Hound of the Baskervilles
Mongrel
Monster Dog
The Omen
The Pack
Pet Sematary 2
Play Dead
Revenge
Zoltan...Hound of Dracula

Killer Dreams
Alias John Preston
Bad Dreams
Blood Rage
Dario Argento's Trauma
Dead of Night▶
Deadly Dreams
Dream No Evil
Freddy's Dead: The Final Nightmare
A Nightmare on Elm Street
A Nightmare on Elm Street 2: Freddy's Revenge
A Nightmare on Elm Street 3: Dream Warriors
A Nightmare on Elm Street 4: Dream Master
A Nightmare on Elm Street 5: Dream Child
Paperhouse▶
Phantasm
Twisted Nightmare

Killer Kats
see also *Cats*
Batman Returns
The Black Cat
Cat People▶
Cat People
Cat Women of the Moon
Claws
The Corpse Grinders
The Creeper
Curse of the Cat People▶
The Leopard Man
Mutator
Night of a Thousand Cats
Pet Sematary
Seven Deaths in the Cat's Eye
Strays
The Uncanny
The Uninvited

Killer Pigs
The Amityville Horror
Evilspeak
Pigs
Razorback

Killer Plants
Attack of the Killer Tomatoes
Attack of the Mushroom People
Body Snatchers
Day of the Triffids▶
Dr. Terror's House of Horrors
The Freakmaker
Invasion of the Body Snatchers▶
Killer Tomatoes Eat France
Killer Tomatoes Strike Back
Little Shop of Horrors▶
Navy vs. the Night Monsters
Please Don't Eat My Mother
Return of the Killer Tomatoes
Seedpeople
Seeds of Evil

Killer Rodents
The Bat
The Bat People

Ben
Deadly Eyes
Food of the Gods
Food of the Gods: Part 2
The Killer Shrews
Of Unknown Origin
Rats
The Rats are Coming! The Werewolves are Here!
Willard

Killer Toys
Black Devil Doll from Hell
Child's Play
Child's Play 2
Child's Play 3
Dance of Death
Demonic Toys
Devil Doll▶
Devil Doll
Devil's Gift
Dollman vs Demonic Toys
Dolls
Dolly Dearest
Halloween 3: Season of the Witch
Magic
Poltergeist▶
Puppet Master
Puppet Master 2
Puppet Master 3: Toulon's Revenge
Puppet Master 4
Silent Night, Deadly Night 5: The Toymaker
Trilogy of Terror
Wired to Kill

Kindness of Strangers
Angels Over Broadway▶
The Big Push
Good Sam
Lilies of the Field▶
Major Barbara▶
Mr. Deeds Goes to Town▶
Mr. Lucky▶
Mr. North
She Couldn't Say No
Sincerely Yours
Toll Gate
Touch & Go
The Vals

King of Beasts (Dogs)
see also *Killer Dogs*
The Accidental Tourist▶
Across the Bridge
The Adventures of Milo & Otis▶
The Adventures of Rex & Rinty
The Adventures of Rin Tin Tin
After the Thin Man▶
All Dogs Go to Heaven
The Amazing Dobermans
Antarctica
The Awful Truth▶
Baxter
Beethoven
Beethoven's 2nd
Behave Yourself!
Benji▶
Benji the Hunted
Benji's Very Own Christmas Story
Big Red
Bingo
Blondie in Society
A Boy Named Charlie Brown▶
Call of the Wild
Captured in Chinatown
Challenge To Be Free
Challenge to Lassie
Challenge to White Fang
A Charlie Brown Celebration
Children of the Wild
Chips, the War Dog
C.H.O.M.P.S.
Clean Slate

Come Back Little Reba
Complex
Cool Hand Luke▶
Courage of Lassie
Courage of Rin Tin Tin
Courage of the North
A Cry in the Dark▶
Cujo
Danny Boy
Daring Dobermans
The Dawson Patrol
Devil Dog: The Hound of Hell
Digby, the Biggest Dog in the World
Dirkham Detective Agency
The Doberman Gang
A Dog of Flanders
Dog Pound Shuffle
The Dog Who Stopped the War
Dogs of Hell
Down and Out in Beverly Hills
Dusty
Elmer
Eyes of Texas
Fabulous Joe
Family Dog: Complete Series
Famous Five Get Into Trouble
Fangs of the Wild
Flaming Signal
For the Love of Benji
The Fox and the Hound▶
Frankenweenie
George!
Git!
God's Country
The Good, the Bad, and Huckleberry Hound
Goodbye, My Lady
Great Adventure
Greyfriars Bobby
Hambone & Hillie
Heart of the Rockies
He's Your Dog, Charlie Brown!
Hollow Gate
Homeward Bound: The Incredible Journey▶
The Hound of the Baskervilles
The Incredible Journey
Inside Information
Iron Will
It's a Dog's Life
It's a Mystery, Charlie Brown
K-9
K-9000
Kavik the Wolf Dog
Lady and the Tramp▶
Lassie
Lassie: Adventures of Neeka
Lassie, Come Home
Lassie: The Miracle
Lassie: Well of Love
Lassie's Great Adventure
Laurel & Hardy: Laughing Gravy
Legend of the Northwest
Life is a Circus, Charlie Brown/You're the Greatest, Charlie Brown
Lightning Warrior
Little Heroes
The Lone Defender
Look Who's Talking Now
Love Leads the Way
Magic of Lassie
Man Trouble
The Man Who Wagged His Tail
Man's Best Friend
The Meeting: Eddie Finds a Home
Million Dollar Haul
Milo & Otis
Mrs. Brown, You've Got a Lovely Daughter
Mr. Superinvisible
Mom, the Wolfman and Me
Mongrel
Monster Dog
My Dog Shep
My Dog, the Thief

The Night Cry
Nikki, the Wild Dog of the North
Oh, Heavenly Dog!
Old Yeller▶
101 Dalmations▶
The Pack
The Painted Hills
The Plague Dogs
Play Dead
Poco
Pound Puppies and the Legend of Big Paw
The Return of Grey Wolf
The Return of Our Gang
Reuben, Reuben▶
Rin Tin Tin, Hero of the West
Rover Dangerfield
The Sandlot▶
Savage Sam
Scruffy
Shadow of the Thin Man▶
The Shaggy D.A.
The Shaggy Dog
Shep Comes Home
Sherlock Hound: Tales of Mystery
Silver Stallion
Skeezer
Skull & Crown
Smoke
Son of Lassie
Song of the Thin Man
Sputnik
Spy with a Cold Nose
Storm in a Teacup
Summerdog
Teddy at the Throttle
The Tender Years
They Only Kill Their Masters
The Thin Man▶
The Thin Man Goes Home
To Dance with the White Dog▶
Toby McTeague
Tom and Jerry: The Movie
Turner and Hooch
The Ugly Dachshund
Umberto D▶
The Underdog
Watchers
Watchers 2
We Think the World of You▶
When Lightning Strikes
Where the Red Fern Grows
Where the Red Fern Grows: Part 2
White Fang 2: The Myth of the White Wolf
White Fang and the Hunter
Whitewater Sam
The Wizard of Oz▶
Wolf Dog
Wolfheart's Revenge
Woof!
Zoltan...Hound of Dracula

Kings
see *Royalty*

Korean War
All the Young Men▶
Battle Circus
The Bridges at Toko-Ri▶
The Canon Operation
Dragonfly Squadron
Field of Honor
For the Boys
The Hunters
Iron Angel
Jet Attack/Paratroop Command
The Last Picture Show▶
MacArthur
The Manchurian Candidate▶
M*A*S*H
M*A*S*H: Goodbye, Farewell & Amen▶
M*A*S*H: The Collector's Edition
Men in War

Men of the Fighting Lady▶
Mission Inferno
Mr. Walkie Talkie
One Minute to Zero
Operation Dames
Operation Inchon
Pork Chop Hill▶
Pueblo Affair▶
Retreat, Hell!
Sabre Jet
Sayonara▶
Sergeant Ryker
The Steel Helmet▶
Torpedo Alley
Wonsan Operation

Kung Fu
see *Martial Arts*

Labor & Unions
see also *Miners & Mining*
Act of Vengeance
Black Fury▶
Blue Collar▶
Boxcar Bertha
Brother John▶
Deadly Stranger
The Devil & Miss Jones▶
The Displaced Person▶
The End of St. Petersburg▶
Fame is the Spur
F.I.S.T.
The $5.20 an Hour Dream
Gung Ho
Hoffa▶
I'm All Right Jack▶
Joyride
Keeping On
Killing Floor
Land of Promise
Last Exit to Brooklyn▶
Mac▶
Man of Iron▶
Man of Marble▶
Matewan▶
Molly Maguires
Moonlighting▶
Never Steal Anything Small
Newsies
Norma Rae▶
North Dallas Forty▶
On the Waterfront▶
Pajama Game▶
Riff Raff▶
Salt of the Earth▶
Singleton's Pluck▶
Sons of Steel
Strike▶
Sweetheart!
Take This Job & Shove It
Teamster Boss: The Jackie Presser Story▶
The Triangle Factory Fire Scandal
Waterfront

Late Bloomin' Love
see also *Growing Older*
Adorable Julia
The African Queen▶
Ali: Fear Eats the Soul▶
Atlantic City▶
Bed & Breakfast
Breakfast in Paris
Brief Encounter▶
Cass Timberlane
Charly▶
Children of Nature
The Christmas Wife
Circle of Two
Cold Sassy Tree▶
Crazy from the Heart▶
Devil in the Flesh▶
Devil in the Flesh
Doctor in Distress
End of August
A Fine Romance
Finnegan Begin Again
Forbidden Love
Foreign Affairs▶

Forty Carats
Gal Young 'Un▶
Gin Game▶
Grumpy Old Men▶
Harold and Maude▶
If Ever I See You Again
La Symphonie Pastorale▶
The Last Winters
Lonely Hearts
The Lonely Passion of Judith
    Hearne▶
Love Among the Ruins▶
Macaroni
A Man and a Woman▶
The Night of the Iguana▶
Other People's Money
The Pamela Principle
Players
Queen of the Stardust
    Ballroom▶
The Rainmaker▶
Roman Spring of Mrs. Stone▶
San Antonio
Shadowlands▶
Shirley Valentine▶
The Shock
The Shop Around the
    Corner▶
Shore Leave▶
A Small Killing
Something in Common
Stay As You Are
Stormy Waters
Stroszek▶
To Love Again
Travelling North
24 Hours in a Woman's Life
Twice in a Lifetime▶
Used People
With Six You Get Eggroll

Law & Lawyers

*see also Order in the
    Court*
Adam's Rib▶
Afterburn▶
Anatomy of a Murder▶
And Justice for All
Angel on My Shoulder
Assault at West Point: The
    Court-Martial of Johnson
    Whittaker
Beyond a Reasonable Doubt
Beyond the Silhouette
Bleak House
Blood Brothers
Brain Donors
Brothers in Law
Brother's Keeper▶
The Candidate▶
Cape Fear▶
Carlito's Way▶
A Case for Murder
A Case of Libel
Chase
Circonstances Attenuantes
Citizen Cohn
Class Action▶
The Client
The Conqueror Worm▶
Criminal Law
Dark Justice
Deadly Matrimony
Death of a Soldier
Defenders of the Law
Dirty Mary Crazy Larry▶
Disorganized Crime
The Divorce of Lady X
Down the Drain
El Fego Baca: Six-Gun Law
The Enforcer
Evelyn Prentice
Eye Witness
False Witness
A Few Good Men▶
Final Verdict
The Firm▶
First Monday in October
The Franchise Affair
A Free Soul
From the Hip
Georgia

Gideon's Trumpet
The Good Fight
Guilty as Sin
Honor Thy Father and Mother:
    The True Story of the
    Menendez Brothers
I Am the Law▶
Illegal
I'm No Angel▶
In the Name of the Father▶
The Incident▶
The Jagged Edge
The Judge
Judge Priest▶
Justice
L.A. Law▶
Last Innocent Man
Legal Eagles
Legend of Billie Jean
Let Freedom Ring
Let's Kill All the Lawyers
Life & Times of Judge Roy
    Bean
Love Crimes
Madame X
The Magnificent Yankee▶
Man from Colorado
Manhattan Melodrama▶
Marked Woman▶
My Cousin Vinny▶
The Narrow Margin▶
Night and the City▶
North▶
Ordeal by Innocence
Original Intent
The Paper Chase▶
The Pelican Brief
Penthouse▶
Perfect Witness
Perry Mason Returns▶
Philadelphia▶
Physical Evidence
Presumed Innocent▶
Promised a Miracle
Reet, Petite and Gone▶
Regarding Henry▶
Road Agent
Rumpole of the Bailey
Rumpole of the Bailey:
    Rumpole's Return▶
Runaway Father
Rustler's Valley
Shoot to Kill
A Simple Twist of Fate
Slightly Honorable
The Star Chamber
State's Attorney
The Sun Shines Bright
To Kill a Mockingbird▶
The Trial
Trial and Error
Trois Couleurs: Rouge▶
True Believer
True Colors
Truth or Die
Twelve Angry Men▶
The Verdict▶
Victim▶
Violent Blood Bath
Web of Deceit
The Winslow Boy▶
The Wistful Widow of Wagon
    Gap
Woman of Desire
The World's Oldest Living
    Bridesmaid
The Young Philadelphians▶

Loneliness

see Only the Lonely

Loner Cops

see also Cops
Above the Law
Action Jackson
Bad Attitude
Bad Lieutenant▶
The Blue Knight
Code of Silence
The Cop & the Girl
Cop in Blue Jeans

Dead Bang
The Dead Pool
Deadly Dancer
Die Hard▶
Die Hard 2: Die Harder▶
Dirty Harry▶
The Enforcer
Excessive Force
Force of One
Heat
In the Heat of the Night▶
Klute▶
Magnum Force
McQ
Nightstick
Northwest Trail
One Good Cop
One Man Jury
Rent-A-Cop
RoboCop▶
Serpico▶
Sharky's Machine
SnakeEater
SnakeEater 2: The Drug
    Buster
SnakeEater 3: His Law
Speed▶
Stick
Stone Cold
Sudden Impact
Ten to Midnight
Year of the Dragon

Lost Worlds

At the Earth's Core
Beyond Atlantis
Brigadoon▶
Creatures the World Forgot
Gold of the Amazon Women
Jane & the Lost City
Journey to the Center of the
    Earth▶
The Land That Time Forgot
The Land Unknown
The Lost Continent
Lost Horizon▶
The Lost World
Mysterious Island▶
Mysterious Island of Beautiful
    Women
The People That Time Forgot
What Waits Below
When Dinosaurs Ruled the
    Earth
Where Time Began

Lovers on the Lam

see also Fugitives
Badlands▶
Bonnie & Clyde▶
The Getaway
Gun Crazy▶
Guncrazy
Kalifornia
Natural Born Killers
The Sugarland Express▶
True Romance
Wild at Heart▶

Macho Men

see also Action Adventure
Abilene Town▶
Aces: Iron Eagle 3
Across the Pacific▶
Action in the North Atlantic
The Adventurers
The Adventures of Captain
    Marvel
The Adventures of Ford
    Fairlane
Alone Against Rome
The Amazing Transplant
American Commandos
American Kickboxer 1
American Ninja
American Ninja 2: The
    Confrontation
American Ninja 4: The
    Annihilation
Atlas
The Avenger

Backdraft
Bad Boys▶
Bail Out
Bail Out at 43,000
The Barbarians
Black Cobra 2
The Black Pirate▶
Blue Blazes Rawden
Bootleg
Brannigan
A Bridge Too Far
Brutal Glory
Buck Rogers in the 25th
    Century
Bulletproof
Cannonball Run
Cannonball Run 2
Captain America
Chasers
Chino
The Cobra
Codename: Terminate
Colossus and the Amazon
    Queen
Combat Killers
Conan the Barbarian▶
Conquest of Mycene
Convoy
Cool Hand Luke▶
Coriolanus, Man without a
    Country
Cyborg Cop
Dead Man Walking
Deadly Spygames
Deathstalker 4: Clash of the
    Titans
Delta Force 3: The Killing
    Game
D.I.
Diamonds are Forever▶
Dick Tracy
Dick Tracy, Detective
Dick Tracy, Detective/The
    Corpse Vanishes
Dick Tracy Meets Gruesome
Dick Tracy Returns
Dick Tracy: The Original
    Serial, Vol. 1▶
Dick Tracy: The Original
    Serial, Vol. 2▶
Dick Tracy vs. Crime Inc.
Dick Tracy vs. Cueball
Dick Tracy's Dilemma
The Dirty Dozen▶
The Dirty Dozen: The Deadly
    Mission
The Dirty Dozen: The Fatal
    Mission
The Dirty Dozen: The Next
    Mission
Dirty Harry▶
Dr. No▶
The Dogs of War
The Dolls
Double Impact
Double Revenge
Duel of Champions
Dune Warriors
Excessive Force
Fearless Tiger
A Few Good Men▶
Firewalker
First Blood
Fist
A Fistful of Dollars▶
For Your Eyes Only▶
Force of One
Forced Vengeance
Fury on Wheels
Futurekick
Gator
Giant▶
The Giant of Marathon
The Giant of Metropolis
The Giants of Thessaly
The Gladiator▶
Gladiator of Rome
Gladiators 7
Goliath Against the Giants
Goliath and the Dragon
Gone with the Wind▶
The Green Hornet▶

Greystoke: The Legend of
    Tarzan, Lord of the Apes
Guns
Hangfire
Hard Knox
Hard Promises
Hard to Kill
Hawkeye
Hell in the Pacific▶
Hellfighters
Hercules
Hercules 2
Hercules Against the Moon
    Men
Hercules and the Princess of
    Troy
Hercules in New York
Hero of Rome
Heroes Three
Highlander 3: The Sorcerer
Hired to Kill
The Hitman
Hooper
Horsemen
Hot Shots! Part Deux
Hustle
I Come in Peace
Infra-Man
The Invaders
Invasion U.S.A.
The Iron Crown
Jackie Chan's Police Force
Judex
Kill and Kill Again
The Killing Zone
Kindergarten Cop
Kinjite: Forbidden Subjects
K2: The Ultimate High
Last Action Hero
Last Flight to Hell
The Last Warrior
Legend of the Lone Ranger
License to Kill▶
The Lion of Thebes▶
Machoman
Maciste in Hell
Mad Wax: The Surf Movie
The Magnificent Matador
The Magnificent Seven▶
Magnum Force
The Mambo Kings▶
A Man Called Rage
The Man with the Golden Gun
The Masked Marvel
Master Blaster
McBain
Medusa Against the Son of
    Hercules
Messalina vs. the Son of
    Hercules
Messenger of Death
Missing in Action
Missing in Action 2: The
    Beginning
Mr. Majestyk
Mobsters
Mole Men Against the Son of
    Hercules
Murphy's Law
Neutron and the Black Mask
Neutron vs. the Amazing Dr.
    Caronte
Neutron vs. the Death Robots
Neutron vs. the Maniac
Never Say Never Again
No Holds Barred
No Way Back
Nomad Riders
One Down, Two to Go!
One-Eyed Jacks▶
One Man Jury
Out for Justice
Partners
Party Animal
Paternity
Patton▶
Prison Planet
Ragin' Cajun
Raging Bull▶
Rambo: First Blood, Part 2
Rambo 3
Raw Deal

Raw Justice
Revolt of the Barbarians
The Road Warrior▶
Robin Hood▶
Rocky▶
Rocky 2
Rocky 3
Rocky 4
Rocky 5
Roland the Mighty
Rollercoaster
The Rookie
The Runaway Barge
Samson Against the Sheik
Samson and His Mighty
    Challenge
Samson and the 7 Miracles of
    the World
Sands of Iwo Jima▶
The Searchers▶
Seven
Seven Magnificent Gladiators
The Seventh Voyage of
    Sinbad▶
The Shadow
Shaft▶
Shaft's Big Score
Sinbad of the Seven Seas
Sirocco
Soldier's Fortune
Son of Sinbad
Sorcerer
Speed▶
Spy Smasher Returns
Stagecoach▶
Steel
Steel Cowboy
Stone Cold
Stormquest
Street Soldiers
A Streetcar Named Desire▶
Suburban Commando
Superargo
Superman: The Movie▶
Superman 2▶
Superman 3
Superman 4: The Quest for
    Peace
Superman & the Mole Men
Swamp Fire
Swashbuckler
The Swordsman
Tango and Cash
Tarzan and the Green
    Goddess
Tarzan, the Ape Man▶
Tarzan, the Ape Man
Tarzan's Revenge
Ten to Midnight
Terror of Rome Against the
    Son of Hercules
Terror of the Steppes
Test Pilot▶
Thief▶
Thieves of Fortune
The 13th Mission
Thor and the Amazon Women
Thunder Warrior 3
Thunderball
Tiger Joe
Too Late the Hero▶
Tor
Total Recall▶
Tough Guy
Triumph of the Son of
    Hercules
Tyrant of Lydia Against the
    Son of Hercules
Under Siege
Venus Against the Son of
    Hercules
Viva Villa!▶
Warlords 3000
Where Eagles Dare▶
White Lightning
The Wild Bunch▶
Windjammer

Mad Scientists

**see also Inventors &
Inventions; Science &
Scientists**

The Ape Man
Atom Age Vampire
Attack of the Swamp Creature
Before I Hang
Bela Lugosi Meets a Brooklyn
    Gorilla
Beverly Hills Bodysnatchers
Bloodbath at the House of
    Death
Bloodlust
The Body Shop
The Brain That Wouldn't Die
Brenda Starr
Bride of Re-Animator
Bride of the Monster
Captain America
Captive Wild Woman
The Cars That Ate Paris▶
Castle of Evil
Castle of the Creeping Flesh
The Cobweb
The Corpse Vanishes
Creator
Creature of the Walking Dead
The Creeper
The Creeping Flesh
The Crime of Dr. Crespi
Crimes of Dr. Mabuse▶
The Curse of the Aztec
    Mummy
Cyborg Cop
The Dead Next Door
Dead Pit
Dead Sleep
Death Warmed Up
Deep Red
Devil Doll▶
Dr. Black, Mr. Hyde
Doctor Blood's Coffin
Doctor Butcher M.D.
Dr. Caligari
Dr. Cyclops
Dr. Death, Seeker of Souls
Dr. Frankenstein's Castle of
    Freaks
Dr. Goldfoot and the Bikini
    Machine
Dr. Jekyll and Mr. Hyde▶
Dr. Jekyll and Mr. Hyde
Dr. Jekyll and Sister Hyde
Dr. Jekyll and the Wolfman
Dr. Jekyll's Dungeon of Death
Dr. No▶
Dr. Orloff's Monster
Doctor Who: The Caves of
    Androzani
Doctor X
Donovan's Brain▶
The Double O Kid
Embryo
Evil Town
The Flesh Eaters
Frankenhooker
Frankenstein
Frankenstein
Frankenstein and the Monster
    from Hell
Frankenstein '80
Frankenstein General Hospital
Frankenstein Unbound▶
Frankenstein's Daughter
Freaked
The Freakmaker
The Giant Spider Invasion
Girl in His Pocket
The Head
Hellmaster
Hideous Sun Demon
House of Frankenstein
Hyena of London
The Immortalizer
The Incredible Two-Headed
    Transplant
The Indestructible Man
Invasion of the Zombies
The Invisible Dr. Mabuse▶
The Invisible Man▶

The Invisible Ray
The Invisible Terror
Island of Dr. Moreau
Island of Lost Souls▶
Jurassic Park▶
The Killing Device
King of Kong Island
King of the Zombies
Lady Frankenstein
The Lawnmower Man
Lightblast
The Living Dead
The Lost City
The Mad Ghoul
Man Made Monster
The Man They Could Not
    Hang
The Man Who Lived Again
The Man with Two Lives
Mandroid
Maniac
The Manster
Master Minds
Metamorphosis
Miami Horror
The Monster▶
The Monster Maker
Monsters Crash the Pajama
    Party
Munster's Revenge
Murders in the Rue Morgue
Nightmare Castle
Nightmare Weekend
Orlak, the Hell of Frankenstein
Philadelphia Experiment 2
The Pink Panther Strikes
    Again▶
The Re-Animator▶
Red Blooded American Girl
Return of the Killer Tomatoes
Revenge of the Zombies
Revolt of the Zombies
Samson in the Wax Museum
Scanner Cop
Science Crazed
Screamers
Severed Ties
Shadow of Chinatown
She Demons
Shock Waves
Silent Killers
Strange Behavior
Strange Case of Dr. Jekyll &
    Mr. Hyde
Superargo
Supersonic Man
Teenage Zombies
Terror is a Man
Testament of Dr. Mabuse
Torture Ship
Transmutations
The Unearthly
The Vampire Bat
Vulture
Werewolf of London
The Worst of Hollywood: Vol.
    1

Made for Television

**see TV Movies; TV Pilot
Movies; TV Series**

Mafia

see Organized Crime

Magic

**see also Genies; Magic
Carpet Rides; Occult**

Alabama's Ghost
The Alchemist
Bedknobs and Broomsticks
Black Magic Terror
The Butcher's Wife
Chandu on the Magic Island
Chandu the Magician
Cthulhu Mansion
The Day the Earth Froze
Death Magic
Deathstalker 3
The Devil Thumbs a Ride/
    Having Wonderful Crime

Doctor Mordrid: Master of the
    Unknown
Escape to Witch Mountain▶
Eternally Yours
Gryphon
Houdini
Lady in Distress
The Linguini Incident
Magic Serpent
The Magician▶
The Magician of Lublin
The Man in the Santa Claus
    Suit
Max Maven's Mindgames
Merlin
Merlin of the Crystal Cave
Mondo Magic
My Chauffeur
The Mysterious Stranger
Penn and Teller Get Killed
Prospero's Books▶
Quicker Than the Eye
Stunt Rock
Sword & the Sorcerer
Teen Witch
Turnaround
Tut & Tuttle
Wedding Band
The Wizard of Gore
Zotz!

Magic Carpet Rides

Aladdin▶
Golden Voyage of Sinbad
1001 Arabian Nights
The Seventh Voyage of
    Sinbad▶
Sinbad and the Eye of the
    Tiger
Sinbad of the Seven Seas
Sinbad the Sailor▶
The Thief of Baghdad▶
Thief of Baghdad
Thief of Baghdad
The Thief of Baghdad

Marriage

**see also Divorce; War
Between the Sexes;
Wedding Bells; Wedding
Hell**

Accused
Across the Wide Missouri
The Adjuster
The Adultress
The Adventures of Mark
    Twain▶
An Affair in Mind
The Age of Innocence▶
Alfredo, Alfredo
All This and Heaven Too▶
Almost You
Always▶
American Matchmaker
Any Wednesday
Arnold
Arrivederci, Baby!
As You Desire Me▶
Ash Wednesday
Ask Any Girl
Assault and Matrimony
Attack of the 50 Ft. Woman
Autumn Leaves
Autumn Marathon
Baby Doll▶
The Baby Maker
Bachelor in Paradise
Bachelor Party
Back to the Wall
Backstreet Dreams
Bad Behavior
Barefoot in the Park▶
Barjo
The Barkleys of Broadway▶
The Bat People
Battle Shock
Bedroom Eyes 2
Best Enemies
Best Friends
The Best Intentions▶
Betrayal

Betsy's Wedding
Big Business Girl
Bill Cosby, Himself
A Black Veil for Lisa
Blindfold: Acts of Obsession
The Bliss of Mrs. Blossom▶
Blonde Venus▶
Blondie
Blondie Hits the Jackpot
Blondie in Society
Blondie Knows Best
Blood of Jesus
Blood Wedding▶
Blue Heaven
Blume in Love▶
Body Chemistry
Brand New Life
The Bride & the Beast
The Bride Walks Out
The Brides Wore Blood
Bulldog Drummond's Bride
Bullwhip
Burn Witch, Burn!▶
The Burning Bed▶
By Love Possessed
By the Light of the Silvery
    Moon
Captain's Paradise▶
Car Trouble
Casanova Brown
Cast a Dark Shadow▶
Cause for Alarm
Chained
A Change of Seasons
Charles & Diana: A Palace
    Divided
Cheaters
Cheatin' Hearts
Child Bride of Short Creek
China Moon
Chinese Roulette
Chloe in the Afternoon▶
The Chocolate Soldier
Choices
Christina
Claire's Knee▶
Clash by Night▶
Coast to Coast
Cold Heaven
Come Back, Little Sheba▶
Coming to America▶
Common Law Wife
Conflict▶
Consenting Adults
Consolation Marriage
Conspiracy of Terror
Country Girl▶
The Cowboy and the Lady
Crazy in Love
Crime & Passion
A Cry in the Night
Cul de Sac▶
Dancing in the Dark
Dangerous Game
Dangerous Liaisons
Danielle Steel's Changes
The Dead▶
Dead in the Water
Dead Mate
Dead On
Death Kiss
Deception
Departamento Compartido
Designing Woman▶
Desire and Hell at Sunset
    Motel
Desire Under the Elms
Despedida de Casada
Desperate Characters▶
Desperate Hours
The Devil in Silk
Diabolically Yours
Dial "M" for Murder▶
Diary of a Mad Housewife▶
Diary of the Dead
Dirty Hands
The Disappearance of
    Christina
Divorce—Italian Style▶
The Divorce of Lady X
Doctors' Wives
Dodsworth▶

Dollar
A Doll's House
A Doll's House▶
Dominique is Dead
Dona Flor and Her Two Husbands▶
Donkey Skin▶
Don't Raise the Bridge, Lower the River
Doomsday
Double Deal
Double Exposure
Double Indemnity▶
Double Standard
Doubting Thomas
Dream Lover
Dressmaker
Drifting Souls
Drowning by Numbers▶
Drums Along the Mohawk▶
East Side, West Side
Easy Living
Eat a Bowl of Tea▶
Eating Raoul▶
Ecstasy
Edward and Mrs. Simpson
Effi Briest▶
Egg and I▶
El: This Strange Passion▶
Elizabeth of Ladymead▶
Ellie
Elvis and Me
Emmanuelle
Emmanuelle, the Queen
Empty Canvas
Encore▶
End of Desire
End of the Road
Enemies, a Love Story▶
Enormous Changes▶
The Entertainer▶
Entre-Nous▶
Erotic Images
Escapade▶
Esposa y Amante
Estate of Insanity
Eternally Yours
Ethan Frome
Eureka!
Evelyn Prentice
Every Breath
Every Girl Should Be Married
Everybody's All American
Ex-Lady
Experiment Perilous▶
The Eyes of Youth
Falling from Grace
Family Upside Down▶
Far Cry from Home
The Farmer's Wife
Fatal Attraction
Father of the Bride▶
Fatty and Mabel Adrift/Mabel, Fatty and the Law
Fearless▶
Femme Fatale
Fergie & Andrew: Behind Palace Doors
Fever
Fictitious Marriage
A Fine Romance
First Affair
Fools
For Keeps
For Love or Money
For Pete's Sake
Fortune's Fool
Fortunes of War▶
Four Days in July
The Four Seasons
Fourth Story▶
Frieda
From the Terrace
Fulfillment
Full of Life
Fun with Dick and Jane
Gaslight▶
A Gathering of Eagles
George Washington
George Washington: The Forging of a Nation
Gertrud▶

Get Out Your Handkerchiefs▶
Getting Up and Going Home
The Ghost and the Guest
Giant▶
The Gift of Love
Girl from Hunan▶
Goin' to Town
The Golden Honeymoon
The Good Wife
Gore Vidal's Lincoln
Grand Isle
Grand Theft Auto
The Grass is Greener
Greed▶
The Greek Tycoon
Grievous Bodily Harm
Group Marriage
Grown Ups
The Guardsman▶
Guess Who's Coming to Dinner▶
Guest Wife
A Guide for the Married Man▶
A Guide for the Married Woman
The Hairdresser's Husband
A Handful of Dust▶
Hard Promises
The Hawk
The Heartbreak Kid▶
Heartburn▶
Hell-Ship Morgan
Here We Go Again!
High Heels
High Society▶
Homecoming▶
Honeymoon
Honeymoon Academy
The Horrible Dr. Hichcock
Hot Spell
Hotel Room
The Householder
How to Break Up a Happy Divorce
How to Commit Marriage
How to Marry a Millionaire
How to Murder Your Wife▶
The Howards of Virginia
Hurry, Charlie, Hurry
Husbands and Lovers
Husbands and Wives▶
I Do! I Do!
I Dood It
I Love My...Wife
I Love You Again▶
I Love You Rosa
I Love You to Death
I Love You...Goodbye
I Married a Vampire
I Married a Woman
I Was a Male War Bride▶
I Will, I Will for Now
I Wonder Who's Killing Her Now?
Il Bell'Antonio
Il Grido
Illicit
Illusions
I'm on My Way/The Non-Stop Kid
Immortal Bachelor
The Imported Bridegroom
In Celebration▶
In Name Only
Indecent Proposal
The Innocent▶
Intersection
Intimate Story
Intimate Strangers
The Invasion of Carol Enders
The Invisible Ghost
It Started with a Kiss
It Takes Two
Java Head▶
Jenny
The Jeweller's Shop
Josepha▶
Ju Dou▶
Jubal
Jubilee Trail
Jude the Obscure
Juliet of the Spirits▶

Just Like Weather▶
Killing Heat
A Kind of Loving▶
Kiss and Be Killed
Kuni Lemel in Tel Aviv
La Bete Humaine▶
La Chienne▶
La Vengeance d'une Femme▶
La Vie Continue
Lady Chatterley's Lover
Lady L
Lady Windermere's Fan
The Last Days of Chez Nous
The Last Married Couple in America
L'Atalante▶
Late Spring▶
Laurel & Hardy: Be Big
Le Beau Mariage▶
Le Bonheur
Le Chat▶
Lesson in Love
Let's Get Married
A Letter to Three Wives▶
Lianna▶
The Liars
Liar's Moon
Life of Oharu▶
Linda
Listen, Darling
A Little Sex
Lonely Wives
The Long Haul
The Long, Long Trailer
Lost Honeymoon
Loulou▶
Love, Cheat & Steal
Love from a Stranger
Love Matters
The Lovers▶
Lovers and Other Strangers▶
Loving Couples
Lucy and Desi: Before the Laughter
Madame Bovary▶
Made for Each Other▶
Made in Heaven
Making Love
The Makioka Sisters▶
Man from Nowhere
Manhattan Murder Mystery▶
Mannequin
Maria Chapdelaine▶
The Marriage Circle▶
Marriage is Alive and Well
Marriage Italian Style▶
The Marriage of Maria Braun▶
Married?
Married to It
Married Too Young
A Married Woman▶
Marty▶
Matrimaniac
Max, Mon Amour
McLintock!▶
The Member of the Wedding
Memories of a Marriage▶
Memory of Us
Men...▶
The Merry Widow
Mexican Spitfire at Sea
Microwave Massacre
Mid-Channel
Midnight Crossing
Miracle of Morgan's Creek▶
Mr. & Mrs. Smith▶
Mr. Love
Mr. Mom▶
Mr. Skeffington▶
Mr. Sycamore
Mr. Wonderful
Mistress▶
Modern Love
The Money Pit
Montana
Moon Over Harlem
Moon's Our Home
Moonstruck▶
Murder at 45 R.P.M.
Murder So Sweet
The Music Lovers
My Dear Secretary

My Favorite Wife▶
My First Wife
My Little Chickadee▶
My Michael▶
My New Gun
My Other Husband
My Sweet Victim
Naked Jungle▶
Niagara
Nightkill
Not Tonight Darling
Nouvelle Vague
Now and Forever
Nudo di Donna
Odd Obsession
O'Hara's Wife
On Approval▶
On Golden Pond▶
On Her Majesty's Secret Service▶
On Valentine's Day
One Night in the Tropics
One of My Wives Is Missing
One Trick Pony
Only with Married Men
Orchestra Wives▶
Overnight Sensation
The Paint Job
Paint Your Wagon
The Painted Veil
Pajama Tops
The Palm Beach Story▶
Paper Marriage
A Paper Wedding▶
Paradise▶
Pardon Mon Affaire▶
Pardon Mon Affaire, Too!
Passion in Paradise
Peggy Sue Got Married
The Penitent
Pennies From Heaven▶
The Perfect Bride
The Perfect Marriage
Period of Adjustment▶
Pete 'n' Tillie
Pete Townshend: White City
Petulia▶
Phaedra
Phfftt!
The Philadelphia Story▶
The Piano▶
A Piece of Pleasure▶
Pipe Dreams
Platinum Blonde▶
Playing Dead
Portrait of Teresa▶
The Postman Always Rings Twice▶
The Postman Always Rings Twice
Praying Mantis
Prelude to a Kiss
The Primitive Lover
Prisoner of Second Avenue
Prisoners of Inertia
Private Life
Private Lives▶
Promises! Promises!
Prowler
The Purchase Price
Quartet▶
Question of Faith
Race for Life
Rachel and the Stranger▶
Raging Bull▶
Raise the Red Lantern▶
Rape and Marriage: The Rideout Case
Rebecca▶
Red Rock West▶
Revenge of the Stepford Wives
Reversal of Fortune▶
Rich and Famous
Rich and Strange
Rider from Tucson
Riptide▶
Risky Business
Rocky 2
Romantic Englishwoman▶
The Roof
Rose of Washington Square

Runaways
Ruthless People▶
Ryan's Daughter
Satan's Black Wedding
Savage Attraction
Say Yes!
Scar of Shame
Scarlet Dawn
Scenes from a Mall
Scenes from a Marriage▶
Scorchers
Season of Fear
Second Chance
Secret Beyond the Door
Secrets of Women▶
Seems Like Old Times
Send Me No Flowers▶
Separate Vacations
Separate Ways
Seven Chances▶
Seven Days Ashore/Hurry, Charlie, Hurry
The Seven Year Itch▶
The Seventeenth Bride
Sex and the Single Girl
Sexpot
Sexual Malice
Shadowlands▶
The Shame▶
Shattered
She and He
She-Devil
She Waits
She's Having a Baby
Shoot the Moon
Shooting Elizabeth
Sibling Rivalry
Silent Tongue
Silent Victim
Sin Takes a Holiday
The Singing Blacksmith
The Single Standard
The Sisters▶
Sketch Artist
Skinner's Dress Suit
The Slugger's Wife
Smash Palace
Smash-Up: The Story of a Woman▶
Smouldering Fires
Snoopy's Getting Married, Charlie Brown
So This is Paris▶
Sofie
The Soft Skin▶
Son-in-Law
Sound of Murder
The Stationmaster's Wife
The Story of Boys & Girls▶
Stromboli
Suspicion▶
Sweet Hearts Dance
Sweet Movie
Sweet Poison
Sweet Revenge
Sweethearts▶
Tell Me a Riddle
Tell Me That You Love Me
Tender Is the Night
The Tender Trap
Test Pilot▶
That Certain Thing
That Uncertain Feeling
Third Walker▶
30 Is a Dangerous Age, Cynthia
Three Broadway Girls▶
Three Daring Daughters
Three Husbands
Thursday's Game▶
Till Death Do Us Part
Till Marriage Do Us Part
Tin Men
To Joy▶
Too Beautiful for You
Torchlight
The Torture of Silence
A Touch of Class▶
Tricks of the Trade
True Lies▶
True Love▶
The Tunnel

Marriage

The Tunnel of Love
Twice a Woman
Two for the Road▶
The Two Mrs. Carrolls
Ulysses
The Unchastened Woman
Under Capricorn
Under the Volcano▶
Undercover Blues
Une Jeunesse▶
Unfaithfully Yours▶
Unfaithfully Yours
Unholy Wife
The Unkissed Bride
Until September
Uptown New York
Vanishing Act
Vasectomy: A Delicate Matter
Violets Are Blue
The Virgin of Nuremberg
Vivacious Lady▶
Voulez-Vous Danser Avec
    Moi?
Voyage to Italy
W
Walk in the Spring Rain
Waltz of the Toreadors▶
War Brides
The Wash▶
Waterland
Way Down East▶
A Wedding
Wedding in Blood▶
A Wedding in Galilee▶
We're Not Married▶
What's Good for the Goose
When a Man Loves a Woman
Where Angels Fear to Tread▶
Where Were You When the
    Lights Went Out?
White Gold▶
Who's Afraid of Virginia
    Woolf?
Who's Got the Action?
Wife Versus Secretary▶
Wifemistress
A Woman Named Jackie
The Woman Next Door▶
Woman of the Year▶
A Woman Under the
    Influence▶
The Women▶
The World is Full of Married
    Men
World's Greatest Lover
Worth Winning
X, Y & Zee
A Year in Provence▶
You Can't Fool Your Wife
Yours, Mine & Ours
You've Got to Have Heart
Zandy's Bride

Martial Arts

Above the Law
Against the Drunken Cat
    Paws
Alley Cat
Aloha Summer
American Kickboxer 1
American Ninja
American Ninja 2: The
    Confrontation
American Ninja 3: Blood Hunt
American Ninja 4: The
    Annihilation
American Samurai
American Shaolin: King of the
    Kickboxers 2
The Amsterdam Connection
Angel of Fury
Angel Town
Assassin
Baby Cart 1: Lend a
    Child...Lend an Arm
Baby Cart at the River Styx
Baby Cart to Hades
Back in Action
Bells of Death
Best of the Best
Best of the Best 2
The Big Brawl

Big Trouble in Little China
Black Belt Jones
Black Dragon
Black Dragon's Revenge
Black Eagle
Black Samurai
Blackbelt 2: Fatal Force
The Blazing Ninja
Blind Fists of Bruce
Blind Fury
Blind Rage
Blood Ring
Blood Warriors
Bloodfight
Bloodfist
Bloodfist 2
Bloodfist 3: Forced to Fight
Bloodfist 4: Die Trying
Bloodfist 5: Human Target
Bloodmatch
Bloodsport
The Bloody Fight
The Bodyguard
Born Invincible
Born Losers
Bounty Tracker
Braddock: Missing in Action 3
Brain Smasher...A Love Story
Breaker! Breaker!
Breathing Fire
Bronson Lee, Champion
The Bronx Executioner
Bruce Lee: Curse of the
    Dragon▶
Bruce Lee Fights Back From
    the Grave
Bruce Lee: The Legend
Bruce Lee's Ways of Kung Fu
Bruce Le's Greatest Revenge
Bruce Li in New Guinea
Bruce Li the Invincible
Bruce the Superhero
Bruce's Deadly Fingers
Bruce's Fists of Vengeance
Buddha Assassinator
The Bushido Blade
Cantonen Iron Kung Fu
Catch the Heat
The Cavalier
Challenge of the Masters
Challenge the Ninja
Champion Operation
China O'Brien
China O'Brien 2
China White
The Chinatown Kid
Chinese Connection
Chinese Connection 2
Circle of Iron
Clash of the Ninja
Cleopatra Jones
Cleopatra Jones & the Casino
    of Gold
Clones of Bruce Lee
The Cobra
Cobra Against Ninja
Cold Blooded Murder
Counter Attack
Crack Shadow Boxers
Dance of Death
Day of the Panther
The Deadliest Art: The Best of
    the Martial Arts Films
Deadly Bet
Death Challenge
Death Machines
Death Mask of the Ninja
Death Ring
Death Warrant
Deathfight
Desert Kickboxer
The Divine Enforcer
Dolemite
Double Impact
Dragon Force
Dragon Princess
The Dragon Returns
Dragon: The Bruce Lee
    Story▶
Dragon the Odds
Dragon vs. Needles of Death

Dragon's Claw
The Dragon's Showdown
Dreadnaught Rivals
Dual Flying Kicks
Duel of Fists
Duel of the Iron Fist
Duel of the Seven Tigers
The Dynamite Brothers
Dynamo
Dynasty
Eagle Claws Champion
Eagle's Shadow
Eighteen Jade Arhats
The Eliminators
Empire of Spiritual Ninja
Empire of the Dragon
Enter the Dragon▶
Enter the Ninja
Enter the Panther
Enter Three Dragons
Exit the Dragon, Enter the
    Tiger
An Eye for an Eye
Fast Fists
The Fate of Lee Khan
Fearless Hyena
Ferocious Female Freedom
    Fighters
Fight for Survival
Fight to the Death
Fighting Black Kings
Fighting Duel of Death
Fighting Life
Final Impact
Firecracker
A Fist Full of Talons
Fist of Fear, Touch of Death
Fist of Steel
The Fist, the Kicks, and the
    Evils
Fists of Blood
Fists of Dragons
Fists of Fury▶
Fists of Fury 2
Five Fighters from Shaolin
Force of One
Forced Vengeance
Forgotten Warrior
The Four Hands of Death:
    Wily Match
Four Robbers
Full Contact
Full Metal Ninja
Furious
The Furious Avenger
Futurekick
The Gambling Samurai
Game of Death
Gang Wars
Ghostwarrior
Golden Exterminators
Golden Ninja Warrior
Golden Sun
Goldfinger▶
Good Guys Wear Black
The Great Hunter
Green Dragon Inn
Gymkata
Half a Loaf of Kung Fu
Hands of Death
Hard to Kill
Hell's Wind Staff
Hero and the Terror
Hot Potato
The Hot, the Cool, and the
    Vicious
Hurricane Sword
Image of Bruce Lee
Immortal Combat
In Your Face
Incredible Master Beggars
Instant Kung-Fu Man
The Instructor
Invasion U.S.A.
Invincible
Iron Dragon Strikes Back
Iron Thunder
Ironheart
Jackie Chan's Police Force
Jaguar Lives
Japanese Connection
Karate Cop

The Karate Kid▶
The Karate Kid: Part 2
The Karate Kid: Part 3
Karate Warrior
Karate Warriors
The Kick Fighter
Kick of Death: The Prodigal
    Boxer
Kickboxer
Kickboxer 2: The Road Back
Kickboxer 3: The Art of War
Kickboxer the Champion
Kill and Kill Again
Kill Factor
Kill Line
Kill or Be Killed
Kill Squad
Kill the Golden Goose
Killer Elephants
King Boxer
King Boxers
The King of the Kickboxers
Kingfisher the Killer
Knights
Kung Fu
Kung Fu Avengers
Kung Fu Commandos
Kung Fu from Beyond the
    Grave
Kung Fu Massacre
Kung Fu of Eight Drunkards
Kung Fu Powerhouse
Kung Fu Rebels
Kung Fu Strongman
Kung Fu Terminator
Kung Fu: The Movie
Kung Fu's Hero
Lady Dragon
Lady Dragon 2
The Last Dragon
Leopard Fist Ninja
Lethal Ninja
Lionheart
Little Dragons
Little Heroes of Shaolin
    Temple
Little Ninjas
Low Blow
Machoman
Mafia vs. Ninja
Magic Kid
Magnum Killers
Man Called Tiger
Manchurian Avenger
Marked for Death
Martial Law
Martial Law 2: Undercover
Martial Outlaw
Marvelous Stunts of Kung Fu
Master Killer
Master Ninja
Master of Kung Fu
Master's Revenge
Militant Eagle
Mission Kiss and Kill
Mission of Justice
My Name Called Bruce
My Samurai
Naked Killer
New Fist of Fury
The Next Karate Kid
Night Master
Night of the Kickfighters
Night of the Warrior
9 1/2 Ninjas
Nine Deaths of the Ninja
Ninja 3: The Domination
Ninja Academy
Ninja: American Warrior
Ninja Brothers of Blood
Ninja Champion
Ninja Checkmate
Ninja Commandments
Ninja Condors
Ninja Connection
Ninja Death Squad
Ninja Demon's Massacre
Ninja Destroyer
Ninja Dragon
Ninja Exterminators
Ninja Fantasy
Ninja Hunt

Ninja Massacre
Ninja Masters of Death
Ninja Mission
Ninja Nightmare
Ninja of the Magnificence
Ninja Operation: Licensed to
    Terminate
Ninja Phantom Heroes
The Ninja Pirates
Ninja Powerforce
Ninja Showdown
Ninja Squad
Ninja Strike Force
Ninja Supremo
Ninja Swords of Death
Ninja Terminator
Ninja the Battalion
Ninja the Protector
Ninja, the Violent Sorcerer
Ninja Turf
Ninja Vengeance
Ninja vs. Bruce Lee
Ninja vs. Ninja
Ninja vs. the Shaolin
Ninja Wars
Ninja's Extreme Weapons
No Retreat, No Surrender
No Retreat, No Surrender 2
No Retreat, No Surrender 3:
    Blood Brothers
The Noble Ninja
Octagon
Of Cooks and Kung-Fu
Omega Cop
The One Arm Swordsmen
One Down, Two to Go!
One-Eyed Swordsman
Only the Strong
Operation Orient
Out for Blood
Out for Justice
Overkill
The Perfect Weapon
Phoenix the Ninja
The Power of the Ninjitsu
Pray for Death
Prodigal Boxer: The Kick of
    Death
Professional Killers 1
Protector
Pursuit
Pushed to the Limit
Queen Boxer
Rage and Honor
Rage and Honor 2: Hostile
    Takeover
Rage of Honor
Rage of Wind
Ragin' Cajun
Rapid Fire
Raw Force
Real Bruce Lee
The Rebellious Reign
Remo Williams: The
    Adventure Begins
Renegade Monk
Renegade Ninja
Retrievers
Return of the Chinese Boxer
Return of the Dragon
Return of the Scorpion
Return of the Tiger
Revenge of the Ninja
Revolt of the Dragon
Ring of Fire
Ring of Fire 2: Blood and Steel
Ring of Steel
Rivals of the Silver Fox
Roller Blade
Sakura Killers
The Samurai
Samurai Blood, Samurai Guts
Samurai Death Bells
Samurai Sword of Justice
Sanshiro Sugata▶
Scorpion
Secret of Tai Chi
Seven Blows of the Dragon
The 7 Brothers Meet Dracula
Shadow Killers
Shaolin Disciple
Shaolin Ex-Monk

Shaolin Executioner
Shaolin Kids
Shaolin Kung Fu Mystagogue
Shaolin Temple Strikes Back
Shaolin Thief
Shaolin Traitor
Shaolin Vengence
Shaolin Warrior
Sharp Fists in Kung Fu
Shinobi Ninja
Shogun's Ninja
Shootfighter: Fight to the
   Death
Showdown
Showdown at the Equator
Showdown in Little Tokyo
Sidekicks
Silent Assassins
Silent Rage
Slaughter in San Francisco
Sloane
Snake in the Eagle's Shadow
   2
Snuff-Bottle Connection
Soul of Samurai
Space Ninja: Sword of the
   Space Ark
Steel Fisted Dragon
Stickfighter
Sting of the Dragon Masters
The Story of Drunken Master
Story of the Dragon
The Stranger and the
   Gunfighter
The Street Fighter's Last
   Revenge
Street Hunter
Street Soldiers
Super Kung Fu Kid
Super Ninja
Super Ninjas
Surf Ninjas
Survival Game
Survival of a Dragon
Sword of Doom▶
Sword of Fury II
Swords of Death
Talons of the Eagle
Taoism Drunkard
Tattoo Connection
Ten Brothers of Shao-lin
They Call Me Bruce?
They Still Call Me Bruce
Thousand Mile Escort
3 Ninjas
3 Ninjas Kick Back
Thundering Ninja
Tiger Claws
Tigershark
Timecop
TNT Jackson
To Be the Best
To Subdue the Evil
To the Death
Tongs: An American
   Nightmare
Tough Guy
Trancers 3: Deth Lives
Triple Impact
The True Game of Death
24 Hours to Midnight
Twister Kicker
Two Assassins in the Dark
Two Dragons Fight Against
   the Tiger
Two Graves to Kung-Fu
The Two Great Cavaliers
Two Wondrous Tigers
The Unbeaten 28
Unmasking the Idol
Vampire Raiders—Ninja
   Queen
Vengeance of the Snowmaid
Venus the Ninja
The Victim
The Warrior
Warrior Within
Warriors of the Sung Dynasty
Way of the Black Dragon
Weapons of Death
When Taekwondo Strikes
The White Butterfly Killer

White Phantom: Enemy of
   Darkness
Wolfen Ninja
The Young Bruce Lee
Young Dragon
Young Hero of Shaolin
The Young Taoism Fighter
Young Tiger
Zatoichi: Master Ichi and a
   Chest of Gold
Zatoichi: The Blind
   Swordsman and the Chess
   Expert
Zatoichi: The Blind
   Swordsman's Vengeance
Zatoichi vs. Yojimbo▶

Martyred Pop Icons

*see also Rock Stars on
Film*
Beatlemania! The Movie
Blue Hawaii
The Buddy Holly Story▶
Bus Stop▶
Clambake
Don't Look Back▶
The Doors
The Doors: Soft Parade, a
   Retrospective
Elvis and Me
The Elvis Files
Elvis in the Movies
Elvis Memories
Elvis on Tour
Elvis: One Night with You
Elvis Presley's Graceland
Elvis: Rare Moments with the
   King
Elvis Stories
Elvis: The Movie
Forever James Dean
Fun in Acapulco
James Dean Story
John & Yoko: A Love Story
King Creole
Kissin' Cousins
La Bamba▶
Lenny▶
Live a Little, Love a Little
Love Me Tender
Marilyn
Marilyn: The Untold Story▶
Paradise, Hawaiian Style
The Real Buddy Holly Story
Rebel Without a Cause▶
The Rose▶
Roustabout
Sgt. Pepper's Lonely Hearts
   Club Band
The Seven Year Itch▶
Speedway
Spinout
Stardust Memories
Stay Away, Joe
This is Elvis
Train to Hollywood▶
The Trouble with Girls (and
   How To Get Into It)▶

Mass Media

*see also Front Page;
Radio*
America
Behind the Rising Sun
Broadcast News▶
A Case of Libel
Chill Factor
The China Syndrome▶
A Cry in the Dark▶
Dead Men Don't Die
Death Watch▶
E. Nick: A Legend in His Own
   Mind
Eternity
Exiled to Shanghai
Eyewitness
A Face in the Crowd▶
France/Tour/Detour/Deux/
   Enfants▶
The Gladiators
The Groove Tube

Groundhog Day▶
Hero▶
Hollywood Scandals and
   Tragedies
I Was a Teenage TV Terrorist
The Image
International House
Lipstick Camera
Live! From Death Row
Livin' Large
The Lost Honor of Katharina
   Blum▶
Loving You
My Favorite Year▶
Natural Born Killers
Network▶
News at Eleven
Nothing Sacred▶
The Passenger▶
Pray TV
Prime Suspect
Ratings Game
Riders of the Storm
Scrooged
The Seduction
Sex Through a Window
S.F.W.
Six Fois Deux/Sur et Sous la
   Communication▶
Soft and Hard
Superstar: The Life and Times
   of Andy Warhol▶
Tabloid!
The Thrill of It All!
Tunnelvision
Zelig▶

The Meaning of Life

Joey Breaker▶
Monty Python's The Meaning
   of Life▶
My Life
My Own Private Idaho▶
The Razor's Edge▶
The Razor's Edge
The Remains of the Day▶
Shadowlands▶
The Sheltering Sky▶

Medieval Romps

*see also Camelot (Old);
Historical Drama; Period
Piece; Swashbucklers*
The Adventures of Robin
   Hood▶
Beatrice▶
Becket▶
Being Human
The Beloved Rogue▶
Camelot
Choice of Weapons
The Company of Wolves▶
Conquest of the Normans
Deathstalker
Deathstalker 2: Duel of the
   Titans
The Decameron▶
Decameron Nights
Diane
Donkey Skin▶
Dragonslayer▶
El Cid▶
Excalibur▶
The Fighting Prince of
   Donegal
Fire and Sword
The Flame & the Arrow▶
Flesh and Blood
Goetz von Berlichingen
Hawk and Castile
Hawk the Slayer
Inquisition
Ivanhoe▶
Ivanhoe
Jabberwocky▶
Jack the Giant Killer▶
King Arthur, the Young
   Warlord
Knights of the Round Table
Kojiro▶
Ladyhawke

Legend
Leonor
The Lion in Winter▶
Lionheart
Magdalene
Magic Serpent
The Magic Sword
Mark of the Devil
Mark of the Devil 2
The Mongols
Monty Python and the Holy
   Grail▶
The Name of the Rose
Naughty Knights
The Navigator▶
Onibaba▶
Pippin▶
The Prince of Thieves
Ran▶
Rashomon▶
The Return of Martin Guerre▶
Rikyu▶
Robin and Marian
Robin Hood▶
Robin Hood: Men in Tights
Robin Hood: Prince of Thieves
Robin Hood...The Legend:
   Herne's Son
Robin Hood...The Legend:
   Robin Hood and the
   Sorcerer
Robin Hood...The Legend:
   The Swords of Wayland
Robin Hood...The Legend:
   The Time of the Wolf
The Scalawag Bunch
The Secret of El Zorro
Seven Samurai▶
The Seventh Seal▶
Skullduggery
Stealing Heaven
Sword & the Dragon
Sword & the Sorcerer
The Sword in the Stone▶
Sword of Lancelot
Sword of Sherwood Forest
Sword of the Valiant
Tales of Robin Hood
Tharus Son of Attila
Time Bandits
Time Trackers
Tor
The Undead▶
Unidentified Flying Oddball
The Vikings
The Warrior & the Sorceress
When Knights were Bold
Wholly Moses!
Wizards of the Lost Kingdom
Young Warlord
The Zany Adventures of
   Robin Hood

Meltdown

see also Disaster Flicks
Above and Beyond▶
Access Code
Amazing Grace & Chuck
Atomic Attack
The Atomic Cafe▶
The Atomic Kid
Black Rain▶
Bombs Away!
Chain Reaction
The China Syndrome▶
Cloak and Dagger
Control
Cyclotrode "X"
The Day After▶
The Day the Earth Caught
   Fire▶
The Death Merchant
Desert Bloom▶
Dick Barton Strikes Back
Disaster at Silo 7
Dr. Strangelove, or: How I
   Learned to Stop Worrying
   and Love the Bomb▶
Enola Gay: The Men, the
   Mission, the Atomic Bomb
Fail-Safe▶
Fat Man and Little Boy

Final Sanction
First Spaceship on Venus▶
First Strike
First Yank into Tokyo
Flight of Black Angel
The Fourth Protocol▶
Full Fathom Five
Future Kill
Glen and Randa
Ground Zero▶
H-Man
Hiroshima Maiden
Hiroshima: Out of the Ashes▶
I Live in Fear▶
In the King of Prussia
Incident at Map-Grid 36-80
A Man Called Rage
The Manhattan Project
Massive Retaliation
Miracle Mile▶
Modern Problems
Nuclear Conspiracy
On the Beach▶
One Night Stand▶
Panic in the Year Zero!
Patriot
Plutonium Incident
Prisoner in the Middle
Rats
Reactor
The Reflecting Skin▶
Refuge of Fear
Rhapsody in August
Rocket Attack U.S.A.
The Sacrifice▶
Seven Days in May▶
The Shoes of the Fisherman
Silkwood▶
Slugs
Special Bulletin▶
Split Second
The Spy Who Loved Me
State of Things
Superman 4: The Quest for
   Peace
TC 2000
Testament▶
This is Not a Test
Threads▶
True Lies▶
The 27 Day
Unknown World
Utopia
Voyage to the Bottom of the
   Sea▶
WarGames
When the Wind Blows▶
Young Lady Chatterly 2

Men

*see also Macho Men;
Repressed Men; War
Between the Sexes*
Bachelor Apartment
Carnal Knowledge▶
City Slickers
Esta Noche Cena Pancho
The Incredible Shrinking
   Man▶
The Men's Club
Mr. Mom▶
90 Days▶
Patti Rocks▶
Planet of the Apes▶
Raging Bull▶
Rate It X
The Saint of Fort Washington
Three Men and a Baby▶
Three Men and a Cradle▶
Thursday's Game▶
Truth or Die
Watch It▶

Men in Prison

*see also Fugitives; Great
Escapes; POW/MIA;
Women in Prison*
American Me▶
Appointment with Crime
Attica▶
Baba▶

Men

Bad Boys▶
Band of the Hand
Behind Prison Walls
Beyond the Walls
Birdman of Alcatraz▶
Black Lemons
Blind Faith
Botany Bay
Boy's Reformatory
Breaker Morant▶
Breakout
The Brig▶
Broken Melody
Brubaker▶
Buried Alive
Buy & Cell
Caged in Paradiso
Chain Gang Killings
The Chair
City Without Men
Club Fed
Coming Out of the Ice▶
The Count of Monte Cristo
The Count of Monte Cristo▶
The Count of Monte Cristo
Crashout
Criminal Code
Cry Danger▶
Das Testament des Dr.
  Mabuse▶
Dead Man Out▶
Dead Right
Deadlock
Death House
Death Warrant
Deathrow Gameshow
The Defiant Ones▶
Devil's Canyon
The Devil's Cargo
The Dirty Dozen▶
The Dirty Dozen: The Deadly
  Mission
The Dirty Dozen: The Fatal
  Mission
The Dirty Dozen: The Next
  Mission
Doin' Time
The Domino Principle
Down by Law▶
Each Dawn I Die
Eagles Attack at Dawn
Embassy
Empire of the Sun▶
Ernest Goes to Jail
Escape from Alcatraz▶
Escape from Death Row
Escape from DS-3
Escape from El Diablo
Escape from New York
Execution of Raymond
  Graham
The Executioner's Song
Fast Walking
Framed
Gang Busters
Gideon's Trumpet
The Glass House▶
Gulag
Hangfire
Hard Frame
Hold 'Em Jail
House Across the Bay
I Am a Fugitive from a Chain
  Gang▶
In Hot Pursuit
An Innocent Man
Invasion
The Invisible Strangler
Jailbreakin'
Jailhouse Rock▶
The Jericho Mile
Johnny Handsome▶
Kansas City Confidential▶
King of the Damned
Kiss of the Spider Woman▶
L'Addition
The Last Detail▶
The Last Mile
The Life of Emile Zola▶
The Line
Little Red Schoolhouse
Live! From Death Row

Lock Up
The Longest Yard
A Man Escaped▶
Man of La Mancha
The Man Who Broke 1,000
  Chains
Maximum Security
McKenzie Break▶
McVicar
Mean Frank and Crazy Tony
Midnight Express▶
Mrs. Soffel
Mr. Frost
Moon 44
Mutiny in the Big House
My Boys are Good Boys
The Night Visitor
984: Prisoner of the Future
Off the Wall
On the Yard
Papillon▶
Pardon Us
Penitentiary
Penitentiary 2
Penitentiary 3
Phantom Empire
Pressure Point▶
Prison
Prison Break
Prison Planet
Prison Train
The Pursuit of Happiness
Real Bullets
Riot
Riot in Cell Block 11▶
Runaway Train▶
Samar
Scum▶
A Sense of Freedom▶
Shoeshine▶
Short Eyes▶
Slaughterhouse Rock
Soul Vengeance
Space Rage
Stir Crazy
Tank
Terminal Island
Terror of the Bloodhunters
Terror on Alcatraz
There was a Crooked Man▶
They Never Come Back
They Went That-a-Way &
  That-a-Way
Tomb of the Undead
Torture Ship
Triumph of the Spirit▶
Truth or Die
Two-Way Stretch
Weeds▶
Women's Prison Massacre
Yol▶

Mental Retardation
see also Physical
  Problems; Savants
Bill▶
Bill: On His Own▶
Charly▶
A Child is Waiting▶
A Dangerous Woman
Dark Night of the Scarecrow
A Day in the Death of Joe
  Egg▶
Dominick & Eugene▶
Family Pictures▶
Homer and Eddie
Larry
Lovey: A Circle of Children 2
Malcolm
Of Mice and Men▶
Rain Man▶
The Rain People▶
Slipping into Darkness
Square Dance
Sweetie▶
Tim
Two of a Kind
What's Eating Gilbert Grape▶
The Wizard
The Woman Who Willed a
  Miracle

Metamorphosis
see also Genetics
An American Werewolf in
  London▶
Cat People▶
Cat People
The Company of Wolves▶
The Curse of the Werewolf
The Fly▶
The Fly 2
The Howling▶
I Was a Teenage Werewolf
The Lair of the White Worm▶
Naked Lunch▶
Silver Bullet
Wolfen▶
The Wolfman
Woof!

Mexico
see also Central America
Across the Bridge
Against All Odds
The Black Scorpion
The Border▶
Borderline
Breakout
A Bullet for the General
Bullfighter & the Lady
Bullfighters
The Cisco Kid
Commando Squad
Crazy from the Heart▶
Danzon▶
Django
Emiliano Zapata
Escape from Cell Block 3
The Falcon in Mexico
Five Giants from Texas
Found Alive
Fun in Acapulco
His Kind of Woman▶
Holiday in Mexico
A Home of Our Own▶
In 'n Out
Interval
Juarez
Los Olvidados▶
Love has Many Faces
The Magnificent Seven▶
The Masked Rider
Mexican Hayride
The Night of the Iguana▶
Octaman
Old Gringo
On the Line
The Pearl▶
The Professionals▶
The Proud Ones
Que Viva Mexico▶
The Scout▶
Shoot the Living, Pray for the
  Dead
Sonny and Jed
South of Santa Fe
Survival Run
Touch of Evil▶
Treasure of the Sierra Madre▶
Two Mules for Sister Sara▶
Valdez is Coming
Vera Cruz
Villa Rides
Viva Villa!▶
Viva Zapata!▶
Warlords from Hell
The White Orchid
Wild Rovers

Middle East
see also Genies; Islam;
  Israel; Persian Gulf War;
  Terrorism
Abbott & Costello Meet the
  Mummy
Ali Baba and the Forty
  Thieves
Ali Baba and the 40 Thieves▶
The Ambassador
The Arab Conspiracy
Arabian Nights

Bloodstone
A Casualty of War
Cleopatra
Counterforce
Cup Final
Eagles Attack at Dawn
The Egyptian
Fictitious Marriage
Glory Boys
The Great Armored Car
  Swindle
The Guns and the Fury
Hamsin▶
Hanna K.
Harum Scarum
Held Hostage
Honeybaby
Hostages▶
The Invincible Six
Iran: Days of Crisis
Iron Eagle
Iron Eagle 2
Ishtar
The Jewel of the Nile
Khartoum
Killing Streets
King Richard and the
  Crusaders
Lawrence of Arabia▶
The Lighthorsemen▶
The Lone Runner
A Matter of WHO
Not Without My Daughter▶
On Wings of Eagles
Paradise
Rescue Force
The Road to Morocco▶
The Robe
Rosebud
Sadat
The Sheik▶
Sirocco
Son of Ali Baba
The Spy Who Loved Me
Three Days in Beirut
Torn Apart
Trident Force
Warbirds
A Wedding in Galilee▶

Military Comedy
see also Comedy; War,
  General
Abbott and Costello in the
  Foreign Legion
Abroad with Two Yanks
Article 99
As You Were
At War with the Army
The Baby and the Battleship
Basic Training
Best Defense
Best Foot Forward
Biloxi Blues
Black and White in Color▶
The Captain from Koepenick
Caught in the Draft▶
Chesty Anderson USN
Clipped Wings
Combat Academy
Don't Go Near the Water
Ensign Pulver
The Flying Deuces▶
Follow That Camel
Follow the Leader
Getting Wasted
G.I. Blues
G.I. Jane
Going Under
Here Come the Marines
Hillbilly Blitzkrieg
Hot Shots!▶
Hot Shots! Part Deux
In the Army Now
Jumping Jacks
Le Gendarme de Saint-Tropez
Leave It to the Marines
A Man Called Sarge
M*A*S*H▶
M*A*S*H: Goodbye, Farewell
  & Amen▶
Miracle of Morgan's Creek▶

Mr. Walkie Talkie
The Mouse That Roared▶
Never Wave at a WAC
No Time for Sergeants▶
The Odd Squad
Off Limits
Operation Dames
Perfect Furlough
Private Benjamin
Private Manoeuvres
Privates on Parade
Renaissance Man
The Sad Sack
She's in the Army Now
Snuffy Smith, Yard Bird
Soldier in the Rain
Stripes
Suppose They Gave a War
  and Nobody Came?
Tanks a Million
Three Legionnaires
23 1/2 Hours Leave
The Virgin Soldiers
Viva Max
Weekend Pass
Weekend Warriors
We're in the Legion Now
We're in the Navy Now
The West Point Story

Miners & Mining
Act of Vengeance
The Adventures of Bullwhip
  Griffin
Angels Die Hard
Ballad of Cable Hogue▶
The Big Man: Crossing the
  Line▶
Black Fury▶
Burning Rage
Challenge to White Fang
The Christmas Coal Mine
  Miracle
Eureka Stockade
Fighting Cowboy
Fighting Valley
Flaming Frontiers
Gangster's Den
Gangsters of the Frontier
Ghost Town Renegades
Girl Rush
Grand Canyon Trail
Green Fire
The Hallelujah Trail
Haunted Gold
Hills of Utah
How Green was My Valley▶
Human Hearts
Kameradschaft▶
King Solomon's Mines
Little Church Around the
  Corner
The Man from Music Mountain
Matewan▶
McCabe & Mrs. Miller▶
Molly Maguires
My Darlin' Clementine
'Neath Canadian Skies
No Man's Law
North to Alaska▶
Paint Your Wagon
Pale Rider▶
Phantom Gold
Poldark▶
The Rainbow Gang
Red Earth
Rider from Tucson
The Ruthless Four
Salt of the Earth▶
Sands of Sacrifice
Silver Bandit
The Spoilers▶
Springhill
The Stars Look Down▶
The Strangeness
The War Wagon▶
Way Out West▶
Where the Green Ants Dream
Where Trails End
Wildrose▶
Xica▶

Missing Persons

see also Hostage!;
Kidnapped!
Adam▶
Agatha
Almost Human
American Nightmare
Anastasia▶
Anastasia: The Mystery of
  Anna
AngKor: Cambodia Express
Big Jake
Bureau of Missing Persons
Cavalcade of the West
Christina
Coming Out Alive
Curse of the Pink Panther
Disappearance
Dying Room Only
The Emerald Forest▶
Empire State
The Empty Beach
Equinox▶
Escapade in Japan
Experiment in Terror▶
Eye Witness
Final Cut
Foxtrap
Frantic▶
From Hollywood to Deadwood
Girl Hunters
Grayeagle
Green Eyes▶
Grievous Bodily Harm
Harem
Harper▶
Heading for Heaven
Hell Squad
Hide in Plain Sight▶
High Road to China
The Hit List
Hollywood Chaos
Home is Where the Hart is
Hurricane Smith
Into Thin Air▶
The Island at the Top of the
  World
Jungle Goddess
Kentucky Jubilee
Kidnap Syndicate
The Lady Vanishes▶
The Lady Vanishes
The Last Winter
Little Miss Millions
Low Down Dirty Shame
Midnight Warning
Misery▶
Missing▶
The Missing Corpse
Murder, My Sweet▶
Nickel & Dime
Night of the Cyclone
Norseman
Old Gringo
Picnic at Hanging Rock▶
The Port of Missing Girls
Prisoner of Zenda▶
The Professionals▶
Psych-Out
Psycho from Texas
Raising Arizona▶
Romancing the Stone▶
Ruthless People▶
Scandalous
Seance on a Wet Afternoon▶
The Searchers▶
Skull: A Night of Terror
Stark
Street Girls
Street Justice
Surfacing
Tarzan the Fearless
Terminal Force
Tokyo Joe
Tony Rome
The Vanishing▶
Wanted: Babysitter
Where Are the Children?
Where's Piccone▶
White Fire
The Wicker Man▶

Without a Trace

Missionaries

see also Nuns & Priests;
Religion; Religious Epics
At Play in the Fields of the
  Lord▶
Beyond the Next Mountain
Black Robe▶
Ethan
Hawaii▶
The Inn of the Sixth
  Happiness▶
The Keys of the Kingdom▶
The Mission▶
Mission to Glory
The Missionary

Misspelled Titles

The 'Burbs
Charly▶
Cheech and Chong: Still
  Smokin'
C.H.O.M.P.S.
Class of Nuke 'Em High
Class of Nuke 'Em High, Part
  2: Subhumanoid Meltdown
The Concentratin' Kid
Doin' Time
Doin' Time on Planet Earth
Feelin' Up
Fightin' Ranch
Fyre
Git Along Little Dogies
Hittin' the Trail
I Dood It
I Live with Me Dad
I Wanna Be a Beauty Queen
Lightnin' Carson Rides Again
Li'l Abner
Livin' Large
Lock 'n' Load
The Mirror Crack'd
Mo' Better Blues
Mo' Money
'Neath Canadian Skies
Nobody's Perfekt
Old Swimmin' Hole
Packin' It In
Peddlin' in Society
Pete 'n' Tillie
Pudd'nhead Wilson
Puss 'n Boots
Rappin'
Rat Pfink a Boo-Boo
Reg'lar Fellers
Ride 'Em Cowgirl
Ridin' on a Rainbow
Ridin' the California Trail
Ridin' the Trail
Roamin' Wild
Roarin' Lead
Rockin' Road Trip
Rockin' Ronnie
Rootin' Tootin' Rhythm
Singin' in the Rain▶
Six Shootin' Sheriff
Smilin' Through
Snowballin'
Spittin' Image
Straight Shootin'
Streetwalkin'
Sweet Sweetback's
  Baadasssss Song▶
Thrashin'
Tol'able David
We're Talkin' Serious Money
Workin' for Peanuts

Mistaken Identity

see also Amnesia; Gender
Bending; Role Reversal
Across the Bridge
The Adventurer
The Adventures of Bullwhip
  Griffin
Along Came Jones▶
Alvin Rides Again
Amore!
Amos and Andrew
Another You

As You Desire Me▶
As You Like It
As Young As You Feel▶
Bachelor Mother▶
The Ballad of Little Jo
The Beautiful Blonde from
  Bashful Bend
Being There▶
Betrayed▶
Billy the Kid Returns
Bittersweet Love
Black Glove
Blackjack
Blame It on the Bellboy
Blind Justice
Blondie Knows Best
Body Snatchers
Borderline
Boy's Reformatory
Brighton Strangler
Broadway Limited
Broken Melody
Bullets or Ballots▶
Bullseye!
Bundle of Joy
Buona Sera, Mrs. Campbell
Butler's Dilemma
Camp Cucamonga: How I
  Spent My Summer
  Vacation
The Capture▶
Caroline?▶
Carry On Admiral
A Case of Deadly Force▶
CB4: The Movie
Center of the Web
The Challengers
Chameleon Street▶
Charade▶
Charley's Aunt
The Chase
Convicted
Convicts at Large
Cornbread, Earl & Me
The Couch Trip
Counterblast
Court Jester▶
Dave▶
Deadwood
The Desert Song
Don't Tell Her It's Me
Double Vision
El Callao
El Mariachi▶
Ernest Goes to Jail
Erotic Touch of Hot Skin
Evergreen
Every Man's Law
Execution of Raymond
  Graham
F/X 2: The Deadly Art of
  Illusion
Family Reunion
Fargo Express
Fatal Exposure
Father
Feet First
Fighting Parson
Gangway
The Gay Divorcee▶
Generale Della Rovere▶
Gentleman Bandit
Get That Man
The Glass Bottom Boat
Good Neighbor Sam▶
The Great Dictator▶
The Gun in Betty Lou's
  Handbag
Gunfire
Gunsmoke Trail
Hell on Frisco Bay
Her Life as a Man
Hero▶
High & Low▶
High Lonesome
Highway 13
His Brother's Ghost
His Wife's Lover▶
Hittin' the Trail
Hollywood Chaos
Hometown Boy Makes Good
Honolulu

A House In The Hills
I Love You
I Want to Live!▶
I Will, I Will for Now
If Looks Could Kill
The Imposter
In Person
In Society
The Inspector General▶
Instant Kung-Fu Man
Invasion of the Body
  Snatchers▶
It! The Terror from Beyond
  Space
Johnny Handsome▶
Johnny Stecchino▶
Kansas City Confidential▶
Keaton's Cop
Killer Dill
The Killing Time
A Kiss Before Dying
Landslide
The Last Contract
The Last Winter
Laughing at Danger
Laurel & Hardy: The Hoose-
  Gow
Law of the Underworld
Life Is a Long Quiet River▶
Lisa
The Little Drummer Girl▶
Little Sister
The Lookalike
Love at Large▶
Lucky Cisco Kid
Made in America
Maid's Night Out
The Man in the Raincoat
The Man on the Box
Man on the Run
The Man with One Red Shoe
The Mark of Zorro▶
Meet the Mob
Mexican Spitfire/Smartest Girl
  in Town
The Misadventures of Mr. Wilt
Mississippi Mermaid▶
Mistaken Identity
Mr. Klein▶
Monsignor Quixote
Monte Carlo Nights
My Geisha
My Man Godfrey▶
My Outlaw Brother
My Twentieth Century▶
Mystery Date
Naughty Marietta
Never a Dull Moment
Next of Kin
The Night We Never Met
Nightfall▶
Nobody's Perfect
North by Northwest▶
The Obsessed
Obsession
One Body Too Many
Opportunity Knocks
Oscar
Out of Bounds
Out on a Limb
Paper Mask
Pardon My Sarong
The Passenger▶
Phantom Fiend
Phantom Killer
Pier 23
The Player▶
The Pope Must Diet
Prelude to a Kiss
Private Life of Don Juan
The Private Secretary
Profile
Ranson's Folly
Rattler Kid
The Red Half-Breed
Red Heat
Red Rock West▶
Return of Jesse James
The Return of Martin Guerre▶
Return of the Tall Blond Man
  With One Black Shoe
River Beat

Romance on the High Seas▶
Running Hot
St. Benny the Dip
The Scar
Scream of Fear▶
The Secret of My Success
The 7th Commandment
The Sinister Invasion
Sister Act
Sister Act 2: Back in the Habit
Six Gun Gospel
Small Kill
Smokey and the Bandit, Part
  3
Social Error
Soldat Duroc...Ca Va Etre Ta
  Fete!
Someone at the Door
Splitting Heirs
Stolen Identity
A Stolen Life
Straight Talk
The Suitors
Supergrass
Support Your Local
  Gunfighter▶
Switched at Birth
10 Rillington Place▶
The Tenth Man
Texas Carnival
Texas Cyclone
They Knew What They
  Wanted▶
The Thin Blue Line▶
Things Change▶
The 39 Steps▶
Tombstone Terror
Top Hat▶
Toto le Heros▶
True Identity
The Unholy Three▶
The Well▶
We're No Angels
West of the Pecos
White Eagle
White of the Eye▶
Who's Harry Crumb?
Withnail and I▶
The Worldly Madonna
The Wrong Guys
Zertigo Diamond Caper

Modern Cowboys

see also Western Comedy;
Westerns
Another Pair of Aces: Three of
  a Kind▶
Barbarosa▶
Bronco Billy
City Slickers▶
City Slickers 2: The Legend of
  Curly's Gold
Coogan's Bluff▶
The Cowboy Way
Dudes
The Electric Horseman
Fool for Love
Lonely are the Brave▶
My Heroes Have Always Been
  Cowboys
Rhinestone
Samurai Cowboy
Sweet Creek County War
True West▶
Wild Horses

Monster Moms

see also Bad Dads;
Parenthood
The Baby
Bellissima▶
Beyond the Door
Big Bad Mama
Big Bad Mama 2
Carrie▶
Die! Die! My Darling!
Flesh Eating Mothers
Gorgo
The Grifters▶
Gypsy
Invaders from Mars

Monster

Ma Barker's Killer Brood
Mad Youth
Mom
Mommie Dearest
Mother's Day
Parents>
The Positively True
  Adventures of the Alleged
  Texas Cheerleader-
  Murdering Mom>
Psycho>
Psycho 2
Psycho 3
Serial Mom>
Sleepwalkers
Small Sacrifices
The Stepmother

Monsters, General

see also *Ghosts, Ghouls,
& Goblins; Giants; Killer
Beasts; Killer Bugs; Killer
Plants; Killer Toys; Mad
Scientists; Robots &
Androids; Sea Critter
Attack; Vampires;
Werewolves; Zombies*

Alligator>
Alligator 2: The Mutation
The Amazing Colossal Man
The Astounding She-Monster
Atlas in the Land of the
  Cyclops
Barn of the Naked Dead
Basket Case>
Basket Case 2
Basket Case 3: The Progeny
The Beast from Haunted Cave
The Beast from 20,000
  Fathoms
Beast in the Cellar
Beast of the Yellow Night
The Beast of Yucca Flats
The Beast Within
Beginning of the End
The Being
The Best of the Monsters
Bio Hazard
Black Roses
Blackenstein
The Blob
The Blob>
Blood Tide
Boggy Creek II
The Boy Who Loved Trolls
Brain of Blood
The Brainiac
The Bride
Bride of the Gorilla
Bride of the Monster
Brides of the Beast
Cameron's Closet
Captain Sinbad
The Capture of Bigfoot
Carry On Screaming
Cast a Deadly Spell>
Castle of Evil
The Cellar
The Channeler
C.H.U.D.
C.H.U.D. 2: Bud the Chud
City of the Walking Dead
Class of Nuke 'Em High
The Crater Lake Monster
Creature of Destruction
Creeping Terror
Creepozoids
Creepshow
The Curse
Curse 2: The Bite
Curse 3: Blood Sacrifice
Curse of the Swamp Creature
Cyclops
Dagora, the Space Monster
The Dark
The Daughter of Dr. Jekyll
Day of the Animals
Deepstar Six
The Demon
Demon of Paradise
Demons

Demons of Ludlow
Demonstone
Demonwarp
Destroy All Monsters
Devil Kiss
Devil Monster
Devil Rider
Dr. Orloff's Invisible Horror
Dr. Orloff's Monster
Doctor Who: Terror of the
  Zygons
Don't Be Afraid of the Dark
Earth vs. the Spider
Emergency>
Endgame
Equinox>
Evil Dead
Evil Dead 2: Dead by Dawn
The Evil of Frankenstein
Evil Town
Fiend Without a Face
Fire Maidens from Outer
  Space
Fire Monsters Against the Son
  of Hercules
Forbidden Planet>
Frankenstein>
Frankenstein
Frankenstein: A Cinematic
  Scrapbook
Frankenstein '80
Frankenstein General Hospital
Frankenstein Island
Frankenstein Meets the
  Wolfman>
Frankenstein Unbound>
Frankenstein's Daughter
Gamera, the Invincible
Gamera vs. Barugon
Gamera vs. Gaos
Gamera vs. Guiron
Gamera vs. Zigra
The Gamma People
Gappa the Trifibian Monster
Gate 2
Geek Maggot Bingo
Ghidrah the Three Headed
  Monster
The Giant Claw
Godzilla, King of the Monsters
Godzilla 1985
Godzilla on Monster Island
Godzilla Raids Again
Godzilla vs. Biollante
Godzilla vs. Megalon
Godzilla vs. Monster Zero
Godzilla vs. Mothra
Godzilla vs. the Cosmic
  Monster
Godzilla vs. the Smog
  Monster
Godzilla's Revenge
Goliath and the Dragon
Gorgo
Half Human
Hideous Sun Demon
Horror Express
Horror of Party Beach
House of Dracula
Howling 6: The Freaks
I Was a Teenage Zombie
The Incredible Two-Headed
  Transplant
Infra-Man
Intruder Within
Invasion of the Animal People
The Invisible Monster
Island Claw
Island of Dr. Moreau
It Came from Beneath the
  Sea>
It's Alive!
Jack the Giant Killer>
Jason and the Argonauts>
Jungle Heat
The Killer Shrews
The Kindred
King of Kong Island
Labyrinth>
Lady Frankenstein
Legend of Boggy Creek
Little Monsters

Mad Doctor of Blood Island
The Mad Monster
Mad Monster Party
Man Beast
Man Made Monster
The Manster
Maxim Xul
Meteor Monster
The Milpitas Monster
Mirror, Mirror
The Monolith Monsters
The Monster and the Stripper
The Monster of Piedras
  Blancas
Monster on the Campus
The Monster Squad
The Monster that Challenged
  the World
Monsters Crash the Pajama
  Party
Mutant
Mutants In Paradise
My Demon Lover
Night of the Living Dead>
The People Under the Stairs
The Phantom Creeps
The Phantom from 10,000
  Leagues
The Prey
The Quatermass Experiment>
The Quest
Rana: The Legend of Shadow
  Lake
Rawhead Rex
The Return of Swamp Thing
Return to Boggy Creek
Revenge of Doctor X
Revolt of the Zombies
Samson in the Wax Museum
Saturday the 14th Strikes
  Back
Science Crazed
Scream Dream
The Screaming Dead
The Sea Serpent
The Secret of the Loch
Seven Doors of Death
Shadowzone
Silent Night, Deadly Night 5:
  The Toymaker
The Slayer
The Slime People
Slithis
The Snake Hunter Strangler
The Snow Creature
Sons of Hercules in the Land
  of Darkness
Space Monster
Squirm
Stay Awake
Stepmonster
The Strangeness
Subspecies
Swamp of the Lost Monster
Tales from the Darkside: The
  Movie
Terror Beneath the Sea
Terror in the Swamp
Terror of Mechagodzilla
Terror of Rome Against the
  Son of Hercules
The Terror Within
The Terror Within 2
The Terrornauts
Them!>
Things
The Time Machine>
Tomb of Torture
The Toxic Avenger
The Toxic Avenger, Part 2
The Toxic Avenger, Part 3:
  The Last Temptation of
  Toxie
Track of the Moonbeast
Transmutations
20 Million Miles to Earth
Varan the Unbelievable
The Video Dead
Voodoo Woman
Voyage to the Planet of
  Prehistoric Women
The War of the Colossal Beast

War of the Gargantuas
Watchers
Watchers 2
Yog, Monster from Space
Yongkari Monster of the Deep

Motor Vehicle Dept.

see also *Bikers; Fast
Cars; Killer Cars*

Action Jackson
American Graffiti>
Back to the Future>
Bail Out
The Betsy
Black Moon Rising
The Blues Brothers
Cadillac Man
Car Trouble
Car Wash
The Chase
Chitty Chitty Bang Bang
Comic Cabby
Corvette Summer
Coupe de Ville
Cry Panic
Dangerous Curves
Dark of the Night
D.C. Cab
Deadline Auto Theft
Dream Machine
Drive-In
Drive-In Massacre
The Driver
Driving Me Crazy
Duel>
Ferris Bueller's Day Off>
Firebird 2015 A.D.
Follow That Car
Ford: The Man & the Machine
Free Ride
Freedom
Freeway
Great American Traffic Jam
Gung Ho
The Hearse
Herbie Rides Again
High Rolling in a Hot Corvette
Hometown U.S.A.
Hot Wire
How I Learned to Love
  Women
Killing Cars
License to Drive
The Love Bug
Maximum Overdrive
Motorama
Motown's Mustang
Moving Violations
My Chauffeur
National Lampoon's
Night on Earth>
One Deadly Owner
Pepper and His Wacky Taxi
Raw Power
Repo Jake
Repo Man>
Roger & Me>
Silkwood>
Smokey & the Hotwire Gang
Steel Arena
Stingray
Sunset Limousine
Superbug Super Agent
This Man Must Die>
Tomboy
Tucker: The Man and His
  Dream>
Used Cars>
The Van
Vanishing Point
Wheels of Terror
Zero to Sixty

Mountaineering

Alpine Fire
The Challenge>
Cliffhanger>
The Climb
The Eiger Sanction
Five Days One Summer

God's Bloody Acre
Heidi
K2: The Ultimate High
The Mountain
My Side of the Mountain
Storm and Sorrow
Third Man on the Mountain
The White Tower>

Movie & TV Trailers

Bikers, Blondes, and Blood
Cinema Shrapnel
Cowboys of the Saturday
  Matinee
Dracula: A Cinematic
  Scrapbook
Frankenstein: A Cinematic
  Scrapbook
Hitchcock Classics Collection:
  Trailers on Tape
Hollywood Uncensored
It Came from Hollywood
Loose Shoes
1939, The Movies' Vintage
  Year: Trailers on Tape
The Professor
To See Such Fun

Mummies

see also *Horror; Zombies*

Abbott & Costello Meet the
  Mummy
Attack of the Mayan Mummy
Awakening
Castle of the Living Dead
The Curse of the Aztec
  Mummy
Curse of the Aztec Mummy/
  Robot vs. the Aztec
  Mummy
Dawn of the Mummy
The Monster Squad
The Mummy>
Mummy & Curse of the Jackal
The Mummy's Curse
The Mummy's Ghost
The Mummy's Hand
The Mummy's Revenge
The Mummy's Tomb
The Robot vs. the Aztec
  Mummy
Sphinx
Wrestling Women vs. the
  Aztec Mummy

Music

see also *Martyred Pop
Icons; Musician Biopics;
Nashville Narratives; Rock
Stars on Film; Struggling
Musicians*

Airheads
Alexander's Ragtime Band>
All You Need Is Cash>
Allegro Non Troppo>
Almost Blue
Amadeus>
American Blue Note
Americathon
The Apple
Backbeat>
Ballad in Blue
Basileus Quartet>
Beach Boys: An American
  Band
Beat Street
The Beatniks
Beethoven
Beethoven Lives Upstairs
Beethoven's Nephew
The Benny Goodman Story
The Best of the Kenny Everett
  Video Show
Big Business Girl
Bird>
Bix
Blame It on the Night
Blink
Bloodhounds of Broadway
Blueberry Hill
The Bodyguard

Born to Boogie
Bound for Glory▶
Broken Strings
Buddy's Song
Bummer
Burglar▶
Captain January
Carmen▶
CB4: The Movie
The Challengers
Coal Miner's Daughter▶
Comeback
The Commitments▶
The Competition▶
The Compleat Beatles▶
Concrete Angels
The Conductor
Cool As Ice
Cool Mikado
The Cotton Club▶
The Courier
Crossroads
Dead Girls
Death Drug
Death Games
Deception▶
Decline of Western Civilization 1▶
Decline of Western Civilization 2: The Metal Years
Diner▶
Disorderlies
Diva▶
Divine Madness
Doctor Duck's Super Secret All-Purpose Sauce
Don't Look Back▶
The Doors
The Doors: Soft Parade, a Retrospective
Double Trouble
Dreaming Lips
Dubeat-E-O
Duet for One
The Duke is the Tops
Dutch Treat
Easyriders Video Magazine
Eddie and the Cruisers
Eddie and the Cruisers 2: Eddie Lives!
The Eddy Duchin Story
Edie in Ciao! Manhattan
Elvis and Me
Elvis Memories
Elvis on Tour
Elvis: One Night with You
Elvis: Rare Moments with the King
Elvis Stories
Elvis: The Lost Performances
Elvis: The Movie
Encounter at Raven's Gate
Escape Me Never
The Eternal Waltz
Eubie!
The Fabulous Baker Boys▶
The Fabulous Dorseys
Face the Music
Fantasia▶
Fastest Guitar Alive
The Fighting Legion
Fighting Mad
Fingers▶
Five Easy Pieces▶
The Five Heartbeats▶
The Five Pennies
FM
Follow Me, Boys!▶
Follow That Dream
For Those About to Rock: Monsters in Moscow
Forget Mozart
Frankie and Johnny
Fugitive Valley
The Gay Ranchero
The Gene Krupa Story
Get Crazy
Getting Over
Giant Steps
The Gig
Gimme Shelter

Give My Regards to Broad Street
The Glenn Miller Story▶
Good Morning, Vietnam▶
Gotta Dance, Gotta Sing
Great Balls of Fire
The Great Waltz▶
Green Card
Hail Caesar
A Hard Day's Night▶
Hear My Song▶
Heartbreak Hotel
Hearts of Fire
Heaven Tonight
Hi-De-Ho
Home Sweet Home
House Party▶
House Party 2: The Pajama Jam
House Party 3
Humoresque▶
I Wanna Hold Your Hand
Identity Crisis
Incident at Channel Q
Irving Berlin's America
It Couldn't Happen Here
I've Always Loved You
The Jacksons: An American Dream
Jazz Singer
Jazzman▶
Joey
Johnny Guitar▶
Johnny Suede
Kid from Gower Gulch
King of Jazz
Knights & Emeralds
Krush Groove
Lady Be Good
Lady Sings the Blues
Las Vegas Hillbillys
The Las Vegas Story
The Last Waltz
Le Cavaleur
Leningrad Cowboys Go America
Let It Be
Let It Rock
Let's Get Lost
Lisztomania
Los Apuros de Dos Gallos
Mahler▶
The Man and the Monster
A Matter of Degrees
Matters of the Heart
The Medium
Melody for Three
Mo' Better Blues
Monkey Grip▶
Monterey Pop▶
Moonlight Sonata
Moscow on the Hudson▶
Mozart: A Childhood Chronicle▶
The Mozart Brothers▶
The Mozart Story
The Music Lovers
The Music Teacher
My Pal Trigger
Mystery in Swing
Netherworld
New York, New York▶
1991: The Year Punk Broke
Not Quite Love
Oklahoma Kid▶
On the Air Live with Captain Midnight
Outlaw Blues
Party! Party!
Pete Kelly's Blues
Peter Pan▶
Phantom of the Paradise
The Piano▶
The Pied Piper of Hamelin
Play Misty for Me▶
Play Murder for Me
Playing for Time▶
Point of Terror
Portfolio
Privates on Parade
Quadrophenia▶

The Real Buddy Holly Story
The Real Patsy Cline
Rhapsody
Rich Girl
River of No Return
Roadkill
Rock & Roll Cowboys
Rock & Rule
Rock & the Money-Hungry Party Girls
Rock, Baby, Rock It
Rock 'n' Roll High School▶
Rock 'n' Roll High School Forever
Rock, Pretty Baby
Rocktober Blood
Round Midnight▶
Running Out of Luck
Satisfaction
Scenes from the Goldmine
Scream Dream
Sepia Cinderella
The Seventh Veil▶
Shock 'Em Dead
Shoot the Piano Player▶
Shout
Sid & Nancy▶
Sinatra
Singles▶
Some Like It Hot▶
Sometimes It Works, Sometimes It Doesn't
Somos Novios
A Song is Born▶
Song of Arizona
A Song to Remember▶
Spellcaster
Splitz
Spring Symphony
A Star is Born▶
Sticky Fingers
Stunt Rock
Sundance
Sunset Strip
Sweet Country Road
Sweet Love, Bitter
Swing High, Swing Low
Swing It, Professor
Tapeheads
Tchaikovsky
Terror on Tour
They Shall Have Music
32 Short Films About Glenn Gould▶
This is Elvis
This is Spinal Tap▶
The Three Caballeros
Thunder Alley
Thunder & Mud
Tougher than Leather
Tous les Matins du Monde▶
Trick or Treat
The Trumpet and I
Twilight in the Sierras
Two-Gun Troubador
Un Coeur en Hiver
Underground U.S.A.
Unfaithfully Yours▶
Unfaithfully Yours
Vagabond Lover
Verdi
Voyage of the Rock Aliens
Wagner: The Complete Epic
Wagner: The Movie
Waltz King
Wayne's World 2
Who's the Man?
Wild Guitar
Wild Orchid 2: Two Shades of Blue
Woodstock▶
World of Henry Orient▶
Yanco
Young Man with a Horn▶
Zachariah

Musical Comedy
see also Musicals
The Affairs of Dobie Gillis
Almost Angels
Amateur Night

Andy Hardy Meets Debutante
April In Paris
Around the World
Artists and Models
Athena
Babes in Arms
Babes on Broadway
Bathing Beauty
Beach Blanket Bingo▶
Beach Party
Because You're Mine
Bert Rigby, You're a Fool
Best Foot Forward
The Best Little Whorehouse in Texas
Bikini Beach
Billy Rose's Jumbo▶
The Blues Brothers
Boardinghouse Blues
The Boy Friend▶
Boy! What a Girl
Broadway Melody of 1936▶
Broadway Rhythm
Bundle of Joy
Bye, Bye, Birdie▶
Cairo
Call Out the Marines
Captain January
Carefree▶
The Cocoanuts
College Swing
Como Dos Gotas de Agua
Copacabana
Court Jester▶
Cover Girl▶
Cry-Baby▶
Dames▶
Dance, Girl, Dance
Dangerous When Wet
Darling Lili
Delightfully Dangerous
The Devil's Brother
Diplomaniacs
Disorderlies
Dixiana
Dixie Jamboree
Doll Face
DuBarry Was a Lady
Duchess of Idaho
Earth Girls are Easy
Easy Come, Easy Go
The Eighties
Escape to Paradise
Evergreen
Everybody Sing
Fashions of 1934
Feel the Motion
Femmes de Paris
Fiesta
Finian's Rainbow▶
The First Nudie Musical
Flirtation Walk
Flower Drum Song
Follow That Dream
Follow That Rainbow
Four Jacks and a Jill
Frankie and Johnny
The French Line
The French Way
Frolics on Ice
Fun in Acapulco
Funny Face▶
A Funny Thing Happened on the Way to the Forum▶
The Gay Divorcee▶
Gentlemen Prefer Blondes▶
George White's Scandals
G.I. Blues
Gigi▶
The Girl Can't Help It
Girl Crazy▶
Girl Happy
The Girl Most Likely
Girl of the Golden West
Girl Rush
Girls! Girls! Girls!
Give a Girl a Break
Glorifying the American Girl
Going Hollywood▶
Going My Way▶
Gold Diggers of 1933▶
Gold Diggers of 1935▶

The Goldwyn Follies
Good News
Grease▶
Grease 2
The Great American Broadcast▶
Guys and Dolls▶
Gypsy▶
Gypsy
Hairspray▶
Hallelujah, I'm a Bum
The Happiest Millionaire
Happy Go Lovely
The Harvey Girls▶
Head▶
The Heat's On
Hello, Dolly!
Help!▶
Here Come the Girls
Here Comes the Groom
High Society▶
Hips, Hips, Hooray
Hit the Deck
Holiday in Havana
Holiday in Mexico
Holiday Inn▶
Hollywood Canteen▶
Honolulu
How to Stuff a Wild Bikini
How to Succeed in Business without Really Trying▶
Huckleberry Finn
I Do! I Do!
I Dood It
I Dream of Jeannie
I Dream Too Much
I Love Melvin
I Married an Angel
In the Good Old Summertime▶
In the Navy
International House
It Happened in Brooklyn
It's a Date
It's a Great Feeling
It's Love Again
Jive Junction
Juke Joint
Jupiter's Darling
Just for You
Keep 'Em Flying
Kid Galahad
Kid Millions
King Kelly of the U.S.A.
King of Jazz
Kiss Me Kate▶
Kissin' Cousins
La Marchanta
Lady Be Good
Latin Lovers
Le Million▶
Les Girls
Let's Dance
Let's Go Collegiate
Life Begins for Andy Hardy▶
Li'l Abner
Lili▶
Lily of Killarney
Little Nellie Kelly
Little Shop of Horrors▶
Live a Little, Love a Little
Look Out Sister▶
Louisiana Purchase
Lovely to Look At▶
Loving You
Lucky Me
Lullaby of Broadway
Make a Wish
Mame
Mamele
A Matter of Degrees
Maytime in Mayfair
Meet Me in Las Vegas
Melody Cruise
The Merry Widow▶
The Merry Widow
Mr. Music
The Muppet Christmas Carol
The Muppet Movie▶
The Muppets Take Manhattan▶
Muscle Beach Party

Musical

My Dream is Yours
My Sister Eileen▶
My Song Goes Round the World
Nancy Goes to Rio
Naughty Marietta
Neptune's Daughter
Never a Dull Moment
New Faces of 1952
Newsies
No Time for Romance
On a Clear Day You Can See Forever
On the Avenue
One from the Heart
One in a Million▶
One Night in the Tropics
One Touch of Venus
The Opposite Sex
Paint Your Wagon
Pajama Game▶
Pajama Party
Pal Joey▶
Panama Hattie
The Perils of Pauline
Phantom of the Paradise
Pin-Up Girl
The Pirate▶
The Pirates of Penzance
Popeye
Presenting Lily Mars
Rebecca of Sunnybrook Farm
The Road to Bali▶
The Road to Lebanon
The Road to Morocco▶
Road to Nashville
The Road to Rio▶
The Road to Singapore
The Road to Utopia▶
The Road to Zanzibar▶
Roadie
Roberta▶
Robin and the Seven Hoods
Rock 'n' Roll High School▶
Rock 'n' Roll High School Forever
Roman Scandals
Romance on the High Seas▶
Royal Wedding
Running Out of Luck
Second Fiddle
Sensations of 1945
Sgt. Pepper's Lonely Hearts Club Band
Seven Brides for Seven Brothers▶
Seven Days' Leave
The Seven Little Foys▶
1776▶
Sextette
Shake, Rattle and Rock
Shall We Dance▶
Ship Ahoy
Shock Treatment
Show Business▶
Silk Stockings▶
Sing Your Worries Away
Singin' in the Rain▶
Sioux City Sue
The Sky's the Limit
Small Town Girl
A Song is Born▶
Song of the Islands
Speedway
Spinout
Spotlight Scandals
Springtime in the Rockies
Starstruck
State Fair▶
State Fair
Step Lively
The Stooge
The Stork Club
Strike Up the Band
Summer Holiday
Summer Stock▶
Sun Valley Serenade
Sunny
Sunny Skies
Sweet Rosie O'Grady
Sweethearts▶
Swing It, Professor

Swing Time▶
Take Me Out to the Ball Game
Tea for Two▶
Texas Carnival
That Girl from Paris
There's No Business Like Show Business▶
Thin Ice▶
Thoroughly Modern Millie
Three Daring Daughters
The Three Musketeers
Tickle Me
Tokyo Pop
Too Many Girls▶
Top Hat▶
23 1/2 Hours Leave
Two Girls and a Sailor▶
Two Tickets to Broadway
Two Weeks with Love
The Unsinkable Molly Brown▶
Up in Arms
Vogues of 1938
Wallaby Jim of the Islands
The West Point Story
White Christmas▶
Whoopee!
A Woman is a Woman▶
Wonder Man
Yes, Giorgio
Yidl Mitn Fidl
Yolanda and the Thief
You Were Never Lovelier▶
You'll Find Out
You'll Never Get Rich▶
Ziegfeld Follies
Zis Boom Bah

Musical Drama

see also **Musicals**

Actor: The Paul Muni Story
The Band Wagon▶
The Barkleys of Broadway▶
Beatlemania! The Movie
The Belle of New York
Bells are Ringing▶
Beware
Blonde Venus▶
Blue Hawaii
Body Moves
Body Rock
Broadway Serenade
The Buddy Holly Story▶
Cabaret▶
Camelot
Can-Can
The Cantor's Son
Carmen Jones▶
Carnival Rock
The Cat and the Fiddle▶
The Chocolate Soldier
A Christmas Carol
Clambake
Club Havana
Coal Miner's Daughter▶
The Complete Showboat
Concrete Angels
Congress Dances
Cool Mikado
The Cotton Club▶
Crossover Dreams
Curly Top
Daddy Long Legs▶
A Damsel in Distress▶
Dance Hall
Dance of Life
Dancing Lady
Dancing Pirate
A Date with Judy
Deadman's Curve
The Deputy Drummer
Dimples
Dogs in Space
Don Quixote▶
Double Trouble
Down Argentine Way▶
The Duke is the Tops
The Farmer Takes a Wife
Fast Forward
Fiddler on the Roof▶
The Firefly
Fisherman's Wharf
The Five Pennies

Flashdance
Footloose
The Forbidden Dance
42nd Street▶
Frankie and Johnny
Funny Girl▶
Funny Lady
Gangway
George Balanchine's The Nutcracker
The Glenn Miller Story▶
Go, Johnny Go!
Goodbye, Mr. Chips
Graffiti Bridge
Great Balls of Fire
The Great Caruso
The Great Waltz▶
The Great Ziegfeld▶
Greek Street
Hard to Hold
The Harder They Come
Harmony Lane
Harum Scarum
Heart's Desire
Hello, Frisco, Hello
Honeysuckle Rose
Honkytonk Nights
I Could Go on Singing
Idolmaker
If You Knew Susie
I'll Cry Tomorrow▶
I'll See You in My Dreams
The In Crowd
It Happened at the World's Fair
It's Always Fair Weather
Jailbird Rock
Jailhouse Rock▶
Jazz Singer
Jesus Christ, Superstar▶
Jolson Sings Again
The Jolson Story▶
The Josephine Baker Story▶
Jubilee
Jungle Patrol
Just Around the Corner
The King and I▶
King Creole
Knights of the City
La Bamba▶
La Cucaracha
Ladies of the Chorus
Lady Sings the Blues
Lambada
Life of Verdi
Light of Day
The Little Colonel▶
Little Miss Broadway
The Littlest Angel
The Littlest Rebel
Los Tres Calaveras
Lottery Bride
Love Me or Leave Me▶
Love Me Tender
Mack the Knife
The Mambo Kings▶
The Man I Love▶
Man of La Mancha
Marco
A Matter of Time
Meet Danny Wilson
Melody Master
Miss Sadie Thompson▶
Motown's Mustang
Murder at the Vanities
Murder with Music
The Music Lovers
The Music Man▶
Musica Proibita
My Fair Lady▶
Never Steal Anything Small
New Moon
New York, New York▶
Night and Day
No, No Nanette
Northwest Outpost
The Old Curiosity Shop
Oliver!▶
The One and Only, Genuine, Original Family Band▶
One Night of Love▶
One Trick Pony

Opera do Malandro
Orchestra Wives▶
An Orphan Boy of Vienna
Paradise, Hawaiian Style
Paradise in Harlem
Paradise Island
Paris Blues
Pennies From Heaven▶
Pete Kelly's Blues
Pete Townshend: White City
Piaf
The Poor Little Rich Girl
Princess Tam Tam▶
Purple Rain
Quadrophenia▶
Rainbow
Rappin'
Reckless
The Red Shoes▶
Rhapsody in Blue▶
Rock, Baby, Rock It
Rock, Rock, Rock
Rooftops
The Rose▶
Rose Marie▶
Rose of Washington Square
Roustabout
Sailing Along
Salsa
Sarafina!▶
Satisfaction
Scrooge
Senora Tentacion
Shining Star
Shout
Show Boat▶
Show Boat
Sincerely Yours
Sing
Smilin' Through
Something to Sing About
Song O' My Heart
Song of Freedom
Song of Norway
Song Without End
Songwriter
The Sound of Music▶
Sparkle
Star!
Stars and Stripes Forever▶
Stay Away, Joe
Stepping Out▶
Stowaway▶
Sunday in the Park with George▶
Sweet Charity▶
Sweet Dreams
Sweetheart of the Navy
Tap
They Shall Have Music
This is the Army
The Three Penny Opera▶
Thunder Alley
Till the Clouds Roll By/A Star Is Born▶
Tommy
Transatlantic Merry-Go-Round
Umbrellas of Cherbourg▶
Una Vez en la Vida
Waltz King
Way Down South
West Side Story▶
What's Love Got to Do With It?
Yankee Doodle Dandy▶
Yentl
Young at Heart
Young Caruso
Young Man with a Horn▶
Ziegfeld Girl▶
Zoot Suit▶
Zou Zou

Musical Fantasy

see also **Musicals**

Alice
Alice in Wonderland
Babes in Toyland
Bedknobs and Broomsticks
Brigadoon▶
Butterfly Ball
Cabin in the Sky▶

Calacan▶
Carousel▶
Chitty Chitty Bang Bang
Cinderella
Cinderella 2000
Comic Book Kids
A Connecticut Yankee in King Arthur's Court
Damn Yankees▶
Doctor Dolittle
Down to Earth
Fairytales
The 5000 Fingers of Dr. T▶
Kismet
La Pastorela
Labyrinth▶
The Little Match Girl
The Little Prince
Magical Mystery Tour
March of the Wooden Soldiers▶
Mary Poppins▶
The New Adventures of Pippi Longstocking
Once Upon a Brothers Grimm
Peter Pan▶
Rumpelstiltskin
Sleeping Beauty
Willy Wonka & the Chocolate Factory▶
The Wizard of Oz▶
Wonderwall: The Movie

Musicals

see also **Animated Musicals; Contemporary Musicals; Disco Musicals; Musical Comedy; Musical Drama; Musical Fantasy**

Alexander's Ragtime Band▶
An American in Paris▶
Anchors Aweigh▶
Annie
Babes in Toyland
Balalaika
Beat Street
Bitter Sweet
Black Tights
Born to Dance
Breaking the Ice
Broadway Melody
Broadway Melody of 1938
Broadway Melody of 1940
By the Light of the Silvery Moon
Calamity Jane▶
Charm of La Boheme
Deep in My Heart
The Desert Song
Dogs in Space
Dos Postolas Gemelas
Easter Parade▶
Easy to Love
Flying Down to Rio
Follies Girl
Follies in Concert
Follow the Fleet▶
Footlight Parade▶
Footlight Serenade
For Me and My Gal
For the First Time
Gaiety
Hair▶
Half a Sixpence
Hands Across the Border
Hans Brinker
Hans Christian Andersen
Happy Landing
Harlem on the Prairie
Harvest Melody
Hats Off
Hawaii Calls
Hi-De-Ho
Higher and Higher
Hillbillies in a Haunted House
Iceland
Incident at Channel Q
Invitation to the Dance
Junction 88
Killer Diller
Krush Groove

The Last Radio Station
Let Freedom Ring
Let's Sing Again
Little Johnny Jones
A Little Night Music
London Melody
Look for the Silver Lining
Madam Satan
Manhattan Merry-Go-Round
Maytime►
Meet Me in St. Louis►
Meet the Navy
Mrs. Brown, You've Got a Lovely Daughter
Moon Over Harlem
Moon Over Miami►
Music in My Heart
Music Shoppe
My Lucky Star
Oh! Calcutta!
Oklahoma!►
On Moonlight Bay
On the Town
Pagan Love Song
Pinocchio
Pippin►
Private Buckaroo
Red Garters
Reet, Petite and Gone►
Rhapsody
Rhythm Parade
Rich, Young and Pretty
Rosalie
Second Chorus
Sepia Cinderella
The Seven Hills of Rome
The Seven Little Foys►
She Shall Have Music
South Pacific►
Stage Door Canteen
Stormy Weather
The Story of Vernon and Irene Castle►
The Student Prince
Sweeney Todd: The Demon Barber of Fleet Street
Sweet Adeline
Swing
Swing Parade of 1946
Take It Big
Taking My Turn
Terror of Tiny Town
Thank Your Lucky Stars►
That Midnight Kiss
That's Dancing!
That's Entertainment
That's Entertainment, Part 2
That's Entertainment 3
That's Singing: The Best of Broadway
Thousands Cheer
Three Little Words
The Threepenny Opera
Thrill of a Romance
Till the Clouds Roll By
Tin Pan Alley
The Toast of New Orleans
Tonight and Every Night
The Trouble with Girls (and How To Get Into It)►
Under the Cherry Moon
Vagabond Lover
The Vampyr
Velnio Nuotaka
Viva Las Vegas
Week-End In Havana
Window Shopping
Wintertime
Words and Music
Yes, Sir, Mr. Bones

Musician Biopics
see also Nashville Narratives
Amadeus►
Bird►
The Buddy Holly Story►
Coal Miner's Daughter►
The Doors
Elvis: The Movie
The Gene Krupa Story
The Glenn Miller Story►

Great Balls of Fire
John & Yoko: A Love Story
La Bamba►
Lady Sings the Blues
Sweet Dreams

Mystery & Suspense
see also Psycho-Thriller
Abduction of St. Anne
Above Suspicion►
Absolution
Accidental Meeting
Accidents
Accomplice
Accused
Ace Crawford, Private Eye
Ace Drummond
Ace of Hearts
Across the Bridge
Across the Pacific►
Acting on Impulse
Adrift
Adventures of a Private Eye
The Adventures of Sherlock Holmes
The Adventures of Sherlock Holmes: Hound of the Baskervilles
An Affair in Mind
The Affair of the Pink Pearl
African Rage
After Dark, My Sweet►
After Pilkington
After the Thin Man►
Agatha
Alias John Preston
All-American Murder
All the Kind Strangers
Alligator Eyes
Almost Partners
The Alphabet Murders
Alphaville►
The Amateur
Amazing Mr. Blunden
The Amazing Mr. X
The Ambassador
The American Friend►
American Gigolo
Amsterdamned
And Soon the Darkness
And Then There Were None►
The Anderson Tapes►
Android
The Andromeda Strain
Angel Heart
Animal Instincts
Another Thin Man
Any Man's Death
Apology
Appointment with Death
Appointment with Fear
Apprentice to Murder
Arabesque
Are You in the House Alone?
Arizona Stagecoach
The Arsenal Stadium Mystery
The Art of Crime
Assassin
The Assassination Run
Assault
At Close Range►
The Atomic City
Autopsy
The Avenging Hand
The Baby Doll Murders
Back from Eternity
Back to Hannibal: The Return of Tom Sawyer and Huckleberry Finn
Back to the Wall
Backfire
Backstab
Backtrack►
B.A.D. Cats
Bad Influence
Bad Ronald►
The Banker
The Barcelona Kill
Basic Instinct
The Bat Whispers
Battle Shock
Bedford Incident

Bedroom Eyes
Bedroom Eyes 2
The Bedroom Window
Before Morning
Behind Locked Doors
Bell from Hell
Bellamy
Benefit of the Doubt
The Berlin Affair
Berlin Express►
Berserk!
Besame
Best Seller►
Betrayal of the Dove
Betrayed
Beyond a Reasonable Doubt
Beyond the Bermuda Triangle
Beyond the Silhouette
Big Deadly Game
The Big Easy►
The Big Fix►
Big Heat►
The Big Hurt
Big News
The Big Sleep►
The Big Sleep
The Big Switch
Big Town After Dark
Bikini Island
The Bird with the Crystal Plumage
Birgitt Haas Must Be Killed
Bits and Pieces
Bitter Harvest
The Black Abbot
Black Bird
Black Box Affair
The Black Cat
Black Cobra
Black Glove
Black Gold
The Black Hand►
Black Hand
Black Ice
Black Limelight
Black Magic Woman
Black Panther
Black Rainbow►
The Black Raven
Black Sunday
Black Tide
Black Tower
A Black Veil for Lisa
Black Widow►
The Black Windmill
Blackmail►
Blackout
Blind Date
Blind Fear
Blind Justice
Blind Man's Bluff
Blind Side
Blind Vision
Blind Witness
Blindfold: Acts of Obsession
Blindside
Blink
Blonde Blackmailer
Blood Frenzy
Blood on the Sun
Blood Relations
Blood Relatives
Blood Simple►
Bloody Avenger
Blow Out►
Blown Away
Blue City
Blue Desert►
Blue Ice
Blue Steel
Blue Tornado
Blue Velvet►
Body Chemistry
Body Chemistry 3: Point of Seduction
Body Double►
Body Heat►
The Body in the Library
Body Language
Body of Influence
Body Parts
Body Shot

The Body Vanished
Borderline
B.O.R.N.
Born to Kill►
The Boston Strangler
Bounty Hunters
The Bourne Identity►
Bowery at Midnight/Dick Tracy vs. Cueball
The Boys from Brazil
Brass Target
Breakheart Pass
Breaking All the Rules
The Bride Wore Black►
Bright Smiler
Brighton Strangler
The Brighton Strangler/Before Dawn
Broken Trust
Brotherly Love
Bulldog Drummond
Bulldog Drummond at Bay
Bulldog Drummond Comes Back
Bulldog Drummond in Africa/Arrest Bulldog Drummond
Bulldog Drummond's Bride
Bulldog Drummond's Peril
Bulldog Drummond's Revenge
Bulldog Drummond's Revenge/Bulldog Drummond's Peril
Bulldog Drummond's Secret Police
Burns
Burndown
Buying Time
By Dawn's Early Light
By Hook or Crook
By the Blood of Others►
Cada Noche un Amor
Calendar Girl Murders
The Caller
Calling Paul Temple
Cambio de Cara
Candles at Nine
Caper of the Golden Bulls
Cardiac Arrest
Caribe
Carnival Lady
Caroline at Midnight
A Case for Murder
Case of the Baby Sitter
The Case of the Lucky Legs
The Case of the Missing Lady
Cast a Dark Shadow►
Cast a Deadly Spell►
Castle in the Desert
Cat and Mouse►
The Cat and the Canary►
The Cat and the Canary
Cat Chaser
The Cat o' Nine Tails
Catacombs
The Catamount Killing
Catch Me a Spy
Caught in the Act
Cause for Alarm
Center of the Web
The Centerfold Girls
Chain of Desire
Challenge of McKenna
Charade►
Charlie Chan and the Curse of the Dragon Queen
Charlie Chan at the Opera►
Charlie Chan at the Wax Museum
The Charlie Chan Collection
Charlie Chan in Paris
Charlie Chan in Rio
Charlie Chan in the Secret Service
Charlie Chan's Secret
Child in the Night
Child of Glass
Chill Factor
The China Lake Murders
China Moon
Chinatown►
The Chinese Cat

Choice of Arms
Christina
City in Panic
City Killer
City of Blood
City of Shadows
City on Fire
The Clay Pigeon
The Clergyman's Daughter
A Climate for Killing
Cloak and Dagger
Clouds Over Europe►
Clown Murders
Clue
The Clutching Hand
The Cobra Strikes
The Cobweb
Code Name Alpha
Code Name: Diamond Head
Codename: Foxfire
Codename: Icarus
Cohen and Tate
Cold Comfort
Cold Eyes of Fear
Cold Sweat
Color Me Dead
Color of Night
Columbo: Murder By the Book
Columbo: Prescription Murder►
Coma►
Coming Out Alive
Compromising Positions
Concrete Beat
The Confession
Confessions of a Hit Man
Confidentially Yours►
Consenting Adults
The Conversation►
Convicted
The Corpse Vanishes
Cosmo Jones, Crime Smasher
Counter Punch
The Cover Girl Murders
Crack-Up
The Crackler
The Cradle Will Fall
Crazy Streets
Criminal Court
Criminal Law
Criminals Within
Criss Cross►
Cross Country
Crow Hollow
The Crucifer of Blood
Cruise into Terror
Cruise Missile
Cruising
Cry Danger►
A Cry in the Night
The Cry of the Owl
Cry Panic
Cry Terror
Curiosity Kills
Curse of the Yellow Snake
Cutter's Way
Cycle Psycho
Dagger Eyes
The Dain Curse
Damned River
Dance Macabre
Dance with Death
Danger Man
Danger on the Air
Danger Zone
Dangerous Appointment
Dangerous Game
Dangerous Heart
Dangerous Love
Dangerous Mission
Dangerous Obsession
Dangerous Summer
Danielle Steel's Kaleidoscope
The Dark Angel►
Dark Corner►
Dark Forces
Dark Night of the Scarecrow
Dark of the Night
Dark Passage
Dark Side of Midnight
The Dark Wind
Darker than Amber

Mystery

The Darkside
Daughter of Horror
The Day of the Jackal▶
Day of the Maniac
Dead Again▶
Dead Certain
Dead Connection
Dead Eyes of London
Dead Heat on a Merry-Go-
  Round▶
Dead in the Water
Dead Lucky
Dead of Winter▶
Dead On
Dead on the Money
Dead Reckoning▶
Dead Reckoning
Dead Women in Lingerie
Dead Zone▶
Deadfall
Deadline
Deadline Assault
Deadline at Dawn
Deadly Business
Deadly Currents
Deadly Dancer
Deadly Embrace
Deadly Exposure
Deadly Fieldtrip
Deadly Force
The Deadly Game
Deadly Games
Deadly Illusion
Deadly Impact
Deadly Innocence
Deadly Intent
Deadly Matrimony
Deadly Passion
Deadly Possession
Deadly Rivals
The Deadly Secret
Deadly Spygames
Deadly Sting
Deadly Strangers
Deadly Surveillance
Dear Dead Delilah
Dear Detective
Death at Love House
Death by Prescription
Death Cruise
Death Dreams
Death from a Distance
Death Games
Death Goes to School
Death in the Shadows
The Death Kiss
Death Kiss
Death Magic
Death of a Scoundrel
Death on the Nile
Death Rage
Death Ray 2000
Death Sentence
Death Train
Death Valley
Death Warrant
Death Weekend
Deathmask
Deathtrap
Deceived
December Flower
Deception
Deceptions
The Deep
Deep Cover
Defense of the Realm▶
Defenseless
Deja Vu
Delusion
Deranged
Descending Angel▶
Desire and Hell at Sunset
  Motel
Desperate
Desperate Hours▶
Desperate Hours
Desperate Motives
Desperately Seeking Susan
The Detective▶
Devil Diamond
The Devil Thumbs a Ride▶

The Devil Thumbs a Ride/
  Having Wonderful Crime
The Devil's Cargo
Devil's Party
The Devil's Undead
Devlin
Diabolically Yours
Dial Help
Dial "M" for Murder▶
Diamond Run
The Diamond Trap
Diamonds
Diamond's Edge
Diamonds on Wheels
Dias de Ilusion
Dick Tracy
Dick Tracy, Detective
Dick Tracy, Detective/The
  Corpse Vanishes
Dick Tracy Double Feature #1
Dick Tracy Double Feature #2
Dick Tracy Meets Gruesome
Dick Tracy Returns
Dick Tracy: The Original
  Serial, Vol. 1▶
Dick Tracy: The Original
  Serial, Vol. 2▶
Dick Tracy: The Spider Strikes
Dick Tracy vs. Crime Inc.
Dick Tracy vs. Cueball
Dick Tracy's Dilemma
Die! Die! My Darling!
Die Screaming, Marianne
Die Sister, Die!
Die Watching
Dinner at the Ritz
Diplomatic Courier▶
Dirkham Detective Agency
Dirty Hands
Dirty Harry▶
Disappearance
The Disappearance of
  Christina
Disconnected
Discretion Assured
Dishonored Lady
Distortions
Disturbance
Diva▶
The Dive
D.O.A.▶
D.O.A.
Dr. Mabuse vs. Scotland Yard
Dr. Tarr's Torture Dungeon
Dog Day
Dog Day Afternoon▶
Dominique is Dead
The Domino Principle
Don't Bother to Knock
Don't Go in the House
Don't Look in the Attic
Don't Look Now▶
Don't Open the Door!
Doomed to Die
The Doomsday Flight
Door with the Seven Locks
Double Agents
Double Cross
Double Exposure
Double Face
Double Identity
Double Indemnity▶
Double Jeopardy
The Double McGuffin
The Double Negative
Double Obsession
Double Threat
Double Vision
The Draughtsman's
  Contract▶
Dream Lover
Dream No Evil
Dress Gray▶
Dressed for Death
Dressed to Kill
The Drifter
Driven to Kill
Driver's Seat
The Dropkick▶
The Drowning Pool
Drums of Jeopardy
Duel▶

The Dummy Talks
Dust to Dust
Dying Room Only
Dying to Remember
The Dying Truth
Dynasty of Fear
Early Frost
Echo Murders
Echoes
Edge of Darkness
The Eiger Sanction
Eight Witnesses
El Libro de Piedra
El Tesoro de Chucho el Roto
Embassy
Emergency▶
Emil and the Detective
Emissary
The Empty Beach
Endangered Species
Endless Night
Enigma
Enrapture
The Equalizer: Memories of
  Manon
Equus
Escapade in Florence
Escape
Escapist
Estate of Insanity
Evelyn Prentice
Even Angels Fall
Everybody Wins
Everybody's Dancin'
Evil Under the Sun
Ex-Mrs. Bradford▶
The Executioner
Experiment in Terror▶
Experiment Perilous▶
Exposed
Exposure
Express to Terror
Exterminator
Eye of the Needle
Eyes of Laura Mars
Eyewitness
Eyewitness to Murder
F/X▶
The Face at the Window
A Face in the Fog
Fade to Black
Fail-Safe▶
Fake Out
The Falcon and the
  Snowman▶
The Falcon in Hollywood
The Falcon in Mexico
Falcon Takes Over/Strange
  Bargain
Falcon's Adventure/Armored
  Car Robbery
The Falcon's Brother
False Identity
Family Plot
The Fan
The Fantasist
Far from Home
Farewell, My Lovely▶
Fatal Bond
Fatal Charm
Fatal Exposure
Fatal Games
The Fatal Hour
The Fatal Image
Fatal Instinct
FBI Girl
Fear
Fear City
Fear in the Night▶
Fearless
Fearmaker
The Female Jungle
Femme Fatale
Fer-De-Lance
Fever
Fiction Makers
The Fifth Floor
52 Pick-Up
The Fighting Westerner
Fin de Fiesta
Final Analysis
Final Assignment

Final Cut
Final Embrace
Final Judgement
Final Notice
The Final Option
Finessing the King
Fingerprints Don't Lie
The Finishing Touch
The Firm▶
Flashpoint
Flatliners
Fleshtone
Flowers in the Attic
Flying from the Hawk
Fog Island
Follow Me Quietly▶
The Fool Killer
Forbidden Sun
Foreign Correspondent▶
Forger of London
Forget Mozart
The Forgotten One
The Formula
Formula for a Murder
Fortress
The Fourth Protocol▶
Fourth Story▶
The Franchise Affair
Frantic▶
The French Detective▶
French Intrigue
French Silk
Frenzy
Frenzy▶
Fresh Kill
Fright
From Hollywood to Deadwood
From the Dead of Night▶
Frozen Alive
Fu Manchu
Full Circle
Full Exposure: The Sex Tape
  Scandals
Full Fathom Five
Funeral in Berlin▶
The Game
A Game of Crime
Game of Seduction
Gangbusters
Gaslight▶
Georgia
Get That Man
Getting Even
The Ghost Camera
Ghost Ship
The Ghost Walks
Girl Hunters
The Girl in a Swing
The Girl in Lover's Lane
A Girl to Kill for
Girls Night Out
Glass
The Glass Key▶
Glass Tomb
Golden Lady
Golden Rendezvous
Gone to Ground
Goodnight God Bless
Gorky Park▶
Gotham▶
The Great Riviera Bank
  Robbery
Green Archer
Green Eyes
Green for Danger
Green Ice
The Green Man▶
Grievous Bodily Harm
Ground Zero
Guest in the House
Guilty as Sin
Gunpowder
Half a Soldier
Hammett
Hands of a Stranger
Hanky Panky
Happily Ever After
Hard-Boiled Mahoney
Harper▶
The Harvest
Hat Box Mystery
The Haunted Castle▶

Haunted: The Ferryman
The Haunting of Barney
  Palmer
Haunting of Harrington House
The Haunting Passion
The Hawk
He Lives: The Search for the
  Evil One
Heads
Hear No Evil
Heartaches
The Heat of the Day
Heat Wave
Heatwave▶
The Heist
Hell Harbor
Hell's Headquarters
Help!▶
Hi-Jacked
Hidden Agenda
Hidden City
Hidden Fears
Hidden Obsession
The Hidden Room▶
Hide in Plain Sight▶
High & Low▶
High Frequency
High Stakes
Highway 13
The Hillside Strangler
The Hit List
Hitchcock Classics Collection:
  Trailers on Tape
Hitchcock Collection
The Hitman
The Holcroft Covenant
Hollywood Stadium Mystery
Home for the Holidays
Homicide▶
The Hooded Terror
The Horse Without a Head
Horseplayer
Hostage
Hostages
Hot Child in the City
Hotel Colonial
Hotel Reserve▶
Hotline
The Hound of the
  Baskervilles▶
The Hound of the Baskervilles
Hour of Decision
A House In The Hills
House of Fear
The House of Lurking Death
House of Mystery
The House of Secrets
House of Shadows
The House of the Arrow▶
House of the Damned
House of the Rising Sun
The House on Carroll Street
House on Marsh Road
The Housekeeper
Human Gorilla
The Human Monster
Hunt the Man Down
Hunt the Man Down/
  Smashing the Rackets
Hunter
The Hunting
Hustle
Hysteria
I Am the Cheese
I Bury the Living▶
I Confess
I Killed That Man
I, Madman
I See a Dark Stranger▶
I Stand Condemned
I, the Jury
I Wake Up Screaming▶
I'd Give My Life
If It's a Man, Hang Up
If Looks Could Kill
I'll Get You
I'll Name the Murderer
Illegal
Illicit Behavior
Illusions
I'm the Girl He Wants to Kill

I'm the One You're Looking For
Image of Death
Impact▶
Impulse
In a Lonely Place▶
In a Moment of Passion
In a Stranger's Hand
In an Old Manor House
In the Cold of the Night
In the Heat of the Night▶
In the Line of Fire▶
In the Secret State
In the Spirit
Indecency
Indecent Behavior
The Indian Scarf
Infamous Crimes
Inheritance▶
The Inheritor
The Inner Circle
Inner Sanctum
The Innocent
Innocent Victim
The Inquiry
Insanity
The Inside Man
Inspiration of Mr. Budd
The Instructor
Interface
Internal Affairs
International Crime
Internecine Project
Interrupted Journey
Intimate Stranger
Into the Fire
Intrigue
Intruder
Invasion of Privacy
Investigation
Invincible Armor
The Invisible Avenger
The Invisible Killer
Invitation to Hell
The Ipcress File▶
Irish Luck
Island
Island Monster
Island of Adventure
Istanbul
It Could Happen to You
It Happened at Nightmare Inn
Jack's Back▶
The Jade Mask
The Jagged Edge
Jailbird's Vacation
Jane Doe
Jaws of Death
Jennifer 8
Jenny Lamour
Jezebel's Kiss
Jigsaw
The Jigsaw Man
Jigsaw Murders
Johnny Angel▶
Johnny Nobody
Journey into Fear▶
Journey into Fear
Joy House
Juggernaut▶
Julia and Julia
Jungle Bride
The Junkman
Just Another Pretty Face
Kafka
Kelly's Heroes
Kemek
The Kennel Murder Case
Kentucky Jubilee
The KGB: The Secret War
Kid
Kidnapped
The Kidnapping of the
   President
Kill Cruise
Killer Fish
Killer Image
A Killer in Every Corner
Killer Likes Candy
Killer with Two Faces
The Killers
A Killing Affair

Killing Cars
The Killing Game
Killing Hour
The Killing Kind
The Killing Mind
Killing Obsession
Killing Stone
The Killing Time
Killjoy
Killpoint
The King Murder Case
A Kiss Before Dying
Kiss Daddy Goodnight
Kiss Me a Killer
Kiss Me, Kill Me
Klute▶
L.A. Goddess
Lady Beware
The Lady Confesses
The Lady from Shanghai▶
Lady in a Cage▶
Lady in Cement
Lady in the Death House
The Lady in White▶
Lady of Burlesque
Lady Scarface
The Lady Vanishes▶
The Lady Vanishes
Ladykiller
Ladykillers
The Lady's Maid's Bell
Laguna Heat
Last Dance
The Last Embrace▶
The Last of Philip Banter
The Last of Sheila
Last Reunion
Last Rites
Last Song
The Late Show▶
Laughing Policeman
Laura▶
Le Corbeau▶
Le Magnifique
Le Secret▶
Left for Dead
Legacy of Lies
The Liars
Liar's Edge
Liebestraum
Lies
Lies Before Kisses
Lifespan
The Lift
The Lightning Incident
Lights! Camera! Murder!
Lily was Here
The Limping Man
Linda
Lipstick Camera
Lisa
Lisbon
The List of Adrian
   Messenger▶
The Little Drummer Girl▶
The Little Girl Who Lives
   Down the Lane
Little Nikita
Living to Die
The Lodger▶
Lonely Hearts
Long Time Gone
Loose Cannons
The Lost Jungle
The Lost Tribe
Love & Murder
Love and Hate: A Marriage
   Made in Hell
Love at Large▶
Love Camp
Love, Cheat & Steal
Love from a Stranger
Love Kills
Love on the Run
Lower Level
Lure of the Islands
Lying Lips
Mackintosh Man
The Mad Executioners
Madame Sin
Madeleine
Madigan▶

Malibu Express
Malice
The Maltese Falcon▶
A Man About the House
Man Bait
Man from Headquarters
The Man in the Mist
The Man Inside
Man on Fire
Man on the Eiffel Tower▶
Man on the Run
Man Outside
The Man Who Haunted
   Himself
The Man Who Knew Too
   Much▶
The Man Who Knew Too
   Much
The Man Who Would Not Die
The Manchurian Candidate▶
The Mandarin Mystery
Manfish
The Manhattan Project
Manhunter▶
Mania
Maniac
Marathon Man▶
Margin for Murder
Marie Galante▶
Mark of Cain
Mark of the Beast
Marked for Murder
Marnie▶
Maroc 7
Mascara
Mask of the Dragon
Masks of Death
Masquerade▶
Master Touch
A Matter of WHO
Maya
The Maze▶
Mazes and Monsters
The McGuffin
Medusa
Meeting at Midnight
Melodie en Sous-Sol
Memories of Murder
Men at Work
Messenger of Death
Miami Blues
Midnight
Midnight at the Wax Museum
Midnight Faces
Midnight Girl
Midnight Lace
Midnight Limited
Midnight Warning
Midnight Witness
Mike's Murder
Million Dollar Haul
Million Dollar Mystery
Mind, Body & Soul
Mind Twister
Mindfield
Mirage▶
The Mirror Crack'd
Mirror Images
Mirror Images 2
Missing Pieces
Mission: Monte Carlo
Mrs. Amworth
Mistaken Identity
Mr. Frost
Mr. Moto's Last Warning▶
Mr. Moto's Last Warning/
   Meeting at Midnight
Mr. Reeder in Room 13
Mr. Scarface
Mr. Wong, Detective
Mr. Wong in Chinatown
Money Madness
Monique
Monsieur Hire▶
The Monster Walks
Moon in Scorpio
Moonlighting
The Morning After
Mortal Passions
The Most Dangerous Game▶
Mother's Boys
Motor Patrol

Motorcycle Squad
Murder▶
Murder Ahoy
Murder at 45 R.P.M.
Murder at Midnight
Murder at the Baskervilles
Murder at the Gallop▶
Murder by Decree▶
Murder by Natural Causes▶
Murder by Night
Murder by Numbers
Murder by Phone
Murder by Television
Murder by the Book
Murder in Space
Murder in the Doll House
Murder in the Footlights
A Murder is Announced
Murder Most Foul▶
Murder, My Sweet▶
Murder of a Moderate Man
Murder on Approval
Murder on the Campus
Murder on the High Seas
Murder on the Midnight
   Express
Murder on the Orient
   Express▶
Murder Once Removed
Murder 101
Murder Over New York
Murder Rap
Murder She Said
Murder So Sweet
Murder Story
Murder: Ultimate Grounds for
   Divorce
Murderer in the Hotel
Murderers' Row
Murderlust
Murderous Vision
Murders at Lynch Cross
Murders in the Rue Morgue
The Murders in the Rue
   Morgue▶
My Man Adam
My Sister, My Love
My Sweet Victim
Mysterious Doctor Satan
The Mysterious Magician
Mysterious Mr. Wong
Mystery at Castle House
Mystery at Fire Island
Mystery in Swing
Mystery Liner
The Mystery Man
Mystery Mansion
Mystery of Mr. Wong
The Mystery of the Mary
   Celeste
Mystery of the Riverboat
Mystery Plane
Mystic Circle Murder
The Naked Edge
The Naked Face
Naked Obsession
The Name of the Rose
Nancy Drew, Reporter
The Narrow Margin▶
Narrow Margin
Nature's Playmates
The Neighbor
Neutron vs. the Maniac
Never Say Die
New Year's Evil
New York Ripper
Newman's Law
The Next Victim
Next Victim
Niagara
Night and the City▶
Night Angel
Night Birds
Night Cries
Night Eyes
Night Eyes 2
Night Eyes 3
A Night for Crime
The Night Has Eyes
Night Moves▶
Night of Terror
Night of the Assassin

Night of the Cyclone
The Night of the Hunter▶
Night of the Juggler
Night Rhythms
Night School
Night Shadow
Night Stalker
Night Terror
A Night to Remember▶
Night Train to Munich▶
The Night Visitor
Night Watch
The Nightcomers
Nighthawks
Nightkill
The Nightman
Nightmare in Badham County
Nightwing
No Comebacks
No Mercy
No Place to Hide
No Problem
No Secrets
No Way Out▶
No Way to Treat a Lady▶
Nocturne
Non-Stop New York
Norman Conquest
North by Northwest▶
Nothing Underneath
Notorious▶
Nowhere to Hide
Nuclear Conspiracy
No. 17▶
The Oblong Box
The Obsessed
Obsession
Obsession: A Taste for Fear
Obsessive Love
The Occult Experience
Octagon
October Man▶
Octopussy
The Odessa File
On Dangerous Ground▶
On the Edge
One Frightened Night
One of My Wives Is Missing
One Shoe Makes It Murder
Open House
Open Secret
Operation Amsterdam
Ordeal by Innocence
Orion's Belt
The Osterman Weekend
Out of Bounds
Out of Order
Out of Sight, Out of Her Mind
Out of the Darkness▶
Out of the Past▶
Out on Bail
The Outside Man
The Oval Portrait
Over Indulgence
Overexposed
Paid to Kill
Paint It Black
The Pamela Principle
Panic in the Streets▶
Panic on the 5:22
Panique▶
The Panther's Claw
Paperhouse▶
Parallax View▶
Paranoia
Paris Belongs to Us
Paris Express
Parker
Party Girls for Sale
Party Line
Passion Flower
Passion in Paradise
Past Midnight
The Payoff
The Pearl of Death
The Pelican Brief
Pendulum
Penthouse▶
The Perfect Bride
Perfect Crime
Perfect Family
A Perfect Spy

Perfect Strangers
Perfect Victims
Peril
Perry Mason Returns▶
Perry Mason: The Case of the Lost Love
Personals
Peter Gunn
The Phantom Broadcast
The Phantom Creeps
Phantom Express
Phantom Fiend
Phantom Killer
The Phantom Light
Phantom of Chinatown
The Phantom of 42nd Street
The Phantom of Soho
Phobia
Phoenix Team
The Phone Call
Photographer
Physical Evidence
Picnic at Hanging Rock▶
Picture Mommy Dead
Pier 23
Plain Clothes
Play Misty for Me▶
Play Nice
Plumber
A Pocketful of Rye
Point Blank
Poor Girl, A Ghost Story
Posed For Murder
Positive I.D.
Postmark for Danger/ Quicksand
Power Play
The Practice of Love
Praying Mantis
President's Mistress
The President's Mystery
The Presidio
Presumed Innocent▶
Prey of the Chameleon
Prime Suspect
Prime Suspect▶
Prime Suspect 2▶
Prison Shadows
The Private Life of Sherlock Holmes▶
The Prize▶
Probe
Project: Eliminator
Project X
Promise to Murder
Prowler
Psychic
Psycho▶
Psycho 2
Psycho 3
Psychomania
Pulp
Pursuit▶
Pursuit to Algiers
Puzzle
Quake
Quicker Than the Eye
Quicksand: No Escape
The Quiller Memorandum▶
Rage
Railroaded
The Rain Killer
Raw Nerve
Rear Window▶
Rebecca▶
Reckless Moment▶
The Red House▶
Red King, White Knight
The Red Raven Kiss-Off
Red Rock West▶
Red Wind
Redneck
Reflections of Murder
Regina
Rehearsal for Murder
Reilly: Ace of Spies▶
The Reincarnation of Peter Proud
Relentless 3
Remember Me
Repulsion▶
Return

The Return of Boston Blackie
Return of Chandu
The Return of Dr. Mabuse
Return of Frank Cannon
Return to Waterloo
Revenge
Revenge of the Stepford Wives
Rich and Strange
Rider on the Rain▶
Riders to the Sea
Rififi▶
Ring of Death
Rising Sun▶
Road Games
Road to Salina
Roaring City
Rogue's Gallery
Rogue's Tavern
Rogue's Yarn
Romeo Is Bleeding
Room 43
Roots of Evil
Rope▶
The Rosary Murders
R.S.V.P.
Rude Awakening
Run If You Can
Runaways
Russian Roulette
Sabotage▶
Saboteur▶
The Saint
Saint in London
The Saint in New York
The Saint Strikes Back
The Saint Strikes Back: Criminal Court
The Saint Takes Over
The Saint's Double Trouble
The Saint's Vacation/The Narrow Margin
The Salamander
The Salzburg Connection
Sanctuary of Fear
Sanders of the River▶
Sapphire▶
Savages
Save Me
Scalp Merchant
Scam
Scandal Man
Scandalous
Scared to Death/Dick Tracy's Dilemma
Scarlet Claw▶
The Scarlet Clue
Scarlet Street▶
Scavengers
Scene of the Crime
Scene of the Crime▶
Scenes from a Murder
Schnelles Geld
Scissors
Scorned
Scorpio
The Scorpio Factor
Scotland Yard Inspector
Scream
Scream Bloody Murder
Scream for Help
Screamer
Sea of Love▶
Seance on a Wet Afternoon▶
Season of Fear
Second Woman
The Secret Adversary
Secret Agent 00
Secret of the Black Trunk
The Secret Passion of Robert Clayton
Seven Doors to Death
Seven Hours to Judgment
The Seven Percent Solution▶
The Seventh Sign
Sexo Y Crimen
Sexpot
Sexton Blake and the Hooded Terror
Sexual Intent
Sexual Malice
Sexual Response

The Shadow
Shadow Dancing▶
The Shadow Man
Shadow of a Doubt▶
Shadow of the Thin Man▶
Shadow Play
The Shadow Strikes
Shadows on the Stairs
Shaft▶
Shallow Grave
The Shanghai Cobra
Shattered
Shattered Silence
She Waits
Sherlock Holmes and the Deadly Necklace
Sherlock Holmes and the Incident at Victoria Falls
Sherlock Holmes and the Secret Weapon▶
Sherlock Holmes Faces Death▶
Sherlock Holmes in Washington
Sherlock Holmes: The Master Blackmailer
Sherlock Holmes: The Sign of Four
Sherlock Holmes: The Silver Blaze
Sherlock Holmes: The Voice of Terror
She's Dressed to Kill
Shock!
Shoot to Kill
A Shot in the Dark
The Shout▶
A Show of Force
Show Them No Mercy▶
Shriek in the Night
Side Show
Sidney Sheldon's Bloodline
The Sign of Four
The Silencer
Silent Assassins
Silent Killers
The Silent Mr. Sherlock Holmes
Silent Motive
The Silent Partner▶
The Silent Passenger
Silhouette
Sins of Desire
Sins of the Night
The Sister-in-Law
Sister, Sister
Sisters of Death
Sketch Artist
Sketches of a Strangler
Sky Liner
Slamdance
The Slasher
Slaughter of the Innocents
Slayground
Sleeping Car to Trieste
Sleepwalk
Sleuth▶
Slightly Honorable
Slightly Scarlet
Slipping into Darkness
Sliver
Slow Burn
Small Kill
Smart-Aleck Kill
Smile, Jenny, You're Dead
Smooth Talker
Snatched
Sneakers
Snow Kill
Snowblind
Sois Belle et Tais-Toi
Soldier of the Night
Somebody Has to Shoot the Picture▶
Someone Behind the Door
Someone to Watch Over Me▶
Song of the Thin Man
Sound of Murder
Spaceways
The Spaniard's Curse
Spare Parts
Special Police

The Specialist
The Speckled Band▶
Spectre of the Rose
Spellbound▶
The Sphinx
Sphinx
Spider Woman▶
Spiders▶
The Spider's Stratagem▶
Sprague
Sputnik
Spy Story
The Spy Who Came in from the Cold▶
S*P*Y*S
The Squeaker
The Squeeze
Stacey
Stage Fright▶
Stamp of a Killer
Star of Midnight
Star Time
State Department File 649
State of Things▶
Station
Stay Tuned for Murder
The Stepmother
Stick
Still Life
Still of the Night
A Stolen Face
Stolen Painting
Stone Cold Dead
Stormy Monday
The Strange Affair of Uncle Harry
The Strange Countess
Strange Shadows in an Empty Room
Strange Tales/Ray Bradbury Theatre
The Stranger▶
A Stranger Among Us
Stranger in Town
A Stranger is Watching
Stranger on the Third Floor▶
The Stranger Within
Strangers
Strangers on a Train▶
The Strangler
Strangler of Blackmoor Castle
Strangler of the Swamp
Strangler of the Tower
Stray Dog▶
Strike Force
Stripped to Kill
Stripped to Kill II: Live Girls
A Study in Scarlet
A Study in Terror▶
The Substitute
Subterfuge
Sucker Money
Sudden Terror
Suddenly▶
Summer Heat
Summer's Children
Sunstroke
Surrogate
Suspect
Suspicion▶
Suspicion
Svengali
Swamp Thing
Swiss Conspiracy
Tag: The Assassination Game
Tagget
Tainted Blood
Take Two
Taking the Heat
Tale of a Vampire
Tales from the Darkside
Tales of the Unexpected
The Tall Blond Man with One Black Shoe▶
Tangiers
Tangled Destinies
Target
The Tattered Web
The Taxi Mystery
The Teacher
Telefon
Ten Days Wonder

Ten Little Indians
10 Rillington Place▶
Tequila Sunrise
Tereza
Terminal Choice
Terminal Entry
The Terror
Terror at London Bridge
Terror by Night
Terror by Night/Meeting at Midnight
Terror Stalks the Class Reunion
Terror Street
Terrorists
There Goes Kelly
They Call Me Mr. Tibbs!
They Meet Again
They Only Kill Their Masters
They Watch
They Won't Believe Me▶
They're Playing with Fire
Thief
Thief▶
Thief of Hearts
The Thin Man▶
The Thin Man Goes Home
Third Degree Burn
The Third Key
The Third Man▶
Third Solution
13th Guest
The Thirteenth Man
The Thirty-Nine Steps
The 39 Steps▶
This is a Hijack
This Lightning Always Strikes Twice
This Man Must Die▶
This Sweet Sickness
Threat
Three by Hitchcock
Three Days of the Condor▶
Thrilled to Death
Thrillkill
Through Naked Eyes
Thundersquad
Tiara Tahiti
Ticket of Leave Man
Tiger Bay▶
Tightrope▶
Till Death Do Us Part
Till There was You
Time for Murder
Time for Revenge
Time is Running Out
A Time to Die
Times to Come▶
To Catch a King
To Catch a Thief▶
To Kill a Clown
To Kill a Stranger
The Todd Killings
Tomorrow at Seven
Tony Rome
Too Scared to Scream
Topaz▶
Torment
Torn Curtain
Total Exposure
Touch Me Not
Touch of Evil▶
Tough Assignment
Tough Guys Don't Dance
Tourist Trap
Town that Dreaded Sundown
Traces of Red
Track 29
Trade Secrets
The Train Killer
The Trap
Trapped
Trauma
Treacherous Crossing
Trespasses
Trial and Error
Trifles
The Triumph of Sherlock Holmes
Tropical Heat
The Trouble with Harry▶
True Believer

Twenty Dollar Star
Twin Peaks
Twisted Obsession
Two by Forsyth
Two Fathers' Justice
The Two Jakes
Two Minute Warning
Ultimate Desires
The Ultimate Imposter
The Ultimate Thrill
The Unbreakable Alibi
Under Capricorn
Under Investigation
Under Suspicion
Uneasy Terms
Unforgotten Crime
Unholy Four
Unholy Wife
Union City
Union Station
Unsane
Unsuitable Job for a Woman
Up in the Air
Urge to Kill
Utz
The Vagrant
Vamping
The Vanishing▶
The Vanishing
Vanishing Act
Vatican Conspiracy
Vegas
Velvet Touch▶
Vertigo▶
The Very Edge
Vicious
The Vicious Circle
Victim of Beauty
Victim of Love
Video Murders
Violette▶
The Vision
Visions
Visiting Hours
Voulez-Vous Danser Avec
    Moi?
Vultures
W
Waikiki
Wanted: Babysitter
Warm Nights on a Slow-
    Moving Train
Warning Sign
Watched
The Way Out
Wayne Murder Case▶
Weep No More My Lady
Whatever Happened to Aunt
    Alice?▶
When a Stranger Calls
When a Stranger Calls Back
When Angels Fly
When the Bough Breaks
Where Are the Children?
Where Sleeping Dogs Lie
A Whisper to a Scream
Whispering City▶
Whispering Shadow
Whispers in the Dark
The Whistle Blower▶
White Fire
White Hot: The Mysterious
    Murder of Thelma Todd
White Mischief▶
White of the Eye▶
White Sands
Who Is the Black Dahlia?▶
Who Killed Baby Azaria?
Who Killed Mary What's 'Er
    Name?
Whodunit
Widow Couderc▶
Widow's Nest
Wild Cactus
Wild West
Wildcard
The Wind
The Window▶
Witchfire
Without Warning
Witness for the Prosecution▶
Woman Condemned

Woman Hunt
The Woman Hunter
Woman in Black
The Woman in Green
Woman of Desire
The Woman Who Came Back
A Woman's Face▶
Wonderland▶
The Word
Writer's Block
The Wrong Man▶
The Wrong Man
Y Donde Esta el Muerto?
    (And... Where Is the Dead)
Yellowstone
Young and Innocent▶
The Young Detectives on
    Wheels
Young Sherlock Holmes
Z▶
Zentropa
Zero Boys
Zertigo Diamond Caper
The Zodiac Killer

Nashville Narratives

see also *American South;*
Musician Biopics;
Southern Belles

Baja Oklahoma
Cassie
The City
Coal Miner's Daughter▶
Falling from Grace
Hard Part Begins
Honeysuckle Rose
Honkytonk Man
Honkytonk Nights
Lady Grey
Nashville▶
Nashville Girl
The Night the Lights Went Out
    in Georgia
Payday
Pure Country
The Real Patsy Cline
Rhinestone
Rikky and Pete
Road to Nashville
A Smoky Mountain Christmas
Songwriter
Sweet Dreams
Tender Mercies▶
The Thing Called Love

Native America

The Abduction of Allison Tate
Across the Wide Missouri
Angry Joe Bass
Apache Blood
Apache Chief
Apache Woman
Bad Lands
The Bears & I
Billy Jack
Black Robe▶
Born Losers
Braveheart
Broken Arrow
The Broken Chain
Buffalo Bill Rides Again
Bugles in the Afternoon
Captain Apache
The Captive: The Longest
    Drive 2
Cavalier of the West
Cavalry Charge
Chato's Land
Cheyenne Autumn
Chuka
Circle of Death
Clearcut
Comancheros▶
Conquest of Cochise
Cotter
Crazy Horse and Custer: "The
    Untold Story"
Crypt of Dark Secrets
Custer's Last Fight
Dakota Incident
Dan Candy's Law

Dances with Wolves▶
The Dark Wind
Demon Warrior
Diplomaniacs
Escape from Fort Bravo
Eyes of Fire
Fish Hawk
Flaming Star▶
Fleshburn
The Gatling Gun
Geronimo
Geronimo▶
Geronimo: An American
    Legend
Ghost Dance
The Glory Trail
Grizzly Mountain
I Heard the Owl Call My Name
I Will Fight No More Forever▶
Incident at Oglala: The
    Leonard Peltier Story▶
The Indian Fighter▶
Island of the Blue Dolphins
Jim Thorpe: All American
Joe Panther▶
Johnny Firecloud
Johnny Tiger
Journey Through Rosebud
Journey to Spirit Island
The Last of His Tribe
The Last of the Mohicans▶
The Last of the Mohicans
The Last of the Mohicans▶
The Last of the Redmen
Legend of Walks Far Woman
The Legend of Wolf Mountain
The Light in the Forest
Little Big Man▶
Lost Legacy: A Girl Called
    Hatter Fox
A Man Called Horse▶
The Manitou
Map of the Human Heart
Mission to Glory
A Mormon Maid
Naked in the Sun
Natas...The Reflection
On Top of the Whale
Poltergeist 2: The Other Side
Powwow Highway▶
The Red Fury
The Red Half-Breed
Renegades
Requiem for a Heavyweight▶
Roanoak
Running Brave
Savage Sam
The Savage Seven
Savage Wilderness
The Secret of Navajo Cave
Shadow of the Wolf
Shadowhunter
Silent Tongue
The Slayer/The Scalps
Smith!
Spirit Rider▶
Terror in the Jungle
Texas John Slaughter:
    Geronimo's Revenge
Three Warriors
Thunder Warrior
Thunder Warrior 2
Thunderheart▶
Tonka
Track of the Moonbeast
Uninvited
The Villain
Wagon Wheels
War Party
Where the Spirit Lives
White Fang 2: The Myth of the
    White Wolf
Windwalker▶

Nazis & Other
Paramilitary Slugs

see also *Germany;*
Holocaust; Judaism;
World War II

All Through the Night▶
Angel of Death

Angel with the Trumpet
Angry Harvest▶
Any Man's Death
Ark of the Sun God
The Assisi Underground
Background to Danger▶
Bedknobs and Broomsticks
The Berlin Affair
Berlin Express▶
Betrayed▶
The Black Klansman
The Boxer and Death▶
The Boys from Brazil
Brady's Escape
Cabaret▶
Cabo Blanco
Casablanca▶
Casablanca Express
Charlie Grant's War
Clipped Wings
Closet Land
Cold Days
Commandos Strike at Dawn
The Conformist▶
Cottage to Let
Counterblast
The Counterfeit Traitor▶
The Cut Throats
Dam Busters▶
Dawn Express
A Day in October
Dead Bang
Death is Called Engelchen▶
The Death of Adolf Hitler
Descending Angel▶
Desert Commandos
The Desert Fox▶
Despair▶
The Devil's Brigade
The Diary of Anne Frank▶
The Dirty Dozen▶
The Dirty Dozen: The Deadly
    Mission
The Dirty Dozen: The Fatal
    Mission
The Dirty Dozen: The Next
    Mission
Dirty Heroes
Edge of Darkness▶
Elves
Enemy of Women
Enigma Secret
Equalizer 2000
Escape from Sobibor▶
Europa, Europa▶
The Execution
Eye of the Needle
The Fallen Sparrow▶
Father
Firewalker
Five Fingers▶
Flesh Feast
Forbidden
Force 10 from Navarone
Foreign Correspondent▶
The Forty-Ninth Parallel▶
Four Bags Full
The Four Horsemen of the
    Apocalypse
A Friendship in Vienna
Goldengirl
Good Evening, Mr.
    Wallenberg
The Great Dictator▶
The Great Escape▶
Hanna's War
Hanussen▶
He Lives: The Search for the
    Evil One
Hell Commandos
Hell Hunters
Hell River
Hell Squad
Heroes in Hell
The Hiding Place
Hitler
Hitler: Dead or Alive
Hitler's Children▶
Hitler's Daughter
Holocaust▶
Hornet's Nest
Hotel Reserve▶

The House on Carroll Street
The House on Garibaldi Street
Ilsa, Harem Keeper of the Oil
    Sheiks
Ilsa, She-Wolf of the SS
In a Glass Cage
The Incredible Mr. Limpet
Indiana Jones and the Last
    Crusade▶
Indiana Jones and the Temple
    of Doom▶
Inside Out
Inside the Third Reich
Into the Homeland
Invisible Agent
Jenny's War
Judgment at Nuremberg▶
Julia▶
Jungle Siren
Kanal▶
Kapo▶
The Keep
The Key to Rebecca
The Klansman
Kojak: The Belarus File
Korczak▶
La Passante▶
Lassiter
The Last Five Days
The Last Metro▶
The Last Train
Law of the Jungle
Les Violons du Bal
Lifeboat▶
The Long Island Four
The Longest Day▶
The Lucifer Complex
Madame Rosa▶
A Man Escaped▶
Marathon Man▶
Massacre in Rome
Master Key
Master Race
The Mediterranean in Flames
Mein Kampf
Mephisto▶
Miracle at Moreaux
Mission Corbari
Mr. Klein▶
The Mortal Storm▶
Music Box
The Nasty Girl▶
Night Ambush
A Night in Casablanca▶
Night of the Fox
Night of the Generals▶
The Night Porter
Night Train to Munich▶
No Dead Heroes
The North Star▶
Northern Pursuit
Notorious▶
Oasis of the Zombies
The Odessa File
Old Gun▶
Once Upon a Honeymoon
One of Our Aircraft Is
    Missing▶
Only Way
Open City▶
Operation Amsterdam
Operation Crossbow▶
Passage to Marseilles▶
The Pedestrian
Pimpernel Smith
A Prayer for Katarina
    Horovitzova▶
Prayer of the Rollerboys
Pressure Point▶
Puppet Master 3: Toulon's
    Revenge
The Quiller Memorandum▶
Raid on Rommel
Raiders of the Lost Ark▶
Reunion in France
The Revolt of Job▶
Rio Rita
River of Death
River of Diamonds
The Rocketeer▶
The Rose Garden
The Salzburg Connection

Savage Attraction
The Scarlet & the Black
Schindler's List▶
Scream and Scream Again
The Secret Code
The Secret War of Harry Frigg
Seven Miles from Alcatraz/
    Flight from Glory
The Seventh Cross▶
Severed Ties
She Demons
Shining Through
Shock Waves
Silent Scream
633 Squadron
Skinheads: The Second
    Coming of Hate
Snow Treasure
So Ends Our Night▶
Soldier of Orange▶
A Soldier's Tale
Son of Lassie
The Sorrow and the Pity▶
The Sound of Music▶
S.S. Experiment Camp 2
S.S. Love Camp No. 27
Stalag 17▶
The Stranger▶
Strangers in Paradise
Sundown
Surf Nazis Must Die
Sweet Light in a Dark Room▶
Swing Kids
A Taxing Woman's Return▶
That Summer of White Roses
They Saved Hitler's Brain
13 Rue Madeleine▶
'38: Vienna Before the Fall
This Land is Mine▶
Tiger Fangs
Tigershark
To Be or Not to Be▶
To Be or Not to Be
To Catch a King
Top Secret!▶
The Tormentors
Transport from Paradise
Triumph of the Spirit▶
Triumph of the Will
True Colors
U-Boat Prisoner
Uranus▶
War & Love
War & Remembrance, Part 1
War & Remembrance, Part 2
War & Remembrance: The
    Final Chapter, Part 8
War & Remembrance: The
    Final Chapter, Part 9
Watch on the Rhine▶
Waterfront
Where Eagles Dare▶
Where Trails End
Wild Geese 2
The Winds of War
Wings Over the Pacific
Wizards
Wooden Horse▶
Yank in Libya
The Yesterday Machine
Zentropa
Zombie Lake
Zone Troopers

Negative Utopia

    see also *Post Apocalypse;*
    Technology-Rampant
Alphaville▶
Animal Farm▶
Brazil▶
El Norte▶
Futureworld
Metropolis▶
Moonraker
The Mosquito Coast
984: Prisoner of the Future
1984▶
The Prisoner: Arrival
Rollerball
Soylent Green
10th Victim▶
THX 1138▶

Whodunit
Zardoz

New Black Cinema

    see also *African America;*
    Blaxploitation
Boyz N the Hood▶
Crooklyn▶
Do the Right Thing▶
The Five Heartbeats▶
Hangin' with the Homeboys▶
Hollywood Shuffle
I'm Gonna Git You Sucka▶
Joe's Bed-Stuy Barbershop:
    We Cut Heads
Jungle Fever▶
Just Another Girl on the I.R.T.
Livin' Large
Menace II Society▶
The Meteor Man
Mo' Better Blues
Poetic Justice
Posse▶
A Rage in Harlem▶
School Daze▶
She's Gotta Have It▶
Straight Out of Brooklyn
Sweet Sweetback's
    Baadasssss Song▶
To Sleep with Anger▶

New Zealand

    see *Down Under*

Newspapers

    see *Front Page*

Nifty '50s

Absolute Beginners
The Affairs of Dobie Gillis
As Summers Die
Back to the Future▶
Back to the Future, Part 2
Badlands▶
Book of Love
The Buddy Holly Story▶
Bye, Bye, Birdie▶
Celia: Child Of Terror
Child Bride of Short Creek
Crazy Mama
Cry-Baby▶
Dance with a Stranger▶
Dead Poets Society▶
Desire and Hell at Sunset
    Motel
Dirty Dancing▶
Elvis: The Movie
Father of the Bride▶
Fellow Traveler▶
For the Boys
The Front▶
Girls' Town
Grease▶
Grease 2
Ground Zero▶
Guilty by Suspicion
The Heart of Dixie
Hometown U.S.A.
Housekeeping▶
The Hudsucker Proxy▶
A King in New York
The Kitchen Toto▶
La Bamba▶
La Notte Brava
Last Exit to Brooklyn▶
The Last Picture Show▶
The Long Day Closes▶
Long Gone
The Long Walk Home▶
The Lords of Flatbush
Lost, Lonely, and Vicious
Loveless
Mac▶
The Man in the Moon▶
Matinee
Mischief
Moscow Does Not Believe in
    Tears▶
My Favorite Year▶
My Michael▶

Newsfront▶
Nightbreaker▶
Oh, What a Night
One Plus One
Ordeal by Innocence
Our Time
Parents▶
Peggy Sue Got Married
Perfect Harmony
Pillow Talk▶
The Playboys▶
Porky's
A Rage in Harlem▶
A Raisin in the Sun▶
The Reflecting Skin
Rock All Night
Rock, Baby, Rock It
Round Midnight▶
School Ties▶
Shag: The Movie▶
Shake, Rattle and Rock
Shout
Sparkle
Stacking
Strange Invaders▶
Superdad
Suzanne
That'll Be the Day
This Boy's Life▶
Trading Hearts
Visitants
The War of the Worlds▶
The Way We Were▶
When Father was Away on
    Business▶
Who Shot Pat?
The Wild One▶
The Wooden Gun
You've Ruined Me, Eddie

Nightclubs

Amateur Night
Animal Instincts
Backbeat▶
Berlin Blues
Black Glove
The Blue Angel▶
The Bride Wore Red
Bucktown
A Bunny's Tale
Bus Stop▶
Cabaret▶
Can-Can
Carnival Rock
Casablanca▶
CB4: The Movie
Club Havana
Copacabana
The Cotton Club▶
Dance, Girl, Dance
Dance Hall Racket
Deadly Revenge
Desperate Cargo
Dick Tracy▶
Dracula Blows His Cool
The Fabulous Baker Boys▶
Fake Out
Femmes de Paris
Flaming Lead
Foxstyle
Framed
French Can-Can▶
The French Way
Fun in Acapulco
G.I. Blues
Girls! Girls! Girls!
Harlem Nights
It Started in Naples▶
Jive Junction
The Killing of a Chinese
    Bookie
King Creole
La Cage aux Folles▶
La Cage aux Folles 2
La Cage aux Folles 3: The
    Wedding
Lambada
Last Night at the Alamo▶
Lenny▶
Lenny Bruce Performance
    Film
Liquid Dreams

Lullaby of Broadway
Mad Dog and Glory▶
The Mambo Kings▶
Marked Woman▶
Martial Law 2: Undercover
Midnight Warrior
Mighty Joe Young
Morocco▶
Night After Night
The Night They Raided
    Minsky's▶
No Surrender▶
Not Quite Love
The Nutty Professor▶
Pete Kelly's Blues
Play Murder for Me
The Public Eye▶
Rebel
Ruby
Ruby's Dream
Sea Racketeers
Sex, Drugs, and Rock-n-Roll
The Shining Hour
Smash-Up: The Story of a
    Woman▶
Suffering Bastards
That Naughty Girl
30 Is a Dangerous Age,
    Cynthia
To Catch a King
Treasure of the Moon
    Goddess
Two Top Bananas
Underground U.S.A.
Uptown Saturday Night
Whistle Stop
A Woman is a Woman▶
Wonderland▶
Xanadu
The Zoo Gang

Ninjitsu

    see *Martial Arts*

No-Exit Motel

    see also *Grand Hotel*
Cheap Shots
Eaten Alive
Motel Hell
Mountaintop Motel Massacre
The Newlydeads
Pink Motel
Poor Pretty Eddie
Psycho▶
Psycho 2
Psycho 3
Psycho 4: The Beginning
Slaughter Hotel

Nuclear Disaster

    see *Disaster Flicks;*
    Meltdown

Nuns & Priests

    see also *Missionaries;*
    Religion; Religious Epics
Absolution
Agnes of God
The Agony and the Ecstasy
Angels with Dirty Faces▶
The Assisi Underground
The Atonement of Gosta
    Berling▶
Becket▶
The Bells of St. Mary's▶
Black Narcissus▶
Black Robe▶
The Bridge of San Luis Rey▶
Camila▶
The Cardinal
Catholic Hour
Change of Habit
Child of Darkness, Child of
    Light
Cold Justice
The Confession
The Confessional
Conspiracy of Hearts▶
The Cross & the Switchblade

Curse 4: The Ultimate
    Sacrifice
Damien: The Leper Priest
Death of an Angel
The Detective▶
The Devils▶
The Devil's Playground▶
Diary of a Country Priest▶
The Divine Enforcer
Dixie: Changing Habits▶
El Callao
Elmer Gantry▶
End of the World
The Exorcist▶
The Exorcist 2: The Heretic
The Father Clements Story
Fighting Father Dunne
First Legion
For Better and For Worse
Forever Young
The Fugitive▶
Gentleman Bandit
Going My Way▶
Goodnight God Bless
A Home of Our Own
Hot Under the Collar
I Confess
I Heard the Owl Call My Name
In the Region of Ice▶
In This House of Brede▶
Jesus of Montreal▶
Judgment▶
The Left Hand of God▶
Leon Morin, Priest
Lilies of the Field▶
Loyola, the Soldier Saint
Mass Appeal
Massacre in Rome
Mission to Glory
Monsignor
Mortal Sins
Most Wanted
The Name of the Rose
Nasty Habits
Nazarin▶
Night of the Assassin
Night of the Demons 2
The Nun
Nuns on the Run
The Nun's Story▶
Pier 23
Pope John Paul II
The Pope Must Diet
The Possessed
Prayer for the Dying
The Prisoner▶
The Rosary Murders
The Runner Stumbles
Saving Grace
The Scarlet & the Black
Second Sight
Secret Ingredient
September Gun
Shattered Vows
The Shoes of the Fisherman
The Singing Nun
Sister Act
Sister Act 2: Back in the Habit
Sisters of Satan
Sorceress▶
The Sound of Music▶
Spirits
Therese▶
To Kill a Priest
Trouble Along the Way
The Trouble with Angels
True Confessions▶
Under Satan's Sun▶
Under the Red Robe
The Unholy
Vatican Conspiracy
We're No Angels
Where Angels Go, Trouble
    Follows
The White Sister▶

Nursploitation!

    see also *Doctors &*
    Nurses; Sexploitation
Candy Stripe Nurses
Emmanuelle in the Country
Hospital of Terror

Inner Sanctum
Naked Massacre
Night Call Nurses
Nurse on Call
Private Duty Nurses
The Sensuous Nurse
The Student Nurses
Tender Loving Care
The Young Nurses
Young Nurses in Love

Occult

see also Demons &
Wizards; Satanism;
Witchcraft
Afterward
Alabama's Ghost
The Amazing Mr. X
The American Scream
Apprentice to Murder
Army of Darkness▶
Bad Dreams
Barbarian Queen
Because of the Cats
The Believers
Beyond Dream's Door
Beyond Evil
Beyond the Door 3
The Black Cat
Black Magic Terror
Black Magic Woman
Blackbeard's Ghost
Blood Diner
The Blood on Satan's Claw▶
Blood Orgy of the She-Devils
Bloodspell
Born of Fire
The Brainiac
Brimstone & Treacle▶
The Brotherhood of Satan
The Burning Court
Cabin in the Sky▶
Cat Girl
Cat in the Cage
The Cellar
Chandu on the Magic Island
Child of Glass
Children Shouldn't Play with
Dead Things
Come Along with Me
Craze
The Curse of the Crying
Woman
Curse of the Demon▶
Curse of the Devil
Damien: Omen 2
Damn Yankees▶
The Dark Secret of Harvest
Home
Dead Men Don't Die
Deathstalker 4: Clash of the
Titans
Deep Red: Hatchet Murders
Demon Possessed
Demon Rage
Demon Warrior
Demon Wind
Demonoid, Messenger of
Death
Demons 2
Demons of Ludlow
The Devil
The Devil & Daniel Webster▶
Devil Dog: The Hound of Hell
Devil Doll▶
Devil Doll
Devil Kiss
The Devils▶
The Devil's Daughter
The Devil's Eye
Devil's Gift
The Devil's Hand
The Devil's Mistress
The Devil's Nightmare
Devil's Rain
Devil's Son-in-Law
Diary of a Madman
Dick Tracy, Detective
Doctor Faustus
Dr. Strange
Dominique is Dead

Dona Flor and Her Two
Husbands▶
Donovan's Brain▶
Don't Be Afraid of the Dark
The Dreaming
Dreamscape
The Dunwich Horror
The Dybbuk▶
The Dying Truth
El Monte de las Brujas
Encounter with the Unknown
The Entity
Equinox▶
Erotic Dreams
Eternal Evil
The Evictors
The Evil
Evil Altar
Evil Dead
Evil Dead 2: Dead by Dawn
The Evil Mind
Evilspeak
Excalibur▶
Exorcism
The Exorcist▶
The Exorcist 2: The Heretic
Eye of the Demon
Eyes of Fire
Feast for the Devil
The Final Conflict
The First Power
The Fish that Saved
Pittsburgh
Fright House
Full Circle
Genie of Darkness
Ghosts That Still Walk
The Girl in a Swing
God Told Me To
Grave Secrets
The Guardian
Half of Heaven▶
Hanussen▶
The Hearse
Horror Hotel
House of the Yellow Carpet
The House on Skull Mountain
The House that Bled to Death
I Don't Want to Be Born
I'm Dangerous Tonight
Inferno
Inner Sanctum
Into the Badlands
The Invasion of Carol Enders
Invasion of the Blood Farmers
Journey into the Beyond
Kill, Baby, Kill▶
Killing Hour
The Kiss
KISS Meets the Phantom of
the Park
La Hora 24
Lady Terminator
The Lady's Maid's Bell
Land of the Minotaur
The Legacy
The Legend of Hell House▶
Leonor
The Living Head
Low Blow
The Magician▶
Making Contact
Manos, the Hands of Fate
Mardi Gras for the Devil
Mardi Gras Massacre
Maxim Xul
Medea
Men of Two Worlds
Midnight
Midnight Cabaret
Mirror, Mirror
Mirror of Death
Mirrors
Mrs. Amworth
The Monster Demolisher
Mystic Circle Murder
Natas...The Reflection
Necromancer: Satan's
Servant
Necropolis
The Night Stalker: Two Tales
of Terror

Ninja, the Violent Sorcerer
The Occult Experience
The Occultist
Omoo Omoo, the Shark God
One Step Beyond
Only You
The Oracle
Orgy of the Dead
Out on a Limb
Phantasm
Phantasm II
Poltergeist▶
Poltergeist 2: The Other Side
Poltergeist 3
Possession: Until Death Do
You Part
The Power
The Psychic
Psychic
Psychic Killer
Psychomania
Puppet Master
Quest of the Delta Knights
Race with the Devil
The Raven▶
A Reflection of Fear
The Reincarnate
Rendez-Moi Ma Peau
Repossessed
Rest In Pieces
Retribution
Return
Return from Witch Mountain
Return of Chandu
Rosemary's Baby▶
Ruby
Run If You Can
The Runestone
Sabaka
Satan's Princess
Satan's Touch
Scared Stiff
Season of the Witch
Second Sight
Seizure
The Sentinel
The Seventh Sign
The Seventh Victim▶
The Shaman
Shock 'Em Dead
Silent Night, Deadly Night 3:
Better Watch Out!
Sorceress
The Spaniard's Curse
Speak of the Devil
The Spellbinder
Spellbound
Spiritism
Student of Prague▶
Summer of Fear
Supergirl
Teen Witch
The Tempter
Terror Beach
Terror Creatures from the
Grave
That Darn Sorceress
Three Sovereigns for Sarah
To the Devil, A Daughter
The Torture Chamber of Dr.
Sadism
The Touch of Satan
Treasure of the Four Crowns
The Undead▶
Unknown Powers
Venus in Furs
Vibes
The Visitor
Warlock Moon
White Gorilla
Who Killed Doc Robbin?
The Wicker Man▶
Wild Man
Witch Who Came from the
Sea
Witchboard
Witchboard 2: The Devil's
Doorway
Witchcraft 2: The Temptress
Witchcraft 4: Virgin Heart
Witchcraft 5: Dance with the
Devil

Witchcraft Through the Ages▶
The Witches of Eastwick
The Witching
Witching Time
The Witchmaker
The Witch's Mirror
The Wizard of Oz▶
Wizards
The Woman Who Came Back
Zapped Again
The Zodiac Killer

Oceans

see Deep Blue; Go Fish;
Scuba; Sea Critter Attack;
Submarines

Oil

see Black Gold

Oil

see Black Gold

Oldest Profession

see also Gigolos; Happy
Hookers; Women in
Prison
Accatone!▶
Alexander: The Other Side of
Dawn
Alien Warrior
The Allnighter
American Justice
American Nightmare
Amor Bandido
The Amsterdam Connection
Angel
Angel 3: The Final Chapter
Anna Christie▶
Anna Christie
Aroused
Auntie
Avenging Angel
Back Roads
Bad Girls
The Balcony▶
Being at Home with Claude
Bellas de Noche
The Best Little Whorehouse in
Texas
Beverly Hills Madam
Beverly Hills Vamp
Blood Money: The Story of
Clinton and Nadine
Blow Out▶
The Blue Hour
Boiling Point
Bordello
Broken Mirrors
Butterfield 8▶
Candy Tangerine Man
Caravaggio▶
Catherine & Co.
Chained Heat 2
The Cheyenne Social Club
Christiane F.▶
Cinderella Liberty▶
Class of 1984
Club Life
Coffy
Confessions of a Vice Baron
The Courtesans of Bombay▶
Crimes of Passion▶
Cross Country
Cry of a Prostitute: Love Kills
Dead End Street
Deadly Sanctuary
Death Shot
Death Target
Dedee d'Anvers
Desperate Crimes
Diary of a Lost Girl▶
Diva▶
Dixie: Changing Habits▶
Doctor Detroit
Dr. Jekyll and Sister Hyde
Double Cross
Dressed to Kill
Drying Up the Streets
East End Hustle

8 Million Ways to Die
Elmer Gantry▶
Emily
Emmanuelle & Joanna
Erendira
Everybody Wins
Fall from Innocence
Firepower
Flesh▶
Fleshpot on 42nd Street
Forever Amber
Foxy Brown
Frankenhooker
Frankie and Johnny
French Quarter
Full Exposure: The Sex Tape
Scandals
Fyre
Get Rita
The Gift
Gigi▶
Girls of the White Orchid
Half Moon Street
The Happy Hooker
The Happy Hooker Goes
Hollywood
The Happy Hooker Goes to
Washington
Hard Vice
Help Wanted Female
High Stakes
Hollywood Chainsaw Hookers
Hollywood Vice Sqaud
Honky Tonk Girl
Hotel Room
Hustle
Hustler Squad
Hustling▶
I Want to Live!▶
Impulse
Irma La Douce
Jack's Back▶
Jamon, Jamon
Just a Gigolo
Justine
Keetje Tippei
Kinjite: Forbidden Subjects
Kiss the Night
Kitty and the Bagman
Klute▶
La Chienne▶
L.A. Crackdown
L.A. Crackdown 2
Ladies of the Lotus
Lady of the Evening
Lady of the House
The Last Prostitute
The Last Temptation of
Christ▶
Life of Oharu▶
A Life of Sin
Little Ladies of the Night
Lola Montes▶
Love by Appointment
Love Strange Love
Mack
Madame Rosa▶
Magdalene
Malibu High
Man of Flowers
Manon
Marriage Italian Style▶
Mayflower Madam
McCabe & Mrs. Miller▶
Miami Blues
Mid Knight Rider
Midnight Auto Supply
Midnight Cop
Midnight Cowboy▶
Miss Sadie Thompson▶
The Missionary
Mona Lisa▶
Murderlust
Murphy's Law
My Life to Live▶
My Mother's Secret Life
My Own Private Idaho▶
My Pleasure Is My Business
Naked Kiss
Nana▶
Nana
Never on Sunday▶

New York's Finest
Night Friend
Night of the Generals▶
Night Shift
Night Slasher
The Night They Robbed Big Bertha's
Nightmare in Badham County
Nights of Cabiria▶
No One Cries Forever
No Prince for My Cinderella
The Nun
Nuts▶
Off Limits
Oldest Profession
Olivia
One Night Only
Out of the Dark
Padre Nuestro
Pandora's Box▶
Panic in Needle Park▶
Party Girls
The Passing of Evil
Pennies From Heaven▶
Personal Services
Poker Alice
Pretty Baby▶
Pretty Woman▶
Prettykill
Prime Cut
The Pyx▶
Queen Kelly▶
Quick, Let's Get Married
Rain
Raw Justice
Reason to Die
Red Kimono
Risky Business▶
Room 43
Roots of Evil
Saint Jack▶
Sandakan No. 8▶
Sansho the Bailiff▶
Scarred
Schnelles Geld
Scorchers
Secret Games
Secrets of a Married Man
Sessions
Sex, Love and Cold Hard Cash
Sharky's Machine
The Silencer
Single Room Furnished
Sisters of Gion▶
Sketches of a Strangler
Skin Art
SS Girls
S.S. Love Camp No. 27
Stone Cold Dead
Storyville
Street Girls
Street of Forgotten Women
Street of Shame▶
Street Smart
Streetwalkin'
The Sun's Burial▶
Sweet Charity▶
Sweet Revenge
Sweet Sweetback's Baadasssss Song▶
Sweet Trash
The Sword and the Cross
Talons of the Eagle
Taxi Driver▶
They Were So Young
Thousand Pieces of Gold▶
Tightrope▶
Tokyo Decadence
Trading Places
Traffic in Souls▶
Train Station Pickups
Tricks of the Trade
Truck Stop Women
Twenty Dollar Star
Twin Peaks: Fire Walk with Me
Ultimate Desires
Uncaged
Utamaro and His Five Women
The Vampire Hookers
Via Appia

Vice Squad
Walk on the Wild Side
Warm Nights on a Slow-Moving Train
Warrior Queen
Waterloo Bridge▶
Whore
Wild Orchid 2: Two Shades of Blue
The Winter of Our Dreams
A Woman in Flames▶
A Woman of Rome
Working Girls
Working Girls▶
The World of Suzie Wong
Wrestling Racket Girls

The Olympics

see also Sports Dramas

Blades of Courage
Chariots of Fire▶
Cool Runnings
Crossbar
Dorf and the First Games of Mount Olympus
The First Olympics: Athens 1896
Going for the Gold: The Bill Johnson Story
International Velvet
The Jesse Owens Story
Life is a Circus, Charlie Brown/You're the Greatest, Charlie Brown
A Million to One
Miracle on Ice
Personal Best▶
Running Brave
Special Olympics
Sword of Gideon
Tokyo Olympiad
21 Hours at Munich▶
Walk, Don't Run
Wilma

On the Rocks

see also Pill Poppin'

Arthur 2: On the Rocks
Barfly▶
The Big Hangover
Blue Heaven
Break of Hearts
Clean and Sober▶
Cocktail
Come Back, Little Sheba▶
Country Girl▶
Country Girl
A Cry for Love
Dance of Life
Danger in the Skies
Dangerous
Days of Wine and Roses
Days of Wine and Roses▶
Desde el Abismo
Desert Bloom▶
The Devil at 4 O'Clock
The Devil Thumbs a Ride▶
The Devil Thumbs a Ride/Having Wonderful Crime
Dona Flor and Her Two Husbands▶
Drunken Angel▶
Educating Rita▶
El Dorado▶
The Electric Horseman
The Entertainer▶
Fat City▶
The Fire Within▶
Fish Hawk
The Flaming Teen-Age
Flesh and Bone▶
Frances▶
A Free Soul
Gervaise▶
The Great Man Votes▶
The Green Man▶
Honkytonk Man
Hot Summer in Barefoot County
I Live with Me Dad
I'll Cry Tomorrow▶

The Informer▶
Ironweed▶
Izzy & Moe
Jack the Bear
Kill Cruise
The Last American Hero▶
Le Beau Serge▶
License to Kill
Long Day's Journey into Night▶
Long Day's Journey into Night
The Lost Weekend▶
M.A.D.D.: Mothers Against Drunk Driving
Marvin & Tige
Mean Dog Blues
The Morning After
My Favorite Year▶
Only When I Laugh▶
Papa's Delicate Condition▶
Police Court
Reuben, Reuben▶
The Robe
Scent of a Woman▶
Shakes the Clown
The Sin of Harold Diddlebock▶
The Singing Blacksmith
Skin Deep
Smash-Up: The Story of a Woman▶
A Star is Born▶
A Star is Born
Straight Up
Stranded
Strange Brew
Tales of Ordinary Madness
Ten Nights in a Bar Room
Ten Nights in a Bar-Room
Termini Station
Under Capricorn
Under the Volcano▶
The Verdict▶
Wagons East
What Price Hollywood?▶
When a Man Loves a Woman
Whiskey Galore▶
White Lightning
Willa
The Winning Team

Only the Lonely

Abducted
The Abduction of Kari Swenson
An Autumn Afternoon▶
The Ballad of Little Jo
Betrayal
Birdman of Alcatraz▶
The Body Shop
Breakfast in Paris
The Browning Version▶
The Cemetery Club
Choose Me▶
A Chorus of Disapproval
A Christmas Without Snow
Citizen Kane▶
Cotter
Cowboys Don't Cry
Cyrano de Bergerac▶
Cyrano de Bergerac
Cyrano de Bergerac▶
A Day in the Country▶
Desperately Seeking Susan
Didn't You Hear?
Dirty Dishes▶
Distant Thunder
Docks of New York▶
Doin' Time on Planet Earth
The Doll
A Doll's House
A Doll's House▶
The Eclipse▶
El Super▶
An Empty Bed▶
Empty Suitcases
The Enchanted Cottage
Escapade in Japan
E.T.: The Extra-Terrestrial▶
Every Man for Himself & God Against All▶
Eye of the Needle

The Final Alliance
Full Moon in Blue Water
Full Moon in Paris
The Game of Love
The Gun in Betty Lou's Handbag
Harold and Maude▶
The Heart is a Lonely Hunter▶
Hell Hounds of Alaska
High Country
Hiroshima, Mon Amour▶
The Hunchback of Notre Dame▶
Husband Hunting
Husbands and Wives▶
I Don't Give a Damn
I Sent a Letter to My Love▶
In the White City▶
Inside Out
La Petite Sirene
La Vie Continue
Lana in Love
The Last Horror Film
Les Bons Debarras
The Lonely Guy
Lonely Hearts▶
The Lonely Passion of Judith Hearne▶
Lonelyhearts
Looking for Mr. Goodbar
Lunatics: A Love Story▶
Luther the Geek
Man of Flowers
Marianela
Marty
Marty▶
The Match Factory Girl▶
Men Don't Leave
Miles to Go Before I Sleep
Mr. Kingstreet's War
Mouchette▶
976-EVIL
None But the Lonely Heart▶
Once Around
Only the Lonely
Only You
Our Miss Brooks
Panic Station
The Passion of Anna▶
Persona▶
Priest of Love
The Prime of Miss Jean Brodie▶
The Prince of Central Park▶
The Pursuit of Happiness
Queen of the Stardust Ballroom▶
The Rachel Papers▶
Rachel, Rachel▶
The Red Desert▶
Red Kimono
Restless
Return Engagement
Robert et Robert▶
Roseland
Samurai 2: Duel at Ichijoji Temple▶
Scene of the Crime▶
The Seagull▶
Secret Life of an American Wife
Seize the Day▶
Separate Tables▶
Separate Tables
September
Shadows in the Storm
Single Bars, Single Women
Sleepless in Seattle▶
Slipstream
The Solitary Man
Someone to Love
South of Reno
Summer▶
Sweetwater
Tales of the Klondike: The Scorn of Women
Tenth Month
Terror at the Opera
That Cold Day in the Park
Tomorrow▶
Too Shy to Try

Turtle Diary▶
Vagabond▶
When Your Lover Leaves
Wildest Dreams
Woman in the Shadows
The Young in Heart▶
Zelly & Me▶

Opera

see also Musicals

Interrupted Melody▶
Musica Proibita
Naughty Marietta
A Night at the Opera▶

Order in the Court

see also Justice Prevails...?; Law & Lawyers

Absence of Malice
The Accused
The Accused▶
Action for Slander
Adam's Rib▶
All God's Children
The Ambush Murders
Anatomy of a Murder▶
And Justice for All
The Andersonville Trial▶
As Summers Die
Assault at West Point: The Court-Martial of Johnson Whittaker
Beyond a Reasonable Doubt
Body of Evidence
The Bramble Bush
Breaker Morant▶
The Caine Mutiny Court Martial▶
Carrington, V.C.▶
A Case of Libel
Clarence Darrow▶
Class Action▶
Clearcut
The Client
Cold Days
Conduct Unbecoming
Conspiracy: The Trial of the Chicago Eight▶
Convicted
Cordelia
The Court Martial of Billy Mitchell▶
Criminal Court
Cross Examination
A Cry in the Dark▶
Death of a Soldier
Death Sentence
The Defender
The Defense Never Rests
Defenseless
Delinquent Parents
The Devil & Daniel Webster▶
Dishonored Lady
The Drake Case
A Dry White Season▶
Ernest Goes to Jail
Eureka!
Evelyn Prentice
A Few Good Men▶
Final Verdict
A Free Soul
From the Hip
Gideon's Trumpet
The Good Father▶
The Good Fight
The Good Mother
Guilty as Sin
Guilty of Innocence
Hard Traveling
Hitz
Honor Thy Father and Mother: The True Story of the Menendez Brothers
How Many Miles to Babylon?
I Want to Live!▶
Illegally Yours
In the Name of the Father▶
Inherit the Wind▶
It Could Happen to You
The Jagged Edge

Jailbait: Betrayed By
    Innocence
The Judge
The Judge and the Assassin▶
Judge Horton and the
    Scottsboro Boys
Judgment at Nuremberg▶
Judgment in Berlin
Justice
A Killing in a Small Town▶
King of the Pecos
Knock on Any Door
L.A. Law▶
Last Innocent Man
The Last Wave▶
Les Assassins de L'Ordre
Little Gloria...Happy at Last
The Long Dark Hall
Madame X
Madeleine
Midnight
Mrs. R's Daughter
Monsieur Beaucaire
Murder▶
Murder or Mercy
Music Box
Naked Lie
Never Forget
Nuts▶
Outrage!
The Paradine Case
Penalty Phase
Perry Mason Returns▶
Perry Mason: The Case of the
    Lost Love
Philadelphia
Presumed Innocent▶
Prisoners of the Sun▶
Question of Silence▶
Rampage
Red Kimono
The Respectful Prostitute
Reversal of Fortune▶
Riverbend
Roe vs. Wade▶
The Rose Garden
Rumpole of the Bailey
Rumpole of the Bailey:
    Rumpole's Return▶
The Runner Stumbles
Sacco & Vanzetti
The Scorpion Woman
The Secret Passion of Robert
    Clayton
Separate But Equal▶
Sergeant Rutledge▶
Sergeant Ryker
Silent Victim
A Simple Twist of Fate
Skullduggery
The Star Chamber
State's Attorney
Stuck on You
Suspect
Swoon▶
They Won't Believe Me▶
To Kill a Mockingbird▶
The Trial
The Trial
Trial of Bernhard Goetz
The Trial of Lee Harvey
    Oswald
Trial of the Catonsville Nine
Twelve Angry Men▶
The Verdict▶
When Every Day was the
    Fourth of July
When Thief Meets Thief
Where Love Has Gone
The Winslow Boy▶
Witness for the Prosecution▶
Wives Under Suspicion
Woman in Brown
A Woman's Face▶
The Young Philadelphians▶

Organized Crime

*see also Crime &
Criminals; Disorganized
Crime; Gangs*
Absence of Malice
Across 110th Street

Action U.S.A.
Agent on Ice
Almost Human
Alphabet City
American Born
The American Gangster
American Justice
The American Soldier
Angels with Dirty Faces▶
Another Stakeout
Armed for Action
Armed Response
Atlantic City▶
Avenging Disco Godfather
Baby on Board
Backtrack▶
Bad Charleston Charlie
Bad Georgia Road
Ball of Fire▶
The Barber Shop▶
The Barcelona Kill
Bellas de Noche
Beverly Hills Bodysnatchers
Big Bad Mama 2
Big Boss
Big Combo▶
Big News
The Big Slice
The Big Sweat
The Big Switch
Big Town After Dark
Billy Bathgate
Black Belt Jones
Black Caesar
Black Godfather
Black Lemons
Black Lizard
Black Rain
Black Shampoo
Blackjack
Blank Check
Blind Fury
Blood Brothers
Blood Ties
Blood Vows: The Story of a
    Mafia Wife
Blown Away
Blue Money
Body Trouble
Born to Run
Boss Foreman
Brighton Rock▶
A Bronx Tale▶
The Brotherhood
Bugsy▶
Bugsy Malone
California Casanova
Camorra: The Naples
    Connection
Capone
Car Crash
Car 54, Where Are You?
The Chinatown Murders: Man
    Against the Mob
Chu Chu & the Philly Flash
The Client
Cobra
Cohen and Tate
Cold Heat
Comfort and Joy▶
Confessions of a Hit Man
Cookie
Cop in Blue Jeans
Cops and Robbersons
Corleone
Corruption
The Cotton Club▶
Courier of Death
Crazy Streets
Crime Killer
Crime Story: The Complete
    Saga
Dagger Eyes
Dangerous Charter
Darker than Amber
Daughter of the Tong
Deadly Matrimony
Deadly Rivals
Deadly Vengeance
Deadly Weapons
Death Force

Death Wish 5: The Face of
    Death
Deja Vu
Delta Fox
Desperate
Desperate Crimes
Dick Tracy▶
Dirty Work
Doctor Detroit
The Don is Dead
Double Deal
Drunken Angel▶
The Enforcer
Ernest Goes to Jail
Eureka!
Excessive Force
The Executioner
The Executioner, Part 2:
    Frozen Scream
Extreme Vengeance
An Eye for an Eye
Faith
Fake Out
The Family
A Family Matter
Fass Black
Fatal Chase
Fear in the City
The Fighting Rookie
Final Justice
Fingers▶
Fireback
The Firm▶
Fist of Honor
Five Miles to Midnight
The Freshman
Gang War
Gangster Wars
Gangsters
Gangster's Law
Get Rita
The Girl Who Had Everything
Gloria
The Godfather▶
The Godfather 1902-1959:
    The Complete Epic▶
The Godfather, Part 2▶
The Godfather, Part 3▶
Goodfellas▶
Gunblast
Hard-Boiled
The Harder They Fall▶
Harlem Nights
Heat
Hell on Frisco Bay
Hell Up in Harlem
Heroes in Blue
Hiding Out
High Stakes
Hired to Kill
Hit Lady
The Hit List
Hit the Dutchman
Hollywood Cop
Hollywood Crime Wave
Hollywood Man
Hong Kong Nights
Honor Thy Father
Hooch
The Hunted Lady
Hurricane Smith
I Died a Thousand Times
I, Mobster
Ice
Innocent Blood
Johnny Stecchino▶
Jornada de Muerte
Kansas City Massacre
Keaton's Cop
Keeper of the City
The Key Man
Kill Me Again
The Kill Reflex
The Killer▶
Killer Bait
Killer Instinct
Killing in the Sun
The Killing of a Chinese
    Bookie
The King of the Roaring '20s:
    The Story of Arnold
    Rothstein

Kiss Tomorrow Goodbye
The Krays▶
L.A. Wars
Ladies of the Lotus
Lady Mobster
Lady of the Evening
Lady Scarface
The Last Contract
Last Exit to Brooklyn▶
Last Rites
Legacy of Lies
Lepke
Lethal Games
Little Caesar▶
Little Vegas
Loan Shark
The Long Good Friday▶
Lucky Luciano
Ma and Pa Kettle Go to Town
Mad Dog and Glory▶
Madigan's Millions
Mafia Princess
Mafia vs. Ninja
Magic Kid
Making the Grade
The Man I Love▶
Man on a String
The Manhandlers
Manhunt
Manhunter
Married to the Mob▶
Mean Machine
Mean Streets▶
Meet Danny Wilson
Men of Respect
The Messenger
Mikey & Nicky
Mr. Majestyk
Mister Mean
Mob Boss
Mobsters
The Monster and the Girl
Moon Over Harlem
Movie...In Your Face
Moving Target
My Blue Heaven
The Narrow Margin▶
Never Steal Anything Small
New Mafia Boss
1931: Once Upon a Time in
    New York
Nitti: The Enforcer
Odd Jobs
Once Upon a Time in
    America▶
Our Family Business
Out for Justice
The Outfit
The Outside Man
Overkill
Palais Royale
The Palermo Connection
Panic Button
Passion for Power
Payoff
Penthouse▶
Perfect Killer
Perfect Witness
The Plot Against Harry▶
Point Blank
The Pope Must Diet
Port of New York
Pray for Death
Prime Target
Prizzi's Honor▶
The Public Eye▶
Pulp Fiction▶
Quick
Rapid Fire
Raw Deal
Red Heat
The Red Light Sting
The Revenger
Ricco
Ring of the Musketeers
The Rise and Fall of Legs
    Diamond
Rock, Baby, Rock It
Romeo Is Bleeding
Ruby
Rulers of the City
Run

Scarface▶
Scarface Mob
Sex, Love and Cold Hard
    Cash
Shaft's Big Score
Shoot to Kill
Sicilian Connection
The Sicilian Connection
Sitting Ducks▶
Sizzle
Slaughter
Slaughter's Big Ripoff
Sloane
Slow Burn
Smokescreen
Sno-Line
Special Investigator
Squizzy Taylor
Stand-In
Stark
State of Grace▶
Stiletto
The Stone Killer
Street Hero
Street People
Street War
Taking the Heat
Target for Killing
Terminal Force
They Call Me Bruce?
They Paid with Bullets:
    Chicago 1929
Thief▶
Things Change▶
This Could Be the Night
The Three Penny Opera▶
The Threepenny Opera
Ticket of Leave Man
The Tongfather
Tony Rome
The Trap
TripleCross
True Identity
True Romance
Ulterior Motives
Underworld, U.S.A.▶
The Untouchables▶
Velvet Smooth
Vendetta for the Saint
Verne Miller
We're Talkin' Serious Money
What! No Beer?
White Heat▶
White Hot: The Mysterious
    Murder of Thelma Todd
White Sands
Who's Got the Action?
Wise Guys
The Wrestler
Zatoichi: The Life and Opinion
    of Masseur Ichi
Zatoichi: Zatoichi's Flashing
    Sword
Zebra Force

Outtakes & Bloopers

Abbott and Costello
    Scrapbook
Bela Lugosi Scrapbook
Cinema Shrapnel
Hollywood Bloopers
Hollywood Outtakes & Rare
    Footage
Hollywood Uncensored
Salute to the "King of the
    Cowboys," Roy Rogers
Star Trek Bloopers
Voice of Hollywood
What Do You Say to a Naked
    Lady?
Zombiethon

Overlooked Gems

Cross Creek
Crossing Delancey▶
Dazed and Confused▶
Diner▶
Dogfight▶
Gallipoli▶
Housekeeping▶
Joey Breaker▶

Overlooked

Johnny Nobody
The Joy Luck Club▶
The Lighthorsemen▶
Local Hero▶
Matewan▶
Metropolitan▶
Miss Firecracker▶
Raising Arizona▶
Road House
Searching for Bobby Fischer▶
Shag: The Movie▶
The Silent Partner▶
Stay Hungry▶
Stealing Home
Strictly Ballroom▶
The Tall Guy▶

Pacific Islands

see also Island Fare

Aloha Summer
Balboa
Blue Hawaii
Carlton Browne of the F.O.
Castaway
Cry of Battle
Dangerous Life
Don't Go Near the Water
Enchanted Island
Ethan
Eye of the Octopus
Fighting Marines
Flaming Signal
Fog Island
Food of the Gods
From Hell to Borneo
From Here to Eternity▶
Hell in the Pacific▶
Hell Raiders
His Majesty O'Keefe
Hula
The Island▶
Island of Dr. Moreau
The Last Flight of Noah's Ark
The Last Warrior
Lt. Robin Crusoe, U.S.N.
Mad Doctor of Blood Island
The Mermaids of Tiburon
Midway
Miss Sadie Thompson▶
Mission Manila
Mr. Robinson Crusoe
Moana, a Romance of the Golden Age▶
Mysterious Island▶
Noon Sunday
Paradise, Hawaiian Style
Pardon My Sarong
Rain
South Pacific▶
Tabu: A Story of the South Seas▶
Till There was You
Tora! Tora! Tora!
Wackiest Ship in the Army
White Shadows in the South Seas
Windom's Way▶
The Year of Living Dangerously▶

Painting

see Art & Artists

Parades & Festivals

see also Carnivals & Circuses

Easter Parade▶
Ferris Bueller's Day Off▶
Miracle on 34th Street▶
National Lampoon's Animal House▶
Sweet Beat

Parenthood

see also Bad Dads; Bringing Up Baby; Monster Moms; Stepparents

Adam▶
Addams Family Values

Alice in the Cities▶
Aliens▶
All the Kind Strangers
Amazing Grace
American Heart▶
An Autumn Afternoon▶
Baby Boom
Baby Girl Scott
Bachelor Mother▶
Backfield in Motion
The Ballad of Narayama▶
Battling for Baby
Being Two Isn't Easy
Between Two Women
Big Girls Don't Cry...They Get Even
The Big Wheel
Blind Fools
Blondie's Blessed Event
Blue City
Boys Town▶
Bush Mama
Cahill: United States Marshal
Careful, He Might Hear You▶
Casanova Brown
Chapter in Her Life
The Children of Times Square
Cody
Cold River
Commissar▶
Cowboys Don't Cry
Crisscross
Crooklyn▶
A Cry in the Dark▶
Da
Daddy Nostalgia▶
Danielle Steel's "Daddy"
Desde el Abismo
Distant Voices, Still Lives▶
Dona Herlinda & Her Son
Donde Duermen Dos...Duermen Tres
Drop-Out Mother
Dutch
East of Eden▶
East of Eden
El Monte de las Brujas
The Emerald Forest▶
Endless Love
Enormous Changes▶
Epitaph
The Equalizer: Memories of Manon
Ernie Kovacs: Between the Laughter
Esposa y Amante
Family Life
Fatal Confinement
Father Figure
Father of the Bride▶
A Fight for Jenny
Fine Things
Flowers in the Attic
Follow That Rainbow
Forbidden Planet▶
Gas Food Lodging▶
Ghost Dad
A Global Affair
God Bless the Child▶
The Good Father▶
The Good Mother
Growing Pains
Guess What We Learned in School Today?
Gypsy▶
Gypsy
Harry & Son
Held for Murder
High Tide▶
A Hole in the Head
Home from the Hill▶
A Home of Our Own
Houseboat
I Accuse My Parents
I Live with Me Dad
I Never Sang For My Father▶
I Remember Mama▶
I'll Do Anything
I'll Take Sweden
Immediate Family
Innocent Victim
Irreconcilable Differences

Journey for Margaret▶
Kiss Daddy Goodbye
The Lady is Willing
Long Time Gone
Lost Angels
Love Under Pressure
Ma and Pa Kettle Back On the Farm
Ma Barker's Killer Brood
Mad Youth
M.A.D.D.: Mothers Against Drunk Driving
Max Dugan Returns
Memory of Us
Mirele Efros
Mrs. R's Daughter
Mr. Mom▶
Misunderstood
Mom
Mom & Dad
Monkey Grip▶
Mother & Daughter: A Loving War
Mother and Son
My Father's Nurse
My Life
My Mom's a Werewolf
National Lampoon's European Vacation
Natural Enemies
Next of Kin
Night Cries
North▶
Nothing in Common
On Golden Pond▶
On the Third Day
One Man's War
Only the Lonely
Only When I Laugh▶
Padre Padrone▶
Parenthood▶
Parents▶
Paris, Texas▶
Poil de Carotte
Psycho 4: The Beginning
Raising Arizona▶
The Red House▶
Red River▶
The Reluctant Debutante▶
Revenge
The Revolt of Mother▶
Rising Son▶
The River Rat
A River Runs Through It▶
Runaway Father
Scream for Help
Sex and the Single Parent
The Shaggy D.A.
Silence of the Heart
A Simple Twist of Fate
A Slightly Pregnant Man
Son of Godzilla
Special Olympics
Speeding Up Time
Stella
Stella Dallas▶
The Strange Love of Molly Louvain
Sunstroke
Superdad
Suzanne
Taken Away
Target
Teen Mothers
Teenage Bad Girl
Tequila Sunrise
Terms of Endearment▶
This Property is Condemned
Three Fugitives
Three Men and a Baby▶
Three Men and a Cradle▶
Throw Momma from the Train▶
The Turning Point
The Unborn 2
Undercover Blues
Unfinished Business
The Unstoppable Man
Wanted: The Perfect Guy
When Wolves Cry
Where Are the Children?
Where's Poppa?▶

Without a Trace
The Woman Who Willed a Miracle
Yours, Mine & Ours

Party Hell

see also Horror

April Fool's Day
Carrie▶
Happy Birthday to Me
Hell Night
Hello Mary Lou: Prom Night 2
Killer Party
Monsters Crash the Pajama Party
Night of the Demons
Prom Night
Prom Night 3: The Last Kiss
Prom Night 4: Deliver Us From Evil
Psycho Girls
Rabid Grannies
The Slumber Party Massacre
Slumber Party Massacre 2
Slumber Party Massacre 3
Twilight Zone: The Movie

Patriotism & Paranoia

see also Propaganda

Amber Waves
Born on the Fourth of July▶
The Chase
The Commies are Coming, the Commies are Coming
The Cosmic Man
Death of a Bureaucrat▶
Delta Force
Dress Gray▶
F/X▶
Fellow Traveler▶
Firefox
First Blood
Guilty by Suspicion
Harry's War
Heroes for Sale▶
Ivan the Terrible, Part 1▶
Ivan the Terrible, Part 2▶
Missing in Action
Mom & Dad
Murrow
Panama Patrol
Paris Belongs to Us
Patton▶
The Prisoner▶
Rambo: First Blood, Part 2
Rambo 3
Red Dawn
The Red Menace
Red Nightmare
Reunion in France
The Sea Hawk▶
The Secret Four
Skinheads: The Second Coming of Hate
Sky High
The Spider's Stratagem▶
Strictly G.I.
Taps
Thirty Seconds Over Tokyo▶
The 27 Day

Peace

The Day the Earth Stood Still▶
The Deserters
Destry Rides Again▶
Diplomaniacs
Firehead
Friendly Persuasion▶
Gandhi▶
Sadat
War and Peace
War and Peace▶

Period Piece

see also Historical Drama; Medieval Romps; Royalty

Abbott and Costello Meet the Keystone Kops

Adventures of Don Juan▶
The Adventures of Marco Polo
The Adventures of Mark Twain▶
The Age of Innocence▶
Al Capone▶
All the Brothers Were Valiant
Allonsanfan▶
Alone Against Rome
Amadeus▶
American Friends
American Graffiti▶
An American Story
The Amorous Adventures of Moll Flanders
Anna and the King of Siam▶
Anna Karenina
Anne of Avonlea▶
Anne of Green Gables▶
Anthony Adverse
The Assassination Bureau▶
Assault at West Point: The Court-Martial of Johnson Whittaker
At Sword's Point▶
The Awful Dr. Orlof
The Babe
The Bachelor▶
Back Home
Back to Hannibal: The Return of Tom Sawyer and Huckleberry Finn
Backbeat▶
The Ballad of Little Jo
Band of Angels
The Barbary Coast
The Barretts of Wimpole Street▶
Barry Lyndon▶
Barton Fink▶
Batman: Mask of the Phantasm
Battle of Valiant
The Bay Boy
Beau Brummel
Beautiful Dreamers
Beauty and the Beast▶
Becoming Colette
Belizaire the Cajun
Belle Epoque▶
Belle of the Nineties
Ben-Hur▶
The Best Intentions▶
Beulah Land
Billy Bathgate
Bix
Black Robe▶
Bleak House
Blood Clan
Blood Red
Bopha!▶
The Bostonians
Botany Bay
Boxcar Bertha
Bram Stoker's Dracula
Brenda Starr
The Bretts▶
Broadway Bound
The Broken Chain
A Bronx Tale▶
Brothers Lionheart
Brutal Glory
Bugsy▶
By the Light of the Silvery Moon
Bye Bye Blues
Calendar Girl
Call of the Wild
The Canterbury Tales
Carlito's Way▶
Carnival in Flanders▶
Carthage in Flames
Cartouche▶
Casanova
Casanova's Big Night
The Castilian
Catherine the Great
The Charge of the Light Brigade▶
The Charge of the Light Brigade
The Charmer

Cheech and Chong's, The
   Corsican Brothers
Chinatown▶
Chips, the War Dog
A Christmas Carol▶
A Christmas Carol
Christopher Columbus
The Cisco Kid
City Boy▶
The Clan of the Cave Bear
Cleopatra
Cold Sassy Tree▶
Colonel Redl▶
The Color of Pomegranates▶
Coming Through
Conduct Unbecoming
The Conqueror Worm▶
Conquest▶
Conquest of Cochise
The Country Diary of an
   Edwardian Lady
Courage Mountain
The Covered Wagon
Crooklyn▶
Crossing the Bridge
Cry of the Banshee
Daisy Miller
Damn the Defiant▶
Dangerous Liaisons▶
A Dangerous Man: Lawrence
   after Arabia▶
Dante's Inferno: Life of Dante
   Gabriel Rossetti
Danton▶
The Dark Angel▶
Dark of the Sun
Daughters of the Dust▶
Dazed and Confused▶
Decameron Nights
The Deceivers
Deja Vu
Delusion
Delusions of Grandeur
Demons of the Mind
Desiree
The Devils▶
Diner▶
The Disappearance of Aimee▶
Disraeli▶
Dr. Bethune▶
Doctor Zhivago▶
The Dollmaker
A Doll's House
A Doll's House▶
DuBarry Was a Lady
Duel of Champions
Duel of Hearts
East of Elephant Rock
Edvard Munch
Effi Briest▶
Eight Men Out▶
1860
Eijanaika▶
El Cid▶
Ele, My Friend
The Elegant Criminal
The Elephant Man▶
Elizabeth of Ladymead▶
Elizabeth, the Queen
The Emigrants▶
Emma's Shadow▶
Empire of the Sun▶
Enchanted April
End of Desire
The Ernest Green Story
Ernesto
Ethan Frome
The Europeans▶
Every Day's a Holiday
Fabiola▶
The Fall of the Roman
   Empire▶
Family Prayers
Fanny and Alexander▶
Fanny Hill: Memoirs of a
   Woman of Pleasure
Far and Away
Far from the Madding
   Crowd▶
The Far Pavilions
Farewell, My Lovely▶
The Farmer Takes a Wife

Fiddler on the Roof▶
The Field▶
55 Days at Peking▶
The Fighting Kentuckian
Fiorile▶
Fire and Sword
The First Olympics: Athens
   1896
F.I.S.T.
Five Corners▶
Five Weeks in a Balloon
The Fixer▶
Flambards
The Flame is Love
The Flame Trees of Thika▶
Flight of the Eagle
Flowers of Reverie
Fools of Fortune
Forest of Little Bear
Forever Amber
Forget Mozart
Fortunes of War▶
The Four Feathers
The Four Feathers
The Four Musketeers▶
Francesco
The Franchise Affair
Frankenstein
Frankie and Johnny
Freedom Road
The French Lieutenant's
   Woman▶
Fulfillment
A Funny Thing Happened on
   the Way to the Forum▶
Gaslight▶
Gate of Hell▶
George Washington
George Washington: The
   Forging of a Nation
Geronimo▶
Geronimo: An American
   Legend
Gervaise▶
The Getting of Wisdom
Gettysburg▶
Glory▶
The Go-Between▶
Gold Diggers of 1933▶
Golden Gate
Good Evening, Mr.
   Wallenberg
Good Morning, Babylon▶
Goodbye, Miss 4th of July
The Gorgeous Hussy
Gothic▶
Grand Isle
Great Expectations
Great Expectations
Great Expectations
Great Expectations: The
   Untold Story
The Great Gatsby
The Great Moment
The Great Train Robbery▶
The Great Waldo Pepper▶
Green Dolphin Street
Greyfriars Bobby
The Grissom Gang▶
The Guns and the Fury
Gypsy
Hamlet▶
Harem
Haunted Summer
Hawaii
Hawk the Slayer
The Hearst and Davies Affair
Heart of Darkness
Heart of Glass▶
Heartland▶
The Heiress▶
Hello, Frisco, Hello
Henry V▶
Hester Street▶
High Road to China
The Hindenburg
Hit the Dutchman
Hobson's Choice▶
Hobson's Choice
Home at Last
The Horse Soldiers
The Hound of the Baskervilles

The House of Eliott
The House on Carroll Street
Howard's End▶
I Remember Mama▶
The Imported Bridegroom
Impromptu▶
In Old Chicago▶
In the Good Old
   Summertime▶
Indochine▶
The Inheritors
The Inkwell
Inside Daisy Clover
The Iron Mask
Iron Will
Ironclads
It Happened in New Orleans
It Runs In the Family▶
It's a Dog's Life
Ivan the Terrible, Part 1▶
Ivan the Terrible, Part 2▶
Ivanhoe▶
Jamaica Inn
Jane Eyre▶
Java Head▶
Jazzman▶
Jeeves & Wooster: Jeeves'
   Arrival
Jezebel▶
Joseph Andrews
Journey of Honor
Jude the Obscure
Kagemusha▶
Keetje Tippei
The Killing Beach
The King and I▶
King of the Hill▶
The King's Rhapsody
The King's Thief
The King's Whore▶
Korczak▶
La Chartreuse de Parme
La Grande Bourgeoise
La Marseillaise▶
La Nuit de Varennes▶
La Ronde▶
Lady Caroline Lamb
Lady for a Night
Lady from Louisiana
Lady L
Land of Promise
Land of the Pharaohs
The Last Days of Pompeii
The Last Emperor▶
The Last of His Tribe
The Last of the Mohicans▶
The Last of the Redmen
The Lawrenceville Stories
A League of Their Own▶
Les Miserables
Life with Father▶
Light at the Edge of the World
The Lighthorsemen▶
Like Water for Chocolate▶
Lillie▶
The Lion in Winter▶
Little Dorrit, Film 1: Nobody's
   Fault▶
Little House on the Prairie▶
Little Minister▶
The Little Princess▶
Little Women▶
Little Women
The Lodger▶
The Long Day Closes▶
The Lords of Discipline
The Lords of Flatbush
Lorna Doone
Lost in Yonkers
Louisiana
The Lovable Cheat
Love Among the Ruins▶
Love and Death▶
Love and Faith▶
Love Field
Love for Lydia▶
The Lover
Lovers: A True Story▶
Loves & Times of
   Scaramouche
The Lower Depths▶
M. Butterfly

The Mad Whirl
Madame Bovary▶
Mademoiselle Fifi
The Magician of Lublin
The Magnificent Ambersons▶
Maids of Wilko
Malcolm X▶
The Mambo Kings▶
A Man for All Seasons▶
The Man from Snowy River
The Man in Grey▶
The Man in the Iron Mask▶
The Man in the Moon▶
Man of Evil
Mania
Mansfield Park
Marie Antoinette
The Mark of Zorro▶
The Marquise
Mary of Scotland▶
Masque of the Red Death
Matinee
A Matter of Time
Mayerling▶
Meet Me in St. Louis▶
Melody Master
Merry-Go-Round▶
Mesmerized
Messalina, Empress of Rome
A Midsummer Night's Sex
   Comedy▶
The Mill on the Floss
Miller's Crossing▶
Miss Rose White▶
Mrs. Soffel
Mr. Corbett's Ghost
Mister Johnson▶
The Moderns▶
Modigliani
Monaco Forever
Monsieur Beaucaire▶
Monsieur Vincent▶
Morning Glory
Much Ado About Nothing▶
The Music Man▶
Mutiny on the Bounty
My Apprenticeship▶
My Childhood▶
My Fair Lady▶
My Twentieth Century▶
My Universities▶
The New Land▶
New Moon
Newsies
Nicholas and Alexandra
Nicholas Nickleby▶
No Drums, No Bugles
No Time for Romance
Northanger Abbey
O Pioneers!
Odd Birds
Of Human Hearts
Old Gringo
Oliver!▶
Oliver Twist▶
Oliver Twist
Oliver Twist▶
Oliver Twist
Omar Khayyam
On a Clear Day You Can See
   Forever
On Moonlight Bay
On Valentine's Day
Once Upon a Time in
   America▶
Orlando▶
Oscar
Our Time
Our Town▶
The Outfit
The Ox
Palais Royale
Pancho Barnes
Pantaloons
Party Girl▶
A Passage to India▶
Passion
Passion in Paradise
Passion of Love▶
Peg O' My Heart
Pelle the Conqueror▶
Peppermint Soda▶

A Perfect World
The Piano▶
Pictures
Pink Strings and Sealing Wax
The Playboys▶
Poldark▶
Pollyanna▶
Portrait of a Lady
Portrait of Jennie▶
Power
The Power of One
Pride and Prejudice▶
Pride and Prejudice
Prince Valiant
Princess Yang Kwei Fei▶
The Private Affairs of Bel
   Ami▶
The Private Life of Henry VIII▶
The Private Lives of Elizabeth
   & Essex▶
The Public Eye▶
Queen Christina▶
Racing with the Moon▶
Rambling Rose▶
Ran▶
Rasputin and the Empress▶
Rebel Love
Red Sorghum▶
The Remains of the Day▶
Rembrandt—1669
The Return of Eliot Ness
The Return of Martin Guerre▶
The Return of the Musketeers
Return to Paradise
The Revolt of Mother▶
Rich Man, Poor Man▶
Richard III▶
The Right Hand Man
Rikyu▶
A River Runs Through It▶
The Road to Yesterday
The Robe
Robin Hood▶
Robin Hood: Prince of Thieves
The Rocketeer▶
Romance
Rome '78
A Room with a View▶
Rosa Luxemburg
The Rose and the Jackal
Rouge
Saga of the Vagabond
The St. Valentine's Day
   Massacre
Salome
Samurai Reincarnation
San Francisco▶
The Sandlot▶
Sansho the Bailiff▶
Sarah, Plain and Tall▶
Savage Messiah▶
The Scent of Green Papaya▶
School for Scandal
School Ties▶
Sea Devils
The Sea Hawk▶
The Secret Garden▶
The Secret Garden
The Seekers
Sense & Sensibility
Senso▶
Sergeant Rutledge▶
Shadow on the Sun
Shadowlands▶
Shag: The Movie▶
Shake Hands with the Devil▶
Sherlock Holmes: The Master
   Blackmailer
Shogun▶
The Shooting Party▶
Shopworn Angel▶
Show Boat
The Sign of Four
Silas Marner▶
Sirens▶
Sister Dora
Skin Game▶
The Sky is Gray▶
Skylark
Smart-Aleck Kill
Sofie
Something for Everyone

Sommersby
Son of Fury▶
Song Without End
Sorceress▶
The Sound and the Silence▶
Splendor in the Grass▶
Spring Symphony
Star!
Stars and Stripes Forever▶
The Stationmaster's Wife
The Stick-Up
The Strange Woman
Sudie & Simpson
A Summer Story▶
Swing Kids
Swing Shift
Swoon▶
Sword of Sherwood Forest
Swords of Death
Tai-Pan
A Tale of Two Cities▶
A Tale of Two Cities▶
A Tale of Two Cities▶
Tales from Avonlea, Vol. 1:
    The Journey Begins▶
Tales from the Gimli Hospital
Tamango
Taras Bulba
Tchaikovsky
Tess▶
That Forsyte Woman
That Night
That'll Be the Day
They Came to Cordura
They Shoot Horses, Don't
    They?▶
Thieves Like Us▶
Three Comrades▶
The Three Musketeers
Throne of Blood▶
The Tigress
Tito and Me▶
Tom Sawyer
Torrents of Spring
Tous les Matins du Monde▶
Trading Hearts
Tune in Tomorrow
20,000 Leagues Under the
    Sea▶
Twenty-Four Eyes▶
The Two Jakes
Two Nights with Cleopatra
Under Capricorn
Under the Biltmore Clock
Under the Volcano▶
An Unfinished Piece for a
    Player Piano▶
Used People
Utamaro and His Five Women
Valentino
Valentino Returns
The Valley of Decision▶
Valmont▶
Van Gogh▶
Victoria Regina
The Vikings
The Virgin Queen▶
Viva Villa!▶
War and Peace
The Warriors
We of the Never Never▶
What's the Matter with Helen?
Where Angels Fear to Tread▶
White Hot: The Mysterious
    Murder of Thelma Todd
The Wicked Lady
Wide Sargasso Sea
Wild Hearts Can't Be Broken▶
Wild Party
A Winner Never Quits
The Wolves▶
Woman in Black
A Woman Rebels
Women in Love▶
Wrangler
Xica▶
Yellow Earth
Yentl
Young Bess▶
Young Sherlock Holmes

Persian Gulf War
The Heroes of Desert Storm
The Human Shield

Philanthropy
    see Kindness of Strangers

Phobias!
Arachnophobia
Body Double▶
High Anxiety
Home Remedy
Inside Out
Vertigo▶

Phone Terror
Are You Lonesome Tonight
Black Sabbath▶
Call Me
Don't Answer the Phone
Lady Beware
Lisa
976-EVIL
976-EVIL 2: The Astral Factor
Party Line
Smooth Talker
Sorry, Wrong Number▶
Sorry, Wrong Number
Telefon
When a Stranger Calls
When a Stranger Calls Back

Photography
    see Shutterbugs

Physical Problems
    *see also Blindness;
    Deafness; Mental
    Retardation; Savants*
Acorn People
The Affair▶
An Affair to Remember
Amy
Autumn Sonata▶
Big Street
Born on the Fourth of July▶
A Brief History of Time▶
Broken Strings
The Brute Man
Chained for Life
Chinese Roulette
Choices
Coming Home▶
Crossbar
A Day in the Death of Joe
    Egg▶
El Cochecito▶
The Elephant Man▶
Endgame
Even Cowgirls Get the Blues
Fighting Life
The Glass Menagerie▶
Hearing Voices
The Hunchback of Notre
    Dame▶
Inside Moves
It's Good to Be Alive
Joni
Knife in the Head
Lightning Jack
Long Journey Back
Love Affair▶
Mac and Me
The Man with the Golden
    Arm▶
The Man Without a Face
Marianela
Mask▶
The Men▶
The Miracle Worker▶
Monkey Shines
My Left Foot▶
Next Victim
Night Monster
Of Human Bondage▶
Off the Mark
One-Eyed Swordsman
The Other Side of the
    Mountain

The Other Side of the
    Mountain, Part 2
Passion Fish▶
Phantom of the Opera▶
The Pit
Ratboy
Reach for the Sky
Rear Window▶
Revolver
Richard III▶
Ride a Wild Pony▶
The River▶
Scent of a Woman▶
The Secret
Seizure: The Story of Kathy
    Morris
The Seventh Veil▶
Silence
Silence Like Glass
Skag▶
The Sky Pilot
The Small Back Room▶
Sound of Love
Special Olympics
The Spiral Staircase▶
Spiral Staircase
The Steel Claw
Stella Maris▶
The Stratton Story▶
Talk to Me
The Terry Fox Story▶
A Test of Love
To All My Friends on Shore▶
Untamed Heart
Walking on Air
The Waterdance▶
What Ever Happened to Baby
    Jane?▶
What's Eating Gilbert Grape▶
Whose Life Is It Anyway?▶
A Winner Never Quits
A Woman's Face▶

Pill Poppin'
    see also On the Rocks
Above the Law
Aces: Iron Eagle 3
The Acid Eaters
Across the Tracks
Adventures in Spying
Air America
All That Jazz▶
Alphabet City
Altered States▶
American Fabulous
Amongst Friends
The Amsterdam Connection
The Amsterdam Kill
And Then You Die▶
Angel's Brigade
Armistead Maupin's Tales of
    the City
Assassin of Youth
Avenging Disco Godfather
Awakenings of the Beast
Back in Action
Bad Lieutenant▶
Bad Medicine
The Beatniks
Beretta's Island
Best Revenge
Bird▶
Black Starlet
Blast-Off Girls
Blind Spot
Blindside
Blood & Concrete: A Love
    Story
Blood Freak
Blood In...Blood Out: Bound
    by Honor
Bloodbath
The Bloody Brood
Blue Sunshine
The Boost
Borderline
Born to Win
Bright Lights, Big City
Brotherhood of Justice
Burning Vengeance
Busting
Camp Double Feature

Captain Blackjack
Captive Rage
Carlito's Way▶
Caroline at Midnight
Cartel
Catch the Heat
Chained Heat 2
Chains of Gold
Chameleon
Cheech and Chong: Still
    Smokin'
Cheech and Chong: Things
    Are Tough All Over
Cheech and Chong's Next
    Movie
Cheech and Chong's Nice
    Dreams
Cheech and Chong's Up in
    Smoke
The Children of Times Square
China White
Chinatown Connection
Christiane F.▶
Chrome Soldiers
Class of 1984
Clean and Sober▶
Club Life
Cocaine Cowboys
Cocaine Fiends
Cocaine: One Man's
    Seduction
Cocaine Wars
Codename: Wildgeese
Coffy
Coldfire
The Colombian Connection
Commando Squad
Comrades in Arms
Conexion Mexico
Confessions of a Vice Baron
The Connection
Contra Company
Contraband
Corridors of Blood
Countryman
Courage▶
Covert Action
Crack House
Crazy Streets
Crossing the Bridge
A Cry for Love
Cut and Run
Dance or Die
Dangerous Game
Dangerous Heart
Day of Atonement
Day of the Cobra
Day of the Maniac
Dazed and Confused▶
Dead Aim
Dead Ringers▶
Deadly Surveillance
Death Drug
The Death of Richie
Death Shot
Death Wish 4: The
    Crackdown
Deep Cover
Delta Heat
Desert Snow
Desperate Lives
The Destructors
The Devil's Harvest
The Devil's Sleep
Dirty Laundry
Dr. Jekyll and Mr. Hyde▶
Dr. Jekyll and Mr. Hyde
Dogs in Space
Dope Mania
Double-Crossed
Down & Dirty▶
Drug Wars 2: The Cocaine
    Cartel
Drugstore Cowboy▶
Drying Up the Streets
Easy Kill
Easy Rider▶
Edge of Sanity
Edie in Ciao! Manhattan
8 Million Ways to Die
Enter the Dragon▶
Exposure

Extreme Prejudice
Fall from Innocence
Fast Money
Fatal Beauty
Fatal Fix
Feelin' Screwy
Fever
The Fifth Floor
Fire Birds
First Born
The Five Heartbeats▶
The Fix
The Flaming Teen-Age
Flashback▶
Flatfoot
Flesh▶
Fletch
Four Friends▶
Frances▶
The French Connection▶
French Connection 2▶
French Intrigue
Fresh Kill
The Fury of the Wolfman
Ganjasaurus Rex
The Gene Krupa Story
The Gift
The Golden Triangle
Goodfellas▶
Gordon's War
Gothic▶
Gunmen
Hallucination
Haunted Summer
Heat▶
Help Wanted Female
A Hero Ain't Nothin' But a
    Sandwich
Heroes for Sale▶
High Crime
High Risk
High School Confidential
Hit!
The Hooked Generation
How Come Nobody's On Our
    Side?
Hussy
I Come in Peace
I Drink Your Blood
I Love You, Alice B. Toklas
I'm Dancing as Fast as I Can
The Imposter
In Hot Pursuit
Inside Edge
Iron Horsemen
Island Monster
Jaguar Lives
Jekyll & Hyde...Together
    Again
Jo Jo Dancer, Your Life is
    Calling
Jumpin' at the Boneyard
Kamikaze Hearts
Kandyland
Kemek
Kickboxer the Champion
Kill or Be Killed
The Killing Zone
Kowloon Assignment
Kung Fu's Hero
La Bamba▶
L.A. Wars
Lady Sings the Blues
Last Flight to Hell
The Last of the Finest
Lenny▶
Less Than Zero
Lethal Obsession
Lethal Weapon▶
Let's Get Harry
Let's Get Lost
License to Kill▶
Light Sleeper
Live and Let Die
Loaded Guns
London Kills Me
Long Day's Journey into
    Night▶
Long Day's Journey into Night
Lost Angels
Lovely...But Deadly
The Man Inside

The Man with the Golden Arm▶
Marihuana
Marked for Death
Martial Outlaw
Maybe I'll Be Home in the Spring
McBain
McQ
The Messenger
Miami Vendetta
Midnight Cop
Midnight Express▶
Mike's Murder
Mindfield
Mission Manila
Mixed Blood
Mob War
Monkey Grip▶
More
Naked Lunch▶
The Narcotics Story
New Jack City
Newman's Law
Night Friend
The Night of the Iguana▶
Ninja Turf
Ninja vs. Ninja
No Escape, No Return
Not My Kid
On the Edge
On the Edge: The Survival of Dana
One False Move▶
The Organization▶
Out of the Rain
Over the Edge▶
Pace That Kills
The Palermo Connection
Panic in Needle Park▶
Passion for Power
The People Next Door
Performance▶
Pharmacist
Platoon the Warriors
Playing with Fire
Point of No Return
Police
The Poppy is also a Flower
Postcards from the Edge▶
Pot, Parents, and Police
Premonition
Pretty Smart
Prime Cut
Private Investigations
Professionals
Protector
Psych-Out
Puppet on a Chain
Question of Honor
Quiet Cool
Rage and Honor
Rapid Fire
Reckless Disregard
Red Blooded American Girl
Red Heat
Red Surf
Reefer Madness
Return of the Tiger
Revenge of the Ninja
Revenge of the Stepford Wives
Rip-Off
River's Edge▶
Rock House
Rodrigo D.: No Future
The Rose▶
Running Scared
Rush▶
Saigon Commandos
Satan's Harvest
Savage Instinct
Scarface▶
Schnelles Geld
Scorchy
Secret Agent Super Dragon
The Seducers
The Seven Percent Solution▶
Severance
Showdown in Little Tokyo
Sicilian Connection
Sid & Nancy▶

Silk
The Slender Thread▶
The Snake People
SnakeEater 2: The Drug Buster
Sno-Line
Sorry, Wrong Number
Stand Alone
Straight Up
Street Girls
Street Hawk
Streetwalkin'
Strike Force
Sugar Hill▶
Sunset Heat
Sunset Strip
Super Bitch
Superfly
The Take
Talons of the Eagle
Target Eagle
Tchao Pantin▶
Teenage Devil Dolls
Tequila Sunrise
The Third Man▶
This Time I'll Make You Rich
Thunder Alley
Timothy and the Angel
To Die Standing
Tombstone▶
The Tong Man
Tongs: An American Nightmare
Torchlight
Toughlove
Toxic Zombies
Traffik▶
Transmutations
Trash
Trespass
The Trip
Tropical Snow
Trouble in Paradise
True Romance
Twenty-One
Twin Peaks: Fire Walk with Me
Undercover
Valley of the Dolls
Vanishing Point
Wait Until Dark▶
Wanda, The Sadistic Hypnotist
Warlords from Hell
Warlords 3000
Watched
Weekend with the Babysitter
Weird World of LSD
What Have I Done to Deserve This?▶
Whispers of White
Who'll Stop the Rain?▶
Wild in the Streets
The Wild Pair
Wild Weed
The Winter of Our Dreams
Wired
Withnail and I▶
Women on the Verge of a Nervous Breakdown▶
Woodstock▶

Poetry
The Barretts of Wimpole Street▶
The Color of Pomegranates▶
Kerouac
Lady Caroline Lamb
Poetic Justice
Tales of Ordinary Madness

Poisons
Arsenic and Old Lace▶
Barracuda
Color Me Dead
The Crazies
D.O.A.▶
D.O.A.
Doomwatch
The Invisible Killer
Juggernaut

Kiss and Kill
Surf 2

Politics

see also Presidency
Access Code
The Act
Advise and Consent▶
Agent on Ice
All the King's Men▶
All the President's Men▶
Amazing Grace & Chuck
The Ambassador
American Roulette
An American Story
Americana
The Americano
Americathon
And the Band Played On▶
Angry Joe Bass
Animal Instincts
Antonio Das Mortes
Article 99
Assassination
The Assignment
Atomic Submarine
Avenging Force
Before the Revolution
Beggars in Ermine
Behold a Pale Horse
Being There▶
Beloved Enemy▶
The Berlin Conspiracy
Best Kept Secrets
The Best Man▶
Beyond Obsession
The Big Hurt
Black God & White Devil
Black Ice
Blaze
Blind Ambition
Blood Money: The Story of Clinton and Nadine
Blow Out▶
Bob Roberts▶
Bootleg
Bopha!▶
Born American
Breaking with Old Ideas
Burgess, Philby, and MacLean: Spy Scandal of the Century
Buried Alive
Burn!▶
Cal▶
Call Him Mr. Shatter
Canadian Bacon
Carry On Emmanuelle
Children in the Crossfire
China Gate▶
Citizen Cohn
Clear and Present Danger▶
The Clockmaker▶
Code Name: Chaos
The Colombian Connection
The Comedians
The Commies are Coming, the Commies are Coming
Complex World
Confessions of a Police Captain
Conspiracy
Conspiracy: The Trial of the Chicago Eight▶
Contra Company
Corporate Affairs
Country▶
Dangerous Life
A Dangerous Man: Lawrence after Arabia▶
Dangerous Moves▶
Danton▶
Dark Forces
Dave▶
Deadly Exposure
Death of a Bureaucrat▶
Defense of the Realm▶
Demonstone
The Devils▶
Devlin
Diary of a Rebel

Disraeli▶
The Distinguished Gentleman
Dr. Syn, Alias the Scarecrow
The Dogs of War
Don's Party▶
Double Cross
Double Edge
Early Days
Earth Entranced
East of Elephant Rock
Echoes of Conflict
Eijanaika▶
El Diputado▶
Elizabeth, the Queen
Eminent Domain
Emissary
The Endless Game
The Everlasting Secret Family
The Evil That Men Do
Executive Action
Exposed
Eye of the Stranger
Fame is the Spur
The Farmer's Daughter▶
Fat and the Lean▶
Fever Mounts at El Pao
Fires Within
First Family
First Monday in October
A Flash of Green
Foreplay
Free Amerika Broadcasting
The French Detective▶
The French Woman
Friday Foster
Funeral for an Assassin
Gabriel Over the White House▶
Germany in Autumn
A Girl on Her Own
The Gorgeous Hussy
Gorky Park▶
The Great McGinty▶
Ground Zero▶
Guilty by Suspicion
Hail
Hangar 18
Hanna K.
Hard to Kill
Head of the Family
Hennessy
Henry V▶
His Girl Friday▶
Hitler's Daughter
The Home and the World▶
Home Town Story
Hoodlum Empire
Hostages▶
Hour of the Assassin
The House of the Spirits
Hungarian Rhapsody▶
I, Mobster
Imagemaker
In the Line of Duty: Ambush in Waco
In the Line of Fire▶
In the Name of the Father▶
In the Name of the Pope-King▶
Independence
Indochine▶
It's a Joke, Son!
JFK▶
JFK: Reckless Youth
John and the Missus
John F. Kennedy
Johnny We Hardly Knew Ye
A Joke of Destiny, Lying in Wait Around the Corner Like a Bandit
Juarez
Jud Suess▶
Julius Caesar▶
Julius Caesar
Just Like Weather▶
Kennedy
Kent State
The Kidnapping of the President
The Killer Elite
Killer Image
The Killing Beach

The Killing Device
Killing of Angel Street
Kiss of the Spider Woman▶
The Kitchen Toto▶
Knife in the Head
Kung Fu Rebels
La Boca del Lobo
La Hija del General
La Passante▶
Lady of the House
Larks on a String▶
The Last Bastion
Last Hurrah
Last Plane Out
Laurel & Hardy: Chickens Come Home
The Lawless Nineties
LBJ: The Early Years▶
Le Complot▶
L'Etat Sauvage▶
The Life and Assassination of the Kingfish
Life is Beautiful
A Lion is in the Streets▶
Lisbon
The Little Drummer Girl▶
Little Nikita
The Living Daylights▶
Lone Star Kid
The Looking Glass War
The Losers
Louisiana Purchase
Love▶
Love and Anarchy▶
M. Butterfly
Made in Argentina
A Man Called Peter▶
The Manchurian Candidate▶
Mandela▶
The Mating Game▶
Meeting Venus
Memories of Underdevelopment
Missiles of October▶
Missing▶
Mission of Justice
Mr. Ace
Mr. Smith Goes to Washington▶
Morgan Stewart's Coming Home
Mussolini & I
My Sweet Charlie
My Universities▶
Naked Obsession
Nancy Astor
Nashville▶
Nightbreaker▶
Nine Days a Queen▶
No Way Out▶
Northern Extremes
Odd Man Out▶
The Official Story▶
One, Two, Three▶
Open Doors▶
Palombella Rossa
Parallax View▶
Paths of Glory▶
Patty Hearst
The Pelican Brief
Perfumed Nightmare▶
Pizza Man
A Place Called Today
Place of Weeping
Plutonium Incident
Portrait of a Rebel: Margaret Sanger
Power
Power Play
A Prayer for Katarina Horovitzova▶
President's Mistress
Presumed Innocent▶
Primary Motive
Prince Jack
Protocol
Quiet Fire
Rage of Angels: The Story Continues
Ramparts of Clay▶
Red King, White Knight
Red Kiss▶

Politics

Relentless 2: Dead On
Repentance▶
The Report on the Party and
   the Guests▶
Report to the Commissioner▶
Requiem for Dominic▶
Roads to the South
Robert Kennedy and His
   Times
Romero
Rosa Luxemburg
The Round Up
Running Mates▶
Sacco & Vanzetti
Saigon: Year of the Cat
Salt of the Earth▶
Salvador▶
Samaritan: The Mitch Snyder
   Story▶
The Sand Pebbles▶
Scandal▶
The Secret
Secret Honor▶
Seduced
The Seduction of Joe Tynan
The Senator was Indiscreet▶
Seven Days in May▶
A Show of Force
Slash
Sleeping Dogs
Soldier in Love
Sotto, Sotto
Special Police
The Spook Who Sat By the
   Door
Stalin
State of Siege▶
State of the Union▶
Stay Tuned for Murder
Storm Over Asia▶
Storyville
Superfly T.N.T.
Tailspin: Behind the Korean
   Airline Tragedy
Tanner '88
Target: Favorite Son
Taxi Blues▶
Ten Days That Shook the
   World▶
Time for Revenge
Timecop
Tito and Me▶
The Trial▶
Trial of the Catonsville Nine
Uncommon Valor
Under Fire▶
Under Western Stars
Unnatural Causes▶
Upper Crust
Vengeance
A Very British Coup▶
Viva Villa!▶
Viva Zapata!▶
The War Room▶
Washington Affair
Washington Mistress
Way He Was
Werewolf of Washington
The Whistle Blower▶
Whoops Apocalypse
The Wilby Conspiracy▶
Wild in the Streets
Will: G. Gordon Liddy
The Wind and the Lion▶
Windom's Way▶
Winter Kills▶
A Woman Called Golda▶
A Woman Named Jackie
A World Apart▶
World War II: When Lions
   Roared
Z▶
Zero Population Growth

Pool

see also *Gambling*
The Baltimore Bullet
The Baron and the Kid
The Color of Money▶
The Hustler▶
Kiss Shot
Pool Hustlers

Pornography

see also *Sex & Sexuality;*
Sexploitation
Body Double▶
Defenseless
Fallen Angel
The Glitter Dome
Hardcore
Heavy Traffic▶
Hi, Mom!▶
Hollywood Vice Sqaud
Inserts
It's Called Murder, Baby
Kamikaze Hearts
Kidnapped
The Last Porno Flick
M'Lady's Court
The Pornographers▶
Rented Lips
The Sinister Urge
South Bronx Heroes
Stripper
Variety

Post Apocalypse

see also *Negative Utopia;*
Technology-Rampant
After the Fall of New York
Aftermath
Battle for the Planet of the
   Apes
Beneath the Planet of the
   Apes
The Blood of Heroes
A Boy and His Dog
Circuitry Man
City Limits
Class of 1999
The Creation of the
   Humanoids
Crime Zone
Cyborg
Damnation Alley
Day of the Dead
Day the World Ended
Daybreak
Dead Man Walking
Deadly Reactor
Def-Con 4
Driving Force
Dune Warriors
The Element of Crime
Endgame
Equalizer 2000
Escape from Safehaven
Exterminators of the Year
   3000
The Final Executioner
Final Sanction
Firefight
First Spaceship on Venus▶
Fortress of Amerikka
Future Hunters
Future Kill
Glen and Randa
The Handmaid's Tale
Hardware
Hell Comes to Frogtown
In the Aftermath
Interzone
Karate Cop
The Killing Edge
Knights
Land of Doom
The Last Man on Earth
The Lawless Land
Le Dernier Combat▶
Lord of the Flies▶
Mad Max▶
Mad Max: Beyond
   Thunderdome
A Man Called Rage
Maniac Warriors
Nemesis
Neon City
Night of the Comet
984: Prisoner of the Future
1990: The Bronx Warriors
Omega Cop
Omega Man
On the Beach▶

Osa
Panic in the Year Zero!
People Who Own the Dark
Phoenix the Warrior
Planet Earth
Planet of the Apes▶
Prayer of the Rollerboys
Prison Planet
The Quiet Earth▶
Quintet
Radioactive Dreams
Raiders of the Sun
Rats
Rebel Storm
Refuge of Fear
The Road Warrior▶
RoboCop▶
Robot Holocaust
Roller Blade
Rush
The Seventh Sign
She
Silent Running▶
The Sisterhood
The Slime People
Steel Dawn
Stephen King's The Stand
Strange New World
Survival Earth
Survival Zone
Survivor
Teenage Caveman
Terminator 2: Judgment Day▶
The Terror Within 2
Testament▶
Things to Come▶
The Time Travelers
Time Troopers
2020 Texas Gladiators
Ultra Warrior
Urban Warriors
Virus
WarCat
Warlords
Warlords of the 21st Century
Warlords 3000
Warriors of the Apocalypse
Warriors of the Wasteland
Wheels of Fire
Where Have All the People
   Gone?
World Gone Wild

Postwar

see also *Veterans*
An American Story
Americana
Back Home
Baltic Deputy▶
Behold a Pale Horse
Berlin Express▶
The Best Years of Our Lives▶
Bitter Rice▶
Black Rain▶
Bloody Trail
The Blum Affair
Born on the Fourth of July▶
Brussels Transit
The Burmese Harp▶
The Bushwackers
Cabo Blanco
Chattahoochee
Cinema Paradiso▶
The Cruel Story of Youth▶
Demons in the Garden▶
Deutschland im Jahre Null▶
Distant Thunder
Distant Voices, Still Lives▶
Dixie Lanes
D.P.
Early Summer▶
Eat a Bowl of Tea▶
Ebony Dreams
Europa '51
Exodus▶
Father▶
The Fighting Kentuckian
First Blood
Foolish Wives▶
Four in a Jeep
Frieda
Grave of the Fireflies▶

Green Eyes▶
Gun Fury
Heroes
Hiroshima, Mon Amour▶
Hiroshima: Out of the Ashes▶
Horizons West
House▶
I Am a Fugitive from a Chain
   Gang▶
I Don't Give a Damn
In a Glass Cage
The Indian Runner
The Innocent
Inside Out
Isn't Life Wonderful▶
It Happened in New Orleans
Jacob's Ladder
Judgment at Nuremberg▶
The Last Reunion
The Last Time I Saw Paris
Le Dernier Combat▶
The Left Hand of God▶
Les Rendez-vous D'Anna
Lilies of the Field▶
The Limping Man
Love is a Many-Splendored
   Thing
Love Nest
MacArthur's Children▶
Man of Marble▶
The Man Who Broke 1,000
   Chains
Manon
Maria's Day▶
Maria's Lovers
The Marriage of Maria Braun▶
Master Race
Mine Own Executioner▶
The Miniver Story
Miss Rose White▶
A Month in the Country▶
Mother▶
My Old Man's Place
Nevil Shute's The Far Country
Night Stage to Galveston
Night Wars
1900▶
Notorious▶
The Odessa File
Panique▶
Plenty
A Private Function
QB VII▶
Quality Street
Rambo: First Blood, Part 2
Random Harvest▶
The Razor's Edge▶
Reunion▶
Rich Man, Poor Man▶
Rio Conchos▶
Robin Hood of the Pecos
The Rose Garden
Savage Dawn
The Search▶
Sergeant Ryker
Shoeshine▶
Sommersby
Sophie's Choice▶
Souvenir
Strategic Air Command
The Teahouse of the August
   Moon
The Third Man▶
Three Comrades▶
Till the End of Time
Time of Indifference
Torpedo Alley
Trained to Kill, U.S.A.
Uranus▶
Verboten!
Vietnam, Texas
We All Loved Each Other So
   Much▶
Who'll Stop the Rain?▶
Wish You Were Here▶
Wolf Lake
The Yakuza
Year of the Quiet Sun▶
Zentropa

POW/MIA

see also *Vietnam War;*
War, General; World War
II
Against the Wind
All My Sons▶
American Commandos
The Andersonville Trial▶
Another Time, Another Place▶
Au Revoir Les Enfants▶
Ay, Carmela!▶
Bat 21
The Beast
Blockhouse
Bomb at 10:10
The Boxer and Death▶
Brady's Escape
The Bridge on the River
   Kwai▶
Bridge to Hell
Bye Bye Blues▶
Captive Heart▶
Captive Hearts
Charlie Bravo
Codename: Terminate
The Colditz Story
Come See the Paradise▶
Cornered▶
Crossfire
The Desert Tigers
Dirty Heroes
The Dunera Boys▶
The Elusive Corporal▶
Empire of the Sun▶
Era Notte a Roma▶
Escape
Escape from Sobibor▶
Escape to Athena
Fighting Mad
The Forgotten
Generale Della Rovere▶
Grand Illusion▶
The Great Escape▶
The Great Escape 2: The
   Untold Story
The Hand
Hanoi Hilton
Hell to Eternity
Heroes in Hell
Homecoming▶
The Human Condition: A
   Soldier's Prayer▶
Hunted
In Gold We Trust
In Love and War
The Incident
The Iron Triangle
Jenny's War
King Rat▶
A Love in Germany
McKenzie Break▶
Merry Christmas, Mr.
   Lawrence▶
Mine Own Executioner▶
Missing in Action
Nam Angels
Night Wars
Objective, Burma!▶
On Wings of Eagles
One That Got Away▶
Operation 'Nam
Operation War Zone
Pacific Inferno
Porridge
P.O.W. Deathcamp
The P.O.W. Escape
Prisoners of the Sun▶
The Purple Heart
Rolling Thunder
The Seventh Cross▶
Stalag 17▶
The Summer of My German
   Soldier▶
Three Came Home▶
Victory
Von Ryan's Express▶
War Victims
When Hell Was in Session▶
Women of Valor
Wooden Horse▶

Presidency

***see also** Camelot (New); Politics*

Abe Lincoln in Illinois▶
Advise and Consent▶
All the President's Men▶
Assassination
The Best Man▶
Black Sunday
Dave▶
Dirty Tricks
Eleanor & Franklin▶
Eleanor: First Lady of the World
Escape from New York
Executive Action
First Family
Foreplay
Gabriel Over the White House▶
Gore Vidal's Lincoln
Guarding Tess
Hail
Imagemaker
In the Line of Fire▶
Indomitable Teddy Roosevelt
JFK▶
The JFK Conspiracy
JFK: Reckless Youth
JFK Remembered
Kennedy
The Kidnapping of the President
Kisses for My President
The Last Bastion
LBJ: A Biography
LBJ: The Early Years▶
Meteor
Missiles of October▶
The President's Analyst▶
President's Mistress
The President's Plane is Missing
Prince Jack
Rockin' Ronnie
Ruby
Sadat
Secret Honor▶
Suddenly▶
Sunrise at Campobello▶
The War Room▶
Wild in the Streets
Wilson▶
Winter Kills▶
Young Mr. Lincoln▶

Price of Fame

***see also** Rags to Riches*

Abraham Lincoln
All About Eve▶
All That Jazz▶
American Blue Note
The Bad and the Beautiful▶
Bert Rigby, You're a Fool
Beyond the Valley of the Dolls
The Big Knife▶
Black Starlet
The Bodyguard
The Buddy Holly Story▶
By the Sword
The Cantor's Son
Cassie
Champion▶
A Chorus Line
Citizen Kane▶
Coal Miner's Daughter▶
Comeback
The Comic▶
The Commitments▶
The Cotton Club▶
Country Girl
Covergirl
Crossover Dreams
Darling▶
Dead Ringers▶
Echo Park
Eddie and the Cruisers
Eddie and the Cruisers 2: Eddie Lives!
Edie in Ciao! Manhattan
Elmer Gantry▶

Elvis and Me
Elvis Presley's Graceland
Elvis: Rare Moments with the King
Elvis: The Echo Will Never Die
Elvis: The Movie
Eureka!
Extra Girl
Fame▶
The Fan
Fellow Traveler▶
The Five Heartbeats▶
Flashdance
Frances▶
Gemini Affair
The Gene Krupa Story
The Goddess▶
Goodbye, Norma Jean
Goodnight, Sweet Marilyn
Gore Vidal's Lincoln
The Gunfighter▶
Hail Caesar
A Hard Day's Night▶
Hard Part Begins
Harvest Melody
Hero at Large
Hollywood Heartbreak
I, Claudius, Vol. 3: Poison is Queen/Some Justice
I, Claudius, Vol. 4: Queen of Heaven/Reign of Terror
I Ought to Be in Pictures
Idolmaker
I'll Cry Tomorrow▶
Imitation of Life▶
Inside Daisy Clover
Irreconcilable Differences
It Should Happen to You▶
The Jacksons: An American Dream
Jacqueline Bouvier Kennedy
James Dean
The Jayne Mansfield Story
Jazz Singer
Jimmy Hollywood
Jo Jo Dancer, Your Life is Calling
John & Yoko: A Love Story
Keep Punching
King of Comedy▶
La Bamba▶
La Dolce Vita▶
Lady Grey
Lady Jane▶
Lady Sings the Blues
The Lady Without Camelias
Lenny▶
Let It Rock
Little Caesar▶
The Lonely Lady
Love Me or Leave Me▶
Lucy and Desi: Before the Laughter
The Magnificent Ambersons▶
Mahogany
The Main Event
The Man Who Would Be King▶
Marilyn: The Untold Story▶
Mephisto▶
Miss All-American Beauty
Mistress
Mommie Dearest
My Fair Lady▶
My Favorite Year▶
Naked in New York
Oh, God! You Devil
The One and Only
One Trick Pony
The Oscar
Payday
Police Court
Postcards from the Edge▶
Prisoner of Rio
Pure Country
Purple Rain
The Queen of Mean
Raging Bull▶
Rocky▶
Rocky 2
Rocky 3
Rocky 4

Rocky 5
The Rose▶
Shadow of China▶
Shakes the Clown
Shop Angel
Show People▶
Sins
Small Town Boy
Smash-Up: The Story of a Woman▶
Smithereens
S.O.B.
Soldier in Love
Star 80
A Star is Born▶
Stardust Memories
Sunset Boulevard▶
Svengali
Sweet Dreams
Sweet Love, Bitter
Sweet Perfection
Sweethearts▶
The Thing Called Love
True Colors
Tucker: The Man and His Dream▶
Twenty Dollar Star
Two Weeks in Another Town
Valley of the Dolls
A Very Private Affair
What Ever Happened to Baby Jane?▶
What Price Hollywood?▶
What's Love Got to Do With It?
While the City Sleeps▶
Winning▶
Wired
A Woman Named Jackie
You Light Up My Life
Ziegfeld Girl▶

Prince/Princess

***see** Royalty*

Prison

***see** Great Escapes; Men in Prison; POW/MIA; Women in Prison*

Propaganda

***see also** Patriotism & Paranoia; Politics*

Air Force▶
Arsenal▶
The Atomic Cafe▶
Aventure Malgache
Baltic Deputy▶
Behind the Rising Sun
The Black King
Blood on the Sun
Bon Voyage
Born American
Breaking with Old Ideas
Chapayev▶
The Commies are Coming, the Commies are Coming
Corregidor
Dangerous Hours
Desperate Journey
The Devil's Harvest
Dope Mania
The End of St. Petersburg▶
Fighting Seabees
The General Line▶
The Green Berets
Guadalcanal Diary
Jud Suess▶
Mrs. Miniver▶
A Mormon Maid
No Greater Love
Passage to Marseilles▶
Que Viva Mexico▶
The Red Menace
Red Nightmare
Reefer Madness
Reunion in France
Rocket Attack U.S.A.
Shack Out on 101▶
Stamp Day for Superman
Strike▶

Teenage Devil Dolls
Ten Days That Shook the World▶
Ten Nights in a Bar-Room
The Thief
Threads▶
To the Shores of Tripoli
Tomorrow's Children
Trapped by the Mormons
Woza Albert!
Zvenigora▶

Prostitutes

***see** Gigolos; Happy Hookers; Oldest Profession*

Psychiatry

***see** Shrinks*

Psycho-Thriller

***see also** Mystery & Suspense*

Afraid of the Dark
After Darkness
After Midnight
Alligator Eyes
Almanac of Fall
Ambition
Anatomy of a Psycho
Apartment Zero▶
Apology
Are You Lonesome Tonight
The Arousers
The Art of Dying▶
The Attic
Awakening of Candra
The Babysitter
Bad Influence
Baffled
The Barretts of Wimpole Street▶
Being at Home with Claude
The Berlin Affair
Betrayal
Beware, My Lovely
Beyond Erotica
Bitter Moon
Bizarre
Black and White as Day and Night
Blow-Up▶
Body Chemistry 2: Voice of a Stranger
Brighton Strangler
Brimstone & Treacle▶
By the Blood of Others▶
Call Me
Cape Fear▶
The Case of the Frightened Lady
Cat's Play
Cause for Alarm
Cold Heaven
Cold Room
The Collector▶
The Comfort of Strangers▶
Conflict▶
The Crush
Cul de Sac▶
Curse of the Stone Hand
Daddy's Gone A-Hunting▶
Dangerous Pursuit
Dark Mirror▶
Dark Past▶
The Dark Ride
Dark Waters
Darkroom
Day of Wrath▶
Dead Again▶
Dead as a Doorman
Dead Calm▶
Deadbolt
Deadly Daphne's Revenge
Deadly Game
Deadly Hero▶
Deadly Sunday
Deranged
Diabolique▶
Disturbance
Disturbed
Don't Answer the Phone

Doppelganger: The Evil Within
Dream Lover
The Dreaming
Dressed for Death
The Drifter
Dynasty of Fear
El: This Strange Passion▶
Entangled
Every Breath
Evil Judgement
Eye of the Storm
Eyes of the Beholder
Fair Game
Falling Down
Fatal Attraction▶
Fear
The Fear Inside
Final Approach
Fingers▶
The Flaming Urge
Force of Evil
Freeway
Frenchman's Farm
Fright
Gaslight▶
Girl in Black Stockings
Girly
Hallucination
The Hand
The Hand that Rocks the Cradle
Hellbent
The Hitch-Hiker▶
Honeymoon
House of Games▶
Hush, Hush, Sweet Charlotte▶
I Never Promised You a Rose Garden▶
In a Glass Cage
In the Heat of Passion
In the Realm of Passion
The Incident
Innocent Prey
Intimate Stranger
Investigation
The Invisible Ghost
Jacob's Ladder
Juggernaut
Julia and Julia
Killer Inside Me
The Killing Mind
Kiss of a Killer
Knife in the Water▶
Knight Moves
La Rupture
La Vengeance d'une Femme
Laser Moon
The Last of Sheila
Le Boucher▶
Love Crimes
Love, Lies and Murder
M▶
Magic
Make Haste to Live
Man on the Eiffel Tower▶
The Man Who Haunted Himself
The Mark▶
Marnie▶
Mayalunta
The Meal
Mean Season
Memories of Murder
Midnight Fear
Midnight Lace
Mind Games
Misery▶
Mortal Sins
The Most Dangerous Game▶
Moving Targets
Murphy's Law
My Brother has Bad Dreams
My Neighborhood
Naked Massacre
A Name for Evil
The Night of the Following Day
The Night Walker
Nightmare at Bittercreek
The Offence▶
One Night Stand

Psycho-Thriller

Opposing Force
Pacific Heights▶
The Paint Job
Panic Station
The Passion of Anna▶
Peeping Tom▶
The Penthouse
Performance▶
Play Misty for Me▶
Playgirl Killer
Poison Ivy
Portrait in Terror
Portrait of Jennie▶
Posed For Murder
Praying Mantis
Pretty Poison▶
Prey of the Chameleon
Psycho 3
Psychomania
Raising Cain
Reason to Die
A Reflection of Fear
Relentless
Repulsion▶
Ricochet▶
Rituals
Room to Let
Rorret▶
Sapphire▶
Savage Abduction
Secret Beyond the Door
Secret Ceremony
Secret Games
Secret Games 2: The Escort
Secrets of Three Hungry
  Wives
Seduced
The Seduction
Shadows in the Storm
The Shining
Siesta
The Silence of the Lambs▶
Single White Female
Sleeping with the Enemy
A Small Killing
Snapdragon
Sorry, Wrong Number▶
Sorry, Wrong Number
The Spiral Staircase▶
Spiral Staircase
Stardust Memories
The Stepfather▶
Stepfather 2: Make Room for
  Daddy
Stepfather 3: Father's Day
Storm
Strange Illusion
The Stranger▶
Striking Distance
Svengali▶
Svengali
Sweet Killing
A Taste for Killing
Tattoo
The Temp
The Tenant▶
Through a Glass Darkly▶
Timebomb
To Play or To Die
Tower of Terror
Trapped
Trauma
The Two Mrs. Carrolls
Unlawful Entry
The Vanishing▶
Vengeance Is Mine▶
Victim of Love
Violated
Voyage
Wait Until Dark▶
Web of Deceit
When Hell Was in Session▶
Where Are the Children?
While I Live
The Wind

Psychotics/
Sociopaths

see also *Roommates from
  Hell*
Accidental Meeting

The Avenger
Bad Ronald
The Bad Seed
Badlands▶
Bellamy
Berserk!
Black Eliminator
Black Panther
Black Pit of Dr. M
Blind Side
Blind Vision
Blue Steel
Body Bags
The Boston Strangler
Boxing Helena
The Boys Next Door
Cape Fear▶
Carrie
The Centerfold Girls
City Killer
Cold Eyes of Fear
Cold Steel
Consenting Adults
Crimes of Dr. Mabuse▶
The Crush
Damned River
Dario Argento's Trauma
Dark Past▶
The Dark Ride
Das Testament des Dr.
  Mabuse▶
Dead as a Doorman
Dead Boyz Can't Fly
Deadbolt
Deadly Daphne's Revenge
Deadly Game
Death of a Soldier
Death Sentence
Demolition Man
Demon Hunter
Deranged▶
Deranged
Desperate Motives
Diary of a Teenage Hitchhiker
Dr. Giggles
Don't Answer the Phone
Doppelganger: The Evil Within
The Drifter
Ed Wood
Ex-Cop
Eyes of the Beholder
Fade to Black
Falling Down
The Fan
Fatal Attraction▶
Fear
Fear City
The Fear Inside
The Fool Killer
Force of Evil
Girl in Black Stockings
Guilty as Sin
Helter Skelter
Homer and Eddie
Honeymoon
The Hostage
Hot Potato
Hot Touch
House of Terror
The Housekeeper
Hush Little Baby, Don't You
  Cry
In the Line of Fire▶
The Invisible Terror
Kalifornia
Killer Inside Me
Killing Obsession
Killzone
Lightning Bolt
The Lightship
The Little Girl Who Lives
  Down the Lane
Live Wire
Lunatic
The Mad Bomber
The Mad Executioners
Mademoiselle
Maniac Warriors
Midnight 2: Sex, Death, and
  Videotape
Midnight Fear
Mommie Dearest

Mondo Balardo
Most Wanted
Mother's Boys
Moving Targets
Murder Elite
Murderlust
The Naked Flame
Naked Massacre
The Neighbor
Past Midnight
Perfect Family
Perfect Victims
Play Nice
Playgirl Killer
Poison Ivy
Pretty Poison▶
Psycho▶
Psycho 2
Psycho 3
Psycho 4: The Beginning
Psycho Girls
Psychos in Love
Quake
Rampage
Relentless
Repulsion▶
Reservoir Dogs▶
Ricochet▶
Roadkill
The Sadist
Savage Abduction
The Sea Wolf▶
Seven Hours to Judgment
The Shining
The Silencer
Single White Female
Small Kill
Speed▶
The Stepfather▶
Stepfather 2: Make Room for
  Daddy
Stepfather 3: Father's Day
Still Life
Stripped to Kill
Sweet Hostage
Tainted Blood
The Taking of Beverly Hills
Ted & Venus
The Temp
The Tenant▶
Tetsuo: The Iron Man
Thirteenth Day of Christmas
Three the Hard Way
Twin Peaks: Fire Walk with
  Me
The Two Mrs. Carrolls
Unlawful Entry
The Vanishing
Vice Squad
Violence at Noon▶
Voyage
What Ever Happened to Baby
  Jane?▶
When a Stranger Calls Back
Whispers
White Heat▶
Writer's Block
The Zombie Army

Puppets

see also *Killer Toys; Toys*
Alice in Wonderland
The Dark Crystal▶
Devil Doll
Early Russian Cinema, Vol. 3:
  Starewicz's Fantasies
Faust
The Great Gabbo
The Great Rupert▶
Lili▶
Magic
Pinocchio▶
Puppet Master
Puppet Master 2
Puppet Master 4

Pure Ego Vehicles

see also *Big Budget
  Stinkers; Macho Men;
  Rock Stars on Film*
The Adventures of Ford
  Fairlane

Air America
Assault of the Rebel Girls
Charade
Conan the Destroyer
The Dead Pool
Harlem Nights
Hello, Dolly!
Hudson Hawk
Jazz Singer
Last Action Hero
Le Repos du Guerrier
Marie Antoinette
Modern Love
On Deadly Ground
Purple Rain
Rambo 3
Richard Petty Story
Running Out of Luck
Sidekicks
SnakeEater
Sophia Loren: Her Own Story
Staying Alive
Sweet Country Road
Tarzan, the Ape Man
Thank Your Lucky Stars▶
To Hell and Back
Torch Song
200 Motels
Under the Cherry Moon
What Comes Around
Wildcats
The Wizard of Speed and
  Time
Yes, Giorgio

Queens

see *Royalty*

Race Against Time

Acceptable Risks
Alien Space Avenger
The Andromeda Strain
Bitter Harvest
Chain Reaction
The China Syndrome▶
Coma▶
D.O.A.▶
D.O.A.
Fail-Safe▶
Germicide
Grand Tour: Disaster in Time
Hell Commandos
Jet Over the Atlantic
Killer on Board
Last Flight Out: A True Story
Lorenzo's Oil▶
Once Upon a Forest
Panic in Echo Park
Panic in the Streets▶
Prisoner in the Middle
Pursuit▶
The Silver Streak
Somebody Has to Shoot the
  Picture▶
The Taking of Beverly Hills
Time is Running Out
Time Lock
WarGames

Radio

see also *Mass Media*
Airheads
Bad Channels
Breakfast in Hollywood
Carefree▶
Choose Me▶
Citizens Band▶
City in Panic
Comfort and Joy▶
The Couch Trip
Danger on the Air
Dirty Mind of Young Sally
Empire of the Air: The Men
  Who Made Radio
The Fisher King▶
FM
Freeway
Girls Night Out
Good Morning, Vietnam▶
The Great American
  Broadcast▶

The Hucksters▶
The Jackpot
The Key Man
Laser Moon
The Last Radio Station
Look Who's Laughing
The Man Who Came to
  Dinner▶
My Dream is Yours
The Next Voice You Hear
Night Rhythms
No Trace
Old Barn Dance
On the Air Live with Captain
  Midnight
Once Upon a Honeymoon
Open House
People Are Funny
People's Choice
The Phantom Broadcast
Pot O' Gold
Psycho 4: The Beginning
Pump Up the Volume
Rachel River
Radio Days▶
Rebecca of Sunnybrook Farm
Sexual Response
Sleepless in Seattle▶
Straight Talk
Strike Up the Band
Talk Radio▶
There Goes Kelly
Up in the Air
Whistling in Brooklyn
Who Done It?
WKRP in Cincinnati, Vol. 1
Zoo Radio

Rags to Riches

see also *Price of Fame;
  Wrong Side of the Tracks*
The Abe Lincoln of Ninth
  Avenue
Aladdin▶
All the King's Men▶
The Amorous Adventures of
  Moll Flanders
Annie
Better Late Than Never
The Beverly Hillbillies
Blank Check
Body Slam
Breaking Glass
Brewster's Millions
The Buddy Holly Story▶
Callie and Son
Can You Hear the Laughter?
  The Story of Freddie Prinze
Christmas in July▶
Citizen Kane▶
Coal Miner's Daughter▶
Covergirl
Craig's Wife▶
Daddy Long Legs▶
Dangerous When Wet
Darling▶
Dodsworth▶
Dreamer
Drifting Souls
Emperor Jones
Fifth Avenue Girl
Footlight Parade▶
For Richer, For Poorer
Forever Amber
Give a Girl a Break
The Great Rupert▶
Hero▶
Honeyboy
The Hudsucker Proxy▶
I Love Melvin
It Could Happen to You
Jailhouse Rock▶
The Jerk
Jimmy Hollywood
Joseph Andrews
Kept Husbands
A Kid for Two Farthings
Kipps▶
La Violetera
Lady for a Day▶
Lady Grey
The Last American Hero▶

The Last Laugh▶
Laurel & Hardy: Below Zero
Lenny▶
Lili▶
Little Lord Fauntleroy▶
Little Lord Fauntleroy
Livin' Large
Lots of Luck
Love Nest
Lucky Partners
Macario
The Mambo Kings▶
The Manions of America
Mannequin
Meet John Doe▶
Miss Melody Jones
Mrs. Parkington
Mr. Billion
Money for Nothing
My Fair Lady▶
New York's Finest
The Object of Beauty▶
One in a Million: The Ron LaFlore Story
Only One Night
The Patsy
The Pearl▶
Peddlin' in Society
Possessed
Power
Pride of the Clan
The Prince and the Pauper▶
The Prince and the Pauper
The Prince and the Showgirl
Princess Tam Tam▶
Pygmalion▶
Rebecca of Sunnybrook Farm
Rocky▶
Scarlet Dawn
Scruples
The Secret of My Success
Sepia Cinderella
The Sin of Harold Diddlebock
The Sin of Madelon Claudet▶
Sing Your Worries Away
Speak Easily
The Stork Club
Straight Talk
Striker's Mountain
Sweet Adeline
Sweet Hearts Dance
The Tall Guy▶
Tennessee Stallion
Three Coins in the Fountain
The Toast of New Orleans
Toast of New York▶
Trading Places
Trois Couleurs: Blanc▶
The Unsinkable Molly Brown▶
What Price Hollywood?▶
Working Girl▶
Ziegfeld Girl▶

Rape

see also *Sexual Abuse*
The Accused▶
Act of Vengeance
The Adventurers
American Commandos
And Justice for All
Awakening of Candra
Backlash
Bad Lieutenant▶
The Beast Within
Blind Justice
Blue Desert▶
Born Innocent
Broken Badge▶
Bullies
Caged Terror
Cast the First Stone
Casualties of War▶
Certain Sacrifice
Chain Gang Women
Class of 1984
Code of Honor
Convicted
Coward of the County
Deadline Assault
Deadly Daphne's Revenge
Deadly Darling
Deadly Twins

Death Blow
Death Wish
Deep in the Heart
Demented
The Desperados
Diary of a Lost Girl
Diary of a Teenage Hitchhiker
Emmanuelle's Daughter
The Entity
Extremities
Flesh and Blood
Forbidden Sun
Forced Entry
Free, White, and 21
From the Life of the Marionettes▶
The Furious Avenger
Gentle Savage
Guncrazy
Hands of a Stranger
Hannie Caulder
Heat of the Flame
His Name was King
Home Before Midnight
The Hooked Generation
The Hotel New Hampshire
I Spit on Your Grave
I'm the One You're Looking For
In Trouble
It's Alive▶
Jackson County Jail
Jailbait: Betrayed By Innocence
Judge Horton and the Scottsboro Boys
Kiss of a Killer
The Ladies Club
Landscape in the Mist▶
Lethal Woman
Lipstick
Liquid Sky▶
Ms. 45▶
Mrs. R's Daughter
Most Wanted
Motor Psycho
Multiple Maniacs
Naked Vengeance
Necromancer: Satan's Servant
Night of the Demon
Northville Cemetery Massacre
Olivier, Olivier▶
Open Doors▶
A Passage to India▶
The Phantom of Soho
Positive I.D.
Purgatory
Rage▶
The Ramrodder
Rape and Marriage: The Rideout Case
Rape of Love
Rashomon▶
Rider on the Rain▶
Screamer
Sex Crimes
Shame
The Shaming
She Came on the Bus
Short Fuse
Silent Witness
Slashed Dreams
A Stranger is Watching
Straw Dogs▶
Streets
Sudden Death
Sudden Impact
Tainted
Time to Kill
To Kill a Mockingbird▶
To Kill a Stranger
The Tormentors
Trespasses
Vengeance of the Snowmaid
Violated
Violent Ones
The Violent Years
When He's Not a Stranger▶
Wild Riders
The Wind▶
The Young One

Rebel With a Cause

see also *Rebel Without a Cause*
Acceptable Risks
The Accused▶
Ace High
The Adventures of Robin Hood▶
Afterburn▶
Alice's Restaurant
American Tiger
Ann Vickers
The Applegates
As Young As You Feel▶
The Attic: The Hiding of Anne Frank
Billy Jack
The Blob
Bloody Che Contra
Blue Collar▶
Born Losers
Boyz N the Hood▶
Brubaker▶
Burglar▶
The Burmese Harp▶
The China Syndrome▶
Courage▶
Courageous Dr. Christian
Crime of Honor
Dark Rider
Daybreak
Dead Poets Society▶
Deadly Business▶
Deadly Stranger
Die Hard▶
Die Hard 2: Die Harder▶
A Dream for Christmas▶
Dust▶
East of Eden▶
East of Eden
Easy Wheels
Exiled in America
The Fighter▶
The Final Alliance
The Firing Line
The $5.20 an Hour Dream
Flesh and the Spur
Flight of the Intruder
The Fugitive▶
The Gambling Samurai
Game of Survival
Gandhi▶
Gorillas in the Mist▶
Guess Who's Coming to Dinner▶
Hair▶
Hardcore
Hidden City
In the Name of the Father▶
Iron Horsemen
Iron Thunder
James Dean Story
Jesse
Joe Kidd
Johnny Firecloud
Katherine
Killing of Randy Webster
Knights of the City
Kung Fu
La Marseillaise▶
The Last American Hero▶
Lawrence of Arabia▶
Legend of Billie Jean
Legend of Earl Durand
Legend of the Lone Ranger
Little Tough Guy
Lois Gibbs and the Love Canal
The Loneliness of the Long Distance Runner▶
Lust for Life▶
Luther
Man of Marble▶
The Manhattan Project
Marie▶
Memories of Underdevelopment
Mr. Smith Goes to Washington▶
Mountain Man
Network▶
Night of Evil

Norma Rae▶
Northern Lights▶
Odd Man Out▶
One-Eyed Jacks▶
One Man Jury
One Man's War
Original Intent
Overdrawn at the Memory Bank
Paths of Glory▶
Patty Hearst
Plutonium Baby
The Principal
Project X
Punk Rock Movie
Quarantine
A Raisin in the Sun▶
Robin Hood: Prince of Thieves▶
Roe vs. Wade▶
Rooster: Spurs of Death!
Sakharov▶
Samaritan: The Mitch Snyder Story▶
The Sand Pebbles▶
Sansho the Bailiff▶
Save the Lady
The Scarlet Pimpernel▶
Serpico▶
The Shock
Silkwood▶
Sins of Rome
Somebody Has to Shoot the Picture▶
Stay Away, Joe
The Stranger Wore a Gun
Sympathy for the Devil
Taffin
This Land is Mine▶
Tin Star▶
To Kill a Priest
Trial of the Catonsville Nine
True Believer
Under Western Stars
Vengeance
WarGames
The Westerner▶
When a Man Rides Alone
Wisdom

Rebel Without a Cause

see also *Rebel With a Cause*
Across the Tracks
All Night Long▶
Badlands▶
A Boy and His Dog
The Boys Next Door
Breathless▶
Breathless
Cheech and Chong's Up in Smoke
A Clockwork Orange▶
Cool As Ice
The Cruel Story of Youth▶
Dino
Easy Rider▶
The Electric Horseman
Ferris Bueller's Day Off▶
Five Easy Pieces▶
The Fugitive Kind
Fury to Freedom: The Life Story of Raul Ries
Girls' Town
Going Places▶
Gore Vidal's Billy the Kid
Great Missouri Raid
Guncrazy
Heart Beat
Hud▶
I Was a Teenage Werewolf
If...▶
James Dean
Just for the Hell of It
Leather Jackets
The Little Valentino
Lost Angels
On the Edge: The Survival of Dana
Over the Edge▶
Petit Con

Presumed Guilty
Pump Up the Volume
Rambo: First Blood, Part 2
Rambo 3
Rebel High
Rebel Rousers
Rebel Without a Cause▶
Reckless
Road House
Rocky 4
September 30, 1955
sex, lies and videotape▶
Snow Kill
Suburbia
Summer Camp Nightmare
That Was Then...This Is Now
3:15—The Moment of Truth
Thunder Road▶
Top Gun
The Violent Years
West Side Story▶
The Wild Angels
The Wild One▶
The Wild Ride

Red Scare

Arsenal▶
Baltic Deputy▶
The Bamboo Saucer
Battle Beneath the Earth
Chapayev▶
China Cry
China, My Sorrow
Coming Out of the Ice▶
Comment Ca Va?
The Commies are Coming, the Commies are Coming
Commissar▶
Comrade X
Conspirator
Death of a Bureaucrat▶
Earth▶
Eminent Domain
Fellow Traveler▶
Golden Gate
The Great Armored Car Swindle
Guilty by Suspicion
Guilty of Treason
Hands Up▶
Hawthorne of the USA
Indochine▶
The Inner Circle▶
The Interrogation▶
Invasion U.S.A.
Jet Pilot
Little World of Don Camillo▶
Man of Iron▶
Man of Marble▶
Mandela▶
Mother Kusters Goes to Heaven▶
Mother of Kings
Never Let Me Go
Nicholas and Alexandra
Night Crossing
Night Flight from Moscow
The Oak
Oh, Bloody Life!
Open Doors▶
The Red Menace
Red Nightmare
Reds▶
Requiem for Dominic▶
Revolution! A Red Comedy▶
The She-Beast
Sideburns
Strike▶
The Theme▶
Thoughts are Free▶
Tito and Me▶
Tobor the Great
The Ugly American
Uranus▶
When Father was Away on Business▶

Religion

see also *Islam; Judaism; Missionaries; Nuns & Priests; Religious Epics; Saints*
Abduction of St. Anne
Absolution
Androcles and the Lion
Angel Baby
Augustine of Hippo▶
Bernadette
The Birch Interval
The Blasphemer
Blood of Jesus
Body and Soul
Brother Sun, Sister Moon
Brothers in Arms
Caligari's Cure▶
Camila▶
Catholics▶
Chariots of Fire▶
The Church
Conquest of Space
The Courageous Mr. Penn
Crimes of Passion▶
Cry from the Mountain
Day of Judgment
Day of Triumph
Def by Temptation
Devi▶
The Devil at 4 O'Clock
The Disappearance of Aimee▶
Dr. Syn
Dr. Syn, Alias the Scarecrow
A Dream for Christmas▶
El Cid▶
El Cristo de los Milagros
El: This Strange Passion▶
Emanon
The Favor, the Watch, & the Very Big Fish
The Fiend
Final Judgement
The Flowers of St. Francis▶
Francesco
Friendly Persuasion▶
The Ghoul
Glory! Glory!▶
Go Down Death
The Godfather, Part 3▶
God's Gun
Greaser's Palace
The Greatest Story Ever Told
Green Pastures▶
The Guyana Tragedy: The Story of Jim Jones
Hail Mary
Hallelujah!▶
Hazel's People
Heavens Above▶
Hellfire
The Hoodlum Priest▶
Household Saints▶
In the Line of Duty: Ambush in Waco
Inherit the Wind▶
The Inquiry
Invasion of the Space Preachers
Iron Horsemen
Jesus
Jesus Christ, Superstar▶
Jesus of Nazareth
Jesus of Nazareth▶
The Jesus Trip
Joan of Arc
Joni
Klondike Annie
La Chartreuse de Parme
The Last Temptation of Christ▶
Laughing Sinners
Leap of Faith
Leaves from Satan's Book
The Light of Faith
Little Buddha
Little Church Around the Corner
The Littlest Angel
Love and Faith▶
Luther

Major Barbara▶
A Man Called Peter▶
Marjoe
Martin Luther
The Meeting: Eddie Finds a Home
The Milky Way▶
The Miracle▶
Miracle in Rome
Miracle of Our Lady of Fatima
Mohammed: Messenger of God
Monsieur Vincent▶
Monsignor Quixote
Monty Python's Life of Brian▶
A Mormon Maid
The Next Voice You Hear
The Night of the Iguana▶
One Man's Way
Ordet▶
Padre Nuestro
Pass the Ammo
The Passion of Joan of Arc▶
The Passover Plot
The Penitent
Pray TV
Prisoner of Rio
The Private Secretary
The Prodigal Planet
Promised a Miracle
Quo Vadis▶
Quo Vadis
Rain
The Rapture
Red Planet Mars
Resurrection▶
Return to Paradise
The Robe
Romero
Sacrilege
St. Benny the Dip
Saint Joan
Salome
Salvation!
Sanctuary of Fear
Sebastiane▶
Shadowlands▶
Shiokari Pass
The Sky Pilot
The Song of Bernadette▶
Susan and God▶
This Stuff'll Kill Ya!
Through a Glass Darkly▶
Tournament
Trapped by the Mormons
The Vision
Where Angels Go, Trouble Follows
Whistle Down the Wind▶
Whistling in the Dark▶
Whitcomb's War
The White Rose▶
Wholly Moses!
The Winter Light▶
Wise Blood▶
Witness▶
The Word
The Worldly Madonna

Religious Epics

see also *Religion*
The Agony and the Ecstasy
The Babylon Story from ''Intolerance''▶
Barabbas
Ben-Hur▶
The Bible...In the Beginning▶
Cleopatra
David and Bathsheba▶
Day of Triumph
Demetrius and the Gladiators
The Egyptian
El Cid▶
Exodus▶
Fourth Wise Man
The Gospel According to St. Matthew▶
Great Leaders of the Bibles
Herod the Great
In the Name of the Pope-King▶
The Inquiry

Jesus Christ, Superstar▶
Jesus of Nazareth
Joseph & His Brethren
Judith of Bethulia▶
King David
King of Kings
The King of Kings▶
The Last Supper▶
Legal Tender
Mary and Joseph: A Story of Faith
The Messiah▶
Moses
Nativity
Nefertiti, Queen of the Nile
The Prodigal
Rachel's Man
The Robe
Salome
Samson and Delilah▶
Samson and Delilah
Saul and David
The Silver Chalice
Sin of Adam & Eve
Sins of Jezebel
Sodom and Gomorrah
Solomon and Sheba
The Song of Bernadette▶
The Story of David▶
The Story of Jacob & Joseph▶
The Story of Ruth
The Sword and the Cross
The Ten Commandments
The Ten Commandments▶

Renegade Body Parts

see also *Horror*
The Addams Family
Addams Family Values
The Beast with Five Fingers
Blood of Ghastly Horror
Body Parts
The Brain That Wouldn't Die
The Crawling Eye
The Crawling Hand
Demonoid, Messenger of Death
Doctor Butcher M.D.
The Hand▶
Hands of a Stranger
The Hands of Orlac
How to Get Ahead in Advertising▶
Mindkiller
Severed Ties
Waxwork 2: Lost in Time

Repressed Men

see also *Men*
The Age of Innocence▶
Bitter Moon
Falling Down
Maurice▶
The Remains of the Day▶
Shadowlands▶
Sirens▶

Rescue Missions

see also *Rescue Missions Involving Time Travel*
Berlin Tunnel 21
Boomerang
Breakout
Caged Fear
The Children
Commando▶
Crossfire
Daredevils of the Red Circle
Dark Mountain
Desperate Women
Die Hard▶
Die Hard 2: Die Harder▶
The Dirty Dozen: The Deadly Mission
Dragonworld
El Zorro Blanco
Ernest Scared Stupid
The Ewok Adventure
Executioner of Venice
Force: Five

Free Willy
Hard Ticket to Hawaii
High Velocity
Hired to Kill
Honeybaby
The Inn of the Sixth Happiness▶
Jenny's War
Killing Streets
The Lone Runner
The Losers
The Magnificent Seven▶
Missing in Action
Missing in Action 2: The Beginning
Navy SEALS
Pray for Death
Raid on Entebbe▶
Rambo: First Blood, Part 2
The Rescue
Rescue Me
Return of Chandu
Revenge of the Barbarians
The Sea Shall Not Have Them
The Searchers▶
Seven Samurai▶
The Slender Thread▶
The Taking of Flight 847: The Uli Derickson Story▶
A Thousand Heroes
Three Days to a Kill
Thunder in Paradise
Uncommon Valor
The Yakuza

Rescue Missions Involving Time Travel

see also *Rescue Missions*
Back to the Future▶
Back to the Future, Part 2
Back to the Future, Part 3▶
Bill & Ted's Excellent Adventure
Maximum Breakout
Millenium
The Navigator▶
Star Trek 4: The Voyage Home▶
Superman: The Movie▶
The Terminator▶
Terminator 2: Judgment Day▶
Time After Time▶
Trancers 2: The Return of Jack Deth

Revenge

see also *Vigilantes*
Act of Aggression
Act of Passion: The Lost Honor of Kathryn Beck
Act of Vengeance
An Actor's Revenge
Adios, Hombre
The Adventurers
Against the Drunken Cat Paws
The Alchemist
Alien Seed
All Dogs Go to Heaven
American Commandos
American Eagle
American Samurai
Anatomy of a Psycho
Angel and the Badman▶
Angel of Destruction
Angel Square
Angels from Hell
Appointment with Crime
Archer: The Fugitive from the Empire
Arizona Terror
Asylum
Attack of the 50 Ft. Woman
Avenged
Avenging Angel
Avenging Force
Back in Action
Back to Back
Ballad of Cable Hogue▶

The Ballad of the Sad Cafe
Bandits
Banzai Runner
The Baron
Basket Case▶
The Beast with Five Fingers
The Beguiled▶
Bell from Hell
Benefit of the Doubt
Best of the Best 2
Big Jake
Black Arrow▶
The Black Arrow
Black Cobra
Black Dragon's Revenge
The Black Hand▶
The Black Klansman
The Black Pirate▶
The Black Raven
The Black Six
Black Sunday▶
A Black Veil for Lisa
Blackbelt 2: Fatal Force
Blind Vengeance
Blood and Guns
Blood for a Silver Dollar
Blood on the Mountain
Blood Red
Blood Ring
Bloodfist
Bloodmatch
Bloody Birthday
The Bloody Fight
The Blue Knight
The Blue Lamp▶
Boiling Point
Border Rangers
Born Invincible
Bounty Hunters
Bounty Tracker
Branded a Coward
Bride of Killer Nerd
Bronze Buckaroo
Brotherhood of Justice
Bruce Li the Invincible
The Brute Man
Bulldance
Bulldog Courage
Bullet for Sandoval
Bullies
The Burning
Bury Me an Angel
Cadillac Man
Caged Terror
Cape Fear▶
The Caravan Trail
Carolina Skeletons
Carson City Kid
Cartouche▶
Certain Sacrifice
Chain Gang Women
The Chair
Challenge
Chan is Missing▶
The Chase
Chisum
Chrome and Hot Leather
Class of 1984
Clayton County Line
Cobra
Cobra Against Ninja
Code Name: Zebra
Code of Honor
Coffy
Cold Eyes of Fear
Cold Justice
Cold Steel
Cold Sweat
Cole Justice
Commando Invasion
Conflict of Interest
Conqueror & the Empress
Cornered▶
The Count of Monte Cristo
The Count of Monte Cristo▶
The Count of Monte Cristo
The Count of the Old Town
The Courier
The Cowboys▶
Crack House
Crazed Cop
Creepers

Crimebusters
The Crow
Cry Danger▶
Cry of the Innocent▶
The Cry of the Owl
Cry Vengeance
Curse of the Devil
Daddy-O
Daddy's Gone A-Hunting▶
Danger Zone 2
Dangerous Obsession
Dangerous Orphans
Dark August
Dark River: A Father's Revenge
Darkman▶
Daughter of the Dragon
DaVinci's War
Dawn Rider
The Day the Women Got Even
Dead Boyz Can't Fly
Dead Man's Revenge
Dead on the Money
Deadly Daphne's Revenge
Deadly Darling
Deadly Game
Deadly Reactor
The Deadly Secret
Deadly Sting
The Deadly Trackers
Deadly Twins
Deadly Vengeance
Deadly Weapon
Death Blow
Death Magic
Death Row Diner
Death Wish
Death Wish 2
Death Wish 3
Deep in the Heart
Demented
Demon Warrior
Demon Witch Child
The Demons
Demonwarp
Despedida de Casada
The Desperados
Desperate Crimes
Devastator
Devil Times Five
Devil Woman
Devil's Canyon
The Devil's Mistress
The Devil's Possessed
Devonsville Terror
The Diabolical Dr. Z
Diamond Ninja Force
Die! Die! My Darling!
Dingaka
Dinner at the Ritz
Diplomatic Immunity
Dirty Harry▶
The Divine Enforcer
Dixie Dynamite
Do or Die
Dr. Syn, Alias the Scarecrow
Dr. Terror's House of Horrors
Dolemite
Double Exposure
The Double Negative
Double Revenge
Driven to Kill
Drums of Jeopardy
Dudes
Duel in the Eclipse
Dynasty
Eagles Attack at Dawn
Easy Kill
Edge of Darkness
The Eiger Sanction
El Barbaro
El Fugitivo
El Hombre de la Furia
El Sabor de la Venganza
El Zorro Vengador
The Eliminators
Emmanuelle, the Queen
The Empire of Passion▶
The Equalizer: Memories of Manon
Escape
The Evil That Men Do

Evilspeak
Ex-Cop
The Execution
The Executioner, Part 2: Frozen Scream
Exterminator
Exterminator 2
Extreme Vengeance
Extremities
An Eye for an Eye
Eye of the Eagle 2
Eye of the Tiger
Fair Game
The Fall of the House of Usher
The Fall of the House of Usher▶
The Fall of the House of Usher
Falling Down
Far Country▶
Fight for Us
Fight for Your Life
The Fighter▶
Fighting Back
The Fighting Legion
Fighting Mad
Final Impact
Final Mission
Fine Gold
Fiorile
Firecracker
Fist Fighter
Fist of Honor
Fists of Blood
Flesh and Blood
Flesh and the Spur
Flesh Feast
Fleshburn
Fog Island
For Your Eyes Only▶
Forbidden Sun
Force of Evil
Forced Vengeance
Forgotten Warrior
The Four Musketeers▶
Frame Up
Framed
Freaks▶
Freeway
Frightmare
Frogs
The Fugitive: The Final Episode
Full Contact
Full Metal Ninja
Funland
The Furious Avenger
Future Kill
''G'' Men
Galloping Dynamite
The Gambling Samurai
Gangs, Inc.
Garringo
Gator Bait 2: Cajun Justice
Gentleman from Dixie
Getting Even
The Ghost
Ghost Dance
The Ghost of Yotsuya
Ghostriders
The Godfather▶
The Godfather 1902-1959: The Complete Epic▶
The Godfather, Part 2▶
God's Gun
Gone with the West
Grave of the Vampire
The Graveyard
The Great Hunter
Green Mansions
Gunplay
Gunsmoke: Return to Dodge
Hamlet▶
Hang 'Em High
Hannie Caulder
Hard to Kill
Hardcase and Fist
The Haunted Palace
HauntedWeen
Hawkeye
He Who Gets Slapped▶
Headless Eyes
Heat Street

The Heist
Hell Hunters
Hell on Frisco Bay
Hellbent
Hello Mary Lou: Prom Night 2
Hell's Angels '69
Hennessy
Hi-Riders
The Hidden Room▶
High Command
High Noon▶
Hired Hand
Hit!
Hit & Run
Hog Wild
Homeboy
Hornet's Nest
Horror Rises from the Tomb
The Horror Show
Hot Lead
Hour of the Gun
House Across the Bay
A House In The Hills
House of Horrors
House of Strangers▶
How to Make a Monster
Human Beasts
The Human Factor
Hunter
I Drink Your Blood
I Married a Witch▶
I Met a Murderer
I Spit on Your Grave
Igor & the Lunatics
Illicit Behavior
I'm the One You're Looking For
In a Glass Cage
In Deadly Heat
In the Realm of Passion
In Your Face
The Indestructible Man
Inn of the Damned
An Innocent Man
Innocent Victim
Inquisition
Instant Justice
The Invisible Man's Revenge
Iron Dragon Strikes Back
Ironheart
Jailbird's Vacation
The Jayhawkers
Jenny Lamour
Jessie's Girls
The Jitters
Johnny Handsome▶
Joshua
Jubal
The Jungle Trap
Kansas City Confidential▶
The Karate Kid: Part 2
Karate Warrior
Kemek
Kickboxer 2: The Road Back
Kid
Kid Colter
Kid Vengeance
Kidnap Syndicate
Kill Alex Kill
Kill Line
Killcrazy
The Killing Kind
The Killing Zone
King Boxer
The King of the Kickboxers
King of the Pecos
Kingfisher the Killer
Kiss Daddy Goodbye
Kuffs
L.A. Bounty
La Choca
L.A. Crackdown
La Generala
L.A. Heat
La Passante▶
La Vengeance d'une Femme
L.A. Vice
The Ladies Club
Lady Avenger
Lady Dragon
Lady Dragon 2
The Lady in White▶

Lady Mobster
Lady Scarface/The Threat
Lady Street Fighter
L'Annee des Meduses
Laserblast
Last Bullet
The Last Days of Dolwyn
The Last Hour
Last House on the Left
The Last Reunion
Last Train from Gun Hill▶
The Late Show▶
Law of the Sea
Legend of the Northwest
License to Kill▶
Lionheart
The Lion's Share
Lipstick
Little Moon & Jud McGraw
The Long Weekend
Lorna Doone
Los Jinetes de la Bruja
Lovely...But Deadly
Lure of the Sila
Macbeth▶
Macbeth
Macho Callahan
Mad Dog
Mad Max▶
Magdalene
Make a Million
Make Haste to Live
The Man from Laramie▶
The Man in the Iron Mask▶
Man in the Wilderness
The Man That Corrupted Hadleyburg
The Man They Could Not Hang
The Manhandlers
Manhunt
Maniac
Manon of the Spring▶
Marathon Man▶
Marvelous Stunts of Kung Fu
The Mask▶
Massacre at Central High
The Match Factory Girl▶
McBain
McQ
Mean Machine
Medea
Memories of Murder
Men...▶
The Messenger
Miami Cops
Miami Vendetta
Midnite Spares
Millie
Mind Trap
Ms. 45▶
Missing Pieces
Mission Inferno
Model by Day
Molly and Gina
The Monster and the Girl
Monte Walsh▶
Mooncussers
Moonshine County Express
Motor Psycho
The Mummy▶
Murder on Lenox Avenue
Murphy's Law
Murphy's War
Nails
The Naked Angels
Naked Vengeance
The Naked Witch
Nasty Hero
Navajo Joe
Necromancer: Satan's Servant
The Nesting
Nevada Smith
Never Pick Up a Stranger
The New Frontier
The New Kids
The Newlydeads
Next of Kin
Nido de Aguilas
Night Creature
The Night Visitor

Nightmare Castle
Nightmare in Wax
Ninja Nightmare
No Safe Haven
Nomad Riders
Nowhere to Run
Obsessed
Offerings
Oklahoma Kid▶
Old Boyfriends
Old Gun▶
Olivia
On Dangerous Ground▶
One Arabian Night▶
One Armed Executioner
One Deadly Summer▶
One-Eyed Jacks▶
One Man's War
One Russian Summer
Orca
Orlak, the Hell of Frankenstein
The Other Side of Midnight
Out for Blood
Out for Justice
Outlaw Force
The Outlaw Josey Wales▶
Outrage!
Overkill
Pathfinder▶
Patriot Games▶
Pay Off
Payback
Payoff
Pecos Kid
Pepi, Luci, Bom and Other Girls on the Heap
The Perfect Bride
The Perfect Weapon
The Phantom Bullet
The Phantom of Soho
Phantom of the Paradise
The Pit
Platoon the Warriors
Play Dead
Pledge Night
Plutonium Baby
Point Blank
Positive I.D.
Posse▶
Possession: Until Death Do You Part
The Power of the Ninjitsu
Premature Burial
President's Target
Prison
Prom Night
The Prowler
Psychic Killer
Psycho Girls
Psychopath
Pumpkinhead
The Punisher
Puppet Master 3: Toulon's Revenge
Pursued▶
Pushed to the Limit
Queen Boxer
The Quick and the Dead
Quiet Cool
Quiet Fire
Rage
Rainbow Ranch
Rapid Fire
The Raven▶
Relentless
Renegade Ninja
Renegades
Reservoir Dogs▶
The Restless Breed
Retribution
Return of Frank James▶
Return of the Evil Dead
The Return of the Musketeers
Return of the Seven
Return of the Vampire
Return of Wildfire
Return to Macon County
Revenge
Revenge of a Kabuki Actor
Revenge of the Barbarians
Revenge of the Nerds

Revenge of the Nerds 2:
  Nerds in Paradise
Revenge of the Radioactive
  Reporter
Revenge of the Red Baron
The Revenge Rider
Revolt of the Zombies
Revolver
Ricco
Ricochet▶
Ride Lonesome
Ride to Glory
Ringside
Rio Lobo
Rip Roarin' Buckaroo
Rock House
Rolling Thunder
Rolling Vengeance
Romola
Rose of Rio Grande
Round Numbers
Ruby Gentry
Rulers of the City
Runaways
Rustler's Paradise
Sacrilege
The Samurai
Samurai Reincarnation
The Satan Killer
Savage Drums
Savage Guns
Savage Instinct
Savage Justice
Savage Run▶
Savage Streets
Scam
Scorned
Scream Dream
Screamer
Search and Destroy
Second Victory
The Secret Four
Seven Hours to Judgment
The Seven-Ups
Severed Ties
Sex Crimes
The Shadow Man
Shame
Shaolin Vengence
Shaolin Warrior
The She-Beast
She-Devil
She Devils in Chains
She-Freak
The Shooting▶
Short Eyes▶
The Showdown
Showdown
Silent Night, Deadly Night 2
Simba▶
Simple Justice
The Sin of Harold Diddlebock
Sisters of Death
Six Shootin' Sheriff
Sizzle
Slaughter
Slaughter's Big Ripoff
Slayground
Sleeping with the Enemy
Sloane
A Small Town in Texas
Smart Money
Smoke in the Wind
SnakeEater
SnakeEater 3: His Law
Soldier Blue
Soldier's Fortune
Sometimes They Come Back
Sons of Katie Elder▶
Sorority Girl
Soul Vengeance
Sound of Murder
Space Ninja: Sword of the
  Space Ark
Special Investigator
Speeding Up Time
The Spoilers▶
Stanley
Star Trek 2: The Wrath of
  Khan▶
Steel and Lace
Steel Fisted Dragon

Steele Justice
The Sting 2
Strange Shadows in an Empty
  Room
Stranger in Paso Bravo
Strangler of the Swamp
Straw Dogs▶
Street Hunter
Street War
Striker
Sudden Death
Sudden Impact
Super Force
The Supernaturals
Sweet Justice
Sweet Poison
Sweet Revenge
Swift Justice
Sword of Gideon
Sword of Venus
Take Two
Talion
Taste the Blood of Dracula
Tattooed Hit Man
Tenement
Terror Creatures from the
  Grave
Texas Kid
Theatre of Blood▶
Things
This Gun for Hire▶
This Man Must Die▶
Thou Shalt Not Kill...Except
Threat
Three Husbands
Three in the Cellar
Thunder in the Desert
Thunder Warrior 3
Tillie's Punctured Romance
A Time of Destiny
Time to Die
To Be the Best
Today We Kill, Tomorrow We
  Die
Tombs of the Blind Dead
Top of the Heap
Tormented
The Tormentors
The Torture Chamber of Dr.
  Sadism
Toy Soldiers
The Trackers
Trapper County War
Trick or Treat
Trigger Tricks
Truck Turner
Turk 182!
24 Hours to Midnight
Twice a Judas
Twilight People
Twisted Brain
Twisted Nightmare
Two by Forsyth
Two Fathers' Justice
Two Graves to Kung-Fu
2000 Maniacs
Under the Gun
Underworld, U.S.A.▶
Unfaithfully Yours▶
Unfaithfully Yours
Unholy Four
The Unstoppable Man
Until They Get Me
Up River
Utu▶
Valmont▶
Vendetta
Vengeance
Vengeance of the Snowmaid
Vengeance of the Zombies
The Vernonia Incident
Vietnam, Texas
The Vigilantes are Coming
Viper
The Virgin Spring▶
Voodoo Black Exorcist
Walking Tall
Walking Tall: Part 2
Walking the Edge
The War Wagon▶
Water Rustlers
Waterfront

Weekend of Shadows▶
The Weirdo
West of Zanzibar
The White Sheik▶
Wild Gypsies
Wild Man
Wild Wheels
Wired to Kill
Without Honors
Wolf
Wolf Lake
The Women▶
Wonder Man
Write to Kill
X Marks the Spot
Young Warriors
Yuma
Zombie Lake
Zombie Nightmare

Revolutionary War
America/The Fall of Babylon▶
The Bastard
George Washington
The Howards of Virginia
John Paul Jones
Johnny Tremain & the Sons of
  Liberty
The Rebels
Revolution
The Seekers
1776▶
Sweet Liberty
The Time of Their Lives

Road Trip
**see also Bikers; Chases;
Fast Cars; Motor Vehicle
Dept.**
The Acid Eaters
Across the Great Divide
The Adventures of Huck
  Finn▶
Alice Doesn't Live Here
  Anymore
Alligator Eyes
Aloha, Bobby and Rose
American Autobahn
American Fabulous
Ariel▶
Armed for Action
Ashik Kerib▶
Bad Company▶
The Big Crimewave
Bingo
Blue De Ville
Blue Murder at St. Trinian's▶
Bolero
Bound for Glory▶
Boxcar Blues
Breaking the Rules
Bright Angel
Bronson's Revenge
Buck and the Preacher
Bustin' Loose▶
Butch Cassidy and the
  Sundance Kid▶
Bye Bye Brazil
Calendar Girl
Camilla▶
Candy Mountain
Cannonball
Cannonball Run
Cannonball Run 2
A Canterbury Tale▶
Changes
The Chase
Chasers
Cheech and Chong: Things
  Are Tough All Over
Clodhopper
Coast to Coast
The Concrete Cowboys
Cooperstown
Coupe de Ville
Crazy Mama
Crossroads
Cycle Vixens
Danzon▶
Delusion
Der Purimshpiler

Detour▶
The Devil Thumbs a Ride▶
The Devil Thumbs a Ride/
  Having Wonderful Crime
Diamonds on Wheels
Down by Law▶
Dutch
The Easy Life▶
Easy Rider▶
End of the Line
Endplay
Every Which Way But Loose
Fandango
Far Out Man
Father Hood
Finders Keepers
Flash & Firecat
Flight of the Innocent
Flim-Flam Man
Goodbye Pork Pie
Great Smokey Roadblock
The Great Texas Dynamite
  Chase
Greedy Terror
Harry and Tonto▶
Having Wonderful Crime
Heart Beat
Hell's Angels on Wheels
High Rolling in a Hot Corvette
Highway 61
Hitcher
Hitchhikers
Hollywood or Bust
Homer and Eddie
Homeward Bound: The
  Incredible Journey▶
Honkytonk Man
Huck and the King of Hearts
Il Sorpasso
The Incredible Journey
Into the Night
Into the West▶
It Takes Two
Jornada de Muerte
Josh and S.A.M.
The Journey of Natty Gann▶
Joy Ride to Nowhere
Joyride
The Judge Steps Out
Kalifornia
Kings of the Road—In the
  Course of Time▶
Kiss My Grits
La Petite Bande
La Strada▶
Ladies on the Rocks
Landscape in the Mist▶
Leaving Normal
Leningrad Cowboys Go
  America
Les Rendez-vous D'Anna
Lion of Africa
The Living End
Loners
The Long Haul
Loose Connections
Lost in America▶
Made in USA
Me and the Kid
Midnight Run▶
Mob Story
More
The Music of Chance
My Own Private Idaho▶
National Lampoon's
  Vacation▶
Natural Born Killers
Neon City
Never on Tuesday
Night on Earth▶
No Place to Run
Out
Over the Hill
Paper Moon▶
The Passing of Evil
Patti Rocks▶
Pee Wee's Big Adventure▶
Pierrot le Fou▶
Pink Cadillac
Planes, Trains & Automobiles
Powwow Highway▶
Prime Target

Prison Train
Rain Man▶
The Rain People▶
Rainbow Bridge
The Reivers▶
Rescue Me
Rich Hall's Vanishing America
Ride in the Whirlwind
Road Games
The Road to Bali▶
The Road to Hong Kong
The Road to Lebanon
The Road to Morocco▶
The Road to Rio▶
The Road to Singapore
The Road to Utopia▶
The Road to Zanzibar▶
The Road Warrior▶
Roadie
Roadkill
Roadside Prophets
Rockin' Road Trip
Round Trip to Heaven
Rubin & Ed
The Runaway Bus
Running Hot
Sawdust & Tinsel▶
Scarecrow
September Gun
Sincerely Charlotte▶
Slither▶
Something Wild
Sorcerer
Spies Like Us
Starlight Hotel
Starman▶
Stay As You Are
Summer City
The Sure Thing▶
Thelma & Louise▶
Those Magnificent Men in
  Their Flying Machines▶
Three for the Road
Thumb Tripping
Tilt
Tokyo Pop
Traveling Man
Trouble Bound
True Romance
Twentieth Century▶
Two for the Road▶
Until The End of The World▶
The Way West
Weekend▶
Where the Eagle Flies
White Line Fever
Wild at Heart▶
The Wizard of Oz▶
The Wrong Man

Roaring '20s
Bare Knees
The Cotton Club▶
Eight Men Out▶
The Great Gatsby
Jazz Singer
Jazzman▶
The Moderns▶
The Roaring Twenties
Thoroughly Modern Millie
The Untouchables▶

Robots & Androids
**see also Technology-
Rampant**
Alien▶
Aliens▶
And You Thought Your
  Parents Were Weird!
Android
A.P.E.X.
Assassin
The Astro-Zombies
Bill & Ted's Bogus Journey
Blade Runner▶
Cherry 2000
Chopping Mall
Class of 1999
Class of 1999 2: The
  Substitute

The Creation of the
  Humanoids
Cyborg
Cyborg 2
Cyborg Cop
Daleks—Invasion Earth 2150
  A.D.
The Day the Earth Stood
  Still▶
Devil Girl from Mars
Dr. Goldfoot and the Bikini
  Machine
Doctor Satan's Robot
Doctor Who: An Unearthly
  Child
Doctor Who and the Daleks
Doctor Who: Cybermen—The
  Early Years
Doctor Who: Day of the
  Daleks
Doctor Who: Death to the
  Daleks
Doctor Who: Earthshock
Doctor Who: Pyramids of
  Mars
Doctor Who: Revenge of the
  Cybermen
Doctor Who: Robots of Death
Doctor Who: Shada
Doctor Who: Spearhead from
  Space
Doctor Who: Terror of the
  Zygons
Doctor Who: The Ark in Space
Doctor Who: The Brain of
  Morbius
Doctor Who: The Curse of
  Fenric
Doctor Who: The Deadly
  Assassin
Doctor Who: The Five Doctors
Doctor Who: The Hartnell
  Years
Doctor Who: The Mind
  Robber
Doctor Who: The Seeds of
  Death
Doctor Who: The Talons of
  Weng-Chiang
Doctor Who: The Three
  Doctors
Doctor Who: The Time
  Warrior
Doctor Who: The Troughton
  Years
Doctor Who: The War Games
Doctor Who: Tomb of the
  Cyberman
The Eliminators
The Empire Strikes Back▶
Eve of Destruction
Forbidden Planet▶
Future Cop
Galaxina
The Hitchhiker's Guide to the
  Galaxy
How to Make a Doll
The Human Duplicators
Humanoid Defender
The Invisible Boy
Knights
Kronos
Light Years
Making Mr. Right
Mandroid
Megaville
Nemesis
Not Quite Human
Not Quite Human 2
Planet Busters
Planets Against Us
Programmed to Kill
Project: Shadowchaser
Prototype▶
Prototype X29A
Return of the Jedi▶
Robo-Chic
RoboCop▶
RoboCop 2
RoboCop 3
Roboman
Robot Holocaust

Robot Jox
Robot Monster
The Robot vs. the Aztec
  Mummy
Robot Wars
R.O.T.O.R.
Runaway
Running Delilah
Short Circuit
Star Crash
Star Wars▶
Steel and Lace
Still Not Quite Human
TC 2000
The Terminator▶
Terminator 2: Judgment Day▶
Terror of Mechagodzilla
Tobor the Great
The Vindicator
War of the Robots
Westworld▶
Wild, Wild Planet

Rock Stars on Film

  see also *Concert Films;*
    Martyred Pop Icons; Pure
    Ego Vehicles
All You Need Is Cash▶
Backbeat▶
Blow-Up▶
Blue Hawaii
The Bodyguard
Breaking Glass
The Bride
Carny▶
Caveman
Charro!
Chuck Berry: Hail! Hail! Rock
  'n' Roll▶
Clambake
Double Trouble
Dune
Easy Come, Easy Go
Flaming Star▶
Follow That Dream
Frankie and Johnny
Freddy's Dead: The Final
  Nightmare
Fun in Acapulco
G.I. Blues
The Gift
The Girl Can't Help It
Girl Happy
Girls! Girls! Girls!
Give My Regards to Broad
  Street
Go, Johnny Go!
A Hard Day's Night▶
The Harder They Come
Harum Scarum
Head▶
Help!▶
How I Won the War
The Hunger
It Happened at the World's
  Fair
Jailhouse Rock▶
Jubilee
Kid Galahad
King Creole
KISS Meets the Phantom of
  the Park
Kissin' Cousins
La Bamba▶
The Last Temptation of
  Christ▶
The Legacy
Let It Be
Lisztomania
Live a Little, Love a Little
Love Me Tender
Loving You
The Magic Christian▶
Magical Mystery Tour
The Man Who Fell to Earth▶
Merry Christmas, Mr.
  Lawrence▶
Mrs. Brown, You've Got a
  Lovely Daughter
Monster Dog
Nomads
One Trick Pony

Paradise, Hawaiian Style
Pat Garrett & Billy the Kid▶
Performance▶
Pink Floyd: The Wall
Poetic Justice
Quadrophenia▶
Rock 'n' Roll High School▶
Roustabout
Speedway
Spinout
Stay Away, Joe
That'll Be the Day
This is Elvis
Tickle Me
Tommy
The Trouble with Girls (and
  How To Get Into It)▶
Viva Las Vegas
Wild in the Country
Woodstock▶
Yellow Submarine▶

Rodeos

  see also *Westerns*
The Adventures of Gallant
  Bess
Arizona Cowboy
The Cowboy Way
Desert Trail
8 Seconds
Feud of the West
Girl from Calgary
Goldenrod
Junior Bonner▶
Kid from Gower Gulch
Lady Takes a Chance▶
Lights of Old Santa Fe
The Lusty Men▶
Luzia
Man from Utah
The Misfits▶
My Heroes Have Always Been
  Cowboys
Never a Dull Moment
Oklahoma Cyclone
Rider from Tucson
Rodeo Girl
Rolling Home
Saddle Buster
Trouble in Texas
Western Double Feature 5
Wild Horse
Wild Horse Rodeo

Role Reversal

  see also *Gender Bending;*
    Identity
Age Isn't Everything
All of Me
Anastasia▶
Anastasia: The Mystery of
  Anna
Angel
Angel on My Shoulder
Angel on My Shoulder
Bad Manners
The Bank Dick▶
Before Morning
Belfast Assassin
Big▶
Biggles
Blood of Dracula
Bloodlink
The Captain from Koepenick
Captive Heart▶
Cheech and Chong's, The
  Corsican Brothers
Christmas in Connecticut▶
Cinderfella
Clambake
Class Act
Cleo/Leo
Coming to America▶
Como Dos Gotas de Agua
Condorman
The Couch Trip
Courage▶
Dave▶
The Deputy Drummer
Desperately Seeking Susan
Devil's Canyon

Dr. Black, Mr. Hyde
Doctor Detroit
Doctor Dolittle
Dr. Heckyl and Mr. Hype
Dr. Jekyll and Mr. Hyde▶
Dr. Jekyll and Mr. Hyde
Doctors and Nurses
Donde Duermen
  Dos...Duermen Tres
Down and Out in Beverly Hills
Dream a Little Dream
A Dream of Passion
18 Again!
Extremities
The $5.20 an Hour Dream
For Ladies Only
48 Hrs.▶
Freaky Friday
Gentleman's Agreement▶
The Gladiator▶
The Grand Duchess and the
  Waiter▶
The Great Gabbo
Greystoke: The Legend of
  Tarzan, Lord of the Apes
Guest Wife
Gunfire
Heart Like a Wheel
Her Life as a Man
Hiding Out
Identity Crisis
The Incredible Mr. Limpet
Iron Maze
Johnny Guitar▶
Just One of the Guys
Kagemusha▶
Kim
Kings and Desperate Men
La Femme Nikita▶
La Ronde▶
The Lady Vanishes▶
The Lady Vanishes
Ladybugs
Law and Order
Liana, Jungle Goddess
Like Father, Like Son
Liquid Sky▶
Lonely Wives
Maid to Order
Male and Female▶
The Man Who Haunted
  Himself
The Man Who Wagged His
  Tail
Man with Two Heads
Monkey Business▶
My Blue Heaven
My Fair Lady▶
My Neighborhood
Now, Voyager▶
Overboard
Panamint's Bad Man
Paris When It Sizzles▶
People's Choice
Performance▶
Persona▶
Pocketful of Miracles▶
Point of No Return
Posse▶
The Prince and the Pauper
The Prince and the Pauper
Prisoner of Zenda▶
Prisoner of Zenda
Psycho▶
Quicksilver
Rabbit Test
The Raggedy Rawney
Raid on Rommel
Red Lion
Red Rock Outlaw
Rendez-Moi Ma Peau
Rider of the Law
The Road to Yesterday
Roman Holiday▶
Satanik
Savages
Scalpel
The Scarlet Pimpernel▶
September Affair
The Shaggy D.A.
The Shaggy Dog
The Shakiest Gun in the West

Showdown in Little Tokyo
Silent Night, Deadly Night
Slapstick of Another Kind
A Slightly Pregnant Man
Small Town Boy
Something Special
Sometimes Aunt Martha Does
  Dreadful Things
Song of Texas
Soul Man
A Stolen Face
Stoogemania
Summer Night with Greek
  Profile, Almond Eyes &
  Scent of Basil
Super Soul Brother
Sweet Revenge
Switch▶
Sylvia Scarlett
Taking Care of Business
A Tale of Two Cities▶
That Man Is Pregnant
That's My Baby!
Tomboy
Tootsie▶
Trading Places
Triple Echo
True Identity
Ultimate Desires
Vice Versa▶
Victor/Victoria▶
Wait Till Your Mother Gets
  Home
Watermelon Man
White Sands
Wonder Man
Yentl
Yidl Mitn Fidl

Romance

  see *Late Bloomin' Love;*
    Lovers on the Lam;
    Romantic Adventures;
    Romantic Comedy;
    Romantic Drama;
    Romantic Triangles

Romantic
Adventures

The African Queen▶
Arabian Nights
Baby...Secret of the Lost
  Legend
Gun Crazy▶
Guncrazy
Gypsy Angels
The Jewel of the Nile
Joe Versus the Volcano
Mogambo▶
Red Dust▶
Romancing the Stone▶
Son of Ali Baba

Romantic Comedy

Abdulla the Great
About Last Night...▶
Acqua e Sapone
Adam's Rib▶
The Admiral Was a Lady
Adorable Julia
The Adventures of Sadie
Aggie Appleby, Maker of Men
Alfredo, Alfredo
All Night Long▶
All Tied Up
The Allnighter
All's Fair
...Almost
Almost an Angel
Almost Pregnant
Almost You
The Ambassador's Daughter
American Dreamer
American Friends
American Matchmaker
Amore!
The Amorous Adventures of
  Moll Flanders
And You Thought Your
  Parents Were Weird!

Romantic

Animal Behavior
Anna Christie
Anna Karenina▶
Annabel Takes a Tour/Maid's
  Night Out
Annie Hall▶
Another Chance
Another Thin Man
The Apartment▶
April Fools
Are Parents People?
Arthur▶
Arthur 2: On the Rocks
Ask Any Girl
Avanti!
Baby Boom
Babycakes
Bachelor Apartment
Bachelor Bait
Bachelor in Paradise
Bachelor Party
Back to the Beach
Bahama Passage
Baja Oklahoma
Ball of Fire▶
The Balloonatic/One Week
Bare Essentials
Barefoot in the Park▶
Barnaby and Me
The Bashful Bachelor
Battling Butler
Beachcomber▶
Bed & Breakfast
Belle Epoque▶
Bells are Ringing▶
Benny & Joon
Best Legs in the 8th Grade
Betsy's Wedding
Beyond Tomorrow
Birds & the Bees
Blame It on Rio
Blind Date
Blonde Crazy
Blue Country
Bobo
Bombshell▶
Boom Town
Boomerang
Born Yesterday▶
Born Yesterday
Boyfriends & Girlfriends
Breakfast at Tiffany's▶
Breath of Scandal
The Bride Came C.O.D.
Bull Durham▶
But Not for Me
The Butcher's Wife
Butterflies
Bye Bye Baby
Cactus Flower
Cafe Romeo
California Casanova
California Suite▶
Came a Hot Friday
The Cameraman▶
Can She Bake a Cherry Pie?
Can't Buy Me Love
Captain's Paradise▶
Car Trouble
Career Opportunities
Cartier Affair
Casanova
Casanova Brown
Casanova '70
The Cemetery Club
Chances Are▶
A Change of Seasons
Charley's Aunt
The Cheerful Fraud
Chilly Scenes of Winter
Christmas in Connecticut▶
Christmas in Connecticut
Class of '44
The Clock▶
Closely Watched Trains▶
Cold Feet
Come Blow Your Horn▶
Comeback Kid
Coming to America▶
Continental Divide
Cool Blue
Couples and Robbers

The Cowboy and the Lady
Crazy in Love
Crazy Moon
Creator
Crocodile Dundee▶
Cross My Heart
Crossing Delancey▶
Curly Sue
Date with an Angel
Dear Brigitte
Decameron Nights
Defending Your Life▶
The Demi-Paradise▶
Designing Woman▶
Desk Set▶
Desperate Moves
Desperately Seeking Susan
The Devil & Miss Jones▶
Different Story
Dirty Rotten Scoundrels▶
The Divorce of Lady X
Doc Hollywood
Doctor in Distress
Dr. Jack/For Heaven's Sake
Does This Mean We're
  Married?
Dollar
Dona Flor and Her Two
  Husbands▶
Dona Herlinda & Her Son
Don't Hang Up
Don't Tell Her It's Me
Dos Esposas en Mi Cama
Dream Date
Dream Trap
Dreams Come True
East and West▶
El Ceniciento
Electric Dreams
Elsa, Elsa
Eversmile New Jersey
Every Girl Should Be Married
Every Which Way But Loose
Face the Music
The Farmer's Daughter▶
The Farmer's Other Daughter
Fate
Father Goose
The Favor
Feelin' Screwy
Feet First
Fifth Avenue Girl
A Fine Romance
First Time
Foolin' Around
For Heaven's Sake▶
For Love of Ivy
For Love or Money
A Forgotten Tune for the
  Flute▶
Forrest Gump▶
Forty Carats
Four Weddings and a
  Funeral▶
Framed
Frankie and Johnny▶
The French Lesson
Fridays of Eternity
Friends, Lovers & Lunatics
Full of Life
Funny About Love
Gabriela
The Gay Lady
Get Out Your Handkerchiefs▶
Getting It Right
The Ghost and the Guest
Gidget
Gidget Goes Hawaiian
Gidget Goes to Rome
Ginger in the Morning
A Girl, a Guy and a Gob
The Girl from Missouri▶
The Girl from Petrovka
The Girl in the Picture
Girl Shy▶
Girl Under the Sheet
The Glass Bottom Boat
The Gold of Naples▶
The Golden Honeymoon
The Goodbye Girl▶
Goodbye, New York

The Grand Duchess and the
  Waiter▶
The Grass is Greener
The Great Gildersleeve
Green Card
Groundhog Day▶
Hammersmith is Out
Hanky Panky
Happy New Year▶
Happy Together
Hardhat & Legs
Having It All
Having Wonderful Crime
Having Wonderful Time
He Said, She Said
Hear My Song▶
Heartaches▶
Heartbeat
Her Alibi
Herbie Goes to Monte Carlo
Hi Diddle Diddle
High Spirits
Higher Education
His First Flame▶
His Wife's Lover▶
Hobson's Choice▶
Hobson's Choice
Honeymoon Academy
Honeymoon in Vegas
Hook, Line and Sinker
The Horizontal Lieutenant
Hot Chocolate
House Calls▶
Houseboat
Housesitter
How to Marry a Millionaire
How U Like Me Now?▶
Hurry, Charlie, Hurry
Hurry Up or I'll Be Thirty
I Don't Buy Kisses Anymore
I Know Where I'm Going▶
I Love Trouble
I Married a Centerfold
I Married a Witch▶
I Married a Woman
I Will, I Will for Now
Idiot's Delight▶
Il Bell'Antonio
I'll Take Sweden
Imposters
Impromptu▶
In Love with an Older Woman
In Person
The Incredible Mr. Limpet
Indiscreet
Indiscreet▶
Indiscreet
Innerspace
Instant Karma
Invitation to the Wedding
Irma La Douce
It
It Could Happen to You
It Happened One Night▶
It Should Happen to You▶
It Started with a Kiss
It Takes Two
It's My Turn
I've Heard the Mermaids
  Singing▶
Jersey Girl
Jock Petersen
Joe Versus the Volcano
Joey Breaker▶
The Judge Steps Out
Julia Has Two Lovers
June Bride▶
Jupiter's Thigh
Just Me & You
Just One of the Girls
Just Tell Me What You Want
Just the Way You Are
Key Exchange
Key to the City
The King on Main Street
King Ralph
A Kiss for Mary Pickford
Kiss Me Goodbye
Kiss Shot
Kuni Lemel in Tel Aviv
La Lectrice
L.A. Story▶

La Vie de Boheme▶
The Lady Eve▶
The Lady is Willing
Lady L
Lady Takes a Chance▶
L'Annee des Meduses
Lassie from Lancashire
The Last Fling
The Last Married Couple in
  America
Late for Dinner
Le Beau Mariage▶
Le Magnifique
Legal Eagles
Lena's Holiday
Let's Make it Legal
Let's Make Love
Lt. Robin Crusoe, U.S.N.
The Linguini Incident
Listen to Your Heart
Little Noises
A Little Romance▶
Little Sister
Little White Lies
The Lonely Guy
Lonely Hearts▶
Lonely in America
Look Who's Talking▶
Look Who's Talking, Too
Loose in New York
Lost and Found
Lost in Yonkers
The Love Affair, or The Case
  of the Missing Switchboard
  Operator▶
Love Among the Ruins▶
Love at First Sight
Love by Appointment
Love Crazy▶
Love Hurts
Love in the Afternoon
Love is Better Than Ever
Love Laughs at Andy Hardy
Love on the Run
Love or Money?
Love Potion #9
Lovelines
Lover Come Back
Loverboy
Lovers and Liars
Lovers Like Us
Lovers' Lovers
Loves & Times of
  Scaramouche
Loving Couples
The Lunatic
Lunatics: A Love Story▶
Made in America
Made in Heaven
Magic on Love Island
The Magnificent Dope
The Maid
Maid's Night Out
The Main Event
Main Street to Broadway
Making Mr. Right
Male and Female▶
Mama, There's a Man in Your
  Bed▶
A Man, a Woman, and a Bank
Man Trouble
The Man Who Loved
  Women▶
The Man Who Loved Women
Manhattan▶
Mannequin
Marriage Italian Style▶
Married?
Married to the Mob▶
The Marrying Man
The Matchmaker▶
Matrimaniac
May Wine
Me, Myself & I
Meeting Venus
Micki & Maude
A Midsummer Night's Dream▶
A Midsummer Night's Dream
Milk Money
Miracle Beach
The Misadventures of Merlin
  Jones

Miss Right
Mr. Boggs Steps Out
Mr. Love
Mr. Lucky▶
Mr. Peabody & the Mermaid
Mr. Wonderful
Modern Love
Modern Romance▶
Monaco Forever
Moon is Blue
Moon Pilot
Moonstruck▶
Morgan!
Much Ado About Nothing▶
Murphy's Romance▶
My Best Friend's Girl
My Brother's Wife
My Dear Secretary
My Girl 2▶
My Love For Yours
My Man Godfrey
My Night at Maud's▶
My Stepmother Is an Alien
My Tutor
Mystery Date
The Mystery Man
Naked in New York
Never on Sunday▶
A New Kind of Love
A New Leaf
Next Time I Marry
Next Year If All Goes Well
Nice Girl Like Me
Nice Girls Don't Explode
Night and Day▶
The Night Club
The Night We Never Met
Ninotchka▶
Nobody's Fool
The Norman Conquests, Part
  1: Table Manners▶
The Norman Conquests, Part
  2: Living Together▶
The Norman Conquests, Part
  3: Round and Round the
  Garden▶
North to Alaska▶
Nothing Personal
Off Beat
Okoge
On Approval▶
Once Around
One Rainy Afternoon
One, Two, Three▶
One Wild Moment
Only the Lonely
Only with Married Men
Only You
The Opposite Sex and How to
  Live With Them
Our Miss Brooks
Outrageous Fortune
Overboard
The Owl and the Pussycat▶
Panama Lady
Pantaloons
Paper Marriage
Pardon Mon Affaire▶
Paris Holiday
Pat and Mike▶
Peggy Sue Got Married
Perfect Match
Perfectly Normal
Personal Property
The Personals
Phffft!
The Pick-Up Artist
Pillow Talk
Play It Again, Sam▶
Playmates
Pool Hustlers
Pool Sharks
Pop Always Pays
Prelude to a Kiss
Pretty Woman▶
Priceless Beauty
The Prince and the Showgirl
The Princess and the Pirate▶
Prisoner of Zenda
Private Lives▶
Probation
Promise Her Anything

Promises! Promises!
Protocol
The Purple Rose of Cairo▶
Quackser Fortune Has a
  Cousin in the Bronx▶
Queens Logic
Quick Change
The Quiet Man▶
The Rage of Paris▶
The Ranch
The Rat Race▶
Rattle of a Simple Man
Reaching for the Moon
Reality Bites
The Reluctant Debutante▶
Rich in Love
The Ritz▶
Road to Ruin
Roads to the South
The Roaring Road
Roman Holiday▶
Romantic Comedy
Roses Bloom Twice
Round Numbers
Roxanne▶
Running Mates▶
Ruthless People▶
Sabrina▶
Sacred Mountain/White
  Flame▶
Saratoga
Scorchers
Seaside Swingers
Secret Admirer
Secret Ingredient
Secret Life of an American
  Wife
The Secret of My Success▶
See You in the Morning
Seems Like Old Times
Send Me No Flowers▶
The Sensual Man
The Sensuous Nurse
Separate Vacations
Seven Days Ashore/Hurry,
  Charlie, Hurry
Seven Minutes in Heaven
The Seven Year Itch▶
Sex and the Single Girl
Sex and the Single Parent
Shanghai Surprise
She Done Him Wrong▶
She's Gotta Have It▶
She's Having a Baby
The Shop Around the
  Corner▶
Shore Leave▶
Short Circuit
The Shrimp on the Barbie
Sibling Rivalry
Singles▶
Sixteen Candles▶
Skin Deep
Sleepless in Seattle▶
Smiles of a Summer Night▶
Smokescreen
Snow: The Movie
Snowballin'
So This is Paris▶
Soapdish▶
The Social Secretary
Soldat Duroc...Ca Va Etre Ta
  Fete!
Something Short of Paradise
Soup for One
Soy un Golfo
Spite Marriage▶
Stand-In▶
State of the Union▶
The Station
The Sterile Cuckoo▶
Stolen Kisses▶
The Story of Boys & Girls▶
Straight Talk
Strictly Ballroom▶
Strictly Business
Stroke of Midnight
Summer School
Sunset Limousine
Surf Party
Surrender
Surviving Desire▶

Suzy
The Swan
The Swan▶
Sweet Lies
Sweet Talker
The Tall Guy▶
The Taming of the Shrew
The Taming of the Shrew
The Taming of the Shrew
Tammy and the Bachelor
Tammy and the Doctor
The Teahouse of the August
  Moon
Ted & Venus
The Tender Trap
That Certain Thing
That Lucky Touch
That Touch of Mink
That Uncertain Feeling
There's a Girl in My Soup
They All Laughed
They Got Me Covered
The Thing Called Love
The Things of Life▶
30 Is a Dangerous Age,
  Cynthia
This Could Be the Night
This Happy Feeling
Thomas Graal's Best Film▶
Thomas Graal's First Child▶
Those Endearing Young
  Charms
Three Broadway Girls▶
Three Coins in the Fountain
Three for Bedroom C
Three Guys Named Mike
Three Husbands
Three of Hearts
Three Way Weekend
Threesome
Tiger and the Pussycat
Till Marriage Do Us Part
Tillie's Punctured Romance
Time of the Gypsies▶
To Paris with Love
Togetherness
Tom, Dick, and Harry
Tom Jones▶
Tomboy
Too Beautiful for You
Topsy Turvy
A Touch of Class▶
Tulips
Tune in Tomorrow
Two-Faced Woman▶
Two Nights with Cleopatra
Two of a Kind
Underground Aces
The Unkissed Bride
Up Your Alley
Utilities
Valley Girl
Victor/Victoria▶
Vivacious Lady▶
Waiting for the Light
Walk, Don't Run
Warm Summer Rain
Watch It▶
We All Loved Each Other So
  Much▶
The Wedding Banquet▶
The Wedding Party
We're Not Married▶
What Happened to Rosa?▶
What's Good for the Goose
What's New Pussycat?▶
When Harry Met Sally...▶
When Ladies Meet
Where the Boys Are
Who Am I This Time?▶
The Whoopee Boys
Wildest Dreams
Wimps
Wishful Thinking
With Six You Get Eggroll
Without Love
Without Reservations
The Woman in Red
Woman of the Year▶
The Women
Working Girl▶

The World's Oldest Living
  Bridesmaid
Worth Winning
You Can't Fool Your Wife
Your Place or Mine
You've Got to Have Heart

Romantic Drama

Aaron Loves Angela
The Accidental Tourist▶
The Adorable Cheat
The Affair▶
An Affair to Remember
After Julius
After Midnight
Against All Odds
The Age of Innocence▶
Algiers▶
Ali: Fear Eats the Soul▶
Alice▶
Alice Adams
All the Vermeers in New
  York▶
All This and Heaven Too▶
Almost Blue
Always
Anatomy of a Seduction
And a Nightingale Sang
And Now My Love
Angel Square
The Animal Kingdom▶
Ann Vickers
Anna Christie▶
Anna Karenina
Annapolis
The Annapolis Story
Anne of Avonlea▶
Another Time, Another Place▶
Anthony Adverse
Arch of Triumph▶
Arch of Triumph
As Is
Aspen Extreme
Atalia
The Atonement of Gosta
  Berling▶
The Average Woman
Back Street
Backstreet Dreams
The Ballad of the Sad Cafe
Band of Angels
Barbarian and the Geisha
The Barretts of Wimpole
  Street▶
Bayou Romance
Beau Revel▶
Beauty and the Beast▶
Beloved Enemy▶
Berlin Blues
The Best Intentions▶
Betty Blue▶
Beware of Pity
The Big Parade▶
Big Street
The Bigamist
Bird of Paradise
Birds of Paradise
Bitter Sweet
The Bitter Tea of General
  Yen▶
The Bitter Tears of Petra von
  Kant
The Black Marble▶
Black Orchid
Blind Husbands▶
Blood and Sand
Blood and Sand/Son of the
  Sheik
Blood Feud
The Blood of Others
The Blue Hour
The Blue Light▶
The Bodyguard
Bolero
Bombay Talkie
Born to Be Bad
The Boss Is Served
Boy Takes Girl
Breakfast in Paris
Breathless▶
The Bride Wore Red

Brief Encounter▶
Buffalo Jump▶
Bullfighter & the Lady
Burning Secret
Buster and Billie
By Love Possessed
Bye Bye Blues
Cabiria
Cabo Blanco
Cactus
Cactus in the Snow
Caddie
Camelia
Camila▶
Camille▶
Camille Claudel▶
Captive Hearts
Carmen▶
Carnival Story
The Carpetbaggers
Casablanca▶
Cash McCall
Casino
Cass Timberlane
Castaway▶
The Castaway Cowboy
Caught▶
Chain Lightning
Chained
Chanel Solitaire
Chapter Two
Charles & Diana: A Palace
  Divided
The Children
Children of a Lesser God▶
Christopher Strong
Cinderella Liberty▶
Circle of Love
Circle of Two
Circus World
City for Conquest▶
City Girl
Claire of the Moon
Clash by Night▶
Close My Eyes
Cobra
Cocktail
A Coeur Joie
Cold Sassy Tree▶
Collector's Item▶
Come See the Paradise▶
The Coming of Amos▶
Coming Through
The Competition▶
Conquest▶
Consolation Marriage
Cool Change
Corregidor
The Cousins▶
Cowboy & the Ballerina
The Cranes are Flying▶
The Crossing
Crystal Heart
The Cutting Edge
Cyrano de Bergerac▶
Damage▶
Dance
Dancers
Dangerous Liaisons▶
Danielle Steel's Changes
Danielle Steel's ''Daddy''
Dark Eyes▶
Dark Journey▶
The Dawning
Daybreak
Days and Nights in the Forest
Deadly Desire
Deception▶
A Dedicated Man
Deja Vu
Desert Hearts▶
Desire
Devil in the Flesh▶
Devil in the Flesh
Devil's Wanton
Devotion
Die Grosse Freiheit Nr. 7
A Different Kind of Love
The Divorcee
Doctor Zhivago▶
Dogfight▶
The Dolls

The Dolphin
Doomsday
Dos Chicas de Revista
A Dream of Kings▶
Dreams Lost, Dreams Found
Dressmaker
Dubarry
Duel of Hearts
Dying Young
Dynasty
East Side, West Side
Ecstasy
Edward and Mrs. Simpson
Effi Briest▶
8 Seconds
84 Charing Cross Road▶
El Diputado▶
El Penon de las Animas
Elena and Her Men▶
Elephant Walk
Eliza's Horoscope
Empty Canvas
Enchanted April
End of August
Endless Love
Escape to Love
Ethan
Ethan Frome
Every Time We Say Goodbye
Everybody's All American
Everything Happens at Night▶
Ex-Lady
The Eyes, the Mouth
Falling in Love
The Family Man
Fanny▶
Far and Away
Far from the Madding
  Crowd▶
The Far Pavilions
A Farewell to Arms▶
The Farmer Takes a Wife
Fatal Attraction
Fergie & Andrew: Behind
  Palace Doors
Fire and Ice
Fire and Sword
Fire with Fire
Fires Within
First Affair
First Love
Five Days One Summer
The Flame is Love
Flor Silvestre
The Flying Fool
Fool for Love
Fools
For Love Alone
For Love or Money
For the Love of Angela
Forbidden
Foreign Affairs▶
Forever
Forever: A Ghost of a Love
  Story
Forever Emmanuelle
Foxfire Light
Franz
The French Lieutenant's
  Woman▶
French Postcards
Fresh Horses
The Fugitive Kind▶
Fulfillment
Full Moon in Paris
Furia Pasional
Gal Young 'Un▶
Gamble on Love
The Game of Love
Georgia, Georgia
Ghost▶
The Gift of Love
Girl in Black
The Girl in Blue
The Go-Between▶
Golden Demon
Golden Gate
Gone with the Wind▶
Goodbye Again
The Gorgeous Hussy
Grand Isle
The Great Lie▶

Romantic

Green Dolphin Street
Green Fields
Green Fire
Green Mansions
Griffin and Phoenix: A Love
    Story
Guitarras Lloren Guitarras
The Hairdresser's Husband
Hanover Street
Harem
Havana
Head Over Heels▶
Hearing Voices
The Hearst and Davies Affair
Heart of Humanity
Heartbreakers▶
Heat and Dust▶
The Heiress▶
Heroes
Hide-Out
His Private Secretary
History is Made at Night▶
Hold the Dream
Holiday Affair
Holocaust
    Survivors...Remembrance
    of Love
The Home and the World▶
Home Before Midnight
Home Sweet Home
Homecoming
Honky
Hotel Room
Humoresque▶
Husbands and Wives▶
I Can't Escape
I Conquer the Sea
I Live in Grosvenor Square
I Love All of You
I Love N.Y.
I Love You
I Never Sang For My Father▶
Ice Castles
Iguana
I'm a Fool
Image of Passion
In a Shallow Grave
In Dangerous Company
In Search of Anna
In Too Deep
An Indecent Obsession
Indecent Proposal
Independence Day
Indiscretion of an American
    Wife
Indochine▶
Interval
Iron Cowboy
Island of Desire
Isle of Secret Passion
I've Always Loved You
Jacko & Lise
Jane Eyre
Jane Eyre▶
Jenny
Johnny Frenchman
Josepha▶
Jude the Obscure
Jules and Jim▶
Jungle Fever▶
Just Between Friends
Kept Husbands
The Key
Killing Heat
Kings Go Forth
The King's Rhapsody
The King's Whore
Kipperbang
Kitty Foyle▶
Knight Without Armour▶
Knights of the Round Table
La Bella Lola
La Carcel de Laredo
La Chartreuse de Parme
La Fuerza Inutil
La Grande Bourgeoise
La Mentira
La Petite Sirene
La Strada▶
Lady Chatterley's Lover
Lady from Louisiana
The Lady in Question

The Lady Refuses
The Lady with the Dog▶
Lagrimas de Amor
Lana in Love
The Last of the Mohicans▶
The Last Prostitute
The Last Time I Saw Paris
The Last Train
The Last Winters
Le Bonheur
Le Repos du Guerrier
A Legacy for Leonette
Leon Morin, Priest
Leopard in the Snow
Letters from the Park▶
Lianna▶
Lies of the Twins
The Life and Loves of Mozart
Life and Nothing But▶
A Life of Her Own
Lilith▶
Linda
Listen to Me
The Little American
Little Dorrit, Film 2: Little
    Dorrit's Story▶
Little Minister▶
Lola▶
Lola
Long Ago Tomorrow
The Long, Hot Summer▶
Lorna Doone
Louisiana
Loulou▶
Love Affair
Love Affair: The Eleanor &
    Lou Gehrig Story▶
Love and Faith▶
Love and the Frenchwoman▶
Love at the Top
A Love in Germany
Love is a Many-Splendored
    Thing
Love Letters▶
The Love of Three Queens
Love on the Run▶
Love Streams
Love with a Perfect Stranger
Love with the Proper
    Stranger▶
Love Without Pity
The Lover
The Lovers▶
Lovers: A True Story▶
The Loves of Carmen
Love's Savage Fury
Lovespell
Lydia▶
Mad Bull
Madame Bovary▶
The Magnificent Matador
Mambo
A Man and a Woman▶
The Man in Grey▶
The Man in the Moon▶
Man is Not a Bird
The Man Who Guards the
    Greenhouse
Mannequin
Manon
Map of the Human Heart
Maria
Maria Chapdelaine▶
Maria Chapdelaine
Marianela
Marjorie Morningstar
Marty
Marty▶
A Matter of Love
Mayerling▶
Medicine Man
Melody
Menschenfrauen
Merry-Go-Round▶
The Mill on the Floss
A Million to One
Mirrors
Mississippi Masala▶
Mississippi Mermaid▶
Mrs. Soffel
Mr. Jones
Model Behavior

Mogambo▶
Moonlight Sonata
Morning Glory
Morocco▶
My Champion
My Forbidden Past
My Man Adam
Mysteries
Nairobi Affair
Nais▶
Naked Sun
Narda or The Summer
Nativity
The Nest
Nevil Shute's The Far Country
New York Nights
Nicole
A Night Full of Rain
Night Games
A Night in Heaven
Night Is My Future
North Shore
Northanger Abbey
Nosotros
Not Quite Paradise
Nouvelle Vague
Now and Forever
O Pioneers!
Of Human Bondage▶
Of Mice and Men▶
An Officer and a Gentleman▶
Old Gringo
Oliver's Story
Once in Paris...
One Brief Summer
One Summer Love
Only Once in a Lifetime
Our Modern Maidens
Our Time
Out of Season
Outcasts of the City
Over the Summer
Oxford Blues
A Paper Wedding
Parrish
Passion of Love▶
A Patch of Blue
Paul and Michelle
The Peasants
Pepe Le Moko▶
The Piano▶
Picnic▶
Pittsburgh
The Playboys▶
Pleasure
Poetic Justice
Poor White Trash
Port of Call▶
Portrait of Jennie▶
Possessed
Pride of the Clan
Princess Yang Kwei Fei▶
The Private Lives of Elizabeth
    & Essex▶
The Prizefighter and the
    Lady▶
The Promise
The Proud Ones
The Public Eye▶
Pure Country
Purple Hearts
The Purple Taxi
Quality Street
Quatorze Juliet
Queen Christina▶
Queen of the Stardust
    Ballroom▶
Rachel, Rachel▶
Rachel's Man
Racing with the Moon▶
Rage of Angels
Rage of Angels: The Story
    Continues
The Railway Station Man▶
The Rainmaker▶
Rebel
Rebel Love
Reckless
Red Headed Woman▶
Red Kiss▶
Red Sorghum▶
Return Engagement

The Return of Martin Guerre▶
Return of the Soldier▶
Return to Paradise
Return to the Blue Lagoon
Return to Two Moon Junction
Reunion in France
The Ring
The Road to Yesterday
Roman Spring of Mrs. Stone▶
Romance
Romance in Manhattan
Romance on the Orient
    Express
Romantic Englishwoman▶
Rome Adventure
Romeo and Juliet
Romeo and Juliet▶
Romper Stomper
Room at the Top▶
A Room with a View▶
The Rose Tattoo▶
Rouge
Running Away
Ryan's Daughter
Sadie Thompson▶
The Sailor Who Fell from
    Grace with the Sea
Same Time, Next Year▶
San Francisco▶
The Sandpiper
Sarah, Plain and Tall▶
Savage Messiah▶
Say Hello to Yesterday
Sayonara▶
Scarlet Dawn
Scenes from the Goldmine
Second Wind
Secret Obsession
Secret of Yolanda
Secret Passions
Sense & Sensibility
September Affair
Shadow of China▶
Shadowlands▶
The Shining Hour
Shining Through
Shoot the Piano Player▶
Shop Angel
Shopworn Angel▶
Silver City
Sin Takes a Holiday
Sincerely Charlotte▶
Sister Dora
A Slave of Love▶
Slipstream
Smilin' Through▶
Snow Country
The Soft Skin▶
A Soldier's Tale
Somewhere I'll Find You▶
Somewhere Tomorrow
Sommersby
A Song to Remember▶
Sooner or Later
The Sorrows of Satan▶
Souvenir
A Special Day▶
Stanley and Iris
Stealing Heaven
Stella
The Stilts▶
Stolen Hours
Stormy Waters
The Story of a Three Day
    Pass
The Story of the Late
    Chrysanthemum▶
The Strange Love of Molly
    Louvain
Strangers Kiss
Strangers When We Meet
Strapless
Street Scene
The Student Prince in Old
    Heidelberg
Summer Affair
Summer Lovers
A Summer Story▶
Summertime▶
Sweet Bird of Youth
Sweet Ecstasy
Sweet Light in a Dark Room▶

Swimming Pool
Tacos al Carbon
A Tale of Two Cities
Talk to Me
Tango Bar
Tarzan Escapes▶
Tears in the Rain
The Tempest▶
The Tempest
Tender Mercies▶
Test Pilot▶
That Night
That Summer of White Roses
They Call It Sin
36 Fillete▶
Three Comrades▶
Tim
Time Out for Love
A Time to Love & a Time to
    Die
To Have & Have Not▶
To Love Again
To the Camp & Back
Today We Live
Together
Tomorrow▶
Tomorrow is Forever
Torn Apart
Torn Between Two Lovers
The Torture of Silence
The Touch
Trapeze▶
Tristana▶
Trouble in Mind▶
True Heart Susie
True Romance
The Tsar's Bride▶
The Tunnel
21 Days
24 Hours in a Woman's Life
Twist & Shout▶
Two Daughters▶
Two English Girls▶
Two Moon Junction
Un Coeur en Hiver
The Unbearable Lightness of
    Being▶
An Unremarkable Life
Untamed Heart
The Valley of Decision▶
Vanity Fair
Verboten!
The Victory
The Virgin and the Gypsy
Voyage of the Heart
Voyager▶
Walk in the Spring Rain
Walk Softly, Stranger
Waltz Across Texas
The Wanderer
War & Love
War and Peace
War and Peace▶
War Lover
Washington Mistress
Waterfront
The Way We Were▶
We the Living
Weather in the Streets
Wedding in Blood▶
The Wedding March▶
When the Time Comes
When Thief Meets Thief
Which Way Home
Whistle Stop
White Cargo
White Light
White Nights▶
White Palace
The White Sister▶
Wide Sargasso Sea
Wife Versus Secretary▶
Wild at Heart▶
Wild Hearts Can't Be Broken▶
Wildfire
Wind
The Wind and the Lion▶
Windmills of the Gods
Windrider
The Winds of Jarrah
Wings
Wings of Desire▶

Winter Flight
Winter People
The Woman He Loved
The Woman Next Door▶
A Woman of Substance,
 Episode 1: Nest of Vipers
A Woman of Substance,
 Episode 2: The Secret is
 Revealed
A Woman of Substance,
 Episode 3: Fighting for the
 Dream
A Woman Without Love▶
The World of Suzie Wong
Wuthering Heights▶
Wuthering Heights
Yanks
Year of the Quiet Sun▶
Yesterday's Hero
You Light Up My Life
The Young and the Guilty
Young Lady Chatterly 2
Youth on Parole

Romantic Triangles

The Age of Innocence▶
Bull Durham▶
Casablanca▶
The Cook, the Thief, His Wife
 & Her Lover▶
Elephant Walk
Ethan Frome
The Favor
Henry & June▶
High Society▶
The Lovers▶
Mildred Pierce▶
Mo' Better Blues
My Favorite Wife▶
The Philadelphia Story▶
A Room with a View▶
Sabrina▶
She's Gotta Have It▶
Sommersby
Summer Lovers
Three of Hearts
Threesome
The Unbearable Lightness of
 Being▶

Roommates from Hell

 *see also Psychotics/
 Sociopaths*
Deadbolt
The Fear Inside
Malice
The Night We Never Met
Pacific Heights▶
Single White Female

Royalty

 *see also Historical
 Drama; Medieval Romps;
 Period Piece*
Abdulla the Great
The Adventures of Marco Polo
Aladdin▶
Alexander Nevsky▶
Ali Baba and the Forty
 Thieves
Ali Baba and the 40 Thieves▶
Anastasia▶
Anastasia: The Mystery of
 Anna
Anna and the King of Siam▶
Anne of the Thousand Days▶
Arabian Nights
Autobiography of a Princess
Balalaika
Barbarian Queen 2: The
 Empress Strikes Back
Becket▶
Bonnie Prince Charlie
Boots & Saddles
Caligula
Carlton Browne of the F.O.
Case of the Baby Sitter
Catherine the Great

Charles & Diana: A Palace
 Divided
Chimes at Midnight▶
Cleopatra
Cobra Woman
The Coming of Amos▶
Coming to America▶
Conquest of the Normans
Court Jester▶
Death Mask of the Ninja
Desiree
Diana: Her True Story
Dr. Syn, Alias the Scarecrow
Donkey Skin▶
DuBarry Was a Lady
East of Borneo
Edward and Mrs. Simpson
Edward II
The Egyptian
El Ceniciento
Elena and Her Men▶
Elizabeth, the Queen
Emperor Jones
Emperor Jones/Paul
 Robeson: Tribute to an
 Artist
The Emperor's New Clothes
Excalibur▶
Fairytales
Fergie & Andrew: Behind
 Palace Doors
The Fifth Musketeer
The Fighting Prince of
 Donegal
Fit for a King
Forever Amber
Goetz von Berlichingen
The Grand Duchess and the
 Waiter▶
Hennessy
Henry IV
Henry V▶
His Majesty, the American
The Iron Mask
Ivan the Terrible, Part 1▶
Ivan the Terrible, Part 2▶
Julius Caesar▶
Julius Caesar
Just Suppose
Kind Hearts and Coronets▶
The King and I▶
A King in New York
King Lear▶
The King on Main Street
King Ralph
King Richard and the
 Crusaders
The King's Rhapsody
The King's Thief
The King's Whore
La Nuit de Varennes▶
Lady Jane▶
The Last Emperor▶
Lillie
The Lion in Winter▶
Lion Man
Lorna Doone
Lost in a Harem
Macbeth▶
Macbeth
The Magic Fountain
A Man for All Seasons▶
The Man in the Iron Mask▶
The Man Who Would Be
 King▶
Mannequin 2: On the Move
Marbella
Marie Antoinette
Mary of Scotland
The Master of Ballantrae
Mayerling▶
A Midsummer Night's Dream▶
Mom and Dad Save the World
Monsieur Beaucaire
My Pal, The King
Nicholas and Alexandra
Nine Days a Queen▶
Once Upon a Time
Options
Peter the Great▶
Phedre
Phoenix

The Polar Bear King
Power
The Prince and the Pauper▶
The Prince and the Pauper
The Prince and the Showgirl
The Princess and the Pea▶
Princess Tam Tam▶
Princess Yang Kwei Fei▶
Prisoner of Zenda▶
Prisoner of Zenda
The Private Life of Henry VIII▶
The Private Lives of Elizabeth
 & Essex▶
Queen Christina▶
Queen Kelly▶
The Rape of the Sabines
Rasputin▶
Rasputin and the Empress▶
The Rebellious Reign
The Return of the Musketeers
Return to Oz
Richard III▶
The Rise of Louis XIV▶
Roman Holiday▶
The Royal Bed
Salome/Queen Elizabeth
Scarlet Empress▶
Shin Heike Monogatari▶
Six Wives of Henry VIII▶
Snow White and the Seven
 Dwarfs▶
Snow White and the Seven
 Dwarfs
Soldier in Love
Solomon and Sheba
Son of Ali Baba
Splitting Heirs
Spy of Napoleon
Storm Over Asia▶
The Story of David▶
Surf Ninjas
The Swan
The Swan
The Sword & the Rose
Sword & the Sorcerer
The Sword of El Cid
The Three Musketeers▶
Throne of Blood▶
The Tower of London
Tower of London
Tower of Screaming Virgins
The Tragedy of King Richard II
Victoria Regina
The Virgin Queen▶
The War Lord▶
The Warriors
The Wedding March▶
Willow
The Woman He Loved
Young Bess▶

Running

Across the Tracks
Billie
College▶
Finish Line
Go for the Gold
The Gold & Glory
Goldengirl
The Jericho Mile
The Jesse Owens Story
Jim Thorpe: All American
The Loneliest Runner
The Loneliness of the Long
 Distance Runner▶
Marathon
Marathon Man▶
Off the Mark
On the Edge
Raw Courage
Running Brave
Sam's Son
See How She Runs▶
A Shining Season
The Terry Fox Story▶

Russia

 see also Red Scare
Anastasia▶
Anastasia: The Mystery of
 Anna

Anna Karenina▶
Anna Karenina
Assassination of Trotsky
Back in the USSR
Balalaika
Baltic Deputy▶
The Battle of Russia
The Battleship Potemkin▶
The Brothers Karamazov▶
Burglar▶
Come and See▶
Coming Out of the Ice▶
The Commies are Coming, the
 Commies are Coming
Commissar▶
Comrade X
Days of Glory
Dersu Uzala▶
Doctor Zhivago▶
Don't Drink the Water
Drums of Jeopardy
The Eagle▶
The End of St. Petersburg▶
The Extraordinary Adventures
 of Mr. West in the Land of
 the Bolsheviks
Final Assignment
Final Warning
First Strike
The Fixer▶
For Those About to Rock:
 Monsters in Moscow
Freeze-Die-Come to Life▶
The Girl from Petrovka
Gulag
I Killed Rasputin
The Ice Runner
The Inner Circle▶
Ivan the Terrible, Part 1▶
Ivan the Terrible, Part 2▶
Kindergarten▶
Laser Mission
Last Command▶
The Light Ahead
Little Vera▶
Love and Death▶
The Man with a Movie
 Camera▶
The Mirror▶
Moscow Does Not Believe in
 Tears▶
Mother▶
The Music Lovers
My Name is Ivan▶
Never Let Me Go
Nicholas and Alexandra
One Day in the Life of Ivan
 Denisovich▶
One Russian Summer
Peter the Great▶
Rasputin▶
Rasputin and the Empress▶
The Red and the White▶
Red Heat
The Russia House
Russian Roulette
Sakharov▶
Scarlet Dawn
Scarlet Empress▶
The Seagull▶
Sideburns
A Slave of Love▶
Solo Voyage: The Revenge
Stalin
Taxi Blues▶
Terminal Velocity
The Ultimate Imposter
War and Peace
War and Peace▶
We the Living
White Nights
World War III
Young Catherine▶

Sail Away

 *see also Deep Blue; Go
 Fish; Scuba; Sea Critter
 Attack; Submarines*
Adrift
Adventure Island
The Adventures of
 Huckleberry Finn▶

An Affair to Remember
The African Queen▶
All the Brothers Were Valiant
And the Ship Sails On▶
Anna Christie
Annapolis
Assault on a Queen
Away All Boats
The Baby and the Battleship
The Battleship Potemkin▶
Beat the Devil
Beyond the Poseidon
 Adventure
Billy Budd▶
Birds of Paradise
Bitter Moon
Blood Voyage
The Boatniks
Botany Bay
The Bounty▶
Boy in Blue
Cabin Boy
The Caine Mutiny▶
The Caine Mutiny Court
 Martial▶
Captain Caution
Captain Horatio Hornblower▶
Captain Ron
Captains Courageous▶
Captain's Paradise▶
The Captain's Table
Carry On Admiral
Carry On Cruising
China Seas▶
Christopher Columbus
The Coast Patrol
Convoy
Cruise into Terror
Cry from the Mountain
Damn the Defiant▶
Dangerous Charter
Dangerous Passage
Dark Tide
Das Boot▶
Day of the Assassin
The Day Will Dawn▶
Dead Ahead: The Exxon
 Valdez Disaster▶
Dead Calm▶
Dead Reckoning
Death Cruise
Death Ship
Death Tide
The Deep
Destroyer▶
Disney's Storybook Classics
Dixie Jamboree
Doctor at Sea
Don Winslow of the Coast
 Guard
The Dove
Down to the Sea in Ships
Ensign Pulver
Erik, the Viking
The Evil Below
Feet First
Fer-De-Lance
Ferry to Hong Kong
The Fighting Sullivans▶
The Final Countdown▶
Flat Top
Flight of the Intruder
Francis in the Navy
Friday the 13th, Part 8: Jason
 Takes Manhattan
Gangway
Geheimakte WB1
Ghost Ship
The Gift Horse
A Girl in Every Port
Going Under
Golden Rendezvous
Goliath Awaits
Gray Lady Down
The Great Lover
Gun Cargo
The Hairy Ape
Haunted Harbor
Hawaii Calls
He is My Brother
Hell-Ship Morgan
History is Made at Night▶

Horror of the Zombies
The Hunt for Red October▶
I Conquer the Sea
In Which We Serve▶
The Incredible Mr. Limpet
The Incredible Petrified World
Ironclads
Isle of Forgotten Sins
Jaws▶
Jaws 2
The Jewel of the Nile
John Paul Jones
Juggernaut▶
Kill Cruise
Killer on Board
King Kelly of the U.S.A.
Knife in the Water▶
The Last of Sheila
The Last Voyage
Law of the Sea
Le Crabe Tambour▶
The Legend of Sea Wolf
The Legend of the Sea Wolf
Lifeboat▶
Light at the Edge of the World
The Lightship
Live and Let Die
Long John Silver
The Long Voyage Home▶
Lord Jim▶
Love Affair▶
Manfish
The Mermaids of Tiburon
Mister Roberts▶
Monkey Business▶
Moon in Scorpio
Moran of the Lady Letty
Murder on the High Seas
Mutiny
The Mutiny of the Elsinore
Mutiny on the Bounty▶
Mutiny on the Bounty
Mystery Liner
The Mystery of the Mary
    Celeste
The Navigator▶
The Navy Comes Through
New Moon
A Night to Remember▶
Old Ironsides
Operation Petticoat▶
Oxford Blues
The Port of Missing Girls
The Poseidon Adventure
PT 109
Pueblo Affair▶
Pursuit of the Graf Spee
Reaching for the Moon
Reap the Wild Wind
Rich and Strange
Roaring Speedboats
Romancing the Stone▶
Run Silent, Run Deep▶
The Sand Pebbles▶
Save the Lady
Sea Chase
Sea Devils
Sea Gypsies
Sea Racketeers
The Sea Wolf▶
The Sea Wolf
Sharks' Treasure
Ship Ahoy
Ship of Fools▶
Ships in the Night
Shipwreck Island
Shout at the Devil
Sinbad the Sailor▶
Sink the Bismarck▶
South Seas Massacre
Steamboat Bill, Jr.▶
Submarine Seahawk
Swashbuckler
Tamango
Task Force
Tentacles of the North
They Were Expendable▶
Three Daring Daughters
Thunder in Paradise
Till There was You
To Have & Have Not▶
Today We Live

Torpedo Run
Transatlantic Merry-Go-Round
Treacherous Crossing
The Treasure of Jamaica Reef
Two Lost Worlds
U-Boat Prisoner
Under Siege
The Unsinkable Molly Brown▶
Up the Creek
Voyage
Voyage of Terror: The Achille
    Lauro Affair
Voyage of the Damned▶
Wake of the Red Witch
Wild Orchids
Wind
Windjammer
Windrider
Witch Who Came from the
    Sea
Woman of Desire
Wonderland Cove
The Wreck of the Mary Deare
Yankee Clipper

Saints

see also Religion
Augustine of Hippo▶
Bernadette
Brother Sun, Sister Moon
The Flowers of St. Francis
Francesco
Joan of Arc
Miracle in Rome
Miracle of Our Lady of Fatima
The Passion of Joan of Arc▶
Saint Joan
Sebastiane▶
The Song of Bernadette▶
Therese▶
A Time for Miracles

Sanity Check

*see also Doctors &
Nurses; Hospitals &
Medicine; Shrinks*
Aguirre, the Wrath of God▶
Alone in the Dark
American Eagle
Amos
An Angel at My Table▶
Anguish
Another Time, Another Place
Appointment with Fear
Arsenic and Old Lace▶
Asylum
Asylum of Satan
Bad Dreams
Beauty on the Beach
Bedlam▶
Behind Locked Doors
The Bell Jar
Bestia Nocturna
Beyond Therapy
A Blade in the Dark
Blood Frenzy
Blood Salvage
Blood Song
Bloody Wednesday
Body Chemistry
Boxing Helena
Buried Alive
Camille Claudel▶
Captain Newman, M.D.
The Carpenter
Cat in the Cage
Cause for Alarm
Chattahoochee
Clockwise
Coast to Coast
The Cobweb
The Collector▶
Committed
The Couch Trip
The Cracker Factory
Crazed
Crazy Fat Ethel II
Crazy People
Crime and Punishment▶
The Crime of Dr. Crespi
Criminally Insane

Crow Hollow
Cutting Class
Dark Obsession
Dark Places
Dark Sanity
Dark Waters
Darkroom
A Day at the Races▶
Dead Man Out▶
Dead of Night▶
Dead Pit
Deadly Innocence
Deadly Intruder
Deadly Strangers
The Deadly Trap
Death Kiss
Death Nurse
Dementia 13
A Demon in My View
Demons of the Mind
Deranged
Despair▶
Desperate Living
Deutschland im Jahre Null▶
Devi▶
The Devil Bat
The Devil Bat's Daughter
Devil Doll▶
The Devil in Silk
Devil in the Flesh
Devil Times Five
Devil Wears White
Diary of a Mad Housewife▶
Diary of a Madman
Diary of a Young Comic
Diary of Forbidden Dreams▶
Dick Barton, Special Agent
Die! Die! My Darling!
Die Screaming, Marianne
Disturbance
Disturbed
The Doctor and the Devils
Doctor Blood's Coffin
Doctor Butcher M.D.
Dr. Caligari
Dr. Frankenstein's Castle of
    Freaks
Dr. Hackenstein
Dr. Jekyll and Mr. Hyde▶
Dr. Jekyll and Mr. Hyde
Dr. Jekyll and the Wolfman
Dr. Mabuse the Gambler▶
Dr. Mabuse vs. Scotland Yard
Dr. Strangelove, or: How I
    Learned to Stop Worrying
    and Love the Bomb▶
Dr. Tarr's Torture Dungeon
Doctor X
Dog Day Afternoon▶
The Doll
Dominique is Dead
Don't Go in the Woods
Don't Look in the Basement
Don't Look Now▶
Don't Mess with My Sister!
Don't Open Till Christmas
Doom Asylum
A Double Life
Dream Lover
Dream No Evil
The Dream Team
Easy Rider▶
Eaten Alive
Echoes
Edge of Sanity
El: This Strange Passion▶
The End of Innocence
End of the Road
Endless Love
Endless Night
Entr'acte
Equus
Escape from Safehaven
Estate of Insanity
Europa '51
Exorcism's Daughter
Eyeball
The Eyes of the Amaryllis
The Fall of the House of Usher
The Fall of the House of
    Usher▶
The Fall of the House of Usher

False Identity
Fat Guy Goes Nutzoid
Fear Strikes Out▶
The Fifth Floor
The Fisher King▶
The Five of Me
Follow Me Quietly▶
Forced March
The 4th Man▶
Frances▶
Fright
From the Life of the
    Marionettes▶
Frozen Terror
The Girl in Room 2A
The Goalie's Anxiety at the
    Penalty Kick▶
The Hairdresser's Husband
Hamlet▶
Hammersmith is Out
Harvey▶
The Haunting▶
Haunting of Sarah Hardy
Haunts
Heart of Midnight
Heat and Sunlight
Henry IV
Heroes
Hider in the House
The Horrible Dr. Hichcock
The Horror Chamber of Dr.
    Faustus▶
Horror Hospital
Horror House on Highway 5
The Hospital▶
Hotline
The Housekeeper
How to Get Ahead in
    Advertising▶
How to Make a Monster
Hush, Hush, Sweet
    Charlotte▶
Hysteria
I Am the Cheese
I Dismember Mama
I Never Promised You a Rose
    Garden▶
Icy Breasts▶
If Things Were Different
Illusions
Impulse
The Incredible Two-Headed
    Transplant
Innocent Victim
Insanity
Interiors▶
The Invisible Ghost
It Happened at Nightmare Inn
It's Alive!
Juggernaut
Keeper
Killer's Moon
The King of Hearts▶
Lassie from Lancashire
The Last of Philip Banter
The Last Ride
Lethal Weapon▶
Lethal Weapon 2▶
Let's Scare Jessica to Death
Lilith▶
The Lonely Sex
Lost Angels
Lower Level
Lunatics: A Love Story▶
Luther the Geek
Mad Love▶
Man Facing Southeast▶
Manhunter▶
Marat/Sade▶
Midnight Warning
Mind Games
Mine Own Executioner▶
Mr. Jones
Morgan!
Mother Kusters Goes to
    Heaven▶
My First Wife
Network▶
Night of Bloody Horror
Night of Terror
The Night Visitor
Night Wars

Night Watch
The Ninth Configuration▶
Nobody's Perfekt
Nuts▶
October Man▶
Offerings
One Flew Over the Cuckoo's
    Nest▶
125 Rooms of Comfort
One Summer Love
The Onion Field▶
Out of Sight, Out of Her Mind
Overexposed
Pale Blood
Paperback Hero
Pay Off
Peeping Tom▶
Performance▶
A Piano for Mrs. Cimino▶
Picture Mommy Dead
Pigs
The Pink Panther Strikes
    Again▶
The Pit and the Pendulum▶
The Pit & the Pendulum
Play Misty for Me▶
Poison▶
The Possessed▶
The President's Analyst▶
Prettykill
Prime Suspect
Private Parts
Psychic Killer
Psycho▶
Psycho 2
Psycho Cop
Psycho Cop 2
Psychos in Love
Question of Silence▶
Raising Cain
Rasputin▶
The Rejuvenator
Remember Me
Return of the Ape Man
Revolt of the Zombies
Richard III▶
Room to Let
The Ruling Class▶
Scarlet Empress▶
Scissors
The Scout▶
Scream Bloody Murder
Scream for Help
Screamer
Seance on a Wet Afternoon▶
Secret Beyond the Door
The Sender
Sessions
Seven Days in May▶
Shadow Play
Shattered
Shattered Silence
Shattered Spirits
The Shining
Shock Corridor▶
The Silence of the Lambs▶
Silent Night, Bloody Night
Sisters▶
Sketches of a Strangler
Slaughter Hotel
Sledgehammer
Sniper▶
Solaris
Sophie's Choice▶
South of Reno
Spectre of the Rose
Spellbound▶
Story of Adele H.▶
Strait-Jacket
Strange Illusion
Street Asylum
A Streetcar Named Desire▶
Strong Medicine
Summer of Secrets
The Survivalist
Svengali
Sybil▶
Tainted Image
Teenage Frankenstein
The Tenant▶
The Testament of Dr.
    Cordelier▶

They Might Be Giants▶
Three Nuts in Search of a Bolt
Torture Train
Touched
Tracks
Trapped in Silence
Twin Peaks: Fire Walk with Me
Twinsanity
Twister
Urge to Kill
Vampire's Kiss▶
Vengeance Is Mine▶
Violated
Ward Six
Watched
What About Bob?▶
What Ever Happened to Baby Jane?▶
Whatever Happened to Susan Jane?
What's the Matter with Helen?
While I Live
White Heat▶
The Wind
Witchfire
Woman in Black
A Woman Under the Influence▶
You are Not I
The Young Ones

Satanism

see also *Demons & Wizards; Devils; Occult*

Alison's Birthday
Amazon Jail
Angel on My Shoulder
Asylum of Satan
Bad Dreams
Beast of the Yellow Night
Beyond the Door 3
The Black Cat▶
Black Roses
Black Sunday
The Blood on Satan's Claw▶
Blood Orgy of the She-Devils
The Bloodsuckers
The Brotherhood of Satan
Child of Darkness, Child of Light
The Chosen
The Crimson Cult
Damien: Omen 2
The Demon Lover
Demonoid, Messenger of Death
The Devil & Daniel Webster▶
Devil Rider
The Devils▶
The Devil's Daughter
The Devil's Eye
The Devil's Mistress
The Devil's Nightmare
The Devil's Partner
The Devil's Possessed
Devil's Rain
Devil's Son-in-Law
The Devil's Web
Disciple of Death
Doctor Faustus
El Monte de las Brujas
Equinox▶
Erotic Dreams
Eternal Evil
Evil Altar
Evilspeak
Exorcism
The Exorcist▶
The Exorcist 2: The Heretic
Eye of the Demon
Fear No Evil
The Final Conflict
Guardian of the Abyss
Hack O'Lantern
Halloween Night
Highway to Hell
House of the Black Death
I Don't Want to Be Born
I Drink Your Blood
Inferno
Invitation to Hell

Jaws of Satan
Land of the Minotaur
Leaves from Satan's Book
The Legend of Hillbilly John
Leonor
The Man and the Monster
Masque of the Red Death/ Premature Burial
Maxim Xul
The Mephisto Waltz▶
Midnight
Midnight Cabaret
Midnight's Child
Mind, Body & Soul
Mysterious Doctor Satan
Necromancer: Satan's Servant
Night Visitor
976-EVIL
976-EVIL 2: The Astral Factor
The Occultist
Oh, God! You Devil
The Omen
Other Hell
Prime Evil
Prince of Darkness
The Pyx▶
Race with the Devil
Rest In Pieces
Revenge
Rosemary's Baby▶
The Satanic Rites of Dracula
Satan's Black Wedding
Satan's Blade
Satan's Cheerleaders
Satan's Princess
Satan's School for Girls
Satan's Touch
Satanwar
The Sentinel
Servants of Twilight
The Seventh Victim▶
Shock 'Em Dead
Sisters of Satan
Speak of the Devil
Specters
The Spellbinder
Sugar Cookies
Suicide Cult
The Tempter
Terror Beach
To the Devil, A Daughter
Tombs of the Blind Dead
The Visitor
Warlock
Warlock: The Armageddon
Witchcraft
Witchcraft 3: The Kiss of Death
Witchcraft 5: Dance with the Devil
Witchcraft 6
WitchTrap

Satire & Parody

see also *Black Comedy; Comedy; Genre Spoofs*

Abbott and Costello Go to Mars
ABC's of Love & Sex, Australia Style
Abduction
The Act
The Adventures of Hairbreadth Harry
The Adventures of Picasso
The Adventures of Sherlock Holmes' Smarter Brother▶
The Affairs of Annabel
Airplane!▶
Airplane 2: The Sequel
Alex in Wonderland
Alien Women
All Through the Night▶
All You Need Is Cash▶
The Alphabet Murders
Amazon Women on the Moon
America 3000
American Tickler
America's Deadliest Home Video
Americathon

Andy Warhol's Dracula▶
Angel City
Animal Farm▶
Any Wednesday
The Apartment▶
As Young As You Feel▶
Attack of the Robots
Auntie Mame▶
Bad Manners
Bad Medicine
Bananas▶
Barjo
Barry McKenzie Holds His Own
Based on an Untrue Story
Basic Training
The Bawdy Adventures of Tom Jones
Beau Pere▶
Being There▶
The Best Man▶
Beyond the Valley of the Dolls
Beyond Therapy
Big Bus
Big Deal on Madonna Street▶
The Big Picture
Big Trouble in Little China
Bill & Ted's Bogus Journey
Bill & Ted's Excellent Adventure
Bingo Inferno
Black and White in Color▶
Black Bird
Bob & Carol & Ted & Alice
Bob Roberts▶
The Bonfire of the Vanities
Born in East L.A.
Boss
Boy Meets Girl▶
Britannia Hospital
Bullshot
Bullshot Crummond
The 'Burbs
Canadian Bacon
The Candidate▶
Carry On Cleo
Carry On Dick
Casino Royale
Caveman
CB4: The Movie
Champagne for Caesar▶
The Cheap Detective▶
Clockwise
A Clockwork Orange▶
Closet Cases of the Nerd Kind
The Coca-Cola Kid▶
Code Name: Chaos
Cold Turkey▶
The Committee
Coup de Grace
Crainquebille▶
Creature from the Haunted Sea
Crimewave
Cry Uncle
Curtain Up
Dark Habits
Dark Star▶
Darktown Strutters
Darling Lili
Dead Men Don't Die
Dead Men Don't Wear Plaid
Deal of the Century
Death of a Bureaucrat▶
Deathrow Gameshow
Diary of a Chambermaid▶
Dirty Dishes▶
The Discreet Charm of the Bourgeoisie▶
Dr. Heckyl and Mr. Hype
Dr. Strangelove, or: How I Learned to Stop Worrying and Love the Bomb▶
Doctors and Nurses
Dope Mania
The Dove▶
Down & Dirty▶
Down and Out in Beverly Hills
Down to Earth
Down Under
Dracula Sucks
Dragnet

E. Nick: A Legend in His Own Mind
Easy Wheels
11 Harrowhouse▶
Ella Cinders▶
Erik the Viking
The Extraordinary Adventures of Mr. West in the Land of the Bolsheviks
The Family Game▶
Fat and the Lean▶
Fatal Instinct
Ferocious Female Freedom Fighters
First Family
The Flaming Teen-Age
Flesh Gordon
Flicks
Footlight Frenzy
The Fortune Cookie▶
Frankenstein General Hospital
Frankenweenie
The French Touch
The Freshman
From Here to Maternity
The Front▶
Funny Money
Gabriel Over the White House▶
Galactic Gigolo
Galaxina
Ganjasaurus Rex
Gas
Geek Maggot Bingo
Genevieve▶
Gentlemen Prefer Blondes▶
Glory! Glory!▶
Going Berserk
Going Places▶
Greaser's Palace
Great American Traffic Jam
The Great Dictator▶
The Great Madcap
Great McGonagall
The Groove Tube
Grunt! The Wrestling Movie
Gulliver
Gumshoe
Gypsy
Hail
Hail the Conquering Hero▶
Hairspray▶
Half a Sixpence
Happiness
Hardware Wars & Other Film Farces
Heaven Can Wait▶
Heavens Above▶
Hell Comes to Frogtown
Hexed
High Anxiety
High Hopes▶
High Season
History of the World: Part 1
The History of White People in America
The History of White People in America: Vol. 2
Hollywood Harry
Home Movies
The Horror of Frankenstein
The Hospital▶
Hot Shots!▶
Hot Shots! Part Deux
The Hound of the Baskervilles
How I Got into College
I Love You, Alice B. Toklas
I Married a Vampire
I Was a Zombie for the FBI
The Icicle Thief▶
I'll Do Anything
I'm All Right Jack▶
I'm Gonna Git You Sucka▶
The Incredible Shrinking Woman
Incredibly Strange Creatures Who Stopped Living and Became Mixed-Up Zombies
The Inspector General
Invasion Earth: The Aliens Are Here!
Is There Sex After Death?▶

It Couldn't Happen Here
It's a Bundyful Life
J-Men Forever!▶
Jabberwocky
Jack and His Friends
Jamon, Jamon
Jekyll & Hyde...Together Again
Jet Benny Show
Johnny Dangerously
A Joke of Destiny, Lying in Wait Around the Corner Like a Bandit
Kentucky Fried Movie▶
The King of Hearts▶
La Casa de Madame Lulu
La Nueva Cigarra
The Ladies' Man
L'Age D'Or▶
The Last Polka▶
Leon the Pig Farmer
Let's Kill All the Lawyers
Lincoln County Incident
Lip Service▶
Look Out Sister▶
Loose Shoes
Love and Death▶
Love at Stake
Mad Mission 3
Mad Monster Party
Man Bites Dog
The Man in the White Suit▶
The Man Who Came to Dinner▶
Man Who Had Power Over Women
The Man with Bogart's Face
The Man with Two Brains▶
Marihuana
Men...▶
The Meteor Man
Mickey
The Milky Way▶
The Missionary
Mob Boss
Modern Times▶
Monster in a Box▶
Monty Python and the Holy Grail▶
Monty Python's Flying Circus
Monty Python's Life of Brian▶
Monty Python's Parrot Sketch Not Included
Monty Python's The Meaning of Life▶
More! Police Squad
The Mouse That Roared▶
Movers and Shakers
Movie, Movie
Murder by Death
Mutant on the Bounty
My Best Friend Is a Vampire
My Best Girl
Myra Breckinridge
The Naked Gun: From the Files of Police Squad▶
Naked Gun 33 1/3: The Final Insult
Naked Gun 2 1/2: The Smell of Fear
Naked in New York
Nasty Habits
National Lampoon Goes to the Movies
National Lampoon's Animal House▶
National Lampoon's Loaded Weapon 1
Natural Born Killers
Night Patrol
99 & 44/100 Dead
Nocturna
Northanger Abbey
The Nutty Professor▶
On the Avenue▶
Oscar
Overdrawn at the Memory Bank
Padre Nuestro
Pajama Tops
Pandemonium
Paramedics

Pardners
Partners
Pass the Ammo
P.C.U.
Personal Services
Phantom of Liberty▶
Pictures
The Pink Chiquitas
The Player▶
Police Squad! Help Wanted!
The Positively True
    Adventures of the Alleged
    Texas Cheerleader-
    Murdering Mom▶
Pray TV
The President's Analyst▶
Prime Time
The Princess Bride▶
Prisoner of Rio
A Private Function
Prize of Peril
The Producers▶
A Propos de Nice▶
Putney Swope▶
The Ramrodder
Rat Pfink a Boo-Boo
Real Men
Really Weird Tales
Red Desert Penitentiary
Red Earth
Red Garters
Rentadick
Repentance▶
The Report on the Party and
    the Guests▶
Repossessed
Return of Captain Invincible
The Return of Spinal Tap
Revolution! A Red Comedy▶
Ricky 1
Ring of the Musketeers
The Road to Lebanon
Robin Hood: Men in Tights
Rockin' Ronnie
The Rocky Horror Picture
    Show▶
Romeo Is Bleeding
Rosalie Goes Shopping▶
The Royal Bed
Rude Awakening
The Ruling Class▶
Running Mates▶
Sallah▶
Salvation!
Sammy & Rosie Get Laid▶
Saturday Night Live
Scenes from the Class
    Struggle in Beverly Hills
School for Scandal
Scrambled Feet
Scrooged
Second Time Lucky
The Secret Diary of Sigmund
    Freud
Seduction of Mimi▶
The Senator was Indiscreet▶
Serial▶
Serial Mom▶
Sex Adventures of the Three
    Musketeers
Sex with a Smile
Shame of the Jungle
Shampoo
A Shock to the System▶
Sideburns
Silent Movie
Simon of the Desert▶
Slammer Girls
Sleeper▶
Smile▶
S.O.B.
Spaced Out
Spaceship
Spirit of '76
State of Things▶
Stay Tuned
Straight to Hell
Strange Invaders▶
Streetfight
Sullivan's Travels▶
Sunset

Suppose They Gave a War
    and Nobody Came?
Surf Nazis Must Die
Sympathy for the Devil
Tanner '88
Tapeheads
Tartuffe
A Taste for Flesh and Blood
That's Adequate
They Call Me Bruce?
They Live
They Still Call Me Bruce
This is Spinal Tap▶
Thorn
Three Ages▶
Three of a Kind
The Thrill of It All!
To Be or Not to Be
Too Many Crooks
Top Secret!▶
Transylvania 6-5000
Trash
Traxx
True Stories▶
Trust Me
Tunnelvision
Turumba▶
Uforia
UHF
Unmasking the Idol
Up from the Depths
Up the Academy
A Very Curious Girl
Victor/Victoria▶
The Villain Still Pursued Her
Virgin High
Voyage of the Rock Aliens
Walker
Watermelon Man
Way He Was
What's Up, Tiger Lily?▶
The Wheeler Dealers▶
When Nature Calls
Where the Buffalo Roam
Where the Bullets Fly
White Mischief▶
The White Sheik▶
Whoops Apocalypse
Who's Who
Wild, Wild West Revisited
Without a Clue
Wolf
World Gone Wild
The Worm Eaters
The Worst of Hollywood: Vol.
    1
The Worst of Hollywood: Vol.
    2
The Worst of Hollywood: Vol.
    3
The Would-Be Gentleman
Yin & Yang of Mr. Go
You'll Find Out
Young Doctors in Love
Young Frankenstein▶
Young Nurses in Love
Zachariah
The Zany Adventures of
    Robin Hood
Zelig▶
Zoo Radio
Zorro, the Gay Blade

Savants
    see also Mental
    Retardation
Being There▶
Champagne for Caesar▶
Charly▶
Doctor Dolittle
Forrest Gump▶
King Lear▶
Malcolm
Rain Man▶
Tony Draws a Horse

Scams, Stings & Cons
    see also Heists
Abbott and Costello Meet the
    Keystone Kops
Adios Amigo

After the Fox
The Amazing Mr. X
Another You
Assault on a Queen
Barnaby and Me
Bedtime Story
Bergonzi Hand
Best of the Badmen
Beyond a Reasonable Doubt
The Big Grab
Big Trouble
Billionaire Boys Club
Birds & the Bees
Black Oak Conspiracy
Blackmail▶
Blackout
Blat
Blonde Crazy
Blood on the Moon
Blue Murder at St. Trinian's▶
Border Phantom
Border Saddlemates
Buffalo Stampede
Buona Sera, Mrs. Campbell
Butterfly Affair
Came a Hot Friday
Candleshoe
Caper of the Golden Bulls
The Captain from Koepenick
Cartier Affair
Catch Me a Spy
Cause for Alarm
Chameleon Street▶
The Charmer
Cheap Shots
Cheech and Chong: Things
    Are Tough All Over
Chinatown▶
Club Fed
Cold Justice
The Color of Money▶
The Con Artists
Con Man
Consenting Adults
The Conversation▶
Convicts at Large
Cops and Robbers
Cotton Comes to Harlem▶
Country Gentlemen
Couples and Robbers
Crack-Up
Curly Sue
Dangerous Summer
Dead Heat on a Merry-Go-
    Round▶
The Dead Pool
Deadfall
Deception
Diggstown
Dirty Rotten Scoundrels▶
The Distinguished Gentleman
Dr. Christian Meets the
    Women
Dollar
Elmer Gantry▶
Every Day's a Holiday
F/X▶
F/X 2: The Deadly Art of
    Illusion
Falcon Takes Over/Strange
    Bargain
Federal Agents vs.
    Underworld, Inc.
A Fish Called Wanda▶
Flim-Flam Man
Forger of London
Formula for a Murder
The Fourth Protocol▶
Framed
Frauds
The Gang's All Here
A Girl in Every Port
Girl Under the Sheet
Glory! Glory!▶
Going to Town
Good Neighbor Sam▶
Great Bank Hoax
The Great Impostor
Green Card
The Grifters▶
Harlem Rides the Range

Harry & Walter Go to New
    York
The Heat's On
Hi Diddle Diddle
Hold Your Man▶
The Honeymoon Machine
Hopscotch▶
The Hot Rock▶
House of Errors
House of Games▶
Housesitter
I Love Melvin
I Love You Again▶
If I Were Rich
In the Soup
Infernal Trio
Invasion of the Space
    Preachers
Kid from Not-So-Big
Killer
The Killing▶
Kind Hearts and Coronets▶
The King and Four Queens
The King of Marvin Gardens
The Lady Eve▶
The Last of Mrs. Cheyney▶
Law and Order
Le Gentleman D'Epsom
Leap of Faith
Les Aventuriers
Let's Do It Again
The Liars
Lies
Life Stinks
Lonely Hearts
Lovers: A True Story▶
The Madwoman of Chaillot
The Magician of Lublin
Malone
Manhattan Melodrama▶
Marshal of Cedar Rock
The Mask of Dijon
Maverick
Me and the Kid
Medicine Man
Mexican Hayride
Mexican Spitfire at Sea
Millions
Mistaken Identity
Mr. Boggs Steps Out
Mr. Lucky▶
Mo' Money
Murder for Sale
Murder on Approval
Murder on the Yukon
Never Give a Sucker an Even
    Break▶
Never Say Never Again
Nickel & Dime
Night and the City▶
No Way Out▶
None But the Lonely Heart▶
Nothing Sacred▶
Old Spanish Custom
One of My Wives Is Missing
Opportunity Knocks
Ossessione▶
Panic Button
Paper Man
Paper Moon▶
Parallax View▶
Parole, Inc.
Pass the Ammo
Phantom Gold
Piece of the Action
The Pope Must Diet
Popi▶
The President's Plane is
    Missing
Prisoner of Rio
The Producers▶
The Promoter▶
Reborn
The Red Light Sting
Remedy for Riches
Risky Business▶
The Road to Zanzibar▶
Roaring Speedboats
Ruthless People▶
Sands of Sacrifice
Save the Tiger▶
Scam

Scandalous
Sexual Intent
Silver Bears
Six Degrees of Separation
Skin Game▶
Sky Hei$t
Slither▶
Small Hotel
Something for Everyone
The Squeeze
Stacy's Knights
Stagecoach to Denver
Stavisky▶
The Sting▶
The Sting 2
Sucker Money
Sunburn
Support Your Local
    Gunfighter▶
Sweet Talker
The Swindle
Swindle
The Switch
Tall in the Saddle
A Taste for Killing
Tax Season
The Ten Million Dollar
    Getaway
Tequila Sunrise
Things Change▶
The Third Key
This is a Hijack
Thrilled to Death
The Tigress
Title Shot
Too Pretty to Be Honest
Tootsie▶
Train Robbers
Tricheurs
Trust Me
Underworld Scandal
The Unholy Three▶
Walpurgis Night▶
The Warrior & the Sorceress
Watch the Birdie
We're Talkin' Serious Money
White Men Can't Jump
Why Me?
Write to Kill

School Daze
    see also Campus Capers;
    Hell High School
Absolution
Accident
All God's Children
American Friends
Amy
Anna and the King of Siam▶
Au Revoir Les Enfants▶
Back to School
Backfield in Motion
The Beguiled▶
The Belles of St. Trinian's▶
The Bells of St. Mary's▶
Beverly Hills 90210: The
    Graduation
Black Narcissus▶
Blue Jeans
Bluffing It
Boarding School
The Broadway Drifter
The Browning Version▶
Buried Alive
Cheers for Miss Bishop
Children of a Lesser God▶
The Children's Hour
The Chocolate War▶
The Club
The Corn is Green▶
Crazy for Love
Crazy from the Heart▶
Dead Poets Society▶
The Devil's Playground▶
Doctor Dolittle
Dream to Believe
Educating Rita▶
Encino Man
The Ernest Green Story
Europa, Europa▶
Eyes Right!
Fame▶

Flirting▶
Forever Mary▶
The French Lesson
French Postcards
Games Girls Play
The George McKenna Story
Getting It On
The Getting of Wisdom
Getting Straight
Getting Wasted
The Girl, the Body and the Pill
The Girl Who Spelled
    Freedom▶
The Girls of Huntington House
The Goodbye Bird
Goodbye, Mr. Chips▶
Goodbye, Mr. Chips
Goodnight God Bless
The Gospel According to Vic
Grease▶
Grown Ups
Guess What We Learned in
    School Today?
The Happiest Days of Your
    Life▶
Hard Knox
Here Come the Co-Eds
High School USA
Homework
Horsemasters
How I Got into College
Impure Thoughts
Iron & Silk
Johnny Tiger
The Kid with the 200 I.Q.
Kindergarten Cop
Lambada
Leader of the Band
Lean on Me▶
L'Ecole Buisoniere
The Little Princess▶
Little Red Schoolhouse
The Long Gray Line▶
The Lords of Discipline
Married to It
A Minor Miracle
Murder in New Hampshire:
    The Pamela Smart Story
Murder 101
Murderer's Wife
National Lampoon's Class
    Reunion
The NeverEnding Story▶
Not Quite Human 2
Oxford Blues
Passion for Life
The People
Perfect Harmony
Platinum High School
Porky's
The Possessed
Prep School
Pride of Jesse Hallum
The Prime of Miss Jean
    Brodie▶
The Principal
The Pure Hell of St. Trinian's
Rachel, Rachel▶
The Rascals
Real Genius▶
Rebel
Renaissance Man
The Sandpiper
Satan's School for Girls
Secret Places
A Separate Peace
September Gun
Shout
Sing
Stand and Deliver▶
Stanley and Iris
Student Confidential
The Student Teachers
The Substitute
Summer School
Summer School Teachers
Tea and Sympathy▶
Teachers
To Sir, with Love
Tom Brown's School Days
Tom Brown's School Days▶
Topaze▶

Toy Soldiers
The Trouble with Angels
Twenty-Four Eyes▶
The Underachievers
Undergrads▶
Up the Academy
Up the Down Staircase▶
Virgin Queen of St. Francis
    High
Vital Signs
Waterland
Why Shoot the Teacher▶
The Winslow Boy▶
With Honors
The Worst Witch
Yentl
The Young Teacher
Zebrahead▶

Sci Fi

see also Fantasy

Abbott and Costello Go to
    Mars
Abraxas: Guardian of the
    Universe
The Abyss▶
Access Code
Aelita: Queen of Mars
After the Fall of New York
Aftermath
Aftershock
Akira
Alien▶
Alien 3
Alien Contamination
The Alien Factor
Alien from L.A.
Alien Intruder
Alien Nation
Alien Predators
Alien Private Eye
Alien Space Avenger
Alien Warrior
Alien Women
Alienator
Aliens▶
Aliens Are Coming
Aliens from Spaceship Earth
The Alpha Incident
Alphaville▶
Altered States▶
The Amazing Colossal Man
Amazing Stories
The Amphibian Man
Android
The Angry Red Planet
Anna to the Infinite Power
A.P.E.X.
Arcade
Arena
Around the World Under the
    Sea
The Arrival
The Asphyx▶
Assassin
Assignment Outer Space
The Astounding She-Monster
The Astro-Zombies
At the Earth's Core
The Atomic Brain
The Atomic Man
Atomic Submarine
Attack of the 50 Foot Woman
Attack of the 50 Ft. Woman
Attack of the Giant Leeches
Attack of the Killer Tomatoes
Attack of the Mushroom
    People
The Aurora Encounter
Bad Channels
Bad Girls from Mars
The Bamboo Saucer
Barbarella
*batteries not included
Battle Beneath the Earth
Battle Beyond the Stars
Battle Beyond the Sun
Battle for the Planet of the
    Apes
Battle of the Worlds
Battlestar Galactica

The Beast from 20,000
    Fathoms
The Beast of Yucca Flats
The Bees
Beginning of the End
Beneath the Planet of the
    Apes
Beneath the Valley of the
    Ultra-Vixens
Beyond the Stars
Beyond the Time Barrier
The Black Hole
Blade Runner▶
Blake of Scotland Yard
Blake's Seven
The Blob
The Blob▶
The Blood of Heroes
Blue Monkey
Body Melt
Body Snatchers
Bog
Boom in the Moon
A Boy and His Dog
The Brain Eaters
The Brain from Planet Arous
Brainstorm
Brainwaves
The Bronx Executioner
The Brother from Another
    Planet▶
Buck Rogers Conquers the
    Universe
Buck Rogers in the 25th
    Century
Bug
Capricorn One▶
Captive Planet
The Castle of Fu Manchu
Cat Women of the Moon
Charly▶
Cherry 2000
Children of the Damned
Cinderella 2000
Circuitry Man
City Limits
Class of 1999
Class of 1999 2: The
    Substitute
Class of Nuke 'Em High, Part
    2: Subhumanoid Meltdown
The Clones
The Clonus Horror
Close Encounters of the Third
    Kind▶
Club Extinction
Cocoon▶
Colossus: The Forbin
    Project▶
Communion
Conquest of Space
Conquest of the Planet of the
    Apes
The Cosmic Man
The Cosmic Monsters
Cosmos: War of the Planets
Crash and Burn
The Crazies
The Creation of the
    Humanoids
Creature
Creatures the World Forgot
Crime Zone
Critters 4
Cyborg
Cyborg 2
D-Day on Mars
Dagora, the Space Monster
Daleks—Invasion Earth 2150
    A.D.
Damnation Alley
Dark Side of the Moon
Dark Universe
Darkman▶
D.A.R.Y.L.
The Day It Came to Earth
Day of the Triffids▶
The Day the Earth Caught
    Fire▶
The Day the Earth Stood
    Still▶
The Day the Sky Exploded

Day Time Ended
Dead End Drive-In
Dead Man Walking
Dead Space
Deadly Harvest
The Deadly Mantis
Deadly Weapon
Death Sport
Death Watch▶
Deep Red
Deep Space
Deepstar Six
Def-Con 4
Deluge
Demolition Man
Demon City Shinjuku
Demon Seed▶
Destination Moon
Destination Moonbase Alpha
Destination Saturn
Destroy All Monsters
Destroy All Planets
Devil Girl from Mars
Dinosaurus!
Doc Savage
Dr. Alien
Dr. Cyclops
Dr. Goldfoot and the Bikini
    Machine
Doctor Mordrid: Master of the
    Unknown
Doctor Satan's Robot
Doctor Who: An Unearthly
    Child
Doctor Who and the Daleks
Doctor Who: Cybermen—The
    Early Years
Doctor Who: Daleks Invasion
    of Earth 2150 A.D.
Doctor Who: Day of the
    Daleks
Doctor Who: Death to the
    Daleks
Doctor Who: Earthshock
Doctor Who: Mawdryn
    Undead
Doctor Who: Pyramids of
    Mars
Doctor Who: Revenge of the
    Cybermen
Doctor Who: Robots of Death
Doctor Who: Shada
Doctor Who: Spearhead from
    Space
Doctor Who: Terror of the
    Zygons
Doctor Who: The Ark in Space
Doctor Who: The Brain of
    Morbius
Doctor Who: The Caves of
    Androzani
Doctor Who: The Curse of
    Fenric
Doctor Who: The Deadly
    Assassin
Doctor Who: The Five Doctors
Doctor Who: The Hartnell
    Years
Doctor Who: The Keeper of
    Traken
Doctor Who: The Masque of
    Mandragora
Doctor Who: The Mind
    Robber
Doctor Who: The Pertwee
    Years
Doctor Who: The Seeds of
    Death
Doctor Who: The Sontaran
    Experiment/The Genesis of
    the Daleks
Doctor Who: The Talons of
    Weng-Chiang
Doctor Who: The Three
    Doctors
Doctor Who: The Time
    Warrior
Doctor Who: The Tom Baker
    Years
Doctor Who: The Troughton
    Years

Doctor Who: The Twin
    Dilemma
Doctor Who: The War Games
Doctor Who: Tomb of the
    Cyberman
The Dog Soldier
Doin' Time on Planet Earth
Donovan's Brain▶
Dune
Dune Warriors
Duplicates
Earth vs. the Flying Saucers
Earth vs. the Spider
The Electronic Monster
The Element of Crime
The Eliminators
Embryo
Empire of the Ants
The Empire Strikes Back▶
Encounter at Raven's Gate
End of the World
Endgame
Endless Descent
Enemy Mine
Equalizer 2000
Escape from Galaxy Three
Escape from New York
Escape from Planet Earth
Escape from the Bronx
Escape from the Planet of the
    Apes▶
Escape 2000
Escapes
E.S.P.
E.T.: The Extra-Terrestrial▶
Eve of Destruction
Explorers
Exterminators of the Year
    3000
The Eye Creatures
Eyes Behind the Stars
Fahrenheit 451▶
Fangs
Fantastic Planet▶
Fantastic Voyage▶
Fiend Without a Face
The Final Executioner
The Final Programme
Fire in the Sky
Fire Maidens from Outer
    Space
The Fire Next Time
Firebird 2015 A.D.
First Man into Space
First Men in the Moon
First Spaceship on Venus▶
Flash Gordon
Flash Gordon Conquers the
    Universe
Flash Gordon: Mars Attacks
    the World
Flash Gordon: Rocketship
Flash Gordon: Vol. 1
Flash Gordon: Vol. 2
Flash Gordon: Vol. 3
The Flesh Eaters
Flight to Mars
The Fly▶
The Fly 2
The Flying Saucer
Forbidden Planet▶
Forbidden World
Forbidden Zone
Force on Thunder Mountain
Fortress
Fortress of Amerikka
Four Sided Triangle
The 4D Man
Frankenstein Meets the Space
    Monster
Freejack
From "Star Wars" to "Jedi":
    The Making of a Saga
From the Earth to the Moon
Frozen Alive
Fugitive Alien
Future Force
Future Hunters
Future Zone
Futurekick
Futureworld
Galactic Gigolo

Galaxy Invader
Galaxy of Terror
Game of Survival
Gamera, the Invincible
Gamera vs. Barugon
Gamera vs. Gaos
Gamera vs. Guiron
Gamera vs. Zigra
The Gamma People
Gappa the Trifibian Monster
Generations: Mind Control-
 From the Future
Ghidrah the Three Headed
 Monster
Ghost Patrol
The Giant Claw
The Giant Gila Monster
The Giant Spider Invasion
The Gladiators
Glen and Randa
Godzilla, King of the Monsters
Godzilla 1985
Godzilla on Monster Island
Godzilla Raids Again
Godzilla vs. Biollante
Godzilla vs. Megalon
Godzilla vs. Monster Zero
Godzilla vs. Mothra
Godzilla vs. the Cosmic
 Monster
Godzilla vs. the Sea Monster
Godzilla vs. the Smog
 Monster
Godzilla's Revenge
Gorath
Gorgo
Grampa's Sci-Fi Hits
Grand Tour: Disaster in Time
The Green Slime
The Groundstar Conspiracy▶
GUY: Awakening of the Devil
The Guyver
H-Man
Half Human
The Handmaid's Tale
Hands of Steel
Hangar 18
Hardware
Heartbeeps
The Hidden▶
The Hidden 2
Hide and Seek
Hideous Sun Demon
High Desert Kill
Highlander 2: The Quickening
The Hitchhiker's Guide to the
 Galaxy
Hollywood Boulevard 2
Homewrecker
Horror Planet
Horrors of the Red Planet
Howard the Duck
The Human Duplicators
The Human Vapor
Humanoid Defender
Hyper-Sapien: People from
 Another Star
I Come in Peace
I Married a Monster from
 Outer Space
Iceman▶
Idaho Transfer
The Illustrated Man▶
In the Aftermath
In the Cold of the Night
Incredible Melting Man
The Incredible Petrified World
The Incredible Shrinking
 Man▶
Infra-Man
Innerspace
Interzone
Intruder Within
Intruders
Invader
The Invaders
Invaders from Mars
Invasion
Invasion Earth: The Aliens Are
 Here!
Invasion of the Animal People
Invasion of the Bee Girls▶

Invasion of the Body
 Snatchers▶
Invasion of the Body Stealers
Invasion of the Girl Snatchers
Invasion of the Space
 Preachers
The Invisible Boy
The Invisible Man Returns▶
The Invisible Terror
Invisible: The Chronicles of
 Benjamin Knight
Island of Terror▶
Island of the Burning Doomed
Island of the Lost
It Came from Beneath the
 Sea▶
It Came From Outer Space▶
It Conquered the World
It! The Terror from Beyond
 Space
Journey Beneath the Desert
Journey into the Beyond
Journey to the Center of the
 Earth▶
Journey to the Center of the
 Earth
Journey to the Center of Time
Journey to the Far Side of the
 Sun▶
Killers from Space
The Killing Edge
Killings at Outpost Zeta
King Dinosaur
King Kong Versus Godzilla
The Kirlian Witness
Knights
Kronos
Krull
Laboratory
The Land That Time Forgot
The Land Unknown
Laserblast
Last Chase
The Last Starfighter
Last War
The Last Woman on Earth
Lathe of Heaven
The Lawless Land
The Lawnmower Man
Leviathan
Lifeforce
Lifepod
Light Years
Liquid Sky▶
The Living Dead
Lobster Man from Mars
Lock 'n' Load
Logan's Run
Looker
Lords of the Deep
The Lost Empire
The Lost Missile
Lost Planet Airmen
The Love Factor
The Lucifer Complex
Making Mr. Right
The Making of The
 Hitchhiker's Guide to the
 Galaxy
A Man Called Rage
The Man from Atlantis
The Man Who Fell to Earth▶
Mandroid
Manhunt of Mystery Island
Maniac Warriors
The Manster
Marooned
Mars Needs Women
The Martian Chronicles: Part 1
The Martian Chronicles: Part 2
The Martian Chronicles: Part 3
Masters of Venus
Mechanical Crabs
Meet the Hollowheads
Megaforce
Megaville
Mesa of Lost Women
Metallica
Metalstorm
Metamorphosis
Meteor Monster

Metropolis▶
Midnight Movie Massacre
Millenium
Mind Snatchers
Mind Trap
Mind Warp
Mindwarp
Misfits of Science
Missile to the Moon
Mission Galactica: The Cylon
 Attack
Mission Mars
Mission Stardust
Mistress of the World
The Mole People
Monkey Boy
Monolith
The Monolith Monsters
Monster a Go-Go!
Monster from Green Hell
Monster from the Ocean Floor
The Monster Maker
The Monster of Piedras
 Blancas
Monster on the Campus
The Monster that Challenged
 the World
Moon 44
Moon Pilot
Moontrap
Mothra▶
Murder by Moonlight
Murder in Space
Mutant Hunt
Mutator
The Mysterians
Mysterious Island▶
Mysterious Planet
Mysterious Two
Navy vs. the Night Monsters
Nemesis
Neon City
The Nest
Neutron and the Black Mask
Neutron vs. the Amazing Dr.
 Caronte
Neutron vs. the Death Robots
The New Gladiators
The New Invisible Man
Next One
Night Beast
Night Caller from Outer Space
Night of the Blood Beast
Nightfall
Nightflyers
984: Prisoner of the Future
1984▶
No Survivors, Please
Norman's Awesome
 Experience
Not of This Earth
Nude on the Moon
Octaman
Official Denial
Omega Man
On the Comet▶
One Million B.C.
The Original Fabulous
 Adventures of Baron
 Munchausen
The Original Flash Gordon
 Collection
The Outer Limits: Galaxy
 Being
Outland
Parasite
Peacemaker
The People
The People That Time Forgot
People Who Own the Dark
The Phantom Empire
Phantom from Space
The Phantom from 10,000
 Leagues
The Phantom Planet
Phase 4
Phenomenal and the Treasure
 of Tutankamen
The Philadelphia Experiment
Philadelphia Experiment 2
Phoenix the Warrior
Plan 9 from Outer Space

Planet Burg
Planet Earth
Planet of Blood
Planet of the Apes▶
Planet of the Dinosaurs
Planet of the Vampires
Planet on the Prowl
Planets Against Us
The Power Within
Predator
Predator 2
Prehistoric Women
Primal Impulse
Primal Scream
Prisoners of the Lost Universe
The Professor
Programmed to Kill
Project A-ko
Project A-ko 2: Plot of the
 Daitokuji Financial Group
Project A-ko 3: Cinderella
 Rhapsody
Project: Alien
Project: Genesis
Project Moon Base
Prototype▶
Prototype X29A
PSI Factor
The Psychotronic Man
Pulse
The Puma Man
The Purple Monster Strikes
Purple People Eater
Quarantine
Quatermass 2▶
Quatermass Conclusion
The Quatermass Experiment▶
Queen of Outer Space
Quest for Love
The Quiet Earth▶
Quintet
Radar Men from the Moon
Radioactive Dreams
Raiders of Atlantis
Rats
Reactor
Rebel Storm
Red Planet Mars
Refuge of Fear
Remote Control
Resurrection of Zachary
 Wheeler
The Return
Return from Witch Mountain
Return of Chandu
The Return of Swamp Thing
Return of the Aliens: The
 Deadly Spawn
Return of the Fly
Return of the Jedi▶
Revenge of the Teenage
 Vixens from Outer Space
Riding with Death
Robinson Crusoe on Mars
Robo-Chic
Roboman
Robot Holocaust
Robot Jox
Robot Monster
Robot Wars
Rock & Roll Cowboys
Rocket Attack U.S.A.
Rocketship
Rocketship X-M
Rocky Jones, Space Ranger
Rocky Jones, Space Ranger:
 Renegade Satellite
Roller Blade
Roller Blade Warriors: Taken
 By Force
Rollerball
R.O.T.O.R.
Runaway
Running Against Time
Running Delilah
The Running Man
Rush
Saturn 3
Scanner Cop
Scream and Scream Again
The Sea Serpent
Search and Destroy

The Secret of the Golden
 Eagle
The Secret of the Telegian
The Sex Machine
Shadowzone
She
Silent Running▶
The Sisterhood
Skeeter
Sky Pirates
Slaughterhouse Five
Slave Girls from Beyond
 Infinity
Sleeper▶
The Slime People
Slipstream
Solar Crisis
Solarbabies
Solaris
Son of Godzilla
Soylent Green
Space Monster
Space Mutiny
Space: 1999
Space: 1999—Alien Attack▶
Space Ninja: Sword of the
 Space Ark
Space Patrol
Space Rage
Space Raiders
Space Soldiers Conquer the
 Universe
Spaceballs
SpaceCamp
Spaced Invaders
Spacehunter: Adventures in
 the Forbidden Zone
Spaceship
Split
Split Second
Sputnik
Stalker▶
Star Crash
Star Crystal
Star Quest
Star Slammer
Star Trek: The Motion Picture
Star Trek 2: The Wrath of
 Khan▶
Star Trek 3: The Search for
 Spock
Star Trek 4: The Voyage
 Home▶
Star Trek 5: The Final Frontier
Star Trek 6: The
 Undiscovered Country
Star Trek Bloopers
Star Trek: The Cage
Star Trek the Next
 Generation: Encounter at
 Farpoint
Star Wars▶
Starchaser: The Legend of
 Orin
Starflight One
Starman▶
Starship
Starship Invasions
Starvengers
Steel and Lace
Stranded
Strange New World
The Stranger
The Stranger from Venus
Strangers in Paradise
Stryker
Sun Ra & His Intergalactic
 Solar Arkestra: Space is
 the Place
Super Force
Superman: The Serial, Vol. 1
Survival Earth
Survival Zone
Survivor
Syngenor
Tarantula▶
A Taste for Flesh and Blood
Teen Alien
Teenage Caveman
Teenagers from Outer Space
10th Victim
The Terminal Man

Terminator 2: Judgment Day▶
Terronauts
Terror Beneath the Sea
Terror is a Man
Terror of Mechagodzilla
The Terror Within 2
The Terrornauts
Test Tube Teens from the Year 2000
Tetsuo: The Iron Man
Them!▶
They
They Came from Beyond Space
The Thing▶
The Thing
Things to Come▶
This is Not a Test
This Island Earth
Those Fantastic Flying Fools
The Three Worlds of Gulliver
THX 1138▶
Ticks
Time After Time▶
Time Fighters
The Time Guardian
The Time Machine▶
Time Machine
Time Runner
Time Trackers
The Time Travelers
Time Troopers
Time Walker
Timecop
Timerider
Timestalkers
Tobor the Great
Total Recall▶
Toward the Terra
Trancers
Trancers 2: The Return of Jack Deth
Trancers 3: Deth Lives
Trancers 4: Jack of Swords
Transatlantic Tunnel
Transformations
The Trial of the Incredible Hulk
Tripods: The White Mountains
Tron
The Trouble with Dick
12:01
20 Million Miles to Earth
The 27 Day
The Twilight Zone
Two Lost Worlds
2001: A Space Odyssey▶
2010: The Year We Make Contact▶
2069: A Sex Odyssey
UFO: Target Earth
Uforia
Ugly Little Boy
The Ultimate Warrior
Undersea Kingdom
The Unearthly Stranger
Unknown World
Unnatural
Until The End of The World▶
The Valley of Gwangi▶
Village of the Damned▶
Village of the Giants
Virus
Visitants
Voyage of the Rock Aliens
Voyage to the Bottom of the Sea▶
Voyage to the Planet of Prehistoric Women
Voyage to the Prehistoric Planet
War in Space
The War of the Colossal Beast
War of the Gargantuas
War of the Robots
War of the Wizards
The War of the Worlds▶
Warlords
Warlords of the 21st Century
Warning from Space
Warrior of the Lost World
Wavelength
Waxwork 2: Lost in Time

Weird Science
Welcome Back Mr. Fox
Westworld▶
What Waits Below
When Dinosaurs Ruled the Earth
When Time Began
When Worlds Collide
Where Time Began
Wild Palms
Wild, Wild Planet
A Wind Named Amnesia
Wired to Kill
Woman in the Moon
Women of the Prehistoric Planet
World Gone Wild
X from Outer Space
X: The Man with X-Ray Eyes▶
Xtro
Xtro 2: The Second Encounter
The Yesterday Machine
Yongkari Monster of the Deep
Zardoz
Zeram
Zero Population Growth
Zombies of the Stratosphere
Zone Troopers
Zontar, the Thing from Venus

Science & Scientists
see also Genetics; Inventors & Inventions; Mad Scientists
Altered States▶
Android
The Andromeda Strain
Around the World Under the Sea
Arrowsmith
Assassin
The Atomic City
The Atomic Man
Attack of the Robots
Beach Party
A Brief History of Time▶
Caravan to Vaccares
Children of the Damned
Dam Busters▶
Dark Star▶
Darkman▶
The Day of the Dolphin
Day One▶
Dead Men Don't Wear Plaid
The Dead Next Door
Deadly Friend
Demon Seed▶
Dick Barton, Special Agent
Dick Tracy, Detective/The Corpse Vanishes
Die Laughing
Die, Monster, Die!
Dirty Games
Dr. Alien
Doctor Dolittle
The Eliminators
Fantastic Voyage▶
Fat Man and Little Boy
Feast for the Devil
The Fly▶
The Fly 2
Forbidden World
Forever Darling
Four Sided Triangle
The 4D Man
From the Earth to the Moon
Geheimakte WB1
Glory Enough for All: The Discovery of Insulin
The Henderson Monster
How to Make a Doll
Human Gorilla
Humanoid Defender
Illegal Entry: Formula for Fear
The Incredible Hulk Returns
International House
The Invisible Man Returns▶
Jurassic Park▶
Last Day of the War
Laughing at Danger
Link
The Lost World
Love Potion #9

The Man with Two Brains▶
Max Fleischer's Documentary Features
Medicine Man
Miracle Mile▶
Mr. Superinvisible
Monkey Boy
Monkey Business▶
Monkey's Uncle
My Science Project
My Stepmother Is an Alien
Neptune Factor
Phantom Empire
Project X
Prototype X29A
The Quiet Earth▶
Real Genius▶
Return of Captain Invincible
Return of the Ape Man
Return of the Fly
The Rocky Horror Picture Show▶
The Secret of the Telegian
The Sex Machine
Shaker Run
Shakma
Simon
Son of Flubber
Spaceways
Stephen King's Golden Years
The Story of Louis Pasteur▶
The Structure of Crystals
Surf 2
Swamp Thing
The Thing
Things to Come▶
This Island Earth
Threshold
Tidal Wave
Time Trackers
The Time Travelers
Tomcat: Dangerous Desires
12:01
Unknown Island
Unknown World
Where Time Began
The Wild and the Free
Woman in the Dunes▶
The Yesterday Machine

Scotland
see also Great Britain
Another Time, Another Place▶
The Big Man: Crossing the Line▶
Blood Clan
Bonnie Prince Charlie
Bonnie Scotland
Brigadoon▶
Challenge to Lassie
Comfort and Joy▶
Devil Girl from Mars
The Devil's Undead
Dreams Lost, Dreams Found
Escape
The Gospel According to Vic
Gregory's Girl▶
Greystoke: The Legend of Tarzan, Lord of the Apes
I Know Where I'm Going▶
Lady of the Lake
Little Minister▶
Local Hero▶
Madeleine
Mary of Scotland▶
The Master of Ballantrae
The Pointsman
Pride of the Clan
The Prime of Miss Jean Brodie▶
Ring of Bright Water▶
Rob Roy—The Highland Rogue
The Secret of the Loch
The Three Lives of Thomasina▶
Tragedy of Flight 103: The Inside Story▶
Trouble in the Glen
Whiskey Galore▶
Year of the Comet

Screwball Comedy
see also Comedy; Slapstick Comedy
All in a Night's Work
Amazing Adventure
Ambassador Bill
America
And Baby Makes Six
Angel on My Shoulder▶
Angel on My Shoulder
Antonio
As You Like It
As You Were
Assault of the Party Nerds
The Associate
Auntie
The Awful Truth▶
The Baby and the Battleship
The Bachelor and the Bobby-Soxer▶
Bachelor Mother▶
Bachelor of Hearts
Back to School
Bank Shot▶
Bedazzled▶
Bedtime Story
Beer
Best of W.C. Fields
Big Business
Blame It on the Bellboy
The Bliss of Mrs. Blossom▶
Blue Murder at St. Trinian's▶
Boeing Boeing
Boss Foreman
Bringing Up Baby▶
Bugs Bunny: Hollywood Legend
Bugs Bunny's Comedy Classics
Bullseye!
Buona Sera, Mrs. Campbell
Camp Cucamonga: How I Spent My Summer Vacation
Carry On Admiral
Chaplin: A Character Is Born
Chaplin: A Character Is Born/Keaton: The Great Stone Face
Chaplin Essanay Book 1
The Chaplin Revue
Charlie Chaplin Carnival, Four Early Shorts
Charlie Chaplin Cavalcade, Mutual Studios Shorts
Charlie Chaplin Centennial Collection
Charlie Chaplin Festival
Charlie Chaplin: Night at the Show▶
Charlie Chaplin: Rare Chaplin
Charlie Chaplin...Our Hero!
Charlie Chaplin's Keystone Comedies #1
Charlie Chaplin's Keystone Comedies #2
Charlie Chaplin's Keystone Comedies #3
Charlie Chaplin's Keystone Comedies #4
Charlie Chaplin's Keystone Comedies #5
The Circus▶
Combat Academy
The Couch Trip
The Count
Crackers
Days of Thrills and Laughter▶
Doctor in the House▶
Dr. Otto & the Riddle of the Gloom Beam
Doctor Takes a Wife▶
Don Juan, My Love▶
Donde Duermen Dos...Duermen Tres
Double Wedding
Doubting Thomas
Down Among the Z Men
Down the Drain
Easy Money
Easy Street▶

Egg and I▶
El Gendarme Desconocido
Everything You Always Wanted to Know About Sex (But Were Afraid to Ask)▶
The Favor, the Watch, & the Very Big Fish
Fireballs
The Fireman
Fit for a King
The Floorwalker
The Floorwalker/By the Sea▶
Forever Darling
Forsaking All Others
Fotografo de Senoras
The Geisha Boy
Get Crazy
Gold Rush/Payday
A Hard Day's Night▶
Harvey▶
Her Husband's Affairs
He's My Girl
Holiday▶
Hot to Trot!
How I Learned to Love Women
How Sweet It Is!
I Love My...Wife
I Love You Again▶
I Wanna Be a Beauty Queen
Inspector Hornleigh
Italian Straw Hat▶
It's the Old Army Game
Joy of Living▶
La Chevre▶
Labyrinth of Passion
The Lady Eve▶
Libeled Lady▶
Life Stinks
Little Rascals Christmas Special
Lobster Man from Mars
The Long, Long Trailer
Lots of Luck
The Love Bug
Love Crazy▶
Lucky Partners
Lunatics & Lovers
Madhouse
Make Mine Mink▶
Malibu Beach
Malibu Bikini Shop
The Marriage Circle▶
The Marx Brothers in a Nutshell▶
The Mating Game▶
Me and Him
Meatballs
Meatballs 2
A Midsummer Night's Sex Comedy▶
Minsky's Follies
Miracle of Morgan's Creek▶
Mr. & Mrs. Smith▶
Modern Girls
The Money Pit
Monkey Business▶
Monkeys, Go Home!
Moon's Our Home
The More the Merrier▶
Morons from Outer Space
Mugsy's Girls
Munster's Revenge
My American Cousin▶
My Chauffeur
My Favorite Brunette
My Favorite Wife▶
My Man Godfrey▶
Naked Is Better
National Lampoon's Christmas Vacation
National Lampoon's European Vacation
National Lampoon's Vacation▶
Nervous Ticks
Noises Off
Not for Publication
Nothing Sacred▶
The Nude Bomb

Ollie Hopnoodle's Haven of Bliss
One Woman or Two
The Palm Beach Story▶
Pink Flamingos
Platinum Blonde▶
Police Academy
Police Academy 2: Their First Assignment
Police Academy 3: Back in Training
Police Academy 4: Citizens on Patrol
Police Academy 5: Assignment Miami Beach
Police Academy 6: City Under Siege
Polyester
Reaching for the Moon
Recruits
The Rink▶
Romance with a Double Bass▶
Running Wild
See No Evil, Hear No Evil
Simon
The Smallest Show on Earth▶
Some Like It Hot▶
Son of Flubber
A Southern Yankee
Spaceballs
Spaced Invaders
Spring Break
Stallion
Stan Without Ollie, Vol. 1
Stan Without Ollie, Vol. 2
Stan Without Ollie, Vol. 3
Stan Without Ollie, Vol. 4
Starhops
Starring Bugs Bunny!
Start the Revolution Without Me▶
The Statue
Stewardess School
Still Not Quite Human
Stir Crazy
Stitches
Stocks and Blondes
The Stoogephile Trivia Movie
Strange Brew
Stripes
Stroker Ace
Stuckey's Last Stand
Student Affairs
The Student Teachers
Summer School Teachers
Sundance
Superdad
Supergrass
Swap Meet
Sweet Revenge
Sweet Young Thing
Swing It, Sailor!
The Swinging Cheerleaders
Swinging Wives
Switching Channels
Takin' It All Off
Talk of the Town▶
Teen Vamp
Teen Witch
Tell It to the Judge
That Naughty Girl
They Went That-a-Way & That-a-Way
Three in the Cellar
The Three Stooges Meet Hercules
Thunder & Mud
Tigers in Lipstick
Tramp & a Woman
Tricks of the Trade
Triple Trouble/Easy Street
Truck Stop
Twist
Two Reelers: Comedy Classics 10
Two Weeks to Live
The Underachievers
The Vagabond
Vibes
Vice Versa▶
Waitress

Waltz of the Toreadors▶
Watch the Birdie
W.C. Fields Comedy Bag
What's Up, Doc?▶
When Women Had Tails
When Women Lost Their Tails
Where Were You When the Lights Went Out?
Which Way Is Up?
Whoops Apocalypse
Who's That Girl?
Wild Women of Wongo
Witches' Brew
Woman of Paris/Sunnyside▶
Work/Police▶
World's Greatest Lover
You Can't Cheat an Honest Man▶
You Can't Take It with You▶
Zotz!

Scuba

see also Deep Blue
The Abyss▶
Beneath the 12-Mile Reef
The Big Blue
Daring Game
The Deep
Easy Come, Easy Go
The Evil Below
ffolkes
Flipper▶
Flipper's New Adventure▶
Full Fathom Five
Isle of Forgotten Sins
Leviathan
The Man from Atlantis
Navy SEALS
Neptune Factor
Never Say Never Again
Night of the Sharks
Oceans of Fire
The Sea Serpent
Thunderball
The Treasure Seekers
Underwater

Sea Critter Attack

see also Deep Blue; Go Fish; Killer Beasts
Alligator▶
Around the World Under the Sea
Attack of the Giant Leeches
Attack of the Swamp Creature
Barracuda
The Beach Girls and the Monster
The Beast from 20,000 Fathoms
Beyond Atlantis
Blood Beach
Bloodstalkers
Creature from Black Lake
Creature from the Black Lagoon▶
Creature from the Haunted Sea
Creature of Destruction
The Creature Walks Among Us
Curse of the Swamp Creature
Deepstar Six
Demon of Paradise
Devil Monster
Devilfish
The Flesh Eaters
Godzilla vs. the Sea Monster
Gorgo
The Great Alligator
Horror of Party Beach
Island Claw
Jason and the Argonauts▶
Jaws▶
Jaws 2
Jaws 3
Jaws of Death
Jaws: The Revenge
Killer Fish
The Loch Ness Horror
The Man from Atlantis

The McConnell Story
Mean Streets▶
Memphis Belle▶
Monster from the Ocean Floor
The Monster of Piedras Blancas
The Monster that Challenged the World
New York, New York▶
None But the Brave
Obsession
Octaman
Orca
The Phantom from 10,000 Leagues
Piranha
Piranha 2: The Spawning
Reap the Wild Wind
Revenge of the Creature
Scorpion with Two Tails
Screams of a Winter Night
The Sea Serpent
Serpent Island
Shark!
Shark's Paradise
The Spawning
Swamp Thing
Tentacles
Terror in the Swamp
Tintorera...Tiger Shark
20,000 Leagues Under the Sea▶
Up from the Depths
What Waits Below

Sea Disasters

see also Air Disasters; Deep Blue; Disaster Flicks
The Abyss▶
Airport '77
Beyond the Poseidon Adventure
Das Boot▶
Deepstar Six
Goliath Awaits
Juggernaut▶
The Last Voyage
Leviathan
A Night to Remember▶
The Poseidon Adventure
Raise the Titanic
The Seducers
S.O.S. Titanic
The Unsinkable Molly Brown▶

Serial Killers

see also Crime & Criminals; Crime Sprees
Addams Family Values
Ambition
Amsterdamned
Aroused
The Awful Dr. Orlof
The Baby Doll Murders
The Banker
Bluebeard▶
Body Parts
The Boston Strangler
Broken Mirrors
Bums
The China Lake Murders
Cold Front
Confessions of a Serial Killer
Cop
Cosh Boy
Dangerous Love
The Dark Ride
Dead Certain
Dead Girls
Deadly Force
Deadly Games
Deadly Neighbor
The Deliberate Stranger▶
A Demon in My View
Destroyer
The Element of Crime
Evil Laugh
Eyes of a Stranger
Eyes of Laura Mars
Eyes of the Beholder
Fatal Charm

Fathers and Sons
Fear
Final Notice
The First Power
The Freeway Maniac
Ghost in the Machine
The Hawk
Henry: Portrait of a Serial Killer▶
Hidden Obsession
The Hillside Strangler
Honeymoon Killers▶
The Horror Show
The Hunt for the Night Stalker
Impulse
Inn on the River
The Invisible Strangler
Jack the Ripper
Jack the Ripper▶
The January Man
Jennifer 8
Kalifornia
L.A. Crackdown 2
Laser Moon
Laughing Policeman
M▶
The Mad Executioners
Man Bites Man▶
Maniac Cop
Mr. Frost
Mortal Sins
Natural Born Killers
Night Shadow
Night Stalker
No Way to Treat a Lady▶
The Paint Job
Pale Blood
Prey of the Chameleon
Prime Suspect▶
Psychic
Relentless 3
The Rosary Murders
The Satan Killer
Serial Mom▶
The Silence of the Lambs▶
Slaughter of the Innocents
Snapdragon
So I Married an Axe Murderer
Split Second
Stamp of a Killer
Star Time
Still Life
Strangler of Blackmoor Castle
Striking Distance
10 Rillington Place▶
Ten to Midnight
Terror at London Bridge
To Catch a Killer▶
The Todd Killings
While the City Sleeps▶
Without Warning
Writer's Block
Zipperface

Serials

Ace Drummond
The Adventures of Captain Marvel
The Adventures of Frank and Jesse James
Adventures of Red Ryder
The Adventures of Rex & Rinty
Adventures of Smilin' Jack
The Adventures of Tarzan
The Adventures of the Flying Cadets
The Adventures of the Masked Phantom
Amazing Stories
Battling with Buffalo Bill
The Black Coin
The Black Widow
Blake of Scotland Yard
Bugs Bunny Superstar
Burn 'Em Up Barnes
Canadian Mounties Vs. Atomic Invaders
Captain America
Carmilla
Casey Jones and Fury (Brave Stallion)

Cheyenne Rides Again
The Clutching Hand
Custer's Last Stand
Cyclotrode ''X''
D-Day on Mars
Daredevils of the Red Circle
Darkest Africa
Daughter of Don Q
Destination Saturn
Devil Horse
Dick Tracy
Dick Tracy Returns
Dick Tracy: The Original Serial, Vol. 1▶
Dick Tracy: The Original Serial, Vol. 2▶
Dick Tracy vs. Crime Inc.
Doctor Satan's Robot
Don Daredevil Rides Again
Don Winslow of the Coast Guard
Don Winslow of the Navy
Drums of Fu Manchu▶
East Side Kids/The Lost City
Federal Agents vs. Underworld, Inc.
Federal Operator 99
Fighting Devil Dogs
Fighting Marines
Fighting with Kit Carson
Flaming Frontiers
Flash Gordon Conquers the Universe
Flash Gordon: Mars Attacks the World
Flash Gordon: Vol. 1
Flash Gordon: Vol. 2
Flash Gordon: Vol. 3
Flying Discman from Mars
G-Men Never Forget
G-Men vs. the Black Dragon
The Galloping Ghost
Genie of Darkness
Government Agents vs. Phantom Legion
Green Archer
The Green Hornet▶
Haunted Harbor
Hawk of the Wilderness
Heroes of the West
Holt of the Secret Service
Hurricane Express
In Old New Mexico
The Invisible Monster
Jesse James Rides Again
Jungle Drums of Africa
Junior G-Men
Junior G-Men of the Air
King of the Congo
King of the Forest Rangers
King of the Kongo
King of the Rocketmen
King of the Texas Rangers
Last Frontier
The Last of the Mohicans
Law of the Wild
A Lawman is Born▶
Lightning Warrior
Little Rascals, Book 4
The Lone Defender
The Lone Ranger
Lone Ranger
The Lost City
Lost City of the Jungle
The Lost Jungle
Lost Planet Airmen
Manhunt in the African Jungle
Manhunt of Mystery Island
Mansfield Park
The Masked Marvel
Master Key
Masters of Venus
The Miracle Rider
Mission: Monte Carlo
The Monster Demolisher
Mysterious Doctor Satan
Mystery Mountain
Mystery of the Riverboat
Mystery Squadron
Mystery Trooper
The New Adventures of Tarzan

Nyoka and the Tigermen
Oregon Trail
The Original Flash Gordon Collection
Overland Mail
The Painted Stallion
The Perils of Pauline
Perils of the Darkest Jungle
The Phantom Creeps
The Phantom Empire
Phantom of the Air
Phantom of the West
The Phantom Rider
Pirates of the High Seas
The Purple Monster Strikes
Queen of the Jungle
Radar Men from the Moon
Radio Patrol
Raiders of Ghost City
Red Barry
Return of Chandu
Riders of Death Valley
Robinson Crusoe of Clipper Island
Robinson Crusoe of Mystery Island
Rustlers of Red Dog
Saturday Night Serials
Savage Fury
Sea Hound
The Secret Code
Shadow of Chinatown
Shadow of the Eagle
Sign of the Wolf
Son of Zorro
S.O.S. Coast Guard
Space Soldiers Conquer the Universe
Spy Smasher Returns
Stone Cold Dead
Sunset on the Desert
Superman: The Serial, Vol. 1
Tailspin Tommy
Tarzan the Tiger
Texas to Bataan
The Three Musketeers
Tim Tyler's Luck
Tom Mix Compilation 1
Tom Mix Compilation 2
Trader Tom of the China Seas
Trail of the Silver Spurs
Trail Riders
Tumbledown Ranch in Arizona
Undersea Kingdom
Vanishing Legion
The Vigilantes are Coming
Whispering Shadow
Winners of the West
Wolf Dog
Woman in Grey
Young Eagles
Zombies of the Stratosphere
Zorro Rides Again
Zorro's Black Whip
Zorro's Fighting Legion

Sex & Sexuality

see also Crimes of Passion; Erotic Thrillers; Pornography; Sexploitation

ABC's of Love & Sex, Australia Style
Accident
Acting on Impulse
The Adjuster
The Adultress
Adventures of a Private Eye
Adventures of a Taxi Driver
The Adventures of Sadie
Alfie
The Allnighter
Almost Pregnant
Alpine Fire
Alvin Purple
Alvin Rides Again
The Amazing Transplant
American Gigolo
The Amorous Adventures of Moll Flanders
The Amy Fisher Story
And God Created Woman

Andy Warhol's Dracula▶
Andy Warhol's Frankenstein
Angel Heart
Angel of H.E.A.T.
Animal Instincts
Any Wednesday
The Apartment▶
Armistead Maupin's Tales of the City
The Arousers
Arrivederci, Baby!
Assault
Baby Doll
The Baby Doll Murders
Baby Face
Baby Love
The Baby Maker
The Bachelor▶
Bachelor in Paradise
Bachelor Party
Bad Girls from Mars
Bad Lieutenant▶
Barbarella
Basic Training
The Bawdy Adventures of Tom Jones
Beach Girls
Becoming Colette
Bedroom Eyes
Bedroom Eyes 2
Being at Home with Claude
Belle Epoque▶
Belle of the Nineties
Beneath the Valley of the Ultra-Vixens
The Berlin Affair
The Best Little Whorehouse in Texas
Betrayal
Betty Blue▶
Beverly Hills Madam
Beyond Erotica
Beyond the Silhouette
The Big Bet
The Big Dis
Bilitis
The Bitch
Bitter Harvest
Bitter Moon
Bitter Rice▶
The Black Room
Black Starlet
Blind Vision
Blindfold: Acts of Obsession
Blood and Sand▶
Bloodbath
Blown Away
The Blue Angel▶
Blue Jeans
The Blue Lagoon
Blue Movies
Blue Velvet▶
Boarding School
Bob & Carol & Ted & Alice
Boccaccio '70
Body Chemistry
Body Chemistry 2: Voice of a Stranger
Body Chemistry 3: Point of Seduction
Body Double▶
Body Waves
Boeing Boeing
Bonjour Tristesse▶
The Boss' Wife
Boxing Helena
A Boy and His Dog
Boy's Night Out▶
Bram Stoker's Dracula
Breathless
The Bride Is Much Too Beautiful
Brides of the Beast
Broken Trust
Buford's Beach Bunnies
Business as Usual
Butterfield 8▶
Butterfly
Bye Bye Baby
Cactus in the Snow
Caligula

Can I Do It...Till I Need Glasses?
The Canterbury Tales
Carnal Crimes
Carnal Knowledge▶
Carnival in Flanders▶
Carry On Emmanuelle
Casanova
Casanova '70
Casual Sex?
Cat on a Hot Tin Roof▶
Cat People
Cave Girl
Cesar & Rosalie▶
Chain of Desire
Champagne for Breakfast
Chatterbox
Cheaters
Cheech and Chong's Up in Smoke
Cherry 2000
The Chicken Chronicles
Chinese Roulette
Choose Me▶
Cinderella 2000
Claire's Knee▶
Class
Class of '63
Class Reunion
Cleo/Leo
Close My Eyes
Closely Watched Trains▶
Cold Sweat
Collector's Item▶
Color of Night
The Comfort of Strangers▶
Compromising Positions
Conspiracy
Contagion
The Cook, the Thief, His Wife & Her Lover▶
The Cool Surface
Cool World
Corruption
The Courtesans of Bombay▶
Crimes of Passion▶
The Cruel Story of Youth▶
Crush
Cry Uncle
Damage▶
Dangerous Game
Dangerous Liaisons▶
The Dark Side of Love
Dark Tide
Daughters of Satan
Dead On
Dear Boys
Death of a Centerfold
The Decameron▶
Decameron Nights
Deceit
Deceptions
The Decline of the American Empire▶
Denial: The Dark Side of Passion
Desire
Desire and Hell at Sunset Motel
Desk Set▶
Devil in the Flesh▶
Devil in the Flesh
The Devils▶
The Devil's Eye
The Devil's Nightmare
The Devil's Playground▶
Devil's Wedding Night
Diary of a Chambermaid▶
Diary of a Mad Housewife▶
Diary of a Mad Old Man
Die Watching
Diner▶
Discretion Assured
Divine Nymph
Divorce—Italian Style▶
Dr. Alien
Dr. Caligari
Dog Day Afternoon▶
Doll Face
Dollar
Domino
Dona Herlinda & Her Son

Don's Party▶
Double Suicide▶
Dracula Sucks
Dreams
Dreams Come True
Dreams of Desire
Driver's Seat
Drum
East End Hustle
Eating Raoul▶
Ebony Tower
Echoes of Paradise
The Eclipse▶
Ecstasy
Eddie Murphy "Delirious"
Eddie Murphy: Raw
Eden
Eden 2
Eden 3
Eden 4
El: This Strange Passion▶
Elmer Gantry▶
Elvira, Mistress of the Dark
Emily
Emmanuelle
Emmanuelle 4
Emmanuelle & Joanna
Emmanuelle in Bangkok
Emmanuelle in Soho
Emmanuelle in the Country
Emmanuelle, the Joys of a Woman
Emmanuelle, the Queen
Emmanuelle's Daughter
End of August
Endless Love
Enemies, a Love Story▶
Enormous Changes▶
Enrapture
Ernesto
Erotic Escape
Erotic Images
Erotic Touch of Hot Skin
Et La Tenoresse?...Bordel!
Every Breath
Everything You Always Wanted to Know About Sex (But Were Afraid to Ask)▶
Evils of the Night
Fairytales
Fanny Hill
Fanny Hill: Memoirs of a Woman of Pleasure
The Fantasist
Fast Food
Fast Times at Ridgemont High▶
Fatal Attraction
Fatal Attraction▶
Fatal Bond
Fatal Charm
Fatal Instinct
The Favor
Feelin' Screwy
Fellini Satyricon▶
Female Trouble
Final Judgement
The Finishing Touch
First Affair
The First Time
First Time
First Turn On
Flesh▶
Flesh Gordon
A Flight of Rainbirds
Foreign Body
Foreplay
Forever Emmanuelle
The 4th Man▶
Foxes
Frankenstein Unbound▶
Frasier the Sensuous Lion
Fraternity Vacation
The French Woman
Frenzy▶
Fritz the Cat▶
The Fugitive Kind
Full Exposure: The Sex Tape Scandals
Fun Down There
Gabriela

Galactic Gigolo
The Game is Over
Games Girls Play
Gas Pump Girls
Gentlemen Prefer Blondes▶
Genuine Risk
Georgy Girl▶
Get Out Your Handkerchiefs▶
Ghosts Can Do It
The Gift
Gilda▶
Ginger Ale Afternoon
The Girl
The Girl on a Motorcycle
Glen or Glenda
Go West, Young Man
The Goddess▶
The Good Mother
Goodbye Emmanuelle
Gorp
Gothic▶
The Graduate▶
The Handmaid's Tale
Happily Ever After
Hardbodies 2
Harrad Experiment
Harrad Summer
Heart of the Stag
Heaven Can Wait▶
Heavy Petting
Hell Comes to Frogtown
Henry & June▶
Higher Education
The Hit List
Hold Me, Thrill Me, Kiss Me
Hollywood Confidential
Homework
Honey
Horseplayer
Hot Child in the City
Hot Spot
Hot Target
Hot Under the Collar
The Hotel New Hampshire
Hotel Paradiso
Hotel Room
How Funny Can Sex Be?
How to Pick Up Girls
How to Seduce a Woman
Hugh Hefner: Once Upon a Time
Husbands and Lovers
I Am Curious (Yellow)
I Posed for Playboy
I Will, I Will for Now
Ilsa, Harem Keeper of the Oil Sheiks
I'm No Angel▶
Impure Thoughts
In Praise of Older Women
In the Heat of Passion
In the Realm of the Senses▶
An Inconvenient Woman
Indecency
Indecent Behavior
Indecent Proposal
Inside Out
Invasion of Privacy
Invasion of the Bee Girls▶
Irezumi▶
Is There Sex After Death?▶
Isadora▶
It
The Italian Stallion
It's Not the Size That Counts
It's Pat
Jailbait
Jamon, Jamon
Justine
Kandyland
Killer Workout
The Killing Game
Kiss Me, Stupid!
Kiss of a Killer
The Knack▶
La Cicada
L.A. Goddess
La Ronde▶
Labyrinth of Passion
Lady Caroline Lamb
Lady Chatterley's Lover
Lady Frankenstein

Lady on the Bus
Ladykiller
Ladykillers
Lake Consequence
L'Annee des Meduses
Last Call
Last of the Red Hot Lovers
Last Resort
Last Summer
Last Tango in Paris▶
Le Boucher▶
Le Cavaleur
Le Sex Shop▶
Les Nuits Fauves▶
Lethal Lolita—Amy Fisher: My Story
Liebestraum
Lies Before Kisses
A Life of Sin
Lifeforce
The Lifetaker
Like Water for Chocolate▶
Lipstick Camera
Liquid Sky▶
Little Darlings
A Little Sex
Lolita▶
Looking for Mr. Goodbar
Loulou▶
The Love Affair, or The Case of the Missing Switchboard Operator▶
The Love Boat
Love Crimes
The Love Goddesses
Love Letters▶
Love Matters
Love Meetings
Loverboy
Lovers: A True Story▶
Lovers' Lovers
The Loves of Irina
Loving Couples
Lunch Wagon
Madame Bovary▶
Mademoiselle
Mae West
Maitresse
Making Love
Malicious
Man Who Had Power Over Women
The Man Who Loved Women▶
The Man Who Loved Women
A Man with a Maid
Maria's Lovers
Marilyn: The Untold Story▶
Married People, Single Sex
A Married Woman▶
Mars Needs Women
Mata Hari
Me and Him
Menage▶
A Midsummer Night's Sex Comedy▶
Millions
Mirror Images
Mirror Images 2
Miss Julie
Miss Right
Miss Sadie Thompson▶
Mistress
Mo' Better Blues
Mondo Trasho
Monsieur Hire▶
Montenegro▶
Monty Python's The Meaning of Life▶
Moon is Blue
Mortal Sins
Movers and Shakers
My Best Friend's Girl
My Chauffeur
My Demon Lover
My Father is Coming
My Life to Live▶
My Wonderful Life
Myra Breckinridge
The Mystery of Alexina
The Naked Country
Naked Lie

Naked Lunch▶
Naked Obsession
Nea
Negatives
New York Nights
Nice Girls Don't Explode
Night and Day▶
Night Games
Night of the Living Babes
Night Zoo
The Nightman
9 1/2 Weeks
No Secrets
Norman Loves Rose
Novel Desires
Nudo di Donna▶
Oh! Calcutta!
Once is Not Enough
One Plus One
Oriane
The Other Side of Midnight
Paddy
Paradisio
Paranoia
Pardon Mon Affaire, Too!
Party Animal
Pauline at the Beach▶
Peeping Tom▶
The Penitent
Pepi, Luci, Bom and Other Girls on the Heap
Performance▶
The Perils of Gwendoline
Peyton Place▶
Picnic▶
Playgirl Killer
Playing with Fire
A Pleasure Doing Business
Point of Terror
Poison Ivy
The Pornographers▶
Portnoy's Complaint
The Postman Always Rings Twice▶
The Postman Always Rings Twice
Power, Passion & Murder
Prep School
Pretty Baby▶
Pretty Woman▶
Private Lessons
Rabbit Test
Rain
The Rainbow▶
Raising Cain
Rambling Rose▶
Red Kiss▶
Red Shoe Diaries
Red Shoe Diaries 2: Double Dare
Red Shoe Diaries 3: Another Woman's Lipstick
Red Shoe Diaries 4: Auto Erotica
The Reincarnation of Golden Lotus▶
Rendez-vous▶
Repo Jake
Repulsion▶
Restless
Return to Peyton Place
Return to Two Moon Junction
Rita, Sue & Bob Too▶
The Rocky Horror Picture Show▶
Rosebud Beach Hotel
R.S.V.P.
Rubdown
The Rue Morgue Massacres
The Sailor Who Fell from Grace with the Sea
Salmonberries
Salome
Sammy & Rosie Get Laid▶
Save Me
Scene of the Crime▶
Scorchy
Scorned
Screwball Academy
Scrubbers
Sea of Love▶

Secret Games 2: The Escort
Secret Life of an American Wife
Secrets
Secrets of Three Hungry Wives
Seduction: The Cruel Woman
The Seniors
Sensations
Sensuous Summer
Separate Vacations
Sex
Sex Crimes
sex, lies and videotape▶
Sex on the Run
Sextette
Sexual Intent
Sexual Malice
Sexual Response
The Shaming
Shampoo
Shattered▶
She's Gotta Have It▶
Sibling Rivalry
The Silence▶
Sinbad
Single Bars, Single Women
Sirens▶
The Sister-in-Law
Sisters of Satan
Ski School
Skin Deep
The Slap
Sliver
Smooth Talker
Snapdragon
Sooner or Later
Splendor in the Grass▶
Star 80
The Stationmaster's Wife
The Statue
The Stilts▶
The Story of O
The Story of O, Part 2
Storyville
Strangers
Strike a Pose
Stripped to Kill
The Stripper
The Stud
Sugarbaby▶
Summer Heat
Summer Lovers
Summer School Teachers
Sunday, Bloody Sunday▶
Super Bitch
Supervixens
Surfacing
Susan Slept Here
Susana▶
Sweet Ecstasy
Sweet Lies
Sweet Movie
Sweet Poison
Sweet Spirits
Swimming Pool
Swindle
Tale of Two Sisters
Talkin' Dirty After Dark
Talking Walls
Tattoo
Taxi zum Klo▶
Tea and Sympathy▶
Tea For Three
Teorema▶
The Terror Within
Test Tube Babies
Texasville
That Obscure Object of Desire▶
Therese & Isabelle
Thief of Hearts
36 Fillete▶
This Property is Condemned
This Sweet Sickness
Three in the Attic
Three in the Cellar
Threesome
Tie Me Up! Tie Me Down!
Tigers in Lipstick
The Tigress
'Tis a Pity She's a Whore

To Sleep with a Vampire
Together
Tokyo Decadence
Tom Jones▶
Tonight for Sure
Traenen in Florenz
Trash
Tropic of Cancer▶
Tropical Heat
Truth About Women
Turkish Delights
Twenty-One
Twin Peaks: Fire Walk with Me
Twins of Evil
Twist
The Ultimate Thrill
The Unbearable Lightness of Being▶
Under Investigation
Under Suspicion
The Underachievers
The Valley Obscured by the Clouds
Valmont▶
A Very Curious Girl
Via Appia
A View to a Kill
Virgin Queen of St. Francis High
The Virgin Soldiers
Wager of Love
Wedding in Blood▶
Weekend Pass
Welcome to L.A.▶
What's Good for the Goose
What's Up Front
When Women Had Tails
Where the Boys Are '84
Where the Hot Wind Blows
A Whisper to a Scream
Whispers in the Dark
Whore
Wide Sargasso Sea
Wild at Heart▶
Wild Orchid
Wild, Wild World of Jayne Mansfield
Wish You Were Here▶
The Witches of Eastwick
A Woman, Her Men and Her Futon
A Woman in Flames▶
The Woman Next Door▶
Woman of Desire
Woman Times Seven
Women in Love▶
Women on the Verge of a Nervous Breakdown▶
Women's Club
Working Girls
Working Girls▶
The World is Full of Married Men
The Wrong Man
X, Y & Zee
Xica▶
Yanks
Yesterday, Today and Tomorrow▶
Young Aphrodites
Young Lady Chatterly 2
Young Love, First Love
Young Nurses in Love
Your Ticket Is No Longer Valid
You've Got to Have Heart
The Yum-Yum Girls
Zabriskie Point▶
Zandalee
Zapped!
Zombie Island Massacre

Sexploitation

see also Erotic Thrillers; Exploitation

The Abductors
The Acid Eaters
Agony of Love
Amazon Jail
Angel 3: The Final Chapter
Aroused
Baby Love

Bad Girls Do Cry
Bad Girls Go to Hell
Barbarian Queen 2: The Empress Strikes Back
Bare Hunt
The Bawdy Adventures of Tom Jones
The Beast that Killed Women
Bedroom Eyes
The Bellboy and the Playgirls
Beneath the Valley of the Ultra-Vixens
Best Buns on the Beach
Beverly Hills Knockouts
The Big Bust Out
The Big Doll House
The Bikini Car Wash Company
The Bikini Car Wash Company 2
Black Venus
Blazing Stewardesses
Blue Ribbon Babes
Body of Evidence
Bolero
Bottoms Up
The Bride Is Much Too Beautiful
Caged Fury
Candy Stripe Nurses
Candy Tangerine Man
Carnal Crimes
Casting Call
Chain Gang Women
Champagne for Breakfast
Cheering Section
The Cheerleaders
Cheerleaders' Wild Weekend
Cherry Hill High
Chesty Anderson USN
Class Reunion
Cleo/Leo
Cool It, Baby
Corruption
The Curious Dr. Humpp
Dandelions
Deadly Embrace
Delinquent School Girls
Devil's Wedding Night
Dinosaur Island
Dirty Mind of Young Sally
Domino
Dracula Sucks
Ecstasy
Emily
Emmanuelle
Emmanuelle 4
Emmanuelle 5
Emmanuelle 6
Emmanuelle & Joanna
Emmanuelle in Bangkok
Emmanuelle in Soho
Emmanuelle in the Country
Emmanuelle on Taboo Island
Emmanuelle, the Joys of a Woman
Erotic Dreams
Erotic Escape
Erotic Touch of Hot Skin
Fanny Hill: Memoirs of a Woman of Pleasure
Fantasies
Feelin' Up
Firehouse
The First Nudie Musical
Flesh Gordon
Fleshpot on 42nd Street
Forever Emmanuelle
The French Woman
Ghosts Can't Do It
Gimme an F
Ginger
The Girl, the Body and the Pill
Good Time with a Bad Girl
Goodbye Emmanuelle
Great Bikini Off-Road Adventure
The Happy Hooker
The Happy Hooker Goes to Washington
Hard to Die
Hardbodies

Help Wanted Female
Hollywood Boulevard 2
Hollywood Erotic Film Festival
Hollywood High
Hollywood High, Part 2
Hollywood Hot Tubs
Hollywood Hot Tubs 2:
   Educating Crystal
Homework
Honkytonk Nights
Hot Moves
Hot T-Shirts
H.O.T.S.
How to Make a Doll
Ilsa, She-Wolf of the SS
Ilsa, the Tigress of Siberia
Ilsa, the Wicked Warden
Inferno in Paradise
Inhibition
Inn of Temptation
Invasion of the Girl Snatchers
The Invisible Maniac
Joy of Sex
Kandyland
Knock Outs
Lady Godiva Rides
Last Dance
Liana, Jungle Goddess
Liquid Dreams
Little Miss Innocence
Love Desperados
The Love Factor
Love Notes
Lust for Freedom
Mistress Pamela
Modern Girls
Mondo Balardo
My Pleasure Is My Business
My Therapist
Mysterious Jane
Naked Killer
The Naked Sword of Zorro
Naked Venus
Nature's Playmates
Naughty Knights
Night Call Nurses
The Night Evelyn Came Out of
   the Grave
The Night Porter
Nine Ages of Nakedness
Nude on the Moon
Nurse on Call
Orgy of the Dead
Pagan Island
Paranoia
Party Favors
Party Plane
Perfect Timing
The Perils of Gwendoline
The Perverse Countess
Please Don't Eat My Mother
Prehistoric Bimbos in
   Armageddon City
Preppies
The Prime Time
Private Duty Nurses
Private Passions
Rebel Vixens
Red Shoe Diaries 2: Double
   Dare
Return to the Blue Lagoon
Revenge of the Cheerleaders
Revenge of the Virgins
Sacrilege
Saturday Night Sleazies, Vol.
   1
Screen Test
Sea of Dreams
The Seducers
Sensual Partners
The Sensuous Teenager
Sex Adventures of the Three
   Musketeers
Sex and Buttered Popcorn
Sex is Crazy
Sex Through a Window
Shanty Tramp
She Came on the Bus
She Devils in Chains
Slammer Girls
Slumber Party Massacre 3
Snake Dancer

Snapshot
Snowballing
Sorority Babes in the Slimeball
   Bowl-A-Rama
Sorority House Party
Spaced Out
The Speed Lovers
S.S. Love Camp No. 27
Stocks and Blondes
The Story of O, Part 2
Strange World of Coffin Joe
Striptease
The Student Nurses
The Student Teachers
Submission
Suburban Roulette
Sugar Cookies
Superchick
Supervixens
Sweater Girls
Sweet Georgia
Sweet Young Thing
The Swinging Cheerleaders
Swinging Wives
Takin' It All Off
Tarzana, the Wild Girl
Tender Loving Care
Test Tube Teens from the
   Year 2000
Texas Layover
Thinkin' Big
Tokyo Decadence
Tomcat: Dangerous Desires
Train Station Pickups
Truck Stop
Truck Stop Women
2069: A Sex Odyssey
Ultimate Desires
The Vampire Hookers
Venus in Furs
Vice Academy
Vice Academy 2
Vice Academy 3
Wanda, The Sadistic
   Hypnotist
Wild Orchid 2: Two Shades of
   Blue
The Wildest Office Party
Witchcraft 2: The Temptress
Witchcraft 3: The Kiss of
   Death
Witchcraft 5: Dance with the
   Devil
World of the Depraved
The Young Nurses
The Zombie Army

Sexual Abuse

see also Rape; Spousal
Abuse

Boxing Helena
The Devils▶
Fall from Innocence
Fortune and Men's Eyes
Heart of the Stag
Ilsa, Harem Keeper of the Oil
   Sheiks
Mesmerized
The Night Porter
Romper Stomper
Twin Peaks: Fire Walk with
   Me

Ships

see Deep Blue; Sail Away;
Submarines

Showbiz Comedies

The Big Picture
Blazing Saddles
Boardinghouse Blues
The Boy Friend▶
Broadway Melody
Broadway Melody of 1936▶
Broadway Melody of 1938
Broadway Melody of 1940
The Comic▶
The Dark Backward
The Day the Women Got Even
Delirious
Dog Pound Shuffle▶

Ella Cinders▶
The Errand Boy
Everybody Sing
Extra Girl
Forever Female▶
Free and Easy
George White's Scandals
Grave Secrets
Gypsy▶
Gypsy
The Hard Way▶
Hear My Song▶
Hollywood Boulevard 2
Hollywood Chaos
Hollywood in Trouble
Hollywood Party
Hollywood Shuffle
Hooper
I'll Do Anything
It's a Date
It's a Great Feeling
Joey Breaker▶
Lady Killer▶
Let's Make Love
Life with Mikey
Main Street to Broadway
Merton of the Movies
Mr. Saturday Night
The Muppet Movie▶
The Muppets Take
   Manhattan▶
My Dream is Yours
My Favorite Year▶
Nancy Goes to Rio
The Night They Raided
   Minsky's▶
Nudity Required
Panama Hattie
Panic Button
The Party▶
Pick a Star
Postcards from the Edge▶
The Prince and the Showgirl
The Producers▶
Prurient Interest
Ratings Game
Salut l'Artiste▶
Second Fiddle
Silent Movie
Soapdish▶
S.O.B.
Tapeheads
There's No Business Like
   Show Business▶
Tune in Tomorrow
Who Framed Roger Rabbit?▶
The Wizard of Speed and
   Time
World's Greatest Lover
Young & Willing

Showbiz Dramas

Actors and Sin
All About Eve▶
American Blue Note
The Ann Jillian Story
Anna▶
The Barefoot Contessa▶
The Big Knife▶
Blast-Off Girls
The Bodyguard
Cancion en el Alma
Cassie
A Chorus Line
The Comic
Concrete Angels
Dangerous
Day for Night▶
The Day of the Locust▶
Doll Face
The Dresser▶
Ernie Kovacs: Between the
   Laughter
Fame▶
For the Boys
Frances▶
Funny Girl▶
Funny Lady
The Girl Said No
Happily Ever After
Hard Part Begins
Hollywood Heartbreak

Hollywood Mystery
The Jacksons: An American
   Dream
King of Comedy▶
La Dolce Vita▶
The Last Metro▶
The Last Tycoon▶
Lenny▶
The Lonely Lady
Lucy and Desi: Before the
   Laughter
A Man Called Adam
Max
Mommie Dearest
Network▶
Once in Paris...
Payday
Postcards from the Edge▶
Pure Country
Sam's Son
Second Coming of Suzanne
Shakespeare Wallah▶
Sidewalks of London▶
Smash-Up: The Story of a
   Woman▶
Something to Sing About
Sparkle
Stage Struck
Star!
Star 80▶
A Star is Born▶
A Star is Born
Sunset Boulevard▶
Targets▶
They Call It Sin
What's Love Got to Do With
   It?
Wired

Showbiz Thrillers

Children Shouldn't Play with
   Dead Things
Dead of Winter▶
The Dead Pool
Destroyer
F/X▶
F/X 2: The Deadly Art of
   Illusion
The House of Seven Corpses
Lady of Burlesque
Return to Horror High
Satan in High Heels
Stage Fright
Strangers Kiss
The Stunt Man▶
Up in the Air
What Ever Happened to Baby
   Jane?▶
The Wizard of Speed and
   Time

Shower & Bath
Scenes

About Last Night...▶
American Gigolo
Body Double▶
Breathless
Bull Durham▶
Club Paradise
Diabolique▶
Dressed to Kill
Fatal Attraction▶
Ghostbusters 2
High Anxiety
Hollywood Hot Tubs
Hollywood Hot Tubs 2:
   Educating Crystal
Jinxed
The Legacy
Married to the Mob▶
Mister Roberts▶
National Lampoon's
   Vacation▶
Porky's
The Postman Always Rings
   Twice
Psycho▶
Psycho 2
St. Elmo's Fire
Schizo
Silkwood▶

Snow White and the Seven
   Dwarfs
Stripes
Tequila Sunrise
Tie Me Up! Tie Me Down!
Valley Girl
Valmont▶

Shrinks

see also Doctors & Nurses

Agnes of God
Beauty on the Beach
Betrayal
Beyond Reason
Beyond Therapy
Blood Frenzy
Body Chemistry 2: Voice of a
   Stranger
Body of Influence
The Brain
Captain Newman, M.D.
The Cobweb
Color of Night
The Couch Trip
Dark Mirror▶
Dead Man Out▶
The Dream Team
Face to Face▶
Fear
Final Analysis
Final Approach
A Fine Madness▶
Future Shock
High Anxiety
Home Movies
Hometown Boy Makes Good
House of Games▶
Human Experiments
I Don't Buy Kisses Anymore
I Never Promised You a Rose
   Garden▶
The Impossible Years
Lies of the Twins
Lovesick
Lovey: A Circle of Children 2
The Man Who Loved Women
Mine Own Executioner▶
Mr. Frost
Mr. Jones
On a Clear Day You Can See
   Forever
One Flew Over the Cuckoo's
   Nest▶
Pressure Point▶
The Prince of Tides▶
Red Wind
The Scar
Schizoid
Shock!
The Sleeping Tiger
Spellbound▶
Still of the Night
The Stranger▶
Sybil▶
They Might Be Giants▶
The Three Faces of Eve▶
Victim of Love
What's New Pussycat?▶
Whispers in the Dark
Wild in the Country

Shutterbugs

see also Front Page

Adventures in Spying
Backbeat▶
Bikini Island
Blow-Up▶
Body Shot
The Corrupt Ones
Dagger Eyes
Darkroom
Dr. Mabuse vs. Scotland Yard
The Dolls
Don't Answer the Phone
Don't Change My World
Double Exposure
Double Exposure: The Story
   of Margaret Bourke-White
The Double Negative
Eyes Behind the Stars
Eyes of Laura Mars

Shutterbugs

Fatal Exposure
Fatal Images
The Favor, the Watch, & the Very Big Fish
Funny Face▶
Heat and Sunlight
High Season
I Love Melvin
Killer Image
Love & Murder
Love Crimes
Mad Dog and Glory▶
Model Behavior
Not for Publication
The Outcasts▶
Peeping Tom▶
Perfect Timing
Photographer
Proof▶
The Public Eye▶
Return to Boggy Creek
Secret File of Hollywood
Shoot
Shoot It Black, Shoot It Blue
Snapshot
Somebody Has to Shoot the Picture▶
Straight for the Heart
Sunset Heat
Sunset Strip
A Time to Die
The Unbearable Lightness of Being▶
Until The End of The World▶
Watch the Birdie

Silent Films

The Adorable Cheat
The Adventurer
The Adventures of Hairbreadth Harry
The Adventures of Tarzan
Aelita: Queen of Mars
All Night Long/Smile Please
America/The Fall of Babylon▶
American Aristocracy
American Pluck
The Americano
The Americano/Variety
Anna Christie▶
Annapolis
April Fool
Are Parents People?
Arsenal▶
Assunta Spina
The Atonement of Gosta Berling▶
Avenging Conscience
The Average Woman
Baby Face Harry Langdon
The Babylon Story from "Intolerance"▶
Backfire
Backstairs
Bakery/Grocery Clerk
The Balloonatic/One Week
Bare Knees
The Bargain
The Bat▶
Battle of Elderbush Gulch
The Battleship Potemkin▶
Battling Bunyon
Battling Butler
Beau Brummel
Beau Revel▶
Bed and Sofa▶
Behind the Front
Bellhop/The Noon Whistle
The Beloved Rogue▶
Below the Deadline
Ben-Hur▶
Ben Turpin: An Eye for an Eye
The Best of Chaplin
The Big Parade▶
Big Stakes
The Birth of a Nation▶
The Black Pirate▶
The Blacksmith/The Balloonatic
The Blacksmith/The Cops
The Blasphemer
Blind Husbands▶

Blood and Sand
Blood and Sand/Son of the Sheik
The Blot
Body and Soul
The Broadway Drifter
Broken Blossoms▶
Broken Hearts of Broadway
The Broken Mask
Burlesque of Carmen
The Busher
Buster Keaton Festival, Vol. 1
Buster Keaton Festival, Vol. 2
Buster Keaton Festival, Vol. 3
Buster Keaton Rides Again/The Railrodder
Buster Keaton: The Golden Years
The Cabinet of Dr. Caligari▶
Cabiria
California Straight Ahead
The Cameraman▶
Campus Knights
Cannon Ball/Eyes Have It
Cannonball/Dizzy Heights and Daring Hearts
Captain Swagger
The Cat and the Canary▶
Champagne
The Champion/His New Job▶
Chaplin Essanay Book 1
The Chaplin Revue
Chapter in Her Life
Charleston▶
Charley's Aunt
Charlie Chaplin Carnival, Four Early Shorts
Charlie Chaplin Cavalcade, Mutual Studios Shorts
Charlie Chaplin Centennial Collection
Charlie Chaplin Festival
Charlie Chaplin: Night at the Show▶
Charlie Chaplin: Rare Chaplin
Charlie Chaplin: The Early Years, Vol. 1
Charlie Chaplin: The Early Years, Vol. 2
Charlie Chaplin: The Early Years, Vol. 3
Charlie Chaplin: The Early Years, Vol. 4
Charlie Chaplin...Our Hero!
Charlie Chaplin's Keystone Comedies #1
Charlie Chaplin's Keystone Comedies #2
Charlie Chaplin's Keystone Comedies #3
Charlie Chaplin's Keystone Comedies #4
Charlie Chaplin's Keystone Comedies #5
Charlie Chase and Ben Turpin
The Cheat▶
The Cheerful Fraud
Child of the Prairie
The Cigarette Girl of Mosselprom
The Circus▶
City Girl
City Lights▶
Civilization▶
Clodhopper
Cobra
College▶
Comedy Classics of Mack Sennett and Hal Roach
The Coming of Amos
The Confession
Cops/One Week
Cord & Dischords/Naughty Nurse
The Count
Count/Adventurer
The Count of Monte Cristo
The Country Kid▶
County Fair
The Covered Wagon
Crainquebille▶
The Crazy Ray▶

Cricket on the Hearth
The Crowd▶
The Cure
Custer's Last Fight
Cyclone Cavalier
Dancing Mothers
Danger Ahead!
Dangerous Hours
Dante's Inferno▶
Days of Thrills and Laughter▶
Desert of the Lost
Desperate Scoundrel/The Pride of Pikeville
Diary of a Lost Girl▶
Disciple
Discontent
Docks of New York▶
Dr. Jack/For Heaven's Sake
Dr. Jekyll and Mr. Hyde▶
Dr. Mabuse the Gambler▶
Dog Star Man▶
Don Juan▶
Don Q., Son of Zorro
Don't Shove/Two Gun Gussie
Doomsday
Down to Earth▶
Down to the Sea in Ships
Dracula/Garden of Eden
The Drake Case
Dream Street
The Dropkick▶
D.W. Griffith Triple Feature
Dynamite Dan
The Eagle▶
Early Cinema Vol. 1
Early Russian Cinema, Vol. 1: Beginnings
Early Russian Cinema, Vol. 2: Folklore & Legend
Early Russian Cinema, Vol. 3: Starewicz's Fantasies
Early Russian Cinema, Vol. 4: Provincial Variations
Early Russian Cinema, Vol. 5: Chardynin's Pushkin
Early Russian Cinema, Vol. 6: Class Distinctions
Early Russian Cinema, Vol. 7: Evgenii Bauer
Early Russian Cinema, Vol. 8: Iakov Protazanov
Early Russian Cinema, Vol. 9: High Society
Early Russian Cinema, Vol. 10: The End of an Era
Early Sound Films
Earth▶
East and West▶
Easy Street▶
Easy Virtue
Ella Cinders▶
The End of St. Petersburg▶
Entr'acte
Extra Girl
The Extraordinary Adventures of Mr. West in the Land of the Bolsheviks
Eyes of Julia Deep
Eyes of Turpin Are Upon You!
The Eyes of Youth
Eyes Right!
Fangs of Fate
The Farmer's Wife
Fatty and Mabel Adrift/Mabel, Fatty and the Law
Faust▶
Feel My Pulse
The Fighting American
Fighting Jack
The Fighting Stallion▶
Final Extra
The Fireman
The First Movie Cowboy
Flesh and Blood
The Flesh and the Devil▶
Flirting with Fate▶
The Floorwalker▶
The Floorwalker/By the Sea▶
The Flying Scotsman
A Fool There Was
Foolish Wives▶
For Heaven's Sake▶

The Forbidden City
Fortune's Fool
The Four Horsemen of the Apocalypse▶
Free to Love
The Freshman▶
The Fugitive: Taking of Luke McVane
The Garden of Eden
The General▶
The General Line▶
Girl Shy▶
The Girl with the Hat Box
A Girl's Folly
Going to Congress/Don't Park There
The Gold Rush▶
Gold Rush/Payday
Golden Age of Comedy
The Grand Duchess and the Waiter▶
Great K & A Train Robbery
The Greatest Question
Greed▶
Grit of the Girl Telegrapher/In the Switch Tower
Gypsy Blood
The Hands of Orlac
Hands Up
Happiness
A Hash House Fraud/The Sultan's Wife
The Haunted Castle▶
Hawthorne of the USA
He Who Gets Slapped▶
Heading Home
Headwinds
Heart of Humanity
Heart of Texas Ryan
Heart's Haven
Hearts of the World▶
Her Silent Sacrifice
His First Flame▶
His Majesty, the American
His Majesty, the Scarecrow of Oz/The Magic Cloak of Oz
His Picture in the Papers
His Royal Slyness/Haunted Spooks
Home Sweet Home
Homecoming▶
Homer Comes Home
Hoodoo Ann
Hot Foot/A Happy Married Couple
Hot Water/Safety Last
Hotel Imperial
Hula
Human Hearts
The Hunchback of Notre Dame▶
The Ice Flood
The Idol Dancer
I'm on My Way/The Non-Stop Kid
The Immigrant▶
In the Days of the Thundering Herd & the Law & the Outlaw
Intolerance▶
Irish Cinderella
The Iron Mask
The Island▶
Isn't Life Wonderful▶
It
Italian
Italian Straw Hat▶
It's the Old Army Game
The Jack Knife Man▶
Jesse James Under the Black Flag
Jesus of Nazareth
Joyless Street▶
Judith of Bethulia▶
Just Suppose
The Kid▶
The Kid Brother
The Kid/Idle Class▶
Kid's Auto Race/Mabel's Married Life
King of Kings
King of the Kongo

King of the Rodeo
King of the Wild Horses▶
The King on Main Street
Kismet▶
The Kiss▶
The Knockout/Dough and Dynamite▶
Kriemhilde's Revenge▶
La Chute de la Maison Usher▶
Lady of the Lake
Lady Windermere's Fan
The Lamb
Last Command▶
The Last Laugh▶
The Last of the Mohicans▶
The Last Outlaw
Laugh with Linder!
Laughfest
Laughing at Danger
Leap Year
The Leatherneck
Leaves from Satan's Book▶
The Leopard Woman
Let 'er Go Gallegher
Let's Go!
The Light of Faith
Linda
The Little American
Little Annie Rooney
Little Church Around the Corner
Little Rascals, Book 18
The Lizzies of Mack Sennett
The Lodger▶
The Lost World
Love 'Em and Leave 'Em▶
The Love Flower
Lucky Devil
Mabel & Fatty
Mack & Carole
Mack Sennett Comedies: Vol. 1
Mack Sennett Comedies: Vol. 2
The Mad Whirl
Male and Female▶
The Man from Beyond
The Man from Painted Post
Man in the Silk Hat
Man in the Silk Hat▶
The Man on the Box
The Man Who Laughs▶
The Man with a Movie Camera▶
Mantrap
The Manxman
Mark of Zorro▶
Marked Money
The Marriage Circle▶
Married?
Master of the House▶
Matrimaniac
Max
Merry-Go-Round▶
Metropolis▶
The Michigan Kid
Mickey
Mid-Channel
Midnight Faces
Moana, a Romance of the Golden Age▶
Modern Times▶
Monsieur Beaucaire
Moran of the Lady Letty
A Mormon Maid
Mother▶
My Best Girl
My Boy
My Lady of Whims
The Mysterious Lady
Mystery of the Leaping Fish/Chess Fever
Napoleon▶
Narrow Trail▶
The Navigator▶
The Nervous Wreck▶
Never Weaken/Why Worry?▶
The Night Club
The Night Cry
The Night Patrol
No Man's Law
Nomads of the North

Nosferatu▶
Old Ironsides▶
Oliver Twist▶
On the Night Stage
One A.M.
One Arabian Night▶
One-Punch O'Day
Orphans of the Storm▶
Othello
Our Dancing Daughters
Our Gang
Our Gang Comedy Festival
Our Gang Comedy Festival 2
Our Hospitality▶
The Outlaw and His Wife
Outside the Law
Pace That Kills
Pandora's Box▶
Passion
The Passion of Joan of Arc▶
Patchwork Girl of Oz
Paths to Paradise▶
Pawnshop
The Peacock Fan
Peck's Bad Boy
Peg O' My Heart
The Phantom Chariot
The Phantom Flyer
Phantom of the Opera▶
Playing Dead
Pollyanna
The Pony Express
Pool Sharks
A Poor Little Rich Girl▶
Pop Goes the Cork
Power
The Prairie King
The Prairie Pirate
Pride of the Clan
The Primitive Lover
A Propos de Nice▶
Q Ships
Queen Kelly▶
Quo Vadis
Ranson's Folly
The Raven
Reaching for the Moon
Rebecca of Sunnybrook Farm
Red Kimono
Red Signals
Reggie Mixes In▶
Renoir Shorts▶
The Return of Boston Blackie
Return of Draw Egan
The Return of Grey Wolf
Riders of the Purple Sage
Riders of the Range
The Ring
The Rink▶
Rink/Immigrant
Risky Business
The Road to Ruin
The Road to Yesterday
Road to Yesterday/The
    Yankee Clipper
The Roaring Road
Robin Hood▶
Robinson Crusoe
Romola
Rounding Up the Law
Running Wild
Sacred Mountain/White
    Flame▶
Sadie Thompson▶
Sailor-Made Man/Grandma's
    Boy▶
Salammbo
Sally of the Sawdust
Salome
Salome/Queen Elizabeth
Sands of Sacrifice
The Saphead
Sawmill/The Dome Doctor
Scar of Shame
The Scarlet Car
Sea Lion
Secrets of a Soul
Seven Chances▶
Seven Years Bad Luck▶
Sex
Shadows
Shattered▶

She
The Sheik▶
Shifting Sands
Ships in the Night
The Shock
Short Films of D.W. Griffith,
    Vol. 1
Short Films of D.W. Griffith,
    Vol. 2
Show People▶
Siegfried▶
Silent Laugh Makers, No. 1▶
Silent Laugh Makers, No. 2▶
Silent Laugh Makers, No. 3
The Silent Mr. Sherlock
    Holmes
Silent Movie
Silent Movies...Just For the
    Fun of It!
The Single Standard
Skinner's Dress Suit
Sky High
Smiling Madame Beudet/The
    Seashell and the
    Clergyman▶
So This is Paris▶
The Social Secretary
Son of a Gun
Son of the Sheik▶
The Sorrows of Satan▶
Soul-Fire
Soul of the Beast
Spangles
Sparrows▶
The Speed Spook
Spiders▶
Spies▶
Spite Marriage▶
The Spoilers
Square Shoulders
Stan Without Ollie, Vol. 1
Stand and Deliver
Steamboat Bill, Jr.▶
Stella Maris▶
Storm Over Asia▶
Story of the Silent Serials Girls
    in Danger
Straight Shootin'
The Street
Street of Forgotten Women
Strike▶
Student of Prague▶
The Student Prince in Old
    Heidelberg
Suds
Sunny Side Up
Sunrise▶
The Swan
Sweet Adeline
Tabu: A Story of the South
    Seas▶
Tale of Two Cities/In the
    Switch Tower
Tarzan of the Apes
Tarzan the Tiger
The Taxi Mystery
Teddy at the Throttle
Teddy at the Throttle/
    Speeding Along
The Tempest▶
The Tempest/The Eagle▶
The Ten Commandments
Ten Days That Shook the
    World▶
Ten Nights in a Bar Room
Tentacles of the North
Test of Donald Norton
That Certain Thing
These Girls Won't Talk
The Thief
The Thief of Baghdad▶
Thomas Graal's Best Film▶
Thomas Graal's First Child▶
Three Ages▶
Three Charlies and One
    Phoney!
The Three Musketeers
The Three Musketeers▶
Three Word Brand
Through the Breakers
Tillie Wakes Up
Tillie's Punctured Romance

Tol'able David
Toll Gate
Tom Mix Compilation 1
Tom Mix Compilation 2
The Tomboy
The Tong Man
Too Wise Wives
The Torture of Silence
Tournament
Traffic in Souls▶
Trailin'
Tramp & a Woman
Trapped by the Mormons
Treasure of Arne
Triple Trouble/Easy Street
True Heart Susie
20,000 Leagues Under the
    Sea▶
Two Men & a Wardrobe
Un Chien Andalou▶
The Unchastened Woman
Uncle Tom's Cabin
The Unholy Three▶
The Unknown▶
The Untamable
Until They Get Me
The Vagabond
Vanishing American
Variety▶
The Virginian
Virtue's Revolt
Wagon Tracks
Walking Back
The Walloping Kid
Warning Shadows▶
Waxworks▶
Way Down East▶
The Wedding March▶
We're in the Navy Now
West-Bound Limited
West of Zanzibar
What Happened to Rosa?▶
When the Clouds Roll By▶
Where East is East
White Gold▶
The White Rose▶
The White Sin
The White Sister▶
White Tiger
Wild Horse Canyon
Wild Orchids
The Wind▶
Wings
The Wishing Ring▶
Witchcraft Through the Ages▶
With Kit Carson Over the
    Great Divide
The Wizard of Oz
Wolf Blood
Wolfheart's Revenge
Woman in Grey
Woman in the Moon
A Woman of Affairs
Woman of Paris/Sunnyside▶
Work/Police▶
Working Winnie/Oh So Simple
The Worldly Madonna
Yankee Clipper
Yankee Doodle in Berlin
Zvenigora▶

**Silent Horror/
Fantasy Classics**

Aelita: Queen of Mars
The Cabinet of Dr. Caligari▶
Dante's Inferno▶
Dr. Jekyll and Mr. Hyde▶
The Golem▶
The Hunchback of Notre
    Dame▶
La Chute de la Maison Usher▶
Metropolis▶
Million Dollar Mystery
The Monster▶
Nosferatu▶
Phantom of the Opera▶
The Thief of Baghdad▶
20,000 Leagues Under the
    Sea▶
Vampyr▶
The Wizard of Oz

Singles

About Last Night...▶
Boy's Night Out▶
Breakfast at Tiffany's▶
Crossing Delancey▶
He Said, She Said
Metropolitan▶
Mr. Wonderful
Mystic Pizza▶
The Opposite Sex and How to
    Live With Them
Pillow Talk▶
Reality Bites
St. Elmo's Fire
Singles▶
Sleepless in Seattle▶
That Touch of Mink
The Thing Called Love
When Harry Met Sally▶
The Wild Life

Sixties

    see Flower Children

Skateboarding

Gleaming the Cube
Skateboard

Skating

    see also Hockey

Airborne
Blades of Courage
Breaking the Ice
The Cutting Edge
Derby▶
Everything Happens at Night▶
Frolics on Ice
Hans Brinker
Happy Landing
Ice Castles
Ice Pawn
Iceland
My Lucky Star
Nutcracker, A Fantasy on Ice▶
One in a Million▶
Roller Boogie
Schizo
Sun Valley Serenade
Unholy Rollers
Wintertime
Xanadu

Skiing

Aspen Extreme
Avalanche
Better Off Dead
Club Med
Downhill Racer
Fire and Ice
Fire, Ice and Dynamite
For Your Eyes Only▶
Going for the Gold: The Bill
    Johnson Story
Hot Dog...The Movie!
Iced
Lost and Found
The Man Who Skied Down
    Everest
On Her Majesty's Secret
    Service▶
One Last Run
The Other Side of the
    Mountain
The Other Side of the
    Mountain, Part 2
Red Snow
Reno and the Doc
Ski Bum
Ski Patrol
Ski School
Ski Troop Attack
Skier's Dream
Snow: The Movie
Snowball Express
Snowballin'
Snowballing
Snowblind
Striker's Mountain
Tales from the Snow Zone

Slapstick Comedy

    see also Comedy;
    Screwball Comedy

Abbott and Costello Go to
    Mars
Abbott and Costello in
    Hollywood
Abbott and Costello in the
    Foreign Legion
Abbott and Costello Meet
    Captain Kidd
Abbott and Costello Meet Dr.
    Jekyll and Mr. Hyde
Abbott and Costello Meet
    Frankenstein▶
Abbott & Costello Meet the
    Invisible Man▶
Abbott and Costello Meet the
    Keystone Kops
Abbott and Costello Meet the
    Killer, Boris Karloff
Abbott & Costello Meet the
    Mummy
Abbott and Costello
    Scrapbook
Abroad with Two Yanks
Ace Crawford, Private Eye
Ace Ventura: Pet Detective
The Adventurer
The Adventures of Buckaroo
    Banzai Across the Eighth
    Dimension▶
The Adventures of the Little
    Rascals
Africa Screams
After the Fox
Air Raid Wardens
All Night Long/Smile Please
All of Me
Alvin Purple
Alvin Rides Again
American Aristocracy
American Pluck
Amos and Andrew
Animal Crackers▶
Any Which Way You Can
Armed and Dangerous
Around the World in 80 Ways
Assault and Matrimony
At the Circus
At War with the Army
Baby's Day Out
The Bad News Bears▶
The Bad News Bears Go to
    Japan
The Bad News Bears in
    Breaking Training
Bakery/Grocery Clerk
The Bank Dick▶
The Barber Shop▶
The Barefoot Executive
The Battle of the Sexes▶
Bedtime for Bonzo
Beethoven
Beethoven's 2nd
The Bellboy
Bellhop/The Noon Whistle
Big Mouth
Big Store
Block-heads▶
Bohemian Girl▶
Bonnie Scotland
Boy, Did I Get a Wrong
    Number!
Brain Donors
Buck Privates
Buck Privates Come Home▶
Bullfighters
Buster Keaton Rides Again/
    The Railrodder
The Caddy
Caddyshack▶
Caddyshack 2
Candleshoe
Cannonball/Dizzy Heights and
    Daring Hearts
Carry On at Your
    Convenience
Carry On Behind
Carry On Cruising
Carry On Doctor▶

Slapstick

Carry On Emmanuelle
Carry On England
Carry On Nurse
Carry On 'Round the Bend
Casanova's Big Night
The Case of the Mukkinese Battle Horn
The Champion/His New Job▶
Charlie Chaplin: The Early Years, Vol. 1
Charlie Chaplin: The Early Years, Vol. 2
Charlie Chaplin: The Early Years, Vol. 3
Charlie Chaplin: The Early Years, Vol. 4
Cheech and Chong: Still Smokin'
Cheech and Chong: Things Are Tough All Over
Cheech and Chong's Next Movie
Cheech and Chong's, The Corsican Brothers
Cheech and Chong's Up in Smoke
Christmas in July▶
A Chump at Oxford
Cinderfella
Classic Comedy Video Sampler
Cockeyed Cavaliers
College▶
Comedy Festival #1
Comedy Reel, Vol. 2
Comin' Round the Mountain
Cord & Dischords/Naughty Nurse
Count/Adventurer
Cracking Up
The Cure
Curse of the Pink Panther
Dance with Me, Henry
A Day at the Races
The Delicate Delinquent
The Dentist▶
Detective School Dropouts
Disorderly Orderly
Don't Raise the Bridge, Lower the River
Don't Shove/Two Gun Gussie
Dorf and the First Games of Mount Olympus
Dorf Goes Auto Racing
Doughboys
Duck Soup▶
Ernest Goes to Camp
Ernest Goes to Jail
Ernest Rides Again
Ernest Scared Stupid
The Errand Boy
Family Jewels
The Fatal Glass of Beer
The Feud
Finders Keepers
A Fine Mess
Flim-Flam Man
The Flying Deuces▶
Folks!
For Auld Lang Syne: The Marx Brothers
Francis Goes to the Races
Francis Joins the WACs
Francis the Talking Mule▶
Free and Easy
The Fuller Brush Girl
Fuller Brush Man
Funny Farm
George Washington Slept Here
Get Smart, Again!
Ghost in the Noonday Sun
Gilligan's Island: Meet the Crew
A Girl in Every Port
The Gods Must Be Crazy▶
The Gods Must Be Crazy 2
Going Bananas
The Gorilla
Great Guns
The Great Lover
Great Race

A Guide for the Married Man▶
Gus
Half-Shot at Sunrise
Hands Up
Hardly Working
A Hash House Fraud/The Sultan's Wife
Here Come the Co-Eds
Hey Abbott!
Hold That Ghost▶
Hollywood or Bust
Home Alone▶
Home Alone 2: Lost in New York
The Horn Blows at Midnight▶
Horse Feathers▶
Hot Lead & Cold Feet
I Hate Blondes
In Society
Ishtar
It's a Mad, Mad, Mad, Mad World
Jack & the Beanstalk
The Jerk
Jour de Fete▶
Julia Misbehaves▶
Jumping Jacks
Kentucky Kernels
The Klutz
The Last Remake of Beau Geste
Laughfest
Laurel & Hardy and the Family
Laurel & Hardy: Another Fine Mess
Laurel & Hardy: At Work
Laurel & Hardy: Be Big
Laurel & Hardy: Below Zero
Laurel & Hardy: Berth Marks
Laurel & Hardy: Blotto
Laurel & Hardy: Brats
Laurel & Hardy: Chickens Come Home
Laurel & Hardy Comedy Classics, Vol. 7
Laurel & Hardy: Hog Wild
Laurel & Hardy: Laughing Gravy
Laurel & Hardy: Men O'War
Laurel & Hardy: Night Owls
Laurel & Hardy On the Lam
Laurel & Hardy: Perfect Day
Laurel & Hardy Spooktacular
Laurel & Hardy: Stan "Helps" Ollie
Laurel & Hardy: The Hoose-Gow
Let's Go!
Little Giant
Lost in a Harem
Lost in Alaska
The Lost Stooges
Love Happy
Ma and Pa Kettle
Ma and Pa Kettle at the Fair
Ma and Pa Kettle Back On the Farm
Ma and Pa Kettle Go to Town
Man's Favorite Sport?
Matilda
Meatballs 3
Meatballs 4
Menage▶
Mexican Hayride
Milky Way
Mr. Bill's Real Life Adventures
Mr. Hulot's Holiday▶
Monkey Business▶
Monkey Trouble
Music Box/Helpmates
My Friend Irma
The Naughty Nineties
The Navigator▶
Never Give a Sucker an Even Break▶
A Night at the Opera▶
A Night in Casablanca▶
The Noose Hangs High▶
The North Avenue Irregulars
Not Quite Human
Not Quite Human 2
Nothing But Trouble

Nuns on the Run
Odd Jobs
Off Limits
Off the Wall
One A.M.
Our Relations▶
Out of the Blue
Pack Up Your Troubles
Pardon My Sarong
Pardon My Trunk
Pardon Us
The Party▶
The Patsy
Pawnshop
Pharmacist
The Pink Panther▶
The Pink Panther Strikes Again▶
Playtime▶
Problem Child 2
Quick, Let's Get Married
Railrodder▶
Return of the Pink Panther
Revenge of the Pink Panther
Rio Rita
The Road to Hong Kong
Robin Hood: Men in Tights
Rockin' Road Trip
Room Service
Saps at Sea
Seven Years Bad Luck▶
A Shot in the Dark▶
Show People▶
Sidewalks of New York
Silent Laugh Makers, No. 1▶
Silent Laugh Makers, No. 2▶
Silent Laugh Makers, No. 3
Slapstick
Slapstick of Another Kind
Snow White and the Three Stooges
Son of the Pink Panther
Sons of the Desert▶
The Speed Spook
Spies Like Us
Stooges Shorts Festival
The Stooges Story▶
Swiss Miss
Take the Money and Run▶
Tanks a Million
30-Foot Bride of Candy Rock
Three Charlies and One Phoney!
Three Stooges Comedy Capers: Vol. 1
Three Stooges Comedy Classics
Three Stooges: Cookoo Cavaliers and Other Nyuks
Three Stooges Festival
Three Stooges: From Nurse to Worse and Other Nyuks
The Three Stooges: Half-Wit's Holiday and Other Nyuks
The Three Stooges: Idiots Deluxe and Other Nyuks
The Three Stooges: Nutty but Nice and Other Nyuks
The Three Stooges: They Stooge to Conga and Other Nyuks
Tillie Wakes Up
Too Shy to Try
Trail of the Pink Panther
A Tribute to the Boys
Two-Way Stretch
Up the Creek
Utopia
Voyage-Suprise▶
Walk Like a Man
W.C. Fields: Flask of Fields
Weekend at Bernie's
Weekend at Bernie's 2
What! No Beer?
Who Done It?
Who Killed Doc Robbin?
Why Me?
Wide Open Faces
A Woman of Distinction
The Wonders of Aladdin
Yankee Doodle in Berlin
The Yellow Cab Man

Yellowbeard

Slavery

see also Civil Rights

The Abductors
The Adventures of Huckleberry Finn
Angel City
The Association
Band of Angels
The Big Bust Out
Brother Future
Buck and the Preacher
Burn!▶
The Civil War, Episode 1: The Cause—1861▶
The Civil War, Episode 2: A Very Bloody Affair—1862▶
The Civil War, Episode 3: Forever Free—1862▶
The Civil War, Episode 4: Simply Murder—1863▶
The Civil War, Episode 5: The Universe of Battle—1863▶
The Civil War, Episode 6: Valley of the Shadow of Death—1864▶
The Civil War, Episode 7: Most Hallowed Ground—1864▶
The Civil War, Episode 8: War is All Hell—1865▶
The Civil War, Episode 9: The Better Angels of Our Nature—1865▶
The Colombian Connection
Dragonard
Gone are the Days
Half Slave, Half Free
Hell's Wind Staff
The House of Dies Drear
The House of 1000 Dolls
Intimate Power
Island of Lost Girls
Lust for Freedom
Man Friday
Man from Deep River
Mandinga
Mandingo
Naked in the Sun
Naked Warriors
Pudd'nhead Wilson
The Road to Morocco▶
The Robe▶
Roots▶
Roots: The Gift
Sansho the Bailiff▶
The Silencer
Skin Game▶
Slave Trade in the World Today
Slavers
Spartacus▶
Sunshine Run
Tamango
Traffic in Souls▶
Uncle Tom's Cabin
Wanda, The Sadistic Hypnotist
White Slave
A Woman Called Moses
Xica▶

Slice of Life

see also True Stories

The Adventures of Huck Finn
The Adventures of Huckleberry Finn▶
Ah, Wilderness!▶
Alice Doesn't Live Here Anymore
All Creatures Great and Small▶
Amarcord▶
American Graffiti
Andy Hardy Gets Spring Fever
Andy Hardy's Double Life
Andy Hardy's Private Secretary
Angie

Avalon▶
Babycakes
Bad Behavior
The Bicycle Thief▶
Billy Galvin
Bloodbrothers
The Blot
Blueberry Hill
Bodies, Rest & Motion
Breaking In▶
Bright Angel
Bus Stop▶
Captains Courageous▶
Car Wash
Cesar▶
Citizens Band▶
Coming Up Roses
Cotter
Courtship▶
Crisscross
Crooklyn▶
Cross Creek
Crossing Delancey▶
The Crowd▶
Dance of Life
A Dangerous Woman
Days of Heaven▶
Delicatessen▶
Desperate Characters▶
Dim Sum: A Little Bit of Heart▶
Diner▶
The Dining Room
Dinner at Eight
Dodes 'ka-den▶
Early Summer▶
Earthworm Tractors
Eat a Bowl of Tea▶
Eating
Echo Park
Edge of the World▶
Egg
El Super▶
An Empty Bed▶
End of the Line
Every Man for Himself & God Against All▶
Everybody's All American
The Family Game▶
Family Secrets
Fanny and Alexander▶
Five Corners
Fleshpot on 42nd Street
The Flintstones
Fried Green Tomatoes▶
The Funeral▶
Girlfriends▶
God's Little Acre▶
The Graduate▶
Grand Canyon▶
Gregory's Girl▶
The Group
Hannah and Her Sisters▶
Heavy Traffic▶
Here Comes Kelly
Hester Street▶
High Hopes▶
Honor Thy Father
The Horse of Pride
How U Like Me Now?▶
I Don't Buy Kisses Anymore
I Remember Mama▶
I Wanna Hold Your Hand
The Inheritors
Ironweed▶
It Runs in the Family▶
Jacknife▶
Joyless Street▶
Judge Priest▶
Key Exchange
Kings Row▶
La Terra Trema▶
The Last American Hero▶
The Last Days of Dolwyn
The Last Picture Show▶
Late Spring▶
Laws of Gravity▶
Le Grand Chemin▶
Leather Boys
Life Begins for Andy Hardy▶
Life with Father▶
The Little Thief▶

Little Women▶
Little Women
Living on Tokyo Time
Local Hero▶
London Kills Me
Look Back in Anger▶
The Lords of Flatbush
Love on the Run▶
Lumiere
Mac▶
MacArthur's Children▶
Madame Sousatzka▶
The Mango Tree
Marius▶
Marty
Mean Streets▶
Meet Me in St. Louis▶
Memories of a Marriage▶
Metropolitan▶
Mississippi Masala▶
Moonrise
Moonstruck▶
More American Graffiti
The Music Man▶
My Sister Eileen▶
Mystic Pizza▶
Naked▶
Nashville▶
1918
90 Days▶
No Fear, No Die
Nobody's Fool
Offnight
Oklahoma!▶
Old Swimmin' Hole
One More Saturday Night
One Third of a Nation
Our Town▶
Our Vines Have Tender
  Grapes▶
The Out-of-Towners▶
Over the Brooklyn Bridge
Papa's Delicate Condition▶
The Paper Chase▶
The Patriots▶
Pete 'n' Tillie
Pharmacist
The Playboys▶
The Pope of Greenwich
  Village
Prisoner of Second Avenue
Queens Logic
Rachel River
Raggedy Man▶
Raging Bull▶
Rainy Day
Rambling Rose▶
Real Life▶
Return of the Secaucus 7▶
Return to Mayberry
Reuben, Reuben▶
Riff Raff▶
A River Runs Through It▶
Room at the Top▶
Rosalie Goes Shopping▶
The Rules of the Game▶
Same Time, Next Year▶
Short Cuts▶
Sinners
Sinners in Paradise
The Smallest Show on Earth▶
Smithereens
Some Came Running▶
The Southerner▶
State Fair▶
State Fair
Steamboat Bill, Jr.▶
Steel Magnolias▶
Stranger than Paradise▶
Strong Medicine
Stroszek▶
Sugarbaby▶
The Sun Shines Bright
Tex
That Sinking Feeling▶
The Time of Your Life▶
Tin Men
To Kill a Mockingbird▶
Toni▶
Tonio Kroger
A Touch of Class▶
The Tree of Wooden Clogs▶

Trouble in the Glen
True Love▶
Twenty Bucks▶
29th Street
Twice in a Lifetime▶
Twist & Shout▶
The Two Sisters
Urban Cowboy
Used People
Walls of Glass
Wanderers▶
Watch It▶
A Wedding
The Whole Shootin' Match▶
Who's That Knocking at My
  Door?▶
Why Shoot the Teacher?▶
Wild Style
Wish You Were Here▶

Soccer

The Club▶
Cup Final
The Goalie's Anxiety at the
  Penalty Kick▶
Gregory's Girl▶
The Hero
Hot Shot
Hothead
Ladybugs
Long Shot
Those Glory, Glory Days
Victory
Yesterday's Hero

South America

see also Central America

Aguirre, the Wrath of God▶
Amazon
The Americano
Americano
At Play in the Fields of the
  Lord▶
Bananas▶
Black Orpheus▶
Bloody Che Contra
Burden of Dreams
Bye Bye Brazil
Catch the Heat
Clear and Present Danger▶
The Colombian Connection
Diplomatic Immunity
800 Leagues Down the
  Amazon
El Muerto
The Emerald Forest▶
Fitzcarraldo▶
Five Came Back
The Fugitive▶
Fury
Green Fire
Green Mansions
The Hour of the Star▶
The House of the Spirits
It's All True
Last Flight to Hell
The Last Movie
Latin Lovers
Let's Get Harry
Mighty Jungle
Miracles
Miss Mary
Missing▶
The Mission▶
Monster
Moon Over Parador
The Muthers
Naked Jungle▶
Nancy Goes to Rio
Night Gallery▶
One Man Out
Only Angels Have Wings▶
The Plague
Quilombo
Rodrigo D.: No Future
Romancing the Stone▶
Salvador▶
Simon Bolivar
The Story of Fausta
Sweet Country
Terror in the Jungle

The Three Caballeros
To Kill a Stranger
Wild Orchid
Xica▶
You Were Never Lovelier▶

Southern Belles

*see also American South;
Nashville Narratives*

Blaze
Cat on a Hot Tin Roof▶
Cat on a Hot Tin Roof
Crimes of the Heart
Dear Dead Delilah
Driving Miss Daisy▶
The Glass Menagerie▶
Gone with the Wind▶
Hush, Hush, Sweet
  Charlotte▶
Jezebel▶
Miss Firecracker▶
Nashville▶
North and South Book 1▶
North and South Book 2▶
Rich in Love
Scorchers
Steel Magnolias▶
A Streetcar Named Desire▶
The Trip to Bountiful▶

Space Operas

*see also Alien Beings—
Benign; Alien Beings—
Vicious*

Alien▶
Assignment Outer Space
Battle Beyond the Stars
Battle Beyond the Sun
Battlestar Galactica
The Black Hole
Buck Rogers Conquers the
  Universe
Capricorn One▶
Cat Women of the Moon
Conquest of Space
Countdown
Creature
Dark Side of the Moon
Dark Star▶
The Day the Sky Exploded
Destination Moon
Destination Moonbase Alpha
Destination Saturn
Doctor Who and the Daleks
Doctor Who: Death to the
  Daleks
Doctor Who: Pyramids of
  Mars
Doctor Who: Spearhead from
  Space
Doctor Who: Terror of the
  Zygons
Doctor Who: The Ark in Space
Escape from Planet Earth
Explorers
Fire Maidens from Outer
  Space
First Men in the Moon
First Spaceship on Venus▶
Flight to Mars
Forbidden Planet▶
From the Earth to the Moon
Galaxy of Terror
The Green Slime
Hangar 18
Heavens Above▶
Horror Planet
Horrors of the Red Planet
Journey to the Far Side of the
  Sun▶
Killings at Outpost Zeta
Laser Mission
The Last Starfighter
Lifepod
Marooned
Megaforce
Mission Galactica: The Cylon
  Attack
Mission Mars
Mom and Dad Save the World
Moon 44

Moonraker
Moontrap
Murder in Space
Mutant on the Bounty
Nude on the Moon
Outland
Planet Burg
Planet of the Apes▶
Planet of the Dinosaurs
Planet of the Vampires
Project Moon Base
PSI Factor
Return of the Jedi▶
Return to Earth
The Right Stuff▶
Robinson Crusoe on Mars
Rocketship X-M
Silent Running▶
Solar Crisis
Solaris
Space Mutiny
Space Rage
Space Raiders
Spaceballs
SpaceCamp
Star Crash
Star Slammer
Star Trek: The Motion Picture
Star Trek 2: The Wrath of
  Khan▶
Star Trek 3: The Search for
  Spock
Star Trek 4: The Voyage
  Home▶
Star Trek 5: The Final Frontier
Star Trek 6: The
  Undiscovered Country
Star Trek the Next
  Generation: Encounter at
  Farpoint
Star Wars▶
Starship
Terronauts
Transformations
2001: A Space Odyssey▶
2010: The Year We Make
  Contact▶
Voyage to the Planet of
  Prehistoric Women
Voyage to the Prehistoric
  Planet
Walking on Air
Warlords of the 21st Century
Woman in the Moon
Women of the Prehistoric
  Planet

Spaghetti Western

*see also Western Comedy;
Westerns*

Ace High
Beyond the Law
Boot Hill
Bullet for Sandoval
Chino
A Fistful of Dollars▶
A Fistful of Dynamite▶
Five Giants from Texas
For a Few Dollars More
The Good, the Bad and the
  Ugly▶
The Grand Duel
Gun Fight at Red Sands
Hang 'Em High
Hellbenders
Linchamiento
A Minute to Pray, A Second to
  Die
My Name is Nobody
Once Upon a Time in the
  West▶
Rough Justice
The Ruthless Four
Spaghetti Western
Straight to Hell
The Stranger and the
  Gunfighter
Stranger in Paso Bravo
Take a Hard Ride
Tramplers
Trinity is Still My Name

You're Jinxed, Friend, You've
  Met Sacramento

Spain

Ay, Carmela!▶
Barcelona▶
The Barcelona Kill
Behold a Pale Horse
Belle Epoque▶
Blood and Sand▶
Caper of the Golden Bulls
The Castilian
I'm the One You're Looking
  For
Marbella
The Naked Maja
The Pride and the Passion
Sand and Blood
Siesta
The Spanish Gardener▶
Surprise Attack
The Sword of El Cid
A Touch of Class▶

Spies & Espionage

*see also Feds; Foreign
Intrigue; Terrorism*

Above Suspicion▶
Access Code
Across the Pacific▶
Action in Arabia
Adventures in Spying
The Adventures of Tartu
Against the Wind
Agent on Ice
Air Raid Wardens
Alamut Ambush
Alien Women
All Through the Night▶
The Amateur
Arabesque
Armored Command
Artists and Models
As If It Were Raining
Assassin
The Assassination Run
The Atomic Kid
Attack of the Robots
Avalanche Express
Aventure Malgache
Background to Danger▶
Bear Island
Behind Enemy Lines
The Berlin Conspiracy
Berlin Express▶
Besame
Betrayed▶
Big Deadly Game
Big Jim McLain
The Big Lift
Black Box Affair
Black Brigade
The Black Dragons
Black Eagle
The Black Windmill
Blue Ice
Bon Voyage
Boris and Natasha: The Movie
The Bourne Identity▶
British Intelligence
Bulldog Drummond at Bay
Bulldog Drummond Escapes
Bulletproof
Burgess, Philby, and
  MacLean: Spy Scandal of
  the Century
Cairo
Call Me Bwana
Canadian Mounties Vs.
  Atomic Invaders
The Canon Operation
Caravan to Vaccares
Carve Her Name with Pride
Casablanca▶
Casino Royale
A Casualty of War
The Charge of the Model T's
Chu Chu & the Philly Flash
Clear and Present Danger▶
Clipped Wings
Cloak and Dagger

Cloak & Dagger
Code Name Alpha
Code Name: Chaos
Code Name: Dancer
Code Name: Diamond Head
Code Name: Emerald
Codename: Foxfire
Codename: Icarus
Codename Kyril
Codename: Wildgeese
Cold War Killers
Company Business
Comrades in Arms
Condorman
Conspirator
Counterblast
The Counterfeit Traitor▶
Cowboy Commandos
Criminals Within
Dandy in Aspic
Danger Man
Daniel
Dark Journey▶
Darling Lili
Dawn Express
The Day and the Hour
A Day in October
The Day of the Dolphin
The Day of the Jackal▶
The Day Will Dawn▶
Dead Aim
Deadly Currents
The Deadly Game
Deadly Recruits
Deadly Rivals
Deadly Spygames
The Deadly Trap
Death Ray 2000
Death Rides the Range
Deathcheaters
Defense Play
Delta Force Commando 2
Desperate Cargo
Diamonds are Forever▶
Diplomatic Courier▶
Dishonored
Dr. No▶
The Doll Squad
Don't Drink the Water
Don't Raise the Bridge, Lower the River
Double Agents
Double Deal
The Double O Kid
Down Among the Z Men
Duck Soup▶
The Dunera Boys▶
Edge of Darkness▶
Edge of Darkness
The Eiger Sanction
Embassy
Emissary
The Endless Game
Enforcer from Death Row
An Englishman Abroad▶
Enigma
Erik
Escape from Fort Bravo
Escape from the KGB
The Executioner
The Experts
Eye of the Needle
Eyewitness
The Falcon and the Snowman▶
The Falcon's Brother
The Fallen Sparrow▶
The Fantastic World of D.C. Collins
Federal Agent
Final Assignment
The Final Option
Fire Over England▶
Firefall
Firefox
Firehead
First Yank into Tokyo
Five Fingers▶
Five for Hell
Flight from Vienna
Flight to Nowhere
Flying Blind

For Your Eyes Only▶
Foreign Correspondent▶
The Foreigner
The Formula
The Fourth Protocol▶
Francis Gary Powers: The True Story of the U-2 Spy
French Intrigue
From Russia with Love▶
Funeral in Berlin▶
The General Died at Dawn▶
A Generation▶
Get Smart, Again!
Girl Hunters
Girls Are for Loving
The Glass Bottom Boat
Golden Earrings
Goldfinger▶
Gotcha!
The Great Armored Car Swindle
Green Inferno
The Groundstar Conspiracy▶
Gunpowder
Hanky Panky
Happy Anniversary 007: 25 Years of James Bond
Hard Ticket to Hawaii
The Heat of the Day
Heroes in Hell
Heroes Stand Alone
Hidden Enemy
Hillbillies in a Haunted House
The Holcroft Covenant
Holt of the Secret Service
Honeybaby
Honeymoon Academy
Hopscotch▶
Hostage
The Hot Line
Hotel Reserve▶
Hour of the Assassin
The House on Carroll Street
The House on Garibaldi Street
The Human Factor
The Hunt for Red October▶
Hunter
I Dood It
I See a Dark Stranger▶
I Stand Condemned
The Ice Runner
Ice Station Zebra
If Looks Could Kill
The Impossible Spy▶
The In-Laws▶
In the Secret State
Incident at Map-Grid 36-80
The Innocent
The Inside Man
Inside the Lines
Internecine Project
Intrigue
Invisible Agent
The Ipcress File▶
Ishtar
It Means That to Me
J-Men Forever!▶
Jakarta
Jet Pilot
The Jigsaw Man
Joan of Paris▶
Journey into Fear▶
Journey into Fear
Jumpin' Jack Flash
Jungle Drums of Africa
Keep Talking Baby
The KGB: The Secret War
Kill Castro
Kill Factor
Kim▶
Koroshi
La Cage aux Folles 2
Ladies Man
Laser Mission
The Last Embrace▶
Le Magnifique
License to Kill
License to Kill▶
Lightning Bolt
Lipstick Camera
Lisbon
The Little Drummer Girl▶

Live and Let Die
The Living Daylights▶
Loaded Guns
The Looking Glass War
Lost Diamond
The Lost One
Love on the Run
M. Butterfly
Mackintosh Man
Madame Sin
Malone
Man from Headquarters
The Man from U.N.C.L.E.
The Man on the Box
The Man Outside
The Man Who Never Was▶
The Man Who Wasn't There
The Man with One Red Shoe
The Man with the Golden Gun
Marie Galante▶
Maroc 7
Mata Hari▶
Mata Hari
The Mediterranean in Flames
The Mercenaries
Mind Trap
Mindfield
Mission Phantom
Mission to Venice
Mr. Superinvisible
The Monocle
Monte Carlo
Moonraker
Morituri▶
Murder for Sale
Murder on the Midnight Express
Murderers' Row
My Favorite Blonde▶
My Favorite Brunette
My Name is Ivan▶
The Mysterious Lady
Mystery Plane
Nasty Rabbit
Never Say Never Again
Never Too Young to Die
Night Flight from Moscow
A Night in Casablanca▶
Night Train to Munich▶
Ninja Champion
No Dead Heroes
No Way Out▶
North by Northwest▶
Notorious▶
The Nude Bomb
Number 1 of the Secret Service
Octopussy
The Odessa File
Old Mother Riley's Ghosts
On Her Majesty's Secret Service▶
On the Edge
Once Upon a Honeymoon
One Against the Wind▶
One Armed Executioner
One of Our Dinosaurs Is Missing
Operation C.I.A.
Operation Crossbow▶
The Osterman Weekend
Overture
The Package
Panama Hattie
Panama Menace
Panama Patrol
Paper Tiger
Paradisio
Pascali's Island▶
Patriot Games▶
The Peking Blond
Pepper
A Perfect Spy
Permission To Kill
The Persuaders
Philby, Burgess and MacLean: Spy Scandal of the Century
Phoenix Team
Picasso Trigger
Pickup on South Street▶
President's Mistress
Prime Risk

The Prize▶
Protocol
Pueblo Affair▶
A Question of Attribution
Qui Etes Vous, Mr. Sorge?
The Quiller Memorandum▶
Ravishing Idiot
Rebel Love
Reilly: Ace of Spies▶
Retrievers
Return of the Man from U.N.C.L.E.
Rio Rita
Robinson Crusoe of Mystery Island
Roboman
Robot Pilot
Running Blind
Running Delilah
Running Scared
The Russia House
Russian Roulette
The Rutanga Tapes
Sabotage▶
Saboteur▶
The Saint's Vacation/The Narrow Margin
Samurai
S.A.S. San Salvador
Scorpio
Sea Devils
Sebastian
Second Best Secret Agent in the Whole Wide World
The Secret Agent▶
Secret Agent
Secret Agent 00
Secret Agent Super Dragon
Secret Weapon
Secret Weapons
Sell Out
Shack Out on 101▶
Shadows Over Shanghai
S*H*E
Shining Through
Ship Ahoy
A Show of Force
Sky High
Sky Liner
Sneakers
Snuff-Bottle Connection
The Soldier
A Southern Yankee
Soviet Spy
Spies▶
Spies, Lies and Naked Thighs
Spy
Spy in Black▶
Spy of Napoleon
Spy Smasher Returns
Spy Story
Spy Trap
The Spy Who Came in from the Cold▶
The Spy Who Loved Me
Spy with a Cold Nose
Spymaker: The Secret Life of Ian Fleming
S*P*Y*S
Stalag 17▶
State Department File 649
Steal the Sky
Stopover Tokyo
The Stranger▶
Strike Commando
Subterfuge
The Tall Blond Man with One Black Shoe▶
The Tamarind Seed
Tangiers
Target for Killing
Telefon
Terminal Entry
Terminal Velocity
Texas to Bataan
There Goes Barder
They Got Me Covered
The Thief
The Third Man▶
13 Rue Madeleine▶
The Thirty-Nine Steps
The 39 Steps▶

Three Days in Beirut
Three Days of the Condor▶
Three Kinds of Heat
Thunderball
Tiffany Jones
To Live and Die in Hong Kong
Tokyo Joe
Top Secret!▶
Topaz▶
Torn Curtain
Trenchcoat
Trident Force
Triple Cross▶
Tripwire
The Trouble with Spies
True Lies▶
The Ultimate Imposter
Undeclared War
Under the Rainbow
Undercover Blues
Up Periscope
The Uranium Conspiracy
A View to a Kill
Viper
Wanted Dead or Alive
Watch on the Rhine▶
Waterfront
What's Up, Tiger Lily?▶
Where Eagles Dare▶
Where the Bullets Fly
The Whistle Blower▶
White Ghost
White Nights
WhiteForce
Wonsan Operation
Yin & Yang of Mr. Go
You Only Live Twice
Young Nurses in Love
Your Turn Darling
Yuri Nosenko, KGB
Zeppelin
Zotz!

Sports

see Baseball; Basketball; Bicycling; Boxing; Fast Cars; Football; Golf; Hockey; The Olympics; Pool; Scuba; Skating; Skiing; Soccer; Sports Comedies; Sports Dramas; Surfing; Swimming; Tennis; Volleyball

Sports Comedies

The Air Up There
Angels in the Outfield
The Bad News Bears▶
The Bad News Bears Go to Japan
The Bad News Bears in Breaking Training
The Best of Times
Billie
Bingo Long Traveling All-Stars & Motor Kings▶
Blue Skies Again
Body Slam
Bowery Blitzkrieg
Bull Durham▶
Comeback Kid
The Comrades of Summer
Cool Runnings
Day the Bookies Wept
Diggstown
D2: The Mighty Ducks
Fast Break
First & Ten
First & Ten: The Team Scores Again
The Fish that Saved Pittsburgh
For Heaven's Sake
The Freshman▶
Goof Balls
Hold 'Em Jail
Hot Dog...The Movie!
Hothead
It Happens Every Spring▶
Jocks
Johnny Be Good

Ladybugs
A League of Their Own▶
Little Big League
The Longest Yard
The Longshot
Major League
Major League 2
The Mighty Ducks
Mr. Baseball
Monty Python's The Meaning
 of Life▶
Necessary Roughness
North Dallas Forty▶
Off the Mark
The One and Only
One-Punch O'Day
Paper Lion
Pat and Mike▶
Prize Fighter
Rookie of the Year
The Sandlot▶
The Scout▶
Semi-Tough
Ski School
Slap Shot▶
Splitz
Spring Fever
Squeeze Play
Swim Team
Trading Hearts
White Men Can't Jump
Wildcats
The World's Greatest Athlete

Sports Dramas

Above the Rim
Airborne
All the Right Moves
American Anthem
American Flyers
American Kickboxer 1
Babe!▶
The Babe
Babe Ruth Story
Bang the Drum Slowly
Bang the Drum Slowly▶
The Big Blue
Big Mo
Billyboy
Blades of Courage
Blue Chips
Body and Soul▶
Body & Soul
Boy in Blue
Breaking Away▶
Brian's Song▶
Brutal Glory
Challenge of a Lifetime
Champion▶
Champions
Chariots of Fire▶
Chasing Dreams
The Club▶
Coach
The Color of Money▶
Crossbar
The Cutting Edge
Dawn!
Days of Thunder
Dempsey
Diving In
Don't Look Back: The Story of
 Leroy "Satchel" Paige
Downhill Racer
Dream to Believe
Dreamer
Dynamite Dan
Eight Men Out▶
8 Seconds
Fat City▶
Field of Dreams▶
Fight for the Title
Final Shot: The Hank Gathers
 Story
Finish Line
The First Olympics: Athens
 1896
Gentleman Jim▶
Gladiator
Go for the Gold
Going for the Gold: The Bill
 Johnson Story

The Gold & Glory
Goldengirl
Grambling's White Tiger
Heart Like a Wheel
Heaven is a Playground
The Hero
Hockey Night
Honeyboy
Hoosiers▶
Hot Shot
The Hustler▶
Ice Castles
Ice Pawn
International Velvet
The Jericho Mile
The Jesse Owens Story
Jim Thorpe: All American
The Joe Louis Story
Kid Galahad▶
Knute Rockne: All American▶
The Last American Hero▶
The Last Fight
The Loneliest Runner
Long Gone
Marciano
Miracle on Ice
My Champion
Nadia
The Natural▶
On the Edge
One in a Million: The Ron
 LaFlore Story
One Last Run
One on One
Over the Top
Paperback Hero
Pastime▶
Personal Best▶
Pistol: The Birth of a Legend
Players
Pride of St. Louis
The Pride of the Yankees▶
The Program
Pulsebeat
Raging Bull▶
Red Line 7000
Red Surf
Requiem for a Heavyweight▶
Rocky▶
Rocky 2
Rocky 3
Rocky 4
Rocky 5
Rudy
Running Brave
Side Out
Skier's Dream
The Spirit of West Point
The Stratton Story▶
Talent for the Game
That Championship Season
This Sporting Life▶
Tiger Town
Touch and Go
21 Hours at Munich▶
Victory
Vision Quest
Wilma
Wind
A Winner Never Quits
The Winning Team
Youngblood

Spousal Abuse

see also Sexual Abuse
The Burning Bed▶
Dangerous Game
Falling Down
Far Cry from Home
Independence Day
Intimate Strangers
Mesmerized
Mortal Thoughts
Olivia
Remember Me
Sleeping with the Enemy
This Boy's Life▶
What's Love Got to Do With
 It?

Star Gazing

Duel in the Eclipse
Eliza's Horoscope
The Fish that Saved
 Pittsburgh
How Come Nobody's On Our
 Side?
Lamp at Midnight
Local Hero▶

Stepparents

*see also Family Ties;
 Parenthood*
Big Girls Don't Cry...They Get
 Even
Cinderella▶
Cinderella
Ellie
Hard Frame
Lassie
Lost
The Orphan
Out on a Limb
Private Passions
Rivals
The Stepfather▶
Stepfather 2: Make Room for
 Daddy
Stepfather 3: Father's Day
The Stepmother
A Summer to Remember▶
This Boy's Life▶

Stewardesses

see also Airborne
Blazing Stewardesses
Stewardess School
Three Guys Named Mike

Storytelling

The Company of Wolves▶
Grim Prairie Tales
Monster in a Box▶
My Dinner with Andre▶
Paper Tiger
The Princess Bride▶
The Story Lady
The Willies
Windwalker▶

Strained Suburbia

*see also Yuppie
 Nightmares*
Adventures in Spying
The Amityville Horror
Amongst Friends
Amos and Andrew
Blue Velvet▶
The 'Burbs
Clown House
Coneheads
Consenting Adults
Deadly Neighbor
Dennis the Menace
Desperate Hours▶
Desperate Hours
Don't Tell Mom the
 Babysitter's Dead
Edward Scissorhands▶
The Graduate▶
Grand Canyon▶
The Grass is Always Greener
 Over the Septic Tank
Hocus Pocus
House▶
How to Beat the High Cost of
 Living
Hush Little Baby, Don't You
 Cry
I Love My...Wife
Jaws▶
Jaws 2
Madhouse
Marked for Death
The Meal
Mr. Blandings Builds His
 Dream House
The Money Pit
My Blue Heaven

My New Gun
Neighbors
Opportunity Knocks
The Osterman Weekend
Over the Edge▶
Parents▶
The People Next Door
Please Don't Eat the Daisies
The Positively True
 Adventures of the Alleged
 Texas Cheerleader-
 Murdering Mom▶
Return of the Living Dead 2
Revenge of the Stepford
 Wives
Serial Mom▶
Shattered Spirits
Short Cuts▶
The Stranger▶
Swimmer▶
Terrorvision
Twice in a Lifetime▶
The Underworld Story
The War of the Roses▶
When Every Day was the
 Fourth of July

Struggling Musicians

see also Music
American Blue Note
Backbeat▶
Beyond the Valley of the Dolls
Bikini Summer
Blast-Off Girls
Breaking Glass
Bye Bye Blues
The Competition▶
Cotton Candy
Crossover Dreams
Crossroads
Dangerous Holiday
Dangerous Moonlight▶
Desperate Teenage Lovedolls
Dogs in Space
Eddie and the Cruisers
Eddie and the Cruisers 2:
 Eddie Lives!
The Eternal Waltz
The Fabulous Dorseys
Falling from Grace
The Five Heartbeats▶
Heaven Tonight
Killing 'em Softly
Knights of the City
Light of Day
A Man Called Adam▶
Mo' Better Blues
Murder Rap
Oh, God! You Devil
One Trick Pony
Purple Rain
The Return of Spinal Tap
Rhinestone
Rock & Rule
The Rose▶
Satisfaction
Sparkle
A Star is Born
Streets of Fire
Tender Mercies▶
This is Spinal Tap▶
You Light Up My Life

Submarines

see also Deep Blue
Above Us the Waves▶
The Abyss▶
Assault on a Queen
Crash Dive
Das Boot▶
The Day Will Dawn▶
Destination Tokyo
Enemy Below▶
First Strike
For Your Eyes Only▶
Full Fathom Five
Going Under
The Hunt for Red October▶
The Inside Man
Mysterious Island▶
Operation Petticoat▶

Q Ships
Run Silent, Run Deep▶
The Spy Who Loved Me
Submarine Seahawk
Torpedo Alley
Torpedo Attack
Torpedo Run
20,000 Leagues Under the
 Sea▶
Up Periscope
Voyage to the Bottom of the
 Sea▶
We Dive at Dawn▶
You Only Live Twice

Subways

see also Trains
Adventures in Babysitting
Carlito's Way▶
Dutchman▶
Eve of Destruction
The French Connection▶
The Fugitive▶
Highlander 2: The Quickening
The Incident
Lethal Weapon 3
Predator 2
Risky Business▶
Speed▶
Subway
The Taking of Pelham One
 Two Three▶
The Warriors

Suicide

*see also Death & the
 Afterlife*
Absence of Malice
Angels Over Broadway▶
The Arrangement
Attack Squadron
Autopsy
Bad Girls Dormitory
Bedazzled▶
The Bell Jar
Better Off Dead
The Big Chill▶
Buddy Buddy
Can You Hear the Laughter?
 The Story of Freddie Prinze
Club Extinction
Crimes of the Heart
Dead Poets Society▶
Death Wish Club
Delinquent Daughters
Demon Witch Child
Deutschland im Jahre Null▶
The Devil in Silk
Docks of New York▶
Dominique is Dead
Double Suicide▶
The End▶
Esposa y Amante
Europa '51
The Eyes, the Mouth
The Fire Within▶
Fuzz
Golden Gate
Goodbye Cruel World
Harold and Maude▶
Heading for Heaven
Heathers▶
The Hudsucker Proxy▶
Hustle
It's a Wonderful Life▶
Kamikaze
Last Cry for Help
Last Tango in Paris▶
Le Corbeau▶
Maedchen in Uniform▶
Memorial Day
Mother Kusters Goes to
 Heaven▶
Mouchette▶
Nais▶
Natural Enemies
'night, Mother
The Odd Job
Ode to Billy Joe
One Flew Over the Cuckoo's
 Nest▶

Ordinary People▶
Pain in the A—▶
Peeping Tom▶
Permanent Record
Retribution
Return of Frank Cannon
Reuben, Reuben▶
Right of Way
Romeo and Juliet▶
Romeo and Juliet
Romeo and Juliet▶
Scent of a Woman▶
Silence of the Heart▶
The Slender Thread▶
Stealing Home
Stella Maris▶
The Tenant▶
Warm Summer Rain
Wetherby▶
Whose Life Is It Anyway?▶

Summer Camp
Addams Family Values
Backwoods
Berserker
The Best Way
The Burning
Camp Cucamonga: How I
    Spent My Summer
    Vacation
Camp Nowhere
Cannibal Campout
Cry from the Mountain
Don't Go in the Woods
Ernest Goes to Camp
Evil Dead
The Final Terror
The Forest
Friday the 13th
Friday the 13th, Part 2
Friday the 13th, Part 3
Friday the 13th, Part 4: The
    Final Chapter
Gimme an F
Gorp
The Great Outdoors
Grim Prairie Tales
The Hills Have Eyes
Hot Resort
Indian Summer
Little Darlings
Meatballs
Meatballs 2
Meatballs 3
Meatballs 4
Nuts in May
Oddballs
Party Camp
Poison Ivy
Princes in Exile
Race with the Devil
Redwood Forest Trail
Rituals
Sleepaway Camp
Sleepaway Camp 2: Unhappy
    Campers
Sleepaway Camp 3: Teenage
    Wasteland
Storm
Stuckey's Last Stand
Summer Camp Nightmare
Three Way Weekend
Ticks
Troop Beverly Hills
The Willies

Super Heroes
The Amazing Spider-Man
Batman
Batman▶
Batman: Mask of the
    Phantasm
Batman Returns
Blankman
Captain America
Captain America 2: Death Too
    Soon
Chinese Web
Cloak & Dagger
Death of the Incredible Hulk
Dr. Strange

El Hombre Contra el Mundo
El Zorro Blanco
The Flash
The Flash 2: Revenge of the
    Trickster
Flash Gordon
The Incredible Hulk
The Incredible Hulk Returns
Infra-Man
The Mask▶
The Meteor Man
The Original Flash Gordon
    Collection
Phenomenal and the Treasure
    of Tutankamen
The Puma Man
The Punisher
Return of Captain Invincible
The Shadow
Spiderman: The Deadly Dust
Super Fuzz
Supergirl
Superman: The Movie▶
Superman 2▶
Superman 3
Superman 4: The Quest for
    Peace
Superman & the Mole Men
Supersonic Man
The Trial of the Incredible Hulk
TV's Best Adventures of
    Superman
Vip, My Brother Superman
The Wild World of Batwoman

**Supernatural
Comedies**
Angels in the Outfield
Beetlejuice▶
Bell, Book and Candle
Bernard and the Genie
Blackbeard's Ghost
Dead Heat
The Devil & Max Devlin
Fridays of Eternity
Ghost Chasers
Ghost Dad
Ghost Fever
The Ghost Goes West▶
The Ghost Train
Ghost Writer
Ghostbusters▶
Ghostbusters 2
Ghosts Can Do It
Ghosts of Berkeley Square
Haunted Honeymoon
Heart and Souls
High Spirits
Hillbillies in a Haunted House
Hocus Pocus
Limit Up
Love at Stake
The Man in the Santa Claus
    Suit
My Best Friend Is a Vampire
Oh, God!
Oh, God! Book 2
Oh, God! You Devil
Rockula
Saturday the 14th
Saturday the 14th Strikes
    Back
She-Devil
Spook Busters
Spooks Run Wild
Teen Wolf
Teen Wolf Too
Topper▶
Topper Returns▶
Topper Takes a Trip▶
Who Killed Doc Robbin?
Wicked Stepmother
Wishful Thinking
A Witch Without a Broom

**Supernatural Cop
Thrillers**
Angel Heart
Apprentice to Murder
The Believers

The Dying Truth
The First Power
God Told Me To
Maniac Cop
Maniac Cop 2
Maniac Cop 3
Split Second
Wolfen▶

Supernatural Horror
*see also Classic Horror;
Horror*
Afterward
Alabama's Ghost
Alison's Birthday
The Amityville Horror
Amityville 2: The Possession
Amityville 3: The Demon
Amityville 4
Amityville: A New Generation
Amityville 1992: It's About
    Time
The Appointment
Audrey Rose
Bad Dreams
The Believers
Beyond Evil
The Black Cat
Blood Orgy of the She-Devils
Bloodbeat
Bloodlust
Born of Fire
The Brainiac
Candyman
Cassandra
Charlie Boy
Children of the Night
Christine
Crimes of Dr. Mabuse▶
Crypt of Dark Secrets
Curse of the Aztec Mummy/
    Robot vs. the Aztec
    Mummy
Curse of the Black Widow
Curse of the Blue Lights
The Curse of the Crying
    Woman
Curse of the Demon▶
Curse of the Headless
    Horseman
Curse of the Living Corpse
Curse of the Stone Hand
The Curse of the Werewolf
The Cursed Mountain Mystery
Damien: Omen 2
Dance of Death
The Dark
Dark Places
The Dark Secret of Harvest
    Home
Dark Tower
The Daughter of Dr. Jekyll
Daughters of Satan
Dawn of the Mummy
Dead and Buried
The Dead Don't Die
The Death Curse of Tartu
Death Ship
Deathdream
Deathhead Virgin
Deathmoon
Deep Red: Hatchet Murders
Def by Temptation
The Demon Lover
Demon of Paradise
Demon Rage
Demon Warrior
Demon Wind
Demon Witch Child
Demonoid, Messenger of
    Death
The Demons
Demons
Demons 2
Demons of Ludlow
Demonstone
Demonwarp
Destroyer
The Devil
Devil Dog: The Hound of Hell
Devil Doll
Devil Woman

The Devil's Daughter
Devil's Gift
The Devil's Hand
The Devil's Nightmare
The Devil's Partner
The Devil's Possessed
Devil's Rain
The Devil's Web
Devil's Wedding Night
Devonsville Terror
The Diabolical Dr. Z
Diary of a Madman
Diary of the Dead
Die, Monster, Die!
Disciple of Death
The Doctor and the Devils
Doctor Butcher M.D.
Dr. Frankenstein's Castle of
    Freaks
Doctor Phibes Rises Again
Dr. Tarr's Torture Dungeon
Dr. Terror's House of Horrors
Don't Be Afraid of the Dark
Don't Go to Sleep
The Dunwich Horror
Dust Devil
Edge of Sanity
El Monte de las Brujas
Equinox▶
The Evil
Evil Altar
Evil Town
Evilspeak
Exorcism
The Exorcist▶
The Exorcist 2: The Heretic
Feast for the Devil
Feet Foremost
The Final Conflict
Firestarter
The First Power
Fright House
From Beyond the Grave
The Gate
Gate 2
The Ghastly Ones
The Ghost
Ghost Dance
Ghost Keeper
The Ghost of Rashmon Hall
The Ghost of Yotsuya
Ghost Stories: Graveyard
    Thriller
Ghost Story
Ghosthouse
Ghostriders
The Ghosts of Hanley House
Ghosts That Still Walk
Giant from the Unknown
God Told Me To
Grave Secrets: The Legacy of
    Hilltop Drive
The Haunted Palace
The Hearse
Hellbound: Hellraiser 2
Hellraiser
Hellraiser 3: Hell on Earth
The Horrible Dr. Hichcock
Horror Express
Horror Hotel
Horror of the Blood Monsters
Horror Rises from the Tomb
The House by the Cemetery
The House in Marsh Road
The House of Seven Corpses
House of the Yellow Carpet
The House on Skull Mountain
The House that Bled to Death
House Where Evil Dwells
The Howling▶
Howling 2: Your Sister is a
    Werewolf
Howling 3: The Marsupials
Howling 4: The Original
    Nightmare
Howling 5: The Rebirth
Howling 6: The Freaks
Immortal Sins
The Indestructible Man
Inferno
Initiation of Sarah
Inquisition

Invasion of the Blood Farmers
Invasion of the Zombies
Invitation to Hell
It's Alive!
Jaws of Satan
J.D.'s Revenge
Jennifer
Judgment Day
Kill and Go Hide
Kill, Baby, Kill▶
The Kiss
Kiss Daddy Goodbye
Kwaidan▶
Land of the Minotaur
The Last Man on Earth
The Legacy
The Legend of Hell House▶
Let's Scare Jessica to Death
Lisa and the Devil
The Living Head
Los Vampiros de Coyacan
The Loves of Irina
Lurkers
Lust for a Vampire
The Man and the Monster
Manhattan Baby
Maniac
The Manitou
Mannikin
Manos, the Hands of Fate
Mardi Gras for the Devil
Mardi Gras Massacre
Mark of the Devil
Mark of the Devil 2
Mary, Mary, Bloody Mary
Maxim Xul
The Medusa Touch
The Mephisto Waltz▶
Meridian: Kiss of the Beast
Messiah of Evil
Midnight
Midnight Cabaret
Midnight's Child
Mirror, Mirror
Mirror of Death
The Monster Demolisher
The Mummy's Revenge
Near Dark▶
Necromancer: Satan's
    Servant
Necropolis
Neon Maniacs
The Nesting
Netherworld
The Night Evelyn Came Out of
    the Grave
Night Life
Night Nurse
Night of Horror
Night of the Death Cult
Night of the Demons
Night of the Demons 2
Night of the Ghouls
Night of the Sorcerers
The Night Stalker: Two Tales
    of Terror
Night Vision
Night Visitor
Nightmare Castle
Nightmare in Blood
Nightmare Sisters
Nightmare Weekend
Nightstalker
Nightwish
Nomads
Nothing But the Night
The Occultist
Of Unknown Origin
The Offspring
The Omen
Omen 4: The Awakening
The Oracle
Orgy of the Dead
Orgy of the Vampires
The Other▶
Other Hell
Out of the Body
The Outing
Patrick
Pet Sematary
Pet Sematary 2
Phantasm

Phantasm II
Phantom of the Ritz
Poltergeist▶
Poltergeist 2: The Other Side
Poltergeist 3
The Possessed
The Possession of Joel
  Delaney
The Premonition
The Psychic
Psychomania
Pumpkinhead
Rawhead Rex
Revolt of the Zombies
The Sleeping Car
Specters
The Supernaturals
Terror Creatures from the
  Grave
They Watch
13 Ghosts
The Turn of the Screw
The Visitors
Witchcraft 4: Virgin Heart
The Wraith

Supernatural Martial Arts

Baby Cart at the River Styx
Baby Cart to Hades
The Crow
Kung Fu from Beyond the
  Grave
Kung Fu Vampire Buster
Ninja, the Violent Sorcerer
Remo Williams: The
  Adventure Begins
The 7 Brothers Meet Dracula
Vampire Raiders—Ninja
  Queen

Supernatural Westerns

Back to the Future, Part 3▶
Billy the Kid Versus Dracula
The Devil's Mistress
Ghostriders
Grim Prairie Tales
Into the Badlands
Jesse James Meets
  Frankenstein's Daughter
Mad at the Moon
Sundown
Timerider

Surfing

see also *Beach Blanket Bingo*
Aloha Summer
Beach Blanket Bingo▶
Beach Party
Big Wednesday
Bikini Beach
California Dreaming
Computer Beach Party
The Endless Summer▶
The Endless Summer 2▶
Follow Me
Gidget
How to Stuff a Wild Bikini
Lauderdale
Mad Wax: The Surf Movie
Muscle Beach Party
North Shore
Point Break
Puberty Blues
Red Surf
Ride the Wild Surf
Summer City
Sundance
Surf Nazis Must Die
Surf Party
Surf 2

Survival

see also *Negative Utopia; Post Apocalypse*
Adrift
Adventure Island

Adventures of Eliza Fraser
The Alaska Wilderness
  Adventure
Alive
Alive: 20 Years Later
Alpine Fire
And I Alone Survived
Antarctica
Attack of the Beast Creatures
The Aviator
Back from Eternity
Bat 21
Benjamin Argumedo
Black Rain▶
Born Killer
The Bridge on the River
  Kwai▶
Buffalo Rider
A Bullet Is Waiting
Caged in Paradiso
Captain January
Challenge To Be Free
Clearcut
Cliffhanger▶
Clown
Cold River
Cool Hand Luke▶
Damned River
Das Boot▶
The Dawson Patrol
The Day After▶
Dead Calm▶
Deadly Harvest
Deadly Prey
Death Hunt
Def-Con 4
Deliverance▶
Delos Adventure
Delusion
The Desert Tigers
Desperate Target
The Devil
The Devil at 4 O'Clock
Diamonds of the Night▶
The Dive
Dust Devil
Earthling
Edge of Honor
Empire of the Sun▶
Endgame
Enemy Mine
Enemy Territory
Erendira▶
Eric▶
Escape from Hell
Escapist
Fearless▶
Fight for Your Life
Firehawk
Five Came Back
Flight from Glory
Flight from Singapore
Flight of the Eagle
The Flight of the Phoenix▶
Fortress
Found Alive
Gas-s-s-s!
The Ghost of Fletcher Ridge
Grave of the Fireflies▶
He is My Brother
Heaven and Earth
Heroes for Sale▶
High Ice
High Noon▶
Hunter's Blood
The Incredible Journey
The Interrogation▶
The Island▶
The Island at the Top of the
  World
Island of the Blue Dolphins
Island of the Lost
Jeremiah Johnson▶
Jungle Inferno
Just Before Dawn
Kameradschaft▶
Killing at Hell's Gate
The Killing Fields▶
King Rat▶
The Land That Time Forgot
The Last Chance▶
Last Exit to Brooklyn▶

The Last Flight of Noah's Ark
Le Dernier Combat▶
Legend of Alfred Packer
The Legend of Wolf Mountain
The Life and Death of Colonel
  Blimp▶
Lifeboat▶
Lily was Here
Little Dorrit, Film 1: Nobody's
  Fault▶
Little Dorrit, Film 2: Little
  Dorrit's Story▶
Lord of the Flies▶
Lord of the Flies
Lost
Love on the Dole▶
Male and Female▶
Man in the Wilderness
Manon
Melody
Merry Christmas, Mr.
  Lawrence▶
Mr. Robinson Crusoe
The Mosquito Coast
The Most Dangerous Game▶
My Side of the Mountain
Mysterious Island▶
The Naked Prey▶
Nightmare at Bittercreek
Nightmare at Noon
Objective, Burma!▶
On the Beach▶
Once Before I Die
Osa
Out of Control
The Overlanders
Packin' It In
Pagan Island
Panic in the Year Zero!
Paradise
Perfect Witness
Phone Call from a Stranger
Pioneer Woman
The Poseidon Adventure
Quest for Fire▶
The Return of Grey Wolf
Return of the Jedi▶
The Revolt of Job▶
Robby
Robinson Crusoe
Sahara▶
Savage Hunger
Savage is Loose
Sea Gypsies
The Sea Shall Not Have Them
Seven Days in May▶
Shadow of the Wolf
She'll Be Wearing Pink
  Pajamas
Silence
Silence of the North
Skyline▶
Sniper
S.O.S. Pacific
Sourdough
SpaceCamp
Springhill
Stagecoach▶
Starbird and Sweet William
Storm and Sorrow
Survival of Spaceship Earth
Survival Quest
Survival Run
The Survivalist
Sweet Sweetback's
  Baadasssss Song▶
The Swiss Family Robinson▶
The Terror
Testament▶
Thief▶
Three Came Home▶
Trouble in Paradise
Tundra
Two Dragons Fight Against
  the Tiger
Unsettled Land
Voyage
The Voyage of the Yes
Wagon Master▶
Warriors of the Apocalypse
The White Dawn
White Fang and the Hunter

White Water Summer

Swashbucklers

see also *Action Adventure; Medieval Romps*
Abbott and Costello Meet
  Captain Kidd
Adventures of Captain Fabian
Adventures of Don Juan▶
The Adventures of Robin
  Hood▶
Against All Flags▶
Ali Baba and the Forty
  Thieves
Ali Baba and the 40 Thieves▶
Anthony Adverse
Arabian Nights
At Sword's Point
The Black Pirate▶
The Black Pirate
Blackbeard the Pirate
Blackbeard's Ghost
Bluebeard
The Bold Caballero
The Buccaneer
Captain Blood▶
Captain Horatio Hornblower▶
Captain Kidd
Captain Kronos: Vampire
  Hunter▶
Captain Ron
Cartouche▶
The Challenge
Cheech and Chong's, The
  Corsican Brothers
China Seas▶
Conqueror & the Empress
Corsair
The Corsican Brothers
The Count of Monte Cristo
The Count of Monte Cristo▶
The Count of Monte Cristo
Court Jester▶
Crimson Pirate▶
Dancing Pirate
Dr. Syn
Dr. Syn, Alias the Scarecrow
Don Q., Son of Zorro
The Elusive Pimpernel
Executioner of Venice
Fearless Tiger
The Fifth Musketeer
Fighting Marines
The Fighting Prince of
  Donegal
A Fist Full of Talons
The Flame & the Arrow▶
The Four Musketeers▶
Ghost in the Noonday Sun
Gun Cargo
Gypsy
Hawk of the Wilderness
Hell Ship Mutiny
Highlander: The Gathering
His Majesty O'Keefe
Hook
The Iron Mask
The Island
Island Trader
Ivanhoe
The King's Thief
Kojiro▶
The Lamb
The Lives of a Bengal
  Lancer▶
Long John Silver
The Man in the Iron Mask▶
Marauder
Mark of Zorro▶
The Mark of Zorro▶
The Master of Ballantrae
Master of Dragonard Hill
Monty Python's The Meaning
  of Life▶
Mooncussers
Moonfleet
Moran of the Lady Letty
Morgan the Pirate
My Favorite Year▶
My Wicked, Wicked Ways
The Naked Sword of Zorro
Nate and Hayes

Naughty Marietta
New Moon
The Ninja Pirates
Old Ironsides▶
The Pirate▶
Pirate Movie
Pirate Warrior
Pirates
The Pirates of Penzance
Pirates of the Coast
Pirates of the Seven Seas
The Princess and the Pirate
The Princess Bride▶
Prisoner of Zenda▶
Prisoner of Zenda
Quest of the Delta Knights
The Return of the Musketeers
Ring of the Musketeers
Robin Hood▶
Romola
Scaramouche▶
The Scarlet Pimpernel▶
The Sea Hawk▶
Sea Hound
The Secret of El Zorro
Shipwrecked
The Sign of Zorro
Sinbad and the Eye of the
  Tiger
Sinbad the Sailor▶
Smuggler's Cove
Son of Ali Baba
Son of Captain Blood
Son of Fury▶
The Son of Monte Cristo
Son of Zorro
South of Pago Pago
South Seas Massacre
The Spanish Main
The Story of Robin Hood &
  His Merrie Men▶
Swashbuckler
The Swiss Family Robinson▶
Sword & the Sorcerer
Sword of Sherwood Forest
The Swordsman
Tharus Son of Attila
Three Amigos
The Three Musketeers
The Three Musketeers▶
The Three Musketeers
The Three Musketeers▶
The Three Musketeers
Tiger of the Seven Seas
Treasure Island▶
Treasure Island
Treasure of the Golden
  Condor
Treasure of the Moon
  Goddess
Two Lost Worlds
Under the Red Robe
Wallaby Jim of the Islands
The Warriors
The Wicked Lady
Yellowbeard
Zorro, the Gay Blade

Swimming

see also *Deep Blue; Go Fish; Island Fare; Pacific Islands; Sea Critter Attack*
Barracuda
Bathing Beauty
Cocoon▶
Dangerous When Wet
Dawn!
Easy to Love
Gremlins▶
Jaws▶
Lifeguard
The Man from Atlantis
Million Dollar Mermaid
Neptune's Daughter
Off the Mark
Swim Team
Swimmer▶
Thrill of a Romance

Swingers

Barfly▶
Bob & Carol & Ted & Alice
A Change of Seasons
Group Marriage
Invasion of the Bee Girls▶
Looking for Mr. Goodbar
9 1/2 Weeks
The Party▶
The Swap
The Swinging Cheerleaders
Swinging Wives

Sword & Sandal

Ali Baba and the Forty
    Thieves
Ali Baba and the 40 Thieves▶
Alone Against Rome
Arabian Nights
The Avenger
Colossus and the Amazon
    Queen
Colossus of the Arena
Coriolanus, Man without a
    Country
Fabiola▶
Fire Monsters Against the Son
    of Hercules
Giants of Rome
Gladiator of Rome
Gladiators 7
Goliath Against the Giants
Goliath and the Barbarians
Goliath and the Dragon
Goliath and the Sins of
    Babylon
Gor
Hercules
Hercules Against the Moon
    Men
Hercules and the Captive
    Women
Hercules and the Princess of
    Troy
Hercules in the Haunted World
Hercules, Prisoner of Evil
Hercules Unchained
Hero of Rome
The Invincible Gladiator
The Last Days of Pompeii
Revenge of the Barbarians
Revolt of the Barbarians
Roland the Mighty
Samson
Samson Against the Sheik
Samson and His Mighty
    Challenge
Samson and the 7 Miracles of
    the World
Sins of Rome
Son of Ali Baba
Sons of Hercules in the Land
    of Darkness
Sword of Venus
Terror of the Steppes
Thor and the Amazon Women

Team Efforts

The Alamo▶
The Bad News Bears Go to
    Japan
The Bad News Bears in
    Breaking Training
Breaking Away▶
The Club▶
Coach
Codename: Foxfire
Codename: Wildgeese
Crossfire
The Cutting Edge
The Dirty Dozen▶
The Dirty Dozen: The Deadly
    Mission
The Dirty Dozen: The Fatal
    Mission
The Dirty Dozen: The Next
    Mission
Dirty Hands
The Doll Squad
D2: The Mighty Ducks
Finger on the Trigger

Force Five
Force 10 from Navarone
The Guns of Navarone▶
Hoosiers▶
Kill and Kill Again
Ladybugs
Let's Get Harry
The Losers
The Magnificent Seven▶
Memphis Belle▶
The Mighty Ducks
Miracle on Ice
Renaissance Man
Seven Magnificent Gladiators
Seven Samurai▶
Silverado▶
Three the Hard Way
Uncommon Valor
The Untouchables▶
Victory
Wild Geese
Wild Geese 2
Wind

Tearjerkers

Acorn People
An Affair to Remember
After the Promise
All Dogs Go to Heaven
All Fall Down
All Mine to Give
Another Time, Another Place
Baby Face
Back Street
Balboa
Ballad in Blue
Bang the Drum Slowly
Bang the Drum Slowly▶
Beaches
Big Bluff
Bittersweet Love
Black Eyes
Blind Spot
Blood of Jesus
Blossoms in the Dust
Bonjour Tristesse▶
Bouquet of Barbed Wire
Breaking the Rules
Brian's Song▶
The Cabin in the Cotton
Carrie▶
Carry On Cruising
Cast the First Stone
The Champ▶
The Champ
Chantilly Lace
The Cheat▶
Chinatown After Dark
Choices
Christmas Comes to Willow
    Creek
City That Never Sleeps
City Without Men
Claudia
Coquette
The Country Kid▶
The Courtney Affair
Craig's Wife▶
Crawlspace
Curly Sue
Dance Fools Dance▶
Dead Wrong
Death Be Not Proud▶
Dedee d'Anvers
Delinquent Parents
A Different Kind of Love
A Dog of Flanders
Dog Pound Shuffle▶
An Early Frost▶
Easy Virtue
The Eddy Duchin Story
Eric▶
Escape Me Never
Fine Things
Fire Down Below
Flamingo Road▶
The Forbidden City
Fortune's Fool
Found Alive
Fourth Wish
Free Willy
Fulfillment

Gangs, Inc.
The Garden of Allah▶
The Gathering
The Gathering: Part 2
Ghost▶
Girl from Chicago
The Girl Who Had Everything
Goodbye, Mr. Chips▶
Goodbye, My Lady
Great Day
The Greatest Question
Griffin and Phoenix: A Love
    Story
Harlow
Hearts of Humanity
Heaven and Earth
Hell-Ship Morgan
Her Silent Sacrifice
High Gear
A Home of Our Own
Honky Tonk▶
Hot Spell
Human Desire
Human Hearts
I Conquer the Sea
I Sent a Letter to My Love▶
Ice Castles
If Ever I See You Again
In This Our Life
Inside Daisy Clover
Intermezzo▶
Jack the Bear
Johnny Belinda▶
Johnny Belinda
Johnny Eager▶
Journey for Margaret▶
Keep Punching
The Kid with the Broken Halo
La Bete Humaine▶
La Chienne▶
Lady Caroline Lamb
The Lady Without Camelias
Le Jour Se Leve▶
Leopard in the Snow
Leper
Letter from an Unknown
    Woman▶
The Little Match Girl
The Little Princess▶
Look Who's Talking Now
Love Affair▶
Love Affair: The Eleanor &
    Lou Gehrig Story▶
Love Butcher
The Love Flower
Love has Many Faces
Love in the Present Tense
Love Songs
Love Story▶
Lovers of Their Time
Loving
Lure of the Sila
Madame X
Magnificent Obsession
Man of Evil
The Manxman
Matters of the Heart
Mildred Pierce▶
Miles to Go
Millie
Mimi
The Miniver Story
Miss Julie
Mrs. Silly
Mr. Skeffington▶
Mistress
Moment in Time
Moon Over Harlem
A Mormon Maid
Mother and Son
Murder on Lenox Avenue
The Nest
The Night Cry
Night Life in Reno
Nomads of the North
Now, Voyager▶
Old Yeller▶
Only Angels Have Wings▶
An Orphan Boy of Vienna
The Other Side of the
    Mountain

The Other Side of the
    Mountain, Part 2
Our Time
The Passing of the Third Floor
    Back
Pattes Blanches
Peg O' My Heart
Penny Serenade▶
A Place in the Sun▶
The Pride of the Yankees▶
The Promise
Question of Faith
A Question of Guilt
Quicksand
The Racket▶
Rage of Angels
The Rains Came
Random Harvest▶
Rebecca of Sunnybrook Farm
Red Kimono
Remolina de Pasiones
Rikisha-Man▶
The Road to Ruin
Romola
Scar of Shame
Secrets of a Married Man
Seizure: The Story of Kathy
    Morris
Sex
Shadowlands▶
She Goes to War
A Shining Season▶
The Shock
Shopworn Angel▶
Silent Night, Lonely Night
The Sin of Madelon Claudet▶
Since You Went Away▶
Six Weeks
Smilin' Through▶
Sommersby
Sooner or Later
Sparrows▶
Steel Magnolias▶
Stella
Stella Dallas▶
Stella Maris▶
Stolen Hours
Strangers: The Story of a
    Mother and Daughter▶
Stromboli
Suds
Summer and Smoke
A Summer Place
Sunny
Sunny Skies
Susan Lenox: Her Fall and
    Rise
Tango
Tell Me That You Love Me
Tender Comrade
Terms of Endearment▶
Test Tube Babies
That Certain Woman
They Drive by Night▶
Things in Their Season
This Boy's Life▶
Three Secrets
Thursday's Child
Tiefland
Time to Live
Tomorrow's Children
The Tong Man
Torch Song
Toute Une Nuit▶
Traffic in Souls▶
Trapped by the Mormons
Under the Roofs of Paris▶
The Underdog
The Unholy Three▶
Untamed Heart
Uptown New York
Walk on the Wild Side
Walpurgis Night▶
Waterfront
Waterloo Bridge▶
Way Down East▶
Welcome Home
West-Bound Limited
West of Zanzibar
When Wolves Cry
Where East is West
Where the Red Fern Grows

The White Cliffs of Dover▶
The White Rose▶
Wide Sargasso Sea
Winter Meeting
Without a Trace
A Woman of Affairs
The World Accuses
The World is Full of Married
    Men
The World Owes Me a Living
Written on the Wind▶
X, Y & Zee.
The Yearling▶

Technology-Rampant

*see also Computers; Killer
Appliances; Robots &
Androids*

A Nous la Liberte▶
Assassin
Attack of the Killer
    Refrigerator
Attack of the Robots
Baby Girl Scott
Back to the Future▶
Best Defense
The Bionic Woman
Black Cobra 3: The Manila
    Connection
The Black Hole
Blade Runner▶
Blades
Bloodlust
Brainscan
Chandu the Magician
Charly▶
Chopping Mall
Circuitry Man
Colossus: The Forbin
    Project▶
Computer Beach Party
Computer Wizard
Crash and Burn
The Creation of the
    Humanoids
Death of the Rat
Death Ray 2000
Defense Play
Demon Seed▶
Diamonds are Forever▶
Dr. Goldfoot and the Bikini
    Machine
Dungeonmaster
Duplicates
Electric Dreams
The Eliminators
Eve of Destruction
Fail-Safe▶
Family Viewing▶
The Final Programme
The Fly▶
The Fly 2
Future Cop
Futureworld
Geheimakte WB1
Ghost in the Machine
Hide and Seek
Improper Channels
Interface
A Joke of Destiny, Lying in
    Wait Around the Corner
    Like a Bandit
A King in New York
The Lift
Lost Legacy: A Girl Called
    Hatter Fox
Maximum Overdrive
Metropolis▶
Microwave Massacre
Modern Times▶
Mon Oncle▶
Moonraker
Munster's Revenge
Murder by Phone
Murder by Television
Mutant Hunt
Night of the Kickfighters
Nightflyers
One Deadly Owner
Out of Order

Panique▶
The Philadelphia Experiment
The Power Within
Project: Eliminator
Project: Shadowchaser
The Quiet Earth▶
Remote
RoboCop▶
RoboCop 2
RoboCop 3
Robot Holocaust
Robot Jox
Rock & Roll Cowboys
R.O.T.O.R.
Runaway
Search and Destroy
Shadowzone
Shaker Run
Shocker
Short Circuit
Short Circuit 2
Sneakers
Space: 1999
Speaking Parts▶
The Spy Who Loved Me
Stay Tuned
Steel and Lace
Strange New World
Terminal Choice
Terminal Entry
The Terminal Man
The Terminator▶
Terrorvision
Things to Come▶
Thrillkill
Tron
12:01
Twisted
2001: A Space Odyssey▶
The Ultimate Imposter
The Unborn
The Vindicator
WarGames
Warning Sign
Weird Science
Westworld▶
Wild Palms
Wired to Kill
Wrestling Women vs. the
    Aztec Ape
Zardoz

Teen Angst

see also Coming of Age;
Hell High School

Above the Rim
Across the Tracks
Adventures in Dinosaur City
Age Isn't Everything
Ah, Wilderness!▶
Airborne
Almos' a Man
American Graffiti▶
An American Summer
Amor Bandido
Andy Hardy Gets Spring Fever
Andy Hardy Meets Debutante
Andy Hardy's Double Life
Andy Hardy's Private
    Secretary
Angel
Angels with Dirty Faces▶
Baby It's You▶
The Bachelor and the Bobby-
    Soxer▶
Backstreet Dreams
Bad Boys▶
Bad Ronald▶
Battle of the Bullies
The Bay Boy
Beach Blanket Bingo▶
Beach House
Beach Party
The Beat
The Beniker Gang
Berserker
The Best Little Girl in the
    World▶
Better Off Dead
Beverly Hills 90210
Beverly Hills 90210: The
    Graduation

Beyond Innocence
The Big Bet
Big Girls Don't Cry...They Get
    Even
Big Town
Bikini Beach
Bill & Ted's Excellent
    Adventure
Blackboard Jungle▶
BMX Bandits
Body Snatchers
Book of Love
Born Innocent
Boy's Reformatory
Boyz N the Hood▶
Brainscan
The Breakfast Club▶
Breaking All the Rules
Breaking Away▶
Brotherhood of Justice
Buffy the Vampire Slayer▶
Burglar▶
Buster and Billie
Buying Time
Bye, Bye, Birdie▶
Cadillac Girls
Can You Feel Me Dancing?
Can't Buy Me Love
Career Opportunities
Carrie▶
Cave Girl
The Chalk Garden▶
The Chicken Chronicles
Children of the Corn 2: The
    Final Sacrifice
China, My Sorrow
Choices
The Choppers
Christine
Class
The Class of Miss MacMichael
Clayton County Line
Condemned to Hell
Coneheads
Corvette Summer
Cotton Candy
The Cruel Story of Youth▶
The Crush
Cry-Baby▶
A Cry in the Wild▶
A Dangerous Age
Dangerous Curves
Dangerously Close
Dario Argento's Trauma
Dark Horse
Date Bait
A Date with Judy
Daughter of Death
Dazed and Confused▶
Dead End▶
Dead Poets Society▶
Deadly Weapon
Death Wish Club
Defense Play
The Defilers
Delinquent Daughters
Delivery Boys
Desert Bloom▶
Desperate Lives
The Devil on Wheels
The Devil's Sleep
The Diary of Anne Frank▶
Diner▶
Dino
Diving In
Dogs in Space
Doin' Time on Planet Earth
Don't Tell Mom the
    Babysitter's Dead
Dream Date
Dream Machine
Dream to Believe
Drive-In
Dudes
Dutch
Dutch Girls
East of Eden▶
East of Eden
East Side Kids
The Effect of Gamma Rays on
    Man-in-the-Moon
    Marigolds▶

Encino Man
Endless Love
The Ernest Green Story
Escape Artist▶
Escape from El Diablo
E.T.: The Extra-Terrestrial▶
Evils of the Night
Eyes of the Panther
Eyes Right!
Fame▶
Fast Talking
Fast Times at Ridgemont
    High▶
Fear No Evil
Fellini's Roma
Ferris Bueller's Day Off▶
Fire with Fire
The First Time
First Turn On
The Flamingo Kid▶
Flirting▶
Fly with the Hawk
Footloose
For Keeps
Force of Impulse
Forever
Foxes
The Franchise Affair
Freeze Frame
Friends
Friends Forever▶
A Friendship in Vienna
Gas Food Lodging▶
Gate 2
Girl from Hunan▶
A Girl of the Limberlost
The Girl, the Body and the Pill
Girlfriend from Hell
Girls Just Want to Have Fun
Gleaming the Cube
The Goodbye Bird
Goodbye, Miss 4th of July
Grease▶
Grease 2
Hadley's Rebellion
Hairspray▶
Halloween▶
Hard Knocks
Hardcore
Harley
Heathers▶
The Heavenly Kid
Hide and Go Shriek
High School Caesar
High School Confidential
High School USA
Hollywood High
Hollywood High, Part 2
A Home of Our Own
Hometown U.S.A.
Homework
Hoosiers▶
Hornet's Nest
Hot Bubblegum
Hot Times
How I Got into College
How to Stuff a Wild Bikini
I Accuse My Parents
I Am the Cheese
I Never Promised You a Rose
    Garden▶
I Wanna Hold Your Hand
I Was a Teenage Werewolf
If...▶
If Looks Could Kill
The Impossible Years
The In Crowd
In the Land of the Owl Turds
Inga
The Inkwell
The Invisible Kid
Jennifer
Junior High School
Just Another Girl on the I.R.T.
Just for the Hell of It
Just One of the Girls
Kansas
Kid Dynamite
King Creole
Knights & Emeralds
La Bamba▶
La Hija del General

La Notte Brava
La Petite Sirene
Lantern Hill
Last Cry for Help
Last Summer
Lauderdale
The Lawrenceville Stories
Les Enfants Terrible▶
Les Mistons▶
Liar's Edge
License to Drive
Life Begins for Andy Hardy▶
Lisa
Little Darlings
A Little Romance▶
Little Sweetheart
The Little Thief▶
The Little Valentino
The Loneliest Runner
The Loneliness of the Long
    Distance Runner▶
Loners
Looking for Miracles
Loose Screws
Losin' It
Lost Angels
The Lost Boys
Love Laughs at Andy Hardy
Love Under Pressure
Lovelines
Lucas▶
Mad About You
Mad Youth
Made in USA
Making the Grade
Malibu Beach
Man from Texas
The Man in the Moon▶
The Manhattan Project
Married Too Young
Meatballs
Meatballs 2
Meatballs 3
Meatballs 4
The Member of the Wedding▶
The Member of the Wedding
Mermaids▶
Metropolitan▶
Mickey Rooney in the Classic
    Mickey McGuire Silly
    Comedies
Min & Bill
The Miracle
Mirror, Mirror
Mischief
Misfits of Science
Miss A & Miss M
Miss Annie Rooney
Mon Oncle Antoine▶
Monika
Monkey Business▶
Morgan Stewart's Coming
    Home
Motorcycle Gang
Mouchette▶
Murder in New Hampshire:
    The Pamela Smart Story
My American Cousin▶
My Best Friend Is a Vampire
My Boyfriend's Back
My Boys are Good Boys
My Father, My Rival
My Father the Hero
My Girl 2▶
My Own Private Idaho▶
My Science Project
Mystery Date
Mystic Pizza▶
Naked Youth
Nice Girls Don't Explode
Nickel Mountain
The Night Before
Night Breed
Night Friend
A Night in the Life of Jimmy
    Reardon
Night Life
Night of Evil
A Nightmare on Elm Street 2:
    Freddy's Revenge

A Nightmare on Elm Street 3:
    Dream Warriors
A Nightmare on Elm Street 4:
    Dream Master
A Nightmare on Elm Street 5:
    Dream Child
1969▶
Ninja Supremo
No Big Deal
Nobody's Perfect
Not My Kid
Nowhere to Run
O.C. and Stiggs
Odd Birds
On the Edge: The Survival of
    Dana
One Crazy Summer
One Dark Night
Only the Strong
Ordinary Magic
Our Time
Outside Chance of Maximillian
    Glick
The Outsiders
Over the Edge▶
Over the Summer
Pajama Party
Palm Springs Weekend
Paradise Motel
Parenthood▶
Party! Party!
Pathfinder▶
Peggy Sue Got Married
The People Next Door
Peppermint Soda▶
Pigeon Feathers
Pin
Pippin▶
Platypus Cove
Playing for Keeps
Playing with Fire
Poison Ivy
Pom Pom Girls
Porky's
Porky's 2: The Next Day
The Positively True
    Adventures of the Alleged
    Texas Cheerleader-
    Murdering Mom▶
Pot, Parents, and Police
Prayer of the Rollerboys
Pretty in Pink
Pretty Smart
The Prime of Miss Jean
    Brodie▶
The Prime Time
Primo Baby
Princes in Exile
Puberty Blues
Pump Up the Volume
Quadrophenia▶
Quarterback Princess
Racing with the Moon▶
Rad
Rambling Rose▶
Raw Power
Rebel Without a Cause▶
Red Kiss▶
Return to Horror High
Return to the Blue Lagoon
Revenge of the Living
    Zombies
River's Edge▶
Roadhouse 66
Rock 'n' Roll High School
    Forever
Rock, Rock, Rock
Rockula
Rodrigo D.: No Future
Romeo and Juliet
Romeo and Juliet▶
Rooftops
Roustabout
Running Mates▶
Say Anything▶
Scarred
Scream for Help
Screen Test
Screwballs
Secret Admirer
Secrets of Sweet Sixteen

Teen

Seizure: The Story of Kathy
    Morris
Senior Trip
Seven Minutes in Heaven
The Seventh Coin
S.F.W.
Shag: The Movie
Shake, Rattle and Rock
Sharma & Beyond
She's Out of Control
Shooting
Shout
Silence of the Heart▶
The Silent One
Sing
Sixteen Candles▶
Skateboard
Smokey Bites the Dust
Smugglers' Cove▶
Snowballing
Solarbabies
Some Kind of Wonderful
Something Special
Sooner or Later
The Spell
Spetters
Spirit Rider▶
Splendor in the Grass▶
Spring Fever
Stand and Deliver▶
Starchaser: The Legend of
    Orin
Sticky Fingers
Still Not Quite Human
Stones of Death
Straight Out of Brooklyn
Straight Up
Strange Illusion
Streets
The Stripper
Student Bodies
Suburbia
Summer Camp Nightmare
Summer Holiday
Summer of '42▶
The Summer of My German
    Soldier▶
Summer School
Sunnyside
Swap Meet
Sweet 16
Swim Team
Swing Kids
A Swingin' Summer
Tainted Blood
Tearaway
Teen Mothers
Teen Wolf
Teenage
Teenage Bad Girl
Teenage Bonnie & Klepto
    Clyde
Teenage Caveman
Teenage Crime Wave
Teenage Mother
Teenage Mutant Ninja Turtles
    2: The Secret of the Ooze
Teenage Strangler
Teenage Wolfpack
Teenager
Teenagers from Outer Space
The Tender Age
Terminal Bliss
Tex
That Night
That Was Then...This Is Now
They Made Me a Criminal
36 Fillete▶
This Boy's Life▶
This Special Friendship
Thrashin'
3:15—The Moment of Truth
Three O'Clock High
Time Stands Still▶
Times Square
To Play or To Die
Tom Brown's School Days▶
Toughlove
Toy Soldiers
Treasure Island
Troop Beverly Hills
The Trouble with Angels

Trust
Twirl
Twist & Shout▶
Twisted
Uncle Buck▶
Under the Boardwalk
Unfinished Business
Up Against the Wall
Uptown Angel
Urusei Yatsura Movie 1: Only
    You
Urusei Yatsura Movie 2:
    Beautiful Dreamer
Urusei Yatsura Movie 3:
    Remember My Love
Valley Girl
The Vals
The Van
Village of the Giants
Virgin High
Vision Quest
The Voyage of the Yes
Walking Back
Wanderers▶
Weird Science
Welcome Home, Roxy
    Carmichael
Welcome to 18
Where Angels Go, Trouble
    Follows
Where the Boys Are '84
Where the Day Takes You
The White Butterfly Killer
The Wild Life
Wild Ones on Wheels
Wild Pony
Wish You Were Here▶
The Wooden Gun
The Wraith
The Year My Voice Broke▶
The Young Graduates
Young Guns
Young Love, First Love
Youngblood
Youth Aflame
Youth on Parole
You've Ruined Me, Eddie
Zebrahead▶
Zero Boys
Zombie Nightmare
The Zoo Gang

Television

see *Mass Media; TV
Movies; TV Pilot Movies;
TV Series*

Tennis

Jocks
Nobody's Perfect
Players
Racquet
Spring Fever

Terror in Tall
Buildings

see also *Mystery &
Suspense*

Blackout
Die Hard▶
Hard to Die
Project: Shadowchaser
Speed▶
Terror on the 40th Floor
Tower of Terror
The Towering Inferno

Terrorism

see also *Crime &
Criminals; Foreign
Intrigue; Spies &
Espionage*

Act of Passion: The Lost
    Honor of Kathryn Beck
Act of Piracy
Airheads
The Amateur
Angel of Fury
The Applegates

The Assassination Run
Assignment Skybolt
Barcelona▶
Belfast Assassin
Black Cobra 2
Black Cobra 3: The Manila
    Connection
Black Sunday
Black Terrorist
Blink of an Eye
Blood on the Badge
Blown Away▶
Captain America 2: Death Too
    Soon
Captive
Captive Rage
The Cassandra Crossing
Children of Rage
C.I.A. 2: Target Alexa
Codename: Vengeance
Commando▶
Contra Company
Could It Happen Here?
Cover-Up
Crash and Burn
Cry of the Innocent▶
The Crying Game▶
Dark Rider
Deadline
Deadly Commando
Death Before Dishonor
The Death Merchant
Death of the Incredible Hulk
Death Ray
Delta Force
Delta Force 3: The Killing
    Game
Delta Force Commando
Delta Force Commando 2
Dick Barton, Special Agent
Die Hard▶
Die Hard 2: Die Harder▶
Dirty Games
Dr. Otto & the Riddle of the
    Gloom Beam
Dog Day Afternoon▶
The Enforcer
The Evil That Men Do
Exposed
Fast Kill
A Father's Revenge
ffolkes
The Final Option
Flashpoint Africa
Fortress of Amerikka
48 Hours to Live
French Quarter Undercover
Full Fathom Five
Galyon
Germicide
The Glass Jungle
Glory Boys
Held Hostage
Hell Squad
Hidden Agenda
Hostage
In the Name of the Father▶
Invasion Force
Invasion U.S.A.
Iran: Days of Crisis
Jericho Fever
Journeys from Berlin/1971
Judgment in Berlin
Juggernaut▶
July Group
Jungle Assault
Kamikaze '89▶
Katherine
The Kidnapping of the
    President
Kings and Desperate Men
L'Anne Sainte
The Little Drummer Girl▶
Live Wire
The Lost Command
The Mad Bomber
Merchants of War
Molly Maguires
Murder on Flight 502
Naked Gun 33 1/3: The Final
    Insult
Navy SEALS

Night of the Assassin
Nightstick
Ninja Connection
Ninja the Battalion
No Dead Heroes
Odd Man Out▶
Omega Syndrome
Operation Thunderbolt
Panic in the Streets▶
Panic on the 5:22
The Passenger▶
Passenger 57
Patriot
Patriot Games▶
Patty Hearst
Programmed to Kill
Project: Alien
Pursuit▶
Python Wolf
Raid on Entebbe▶
The Railway Station Man▶
Rebel
Rescue Force
Rollercoaster
Rosebud
Running Delilah
The Rutanga Tapes
Secret Agent 00
Secret Agent Super Dragon
Skeleton Coast
Skull: A Night of Terror
Special Bulletin▶
Stalking Danger
Summer Night
The Taking of Flight 847: The
    Uli Derickson Story▶
The Taking of Pelham One
    Two Three▶
Terminal Entry
Terror in Beverly Hills
Terror in Paradise
Terror Squad
The Terrorists
Terrorists
Thunder Run
Thunderball
A Town Called Hell
Toy Soldiers
The Tragedy of a Ridiculous
    Man
Tragedy of Flight 103: The
    Inside Story▶
Trained to Kill, U.S.A.
Treasure of the Lost Desert
Trident Force
Troma's War
True Lies▶
Turk 182!
21 Hours at Munich▶
Undeclared War
The Vernonia Incident
Viper
Voyage of Terror: The Achille
    Lauro Affair
Wanted Dead or Alive
Women on the Verge of a
    Nervous Breakdown▶
Wrong is Right
Year of the Gun
You Only Live Twice

This is Your Life

see also *Musician Biopics;
Nashville Narratives*
Abe Lincoln in Illinois▶
Above and Beyond▶
Abraham Lincoln
Actor: The Paul Muni Story
The Adventures of Mark
    Twain▶
Agatha
Al Capone▶
Alex in Wonderland
Alexander the Great
All That Jazz▶
Amadeus▶
Amarcord▶
The Amazing Howard Hughes
American Graffiti▶
Amin: The Rise and Fall
An Angel at My Table▶
Anita, Dances of Vice

The Ann Jillian Story
Annie Oakley▶
Annie Oakley
Antony and Cleopatra
Au Revoir Les Enfants▶
The Autobiography of Miss
    Jane Pittman▶
Babe!▶
The Babe
Babe Ruth Story
Backbeat▶
Barefoot in Athens
Barnum
The Barretts of Wimpole
    Street▶
Becoming Colette
Beethoven
Beethoven Lives Upstairs
The Benny Goodman Story
The Best Intentions▶
Bethune
Big Mo
The Big Red One▶
Bird▶
Bix
Blades of Courage
Blaze
Blind Ambition
Blossoms in the Dust
Bluebeard▶
Bogie
Bonnie & Clyde▶
Bonnie Prince Charlie
Born Again
Born on the Fourth of July▶
Bound for Glory▶
Boy in Blue
Bruce Lee: Curse of the
    Dragon▶
Bruce Lee: The Legend
The Buccaneer
Bud and Lou
The Buddy Holly Story▶
Bugsy▶
Buster Keaton Rides Again/
    The Railrodder
Cabeza de Vaca▶
Caddie
Calamity Jane
Camille Claudel▶
Can You Hear the Laughter?
    The Story of Freddie Prinze
Caravaggio▶
Casanova
Casimir the Great
Cast a Giant Shadow
Catherine the Great
Catholic Hour
Celeste▶
Chain Lightning
Champions
Chanel Solitaire
Chapayev▶
Chaplin▶
Chariots of Fire▶
Christopher Columbus
Christopher Columbus: The
    Discovery
Churchill and the Generals
Citizen Cohn
Coal Miner's Daughter▶
The Color of Pomegranates▶
Coming Through
Conrack▶
The Country Diary of an
    Edwardian Lady
The Courageous Mr. Penn
The Court Martial of Jackie
    Robinson▶
Crime Lords
Cromwell
Cross Creek
Damien: The Leper Priest
Dance with a Stranger▶
A Dangerous Man: Lawrence
    after Arabia▶
Daniel Boone
Dante's Inferno: Life of Dante
    Gabriel Rossetti
Dawn!▶
The Death of Adolf Hitler
Deep in My Heart

Dempsey
The Desert Fox▶
Diana: Her True Story
The Diary of Anne Frank▶
Dick Turpin
Dillinger▶
Dillinger
The Disappearance of Aimee▶
Disraeli▶
The Doctor
Dr. Bethune▶
Don't Look Back: The Story of
    Leroy "Satchel" Paige
The Doors
Double Exposure: The Story
    of Margaret Bourke-White
Dragon: The Bruce Lee
    Story▶
Dreamchild▶
Ed Wood
The Eddy Duchin Story
Edie in Ciao! Manhattan
Edison the Man
Edith & Marcel
The Education of Sonny
    Carson
Edvard Munch
Edward and Mrs. Simpson
8 Seconds
Eleanor & Franklin▶
Eleanor: First Lady of the
    World
The Elegant Criminal
The Elephant Man▶
Elizabeth, the Queen
Elvis and Me
Elvis in the Movies
Elvis Memories
Elvis Presley's Graceland
Elvis: Rare Moments with the
    King
Elvis Stories
Elvis: The Echo Will Never Die
Elvis: The Movie
Enemy of Women
Enter Laughing
Ernie Kovacs: Between the
    Laughter
The Eternal Waltz
Eubie!
Europa, Europa▶
Evel Knievel
Exit the Dragon, Enter the
    Tiger
F. Scott Fitzgerald in
    Hollywood
The Fabulous Dorseys
Fallen Champ: The Untold
    Story of Mike Tyson▶
Fanny and Alexander▶
Fast Company
Final Shot: The Hank Gathers
    Story
The Five of Me
The Five Pennies
For Us, the Living
Forbidden Passion: The Oscar
    Wilde Movie
Ford: The Man & the Machine
Forever James Dean
The Fountainhead▶
1492: Conquest of Paradise
Francesco
Frida
Funny Girl▶
Funny Lady
The Gallant Hours▶
Gandhi▶
The Gathering Storm
The Gene Krupa Story
Gentleman Jim▶
George Washington
George Washington: The
    Forging of a Nation
Geronimo▶
Give 'Em Hell, Harry!
The Glenn Miller Story▶
The Goddess▶
Going for the Gold: The Bill
    Johnson Story
Goodbye, Norma Jean
Goodnight, Sweet Marilyn

Gore Vidal's Lincoln
The Gorgeous Hussy
Gorillas in the Mist▶
Grambling's White Tiger
Greased Lightning
Great Balls of Fire
The Great Caruso
The Great Impostor
Great Missouri Raid
The Great Moment
The Great Wallendas
The Great Waltz▶
The Great White Hope
The Great Ziegfeld▶
The Greatest
The Greatest Story Ever Told
The Greek Tycoon
Gypsy▶
Gypsy
Hammett
The Happy Hooker Goes
    Hollywood
Harlow
Harmon of Michigan
Harmony Lane
Haunted Summer
Heading Home
Heart Beat
Heart Like a Wheel
Heart of a Champion: The Ray
    Mancini Story
Heaven and Earth
Hedda Hopper's Hollywood
Henry & June▶
Hitler
Hitler: The Last Ten Days
Hoffa
Holy Terror
Home Sweet Home
The Hoodlum Priest▶
Hoodoo Ann
Houdini
Hugh Hefner: Once Upon a
    Time
Hughes & Harlow: Angels in
    Hell
The Hunter
I Am a Fugitive from a Chain
    Gang▶
I Dream of Jeannie
I Shot Billy the Kid
Ike
I'll Cry Tomorrow▶
I'll See You in My Dreams
Imperial Venus
In Love and War
The Incredible Sarah
The Inn of the Sixth
    Happiness▶
Inside the Third Reich
Interrupted Melody▶
Invincible Mr. Disraeli
Iris
The Iron Duke
Isadora▶
It's Good to Be Alive
J. Edgar Hoover
Jack Frost
Jack London
The Jackie Robinson Story▶
The Jacksons: An American
    Dream
Jacqueline Bouvier Kennedy
James Dean
James Dean Story
James Dean: The First
    American Teenager
James Joyce: A Portrait of the
    Artist as a Young Man
James Joyce's Women▶
Janis: A Film
The Jayne Mansfield Story
Jesse James Under the Black
    Flag
The Jesse Owens Story
Jesus
Jesus Christ, Superstar▶
JFK: Reckless Youth
Jim Thorpe: All American
Joan of Arc
The Joe Louis Story
John & Yoko: A Love Story

John F. Kennedy
John Paul Jones
Johnny We Hardly Knew Ye
Jolson Sings Again
The Jolson Story▶
Joni
The Josephine Baker Story▶
Juarez
Judith of Bethulia▶
Kennedy
King▶
The King of Kings▶
The King of the Roaring '20s:
    The Story of Arnold
    Rothstein
Knute Rockne: All American▶
Korczak▶
La Bamba
La Signora di Tutti▶
Lady Jane▶
Lady Sings the Blues
Lamp at Midnight
Last Days of Frank & Jesse
    James
The Last Days of Patton
The Last Emperor▶
Last Four Days
The Last of Mrs. Lincoln
Lawrence of Arabia▶
LBJ: The Early Years▶
The Learning Tree
The Left-Handed Gun▶
Legend of Valentino
The Legend of Valentino
Lenny▶
Lepke
Let's Get Lost
The Life and Assassination of
    the Kingfish
The Life and Loves of Mozart
Life & Times of Captain Lou
    Albano
The Life of Emile Zola▶
Life of Verdi
The Light in the Jungle
Lightning Over Water
Lillie▶
Lisztomania
The Loneliest Runner
The Long Gray Line▶
Long Journey Back
Look for the Silver Lining
Love Affair: The Eleanor &
    Lou Gehrig Story▶
Love Me or Leave Me▶
The Loves of Edgar Allen Poe
Loyola, the Soldier Saint
Lucky Luciano
Lucy and Desi: Before the
    Laughter
Lust for Life▶
MacArthur
Madame Curie▶
Madman
Mae West
Mafia Princess
Magnificent Adventurer
The Magnificent Yankee▶
Mahler▶
Malcolm X▶
A Man Called Peter▶
Man of a Thousand Faces▶
Mandela▶
Marciano
Marco
Marie Antoinette
Marilyn
Marilyn: The Untold Story▶
Marjoe
Marlon Brando
Martin Luther
Mary of Scotland▶
Mary White
A Matter of Life and Death
McVicar
Melody Master
The Miracle Worker▶
Mishima: A Life in Four
    Chapters▶
Mo' Better Blues
Modigliani
Mommie Dearest

Monsieur Vincent▶
Moulin Rouge▶
Mozart: A Childhood
    Chronicle▶
The Mozart Story
Murderers Among Us: The
    Simon Wiesenthal Story▶
Murrow
The Music Lovers
Mussolini & I
My Apprenticeship▶
My Childhood▶
My Father's Glory▶
My Left Foot▶
My Universities▶
My Wicked, Wicked Ways
Nadia
The Naked Civil Servant▶
The Naked Maja
Nancy Astor
Napoleon▶
Napoleon
Ned Kelly
Nicholas and Alexandra
Night and Day
Nijinsky
Nurse Edith Cavell▶
Onassis
One in a Million: The Ron
    LaFlore Story
One Man's Way
The Outlaw
Padre Padrone▶
Pancho Barnes
Pancho Villa
Papa's Delicate Condition▶
Patton▶
Patty Hearst
Paul Robeson
Perfumed Nightmare▶
The Perils of Pauline
Personal Services
Peter the Great▶
Piaf
Pistol: The Birth of a Legend
Poor Little Rich Girl: The
    Barbara Hutton Story
Pope John Paul II
Portrait of a Rebel: Margaret
    Sanger
Prick Up Your Ears▶
Pride of St. Louis
The Pride of the Yankees▶
Priest of Love
Prince Jack
PT 109
The Queen of Mean
Queenie
Raging Bull▶
Rainbow
Rasputin▶
The Raven
A Real American Hero
The Real Buddy Holly Story
The Real Patsy Cline
Reilly: Ace of Spies▶
Rembrandt▶
Rembrandt—1669
Return to Earth
Rhapsody in Blue▶
Rhodes
Richard Petty Story
Riel
Ring of Bright Water▶
The Rise and Fall of Legs
    Diamond
The Rise of Louis XIV▶
Rita Hayworth: The Love
    Goddess
Road to 1984
Robert Kennedy and His
    Times
Rodeo Girl
Romero
Rosa Luxemburg
Rosie: The Rosemary Clooney
    Story
Ruby
Rush▶
Sadat
Sakharov▶

Samaritan: The Mitch Snyder
    Story▶
Savage Messiah▶
Schindler's List▶
Sebastiane▶
The Secret Diary of Sigmund
    Freud
Secret Honor▶
A Sense of Freedom▶
The Seven Little Foys▶
Shadow on the Sun
Shadowlands▶
The Sicilian
Sid & Nancy
Silent Victory: The Kitty O'Neil
    Story▶
Simon Bolivar
Sinatra
Sister Kenny▶
Six Wives of Henry VIII▶
Soldier in Love
Somebody Up There Likes
    Me▶
Song of Norway
A Song to Remember▶
Song Without End
Sophia Loren: Her Own Story
The Sound and the Silence
The Spectre of Edgar Allen
    Poe
Spirit of St. Louis▶
Spitfire▶
Spring Symphony
Spymaker: The Secret Life of
    Ian Fleming
Squizzy Taylor
Stalin
Star!
Stars and Stripes Forever▶
Stevie
Story of Adele H.▶
The Story of Louis Pasteur▶
The Story of Vernon and Irene
    Castle▶
The Stratton Story▶
Striker's Mountain
Sunrise at Campobello▶
Sweet Dreams
Sweet Love, Bitter
Sweetheart!
Sylvia
Taxi zum Klo▶
Tchaikovsky
Teamster Boss: The Jackie
    Presser Story▶
The Ten Commandments▶
The Testament of Orpheus▶
That Hamilton Woman▶
Therese▶
32 Short Films About Glenn
    Gould▶
This Boy's Life▶
This is Elvis
Three Came Home▶
Three Little Words
Till the Clouds Roll By
Till the Clouds Roll By/A Star
    Is Born▶
A Time for Miracles
To Hell and Back
To Kill a Priest
To Race the Wind
Tom Edison: The Boy Who Lit
    Up the World
Tom Horn
Valentino
Van Gogh▶
Veronika Voss▶
Victoria Regina
Vincent & Theo▶
Vincent: The Life and Death of
    Vincent van Gogh
The Virgin Queen▶
The Virginia Hill Story
Viva Villa!▶
Viva Zapata!▶
A Voyage 'Round My Father▶
Wagner: The Complete Epic
Wagner: The Movie
Wait Until Spring, Bandini
Waiting for the Moon
Waltz King

Weeds▶
What's Love Got to Do With It?
White Hunter, Black Heart▶
Who's That Knocking at My Door?▶
Wild Hearts Can't Be Broken▶
Wild, Wild World of Jayne Mansfield
Will: G. Gordon Liddy
Wilma
Wilson▶
Winds of Kitty Hawk
Wings of Eagles
A Winner Never Quits
The Winning Team
Wired
Without Warning: The James Brady Story▶
The Wolf at the Door
A Woman Called Golda▶
A Woman Called Moses
The Woman He Loved
A Woman Named Jackie
The Wonderful World of the Brothers Grimm
Words and Music
Wyatt Earp▶
Yankee Doodle Dandy▶
Young Bill Hickok
Young Buffalo Bill
Young Caruso
Young Charlie Chaplin
Young Mr. Lincoln▶
Young Tom Edison
Young Winston▶
Zora Is My Name!

3-D Flicks

Amityville 3: The Demon
Andy Warhol's Frankenstein
Cat Women of the Moon
Creature from the Black Lagoon▶
The Creature Walks Among Us
Devil's Canyon
Dogs of Hell
Dynasty
Flesh and Blood Show
The French Line
Friday the 13th, Part 3
Gun Fury
House of Wax▶
It Came From Outer Space▶
Jaws 3
Kiss Me Kate▶
The Man Who Wasn't There
The Mask
Miss Sadie Thompson▶
Paradisio
Parasite
Revenge of the Creature
Robot Monster
Spacehunter: Adventures in the Forbidden Zone
Starchaser: The Legend of Orin
The Stranger Wore a Gun

Time Travel

see also Rescue Missions Involving Time Travel
Adventures in Dinosaur City
Amazing Mr. Blunden
A.P.E.X.
Army of Darkness▶
The Arrival
Back to the Future▶
Back to the Future, Part 2
Back to the Future, Part 3▶
Beastmaster 2: Through the Portal of Time
Being Human
Beyond the Time Barrier
Biggles
Bill & Ted's Bogus Journey
Bill & Ted's Excellent Adventure
The Blue Yonder
Brother Future

Buck Rogers in the 25th Century
Doctor Mordrid: Master of the Unknown
Doctor Who: An Unearthly Child
Doctor Who and the Daleks
Doctor Who: Cybermen—The Early Years
Doctor Who: Daleks Invasion of Earth 2150 A.D.
Doctor Who: Day of the Daleks
Doctor Who: Death to the Daleks
Doctor Who: Earthshock
Doctor Who: Mawdryn Undead
Doctor Who: Pyramids of Mars
Doctor Who: Revenge of the Cybermen
Doctor Who: Robots of Death
Doctor Who: Shada
Doctor Who: Spearhead from Space
Doctor Who: Terror of the Zygons
Doctor Who: The Ark in Space
Doctor Who: The Brain of Morbius
Doctor Who: The Caves of Androzani
Doctor Who: The Curse of Fenric
Doctor Who: The Deadly Assassin
Doctor Who: The Five Doctors
Doctor Who: The Hartnell Years
Doctor Who: The Keeper of Traken
Doctor Who: The Masque of Mandragora
Doctor Who: The Mind Robber
Doctor Who: The Pertwee Years
Doctor Who: The Seeds of Death
Doctor Who: The Sontaran Experiment/The Genesis of the Daleks
Doctor Who: The Talons of Weng-Chiang
Doctor Who: The Three Doctors
Doctor Who: The Time Warrior
Doctor Who: The Tom Baker Years
Doctor Who: The Troughton Years
Doctor Who: The Twin Dilemma
Doctor Who: The War Games
Doctor Who: Tomb of the Cyberman
The Eliminators
Escape from the Planet of the Apes▶
Escapes
The Final Countdown▶
Frankenstein Unbound▶
Freejack
Future Zone
Grand Tour: Disaster in Time
Groundhog Day▶
Hercules in New York
Highlander 2: The Quickening
Idaho Transfer
The Jetsons Meet the Flintstones
Lords of Magick
Mannequin 2: On the Move
Millennium
The Navigator▶
Next One
Night of Dark Shadows
Peggy Sue Got Married
The Philadelphia Experiment
Philadelphia Experiment 2

Roman Scandals
Running Against Time
Spirit of '76
The Swordsman
Teenage Mutant Ninja Turtles 3
Terminator 2: Judgment Day▶
Test Tube Teens from the Year 2000
The Three Stooges Meet Hercules
Time After Time▶
Time Bandits
The Time Guardian
The Time Machine▶
Time Machine
Time Runner
Time Trackers
Timecop
Timestalkers
Trancers
Trancers 2: The Return of Jack Deth
Trancers 3: Deth Lives
Trancers 4: Jack of Swords
12:01
Unidentified Flying Oddball
Warlock
Waxwork 2: Lost in Time
A Witch Without a Broom

Toilets

see Shower & Bath Scenes

Torrid Love Scenes

see also Sex & Sexuality; Sexploitation
The Adventurers
Against All Odds
Alien Prey
Angel Heart
Atlantic City▶
Basic Instinct
The Berlin Affair
Betty Blue▶
The Big Easy▶
Bitter Moon
Black Ice
Blue Velvet▶
Body Double▶
Body Heat▶
Body of Evidence
Bram Stoker's Dracula
Breathless
Bull Durham▶
Cat Chaser
Cat on a Hot Tin Roof▶
Close My Eyes
The Cook, the Thief, His Wife & Her Lover▶
Crimes of Passion▶
Dark Obsession
Deadly Desire
The Dolphin
Dona Flor and Her Two Husbands▶
Don't Look Now▶
The Executioner's Song
The Fabulous Baker Boys▶
Fatal Attraction▶
Five Easy Pieces▶
From Here to Eternity▶
Green Fire
The Harvest
Heat of Desire
Henry & June▶
The Hunting
In the Realm of the Senses▶
Kiss Me a Killer
Lady Godiva Rides
Last Tango in Paris▶
Law of Desire▶
The Lawnmower Man
The Lover
The Lovers▶
Mad Dog and Glory▶
The Mambo Kings▶
Men in Love
Moon in the Gutter

Moonstruck▶
Night Eyes 2
Night Eyes 3
9 1/2 Weeks
1900▶
An Officer and a Gentleman▶
The Pamela Principle
The Postman Always Rings Twice
Prizzi's Honor▶
Pyrates
Rage of Angels
Revenge
Risky Business▶
Sea of Love▶
Secrets
Sexual Response
Siesta
Sliver
Something Wild
The Story of O
Swept Away...▶
Tattoo
Tequila Sunrise
Threesome
The Unbearable Lightness of Being▶
White Palace
Wild at Heart▶
Wild Orchid
Wild Orchid 2: Two Shades of Blue
The Woman Next Door▶
Women & Men: In Love There Are No Rules
Women in Love▶
Year of the Gun
Zandalee

Toys

see also Killer Toys
Babes in Toyland
Child's Play 2
Dance of Death
Demonic Toys
Devil Doll▶
Dolls
Dolly Dearest
Not Quite Human
Silent Night, Deadly Night 5: The Toymaker
The Toy
Toys
Wired to Kill

Tragedy

see also Drama; Tearjerkers
Angel with the Trumpet
Anna Karenina▶
Baba▶
Bitter Sweet
Camille▶
Celebrity
Charly▶
The Crucified Lovers▶
Damage▶
Deadman's Curve
Deep End▶
A Different Kind of Love
The Discovery Program
Dying Young
East of Eden▶
East of Eden
Effi Briest▶
El Amor Brujo▶
El Bruto
End of the Road
Enemies, a Love Story▶
Ernie Kovacs: Between the Laughter
Ethan Frome
Everybody's All American
The Fighting Sullivans▶
Flowers of Reverie
Franz
The French Lieutenant's Woman▶
Gate of Hell▶
Girl in Black
Golden Boy▶

Hamlet▶
Hamlet
Harmony Lane
Henry IV
House of Cards
Howard's End▶
I, Claudius, Vol. 6: Fool's Luck/A God in Colchester
Il Grido
In Memoriam
Jude the Obscure
Jules and Jim▶
Julius Caesar▶
Julius Caesar
King Lear▶
King Lear
Law of Desire▶
Love is a Many-Splendored Thing
Love Story▶
Lovespell
Macbeth▶
Macbeth
Madame Bovary▶
Maria Candelaria
Mary of Scotland▶
Medea
The Merchant of Venice▶
The Mummy▶
The Nest
Oedipus Rex
Oedipus Rex▶
Othello
Othello▶
Our Time
Pennies From Heaven▶
Phaedra
Piece of Cake
A Place in the Sun▶
Princess Yang Kwei Fei▶
Ran▶
Romeo and Juliet▶
Romeo and Juliet
Romeo and Juliet▶
Shadowlands▶
Shadows of Forgotten Ancestors▶
Shattered▶
The Shooting Party
Silent Tongue
Stella
Sure Fire
Tess▶
Three Comrades▶
Throne of Blood▶
Tragedy of Flight 103: The Inside Story▶
Trois Couleurs: Bleu▶
Trojan Women
Turkish Delights
Variety▶
A Very Private Affair
The Virgin Spring▶
Voyager▶
Where Angels Fear to Tread▶
The White Cliffs of Dover▶
The White Sister▶
The Woman Next Door▶
The World According to Garp▶

Trains

see also Subways
Across the Bridge
Alberto Express
Avalanche Express
Berlin Express▶
Blood and Steel
Boxcar Bertha
The Brain
Breakheart Pass
Cafe Express
Cajon Pass
The Cassandra Crossing
Chattanooga Choo Choo
Closely Watched Trains▶
Dakota
Danger Ahead!
Danger Lights
Death Train
The Denver & Rio Grande
Detonator

The Dirty Dozen: The Fatal Mission
End of the Line
Express to Terror
Finders Keepers
Flame Over India▶
The Flying Scotsman
From Russia with Love▶
The Fugitive
The General▶
The Ghost Train
The Glory Trail
Go Kill and Come Back
Great K & A Train Robbery
The Great Locomotive Chase
The Great Train Robbery▶
The Grey Fox▶
Grit of the Girl Telegrapher/In the Switch Tower
The Harvey Girls▶
Helltrain
Horror Express
Hot Lead & Cold Feet
The Illusion Travels by Streetcar▶
Indiscretion of an American Wife
Inner Sanctum
Interrupted Journey
Jesse James at Bay
La Bete Humaine▶
The Lady Eve▶
The Lady Vanishes▶
The Lady Vanishes
Malcolm
Man Who Loved Cat Dancing
Man Without a Star▶
Midnight Limited
Murder on the Midnight Express
Murder on the Orient Express▶
My Twentieth Century▶
Mystery Mountain
Narrow Margin
Night Train to Munich▶
Night Train to Terror
No. 17▶
The Odyssey of the Pacific
Oh, Mr. Porter
Once Upon a Time in the West▶
Panic on the 5:22
Paris Express
Phantom Express
Plunder Road
Prison Train
Railroaded
Railrodder▶
Red Signals
The Return of Casey Jones
The Road to Yesterday
Robbery
Romance on the Orient Express
Runaway Train▶
Running Scared
The Saint's Vacation/The Narrow Margin
Shanghai Express▶
The Silver Streak
The Silver Streak▶
The Sleeping Car
Sleeping Car to Trieste
Some Like It Hot▶
Strangers on a Train▶
Subway
Terror Train
Three for Bedroom C
3:10 to Yuma▶
Throw Momma from the Train▶
Thunder Over Texas
Torture Train
Tough Guys
Tracks
The Train▶
The Train Killer
Train Robbers
Train to Tombstone
Two Weeks to Live
Von Ryan's Express▶

Warm Nights on a Slow-Moving Train
Wild Engine/Mistaken Orders
Without Reservations
Zentropa

Transportation
see also Airborne; Buses; Fast Cars; Motor Vehicle Dept.; Subways; Trains

Transvestites & Transsexuals
see Gender Bending

Trapped with a Killer!
Adrift
Blind Witness
Blink
Blood at Sundown
Blood Bride
Dead Calm▶
Deadbolt
Extremities
Eye of the Needle
Eyes of the Beholder
Fatal Attraction▶
Hider in the House
Kalifornia
Lifepod
Manhunter▶
Misery▶
Narrow Margin
Pacific Heights▶
The Penthouse
The Shining
The Silence of the Lambs▶
Slaughter of the Innocents
The Terror
Voyage
Wait Until Dark▶
What's the Matter with Helen?
When a Stranger Calls
When a Stranger Calls Back

Treasure Hunt
Abbott & Costello Meet the Mummy
Adventure of the Action Hunters
The Adventurers
All the Brothers Were Valiant
The Bloody Tattoo
Blue Jeans and Dynamite
Cabo Blanco
Call of the Wild
City Slickers 2: The Legend of Curly's Gold
Comin' Round the Mountain
Curse of the Crystal Eye
Enemy Gold
Ernest Rides Again
Finger on the Trigger
Girls in Prison
Greedy
Green Fire
Hear No Evil
Hunters of the Golden Cobra
Inside Out
The Jewel of the Nile
Kelly's Heroes
Klondike Fever
Les Aventuriers
Lust in the Dust▶
The Mermaids of Tiburon
One-Eyed Soldiers
The Phantom of the Range
Romancing the Stone▶
The Secret of the Golden Eagle
Secret of the Ice Cave
Shadow of Chikara
Tarzan's Secret Treasure
Terror on Alcatraz
That Man from Rio
There Goes the Neighborhood
Thieves of Fortune
Treasure Island▶

Treasure Island
The Treasure of Jamaica Reef
The Treasure of Matecumbe
The Treasure of the Amazon
Treasure of the Four Crowns
Treasure of the Golden Condor
Treasure of the Sierra Madre▶
Treasure of the Yankee Zephyr
The Treasure Seekers
Trespass
Uninvited
Whistling in Dixie
The Wrong Road

Trees & Forests
see also Good Earth; Wilderness
Big Trees▶
Dr. Tarr's Torture Dungeon
Equinox▶
Evil Dead
Himatsuri
The Ice Flood
King of the Forest Rangers
Lassie: Adventures of Neeka
Les Grandes Gueules
Lunatic
Mr. Sycamore
The Night Brings Charlie
Redwood Forest Trail
Surfacing
The Wizard of Oz▶

True Crime
see also Crime & Criminals; This is Your Life; True Stories
At Close Range▶
Ballad of Gregorio Cortez
Beyond Reasonable Doubt
Billionaire Boys Club
Black Oak Conspiracy
Black Panther
Bluebeard▶
The Boston Strangler
Cordelia
Dead Wrong: The John Evans Story
Death Scream
The Deliberate Stranger▶
Dick Turpin
Dillinger
Double-Crossed
Echoes in the Darkness
The Elegant Criminal
The Executioner's Song
The Falcon and the Snowman▶
Great Gold Swindle
Helter Skelter
The Hillside Strangler
Honor Thy Father and Mother: The True Story of the Menendez Brothers
Mad Dog Morgan
McVicar
Mrs. Soffel
Money Movers
Murder in Coweta County
Murder in New Hampshire: The Pamela Smart Story
Murder in Texas▶
Murder So Sweet
Murph the Surf
Nowhere to Run
The People vs. Jean Harris
The Preppie Murder
The Pursuit of D.B. Cooper
Rampage
Squizzy Taylor
Sweetheart!
Swoon▶
Triple Cross▶
Undercover Cop
The Untouchables▶
Verne Miller
The Zodiac Killer

True Stories
see also This is Your Life; True Crime
The Abduction of Kari Swenson
Above and Beyond▶
The Accused▶
Act of Vengeance
Adam▶
The Adventures of Nellie Bly
After the Promise
After the Shock
Afterburn▶
Al Capone▶
The Alamo▶
Alamo Bay
Alive
All Mine to Give
All the President's Men▶
Alvarez Kelly
The Ambush Murders
An American Story
The Amityville Horror
Amor Bandido
The Amy Fisher Story
And I Alone Survived
And the Band Played On▶
Andre
The Ann Jillian Story
Anna and the King of Siam▶
Apprentice to Murder
Archer's Adventure
Assault at West Point: The Court-Martial of Johnson Whittaker
The Assisi Underground
At Close Range▶
The Attic: The Hiding of Anne Frank
Attica▶
Au Revoir Les Enfants▶
Awakening of Candra
Awakenings▶
Away All Boats
Backbeat▶
Bad Blood
Badge of the Assassin
Badlands▶
Ballad in Blue
Ballad of Gregorio Cortez▶
The Ballad of Little Jo
Bataan
Battle Hell
Battle of the Eagles
Beautiful Dreamers
Benjamin Argumedo
Beyond Reasonable Doubt
Beyond the Next Mountain
Big Mo
The Big Red One▶
Bill▶
Bill: On His Own▶
Bitter Harvest▶
Black Oak Conspiracy
Black Panther
Blind Ambition
Blood Clan
Bonnie & Clyde▶
The Boston Strangler
The Bridge at Remagen
Brink's Job▶
Brutal Glory
Burke & Wills
The Burning Bed▶
Cabeza de Vaca▶
Call Northside 777▶
Camel Boy
Camila▶
Can You Hear the Laughter? The Story of Freddie Prinze
The Canon Operation
The Cantor's Son
The Captain from Koepenick
Carve Her Name with Pride
A Case of Deadly Force▶
Cast the First Stone
Castaway
Casualties of Love: The "Long Island Lolita" Story
Casualties of War▶
Chameleon Street▶

Champions
Chariots of Fire▶
Charlie Grant's War
Charlotte Forten's Mission: Experiment in Freedom▶
The Chase
Chattahoochee
Cheyenne Autumn
The Children of An Lac
China Cry
Christabel
Christian the Lion
Christiane F.▶
Churchill and the Generals
Circle of Power
The Climb
Coming Out of the Ice▶
Coming Through
Communion
Confessions of a Serial Killer
Confessions of Tom Harris
Conrack▶
Convicted
Cool Runnings
Cordelia
The Counterfeit Traitor▶
Courage▶
The Court Martial of Billy Mitchell▶
The Court Martial of Jackie Robinson▶
The Crash of Flight 401
Crime of Honor
Cry Freedom
A Cry in the Dark▶
Dance with a Stranger▶
Dangerous Life
David and Lisa▶
Dawn!
Day One▶
Dead Ahead: The Exxon Valdez Disaster▶
Dead Ringers▶
Dead Wrong: The John Evans Story
Deadly Business▶
Deadly Matrimony
Death of a Centerfold
Death of a Soldier
The Death of Adolf Hitler
The Death of Richie
Death Scream
The Deliberate Stranger▶
Delta Force
Deranged▶
The Diary of Anne Frank▶
Dillinger▶
Dillinger
The Doctor
Dr. Bethune▶
Dog Day Afternoon▶
Donner Pass: The Road to Survival
Don't Cry, It's Only Thunder
Double-Crossed
Double Exposure: The Story of Margaret Bourke-White
The Dove
Drugstore Cowboy▶
Drum Beat
Echoes in the Darkness
Eddie Macon's Run
Edie in Ciao! Manhattan
Edison the Man
The Education of Sonny Carson
Edward and Mrs. Simpson
Egg and I▶
Eight Men Out▶
84 Charing Cross Road▶
Eleni
The Elephant Man▶
Elvira Madigan▶
Elvis and Me
Elvis in the Movies
Elvis Memories
Elvis: Rare Moments with the King
Elvis: The Echo Will Never Die
Elvis: The Movie
The Emerald Forest▶
Eminent Domain

Empire of the Sun
Encounter with the Unknown
Endangered Species
Enemy of Women
The Enforcer
An Englishman Abroad▶
Enigma Secret
Enola Gay: The Men, the Mission, the Atomic Bomb
Enter Laughing
The Entity
Eric▶
The Ernest Green Story
Escape from Sobibor▶
Europa, Europa
Evel Knievel
Every Man for Himself & God Against All▶
The Execution of Private Slovik▶
Execution of Raymond Graham
The Executioner's Song
Exodus▶
Extreme Justice
Eye of the Octopus
Eye on the Sparrow
The Falcon and the Snowman▶
False Arrest
Fast Company
Fat Man and Little Boy
Fatal Vision
The Father Clements Story
The FBI Murders▶
The FBI Story▶
Fear Strikes Out▶
Fifth Day of Peace
Fighting Father Dunne
Fighting Seabees
The Fighting Sullivans▶
Final Warning
Fire and Rain
Fire in the Sky
Fitzcarraldo▶
The Fixer▶
Flight of the Eagle
Forty Days of Musa Dagh
Foul Play
Frances▶
Francis Gary Powers: The True Story of the U-2 Spy
Gaby: A True Story▶
Gentleman Bandit
The George McKenna Story
Geronimo▶
Gideon's Trumpet
The Girl Who Spelled Freedom▶
Girls of the White Orchid
Glory Enough for All: The Discovery of Insulin
Going for the Gold: The Bill Johnson Story
Going Home
Good Evening, Mr. Wallenberg
Goodbye, Miss 4th of July
Goodfellas▶
Grain of Sand
Grambling's White Tiger
Grave Secrets: The Legacy of Hilltop Drive
The Great Escape▶
Great Gold Swindle
The Great Impostor
The Great Locomotive Chase
The Great Riviera Bank Robbery
The Great Train Robbery▶
The Great Wallendas
The Greek Tycoon
The Grey Fox▶
Guilty of Innocence
Guns of War
The Guyana Tragedy: The Story of Jim Jones
Hanna's War
Hard Choices
The Hatfields & the McCoys
He Walked by Night▶
He Who Walks Alone

Heart Like a Wheel▶
Heartland▶
Heaven's Heroes
Held Hostage
Hell to Eternity
Hellcats of the Navy
Helter Skelter
Henry & June▶
Henry: Portrait of a Serial Killer▶
Hide in Plain Sight▶
The Hiding Place
The Highest Honor
The Hindenburg
Holy Terror
A Home of Our Own
Honeymoon Killers
Honor Thy Father
Hoodlum Empire
The Hoodlum Priest▶
The Horse Soldiers
Hostages▶
The House on Garibaldi Street
The Hunt for the Night Stalker
The Hunter
I Am a Fugitive from a Chain Gang▶
I Love You to Death
I Will Fight No More Forever▶
If You Could See What I Hear
I'm Dancing as Fast as I Can
The Impossible Spy▶
In Cold Blood▶
In the Line of Duty: Ambush in Waco
In the Mood
In the Name of the Father▶
In Which We Serve▶
Infernal Trio
Inherit the Wind▶
The Inn of the Sixth Happiness▶
The Inner Circle▶
Inside the Third Reich
Interrupted Melody▶
Iron Will
Ironclads
Island of the Blue Dolphins
It's Good to Be Alive
Izzy & Moe
The Jayne Mansfield Story
Jenny's War
The Jesse Owens Story
Jesus Christ, Superstar▶
JFK▶
Jo Jo Dancer, Your Life is Calling
Joni
Journey of Hope▶
Journeys from Berlin/1971
Judge Horton and the Scottsboro Boys
Judgment in Berlin
Julia▶
Justin Morgan Had a Horse
Kidco
The Killing Fields▶
A Killing in a Small Town▶
King of the Wind
Knute Rockne: All American▶
Korczak▶
The Krays▶
Ladies They Talk About
Lady Jane▶
Lady of the House
Larry
The Last American Hero▶
The Last Days of Dolwyn
The Last Five Days
Last Flight Out: A True Story
The Last Supper▶
Lean on Me▶
The Legend of Blood Castle
Legend of Boggy Creek
Let Him Have It▶
Lethal Lolita—Amy Fisher: My Story
Life & Times of Grizzly Adams
Little Boy Lost
Little Gloria...Happy at Last
Little Heroes
Little Laura & Big John

Lone Star Kid
The Long Island Four
Lorenzo's Oil▶
Lost
The Lost One
Love Leads the Way
Love, Lies and Murder
Lovey: A Circle of Children 2
M. Butterfly
Ma Barker's Killer Brood
Machine Gun Kelly
Mad Dog Morgan
M.A.D.D.: Mothers Against Drunk Driving
Madeleine
Madman
Malaya
A Man Escaped▶
The Man Who Never Was▶
Manhunt for Claude Dallas
Marciano
Marie▶
Mark Twain and Me
Marked Woman▶
Mary White
Mask▶
Massacre in Rome
Mata Hari▶
Matewan▶
A Matter of Life and Death
Mayerling▶
The McConnell Story
Melvin and Howard▶
Memphis Belle▶
Midnight Express▶
Miracle of Our Lady of Fatima
The Miracle Worker▶
Missing▶
Mission of the Shark▶
Mrs. R's Daughter
Mrs. Soffel▶
Mr. Horn
Molly Maguires
Money for Nothing
Money Movers
Mountain Man
The Mozart Story
Murder in Coweta County
Murder in the Old Red Barn
The Murder of Mary Phagan▶
Murder One
Murder Ordained
Murph the Surf
Mutiny on the Bounty▶
My Darling Clementine▶
My Left Foot▶
My Pleasure Is My Business
The Mystery of Alexina
The Mystery of the Mary Celeste
Naked in the Sun
Nancy Astor
The Nasty Girl▶
The Neon Empire
Night Ambush
Night Crossing
A Night to Remember▶
Nightmare at 43 Hillcrest
Nitti: The Enforcer
Norma Rae▶
Not Without My Daughter
Nowhere to Run
Nurse Edith Cavell▶
Old Gringo
Olivier, Olivier▶
On Wings of Eagles
One Against the Wind▶
One in a Million: The Ron LaFlore Story
One That Got Away▶
The Onion Field▶
Operation Amsterdam
Operation Haylift
Operation Thunderbolt
Opposing Force
The Ordeal of Dr. Mudd▶
The Other Side of the Mountain
The Ox
Pancho Barnes
Passion in Paradise
The Passion of Joan of Arc▶

Pat Garrett & Billy the Kid▶
Paths of Glory▶
Patton▶
Patty Hearst
Pete Townshend: White City
Phar Lap
Philby, Burgess and MacLean: Spy Scandal of the Century
Playing for Time▶
Portrait of a Rebel: Margaret Sanger
The Positively True Adventures of the Alleged Texas Cheerleader-Murdering Mom▶
The Preppie Murder
Pressure Point▶
Prick Up Your Ears▶
Prince of the City▶
A Private Matter▶
The Prize Pulitzer
Promised a Miracle
PT 109
Quarterback Princess
A Question of Attribution
Question of Faith
Question of Honor
Qui Etes Vous, Mr. Sorge?
Quilombo
Raid on Entebbe▶
Rainbow Drive
Rape and Marriage: The Rideout Case
Reach for the Sky
A Real American Hero
Reckless Disregard
Reds▶
Reilly: Ace of Spies▶
The Return of Martin Guerre▶
Reversal of Fortune▶
Ring of Bright Water▶
Ring of Terror
Riot in Cell Block 11▶
River's Edge▶
Rodeo Girl
Roe vs. Wade▶
Ruby
Rudy
The Rumor Mill
A Rumor of War▶
Runaway Father
The Runner Stumbles
Running Brave
Sacco & Vanzetti
Sadat
St. Helen's, Killer Volcano
The St. Valentine's Day Massacre
Sakharov▶
Samaritan: The Mitch Snyder Story▶
Samurai 1: Musashi Miyamoto▶
Samurai 2: Duel at Ichijoji Temple▶
Samurai 3: Duel at Ganryu Island▶
Savage Attraction
Scandal▶
The Scarlet & the Black
Schindler's List▶
Sea Gypsies
Sea Wolves
The Search for Bridey Murphy
Searching for Bobby Fischer▶
Secret Weapon
Seizure: The Story of Kathy Morris
Separate But Equal▶
Sergeant Matlovich vs. the U.S. Air Force
Sergeant York▶
Sexual Intent
Shadow on the Sun
Shadowlands▶
Shattered Vows
A Shining Season▶
Shout at the Devil
The Sicilian
Sid & Nancy▶
Silence of the North
Silent Victim

Silent Victory: The Kitty O'Neil Story▶
Silkwood▶
The Singing Nun
Six Degrees of Separation
633 Squadron
Skeezer
The Slender Thread▶
Small Sacrifices
Sniper▶
Soldier Blue
The Sound of Music▶
Spartacus▶
Spirit of St. Louis▶
The Spirit of West Point
Springfield Rifle
Springhill
Squizzy Taylor
Stand and Deliver▶
Star 80
Stealing Heaven
Stevie
Storm and Sorrow
The Stratton Story▶
Street Smart
The Sugarland Express▶
Switched at Birth
The Taking of Flight 847: The Uli Derickson Story▶
Teamster Boss: The Jackie Presser Story▶
The Ten Million Dollar Getaway
10 Rillington Place▶
Ten Who Dared
The Terry Fox Story▶
The Thin Blue Line▶
Thirty Seconds Over Tokyo▶
A Thousand Heroes
Thousand Pieces of Gold▶
Three Came Home▶
The Three Faces of Eve▶
Till Death Do Us Part
Till the Clouds Roll By
Time Flies When You're Alive
To Catch a Killer▶
To Heal a Nation
To Kill a Priest
Toast of New York▶
Tom Edison: The Boy Who Lit Up the World
Touched by Love
Town that Dreaded Sundown
Tragedy of Flight 103: The Inside Story▶
The Triangle Factory Fire Scandal
Triple Cross▶
Triumph of the Spirit▶
True Confessions▶
29th Street
Vengeance Is Mine▶
Violette▶
Voyage of Terror: The Achille Lauro Affair
Voyage of the Damned▶
Walking Tall
Walking Tall: Part 2
Walking Tall: The Final Chapter
Walking Through the Fire
The Wall▶
The Wannsee Conference▶
Wedding in Blood▶
Weeds▶
What's Love Got to Do With It?
When Hell Was in Session▶
White Mischief▶
The White Rose▶
The Wild Child▶
Wild Hearts Can't Be Broken▶
Will: G. Gordon Liddy
A Winner Never Quits
Without a Trace
A Woman Called Golda▶
The Woman He Loved
Wooden Horse▶
A World Apart▶
The Wrong Man▶
Yours, Mine & Ours
Yuri Nosenko, KGB

The Zodiac Killer
Zoot Suit▶
Zulu

TV Movies

ABC Stage 67: Truman
    Capote's A Christmas
    Memory
The Abduction of Kari
    Swenson
Abduction of St. Anne
Acceptable Risks
Acorn People
Act of Passion: The Lost
    Honor of Kathryn Beck
Act of Vengeance
Acting on Impulse
Adam▶
Adrift
The Adultress
The Adventures of
    Huckleberry Finn
The Adventures of Nellie Bly
The Adventures of Tom
    Sawyer
The Affair▶
An Affair in Mind
The Affair of the Pink Pearl
African Journey
After Pilkington
After the Promise
After the Rehearsal▶
After the Shock
Afterburn▶
Afterward
Air Hawk
The Alamo: Thirteen Days to
    Glory
Alexander: The Other Side of
    Dawn
Alice to Nowhere
Aliens Are Coming
All God's Children
All My Sons▶
All Quiet on the Western Front
All the Kind Strangers
All the Rivers Run
All You Need Is Cash▶
Almost Partners
Alone in the Neon Jungle
The Amazing Howard Hughes
The Amazing Spider-Man
Amazing Stories
The Amazons
Amber Waves
The Ambush Murders
An American Christmas Carol
Amityville 4
Amos
The Amy Fisher Story
Anastasia: The Mystery of
    Anna
Anatomy of a Seduction
Anatomy of Terror
And a Nightingale Sang
And Baby Makes Six
And I Alone Survived
And the Band Played On▶
And the Children Shall Lead
The Andersonville Trial▶
An Angel at My Table▶
Angel City
Angel on My Shoulder
The Ann Jillian Story
Anna Karenina
Anne of Avonlea▶
Anne of Green Gables▶
Annie Oakley
Another Pair of Aces: Three of
    a Kind▶
Antonia and Jane▶
Ants
Anzacs: The War Down
    Under▶
Apology
Arch of Triumph
Archer: The Fugitive from the
    Empire
Are You in the House Alone?
Are You Lonesome Tonight
As Is
As Summers Die

Assassin
The Assassination Run
Assault and Matrimony
Assault at West Point: The
    Court-Martial of Johnson
    Whittaker
Attack of the 50 Ft. Woman
The Attic: The Hiding of Anne
    Frank
Attica▶
The Autobiography of Miss
    Jane Pittman▶
Awakening of Candra
Babe!▶
Babes in Toyland
Baby Girl Scott
Baby of the Bride
Babycakes
The Babysitter
Back Home
Back to Hannibal: The Return
    of Tom Sawyer and
    Huckleberry Finn
Backfield in Motion
Backtrack▶
Bad Ronald▶
The Bad Seed
Badge of the Assassin
Baffled
Baja Oklahoma
Bang the Drum Slowly
Barbarians at the Gate▶
The Barbary Coast
Bare Essentials
Barefoot in Athens
The Baron and the Kid
Based on an Untrue Story
The Bastard
Battle of the Bullies
Battling for Baby
Beauty and the Beast
Behind Enemy Lines
The Beniker Gang
Berlin Alexanderplatz▶
Berlin Tunnel 21
The Best Little Girl in the
    World▶
The Best of Abbott & Costello
    Live
Best of Comic Relief
The Best of John Candy on
    SCTV
The Best of the Kenny Everett
    Video Show
The Best of the Monsters
Betrayal
Better Late Than Never
Between Friends
Between Two Women
Beulah Land
Beverly Hills Madam
Bewitched
Beyond the Bermuda Triangle
Big Valley
Bill▶
Bill: On His Own▶
Billionaire Boys Club
Billy Crystal: Don't Get Me
    Started
Billy: Portrait of a Street Kid
Birds of Prey
Birthday Boy
Bitter Harvest▶
The Black Arrow
Black Magic
Black Water Gold
Blackout
Blades of Courage
Blaise Pascal▶
Blat
Bleak House
Blind Ambition
Blind Justice
Blind Man's Bluff
Blind Side
Blind Spot
Blind Vengeance
Blind Witness
Blinded by the Light
Blood Money: The Story of
    Clinton and Nadine
The Blood of Others

Blood Ties
Blood Vows: The Story of a
    Mafia Wife
The Blue and the Gray
Blue Ice
The Blue Knight
The Blue Lightning
Blue Money
Bluffing It
Body Bags
Bogie
Bon Voyage, Charlie Brown▶
Bordello
Born Beautiful
Born Innocent
Born to Run
The Borrowers▶
The Bounty Man
The Bourne Identity▶
The Boy in the Plastic Bubble
The Boy Who Left Home to
    Find Out About the Shivers
The Boy Who Loved Trolls
Brady's Escape
Brand New Life
Breaking Home Ties
Breaking Up
Breaking Up Is Hard to Do
The Bretts▶
Brian's Song▶
Brideshead Revisited▶
Bridge to Silence
Bridge to Terabithia
Bright Smiler
Broadway Bound
Broken Angel
Broken Badge▶
The Broken Chain
Brother Future
Brotherhood of Justice
The Brotherhood of the Rose
Brotherly Love
Buck Rogers in the 25th
    Century
Bud and Lou
Buried Alive
The Burning Bed▶
Burning Rage
Butterflies
By Dawn's Early Light
Cafe Romeo
The Caine Mutiny Court
    Martial▶
Calamity Jane
Calendar Girl Murders
California Gold Rush
Call of the Wild
Callie and Son
Camp Cucamonga: How I
    Spent My Summer
    Vacation
The Canterville Ghost
Capone
Captain America
Captain America 2: Death Too
    Soon
The Captive: The Longest
    Drive 2
The Capture of Grizzly Adams
Carmilla
Caroline?▶
Cartier Affair
Casanova
A Case of Deadly Force▶
A Case of Libel
Casey at the Bat
Casino
Cast a Deadly Spell▶
Cast the First Stone
Casualties of Love: The
    "Long Island Lolita" Story
A Casualty of War
Catholics▶
Caught in the Act
Celebrity
Chains of Gold
Chantilly Lace
Charles & Diana: A Palace
    Divided
Charlie and the Great Balloon
    Chase

Charlotte Forten's Mission:
    Experiment in Freedom▶
The Charmer
Chase
The Chase
Chiefs
Child Bride of Short Creek
Child in the Night
Child of Darkness, Child of
    Light
Child of Glass
Children in the Crossfire
The Children of An Lac
Children of Divorce
The Children of Times Square
Children's Carol
Chips, the War Dog
The Choice
Choices
Christabel
The Christmas Coal Mine
    Miracle
Christmas Comes to Willow
    Creek
Christmas in Connecticut
Christmas Lilies of the Field
A Christmas to Remember
The Christmas Wife
A Christmas Without Snow
Christopher Columbus
The Chronicles of Narnia
Cinderella
The Cisco Kid
Citizen Cohn
The City
City in Fear▶
City Killer
Clarence
Clarence Darrow▶
Class of '63
The Clergyman's Daughter
Cloud Waltzing
Clowning Around
The Clowns▶
Cocaine: One Man's
    Seduction
Code Name: Dancer
Code Name: Diamond Head
Code Name: Emerald
Code of Honor
Codename: Foxfire
Codename: Icarus
Codename Kyril
Cold Comfort
Cold Room
Columbo: Murder By the Book
Columbo: Prescription
    Murder▶
Come Along with Me
Comeback Kid
Coming Out of the Ice▶
Coming Through
The Comrades of Summer
Conagher
Concrete Beat
The Connection
Consenting Adult
A Conspiracy of Love
Control
Convicted
Convicted: A Mother's Story
Cooperstown
Cotton Candy
Country Girl
Courage▶
The Court Martial of Jackie
    Robinson▶
The Courtesans of Bombay▶
Courtship▶
Coward of the County
Cowboy & the Ballerina
The Cracker Factory
The Crackler
The Cradle Will Fall
The Crash of Flight 401
Crazy from the Heart▶
Crazy in Love
Criminal Justice▶
Crisis at Central High▶
The Crucifer of Blood
Cruise into Terror
A Cry in the Night

Cry Panic
Cry Terror
Curiosity Kills
The Curse of King Tut's Tomb
Curse of the Black Widow
Cyrano de Bergerac
The Dain Curse
Damien: The Leper Priest
The Dancing Princesses
Danger in the Skies
Danger UXB
A Dangerous Man: Lawrence
    after Arabia▶
Dangerous Relations
Daniel and the Towers
Danielle Steel's Changes
Danielle Steel's "Daddy"
Danielle Steel's Kaleidoscope
The Dark Angel▶
Dark Night of the Scarecrow
The Dark Secret of Harvest
    Home
David Copperfield
The Day After▶
A Day for Thanks on Walton's
    Mountain
Day One▶
The Day the Women Got Even
Daybreak
Days of Wine and Roses
Dead Ahead: The Exxon
    Valdez Disaster▶
The Dead Don't Die
Dead on the Money
Deadlock
Deadly Business▶
Deadly Matrimony
Deadly Surveillance
Deadman's Curve
Dear America: Letters Home
    from Vietnam▶
Dear Detective
Death at Love House
Death Be Not Proud▶
Death Cruise
Death Dreams
Death of a Salesman▶
The Death of Adolf Hitler
The Death of Richie
Death of the Incredible Hulk
Death Race 2000
Death Ray 2000
Death Scream
Death Sentence
The Death Squad
Death Stalk
Deathmoon
The Defender
The Defense Never Rests
The Deliberate Stranger▶
Dempsey
Desperate Lives
Desperate Women
Detective Sadie & Son
Detonator
Devil Dog: The Hound of Hell
Devlin
The Diamond Trap
Diana: Her True Story
The Dining Room
Dinner at Eight
The Dirty Dozen: The Deadly
    Mission
The Dirty Dozen: The Fatal
    Mission
The Dirty Dozen: The Next
    Mission
The Disappearance of Aimee▶
Disaster at Silo 7
The Displaced Person▶
Divorce His, Divorce Hers
Dixie: Changing Habits▶
Dr. Syn, Alias the Scarecrow
The Dollmaker
A Doll's House
Don't Be Afraid of the Dark
Don't Go to Sleep
Don't Look Back: The Story of
    Leroy "Satchel" Paige
The Doomsday Flight
Door to Door

Double Exposure: The Story
of Margaret Bourke-White
Double Jeopardy
Double Standard
D.P.
Dracula
Draw!
A Dream for Christmas▶
Dreams Lost, Dreams Found
Dress Gray▶
Drop-Out Mother
Drug Wars 2: The Cocaine
Cartel
Duel▶
Duel of Hearts
Dumb Waiter
Dust to Dust
Dying Room Only
Dynamite and Gold
An Early Frost▶
East of Eden
Eat a Bowl of Tea▶
Ebony Tower
Echoes in the Darkness
Eden
Eden 2
Eden 3
Eden 4
Edge of Darkness
Edward and Mrs. Simpson
El Diablo
Eleanor & Franklin▶
Eleanor: First Lady of the
World
Elizabeth, the Queen
Elvis and Me
Elvis: The Movie
Embassy
The Emperor's New Clothes
An Englishman Abroad▶
Enola Gay: The Men, the
Mission, the Atomic Bomb
Eric▶
The Ernest Green Story
Ernie Kovacs: Between the
Laughter
Escape from Sobibor▶
The Ewok Adventure
The Ewoks: Battle for Endor
The Execution
The Execution of Private
Slovik▶
Execution of Raymond
Graham
The Executioner's Song
Experience Preferred... But
Not Essential
Eye of the Demon
Eye on the Sparrow
F. Scott Fitzgerald in
Hollywood
Face to Face▶
Fallen Angel
Fallen Angels 1▶
Fallen Angels 2▶
Fallen Champ: The Untold
Story of Mike Tyson▶
False Arrest
False Witness
Family Life
The Family Man
A Family Matter
Family Pictures▶
Family Secrets
Family Sins
Family Upside Down▶
The Fantastic World of D.C.
Collins
Fantasy Island
The Far Pavilions
Fatal Chase
Fatal Exposure
The Fatal Image
Fatal Vision
The Father Clements Story
Father Figure
A Father's Revenge
The FBI Murders▶
Fear
The Fear Inside
Feet Foremost
Fellow Traveler▶

Fer-De-Lance
Fergie & Andrew: Behind
Palace Doors
Fever
A Few Moments with Buster
Keaton and Laurel and
Hardy▶
The Fig Tree
A Fight for Jenny
Final Shot: The Hank Gathers
Story
Final Verdict
Final Warning
Fine Things
Finessing the King
Finish Line
Finnegan Begin Again
Fire
Fire and Rain
The Fire Next Time
Fireball Forward
Firehouse
Firesign Theatre Presents
Nick Danger in the Case of
the Missing Yolks
First Affair
First & Ten
First & Ten: The Team Scores
Again
The First Olympics: Athens
1896
Five Miles to Midnight
The Five of Me
The $5.20 an Hour Dream
The Flame is Love
The Flame Trees of Thika▶
A Flash of Green
Flatbed Annie and Sweetiepie:
Lady Truckers
Flight of Black Angel
Flood!
Florida Straits
For Heaven's Sake
For Ladies Only
For Love or Money
For Richer, For Poorer
For the Love of It
For Us, the Living▶
For Your Love Only
Forbidden
Forbidden Love
Force Five
Force of Evil
Foreign Affairs▶
Forever
Forever Young
The Forgotten
Forgotten Prisoners
Fortress
Fortunes of War▶
Four Eyes and Six Guns
The Four Feathers
Foxfire▶
France/Tour/Detour/Deux/
Enfants▶
The Franchise Affair
Francis Gary Powers: The
True Story of the U-2 Spy
Frankenstein
Freedom Road
French Silk
Friendly Fire
A Friendship in Vienna
Frog
Frogs!
From Here to Eternity
From Here to Maternity
From the Dead of Night▶
Fulfillment
Full Exposure: The Sex Tape
Scandals
Future Cop
The Gambler Returns: The
Luck of the Draw
Gangster Wars
The Gathering
The Gathering: Part 2
Gentleman Bandit
The George McKenna Story
George Washington
George Washington: The
Forging of a Nation

Geronimo▶
Get Christie Love!
Get Smart, Again!
Getting Physical
Ghostwriter
Gideon's Trumpet
The Gift of Love
A Girl of the Limberlost
The Girl Who Spelled
Freedom▶
The Girls of Huntington House
Girls of the White Orchid
The Gladiator
The Glass House▶
The Glitter Dome
Glitz
Glory Enough for All: The
Discovery of Insulin
God Bless the Child▶
Gold of the Amazon Women
The Golden Honeymoon
Goldenrod
Goliath Awaits
Gone are the Days
The Good Father▶
The Good Fight
Goodbye, Miss 4th of July
Gore Vidal's Billy the Kid
Gore Vidal's Lincoln
Gotham▶
Grambling's White Tiger
Grand Isle
Grand Tour: Disaster in Time
The Grass is Always Greener
Over the Septic Tank
Great American Traffic Jam
The Great Escape 2: The
Untold Story
Great Expectations
Great Expectations▶
The Great Los Angeles
Earthquake
Great Movie Stunts & the
Making of Raiders of the
Lost Ark
The Great Wallendas
Green Eyes▶
Griffin and Phoenix: A Love
Story
Gryphon
The Guardian
A Guide for the Married
Woman
Guilty of Innocence
Gulag
A Gun in the House
Gunsmoke: Return to Dodge
The Guyana Tragedy: The
Story of Jim Jones
Gypsy
The Gypsy Warriors
Half Slave, Half Free
Halloween with the Addams
Family
Hands of a Stranger
The Hanged Man
Happily Ever After
Happy Since I Met You▶
Hard Frame
Hard Knox
Hard Rain-The Tet 1968
Hardhat & Legs
Harem
The Hatfields & the McCoys
The Haunting of Barney
Palmer
Haunting of Harrington House
Haunting of Sarah Hardy
The Haunting Passion
Haunts of the Very Rich
Having It All
He Who Walks Alone
The Hearst and Davies Affair
Heart of a Champion: The Ray
Mancini Story
Heart of Darkness
Heartbreak House
Heat Wave▶
Hector's Bunyip
Heidi
Heidi▶
The Heist

Held Hostage
Help Wanted: Male
Helter Skelter
The Henderson Monster
Her Life as a Man
Hercules, Prisoner of Evil
Hi-Di-Hi
High Desert Kill
High Noon: Part 2
High School USA
Hill Number One
The Hillside Strangler
Hired Hand
Hiroshima Maiden
The History of White People in
America
The History of White People in
America: Vol. 2
Hit Lady
Hit Woman: The Double Edge
Hitchhiker 2
Hitchhiker 3
Hitchhiker 4
Hitler's Daughter
The Hobbit▶
The Hoboken Chicken
Emergency
Hobo's Christmas
Hobson's Choice
Hold the Dream
The Hollywood Detective
Holocaust▶
Holocaust
Survivors...Remembrance
of Love
Home at Last
Home for Christmas
Home for the Holidays
Home to Stay
Homecoming: A Christmas
Story
Homeward Bound
Honeyboy
Honor Thy Father
Honor Thy Father and Mother:
The True Story of the
Menendez Brothers
The Horse Without a Head
Horsemasters
The Hostage Tower
Hostages▶
Hotel du Lac
Hotel Room
Hotline
The House of Dies Drear
The House of Eliott
The House of Lurking Death
The House on Garibaldi Street
A House Without a Christmas
Tree
How Many Miles to Babylon?
How to Be a Perfect Person in
Just Three Days
How to Break Up a Happy
Divorce
How to Pick Up Girls
Huckleberry Finn
Hullabaloo Over Georgie &
Bonnie's Pictures
Humanoid Defender
The Hunchback of Notre
Dame▶
The Hunt for the Night Stalker
Hunter
Hurricane
Hush Little Baby, Don't You
Cry
Hustling▶
I, Claudius, Vol. 1: A Touch of
Murder/Family Affairs
I, Claudius, Vol. 2: Waiting in
the Wings/What Shall We
Do With Claudius?
I, Claudius, Vol. 3: Poison is
Queen/Some Justice
I, Claudius, Vol. 4: Queen of
Heaven/Reign of Terror
I, Claudius, Vol. 5: Zeus, By
Jove!/Hail Who?
I, Claudius, Vol. 6: Fool's
Luck/A God in Colchester

I, Claudius, Vol. 7: Old King
Log
I Heard the Owl Call My Name
I Know Why the Caged Bird
Sings▶
I Married a Centerfold
I Posed for Playboy
I Will Fight No More Forever▶
Ike
I'm a Fool
The Image
The Impossible Spy▶
The Imposter
In a Stranger's Hand
In Love with an Older Woman
In the Custody of Strangers▶
In the Line of Duty: Ambush in
Waco
In This House of Brede▶
The Incident▶
An Inconvenient Woman
The Incredible Hulk Returns
The Incredible Journey of Dr.
Meg Laurel▶
The Incredible Rocky
Mountain Race
Indiscreet
Initiation of Sarah
Inside the Third Reich
Intimate Contact▶
Intimate Power
Intimate Strangers
Intimate Strangers
Into the Badlands
Into the Homeland
Into Thin Air▶
Intrigue
Intruder Within
Invasion of Privacy
Invincible Mr. Disraeli
Invitation to Hell
Iran: Days of Crisis
Ironclads
Islands
It Came Upon a Midnight
Clear
It's a Bundyful Life
It's Good to Be Alive
Ivanhoe
Ivory Hunters
Izzy & Moe
J. Edgar Hoover
Jack the Ripper▶
Jackson County Jail
The Jacksons: An American
Dream
Jacob Have I Loved
Jacqueline Bouvier Kennedy
Jailbait: Betrayed By
Innocence
Jamaica Inn
James Dean
Jane Doe
Jane Eyre▶
The Jayne Mansfield Story
Jealousy
Jenny's War
The Jericho Mile
Jesse
The Jesse Owens Story
Jesus of Nazareth▶
The Jewel in the Crown
The JFK Conspiracy
JFK: Reckless Youth
John & Yoko: A Love Story
Johnny Appleseed
Johnny Belinda
Johnny Shiloh
Johnny We Hardly Knew Ye
Judge Horton and the
Scottsboro Boys
Judgment▶
Just Me & You
Justice
K-9000
Kansas City Massacre
Katherine
Kavik the Wolf Dog
Keep the Change
Keeping On
Kennedy
Kenny Rogers as the Gambler

Kenny Rogers as the Gambler, Part 2: The Adventure Continues
Kenny Rogers as the Gambler, Part 3: The Legend Continues
Kent State
The Key to Rebecca
Kicks
The Kid from Left Field
The Kid Who Loved Christmas
The Kid with the 200 I.Q.
Killer on Board
Killer with Two Faces
Killing at Hell's Gate
Killing Floor
A Killing in a Small Town
The Killing Mind
Killing Stone
Killjoy
King▶
Kiss of a Killer
Kojak: The Belarus File
Konrad
Kung Fu: The Movie
Kurt Vonnegut's Monkey House
Lady from Yesterday
Lady Mobster
Laguna Heat
Lantern Hill
Larry
Lassie: The Miracle
Lassie's Great Adventure
Last Chase
Last Cry for Help
Last Days of Frank & Jesse James
The Last Days of Patton
The Last Fling
Last Innocent Man
Last Light
The Last of His Tribe
The Last of Mrs. Lincoln
The Last of the Mohicans
The Last Outlaw
The Last Polka
The Last Prostitute
The Last Ride of the Dalton Gang
Lathe of Heaven
Laurel Avenue
Law of the Land
The Lawrenceville Stories
LBJ: The Early Years▶
Leave 'Em Laughing
Legacy of Lies
The Legend of Sleepy Hollow
Legend of Valentino
Legend of Walks Far Woman
Legs
Les Miserables▶
Lethal Lolita—Amy Fisher: My Story
Letters from the Park▶
Letting Go
License to Kill
A Life in the Theater
Life of Verdi
Lifeguard
Lifepod
Lillie▶
Lily in Love
The Lindbergh Kidnapping Case▶
Lion of Africa
Lip Service▶
Listen to Your Heart
Little Gloria...Happy at Last
Little Lord Fauntleroy
The Little Mermaid
The Little Princess
Little Red Riding Hood▶
Little White Lies
Little Women
The Littlest Angel
Live Wire
Lois Gibbs and the Love Canal
The Loneliest Runner
Lonesome Dove▶
The Long Days of Summer
Long Gone

The Long, Hot Summer▶
Long Journey Back
Long Time Gone
A Long Way Home
The Longest Drive
Longtime Companion▶
Look Back in Anger▶
The Lookalike
The Lord of the Rings
Lorna Doone
The Lost Capone▶
Lost Legacy: A Girl Called Hatter Fox
Lots of Luck
Louisiana
Love Affair: The Eleanor & Lou Gehrig Story▶
Love Among the Ruins▶
Love and Hate: A Marriage Made in Hell
Love by Appointment
Love, Cheat & Steal
Love for Lydia▶
Love, Lies and Murder
Love on the Run
Love's Savage Fury
Loving
Lucy and Desi: Before the Laughter
Ma Barker's Killer Brood
Macbeth
Mad Death
Madame Sin
M.A.D.D.: Mothers Against Drunk Driving
Mae West
Mafia Princess
Magee and the Lady
The Magic Flute▶
Magical Mystery Tour
Make Me an Offer
A Man for All Seasons▶
The Man from Atlantis
The Man in the Iron Mask▶
The Man in the Mist
The Man in the Santa Claus Suit
Man on a String
The Man That Corrupted Hadleyburg
The Man Upstairs
The Man Who Broke 1,000 Chains
Mandela▶
The Manhunt
Manhunt for Claude Dallas
Manhunter
The Manions of America
Mansfield Park
Marathon
Marciano
Margin for Murder
Maricela
Marilyn: The Untold Story▶
Mark Twain and Me
The Marquise
Marriage is Alive and Well
A Married Man
The Martian Chronicles: Part 1
The Martian Chronicles: Part 2
The Martian Chronicles: Part 3
Marty
Mary and Joseph: A Story of Faith
Mary White
M*A*S*H: Goodbye, Farewell & Amen▶
Master Harold and the Boys▶
Mating Season
A Matter of Life and Death
Matters of the Heart
Max and Helen
Maybe I'll Be Home in the Spring
Mayflower Madam
The Maze▶
Mazes and Monsters
Medium Cool▶
Melvin Purvis: G-Man
The Member of the Wedding
Memorial Day
Memphis

Merlin of the Crystal Cave
MGM: When the Lion Roars
Miami Vice 2: The Prodigal Son
The Midnight Hour
The Mighty Pawns
Miles to Go
Miles to Go Before I Sleep
Miracle at Moreaux
Miracle in Rome
Miracle of the Heart: A Boys Town Story
Miracle on Ice
The Miracle Worker▶
Mirrors
Miss All-American Beauty
Miss Rose White▶
Missiles of October▶
Missing Pieces
Mission Galactica: The Cylon Attack
Mission: Monte Carlo
Mission of the Shark▶
Mrs. R's Daughter
Mr. Bill's Real Life Adventures
Mr. Corbett's Ghost
Mr. Horn
Mr. Inside, Mr. Outside
Mistral's Daughter
Mistress
Mom, the Wolfman and Me
Montana
Monte Carlo
Moon of the Wolf
More! Police Squad
More Wild, Wild West
Most Wanted
Mother & Daughter: A Loving War
Munster's Revenge
Murder by Moonlight
Murder by Natural Causes▶
Murder by Night
Murder by the Book
Murder in Coweta County
Murder in New Hampshire: The Pamela Smart Story
Murder in Space
Murder in Texas▶
A Murder is Announced
Murder Motel
The Murder of Mary Phagan▶
Murder on Flight 502
Murder on the Bayou▶
Murder on the Midnight Express
Murder Once Removed
Murder or Mercy
Murder Ordained
Murder So Sweet
Murderers Among Us: The Simon Wiesenthal Story▶
Murderous Vision
Murders at Lynch Cross
The Murders in the Rue Morgue▶
Murrow
Mussolini & I
My Brother's Wife
My Darlin' Clementine
My Father's House
My Mother's Secret Life
My Old Man
My Sweet Charlie
My Wicked, Wicked Ways
Mysterious Island of Beautiful Women
Mysterious Two
Nadia
Nails
Nairobi Affair
Naked Lie
Nativity
Necessary Parties
The Neon Empire
Never Forget
Nevil Shute's The Far Country
News at Eleven
Night Cries
Night Nurse
Night of Dark Shadows
Night of the Fox

Night of the Wilding
Night Partners
The Night Stalker: Two Tales of Terror
Night Terror
The Night the City Screamed
The Night Train to Kathmandu
Nightfall
The Nightingale
Nightlife
The Nightman
Nightmare at Bittercreek
Nightmare in Badham County
Nightmare on the 13th Floor
Nitti: The Enforcer
No Comebacks
No Place to Hide
No Place to Run
No Room to Run
Noon Wine▶
North and South Book 1▶
North and South Book 2▶
Northanger Abbey
Not My Kid
Not Quite Human
Not Quite Human 2
Nurse
Nutcracker, A Fantasy on Ice
O Pioneers!
Obsessive Love
Of Mice and Men▶
Official Denial
O'Hara's Wife
Oliver Twist▶
Oliver Twist
Ollie Hopnoodle's Haven of Bliss
On the Edge: The Survival of Dana
On Valentine's Day
On Wings of Eagles
Onassis
One Against the Wind▶
One Cooks, the Other Doesn't
One Deadly Owner
One Night Stand
One of My Wives Is Missing
One Shoe Makes It Murder
Open All Hours
The Oppermann Family
The Ordeal of Dr. Mudd▶
Orphan Train▶
Orpheus Descending
Our Town▶
Out of the Darkness▶
Out on a Limb
Outrage!
Outside Chance
Overture
The Ox-Bow Incident▶
Pacific Inferno
Pair of Aces
Pals
Pancho Barnes
Panic in Echo Park
Panic on the 5:22
Paper Man
Paris Trout
The Park is Mine
Passion Flower
Passion in Paradise
Paul Robeson
Paul's Case
Pecos Bill
The Pee Wee Herman Show
Pee Wee's Playhouse Christmas Special
Pee Wee's Playhouse Festival of Fun
Penalty Phase
The People
The People Next Door
The People vs. Jean Harris▶
The Perfect Bride
Perfect Family
Perfect Harmony
A Perfect Little Murder
A Perfect Spy
Perfect Witness
Perry Mason: The Case of the Lost Love
Personals

Peter Gunn
Peter Lundy and the Medicine Hat Stallion
Peter Pan▶
Peter the Great▶
A Piano for Mrs. Cimino
Picture of Dorian Gray▶
Piece of Cake
The Pied Piper of Hamelin
Pilgrim, Farewell
Pinocchio
Pioneer Woman
Planet Earth
Play It Again, Charlie Brown
Playing for Time▶
Playmates
Pleasure Palace
Plumber
Plutonium Incident
A Pocketful of Rye
The Point
Poison Ivy
Poker Alice
Police Squad! Help Wanted!
Policewoman Centerfold
Poor Little Rich Girl: The Barbara Hutton Story
Pope John Paul II
The Poppy is also a Flower
The Portrait▶
Portrait of a Showgirl
Portrait of a Stripper
Portrait of a White Marriage
The Positively True Adventures of the Alleged Texas Cheerleader-Murdering Mom▶
The Possessed
Powder Keg
The Power Within
Pray for the Wildcats
Pray TV
Praying Mantis
The Preppie Murder
The President's Plane is Missing
Pride and Prejudice
Pride of Jesse Hallum
Prime Suspect
Prime Suspect▶
Prime Suspect 2▶
Prince of Bel Air
The Prince of Central Park▶
The Princess and the Pea▶
Princess Daisy
The Princess Who Never Laughed▶
Prison Stories: Women on the Inside▶
Prisoner of Rio
Prisoners of the Lost Universe
Private Contentment
A Private Matter▶
The Prize Pulitzer
Project Moon Base
Promise to Murder
Promised a Miracle
Prototype▶
Proud Men
Psycho 4: The Beginning
Pudd'nhead Wilson
Pueblo Affair▶
Puss 'n Boots
Puzzle
Python Wolf
QB VII▶
Quarterback Princess
The Queen of Mean
Queen of the Stardust Ballroom▶
Queenie
A Question of Attribution
A Question of Guilt
Question of Honor
A Question of Love▶
The Quick and the Dead
Quo Vadis
Rage▶
Rage of Angels
Rage of Angels: The Story Continues
Raid on Entebbe▶

The Railway Station Man▶
Rainbow
Rainbow Drive
A Raisin in the Sun▶
Rape and Marriage: The
Rideout Case
Rappaccini's Daughter
Ratings Game
Rattlers
A Real American Hero
The Rebels
Reckless Disregard
Red Alert
Red Flag: The Ultimate Game
Red King, White Knight
The Red Pony▶
Red Shoe Diaries
Red Shoe Diaries 3: Another
Woman's Lipstick
Red Shoe Diaries 4: Auto
Erotica
Reflections of Murder
Rehearsal for Murder
Reilly: Ace of Spies▶
The Return of Eliot Ness
Return of Frank Cannon
The Return of the King
Return of the Man from
U.N.C.L.E.
Return of the Rebels
Return to Earth
Return to Fantasy Island
Return to Lonesome Dove
Return to Mayberry
Revenge of the Stepford
Wives
Rich Man, Poor Man▶
Ride the Wind
Riding High
Right of Way
Rio Diablo
The Rise & Rise of Daniel
Rocket
The Rise of Louis XIV▶
Rising Son▶
Rita Hayworth: The Love
Goddess
Riverbend
Robbers of the Sacred
Mountain
Robin Hood▶
Robin Hood...The Legend:
Herne's Son
Robin Hood...The Legend:
Robin Hood and the
Sorcerer
Robin Hood...The Legend:
The Swords of Wayland
Robin Hood...The Legend:
The Time of the Wolf
Rocket to the Moon
Rodeo Girl
Roe vs. Wade▶
Roll of Thunder, Hear My Cry
Romance on the Orient
Express
The Room
Roommate
Roots▶
Roots: The Gift
Roots: The Next Generation▶
The Rose and the Jackal
Rosie: The Rosemary Clooney
Story
Roughnecks
The Rousters
Rudolph the Red-Nosed
Reindeer
The Rumor Mill
A Rumor of War▶
Runaway
The Runaway Barge
Runaway Father
Running Against Time
Running Mates▶
The Sacketts
Sadat
Saigon: Year of the Cat
Sakharov▶
Samaritan: The Mitch Snyder
Story▶
Samson and Delilah

Sarah, Plain and Tall▶
Satan's School for Girls
The Savage Bees
Savage Run▶
Savages
Say Goodbye, Maggie Cole
Scandal in a Small Town
The Scarlet & the Black
The Scarlet Pimpernel▶
Scene of the Crime
Scout's Honor
Scruples
The Sea Wolf
Second Chance
The Secret Garden
The Secret Garden▶
Secret Passions
Secret Weapon
Secret Weapons
Secrets
Secrets of a Married Man
Secrets of Three Hungry
Wives
Seduced
See How She Runs▶
The Seekers
Senior Trip
Sense & Sensibility
Separate But Equal▶
Separate Tables
September Gun
Sergeant Matlovich vs. the
U.S. Air Force
Servants of Twilight
Sessions
Sex and the Single Parent
The Shadow Box▶
The Shadow Riders
Shame
Shattered Silence
Shattered Vows
S*H*E
She Waits
The Shell Seekers
Sherlock Holmes: The Master
Blackmailer
She's Dressed to Kill
A Shining Season▶
Shogun▶
Shooting Stars
Side Show
Silas Marner▶
Silent Night, Lonely Night
Silent Victory: The Kitty O'Neil
Story▶
Silent Witness
Silhouette
Sinatra
Single Bars, Single Women
The Sins of Dorian Gray
Six Fois Deux/Sur et Sous la
Communication▶
Six Wives of Henry VIII▶
Sizzle
Skeezer
Sketch Artist
Sketches of a Strangler
Sky Hei$t
The Sky is Gray▶
Slow Burn
A Small Killing
Small Sacrifices
Smoke
A Smoky Mountain Christmas
Smooth Talk▶
Snatched
Sniper▶
The Snow Queen
Snow White and the Seven
Dwarfs
Snowbeast
Snowblind
Soft and Hard
Soldier in Love
The Solitary Man
Someone I Touched
Something in Common
Sometimes They Come Back
Son of the Morning Star▶
Sooner or Later
Sophia Loren: Her Own Story
Sophisticated Gents▶

Sorry, Wrong Number
S.O.S. Titanic
The Sound and the Silence
Special Bulletin▶
Special Olympics
The Spell
Spiderman: The Deadly Dust
Spiral Staircase
Spy
Spymaker: The Secret Life of
Ian Fleming
Stagecoach
Stalin
Stamp of a Killer
Standing Tall
Star Trek Bloopers
Starflight One
State of Emergency
Steal the Sky
Steel Cowboy
Stephen King's Golden Years
Stephen King's It
Stephen King's The Stand
Stephen King's The
Tommyknockers
Stigma
Still Not Quite Human
Stone Fox
The Story of David▶
The Story of Jacob &
Joseph▶
A Strange and Deadly
Occurence
Strange Case of Dr. Jekyll &
Mr. Hyde
Strange Interlude
The Stranger
A Stranger is Watching
The Stranger Who Looks Like
Me
The Stranger Within
Strangers: The Story of a
Mother and Daughter▶
Strapped
A Streetcar Named Desire▶
The Streets of L.A.
Strike Force
Sudie & Simpson▶
Summer Fantasy
Summer of Fear
The Summer of My German
Soldier▶
Summer Solstice
A Summer to Remember
Sunburn
Svengali
Sweet Bird of Youth
Sweet 15
Sweet Hostage
Swimsuit: The Movie
Switched at Birth
Sword of Gideon
Sybil▶
T Bone N Weasel
Tagget
Tailspin: Behind the Korean
Airline Tragedy
Take Your Best Shot
Taken Away
The Taking of Flight 847: The
Uli Derickson Story▶
Taking the Heat
A Tale of Two Cities
A Tale of Two Cities▶
Tales from the Crypt
Tales from the Crypt, Vol. 3
Tarantulas: The Deadly Cargo
Target: Favorite Son
The Tattered Web
Teamster Boss: The Jackie
Presser Story▶
Tears in the Rain
Tell Me Where It Hurts
The Ten Million Dollar
Getaway
Tender Is the Night
The Tenth Man
Tenth Month
Terror at London Bridge
Terror Out of the Sky
The Terry Fox Story▶

The Testament of Dr.
Cordelier▶
Texas Guns
Texas John Slaughter:
Geronimo's Revenge
Texas John Slaughter:
Stampede at Bitter Creek
They Watch
Thief
The Thief of Baghdad
Third Degree Burn
Thirteenth Day of Christmas
This Lightning Always Strikes
Twice
Thompson's Last Run
The Thorn Birds▶
Threads▶
The Three Little Pigs
Three of a Kind
Through Naked Eyes
Thumbelina▶
Thursday's Game▶
Tidy Endings
Tiger Town
Till Death Do Us Part
Time Flies When You're Alive
A Time for Miracles
Time for Murder
Time to Live
Timestalkers
To All My Friends on Shore▶
To Catch a Killer▶
To Catch a King
To Dance with the White
Dog▶
To Heal a Nation
To Race the Wind
Tomorrow's Child
Torn Between Two Lovers
Toughlove
A Town Like Alice
The Tracker
The Trackers
Traffik▶
The Tragedy of King Richard II
Trapped
Trapped in Silence
Traveling Man
Treasure Island
The Trial of Lee Harvey
Oswald
The Trial of the Incredible Hulk
The Triangle Factory Fire
Scandal
Tribes
Tricks of the Trade
Trilogy of Terror
Trouble in Paradise
True West▶
Truth or Die
12:01
21 Hours at Munich▶
24 Hours in a Woman's Life
Twin Peaks
Twirl
Two Fathers' Justice
Two Kinds of Love
Two of a Kind
The Two Worlds of Jenny
Logan
The Ultimate Imposter
The Unbreakable Alibi
Uncle Tom's Cabin
Under the Biltmore Clock
Undergrads▶
Unexplained Laughter
Unnatural Causes▶
Uphill All the Way
Urge to Kill
Users
Vanishing Act
The Vegas Strip Wars
Vendetta for the Saint
Vengeance
A Very Brady Christmas
A Very British Coup▶
Victim of Beauty
Victim of Love
Victoria Regina
Vietnam War Story 1
Vietnam War Story 2
Vietnam War Story 3

The Virginia Hill Story
Voyage
Voyage of Terror: The Achille
Lauro Affair
The Voyage of the Yes
A Voyage' Round My Father▶
Wagner: The Complete Epic
Wagner: The Movie
Wait Till Your Mother Gets
Home
Waiting for the Moon
Walking on Air
Walking Through the Fire
A Waltz Through the Hills
War & Remembrance, Part 1
War & Remembrance, Part 2
War & Remembrance: The
Final Chapter, Part 8
War & Remembrance: The
Final Chapter, Part 9
War Between the Tates
Washington Mistress
We are the Children
Web of Deceit
Weekend War
Welcome Home
Wet Gold
Whale for the Killing
When a Stranger Calls Back
When Every Day was the
Fourth of July
When Hell Was in Session▶
When He's Not a Stranger▶
When the Bough Breaks
When the Time Comes
When Your Lover Leaves
Where the Spirit Lives
Which Way Home
White Hot: The Mysterious
Murder of Thelma Todd
White Mama▶
Who Am I This Time?▶
Who Is the Black Dahlia?▶
Who Killed Baby Azaria?
Who'll Save Our Children?▶
Whoops Apocalypse
The Widow
The Wild and the Free
Wild & Wooly
Wild Horses
Wild Palms
Wild Times
Wild, Wild West Revisited
Wild Women
Wildflower▶
Will: G. Gordon Liddy
Willa
Wilma
Windmills of the Gods
Winds of Kitty Hawk
The Winds of War
A Winner Never Quits
Without Warning: The James
Brady Story▶
A Woman Called Golda▶
A Woman Called Moses
The Woman He Loved
The Woman Hunter
Woman in Black
A Woman Named Jackie
A Woman of Substance,
Episode 1: Nest of Vipers
A Woman of Substance,
Episode 2: The Secret is
Revealed
A Woman of Substance,
Episode 3: Fighting for the
Dream
The Woman Who Willed a
Miracle
Women & Men: Stories of
Seduction
Women of Valor
Words by Heart
World War II: When Lions
Roared
World War III
The World's Oldest Living
Bridesmaid
The Wrestler
Writer's Block
The Wrong Man

A Year in Provence▶
You Must Remember This
Young Catherine▶
Young Charlie Chaplin
Young Love, First Love
The Young Ones
Your Place or Mine
Yuri Nosenko, KGB
The Zany Adventures of
  Robin Hood

TV Pilot Movies

Africa Texas Style
American Dream▶
The Art of Crime
Balboa
Battlestar Galactica
Beverly Hills 90210
The Bionic Woman
Blade in Hong Kong
Blue De Ville
Brass
Buck Rogers in the 25th
  Century
Call to Glory
China Beach
The Concrete Cowboys
Conspiracy of Terror
Daring Game
Death Ray 2000
Destination Moonbase Alpha
Doctor Quinn, Medicine
  Woman
Dr. Strange
Express to Terror
The Flash
Force Five
The Gunfighters
Hercules and the Princess of
  Troy
Highlander: The Gathering
The Hunted Lady
Hunter
The Incredible Hulk
Jigsaw
The Kid with the Broken Halo
Kung Fu
L.A. Law▶
Loving
Miami Vice
Misfits of Science
Moonlighting
Nick Knight
Night Gallery▶
Our Family Business
Probe
Rags to Riches
Riding with Death
Sanctuary of Fear
Scarface Mob
Search for the Gods
The Secret Adversary
She's in the Army Now
Skag▶
Smile, Jenny, You're Dead
Space: 1999—Alien Attack▶
Sprague
Stalk the Wild Child
Stark
Strange New World
The Streets of San
  Francisco▶
Strike Force
Superman & the Mole Men
Terraces
Tour of Duty
Vegas
Waikiki
Walker: Texas Ranger: One
  Riot, One Ranger
The Women of Brewster
  Place▶

TV Series

The Addams Family
Adventures of Kit Carson
Adventures of Ozzie & Harriet
The Adventures of Robin
  Hood

The Adventures of Sherlock
  Holmes: Hound of the
  Baskervilles
The Affair of the Pink Pearl
And Now for Something
  Completely Different▶
Andy Griffith Show
Beauty and the Beast: Once
  Upon a Time in New York
Best of Eddie Murphy
Best of Ernie Kovacs
The Best of Soap: Jessica's
  Wonderful Life
The Best of Soap: Who Killed
  Peter?
The Best of the Kids in the
  Hall
The Best of the Two Ronnies
The Beverly Hillbillies
Beverly Hills 90210
Beverly Hills 90210: The
  Graduation
Blake's Seven
Bonanza
The Brady Bunch, Vol. 1
The Burns and Allen Show
Car 54, Where Are You?
The Cisco Kid
Combat!
Crime Story: The Complete
  Saga
Danger Man
Dark Justice
Dark Shadows
Davy Crockett and the River
  Pirates
Davy Crockett, King of the
  Wild Frontier▶
Death Valley Days: No Gun
  Behind His Badge
The Defender
Devlin Connection
Doctor Who: An Unearthly
  Child
Doctor Who: Cybermen—The
  Early Years
Doctor Who: Daleks Invasion
  of Earth 2150 A.D.
Doctor Who: Day of the
  Daleks
Doctor Who: Death to the
  Daleks
Doctor Who: Earthshock
Doctor Who: Mawdryn
  Undead
Doctor Who: Pyramids of
  Mars
Doctor Who: Revenge of the
  Cybermen
Doctor Who: Robots of Death
Doctor Who: Shada
Doctor Who: Spearhead from
  Space
Doctor Who: Terror of the
  Zygons
Doctor Who: The Ark in Space
Doctor Who: The Brain of
  Morbius
Doctor Who: The Caves of
  Androzani
Doctor Who: The Curse of
  Fenric
Doctor Who: The Deadly
  Assassin
Doctor Who: The Five Doctors
Doctor Who: The Hartnell
  Years
Doctor Who: The Keeper of
  Traken
Doctor Who: The Masque of
  Mandragora
Doctor Who: The Mind
  Robber
Doctor Who: The Pertwee
  Years
Doctor Who: The Seeds of
  Death
Doctor Who: The Sontaran
  Experiment/The Genesis of
  the Daleks
Doctor Who: The Talons of
  Weng-Chiang

Doctor Who: The Three
  Doctors
Doctor Who: The Time
  Warrior
Doctor Who: The Tom Baker
  Years
Doctor Who: The Troughton
  Years
Doctor Who: The Twin
  Dilemma
Doctor Who: The War Games
Doctor Who: Tomb of the
  Cyberman
Dragnet
El Fego Baca: Six-Gun Law
The Equalizer: Memories of
  Manon
Family Dog: Complete Series
Fawlty Towers
The Flash 2: Revenge of the
  Trickster
Fu Manchu
The Fugitive: Premiere
  Episode
The Fugitive: The Final
  Episode
Gilligan's Island: Meet the
  Crew
Gunfight at Sandoval
Hey Abbott!
Hill Street Blues, Vol. 1: Hill
  Street Station
The Hitchhiker
The Honeymooners "Classic
  39": TV or Not TV/
  Honeymooners Highlights
Honeymooners Hidden
  Episodes, Vol. 1
I Love Lucy
The Invaders
Jeeves & Wooster: Jeeves'
  Arrival
Judge Roy Bean
Little House on the Prairie▶
Little Rascals, Book 1
Little Rascals, Book 2
Little Rascals, Book 3
Little Rascals, Book 4
Little Rascals, Book 5
Little Rascals, Book 6
Little Rascals, Book 7
Little Rascals, Book 8
Little Rascals, Book 9
Little Rascals, Book 10
Little Rascals, Book 11
Little Rascals, Book 12
Little Rascals, Book 13
Little Rascals, Book 14
Little Rascals, Book 15
Little Rascals, Book 16
Little Rascals, Book 17
Little Rascals: Choo Choo/
  Fishy Tales
Little Rascals Comedy
  Classics, Vol. 1
Little Rascals Comedy
  Classics, Vol. 2
Little Rascals: Fish Hooky/
  Spooky Hooky
Little Rascals: Honkey
  Donkey/Sprucin' Up
Little Rascals: Little Sinner/
  Two Too Young
Little Rascals: Mush and Milk/
  Three Men in a Tub
Little Rascals on Parade
Little Rascals: Pups is Pups/
  Three Smart Boys
Little Rascals: Spanky/Feed
  'Em and Weep
Little Rascals: The Pinch
  Singer/Framing Youth
Little Rascals Two Reelers,
  Vol. 1
Little Rascals Two Reelers,
  Vol. 2
Little Rascals Two Reelers,
  Vol. 3
Little Rascals Two Reelers,
  Vol. 4
Little Rascals Two Reelers,
  Vol. 5

Little Rascals Two Reelers,
  Vol. 6
Lone Ranger and the Lost
  City of Gold
The Loretta Young Show
The Love Boat
The Man from U.N.C.L.E.
M*A*S*H: The Collector's
  Edition
Maverick: The Collector's
  Edition
Medic
The Mod Squad
Monty Python's Flying Circus
Murderer's Wife
An Occurrence at Owl Creek
  Bridge▶
One Step Beyond
Our Gang Comedies
The Outer Limits: Galaxy
  Being
Ozzie & Harriet
The Prisoner: Arrival
Prisoner Cell Block H
Professionals
Queen for a Day
Remington Steele, Vol. 1:
  License to Steele
Requiem for a Heavyweight▶
Ripping Yarns
Rising Damp
Robin Hood: The Movie
Rocky Jones, Space Ranger
Rocky Jones, Space Ranger:
  Renegade Satellite
Rumpole of the Bailey
Saturday Night Live
Saturday Night Live: Best of
  Robin Williams
Secret Agent
Smart-Aleck Kill
Space: 1999
Space Patrol
Star Trek: The Cage
Star Trek the Next
  Generation: Encounter at
  Farpoint
Star Trek 25th Anniversary
  Special
Tales from Avonlea, Vol. 1:
  The Journey Begins▶
Tales from the Darkside
Thanksgiving Story
The Trouble with Father
TV's Best Adventures of
  Superman
The Twilight Zone
Twin Peaks
The Waltons: A Thanksgiving
  Story
Wanted: Dead or Alive
The White Shadow, Vol. 1
Wild, Wild West Revisited
WKRP in Cincinnati, Vol. 1
Your Show of Shows

Twins

After Darkness
Basket Case▶
Basket Case 2
Basket Case 3: The Progeny
Big Business
Bloodlink
Brotherly Love
Chained for Life
City of Shadows
Cobra Woman
Como Dos Gotas de Agua
The Corsican Brothers
Dead Ringers▶
Deadly Twins
Devil's Wedding Night
The Double Life of Veronique
Double Trouble
Double Vision
Dual Alibi
Equinox
The Eyes, the Mouth
Instant Kung-Fu Man
Invitation au Voyage
Lies of the Twins
Lost Honeymoon

The Man in the Iron Mask▶
Mirror Images
Mirror Images 2
Mother Lode
Mountain Fury
Nukie
The Other▶
Out on a Limb
The Parent Trap
The Sphinx
Start the Revolution Without
  Me▶
A Stolen Life
Twins
Twins of Evil
Twinsanity
The Worldly Madonna

UFOs

see Alien Beings—Benign;
  Alien Beings—Vicious;
  Space Operas

Underground

see Avant-Garde

Unexplained
Phenomena

The Adventures of Sherlock
  Holmes: Hound of the
  Baskervilles
The Amityville Curse
Angel Baby
Beyond the Bermuda Triangle
Black Rainbow▶
Blue Tornado
The Carpathian Eagle
The Carpenter
Carrie▶
Catacombs
Daffy Duck's Quackbusters
Dead Again▶
Dead Zone▶
Delusion
Die, Monster, Die!
Dying to Remember
El Libro de Piedra
Encounter with the Unknown
Endgame
The Entity
Escapes
E.S.P.
Eternal Evil
The Evil Mind
Eyes of Laura Mars
Fire in the Sky
Firestarter
The 4D Man
The Fury
Ghost Chasers
Ghost Town
The Ghosts of Hanley House
Grandma's House
Hangar 18
The Haunting Passion
The House of Seven Corpses
Lisa and the Devil
Lurkers
Maximum Overdrive
Miracle in Rome
Miracle of Our Lady of Fatima
Mondo Balardo
Murphy's Fault
A Name for Evil
The Night Stalker: Two Tales
  of Terror
Nomads
Psychic
The Psychotronic Man
Retribution
Return from Witch Mountain
Salem's Lot
Scared Stiff▶
Shattered Silence
The Sleeping Car
Spook Busters
The Stranger
Things Happen at Night
The Three Lives of
  Thomasina▶

Unexplained

The Tin Drum▶
Truly, Madly, Deeply▶
Twin Peaks
The Undead
Visions
Visions of Evil
Waiting for the Light
Web of the Spider
X: The Man with X-Ray Eyes▶

Urban Drama

Above the Rim
American Heart▶
American Me▶
The Asphalt Jungle▶
Bad Attitude
Bad Lieutenant▶
Boyz N the Hood▶
The Bronx War
Carlito's Way▶
Crossing the Bridge
Dead Boyz Can't Fly
Do the Right Thing▶
The George McKenna Story
Grand Canyon▶
Heaven is a Playground
Juice
Just Another Girl on the I.R.T.
Love Your Mama
Menace II Society▶
Mi Vida Loca
Money for Nothing
Naked▶
New Jack City
Poetic Justice
South Central
Straight Out of Brooklyn
Strapped
Sugar Hill▶
Zebrahead▶

Vacations

American Gothic
The American Scream
An American Werewolf in
   London▶
Backwoods
Beyond the Door 3
Blame It on Rio
Blondie Takes a Vacation
Body Trouble
Cabin Boy
California Suite▶
Cancel My Reservation
Captain Ron
Casual Sex?
City Slickers▶
Claire's Knee▶
Deadly Intruder
Death Stalk
Death Weekend
Deliverance▶
Demon Lust
Devil Wears White
Dirty Dancing▶
Don't Drink the Water
Enchanted April
Far from Home
A Far Off Place
The Fatal Image
Frantic▶
Fraternity Vacation
Gidget Goes Hawaiian
Gidget Goes to Rome
Grotesque
Harry and the Hendersons
The Hills Have Eyes
Home Alone▶
Home Alone 2: Lost in New
   York
Hot Pursuit
Judgment Day
Killing at Hell's Gate
Lena's Holiday
The Long, Long Trailer
The Lunatic
Magic Kid
The Man Who Knew Too
   Much▶
The Man Who Knew Too
   Much

Mr. Hobbs Takes a Vacation▶
Mr. Hulot's Holiday▶
My Father the Hero
My Grandpa is a Vampire
National Lampoon's
   Christmas Vacation
National Lampoon's European
   Vacation
National Lampoon's
   Vacation▶
Nightmare at Bittercreek
Ollie Hopnoodle's Haven of
   Bliss
The Out-of-Towners▶
Pauline at the Beach▶
Poor White Trash 2
Russian Roulette
The Slayer/The Scalps
Spring Break
Summer Rental
Target
Terror at Red Wolf Inn
Terror at Tenkiller
Twitch of the Death Nerve
The Two Faces of Evil
Week-End In Havana
Weekend at Bernie's
Welcome to Spring Break
Where the Boys Are '84
The Wild Life
Witchery

Vampire Babes

see also Vampires

The Brides of Dracula
Captain Kronos: Vampire
   Hunter▶
The Craving
Crypt of the Living Dead
Daughters of Darkness▶
Demon Queen
Dracula's Daughter▶
Fangs of the Living Dead
The Fearless Vampire Killers▶
Fright Night
The Kiss
Lemora, Lady Dracula
Lust for a Vampire
Mary, Mary, Bloody Mary
Night of the Sorcerers
Nightlife
Once Bitten
Twins of Evil
Vamp
The Vampire Lovers
Vampyres
The Velvet Vampire

Vampire Spoof

see also Horror Comedy;
Vampires

Andy Warhol's Dracula▶
Beverly Hills Vamp
Buffy the Vampire Slayer▶
Dracula & Son
Dracula Blows His Cool
Dracula Sucks
Dracula: Up in Harlem
Dracula vs. Frankenstein
The Fearless Vampire Killers▶
Gore-Met Zombie Chef From
   Hell
I Married a Vampire
Kung Fu Vampire Buster
Love at First Bite
The Malibu Beach Vampires
My Best Friend Is a Vampire
My Grandpa is a Vampire
Near Dark▶
Once Bitten
A Polish Vampire in Burbank
Rockula
Teen Vamp
Vamp
The Vampire Happening

Vampires

Alien Massacre
The Bat People
Beast of Morocco
Bela Lugosi Scrapbook

Billy the Kid Versus Dracula
Black Sabbath▶
Black Vampire
Blacula
Blood and Roses
Blood Freak
Blood of Dracula's Castle
Blood of the Vampire
The Blood Spattered Bride
Blood Thirst
Blood Ties
Bloodlust: Subspecies 3
Bloodstone: Subspecies 2
The Bloodsuckers
Bloodsuckers from Outer
   Space
The Bloody Vampire
Body Snatcher from Hell
Bram Stoker's Dracula
The Brides of Dracula
The Brides Wore Blood
Bring Me the Vampire
Buffy the Vampire Slayer▶
Captain Kronos: Vampire
   Hunter▶
Carmilla
Cave of the Living Dead
Children of the Night
Condemned to Live
Count Dracula
Count Yorga, Vampire
The Craving
Crypt of the Living Dead
Dance of the Damned
Dark Shadows
Daughters of Darkness▶
Dead Men Walk
Demon Queen
The Devil Bat
The Devil Bat's Daughter
Devil's Wedding Night
Dr. Terror's House of Horrors
Dracula▶
Dracula
Dracula: A Cinematic
   Scrapbook
Dracula/Garden of Eden
Dracula Has Risen from the
   Grave
Dracula Rising
Dracula (Spanish Version)
Dracula vs. Frankenstein
Dracula's Daughter▶
Dracula's Great Love
Dracula's Last Rites
Dracula's Widow
Elvira, Mistress of the Dark
Evil's Commandment
Evils of the Night
Fangs of the Living Dead
Fright Night
Fright Night 2
Genie of Darkness
Ghost Stories: Graveyard
   Thriller
Grave of the Vampire
Graveyard Shift
Heartstopper
The Horror of Dracula▶
Horror of the Blood Monsters
House of Dark Shadows
House of Frankenstein
The House that Dripped Blood
Howling 6: The Freaks
The Hunger
I Like Bats
Innocent Blood
Invasion of the Vampires
Isle of the Dead
The Last Man on Earth
Lemora, Lady Dracula
Let's Scare Jessica to Death
Lifeforce
Los Vampiros de Coyacan
The Lost Boys
The Lost Platoon
The Loves of Irina
Lust for a Vampire
Mark of the Vampire▶
Martin▶
Mary, Mary, Bloody Mary
Midnight Kiss

Mrs. Amworth
The Monster Club
The Monster Demolisher
The Monster Squad
My Grandpa is a Vampire
My Son, the Vampire
Near Dark▶
Nick Knight
Night of Dark Shadows
Night of the Sorcerers
The Night Stalker: Two Tales
   of Terror
Nightlife
Nightmare in Blood
Ninja, the Violent Sorcerer
Nocturna
Not of This Earth
Once Bitten
Orgy of the Vampires
Pale Blood
Planet of Blood
Planet of the Vampires
Rabid
Red Blooded American Girl
The Reflecting Skin
The Return of Count Yorga
Return of the Vampire
Return to Salem's Lot
The Saga of the Draculas
Salem's Lot
Samson vs. the Vampire
   Women
The Satanic Rites of Dracula
The Scars of Dracula
Scream Blacula Scream
The 7 Brothers Meet Dracula
The Slaughter of the Vampires
Sleepwalkers
Son of Dracula▶
Subspecies
Sundown
Tale of a Vampire
Taste the Blood of Dracula
Theatre of Death
Thirst
The Thirsty Dead
To Die for
To Die for 2
To Sleep with a Vampire
Track of the Vampire
Transylvania Twist
Twins of Evil
Uncle Was a Vampire
Understudy: The Graveyard
   Shift 2
The Unearthing
Vamp
The Vampire
Vampire at Midnight
The Vampire Bat
Vampire Circus
Vampire Cop
The Vampire Happening
The Vampire Hookers
The Vampire Lovers
The Vampire People
The Vampire's Coffin
The Vampire's Ghost
Vampire's Kiss▶
Vampyr▶
The Vampyr
Vampyres
The Velvet Vampire
The Werewolf vs. the Vampire
   Woman
The Wicked
World of the Vampires
Zoltan...Hound of Dracula

Variety

Doctor Duck's Super Secret
   All-Purpose Sauce
Flying Karamazov Brothers
   Comedy Hour
Give a Girl a Break
Heller in Pink Tights
Hollywood Goes to War
Hollywood Varieties
I Wanna Be a Beauty Queen
If You Don't Stop It...You'll Go
   Blind
In the Money

International House
Minsky's Follies
Mr. Mike's Mondo Video
Parade▶
The Pee Wee Herman Show
Pee Wee's Playhouse
   Christmas Special
Pee Wee's Playhouse Festival
   of Fun
Ripley's Believe It or Not!
Sleazamania
Strictly G.I.
That's Dancing!
That's Singing: The Best of
   Broadway
Two Top Bananas
Varieties on Parade
Your Show of Shows
Ziegfeld Follies

Veterans

see also Postwar

Alamo Bay
American Eagle
Americana
Anatomy of Terror
Angels from Hell
The Annihilators
Article 99
Ashes and Embers
Backfire
Bad Company▶
Bell Diamond
The Best Years of Our Lives▶
Billy Jack
Birds of Prey
Birdy▶
The Black Six
Braddock: Missing in Action 3
The Bushwackers
The Cage
Cease Fire
Chattahoochee
Child Bride of Short Creek
Chrome Soldiers
Combat Shock
Cry of the Innocent▶
Dark Before Dawn
Distant Thunder
The Enchanted Cottage
Fear
Fireback
First Blood
Fleshburn
Forced Vengeance
The Forgotten
Ghetto Revenge
G.I. Executioner
The Great American
   Broadcast▶
Heated Vengeance
Heroes
Heroes for Sale▶
House▶
Identity Unknown
In a Shallow Grave
In Country
Jud
Jungle Assault
Kill Alex Kill
Killcrazy
The Killer's Edge
Killzone
Last Mercenary
Lethal Weapon▶
Liberty & Bash
The Line
Memorial Day
Mr. Majestyk
Moon in Scorpio
The Park is Mine
Rambo 3
Red, White & Busted
Ride in a Pink Car
Riders of the Storm
Robbery
Rolling Thunder
Savage Dawn
Scent of a Woman▶
Shark River
Skin Art
Soldier's Revenge

Stand Alone
Stanley
Steele Justice
Tagget
To Heal a Nation
To Kill a Clown
Tracks
Who'll Stop the Rain?▶
The Woman Inside

Vietnam War

see also *Postwar; POW/MIA*

After the Fall of Saigon
Air America
American Commandos
Americana
The Annihilators
Apocalypse Now▶
Ashes and Embers
Autopsy
Bat 21
Bell Diamond
Beyond the Call of Duty
Birdy▶
The Black Six
Born on the Fourth of July▶
The Boys in Company C
Braddock: Missing in Action 3
Cactus in the Snow
Casualties of War▶
Cease Fire
Charlie Bravo
The Children of An Lac
China Beach▶
China Gate▶
Combat Shock
Coming Home▶
Commando Invasion
Conspiracy: The Trial of the
   Chicago Eight▶
Crossfire
Dear America: Letters Home
   from Vietnam▶
Deathdream
The Deer Hunter▶
The Deserters
Dogfight▶
Don't Cry, It's Only Thunder
84 Charlie Mopic▶
Explosion
Eye of the Eagle
Eye of the Eagle 2
Eye of the Eagle 3
Fatal Mission
Fear
Fighting Mad
Firehawk
First Blood
Flight of the Intruder
For the Boys
The Forgotten
Forgotten Warrior
Four Friends
Friendly Fire▶
Full Metal Jacket▶
Gardens of Stone
Ghetto Revenge
Go Tell the Spartans▶
Good Morning, Vietnam▶
The Green Berets
Green Eyes▶
Hail, Hero!
Hair▶
Hamburger Hill
Hanoi Hilton
Hard Rain-The Tet 1968
Heated Vengeance
Heaven and Earth
In Country
In Gold We Trust
In Love and War
Invasion of the Flesh Hunters
The Iron Triangle
Jacknife▶
Jacob's Ladder
Jenny
Jud
Jungle Assault
Kent State
The Killing Fields▶
Lady from Yesterday

Last Flight Out: A True Story
The Last Hunter
Memorial Day
Missing in Action
Missing in Action 2: The
   Beginning
More American Graffiti
Nam Angels
Night Wars
1969▶
No Dead Heroes
The Odd Angry Shot
Off Limits
Once Upon a Time in Vietnam
Operation C.I.A.
Operation 'Nam
Operation War Zone
Ordinary Heroes
Platoon▶
Platoon Leader
P.O.W. Deathcamp
The P.O.W. Escape
Primary Target
Private War
Purple Hearts
Rambo: First Blood, Part 2
Rambo 3
Red, White & Busted
Return of the Secaucus 7▶
Ride in a Pink Car
Rolling Thunder
A Rumor of War▶
Running on Empty▶
Saigon Commandos
Saigon: Year of the Cat
Search and Destroy
The Siege of Firebase Gloria
Skin Art
Soldier's Revenge
Some Kind of Hero
Streamers
Strike Commando
Summertree
Thou Shalt Not Kill...Except
To Heal a Nation
To the Shores of Hell
Tornado
Tour of Duty
Trial of the Catonsville Nine
Twilight's Last Gleaming
Uncommon Valor
Unnatural Causes▶
Vietnam: Chronicle of a War
Vietnam War Story 1
Vietnam War Story 2
Vietnam War Story 3
Warbus
Wardogs
Welcome Home
When Hell Was in Session▶
Which Way Home
The Wild Aces
Winner Takes All
Woodstock▶

Vigilantes

see also *Revenge*

American Commandos
Avenged
Combat Shock
The Death Squad
Death Wish
Death Wish 2
Death Wish 3
Death Wish 5: The Face of
   Death
Defiance
Dirty Harry▶
Falling Down
Force Five
Jimmy Hollywood
Keeper of the City
One Man Jury
Out for Blood
The Outlaw Josey Wales▶
Quiet Cool
Raw Deal
Self-Defense
Shadows and Fog
SnakeEater
SnakeEater 2: The Drug
   Buster

The Sniper
Soldier of the Night
Steele Justice
The Stranger Wore a Gun
Street Hunter
Target Eagle
To Protect and Serve
Zebra Force

Viva Las Vegas!

see also *Gambling*

Gamble on Love
Happily Ever After
Hard Vice
Hell Squad
Honeymoon in Vegas
Indecent Proposal
Jinxed
Jocks
Kiss Me, Stupid!
Lady Cocoa
Las Vegas Hillbillys
Las Vegas Lady
Las Vegas Serial Killer
The Las Vegas Story
Las Vegas Weekend
Meet Me in Las Vegas
Rock-a-Doodle
Sister Act
The Vegas Strip Wars
Viva Las Vegas

Volcanoes

see also *Disaster Flicks*

The Devil at 4 O'Clock
Joe Versus the Volcano
Last Days of Pompeii
The Last Days of Pompeii
Nutcase
St. Helen's, Killer Volcano
When Time Ran Out

Volleyball

Side Out

Voodoo

Angel Heart
Asylum
Beyond the Carribean
Black Devil Doll from Hell
Black Magic Woman
Caribe
Curse 3: Blood Sacrifice
Curse of the Living Dead
The Devil's Daughter
Dr. Terror's House of Horrors
Headhunter
The House on Skull Mountain
Household Saints▶
How to Stuff a Wild Bikini
I Walked with a Zombie▶
Jungle Drums of Africa
Live and Let Die
Macumba Love
The Offspring
The Possession of Joel
   Delaney
Scared Stiff
Scream Blacula Scream
The Serpent and the Rainbow
The Snake People
Theatre of Death
Voodoo Black Exorcist
Voodoo Dawn
Weekend at Bernie's 2

Waitresses

Alice Doesn't Live Here
   Anymore
Atlantic City▶
Come Back to the Five &
   Dime Jimmy Dean, Jimmy
   Dean▶
Five Easy Pieces▶
Frankie and Johnny▶
It Could Happen to You
Joey Breaker▶
Mystic Pizza▶
The Postman Always Rings
   Twice▶

The Postman Always Rings
   Twice
Thelma & Louise▶
Untamed Heart
Waitress
White Palace

War Between the Sexes

see also *Divorce;
   Marriage; Singles*

About Last Night...▶
Adam's Rib▶
The Adventures of Robin
   Hood▶
The African Queen▶
All of Me
All Tied Up
All's Fair
Alternative
Always▶
America 3000
Anita de Montemar
Annie Hall▶
Around the World Under the
   Sea
Autumn Marathon
The Awful Truth▶
The Ballad of the Sad Cafe
Bare Essentials
Basic Training
Behind Office Doors
The Best Intentions▶
Beware of Pity
The Bigamist
Blood and Sand▶
Blue Paradise
The Bodyguard
Boomerang
The Bride Walks Out
Bringing Up Baby▶
Buffalo Jump▶
Bull Durham▶
Cannibal Women in the
   Avocado Jungle of Death
Carmen▶
Carmen Jones▶
Carrington, V.C.▶
Carry On Nurse
Casablanca▶
Casanova's Big Night
Castaway
Casual Sex?
Chained
Cold Heat
Concrete Beat
The Cry of the Owl
The Cutting Edge
Dangerous Liaisons
Dear Murderer
Dear Wife
Designing Woman▶
Divorce His, Divorce Hers
Divorce—Italian Style▶
Dogfight▶
Don Juan, My Love▶
Easy Wheels
El Forastero Vengador
El: This Strange Passion▶
Far and Away
The Favor
The Female Bunch
Fever
The Fighting Sheriff
First Monday in October
Forever Darling
Frankie and Johnny▶
Fury is a Woman▶
A Girl in a Million
Gone with the Wind▶
The Good Father▶
Goodbye Love
Guarding Tess
The Happy Ending
Hardhat & Legs
Having It All
He Said, She Said
Hearing Voices
Heartburn▶
His Girl Friday▶
Hotel Room

Housesitter
I, Claudius, Vol. 1: A Touch of
   Murder/Family Affairs
I Live My Life
I Love All of You
I Love My...Wife
I Love Trouble
I Love You
In the Good Old
   Summertime▶
In the Line of Fire▶
Intimate Story
Irreconcilable Differences
It Happened One Night▶
The Jewel of the Nile
Juliet of the Spirits▶
June Bride▶
Just Tell Me What You Want
Key Exchange
Kill My Wife...Please!
The King and I▶
Kiss Me Kate▶
Kramer vs. Kramer▶
La Diosa Arrodillada
La Discrete▶
L.A. Story▶
The Lady Says No
The Last Woman on Earth
Le Chat▶
Legion of Iron
Letters to an Unknown Lover
Lily in Love
The Lion in Winter▶
Love Crazy▶
Love in the Afternoon
Love Nest
Lover Come Back
Loyalties
Lucky Partners
Man of Destiny
The Man Who Guards the
   Greenhouse
Manhattan▶
Maria's Lovers
The Marriage of Maria Braun▶
The Marrying Man
A Matter of Love
Maverick
McLintock!▶
Men...▶
Menschenfrauen
A Midsummer Night's Dream▶
Moonlighting
Moonstruck▶
Mortal Thoughts
Much Ado About Nothing▶
Murphy's Law
My Brilliant Career▶
Near Misses
A New Leaf
9 to 5
Nothing in Common
One Woman or Two
The Opposite Sex and How to
   Live With Them
Pajama Tops
Pat and Mike▶
Patti Rocks▶
Pauline at the Beach▶
A Piece of Pleasure▶
Pillow Talk▶
Places in the Heart▶
Portrait of Teresa▶
The Practice of Love
Private Lives▶
Prizzi's Honor▶
Public Enemy▶
Queen of Outer Space
Question of Silence▶
The Quiet Man▶
Ramrod
The Ref▶
Romancing the Stone▶
Rooster Cogburn
Running Mates▶
Sabrina▶
Scenes from a Mall
Seance on a Wet Afternoon▶
The Sensual Man
Sex and the College Girl
She-Devil
Shore Leave▶

The Single Standard
The Social Secretary
Sotto, Sotto
Speedtrap
Spies, Lies and Naked Thighs
Star 80
The Story of Fausta
Summer Night with Greek
   Profile, Almond Eyes &
   Scent of Basil
Switch▶
Switching Channels
The Taming of the Shrew
The Taming of the Shrew
The Taming of the Shrew
A Taxing Woman▶
Teacher's Pet▶
Ted & Venus
That's My Baby!
Thelma & Louise▶
The Thing▶
Thor and the Amazon Women
Three of Hearts
Thunder in the Pines
Tiger and the Pussycat
To Have & Have Not▶
Tony Draws a Horse
True Love▶
Two-Faced Woman▶
Vasectomy: A Delicate Matter
War Between the Tates
The War of the Roses▶
When Harry Met Sally▶
When Ladies Meet
When Women Lost Their Tails
Who's Afraid of Virginia
   Woolf?▶
Wife Versus Secretary▶
The Witches of Eastwick
Without Love
A Woman of Distinction▶
Woman of the Year▶
Women & Men: In Love There
   Are No Rules
Women & Men: Stories of
   Seduction
Women on the Verge of a
   Nervous Breakdown▶
The World According to
   Garp▶
Year of the Comet
Yesterday, Today and
   Tomorrow▶
You're a Big Boy Now▶

War, General

*see also Anti-War War
Movies; Big Battles; Civil
War; Korean War;
Persian Gulf War;
Postwar; POW/MIA;
Revolutionary War;
Terrorism; Veterans;
Vietnam War; World War
I; World War II*
The Adventures of the Flying
   Cadets
The Alamo▶
The Alamo: Thirteen Days to
   Glory
Alexander Nevsky▶
Alexander the Great
Alone Against Rome
Alsino and the Condor▶
Anna Karenina
Atlas
The Avenger
Ay, Carmela!▶
Ballad of a Soldier▶
Battle Hell
The Battle of Algiers▶
The Battle of Austerlitz
The Beast
Beau Geste▶
Behind the Front
Behold a Pale Horse
Benjamin Argumedo
The Bitter Tea of General
   Yen▶
The Buccaneer
Bugles in the Afternoon

A Bullet for the General
By Dawn's Early Light
Captain Caution
Captain Horatio Hornblower▶
Carthage in Flames
Cast a Giant Shadow
Cavalry Command
Chapayev▶
The Charge of the Light
   Brigade▶
The Charge of the Light
   Brigade
Civilization▶
Codename: Terminate
Colonel Wolodyjowski
The Conqueror
Conquest of the Normans
Coup de Grace
The Court Martial of Billy
   Mitchell▶
Cromwell
Cup Final
Danton▶
Days of Hell
Deadline
The Desert of the Tartars
Devil Wears White
Distant Drums
Doctor Zhivago▶
Dragon Seed
Eagles Attack at Dawn
1860
El Cid▶
El Paso Stampede
El Rey
Elizabeth of Ladymead▶
Emissary
The Enchanted Cottage
The End of St. Petersburg▶
The Expendables
The Fall of the Roman
   Empire▶
Field of Honor
The Fighter▶
Fighting Marines
Fighting Pilot
The Fighting Prince of
   Donegal
The Finest Hour
Fire Over England▶
The Firing Line
Flor Silvestre
Flowers of Reverie
Forever and a Day▶
Fort Apache▶
Forty Days of Musa Dagh
The Four Feathers▶
The Four Feathers
F.P. 1
Funny, Dirty Little War
Guerilla Brigade
Gunga Din▶
Guns at Batasi
Hail the Conquering Hero▶
Harry's War
Heart of a Nation▶
Heartbreak Ridge▶
Hearts & Armour
Heaven & Earth▶
Hell in the Pacific▶
Hell on the Battleground
Hell Raiders
Henry V▶
Hero Bunker
The Hidden Fortress▶
Hill 24 Doesn't Answer▶
Holy Terror
Homecoming▶
How I Won the War
In the Name of the Pope-
   King▶
The Informer▶
The Invincible Gladiator
Johnny Got His Gun
Judith of Bethulia▶
Khartoum
Killers
Kolberg
La Chamuscada
La Marseillaise▶
La Nuit de Varennes▶
La Trinchera

La Venganza del Rojo
The Last Command
The Last of the Mohicans
The Last of the Mohicans▶
The Last Valley
Late Summer Blues
Latino
Laughing at Life
Legion of Missing Men
The Life and Death of Colonel
   Blimp▶
Lion of the Desert▶
The Longest Day▶
The Lost Command
The Lost Idol/Shock Troop
Mademoiselle Fifi
Man from the Alamo▶
Man with a Cross
Massive Retaliation
Megaforce
Mercenary Fighters
Mission to Glory
Mission to Kill
The Mongols
The Moonraker
Mother▶
Mountain Fury
The Mouse That Roared▶
Napoleon▶
An Occurrence at Owl Creek
   Bridge/Coup de Grace
Old Gringo
One Night Stand▶
Orphans of the Storm▶
The Phantom Planet
Port Arthur
Prehistoric Bimbos in
   Armageddon City
The Pride and the Passion
Project: Alien
Rage to Kill
The Rape of the Sabines
The Real Glory▶
A Reason to Live, A Reason
   to Die
The Rebellious Reign
The Red and the Black▶
The Red and the White▶
Red Dawn
Reds▶
Reign of Terror
Revenge of the Barbarians
Rhodes
Ride to Glory
River of Unrest
Ryan's Daughter
Saga of the Vagabond
Salome, Where She Danced
Sanders of the River▶
Scarlet Dawn
Senso▶
Seven Indignant
The Seventeenth Bride
Shake Hands with the Devil▶
The Shame▶
She Wore a Yellow Ribbon▶
Simon Bolivar
Sinai Commandos
Smugglers
Something of Value▶
Storm Over Asia▶
Striker
Surprise Attack
The Tempest/The Eagle▶
This Island Earth
The 317th Platoon▶
Tiger Joe
Time to Kill
Torn Allegiance
Treasure of the Lost Desert
The Ugly American
Under Fire▶
The Uprising▶
Vera Cruz
Villa Rides
Walker
War and Peace
War and Peace▶
War Bus Commando
Warbirds
Waterloo
Weekend War

Wild Geese 2
The World Owes Me a Living
World War III
Yank in Libya
Young Winston▶
Zulu Dawn▶

Wedding Bells

*see also Marriage;
Wedding Hell*
Betsy's Wedding
The Bride Came C.O.D.
The Bride Walks Out
Date Bait
Easy Money
Father of the Bride▶
Father of the Bride
Foolin' Around
For Better and For Worse
Four Weddings and a
   Funeral▶
Full of Life
Hard Promises
Honeymoon in Vegas
House Party 3
Housesitter
The Jewel of the Nile
Lovers and Other Strangers▶
Murders in the Rue Morgue
The Philadelphia Story▶
Prelude to a Kiss
Royal Wedding▶
She's Having a Baby
30-Foot Bride of Candy Rock
A Wedding
Wedding Band
The Wedding March▶
The Wedding Party
Wedding Rehearsal
When Harry Met Sally▶
The World's Oldest Living
   Bridesmaid

Wedding Hell

*see also Marriage;
Wedding Bells*
Black Vampire
Blood Bride
The Blood Spattered Bride
The Bride
The Bride & the Beast
The Bride of Frankenstein▶
Bride of Killer Nerd
Bride of Re-Animator
Bride of the Gorilla
Bride of the Monster
The Bride Wore Black▶
Brides of the Beast
The Brides Wore Blood
The Catered Affair▶
Cheatin' Hearts
The Graduate▶
He Knows You're Alone
Highway to Hell
Honeymoon
Honeymoon Horror
Honeymoon Killers▶
I Married a Monster from
   Outer Space
My New Gun
The Newlydeads
Niagara
The Perfect Bride
True Love▶
The Wedding Banquet▶
Wedding in Blood▶
Wedding in White

Werewolves

An American Werewolf in
   London▶
Black Werewolf
Blood of Dracula's Castle
Bride of the Gorilla
Children of the Full Moon
The Company of Wolves▶
The Craving
Cry of the Werewolf
Curse of the Devil
Curse of the Queerwolf
The Curse of the Werewolf

Deathmoon
Dr. Jekyll and the Wolfman
Dr. Jekyll vs. the Werewolf
Dr. Terror's House of Horrors
Dracula vs. Frankenstein
Face of the Screaming
   Werewolf
Frankenstein Meets the
   Wolfman▶
Full Eclipse
The Fury of the Wolfman
Hercules, Prisoner of Evil
House of Frankenstein
The Howling▶
Howling 2: Your Sister is a
   Werewolf
Howling 3: The Marsupials
Howling 4: The Original
   Nightmare
Howling 6: The Freaks
I Was a Teenage Werewolf
Legend of the Werewolf
The Legend of the Wolf
   Woman
Lone Wolf
The Mad Monster
Meridian: Kiss of the Beast
Monster Dog
The Monster Squad
Moon of the Wolf
My Mom's a Werewolf
Night of the Howling Beast
Orgy of the Dead
The Rats are Coming! The
   Werewolves are Here!
Return of the Vampire
Silver Bullet
Teen Wolf
Teen Wolf Too
The Undying Monster
Werewolf in a Girl's Dormitory
Werewolf of London
Werewolf of Washington
The Werewolf vs. the Vampire
   Woman
Werewolves on Wheels
Wolf
Wolf Blood
The Wolf Man▶
Wolfen▶
The Wolfman

Western Comedy

*see also Comedy;
Westerns*
Adios Amigo
Along Came Jones▶
The Apple Dumpling Gang
The Apple Dumpling Gang
   Rides Again
Bad Man's River
Ballad of Cable Hogue▶
Bang Bang Kid
The Beautiful Blonde from
   Bashful Bend
Blazing Saddles▶
Bordello
Border Phantom
Boss
Bowery Buckaroos
Branded Men
Bronco Billy
Bus Stop▶
Carry On Cowboy
Cat Ballou▶
Catlow
Check & Double Check
The Cheyenne Social Club
The Cisco Kid
City Slickers▶
City Slickers 2: The Legend of
   Curly's Gold
Cold Feet
The Cowboy Way
Desperate Women
Destry Rides Again▶
The Duchess and the
   Dirtwater Fox
El Diablo Rides
Four Eyes and Six Guns
Four for Texas
The Frisco Kid

From Noon Till Three
Go West
Goin' South▶
Gold Raiders
The Good Guys and the Bad Guys
Greaser's Palace
Great Scout & Cathouse Thursday
Gun Crazy
The Hallelujah Trail
Hangman's Knot
Hearts of the West▶
I'm from Arkansas
The Incredible Rocky Mountain Race
The Kid Brother▶
Life & Times of Judge Roy Bean
Lightning Jack
Lincoln County Incident
Local Badman
Maverick
McLintock!▶
More Wild, Wild West
The Nervous Wreck▶
Oklahoma Kid▶
The Paleface
Pardners
Pocket Money
Rancho Deluxe▶
Ride 'Em Cowboy
The Rounders
Rustler's Rhapsody
Samurai Cowboy
The Scalphunters
Scandalous John
September Gun
The Shakiest Gun in the West
Shame, Shame on the Bixby Boys
Son of Paleface▶
Sting of the West
Support Your Local Gunfighter▶
Support Your Local Sheriff▶
Take Me Back to Oklahoma
Texas▶
Texas Across the River
Texas Layover
There was a Crooked Man▶
They Call Me Trinity
Three Godfathers▶
Ticket to Tomahawk
Trinity is Still My Name
Under Montana Skies
The Villain
Wackiest Wagon Train in the West
Wagons East
Waterhole #3
Way Out West▶
Wild & Wooly
Wild Horse Phantom
Wild Rovers
The Wistful Widow of Wagon Gap
Yellow Hair & the Fortress of Gold

Westerns

see also Spaghetti Western; Western Comedy
Abilene Town▶
Aces and Eights
Aces Wild
Across the Plains
Adios Gringo
Adios, Hombre
The Adventures of Gallant Bess
Adventures of Kit Carson
Adventures of Red Ryder
Against A Crooked Sky
The Alamo▶
Alias Billy the Kid
Alias John Law
Allegheny Uprising
Along the Great Divide
Along the Sundown Trail
Alvarez Kelly
Ambush at Tomahawk Gap

Ambush Trail
American Empire
Americano
And God Said to Cain
Angel and the Badman▶
Animal Called Man
Annie Oakley▶
Another Man, Another Chance
Another Pair of Aces: Three of a Kind▶
Any Gun Can Play
Apache
Apache Blood
Apache Chief
Apache Kid's Escape
Apache Rose
Apache Uprising
Apache Woman
Apaches Last Battle
Apocalipsis Joe
The Appaloosa
Arizona
Arizona Badman
Arizona Bound
Arizona Bushwackers
Arizona Cowboy
Arizona Days
Arizona Gangbusters
Arizona Kid
Arizona Mahoney
Arizona Raiders
Arizona Roundup
Arizona Stagecoach
Arizona Terror
Arizona Whirlwind
Arrowhead
At Gunpoint
Backfire
Bad Company▶
Bad Day at Black Rock▶
Bad Girls
Bad Guys
Bad Jim
Bad Lands
Bad Man of Deadwood
Bad Men of the Border
The Badlanders
Badman's Territory▶
Badmen of Nevada
Ballad of a Gunfighter
Ballad of Gregorio Cortez▶
The Ballad of Little Jo
Bandera Bandits
Bandit King of Texas
Bandit Queen
Bandits
Bandolero!
Bar-20
Barbarosa▶
The Bargain
Baron of Arizona▶
Battle of Elderbush Gulch
Battling Marshal
Battling Outlaws
Battling with Buffalo Bill
Belle Starr
Bells of Coronado
Bells of Rosarita
Bells of San Angelo
Bells of San Fernando
Below the Border
Bend of the River▶
Beneath Arizona Skies/ Paradise Canyon
Best of the Badmen
Between Fighting Men
Between God, the Devil & a Winchester
Between Men
Beyond the Law
Beyond the Rockies
Big Calibre
The Big Cat
Big Country
A Big Hand for the Little Lady
Big Jake
Big Show
The Big Sky▶
The Big Sombrero
Big Stakes
The Big Stampede

Big Trail▶
Big Valley
Billy the Kid
Billy the Kid in Texas
Billy the Kid Returns
Billy the Kid Trapped
Bite the Bullet▶
Black Hills
The Black Lash
Black Market Rustlers
Blazing Guns
Blood at Sundown
Blood for a Silver Dollar
Blood on the Moon
Bloody Trail
Blue
Blue Canadian Rockies
Blue Steel
Boiling Point
The Boldest Job in the West
Bonanza
Bonanza: The Return
Boot Hill Bandits
Boothill Brigade
Boots & Saddles
Boots of Destiny
Border Badmen
Border Bandits
Border Caballero
Border Devils
Border Feud
Border Law
The Border Legion
Border Patrol
Border Rangers
Border Romance
Border Roundup
Border Saddlemates
Border Shootout
Border Vengeance
Border Vigilantes
Bordertown Gunfighters
Born in America
Boss Cowboy
Boss of Bullion City
Boss of Rawhide
The Bounty Man
Brand of Fear
Brand of Hate
Brand of the Outlaws
Branded
Branded a Coward
Brandy Sheriff
The Bravados▶
Breakheart Pass
Breed of the Border
Broadway to Cheyenne
Broken Arrow
Broken Lance▶
Bronson's Revenge
Bronze Buckaroo
Brothers of the West
Brothers O'Toole
Buck and the Preacher
Buckeye and Blue
Buckskin
Buckskin Frontier
Buffalo Bill
Buffalo Bill & the Indians▶
Buffalo Bill Rides Again
Buffalo Rider
Buffalo Stampede
Bugles in the Afternoon
Bull of the West
Bulldog Courage
Bullet Code
Bullet for Sandoval
A Bullet for the General
Bullwhip
The Burning Hills
Bury Me Not On the Lone Prairie
The Bushwackers
Butch and Sundance: The Early Days
Butch Cassidy and the Sundance Kid▶
Buzzy Rides the Range
Cahill: United States Marshal
Cain's Cutthroats
Calamity Jane
California Joe

Call of the Canyon
Call of the Forest
Call of the Rockies
Calling Wild Bill Elliott
Captain Apache
The Captive: The Longest Drive 2
The Capture▶
The Caravan Trail
The Cariboo Trail
Carson City Kid
Cattle Queen of Montana
Cavalcade of the West
Cavalier of the West
Cavalry
Cavalry Charge
Cavalry Command
Challenge of McKenna
Charro!
Chato's Land
Check Your Guns
Cheyenne Autumn
Cheyenne Kid
Cheyenne Rides Again
Cheyenne Takes Over
Child of the Prairie
Chino
The Chisholms
Chisum
The Christmas Kid
Chuka
Cimarron
Circle Canyon
Circle of Death
The Cisco Kid
Clearing the Range
Code of the Fearless
Colorado
Colorado Serenade
Colorado Sundown
Colt Comrades
Colt is My Law
Comancheros▶
Come On, Cowboys
Come On Danger!
Come On Rangers
Come On Tarzan
Comes a Horseman
Conagher
The Concentratin' Kid
Conquest of Cochise
Copper Canyon
Coroner Creek
Cotter
Courage of the North
Courageous Avenger
Courtin' Wildcats
The Covered Wagon
Covered Wagon Days
Covered Wagon Trails
Cow Town
Cowboy
Cowboy & the Bandit
Cowboy & the Senorita
Cowboy Commandos
Cowboy Counselor
Cowboy Millionaire
The Cowboys▶
Cowboys from Texas
Cowboys of the Saturday Matinee
Coyote Trails
Crazy Horse and Custer: "The Untold Story"
The Crimson Trail
Crooked Trail
Crossfire
Culpepper Cattle Co.
Custer's Last Fight
Custer's Last Stand
Cyclone of the Saddle
Dakota
Dakota Incident
Dan Candy's Law
Danger Ahead
Danger Trails
Daniel Boone
Daniel Boone: Trail Blazer
Daring Danger
Dark Command▶
Dawn on the Great Divide
Dawn Rider

Dawn Rider/Frontier Horizon
Dead for a Dollar
Dead Man's Revenge
Dead or Alive
Deadly Companions
The Deadly Trackers
Deadwood
Deadwood Pass
Death of a Gunfighter
Death Rides the Plains
Death Rides the Range
Death Valley
Death Valley Manhunt
Death Valley Rangers
The Deerslayer
Demon for Trouble
The Denver & Rio Grande
Deputy Marshall
Desert Gold
Desert Guns/Six-Shootin' Sheriff
Desert Phantom
Desert Snow
Desert Trail
Desperados
The Desperados
Devil & Leroy Basset
Devil Horse
Devil Riders
Devil's Canyon
The Devil's Mistress
Diamond Trail
Disciple
Distant Drums
Django
Django Shoots First
Doctor Quinn, Medicine Woman
Dodge City▶
Don Amigo/Stage to Chino
Don Daredevil Rides Again
Donner Pass: The Road to Survival
The Doolins of Oklahoma
Doomed at Sundown
Doomed Caravan▶
Down Dakota Way
Down Mexico Way
Down Texas Way
Down the Wyoming Trail
Draw!
Drift Fence
The Drifter
The Driftin' Kid
Driftin' River
Drum Beat
Drum Taps
Drums Along the Mohawk▶
Dude Bandit
Dude Ranger
Duel at Diablo▶
Duel in the Eclipse
Duel in the Sun▶
Duelo en el Dorado
Duke: The Films of John Wayne
Durango Valley Raiders
Dynamite and Gold
Dynamite Canyon
Dynamite Pass
Dynamite Ranch
Eagle's Wing
El Ametralladora
El Ciclon
El Condor
El Diablo
El Dorado▶
El Forastero Vengador
El Fugitivo
El Gallo de Oro
El Gavilan Pollero
El Hombre de la Furia
El Paso Stampede
El Robo al Tren Correo
El Sabor de la Venganza
El Zorro Vengador
The Electric Horseman
Enemy of the Law
Escape from Fort Bravo
Every Man's Law
Extreme Prejudice
Eyes of Texas

Westerns

False Colors
Fangs of Fate
Far Country▶
Far Frontier
Fargo Express
Fast Bullets
Fastest Guitar Alive
Fastest Gun Alive▶
Feud Maker
Feud of the Trail
Feud of the West
The Fiddlin' Buckaroo
$50,000 Reward
Fight for Gold
Fightin' Ranch
Fighting Caballero
Fighting Caravans
Fighting Champ
Fighting Cowboy
Fighting Fists of Shanghai Joe
Fighting Fool
Fighting Jack
The Fighting Kentuckian
The Fighting Legion
Fighting Mad
The Fighting Marshal
Fighting Parson
The Fighting Redhead
Fighting Renegade
Fighting Shadows
The Fighting Sheriff
The Fighting Stallion▶
Fighting Texans
Fighting Thru
The Fighting Trooper
Fighting Valley
Fighting Vigilantes
Fighting with Kit Carson
Finger on the Trigger
Firecreek
The First Movie Cowboy
Fistful of Death
Five Card Stud
Flame of the Barbary Coast
Flaming Bullets
Flaming Frontiers
Flaming Lead
Flaming Star▶
Flesh and the Spur
Forbidden Trails
Forlorn River
Fort Apache▶
The Forty-Niners
Four Faces West
Four Rode Out
Frontier Days
Frontier Fugitives
Frontier Horizon
Frontier Justice
Frontier Law
Frontier Outlaws
Frontier Pony Express
Frontier Scout
Frontier Uprising
Frontier Vengeance
The Frontiersman
Fuerte Perdido
The Fugitive: Taking of Luke McVane
Fugitive Valley
The Gallant Fool
Galloping Dynamite
Galloping Romeo
The Gambler Returns: The Luck of the Draw
The Gambling Terror
Gangster's Den
Gangsters of the Frontier
Garringo
The Gatling Gun
The Gay Ranchero
Gene Autry Matinee Double Feature #1
Gene Autry Matinee Double Feature #2
Gene Autry Matinee Double Feature #3
Gentle Savage
The Gentleman from California
Gentleman from Dixie
Gentleman from Texas

The Gentleman Killer
Geronimo
Geronimo: An American Legend
Geronimo's Revenge
Get That Girl
Ghost City
Ghost Patrol
Ghost Rider
Ghost Town
Ghost Town Gold
Ghost Town Law
Ghost Town Renegades
Ghost Town Riders
Ghost Valley
Ghostriders
Girl from Calgary
Girl of the Golden West
Git Along Little Dogies
The Glory Trail
God's Country and the Man
God's Gun
The Golden Stallion
Gone with the West
The Good, the Bad and the Ugly▶
Gore Vidal's Billy the Kid
Grand Canyon Trail
The Grand Duel
Grayeagle
Great Day in the Morning
The Great Gundown
Great Jesse James Raid
Great Missouri Raid
The Great Northfield Minnesota Raid
Great Treasure Hunt
Gun Code
Gun Fight at Red Sands
Gun Fury
Gun Glory
Gun Grit
Gun Law
Gun Lords of Stirrup Basin
Gun Packer
Gun Play
The Gun Ranger
Gun Riders
Gun Smugglers/Hot Lead
A Gunfight
Gunfight at Sandoval
Gunfight at the O.K. Corral▶
The Gunfighter▶
The Gunfighters
Gunfire
Gunman from Bodie
Gunners & Guns
Gunplay
Guns for Dollars
Guns in the Dark
Guns of Diablo
Guns of Fury
Guns of Justice
Guns of the Law
Guns of the Magnificent Seven
The Gunslinger
Gunslinger
Gunsmoke: Return to Dodge
Gunsmoke Trail
The Half-Breed
Hands Across the Border
The Hanged Man
The Hanging Tree▶
Hannie Caulder
Hard Hombre
Harlem on the Prairie
Harlem Rides the Range
Harmony Trail
Harry Tracy
The Harvey Girls▶
Haunted Gold
Haunted Ranch
Hawaiian Buckaroo
The Hawk of Powder River
Hawken's Breed
Headin' for the Rio Grande
Heart of Texas Ryan
Heart of the Golden West
Heart of the Rio Grande
Heart of the Rockies
Heaven's Gate

Hell Fire Austin
Helldorado
Heller in Pink Tights
Hellfire
Hell's Hinges
Helltown
Heritage of the Desert
Heroes of the Alamo
Heroes of the Hills
Heroes of the West
Hidden Gold
Hidden Guns▶
Hidden Valley
High Lonesome
High Noon▶
High Noon: Part 2
High Plains Drifter
Hills of Oklahoma
Hills of Utah
Hired Hand
His Brother's Ghost
His Fighting Blood
His Name was King
Historia de un Gran Amor
Hit the Saddle
Hittin' the Trail
Hombre▶
Home in Oklahoma
Homesteaders of Paradise Valley
Honor of the Range
Hopalong Cassidy▶
Hopalong Cassidy: Borrowed Trouble
Hopalong Cassidy: Dangerous Venture
Hopalong Cassidy: False Paradise
Hopalong Cassidy: Hoppy's Holiday
Hopalong Cassidy: Renegade Trail
Hopalong Cassidy: Riders of the Deadline
Hopalong Cassidy: Silent Conflict
Hopalong Cassidy: Sinister Journey
Hopalong Cassidy: The Dead Don't Dream
Hopalong Cassidy: The Devil's Playground
Hopalong Cassidy: The Marauders
Hopalong Cassidy: Unexpected Guest
Hoppy Serves a Writ
Horizons West
Hostile Guns
Hot Lead
Hour of the Gun
How the West was Won▶
Hurricane Express
I Shot Billy the Kid
I Shot Jesse James▶
I Will Fight No More Forever▶
Idaho
In Old Caliente
In Old California
In Old Cheyenne
In Old Colorado
In Old Montana
In Old New Mexico
In Old Santa Fe
In the Days of the Thundering Herd & the Law & the Outlaw
The Indian Fighter▶
Indian Paint
Indian Uprising
Into the Badlands
Invitation to a Gunfighter
The Jayhawkers
Jeremiah Johnson▶
Jesse James▶
Jesse James at Bay
Jesse James Meets Frankenstein's Daughter
Jesse James Rides Again
Jesse James Under the Black Flag
Joe Kidd

John Wayne Anthology: Star Packer/Lawless Range
Johnny Guitar▶
Johnny Reno
Jory
Joshua
Jubal
Jubilee Trail
Judge Roy Bean
Junior Bonner▶
Justice of the West
Justice Rides Again
Justicia para los Mexicanos
The Kansan
Kansas Pacific
The Kansas Terrors
Keep the Change
Kenny Rogers as the Gambler
Kenny Rogers as the Gambler, Part 2: The Adventure Continues
Kenny Rogers as the Gambler, Part 3: The Legend Continues
The Kentuckian
Kentucky Rifle
Kid Courageous
Kid from Gower Gulch
Kid Ranger
Kid Vengeance
Kid's Last Ride
The King and Four Queens
King of the Bullwhip
King of the Cowboys
King of the Grizzlies
King of the Pecos
King of the Rodeo
King of the Sierras
King of the Stallions
King of the Texas Rangers
King of the Wild Horses▶
Kit Carson
Knights of the Range
La Ley del Revolver
The Lamb
Land of Hunted Men
Land of the Lawless
Land Raiders
Laramie Kid
Last Bullet
The Last Command
Last Days of Frank & Jesse James
Last Frontier
Last Gun
The Last Hunt
Last of the Clintons
Last of the Comanches
The Last of the Mohicans
Last of the Pony Riders
Last of the Warrens
Last of the Wild Horses
The Last Outlaw
Last Outlaw
The Last Outlaw
The Last Ride of the Dalton Gang
The Last Tomahawk
Last Train from Gun Hill▶
The Law and Jake Wade
Law and Lawless
Law and Order
Law of the Land
Law of the Lash
Law of the Pampas
Law of the Saddle
Law of the Texan
The Law Rides
The Law Rides Again
Law West of Tombstone
Lawless Frontier
Lawless Range
A Lawless Street
Lawman▶
A Lawman is Born▶
Lawmen
Leather Burners
The Left-Handed Gun▶
Legend of Alfred Packer
Legend of Earl Durand
The Legend of Frank Woods
Legend of Frenchie King

The Legend of Jedediah Carver
Legend of the Lone Ranger
Legion of the Lawless
The Light of Western Stars
Lightnin' Carson Rides Again
Lightning Bill
Lightning Bill Crandall
Lightning Raiders
Lightning Range
Lightning Strikes West
Lightning Warrior
Lights of Old Santa Fe
Lion's Den
Little Big Horn
Little Big Man▶
Little Moon & Jud McGraw
Loaded Pistols
The Lone Avenger
Lone Bandit
The Lone Defender
Lone Justice
The Lone Ranger
Lone Ranger
Lone Ranger and the Lost City of Gold
The Lone Rider in Cheyenne
The Lone Rider in Ghost Town
Lone Star
Lone Star Law Men
The Lone Star Ranger
Lone Wolf McQuade
Lonely are the Brave▶
Lonely Man
Lonely Trail/Three Texas Steers
Lonesome Dove▶
Lonesome Trail
The Long Riders▶
The Longest Drive
Los Apuros de Dos Gallos
Los Asesinos
Los Hermanos Centella
Los Hermanos Diablo
Los Jinetes de la Bruja
Los Sheriffs de la Frontera
Lost Canyon
Love Desperados
Lucky Cisco Kid
Lucky Luke: Daisy Town
Lucky Luke: The Ballad of the Daltons
Lucky Terror
Lucky Texan
Lust for Gold
The Lusty Men▶
Macho Callahan
MacKenna's Gold
Madron
The Magnificent Seven▶
Major Dundee
A Man Alone
Man & Boy
A Man Called Horse▶
A Man Called Sledge
Man from Button Willow
Man from Cheyenne
Man from Colorado
The Man from Gun Town
The Man from Hell
Man from Hell's Edges
The Man from Laramie▶
Man from Montana
Man from Monterey
The Man from Music Mountain
The Man from Painted Post
The Man from Snowy River
Man from Texas
Man from the Alamo▶
The Man from Thunder River
Man from Utah
Man of Action
Man of the Forest
Man of the West
Man or Gun
Man Who Loved Cat Dancing
The Man Who Shot Liberty Valance▶
Man Without a Star▶
Manchurian Avenger
The Manhunt

Manos Torpes
Man's Country
Man's Land
Mariachis
Mark of the Spur
Marked for Murder
Marked Trails
Marshal of Cedar Rock
Marshal of Heldorado
The Marshal's Daughter
The Masked Rider
Mason of the Mounted
Maverick Queen
Maverick: The Collector's Edition
McCabe & Mrs. Miller▶
The McMasters
The Meanest Men in the West
Melody of the Plains
Melody Ranch
Melody Trail
Mesquite Buckaroo
Minnesota Clay
Miracle in the Wilderness
The Miracle Rider
Missouri Breaks
Missourians
Mr. Horn
Mohawk
Molly & Lawless John
Montana
Montana Belle
Monte Walsh▶
Mosby's Marauders
Mountain Justice
The Mountain Men
Murder on the Yukon
My Darling Clementine▶
My Heroes Have Always Been Cowboys
My Outlaw Brother
My Pal, The King
My Pal Trigger
Mysterious Desperado
Mysterious Desperado/Rider From Tucson
The Mysterious Rider
Mystery Man
Mystery Mountain
Mystery of the Hooded Horseman
Mystery Ranch
Mystery Trooper
Naked Hills
Naked in the Sun
The Naked Spur▶
Narrow Trail▶
Navajo Joe
Near the Rainbow's End
'Neath Canadian Skies
'Neath the Arizona Skies
Ned Kelly
Nevada
Nevada City
Nevada Smith
The Nevadan
The New Frontier
Nido de Aguilas
Night of the Grizzly
Night Rider
Night Riders of Montana
Night Stage to Galveston
Night Time in Nevada
The Nine Lives of Elfego Baca
No Man's Law
No Man's Range
North of the Border
North of the Great Divide
Oath of Vengeance
Oh Susannah
Oklahoma Annie
Oklahoma Badlands
Oklahoma Cyclone
The Oklahoman
Old Barn Dance
Old Corral
On the Night Stage
On the Old Spanish Trail
On Top of Old Smoky
One-Eyed Jacks▶
100 Rifles
One Little Indian

Only the Valiant
Oregon Trail
Outcast
The Outlaw
Outlaw Country
The Outlaw Deputy
Outlaw Express
Outlaw Fury
Outlaw Gang
The Outlaw Josey Wales▶
Outlaw Justice
Outlaw of the Plains
Outlaw Roundup
Outlaw Rule
The Outlaw Tamer
Outlaw Trail
Outlaw Women
Outlaws of Sonora
Outlaws of the Desert
Outlaws of the Range
Outlaw's Paradise
Overland Mail
Overland Stage Raiders▶
The Ox-Bow Incident▶
Painted Desert
The Painted Stallion
Pair of Aces
Pale Rider▶
Pals of the Range
Pals of the Saddle
Panamint's Bad Man
Pancho Villa
Pancho Villa Returns
Pardon My Gun
Paroled to Die
Partners of the Trail
Passion
Pat Garrett & Billy the Kid▶
Pecos Kid
Peter Lundy and the Medicine Hat Stallion
The Phantom Bullet
The Phantom Empire
Phantom Gold
The Phantom of the Range
Phantom of the West
Phantom Patrol
Phantom Rancher
Phantom Ranger
The Phantom Rider
Phantom Thunderbolt
Pinto Canyon
Pinto Rustlers
Pioneer Marshal
Pioneer Woman
The Pioneers
Pistoleros Asesinos
A Place Called Glory
The Plainsman
The Pocatello Kid
The Pony Express
Pony Express▶
Pony Express Rider▶
Pony Post
Posse▶
Powdersmoke Range
Prairie Badmen
The Prairie King
Prairie Moon
Prairie Pals
The Prairie Pirate
The Professionals▶
The Proud and the Damned
Proud Men
Proud Rebel▶
Public Cowboy No. 1
Purple Vigilantes
Pursued▶
The Quick and the Dead
Quigley Down Under
Racketeers of the Range
Rage at Dawn
Raiders of Red Gap
Raiders of Sunset Pass
Raiders of the Border
Rainbow Ranch
Rainbow's End
Ramrod
The Ramrodder
Rancho Notorious▶
Randy Rides Alone
Range Busters

Range Feud
The Range Feud/Two Fisted Law
Range Law
Range Renegades
Range Rider
Range Riders
Rangeland Empire
Rangeland Racket
Ranger and the Lady
Ranger's Roundup
The Rangers Step In
Rangers Take Over
The Rare Breed
Rattler Kid
Rawhide
Rawhide▶
Rawhide Mail
Rawhide Romance
A Reason to Live, A Reason to Die
Red Desert
Red Garters
Red Headed Stranger
Red River▶
Red River Valley
Red Rock Outlaw
The Red Rope
Red Sun
Redwood Forest Trail
Renegade Girl
Renegade Ranger/Scarlet River
Renegade Trail
Renfrew of the Royal Mounted
Renfrew on the Great White Trail
The Restless Breed
The Return of a Man Called Horse
Return of Draw Egan
Return of Frank James▶
Return of Jesse James
The Return of Josey Wales
Return of the Bad Men
Return of the Lash
Return of the Seven
Return of Wildfire
Return to Lonesome Dove
Return to Snowy River▶
Revenge of the Virgins
The Revenge Rider
Ride 'Em Cowgirl
Ride Him, Cowboy▶
Ride in the Whirlwind
Ride Lonesome
Ride, Ranger, Ride
Ride the High Country▶
Ride the Man Down
Ride the Wind
Ride to Glory
Rider from Tucson
Rider of the Law
Riders of Death Valley
Riders of Destiny
Riders of Pasco Basin
Riders of the Desert
Riders of the Purple Sage
Riders of the Range
Riders of the Range/Storm Over Wyoming
Riders of the Rockies
Riders of the Timberline
Riders of the West
Riders of the Whistling Pines
Riders of the Whistling Skull
Ridin' Down the Canyon
Ridin' on a Rainbow
Ridin' the California Trail
Ridin' the Lone Trail
Ridin' the Trail
Ridin' Thru
The Riding Avenger
Riding On
Riding Speed
Riding the Sunset Trail▶
The Riding Tornado
Rim of the Canyon
Rimfire
Rin Tin Tin, Hero of the West
Rio Bravo▶

Rio Conchos▶
Rio Diablo
Rio Grande▶
Rio Grande Raiders
Rio Hondo
Rio Lobo
Rio Rattler
River of No Return
Road Agent
The Roamin' Cowboy
Roamin' Wild
Roarin' Lead
Roaring Guns
Roaring Ranch
Roaring Six Guns
Robbery Under Arms
Robin Hood of Texas
Robin Hood of the Pecos
Rock River Renegades
Rockwell: A Legend of the Wild West
Rocky Mountain Rangers
Rodeo Girl
Rogue of the Range
Rogue of the Rio Grande
Roll Along Cowboy
Roll on Texas Moon
Roll, Wagons, Roll
Rollin' Plains
Romance on the Range
Rooster Cogburn
Rootin' Tootin' Rhythm
Rose of Rio Grande
Rough Night in Jericho
Rough Riders of Cheyenne
Rough Riders' Roundup
Rough Ridin' Rhythm
Rough Riding Rangers
Round-Up Time in Texas
Rounding Up the Law
Run of the Arrow
Running Wild
Rustler's Hideout
Rustlers of Red Dog
Rustler's Paradise
Rustler's Valley
The Sacketts
Sacred Ground
Saddle Buster
Saddle Mountain Round-Up
Saga of Death Valley
Sagebrush Law
Sagebrush Trail▶
Salute to the "King of the Cowboys," Roy Rogers
San Antonio
San Fernando Valley
Sandflow
Santa Fe Bound
Santa Fe Marshal
Santa Fe Stampede
Santa Fe Trail
Santa Fe Uprising
Santee
Sartana's Here...Trade Your Pistol for a Coffin
Savage Guns
Savage Journey
Savage Wilderness
Scalps
The Searchers▶
Sergeant Rutledge▶
Seven Cities of Gold
Seven Sixgunners
Seventh Cavalry
The Shadow Riders
Shadows of Death
Shalako
Shane▶
She Wore a Yellow Ribbon▶
Sheriff of Tombstone
Shine on, Harvest Moon
Shoot the Living, Pray for the Dead
Shoot the Sun Down
The Shooting▶
The Shootist▶
Shotgun
The Showdown
Showdown
Showdown at Boot Hill
Showdown at Williams Creek

Silent Code
Silent Tongue
Silent Valley
Silver Bandit
Silver City Bonanza
Silver City Kid
Silver Lode
Silver Queen
Silver River
Silver Spurs
Silver Stallion
Silver Star
Silverado▶
Sing, Cowboy, Sing
Singing Buckaroo
Six Gun Gospel
Six Gun Rhythm
Six Shootin' Sheriff
Sky Bandits
Sky High
Slaughter Trail
Smoke in the Wind
Smokey Smith
Soldier Blue
The Sombrero Kid
Somewhere in Sonora
Son of a Gun
Son of God's Country
Son of the Morning Star▶
Song of Arizona
Song of Nevada
Song of Old Wyoming
Song of Texas
Song of the Gringo
Song of the Trail
Songs and Bullets
Sonora Stagecoach
Sons of Katie Elder▶
Sons of the Pioneers
South of Monterey
South of St. Louis
South of Santa Fe
South of the Border
South of the Rio Grande
Southward Ho!
Spirit of the West
Springfield Rifle
Springtime in the Rockies
Springtime in the Sierras
Spurs
Square Dance Jubilee
Stage to Mesa City
Stagecoach▶
Stagecoach
Stagecoach to Denver
The Stalking Moon
Standing Tall
The Star Packer
Station West▶
Storm Over Wyoming
Storm Rider
Stormy Trails
Straight Shooter
Straight Shootin'
The Stranger from Pecos
The Stranger Wore a Gun
Stranger's Gold
Strawberry Roan
Sudden Death
Sundance and the Kid
Sundown Fury
Sundown Kid
Sundown Riders
Sundown Saunders
Sunrise Trail
Sunset
Sunset in El Dorado
Sunset on the Desert
Sunset Range
Sunset Serenade
Sunset Trail
Susanna Pass
Sweet Georgia
Swifty
Talion
Tall in the Saddle
The Tall Men
The Tall T
Taste of Death
Telegraph Trail
Tell Them Willie Boy Is Here▶
Ten Wanted Men

Tennessee's Partner
Tension at Table Rock
Terror of Tiny Town
Terror Trail
Test of Donald Norton
Tex Rides with the Boy
  Scouts
Texas Bad Man
Texas Buddies
Texas Cyclone
Texas Gunfighter
Texas Guns
Texas Jack
Texas John Slaughter:
  Geronimo's Revenge
Texas John Slaughter:
  Stampede at Bitter Creek
Texas Justice
Texas Kid
Texas Lady
Texas Legionnaires
Texas Masquerade
Texas Pioneers
The Texas Rangers
Texas Terror
Texas to Bataan
Texas Trouble
Texas Wildcats
They Died with Their Boots
  On▶
Thousand Pieces of Gold▶
Three Bullets for a Long Gun
Three Desperate Men
Three Faces West
Three in the Saddle
3:10 to Yuma▶
Three Texas Steers
Three Violent People
Three Word Brand
The Throwback
Thunder in God's Country
Thunder in the Desert
Thunder Mountain
Thunder Over Texas
Thunder Pass
Thunder River Feud
Thundering Gunslingers
Thundering Trail
Timber Terrors
Tin Star▶
The Tioga Kid
To the Last Man
Today We Kill, Tomorrow We
  Die
Toll Gate
Toll of the Desert
Tom Horn
Tom Mix Compilation 1
Tom Mix Compilation 2
Tombstone▶
Tombstone Canyon
Tombstone Terror
Tonto Basin Outlaws
The Tonto Kid
The Topeka Terror
The Tracker
The Trackers
Trail Beyond
Trail Drive
Trail of Robin Hood
Trail of Terror
Trail of the Hawk
Trail of the Mounties
Trail of the Silver Spurs
Trail Riders
Trail Street
Trailin'
Trailing Double Trouble
Trailing Trouble
Trails West
Train Robbers
Train to Tombstone
The Traitor
Tramplers
Treasure of Pancho Villa
Tribute to a Bad Man▶
Trigger, Jr.
Trigger Men
Trigger Pals
Trigger Tricks
The Trigger Trio

Triumphs of a Man Called
  Horse
Trouble Busters
Trouble in Texas
True Grit▶
Tulsa▶
Tumbledown Ranch in
  Arizona
Tumbleweed Trail
Tumbleweeds▶
Twice a Judas
Twilight in the Sierras
Twilight on the Rio Grande
Twilight on the Trail
Two Fisted Justice
Two-Fisted Justice
Two-Fisted Law
Two Gun Man
Two-Gun Man from Harlem
Two-Gun Troubador
Two Mules for Sister Sara▶
Two Rode Together
Ulzana's Raid▶
The Undefeated
Under California Stars
Under Nevada Skies
Under Western Stars
Undercover Man
Underground Rustlers
The Unforgiven▶
Unforgiven▶
Uninvited
The Unknown Ranger
Up River
Utah
Utah Trail
Valdez is Coming
Valley of Fire
Valley of Terror
Valley of the Lawless
Valley of the Sun▶
Vanishing American
Vanishing Legion
The Vanishing Westerner
Vengeance Valley
Vigilantes of Boom Town
Villa Rides
The Violent Men
Virginia City▶
The Virginian
The Virginian
Wagon Master▶
Wagon Tracks
Wagon Trail
Wagon Wheels
Wall Street Cowboy
The Walloping Kid
Wanda Nevada
Wanted: Dead or Alive
War of the Wildcats
The War Wagon▶
Warlock▶
Water Rustlers
Way of the West
The Way West
Welcome to Blood City
West of Nevada
West of Pinto Basin
West of the Divide
West of the Law
West of the Pecos
West to Glory
Western Double Feature 1
Western Double Feature 1:
  Wild Bill & Sunset Carson
Western Double Feature 2
Western Double Feature 2:
  Wayne & Hale
Western Double Feature 3
Western Double Feature 3:
  Rogers & Allen
Western Double Feature 4
Western Double Feature 4:
  Rogers & Evans
Western Double Feature 5
Western Double Feature 5:
  Rogers & Autry
Western Double Feature 6:
  Rogers & Trigger
Western Double Feature 7:
  Wild Bill & Crabbe

Western Double Feature 8:
  Hale & Carradine
Western Double Feature 9:
  LaRue & Beery
Western Double Feature 10:
  Roy, Dale, & Trigger
Western Double Feature 11
Western Double Feature 12
Western Double Feature 13
Western Double Feature 14
Western Double Feature 15
Western Double Feature 16
Western Double Feature 17
Western Double Feature 18
Western Double Feature 19
Western Double Feature 20
Western Double Feature 21
Western Double Feature 22
Western Double Feature 23
Western Double Feature 24
Western Double Feature 25
Western Frontier
Western Justice
Western Mail
Western Pacific Agent
Western Trails
Western Union▶
The Westerner▶
Westward Ho
Westward Ho, the Wagons!
Westward the Women▶
When a Man Rides Alone
When a Man Sees Red
When the Legends Die▶
When the West Was Young
Where the North Begins
Where Trails Divide
Where Trails End
Whirlwind Horseman
Whistlin' Dan
Whistling Bullets
White Apache
The White Buffalo
White Comanche
White Eagle
White Gold▶
The Wild Bunch▶
Wild Country
The Wild Country
Wild Frontier
Wild Horse
Wild Horse Canyon
Wild Horse Rodeo
Wild Mustang
Wild Times
Wild West
Wild, Wild West Revisited
Wild Women
Wildfire
Will Penny▶
Winchester '73▶
The Wind▶
Winds of the Wasteland
Winners of the West
Winning of the West
With Kit Carson Over the
  Great Divide
Without Honors
Wolf Call
Wolfheart's Revenge
The Woman of the Town
Wrangler
Wyatt Earp▶
Wyoming Outlaw
Yellow Dust
The Yellow Rose of Texas
Yodelin' Kid From Pine Ridge
Young Bill Hickok
Young Blood
Young Buffalo Bill
Young Guns
Young Guns 2
Yukon Flight
Yuma
Zachariah
Zandy's Bride
Zorro Rides Again
Zorro's Black Whip
Zorro's Fighting Legion

Wild Kingdom

see also *Birds; Cats;*
Dinosaurs; Insects; Killer
Beasts; Killer Bugs; King
of Beasts (Dogs); Sea
Critter Attack; Wilderness
The Adventures of Tarzan
Africa Texas Style
All Creatures Great and
  Small▶
Andre
Animal Farm▶
Bambi▶
The Barefoot Executive
The Bear▶
The Bears & I
The Beast that Killed Women
Beastmaster
Beastmaster 2: Through the
  Portal of Time
Beasts
Bedtime for Bonzo
The Belstone Fox
Black Cobra
Bless the Beasts and Children
Born Free▶
The Brave One▶
A Breed Apart
Bringing Up Baby▶
Buffalo Rider
Bugs Bunny Superstar
Call of the Wild
Captive Wild Woman
The Carnivores
Catch as Catch Can
Charlie, the Lonesome Cougar
Cheetah
Christian the Lion
The Chronicles of Narnia
Clarence, the Cross-eyed
  Lion▶
Courage of the North
A Cry in the Dark▶
A Cry in the Wild▶
Dark Age
Darkest Africa
Day of the Animals
The Day of the Dolphin
Doctor Dolittle
Dumbo▶
Eaten Alive
Ele, My Friend
The Electric Horseman
Elephant Boy▶
Every Which Way But Loose
Eyes of the Panther
The Fifth Monkey
Flight of the Grey Wolf
Flipper▶
The Fox and the Hound▶
Francis Goes to the Races
Francis in the Navy
Francis Joins the WACs
Francis the Talking Mule▶
Frasier the Sensuous Lion
Free Willy
Futz
Gaiety
Gentle Giant
Going Ape!
Going Bananas
The Golden Seal
Goldy: The Last of the Golden
  Bears
Goldy 2: The Saga of the
  Golden Bear
Goliathon
Gorilla
Gorillas in the Mist▶
The Great Adventure▶
The Great Rupert▶
Grizzly Adams: The Legend
  Continues
Gus
Harry and the Hendersons
Hatari!▶
Hawmps!
High Country Calling
In the Shadow of Kilimanjaro
Island of Lost Souls▶
Island of the Blue Dolphins

Jungle
The Jungle Book▶
Jungle Drums of Africa
King Kung Fu
King of the Grizzlies
Lassie, Come Home
Lassie: The Miracle
The Last Safari
Legend of Lobo
Leonard Part 6
The Lion King▶
Living Free
Matilda
Max, Mon Amour
The Misadventures of Merlin
  Jones
Mr. Kingstreet's War
Monkeys, Go Home!
Monkey's Uncle
The Monster and the Girl
Mountain Family Robinson
Mountain Man
Mouse and His Child
Murders in the Rue Morgue
My Sister, My Love
Napoleon and Samantha▶
Never Cry Wolf▶
Night of the Grizzly
Nikki, the Wild Dog of the
  North
Once Upon a Forest
Operation Haylift
Pardon My Trunk
Pet Sematary 2
Pippi Longstocking
Planet of the Apes▶
The Polar Bear King
Project X
Razorback
Red Earth
The Rescuers▶
The Rescuers Down Under
Ring of Bright Water▶
Rock-a-Doodle
Rogue Lion
Rub a Dub Dub
The Runaways
Sammy, the Way-Out Seal
The Secret of NIMH▶
Shakma
Shaolin Traitor
The Silver Streak▶
Soul of the Beast
Stalk the Wild Child
Starring Bugs Bunny!
A Summer to Remember
Super Seal
Survival of Spaceship Earth
Tarka the Otter
The Tender Warrior
Those Calloways
Thumbelina▶
A Tiger Walks
Time of the Apes
Tomboy & the Champ
Trap on Cougar Mountain
Vampire Circus
Vanishing Wilderness
Walk Like a Man
Watership Down
Whale of a Tale
When the North Wind Blows
When the Whales Came
The White Buffalo
White Gorilla
White Pongo
Wild Horses
Wolfen Ninja
The Yearling▶
Zebra in the Kitchen

Wilderness

see also *Good Earth;*
Trees & Forests
Abducted
Across the Great Divide
The Adventures of Frontier
  Fremont
The Adventures of the
  Wilderness Family
The Alaska Wilderness
  Adventure

All Mine to Give
Backwoods
Beyond Fear
Black Robe▶
Blood Brothers
The Bridge to Nowhere
Bullies
Cajon Pass
The Capture of Grizzly Adams
Claws
Clearcut
Cold River
Continental Divide
Davy Crockett and the River
   Pirates
Davy Crockett, King of the
   Wild Frontier▶
Death Hunt
Earthling
Edge of Honor
Eyes of Fire
The Fatal Glass of Beer
Ferngully: The Last Rain
   Forest
Flight from Glory
Further Adventures of the
   Wilderness Family, Part 2
God's Country
Goldy 2: The Saga of the
   Golden Bear
Great Adventure
The Great Outdoors
Grizzly
Grizzly Adams: The Legend
   Continues
Heaven on Earth
Hunter's Blood
Ice Palace
Jeremiah Johnson▶
Just Before Dawn
Kid Colter
The Legend of Wolf Mountain
Life & Times of Grizzly Adams
Lost
Lost in the Barrens
Man in the Wilderness
Mountain Charlie
Mountain Family Robinson
Mountain Man
Napoleon and Samantha▶
Northwest Passage▶
Northwest Trail
Orion's Belt
Orphans of the North
Quest for Fire▶
Shoot to Kill▶
Silence
Silence of the North
Slashed Dreams
Sourdough
Spirit of the Eagle
Starbird and Sweet William
The Tale of Ruby Rose▶
Tales of the Klondike: In a Far
   Country
Tales of the Klondike: Race
   for Number One
Tales of the Klondike: The
   Scorn of Women
Tales of the Klondike: The
   Unexpected
Timber Queen
Tundra
Vanishing Prairie▶
Vanishing Wilderness
Violent Zone
The Voyage of Tanai
White Fang▶
White Fang and the Hunter
The White Tower▶
White Water Summer
Whitewater Sam
Young & Free

Witchcraft

   see also **Demons &**
   Wizards; Occult
Bell, Book and Candle
Bewitched
Beyond Darkness
Black Magic
Black Sunday▶

Burn Witch, Burn!▶
Cast a Deadly Spell▶
The Conqueror Worm▶
Cry of the Banshee
The Curse of the Crying
   Woman
Curse of the Devil
Daughters of Satan
Day of Wrath▶
The Day the Earth Froze
Demon Witch Child
The Demons
The Devils▶
Devonsville Terror
Dr. Strange
Eye of the Demon
Eyes of Fire
The Haunted Palace
The Haunting of Morella
Hercules, Prisoner of Evil
Hocus Pocus
Horror Hotel
Horror Rises from the Tomb
The Hospital▶
I Married a Witch▶
Inquisition
Kill, Baby, Kill▶
Lisa and the Devil
Lost Legacy: A Girl Called
   Hatter Fox
Love at Stake
Maciste in Hell
Mark of the Devil
Mark of the Devil 2
My Little Pony: The Movie
The Naked Witch
Netherworld
The Polar Bear King
The Resurrected
Return to Oz
Season of the Witch
The She-Beast
The Shrieking
Something Weird
Sorceress▶
The Terror
Terror Beach
That Darn Sorceress
Three Sovereigns for Sarah
The Touch of Satan
Troll 2
The Undead▶
The Virgin Witch
Warlock
Warlock Moon
Warlock: The Armageddon
The Werewolf vs. the Vampire
   Woman
Wicked Stepmother
The Witch
Witch Who Came from the
   Sea
A Witch Without a Broom
Witchcraft
Witchcraft 3: The Kiss of
   Death
Witchcraft 4: Virgin Heart
Witchery
The Witches▶
Witches' Brew
Witches' Mountain
The Witches of Eastwick
The Witchmaker
The Witch's Mirror
WitchTrap
The Wizard of Oz▶
The Woman Who Came Back
The Worst Witch

Women

   see also **Dream Girls;**
   Femme Fatale; Women in
   Prison; Wonder Women
Accidental Meeting
Alice Doesn't Live Here
   Anymore
Anna▶
Another Way▶
Another Woman▶
Antonia and Jane▶
Arizona

The Astounding She-Monster
Bachelor Mother▶
The Ballad of Little Jo
Beaches▶
Blood and Sand▶
Blood Games
Blue De Ville
Born in Flames
The Bostonians
A Bunny's Tale
Business as Usual
Camilla▶
Cave Girls
Certain Fury
Challenge of a Lifetime
Chantilly Lace
The Children's Hour
China Beach▶
City Without Men
Claire of the Moon
The Color Purple▶
Come Back to the Five &
   Dime Jimmy Dean, Jimmy
   Dean▶
Commissar▶
Crazy Mama
Crimes of the Heart
Cry of the Werewolf
Daisy Miller
A Dangerous Woman
Darktown Strutters
Daughters of the Dust▶
The Day the Women Got Even
Defenseless
Dirty Dishes▶
Doctor Quinn, Medicine
   Woman
A Doll's House
A Doll's House▶
Double Obsession
Dreams
Early Summer▶
Easy Virtue
Eating
Ebony Dreams
Eleanor: First Lady of the
   World
Empty Suitcases
Enchanted April
Enid is Sleeping
Enormous Changes▶
Even Cowgirls Get the Blues
The Execution
Family Secrets
Feds
Fire in the Night
Flatbed Annie and Sweetiepie:
   Lady Truckers
Fran
Francis Joins the WACs
Fried Green Tomatoes▶
Gangs, Inc.
Gas Food Lodging▶
A Geisha▶
Gentlemen Prefer Blondes▶
Girlfriends▶
The Group
The Happy Ending
Hard Country
Head of the Family
Heat and Dust▶
Heaven and Earth
Hellcats
Horror of the Zombies
House of Whipcord
Household Saints▶
How to Marry a Millionaire
In This House of Brede▶
The Insect Woman▶
Island of Lost Girls
Jamon, Jamon
Je Tu Il Elle
The Joy Luck Club▶
Joy Ride to Nowhere
Juliet of the Spirits▶
Just Another Girl on the I.R.T.
Kamikaze Hearts
Keetje Tippei
The Ladies Club
Ladies on the Rocks
Late Chrysanthemums
A League of Their Own▶

Leaving Normal
The Legend of Blood Castle
Little Women▶
Little Women
Lola Montes▶
The Love Goddesses
Lumiere
Madame Bovary▶
Mademoiselle Striptease
Maedchen in Uniform▶
The Magic Bubble
Malou
Marilyn: The Untold Story▶
Mars Needs Women
Memories of Murder
Mi Vida Loca
Miles to Go
Miss All-American Beauty
Miss Firecracker▶
Monkey Grip▶
Mortal Thoughts
Moscow Does Not Believe in
   Tears▶
Mother & Daughter: A Loving
   War
My Brilliant Career▶
My Twentieth Century▶
9 to 5
Nomugi Pass
The Nun
One Sings, the Other Doesn't
The Opposite Sex
Oriane
Osaka Elegy
Overseas: Three Women with
   Man Trouble▶
Pancho Barnes
Passion Fish▶
Patti Rocks▶
Perfume
Poetic Justice
Poor Little Rich Girl: The
   Barbara Hutton Story
Portrait of a Showgirl
Portrait of Teresa▶
Prime Suspect▶
Prime Suspect 2▶
Pumping Iron 2: The Women
Queen of Diamonds
Question of Silence▶
Revenge of the Teenage
   Vixens from Outer Space
Rich and Famous
Rosa Luxemburg
Ruby in Paradise▶
Salmonberries
Samson vs. the Vampire
   Women
The Scent of Green Papaya▶
Sexual Intent
She-Devil
Sifted Evidence
The Sisterhood
Snapdragon
Sorceress▶
Spices▶
Stage Door▶
Star!
Steaming
Steel and Lace
Steel Magnolias▶
The Story of Qui Ju▶
The Story of Women▶
Strangers in Good Company▶
Strangers: The Story of a
   Mother and Daughter▶
Street of Shame▶
Stripper
Sudden Death
Sunset Strip
The Taxi Mystery
Tell Me Where It Hurts
Tender Comrade
Three Secrets
Tomorrow's Children
Trojan Women
Twenty-One
An Unmarried Woman▶
Unnatural
Utamaro and His Five Women
Visiting Hours
Viva Maria!

Walpurgis Night▶
Westward the Women▶
What's Love Got to Do With
   It?
When a Woman Ascends the
   Stairs
Whose Child Am I?
Widow's Peak
Wildrose▶
Witchfire
A Woman and a Woman
A Woman Named Jackie
A Woman Rebels
The Women▶
The Women of Brewster
   Place▶
Women on the Verge of a
   Nervous Breakdown▶
Working Girl▶
Working Girls▶

Women Cops

   see also **Cops**
Arizona Heat
Black Widow▶
Blue Steel
China O'Brien
Dear Detective
Do or Die
The Enforcer
Fatal Beauty
Get Christie Love!
L.A. Crackdown
L.A. Crackdown 2
Policewoman Centerfold
Policewomen
Prey of the Chameleon
Scorchy
The Silence of the Lambs▶
Silk 2
A Stranger Among Us
Tereza▶
V.I. Warshawski

Women in Prison

   see also **Exploitation;**
   Men in Prison;
   Sexploitation
Alien 3
Amazon Jail
Bad Girls Dormitory
Bad Girls in the Movies
The Big Bird Cage
The Big Bust Out
The Big Doll House
Born Innocent
Caged Fear
Caged Fury
Caged Heat
Caged in Paradiso
Caged Women
Chained Heat
Chained Heat 2
Chasers
The Concrete Jungle
Condemned to Hell
Convicted: A Mother's Story
Deadlock
Desperate Women
Escape from Cell Block 3
Escape from Hell
False Arrest
Girl on a Chain Gang
Girls in Chains
Girls in Prison
Girls Riot
Hot Box
Human Experiments
I Want to Live!▶
Ilsa, the Wicked Warden
Jailbird Rock
Ladies They Talk About
Lady in the Death House
Love Child
Lust for Freedom
Me & Veronica
Midnight
The Muthers
Naked Cage
Nightmare in Badham County
99 Women

Women

Off the Wall
Outside Chance
Playing for Time▶
Prison Stories: Women on the
  Inside▶
Prisoner Cell Block H
Purgatory
Red Heat
Reform School Girl
Reform School Girls
Savage Island
Scrubbers
Slammer Girls
Star Slammer
Sweet Sugar
10 Violent Women
Terminal Island
Vendetta
Violent Women
Women in Cell Block 7
Women in Fury
Women Unchained
Women's Prison Escape
Women's Prison Massacre

Wonder Women

see also Dream Girls

The Abductors
Act of Vengeance
Alien▶
Alien 3
Aliens▶
Alley Cat
The Amazons
Amazons
The American Angels:
  Baptism of Blood
Angel's Brigade
Annie Oakley
Attack of the 50 Foot Woman
Attack of the 50 Ft. Woman
Bad Georgia Road
Barbarian Queen
Barbarian Queen 2: The
  Empress Strikes Back
Basic Training
Batman Returns
Beauty for the Asking
Belle Starr
Big Bad Mama 2
The Big Bust Out
Billie
Bimini Code
The Bionic Woman
Blonde in Black Leather
Blonde Savage
Born in Flames
Buffy the Vampire Slayer▶
Bury Me an Angel
Business as Usual
China O'Brien 2
Chopper Chicks in
  Zombietown
The Clan of the Cave Bear
Cleopatra
Cleopatra Jones
Colossus and the Amazon
  Queen
Comes a Horseman
Conexion Mexico
Dance of Death
Danger Zone
The Deadly and the Beautiful
Deadly Weapons
Do or Die
The $5.20 an Hour Dream
Get Christie Love!
Girl from Calgary
Golden Lady
Golden Ninja Warrior
Grand Larceny
The Great Texas Dynamite
  Chase
Heartland▶
Hot Box
Hundra
I Spit on Your Grave
Invincible Barbarian
Kilma, Queen of the Amazons
Kisses for My President
L.A. Crackdown
La Femme Nikita▶

Lady Scarface
Lethal Woman
The Lost Empire
Mae West
Mame
Mankillers
Marie▶
Mind Trap
Mission of Justice
Mistress of the Apes
Moonshine County Express
Nancy Drew, Reporter
Night Partners
Not Without My Daughter
Nyoka and the Tigermen
Panther Squad
The Perils of Pauline
Phoenix the Warrior
Point of No Return
Prehistoric Women
Queen Boxer
Queen of the Road
Raiders of Sunset Pass
Resurrection▶
Roller Blade
Runaway Nightmare
Running Delilah
Sara Dane
Savage Beach
The Savage Girl
Savage Streets
See How She Runs▶
S*H*E
Sheena
She'll Be Wearing Pink
  Pajamas
She's in the Army Now
The Silence of the Lambs▶
Sister Kenny▶
Stormquest
Supergirl
Sweet Revenge
Switchblade Sisters
Terminal Velocity
Thor and the Amazon Women
Tiffany Jones
Trapped
Tulsa▶
Uncaged
Velvet Smooth
Venus the Ninja
Wild Women
The Wild World of Batwoman
Wolfen Ninja
A Woman Rebels
Wrestling Women vs. the
  Aztec Ape
Wrestling Women vs. the
  Aztec Mummy
Zorro's Black Whip

World War I

Ace of Aces
The African Queen▶
All Quiet on the Western
  Front▶
All Quiet on the Western Front
Anzacs: The War Down
  Under▶
Arsenal▶
The Big Parade▶
Biggles
The Blue Max
The Chaplin Revue
The Charge of the Model T's
Courage Mountain
Crimson Romance
Dark Journey▶
Darling Lili
Dawn Patrol▶
The Day that Shook the World
Devil in the Flesh▶
Dishonored
Dr. Mabuse the Gambler▶
Doughboys
Elizabeth of Ladymead▶
The End of St. Petersburg▶
A Farewell to Arms▶
Fifth Day of Peace
The Fighting 69th▶
Flambards
For Me and My Gal

The Four Horsemen of the
  Apocalypse▶
Gallipoli▶
Going Home
Grand Illusion▶
The Great War
Half-Shot at Sunrise
Heart of Humanity
Hearts of the World▶
Hell's Angels▶
Hotel Imperial
How Many Miles to Babylon?
An Indecent Obsession
Inside the Lines
The Iron Major
Island
Isn't Life Wonderful▶
Killing Floor
The King of Hearts▶
Lafayette Escadrille
The Land That Time Forgot
Lawrence of Arabia▶
The Life and Death of Colonel
  Blimp▶
Life and Nothing But▶
The Lighthorsemen▶
The Little American
The Lost Patrol▶
Man of Legend
Mata Hari▶
Mata Hari
Miracle of Our Lady of Fatima
Nicholas and Alexandra
1918
Nurse Edith Cavell▶
Paths of Glory▶
The Patriots▶
Q Ships
Return of the Soldier▶
Revolt of the Zombies
She Goes to War
Shopworn Angel▶
Shout at the Devil
Spy in Black▶
Suzy
Three Legionnaires
Tin Pan Alley
Today We Live
Tomorrow is Forever
Waterloo Bridge▶
Westfront 1918▶
What Price Glory?▶
When the Whales Came
The White Cliffs of Dover▶
Wilson▶
Wings
Wings of Eagles
Yankee Doodle in Berlin
Zeppelin

World War II

*see also Postwar; POW/
MIA*

Above and Beyond▶
Above Suspicion▶
Above Us the Waves▶
Abroad with Two Yanks
Across the Pacific▶
Action in Arabia
Action in the North Atlantic
Adventures of Smilin' Jack
Against the Wind
Air Force▶
Air Raid Wardens
Alan & Naomi
All My Sons▶
All Through the Night▶
The Americanization of
  Emily▶
And a Nightingale Sang
Angels One Five
Angry Harvest▶
The Annapolis Story
Another Time, Another Place
Another Time, Another Place▶
Anzio
Arch of Triumph▶
Arch of Triumph
Armored Command
Around the World
Ashes and Diamonds▶
The Assault▶

Assault on Agathon
The Assisi Underground
Attack Force Z
Attack Squadron
The Attic: The Hiding of Anne
  Frank
Au Revoir Les Enfants▶
Aventure Malgache
Away All Boats
Back Home
Back to Bataan
Background to Danger▶
Balkan Express
Bataan
Battle Cry▶
The Battle of Blood Island
Battle of Britain
Battle of China
The Battle of El Alamein
Battle of Neretva
The Battle of Russia
The Battle of San Pietro
Battle of the Bulge
Battle of the Commandos
Battle of the Eagles
The Battle of the Japan Sea
Battleforce
Battleground▶
Bear Island
Bedknobs and Broomsticks
Behind Enemy Lines
Berlin Express▶
The Best Years of Our Lives▶
Betrayal from the East
Betrayed▶
Between Heaven and Hell▶
The Big Lift
The Big Red One▶
Black Brigade
The Black Dragons
Black Rain▶
Blockhouse
The Blood of Others▶
Blood on the Sun
The Boat is Full▶
Bomb at 10:10
Bombardier
Bon Voyage
Border Street
The Boxer and Death▶
Brady's Escape
Brass Target
The Brave Bunch
Breakthrough
The Bridge at Remagen
The Bridge on the River
  Kwai▶
Bridge to Hell
A Bridge Too Far
Brief Encounter▶
Bugs & Daffy: The Wartime
  Cartoons
The Burmese Harp▶
Bye Bye Blues
The Caine Mutiny▶
Cairo
Campaign in Poland
A Canterbury Tale▶
The Canterville Ghost
Captain Newman, M.D.
Captains of the Clouds
Captive Heart▶
Captive Hearts
Carry On England
Carve Her Name with Pride
Casablanca▶
Casablanca Express
Catch-22▶
Caught in the Draft▶
Chain Lightning
Charlie Grant's War
Chicago Joe & the Showgirl
Children's Island
China Sky
Chips, the War Dog
Christ Stopped at Eboli▶
Christabel
Churchill and the Generals
Class of '44
Cloak and Dagger
The Clock▶
Closely Watched Trains▶

Code Name: Emerald
Cold Days
The Colditz Story
Combat!
Combat Killers
Come and See▶
Come See the Paradise▶
Command Decision
Commando Attack
Commando Squad
Commandos
Commandos Strike at Dawn
Conspiracy of Hearts▶
Convoy
Cornered▶
Corregidor
Cottage to Let
The Counterfeit Traitor▶
Cowboy Commandos
The Cranes are Flying▶
Crash Dive
Cross of Iron
Cruel Sea▶
Cry of Battle
D-Day, the Sixth of June▶
Dam Busters▶
Danger UXB
Dangerous Moonlight▶
Darby's Rangers
Das Boot▶
David▶
Dawn Express
The Day and the Hour
A Day in October
Day One▶
The Day Will Dawn▶
Days of Glory
Deadly Mission
Death is Called Engelchen▶
Death of a Soldier
The Death of Adolf Hitler
December
December 7th: The Movie
Deep Six
Desert Commandos
The Desert Fox▶
The Desert Rats▶
The Desert Tigers
Despair▶
Desperate Journey
Destination Tokyo
Destroyer▶
The Devil's Brigade
Diamonds of the Night▶
The Diary of Anne Frank▶
The Dirty Dozen▶
The Dirty Dozen: The Deadly
  Mission
The Dirty Dozen: The Fatal
  Mission
The Dirty Dozen: The Next
  Mission
Dirty Heroes
Distant Thunder▶
Distant Voices, Still Lives▶
Dive Bomber▶
The Dresser▶
Dressmaker
The Dunera Boys▶
The Eagle Has Landed▶
Ebony Dreams
Edge of Darkness▶
Elizabeth of Ladymead▶
The Elusive Corporal▶
Empire of the Sun▶
Enemy Below▶
Enemy of Women
Enigma Secret
Enola Gay: The Men, the
  Mission, the Atomic Bomb
Ensign Pulver
Era Notte a Roma▶
Escape from Sobibor▶
Escape to Athena
Europa, Europa▶
Every Time We Say Goodbye
The Execution
The Execution of Private
  Slovik▶
Eye of the Needle
Farewell to the King
Fat Man and Little Boy

Father▶
Father Goose
The Fifth Seal
Fight for the Title
Fight to the Death
Fighter Attack
Fighting Seabees
The Fighting Sullivans▶
Films by Peter Thompson
The Final Countdown▶
Fireball Forward
Fires on the Plain▶
First Yank into Tokyo
Five Fingers▶
Five for Hell
Flame to the Phoenix
Flat Top
Flying Leathernecks▶
Flying Tigers
For the Boys
Forbidden
Forbidden Games▶
Force 10 from Navarone
Foreign Correspondent
The Foreman Went to France
Fortunes of War▶
The Forty-Ninth Parallel▶
Forty Thousand Horsemen
Four Bags Full
The Four Horsemen of the
    Apocalypse
Four in a Jeep
Foxtrot
Frieda
A Friendship in Vienna
From Hell to Victory
From Here to Eternity▶
From Here to Eternity
G-Men vs. the Black Dragon
The Gallant Hours▶
Garden of the Finzi-Continis▶
Geheimakte WB1
Generale Della Rovere▶
A Generation▶
The Gift Horse
Go for Broke!
Golden Earrings
Great Day
The Great Escape▶
The Great Escape 2: The
    Untold Story
Green for Danger
The Green Glove
Greta▶
Guadalcanal Diary
Gung Ho!
The Guns of Navarone▶
Guns of War
A Guy Named Joe
The Gypsy Warriors
The Halls of Montezuma
The Hand
Hanna's War
Hanover Street
The Hasty Heart
The Heat of the Day
Hell Commandos
Hell is for Heroes▶
Hell River
Hell Squad
Hell to Eternity
Hellcats of the Navy
Hell's Brigade: The Final
    Assault
Heroes Die Young
Heroes in Hell
The Hiding Place
The Highest Honor
Hillbilly Blitzkrieg
Hiroshima Maiden
Hiroshima: Out of the Ashes▶
Hitler
Hitler: The Last Ten Days
Hitler's Children▶
Hollywood Canteen▶
Holocaust▶
Homecoming
Hope and Glory▶
The Horizontal Lieutenant
Hornet's Nest
Hotel Reserve▶
The Human Comedy▶

The Human Condition: A
    Soldier's Prayer▶
The Human Condition: No
    Greater Love▶
The Human Condition: Road
    to Eternity▶
Hunted!
Hunted
Hunters of the Golden Cobra
Hustler Squad
I See a Dark Stranger▶
I Was a Male War Bride▶
Identity Unknown
Ike
Immortal Battalion▶
Immortal Sergeant
The Imperial Japanese Empire
Imperial Navy
In a Shallow Grave
In Harm's Way
In Which We Serve▶
The Incident▶
The Incredible Mr. Limpet
The Inheritors
Inside the Third Reich
Is Paris Burning?▶
Jenny's War
Jet Attack/Paratroop
    Command
Jive Junction
Joan of Paris▶
Journey for Margaret▶
Journey into Fear▶
Judgment at Nuremberg▶
Julia▶
Jungle Patrol
Kamikaze
Kanal▶
Kapo▶
Kelly's Heroes
The Key
The Key to Rebecca
Kindergarten▶
King Rat▶
Kings Go Forth
La Grande Vadrouille▶
Lassiter
The Last Bastion
The Last Chance▶
Last Day of the War
The Last Days of Patton
The Last Five Days
The Last Metro▶
The Last Train
The Last Warrior
Law of the Jungle
A League of Their Own▶
Leon Morin, Priest
Les Violons du Bal
Letters to an Unknown Lover
The Life and Death of Colonel
    Blimp▶
Lifeboat▶
The Lion Has Wings
The Little Thief▶
The Long Island Four
The Longest Day▶
The Lost One
A Love in Germany
MacArthur
MacArthur's Children▶
Malaya
Malta Story
A Man Called Sarge
A Man Escaped▶
The Man Who Never Was▶
Manhunt in the African Jungle
Manon
Map of the Human Heart
Maria's Lovers
Marine Raiders
Massacre in Rome
Max and Helen
The McConnell Story
McKenzie Break▶
The Mediterranean in Flames
Mediterraneo▶
Meet Sexton Blake
Mein Kampf
Memories of Hell
Memphis Belle▶

Memphis Belle: A Story of a
    Flying Fortress
The Men▶
Mephisto▶
Merrill's Marauders
Merry Christmas, Mr.
    Lawrence▶
A Midnight Clear▶
Midway
Miracle at Moreaux
The Miracle of the White
    Stallions
The Mirror▶
The Misfit Brigade
Mission Batangas
Mission Corbari
Mission of the Shark▶
Mrs. Miniver▶
Mr. Kingstreet's War
Mr. Klein▶
Mister Roberts▶
Mr. Skeffington▶
Mr. Winkle Goes to War
Monte Carlo
The More the Merrier▶
Morituri▶
The Mortal Storm▶
Mother of Kings
The Mountain Road
Murderers Among Us: The
    Simon Wiesenthal Story▶
Murphy's War
Music Box
Mussolini & I
My Name is Ivan▶
The Naked and the Dead
The Nasty Girl▶
The Navy Comes Through
Navy Way
Never So Few
Never Wave at a WAC
Night Ambush
Night of the Fox
The Night of the Shooting
    Stars▶
The Nightmare Years
No Greater Love
No Regrets for Our Youth▶
None But the Brave
The North Star▶
Nous N'Irons Plus au Bois
The Nun's Story▶
Objective, Burma!▶
The Odd Squad
Once Before I Die
Once Upon a Honeymoon
One Against the Wind▶
One of Our Aircraft Is
    Missing▶
One That Got Away▶
Only Way
Open City▶
Operation Amsterdam
Operation Cross Eagles
Operation Crossbow▶
The Oppermann Family
Overlanders▶
Pacific Inferno
Paisan▶
Panama Hattie
Passage to Marseilles▶
Patton▶
The Pawnbroker▶
The Philadelphia Experiment
Piece of Cake
Pimpernel Smith
Pin-Up Girl
Place in Hell
Playing for Time▶
Prelude to War
Prisoners of the Sun▶
Private Buckaroo
Private Contentment
PT 109
The Purple Heart
Pursuit of the Graf Spee
Qui Etes Vous, Mr. Sorge?
Racing with the Moon▶
Rage of Wind
Raggedy Man▶
Raid on Rommel
Raiders in Action

Raiders of Sunset Pass
Reach for the Sky
Rebel
The Reflecting Skin
Reunion▶
Reunion in France
The Revolt of Job▶
Rise and Fall of the Third
    Reich
Robot Pilot
Run Silent, Run Deep▶
Running Away
Saboteur▶
Sahara▶
Salo, or the 120 Days of
    Sodom
Salute John Citizen▶
San Demetrio, London
Sands of Iwo Jima▶
The Scarlet & the Black
Schindler's List▶
Sea Chase
The Sea Shall Not Have Them
Sea Wolves
The Search▶
Second Victory
The Secret Code
The Secret War of Harry Frigg
Seven Beauties▶
Seven Days' Leave
The Seventh Cross▶
Shadows Over Shanghai
Shell Shock
Sherlock Holmes and the
    Secret Weapon▶
Sherlock Holmes: The Voice
    of Terror
Shining Through
Ship of Fools▶
The Shop on Main Street▶
The Silent Enemy
Silent Raiders
Since You Went Away▶
Sink the Bismarck▶
633 Squadron
Ski Troop Attack
The Small Back Room▶
Snow Treasure
So This is Washington
Soldat Duroc...Ca Va Etre Ta
    Fete!
Soldier of Orange▶
A Soldier's Story▶
A Soldier's Tale
Somewhere I'll Find You▶
Son of Lassie
The Sorrow and the Pity▶
The Sound of Music▶
South Pacific
Special Forces
Spitfire▶
Spy Smasher Returns
S.S. Experiment Camp 2
SS Girls
Stage Door Canteen
Stalag 17▶
The Steel Claw
Strictly G.I.
Submarine Seahawk
Suicide Battalion/Hell Squad
Suicide Patrol
The Summer of My German
    Soldier▶
Sundown
Sweet Light in a Dark Room▶
Swing Shift
Tank Commando
Task Force
A Taste of Hell
The Teahouse of the August
    Moon
Tender Comrade
The Tenth Man
Thank Your Lucky Stars▶
That Long Night in '43
That Summer of White Roses
They Were Expendable▶
13 Rue Madeleine▶
Thirty Seconds Over Tokyo▶
Thirty-Six Hours of Hell
This is the Army
This Land is Mine▶

Thousands Cheer
Three Came Home▶
Tides of War
Tiger Fangs
A Time of Destiny
A Time to Love & a Time to
    Die
The Tin Drum▶
To Be or Not to Be▶
To Be or Not to Be
To Have & Have Not▶
To Hell and Back
To the Shores of Tripoli
Tobruk
Tomorrow is Forever
Tonight and Every Night
Too Late the Hero▶
Tora! Tora! Tora!
Torpedo Attack
Torpedo Run
Tower of Terror
The Train▶
Transport from Paradise
Triple Cross▶
Triple Echo
Triumph of the Spirit▶
Triumph of the Will
True Colors
Twelve O'Clock High▶
25 Fireman's Street▶
Two Girls and a Sailor▶
Two of Us▶
Two Women▶
U-Boat Prisoner
Under the Earth▶
The Underdog
Until They Sail
Up in Arms
Up Periscope
Victory
Von Ryan's Express▶
Voyage of the Damned▶
W Hour
Wackiest Ship in the Army
Wake Island▶
A Walk in the Sun▶
The Wannsee Conference▶
War & Love
War & Remembrance, Part 1
War & Remembrance, Part 2
War & Remembrance, Part 3
War & Remembrance, Part 4
War & Remembrance, Part 5
War & Remembrance, Part 6
War & Remembrance, Part 7
War & Remembrance: The
    Final Chapter, Part 8
War & Remembrance: The
    Final Chapter, Part 9
War & Remembrance: The
    Final Chapter, Part 10
War & Remembrance: The
    Final Chapter, Part 11
War & Remembrance: The
    Final Chapter, Part 12
The War Boy
War in the Sky▶
War Lover
War Victims
Warkill
Watch on the Rhine▶
Waterfront
We Dive at Dawn▶
We Will Not Enter the Forest▶
Wedding in White
Well-Digger's Daughter▶
What Did You Do in the War,
    Daddy?
When Hell Broke Loose
When Taekwondo Strikes
Where Eagles Dare▶
The White Cliffs of Dover▶
The White Rose▶
The Winds of War
A Wing and a Prayer▶
Wings Over the Pacific
The Wizard of Loneliness
Women of Valor
Wooden Horse▶
World War II: When Lions
    Roared
A Yank in Australia

A Yank in the R.A.F.
Yanks
You'll Never Get Rich▶
The Young Lions▶
Zero
Zero Pilot
Zone Troopers

Wrestling

...All the Marbles
The American Angels:
    Baptism of Blood
Bad Guys
Below the Belt
Body Slam
Grunt! The Wrestling Movie
Hadley's Rebellion
Invasion of the Zombies
La Corona de un Campeon
Life & Times of Captain Lou
    Albano
Mad Bull
Mugsy's Girls
My Breakfast with Blassie
No Holds Barred
The One and Only
Paradise Alley
Pin Down Girls
Samson in the Wax Museum
Summer's Games
Superargo
Take Down
Thunder & Mud
Vision Quest
Women in Love▶
The World According to
    Garp▶
The Wrestler
Wrestling Racket Girls
Wrestling Women vs. the
    Aztec Ape
Wrestling Women vs. the
    Aztec Mummy

Wrong Side of the Tracks

see also Rags to Riches
Aaron Loves Angela
Algiers▶
Alice Adams
Angel and the Badman▶
Angels with Dirty Faces▶
Anna Christie
Bachelor Party
Back Door to Heaven▶
Breaking Away▶
The Bride Wore Red
Camille▶
Cannery Row
Captains Courageous▶
Carbon Copy
Careful, He Might Hear You▶
Carrie▶
Cat Ballou▶
Chains
China Girl
Claudia
Cool As Ice
The Courtney Affair
Courtship▶
The Crucified Lovers▶
Cry-Baby▶
The Dark Side of Love
Diary of a Chambermaid▶
Dirty Dancing
Dr. Jack/For Heaven's Sake
Eegah!
Far and Away
Fire with Fire
The Flamingo Kid▶
Foxfire Light
Fresh Horses
Future Kill
Grease▶
The Great Gatsby
The Hairy Ape
Hearts of Humanity
Historia de un Gran Amor
Iron Maze
It
It Could Happen to You

It Happened One Night▶
Jersey Girl
Jungle Fever▶
King Ralph
The Lacemaker▶
Last Exit to Brooklyn▶
Liar's Moon
Little Minister▶
The Loves of Carmen
Luzia
The Man from Snowy River▶
Manhattan Melodrama▶
Masquerade▶
A Million to One
Min & Bill
My Forbidden Past
My Man Godfrey▶
Naked Youth
Night Beat
Nosotros
Off Beat
Outpost in Morocco
Over the Brooklyn Bridge
The Phantom in the House
Phantom of the Opera▶
Picnic on the Grass
A Place in the Sun▶
Pretty in Pink
Primrose Path
Princess Tam Tam▶
Probation
Pygmalion▶
Reckless
Reform School Girl
Return to Snowy River▶
Rich Girl
Riff Raff▶
Rocky▶
Room at the Top▶
Ruby Gentry
Rumble Fish▶
San Francisco▶
The Servant▶
sex, lies and videotape▶
Show People▶
Snow Country
Some Kind of Wonderful
Somebody Up There Likes
    Me▶
Stay Hungry▶
The Story of the Late
    Chrysanthemum▶
Suburbia
The Swan
The Swan▶
Sweet Light in a Dark Room▶
The Tamarind Seed
Tango
That Night
This Sporting Life▶
Tortilla Flat▶
A Tree Grows in Brooklyn▶
Under the Boardwalk
Uptown Angel
Valley Girl
The Valley of Decision▶
Virtue's Revolt
Vivacious Lady▶
Waterloo Bridge▶
White Palace
The White Sin
The World of Suzie Wong
The Young Philadelphians▶

You Lose, You Die

see also Post Apocalypse
Arena
Death Race 2000
Deathrow Gameshow
Mad Max: Beyond
    Thunderdome
Naked Warriors
Prayer of the Rollerboys
Robot Jox
Roller Blade
Roller Blade Warriors: Taken
    By Force
Rollerball
The Running Man
Solarbabies
Tron

Yuppie Nightmares

**see also Strained
    Suburbia**
Addams Family Values
Alice▶
Almost You
Amos and Andrew
Baby Boom
Bad Influence
Barbarians at the Gate▶
Bare Essentials
Bedroom Eyes
Beetlejuice▶
The Big Chill▶
Blind Date
Blind Side
The Boost
Bright Lights, Big City
Cape Fear▶
City of Hope▶
Clara's Heart
Clean and Sober▶
Coma▶
Consenting Adults
Curly Sue
Dead Calm▶
Desperately Seeking Susan
Diary of a Mad Housewife▶
Down and Out in Beverly Hills
Drop Dead Fred
Edge of Honor
The End of Innocence
Eye of the Demon
Fatal Attraction▶
The Fisher King▶
Folks!
Fun with Dick and Jane
The Further Adventures of
    Tennessee Buck
Goodbye, New York
The Guardian
The Hand that Rocks the
    Cradle
The Hard Way▶
He Said, She Said
Heartburn▶
Hiding Out
In the Spirit
Indian Summer
Jungle Fever▶
Key Exchange
Kicks
L.A. Story▶
Let's Kill All the Lawyers
Limit Up
Looking for Mr. Goodbar
Lost in America▶
Love or Money?
Madhouse
Maid to Order
The Malibu Beach Vampires
Maniac
Micki & Maude
The Mighty Ducks
The Money Pit
Mother's Boys
Moving
My Daughter's Keeper
My New Gun
Neighbors
New Year's Day▶
Night of the Living Babes
Nothing But Trouble
Nothing in Common
Oasis of the Zombies
The Object of Beauty▶
Pacific Heights▶
Perfect Family
Permanent Vacation
Preppies
Private Benjamin
Quicksilver
Reversal of Fortune▶
Roadhouse 66
Rude Awakening
Ruthless People▶
St. Elmo's Fire
The Secret of My Success
September
sex, lies and videotape▶
Shattered

A Shock to the System▶
Six Degrees of Separation
Something Wild
Stay Tuned
Straw Dogs▶
Summer Rental
Taking Care of Business
Taking the Heat
The Temp
Three Men and a Little Lady
The Toxic Avenger, Part 3:
    The Last Temptation of
    Toxie
Trading Places
Trapped
Unlawful Entry
The Vagrant
Video Americana
Voodoo Dawn
Wall Street▶
The War of the Roses▶
Westworld▶
What About Bob?▶
When a Man Loves a Woman
Windy City
Wolf

Zombie Soldiers

see also Zombies
Akira Kurosawa's Dreams
The Dark Power
Deathdream
Hard Rock Zombies
Oasis of the Zombies
Revenge of the Zombies
Revolt of the Zombies
Scream and Scream Again
She Demons
Shock Waves
The Supernaturals
They Saved Hitler's Brain
The Zombie Army
Zombie Lake

Zombies

**see also Death & the
    Afterlife; Ghosts, Ghouls,
    & Goblins; Zombie
    Soldiers**
The Alchemist
Alien Massacre
The Astro-Zombies
Bowery at Midnight
Bride of Re-Animator
Carnival of Souls
Cast a Deadly Spell▶
Children Shouldn't Play with
    Dead Things
The Chilling
Chopper Chicks in
    Zombietown
C.H.U.D. 2: Bud the Chud
City of the Walking Dead
Creature of the Walking Dead
The Curse of the Aztec
    Mummy
Curse of the Screaming Dead
Dawn of the Dead▶
Dawn of the Mummy
Day of the Dead
Dead Alive
The Dead Don't Die
Dead Heat
Dead Men Don't Die
The Dead Next Door
Dead Pit
Death Becomes Her▶
The Death Curse of Tartu
Deathdream
Demon Wind
Destroyer
Devil Kiss
Ed and His Dead Mother
Evil Town
The Ghoul
The Hanging Woman
Haunting Fear
Hellgate
The Hereafter
Horror of the Zombies
Horror Rises from the Tomb

The House of Seven Corpses
House of the Dead
I Eat Your Skin
I Walked with a Zombie▶
Isle of the Dead
The Jitters
King of the Zombies
Kiss Daddy Goodbye
The Mad Ghoul
Messiah of Evil
The Mummy▶
Mummy & Curse of the Jackal
The Mummy's Revenge
My Boyfriend's Back
Neon Maniacs
Night Life
Night of Horror
Night of the Comet
Night of the Creeps
Night of the Death Cult
Night of the Ghouls
Night of the Living Babes
Night of the Living Dead▶
Night of the Living Dead
Night of the Living Dead, 25th
    Anniversary Documentary
Nightmare Weekend
Oasis of the Zombies
Orgy of the Dead
The Outing
Pet Sematary 2
Plan 9 from Outer Space
Prison
Quatermass 2▶
The Re-Animator▶
Redneck Zombies
Return of the Evil Dead
Return of the Living Dead
Return of the Living Dead 2
Return of the Living Dead 3
Revenge of the Dead
Revenge of the Living
    Zombies
Revenge of the Zombies
Revolt of the Zombies
The Robot vs. the Aztec
    Mummy
Seedpeople
Seven Doors of Death
Shock Waves
Sole Survivor
Steps from Hell
The Stuff
Svengali▶
Teenage Zombies
Tomb of the Undead
Tombs of the Blind Dead
Torture Chamber of Baron
    Blood
The Vampire's Ghost
Vengeance of the Zombies
Virgin Among the Living Dead
Voodoo Dawn
Voodoo Woman
The White Zombie▶
Winterbeast
Zombie
The Zombie Army
Zombie High
Zombie Island Massacre
Zombie Lake
Zombie Nightmare
Zombies of Moratau
Zombies of the Stratosphere
Zombies on Broadway
Zombiethon

The **KIBBLES INDEX** presents over 250 categories that defy traditional classification—it's a potpourri of movie trivia listing selected authors, playwrights, producers, special effects wizards, and composers, as well as miscellaneous categories like Amy Fisher biopics, top grossing films, four-bone delights, and "the so bad they're almost good" *Woof!* features. Like the category index, the terms are listed alphabetically. Following is a complete list of the categories:

Films Adapted from:
a Book
a Cartoon
a Fairy Tale
a Game
a Play or Musical
a Poem
a Song
a Story
an Article
an Opera
Memoirs or Diaries
Television
the Radio

Books to Film:
Louisa May Alcott
Eric Ambler
Hans Christian Andersen
Maya Angelou
Isaac Asimov
Jane Austen
Clive Barker
J.M. Barrie
Ambrose Bierce
Robert Bloch
Judy Blume
Ray Bradbury
Barbara Taylor Bradford
Pearl S. Buck
Frances Hodgson Burnett
Edgar Rice Burroughs
William Burroughs
Truman Capote
Barbara Cartland
Willa Cather

Raymond Chandler
Paddy Chayefsky
John Cheever
Anton Chekhov
Agatha Christie
Tom Clancy
Mary Higgins Clark
Arthur C. Clarke
James Clavell
Jackie Collins
Joseph Conrad
Pat Conroy
Robin Cook
James Fenimore Cooper
Stephen Crane
Michael Crichton
Clive Cussler
Miguel de Cervantes
Guy de Maupassant
Daniel Defoe
Charles Dickens
E.L. Doctorow
Fyodor Dostoyevski
Sir Arthur Conan Doyle
Daphne Du Maurier
Alexandre Dumas
Dominick Dunne
Bret Easton Ellis
Howard Fast
William Faulkner
Henry Fielding
F. Scott Fitzgerald
Gustov Flaubert
Ian Fleming
E.M. Forster
Frederick Forsyth

Rumer Godden
Nikolai Gogol
William Goldman
Elizabeth Goudge
Kenneth Grahame
Graham Greene
Zane Grey
John Grisham
Arthur Hailey
Alex Haley
Dashiell Hammett
Thomas Hardy
Harlequin Romances
Nathaniel Hawthorne
Ernest Hemingway
O. Henry
S.E. Hinton
Victor Hugo
Fanny Hurst
John Irving
Washington Irving
Susan Isaacs
Rona Jaffe
John Jakes
Henry James
James Jones
James Joyce
Franz Kafka
Stephen King
Rudyard Kipling
Dean R. Koontz
Judith Krantz
Louis L'Amour
D.H. Lawrence
John Le Carre
Harper Lee

Elmore Leonard
Sinclair Lewis
Astrid Lindgren
Jack London
H.P. Lovecraft
Robert Ludlum
Peter Maas
Alistair MacLean
Norman Mailer
W. Somerset Maugham
Colleen McCullough
Larry McMurtry
Herman Melville
James Michener
L.M. Montgomery
Vladimir Nabokov
Joyce Carol Oates
Marcel Pagnol
Edgar Allan Poe
Katherine Anne Porter
Mario Puzo
Harold Robbins
Sir Walter Scott
Sidney Sheldon
Mary Shelley
Danielle Steele
John Steinbeck
Stendahl
Robert Louis Stevenson
Bram Stoker
Harriet Beecher Stowe
Jacqueline Susann
Paul Theroux
James Thurber
J.R.R. Tolkien
Leo Tolstoy
Scott Turow
Mark Twain

John Updike
Leon Uris
Jules Verne
Kurt Vonnegut
Alice Walker
Edgar Wallace
Joseph Wambaugh
Evelyn Waugh
H.G. Wells
Edith Wharton
William Wharton
Oscar Wilde
Thornton Wilder
Virginia Woolfe
Herman Wouk

Plays to Film:
Horton Foote
Beth Henley
Eugene O'Neill
William Shakespeare
George Bernard Shaw
Neil Simon
Tom Stoppard
Tennessee Williams

Producers:
Robert Altman
William Castle
Coppola/American Zoetrope
Roger Corman/New World
Val Lewton
George Lucas
Merchant Ivory
Steven Spielberg
Troma Films
Andy Warhol
Universal Studios' Classic Horror

Special Effects:
Special FX Extravaganzas
Special FX Extravaganzas: Make-Up
Rick Baker
Rob Bottin
Anton Furst
Ray Harryhausen
Herschell Gordon Lewis
Tom Savini
Dick Smith
Douglas Trumball

Quality Check:
Classics
Disney Animated Movies
Disney Family Movies
4 Bones
Letterboxed Editions
Modern Shakespeare
Trash
Woofs!

Rip-Offs:
Alien & Rip-Offs
Basic Instinct & Rip-Offs
E.T. & Rip-Offs
Gremlins & Rip-Offs
Road Warrior & Rip-Offs

Miscellaneous:
Amy Fisher
BBC TV Productions
Family Viewing
Live Action/Animation Combos
Top Grossing Films of 1939-1992

KIBBLES INDEX

20 Highest Grossing Films of All Time

Back to the Future▶
Batman▶
Batman Returns
Beverly Hills Cop
The Empire Strikes Back▶
E.T.: The Extra-Terrestrial▶
The Exorcist▶
Ghost▶
Ghostbusters▶
Grease▶
Home Alone▶
Home Alone 2: Lost in New York
Indiana Jones and the Last Crusade▶
Indiana Jones and the Temple of Doom▶
Jaws▶
Raiders of the Lost Ark▶
Return of the Jedi▶
Star Wars▶
Terminator 2: Judgment Day▶
Tootsie▶

Adapted from a Book

Abduction
About Last Night...▶
Absolute Beginners
Accident
The Accidental Tourist▶
Acorn People
Across the Pacific▶
Act of Passion: The Lost Honor of Kathryn Beck
Adam Had Four Sons
Adorable Julia
Adventure
The Adventurers
The Adventures of Huck Finn▶
The Adventures of Huckleberry Finn
The Adventures of Huckleberry Finn
The Adventures of Robin Hood▶
The Adventures of Sadie
The Adventures of Sherlock Holmes: Hound of the Baskervilles
The Adventures of Tom Sawyer▶
The Adventures of Tom Sawyer▶
Advise and Consent▶
The African Queen▶
After Dark, My Sweet▶

After Julius
After the Thin Man▶
The Age of Innocence▶
The Agency
The Agony and the Ecstasy
Airport▶
Alan & Naomi
Ali Baba and the 40 Thieves▶
Alice▶
Alice Adams
Alice in Wonderland
Alice Through the Looking Glass
Alice to Nowhere
Alive
All About Eve▶
All Creatures Great and Small▶
All of Me
All Quiet on the Western Front▶
All Quiet on the Western Front
All the Brothers Were Valiant
All the King's Men▶
All the President's Men▶
All This and Heaven Too▶
Allan Quartermain and the Lost City of Gold
Altered States▶
Amazing Mr. Blunden
The Ambassador
The Ambush Murders
The American Friend▶
The Americanization of Emily▶
The Amityville Horror
The Amorous Adventures of Moll Flanders
Anastasia: The Mystery of Anna
Anatomy of a Murder▶
And the Band Played On▶
And Then There Were None▶
The Anderson Tapes▶
The Andersonville Trial▶
The Andromeda Strain
An Angel at My Table▶
Angel Heart
Angela▶
Angie
Animal Farm▶
Ann Vickers
Anna and the King of Siam▶
Anna Karenina▶
Anna Karenina
Anna to the Infinite Power
Anne of Avonlea▶
Anne of Green Gables▶
Another Thin Man▶
Anthony Adverse
Any Number Can Play
Anzio

Apocalypse Now▶
Appointment with Death
The Apprenticeship of Duddy Kravitz▶
Arch of Triumph▶
Arch of Triumph
Are You in the House Alone?
Armistead Maupin's Tales of the City
Around the World in 80 Days▶
The Arrangement
Arrowsmith
As Summers Die
Ashes and Diamonds▶
The Asphalt Jungle▶
The Assault▶
Assault at West Point: The Court-Martial of Johnson Whittaker
At Play in the Fields of the Lord▶
At Sword's Point
At the Earth's Core
The Atonement of Gosta Berling▶
The Attic: The Hiding of Anne Frank
Attica▶
Audrey Rose
Auntie Mame▶
The Autobiography of Miss Jane Pittman▶
Avalanche Express
Awakenings▶
Babar: The Movie
The Bachelor▶
Back Street
Background to Danger▶
Bad Day at Black Rock▶
Bad Ronald▶
Bambi▶
Band of Angels
Bang the Drum Slowly
Bang the Drum Slowly▶
Bank Shot▶
Barabbas
Barbarians at the Gate▶
Barjo
Barry Lyndon▶
The Bastard
The Bat▶
The Bat
The Bat Whispers
Battle Beyond the Stars
Battle Cry▶
The Bawdy Adventures of Tom Jones
Beachcomber▶
Beaches▶

The Bear▶
The Beast Within
Beau Geste▶
Being There▶
The Bell Jar
Ben-Hur▶
Berlin Alexanderplatz▶
The Best Years of Our Lives▶
Betrayal
The Betsy
Betty Blue▶
Between Friends
Beyond Innocence
Beulah Land
Bhowani Junction
The Bicycle Thief▶
The Big Fix▶
The Big Man: Crossing the Line▶
The Big Sky▶
The Big Sleep▶
Big Street
Billionaire Boys Club
Billy Bathgate
Billy Budd▶
Birdy▶
The Birth of a Nation▶
The Bitch
Bitter Moon
The Bitter Tea of General Yen▶
Black Arrow▶
Black Beauty▶
Black Like Me
The Black Marble▶
Black Narcissus▶
Black Robe▶
The Black Stallion▶
The Black Stallion Returns
Black Sunday
Blackboard Jungle▶
Blade Runner▶
Bless the Beasts and Children
Blockhouse
Blood and Roses
Blood and Sand
Blood Island
The Blood of Others▶
Blood on the Moon
Blood Relatives
Blue City
The Blue Max▶
The Body in the Library
Body Parts
The Body Snatcher▶
Boiling Point
The Bonfire of the Vanities▶
Bonjour Tristesse▶
Book of Love
Born Free▶

Born on the Fourth of July▶
The Borrowers▶
Borsalino▶
The Boston Strangler
Botany Bay
The Bourne Identity▶
Boxcar Bertha
The Boys from Brazil
Bram Stoker's Dracula
The Bramble Bush
Breakheart Pass
Brewster's Millions
The Bride of Frankenstein▶
The Bride of San Luis Rey▶
The Bridge on the River Kwai▶
The Bridges at Toko-Ri▶
A Brief History of Time▶
Bright Lights, Big City
Brighton Rock▶
The Brothers Karamazov▶
Buddy's Song
Bugsy▶
Bulldog Drummond
Bulldog Drummond's Secret Police
Bullitt▶
A Bunny's Tale
The Burning Hills
Burnt Offerings
Butterfield 8▶
Butterfly Ball
Cabeza de Vaca▶
Cadence
Call of the Wild
Camelot
Camille▶
Cancel My Reservation
Cannery Row
A Canterbury Tale▶
The Canterbury Tales
The Canterville Ghost
Cape Fear▶
Captain Blood▶
The Captain from Koepenick
Captain Horatio Hornblower▶
Captain Newman, M.D.
Captains Courageous▶
The Cardinal
Carlito's Way▶
Caroline?▶
The Carpetbaggers
Carrie▶
The Case of the Missing Lady
Cash McCall
Casino Royale
Cass Timberlane
The Castle▶
Cat Chaser

▲ 1179 • KIBBLES INDEX

Adapted

Catch-22►
Catholics►
Catlow
Celebrity
Chamber of Horrors
Champion►
Chapayev►
Charlotte's Web
Charly►
Cheech and Chong's, The Corsican Brothers
Cheers for Miss Bishop
Cheyenne Autumn
Child of Darkness, Child of Light
The Children
Children of Sanchez
Children of the Corn
Children of the Damned
Chilly Scenes of Winter
China Cry
China Seas►
China Sky
Chitty Chitty Bang Bang
The Chocolate War►
The Choirboys
Christ Stopped at Eboli►
Christine
A Christmas Carol
A Christmas Carol
The Christmas Wife
The Chronicles of Narnia
Cimarron
Cinderella
Circle of Two
The Citadel►
Citizen Cohn
The City and the Dogs►
City Boy►
City of Joy
Civil War Diary
The Clan of the Cave Bear
The Class of Miss MacMichael
Clear and Present Danger►
The Clergyman's Daughter
The Client
A Clockwork Orange►
Closely Watched Trains►
Cold Heaven
Cold Room
The Collector►
Colonel Wolodyjowski
The Color Purple►
Colossus: The Forbin Project►
Columbo: Prescription Murder►
Coma►
Come Along with Me
Come and Get It►
The Comedians
The Comfort of Strangers►
Commandos Strike at Dawn
Communion
Compromising Positions
Conagher
Confidentially Yours►
A Connecticut Yankee►
A Connecticut Yankee in King Arthur's Court
Conrack►
Consenting Adult
Conspirator
Contempt►
Cool Hand Luke►
Cop
The Corsican Brothers
Cotton Comes to Harlem►
Count Dracula
The Count of Monte Cristo
The Count of Monte Cristo
The Count of Monte Cristo
The Country Diary of an Edwardian Lady
Coup de Grace
The Courtship of Eddie's Father►
The Crackler
The Cradle Will Fall
Crainquebille►
Crazy in Love
Crime and Punishment
Crime and Punishment
Crimes at the Dark House►

Crisis at Central High►
Crooked Hearts►
Crossing Delancey►
The Crucifer of Blood
Crusoe►
A Cry for Love
A Cry in the Dark►
A Cry in the Night
The Cry of the Owl
Cry, the Beloved Country►
Cthulhu Mansion
Cujo
The Curse of Frankenstein►
Curse of the Demon►
Curse of the Headless Horseman
Curse of the Yellow Snake
Cyrano de Bergerac►
D-Day, the Sixth of June►
Dad
Daddy Long Legs►
The Dain Curse
Damage►
Damnation Alley
Dances with Wolves►
Dandy in Aspic
Dangerous Liaisons►
A Dangerous Woman
Daniel
Danielle Steel's Changes
Danielle Steel's "Daddy"
Dark Age
The Dark Angel►
The Dark Half
The Dark Hour
Dark of the Sun
The Dark Secret of Harvest Home
The Dark Wind
Das Boot►
David►
David and Lisa►
David Copperfield►
The Dawning
The Day of the Jackal►
The Day of the Locust►
Day of the Triffids►
Day One►
Dead Calm►
Dead Eyes of London
Dead Lucky
Dead Ringers►
Dead Solid Perfect
Dead Zone►
Deadline at Dawn
Deadly Currents
Dear Boys
Dear Brigitte
Death Be Not Proud►
Death Dreams
Death in Venice►
The Death of Richie
Death on the Nile
Death Race 2000
Decoration Day►
The Deerslayer
The Deliberate Stranger►
Deliverance►
Delusions of Grandeur
Dempsey
Desert Bloom►
Desert Gold
Desiree
Despair►
Desperate Hours►
Desperate Hours
The Detective►
Detonator
Devil in the Flesh►
The Devils►
Diamond Head
Diamonds are Forever►
Diana: Her True Story
Diane
Diary of a Chambermaid►
Diary of a Lost Girl►
Die Hard►
Die Hard 2: Die Harder►
Die, Monster, Die!
A Different Kind of Love
Diggstown►
Dirty Gertie from Harlem U.S.A.

Doc Hollywood
Doc Savage
The Doctor
Doctor Dolittle
Doctor Faustus
Dr. Jekyll and Mr. Hyde►
Dr. Jekyll and Mr. Hyde
Dr. No►
Dr. Strangelove, or: How I Learned to Stop Worrying and Love the Bomb►
Doctor Zhivago►
Doctors' Wives
Dodsworth►
The Dogs of War
The Dollmaker
Don Quixote►
Dona Flor and Her Two Husbands►
Donovan's Brain►
Don't Go Near the Water
Don't Look Back: The Story of Leroy "Satchel" Paige
Don't Look Now►
Don't Tell Her It's Me
Dorian Gray
Double Indemnity►
The Double Negative
Down and Out in Beverly Hills
Dracula►
Dracula
Dracula (Spanish Version)
Dragon: The Bruce Lee Story►
A Dream of Kings►
Dress Gray►
Dressed to Kill
Driver's Seat
The Drowning Pool
Drugstore Cowboy►
Drums Along the Mohawk►
Dubarry
Dude Ranger
Duel in the Sun►
Duel of Hearts
The Duellists►
Dune
The Dunwich Horror
Dusty
The Dybbuk►
Dynasty
The Eagle Has Landed►
East of Eden►
East of Eden
East Side, West Side
Easy Living
Ebony Tower
Echo Murders
Echoes in the Darkness
Edge of Darkness►
The Education of Sonny Carson
Effi Briest►
Egg and I►
The Eiger Sanction►
800 Leagues Down the Amazon
Eight Men Out►
8 Million Ways to Die
El Amor Brujo►
Eleanor & Franklin►
Eleni
Elmer Gantry►
The Elusive Pimpernel
The Emigrants►
Emil and the Detective
Empire of the Ants
Empire of the Sun►
Empty Canvas
Enchanted April
Enchanted Island
Encore►
End of August
End of Desire
End of the Road
Endless Love
Endless Night
Endplay
Enemies, a Love Story►
Enola Gay: The Men, the Mission, the Atomic Bomb
Enormous Changes►
Entangled

Enter Laughing
Erendira
Eric►
Escape Me Never
Escape to Witch Mountain►
Ethan Frome
Eureka!
The Europeans►
Evelyn Prentice
Even Cowgirls Get the Blues
Everybody's All American
Everything You Always Wanted to Know About Sex (But Were Afraid to Ask)►
The Evil That Men Do
Evil Under the Sun
The Execution of Private Slovik►
The Executioner's Song
Exodus►
Extremities
Eye of the Needle►
Eyes Right!
Fahrenheit 451►
The Fall of the House of Usher
The Fall of the House of Usher►
The Fall of the House of Usher
False Witness
Family Pictures►
Fanny►
Far from the Madding Crowd►
A Far Off Place
The Far Pavilions
Farewell My Concubine
Farewell, My Lovely►
A Farewell to Arms►
Farewell to the King
Fatal Vision
Father Figure
Father of the Bride
Faust►
Fearless►
Fellini Satyricon►
Field of Dreams►
52 Pick-Up
The Fighting Prince of Donegal
A Fine Madness►
Fine Things
Finessing the King
The Fire in the Stone
The Fire Within►
Firestarter
The Firm►
First Blood
The First Deadly Sin
Fitzcarraldo►
Five Card Stud
Five Fingers►
The Five of Me
Five Weeks in a Balloon
The Fixer►
Flambards
The Flame is Love
A Flash of Green
Fletch
Fletch Lives
Flowers in the Attic
Follow That Dream
Food of the Gods: Part 2
For Us, the Living
For Your Eyes Only►
Forbidden
Forbidden Passion: The Oscar Wilde Movie
Ford: The Man & the Machine
Foreign Affairs►
Foreign Body
Forever
Forever Amber
Forlorn River
The Formula
Fortunes of War►
Forty Days of Musa Dagh
The Fountainhead►
Four Daughters►
The Four Feathers►
The Four Horsemen of the Apocalypse►
The Four Horsemen of the Apocalypse
The Fourth Protocol►

The Franchise Affair
Frankenstein►
Frankenstein
Frankenstein Unbound►
Freaky Friday
Freedom Road
Freejack
The French Lieutenant's Woman►
Fried Green Tomatoes►
Friendly Persuasion
A Friendship in Vienna
From Beyond►
From the Dead of Night►
From the Terrace
Fulfillment
Full Metal Jacket►
Gabriela
Gal Young 'Un►
Garden of the Finzi-Continis►
Gas Food Lodging►
A Generation►
George Balanchine's The Nutcracker
George Washington
Georgia, Georgia
Georgy Girl►
Gervaise►
The Getaway
Getting It Right
The Getting of Wisdom
Getting Up and Going Home
Gettysburg►
The Ghost and Mrs. Muir►
Ghost Story
Giant►
Gideon's Trumpet
Gidget
Gigi►
Girl Hunters
The Girl in a Swing
Girl in His Pocket
A Girl of the Limberlost
The Girl Who Had Everything
The Glass Key►
Glitz
Glory►
Glory Enough for All: The Discovery of Insulin
Gnome-Mobile
Go Tell the Spartans►
The Goalie's Anxiety at the Penalty Kick►
The Godfather►
The Godfather 1902-1959: The Complete Epic►
The Godfather, Part 2►
The Godfather, Part 3►
God's Little Acre►
Golden Demon
Golden Earrings
The Golden Honeymoon
Golden Rendezvous
The Golden Salamander
Gone with the Wind►
The Good Mother
Goodbye Again
Goodbye Columbus►
Goodbye, Mr. Chips►
Goodbye, My Lady
Goodfellas►
Gore Vidal's Lincoln
Gorky Park►
The Graduate►
Grambling's White Tiger
Grand Hotel►
Grand Isle
The Grapes of Wrath►
The Grass is Always Greener Over the Septic Tank
Grave of the Fireflies►
Graveyard Shift
The Great Escape►
Great Expectations►
Great Expectations
Great Expectations
The Great Gabbo
The Great Gatsby
The Great Mouse Detective►
The Great Santini►
The Great Train Robbery►
Greed►

The Green Berets
Green Dolphin Street
Green Eyes
Green Fields
The Green Man▶
Green Mansions
The Green Room
The Grifters▶
The Groundstar Conspiracy▶
The Group
Guadalcanal Diary
The Guardian
A Guide for the Married Man▶
Gulliver's Travels
Gun Glory
The Guns of Navarone▶
Hail, Hero!
Half a Sixpence
Half Moon Street
The Handmaid's Tale
Hands of a Stranger
The Hands of Orlac
The Happiest Millionaire
Hard Traveling
The Harder They Fall▶
Harrad Experiment
Harvest▶
The Haunted Palace
Haunted Summer
Haunted: The Ferryman
The Haunting▶
The Haunting of Barney Palmer
Hawaii▶
The Hawk
Hazel's People
The Heart is a Lonely Hunter▶
Heart of Darkness
Heartburn▶
Hearts & Armour
Heat
Heat and Dust▶
Heaven and Earth
Heidi
Heidi▶
Heidi
Heidi▶
The Heiress▶
Heller in Pink Tights
Hellraiser 3: Hell on Earth
Helltown
Helter Skelter
Here Come the Littles: The
    Movie
A Hero Ain't Nothin' But a
    Sandwich
Hidden Fears
The Hideaways
The Hiding Place
High & Low▶
High Sierra▶
Hiroshima, Mon Amour▶
His Fighting Blood
The Hitchhiker's Guide to the
    Galaxy
The Hobbit▶
The Holcroft Covenant
Hombre▶
The Home and the World▶
Homecoming: A Christmas
    Story
Honor Thy Father
Honor Thy Father and Mother:
    The True Story of the
    Menendez Brothers
Hook
Hoppy Serves a Writ
The Horizontal Lieutenant
The Horror of Dracula▶
The Horse's Mouth▶
Hostage
The Hot Rock▶
Hotel
Hotel du Lac
The Hotel New Hampshire
Hotel Reserve▶
The Hound of the Baskervilles▶
The Hound of the Baskervilles
The Hour of the Star▶
The House of Lurking Death
House of Strangers▶
The House of the Arrow▶
The House of the Spirits

The House that Dripped Blood
Household Saints▶
Housekeeping▶
How Green was My Valley▶
How to Be a Perfect Person in
    Just Three Days
How to Pick Up Girls
How to Succeed in Business
    without Really Trying▶
Howard's End▶
Huck and the King of Hearts
Huckleberry Finn
The Human Comedy▶
Human Desire
The Human Factor
The Human Monster
The Hunchback of Notre
    Dame▶
Hunger
The Hunt for Red October▶
Hustling▶
I Am a Camera▶
I Am a Fugitive from a Chain
    Gang▶
I Am the Cheese
I Died a Thousand Times
I Heard the Owl Call My Name
I Know Why the Caged Bird
    Sings▶
I Never Promised You a Rose
    Garden▶
I Was a Male War Bride▶
Ice Palace
Ice Station Zebra
The Idiot▶
The Illustrated Man▶
Imitation of Life▶
In a Lonely Place▶
In Cold Blood▶
In Country
In Love with an Older Woman
In Name Only
In Praise of Older Women▶
In This House of Brede▶
In This Our Life
An Inconvenient Woman
The Incredible Journey
The Incredible Mr. Limpet
An Indecent Obsession
Indecent Proposal
The Informer▶
The Innocent
Internecine Project
The Interns
Interrupted Melody▶
Intruder in the Dust▶
Invasion of the Body
    Snatchers▶
The Invisible Man▶
Invitation au Voyage
The Ipcress File▶
Iron & Silk
The Iron Mask
Ironweed▶
Is Paris Burning?▶
The Island
Island in the Sun
Island of Dr. Moreau
Island of Lost Souls▶
Island of the Blue Dolphins
Islands in the Stream
Isle of Secret Passion
It
It Came From Outer Space▶
Ivanhoe▶
J. Edgar Hoover
Jack London
Jack the Bear
Jacob Have I Loved
Jamaica Inn
James Joyce: A Portrait of the
    Artist as a Young Man
Jane Eyre
Jane Eyre▶
Java Head▶
Jaws▶
Jaws 2
Jean de Florette▶
Jeeves & Wooster: Jeeves'
    Arrival
Jekyll & Hyde...Together Again
Jenny's War

The Jewel in the Crown
The Jeweller's Shop
JFK: Reckless Youth
John and the Missus
Johnny Got His Gun
Joni
Joseph Andrews
Journey for Margaret▶
Journey into Fear▶
Journey of Honor
Journey to the Center of the
    Earth▶
Journey to the Center of the
    Earth
The Joy Luck Club▶
Jude the Obscure
Judge Priest▶
Jules and Jim▶
Julia Misbehaves▶
The Jungle Book▶
Jurassic Park▶
Just for You
Just William's Luck
Justine
Kangaroo▶
Keep the Change
Keeper of the City
The Key
The Keys of the Kingdom▶
Kidnapped
The Kidnapping of the
    President
Killer Inside Me
The Killing▶
A Killing Affair
The Killing Beach
Killing Heat
Kind Hearts and Coronets▶
King Creole
King of the Gypsies
King of the Hill▶
The King of the Roaring '20s:
    The Story of Arnold
    Rothstein
King, Queen, Knave▶
King Rat▶
King Richard and the
    Crusaders
King Solomon's Mines▶
King Solomon's Mines
Kings Go Forth
Kings Row▶
Kipps▶
Kiss of a Killer
Kiss of the Spider Woman▶
Kiss Tomorrow Goodbye
Kitty Foyle▶
Knights of the Round Table
Kramer vs. Kramer▶
Kwaidan▶
La Belle Noiseuse▶
La Bete Humaine▶
La Chartreuse de Parme
La Chienne▶
La Mentira
La Rupture
La Symphonie Pastorale▶
La Vengeance d'une Femme
La Vie de Boheme▶
The Lacemaker▶
Lady Chatterley's Lover
Lady for a Day▶
Lady L
Lady of Burlesque
The Lady Vanishes▶
The Lady Vanishes
Lady Windermere's Fan
Laguna Heat
The Lair of the White Worm▶
The Land of Faraway
Land of Promise
The Land That Time Forgot
Lantern Hill
Last Days of Pompeii
The Last Detail▶
Last Exit to Brooklyn▶
The Last Hit
The Last Hunt
Last Hurrah
The Last of the Mohicans▶
The Last of the Mohicans
The Last of the Mohicans▶

The Last of the Redmen
The Last Safari
Last Summer
The Last Temptation of Christ▶
The Last Tycoon▶
Lathe of Heaven
Laughing Policeman
Laura▶
A Lawless Street
The Learning Tree
A Legacy for Leonette
The Legend of Hell House▶
The Legend of Sea Wolf
The Legend of Sleepy Hollow
The Legend of the Sea Wolf
Legend of Walks Far Woman
Lensman
Leon Morin, Priest▶
The Leopard Man
Les Miserables▶
Les Miserables
Les Miserables
Les Miserables
Less Than Zero
L'Etat Sauvage▶
The Letter▶
A Letter to Three Wives▶
A Life of Her Own
Life of Oharu▶
Life with Father▶
Lifeboat▶
The Light in the Forest
Light Years
Like Water for Chocolate▶
Linda
Little Big Man▶
The Little Colonel▶
The Little Drummer Girl▶
Little Gloria...Happy at Last
Little House on the Prairie▶
The Little Match Girl
Little Men
The Little Mermaid▶
The Little Mermaid▶
Little Minister▶
The Little Princess
A Little Romance▶
Little Women▶
Little Women
Living Free
The Lodger▶
Logan's Run
Lola Montes▶
Lolita▶
Lonely are the Brave▶
The Lonely Guy
The Lonely Lady
The Lonely Passion of Judith
    Hearne▶
Lonelyhearts
The Long, Hot Summer▶
The Longest Day▶
The Lookalike
Looking for Miracles
Looking for Mr. Goodbar
Lord Jim▶
Lord of the Flies▶
Lord of the Flies
The Lord of the Rings
The Lords of Discipline
Lorna Doone
The Lost Command
The Lost Honor of Katharina
    Blum▶
Lost Horizon▶
Lost in the Barrens
The Lost Language of Cranes▶
The Lost Patrol▶
Love for Lydia▶
Love in the Present Tense
The Lover
The Loves of Carmen
Lucky Jim
Lust for Life▶
The Mad Executioners
Madame Bovary▶
Madigan▶
Mafia Princess
Magic
The Magnificent Ambersons▶
Magnificent Obsession
Make Me an Offer

Malarek
Malcolm X▶
The Maltese Falcon▶
The Mambo Kings▶
Man Friday
Man from Nowhere
The Man I Love▶
The Man in the Gray Flannel
    Suit
The Man in the Iron Mask▶
The Man in the Mist
Man of Destiny
Man of Evil
Man of the Forest
Man on the Eiffel Tower▶
The Man Outside
The Man That Corrupted
    Hadleyburg
The Man Who Fell to Earth▶
The Man Who Never Was▶
The Man Who Would Be King▶
The Man Who Would Not Die
The Man with the Golden Arm▶
The Man Without a Face
The Manchurian Candidate▶
Mandingo
Manhunt for Claude Dallas
Manhunter▶
Mannikin
Manon
Manon of the Spring▶
Mansfield Park
Marathon Man▶
Margin for Murder
Marie▶
Marie Antoinette
Marilyn: The Untold Story▶
The Mark of Zorro▶
The Martian Chronicles: Part 1
The Martian Chronicles: Part 3
Mary Poppins▶
Masada▶
M*A*S*H▶
The Mask of Fu Manchu
The Master of Ballantrae
Master of the World
Matewan▶
Matters of the Heart
Mazes and Monsters
McCabe & Mrs. Miller▶
McKenzie Break▶
McVicar
Memphis
The Men's Club
Mephisto▶
The Mephisto Waltz▶
Merry Christmas, Mr.
    Lawrence▶
Midnight
A Midnight Clear▶
Midnight Cowboy▶
Mildred Pierce▶
Mimi
Mindwalk: A Film for
    Passionate Thinkers▶
Miracle at Moreaux
Miracle in the Wilderness
The Miracle of the Bells
The Mirror Crack'd
Misery▶
Miss Sadie Thompson▶
Missing Pieces
Mission Stardust
Missouri Traveler▶
Mrs. Doubtfire
Mrs. Miniver▶
Mrs. Parkington
Mr. & Mrs. Bridge▶
Mr. Horn
Mister Johnson▶
Mr. North
Mr. Peabody & the Mermaid
Mr. Skeffington▶
Mr. Winkle Goes to War
Mistral's Daughter
Mistress Pamela
Misty
Moby Dick▶
Monkey Boy
Monkey Grip▶
Monkey Shines
Monsieur Beaucaire▶

Adapted

Monsignor
Monsignor Quixote
Monte Walsh▶
A Month in the Country▶
The Moon and Sixpence▶
Moonfleet
Morning Glory
Morocco▶
The Mortal Storm▶
The Mosquito Coast
Mother▶
Mother's Boys
The Mountain
Mountain Fury
Mountains of the Moon▶
The Mouse That Roared▶
The Muppet Christmas Carol
Murder by the Book
Murder in Coweta County
Murder in Texas▶
A Murder is Announced
Murder, My Sweet▶
Murder of a Moderate Man
Murder on the Bayou▶
The Music of Chance
The Mutiny of the Elsinore
Mutiny on the Bounty▶
Mutiny on the Bounty
My African Adventure
My Brilliant Career▶
My Father's Glory▶
My Friend Walter
My Girl Tisa
My Man Godfrey▶
My Man Godfrey
My Michael▶
My Old Man
Myra Breckinridge
Mysteries
Mysterious Island▶
The Mysterious Stranger
The Naked and the Dead
The Naked Edge
The Naked Face
Naked Lunch▶
The Name of the Rose
Nana▶
Nana
Nasty Habits
National Velvet▶
Native Son
The Natural▶
Necessary Parties
Needful Things
Neighbors
The Neon Empire
Never Cry Wolf▶
Never Let Me Go
Never Love a Stranger
Never Say Never Again
Never So Few
The NeverEnding Story▶
Nevil Shute's The Far Country
The New Adventures of Pippi
  Longstocking
The New Invisible Man
The New Land▶
Nice Girl Like Me
Nicholas and Alexandra
Nicholas Nickleby▶
Nickel Mountain
Night After Night
Night Ambush
Night and the City▶
Night Breed
A Night in the Life of Jimmy
  Reardon
'night, Mother
The Night of the Following Day
Night of the Generals▶
The Night of the Hunter▶
A Night to Remember▶
Night Train to Munich▶
Nikki, the Wild Dog of the North
1984▶
92 in the Shade▶
No Escape
No Love for Johnnie▶
North▶
North and South Book 1▶
North and South Book 2▶
North Dallas Forty▶

North to Alaska▶
Northanger Abbey
Northern Pursuit
Northwest Passage▶
Nosferatu▶
Not as a Stranger
Not Quite Human
Now and Forever
Now, Voyager▶
The Nun's Story▶
O Pioneers!
The Oak
Oblomov▶
Octopussy
The Odessa File
Of Human Bondage▶
Of Human Bondage
Of Mice and Men▶
The Old Curiosity Shop
The Old Dark House▶
Old Gringo
The Old Maid▶
Oliver!▶
Oliver Twist▶
Oliver Twist
Oliver Twist▶
Oliver Twist
Omega Man
The Omen
On the Beach▶
On the Comet▶
On Wings of Eagles
Onassis
One Day in the Life of Ivan
  Denisovich▶
One Deadly Summer▶
One Flew Over the Cuckoo's
  Nest▶
One in a Million: The Ron
  LaFlore Story
One Man's Way
One Night in the Tropics
One Russian Summer
One Shoe Makes It Murder
Ordeal by Innocence
Ordinary Magic
Orlando▶
Orphan Train▶
The Osterman Weekend
The Other▶
The Other Side of Midnight
Our Vines Have Tender
  Grapes▶
Out
Out of Africa▶
Out of the Past▶
Out on a Limb
The Outlaw Josey Wales▶
Outlaw of Gor
Outrage!
The Outsiders
Overnight Sensation
The Ox-Bow Incident▶
The Painted Veil
Pal Joey▶
Panique▶
Papa's Delicate Condition▶
The Paper Chase▶
Paper Moon▶
Paperhouse▶
The Paradine Case
Paris Express
Paris Trout
Parrish
A Passage to India▶
Paths of Glory▶
Patriot Games▶
Patty Hearst
The Pawnbroker▶
The Pearl▶
The Peasants
The Pelican Brief
Pelle the Conqueror▶
The Penthouse
The People
A Perfect Spy
Peril
Pet Sematary
Pete 'n' Tillie
Peter Pan▶
Petulia▶

Phantom Fiend
Phantom of the Opera▶
The Phantom of the Opera
Phantom Tollbooth▶
The Pickwick Papers
Picnic at Hanging Rock▶
Picture of Dorian Gray▶
Piece of Cake
Pigeon Feathers
Pinky▶
Pippi Goes on Board
Pippi Longstocking
Pippi on the Run
A Place in the Sun▶
The Plague
The Plague Dogs
Planet of the Apes▶
The Player▶
A Pocketful of Rye
Poldark▶
Police
Pollyanna▶
Poor Little Rich Girl: The
  Barbara Hutton Story
The Poppy is also a Flower
Portnoy's Complaint
Portrait of a Lady
Postcards from the Edge▶
The Postman Always Rings
  Twice▶
The Postman Always Rings
  Twice
Power
The Power of One
A Prayer for Katarina
  Horovitzova▶
Presenting Lily Mars
The President's Mystery
Pride and Prejudice
Pride and Prejudice
Prime Suspect▶
The Prince and the Pauper▶
The Prince and the Pauper
The Prince of Central Park▶
The Prince of Thieves
The Prince of Tides▶
The Princess and the Goblin
The Princess Bride▶
Princess Daisy
Prisoner of Zenda▶
Prisoner of Zenda
The Private Affairs of Bel Ami▶
The Private History of a
  Campaign That Failed
Private War
The Prize▶
The Prize Pulitzer
Prizzi's Honor▶
Promised a Miracle
The Proud Ones
Prudential Family Playhouse
Psycho▶
Puppet on a Chain
The Purple Taxi
Pursuit▶
Quartet▶
Queenie
Querelle
Question of Honor
The Quick and the Dead
Quick Change
The Quiller Memorandum▶
Quo Vadis▶
Quo Vadis
Rachel, Rachel▶
A Rage in Harlem▶
Rage of Angels
Rage of Angels: The Story
  Continues
Ragtime▶
Railway Children▶
The Railway Station Man▶
Rain
Rainbow
The Rainbow▶
Rainbow Drive
The Rains Came
Raintree County
Raise the Titanic
Rampage
The Razor's Edge▶
The Razor's Edge

Rebecca▶
Rebecca of Sunnybrook Farm
The Rebels
The Red and the Black▶
The Red Badge of Courage▶
The Red House▶
The Red Pony▶
The Red Raven Kiss-Off
Reflections in a Golden Eye
The Reincarnation of Peter
  Proud
The Reivers▶
The Remains of the Day▶
Remo Williams: The Adventure
  Begins
The Resurrected
The Return of the King
The Return of the Musketeers
Return of the Soldier▶
Return to Earth
Return to Oz
Reuben, Reuben▶
Reunion
Revenge
Reversal of Fortune▶
Rhapsody
Rhapsody in August
Rich in Love
Rich Man, Poor Man▶
The Riddle of the Sands
Ride a Wild Pony▶
Riders of the Purple Sage
The Right Stuff▶
Ring of Bright Water▶
Rip van Winkle
Rising Sun▶
A River Runs Through It▶
The Robe
Robert Kennedy and His Times
Robin Hood▶
Robinson Crusoe
Roll Along Cowboy
Roll of Thunder, Hear My Cry
Room Service
A Room with a View▶
Roots▶
Roots: The Gift
Roots: The Next Generation▶
The Rosary Murders
Rosebud
Rosemary's Baby▶
Roxanne▶
Rumble Fish▶
The Rumor Mill
A Rumor of War▶
Rumpole of the Bailey
Runaway
Running Against Time
The Running Man
Rush▶
The Russia House
The Russians are Coming, the
  Russians are Coming▶
The Sacketts
Sadie Thompson▶
The Sailor Who Fell from Grace
  with the Sea
The Saint
Saint Jack▶
Salo, or the 120 Days of
  Sodom
Salome
The Salzburg Connection
Sanctuary of Fear
Sarah, Plain and Tall▶
Satan Met a Lady
Savage Wilderness
Sayonara▶
The Scar
The Scarlet & the Black
Scarlet Dawn
The Scarlet Letter
The Scarlet Letter▶
The Scarlet Pimpernel▶
Schindler's List▶
Scrooge▶
Scrooge
Scruples
The Sea Wolf▶
The Sea Wolf
The Search for Bridey Murphy
Searching for Bobby Fischer▶

Second Victory
The Secret Adversary
The Secret Four
The Secret Garden▶
The Secret Garden
The Secret Garden▶
The Secret Garden
The Secret of NIMH▶
Seduction: The Cruel Woman
The Seekers
Seize the Day▶
Sense & Sensibility
A Sense of Freedom▶
A Separate Peace
Sergeant Rutledge▶
The Serpent and the Rainbow
Serpico▶
The Servant▶
Servants of Twilight
Seven Blows of the Dragon
Seven Faces of Dr. Lao▶
The Seven Percent Solution▶
Seven Sixgunners
Seven Thieves▶
The Seventh Cross▶
S.F.W.
Shadow of China▶
Shadow of the Thin Man▶
Shadow of the Wolf
The Shadow Riders
Shaft▶
Shalako
Shane▶
Sharky's Machine
Shattered Vows
She
She Came to the Valley
She-Devil
The Shell Seekers
The Sheltering Sky▶
Sherlock Holmes: The Silver
  Blaze
Sherlock Holmes: The Voice of
  Terror
Sherlock Hound: Tales of
  Mystery
The Shining
Shining Through
Ship of Fools▶
Shipwrecked
A Shock to the System▶
The Shoes of the Fisherman
Shogun▶
The Shooting Party▶
The Shootist▶
The Shout▶
Shout at the Devil
Sidney Sheldon's Bloodline
Silas Marner▶
The Silence of the Lambs▶
The Silk Road
Silver Bears
Silver Bullet
The Silver Chalice
Silver River
The Silver Stallion: King of the
  Wild Brumbies
A Simple Twist of Fate
Single White Female
The Sins of Dorian Gray
The Sisters▶
Ski Bum
Skyscraper Souls▶
Slapstick of Another Kind
Slaughterhouse Five
Slaves of New York
Slightly Honorable
Sliver
Slow Burn
A Small Killing
Smart-Aleck Kill
Smith!
The Snake Pit▶
SnakeEater 3: His Law
The Snapper▶
Snow Country
Snow Treasure
Sofie
Solaris
Soldier Blue
Soldier in the Rain
Solomon and Sheba

Something of Value▶
Something Wicked This Way Comes
Sometimes a Great Notion▶
Somewhere in Sonora
Son of Fury▶
Son of the Morning Star▶
Sophie's Choice▶
Sounder▶
South Central
South Pacific
The Spanish Gardener▶
Special Investigator
Spencer's Mountain
Spirit Rider▶
Spirits of the Dead▶
The Spoilers▶
The Spook Who Sat By the Door
Spy in Black▶
Spy of Napoleon
Spy Story
The Spy Who Came in from the Cold▶
The Squeaker
Stars and Bars
Stars in My Crown▶
The Stars Look Down▶
State Fair▶
State Fair
Staying On
Steaming
Stella
Stella Dallas▶
Stephen King's The Stand
Stephen King's The Tommyknockers
Steppenwolf
Stick
Stiletto
Stopover Tokyo
Storm and Sorrow
The Story of O
The Story of Qui Ju▶
Straight Time▶
Strange Case of Dr. Jekyll & Mr. Hyde
Strange Fruit
Strange Tales/Ray Bradbury Theatre
The Stranger Wore a Gun
Strangers on a Train▶
Strangers When We Meet
The Streets of San Francisco▶
Studs Lonigan
The Stunt Man▶
Sudie & Simpson▶
Summer Heat
The Summer of My German Soldier▶
A Summer Place
The Sundowners▶
Suzy
Svengali▶
Svengali
Swann in Love
Sweet Hostage
Sweet Killing
Sweet Love, Bitter
The Swiss Family Robinson▶
Sword of Gideon
Tai-Pan
A Tale of Two Cities▶
A Tale of Two Cities
A Tale of Two Cities▶
Tall Story
Taras Bulba
Tarzan, the Ape Man▶
Tarzan, the Ape Man
Ten Days That Shook the World▶
Ten Days Wonder
Ten Little Indians
Ten North Frederick
The Tenant▶
Tender Is the Night
The Tenth Man
10th Victim
The Terminal Man
Terror is a Man
Terror Stalks the Class Reunion

Tess▶
Tex
That Darn Cat
That Forsyte Woman
That Night
That Obscure Object of Desire▶
That Was Then...This Is Now
They Call It Sin
They Came to Cordura
They Live by Night▶
They Won't Forget▶
The Thief Who Came to Dinner
Thieves Like Us▶
The Thing▶
Things to Come▶
The Third Man▶
Third Man on the Mountain
This Gun for Hire
This Sweet Sickness
The Thorn Birds▶
Those Calloways
Three Came Home▶
Three Comrades▶
Three Days of the Condor▶
The Three Musketeers
The Three Musketeers
The Three Musketeers
The Three Musketeers▶
3:10 to Yuma▶
The Three Worlds of Gulliver
Thumbelina▶
Thunder Mountain
Thunder Pass
Till Death Do Us Part
Till the End of Time
Tim
Time for Murder
The Time Machine▶
Time Machine
Time of Indifference
A Time to Love & a Time to Die
The Tin Drum▶
To Catch a Thief▶
To Dance with the White Dog▶
To Have & Have Not▶
To Hell and Back
To Kill a Mockingbird▶
To Sir, with Love
To the Devil, A Daughter
To the Last Man
To the Lighthouse
Tokyo Decadence
Tom Brown's School Days
Tom Brown's School Days▶
Tom Jones▶
Tom Sawyer
Tomb
Topaz▶
Topkapi▶
Torn Apart
Tortilla Flat▶
Total Recall▶
Tough Guys Don't Dance
A Town Like Alice
Toy Soldiers
Trader Horn
Transport from Paradise
Treasure Island▶
Treasure Island
Treasure of the Sierra Madre▶
A Tree Grows in Brooklyn▶
Trespasser
The Trial▶
The Trial
Triple Cross▶
Tristana▶
The Triumph of Sherlock Holmes
Trojan Women
Tropic of Cancer▶
True Confessions▶
True Grit▶
True West▶
Tune in Tomorrow
Tunes of Glory▶
20,000 Leagues Under the Sea▶
The 27 Day
29th Street
Twice-Told Tales▶
Twilight's Last Gleaming

Two English Girls▶
Two Kinds of Love
2001: A Space Odyssey▶
2010: The Year We Make Contact▶
Two to Tango
The Two Worlds of Jenny Logan
Ugetsu▶
The Ugly American
Ulysses
The Unbearable Lightness of Being▶
The Unbreakable Alibi
Uncle Moses
Uncle Tom's Cabin
Under Capricorn
Under Satan's Sun▶
Under the Volcano▶
Uneasy Terms
The Unnamable
The Unsinkable Molly Brown▶
Unsuitable Job for a Woman
Until They Sail
Up the Down Staircase▶
Users
Utz
The Valley of Decision▶
Valley of the Dolls
Valmont▶
The Vampire Lovers
Vampyr▶
The Vanishing
Vanity Fair
A Very Old Man with Enormous Wings
V.I. Warshawski
Village of the Damned▶
Village of the Giants
The Violent Men
The Virgin and the Gypsy
The Virgin Soldiers
The Virginian
The Virginian▶
Vision Quest
Viva Zapata!▶
Voyage of the Damned▶
Voyager▶
Wages of Fear▶
Wagon Wheels
Walk on the Wild Side
Walking on Air
Wanderers▶
War & Love
War and Peace
War and Peace▶
War & Remembrance, Part 1
War & Remembrance, Part 2
War & Remembrance, Part 3
War & Remembrance, Part 4
War & Remembrance, Part 5
War & Remembrance, Part 6
War & Remembrance, Part 7
War & Remembrance: The Final Chapter, Part 8
War & Remembrance: The Final Chapter, Part 9
War & Remembrance: The Final Chapter, Part 10
War & Remembrance: The Final Chapter, Part 11
War & Remembrance: The Final Chapter, Part 12
War Between the Tates
War Lover
The War of the Roses▶
The War of the Worlds▶
The War Wagon▶
Warlock▶
Warriors of the Sung Dynasty
Watchers
Waterland
Watership Down
The Way We Were▶
The Way West
We the Living
We Think the World of You▶
Weep No More My Lady
We're Back! A Dinosaur's Story
West of the Pecos
Whale for the Killing
What Price Hollywood?▶

What's Eating Gilbert Grape▶
What's Love Got to Do With It?
When the Bough Breaks
When the West Was Young
When the Whales Came
When the Wind Blows▶
Where Angels Fear to Tread▶
Where Are the Children?
Where the Buffalo Roam
Where the Lilies Bloom▶
Where the Red Fern Grows
Where the Red Fern Grows: Part 2
Where Time Began
Where's Poppa?▶
Whispers
Whistle Down the Wind▶
White Cargo
White Fang▶
White Fang and the Hunter
White Hot: The Mysterious Murder of Thelma Todd
White Lie
White Nights▶
Who Am I This Time?▶
Who Framed Roger Rabbit?▶
Who is Killing the Great Chefs of Europe?▶
Who'll Stop the Rain?▶
Why Shoot the Teacher▶
The Wicked Lady
Wide Sargasso Sea
The Widow
The Wild Country
Wild Times
Wildflower▶
Will: G. Gordon Liddy
The Wind▶
Windom's Way▶
The Winds of Jarrah
Winter People
Wise Blood▶
The Witches of Eastwick
Without Reservations
Without Warning: The James Brady Story▶
Witness for the Prosecution▶
The Wizard of Loneliness
The Wizard of Oz▶
Wolf Call
Wolfen▶
A Woman Called Moses
Woman in Black
Woman in the Shadows
A Woman Named Jackie
A Woman of Substance, Episode 1: Nest of Vipers
A Woman of Substance, Episode 2: The Secret is Revealed
A Woman of Substance, Episode 3: Fighting for the Dream
A Woman Rebels
Women in Love▶
Wooden Horse▶
Words by Heart
The World According to Garp▶
The World is Full of Married Men
The World of Apu▶
World of Henry Orient▶
A World of Strangers▶
The World Owes Me a Living
The Worst Witch
The Wreck of the Mary Deare
The Wrong Box▶
The Wrong Move
Wuthering Heights▶
Wuthering Heights
A Year in Provence▶
Year of the Dragon
The Yearling▶
Yentl
Yesterday's Hero
You Only Live Twice
Young at Heart
Young Bess▶
The Young in Heart▶
Young Lady Chatterly 2
Young Man with a Horn▶
Young Winston▶

Your Ticket Is No Longer Valid
Zandy's Bride
Zatoichi: Master Ichi and a Chest of Gold
Zotz!

Adapted from a Cartoon

The Addams Family
Addams Family Values
The Adventures of Captain Marvel
Adventures of Red Ryder
Adventures of Smilin' Jack
The Amazing Spider-Man
Annie
Arcadia of My Youth
Batman
Batman▶
Batman Returns
The Belles of St. Trinian's▶
Big Zapper
Blondie
Blondie Has Trouble
Blondie Hits the Jackpot
Blondie in Society
Blondie Knows Best
Blondie Takes a Vacation
Blondie's Blessed Event
Brenda Starr
Captain America
The Crow
Dennis the Menace
Dennis the Menace: Dinosaur Hunter
Dick Tracy
Dick Tracy▶
Dick Tracy vs. Cueball
Dick Tracy's Dilemma
Dr. Strange
Fatty Finn
The Fighting Redhead
The Flash
The Flash 2: Revenge of the Trickster
Flash Gordon
Friday Foster
The Great St. Trinian's Train Robbery
The Guyver
Hillbilly Blitzkrieg
Howard the Duck
The Incredible Hulk
It's a Great Life
Kowloon Assignment
Li'l Abner
Little Nemo: Adventures in Slumberland
Little Orphan Annie
Los Caciques
The Mask▶
The Perils of Gwendoline
Petit Con
Prince Valiant
The Pure Hell of St. Trinian's
Reg'lar Fellers
The Return of Swamp Thing
The Sad Sack
Superman: The Movie▶
Superman 2▶
Superman 3
Superman 4: The Quest for Peace
Tales from the Crypt▶
Teenage Mutant Ninja Turtles: The Movie
Teenage Mutant Ninja Turtles 2: The Secret of the Ooze
Teenage Mutant Ninja Turtles 3
Timecop
Tom and Jerry: The Movie
Vault of Horror
Wild Palms
The Wild World of Batwoman

Adapted from a Fairy Tale

Aladdin
Aladdin▶

Adapted

Aladdin and His Wonderful Lamp
Alice in Wonderland
Alice's Adventures in Wonderland
Beauty and the Beast▶
Beauty and the Beast
Beauty and the Beast
The Blue Light▶
The Boy Who Left Home to Find Out About the Shivers
Butterfly Ball
Cannon Movie Tales: Red Riding Hood
Cannon Movie Tales: Sleeping Beauty
Cannon Movie Tales: Snow White▶
Cannon Movie Tales: The Emperor's New Clothes
Casey at the Bat
Cinderella
Cinderella
Cinderella 2000
Cinderfella
The Company of Wolves▶
The Dancing Princesses
Deadtime Stories
Donkey Skin▶
Dos Cruces en Danger Pass▶
Elle Voit des Nains Partout
The Emperor's New Clothes
Fairytales
Frog
Fun & Fancy Free
George Balanchine's The Nutcracker
The Glass Slipper
Goldilocks & the Three Bears
Hans Christian Andersen
Hansel and Gretel
Happily Ever After
A Hungarian Fairy Tale▶
Irish Cinderella
Jack & the Beanstalk
La Petite Sirene
Les Visiteurs du Soir▶
The Little Match Girl
The Little Mermaid
The Little Mermaid▶
Little Red Riding Hood▶
The Magic Fountain
The Magic Legend of the Golden Goose
The Magic Sword
Magical Wonderland
March of the Wooden Soldiers▶
Mother Goose Rock 'n' Rhyme
The NeverEnding Story▶
The Nightingale
Nutcracker, A Fantasy on Ice
The Nutcracker Prince
Nutcracker: The Motion Picture
Once Upon a Brothers Grimm
Peter Pan▶
Pied Piper of Hamelin
The Pied Piper of Hamelin
Pinocchio▶
Pinocchio
Pinocchio's Storybook Adventures
The Princess and the Pea▶
The Princess and the Swineherd
The Princess Bride▶
Princess Cinderella
The Princess Who Never Laughed▶
Puss 'n Boots
Rapunzel
Red Riding Hood
The Red Shoes
Rip van Winkle
Rub a Dub Dub
Rudyard Kipling's Classic Stories
Rumpelstiltskin
The Scalawag Bunch
Sleeping Beauty▶
Sleeping Beauty
The Snow Queen

Snow White and the Seven Dwarfs
Snow White and the Three Stooges
Storytime Classics
The Swan▶
The Tale of the Frog Prince▶
The Three Little Pigs
Thumbelina▶
Thumbelina
Tom Thumb
Who Slew Auntie Roo?
The Wishmaker
The Witches▶
The Wonderful World of the Brothers Grimm
The Wonders of Aladdin

Adapted from a Game

Clue
Super Mario Bros.
Tag: The Assassination Game

Adapted from a Play or Musical

Abe Lincoln in Illinois▶
The Adventures of Robin Hood▶
Age Old Friends▶
Agnes of God
Ah, Wilderness!▶
Alfie▶
Alice
All My Sons▶
Amadeus▶
Anastasia
Animal Crackers▶
The Animal Kingdom▶
Anna Christie▶
Anna Christie
Annie
Another Country
Any Wednesday
Arsenic and Old Lace▶
As Is
As You Desire Me▶
The Avenger
The Awful Truth▶
Babes in Arms
Babes in Toyland
Baby Doll▶
Baby, the Rain Must Fall
The Bacchantes
The Bad Seed
The Balcony▶
The Ballad of the Sad Cafe
Barefoot in the Park▶
Beatlemania! The Movie
Beau Brummel
Beau Brummel▶
Becket▶
Becky Sharp
Being at Home with Claude
Bells are Ringing▶
Best Foot Forward
The Best Little Whorehouse in Texas
The Best Man▶
Betrayal
Beyond Therapy
The Big Knife▶
Big News
Billie
Biloxi Blues
The Birth of a Nation▶
Bitter Sweet
Black Limelight
Black Lizard
Black Orpheus▶
Blessed Event▶
Blithe Spirit▶
Blood Wedding▶
Bodies, Rest & Motion
Bopha!▶
Born Yesterday▶
Born Yesterday
Boy Meets Girl▶
The Boys in the Band

Breath of Scandal
The Brig▶
Brigadoon▶
Brighton Beach Memoirs▶
Broadway Bound
A Bronx Tale▶
The Browning Version▶
Bus Stop▶
Butterflies Are Free▶
Bye, Bye, Birdie▶
Cabaret▶
Cactus Flower
Caesar and Cleopatra
California Suite▶
Can-Can
Casablanca▶
Casanova Brown
Cast a Dark Shadow▶
Casual Sex?
Cat on a Hot Tin Roof▶
Cat on a Hot Tin Roof
Cavalcade▶
Cease Fire
Ceiling Zero▶
The Chalk Garden▶
Chapter Two
Charm of La Boheme
The Chase
The Cheap Detective▶
Children of a Lesser God▶
The Children's Hour
Chimes at Midnight▶
The Chocolate Soldier
A Chorus Line
A Chorus of Disapproval
Circle of Love
Clarence Darrow▶
Clarence, the Cross-eyed Lion▶
Clash by Night▶
Come Back, Little Sheba▶
Come Back to the Five & Dime Jimmy Dean, Jimmy Dean▶
Come Blow Your Horn▶
Command Decision
Conduct Unbecoming
The Connection▶
Cool Mikado
Coquette
The Corn is Green▶
The Count of the Old Town
Country Girl▶
County Fair
Craig's Wife▶
Crimes of the Heart▶
Cyrano de Bergerac▶
Cyrano de Bergerac▶
Da
Daddy's Dyin'...Who's Got the Will?
Damn Yankees▶
A Day in the Death of Joe Egg▶
Day of Wrath▶
Daybreak
Dead End▶
Death of a Salesman▶
Deathtrap
The Desert Song
Desire Under the Elms▶
Desk Set▶
Desperate Hours▶
Detective Story▶
The Devil's Brother
The Devil's Disciple▶
Dial "M" for Murder▶
Diary of a Hitman
The Dining Room
Dinner at Eight▶
Disraeli▶
The Divorce of Lady X
The Doctor and the Devils
Doll Face
A Doll's House
A Doll's House▶
Don't Drink the Water
Double Wedding▶
The Dresser▶
Driving Miss Daisy▶
DuBarry Was a Lady
Duet for One
Dumb Waiter
Dutchman▶

Easy Virtue
Educating Rita▶
Edward II
The Effect of Gamma Rays on Man-in-the-Moon Marigolds▶
Emperor Jones
Emperor Jones/Paul Robeson: Tribute to an Artist
Employees' Entrance▶
The Enchanted Cottage
Ensign Pulver
The Entertainer▶
Entertaining Mr. Sloane
Equus
Escapade▶
Escape Me Never▶
Everybody Wins
The Farmer Takes a Wife
The Farmer's Wife
A Few Good Men▶
Fiddler on the Roof▶
The Field▶
A Fine Romance
Finian's Rainbow▶
Flower Drum Song
Follies in Concert
Fool for Love
Footlight Serenade
Forbidden Planet▶
Forever Female▶
Fortune and Men's Eyes
Forty Carats
Foxfire▶
Frankie and Johnny▶
The Front Page▶
The Fugitive Kind
A Funny Thing Happened on the Way to the Forum▶
Fury is a Woman▶
Futz
Gaslight▶
The Gay Divorcee▶
The Gazebo▶
Generation
Gentlemen Prefer Blondes▶
George Washington Slept Here▶
George White's Scandals
The Ghost Breakers▶
The Glass Menagerie▶
Glengarry Glen Ross▶
Golden Boy▶
The Golden Coach▶
Gone are the Days
The Goodbye Girl▶
The Gorilla
Grease▶
Grease 2
The Great White Hope
Green Pastures▶
Grown Ups
The Guardsman▶
Gypsy▶
Gypsy
Hair▶
The Hairy Ape
Hamlet▶
Hamlet
Hamlet▶
The Happiest Days of Your Life▶
Happy Birthday, Gemini
He Who Gets Slapped▶
Heartbreak House
Heaven Can Wait▶
Hedda
Hello, Dolly!
Henry IV
Henry V▶
His Double Life
His Girl Friday▶
Hit the Deck
Holiday▶
The Honey Pot
Hotel Paradiso
I Confess
I Do! I Do!
I Married an Angel
I Never Sang For My Father▶
I Ought to Be in Pictures
I Remember Mama▶

Idiot's Delight▶
Illicit
Illusions
The Impossible Years
In Celebration▶
In Search of the Castaways▶
In the Good Old Summertime▶
Indiscreet
Inherit the Wind▶
Iphigenia▶
Irma La Douce
Italian Straw Hat▶
Jacknife▶
Jesus Christ, Superstar▶
Joan of Arc
Johnny Belinda
Jubal
Julius Caesar▶
Julius Caesar
Key Exchange
Key Largo▶
The Killing of Sister George
The King and I▶
King Lear▶
King Lear
Kiss Me Kate▶
Kiss Me, Stupid!
The Knack▶
K2: The Ultimate High
La Cage aux Folles▶
La Cage aux Folles 2
La Cage aux Folles 3: The Wedding
La Pastorela
La Ronde▶
Ladies They Talk About
Lady Be Good
The Last of Mrs. Cheney▶
Last of the Red Hot Lovers
Laughing Sinners
Lenny▶
Les Enfants Terrible▶
A Life in the Theater
Li'l Abner
The Lion in Winter▶
The Little Foxes▶
Little Johnny Jones
Little Murders▶
A Little Night Music
Little Shop of Horrors▶
Long Day's Journey into Night▶
Long Day's Journey into Night
The Long Voyage Home▶
Look Back in Anger▶
Look Back in Anger
Look Back in Anger▶
Loot...Give Me Money, Honey!
Lost in Yonkers
Louisiana Purchase
The Lovable Cheat
The Lower Depths▶
M. Butterfly
Macbeth▶
Macbeth
Madame X
The Madwoman of Chaillot
The Magnificent Yankee▶
The Mahabharata
Major Barbara▶
Male and Female▶
Mame
A Man for All Seasons▶
Man of La Mancha
The Man Who Came to Dinner▶
Marat/Sade▶
Marius▶
Marriage Italian Style▶
Mary of Scotland▶
Mass Appeal
Master Harold and the Boys▶
The Matchmaker▶
Maytime▶
Medea
The Merry Widow▶
The Merry Widow
Merton of the Movies
Mexican Hayride
Midnight Lace
A Midsummer Night's Dream▶
A Midsummer Night's Dream

The Miracle Worker▶
Miss Firecracker▶
Miss Julie
Miss Rose White▶
Mr. Music
Mister Roberts▶
Monster in a Box▶
Morning Glory
Much Ado About Nothing▶
Murder▶
Murder at the Vanities
Murder by Death
The Music Man▶
My Brother's Wife
My Fair Lady▶
My Sister Eileen▶
Never Steal Anything Small
Never Too Late to Mend
New Faces of 1952
New Moon
The Night of the Iguana▶
No, No Nanette
No Time for Sergeants▶
Noises Off
The Norman Conquests, Part 1: Table Manners▶
The Norman Conquests, Part 2: Living Together▶
The Norman Conquests, Part 3: Round and Round the Garden▶
Norman, Is That You?
No. 17▶
The Odd Couple▶
Oedipus Rex
Oedipus Rex▶
Oh! Calcutta!
Oh, Poor Dad (Momma's Hung You in the Closet & I'm Feeling So Sad)
Oklahoma!▶
On a Clear Day You Can See Forever
On Approval▶
On Borrowed Time▶
On Golden Pond▶
On the Town▶
One of My Wives Is Missing
One Touch of Venus
One Trick Pony
Only When I Laugh▶
Opera do Malandro
Ordet▶
Orphans▶
Orphans of the Storm▶
Orpheus Descending
Oscar
Othello
Othello▶
Other People's Money
Our Town▶
Out of Season
The Owl and the Pussycat▶
Paint Your Wagon
Pajama Game▶
Panama Hattie
The Passing of the Third Floor Back
Patterns▶
People Will Talk▶
The Perfect Marriage
Period of Adjustment▶
Personal Property
Petrified Forest▶
Phaedra
Phantom of the Paradise
The Philadelphia Story▶
Pippin▶
The Pirates of Penzance▶
Play It Again, Sam▶
Playboy of the Western World
Plaza Suite▶
Plenty
The Portrait▶
Prelude to a Kiss
The Prime of Miss Jean Brodie▶
Princess Tam Tam▶
Prisoner of Second Avenue
Private Lives▶
The Private Secretary
Privates on Parade

Purlie Victorious
Pygmalion▶
Quality Street
A Question of Attribution
Quiet Day In Belfast▶
The Rainmaker▶
A Raisin in the Sun▶
Ran▶
Rap Master Ronnie
Red Planet Mars
The Return of Peter Grimm▶
Richard III▶
Riders to the Sea
The Ritz▶
Roman Spring of Mrs. Stone▶
Romance
Romantic Comedy
Romeo and Juliet▶
Romeo and Juliet
Romeo and Juliet▶
The Room
Rope▶
Rosencrantz & Guildenstern Are Dead
Ruby
The Runner Stumbles
Sabrina▶
Saint Joan
Same Time, Next Year▶
The Saphead
Sarafina!▶
School for Scandal
Scorchers
Scum▶
The Seagull▶
Secret Honor▶
Separate Tables▶
Separate Tables
1776▶
Sextette
The Shadow Box▶
Shadowlands▶
The Shanghai Gesture
Shirley Valentine▶
The Shop Around the Corner▶
Short Eyes▶
Show Boat▶
Show Boat
The Show-Off▶
The Sicilian
Silent Night, Lonely Night
Silk Stockings▶
Sinful Life
The Singing Blacksmith
Six Degrees of Separation
Skin Game
Sleuth▶
Small Hotel
So Ends Our Night▶
A Soldier's Story▶
South Pacific▶
Stage Door▶
Star Spangled Girl
State of the Union▶
Stevie
Stolen Hours
Strange Interlude▶
Strange Interlude
The Strange Love of Molly Louvain
Streamers
Street Scene▶
A Streetcar Named Desire▶
The Stripper
Suddenly, Last Summer▶
Summer and Smoke▶
Summertime▶
Summertree
Sunday in the Park with George▶
Sunrise at Campobello▶
The Sunshine Boys▶
Susan Slept Here
Sweeney Todd: The Demon Barber of Fleet Street
Sweet Bird of Youth▶
Sweet Bird of Youth
Sweet Charity▶
Sylvia and the Phantom▶
Talk Radio▶
Tall Story
The Taming of the Shrew

The Taming of the Shrew▶
The Taming of the Shrew
Tartuffe
A Taste of Honey▶
Tea and Sympathy▶
Tea for Two
The Teahouse of the August Moon
The Tempest
The Tempest▶
The Terror
That Championship Season
That's Singing: The Best of Broadway
There's a Girl in My Soup
These Three▶
They Knew What They Wanted▶
Thin Ice▶
This Happy Breed▶
This is the Army
This Property is Condemned
Thoroughly Modern Millie
Those Endearing Young Charms
A Thousand Clowns▶
Three Daring Daughters
Three Men on a Horse▶
The Three Penny Opera▶
The Threepenny Opera
Throne of Blood
Tidy Endings
Time Lock
The Time of Your Life▶
Too Many Girls
Topaze▶
Torch Song Trilogy
Tough Guy
Toys in the Attic
The Tragedy of King Richard II
The Trip to Bountiful▶
The Tunnel of Love
Twelve Angry Men▶
21 Days
Two Can Play
Two for the Seesaw▶
The Unapproachable
Under Milk Wood
Under the Biltmore Clock
An Unfinished Piece for a Player Piano▶
Velnio Nuotaka
Volpone▶
A Voyage' Round My Father▶
Wait Until Dark▶
The War Lord▶
Watch on the Rhine▶
Waterfront
Weekend at the Waldorf▶
We're No Angels
West Side Story▶
The Whales of August▶
Where Were You When the Lights Went Out?
Whoopee!
Who's Afraid of Virginia Woolf?▶
Whose Life Is It Anyway?▶
The Wild Duck
Window Shopping
The Winslow Boy▶
Winterset
Without Love▶
The Wiz
The Women▶
Woyzeck▶
Woza Albert!
Yellow Dust
You Can't Take It with You▶
Young & Willing
You're a Good Man, Charlie Brown
Zoot Suit▶

Adapted from a Poem

Casey at the Bat
The Castilian
Gunga Din▶
The Man from Snowy River

Old Ironsides▶
The Set-Up▶
Ulysses
The White Cliffs of Dover▶
Wild Party

Adapted from a Song

Alice's Restaurant
The Baron and the Kid
Born in East L.A.
Convoy
Coward of the County
Frankie and Johnny
The Gambler Returns: The Luck of the Draw
Girls Just Want to Have Fun
The Indian Runner
Kenny Rogers as the Gambler
Kenny Rogers as the Gambler, Part 2: The Adventure Continues
Kenny Rogers as the Gambler, Part 3: The Legend Continues
Love Potion #9
My Darlin' Clementine
The Night the Lights Went Out in Georgia
Ode to Billy Joe
Purple People Eater
Single Bars, Single Women
Take This Job & Shove It
Yellow Submarine▶
You Light Up My Life

Adapted from a Story

ABC Stage 67: Truman Capote's A Christmas Memory
The Adventures of Ichabod and Mr. Toad▶
The Affair of the Pink Pearl
Alice in Wonderland
Alice in Wonderland
Ambassador Bill
Androcles and the Lion
Angels in the Outfield▶
Angels with Dirty Faces▶
Appointment with Crime
Arizona Bushwackers
As Young As You Feel▶
Ashik Kerib▶
The Assassination Bureau▶
Babette's Feast▶
The Ballad of the Sad Cafe
Bartleby
The Beast from 20,000 Fathoms▶
Benefit of the Doubt
Big Business Girl
The Big Stampede
Billy the Kid
The Birds▶
The Black Abbot
Blackmail▶
Boots of Destiny
Border Caballero
Boss of Bullion City
A Boy and His Dog
Boy's Night Out▶
Breakfast at Tiffany's▶
Brief Encounter▶
Bright Angel
Bury Me Not On the Lone Prairie
By the Light of the Silvery Moon
Call of the Wild
The Canterville Ghost
Carmilla
Casanova's Big Night
Cat's Eye
Caught in the Draft▶
Charade▶
Cinderella
Cinderella 2000
The Cisco Kid
College Swing
Comrade X
Country Lovers, City Lovers

Crash Dive
Creature from the Black Lagoon▶
Creature with the Blue Hand
Cricket on the Hearth
Cult of the Cobra
Dark Eyes▶
Daughter of the Dragon
David and Bathsheba▶
A Day in the Country▶
The Dead▶
The Decameron▶
Decameron Nights
Department Store
The Devil & Daniel Webster▶
Diary of a Madman
The Displaced Person▶
Dive Bomber▶
Doomed at Sundown
Door with the Seven Locks
Double Trouble
Double Vision
D.P.
Drift Fence
The Dropkick▶
Eat a Bowl of Tea▶
The Eyes of the Amaryllis
Eyes of the Panther
A Face in the Crowd▶
Face to Face
Fallen Angels 1▶
Fallen Angels 2▶
Feud Maker
The Fig Tree
The Fighter▶
Fighting Caravans
First Love
Five Days One Summer
The 5000 Fingers of Dr. T▶
Flirtation Walk
Forger of London
Frontier Uprising
Galloping Romeo
Gangway
The Ghost of Frankenstein▶
Ghost Valley
The Gift of Love
The Glass House▶
The Go-Between▶
Great Adventure
Gunfight at the O.K. Corral▶
Guys and Dolls▶
The Hard Way▶
Haunting Fear
The Haunting of Morella
Highlander▶
Hills of Oklahoma
Homecoming
Hostile Guns
The House of Usher
How the Grinch Stole Christmas▶
I'm a Fool
Importance of Being Earnest▶
In Old Chicago▶
The Incredible Sarah
The Indian Scarf
The Invisible Boy
The Invisible Woman▶
Isle of Forgotten Sins
It's a Date
It's a Dog's Life
Jigsaw
Johnny Eager▶
Johnny Reno
Jonathan Livingston Seagull
Judgment Night
The Jungle Book
Kaos▶
Key to the City
Kim▶
Kurt Vonnegut's Monkey House
La Chute de la Maison Usher▶
La Merveilleuse Visite
The Lady Eve▶
Lady Killer▶
The Lady with the Dog▶
The Lady's Maid's Bell
The Land Unknown
Late Chrysanthemums
The Lawnmower Man

Adapted

The Lawrenceville Stories
Le Plaisir
The Leech Woman
Life on a String
Little Miss Marker
The Little Prince
Lone Star
The Lost World
Love on the Run
Loyalties
Lurking Fear
The Magic Fountain
The Magic Legend of the
  Golden Goose
The Magnificent Dope
Main Street to Broadway
Manfish
The Marquise
Marty
The Masked Rider
Masque of the Red Death▶
Masque of the Red Death
Maximum Overdrive
Menace II Society▶
Mr. Reeder in Room 13
The Most Dangerous Game▶
The Mummy's Curse
The Mummy's Tomb
Murders in the Rue Morgue
The Murders in the Rue
  Morgue▶
My Apprenticeship▶
My Childhood▶
My Favorite Blonde▶
My Lucky Star
My Mother's Castle▶
My Sister Eileen▶
My Universities▶
The Mysterious Magician
Mystic Circle Murder
Naked Jungle▶
The Naked Maja
Nevada
Nightfall
Nightflyers
No Comebacks
Noon Wine▶
O Youth and Beauty
Objective, Burma!▶
The Oblong Box
O.C. and Stiggs
An Occurrence at Owl Creek
  Bridge▶
An Occurrence at Owl Creek
  Bridge/Coup de Grace
Of Human Hearts
On Moonlight Bay
Our Modern Maidens
Our Relations▶
The Outlaw Deputy
The Oval Portrait
Paul's Case
Peck's Bad Boy
The Pied Piper of Hamelin
The Pit and the Pendulum
The Pit & the Pendulum
Pittsburgh
Play Misty for Me▶
Pocketful of Miracles▶
The Possessed▶
Premature Burial
The Prince and the Pauper
The Princess and the
  Swineherd
Pudd'nhead Wilson
The Purchase Price
The Queen of Spades▶
Quest for Love
Rappaccini's Daughter
Rawhead Rex
The Re-Animator▶
Rear Window▶
Red Balloon/Occurrence at Owl
  Creek Bridge▶
The Red Shoes
The Red Shoes
The Reluctant Dragon
The Report on the Party and
  the Guests▶
Return to Paradise
Return to the Lost World
Revenge of the Creature

Ride Him, Cowboy▶
Ridin' Down the Canyon
Ridin' the Lone Trail
Robbers of the Sacred
  Mountain
Rocket to the Moon
The Rocking Horse Winner
Roman Holiday▶
Roommate
Rough Ridin' Rhythm
The Ruggles of Red Gap▶
Rumpelstiltskin
Sabotage▶
Salome
Saturday Night Fever
Secret of the Black Trunk
Seven Brides for Seven
  Brothers▶
The Seven Hills of Rome
Shadow of a Doubt▶
Shanghai Express▶
Sherlock Holmes: The Master
  Blackmailer
Shinbone Alley
The Shooting Party
Shopworn Angel▶
Short Cuts▶
The Skull
The Sky is Gray▶
Sleep of Death
Sleeping Car to Trieste
Smooth Talk▶
The Snow Queen
Snow White and the Seven
  Dwarfs▶
The Snows of Kilimanjaro▶
Somewhere I'll Find You▶
Song of the Thin Man
Sorrows of Gin
Sorry, Wrong Number
The Southerner▶
The Spectre of Edgar Allen Poe
Stagecoach▶
Station West▶
The Strange Countess
A Summer Story▶
A Summer to Remember
Sunset Boulevard▶
Swimmer▶
Tales from Avonlea, Vol. 1: The
  Journey Begins▶
Tales from the Darkside: The
  Movie
Tales of Terror
Tales of the Klondike: In a Far
  Country
Tales of the Klondike: Race for
  Number One
Tales of the Klondike: The
  Scorn of Women
Tales of the Klondike: The
  Unexpected
The Tell-Tale Heart
Tennessee's Partner
They Met in Bombay
They Watch
The Thin Man▶
The Thin Man Goes Home
The Thing
Three Brothers▶
The Three Little Pigs
Thunder Pass
Today We Live
Tomb of Ligeia▶
Tomorrow▶
Tonto Basin Outlaws
The Topeka Terror
Torture Garden
Torture Ship
Trailin'
Transmutations
Tribute to a Bad Man▶
Trio▶
Tropical Heat
Twelve Chairs▶
12:01
Two by Forsyth
Two Evil Eyes
Vanina Vanini▶
Ward Six
Wee Willie Winkie▶
Who Slew Auntie Roo?

Who's the Man?
The Window▶
Wintertime
A Woman Without Love▶
Women & Men: In Love There
  Are No Rules
Women & Men: Stories of
  Seduction
Young at Heart
The Young One
Youth Aflame

Adapted from an Article

All Mine to Give
Christiane F.▶
The Last American Hero▶
Olivier, Olivier▶
Streetwise▶

Adapted from an Opera

Aria
Balalaika
Baritone
Broken Melody
Burlesque of Carmen
Carmen▶
Carmen Jones▶
The Chocolate Soldier
Farewell My Concubine
Faust
Fitzcarraldo▶
For the First Time
The Great Caruso
The Great Waltz▶
Gypsy Blood
I Dream Too Much
Jesus Christ, Superstar▶
La Grande Vadrouille▶
Life of Verdi
The Magic Flute▶
The Medium
Meeting Venus
Midnight Girl
The Mozart Brothers▶
Otello▶
The Panther's Claw
Phantom of the Opera▶
Rose Marie▶
The Tales of Hoffmann
Terror at the Opera
The Toast of New Orleans
The Tsar's Bride▶
The Vampyr
Verdi
Wagner: The Complete Epic
Wagner: The Movie

Adapted from Memoirs or Diaries

Celeste▶
Churchill and the Generals
Danger UXB
The Diary of Anne Frank▶
Edvard Munch
The Elegant Criminal
The Flame Trees of Thika▶
A Free Soul
The Gathering Storm
Goodbye, Miss 4th of July
Gypsy▶
The Happy Hooker
The Happy Hooker Goes
  Hollywood
The Happy Hooker Goes to
  Washington
Heart Beat
Heartland▶
Henry & June▶
I Remember Mama▶
I'll Cry Tomorrow▶
I'm Dancing as Fast as I Can
In the Name of the Father▶
Inside the Third Reich
Jacquot
Julia▶

Maids of Wilko
Meetings with Remarkable Men
Mommie Dearest
Sister Kenny▶
Stars and Stripes Forever▶
This Boy's Life▶
What's Love Got to Do With It?
Wish You Were Here▶

Adapted from Television

The Addams Family
Addams Family Values
Batman
Batman: Mask of the Phantasm
The Beverly Hillbillies
Bonanza: The Return
Boris and Natasha: The Movie
Car 54, Where Are You?
Coneheads
Cooley High▶
The Crawling Eye
Days of Wine and Roses▶
Dennis the Menace
Dragnet
The Flintstones
The Fugitive▶
Get Smart, Again!
Gunfight at Sandoval
Here Come the Littles: The
  Movie
It's Pat
Jetsons: The Movie
The Key to Rebecca
Lassie
The Left-Handed Gun▶
Maverick
The Naked Gun: From the Files
  of Police Squad▶
Naked Gun 33 1/3: The Final
  Insult
Naked Gun 2 1/2: The Smell of
  Fear
The Nude Bomb
One Night Stand
Our Miss Brooks
Pennies From Heaven▶
The People Next Door
Queen for a Day
The Saint
Sergeant Ryker
Star Trek: The Motion Picture
Star Trek 2: The Wrath of
  Khan▶
Star Trek 3: The Search for
  Spock
Star Trek 4: The Voyage
  Home▶
Star Trek 5: The Final Frontier
Star Trek 6: The Undiscovered
  Country
Twin Peaks: Fire Walk with Me
The Untouchables▶
Wackiest Wagon Train in the
  West
Wayne's World▶
Wayne's World 2

Adapted from the Radio

Behind the Mask
Big Town
Check & Double Check
Cosmo Jones, Crime Smasher
The Devil's Eye
Dreaming Out Loud
Gang Busters
Gangbusters
Going to Town
Goon Movie
The Great Gildersleeve
Here We Go Again!
Inner Sanctum
International Crime
The Invisible Avenger
Mr. Arkadin▶
My Friend Irma
Queen for a Day
Renfrew of the Royal Mounted

The Shadow
The Shadow Strikes
Sorry, Wrong Number▶
Treacherous Crossing
The War of the Worlds▶

"Alien" & Rip-Offs

Alien▶
Alien 3
Alien Prey
Alien Seed
Alien Space Avenger
Aliens▶
Creature
Deep Space
Deepstar Six
Forbidden World
Galaxy of Terror
Horror Planet
Leviathan
Nightflyers
Predator
Star Crystal
Xtro 2: The Second Encounter

Amy Fisher

The Amy Fisher Story
Casualties of Love: The "Long
  Island Lolita" Story
Lethal Lolita—Amy Fisher: My
  Story

"Basic Instinct" & Rip-Offs

Basic Instinct
Fatal Instinct
Sliver

BBC TV Productions

An Affair in Mind
After Pilkington
And a Nightingale Sang
And Now for Something
  Completely Different▶
The Assassination Run
The Borrowers▶
Christabel
The Chronicles of Narnia
Danger Man
The Dark Angel▶
Doctor Who: Cybermen—The
  Early Years
Doctor Who: Daleks Invasion of
  Earth 2150 A.D.
Doctor Who: Earthshock
Doctor Who: Mawdryn Undead
Doctor Who: Shada
Doctor Who: The Caves of
  Androzani
Doctor Who: The Curse of
  Fenric
Doctor Who: The Five Doctors
Doctor Who: The Hartnell
  Years
Doctor Who: The Keeper of
  Traken
Doctor Who: The Masque of
  Mandragora
Doctor Who: The Mind Robber
Doctor Who: The Pertwee
  Years
Doctor Who: The Seeds of
  Death
Doctor Who: The Sontaran
  Experiment/The Genesis of
  the Daleks
Doctor Who: The Talons of
  Weng-Chiang
Doctor Who: The Three
  Doctors
Doctor Who: The Time Warrior
Doctor Who: The Tom Baker
  Years
Doctor Who: The Troughton
  Years
Doctor Who: The Twin Dilemma

Doctor Who: The War Games
Doctor Who: Tomb of the
    Cyberman
Edge of Darkness
An Englishman Abroad▶
The Flame Trees of Thika▶
Fortunes of War▶
The Franchise Affair
The Hitchhiker's Guide to the
    Galaxy
The House of Eliott
How Many Miles to Babylon?
Jude the Obscure
The Lost Language of Cranes▶
The Making of The Hitchhiker's
    Guide to the Galaxy
Mansfield Park
Maria's Child
Merlin of the Crystal Cave
Northanger Abbey
A Perfect Spy
Poldark▶
Portrait of a Lady
A Question of Attribution
Robin Hood...The Legend:
    Herne's Son
Robin Hood...The Legend:
    Robin Hood and the
    Sorcerer
Robin Hood...The Legend: The
    Swords of Wayland
Robin Hood...The Legend: The
    Time of the Wolf
School for Scandal
The Secret Garden
Sense & Sensibility
Shadowlands▶
Six Wives of Henry VIII▶
A Tale of Two Cities▶
The Vampyr
A Year in Provence▶

Books to Film: Louisa May Alcott

Little Men
Little Women▶
Little Women

Books to Film: Eric Ambler

Background to Danger▶
Hotel Reserve▶
Journey into Fear▶

Books to Film: Hans Christian Andersen

The Red Shoes▶
The Red Shoes

Books to Film: Maya Angelou

Georgia, Georgia
I Know Why the Caged Bird
    Sings▶

Books to Film: Isaac Asimov

Nightfall

Books to Film: Jane Austen

Mansfield Park
Northanger Abbey
Pride and Prejudice
Pride and Prejudice
Sense & Sensibility

Books to Film: Clive Barker

Candyman

Hellbound: Hellraiser 2
Hellraiser
Hellraiser 3: Hell on Earth
Night Breed
Rawhead Rex
Transmutations

Books to Film: J.M. Barrie

Hook
Peter Pan▶

Books to Film: Ambrose Bierce

Eyes of the Panther
An Occurrence at Owl Creek
    Bridge▶
An Occurrence at Owl Creek
    Bridge/Coup de Grace▶
Red Balloon/Occurrence at Owl
    Creek Bridge▶

Books to Film: Robert Bloch

Mannikin
The Skull
Torture Garden

Books to Film: Judy Blume

Forever

Books to Film: Ray Bradbury

The Beast from 20,000
    Fathoms
Fahrenheit 451▶
The Illustrated Man▶
It Came From Outer Space▶
The Martian Chronicles: Part 1
The Martian Chronicles: Part 2
The Martian Chronicles: Part 3
Something Wicked This Way
    Comes
Strange Tales/Ray Bradbury
    Theatre
Walking on Air

Books to Film: Barbara Taylor Bradford

Hold the Dream
A Woman of Substance,
    Episode 1: Nest of Vipers
A Woman of Substance,
    Episode 2: The Secret is
    Revealed
A Woman of Substance,
    Episode 3: Fighting for the
    Dream

Books to Film: Pearl S. Buck

China Sky
Dragon Seed
The Good Earth▶

Books to Film: Frances Hodgson Burnett

Little Lord Fauntleroy▶
Little Lord Fauntleroy▶
The Little Princess▶
The Little Princess
The Secret Garden▶
The Secret Garden
The Secret Garden▶

The Secret Garden

Books to Film: Edgar Rice Burroughs

At the Earth's Core
Greystoke: The Legend of
    Tarzan, Lord of the Apes
The Land That Time Forgot
The People That Time Forgot
Tarzan and His Mate▶
Tarzan and the Green Goddess
Tarzan and the Trappers
Tarzan Escapes▶
Tarzan Finds a Son▶
Tarzan, the Ape Man▶
Tarzan, the Ape Man
Tarzan the Fearless
Tarzan's New York Adventure
Tarzan's Revenge
Tarzan's Secret Treasure

Books to Film: William Burroughs

Kerouac
Naked Lunch▶

Books to Film: Truman Capote

ABC Stage 67: Truman
    Capote's A Christmas
    Memory
Breakfast at Tiffany's▶
The Glass House▶
In Cold Blood▶

Books to Film: Barbara Cartland

Duel of Hearts
The Flame is Love

Books to Film: Willa Cather

O Pioneers!
Paul's Case

Books to Film: Raymond Chandler

The Big Sleep▶
The Big Sleep
Double Indemnity▶
Farewell, My Lovely▶
The Finger Man
Lady in the Lake
The Long Goodbye▶
Marlowe
Murder, My Sweet▶
Smart-Aleck Kill
Strangers on a Train▶

Books to Film: Paddy Chayefsky

Altered States▶
As Young As You Feel▶
The Catered Affair▶
Marty

Books to Film: John Cheever

Sorrows of Gin
Swimmer▶

Books to Film: Anton Chekhov

The Lady with the Dog▶
The Seagull
The Shooting Party

Ward Six

Books to Film: Agatha Christie

The Affair of the Pink Pearl
The Alphabet Murders
And Then There Were None▶
Appointment with Death
The Body in the Library
The Case of the Missing Lady
The Clergyman's Daughter
The Crackler
Death on the Nile
Endless Night
Evil Under the Sun
Finessing the King
The House of Lurking Death
Love from a Stranger
The Man in the Mist
The Mirror Crack'd
Murder Ahoy
Murder at the Gallop▶
A Murder is Announced
Murder Most Foul▶
Murder on the Orient Express▶
Murder She Said
Ordeal by Innocence
A Pocketful of Rye
The Secret Adversary
Ten Little Indians
The Unbreakable Alibi
Witness for the Prosecution▶

Books to Film: Tom Clancy

Clear and Present Danger▶
The Hunt for Red October▶
Patriot Games▶

Books to Film: Mary Higgins Clark

The Cradle Will Fall
A Cry in the Night
Double Vision
Terror Stalks the Class
    Reunion

Books to Film: Arthur C. Clarke

2001: A Space Odyssey▶
2010: The Year We Make
    Contact▶

Books to Film: James Clavell

King Rat▶
Shogun▶
Tai-Pan▶

Books to Film: Jackie Collins

The Bitch
The World is Full of Married
    Men
Yesterday's Hero

Books to Film: Joseph Conrad

Apocalypse Now▶
The Duellists▶
Face to Face
Heart of Darkness
Lord Jim▶

Books to Film: Pat Conroy

Conrack▶
The Great Santini▶

The Lords of Discipline
The Prince of Tides▶

Books to Film: Robin Cook

Coma▶
Sphinx

Books to Film: James Fenimore Cooper

The Deerslayer
The Last of the Mohicans▶
The Last of the Mohicans
The Last of the Mohicans▶
The Last of the Redmen

Books to Film: Stephen Crane

Face to Face
The Red Badge of Courage▶

Books to Film: Michael Crichton

The Andromeda Strain
The Great Train Robbery▶
Jurassic Park▶
Rising Sun▶
The Terminal Man
Westworld▶

Books to Film: Clive Cussler

Raise the Titanic

Books to Film: Miguel de Cervantes

Don Quixote▶
Man of La Mancha

Books to Film: Guy de Maupassant

A Day in the Country▶
Diary of a Madman▶
Le Plaisir
The Private Affairs of Bel Ami▶
A Woman Without Love▶

Books to Film: Daniel Defoe

The Amorous Adventures of
    Moll Flanders
Crusoe
Man Friday
Robinson Crusoe
Robinson Crusoe on Mars

Books to Film: Charles Dickens

An American Christmas Carol
Bleak House
A Christmas Carol▶
A Christmas Carol
Cricket on the Hearth
David Copperfield▶
David Copperfield
Great Expectations▶
Great Expectations
Great Expectations▶
Great Expectations: The Untold
    Story
Little Dorrit, Film 1: Nobody's
    Fault▶
Little Dorrit, Film 2: Little
    Dorrit's Story▶
The Muppet Christmas Carol
Nicholas Nickleby▶

Books

The Old Curiosity Shop
Oliver!▶
Oliver Twist▶
Oliver Twist
Oliver Twist▶
Oliver Twist
The Pickwick Papers
Scrooge▶
Scrooge
A Tale of Two Cities▶
A Tale of Two Cities
A Tale of Two Cities▶
Tale of Two Cities/In the Switch
   Tower

Books to Film: E.L. Doctorow

Billy Bathgate
Daniel
Ragtime▶

Books to Film: Fyodor Dostoyevski

The Brothers Karamazov▶
Crime and Punishment▶
Crime and Punishment
La Vengeance d'une Femme
White Nights▶

Books to Film: Sir Arthur Conan Doyle

The Adventures of Sherlock
   Holmes
The Adventures of Sherlock
   Holmes: Hound of the
   Baskervilles
The Crucifer of Blood
Dressed to Kill
The Hound of the Baskervilles▶
The Hound of the Baskervilles
House of Fear
The Lost World
Masks of Death
Murder at the Baskervilles
The Pearl of Death
Return to the Lost World
Robbers of the Sacred
   Mountain
Scarlet Claw▶
Sherlock Holmes and the
   Deadly Necklace
Sherlock Holmes and the
   Secret Weapon▶
Sherlock Holmes: The Master
   Blackmailer
Sherlock Hound: Tales of
   Mystery
The Sign of Four
The Silent Mr. Sherlock Holmes
Tales from the Darkside: The
   Movie
The Triumph of Sherlock
   Holmes
The Woman in Green

Books to Film: Daphne Du Maurier

The Birds▶
Don't Look Now▶
Jamaica Inn
Rebecca▶

Books to Film: Alexandre Dumas

At Sword's Point
Black Magic
Camille▶
The Corsican Brothers
The Count of Monte Cristo
The Count of Monte Cristo
The Count of Monte Cristo
The Four Musketeers▶
The Iron Mask

The Man in the Iron Mask▶
Mountain Fury
The Prince of Thieves
The Return of the Musketeers
Robin Hood▶
Sword of Monte Cristo
The Three Musketeers
The Three Musketeers▶
The Three Musketeers
The Three Musketeers

Books to Film: Dominick Dunne

An Inconvenient Woman

Books to Film: George Eliot

The Mill on the Floss
Silas Marner▶

Books to Film: Bret Easton Ellis

Less Than Zero

Books to Film: Howard Fast

Freedom Road

Books to Film: William Faulkner

Intruder in the Dust▶
The Long, Hot Summer▶
The Reivers▶
Today We Live
Tomorrow▶

Books to Film: Henry Fielding

Joseph Andrews
Tom Jones▶

Books to Film: F. Scott Fitzgerald

The Great Gatsby
The Last Time I Saw Paris
The Last Tycoon▶
Tender Is the Night

Books to Film: Gustov Flaubert

Madame Bovary▶
Salammbo

Books to Film: Ian Fleming

Casino Royale
Chitty Chitty Bang Bang
Diamonds are Forever▶
Dr. No▶
For Your Eyes Only▶
From Russia with Love▶
Goldfinger▶
License to Kill▶
Live and Let Die
The Living Daylights▶
The Man with the Golden Gun
Moonraker
Never Say Never Again
Octopussy
On Her Majesty's Secret
   Service▶
The Poppy is also a Flower
The Spy Who Loved Me
Thunderball
A View to a Kill
You Only Live Twice

Books to Film: E.M. Forster

Howard's End▶
Maurice▶
A Passage to India▶
A Room with a View▶
Where Angels Fear to Tread▶

Books to Film: Frederick Forsyth

The Day of the Jackal▶
The Dogs of War
The Fourth Protocol▶
No Comebacks
The Odessa File
Two by Forsyth

Books to Film: Rumer Godden

Black Narcissus▶
In This House of Brede▶
The River▶

Books to Film: Nikolai Gogol

The Overcoat▶
Taras Bulba

Books to Film: William Goldman

Heat
Magic
Marathon Man▶
Mr. Horn
The Princess Bride▶

Books to Film: Elizabeth Goudge

Green Dolphin Street

Books to Film: Kenneth Grahame

The Adventures of Ichabod and
   Mr. Toad▶
The Reluctant Dragon

Books to Film: Graham Greene

Across the Bridge
Beyond the Limit
Brighton Rock▶
The Fallen Idol▶
The Fugitive▶
The Human Factor
Monsignor Quixote
Strike It Rich
The Tenth Man
The Third Man▶
This Gun for Hire▶
This Gun for Hire
Travels with My Aunt

Books to Film: Zane Grey

Arizona Mahoney
The Border Legion
Desert Gold
Drift Fence
Dude Ranger
Fighting Caravans
Forlorn River
Helltown
The Light of Western Stars
Man of the Forest
Nevada
Riders of the Purple Sage
Roll Along Cowboy

Thunder Mountain
Thunder Pass
To the Last Man
Wagon Wheels
West of the Pecos
When the West Was Young

Books to Film: John Grisham

The Client
The Firm▶
The Pelican Brief

Books to Film: H. Rider Haggard

Allan Quartermain and the Lost
   City of Gold
King Solomon's Mines▶
King Solomon's Mines
She

Books to Film: Arthur Hailey

Airport▶
Hotel
Time Lock

Books to Film: Alex Haley

Malcolm X▶
Roots▶
Roots: The Gift
Roots: The Next Generation▶

Books to Film: Dashiell Hammett

After the Thin Man▶
Another Thin Man
The Dain Curse
Hammett
The Maltese Falcon▶
Satan Met a Lady
Shadow of the Thin Man▶
Song of the Thin Man
The Thin Man▶
The Thin Man Goes Home
Woman in the Shadows

Books to Film: Thomas Hardy

Far from the Madding Crowd▶
Jude the Obscure
Tess▶

Books to Film: Harlequin Romances

Dreams Lost, Dreams Found
Love with a Perfect Stranger
The Winds of Jarrah

Books to Film: Nathaniel Hawthorne

Rappaccini's Daughter
The Scarlet Letter▶
Twice-Told Tales▶

Books to Film: Ernest Hemingway

A Farewell to Arms▶
Islands in the Stream
The Killers
My Old Man
The Snows of Kilimanjaro▶
To Have & Have Not▶
Women & Men: Stories of
   Seduction

Books to Film: O. Henry

The Cisco Kid
The Gift of Love
Ruthless People▶

Books to Film: S.E. Hinton

The Outsiders
Rumble Fish▶
Tex
That Was Then...This Is Now

Books to Film: Victor Hugo

Delusions of Grandeur
The Hunchback of Notre
   Dame▶
Les Miserables▶
Les Miserables
Les Miserables▶

Books to Film: Fanny Hurst

Back Street
The Castle▶
Imitation of Life▶
Young at Heart

Books to Film: John Irving

The Hotel New Hampshire
The World According to Garp▶

Books to Film: Washington Irving

The Adventures of Ichabod and
   Mr. Toad▶
The Legend of Sleepy Hollow
Rip van Winkle

Books to Film: Susan Isaacs

Compromising Positions
Shining Through

Books to Film: Rona Jaffe

Mazes and Monsters

Books to Film: John Jakes

The Bastard
North and South Book 1▶
North and South Book 2▶
The Rebels
The Seekers

Books to Film: Henry James

The Bostonians
Daisy Miller
The Europeans▶
The Green Room
The Heiress▶
Lost Moment
The Nightcomers
Portrait of a Lady
Some Came Running▶
The Turn of the Screw

Books to Film: James Jones

From Here to Eternity▶

From Here to Eternity

Books to Film: James Joyce

The Dead
James Joyce: A Portrait of the
    Artist as a Young Man
Ulysses

Books to Film: Franz Kafka

The Trial▶
The Trial

Books to Film: Stephen King

Carrie▶
Cat's Eye
Children of the Corn
Christine
Creepshow
Creepshow 2
Cujo
The Dark Half
Dead Zone▶
Firestarter
Graveyard Shift
The Lawnmower Man
Maximum Overdrive
Misery▶
Needful Things
Pet Sematary
Return to Salem's Lot
The Running Man
Salem's Lot
The Shining
Silver Bullet
Sleepwalkers
Sometimes They Come Back
Stand By Me▶
Stephen King's Golden Years
Stephen King's It
Stephen King's The Stand
Stephen King's The
    Tommyknockers
Tales from the Darkside: The
    Movie

Books to Film: Rudydard Kipling

Captains Courageous▶
A Fool There Was
Gunga Din▶
The Jungle Book
Kim▶
The Man Who Would Be King▶
They Watch
Wee Willie Winkie▶

Books to Film: Dean R. Koontz

Servants of Twilight
Watchers
Whispers

Books to Film: Judith Krantz

Mistral's Daughter
Princess Daisy
Scruples

Books to Film: Louis L'Amour

The Burning Hills
Cancel My Reservation
Conagher
Heller in Pink Tights
The Quick and the Dead
The Sacketts
The Shadow Riders

Shalako

Books to Film: D.H. Lawrence

Kangaroo
Lady Chatterley's Lover
The Rainbow▶
The Rocking Horse Winner
Trespasser
The Virgin and the Gypsy
Women in Love▶
Young Lady Chatterly 2

Books to Film: John Le Carre

The Little Drummer Girl▶
The Looking Glass War
A Perfect Spy
The Russia House
The Spy Who Came in from the
    Cold▶

Books to Film: Harper Lee

To Kill a Mockingbird▶

Books to Film: Elmore Leonard

The Ambassador
Cat Chaser
52 Pick-Up
Glitz
Hombre▶
Stick
3:10 to Yuma▶
Valdez is Coming

Books to Film: Sinclair Lewis

Ann Vickers
Arrowsmith
Dodsworth▶
Elmer Gantry▶

Books to Film: Astrid Lindgren

The Land of Faraway
The New Adventures of Pippi
    Longstocking
Pippi Goes on Board
Pippi in the South Seas
Pippi Longstocking
Pippi on the Run

Books to Film: Jack London

The Assassination Bureau▶
Call of the Wild
The Fighter▶
Great Adventure
The Legend of Sea Wolf
The Legend of the Sea Wolf
The Mutiny of the Elsinore
The Sea Wolf▶
The Sea Wolf
Tales of the Klondike: In a Far
    Country
Tales of the Klondike: Race for
    Number One
Tales of the Klondike: The
    Scorn of Women
Tales of the Klondike: The
    Unexpected
Torture Ship
White Fang
White Fang and the Hunter
Wolf Call

Books to Film: H.P. Lovecraft

Blood Island
Bride of Re-Animator
Cthulhu Mansion
The Curse
Die, Monster, Die!
The Dunwich Horror
From Beyond▶
The Haunted Palace
Lurking Fear
The Re-Animator▶
The Resurrected
The Sinister Invasion
The Unnamable
The Unnamable 2: The
    Statement of Randolph
    Carter

Books to Film: Robert Ludlum

The Bourne Identity▶
The Holcroft Covenant
The Osterman Weekend

Books to Film: Peter Maas

King of the Gypsies
Marie▶
Serpico▶

Books to Film: Alistair MacLean

Bear Island
Breakheart Pass
Caravan to Vaccares
Detonator
Force 10 from Navarone
Golden Rendezvous
The Guns of Navarone▶
Ice Station Zebra
Puppet on a Chain
River of Death
Where Eagles Dare▶

Books to Film: Norman Mailer

The Executioner's Song
Marilyn: The Untold Story▶
The Naked and the Dead
Pursuit
Tough Guys Don't Dance

Books to Film: W. Somerset Maugham

Adorable Julia
Beachcomber▶
Dirty Gertie from Harlem U.S.A.
Encore▶
The Letter▶
Miss Sadie Thompson▶
The Moon and Sixpence▶
Of Human Bondage▶
Of Human Bondage
Overnight Sensation
The Painted Veil
Rain
The Razor's Edge▶
The Razor's Edge
Sadie Thompson▶
Trio▶

Books to Film: Colleen McCullough

An Indecent Obsession
The Thorn Birds▶
Tim

Books to Film: Larry McMurtry

The Best Little Whorehouse in
    Texas
The Last Picture Show▶
Lonesome Dove▶
Terms of Endearment▶
Texasville

Books to Film: Herman Melville

Bartleby
Enchanted Island
Moby Dick▶

Books to Film: James Michener

The Bridges at Toko-Ri▶
Dynasty
Hawaii▶
Return to Paradise
Sayonara▶
Until They Sail

Books to Film: L.M. Montgomery

Anne of Avonlea▶
Anne of Green Gables▶
Lantern Hill
Tales from Avonlea, Vol. 1: The
    Journey Begins▶

Books to Film: Vladimir Nabokov

Despair▶
Lolita▶

Books to Film: Joyce Carol Oates

Smooth Talk▶

Books to Film: Marcel Pagnol

The Baker's Wife▶
Fanny▶
Jean de Florette▶
Manon of the Spring▶
Marius▶
My Father's Glory▶
My Mother's Castle▶
Topaze▶

Books to Film: Edgar Allan Poe

The Black Cat▶
The Black Cat
Dr. Tarr's Torture Dungeon
The Fall of the House of Usher
The Fall of the House of
    Usher▶
The Fall of the House of Usher
The Haunted Palace
Haunting Fear
The Haunting of Morella
The House of Usher
Jaws of Justice
La Chute de la Maison Usher▶
The Living Coffin
Manfish
Masque of the Red Death▶
Masque of the Red Death
Murders in the Rue Morgue
The Murders in the Rue
    Morgue▶
The Oblong Box
The Oval Portrait
The Pit and the Pendulum▶
The Pit & the Pendulum
Premature Burial

The Raven
The Raven▶
The Spectre of Edgar Allen Poe
Spirits of the Dead▶
Tales of Terror
The Tell-Tale Heart
Tomb of Ligeia▶
The Torture Chamber of Dr.
    Sadism
Two Evil Eyes
Web of the Spider

Books to Film: Katherine Anne Porter

Noon Wine▶
Ship of Fools▶

Books to Film: Mario Puzo

The Godfather▶
The Godfather, Part 2▶
The Godfather, Part 3▶
The Sicilian

Books to Film: Harold Robbins

The Adventurers
The Betsy
The Carpetbaggers
King Creole
The Lonely Lady
Nevada Smith
Never Love a Stranger
Stiletto
Where Love Has Gone

Books to Film: Sir Walter Scott

Ivanhoe▶
Ivanhoe
King Richard and the
    Crusaders

Books to Film: Sidney Sheldon

The Naked Face
The Other Side of Midnight
Rage of Angels
Rage of Angels: The Story
    Continues
Sidney Sheldon's Bloodline
Windmills of the Gods

Books to Film: Mary Shelley

The Bride of Frankenstein▶
Frankenstein▶
Frankenstein
Frankenstein Unbound▶

Books to Film: Danielle Steel

Danielle Steel's Changes
Danielle Steel's ''Daddy''
Danielle Steel's Kaleidoscope
Fine Things
Now and Forever
The Promise

Books to Film: John Steinbeck

Cannery Row
East of Eden
East of Eden
The Grapes of Wrath▶
Lifeboat▶
Of Mice and Men▶

Books

The Pearl▶
The Red Pony▶
Tortilla Flat▶

Books to Film: Stendhal

La Chartreuse de Parme
The Red and the Black▶
Vanina Vanini▶

Books to Film: Robert Louis Stevenson

Abbott and Costello Meet Dr.
   Jekyll and Mr. Hyde
Adventure Island
Black Arrow▶
The Body Snatcher
Dr. Jekyll and Mr. Hyde▶
Dr. Jekyll and Mr. Hyde
Dr. Jekyll and Sister Hyde
Jekyll & Hyde...Together Again
Kidnapped
Man with Two Heads
The Master of Ballantrae
Strange Case of Dr. Jekyll &
   Mr. Hyde
Treasure Island▶
Treasure Island
The Wrong Box▶

Books to Film: Bram Stoker

Count Dracula
Dracula▶
Dracula
Dracula (Spanish Version)
The Horror of Dracula▶
The Lair of the White Worm▶
Nosferatu▶
Tomb

Books to Film: Harriet Beecher Stowe

Uncle Tom's Cabin

Books to Film: Jacqueline Susann

The Love Machine
Once is Not Enough

Books to Film: Jonathan Swift

Gulliver's Travels
The Three Worlds of Gulliver

Books to Film: Paul Theroux

Half Moon Street
The Mosquito Coast
Saint Jack▶

Books to Film: James Thurber

The Battle of the Sexes▶
Billy Liar▶
The Secret Life of Walter
   Mitty▶

Books to Film: J.R.R. Tolkien

The Hobbit▶
The Lord of the Rings
The Return of the King

Books to Film: Leo Tolstoy

War and Peace▶

Books to Film: Scott Turow

Presumed Innocent▶

Books to Film: Mark Twain

The Adventures of Huck Finn▶
The Adventures of Huckleberry
   Finn▶
The Adventures of Huckleberry
   Finn
The Adventures of Tom
   Sawyer▶
The Adventures of Tom Sawyer
A Connecticut Yankee▶
A Connecticut Yankee in King
   Arthur's Court
Huck and the King of Hearts
Huckleberry Finn
The Innocents Abroad
The Man That Corrupted
   Hadleyburg
The Mysterious Stranger▶
The Prince and the Pauper▶
The Prince and the Pauper
The Private History of a
   Campaign That Failed
Pudd'nhead Wilson
Tom Sawyer▶
Tom Sawyer
Unidentified Flying Oddball

Books to Film: John Updike

Pigeon Feathers
Roommate
The Witches of Eastwick

Books to Film: Leon Uris

Battle Cry▶
Exodus▶
QB VII▶
Topaz▶

Books to Film: Jules Verne

Around the World in 80 Days▶
800 Leagues Down the
   Amazon
Five Weeks in a Balloon
From the Earth to the Moon
In Search of the Castaways▶
Journey to the Center of the
   Earth▶
Journey to the Center of the
   Earth
Light at the Edge of the World
Master of the World▶
Mysterious Island▶
On the Comet▶
Those Fantastic Flying Fools
20,000 Leagues Under the
   Sea▶
Where Time Began

Books to Film: Kurt Vonnegut

D.P.
Slapstick of Another Kind
Slaughterhouse Five
Who Am I This Time?▶

Books to Film: Alice Walker

The Color Purple▶

Books to Film: Edgar Wallace

The Black Abbot
Chamber of Horrors
Creature with the Blue Hand
Curse of the Yellow Snake
Dead Eyes of London
Door with the Seven Locks
Forger of London
The Human Monster
The Indian Scarf
Mr. Reeder in Room 13
The Mysterious Magician
The Secret Four
Secret of the Black Trunk
The Squeaker
The Strange Countess
The Terror

Books to Film: Joseph Wambaugh

The Black Marble▶
The Choirboys
Echoes in the Darkness
The Glitter Dome
The New Centurions
The Onion Field▶

Books to Film: Evelyn Waugh

Brideshead Revisited▶
A Handful of Dust▶
The Loved One▶

Books to Film: H.G. Wells

Empire of the Ants
First Men in the Moon
Food of the Gods
Food of the Gods: Part 2
Half a Sixpence
The Invisible Man▶
The Invisible Man's Revenge
Island of Dr. Moreau
Kipps▶
La Merveilleuse Visite
The Man Who Could Work
   Miracles▶
The New Invisible Man
Terror is a Man
Things to Come▶
The Time Machine▶
Time Machine
Village of the Giants
The War of the Worlds▶

Books to Film: Edith Wharton

The Age of Innocence▶
The Children
Ethan Frome
The Lady's Maid's Bell
The Old Maid▶

Books to Film: William Wharton

Birdy▶
Dad
A Midnight Clear▶

Books to Film: Oscar Wilde

The Canterville Ghost
Dorian Gray
Importance of Being Earnest▶

Lady Windermere's Fan
Picture of Dorian Gray▶
Salome
The Sins of Dorian Gray

Books to Film: Thornton Wilder

The Bridge of San Luis Rey▶
Hello, Dolly!
The Matchmaker▶
Mr. North
Our Town▶

Books to Film: Virginia Woolf

To the Lighthouse

Books to Film: Herman Wouk

The Caine Mutiny▶
The Caine Mutiny Court
   Martial▶
Marjorie Morningstar
War & Remembrance, Part 1
War & Remembrance, Part 2
War & Remembrance, Part 3
War & Remembrance, Part 4
War & Remembrance, Part 5
War & Remembrance, Part 6
War & Remembrance, Part 7
War & Remembrance: The
   Final Chapter, Part 8
War & Remembrance: The
   Final Chapter, Part 9
War & Remembrance: The
   Final Chapter, Part 10
War & Remembrance: The
   Final Chapter, Part 11
War & Remembrance: The
   Final Chapter, Part 12
The Winds of War

Classics

A Nous la Liberte▶
Abe Lincoln in Illinois▶
Across the Pacific▶
Adam's Rib▶
The Adventures of Robin
   Hood▶
The Adventures of Tarzan
The Adventures of Tom
   Sawyer▶
The African Queen▶
Aguirre, the Wrath of God▶
Airplane!▶
Alexander Nevsky▶
Alice in Wonderland▶
All About Eve▶
All Quiet on the Western Front▶
All the King's Men▶
All This and Heaven Too▶
Amarcord▶
American Graffiti▶
An American in Paris▶
Anastasia▶
Anatomy of a Murder▶
Anchors Aweigh▶
Angels with Dirty Faces▶
Animal Crackers▶
Anna Christie
Anna Karenina▶
Annie Hall▶
The Apartment▶
Apocalypse Now▶
Applause▶
Arsenal▶
Arsenic and Old Lace▶
The Asphalt Jungle▶
At the Circus
Avenging Conscience
The Awful Truth▶
Baby Face
The Bad and the Beautiful▶
Badlands▶
Bahama Passage
Bambi▶

The Bank Dick▶
Bathing Beauty
The Battleship Potemkin▶
Beau Geste▶
Beauty and the Beast▶
Ben-Hur▶
The Best Years of Our Lives▶
Beyond the Forest
The Bicycle Thief▶
The Big Parade▶
The Big Sleep▶
Big Trail▶
The Birth of a Nation▶
Black Beauty▶
The Black Cat▶
The Black Pirate▶
Blade Runner▶
Blind Husbands▶
Block-heads▶
Blood and Sand
The Blood of a Poet▶
Blow-Up▶
The Blue Angel▶
Body and Soul▶
Bonnie & Clyde▶
Born Yesterday▶
Boudu Saved from Drowning▶
Bowery Blitzkrieg
Boys Town▶
Breathless▶
The Bride Came C.O.D.
The Bride of Frankenstein▶
The Bridge on the River Kwai▶
Broken Blossoms▶
The Burmese Harp▶
But Not for Me
Butch Cassidy and the
   Sundance Kid▶
The Cabinet of Dr. Caligari▶
Caddyshack▶
The Caine Mutiny▶
The Cameraman▶
Camille▶
Carefree▶
Casablanca▶
Cat People▶
The Catered Affair▶
Cesar▶
Challenge to Lassie
The Champ▶
The Cheat▶
Children of Paradise▶
Chimes at Midnight▶
Chinatown▶
A Christmas Carol▶
Cinderella▶
The Circus▶
Citizen Kane▶
City Lights▶
Claire's Knee▶
College▶
Condemned to Live
The Crazy Ray▶
Creature from the Black
   Lagoon▶
The Crime of Monsieur Lange▶
The Criminal Life of Archibaldo
   de la Cruz▶
The Crowd▶
Curly Top▶
Curse of the Cat People▶
Cyrano de Bergerac▶
Dance Fools Dance▶
Dancing Lady
A Day in the Country▶
The Day the Earth Stood Still▶
The Dentist▶
Desperate Scoundrel/The Pride
   of Pikeville
Detour▶
Deutschland im Jahre Null▶
Diabolique▶
Dial ''M'' for Murder▶
Diary of a Country Priest▶
Diary of a Lost Girl▶
Dimples
Dinner at Eight▶
The Divorcee
D.O.A.▶
Docks of New York▶
Dr. Jekyll and Mr. Hyde▶
Dr. Mabuse the Gambler▶

Dr. Strangelove, or: How I Learned to Stop Worrying and Love the Bomb▶
Doctor X
Don Juan▶
Don Quixote▶
Double Indemnity▶
Down Argentine Way▶
Dracula▶
Drums Along the Mohawk▶
Duck Soup▶
Dumbo▶
The Dybbuk▶
Each Dawn I Die
The Eagle▶
The Earrings of Madame De...▶
Earth▶
East of Eden▶
Easter Parade▶
Easy Street▶
The Eclipse▶
Edge of the World▶
8 1/2▶
Elephant Walk
Elmer Gantry▶
Emperor Jones▶
The End of St. Petersburg▶
Entr'acte
E.T.: The Extra-Terrestrial▶
The Exorcist▶
The Exterminating Angel▶
A Face in the Crowd▶
Fahrenheit 451▶
Fame is the Spur
Fanny▶
Fantasia▶
Father of the Bride▶
Faust▶
Five Easy Pieces▶
Foolish Wives▶
Forbidden Games▶
Forbidden Planet▶
Foreign Correspondent▶
Fort Apache▶
42nd Street▶
The Four Horsemen of the Apocalypse▶
The 400 Blows▶
Frankenstein▶
The French Connection▶
Frenzy▶
The Freshman▶
From Here to Eternity▶
Fury▶
Gandhi▶
Gaslight▶
The Gay Divorcee▶
The General▶
The General Line▶
Gertrud▶
Giant▶
Gigi▶
Give a Girl a Break
The Godfather▶
The Godfather, Part 2▶
Going My Way▶
The Gold Rush▶
The Golem▶
Gone with the Wind▶
The Good Earth▶
Goodbye, Mr. Chips▶
The Gospel According to St. Matthew▶
The Graduate▶
Grand Illusion▶
The Grapes of Wrath▶
Grease▶
The Great Dictator▶
Great Expectations▶
Greed▶
Gun Crazy▶
Hail the Conquering Hero▶
Half a Sixpence
Hamlet▶
Harold and Maude▶
Harvest▶
Harvey▶
Hearts of the World▶
High Noon▶
Hiroshima, Mon Amour▶
His Girl Friday▶
Holiday▶

The Home and the World▶
Horse Feathers▶
How Green was My Valley▶
How the Grinch Stole Christmas▶
The Hunchback of Notre Dame▶
The Hustler▶
I Am a Fugitive from a Chain Gang▶
I Remember Mama▶
I Want to Live!▶
I Was a Teenage Werewolf
If...▶
Ikiru▶
The Immigrant▶
In a Lonely Place▶
In the Heat of the Night▶
In Which We Serve▶
The Incredible Shrinking Man▶
The Informer▶
Inherit the Wind▶
Intermezzo▶
Intolerance▶
Invaders from Mars
Invasion of the Body Snatchers▶
The Invisible Man▶
It Happened in Brooklyn▶
It Happened One Night▶
Italian Straw Hat▶
It's A Gift▶
It's a Great Feeling▶
It's a Wonderful Life▶
Ivan the Terrible, Part 1▶
Ivan the Terrible, Part 2▶
Ivanhoe▶
Jazz Singer▶
Jezebel▶
Johnny Belinda▶
Jour de Fete▶
Joyless Street▶
Judgment at Nuremberg▶
Jules and Jim▶
Juliet of the Spirits▶
Julius Caesar▶
Juno and the Paycock
Kameradschaft▶
Kanal▶
Kentucky Kernels
Key Largo▶
The Kid▶
The Kid Brother▶
The King and I▶
King Kong▶
King Solomon's Mines▶
Kings Row▶
The Kiss▶
Kriemhilde's Revenge▶
La Bete Humaine▶
La Chienne▶
La Chute de la Maison Usher▶
La Cucaracha▶
La Dolce Vita▶
La Marseillaise▶
La Ronde▶
La Strada▶
La Terra Trema▶
Lady and the Tramp▶
Lady Be Good
The Lady Eve▶
The Lady Vanishes▶
L'Age D'Or▶
Lassie, Come Home
Last Command▶
Last Days of Pompeii
The Last Laugh▶
L'Atalante▶
Laura▶
Lawrence of Arabia▶
Le Million▶
Les Visiteurs du Soir▶
Let's Dance
The Letter▶
A Letter to Three Wives▶
Life of Oharu▶
The Light of Faith
Little Caesar▶
Little Women▶
The Lodger▶
Lola Montes▶
Lost Horizon▶

The Lost Patrol▶
The Lost Weekend▶
Louisiana Story▶
Love Affair▶
Love Crazy▶
Lovely to Look At▶
M▶
Mad Max▶
The Magnificent Ambersons▶
The Magnificent Seven▶
The Maltese Falcon▶
Man in the Silk Hat▶
The Man Who Came to Dinner▶
The Man Who Could Work Miracles▶
The Man Who Knew Too Much▶
The Man Who Would Be King▶
The Manchurian Candidate▶
Manhattan▶
Marius▶
Mark of the Vampire▶
Marnie▶
Mary of Scotland▶
M*A*S*H▶
The Matchmaker▶
McCabe & Mrs. Miller▶
Mean Streets▶
Meet Me in Las Vegas
The Merry Widow▶
Metropolis▶
Mighty Joe Young
Mildred Pierce▶
Miracle of Morgan's Creek▶
Miracle on 34th Street▶
Mrs. Miniver▶
Mr. Blandings Builds His Dream House▶
Mr. Deeds Goes to Town▶
Mr. Hulot's Holiday▶
Mister Roberts▶
Mr. Smith Goes to Washington▶
Moana, a Romance of the Golden Age▶
Modern Times▶
Monkey Business▶
Moonstruck▶
Morocco▶
Mother▶
Mothra▶
The Mummy▶
The Muppet Movie▶
Murder, My Sweet▶
Mutiny on the Bounty▶
My Darling Clementine▶
My Life to Live▶
My Man Godfrey▶
Mysterious Island▶
Mystery of the Wax Museum▶
Napoleon▶
Narrow Trail▶
Nashville▶
National Lampoon's Animal House▶
National Velvet▶
Next Time I Marry
Nicholas Nickleby▶
A Night at the Opera▶
The Night Club
A Night in Casablanca▶
The Night of the Hunter▶
Night of the Living Dead▶
Nights of Cabiria▶
North by Northwest▶
Nosferatu▶
Nothing But a Man▶
Now, Voyager▶
Of Human Bondage▶
Of Mice and Men▶
Old Yeller▶
Oliver Twist▶
On the Waterfront▶
Once Upon a Time in the West▶
One Flew Over the Cuckoo's Nest▶
101 Dalmations▶
Only Angels Have Wings▶
Open City▶
Ordet▶

Orpheus▶
Our Hospitality▶
Our Relations▶
Out of the Past▶
Pandora's Box▶
Pardon Us▶
Passion
The Passion of Joan of Arc▶
Father Panchali▶
Paths of Glory▶
Patton▶
Pelle the Conqueror▶
Pepe Le Moko▶
Persona▶
Peyton Place▶
Phantom of the Opera▶
The Philadelphia Story▶
Pickpocket▶
Pickup on South Street▶
Picture of Dorian Gray▶
Pinocchio▶
The Pit and the Pendulum▶
Planet of the Apes▶
Possessed
The Postman Always Rings Twice▶
Pride and Prejudice▶
The Private Life of Henry VIII▶
Psycho▶
Public Enemy▶
Pygmalion▶
Que Viva Mexico▶
Queen Kelly▶
The Quiet Man▶
Raging Bull▶
Ran▶
Rashomon▶
Rebel Without a Cause▶
Red Dust▶
Red Headed Woman▶
The Red Pony▶
Red River▶
The Red Shoes▶
Revenge of the Zombies▶
Ride the High Country▶
The Rink▶
Rio Bravo▶
Romeo and Juliet▶
Rope▶
The Ruggles of Red Gap▶
The Rules of the Game▶
San Francisco▶
Sansho the Bailiff▶
Sawdust & Tinsel▶
Scaramouche▶
The Scarlet Pimpernel▶
Scrooge▶
Seance on a Wet Afternoon▶
The Searchers▶
Seven Chances▶
Seven Samurai▶
The Seventh Seal▶
Shadow of a Doubt▶
Shane▶
She Done Him Wrong▶
She Wore a Yellow Ribbon▶
The Sheik▶
Shoeshine▶
Siegfried▶
Silk Stockings▶
The Sin of Madelon Claudet▶
Singin' in the Rain▶
The Single Standard▶
Sleeping Beauty▶
Sodom and Gomorrah
Son of the Sheik▶
The Sound of Music▶
Spies▶
Spite Marriage▶
The Spy Who Came in from the Cold▶
Stagecoach▶
A Star is Born▶
Star Wars▶
The Stars Look Down▶
Steamboat Bill, Jr.▶
Stella Dallas▶
Storm Over Asia▶
Strangers on a Train▶
Street of Shame▶
A Streetcar Named Desire▶
Strike▶

Student of Prague▶
A Sunday in the Country▶
Sunrise▶
Suspicion▶
Svengali▶
Sweet Smell of Success▶
Tabu: A Story of the South Seas▶
Tarzan, the Ape Man▶
The Ten Commandments▶
Ten Days That Shook the World▶
These Three▶
They Were Expendable▶
Thief of Baghdad▶
The Thin Man▶
The Thing▶
The Third Man▶
The Thirteenth Man
Thirty Seconds Over Tokyo▶
Three Charlies and One Phoney!
The Three Musketeers▶
Three on a Match▶
Throne of Blood▶
Tin Star▶
The Tip-Off
To Have & Have Not▶
To Kill a Mockingbird▶
Tom Sawyer▶
Topper▶
Touch of Evil▶
Tramp & a Woman
Treasure of the Sierra Madre▶
True Heart Susie
Tumbleweeds▶
Twentieth Century▶
Ugetsu▶
Un Chien Andalou▶
Under the Roofs of Paris▶
The Vagabond▶
Vampyr▶
Variety▶
Vertigo▶
The Virginian▶
Wages of Fear▶
The War of the Worlds▶
Warning Shadows▶
Waxworks▶
Way Down East▶
The Wedding March▶
West Side Story▶
Westfront 1918▶
When Ladies Meet▶
White Christmas▶
The White Zombie▶
The Wild Bunch▶
The Wild One▶
Wild Strawberries▶
The Wind▶
Wings
The Wizard of Oz▶
A Woman of Affairs▶
Woman of the Year▶
The World of Apu▶
Wuthering Heights▶
Yankee Doodle Dandy▶
The Yearling▶
Yojimbo▶
You Can't Cheat an Honest Man▶
Young Mr. Lincoln▶
Zero for Conduct▶
Zvenigora▶

Disney Animated Movies

Aladdin▶
Alice in Wonderland▶
Bambi▶
Beauty and the Beast▶
Cinderella▶
DuckTales the Movie: Treasure of the Lost Lamp▶
Dumbo▶
Fantasia▶
The Fox and the Hound▶
The Great Mouse Detective▶
The Jungle Book▶
Lady and the Tramp▶

Disney

The Lion King▶
The Little Mermaid▶
The Nightmare Before
  Christmas▶
101 Dalmations▶
Peter Pan▶
Pinocchio▶
The Rescuers▶
The Rescuers Down Under
The Return of Jafar
Robin Hood▶
Sleeping Beauty▶
Snow White and the Seven
  Dwarfs▶
The Sword in the Stone▶
The Three Caballeros

Disney Family Movies

The Absent-Minded Professor▶
The Adventures of Bullwhip
  Griffin
The Adventures of Huck Finn▶
The Adventures of Ichabod and
  Mr. Toad▶
The Air Up There
Almost Angels
Amy
Angels in the Outfield
The Apple Dumpling Gang
The Apple Dumpling Gang
  Rides Again
Babes in Toyland
The Barefoot Executive
The Bears & I
Bedknobs and Broomsticks
Benji the Hunted
Big Red
Black Arrow▶
The Black Arrow
The Black Hole
Blackbeard's Ghost
Blank Check
The Blue Yonder
Bon Voyage!
Born to Run
Breakin' Through
Candleshoe
The Castaway Cowboy
The Cat from Outer Space
Charley and the Angel
Charlie, the Lonesome Cougar
Cheetah
Child of Glass
The Computer Wore Tennis
  Shoes
Condorman
Darby O'Gill & the Little
  People▶
Davy Crockett and the River
  Pirates
Davy Crockett, King of the Wild
  Frontier▶
The Devil & Max Devlin
Diamonds on Wheels
Dr. Syn, Alias the Scarecrow
Emil and the Detective
Escapade in Florence
Escape to Witch Mountain▶
A Far Off Place
The Fighting Prince of Donegal
Flight of the Grey Wolf
Flight of the Navigator
Freaky Friday
Fun & Fancy Free
The Girl Who Spelled
  Freedom▶
Gnome-Mobile
Gone are the Days
The Great Locomotive Chase
Greyfriars Bobby
Gus
Herbie Goes Bananas
Herbie Goes to Monte Carlo
Herbie Rides Again
Homeward Bound: The
  Incredible Journey
Honey, I Blew Up the Kid
Honey, I Shrunk the Kids

The Horse in the Gray Flannel
  Suit
The Horse Without a Head
Horsemasters
Hot Lead & Cold Feet
In Search of the Castaways▶
The Incredible Journey
Iron Will
The Island at the Top of the
  World
Johnny Shiloh
Johnny Tremain & the Sons of
  Liberty
The Journey of Natty Gann▶
Justin Morgan Had a Horse
King of the Grizzlies
The Last Flight of Noah's Ark
Lt. Robin Crusoe, U.S.N.
The Light in the Forest
The Littlest Horse Thieves
The Littlest Outlaw
Lots of Luck
The Love Bug
Love Leads the Way
Mary Poppins
Menace on the Mountain
Mickey's Christmas Carol▶
Million Dollar Duck
Miracle Down Under
The Miracle of the White
  Stallions
The Misadventures of Merlin
  Jones
Monkeys, Go Home!
Monkey's Uncle
Moon Pilot
The Moon-Spinners
Mooncussers
Mosby's Marauders
My Dog, the Thief
Napoleon and Samantha▶
Never a Dull Moment
Newsies
Night Crossing
Nikki, the Wild Dog of the North
The Nine Lives of Elfego Baca
No Deposit, No Return
The North Avenue Irregulars
Now You See Him, Now You
  Don't
Old Yeller▶
The One and Only, Genuine,
  Original Family Band▶
One Little Indian
One Magic Christmas
One of Our Dinosaurs Is
  Missing
The Parent Trap
Pete's Dragon
Pollyanna▶
Return from Witch Mountain
Return to Oz
Ride a Wild Pony▶
Rob Roy—The Highland Rogue
The Rocketeer▶
Sammy, the Way-Out Seal
Savage Sam
Scandalous John
The Secret of El Zorro
The Shaggy D.A.
The Shaggy Dog
The Sign of Zorro
Smith!
Smoke
Snowball Express
So Dear to My Heart▶
Son of Flubber
The Story of Robin Hood & His
  Merrie Men▶
Summer Magic
Superdad
The Swiss Family Robinson▶
The Sword & the Rose
Ten Who Dared
That Darn Cat
Third Man on the Mountain
Those Calloways
The Three Lives of
  Thomasina▶
3 Ninjas
3 Ninjas Kick Back
A Tiger Walks

Toby Tyler▶
Tonka
Treasure Island▶
The Treasure of Matecumbe
20,000 Leagues Under the
  Sea▶
The Ugly Dachshund
Undergrads▶
Unidentified Flying Oddball
Waltz King
The Watcher in the Woods
Westward Ho, the Wagons!
White Fang▶
White Fang 2: The Myth of the
  White Wolf
The Wild Country
Wild Hearts Can't Be Broken▶
The World's Greatest Athlete

"E.T." & Rip-Offs

E.T.: The Extra-Terrestrial▶
Mac and Me

Family Viewing

The Absent-Minded Professor▶
Adventures in Dinosaur City
Adventures in Spying
The Adventures of Bullwhip
  Griffin
The Adventures of Huckleberry
  Finn
The Adventures of Mark
  Twain▶
African Journey
Aladdin▶
Aladdin and His Wonderful
  Lamp
Almos' a Man
Almost Partners
The Amazing Dobermans
An American Tail
An American Tail: Fievel Goes
  West
Amy
And the Children Shall Lead
And You Thought Your Parents
  Were Weird!
Andre
Angels in the Outfield
Anne of Avonlea▶
Anne of Green Gables▶
Annie Oakley
The Apple Dumpling Gang
The Apple Dumpling Gang
  Rides Again
Babar: The Movie
Babes in Toyland
Baby's Day Out
Back to Hannibal: The Return
  of Tom Sawyer and
  Huckleberry Finn
The Ballad of Paul Bunyan
Bambi▶
The Barefoot Executive
Batman▶
Be My Valentine, Charlie Brown
Beauty and the Beast▶
Beethoven
Beethoven's 2nd
Behave Yourself!
Bell, Book and Candle
Benji▶
Benji the Hunted
Benji's Very Own Christmas
  Story
Bernard and the Genie
The Best Christmas Pageant
  Ever
Big Red
The Billion Dollar Hobo
Bingo
The Black Arrow
Black Beauty
Black Beauty/Courage of Black
  Beauty
The Black Hole
Blackbeard's Ghost
The Blue Yonder
Bon Voyage!
Born Free▶

Born to Run
The Borrowers▶
A Boy Named Charlie Brown▶
The Boy Who Loved Trolls
The Brain
Breakin' Through
Brewster's Millions
Bridge to Terabithia
Brother Future
Bugs Bunny: Hollywood
  Legend
Bugs Bunny's Comedy
  Classics
The Bulldozer Brigade
Calacan▶
Candleshoe
The Canterville Ghost
The Capture of Grizzly Adams
The Care Bears Movie
The Care Bears Movie 2: A
  New Generation
Casey at the Bat
The Castaway Cowboy
The Cat from Outer Space
Challenge to Lassie
The Challengers
Charley and the Angel
A Charlie Brown Christmas
Charlie Brown's All-Stars
Charlie, the Lonesome Cougar
Cheetah
Child of Glass
Chips, the War Dog
The Chronicles of Narnia
Cinderella▶
Clarence
Clarence, the Cross-eyed
  Lion▶
Clowning Around
The Computer Wore Tennis
  Shoes
Condorman
Courage Mountain
Courage of Lassie
Cross Creek
Cry from the Mountain
Daniel and the Towers
Darby O'Gill & the Little
  People▶
The Dark Crystal▶
Davy Crockett and the River
  Pirates
Davy Crockett, King of the Wild
  Frontier▶
A Day for Thanks on Walton's
  Mountain
The Devil & Max Devlin
Diamond's Edge
Diamonds on Wheels
Disney's Storybook Classics
Dr. Syn, Alias the Scarecrow
A Dog of Flanders
The Dog Who Stopped the War
Donner Pass: The Road to
  Survival
D2: The Mighty Ducks
DuckTales the Movie: Treasure
  of the Lost Lamp
Dumbo▶
Dusty
Ele, My Friend
Emil and the Detective
The Enchanted Forest
Escapade in Florence
Escape to Witch Mountain▶
Father of the Bride
Felix the Cat: The Movie
Ferngully: The Last Rain Forest
The Fig Tree
The Fighting Prince of Donegal
Flight of the Grey Wolf
Flight of the Navigator
Flipper▶
Flipper's New Adventure▶
Flipper's Odyssey
Follow Me, Boys!▶
For the Love of Benji
The Fox and the Hound▶
Freaky Friday
Free Willy
Freeze Frame
Frog

Frogs!
Gay Purr-ee
George's Island▶
The Gift of Love
A Girl of the Limberlost
The Girl Who Spelled
  Freedom▶
Gnome-Mobile
Goin' Coconuts
Gone are the Days
The Good, the Bad, and
  Huckleberry Hound
The Great Land of Small
The Great Locomotive Chase
Greyfriars Bobby
Gryphon
Gus
Happily Ever After
The Haunting of Barney Palmer
Hector's Bunyip
Heidi
Heidi▶
Herbie Goes Bananas
Herbie Goes to Monte Carlo
Herbie Rides Again
Here Comes Santa Claus
He's Your Dog, Charlie Brown!
The Hideaways
The Hills of Home▶
Hiroshima Maiden
The Hoboken Chicken
  Emergency
Hockey Night
Home Alone▶
Home at Last
Home for Christmas
Honey, I Blew Up the Kid
Honey, I Shrunk the Kids
The Horse in the Gray Flannel
  Suit
The Horse Without a Head
Horsemasters
Hot Lead & Cold Feet
The House of Dies Drear
How to Be a Perfect Person in
  Just Three Days
Huck and the King of Hearts
Huckleberry Finn
Hugo the Hippo
I Love Lucy
The Incredible Journey
Into the West▶
The Invisible Boy
Is This Goodbye, Charlie
  Brown?
The Island at the Top of the
  World
It Was a Short Summer, Charlie
  Brown
It's an Adventure, Charlie
  Brown!
It's the Great Pumpkin, Charlie
  Brown
Jack & the Beanstalk
Jacob Have I Loved
The Jetsons Meet the
  Flintstones
Joe Panther▶
Johnny Appleseed
Johnny Shiloh
Johnny Tremain & the Sons of
  Liberty
Journey Back to Oz
The Journey of Natty Gann▶
Journey to Spirit Island
The Jungle Book
The Jungle Book▶
Justin Morgan Had a Horse
Kid Colter
A Kid for Two Farthings
The Kid Who Loved Christmas
King of the Grizzlies
King of the Wind
Konrad
The Land Before Time: The
  Great Valley Adventure
The Land of Faraway
Lantern Hill
Lassie: Adventures of Neeka
Lassie: Well of Love
The Last Flight of Noah's Ark
The Lawrenceville Stories

Legend of Lobo
The Legend of Sleepy Hollow
Lt. Robin Crusoe, U.S.N.
The Light in the Forest
The Lion King▶
Little Heroes
Little Miss Marker▶
Little Nemo: Adventures in Slumberland
The Little Princess▶
The Little Princess
The Little Rascals▶
Little Rascals Collector's Edition, Vol. 1-6
Little Rascals Comedy Classics, Vol. 1
Little Rascals Comedy Classics, Vol. 2
Little Rascals: Fish Hooky/Spooky Hooky
Little Rascals: Honkey Donkey/Sprucin' Up
Little Rascals: Little Sinner/Two Too Young
Little Rascals: Mush and Milk/Three Men in a Tub
Little Rascals on Parade
Little Rascals: Pups is Pups/Three Smart Boys
Little Rascals: Readin' and Writin'/Mail and Female
Little Rascals: Reunion in Rhythm/Mike Fright
Little Rascals: Spanky/Feed 'Em and Weep
Little Rascals: The Pinch Singer/Framing Youth
Little Rascals Two Reelers, Vol. 1
Little Rascals Two Reelers, Vol. 2
Little Rascals Two Reelers, Vol. 3
Little Rascals Two Reelers, Vol. 4
Little Rascals Two Reelers, Vol. 5
Little Rascals Two Reelers, Vol. 6
Little Rascals, Vol. 1
Little Rascals, Vol. 2
The Littlest Horse Thieves
The Littlest Outlaw
Lone Star Kid
Look Who's Talking Now
Looking for Miracles
Lots of Luck
The Love Bug
Love Leads the Way
Magic of Lassie
The Magic Sword
Magical Wonderland
Maricela
Mark Twain and Me
Mary Poppins▶
Max Maven's Mindgames
Men of Boys Town
Menace on the Mountain
Mickey's Christmas Carol▶
The Mighty Ducks
The Mighty Pawns
Million Dollar Duck
Miracle at Moreaux
Miracle Down Under
The Miracle of the White Stallions
The Misadventures of Merlin Jones
Mr. Superinvisible
Misty
Monkey Trouble
Monkeys, Go Home!
Monkey's Uncle
Moon Pilot
The Moon-Spinners
Mooncussers
Mosby's Marauders
Mother Goose Rock 'n' Rhyme
Munchie
The Muppet Movie▶
The Muppets Take Manhattan▶
My Darlin' Clementine

My Dog, the Thief
My Friend Flicka
My Neighbor Totoro
The Mysterious Stranger
Napoleon and Samantha▶
Necessary Parties
Never a Dull Moment
The NeverEnding Story▶
The NeverEnding Story 2: Next Chapter
Newsies
Night Crossing
The Nightingale
Nikki, the Wild Dog of the North
The Nine Lives of Elfego Baca
No Deposit, No Return
No Grumps Allowed!
The North Avenue Irregulars
Not Quite Human
Not Quite Human 2
Now You See Him, Now You Don't
Nukie
The Nutcracker Prince
Old Yeller▶
Ollie Hopnoodle's Haven of Bliss
Once Upon a Forest
The One and Only, Genuine, Original Family Band▶
101 Dalmations
One Little Indian
One Magic Christmas
One of Our Dinosaurs Is Missing
The Out-of-Towners▶
Pecos Bill
Pete's Dragon
Pinocchio▶
Pippi Goes on Board
Pippi in the South Seas
Pippi Longstocking
Pippi on the Run
Pistol: The Birth of a Legend
Poco
Pollyanna▶
Prancer
Primo Baby
Prince and the Great Race
The Princess and the Goblin
A Rare Breed
The Red Pony▶
The Red Fury
The Reluctant Dragon
The Rescuers▶
The Rescuers Down Under
Return from Witch Mountain
The Return of the King
Return to Oz
Ride a Wild Pony▶
Ring of Bright Water▶
Rob Roy—The Highland Rogue
Rock-a-Doodle
The Rocketeer▶
Rover Dangerfield
Rudolph the Red-Nosed Reindeer
Rumpelstiltskin
Run for the Roses
Runaway
Runaway Island, Part 1
Runaway Island, Part 2
Runaway Island, Part 3
Runaway Island, Part 4
The Runaways
Sammy, the Way-Out Seal
Santa Claus
Santa Claus is Coming to Town
Santa Claus: The Movie
Sarah, Plain and Tall
Savage Sam
Savannah Smiles
Save the Lady
Scandalous John
The Secret Garden▶
The Secret Garden
The Secret of El Zorro
The Secret of Navajo Cave
The Secret of the Golden Eagle
Seven Alone
The Shaggy D.A.
The Shaggy Dog

She's a Good Skate, Charlie Brown
The Sign of Zorro
The Silver Stallion: King of the Wild Brumbies
Skeezer
Sleeping Beauty▶
Sleeping Beauty
Smith!
Smoke
A Smoky Mountain Christmas
Snoopy, Come Home!
Snow White and the Seven Dwarfs▶
Snowball Express
Solo
Son of Flubber
Spirit of the Eagle
Spy Trap
Starbird and Sweet William
Starring Bugs Bunny!
Still Not Quite Human
Stone Fox
The Story Lady
The Story of Robin Hood & His Merrie Men▶
Summer Magic
A Summer to Remember
The Sun Comes Up
Superdad
Sweet 15
The Swiss Family Robinson▶
The Sword & the Rose
The Sword in the Stone▶
Tales from Avonlea, Vol. 1: The Journey Begins
Ten Who Dared
That Darn Cat
Thief of Baghdad▶
Third Man on the Mountain
Those Calloways
The Three Little Pigs
The Three Lives of Thomasina▶
Thumbelina
Tiger Town
A Tiger Walks
Toby Tyler▶
Tom and Jerry: The Movie
Tom Sawyer▶
Tom Sawyer
Tonka
Treasure Island▶
The Treasure of Matecumbe
The Ugly Dachshund
Unidentified Flying Oddball
Up Against the Wall
A Very Brady Christmas
Walking on Air
The Waltons: A Thanksgiving Story
Waltz King
A Waltz Through the Hills
The Watcher in the Woods
Westward Ho, the Wagons!
What the Moon Saw
Where the Lilies Bloom▶
Where the Red Fern Grows
Where the Red Fern Grows: Part 2
White Fang▶
White Fang 2: The Myth of the White Wolf
Whitewater Sam
Who Has Seen the Wind?
The Wild Country
Wild Hearts Can't Be Broken▶
Wild Horse Hank
The Witches▶
Woof!
Words by Heart
The World's Greatest Athlete
The Yearling▶
You Must Remember This
The Young Detectives on Wheels

4 Bones

A Nous la Liberté▶
Abe Lincoln in Illinois▶
Adam's Rib▶

The Adventures of Robin Hood▶
The African Queen▶
All About Eve▶
All Quiet on the Western Front▶
All the King's Men▶
An American in Paris▶
Anatomy of a Murder▶
Andrei Rublev▶
An Angel at My Table▶
Angels with Dirty Faces▶
Annie Hall▶
Apocalypse Now▶
The Asphalt Jungle▶
Au Revoir Les Enfants▶
The Awful Truth▶
The Ballad of Narayama▶
Bambi▶
The Bank Dick▶
The Battleship Potemkin▶
Beauty and the Beast▶
Ben-Hur▶
The Best Years of Our Lives▶
The Bicycle Thief▶
The Big Parade▶
The Big Sleep▶
The Birth of a Nation▶
The Blue Angel▶
Breathless▶
Brian's Song▶
The Bride of Frankenstein▶
The Bridge on the River Kwai▶
Brief Encounter▶
Bringing Up Baby▶
The Burmese Harp▶
Butch Cassidy and the Sundance Kid▶
The Cabinet of Dr. Caligari▶
The Caine Mutiny▶
The Cameraman▶
Casablanca▶
Cesar▶
Children of Paradise▶
Chimes at Midnight▶
Chinatown▶
Christ Stopped at Eboli▶
A Christmas Carol▶
Citizen Kane▶
City Lights▶
The Civil War, Episode 1: The Cause—1861▶
The Civil War, Episode 2: A Very Bloody Affair—1862▶
The Civil War, Episode 3: Forever Free—1862▶
The Civil War, Episode 4: Simply Murder—1863▶
The Civil War, Episode 5: The Universe of Battle—1863▶
The Civil War, Episode 6: Valley of the Shadow of Death—1864▶
The Civil War, Episode 7: Most Hallowed Ground—1864▶
The Civil War, Episode 8: War is All Hell—1865▶
The Civil War, Episode 9: The Better Angels of Our Nature—1865▶
A Clockwork Orange▶
Close Encounters of the Third Kind▶
Colonel Redl▶
Come and See▶
Commissar▶
The Conformist▶
Crime and Punishment▶
The Crowd▶
Cyrano de Bergerac▶
Danton▶
Das Boot▶
David Copperfield▶
Day for Night▶
Day of Wrath▶
Dead of Night▶
The Deer Hunter▶
Deliverance▶
Destry Rides Again▶
Diamonds of the Night▶
Dinner at Eight▶
The Discreet Charm of the Bourgeoisie▶

Dr. Strangelove, or: How I Learned to Stop Worrying and Love the Bomb▶
Don Quixote▶
Double Indemnity▶
Duck Soup▶
Dumbo▶
The Earrings of Madame De...▶
Earth▶
East of Eden▶
8 1/2▶
El Norte▶
The Elephant Man▶
The Empire Strikes Back▶
E.T.: The Extra-Terrestrial▶
Every Man for Himself & God Against All▶
Fanny▶
Fanny and Alexander▶
Fantasia▶
Fitzcarraldo▶
Five Easy Pieces▶
Forbidden Games▶
Foreign Correspondent▶
Forever and a Day▶
42nd Street▶
The Four Feathers▶
The 400 Blows▶
Frankenstein▶
The Freshman▶
From Here to Eternity▶
The Fugitive▶
Gallipoli▶
Garden of the Finzi-Continis▶
The General▶
The General Line▶
Gigi▶
The Godfather▶
The Godfather 1902-1959: The Complete Epic▶
The Godfather, Part 2▶
The Gold Rush▶
Gone with the Wind▶
Goodfellas▶
The Gospel According to St. Matthew▶
The Graduate▶
Grand Illusion▶
The Great Dictator▶
Great Expectations▶
Greed▶
Gunga Din▶
Hamlet▶
Harold and Maude▶
Harvest▶
Hearts of Darkness: A Filmmaker's Apocalypse▶
Henry V▶
Henry: Portrait of a Serial Killer▶
Here Comes Mr. Jordan▶
High Noon▶
Hiroshima, Mon Amour▶
His Girl Friday▶
Hollywood Canteen▶
How Green was My Valley▶
Howard's End▶
Hud▶
The Hunchback of Notre Dame▶
The Hustler▶
I Am a Fugitive from a Chain Gang▶
The Idiot▶
If...▶
Ikiru▶
The Informer▶
Intolerance▶
The Invisible Man▶
Isn't Life Wonderful▶
It Happened One Night▶
It's a Wonderful Life▶
Ivan the Terrible, Part 1▶
Ju Dou▶
Judgment at Nuremberg▶
Jules and Jim▶
The King and I▶
King Kong▶
Knife in the Water▶
Koyaanisqatsi▶
Kriemhilde's Revenge▶
Kwaidan▶

La Chienne▶
La Dolce Vita▶
La Strada▶
Lady and the Tramp▶
The Lady Eve▶
The Lady Vanishes▶
L'Age D'Or▶
Last Command▶
The Last Detail▶
The Last Emperor▶
The Last Picture Show▶
Late Spring▶
Laura▶
Lawrence of Arabia▶
Les Miserables▶
The Letter▶
A Letter to Three Wives▶
The Life and Death of Colonel
     Blimp▶
The Lion in Winter▶
Little Women▶
The Lives of a Bengal Lancer▶
Local Hero▶
Lola Montes▶
Long Day's Journey into
     Night▶
Lost Horizon▶
The Lost Weekend▶
M▶
The Magnificent Ambersons▶
The Magnificent Seven▶
Male and Female▶
The Maltese Falcon▶
A Man for All Seasons▶
The Man Who Would Be King▶
The Manchurian Candidate▶
Manhattan▶
Marius▶
The Marriage of Maria Braun▶
M*A*S*H▶
McCabe & Mrs. Miller▶
Mean Streets▶
Metropolis▶
Miracle of Morgan's Creek▶
Miracle on 34th Street▶
Mrs. Miniver▶
Mr. & Mrs. Bridge▶
Mister Roberts▶
Mr. Smith Goes to
     Washington▶
Modern Times▶
Mon Oncle▶
The Music Man▶
Mutiny on the Bounty▶
My Left Foot▶
My Life as a Dog▶
My Life to Live▶
My Man Godfrey▶
Napoleon▶
Nashville▶
National Velvet▶
A Night at the Opera▶
The Night of the Hunter▶
The Night of the Shooting
     Stars▶
North by Northwest▶
Nosferatu▶
Notorious▶
O Lucky Man!▶
Objective, Burma!▶
Of Mice and Men▶
Oliver Twist▶
On the Waterfront▶
One Flew Over the Cuckoo's
     Nest▶
Only Angels Have Wings▶
Open City▶
Our Hospitality▶
The Ox-Bow Incident▶
Pandora's Box▶
The Passion of Joan of Arc▶
Pather Panchali▶
Paths of Glory▶
Pelle the Conqueror▶
Persona▶
Petulia▶
The Philadelphia Story▶
Pinocchio▶
Pixote▶
Poltergeist▶
The Private Life of Henry VIII▶
Psycho▶

The Quiet Man▶
Raging Bull▶
Raiders of the Lost Ark▶
A Raisin in the Sun▶
Ran▶
Rashomon▶
Rear Window▶
Rebecca▶
Rebel Without a Cause▶
Red River▶
The Red Shoes▶
The Reincarnation of Golden
     Lotus▶
The Report on the Party and
     the Guests▶
Ride the High Country▶
The River▶
A Room with a View▶
Roots▶
Rosemary's Baby▶
The Ruggles of Red Gap▶
The Rules of the Game▶
Sansho the Bailiff▶
Scenes from a Marriage▶
Schindler's List▶
The Searchers▶
Sergeant York▶
Seven Beauties▶
Seven Samurai▶
The Seventh Seal▶
Shane▶
Shin Heike Monogatari▶
Shoeshine▶
Shoot the Piano Player▶
The Shop on Main Street▶
Show Boat▶
Siegfried▶
Singin' in the Rain▶
Small Change▶
Snow White and the Seven
     Dwarfs▶
Some Like It Hot▶
The Sound of Music▶
Sounder▶
The Southerner▶
Spartacus▶
Stagecoach▶
Stalag 17▶
Star Wars▶
Storm Over Asia▶
Strangers on a Train▶
A Streetcar Named Desire▶
The Stunt Man▶
Sullivan's Travels▶
Sunrise▶
A Tale of Two Cities▶
The Third Man▶
The 39 Steps▶
Throne of Blood▶
The Tin Drum▶
To Kill a Mockingbird▶
Tokyo Story▶
Tom Jones▶
Tootsie▶
Top Hat▶
Touch of Evil▶
The Train▶
Treasure of the Sierra Madre▶
Tristana▶
Twelve Angry Men▶
Twentieth Century▶
2001: A Space Odyssey▶
Two Women▶
Umberto D▶
Un Chien Andalou▶
Vampyr▶
Variety▶
Vertigo▶
Viridiana▶
Viva Zapata!▶
Wages of Fear▶
The Wedding March▶
Who's Afraid of Virginia
     Woolf?▶
The Wild Bunch▶
Wild Strawberries▶
The Wind▶
The Wizard of Oz▶
Woman in the Dunes▶
Woman of the Year▶
Woodstock▶
The World of Apu▶

Wuthering Heights▶
Yankee Doodle Dandy▶
Yojimbo▶
Young Frankenstein▶
Z▶
Zero for Conduct▶
Zvenigora▶

"Gremlins" & Rip-Offs

Critters
Critters 2: The Main Course
Critters 3
Critters 4
Ghoulies
Ghoulies 2
Ghoulies 3: Ghoulies Go to
     College
Gremlins▶
Gremlins 2: The New Batch▶
Munchie
Munchies
Spookies

Hammer Films: Horror

Asylum
Blood of the Vampire
The Blood on Satan's Claw▶
The Brides of Dracula
Captain Kronos: Vampire
     Hunter▶
Count Dracula's Great Love
The Creeping Flesh
The Curse of Frankenstein
The Curse of the Werewolf
Die Screaming, Marianne
Dr. Jekyll and Sister Hyde
Dracula Has Risen from the
     Grave
The Evil of Frankenstein
Frankenstein and the Monster
     from Hell
The Ghoul
The Gorgon
Hands of the Ripper
The Horror of Dracula▶
The Horror of Frankenstein
The Hound of the Baskervilles
Hysteria
Lust for a Vampire
Maniac
The Mummy▶
The Satanic Rites of Dracula
The Scars of Dracula
The 7 Brothers Meet Dracula
Tales from the Crypt▶
Tales That Witness Madness
Taste the Blood of Dracula
Theatre of Blood▶
To the Devil, A Daughter
Twins of Evil
Vampire Circus
The Vampire Lovers
Vault of Horror

Hammer Films: Sci Fi & Fantasy

Creatures the World Forgot
Four Sided Triangle
Men of Sherwood Forest
Quatermass 2▶
The Quatermass Experiment▶
Spaceways
Sword of Sherwood Forest
When Dinosaurs Ruled the
     Earth

Letterboxed Editions

The Abyss▶
The Accidental Tourist▶
The Addams Family
Addams Family Values
The Adventures of Ford
     Fairlane
The Adventures of Huck Finn▶

The Adventures of Robin
     Hood▶
An Affair to Remember
After Hours▶
Against All Odds
The Age of Innocence▶
Akira Kurosawa's Dreams
The Alamo▶
Alexander the Great
Alice Doesn't Live Here
     Anymore
Alien 3
Aliens▶
Alive
All That Jazz▶
All the President's Men▶
All the Vermeers in New York▶
Always
An American Tail: Fievel Goes
     West
The Americanization of Emily▶
Amsterdamned
Anastasia▶
Annie
Annie Hall▶
The Apartment▶
Apocalypse Now▶
Arabian Nights▶
Arachnophobia
Army of Darkness▶
Auntie Mame▶
Avalon▶
The Awful Dr. Orlof
Baby Cart to Hades
Back to the Future▶
Back to the Future, Part 2
Back to the Future, Part 3▶
Backdraft
Bad Day at Black Rock▶
Barbarella
Barry Lyndon▶
Batman▶
Batman: Mask of the Phantasm
Battle Cry▶
Battle of Britain
Battle of the Bulge
The Bear▶
Beautiful Dreamers
Beauty and the Beast▶
Becket▶
Bedazzled▶
Beethoven's 2nd
The Bellboy
Bells are Ringing▶
Ben-Hur▶
Beneath the Planet of the Apes
Beneath the 12-Mile Reef
Benny & Joon
The Best Little Whorehouse in
     Texas
Best of the Best 2
Bhowani Junction
The Big Chill▶
Big Jake
Big Trouble in Little China
Big Wednesday
Billie
Billy Bathgate
Billy Rose's Jumbo▶
Bird on a Wire
Black Rain
Black Robe▶
Blade Runner▶
Blink
The Blob
Blood Alley
Blood & Concrete: A Love
     Story
Bloodhounds of Broadway
Blow-Up▶
The Blue Max
Blue Thunder
Blue Velvet▶
Bobo
Body Double▶
Body of Evidence
Body Parts
Boiling Point
The Bonfire of the Vanities▶
Boomerang

Born on the Fourth of July▶
Born Yesterday
Boyz N the Hood▶
Brain Donors
Brainstorm
Bram Stoker's Dracula
Brazil▶
Brewster McCloud▶
The Bridge on the River Kwai▶
A Bridge Too Far
Brigadoon▶
Broken Lance▶
Buona Sera, Mrs. Campbell
Burn!▶
The Butcher's Wife
Butterfield 8▶
Bye, Bye, Birdie▶
Cahill: United States Marshal
Camelot
Can-Can
Candyman
Cape Fear▶
The Cardinal
Carlito's Way▶
Carmen Jones▶
Carnal Knowledge▶
Casualties of War▶
Cat People
CB4: The Movie
The Champ
Chaplin▶
The Chase
Chasers
Chinatown▶
Chinese Connection
Chinese Roulette
Chisum
Cimarron
Circuitry Man
Circus World
City of Joy
City Slickers▶
Clash of the Titans
Class Act
Clean and Sober▶
Cleopatra
Cliffhanger▶
A Clockwork Orange▶
Close Encounters of the Third
     Kind▶
The Color Purple▶
Comancheros▶
Come See the Paradise▶
Conan the Barbarian▶
The Cook, the Thief, His Wife &
     Her Lover▶
Cop and a Half
The Court Martial of Billy
     Mitchell▶
The Cowboys▶
The Cranes are Flying▶
Cria▶
The Crush
The Crying Game▶
Cyborg
Daddy Long Legs▶
Damage▶
Damien: Omen 2
Dances with Wolves▶
Dandy in Aspic
Dangerous Liaisons▶
The Dark Backward
Dark Habits
Dark Star▶
Dave▶
Day of the Triffids▶
Day the World Ended
Days of Thunder
Dazed and Confused▶
Dead Again▶
Dead Calm
Death Becomes Her▶
The Decameron▶
The Deep
Deep Cover
The Deer Hunter▶
Defending Your Life▶
Deliverance▶
Delusion
Demolition Man
Dennis the Menace
Designing Woman▶

Desiree
The Detective►
Diamonds are Forever►
Diane
The Diary of Anne Frank►
Diary of Forbidden Dreams►
Dick Tracy►
Die Hard►
Die Hard 2: Die Harder►
Diner►
The Dirty Dozen►
Dirty Harry►
Doc Hollywood►
The Doctor
Doctor Dolittle
Dr. Giggles
Dr. No►
Dr. Strangelove, or: How I
    Learned to Stop Worrying
    and Love the Bomb►
Doctor Zhivago►
The Doors
Dracula►
Dragon: The Bruce Lee Story►
Dressed to Kill►
Driving Miss Daisy►
The Duellists►
East of Eden►
The Eddy Duchin Story
The Eiger Sanction
8 1/2►
The Electric Horseman
Empire of the Sun►
The Empire Strikes Back►
Enter the Dragon►
Equinox
The Errand Boy
Escape from the Planet of the
    Apes►
E.T.: The Extra-Terrestrial►
Excalibur►
The Fall of the Roman Empire►
Falling Down
Fantastic Voyage►
Far and Away
Far from the Madding Crowd►
A Far Off Place
Fatal Attraction►
Father of the Bride
Fearless►
The Fearless Vampire Killers►
Fellini Satyricon►
Fellini's Roma
A Few Good Men►
Fiddler on the Roof►
Field of Dreams►
55 Days at Peking►
Final Approach
The Final Conflict
Finian's Rainbow►
Fire in the Sky
The Firm►
First Blood
First Men in the Moon
The Fisher King►
A Fistful of Dollars►
A Fistful of Dynamite►
Five Easy Pieces►
Five Weeks in a Balloon
Flash Gordon
Flatliners
Flight of the Intruder
FM
Follow That Dream
For a Few Dollars More►
For Your Eyes Only►
Forbidden Planet►
Forever Young
Fort Apache, the Bronx►
The Fortune Cookie►
The 400 Blows►
1492: Conquest of Paradise
Frankie and Johnny►
Free Willy
Freebie & the Bean
Freejack►
The Freshman
From Russia with Love►
The Funhouse
Funny Face►
Funny Girl►
Funny Lady

Fury is a Woman►
Game of Death
Gandhi►
Gas Food Lodging►
Geronimo
Gettysburg►
Ghost►
Ghostbusters►
Ghostbusters 2
Gigi►
The Glass Bottom Boat
Glengarry Glen Ross►
Glory►
Going Places►
Goldfinger►
Gonza the Spearman
The Good, the Bad and the
    Ugly►
Goodbye, Mr. Chips►
Goodbye, Mr. Chips
Goodfellas►
The Goonies
The Gospel According to St.
    Matthew►
The Graduate►
Grand Prix
The Grass is Greener►
Grave of the Fireflies►
The Great Escape►
Great Race
The Greatest Story Ever Told
Greedy
The Green Berets►
Gremlins►
Gremlins 2: The New Batch►
Greystoke: The Legend of
    Tarzan, Lord of the Apes►
Grumpy Old Men►
Guilty as Sin
Guilty by Suspicion
The Guns of Navarone►
Gypsy►
Hair►
The Hallelujah Trail
Hamlet►
Hard Target
The Hard Way►
The Harder They Come
Harlem Nights
Harper►
Hawaii►
The Hawks & the Sparrows
He Said, She Said
Heart and Souls
Heaven and Earth
Heaven's Gate
Hellfighters
Henry V►
Henry & June►
Hercules
Hero►
The Hidden Fortress►
High & Low►
High Plains Drifter
High Society►
The Hindenburg
History of the World: Part 1
Hit the Deck
Hoffa►
A Hole in the Head
Hombre►
Home Alone►
Home from the Hill►
Homeward Bound: The
    Incredible Journey►
Honey, I Blew Up the Kid
The Hot Rock►
How the West was Won►
How to Succeed in Business
    without Really Trying►
Howard's End►
Huckleberry Finn
The Hunger
The Hunt for Red October►
Hunter in the Dark
Husbands and Wives►
I Could Go on Singing
I Died a Thousand Times
I Love You to Death
Ice Station Zebra
In Like Flint
In the Line of Fire►

In the Name of the Father►
In the Navy
The Indian Runner
Indiana Jones and the Last
    Crusade►
Indochine►
Innocent Blood
Inside Daisy Clover
Invasion of the Body
    Snatchers►
Irma La Douce
Islands in the Stream
It's a Mad, Mad, Mad, Mad
    World
It's Always Fair Weather
Ivan the Terrible, Part 1►
Ivan the Terrible, Part 2►
Jack the Bear
The Jagged Edge
Jailhouse Rock►
Jaws►
Jaws 2
Jennifer 8
Jesus Christ, Superstar►
JFK►
Joe Kidd
Joe Versus the Volcano
Journey of Honor
The Joy Luck Club►
The Judge and the Assassin►
Jules and Jim►
Jupiter's Darling
Kafka
Kagemusha►
Kalifornia
The Karate Kid: Part 3
The Keep
Kelly's Heroes
Khartoum
Kid Galahad
The Killing Fields►
The King and I►
The King of Hearts►
The King of Kings►
King of the Hill►
Kismet
Kiss Me, Stupid!
Klute►
Knights of the Round Table
Kramer vs. Kramer►
The Krays►
Kwaidan►
La Dolce Vita►
Labyrinth of Passion
The Lacemaker►
Ladyhawke
Land of the Pharaohs
The Last Boy Scout
Last Exit to Brooklyn►
The Last of the Mohicans►
The Last Picture Show►
Last Tango in Paris►
L'Avventura►
Lawrence of Arabia►
Le Complot►
Le Crabe Tambour►
Le Mans►
A League of Their Own►
Leap of Faith
Leningrad Cowboys Go
    America
Les Girls
L'Etat Sauvage►
Lethal Weapon►
Lethal Weapon 2►
Leviathan
License to Kill►
Liebestraum
Life & Times of Judge Roy
    Bean
Life with Mikey
Lisztomania
Little Big Man►
Little Nemo: Adventures in
    Slumberland
A Little Romance►
Live and Let Die
The Living Daylights►
Logan's Run
Lola Montes►
Lolita►
The Long Goodbye►

The Longest Day►
Lorenzo's Oil►
The Lost Boys
Lost Horizon►
Lost in America►
Lost in Yonkers
Love Me or Leave Me►
Love Meetings
The Lover
Lucky Me
Lust for Life►
M. Butterfly
Mac►
Mad Dog and Glory►
Mad Max: Beyond
    Thunderdome
Made in America
The Madwoman of Chaillot
The Magnificent Seven►
Major League 2
Malcolm X►
Mame
A Man Called Horse►
The Man from Snowy River
Man of a Thousand Faces►
Man Trouble
The Man Who Fell to Earth►
The Man Who Would Be King►
The Man with the Golden Gun►
Manhattan►
Manhunter►
Maniac Cop 2
Mary Poppins►
M*A*S*H►
Matador
McCabe & Mrs. Miller►
Meet Me in Las Vegas
Men of Respect
The Meteor Man
Midnight Cowboy►
Midnight Express►
Midway
The Mission►
Mississippi Mermaid►
Mrs. Soffel
Mr. Baseball
Mr. Jones
Mr. Wonderful
Mo' Money
Monty Python and the Holy
    Grail►
Moonraker►
Moonstruck►
Mortal Thoughts
The Mosquito Coast
Music Box
The Music Lovers
The Music Man►
Mutiny on the Bounty
My Fair Lady►
My Favorite Year►
My New Gun
My Own Private Idaho►
Mystery Train►
Naked Gun 2 1/2: The Smell of
    Fear
Naked Killer
Naked Kiss
Narrow Margin
The Natural►
Necessary Roughness
Nemesis
Never So Few
The NeverEnding Story►
The NeverEnding Story 2: Next
    Chapter
New York, New York►
Nicholas and Alexandra
A Night at the Opera►
The Night of the Iguana►
Night on Earth►
9 1/2 Weeks
Noises Off
North by Northwest►
North to Alaska►
Ocean's 11
Octopussy
Oklahoma!►
Old Gringo
Oliver!►
The Omen

On Her Majesty's Secret
    Service►
One, Two, Three►
Only the Lonely
The Opposite Sex
Orlando►
Other People's Money
The Other Side of Midnight
Our Man Flint
Out for Justice
Outland
The Outsiders
Overboard
Party Girl►
Passenger 57
Passion Fish►
Past Midnight
Pat Garrett & Billy the Kid►
Patton►
The Pelican Brief
A Perfect World
Pete Kelly's Blues
Peyton Place►
The Pickle
Picnic►
Pierrot le Fou►
Pillow Talk►
Pink Floyd: The Wall
The Pink Panther►
Planet of the Apes►
The Player►
Please Don't Eat the Daisies
Pocketful of Miracles►
Point Blank
Point Break
Point of No Return
Poltergeist►
Poltergeist 2: The Other Side
The Poseidon Adventure
Predator
Predator 2
Presumed Innocent►
The Princess Bride►
Prisoner of Second Avenue
The Producers►
The Professionals►
PT 109
The Public Eye►
Pure Country
Quest for Fire►
Quigley Down Under
Rage and Honor
Raging Bull►
Raintree County
Raising Cain
Ran►
The Real McCoy
Reality Bites
Rebel Without a Cause►
The Red and the White►
Red Beard►
Red Dawn
Regarding Henry►
The Reluctant Debutante►
The Remains of the Day►
Reservoir Dogs►
Return of the Dragon►
Return of the Jedi►
Revenge
Revenge of the Pink Panther
Rich in Love
Richard III►
Ride the High Country►
The Right Stuff►
Rising Sun►
Risky Business►
A River Runs Through It►
Road House
The Road Warrior►
The Robe
Robin and the Seven Hoods►
Robin Hood: Prince of Thieves
RoboCop►
Rocco and His Brothers►
The Rocketeer►
Rollerball
Rollercoaster
Romancing the Stone►
The Rookie
Rose Marie►
Runaway Train►
Running Scared

Letterboxed

The Russia House
Ryan's Daughter
The Sacrifice
The Saint of Fort Washington
The Sandlot▶
Scarface▶
Scent of a Woman▶
Schindler's List▶
School Ties▶
Sea Chase
Sea of Love▶
The Searchers▶
Seven Brides for Seven Brothers▶
Seven Faces of Dr. Lao▶
1776▶
sex, lies and videotape▶
Shadow of the Wolf
The Shakiest Gun in the West
Shampoo
Shattered
The Sheltering Sky▶
Shipwrecked
Shock Corridor▶
The Shoes of the Fisherman
Shoot the Piano Player▶
A Shot in the Dark▶
The Silence of the Lambs▶
Silk Stockings▶
Silverado▶
Singles▶
Sister Act
Sleepless in Seattle▶
Sliver
Sneakers▶
Sniper
Soapdish▶
S.O.B.
Sofie
Solar Crisis
Solaris
Solomon and Sheba
Some Came Running▶
Some Like It Hot▶
Sommersby
The Sound of Music▶
South Central
South Pacific▶
Spartacus▶
A Special Day▶
The Spy Who Loved Me
Stanley and Iris
Star!
Star Trek 2: The Wrath of Khan▶
Star Trek 3: The Search for Spock
Star Trek 4: The Voyage Home▶
Star Trek 5: The Final Frontier
Star Wars▶
Starman▶
A Stranger Among Us
Sudden Impact
The Sugarland Express▶
Summer and Smoke
Sunday, Bloody Sunday▶
Super Mario Bros.
Superman: The Movie▶
Suspiria▶
Swashbuckler
Sweet Bird of Youth▶
The Swiss Family Robinson▶
The Taking of Beverly Hills
Tampopo▶
Tango and Cash
Taras Bulba
Taxi Driver▶
Tea and Sympathy▶
The Teahouse of the August Moon
Teenage Mutant Ninja Turtles 3
Tell Them Willie Boy Is Here▶
The Temp
The Ten Commandments▶
The Tender Trap
The Terminator▶
That Obscure Object of Desire▶
That Touch of Mink▶
That's Entertainment
Thelma & Louise▶

There's No Business Like Show Business▶
The Thing▶
The Things of Life▶
Third Solution
This Boy's Life▶
This Could Be the Night
Those Magnificent Men in Their Flying Machines▶
Three Days of the Condor▶
Thumbelina
Thunderball
Thunderbolt & Lightfoot▶
THX 1138▶
Tie Me Up! Tie Me Down!
The Time Machine▶
Tokyo Olympiad
Tom Sawyer
Tootsie▶
The Towering Inferno
Trading Places
The Train▶
Train Robbers
Trapeze▶
Travels with My Aunt
Trespass
Tucker: The Man and His Dream▶
The Tunnel of Love
20,000 Leagues Under the Sea▶
Twin Peaks: Fire Walk with Me
Two for the Road▶
Two for the Seesaw▶
The Two Jakes
2001: A Space Odyssey▶
2010: The Year We Make Contact▶
Two Weeks in Another Town
Ulysses
Umberto D▶
Under Siege
Undercover Blues
The Unforgiven▶
Unforgiven▶
Unlawful Entry
The Unsinkable Molly Brown▶
Untamed Heart
The Untouchables▶
Up Periscope
Used People
Victor/Victoria▶
A View to a Kill
The Vikings
Vincent, Francois, Paul and the Others▶
The Violent Men
Viva Las Vegas
Von Ryan's Express▶
Voyage to the Bottom of the Sea▶
The War of the Roses▶
The War Wagon▶
Waterland
The Way We Were▶
West Side Story▶
Westworld▶
What Ever Happened to Baby Jane?▶
What's New Pussycat?▶
When Harry Met Sally▶
Where Eagles Dare▶
Where the Boys Are
Where the Day Takes You
Whispers in the Dark
White Christmas▶
White Nights
Who Framed Roger Rabbit?▶
Who's Afraid of Virginia Woolf?▶
Wild at Heart▶
Wild Rovers
Wilder Napalm
Wind
The Wind and the Lion▶
Winning▶
Witness for the Prosecution
The Wiz
Wolfen▶
The Wolves▶
Women on the Verge of a Nervous Breakdown▶

The Wonderful World of the Brothers Grimm
Woodstock▶
World of Henry Orient▶
Wrangler
The Wreck of the Mary Deare
The Yakuza
The Year of Living Dangerously▶
Yojimbo▶
You Only Live Twice
Young Guns 2
The Young Lions▶
Zardoz▶
Zulu

Live Action/ Animation Combos

Alice▶
Alice in Wonderland
Anchors Aweigh▶
Bedknobs and Broomsticks
Butterfly Ball
Cool World
Dangerous When Wet
Fabulous Adventures of Baron Munchausen
Freddie as F.R.O.7
Fun & Fancy Free
Hollywood Party
The Incredible Mr. Limpet
Mary Poppins▶
So Dear to My Heart▶
The Three Caballeros
Volere Volare
Who Framed Roger Rabbit?▶
Xanadu

MGM Musicals

An American in Paris▶
Anchors Aweigh▶
Athena
The Band Wagon▶
The Barkleys of Broadway▶
Because You're Mine
Bells are Ringing▶
Big Store
Born to Dance
Broadway Melody
Broadway Melody of 1936▶
Broadway Melody of 1938
Broadway Melody of 1940
Broadway Rhythm
Broadway Serenade
The Chocolate Soldier
The Complete Showboat
Dancing Lady
Deep in My Heart
Double Trouble
Duchess of Idaho
Easter Parade▶
Easy to Love
Everybody Sing
The Firefly
For Me and My Gal
Gigi▶
Girl of the Golden West
Give a Girl a Break
Going Hollywood▶
Good News
Goodbye, Mr. Chips
The Great Ziegfeld▶
Harum Scarum
Holiday in Mexico
Honolulu
I Love Melvin
I Married an Angel
In the Good Old Summertime▶
It Happened at the World's Fair
It Happened in Brooklyn
Judy Garland: The Golden Years at MGM
Lady Be Good
Les Girls
Little Nellie Kelly
Live a Little, Love a Little
Love Me or Leave Me▶
Lovely to Look At▶
Madam Satan

Maytime▶
Meet Me in Las Vegas
Meet Me in St. Louis▶
The Merry Widow▶
The Merry Widow
Million Dollar Mermaid
Mrs. Brown, You've Got a Lovely Daughter
On an Island with You
On the Town▶
Pagan Love Song
Rich, Young and Pretty
Rosalie
Rose Marie▶
Royal Wedding▶
Seven Brides for Seven Brothers▶
Ship Ahoy
Show Boat
Singin' in the Rain▶
Skirts Ahoy!
Small Town Girl
Spinout
Stay Away, Joe
Strike Up the Band
The Student Prince
Summer Stock▶
Sweethearts▶
Take Me Out to the Ball Game
Texas Carnival
That Midnight Kiss
That's Dancing!
That's Entertainment
That's Entertainment, Part 2
That's Entertainment 3
Three Little Words
Thrill of a Romance
Till the Clouds Roll By
Till the Clouds Roll By/A Star Is Born▶
The Toast of New Orleans
The Trouble with Girls (and How To Get Into It)▶
The Unsinkable Molly Brown▶
Viva Las Vegas
The Wizard of Oz▶
Words and Music
Yankee Doodle Dandy▶
Yolanda and the Thief
Ziegfeld Follies
Ziegfeld Girl▶

Modern Shakespeare

Chimes at Midnight▶
A Double Life▶
Forbidden Planet▶
Fury is a Woman▶
The Godfather▶
The Godfather, Part 2▶
The Godfather, Part 3▶
Jubal
King Lear
Kiss Me Kate▶
Men are not Gods
Men of Respect
A Midsummer Night's Sex Comedy▶
My Own Private Idaho▶
Otello▶
Prospero's Books▶
Ran▶
Ring of Fire
Rosencrantz & Guildenstern Are Dead
Shakespeare Wallah
Throne of Blood▶
West Side Story▶

Plays to Film: Horton Foote

Baby, the Rain Must Fall
The Chase
Courtship▶
1918
The Trip to Bountiful▶

Plays to Film: Beth Henley

Crimes of the Heart
Nobody's Fool
True Stories▶

Plays to Film: Eugene O'Neill

Ah, Wilderness!▶
Anna Christie▶
Anna Christie
Desire Under the Elms
Emperor Jones
Emperor Jones/Paul Robeson: Tribute to an Artist
The Hairy Ape
Long Day's Journey into Night▶
Long Day's Journey into Night
The Long Voyage Home▶
On Borrowed Time▶
Strange Interlude
Strange Interlude
Summer Holiday

Plays to Film: William Shakespeare

Antony and Cleopatra
As You Like It
Carry On Cleo
Hamlet
Hamlet
Hamlet▶
Henry V▶
Julius Caesar▶
Julius Caesar
King Lear▶
King Lear
Macbeth▶
Macbeth
The Merchant of Venice▶
A Midsummer Night's Dream▶
A Midsummer Night's Dream
Much Ado About Nothing▶
Othello
Othello▶
Prospero's Books▶
Ran▶
Richard III▶
Romeo and Juliet
Romeo and Juliet
Romeo and Juliet▶
The Taming of the Shrew
The Taming of the Shrew
The Taming of the Shrew
The Tempest
The Tempest▶
The Tragedy of King Richard II
West Side Story▶

Plays to Film: George Bernard Shaw

Androcles and the Lion
Caesar and Cleopatra
The Devil's Disciple▶
Heartbreak House
Major Barbara▶

Plays to Film: Neil Simon

Barefoot in the Park▶
Biloxi Blues
Brighton Beach Memoirs
Broadway Bound
California Suite▶
Chapter Two
The Cheap Detective▶
Come Blow Your Horn▶
The Goodbye Girl▶
The Heartbreak Kid▶
I Ought to Be in Pictures
Last of the Red Hot Lovers
Lost in Yonkers
The Marrying Man

Max Dugan Returns
Murder by Death
The Odd Couple▶
One Trick Pony
Only When I Laugh▶
The Out-of-Towners▶
Plaza Suite▶
Prisoner of Second Avenue
Seems Like Old Times
The Slugger's Wife
Star Spangled Girl
The Sunshine Boys▶
Sweet Charity▶

Plays to Film: Tom Stoppard

Rosencrantz & Guildenstern Are Dead

Plays to Film: Tennessee Williams

Baby Doll▶
Cat on a Hot Tin Roof▶
Cat on a Hot Tin Roof
The Fugitive Kind
The Glass Menagerie▶
The Night of the Iguana▶
Orpheus Descending
Period of Adjustment
Roman Spring of Mrs. Stone▶
The Rose Tattoo▶
A Streetcar Named Desire▶
Suddenly, Last Summer▶
Summer and Smoke
Sweet Bird of Youth
Sweet Bird of Youth
This Property is Condemned

Producers: Robert Altman

Buffalo Bill & the Indians▶
James Dean Story
The Late Show▶
Nashville▶
Quintet
Rich Kids
A Wedding
Welcome to L.A.▶

Producers: William Castle

Bug
House on Haunted Hill
Macabre
Riot
Rosemary's Baby▶
Strait-Jacket
13 Ghosts
Zotz!

Producers: Coppola/ American Zoetrope

American Graffiti▶
The Black Stallion▶
The Conversation▶
Escape Artist▶
The Godfather, Part 2▶
Hammett

Producers: Roger Corman/New World

Atlas
Attack of the Giant Leeches
Avalanche
Battle Beyond the Stars
Battle Beyond the Sun
Beyond the Call of Duty
Big Bad Mama
Big Bad Mama 2
The Big Bird Cage
The Big Doll House
Bloodfist

Bloodfist 2
Bloody Mama
Body Waves
Boxcar Bertha
A Bucket of Blood▶
Caged Heat
Candy Stripe Nurses
Carnival Rock
Cocaine Wars
Cockfighter▶
Crazy Mama
Daddy's Boys
Day the World Ended
Death Race 2000
Death Sport
Dementia 13
Dinosaur Island
The Dunwich Horror
Eat My Dust
Eye of the Eagle 3
The Fall of the House of Usher▶
Field of Fire
Fighting Mad
Firehawk
Forbidden World
Futurekick
Galaxy of Terror
Gas-s-s-s!
Grand Theft Auto
The Gunslinger
The Haunted Palace
Humanoids from the Deep
I, Mobster
I Never Promised You a Rose Garden▶
In the Heat of Passion
It Conquered the World
Jackson County Jail
Lady in Red
The Last Woman on Earth
Little Shop of Horrors▶
Lords of the Deep
Lumiere
Machine Gun Kelly
Masque of the Red Death▶
Masque of the Red Death
Monster from the Ocean Floor
Munchies
Nam Angels
Night of the Blood Beast
Piranha
The Pit and the Pendulum▶
Premature Burial
Primary Target
Private Duty Nurses
Raiders of the Sun
The Raven▶
Rock 'n' Roll High School Forever
The St. Valentine's Day Massacre
Ski Troop Attack
Small Change▶
Smokey Bites the Dust
Stripped to Kill
The Student Nurses
T-Bird Gang
Tales of Terror
Targets▶
Teenage Caveman
The Terror
Thunder and Lightning
Time Trackers
Tomb of Ligeia▶
Too Hot to Handle
The Trip
The Undead▶
Unholy Rollers
Voyage to the Planet of Prehistoric Women
The Wasp Woman
The Wild Angels
The Wild Ride
X: The Man with X-Ray Eyes▶
The Young Nurses

Producers: Val Lewton

Bedlam▶

Cat People▶
Isle of the Dead

Producers: George Lucas

The Empire Strikes Back▶
The Ewok Adventure
More American Graffiti
Raiders of the Lost Ark▶
Return of the Jedi▶

Producers: Merchant Ivory

Autobiography of a Princess
The Ballad of the Sad Cafe
Bombay Talkie
The Courtesans of Bombay▶
The Europeans▶
Fast Talking
Howard's End▶
Hullabaloo Over Georgie & Bonnie's Pictures
Jane Austen in Manhattan
Maurice▶
Mr. & Mrs. Bridge▶
The Remains of the Day▶
A Room with a View▶
Roseland▶
Shakespeare Wallah▶

Producers: Steven Spielberg

Amazing Stories
An American Tail
An American Tail: Fievel Goes West
Back to the Future▶
The Color Purple▶
Empire of the Sun▶
The Goonies
Gremlins▶
Honey, I Shrunk the Kids
Innerspace
Jurassic Park▶
Poltergeist▶
Twilight Zone: The Movie
Who Framed Roger Rabbit?▶
Young Sherlock Holmes

Producers: Andy Warhol

Andy Warhol's Bad▶
Cocaine Cowboys
Flesh▶
Heat▶
Trash

Restored Footage

Beau Revel
Crimes of Passion▶
Dr. Jekyll and Mr. Hyde▶
Foolish Wives▶
Frankenstein▶
Isadora▶
Lawrence of Arabia▶
Lost Horizon▶
The Lost World
New York, New York▶
Othello▶
Que Viva Mexico▶
Red River▶
The Rules of the Game▶
Sadie Thompson▶
Spartacus▶
Spiders▶
A Star is Born▶
Star Trek: The Motion Picture
Star Trek: The Cage
Sunny Side Up
Tarzan and His Mate▶
Twelve O'Clock High▶
Two English Girls▶
Wages of Fear▶
When Time Ran Out

"Road Warrior" & Rip-Offs

City Limits
Dead Man Walking
Driving Force
Dune Warriors
Endgame
Escape from Safehaven
Exterminators of the Year 3000
Firefight
Future Hunters
Future Kill
The Killing Edge
Never Too Young to Die
Phoenix the Warrior
Prison Planet
Radioactive Dreams
The Road Warrior▶
Solarbabies
Steel Dawn
Survival Zone
2020 Texas Gladiators
Ultra Warrior
Warlords 3000
Warriors of the Apocalypse
Warriors of the Wasteland
Wheels of Fire
World Gone Wild

Special FX Extravaganzas

The Abyss▶
Aliens▶
Batman▶
Beetlejuice▶
Big Trouble in Little China
The Black Hole
Blithe Spirit▶
Captain Sinbad
Crash Dive
The Ewok Adventure
The Exorcist▶
The Exorcist 2: The Heretic
Fantastic Voyage▶
Forbidden Planet▶
Highlander 3: The Sorcerer
Innerspace
Jurassic Park▶
Lifeforce
The Mask▶
Poltergeist▶
The Rains Came
Return of the Jedi▶
The Shadow
Solar Crisis
Star Trek 2: The Wrath of Khan▶
Star Trek 4: The Voyage Home▶
Star Wars▶
Superman 2▶
The Terminator▶
Terminator 2: Judgment Day▶
The Thing
Total Recall▶
2001: A Space Odyssey▶
2010: The Year We Make Contact▶
Who Framed Roger Rabbit?▶
Wolfen▶

Special FX Extravaganzas: Make-Up

An American Werewolf in London▶
Battle for the Planet of the Apes
Beetlejuice▶
Beneath the Planet of the Apes
Body Melt
Conquest of the Planet of the Apes
Dawn of the Dead▶
Day of the Dead
Escape from the Planet of the Apes▶

The Exorcist▶
The Fly▶
The Fly 2
Freaked
Hocus Pocus
The Howling▶
The Man Without a Face
Planet of the Apes▶
Scanner Cop
Scanners
The Thing
Wolf

Special FX Wizards: Rick Baker

An American Werewolf in London▶
Food of the Gods
The Funhouse
The Fury
Greystoke: The Legend of Tarzan, Lord of the Apes
Incredible Melting Man
The Incredible Shrinking Woman
It's Alive▶
King Kong
Octaman
Schlock
Squirm
Star Wars▶
Tanya's Island
Track of the Moonbeast
Videodrome
Wolf

Special FX Wizards: Rob Bottin

Bugsy▶
Explorers
The Fog
The Howling▶
Humanoids from the Deep
Innerspace
Legend
RoboCop▶
Tanya's Island
The Thing
Twilight Zone: The Movie
The Witches of Eastwick

Special FX Wizards: Anton Furst

Alien▶
Batman▶
The Company of Wolves▶
Full Metal Jacket▶
Moonraker
Star Wars▶

Special FX Wizards: Ray Harryhausen

The Beast from 20,000 Fathoms
Clash of the Titans
Earth vs. the Flying Saucers
First Men in the Moon
Golden Voyage of Sinbad
It Came from Beneath the Sea▶
Jason and the Argonauts▶
Mighty Joe Young
Mysterious Island▶
The Seventh Voyage of Sinbad▶
Sinbad and the Eye of the Tiger
The Three Worlds of Gulliver
20 Million Miles to Earth
The Valley of Gwangi▶

Special FX Wizards: Herschell Gordon Lewis

Blood Feast▶

Special

Color Me Blood Red
Gruesome Twosome
Just for the Hell of It
Moonshine Mountain
The Psychic
She-Devils on Wheels
Suburban Roulette
This Stuff'll Kill Ya!
2000 Maniacs
The Wizard of Gore

Special FX Wizards: Tom Savini

Creepshow
Dawn of the Dead▶
Day of the Dead
Deathdream
Deranged▶
Friday the 13th
Friday the 13th, Part 4: The Final Chapter
Knightriders
Maniac
Martin▶
Midnight
Monkey Shines
The Prowler
The Ripper
Texas Chainsaw Massacre, Part 2

Special FX Wizards: Dick Smith

Altered States▶
Amadeus▶
The Exorcist▶
Ghost Story
The Godfather▶
House of Dark Shadows
Little Big Man▶
Marathon Man▶
Midnight Cowboy▶
Scanners
The Sentinel
Spasms
The Sunshine Boys▶
Taxi Driver▶
World of Henry Orient▶

Special FX Wizards: Douglas Trumball

The Andromeda Strain▶
Blade Runner▶
Brainstorm
Close Encounters of the Third Kind▶
Silent Running▶
Star Trek: The Motion Picture
2001: A Space Odyssey▶

Top Grossing Films of 1939

Gone with the Wind▶
The Hunchback of Notre Dame▶
Jesse James▶
Mr. Smith Goes to Washington▶
The Wizard of Oz▶

Top Grossing Films of 1940

Boom Town
Fantasia▶
Pinocchio▶
Rebecca▶
Santa Fe Trail

Top Grossing Films of 1941

Honky Tonk▶
The Philadelphia Story▶

Sergeant York▶
A Yank in the R.A.F.

Top Grossing Films of 1942

Bambi▶
Casablanca▶
Mrs. Miniver▶
Random Harvest▶
Yankee Doodle Dandy▶

Top Grossing Films of 1943

The Outlaw
The Song of Bernadette▶
Stage Door Canteen
This is the Army

Top Grossing Films of 1944

Going My Way▶
Meet Me in St. Louis▶
Since You Went Away▶
Thirty Seconds Over Tokyo▶

Top Grossing Films of 1945

Anchors Aweigh▶
The Bells of St. Mary's▶
Spellbound▶
Weekend at the Waldorf▶

Top Grossing Films of 1946

The Best Years of Our Lives▶
Duel in the Sun▶
The Jolson Story▶

Top Grossing Films of 1947

Egg and I▶
Life with Father▶

Top Grossing Films of 1948

Johnny Belinda▶
On an Island with You
The Paleface▶
Red River▶
The Red Shoes▶
The Three Musketeers

Top Grossing Films of 1949

Battleground▶
Jolson Sings Again
Samson and Delilah▶
Sands of Iwo Jima▶

Top Grossing Films of 1950

Cinderella▶
Father of the Bride▶
King Solomon's Mines▶

Top Grossing Films of 1951

Alice in Wonderland▶
David and Bathsheba▶
The Great Caruso▶
Quo Vadis▶
Show Boat

Top Grossing Films of 1952

The Greatest Show on Earth▶
Hans Christian Andersen▶
Ivanhoe▶
The Snows of Kilimanjaro▶

Top Grossing Films of 1953

From Here to Eternity▶
How to Marry a Millionaire
Peter Pan▶
The Robe▶
Shane▶

Top Grossing Films of 1954

The Caine Mutiny▶
The Glenn Miller Story▶
Rear Window▶
20,000 Leagues Under the Sea▶
White Christmas▶

Top Grossing Films of 1955

Battle Cry▶
Lady and the Tramp▶
Mister Roberts▶
Oklahoma!▶

Top Grossing Films of 1956

Around the World in 80 Days▶
Giant▶
The King and I▶
The Ten Commandments▶

Top Grossing Films of 1957

The Bridge on the River Kwai▶
Old Yeller▶
Peyton Place▶
Raintree County
Sayonara▶

Top Grossing Films of 1958

Auntie Mame▶
Cat on a Hot Tin Roof▶
Gigi▶
No Time for Sergeants▶
South Pacific▶

Top Grossing Films of 1959

Ben-Hur▶
Darby O'Gill & the Little People▶
Operation Petticoat▶
The Shaggy Dog
Sleeping Beauty▶

Top Grossing Films of 1960

The Alamo▶
Exodus▶
Psycho▶
Spartacus▶
The Swiss Family Robinson▶

Top Grossing Films of 1961

The Absent-Minded Professor▶
El Cid▶

The Guns of Navarone▶
West Side Story▶

Top Grossing Films of 1962

How the West was Won▶
In Search of the Castaways▶
Lawrence of Arabia▶
The Longest Day▶
The Music Man▶

Top Grossing Films of 1963

Cleopatra
Irma La Douce
It's a Mad, Mad, Mad, Mad World
The Sword in the Stone▶
Tom Jones▶

Top Grossing Films of 1964

The Carpetbaggers▶
From Russia with Love▶
Goldfinger▶
Mary Poppins▶
My Fair Lady▶

Top Grossing Films of 1965

Doctor Zhivago▶
The Sound of Music▶
That Darn Cat
Those Magnificent Men in Their Flying Machines▶
Thunderball

Top Grossing Films of 1966

The Bible...In the Beginning▶
Hawaii▶
Lt. Robin Crusoe, U.S.N.
A Man for All Seasons▶
Who's Afraid of Virginia Woolf?▶

Top Grossing Films of 1967

Bonnie & Clyde▶
The Dirty Dozen▶
The Graduate▶
Guess Who's Coming to Dinner▶
The Jungle Book▶

Top Grossing Films of 1968

Bullitt▶
Funny Girl▶
The Odd Couple▶
Romeo and Juliet▶
2001: A Space Odyssey▶

Top Grossing Films of 1969

Butch Cassidy and the Sundance Kid▶
Easy Rider▶
Hello, Dolly!▶
The Love Bug
Midnight Cowboy▶

Top Grossing Films of 1970

Airport▶
Love Story▶

M*A*S*H▶
Patton▶

Top Grossing Films of 1971

Billy Jack
Diamonds are Forever▶
Fiddler on the Roof▶
The French Connection▶
Summer of '42▶

Top Grossing Films of 1972

Deliverance▶
The Godfather▶
Jeremiah Johnson▶
The Poseidon Adventure▶
What's Up, Doc?▶

Top Grossing Films of 1973

American Graffiti▶
The Exorcist▶
Papillon▶
The Sting▶
The Way We Were▶

Top Grossing Films of 1974

Blazing Saddles▶
Earthquake
The Towering Inferno▶
The Trial of Billy Jack
Young Frankenstein▶

Top Grossing Films of 1975

Dog Day Afternoon▶
Jaws▶
One Flew Over the Cuckoo's Nest▶

Top Grossing Films of 1976

All the President's Men▶
King Kong
Rocky▶
The Silver Streak▶
A Star is Born

Top Grossing Films of 1977

Close Encounters of the Third Kind▶
The Goodbye Girl▶
Saturday Night Fever
Smokey and the Bandit
Star Wars▶

Top Grossing Films of 1978

Every Which Way But Loose
Grease▶
Jaws 2
National Lampoon's Animal House▶
Superman: The Movie▶

Top Grossing Films of 1979

Alien▶
The Jerk
Kramer vs. Kramer▶
Rocky 2
Star Trek: The Motion Picture

Top Grossing Films of 1980

Airplane!▶
Any Which Way You Can
The Empire Strikes Back▶
9 to 5
Stir Crazy

Top Grossing Films of 1981

Arthur▶
Cannonball Run
On Golden Pond▶
Stripes
Superman 2▶

Top Grossing Films of 1982

E.T.: The Extra-Terrestrial▶
An Officer and a Gentleman▶
Porky's
Rocky 3

Top Grossing Films of 1983

Return of the Jedi▶
Superman 3
Terms of Endearment▶
Trading Places
WarGames

Top Grossing Films of 1984

Beverly Hills Cop
Ghostbusters▶
Gremlins▶
Indiana Jones and the Temple of Doom▶
The Karate Kid▶

Top Grossing Films of 1985

Back to the Future▶
The Color Purple▶
Out of Africa▶
Rambo: First Blood, Part 2
Rocky 4

Top Grossing Films of 1986

Crocodile Dundee▶
The Karate Kid: Part 2
Platoon▶
Star Trek 4: The Voyage Home▶
Top Gun

Top Grossing Films of 1987

Beverly Hills Cop 2
Fatal Attraction▶
Good Morning, Vietnam▶
Lethal Weapon▶
Three Men and a Baby▶
The Untouchables▶

Top Grossing Films of 1988

Coming to America▶
Crocodile Dundee 2
Die Hard▶
Rain Man▶
Twins
Who Framed Roger Rabbit?▶

Top Grossing Films of 1989

Batman▶
Driving Miss Daisy▶
Ghostbusters 2
Honey, I Shrunk the Kids
Indiana Jones and the Last Crusade▶
Lethal Weapon 2▶

Top Grossing Films of 1990

Dances with Wolves▶
Dick Tracy▶
Die Hard 2: Die Harder▶
Ghost▶
Home Alone▶
The Hunt for Red October▶
Pretty Woman▶
Teenage Mutant Ninja Turtles: The Movie▶
Total Recall▶

Top Grossing Films of 1991

The Addams Family
Backdraft
Boyz N the Hood▶
City Slickers▶
Doc Hollywood
Dying Young
Hot Shots!▶
Naked Gun 2 1/2: The Smell of Fear
New Jack City
101 Dalmations▶
Robin Hood: Prince of Thieves
The Rocketeer▶
The Silence of the Lambs▶
Sleeping with the Enemy
Teenage Mutant Ninja Turtles 2: The Secret of the Ooze
Terminator 2: Judgment Day▶
What About Bob?▶

Top Grossing Films of 1992

Aladdin▶
Alien 3
Basic Instinct
Batman Returns
The Bodyguard
Boomerang
Bram Stoker's Dracula
Fried Green Tomatoes▶
The Hand that Rocks the Cradle
Home Alone 2: Lost in New York
The Last of the Mohicans▶
A League of Their Own▶
Lethal Weapon 3
Patriot Games▶
Sister Act
Under Siege
Unforgiven▶
Wayne's World▶
White Men Can't Jump

Top Grossing Films of 1993

Aladdin▶
Cliffhanger▶
A Few Good Men▶
The Firm▶
Free Willy
The Fugitive▶
In the Line of Fire▶
Indecent Proposal
Jurassic Park▶
Sleepless in Seattle▶

Trash

Alien Massacre
Alien Prey
All the Lovin' Kinfolk
The Allnighter
Alone in the T-Shirt Zone
America
American Tickler
Andy Warhol's Bad▶
Andy Warhol's Dracula▶
Andy Warhol's Frankenstein
Angel of H.E.A.T.
Assassin of Youth
Assault of the Killer Bimbos
The Astounding She-Monster
The Astro-Zombies
Attack of the Beast Creatures
Attack of the Giant Leeches
Attack of the Killer Tomatoes
Bad Girls Go to Hell
Barn of the Naked Dead
The Beast of Yucca Flats
Bela Lugosi Meets a Brooklyn Gorilla
The Bellboy and the Playgirls
Best Buns on the Beach
Beverly Hills Bodysnatchers
Beverly Hills Knockouts
The Big Gag
The Bitch
Black Venus
Blazing Stewardesses
Blood Freak
Blood of Ghastly Horror
Bloodlust
Bloodsucking Freaks
Body of Evidence
Bottoms Up
Brain of Blood
Camp Double Feature
Candy Tangerine Man
The Carpetbaggers
Casting Call
The Castle of Fu Manchu
Cheerleader Camp
Cocaine Fiends
The Commies are Coming, the Commies are Coming
Corruption
Creeping Terror
Curse of the Blue Lights
Curse of the Living Dead
Cyborg
Cycle Vixens
Dead Aim
The Dead Next Door
Delinquent School Girls
Demons
Desperate Living
Desperate Teenage Lovedolls
Detour to Danger
Dolemite
Dolemite 2: Human Tornado
Drop Dead Fred
Drum
Drums O'Voodoo
Eegah!
Escape from Planet Earth
Faces of Death, Part 1
Faces of Death, Part 2
Fat Guy Goes Nutzoid
Female Trouble
The Fifth Floor
Film House Fever
Five Minutes to Love
Flesh and Blood Show
Frankenstein Meets the Space Monster
Fun Down There
Ghoul School
Glen or Glenda
Gore-Met Zombie Chef From Hell
Gun Cargo
Heartstopper
Hitchhikers
Hold Me, Thrill Me, Kiss Me
Hollywood After Dark
Hollywood Chainsaw Hookers
The Hollywood Strangler Meets the Skid Row Slasher

Honkytonk Nights
Horror of Party Beach
The House of Usher
I Spit on Your Grave
I Was a Zombie for the FBI
Ilsa, Harem Keeper of the Oil Sheiks
Ilsa, She-Wolf of the SS
Ilsa, the Tigress of Siberia
Impulse
In the Cold of the Night
Incredibly Strange Creatures Who Stopped Living and Became Mixed-Up Zombies
Infra-Man
Invasion of the Bee Girls▶
Island of Lost Girls
It's Not the Size That Counts
Jail Bait
Jungle Master
Killer Tomatoes Eat France
Killer Tomatoes Strike Back
Kung Fu Vampire Buster
The Last Season
The Lonely Lady
Lost, Lonely, and Vicious
The Loves of Hercules
Man with Two Heads
Manos, the Hands of Fate
Master Blaster
Microwave Massacre
Midnight 2: Sex, Death, and Videotape
Mind Trap
Mondo Balardo
Mondo Trasho
Motel Hell
Multiple Maniacs
The Naked Flame
A Night in Heaven
Night of the Cobra Woman
Night of the Demon
Night of the Ghouls
Nightmare
Oasis of the Zombies
Once is Not Enough
Orgy of the Dead
Out of the Body
The Outcast
Pagan Island
The Perverse Countess
Phantasm
Pink Flamingos
Plan 9 from Outer Space
Please Don't Eat My Mother
Pot, Parents, and Police
The Power
The Psychic
Queen of Outer Space
Rabid Grannies
Rat Pfink a Boo-Boo
The Rats are Coming! The Werewolves are Here!
Reform School Girl
Return of the Family Man
Return of the Killer Tomatoes
Return to the Blue Lagoon
Revenge of the Virgins
Robot Monster
Rush
Satan in High Heels
Satan's Cheerleaders
Saturday the 14th Strikes Back
Savage Intruder
Screen Test
She Demons
She-Devils on Wheels
The Sinister Invasion
The Sinister Urge
Slaves in Bondage
Sleazemania III: The Good, the Bad & the Sleazy
Some Call It Loving
Sorority Girl
Space Monster
The Speed Lovers
Streetfight
Sweet Trash
Tarzan, the Ape Man
Teenage Gang Debs
Teenage Mother
Teenage Strangler

Teenagers from Outer Space
Terror in the Jungle
Texas Layover
They Saved Hitler's Brain
Tomboy
Torture Dungeon
Train Station Pickups
The Trial of Billy Jack
Troma's War
Unholy Rollers
Valley of the Dolls
Victims
Violated
The Violent Years
White Pongo
Wild Ones on Wheels
Wild Women of Wongo
Winterbeast
World of the Depraved
The Worst of Faces of Death
Youth Aflame
You've Ruined Me, Eddie
The Zombie Army

Troma Films

Blades
Bloodsucking Freaks
Chopper Chicks in Zombietown
Class of Nuke 'Em High
Class of Nuke 'Em High, Part 2: Subhumanoid Meltdown
Combat Shock
Deadly Daphne's Revenge
Evil Clutch
Ferocious Female Freedom Fighters
I Married a Vampire
I Was a Teenage TV Terrorist
Monster in the Closet
Rabid Grannies
Redneck Zombies
Sizzle Beach U.S.A.
Splatter University
Squeeze Play
Stuck on You
Student Confidential
Surf Nazis Must Die
The Toxic Avenger
The Toxic Avenger, Part 2
The Toxic Avenger, Part 3: The Last Temptation of Toxie
Troma's War

Universal Studios' Classic Horror

Abbott and Costello Meet Dr. Jekyll and Mr. Hyde
Abbott and Costello Meet Frankenstein▶
Abbott and Costello Meet the Killer, Boris Karloff
The Black Cat▶
The Bride of Frankenstein▶
Creature from the Black Lagoon▶
The Creature Walks Among Us
Dracula▶
Dracula (Spanish Version)
Dracula's Daughter▶
Frankenstein▶
Frankenstein Meets the Wolfman▶
The Ghost of Frankenstein
House of Dracula
House of Frankenstein
The Hunchback of Notre Dame▶
Invisible Agent
The Invisible Man▶
The Invisible Man Returns▶
The Invisible Woman▶
Island of Lost Souls▶
The Mummy▶
The Mummy's Curse
The Mummy's Ghost
The Mummy's Hand
The Mummy's Tomb
Murders in the Rue Morgue
Phantom of the Opera▶

Universal

The Raven▶
Revenge of the Creature
Son of Dracula▶
Son of Frankenstein▶
Werewolf of London
The Wolf Man▶

Woofs!

The Adventurers
Adventures of a Taxi Driver
The Adventures of Ford
  Fairlane
The Adventurous Knights
After the Fall of New York
Albino
The Alchemist
Alien Contamination
Alien from L.A.
Alien Massacre
Alien Predators
Alien Warrior
Almost Human
The Amazing Transparent Man
The Amazing Transplant
The Ambushers
American Gothic
American Ninja 3: Blood Hunt
American Ninja 4: The
  Annihilation
Americathon
Amin: The Rise and Fall
Amityville 2: The Possession
The Amityville Curse
Angel 3: The Final Chapter
Angel of Death
Angel of H.E.A.T.
Angels' Wild Women
The Annihilators
A*P*E*
The Appointment
The Astounding She-Monster
The Astro-Zombies
Atlas in the Land of the Cyclops
Atom Age Vampire
The Atomic Brain
Ator the Fighting Eagle
Attack of the Beast Creatures
Attack of the Killer Refrigerator
Attack of the Killer Tomatoes
Attack of the Mayan Mummy
Attack of the Swamp Creature
Auntie
Avenging Angel
Awakening of Candra
Baby Love
Bad Charleston Charlie
Bad Girls Do Cry
Bad Girls from Mars
Bad Girls Go to Hell
Bad Medicine
Balboa
Bananas Boat
Bandera Bandits
Barn of the Naked Dead
Barracuda
Basic Training
Battle of the Bullies
Beaks: The Movie
Beast of the Yellow Night
The Beast of Yucca Flats
The Bees
Bela Lugosi Meets a Brooklyn
  Gorilla
The Bellboy and the Playgirls
Best Buns on the Beach
Beyond Atlantis
Beyond Evil
Beyond the Door
Beyond the Door 3
The Big Bust Out
Big Foot
The Bikini Car Wash Company
Birds of Paradise
The Bitch
The Black Cat
Black Cobra
The Black Cobra
Black Gestapo
Black Magic Woman
The Black Maid
Black Shampoo

Black Venus
Blackenstein
Blade of the Ripper
Blastfighter
The Blazing Ninja
Blazing Stewardesses
Blockhouse
Blood Beach
Blood Diner
Blood Freak
Blood Games
Blood Lake
Blood of Ghastly Horror
Blood Orgy of the She-Devils
Blood Rage
Blood Screams
Blood Sisters
Blood Voyage
Bloodmoon
Bloodstalkers
Bloodsuckers from Outer
  Space
Bloodsucking Freaks
Bloodsucking Pharoahs of
  Pittsburgh
The Bloody Brood
Bloody Moon
The Blue Lagoon
Blue Movies
Blue Paradise
Blue Ribbon Babes
The Body Beneath
Body of Evidence
Body Rock
The Body Shop
Bolero
Boogey Man 2
Boom in the Moon
Boss Foreman
Bottoms Up
Brain of Blood
The Bride & the Beast
Bride of the Monster
Brides of the Beast
The Brides Wore Blood
Brujo Luna
Bug
Bullies
Bummer
Cabin Boy
Caged Terror
California Casanova
Caligula
Can I Do It...Till I Need
  Glasses?
Can't Stop the Music
Cartel
Castle of Evil
Castle of the Creeping Flesh
Cave Girl
Cave of the Living Dead
Cellar Dweller
The Centerfold Girls
Chain Gang Women
Chained for Life
Challenge
Cheaper to Keep Her
Cheech and Chong's, The
  Corsican Brothers
Cheering Section
Cheerleader Camp
The Cheerleaders
Cheerleaders' Wild Weekend
Cherry Hill High
The Children
Child's Play 2
The Chilling
The Chosen
Chu Chu & the Philly Flash
C.H.U.D.
C.H.U.D. 2: Bud the Chud
City on Fire
Clash of the Titans
Class of 1984
Class Reunion
Class Reunion Massacre
Claws
Clifford
Color Me Blood Red
Comic Cabby
Condemned to Hell
Confidential

The Conqueror
Conqueror & the Empress
Conqueror of the World
Copkillers
The Corpse Grinders
Corruption
Cosh Boy
Cosmos: War of the Planets
The Cradle Will Fall
The Crater Lake Monster
The Crawling Hand
Crazed
Crazy Fat Ethel II
The Creation of the Humanoids
Creatures the World Forgot
Creeping Terror
The Cremators
Crocodile
Crucible of Terror
Cruise into Terror
Crypt of the Living Dead
Cthulhu Mansion
Curse of the Alpha Stone
The Curse of the Aztec Mummy
Curse of the Aztec Mummy/
  Robot vs. the Aztec Mummy
Curse of the Blue Lights
Curse of the Screaming Dead
Curse of the Stone Hand
Curtains
Cycle Psycho
Cycle Vixens
Dagora, the Space Monster
Dance of Death
Danger Zone
Dangerous Love
Dark Sanity
Dawn of the Mummy
The Day It Came to Earth
Dead Aim
Dead Pit
Dead Women in Lingerie
Deadly Darling
Deadly Embrace
Deadly Encounter
Deadly Prey
Deadly Sanctuary
Deadly Twins
The Death Curse of Tartu
Death Spa
Death Wish 2
Death Wish 5: The Face of
  Death
Deathstalker
Delinquent School Girls
Delirium
The Demon Lover
Demon of Paradise
Demon Witch Child
Demonwarp
Detour to Danger
Devil Woman
Devil's Gift
The Devil's Harvest
Devil's Son-in-Law
Devil's Wedding Night
Diamond Ninja Force
Die Laughing
Digging Up Business
Dirty Laundry
Dirty Mind of Young Sally
Doctor Butcher M.D.
Dr. Orloff's Monster
Dr. Tarr's Torture Dungeon
The Dolls
Don't Go in the Woods
Don't Look in the Attic
Don't Open the Door!
Don't Open Till Christmas
Doom Asylum
Dorm That Dripped Blood
Dracula: Up in Harlem
Dracula vs. Frankenstein
Dracula's Great Love
Dracula's Last Rites
Driller Killer
Drive-In
Drive-In Massacre
Driver's Seat
Drop Dead Fred
Drum
Drums O'Voodoo

Dutch Girls
Ecstasy
Eegah!
Emily
Empire of Spiritual Ninja
End of the World
Endless Descent
Erotic Dreams
Erotic Images
Escape from Hell
Escape from Safehaven
Escape from the KGB
Escape 2000
Escapist
Eve of Destruction
The Evictors
Evil Laugh
Evilspeak
Exterminators of the Year 3000
Eyeball
Eyes of a Stranger
Faces of Death, Part 2
Fade to Black
Fair Game
Fanny Hill: Memoirs of a
  Woman of Pleasure
Fantasies
Far Out Man
Fat Guy Goes Nutzoid
Fatal Pulse
The Fear Chamber
Feelin' Up
The Female Bunch
Fever Pitch
Fiend
The Fiendish Plot of Dr. Fu
  Manchu
The Fifth Floor
Final Exam
Flesh Feast
Flight to Nowhere
Food of the Gods
Food of the Gods: Part 2
The Forbidden Dance
Forbidden World
Foreplay
Fowl Play
Frankenstein '80
Frankenstein General Hospital
Frankenstein Island
Frankenstein Meets the Space
  Monster
Frankenstein's Great Aunt Tillie
Friday the 13th, Part 2
Friday the 13th, Part 3
Friday the 13th, Part 4: The
  Final Chapter
Friday the 13th, Part 5: A New
  Beginning
Friday the 13th, Part 6: Jason
  Lives
Friday the 13th, Part 7: The
  New Blood
Fugitive Alien
Fun Down There
Galactic Gigolo
The Gamma People
Gangster's Law
The Garbage Pail Kids Movie
Gas
Gates of Hell
The Ghastly Ones
Ghost Fever
Ghost in the Noonday Sun
Ghoulies 3: Ghoulies Go to
  College
Giant from the Unknown
Giants of Rome
Gimme an F
The Girl in Room 2A
Girl on a Chain Gang
Glen or Glenda
The Glory Stompers
Goblin
God's Bloody Acre
Godzilla vs. the Sea Monster
Goliath and the Dragon
Goliathon
Goof Balls
Gore-Met Zombie Chef From
  Hell
Gorp

The Green Berets
The Green Slime
Grotesque
Grunt! The Wrestling Movie
Guess What We Learned in
  School Today?
H-Bomb
H-Man
Halloween with the Addams
  Family
Hallucination
Hands of Steel
Hangmen
Hardbodies 2
Hawmps!
The Hearse
Heavenly Bodies
Hell Night
Hell Up in Harlem
Hellcats
Hellgate
Hellriders
Hell's Brigade: The Final
  Assault
Helltrain
Hillbillies in a Haunted House
The Hills Have Eyes
His Name was King
Hitchhikers
The Hollywood Strangler Meets
  the Skid Row Slasher
Hollywood Zap
Hometown U.S.A.
Horror House on Highway 5
Horror of Party Beach
Horror of the Blood Monsters
Horror Planet
Hospital Massacre
Hot Box
Hot T-Shirts
Hot Touch
The Hound of the Baskervilles
House of Psychotic Women
House of Whipcord
House on the Edge of the Park
How to Seduce a Woman
Humanoids from the Deep
Humongous
Hurricane
I Dismember Mama
I Eat Your Skin
I Spit on Your Corpse
I Spit on Your Grave
I Was a Teenage TV Terrorist
Icebox Murders
Idaho Transfer
Ilsa, Harem Keeper of the Oil
  Sheiks
Ilsa, She-Wolf of the SS
Ilsa, the Tigress of Siberia
Ilsa, the Wicked Warden
Impulse
In Search of Anna
In the Shadow of Kilimanjaro
In Trouble
Incredible Melting Man
The Incredible Petrified World
The Incredible Two-Headed
  Transplant
Incredibly Strange Creatures
  Who Stopped Living and
  Became Mixed-Up Zombies
Incubus
Infra-Man
Inner Sanctum
Invasion of the Animal People
Invasion of the Blood Farmers
Invasion of the Body Stealers
Invasion of the Flesh Hunters
Invasion of the Girl Snatchers
Invincible Barbarian
Invincible Gladiators
The Invisible Maniac
Invitation to Hell
The Island
Island Claw
Island of Lost Girls
It's Alive 2: It Lives Again
It's Not the Size That Counts
Jason Goes to Hell: The Final
  Friday
Jaws of Satan

Jazz Singer
Joy Sticks
Junior
Just for the Hell of It
Kidnapped
Kill Alex Kill
Killer Party
Killers from Space
Kilma, Queen of the Amazons
King of Kong Island
The King of the Kickboxers
King of the Zombies
King's Ransom
Kung Fu Vampire Buster
Las Vegas Serial Killer
The Las Vegas Story
Laserblast
The Last Horror Film
Last House on Dead End Street
Last Mercenary
The Last Season
The Last Slumber Party
The Last Woman on Earth
Lauderdale
A Legacy for Leonette
Legacy of Horror
Legend of the Dinosaurs
Leprechaun
The Lifetaker
Link
Lipstick
Lisa and the Devil
Lisztomania
Little Darlings
Loaded Guns
The Loch Ness Horror
The Lone Runner
The Lonely Lady
The Longshot
Lords of the Deep
Love Thrill Murders
The Loves of Hercules
Love's Savage Fury
Lurkers
Luther the Geek
Mack the Knife
Mad About You
The Mad Bomber
Mad Doctor of Blood Island
Mad Dog
Mad Youth
Madigan's Millions
Mama Dracula
A Man Called Rage
Man from Deep River
Maniac
Mannequin 2: On the Move
Manos, the Hands of Fate
Mardi Gras Massacre
A Matter of Time
Maximum Thrust
Maya
Meatballs 3
The Meateater
Mechanical Crabs
The Medal of Honor
Megaforce
Mesa of Lost Women
Meteor
Meteor Monster
Midnight Cabaret
Mistress of the Apes
Mob War
Mondo Trasho
Mongrel
Monsignor
Monster a Go-Go!
Monster Dog
The Monster of Piedras Blancas
Moonshine Mountain
Moses
Mountaintop Motel Massacre
Mummy & Curse of the Jackal
Murderer's Keep
Murderlust
Mutant Hunt
Mutants In Paradise
The Mutilator
My African Adventure
My Therapist
Myra Breckinridge

Nail Gun Massacre
Naked Cage
The Naked Flame
Naked Vengeance
Naked Youth
The Narcotics Story
National Lampoon's Class Reunion
Navy vs. the Night Monsters
Neon Maniacs
The New Gladiators
New Year's Evil
New York Ripper
The Night God Screamed
A Night in Heaven
Night of Dark Shadows
Night of the Bloody Apes
Night of the Bloody Transplant
Night of the Demon
Night of the Ghouls
Night of the Living Babes
Night of the Sharks
Night of the Sorcerers
Night of the Zombies
Night Patrol
Night Train to Terror
Nightmare
Nightmare in Red China
Nightmare Sisters
Nightstalker
Nine Deaths of the Ninja
1990: The Bronx Warriors
Ninja Champion
Ninja Exterminators
Ninja Fantasy
Ninja Hunt
Ninja Terminator
Ninja Wars
No One Cries Forever
Nobody's Perfekt
Nocturna
Norman's Awesome Experience
Nude on the Moon
The Occultist
Ocean Drive Weekend
Oddballs
On Deadly Ground
On the Edge: The Survival of Dana
One Brief Summer
One Down, Two to Go!
One Russian Summer
Orca
Orgy of the Dead
The Other Side of Midnight
Parasite
Party Favors
People Who Own the Dark
Perfect Timing
Phobia
Pieces
Pink Motel
Plan 9 from Outer Space
Please Don't Eat My Mother
Police Academy 5: Assignment Miami Beach
Prehistoric Bimbos in Armageddon City
Prehistoric Women
Pretty Smart
Prettykill
The Prime Time
Private Manoeuvres
The Psychic
Psychos in Love
Pulsebeat
The Puma Man
Queen of Outer Space
Quick, Let's Get Married
Rabid Grannies
Raise the Titanic
The Rape of the Sabines
Rat Pfink a Boo-Boo
The Rats are Coming! The Werewolves are Here!
Rebel Vixens
The Red Menace
The Return
Revenge
Revenge of Doctor X
Ridin' the Lone Trail

The Ripper
The Robot vs. the Aztec Mummy
Rocket Attack U.S.A.
Roller Boogie
Rooster: Spurs of Death!
Sahara
Santa Claus
Sasquatch
Satan's Blade
Satan's Cheerleaders
Satan's Touch
Satanwar
Savage!
Savage is Loose
Savage Weekend
Scarlet Spear
Scream Bloody Murder
Scream of the Demon Lover
Screen Test
Secrets of Sweet Sixteen
Senior Week
Sensual Partners
The Sensuous Teenager
The Serpent and the Rainbow
The Severed Arm
Sex Adventures of the Three Musketeers
Sex, Drugs, and Rock-n-Roll
The Sex Machine
Sex on the Run
Sextette
Sharp Fists in Kung Fu
She Came on the Bus
She Demons
She-Devils on Wheels
Sheena
Shriek of the Mutilated
Sidney Sheldon's Bloodline
The Simple Truth
Sincerely Yours
The Sinister Urge
Sinner's Blood
Skinned Alive
Skullduggery
Sky Pirates
Slashdance
The Slasher
The Slaughter of the Vampires
Slaughterhouse
Slaughterhouse Rock
Slave of the Cannibal God
The Slayer
Sledgehammer
Sleepaway Camp 3: Teenage Wasteland
The Slime People
Slithis
Sloane
Slugs
Slumber Party Massacre 2
Slumber Party Massacre 3
Smooth Talker
The Snow Creature
Something Weird
Sonny Boy
Sorceress
Sorority House Massacre
Sorority House Massacre 2: Nighty Nightmare
Soul Hustler
South Seas Massacre
Space Monster
Space Riders
Spaced Out
Spare Parts
Spasms
Sphinx
Splatter University
Splitz
Spookies
The Sporting Club
The Squeeze
Squeeze Play
SS Girls
Stepsisters
Stewardess School
Stocks and Blondes
Stone Cold
Stormquest
The Strangeness
The Stranger from Venus

Street Hero
Street Hunter
Street People
Street Trash
Street Warriors
Street Warriors, Part 2
Strike Commando
Stroker Ace
Stryker
The Stud
Student Affairs
Student Bodies
Sugar Cookies
Suicide Cult
Summer School Teachers
Sunnyside
Sunset Strip
Superchick
Superfly T.N.T.
Supersonic Man
Surf 2
Surfacing
Survival Zone
Sweater Girls
Sweet Spirits
Sweet Trash
Switchblade Sisters
Tarzan, the Ape Man
Teenage Mother
Teenage Strangler
Teenage Zombies
Teenagers from Outer Space
The Telephone
The Temp
10 Violent Women
Tentacles
Terronauts
The Terror
Terror in Beverly Hills
Terror in the Wax Museum
Terror on Tour
Terrorvision
Test Tube Babies
Texas Chainsaw Massacre, Part 2
Texas Layover
They Saved Hitler's Brain
They Went That-a-Way & That-a-Way
They're Playing with Fire
Thieves of Fortune
The Thirsty Dead
This Stuff'll Kill Ya!
Three on a Meathook
Threesome
The Thrill Killers
Throne of Fire
Tintorera...Tiger Shark
TNT Jackson
To All a Goodnight
Tomb of Torture
Tomboy
The Tormentors
Torso
Tower of Evil
Treasure of the Moon Goddess
The Trial of Billy Jack
Trick or Treats
Troma's War
Twice Dead
Twilight People
Two Lost Worlds
2020 Texas Gladiators
The Uncanny
Under the Rainbow
Underground Aces
The Uninvited
Unknown Island
Unknown Powers
Vampire Raiders—Ninja Queen
Vasectomy: A Delicate Matter
Vengeance Is Mine
Venom
Vice Academy 3
Vice Squad
The Video Dead
Video Wars
Vigilante
Violated
Violent Ones
The Violent Years
Viva Knievel

Voyage to the Planet of Prehistoric Women
Vulcan God of Fire
Wacko
Waitress
Wanted: Babysitter
Warlords from Hell
Warrior of the Lost World
Warriors of the Apocalypse
Warriors of the Wasteland
Weekend with the Babysitter
Werewolves on Wheels
When Lightning Strikes
When Nature Calls
Where the Boys Are '84
White Cannibal Queen
White Gorilla
White Pongo
Wholly Moses!
The Wild Beasts
Wild Guitar
Wild Ones on Wheels
Wild Orchid 2: Two Shades of Blue
Wild Riders
Wild Wheels
The Wildest Office Party
Wired to Kill
Witchcraft
The Witching
Woman Hunt
Women in Cell Block 7
Women in Fury
Women of the Prehistoric Planet
Women Unchained
Women's Prison Massacre
Woodchipper Massacre
The World is Full of Married Men
World of the Vampires
The Worm Eaters
The Worst of Faces of Death
Wrestling Racket Girls
Wrestling Women vs. the Aztec Ape
Wrestling Women vs. the Aztec Mummy
Xanadu
Xtro
The Yesterday Machine
You Light Up My Life
Youth Aflame
Zandalee
Zero Boys
Zero Pilot
Zombie Nightmare
Zombies of Moratau

SERIES & PARTNERSHIPS INDEX

The **SERIES INDEX** provides 68 concise listings of major movie series, from James Bond to the Raiders of the Lost Ark to Dirty Harry, as well as recurring and notable cinematic partnerships, including the Three Stooges, Hepburn and Tracy, and Zucker/Abrahams/Zucker. It follows the arrangement of the Category Index, with series names arranged alphabetically. The categories are as follows:

Abbott & Costello
Andy Hardy
Astaire & Rogers
Beach Party
Billy the Kid
The Bowery Boys
Bulldog Drummond
Charlie Brown and the Peanuts
  Gang
Charlie Chan
Cheech & Chong
Corman's Mama
Dirty Harry
Dr. Christian
Dr. Mabuse
Dr. Seuss
Dracula
Eddy & MacDonald
Elvisfilm
Faerie Tale Theatre
The Falcon
Frankenstein
Godzilla and Friends

Hallmark Hall of Fame
Hepburn & Tracy
Hopalong Cassidy
Hope & Crosby
Jack the Ripper
James Bond
James Bond Spoofs
Jesse James
Lassie
Laurel & Hardy
The Lone Rider
Martin & Lewis
The Marx Brothers
Mike Hammer
Mr. Wong
Monty Python
Muppets
National Lampoon
A Night at the Movies
Our Gang
The Pink Panther
Planet of the Apes
Raiders of the Lost Ark

Rambo
The Rangebusters
Redford & Newman
Renfrew of the Mounties
The Ritz Brothers
The Rough Riders
The Saint
Sexton Blake
Shelly Duvall's Tall Tales and
  Legends
Sherlock Holmes
Star Wars
Tarzan
The Texas Rangers
The Thin Man
The Three Mesquiteers
The 3 Stooges
The Trail Blazers
Turner & Douglas
Wonderworks Family Movies
Wyatt Earp
Zucker/Abrahams/Zucker

SERIES & PARTNERSHIPS INDEX

Abbott & Costello

Abbott and Costello Go to Mars
Abbott and Costello in Hollywood
Abbott and Costello in the Foreign Legion
Abbott and Costello Meet Captain Kidd
Abbott and Costello Meet Dr. Jekyll and Mr. Hyde
Abbott and Costello Meet Frankenstein▶
Abbott & Costello Meet the Invisible Man▶
Abbott and Costello Meet the Keystone Kops
Abbott and Costello Meet the Killer, Boris Karloff
Abbott & Costello Meet the Mummy
Africa Screams
The Best of Abbott & Costello Live
Buck Privates
Buck Privates Come Home▶
Comin' Round the Mountain
Dance with Me, Henry
Here Come the Co-Eds
Hey Abbott!
Hit the Ice
Hold That Ghost▶
In Society
In the Navy
Jack & the Beanstalk
Keep 'Em Flying
Little Giant
Lost in a Harem
Lost in Alaska
Mexican Hayride
The Naughty Nineties
The Noose Hangs High▶
One Night in the Tropics
Pardon My Sarong
Ride 'Em Cowboy
Rio Rita
30-Foot Bride of Candy Rock
The Time of Their Lives
Who Done It?
The Wistful Widow of Wagon Gap

Andy Hardy

Andy Hardy Gets Spring Fever
Andy Hardy Meets Debutante
Andy Hardy's Double Life
Andy Hardy's Private Secretary
Life Begins for Andy Hardy▶
Love Finds Andy Hardy▶
Love Laughs at Andy Hardy

Astaire & Rogers

The Barkleys of Broadway▶
Carefree▶
Flying Down to Rio
Follow the Fleet▶
The Gay Divorcee▶
Roberta▶
The Story of Vernon and Irene Castle▶
Swing Time▶
Top Hat▶

Beach Party

Back to the Beach
Beach Blanket Bingo▶
Beach Party
Bikini Beach
How to Stuff a Wild Bikini
Muscle Beach Party
Pajama Party

Billy the Kid

Billy the Kid
Billy the Kid in Texas
Billy the Kid Returns
Billy the Kid Trapped
Billy the Kid Versus Dracula
Border Badmen
Deadwood
Devil Riders
Frontier Outlaws
Gangster's Den
Gore Vidal's Billy the Kid
I Shot Billy the Kid
Law and Order
The Left-Handed Gun▶
The Mysterious Rider
Oath of Vengeance
Outlaw of the Plains
Pat Garrett & Billy the Kid▶
Prairie Badmen
Rustler's Hideout
Shadows of Death
Thundering Gunslingers
Trigger Men
Wild Horse Phantom
Young Guns
Young Guns 2

The Bowery Boys

Angels with Dirty Faces▶
Blues Busters
Bowery Blitzkrieg
Bowery Buckaroos
Boys of the City
Clipped Wings
Dead End▶
East Side Kids
East Side Kids/The Lost City
Flying Wild
Follow the Leader
Ghost Chasers
Hard-Boiled Mahoney
Here Come the Marines
Kid Dynamite
Let's Get Tough
Little Tough Guy
Master Minds
Million Dollar Kid
Mr. Wise Guy
'Neath Brooklyn Bridge
Pride of the Bowery
Smart Alecks
Smugglers' Cove▶
Spook Busters
Spooks Run Wild
That Gang of Mine
They Made Me a Criminal

Bulldog Drummond

Arrest Bulldog Drummond
Bulldog Drummond
Bulldog Drummond at Bay
Bulldog Drummond Comes Back
Bulldog Drummond Escapes
Bulldog Drummond in Africa/Arrest Bulldog Drummond
Bulldog Drummond's Bride
Bulldog Drummond's Peril
Bulldog Drummond's Revenge
Bulldog Drummond's Revenge/Bulldog Drummond's Peril
Bulldog Drummond's Secret Police
Bulldog Jack▶

Charlie Brown and the Peanuts Gang

Be My Valentine, Charlie Brown
Bon Voyage, Charlie Brown▶
A Boy Named Charlie Brown▶
A Charlie Brown Celebration
A Charlie Brown Christmas
A Charlie Brown Thanksgiving
Charlie Brown's All-Stars
He's Your Dog, Charlie Brown!
It Was a Short Summer, Charlie Brown
It's a Mystery, Charlie Brown
It's Arbor Day, Charlie Brown
It's the Great Pumpkin, Charlie Brown
Play It Again, Charlie Brown
Race for Your Life, Charlie Brown
Snoopy, Come Home▶
Snoopy's Getting Married, Charlie Brown
Someday You'll Find Her, Charlie Brown
There's No Time for Love, Charlie Brown
You're a Good Man, Charlie Brown
You're in Love, Charlie Brown

Charlie Chan

Castle in the Desert
Charlie Chan and the Curse of the Dragon Queen
Charlie Chan at the Opera▶
Charlie Chan at the Wax Museum
The Charlie Chan Collection
Charlie Chan in Paris
Charlie Chan in Rio
Charlie Chan in the Secret Service
Charlie Chan's Secret
The Chinese Cat
The Jade Mask
Meeting at Midnight
Murder Over New York
The Scarlet Clue
The Shanghai Cobra
Terror by Night/Meeting at Midnight

Cheech & Chong

After Hours▶
Cheech and Chong: Still Smokin'
Cheech and Chong: Things Are Tough All Over
Cheech and Chong's Next Movie
Cheech and Chong's Nice Dreams
Cheech and Chong's, The Corsican Brothers
Cheech and Chong's Up in Smoke

Corman's Mama

Big Bad Mama
Big Bad Mama 2
Bloody Mama
Crazy Mama

Dirty Harry

The Dead Pool
Dirty Harry▶
The Enforcer
Magnum Force
Sudden Impact

Dr. Christian

Courageous Dr. Christian
Dr. Christian Meets the Women
Meet Dr. Christian
Melody for Three
Remedy for Riches
They Meet Again

Dr. Mabuse

Das Testament des Dr. Mabuse▶
Dr. Mabuse the Gambler▶
Dr. Mabuse vs. Scotland Yard
The Invisible Dr. Mabuse▶
The Return of Dr. Mabuse
The Thousand Eyes of Dr. Mabuse

Dr. Seuss

The 5000 Fingers of Dr. T▶
How the Grinch Stole Christmas▶

Dracula

Abbott and Costello Meet Frankenstein▶
Bela Lugosi Scrapbook
The Best of the Two Ronnies
Blood of Dracula
Blood of Dracula's Castle
Bram Stoker's Dracula
The Brides of Dracula
Count Dracula
Count Dracula's Great Love
Dracula▶
Dracula
Dracula: A Cinematic Scrapbook
Dracula & Son

Dracula

Dracula/Garden of Eden
Dracula Has Risen from the Grave
Dracula Rising
Dracula (Spanish Version)
Dracula Sucks
Dracula: Up in Harlem
Dracula vs. Frankenstein
Dracula's Daughter▶
Dracula's Great Love
Dracula's Last Rites
Dracula's Widow
The Horror of Dracula
House of Dracula
House of Frankenstein
Hysterical
Love at First Bite
The Monster Squad
Nocturna
Return of Dracula
Return of the Vampire
The Satanic Rites of Dracula
The Scars of Dracula
The Screaming Dead
Son of Dracula▶
Taste the Blood of Dracula
To Die for
Transylvania 6-5000
Vampire Circus
Waxwork
Zoltan...Hound of Dracula

Eddy & McDonald

Girl of the Golden West
I Married an Angel
Maytime▶
Naughty Marietta
New Moon
Rose Marie▶
Sweethearts▶

Elvisfilm

Blue Hawaii
Change of Habit
Charro!
Clambake
Double Trouble
Easy Come, Easy Go
Elvis and Me
The Elvis Files
Elvis in Hollywood▶
Elvis in the Movies
Elvis Memories
Elvis on Tour
Elvis: One Night with You
Elvis Presley's Graceland
Elvis: Rare Moments with the King
Elvis Stories
Elvis: The Echo Will Never Die
Elvis: The Lost Performances
Elvis: The Movie
Flaming Star▶
Follow That Dream
Frankie and Johnny
Fun in Acapulco
G.I. Blues
Girl Happy
Girls! Girls! Girls!
Harum Scarum
Heartbreak Hotel
Honeymoon in Vegas
It Happened at the World's Fair
Jailhouse Rock▶
Kid Galahad
King Creole
Kissin' Cousins
Live a Little, Love a Little
Love Me Tender
Loving You
Paradise, Hawaiian Style
Rock-a-Doodle
Roustabout
Speedway
Spinout
Stay Away, Joe
This is Elvis
Tickle Me
Top Secret!▶

The Trouble with Girls (and How To Get Into It)▶
Viva Las Vegas
Wild in the Country

Faerie Tale Theatre

Aladdin and His Wonderful Lamp
Beauty and the Beast
The Boy Who Left Home to Find Out About the Shivers
Cinderella
The Dancing Princesses
The Emperor's New Clothes
Goldilocks & the Three Bears
Hansel and Gretel
Jack & the Beanstalk
The Little Mermaid
Little Red Riding Hood▶
The Nightingale
The Pied Piper of Hamelin
Pinocchio
The Princess and the Pea▶
The Princess Who Never Laughed▶
Puss 'n Boots
Rapunzel
Rip van Winkle
Rumpelstiltskin
Sleeping Beauty
The Snow Queen
Snow White and the Seven Dwarfs
The Tale of the Frog Prince▶
The Three Little Pigs
Thumbelina▶

The Falcon

The Amityville Curse
The Devil's Cargo
The Falcon in Hollywood
The Falcon in Mexico
Falcon Takes Over/Strange Bargain
Falcon's Adventure/Armored Car Robbery
The Falcon's Brother

Frankenstein

Abbott and Costello Meet Frankenstein▶
Andy Warhol's Frankenstein
Blackenstein
The Bride
The Bride of Frankenstein▶
The Curse of Frankenstein
Dr. Frankenstein's Castle of Freaks
Dracula vs. Frankenstein
The Evil of Frankenstein
Frankenstein▶
Frankenstein
Frankenstein: A Cinematic Scrapbook
Frankenstein and the Monster from Hell
Frankenstein '80
Frankenstein General Hospital
Frankenstein Island
Frankenstein Meets the Space Monster
Frankenstein Meets the Wolfman▶
Frankenstein Unbound▶
Frankenstein's Daughter
Frankenstein's Great Aunt Tillie
Frankenweenie
The Ghost of Frankenstein
Gothic▶
The Horror of Frankenstein
House of Frankenstein
Jesse James Meets Frankenstein's Daughter
Lady Frankenstein
Munster's Revenge
Nosferatu▶
Orlak, the Hell of Frankenstein
Prototype▶

The Screaming Dead
Son of Frankenstein▶
Teenage Frankenstein
The Vindicator
Young Frankenstein▶

Godzilla and Friends

Dagora, the Space Monster
Destroy All Monsters
Destroy All Planets
Gamera, the Invincible
Gamera vs. Barugon
Gamera vs. Gaos
Gamera vs. Guiron
Gamera vs. Zigra
Gappa the Trifibian Monster
Ghidrah the Three Headed Monster
Godzilla, King of the Monsters
Godzilla 1985
Godzilla on Monster Island
Godzilla Raids Again
Godzilla vs. Biollante
Godzilla vs. Megalon
Godzilla vs. Monster Zero
Godzilla vs. Mothra
Godzilla vs. the Cosmic Monster
Godzilla vs. the Sea Monster
Godzilla vs. the Smog Monster
Godzilla's Revenge
King Kong Versus Godzilla
Mothra▶
Rodan
Son of Godzilla
Terror of Mechagodzilla
Varan the Unbelievable
War of the Gargantuas
X from Outer Space
Yog, Monster from Space

Hallmark Hall of Fame

An American Story
Blind Spot
Caroline?▶
Decoration Day▶
Foxfire▶
Miss Rose White▶
O Pioneers!
One Against the Wind▶
Sarah, Plain and Tall▶
The Secret Garden▶
The Shell Seekers
Skylark
To Dance with the White Dog▶

Hepburn & Tracy

Adam's Rib▶
Hepburn & Tracy
Pat and Mike▶
State of the Union▶
Without Love
Woman of the Year▶

Hopalong Cassidy

Bar-20
Border Patrol
Border Vigilants
Colt Comrades
Doomed Caravan▶
False Colors
The Frontiersman
Hopalong Cassidy▶
Hopalong Cassidy: Borrowed Trouble
Hopalong Cassidy: Dangerous Venture
Hopalong Cassidy: False Paradise
Hopalong Cassidy: Hoppy's Holiday
Hopalong Cassidy: Renegade Trail
Hopalong Cassidy: Riders of the Deadline

Hopalong Cassidy: Silent Conflict
Hopalong Cassidy: Sinister Journey
Hopalong Cassidy: The Dead Don't Dream
Hopalong Cassidy: The Devil's Playground
Hopalong Cassidy: The Marauders
Hopalong Cassidy: Unexpected Guest
Hoppy Serves a Writ
In Old Colorado
Law of the Pampas
Leather Burners
Lost Canyon
Mystery Man
Outlaws of the Desert
Renegade Trail
Riders of the Timberline
Rustler's Valley
Santa Fe Marshal
The Showdown
Texas Masquerade
Twilight on the Trail
Undercover Man

Hope & Crosby

My Favorite Brunette
The Road to Bali▶
The Road to Hong Kong
The Road to Morocco▶
The Road to Rio▶
The Road to Singapore
The Road to Utopia▶
The Road to Zanzibar▶

Jack the Ripper

Blade of the Ripper
Cosh Boy
Hands of the Ripper
He Kills Night After Night After Night
Jack the Ripper
Jack the Ripper▶
Jack's Back▶
The Lodger
The Monster of London City
Murder by Decree▶
Night Ripper
Phantom Fiend
The Ripper
Room to Let
A Study in Terror▶
Terror at London Bridge
Terror in the Wax Museum
Time After Time▶

James Bond

Diamonds are Forever▶
Dr. No▶
For Your Eyes Only▶
From Russia with Love▶
Goldfinger▶
License to Kill▶
Live and Let Die
The Living Daylights▶
The Man with the Golden Gun
Moonraker
Never Say Never Again
Octopussy
On Her Majesty's Secret Service▶
The Spy Who Loved Me
Thunderball
A View to a Kill
You Only Live Twice

James Bond Spoofs

The Ambushers
Casino Royale
If Looks Could Kill
In Like Flint
Murderers' Row
Number 1 of the Secret Service
Our Man Flint

Second Best Secret Agent in the Whole Wide World
Where the Bullets Fly

Jesse James

I Shot Jesse James▶
Jesse James▶
Jesse James at Bay
Jesse James Meets Frankenstein's Daughter
Jesse James Rides Again
Last Days of Frank & Jesse James
The Long Riders▶
Return of Jesse James

Lassie

Challenge to Lassie
Courage of Lassie
The Hills of Home▶
Lassie: Adventures of Neeka
Lassie, Come Home
Lassie: The Miracle
Lassie: Well of Love
Lassie's Great Adventure
Magic of Lassie
The Painted Hills
Son of Lassie
The Sun Comes Up

Laurel & Hardy

Air Raid Wardens
Bellhop/The Noon Whistle
Block-heads
Bohemian Girl▶
Bonnie Scotland
Bullfighters
A Chump at Oxford
The Devil's Brother
A Few Moments with Buster Keaton and Laurel and Hardy▶
The Flying Deuces▶
Golden Age of Comedy
Great Guns
Hollywood Party
Laurel & Hardy and the Family
Laurel & Hardy: Another Fine Mess
Laurel & Hardy: At Work
Laurel & Hardy: Be Big
Laurel & Hardy: Below Zero
Laurel & Hardy: Berth Marks
Laurel & Hardy: Blotto
Laurel & Hardy: Brats
Laurel & Hardy: Chickens Come Home
Laurel & Hardy Comedy Classics, Vol. 1
Laurel & Hardy Comedy Classics, Vol. 2
Laurel & Hardy Comedy Classics, Vol. 3
Laurel & Hardy Comedy Classics, Vol. 4
Laurel & Hardy Comedy Classics, Vol. 5
Laurel & Hardy Comedy Classics, Vol. 6
Laurel & Hardy Comedy Classics, Vol. 7
Laurel & Hardy Comedy Classics, Vol. 8
Laurel & Hardy Comedy Classics, Vol. 9
Laurel & Hardy: Hog Wild
Laurel & Hardy: Laughing Gravy
Laurel & Hardy: Men O'War
Laurel & Hardy: Night Owls
Laurel & Hardy On the Lam
Laurel & Hardy: Perfect Day
Laurel & Hardy Special
Laurel & Hardy Spooktacular
Laurel & Hardy: Stan "Helps" Ollie
Laurel & Hardy: The Hoose-Gow

Nothing But Trouble
Our Relations▶
Pack Up Your Troubles
Pardon Us
Pick a Star
Saps at Sea
Silent Laugh Makers, No. 1▶
Sons of the Desert▶
Swiss Miss
A Tribute to the Boys
Utopia
Way Out West▶

The Lone Rider

Border Roundup
Death Rides the Plains
Law of the Saddle
The Lone Rider in Cheyenne
The Lone Rider in Ghost Town
Raiders of Red Gap
Rangeland Racket

Martin & Lewis

Artists and Models
At War with the Army
The Caddy
Hollywood or Bust
Jumping Jacks
My Friend Irma
Pardners
Scared Stiff▶
The Stooge

The Marx Brothers

Animal Crackers▶
At the Circus
Big Store
The Cocoanuts
A Day at the Races▶
Duck Soup▶
Go West
Horse Feathers▶
Love Happy
The Marx Brothers in a
    Nutshell▶
Monkey Business▶
A Night at the Opera▶
A Night in Casablanca▶
Room Service

Mike Hammer

Girl Hunters
I, the Jury
Kiss Me Deadly▶
Margin for Murder

Mr. Wong

Doomed to Die
The Fatal Hour
Mr. Wong, Detective
Mr. Wong in Chinatown
Mysterious Mr. Wong
Mystery of Mr. Wong
Phantom of Chinatown

Monty Python

The Adventures of Baron
    Munchausen▶
All You Need Is Cash▶
And Now for Something
    Completely Different▶
Brazil▶
Clockwise
Consuming Passions
Down Among the Z Men
Erik the Viking
A Fish Called Wanda▶
The Fisher King▶
Jabberwocky
The Missionary
Monty Python and the Holy
    Grail▶
Monty Python Live at the
    Hollywood Bowl▶

Monty Python's Life of Brian▶
Monty Python's Parrot Sketch
    Not Included
Monty Python's The Meaning
    of Life▶
Nuns on the Run
The Odd Job
Personal Services
A Private Function
Privates on Parade
Rentadick
Ripping Yarns
Romance with a Double Bass▶
The Secret Policeman's Other
    Ball▶
Secret Policeman's Private
    Parts
Time Bandits
Whoops Apocalypse
Yellowbeard

Muppets

The Adventures of a Gnome
    Named Gnorm
The Great Muppet Caper▶
Labyrinth▶
The Muppet Christmas Carol
The Muppet Movie▶
The Muppets Take Manhattan▶
Sesame Street Presents:
    Follow That Bird

National Lampoon

National Lampoon's Animal
    House▶
National Lampoon's Christmas
    Vacation
National Lampoon's Class of
    '86
National Lampoon's Class
    Reunion
National Lampoon's European
    Vacation
National Lampoon's Vacation▶

A Night at the Movies

Auntie Mame▶
Battle Cry▶
Days of Wine and Roses▶
Dial "M" for Murder▶
Fanny▶
Ocean's 11
The Prince and the Showgirl
PT 109
The Wrong Man▶
The Young Philadelphians▶

Our Gang

General Spanky
The Little Rascals▶
Little Rascals, Book 1
Little Rascals, Book 2
Little Rascals, Book 3
Little Rascals, Book 4
Little Rascals, Book 5
Little Rascals, Book 6
Little Rascals, Book 7
Little Rascals, Book 8
Little Rascals, Book 9
Little Rascals, Book 10
Little Rascals, Book 11
Little Rascals, Book 12
Little Rascals, Book 13
Little Rascals, Book 14
Little Rascals, Book 15
Little Rascals, Book 16
Little Rascals, Book 17
Little Rascals, Book 18
Little Rascals: Choo Choo/
    Fishy Tales
Little Rascals Christmas
    Special
Little Rascals Collector's
    Edition, Vol. 1-6
Little Rascals Comedy
    Classics, Vol. 1

Little Rascals Comedy
    Classics, Vol. 2
Little Rascals: Fish Hooky/
    Spooky Hooky
Little Rascals: Honkey Donkey/
    Sprucin' Up
Little Rascals: Little Sinner/Two
    Too Young
Little Rascals: Mush and Milk/
    Three Men in a Tub
Little Rascals on Parade
Little Rascals: Pups is Pups/
    Three Smart Boys
Little Rascals: Readin' and
    Writin'/Mail and Female
Little Rascals: Reunion in
    Rhythm/Mike Fright
Little Rascals: Spanky/Feed
    'Em and Weep
Little Rascals: The Pinch
    Singer/Framing Youth
Little Rascals Two Reelers, Vol.
    1
Little Rascals Two Reelers, Vol.
    2
Little Rascals Two Reelers, Vol.
    3
Little Rascals Two Reelers, Vol.
    4
Little Rascals Two Reelers, Vol.
    5
Little Rascals Two Reelers, Vol.
    6
Little Rascals, Vol. 1
Little Rascals, Vol. 2
Our Gang
Our Gang Comedies
Our Gang Comedy Festival
Our Gang Comedy Festival 2
Rascal Dazzle
The Return of Our Gang

Pink Panther

Curse of the Pink Panther
The Pink Panther▶
The Pink Panther Strikes
    Again▶
Return of the Pink Panther
Revenge of the Pink Panther
A Shot in the Dark▶
Son of the Pink Panther
Trail of the Pink Panther

Planet of the Apes

Battle for the Planet of the
    Apes
Beneath the Planet of the Apes
Conquest of the Planet of the
    Apes
Escape from the Planet of the
    Apes▶
Planet of the Apes▶

**Raiders of the Lost
Ark**

Indiana Jones and the Last
    Crusade▶
Indiana Jones and the Temple
    of Doom▶
Raiders of the Lost Ark▶

Rambo

First Blood
Rambo: First Blood, Part 2
Rambo 3

The Rangebusters

Arizona Stagecoach
Black Market Rustlers
Boot Hill Bandits
Cowboy Commandos
Fugitive Valley
Haunted Ranch
Kid's Last Ride
Land of Hunted Men

Range Busters
Rock River Renegades
Saddle Mountain Round-Up
Texas to Bataan
Thunder River Feud
Tonto Basin Outlaws
Trail of the Silver Spurs
Trail Riders
Trailing Double Trouble
Tumbledown Ranch in Arizona
Two-Fisted Justice
Underground Rustlers
West of Pinto Basin

Redford & Newman

Butch Cassidy and the
    Sundance Kid▶
The Sting▶

**Renfrew of the
Mounties**

Danger Ahead
Fighting Mad
Murder on the Yukon
Renfrew of the Royal Mounted
Renfrew on the Great White
    Trail
Sky Bandits
Yukon Flight

The Ritz Brothers

Blazing Stewardesses
The Goldwyn Follies
The Gorilla

The Rough Riders

Arizona Bound
Below the Border
Down Texas Way
Forbidden Trails
Ghost Town Law
Gunman from Bodie
Riders of the West

The Saint

The Saint
Saint in London
The Saint in New York
The Saint Strikes Back
The Saint Takes Over
The Saint's Double Trouble
The Saint's Vacation/The
    Narrow Margin
Vendetta for the Saint

Sexton Blake

Echo Murders
Meet Sexton Blake
Sexton Blake and the Hooded
    Terror
Stage Struck

**Shelly Duvall's Tall
Tales & Legends**

Annie Oakley
Casey at the Bat
Johnny Appleseed
The Legend of Sleepy Hollow
My Darlin' Clementine
Pecos Bill

Sherlock Holmes

The Adventures of Sherlock
    Holmes
The Adventures of Sherlock
    Holmes: Hound of the
    Baskervilles
The Adventures of Sherlock
    Holmes' Smarter Brother▶
The Crucifer of Blood
Dressed to Kill

The Hound of the Baskervilles▶
The Hound of the Baskervilles
House of Fear
Masks of Death
Murder at the Baskervilles
Murder by Decree▶
The Pearl of Death
The Private Life of Sherlock
    Holmes▶
Pursuit to Algiers
Scarlet Claw▶
The Seven Percent Solution▶
Sherlock Holmes and the
    Deadly Necklace
Sherlock Holmes and the
    Incident at Victoria Falls
Sherlock Holmes and the
    Secret Weapon▶
Sherlock Holmes Faces
    Death▶
Sherlock Holmes in
    Washington
Sherlock Holmes: The Master
    Blackmailer
Sherlock Holmes: The Sign of
    Four
Sherlock Holmes: The Silver
    Blaze
Sherlock Holmes: The Voice of
    Terror
The Sign of Four
The Silent Mr. Sherlock Holmes
The Speckled Band▶
Spider Woman▶
The Strange Case of the End of
    Civilization as We Know It
A Study in Scarlet
A Study in Terror▶
Terror by Night
Terror by Night/Meeting at
    Midnight
They Might Be Giants▶
The Triumph of Sherlock
    Holmes
Without a Clue
The Woman in Green
Young Sherlock Holmes

Star Wars

The Empire Strikes Back▶
The Ewok Adventure
The Ewoks: Battle for Endor
Return of the Jedi▶
Star Wars▶

Tarzan

Greystoke: The Legend of
    Tarzan, Lord of the Apes
The New Adventures of Tarzan
Tarzan and His Mate▶
Tarzan and the Green Goddess
Tarzan and the Trappers
Tarzan Escapes▶
Tarzan Finds a Son▶
Tarzan of the Apes
Tarzan, the Ape Man▶
Tarzan, the Ape Man
Tarzan the Fearless
Tarzan the Tiger
Tarzan's New York Adventure
Tarzan's Revenge
Tarzan's Secret Treasure
Walk Like a Man

The Texas Rangers

Boss of Rawhide
Dead or Alive
Enemy of the Law
Fighting Valley
Flaming Bullets
Frontier Fugitives
Gangsters of the Frontier
Guns of the Law
Marked for Murder
Outlaw Roundup
Ranger's Roundup
Rangers Take Over
Three in the Saddle

Texas

Wild West

The Thin Man

After the Thin Man▶
Another Thin Man
Shadow of the Thin Man▶
Song of the Thin Man
The Thin Man▶
The Thin Man Goes Home

The Three Mesquiteers

Come On, Cowboys
Covered Wagon Days
Cowboys from Texas
Frontier Horizon
Ghost Town Gold
Heart of the Rockies
Heroes of the Hills
Hit the Saddle
The Kansas Terrors
Lonely Trail/Three Texas
   Steers
Outlaws of Sonora
Overland Stage Raiders▶
Pals of the Saddle
Powdersmoke Range
Purple Vigilantes
Riders of the Whistling Skull
Roarin' Lead
Rocky Mountain Rangers
Santa Fe Stampede
Three Texas Steers
The Trigger Trio
Wild Horse Rodeo
Wyoming Outlaw

The Three Musketeers

The Three Musketeers

3 Stooges

Dancing Lady
Gold Raiders
Hollywood Party
It's a Mad, Mad, Mad, Mad
   World
The Lost Stooges
Snow White and the Three
   Stooges
Stoogemania
The Stoogephile Trivia Movie
Stooges Shorts Festival
The Stooges Story▶
Three Stooges Comedy
   Capers: Vol. 1
Three Stooges Comedy
   Classics
Three Stooges: Cookoo
   Cavaliers and Other Nyuks
Three Stooges Festival
Three Stooges: From Nurse to
   Worse and Other Nyuks
The Three Stooges: Half-Wit's
   Holiday and Other Nyuks
The Three Stooges: Idiots
   Deluxe and Other Nyuks
The Three Stooges Meet
   Hercules
The Three Stooges: Nutty but
   Nice and Other Nyuks
The Three Stooges: They
   Stooge to Conga and Other
   Nyuks

The Trail Blazers

Arizona Whirlwind
Death Valley Rangers
The Law Rides Again
Outlaw Trail

Turner & Douglas

The Jewel of the Nile

Romancing the Stone▶
The War of the Roses▶

Wonderworks Family Movies

African Journey
Almost Partners
And the Children Shall Lead
Anne of Avonlea▶
Anne of Green Gables▶
The Boy Who Loved Trolls
Bridge to Terabithia
Brother Future
The Canterville Ghost
The Chronicles of Narnia
City Boy▶
Clowning Around
Clowning Around 2
Daniel and the Towers
The Fig Tree
Frog
Frogs!
A Girl of the Limberlost
Gryphon
The Haunting of Barney Palmer
Hector's Bunyip
Hiroshima Maiden
The Hoboken Chicken
   Emergency
Home at Last
The House of Dies Drear
How to Be a Perfect Person in
   Just Three Days
Jacob Have I Loved
Konrad
Lantern Hill
The Little Princess
Lone Star Kid
Looking for Miracles
Maricela
The Mighty Pawns
Miracle at Moreaux
My Friend Walter
Necessary Parties
Runaway
Spirit Rider▶
Sweet 15
Walking on Air
A Waltz Through the Hills
Words by Heart
You Must Remember This

Wyatt Earp

Cheyenne Autumn
Four Eyes and Six Guns
Gunfight at the O.K. Corral▶
Hour of the Gun
My Darling Clementine▶
Sunset
Tombstone▶
Wyatt Earp▶

Zucker/Abrahams/ Zucker

Airplane!▶
Kentucky Fried Movie▶
More! Police Squad
The Naked Gun: From the Files
   of Police Squad▶
Naked Gun 33 1/3: The Final
   Insult
Naked Gun 2 1/2: The Smell of
   Fear
Police Squad! Help Wanted!
Top Secret!▶

The **CAST INDEX** lists the video accomplishments of over 12,000 actors in a straight alphabetical format by last name (names are presented in a first name, last name format, but alphabetization begins with the last name). Every cast member credited in the main review section with more than one video credit is indexed here, creating an intriguing array of videographies for the famous and the not-so-famous. The **Director, Writer, and Composer Indexes** immediately follow this index.

Beverly Aadland
Assault of the Rebel Girls '59
Raiders of Sunset Pass '43

Lee Aaker
The Atomic City '52
Courage of Rin Tin Tin '83
Rin Tin Tin, Hero of the West '55

Angela Aames
Bachelor Party '84
Basic Training '86
The Lost Empire '83

Willie Aames
Cut and Run '85
Frankenstein '73
Paradise '82
Scavenger Hunt '79
Zapped! '82

Caroline Aaron
Alice '90
Crimes & Misdemeanors '89
Edward Scissorhands '90
Heartburn '86

Judith Abarbanel
American Matchmaker '40
The Cantor's Son '37
Uncle Moses '32

Bruce Abbott
Bad Dreams '88
Bride of Re-Animator '89
Interzone '88
The Re-Animator '85
Summer Heat '87
Trapped '89

Bud Abbott
Abbott and Costello Go to Mars '53
Abbott and Costello in Hollywood '45
Abbott and Costello in the Foreign Legion '50
Abbott and Costello Meet Captain Kidd '52
Abbott and Costello Meet Dr. Jekyll and Mr. Hyde '52
Abbott and Costello Meet Frankenstein '48
Abbott & Costello Meet the Invisible Man '51
Abbott & Costello Meet the Keystone Kops '54
Abbott and Costello Meet the Killer, Boris Karloff '49
Abbott & Costello Meet the Mummy '55
Abbott and Costello Scrapbook '70s
Africa Screams '49
The Best of Abbott & Costello Live '54
Buck Privates '41

Buck Privates Come Home '47
Classic Comedy Video Sampler '49
Comin' Round the Mountain '51
Dance with Me, Henry '56
Here Come the Co-Eds '45
Hey Abbott! '78
Hit the Ice '43
Hold That Ghost '41
Hollywood Clowns '85
Hollywood Goes to War '54
In Society '44
In the Navy '41
Jack & the Beanstalk '52
Keep 'Em Flying '41
Little Giant '46
Lost in a Harem '44
Lost in Alaska '52
Mexican Hayride '48
The Naughty Nineties '45
The Noose Hangs High '48
One Night in the Tropics '40
Pardon My Sarong '42
Ride 'Em Cowboy '42
Rio Rita '42
The Time of Their Lives '46
Who Done It? '42
The Wistful Widow of Wagon Gap '47

Diahnne Abbott
Jo Jo Dancer, Your Life is Calling '86
King of Comedy '82
Love Streams '84
New York, New York '77

John Abbott
Adventure Island '47
Anna and the King of Siam '46
Cry of the Werewolf '44
Deception '46
The Falcon in Hollywood '44
Humoresque '46
The Merry Widow '52
Pursuit to Algiers '45
U-Boat Prisoner '44
The Vampire's Ghost '45

Phillip Abbott
The Fantastic World of D.C. Collins '84
Hangar 18 '80
The Invisible Boy '57

Kareem Abdul-Jabbar
Chuck Berry: Hail! Hail! Rock 'n' Roll '87
The Deadliest Art: The Best of the Martial Arts Films '90
The Fish that Saved Pittsburgh '79
Fletch '85
Game of Death '79

Pee Wee's Playhouse Christmas Special '88
Purple People Eater '88

Alfred Abel
Dr. Mabuse the Gambler '22
Metropolis '26

Walter Abel
Curley '47
Fabulous Joe '47
Fury '36
Grace Quigley '84
Holiday Inn '42
The Indian Fighter '55
Kid from Brooklyn '46
Law of the Underworld '38
Mirage '66
Mr. Skeffington '44
Prudential Family Playhouse '50
Quick, Let's Get Married '71
Raintree County '57
Silent Night, Bloody Night '73
13 Rue Madeleine '46
The Three Musketeers '35
Wake Island '42

Jim Abele
Student Affairs '88
Wimps '87

Ian Abercrombie
Army of Darkness '92
Catacombs '89
Curse 4: The Ultimate Sacrifice '92
Kicks '85
Puppet Master 3: Toulon's Revenge '91
Test Tube Teens from the Year 2000 '93
Zandalee '91

Keith Aberdein
Smash Palace '82
Wild Horses '82

Abigail
Adventures of Eliza Fraser '76
Breaking Loose '90

F. Murray Abraham
All the President's Men '76
Amadeus '84
Beyond the Stars '89
The Big Fix '78
By the Sword '93
An Innocent Man '89
Intimate Power '89
Last Action Hero '93
Madman '79
Mobsters '91
The Name of the Rose '86
Prisoner of Second Avenue '74
The Ritz '76
Scarface '83
Serpico '73

Slipstream '89
The Sunshine Boys '75
Surviving the Game '94
Sweet Killing '93
They Might Be Giants '71
Third Solution '89

Ken Abraham
Creepozoids '87
Deadly Embrace '88
Marked for Murder '89
Vice Academy '88

Michele Abrams
Buffy the Vampire Slayer '92
Cool World '92

Victoria Abril
After Darkness '85
Esposa y Amante '70s
High Heels '91
Jimmy Hollywood '94
L'Addition '85
Lovers: A True Story '90
Max, Mon Amour '86
Moon in the Gutter '83
On the Line '83
Padre Nuestro '85
Tie Me Up! Tie Me Down! '90

Sharon Acker
The Hanged Man '74
Off Your Rocker '80
The Stranger '73

Leslie Ackerman
Blame It on the Night '84
Joy Ride to Nowhere '78
Law and Disorder '74
Shattered Vows '84
Skag '79
Young Love, First Love '79

Joss Ackland
The Apple '80
Bill & Ted's Bogus Journey '91
Codename Kyril '91
The House that Dripped Blood '71
The Hunt for Red October '90
It Couldn't Happen Here '88
Lady Jane '85
Lethal Weapon 2 '89
The Mighty Ducks '92
Mind Snatchers '72
Mother's Boys '94
Nowhere to Run '93
The Object of Beauty '91
Once Upon a Crime '92
The Palermo Connection '91
Project: Shadowchaser '92
Queenie '87
Rough Cut '80
Saint Jack '79
Shadowlands '85
The Sicilian '87
Silver Bears '78

Spymaker: The Secret Life of Ian Fleming '90
S*P*Y*S '74
To Kill a Priest '89
White Mischief '88
Who is Killing the Great Chefs of Europe? '78
A Woman Named Jackie '91
A Zed & Two Noughts '88

David Ackroyd
And I Alone Survived '78
The Children of Times Square '86
Cocaine: One Man's Seduction '83
The Dark Secret of Harvest Home '78
Dead On '93
The Fear Inside '92
A Gun in the House '81
Love, Cheat & Steal '94
Memories of Me '88
Poor Little Rich Girl: The Barbara Hutton Story '87
A Smoky Mountain Christmas '86
When Your Lover Leaves '83
Windmills of the Gods '88

Rodolfa Acosta
Drum Beat '54
Pancho Villa Returns '50
Savage Run '70

Jay Acovone
Born to Run '93
Doctor Mordrid: Master of the Unknown '92
Quicksand: No Escape '91

Acquanetta
Captive Wild Woman '43
Grizzly Adams: The Legend Continues '90
The Lost Continent '51

Eddie Acuff
G-Men Never Forget '48
Law of the Underworld '38

Deborah Adair
Endless Descent '90
Gore Vidal's Lincoln '88

Dick Adair
Blind Rage '78
Pay or Die '80

Robert Adair
The Face at the Window '39
Norman Conquest '53

Betty Adams
Blazing Guns '50
Outlaw Gang '49
Sudden Death '50

Beverly Adams
Devil's Angels '67

Adams ►cont.

How to Stuff a Wild Bikini '65
Murderers' Row '66
Roustabout '64
Torture Garden '67

Brandon Adams
Ghost in the Machine '93
The People Under the Stairs '91
The Sandlot '93

Brooke Adams
Almost You '85
Cuba '79
Days of Heaven '78
Dead Zone '83
Gas Food Lodging '92
The Innocents Abroad '84
Invasion of the Body Snatchers '78
James Dean '76
Key Exchange '85
The Last Hit '93
The Lion of Africa '87
A Man, a Woman, and a Bank '79
Man on Fire '87
Shock Waves '77
Sometimes They Come Back '91
The Stuff '85
Tell Me a Riddle '80
The Unborn '91
Utilities '83

Casey Adams
Bus Stop '56
The Indestructible Man '56
The Monster that Challenged the World '57
Niagara '52
Summer and Smoke '61
What Price Glory? '52

Catlin Adams
The Jazz Singer '80
The Jerk '79
Panic in Echo Park '77

Claire Adams
The Big Parade '25
Heart's Haven '22

Don Adams
Back to the Beach '87
Get Smart, Again! '89
Jimmy the Kid '82
The Nude Bomb '80
Two Top Bananas '87

Dorothy Adams
Laura '44
The Prodigal '55
Streets of Sin '49

Edie Adams
Adventures Beyond Belief '87
The Apartment '60
The Best Man '64
Best of Ernie Kovacs '56
Call Me Bwana '63
Cheech and Chong's Up in Smoke '79
Haunting of Harrington House '82
The Honey Pot '67
It's a Mad, Mad, Mad, Mad World '63
Love with the Proper Stranger '63
Lover Come Back '61
The Oscar '66
Racquet '79
The Seekers '79
Shooting Stars '85

Ernie Adams
Beyond the Rockies '32
Breed of the Border '33
The Fighting Legion '30
Galloping Romeo '33
Gun Lords of Stirrup Basin '37
The Gun Ranger '34
Lightning Bill Crandall '37
Ridin' the Lone Trail '37
Sagebrush Law '43
The Tip-Off '31
Wings Over the Pacific '43

Jane Adams
The Brute Man '46
House of Dracula '45

Lost City of the Jungle '45
Rising Son '90
Vital Signs '90

Julie Adams
Away All Boats '56
Backtrack '89
Black Roses '88
Creature from the Black Lagoon '54
Francis Joins the WACs '54
Horizons West '52
The Last Movie '71
Man from the Alamo '53
McQ '74
Psychic Killer '75
Tickle Me '65
The Trackers '71

Lynne Adams
Blood Relations '87
The Carpenter '89
Night Zoo '87

Mason Adams
Adam '83
F/X '86
Half Slave, Half Free '85
The Kid with the Broken Halo '82
Rage of Angels: The Story Continues '86
Revenge of the Stepford Wives '80
A Shining Season '79
Son-in-Law '93

Maud Adams
Angel 3: The Final Chapter '88
Deadly Intent '88
The Girl in Blue '74
Hell Hunters '86
The Hostage Tower '80
Intimate Power '89
Jane & the Lost City '87
The Kill Reflex '89
Killer Force '75
A Man of Passion '90s
The Man with the Golden Gun '74
Nairobi Affair '88
Octopussy '83
Playing for Time '80
Rollerball '75
Silent Night, Deadly Night 4: Initiation '90
Target Eagle '84
Tattoo '81
Women's Club '87

Nick Adams
Die, Monster, Die! '65
The FBI Story '59
Godzilla vs. Monster Zero '68
Hell is for Heroes '62
The Interns '62
Los Asesinos '68
Mission Mars '67
Mister Roberts '55
Mosby's Marauders '66
No Time for Sergeants '58
Our Miss Brooks '56
Picnic '55
Pillow Talk '59
Rebel Without a Cause '55
Teacher's Pet '58

Peter Adams
Alternative '76
Bullwhip '58

Stanley Adams
Hell Ship Mutiny '57
Lilies of the Field '63
The Passing of Evil '70

Ted Adams
Arizona Gunfighter '37
Billy the Kid '41
Border Caballero '36
Desert Phantom '36
Ghost Valley '32
Lightnin' Carson Rides Again '38
The Lion Man '36
Outlaw Country '49
Outlaw's Paradise '39
Pals of the Saddle '38
Pinto Canyon '40
The Savage Girl '32
Toll of the Desert '35
Undercover Man '36

Tom Adams
Fast Kill '73

The Fighting Prince of Donegal '66
The House that Dripped Blood '71
Second Best Secret Agent in the Whole Wide World '65
Where the Bullets Fly '66

Dawn Addams
Alien Women '69
Ballad in Blue '66
A King in New York '57
The Liars '64
The Robe '53
The Silent Enemy '58
The Thousand Eyes of Dr. Mabuse '60
The Vampire Lovers '70
Vault of Horror '73
Where the Bullets Fly '66

Nancy Addison
The Dain Curse '78
Somewhere Tomorrow '85

Wesley Addy
The Big Knife '55
The Bostonians '84
The Europeans '79
The Grissom Gang '71
Kiss Me Deadly '55
Network '76
Tora! Tora! Tora! '70

Isabelle Adjani
Camille Claudel '89
The Driver '78
Ishtar '87
Next Year If All Goes Well '83
One Deadly Summer '83
Possession '81
Quartet '81
The Slap '74
Story of Adele H. '75
Subway '85
The Tenant '76

Bill Adler
Pom Pom Girls '76
Van Nuys Blvd. '79

Jay Adler
Crime of Passion '57
Grave of the Vampire '72

Jerry Adler
Manhattan Murder Mystery '93
The Public Eye '92

Luther Adler
Absence of Malice '81
The Brotherhood '68
Cornered '45
Crashout '55
The Desert Fox '51
D.O.A. '49
Hoodlum Empire '52
House of Strangers '49
Kiss Tomorrow Goodbye '50
The Last Angry Man '59
The Loves of Carmen '48
Mean Johnny Barrows '75
Murph the Surf '75
Voyage of the Damned '76
Wake of the Red Witch '49

Matt Adler
Diving In '90
Doin' Time on Planet Earth '88
Flight of the Navigator '86
North Shore '87
White Water Summer '87

Edvin Adolphson
Boy of Two Worlds '70
The Count of the Old Town '34
Dollar '38
Only One Night '42

Renee Adoree
The Big Parade '25
The Michigan Kid '28

Mario Adorf
Hired to Kill '73
Hit Men '73
The Holcroft Covenant '85
Invitation au Voyage '82
The Lost Honor of Katharina Blum '75
Manhunt '73
Paralyzed '70s
The Tin Drum '79

Iris Adrian
Blue Hawaii '62
The Fast and the Furious '54

G.I. Jane '51
I Killed That Man '42
I'm from Arkansas '44
Infamous Crimes '47
The Lovable Cheat '49
Million Dollar Kid '44
The Paleface '48
The Road to Zanzibar '41
Shake Hands with Murder '44
Stop That Cab '51
The Stork Club '45
Varieties on Parade '52

Max Adrian
The Boy Friend '71
The Devils '71
The Music Lovers '71

Patricia Adriani
I'm the One You're Looking For '88
The Nest '80

John Agar
Along the Great Divide '51
Body Bags '93
The Brain from Planet Arous '57
Cavalry Command '63
Curse of the Swamp Creature '66
The Daughter of Dr. Jekyll '57
Fear '90
Flesh and the Spur '57
Fort Apache '48
Hell Raiders '68
Jet Attack/Paratroop Command '58
Johnny Reno '66
Miracle Mile '89
The Mole People '56
Revenge of the Creature '55
Sands of Iwo Jima '49
She Wore a Yellow Ribbon '49
Tarantula '55
Zontar, the Thing from Venus '66

Tetchie Agbayani
Deathfight '93
The Dolls '83
Gymkata '85
Rikky and Pete '88

Carlos Agosti
The Bloody Vampire '62
El Zorro Blanco '87
Invasion of the Vampires '61

Pierre Agostino
The Hollywood Strangler Meets the Skid Row Slasher '79
Las Vegas Serial Killer '86

Janet Agren
Aladdin '86
Emerald Jungle '80
Gates of Hell '83
Hands of Steel '86
Magdalene '88
Night of the Sharks '89
Panic '83
Perfect Crime '78
The Uranium Conspiracy '78

Antonio Aguilar
Benjamin Argumedo '78
El Rey '87
Emiliano Zapata '87
Simon Blanco '87
The Undefeated '69
Volver, Volver, Volver! '87

Kris Aguilar
Bloodfist '89
Fist of Steel '93

Luis Aguilar
Duelo en el Dorado
El Fugitivo '65
El Zorro Vengador '47
Los Tres Amores de Losa '47
Stallion '88

Hilda Aguirre
Diamante, Oro y Amor '87
El Zorro Blanco '87
Stallion '88

Jenny Agutter
An American Werewolf in London '81
Amy '81
Child's Play 2 '90
Dark Tower '87
Darkman '90
Dominique is Dead '79

The Eagle Has Landed '77
Equus '77
Gunfire '78
Logan's Run '76
The Man in the Iron Mask '77
Railway Children '70
The Riddle of the Sands '79
Secret Places '85
Silas Marner '85
Star! '68
Survivor '80
Sweet William '79

Brian Aherne
Beloved Enemy '36
A Bullet Is Waiting '54
Forever and a Day '43
I Confess '53
I Live My Life '35
The Lady in Question '40
A Night to Remember '42
Prince Valiant '54
Smilin' Through '41
The Swan '56
Sword of Lancelot '63
Sylvia Scarlett '35
Waltz King '63

Philip Ahn
Back to Bataan '45
Betrayal from the East '44
China Sky '44
The General Died at Dawn '36
Hawaii Calls '38
His Majesty O'Keefe '53
Paradise, Hawaiian Style '66
Shock Corridor '63

Charles Aidman
Adam at 6 A.M. '70
The Barbary Coast '74
Countdown '68
Hour of the Gun '67
House of the Dead '80
The Invasion of Carol Enders '74
Menace on the Mountain '70
Picture of Dorian Gray '74
Prime Suspect '82
Zone of the Dead '78
Zoot Suit '81

Danny Aiello
Alone in the Neon Jungle '87
Bang the Drum Slowly '73
Bloodbrothers '78
The Cemetery Club '93
Chu Chu & the Philly Flash '81
The Closer '91
Deathmask '69
Defiance '79
Do the Right Thing '89
Fingers '78
Fort Apache, the Bronx '81
The Front '76
The Godfather, Part 2 '74
Harlem Nights '89
Hide in Plain Sight '80
Hooch '76
Hudson Hawk '91
Jacob's Ladder '90
The January Man '89
Key Exchange '85
The Lost Idol/Shock Troop '80s
Man on Fire '87
Me and the Kid '93
Mistress '91
Moonstruck '87
Old Enough '84
Once Around '91
Once Upon a Time in America '84
The Pick-Up Artist '87
The Pickle '93
The Preppie Murder '89
Protector '85
The Purple Rose of Cairo '85
Question of Honor '80
Radio Days '87
Ruby '92
The Stuff '85
Third Solution '89
29th Street '91
White Hot '88

Rick Aiello
The Closer '91
29th Street '91

Anouk Aimee
Dr. Bethune '90
8 1/2 '63
The Golden Salamander '51

Justine '69
La Dolce Vita '60
Lola '61
A. Man and a Woman '66
A Man and a Woman: 20 Years
  Later '86
Modigliani '58
Paris Express '53
Sodom and Gomorrah '62
Success is the Best Revenge
  '84
The Tragedy of a Ridiculous
  Man '81

Richard Ainley
I Dood It '43
White Cargo '42

Holly Aird
The Flame Trees of Thika '80s
Over Indulgence '87

Michael Aitkens
The Highest Honor '84
Moving Targets '87

Franklin Ajaye
Car Wash '76
Convoy '78
Fraternity Vacation '85
The Jazz Singer '80
The Wrong Guys '88

Chantal Akerman
Akermania, Vol. 1 '92
Je Tu Il Elle '74

Andra Akers
Desert Hearts '86
E. Nick: A Legend in His Own
  Mind '84

Karen Akers
Heartburn '86
The Purple Rose of Cairo '85

Claude Akins
Battle for the Planet of the
  Apes '73
The Big Push '75
The Caine Mutiny '54
The Concrete Cowboys '79
The Curse '87
The Death Squad '73
The Devil's Brigade '68
Eric '75
Falling from Grace '92
From Here to Eternity '53
The Gambler Returns: The
  Luck of the Draw '93
Killer on Board '77
The Killers '64
A Man Called Sledge '71
Manhunt for Claude Dallas '86
Merrill's Marauders '62
Monster in the Closet '86
Pecos Bill '86
Return of the Seven '66
Rio Bravo '59
Sea Chase '55
Tarantulas: The Deadly Cargo
  '77
Waterhole #3 '67

Marc Alaimo
Archer: The Fugitive from the
  Empire '81
Arena '88
Quicksand: No Escape '91
Tango and Cash '89

Steve Alaimo
Alligator Alley '72
The Hooked Generation '69
Wild Rebels '71

Maria Alba
Chandu on the Magic Island '34
Mr. Robinson Crusoe '32
Return of Chandu '34

Captain Lou Albano
Body Slam '87
Life & Times of Captain Lou
  Albano '85
Wise Guys '86

Josh Albee
The Adventures of Tom Sawyer
  '73
The Runaways '75

Anna Maria Alberghetti
Cinderfella '60
Here Comes the Groom '51
The Last Command '55
The Medium '51

Luis Alberni
The Big Stampede '32
Dancing Pirate '36
Goodbye Love '34
The Great Man Votes '38
Harvest Melody '43
Hats Off '37
Man from Monterey '33
One Night of Love '34
The Sphinx '33

Hans Albers
Baron Munchausen '43
The Blue Angel '30
Die Grosse Freiheit Nr. 7 '45
F.P. 1 Doesn't Answer '33

Eddie Albert
The Act '82
Actors and Sin '52
Beulah Land '80
The Big Picture '89
The Birch Interval '78
Bombardier '43
Brenda Starr '86
Burning Rage '84
Captain Newman, M.D. '63
Carrie '52
The Concorde: Airport '79 '79
The Crash of Flight 401 '78
Devil's Rain '75
Dreamscape '84
Dress Gray '86
Escape to Witch Mountain '75
Fireball Forward '72
Foolin' Around '80
The Fuller Brush Girl '50
Goliath Awaits '81
Head Office '86
The Heartbreak Kid '72
How to Beat the High Cost of
  Living '80
I'll Cry Tomorrow '55
The Longest Day '62
The Longest Yard '74
McQ '74
The Miracle of the White
  Stallions '63
Moving Violation '76
Oklahoma! '55
Out of Sight, Out of Her Mind
  '89
The Perfect Marriage '46
Roman Holiday '53
Smash-Up: The Story of a
  Woman '47
Stitches '85
Take This Job & Shove It '81
The Teahouse of the August
  Moon '56
Turnaround '87
The Victory '88
Whiffs '75
Who's Got the Action? '63
The Word '78
Yes, Giorgio '82

Edward Albert
Accidents '89
Body Language '92
Broken Trust '93
Butterflies Are Free '72
Butterfly '82
Death Cruise '74
Distortions '87
The Domino Principle '77
Ellie '84
Exiled in America '90
Fist Fighter '88
The Fool Killer '65
Forty Carats '73
Galaxy of Terror '81
Getting Even '86
The Greek Tycoon '78
Guarding Tess '94
The Heist '88
House Where Evil Dwells '82
The Ice Runner '93
Mind Games '89
Night School '81
The Purple Taxi '77
The Rescue '88
The Rip Off '78
Sexual Malice '93
Shootfighter: Fight to the Death
  '93
Silent Victory: The Kitty O'Neil
  Story '79
The Squeeze '80
Terminal Entry '87
Time to Die '83

The Underachievers '88
When Time Ran Out '80
Wild Zone '89

Laura Albert
Blood Games '90
Death by Dialogue '88
Dr. Caligari '89

Guido Alberti
Casanova '70 '65
Ten Days Wonder '72

Frank Albertson
Ah, Wilderness! '35
Big Business Girl '31
Fury '36
Hollywood Mystery '34
It's a Wonderful Life '46
Killer Dill '47
Louisiana Purchase '41
Man Made Monster '41
Navy Blue and Gold '37
Nightfall '56
Psycho '60
Room Service '38
Way Back Home '32

Jack Albertson
Changes '69
Charlie and the Great Balloon
  Chase '82
Days of Wine and Roses '62
Dead and Buried '81
Flim-Flam Man '67
How to Murder Your Wife '64
Justine '69
Kissin' Cousins '64
Lover Come Back '61
Marriage is Alive and Well '80
Miracle on 34th Street '47
The Patsy '64
Period of Adjustment '62
The Poseidon Adventure '72
Roustabout '64
Where the Eagle Flies '72
Who's Got the Action? '63
Willy Wonka & the Chocolate
  Factory '71

Hardie Albright
Champagne for Breakfast '35
The Jade Mask '45
Mom & Dad '47
The Purchase Price '32
The Scarlet Letter '34
Sing Sing Nights '35
Sunset in El Dorado '45

Lola Albright
Champion '49
The Impossible Years '68
Joy House '64
Kid Galahad '62
The Monolith Monsters '57
The Tender Trap '55
The Way West '67
Where Were You When the
  Lights Went Out? '68

Victor Alcocer
It Happened at Nightmare Inn
  '70
Pistoleros Asesinos '87

Alan Alda
And the Band Played On '93
Betsy's Wedding '90
California Suite '78
Canadian Bacon '94
Crimes & Misdemeanors '89
The Four Seasons '81
The Glass House '72
Gone are the Days '63
Jenny '70
Manhattan Murder Mystery '93
M*A*S*H: Goodbye, Farewell &
  Amen '83
M*A*S*H: The Collector's
  Edition '72
The Mephisto Waltz '71
A New Life '88
Paper Lion '68
Playmates '72
Purlie Victorious '63
Same Time, Next Year '78
The Seduction of Joe Tynan '79
Sweet Liberty '86
To Kill a Clown '72
Whispers in the Dark '92

Antony Alda
Homeboy '88
The Killing Device '92
Movie Maker '86

Robert Alda
The Beast with Five Fingers '46
Bittersweet Love '76
Cloak and Dagger '46
The Devil's Hand '61
Every Girl Should Have One '78
Express to Terror '79
Force of Impulse '60
The Heist '88
Hollywood Varieties '50
I Will, I Will for Now '76
Lisa and the Devil '75
Love by Appointment '76
The Man I Love '46
Night Flight from Moscow '73
Revenge of the Barbarians '64
Rhapsody in Blue '45
The Rip Off '78
The Squeeze '80

Rutanya Alda
Amityville 2: The Possession
  '82
Article 99 '92
Black Widow '87
The Dark Half '91
The Deer Hunter '78
Girls Night Out '83
Leaving Normal '92
Mommie Dearest '81
Prancer '89
Racing with the Moon '84
Vigilante '83

Mary Alden
April Fool '26
Strange Interlude '32

Priscilla Alden
Crazy Fat Ethel II '85
Criminally Insane '75
Death Nurse '87

John Alderman
The Alpha Incident '76
Little Miss Innocence '73

Mari Aldon
Distant Drums '51
Race for Life '55

Tom Aldredge
The Adventures of Huck Finn
  '93
Gentleman Bandit '81
O Pioneers! '91
Other People's Money '91
What About Bob? '91

Kay Aldridge
Haunted Harbor '44
Nyoka and the Tigermen '42
The Phantom of 42nd Street
  '45

Kitty Aldridge
An African Dream '90
American Roulette '88
Slipstream '89

Michael Aldridge
Bullshot '83
Footlight Frenzy '84
Love for Lydia '79

Norma Aleandro
Cousins '89
Gaby: A True Story '87
The Official Story '85
One Man's War '90
Vital Signs '90

Julio Aleman
Diamante, Oro y Amor '87
The Green Wall '70
La Hora 24 '87
La Trinchera '87
Marcados por el Destino '87
Neutron and the Black Mask
  '61
Neutron vs. the Amazing Dr.
  Caronte '61
Neutron vs. the Death Robots
  '62
Patsy, Mi Amor '87

Aki Aleong
Braddock: Missing in Action 3
  '88
Farewell to the King '89
Hanoi Hilton '87

Barbara Lee Alexander
Hired to Kill '91
Illegal Entry: Formula for Fear
  '93

Psycho Cop 2 '94

Ben Alexander
All Quiet on the Western Front
  '30
Criminals Within '41
Dragnet '54
Hearts of the World '18
Legion of Missing Men '37

Jace Alexander
City of Hope '91
Mistress '91

Jane Alexander
All the President's Men '76
The Betsy '78
Brubaker '80
Calamity Jane '82
City Heat '84
Death Be Not Proud '75
Eight Men Out '88
Eleanor & Franklin '76
A Friendship in Vienna '88
Glory '89
The Great White Hope '70
A Gunfight '71
In Love and War '91
In the Custody of Strangers '82
Kramer vs. Kramer '79
Lovey: A Circle of Children 2
  '82
The New Centurions '72
Night Crossing '81
Playing for Time '80
A Question of Love '78
The Rumor Mill '87
Square Dance '87
Sweet Country '87
Testament '83

Jason Alexander
Blankman '94
Brighton Beach Memoirs '86
The Burning '82
Coneheads '93
I Don't Buy Kisses Anymore '92
Jacob's Ladder '90
The Mosquito Coast '86
North '94
The Paper '94
Pretty Woman '90
White Palace '90

Jeff Alexander
Curse of the Swamp Creature
  '66
Twisted Brain '74

John Alexander
Arsenic and Old Lace '44
Fancy Pants '50
The Horn Blows at Midnight '45
The Jolson Story '46
Mr. Skeffington '44
A Tree Grows in Brooklyn '45

Katherine Alexander
The Barretts of Wimpole Street
  '34
Dance, Girl, Dance '40
The Great Man Votes '38
That Certain Woman '37

Khandi Alexander
CB4: The Movie '93
Greedy '94
Sugar Hill '94
What's Love Got to Do With It?
  '93

Richard Alexander
Daring Danger '32
The Kansas Terrors '39
The Mysterious Lady '28
Renfrew on the Great White
  Trail '38
Scarlet Dawn '32
Texas Bad Man '32

Graciela Alfano
Departamento Compartido '85
Fotografo de Senoras '85

Lidia Alfonsi
Black Sabbath '64
Open Doors '89

Chuck Alford
Commando Squad '76
The Hollywood Strangler Meets
  the Skid Row Slasher '79

Hans Alfredson
The Adventures of Picasso '80
The New Land '73
The Shame '68

Muhammad Ali
Body & Soul '81
Doin' Time '85
Freedom Road '79
The Greatest '77

Mary Alice
Charlotte Forten's Mission: Experiment in Freedom '85
He Who Walks Alone '78
Laurel Avenue '93
Sparkle '76
To Sleep with Anger '90
The Women of Brewster Place '89

Ana Alicia
Coward of the County '81
Romero '89

Lisa Aliff
Damned River '89
Playroom '90

Jeff Alin
American Tickler '76
A Matter of Love '78

Elizabeth Allan
Ace of Aces '33
Camille '36
Donovan's Reef '63
The Haunted Strangler '58
Java Head '35
Mark of the Vampire '35
Phantom Fiend '35
The Shadow '36
Star Spangled Girl '71
A Tale of Two Cities '35
A Woman Rebels '36

Jed Allan
Lassie: Adventures of Neeka '68
Man from Clover Grove '78

Louise Allbritton
The Doolins of Oklahoma '49
Egg and I '47
Pittsburgh '42
Son of Dracula '43
Who Done It? '42

Michael Alldredge
About Last Night... '86
Robot Jox '89

Bambi Allen
Outlaw Riders '72
Satan's Sadists '69

Chad Allen
Camp Cucamonga: How I Spent My Summer Vacation '90
Murder in New Hampshire: The Pamela Smart Story '91
Praying Mantis '93
Straight Up '90

Corey Allen
Darby's Rangers '58
Party Girl '58
Rebel Without a Cause '55

Debbie Allen
The Fish that Saved Pittsburgh '79
Jo Jo Dancer, Your Life is Calling '86
Ragtime '81
Roots: The Next Generation '79

Fred Allen
It's in the Bag '45
We're Not Married '52

Ginger Lynn Allen
Bound and Gagged: A Love Story '93
Buried Alive '89
Cleo/Leo '89
Hollywood Boulevard 2 '89
Leather Jackets '90
Mind, Body & Soul '92
Vice Academy '88
Vice Academy 2 '90
Vice Academy 3 '91
Wild Man '89
Young Guns 2 '90

Gracie Allen
College Swing '38
A Damsel in Distress '37
Honolulu '39
International House '33
Two Girls and a Sailor '44

Jeffrey Allen
Moonshine Mountain '64
This Stuff'll Kill Ya! '71
2000 Maniacs '64

Joan Allen
All My Sons '86
Ethan Frome '92
Fat Guy Goes Nutzoid '86
In Country '89
Josh and S.A.M. '93
Manhunter '86
Peggy Sue Got Married '86
Searching for Bobby Fischer '93
Tucker: The Man and His Dream '88
Without Warning: The James Brady Story '91

Jonelle Allen
Grave Secrets: The Legacy of Hilltop Drive '92
The Midnight Hour '86
Penalty Phase '86
The River Niger '76

Judith Allen
Boots & Saddles '37
Bright Eyes '34
Dancing Man '33
Git Along Little Dogies '37
Healer '36
The Port of Missing Girls '38
Tough Kid '39
Train to Tombstone '50

Karen Allen
Animal Behavior '89
Backfire '88
Cruising '80
East of Eden '80
Ghost in the Machine '93
The Glass Menagerie '87
King of the Hill '93
Manhattan '79
National Lampoon's Animal House '78
Raiders of the Lost Ark '81
The Sandlot '93
Scrooged '88
Secret Weapon '90
Shoot the Moon '82
A Small Circle of Friends '80
Split Image '82
Starman '84
Sweet Talker '91
Until September '84
Voyage '93
Wanderers '79

Keith Allen
Chicago Joe & the Showgirl '90
Small Time '91

Marty Allen
Harrad Summer '74
Whale of a Tale '76

Mike Allen
Death Driver '78
Hooch '76

Nancy Allen
Acting on Impulse '93
Blow Out '81
The Buddy System '83
Carrie '76
Dressed to Kill '80
Forced Entry '75
The Gladiator '86
Home Movies '79
I Wanna Hold Your Hand '78
The Last Detail '73
Limit Up '89
Memories of Murder '90
1941 '79
Not for Publication '84
The Philadelphia Experiment '84
Poltergeist 3 '88
RoboCop '87
RoboCop 2 '90
RoboCop 3 '93
Strange Invaders '83
Sweet Revenge '87

Patrick Allen
Flight from Singapore '62
Full Metal Ninja '89
Invasion of the Body Stealers '69
Island of the Burning Doomed '67
The Long Haul '57

**Puppet on a Chain '72
Thirteenth Day of Christmas '85
When Dinosaurs Ruled the Earth '70**

Rex Allen
Arizona Cowboy '49
Border Saddlemates '52
Colorado Sundown '52
Hills of Oklahoma '50
I Dream of Jeannie '52
Redwood Forest Trail '50
Silver City Bonanza '51
Thunder in God's Country '51
Trail of Robin Hood '50
Western Double Feature 3: Rogers & Allen '50

Robert Allen
The Awful Truth '37
The Black Room '35
Crime and Punishment '35
Fighting Shadows '35
The Perils of Pauline '34
The Rangers Step In '37
The Revenge Rider '35
The Unknown Ranger '36

Ronald Allen
Eat the Rich '87
Supergrass '87

Rosalind Allen
Children of the Corn 2: The Final Sacrifice '92
Ticks '93
To Die for 2 '91

Sheila Allen
The Alphabet Murders '65
Bouquet of Barbed Wire '76
Children of the Damned '63
Pascali's Island '88

Steve Allen
Amazon Women on the Moon '87
The Benny Goodman Story '55
Best of Comic Relief '86
Great Balls of Fire '89
Heart Beat '80
Hey Abbott! '78
Kerouac '84
Ratings Game '84
Where Were You When the Lights Went Out? '68

Todd Allen
Brothers in Arms '88
Storm and Sorrow '90
Witchboard '87
Wyatt Earp '94

Woody Allen
Annie Hall '77
Bananas '71
Broadway Danny Rose '84
Casino Royale '67
Crimes & Misdemeanors '89
Everything You Always Wanted to Know About Sex (But Were Afraid to Ask) '72
The Front '76
Hannah and Her Sisters '86
Husbands and Wives '92
King Lear '87
Love and Death '75
Manhattan '79
Manhattan Murder Mystery '93
A Midsummer Night's Sex Comedy '82
New York Stories '89
Play It Again, Sam '72
Scenes from a Mall '91
Shadows and Fog '92
Sleeper '73
Stardust Memories '80
Take the Money and Run '69
What's New Pussycat? '65
What's Up, Tiger Lily? '66
Zelig '83

Fernando Allende
Frontera
Heartbreaker '83
La Virgen de Guadalupe '87
Maria '71

Kirstie Alley
Blind Date '84
A Bunny's Tale '85
Champions '84
Look Who's Talking '89
Look Who's Talking Now '93
Look Who's Talking, Too '90
Loverboy '89

**Madhouse '90
North and South Book 1 '85
North and South Book 2 '86
One More Chance '90
Prince of Bel Air '87
Runaway '84
Shoot to Kill '88
Sibling Rivalry '90
Star Trek 2: The Wrath of Khan '82
Summer School '87**

Sara Allgood
The Accused '48
Blackmail '29
Challenge to Lassie '49
City Without Men '43
The Fabulous Dorseys '47
How Green was My Valley '41
Jane Eyre '44
Juno and the Paycock '30
The Keys of the Kingdom '44
The Lodger '44
The Spiral Staircase '46
Storm in a Teacup '37
The Strange Affair of Uncle Harry '45
That Hamilton Woman '41

Dorothy Allison
Rikky and Pete '88
See No Evil '71
The Third Key '57

Gregg Allman
Rush '91
Rush Week '88

Christopher Allport
Circle of Power '83
News at Eleven '86
Savage Weekend '80
Special Bulletin '83

Astrid Allwyn
Beggars in Ermine '34
Charlie Chan's Secret '35
International Crime '37
It Could Happen to You '37
Love Affair '39
Monte Carlo Nights '34
Mystery Liner '34
Stowaway '36

June Allyson
Battle Circus '53
Best Foot Forward '43
Blackout '78
Curse of the Black Widow '77
Executive Suite '54
Girl Crazy '43
The Glenn Miller Story '54
Good News '47
The Kid with the Broken Halo '82
Little Women '49
The McConnell Story '55
My Man Godfrey '57
The Opposite Sex '56
Strategic Air Command '55
The Stratton Story '49
They Only Kill Their Masters '72
Thousands Cheer '43
The Three Musketeers '48
Till the Clouds Roll By '46
Two Girls and a Sailor '44
Vegas '78
Words and Music '48

Ferdinando Almada
La Venganza del Rojo '87
Los Jinetes de la Bruja '76

Mario Almada
El Sabor de la Venganza '65
Emiliano Zapata '87
La Fuga del Rojo '87
La Venganza del Rojo '87
Los Jinetes de la Bruja '76
Nido de Aguilas '76
Simon Blanco '87
Sin Salida '87

Gila Almagor
Every Time We Say Goodbye '86
Hide and Seek '80
The House on Chelouche Street '73
Sallah '63

Chelo Alonso
Atlas in the Land of the Cyclops '61
Girl Under the Sheet '60s

**The Good, the Bad and the Ugly '67
Son of Samson '62**

Ernesto Alonso
The Criminal Life of Archibaldo de la Cruz '55
Wuthering Heights '53

Jose Alonso
El Diputado '78
Murderer in the Hotel '83

Maria Conchita Alonso
Blood Ties '87
Colors '88
Extreme Prejudice '87
Fear City '85
A Fine Mess '86
The House of the Spirits '93
McBain '91
Moscow on the Hudson '84
Predator 2 '90
The Running Man '87
Teamster Boss: The Jackie Presser Story '92
Touch and Go '86
Vampire's Kiss '88

Corinne Alphen
C.O.D. '83
Hot T-Shirts '79
New York Nights '84
Spring Break '83

Carol Alt
Beyond Justice '92
Bye Bye Baby '88
A Family Matter '91
Millions '90
My Wonderful Life '90
Portfolio '83
Ring of Steel '94
Thunder in Paradise '93

John Altamura
New York's Finest '87
The Toxic Avenger, Part 2 '89
The Toxic Avenger, Part 3: The Last Temptation of Toxie '89

Hector Alterio
Basileus Quartet '82
Camila '84
Fridays of Eternity '81
The Nest '80
The Official Story '85

Bruce Altman
The Favor, the Watch, & the Very Big Fish '92
Glengarry Glen Ross '92
Mr. Jones '93
My New Gun '92

Jeff Altman
Doin' Time '85
In Love with an Older Woman '82
Russian Roulette '93

Walter George Alton
Heavenly Bodies '84
The Puma Man '80

Crox Alvarado
The Curse of the Aztec Mummy '59
Curse of the Aztec Mummy/Robot vs. the Aztec Mummy '59
La Corona de un Campeon '87
The Robot vs. the Aztec Mummy '59

Magali Alvarado
Mi Vida Loca '94
Salsa '88

Trini Alvarado
American Blue Note '89
American Friends '91
The Babe '92
The Chair '87
Mrs. Soffel '84
A Movie Star's Daughter '79
Nitti: The Enforcer '88
Private Contentment '83
Rich Kids '79
Satisfaction '88
Stella '89
Sweet Lorraine '87
Times Square '80

Anicee Alvina
Friends '71
Paul and Michelle '74**

Kirk Alyn
Daughter of Don Q '46
Federal Agents vs. Underworld,
Inc. '49
Superman: The Serial, Vol. 1
'48

Lyle Alzado
Club Fed '90
Comrades in Arms '91
Destroyer '88
Ernest Goes to Camp '87
The Lost Idol/Shock Troop '80s
Neon City '91
Oceans of Fire '86
Tapeheads '89
Tough Guys '86
Who's Harry Crumb? '89
Zapped Again '89

Shigeru Amachi
The Ghost of Yotsuya '58
Zatoichi: The Blind
Swordsman's Vengeance
'66
Zatoichi: The Life and Opinion
of Masseur Ichi '62

Betty Amann
Nancy Drew, Reporter '39
Rich and Strange '32

Andriana Ambesi
Fangs of the Living Dead '68
Secret Agent Super Dragon '66
Stranger in Paso Bravo '73

Don Ameche
Alexander's Ragtime Band '38
The Boatniks '70
Cocoon '85
Cocoon: The Return '88
Coming to America '88
Corrina, Corrina '94
Down Argentine Way '40
Folks! '92
Guest Wife '45
Happy Landing '38
Harry and the Hendersons '87
Heaven Can Wait '43
In Old Chicago '38
It's in the Bag '45
The Magnificent Dope '42
Moon Over Miami '41
Oddball Hall '91
One in a Million '36
Pals '87
Picture Mommy Dead '66
Sunstroke '80
Suppose They Gave a War and
Nobody Came? '70
Things Change '88
The Three Musketeers '39
Trading Places '83
A Wing and a Prayer '44

Sonia Amelio
Fearmaker '89
Tacos al Carbon '87

**George American
Horse**
Kenny Rogers as the Gambler,
Part 3: The Legend
Continues '87
Son of the Morning Star '91

Adrienne Ames
The Death Kiss '33
Harmony Lane '35
Panama Patrol '39

Heather Ames
Blood of Dracula '57
How to Make a Monster '58

Leon Ames
The Absent-Minded Professor
'61
Battleground '49
The Big Hangover '50
The Big Push '75
By the Light of the Silvery
Moon '53
Claws '77
A Date with Judy '48
Deadly Encounter '78
East Side Kids '40
From the Terrace '60
Get That Man '35
The Iron Major '43
Lady in the Lake '46
The Meal '75
Merton of the Movies '47

**The Misadventures of Merlin
Jones '65**
Monkey's Uncle '65
Murders in the Rue Morgue '32
On an Island with You '48
On Moonlight Bay '51
Panama Patrol '39
Peggy Sue Got Married '86
Peyton Place '57
The Postman Always Rings
Twice '46
The Show-Off '46
Son of Flubber '63
Son of Lassie '45
Song of the Thin Man '47
They Were Expendable '45
Thirty Seconds Over Tokyo '44
Tora! Tora! Tora! '70
Velvet Touch '48
Watch the Birdie '50
Weekend at the Waldorf '45
Yolanda and the Thief '45

Robert Ames
Behind Office Doors '31
Millie '31

Madchen Amick
Don't Tell Her It's Me '90
Dream Lover '93
I'm Dangerous Tonight '90
Love, Cheat & Steal '93
Sleepwalkers '92
Twin Peaks '90

Soudad Amidou
Petit Con '84
Sorcerer '77

Suzy Amis
The Ballad of Little Jo '93
Big Town '87
Blown Away '94
Fandango '85
Plain Clothes '88
Rich in Love '93
Rocket Gibraltar '88
Twister '89
Watch It '93
Where the Heart Is '90

Christine Amor
Bloodmoon '90
Now and Forever '82

John Amos
American Flyers '85
Beastmaster '82
Coming to America '88
Die Hard 2: Die Harder '90
Future Cop '76
Let's Do It Again '75
Lock Up '89
Mac '93
Mardi Gras for the Devil '93
Ricochet '91
Sweet Sweetback's
Baadasssss Song '71
Touched by Love '80
Willa '79
The World's Greatest Athlete
'73

John Amplas
Martin '77
Midnight '81

Morey Amsterdam
Beach Party '63
Machine Gun Kelly '58
Muscle Beach Party '64
Sooner or Later '78

Richard Anconina
Police '85
Tchao Pantin '84

Jacqueline Andere
The Exterminating Angel '62
Simon Blanco '87

Avalon Anders
Bikini Summer 2 '92
Great Bikini Off-Road
Adventure '94
Sorority House Party '92

Glenn Anders
The Lady from Shanghai '48
Nancy Goes to Rio '50

Luana Anders
Border Radio '88
Dementia 13 '63
Goin' South '78
Irreconcilable Differences '84
The Killing Kind '73

Limit Up '89
Manipulator '71
Movers and Shakers '85
Night Tide '63
The Pit and the Pendulum '61
Sex and the College Girl '64

Merry Anders
Blood Legacy '73
Phffft! '54
The Time Travelers '64
Women of the Prehistoric
Planet '66

Rudolph Anders
Phantom from Space '53
Under Nevada Skies '46

Elga Andersen
Le Mans '71
Night Flight from Moscow '73
Your Turn Darling '63

Billy Anderson
The Champion/His New Job '15
The Great Train Robbery:
Cinema Begins '03
Son of a Gun '19

Bridgette Anderson
Between Two Women '86
Fever Pitch '85
Hansel and Gretel '82
Savannah Smiles '82
A Summer to Remember '84

Cheryl Anderson
Acorn People '82
Rosie: The Rosemary Clooney
Story '82
Writer's Block '91

Donna Anderson
On the Beach '59
Werewolves on Wheels '71

Eddie Anderson
Brewster's Millions '45
Broadway Rhythm '44
Cabin in the Sky '43
False Faces '32
Gone with the Wind '39
Green Pastures '36
Honolulu '39
It's a Mad, Mad, Mad, Mad
World '63
Jezebel '38
The Show-Off '46
Topper Returns '41
You Can't Cheat an Honest
Man '39
You Can't Take It with You '38

Erich Anderson
Bat 21 '88
Friday the 13th, Part 4: The
Final Chapter '84
Love Kills '91

Erika Anderson
Quake '91
Zandalee '91

G.M. Anderson
The First Movie Cowboy '13
The Long Haul '57

Harry Anderson
Rich Hall's Vanishing America
'86
Spies, Lies and Naked Thighs
'91
Stephen King's It '90

James Anderson
The Connection '61
The Freshman '25

Jean Anderson
Back Home '90
Screamtime '83

John Anderson
Ashes and Embers '82
Cotton Comes to Harlem '70
The Deerslayer '78
The Desperados '80s
Donner Pass: The Road to
Survival '84
Eight Men Out '88
Executive Action '73
Firehouse '87
Five Card Stud '68
Geronimo '62
Namu, the Killer Whale '66
Psycho '60
Ride the High Country '62
Smile, Jenny, You're Dead '74
The Specialist '75

The Stepmother '71
Zoot Suit '81

Judith Anderson
All Through the Night '42
And Then There Were None '45
Cat on a Hot Tin Roof '58
Cinderfella '60
Diary of a Chambermaid '46
Edge of Darkness '43
Elizabeth, the Queen '68
Inn of the Damned '74
Kings Row '41
Lady Scarface '41
Lady Scarface/The Threat '49
Laura '44
A Man Called Horse '70
Medea '59
Pursued '47
Rebecca '40
The Red House '47
Salome '53
Spectre of the Rose '46
Stage Door Canteen '43
Star Trek 3: The Search for
Spock '84
The Strange Love of Martha
Ivers '46
The Ten Commandments '56
Tycoon '47

Kevin Anderson
Hoffa '92
In Country '89
Liebestraum '91
Miles from Home '88
The Night We Never Met '93
Orphans '87
Orpheus Descending '91
Pink Nights '87
Rising Son '90
Risky Business '83
Sleeping with the Enemy '91
The Wrong Man '93

Lindsay Anderson
Blame It on the Bellboy '92
Chariots of Fire '81
Look Back in Anger '80
Prisoner of Honor '91

Loni Anderson
Blown Away '90
The Jayne Mansfield Story '80
Munchie '92
My Mother's Secret Life '84
Sizzle '81
Sorry, Wrong Number '89
Stroker Ace '83
White Hot: The Mysterious
Murder of Thelma Todd '91
WKRP in Cincinnati, Vol. 1 '78

Louie Anderson
Coming to America '88
Quicksilver '86
The Wrong Guys '88

Mary Anderson
Lifeboat '44
The Underworld Story '50
Whispering City '47
Wilson '44

**Melissa Sue
Anderson**
Chattanooga Choo Choo '84
The Equalizer: Memories of
Manon '88
First Affair '83
Happy Birthday to Me '81
Little House on the Prairie '74
The Loneliest Runner '76
On the Edge: The Survival of
Dana '79

Melody Anderson
Beverly Hills Madam '86
Dead and Buried '81
Ernie Kovacs: Between the
Laughter '84
Final Notice '89
Firewalker '86
Flash Gordon '80
Hitler's Daughter '90
Landslide '92
Policewoman Centerfold '83
Speed Zone '88

**Michael Anderson,
Jr.**
The Great Land of Small '86
In Search of the Castaways '62
A Legacy for Leonette '85

Sons of Katie Elder '65
The Sundowners '60
Sunset Grill '92

Mitchell Anderson
Back to Hannibal: The Return
of Tom Sawyer and
Huckleberry Finn '90
Deadly Dreams '88
Goodbye, Miss 4th of July '88

Pamela Anderson
Raw Justice '93
Snapdragon '93

Pat Anderson
Cover Girl Models '75
Summer School Teachers '75

Richard Anderson
The Bionic Woman '75
Escape from Fort Bravo '53
Forbidden Planet '56
Give a Girl a Break '53
Hit the Deck '55
I Love Melvin '53
The Long, Hot Summer '58
The Magnificent Yankee '50
Murder by Natural Causes '79
Paths of Glory '57
Perry Mason Returns '85
Rich, Young and Pretty '51
Scaramouche '52
The Search for Bridey Murphy
'56
The Vanishing Westerner '50

Robert Anderson
The Tall T '57
White Shadows in the South
Seas '28

Stanley Anderson
He Said, She Said '91
Son of the Morning Star '91

Susy Anderson
Black Sabbath '64
Gangster's Law '86
Thor and the Amazon Women
'60

Warner Anderson
Abbott and Costello in
Hollywood '45
Armored Command '61
Blackboard Jungle '55
Destination Moon '50
Destination Tokyo '43
Detective Story '51
Drum Beat '54
Go for Broke! '51
A Lawless Street '55
A Lion is in the Streets '53
Objective, Burma! '45
Song of the Thin Man '47
Weekend at the Waldorf '45

Bibi Andersson
Babette's Feast '87
Brink of Life '57
The Concorde: Airport '79 '79
The Devil's Eye '60
Duel at Diablo '66
Exposed '83
Germicide '74
I Never Promised You a Rose
Garden '77
Law of Desire '86
The Magician '58
The Passion of Anna '70
Persona '66
Quintet '79
Scenes from a Marriage '73
The Seventh Seal '56
The Touch '71
Twice a Woman '79
Wild Strawberries '57

Harriet Andersson
Cries and Whispers '72
Dreams '55
Fanny and Alexander '83
Lesson in Love '54
Monika '52
Sawdust & Tinsel '53
Smiles of a Summer Night '55
Through a Glass Darkly '61

Keith Andes
Away All Boats '56
Back from Eternity '56
Blackbeard the Pirate '52
The Ultimate Imposter '79

Eiko Ando
Barbarian and the Geisha '58

Ando ▶*cont.*

Paper Tiger '74
Peter Andorai
Mephisto '81
My Twentieth Century '90
Annette Andre
A Funny Thing Happened on
the Way to the Forum '66
Mission: Monte Carlo '75
Gaby Andre
The Cosmic Monsters '58
East of Kilimanjaro '59
Goliath and the Dragon '61
The Green Glove '52
Lona Andre
Custer's Last Stand '36
The Mysterious Rider '33
Slaves in Bondage '37
Marcel Andre
Beauty and the Beast '46
Maniac '34
Andre the Giant
Micki & Maude '84
The Princess Bride '87
Starr Andreeff
Dance of the Damned '88
Out of the Dark '88
Syngenor '90
The Terror Within '88
Ursula Andress
The Blue Max '66
Casino Royale '67
The Chinatown Murders: Man
Against the Mob '92
Clash of the Titans '81
Dr. No '62
The Fifth Musketeer '79
Four for Texas '63
Fun in Acapulco '63
Loaded Guns '75
Loves & Times of
Scaramouche '76
Once Before I Die '65
Peter the Great '86
Red Sun '71
The Sensuous Nurse '76
Slave of the Cannibal God '79
Stateline Motel '75
10th Victim '65
Tigers in Lipstick '80
What's New Pussycat? '65
Simon Andrew
The Barcelona Kill '77
Blood and Sand '89
The Blood Spattered Bride '72
Blue Jeans and Dynamite '80s
Fist Fighter '88
Night of the Sorcerers '70
Surprise Attack '70s
Anthony Andrews
Brideshead Revisited '81
Danger UXB '81
Hanna's War '88
The Holcroft Covenant '85
Ivanhoe '82
The Lighthorsemen '87
The Scarlet Pimpernel '82
Second Victory '87
Strange Case of Dr. Jekyll &
Mr. Hyde '89
Suspicion '87
Under the Volcano '84
The Woman He Loved '88
Barry Andrews
The Blood on Satan's Claw '71
Dracula Has Risen from the
Grave '68
Dana Andrews
Airport '75 '75
Ball of Fire '41
Battle of the Bulge '65
The Best Years of Our Lives
'46
Beyond a Reasonable Doubt
'56
Born Again '78
The Cobra '68
Crash Dive '43
Curse of the Demon '57
Danger in the Skies '79
The Devil's Brigade '68
Elephant Walk '54

Enchanted Island '58
Ike '79
In Harm's Way '65
Johnny Reno '66
Kit Carson '40
The Last Tycoon '76
Laura '44
The Loved One '65
Lucky Cisco Kid '40
The North Star '43
The Ox-Bow Incident '43
Prince Jack '83
The Purple Heart '44
State Fair '45
Up in Arms '44
A Walk in the Sun '46
The Westerner '40
While the City Sleeps '56
A Wing and a Prayer '44
David Andrews
Cherry 2000 '88
Graveyard Shift '90
Wild Horses '84
Wyatt Earp '94
Edward Andrews
Advise and Consent '62
Avanti! '72
Elmer Gantry '60
The Glass Bottom Boat '66
Kisses for My President '64
Sixteen Candles '84
Tea and Sympathy '56
The Thrill of It All! '63
A Tiger Walks '64
The Trouble with Girls (and
How To Get Into It) '69
Harry Andrews
The Agony and the Ecstasy '65
Alexander the Great '55
The Big Sleep '78
The Charge of the Light
Brigade '68
The Curse of King Tut's Tomb
'80
Dandy in Aspic '68
Death on the Nile '78
The Devil's Disciple '59
Entertaining Mr. Sloane '70
Equus '77
The Final Programme '73
The Four Feathers '78
Hawk the Slayer '81
Horrors of Burke & Hare '71
I Want What I Want '72
Internecine Project '73
Mackintosh Man '73
Man of La Mancha '72
The Medusa Touch '78
Mesmerized '86
Moby Dick '56
Nice Girl Like Me '69
Nicholas and Alexandra '71
The Passover Plot '75
The Ruling Class '72
Saint Joan '57
633 Squadron '64
Sky Riders '76
S.O.S. Titanic '79
The Story of Jacob & Joseph
'74
Too Late the Hero '70
Wuthering Heights '70
Julie Andrews
The Americanization of Emily
'64
Darling Lili '70
Duet for One '86
A Fine Romance '92
Hawaii '66
Little Miss Marker '80
The Man Who Loved Women
'83
Mary Poppins '64
S.O.B. '81
The Sound of Music '65
Star! '68
The Tamarind Seed '74
10 '79
That's Life! '86
Thoroughly Modern Millie '67
Torn Curtain '66
Victor/Victoria '82
The Andrews Sisters
In the Navy '41
Private Buckaroo '42
The Road to Rio '47

Slim Andrews
The Driftin' Kid '41
Riding the Sunset Trail '41
Stanley Andrews
The Adventures of Frank and
Jesse James '48
Blondie '38
Crash Dive '43
In Old Colorado '41
Shine on, Harvest Moon '38
Anemone
Le Grand Chemin '87
Twisted Obsession '90
Julie Ange
Girl on a Chain Gang '65
Teenage Mother '67
Heather Angel
Arrest Bulldog Drummond '38
The Bold Caballero '36
Bulldog Drummond Escapes
'37
Bulldog Drummond's Bride '39
Bulldog Drummond's Secret
Police '39
Daniel Boone '34
Half a Soldier '40
Headline Woman '35
The Informer '35
The Last of the Mohicans '36
Premature Burial '62
Shadows on the Stairs '41
Suspicion '41
The Three Musketeers '35
The Undying Monster '42
Vanessa Angel
The Cover Girl Murders '93
Homicidal Impulse '92
Pier Angeli
Battle of the Bulge '65
Octaman '71
One Step to Hell '68
The Silver Chalice '54
Sodom and Gomorrah '62
Somebody Up There Likes Me
'56
S.O.S. Pacific '60
Muriel Angelus
The Great McGinty '40
Night Birds '31
Angelyne
Earth Girls are Easy '89
The Malibu Beach Vampires
'91
Jean-Hughes
Anglade
Betty Blue '86
La Femme Nikita '91
L'Homme Blesse '83
Philip Anglim
Deadly Currents '93
Haunted Summer '88
Sally Anglim
Thundering Trail '51
Yes, Sir, Mr. Bones '51
Ira Angustain
Can You Hear the Laughter?
The Story of Freddie Prinze
'79
The White Shadow, Vol. 1 '78
Christien Anholt
One Against the Wind '91
Reunion '88
Paul Anka
Girls' Town '59
The Longest Day '62
Evelyn Ankers
Black Beauty '46
Captive Wild Woman '43
Flight to Nowhere '46
The Ghost of Frankenstein '42
The Invisible Man's Revenge
'44
The Last of the Redmen '47
The Mad Ghoul '43
Parole, Inc. '49
The Pearl of Death '44
Sherlock Holmes: The Voice of
Terror '42
Son of Dracula '43
The Wolf Man '41
Morris Ankrum
Beginning of the End '57

Border Vigilantes '41
Borderline '50
Doomed Caravan '41
Earth vs. the Flying Saucers '56
The Giant Claw '57
Half Human '58
How to Make a Monster '58
In Old Colorado '41
The Light of Western Stars '40
The Showdown '40
Ann-Margret
Bye, Bye, Birdie '63
Carnal Knowledge '71
The Cheap Detective '78
Chrome Hearts '70
The Cincinnati Kid '65
52 Pick-Up '86
Grumpy Old Men '93
Hollywood Home Movies '87
I Ought to Be in Pictures '82
Joseph Andrews '77
The Last Remake of Beau
Geste '77
Lookin' to Get Out '82
Magic '78
Middle Age Crazy '80
Murderers' Row '66
A New Life '88
Newsies '92
The Outside Man '73
Pocketful of Miracles '61
Return of the Soldier '82
R.P.M.* (*Revolutions Per
Minute) '70
State Fair '62
A Streetcar Named Desire '84
Tiger and the Pussycat '67
A Tiger's Tale '87
Tommy '75
Train Robbers '73
Twice in a Lifetime '85
Twist '76
The Villain '79
Viva Las Vegas '63
Annabella
Dinner at the Ritz '37
Le Million '31
13 Rue Madeleine '46
Under the Red Robe '36
Frank Annese
Another Chance '88
House of the Rising Sun '87
Francesca Annis
The Affair of the Pink Pearl '84
The Case of the Missing Lady
'83
The Clergyman's Daughter '84
Coming Out of the Ice '82
The Crackler '84
Dune '84
Finessing the King '84
Flipper's New Adventure '64
The House of Lurking Death
'84
Krull '83
Lillie '79
Macbeth '71
The Man in the Mist '83
The Maze '85
Onassis '88
The Secret Adversary '83
The Unbreakable Alibi '83
Under the Cherry Moon '86
Michael Ansara
Abbott & Costello Meet the
Mummy '55
Access Code '84
Action in Arabia '44
And Now Miguel '66
Assassination '87
The Barbary Coast '74
Bayou Romance '86
The Bears & I '74
Border Shootout '90
Daring Game '68
Day of the Animals '77
Dear Dead Delilah '72
Diane '55
The Doll Squad '73
The Fantastic World of D.C.
Collins '84
The Guns and the Fury '83
Guns of the Magnificent Seven
'69
Harum Scarum '65
Hill Number One '51
It's Alive '74
Jupiter's Darling '55

The KGB: The Secret War '86
Knights of the City '85
The Manitou '78
Mission to Glory '80
Mohammed: Messenger of God
'77
Powder Keg '70
Quick, Let's Get Married '71
Texas Across the River '66
Voyage to the Bottom of the
Sea '61
Zachary Ansley
Christmas Comes to Willow
Creek '87
Princes in Exile '90
This Boy's Life '93
Susan Anspach
Back to Back '90
The Big Fix '78
Blood Red '88
Blue Monkey '87
Blume in Love '73
Deadly Encounter '72
The Devil & Max Devlin '81
Five Easy Pieces '70
Gas '81
Gone are the Days '84
Hitchhiker 2 '85
Into the Fire '88
Mad Bull '77
Misunderstood '84
Montenegro '81
Play It Again, Sam '72
The Rutanga Tapes '90
Adam Ant
Acting on Impulse '93
Cold Steel '87
Nomads '86
Slamdance '87
Spellcaster '91
Sunset Heat '92
Trust Me '89
World Gone Wild '88
Gerald Anthony
Secret of the Ice Cave '89
To Die Standing '91
Lysette Anthony
The Bretts '88
Face the Music '92
Husbands and Wives '92
Ivanhoe '82
Krull '83
Look Who's Talking Now '93
Oliver Twist '82
Save Me '93
Without a Clue '88
Ray Anthony
The Girl Can't Help It '56
Girls' Town '59
High School Confidential '58
Tony Anthony
Force of Impulse '60
Treasure of the Four Crowns
'82
Steve Antin
The Accused '88
Inside Monkey Zetterland '93
Last American Virgin '82
Penitentiary 3 '87
Survival Quest '89
Susan Anton
The Boy Who Loved Trolls '84
Cannonball Run 2 '84
Goldengirl '79
Lena's Holiday '90
Making Mr. Right '86
Spring Fever '81
Laura Antonelli
Collector's Item '89
Divine Nymph '71
High Heels '72
How Funny Can Sex Be? '76
The Innocent '76
Malicious '74
A Man Called Sledge '71
Passion of Love '82
Swashbuckler '84
Tigers in Lipstick '80
Till Marriage Do Us Part '74
Wifemistress '79
Omero Antonutti
Basileus Quartet '82
Good Morning, Babylon '87
Kaos '85

The Night of the Shooting Stars '82
Padre Padrone '77

Gabrielle Anwar
Body Snatchers '93
Fallen Angels 2 '93
For Love or Money '93
If Looks Could Kill '91
Scent of a Woman '92
The Three Musketeers '93
Wild Hearts Can't Be Broken '91

Rocky Aoki
For Us, the Living '88
Midnight Faces '26
A Public Affair '62
That's Adequate '90

Oscar Apfel
Bulldog Edition '36
Rainbow's End '35

Apollonia
Back to Back '90
Black Magic Woman '91
Heartbreaker '83
Ministry of Vengeance '89
Purple Rain '84
Tricks of the Trade '88

Noel Appleby
My Grandpa is a Vampire '92
The Navigator '88

Christina Applegate
Don't Tell Mom the Babysitter's Dead '91
It's a Bundyful Life '92
Jaws of Satan '81
Streets '90

Royce D. Applegate
Gettysburg '93
Outside Chance '78

John Aprea
The Arousers '70
The Godfather, Part 2 '74
Idolmaker '80
Picasso Trigger '89
Savage Beach '89

Amy Aquino
Alan & Naomi '92
Descending Angel '90

Tomas Arana
The Bodyguard '92
The Church '90
The Devil's Daughter '91
Domino '88
The Last Temptation of Christ '88

Michiyo Aratama
The Gambling Samurai '60
The Human Condition: A Soldier's Prayer '61
The Human Condition: No Greater Love '58
The Human Condition: Road to Eternity '64
Kwaidan '64
Saga of the Vagabond '59

Alfonso Arau
Dynamite and Gold '88
Posse '75
Romancing the Stone '84
Scandalous John '71
Three Amigos '86

Fatty Arbuckle
Charlie Chaplin's Keystone Comedies #4 '14
Fatty and Mabel Adrift/Mabel, Fatty and the Law '16
The Knockout/Dough and Dynamite '14
Leap Year '21
The Lizzies of Mack Sennett '15
Mabel & Fatty '16
Mack Sennett Comedies: Vol. 2 '16

Allan Arbus
Coffy '73
Daniel and the Towers '90s
Greaser's Palace '72
The Young Nurses '73

Anne Archer
Body of Evidence '92
Cancel My Reservation '72
Check Is in the Mail '85
Clear and Present Danger '94

Eminent Domain '91
Family Prayers '91
Fatal Attraction '87
Good Guys Wear Black '78
Green Ice '81
Hero at Large '80
The Last of His Tribe '92
Lifeguard '75
Love at Large '89
Nails '92
The Naked Face '84
Narrow Margin '90
Paradise Alley '78
Patriot Games '92
Question of Faith '93
Raise the Titanic '80
Short Cuts '93
Too Scared to Scream '85
Waltz Across Texas '83

John Archer
Best of the Badmen '50
Blue Hawaii '62
Crash Dive '43
Gangs, Inc. '41
Hello, Frisco, Hello '43
High Lonesome '50
King of the Zombies '41
Overland Stage Raiders '38
Sherlock Holmes in Washington '43

Fanny Ardant
Afraid of the Dark '91
Confidentially Yours '83
The Family '87
Next Summer '84
Swann in Love '84
The Woman Next Door '81

Eve Arden
Anatomy of a Murder '59
At the Circus '39
Cinderella '84
Comrade X '40
Cover Girl '44
Eternally Yours '39
Grease '78
Grease 2 '82
A Guide for the Married Woman '78
Having Wonderful Time '38
Kid from Brooklyn '46
Letter of Introduction '38
Mildred Pierce '45
My Dream is Yours '49
Night and Day '46
No, No Nanette '40
One Touch of Venus '48
Our Miss Brooks '56
Pandemonium '82
Phone Call from a Stranger '52
Slightly Honorable '40
Stage Door '37
Tea for Two '50
That Uncertain Feeling '41
Three Husbands '50
Under the Rainbow '81
We're Not Married '52
Whistling in the Dark '41
Ziegfeld Girl '41

George Ardisson
Hercules in the Haunted World '64
The Invaders '63

Rosita Arenas
The Curse of the Aztec Mummy '59
Curse of the Aztec Mummy/Robot vs. the Aztec Mummy '59
The Curse of the Crying Woman '61
El Bruto '52
Neutron and the Black Mask '61
Neutron vs. the Amazing Dr. Caronte '61
Neutron vs. the Death Robots '62
The Robot vs. the Aztec Mummy '57
The Witch's Mirror '60

Eddi Arent
Circus of Fear '67
Dead Eyes of London '61
Door with the Seven Locks '62
Forger of London '61
The Mysterious Magician '65
The Squeaker '65

Joey Aresco
Circle of Fear '89
Primary Target '89

Niels Arestrup
Je Tu Il Elle '74
Meeting Venus '91
Sincerely Charlotte '86

Asia Argento
Dario Argento's Trauma '93
Demons 2 '87

Fiore Argento
Creepers '85
Demons '86

Carmen Argenziano
The Accused '88
Death Force '78
Red Scorpion '89
Unlawful Entry '92

Allison Argo
Cry from the Mountain '85
Return of Frank Cannon '80

Victor Argo
Bad Lieutenant '92
Household Saints '93
King of New York '90
Quick Change '90

David Argue
Backlash '86
BMX Bandits '83
Gallipoli '81
Snow: The Movie '83

Imanol Arias
Camila '84
Demons in the Garden '82
Labyrinth of Passion '82

Ineko Arima
Equinox Flower '58
The Human Condition: No Greater Love '58

Adam Arkin
The Doctor '91
Fourth Wise Man '85
Heat Wave '90
Necessary Parties '88
Tom Edison: The Boy Who Lit Up the World '78

Alan Arkin
Bad Medicine '85
Big Trouble '86
Catch-22 '70
Chu Chu & the Philly Flash '81
Cooperstown '93
Coupe de Ville '90
Deadly Business '86
Edward Scissorhands '90
The Emperor's New Clothes '84
Escape from Sobibor '87
Fourth Wise Man '85
Freebie & the Bean '74
Glengarry Glen Ross '92
Havana '90
The Heart is a Lonely Hunter '68
Hearts of the West '75
Improper Channels '82
The In-Laws '79
Indian Summer '93
Joshua Then and Now '85
Last of the Red Hot Lovers '72
Little Murders '71
The Magician of Lublin '79
A Matter of Principle '83
Necessary Parties '88
North '94
Popi '69
Rafferty & the Gold Dust Twins '75
Return of Captain Invincible '83
The Rocketeer '91
The Russians are Coming, the Russians are Coming '66
The Seven Percent Solution '76
Simon '80
Taking the Heat '93
Wait Until Dark '67
Woman Times Seven '67

David Arkin
The Long Goodbye '73
Nashville '75

Richard Arlen
Accomplice '46
Apache Uprising '66
Behind the Front '26

Blonde Blackmailer '58
Buffalo Bill Rides Again '47
Cavalry Command '63
The Crawling Hand '63
Feel My Pulse '28
Flying Blind '41
Hidden Guns '56
The Human Duplicators '64
Identity Unknown '45
Island of Lost Souls '32
Johnny Reno '66
Let 'Em Have It '35
The Light of Western Stars '30
The Mountain '56
Return of Wildfire '48
Road to Nashville '66
Sex and the College Girl '64
Timber Queen '44
The Virginian '29
Warlock '59
Wildcat '42
Wings '27

Arletty
Children of Paradise '44
Circonstances Attenuantes '36
Le Jour Se Leve '39
Les Visiteurs du Soir '42
The Longest Day '62

Dimitra Arliss
Eleni '85
Ski Bum '75

George Arliss
Disraeli '29
Dr. Syn '37
The Iron Duke '34
Transatlantic Tunnel '35

Pedro Armendariz, Jr.
The Deadly Trackers '73
Don't Be Afraid of the Dark '73
La Chevre '81
Los Asesinos '68
Old Gringo '89
Tombstone '93

Pedro Armendariz, Sr.
Captain Sinbad '63
The Conqueror '56
Diane '55
El Bruto '52
Flor Silvestre '58
Fort Apache '48
From Russia with Love '63
The Fugitive '48
The Littlest Outlaw '54
Los Caciques '87
Maria Candelaria '46
The Pearl '48
Three Godfathers '48
Tulsa '49

Henry Armetta
The Black Cat '34
Boss Foreman '39
Fisherman's Wharf '39
Let's Sing Again '36
The Merry Widow '34
Speak Easily '32
What! No Beer? '33

Armida
Bad Men of the Border '45
Border Romance '30
Fiesta '47
Gaiety '43
Jungle Goddess '49

Russell Arms
By the Light of the Silvery Moon '53
Captains of the Clouds '42
Fighting Vigilantes '47
Stage to Mesa City '48

Alun Armstrong
Black Beauty '94
Split Second '92
White Hunter, Black Heart '90

Bess Armstrong
Dream Lover '93
The Four Seasons '81
High Road to China '83
How to Pick Up Girls '78
Jaws 3 '83
Jekyll & Hyde...Together Again '82
Nothing in Common '86
Second Sight '89
The Skateboard Kid '93

Walking Through the Fire '80

Billy Armstrong
Charlie Chaplin: Rare Chaplin '15
Work/Police '16

Curtis Armstrong
The Adventures of Huck Finn '93
Bad Medicine '85
Better Off Dead '85
One Crazy Summer '86
Revenge of the Nerds '84
Revenge of the Nerds 2: Nerds in Paradise '87
Revenge of the Nerds 3: The Next Generation '92
Risky Business '83

Jack Armstrong
Eden '92
Eden 2 '93
Eden 3 '93
Eden 4 '93

Katherine Armstrong
Ambition '91
Street Soldiers '91

Kerry Armstrong
The Hunting '92
Prisoner Cell Block H '80

Louis Armstrong
Cabin in the Sky '43
The Five Pennies '59
The Glenn Miller Story '54
Hello, Dolly! '69
High Society '56
A Man Called Adam '66
Paris Blues '61

Melinda Armstrong
Bikini Summer '91
Bikini Summer 2 '92

R.G. Armstrong
Angels Die Hard '84
Boss '88
Bulletproof '88
Children of the Corn '84
Dear Detective '78
Dick Tracy '90
Dixie Dynamite '76
El Dorado '67
Evilspeak '82
Final Comedown '72
The Fugitive Kind '60
Ghetto Blaster '89
The Great Northfield Minnesota Raid '72
The Great White Hope '70
My Name is Nobody '74
The Pack '77
Predator '87
Reflections of Murder '74
Ride the High Country '62
The Shadow Riders '82
Steel '80
Texas Detour '77
The Twilight Zone '61
Warlock: The Armageddon '93

Robert Armstrong
Action in Arabia '44
Baby Face Morgan '42
Big News '29
Blood on the Sun '45
Criminal Court '46
Danger Lights '30
Dive Bomber '41
Ex-Mrs. Bradford '36
The Fugitive '48
"G" Men '35
Gangbusters '38
The Girl Said No '37
King Kong '33
The Mad Ghoul '43
Mighty Joe Young '49
Mr. Winkle Goes to War '44
The Most Dangerous Game '32
The Mystery Man '35
The Paleface '48
Palooka '34
The Racketeer '29
Son of Kong '33
Three Legionnaires '37
The Tip-Off '31
Wings Over the Pacific '43

Todd Armstrong
Dead Heat on a Merry-Go-Round '66

Armstrong ▶cont.

Jason and the Argonauts '63

Desi Arnaz, Jr.
Fake Out '82
Great American Traffic Jam '80
House of the Long Shadows '82
How to Pick Up Girls '78
Joyride '77
The Mambo Kings '92
Marco '73
The Voyage of the Yes '72
A Wedding '78

Desi Arnaz, Sr.
Bataan '43
The Escape Artist '82
Forever Darling '56
Four Jacks and a Jill '41
Holiday in Havana '49
The Long, Long Trailer '54
The Navy Comes Through '42
Too Many Girls '40

Lucie Arnaz
Death Scream '75
The Jazz Singer '80
Mating Season '81
Second Thoughts '83
Washington Mistress '81
Who Is the Black Dahlia? '75

Adelheid Arndt
Chinese Boxes '84
Rosa Luxemburg '86

Peter Arne
The Atomic Man '56
Battle Beneath the Earth '68
The Hellfire Club '61
The Moonraker '58
The Oblong Box '69

James Arness
The Alamo: Thirteen Days to Glory '87
Big Jim McLain '52
The Farmer's Daughter '47
Flame of the Islands '55
Gunsmoke: Return to Dodge '87
Horizons West '52
Sea Chase '55
Stars in My Crown '50
Them! '54
The Thing '51
Two Lost Worlds '50
Wagon Master '50

Jeanetta Arnetta
Ladybugs '92
The Redeemer '76
The Shadow Riders '82

Stefan Arngrim
Class of 1984 '82
Fear No Evil '80

Alice Arno
The Loves of Irina '80s
The Perverse Countess '73

Edward Arnold
The Ambassador's Daughter '56
City That Never Sleeps '53
Come and Get It '36
Crime and Punishment '35
Dear Wife '49
The Devil & Daniel Webster '41
Hide-Out '34
The Hucksters '47
Idiot's Delight '39
I'm No Angel '33
Johnny Apollo '40
Johnny Eager '42
Let Freedom Ring '39
Meet John Doe '41
Mrs. Parkington '44
Mr. Smith Goes to Washington '39
Rasputin and the Empress '32
Roman Scandals '33
Sadie McKee '34
Slightly Honorable '40
Take Me Out to the Ball Game '49
Three Daring Daughters '48
Toast of New York '37
Weekend at the Waldorf '45
The Yellow Cab Man '50
You Can't Take It with You '38

Ziegfeld Follies '46

Mark Arnold
Threesome '94
Trancers 4: Jack of Swords '93

Roseanne (Barr) Arnold
Backfield in Motion '91
Freddy's Dead: The Final Nightmare '91
She-Devil '89

Tom Arnold
Backfield in Motion '91
Hero '92
True Lies '94
Undercover Blues '93

Mark Arnott
Not Quite Human 2 '89
Return of the Secaucus 7 '80

Francoise Arnoul
French Can-Can '55
The Little Theatre of Jean Renoir '71

Charles Arnt
Big Town '47
Gambler's Choice '44
The Great Gildersleeve '43
Strange Illusion '45
That Brennan Girl '46

Michael J. Aronin
Getting Even '87
The Lone Runner '88
Miami Cops '89

Judie Aronson
American Ninja '85
Desert Kickboxer '92
Friday the 13th, Part 4: The Final Chapter '84
The Sleeping Car '90

Alexis Arquette
Down and Out in Beverly Hills '86
Jumpin' at the Boneyard '92
Miracle Beach '92
Threesome '94

David Arquette
Buffy the Vampire Slayer '92
Where the Day Takes You '92

Lewis Arquette
Attack of the 50 Ft. Woman '93
Book of Love '91
The Linguini Incident '92
Syngenor '90

Patricia Arquette
Ed Wood '94
Ethan Frome '92
Far North '88
The Indian Runner '91
Inside Monkey Zetterland '93
A Nightmare on Elm Street 3: Dream Warriors '87
Prayer of the Rollerboys '91
Pretty Smart '87
Trouble Bound '92
True Romance '93
Wildflower '91

Rosanna Arquette
After Hours '85
...Almost '90
Amazon Women on the Moon '87
The Aviator '85
Baby It's You '82
The Big Blue '88
Black Rainbow '91
The Dark Secret of Harvest Home '78
Desperately Seeking Susan '85
Don't Hang Up '90
8 Million Ways to Die '85
The Executioner's Song '82
Fathers and Sons '92
Flight of the Intruder '90
Gorp '80
Johnny Belinda '82
The Linguini Incident '92
A Long Way Home '81
New York Stories '89
Nobody's Fool '86
Nowhere to Run '93
Off the Wall '82
One Cooks, the Other Doesn't '83
Promised a Miracle '88
Pulp Fiction '94

Silverado '85
S.O.B. '81
Son of the Morning Star '91
Sweet Revenge '90
The Wrong Man '93

Rod Arrants
A*P*E* '76
Vamping '84

Jeri Arrendondo
Silent Tongue '92
Spirit of the Eagle '90

Carlos Arruza
The Alamo '60
Torero '56

Antonin Artaud
Napoleon '27
The Passion of Joan of Arc '28

Beatrice Arthur
History of the World: Part 1 '81
How to Commit Marriage '69
Lovers and Other Strangers '70
Mame '74

Jean Arthur
Arizona '40
Danger Lights '30
The Devil & Miss Jones '41
Ex-Mrs. Bradford '36
History is Made at Night '37
Lady Takes a Chance '43
The Making of a Legend: "Gone With the Wind" '89
Mr. Deeds Goes to Town '36
Mr. Smith Goes to Washington '39
The More the Merrier '43
Only Angels Have Wings '39
The Plainsman '36
Shane '53
Talk of the Town '42
You Can't Take It with You '38

Johnny Arthur
Danger on the Air '38
The Ghost Walks '34
The Masked Marvel '43
The Monster '25
The Road to Singapore '40

Maureen Arthur
How to Succeed in Business without Really Trying '67
The Love Machine '71

Robert Arthur
Hellcats of the Navy '57
Just for You '52
Naked Youth '59
The Ring '52
September Affair '50

Oscar Asche
Don Quixote '35
The Private Secretary '35
Scrooge '35

Leslie Ash
Curse of the Pink Panther '83
Murder: Ultimate Grounds for Divorce '85
Quadrophenia '79
Shadey '87

Dana Ashbrook
Ghost Dad '90
Girlfriend from Hell '89
Return of the Living Dead 2 '88
Twin Peaks: Fire Walk with Me '92
Waxwork '88

Daphne Ashbrook
Intruders '92
Murder So Sweet '93
Quiet Cool '86
Sunset Heat '92

Linden Ashby
The Perfect Bride '91
Wyatt Earp '94

Peggy Ashcroft
The Heat of the Day '91
Hullabaloo Over Georgie & Bonnie's Pictures '78
The Jewel in the Crown '84
Madame Sousatzka '88
The Nun's Story '59
A Passage to India '84
The Pedestrian '73
Rhodes '35
Secret Ceremony '69
The 39 Steps '35

Jane Asher
Deep End '70
Dreamchild '85
Masque of the Red Death '65
Masque of the Red Death/ Premature Burial '65
The Prince and the Pauper '62
Success is the Best Revenge '84
A Voyage' Round My Father '89

Edward Ashley
Beyond the Next Mountain '87
Bitter Sweet '40
Nocturne '46

Elizabeth Ashley
The Carpetbaggers '64
Coma '78
Dangerous Curves '88
Dragnet '87
Great Scout & Cathouse Thursday '76
A Man of Passion '90s
One of My Wives Is Missing '76
Paperback Hero '73
Paternity '81
Rancho Deluxe '75
Shattered Silence '71
Ship of Fools '65
Stagecoach '86
Svengali '83
Vampire's Kiss '88
War Between the Tates '76
Windows '80

Jennifer Ashley
Barn of the Naked Dead '73
Hell on Wheels '67
Horror Planet '80
Pom Pom Girls '76
Tintorera...Tiger Shark '78

John Ashley
Beach Blanket Bingo '65
Beach Party '63
Beast of the Yellow Night '70
Beyond Atlantis '73
Bikini Beach '64
Brides of the Beast '68
Dragstrip Girl '57
The Eye Creatures '65
Frankenstein's Daughter '58
Hell on Wheels '67
High School Caesar '56
How to Make a Monster '58
How to Stuff a Wild Bikini '65
Hud '63
Mad Doctor of Blood Island '69
Motorcycle Gang '57
Muscle Beach Party '64
Revenge of Doctor X '80s
Smoke in the Wind '75
Suicide Battalion/Hell Squad '58
Twilight People '72
Woman Hunt '72

John Ashton
Beverly Hills Cop '84
Beverly Hills Cop 2 '87
The Deliberate Stranger '86
Dirty Work '92
King Kong Lives '86
L.A. Gangs Rising '89
Little Big League '94
Love, Lies and Murder '91
Midnight Run '88
She's Having a Baby '88
Some Kind of Wonderful '87
Stephen King's The Tommyknockers '93

Luke Askew
Back to Back '90
The Devil's Brigade '68
Dune Warriors '91
The Great Northfield Minnesota Raid '72
Kung Fu: The Movie '86
The Longest Drive '76
Posse '75
Wanda Nevada '79
The Warrior & the Sorceress '84

Leon Askin
Dr. Death, Seeker of Souls '73
Savage Island '85
Sherlock Holmes and the Deadly Necklace '62

Robin Askwith
Flesh and Blood Show '73
Hans Brinker '69
Horror Hospital '73

Gregoire Aslan
Golden Voyage of Sinbad '73
Paris When It Sizzles '64

Ed Asner
A Case of Libel '83
Change of Habit '69
Daniel '83
Death Scream '75
The Doomsday Flight '66
El Dorado '67
The Family Man '79
Fort Apache, the Bronx '81
A Friendship in Vienna '88
The Gathering '77
Gus '83
Gypsy '93
Haunts of the Very Rich '72
Heads '93
JFK '91
Kid Galahad '62
The Life and Assassination of the Kingfish '76
Moon Over Parador '88
My Darlin' Clementine '86
O'Hara's Wife '82
Rich Man, Poor Man '76
Roots '77
Silent Motive '91
Skin Game '71
A Small Killing '81
Switched at Birth '91
They Call Me Mr. Tibbs! '70
The Todd Killings '71
The Wrestler '73

Patricia Aspillaga
Emiliano Zapata '87
La Hija del General '84

Armand Assante
Animal Behavior '89
Belizaire the Cajun '86
Deadly Business '86
Eternity '90
Fatal Instinct '93
Fever '91
1492: Conquest of Paradise '92
Hands of a Stranger '87
Hoffa '92
I, the Jury '82
Jack the Ripper '88
Lady of the House '78
Little Darlings '80
The Lords of Flatbush '74
The Mambo Kings '92
The Marrying Man '91
Paradise Alley '78
Passion in Paradise '89
The Penitent '88
Private Benjamin '80
Prophecy '79
Q & A '90
Rage of Angels '83
Sophia Loren: Her Own Story '80
Unfaithfully Yours '84

Pat Ast
Heat '72
Reform School Girls '86

Fred Astaire
The Amazing Dobermans '76
The Band Wagon '53
The Barkleys of Broadway '49
The Belle of New York '52
Broadway Melody of 1940 '40
Carefree '38
Daddy Long Legs '55
A Damsel in Distress '37
Dancing Lady '33
Easter Parade '48
Family Upside Down '78
Finian's Rainbow '68
Flying Down to Rio '33
Follow the Fleet '36
Funny Face '57
The Gay Divorcee '34
Ghost Story '81
Gotta Dance, Gotta Sing '84
Holiday Inn '42
Irving Berlin's America '86
Let's Dance '50
The Man in the Santa Claus Suit '79
On the Beach '59
Paris When It Sizzles '64

The Purple Taxi '77
Roberta '35
Royal Wedding '51
Second Chorus '40
Shall We Dance '37
Silk Stockings '57
The Sky's the Limit '43
The Story of Vernon and Irene Castle '39
Swing Time '36
That's Dancing! '85
That's Entertainment '74
That's Entertainment, Part 2 '76
Three Little Words '50
Top Hat '35
The Towering Inferno '74
Yolanda and the Thief '45
You Were Never Lovelier '42
You'll Never Get Rich '41
Ziegfeld Follies '46

Nils Asther
The Bitter Tea of General Yen '33
Bluebeard '44
Make-Up '37
Night Monster '42
Our Dancing Daughters '28
The Single Standard '29
Son of Lassie '45
Wild Orchids '28

Adrianna Asti
Before the Revolution '65
Phantom of Liberty '68

John Astin
Adventures Beyond Belief '87
The Barcelona Kill '77
Body Slam '87
Brothers O'Toole '73
Halloween with the Addams Family '79
Huck and the King of Hearts '93
Killer Tomatoes Eat France '91
Killer Tomatoes Strike Back '90
National Lampoon's European Vacation '85
Night Life '90
Only with Married Men '74
Pepper and His Wacky Taxi '72
Return of the Killer Tomatoes '88
Stepmonster '92
Teen Wolf Too '87
That Touch of Mink '62
Viva Max '69
The Wheeler Dealers '63

MacKenzie Astin
The Garbage Pail Kids Movie '87
Iron Will '93

Sean Astin
Encino Man '92
The Goonies '85
Like Father, Like Son '87
Memphis Belle '90
Rudy '93
Staying Together '89
Toy Soldiers '91
The War of the Roses '89
Where the Day Takes You '92
White Water Summer '87
The Willies '90

Gertrude Astor
After Midnight '33
The Cat and the Canary '27
The Cheerful Fraud '27
Strong Man '26

Mary Astor
Across the Pacific '42
Any Number Can Play '49
Beau Brummel '24
Behind Office Doors '31
The Best of Bogart '43
Cass Timberlane '47
Dodsworth '36
Don Juan '26
Don Q., Son of Zorro '25
The Fighting American '24
The Great Lie '41
Hurricane '37
Hush, Hush, Sweet Charlotte '65
The Kennel Murder Case '33
Lady from Nowhere '36
Listen, Darling '38
Little Women '49
The Maltese Falcon '41

Meet Me in St. Louis '44
The Palm Beach Story '42
Prisoner of Zenda '37
Red Dust '32
Return to Peyton Place '61
The Royal Bed '31
This Happy Feeling '58
Thousands Cheer '43

Patti Astor
The Foreigner '78
Underground U.S.A. '84

Hooper Atchley
Clearing the Range '31
I Can't Escape '34
Midnight Warning '32
Spirit of the West '32

Roscoe Ates
Black Hills '48
The Champ '31
Check Your Guns '48
Cheyenne Kid '33
Cimarron '30
Colorado Serenade '46
Come On Danger! '32
Driftin' River '46
Freaks '32
The Hawk of Powder River '48
Hills of Oklahoma '50
Reg'lar Fellers '41
Robin Hood of the Pecos '41
Three Texas Steers '39
Thunder in the Pines '49
The Tioga Kid '48
West to Glory '47
What! No Beer? '33
Wild Country '47
Wild West '46
Woman in the Shadows '34

William Atherton
Buried Alive '90
Chrome Soldiers '92
Class of '44 '73
The Day of the Locust '75
Die Hard '88
Die Hard 2: Die Harder '90
A Fight for Jenny '90
Ghostbusters '84
Grim Prairie Tales '89
The Hindenburg '75
Intrigue '90
Looking for Mr. Goodbar '77
No Mercy '86
The Pelican Brief '93
Real Genius '85
The Sugarland Express '74
Tomorrow's Child '82

Harvey Atkin
Meatballs '79
SnakeEater 2: The Drug Buster '89

Christopher Atkins
Beaks: The Movie '87
The Blue Lagoon '80
Child Bride of Short Creek '81
Die Watching '93
Dracula Rising '93
Fatal Charm '92
King's Ransom '91
Listen to Me '89
Mortuary Academy '91
A Night in Heaven '83
Pirate Movie '82
Secret Weapons '85
Shakma '89
Shoot '92

David Atkins
Personal Services '87
Prick Up Your Ears '87
Squizzy Taylor '84

Eileen Atkins
Bewitched '85
The Dresser '83
I Don't Want to Be Born '75
Let Him Have It '91
The Lost Language of Cranes '92
Oliver Twist '82
The Vision '87
Wolf '94

Tom Atkins
Blind Justice '86
Dead Man Out '89
Desperate Lives '82
Halloween 3: Season of the Witch '82
Lethal Weapon '87

Maniac Cop '88
Night of the Creeps '86
Skeezer '82
Special Delivery '76
Tarantulas: The Deadly Cargo '77

Rowan Atkinson
Bernard and the Genie '90s
Four Weddings and a Funeral '93
Hot Shots! Part Deux '93
Never Say Never Again '83
The Tall Guy '89
The Witches '90

Richard Attenborough
The Baby and the Battleship '56
The Bliss of Mrs. Blossom '68
Brannigan '75
Brighton Rock '47
Brothers in Law '57
Conduct Unbecoming '75
David Copperfield '70
Doctor Dolittle '67
The Flight of the Phoenix '65
The Gift Horse '52
The Great Escape '63
Guns at Batasi '64
The Human Factor '79
In Which We Serve '43
Jurassic Park '93
The League of Gentlemen '60
Loot...Give Me Money, Honey! '70
The Magic Christian '69
Only Two Can Play '62
Rosebud '75
The Sand Pebbles '66
Seance on a Wet Afternoon '64
S.O.S. Pacific '60
Ten Little Indians '75
10 Rillington Place '71

Malcolm Atterbury
Blood of Dracula '57
Crime of Passion '57
How to Make a Monster '58
I Was a Teenage Werewolf '57

Edith Atwater
The Body Snatcher '45
Die Sister, Die! '74
It Happened at the World's Fair '63
The Love Machine '71
Our Time '74

Lionel Atwill
Balalaika '39
Beggars in Ermine '34
Boom Town '40
Cairo '42
Captain America '44
Captain Blood '35
Doctor X '32
Fog Island '45
Frankenstein Meets the Wolfman '42
The Ghost of Frankenstein '42
The Gorilla '39
The Great Waltz '38
High Command '37
The Horror of It All '91
The Hound of the Baskervilles '39
House of Dracula '45
House of Frankenstein '44
Johnny Apollo '40
Lady in the Death House '44
Lost City of the Jungle '45
Man Made Monster '41
Mystery of the Wax Museum '33
Night Monster '42
Pardon My Sarong '42
Raiders of Ghost City '44
Sherlock Holmes and the Secret Weapon '42
Son of Frankenstein '39
The Sphinx '33
Three Comrades '38
The Three Musketeers '39
To Be or Not to Be '42
The Vampire Bat '32
The Wrong Road '37

Anat Atzman
Dead End Street '83
Double Edge '92

Every Time We Say Goodbye '86

Rene Auberjonois
The Ballad of Little Jo '93
Brewster McCloud '70
The Dark Secret of Harvest Home '78
Eyes of Laura Mars '78
The Feud '90
Gore Vidal's Billy the Kid '89
King Kong '76
Lone Justice '93
M*A*S*H '70
McCabe & Mrs. Miller '71
My Best Friend Is a Vampire '88
Once Upon a Midnight Scary '90
Pete 'n' Tillie '72
Petulia '68
Police Academy 5: Assignment Miami Beach '88
A Smoky Mountain Christmas '86
3:15—The Moment of Truth '86
Walker '87
Wild, Wild West Revisited '79
Wildcard '92

Lenore Aubert
Abbott and Costello Meet Frankenstein '48
Abbott and Costello Meet the Killer, Boris Karloff '49
Action in Arabia '44
Having Wonderful Crime '45

James Aubrey
Bouquet of Barbed Wire '76
Forever Young '85
Home Before Midnight '84
Legion of Missing Men '37
Lord of the Flies '63
Riders of the Storm '88
The Terror '79

Jimmy Aubrey
Aces and Eights '36
Courage of the North '35

Danielle Aubry
Bikini Beach '64
Operation C.I.A. '65

Jacques Aubuchon
Gun Glory '57
Thunder Road '58

Michel Auclair
Beauty and the Beast '46
Manon '50
Murder at 45 R.P.M. '65
The Story of a Love Story '73
Swashbuckler '84

Maxine Audley
A King in New York '57
Peeping Tom '63

Stephane Audran
Babette's Feast '87
The Big Red One '80
Black Bird '75
The Blood of Others '84
Blood Relatives '77
Brideshead Revisited '81
Coup de Torchon '81
The Discreet Charm of the Bourgeoisie '72
Eagle's Wing '79
La Cage aux Folles 3: The Wedding '86
La Rupture '70
Le Boucher '69
Les Biches '68
Poor Little Rich Girl: The Barbara Hutton Story '87
Silver Bears '78
Six in Paris '68
Ten Little Indians '75
The Turn of the Screw '92
Twist '76
Vincent, Francois, Paul and the Others '75
Violette '78
Wedding in Blood '74

Mischa Auer
And Then There Were None '45
Around the World '43
Arrivederci, Baby! '66
Brewster's Millions '45
The Christmas That Almost Wasn't '66
Condemned to Live '35

Destry Rides Again '39
Drums of Jeopardy '31
Flaming Signal '33
Hold That Ghost '41
I Dream Too Much '35
Inside the Lines '30
Mr. Arkadin '55
The Monster Walks '32
My Man Godfrey '36
Pick a Star '37
The Rage of Paris '38
Seven Sinners '40
Sputnik '61
Sucker Money '34
Sweethearts '38
That Girl from Paris '36
Vogues of 1938 '37
Woman Condemned '33
You Can't Take It with You '38

Claudine Auger
The Associate '82
Head of the Family '71
The Killing Game '67
Lobster for Breakfast '82
Ricco '74
The Road to Lebanon '60
Secret Places '85
Thunderball '65
Triple Cross '67
Twitch of the Death Nerve '71

Robert August
The Endless Summer '66
The Endless Summer 2 '94

Ewa Aulin
The Legend of Blood Castle '72
Start the Revolution Without Me '70

Jean-Pierre Aumont
Becoming Colette '92
Blackout '78
The Blood of Others '84
Cat and Mouse '78
Catherine & Co. '76
Cauldron of Blood '67
Day for Night '73
The Devil at 4 O'Clock '61
Don't Look in the Attic '81
The Happy Hooker '75
Heartbeat '46
The Horse Without a Head '63
John Paul Jones '59
Lili '53
Mahogany '75
Maria Chapdelaine '34
Nana '82
Napoleon '55
Something Short of Paradise '79
Sweet Country '87
A Tale of Two Cities '91
A Time for Miracles '80
Windmills of the Gods '88

Michel Aumont
Alberto Express '92
Grain of Sand '84
Hothead '78
La Vie Continue '82
Les Comperes '83
One Woman or Two '85
Spoiled Children '77
A Sunday in the Country '84

Tina Aumont
La Grande Bourgeoise '74
Lifespan '75
Malicious '74
Man of Legend '71
A Matter of Time '76
Partner '68
Texas Across the River '66
Torso '73

Albert Austin
Charlie Chaplin: The Early Years, Vol. 2 '17
Charlie Chaplin: The Early Years, Vol. 3 '16
Charlie Chaplin: The Early Years, Vol. 4 '16
The Cure '17
Three Charlies and One Phoney! '18
The Vagabond '16

Charlotte Austin
The Bride & the Beast '58
Daddy Long Legs '55

Julie Austin
Elves '89

Austin ▶cont.

Fatal Exposure '90
Karen Austin
Assassin '86
Far from Home '89
A Girl to Kill for '90
The Jagged Edge '85
The Ladies Club '86
Summer Rental '85
When a Stranger Calls Back '93
When the Time Comes '91
Terri Austin
False Witness '89
The Vindicator '85
Daniel Auteuil
The Elegant Criminal '92
Jean de Florette '87
Le Sex Shop '73
Mama, There's a Man in Your Bed '89
Manon of the Spring '87
Un Coeur en Hiver '93
Alan Autry
At Close Range '86
Blue De Ville '86
Proud Men '87
Gene Autry
Bad Girls in the Movies '86
Big Show '37
The Big Sombrero '49
Blue Canadian Rockies '52
Boots & Saddles '37
Call of the Canyon '42
Cow Town '50
Cowboys of the Saturday Matinee '84
Down Mexico Way '41
Gene Autry Matinee Double Feature #1 '53
Gene Autry Matinee Double Feature #2 '53
Gene Autry Matinee Double Feature #3 '53
Git Along Little Dogies '37
Heart of the Rio Grande '42
Hills of Utah '51
In Old Santa Fe '34
Last of the Pony Riders '53
Loaded Pistols '48
The Man from Music Mountain '38
Manhattan Merry-Go-Round '37
Melody Ranch '40
Melody Trail '35
Mystery Mountain '34
Night Stage to Galveston '52
Oh Susannah '38
Old Barn Dance '38
Old Corral '36
On Top of Old Smoky '53
The Phantom Empire '35
Prairie Moon '38
Public Cowboy No. 1 '37
Red River Valley '36
Ride, Ranger, Ride '36
Riders of the Whistling Pines '49
Ridin' on a Rainbow '41
Rim of the Canyon '49
Robin Hood of Texas '47
Rootin' Tootin' Rhythm '38
Round-Up Time in Texas '37
Saturday Night Serials '40
Sioux City Sue '46
South of the Border '39
Springtime in the Rockies '37
Twilight on the Rio Grande '41
Valley of Fire '51
Western Double Feature 1 '38
Western Double Feature 4 '37
Western Double Feature 5: Rogers & Autry '37
Western Double Feature 16 '46
Western Double Feature 20 '53
Winning of the West '53
Yodelin' Kid From Pine Ridge '37
Frankie Avalon
The Alamo '60
Back to the Beach '87
Beach Blanket Bingo '65
Beach Party '63
Bikini Beach '64

Blood Song '82
The Castilian '63
Dr. Goldfoot and the Bikini Machine '66
Grease '78
How to Stuff a Wild Bikini '65
I'll Take Sweden '65
Muscle Beach Party '64
Panic in the Year Zero! '62
Pee Wee's Playhouse Christmas Special '88
Voyage to the Bottom of the Sea '61
Phillip Avalon
The Cursed Mountain Mystery '93
Summer City '77
Luis Avalos
Ghost Fever '87
Lone Justice '93
Loren Avedon
The King of the Kickboxers '91
No Retreat, No Surrender 2 '89
No Retreat, No Surrender 3: Blood Brothers '91
Brian Avery
Forced to Kill '93
The Graduate '67
James Avery
Beastmaster 2: Through the Portal of Time '91
Kicks '85
Linda Avery
Hitchhikers '72
Noon Sunday '71
Margaret Avery
Blueberry Hill '88
The Color Purple '85
The Fish that Saved Pittsburgh '79
For Us, the Living '88
Heat Wave '90
Hell Up in Harlem '73
The Jacksons: An American Dream '92
Lathe of Heaven '80
Mardi Gras for the Devil '93
Return of Superfly '90
Riverbend '90
The Sky is Gray '80
Terror at Red Wolf Inn '72
Which Way Is Up? '77
Val Avery
Black Caesar '72
Choices '81
Continental Divide '81
Courage '86
A Dream of Kings '69
Firehouse '72
Rick Aviles
Ghost '90
Mystery Train '89
The Saint of Fort Washington '93
Spike of Bensonhurst '88
Stephen King's The Stand '94
Chikage Awashima
Early Summer '51
The Human Condition: No Greater Love '58
Eddie Axberg
The Emigrants '72
The New Land '73
Nina Axelrod
Cross Country '83
Motel Hell '80
Hanne Axman
Five Fingers '52
The Red Menace '49
Hoyt Axton
Act of Vengeance '86
Buried Alive '90
Christmas Comes to Willow Creek '87
Deadline Auto Theft '83
Disorganized Crime '89
Dixie Lanes '88
Endangered Species '82
Goldilocks & the Three Bears '83
Gremlins '84
Guilty of Innocence '87
Heart Like a Wheel '83
The Junkman '82

Retribution '88
The Rousters '90
We're No Angels '89
Anne Ayars
Fiesta '47
Gaiety '43
Reunion in France '42
Dan Aykroyd
All You Need Is Cash '78
The Blues Brothers '80
Caddyshack 2 '88
Chaplin '92
Coneheads '93
The Couch Trip '87
Doctor Detroit '83
Dragnet '87
Driving Miss Daisy '89
Ghostbusters '84
Ghostbusters 2 '89
The Great Outdoors '88
Into the Night '85
Loose Cannons '90
Love at First Sight '76
The Masters of Menace '90
Mr. Mike's Mondo Video '79
My Girl '91
My Girl 2 '94
My Stepmother Is an Alien '88
Neighbors '81
1941 '79
North '94
Nothing But Trouble '91
Sneakers '92
Spies Like Us '85
This is My Life '92
Trading Places '83
Twilight Zone: The Movie '83
Peter Aykroyd
The Funny Farm '82
Gas '81
Felix Aylmer
Action for Slander '38
Alice in Wonderland '50
As You Like It '36
The Case of the Frightened Lady '39
The Chalk Garden '64
Dreaming Lips '37
The Evil Mind '34
Exodus '60
Eye Witness '49
From the Terrace '60
Ghosts of Berkeley Square '47
Hamlet '48
The Hands of Orlac '60
Henry V '44
The Iron Duke '34
Ivanhoe '52
Knights of the Round Table '53
A Man About the House '47
The Master of Ballantrae '53
Mr. Emmanuel '44
The Mummy '59
Nine Days a Queen '34
October Man '48
Paris Express '53
Quo Vadis '51
Saint Joan '57
School for Scandal '65
Separate Tables '58
The Shadow '36
Spellbound '41
Trio '50
Victoria Regina '61
The Wicked Lady '45
Agnes Ayres
The Sheik '21
Son of the Sheik '26
Leah Ayres
Bloodsport '88
The Burning '82
Eddie Macon's Run '83
Lew Ayres
Advise and Consent '62
All Quiet on the Western Front '30
Battle for the Planet of the Apes '73
Big News '29
Broadway Serenade '39
The Capture '50
The Carpetbaggers '64
Cast the First Stone '89
Damien: Omen 2 '78
Dark Mirror '46
Dr. Kildare's Strange Case '40
Donovan's Brain '53

End of the World '77
Francis Gary Powers: The True Story of the U-2 Spy '76
Holiday '38
Johnny Belinda '48
The Kiss '29
Of Mice and Men '81
Salem's Lot '79
The Stranger '73
Robert Ayres
Battle Beneath the Earth '68
Cat Girl '57
River Beat '54
Sabine Azema
Life and Nothing But '89
A Sunday in the Country '84
Tony Azito
Bloodhounds of Broadway '89
Chattanooga Choo Choo '84
Private Resort '84
Shabana Azmi
City of Joy '92
Madame Sousatzka '88
Son of the Pink Panther '93
Charles Aznavour
The Adventurers '70
Blockhouse '73
Edith & Marcel '83
Shoot the Piano Player '62
Sky Riders '76
Ten Little Indians '75
The Testament of Orpheus '59
The Tin Drum '79
Twist '76
Candice Azzara
Doin' Time on Planet Earth '88
Easy Money '83
Fatso '80
House Calls '78
Karin Baal
Berlin Alexanderplatz '80
Dead Eyes of London '61
Teenage Wolfpack '57
Obba Babatunde
God Bless the Child '88
Miami Blues '90
Philadelphia '93
Undercover Blues '93
Barbara Babcock
The Black Marble '79
The Christmas Coal Mine Miracle '77
Far and Away '92
Happy Together '89
The Heart of Dixie '89
Hill Street Blues, Vol. 1: Hill Street Station '81
The Lords of Discipline '83
News at Eleven '86
On the Edge: The Survival of Dana '79
That Was Then...This Is Now '85
Lauren Bacall
All I Want for Christmas '91
Appointment with Death '88
The Big Sleep '46
Blood Alley '55
The Cobweb '55
Dark Passage '47
Designing Woman '57
Dinner at Eight '89
The Fan '81
Flame Over India '60
Harper '66
Hollywood Bloopers '50s
How to Marry a Millionaire '53
Innocent Victim '48
Key Largo '48
Misery '90
Mr. North '88
Murder on the Orient Express '74
The Portrait '93
Sex and the Single Girl '64
The Shootist '76
To Have & Have Not '44
Written on the Wind '56
Young Man with a Horn '50
Barbara Bach
Caveman '81
Force 10 from Navarone '78
Give My Regards to Broad Street '84
The Great Alligator '81

Jaguar Lives '79
The Legend of Sea Wolf '75
Princess Daisy '83
Screamers '80
The Spy Who Loved Me '77
Stateline Motel '75
Street Law '79
The Unseen '80
Up the Academy '80
Catherine Bach
Cannonball Run 2 '84
Criminal Act '88
Driving Force '88
The Masters of Menace '90
Nicole '72
Rage and Honor '92
Strange New World '75
Street Justice '89
John Bach
Georgia '87
The Lost Tribe '89
The Sound and the Silence '93
Wild Horses '82
Hans Bachman
Invader '91
Star Quest '89
Brian Backer
Fast Times at Ridgemont High '82
Moving Violations '85
Talk to Me '82
Jim Backus
Above and Beyond '53
Angel's Brigade '79
Ask Any Girl '59
Billie '65
C.H.O.M.P.S. '79
Crazy Mama '75
Don't Bother to Knock '52
Francis in the Navy '55
Gilligan's Island: Meet the Crew '64
The Great Lover '49
His Kind of Woman '51
The Horizontal Lieutenant '62
I Love Melvin '53
Ice Palace '60
I'll See You in My Dreams '51
It's a Mad, Mad, Mad, Mad World '63
Man of a Thousand Faces '57
Meet Me in Las Vegas '56
Myra Breckinridge '70
Naked Hills '56
Now You See Him, Now You Don't '72
Pat and Mike '52
Pete's Dragon '77
Pied Piper of Hamelin '57
Rebel Without a Cause '55
The Rebels '79
Slapstick of Another Kind '84
The Wheeler Dealers '63
Where Were You When the Lights Went Out? '68
The Wonderful World of the Brothers Grimm '62
Zotz! '62
Olga Baclanova
Docks of New York '28
Freaks '32
The Man Who Laughs '27
Irving Bacon
The Bashful Bachelor '42
Blondie Has Trouble '40
Blondie Takes a Vacation '39
Blondie's Blessed Event '42
Branded Men '31
Caught in the Draft '41
Cause for Alarm '51
Dreaming Out Loud '40
Dynamite '49
The Howards of Virginia '40
It's a Great Life '43
Monsieur Verdoux '47
Western Union '41
Kevin Bacon
The Air Up There '94
The Big Picture '89
Criminal Law '89
Diner '82
End of the Line '88
Enormous Changes '83
A Few Good Men '92
Flatliners '90
Footloose '84
Friday the 13th '80

He Said, She Said '91
Hero at Large '80
JFK '91
National Lampoon's Animal House '78
Only When I Laugh '81
Planes, Trains & Automobiles '87
Pyrates '91
Queens Logic '91
Quicksilver '86
She's Having a Baby '88
Starting Over '79
Tremors '89
Trumps '88
White Water Summer '87

Lloyd Bacon
Charlie Chaplin: The Early Years, Vol. 4 '16
Charlie Chaplin...Our Hero! '15
Wagon Tracks '19

Hermione Baddeley
The Belles of St. Trinian's '53
Brighton Rock '47
A Christmas Carol '51
Mary Poppins '64
Passport to Pimlico '49
The Pickwick Papers '54
Room at the Top '59
The Unsinkable Molly Brown '64

Alan Badel
The Adventurers '70
Children of the Damned '63
The Day of the Jackal '73
Luther '74
The Medusa Touch '78
Nijinsky '80
The Riddle of the Sands '79
This Sporting Life '63

Rupert Baderman
1984 '84
Shadowlands '85

Mary Badham
This Property is Condemned '66
To Kill a Mockingbird '62

Jane Badler
Easy Kill '89
Fine Gold

Antonio Badu
El Gavilan Pollero '47
Mariachis '49

Buddy Baer
The Big Sky '52
Giant from the Unknown '58
Jack & the Beanstalk '52
Quo Vadis '51

Harry Baer
Big Boss '77
Fox and His Friends '75
Mr. Scarface '77
Rulers of the City '71

John Baer
Indian Uprising '51
Night of the Blood Beast '58

Max Baer, Sr.
Buckskin Frontier '43
The Harder They Fall '56
The Navy Comes Through '42
The Prizefighter and the Lady '33

Meredith Baer
The Chicken Chronicles '77
The Sister-in-Law '74

Parley Baer
The Adventures of Huckleberry Finn '60
Cash McCall '60
Dave '93
Gypsy '62
Rodeo Girl '80
Sixteen '72
The Ugly Dachshund '65

Joan Baez
Dynamite Chicken '70
Woodstock '70

Carol Bagdasarian
The Aurora Encounter '85
The Charge of the Model T's '76

Vernel Bagneris
Down by Law '86

Blake Bahner
Blackbelt 2: Fatal Force '93
Deadly Breed '89
Fatal Exposure '90
Sensations '87
Thrilled to Death '88

Chuck Bail
L.A. Bad '85
The Stunt Man '80

Bill Bailey
Fighting Jack '26
Heat and Sunlight '87
On the Edge '86

Bunty Bailey
Dolls '87
Spellcaster '91

G.W. Bailey
An American Story '92
Burglar '87
Double-Crossed '91
Held Hostage '91
Mannequin '87
Police Academy 6: City Under Siege '89
Rustler's Rhapsody '85
A Winner Never Quits '86
Write to Kill '91

Jim Bailey
Penitentiary 3 '87
Vultures '84

Mark Bailey
Simple Men '92
The Unbelievable Truth '90

Pearl Bailey
Carmen Jones '54
The Member of the Wedding '83
Norman, Is That You? '76
Peter Gunn '89

Raymond Bailey
The Gallant Hours '60
The Incredible Shrinking Man '57
Picnic '55
Vertigo '58

Richard Bailey
Forever Amber '47
Manhunt of Mystery Island '45

Robin Bailey
Screamtime '83
See No Evil '71

Barbara Bain
Destination Moonbase Alpha '75
Murder Once Removed '71
Skinheads: The Second Coming of Hate '88
Space: 1999—Alien Attack '79
Spirit of '76 '91
Trust Me '89

Conrad Bain
Bananas '71
Child Bride of Short Creek '81
C.H.O.M.P.S. '79
A Pleasure Doing Business '79
Postcards from the Edge '90
Who Killed Mary What's 'Er Name? '71

Cynthia Bain
Danielle Steel's Changes '91
Hometown Boy Makes Good '93
Pumpkinhead '88
Spontaneous Combustion '89
Vietnam War Story 2 '88

Sherry Bain
Pipe Dreams '76
Wild & Wooly '78
Wild Riders '71

Fay Bainter
Babes on Broadway '41
The Children's Hour '61
Dark Waters '44
The Human Comedy '43
Jezebel '38
Journey for Margaret '42
June Bride '48
Kid from Brooklyn '46
Our Town '40
Presenting Lily Mars '43
Quality Street '37

The Secret Life of Walter Mitty '47
The Shining Hour '38
State Fair '45
Woman of the Year '42
Young Tom Edison '40

Jimmy Baio
The Bad News Bears in Breaking Training '77
Kiss and Be Killed '91
Playing for Keeps '86

Scott Baio
Bugsy Malone '76
Foxes '80
I Love N.Y. '87
Senior Trip '81
Zapped! '82

Harry Baird
The Oblong Box '69
The Story of a Three Day Pass '68
Tor '64

Jimmie Baird
Black Orchid '59
Brass '85
Return of Dracula '58

Richard Bakalayan
The Computer Wore Tennis Shoes '69
Jet Attack/Paratroop Command '58
The St. Valentine's Day Massacre '67
Up Periscope '59

Art Baker
Homecoming '48
A Southern Yankee '48
Task Force '49
The Underworld Story '50

Blanche Baker
Awakening of Candra '81
Cold Feet '84
Embassy '85
French Postcards '79
The Handmaid's Tale '90
Livin' Large '91
Mary and Joseph: A Story of Faith '79
Shakedown '88
Sixteen Candles '84

Bob Baker
Ghost Town Riders '38
Outlaw Express '38
Riders of Pasco Basin '40
Western Trails '38

Carroll Baker
Andy Warhol's Bad '77
Baby Doll '56
Big Country '58
Bloodbath
But Not for Me '59
Captain Apache '71
The Carpetbaggers '64
Cheyenne Autumn '64
Easy to Love '53
Giant '56
The Greatest Story Ever Told '65
Harlow '65
How the West was Won '63
Ironweed '87
Kindergarten Cop '90
Kiss Me, Kill Me '69
Native Son '86
Next Victim '74
Paranoia '69
Private Lessons
The Secret Diary of Sigmund Freud '84
Star 80 '83
The Watcher in the Woods '81
The World is Full of Married Men '80
You've Got to Have Heart '77

Diane Baker
Baker's Hawk '76
The Closer '91
Danger in the Skies '79
The Diary of Anne Frank '59
The Horse in the Gray Flannel Suit '68
Journey to the Center of the Earth '59
The Joy Luck Club '93
Marnie '64
Mirage '66

The Prize '63
The Silence of the Lambs '91
Stolen Hours '63
Strait-Jacket '64
Twenty Bucks '93

Dylan Baker
Delirious '91
The Long Walk Home '89
Love Potion #9 '92
Planes, Trains & Automobiles '87
The Wizard of Loneliness '88

Frank Baker
The New Adventures of Tarzan '35
Tarzan and the Green Goddess '38

George Baker
The Charmer '89
Goodbye, Mr. Chips '69
The Moonraker '58
Robin Hood...The Legend: Herne's Son '85
Sword of Lancelot '63

Jay Baker
April Fool's Day '86
Storm and Sorrow '90

Joe Don Baker
The Abduction of Kari Swenson '87
Adam at 6 A.M. '70
Cape Fear '91
Charley Varrick '73
The Children '90
Citizen Cohn '92
Cool Hand Luke '67
Criminal Law '89
The Distinguished Gentleman '92
Edge of Darkness '86
Final Justice '84
Fletch '85
Framed '75
Getting Even '86
Guns of the Magnificent Seven '69
Joy Sticks '83
Junior Bonner '72
The Killing Time '87
Leonard Part 6 '87
The Living Daylights '87
Mitchell '75
The Natural '84
The Pack '77
Reality Bites '94
Ring of Steel '94
Shadow of Chikara '77
Speedtrap '78
Wacko '83
Walking Tall '73
Wild Rovers '71

Jolyon Baker
Duel of Hearts '92
Final Analysis '92

Josephine Baker
The French Way '40
Princess Tam Tam '35
Zou Zou '34

Kai Baker
American Eagle '90
Stormquest '87

Kathy Baker
Article 99 '92
Clean and Sober '88
Dad '89
Edward Scissorhands '90
The Image '89
Jacknife '89
Jennifer 8 '92
A Killing Affair '85
Mad Dog and Glory '93
Mr. Frost '89
Permanent Record '88
The Right Stuff '83
Street Smart '87

Kenny Baker
The Elephant Man '80
The Empire Strikes Back '80
Return of the Jedi '83
Star Wars '77
Time Bandits '81

Kenny L. Baker
Amadeus '84
At the Circus '39

Cannon Movie Tales: Sleeping Beauty '89
The Harvey Girls '46

Kirsten Baker
Gas Pump Girls '79
Girls Next Door '79

Ray Baker
Camp Nowhere '94
Everybody's All American '88
Heart Condition '90

Scott Thompson Baker
Cleo/Leo '89
New York's Finest '87
Rest In Pieces '87

Sharon Baker
Captive Planet '78
Metallica '85

Stanley Baker
Accident '67
Butterfly Affair '71
Cruel Sea '53
Dingaka '65
The Guns of Navarone '61
Knights of the Round Table '53
Queen of Diamonds '80s
Richard III '55
Robbery '67
Sodom and Gomorrah '62
Zulu '64

Timothy Baker
Bloodfist 2 '90
Out for Blood '93

Tom Baker
Angels Die Hard '84
Candy Stripe Nurses '74
The Chronicles of Narnia '89
The Freakmaker '73
Fyre '78
Golden Voyage of Sinbad '73
Nicholas and Alexandra '71
Vault of Horror '73
The Zany Adventures of Robin Hood '84

William "Billy" Bakewell
Annapolis '28
The Capture '50
Dance Fools Dance '31
Davy Crockett, King of the Wild Frontier '55
Dawn Express '42
Exiled to Shanghai '37
Gone with the Wind '39
Lucky Me '54
Radar Men from the Moon '52
Roaring Speedboats '37
Romance on the High Seas '48
Sons of Steel '35

Brenda Bakke
Dangerous Love '87
Death Spa '87
Fist Fighter '88
Hardbodies 2 '86
Hot Shots! Part Deux '93
Scavengers '87

Brigitte Bako
Dark Tide '93
Red Shoe Diaries '92

Muhamad Bakri
Beyond the Walls '84
Double Edge '92
Hanna K. '83

Scott Bakula
Color of Night '94
The Last Fling '86
Necessary Roughness '91
Sibling Rivalry '90

Bob Balaban
Absence of Malice '81
Alice '90
Altered States '80
Amos and Andrew '93
Bank Shot '74
Close Encounters of the Third Kind '77
Dead Bang '89
End of the Line '88
For Love or Money '93
Girlfriends '78
Greedy '94
Midnight Cowboy '69
The Strawberry Statement '70

Balaban ▶cont.

2010: The Year We Make
  Contact '84
Whose Life Is It Anyway? '81

Belinda Balaski
The Howling '81
Proud Men '87

Adam Baldwin
Bad Guys '86
Bitter Harvest '93
The Chocolate War '88
Cohen and Tate '88
Cold Sweat '93
D.C. Cab '84
Deadbolt '92
800 Leagues Down the
  Amazon '90s
Full Metal Jacket '87
Guilty by Suspicion '91
Hadley's Rebellion '84
Love on the Run '85
My Bodyguard '80
Next of Kin '84
Ordinary People '80
Predator 2 '90
Radio Flyer '92
Reckless '84
3:15—The Moment of Truth '86
Where the Day Takes You '92
Wyatt Earp '94

Alec Baldwin
The Alamo: Thirteen Days to
  Glory '87
Alice '90
Beetlejuice '88
Code of Honor '84
Crazy Streets '80s
Dress Gray '86
Forever, Lulu '87
The Getaway '93
Glengarry Glen Ross '92
Great Balls of Fire '89
The Hunt for Red October '90
Malice '93
Married to the Mob '88
The Marrying Man '91
Miami Blues '90
Prelude to a Kiss '92
The Shadow '94
She's Having a Baby '88
Talk Radio '88
Working Girl '88

Daniel Baldwin
Attack of the 50 Ft. Woman '93
Car 54, Where Are You? '94
Harley Davidson and the
  Marlboro Man '91
The Heroes of Desert Storm
  '91
Knight Moves '93
Lone Justice '93

Janet Baldwin
Gator Bait '73
Humongous '82
Ruby '77

Robert Baldwin
Courageous Dr. Christian '40
Meet Dr. Christian '39

Stephen Baldwin
The Beast '88
Bitter Harvest '93
Born on the Fourth of July '89
Crossing the Bridge '92
8 Seconds '94
Last Exit to Brooklyn '90
The Lawrenceville Stories '80s
Posse '93
A Simple Twist of Fate '94
Threesome '94

Walter Baldwin
Interrupted Melody '55
Winter Meeting '48

William Baldwin
Backdraft '91
Flatliners '90
Internal Affairs '90
The Preppie Murder '89
Sliver '93
Three of Hearts '93

Christian Bale
Empire of the Sun '87
Henry V '89
The Land of Faraway '87

Newsies '92
Swing Kids '93
Treasure Island '89

Rafael Baledon
La Fuerza Inutil '87
Los Hermanos Diablo '65

Betty Balfour
Champagne '28
Evergreen '34

Michael Balfour
The Canterbury Tales '71
Fiend Without a Face '58
Mania '63
Moulin Rouge '52
Murder on Approval '56
Quatermass 2 '57

Jennifer Balgobin
City Limits '85
Dr. Caligari '89
Repo Man '83
Roadside Prophets '92

Ina Balin
Black Orchid '59
Charro! '69
The Children of An Lac '80
The Comancheros '61
The Don is Dead '73
From the Terrace '60
Galyon '77
Panic on the 5:22 '74
The Patsy '64
The Projectionist '71
Vasectomy: A Delicate Matter
  '86

Andras Balint
Colonel Redl '84
Father '67
A Happy New Year! '79
Love Film '70
Stalin '92

Eszter Balint
Bail Jumper '89
The Linguini Incident '91
Stranger than Paradise '84

Fairuza Balk
Gas Food Lodging '92
Outside Chance of Maximillian
  Glick '88
Return to Oz '85
Shame '92
Valmont '89
The Worst Witch '86

Frank Ball
Boothill Brigade '37
Feud Maker '38
The Forty-Niners '32
Galloping Romeo '33
Gun Lords of Stirrup Basin '37
When a Man Rides Alone '33

Lucille Ball
Abbott and Costello in
  Hollywood '45
The Affairs of Annabel '38
Annabel Takes a Tour/Maid's
  Night Out '38
Beauty for the Asking '39
Best Foot Forward '43
Big Street '42
Comedy Classics '35
Dance, Girl, Dance '40
Dark Corner '46
DuBarry Was a Lady '43
Easy Living '49
Fancy Pants '50
Five Came Back '39
Follow the Fleet '36
Forever Darling '56
The Fuller Brush Girl '50
A Girl, a Guy and a Gob '41
Having Wonderful Time '38
Having Wonderful Time/
  Carnival Boat '38
Hedda Hopper's Hollywood '42
Her Husband's Affairs '47
I Dream Too Much '35
Joy of Living '38
The Long, Long Trailer '54
Look Who's Laughing '41
Mame '74
Miss Grant Takes Richmond
  '49
Next Time I Marry '38
Panama Lady '39
Roberta '35
Roman Scandals '33
Room Service '38

Seven Days' Leave '42
Sorrowful Jones '49
Stage Door '37
That Girl from Paris '36
Thousands Cheer '43
Too Many Girls '40
Top Hat '35
Valley of the Sun '42
Without Love '45
You Can't Fool Your Wife '40
Yours, Mine & Ours '68
Ziegfeld Follies '46

Nicholas Ball
Claudia '85
The House that Bled to Death
  '81
Lifeforce '85

Vincent Ball
Blonde Blackmailer '58
Blood of the Vampire '58
Dead Lucky '60
Demolition '77
A Matter of WHO '62
Not Tonight Darling '72
Sirens '94
Terror Ship '54

Carl Ballantine
Hollywood Chaos '89
Mr. Saturday Night '92
Revenge of the Cheerleaders
  '76
Speedway '68
World's Greatest Lover '77

Kaye Ballard
Eternity '90
Fate '90
The Girl Most Likely '57
Modern Love '90
The Ritz '76
Tiger Warsaw '87

Smith Ballew
Gun Cargo '49
Hawaiian Buckaroo '38
Panamint's Bad Man '38
Rawhide '38
Roll Along Cowboy '37

Jean-Francois Balmer
Madame Bovary '91
Window Shopping '86

Martin Balsam
After the Fox '66
Al Capone '59
All the President's Men '76
The Anderson Tapes '71
Bedford Incident '65
Brand New Life '72
Breakfast at Tiffany's '61
Cape Fear '61
The Carpetbaggers '64
Catch-22 '70
Confessions of a Police
  Captain '72
Death Rage '77
Death Wish 3 '85
The Defender '57
Delta Force '86
Eyes Behind the Stars '72
The Good Guys and the Bad
  Guys '69
The Goodbye People '83
Grown Ups '86
Hard Frame '70
Harlow '65
Hombre '67
The House on Garibaldi Street
  '79
Innocent Prey '88
The Lindbergh Kidnapping
  Case '76
Little Big Man '70
Little Gloria...Happy at Last '84
Marjorie Morningstar '58
Miles to Go Before I Sleep '74
Mitchell '75
Murder in Space '85
Murder on the Orient Express
  '74
The People vs. Jean Harris '81
P.I. Private Investigations '87
Psycho '60
Queenie '87
Raid on Entebbe '77
St. Elmo's Fire '85
The Salamander '82
Season for Assassins '71
Silver Bears '78

Spaghetti Western '69
The Stone Killer '73
Summer Wishes, Winter
  Dreams '73
The Taking of Pelham One Two
  Three '74
A Thousand Clowns '65
Tora! Tora! Tora! '70
Twelve Angry Men '57
Two Minute Warning '76
The Warning '80

Talia Balsam
Calamity Jane '82
Consenting Adult '85
Crawlspace '86
In the Mood '87
Kent State '81
The Kindred '87
Mass Appeal '84
Nadia '84
On the Edge: The Survival of
  Dana '79
Private Investigations '87
Sunnyside '79
Trust Me '89

Kirk Baltz
Reservoir Dogs '92
Skin Art '93

Gerry Bamman
The Chase '91
Home Alone 2: Lost in New
  York '92
Lightning Over Water '80
Lorenzo's Oil '92
The Ten Million Dollar Getaway
  '91

Anne Bancroft
Agnes of God '85
The Bell Jar '79
Bert Rigby, You're a Fool '89
Broadway Bound '92
Demetrius and the Gladiators
  '54
Don't Bother to Knock '52
84 Charing Cross Road '86
The Elephant Man '80
Fatso '80
Garbo Talks '84
Girl in Black Stockings '57
The Graduate '67
The Hindenburg '75
Honeymoon in Vegas '92
Jesus of Nazareth '77
Lipstick '76
Malice '93
The Miracle Worker '62
Mr. Jones '93
'night, Mother '86
Nightfall '56
Point of No Return '93
Prisoner of Second Avenue '74
The Restless Breed '58
Savage Wilderness '55
Silent Movie '76
The Slender Thread '65
To Be or Not to Be '83
Torch Song Trilogy '88
Treasure of the Golden Condor
  '53
The Turning Point '77
Young Winston '72

Bradford Bancroft
Damned River '89
A Time to Die '91

George Bancroft
Angels with Dirty Faces '38
Docks of New York '28
Each Dawn I Die '39
Hell-Ship Morgan '36
Little Men '40
Mr. Deeds Goes to Town '36
Old Ironsides '26
The Pony Express '25
Stagecoach '39
Texas '41
Whistling in Dixie '42
White Gold '28
Young Tom Edison '40

Antonio Banderas
The House of the Spirits '93
Labyrinth of Passion '82
Law of Desire '86
The Mambo Kings '92
Matador '86
Philadelphia '93
Tie Me Up! Tie Me Down! '90

Women on the Verge of a
  Nervous Breakdown '88

Kanu Banerjee
Aparajito '58
Pather Panchali '54

Karuna Banerjee
Aparajito '58
Pather Panchali '54

Victor Banerjee
Bitter Moon '92
Foreign Body '86
The Home and the World '84
Hullabaloo Over Georgie &
  Bonnie's Pictures '78
A Passage to India '84

Lisa Banes
Cocktail '88
The Hotel New Hampshire '84
Look Back in Anger '80
Marie '85

Joy Bang
Messiah of Evil '74
Night of the Cobra Woman '72
Play It Again, Sam '72

Tallulah Bankhead
Die! Die! My Darling! '65
Lifeboat '44
The Making of a Legend:
  ''Gone With the Wind'' '89
Stage Door Canteen '43

Aaron Banks
The Bodyguard '76
Fist of Fear, Touch of Death '77

Jonathan Banks
Armed and Dangerous '86
Assassin '86
Beverly Hills Cop '84
Boiling Point '93
Cold Steel '87
Freejack '92
Nadia '84
There Goes the Neighborhood
  '92

Leslie Banks
The Arsenal Stadium Mystery
  '39
Chamber of Horrors '40
Cottage to Let '41
Eye Witness '49
Fire Over England '37
Henry V '44
Jamaica Inn '39
Madeleine '50
The Man Who Knew Too Much
  '34
The Most Dangerous Game '32
Sanders of the River '35
Transatlantic Tunnel '35
21 Days '37

Vilma Banky
Blood and Sand/Son of the
  Sheik '26
The Eagle '25
Son of the Sheik '26

Ian Bannen
The Big Man: Crossing the Line
  '91
Bite the Bullet '75
Blue Ice '92
Carlton Browne of the F.O. '59
The Courier '88
Damage '92
Defense of the Realm '85
Doomwatch '72
Driver's Seat '73
Eye of the Needle '81
The Flight of the Phoenix '65
Fright '71
From Beyond the Grave '73
The Gathering Storm '74
George's Island '91
Ghost Dad '90
Hope and Glory '87
Mackintosh Man '73
The Offence '73
The Prodigal '83
Ride to Glory '71
The Sound and the Silence '93
A Tale of Two Cities '58
The Third Key '57
Too Late the Hero '70
The Watcher in the Woods '81

John Banner
The Fallen Sparrow '43
Guilty of Treason '50

Togetherness '70

Reggie Bannister
Phantasm '79
Phantasm II '88
Silent Night, Deadly Night 4: Initiation '90
Survival Quest '89

Jack Bannon
DaVinci's War '92
Miracle of the Heart: A Boys Town Story '86
Take Your Best Shot '82

Jim Bannon
The Fighting Redhead '50
Man from Colorado '49
Unknown World '51

Ildiko Bansagi
Meeting Venus '91
Mephisto '81

Nina Bara
Black Hills '48
Missile to the Moon '59

Theda Bara
A Fool There Was '14
The Love Goddesses '65
The Unchastened Woman '25

John Baragrey
Gamera, the Invincible '66
Pardners '56

Christine Baranski
Addams Family Values '93
Crackers '84
The Night We Never Met '93
9 1/2 Weeks '86
The Ref '93
Reversal of Fortune '90
To Dance with the White Dog '93

Olivia Barash
Child of Glass '78
Dr. Alien '88
Grave Secrets '89
Repo Man '83
Tuff '85

Richie Barathy
Body Trouble '92
Caged Fury '90

Luca Barbareschi
Bye Bye Baby '88
Private Affairs '89

Adrienne Barbeau
Back to School '86
Cannibal Women in the Avocado Jungle of Death '89
Cannonball Run '81
Charlie and the Great Balloon Chase '82
The Crash of Flight 401 '78
Creepshow '82
Double-Crossed '91
Escape from New York '81
The Fog '79
Magic on Love Island '80
Next One '84
Open House '86
Red Alert '77
Return to Fantasy Island '77
Seduced '85
Swamp Thing '82
Terror at London Bridge '85
Two Evil Eyes '90

Ellen Barber
Blood Bride
Born Beautiful '82
The Premonition '75

Frances Barber
Castaway '87
Pete Townshend: White City '85
Prick Up Your Ears '87
Sammy & Rosie Get Laid '87
We Think the World of You '88
A Zed & Two Noughts '88

Glynis Barber
Edge of Sanity '89
The Wicked Lady '83
Yesterday's Hero '79

Katie Barberi
The Garbage Pail Kids Movie '87
Not Quite Human 2 '89

Urbano Barberini
Demons '86

Gor '88
Outlaw of Gor '87
Terror at the Opera '88
Torrents of Spring '90

George Barbier
The Adventures of Marco Polo '38
Little Miss Broadway '38
The Man Who Came to Dinner '41
The Merry Widow '34
My Lucky Star '38
On the Avenue '37
Week-End In Havana '41
Wife Versus Secretary '36

Don Barclay
Border Phantom '37
Outlaw Express '38
Sweetheart of the Navy '37
Thunder in the Desert '38

Joan Barclay
The Black Dragons '42
Blake of Scotland Yard '36
The Corpse Vanishes '42
Feud of the West '36
Finishing School '33
Flying Wild '41
The Glory Trail '36
Lightnin' Carson Rides Again '38
Outlaw's Paradise '39
Phantom Patrol '36
Prison Shadows '36
Sagebrush Law '43
Shadow of Chinatown '36
The Shanghai Cobra '45
West of Nevada '36
Whirlwind Horseman '38

Roy Barcroft
Arizona Cowboy '49
Bells of Rosarita '45
Below the Border '42
Billy the Kid Versus Dracula '66
Calling Wild Bill Elliott '43
D-Day on Mars '45
Dawn on the Great Divide '42
Don Amigo/Stage to Chino '40s
Don Daredevil Rides Again '51
Down Dakota Way '49
Eyes of Texas '48
Federal Agents vs. Underworld, Inc. '49
The Frontiersman '38
G-Men Never Forget '48
Haunted Harbor '44
Hoodlum Empire '52
Hopalong Cassidy: Renegade Trail '39
Hoppy Serves a Writ '43
Jesse James Rides Again '47
The Last Hunt '56
Manhunt of Mystery Island '45
Marshal of Cedar Rock '53
North of the Great Divide '50
The Purple Monster Strikes '45
Radar Men from the Moon '52
Raiders of Sunset Pass '43
Renegade Trail '39
Sagebrush Law '43
The Showdown '40
Six Gun Gospel '43
Son of Zorro '47
Stagecoach to Denver '46
Sunset in El Dorado '45
Sunset on the Desert '42
The Topeka Terror '45
The Vanishing Westerner '50
Vigilantes of Boom Town '46

Trevor Bardette
Doomed Caravan '41
Gun Crazy '49
Hills of Oklahoma '50
The Monolith Monsters '57
Omoo Omoo, the Shark God '49
The Secret Code '42
Thunder Road '58

Aleksander Bardini
The Double Life of Veronique '91
No End '84

Brigitte Bardot
And God Created Woman '57
The Bride Is Much Too Beautiful '58
A Coeur Joie '67
Contempt '64

Crazy for Love '52
Dear Brigitte '65
Doctor at Sea '56
Head Over Heels '67
Le Repos du Guerrier '62
Legend of Frenchie King '71
Mademoiselle Striptease '57
Ravishing Idiot '64
Shalako '68
Spirits of the Dead '68
That Naughty Girl '58
A Very Private Affair '62
Viva Maria! '65
Voulez-Vous Danser Avec Moi? '59
The Women '69

Edda Barends
Broken Mirrors '85
Question of Silence '83

Lynn Bari
Abbott and Costello Meet the Keystone Kops '54
The Amazing Mr. X '48
The Bridge of San Luis Rey '44
El Fego Baca: Six-Gun Law '54
Francis Joins the WACs '54
Hello, Frisco, Hello '43
I Dream of Jeannie '52
Kit Carson '40
The Magnificent Dope '42
Nocturne '46
Orchestra Wives '42
Shock! '46
Sun Valley Serenade '41
Trauma '62

Sophie Barjac
Alice '86
Holiday Hotel '77

Jess Barker
Dragonfly Squadron '54
Kentucky Rifle '55

Lex Barker
Apaches Last Battle '64
Away All Boats '56
The Black Devils of Kali '55
Executioner of Venice '63
The Farmer's Daughter '47
Girl in Black Stockings '57
The Invisible Dr. Mabuse '62
La Dolce Vita '60
Mission in Morocco '59
Mr. Blandings Builds His Dream House '48
Pirates of the Coast '61
A Place Called Glory '66
The Return of Dr. Mabuse '61
Strange Awakening '58
The Torture Chamber of Dr. Sadism '69
Velvet Touch '48
Woman Times Seven '67

Ronnie Barker
The Best of the Two Ronnies '70s
The Man Outside '68
Open All Hours '83
Porridge '91

Steve Barkett
Dark Universe '93
Dinosaur Island '93

Ellen Barkin
Act of Vengeance '86
The Adventures of Buckaroo Banzai Across the Eighth Dimension '84
The Big Easy '87
Blood Money: The Story of Clinton and Nadine '88
Daniel '83
Desert Bloom '86
Diner '82
Down by Law '86
Eddie and the Cruisers '83
Enormous Changes '83
Harry & Son '84
Into the West '92
Johnny Handsome '89
Kent State '81
Mac '93
Man Trouble '92
The Princess Who Never Laughed '84
Sea of Love '89
Siesta '87
Switch '91
Tender Mercies '83
Terminal Choice '85

This Boy's Life '93
Trumps '88

Peter Barkworth
Champions '83
The Littlest Horse Thieves '76

Binnie Barnes
The Adventures of Marco Polo '38
Call Out the Marines '42
Decameron Nights '53
The Divorce of Lady X '38
Forty Carats '73
Holiday '38
I Married an Angel '42
In Old California '42
It's in the Bag '45
The Last of the Mohicans '36
Melody Master '41
Private Life of Don Juan '34
The Private Life of Henry VIII '33
The Spanish Main '45
The Three Musketeers '39
The Time of Their Lives '46
The Trouble with Angels '66
Where Angels Go, Trouble Follows '68

Christopher Barnes
Angel of Fury '93
Battle of the Bullies '85
Tut & Tuttle '82

Joanna Barnes
I Wonder Who's Killing Her Now? '76
Kill My Wife...Please!
Spartacus '60
The War Wagon '67

Priscilla Barnes
Beyond Reason '77
Body Trouble '92
Delta Fox '77
The Last Married Couple in America '80
License to Kill '89
Lords of the Deep '89
The Seniors '78
Stepfather 3: Father's Day '92
Talons of the Eagle '92
Texas Detour '77
Time Machine '78
Traxx '87

Charlie Barnett
D.C. Cab '84
My Man Adam '86

Chester Barnett
Trilby '17
The Wishing Ring '14

Vince Barnett
Baby Face Morgan '42
Boots of Destiny '37
Captive Wild Woman '43
Charade '53
The Corpse Vanishes '42
Crimson Romance '34
The Death Kiss '33
East Side Kids/The Lost City '35
Gangs, Inc. '41
I Killed That Man '42
I Live My Life '35
The Prizefighter and the Lady '33
Red Planet Mars '52
Ride 'Em Cowgirl '41
Shoot to Kill '47
Thunder in the Pines '48
We're in the Legion Now '37
X Marks the Spot '42
Yellow Cargo '36

Bruce Baron
Challenge the Ninja '80s
Fireback '78
Ninja Champion '80s
Ninja Destroyer '70s
Ninja Hunt '80s

Sandy Baron
Birdy '84
Broadway Danny Rose '84
If It's Tuesday, This Must Be Belgium '69
Leprechaun 2 '94
Motorama '91
The Out-of-Towners '70

Byron Barr
Big Town '47

Double Indemnity '44
Down Dakota Way '49
Pitfall '48

Jean-Marc Barr
The Big Blue '88
Hope and Glory '87
The Plague '92
Zentropa '92

Patrick Barr
The Case of the Frightened Lady '39
Flesh and Blood Show '73
The Godsend '79
House of Whipcord '75
Sailing Along '38
The Satanic Rites of Dracula '73

Sharon Barr
Archer: The Fugitive from the Empire '81
Spittin' Image '83

Maria Barranco
Don Juan, My Love '90
Tie Me Up! Tie Me Down! '90
Women on the Verge of a Nervous Breakdown '88

Robert Barrat
The Adventures of Mark Twain '44
Bad Lands '39
Captain Caution '40
Devil Dogs of the Air '35
Distant Drums '51
Heroes for Sale '33
Mary of Scotland '36
Northwest Passage '40
Shadows Over Shanghai '38
Strangler of the Swamp '46

Jean-Louis Barrault
Beethoven '36
Children of Paradise '44
La Nuit de Varennes '82
La Ronde '51
The Longest Day '62
The Testament of Dr. Cordelier '59

Marie-Christine Barrault
Chloe in the Afternoon '72
Cousin, Cousine '76
The Daydreamer '75
Jesus of Montreal '89
L'Etat Sauvage '78
The Medusa Touch '78
My Night at Maud's '69
Stardust Memories '80
Swann in Love '84
Table for Five '83

Edith Barrett
I Walked with a Zombie '43
Jane Eyre '44
Lady for a Night '42

Jane Barrett
Eureka Stockade '49
The Sword & the Rose '53

John Barrett
American Kickboxer 1 '91
Lights! Camera! Murder! '89
To the Death '93

Judith Barrett
The Road to Singapore '40
Yellowstone '36

Nancy Barrett
Belizaire the Cajun '86
House of Dark Shadows '70
Night of Dark Shadows '71

Nitchie Barrett
Preppies '82
A Time to Die '91

Ray Barrett
Rebel '85
Revenge '71
Waterfront '83
Where the Green Ants Dream '84

Barbara Barrie
The Bell Jar '79
Breaking Away '79
Child of Glass '78
End of the Line '88
The Execution '85
Private Benjamin '80
Real Men '87

Barrie ►cont.

To Race the Wind '80
Two of a Kind '82

Judith Barrie
Hidden Gold '33
Party Girls '29

Mona Barrie
Cass Timberlane '47
Dawn on the Great Divide '42
One Night of Love '34
Today I Hang '42

Wendy Barrie
Dead End '37
Five Came Back '39
Follies Girl '43
The Hound of the Baskervilles '39
I Am the Law '38
If I Were Rich '33
The Private Life of Henry VIII '33
The Saint Strikes Back '39
The Saint Strikes Back: Criminal Court '46
The Saint Takes Over '40
Vengeance '37
Wedding Rehearsal '32

Edgar Barrier
Arabian Nights '42
Cobra Woman '44
The Giant Claw '57
The Phantom of the Opera '43

Pat Barringer
The Acid Eaters '67
Orgy of the Dead '65

Phyliss Barrington
The Drifter '32
Sucker Money '34

Bob Barron
Ballad of a Gunfighter '64
Song of Old Wyoming '45

Keith Barron
Baby Love '69
Con Man '92
Nothing But the Night '72

Robert Barron
Bill & Ted's Excellent Adventure '89
The Caravan Trail '46
Guns of the Law '44
Sea Hound '47
Tank Commando '59

Bruce Barry
The Good Wife '86
Plunge Into Darkness '77

Donald (Don "Red") Barry
Adventures of Red Ryder '40
Blazing Stewardesses '75
Border Rangers '50
California Joe '43
Frontier Vengeance '40
Gunfire '50
Hard Frame '70
I Shot Billy the Kid '50
Iron Angel '64
Outlaw Gang '49
Panama Patrol '39
The Purple Heart '44
Red Desert '50
Ringside '49
Saga of Death Valley '39
The Shakiest Gun in the West '68
Sinners in Paradise '38
The Sombrero Kid '42
Square Dance Jubilee '51
Sundown Fury '42
Sundown Kid '43
Texas Layover '75
Tough Assignment '49
Trail of the Mounties '47
Train to Tombstone '50
Western Double Feature 9: LaRue & Beery '40s
Western Double Feature 15 '50
Wyoming Outlaw '39

Gene Barry
The Adventures of Nellie Bly '81
The Atomic City '52
Back from Eternity '56

China Gate '57
Columbo: Prescription Murder '67
A Cry for Love '80
The Gambler Returns: The Luck of the Draw '93
Maroc 7 '67
Perry Mason: The Case of the Lost Love '87
Red Garters '54
Second Coming of Suzanne '80
Soldier of Fortune '55
Subterfuge '68
Suzanne '80
Thunder Road '58
The 27 Day '57
The War of the Worlds '53

Leon Barry
King of the Wild Horses '24
The Three Musketeers '21

Neill Barry
Joey '85
O.C. and Stiggs '87
Old Enough '84

Patricia Barry
Bogie: The Last Hero '80
Sammy, the Way-Out Seal '62
Twilight Zone: The Movie '83

Phyllis Barry
Goodbye Love '34
What! No Beer? '33

Raymond J. Barry
Born on the Fourth of July '89
Cool Runnings '93
Cop '88
Daddy's Boys '87
Falling Down '93
K2: The Ultimate High '92
Rapid Fire '92
Year of the Dragon '85

Tony Barry
Goodbye Pork Pie '81
Hard Knocks '80
Little Boy Lost '78
The Quest '86
Shame '87
We of the Never Never '82

Wesley Barry
Battling Bunyon '24
The Country Kid '23
Sunny Skies '30

Drew Barrymore
Altered States '80
The Amy Fisher Story '93
Babes in Toyland '86
Bad Girls '94
Cat's Eye '85
A Conspiracy of Love '87
Doppelganger: The Evil Within '90
E.T.: The Extra-Terrestrial '82
Far from Home '89
Firestarter '84
Guncrazy '92
Irreconcilable Differences '84
Motorama '91
Poison Ivy '92
See You in the Morning '89
Sketch Artist '92
Strange Tales/Ray Bradbury Theatre '86
Wayne's World 2 '93

Ethel Barrymore
The Farmer's Daughter '47
Just for You '52
Moonrise '48
None But the Lonely Heart '44
The Paradine Case '47
Pinky '49
Portrait of Jennie '48
Rasputin and the Empress '32
The Spiral Staircase '46
That Midnight Kiss '49
Young at Heart '54

John Barrymore
Beau Brummel '24
The Beloved Rogue '27
A Bill of Divorcement '32
Bulldog Drummond Comes Back '37
Bulldog Drummond's Peril '38
Bulldog Drummond's Revenge '37
Bulldog Drummond's Revenge/ Bulldog Drummond's Peril '38

Dinner at Eight '33
Dr. Jekyll and Mr. Hyde '20
Don Juan '26
Grand Hotel '32
The Great Man Votes '38
The Horror of It All '91
The Invisible Woman '40
Marie Antoinette '38
Maytime '37
Playmates '41
Rasputin and the Empress '32
Romeo and Juliet '36
State's Attorney '31
Svengali '31
The Tempest '28
The Tempest/The Eagle '27
Topaze '33
Twentieth Century '34

John Blythe Barrymore, Jr.
Americana '81
A Game of Crime '60
High Lonesome '50
High School Confidential '58
Never Love a Stranger '58
Smokey Bites the Dust '81

Lionel Barrymore
Ah, Wilderness! '35
America/The Fall of Babylon '24
Camille '36
Captains Courageous '37
David Copperfield '35
Devil Doll '36
Dinner at Eight '33
Dr. Kildare's Strange Case '40
Duel in the Sun '46
A Free Soul '31
The Girl from Missouri '34
The Gorgeous Hussy '36
Grand Hotel '32
A Guy Named Joe '44
It's a Wonderful Life '46
Key Largo '48
Lady Be Good '41
Let Freedom Ring '39
The Little Colonel '35
Lone Star '52
Malaya '49
Mark of the Vampire '35
Mata Hari '32
Navy Blue and Gold '37
On Borrowed Time '39
Rasputin and the Empress '32
The Return of Peter Grimm '35
Sadie Thompson '28
Saratoga '37
Short Films of D.W. Griffith, Vol. 2 '09
Since You Went Away '44
Test Pilot '38
Thousands Cheer '43
Treasure Island '34
The Valley of Decision '45
West of Zanzibar '28
You Can't Take It with You '38

Paul Bartel
Amazon Women on the Moon '87
Chopping Mall '86
Desire and Hell at Sunset Motel '92
Eating Raoul '82
Far Out Man '89
Frankenweenie '84
Hollywood Boulevard '76
Killer Party '86
Liquid Dreams '92
Mortuary Academy '91
Out of the Dark '88
Piranha '78
The Pope Must Diet '91
Pucker Up and Bark Like a Dog '89
Rock 'n' Roll High School '79
Scenes from the Class Struggle in Beverly Hills '89

Eddie Barth
Thunder and Lightning '77
Twenty Dollar Star '91

Richard Barthelmess
Broken Blossoms '19
The Cabin in the Cotton '32
The Dropkick '27
Heroes for Sale '33
The Idol Dancer '20
Just Suppose '26

The Love Flower '20
Only Angels Have Wings '39
Ranson's Folly '26
Shore Leave '25
Soul-Fire '25
The Spoilers '42
Spy of Napoleon '36
Tol'able David '21
Way Down East '20

Freddie Bartholomew
Anna Karenina '35
Captains Courageous '37
David Copperfield '35
Listen, Darling '38
Little Lord Fauntleroy '36
St. Benny the Dip '51
Sepia Cinderella '47
Tom Brown's School Days '40

Bennie Bartlett
Clipped Wings '53
Master Minds '49

Bonnie Bartlett
Dave '93
The Deliberate Stranger '86
Dempsey '83
A Long Way Home '81
Love Letters '83
Rape and Marriage: The Rideout Case '80
Twins '88

Robin Bartlett
Alice '90
Baby Boom '87
Deceived '91
Fallen Angels 1 '93
If Looks Could Kill '91
Lean on Me '89
Regarding Henry '91

Eva Bartok
Blood and Black Lace '64
Crimson Pirate '52
The Gamma People '56
Naked in the Night '58
Norman Conquest '53
Operation Amsterdam '60
S.O.S. Pacific '60
Spaceways '53

Luciano Bartoli
Bizarre '87
Henry IV '85

Buzz Barton
Apache Kid's Escape '30
Feud of the West '35
The Lone Defender '32
Mystery Trooper '32
Powdersmoke Range '35
The Riding Avenger '36
The Tonto Kid '35

Diana Barton
Body of Influence '93
Sexual Malice '93

Gregg Barton
Silver City Bonanza '51
West to Glory '47

James Barton
Here Comes the Groom '51
The Misfits '61
Naked Hills '56
The Time of Your Life '48

Peter Barton
Friday the 13th, Part 4: The Final Chapter '84
Hell Night '81

Billy Barty
Ace Crawford, Private Eye
The Amazing Dobermans '76
Body Slam '87
Cannon Movie Tales: Snow White '89
The Day of the Locust '75
Digging Up Business '91
Foul Play '78
Harum Scarum '65
Legend '85
Life Stinks '91
Masters of the Universe '87
Mickey the Great '39
A Midsummer Night's Dream '35
Night Patrol '85
Roustabout '64
Rumpelstiltskin '86
Tough Guys '86

Under the Rainbow '81
Willow '88
Wishful Thinking '92

Mikhail Baryshnikov
Company Business '91
Dancers '87
That's Dancing! '85
The Turning Point '77
White Nights '85

Gary Basaraba
Fried Green Tomatoes '91
One Magic Christmas '85

Richard Basehart
The Andersonville Trial '70
Being There '79
The Bounty Man '72
The Brothers Karamazov '58
Chato's Land '71
Flood! '76
Great Bank Hoax '78
Hans Brinker '69
He Walked by Night '48
Hitler '62
Island of Dr. Moreau '77
La Strada '54
Marilyn: The Untold Story '80
Moby Dick '56
Rage '72
The Rebels '79
Reign of Terror '49
The Swindle '55

Toni Basil
Angel 3: The Final Chapter '88
Easy Rider '69
Eating '90
Mother, Jugs and Speed '76
Pajama Party '64
Rockula '90
Slaughterhouse Rock '88

Kim Basinger
Batman '89
Blind Date '87
Cool World '92
Final Analysis '92
Fool for Love '86
From Here to Eternity '79
The Getaway '93
Hard Country '81
Killjoy '81
The Man Who Loved Women '83
The Marrying Man '91
My Stepmother Is an Alien '88
Nadine '87
The Natural '84
Never Say Never Again '83
9 1/2 Weeks '86
No Mercy '86
The Real McCoy '93
Wayne's World 2 '93

Elya Baskin
Enemies, a Love Story '89
Moscow on the Hudson '84
The Name of the Rose '86
Spy Trap '92

Marianne Basler
Overseas: Three Women with Man Trouble '90
A Soldier's Tale '91

Lena Basquette
Hard Hombre '31
A Night for Crime '42
Pleasure '31
Rose of Rio Grande '38

Alfie Bass
The Fearless Vampire Killers '67
The Lavender Hill Mob '51
Man on the Run '49

Albert Basserman
Foreign Correspondent '40
Invisible Agent '42
Madame Curie '43
Melody Master '41
The Moon and Sixpence '42
The Private Affairs of Bel Ami '47
The Red Shoes '48
Reunion in France '42
Rhapsody in Blue '45
The Shanghai Gesture '42
Since You Went Away '44
A Woman's Face '41

Angela Bassett
Boyz N the Hood '91

City of Hope '91
Critters 4 '91
The Heroes of Desert Storm '91
The Jacksons: An American Dream '92
Malcolm X '92
Passion Fish '92
What's Love Got to Do With It? '93

Alexandra Bastedo
The Blood Spattered Bride '72
Draw! '81
Find the Lady '75
The Ghoul '75
Kashmiri Run '69

Michal Bat-Adam
Atalia '85
The House on Chelouche Street '73
I Love You Rosa '72
The Impossible Spy '87

Sylvia Bataille
The Crime of Monsieur Lange '36
A Day in the Country '46

Alexei Batalov
The Cranes are Flying '57
The Lady with the Dog '59
Moscow Does Not Believe in Tears '80

Nikolai Batalov
Bed and Sofa '27
Mother '26

Pierre Batcheff
Napoleon '27
Un Chien Andalou '28

Anthony Bate
Madhouse Mansion '74
Philby, Burgess and MacLean: Spy Scandal of the Century '84

Jason Bateman
Breaking the Rules '92
Can You Feel Me Dancing? '85
Necessary Roughness '91
A Taste for Killing '92
Teen Wolf Too '87

Justine Bateman
Can You Feel Me Dancing? '85
The Closer '91
Deadbolt '92
The Fatal Image '90
The Night We Never Met '93
Primary Motive '92
Satisfaction '88

Alan Bates
Britannia Hospital '82
Club Extinction '89
A Day in the Death of Joe Egg '71
Duet for One '86
An Englishman Abroad '83
The Entertainer '60
Far from the Madding Crowd '67
The Fixer '68
Georgy Girl '66
The Go-Between '71
Hamlet '90
In Celebration '75
A Kind of Loving '62
The King of Hearts '66
Mr. Frost '89
Nijinsky '80
Prayer for the Dying '87
Quartet '81
Return of the Soldier '82
The Rose '79
Separate Tables '83
The Shout '78
Silent Tongue '92
The Story of a Love Story '73
Trespasser '85
An Unmarried Woman '78
A Voyage 'Round My Father '89
We Think the World of You '88
Whistle Down the Wind '62
The Wicked Lady '83
Women in Love '70
Zorba the Greek '64

Barbara Bates
The Caddy '53
The Inspector General '49

June Bride '48
Let's Make it Legal '51
Rhapsody '54

Florence Bates
The Chocolate Soldier '41
Diary of a Chambermaid '46
Heaven Can Wait '43
I Remember Mama '48
The Judge Steps Out '49
A Letter to Three Wives '49
Love Crazy '41
Lullaby of Broadway '51
Mexican Spitfire at Sea '42
Mr. Lucky '43
The Moon and Sixpence '43
My Dear Secretary '49
Portrait of Jennie '48
Rebecca '40
Road Show '41
San Antonio '45
The Secret Life of Walter Mitty '47
Since You Went Away '44
The Son of Monte Cristo '41
The Tuttles of Tahiti '42
Winter Meeting '48

Granville Bates
The Great Man Votes '38
Next Time I Marry '38

Jeanne Bates
Eraserhead '78
The Mask of Dijon '46
Mom '84
Sabaka '55
The Strangler '64

Kathy Bates
At Play in the Fields of the Lord '91
Come Back to the Five & Dime Jimmy Dean, Jimmy Dean '82
Dick Tracy '90
Fried Green Tomatoes '91
High Stakes '89
A Home of Our Own '93
Hostages '93
Men Don't Leave '89
Misery '90
The Morning After '86
Murder Ordained '87
North '94
Prelude to a Kiss '92
Roe vs. Wade '89
Shadows and Fog '92
Signs of Life '89
Straight Time '78
Summer Heat '87
Used People '92
White Palace '90

Michael Bates
Bedazzled '68
A Clockwork Orange '71
Patton '70

Paul Bates
Coming to America '88
Crazy People '90

Ralph Bates
Dr. Jekyll and Sister Hyde '71
Dynasty of Fear '72
The Graveyard '74
The Horror of Frankenstein '70
I Don't Want to Be Born '75
Letters to an Unknown Lover '84
Lust for a Vampire '71
Murder Motel '74
Poldark '75
Second Chance '80
Taste the Blood of Dracula '70

Randall Batinkoff
Buffy the Vampire Slayer '92
For Keeps '88
The Player '92
School Ties '92
Streetwalkin' '85

Rick Battaglia
Cold Steel for Tortuga '65
Roland the Mighty '58
'Tis a Pity She's a Whore '73

Patrick Bauchau
And the Band Played On '93
Blood Ties '93
Chain of Desire '93
Creepers '85
Double Identity '89
Emmanuelle 4 '84

Every Breath '93
The Music Teacher '88
The Rapture '91
State of Things '82

Belinda Bauer
Archer: The Fugitive from the Empire '81
A Case for Murder '93
Flashdance '83
The Game of Love '90
RoboCop 2 '90
The Rosary Murders '87
Samson and Delilah '84
Servants of Twilight '91
The Sins of Dorian Gray '82
Timerider '83
Winter Kills '79

Michelle (McClellan) Bauer
Deadly Embrace '88
Death Row Diner '88
Evil Toons '90
Hollywood Chainsaw Hookers '88
Night of the Living Babes '87
Nightmare Sisters '87
Phantom Empire '87
Tomb '86
Wild Man '89

Steven Bauer
The Beast '88
A Climate for Killing '91
False Arrest '91
Gleaming the Cube '89
Raising Cain '92
Red Shoe Diaries 2: Double Dare '92
Running Scared '86
Scarface '83
Snapdragon '93
Sweet Poison '91
Sword of Gideon '86
Thief of Hearts '84
Wildfire '88
Woman of Desire '93

Ricardo Bauleo
The Curious Dr. Humpp '70
Lost Diamond '74

Erna Martha Bauman
Invasion of the Vampires '61
World of the Vampires '60

Katherine Baumann
Chrome and Hot Leather '71
Slashed Dreams '74

Harry Baur
Beethoven '36
Crime and Punishment '35
Poil de Carotte '31
Volpone '39

Francis Bavier
The Day the Earth Stood Still '51
Horizons West '52
It Started with a Kiss '59
The Lady Says No '51
The Stooge '51

Barbara Baxley
All Fall Down '62
Come Along with Me '84
Countdown '71
Nashville '75
A Shock to the System '90

Alan Baxter
Abe Lincoln in Illinois '40
Behind Prison Walls '43
Each Dawn I Die '39
It Could Happen to You '37
Saboteur '42
The Set-Up '49
Shadow of the Thin Man '41
Wide Open Faces '38
Wild Weed '49

Anne Baxter
All About Eve '50
Angel on My Shoulder '46
Carnival Story '54
Cimarron '60
Crash Dive '43
East of Eden '80
The Fighting Sullivans '42
Guest in the House '45
Homecoming '48
I Confess '53
Jane Austen in Manhattan '80

The Magnificent Ambersons '42
Masks of Death '86
The North Star '43
The Razor's Edge '46
The Ten Commandments '56
Three Violent People '57
Ticket to Tomahawk '50
Walk on the Wild Side '62

Meredith Baxter Birney
Ben '72
Beulah Land '80
Bittersweet Love '76
Broken Badge '85
The Family Man '79
The Invasion of Carol Enders '74
Jezebel's Kiss '90
The Kissing Place '90
Little Women '78
The Stranger Who Looks Like Me '74
Take Your Best Shot '82

Keith Baxter
Ash Wednesday '73
Berlin Blues '89
Chimes at Midnight '67

Lynsey Baxter
The French Lieutenant's Woman '81
The Girl in a Swing '89
To the Lighthouse '83

Warner Baxter
Adam Had Four Sons '41
Broadway Bill '34
42nd Street '33
Linda '29
Penthouse '33
Stand Up and Cheer '34
Vogues of 1938 '37
West of Zanzibar '28

Francis Bay
The Attic '80
Critters 3 '91
The Neighbor '93
The Pit & the Pendulum '91
Single White Female '92

Nathalie Baye
And the Band Played On '93
Beau Pere '81
Beethoven's Nephew '88
Day for Night '73
The Green Room '78
Honeymoon '87
La Balance '82
The Man Inside '90
The Return of Martin Guerre '83

Gary Bayer
Not My Kid '85
Promised a Miracle '88
Will: G. Gordon Liddy '82

Geoffrey Bayldon
The Bushbaby '70
Madame Sousatzka '88
Porridge '79

Lawrence Bayne
Black King '85
A Whisper to a Scream '88

Michael Beach
Cadence '89
In a Shallow Grave '88
Internal Affairs '90
Lean on Me '89
One False Move '91
Weekend War '88

Stephanie Beacham
And Now the Screaming Starts '73
The Confessional '75
The Dying Truth '91
Foreign Affairs '93
Horror Planet '80
The Nightcomers '72
Super Bitch '89
Troop Beverly Hills '89

John Beal
Amityville 3: The Demon '83
Break of Hearts '35
Double Wedding '37
Edge of Darkness '43
The Firm '93
The Great Commandment '41

I Am the Law '38
The Kid Who Loved Christmas '90
Les Miserables '35
Little Minister '34
Madame X '37
Ten Who Dared '60

Jennifer Beals
Blood & Concrete: A Love Story '90
The Bride '85
Cinderella '84
Club Extinction '89
Day of Atonement '93
Flashdance '83
The Gamble '88
In the Soup '92
Indecency '92
Split Decisions '88
Terror Stalks the Class Reunion '93
That's Dancing! '85
Vampire's Kiss '88

Orson Bean
Anatomy of a Murder '59
Final Judgement '92
Innerspace '87
Instant Karma '90
Lola '69
Movie Maker '86

Robert Bean
Creature from the Haunted Sea '60
The Wild Ride '60

Sean Bean
Black Beauty '94
Caravaggio '86
The Field '90
Lorna Doone '90
Patriot Games '92
Stormy Monday '88

Matthew "Stymie" Beard
Broken Strings '40
East of Eden '80
Little Rascals, Book 1 '30s
Little Rascals, Book 2 '30s
Little Rascals, Book 3 '38
Little Rascals, Book 4 '30s
Little Rascals, Book 5 '30s
Little Rascals, Book 6 '30s
Little Rascals, Book 7 '30s
Little Rascals, Book 9 '30s
Little Rascals, Book 16 '30s
Little Rascals: Choo Choo/ Fishy Tales '32
Little Rascals Christmas Special '79
Little Rascals Collector's Edition, Vol. 1-6
Little Rascals Comedy Classics, Vol. 1
Little Rascals Comedy Classics, Vol. 2
Little Rascals: Fish Hooky/ Spooky Hooky '33
Little Rascals: Honkey Donkey/ Sprucin' Up '34
Little Rascals: Little Sinner/Two Too Young '35
Little Rascals: Mush and Milk/ Three Men in a Tub '33
Little Rascals: Pups is Pups/ Three Smart Boys '30
Little Rascals: Readin' and Writin'/Mail and Female '31
Little Rascals: Reunion in Rhythm/Mike Fright '37
Little Rascals: Spanky/Feed 'Em and Weep '32
Little Rascals: The Pinch Singer/Framing Youth '36
Little Rascals Two Reelers, Vol. 1 '29
Little Rascals Two Reelers, Vol. 2 '33
Little Rascals Two Reelers, Vol. 3 '36
Little Rascals Two Reelers, Vol. 4 '30
Little Rascals Two Reelers, Vol. 5 '34
Little Rascals Two Reelers, Vol. 6 '36
Little Rascals, Vol. 1 '29
Two-Gun Man from Harlem '38

Amanda Bearse
Fraternity Vacation '85
Fright Night '85
It's a Bundyful Life '92
Protocol '84

Emmanuelle Beart
Date with an Angel '87
La Belle Noiseuse '90
Manon of the Spring '87
Un Coeur en Hiver '93

Allyce Beasley
Moonlighting '85
Motorama '91
Silent Night, Deadly Night 4: Initiation '90
Stephen King's The Tommyknockers '93

Norman Beaton
Growing Pains '82
The Mighty Quinn '89
Playing Away '87

Clyde Beatty
Africa Screams '49
Darkest Africa '36
The Lost Jungle '34

Ned Beatty
All God's Children '80
Angel Square '92
Back to Hannibal: The Return of Tom Sawyer and Huckleberry Finn '90
Back to School '86
Big Bad John '90
The Big Bus '76
The Big Easy '87
Blind Vision '91
Captain America '89
Charlotte Forten's Mission: Experiment in Freedom '85
Chattahoochee '89
A Cry in the Wild '90
Deliverance '72
Dying Room Only '73
Ed and His Dead Mother '93
The Execution of Private Slovik '74
The Exorcist 2: The Heretic '77
The Fourth Protocol '87
Friendly Fire '79
Going Under '91
Gray Lady Down '77
Great Bank Hoax '78
The Guyana Tragedy: The Story of Jim Jones '80
The Haunting of Barney Palmer '90s
Hear My Song '91
Hopscotch '80
Illusions '91
The Incredible Shrinking Woman '81
Konrad '90s
The Last American Hero '73
Midnight Crossing '87
Mikey & Nicky '76
Ministry of Vengeance '89
Nashville '75
Network '76
1941 '79
Our Town '77
Physical Evidence '89
Pray TV '82
Prelude to a Kiss '92
Promises in the Dark '79
Purple People Eater '88
A Question of Love '78
Repossessed '90
Robert Kennedy and His Times '90
Rolling Vengeance '87
Rudy '93
Rumpelstiltskin '87
Shadows in the Storm '88
The Silver Streak '76
Sniper '93
Spy '89
Stroker Ace '83
Superman: The Movie '78
Superman 2 '80
Switching Channels '88
The Thief Who Came to Dinner '73
Time Trackers '88
Touched '82
The Toy '82
Tragedy of Flight 103: The Inside Story '91

The Trouble with Spies '87
The Unholy '88
White Lightning '73
Wise Blood '79
A Woman Called Golda '82

Robert Beatty
Against the Wind '48
Appointment with Crime '45
Captain Horatio Hornblower '51
Counterblast '48
The Love of Three Queens '54
Postmark for Danger '56
Postmark for Danger/ Quicksand '56
San Demetrio, London '47
Time Lock '57
Where Eagles Dare '68
Wings of Danger '52

Warren Beatty
All Fall Down '62
Bonnie & Clyde '67
Bugsy '91
Dick Tracy '90
Dollars '71
Heaven Can Wait '78
Ishtar '87
Lilith '64
McCabe & Mrs. Miller '71
Parallax View '74
Promise Her Anything '66
Reds '81
Roman Spring of Mrs. Stone '61
Shampoo '75
Splendor in the Grass '61

Hugh Beaumont
Danger Zone '91
The Fallen Sparrow '43
The Human Duplicators '64
The Lady Confesses '45
The Lost Continent '51
The Mole People '56
Money Madness '47
Objective, Burma! '45
Panama Menace '41
Phone Call from a Stranger '52
Pier 23 '51
Railroaded '47
Roaring City '51
The Seventh Victim '43
To the Shores of Tripoli '42

Lucy Beaumont
Condemned to Live '35
The Crowd '28
A Free Soul '31

Nicholas Beauvy
Rage '72
The Toolbox Murders '78

Terry Beaver
Impure Thoughts '86
To Dance with the White Dog '93

Louise Beavers
Big Street '42
Bullets or Ballots '38
Coquette '29
Delightfully Dangerous '45
Dixie Jamboree '44
DuBarry Was a Lady '43
General Spanky '36
Goodbye, My Lady '56
In the Money '34
The Jackie Robinson Story '50
Mr. Blandings Builds His Dream House '48
Reap the Wild Wind '42
She Done Him Wrong '33
Tammy and the Bachelor '57
Tell It to the Judge '49

Jennifer Beck
Gypsy '62
Tightrope '84

John Beck
Audrey Rose '77
The Big Bus '76
A Climate for Killing '91
Deadly Illusion '87
Fire and Rain '89
Great American Traffic Jam '80
Honor Thy Father and Mother: The True Story of the Menendez Brothers '94
In the Cold of the Night '89
King of the Pecos '36
Lawman '71
The Other Side of Midnight '77

Paperback Hero '73
Sky Riders '76
Sleeper '73
Three in the Attic '68
Time Machine '78

Julian Beck
Emergency '68
Oedipus Rex '67
Poltergeist 2: The Other Side '86
Signals Through the Flames '83

Kimberly Beck
Friday the 13th, Part 4: The Final Chapter '84
Massacre at Central High '76
Nightmare at Noon '87
Private War '90
Roller Boogie '79

Michael Beck
Blackout '85
Celebrity '85
Deadly Game '91
Fade to Black '93
The Golden Seal '83
Holocaust '78
Madman '79
Megaforce '82
Warlords of the 21st Century '82
The Warriors '79
Xanadu '80

Thomas Beck
Charlie Chan at the Opera '36
Charlie Chan in Paris '35

Graham Beckel
Hazel's People '75
Jennifer 8 '92
Lost Angels '89
The Money '75
O Pioneers! '91
The Paper Chase '73
Rising Son '91
Separate But Equal '91

Gerry Becker
Legacy of Lies '92
The Public Eye '92

Gretchen Becker
Firehead '90
Huck and the King of Hearts '93
Maniac Cop 3 '93

Hartmut Becker
Escape from Sobibor '87
Jenny's War '85

Scotty Beckett
Ali Baba and the Forty Thieves '43
Anthony Adverse '36
Battleground '49
The Charge of the Light Brigade '36
Conquest '37
Devil's Party '38
Heaven Can Wait '43
I Dream Too Much '35
The Jolson Story '46
Kings Row '41
Listen, Darling '38
Little Rascals, Book 7 '30s
Love Affair '39
Marie Antoinette '38
My Favorite Wife '40
Nancy Goes to Rio '50
The Oklahoman '56
Stand Up and Cheer '34

Kate Beckinsale
Much Ado About Nothing '93
One Against the Wind '91

Tony Beckley
Assault '70
The Fiend '71
The Italian Job '69

Henry Beckman
Family Reunion '88
The Man Upstairs '93

Reginald Beckwith
Burn Witch, Burn! '62
Men of Sherwood Forest '57

William Beckwith
Escape from Safehaven '88
Prime Evil '88

Don Beddoe
Buck Privates Come Home '47
The Enforcer '51

Golden Boy '39
Jack the Giant Killer '62
The Narrow Margin '52
Nickel Mountain '85
The Night of the Hunter '55

Bonnie Bedelia
The Big Fix '78
The Boy Who Could Fly '86
Death of an Angel '86
Die Hard '88
Die Hard 2: Die Harder '90
Fallen Angels 2 '93
Fat Man and Little Boy '89
The Fire Next Time '93
Heart Like a Wheel '83
Lady from Yesterday '85
Lovers and Other Strangers '70
Memorial Day '83
Needful Things '93
Presumed Innocent '90
Prince of Pennsylvania '88
A Question of Love '78
Salem's Lot '79
Somebody Has to Shoot the Picture '90
The Stranger '87
Switched at Birth '91
They Shoot Horses, Don't They? '69
Violets Are Blue '86
Walking Through the Fire '80
When the Time Comes '91

Barbara Bedford
The Broken Mask '28
Found Alive '34
The Last of the Mohicans '20
The Mad Whirl '25
Mockery '27
Tumbleweeds '25

Kabir Bedi
Archer: The Fugitive from the Empire '81
The Beast '88
Demon Rage '82
Octopussy '83
Terminal Entry '87

Guy Bedos
Pardon Mon Affaire '76
Pardon Mon Affaire, Too! '77

Alfonso Bedoya
The Stranger Wore a Gun '53
Treasure of the Sierra Madre '48

Janet Beecher
I'd Give My Life '36
The Mark of Zorro '40

David Beecroft
The Rain Killer '90
Shadowzone '90

Daniel Beer
Creepshow 2 '87
Point Break '91

Noah Beery, Jr.
Ace Drummond '36
The Avenging Hand '43
Bad Lands '39
The Bastard '78
The Capture of Grizzly Adams '82
The Doolins of Oklahoma '49
Fastest Gun Alive '56
Fighting with Kit Carson '33
Francis Gary Powers: The True Story of the U-2 Spy '76
Great American Traffic Jam '80
Great Chase '63
Gung Ho! '43
Heroes of the West '32
Jubal '56
Million Dollar Kid '44
Mysterious Two '82
'Neath Brooklyn Bridge '42
Of Mice and Men '39
Only Angels Have Wings '39
Red River '48
Richard Petty Story '72
Rocketship X-M '50
Savage Fury '33
Savages '73
Sergeant York '41
Seven Faces of Dr. Lao '63
Tailspin Tommy '34
Tanks a Million '41
The Texas Rangers '51
Walking Tall '73
Walking Tall: Part 2 '75

Noah Beery, Sr.
Adventures of Red Ryder '40
The Big Stampede '32
Buffalo Stampede '33
The Coming of Amos '25
Devil Horse '32
The Drifter '32
Fighting with Kit Carson '33
Flaming Signal '33
Kentucky Kernels '34
King of the Damned '36
Linda '29
Man of the Forest '33
Mark of Zorro '20
A Mormon Maid '17
Mystery Liner '34
Panamint's Bad Man '38
She Done Him Wrong '33
Soul of the Beast '23
To the Last Man '33
Trail Beyond '34
Vanishing American '26
Western Double Feature 9: LaRue & Beery '40s
Zorro Rides Again '37

Wallace Beery
Ah, Wilderness! '35
Behind the Front '26
The Big House '30
The Champ '31
Charlie Chase and Ben Turpin '21
China Seas '35
A Date with Judy '48
Dinner at Eight '33
The Four Horsemen of the Apocalypse '21
Grand Hotel '32
The Last of the Mohicans '20
The Lost World '25
Min & Bill '30
The Night Club '25
Old Ironsides '26
The Pony Express '25
Robin Hood '22
Story of the Silent Serials Girls in Danger
Teddy at the Throttle '16
Teddy at the Throttle/Speeding Along '17
Three Ages '23
Treasure Island '34
Viva Villa! '34
We're in the Navy Now '27
White Tiger '23

Ed Begley, Jr.
The Accidental Tourist '88
The Applegates '89
Blue Collar '78
Cat People '82
Citizens Band '77
Cooperstown '93
Dark Horse '92
Dead of Night '77
Eating Raoul '82
Elvis: The Movie '79
Get Crazy '83
Goin' South '78
The Great Los Angeles Earthquake '91
Greedy '94
The In-Laws '79
The Legend of Sleepy Hollow '86
Protocol '84
Renaissance Man '94
Running Mates '92
Scenes from the Class Struggle in Beverly Hills '89
She-Devil '89
A Shining Season '79
Showdown '73
Spies, Lies and Naked Thighs '91
The Story Lady '93
Streets of Fire '84
This is Spinal Tap '84
Transylvania 6-5000 '85
World War II: When Lions Roared '94

Ed Begley, Sr.
Boots Malone '52
The Dunwich Horror '70
Firecreek '68
Hang 'Em High '67
It Happens Every Spring '49
Lone Star '52
On Dangerous Ground '51

The Oscar '66
Patterns '56
Road to Salina '68
Sorry, Wrong Number '48
Stars in My Crown '50
The Street with No Name '48
Sweet Bird of Youth '62
Tulsa '49
Twelve Angry Men '57
The Unsinkable Molly Brown '64
Wild in the Streets '68

Brionny Behets
Alvin Rides Again '74
Cassandra '87

Sam Behrens
Alive '93
American Blue Note '89
And You Thought Your Parents Were Weird! '91
Murder by Numbers '89

Richard Bekins
George Washington: The Forging of a Nation '86
Model Behavior '82

Barbara Bel Geddes
Blood on the Moon '48
Caught '49
The Five Pennies '59
I Remember Mama '48
Panic in the Streets '50
Summertree '71
The Todd Killings '71
Vertigo '58

Doris Belack
Opportunity Knocks '90
What About Bob? '91

Shari Belafonte-Harper
Fire, Ice and Dynamite '91
French Silk '91
If You Could See What I Hear '82
The Midnight Hour '86
Murder by Numbers '89
Overnight Sensation '83
Speed Zone '88

Harry Belafonte
Buck and the Preacher '72
Carmen Jones '54
Grambling's White Tiger '81
Island in the Sun '57
Uptown Saturday Night '74

Leon Belasco
Abbott and Costello in the Foreign Legion '50
Can-Can '60
Fisherman's Wharf '39
Infamous Crimes '47
It's a Date '40

Christine Belford
The Groundstar Conspiracy '72
Kenny Rogers as the Gambler '80
Pocket Money '72

Ann Bell
Champions '84
The Statue '71

Christopher Bell
Sarah, Plain and Tall '91
Skylark '93
Without Warning: The James Brady Story '91

Edward Bell
Image of Passion '86
The Premonition '75

Hank Bell
Beyond the Rockies '32
The Big Stampede '32
Border Vengeance '35
The Fiddlin' Buckaroo '33
South of Santa Fe '42
Valley of the Sun '42
Whistlin' Dan '32

James Bell
A Lawless Street '55
The Leopard Man '43
My Friend Flicka '43
Teenage Crime Wave '55
Tribute to a Bad Man '56

Jeanne Bell
Fass Black '77
The Muthers '76

Policewomen '73
TNT Jackson '75

Marie Bell
Hotel Paradiso '66
Phedre '68

Marshall Bell
Air America '90
The Heroes of Desert Storm '91
Johnny Be Good '88
Leather Jackets '90
No Way Out '87
Total Recall '90
Tucker: The Man and His Dream '88
Twins '88
The Vagrant '92
Wildfire '88

Rex Bell
Battling with Buffalo Bill '31
Broadway to Cheyenne '32
Diamond Trail '33
Fighting Texans '33
Law of the Sea '38
Rainbow Ranch '33
Stormy Trails '36
The Tonto Kid '35
West of Nevada '36

Tobin Bell
False Identity '90
The Firm '93
Ruby '92

Tom Bell
Ballad in Blue '66
Dressed for Death '74
Let Him Have It '91
Prime Suspect '92
Prospero's Books '91
Quest for Love '71
Wish You Were Here '87

Vanessa Bell
Coming to America '88
Memphis '91

Madge Bellamy
Lorna Doone '22
Northwest Trail '46
Soul of the Beast '23
The White Sin '24
The White Zombie '32

Ned Bellamy
Carnosaur '93
Writer's Block '91

Ralph Bellamy
Ace of Aces '33
The Awful Truth '37
The Boy in the Plastic Bubble '76
Boy Meets Girl '38
Brother Orchid '40
Cancel My Reservation '72
Carefree '38
The Court Martial of Billy Mitchell '55
Dance, Girl, Dance '40
The Defender '57
Delightfully Dangerous '45
Disorderlies '87
Dive Bomber '41
Doctors' Wives '70
Fourth Wise Man '85
The Ghost of Frankenstein '42
The Good Mother '88
Guest in the House '45
Healer '36
His Girl Friday '40
Love Leads the Way '84
Missiles of October '74
Murder on Flight 502 '75
Nightmare in Badham County '76
Oh, God! '77
Pretty Woman '90
The Professionals '66
Return to Earth '76
Rosemary's Baby '68
Search for the Gods '75
Spitfire '34
Sunrise at Campobello '60
Trading Places '83
War & Remembrance, Part 1 '88
War & Remembrance, Part 2 '89
War & Remembrance: The Final Chapter, Part 8 '89
The Winds of War '83

The Wolf Man '41
Woman in the Shadows '34

Annie Belle
House on the Edge of the Park '84
Naked Paradise '78

Kathleen Beller
Are You in the House Alone? '78
The Betsy '78
Cloud Waltzing '87
Fort Apache, the Bronx '81
The Godfather, Part 2 '74
The Manions of America '81
Mary White '77
Mother & Daughter: A Loving War '80
No Place to Hide '81
Promises in the Dark '79
Rappaccini's Daughter '80
Surfacing '84
Sword & the Sorcerer '82
Time Trackers '88
Touched '82

Agostina Belli
The Chosen '77
The Sex Machine '76

Roxana Bellini
Dos Esposas en Mi Cama '87
Samson in the Wax Museum '63

Cynthia Belliveau
The Dark '94
The Dream Team '89
A New Life '88

Pamela Bellwood
Cellar Dweller '87
Cocaine: One Man's Seduction '83
Deadman's Curve '78
Double Standard '88
Hangar 18 '80

Jean-Paul Belmondo
Borsalino '70
The Brain '69
Breathless '59
Cartouche '62
Casino Royale '67
High Heels '72
Is Paris Burning? '68
Le Doulos '61
Le Magnifique '76
Leon Morin, Priest '61
Love and the Frenchwoman '60
Mississippi Mermaid '69
Pierrot le Fou '65
Scoumoune '74
Sois Belle et Tais-Toi '58
Stavisky '74
Stuntwoman '81
Swashbuckler '84
That Man from Rio '64
Two Women '61
Un Singe en Hiver '62
A Woman is a Woman '60

Robert Beltran
Bugsy '91
The Chase '91
Eating Raoul '82
El Diablo '90
Gaby: A True Story '87
Kiss Me a Killer '91
La Pastorela '92
Latino '85
Night of the Comet '84
Scenes from the Class Struggle in Beverly Hills '89
To Die Standing '91

James Belushi
About Last Night... '86
Best Legs in the 8th Grade '84
Birthday Boy '85
Curly Sue '91
Diary of a Hitman '91
Homer and Eddie '89
Jumpin' Jack Flash '86
K-9 '89
Little Shop of Horrors '86
The Man with One Red Shoe '85
The Masters of Menace '90
Mr. Destiny '90
Mutant Video '86
Once Upon a Crime '92
Only the Lonely '91
The Palermo Connection '91

The Principal '87
Real Men '87
Red Heat '88
Salvador '86
Taking Care of Business '90
Thief '81
Traces of Red '92
Trading Places '83
Wedding Band '89
Who's Harry Crumb? '89
Wild Palms '93

John Belushi
All You Need Is Cash '78
The Blues Brothers '80
Continental Divide '81
Goin' South '78
National Lampoon's Animal House '78
Neighbors '81
1941 '79
Old Boyfriends '79

Richard Belzer
America '86
The Big Picture '89
Fame '80
The Flash 2: Revenge of the Trickster '91
Flicks '85
Freeway '88
The Groove Tube '72
Mad Dog and Glory '93
Night Shift '82
The Wrong Guys '88

Brian Benben
Clean and Sober '88
Gangster Wars '81
I Come in Peace '90
Mortal Sins '90

Robert Benchley
China Seas '35
Foreign Correspondent '40
It's in the Bag '45
The Road to Utopia '46
The Sky's the Limit '43
The Stork Club '45
Weekend at the Waldorf '45
You'll Never Get Rich '41
Young & Willing '42

Russ Bender
The Amazing Colossal Man '57
Anatomy of a Psycho '61
It Conquered the World '56
Navy vs. the Night Monsters '66
Suicide Battalion/Hell Squad '58
The War of the Colossal Beast '58

William Bendix
Abroad with Two Yanks '44
Babe Ruth Story '48
Big Steal '49
Blackbeard the Pirate '52
A Connecticut Yankee in King Arthur's Court '49
Crashout '55
Dangerous Mission '54
Dark Corner '46
Deep Six '58
Detective Story '51
For Love or Money '63
A Girl in Every Port '52
The Glass Key '42
Guadalcanal Diary '43
The Hairy Ape '44
It's in the Bag '45
Johnny Nobody '61
Lifeboat '44
Macao '52
The Time of Your Life '48
Wake Island '42
Who Done It? '42
Woman of the Year '42

Billy Benedict
Bowery Buckaroos '47
Follow the Leader '44
Ghost Chasers '51
Hard-Boiled Mahoney '47
Master Minds '49
Spook Busters '46
Wildcat '42

Brooks Benedict
The Dropkick '27
The Freshman '25
Ranson's Folly '26

Dirk Benedict
Battlestar Galactica '78
Blue Tornado '90
Body Slam '87
Cruise into Terror '78
Follow That Car '80
Georgia, Georgia '72
Mission Galactica: The Cylon Attack '79
Official Denial '93
Ruckus '81
Scavenger Hunt '79
Shadow Force '92
Underground Aces '80
W '74

Paul Benedict
The Addams Family '91
Attack of the 50 Ft. Woman '93
Babycakes '89
The Chair '87
Cocktail '88
Desperate Moves '86
The Freshman '90
Mandingo '75

Richard Benedict
Beginning of the End '57
Breakdown '52
Omoo Omoo, the Shark God '49

Yves Beneyton
The Lacemaker '77
Letters to an Unknown Lover '84
Weekend '67

John Benfield
Hidden Agenda '90
In the Name of the Father '93

Wilson Benge
The Bat Whispers '30
Robin Hood '22

Norman Bengell
Hellbenders '67
Planet of the Vampires '65

Jean Benguigui
Buffet Froid '79
Control '87

Roberto Benigni
Down by Law '86
Johnny Stecchino '92
Night on Earth '91
Son of the Pink Panther '93

Annette Bening
Bugsy '91
The Great Outdoors '88
The Grifters '90
Guilty by Suspicion '91
Postcards from the Edge '90
Regarding Henry '91
Valmont '89

Paul Benjamin
Across 110th Street '72
The Deadly Trackers '73
The Education of Sonny Carson '74
The Five Heartbeats '91
I Know Why the Caged Bird Sings '79

Richard Benjamin
Catch-22 '70
Diary of a Mad Housewife '70
First Family '80
Goodbye Columbus '69
House Calls '78
How to Beat the High Cost of Living '80
The Last Married Couple in America '80
The Last of Sheila '73
Love at First Bite '79
No Room to Run '78
Packin' It In '83
Portnoy's Complaint '72
Saturday the 14th '81
Scavenger Hunt '79
The Steagle '71
The Sunshine Boys '75
Westworld '73
Witches' Brew '79

Benji
Benji '74
Benji the Hunted '87
For the Love of Benji '77

David Bennent
Legend '86

Bennent ▶cont.

The Tin Drum '79

Heinz Bennent
From the Life of the
    Marionettes '80
The Last Metro '80
Nea '78
Possession '81
The Tin Drum '79

**Bruce (Herman Brix)
Bennett**
Angels in the Outfield '51
Before I Hang '40
The Cosmic Man '59
Daniel Boone: Trail Blazer '56
Daredevils of the Red Circle '38
Dark Passage '47
Dragonfly Squadron '54
Hidden Guns '56
I'm from Arkansas '44
The Man I Love '46
Mildred Pierce '45
A Million to One '37
The More the Merrier '43
The New Adventures of Tarzan
    '35
Sahara '43
Shadow of Chinatown '36
Silver River '48
A Stolen Life '46
Tarzan and the Green Goddess
    '38
Task Force '49
Three Violent People '57
Treasure of the Sierra Madre
    '48
U-Boat Prisoner '44

Constance Bennett
As Young As You Feel '51
Madame X '66
Married? '26
Sin Takes a Holiday '30
Topper '37
Topper Takes a Trip '39
Two-Faced Woman '41
What Price Hollywood? '32

Hywel Bennett
Deadline '87
Endless Night '71
Loot...Give Me Money, Honey!
    '70
Murder Elite '86
The Virgin Soldiers '69

Jill Bennett
The Charge of the Light
    Brigade '68
For Your Eyes Only '81
Full Circle '77
Hawks '89
I Want What I Want '72
Lust for Life '56
Murders at Lynch Cross '85
The Old Curiosity Shop '75
The Sheltering Sky '90
The Skull '65

Joan Bennett
Bulldog Drummond '29
Colonel Effingham's Raid '45
Disraeli '29
Father of the Bride '50
Father's Little Dividend '51
House Across the Bay '40
House of Dark Shadows '70
Little Women '33
The Making of a Legend:
    "Gone With the Wind" '89
The Man in the Iron Mask '39
Power '28
Reckless Moment '49
The Scar '48
Scarlet Street '45
Secret Beyond the Door '48
The Son of Monte Cristo '41
Suspiria '77
Vogues of 1938 '37
We're No Angels '55

John Bennett
Antonia and Jane '91
The House that Dripped Blood
    '71
It Takes a Thief '59

Marjorie Bennett
Kiss Me Deadly '55

Stacey '73

Ray Bennett
Border Badmen '45
Death Rides the Plains '44
Lovers' Lovers '94
Thundering Trail '51

Tony Bennett
The Oscar '66
The Scout '94

Jack Benny
Broadway Melody of 1936 '35
George Washington Slept Here
    '42
Hollywood Canteen '44
The Horn Blows at Midnight '45
It's a Mad, Mad, Mad, Mad
    World '63
It's in the Bag '45
Medicine Man '30
To Be or Not to Be '42
Transatlantic Merry-Go-Round
    '34

Amber Benson
The Crush '93
King of the Hill '93

Deborah Benson
Just Before Dawn '80
Mutant on the Bounty '89
September 30, 1955 '77

George Benson
Convoy '40
The Creeping Flesh '72

Lucille Benson
Cactus in the Snow '72
Duel '71
Huckleberry Finn '74
Private Parts '72
Reflections of Murder '74

Martin Benson
The Cosmic Monsters '58
Exodus '60
The King and I '56
A Matter of WHO '62
Tiffany Jones '75

Robby Benson
All the Kind Strangers '74
City Limits '85
Deadly Exposure '93
Death Be Not Proud '75
The Death of Richie '76
Die Laughing '80
The End '78
Harry & Son '84
Homewrecker '92
Ice Castles '79
Invasion of Privacy '92
Jory '72
The Last of Mrs. Lincoln '76
Modern Love '90
National Lampoon Goes to the
    Movies '81
Ode to Billy Joe '76
One on One '77
Our Town '77
Rent-A-Cop '88
Running Brave '83
Tribute '80
Two of a Kind '82
The Virginia Hill Story '76
White Hot '89

Michael Bentine
Down Among the Z Men '52
Rentadick '72

Dana Bentley
Karate Cop '93
Sorority House Massacre 2:
    Nighty Nightmare '92

John Bentley
Calling Paul Temple '48
The Chair '87
Flight from Vienna '58
The Happiest Days of Your Life
    '50
Profile '54
River Beat '54
Scarlet Spear '54
Submarine Seahawk '59
The Way Out '73
White Huntress '57

Barbi Benton
Deathstalker '83
For the Love of It '80
Hospital Massacre '81

Jerome Benton
Graffiti Bridge '90
Under the Cherry Moon '86

Suzanne Benton
A Boy and His Dog '75
That Cold Day in the Park '69

Daniel Benzali
A Day in October '92
The Last of His Tribe '92
Messenger of Death '88

John Beradino
Don't Look Back: The Story of
    Leroy "Satchel" Paige '81
Moon of the Wolf '72

Ady Berber
Dead Eyes of London '61
Door with the Seven Locks '62

Luca Bercovici
American Flyers '85
Clean and Sober '88
Frightmare '81
K2: The Ultimate High '92
Mirror Images 2 '93
Mission of Justice '92
Mortal Passions '90
Pacific Heights '90
Parasite '81
Scanner Cop '94

Tom Berenger
At Play in the Fields of the Lord
    '91
Betrayed '88
Beyond Obsession '82
The Big Chill '83
Born on the Fourth of July '89
Butch and Sundance: The Early
    Days '79
Chasers '94
The Dogs of War '81
Eddie and the Cruisers '83
Fear City '85
The Field '90
Gettysburg '93
In Praise of Older Women '78
Johnny We Hardly Knew Ye '77
Last Rites '88
Looking for Mr. Goodbar '77
Love at Large '90
Major League '89
Major League 2 '94
Platoon '86
Rush '77
Rustler's Rhapsody '85
The Sentinel '76
Shattered '91
Shoot to Kill '88
Sliver '93
Sniper '92
Someone to Watch Over Me
    '87

Marisa Berenson
Barry Lyndon '75
Cabaret '72
Death in Venice '71
Killer Fish '79
Night of the Cyclone '90
The Secret Diary of Sigmund
    Freud '84
Sex on the Run '78
S.O.B. '81
Trade Secrets '90s
White Hunter, Black Heart '90

Peter Berg
Aspen Extreme '93
A Case for Murder '93
Crooked Hearts '91
Fire in the Sky '93
Genuine Risk '89
Late for Dinner '91
A Midnight Clear '92
Never on Tuesday '88
Race for Glory '89
Shocker '89

Judith-Marie Bergan
Abduction '75
Never Pick Up a Stranger '79

Francine Berge
Circle of Love '64
Judex '64
The Nun '66

Candice Bergen
The Adventurers '70
Bite the Bullet '75
Carnal Knowledge '71
The Domino Principle '77

11 Harrowhouse '74
Gandhi '82
Getting Straight '70
The Group '66
Mayflower Madam '87
Merlin and the Sword '85
My Sweet Victim '85
A Night Full of Rain '78
Oliver's Story '78
Rich and Famous '81
The Sand Pebbles '66
Soldier Blue '70
Starting Over '79
Stick '85
The Wind and the Lion '75

Edgar Bergen
Fun & Fancy Free '47
The Goldwyn Follies '38
Here We Go Again! '42
Homecoming: A Christmas
    Story '71
I Remember Mama '48
Letter of Introduction '38
Look Who's Laughing '41
You Can't Cheat an Honest
    Man '39

Frances Bergen
Eating '90
The Morning After '86

Polly Bergen
Anatomy of Terror '74
At War with the Army '50
Born Beautiful '82
Cape Fear '61
Cry-Baby '90
Death Cruise '74
Escape from Fort Bravo '53
Haunting of Sarah Hardy '89
How to Pick Up Girls '78
Kisses for My President '64
The Lightning Incident '91
Making Mr. Right '86
Murder on Flight 502 '75
My Brother's Wife '89
The Stooge '51
War & Remembrance, Part 1
    '88
War & Remembrance, Part 2
    '89
War & Remembrance, Part 3
    '88
War & Remembrance, Part 4
    '88
War & Remembrance, Part 5
    '88
War & Remembrance, Part 6
    '88
War & Remembrance, Part 7
    '88
War & Remembrance: The
    Final Chapter, Part 8 '89
War & Remembrance: The
    Final Chapter, Part 9 '89
War & Remembrance: The
    Final Chapter, Part 10 '89
War & Remembrance: The
    Final Chapter, Part 11 '89
War & Remembrance: The
    Final Chapter, Part 12 '89
The Winds of War '83

Tushka Bergen
Barcelona '94
Swing Kids '93
Wrangler '88

Deborah Berger
La Merveilleuse Visite '74
Rosebud '75

Helmut Berger
Ash Wednesday '73
Battleforce '87
Code Name: Emerald '85
Conversation Piece '75
The Damned '69
Deadly Game '83
Dorian Gray '70
Fatal Fix '80s
The Garden of the Finzi-
    Continis '71
The Godfather, Part 3 '90
Mad Dog '84
Order to Kill '73
Romantic Englishwoman '75

Joachim Berger
Carpet of Horror '64
Curse of the Yellow Snake '63

Katya Berger
Nana '82

Tales of Ordinary Madness '83

Nicole Berger
Shoot the Piano Player '62
The Story of a Three Day Pass
    '68

Senta Berger
The Ambushers '67
The Boss Is Served '60s
Cast a Giant Shadow '66
Cobra '71
Cross of Iron '76
Diabolically Yours '67
Full Hearts & Empty Pockets
    '63
Killing Cars '85
Mother Doesn't Always Know
    Best '60s
The Quiller Memorandum '66
The Scarlet Letter '73
Secret of the Black Trunk '62
Sherlock Holmes and the
    Deadly Necklace '62
Smugglers '75
Swiss Conspiracy '77
Testament of Dr. Mabuse '62
Waltz King '63
When Women Had Tails '70
When Women Lost Their Tails
    '75

William Berger
Day of the Cobra '84
Hell Hunters '87
Hercules '83
Hercules 2 '85
Oil '78
Slaughterday '77
Superfly T.N.T. '73
Today We Kill, Tomorrow We
    Die '71
What a Way to Die '70

Thommy Berggren
The Adventurers '70
Elvira Madigan '67

Herbert Berghof
Five Fingers '52
Master Mind '73
Red Planet Mars '52

Patrick Bergin
The Courier '88
Frankenstein '93
Highway to Hell '92
Love Crimes '92
Map of the Human Heart '93
Mountains of the Moon '90
Patriot Games '92
Robin Hood '91
Sleeping with the Enemy '91
Taffin '88
They Watch '93

Erik Berglund
Only One Night '42
Walpurgis Night '41

Henry Bergman
Charlie Chaplin Festival '17
Charlie Chaplin: The Early
    Years, Vol. 2 '17
City Lights '31
Modern Times '36

Ingrid Bergman
Adam Had Four Sons '41
Anastasia '56
Arch of Triumph '48
Autumn Sonata '78
The Bells of St. Mary's '45
The Best of Bogart '43
Cactus Flower '69
The Cary Grant Collection '90
Casablanca '42
The Count of the Old Town '34
Dr. Jekyll and Mr. Hyde '41
Dollar '38
Elena and Her Men '56
Europa '51 '52
Gaslight '44
Goodbye Again '61
The Hideaways '73
Indiscreet '58
The Inn of the Sixth Happiness
    '58
Intermezzo '36
Intermezzo '39
Joan of Arc '48
June Night '40
A Matter of Time '76
Murder on the Orient Express
    '74

Notorious '46
Only One Night '42
Spellbound '45
Stromboli '50
Swedenhielms '35
24 Hours in a Woman's Life '61
Under Capricorn '49
Voyage to Italy '53
Walk in the Spring Rain '70
Walpurgis Night '41
A Woman Called Golda '82
A Woman's Face '38

Peter Bergman
Firesign Theatre Presents Nick
    Danger in the Case of the
    Missing Yolks '83
J-Men Forever! '79
Phantom of the Ritz '88

Sandahl Bergman
Airplane 2: The Sequel '82
All That Jazz '79
Body of Influence '93
Conan the Barbarian '82
Getting Physical '84
Hell Comes to Frogtown '88
Kandyland '87
Lipstick Camera '93
Programmed to Kill '86
Raw Nerve '91
Red Sonja '85
She '83
Stewardess School '86
Xanadu '80

Elisabeth Bergner
As You Like It '36
Catherine the Great '34
Cry of the Banshee '70
Dreaming Lips '37
The Pedestrian '73

Luis Beristain
El: This Strange Passion '52
The Exterminating Angel '62

Busby Berkeley
Babes on Broadway '41
Fashions of 1934 '34
42nd Street '33
Million Dollar Mermaid '52
Roman Scandals '33

Xander Berkeley
Assassin '89
Attack of the 50 Ft. Woman '93
Candyman '92
Deadly Dreams '88
A Few Good Men '92
The Gun in Betty Lou's
    Handbag '92
The Lawless Land '88
Short Time '90

Steven Berkoff
Beverly Hills Cop '84
A Clockwork Orange '71
Intruders '92
The Krays '90
The Passenger '75
Prisoner of Rio '89
Rambo: First Blood, Part 2 '85
Revolution '85
Transmutations '85
War & Remembrance, Part 1
    '88
War & Remembrance: The
    Final Chapter, Part 8 '89

Terri Berland
Pink Motel '82
The Strangeness '85

Milton Berle
Broadway Danny Rose '84
Cracking Up '83
Driving Me Crazy '91
It's a Mad, Mad, Mad, Mad
    World '63
Legend of Valentino '75
Lepke '75
Let's Make Love '60
The Loved One '65
Off Your Rocker '80
The Oscar '66
Side By Side '88
Sun Valley Serenade '41
Who's Minding the Mint? '67

Francois Berleand
Au Revoir Les Enfants '87
May Fools '90

Jeannie Berlin
The Baby Maker '70

Getting Straight '70
The Heartbreak Kid '72
Housewife '72
In the Spirit '90
Portnoy's Complaint '72
The Strawberry Statement '70

Warren Berlinger
Billie '65
Four Deuces '75
Hero '73
The Long Goodbye '73
Platinum High School '60
Sex and the Single Parent '82
Spinout '66
Take Two '87
The World According to Garp
    '82

Shelley Berman
The Best Man '64
Motorama '91
Rented Lips '88
Son of Blob '72
Think Dirty '70
The Wheeler Dealers '63

Ed Bernard
Across 110th Street '72
Reflections of Murder '74
The White Shadow, Vol. 1 '78

Susan Bernard
Faster Pussycat! Kill! Kill! '66
Teenager '74

Herschel Bernardi
Actor: The Paul Muni Story '78
The Front '76
Green Fields '37
Irma La Douce '63
Love with the Proper Stranger
    '63
No Place to Run '72
The Story of Jacob & Joseph
    '74

Sandra Bernhard
Heavy Petting '89
Hudson Hawk '91
Inside Monkey Zetterland '93
King of Comedy '82
Sesame Street Presents:
    Follow That Bird '85
Track 29 '88

Kevin Bernhardt
Counterforce '87
Hellraiser 3: Hell on Earth '92
Midnight Warrior '89

Mara Berni
The Fury of Hercules '61
Samson '61

Corbin Bernsen
Bert Rigby, You're a Fool '89
Dead Aim '87
Dead on the Money '91
Disorganized Crime '89
Eat My Dust '76
Frozen Assets '92
Hello Again '87
L.A. Law '86
Major League '89
Major League 2 '94
Ring of the Musketeers '93
Shattered '91

Claude Berri
Le Sex Shop '73
Marry Me, Marry Me '69

Elizabeth Berridge
Amadeus '84
Five Corners '88
The Funhouse '81
Montana '90

Chuck Berry
Chuck Berry: Hail! Hail! Rock
    'n' Roll '87
Go, Johnny Go! '59
Rock, Rock, Rock '56

Halle Berry
Boomerang '92
Father Hood '93
The Flintstones '94
Jungle Fever '91
The Last Boy Scout '91
The Program '93
Strictly Business '91

Jules Berry
The Crime of Monsieur Lange
    '36
Le Jour Se Leve '39

Les Visiteurs du Soir '42

Ken Berry
The Cat from Outer Space '78
Herbie Rides Again '74
Mountain Man '77

Richard Berry
Day of Atonement '93
Honeymoon '85
L'Addition '85
A Man and a Woman: 20 Years
    Later '86
Special Police '85

Dorothee Berryman
The Decline of the American
    Empire '86
A Paper Wedding '89
Scanners 2: The New Order '91

Michael Berryman
Aftershock '88
Auntie Lee's Meat Pies '92
The Barbarians '87
Beastmaster 2: Through the
    Portal of Time '91
Cut and Run '85
Evil Spirits '91
The Guyver '91
Haunting Fear '91
The Hills Have Eyes '77
The Hills Have Eyes, Part 2 '84
One Flew Over the Cuckoo's
    Nest '75
The Secret of the Golden Eagle
    '91
Teenage Exorcist '93
Voyage of the Rock Aliens '87

Dehl Berti
Bullies '84
Sweet Hostage '75

Roland Bertin
Cyrano de Bergerac '90
Diva '82
The Hairdresser's Husband '92
L'Homme Blesse '84

Valerie Bertinelli
Aladdin and His Wonderful
    Lamp '84
C.H.O.M.P.S. '79
Number One with a Bullet '87
Ordinary Heroes '85
Pancho Barnes '88
Shattered Vows '84
Silent Witness '85
Taken Away '89
Young Love, First Love '79

Juliet Berto
The Joy of Knowledge '65
Le Sex Shop '73

Bibi Besch
The Beast Within '82
Betsy's Wedding '90
Crazy from the Heart '91
Date with an Angel '87
Death of a Centerfold '81
Kill Me Again '89
The Lonely Lady '83
Peter Lundy and the Medicine
    Hat Stallion '77
Tremors '89

Ted Bessell
Acorn People '82
Billie '65
Breaking Up Is Hard to Do '79
Don't Drink the Water '69

Joe Besser
Africa Screams '49
Hey Abbott! '78
Savage Intruder '68

Eugene Besserer
Anna Christie '23
The Flesh and the Devil '27
The Greatest Question '19
The Jazz Singer '27
What Happened to Rosa? '21

Edna Best
The Ghost and Mrs. Muir '47
Intermezzo '39
The Man Who Knew Too Much
    '34

James Best
The Killer Shrews '59
Ma and Pa Kettle at the Fair '52
Mind Warp '72
The Naked and the Dead '58
Ode to Billy Joe '76

Ride Lonesome '59
The Runaway Barge '75
Savage Run '70
Shock Corridor '63
Sounder '72
Verboten! '59

Willie Best
The Bride Walks Out '36
The Ghost Breakers '40
Kentucky Kernels '34
The Littlest Rebel '35
The Monster Walks '32
Two Reelers: Comedy Classics
    1 '33

Martine Beswick
Balboa '82
A Bullet for the General '68
Cyclone '87
Dr. Jekyll and Sister Hyde '71
Evil Spirits '91
From Russia with Love '63
The Happy Hooker Goes
    Hollywood '80
Miami Blues '90
The Offspring '87
Strange New World '75
Thunderball '65
Trancers 2: The Return of Jack
    Deth '91
Wide Sargasso Sea '92

Sabine Bethmann
Dr. Mabuse vs. Scotland Yard
    '64
Journey to the Lost City '58

Lyle Bettger
Carnival Story '54
Johnny Reno '66
Lone Ranger '56
Sea Chase '55
Union Station '50

Laura Betti
Allonsanfan '73
The Canterbury Tales '71
Hatchet for the Honeymoon '70
Lovers and Liars '81
1900 '76
Sonny and Jed '73
Teorema '68

Robert Bettles
Fourth Wish '75
Ride a Wild Pony '75

Franca Bettoya
The Last Man on Earth '64
Marauder '65

Jack Betts
The Bloody Brood '59
Dead Men Don't Die '91

Carl Betz
Deadly Encounter '78
The Meal '75
Spinout '66

Matthew Betz
The Black Coin '36
Broadway to Cheyenne '32
The Fighting Marshal '32
Tarzan the Fearless '33
The Unholy Three '25
The Wedding March '28

Billy Bevan
Cavalcade '33
Comedy Classics '35
Girl of the Golden West '38
High Voltage '29
The Lizzies of Mack Sennett
    '15
Silent Laugh Makers, No. 2 '17
Two Reelers: Comedy Classics
    8 '33
Vanity Fair '32
The White Sin '24
The Woman in Green '45
The Wrong Road '37

Clem Bevans
Abe Lincoln in Illinois '40
Gold Raiders '51
Highway 13 '48
Rim of the Canyon '49
Silver City Bonanza '51

Helen Beverly
Green Fields '37
The Light Ahead '39
Meeting at Midnight '44
Overture to Glory '40

Turhan Bey
Ali Baba and the Forty Thieves
    '43
The Amazing Mr. X '48
Arabian Nights '42
Background to Danger '43
Dragon Seed '44
Falcon Takes Over/Strange
    Bargain '49
The Mad Ghoul '43
The Mummy's Tomb '42
Out of the Blue '47
Parole, Inc. '49
Shadows on the Stairs '41

Troy Beyer
Rooftops '91
Weekend at Bernie's 2 '93

Richard Beymer
Cross Country '83
The Diary of Anne Frank '59
Free Grass '69
Indiscretion of an American
    Wife '54
Johnny Tremain & the Sons of
    Liberty '58
The Longest Day '62
Silent Night, Deadly Night 3:
    Better Watch Out! '89
The Stripper '63
Twin Peaks '90
Under Investigation '93
West Side Story '61

Didier Bezace
Between Heaven and Earth '93
The Little Thief '89

Daniela Bianchi
Dirty Heroes '71
From Russia with Love '63
Secret Agent 00 '67
The Sword of El Cid '62

Charles K. Bibby
Order of the Black Eagle '87
Unmasking the Idol '86

Abner Biberman
Betrayal from the East '44
Elephant Walk '54
Gunga Din '39
His Girl Friday '40
The Keys of the Kingdom '44
Panama Patrol '39
The Rains Came '39

Charles Bickford
Anna Christie '30
Babe Ruth Story '48
A Big Hand for the Little Lady
    '66
Branded '50
Command Decision '48
The Court Martial of Billy
    Mitchell '55
Days of Wine and Roses '62
Duel in the Sun '46
East of Borneo '31
The Farmer Takes a Wife '35
The Farmer's Daughter '47
Fatal Confinement '64
Four Faces West '48
Guilty of Treason '50
Jim Thorpe: All American '51
Johnny Belinda '48
Little Miss Marker '34
Mr. Lucky '43
Mutiny in the Big House '39
Not as a Stranger '55
Of Mice and Men '39
The Plainsman '37
Reap the Wild Wind '42
The Song of Bernadette '43
A Star is Born '54
Tarzan's New York Adventure
    '42
Thunder Pass '37
The Unforgiven '60
A Wing and a Prayer '44

Michael Biehn
The Abyss '89
Aliens '86
Coach '78
Deadfall '93
Deep Red '94
The Fan '81
Hog Wild '80
In a Shallow Grave '88
K2: The Ultimate High '92
The Lords of Discipline '83
Navy SEALS '90

Biehn ▶cont.

Rampage '87
The Seventh Sign '88
Strapped '93
A Taste for Killing '92
The Terminator '84
Timebomb '91
Tombstone '93

Dick Biel
Slime City '89
Splatter University '84

Josef Bierbichler
Heart of Glass '74
Woyzeck '78

Ramon Bieri
A Christmas Without Snow '80
The Frisco Kid '79
Grandview U.S.A. '84
Love Affair: The Eleanor & Lou Gehrig Story '77
Love, Lies and Murder '91
A Matter of Life and Death '81
Nicole '72
Panic in Echo Park '77
The Passing of Evil '70
Sorcerer '77

Adam Biesk
The Applegates '89
Leprechaun 2 '94

Claudio Bigagli
Fiorile '93
Kaos '85
Mediterraneo '91
The Night of the Shooting Stars '82

Roxann Biggs
Broken Angel '88
Dirty Work '92
Guilty by Suspicion '91
Midnight's Child '93

Theodore Bikel
Above Us the Waves '56
The African Queen '51
Benefit of the Doubt '93
Dark Tower '87
Darker than Amber '70
The Defiant Ones '58
A Dog of Flanders '59
Enemy Below '57
Flight from Vienna '58
I Bury the Living '58
I Want to Live! '58
Murder on Flight 502 '75
My Fair Lady '64
My Side of the Mountain '69
Never Let Me Go '53
The Russians are Coming, the Russians are Coming '66
See You in the Morning '89
Shattered '91
Very Close Quarters '84

Fernando Bilbao
Apocalipsis Joe '65
Fangs of the Living Dead '68
The Screaming Dead '72

Tony Bill
Are You in the House Alone? '78
Come Blow Your Horn '63
Haunts of the Very Rich '72
Heart Beat '80
Ice Station Zebra '68
Initiation of Sarah '78
The Killing Mind '90
Little Dragons '80
Never a Dull Moment '68
None But the Brave '65
Pee Wee's Big Adventure '85
Shampoo '75
Soldier in the Rain '63
Washington Mistress '81
You're a Big Boy Now '66

Raoul Billerey
Le Grand Chemin '87
The Little Thief '89

Dawn Ann Billings
Trancers 3: Deth Lives '92
Warlock: The Armageddon '93

Earl Billings
One False Move '91
Stakeout '87

Barbara Billingsley
Back to the Beach '87
Eye of the Demon '87

Jennifer Billingsley
Chrome Hearts '70
Hollywood Man '76
Lady in a Cage '64
The Thirsty Dead '74
White Lightning '73

Peter Billingsley
Arcade '93
Beverly Hills Brats '89
A Christmas Story '83
Death Valley '81
Dirt Bike Kid '86
The Hoboken Chicken Emergency '84
Russkies '87

Sybilla Binder
Counterblast '48
The Golden Salamander '51

Herman Bing
Bitter Sweet '40
Crimson Romance '34
Every Day's a Holiday '38
The Great Waltz '38
The Guardsman '31
Maytime '37
The Merry Widow '34
Tango '36
That Girl from Paris '36

Barbara Bingham
Beyond Darkness '92
Friday the 13th, Part 8: Jason Takes Manhattan '89
Soldier's Fortune '91

Geoffrey Binney
Hot Potato '76
Raw Force '81

Edward Binns
The Americanization of Emily '64
Beyond a Reasonable Doubt '56
Danger in the Skies '79
Hunter '73
Night Moves '75
Oliver's Story '78
A Public Affair '62
Return to Eden '89
Twelve Angry Men '57
Without Warning '52

Juliette Binoche
Damage '92
Hail Mary '85
Rendez-vous '85
Trois Couleurs: Bleu '93
The Unbearable Lightness of Being '88
Women & Men: In Love There Are No Rules '90

Thelma Biral
Desde el Abismo
El Muerto '75
Fridays of Eternity '81

Paul Birch
Apache Woman '55
Day the World Ended '55
Queen of Outer Space '58

Thora Birch
All I Want for Christmas '91
Clear and Present Danger '94
Hocus Pocus '93
Monkey Trouble '94
Paradise '91
Patriot Games '92

Billie Bird
Dennis the Menace '93
The End of Innocence '90
Ernest Saves Christmas '88
Home Alone '90

Jesse Birdsall
Getting It Right '89
Wish You Were Here '87

Tala Birell
Crime and Punishment '35
The Purple Heart '44
The White Legion '36

Jane Birkin
Beethoven's Nephew '88
Blow-Up '66
Catherine & Co. '76
Daddy Nostalgia '90

Death on the Nile '78
Dust '85
Evil Under the Sun '82
French Intrigue
La Belle Noiseuse '90
Le Petit Amour '87
Make Room for Tomorrow '81
Romance of a Horsethief '71
Seven Deaths in the Cat's Eye '72
Swimming Pool '70
Too Pretty to Be Honest '72
Wonderwall: The Movie '69

Len Birman
Captain America '79
Captain America 2: Death Too Soon '79
Lies My Father Told Me '75
Undergrads '85
Web of Deceit '90

Serafina Birman
The Girl with the Hat Box '27
Ivan the Terrible, Part 1 '44
Ivan the Terrible, Part 2 '46

David Birney
Caravan to Vaccares '74
Choice of Weapons '76
The Five of Me '81
Mom, the Wolfman and Me '80
Murder or Mercy '74
Nightfall '88
Oh, God! Book 2 '80
Only with Married Men '74
Prettykill '87
The Tragedy of King Richard II '82

Reed Birney
Crimewave '85
Four Friends '81

Debbie Bishop
Scrubbers '82
Sid & Nancy '86

Ed Bishop
Brass Target '78
The Devil's Web '74
Journey to the Far Side of the Sun '69
Saturn 3 '80

Jennifer Bishop
The Female Bunch '69
Horror of the Blood Monsters '70
House of Terror '87
Impulse '74
Jaws of Death '76
Jessie's Girls '75

Joey Bishop
Betsy's Wedding '90
Deep Six '58
Delta Force '86
The Naked and the Dead '58
Texas Across the River '66
Valley of the Dolls '67
Who's Minding the Mint? '67

Julie Bishop
Action in the North Atlantic '43
The Last of the Redmen '47
Northern Pursuit '43
Rhapsody in Blue '45
Westward the Women '51

Kelly Bishop
Dirty Dancing '87
Queens Logic '91

Larry Bishop
How Come Nobody's On Our Side? '73
The Savage Seven '68
Soul Hustler '76

Pat Bishop
Don's Party '76
Women of Valor '86

Wes Bishop
Chrome and Hot Leather '71
Dixie Dynamite '76

Steve Bisley
Chain Reaction '80
Fast Talking '86
The Highest Honor '84
Mad Max '80

Whit Bissell
Boots Malone '52
Creature from the Black Lagoon '54
Devil's Canyon '53

He Walked by Night '48
I Was a Teenage Werewolf '57
The Lost Continent '51
Shack Out on 101 '55
Spencer's Mountain '63
Teenage Frankenstein '58
The Time Machine '60

Jacqueline Bisset
Airport '70
Anna Karenina '85
Bullitt '68
Casino Royale '67
Choices '86
Class '83
Cul de Sac '66
Day for Night '73
The Deep '77
The Detective '68
The First Time '69
Forbidden '85
The Greek Tycoon '78
High Season '88
Le Magnifique '76
Life & Times of Judge Roy Bean '72
The Maid '90
The Mephisto Waltz '71
Murder on the Orient Express '74
The Passing of Evil '70
Rich and Famous '81
St. Ives '76
Scenes from the Class Struggle in Beverly Hills '89
Secrets '71
Spiral Staircase '75
The Thief Who Came to Dinner '73
Together? '79
Two for the Road '67
Under the Volcano '84
When Time Ran Out '80
Who is Killing the Great Chefs of Europe? '78
Wild Orchid '90

Josie Bisset
All-American Murder '91
Book of Love '91
Mikey '92

Bill Bixby
The Apple Dumpling Gang '75
The Barbary Coast '74
Clambake '67
Death of the Incredible Hulk '90
Fantasy Island '76
The Incredible Hulk '77
The Incredible Hulk Returns '88
Kentucky Fried Movie '77
Rich Man, Poor Man '76
Speedway '68
The Trial of the Incredible Hulk '89

Anita Bjork
Miss Julie '50
Secrets of Women '52

Halvar Bjork
Autumn Sonata '78
The New Land '73

Anna Bjorn
More American Graffiti '79
Sword & the Sorcerer '82

Gunnar Bjornstrand
Autumn Sonata '78
Dreams '55
Face to Face '76
Lesson in Love '54
The Magician '58
Persona '66
The Seventh Seal '56
The Shame '68
Smiles of a Summer Night '55
Through a Glass Darkly '61
Wild Strawberries '57
The Winter Light '62

Karen Black
Airport '75 '75
Auntie Lee's Meat Pies '92
Bad Manners '84
Born to Win '71
Bound and Gagged: A Love Story '93
Burnt Offerings '76
Caged Fear '92
Can She Bake a Cherry Pie? '83
Capricorn One '78
Chanel Solitaire '81

The Children '90
Children of the Night '92
Club Fed '90
Come Back to the Five & Dime Jimmy Dean, Jimmy Dean '82
Crime & Passion '75
Cut and Run '85
The Day of the Locust '75
Dixie Lanes '88
The Double O Kid '92
Easy Rider '69
Eternal Evil '87
Evil Spirits '91
Family Plot '76
Final Judgement '92
Five Easy Pieces '70
The Great Gatsby '74
A Gunfight '71
Haunting Fear '91
The Heist '88
Hitz '92
Homer and Eddie '89
Hostage '87
In Praise of Older Women '78
Invaders from Mars '86
The Invisible Kid '88
It's Alive 3: Island of the Alive '87
Killer Fish '79
The Killer's Edge '90
Killing Heat '84
The Last Word '80
Law and Disorder '74
Little Laura & Big John '73
The Little Mermaid '84
Love Under Pressure '80s
Martin's Day '85
Mirror, Mirror '90
Miss Right '81
Mr. Horn '79
Nashville '75
Night Angel '90
Out of the Dark '88
Overexposed '90
Portnoy's Complaint '72
The Prime Time '60
The Pyx '73
Quiet Fire '91
The Rip Off '78
Rubin & Ed '92
Savage Dawn '84
Separate Ways '82
The Squeeze '80
Trilogy of Terror '75
Twisted Justice '89
You're a Big Boy Now '66
Zapped Again '89

Maurice Black
Marked Money '28
Sixteen Fathoms Deep '34

Honor Blackman
The Cat and the Canary '79
Conspirator '49
The First Olympics: Athens 1896 '84
Fright '71
Glass Tomb '55
Goldfinger '64
Green Grow the Rushes '51
Jason and the Argonauts '63
Lola '69
A Matter of WHO '62
A Night to Remember '58
Shalako '68
Suspended Alibi '57
To the Devil, A Daughter '76
The Virgin and the Gypsy '70

Joan Blackman
Blue Hawaii '61
Career '59
Daring Game '68
Kid Galahad '62
Macon County Line '74

Sidney Blackmer
Beyond a Reasonable Doubt '56
Buffalo Bill '44
The Count of Monte Cristo '34
Deluge '33
Goodbye Love '34
High Society '56
The House of Secrets '37
How to Murder Your Wife '64
In Old Chicago '38
Law of the Pampas '39
Little Caesar '30
The Little Colonel '35

Love Crazy '41
The Panther's Claw '42
People Will Talk '51
The President's Mystery '36
Rosemary's Baby '68
Tammy and the Bachelor '57
Transatlantic Merry-Go-Round '34
War of the Wildcats '43
Wilson '44

Taurean Blacque
Deepstar Six '89
The $5.20 an Hour Dream '80
Hill Street Blues, Vol. 1: Hill Street Station '81

Ruben Blades
Color of Night '94
Crazy from the Heart '91
Critical Condition '86
Crossover Dreams '85
Dead Man Out '89
Disorganized Crime '89
Fatal Beauty '87
Homeboy '88
The Josephine Baker Story '90
The Last Fight '82
The Lemon Sisters '90
The Milagro Beanfield War '88
Mo' Better Blues '90
One Man's War '90
Predator 2 '90
The Super '91
The Two Jakes '90

Estella Blain
The Diabolical Dr. Z '65
Pirates of the Coast '61

Gerard Blain
The American Friend '77
The Cousins '59
Hatari '62
Le Beau Serge '58

Vivian Blaine
The Cracker Factory '79
The Dark '79
Doll Face '46
Guys and Dolls '55
Parasite '81
Skirts Ahoy! '52
State Fair '45

Betsy Blair
Il Grido '57
Marty '55

Janet Blair
Black Arrow '48
Boy's Night Out '62
Burn Witch, Burn! '62
The Fabulous Dorseys '47
Fuller Brush Man '48
The One and Only, Genuine, Original Family Band '68
Tonight and Every Night '45

Kevin Blair
Bloodlust: Subspecies 3 '93
Bloodstone: Subspecies 2 '93
Friday the 13th, Part 7: The New Blood '88
The Hills Have Eyes, Part 2 '84

Linda Blair
Airport '75 '75
Bail Out '90
Bedroom Eyes 2 '89
Born Innocent '74
Chained Heat '83
The Chilling '89
Dead Sleep '91
The Exorcist '73
The Exorcist 2: The Heretic '77
Fatal Bond '91
Grotesque '87
Hell Night '81
Moving Target '89
Night Patrol '85
Nightforce '86
Red Heat '85
Repossessed '90
Roller Boogie '79
Ruckus '81
Savage Island '85
Savage Streets '83
Silent Assassins '88
The Sporting Club '72
Summer of Fear '78
Sweet Hostage '75
Up Your Alley '89
Wild Horse Hank '79
Witchery '88

A Woman Obsessed '88
Zapped Again '89

Tom Blair
The Game '89
Sure Fire '90

Deborah Blaisdell
Student Affairs '88
Wildest Dreams '90
Wimps '87

Amanda Blake
Betrayal '74
The Boost '88
B.O.R.N. '88
Duchess of Idaho '50
The Glass Slipper '55
Gunsmoke: Return to Dodge '87
Sabre Jet '53
Stars in My Crown '50

Andre B. Blake
Philadelphia '93
Who's the Man? '93

Geoffrey Blake
The Abduction of Kari Swenson '87
Fatal Exposure '91
Philadelphia Experiment 2 '93

Jon Blake
Anzacs: The War Down Under '85
Early Frost '84
Freedom '81
The Lighthorsemen '87

Julia Blake
Father '90
Georgia '87
Lonely Hearts '82
Man of Flowers '84
Travelling North '87
Under Capricorn '82

Marie Blake
Love Finds Andy Hardy '38
Sensations of 1945 '44

Pamela Blake
Border Rangers '50
Case of the Baby Sitter '47
Gunfire '50
Hat Box Mystery '47
Highway 13 '48
Kid Dynamite '43
Rolling Home '48
Sea Hound '47
Sky Liner '49
Son of God's Country '48

Robert (Bobby) Blake
The Adventures of Rin Tin Tin '47
Andy Hardy's Double Life '42
Busting '74
Coast to Coast '80
Counter Punch '71
Electra Glide in Blue '73
Heart of a Champion: The Ray Mancini Story '85
Homesteaders of Paradise Valley '47
Humoresque '46
In Cold Blood '67
Of Mice and Men '81
Our Gang Comedies '40s
Pork Chop Hill '59
PT 109 '63
Santa Fe Uprising '46
Stagecoach to Denver '46
Tell Them Willie Boy Is Here '69
This Property Is Condemned '66
Treasure of the Golden Condor '53
Treasure of the Sierra Madre '48
Vigilantes of Boom Town '46
Western Double Feature 12 '44
Western Double Feature 13 '40s
Western Double Feature 21 '40s

Colin Blakely
The Big Sleep '78
The Dogs of War '81
Equus '77
Evil Under the Sun '82
Little Lord Fauntleroy '80
Loophole '83

Love Among the Ruins '75
Murder on the Orient Express '74
Nijinsky '80
Operation Julie '85
The Pink Panther Strikes Again '76
The Private Life of Sherlock Holmes '70
Shattered '72
This Sporting Life '63

Donald Blakely
In the Shadow of Kilimanjaro '86
Short Eyes '79
Strike Force '75

Susan Blakely
Blackmail '91
Broken Angel '88
The Concorde: Airport '79 '79
A Cry for Love '80
Dead Reckoning '89
Dreamer '79
Hiroshima Maiden '88
Honor Thy Father and Mother: The True Story of the Menendez Brothers '94
The Incident '89
Intruders '92
Ladykillers '88
The Lords of Flatbush '74
Make Me an Offer '80
My Mom's a Werewolf '89
Out of Sight, Out of Her Mind '89
Over the Top '86
Report to the Commissioner '74
Rich Man, Poor Man '76
Russian Roulette '93
Savages '72
Secrets '77
The Survivalist '87
The Towering Inferno '74
Wildflower '91

Olive Blakeney
Billy the Kid '41
Gangway '37

Ronee Blakley
The Baltimore Bullet '80
Desperate Women '78
The Driver '78
Lightning Over Water '80
Mannikin '77
Murder by Numbers '89
Nashville '75
A Nightmare on Elm Street '84
The Private Files of J. Edgar Hoover '77
Return to Salem's Lot '87
She Came to the Valley '77
Someone to Love '87
Student Confidential '87

Dominique Blanc
Indochine '92
May Fools '90

Erika Blanc
The Devil's Nightmare '71
Kill, Baby, Kill '66
Mark of the Devil 2 '72
The Night Evelyn Came Out of the Grave '71
Sartana's Here...Trade Your Pistol for a Coffin '70
Special Forces '68
Sweet Spirits '80s

Mel Blanc
Kiss Me, Stupid! '64
Neptune's Daughter '49

Michel Blanc
The Favor, the Watch, & the Very Big Fish '92
Menage '86
Monsieur Hire '89
Prospero's Books '91
Uranus '91

Jewel Blanch
Against A Crooked Sky '75
Baffled '72

Pierre Blanchar
Crime and Punishment '35
La Symphonie Pastorale '46
Man from Nowhere '37

Mari Blanchard
Abbott and Costello Go to Mars '53
Son of Sinbad '55

Susan Blanchard
President's Mistress '78
She's in the Army Now '81

Dorothee Blanck
Cleo from 5 to 7 '61
Umbrellas of Cherbourg '64

Peter Bland
Came a Hot Friday '85
Dangerous Orphans '86
Tearaway '87

Clara Blandick
The Adventures of Tom Sawyer '38
The Bitter Tea of General Yen '33
Dreaming Out Loud '40
The Girl from Missouri '34
Infamous Crimes '47
Murder at Midnight '31
Romance '30
Small Town Boy '37
The Wizard of Oz '39

Sally Blane
Cross Examination '32
Fighting Mad '39
Heritage of the Desert '33
Law of the Sea '38
Night of Terror '33
Phantom Express '32
Probation '30
The Silver Streak '34
Vagabond Lover '29
Way Down South '39
When the West Was Young '32

Mark Blankfield
Angel 3: The Final Chapter '88
Frankenstein General Hospital '88
Jack & the Beanstalk '83
Jekyll & Hyde...Together Again '82
The Midnight Hour '86
Robin Hood: Men in Tights '93

Billy Blanks
Back in Action '94
Bloodfist '89
The King of the Kickboxers '91
Showdown '93
Talons of the Eagle '92
TC 2000 '93
Timebomb '91

Arell Blanton
House of Terror '87
Wild Riders '71

Hans-Christian Blech
The Blum Affair '48
Colonel Redl '84
Dirty Hands '76
The Scarlet Letter '73
The Wrong Move '78

Debra Blee
Beach Girls '82
Malibu Bikini Shop '86
Savage Streets '83
Sloane '84

Brian Blessed
Back in the USSR '92
Flash Gordon '80
Henry V '89
High Road to China '83
The Hound of the Baskervilles '83
I, Claudius, Vol. 1: A Touch of Murder/Family Affairs '91
I, Claudius, Vol. 2: Waiting in the Wings/What Shall We Do With Claudius? '80
I, Claudius, Vol. 3: Poison is Queen/Some Justice '80
King Arthur, the Young Warlord '75
Man of La Mancha '72
Much Ado About Nothing '93
Prisoner of Honor '91
Robin Hood: Prince of Thieves '91
Trojan Women '71
Young Warlord '75

Billy Bletcher
Branded Men '31

God's Country and the Man '37

Brenda Blethyn
Grown Ups '80
A River Runs Through It '92
The Witches '90

Jason Blicker
African Journey '89
American Boyfriends '89

Bernard Blier
Buffet Froid '79
Casanova '70 '65
Catch Me a Spy '71
The Daydreamer '75
Dedee d'Anvers '49
Jenny Lamour '47
Les Miserables '57
The Man in the Raincoat '57
Passion for Life '48
The Tall Blond Man with One Black Shoe '72

Hunt Block
The Dirty Dozen: The Fatal Mission '88
Secret Weapons '85

Dan Blocker
The Errand Boy '61
Lady in Cement '68
Ride the Wind '66

Michael Blodgett
The Ultimate Thrill '74
The Velvet Vampire '71

Joan Blondell
Adventure '45
Angel Baby '61
The Baron '88
Big Business Girl '31
Blonde Crazy '31
Bullets or Ballots '38
The Champ '79
The Cincinnati Kid '65
Dames '34
The Dead Don't Die '75
Death at Love House '75
Desk Set '57
Footlight Parade '33
The Glove '78
Gold Diggers of 1933 '33
Hollywood Bloopers '50s
Illicit '31
Lady for a Night '42
Millie '31
Night Nurse '31
Opening Night '77
The Opposite Sex '56
Public Enemy '31
The Rebels '79
Stand-In '37
Stay Away, Joe '68
Support Your Local Gunfighter '71
This Could Be the Night '57
Three Broadway Girls '32
Three Men on a Horse '36
Three on a Match '32
Topper Returns '41
A Tree Grows in Brooklyn '45
Waterhole #3 '67
The Woman Inside '83

Anne Bloom
Dirt Bike Kid '86
That's Adequate '90

Brian Bloom
Voyage of Terror: The Achille Lauro Affair '90
Walls of Glass '85

Claire Bloom
Alexander the Great '55
Anastasia: The Mystery of Anna '86
Brideshead Revisited '81
The Brothers Karamazov '58
The Buccaneer '58
Charly '68
Clash of the Titans '81
Crimes & Misdemeanors '89
Deja Vu '84
A Doll's House '89
Ghostwriter '84
The Haunting '63
The Illustrated Man '69
Innocents in Paris '53
Intimate Contact '87
Islands in the Stream '77
Limelight '52
Look Back in Anger '58
Queenie '87

Bloom ▶cont.

Richard III '55
Sammy & Rosie Get Laid '87
Separate Tables '83
Shadow on the Sun '88
Shadowlands '85
Soldier in Love '67
The Spy Who Came in from the Cold '65
This Lightning Always Strikes Twice '85
The Wonderful World of the Brothers Grimm '62

John Bloom
Bachelor Party '84
Brain of Blood '71
Dracula vs. Frankenstein '71
The Hills Have Eyes, Part 2 '84
The Incredible Two-Headed Transplant '71

Lindsay Bloom
Cover Girl Models '75
French Quarter '78
Hughes & Harlow: Angels in Hell '77
Texas Detour '77

Verna Bloom
After Hours '85
Badge 373 '73
The Blue Knight '75
High Plains Drifter '73
Hired Hand '71
Honkytonk Man '82
The Journey of Natty Gann '85
The Last Temptation of Christ '88
Medium Cool '69
National Lampoon's Animal House '78
Playing for Time '80
Where Have All the People Gone? '74

Eric Blore
Ex-Mrs. Bradford '36
Fancy Pants '50
Flying Down to Rio '33
The Gay Divorcee '34
I Dream Too Much '35
I Live My Life '35
Joy of Living '38
The Lady Eve '41
Lady Scarface '41
Lady Scarface/The Threat '49
The Moon and Sixpence '43
Music in My Heart '40
Quality Street '37
The Road to Zanzibar '41
Romance on the High Seas '48
Shall We Dance '37
The Shanghai Gesture '42
Sullivan's Travels '41
Swing Time '36
Swiss Miss '38
Top Hat '35

Roberts Blossom
Always '89
Candy Mountain '87
Citizens Band '77
Deranged '74
Doc Hollywood '91
Escape from Alcatraz '79
Flashpoint '84
Home Alone '90
Johnny Belinda '82
The Last Temptation of Christ '88
The Quick and the Dead '94
Resurrection '80
Reuben, Reuben '83
Vision Quest '85

Lisa Blount
An American Story '92
Blind Fury '90
Cease Fire '85
Cut and Run '85
Dead and Buried '81
Femme Fatale '90
Great Balls of Fire '89
Nightflyers '87
An Officer and a Gentleman '82
Prince of Darkness '87
Radioactive Dreams '86
September 30, 1955 '77
South of Reno '87

What Waits Below '83

Ben Blue
Broadway Rhythm '44
College Swing '38
For Me and My Gal '42
Panama Hattie '42
The Russians are Coming, the Russians are Coming '66
Two Girls and a Sailor '44
Where Were You When the Lights Went Out? '68

Monte Blue
Desert Gold '36
The Lives of a Bengal Lancer '35
The Man from Painted Post '17
The Marriage Circle '24
A Million to One '37
Orphans of the Storm '21
Prison Shadows '36
Ride, Ranger, Ride '36
Rootin' Tootin' Rhythm '38
Silver River '48
So This is Paris '26
Song of the Gringo '36
Thunder Pass '37
White Shadows in the South Seas '28

Jack Blum
Happy Birthday to Me '81
SnakeEater 2: The Drug Buster '89

Mark Blum
Blind Date '87
Crocodile Dundee '86
Desperately Seeking Susan '85
The Presidio '88
Worth Winning '89

Alan Blumenfeld
Dark Side of the Moon '90
Instant Karma '90
Night Life '90
Problem Child 2 '91
Worth Winning '89

Graeme Blundell
Alvin Purple '73
Alvin Rides Again '74
Doctors and Nurses '82
Weekend of Shadows '77
The Year My Voice Broke '87

Lothaire Bluteau
Black Robe '91
Jesus of Montreal '89
Orlando '92

Margaret Blye
Ash Wednesday '73
The Italian Job '69
Little Darlings '80
Melvin Purvis: G-Man '74
Mischief '85
Silhouette '91
The Sporting Club '72
Waterhole #3 '67

Stanley Blystone
The Fighting Legion '30
Fighting Parson '35
Man of Action '33

Ann Blyth
All the Brothers Were Valiant '53
The Great Caruso '51
The King's Thief '55
Kismet '55
Mildred Pierce '45
Mr. Peabody & the Mermaid '48
One Minute to Zero '52
Rose Marie '54
The Student Prince '54

Betty Blythe
Dawn on the Great Divide '42
Honky Tonk '41
House of Errors '42
Miracle Kid '42
Nomads of the North '20
The Scarlet Letter '34
She '21

Janus Blythe
The Hills Have Eyes, Part 2 '84
Soldier's Fortune '91

Bruce Boa
Murder Story '89
The Neighbor '93
White Light '90

Eleanor Boardman
The Crowd '28
She Goes to War '29

Virginia True Boardman
Brand of the Outlaws '36
Test of Donald Norton '26

Michael Boatman
China Beach '88
Hamburger Hill '87

Anne Bobby
Baby of the Bride '91
Night Breed '90

Hart Bochner
Apartment Zero '88
Die Hard '88
East of Eden '80
Fellow Traveler '89
Having It All '82
The Innocent '93
Mad at the Moon '92
Making Mr. Right '86
Mr. Destiny '90
Rich and Famous '81
Supergirl '84
Terror Train '80
War & Remembrance, Part 1 '88
War & Remembrance, Part 2 '89
War & Remembrance, Part 3 '88
War & Remembrance, Part 4 '88
War & Remembrance, Part 5 '88
War & Remembrance, Part 6 '88
War & Remembrance, Part 7 '88
War & Remembrance: The Final Chapter, Part 8 '89
War & Remembrance: The Final Chapter, Part 9 '89
War & Remembrance: The Final Chapter, Part 10 '89
War & Remembrance: The Final Chapter, Part 11 '89
War & Remembrance: The Final Chapter, Part 12 '89
The Wild Life '84

Lloyd Bochner
Crystal Heart '87
The Dunwich Horror '70
Fine Gold
The Horse in the Gray Flannel Suit '68
Landslide '92
The Lonely Lady '83
Louisiana '87
Mary and Joseph: A Story of Faith '79
Mazes and Monsters '82
Millenium '89
Morning Glory '93
Naked Gun 2 1/2: The Smell of Fear '91
The Night Walker '64
Point Blank '67
Satan's School for Girls '73
Terraces '77
Tony Rome '67
Ulzana's Raid '72

Wolfgang Bodison
A Few Good Men '92
Little Big League '94

Erika Bodnar
Almanac of Fall
A Happy New Year! '79

Karl-Heinz Boehm
Fox and His Friends '75
Peeping Tom '63
Unnatural '52
The Wonderful World of the Brothers Grimm '62

Dirk Bogarde
Accident '67
The Blue Lamp '49
A Bridge Too Far '77
Cast a Dark Shadow '55
Daddy Nostalgia '90
Damn the Defiant '62
The Damned '69
Darling '65
Death in Venice '71

Despair '78
Doctor at Large '57
Doctor at Sea '56
Doctor in Distress '63
Doctor in the House '53
The Fixer '68
I Could Go on Singing '63
Justine '69
Night Ambush '57
Night Flight from Moscow '73
The Night Porter '74
Permission To Kill '75
Providence '77
The Sea Shall Not Have Them '55
Sebastian '68
The Servant '63
Simba '55
The Sleeping Tiger '54
Song Without End '60
The Spanish Gardener '57
A Tale of Two Cities '58
To See Such Fun '81
Victim '62
The Vision '87

Humphrey Bogart
Across the Pacific '42
Action in the North Atlantic '43
The African Queen '51
All Through the Night '42
Angels with Dirty Faces '38
The Barefoot Contessa '54
Battle Circus '53
Beat the Devil '53
The Best of Bogart '43
The Big Sleep '46
Brother Orchid '40
Bullets or Ballots '38
The Caine Mutiny '54
Casablanca '42
Chain Lightning '50
Conflict '45
Dark Passage '47
Dark Victory '39
Dead End '37
Dead Reckoning '47
Desperate Hours '55
The Enforcer '51
The Harder They Fall '56
High Sierra '41
Hollywood Outtakes & Rare Footage '83
In a Lonely Place '50
Key Largo '48
Kid Galahad '37
Knock on Any Door '49
The Left Hand of God '55
The Maltese Falcon '41
Marked Woman '37
Midnight '34
Oklahoma Kid '39
Passage to Marseilles '44
Petrified Forest '36
The Roaring Twenties '39
Sabrina '54
Sahara '43
Sirocco '51
Stand-In '37
Thank Your Lucky Stars '43
They Drive by Night '40
Three on a Match '32
To Have & Have Not '44
Tokyo Joe '49
Treasure of the Sierra Madre '48
The Two Mrs. Carrolls '47
Virginia City '40
We're No Angels '55

Eric Bogosian
The Caine Mutiny Court Martial '88
Last Flight Out: A True Story '90
Sex, Drugs, Rock & Roll: Eric Bogosian '91
Special Effects '85
Suffering Bastards '90
Talk Radio '88

Roman Bohnen
The Best Years of Our Lives '46
The Hairy Ape '44
Open Secret '48

Corinne Bohrer
Dead Solid Perfect '88
Stewardess School '86
Vice Versa '88

Richard Bohringer
Barjo '93
Diva '82
L'Addition '85
Le Grand Chemin '87
Peril '85

Curt Bois
Bitter Sweet '40
The Boat is Full '81
Boom Town '40
Caught '49
The Great Waltz '38
The Hunchback of Notre Dame '39
The Lady in Question '40
The Tuttles of Tahiti '42
Wings of Desire '88

Christine Boisson
Sorceress '88
Unsettled Land '87

James Bolam
Crucible of Terror '72
Dressed for Death '74
In Celebration '75
The Loneliness of the Long Distance Runner '62
The Maze '85

Mary Boland
Julia Misbehaves '48
New Moon '40
Nothing But Trouble '44
One Night in the Tropics '40
Pride and Prejudice '40
The Ruggles of Red Gap '35
The Women '39

John Boles
Craig's Wife '36
Curly Top '35
Frankenstein '31
King of Jazz '30
The Littlest Rebel '35
Sinners in Paradise '38
Stand Up and Cheer '34
Stella Dallas '37
Thousands Cheer '43

Ray Bolger
April In Paris '52
Babes in Toyland '61
For Heaven's Sake '79
Four Jacks and a Jill '41
The Great Ziegfeld '36
The Harvey Girls '46
Judy Garland: The Golden Years at MGM
Look for the Silver Lining '49
Rosalie '38
The Runner Stumbles '79
Stage Door Canteen '43
Sunny '41
Sweethearts '38
That's Dancing! '85
The Wizard of Oz '39

Florinda Bolkan
Acqua e Sapone '83
Black Lemons '80s
Collector's Item '89
The Day that Shook the World '78
The Last Valley '71
Master Touch '74
Ring of Death '72
Some Girls '88
The Word '78

Tiffany Bolling
Bonnie's Kids '73
The Centerfold Girls '74
Ecstasy '84
Kingdom of the Spiders '77
Wild Party '74

Joseph Bologna
Alligator 2: The Mutation '90
The Big Bus '76
Blame It on Rio '84
Chapter Two '79
Citizen Cohn '92
Cops and Robbers '73
Coupe de Ville '92
Deadly Rivals '92
Honor Thy Father '73
Jersey Girl '92
My Favorite Year '82
Not Quite Human '87
One Cooks, the Other Doesn't '83
Rags to Riches '87
Torn Between Two Lovers '79

Transylvania 6-5000 '85
The Woman in Red '84

Paolo Bonacelli
Christ Stopped at Eboli '79
Henry IV '85
Johnny Stecchino '92
Night on Earth '91
Salo, or the 120 Days of
  Sodom '75

Danny Bonaduce
America's Deadliest Home
  Video '92
H.O.T.S. '79

Louie Bonanno
Night of the Living Babes '87
Student Affairs '88
Wimps '87

Fortuna Bonanova
An Affair to Remember '57
Ali Baba and the Forty Thieves
  '43
Double Indemnity '44

Ivan Bonar
The Haunting Passion '83
MacArthur '77

Derek Bond
Black Tide '56
The Hand '60
Inheritance '47
Nicholas Nickleby '46
Rogue's Yarn '56
Scott of the Antarctic '48
The Stranger from Venus '54
Svengali '55
Tony Draws a Horse '51

James Bond, III
Def by Temptation '90
The Fish that Saved Pittsburgh
  '79
The Sky is Gray '80

Renee Bond
Class Reunion '87
Please Don't Eat My Mother '72

Steve Bond
Gas Pump Girls '79
H.O.T.S. '79
L.A. Gangs Rising '89
Magdalene '89
Massacre at Central High '76
Picasso Trigger '89
The Prey '80
To Die for '89
To Die for 2 '91

Sudie Bond
Come Back to the Five & Dime
  Jimmy Dean, Jimmy Dean
  '82
I Am the Cheese '83
Tomorrow '83
Where the Lilies Bloom '74

**Tommy "Butch"
Bond**
Little Rascals, Book 15 '30s
Our Gang Comedies '40s
Superman: The Serial, Vol. 1
  '48

Ward Bond
Big Trail '30
Blowing Wild '54
Born to Be Wild '38
Bringing Up Baby '38
The Crimson Trail '35
Dakota '45
Dakota Incident '56
Devil Dogs of the Air '35
Drums Along the Mohawk '39
Falcon Takes Over/Strange
  Bargain '49
Fighting Shadows '35
The Fighting Sullivans '42
Fort Apache '48
The Fugitive '48
Gentleman Jim '42
Gone with the Wind '39
Great Missouri Raid '51
A Guy Named Joe '44
Gypsy Colt '54
Hawaii Calls '38
Hello, Frisco, Hello '43
Heroes for Sale '33
Hitler: Dead or Alive '43
It Happened One Night '34
It's a Wonderful Life '46
Johnny Guitar '53

Kiss Tomorrow Goodbye '50
Kit Carson '40
The Long Gray Line '55
The Making of a Legend:
  "Gone With the Wind" '89
The Maltese Falcon '41
A Man Alone '55
Mister Roberts '55
My Darling Clementine '46
Oklahoma Kid '39
On Dangerous Ground '51
Only the Valiant '50
Prison Break '38
The Quiet Man '52
Rio Bravo '59
The Searchers '56
Sergeant York '41
Tall in the Saddle '44
They Were Expendable '45
Three Godfathers '48
The Time of Your Life '48
Wagon Master '50
Waterfront '39
White Eagle '32
Wings of Eagles '57
You Only Live Once '37
Young Mr. Lincoln '39

Sergei Bondarchuk
Battle of Neretva '69
A Summer to Remember '61
War and Peace '68

Beulah Bondi
Back to Bataan '45
Baron of Arizona '51
Breakfast in Hollywood '46
Finishing School '33
The Invisible Ray '36
It's a Wonderful Life '46
Latin Lovers '53
Lone Star '52
Mr. Smith Goes to Washington
  '39
Moon's Our Home '38
Of Human Hearts '38
On Borrowed Time '39
Our Town '40
Penny Serenade '41
Rain '32
Sister Kenny '46
The Sisters '38
The Snake Pit '48
So Dear to My Heart '49
The Southerner '45
Street Scene '31
A Summer Place '59
Unholy Wife '57
Vivacious Lady '38
Watch on the Rhine '43
The Wonderful World of the
  Brothers Grimm '62

Peter Bonerz
The Committee '68
How to Break Up a Happy
  Divorce '76
Medium Cool '69
Serial '80
A Session with the Committee
  '69
Your Place or Mine '83

Ken Bones
Bellman and True '88
Jack the Ripper '88

Charles Bonet
Black Dragon's Revenge '75
Death Promise '78
Way of the Black Dragon '81

Lisa Bonet
Angel Heart '87
Dead Connection '94

Nai Bonet
Devil's Angels '67
Fairytales '79
Gangsters '79
Nocturna '79
Soul Hustler '76

Massimo Bonetti
Kaos '85
The Night of the Shooting Stars
  '82
The Story of Boys & Girls '91

**Helena Bonham
Carter**
Francesco '93
Getting It Right '89
Hamlet '90
Howard's End '92

Lady Jane '85
Maurice '87
A Room with a View '86
The Vision '87
Where Angels Fear to Tread
  '91

Sandrine Bonnaire
La Puritaine '86
Monsieur Hire '89
A Nos Amours '84
The Plague '92
Police '85
Under Satan's Sun '87
Vagabond '85

Lee Bonnell
Look Who's Laughing '41
The Navy Comes Through '42

Vivian Bonnell
Christmas in Connecticut '92
The Josephine Baker Story '90

Bill Bonner
Outlaw Riders '72
Satan's Sadists '69

Frank Bonner
Equinox '71
WKRP in Cincinnati, Vol. 1 '78
You Can't Hurry Love '88

Tony Bonner
Alternative '78
Creatures the World Forgot '70
Dead Sleep '91
Hurricane Smith '92
Inn of the Damned '74
The Lighthorsemen '87
Money Movers '78
Quigley Down Under '90
Sudden Terror '70

Sonny Bono
Airplane 2: The Sequel '82
Balboa '82
Dirty Laundry '87
Escape to Athena '79
Hairspray '88
Murder on Flight 502 '75
Troll '85
Under the Boardwalk '89
The Vals '85

Brian Bonsall
Blank Check '93
Desperate Motives '92
Father Hood '93
Mikey '92

Sorrell Booke
Bank Shot '74
Devil Times Five '74
Gone are the Days '63
The Other Side of Midnight '77
Special Delivery '76
Up the Down Staircase '67

Pat Boone
The Cross & the Switchblade
  '72
Journey to the Center of the
  Earth '59
Roger & Me '89
State Fair '62

Richard Boone
Against A Crooked Sky '75
The Alamo '60
The Arrangement '69
Away All Boats '56
Beneath the 12-Mile Reef '53
Big Jake '71
The Big Sleep '78
The Bushido Blade '80
Dragnet '54
God's Gun '75
The Halls of Montezuma '50
Hombre '67
I Bury the Living '58
Madron '70
The Night of the Following Day
  '69
Rio Conchos '64
The Robe '53
The Shootist '76
The Tall T '57
Ten Wanted Men '54
The War Lord '65
Winter Kills '79

Charley Boorman
Deliverance '72
The Emerald Forest '85
Excalibur '81
Hope and Glory '87

Katrine Boorman
Camille Claudel '89
Hope and Glory '87

Adrian Booth
Captain America '44
Daughter of Don Q '46
Son of God's Country '48

Connie Booth
American Friends '91
Hawks '89
John Cleese on How to Irritate
  People '68
Leon the Pig Farmer '93
Little Lord Fauntleroy '80
Monty Python and the Holy
  Grail '75
Nairobi Affair '88
Romance with a Double Bass
  '74
The Strange Case of the End of
  Civilization as We Know It
  '93

Edwina Booth
The Last of the Mohicans '32
Trader Horn '31

James Booth
American Ninja 4: The
  Annihilation '91
Bad Guys '86
The Bliss of Mrs. Blossom '68
Brannigan '75
Darker than Amber '70
Hotline '82
Man Who Had Power Over
  Women '70
Pray for Death '85
Programmed to Kill '86
Rentadick '72
Revenge '71
Robbery '67

Shirley Booth
Come Back, Little Sheba '52
Hot Spell '58
The Matchmaker '58

Powers Boothe
A Breed Apart '84
By Dawn's Early Light '89
Cruising '80
A Cry for Love '80
The Emerald Forest '85
Extreme Prejudice '87
The Guyana Tragedy: The
  Story of Jim Jones '80
Into the Homeland '87
Plutonium Incident '82
Rapid Fire '92
Red Dawn '84
Skag '79
Smart-Aleck Kill '85
Southern Comfort '81
Tombstone '93
Wildcard '92

Lynn Borden
Frogs '72
This is a Hijack '75

Carla Borelli
Asylum of Satan '72
Charlotte Forten's Mission:
  Experiment in Freedom '85

Veda Ann Borg
Accomplice '46
The Alamo '60
The Bachelor and the Bobby-
  Soxer '47
Big Jim McLain '52
Big Town '47
Blonde Savage '47
The Corsican Brothers '42
Dr. Christian Meets the Women
  '40
The Falcon in Hollywood '44
False Faces '32
Fog Island '45
Guys and Dolls '55
Honky Tonk '41
I Married an Angel '42
I Take This Oath '40
I'll Cry Tomorrow '55
Isle of Forgotten Sins '43
Julia Misbehaves '48
Kid Galahad '37
Love Me or Leave Me '55
Marked Trails '44
Melody Ranch '40
Revenge of the Zombies '43
Rider from Tucson '50

Treasure of Fear '45
Wings of Eagles '57

Sal Borgese
Flight of the Innocent '93
Thundersquad '85

Ernest Borgnine
The Adventurers '70
All Quiet on the Western Front
  '79
Any Man's Death '90
Bad Day at Black Rock '54
The Badlanders '58
Barabbas '62
The Black Hole '79
Bullet for Sandoval '70
The Catered Affair '56
Chuka '67
Codename: Wildgeese '84
Convoy '78
Counter Punch '71
Deadly Blessing '81
Demetrius and the Gladiators
  '54
Devil's Rain '75
The Dirty Dozen '67
The Dirty Dozen: The Deadly
  Mission '87
The Dirty Dozen: The Fatal
  Mission '88
The Dirty Dozen: The Next
  Mission '85
The Double McGuffin '79
Escape from New York '81
Fire '77
The Flight of the Phoenix '65
From Here to Eternity '53
Future Cop '76
The Greatest '77
Hannie Caulder '72
High Risk '76
Ice Station Zebra '68
Jesus of Nazareth '77
Johnny Guitar '53
Jubal '56
Laser Mission '90
The Last Command '55
Law and Disorder '74
Love by Appointment '76
Love Leads the Way '84
The Manhunt '86
Marty '55
Moving Target '89
Neptune Factor '73
The Opponent '89
The Oscar '66
The Poseidon Adventure '72
The Prince and the Pauper '78
Shoot '85
Skeleton Coast '89
Spike of Bensonhurst '88
The Stranger Wore a Gun '53
Super Fuzz '81
Suppose They Gave a War and
  Nobody Came? '70
Torpedo Run '58
The Trackers '71
Vengeance Is Mine '84
Vera Cruz '54
The Vikings '58
When Time Ran Out '80
The Wild Bunch '69
Willard '71
Young Warriors '83

Roscoe Born
Haunting of Sarah Hardy '89
Lady Mobster '88

Katherine Borowitz
Fellow Traveler '89
Mac '93
Men of Respect '91

Jesse Borrego
Blood In...Blood Out: Bound by
  Honor '93
Mi Vida Loca '94

Dieter Borsche
Ali Baba and the 40 Thieves '54
The Black Abbot '63
Dead Eyes of London '61
The Mad Executioners '65
The Phantom of Soho '64

Jean-Mark Bory
Le Repos du Guerrier '62
The Lovers '59

Frank Borzage
Grit of the Girl Telegrapher/In
  the Switch Tower '15
A Mormon Maid '17

Borzage ►*cont.*

Tale of Two Cities/In the Switch
Tower '15

Philip Bosco
Angie '94
Another Woman '88
Blue Steel '90
Children of a Lesser God '86
The Dream Team '89
F/X 2: The Deadly Art of Illusion
'91
Heaven Help Us '85
The Mission '86
The Money Pit '86
Quick Change '90
The Return of Eliot Ness '91
Shadows and Fog '92
Straight Talk '92
Suspect '87
Three Men and a Baby '87
Walls of Glass '85
Working Girl '88

Lucia Bose
The Legend of Blood Castle '72
Lumiere '76

Andrea Bosic
Hornet's Nest '70
Maciste in Hell '60
Pirates of the Seven Seas '62

Tom Bosley
Bang Bang Kid '67
The Bastard '78
Death Cruise '74
Fire and Rain '89
For the Love of It '80
Gus '76
The Jesse Owens Story '84
Love with the Proper Stranger
'63
Million Dollar Mystery '87
Night Gallery '69
O'Hara's Wife '82
The Rebels '79
The Secret War of Harry Frigg
'68
The Streets of San Francisco
'72
The Triangle Factory Fire
Scandal '79
Wicked Stepmother '89
The World of Henry Orient '64
Yours, Mine & Ours '68

Barbara Bosson
The Committee '68
The Last Starfighter '84
Little Sweetheart '90
A Session with the Committee
'69

Barry Bostwick
800 Leagues Down the
Amazon '90s
George Washington '84
George Washington: The
Forging of a Nation '86
Hitchhiker 3 '87
Jailbait: Betrayed By Innocence
'86
Megaforce '82
Movie, Movie '78
Murder by Natural Causes '79
Praying Mantis '93
Red Flag: The Ultimate Game
'81
The Rocky Horror Picture
Show '75
Russian Roulette '93
Scruples '80
War & Remembrance, Part 1
'88
War & Remembrance, Part 2
'89
Weekend at Bernie's 2 '93
A Woman of Substance,
Episode 1: Nest of Vipers
'84
A Woman of Substance,
Episode 2: The Secret is
Revealed '84
A Woman of Substance,
Episode 3: Fighting for the
Dream '84

Hobart Bosworth
Abraham Lincoln '30
Annapolis '28

The Big Parade '25
The Dark Hour '36
Dubarry '30
King of the Sierras '38
The Last of the Mohicans '32
Little Church Around the
Corner '23
A Mormon Maid '17
The Nervous Wreck '26
Phantom Express '32
Sea Lion '21
Spangles '26
A Woman of Affairs '28

Wade Boteler
Big News '29
Come On Danger! '32
The Green Hornet '39
Let 'er Go Gallegher '28
The Mandarin Mystery '37

Sara Botsford
By Design '82
Deadly Eyes '82
The Gunrunner '84
Murder by Phone '82
Still of the Night '82

Benjamin Bottoms
A Shining Season '79
Stalk the Wild Child '76

Joseph Bottoms
The Black Hole '79
Blind Date '84
Born to Race '88
Celebrity '85
Cloud Dancer '80
Crime & Passion '75
The Dove '74
High Rolling in a Hot Corvette
'77
Holocaust '78
Inner Sanctum '91
Intruder Within '81
King of the Mountain '81
Liar's Edge '92
Open House '86
Return Engagement '78
The Sins of Dorian Gray '82
Stalk the Wild Child '76
Surfacing '84
Treacherous Crossing '92

Sam Bottoms
Apocalypse Now '79
Bronco Billy '80
Class of '44 '73
Desperate Lives '82
Dolly Dearest '92
East of Eden '80
Gardens of Stone '87
Hearts of Darkness: A
Filmmaker's Apocalypse '91
Hunter's Blood '87
In 'n Out '86
The Last Picture Show '71
The Outlaw Josey Wales '76
Prime Risk '84
Ragin' Cajun '90
Return to Eden '89
Savages '75
Up from the Depths '79
Zandy's Bride '74

Timothy Bottoms
The Drifter '88
East of Eden '80
The Fantasist '89
The Gift of Love '90
Hambone & Hillie '84
High Country '81
Hurricane '79
Husbands, Wives, Money, and
Murder '86
In the Shadow of Kilimanjaro
'86
Invaders from Mars '86
Istanbul '90
Johnny Got His Gun '71
The Land of Faraway '87
The Last Picture Show '71
Love Leads the Way '84
The Other Side of the
Mountain, Part 2 '78
The Paper Chase '73
Rollercoaster '77
The Sea Serpent '85
A Shining Season '79
A Small Town in Texas '76
The Story of David '76
Texasville '90
Tin Man '83

What Waits Below '83
The White Dawn '75

Barbara Bouchet
Cry of a Prostitute: Love Kills
'72
In Harm's Way '65
Mean Machine '73
Rogue '76
Surabaya Conspiracy '75

Patrick Bouchitey
The Best Way '77
Life Is a Long Quiet River '88

Jean Bouise
Hothead '78
La Femme Nikita '91
Le Dernier Combat '84
Old Gun '76

Ingrid Boulting
Deadly Passion '85
The Last Tycoon '76

Carol Bouquet
Buffet Froid '79
Dagger Eyes '80s
For Your Eyes Only '81
New York Stories '89
Special Police '85
That Obscure Object of Desire
'77
Too Beautiful for You '88

Michel Bouquet
Borsalino '70
The Bride Wore Black '68
La Rupture '70
Le Complot '73
Mississippi Mermaid '69
Pattes Blanches '49
This Special Friendship '67
Toto le Heros '91
Tous les Matins du Monde '92

Bourvil
The Brain '69
Crazy for Love '52
Four Bags Full '56
Jailbird's Vacation '65
La Grande Vadrouille '66
Les Grandes Gueules '65
Les Miserables '57
Mr. Peek-A-Boo '50

Dennis Boutsikaris
*batteries not included '87
The Dream Team '89

Brunella Bova
Miracle in Milan '51
The White Sheik '52

Julie Bovasso
Article 99 '92
Betsy's Wedding '90
Gentleman Bandit '81
Moonstruck '87
Willie & Phil '80
Wise Guys '86

Clara Bow
Dancing Mothers '26
Down to the Sea in Ships '22
Free to Love '25
Hula '28
It '27
Mantrap '26
My Lady of Whims '25
Wings '27

Dorris Bowdon
Drums Along the Mohawk '39
The Grapes of Wrath '40

Dennis Bowen
Gas Pump Girls '79
Van Nuys Blvd. '79

Michael Bowen
The Abduction of Kari Swenson
'87
Casualties of Love: The "Long
Island Lolita" Story '93
Echo Park '86
Iron Eagle '86
Mortal Passions '89
Night of the Comet '84
Season of Fear '89
The Taking of Beverly Hills '91

Roger Bowen
M*A*S*H '70
What About Bob? '91
Zapped! '82

Malick Bowens
The Believers '87

Bopha! '93
Out of Africa '85

Antoinette Bower
Blood Song '82
Die Sister, Die! '74
The Evil That Men Do '84

Tom Bower
Ballad of Gregorio Cortez '83
Family Sins '87
The Lightship '86
Love, Lies and Murder '91
Massive Retaliation '85
Promised a Miracle '88
Raising Cain '92
Relentless 3 '93
River's Edge '87
True Believer '89
Wildrose '85

John Bowers
Lorna Doone '22
The Sky Pilot '21
The White Sin '24

David Bowie
Absolute Beginners '86
Christiane F. '82
The Hunger '83
Into the Night '85
Just a Gigolo '79
Labyrinth '86
The Last Temptation of Christ
'88
The Linguini Incident '92
The Man Who Fell to Earth '76
Merry Christmas, Mr. Lawrence
'83
UHF '89
Yellowbeard '83

Judi Bowker
Anna Karenina '85
Brother Sun, Sister Moon '73
Clash of the Titans '81
East of Elephant Rock '76
The Shooting Party '85

Peter Bowles
The Charge of the Light
Brigade '68
A Day in the Death of Joe Egg
'71
Endless Night '71
The Offence '73

Laura Bowman
Drums O'Voodoo '34
Son of Ingagi '40

Lee Bowman
Bataan '43
Cover Girl '44
Love Affair '39
My Dream is Yours '49
Next Time I Marry '38
Smash-Up: The Story of a
Woman '47
Tonight and Every Night '45

Bruce Boxleitner
The Babe '92
The Baltimore Bullet '80
Diplomatic Immunity '91
Double Jeopardy '92
East of Eden '80
From the Dead of Night '89
Kenny Rogers as the Gambler
'80
Kenny Rogers as the Gambler,
Part 2: The Adventure
Continues '83
Kenny Rogers as the Gambler,
Part 3: The Legend
Continues '87
Kuffs '92
Murderous Vision '91
Passion Flower '86
Perfect Family '92
The Secret '93
Tron '82

Beverly Boyd
Ghost Rider '43
Jive Junction '43

Blake Boyd
Dune Warriors '91
Raiders of the Sun '92

Guy Boyd
Body Double '84
Eyes of Fire '84
The Eyes of the Amaryllis '82
The Jagged Edge '85
Keeping On '81

Kiss Me a Killer '91
The Last of the Finest '90
Murder Ordained '87
Past Midnight '92

Stephen Boyd
Ben-Hur '59
The Bible...In the Beginning '66
Billy Rose's Jumbo '62
Black Brigade '69
The Bravados '58
Caper of the Golden Bulls '67
The Fall of the Roman Empire
'64
Fantastic Voyage '66
Hannie Caulder '72
Imperial Venus '71
The Man Who Never Was '55
The Oscar '66
Shalako '68
The Squeeze '77
The Treasure of Jamaica Reef
'74

William Boyd
Along the Sundown Trail '42
Bar-20 '43
Border Patrol '43
Border Vigilantes '41
Colt Comrades '43
Doomed Caravan '41
East Side Kids/The Lost City
'35
False Colors '43
Federal Agent '36
The Flying Fool '29
The Frontiersman '38
Having Wonderful Time/
Carnival Boat '38
High Voltage '29
His First Command '29
Hopalong Cassidy '35
Hopalong Cassidy: Borrowed
Trouble '48
Hopalong Cassidy: Dangerous
Venture '48
Hopalong Cassidy: False
Paradise '48
Hopalong Cassidy: Hoppy's
Holiday '47
Hopalong Cassidy: Renegade
Trail '39
Hopalong Cassidy: Riders of
the Deadline '43
Hopalong Cassidy: Silent
Conflict '48
Hopalong Cassidy: Sinister
Journey '48
Hopalong Cassidy: The Dead
Don't Dream '48
Hopalong Cassidy: The Devil's
Playground '46
Hopalong Cassidy: The
Marauders '47
Hopalong Cassidy: Unexpected
Guest '47
Hoppy Serves a Writ '43
In Old Colorado '41
King of Kings '27
Laughing at Life '33
Law of the Pampas '39
Leather Burners '43
The Leatherneck '28
Lost Canyon '43
The Lost City '34
Midnight Warning '32
Mystery Man '44
Oliver Twist '33
Outlaws of the Desert '41
Painted Desert '31
Power '28
Prairie Pals '42
Racing Luck '35
Renegade Trail '39
Riders of the Timberline '41
The Road to Yesterday '25
Road to Yesterday/The Yankee
Clipper '27
Rustler's Valley '37
Santa Fe Marshal '40
The Showdown '40
State's Attorney '31
Texas Masquerade '44
Tumbleweed Trail '42
Twilight on the Trail '41
Yankee Clipper '27

Sally Boyden
Barnaby and Me '77
Little Dragons '80

Charles Boyer
Adorable Julia '62
Algiers '38
All This and Heaven Too '40
April Fools '69
Arch of Triumph '48
Around the World in 80 Days '56
Barefoot in the Park '67
Break of Hearts '35
The Buccaneer '58
Casino Royale '67
The Cobweb '55
Conquest '37
The Earrings of Madame De... '54
Fanny '61
First Legion '51
The Four Horsemen of the Apocalypse '62
The Garden of Allah '36
Gaslight '44
History is Made at Night '37
The Hot Line '69
Is Paris Burning? '68
Liliom '35
Love Affair '39
The Madwoman of Chaillot '69
A Matter of Time '76
Mayerling '36
Nana '55
Red Headed Woman '32
Stavisky '74

Katy Boyer
Long Gone '87
Tapeheads '89
Trapped '89

Miriam Boyer
Jonah Who Will Be 25 in the Year 2000 '76
Tous les Matins du Monde '92
Un Coeur en Hiver '93
Window Shopping '86

Sully Boyer
Car Wash '76
The Manhattan Project '86

Lara Flynn Boyle
Baby's Day Out '94
The Dark Backward '91
Dead Poets Society '89
Equinox '93
Eye of the Storm '91
How I Got into College '89
May Wine '90
Mobsters '91
Poltergeist 3 '88
The Preppie Murder '89
Red Rock West '93
The Rookie '90
The Temp '93
Threesome '94
Twin Peaks '90
Wayne's World '92
Where the Day Takes You '92

Peter Boyle
Beyond the Poseidon Adventure '79
Brink's Job '78
The Candidate '72
Conspiracy: The Trial of the Chicago Eight '87
Disaster at Silo 7 '88
The Dream Team '89
Echoes in the Darkness '87
F.I.S.T. '78
From Here to Eternity '79
Ghost in the Noonday Sun '74
Hammett '82
Hardcore '79
Honeymoon in Vegas '92
Joe '70
Johnny Dangerously '84
Kickboxer 2: The Road Back '90
Men of Respect '91
Nervous Ticks '93
Outland '81
Red Heat '88
The Shadow '94
Slither '73
Solar Crisis '92
Speed Zone '88
Steelyard Blues '73
Surrender '87
Swashbuckler '76
Taking the Heat '93
Taxi Driver '76

Tragedy of Flight 103: The Inside Story '91
Turk 182! '85
Walker '87
Where the Buffalo Roam '80
Yellowbeard '83
Young Frankenstein '74

Max Bozyk
The Jolly Paupers '38
Mamele '38
Yidl Mitn Fidl '36

Marcel Bozzuffi
The French Connection '71
La Cage aux Folles 2 '81
Z '69

Teda Bracci
The Big Bird Cage '72
Chrome Hearts '70

Elizabeth Bracco
In the Soup '92
Money for Nothing '93
Mystery Train '89

Lorraine Bracco
Being Human '94
Camorra: The Naples Connection '85
The Dream Team '89
Even Cowgirls Get the Blues '94
Goodfellas '90
Medicine Man '92
The Pick-Up Artist '87
Radio Flyer '92
Scam '93
Sing '89
Someone to Watch Over Me '87
Switch '91
Talent for the Game '91
Traces of Red '92

Eddie Bracken
Caught in the Draft '41
Hail the Conquering Hero '44
Home Alone 2: Lost in New York '92
Miracle of Morgan's Creek '44
National Lampoon's Vacation '83
Summer Stock '50
Too Many Girls '40
We're Not Married '52
Young & Willing '42

Sidney Bracy
The Cameraman '28
Tangled Destinies '32

Lane Bradbury
Maybe I'll Be Home in the Spring '70
The Ultimate Warrior '75

Kim Braden
Billyboy '79
Bloodsuckers from Outer Space '83

Greg Bradford
Lovelines '84
Zapped! '82

Lane Bradford
Bandit King of Texas '49
The Fighting Redhead '50
Gun Glory '57
The Hawk of Powder River '48
The Invisible Monster '50

Richard Bradford
Ambition '91
Badge of the Assassin '85
The Chinatown Murders: Man Against the Mob '92
Cold Heaven '92
Goin' South '78
The Heart of Dixie '89
Internal Affairs '90
Legend of Billie Jean '85
Little Nikita '88
Mean Season '85
The Milagro Beanfield War '88
More American Graffiti '79
Permanent Record '88
A Rumor of War '80
Running Hot '83
Servants of Twilight '91
Sunset '88
The Trip to Bountiful '85
The Untouchables '87

David Bradley
American Ninja 3: Blood Hunt '89
American Ninja 4: The Annihilation '91
American Samurai '92
Blood Warriors '93
Cyborg Cop '93
Lower Level '91

Doug Bradley
Hellbound: Hellraiser 2 '88
Hellraiser 3: Hell on Earth '92

Carl Bradshaw
The Harder They Come '72
The Lunatic '92

Alice Brady
The Gay Divorcee '34
Go West, Young Man '36
Gold Diggers of 1935 '35
Her Silent Sacrifice '18
In Old Chicago '38
Joy of Living '38
My Man Godfrey '36
Young Mr. Lincoln '39

Pat Brady
Bells of Coronado '50
Call of the Canyon '42
Down Dakota Way '49
The Golden Stallion '49
Song of Texas '43
Sunset on the Desert '42
Texas Legionnaires '43
Trigger, Jr. '50
Twilight in the Sierras '50
Western Double Feature 19 '45

Scott Brady
Arizona Bushwackers '67
Bonnie's Kids '73
Cain's Cutthroats '71
Castle of Evil '66
The China Syndrome '79
Dollars '71
Gun Riders '69
He Walked by Night '48
Johnny Guitar '53
Journey to the Center of Time '67
Kansas City Massacre '75
Loners '72
Maverick Queen '55
Mohawk '56
Montana Belle '52
Party Girls for Sale '54
Port of New York '49
The Restless Breed '58
Satan's Sadists '69
Storm Rider '57
Strange Behavior '81
They Were So Young '55
When Every Day was the Fourth of July '78
White Fire '53

Eric (Hans Gudegast) Braeden
The Adultress '77
Aliens Are Coming '80
The Ambulance '90
Colossus: The Forbin Project '70
Dayton's Devils '68
Death Scream '75
Escape from the Planet of the Apes '71
Happily Ever After '82
Lady Ice '73
The Power Within '79
The Ultimate Thrill '74

Sonia Braga
Dona Flor and Her Two Husbands '78
Gabriela '84
I Love You '81
Kiss of the Spider Woman '85
Lady on the Bus '78
The Last Prostitute '91
The Man Who Broke 1,000 Chains '87
The Milagro Beanfield War '88
Moon Over Parador '88
The Rookie '90

Wilfrid Brambell
The Adventures of Picasso '78
The Conqueror Worm '68
Sword of the Valiant '83

Francisco (Frank) Brana
Crypt of the Living Dead '73
Cthulhu Mansion '91
Graveyard of Horror '71
Street Warriors '87

Kenneth Branagh
Coming Through '90
Dead Again '91
Fortunes of War '87
Henry V '89
High Season '88
Look Back in Anger '89
A Month in the Country '87
Much Ado About Nothing '93
Peter's Friends '92
Swing Kids '93

Lillo Brancato
A Bronx Tale '93
Renaissance Man '94

Neville Brand
The Adventures of Huckleberry Finn '74
The Barbary Coast '74
Birdman of Alcatraz '62
Cahill: United States Marshal '73
The Deadly Trackers '73
Death Stalk '74
Desperados '69
D.O.A. '49
Eaten Alive '76
Evils of the Night '85
The Halls of Montezuma '50
Hi-Riders '77
Kansas City Confidential '52
Lonely Man '57
The Longest Drive '76
Love Me Tender '56
The Mad Bomber '72
Mohawk '56
The Ninth Configuration '79
No Place to Run '72
Only the Valiant '50
The Prodigal '55
Psychic Killer '75
The Return '80
Riot in Cell Block 11 '54
Scarface Mob '62
The Seekers '79
Stalag 17 '53
That Darn Cat '65
This is a Hijack '75
The Tin Star '57

Klaus Maria Brandauer
Becoming Colette '92
Burning Secret '89
Colonel Redl '84
Hanussen '88
Kindergarten '84
The Lightship '86
Mephisto '81
Never Say Never Again '83
Out of Africa '85
Quo Vadis '85
The Russia House '90
The Salzburg Connection '72
Streets of Gold '86
White Fang '91

Larry Brandenburg
Mo' Money '92
Victimless Crimes '90

Leslie Brander
Malibu Hot Summer '81
Sizzle Beach U.S.A. '86

Walter Brandi
The Bloody Pit of Horror '65
The Slaughter of the Vampires '62
Terror Creatures from the Grave '66

Jonathan Brandis
Ladybugs '92
NeverEnding Story 2: The Next Chapter '91
Sidekicks '93
Stepfather 2: Make Room for Daddy '89

Jocelyn Brando
Big Heat '53
Nightfall '56
A Question of Love '78
Ten Wanted Men '54

Luisina Brando
Dias de Ilusion '80
The Lion's Share '79

Marlon Brando
Apocalypse Now '79
The Appaloosa '66
Bedtime Story '63
Burn! '70
The Chase '66
Christopher Columbus: The Discovery '92
Desiree '54
A Dry White Season '89
The Formula '80
The Freshman '90
The Fugitive Kind '60
The Godfather '72
The Godfather 1902-1959: The Complete Epic '81
Guys and Dolls '55
Julius Caesar '53
Last Tango in Paris '73
Marlon Brando '85
The Men '50
Missouri Breaks '76
Morituri '65
Mutiny on the Bounty '62
The Night of the Following Day '69
The Nightcomers '72
On the Waterfront '54
One-Eyed Jacks '61
Reflections in a Golden Eye '67
Sayonara '57
A Streetcar Named Desire '51
Superman: The Movie '78
The Teahouse of the August Moon '56
The Ugly American '63
Viva Zapata! '52
The Wild One '54
The Young Lions '58

Rikki Brando
The Bikini Car Wash Company 2 '92
Buford's Beach Bunnies '92

Clark Brandon
Fast Food '89
My Tutor '83

David Brandon
Beyond Darkness '92
Good Morning, Babylon '87
Naked Sun
Stagefright '87

Henry Brandon
Assault on Precinct 13 '76
Drums of Fu Manchu '40
The Land Unknown '57
The Searchers '56
When the North Wind Blows '74

Michael Brandon
A Change of Seasons '80
James Dean '76
Lovers and Other Strangers '70
Promises in the Dark '79
Red Alert '77
Rich and Famous '81

Carolyn Brandt
The Hollywood Strangler Meets the Skid Row Slasher '79
Incredibly Strange Creatures Who Stopped Living and Became Mixed-Up Zombies '63
Rat Pfink a Boo-Boo '66
The Thrill Killers '65

Betsy Brantley
Another Country '84
Dreams Lost, Dreams Found '87
Five Days One Summer '82
The Fourth Protocol '87
Havana '90
I Come in Peace '90

Nicoletta Braschi
Down by Law '86
Johnny Stecchino '92
Mystery Train '89

Keefe Brasselle
Skirts Ahoy! '52
Streets of Sin '49

Claude Brasseur
Act of Aggression '73
Band of Outsiders '64
The Elusive Corporal '62

Brasseur ►cont.

Josepha '82
La Boum '81
L'Etat Sauvage '78
Lobster for Breakfast '82
Pardon Mon Affaire '76
Pardon Mon Affaire, Too! '77
A Simple Story '79

Pierre Brasseur
Carthage in Flames '60
Children of Paradise '44
The Horror Chamber of Dr.
    Faustus '59
Il Bell'Antonio '61

Benjamin Bratt
Blood In...Blood Out: Bound by
    Honor '93
Bright Angel '91
One Good Cop '91

Andre Braugher
The Court Martial of Jackie
    Robinson '90
Glory '89
Somebody Has to Shoot the
    Picture '93
Striking Distance '93

Pinkas Braun
The Man Outside '68
Mission Stardust '68
Praying Mantis '83

Asher Brauner
American Eagle '90
B.A.D. Cats '80
Boss' Son '79
Living to Die '90
Merchants of War '90
Treasure of the Moon Goddess
    '88

Bart Braverman
The Great Texas Dynamite
    Chase '76
Hollywood Hot Tubs 2:
    Educating Crystal '89

Tony Bravo
Caches de Oro
East L.A. Warriors '89

Rossano Brazzi
The Adventurers '70
The Barefoot Contessa '54
Bobo '67
The Christmas That Almost
    Wasn't '66
Dr. Frankenstein's Castle of
    Freaks '74
The Far Pavilions '84
Fear City '85
The Final Conflict '81
Final Justice '84
Formula for a Murder '85
The Italian Job '69
Legend of the Lost '57
Mr. Kingstreet's War '71
One Step to Hell '68
Rome Adventure '62
South Pacific '58
Summertime '55
Third Solution '89
Three Coins in the Fountain '54
A Time for Miracles '80
We the Living '42
Woman Times Seven '67

Peter Breck
The Beatniks '60
Benji '74
The Crawling Hand '63
Highway 61 '91
Shock Corridor '63

Larry Breeding
A Matter of Life and Death '81
Street Music '81

Bobby Breen
Breaking the Ice '38
Escape to Paradise '39
Fisherman's Wharf '39
Hawaii Calls '38
It Happened in New Orleans '36
Let's Sing Again '36
Make a Wish '37
Way Down South '39

Patrick Breen
Fallen Angels 2 '93
For Love or Money '93

Nobody's Perfect '90
Passed Away '92

Paulette Breen
The Clonus Horror '79
The Wizard of Speed and Time
    '88

Tracy Bregman
The Concrete Jungle '82
Happy Birthday to Me '81

Jana Brejchova
Fabulous Adventures of Baron
    Munchausen '61
Loves of a Blonde '65
The Original Fabulous
    Adventures of Baron
    Munchausen '61

Jacques Brel
Franz '72
Les Assassins de L'Ordre '71
Pain in the A— '77

Lucille Bremer
Behind Locked Doors '48
Human Gorilla '48
Meet Me in St. Louis '44
Till the Clouds Roll By '46
Till the Clouds Roll By/A Star is
    Born '46
Yolanda and the Thief '45
Ziegfeld Follies '46

El Brendel
The Beautiful Blonde from
    Bashful Bend '49
Big Trail '30
Happy Landing '38
I'm from Arkansas '44

Eileen Brennan
Babes in Toyland '86
Blood Vows: The Story of a
    Mafia Wife '87
The Cheap Detective '78
Clue '85
Daisy Miller '74
The Death of Richie '76
FM '78
Fourth Wise Man '85
The Funny Farm '82
Great Smokey Roadblock '76
I Don't Buy Kisses Anymore '92
The Last Picture Show '71
Murder by Death '76
Murder So Sweet '93
My Father's House '75
My Old Man '79
The New Adventures of Pippi
    Longstocking '88
Pandemonium '82
Playmates '72
Private Benjamin '80
Rented Lips '88
Scarecrow '73
Stella '89
Sticky Fingers '88
The Sting '73
Texasville '90
White Palace '90

Walter Brennan
The Adventures of Tom Sawyer
    '38
Along the Great Divide '51
At Gunpoint '55
Bad Day at Black Rock '54
Barbary Coast '35
Best of the Badmen '50
Blood on the Moon '48
Come and Get It '38
The Cowboy and the Lady '38
Dakota '45
Far Country '55
Fury '36
Glory '56
The Gnome-Mobile '67
Goodbye, My Lady '56
The Green Promise '49
Home for the Holidays '72
How the West was Won '63
Man of Action '33
Meet John Doe '41
Moon's Our Home '36
My Darling Clementine '46
The North Star '43
Northwest Passage '40
The One and Only, Genuine,
    Original Family Band '68
The Oscar '66
Phantom of the Air '33
The Pride of the Yankees '42
The Princess and the Pirate '44

The Range Feud/Two Fisted
    Law '31
Red River '48
Rio Bravo '59
Sergeant York '41
The Showdown '50
Smoke in the Wind '75
Stanley and Livingstone '39
A Stolen Life '46
The Story of Vernon and Irene
    Castle '39
Support Your Local Sheriff '69
Tammy and the Bachelor '57
Task Force '49
Texas Cyclone '32
These Three '36
They Shall Have Music '39
Those Calloways '65
Ticket to Tomahawk '50
To Have & Have Not '44
Two-Fisted Law '32
The Westerner '40
Who's Minding the Mint? '67

Dori Brenner
Altered States '80
Baby Boom '87
For the Boys '91
Sex and the Single Parent '82
Silent Victim '92
Summer Wishes, Winter
    Dreams '73

Evelyn Brent
Daughter of the Tong '39
Holt of the Secret Service '42
Last Command '28
Law West of Tombstone '38
Love 'Em and Leave 'Em '26
Panama Lady '39
The Payoff '43
The President's Mystery '36
Robot Pilot '41
The Seventh Victim '43
Song of the Trail '36
Trapped by the Mormons '22

George Brent
Baby Face '33
Born Again '78
Dark Victory '39
Experiment Perilous '45
FBI Girl '52
Female '33
The Fighting 69th '40
42nd Street '33
The Great Lie '41
In Person '35
In This Our Life '42
Jezebel '38
Lightning Warrior '31
Man Bait '52
Montana Belle '52
The Old Maid '39
Out of the Blue '47
The Painted Veil '34
The Purchase Price '32
The Rains Came '39
Silver Queen '42
The Spiral Staircase '46
They Call It Sin '32
Tomorrow is Forever '46

Linda Brent
Below the Border '42
Death Valley Rangers '44

Romney Brent
Adventures of Don Juan '49
Dreaming Lips '37
The Sign of Zorro '60
Under the Red Robe '36
The Virgin Queen '55

Timothy Brent
Escape from the Bronx '85
Sting of the West '76
Tornado '83
Warriors of the Wasteland '83

Edmund Breon
Casanova Brown '44
Dressed to Kill '46
Forever Amber '47
Gaslight '44

Bobbie Bresee
Evil Spawn '87
Ghoulies '85
Mausoleum '83
Surf Nazis Must Die '87

Felix Bressart
Bitter Sweet '40
Blossoms in the Dust '41

Comrade X '40
Edison the Man '40
Iceland '42
Ninotchka '39
Portrait of Jennie '48
The Seventh Cross '44
The Shop Around the Corner
    '40
A Song is Born '48
To Be or Not to Be '42
Without Love '45
Ziegfeld Girl '41

Jean Bretonniere
The Green Glove '52
That Naughty Girl '58

Jeremy Brett
The Adventures of Sherlock
    Holmes: Hound of the
    Baskervilles '89
Haunted: The Ferryman '74
The Medusa Touch '78
The Merchant of Venice '73
My Fair Lady '64
One Deadly Owner '74
Sherlock Holmes: The Master
    Blackmailer '92
The Very Edge '63

Diane Brewster
Courage of Black Beauty '57
The Invisible Boy '57
Torpedo Run '58

Maia Brewton
Adventures in Babysitting '87
Back to the Future '85

Tom Breznahan
The Brain '88
Ski School '91
Twice Dead '88

Jean-Claude Brialy
The Bride Wore Black '68
The Burning Court '62
Catherine & Co. '76
Circle of Love '64
Claire's Knee '71
Cleo from 5 to 7 '61
The Cousins '59
The 400 Blows '59
The Judge and the Assassin
    '75
La Nuit de Varennes '82
L'Anne Sainte '78
Le Beau Serge '58
No Fear, No Die '90
Paris Belongs to Us '60
Phantom of Liberty '68
Robert et Robert '79
Tonio Kroger '65
A Woman is a Woman '60

David Brian
Ambush at Tomahawk Gap '53
Beyond the Forest '49
Castle of Evil '66
Confessions of Tom Harris '72
Flamingo Road '49
Intruder in the Dust '49
Million Dollar Mermaid '52
Pocketful of Miracles '61
Springfield Rifle '52

Mary Brian
Amazing Adventure '37
Behind the Front '26
Blessed Event '32
Charlie Chan in Paris '35
The Light of Western Stars '30
Monte Carlo Nights '34
Running Wild '27

Shane Briant
Captain Kronos: Vampire
    Hunter '74
Cassandra '87
Demons of the Mind '72
Dressed for Death '74
The Flame is Love '79
Frankenstein and the Monster
    from Hell '74
Lady Chatterley's Lover '81
Moving Targets '87
Picture of Dorian Gray '74
Till There was You '91
True Colors '87
Wrangler '88

Fanny Brice
Everybody Sing '38
Ziegfeld Follies '46

Pierre Brice
Apaches Last Battle '64
The Bacchantes '63
Mill of the Stone Women '60
A Place Called Glory '66
Sweet Ecstasy '62

Beth Brickell
The Only Way Home '72
Seducers '77

Alan Bridge
Broadway to Cheyenne '32
The Forty-Niners '32
Gene Autry Matinee Double
    Feature #2 '53
Man's Land '32
Miracle of Morgan's Creek '44
Outlaw Rule '35
Sullivan's Travels '41
When a Man Rides Alone '33

Beau Bridges
Daddy's Dyin'...Who's Got the
    Will? '90
The Fabulous Baker Boys '89
The Fifth Musketeer '79
For Love of Ivy '68
The Four Feathers '78
Greased Lightning '77
Hammersmith is Out '72
Heart Like a Wheel '83
Honky Tonk Freeway '81
The Hotel New Hampshire '84
The Incident '67
The Iron Triangle '89
The Killing Time '87
Love Child '82
Married to It '93
Mutual Respect '77
Night Crossing '81
Norma Rae '79
One Summer Love '76
The Other Side of the Mountain
    '75
Outrage! '86
The Positively True Adventures
    of the Alleged Texas
    Cheerleader-Murdering
    Mom '93
President's Mistress '78
The Red Light Sting '84
The Red Pony '49
The Runner Stumbles '79
Seven Hours to Judgment '88
Sidekicks '93
Signs of Life '89
Silver Dream Racer '83
The Stranger Who Looks Like
    Me '74
Swashbuckler '76
Two Minute Warning '76
Village of the Giants '65
The Wild Pair '87
Wildflower '91
Without Warning: The James
    Brady Story '91
The Wizard '89
Women & Men: Stories of
    Seduction '90

Jeff Bridges
Against All Odds '84
American Heart '92
Bad Company '72
Blown Away '94
Cutter's Way '81
8 Million Ways to Die '85
The Fabulous Baker Boys '89
Fat City '72
Fearless '93
The Fisher King '91
Hearts of the West '75
Heaven's Gate '81
The Jagged Edge '85
King Kong '76
Kiss Me Goodbye '82
The Last American Hero '73
The Last Picture Show '71
The Morning After '86
Nadine '87
Rancho Deluxe '75
Rapunzel '82
See You in the Morning '89
Silent Night, Lonely Night '69
Starman '84
Stay Hungry '76
Texasville '90
Thunderbolt & Lightfoot '74
Tron '82
Tucker: The Man and His
    Dream '88

The Vanishing '93
Winter Kills '79
Yin & Yang of Mr. Go '71

Lloyd Bridges
Abilene Town '46
Airplane! '80
Airplane 2: The Sequel '82
Apache Woman '55
Around the World Under the Sea '65
Bear Island '80
Big Deadly Game '54
Blown Away '94
The Blue and the Gray '85
Cousins '89
Daring Game '68
Devlin '92
Dress Gray '86
East of Eden '80
Force of Evil '77
George Washington '84
The Goddess '58
The Great Wallendas '78
The Happy Ending '69
Harmon of Michigan '41
Haunts of the Very Rich '72
The Heat's On '43
High Noon '52
Home of the Brave '49
Honey, I Blew Up the Kid '92
Hot Shots! '91
Hot Shots! Part Deux '93
Joe Versus the Volcano '90
Last of the Comanches '52
The Limping Man '53
Little Big Horn '51
Loving '84
Master Race '44
Mission Galactica: The Cylon Attack '79
Moonrise '48
Mutual Respect '77
North and South Book 2 '86
The Queen of Mean '90
The Rainmaker '56
Ramrod '47
Rocketship X-M '50
Roots '77
Running Wild '73
Sahara '43
Silent Night, Lonely Night '69
Tall Texan '53
The Tattered Web '71
Trapped '49
Try and Get Me '50
Tucker: The Man and His Dream '88
A Walk in the Sun '46
Weekend Warriors '86
The White Tower '50
The Wild Pair '87
Winter People '89

Todd Bridges
Homeboys '92
Twice Dead '88

Richard Briers
A Chorus of Disapproval '89
Henry V '89
A Matter of WHO '62
The Norman Conquests, Part 1: Table Manners '80
The Norman Conquests, Part 2: Living Together '80
The Norman Conquests, Part 3: Round and Round the Garden '80
Peter's Friends '92
Rentadick '72

Richard Bright
The Ambulance '90
The Godfather, Part 3 '90
Idolmaker '80
Panic in Needle Park '75
Rancho Deluxe '75
Red Heat '88
Who's the Man? '93

Charlie Brill
Bail Out '90
Bloodstone '88

Fran Brill
Look Back in Anger '80
Old Enough '84
What About Bob? '91

Patti Brill
Girl Rush '44
Hard-Boiled Mahoney '47

Steven Brill
The Mighty Ducks '92
sex, lies and videotape '89

Nick Brimble
Frankenstein Unbound '90
Robin Hood: Prince of Thieves '91

Cynthia Brimhall
Fit to Kill '93
Hard Hunted '92
Hard Ticket to Hawaii '87

Wilford Brimley
Absence of Malice '81
Act of Vengeance '86
American Justice '86
Borderline '80
The China Syndrome '79
Cocoon '85
Cocoon: The Return '88
Country '84
Death Valley '81
The Electric Horseman '79
End of the Line '88
Eternity '89
The Ewoks: Battle for Endor '85
The Firm '93
Gore Vidal's Billy the Kid '89
Hard Target '93
Harry & Son '84
High Road to China '83
The Hotel New Hampshire '84
Murder in Space '85
The Natural '84
Remo Williams: The Adventure Begins '85
Rodeo Girl '80
Roughnecks '80
The Stone Boy '84
Ten to Midnight '83
Tender Mercies '83
The Thing '82
Thompson's Last Run '90
Tough Enough '83
Where the Red Fern Grows: Part 2 '92

Michele Brin
Secret Games '92
Sexual Intent '94

Paul Brinegar
Charro! '69
How to Make a Monster '58

Ritch Brinkley
Cabin Boy '94
Silhouette '91

Charles Brinley
The Crimson Trail '35
Moran of the Lady Letty '22

Breezy Brisbane
Little Rascals, Book 5 '30s
Little Rascals, Book 6 '30s
Little Rascals, Book 7 '30s

Danielle Brisebois
Big Bad Mama 2 '87
Killcrazy '89
Mom, the Wolfman and Me '80
The Premonition '75

Carl Brisson
The Manxman '29
Murder at the Vanities '34
The Ring '27

May Britt
Haunts '77
The Hunters '58
There Goes Barder '64

Morgan Brittany
Initiation of Sarah '78
LBJ: The Early Years '88
The Prodigal '83
Sundown '91

Barbara Britton
Bandit Queen '51
Captain Kidd '45
Champagne for Caesar '50
Dragonfly Squadron '54
I Shot Jesse James '49
Loaded Pistols '48
Louisiana Purchase '41
Mrs. Wiggs of the Cabbage Patch '42
Reap the Wild Wind '42
Ride the Man Down '53
Wake Island '42
Young & Willing '42

Pamela Britton
Anchors Aweigh '45
D.O.A. '49
If It's Tuesday, This Must Be Belgium '69

Tony Britton
Agatha '79
The Day of the Jackal '73
Dr. Syn, Alias the Scarecrow '64
Horsemasters '61
Operation Amsterdam '60

Herman Brix
Fighting Devil Dogs '38
Hawk of the Wilderness '38

Jim Broadbent
The Crying Game '92
Enchanted April '92
The Good Father '87
Life is Sweet '91
Widow's Peak '94

Peter Brocco
The Balcony '63
Homebodies '74
One Flew Over the Cuckoo's Nest '75

Anne Brochet
Barjo '90
Cyrano de Bergerac '90
Tous les Matins du Monde '92

Phil Brock
A Climate for Killing '91
Dollman vs Demonic Toys '93

Stan Brock
Galyon '77
Return to Africa '89
Tin Men '87

Roy Brocksmith
Arachnophobia '90
Big Business '88
Bill & Ted's Bogus Journey '91
Killer Fish '79
King of the Gypsies '78
Nickel & Dime '92
Tales of Ordinary Madness '83
Total Recall '90

Gladys Brockwell
The Drake Case '29
Oliver Twist '22
Spangles '26

Beth Broderick
Are You Lonesome Tonight '92
Thousand Pieces of Gold '91

Helen Broderick
The Bride Walks Out '36
The Rage of Paris '38
Swing Time '36
Top Hat '35

James Broderick
Alice's Restaurant '69
Dog Day Afternoon '75
The Group '66
Keeping On '81
The Shadow Box '80
The Taking of Pelham One Two Three '74

Matthew Broderick
Biloxi Blues '88
Cinderella '84
Family Business '89
Ferris Bueller's Day Off '86
The Freshman '90
Glory '89
Ladyhawke '85
A Life in the Theater '93
Master Harold and the Boys '84
Max Dugan Returns '83
The Night We Never Met '93
1918 '85
On Valentine's Day '86
Out on a Limb '92
Project X '87
Torch Song Trilogy '88
WarGames '83

Steve Brodie
The Admiral Was a Lady '50
Armored Car Robbery '50
Badman's Territory '46
The Beast from 20,000 Fathoms '53
Blue Hawaii '62
Criminal Court '46
Desperate '47
Donovan's Brain '53

The Giant Spider Invasion '75
Kiss Tomorrow Goodbye '50
Out of the Past '47
Roustabout '64
The Saint Strikes Back: Criminal Court '46
The Steel Helmet '51
Three for Bedroom C '52
Tough Assignment '49
Treasure of Monte Cristo '49
The Wild World of Batwoman '66
The Wizard of Speed and Time '88

Adrien Brody
Home at Last '88
King of the Hill '93

Harry Brogan
Broth of a Boy '59
Shake Hands with the Devil '59

James Brolin
The Ambush Murders '82
The Amityville Horror '79
Backstab '90
Bad Jim '89
The Boston Strangler '68
Capricorn One '78
Cheatin' Hearts '93
City Boy '93
Class of '63 '73
Fantastic Voyage '66
Finish Line '89
Gas Food Lodging '92
High Risk '76
Hold the Dream '85
Mae West '84
Night of the Juggler '80
Nightmare on the 13th Floor '90
Our Man Flint '66
Pee Wee's Big Adventure '85
Steel Cowboy '78
Ted & Venus '93
Von Ryan's Express '65
Westworld '73

Josh Brolin
Finish Line '89
The Goonies '85
Thrashin' '86

J. Edward Bromberg
Cloak and Dagger '46
Invisible Agent '42
The Mark of Zorro '40
The Missing Corpse '45
The Phantom of the Opera '43
Queen of the Amazons '47
Return of Frank James '40
Reunion in France '42
Son of Dracula '43
A Song is Born '48
Strange Cargo '40

John Bromfield
Big Bluff '55
Easy to Love '53
Flat Top '52
Manfish '56
Revenge of the Creature '55

Valri Bromfield
Home is Where the Hart is '88
Mr. Mom '83
Nothing But Trouble '91
Who's Harry Crumb? '89

Sheila Bromley
Nancy Drew, Reporter '39
Torture Ship '39
Waterfront '39

Sydney Bromley
Crystalstone '88
The NeverEnding Story '84

Eleanor Bron
The Attic: The Hiding of Anne Frank '88
Bedazzled '68
Black Beauty '94
Help! '65
Intrigue '90
Little Dorrit, Film 1: Nobody's Fault '88
Little Dorrit, Film 2: Little Dorrit's Story '88
Turtle Diary '86
Two for the Road '67
Women in Love '70

Betty Bronson
Are Parents People? '25
Ben-Hur '26

Medicine Man '30
Naked Kiss '64
Yodelin' Kid From Pine Ridge '37

Charles Bronson
Act of Vengeance '86
Assassination '87
Battle of the Bulge '65
Borderline '80
Breakheart Pass '76
Breakout '75
Bull of the West '89
Cabo Blanco '81
Chato's Land '71
Chino '73
Cold Sweat '74
Death Hunt '81
Death Wish '74
Death Wish 2 '82
Death Wish 3 '85
Death Wish 4: The Crackdown '87
Death Wish 5: The Face of Death '94
The Dirty Dozen '67
Drum Beat '54
The Evil That Men Do '84
The Family '73
Four for Texas '63
From Noon Till Three '76
The Great Escape '63
Guns of Diablo '64
Hard Times '75
Honor Among Thieves '68
House of Wax '53
The Indian Runner '91
Jubal '56
Kid Galahad '62
Kinjite: Forbidden Subjects '89
Lola '69
Love and Bullets '79
Machine Gun Kelly '58
The Magnificent Seven '60
Master of the World '61
The Meanest Men in the West '76
The Mechanic '72
Messenger of Death '88
Miss Sadie Thompson '53
Mr. Majestyk '74
Murphy's Law '86
Never So Few '59
Once Upon a Time in the West '68
Pat and Mike '52
Raid on Entebbe '77
Red Sun '71
Rider on the Rain '70
Run of the Arrow '56
St. Ives '76
The Sandpiper '65
The Sea Wolf '93
Showdown at Boot Hill '58
Someone Behind the Door '71
The Stone Killer '73
Telefon '77
Ten to Midnight '83
This Property is Condemned '66
Vera Cruz '53
Villa Rides '68
When Hell Broke Loose '58
The White Buffalo '77
Wild West '87

Lillian Bronson
The Next Voice You Hear '50
Spencer's Mountain '63

Claudio Brook
The Bees '78
Daniel Boone: Trail Blazer '56
Dr. Tarr's Torture Dungeon '75
La Mansion de la Locura '87
Neutron and the Black Mask '61
The Peking Blond '68
Samson in the Wax Museum '63
Sisters of Satan '75
Viva Maria! '65
The Young One '61

Clive Brook
Action for Slander '38
Cavalcade '33
Convoy '40
Hula '28
On Approval '44
Shanghai Express '32

Faith Brook
After Julius '78
Bloodbath
To Sir, with Love '67
Uneasy Terms '48

Irina Brook
Captive '87
The Girl in the Picture '86
Transmutations '85

Jayne Brook
Clean Slate '94
Kindergarten Cop '90

Elwyn Brook-Jones
Bonnie Prince Charlie '48
The Gilded Cage '54
Rogue's Yarn '56

Lyndon Brook
Above Us the Waves '56
Invasion '65
The Spanish Gardener '57

Hillary Brooke
Abbott and Costello Meet
    Captain Kidd '52
Africa Screams '49
Big Town '47
Big Town After Dark '47
The Enchanted Cottage '45
Heat Wave '54
Jane Eyre '44
The Lost Continent '51
The Man Who Knew Too Much
    '56
Never Wave at a WAC '52
The Philadelphia Story '40
Rangeland Racket '41
The Road to Utopia '46
Sherlock Holmes Faces Death
    '43
Sherlock Holmes: The Voice of
    Terror '42
The Strange Woman '46
To the Shores of Tripoli '42
Underworld Scandal '47
The Woman in Green '45

Sandy Brooke
Crazed Cop '88
Miami Vendetta '87
Star Slammer '87
Terror on Alcatraz '86

Walter Brooke
Conquest of Space '55
The Return of Count Yorga '71

Richard Brooker
Deathstalker '83
Friday the 13th, Part 3 '82

Jacqueline Brookes
Hardhat & Legs '80
Naked Gun 2 1/2: The Smell of
    Fear '91
Rodeo Girl '80
Silent Witness '85

Aimee Brooks
Critters 3 '91
Say Anything '89

Albert Brooks
Broadcast News '87
Defending Your Life '91
I'll Do Anything '93
Lost in America '85
Modern Romance '81
Private Benjamin '80
Real Life '79
The Scout '94
Taxi Driver '76
Twilight Zone: The Movie '83
Unfaithfully Yours '84

Avery Brooks
The Ernest Green Story '93
Half Slave, Half Free '85
Roots: The Gift '88
Uncle Tom's Cabin '87

Clarence Brooks
Bronze Buckaroo '39
Harlem Rides the Range '39

Elisabeth Brooks
The Forgotten One '89
The Howling '81

Foster Brooks
Cracking Up '83
Oddballs '84
Super Seal '77
The Villain '79

Geraldine Brooks
Challenge to Lassie '49
The Green Glove '52
Johnny Tiger '66
The Possessed '47
Reckless Moment '49

Jean Brooks
Boot Hill Bandits '42
Boss of Big Town '43
The Leopard Man '43
The Seventh Victim '43

Joel Brooks
Are You Lonesome Tonight '92
Indecent Proposal '93

Leslie Brooks
City Without Men '43
The Cobra Strikes '48
Romance on the High Seas '48
The Scar '48
Tonight and Every Night '45
You Were Never Lovelier '42

Louise Brooks
Diary of a Lost Girl '29
It's the Old Army Game '26
Love 'Em and Leave 'Em '26
Overland Stage Raiders '38
Pandora's Box '28
Prix de Beaute '30

Mel Brooks
Blazing Saddles '74
High Anxiety '77
History of the World: Part 1 '81
Life Stinks '91
Putney Swope '69
Robin Hood: Men in Tights '93
Silent Movie '76
Spaceballs '87
To Be or Not to Be '83
Twelve Chairs '70

Phyllis Brooks
Dangerous Passage '44
In Old Chicago '38
Little Miss Broadway '38
Rebecca of Sunnybrook Farm
    '38
The Shanghai Gesture '42
Silver Spurs '43
Slightly Honorable '40

Rand Brooks
Gone with the Wind '39
Hopalong Cassidy: Borrowed
    Trouble '48
Hopalong Cassidy: Dangerous
    Venture '48
Hopalong Cassidy: False
    Paradise '48
Hopalong Cassidy: Hoppy's
    Holiday '47
Hopalong Cassidy: Silent
    Conflict '48
Hopalong Cassidy: Sinister
    Journey '48
Hopalong Cassidy: The Dead
    Don't Dream '48
Hopalong Cassidy: The Devil's
    Playground '46
Hopalong Cassidy: The
    Marauders '47
Hopalong Cassidy: Unexpected
    Guest '47
Ladies of the Chorus '49
The Sombrero Kid '42
The Vanishing Westerner '50

Randi Brooks
Colors '88
Cop '88
Forbidden Love '82
Hamburger...The Motion
    Picture '86
Tightrope '84

Ray Brooks
Daleks—Invasion Earth 2150
    A.D. '66
Flesh and Blood Show '73
House of Whipcord '75
The Knack '65
Office Romances '86
Tiffany Jones '75

Richard Brooks
84 Charlie Mopic '89
The Hidden '87
Memphis '91
Shakedown '88
Shocker '89
Short Fuse '88

To Sleep with Anger '90

Edward Brophy
The Cameraman '28
The Champ '31
Cover Girl '44
Dance, Girl, Dance '40
Destroyer '43
Doughboys '30
Evelyn Prentice '34
Great Guy '36
Hide-Out '34
The Invisible Woman '40
Kelly the Second '36
Last Hurrah '58
Mad Love '35
Renegade Girl '46
Roaring City '51
Show Them No Mercy '35
Speak Easily '32
Swing Parade of 1946 '46
The Thin Man Goes Home '44
What! No Beer? '33

Kevin Brophy
Delos Adventure '86
Hell Night '81
The Seduction '82

Pierce Brosnan
The Broken Chain '93
The Carpathian Eagle '81
The Deceivers '88
Detonator '93
Entangled '93
The Fourth Protocol '87
The Heist '89
The Lawnmower Man '92
Live Wire '92
The Long Good Friday '79
The Manions of America '81
The Mirror Crack'd '80
Mrs. Doubtfire '93
Mister Johnson '91
Murder 101 '91
Nomads '86
Remington Steele, Vol. 1:
    License to Steele '82
Taffin '88
Victim of Love '91

Dr. Joyce Brothers
Desperate Lives '82
The Lonely Guy '84

Amelda Brown
Little Dorrit, Film 1: Nobody's
    Fault '88
Little Dorrit, Film 2: Little
    Dorrit's Story '88

Barbara Brown
The Fighting Sullivans '42
Hollywood Canteen '44
Home Town Story '51
Ma and Pa Kettle Back On the
    Farm '51
Ma and Pa Kettle Go to Town
    '50
My Sister Eileen '55

Barry Brown
Bad Company '72
The Disappearance of Aimee
    '76
He Who Walks Alone '78
The Ultimate Thrill '74

Blair Brown
Altered States '80
And I Alone Survived '78
The Bad Seed '85
The Choirboys '77
Continental Divide '81
A Flash of Green '85
Hands of a Stranger '87
Kennedy '83
One Trick Pony '80
Passed Away '72
Stealing Home '88
Strapless '90

Bryan Brown
Blame It on the Bellboy '92
Blood Money '80
Breaker Morant '80
Cocktail '88
Dead in the Water '91
Devlin '92
The Empty Beach '85
F/X '86
F/X 2: The Deadly Art of Illusion
    '91
Far East '85

Give My Regards to Broad
    Street '84
The Good Wife '86
Gorillas in the Mist '88
The Irishman '78
The Last Hit '93
Money Movers '78
Newsfront '78
Palm Beach '79
Parker '84
Prisoners of the Sun '91
Rebel '85
Sweet Talker '91
Tai-Pan '86
The Thorn Birds '83
A Town Like Alice '85
The Winter of Our Dreams '82

Charles D. Brown
Brother Orchid '40
Dance of Life '29
Follow Me Quietly '49
Merton of the Movies '47
Old Swimmin' Hole '40
Shopworn Angel '38

Clancy Brown
Ambition '91
Bad Boys '83
Blue Steel '90
The Bride '85
Cast a Deadly Spell '91
Highlander '86
Last Light '93
Love, Lies and Murder '91
Past Midnight '92
Pet Sematary 2 '92
Season of Fear '89
Shoot to Kill '88

David G. Brown
Chasing Dreams '81
Deadly Harvest '72

D.W. Brown
Mischief '85
Weekend Pass '84

Dwier Brown
The Cutting Edge '92
The Guardian '90
Mom and Dad Save the World
    '92

Eric Brown
Private Lessons '81
They're Playing with Fire '84
Video Murders '87

Gary Brown
Glory Boys '84
Invasion of the Space
    Preachers '90

**Georg Stanford
Brown**
Alone in the Neon Jungle '87
Dayton's Devils '68
House Party 2: The Pajama
    Jam '91
The Jesse Owens Story '84
The Kid with the Broken Halo
    '82
The Night the City Screamed
    '80
North and South Book 1 '85
Roots: The Next Generation '79

Georgia Brown
Actor: The Paul Muni Story '78
The Fixer '68
Long Ago Tomorrow '71
Love at Stake '87
Nothing But the Night '72
Tales That Witness Madness
    '73
Victim of Love '91

James Brown
Adios Amigo '75
The Blues Brothers '80
Courage of Rin Tin Tin '83
Doctor Detroit '83
Objective, Burma! '45
Rin Tin Tin, Hero of the West
    '55
Targets '69

Jim Brown
Crack House '89
Dark of the Sun '68
The Dirty Dozen '67
The Divine Enforcer '91
El Condor '70
Fingers '78
Ice Station Zebra '68

I'm Gonna Git You Sucka '88
Kid Vengeance '75
L.A. Heat '88
L.A. Vice '89
One Down, Two to Go! '82
100 Rifles '69
Pacific Inferno '85
The Passing of Evil '70
Rio Conchos '64
Riot '69
Slaughter '72
Slaughter's Big Ripoff '73
Take a Hard Ride '75
Three the Hard Way '74
Twisted Justice '89

Joe E. Brown
Around the World in 80 Days
    '56
The Comedy of Terrors '64
Earthworm Tractors '36
Fit for a King '37
The Gladiator '38
It's a Mad, Mad, Mad, Mad
    World '63
Lottery Bride '30
A Midsummer Night's Dream
    '35
Pin-Up Girl '44
Riding on Air '37
Show Boat '51
Some Like It Hot '59
The Tender Years '47
When's Your Birthday? '37
Wide Open Faces '38

Johnny Mack Brown
Annapolis '28
Apache Uprising '66
Belle of the Nineties '34
Between Men '35
Boothill Brigade '37
Border Bandits '46
Boss of Bullion City '41
Branded a Coward '35
Bury Me Not On the Lone
    Prairie '41
Coquette '29
Courageous Avenger '35
Crooked Trail '36
Desert Phantom '36
Every Man's Law '35
Female '33
Fighting with Kit Carson '33
Fire Alarm '38
Flaming Frontiers '38
The Gambling Terror '37
Gentleman from Texas '46
Ghost Rider '43
Guns in the Dark '37
A Lawman is Born '37
Lawmen '41
Man from Montana '41
The Masked Rider '41
Oregon Trail '39
Our Dancing Daughters '28
Partners of the Trail '44
Pony Post '40
Raiders of the Border '44
Range Law '44
Ride 'Em Cowboy '42
Riders of Pasco Basin '40
Rogue of the Range '36
Rustlers of Red Dog '35
The Single Standard '29
Six Gun Gospel '43
The Stranger from Pecos '45
Texas Kid '43
Undercover Man '36
Valley of the Lawless '36
Voice of Hollywood '29
Western Double Feature 3 '36
A Woman of Affairs '28

Juanita Brown
Black Starlet '74
Caged Heat '74

Judy Brown
The Big Doll House '71
The Manhandlers '73

Julie Brown
Bloody Birthday '80
Earth Girls are Easy '89
Nervous Ticks '93
The Opposite Sex and How to
    Live With Them '93
Shakes the Clown '92
Spirit of '76 '91

Lou Brown
Alison's Birthday '79

Death Games '82
The Irishman '78

Pamela Brown
Alice in Wonderland '50
Cleopatra '63
I Know Where I'm Going '45
Lust for Life '56
One of Our Aircraft Is Missing '41
Secret Ceremony '69
Victoria Regina '61
Wuthering Heights '70

Paul Brown
Morons from Outer Space '85
Transmutations '85

Peter Brown
Act of Vengeance '74
The Aurora Encounter '85
Chrome and Hot Leather '71
The Commies are Coming, the Commies are Coming '57
The Concrete Jungle '82
Darby's Rangers '58
Eagles Attack at Dawn '74
Hard Frame '70
Memory of Us '74
Merrill's Marauders '62
Red Nightmare '62
Ride the Wild Surf '64
Slashed Dreams '74
A Tiger Walks '64

Phil Brown
The Hidden Room '49
Operation Cross Eagles '69
Tropic of Cancer '70
Without Reservations '46

Philip Brown
Eye of the Needle '81
Special Olympics '78
Wild Zone '89

Ralph Brown
Alien 3 '92
Buster '88
The Crying Game '92
Impromptu '90
Wayne's World 2 '93

Reb Brown
The Cage '89
Captain America '79
Captain America 2: Death Too Soon '79
Death of a Soldier '85
The Firing Line '91
Howling 2: Your Sister is a Werewolf '85
Last Flight to Hell
Mercenary Fighters '88
Space Mutiny '88
Street Hunter '90
Strike Commando '87
Uncommon Valor '83
White Ghost '88
Yor, the Hunter from the Future '83

Ritza Brown
Ator the Fighting Eagle '83
The McGuffin '85

Robert Brown
The Living Daylights '87
Pilgrim, Farewell '80
Shake Hands with the Devil '59
Tower of London '62

Roger Brown
Don't Cry, It's Only Thunder '82
Paper Lion '68
Venus Against the Son of Hercules '62

Ron Brown
Charlie, the Lonesome Cougar '67
The Legend of Black Thunder Mountain '79

Sara Suzanne Brown
Secret Games 2: The Escort '93
Test Tube Teens from the Year 2000 '93

Stephen Brown
Beyond Darkness '92
Metamorphosis '90

Thomas Wilson Brown
Diggstown '92
Honey, I Shrunk the Kids '89

Welcome Home '89

Tim Brown
Code Name: Zebra '84
Pacific Inferno '85
A Place Called Today '72

Timothy Brown
The Dynamite Brothers
Girls Are for Loving '73
Sweet Sugar '72

Tom Brown
Adventures of Smilin' Jack '43
Anne of Green Gables '34
Buck Privates Come Home '47
The Choppers '61
I'd Give My Life '36
In Old Chicago '38
Maytime '37
Navy Blue and Gold '37
Operation Haylift '50
The Payoff '43
Ringside '49

Vanessa Brown
The Fighter '52
The Ghost and Mrs. Muir '47
Three Husbands '50
Witch Who Came from the Sea '76

Wally Brown
Girl Rush '44
Zombies on Broadway '44

Woody Brown
The Accused '88
Alligator 2: The Mutation '90
The Rain Killer '90

Charles A. Browne
Federal Agent '36
Tailspin Tommy '34

Coral Browne
American Dreamer '84
Auntie Mame '58
The Courtney Affair '47
Dreamchild '85
Eleanor: First Lady of the World '82
An Englishman Abroad '83
The Killing of Sister George '69
The Ruling Class '72

Leslie Browne
Dancers '87
Nijinsky '80
The Turning Point '77

Lucille Browne
Brand of Hate '34
Cheyenne Rides Again '38
The Devil's Brother '33
Law of the Wild '34
Mystery Squadron '33
Texas Terror '35
Western Frontier '35

Roscoe Lee Browne
Black Like Me '64
The Connection '61
The Cowboys '72
For Us, the Living '88
Haunting of Harrington House '82
King '78
Legal Eagles '86
The Liberation of L.B. Jones '70
Logan's Run '76
The Mambo Kings '92
Moon 44 '90
Naked in New York '93
Nothing Personal '80
Superfly T.N.T. '73
Twilight's Last Gleaming '77
Unknown Powers '80
The World's Greatest Athlete '73

Suzanne Browne
The Bikini Car Wash Company '90
The Bikini Car Wash Company 2 '92

Ricou Browning
Creature from the Black Lagoon '54
Flipper's New Adventure '64

Brenda Bruce
Antonia and Jane '91
Back Home '90
Peeping Tom '63
Splitting Heirs '93

The Tenth Man '88

Cheryl Lynn Bruce
Daughters of the Dust '92
Music Box '89
Victimless Crimes '90

Colin Bruce
Chicago Joe & the Showgirl '90
Crusoe '89
Gotham '88

David Bruce
Jungle Hell '55
The Mad Ghoul '43
Pier 23 '51
Salome, Where She Danced '45
The Sea Wolf '41

Kate Bruce
The Idol Dancer '20
Judith of Bethulia '14
Short Films of D.W. Griffith, Vol. 2 '09

Lenny Bruce
Dance Hall Racket '58
Dynamite Chicken '70
Lenny Bruce Performance Film '68

Nigel Bruce
The Adventures of Sherlock Holmes '39
Becky Sharp '35
The Blue Bird '40
The Charge of the Light Brigade '36
The Chocolate Soldier '41
The Corn is Green '45
Dressed to Kill '46
The Hound of the Baskervilles '39
House of Fear '45
Journey for Margaret '42
Julia Misbehaves '48
Lassie, Come Home '43
The Last of Mrs. Cheyney '37
Limelight '52
The Pearl of Death '44
Pursuit to Algiers '45
The Rains Came '39
Rebecca '40
Scarlet Claw '44
Sherlock Holmes and the Secret Weapon '42
Sherlock Holmes Faces Death '43
Sherlock Holmes in Washington '43
Sherlock Holmes: The Voice of Terror '42
Son of Lassie '45
Spider Woman '44
Stand Up and Cheer '34
Susan and God '40
Suspicion '41
Terror by Night '46
Terror by Night/Meeting at Midnight '46
Thunder in the City '37
Treasure Island '34
The Two Mrs. Carrolls '47
The Woman in Green '45

Virginia Bruce
Action in Arabia '44
Born to Dance '36
The Great Ziegfeld '36
The Invisible Woman '40
Jane Eyre '34
Let 'Em Have It '35
Let Freedom Ring '39
Pardon My Sarong '42
State Department File 649 '49
Strangers When We Meet '60

Patrick Bruel
Bandits '86
Secret Obsession '88

Eddie Brugman
Broken Mirrors '85
Keetje Tippel '75

Beau Brummel
Three Bullets for a Long Gun '73
Village of the Giants '65

Bo Brundin
Headless Eyes '83
Russian Roulette '75
Shoot the Sun Down '81

Fernando Bruno
Time Out for Love '61

Two Nights with Cleopatra '54

Philip Bruns
Dead Men Don't Die '91
The Opposite Sex and How to Live with Them '93
Return of the Living Dead 2 '88
The Stunt Man '80

Dora Bryan
The Great St. Trinian's Train Robbery '66
My Son, the Vampire '52
No Trace '50
Screamtime '83
Small Hotel '57
A Taste of Honey '61

Jane Bryan
Each Dawn I Die '39
Kid Galahad '37
Marked Woman '37
The Old Maid '39
The Sisters '38

Joyce Bryant
Across the Plains '39
East Side Kids '40

Michael Bryant
Girly '70
Goodbye, Mr. Chips '69
Sakharov '84

Nana Bryant
Big Town '47
Eyes of Texas '48
Harvey '50
Inner Sanctum '48
Ladies of the Chorus '49
The Possessed '47
Sinners in Paradise '38

Pamela Bryant
Lunch Wagon '81
Tigershark '87

Virginia Bryant
The Barbarians '87
Demons 2 '87

William Bryant
Corvette Summer '78
Mountain Family Robinson '79

Andrew Bryniarski
Batman Returns '92
The Program '93

Yul Brynner
Anastasia '56
Battle of Neretva '69
The Brothers Karamazov '58
The Buccaneer '58
Cast a Giant Shadow '66
Catlow '71
Death Rage '77
Futureworld '76
Fuzz '72
Invitation to a Gunfighter '64
The King and I '56
Light at the Edge of the World '71
The Madwoman of Chaillot '69
The Magic Christian '69
The Magnificent Seven '60
Morituri '65
Night Flight from Moscow '73
The Poppy is also a Flower '66
Port of New York '49
Return of the Seven '66
Romance of a Horsethief '71
Solomon and Sheba '59
Taras Bulba '62
The Ten Commandments '56
The Testament of Orpheus '59
Triple Cross '67
The Ultimate Warrior '75
Villa Rides '68
Westworld '73

Edgar Buchanan
Abilene Town '46
Arizona '40
The Big Hangover '50
Big Trees '52
Black Arrow '48
Buffalo Bill '44
City Without Men '43
Coroner Creek '48
Destroyer '43
The Devil's Partner '58
Human Desire '54
It Started with a Kiss '59
Lust for Gold '49
Make Haste to Live '54
Man from Colorado '49

McLintock! '63
Penny Serenade '41
Rage at Dawn '55
Rawhide '51
Ride the High Country '62
The Rounders '65
Shane '53
She Couldn't Say No '52
Silver Star '55
Talk of the Town '42
Texas '41
Yuma '71

Ian Buchanan
The Cool Surface '91
Double Exposure '93

Jack Buchanan
The Band Wagon '53
When Knights were Bold '36

Miles Buchanan
Dangerous Game '90
Runaway Island, Part 1
Runaway Island, Part 2
Runaway Island, Part 3
Runaway Island, Part 4

Sherry Buchanan
Emmanuelle & Joanna '86
Eyes Behind the Stars '72

Simone Buchanan
Run, Rebecca, Run '81
Runaway Island, Part 1
Runaway Island, Part 2
Runaway Island, Part 3
Runaway Island, Part 4
Shame '87

Horst Buchholz
Aces: Iron Eagle 3 '92
Avalanche Express '79
Berlin Tunnel 21 '81
The Catamount Killing '74
Code Name: Emerald '85
Empty Canvas '64
Fanny '61
Faraway, So Close! '93
From Hell to Victory '79
The Magnificent Seven '60
One, Two, Three '61
Raid on Entebbe '77
Return to Fantasy Island '77
Sahara '83
The Savage Bees '76
Teenage Wolfpack '57
Tiger Bay '59

Buck
Robinson Crusoe of Clipper Island '36
Robinson Crusoe of Mystery Island '36

Frank Buck
Jacare '42
Tiger Fangs '43

John Buckler
The Black Room '35
Tarzan Escapes '36

Betty Buckley
Another Woman '88
Babycakes '89
Carrie '76
Frantic '88
Tender Mercies '83
Wild Thing '87
Wyatt Earp '94

Keith Buckley
Half Moon Street '86
The Virgin Witch '70

Helen Buday
For Love Alone '86
Mad Max: Beyond Thunderdome '85

Jack Buetel
Best of the Badmen '50
The Half-Breed '51

Buffalo Bill, Jr.
Deadwood Pass '33
Fighting Cowboy '33
Lightning Bill '35
Powdersmoke Range '35
Rawhide Romance '34
Riding Speed '35
Terror Trail '33

Jimmy Buffett
Doctor Duck's Super Secret All-Purpose Sauce '85
FM '78
Rancho Deluxe '75

Joe Bugner
The Cursed Mountain Mystery '93
Fatal Bond '91

Valerie Buhagiar
Highway 61 '91
Roadkill '89

Genevieve Bujold
Anne of the Thousand Days '69
Another Man, Another Chance '77
Choose Me '84
Coma '78
The Dance Goes On '92
Dead Ringers '88
Earthquake '74
False Identity '90
Final Assignment '80
Journey '77
The King of Hearts '66
The Last Flight of Noah's Ark '80
The Moderns '88
Monsignor '82
Murder by Decree '79
Obsession '76
Oh, What a Night '92
A Paper Wedding '89
Swashbuckler '76
Tightrope '84
Trojan Women '71
Trouble in Mind '86

Donald Buka
Stolen Identity '53
The Street with No Name '48

Raymond Buktenica
The Adventures of Nellie Bly '81
The Jayne Mansfield Story '80
My Girl '91
Wait Till Your Mother Gets Home '83

Peter Bull
The African Queen '51
A Christmas Carol '51
Doctor Dolittle '67
Dr. Strangelove, or: How I Learned to Stop Worrying and Love the Bomb '64
Marie Antoinette '38
Second Best Secret Agent in the Whole Wide World '65
Tom Jones '63

Richard Bull
Different Story '78
Lawman '71

Sandra Bullock
Demolition Man '93
Love Potion #9 '92
Speed '94
The Thing Called Love '93
The Vanishing '93
Who Shot Pat? '92
Wrestling Ernest Hemingway '93

William Bumiller
Death Spa '87
The Heroes of Desert Storm '91

Brooke Bundy
Beverly Hills Bodysnatchers '89
The Crash of Flight 401 '78
Explorers '85
Francis Gary Powers: The True Story of the U-2 Spy '76
A Nightmare on Elm Street 4: Dream Master '88
Twice Dead '88
Two Fathers' Justice '85

Avis Bunnage
Forbidden '85
The Loneliness of the Long Distance Runner '62
No Surrender '86

Cara Buono
The Cowboy Way '94
Gladiator '92
Waterland '92

Victor Buono
Arnold '73
Beneath the Planet of the Apes '70
Better Late Than Never '79
Boot Hill '69

The Evil '78
Four for Texas '63
The Mad Butcher '72
The Man from Atlantis '77
The Man with Bogart's Face '80
More Wild, Wild West '80
Northeast of Seoul '72
The Strangler '64
What Ever Happened to Baby Jane? '62

Sonny Bupp
Citizen Kane '41
Hopalong Cassidy: Renegade Trail '39
Renegade Trail '39
Three Faces West '40

Hugh Burden
Fame is the Spur '47
Ghost Ship '53

Suzanne Burden
Office Romances '86
Sharma & Beyond '84
Strapless '90

Kim Burfield
The Hero '71
Treasure Island '72

Christopher Burgard
84 Charlie Mopic '89
Twice Dead '88

Gregg Burge
A Chorus Line '85
School Daze '88

Dorothy Burgess
Girls in Chains '43
Hold Your Man '33
Ladies They Talk About '33

Gary Burghoff
Casino '80
The Man in the Santa Claus Suit '79
M*A*S*H '70
M*A*S*H: The Collector's Edition '72
Small Kill '93

Alfred Burke
Children of the Damned '63
Dead Lucky '60
The House on Garibaldi Street '79
Night Caller from Outer Space '66
One Day in the Life of Ivan Denisovich '71

Billie Burke
The Barkleys of Broadway '49
Becky Sharp '35
A Bill of Divorcement '32
Breakfast in Hollywood '46
The Bride Wore Red '37
Christopher Strong '33
Craig's Wife '36
Dinner at Eight '33
Doubting Thomas '35
Eternally Yours '39
Everybody Sing '38
Father of the Bride '50
Father's Little Dividend '51
Finishing School '33
Forsaking All Others '35
In This Our Life '42
The Man Who Came to Dinner '41
Navy Blue and Gold '37
Sergeant Rutledge '60
Small Town Girl '53
Topper '37
Topper Returns '41
Topper Takes a Trip '39
The Wizard of Oz '39
The Young in Heart '38
The Young Philadelphians '59

Delta Burke
A Bunny's Tale '85
Dynamite and Gold '88
First & Ten '85
First & Ten: The Team Scores Again '85
The Seekers '79

J. Frank Burke
Angels with Dirty Faces '38
Italian '15

James Burke
Down to Earth '47

Lady by Choice '34
Lucky '54
The Mystery Man '35
The Ruggles of Red Gap '35

Kathleen Burke
Island of Lost Souls '32
The Lives of a Bengal Lancer '35

Michelle Burke
Coneheads '93
Dazed and Confused '93
Major League 2 '94

Paul Burke
Anatomy of Terror '74
Daddy's Gone A-Hunting '69
Fatal Confinement '64
Francis in the Navy '55
Psychic Killer '75
The Red Light Sting '84
Valley of the Dolls '67
Wild & Wooly '78

Robert Burke
Dust Devil '93
A Far Off Place '93
Rambling Rose '91
RoboCop 3 '91
Simple Men '92
Tombstone '93
The Unbelievable Truth '90

Simon Burke
The Devil's Playground '76
The Irishman '78
Slate, Wyn & Me '87

Laura Burkett
Daddy's Boys '87
Overkill '86

Dennis Burkley
Bummer '73
The Doors '91
Lambada '89
Murphy's Romance '85
Pass the Ammo '88
Son-in-Law '93
Stop! or My Mom Will Shoot '92

Tom Burlinson
Flesh and Blood '85
Landslide '92
The Man from Snowy River '82
Phar Lap '84
Piece of Cake '90
Return to Snowy River '88
Showdown at Williams Creek '91
The Time Guardian '87
Windrider '86

Leo Burmester
The Abyss '89
Passion Fish '92
A Perfect World '93

Caesar Burner
Green Inferno '80s
Tombs of the Blind Dead '72

Carol Burnett
Annie '82
Between Friends '83
Chu Chu & the Philly Flash '81
Follies in Concert '85
The Four Seasons '81
Friendly Fire '79
The Front Page '74
The Grass is Always Greener Over the Septic Tank '78
Noises Off '92
Pete 'n' Tillie '72
Tenth Month '79
A Wedding '78

Smiley Burnette
The Adventures of Rex & Rinty '35
A Betrayed Man '36
Big Show '37
Billy the Kid Returns '38
Boots & Saddles '37
Call of the Canyon '42
Call of the Rockies '44
Dick Tracy '37
Dick Tracy: The Original Serial, Vol. 1 '37
Dick Tracy: The Original Serial, Vol. 2 '37
Down Mexico Way '41
Dude Ranger '34
Gene Autry Matinee Double Feature #2 '53

Gene Autry Matinee Double Feature #3 '53
Git Along Little Dogies '37
Harmony Lane '35
Heart of the Golden West '42
Heart of the Rio Grande '42
Hollywood Stadium Mystery '38
Idaho '43
In Old Santa Fe '34
King of the Cowboys '43
Last of the Pony Riders '53
The Man from Music Mountain '38
Melody Trail '35
Mystery Mountain '34
Oh Susannah '38
Old Barn Dance '38
Old Corral '36
On Top of Old Smoky '53
The Phantom Empire '35
Prairie Moon '38
Raiders of Sunset Pass '43
Red River Valley '36
Ride, Ranger, Ride '36
Ridin' on a Rainbow '41
Rootin' Tootin' Rhythm '38
Round-Up Time in Texas '37
Silver Spurs '43
South of the Border '39
Springtime in the Rockies '37
Under Western Stars '45
Western Double Feature 1 '38
Western Double Feature 4 '37
Western Double Feature 5: Rogers & Autry '37
Western Double Feature 16 '46
Winning of the West '53
Yodelin' Kid From Pine Ridge '37

Carol Burns
Bad Blood '87
Dusty '85
Prisoner Cell Block H '80

Edmund Burns
Made for Love '26
Sea Devils '31
Sunny Side Up '28

George Burns
College Swing '38
A Damsel in Distress '37
18 Again! '88
Going in Style '79
Honolulu '39
International House '33
Oh, God! '77
Oh, God! Book 2 '80
Oh, God! You Devil '84
Sgt. Pepper's Lonely Hearts Club Band '78
The Sunshine Boys '75
Two of a Kind '82

Jere Burns
The Gambler Returns: The Luck of the Draw '93
Greedy '94
Wired '89

Marilyn Burns
Eaten Alive '76
Future Kill '85
Helter Skelter '76
Kiss Daddy Goodbye '81
The Texas Chainsaw Massacre '74

Marion Burns
Dawn Rider '35
Dawn Rider/Frontier Horizon '39
Paradise Canyon '35

Mark Burns
The Charge of the Light Brigade '68
Death in Venice '71
House of the Living Dead '73
The Virgin and the Gypsy '70

Michael Burns
That Cold Day in the Park '69
Thumb Tripping '72

Robert Burns
Confessions of a Serial Killer '87
Gun Law '33
South of Santa Fe '32
Terror in the Jungle '68
Western Trails '34

Raymond Burr
Adventures of Don Juan '49

Airplane 2: The Sequel '82
Black Magic '49
Borderline '50
Bride of the Gorilla '51
Casanova's Big Night '54
Crime of Passion '57
The Curse of King Tut's Tomb '80
The Defense Never Rests '90
Delirious '91
Desperate '47
FBI Girl '52
Godzilla, King of the Monsters '56
Godzilla 1985 '85
Great Day in the Morning '56
His Kind of Woman '51
Horizons West '52
Key to the City '50
Love Happy '50
Love's Savage Fury '79
A Man Alone '55
Meet Danny Wilson '52
The Night the City Screamed '80
Out of the Blue '80
The Ox-Bow Incident '55
Party Girls for Sale '54
Passion '54
Perry Mason Returns '85
Perry Mason: The Case of the Lost Love '87
Pitfall '48
A Place in the Sun '51
Rear Window '54
The Return '80
Showdown at Williams Creek '91
Station West '48
They Were So Young '55
Thunder Pass '54
Tomorrow Never Comes '77

Robert Burr
Netherworld '91
The Possession of Joel Delaney '72

Jackie Burroughs
Anne of Green Gables '85
Careful '94
Final Notice '89
The Grey Fox '83
The Housekeeper '86
John and the Missus '87
125 Rooms of Comfort '83
Undergrads '85

William S. Burroughs
Bloodhounds of Broadway '89
Drugstore Cowboy '89
Kerouac '84
Wax, or the Discovery of Television Among the Bees '93

Darren E. Burrows
Class of 1999 '90
Cry-Baby '90

Ellen Burstyn
Act of Vengeance '86
Alex in Wonderland '70
Alice Doesn't Live Here Anymore '74
The Ambassador '84
The Cemetery Club '93
A Dream of Passion '78
Dying Young '91
The Exorcist '73
Grand Isle '92
Hanna's War '88
Harry and Tonto '74
Into Thin Air '85
The King of Marvin Gardens '72
The Last Picture Show '71
The People vs. Jean Harris '81
Providence '77
Resurrection '80
Same Time, Next Year '78
Silence of the North '81
Something in Common '86
Thursday's Game '74
Tropic of Cancer '70
Twice in a Lifetime '85
When a Man Loves a Woman '94

Benny Burt
Hawaiian Buckaroo '38
Sea Racketeers '37

Kate Burton
Big Trouble in Little China '86
Love Matters '93
Uncle Tom's Cabin '87

LeVar Burton
Acorn People '82
Almos' a Man '78
And the Children Shall Lead '85
Billy: Portrait of a Street Kid '77
Grambling's White Tiger '81
The Guyana Tragedy: The Story of Jim Jones '80
The Hunter '80
The Jesse Owens Story '84
The Midnight Hour '86
One in a Million: The Ron LaFlore Story '78
Roots '77
Roots: The Gift '88
Star Trek the Next Generation: Encounter at Farpoint '87
The Supernaturals '86

Norman Burton
Attack of the Mayan Mummy '63
Bad Guys '86
Bloodsport '88
Crimes of Passion '84
Diamonds are Forever '71
Fright '56
Jud '71
Mausoleum '83
Save the Tiger '73
Simon, King of the Witches '71
The Terminal Man '74

Richard Burton
Absolution '81
Alexander the Great '55
Anne of the Thousand Days '69
Assassination of Trotsky '72
Becket '64
Bluebeard '72
The Bramble Bush '60
Breakthrough '78
Circle of Two '80
Cleopatra '63
The Comedians '67
The Desert Rats '53
Divorce His, Divorce Hers '72
Doctor Faustus '68
Equus '77
The Exorcist 2: The Heretic '77
The Gathering Storm '74
Green Grow the Rushes '51
Hammersmith is Out '72
Ice Palace '60
The Klansman '74
The Last Days of Dolwyn '49
The Longest Day '62
Look Back in Anger '58
Lovespell '79
Massacre in Rome '73
The Medusa Touch '78
The Night of the Iguana '64
1984 '84
Raid on Rommel '71
The Robe '53
The Sandpiper '65
The Spy Who Came in from the Cold '65
The Taming of the Shrew '67
The Tempest '63
Under Milk Wood '73
The V.I.P.'s '63
Wagner: The Complete Epic '85
Wagner: The Movie '85
Where Eagles Dare '68
Who's Afraid of Virginia Woolf? '66
Wild Geese '78

Robert Burton
Above and Beyond '52
All the Brothers Were Valiant '53
The Gallant Hours '60
The Girl Who Had Everything '53
Invasion of the Animal People '62
A Man Called Peter '55
A Reason to Live, A Reason to Die '73
The Slime People '63
The Tall T '57
Teenage Frankenstein '58
Trilogy of Terror '75

Tony Burton
Armed and Dangerous '86
Assault on Precinct 13 '76
Blackjack '78
House Party 2: The Pajama Jam '91
Mission of Justice '92
Oceans of Fire '86

Wendell Burton
East of Eden '80
Fortune and Men's Eyes '71
The Sterile Cuckoo '69

Sean Bury
Friends '71
Paul and Michelle '74

Steve Buscemi
Airheads '94
Barton Fink '91
Billy Bathgate '91
Crisscross '92
Ed and His Dead Mother '93
Heart '87
In the Soup '92
King of New York '90
The Last Outlaw '93
Mystery Train '89
New York Stories '89
Parting Glances '86
Reservoir Dogs '92
Twenty Bucks '93

Mae Busch
Bohemian Girl '36
Defenders of the Law '31
Foolish Wives '22
Laurel & Hardy Comedy Classics, Vol. 1 '33
Laurel & Hardy Comedy Classics, Vol. 3 '34
Laurel & Hardy Comedy Classics, Vol. 6 '35
Laurel & Hardy Comedy Classics, Vol. 7 '30s
The Mad Monster '42
Marie Antoinette '38
Sons of the Desert '33
Sucker Money '34
The Unholy Three '25
Without Honors '32
Ziegfeld Girl '41

Gary Busey
Act of Piracy '89
Angels Hard as They Come '71
Barbarosa '82
Big Wednesday '78
The Buddy Holly Story '78
Bulletproof '88
Canvas: The Fine Art of Crime '92
Carny '80
Chrome Soldiers '92
Dangerous Life '89
D.C. Cab '84
Didn't You Hear? '83
The Execution of Private Slovik '74
Eye of the Tiger '86
Fallen Angels 1 '93
The Firm '93
Foolin' Around '80
Gumball Rally '76
Half a Lifetime '86
Hider in the House '90
Insignificance '85
The Last American Hero '73
Lethal Weapon '87
Let's Get Harry '87
My Heroes Have Always Been Cowboys '91
The Neon Empire '89
Point Break '91
Predator 2 '90
Rookie of the Year '93
The Shrieking '73
Silver Bullet '85
South Beach '92
A Star is Born '76
Straight Time '78
Surviving the Game '94
Thunderbolt & Lightfoot '74
Under Siege '92

Jake Busey
P.C.U. '94
S.F.W. '94

Timothy Busfield
Fade to Black '93
Field of Dreams '89
Little Big League '94

Revenge of the Nerds '84
Revenge of the Nerds 2: Nerds in Paradise '87
The Skateboard Kid '93
Sneakers '92
Strays '91
Striking Distance '93

Billy Green Bush
Alice Doesn't Live Here Anymore '74
Conagher '91
Critters '86
Culpepper Cattle Co. '72
The Deliberate Stranger '86
Electra Glide in Blue '73
Elvis and Me '88
Five Easy Pieces '70
Jason Goes to Hell: The Final Friday '93
The River '84
Tom Horn '80

Grand Bush
Blind Vengeance '90
Colors '88
Freejack '92
Streets of Fire '84

James Bush
Beggars in Ermine '34
Crimson Romance '34
The Glory Trail '36
King of the Cowboys '43
The Return of Peter Grimm '35
A Shot in the Dark '35

Jovita Bush
The Cheerleaders '72
Foxstyle '73

Anthony Bushell
Angel with the Trumpet '50
The Arsenal Stadium Mystery '39
Dark Journey '37
Disraeli '29
The Ghoul '34
The Miniver Story '50
A Night to Remember '58
The Royal Bed '31
The Scarlet Pimpernel '34
The Small Back Room '49
Vanity Fair '32

Francis X. Bushman
Ben-Hur '26
David and Bathsheba '51
Dick Tracy: The Original Serial, Vol. 1 '37
Dick Tracy: The Original Serial, Vol. 2 '37
Dick Tracy: The Spider Strikes '37
Eyes Right! '26
Honky Tonk '41
Last Frontier '32
Midnight Faces '26
The Phantom Planet '61
Sabrina '54
When Lightning Strikes '34

Akosua Busia
The Color Purple '85
The Final Terror '83
The George McKenna Story '86
Native Son '86
The Seventh Sign '88

Marion Busia
Deadline Auto Theft '83
Gone in 60 Seconds '74

Narciso Busquets
El Gallo de Oro '65
El Hombre Contra el Mundo '87

Raymond Bussieres
Jonah Who Will Be 25 in the Year 2000 '76
Paris When It Sizzles '64

Sergio Bustamante
Conexion Mexico '87
Lagrimas de Amor '87

Budd Buster
Border Badmen '45
Covered Wagon Trails '40
Cowboy Commandos '43
Feud Maker '38
Frontier Outlaws '44
Gun Grit '36
The Gun Ranger '34
The Lone Rider in Ghost Town '41
Outlaw of the Plains '46

Pinto Canyon '40
Raiders of Sunset Pass '43
Songs and Bullets '38
Texas Jack '35
Thunder in the Desert '38
Trigger Men '41

Dick Butkus
Cracking Up '83
Deadly Games '80
Hamburger...The Motion Picture '86
Johnny Dangerously '84
The Legend of Sleepy Hollow '79
Mother, Jugs and Speed '76

Calvin Butler
Drying Up the Streets '76
July Group '70s

Cindy Butler
Boggy Creek II '83
Grayeagle '77

David Butler
County Fair '20
The Man on the Box '25
Prey for the Hunter '92
The Sky Pilot '21

Dean Butler
Desert Hearts '86
Forever '78
The Kid with the 200 I.Q. '83

Frank Butler
King of the Wild Horses '24
Made for Love '26

Lois Butler
High Lonesome '50
Mickey '48

Paul Butler
Crime Story: The Complete Saga '86
Romeo Is Bleeding '93
To Sleep with Anger '90
Zebrahead '92

Tom Butler
Confidential '86
Ernest Rides Again '93
Scanners 2: The New Order '91
Tales of the Klondike: The Scorn of Women '87

William Butler
Inner Sanctum '91
Leatherface: The Texas Chainsaw Massacre 3 '89

Yancy Butler
Hard Target '93
The Hit List '93

Merritt Butrick
Code of Honor '84
Death Spa '87
From the Dead of Night '89
Shy People '87
Star Trek 2: The Wrath of Khan '82
Star Trek 3: The Search for Spock '84
When the Bough Breaks '86
Wired to Kill '86
Zapped! '82

Lawson Butt
Dante's Inferno '24
Lady of the Lake '28

Charles Butterworth
The Cat and the Fiddle '34
Dixie Jamboree '44
Every Day's a Holiday '38
Forsaking All Others '35
Hollywood Party '34
Illicit '31
Let Freedom Ring '39
Moon's Our Home '36
Penthouse '33
Road Show '41
Second Chorus '40
Swing High, Swing Low '37

Donna Butterworth
Family Jewels '65
Paradise, Hawaiian Style '66

Red Buttons
The Ambulance '90
C.H.O.M.P.S. '79
18 Again! '88
Five Weeks in a Balloon '62
Harlow '65
Hatari '62

It Could Happen to You '94
Leave 'Em Laughing '81
The Longest Day '62
Movie, Movie '78
Off Your Rocker '80
Pete's Dragon '77
The Poseidon Adventure '72
Sayonara '57
Side Show '84
They Shoot Horses, Don't They? '69
13 Rue Madeleine '46
Users '78
Viva Knievel '77
When Time Ran Out '80
Who Killed Mary What's 'Er Name? '71

Pat Buttram
Back to the Future, Part 3 '90
Blue Canadian Rockies '52
The Gatling Gun '72
Hills of Utah '51
Night Stage to Galveston '52
Roustabout '64
Valley of Fire '51

Sarah Buxton
Primal Rage '90
Rock 'n' Roll High School Forever '91

Ruth Buzzi
Bad Guys '86
The Being '83
Chu Chu & the Philly Flash '81
Digging Up Business '91
Dixie Lanes '88
Freaky Friday '76
My Mom's a Werewolf '89
The North Avenue Irregulars '79
Once Upon a Brothers Grimm '77
Scavenger Hunt '79
Surf 2 '84
Up Your Alley '89
The Villain '79
Wishful Thinking '92

Bobbie Byers
Savages from Hell '68
Wild Rebels '71

Spring Byington
Ah, Wilderness! '35
Angels in the Outfield '51
Because You're Mine '52
The Big Wheel '49
The Blue Bird '40
The Devil & Miss Jones '41
The Enchanted Cottage '45
Heaven Can Wait '43
In the Good Old Summertime '49
Jezebel '38
Little Women '33
Lucky Partners '40
Meet John Doe '41
Mutiny on the Bounty '35
Please Don't Eat the Daisies '60
Thrill of a Romance '45
Walk Softly, Stranger '50
Werewolf of London '35
When Ladies Meet '41
You Can't Take It with You '38

Rolan Bykov
Commissar '77
The Overcoat '59

John Byner
Great Smokey Roadblock '76
The Man in the Santa Claus Suit '79
A Pleasure Doing Business '79
Transylvania 6-5000 '85

Ralph Byrd
Blake of Scotland Yard '36
Border Caballero '36
Born to Be Wild '38
Desperate Cargo '41
Dick Tracy '37
Dick Tracy Double Feature #1 '45
Dick Tracy Double Feature #2 '47
Dick Tracy Meets Gruesome '47
Dick Tracy Returns '38
Dick Tracy: The Original Serial, Vol. 1 '37

Byrd ▶cont.

Dick Tracy: The Original Serial, Vol. 2 '37
Dick Tracy: The Spider Strikes '37
Dick Tracy vs. Crime Inc. '41
Dick Tracy's Dilemma '47
Guadalcanal Diary '43
Hell-Ship Morgan '36
The Howards of Virginia '40
The Jungle Book '42
Jungle Goddess '49
Life Begins for Andy Hardy '41
Radar Secret Service '50
Scared to Death/Dick Tracy's Dilemma '47
The Son of Monte Cristo '41
S.O.S. Coast Guard '37
Thunder in the Pines '49
The Trigger Trio '37

Anne Byrne
Manhattan '79
A Night Full of Rain '78

Barbara Byrne
Mystery at Fire Island '81
Sunday in the Park with George '86
Svengali '83

David Byrne
Heavy Petting '89
True Stories '86

Gabriel Byrne
Christopher Columbus '85
Cool World '92
The Courier '88
A Dangerous Woman '93
Dark Obsession '90
Defense of the Realm '85
Excalibur '81
Gothic '87
Hanna K. '83
Hello Again '87
Into the West '92
Julia and Julia '87
The Keep '83
Lionheart '87
Miller's Crossing '90
Point of No Return '93
Shipwrecked '90
Siesta '87
A Simple Twist of Fate '94
A Soldier's Tale '91

Martha Byrne
Anna to the Infinite Power '84
The Eyes of the Amaryllis '82

Michael Byrne
The Good Father '87
Indiana Jones and the Last Crusade '89
Over Indulgence '87

Edd Byrnes
Any Gun Can Play '67
Back to the Beach '87
Darby's Rangers '58
Erotic Images '85
Go Kill and Come Back '68
Mankillers '87
Troop Beverly Hills '89
Twirl '81

David Byron
Fade to Black '93
My Brother's Wife '89

Jeffrey Byron
Dungeonmaster '85
Metalstorm '83
The Seniors '78

Kathleen Byron
Black Narcissus '47
Burn Witch, Burn! '62
The Gambler & the Lady '52
Profile '54
The Small Back Room '49
Twins of Evil '71
Young Bess '53

Marion Byron
Breed of the Border '33
Steamboat Bill, Jr. '28

Walter Byron
Mr. Boggs Steps Out '38
Queen Kelly '29
The Savage Girl '32
Vanity Fair '32

James Caan
Alien Nation '88
Another Man, Another Chance '77
Bolero '82
Brian's Song '71
A Bridge Too Far '77
Chapter Two '79
Cinderella Liberty '73
Comes a Horseman '78
Countdown '68
The Dark Backward '91
Dick Tracy '90
El Dorado '67
Flesh and Bone '93
For the Boys '91
Freebie & the Bean '74
Funny Lady '75
The Gambler '74
Gardens of Stone '87
The Godfather '72
The Godfather 1902-1959: The Complete Epic '81
The Godfather, Part 2 '74
Gone with the West '72
Harry & Walter Go to New York '76
Hide in Plain Sight '80
Honeymoon in Vegas '92
The Killer Elite '75
Kiss Me Goodbye '82
Lady in a Cage '64
Little Moon & Jud McGraw '78
Misery '90
The Program '93
The Rain People '69
Red Line 7000 '65
Rollerball '75
Silent Movie '76
Slither '73
Thief '81

Bruce Cabot
Angel and the Badman '47
Ann Vickers '33
Best of the Badmen '50
Captain Caution '40
Chisum '70
The Comancheros '61
Diamonds are Forever '71
Dodge City '39
Fancy Pants '50
Finishing School '33
Fury '36
Goliath and the Barbarians '60
Goliath and the Dragon '61
Hatari '62
Hellfighters '68
In Harm's Way '65
John Paul Jones '59
King Kong '33
The Last of the Mohicans '36
Let 'Em Have It '35
Lost in Alaska '52
McLintock! '63
Renegade Ranger/Scarlet River '38
Show Them No Mercy '35
Silver Queen '42
Sinners in Paradise '38
Sorrowful Jones '49
Sundown '41
Susan and God '40
The Undefeated '69
The War Wagon '67

Sebastian Cabot
Captain's Paradise '53
Dick Barton Strikes Back '48
Dual Alibi '47
Family Jewels '65
Johnny Tremain & the Sons of Liberty '58
Omar Khayyam '57
Romeo and Juliet '54
The Time Machine '60
Twice-Told Tales '63
Westward Ho, the Wagons! '56

Susan Cabot
Carnival Rock '57
Machine Gun Kelly '58
Son of Ali Baba '52
Sorority Girl '57
The Wasp Woman '59

Jean Cadell
Love from a Stranger '37
The Obsessed '51

Adolph Caesar
Club Paradise '86

The Color Purple '85
Fist of Fear, Touch of Death '77
Fortune Dane '86
The Hitter '79
A Soldier's Story '84

Harry Caesar
Ghetto Blaster '89
The Offspring '87

Sid Caesar
Airport '75 '75
Barnaby and Me '77
Best of Comic Relief '86
Cannon Movie Tales: The Emperor's New Clothes '89
Cannonball Run 2 '84
The Cheap Detective '78
Curse of the Black Widow '77
The Fiendish Plot of Dr. Fu Manchu '80
Grease '78
Grease 2 '82
History of the World: Part 1 '81
It's a Mad, Mad, Mad, Mad World '63
Munster's Revenge '81
Over the Brooklyn Bridge '83
Side By Side '88
Silent Movie '76
Stoogemania '85

Cheri Caffaro
The Abductors '72
Ginger '72
Girls Are for Loving '73
A Place Called Today '72
Too Hot to Handle '76

Stephen Caffrey
The Babe '92
Hard Rain-The Tet 1968 '89
Longtime Companion '90
Tour of Duty '87

Andrea Cagan
Hot Box '72
Teenager '74

Nicolas Cage
Amos and Andrew '93
Birdy '84
Boy in Blue '86
The Cotton Club '84
Deadfall '93
Fire Birds '90
Guarding Tess '94
Honeymoon in Vegas '92
It Could Happen to You '94
Moonstruck '87
Peggy Sue Got Married '86
Racing with the Moon '84
Raising Arizona '87
Red Rock West '93
Rumble Fish '83
Time to Kill '89
Valley Girl '83
Vampire's Kiss '89
Wild at Heart '90
Zandalee '91

James Cagney
Angels with Dirty Faces '38
Blonde Crazy '31
Blood on the Sun '45
Boy Meets Girl '38
The Bride Came C.O.D. '41
Captains of the Clouds '42
Ceiling Zero '35
City for Conquest '40
Devil Dogs of the Air '35
Each Dawn I Die '39
The Fighting 69th '40
Footlight Parade '33
''G'' Men '35
The Gallant Hours '60
Great Guy '36
Johnny Come Lately '43
Kiss Tomorrow Goodbye '50
Lady Killer '33
A Lion is in the Streets '53
Love Me or Leave Me '55
Man of a Thousand Faces '57
A Midsummer Night's Dream '35
Mister Roberts '55
Never Steal Anything Small '59
Oklahoma Kid '39
One, Two, Three '61
Public Enemy '31
Ragtime '81
The Roaring Twenties '39
The Seven Little Foys '55
Shake Hands with the Devil '59

Something to Sing About '36
Strawberry Blonde '41
13 Rue Madeleine '46
The Time of Your Life '48
Tribute to a Bad Man '56
The West Point Story '50
What Price Glory? '52
White Heat '49
Yankee Doodle Dandy '42

Jeanne Cagney
Don't Bother to Knock '52
Kentucky Rifle '55
A Lion is in the Streets '53
Postmark for Danger/Quicksand '56
Quicksand '50
The Time of Your Life '48
Yankee Doodle Dandy '42

William Cagney
Ace of Aces '33
Palooka '34

Howard Caine
Pressure Point '62
Watermelon Man '70

Michael Caine
Alfie '66
Ashanti, Land of No Mercy '79
Battle of Britain '69
Beyond the Limit '83
Beyond the Poseidon Adventure '79
The Black Windmill '74
Blame It on Rio '84
Blue Ice '92
A Bridge Too Far '77
Bullseye! '90
California Suite '78
Death Becomes Her '92
Deathtrap '82
The Destructors '74
Dirty Rotten Scoundrels '88
Dressed to Kill '80
The Eagle Has Landed '77
Educating Rita '83
The Fourth Protocol '87
Funeral in Berlin '66
Gambit '66
Half Moon Street '86
The Hand '81
Hannah and Her Sisters '86
Harry & Walter Go to New York '76
The Holcroft Covenant '85
The Ipcress File '65
The Island '80
The Italian Job '69
Jack the Ripper '88
Jaws: The Revenge '87
The Jigsaw Man '84
The Last Valley '71
The Man Who Would Be King '75
Mr. Destiny '90
Mona Lisa '86
The Muppet Christmas Carol '92
Noises Off '92
On Deadly Ground '94
Pulp '72
Romantic Englishwoman '75
Room 43 '58
A Shock to the System '90
Silver Bears '78
Sleuth '72
Surrender '87
The Swarm '78
Sweet Liberty '86
Too Late the Hero '70
Victory '81
Water '85
The Whistle Blower '87
The Wilby Conspiracy '75
Without a Clue '88
Woman Times Seven '67
World War II: When Lions Roared '94
The Wrong Box '66
X, Y & Zee '72
Zulu '64

Juan Carlos Calabro
Donde Duermen Dos...Duermen Tres '80s
Gran Valor en la Facultad de Medicina '80s

Anna Calder-Marshall
The Two Faces of Evil '82

Wuthering Heights '70

Sergio Calderon
Border Shootout '90
Old Gringo '89

Paul Calderone
Bad Lieutenant '92
Crisscross '92
Q & A '90

Zoe Caldwell
Lantern Hill '90
Medea '59
The Purple Rose of Cairo '85

Don Calfa
Chopper Chicks in Zombietown '91
E. Nick: A Legend in His Own Mind '84
Me, Myself & I '92
The Rainbow Gang '73
Return of the Living Dead '85
Treasure of the Moon Goddess '88
Weekend at Bernie's '89

Louis Calhern
Arch of Triumph '48
The Asphalt Jungle '50
Athena '54
Betrayed '54
Blackboard Jungle '55
Blonde Crazy '31
The Blot '21
The Bridge of San Luis Rey '44
The Count of Monte Cristo '34
Duck Soup '33
Executive Suite '54
Forever Darling '56
The Gorgeous Hussy '36
Heaven Can Wait '43
High Society '56
Julius Caesar '53
Last Days of Pompeii '35
Latin Lovers '53
A Life of Her Own '50
The Magnificent Yankee '50
Men of the Fighting Lady '54
Nancy Goes to Rio '50
Night After Night '32
Notorious '46
Prisoner of Zenda '52
The Prodigal '55
The Red Pony '49
Rhapsody '54
The Student Prince '54
Sweet Adeline '35
They Call It Sin '32
Too Wise Wives '21
Two Weeks with Love '50
Up in Arms '44
We're Not Married '52
The World Gone Mad '33

Alice Calhoun
The Man on the Box '25
Tentacles of the North '26

Rory Calhoun
Adventure Island '47
Angel '84
Apache Uprising '66
Avenging Angel '85
Bad Jim '89
A Bullet Is Waiting '54
Dayton's Devils '68
Emerald of Artama '67
Finger on the Trigger '65
Flatbed Annie and Sweetiepie: Lady Truckers '79
Hard Drivin' '60
Hell Comes to Frogtown '88
Midnight Auto Supply '78
Mission to Glory '80
Motel Hell '80
Operation Cross Eagles '69
Pure Country '92
The Rebels '79
The Red House '47
River of No Return '54
Roller Blade Warriors: Taken By Force '90
Ticket to Tomahawk '50
Treasure of Pancho Villa '55

Joseph Cali
The Competition '80
The Lonely Lady '83

Brandon Call
The Adventures of Ford Fairlane '90
Blind Fury '90

For the Boys '91
R.D. Call
Other People's Money '91
Stephen King's Golden Years '91
Young Guns 2 '90
James Callahan
Outlaw Blues '77
Tropic of Cancer '70
K. Callan
Frankie and Johnny '91
A Touch of Class '73
The Unborn '91
Michael Callan
Bon Voyage! '62
The Cat and the Canary '79
Cat Ballou '65
Donner Pass: The Road to Survival '84
Double Exposure '82
Frasier the Sensuous Lion '73
Freeway '88
Gidget Goes Hawaiian '61
The Interns '62
Lepke '75
Mysterious Island '61
Photographer '75
Tom Edison: The Boy Who Lit Up the World '78
Joseph Calleia
After the Thin Man '36
Algiers '38
Branded '50
The Caddy '53
Deadline at Dawn '46
Five Came Back '39
Gilda '46
The Glass Key '42
Golden Boy '39
The Jungle Book '42
The Light in the Forest '58
The Littlest Outlaw '54
Marie Antoinette '38
The Monster and the Girl '41
My Little Chickadee '40
The Noose Hangs High '48
Riff Raff '35
Sundown '41
Touch of Evil '58
Simon Callow
Amadeus '84
The Crucifer of Blood '91
Four Weddings and a Funeral '93
The Good Father '87
Maurice '87
Mr. & Mrs. Bridge '91
A Room with a View '86
Cab Calloway
The Blues Brothers '80
The Cincinnati Kid '65
Hi-De-Ho '35
International House '33
The Littlest Angel '69
Manhattan Merry-Go-Round '37
Sensations of 1945 '44
Stormy Weather '43
Kirk Calloway
Cinderella Liberty '73
Summertree '71
Donald Calthrop
No. 17 '32
The Phantom Light '35
Scrooge '35
Bill Calvert
Body Waves '92
C.H.U.D. 2: Bud the Chud '89
Terror Squad '87
Phyllis Calvert
Indiscreet '58
Kipps '41
The Man in Grey '45
Man of Evil '48
Mandy '53
Men of Two Worlds '46
The Woman He Loved '88
The Young and the Guilty '58
Corinne Calvet
Apache Uprising '66
Dr. Heckyl and Mr. Hype '80
Far Country '55
Too Hot to Handle '76
What Price Glory? '52

Henry Calvin
The Sign of Zorro '60
Toby Tyler '59
John Calvin
California Dreaming '79
Dragonworld '94
Ghostwarrior '86
The Magic Bubble '93
Primary Target '89
Armando Calvo
Ni Chana Ni Juana '87
Orlak, the Hell of Frankenstein '60
Satanik '69
The Witch's Mirror '60
Godfrey Cambridge
Cotton Comes to Harlem '70
Friday Foster '75
Gone are the Days '63
The President's Analyst '67
Purlie Victorious '63
Son of Blob '72
Watermelon Man '70
Whiffs '75
Ji Tu Cambuka
Glitch! '88
Mandingo '75
Juan Jose Camero
El Muerto '75
Far Away and Long Ago '74
Veronico Cruz '87
Dean Cameron
Bad Dreams '88
Miracle Beach '92
Rockula '90
Ski School '91
Summer School '87
Jane Cameron
Pair of Aces '90
The Unborn '91
Kirk Cameron
The Best of Times '86
Like Father, Like Son '87
Listen to Me '89
Rod Cameron
The Electronic Monster '57
Evel Knievel '72
G-Men vs. the Black Dragon '43
Jungle '52
The Last Movie '71
Manhunt in the African Jungle '54
Midnight Auto Supply '78
The Monster and the Girl '41
Psychic Killer '75
Ride the Man Down '53
Salome, Where She Danced '45
Wake Island '42
Colleen Camp
Apocalypse Now '79
Backfield in Motion '91
Cat in the Cage '68
Cloud Dancer '80
Clue '85
D.A.R.Y.L. '85
Deadly Games '80
Doin' Time '85
Game of Death '79
Greedy '94
Illegally Yours '87
Joy of Sex '84
Lady of the House '78
The Last Porno Flick '74
The Magic Bubble '93
Midnight Auto Supply '78
Police Academy 2: Their First Assignment '85
Police Academy 4: Citizens on Patrol '87
Rosebud Beach Hotel '85
Screwball Academy '86
Seducers '77
The Seduction '82
She Devils in Chains
Sliver '93
Smile '75
Smokey and the Bandit, Part 3 '83
The Swinging Cheerleaders '74
They All Laughed '81
Track 29 '88
Valley Girl '83
Walk Like a Man '87
Wayne's World '92

Wicked Stepmother '89
Hamilton Camp
Arena '88
Attack of the 50 Ft. Woman '93
Casey at the Bat '85
Meatballs 2 '84
Rosebud Beach Hotel '85
Under Fire '83
Frank Campanella
Blood Red '88
Chesty Anderson USN '76
Joseph Campanella
Ben '72
Body Chemistry '90
Club Fed '90
Comic Book Kids '82
Down the Drain '89
Hangar 18 '80
Last Call '90
Magic Kid '92
Meteor '79
Murder Once Removed '71
No Retreat, No Surrender 3: Blood Brothers '91
Original Intent '91
Plutonium Incident '82
The President's Plane is Missing '71
Return to Fantasy Island '77
The St. Valentine's Day Massacre '67
Sky Hei$t '75
Steele Justice '87
Terror on the 40th Floor '74
Beatrice Campbell
Last Holiday '50
The Master of Ballantrae '53
Bill Campbell
Bram Stoker's Dracula '92
Crime Story: The Complete Saga '86
The Night We Never Met '93
The Rocketeer '91
Bruce Campbell
Army of Darkness '92
Crimewave '85
Evil Dead '83
Evil Dead 2: Dead by Dawn '87
Going Back '83
Lunatics: A Love Story '92
Maniac Cop '88
Maniac Cop 2 '90
Mindwarp '91
Moontrap '89
Sundown '91
Waxwork 2: Lost in Time '91
Cheryl Campbell
Chariots of Fire '81
Greystoke: The Legend of Tarzan, Lord of the Apes '84
Lillie '79
McVicar '80
The Shooting Party '85
Christian Campbell
Born to Run '93
City Boy '93
David James Campbell
Killer Workout '86
Killzone '85
Eric Campbell
Charlie Chaplin Festival '17
Charlie Chaplin: The Early Years, Vol. 1 '17
Charlie Chaplin: The Early Years, Vol. 2 '17
Charlie Chaplin: The Early Years, Vol. 3 '16
Charlie Chaplin: The Early Years, Vol. 4 '16
Count/Adventurer '17
The Cure '17
The Fireman '16
The Floorwalker/By the Sea '15
Triple Trouble/Easy Street '18
The Vagabond '16
Glen Campbell
True Grit '69
Uphill All the Way '85
Judy Campbell
Bonnie Prince Charlie '48
Convoy '40
Dust to Dust '85

The World Owes Me a Living '47
Julia Campbell
Livin' Large '91
Lone Justice '93
Opportunity Knocks '90
Kate Campbell
Ghost Valley '32
Monte Carlo Nights '34
Ken Campbell
Joshua Then and Now '85
Letter to Brezhnev '86
Smart Money '88
Louise Campbell
Bulldog Drummond Comes Back '37
Bulldog Drummond's Peril '38
Bulldog Drummond's Revenge '37
Bulldog Drummond's Revenge/ Bulldog Drummond's Peril '38
Nicholas Campbell
The Big Slice '90
Certain Fury '85
Fast Company '78
Going Home '86
July Group '70s
Knights of the City '85
Naked Lunch '91
Rampage '87
The Victory '88
Peggy Campbell
Big Calibre '35
When a Man Sees Red '34
Tisha Campbell
Boomerang '92
House Party '90
House Party 2: The Pajama Jam '91
House Party 3 '94
Rags to Riches '87
Rooftops '89
School Daze '88
Torquil Campbell
The Golden Seal '83
Heaven on Earth '89
William Campbell
Armistead Maupin's Tales of the City '93
Battle Circus '53
Dementia 13 '63
Escape from Fort Bravo '53
Man Without a Star '55
Night of Evil '62
Portrait in Terror '66
Track of the Vampire '66
Frank Campeau
His Majesty, the American '19
The Man from Painted Post '17
When the Clouds Roll By '19
Cris Campion
Field of Honor '87
Pirates '86
Wally Campo
The Beast from Haunted Cave '60
Hell Squad '58
Machine Gun Kelly '58
Suicide Battalion/Hell Squad '58
Tank Commando '59
Rafael Campos
The Astro-Zombies '67
The Hanged Man '74
Lady in a Cage '64
The Return of Josey Wales '86
Slumber Party '57 '76
A Streetcar Named Desire '51
This Could Be the Night '57
Giana Maria Canale
The Devil's Commandment '56
Evil's Commandment '56
Go for Broke! '51
Hercules '58
Man from Cairo '54
Marauder '65
Sins of Rome '54
Tiger of the Seven Seas '62
Lee Canalito
The Glass Jungle '88
Paradise Alley '78

David Canary
Johnny Firecloud '75
Melvin Purvis: G-Man '74
Posse '75
Sharks' Treasure '75
John Candy
Armed and Dangerous '86
Best of Comic Relief '86
The Best of John Candy on SCTV '80s
The Blues Brothers '80
Brewster's Millions '85
Canadian Bacon '94
Class of '44 '73
Clown Murders '83
Cool Runnings '93
Delirious '91
The Double Negative '80
Find the Lady '75
Going Berserk '83
The Great Outdoors '88
Home Alone '90
JFK '91
The Last Polka '84
Little Shop of Horrors '86
Lost and Found '79
The Masters of Menace '90
National Lampoon's Vacation '83
1941 '79
Nothing But Trouble '91
Once Upon a Crime '92
Only the Lonely '91
Planes, Trains & Automobiles '87
Really Weird Tales '86
Second City Insanity '81
Sesame Street Presents: Follow That Bird '85
The Silent Partner '78
Spaceballs '87
Speed Zone '88
Splash '84
Stripes '81
Summer Rental '85
Tales of the Klondike: The Unexpected '83
Tunnelvision '76
Uncle Buck '89
Volunteers '85
Wagons East '94
Who's Harry Crumb? '89
Charles Cane
Dead Reckoning '47
Lucky Me '54
Native Son '51
Roberto Canedo
Bestia Nocturna '86
Wrestling Women vs. the Aztec Ape '62
Dyan Cannon
The Anderson Tapes '71
Author! Author! '82
Based on an Untrue Story '93
Bob & Carol & Ted & Alice '69
Caddyshack 2 '88
Christmas in Connecticut '92
Coast to Coast '80
Deathtrap '82
Doctors' Wives '70
The End of Innocence '90
Having It All '82
Heaven Can Wait '78
Honeysuckle Rose '80
Jenny's War '85
Lady of the House '78
The Last of Sheila '73
The Love Machine '71
Merlin and the Sword '85
The Pickle '93
Revenge of the Pink Panther '78
Shamus '73
The Virginia Hill Story '76
J.D. Cannon
The Adventures of Nellie Bly '81
Cool Hand Luke '67
Cotton Comes to Harlem '70
Death Wish 2 '82
Killing Stone '78
Lawman '71
Pleasure Palace '80
Raise the Titanic '80
Scorpio '73
Street Justice '89
Walking Through the Fire '80

Kathy Cannon
High Noon: Part 2 '80
Matters of the Heart '90
Private Duty Nurses '71
The Red Fury '70s
Will: G. Gordon Liddy '82

Diana Canova
The First Nudie Musical '75
Night Partners '83

Judy Canova
The Adventures of Huckleberry
Finn '60
Oklahoma Annie '51

Antonio Cantafora
Gabriela '84
Intervista '87

Luis Aceves Canteneda
Curse of the Aztec Mummy/
Robot vs. the Aztec Mummy
'59
The Robot vs. the Aztec
Mummy '59

Cantinflas
Around the World in 80 Days
'56
El Gendarme Desconocido '41

Eddie Cantor
Glorifying the American Girl '30
Hollywood Canteen '44
Hollywood Goes to War '54
If You Knew Susie '48
Kid Millions '34
Roman Scandals '33
Show Business '44
Thank Your Lucky Stars '43
Whoopee! '30

Yakima Canutt
Branded a Coward '35
Calling Wild Bill Elliott '43
Circle of Death '35
Cyclone of the Saddle '35
Dawn Rider '35
The Fighting Stallion '26
Gone with the Wind '39
Heart of the Rockies '37
Hit the Saddle '37
The Kansas Terrors '39
King of the Pecos '36
Last Frontier '32
Lucky Texan '34
The Man from Hell '34
Man from Utah '34
Outlaw Rule '36
Overland Stage Raiders '38
The Painted Stallion '37
Paradise Canyon '35
Riders of the Rockies '37
Riders of the Whistling Skull '37
Sagebrush Trail '33
Santa Fe Stampede '38
The Showdown '50
The Star Packer '34
Telegraph Trail '33
Trouble in Texas '37
West of the Divide '34
Wild Horse Canyon '25
Winds of the Wasteland '36
Wyoming Outlaw '39

Peter Capaldi
Dangerous Liaisons '88
John & Yoko: A Love Story '85
The Lair of the White Worm '88
Local Hero '83

Jad Capelja
Freedom '81
Puberty Blues '81

Virginia Capers
Ferris Bueller's Day Off '86
Jo Jo Dancer, Your Life is
Calling '86
The North Avenue Irregulars
'79
White Mama '80

Manuel Capetillo
Passion for Power '85
Vivo o Muerto '87

Carmine Capobianco
Galactic Gigolo '87
Psychos in Love '87

John Capodice
The Hard Way '91
Honeymoon in Vegas '92

Lino Capolicchio
Fiorile '93
The Garden of the Finzi-
Continis '71

Nadia Capone
Skull: A Night of Terror '88
A Whisper to a Scream '88

Carl Capotorto
American Blue Note '89
Mac '93

Jordanna Capra
Hired to Kill '91
Watch It '93

Anna Capri
The Brotherhood of Satan '71
Darker than Amber '70
Payday '72
The Specialist '75

Kate Capshaw
Best Defense '84
Black Rain '89
Code Name: Dancer '87
Dreamscape '84
Indiana Jones and the Temple
of Doom '84
A Little Sex '82
Love at Large '89
My Heroes Have Always Been
Cowboys '91
Power '86
Private Affairs '89
The Quick and the Dead '87
SpaceCamp '86
Windy City '84

Capucine
The Con Artists '80
Curse of the Pink Panther '83
Fellini Satyricon '69
From Hell to Victory '79
The Honey Pot '67
Jaguar Lives '79
North to Alaska '60
The Pink Panther '64
Scandalous '88
Song Without End '60
The Switch '89
Trail of the Pink Panther '82
Walk on the Wild Side '62
What's New Pussycat? '65

Irene Cara
Aaron Loves Angela '75
Busted Up '86
Caged in Paradiso '89
Certain Fury '85
City Heat '84
D.C. Cab '84
Fame '80
For Us, the Living '88
Killing 'em Softly '85
Roots: The Next Generation '79
Sparkle '76

Paul Carafotes
Choices '81
Journey to the Center of the
Earth '88

Antony Carbone
A Bucket of Blood '59
Creature from the Haunted Sea
'60
The Last Porno Flick '74
The Last Woman on Earth '61
Sex Through a Window '72
Skateboard '77

Elsa Cardenas
Fun in Acapulco '63
Los Asesinos '68
Mision Suicida '87
Rio Hondo '47

Pat Cardi
And Now Miguel '66
Twisted Brain '74

Tantoo Cardinal
Black Robe '91
Dances with Wolves '90
The Lightning Incident '91
Loyalties '86
Silent Tongue '92
Spirit Rider '93

Claudia Cardinale
The Battle of Austerlitz '60
Big Deal on Madonna Street
'58
Blonde in Black Leather '77
Blood Brothers '74

Butterfly Affair '71
Cartouche '62
Circus World '64
Conversation Piece '75
Corleone '79
8 1/2 '63
Escape to Athena '79
Fitzcarraldo '82
The Gift '82
Henry IV '85
Il Bell'Antonio '60
Immortal Bachelor '80
Jesus of Nazareth '77
Legend of Frenchie King '71
The Lost Command '66
L'Udienza '71
A Man in Love '87
Next Summer '84
Once Upon a Time in the West
'68
One Russian Summer '73
The Pink Panther '64
Princess Daisy '83
The Professionals '66
Queen of Diamonds '80s
Red Tent '69
Rocco and His Brothers '60
The Salamander '82
Scoumoune '74
The Sniper '87
Son of the Pink Panther '93
Time of Indifference '64

John Cardos
Blood of Dracula's Castle '69
Satan's Sadists '69

James B. Cardwell
The Devil on Wheels '47
Down Dakota Way '49
Fear '46
The Fighting Sullivans '42
The Shanghai Cobra '45

Roger Carel
Soldat Duroc...Ca Va Etre Ta
Fete! '80
The Two of Us '68

Annette Carell
The Tell-Tale Heart '62
Vulture '67

Julien Carette
Grand Illusion '37
La Bete Humaine '38
The Rules of the Game '39

Harry Carey, Sr.
Aces Wild '37
Air Force '43
Angel and the Badman '47
Beyond Tomorrow '40
Border Devils '32
Buffalo Stampede '33
Cavalier of the West '31
Devil Horse '32
Duel in the Sun '46
Ghost Town '37
The Great Moment '44
Judith of Bethulia '14
Kid Galahad '37
Last of the Clintons '35
The Last of the Mohicans '32
Last Outlaw '36
Law West of Tombstone '38
Man of the Forest '33
Mr. Smith Goes to Washington
'39
Night Rider '32
The Port of Missing Girls '38
Powdersmoke Range '35
The Prairie Pirate '25
Red River '48
Rustler's Paradise '35
Short Films of D.W. Griffith,
Vol. 2 '09
So Dear to My Heart '49
The Spoilers '42
Straight Shootin' '17
Sundown '41
They Knew What They Wanted
'40
Trader Horn '31
Vanishing Legion '31
Wagon Trail '35
Wild Mustang '35
Without Honors '32

Harry Carey, Jr.
Alvarez Kelly '66
Back to the Future, Part 3 '90
Bad Jim '89
Bandolero! '68

Billy the Kid Versus Dracula '66
Breaking In '89
Cahill: United States Marshal
'73
Challenge to White Fang '86
Copper Canyon '50
Crossroads '86
Endangered Species '82
The Long Riders '80
Mask '85
Mister Roberts '55
Moonrise '48
A Public Affair '62
Pursued '47
Red River '48
Rio Grande '50
The Searchers '56
Seventh Cavalry '56
She Wore a Yellow Ribbon '49
Three Godfathers '48
Tombstone '93
Trinity is Still My Name '75
The Undefeated '69
Wagon Master '50
The Whales of August '87

Joyce Carey
Blithe Spirit '45
Brief Encounter '46
Cry, the Beloved Country '51
October Man '48

MacDonald Carey
Access Code '84
Copper Canyon '50
End of the World '77
Great Missouri Raid '51
It's Alive 3: Island of the Alive
'87
John Paul Jones '59
Let's Make it Legal '51
Man or Gun '58
The Rebels '79
Shadow of a Doubt '43
Tammy and the Doctor '63
Wake Island '42
Who Is the Black Dahlia? '75

Michele Carey
Changes '69
The Desperados '80s
El Dorado '67
In the Shadow of Kilimanjaro
'86
Live a Little, Love a Little '68
Scandalous John '71

Phil Carey
Fighting Mad '76
Gun Fury '53
The Long Gray Line '55
Mister Roberts '55
Monster '78
Springfield Rifle '52
The Time Travelers '64
Tonka '58

Roland Carey
The Giants of Thessaly '60
Revolt of the Barbarians '64
The Sword of El Cid '62

Ron Carey
Fatso '80
High Anxiety '77
History of the World: Part 1 '81
Who Killed Mary What's 'Er
Name? '71

Timothy Carey
Beach Blanket Bingo '65
Bikini Beach '64
Echo Park '86
Fast Walking '82
The Finger Man '55
The Killing '56
The Killing of a Chinese Bookie
'76
The Mermaids of Tiburon '62
One-Eyed Jacks '61
Paths of Glory '57
Poor White Trash '57
Speedtrap '78

Timothy Carhart
Beverly Hills Cop 3 '94
Party Animal '83
Pink Cadillac '89
Quicksand: No Escape '91
Red Rock West '93
Thelma & Louise '91

Gia Carides
Backlash '86
Midnite Spares '85

Strictly Ballroom '92

Carmine Caridi
Life Stinks '91
Split Decisions '88

Len Cariou
Drying Up the Streets '76
The Four Seasons '81
The Lady in White '88
A Little Night Music '77
Louisiana '87
Who'll Save Our Children? '82

Richard Carle
The Ghost Walks '34
Mistaken Identity '36
Sin Takes a Holiday '30

Claire Carleton
The Devil's Partner '58
The Fighter '52

George Carlin
Best of Comic Relief '86
Bill & Ted's Bogus Journey '91
Bill & Ted's Excellent
Adventure '89
Car Wash '76
Outrageous Fortune '87
The Prince of Tides '91

Gloria Carlin
Goldenrod '77
Hanoi Hilton '87

Lynn Carlin
Deathdream '72
Forbidden Love '82
Silent Night, Lonely Night '69
Superstition '82
Wild Rovers '71

Anne Carlisle
Liquid Sky '83
Perfect Strangers '84
The Suicide Club '88

Mary Carlisle
Baby Face Morgan '42
Champagne for Breakfast '35
Dance, Girl, Dance '40
Dead Men Walk '43
Held for Murder '32
Kentucky Kernels '34
One Frightened Night '35

Kitty Carlisle Hart
Murder at the Vanities '34
A Night at the Opera '35
Radio Days '87
Six Degrees of Separation '93

June Carlson
Delinquent Daughters '44
The Hawk of Powder River '48
Mom & Dad '47

Karen Carlson
American Dream '81
Black Oak Conspiracy '77
Brotherly Love '85
The Candidate '72
Fleshburn '84
In Love with an Older Woman
'82
Octagon '80
On Wings of Eagles '86
The Student Nurses '70
Teen Vamp '88
Wild Horses '84

Richard Carlson
The Amazing Mr. X '48
Behind Locked Doors '48
Beyond Tomorrow '40
Creature from the Black
Lagoon '54
The Doomsday Flight '66
Flat Top '52
The Ghost Breakers '40
Hold That Ghost '41
The Howards of Virginia '40
Human Gorilla '48
Hunted '88
It Came From Outer Space '53
King Solomon's Mines '50
The Last Command '55
The Little Foxes '41
No, No Nanette '40
Presenting Lily Mars '43
Retreat, Hell! '52
Saturday Night Shockers, Vol.
2 '58
Too Many Girls '40
Tormented '60
Try and Get Me '50

The Valley of Gwangi '69
White Cargo '42
The Young in Heart '38
Karin Carlsson
Walpurgis Night '41
A Woman's Face '38
Hope Marie Carlton
Bloodmatch '91
Hard Ticket to Hawaii '87
Picasso Trigger '89
Round Numbers '91
Savage Beach '89
Slaughterhouse Rock '88
Slumber Party Massacre 3 '90
Terminal Exposure '89
Roger C. Carmel
Gambit '66
Hardly Working '81
My Dog, the Thief '69
Skullduggery '70
Thunder and Lightning '77
Jeanne Carmen
In Old Montana '39
The Monster of Piedras Blancas '57
Jewel Carmen
American Aristocracy '17
The Bat '26
Flirting with Fate '16
Julie Carmen
Blue City '86
Can You Hear the Laughter? The Story of Freddie Prinze '79
Deadly Currents '93
Drug Wars 2: The Cocaine Cartel '92
Fright Night 2 '88
Gloria '80
Gore Vidal's Billy the Kid '89
The Hunt for the Night Stalker '91
Kiss Me a Killer '91
Last Plane Out '83
The Milagro Beanfield War '88
The Neon Empire '89
Night of the Juggler '80
Paint It Black '89
The Penitent '88
She's in the Army Now '81
Jean Carmet
Black and White in Color '76
Buffet Froid '79
La Rupture '70
The Little Theatre of Jean Renoir '71
Return of the Tall Blond Man With One Black Shoe '74
Secret Obsession '88
Sorceress '88
The Tall Blond Man with One Black Shoe '72
Violette '78
Hoagy Carmichael
The Best Years of Our Lives '46
Johnny Angel '45
The Las Vegas Story '52
To Have & Have Not '44
Topper '37
Young Man with a Horn '50
Ian Carmichael
Betrayed '54
Brothers in Law '57
The Colditz Story '55
Dark Obsession '90
Heavens Above '63
I'm All Right Jack '59
Lucky Jim '58
Tullio Carminati
London Melody '37
One Night of Love '34
Roman Holiday '53
Michael Carmine
Band of the Hand '86
*batteries not included '87
Leviathan '89
Judy Carne
The Americanization of Emily '64
Only with Married Men '74
Primo Carnera
Hercules Unchained '59

The Prizefighter and the Lady '33
Alan Carney
Girl Rush '44
Roadie '80
Zombies on Broadway '44
Art Carney
Better Late Than Never '83
Bitter Harvest '81
The Blue Yonder '86
Death Scream '75
Defiance '79
The Emperor's New Clothes '84
Firestarter '84
Going in Style '79
Harry and Tonto '74
House Calls '78
Izzy & Moe '85
Katherine '75
Last Action Hero '93
The Late Show '77
Miracle of the Heart: A Boys Town Story '86
Movie, Movie '78
The Naked Face '84
Night Friend '87
The Night They Saved Christmas '87
Pot O' Gold '41
Roadie '80
St. Helen's, Killer Volcano '82
Steel '80
Sunburn '79
Take This Job & Shove It '81
Undergrads '85
George Carney
Brighton Rock '47
Love on the Dole '41
Morris Carnovsky
Cyrano de Bergerac '50
Dead Reckoning '47
Gun Crazy '49
Joe's Bed-Stuy Barbershop: We Cut Heads '83
Our Vines Have Tender Grapes '45
Rhapsody in Blue '45
Alicia Caro
El Cenizeiento '47
Maria '71
Cindy Carol
Dear Brigitte '65
Gidget Goes to Rome '63
Linda Carol
Carnal Crimes '91
Future Hunters '88
Reform School Girls '86
Martine Carol
Around the World in 80 Days '56
The Battle of Austerlitz '60
Lola Montes '55
Nana '55
Voyage-Surprise '46
Sheila Carol
The Beast from Haunted Cave '60
Ski Troop Attack '60
Sue Carol
Captain Swagger '25
The Lone Star Ranger '39
Walking Back '26
Leslie Caron
An American in Paris '51
The Battle of Austerlitz '60
The Cary Grant Collection '90
Courage Mountain '89
Daddy Long Legs '55
Damage '92
Dangerous Moves '84
Fanny '61
Father Goose '64
Gigi '58
The Glass Slipper '55
Goldengirl '79
Head of the Family '71
Is Paris Burning? '68
Lili '53
Madron '70
The Man Who Loved Women '77
Nicole '72
Promise Her Anything '66
QB VII '74

The Unapproachable '82
Valentino '77
Carleton Carpenter
Summer Stock '50
Two Weeks with Love '50
Up Periscope '59
Horace Carpenter
Maniac '34
The Worst of Hollywood: Vol. 1 '90
John Carpenter
Body Bags '93
Night of the Ghouls '59
Song of Old Wyoming '45
Paul Carpenter
Call Me Bwana '63
Fire Maidens from Outer Space '56
Heat Wave '54
Paid to Kill '54
Unholy Four '54
Peter Carpenter
Blood Mania '70
Point of Terror '71
Camilla Carr
Don't Look in the Basement '73
Keep My Grave Open '80
Logan's Run '76
Making Love '82
Poor White Trash 2 '75
Carole Carr
Down Among the Z Men '52
Scream Dream '89
Mary Carr
The Fighting Marshal '32
Gun Law '33
Kept Husbands '31
The Night Patrol '26
Red Kimono '25
The World Accuses '35
Paul Carr
The Bat People '74
Dirt Gang '71
The Severed Arm '73
Sisters of Death '76
Sniper '75
Truck Stop Women '74
Thomas Carr
The Idol Dancer '20
Superman: The Serial, Vol. 1 '48
David Carradine
Americana '81
Animal Instincts '92
Armed Response '86
Bad Girls in the Movies '86
The Bad Seed '85
Bird on a Wire '90
Bound for Glory '76
Boxcar Bertha '72
Cannonball '76
Circle of Iron '78
Cloud Dancer '80
Crime Zone '88
Deadly Surveillance '91
Death Race 2000 '75
Death Sport '78
Double Trouble '91
Dune Warriors '91
The Dying Truth '91
Evil Toons '90
Field of Fire '92
Future Force '89
Future Zone '90
The Gambler Returns: The Luck of the Draw '93
The Good Guys and the Bad Guys '69
Gray Lady Down '77
High Noon: Part 2 '80
Jealousy '84
Karate Cop '93
Kung Fu '72
Kung Fu: The Movie '86
Lone Wolf McQuade '83
The Long Riders '80
Macho Callahan '70
Martial Law '90
Maybe I'll Be Home in the Spring '70
The McMasters '70
Mean Streets '73
Midnight Fear '90
The Misfit Brigade '87
Mr. Horn '79

Night Children '89
Night Rhythms '92
North and South Book 1 '85
Nowhere to Run '88
Oceans of Fire '86
On the Line '83
The P.O.W. Escape '86
Project: Eliminator '91
Q (The Winged Serpent) '82
Roadside Prophets '92
Safari 3000 '82
The Serpent's Egg '78
Sonny Boy '87
Sundown '91
Think Big '90
Thunder and Lightning '77
Trick or Treats '82
Tropical Snow '88
Violent Ones '68
Warlords '88
The Warrior & the Sorceress '84
Wizards of the Lost Kingdom 2 '89
John Carradine
The Adventures of Huckleberry Finn '60
The Adventures of Mark Twain '44
Alexander's Ragtime Band '38
Alien Massacre '67
Around the World in 80 Days '56
The Astro-Zombies '67
Autopsy of a Ghost '67
Bad Charleston Charlie '73
The Bees '78
Big Foot '72
Billy the Kid Versus Dracula '66
Blood and Sand '41
Blood Legacy '73
Blood of Dracula's Castle '69
Blood of Ghastly Horror '72
Bluebeard '44
The Boogey Man '80
Boogey Man 2 '83
Boxcar Bertha '72
The Bride of Frankenstein '35
Buried Alive '89
The C-Man '49
Cain's Cutthroats '71
Captain Kidd '45
Captains Courageous '37
Captive Wild Woman '43
Casanova's Big Night '54
Cheyenne Autumn '64
The Christmas Coal Mine Miracle '77
The Cosmic Man '59
Court Jester '56
Curse of the Stone Hand '64
Daniel Boone '34
Death at Love House '75
Demon Rage '82
Dimples '36
Drums Along the Mohawk '39
The Egyptian '54
Everything You Always Wanted to Know About Sex (But Were Afraid to Ask) '72
Evil Spawn '87
Evils of the Night '85
The Female Jungle '56
Five Came Back '39
Frankenstein Island '81
The Garden of Allah '36
The Gatling Gun '72
Golden Rendezvous '77
Goliath Awaits '81
The Good Guys and the Bad Guys '69
The Grapes of Wrath '40
Gun Riders '69
Half Human '58
Hell Ship Mutiny '57
Hidden Guns '56
Hillbillies in a Haunted House '67
The Horror of It All '91
Horror of the Blood Monsters '70
Horrors of the Red Planet '64
The Hostage '67
The Hound of the Baskervilles '39
House of Dracula '45
House of Frankenstein '44
The House of Seven Corpses '73

House of the Black Death '65
House of the Long Shadows '82
The Howling '81
Ice Pirates '84
The Incredible Petrified World '58
Invasion of the Animal People '62
The Invisible Man's Revenge '44
Isle of Forgotten Sins '43
Johnny Guitar '53
The Kentuckian '55
Killer Inside Me '76
Last Hurrah '58
The Last Tycoon '76
Les Miserables '35
The Man Who Shot Liberty Valance '62
Mary, Mary, Bloody Mary '76
Mary of Scotland '36
The McMasters '70
Mr. Moto's Last Warning '39
Monster '78
The Monster Club '85
Monster in the Closet '86
Mummy & Curse of the Jackal '67
The Mummy's Ghost '44
Myra Breckinridge '70
The Nesting '80
Nocturna '79
Of Human Hearts '38
The Patsy '64
Peggy Sue Got Married '86
The Private Affairs of Bel Ami '47
Return of Frank James '40
Return of the Ape Man '44
Reunion in France '42
Revenge '86
Revenge of the Zombies '43
Satan's Cheerleaders '77
The Seekers '79
The Sentinel '76
Shock Waves '77
The Shootist '76
Showdown at Boot Hill '58
The Shrieking '73
Silent Night, Bloody Night '73
Silver Spurs '43
Son of Fury '42
Stagecoach '39
Star Slammer '87
The Ten Commandments '56
Terror in the Wax Museum '73
The Three Musketeers '39
Thunder Pass '54
To the Last Man '33
Tomb '86
The Trouble with Girls (and How To Get Into It) '69
The Unearthly '57
The Vals '85
The Vampire Hookers '78
Waterfront '44
Western Double Feature 8: Hale & Carradine '40s
Western Union '41
The White Buffalo '77
Winterset '36
Keith Carradine
An Almost Perfect Affair '79
Andre '94
The Bachelor '93
Backfire '88
The Ballad of the Sad Cafe '91
Blackout '89
Capone '89
Chiefs '83
Choose Me '84
Cold Feet '89
Crisscross '92
Daddy's Dyin'...Who's Got the Will? '90
The Duellists '77
Eye on the Sparrow '91
The Forgotten '89
A Gunfight '71
Half a Lifetime '86
Idaho Transfer '73
The Inquiry '91
Judgment '90
Kung Fu '72
The Long Riders '80
Lumiere '74
Man on a String '71
Maria's Lovers '84

Carradine ▶cont.

McCabe & Mrs. Miller '71
The Moderns '88
Murder Ordained '87
Nashville '75
Old Boyfriends '79
Payoff '91
Pretty Baby '78
A Rumor of War '80
The Shrieking '73
Southern Comfort '81
Thieves Like Us '74
Trouble in Mind '86
Welcome to L.A. '77
A Winner Never Quits '86

Robert Carradine
Aladdin and His Wonderful
   Lamp '84
All's Fair '89
Aloha, Bobby and Rose '74
As Is '85
The Big Red One '80
Blackout '78
Body Bags '93
Buy & Cell '89
Cannonball '76
Clarence '91
Coming Home '78
Conspiracy: The Trial of the
   Chicago Eight '87
The Cowboys '72
The Disappearance of Christina
   '93
Double-Crossed '91
Heartaches '82
Illusions '91
The Incident '89
Jackson County Jail '76
Joyride '77
Just the Way You Are '84
The Long Riders '80
Massacre at Central High '76
Mean Streets '73
Monte Carlo '86
Number One with a Bullet '87
On the Edge: The Survival of
   Dana '79
Pom Pom Girls '76
Revenge of the Nerds '84
Revenge of the Nerds 2: Nerds
   in Paradise '87
Revenge of the Nerds 3: The
   Next Generation '92
Rude Awakening '89
Somebody Has to Shoot the
   Picture '90
Stephen King's The
   Tommyknockers '93
Tag: The Assassination Game
   '82
Tales of the Klondike: In a Far
   Country '87
Wavelength '83

Barbara Carrera
Condorman '81
Embryo '76
I, the Jury '82
Island of Dr. Moreau '77
Lone Wolf McQuade '83
Love at Stake '87
Loverboy '89
Masada '81
Never Say Never Again '83
Point of Impact '93
The Underachievers '88
When Time Ran Out '80
Wicked Stepmother '89
Wild Geese 2 '85

Tia Carrere
Aloha Summer '88
Fatal Mission '89
Quick '93
Rising Sun '93
Showdown in Little Tokyo '91
True Lies '94
Wayne's World '92
Wayne's World 2 '93
Zombie Nightmare '86

Jim Carrey
Ace Ventura: Pet Detective '93
Club Med '83
Earth Girls are Easy '89
Finders Keepers '84
The Mask '94
Once Bitten '85

Peggy Sue Got Married '86
Pink Cadillac '89

Corey Carrier
After Dark, My Sweet '90
Men Don't Leave '89

Matthieu Carriere
The Bay Boy '85
Christopher Columbus: The
   Discovery '92
Coup de Grace '78
La Passante '83
Naked Massacre '80s
An Occurrence at Owl Creek
   Bridge/Coup de Grace '62
A Woman in Flames '84

Elpidia Carrillo
Assassin '89
Beyond the Limit '83
The Border '82
Let's Get Harry '87
The Lightning Incident '91
Predator '87
Salvador '86

Leo Carrillo
American Empire '42
Before Morning '33
Don Amigo/Stage to Chino '40s
Fisherman's Wharf '39
Fit for a King '37
The Fugitive '48
Girl of the Golden West '38
History is Made at Night '37
Manhattan Melodrama '34
One Night in the Tropics '40
Pancho Villa Returns '50
The Phantom of the Opera '43
Riders of Death Valley '41
Too Hot to Handle '38
Viva Villa! '34

**Debbie Lee
Carrington**
Club Fed '90
Spaced Invaders '90

Regina Carrol
Angels' Wild Women '72
Blazing Stewardesses '75
Blood of Ghastly Horror '72
Brain of Blood '71
Dracula vs. Frankenstein '71
The Female Bunch '69
Jessie's Girls '75
Satan's Sadists '69
Texas Layover '75

Barbara Carroll
Goliath Against the Giants '63
The Last Days of Pompeii '60

Brandon Carroll
Hell Squad '58
Suicide Battalion/Hell Squad
   '58

Diahann Carroll
Carmen Jones '54
Death Scream '75
The Five Heartbeats '89
From the Dead of Night '89
Goodbye Again '61
I Know Why the Caged Bird
   Sings '79
Paris Blues '61

Helen Carroll
The Dead '87
The Man Upstairs '93

Janet Carroll
Bluffing It '87
Family Business '89
Memories of Me '88
Risky Business '83

John Carroll
The Farmer Takes a Wife '53
Flying Tigers '42
Go West '40
Lady Be Good '41
Only Angels Have Wings '39
Rio Rita '42
Rock, Baby, Rock It '57
Rose of Rio Grande '38
Sunny '41
Susan and God '40
Wolf Call '39
Zorro Rides Again '37

Leo G. Carroll
Bahama Passage '41
Bulldog Drummond's Secret
   Police '39

A Christmas Carol '38
Father of the Bride '50
First Legion '51
Forever Amber '47
North by Northwest '59
One Plus One '61
The Paradine Case '47
The Parent Trap '61
The Private Lives of Elizabeth &
   Essex '39
The Prize '63
Rebecca '40
The Snows of Kilimanjaro '52
Spellbound '45
Strangers on a Train '51
Suspicion '41
Tarantula '55
The Tower of London '39
Treasure of the Golden Condor
   '53
We're No Angels '55
Wuthering Heights '39

Madeleine Carroll
Bahama Passage '42
The General Died at Dawn '36
Hitchcock Collection '87
My Favorite Blonde '42
My Love For Yours '39
On the Avenue '37
Prisoner of Zenda '37
The Secret Agent '36
The 39 Steps '35

Nancy Carroll
Dance of Life '29
Scarlet Dawn '32
Transatlantic Merry-Go-Round
   '34

Pat Carroll
Brothers O'Toole '73
With Six You Get Eggroll '68

Peter Carroll
Cass '78
Who Killed Baby Azaria? '83

Charles Carson
Beau Brummel '54
Broken Melody '34
The Courageous Mr. Penn '41
Cry, the Beloved Country '51
Dreaming Lips '37

Crystal Carson
Killer Tomatoes Strike Back '90
Kiss and Be Killed '91

Glen Carson
Ninja Death Squad '87
Ninja Phantom Heroes '87

Hunter Carson
Invaders from Mars '86
Mr. North '88
Paris, Texas '83

Jack Carson
Arsenic and Old Lace '44
The Bramble Bush '60
The Bride Came C.O.D. '41
Carefree '38
Cat on a Hot Tin Roof '58
Dangerous When Wet '53
Destry Rides Again '39
Gentleman Jim '42
Hollywood Canteen '44
It's a Great Feeling '49
The King of the Roaring '20s:
   The Story of Arnold
   Rothstein '61
Love Crazy '41
Lucky Partners '40
Mildred Pierce '45
Mr. & Mrs. Smith '41
Mr. Smith Goes to Washington
   '39
My Dream is Yours '49
Phffft! '54
Red Garters '54
Romance on the High Seas '48
The Saint in New York '38
Stage Door '37
Stand-In '37
A Star is Born '54
Strawberry Blonde '41
Thank Your Lucky Stars '43
Vivacious Lady '38

John Carson
An African Dream '90
After Julius '78
Captain Kronos: Vampire
   Hunter '74
Taste the Blood of Dracula '70

John David Carson
The Charge of the Model T's
   '76
Creature from Black Lake '76
Empire of the Ants '77
Savage is Loose '74

L.M. Kit Carson
David Holzman's Diary '67
Running on Empty '88

Sunset Carson
Alias Billy the Kid '46
Battling Marshal '48
Bells of Rosarita '45
Call of the Rockies '44
Rio Grande Raiders '46
Rough Riders of Cheyenne '45
Stage Door Canteen '43
Western Double Feature 1: Wild
   Bill & Sunset Carson '40s
Western Double Feature 17
   '40s

Peter Carsten
Black Lemons '80s
Dark of the Sun '68
Secret of the Black Trunk '62
Web of the Spider '70
Zeppelin '71

Margit Carstensen
Angry Harvest '85
The Bitter Tears of Petra von
   Kant '72
Chinese Roulette '86
Mother Kusters Goes to
   Heaven '76
Possession '81

Alice Carter
Dangerous Heart '93
Gross Anatomy '89

Ann Carter
Curse of the Cat People '44
The Two Mrs. Carrolls '47

Ben Carter
Crash Dive '43
Kentucky Blue Streak '35

Bill Carter
Battle of the Worlds '61
Flatbed Annie and Sweetiepie:
   Lady Truckers '79

Finn Carter
How I Got into College '89
Sweet Justice '92
Tremors '89

Gary Carter
Cobra Against Ninja '80s
Ninja Strike Force '88

Helena Carter
Bugles in the Afternoon '52
Invaders from Mars '53
Kiss Tomorrow Goodbye '50

Jack Carter
Alligator '80
The Amazing Dobermans '76
Arena '89
Deadly Embrace '88
Death Blow '87
The Devil's Daughter '39
Ecstasy '84
The Glove '78
Hambone & Hillie '84
The Happy Hooker Goes to
   Washington '77
Heartbeeps '81
History of the World: Part 1 '81
The Horizontal Lieutenant '62
In the Heat of Passion '91
Octagon '80
Rainbow '78
Red Nights '87
Resurrection of Zachary
   Wheeler '71
Robo-Chic '89
Sexpot '88
Viva Las Vegas '63

Janis Carter
Flying Leathernecks '51
The Half-Breed '51
I Married an Angel '42
Lady of Burlesque '43
Miss Grant Takes Richmond
   '49

Jim Carter
Black Beauty '94
Haunted Honeymoon '86
A Month in the Country '87

Stalin '92

Karen Carter
The Big Bust Out '73
The Legend of the Wolf Woman
   '77

Lynda Carter
Bobbie Jo and the Outlaw '76
Danielle Steel's ''Daddy'' '92
Hotline '82
I Posed for Playboy '91
Last Song '80
Rita Hayworth: The Love
   Goddess '83

Nell Carter
Final Shot: The Hank Gathers
   Story '92
Modern Problems '81

Terry Carter
Battlestar Galactica '78
Black Force 2 '78
Foxy Brown '74
Man on the Run '74

Thomas Carter
Monkey Hustle '77
The White Shadow, Vol. 1 '78
Whose Life Is It Anyway? '81

T.K. Carter
Doctor Detroit '83
He's My Girl '87
A Rage in Harlem '91
Runaway Train '85
Seems Like Old Times '80
Ski Patrol '90
Southern Comfort '81
The Thing '82

Anna Carteret
The Heat of the Day '91
The Shell Seekers '89

Gabrielle Carteris
Beverly Hills 90210: The
   Graduation '93
Raising Cain '92

Angela Cartwright
High School USA '84
Scout's Honor '80
The Sound of Music '65

Veronica Cartwright
Alien '79
The Birds '63
The Children's Hour '61
Dead in the Water '91
False Identity '90
Flight of the Navigator '86
Goin' South '78
Hitler's Daughter '90
Inserts '76
Invasion of the Body Snatchers
   '78
Kid from Not-So-Big '78
Man Trouble '92
My Man Adam '86
Nightmares '83
One Man's Way '63
Prime Suspect '82
The Right Stuff '83
Robert Kennedy and His Times
   '90
Spencer's Mountain '63
Valentino Returns '88
Wisdom '87
The Witches of Eastwick '87

Anthony Caruso
The Asphalt Jungle '50
Cattle Queen of Montana '54
Claws '77
Drum Beat '54
Legend of Earl Durand '74
Objective, Burma! '45
When Gangland Strikes '56
Zebra Force '76

David Caruso
Blue City '86
China Girl '87
First Blood '82
King of New York '90
Mad Dog and Glory '93
An Officer and a Gentleman '82
Rainbow Drive '90

Betty Carvalho
Best of the Best 2 '93
Halloween 5: The Revenge of
   Michael Myers '89

Brent Carver
Crossbar '79

Millenium '89
One Night Stand '77

Lynne Carver
The Adventures of Huckleberry
Finn '39
The Bride Wore Red '37
A Christmas Carol '38
Everybody Sing '38
Madame X '37
Maytime '37
Sunset on the Desert '42

Dana Carvey
Clean Slate '94
Moving '88
Opportunity Knocks '90
Racing with the Moon '84
This is Spinal Tap '84
Tough Guys '86
Wayne's World '92
Wayne's World 2 '93

Gregorio Casal
La Choca '73
Los Dos Hermanos '87

Fernando Casanova
Caches de Oro
Hijazo de Mi Vidaza '70s
Los Sheriffs de la Frontera '47
Mariachis '49

Maria Casares
Children of Paradise '44
La Chartreuse de Parme '48
La Lectrice '88
Orpheus '49
Sand and Blood '87
The Testament of Orpheus '59

Antonio Casas
Blood at Sundown
Brandy Sheriff '78
Tristana '70

Salvatore Cascio
Cinema Paradiso '88
Everybody's Fine '90
The Pope Must Diet '91

Nicholas Cascone
84 Charlie Mopic '89
Vietnam War Story 1 '88

Kathleen Case
Human Desire '54
Last of the Pony Riders '53

Chiara Caselli
Fiorile '93
My Own Private Idaho '91

Bernie Casey
Another 48 Hrs. '90
Ants '77
Backfire '88
Big Mo '73
Bill & Ted's Excellent
Adventure '89
The Cemetery Club '93
Chains of Gold '92
Cleopatra Jones '73
Cornbread, Earl & Me '75
Dr. Black, Mr. Hyde '76
The Fantastic World of D.C.
Collins '84
Guns of the Magnificent Seven
'69
I'm Gonna Git You Sucka '88
The Man Who Fell to Earth '76
The Martian Chronicles: Part 1
'79
The Martian Chronicles: Part 2
'79
The Martian Chronicles: Part 3
'79
Never Say Never Again '83
Panic on the 5:22 '74
Rent-A-Cop '88
Revenge of the Nerds '84
Sharky's Machine '81
Sophisticated Gents '81
Spies Like Us '85
Steele Justice '87
Street Knight '93

Lawrence Casey
The Hunted Lady '77
The Student Nurses '70

Johnny Cash
The Baron and the Kid '84
Door to Door Maniac '61
A Gunfight '71
Last Days of Frank & Jesse
James '86

Murder in Coweta County '83
North and South Book 1 '85
Pride of Jesse Hallum '81
Road to Nashville '67
Stagecoach '86

June Carter Cash
The Baron and the Kid '84
Last Days of Frank & Jesse
James '86
Murder in Coweta County '83

Rosalind Cash
The Adventures of Buckaroo
Banzai Across the Eighth
Dimension '84
Amazing Grace '74
The Class of Miss MacMichael
'78
Cornbread, Earl & Me '75
Death Drug '83
Dr. Black, Mr. Hyde '76
Keeping On '81
The Mighty Pawns '87
Monkey Hustle '77
The Offspring '87
Omega Man '71
Sophisticated Gents '81
Wrong is Right '82

Isadore Cashier
The Cantor's Son '37
His Wife's Lover '31
The Light Ahead '39

Philip Casnoff
Gorp '80
Hands of a Stranger '87
Ironclads '90
North and South Book 2 '86
Red Wind '91
Sinatra '92

John Cason
Jungle Drums of Africa '53
Last Bullet '50
Outlaw of the Plains '46
Rangeland Empire '50

Katrina Caspary
Mac and Me '88
My Mom's a Werewolf '89

Maurice Cass
Spook Busters '46
Thin Ice '37

Peggy Cass
Auntie Mame '58
Cheaters '84
Gidget Goes Hawaiian '61
If It's Tuesday, This Must Be
Belgium '69
Paddy '70

John Cassavetes
Brass Target '78
Devil's Angels '67
The Dirty Dozen '67
The Fury '78
Incubus '82
The Killers '64
Love Streams '84
Marvin & Tige '84
Mikey & Nicky '76
Opening Night '77
Rosemary's Baby '68
The Tempest '82
Two Minute Warning '76
Whose Life Is It Anyway? '81

Nick Cassavetes
Backstreet Dreams '90
Blind Fury '90
Body of Influence '93
Broken Trust '93
Class of 1999 2: The Substitute
'93
Delta Force 3: The Killing Game
'91
Sins of Desire '92
Sins of the Night '93
The Wraith '87

Jean-Pierre Cassel
Alice '86
Between Heaven and Earth '93
The Discreet Charm of the
Bourgeoisie '72
The Elusive Corporal '62
The Fatal Image '90
The Favor, the Watch, & the
Very Big Fish '92
The Four Musketeers '75
From Hell to Victory '79
Is Paris Burning? '68

The Killing Game '67
The Killing of a Chinese Bookie
'76
La Rupture '70
La Truite '83
La Vie Continue '82
Les Rendez-vous D'Anna '78
The Maid '90
Mr. Frost '89
Murder on the Orient Express
'74
Nudo di Donna '83
The Return of the Musketeers
'89
That Lucky Touch '75
Those Magnificent Men in Their
Flying Machines '65
The Three Musketeers '74
Twist '76
Who is Killing the Great Chefs
of Europe? '78

Seymour Cassel
Adventures in Spying '92
Best Seller '87
Black Oak Conspiracy '77
Boiling Point '93
California Dreaming '79
Chain of Desire '93
Diary of a Hitman '91
Dick Tracy '90
Double Exposure '82
Eye of the Tiger '86
Honeymoon in Vegas '92
In the Soup '92
Indecent Proposal '93
It Could Happen to You '94
Johnny Be Good '88
Love Streams '84
The Mountain Men '80
Plain Clothes '88
Seducers '77
Survival Game '87
Sweet Bird of Youth '89
Tin Men '87
Track 29 '88
Trouble Bound '92
Valentino '77
White Fang '91
Wicked Stepmother '89

Alan Cassell
The Club '81
Money Movers '78
Squizzy Taylor '84

Wally Cassell
Breakdown '53
Until They Sail '57

Andrew Cassese
Revenge of the Nerds '84
Revenge of the Nerds 2: Nerds
in Paradise '87

David Cassidy
Instant Karma '90
The Night the City Screamed
'80
Spirit of '76 '91

Edward Cassidy
Aces Wild '37
Boothill Brigade '37
Boots of Destiny '37
Buffalo Bill Rides Again '47
Devil Riders '44
A Face in the Fog '36
Feud of the West '35
Frontier Outlaws '44
Roaring Six Guns '37
Rustler's Hideout '44
Sagebrush Law '43
Santa Fe Bound '37
Son of Zorro '47
Toll of the Desert '35
Wild Horse Phantom '44

Jack Cassidy
The Andersonville Trial '70
Columbo: Murder By the Book
'71
The Eiger Sanction '75

Joanna Cassidy
All-American Murder '91
Bank Shot '74
Barbarians at the Gate '93
Blade Runner '82
The Children of Times Square
'86
Club Paradise '86
Codename: Foxfire '85
Don't Tell Mom the Babysitter's
Dead '91

A Father's Revenge '88
The Fourth Protocol '87
A Girl of the Limberlost '90
The Glove '78
Invitation to Hell '84
Landslide '92
The Late Show '77
Live! From Death Row '92
Lonely Hearts '81
May Wine '90
Night Games '80
Nightmare at Bittercreek '91
1969 '89
The Package '89
Perfect Family '92
Stephen King's The
Tommyknockers '93
Stunts '77
Under Fire '83
Wheels of Terror '90
Where the Heart Is '90
Who Framed Roger Rabbit? '88

Patrick Cassidy
Dress Gray '86
Fever Pitch '85
Hitler's Daughter '90
Just the Way You Are '84
Longtime Companion '90
Love at Stake '87
Nickel Mountain '85
Off the Wall '82
Something in Common '86

Shaun Cassidy
Roots: The Gift '88
Texas Guns '90

Ted Cassidy
Butch Cassidy and the
Sundance Kid '69
Goin' Coconuts '78
Halloween with the Addams
Family '79
MacKenna's Gold '69
Planet Earth '74
Poor Pretty Eddie '73
Sunshine Run '79
Thunder County '74
Women's Prison Escape

Claudio Cassinelli
Allonsanfan '73
Hands of Steel '86
Hercules 2 '85
The New Gladiators '87
Slave of the Cannibal God '79

Nadia Cassini
Pulp '72
Star Crash '78

John Cassisi
Bugsy Malone '76
Man's Best Friend '93

Jean-Pierre Castaldi
A Fine Romance '92
La Merveilleuse Visite '74

Lou Castel
A Bullet for the General '68
The Eyes, the Mouth '83
Paranoia '69
Rorret '87
The Scarlet Letter '73

Dan Castellaneta
Nothing in Common '86
The War of the Roses '89

Richard Castellano
The Godfather '72
The Godfather 1902-1959: The
Complete Epic '81
Honor Thy Father '73
Lovers and Other Strangers '70
Night of the Juggler '80

Sergio Castellitto
Alberto Express '92
The Big Blue '88

Willy Castello
Confessions of a Vice Baron
'42
Mad Youth '40

Joanna Cassidy →
Christopher Castile
Beethoven '92
Beethoven's 2nd '93

Gloria Castillo
Invasion of the Saucer Men '57
Meteor Monster '57
Reform School Girl '57

Don Castle
Motor Patrol '50

Who Killed Doc Robbin? '48

John Castle
The Bretts '88
The Crucifer of Blood '91
Lillie '79
The Lion in Winter '68
Man of La Mancha '72
RoboCop 3 '91

Peggy Castle
Beginning of the End '57
The Finger Man '55
The Seven Hills of Rome '58
The White Orchid '54

Roy Castle
Alice Through the Looking
Glass '66
Doctor Who and the Daleks '65

William Castle
Bug '75
Rosemary's Baby '68
Shampoo '75

Phoebe Cates
Bodies, Rest & Motion '93
Bright Lights, Big City '88
Date with an Angel '87
Drop Dead Fred '91
Fast Times at Ridgemont High
'82
Gremlins '84
Gremlins 2: The New Batch '90
The Heart of Dixie '89
Paradise '82
Private School '83
Shag: The Movie '89

Brigitte Catillon
La Lectrice '88
Un Coeur en Hiver '93

Walter Catlett
Bringing Up Baby '38
Every Day's a Holiday '38
The Front Page '31
The Inspector General '49
Mr. Deeds Goes to Town '36
On the Avenue '37
Pop Always Pays '40
Rain '32
Remedy for Riches '40
A Tale of Two Cities '35
They Got Me Covered '43
Yankee Doodle Dandy '42

Victoria Catlin
Howling 5: The Rebirth '89
Mutant on the Bounty '89

Juliette Caton
Courage Mountain '89
The Last Temptation of Christ
'88

Christine Cattall
Bedroom Eyes '86
Screwball Academy '86

Kim Cattrall
The Bastard '78
Big Trouble in Little China '86
The Bonfire of the Vanities '90
City Limits '85
Deadly Harvest '92
Double Vision '92
Goodnight, Michelangelo '89
Honeymoon Academy '89
Mannequin '87
Masquerade '88
Midnight Crossing '87
Miracle in the Wilderness '91
Palais Royale '88
Police Academy '84
Porky's '82
The Rebels '79
The Return of the Musketeers
'89
Rosebud '92
Running Delilah '93
Scruples '80
Smokescreen '90
Split Second '92
Star Trek 6: The Undiscovered
Country '91
Ticket to Heaven '81
Tribute '80
Turk 182! '85
Wild Palms '93

Philippe Caubere
My Father's Glory '91
My Mother's Castle '91

Lane Caudell
Archer: The Fugitive from the Empire '81
Hanging on a Star '78

Joan Caulfield
Buckskin '68
Daring Dobermans '73
Dear Wife '49
The Lady Says No '51
Monsieur Beaucaire '46
Pony Express Rider '76

Maxwell Caulfield
Alien Intruder '93
Animal Instincts '92
The Boys Next Door '85
Dance with Death '91
Electric Dreams '84
Exiled in America '90
Gettysburg '93
Grease 2 '82
In a Moment of Passion '93
Midnight Witness '93
Mind Games '89
No Escape, No Return '93
Project: Alien '89
Sundown '91
The Supernaturals '86

Victor Cavallo
Dial Help '88
The Tragedy of a Ridiculous Man '81

Megan Cavanagh
A League of Their Own '92
Robin Hood: Men in Tights '93

Paul Cavanagh
A Bill of Divorcement '32
Black Arrow '48
Bride of the Gorilla '51
Captains of the Clouds '42
Charade '53
Goin' to Town '35
Hi-Jacked '50
House of Fear '45
House of Wax '53
Humoresque '46
The Prodigal '55
Shadows on the Stairs '41
Tarzan and His Mate '34
The Woman in Green '45

Hobart Cavanaugh
I Cover the Waterfront '33
The Magnificent Dope '42
Rose of Washington Square '39
Wife Versus Secretary '36

Elise Cavanna
The Barber Shop '33
Best of W.C. Fields '33
The Dentist '32
Pharmacist '32
W.C. Fields: Flask of Fields '30

Ingrid Caven
Malou '83
Mother Kusters Goes to Heaven '76

Dick Cavett
Beetlejuice '88
The Marx Brothers in a Nutshell '90
Moon Over Parador '88
A Nightmare on Elm Street 3: Dream Warriors '87

Joseph Cawthorn
Harmony Lane '35
Sweet Adeline '35
The Taming of the Shrew '29
They Call It Sin '32

Elizabeth Cayton
Necromancer: Satan's Servant '88
Silent Night, Deadly Night 2 '87
Slave Girls from Beyond Infinity '87

John Cazale
The Conversation '74
The Deer Hunter '78
Dog Day Afternoon '75
The Godfather '72
The Godfather 1902-1959: The Complete Epic '81
The Godfather, Part 2 '74

Christopher Cazenove
Aces: Iron Eagle 3 '92

Children of the Full Moon '84
East of Elephant Rock '76
Eye of the Needle '81
The Fantasist '89
Heat and Dust '82
Jenny's War '85
The Man Who Guards the Greenhouse '88
Mata Hari '85
Souvenir '88
Tears in the Rain '88
Three Men and a Little Lady '90
Until September '84
Windmills of the Gods '88

Daniel Ceccaldi
Charles et Lucie '79
Chloe in the Afternoon '72
Holiday Hotel '77
Twisted Obsession '90

Edward Cecil
Desert of the Lost '27
Wild Horse Canyon '25

Jon Cedar
Day of the Animals '77
Kiss Daddy Goodbye '81

Larry Cedar
Boris and Natasha: The Movie '92
C.H.U.D. 2: Bud the Chud '89
Feds '87

Violeta Cela
Conquest '83
El Barbaro '84

Clementine Celarie
Betty Blue '86
Sand and Blood '87

Henry Cele
Curse 3: Blood Sacrifice '90
Rage to Kill '88
The Rutanga Tapes '90
Shaka Zulu '83

Adriano Celentano
The Con Artists '80
The Switch '89

Adolfo Celi
The Agony and the Ecstasy '65
The Arab Conspiracy '76
Bobo '67
Cafe Express '83
Cambio de Cara '71
Dirty Heroes '71
Hired to Kill '73
Hit Men '73
Hitler: The Last Ten Days '73
The Honey Pot '67
Intruder '77
The King of Hearts '66
Murders in the Rue Morgue '71
1931: Once Upon a Time in New York '70
Phantom of Liberty '68
Ring of Death '72
Secret Agent 00 '67
Target for Killing '66
Ten Little Indians '75
Thunderball '65
Von Ryan's Express '65

Teresa Celli
The Asphalt Jungle '50
The Black Hand '50

Antoinette Cellier
Late Extra '35
River of Unrest '37

Caroline Cellier
Pain in the A— '77
Petit Con '84
This Man Must Die '70

Frank Cellier
Cottage to Let '41
The Man Who Lived Again '36
Non-Stop New York '37
O.H.M.S. '37
The Passing of the Third Floor Back '36
Rhodes '36

Peter Cellier
And the Ship Sails On '83
Fergie & Andrew: Behind Palace Doors '93
Man Friday '75
Sister Dora '77

Nicholas Celozzi
Hidden Obsession '92
Slaughterhouse Rock '88

Gino Cervi
Fabiola '48
Full Hearts & Empty Pockets '63
Les Miserables '52
Little World of Don Camillo '51
Mistress of the World '59
The Naked Maja '59

Renzo Cesana
For the First Time '59
The Naked Maja '59
Stromboli '50

Michael Ceveris
Rock 'n' Roll High School Forever '91
A Woman, Her Men and Her Futon '92

June Chadwick
The Evil Below '87
Forbidden World '82
Golden Lady '79
Headhunter '89
Quiet Thunder '87
Rebel Storm '90
This is Spinal Tap '84

Suzy Chaffee
Fire and Ice '87
Snowblind '78

Angelica Chain
La Virgen de Guadalupe '87
The Neighborhood Thief '83

George Chakiris
Diamond Head '62
The Hot Line '69
Is Paris Burning? '68
Pale Blood '91
Return to Fantasy Island '77
633 Squadron '64
West Side Story '61

Feodor Chaliapin
The Church '90
Don Quixote '35
The King's Whore '90
Moonstruck '87
The Name of the Rose '86
Stanley and Iris '90

Georges Chamarat
Fernandel the Dressmaker '57
The French Touch '54

Richard Chamberlain
Allan Quartermain and the Lost City of Gold '86
The Bourne Identity '88
Casanova '87
The Count of Monte Cristo '74
The Four Musketeers '75
Julius Caesar '70
King Solomon's Mines '85
Lady Caroline Lamb '73
The Last Wave '77
The Madwoman of Chaillot '69
The Man in the Iron Mask '77
Murder by Phone '82
The Music Lovers '71
Petulia '68
Portrait of a Lady '67
The Return of the Musketeers '89
Shogun '80
The Swarm '78
The Thorn Birds '83
The Three Musketeers '74
The Towering Inferno '74

Wilt Chamberlain
Conan the Destroyer '84
Rich Hall's Vanishing America '86

Carrie Chambers
The Divine Enforcer '91
Karate Cop '93

Marilyn Chambers
Angel of H.E.A.T. '82
Cassie '87
My Therapist '84
Party Incorporated '89
Rabid '77

Michael "Boogaloo Shrimp" Chambers
Breakin' '84
Breakin' 2: Electric Boogaloo '84

Gower Champion
Give a Girl a Break '53
Jupiter's Darling '55
Lovely to Look At '52
Mr. Music '50
Show Boat '51

Marge Champion
Give a Girl a Break '53
Jupiter's Darling '55
Lovely to Look At '52
Mr. Music '50
The Party '68
Swimmer '68

Michael Champion
The Heroes of Desert Storm '91
One Man Out '89
Private Wars '93
The Swordsman '92

Irene Champlin
Flash Gordon: Vol. 1 '53
Flash Gordon: Vol. 2 '53

Dennis Chan
Kickboxer '89
Kickboxer 3: The Art of War '92

Jackie Chan
The Armour of God '86
The Big Brawl '80
The Deadliest Art: The Best of the Martial Arts Films '90
Eagle's Shadow '84
Half a Loaf of Kung Fu '85
Jackie Chan's Police Force '85
New Fist of Fury '85
Protector '85
The World of Suzie Wong '60
Young Tiger '80

Kim Chan
American Shaolin: King of the Kickboxers 2 '92
Who's the Man? '93

Michael Paul Chan
Falling Down '93
The Joy Luck Club '93
Rapid Fire '92
Thousand Pieces of Gold '91

Naomi Chance
The Gambler & the Lady '52
Terror Ship '54
Three Stops to Murder '53
Wings of Danger '52

Chick Chandler
Baby Face Morgan '42
Blondie in Society '41
The Lost Continent '51
Melody Cruise '32
Mistaken Identity '36
Rhythm Parade '43
Seven Doors to Death '44
Tango '36

George Chandler
Arizona '40
Behind the Mask '37
The Fatal Glass of Beer '33
Lady Killer '33
The Light of Western Stars '30
The Next Voice You Hear '50
W.C. Fields Comedy Bag '33
Westward the Women '51

Helen Chandler
Christopher Strong '33
Dracula '31
Mr. Boggs Steps Out '38

Janet Chandler
Million Dollar Haul '35
Rough Riding Rangers '35

Jeff Chandler
Away All Boats '56
Broken Arrow '50
The Jayhawkers '59
Merrill's Marauders '62
Return to Peyton Place '61

John Davis Chandler
Alligator Alley '72
The Ultimate Thrill '74

Karen Mayo Chandler
Death Feud '89
Stripped to Kill II: Live Girls '89

Lane Chandler
Deluge '33
Heroes of the Alamo '37

Laura '44
The Lawless Nineties '36
Lone Bandit '33
The Outlaw Tamer '33
Pony Post '40
Rustler's Hideout '44
Sea Racketeers '37
The Single Standard '29
Trouble Busters '33
Wild Horse Phantom '44
Winds of the Wasteland '36

Helene Chanel
Maciste in Hell '60
Place in Hell '65
Samson and the 7 Miracles of the World '62

Lon Chaney, Sr.
The Bushwackers '52
Flesh and Blood '22
He Who Gets Slapped '24
The Horror of It All '91
The Hunchback of Notre Dame '23
The Light of Faith '22
Mockery '27
The Monster '25
Nomads of the North '20
Oliver Twist '22
Oubliette '14
Outside the Law '21
The Phantom of the Opera '25
The Scarlet Car '17
Shadows '22
The Shock '23
The Trap '22
The Unholy Three '25
The Unholy Three '30
The Unknown '27
West of Zanzibar '28
Where East is East '29

Lon Chaney, Jr.
Abbott and Costello Meet Frankenstein '48
Alien Massacre '67
Apache Uprising '66
Behave Yourself! '52
Big Chase '54
Billy the Kid '41
Bird of Paradise '32
Bride of the Gorilla '51
Buckskin '68
Cheyenne Rides Again '38
Cobra Woman '44
Cyclops '56
Daniel Boone: Trail Blazer '56
The Defiant Ones '58
Dracula vs. Frankenstein '71
Face of the Screaming Werewolf '59
The Female Bunch '69
Film House Fever '86
Frankenstein Meets the Wolfman '42
The Ghost of Frankenstein '42
The Haunted Palace '63
Here Come the Co-Eds '45
High Noon '52
Hillbillies in a Haunted House '67
House of Dracula '45
House of Frankenstein '44
House of the Black Death '65
I Died a Thousand Times '55
The Indestructible Man '56
The Indian Fighter '55
Johnny Reno '66
Last Frontier '56
A Lion in the Streets '53
Man Made Monster '41
Manfish '56
The Mummy's Curse '44
The Mummy's Ghost '44
The Mummy's Tomb '42
My Favorite Brunette '47
Not as a Stranger '55
Of Mice and Men '39
One Million B.C. '40
Only the Valiant '50
Overland Mail '41
Pardners '56
Passion '54
Renegade Ranger/Scarlet River '38
Riders of Death Valley '41
Saturday Night Serials '40
Sixteen Fathoms Deep '34
Son of Dracula '43
Spider Baby '64
Springfield Rifle '52

The Three Musketeers '33
Undersea Kingdom '36
The Wolf Man '41

Stockard Channing
The Applegates '89
The Big Bus '76
The Cheap Detective '78
Echoes in the Darkness '87
The Fish that Saved Pittsburgh '79
Grease '78
Heartburn '86
The Hospital '71
Married to It '93
The Men's Club '86
Not My Kid '85
Perfect Witness '89
Safari 3000 '82
Silent Victory: The Kitty O'Neil Story '79
Six Degrees of Separation '93
Staying Together '89
Table Settings '84
Tidy Endings '88
A Time of Destiny '88
Without a Trace '83

Rosalind Chao
The Big Brawl '80
Chinese Web '78
The Joy Luck Club '93
Memoirs of an Invisible Man '92
The Terry Fox Story '83
Thousand Pieces of Gold '91
Twirl '81
White Ghost '88

Billy Chapin
The Night of the Hunter '55
Tobor the Great '54

Michael Chapin
Call Northside 777 '48
Murderer's Wife

Miles Chapin
Bless the Beasts and Children '71
French Postcards '79
The Funny Farm '82
Pandemonium '82

Charles Chaplin, Jr.
Fangs of the Wild '54
Girls' Town '59
High School Confidential '58

Charlie Chaplin
The Adventurer '17
The Best of Chaplin '18
Burlesque of Carmen '16
The Champion/His New Job '15
Chaplin: A Character Is Born '79
Chaplin: A Character Is Born/Keaton: The Great Stone Face
Chaplin Essanay Book 1 '15
The Chaplin Revue '58
Charlie Chaplin Carnival, Four Early Shorts '16
Charlie Chaplin Cavalcade, Mutual Studios Shorts '16
Charlie Chaplin Centennial Collection '10s
Charlie Chaplin Festival '17
Charlie Chaplin Festival '17
Charlie Chaplin: Night at the Show '15
Charlie Chaplin: Rare Chaplin '15
Charlie Chaplin: The Early Years, Vol. 1 '17
Charlie Chaplin: The Early Years, Vol. 2 '16
Charlie Chaplin: The Early Years, Vol. 3 '16
Charlie Chaplin: The Early Years, Vol. 4 '16
Charlie Chaplin...Our Hero! '15
Charlie Chaplin's Keystone Comedies #1 '14
Charlie Chaplin's Keystone Comedies #2 '14
Charlie Chaplin's Keystone Comedies #3 '14
Charlie Chaplin's Keystone Comedies #4 '14
Charlie Chaplin's Keystone Comedies #5 '14
The Circus '19
City Lights '31

The Count '16
Count/Adventurer '17
The Cure '17
Days of Thrills and Laughter '61
Easy Street '16
The Fireman '16
The Floorwalker '17
The Floorwalker/By the Sea '15
The Gold Rush '25
Gold Rush/Payday '25
The Great Dictator '40
His Prehistoric Past/The Bank '15
Hollywood Clowns '85
The Immigrant '17
The Kid '21
The Kid/Idle Class '21
Kid's Auto Race/Mabel's Married Life '15
A King in New York '57
The Knockout/Dough and Dynamite '14
Laughfest '10s
Limelight '52
Man in the Silk Hat '83
Modern Times '36
Monsieur Verdoux '47
One A.M. '16
Pawnshop '16
The Rink '16
Rink/Immigrant '10s
Silent Laugh Makers, No. 1 '15
Slapstick '30s
Three Charlies and One Phoney! '18
Tillie's Punctured Romance '14
Tramp & a Woman '15
Triple Trouble/Easy Street '18
The Vagabond '16
When Comedy was King '59
Work/Police '16

Geraldine Chaplin
The Age of Innocence '93
Bolero '82
Buffalo Bill & the Indians '76
Chaplin '92
The Children '90
Cria '76
Doctor Zhivago '65
Duel of Hearts '92
The Four Musketeers '75
I Killed Rasputin '67
In Memoriam '77
Mama Turns a Hundred '79
The Mirror Crack'd '80
The Moderns '88
Nashville '75
The Return of the Musketeers '89
Roseland '77
The Three Musketeers '74
A Wedding '78
Welcome to L.A. '77
White Mischief '88
The Word '79
Zero Population Growth '72

Josephine Chaplin
The Canterbury Tales '71
Escape to the Sun '72
Jack the Ripper '80
L'Odeur des Fauves '66
Shadow Man '75

Sydney Chaplin
Abdulla the Great '55
The Chaplin Revue '58
Charley's Aunt '25
Land of the Pharaohs '55
The Man on the Box '25
Satan's Cheerleaders '77
The Sibling '72
Three Charlies and One Phoney! '18
The Woman Hunter '72

Daniel Chapman
Death Collector '89
Exquisite Corpses '88
Philadelphia '93

Edward Chapman
Bhowani Junction '56
Convoy '40
Juno and the Paycock '30
Man on the Run '49
October Man '48
The Young and the Guilty '58

Graham Chapman
And Now for Something Completely Different '72
John Cleese on How to Irritate People '68
The Magic Christian '69
Monty Python and the Holy Grail '75
Monty Python Live at the Hollywood Bowl '82
Monty Python Meets Beyond the Fringe
Monty Python's Life of Brian '79
Monty Python's Parrot Sketch Not Included '90
Monty Python's The Meaning of Life '83
The Odd Job '78
The Secret Policeman's Other Ball '82
Yellowbeard '83

Helen Chapman
Hopalong Cassidy: Borrowed Trouble '48
Outlaw Roundup '44

Judith Chapman
And God Created Woman '88
Dead Space '90
Scalpel '76

Loni Chapman
Alexander: The Other Side of Dawn '77
The China Lake Murders '90
52 Pick-Up '86
He Who Walks Alone '78
Moving Violation '76
Where the Red Fern Grows '74
Witch Who Came from the Sea '76

Marguerite Chapman
The Amazing Transparent Man '60
Charlie Chan at the Wax Museum '40
Coroner Creek '48
Destroyer '43
Flight to Mars '52
The Green Promise '49
Man Bait '52
Spy Smasher Returns '42

Sean Chapman
Hellbound: Hellraiser 2 '88
Hellraiser '87

Patricia Charbonneau
Brain Dead '89
Call Me '88
Desert Hearts '86
Disaster at Silo 7 '88
K2: The Ultimate High '92
RoboCop 2 '90
Shakedown '88
Stalking Danger '86

Cyd Charisse
The Band Wagon '53
Brigadoon '54
Deep in My Heart '54
The Harvey Girls '46
It's Always Fair Weather '55
Judy Garland: The Golden Years at MGM
Maroc 7 '67
Meet Me in Las Vegas '56
On an Island with You '48
Party Girl '58
Silk Stockings '57
Singin' in the Rain '52
Swimsuit: The Movie '89
That's Dancing! '85
Till the Clouds Roll By/A Star Is Born '44
Two Weeks in Another Town '62
Words and Music '48

Josh Charles
Cooperstown '93
Crossing the Bridge '92
Dead Poets Society '89
Don't Tell Mom the Babysitter's Dead '91
Threesome '94

Ray Charles
Ballad in Blue '66
The Blues Brothers '80

Limit Up '89

Ian Charleson
Car Trouble '86
Chariots of Fire '81
Codename Kyril '91
Gandhi '82
Greystoke: The Legend of Tarzan, Lord of the Apes '84
Louisiana '87
Terror at the Opera '88

Charo
The Concorde: Airport '79 '79
Moon Over Parador '88
Pee Wee's Playhouse Christmas Special '88

Charpin
The Baker's Wife '33
Cesar '36
Fanny '32
Marius '31
Well-Digger's Daughter '46

Henri Charriere
Butterfly Affair '71
Queen of Diamonds '80s

Spencer Charters
The Bat Whispers '30
The Ghost Walks '34
Lady from Nowhere '36
Mr. Boggs Steps Out '38
Three Comrades '38

Melanie Chartoff
Doin' Time '85
Having It All '82
Kenny Rogers as the Gambler, Part 3: The Legend Continues '87
Stoogemania '85

Alden Chase
Buried Alive '39
Cowboy Millionaire '35

Annazette Chase
Fist '79
Truck Turner '74

Charley Chase
Block-heads '38
Charley Chase Festival, Vol. 1 '23
Charlie Chase and Ben Turpin '21
Kelly the Second '36
King of the Wild Horses '24
Silent Laugh Makers, No. 1 '15
Silent Laugh Makers, No. 2 '17
Slapstick '30s
Sons of the Desert '33
Three Charlies and One Phoney! '18

Chevy Chase
Caddyshack '80
Caddyshack 2 '88
Cops and Robbersons '94
Deal of the Century '83
Fletch '85
Fletch Lives '89
Foul Play '78
Funny Farm '88
The Groove Tube '72
Hero '92
Memoirs of an Invisible Man '92
Modern Problems '81
National Lampoon's Christmas Vacation '89
National Lampoon's European Vacation '85
National Lampoon's Vacation '83
Nothing But Trouble '91
Oh, Heavenly Dog! '80
Seems Like Old Times '80
Sesame Street Presents: Follow That Bird '85
Spies Like Us '85
Three Amigos '86
Tunnelvision '76
Under the Rainbow '81

Ilka Chase
The Animal Kingdom '32
The Big Knife '55

Jennifer Chase
Balboa '82
Death Screams '83
House of Death '82

Stephan Chase
The Black Arrow '84
The Dying Truth '91

Steve Chase
Eden '93
Eden 2 '93
Eden 3 '93
Eden 4 '93

Soumitra Chatterjee
Devi '60
Distant Thunder '73
The Home and the World '84
The World of Apu '59

Ruth Chatterton
Dodsworth '36
Female '33
Prudential Family Playhouse '50

Daniel Chatto
Little Dorrit, Film 1: Nobody's Fault '88
Little Dorrit, Film 2: Little Dorrit's Story '88

Francois Chau
Teenage Mutant Ninja Turtles 2: The Secret of the Ooze '91
Vietnam War Story 3 '89

Emmanuelle Chaulet
All the Vermeers in New York '91
Boyfriends & Girlfriends '88

Lilyan Chauvin
Bloodlust '59
Lost, Lonely, and Vicious '59
Silent Night, Deadly Night '84

Richard Chaves
Night Eyes 2 '91
Predator '87

Maury Chaykin
The Adjuster '91
Breaking In '89
Camilla '94
Cold Comfort '90
Dances with Wolves '90
Def-Con 4 '85
George's Island '91
Hero '92
Higher Education '88
Iron Eagle 2 '88
July Group '70s
Leaving Normal '92
Millenium '89
Mrs. Soffel '84
Mr. Destiny '90
Money for Nothing '93
Northern Extremes '93
Sommersby '93
Stars and Bars '88
Sweetheart!
Wild Thing '87

Don Cheadle
Colors '88
Hamburger Hill '87

Andrea Checchi
Black Sunday '60
The Invaders '63

Micheline Cheirel
Carnival in Flanders '35
Cornered '45

Michael Chekhov
Rhapsody '54
Spectre of the Rose '46
Spellbound '45

Tsilla Chelton
Peppermint Soda '77
Tatie Danielle '91

Joan Chen
The Blood of Heroes '89
Deadlock '91
Dim Sum: A Little Bit of Heart '85
Golden Gate '93
Heaven and Earth '93
The Killing Beach '93
The Last Emperor '87
Night Stalker '87
On Deadly Ground '94
Strangers '91
Tai-Pan '86
Twin Peaks '90

Tina Chen
Lady from Yesterday '85

Chen ▶cont.

Paper Man '71

Jacky Cheng
Ninja Exterminators '81
Of Cooks and Kung-Fu '80s

Cher
Come Back to the Five & Dime Jimmy Dean, Jimmy Dean '82
Mask '85
Mermaids '90
Moonstruck '87
Silkwood '83
Suspect '87
The Witches of Eastwick '87

Patrice Chereau
Danton '82
The Last of the Mohicans '92

Nikolai Cherkassov
Alexander Nevsky '38
Baltic Deputy '37
Don Quixote '57
Ivan the Terrible, Part 1 '44
Ivan the Terrible, Part 2 '46

Virginia Cherrill
City Lights '31
Late Extra '35

George Cheseboro
Check Your Guns '48
Cheyenne Takes Over '47
Devil Riders '44
Fighting Champ '33
Fighting Vigilantes '47
Holt of the Secret Service '42
In Old Santa Fe '34
Laramie Kid '35
The Miracle Rider '35
Red River Valley '36
Return of the Lash '47
Roamin' Wild '36
Stage to Mesa City '48
Trigger Men '41
Wolf Blood '25

Morris Chestnut
Boyz N the Hood '91
The Ernest Green Story '93

Leslie Cheung
A Better Tomorrow '86
A Better Tomorrow, Part 2 '88
Farewell My Concubine '93
Rouge '87

Maggie Cheung
Jackie Chan's Police Force '85
Paper Marriage '88
Song of the Exile '90

Philip Cheung
The Blazing Ninja
Bruce Lee's Ways of Kung Fu '80s

Kevin Timothy Chevalia
Folks! '92
Homeward Bound: The Incredible Journey '93

Maurice Chevalier
Breath of Scandal '60
Can-Can '60
Fanny '61
Gigi '58
In Search of the Castaways '62
Love in the Afternoon '57
The Merry Widow '34
Monkeys, Go Home! '66
A New Kind of Love '63
Panic Button '62

Laureen Chew
Chan is Missing '82
Dim Sum: A Little Bit of Heart '85

Cheng Tien Chi
Super Ninjas '80s
The Warrior

Yuen Man Chi
Bruce's Deadly Fingers '80
Young Dragon '77

Sun Chia-Lin
Eighteen Jade Arhats '84
The Hot, the Cool, and the Vicious '80s

Liu Chia-Yung
Challenge of the Masters '89
Two Graves to Kung-Fu '82

Minoru Chiaki
Godzilla Raids Again '59
The Hidden Fortress '58
The Human Condition: Road to Eternity '59
Seven Samurai '54
Throne of Blood '57

Dominic Chianese
The Night We Never Met '93
The Public Eye '92

David Chiang
Duel of Fists '89
Duel of the Iron Fist '72
Seven Blows of the Dragon '73

Walter Chiari
Bonjour Tristesse '57
Girl Under the Sheet '60s
Husband Hunting '60s

Sofiko Chiaureli
Ashik Kerib '88
The Color of Pomegranates '69

Sonny Chiba
Aces: Iron Eagle 3 '92
Assassin '79
The Bodyguard '76
Dragon Princess '70s
Hunter in the Dark '80
Immortal Combat '94
Karate Warriors '70s
Kowloon Assignment '77
Shogun's Ninja '83
The Street Fighter's Last Revenge '79
Terror Beneath the Sea '66
Virus '82

Etienne Chicot
Osa '85
36 Fillete '88

Linden Chiles
Deadline Assault '90
Death Be Not Proud '75
Forbidden World '82
Red Flag: The Ultimate Game '81
Texas Across the River '66
To Heal a Nation '88
Who Is the Black Dahlia? '75

Lois Chiles
Broadcast News '87
Coma '78
Creepshow 2 '87
Death on the Nile '78
Diary of a Hitman '91
Moonraker '79
Raw Courage '84
Twister '89

Simon Chilvers
The Big Hurt '87
The Dunera Boys '85
Ground Zero '88
Windrider '86

Joey Chin
China Girl '87
King of New York '90

Tsai Chin
The Castle of Fu Manchu '68
Enter the Panther '79
Invasion '65
The Joy Luck Club '93
Kiss and Kill '68
The Virgin Soldiers '69
You Only Live Twice '67

William Ching
Give a Girl a Break '53
Never Wave at a WAC '52
Pat and Mike '52
Terror in the Haunted House '58
The Wistful Widow of Wagon Gap '47

Kieu Chinh
The Children of An Lac '80
The Girl Who Spelled Freedom '86
The Joy Luck Club '93
Operation C.I.A. '65

Nicholas Chinlund
The Ambulance '90
Red Shoe Diaries 4: Auto Erotica '93

Anna Chlumsky
My Girl '91
My Girl 2 '94

Tim Choate
Blind Witness '89
Def-Con 4 '85
First Time '82
Spy '89

Jun Chong
Ninja Turf '86
Silent Assassins '88
Street Soldiers '91

Rae Dawn Chong
Amazon '90
American Flyers '85
Badge of the Assassin '85
Beat Street '84
The Borrower '89
Cheech and Chong's, The Corsican Brothers '84
Choose Me '84
City Limits '85
The Color Purple '85
Commando '85
Common Bonds '91
Curiosity Kills '90
Dangerous Relations '93
Denial: The Dark Side of Passion '93
Far Out Man '89
Fear City '85
The Principal '87
Prison Stories: Women on the Inside '91
Quest for Fire '82
Running Out of Luck '86
Soul Man '86
The Squeeze '87
Tales from the Darkside: The Movie '90
Time Runner '92

Thomas Chong
Cheech and Chong: Still Smokin' '83
Cheech and Chong: Things Are Tough All Over '82
Cheech and Chong's Next Movie '80
Cheech and Chong's Nice Dreams '81
Cheech and Chong's, The Corsican Brothers '84
Cheech and Chong's Up in Smoke '79
Far Out Man '89
Spirit of '76 '91
Tripwire '89
Yellowbeard '83

Yuen Tat Chor
Taoism Drunkard
The Young Taoism Fighter

Etchika Choreau
Darby's Rangers '58
Lafayette Escadrille '58

Sarita Choudhury
The House of the Spirits '93
Mississippi Masala '92

Navin Chowdhry
Madame Sousatzka '88
The Seventh Coin '92

Ranjit Chowdhry
Lonely in America '90
Mississippi Masala '92
The Night We Never Met '93

Claudia Christian
Arena '88
Clean and Sober '88
The Dark Backward '91
Hexed '93
The Hidden '87
Mad About You '90
Maniac Cop 2 '90
Mom '89
Never on Tuesday '88
Strays '91
Tale of Two Sisters '89

John Christian
Comrades in Arms '91
Covert Action '88
Mob War '88
The Outfit '93

Linda Christian
Athena '54
The Devil's Hand '61

Full Hearts & Empty Pockets '63
The V.I.P.'s '63

Michael Christian
Hard Knocks
The Legend of Frank Woods '77
Mid Knight Rider '84
Poor Pretty Eddie '73

Paul Christian
The Beast from 20,000 Fathoms '53
Journey to the Lost City '58

Mady Christians
Letter from an Unknown Woman '48
Tender Comrade '43

Audrey Christie
Frankie and Johnny '65
Harper Valley P.T.A. '78
Splendor in the Grass '61

Julie Christie
Billy Liar '63
Darling '65
Demon Seed '77
Doctor Zhivago '65
Don't Look Now '73
Fahrenheit 451 '66
Far from the Madding Crowd '67
Fools of Fortune '90
The Go-Between '71
Heat and Dust '82
Heaven Can Wait '78
McCabe & Mrs. Miller '71
Miss Mary '86
Petulia '68
Power '86
The Railway Station Man '92
Return of the Soldier '82
Secret Obsession '88
Separate Tables '83
Shampoo '75

Katia Christine
Cosmos: War of the Planets '80
Spirits of the Dead '68

Virginia Christine
Billy the Kid Versus Dracula '66
The Cobweb '55
The Inner Circle '46
The Mummy's Curse '44
One Man's Way '63

Eric Christmas
The Challengers '93
Child of Darkness, Child of Light '91
Home is Where the Hart is '88
Middle Age Crazy '80
The Philadelphia Experiment '84

Francoise Christophe
Borsalino '70
The Invaders '63
The King of Hearts '66
Walk into Hell '57

Bojesse Christopher
Meatballs 4 '92
Point Break '91

Dennis Christopher
Alien Predators '80
Breaking Away '79
California Dreaming '79
Chariots of Fire '81
Circuitry Man '90
Didn't You Hear? '83
Don't Cry, It's Only Thunder '82
Doppelganger: The Evil Within '90
Elvis: The Movie '79
Fade to Black '80
False Arrest '92
Jack & the Beanstalk '83
Jake Speed '86
The Last Word '80
September 30, 1955 '77
Sinful Life '89
Stephen King's It '90
A Wedding '78
The Young Graduates '71

Kay Christopher
Dick Tracy's Dilemma '47
Scared to Death/Dick Tracy's Dilemma '47

Thom Christopher
Deathstalker 3 '89
Wizards of the Lost Kingdom '85

William Christopher
For the Love of It '80
M*A*S*H: Goodbye, Farewell & Amen '83
M*A*S*H: The Collector's Edition '72
With Six You Get Eggroll '68

Dorothy Christy
Big Business Girl '31
Convicted '32
Night Life in Reno '31
Sons of the Desert '33

Lung Chun-Eng
Shaolin Traitor '82
Two Assassins in the Dark '80s

David Chung
The Ballad of Little Jo '93
Combination Platter '93

Berton Churchill
The Big Stampede '32
Danger on the Air '38
The Dark Hour '36
Dimples '36
False Faces '32
In Old Chicago '38
Mistaken Identity '36
The Mysterious Rider '33
Sing Sing Nights '35
Stagecoach '39
Wide Open Faces '38

Marguerite Churchill
Ambassador Bill '31
Big Trail '30
Dracula's Daughter '36

Julien Ciamaca
My Father's Glory '91
My Mother's Castle '91

Jo Ciampa
The Family '87
Salome '85

Eduardo Ciannelli
Bulldog Drummond's Bride '39
Cairo '42
The Creeper '48
Doctor Satan's Robot '40
Foreign Correspondent '40
Gunga Din '39
Heartbeat '46
Houseboat '58
Kitty Foyle '40
Law of the Underworld '38
MacKenna's Gold '69
Mambo '55
Marked Woman '37
Monster from Green Hell '58
The Mummy's Hand '40
Mysterious Doctor Satan '40
Passage to Marseilles '44
Strange Cargo '40
They Got Me Covered '43
They Met in Bombay '41

Jude Ciccolella
Glengarry Glen Ross '92
Shakedown '88

Diane Cilento
The Agony and the Ecstasy '65
Hombre '67
The Naked Edge '61
Negatives '68
Rattle of a Simple Man '64
Tom Jones '63
The Wicker Man '75
Winner Takes All '86
Zero Population Growth '72

Kelly Cinnante
Christmas in Connecticut '92
True Love '89

Charles Cioffi
The Arab Conspiracy '76
The Don is Dead '73
Klute '71
Missing '82
Newsies '92
Peter Gunn '89
Return to Earth '76
Shaft '71
The Thief Who Came to Dinner '73
Time After Time '79
Used People '92

Franco Citti
Accatone! '61
The Decameron '70
Oedipus Rex '67
Porcile '69

Jany Clair
Conquest of Mycene '63
Hercules Against the Moon Men '64
Planets Against Us '61

Cyrielle Claire
Code Name: Emerald '85
Control '87
Sword of the Valiant '83

Ina Claire
Ninotchka '39
Three Broadway Girls '32

Rony Clanton
Def by Temptation '90
The Education of Sonny Carson '74

Gordon Clapp
Eight Men Out '88
Return of the Secaucus 7 '80
Small Sacrifices '89
Termini Station '89

Eric Clapton
Chuck Berry: Hail! Hail! Rock 'n' Roll '87
The Last Waltz '78
The Secret Policeman's Other Ball '82
Tommy '75

Diane Clare
Murder on the Campus '52
The Reluctant Debutante '58
Vulture '67

Mary Clare
Mambo '55
The Mill on the Floss '37
The Night Has Eyes '42
Power '34
The Three Weird Sisters '48

O.B. Clarence
The Courageous Mr. Penn '41
A Shot in the Dark '33

Aime Clariomond
La Marseillaise '37
Monsieur Vincent '48

Angela Clark
Houdini '53
Miracle of Our Lady of Fatima '52
The Seven Little Foys '55

Anthony Clark
Colt is My Law
Dogfight '91
The Thing Called Love '93

Blake Clark
Grave Secrets: The Legacy of Hilltop Drive '92
Johnny Handsome '89
Ladybugs '92
Shakes the Clown '92

Bobby Clark
Clark & McCullough '33
The Goldwyn Follies '38
Satan's Sadists '69

Brett Clark
Alien Warrior '85
Eye of the Eagle '87
Inner Sanctum '91

Brian Patrick Clark
Private Wars '93
Sleepaway Camp 2: Unhappy Campers '88

Candy Clark
American Graffiti '73
Amityville 3: The Demon '83
At Close Range '86
The Big Sleep '78
The Blob '88
Blue Thunder '83
Buffy the Vampire Slayer '92
Cat's Eye '85
Citizens Band '77
Cool As Ice '91
Fat City '72
Hambone & Hillie '84
James Dean '76
Johnny Belinda '82
The Man Who Fell to Earth '76

More American Graffiti '79
National Lampoon Goes to the Movies '81
Original Intent '91
Q (The Winged Serpent) '82
Rodeo Girl '80

Dane Clark
Action in the North Atlantic '43
Blackout '54
Blood Song '82
Destination Tokyo '43
The Gambler & the Lady '52
The Glass Key '42
Hollywood Canteen '44
James Dean '76
Last Rites '88
The McMasters '70
Moonrise '48
Murder on Flight 502 '75
Paid to Kill '54
Say Goodbye, Maggie Cole '72
A Stolen Life '46
Thunder Pass '54

Dave Clark
Time is Running Out '52
The Woman Inside '83

Davison Clark
Dishonored '31
Rogue's Gallery '44

Dick Clark
Deadman's Curve '78
Elvis Memories '85

Frank Clark
Roaring Ranch '30
The Spoilers '14

Fred Clark
Abbott and Costello Meet the Keystone Kops '54
Bells are Ringing '60
The Caddy '53
The Court Martial of Billy Mitchell '55
Daddy Long Legs '55
Dr. Goldfoot and the Bikini Machine '66
Don't Go Near the Water '57
Flamingo Road '49
Here Come the Girls '53
The Horse in the Gray Flannel Suit '68
It Started with a Kiss '59
The Jackpot '50
The Lemon Drop Kid '51
The Mating Game '59
Passionate Thief '60
Sunset Boulevard '50
Three for Bedroom C '52
Zotz! '62

Greydon Clark
Bad Bunch '76
Satan's Sadists '69

Harvey Clark
Peck's Bad Boy '34
Red Headed Woman '32
Shriek in the Night '33

Judy Clark
Kid Sister '45
South of Santa Fe '42

Kenneth Clark
Between Heaven and Hell '56
Desert Commandos '60s
Tarzana, the Wild Girl '72

Liddy Clark
Deadly Possession '88
Kitty and the Bagman '82

Marlene Clark
The Baron '88
Black Vampire '72
Night of the Cobra Woman '72
Slaughter '72

Matt Clark
Back to the Future, Part 3 '90
Barbarians at the Gate '93
Blind Witness '89
Brubaker '80
Chasing Dreams '81
Class Action '91
Country '84
The Driver '78
The Execution of Private Slovik '74
An Eye for an Eye '81
Frozen Assets '92

The Great Northfield Minnesota Raid '72
The Harvest '92
The Horror Show '89
In the Custody of Strangers '82
Kansas City Massacre '75
Kenny Rogers as the Gambler, Part 3: The Legend Continues '87
Legend of the Lone Ranger '81
Let's Get Harry '87
Love Letters '83
Melvin Purvis: G-Man '74
Out of the Darkness '85
The Outlaw Josey Wales '76
The Quick and the Dead '87
Return to Oz '85
Ruckus '81
Tuff Turf '85

Oliver Clark
Ernest Saves Christmas '88
Mikey & Nicky '76
Nightlife '90
One Cooks, the Other Doesn't '83
A Star is Born '76

Petula Clark
Finian's Rainbow '68
Goodbye, Mr. Chips '69
Made in Heaven '52
The Promoter '52
The Runaway Bus '54

Roger Clark
Girls in Chains '43
The Lady is Willing '42
Monster '78

Steve Clark
Boothill Brigade '37
Border Bandits '46
Fighting Vigilantes '47
Gun Lords of Stirrup Basin '37
Pinto Canyon '40
Range Law '44
Range Renegades '48
The Stranger from Pecos '45
West of Nevada '36

Susan Clark
Airport '75 '75
The Apple Dumpling Gang '75
Babe! '75
The Choice '81
City on Fire '78
Colossus: The Forbin Project '70
Coogan's Bluff '68
The Double Negative '80
Madigan '68
Murder by Decree '79
Night Moves '75
Nobody's Perfekt '79
The North Avenue Irregulars '79
Promises in the Dark '79
Showdown '73
Skin Game '71
Skullduggery '70
Tell Them Willie Boy Is Here '69
Valdez is Coming '71

Wallis Clark
Postal Inspector '36
Star Reporter '39

Andrew Clarke
Anzacs: The War Down Under '85
Les Patterson Saves the World '90

Caitlin Clarke
Dragonslayer '81
Penn and Teller Get Killed '90

Gary Clarke
Confessions of Tom Harris '72
Date Bait '60
How to Make a Monster '58
Missile to the Moon '59

Mae Clarke
Flying Tigers '42
Frankenstein '31
The Front Page '31
Great Guy '36
Hats Off '37
King of the Rocketmen '49
Lady Killer '33
Lost Planet Airmen '49
Pat and Mike '52
Penthouse '33
Public Enemy '31

Mindy Clarke
Hot Under the Collar '91
Return of the Living Dead 3 '93
Return to Two Moon Junction '93

Robert Clarke
Alienator '89
The Astounding She-Monster '58
Beyond the Time Barrier '60
The Enchanted Cottage '45
Hideous Sun Demon '59
Midnight Movie Massacre '88
Secret File of Hollywood '62
Sword of Venus '53
Tales of Robin Hood '52
Terror of the Bloodhunters '62

Warren Clarke
A Clockwork Orange '71
Cold Room '84
Enigma '82
Firefox '82
The Great Riviera Bank Robbery '79
Gulag '85
Lassiter '84
Mandela '87
O Lucky Man! '73

Lana Clarkson
Barbarian Queen '85
Barbarian Queen 2: The Empress Strikes Back '89
Blind Date '84
Deathstalker '83
The Haunting of Morella '91
Wizards of the Lost Kingdom 2 '89

Patricia Clarkson
An American Story '92
Blind Man's Bluff '91
Caught in the Act '93
The Dead Pool '88
Four Eyes and Six Guns '93
Legacy of Lies '92
Rocket Gibraltar '88
Tune in Tomorrow '90

Robert Clary
Holocaust Survivors...Remembrance of Love '83
New Faces of 1952 '54

Andrew Dice Clay
The Adventures of Ford Fairlane '90
Amazon Women on the Moon '87
Brain Smasher...A Love Story '93
Casual Sex? '88
Making the Grade '84
Night Patrol '85
Pretty in Pink '86
Private Resort '84
Wacko '83

Nicholas Clay
Cannon Movie Tales: Sleeping Beauty '89
Evil Under the Sun '82
Excalibur '81
The Hound of the Baskervilles '83
Lady Chatterley's Lover '81
Lionheart '87
Lovespell '79
Sleeping Beauty '89

Jill Clayburgh
The Art of Crime '75
Day of Atonement '93
First Monday in October '81
Griffin and Phoenix: A Love Story '76
Hanna K. '83
Honor Thy Father and Mother: The True Story of the Menendez Brothers '94
Hustling '75
I'm Dancing as Fast as I Can '82
It's My Turn '80
Miles to Go '86
Naked in New York '93
Portnoy's Complaint '72
Rich in Love '93
Semi-Tough '77
Shy People '87
The Silver Streak '76

Starting Over '79
The Terminal Man '74
The Thief Who Came to Dinner '73
An Unmarried Woman '78
The Wedding Party '69
Where Are the Children? '85
Whispers in the Dark '92

John Clayton
Freedom '81
High Tide '87
Warm Nights on a Slow-Moving Train '87

John Cleese
And Now for Something Completely Different '72
The Big Picture '89
The Bliss of Mrs. Blossom '68
Bullseye! '90
Clockwise '86
Erik the Viking '89
A Fish Called Wanda '88
John Cleese on How to Irritate People '68
The Magic Christian '69
Monty Python and the Holy Grail '75
Monty Python Live at the Hollywood Bowl '82
Monty Python Meets Beyond the Fringe
Monty Python's Life of Brian '79
Monty Python's Parrot Sketch Not Included '90
Monty Python's The Meaning of Life '83
Privates on Parade '84
Romance with a Double Bass '74
The Secret Policeman's Other Ball '82
Secret Policeman's Private Parts '81
Silverado '85
Splitting Heirs '93
The Statue '71
The Strange Case of the End of Civilization as We Know It '93
Time Bandits '81
Whoops Apocalypse '83
Yellowbeard '83

Paul Clemens
The Beast Within '82
The Family Man '79
Promises in the Dark '79
They're Playing with Fire '84

Christian Clemenson
And the Band Played On '93
Bad Influence '90
Hero '92

Aurore Clement
The Eighties '83
Invitation au Voyage '82
Le Crabe Tambour '77
Les Rendez-vous D'Anna '78
Paris, Texas '83
Toute Une Nuit '82

Pierre Clementi
The Conformist '71
Partner '68
Porcile '69
Sweet Movie '75

Hal Clements
Grit of the Girl Telegrapher/In the Switch Tower '15
Let's Go! '23

John Clements
Convoy '40
The Four Feathers '39
The Silent Enemy '39
Train of Events '49

David Clennon
Conspiracy: The Trial of the Chicago Eight '87
The Couch Trip '87
Falling in Love '84
Go Tell the Spartans '78
Hanna K. '83
Legal Eagles '86
Light Sleeper '92
Man Trouble '92
Matinee '92
Missing '82
The Right Stuff '83

Clennon ▶cont.

Star 80 '83
Sweet Dreams '85
The Thing '82
Corinne Clery
The Con Artists '80
Dangerous Obsession '88
Fatal Fix '80s
Insanity '82
Love by Appointment '76
Moonraker '79
The Story of O '75
The Switch '89
Yor, the Hunter from the Future '83
Carol Cleveland
Monty Python and the Holy Grail '75
Monty Python's The Meaning of Life '83
George Cleveland
The Abe Lincoln of Ninth Avenue '39
Abroad with Two Yanks '44
Drums of Fu Manchu '40
Ghost Town Riders '38
Hidden Enemy '40
I Conquer the Sea '36
Little Giant '46
Midnight Limited '40
Miss Grant Takes Richmond '49
Monte Carlo Nights '34
Mutiny in the Big House '39
Playmates '41
Revolt of the Zombies '36
The Show-Off '46
Texas Legionnaires '43
Two-Faced Woman '41
Valley of the Sun '42
The Wistful Widow of Wagon Gap '47
Jimmy Cliff
Club Paradise '86
The Harder They Come '72
Jack Clifford
King of the Pecos '36
The Man from Gun Town '36
The Revenge Rider '36
South of Santa Fe '32
Sunrise Trail '31
Sweet Adeline '26
Faith Clift
Cataclysm '81
Savage Journey '83
Montgomery Clift
The Big Lift '50
From Here to Eternity '53
The Heiress '49
I Confess '53
Indiscretion of an American Wife '54
Judgment at Nuremberg '61
Lonelyhearts '58
The Misfits '61
A Place in the Sun '51
Raintree County '57
Red River '48
The Search '48
Suddenly, Last Summer '59
The Young Lions '58
Elmer Clifton
America/The Fall of Babylon '24
Intolerance '16
Renee Cline
Fatal Exposure '90
Invasion Force '90
Colin Clive
The Bride of Frankenstein '35
Christopher Strong '33
Frankenstein '31
History is Made at Night '37
Jane Eyre '34
Mad Love '35
E.E. Clive
The Adventures of Sherlock Holmes '39
Arrest Bulldog Drummond '38
The Bride of Frankenstein '35
Bulldog Drummond Escapes '37

Bulldog Drummond's Bride '39
Bulldog Drummond's Peril '38
Bulldog Drummond's Revenge/Bulldog Drummond's Peril '38
Bulldog Drummond's Secret Police '39
The Charge of the Light Brigade '36
The Dark Hour '36
The Hound of the Baskervilles '39
The Invisible Man '33
Libeled Lady '36
The Little Princess '39
Personal Property '37
Teagan Clive
Alienator '89
Sinbad of the Seven Seas '89
Vice Academy 2 '90
Al Cliver
Big Boss '77
The Black Cat '81
Forever Emmanuelle '82
Mr. Scarface '77
Rulers of the City '71
2020 Texas Gladiators '85
Zombie '80
George Clooney
Red Surf '90
Return of the Killer Tomatoes '88
Rosemary Clooney
Deep in My Heart '54
Here Come the Girls '53
Red Garters '54
White Christmas '54
Del Close
Ferris Bueller's Day Off '86
Opportunity Knocks '90
Glenn Close
The Big Chill '83
Dangerous Liaisons '88
Fatal Attraction '87
Hamlet '90
The House of the Spirits '93
Immediate Family '89
The Jagged Edge '85
Maxie '85
Meeting Venus '91
The Natural '84
Orphan Train '79
The Paper '94
Reversal of Fortune '90
Sarah, Plain and Tall '91
Skylark '93
The Stone Boy '84
The World According to Garp '82
John Scott Clough
Fast Forward '84
Gross Anatomy '89
Vera Clouzot
Diabolique '55
Wages of Fear '55
David Clover
Ten Speed '76
Zipperface '92
Francois Cluzet
Chocolat '88
The Horse of Pride '80
Olivier, Olivier '92
Round Midnight '86
The Story of Women '88
Andy Clyde
Annie Oakley '35
Bad Lands '39
Bar-20 '43
Border Patrol '43
Border Vigilantes '41
Colt Comrades '43
Comedy Festival #1 '30s
Comedy Festival #2 '30s
Comedy Festival #4 '30s
Doomed Caravan '41
False Colors '43
Hopalong Cassidy: Borrowed Trouble '48
Hopalong Cassidy: Dangerous Venture '48
Hopalong Cassidy: False Paradise '48
Hopalong Cassidy: Hoppy's Holiday '47

Hopalong Cassidy: Riders of the Deadline '43
Hopalong Cassidy: Silent Conflict '48
Hopalong Cassidy: Sinister Journey '48
Hopalong Cassidy: The Dead Don't Dream '48
Hopalong Cassidy: The Devil's Playground '46
Hopalong Cassidy: The Marauders '47
Hopalong Cassidy: Unexpected Guest '47
Hoppy Serves a Writ '43
In Old Colorado '41
Leather Burners '43
Lost Canyon '43
Mystery Man '44
Outlaws of the Desert '41
Riders of the Timberline '41
Ships in the Night '28
Shirley Temple Festival '33
Sundown Riders '48
Texas Masquerade '44
Twilight on the Trail '41
Yellow Dust '36
June Clyde
Behind the Mask '37
Branded Men '31
Hollywood Mystery '34
Make-Up '37
Morals for Women '31
Seven Doors to Death '44
She Shall Have Music '36
A Study in Scarlet '33
Wayne Murder Case '38
Kim Coates
The Amityville Curse '90
Blind Fear '89
The Club '94
Cold Front '89
Innocent Blood '92
Red Blooded American Girl '90
Smokescreen '90
Phyllis Coates
Blues Busters '50
El Paso Stampede '53
The Incredible Petrified World '58
Jungle Drums of Africa '53
Marshal of Cedar Rock '53
Superman & the Mole Men '51
Teenage Frankenstein '58
Edmund Cobb
Buffalo Bill Rides Again '47
Danger Trails '35
Gun Law '33
Gunners & Guns '34
Riders of the Range '24
Rustler's Paradise '35
Sunset in El Dorado '45
Texas Kid '43
Tonto Basin Outlaws '41
Wild Horse '31
Joe Cobb
Little Rascals, Book 1 '30s
Little Rascals, Book 18 '29
Our Gang '26
Our Gang Comedy Festival '88
Our Gang Comedy Festival 2 '89
The Return of Our Gang '25
Lee J. Cobb
Anna and the King of Siam '46
The Brothers Karamazov '58
Buckskin Frontier '43
Bull of the West '89
But Not for Me '59
Call Northside 777 '48
Come Blow Your Horn '63
Coogan's Bluff '68
Danger on the Air '38
The Dark Past '49
Day of Triumph '54
Exodus '60
The Exorcist '73
The Fighter '52
The Four Horsemen of the Apocalypse '62
Golden Boy '39
Green Mansions '59
How the West was Won '63
In Like Flint '67
Lawman '71
The Left Hand of God '55

The Liberation of L.B. Jones '70
Macho Callahan '70
MacKenna's Gold '69
The Man in the Gray Flannel Suit '56
Man of the West '58
Man Who Loved Cat Dancing '73
The Meanest Men in the West '76
Men of Boys Town '41
The Miracle of the Bells '48
On the Waterfront '54
Our Man Flint '66
Party Girl '58
The Racers '55
Rustler's Valley '37
Sirocco '51
The Song of Bernadette '43
Tall Texan '53
That Lucky Touch '75
The Three Faces of Eve '57
The Trap '59
Twelve Angry Men '57
Randall "Tex" Cobb
Blind Fury '90
Buy & Cell '89
Diggstown '92
Ernest Goes to Jail '90
The Golden Child '86
Raising Arizona '87
Raw Nerve '91
Uncommon Valor '83
Bill Cobbs
The Bodyguard '92
Carolina Skeletons '92
Decoration Day '90
Dominick & Eugene '88
The Hudsucker Proxy '93
Roberto Cobo
Cabeza de Vaca '90
Los Olvidados '50
Charles Coburn
Around the World in 80 Days '56
Bachelor Mother '39
Colonel Effingham's Raid '45
The Devil & Miss Jones '41
Edison the Man '40
Gentlemen Prefer Blondes '53
George Washington Slept Here '42
Heaven Can Wait '43
In This Our Life '42
John Paul Jones '59
Kings Row '41
The Lady Eve '41
Made for Each Other '39
Mr. Music '50
Monkey Business '52
The More the Merrier '43
Of Human Hearts '38
The Paradine Case '47
Rhapsody in Blue '45
The Road to Singapore '40
Stanley and Livingstone '39
Three Faces West '40
Trouble Along the Way '53
Vivacious Lady '38
Wilson '44
James Coburn
The Americanization of Emily '64
The Baltimore Bullet '80
Bite the Bullet '75
Bruce Lee: The Legend '84
Charade '63
Cross of Iron '76
Crossover '82
The Dain Curse '78
Dead Heat on a Merry-Go-Round '66
Deadfall '93
Death of a Soldier '85
Draw! '81
Firepower '79
A Fistful of Dynamite '72
Goldengirl '79
The Great Escape '63
Hard Times '75
Hell is for Heroes '62
High Risk '76
The Hit List '93
Hudson Hawk '91
In Like Flint '67
Internecine Project '73
The Last of Sheila '73

Looker '81
The Loved One '65
Loving Couples '80
The Magnificent Seven '60
Major Dundee '65
Martin's Day '85
Maverick '94
Midway '76
Our Man Flint '66
Pat Garrett & Billy the Kid '73
Pinocchio '83
The President's Analyst '67
A Reason to Live, A Reason to Die '73
Ride Lonesome '59
Sister Act 2: Back in the Habit '93
Sky Riders '76
A Thousand Heroes '94
Waterhole #3 '67
What Did You Do in the War, Daddy? '66
Young Guns 2 '90
Michael Coby
The Bitch '78
Supersonic Man '78
Imogene Coca
National Lampoon's Vacation '83
Rabbit Test '78
Robert Cochran
I Stand Condemned '36
Sanders of the River '35
Scrooge '35
Steve Cochran
The Best Years of Our Lives '46
Carnival Story '54
The Chase '46
Copacabana '47
Deadly Companions '61
The Desert Song '53
I, Mobster '58
Il Grido '57
Jim Thorpe: All American '51
Private Hell 36 '54
Shark River '53
A Song is Born '48
White Heat '49
Wonder Man '45
Rory Cochrane
Dazed and Confused '93
Fathers and Sons '92
James Coco
The Chair '87
The Cheap Detective '78
End of the Road '70
Ensign Pulver '64
Generation '69
Hunk '87
Man of La Mancha '72
Murder by Death '76
A New Leaf '71
Only When I Laugh '81
Scavenger Hunt '79
The Strawberry Statement '70
That's Adequate '90
Wholly Moses! '80
Wild Party '74
You Can't Take It with You '84
Jean Cocteau
The Blood of a Poet '30
Les Enfants Terrible '50
The Testament of Orpheus '59
Camille Coduri
Hawks '89
King Ralph '91
Nuns on the Run '90
Strapless '90
Bill Cody
Frontier Days '34
Ghost City '32
Mason of the Mounted '32
Outlaws of the Range '36
Texas Pioneers '32
Iron Eyes Cody
Bowery Buckaroos '47
El Condor '70
Ernest Goes to Camp '87
Grayeagle '77
King of the Stallions '42
The Longest Drive '76
The Road to Yesterday '25
Son of Paleface '52
Spirit of '76 '91
Under Nevada Skies '46

Whistlin' Dan '32

Kathleen Cody
Charley and the Angel '73
Girls on the Road '73
Superdad '73

Lew Cody
Dishonored '31
Mickey '17

Barry Coe
The Bravados '58
But Not for Me '59
The Cat '66
Dr. Death, Seeker of Souls '73
Love Me Tender '56
The Oval Portrait '88
Peyton Place '57

George Coe
Best Seller '87
Blind Date '87
Bustin' Loose '81
The End of Innocence '90
A Flash of Green '85
The Hollywood Detective '89
Rage of Angels '83
Red Flag: The Ultimate Game '81
Sessions '83
Uncle Tom's Cabin '87

Peter Coe
House of Frankenstein '44
The Mummy's Curse '44

Paul Coeur
Cool Runnings '93
White Fang 2: The Myth of the White Wolf '94

Scott Coffey
Dream Lover '93
Montana '90
Satisfaction '88
Shag: The Movie '89
Shout '91
The Temp '93
Zombie High '87

Frederick Coffin
The Bedroom Window '87
Hard to Kill '90
Manhunt for Claude Dallas '86
One Summer Love '76
Shoot to Kill '88

Tristram Coffin
The Corpse Vanishes '42
Dick Tracy, Detective/The Corpse Vanishes '42
Holt of the Secret Service '42
Jesse James Rides Again '47
King of the Rocketmen '49
Land of the Lawless '47
Lost Planet Airmen '51
Ma Barker's Killer Brood '60
Meet the Mob '42
Pirates of the High Seas '50
Queen for a Day '51
Spy Smasher Returns '42
Tonto Basin Outlaws '41
Under Nevada Skies '46
Up in the Air '40

Nikki Coghill
Dark Age '88
The Time Guardian '87

Frank "Junior" Coghlan
The Adventures of Captain Marvel '41
Drum Taps '33
Hell's House '32
In the Money '34
Kentucky Blue Streak '35
The Last of the Mohicans '32
Let 'er Go Gallegher '28
Little Red Schoolhouse '36
Marked Money '28
Square Shoulders '29
Yankee Clipper '27

Emma Cohen
Bronson's Revenge '79
Horror Rises from the Tomb '72

J.J. Cohen
Back to the Future '85
Back to the Future, Part 2 '89
Back to the Future, Part 3 '90
The Principal '87

Nicholas Colasanto
Fat City '72

Mad Bull '77
Raging Bull '80

Catero Colbert
Sweet Perfection '90
Up Against the Wall '91

Claudette Colbert
Boom Town '40
Cleopatra '34
Drums Along the Mohawk '39
Egg and I '47
Guest Wife '45
I Cover the Waterfront '33
It Happened One Night '34
Let's Make it Legal '51
The Love Goddesses '65
The Palm Beach Story '42
Parrish '61
Since You Went Away '44
Texas Lady '56
Three Came Home '50
Tomorrow is Forever '46
Without Reservations '46

Dennis Cole
Amateur Night '85
The Barbary Coast '74
The Connection '73
Dead End City '88
Death House
Powder Keg '70
Pretty Smart '87

Gary Cole
Echoes in the Darkness '87
Fatal Vision '84
In the Line of Fire '93
Son of the Morning Star '91

George Cole
The Adventures of Sadie '55
The Belles of St. Trinian's '54
Blue Murder at St. Trinian's '56
A Christmas Carol '51
Cottage to Let '41
Deadline Auto Theft '83
Dr. Syn, Alias the Scarecrow '64
Fright '71
Gone in 60 Seconds '74
The Pure Hell of St. Trinian's '61
Too Many Crooks '59
The Vampire Lovers '70

Jacqulin Cole
Bad Bunch '76
Satan's Cheerleaders '77

Michael Cole
Chuka '67
Nickel Mountain '85

Nat King Cole
Cat Ballou '65
China Gate '57
Killer Diller '48
Small Town Girl '53

Olivia Cole
The Fig Tree '87
North and South Book 1 '85
The Sky is Gray '80
Some Kind of Hero '82
The Women of Brewster Place '89

Robert Coleby
The Blue Lightning '86
Great Expectations: The Untold Story '87
Hector's Bunyip '86
Now and Forever '82
Plumber '79

Charles Coleman
Bachelor Apartment '31
Grand Canyon Trail '48

Dabney Coleman
Amos and Andrew '93
The Applegates '89
Bad Ronald '74
The Beverly Hillbillies '93
Bite the Bullet '75
Callie and Son '81
Cinderella Liberty '73
Clifford '92
Cloak & Dagger '84
The Dove '74
Downhill Racer '69
Dragnet '87
Dying Room Only '73
Fist '79
Guilty of Innocence '87
Homeboy '80s

Hot to Trot! '88
How to Beat the High Cost of Living '80
The Man with One Red Shoe '85
Melvin and Howard '80
Modern Problems '81
Murrow '86
Never Forget '91
9 to 5 '80
North Dallas Forty '79
Nothing Personal '80
On Golden Pond '81
The Other Side of the Mountain '75
Pray TV '80
The President's Plane is Missing '71
The Scalphunters '68
Short Time '90
There Goes the Neighborhood '92
Tootsie '82
The Trouble with Girls (and How To Get Into It) '69
Viva Knievel '77
WarGames '83
Where the Heart Is '90
Young Doctors in Love '82

Gary Coleman
The Fantastic World of D.C. Collins '84
Jimmy the Kid '82
The Kid from Left Field '79
The Kid with the Broken Halo '82
The Kid with the 200 I.Q. '83
On the Right Track '81
Scout's Honor '80

Jack Coleman
The Return of Eliot Ness '91
Rubdown '93

Nancy Coleman
Desperate Journey '42
Edge of Darkness '43
Kings Row '41

Renee Coleman
A League of Their Own '92
Return to Eden '89
Who's Harry Crumb? '89

Mildred Coles
Lady Scarface '41
Oklahoma Badlands '48
Seven Days Ashore/Hurry, Charlie, Hurry '44

John Colicos
Anne of the Thousand Days '69
Battlestar Galactica '78
Doctors' Wives '70
Love and Hate: A Marriage Made in Hell '90
Murder on Approval '56
The Postman Always Rings Twice '81
Raid on Rommel '71
Scorpio '73
Shadow Dancing '88

David Colin, Jr.
Beyond the Door '75
Beyond the Door 2 '79

Ian Colin
Late Extra '35
Never Too Late to Mend '37

Margaret Colin
Amos and Andrew '93
The Butcher's Wife '91
Like Father, Like Son '87
Martians Go Home! '90
Pretty in Pink '86
Something Wild '86
Three Men and a Baby '87
Traveling Man '89
True Believer '89

Christopher Collet
First Born '84
The Manhattan Project '86
Pigeon Feathers '88
Prayer of the Rollerboys '91
Sleepaway Camp '83

Kenneth Colley
And Nothing But the Truth '82
Casanova '87
Firefox '82
The Music Lovers '71
Prisoner of Honor '91

The Rainbow '89
Return to Waterloo '85
A Summer Story '88

Constance Collier
Dark Corner '46
Monsieur Beaucaire '46
The Perils of Pauline '47
Rope '48
Thunder in the City '37
Wee Willie Winkie '37

Lois Collier
Cobra Woman '44
The Naughty Nineties '45

William Collier, Jr.
Cimarron '30
Phantom Express '32
Street Scene '31

John Collin
Star! '68
Tess '80

Patricia Collinge
Casanova Brown '44
Tender Comrade '43

Anne Collings
The Mask '61
Return to Africa '89

Alan Collins
Ark of the Sun God '82
Exterminators of the Year 3000 '83
Hunters of the Golden Cobra '82
The Last Hunter '80
Tiger Joe '85
Tornado '83

Cora Sue Collins
Evelyn Prentice '34
The Scarlet Letter '34
The World Accuses '35

Eddie Collins
The Blue Bird '40
Drums Along the Mohawk '39
Young Mr. Lincoln '39

Joan Collins
The Adventures of Sadie '55
The Bawdy Adventures of Tom Jones '76
The Big Sleep '78
The Bitch '78
The Bravados '58
Cartier Affair '84
Cosh Boy '61
Dark Places '73
Decameron Nights '53
Dynasty of Fear '72
Empire of the Ants '77
The Executioner '70
Fearless '78
Five Miles to Midnight '80
Game for Vultures '86
Great Adventure '75
Hansel and Gretel '82
Her Life as a Man '83
Homework '82
I Don't Want to Be Born '75
Land of the Pharaohs '55
Monte Carlo '86
Nutcracker Sweet '84
Oh, Alfie '75
The Opposite Sex '56
The Persuaders '71
Quest for Love '71
Revenge '71
The Road to Hong Kong '62
Seven Thieves '60
Sins '85
Stopover Tokyo '57
The Stud '78
Subterfuge '68
Sunburn '79
Tales from the Crypt '72
Tales That Witness Madness '73
Three in the Cellar '70
Tough Guy '53
The Virgin Queen '55
Zero to Sixty '78

Lewis Collins
Codename: Wildgeese '84
The Final Option '82
Jack the Ripper '88
Professionals '76

Monty Collins
Comedy Classics '35
Midnight Limited '40

Patrick Collins
Dirt Bike Kid '86
The Juggler of Notre Dame '84

Pauline Collins
City of Joy '92
Shirley Valentine '89

Phil Collins
Buster '88
Frauds '93
Hook '91

Ray Collins
The Bachelor and the Bobby-Soxer '47
Citizen Kane '41
Commandos Strike at Dawn '43
Crack-Up '46
The Desert Song '53
A Double Life '47
The Fountainhead '49
Francis the Talking Mule '49
Good Sam '48
Homecoming '48
The Human Comedy '43
It Happens Every Spring '49
Ma and Pa Kettle Back On the Farm '51
Ma and Pa Kettle Go to Town '50
The Magnificent Ambersons '42
Man from Colorado '49
The Navy Comes Through '42
The Racket '51
The Seventh Cross '44
Summer Stock '50
Whistling in Brooklyn '43

Rick Collins
The Toxic Avenger, Part 2 '89
The Toxic Avenger, Part 3: The Last Temptation of Toxie '89

Roberta Collins
The Arousers '70
The Big Doll House '71
Caged Heat '74
The Deadly and the Beautiful '73
Hardbodies '84
Unholy Rollers '72
Whiskey Mountain '77

Russell Collins
Enemy Below '57
The Matchmaker '58
Savage Wilderness '55
Soldier of Fortune '55

Ruth Collins
Cemetery High '89
Dead Boyz Can't Fly '93
Death Collector '89
Doom Asylum '88
Exquisite Corpses '88
Galactic Gigolo '87
New York's Finest '87
Sexpot '88
Wildest Dreams '90

Stephen Collins
All the President's Men '76
Between the Lines '77
The Big Picture '89
Brewster's Millions '85
Chiefs '83
Choke Canyon '86
The Henderson Monster '80
Hitchhiker 3 '87
Hold the Dream '85
Inside the Third Reich '82
Jumpin' Jack Flash '86
Loving Couples '80
My New Gun '92
The Promise '78
Star Trek: The Motion Picture '80
Stella '89
Summer Solstice '81
Weekend War '88
A Woman Named Jackie '91

Madeleine Collinson
The Love Machine '71
Twins of Evil '71

Mary Collinson
The Love Machine '71
Twins of Evil '71

Frank Collison
Dollman '91
Wired to Kill '86

Mark Collver
Bix '90
There's Nothing Out There '90

June Collyer
Drums of Jeopardy '31
A Face in the Fog '36
The Ghost Walks '34

Pamela Collyer
Evil Judgement '85
The Kiss '88

Ronald Colman
Around the World in 80 Days '56
Arrowsmith '31
Bulldog Drummond '29
Champagne for Caesar '50
A Double Life '47
Lady Windermere's Fan '26
Lost Horizon '37
Lucky Partners '40
Prisoner of Zenda '37
Random Harvest '42
Romola '25
A Tale of Two Cities '35
Talk of the Town '42
The White Sister '23

Scott Colomby
Are You in the House Alone? '78
Porky's '82
Porky's 2: The Next Day '83
Porky's Revenge '85

Alex Colon
Death of an Angel '86
Invasion U.S.A. '85

Jerry Colonna
Kentucky Jubilee '51
Meet Me in Las Vegas '56
The Road to Singapore '40
Rosalie '38
Strictly G.I. '44

Vince Colosimo
Moving Out '83
Street Hero '84

Louisa Colpeyn
Band of Outsiders '64
Marry Me, Marry Me '69

Marshall Colt
Beverly Hills Madam '86
Guilty of Innocence '87
The Jagged Edge '85
To Heal a Nation '88

Robbie Coltrane
The Adventures of Huck Finn '93
Bert Rigby, You're a Fool '89
Chinese Boxes '84
Defense of the Realm '85
Henry V '89
Let It Ride '89
Loose Connections '87
Mona Lisa '86
Nuns on the Run '90
Oh, What a Night '92
Perfectly Normal '91
The Pope Must Diet '91
Slipstream '88
Wonderland '88

Coluche
My Best Friend's Girl '84
Tchao Pantin '84

Franco Columbo
Last Man Standing '87
Pumping Iron '76

Franco Columbu
Beretta's Island '92
Desperate Crimes '93

Jack Colvin
Child's Play '88
The Incredible Hulk '77
The Incredible Hulk Returns '88

Michael Colyar
Hot Shots! Part Deux '93
House Party 3 '94

Holly Marie Combs
Dr..Giggles '92
Sweet Hearts Dance '88

Jeffrey Combs
Bride of Re-Animator '89
Cellar Dweller '87
Cyclone '87
Dead Man Walking '88

Doctor Mordrid: Master of the Unknown '92
From Beyond '86
The Guyver '91
Lurking Fear '94
Phantom Empire '87
The Pit & the Pendulum '91
The Re-Animator '85
Trancers 2: The Return of Jack Deth '91

Anjanette Comer
The Appaloosa '66
The Baby '72
Dead of Night '77
Death Stalk '74
The Loved One '65
Netherworld '91
Night of a Thousand Cats '72
Terror on the 40th Floor '74

Dorothy Comingore
Citizen Kane '41
The Hairy Ape '44

Perry Como
Doll Face '46
Words and Music '48

Betty Compson
Bulldog Edition '36
Docks of New York '28
God's Country and the Man '37
The Great Gabbo '29
Hard-Boiled Mahoney '47
Hot Foot/A Happy Married Couple '20
Inside the Lines '30
The Lady Refuses '31
Mad Youth '40
Mystic Circle Murder '39
Paths to Paradise '25
The Pony Express '25
The Port of Missing Girls '38
These Girls Won't Talk '20s
Two Reelers: Comedy Classics 9 '34

Fay Compton
The Mill on the Floss '37
Othello '52

Joyce Compton
The Awful Truth '37
Balalaika '39
Christmas in Connecticut '45
Country Gentlemen '36
Escape to Paradise '39
False Faces '32
I Take This Oath '40
King Kelly of the U.S.A. '34
Let 'Em Have It '35
Rose of Washington Square '39
Rustlers of Red Dog '35
Scared to Death '47
Sea Racketeers '37
Silver Spurs '43
Small Town Boy '37
A Southern Yankee '48

Oliver Conant
Class of '44 '73
Summer of '42 '71

Cristi Conaway
Attack of the 50 Ft. Woman '93
Batman Returns '92

Jeff Conaway
Almost Pregnant '91
The Banker '89
Bikini Summer 2 '92
Breaking Up Is Hard to Do '79
Covergirl '83
The Dirty Dozen: The Fatal Mission '88
Elvira, Mistress of the Dark '88
For the Love of It '80
Ghost Writer '89
Grease '78
L.A. Goddess '92
Mirror Images '91
The Patriot '86
Pete's Dragon '77
The Sleeping Car '90
Sunset Strip '92
Tale of Two Sisters '89
A Time to Die '91
Total Exposure '91

James Congdon
The 4D Man '59
Summerdog '78

Terry Congie
Malibu Hot Summer '81
Sizzle Beach U.S.A. '86

Chester Conklin
Anna Christie '23
Battling Bunyon '24
Behind the Front '26
Cannon Ball/Eyes Have It '15
Cannonball/Dizzy Heights and Daring Hearts '16
Charlie Chaplin...Our Hero! '15
Charlie Chaplin's Keystone Comedies #3 '14
Charlie Chaplin's Keystone Comedies #4 '14
Forlorn River '37
Greed '24
Hallelujah, I'm a Bum '33
Harmon of Michigan '41
A Hash House Fraud/The Sultan's Wife '15
The Lizzies of Mack Sennett '15
Mack Sennett Comedies: Vol. 1 '21
Miracle of Morgan's Creek '44
Modern Times '36
The Nervous Wreck '26
Sullivan's Travels '41
Tillie's Punctured Romance '14
The Virginian '29

Joe Conley
Children's Carol '80
A Day for Thanks on Walton's Mountain '82

Jimmy Conlin
Dick Tracy's Dilemma '47
Miracle of Morgan's Creek '44
Sullivan's Travels '41

Didi Conn
Grease 2 '82
You Light Up My Life '77

Christopher Connelly
Benji '74
The Crash of Flight 401 '78
Fantastic Seven '82
Foxtrap '85
Hawmps! '76
The Incredible Rocky Mountain Race '77
The Invasion of Carol Enders '74
Jungle Raiders '85
Liar's Moon '82
Manhattan Baby '82
The Martian Chronicles: Part 3 '79
The Messenger '87
Mines of Kilimanjaro '87
Night of the Sharks '89
1990: The Bronx Warriors '83
Norseman '78
Operation 'Nam '85
The Other '72
Raiders of Atlantis '83
Return of the Rebels '81
Strike Commando '87
They Only Kill Their Masters '72

Edward Connelly
The Mysterious Lady '28
The Saphead '20

Jennifer Connelly
Career Opportunities '91
Creepers '85
Hot Spot '90
Labyrinth '86
Once Upon a Time in America '84
The Rocketeer '91
Seven Minutes in Heaven '86
Some Girls '88

Marc Connelly
Spirit of St. Louis '57
Tall Story '60

Jason Connery
Bye Bye Baby '88
Casablanca Express '89
Double Cross '92
The First Olympics: Athens 1896 '84
Robin Hood...The Legend: Herne's Son '85
Robin Hood...The Legend: The Time of the Wolf '85

Spymaker: The Secret Life of Ian Fleming '90
Winner Takes All '86

Sean Connery
The Anderson Tapes '71
Another Time, Another Place '58
The Arab Conspiracy '76
A Bridge Too Far '77
Cuba '79
Darby O'Gill & the Little People '59
Diamonds are Forever '71
Dr. No '62
Family Business '89
A Fine Madness '66
Five Days One Summer '82
From Russia with Love '63
Goldfinger '64
The Great Train Robbery '79
Happy Anniversary 007: 25 Years of James Bond '87
Highlander '86
Highlander 2: The Quickening '91
The Hunt for Red October '90
Indiana Jones and the Last Crusade '89
The Longest Day '62
The Man Who Would Be King '75
Marnie '64
Medicine Man '92
Memories of Me '88
Meteor '79
Molly Maguires '70
Murder on the Orient Express '74
The Name of the Rose '86
Never Say Never Again '83
The Offence '73
Outland '81
The Presidio '88
Red Tent '69
Rising Sun '93
Robin and Marian '76
The Russia House '90
Shalako '68
Sword of the Valiant '83
The Terrorists '74
Thunderball '65
Time Bandits '81
Time Lock '57
The Untouchables '87
The Wind and the Lion '75
Wrong is Right '82
You Only Live Twice '67
Zardoz '73

Harry Connick, Jr.
Little Man Tate '91
Memphis Belle '90

Billy Connolly
Absolution '81
The Big Man: Crossing the Line '91
Blue Money '84
Indecent Proposal '93
The Return of the Musketeers '89
The Secret Policeman's Other Ball '82

Kevin Connolly
Alan & Naomi '92
The Beverly Hillbillies '93

Walter Connolly
The Adventures of Huckleberry Finn '39
The Bitter Tea of General Yen '33
Broadway Bill '34
Fifth Avenue Girl '39
The Good Earth '37
It Happened One Night '34
Lady by Choice '34
Lady for a Day '33
Libeled Lady '36
Nothing Sacred '37
Too Hot to Handle '38
Twentieth Century '34

Kenneth Connor
Carry On Cleo '65
Carry On England '51
Carry On Nurse '59
What a Carve-Up! '62

Chuck Connors
Airplane 2: The Sequel '82
Balboa '82

Big Country '58
Bordello '79
The Capture of Grizzly Adams '82
Day of the Assassin '81
Designing Woman '57
Embassy '72
Flipper '63
The Gambler Returns: The Luck of the Draw '93
Geronimo '62
High Desert Kill '90
Hot Rod Girl '56
Last Flight to Hell
The Legend of Sea Wolf '75
The Mad Bomber '72
Nightmare in Badham County '76
99 & 44/100 Dead '74
Old Yeller '57
One Last Run '89
Pancho Villa '72
Pat and Mike '52
The Proud and the Damned '72
Ride to Glory '71
Roots '77
Sakura Killers '86
Skinheads: The Second Coming of Hate '88
Soylent Green '73
Summer Camp Nightmare '86
Target Eagle '84
Terror Squad '87
Texas Guns '90
Three Days to a Kill '91
Tourist Trap '79
The Vals '85
Virus '82

Mike Connors
Avalanche Express '79
Casino '80
Fist Fighter '88
Flesh and the Spur '57
Good Neighbor Sam '64
Harlow '65
Long Journey Back '78
Nightkill '80
Panic Button '62
Shake, Rattle and Rock '57
Suicide Battalion/Hell Squad '58
Swamp Women '55
Too Scared to Scream '85
Voodoo Woman '57

Michael Conrad
Bordello '79
Gone with the West '72
Hill Street Blues, Vol. 1: Hill Street Station '81
Scream Blacula Scream '73
Thumb Tripping '72
The War Lord '65

Mikel Conrad
Check Your Guns '48
The Flying Saucer '50

Robert Conrad
Assassin '86
Bandits '73
Breaking Up Is Hard to Do '79
The Commies are Coming, the Commies are Coming '57
Crossfire '67
Hard Knox '83
Lady in Red '79
More Wild, Wild West '80
Murph the Surf '75
Palm Springs Weekend '63
Samurai Cowboy '93
Sudden Death '77
Two Fathers' Justice '85
Wild, Wild West Revisited '79
Will: G. Gordon Liddy '82
Wrong is Right '82

William Conrad
Body and Soul '47
The Conqueror '56
Cry Danger '51
The Desert Song '53
Killing Cars '85
Moonshine County Express '77
Naked Jungle '54
Night Cries '78
The Racket '51
Return of Frank Cannon '80
Vengeance '89

Hans Conried
The Affairs of Dobie Gillis '53

Behave Yourself! '52
Birds & the Bees '56
Blondie's Blessed Event '42
Brothers O'Toole '73
Bus Stop '56
Davy Crockett, King of the Wild Frontier '55
Falcon Takes Over/Strange Bargain '42
The 5000 Fingers of Dr. T '53
Hitler's Children '43
Jet Pilot '57
The Monster that Challenged the World '57
My Friend Irma '49
Nancy Goes to Rio '50
Oh, God! Book 2 '80
The Patsy '64
Rich, Young and Pretty '51
The Senator was Indiscreet '47
Summer Stock '55
Three for Bedroom C '52
Tut & Tuttle '82

Frances Conroy
The Adventures of Huck Finn '93
Another Woman '88
Rocket Gibraltar '88
Scent of a Woman '92

Frank Conroy
Ace of Aces '33
The Bramble Bush '60
Crash Dive '43
I Live My Life '35
Manhattan Melodrama '34
The Ox-Bow Incident '43

John Considine
Choose Me '84
Circle of Power '83
Dixie: Changing Habits '85
Dr. Death, Seeker of Souls '73
Endangered Species '82
Forbidden Love '82
The Late Show '77
Opposing Force '87
Reunion in France '42
Rita Hayworth: The Love Goddess '83
See How She Runs '78
The Shadow Box '80
The Thirsty Dead '74
Trouble in Mind '86
A Wedding '78
Welcome to L.A. '77

Tim Considine
Clown '53
Daring Dobermans '73
Patton '70
The Shaggy Dog '59

Eddie Constantine
Alphaville '65
As If It Were Raining '63
Attack of the Robots '66
Cleo from 5 to 7 '61
It Means That to Me '63
It's Alive 2: It Lives Again '78
Keep Talking Baby '61
Ladies Man '62
License to Kill '64
The Long Good Friday '79
Room 43 '58
S.O.S. Pacific '60
There Goes Barder '64
Your Turn Darling '63
Zentropa '92

Michael Constantine
Billy: Portrait of a Street Kid '77
Conspiracy of Terror '75
Death Cruise '74
Dirty Heroes '71
Don't Drink the Water '69
Fear in the City '81
Forty Days of Musa Dagh '85
The Hustler '61
If It's Tuesday, This Must Be Belgium '69
In the Mood '87
Justine '69
Killing in the Sun
My Life '93
The North Avenue Irregulars '79
Prancer '89
Question of Faith '93
The Reivers '69
Say Goodbye, Maggie Cole '72
Silent Rebellion '82

John Conte
Lost in a Harem '44
The Man with the Golden Arm '55
Trauma '62

Richard Conte
Assault on a Queen '66
Big Combo '55
Call Northside 777 '48
Circus World '64
Explosion '69
The Fighter '52
Full of Life '56
The Godfather '72
The Godfather 1902-1959: The Complete Epic '81
Guadalcanal Diary '43
Hotel '67
House of Strangers '49
I'll Cry Tomorrow '55
Lady in Cement '68
1931: Once Upon a Time in New York '72
Operation Cross Eagles '69
The Purple Heart '44
Race for Life '55
They Came to Cordura '59
13 Rue Madeleine '46
Tony Rome '67
Violent Professionals '82
A Walk in the Sun '46

Steve Conte
Attack of the Mayan Mummy '63
Terror of the Bloodhunters '62

Catherine Conti
Cry of the Black Wolves '70s
2069: A Sex Odyssey '78

Tom Conti
American Dreamer '84
Beyond Therapy '86
Deep Cover '88
The Duellists '77
Dumb Waiter '87
Full Circle '77
The Gospel According to Vic '87
Merry Christmas, Mr. Lawrence '83
Miracles '86
The Norman Conquests, Part 1: Table Manners '80
The Norman Conquests, Part 2: Living Together '80
The Norman Conquests, Part 3: Round and Round the Garden '80
The Princess and the Pea '83
The Quick and the Dead '87
Reuben, Reuben '83
Saving Grace '86
Shirley Valentine '89
That Summer of White Roses '90

Chantal Contouri
Goodbye, Miss 4th of July '88
The Night After Halloween '83
Thirst '79

Patricio Contreras
The Official Story '85
Old Gringo '89

Frank Converse
Alone in the Neon Jungle '87
Anne of Avonlea '87
Brother Future '91
The Bushido Blade '80
Cruise into Terror '78
Danger in the Skies '79
Everybody Wins '90
Home at Last '88
Killer on Board '77
Marilyn: The Untold Story '80
A Movie Star's Daughter '79
Mystery at Fire Island '81
Sergeant Matlovich vs. the U.S. Air Force '78
Tales of the Unexpected '91
The Tattered Web '71
Uncle Tom's Cabin '87

William Converse-Roberts
Courtship '87
The Fig Tree '87
1918 '85
On Valentine's Day '86

Bert Convy
A Bucket of Blood '59
Cannonball Run '81
Help Wanted: Male '82
Hero at Large '80
Jennifer '78
The Love Bug '68
The Man in the Santa Claus Suit '79
Racquet '79
Semi-Tough '77

Dan Conway
Blast-Off Girls '67
Things Change '88

Gary Conway
American Ninja 2: The Confrontation '87
How to Make a Monster '58
Liberty & Bash '90
Teenage Frankenstein '58

Kevin Conway
F.I.S.T. '78
Gettysburg '93
Homeboy '88
Jennifer 8 '92
Johnny We Hardly Knew Ye '77
Lathe of Heaven '80
One Good Cop '91
Paradise Alley '78
The Quick and the Dead '94
Rage of Angels '83
Rambling Rose '91

Morgan Conway
Bowery at Midnight/Dick Tracy vs. Cueball '42
Dick Tracy, Detective '45
Dick Tracy, Detective/The Corpse Vanishes '42
Dick Tracy Double Feature #1 '45
Dick Tracy Double Feature #2 '47
Dick Tracy vs. Cueball '46
The Saint Takes Over '40
Sinners in Paradise '38

Pat Conway
Brighty of the Grand Canyon '67
The Deadly Mantis '57
Geronimo '62

Tim Conway
Ace Crawford, Private Eye
The Apple Dumpling Gang '75
The Apple Dumpling Gang Rides Again '79
The Billion Dollar Hobo '78
Dorf and the First Games of Mount Olympus '87
Dorf Goes Auto Racing '89
Gus '76
The Longshot '86
The Private Eyes '80
Prize Fighter '79
The Shaggy D.A. '76
They Went That-a-Way & That-a-Way '79
The World's Greatest Athlete '73

Tom Conway
Bride of the Gorilla '51
Cat People '42
Criminal Court '46
The Falcon in Hollywood '44
The Falcon in Mexico '44
Falcon's Adventure/Armored Car Robbery '50
The Falcon's Brother '42
I Walked with a Zombie '43
Lady Be Good '41
Mrs. Miniver '42
Murder on Approval '56
Norman Conquest '53
One Touch of Venus '48
Rio Rita '42
The Saint Strikes Back: Criminal Court '46
The Seventh Victim '43
Tarzan's Secret Treasure '41
Three Stops to Murder '53
Voodoo Woman '57

Jackie Coogan
College Swing '38
Dr. Heckyl and Mr. Hype '80
The Escape Artist '82
Girl Happy '65

Halloween with the Addams Family '79
High School Confidential '58
Human Experiments '79
The Kid '21
The Kid/Idle Class '21
Lonelyhearts '58
Mesa of Lost Women '52
My Boy '21
Oliver Twist '22
Outlaw Women '52
Peck's Bad Boy '21
The Prey '80
The Shakiest Gun in the West '68
Tom Sawyer '30
Varieties on Parade '52

Keith Coogan
Adventures in Babysitting '87
Book of Love '91
Cheetah '89
Cousins '89
Don't Tell Mom the Babysitter's Dead '91
Forever: A Ghost of a Love Story '92
Hiding Out '87
Toy Soldiers '91
Under the Boardwalk '89

Carole Cook
The Incredible Mr. Limpet '64
Sixteen Candles '84

Clyde Cook
Through the Breakers '28
White Cargo '42
White Gold '28

Dale "Apollo" Cook
Blood Ring '91
Fist of Steel '93
Triple Impact '92

Donald Cook
Baby Face '33
Confidential '35
Here Come the Co-Eds '45
Show Boat '36
Viva Villa! '34

Elisha Cook, Jr.
Behave Yourself! '52
The Big Sleep '46
Black Bird '75
Born to Kill '47
Carny '80
The Champ '79
Dark Mountain '44
Dark Waters '44
Dillinger '45
Don't Bother to Knock '52
Drum Beat '54
El Condor '70
Electra Glide in Blue '73
The Great Northfield Minnesota Raid '72
Hammett '82
The Haunted Palace '63
The Indian Fighter '55
The Killing '56
Leave 'Em Laughing '81
The Maltese Falcon '41
Messiah of Evil '74
1941 '79
One-Eyed Jacks '61
Papa's Delicate Condition '63
Platinum High School '60
Plunder Road '57
Rosemary's Baby '68
St. Ives '76
Salem's Lot '79
Shane '53
Stranger on the Third Floor '40
They Won't Forget '37
Tin Pan Alley '40
Wildcat '42

Peter Cook
Bedazzled '68
Black Beauty '94
Dandy in Aspic '68
Find the Lady '75
Getting It Right '89
Great Balls of Fire '89
The Hound of the Baskervilles '77
The Princess Bride '87
Those Daring Young Men in Their Jaunty Jalopies '69
Whoops Apocalypse '88
Without a Clue '88
The Wrong Box '66

Yellowbeard '83

Roderick Cook
9 1/2 Weeks '86
Our Time '74

Tommy Cook
Missile to the Moon '59
Teenage Crime Wave '55

Jennifer Cooke
Friday the 13th, Part 6: Jason Lives '86
Gimme an F '85

Keith Cooke
China O'Brien '88
China O'Brien 2 '89
The King of the Kickboxers '91

Peter Cookson
Black Tower '50
Fear '46

Spade Cooley
Everybody's Dancin' '50
Kid from Gower Gulch '47
Silver Bandit '47

Alice Cooper
Decline of Western Civilization 2: The Metal Years '88
Freddy's Dead: The Final Nightmare '91
Monster Dog '82
Roadie '80
Sextette '78

Cami Cooper
The Applegates '89
Shocker '89

Chris Cooper
City of Hope '91
Guilty by Suspicion '91
Lone Justice '93
Matewan '87
Return to Lonesome Dove '93
This Boy's Life '93
Thousand Pieces of Gold '91

Clancy Cooper
Girls in Chains '43
Naked Youth '59
The Secret Code '42

Gary Cooper
Dark Before Dawn '89
Naked Gun 33 1/3: The Final Insult '94

Gary Cooper
The Adventures of Marco Polo '38
Along Came Jones '45
Ball of Fire '41
Beau Geste '39
Blowing Wild '54
Casanova Brown '44
Cloak and Dagger '46
The Court Martial of Billy Mitchell '55
The Cowboy and the Lady '38
Distant Drums '51
Doomsday '28
A Farewell to Arms '32
Fighting Caravans '31
The Fountainhead '49
Friendly Persuasion '56
The General Died at Dawn '36
Good Sam '48
The Hanging Tree '59
Hedda Hopper's Hollywood '42
High Noon '52
It '27
It's a Great Feeling '49
Kings, Queens, Jokers '30s
The Last Outlaw '27
The Lives of a Bengal Lancer '35
Love in the Afternoon '57
Man of the West '58
Meet John Doe '41
Mr. Deeds Goes to Town '36
Morocco '30
The Naked Edge '61
The Plainsman '37
The Pride of the Yankees '42
The Real Glory '39
Return to Paradise '53
Sergeant York '41
Springfield Rifle '52
Task Force '49
Ten North Frederick '58
They Came to Cordura '59
Today We Live '33
Vera Cruz '53

Cooper ▶cont.

The Virginian '29
The Westerner '40
Wings '27
The Wreck of the Mary Deare '59

George Cooper
Federal Agent '36
Little Church Around the Corner '23
Smouldering Fires '25
Uptown New York '32

Gladys Cooper
Beware of Pity '46
The Bishop's Wife '47
Homecoming '48
The Iron Duke '34
Kitty Foyle '40
Madame Bovary '49
Mrs. Parkington '44
Mr. Lucky '43
My Fair Lady '64
Nice Girl Like Me '69
Now, Voyager '42
The Pirate '48
Rebecca '40
The Secret Garden '49
Separate Tables '58
The Song of Bernadette '43
That Hamilton Woman '41
The Twilight Zone '61
The Valley of Decision '45
The White Cliffs of Dover '44

Inez Cooper
I Married an Angel '42
'Neath Canadian Skies '46
North of the Border '46
Wings Over the Pacific '43

Jack Cooper
All Night Long/Smile Please '24
Cord & Dischords/Naughty Nurse '28

Jackie Cooper
The Abe Lincoln of Ninth Avenue '39
The Champ '31
Little Rascals, Book 9 '30s
Little Rascals, Book 10 '30s
Little Rascals, Book 12 '37
Little Rascals, Book 13 '37
The Love Machine '71
Maybe I'll Be Home in the Spring '70
The Navy Comes Through '42
Peck's Bad Boy '34
Return of Frank James '40
Superman: The Movie '78
Superman 2 '80
Superman 3 '83
Surrender '87
Treasure Island '34
Ziegfeld Girl '41

Jeanne Cooper
Plunder Road '57
Red Nightmare '62
Shame '61
Sweet Hostage '75

Jeff Cooper
Circle of Iron '78
Fantastic Balloon Voyage '80s
The Impossible Years '68

Maggie Cooper
And Baby Makes Six '79
Death Ray 2000 '81
An Eye for an Eye '81

Melville Cooper
The Adventures of Robin Hood '38
Dawn Patrol '38
Heartbeat '46
Immortal Sergeant '43
The King's Thief '55
The Lady Eve '41
Let's Dance '50
Murder Over New York '40
Private Life of Don Juan '34
Rebecca '40
Thin Ice '37
13 Rue Madeleine '46
The Underworld Story '50

Ralph Cooper
The Duke is the Tops '38
Gang War '40

Stan Cooper
Great Treasure Hunt '70s
The Hanging Woman '72
Hell Commandos '69

Robert Coote
Alice Through the Looking Glass '66
Bad Lands '39
Commandos Strike at Dawn '43
The Elusive Pimpernel '50
Forever Amber '47
The Ghost and Mrs. Muir '47
Gunga Din '39
The Horse's Mouth '58
Macbeth '48
The Merry Widow '52
Mr. Moto's Last Warning '39
My Fair Lady '64
Nurse Edith Cavell '39
Othello '52
Scaramouche '52
The Three Musketeers '48
Tunes of Glory/Horse's Mouth '60
You Can't Fool Your Wife '40

Joan Copeland
Happy New Year '87
Her Alibi '89
Roseland '77

Teri Copley
Brain Donors '92
Down the Drain '89
The FBI Murders '88
Frozen Assets '92
I Married a Centerfold '84
Transylvania Twist '89

David Copperfield
Terror Train '80
Three of a Kind '80s

Sofia Coppola
The Godfather '72
The Godfather, Part 3 '90
Inside Monkey Zetterland '93
Peggy Sue Got Married '86

Glenn Corbett
All the Young Men '60
Chisum '70
The Mountain Road '60
Ride in a Pink Car '74
Shadow Force '92
Shenandoah '65
The Stranger '73
The Violent Years '56

Gretchen Corbett
Jaws of Satan '81
Let's Scare Jessica to Death '71
PSI Factor '80
The Savage Bees '76
Secrets of Three Hungry Wives '78

Harry H. Corbett
Carry On Screaming '66
Rattle of a Simple Man '64
Silver Dream Racer '83
The Unstoppable Man '59

Barry Corbin
Ballad of Gregorio Cortez '83
Bitter Harvest '81
Career Opportunities '91
The Chase '91
Conagher '91
Critters 2: The Main Course '88
Hard Traveling '85
Hot Spot '90
It Takes Two '88
LBJ: The Early Years '88
My Science Project '85
Nothing in Common '86
Permanent Record '88
Prime Suspect '82
Short Time '90
Six Pack '82
Undercover '87
Urban Cowboy '80
What Comes Around '85
Who's Harry Crumb? '89

Ellen Corby
All Mine to Give '56
Angels in the Outfield '51
A Day for Thanks on Walton's Mountain '82
Forever Amber '47
The Glass Bottom Boat '66

Homecoming: A Christmas Story '71
I Remember Mama '48
Illegal '55
It's a Wonderful Life '46
Ma and Pa Kettle Go to Town '50
On Moonlight Bay '51
The Strangler '64
Support Your Local Gunfighter '71
Thanksgiving Story '73
Vertigo '58
The Waltons: A Thanksgiving Story '73

Donna Corcoran
Angels in the Outfield '51
Don't Bother to Knock '52
Gypsy Colt '54

Kevin Corcoran
Johnny Shiloh '63
Mooncussers '62
Old Yeller '57
Pollyanna '60
Savage Sam '63
The Shaggy Dog '59
A Tiger Walks '64
Toby Tyler '59

Alex Cord
The Brotherhood '68
C.I.A.: Code Name Alexa '92
The Dirty Dozen: The Fatal Mission '88
Fire '77
A Girl to Kill for '90
Goliath Awaits '81
Grayeagle '77
Inn of the Damned '74
Jungle Warriors '84
A Minute to Pray, A Second to Die '67
Roots of Evil '91
Sidewinder One '77
Stiletto '69
Street Asylum '90
To Be the Best '93
The Uninvited '88

Mara Corday
The Black Scorpion '57
Francis Joins the WACs '54
The Giant Claw '57
Tarantula '55

Paula Corday
Because You're Mine '52
Sword of Monte Cristo '51

Rita Corday
The Body Snatcher '45
The Falcon in Hollywood '44
The Leopard Man '43
West of the Pecos '45

Joaquin Cordero
Dos Esposas en Mi Cama '87
El Libro de Piedra '68
El Tesoro de Chucho el Roto '47
La Justicia Tiene Doce Anos '87
Los Amores de Marieta '87
Los Tres Calaveras '64
Orlak, the Hell of Frankenstein '60
Patsy, Mi Amor '87

Allan Cordunner
Heart of Darkness '93
Mandela '87
Yentl '83

Annie Cordy
La Rupture '70
Le Chat '75

Brigitte Corey
The Fury of Hercules '61
Samson '61

Prof. Irwin Corey
Fairytales '79
How to Commit Marriage '69
Stuck on You '84

Isabel Corey
Bob le Flambeur '55
The Invincible Gladiator '63

Jeff Corey
The Balcony '63
Beneath the Planet of the Apes '70
The Boston Strangler '68

Butch and Sundance: The Early Days '79
Butch Cassidy and the Sundance Kid '69
Catlow '71
Conan the Destroyer '84
Creator '85
Curse of the Black Widow '77
Deception '92
Follow Me Quietly '49
Getting Straight '70
Home of the Brave '49
Hopalong Cassidy: Hoppy's Holiday '47
Lady in a Cage '64
Little Big Man '70
Messenger of Death '88
Moonshine County Express '77
My Friend Flicka '43
The Nevadan '50
The Next Voice You Hear '50
Oh, God! '77
Payoff '91
The Premonition '75
Rawhide '51
Secret Ingredient '92
Sinatra '92
A Southern Yankee '48
Superman & the Mole Men '51
Surviving the Game '94
Sword & the Sorcerer '82
They Call Me Mr. Tibbs! '70
Up River '79
Wild Geese '78

Wendell Corey
The Accused '48
Any Number Can Play '49
The Astro-Zombies '67
The Big Knife '55
Buckskin '68
Great Missouri Raid '51
Holiday Affair '49
The Light in the Forest '58
Loving You '57
The Rainmaker '56
Rear Window '54
Rich, Young and Pretty '51
The Search '48
Sorry, Wrong Number '48
Women of the Prehistoric Planet '66

Danny Corkill
Between Two Women '86
Mrs. Soffel '84

Anthony Corlan
Something for Everyone '70
Vampire Circus '71

Al Corley
Incident at Channel Q '86
Squeeze Play '79
Torchlight '85

Pat Corley
Mr. Destiny '90
Night Shift '82
Of Mice and Men '81
Poker Alice '87
Silent Witness '85
The Two Worlds of Jenny Logan '79

Maddie Corman
The Adventures of Ford Fairlane '90
My New Gun '92
Seven Minutes in Heaven '86

Roger Corman
The Godfather 1902-1959: The Complete Epic '81
The Godfather, Part 2 '74
Philadelphia '93
The Silence of the Lambs '91
State of Things '82
Swing Shift '84

Don Cornelius
No Way Back '76
Tapeheads '89

Ellie Cornell
Chips, the War Dog '90
Halloween 4: The Return of Michael Myers '88
Halloween 5: The Revenge of Michael Myers '89

Charlotte Cornwell
The Krays '90
White Hunter, Black Heart '90

Judy Cornwell
Santa Claus: The Movie '85
Think Dirty '70
Wuthering Heights '70

Georges Corraface
Christopher Columbus: The Discovery '92
Impromptu '91
Not Without My Daughter '90

Mady Correll
Monsieur Verdoux '47
Texas Masquerade '44

Adrienne Corri
Blat
A Clockwork Orange '71
Corridors of Blood '58
Devil Girl from Mars '54
The Hellfire Club '61
Madhouse '74
Make Me an Offer '55
The River '51
Rosebud '75
The Tell-Tale Heart '62
Vampire Circus '71

Nick Corri
Gotcha! '85
In the Heat of Passion '91
The Lawless Land '88
A Nightmare on Elm Street '84
Slaves of New York '89
Tropical Snow '88

Lloyd Corrigan
Blondie Hits the Jackpot '49
Captive Wild Woman '43
The Chase '46
Gambler's Choice '44
Ghost Chasers '51
A Girl, a Guy and a Gob '41
Hitler's Children '43
The Lady in Question '40
Since You Went Away '44
The Thin Man Goes Home '44
Young Tom Edison '40

Ray Corrigan
Arizona Stagecoach '42
Black Market Rustlers '43
Boot Hill Bandits '42
Come On, Cowboys '37
Country Gentlemen '36
Cowboy Commandos '43
Frontier Horizon '39
Fugitive Valley '41
Ghost Town Gold '36
Heart of the Rockies '37
Heroes of the Hills '38
Hit the Saddle '37
It! The Terror from Beyond Space '58
Kid's Last Ride '41
Land of Hunted Men '43
Lonely Trail/Three Texas Steers '39
Outlaws of Sonora '38
Overland Stage Raiders '38
The Painted Stallion '38
Pals of the Saddle '38
Purple Vigilantes '38
Range Busters '40
Renegade Girl '46
Riders of the Whistling Skull '37
Roarin' Lead '37
Rock River Renegades '42
Saddle Mountain Round-Up '41
Santa Fe Stampede '38
Saturday Night Serials '40
Three Texas Steers '39
Thunder River Feud '42
Tonto Basin Outlaws '41
Trail of Robin Hood '50
Trail of the Silver Spurs '41
Trailing Double Trouble '40
The Trigger Trio '37
Tumbledown Ranch in Arizona '41
Underground Rustlers '41
Undersea Kingdom '36
West of Pinto Basin '40
White Gorilla '47
Wild Horse Rodeo '37
Wyoming Outlaw '39

Shirley Corrigan
The Devil's Nightmare '71
Dr. Jekyll and the Wolfman '71

Aneta Corseaut
The Blob '58
Return to Mayberry '85

The Toolbox Murders '78

Bud Cort
Brain Dead '89
Brewster McCloud '70
The Chocolate War '88
Die Laughing '80
Electric Dreams '84
Gas-s-s-s! '70
Going Under '91
Harold and Maude '71
Hysterical '83
Invaders from Mars '86
Love at Stake '87
Love Letters '83
Maria's Lovers '84
M*A*S*H '70
The Nightingale '83
Out of the Dark '88
Rumpelstiltskin '82
The Secret Diary of Sigmund
    Freud '84
The Strawberry Statement '70
Sweet Charity '69
Ted & Venus '93
Why Shoot the Teacher '79

Mapita Cortes
Black Pit of Dr. M '47
El Gendarme Desconocido '41

Rowena Cortes
Heroes Three '84
To Live and Die in Hong Kong
    '89

Joe Cortese
Assault and Matrimony '87
Born to Run '93
The Closer '91
Deadly Illusion '87
Evilspeak '82
Family Enforcer '76
Letting Go '85
Python Wolf '88
Ruby '92
Stalking Danger '86
To Protect and Serve '92
Windows '80

Valentina Cortese
The Adventures of Baron
    Munchausen '89
Assassination of Trotsky '72
The Barefoot Contessa '54
Brother Sun, Sister Moon '73
Day for Night '73
First Love '77
Juliet of the Spirits '65
Kidnap Syndicate '76
Les Miserables '52
Malaya '49
When Time Ran Out '80
Widow's Nest '77

Bella Cortez
The Giant of Metropolis '61
Tor '64
Vulcan God of Fire

Carlos Cortez
El Robo al Tren Correo '47
Postal Inspector '36
Rio Hondo '47

Ricardo Cortez
Behind Office Doors '31
Big Business Girl '31
The Gentleman from California
    '37
I Killed That Man '42
Illicit '31
The Inner Circle '46
Last Hurrah '58
Lost Zeppelin '29
The Maltese Falcon '31
Mr. Moto's Last Warning '39
Mockery '27
Murder Over New York '40
The Phantom in the House '29
The Pony Express '25
The Sorrows of Satan '26
The Swan '25

Bill Cosby
Bill Cosby, Himself '81
California Suite '78
The Devil & Max Devlin '81
Ghost Dad '90
Leonard Part 6 '87
Let's Do It Again '75
Man & Boy '71
Mother, Jugs and Speed '76
Piece of the Action '77
To All My Friends on Shore '71

Uptown Saturday Night '74

Howard Cosell
Bananas '71
Broadway Danny Rose '84
Casey at the Bat '85
Sleeper '73

Ernest Cossart
The Great Ziegfeld '36
Kings Row '41
Kitty Foyle '40
Love from a Stranger '47

James Cossins
Dynasty of Fear '72
Wuthering Heights '70

Marina Costa
The Final Executioner '83
Jungle Raiders '85

Robert Costanzo
The Cemetery Club '93
Delusion '91
Die Hard 2: Die Harder '90
Honeyboy '82
Honeymoon in Vegas '92
Man's Best Friend '93
Relentless 3 '93
The Vegas Strip Wars '84

Dolores Costello
Breaking the Ice '38
Little Lord Fauntleroy '36
The Magnificent Ambersons
    '42

Don Costello
Mystery Man '44
Texas Masquerade '44
Whistling in the Dark '41

Elvis Costello
Americathon '79
No Surrender '86
Straight to Hell '87

Helene Costello
Don Juan '26
The Man on the Box '25

Lou Costello
Abbott and Costello Go to Mars
    '53
Abbott and Costello in
    Hollywood '45
Abbott and Costello in the
    Foreign Legion '50
Abbott and Costello Meet
    Captain Kidd '52
Abbott and Costello Meet Dr.
    Jekyll and Mr. Hyde '52
Abbott and Costello Meet
    Frankenstein '48
Abbott & Costello Meet the
    Invisible Man '51
Abbott and Costello Meet the
    Keystone Kops '54
Abbott and Costello Meet the
    Killer, Boris Karloff '49
Abbott & Costello Meet the
    Mummy '55
Abbott and Costello Scrapbook
    '70s
Africa Screams '49
The Best of Abbott & Costello
    Live '54
Buck Privates '41
Buck Privates Come Home '47
Classic Comedy Video Sampler
    '49
Comin' Round the Mountain '51
Dance with Me, Henry '56
Here Come the Co-Eds '45
Hey Abbott! '78
Hit the Ice '43
Hold That Ghost '41
Hollywood Clowns '85
Hollywood Goes to War '54
In Society '44
In the Navy '41
Jack & the Beanstalk '52
Keep 'Em Flying '41
Little Giant '46
Lost in a Harem '44
Lost in Alaska '52
Mexican Hayride '48
The Naughty Nineties '45
The Noose Hangs High '48
One Night in the Tropics '40
Pardon My Sarong '42
Ride 'Em Cowboy '42
Rio Rita '42
30-Foot Bride of Candy Rock
    '59

The Time of Their Lives '46
Who Done It? '42
The Wistful Widow of Wagon
    Gap '47

Mariclare Costello
All God's Children '80
Conspiracy of Terror '75
Coward of the County '81
The Execution of Private Slovik
    '74
Heart of a Champion: The Ray
    Mancini Story '85
Skeezer '82

Ward Costello
The City '76
The Gallant Hours '60
MacArthur '77

Nicholas Coster
Betsy's Wedding '90
The Electric Horseman '79
MacArthur '77
The Solitary Man '82
The Sporting Club '72
Stir Crazy '80

George Costigan
The Hawk '93
Rita, Sue & Bob Too '87

Kevin Costner
Amazing Stories '85
American Flyers '85
The Bodyguard '92
Bull Durham '88
Chasing Dreams '81
Dances with Wolves '90
Fandango '85
Field of Dreams '89
The Gunrunner '84
JFK '91
Night Shift '82
No Way Out '87
A Perfect World '93
Revenge '90
Robin Hood: Prince of Thieves
    '91
Shadows Run Black '84
Silverado '85
Sizzle Beach U.S.A. '86
Stacy's Knights '83
Table for Five '83
Testament '83
The Untouchables '87
Wyatt Earp '94

Kami Cotler
Children's Carol '80
A Day for Thanks on Walton's
    Mountain '82
The Waltons: A Thanksgiving
    Story '73

Joseph Cotten
The Abominable Dr. Phibes '71
Airport '77 '77
Beyond the Forest '49
The Big Push '75
Brighty of the Grand Canyon
    '67
Casino '80
Churchill and the Generals '81
Citizen Kane '41
Delusion '84
Duel in the Sun '46
The Farmer's Daughter '47
From the Earth to the Moon '58
Gaslight '44
The Hearse '80
Heaven's Gate '81
Hellbenders '67
Hush, Hush, Sweet Charlotte
    '65
Journey into Fear '42
Lady Frankenstein '72
The Lindbergh Kidnapping
    Case '76
Lydia '41
The Magnificent Ambersons
    '42
Niagara '52
The Oscar '66
Othello '52
The Passing of Evil '70
Perfect Crime '78
Petulia '68
Portrait of Jennie '48
Return to Fantasy Island '77
Screamers '80
September Affair '50
Shadow of a Doubt '43
Since You Went Away '44

Soylent Green '73
Survivor '80
The Third Man '49
Tora! Tora! Tora! '70
Torture Chamber of Baron
    Blood '66
Tramplers '66
Twilight's Last Gleaming '77
Under Capricorn '49
Walk Softly, Stranger '50
White Comanche '67

Fanny Cottencon
Special Police '85
Window Shopping '86

Catherine Cotter
Outlaws of the Range '36
Pinto Rustlers '36

Ralph Cotterill
Burke & Wills '85
Howling 3: The Marsupials '87
Starship '87

Oliver Cotton
Christopher Columbus: The
    Discovery '85
Eleni '85
Robin Hood...The Legend:
    Herne's Son '85

Paul Coufos
Boxcar Blues '90
Busted Up '86
City of Shadows '86
Dragonfight '92
Food of the Gods: Part 2 '88
The Lost Empire '83
Thunderground '89

George Coulouris
Arabesque '66
Citizen Kane '41
Doctor in the House '53
The Lady in Question '40
The Long Good Friday '79
Master Race '44
Mr. Skeffington '44
Murder on the Orient Express
    '74
None But the Lonely Heart '44
Papillon '73
Race for Life '55
The Runaway Bus '54
The Skull '65
A Song to Remember '45
A Southern Yankee '48
The Stranger '73
The Tempter '74
This Land is Mine '43
Tower of Evil '72
Watch on the Rhine '43

Bernie Coulson
The Accused '88
Adventures in Spying '92
Eddie and the Cruisers 2: Eddie
    Lives! '89

**Country Joe & the
Fish**
Woodstock '70
Zachariah '70

Nicole Courcel
Le Cas du Dr. Laurent '57
Sundays & Cybele '62

Hazel Court
The Curse of Frankenstein '57
Dear Murderer '47
Devil Girl from Mars '54
Doctor Blood's Coffin '60
Ghost Ship '52
Hour of Decision '57
Masque of the Red Death '65
Masque of the Red Death/
    Premature Burial '65
Premature Burial '62
The Raven '63

Jason Court
Grandview U.S.A. '84
A Night in the Life of Jimmy
    Reardon '88

Tom Courtenay
Billy Liar '63
Catch Me a Spy '71
Dandy in Aspic '68
Doctor Zhivago '65
The Dresser '83
Happy New Year '87
I Heard the Owl Call My Name
    '73

King Rat '65
Leonard Part 6 '87
Let Him Have It '91
The Loneliness of the Long
    Distance Runner '62
Night of the Generals '67
One Day in the Life of Ivan
    Denisovich '71
Operation Crossbow '65

Jerome Courtland
Battleground '49
Man from Colorado '49
The Texas Rangers '51
Tharus Son of Attila '87
Tokyo Joe '49
Tonka '58

Alex Courtney
Enter the Ninja '81
Fatal Pulse '88

Chuck Courtney
Billy the Kid Versus Dracula '66
Meteor Monster '57

Inez Courtney
Let's Sing Again '36
The Reckless Way '36
Suzy '26
The Thirteenth Man '37

Brian Cousins
Invisible: The Chronicles of
    Benjamin Knight '93
Longtime Companion '90
Mandroid '93

Jerome Cowan
Blondie Hits the Jackpot '49
Blondie Knows Best '46
Fog '45
The Great Lie '41
June Bride '48
The Maltese Falcon '41
The Perfect Marriage '46
Riff-Raff '47
The Saint Strikes Back '39
Silver Spurs '43
The West Point Story '50
Who Done It? '42

Noel Coward
Hearts of the World '18
In Which We Serve '43
The Italian Job '69
Paris When It Sizzles '64

Bruce Cowling
Battleground '49
Cause for Alarm '51
The Painted Hills '51
The Stratton Story '49

Nicola Cowper
Dreamchild '85
Journey to the Center of the
    Earth '88
Lionheart '87
Transmutations '85
Winter Flight '84

Brian Cox
Hidden Agenda '90
In Celebration '75
The Lost Language of Cranes
    '92
Manhunter '86
Murder by Moonlight '91
Pope John Paul II '84
Secret Weapon '90
Silent Scream '84

Courteney Cox
Ace Ventura: Pet Detective '93
Battling for Baby '92
Blue Desert '91
Cocoon: The Return '88
Curiosity Kills '90
Down Twisted '89
Masters of the Universe '87
Misfits of Science '85
Mr. Destiny '90
The Opposite Sex and How to
    Live With Them '93
The Prize Pulitzer '89
Shaking the Tree '92

Mitch Cox
A.P.E.X. '94
Red Snow '91

Richard Cox
King of the Mountain '81
Street Justice '89
The Vindicator '85
Zombie High '87

Ronny Cox
The Abduction of Kari Swenson '87
The Beast Within '82
Beverly Hills Cop '84
Beverly Hills Cop 2 '87
Bound for Glory '76
Captain America '89
The Connection '73
Deliverance '72
Fallen Angel '81
The FBI Murders '88
Gray Lady Down '77
Harper Valley P.T.A. '78
Hollywood Vice Sqaud '86
Kavik the Wolf Dog '84
Last Song '80
Loose Cannons '90
Lost Legacy: A Girl Called Hatter Fox '77
Martians Go Home! '90
Mind Snatchers '72
One Man Force '89
The Onion Field '79
Our Town '77
Raw Courage '84
Reckless Disregard '84
RoboCop '87
Scandal in a Small Town '88
Scissors '91
Some Kind of Hero '82
Steele Justice '87
Tangiers '83
Taps '81
Target: Favorite Son '87
Total Recall '90
Two of a Kind '82
Vision Quest '85
When Hell Was in Session '82
Who Is the Black Dahlia? '75

Ruth Cox
The Attic '80
Swap Meet '79

Wally Cox
The Barefoot Executive '71
Bedford Incident '65
The Boatniks '70
Morituri '65
The One and Only, Genuine, Original Family Band '68
Spencer's Mountain '63
State Fair '62

Peter Coyote
Baja Oklahoma '87
Best Kept Secrets '88
Bitter Moon '92
The Blue Yonder '86
Crooked Hearts '91
Cross Creek '83
Die Laughing '80
Echoes in the Darkness '87
Endangered Species '82
E.T.: The Extra-Terrestrial '82
Exposure '91
Heart of Midnight '89
Heartbreakers '84
Hitchhiker 2 '85
The Jagged Edge '85
Keeper of the City '92
Legend of Billie Jean '85
A Man in Love '87
The Man Inside '90
Out '88
Outrageous Fortune '87
The People vs. Jean Harris '81
Slayground '84
Southern Comfort '81
Stacking '87
Strangers Kiss '83
Tell Me a Riddle '80
Timerider '83

Buster Crabbe
Alien Dead '85
Arizona Raiders '65
Billy the Kid Trapped '42
Border Badmen '45
Buck Rogers Conquers the Universe '39
Buffalo Stampede '33
Desert Gold '36
Destination Saturn '39
Devil Riders '44
Drift Fence '36
Flash Gordon Conquers the Universe '40
Flash Gordon: Mars Attacks the World '38
Flash Gordon: Rocketship '36

Forlorn River '37
Frontier Outlaws '44
Gangster's Den '45
His Brother's Ghost '45
Jungle Siren '42
King of the Congo '52
The Last of the Redmen '47
Law and Order '42
Lightning Raiders '45
The Mysterious Rider '42
Nabonga '44
Oath of Vengeance '44
The Original Flash Gordon Collection '91
Outlaw of the Plains '46
Pirates of the High Seas '50
Prairie Badmen '46
Red Barry '38
Rocketship '36
Rustler's Hideout '44
Sea Hound '47
Shadows of Death '45
Space Soldiers Conquer the Universe '40
Swamp Fire '46
Swim Team '79
Tarzan the Fearless '33
Thundering Gunslingers '40
To the Last Man '33
Western Double Feature 7: Wild Bill & Crabbe '45
Wild Horse Phantom '44
Wildcat '42

Ruth Cracknell
Alice to Nowhere '86
Island Trader '71

Diane Craig
All the Rivers Run '84
The Mango Tree '77
Ned Kelly '70
Roses Bloom Twice '77

Helen Craig
The Snake Pit '48
They Live by Night '49

James Craig
Cyclops '56
The Devil & Daniel Webster '41
The Devil's Brigade '68
Drums in the Deep South '51
The Human Comedy '43
Kitty Foyle '40
Man or Gun '58
Naked in the Sun '57
Our Vines Have Tender Grapes '45
Seven Miles from Alcatraz/ Flight from Glory '43
The Tormentors '80s
Valley of the Sun '42
Winners of the West '40

Michael Craig
Escape 2000 '81
Inn of the Damned '74
The Irishman '78
Lola '82
Mysterious Island '61
Night of the Assassin '77
Ride a Wild Pony '75
Robin Hood...The Legend: Herne's Son '85
Roses Bloom Twice '77
Sapphire '59
The Silent Enemy '58
Star! '68
Stolen Hours '63
Vault of Horror '73

Yvonne Craig
Digging Up Business '91
It Happened at the World's Fair '63
Kissin' Cousins '64
Mars Needs Women '66

Jeanne Crain
Fastest Gun Alive '56
A Letter to Three Wives '49
Man Without a Star '55
Nefertiti, Queen of the Nile '64
The Night God Screamed '80s
People Will Talk '51
Pinky '49
State Fair '45

Grant Cramer
Hardbodies '84
Killer Klowns from Outer Space '88

Joey Cramer
Flight of the Navigator '86
Stone Fox '87

Marc Cramer
First Yank into Tokyo '45
Isle of the Dead '45

Richard Cramer
The Fatal Glass of Beer '33
Frontier Justice '35
Santa Fe Bound '37
Saps at Sea '40
Speed Reporter '36

Barbara Crampton
Body Double '84
Chopping Mall '86
Fraternity Vacation '85
From Beyond '86
Kidnapped '87
Puppet Master '89
The Re-Animator '85
Robot Wars '93
Trancers 2: The Return of Jack Deth '91

Bob Crane
Gus '76
Return to Peyton Place '61
Superdad '73

Norma Crane
Fiddler on the Roof '71
Tea and Sympathy '56
They Call Me Mr. Tibbs! '70

Richard Crane
The Devil's Partner '58
Dynamite '49
Guns Don't Argue '57
Winning of the West '53

Kenneth Cranham
Brother Sun, Sister Moon '73
Chocolat '88
Danger UXB '81
Hellbound: Hellraiser 2 '88
Monkey Boy '90
Prospero's Books '91
Stealing Heaven '88
Tale of a Vampire '92
Under Suspicion '92

Nick Cravat
Crimson Pirate '52
The Flame & the Arrow '50
The Scalphunters '68

Frank Craven
City for Conquest '40
Dreaming Out Loud '40
In This Our Life '42
Jack London '44
Our Town '40
Pittsburgh '42
Son of Dracula '43

James Craven
D-Day on Mars '45
Green Archer '40
Sherlock Holmes and the Secret Weapon '42
Today I Hang '42

Matt Craven
Agent on Ice '86
Chattahoochee '89
A Few Good Men '92
Happy Birthday to Me '81
Indian Summer '93
Jacob's Ladder '90
K2: The Ultimate High '92
Palais Royale '88
Smokescreen '90
Till Death Do Us Part '72

Andrew Crawford
Dear Murderer '47
The Gay Lady '49

Anne Crawford
Knights of the Round Table '53
Night Beat '48
Tony Draws a Horse '51

Broderick Crawford
All the King's Men '49
Between Heaven and Hell '56
Born Yesterday '50
The Castilian '63
Dark Forces '83
Embassy '72
Eternally Yours '39
Express to Terror '79
Fastest Gun Alive '56
Goliath and the Dragon '61
Human Desire '54

Hunter '77
I Married a Witch '42
Last of the Comanches '52
A Little Romance '79
Lone Star '52
Not as a Stranger '55
The Oscar '66
The Private Files of J. Edgar Hoover '77
Proof of the Man '84
Ransom Money '88
The Real Glory '39
Seven Sinners '40
Slightly Honorable '40
The Swindle '55
The Tattered Web '71
Terror in the Wax Museum '73
The Time of Your Life '48
Upper Crust '88
Vulture '67
Yin & Yang of Mr. Go '71

H. Marion Crawford
The Castle of Fu Manchu '68
Kiss and Kill '68
Man on the Run '49

Joan Crawford
Above Suspicion '43
Autumn Leaves '56
Berserk! '67
The Bride Wore Red '37
Chained '34
Dance Fools Dance '31
Dancing Lady '33
Fatal Confinement '64
Flamingo Road '49
Forsaking All Others '35
The Gorgeous Hussy '36
Grand Hotel '32
Hollywood Canteen '44
Hollywood Outtakes & Rare Footage '83
Humoresque '46
I Live My Life '35
It's a Great Feeling '49
Johnny Guitar '53
Kings, Queens, Jokers '30s
The Last of Mrs. Cheyney '37
Laughing Sinners '31
The Lost Stooges '33
Love on the Run '36
Mannequin '37
Mildred Pierce '45
Night Gallery '69
Our Dancing Daughters '28
Our Modern Maidens '29
Possessed '31
The Possessed '47
Rain '32
Reunion in France '42
Sadie McKee '34
The Shining Hour '38
Strait-Jacket '64
Strange Cargo '40
Susan and God '40
Today We Live '33
Torch Song '53
The Unknown '27
What Ever Happened to Baby Jane? '62
When Ladies Meet '41
A Woman's Face '41
The Women '39

John Crawford
Hard Knocks
The Invisible Monster '50
John Paul Jones '59
Red Line 7000 '65
The Severed Arm '73
Zombies of the Stratosphere '52

Johnny Crawford
Black Beauty/Courage of Black Beauty '57
Courage of Black Beauty '57
El Dorado '67
The Gambler Returns: The Luck of the Draw '93
The Great Texas Dynamite Chase '76
Indian Paint '64
Kenny Rogers as the Gambler, Part 2: The Adventure Continues '83
Outlaw Blues '77
Village of the Giants '65

Katherine Crawford
The Doomsday Flight '66
Riding with Death '76

Walk in the Spring Rain '70

Kathryn Crawford
The Concentratin' Kid '30
King of the Rodeo '28
Mountain Justice '30

Michael Crawford
Condorman '81
A Funny Thing Happened on the Way to the Forum '66
Hello, Dolly! '69
How I Won the War '67
The Knack '65

Wayne Crawford
Barracuda '78
Crime Lords '91
The Evil Below '87
Headhunter '89
Jake Speed '86
Quiet Thunder '87
Rebel Storm '90
White Ghost '88

Laird Cregar
Heaven Can Wait '43
Hello, Frisco, Hello '43
I Wake Up Screaming '41
Joan of Paris '42
The Lodger '44
This Gun for Hire '42

Joseph Crehan
Hands Across the Border '43
Meeting at Midnight '44
Music in My Heart '40
Night Time in Nevada '48
Red Desert '50
Stanley and Livingstone '39
Star Reporter '39

Francis Creighton
Barcelona '94
The Malibu Beach Vampires '91

Bruno Cremer
Is Paris Burning? '68
Josepha '82
Menage '86
A Simple Story '79
Sorcerer '77
The 317th Platoon '65

Richard Crenna
Body Heat '81
Breakheart Pass '76
Broken Badge '85
A Case of Deadly Force '86
Catlow '71
Death Ship '80
Devil Dog: The Hound of Hell '78
Doctors' Wives '70
The Evil '78
First Blood '82
The Flamingo Kid '84
The Hillside Strangler '89
Hot Shots! Part Deux '93
Intruders '92
Last Flight Out: A True Story '90
Leviathan '89
Marooned '69
Montana '90
On Wings of Eagles '86
Our Miss Brooks '56
Pride of St. Louis '52
Rambo: First Blood, Part 2 '85
Rambo 3 '88
Ride to Glory '71
The Sand Pebbles '66
Star! '68
Stone Cold Dead '80
Summer Rental '85
Table for Five '83
Thief '71
Wait Until Dark '67
War Between the Tates '76
Wild Horse Hank '79

Laura Hope Crews
Camille '36
Gone with the Wind '39
The Rains Came '39

Wendy Crewson
Buffalo Jump '90
Corrina, Corrina '94
The Doctor '91
Folks! '92
The Good Son '93
Hobo's Christmas '87
Mark of Cain '84
Mazes and Monsters '82

Skullduggery '79
Spies, Lies and Naked Thighs '91

Bernard Cribbins
The Adventures of Picasso '80
Railway Children '70
The Wrong Arm of the Law '63

Ed Crick
Eye of the Eagle '87
Future Hunters '88

Lawrence Criner
Gang War '40
Miracle in Harlem '48

Donald Crisp
The Adventures of Mark Twain '44
Beloved Enemy '36
The Birth of a Nation '15
The Black Pirate '26
Broken Blossoms '19
Brother Orchid '40
Challenge to Lassie '49
The Charge of the Light Brigade '36
City for Conquest '40
Dawn Patrol '38
Dr. Jekyll and Mr. Hyde '41
A Dog of Flanders '59
Greyfriars Bobby '61
The Hills of Home '48
Home Sweet Home '14
Home Town Story '51
How Green was My Valley '41
Jezebel '38
Knute Rockne: All American '40
Lassie, Come Home '43
Last Hurrah '58
Little Minister '34
The Long Gray Line '55
The Man from Laramie '55
Mutiny on the Bounty '35
National Velvet '44
Oklahoma Kid '39
The Old Maid '39
Pollyanna '60
Prince Valiant '54
The Private Lives of Elizabeth & Essex '39
Ramrod '47
Red Dust '32
The Sea Hawk '40
The Sisters '38
Son of Lassie '45
Spencer's Mountain '63
Stand and Deliver '28
Svengali '31
That Certain Woman '37
The Uninvited '44
The Valley of Decision '45
A Woman Rebels '36
Wuthering Heights '39

Linda Cristal
The Dead Don't Die '75
Hughes & Harlow: Angels in Hell '77
Midnight Auto Supply '78
Mr. Majestyk '74
Perfect Furlough '59
Two Rode Together '61

Perla Cristal
The Christmas Kid '68
The Fury of the Wolfman '70
White Comanche '67
A Witch Without a Broom '68

Criswell
Night of the Ghouls '59
Orgy of the Dead '65

Karlene Crockett
Eyes of Fire '84
Massive Retaliation '85
Return '88

Peter Croft
King of the Damned '36
O.H.M.S. '37

Jonathan Crombie
Anne of Avonlea '87
Anne of Green Gables '85
Bullies '86
Cafe Romeo '91
The Good Fight '92
The Housekeeper '86

James Cromwell
The Babe '92
A Christmas Without Snow '80
Romeo Is Bleeding '93

Sprague '84

Richard Cromwell
Baby Face Morgan '42
The Lives of a Bengal Lancer '35
Riot Squad '41
The Strange Love of Molly Louvain '32
The Wrong Road '37
Young Mr. Lincoln '39

Claudia Cron
Hit & Run '82
Running Brave '83

Laurel Cronin
Beethoven '92
Housesitter '92

Hume Cronyn
Age Old Friends '89
The Arrangement '69
*batteries not included '87
Brewster's Millions '85
Broadway Bound '92
Camilla '94
Cleopatra '63
Cocoon '85
Cocoon: The Return '88
Conrack '74
Day One '89
A Doll's House '59
Foxfire '87
Gin Game '84
Honky Tonk Freeway '81
Impulse '84
Lifeboat '44
Parallax View '74
People Will Talk '51
The Phantom of the Opera '43
The Postman Always Rings Twice '46
Rollover '81
The Seventh Cross '44
Shadow of a Doubt '43
Sunrise at Campobello '60
There was a Crooked Man '70
To Dance with the White Dog '93
The World According to Garp '82
Ziegfeld Follies '46

Tandy Cronyn
Age Old Friends '89
Twisted '86

Leland Crooke
Dead Man Walking '88
Scorchers '92

Annette Crosbie
Ordeal by Innocence '84
Six Wives of Henry VIII '70s

Bing Crosby
The Bells of St. Mary's '45
A Connecticut Yankee in King Arthur's Court '49
Country Girl '54
Going Hollywood '33
Going My Way '44
Here Comes the Groom '51
High Society '56
Holiday Inn '42
Hollywood Goes to War '54
Just for You '52
King of Jazz '30
Let's Make Love '60
Mr. Music '50
My Favorite Brunette '47
Reaching for the Moon '31
The Road to Bali '53
The Road to Hong Kong '62
The Road to Lebanon '60
The Road to Morocco '42
The Road to Rio '47
The Road to Singapore '40
The Road to Utopia '46
The Road to Zanzibar '41
Robin and the Seven Hoods '64
Strictly G.I. '44
That's Entertainment '74
White Christmas '54

Cathy Crosby
El Cuarto Chino '71
Girls' Town '59

Cathy Lee Crosby
Coach '78
The Dark '79
Roughnecks '80
World War III '86

David Crosby
Backdraft '91
Thunderheart '92
Woodstock '70

Denise Crosby
Arizona Heat '87
Curse of the Pink Panther '83
Desert Hearts '86
Desperate Crimes '93
Dolly Dearest '92
The Eliminators '86
48 Hrs. '82
Miracle Mile '89
Pet Sematary '89
Red Shoe Diaries 2: Double Dare '92
Skin Deep '89
Star Trek the Next Generation: Encounter at Farpoint '87

Gary Crosby
Chill Factor '90
Girl Happy '65
Justin Morgan Had a Horse '81
Music Shoppe '82
Night Stalker '87

Lucinda Crosby
Blue Movies '88
Naked Cage '86

Mary Crosby
The Berlin Conspiracy '91
Body Chemistry '90
Corporate Affairs '90
Deadly Innocence '88
Desperate Motives '92
Eating '90
Ice Pirates '84
Last Plane Out '83
Quicker Than the Eye '88
Stagecoach '86
Tapeheads '89

Henrietta Crosman
Charlie Chan's Secret '35
Personal Property '37

Ben Cross
The Assisi Underground '84
Chariots of Fire '81
Cold Sweat '93
Coming Out of the Ice '82
Diamond Fleece '92
The Far Pavilions '84
The Flame Trees of Thika '80s
The Jeweller's Shop '90
Live Wire '92
Nightlife '89
Paperhouse '89
Steal the Sky '88
The Unholy '88

Dennis Cross
Crime of Passion '57
How to Make a Monster '58

Harley Cross
The Believers '87
Cohen and Tate '88
The Fly 2 '89
Stanley and Iris '90
To Dance with the White Dog '93
Where Are the Children? '85

Syd Crossley
The Deputy Drummer '35
That Certain Thing '28

Scatman Crothers
Between Heaven and Hell '56
Black Belt Jones '74
Bloody Mama '70
Bronco Billy '80
Chesty Anderson USN '76
Deadly Eyes '82
Detroit 9000 '73
The Great White Hope '70
The Journey of Natty Gann '85
The King of Marvin Gardens '72
Lady in a Cage '64
Mean Dog Blues '78
One Flew Over the Cuckoo's Nest '75
The Patsy '64
Scavenger Hunt '79
The Shining '80
The Shootist '76
The Silver Streak '76
Stay Hungry '76
Streetfight '75
Truck Turner '74

Twilight Zone: The Movie '83
Two of a Kind '83
Yes, Sir, Mr. Bones '51
Zapped! '82

Lindsay Crouse
All the President's Men '76
Being Human '94
Between the Lines '77
Chantilly Lace '93
Communion '89
Daniel '83
Desperate Hours '90
Eleanor & Franklin '76
House of Games '87
Iceman '84
Paul's Case '80
Places in the Heart '84
Prince of the City '81
Slap Shot '77
Summer Solstice '81
The Verdict '82

Emilia Crow
Grand Tour: Disaster in Time '92
Hitz '92

Graham Crowden
Britannia Hospital '82
Code Name: Emerald '85
The Company of Wolves '85
If... '69
Monsignor Quixote '91
Naughty Knights '71
Out of Africa '85
Romance with a Double Bass '74

Russell Crowe
The Crossing '92
The Efficiency Expert '92
Proof '91
The Quick and the Dead '94
Romper Stomper '92
The Silver Stallion: King of the Wild Brumbies '94

Josephine Crowell
The Greatest Question '19
Hearts of the World '18
The Man Who Laughs '27

Kathleen Crowley
The Female Jungle '56
The Rebel Set '59
Westward Ho, the Wagons! '56

Pat Crowley
Force of Evil '77
Forever Female '53
Hollywood or Bust '56
Red Garters '54
Return to Fantasy Island '77
Wild Women of Wongo '59

Tom Cruise
All the Right Moves '83
Born on the Fourth of July '89
Cocktail '88
The Color of Money '86
Days of Thunder '90
Endless Love '81
Far and Away '92
A Few Good Men '92
The Firm '93
Legend '86
Losin' It '82
The Outsiders '83
Rain Man '88
Risky Business '83
Taps '81
Top Gun '86

Rosalie Crutchley
Creatures the World Forgot '70
Eleni '85
The Franchise Affair
The Hunchback of Notre Dame '82
Make Me an Offer '55
Monsignor Quixote '91
Night of the Laughing Dead '75
Six Wives of Henry VIII '70s
Wuthering Heights '70

Abigail Cruttenden
Intimate Contact '87
Kipperbang '82

Penelope Cruz
Belle Epoque '92
Jamon, Jamon '93

Raymond Cruz
Clear and Present Danger '94
Vietnam War Story 3 '89

Jon Cryer
Dudes '87
Heads '93
Hiding Out '87
Hot Shots! '91
Morgan Stewart's Coming Home '87
No Small Affair '84
Noon Wine '84
O.C. and Stiggs '87
Pretty in Pink '86
Rap Master Ronnie '88
Superman 4: The Quest for Peace '87

Billy Crystal
Best of Comic Relief '86
Billy Crystal: A Comic's Line '83
Billy Crystal: Don't Get Me Started '86
Billy Crystal: Midnight Train to Moscow '89
Breaking Up Is Hard to Do '79
City Slickers '91
City Slickers 2: The Legend of Curly's Gold '94
Enola Gay: The Men, the Mission, the Atomic Bomb '80
Memories of Me '88
Mr. Saturday Night '92
The Princess Bride '87
Rabbit Test '78
Running Scared '86
The Three Little Pigs '84
Throw Momma from the Train '87
When Harry Met Sally '89

Gyorgy Cserhalmi
Hungarian Rhapsody '78
Mephisto '81

Enrique Cuenca
El Aviso Inoportuno '87
Hijazo de Mi Vidaza '70s

Xavier Cugat
A Date with Judy '48
Holiday in Mexico '46
Neptune's Daughter '49
Two Girls and a Sailor '44
You Were Never Lovelier '42

Kieran Culkin
Father of the Bride '91
Home Alone '90
Home Alone 2: Lost in New York '92
It Runs in the Family '94
Nowhere to Run '93

Macaulay Culkin
George Balanchine's The Nutcracker '93
Getting Even with Dad '94
The Good Son '93
Home Alone '90
Home Alone 2: Lost in New York '92
Jacob's Ladder '90
My Girl '91
Only the Lonely '91
Rocket Gibraltar '88
See You in the Morning '89
Uncle Buck '89

Brett Cullen
Dead Solid Perfect '88
In a Stranger's Hand '92
Leaving Normal '92
Prehysteria '93

Max Cullen
Hard Knocks '82
Lightning Jack '94

John Cullum
Ambition '91
Glory '89
Marie '85
Morgan Stewart's Coming Home '87
The Prodigal '83
Sweet Country '87

Joseph Culp
The Arrival '90
Dream Lover '85

Robert Culp
Big Bad Mama 2 '87
The Blue Lightning '86
Bob & Carol & Ted & Alice '69
Calendar Girl Murders '84
The Castaway Cowboy '74

Culp ►cont.

Demon with a Glass Hand '64
Flood! '90
The Gladiator '86
Goldengirl '79
Great Scout & Cathouse Thursday '76
Hannie Caulder '72
Her Life as a Man '83
Hot Rod '79
Inside Out '75
The Key to Rebecca '85
Killjoy '81
Murderous Vision '91
A Name for Evil '70
The Night the City Screamed '80
The Pelican Brief '93
PT 109 '63
Pucker Up and Bark Like a Dog '89
Sammy, the Way-Out Seal '62
Silent Night, Deadly Night 3: Better Watch Out! '89
Sky Riders '76
Timebomb '91
Turk 182! '85
Voyage of Terror: The Achille Lauro Affair '90

Michael Culver
Alamut Ambush '86
Conduct Unbecoming '75
Deadly Recruits '86
The Devil's Web '74
Fast Kill '73
The Green Man '91
Philby, Burgess and MacLean: Spy Scandal of the Century '84

Roland Culver
Betrayed '54
The Day Will Dawn '42
Dead of Night '45
Down to Earth '47
Encore '52
The Great Lover '49
The Obsessed '51
On Approval '44

Dorothy Cumming
Applause '29
King of Kings '27
The Wind '28

Constance Cummings
The Battle of the Sexes '60
Blithe Spirit '45
Criminal Code '31
The Foreman Went to France '42
Night After Night '32

Irving Cummings
The Saphead '21
Sex '20
Uncle Tom's Cabin '14

Quinn Cummings
The Babysitter '80
The Goodbye Girl '77
Intimate Strangers '77
Night Terror '76

Robert Cummings
The Accused '48
Arizona Mahoney '36
Beach Party '63
The Carpetbaggers '64
The Chase '46
Desert Gold '36
The Devil & Miss Jones '41
Dial ''M'' for Murder '54
Everything Happens at Night '39
Five Golden Dragons '67
Forever and a Day '43
Kings Row '41
Lost Moment '47
Lucky Me '54
Moon Over Miami '41
My Geisha '62
One Night in the Tropics '40
Promise Her Anything '66
Reign of Terror '49
Saboteur '42
Tell It to the Judge '49

Susan Cummings
Swamp Women '55
Verboten! '59

Eli Cummins
Dakota '88
Harley '90

Greg Cummins
Action U.S.A. '89
Caged Fury '90
Dead End City '88

Juliette Cummins
Deadly Dreams '88
Friday the 13th, Part 5: A New Beginning '85
Running Hot '83
Slumber Party Massacre 2 '87

Peggy Cummins
The Captain's Table '60
Carry On Admiral '57
Curse of the Demon '57
Gun Crazy '49
Salute John Citizen '42

Peter Cummins
Blue Fire Lady '78
Ground Zero '88

Liam Cundill
Reason to Die '90
Return of the Family Man '80

John Cunningham
Lost and Found '79
Twisted '86

Peter ''Sugarfoot'' Cunningham
Bloodfist 3: Forced to Fight '92
Bloodmatch '91

Alain Cuny
Basileus Quartet '82
Camille Claudel '89
Christ Stopped at Eboli '79
Emmanuelle '74
La Dolce Vita '60
Les Visiteurs du Soir '42
The Lovers '59
The Milky Way '68

Barbara Cupisti
Stagefright '87
Terror at the Opera '88

Lynette Curran
Bliss '85
The Year My Voice Broke '87

Cherie Currie
Foxes '80
Parasite '81
Rosebud Beach Hotel '85
Twilight Zone: The Movie '83
Wavelength '83

Finlay Currie
The Adventures of Huckleberry Finn '60
Ben-Hur '59
Big Deadly Game '54
Billy Liar '63
Bonnie Prince Charlie '48
Corridors of Blood '58
The Day Will Dawn '42
Edge of the World '37
The Forty-Ninth Parallel '41
Great Expectations '46
I Know Where I'm Going '45
Ivanhoe '52
The King's Rhapsody '55
Make Me an Offer '55
People Will Talk '51
Quo Vadis '51
Sleeping Car to Trieste '45
Stars and Stripes Forever '52
Treasure Island '50
Trio '50

Louise Currie
The Adventures of Captain Marvel '41
The Bashful Bachelor '42
The Masked Marvel '43
Million Dollar Kid '44
Wild West '46

Michael Currie
The Dead Pool '88
Pray TV '82

Sondra Currie
The Concrete Jungle '82
Jessie's Girls '75
Mama's Dirty Girls '74
Policewomen '73
Runaways '84

Tim Curry
Annie '82
Blue Money '84
Clue '85
Home Alone 2: Lost in New York '92
The Hunt for Red October '90
Legend '86
National Lampoon's Loaded Weapon 1 '93
Oliver Twist '82
Pass the Ammo '88
Passed Away '92
The Ploughman's Lunch '83
The Rocky Horror Picture Show '75
The Shadow '94
The Shout '78
Stephen King's It '90
The Three Musketeers '93
Times Square '80
The Worst Witch '86

Jane Curtin
Coneheads '93
How to Beat the High Cost of Living '80
Mr. Mike's Mondo Video '79
O.C. and Stiggs '87
Suspicion '87

Valerie Curtin
Big Trouble '86
A Christmas Without Snow '80
Different Story '78
Down and Out in Beverly Hills '86
Maxie '85

Alan Curtis
Apache Chief '50
Buck Privates '41
Flight to Nowhere '46
Gung Ho! '43
The Invisible Man's Revenge '44
Last Outlaw '36
Mannequin '37
Melody Master '41
The Naughty Nineties '45
Renegade Girl '46
Shopworn Angel '38

Dick Curtis
Billy the Kid '41
Boothill Brigade '37
Government Agents vs. Phantom Legion '51
A Lawman is Born '37
Motel Hell '80
Racing Luck '35
Valley of Terror '38

Donald Curtis
The Amazing Mr. X '48
Criminals Within '41
Earth vs. the Flying Saucers '56
It Came from Beneath the Sea '55
Seventh Cavalry '56
Son of Lassie '45

Vondie Curtis-Hall
Coming to America '88
Crooklyn '94
Fallen Angels 2 '93
Falling Down '93
In a Stranger's Hand '92
The Mambo Kings '92
Passion Fish '92
Sugar Hill '94

Jamie Lee Curtis
The Adventures of Buckaroo Banzai Across the Eighth Dimension '84
Amazing Grace & Chuck '87
Annie Oakley '85
As Summers Die '86
Blue Steel '90
Death of a Centerfold '81
Dominick & Eugene '88
Film House Fever '86
A Fish Called Wanda '88
The Fog '79
Forever Young '92
Grandview U.S.A. '84
Halloween '78
Halloween 2: The Nightmare Isn't Over! '81
Love Letters '83
A Man in Love '87
Mother's Boys '94
My Girl '91

My Girl 2 '94
Perfect '85
Prom Night '80
Queens Logic '91
Road Games '81
She's in the Army Now '81
Terror Train '80
Trading Places '83
True Lies '94

Keene Curtis
The Buddy System '83
Sliver '93
Strange New World '75

Ken Curtis
California Gold Rush '81
Call of the Forest '49
Conagher '91
Don Daredevil Rides Again '51
The Killer Shrews '59
Lost '83
Mister Roberts '55
Pony Express Rider '76
The Quiet Man '52
Texas Guns '90
Wings of Eagles '57

Liane Curtis
Critters 2: The Main Course '88
Girlfriend from Hell '89
Hard Choices '84
Sixteen Candles '84
Wild Orchid 2: Two Shades of Blue '92

Robin Curtis
Star Trek 3: The Search for Spock '84
The Unborn 2 '94

Tony Curtis
Arrivederci, Baby! '66
The Bad News Bears Go to Japan '78
Balboa '82
Boeing Boeing '65
The Boston Strangler '68
Brainwaves '82
Captain Newman, M.D. '63
The Cary Grant Collection '90
Center of the Web '92
Christmas in Connecticut '92
Club Life '86
The Count of Monte Cristo '74
Criss Cross '49
The Defiant Ones '58
Five Miles to Midnight '80
Francis the Talking Mule '49
The Great Impostor '61
Great Race '65
Houdini '53
Insignificance '85
It Rained All Night the Day I Left '78
Kings Go Forth '58
The Last of Philip Banter '87
The Last Tycoon '76
Lepke '75
Little Miss Marker '80
Lobster Man from Mars '89
Mafia Princess '86
The Manitou '78
Midnight '89
The Mirror Crack'd '80
Mission: Monte Carlo '75
Naked in New York '93
Operation Petticoat '59
Overture '75
Paris When It Sizzles '64
Perfect Furlough '59
The Persuaders '71
Portrait of a Showgirl '82
Prime Target '91
The Rat Race '60
Sex and the Single Girl '64
Sex on the Run '78
Sextette '78
Some Like It Hot '59
Son of Ali Baba '52
Spartacus '60
Suppose They Gave a War and Nobody Came? '70
Sweet Smell of Success '57
Taras Bulba '62
Those Daring Young Men in Their Jaunty Jalopies '69
Title Shot '81
Trapeze '56
Users '78
Vegas '78
The Vikings '58
Winchester '73 '50

George Curzan
Java Head '35
The Living Dead '36

Pierre Curzi
Maria Chapdelaine '84
Pouvoir Intime '87

Cyril Cusack
All the Way, Boys '73
Children of Rage '75
Cry of the Innocent '80
David Copperfield '70
The Day of the Jackal '73
The Elusive Pimpernel '50
Fahrenheit 451 '66
Far and Away '92
Harold and Maude '71
Johnny Nobody '61
King Lear '71
Late Extra '35
Les Miserables '78
Little Dorrit, Film 1: Nobody's Fault '88
Little Dorrit, Film 2: Little Dorrit's Story '88
Lovespell '79
My Left Foot '89
Night Ambush '57
1984 '84
No Comebacks '85
Odd Man Out '47
Sacco & Vanzetti '71
The Small Back Room '49
The Spanish Gardener '57
The Spy Who Came in from the Cold '65
Street War '70s
The Taming of the Shrew '67
The Tenth Man '88
True Confessions '81
Two by Forsyth '86
Waltz of the Toreadors '62

Joan Cusack
Addams Family Values '93
The Allnighter '87
Broadcast News '87
Grandview U.S.A. '84
Hero '92
Married to the Mob '88
Men Don't Leave '89
My Blue Heaven '90
My Bodyguard '80
Say Anything '89
Sixteen Candles '84
Stars and Bars '88
Toys '92
Working Girl '88

John Cusack
Better Off Dead '85
Class '83
Eight Men Out '88
Elvis Stories '89
Fat Man and Little Boy '89
Grandview U.S.A. '84
The Grifters '90
Hot Pursuit '87
The Journey of Natty Gann '85
Map of the Human Heart '93
Money for Nothing '93
One Crazy Summer '86
Say Anything '89
Shadows and Fog '92
Sixteen Candles '84
Stand By Me '86
Stars and Bars '88
The Sure Thing '85
Tapeheads '89
True Colors '91

Sinead Cusack
Bad Behavior '92
Cyrano de Bergerac '85
Revenge '91
Rocket Gibraltar '88
Waterland '92

Peter Cushing
Alexander the Great '55
And Now the Screaming Starts '73
Asylum '72
At the Earth's Core '76
Biggles '85
Black Werewolf '75
Blood Beast Terror '67
The Bloodsuckers '70
The Brides of Dracula '60
Call Him Mr. Shatter '74
Choice of Weapons '76
A Chump at Oxford '40

The Creeping Flesh '72
The Curse of Frankenstein '57
Daleks—Invasion Earth 2150 A.D. '66
The Devil's Undead '75
Doctor Phibes Rises Again '72
Dr. Terror's House of Horrors '65
Doctor Who and the Daleks '65
Dynasty of Fear '72
The Evil of Frankenstein '64
Frankenstein and the Monster from Hell '74
From Beyond the Grave '73
The Ghoul '75
The Gorgon '64
Hamlet '48
The Hellfire Club '61
Horror Express '72
The Horror of Dracula '58
The Hound of the Baskervilles '59
House of the Long Shadows '82
The House that Dripped Blood '71
Island of Terror '66
Island of the Burning Doomed '67
John Paul Jones '59
Land of the Minotaur '77
Legend of the Werewolf '75
Madhouse '74
Mania '60
Masks of Death '86
Moulin Rouge '52
The Mummy '59
The Naked Edge '61
Nothing But the Night '72
The Satanic Rites of Dracula '73
Scream and Scream Again '70
The 7 Brothers Meet Dracula '73
Shock Waves '77
Silent Scream '84
The Skull '65
Star Wars '77
Sword of Sherwood Forest '60
Sword of the Valiant '83
A Tale of Two Cities '80
Tales from the Crypt '72
Top Secret! '84
Torture Garden '67
Twins of Evil '71
The Uncanny '78
The Vampire Lovers '70

Bob Custer
Law of the Wild '34
Mark of the Spur '32

Iain Cuthbertson
Danger UXB '81
Gorillas in the Mist '88
Railway Children '70

Lise Cutter
Buy & Cell '89
Fleshtone '94
Havana '90
Nickel & Dime '92
Shadow Force '92

Zbigniew Cybulski
Ashes and Diamonds '58
A Generation '54

Jon Cypher
Accidents '89
Elvis and Me '88
Food of the Gods '76
Kid and the Killers '80s
Memory of Us '74
Off the Mark '87
Spontaneous Combustion '89
Valdez is Coming '71

Charles Cyphers
Halloween 2: The Nightmare Isn't Over! '81
Major League '89

Henry Czerny
Clear and Present Danger '94
Northern Extremes '93

Chris D
Border Radio '88
No Way Out '87

Howard da Silva
Abe Lincoln in Illinois '40
David and Lisa '62
Garbo Talks '84

The Great Gatsby '74
The Lost Weekend '45
Missiles of October '74
Mommie Dearest '81
Reunion in France '42
The Sea Wolf '41
1776 '72
Smile, Jenny, You're Dead '74
They Live by Night '49
Three Husbands '50
The Underworld Story '50

Augusta Dabney
The Portrait '93
Running on Empty '88
Violets Are Blue '86

Maryam D'Abo
Double Obsession '93
Immortal Sins '91
Leon the Pig Farmer '93
The Living Daylights '87
Nightlife '90
Red Shoe Diaries 3: Another Woman's Lipstick '93
Shootfighter: Fight to the Death '93
Tomcat: Dangerous Desires '93
Tropical Heat '93
Xtro '83

Olivia D'Abo
Beyond the Stars '89
Bolero '84
Bullies '86
Clean Slate '94
Conan the Destroyer '84
Dream to Believe '85
Greedy '94
Into the Fire '88
Midnight's Child '93
Mission to Kill '85
Point of No Return '93
Spirit of '76 '91
Wayne's World 2 '93

Mark Dacascos
American Samurai '92
Only the Strong '93

Andrew Daddo
Body Melt '93
A Kink in the Picasso '90

Willem Dafoe
Body of Evidence '92
Born on the Fourth of July '89
Clear and Present Danger '94
Cry-Baby '90
Faraway, So Close! '93
Flight of the Intruder '90
Hitchhiker 3 '87
The Hunger '83
The Last Temptation of Christ '88
Light Sleeper '92
Loveless '83
Mississippi Burning '88
New York Nights '84
Off Limits '87
Platoon '86
Roadhouse 66 '84
Streets of Fire '84
To Live & Die in L.A. '85
Triumph of the Spirit '89
White Sands '92
Wild at Heart '90

Jean-Michel Dagory
Clowning Around '92
Clowning Around 2 '93

Lil Dagover
The Cabinet of Dr. Caligari '19
Dr. Mabuse the Gambler '22
The Pedestrian '73
Spiders '18
The Strange Countess '61

Arlene Dahl
Here Come the Girls '53
Journey to the Center of the Earth '59
Kisses for My President '64
Land Raiders '69
Night of the Warrior '91
Reign of Terror '49
Slightly Scarlet '56
A Southern Yankee '48
Three Little Words '50
Watch the Birdie '50

Eva Dahlbeck
Brink of Life '57
The Counterfeit Traitor '62
Dreams '55

Lesson in Love '54
Secrets of Women '52
Smiles of a Summer Night '55

Paul Dahlke
The Head '59
The Third Sex '59

Dan Dailey
It's Always Fair Weather '55
Lady Be Good '41
Meet Me in Las Vegas '56
Panama Hattie '42
Pride of St. Louis '52
The Private Files of J. Edgar Hoover '77
There's No Business Like Show Business '54
What Price Glory? '52
Wings of Eagles '57
Ziegfeld Girl '41

Bill Daily
Alligator 2: The Mutation '90
Magic on Love Island '80

Elizabeth Daily
Bad Dreams '88
Fandango '85
Funny Money '82
No Small Affair '84
Pee Wee's Big Adventure '85
Street Music '81
Streets of Fire '84

Esther Dale
The Awful Truth '37
Blondie Has Trouble '40
Curly Top '35
Holiday Affair '49
Ma and Pa Kettle '49
Ma and Pa Kettle at the Fair '52
Ma and Pa Kettle Go to Town '50
On Moonlight Bay '51
A Stolen Life '46

Jennifer Dale
The Adjuster '91
Cadillac Girls '93
Of Unknown Origin '83
Separate Vacations '86
When Angels Fly '82

Jim Dale
The Adventures of Huckleberry Finn '85
Carry On Cleo '65
Carry On Cowboy '66
Carry On Doctor '68
Carry On Screaming '66
Digby, the Biggest Dog in the World '73
Follow That Camel '67
Hot Lead & Cold Feet '78
Joseph Andrews '77
Pete's Dragon '77
Scandalous '84
Unidentified Flying Oddball '79

Virginia Dale
Danger Zone '51
Holiday Inn '42

Fabienne Dali
Erotic Touch of Hot Skin '65
Kill, Baby, Kill '66

David Dalie
Mighty Jungle '64
Virgin Sacrifice '59

Marcel Dalio
Beethoven '36
Can-Can '60
Captain Blackjack '51
Casablanca '42
China Gate '57
Dedee d'Anvers '49
Grand Illusion '37
How Sweet It Is! '68
Lady L '65
Lafayette Escadrille '58
Lovely to Look At '52
Lucky Me '54
The Merry Widow '64
The Monocle '64
Rich, Young and Pretty '51
The Rules of the Game '39
Sabrina '54
The Snows of Kilimanjaro '52
To Have & Have Not '44

John Dall
Atlantis, the Lost Continent '61
The Corn is Green '45
Gun Crazy '49

Rope '48

Charlene Dallas
Criminal Act '88
Rancho Deluxe '75

Beatrice Dalle
Betty Blue '86
La Vengeance d'une Femme '89
Night on Earth '91

Joe Dallesandro
Andy Warhol's Dracula '74
Andy Warhol's Frankenstein '74
The Cotton Club '84
Cry-Baby '90
Double Revenge '89
Flesh '68
Guncrazy '92
Heat '72
The Hollywood Detective '89
Private War '90
Season for Assassins '71
Seeds of Evil '76
Sugar Hill '94
Sunset '88
Trash '70
Wild Orchid 2: Two Shades of Blue '91

Abby Dalton
Rock All Night '57
Roller Blade Warriors: Taken By Force '89
Whale of a Tale '76

Audrey Dalton
Casanova's Big Night '54
The Monster that Challenged the World '57
The Prodigal '55

Darren Dalton
Brotherhood of Justice '86
Montana '90

Dorothy Dalton
Disciple '15
Moran of the Lady Letty '22
The Three Musketeers '16

Timothy Dalton
Agatha '79
Brenda Starr '86
Chanel Solitaire '81
Cromwell '70
The Doctor and the Devils '85
The Flame is Love '79
Flash Gordon '80
Happy Anniversary 007: 25 Years of James Bond '87
Hawks '89
Jane Eyre '83
The King's Whore '90
License to Kill '89
The Lion in Winter '68
The Living Daylights '87
Mistral's Daughter '84
Naked in New York '93
Permission to Kill '75
The Rocketeer '91
Sextette '78
Sins '85
Wuthering Heights '70

Roger Daltrey
Buddy's Song '91
Cold Justice '89
Forgotten Prisoners '90
If Looks Could Kill '91
The Legacy '79
Lightning Jack '94
Lisztomania '75
The Little Match Girl '87
Mack the Knife '89
McVicar '80
Monterey Pop '68
Murder: Ultimate Grounds for Divorce '85
Tommy '75
Woodstock '70

Candice Daly
Hell Hunters '87
Liquid Dreams '92

James Daly
The Court Martial of Billy Mitchell '55
Planet of the Apes '68
Resurrection of Zachary Wheeler '71
Tender Is the Night '55

Timothy Daly
Caroline at Midnight '93
Dangerous Heart '93
Diner '82
For Love or Money '88
I Married a Centerfold '84
In the Line of Duty: Ambush in Waco '93
Just the Way You Are '84
Love or Money? '88
Made in Heaven '87
Mirrors '85
The Rise & Rise of Daniel Rocket '86
The Spellbinder '88
Year of the Comet '92

Tyne Daly
The Adultress '77
The Aviator '85
Better Late Than Never '79
The Enforcer '76
Intimate Strangers '77
Larry '74
A Matter of Life and Death '81
Movers and Shakers '85
On the Town '91
Speedtrap '78
Telefon '77
Your Place or Mine '83
Zoot Suit '81

Jacqueline Dalya
Behind Prison Walls '43
Miss Melody Jones '73

William Dame
In Deadly Heat '87
Stuff Stephanie in the Incinerator '89

Cathryn Damon
First Time '82
How to Beat the High Cost of Living '80
She's Having a Baby '88

Gabriel Damon
Call to Glory '84
Iron Maze '91
Journey to Spirit Island '92
RoboCop 2 '90

Mark Damon
Anzio '68
Between Heaven and Hell '56
Black Sabbath '64
Crypt of the Living Dead '73
Devil's Wedding Night '73
The Fall of the House of Usher '60
Great Treasure Hunt '70s
The Scalawag Bunch '75

Matt Damon
Geronimo: An American Legend '93
Rising Son '90
School Ties '92

Vic Damone
Athena '54
Hell to Eternity '60
Hit the Deck '55
Kismet '55
Rich, Young and Pretty '51

Barbara Dana
A Matter of Principle '83
Necessary Parties '88

Bill Dana
Harrad Summer '74
I Wonder Who's Killing Her Now? '76
Kill My Wife...Please!
Lena's Holiday '90

Leora Dana
Amityville 3: The Demon '83
Baby It's You '82
Kings Go Forth '58

Viola Dana
The Ice Flood '26
That Certain Thing '28

Malcolm Danare
The Curse '87
Heaven Help Us '85
Popcorn '89

Charles Dance
Alien 3 '92
China Moon '91
For Your Eyes Only '81
The Golden Child '86
Good Morning, Babylon '87

Dance

Dance ►cont.

Hidden City '87
The Jewel in the Crown '84
Last Action Hero '93
The McGuffin '85
Out on a Limb '87
Pascali's Island '88
Plenty '85
Tales of the Unexpected '91
This Lightning Always Strikes Twice '85
White Mischief '88

Tom D'Andrea
Dark Passage '47
Humoresque '46
The Next Voice You Hear '50
Silver River '48

Dorothy Dandridge
Carmen Jones '54
Island in the Sun '57
Lady from Louisiana '42
Since You Went Away '44
Sun Valley Serenade '41
Sundown '41
Tamango '59

Karl Dane
The Big House '30
The Big Parade '25

Lawrence Dane
Clown Murders '83
Fatal Attraction '80
Find the Lady '75
The Good Fight '92
Lethal Lolita—Amy Fisher: My Story '92
Of Unknown Origin '83
Rituals '79
Rolling Vengeance '87
Scanners '81

Patricia Dane
I Dood It '43
Johnny Eager '42
Rio Rita '42
Somewhere I'll Find You '42

Beverly D'Angelo
Annie Hall '77
Aria '88
Big Trouble '86
Coal Miner's Daughter '80
Cold Front '89
Daddy's Dyin'...Who's Got the Will? '90
Every Which Way But Loose '78
Finders Keepers '84
First Love '77
Hair '79
Hands of a Stranger '87
High Spirits '88
Highpoint '80
Honky Tonk Freeway '81
In the Mood '87
The Legend of Sleepy Hollow '86
Lightning Jack '94
Lonely Hearts '91
Maid to Order '87
Man Trouble '92
The Miracle '91
National Lampoon's Christmas Vacation '89
National Lampoon's European Vacation '85
National Lampoon's Vacation '83
Pacific Heights '90
Paternity '81
The Pope Must Diet '91
The Sentinel '76
Sleeping Beauty '83
Slow Burn '86
A Streetcar Named Desire '84
Trading Hearts '87

Carlo D'Angelo
The Devil's Commandment '56
Secret Agent Super Dragon '66

Rodney Dangerfield
Back to School '86
Caddyshack '80
Easy Money '83
Ladybugs '92
Moving '88
Natural Born Killers '94
The Projectionist '71

Henry Daniell
All This and Heaven Too '40
The Body Snatcher '45
Camille '36
Castle in the Desert '42
Diane '55
The Egyptian '54
The Firefly '37
The Great Dictator '40
Jane Eyre '44
Les Girls '57
Lust for Life '56
Madame X '37
The Man in the Gray Flannel Suit '56
The Philadelphia Story '40
The Prodigal '55
Reunion in France '42
The Sea Hawk '40
Sherlock Holmes in Washington '43
Wake of the Red Witch '49
Watch on the Rhine '43
Witness for the Prosecution '57
The Woman in Green '45
A Woman's Face '41

Suzanne Danielle
The Carpathian Eagle '81
Carry On Emmanuelle '78
Golden Lady '79

Anthony Daniels
The Empire Strikes Back '80
Return of the Jedi '83
Star Wars '77

Bebe Daniels
Dixiana '30
Don't Shove/Two Gun Gussie '19
Feel My Pulse '28
42nd Street '33
I'm on My Way/The Non-Stop Kid '18
Male and Female '19
The Maltese Falcon '31
Monsieur Beaucaire '24
Reaching for the Moon '31
Silent Laugh Makers, No. 3 '19

Gary Daniels
Firepower '93
Knights '93

Jeff Daniels
Arachnophobia '90
The Butcher's Wife '91
The Caine Mutiny Court Martial '88
Checking Out '89
Gettysburg '93
Grand Tour: Disaster in Time '92
Heartburn '86
The House on Carroll Street '88
Love Hurts '91
Love Notes '88
Marie '85
The Purple Rose of Cairo '85
Radio Days '87
Ragtime '81
A Rumor of War '80
Something Wild '86
Speed '94
Sweet Hearts Dance '88
Teamster Boss: The Jackie Presser Story '92
Terms of Endearment '83
There Goes the Neighborhood '92
Welcome Home, Roxy Carmichael '90

John Daniels
Bare Knuckles '77
Black Shampoo '76
Candy Tangerine Man '75
Getting Over '81

Mickey Daniels
The Adventurous Knights '35
The Great Ziegfeld '36
Our Gang '26
Our Gang Comedy Festival '88
Our Gang Comedy Festival 2 '89
The Return of Our Gang '25

Phil Daniels
Bad Behavior '92
Breaking Glass '80
The Bride '85
Quadrophenia '79

Scum '79

William Daniels
All Night Long '81
The Bastard '78
Black Sunday '77
Blind Date '87
The Blue Lagoon '80
City in Fear '80
Damien: The Leper Priest '80
The Graduate '67
Her Alibi '88
Killer on Board '77
Marlowe '69
Oh, God! '77
The One and Only '78
Parallax View '74
The President's Analyst '67
The Rebels '79
Reds '81
Rehearsal for Murder '82
Sergeant Matlovich vs. the U.S. Air Force '78
1776 '72
Sunburn '79
A Thousand Clowns '65
Two for the Road '67

Lynn Danielson
Mortuary Academy '91
Nickel & Dime '92
Out of the Dark '88

Eli Danker
The Flight '89
Impulse '90
The Taking of Flight 847: The Uli Derickson Story '88

Blythe Danner
Alice '90
Another Woman '88
Are You in the House Alone? '78
Brighton Beach Memoirs '86
Futureworld '76
Getting Up and Going Home '92
The Great Santini '80
Hearts of the West '75
Husbands and Wives '92
Inside the Third Reich '82
Judgment '90
Love Affair: The Eleanor & Lou Gehrig Story '77
Man, Woman & Child '83
Mr. & Mrs. Bridge '91
Never Forget '91
The Prince of Tides '91
1776 '72
To Kill a Clown '72

Sybil Danning
Albino '76
Amazon Women on the Moon '87
Battle Beyond the Stars '80
Bluebeard '72
Cat in the Cage '68
Chained Heat '83
The Concorde: Airport '79 '79
Daughter of Death '82
Day of the Cobra '84
God's Gun '75
Hercules '83
Hitchhiker 4 '87
Howling 2: Your Sister is a Werewolf '85
Jungle Warriors '84
Kill Castro '80
L.A. Bounty '89
Malibu Express '85
The Man with Bogart's Face '80
The Mercenaries '80
Nightkill '80
Panther Squad '84
Phantom Empire '87
The Prince and the Pauper '78
Private Passions '85
Reform School Girls '86
The Salamander '82
Separate Ways '82
Seven Magnificent Gladiators '84
They're Playing with Fire '84
Tomb '87
Warrior Queen '87
Young Lady Chatterly 2 '85

Royal Dano
The Adventures of Huckleberry Finn '60

All Mine to Give '56
Bad Georgia Road '77
Bend of the River '52
Big Bad Mama '74
Cocaine Wars '86
Crime of Passion '57
The Dark Half '91
Electra Glide in Blue '73
Ghoulies 2 '88
House 2: The Second Story '87
Huckleberry Finn '75
Hughes & Harlow: Angels in Hell '77
Johnny Guitar '53
Killer Klowns from Outer Space '88
Man of the West '58
Messiah of Evil '74
The Red Badge of Courage '51
The Right Stuff '83
Spaced Invaders '90
Teachers '84
Texas Guns '90
Tribute to a Bad Man '56
The Trouble with Harry '55
Wild Party '74

Cesare Danova
Boy, Did I Get a Wrong Number! '66
Gidget Goes to Rome '63
Mean Streets '73
St. Helen's, Killer Volcano '82
Scorchy '76
Tentacles '77
Viva Las Vegas '63

Ted Danson
Body Heat '81
Chinese Web '79
Cousins '89
Creepshow '82
Dad '89
A Fine Mess '86
Getting Even with Dad '94
Just Between Friends '86
Little Treasure '85
Made in America '93
The Onion Field '79
Our Family Business '81
Three Men and a Baby '87
Three Men and a Little Lady '90
We are the Children '87
When the Bough Breaks '86

Michael Dante
Beyond Evil '80
Big Score '83
The Cage '89
Crazy Horse and Custer: "The Untold Story" '90
Cruise Missile '78
Naked Kiss '64

Helmut Dantine
Alexander the Great '55
Bring Me the Head of Alfredo Garcia '74
Casablanca '42
Desperate Journey '42
Edge of Darkness '43
The Fifth Musketeer '79
Hollywood Canteen '44
The Killer Elite '75
Mrs. Miniver '42
The Navy Comes Through '42
Northern Pursuit '43
Operation Crossbow '65
Passage to Marseilles '44
The Stranger from Venus '54
To Be or Not to Be '42
War and Peace '56
Watch on the Rhine '43
Whispering City '47
The Wilby Conspiracy '75

Ray Danton
Apache Blood '75
The Centerfold Girls '74
Conqueror & Empress '64
I'll Cry Tomorrow '55
The Longest Day '62
The Rise and Fall of Legs Diamond '60
Secret Agent Super Dragon '66

Tony Danza
Angels in the Outfield '94
Going Ape! '81
She's Out of Control '89
Single Bars, Single Women '84
Truth or Die '86

Maia Danzinger
Dr. Heckyl and Mr. Hype '80
Last Exit to Brooklyn '90

Ho Chung Dao
Bruce Li in New Guinea '80
Bruce Li the Invincible '80
Invincible '80

Patti D'Arbanville
Big Wednesday '78
Bilitis '77
Blind Spot '93
The Boys Next Door '85
Call Me '88
Deadly Conspiracy '91
The Fifth Floor '80
Flesh '68
Fresh Horses '88
Hog Wild '80
Modern Problems '81
Real Genius '85
Snow Kill '90
Time After Time '79
Wired '89

Patrika Darbo
Daddy's Dyin'...Who's Got the Will? '90
Leaving Normal '92

Kim Darby
Better Off Dead '79
The Capture of Grizzly Adams '82
Don't Be Afraid of the Dark '73
Embassy '85
Enola Gay: The Men, the Mission, the Atomic Bomb '80
Flatbed Annie and Sweetiepie: Lady Truckers '79
Generation '69
The Grissom Gang '71
The One and Only '78
The People '71
Rich Man, Poor Man '76
The Strawberry Statement '70
The Streets of San Francisco '72
Teen Wolf Too '87
True Grit '69

Mireille Darc
Icy Breasts '75
Intruder '77
The Peking Blond '68
Return of the Tall Blond Man With One Black Shoe '74
The Tall Blond Man with One Black Shoe '72
Weekend '67

Denise Darcel
Thunder in the Pines '49
Vera Cruz '53
Westward the Women '51

Alexander D'Arcy
The Awful Truth '37
Blood of Dracula's Castle '69
Fanny Hill: Memoirs of a Woman of Pleasure '64
Horrors of Spider Island '59
Prisoner of Zenda '37
Soldier of Fortune '55

Jake D'Arcy
Gregory's Girl '80
A Sense of Freedom '78

Roy D'Arcy
Legion of Missing Men '37
Revolt of the Zombies '36

Sheila Darcy
Irish Luck '39
Tumbledown Ranch in Arizona '41
Zorro's Fighting Legion '39

Severn Darden
Back to School '86
Battle for the Planet of the Apes '73
Conquest of the Planet of the Apes '72
The Day of the Dolphin '73
Dead Heat on a Merry-Go-Round '66
The Disappearance of Aimee '76
Hired Hand '71
Jackson County Jail '76
The Legend of Hillbilly John '73

Once Upon a Midnight Scary '90
Playmates '72
The President's Analyst '67
Real Genius '85
Saturday the 14th '81
Vanishing Point '71
Wanda Nevada '79
Werewolves on Wheels '71

Bobby Darin
Captain Newman, M.D. '63
The Happy Ending '69
Hell is for Heroes '62
Pressure Point '62
Run, Stranger, Run '73
State Fair '62

Johnny Dark
Rip-Off '71
Up Your Alley '89
Wishful Thinking '92

Jean Darling
Little Rascals, Book 17 '31
March of the Wooden Soldiers '34

Joan Darling
Sunnyside '79
The Two Worlds of Jenny Logan '79

Linda Darlow
The Amy Fisher Story '93
Immediate Family '89

Gerard Darmon
Betty Blue '86
Diva '82
Obsession: A Taste for Fear '89

Linda Darnell
Anna and the King of Siam '46
Blackbeard the Pirate '52
Blood and Sand '41
Buffalo Bill '44
City Without Men '43
Dakota Incident '56
Forever Amber '47
Island of Desire '52
A Letter to Three Wives '49
The Loves of Edgar Allen Poe '42
The Mark of Zorro '40
My Darling Clementine '46
Second Chance '53
Unfaithfully Yours '48

Steve Darrell
The Adventures of Frank and Jesse James '48
Lightning Raiders '45

James Darren
All the Young Men '60
Boss' Son '79
Diamond Head '62
The Gene Krupa Story '59
Gidget '59
Gidget Goes Hawaiian '61
Gidget Goes to Rome '63
The Guns of Navarone '61
Venus in Furs '70

Danielle Darrieux
Alexander the Great '55
Bluebeard '63
The Earrings of Madame De... '54
Five Fingers '52
La Ronde '51
Lady Chatterley's Lover '55
L'Anne Sainte '78
Le Cavaleur '78
Le Plaisir '52
Mayerling '36
Murder at 45 R.P.M. '65
The Rage of Paris '38
The Red and the Black '57
Rich, Young and Pretty '51
Scene of the Crime '87

Frankie Darro
Anything for a Thrill '37
Black Gold '36
Boy's Reformatory '39
Broadway Bill '34
Burn 'Em Up Barnes '34
Devil Diamond '37
Devil Horse '32
The Gang's All Here '41
Irish Luck '39
Let's Go Collegiate '41
Lightning Warrior '31
The Phantom Empire '35
Tough Kid '39
Tough to Handle '37
Up in the Air '40
Valley of Wanted Men '35
Vanishing Legion '31
Westward the Women '51
Wolf Dog '33

Henry Darrow
Computer Wizard '77
Death Blow '87
In Dangerous Company '88
L.A. Bounty '89
The Last of the Finest '90
Where's Willie? '77

John Darrow
Hell's Angels '30
The Lady Refuses '31
Monte Carlo Nights '34
Ten Nights in a Bar-Room '31

Oliver Darrow
Bad Girls from Mars '90
The Channeler '89
Spirits '90

Lili Darvas
Love '71
Meet Me in Las Vegas '56
24 Hours in a Woman's Life '61

Bella Darvi
The Egyptian '54
The Racers '55

Jane Darwell
All Through the Night '42
The Bigamist '53
Captain January '36
Craig's Wife '36
Curly Top '35
The Devil & Daniel Webster '41
Finishing School '33
Girls in Prison '56
Gone with the Wind '39
The Grapes of Wrath '40
The Great Gildersleeve '43
I Live in Grosvenor Square '46
Jesse James '39
Last Hurrah '58
The Lemon Drop Kid '51
Little Miss Broadway '38
The Loves of Edgar Allen Poe '42
One Night of Love '34
The Ox-Bow Incident '43
The Poor Little Rich Girl '36
The Rains Came '39
The Red Stallion '47
Redwood Forest Trail '50
Tender Comrade '43
Three Godfathers '48
Three Husbands '50
Wagon Master '50
We're Not Married '52

Stacey Dash
Mo' Money '92
Moving '88
Renaissance Man '94

Jules Dassin
Never on Sunday '60
Rififi '54

Jean Daste
Boudu Saved from Drowning '32
The Crime of Monsieur Lange '36
Grand Illusion '37
The Green Room '78
L'Atalante '34
Zero for Conduct '33

Alex Datcher
Body Bags '93
Passenger 57 '92
Rage and Honor '92

Kristin Datillo
Child of Darkness, Child of Light '91
Mirror, Mirror '90
Pyrates '91

James Daughton
Blind Date '84
Girlfriend from Hell '89
Malibu Beach '78
Swim Team '79

Claude Dauphin
April In Paris '52
Is Paris Burning? '68
Lady L '65
Le Plaisir '52
Les Miserables '78
Madame Rosa '77
The Madwoman of Chaillot '69
Rosebud '75
Tiara Tahiti '62
Two for the Road '67

Elyssa Davalos
Jericho Fever '93
Wild & Wooly '78

Richard Davalos
Cool Hand Luke '67
East of Eden '54
Sea Chase '55
Something Wicked This Way Comes '83

Harry Davenport
All This and Heaven Too '40
The Bachelor and the Bobby-Soxer '47
Courage of Lassie '46
The Cowboy and the Lady '38
December 7th: The Movie '91
The Enchanted Forest '45
The Farmer's Daughter '47
Fit for a King '37
Foreign Correspondent '40
Gone with the Wind '39
Home Movies '79
The Hunchback of Notre Dame '39
Jack London '44
Kings Row '41
Lucky Partners '40
Marie Antoinette '38
Meet Me in St. Louis '44
The Ox-Bow Incident '43
Son of Fury '42
Tell It to the Judge '49
That Forsyte Woman '50
That Uncertain Feeling '41
The Thin Man Goes Home '44
Three Daring Daughters '48
You Can't Take It with You '38

Nigel Davenport
Chariots of Fire '81
Cry of the Innocent '80
Death by Prescription '80s
Dracula '79
Greystoke: The Legend of Tarzan, Lord of the Apes '84
Island of Dr. Moreau '77
The Last Valley '71
Living Free '72
A Man for All Seasons '66
Nighthawks '81
The Ordeal of Dr. Mudd '80
Peeping Tom '63
Phase 4 '74
Picture of Dorian Gray '74
Sebastian '68
Soul Patrol '80
Upper Crust '88
The Virgin Soldiers '69
Without a Clue '88
Zulu Dawn '79

Robert Davi
Amazon '90
Center of the Web '92
Christopher Columbus: The Discovery '92
Cops and Robbersons '94
Die Hard '88
The $5.20 an Hour Dream '80
Gangster Wars '81
The Goonies '85
Illicit Behavior '91
Legal Tender '90
License to Kill '89
Maniac Cop 2 '90
Maniac Cop 3 '93
Mardi Gras for the Devil '93
Peacemaker '90
Predator 2 '90
Quick '93
Son of the Pink Panther '93
The Taking of Beverly Hills '91
Traxx '87
White Hot: The Mysterious Murder of Thelma Todd '91
Wild Orchid 2: Two Shades of Blue '92
Wild Thing '87

Angel David
The Crow '93
Mixed Blood '84

Clifford David
Agent on Ice '86
Matters of the Heart '90
Resurrection '80

Eleanor David
Comfort and Joy '84
84 Charing Cross Road '86
The Scarlet Pimpernel '82
Slipstream '89
Sylvia '86

Keith David
Always '89
Article 99 '92
Bird '88
Final Analysis '92
The Last Outlaw '93
Marked for Death '90
Men at Work '90
Off Limits '87
Platoon '86
The Quick and the Dead '94
They Live '88
The Thing '82

Lolita David
Adventures in Babysitting '87
Blindside '88
Recruits '86

Thayer David
The Duchess and the Dirtwater Fox '76
The Eiger Sanction '75
House of Dark Shadows '70
Journey to the Center of the Earth '59
The Legend of the Sea Wolf '58
Savages '72
Save the Tiger '73
The Story of Ruth '60

Lolita Davidovich
Blaze '89
Boiling Point '93
The Inner Circle '91
Intersection '93
Keep the Change '92
Leap of Faith '92
The Object of Beauty '91
Prison Stories: Women on the Inside '91
Raising Cain '92

Ben Davidson
The Black Six '74
Conan the Barbarian '82

Davey Davidson
No Drums, No Bugles '71
When the Line Goes Through '71

Diana Davidson
Around the World in 80 Ways '86
Scared to Death '80

Eileen Davidson
Easy Wheels '89
Eternity '89
The House on Sorority Row '83

John Davidson
The Concorde: Airport '79 '79
Edward Scissorhands '90
The Happiest Millionaire '67
Monsieur Beaucaire '24
The Squeeze '87
Tailspin Tommy '34

Max Davidson
Daring Danger '32
Hotel Imperial '27
Roamin' Wild '36

William B. Davidson
Held for Murder '32
I'm No Angel '33
Vice Squad '31

Embeth Davidtz
Army of Darkness '92
Deadly Matrimony '92
Schindler's List '93

Betty Ann Davies
Alias John Preston '56
Blackout '54
The Blue Lamp '49

Jackson Davies
Dead Ahead: The Exxon Valdez Disaster '92
Dead Wrong '83
Jane Doe '83

James Davies
Wildest Dreams '90
Young Nurses in Love '89

John Davies
Interface '84
Positive I.D. '87

John Howard Davies
Oliver Twist '48
The Rocking Horse Winner '49
Tom Brown's School Days '51

Marion Davies
Going Hollywood '33
Show People '28

Rudi Davies
The Lonely Passion of Judith Hearne '87
Maria's Child '93
The Object of Beauty '91

Rupert Davies
The Conqueror Worm '68
The Crimson Cult '68
Dracula Has Risen from the Grave '68
Frightmare '74
The Spy Who Came in from the Cold '65
Waterloo '71
Zeppelin '71

Stephen Davies
The Berlin Conspiracy '91
Hanoi Hilton '87
The Nest '88

Luis Davila
Como Dos Gotas de Agua '70s
Pancho Villa '72
The Scalawag Bunch '75

Ann B. Davis
The Brady Bunch, Vol. 1 '69
Lover Come Back '61
A Very Brady Christmas '88

Art Davis
Along the Sundown Trail '42
Phantom Gold '38
Prairie Pals '42
Tumbleweed Trail '42

Bette Davis
All About Eve '50
All This and Heaven Too '40
As Summers Die '86
Beyond the Forest '49
The Bride Came C.O.D. '41
Bureau of Missing Persons '33
Burnt Offerings '76
The Cabin in the Cotton '32
The Catered Affair '56
The Corn is Green '45
Dangerous '35
The Dark Secret of Harvest Home '78
Dark Victory '39
Death on the Nile '78
Deception '46
The Disappearance of Aimee '76
Empty Canvas '64
Ex-Lady '33
Fashions of 1934 '34
The Great Lie '41
Hell's House '32
Hollywood Canteen '44
Hollywood Outtakes & Rare Footage '83
Hush, Hush, Sweet Charlotte '65
In This Our Life '42
Jezebel '38
Juarez '39
June Bride '48
Kid Galahad '37
The Letter '40
The Little Foxes '41
Little Gloria...Happy at Last '84
Madame Sin '71
The Man Who Came to Dinner '41
Marked Woman '37
Mr. Skeffington '44
Now, Voyager '42
Of Human Bondage '34
The Old Maid '39
Petrified Forest '36
Phone Call from a Stranger '52
A Piano for Mrs. Cimino '82
Pocketful of Miracles '61

Davis ►cont.

The Private Lives of Elizabeth & Essex '39
Return from Witch Mountain '78
Right of Way '84
Satan Met a Lady '36
The Sisters '38
A Stolen Life '46
Strangers: The Story of a Mother and Daughter '79
Thank Your Lucky Stars '43
That Certain Woman '37
Three on a Match '32
The Virgin Queen '55
Watch on the Rhine '43
The Watcher in the Woods '81
Way Back Home '32
The Whales of August '87
What Ever Happened to Baby Jane? '62
Where Love Has Gone '64
White Mama '80
Wicked Stepmother '89
Winter Meeting '48

Brad Davis
Blood Ties '87
The Caine Mutiny Court Martial '88
The Campus Corpse '77
Chariots of Fire '81
Chiefs '83
Child of Darkness, Child of Light '91
Cold Steel '87
Hangfire '91
Heart '87
Midnight Express '78
Querelle '83
Robert Kennedy and His Times '90
Rosalie Goes Shopping '89
A Rumor of War '80
A Small Circle of Friends '80
Sybil '76
Vengeance '89
When the Time Comes '91

Carole Davis
C.O.D. '83
The Flamingo Kid '84
If Looks Could Kill '91
Mannequin '87
Princess Academy '87
The Shrimp on the Barbie '90

Chet Davis
The Eye Creatures '65
Yes, Sir, Mr. Bones '51

Clifton Davis
Don't Look Back: The Story of Leroy ''Satchel'' Paige '81
Dream Date '93
Little Ladies of the Night '77
The Night the City Screamed '80

Duane Davis
Diggstown '92
Final Shot: The Hank Gathers Story '92
The Program '93

Eddie Davis
Fighting Pilot '35
Gunners & Guns '34

Gail Davis
Blue Canadian Rockies '52
Brand of Fear '49
Cow Town '50
On Top of Old Smoky '53
Valley of Fire '51
Winning of the West '53

Geena Davis
The Accidental Tourist '88
Angie '94
Beetlejuice '88
Earth Girls are Easy '89
Fletch '85
The Fly '86
Hero '92
A League of Their Own '92
Quick Change '90
Secret Weapons '85
Thelma & Louise '91
Tootsie '82
Transylvania 6-5000 '85

Gene Davis
Messenger of Death '88
Night Games '80

Jack Davis
Endgame '85
The Return of Our Gang '25

Jim Davis
Bad Company '72
Big Chase '54
The Big Sky '52
The Choirboys '77
Comes a Horseman '78
Day Time Ended '80
Don't Look Back: The Story of Leroy ''Satchel'' Paige '81
Dracula vs. Frankenstein '71
El Dorado '67
Frontier Uprising '61
Gun Riders '69
Guns Don't Argue '57
Hellfire '48
Hi-Jacked '50
Inferno in Paradise '88
Iron Angel '64
Jesse James Meets Frankenstein's Daughter '65
Killing Stone '78
Law of the Land '76
Little Big Horn '51
Maverick Queen '55
Monster from Green Hell '58
Monte Walsh '70
Outcast '54
The Restless Breed '58
The Runaway Barge '75
The Showdown '50
Three Desperate Men '50
The Trackers '71
Zebra in the Kitchen '65

Joan Davis
Around the World '43
George White's Scandals '45
Hold That Ghost '41
If You Knew Susie '48
Just Around the Corner '38
My Lucky Star '38
On the Avenue '37
Outcast '54
Show Business '44
Sun Valley Serenade '41
Thin Ice '37

Judy Davis
Alice '90
Barton Fink '91
The Final Option '82
Georgia '81
Heatwave '83
High Rolling in a Hot Corvette '77
High Tide '87
Husbands and Wives '92
Impromptu '90
Kangaroo '86
My Brilliant Career '79
Naked Lunch '91
One Against the Wind '91
A Passage to India '84
The Ref '93
Rocket to the Moon '86
Where Angels Fear to Tread '91
The Winter of Our Dreams '82
A Woman Called Golda '82

Mac Davis
Blackmail '91
Cheaper to Keep Her '80
North Dallas Forty '79
The Sting 2 '83

Nancy Davis
Donovan's Brain '53
East Side, West Side '49
Hellcats of the Navy '57
The Next Voice You Hear '50

Nathan Davis
Code of Silence '85
Shaking the Tree '92

Ossie Davis
All God's Children '80
Avenging Angel '85
Billy: Portrait of a Street Kid '77
The Client '94
Do the Right Thing '89
Don't Look Back: The Story of Leroy ''Satchel'' Paige '81
The Ernest Green Story '93
Gladiator '92

Gone are the Days '63
Grumpy Old Men '93
Harry & Son '84
Hot Stuff '80
Joe Versus the Volcano '90
Jungle Fever '91
King '78
Let's Do It Again '75
A Man Called Adam '66
Night Gallery '69
Purlie Victorious '63
The Scalphunters '68
School Daze '88
Stephen King's The Stand '94

Owen Davis, Jr.
It Could Happen to You '37
Special Investigator '36

Patricia Davis
For Ladies Only '81
Night Partners '83

Philip Davis
The Bounty '84
Grown Ups '80
High Hopes '89
Howling 5: The Rebirth '89
Quadrophenia '79
Who's Who '78

Phyllis E. Davis
Sweet Sugar '72
Terminal Island '73

Roger Davis
Flash & Firecat '75
House of Dark Shadows '70
Ruby '77

Sammy Davis, Jr.
Billy Crystal: Don't Get Me Started '86
Cannonball Run '81
Cannonball Run 2 '84
Cracking Up '83
Gone with the West '72
James Dean: The First American Teenager '76
The Kid Who Loved Christmas '90
Little Moon & Jud McGraw '78
A Man Called Adam '66
Moon Over Parador '88
Ocean's 11 '60
Robin and the Seven Hoods '64
Sweet Charity '69
Tap '89
That's Dancing! '85
The Three Penny Opera '62
The Trackers '71

Scott Davis
The Abomination '88
Tabloid! '88

Sonny Carl Davis
Fast Money '83
Last Night at the Alamo '83
Pair of Aces '90
Seedpeople '92
Verne Miller '88
The Whole Shootin' Match '79

Tom Davis
One More Saturday Night '86
Tunnelvision '76

Viveka Davis
A Dangerous Woman '93
The End of Innocence '90
Man Trouble '92
Morgan Stewart's Coming Home '87
Not My Kid '85
Shoot the Moon '82

Sammi Davis-Voss
Consuming Passions '88
Final Warning '90
Hope and Glory '87
Horseplayer '91
Indecency '92
The Lair of the White Worm '88
Mona Lisa '86
The Perfect Bride '91
Prayer for the Dying '87
The Rainbow '89
Shadow of China '91

Warwick Davis
The Ewok Adventure '84
The Ewoks: Battle for Endor '85
Leprechaun '93
Leprechaun 2 '94
Willow '88

Bruce Davison
The Affair '73
Brass Target '78
Crimes of Passion '84
Deadman's Curve '78
French Quarter '78
The Gathering '77
The Gathering: Part 2 '79
High Risk '76
Kiss My Grits '82
The Ladies Club '86
Last Summer '69
Lathe of Heaven '80
Lies '83
Live! From Death Row '92
Longtime Companion '90
Mame '74
The Misfit Brigade '87
Mother, Jugs and Speed '76
Poor Little Rich Girl: The Barbara Hutton Story '87
Portrait of Grandpa Doc '77
Short Cuts '93
Short Eyes '79
Six Degrees of Separation '93
Spies Like Us '85
Steel and Lace '90
The Strawberry Statement '70
The Summer of My German Soldier '78
Tomorrow's Child '82
Ulzana's Raid '72
Willard '71

Peter Davison
Black Beauty '94
Love for Lydia '79

Ninetto Davoli
Arabian Nights '74
The Canterbury Tales '71
The Decameron '70
The Hawks & the Sparrows '67

Evelyn Daw
Panamint's Bad Man '38
Something to Sing About '36

Marjorie Daw
His Majesty, the American '19
Rebecca of Sunnybrook Farm '17

Pam Dawber
Holocaust Survivors...Remembrance of Love '83
The Little Mermaid '84
Stay Tuned '92
Through Naked Eyes '87
Wild Horses '84

Sugar Dawn
Arizona Roundup '42
Dynamite Canyon '41
Lone Star Law Men '42
Riding the Sunset Trail '41

Anthony M. (Antonio Marghereti) Dawson
The Curse of the Werewolf '61
Dial ''M'' for Murder '54
Dr. No '62
The Haunted Strangler '58
Hour of Decision '57
The Long Dark Hall '51
The Queen of Spades '49

Richard Dawson
The Devil's Brigade '68
How to Pick Up Girls '78
The Running Man '87

Vicky Dawson
Carbon Copy '81
The Prowler '81

Doris Day
April In Paris '52
Billy Rose's Jumbo '62
By the Light of the Silvery Moon '53
Calamity Jane '53
The Glass Bottom Boat '66
I'll See You in My Dreams '51
It's a Great Feeling '49
Lady Be Good '41
Love Me or Leave Me '55
Lover Come Back '61
Lucky Me '54
Lullaby of Broadway '51
The Man Who Knew Too Much '56
Midnight Lace '60
My Dream is Yours '49

On Moonlight Bay '51
Pajama Game '57
Pillow Talk '59
Please Don't Eat the Daisies '60
Romance on the High Seas '48
Saga of Death Valley '39
Send Me No Flowers '64
Tea for Two '50
Teacher's Pet '58
That Touch of Mink '62
The Thrill of It All! '63
The Tunnel of Love '58
Turf Boy '49
The West Point Story '50
Where Were You When the Lights Went Out? '68
The Winning Team '52
With Six You Get Eggroll '68
Young at Heart '54
Young Man with a Horn '50

Josette Day
Beauty and the Beast '46
Well-Digger's Daughter '46

Laraine Day
Dr. Kildare's Strange Case '40
Doomed at Sundown '37
Foreign Correspondent '40
Journey for Margaret '42
Mr. Lucky '43
Murder on Flight 502 '75
My Dear Secretary '49
Return to Fantasy Island '77
Those Endearing Young Charms '45
Tycoon '47

Marceline Day
The Beloved Rogue '27
Broadway to Cheyenne '32
The Cameraman '28
Fighting Fool '32
Fighting Parson '35
Flaming Signal '33
The King Murder Case '32
Paradise Island '30
The Pocatello Kid '31
Sunny Skies '30
Telegraph Trail '33

Morris Day
The Adventures of Ford Fairlane '90
Graffiti Bridge '90
Purple Rain '84

Patrick Day
The Adventures of Huckleberry Finn '85
Hollywood Hot Tubs 2: Educating Crystal '89

Stuart Garrison Day
Covert Action '88
Search and Destroy '88

Vera Day
Quatermass 2 '57
Up the Creek '58

Daniel Day-Lewis
The Age of Innocence '93
The Bounty '84
Eversmile New Jersey '89
Gandhi '82
How Many Miles to Babylon? '82
In the Name of the Father '93
The Last of the Mohicans '92
My Beautiful Laundrette '85
My Left Foot '89
A Room with a View '86
Stars and Bars '88
Sunday, Bloody Sunday '71
The Unbearable Lightness of Being '88

Assaf Dayan
Operation Thunderbolt '77
The Uranium Conspiracy '78

Margit Dayka
Cat's Play '74
Nice Neighbor '79

Pedro de Aguillon
El Aviador Fenomeno '47
The Living Coffin '58
Orlak, the Hell of Frankenstein '60

Joaquim de Almeida
Clear and Present Danger '94
Good Morning, Babylon '87
Only You '94

Maria de Aragon
Blood Mania '70
The Cremators '72
The Deadly and the Beautiful '73

Isaach de Bankole
Chocolat '88
Heart of Darkness '93
No Fear, No Die '90

Brenda de Banzie
The Entertainer '60
Hobson's Choice '53
The Man Who Knew Too Much '56
The Mark '61
The Pink Panther '64
Too Many Crooks '59

Burr de Benning
Incredible Melting Man '77
Iron Horsemen '71

Andre de Beranger
The Bat '26
So This is Paris '26

Nigel de Brulier
Ben-Hur '26
The Four Horsemen of the Apocalypse '21
The Iron Mask '29
Salome/Queen Elizabeth '23
The Three Musketeers '21

Celia de Burgh
Phar Lap '84
Sound of Love '77

Yvonne De Carlo
American Gothic '88
Arizona Bushwackers '67
Bad Girls in the Movies '86
Band of Angels '57
Blazing Stewardesses '75
Captain's Paradise '53
Cellar Dweller '87
Criss Cross '48
Death of a Scoundrel '56
Flame of the Islands '55
A Global Affair '63
Hostile Guns '67
House of Shadows '83
McLintock! '63
Mirror, Mirror '90
Munster's Revenge '81
Nocturna '79
Passion '54
Play Dead '81
Rhythm Parade '43
The Road to Morocco '42
Salome, Where She Danced '45
Satan's Cheerleaders '77
Sea Devils '53
Shotgun '55
Silent Scream '80
The Sword and the Cross '58
The Ten Commandments '56
Texas Layover '75
Vultures '84

Pedro de Cordoba
Condemned to Live '35
The Ghost Breakers '40
In Old New Mexico '45
Law of the Pampas '39
Mexican Hayride '48
Omoo Omoo, the Shark God '49
Son of Fury '42
Swamp Fire '46

Arturo de Cordova
El: This Strange Passion '52
La Diosa Arrodillada '47
The New Invisible Man '58

Ted de Corsia
Dance with Me, Henry '56
The Enforcer '51
It Happens Every Spring '49
The Killing '56
The Lady from Shanghai '48
The Naked City '48
Neptune's Daughter '49
The Outside Man '73
Slightly Scarlet '56

Eduardo de Filippo
The Gold of Naples '54
Seven Deadly Sins '53

Louis de Funes
Delusions of Grandeur '76
Femmes de Paris '53

Four Bags Full '56
La Grande Vadrouille '66
Le Gendarme de Saint-Tropez '67
Seven Deadly Sins '53
The Sheep Has Five Legs '54

Julio de Grazia
Deadly Revenge '83
Funny, Dirty Little War '83
The Lion's Share '79
The Stranger '87
Time for Revenge '82

Gloria De Haven
Best Foot Forward '43
Bog '84
Broadway Rhythm '44
Modern Times '36
Step Lively '44
Summer Holiday '48
Summer Stock '50
Susan and God '40
The Thin Man Goes Home '44
Three Little Words '50
Two Girls and a Sailor '44
Two Tickets to Broadway '51
The Yellow Cab Man '50

Consuelo de Haviland
Barjo '93
Betty Blue '86

Olivia de Havilland
The Adventurers '70
The Adventures of Robin Hood '38
Airport '77 '77
The Ambassador's Daughter '56
Anastasia: The Mystery of Anna '86
Anthony Adverse '36
Captain Blood '35
The Charge of the Light Brigade '36
Dark Mirror '46
Dodge City '39
The Fifth Musketeer '79
Gone with the Wind '39
The Heiress '49
Hush, Hush, Sweet Charlotte '65
In This Our Life '42
Lady in a Cage '64
The Making of a Legend: "Gone With the Wind" '89
A Midsummer Night's Dream '35
Not as a Stranger '55
The Private Lives of Elizabeth & Essex '39
Proud Rebel '58
Roots: The Next Generation '79
Santa Fe Trail '40
The Snake Pit '48
Strawberry Blonde '41
The Swarm '78
Thank Your Lucky Stars '43
They Died with Their Boots On '41
The Woman He Loved '88

Frank De Kova
Atlantis, the Lost Continent '61
Cat in the Cage '68
Frasier the Sensuous Lion '73
The Jayhawkers '59
Jive Turkey '76
Johnny Firecloud '75
Machine Gun Kelly '58
Teenage Caveman '58

Simon de la Brosse
The Little Thief '89
Strike It Rich '90

Marguerite de la Motte
Final Extra '27
The Iron Mask '29
Mark of Zorro '20

Danny De La Paz
American Me '92
Boulevard Nights '79
Miracle Mile '89
3:15—The Moment of Truth '86

George de la Pena
Brain Donors '92
The Cowboy & the Ballerina '84
Kuffs '92

Nijinsky '80

John de Lancie
Arcade '93
Deep Red '94
Fearless '93
The Fisher King '91
The Hand that Rocks the Cradle '91

Derek De Lint
The Assault '86
Diary of a Mad Old Man '88
The Endless Game '89
Mascara '87
Stealing Heaven '88
Three Men and a Baby '87
The Unbearable Lightness of Being '88

Terence de Marney
Beast of Morocco '66
Dual Alibi '47

Maria de Medeiros
Akermania, Vol. 1 '92
Henry & June '90
Meeting Venus '91
Pulp Fiction '94

Carlo De Meyo
Other Hell '85
The Outside Man '73

Robert De Niro
America at the Movies '76
Angel Heart '87
Awakenings '90
Backdraft '91
Bang the Drum Slowly '73
Bloody Mama '70
Born to Win '71
Brazil '85
A Bronx Tale '93
Cape Fear '91
The Deer Hunter '78
Falling in Love '84
The Godfather 1902-1959: The Complete Epic '81
The Godfather, Part 2 '74
Goodfellas '90
Greetings '68
Guilty by Suspicion '91
Hi, Mom! '70
Jacknife '89
King of Comedy '82
The Last Tycoon '76
Mad Dog and Glory '93
Mean Streets '73
Midnight Run '88
The Mission '86
Mistress '91
New York, New York '77
Night and the City '92
1900 '76
Once Upon a Time in America '84
Raging Bull '80
Stanley and Iris '90
The Swap '71
Taxi Driver '76
This Boy's Life '93
True Confessions '81
The Untouchables '87
The Wedding Party '69
We're No Angels '89

Rossy De Palma
Don Juan, My Love '90
Tie Me Up! Tie Me Down! '90
Women on the Verge of a Nervous Breakdown '88

Lya de Putti
Othello '22
The Sorrows of Satan '26
Variety '25

Anthony De Sando
Grand Isle '92
The Return of Eliot Ness '91

Joe De Santis
Al Capone '59
And Now Miguel '65
Blue '68
Marty '55

Lorraine De Selle
Caged Women '84
House on the Edge of the Park '84
The Wild Beasts '85
Women's Prison Massacre '85

Christian de Sica
An Almost Perfect Affair '79

Detective School Dropouts '85

Vittorio De Sica
The Amorous Adventures of Moll Flanders '65
Andy Warhol's Dracula '74
Angel in a Taxi '59
The Battle of Austerlitz '60
Bellissimo: Images of the Italian Cinema '87
The Earrings of Madame De... '54
Generale Della Rovere '60
The Gold of Naples '54
It Started in Naples '60
L'Odeur des Fauves '66
Pardon My Trunk '52
Peddlin' in Society '47
The Shoes of the Fisherman '68
The Wonders of Aladdin '61

Guiliana de Sio
Pool Hustlers '83
Private Affairs '89

Rosana De Soto
Ballad of Gregorio Cortez '83
Family Business '89
The In-Laws '79
La Bamba '87
Stand and Deliver '88
Star Trek 6: The Undiscovered Country '91

Jose-Luis De Villalonga
Blood and Sand '89
The Lovers '59

Brandon de Wilde
All Fall Down '62
Goodbye, My Lady '56
Hud '63
In Harm's Way '65
The Member of the Wedding '52
Missouri Traveler '58
Shane '53
Those Calloways '65

Brian Deacon
Jesus '79
Triple Echo '77
Vampyres '74
A Zed & Two Noughts '88

Richard Deacon
Abbott & Costello Meet the Mummy '55
Bad Manners '84
Billie '65
Blackbeard's Ghost '67
Carousel '56
The Gnome-Mobile '67
The One and Only, Genuine, Original Family Band '68
The Patsy '64

Lucy Deakins
The Boy Who Could Fly '86
Cheetah '89
The Great Outdoors '88
Little Nikita '88

Allison Dean
Coming to America '88
Ruby in Paradise '93

Eddie Dean
Black Hills '47
The Caravan Trail '46
Check Your Guns '48
Colorado Serenade '46
Driftin' River '46
The Hawk of Powder River '48
Knights of the Range '40
Law of the Pampas '39
Renegade Trail '39
Santa Fe Marshal '40
Song of Old Wyoming '45
The Tioga Kid '48
West to Glory '47
Western Double Feature 24 '40s
Wild Country '47
Wild West '46

James Dean
America at the Movies '76
East of Eden '54
Forever James Dean '88
Giant '56
Hill Number One '51
Hollywood Outtakes & Rare Footage '83

James Dean '85
James Dean Story '57
James Dean: The First American Teenager '76
Rebel Without a Cause '55

Jimmy Dean
Big Bad John '90
The City '76
Diamonds are Forever '71

Loren Dean
Billy Bathgate '91
1492: Conquest of Paradise '92
JFK: Reckless Youth '93
Say Anything '89

Margia Dean
Fangs of the Wild '54
The Quatermass Experiment '56
Rimfire '49

Priscilla Dean
Law of the Sea '38
Outside the Law '21
White Tiger '23

Rick Dean
Bloodfist 3: Forced to Fight '92
Heroes Stand Alone '89
Naked Obsession '91
Raiders of the Sun '92

Ron Dean
Above the Law '88
Big Score '83
Cocktail '88
Cold Justice '89
Legacy of Lies '92
Rudy '93

Leslie Deane
Freddy's Dead: The Final Nightmare '91
Girlfriend from Hell '89
976-EVIL '88
To Protect and Serve '92

Justin Deas
Dream Lover '85
Montana '90

Kristine DeBell
Cheerleaders' Wild Weekend '85
Lifepod '80
Rooster: Spurs of Death! '83
Tag: The Assassination Game '82
Willie & Phil '80

Dorothy DeBorba
Little Rascals, Book 3 '30s
Little Rascals, Book 6 '30s

Jean Debucourt
The Earrings of Madame De... '54
La Chute de la Maison Usher '28
Seven Deadly Sins '53

Rosemary DeCamp
By the Light of the Silvery Moon '53
Cheers for Miss Bishop '41
Commandos Strike at Dawn '43
The Jungle Book '42
Look for the Silver Lining '49
Main Street to Broadway '53
On Moonlight Bay '51
Rhapsody in Blue '45
The Story of Seabiscuit '49
13 Ghosts '60
Yankee Doodle Dandy '42

Eugene Deckers
Flame Over India '60
The Golden Salamander '51
Lady L '65

Guy Decomble
The 400 Blows '59
Jour de Fete '48

A. Dedinstev
Stalag 17 '53
Storm Over Asia '28

Catherine Dee
In Deadly Heat '87
Stuff Stephanie in the Incinerator '89

Frances Dee
Becky Sharp '35
Finishing School '33
Four Faces West '48
Gypsy Colt '54

Dee ►*cont.*

I Walked with a Zombie '43
Little Women '33
Of Human Bondage '34
The Private Affairs of Bel Ami '47
So Ends Our Night '41
Wheel of Fortune '41

Ruby Dee
All God's Children '80
The Balcony '63
Buck and the Preacher '72
Cat People '82
Cop and a Half '93
The Court Martial of Jackie Robinson '90
Decoration Day '90
Do the Right Thing '89
The Ernest Green Story '93
Gone are the Days '63
Gore Vidal's Lincoln '88
I Know Why the Caged Bird Sings '79
The Incident '67
It's Good to Be Alive '74
The Jackie Robinson Story '50
Jungle Fever '91
Love at Large '90
Purlie Victorious '63
A Raisin in the Sun '61
Roots: The Next Generation '79
Stephen King's The Stand '94
Windmills of the Gods '88
Zora Is My Name! '90

Sandra Dee
The Dunwich Horror '70
Fantasy Island '76
Gidget '59
Imitation of Life '59
Lost '83
The Reluctant Debutante '58
A Summer Place '59
Tammy and the Doctor '63
Until They Sail '57

Eddie Deezen
Beverly Hills Vamp '88
Desperate Moves '86
Hollywood Boulevard 2 '89
I Wanna Hold Your Hand '78
Midnight Madness '80
Million Dollar Mystery '87
Mugsy's Girls '85
A Polish Vampire in Burbank '80
Rosebud Beach Hotel '85
Surf 2 '84
Teenage Exorcist '93

Don DeFore
A Girl in Every Port '52
Jumping Jacks '52
Killer Bait '49
My Friend Irma '49
Ramrod '47
A Rare Breed '81
Romance on the High Seas '48
The Stork Club '45
Too Late for Tears '49
Without Reservations '46

Calvert Deforest
Heaven Help Us '85
Leader of the Band '87

Pia Degermark
Elvira Madigan '67
The Looking Glass War '69

Sam DeGrasse
Robin Hood '22
The Scarlet Car '17

John Dehner
California Gold Rush '81
Creator '85
The Day of the Dolphin '73
Fastest Gun Alive '56
Girl in Black Stockings '57
Hot Lead '51
The Jagged Edge '85
Killer Inside Me '76
The King's Thief '55
The Left-Handed Gun '58
Man of the West '58
Mountain Man '77
Nothing Personal '80
The Prodigal '55
Support Your Local Gunfighter '71

Vigilantes of Boom Town '46

David DeKeyser
Leon the Pig Farmer '93
Valentino '77
Yentl '83

Albert Dekker
As Young As You Feel '51
Buckskin Frontier '43
Cass Timberlane '47
Dr. Cyclops '40
East of Eden '54
Experiment Perilous '45
Gamera, the Invincible '66
Gentleman's Agreement '47
The Great Commandment '41
Honky Tonk '41
Illegal '55
In Old California '42
The Kansan '43
Kiss Me Deadly '55
Marie Antoinette '38
Once Upon a Honeymoon '42
Seven Sinners '40
Strange Cargo '40
Suddenly, Last Summer '59
Wake Island '42
War of the Wildcats '43
The Wild Bunch '69
The Woman of the Town '44

Louis Del Grande
Northern Extremes '93
Of Unknown Origin '83

Angel del Pozo
La Ley del Revolver '78
Pancho Villa '72

Dulio Del Prete
Alfredo, Alfredo '72
How Funny Can Sex Be? '76
Redneck '73
The Sensuous Nurse '76

Isobel Del Puerto
Captain Scarlett '53
Mariachis '49

Dolores Del Rio
Accused '36
Bird of Paradise '32
Cheyenne Autumn '64
Children of Sanchez '79
Flaming Star '60
Flor Silvestre '58
Flying Down to Rio '33
The Fugitive '48
Journey into Fear '42
Maria Candelaria '46
Torero '56

Laura Del Sol
Carmen '83
El Amor Brujo '86
The Hit '85
The Stilts '84

Benicio Del Toro
China Moon '91
Christopher Columbus: The Discovery '92
Fearless '93
License to Kill '89
Money for Nothing '93

Carmen Del Valle
Frontera Sin Ley
La Fuga del Rojo '87
La Venganza del Rojo '87

Suzy Delair
Fernandel the Dressmaker '57
Gervaise '56
Is Paris Burning? '68
Jenny Lamour '47
Pattes Blanches '49
Utopia '51

Lisa Delamare
Baxter '89
La Marseillaise '37
Monsieur Vincent '48

Cassandra Delaney
Hurricane Smith '92
One Night Stand '84

Charles Delaney
Captured in Chinatown '35
Hearts of Humanity '32

Joan Delaney
Don't Drink the Water '69
The President's Analyst '67

Kim Delaney
Body Parts '91

Campus Man '87
Christmas Comes to Willow Creek '87
Delta Force '86
The Disappearance of Christina '93
The Drifter '88
Hangfire '91
Hunter's Blood '87
That Was Then...This Is Now '85

Michael Delano
Catlow '71
Out for Blood '93
Private Wars '93
Ring of Fire '91
Ring of Fire 2: Blood and Steel '92

Dana Delany
Almost You '85
China Beach '88
Housesitter '92
Light Sleeper '92
Masquerade '88
Moon Over Parador '88
Patty Hearst '88
Tombstone '93
Wild Palms '93
A Winner Never Quits '86

Debra Deliso
Iced '88
The Slumber Party Massacre '82

Claudia Dell
Bachelor Apartment '31
Boots of Destiny '37
Hearts of Humanity '32
The Lost City '34
Midnight Warning '32
Woman Condemned '33
Yellow Cargo '36

Gabriel Dell
Angels with Dirty Faces '38
Blues Busters '50
Bowery Buckaroos '47
The Escape Artist '82
Follow the Leader '44
Framed '75
Hard-Boiled Mahoney '47
Kid Dynamite '43
Let's Get Tough '42
Little Tough Guy '38
Master Minds '49
Million Dollar Kid '44
'Neath Brooklyn Bridge '42
Pride of the Bowery '41
Smart Alecks '42
Smugglers' Cove '48
Spook Busters '46

Myrna Dell
The Bushwackers '52
Fighting Father Dunne '48
The Judge Steps Out '49
Ma Barker's Killer Brood '60
Naked Hills '56
Nocturne '46

Michael DellaFemina
Bloodlust: Subspecies 3 '93
Invisible: The Chronicles of Benjamin Knight '93
Mandroid '93

Edouard Delmont
Angele '34
Harvest '37
Passion for Life '48
The Sheep Has Five Legs '54
Toni '34

Genevieve Deloir
The Red Half-Breed '70
The Screaming Dead '72

Alain Delon
Assassination of Trotsky '72
The Big Grab '63
Boomerang '76
Borsalino '70
The Concorde: Airport '79 '79
Diabolically Yours '67
The Eclipse '66
The Girl on a Motorcycle '68
Godson '72
Gypsy '75
Honor Among Thieves '68
Icy Breasts '75
Is Paris Burning? '68
Joy House '64
Les Aventuriers '77

The Lost Command '66
Melodie en Sous-Sol '63
Mr. Klein '75
Nouvelle Vague '90
Red Sun '71
Rocco and His Brothers '60
Scorpio '73
Sois Belle et Tais-Toi '58
Spirits of the Dead '68
Swann in Love '84
Swimming Pool '70
Texas Across the River '66
Widow Couderc '74

Nathalie Delon
Bluebeard '72
Eyes Behind the Stars '72
Game of Seduction '86
Godson '72
Le Sex Shop '73

Jennifer Delora
Bedroom Eyes 2 '89
Deranged '87
New York's Finest '87
Robot Holocaust '87
Sensations '87

Daniele Delorme
Les Miserables '57
Pardon Mon Affaire '76

Julie Delpy
Beatrice '88
The Three Musketeers '93
Trois Couleurs: Blanc '94
Voyager '91

Rene Deltgen
Journey to the Lost City '58
The Mozart Story '48
Tromba, the Tiger Man '52

Rudy DeLuca
Life Stinks '91
The Return of Count Yorga '71

Dom DeLuise
The Adventures of Sherlock Holmes' Smarter Brother '78
Almost Pregnant '91
The Best Little Whorehouse in Texas '82
Blazing Saddles '74
Cannonball Run '81
Cannonball Run 2 '84
The Cheap Detective '78
Diary of a Young Comic '79
Driving Me Crazy '91
The End '78
Fail-Safe '64
Fatso '80
The Glass Bottom Boat '66
Going Bananas '88
Haunted Honeymoon '86
History of the World: Part 1 '81
Hot Stuff '80
Johnny Dangerously '84
The Last Married Couple in America '80
Loose Cannons '90
My African Adventure '87
Sextette '78
Silent Movie '76
Smokey and the Bandit, Part 2 '80
Spaceballs '87
Twelve Chairs '70
Wholly Moses! '80
World's Greatest Lover '77

Peter DeLuise
Children of the Night '92
Free Ride '86
The Midnight Hour '86
Rescue Me '93

Gordon DeMain
Fighting Texans '33
High Gear '33
The Mad Monster '42
Rainbow Ranch '33

William Demarest
All Through the Night '41
Along Came Jones '45
Behave Yourself! '52
Charlie Chan at the Opera '36
Christmas in July '40
Dangerous When Wet '53
The Devil & Miss Jones '41
Don't Be Afraid of the Dark '73
Escape from Fort Bravo '53
First Legion '51
The Great Man Votes '38
The Great McGinty '40

The Great Moment '44
The Great Ziegfeld '36
Hail the Conquering Hero '44
Hell on Frisco Bay '55
Here Come the Girls '53
It's a Mad, Mad, Mad, Mad World '63
The Jazz Singer '27
Jolson Sings Again '49
The Jolson Story '46
Jupiter's Darling '55
The Lady Eve '41
Love on the Run '36
Miracle of Morgan's Creek '44
The Mountain '56
Never a Dull Moment '50
The Palm Beach Story '42
Pardon My Sarong '42
The Perils of Pauline '47
Rebecca of Sunnybrook Farm '38
Sincerely Yours '56
Sorrowful Jones '49
Sullivan's Travels '41
Viva Las Vegas '63
What Price Glory? '52

Derrick DeMarney
Dangerous Moonlight '41
Frenzy '46
Inheritance '47
Things to Come '36
Young and Innocent '37

Orane Demazis
Angele '34
Cesar '36
Fanny '32
Harvest '37
Marius '31

Alla Demidova
The Seagull '71
Tchaikovsky '71

Katherine DeMille
Belle of the Nineties '34
The Black Room '35
Drift Fence '36
The Gentleman from California '37
The Judge '49
Viva Villa! '34

Mylene Demongeot
Bonjour Tristesse '57
The Giant of Marathon '60
Just Another Pretty Face '58
The Rape of the Sabines '61
Sois Belle et Tais-Toi '58
12 Plus 1 '70
Uncle Tom's Cabin '69

Rebecca DeMornay
And God Created Woman '88
Backdraft '91
Blind Side '93
By Dawn's Early Light '89
Dealers '89
Feds '88
Guilty as Sin '93
The Hand that Rocks the Cradle '92
An Inconvenient Woman '91
The Murders in the Rue Morgue '86
One from the Heart '82
Pecos Bill '86
Risky Business '83
Runaway Train '85
The Slugger's Wife '85
Testament '83
The Three Musketeers '93
The Trip to Bountiful '85

Darcy Demoss
Eden '92
Eden 2 '93
Eden 3 '93
Eden 4 '93
Living to Die '91
Pale Blood '91

Patrick Dempsey
Can't Buy Me Love '87
Coupe de Ville '90
Face the Music '92
For Better and For Worse '92
Happy Together '89
Heaven Help Us '85
In a Shallow Grave '88
In the Mood '87
JFK: Reckless Youth '93
Loverboy '89
Meatballs 3 '87

Mobsters '91
Run '91
Some Girls '88
With Honors '94

Carol Dempster
Dream Street '21
Isn't Life Wonderful '24
The Love Flower '20
Sally of the Sawdust '25
The Sorrows of Satan '26
The White Rose '23

Jeffrey DeMunn
Barbarians at the Gate '93
Blaze '89
The Blob '88
Gore Vidal's Lincoln '88
Hitcher '86
Sessions '93
Terror in Toyland '85
A Time to Live '85
Treacherous Crossing '92
Windmills of the Gods '88
Windy City '84

Judi Dench
84 Charing Cross Road '86
A Handful of Dust '88
Henry V '89
A Midsummer Night's Dream '68
A Room with a View '86
Saigon: Year of the Cat '87
A Study in Terror '66
Wetherby '85

Catherine Deneuve
Act of Aggression '73
April Fools '69
Choice of Arms '83
Donkey Skin '70
Dos Cruces en Danger Pass '71
The Hunger '83
Hustle '75
I Love All of You '83
Indochine '92
La Grande Bourgeoise '74
The Last Metro '80
Love Songs '85
Lovers Like Us '75
March or Die '77
Mississippi Mermaid '69
Repulsion '65
Scene of the Crime '87
A Slightly Pregnant Man '79
Tristana '70
Umbrellas of Cherbourg '64

Jake Dengel
Bloodsucking Pharoahs of Pittsburgh '90
Ironweed '87
Prayer of the Rollerboys '91

Maurice Denham
The Alphabet Murders '65
Curse of the Demon '57
Damn the Defiant '62
84 Charing Cross Road '86
Hysteria '64
The Mark '61
Mr. Love '86
Monsignor Quixote '91
Negatives '68
Night Caller from Outer Space '66
Sink the Bismarck '60

Lydie Denier
Blood Relations '87
Invasion of Privacy '92
Mardi Gras for the Devil '93
Midnight Cabaret '90
Red Shoe Diaries 3: Another Woman's Lipstick '93
Satan's Princess '90
Under Investigation '93

Jacques Denis
The Clockmaker '76
Jonah Who Will Be 25 in the Year 2000 '76

Anthony John Denison
The Amy Fisher Story '93
Child of Darkness, Child of Light '91
City of Hope '91
Crime Story: The Complete Saga '86
Full Eclipse '93

Full Exposure: The Sex Tape Scandals '89
The Great Escape 2: The Untold Story '88
The Harvest '92
Little Vegas '90
Sex, Love and Cold Hard Cash '93

Leslie Denison
Sherlock Holmes and the Secret Weapon '42
The Snow Creature '54

Michael Denison
Angels One Five '54
The Franchise Affair '52
Importance of Being Earnest '52
Shadowlands '93

Brian Dennehy
Acceptable Risks '86
Annie Oakley '85
Ants '77
The Belly of an Architect '91
Best Seller '87
Butch and Sundance: The Early Days '79
Check Is in the Mail '85
Cocoon '85
Cocoon: The Return '88
Day One '89
Deadly Matrimony '92
Diamond Fleece '92
F/X '86
F/X 2: The Deadly Art of Illusion '91
A Father's Revenge '88
Finders Keepers '84
First Blood '82
F.I.S.T. '78
Foreign Affairs '93
Foul Play '78
Gladiator '92
Gorky Park '83
Indio '92
The Jericho Mile '79
Johnny We Hardly Knew Ye '77
A Killing in a Small Town '90
The Last of the Finest '90
Legal Eagles '86
The Lion of Africa '87
The Little Mermaid '84
Little Miss Marker '80
Miles from Home '88
Never Cry Wolf '83
North Dallas Forty '79
Perfect Witness '89
Presumed Innocent '90
A Real American Hero '78
Return to Snowy River '88
Rising Son '90
The River Rat '84
A Rumor of War '80
Semi-Tough '77
Silent Victory: The Kitty O'Neil Story '79
Silverado '85
Split Image '82
Teamster Boss: The Jackie Presser Story '92
10 '79
To Catch a Killer '92
To Love Again '80
Twice in a Lifetime '85

Charles Denner
Bluebeard '63
The Holes '72
Les Assassins de L'Ordre '71
Mado '76
The Man Who Loved Women '77
Robert et Robert '79
The Two of Us '68
Window Shopping '86
Z '69

Richard Denning
Adam Had Four Sons '41
An Affair to Remember '57
Alice Through the Looking Glass '66
Black Beauty '46
The Black Scorpion '57
Creature from the Black Lagoon '54
Day the World Ended '55
Double Deal '50
Girls in Prison '56
The Glass Key '42
Hangman's Knot '52

Unknown Island '48

Sandy Dennis
Another Woman '88
Come Back to the Five & Dime Jimmy Dean, Jimmy Dean '82
The Execution '85
The Four Seasons '81
God Told Me To '76
The Indian Runner '91
Mr. Sycamore '74
Nasty Habits '77
976-EVIL '88
The Out-of-Towners '70
Parents '89
Splendor in the Grass '61
That Cold Day in the Park '69
Up the Down Staircase '67
Who's Afraid of Virginia Woolf? '66

Reginald Denny
Abbott and Costello Meet Dr. Jekyll and Mr. Hyde '52
Anna Karenina '35
Arrest Bulldog Drummond '38
Assault on a Queen '66
Bulldog Drummond Comes Back '37
Bulldog Drummond Escapes '37
Bulldog Drummond's Bride '39
Bulldog Drummond's Peril '38
Bulldog Drummond's Revenge '37
Bulldog Drummond's Revenge/Bulldog Drummond's Peril '38
Bulldog Drummond's Secret Police '39
California Straight Ahead '25
Captains of the Clouds '42
Cat Ballou '65
The Cheerful Fraud '27
Dancing Man '33
Escape Me Never '47
Escape to Burma '55
The Lost Patrol '34
Madam Satan '30
The Midnight Phantom '35
Mr. Blandings Builds His Dream House '48
My Favorite Brunette '47
Of Human Bondage '34
Parlor, Bedroom and Bath '31
Private Lives '31
Rebecca '40
Sabaka '55
Sherlock Holmes: The Voice of Terror '42
Skinner's Dress Suit '26
We're in the Legion Now '37

Vernon Dent
Baby Face Harry Langdon '26
The Cameraman '28
Extra Girl '23
His First Flame '26
Texas Cyclone '32
Two Reelers: Comedy Classics 10 '31

Christa Denton
Convicted: A Mother's Story '87
The Gate '87
Scandal in a Small Town '88

Donna Denton
Death Blow '87
Glory Years '87
Outlaw of Gor '87
Slaughterhouse Rock '88

Bob Denver
Back to the Beach '87
Gilligan's Island: Meet the Crew '64
High School USA '84
Wackiest Wagon Train in the West '77
Who's Minding the Mint? '67

John Denver
Foxfire '87
Oh, God! '77

Elisabeth Depardieu
Jean de Florette '87
Tartuffe '84

Gerard Depardieu
Buffet Froid '79
Camille Claudel '89

Choice of Arms '83
Cyrano de Bergerac '90
Danton '82
1492: Conquest of Paradise '92
Get Out Your Handkerchiefs '78
Going Places '74
Green Card '90
The Holes '72
I Love All of You '83
Jean de Florette '87
La Chevre '81
The Last Metro '80
Les Comperes '83
Loulou '80
Maitresse '76
Menage '76
Mon Oncle D'Amerique '80
Moon in the Gutter '83
My Father the Hero '93
1900 '76
One Woman or Two '85
Police '85
The Return of Martin Guerre '83
Stavisky '74
Tartuffe '84
This Sweet Sickness '77
Too Beautiful for You '88
Tous les Matins du Monde '92
Under Satan's Sun '87
Uranus '91
Vincent, Francois, Paul and the Others '76
The Woman Next Door '81

Johnny Depp
Benny & Joon '93
Cry-Baby '90
Ed Wood '94
Edward Scissorhands '90
Freddy's Dead: The Final Nightmare '91
A Nightmare on Elm Street '84
Platoon '86
Private Resort '84
What's Eating Gilbert Grape '93

Bo Derek
Bolero '84
A Change of Seasons '80
Fantasies '73
Ghosts Can't Do It '90
Hot Chocolate '92
Orca '77
Tarzan, the Ape Man '81
10 '79
Woman of Desire '93

John Derek
All the King's Men '49
Ambush at Tomahawk Gap '53
The Annapolis Story '55
Exodus '60
Knock on Any Door '49
Omar Khayyam '57
Once Before I Die '65
Outcast '54
The Ten Commandments '56

Joe DeRita
It's a Mad, Mad, Mad, Mad World '63
The Three Stooges Meet Hercules '61

Edouard Dermithe
Les Enfants Terrible '50
The Testament of Orpheus '59

Bruce Dern
After Dark, My Sweet '90
Big Town '87
Black Sunday '77
Bloody Mama '70
The 'Burbs '89
Carolina Skeletons '92
Coming Home '78
The Court Martial of Jackie Robinson '90
The Cowboys '72
Dead Man's Revenge '93
Diggstown '92
The Driver '78
Family Plot '76
The Great Gatsby '74
Harry Tracy '83
Hush, Hush, Sweet Charlotte '65
The Incredible Two-Headed Transplant '71
Into the Badlands '92

The King of Marvin Gardens '72
The Laughing Policeman '74
Marnie '64
Middle Age Crazy '80
1969 '89
On the Edge '86
Posse '75
Psych-Out '68
Rebel Rousers '69
The St. Valentine's Day Massacre '67
Silent Running '71
Smile '75
Support Your Local Sheriff '69
Tattoo '81
That Championship Season '82
They Shoot Horses, Don't They? '69
Thumb Tripping '72
Toughlove '85
The Trip '67
Twist '76
Uncle Tom's Cabin '87
The War Wagon '67
Waterhole #3 '67
The Wild Angels '66
Will Penny '67
World Gone Wild '88

Laura Dern
Afterburn '92
Blue Velvet '86
Fallen Angels 1 '93
Fat Man and Little Boy '89
Foxes '80
Haunted Summer '88
Jurassic Park '93
Mask '85
A Perfect World '93
Rambling Rose '91
Smooth Talk '85
Strange Case of Dr. Jekyll & Mr. Hyde '89
Teachers '84
Wild at Heart '90

Barbara DeRossi
Blood Ties '87
Mussolini & I '85
Quo Vadis '85

Richard Derr
Adam at 6 A.M. '70
Castle in the Desert '42
Guilty of Treason '50
The Invisible Avenger '58
Terror is a Man '59
When Worlds Collide '51

Cleavant Derricks
Bluffing It '87
Moscow on the Hudson '84
Off Beat '86

Michael Des Barres
Midnight Cabaret '90
Nightflyers '87
Pink Cadillac '89
A Simple Twist of Fate '94
Waxwork 2: Lost in Time '91

Jean Desailly
Assassination of Trotsky '72
La Symphonie Pastorale '46
The Soft Skin '64

Anne DeSalvo
Bad Manners '84
Burglar '87
Casualties of Love: The "Long Island Lolita" Story '93
Compromising Positions '85
D.C. Cab '84
Dead in the Water '91
My Favorite Year '82
Perfect '85
Spike of Bensonhurst '88
Taking Care of Business '90

Stanley DeSantis
Armistead Maupin's Tales of the City '93
Candyman '92

Mary Jo Deschanel
The Right Stuff '83
2010: The Year We Make Contact '84

Sandy Descher
The Cobweb '55
The Prodigal '55

Robert Desiderio
Gross Anatomy '89

Desiderio ▶cont.

Maximum Security '87
Oh, God! You Devil '84

William Desmond
Blood and Steel '25
Courage of the North '35
Cowboy & the Bandit '35
Cyclone of the Saddle '35
Phantom of the Air '33
Phantom of the West '31
Powdersmoke Range '35
Rustlers of Red Dog '35
Tailspin Tommy '34
Way of the West '35

Ivan Desny
Berlin Alexanderplatz '80
End of Desire '62
Escapade in Florence '62
Escape from the KGB '87
Lola Montes '55
Madeleine '50
The Marriage of Maria Braun '79
Quicker Than the Eye '88
The Respectful Prostitute '52
Sherlock Holmes and the Deadly Necklace '62
The Snake Hunter Strangler '66
Song Without End '60
Touch Me Not '74

Nada Despotovich
Babycakes '89
Taken Away '89

Maruschka Detmers
Devil in the Flesh '87
First Name: Carmen '83
Hanna's War '88
The Mambo Kings '92

Geoffrey Deuel
Amateur Night '85
Chisum '70

William Devane
The Bad News Bears in Breaking Training '77
Chips, the War Dog '90
The Dark '79
Family Plot '76
From Here to Eternity '79
Hadley's Rebellion '84
Honky Tonk Freeway '81
Jane Doe '83
Marathon Man '76
McCabe & Mrs. Miller '71
Missiles of October '74
My Old Man's Place '71
The Preppie Murder '89
Red Alert '77
Red Flag: The Ultimate Game '81
Rolling Thunder '77
Rubdown '93
Testament '83
Timestalkers '87
Urge to Kill '84
Vital Signs '90
A Woman Named Jackie '91
Yanks '79

Alan Deveau
Loose Screws '85
Recruits '86

Renee Devillers
The French Touch '54
Heart of a Nation '43
J'Accuse '37

Andy Devine
The Adventures of Huckleberry Finn '60
Ali Baba and the Forty Thieves '43
Eyes of Texas '48
Far Frontier '48
The Gay Ranchero '42
Grand Canyon Trail '48
How the West was Won '63
In Old Chicago '38
The Man Who Shot Liberty Valance '62
Montana Belle '52
Myra Breckinridge '70
Never a Dull Moment '50
Night Time in Nevada '48
On the Old Spanish Trail '47
The Red Badge of Courage '51

Slaughter Trail '51
Smoke '70
Springtime in the Sierras '47
Stagecoach '39
A Star is Born '37
Thunder Pass '54
Till the Clouds Roll By/A Star Is Born '46
Two Rode Together '61
Under California Stars '48
Western Double Feature 18 '40s
Western Double Feature 25
Whale of a Tale '76
Yellowstone '36
Zebra in the Kitchen '65

Loretta Devine
Caged Fear '92
Stanley and Iris '90

Danny DeVito
Amazing Stories '85
Batman Returns '92
Goin' South '78
Going Ape! '81
Head Office '86
Hoffa '92
Hurry Up or I'll Be Thirty '73
Jack the Bear '93
The Jewel of the Nile '85
Johnny Dangerously '84
The Money '75
One Flew Over the Cuckoo's Nest '75
Other People's Money '91
Ratings Game '84
Renaissance Man '94
Romancing the Stone '84
Ruthless People '86
Terms of Endearment '83
Throw Momma from the Train '87
Tin Men '87
Twins '88
The Van '77
The War of the Roses '89
Wise Guys '86

Alan Devlin
The Lonely Passion of Judith Hearne '87
The Playboys '92

J.G. Devlin
The Miracle '91
The Raggedy Rawney '90

Richard Devon
The Battle of Blood Island '60
The Prodigal '55

Dorothy Devore
Silent Movies...Just For the Fun of It! '26
The Tomboy '24

Jon DeVries
Act of Passion: The Lost Honor of Kathryn Beck '83
The 4th Man '92
Grand Isle '92
Lianna '83
Rachel River '89
Sarah, Plain and Tall '91
Skylark '93
Truth or Die '86

Elaine Devry
The Cheyenne Social Club '70
A Guide for the Married Man '67

Eddie Dew
Pagan Island '60
Raiders of Sunset Pass '43
Six Gun Gospel '43

Patrick Dewaere
Beau Pere '81
The Best Way '82
Catherine & Co. '76
The French Detective '75
Get Out Your Handkerchiefs '78
Going Places '74
Heat of Desire '84
Hothead '78

Colleen Dewhurst
And Baby Makes Six '79
Anne of Avonlea '87
Anne of Green Gables '85
Annie Hall '77
Bed & Breakfast '92
Between Two Women '86

The Blue and the Gray '85
The Boy Who Could Fly '86
The Cowboys '72
Danielle Steel's Kaleidoscope '92
Dead Zone '83
Dying Young '91
Final Assignment '80
A Fine Madness '66
The Glitter Dome '84
The Guyana Tragedy: The Story of Jim Jones '80
Ice Castles '79
Lantern Hill '90
Mary and Joseph: A Story of Faith '79
McQ '74
Medea '59
The Nun's Story '59
Obsessed '88
Silent Victory: The Kitty O'Neil Story '79
The Story of Jacob & Joseph '74
Sword of Gideon '86
Termini Station '89
Third Walker '79
When a Stranger Calls '79
You Can't Take It with You '84

Billy DeWolfe
Billie '65
Dear Wife '49
Lullaby of Broadway '51
The Perils of Pauline '47
Tea for Two '50

Anthony Dexter
Fire Maidens from Outer Space '56
Married Too Young '62

Brad Dexter
Between Heaven and Hell '56
The Las Vegas Story '52
Last Train from Gun Hill '59
The Magnificent Seven '60
None But the Brave '65
The Oklahoman '56
Run Silent, Run Deep '58
Secret Ingredient '92
Von Ryan's Express '65
Winter Kills '79

Susan Dey
Comeback Kid '80
Echo Park '86
First Love '77
L.A. Law '86
Little Women '78
Looker '81
Love Leads the Way '84
Sunset Limousine '83
That's Adequate '90
The Trouble with Dick '88

Cliff DeYoung
Annie Oakley '85
Awakening of Candra '81
Bulldance '88
Code Name: Dancer '87
Dr. Giggles '92
F/X '86
Fear '88
Flashback '89
Flight of the Navigator '86
Forbidden Sun '89
Fourth Story '90
The Hunger '83
Immortal Sins '91
In Dangerous Company '88
Independence Day '83
King '78
The Lindbergh Kidnapping Case '76
Nails '92
Protocol '84
Pulse '88
Reckless '84
Revenge of the Red Baron '93
Robert Kennedy and His Times '90
Rude Awakening '89
Secret Admirer '85
Shock Treatment '81
Stephen King's The Tommyknockers '93
The Survivalist '87
To Die Standing '91

Dalia di Lazzaro
Andy Warhol's Frankenstein '74

Creepers '85

Neil Diamond
The Jazz Singer '80
The Last Waltz '78

Reed Edward Diamond
Blind Spot '93
Ironclads '90
Memphis Belle '90
O Pioneers! '91

Selma Diamond
All of Me '84
Bang the Drum Slowly '73
Twilight Zone: The Movie '83

John DiAquino
Pumpkinhead '88
Slipping into Darkness '88

Vic Diaz
Beast of the Yellow Night '70
The Children of An Lac '80
The Deadly and the Beautiful '73
Deathhead Virgin '74
Flight to Fury '66
Night of the Cobra Woman '72
Savage! '73
Too Hot to Handle '76

Leonardo DiCaprio
Critters 3 '91
The Quick and the Dead '94
This Boy's Life '93
What's Eating Gilbert Grape '93

George DiCenzo
About Last Night... '86
Back to the Future '85
18 Again! '88
The Equalizer: Memories of Manon '88
The Exorcist 3 '90
The Frisco Kid '79
Helter Skelter '76
The New Adventures of Pippi Longstocking '88
The Night the City Screamed '80
The Ninth Configuration '79
Omega Syndrome '87
Sing '89
Walk Like a Man '87

Bobby DiCicco
Frame Up '91
I Wanna Hold Your Hand '78
The Last Hour '91
Night Shift '82
The Philadelphia Experiment '84
Splash '84
Tiger Warsaw '87

Douglas Dick
The Accused '48
The Oklahoman '56
The Red Badge of Courage '51

Beach Dickerson
Creature from the Haunted Sea '60
T-Bird Gang '59

George Dickerson
After Dark, My Sweet '90
Blue Velvet '86
Cutter's Way '81
Death Warrant '90

Lucinda Dickey
Breakin' '84
Breakin' 2: Electric Boogaloo '84
Cheerleader Camp '88
Ninja 3: The Domination '84

Angie Dickinson
Big Bad Mama '74
Big Bad Mama 2 '87
The Bramble Bush '60
Captain Newman, M.D. '63
Cast a Giant Shadow '66
Charlie Chan and the Curse of the Dragon Queen '81
The Chase '66
China Gate '57
Death Hunt '81
Dressed to Kill '80
Even Cowgirls Get the Blues '94
Fire and Rain '89
Hidden Guns '56
Jealousy '84

The Killers '64
Klondike Fever '79
Lucky Me '54
Ocean's 11 '60
One Shoe Makes It Murder '82
The Outside Man '73
Point Blank '67
The Poppy is also a Flower '66
Pray for the Wildcats '74
Resurrection of Zachary Wheeler '71
Rio Bravo '59
Rome Adventure '62
Texas Guns '90
Thief '71
Treacherous Crossing '92
Wild Palms '93

Neil Dickson
Biggles '85
It Couldn't Happen Here '88
The Murders in the Rue Morgue '86

Bo Diddley
Chuck Berry: Hail! Hail! Rock 'n' Roll '87
Hell's Angels Forever '83
Rockula '90

Gabino Diego
Ay, Carmela! '90
Belle Epoque '92

Juan Diego
Cabeza de Vaca '90
Jamon, jamon '92

John Diehl
Angel '84
A Climate for Killing '91
Cool Blue '88
Dark Side of the Moon '90
Falling Down '93
Glitz '88
Kickboxer 2: The Road Back '90
Madhouse '90
Miami Vice '84
Mikey '92
Mo' Money '92
Motorama '91
Remote '93

John Dierkes
The Daughter of Dr. Jekyll '57
The Haunted Palace '63

Charles Dierkop
Banzai Runner '86
The Fix '84
Roots of Evil '91

Gustav Diesl
Crimes of Dr. Mabuse '32
Das Testament des Dr. Mabuse '33
Westfront 1918 '30

William Dieterle
Backstairs '21
Waxworks '24

Marlene Dietrich
Blonde Venus '32
The Blue Angel '30
Destry Rides Again '39
Dishonored '31
The Garden of Allah '36
Golden Earrings '47
Judgment at Nuremberg '61
Just a Gigolo '79
Knight Without Armour '37
The Lady is Willing '42
The Love Goddesses '65
Morocco '30
Paris When It Sizzles '64
Pittsburgh '42
Rancho Notorious '52
Scarlet Empress '34
Seven Sinners '40
Shanghai Express '32
The Spoilers '42
Stage Fright '50
Touch of Evil '58
Witness for the Prosecution '57

Frank Dietz
The Jitters '88
Zombie Nightmare '86

Anton Diffring
Black Werewolf '75
Call Him Mr. Shatter '74
Circus of Horrors '60
The Colditz Story '55
Fahrenheit 451 '66

Mark of the Devil 2 '72
Seven Deaths in the Cat's Eye '72
Valentino '77
Where Eagles Dare '68
The Winds of War '83
Zeppelin '71

Dudley Digges
China Seas '35
Devotion '31
Emperor Jones '33
Emperor Jones/Paul Robeson: Tribute to an Artist '33
The General Died at Dawn '36
The Invisible Man '33
The Maltese Falcon '31
Mutiny on the Bounty '35
Son of Fury '42

Arthur Dignam
Between Wars '74
The Devil's Playground '76
The Everlasting Secret Family '88
The Right Hand Man '87
Strange Behavior '81
We of the Never Never '82
The Wild Duck '84

Victoria Dillard
Deep Cover '92
Ricochet '91

Phyllis Diller
The Bone Yard '90
Boy, Did I Get a Wrong Number! '66
Maniac '34
Minsky's Follies '83
Pink Motel '82
A Pleasure Doing Business '79
Splendor in the Grass '61
The Worst of Hollywood: Vol. 1 '90

Bradford Dillman
The Amsterdam Kill '78
Black Water Gold '69
The Bridge at Remagen '69
Brother John '70
Bug '75
Death in Deep Water '74
The Enforcer '76
Escape from the Planet of the Apes '71
Force Five '80
Heroes Stand Alone '89
Legend of Walks Far Woman '82
Lords of the Deep '89
Love and Bullets '79
Man Outside '88
Master Mind '73
The Mephisto Waltz '71
Moon of the Wolf '72
Murder or Mercy '74
99 & 44/100 Dead '74
One Away '80
Piranha '78
Resurrection of Zachary Wheeler '71
Running Scared '79
Sergeant Ryker '68
Sudden Impact '83
Suppose They Gave a War and Nobody Came? '70
The Swarm '78
The Treasure of the Amazon '84
The Way We Were '73
The Widow '76

Kevin Dillon
The Blob '88
The Doors '91
Heaven Help Us '85
Immediate Family '89
A Midnight Clear '92
No Big Deal '83
No Escape '94
Platoon '86
Remote Control '88
The Rescue '88
War Party '89
When He's Not a Stranger '89

Matt Dillon
Big Town '87
Bloodhounds of Broadway '89
Drugstore Cowboy '89
The Flamingo Kid '84
Golden Gate '93
Kansas '88

A Kiss Before Dying '91
Liar's Moon '82
Little Darlings '80
Mr. Wonderful '93
My Bodyguard '80
Native Son '86
The Outsiders '83
Over the Edge '79
Rebel '85
Rumble Fish '83
The Saint of Fort Washington '93
Singles '92
Target '85
Tex '82
Women & Men: In Love There Are No Rules '91

Melinda Dillon
Absence of Malice '81
Bound for Glory '76
Captain America '89
A Christmas Story '83
Close Encounters of the Third Kind '77
Fallen Angel '81
F.I.S.T. '78
Harry and the Hendersons '87
The Juggler of Notre Dame '84
Marriage is Alive and Well '80
Nightbreaker '89
The Prince of Tides '91
Right of Way '84
The Shadow Box '80
Shattered Spirits '91
Slap Shot '77
Songwriter '84
Spontaneous Combustion '89
Staying Together '89

Paul Dillon
The Beat '88
Blink '93
Kiss Daddy Goodnight '87

Stephen Dillon
An Affair in Mind '89
Christabel '89

Tom Dillon
Dressed to Kill '46
Night Tide '63

Alan Dinehart
After Midnight '33
Baby, Take a Bow '34
Everything Happens at Night '39
The Heat's On '43
It's a Great Life '43
Second Fiddle '39
A Study in Scarlet '33
Sweet Rosie O'Grady '43

Charles Dingle
The Beast with Five Fingers '46
The Court Martial of Billy Mitchell '55
Guest Wife '45
Here Come the Co-Eds '45
If You Knew Susie '48
Johnny Eager '42
The Little Foxes '41
Somewhere I'll Find You '42
A Southern Yankee '48

Ernie Dingo
Clowning Around '92
Clowning Around 2 '93
Crocodile Dundee 2 '88
The Fringe Dwellers '86
Until The End of The World '91
A Waltz Through the Hills '88

Reece Dinsdale
Threads '85
Winter Flight '84
Young Catherine '91

Rose Dione
Salome '22
Suds '20

Bob Dishy
Brighton Beach Memoirs '86
I Wonder Who's Killing Her Now? '76
Kill My Wife...Please!
Lovers and Other Strangers '70
My Boyfriend's Back '93
Used People '92

Divine
Divine '90
Female Trouble '74
Hairspray '88

I Wanna Be a Beauty Queen '85
Lust in the Dust '85
Mondo Trasho '69
Multiple Maniacs '70
Out of the Dark '88
Pink Flamingos '72
Polyester '81
Trouble in Mind '86

Andrew Divoff
Back in the USSR '92
Interceptor '92
Low Down Dirty Shame '94
Running Cool '93
Toy Soldiers '91

Richard Dix
Ace of Aces '33
American Empire '42
Archer: The Fugitive from the Empire '81
Buckskin Frontier '43
Cimarron '30
The Kansan '43
Lost Squadron '32
Lucky Devil '25
Special Investigator '36
The Ten Commandments '23
Transatlantic Tunnel '35
Vanishing American '26
Yellow Dust '36

Robert Dix
Blood of Dracula's Castle '69
Cain's Cutthroats '71
Deadwood '65
Horror of the Blood Monsters '70
Killers '88
Satan's Sadists '69
Wild Wheels '75

Donna Dixon
Beverly Hills Madam '86
The Couch Trip '87
Doctor Detroit '83
Lucky Stiff '88
Margin for Murder '81
Speed Zone '88
Spies Like Us '85
Wayne's World '92

Ivan Dixon
Car Wash '76
Fer-De-Lance '74
Nothing But a Man '64
A Patch of Blue '65
A Raisin in the Sun '61
Suppose They Gave a War and Nobody Came? '70

James Dixon
It's Alive '74
It's Alive 3: Island of the Alive '87
Return to Salem's Lot '87

Joan Dixon
Gunplay '51
Hot Lead '51

MacIntyre Dixon
Funny Farm '88
Ghostwriter '84

Pamela Dixon
Chance '89
C.I.A.: Code Name Alexa '92
C.I.A. 2: Target Alexa '94
Hollywood in Trouble '87
L.A. Crackdown '87
L.A. Crackdown 2 '88
Magic Kid '92
Mayhem '87

Badja Djola
An Innocent Man '89
Mississippi Burning '88
A Rage in Harlem '91
The Serpent and the Rainbow '87
Who's the Man? '93

Mauricio Do Valle
Amazon Jail '85
Antonio Das Mortes '68

Heidi Dobbs
Death Journey '76
Jornada de Muerte '80s

Valeria D'Obici
Escape from the Bronx '85
Passion of Love '82

Alan Dobie
The Charge of the Light Brigade '68
White Mischief '88

Lawrence Dobkin
Geronimo '62
Patton '70

Gosia Dobrowolska
Around the World in 80 Ways '86
Careful '94
Silver City '84
A Woman's Tale '92

Kevin Dobson
All Night Long '81
Code of Honor '84
Dirty Work '92
Hardhat & Legs '80
Margin for Murder '81
Midway '76
Orphan Train '79

Peter Dobson
The Marrying Man '91
Sing '89
Where the Day Takes You '92

Tamara Dobson
The Amazons '84
Chained Heat '83
Cleopatra Jones '73
Cleopatra Jones & the Casino of Gold '75
Norman, Is That You? '76

Vernon Dobtcheff
The Assassination Bureau '69
Darling Lili '70
M. Butterfly '93
Nijinsky '80
Pascali's Island '88

Jack Dodson
A Climate for Killing '91
The Getaway '72
Return to Mayberry '85

John Doe
Great Balls of Fire '89
A Matter of Degrees '90
Pure Country '92
Roadside Prophets '92
Slamdance '87

Matt Doherty
The Mighty Ducks '92
So I Married an Axe Murderer '93

Shannen Doherty
Beverly Hills 90210: The Graduation '94
Blindfold: Acts of Obsession '94
Freeze Frame '92
Girls Just Want to Have Fun '85
Heathers '89
Night Shift '82

Michael Dolan
Biloxi Blues '88
Hamburger Hill '87
Light of Day '87

Guy Doleman
The Ipcress File '65
Thunderball '65

Ami Dolenz
Children of the Night '92
Faith '92
Miracle Beach '92
Rescue Me '93
Stepmonster '92
Ticks '93
Witchboard 2: The Devil's Doorway '93

Mickey Dolenz
Head '68
Night of the Strangler '73

Dora Doll
Black and White in Color '76
Boomerang '76

Patrick Dollaghan
Circle of Fear '89
Kill Slade '89
Murphy's Fault '88

Larry Domasin
Fun in Acapulco '63
Island of the Blue Dolphins '64

Arielle Dombasle
The Boss' Wife '86

Le Beau Mariage '82
Pauline at the Beach '83
Trade Secrets '90s
Twisted Obsession '90

Faith Domergue
The Atomic Man '56
Blood Legacy '73
Cult of the Cobra '55
The House of Seven Corpses '73
It Came from Beneath the Sea '55
The Sibling '72
This Island Earth '55
Voyage to the Prehistoric Planet '65

Arturo Dominici
Black Sunday '60
Hercules '58

Solveig Dommartin
Faraway, So Close! '93
No Fear, No Die '90
Until The End of The World '91
Wings of Desire '88

Angelica Domrose
Girls Riot '88
The Scorpion Woman '89

Linda Dona
Delta Heat '92
Final Embrace '92

Elinor Donahue
Freddy's Dead: The Final Nightmare '91
Girls' Town '59
High School USA '84
Love is Better Than Ever '52
Pretty Woman '90
Three Daring Daughters '48

Troy Donahue
Assault of the Party Nerds '89
The Chilling '89
Cockfighter '74
Cry-Baby '90
Cyclone '87
Deadly Diamonds '91
Deadly Prey '87
Deadly Spygames '89
Dr. Alien '88
The Godfather 1902-1959: The Complete Epic '81
The Godfather, Part 2 '74
Grandview U.S.A. '84
Hawkeye '88
Hollywood Cop '87
Imitation of Life '59
The Legend of Frank Woods '77
Love Thrill Murders '71
Monster on the Campus '59
Nudity Required '90
Omega Cop '90
Palm Springs Weekend '63
The Pamela Principle '91
Parrish '61
Rome Adventure '62
Sexpot '88
Shock 'Em Dead '90
Showdown '73
Sounds of Silence '91
South Seas Massacre '59
A Summer Place '59
Terminal Force '88
Those Fantastic Flying Fools '67
Tin Man '83
A Woman Obsessed '88

James Donald
Beau Brummel '54
The Big Sleep '78
The Bridge on the River Kwai '57
Cast a Giant Shadow '66
The Gay Lady '49
The Great Escape '63
Immortal Battalion '44
In Which We Serve '43
King Rat '65
Lust for Life '56
The Pickwick Papers '54
Third Man on the Mountain '59
Victoria Regina '61
The Vikings '58

Ted Donaldson
The Red Stallion '47
A Tree Grows in Brooklyn '45

Peter Donat
The Babe '92
The Bay Boy '85
The China Syndrome '79
Different Story '78
F.I.S.T. '78
Honeymoon '87
Massive Retaliation '85
Mazes and Monsters '82
Mirrors '78
Return Engagement '78
School Ties '92
Tucker: The Man and His
Dream '88
The War of the Roses '89

Robert Donat
The Adventures of Tartu '43
The Citadel '38
The Count of Monte Cristo '34
The Ghost Goes West '36
Goodbye, Mr. Chips '39
Hitchcock Collection '87
If I Were Rich '33
The Inn of the Sixth Happiness
'58
Knight Without Armour '37
The Private Life of Henry VIII
'33
The 39 Steps '35
The Winslow Boy '48

Ludwig Donath
The Jolson Story '46
The Lovable Cheat '49
The Secret Code '42

Manuel Donde
Savage Wilderness '55
Swamp of the Lost Monster '65

Yolande Donlan
The Adventurers '70
The Devil Bat '41

Brian Donlevy
Allegheny Uprising '39
Arizona Bushwackers '67
Barbary Coast '35
Beau Geste '39
Big Combo '55
Billy the Kid '41
Command Decision '48
Destry Rides Again '39
The Errand Boy '61
Five Golden Dragons '67
Gamera, the Invincible '66
The Glass Key '42
The Great McGinty '40
Hoodlum Empire '52
How to Stuff a Wild Bikini '65
Impact '49
In Old Chicago '38
Jesse James '39
Kiss of Death '47
Miracle of Morgan's Creek '44
Quatermass 2 '57
The Quatermass Experiment
'56
Ride the Man Down '53
Slaughter Trail '51
A Southern Yankee '48
Wake Island '42

Steve Donmyer
Glitch! '91
Terminal Exposure '89

**Barnard Pierre
Donnadieu**
Beatrice '88
The Return of Martin Guerre
'83
The Vanishing '88

Jeff Donnell
Because You're Mine '52
The Fuller Brush Girl '50
Gidget Goes to Rome '63
In a Lonely Place '50
My Man Godfrey '57
Redwood Forest Trail '50
Three Guys Named Mike '51
Walk Softly, Stranger '50

Donal Donnelly
The Dead '87
The Godfather, Part 3 '90
The Knack '65
Waterloo '71

James Donnelly
And Nothing But the Truth '82
Sea Devils '31

Ruth Donnelly
The Affairs of Annabel '38
Annabel Takes a Tour/Maid's
Night Out '38
Blessed Event '32
Bureau of Missing Persons '33
Female '33
Footlight Parade '33
Holiday '38
Ladies They Talk About '33
A Lawless Street '55
Mr. Deeds Goes to Town '36

Tim Donnelly
The Clonus Horror '79
The Toolbox Murders '78

Robert Donner
Lassie: Well of Love '90
Man Who Loved Cat Dancing
'73
Under the Rainbow '81
Vanishing Point '71

Vincent D'Onofrio
Adventures in Babysitting '87
Being Human '94
The Blood of Heroes '89
Crooked Hearts '91
Desire '93
Dying Young '91
Ed Wood '94
Fires Within '91
First Turn On '83
Full Metal Jacket '87
Household Saints '93
JFK '91
Mr. Wonderful '93
Mystic Pizza '88
The Player '92
Signs of Life '89

Amanda Donohoe
An Affair in Mind '89
Castaway '87
Dark Obsession '90
Double Cross '92
Foreign Body '86
The Lair of the White Worm '88
Paper Mask '91
The Rainbow '89
Shame '88
The Substitute '93

King Donovan
Easy to Love '53
The Enforcer '51
Forever Female '53
The Hanging Tree '59
Invasion of the Body Snatchers
'56
The Merry Widow '52
Singin' in the Rain '52

Martin Donovan
Quick '93
Simple Men '92
Surviving Desire '91
Trust '91

Tate Donovan
Clean and Sober '88
Dangerous Curves '88
Dead Bang '89
Equinox '93
Ethan Frome '92
Inside Monkey Zetterland '93
Into Thin Air '85
Little Noises '91
Love Potion #9 '92
Memphis Belle '90
Not My Kid '85
SpaceCamp '86
Vietnam War Story 2 '88

Terence Donovan
The Man from Snowy River '82
Money Movers '78
The Winds of Jarrah '83

Alison Doody
Duel of Hearts '92
Indiana Jones and the Last
Crusade '89
Major League 2 '94
Prayer for the Dying '88
Ring of the Musketeers '93
Taffin '88

James Doohan
Amore! '93
Double Trouble '91
Man in the Wilderness '71
Star Trek: The Motion Picture
'80

Star Trek 2: The Wrath of Khan
'82
Star Trek 3: The Search for
Spock '84
Star Trek 4: The Voyage Home
'86
Star Trek 5: The Final Frontier
'89
Star Trek 6: The Undiscovered
Country '91
Star Trek Bloopers '69

Paul Dooley
Armistead Maupin's Tales of
the City '93
Big Trouble '86
Breaking Away '79
Cooperstown '93
The Court Martial of Jackie
Robinson '90
A Dangerous Woman '93
Endangered Species '82
Flashback '89
Going Berserk '83
Hansel and Gretel '82
Kiss Me Goodbye '82
Last Rites '88
Lip Service '88
The Murder of Mary Phagan
'87
My Boyfriend's Back '93
O.C. and Stiggs '87
Paternity '81
Popeye '80
Rich Kids '79
Rumpelstiltskin '82
Shakes the Clown '92
Sixteen Candles '84
State of Emergency '94
Strange Brew '83
A Wedding '78
When He's Not a Stranger '89
White Hot: The Mysterious
Murder of Thelma Todd '91

Lucinda Dooling
The Alchemist '81
Lovely...But Deadly '82
Miracle on Ice '81

Patric Doonan
Blackout '50
The Blue Lamp '49
Train of Events '49

Robert DoQui
Coffy '73
A Dream for Christmas '73
Miracle Mile '89
Nashville '75
Original Intent '91
RoboCop '87
Short Fuse '88

Karin Dor
Carpet of Horror '64
Die Screaming, Marianne '73
Dracula vs. Frankenstein '69
Forger of London '61
The Invisible Dr. Mabuse '62
The Last Tomahawk '65
Prisoner in the Middle '74
Strangler of Blackmoor Castle
'63
Topaz '69
The Torture Chamber of Dr.
Sadism '69
You Only Live Twice '67

Ann Doran
The Accused '48
Blondie '38
Criminals Within '41
Fear in the Night '47
Holiday in Havana '49
It! The Terror from Beyond
Space '58
Little Red Schoolhouse '36
Love is Better Than Ever '52
Meet John Doe '41
Mr. Wise Guy '42
The More the Merrier '43
Never a Dull Moment '50
The Painted Hills '51
Pitfall '48
Rebel Without a Cause '55

Jesse Doran
Heart '87
Street Asylum '90

Mary Doran
Broadway Melody '29
Criminal Code '31
The Divorcee '30

Sing Sing Nights '35
The Strange Love of Molly
Louvain '32

Johnny Dorelli
How to Kill 400 Duponts '65
The Odd Squad '86

Stephen Dorff
Backbeat '94
The Gate '87
Judgment Night '93
The Power of One '92
Rescue Me '93
S.F.W. '94

Pierre Doris
Overseas: Three Women with
Man Trouble '90
The Story of a Three Day Pass
'68

Francoise Dorleac
Cul de Sac '66
The Soft Skin '64
That Man from Rio '64

Dolores Dorn
Lucky Me '54
Truck Stop Women '74
Underworld, U.S.A. '60

Michael Dorn
The Jagged Edge '85
Star Trek 6: The Undiscovered
Country '91
Star Trek the Next Generation:
Encounter at Farpoint '87

Philip Dorn
The Fighting Kentuckian '49
I've Always Loved You '46
Random Harvest '42
Reunion in France '42
Tarzan's Secret Treasure '41
Ziegfeld Girl '41

Robert Dornan
Hell on Wheels '67
The Starfighters '63

Sandra Dorne
Alias John Preston '56
Eat the Rich '87
The House in Marsh Road '60
Roadhouse Girl '53

Lester Dorr
Meet the Mob '42
Panama Menace '41

Diana Dors
Adventures of a Taxi Driver '76
Amazing Mr. Blunden '72
Baby Love '69
Berserk! '67
Children of the Full Moon '84
Craze '74
Deep End '70
The Devil's Web '74
From Beyond the Grave '73
Hannie Caulder '72
I Married a Woman '56
The King of the Roaring '20s:
The Story of Arnold
Rothstein '61
The Long Haul '57
Man Bait '52
A Man with a Maid '73
Nothing But the Night '72
Oliver Twist '48
Room 43 '58
Steaming '86
Theatre of Blood '73
There's a Girl in My Soup '70
Unholy Wife '57
Unicorn '83

Fifi d'Orsay
Delinquent Daughters '44
The Gangster '47
Girl from Calgary '32
Going Hollywood '33
Nabonga '44
Three Legionnaires '37

Jimmy Dorsey
The Fabulous Dorseys '47
Hollywood Canteen '44

Tommy Dorsey
The Fabulous Dorseys '47
Presenting Lily Mars '43

Susana Dosamantes
Counterforce '87
Remolina de Pasiones '87
Target Eagle '84

John Dossett
Longtime Companion '90
That Night '93

Karen Dotrice
The Gnome-Mobile '67
The Thirty-Nine Steps '79
The Three Lives of Thomasina
'63

Michele Dotrice
And Soon the Darkness '70
The Blood on Satan's Claw '71

Roy Dotrice
Amadeus '84
Carmilla '89
Cheech and Chong's, The
Corsican Brothers '84
The Cutting Edge '92
The Dancing Princesses '84
The Eliminators '86
Space: 1999—Alien Attack '79
Suburban Commando '91

John Doucette
Fighting Mad '76
Paradise, Hawaiian Style '66
Seven Cities of Gold '55

Doug E. Doug
Class Act '91
Cool Runnings '93
Hangin' with the Homeboys '91

Angela Douglas
The Cariboo Trail '50
Carry On Screaming '66
Digby, the Biggest Dog in the
World '73

Brandon Douglas
The Children of Times Square
'86
Chips, the War Dog '90
Journey to Spirit Island '92

Burt Douglas
High School Confidential '58
Hush Little Baby, Don't You Cry
'86
The Law and Jake Wade '58

Don Douglas
Behind the Rising Sun '43
Club Havana '46
The Great Gabbo '29
Law of the Texan '38
Tomorrow's Children '34
Whistling in the Dark '41

Donna Douglas
Career '59
Frankie and Johnny '65

Eric Douglas
Delta Force 3: The Killing Game
'91
Student Confidential '87
Tomboy '85

Illeana Douglas
Alive '93
Cape Fear '91
Household Saints '93

John Douglas
Hell's Brigade: The Final
Assault '80
Violent Zone '89

Kirk Douglas
Along the Great Divide '51
Amos '85
The Arrangement '69
The Bad and the Beautiful '52
The Big Sky '52
Big Trees '52
The Brotherhood '68
Cast a Giant Shadow '66
Catch Me a Spy '71
Champion '49
The Chosen '77
Detective Story '51
The Devil's Disciple '59
Dr. Jekyll and Mr. Hyde '73
Draw! '81
Eddie Macon's Run '83
The Final Countdown '80
For Love or Money '63
The Fury '78
Greedy '94
A Gunfight '71
Gunfight at the O.K. Corral '57
Hollywood Bloopers '50s
Holocaust
Survivors...Remembrance of
Love '83

Home Movies '79
In Harm's Way '65
The Indian Fighter '55
Is Paris Burning? '68
Last Train from Gun Hill '59
A Letter to Three Wives '49
Light at the Edge of the World '71
The List of Adrian Messenger '63
Lonely are the Brave '62
Lust for Life '56
The Man from Snowy River '82
Man Without a Star '55
Master Touch '74
My Dear Secretary '49
Once is Not Enough '75
Out of the Past '47
Paths of Glory '57
Posse '75
Queenie '87
The Racers '55
Saturn 3 '80
The Secret '93
Seven Days in May '64
Spartacus '60
The Strange Love of Martha Ivers '46
Strangers When We Meet '60
There was a Crooked Man '70
Tough Guys '86
20,000 Leagues Under the Sea '54
Two Weeks in Another Town '62
Ulysses '55
The Vikings '58
The Villain '79
The War Wagon '67
The Way West '67
Young Man with a Horn '50

Mark Douglas
Moonshine Mountain '64
2000 Maniacs '64

Melvyn Douglas
The Americanization of Emily '64
Annie Oakley '35
As You Desire Me '32
Being There '79
Billy Budd '62
The Candidate '72
Captains Courageous '37
The Changeling '80
The Death Squad '73
Ghost Story '81
The Gorgeous Hussy '36
Hard Frame '70
Hot Touch '80s
Hotel '67
Hud '63
I Never Sang For My Father '70
Lamp at Midnight '66
The Making of a Legend: "Gone With the Wind" '89
Mr. Blandings Builds His Dream House '48
Murder or Mercy '74
My Forbidden Past '51
Ninotchka '39
The Old Dark House '32
Portrait of Grandpa Doc '77
The Seduction of Joe Tynan '79
The Shining Hour '38
Tell Me a Riddle '80
The Tenant '76
That Uncertain Feeling '41
Twilight's Last Gleaming '77
Two-Faced Woman '41
The Vampire Bat '32
Woman in the Shadows '34
A Woman's Face '41
A Woman's Secret '49

Michael Douglas
Adam at 6 A.M. '70
Basic Instinct '92
Black Rain '89
The China Syndrome '79
A Chorus Line '85
Coma '78
Falling Down '93
Fatal Attraction '87
Hail, Hero! '69
It's My Turn '80
The Jewel of the Nile '85
Napoleon and Samantha '72
Romancing the Stone '84
Shattered Silence '71
Shining Through '92

The Star Chamber '83
The Streets of San Francisco '72
Summertree '71
Wall Street '87
The War of the Roses '89

Paul Douglas
Angels in the Outfield '51
The Big Lift '50
Clash by Night '52
Executive Suite '54
Forever Female '53
The Gamma People '56
Green Fire '55
It Happens Every Spring '49
A Letter to Three Wives '49
The Mating Game '59
Never Wave at a WAC '52
Panic in the Streets '50
This Could Be the Night '57
We're Not Married '52

Robert Douglas
Adventures of Don Juan '49
At Sword's Point '51
The Challenge '38
The Desert Rats '53
The Flame & the Arrow '50
King Richard and the Crusaders '54
London Melody '37

Sarah Douglas
The Art of Dying '90
Beastmaster 2: Through the Portal of Time '91
Conan the Destroyer '84
The Final Programme '73
Meatballs 4 '92
Nightfall '88
The People That Time Forgot '77
Puppet Master 3: Toulon's Revenge '91
The Return of Swamp Thing '89
Solarbabies '86
Steele Justice '87
Superman: The Movie '78
Superman 2 '80
Tagget '90

Shirley Douglas
Dead Ringers '88
Shadow Dancing '88

Warren Douglas
The Inner Circle '46
The Man I Love '46

Robyn Douglass
Freeze Frame '92
Her Life as a Man '83
The Lonely Guy '84
Partners '82

Brad Dourif
Amos and Andrew '93
Blue Velvet '86
Body Parts '91
Child's Play '88
Color of Night '94
Common Bonds '91
Critters 4 '91
Dario Argento's Trauma '93
Dead Certain '92
Dune '84
The Exorcist 3 '90
Eyes of Laura Mars '78
Fatal Beauty '87
Final Judgement '92
Graveyard Shift '90
Grim Prairie Tales '89
The Guyana Tragedy: The Story of Jim Jones '80
Heaven's Gate '81
Hidden Agenda '90
Horseplayer '91
Impure Thoughts '86
Istanbul '85
Jungle Fever '91
London Kills Me '91
Mississippi Burning '88
One Flew Over the Cuckoo's Nest '75
Rage of Angels: The Story Continues '86
Ragtime '81
Sergeant Matlovich vs. the U.S. Air Force '78
Sonny Boy '87
Spontaneous Combustion '89
Vengeance '89
Wild Palms '93

Wise Blood '79

Billie Dove
All the Brothers Were Valiant '53
The Black Pirate '26

Tony Dow
Back to the Beach '87
Death Scream '75
High School USA '84

Ann Dowd
It Could Happen to You '94
Philadelphia '93

Don Dowe
Evil Toons '90
Test Tube Teens from the Year 2000 '93

Raye Dowell
Landlord Blues '87
She's Gotta Have It '86

Garrick Dowhen
Appointment with Fear '85
Land of Doom '84

Doris Dowling
The Lost Weekend '45
Othello '52

Joan Dowling
Hue and Cry '47
Train of Events '49

Lesley-Anne Down
Arch of Triumph '85
Assault '70
The Betsy '78
Brannigan '75
Death Wish 5: The Face of Death '94
From Beyond the Grave '73
The Great Train Robbery '79
Hanover Street '79
The Hunchback of Notre Dame '82
Indiscreet '88
Ladykillers '88
A Little Night Music '77
Mardi Gras for the Devil '93
Nomads '86
North and South Book 1 '85
North and South Book 2 '86
The Pink Panther Strikes Again '76
Rough Cut '80
Scenes from the Goldmine '87
Sphinx '81

Morton Downey, Jr.
Body Chemistry 2: Voice of a Stranger '91
Driving Me Crazy '91
Legal Tender '90
Predator 2 '90
Revenge of the Nerds 3: The Next Generation '92
The Silencer '92

Robert Downey, Jr.
Air America '90
America '86
Baby It's You '82
Back to School '86
Chances Are '89
Chaplin '92
First Born '84
Hail Caesar '94
Heart and Souls '93
Johnny Be Good '88
Less Than Zero '87
Natural Born Killers '94
1969 '89
Only You '94
The Pick-Up Artist '87
Rented Lips '88
Short Cuts '93
Soapdish '91
To Live & Die in L.A. '85
Too Much Sun '90
True Believer '89
Tuff Turf '85
Weird Science '85

Roma Downey
Devlin '92
Getting Up and Going Home '92
A Woman Named Jackie '91

J. Downing
Ghoulies 2 '88
Robot Wars '93

Cathy Downs
The Amazing Colossal Man '57
Dark Corner '46
The Flaming Urge '53
Kentucky Rifle '55
Missile to the Moon '59
The Noose Hangs High '48
The Phantom from 10,000 Leagues '56

Johnny Downs
The Adventures of the Flying Cadets '44
Bad Boy '39
Harvest Melody '43
The Mad Monster '42
March of the Wooden Soldiers '34
Rhapsody in Blue '45

David Doyle
The Comeback '77
Ghost Writer '89
The Line '80
Love or Money? '88
My Boys are Good Boys '78
Paper Lion '68
Wait Till Your Mother Gets Home '83
Who Killed Mary What's 'Er Name? '71
Wild & Wooly '78

John Doyle
Contagion '87
Rock & Roll Cowboys '92
The Wicked '89

Maxine Doyle
Condemned to Live '35
The Mystery Man '35
S.O.S. Coast Guard '37

Brian Doyle-Murray
Bob Roberts '92
Cabin Boy '94
Caddyshack '80
Club Paradise '86
The Experts '89
Groundhog Day '93
How I Got into College '89
JFK '91
Modern Problems '81
National Lampoon's Christmas Vacation '89
National Lampoon's Vacation '83
The Razor's Edge '84
Scrooged '88
Sixteen Candles '84
Wayne's World '92

Tony Doyle
Adventures in Dinosaur City '92
Eat the Peach '86
The Final Option '82

Heinz Drache
The Avenger '60
Circus of Fear '67
Door with the Seven Locks '62
The Indian Scarf '63
The Mysterious Magician '65
The Squeaker '65

Billy Drago
China White '91
Cyborg 2 '93
Dark Before Dawn '89
Death Ring '93
Delta Force 2: Operation Stranglehold '90
Diplomatic Immunity '91
Freeway '88
Guncrazy '92
Hero and the Terror '88
Invasion U.S.A. '85
Lady Dragon 2 '93
Martial Law 2: Undercover '91
The Outfit '93
Prime Suspect '88
Secret Games '92
The Untouchables '87

Betsy Drake
Clarence, the Cross-eyed Lion '65
Every Girl Should Be Married '48
Second Woman '51

Charles Drake
Air Force '43
Bleak House '85
Conflict '45

Hail, Hero! '69
Harvey '50
It Came From Outer Space '53
A Night in Casablanca '46
The Tender Years '47
Tobor the Great '54
Until They Sail '57
Valley of the Dolls '67
Winchester '73 '50

Claudia Drake
Border Patrol '43
Detour '46
Enemy of Women '44
Gentleman from Texas '46
The Lady Confesses '45

Dona Drake
Louisiana Purchase '41
The Road to Morocco '42

Frances Drake
Forsaking All Others '35
I'd Give My Life '36
The Invisible Ray '36
Les Miserables '35
Mad Love '35

Larry Drake
Dark Night of the Scarecrow '81
Darkman '90
Dr. Giggles '92
Murder in New Hampshire: The Pamela Smart Story '91
Tales from the Crypt '89

Tom Drake
The Bramble Bush '60
Cass Timberlane '47
Courage of Lassie '46
Cycle Psycho
Cyclops '56
FBI Girl '52
The Great Rupert '50
The Hills of Home '48
House of the Black Death '65
The Howards of Virginia '40
Johnny Reno '66
Meet Me in St. Louis '44
Savage Abduction '73
The Singing Nun '66
The Spectre of Edgar Allen Poe '73
Two Girls and a Sailor '44
Warkill '65
The White Cliffs of Dover '44
Words and Music '48

Polly Draper
Making Mr. Right '86
The Pick-Up Artist '87

Milena Dravic
Man is Not a Bird '65
WR: Mysteries of the Organism '71

Alfred Drayton
Nicholas Nickleby '46
Things Happen at Night '48

Alex Dreier
Lady Cocoa '75
Loners '72

Fran Drescher
Cadillac Man '90
Car 54, Where Are You? '94
Doctor Detroit '83
Rosebud Beach Hotel '85
Wedding Band
We're Talkin' Serious Money '92

Sonia Dresdel
The Fallen Idol '49
While I Live '47

Curly Dresden
Arizona Gangbusters '40
Fighting Valley '43
Pals of the Saddle '38
Rough Ridin' Rhythm '37
Santa Fe Stampede '38
Trigger Men '41
Wyoming Outlaw '39

John Dresden
Final Mission '84
No Dead Heroes '87
Raw Force '81

Louise Dresser
Dracula/Garden of Eden '28
The Eagle '25
The Garden of Eden '28
Scarlet Empress '34

Dresser ►cont.

The Tempest/The Eagle '27

Lieux Dressler
Grave of the Vampire '72
Truck Stop Women '74

Marie Dressler
Anna Christie '30
Dinner at Eight '33
Kings, Queens, Jokers '30s
Min & Bill '30
Tillie Wakes Up '17
Tillie's Punctured Romance '14
Vagabond Lover '29

Ellen Drew
Baron of Arizona '51
China Sky '44
Christmas in July '40
Dark Mountain '44
Great Missouri Raid '51
Isle of the Dead '45
Man from Colorado '49
The Monster and the Girl '41
Stars in My Crown '50

Gene Drew
Steel Arena '72
Truck Stop Women '74

Sidney Drew
Early Cinema Vol. 1 '19
Playing Dead '15

Nancy Drexel
Man from Hell's Edges '32
Mason of the Mounted '32
Texas Buddies '32

Lorin Dreyfuss
Detective School Dropouts '85
Dutch Treat '86

Richard Dreyfuss
Always '89
American Graffiti '73
Another Stakeout '93
The Apprenticeship of Duddy
    Kravitz '74
The Big Fix '78
The Buddy System '83
Close Encounters of the Third
    Kind '77
The Competition '80
Dillinger '73
Down and Out in Beverly Hills
    '86
The Goodbye Girl '77
The Graduate '67
Inserts '76
Jaws '75
Let It Ride '89
Lost in Yonkers '93
Moon Over Parador '88
Nuts '87
Once Around '93
Postcards from the Edge '90
Prisoner of Honor '91
Rosencrantz & Guildenstern
    Are Dead '90
Second Coming of Suzanne '80
Stakeout '87
Stand By Me '86
Suzanne '80
Tin Men '87
What About Bob? '91
Whose Life Is It Anyway? '81

Moosie Drier
Ants '77
Charlie and the Great Balloon
    Chase '82
Homeward Bound '80

Deborah Driggs
Night Rhythms '92
Total Exposure '91

Bobby Driscoll
The Fighting Sullivans '42
Identity Unknown '45
So Dear to My Heart '49
Treasure Island '50
The Window '49

Jean-Claude Drouot
La Rupture '70
Le Bonheur '65

Joanne Dru
All the King's Men '49
Hell on Frisco Bay '55
The Light in the Forest '58
Pride of St. Louis '52

Red River '48
She Wore a Yellow Ribbon '49
Sincerely Yours '56
Super Fuzz '81
Thunder Bay '53
Vengeance Valley '51
Wagon Master '50
The Warriors '55

James Drury
The Gambler Returns: The
    Luck of the Draw '93
Love Me Tender '56
The Meanest Men in the West
    '76
Ride the High Country '62
Ten Who Dared '60
The Tender Trap '55
Walker: Texas Ranger: One
    Riot, One Ranger '93

Fred Dryer
Death Before Dishonor '87
The Fantastic World of D.C.
    Collins '84

Robert Dryer
Heartbreaker '83
Savage Streets '83

Gerald du Maurier
The Living Dead '36
Power '34

Carmen Du Sautoy
Deadly Recruits '86
It Couldn't Happen Here '88
Praying Mantis '83

Michael Duane
City Without Men '43
The Prince of Thieves '48

Frances Dubay
The Body Vanished '39
Wild Women '53

Don Dubbins
D.I. '57
From the Earth to the Moon '58
The Illustrated Man '69
Savage Run '70
Tribute to a Bad Man '56

Jessica Dublin
The Rejuvenator '88
The Toxic Avenger, Part 3: The
    Last Temptation of Toxie '89

Ja'net DuBois
Heart Condition '90
I'm Gonna Git You Sucka '88
Piece of the Action '77

Marie DuBois
Circle of Love '64
Jailbird's Vacation '65
Jules and Jim '62
La Petite Sirene '81
Les Grandes Gueules '65
Mon Oncle D'Amerique '80
Night Flight from Moscow '73
Shoot the Piano Player '62
A Woman is a Woman '60

Marta DuBois
Boulevard Nights '79
Fear '90
The Trial of the Incredible Hulk
    '89

Paulette Dubost
The Last Metro '80
May Fools '90
The Rules of the Game '39
The Sheep Has Five Legs '54
Viva Maria! '65

Paul Dubov
Apache Woman '55
China Gate '57
Day the World Ended '55
Ma Barker's Killer Brood '60
Underworld, U.S.A. '60
Verboten! '59

Kristie Ducati
The Bikini Car Wash Company
    '90
The Bikini Car Wash Company
    2 '92

Michael Duchaussoy
The Killing Game '67
May Fools '90
Return of the Tall Blond Man
    With One Black Shoe '74
Road to Ruin '91
This Man Must Die '70

David Duchovny
Beethoven '92
Chaplin '92
Julia Has Two Lovers '91
Kalifornia '93
New Year's Day '89
The Rapture '91
Red Shoe Diaries '92
Red Shoe Diaries 2: Double
    Dare '92
Red Shoe Diaries 3: Another
    Woman's Lipstick '93
Red Shoe Diaries 4: Auto
    Erotica '93
Ruby '92

Rick Ducommun
Blank Check '93
The 'Burbs '89
Class Act '91
Die Hard '88
Encino Man '92
Ghost in the Machine '93
Little Monsters '89
No Small Affair '84

Louis Ducreux
The Double Life of Veronique
    '91
The Story of Women '88
A Sunday in the Country '84

Michael Dudikoff
American Ninja '85
American Ninja 2: The
    Confrontation '87
American Ninja 4: The
    Annihilation '91
Avenging Force '86
Bachelor Party '84
The Black Marble '79
Bloody Birthday '80
The Human Shield '92
I Ought to Be in Pictures '82
Making Love '82
Platoon Leader '87
Radioactive Dreams '86
Rescue Me '93
River of Death '90

William Duell
Grace Quigley '84
Police Squad! Help Wanted! '82

Denice Duff
Bloodfist 5: Human Target '93
Bloodlust: Subspecies 3 '93
Bloodstone: Subspecies 2 '93

Howard Duff
Boy's Night Out '62
The Double Negative '80
East of Eden '80
Flame of the Islands '55
Kramer vs. Kramer '79
Love on the Run '85
Magic on Love Island '80
Monster in the Closet '86
The Naked City '48
No Way Out '87
Oh, God! Book 2 '80
Private Hell 36 '54
Snatched '72
Snowblind '78
Spaceways '53
A Wedding '78
While the City Sleeps '56

Kevin Duffis
The Expendables '89
Nam Angels '88

Julia Duffy
Children in the Crossfire '84
Night Warning '82

Patrick Duffy
Danielle Steel's "Daddy" '92
Enola Gay: The Men, the
    Mission, the Atomic Bomb
    '80
The Last of Mrs. Lincoln '76
The Man from Atlantis '77
Vamping '84

Thomas F. Duffy
Eye of the Stranger '93
Wagons East '94

Jacques Dufilho
Black and White in Color '76
The Horse of Pride '80
Le Crabe Tambour '77

Dennis Dugan
Can't Buy Me Love '87

The Howling '81
The New Adventures of Pippi
    Longstocking '88
Night Call Nurses '72
Night Moves '75
Norman, Is That You? '76
Parenthood '89
She's Having a Baby '88
Unidentified Flying Oddball '79

Tom Dugan
Accomplice '46
Blessed Event '32
The Galloping Ghost '31
Gambler's Choice '44
Medicine Man '30
Perfect Victims '87
Pick a Star '37
Take Me Out to the Ball Game
    '49
To Be or Not to Be '42

Andrew Duggan
The Bears & I '74
The Commies are Coming, the
    Commies are Coming '57
Doctor Detroit '83
Firehouse '72
Frankenstein Island '81
Housewife '72
The Hunted Lady '77
In Like Flint '67
The Incredible Mr. Limpet '64
It's Alive '74
It's Alive 2: It Lives Again '78
J. Edgar Hoover '87
Jigsaw '71
The Long Days of Summer '80
Merrill's Marauders '62
Palm Springs Weekend '63
Pueblo Affair '73
Return to Salem's Lot '87
The Secret War of Harry Frigg
    '68
Skin Game '71
The Streets of San Francisco
    '72
Time Machine '78
The Winds of War '83

Olympia Dukakis
Armistead Maupin's Tales of
    the City '93
The Cemetery Club '93
Dad '89
Death Wish '74
Idolmaker '80
In the Spirit '90
Look Who's Talking '89
Look Who's Talking Now '93
Look Who's Talking, Too '90
Moonstruck '87
Over the Hill '93
Rich Kids '79
Sinatra '92
Steel Magnolias '89
Walls of Glass '85
Working Girl '88

Bill Duke
Bird on a Wire '90
Commando '85
Killing Floor '85
Menace II Society '93
Predator '87

Patty Duke
Amityville '89
The Babysitter '80
Best Kept Secrets '88
Billie '65
By Design '82
Curse of the Black Widow '77
Family Upside Down '78
Fire '77
The 4D Man '59
George Washington '84
George Washington: The
    Forging of a Nation '86
The Goddess '58
Grave Secrets: The Legacy of
    Hilltop Drive '92
Killer on Board '77
The Miracle Worker '62
The Miracle Worker '79
Mom, the Wolfman and Me '80
My Sweet Charlie '70
Prelude to a Kiss '92
September Gun '83
She Waits '71
Something Special '86
The Swarm '78
Valley of the Dolls '67

Robin Duke
Best of Eddie Murphy '89
Club Paradise '86
The Last Polka '84
Motorama '91

David Dukes
Cat on a Hot Tin Roof '84
Catch the Heat '87
Date with an Angel '87
The First Deadly Sin '80
George Washington '91
Held Hostage '91
The Josephine Baker Story '90
The Men's Club '86
Miss All-American Beauty '82
My Darlin' Clementine '86
Only When I Laugh '81
Portrait of a Rebel: Margaret
    Sanger '82
Rawhead Rex '87
The Rutanga Tapes '90
See You in the Morning '89
Snow Kill '90
Strange Interlude '90
The Strawberry Statement '70
The Triangle Factory Fire
    Scandal '79
War & Remembrance, Part 1
    '88
War & Remembrance, Part 2
    '89
War & Remembrance, Part 3
    '88
War & Remembrance, Part 4
    '88
War & Remembrance, Part 5
    '88
War & Remembrance, Part 6
    '88
War & Remembrance, Part 7
    '88
War & Remembrance: The
    Final Chapter, Part 8 '89
War & Remembrance: The
    Final Chapter, Part 9 '89
War & Remembrance: The
    Final Chapter, Part 10 '89
War & Remembrance: The
    Final Chapter, Part 11 '89
War & Remembrance: The
    Final Chapter, Part 12 '89
Wild Party '74
The Winds of War '83
Without a Trace '83

Caitlin Dulany
Class of 1999 2: The Substitute
    '93
Maniac Cop 3 '93

Keir Dullea
Black Christmas '75
Black Water Gold '69
Blind Date '84
Brainwaves '82
David and Lisa '62
Full Circle '77
The Hoodlum Priest '61
The Hostage Tower '80
Leopard in the Snow '78
Love Under Pressure '80s
Madame X '66
Mannikin '77
Next One '84
No Place to Hide '81
Oh, What a Night '92
Paperback Hero '73
Paul and Michelle '74
2001: A Space Odyssey '68
2010: The Year We Make
    Contact '84
Welcome to Blood City '77

Douglass Dumbrille
Abbott and Costello in the
    Foreign Legion '50
Baby Face '33
Blonde Savage '47
Castle in the Desert '42
Crime and Punishment '35
A Day at the Races '37
The Firefly '37
Heroes for Sale '33
I Married an Angel '42
Jupiter's Darling '55
The Lives of a Bengal Lancer
    '35
Lost in a Harem '44
Mr. Deeds Goes to Town '36
The Mysterious Rider '38
Naughty Marietta '35

Ride 'Em Cowboy '42
The Road to Utopia '46
Shake, Rattle and Rock '57
Son of Paleface '52
Spook Busters '46
The Ten Commandments '56
The Three Musketeers '39
Treasure Island '34
Under Nevada Skies '46
Virginia City '40

Denise Dumont
Heart of Midnight '89
Kiss of the Spider Woman '85

Margaret Dumont
Animal Crackers '30
At the Circus '39
Big Store '41
The Cocoanuts '29
A Day at the Races '37
Duck Soup '33
The Horn Blows at Midnight '45
Never Give a Sucker an Even Break '41
A Night at the Opera '35
Rhythm Parade '42
Seven Days Ashore/Hurry, Charlie, Hurry '44
Shake, Rattle and Rock '57
Sing Your Worries Away '42
Three for Bedroom C '52
Up in Arms '44
The Women '39

Ulises Dumont
The Lion's Share '79
Time for Revenge '82

Dennis Dun
Big Trouble in Little China '86
The Last Emperor '87
Prince of Darkness '87
Thousand Pieces of Gold '91

Steffi Duna
Dancing Pirate '36
I Conquer the Sea '36
La Cucaracha '34
Law of the Pampas '39
Way Down South '39

Faye Dunaway
The Arrangement '69
Barfly '87
Beverly Hills Madam '86
Bonnie & Clyde '67
Burning Secret '89
Casanova '87
The Champ '79
Chinatown '74
Christopher Columbus '85
Cold Sassy Tree '89
Country Girl '82
The Deadly Trap '71
The Disappearance of Aimee '76
Double Edge '92
Eyes of Laura Mars '78
The First Deadly Sin '80
The Four Musketeers '75
The Gamble '88
The Handmaid's Tale '90
Little Big Man '70
Midnight Crossing '87
Mommie Dearest '81
Network '76
Oklahoma Crude '73
Ordeal by Innocence '84
Scorchers '92
Silhouette '91
Supergirl '84
The Temp '93
Thomas Crown Affair '68
Three Days of the Condor '75
The Three Musketeers '74
The Towering Inferno '74
Voyage of the Damned '76
Wait Until Spring, Bandini '90
The Wicked Lady '83

Adrian Dunbar
The Crying Game '92
Hear My Song '91
My Left Foot '89
The Playboys '92
Widow's Peak '94

Andrew Duncan
The Gig '85
Morgan Stewart's Coming Home '87

Angus Duncan
Hard Frame '70

How to Seduce a Woman '74

Arletta Duncan
Fighting Champ '33
The Gallant Fool '33
Roaring Speedboats '37

Bob Duncan
Border Feud '47
Colorado Serenade '46

Bud Duncan
Hillbilly Blitzkrieg '42
Snuffy Smith, Yard Bird '42

Carmen Duncan
Dark Forces '83
Moving Targets '87
Now and Forever '82

Julie Duncan
Along the Sundown Trail '42
Fugitive Valley '41
Haunted Ranch '43

Kenne Duncan
The Astounding She-Monster '58
Cyclotrode "X" '46
Dynamite Canyon '41
Flesh and the Spur '57
Make-Up '37
Manhunt of Mystery Island '45
Night of the Ghouls '59
Pinto Canyon '41
Raiders of Sunset Pass '43
Riding the Sunset Trail '41
The Sinister Urge '60

Lindsay Duncan
Body Parts '91
Grown Ups '80
Loose Connections '87
Prick Up Your Ears '87
The Reflecting Skin '91
Traffik '90
A Year in Provence '89

Mary Duncan
City Girl '30
Morning Glory '33

Neil Duncan
Murder on Line One '90
Split Second '92

Peter Duncan
The Lifetaker '89
The Old Curiosity Shop '75

Sandy Duncan
The Cat from Outer Space '78
Million Dollar Duck '71
Pinocchio '76
Roots '77
Star Spangled Girl '71

Jennie Dundas
The Beniker Gang '83
Heaven Help Us '85
Legal Eagles '86
Mrs. Soffel '84

Robert Dunham
Godzilla vs. Megalon '76
The Green Slime '68

Dawn Dunlap
Barbarian Queen '85
Forbidden World '82
Heartbreaker '83

Lesley Dunlop
The Dying Truth '91
Haunted: The Ferryman '74

Vic Dunlop
Jud '71
Martians Go Home! '90
Wishful Thinking '92

Carolyn Dunn
Breaking All the Rules '85
Hitler's Daughter '90

Eddie Dunn
Billy the Kid '41
Call Northside 777 '48
Mexican Spitfire at Sea '42
South of Santa Fe '42
Sunrise Trail '31

Emma Dunn
Blessed Event '32
Hell's House '32
Madame X '37
Morals for Women '31
Son of Frankenstein '39
Talk of the Town '42
You Can't Fool Your Wife '40

James Dunn
Baby, Take a Bow '34
The Bramble Bush '60
Bright Eyes '34
El Fego Baca: Six-Gun Law '62
The Ghost and the Guest '43
The Oscar '66
Shadows Over Shanghai '38
Stand Up and Cheer '34
That Brennan Girl '46
A Tree Grows in Brooklyn '45

Josephine Dunn
Between Fighting Men '32
Our Modern Maidens '29

Kevin Dunn
Chaplin '92
Dave '93
Hot Shots! '91
Little Big League '94
Mississippi Burning '88
Only the Lonely '91
Taken Away '89

Michael Dunn
Dr. Frankenstein's Castle of Freaks '74
The Freakmaker '73
House of the Damned '63
Madigan '68
Murders in the Rue Morgue '71
Ship of Fools '65
Teen Alien '88
You're a Big Boy Now '66

Nora Dunn
Born Yesterday '93
How I Got into College '89
Miami Blues '90
Passion Fish '92
Stepping Out '91
Working Girl '88

Dominique Dunne
Haunting of Harrington House '82
Magic on Love Island '80
Poltergeist '82
The Shadow Riders '82

Griffin Dunne
After Hours '85
Almost You '85
Amazon Women on the Moon '87
An American Werewolf in London '81
The Big Blue '88
Big Girls Don't Cry...They Get Even '92
Chilly Scenes of Winter '79
Cold Feet '84
The Fan '81
From Here to Maternity '85
Hotel Room '93
Johnny Dangerously '84
Lip Service '88
Love Matters '93
Me and Him '89
My Girl '91
Once Around '91
The Other Side of the Mountain '75
Secret Weapon '90
Straight Talk '92
White Palace '90
Who's That Girl? '87

Irene Dunne
Ann Vickers '33
Anna and the King of Siam '46
The Awful Truth '37
Bachelor Apartment '31
Cimarron '30
Consolation Marriage '31
A Guy Named Joe '44
I Remember Mama '48
Joy of Living '38
Life with Father '47
Love Affair '39
My Favorite Wife '40
Never a Dull Moment '50
Penny Serenade '41
Roberta '35
Show Boat '36
Sweet Adeline '35
The White Cliffs of Dover '44

Steve Dunne
The Big Sombrero '49
The Underworld Story '50

Mildred Dunnock
And Baby Makes Six '79

Baby Doll '56
Behold a Pale Horse '64
Brand New Life '72
Butterfield 8 '60
The Corn is Green '45
Love Me Tender '56
Murder or Mercy '74
The Nun's Story '59
One Summer Love '76
Peyton Place '57
The Pick-Up Artist '87
Spiral Staircase '75
Sweet Bird of Youth '62
The Trouble with Harry '55
Viva Zapata! '52
Whatever Happened to Aunt Alice? '69

Rosemary Dunsmore
After the Promise '87
Anne of Avonlea '87
Blades of Courage '88
Dancing in the Dark '86
Personals '90

Wilson Dunster
The Rutanga Tapes '90
Swift Justice '88

Anny Duperey
Bobby Deerfield '77
From Hell to Victory '79
Les Comperes '83
Pardon Mon Affaire '76
Stavisky '74

Starletta DuPois
Hollywood Shuffle '87
A Raisin in the Sun '89

June Duprez
And Then There Were None '45
Brighton Strangler '45
The Brighton Strangler/Before Dawn '45
The Four Feathers '39
The Lion Has Wings '40
None But the Lonely Heart '44
Spy in Black '39
That Brennan Girl '46
Thief of Baghdad '40
Tiger Fangs '43

Roy Dupuis
Being at Home with Claude '92
Entangled '93

David Durand
Boy's Reformatory '39
Viva Villa! '34

Christopher Durang
The Butcher's Wife '91
Heaven Help Us '85
Housesitter '92
In the Spirit '90
Mr. North '88

Jimmy Durante
Alice Through the Looking Glass '66
Billy Rose's Jumbo '62
The Great Rupert '50
Hollywood Goes to War '54
Hollywood Party '34
It Happened in Brooklyn '47
It's a Mad, Mad, Mad, Mad World '63
Little Miss Broadway '38
The Lost Stooges '33
The Man Who Came to Dinner '41
Melody Ranch '40
On an Island with You '48
Palooka '34
Speak Easily '32
Two Girls and a Sailor '44
What! No Beer? '33
Ziegfeld Follies '46

Deanna Durbin
It's a Date '40
Summer Stock '50

John Durbin
Dr. Caligari '89
King of the Hill '93

Minta Durfee
Fatty and Mabel Adrift/Mabel, Fatty and the Law '16
Mack Sennett Comedies: Vol. 1 '21
Mickey '17
Miracle Kid '42
Savage Intruder '68

Anna Marie Duringer
The Lacemaker '77
Veronika Voss '82

Charles Durning
Attica '80
The Best Little Girl in the World '81
The Best Little Whorehouse in Texas '82
Big Trouble '86
Breakheart Pass '76
Brenda Starr '86
Cat Chaser '90
The Choirboys '77
The Connection '73
Cop '88
Crisis at Central High '80
Dark Night of the Scarecrow '81
Death of a Salesman '86
Dick Tracy '90
Die Laughing '80
Dinner at Eight '89
Dog Day Afternoon '75
Far North '88
The Final Countdown '80
The Front Page '74
The Fury '78
Hadley's Rebellion '84
Happy New Year '87
Harry & Walter Go to New York '76
The Hindenburg '75
The Hudsucker Proxy '93
Kenny Rogers as the Gambler, Part 3: The Legend Continues '87
The Legend of Sleepy Hollow '86
The Man Who Broke 1,000 Chains '87
The Man with One Red Shoe '85
Mass Appeal '84
The Music of Chance '93
North Dallas Forty '79
Project: Alien '89
Queen of the Stardust Ballroom '75
The Return of Eliot Ness '91
The Rosary Murders '87
Sharky's Machine '81
Sisters '73
Solarbabies '86
Special Olympics '78
Stand Alone '85
Stick '85
The Sting '73
The Story Lady '93
A Tiger's Tale '87
Tilt '78
To Be or Not to Be '83
Tootsie '82
Tough Guys '86
True Confessions '81
Twilight's Last Gleaming '77
Two of a Kind '83
V.I. Warshawski '91
When a Stranger Calls '79
When a Stranger Calls Back '93
Where the River Runs Black '86

Ian Dury
The Raggedy Rawney '90
Split Second '92

Dan Duryea
Along Came Jones '45
Ball of Fire '41
The Bamboo Saucer '68
Criss Cross '49
Five Golden Dragons '67
The Flight of the Phoenix '65
Great Flamarion '45
Gunfight at Sandoval '59
Killer Bait '49
The Little Foxes '41
None But the Lonely Heart '44
Platinum High School '60
The Pride of the Yankees '42
Sahara '43
Scarlet Street '45
Silver Lode '54
Terror Street '54
Thunder Bay '53
Too Late for Tears '49
The Underworld Story '50
The Valley of Decision '45
Winchester '73 '50

George Duryea
Marked Money '28
Pardon My Gun '30

Marj Dusay
Made in Heaven '87
Pendulum '69

Ann Dusenberry
Basic Training '86
Cutter's Way '81
Desperate Women '78
Heart Beat '80
Killjoy '81
Lies '83
Little Women '78
Long Time Gone '86
The Men's Club '86
The Possessed '77

Eliza Dushku
That Night '93
This Boy's Life '93
True Lies '94

Andre Dussollier
And Now My Love '74
Le Beau Mariage '82
Sand and Blood '87
Three Men and a Cradle '85
Un Coeur en Hiver '93

Jacques Dutronc
L'Etat Sauvage '78
Tricheurs '84
Van Gogh '92

Charles S. Dutton
Alien 3 '92
Cat's Eye '85
Crocodile Dundee 2 '88
The Distinguished Gentleman '92
Jacknife '89
Low Down Dirty Shame '94
Menace II Society '93
Mississippi Masala '92
The Murder of Mary Phagan '87
Q & A '90
Rudy '93
Runaway '89
Surviving the Game '94
An Unremarkable Life '89

Josey Duval
New York's Finest '87
Sex, Drugs, and Rock-n-Roll '84

Maria Duval
The Living Coffin '58
Samson vs. the Vampire Women '61

Robert Duvall
Apocalypse Now '79
Badge 373 '73
Belizaire the Cajun '86
The Betsy '78
Breakout '75
Bullitt '68
Captain Newman, M.D. '63
The Chase '66
Colors '88
The Conversation '74
Countdown '68
Days of Thunder '90
The Detective '68
The Eagle Has Landed '77
Falling Down '93
Geronimo: An American Legend '93
The Godfather '72
The Godfather 1902-1959: The Complete Epic '81
The Godfather, Part 2 '74
The Great Northfield Minnesota Raid '72
The Great Santini '80
The Greatest '77
The Handmaid's Tale '90
Hearts of Darkness: A Filmmaker's Apocalypse '91
Hotel Colonial '88
Ike '79
Joe Kidd '72
The Killer Elite '75
Lady Ice '73
Lawman '71
Let's Get Harry '87
The Lightship '86
Lonesome Dove '89
M*A*S*H '70
The Natural '84

Network '76
Newsies '92
The Paper '94
The Plague '92
The Pursuit of D.B. Cooper '81
The Rain People '69
Rambling Rose '91
The Seven Percent Solution '76
A Show of Force '90
Stalin '92
The Stone Boy '84
Tender Mercies '83
The Terry Fox Story '83
THX 1138 '71
To Kill a Mockingbird '62
Tomorrow '83
True Confessions '81
True Grit '69
Wrestling Ernest Hemingway '93

Shelley Duvall
Annie Hall '77
Brewster McCloud '70
Frankenweenie '84
Frog '89
Frogs! '90s
McCabe & Mrs. Miller '71
My Darlin' Clementine '86
Nashville '75
Popeye '80
Rapunzel '82
Roxanne '87
Rumpelstiltskin '82
The Shining '80
Suburban Commando '91
Thieves Like Us '74
Time Bandits '81

Wayne Duvall
Final Approach '91
Warlords 3000 '93

Pierre Dux
The Day and the Hour '63
La Lectrice '88
La Vie Continue '82

Ann Dvorak
Abilene Town '46
Flame of the Barbary Coast '45
"G" Men '35
The Guardsman '31
A Life of Her Own '50
Manhattan Merry-Go-Round '37
Out of the Blue '47
The Private Affairs of Bel Ami '47
Return of Jesse James '50
Scarface '31
The Strange Love of Molly Louvain '32
Three on a Match '32

Peter Dvorsky
The Kiss '88
Videodrome '83

Dorothy Dwan
The Fighting Legion '30
Great K & A Train Robbery '26
Sawmill/Dome Doctor '22
The Wizard of Oz '25

Earl Dwire
Between Men '35
Big Calibre '35
Cavalcade of the West '36
Lawless Frontier '35
Lawless Range '35
Lightning Bill Crandall '37
Riding On '37
The Star Packer '34
Toll of the Desert '35
Trouble in Texas '37

Hilary Dwyer
The Conqueror Worm '68
Cry of the Banshee '70
The Oblong Box '69
Wuthering Heights '70

Leslie Dwyer
Hi-Di-Hi '88
Roadhouse Girl '53

Valentine Dyall
Frenzy '46
The Ghost of Rashmon Hall '47
The Golden Salamander '51
Horror Hotel '60
Hotel Reserve '44
Room to Let '49
Suspended Alibi '56

Cameron Dye
Body Rock '84
Fraternity Vacation '85
Heated Vengeance '87
Joy of Sex '84
The Last Starfighter '84
Out of the Dark '88
Scenes from the Goldmine '87
Stranded '87

Dale Dye
Fire Birds '90
Heaven and Earth '93

John Dye
Best of the Best '89
Campus Man '87

Bob Dylan
Backtrack '89
Hearts of Fire '87
The Last Waltz '78
Pat Garrett & Billy the Kid '73

Peter Dyneley
Beau Brummel '54
The Manster '59
Soul Patrol '80
Strange Awakening '58

Richard Dysart
The Autobiography of Miss Jane Pittman '74
Back to the Future, Part 3 '90
Being There '79
Bitter Harvest '81
Bogie: The Last Hero '80
Churchill and the Generals '81
The Day of the Locust '75
Day One '89
The Falcon and the Snowman '85
The Hindenburg '75
The Hospital '71
L.A. Law '86
The Last Days of Patton '86
Mask '85
Meteor '79
The Ordeal of Dr. Mudd '80
Pale Rider '85
The People vs. Jean Harris '81
Petulia '68
Prophecy '79
Riding with Death '76
The Rumor Mill '86
The Terminal Man '74
The Thing '82
Wall Street '87
Warning Sign '85

Dick Dyszel
The Alien Factor '78
Night Beast '83

George Dzundza
Act of Passion: The Lost Honor of Kathryn Beck '83
Basic Instinct '92
The Beast '88
Best Defense '84
Broken Badge '85
Brotherly Love '85
The Butcher's Wife '91
The Deer Hunter '78
Glory Years '87
Impulse '90
A Long Way Home '81
No Mercy '86
No Way Out '87
Streamers '83
White Hunter, Black Heart '90

Nicholas Eadie
Celia: Child Of Terror '89
Return to Snowy River '88

Edward Earle
The Revenge Rider '35
Spite Marriage '29
The Wind '28

Harry Earles
Freaks '32
The Unholy Three '25
The Unholy Three '30

Carlos East
The Fear Chamber '68
Fearmaker '89
The Snake People '68

Jeff East
Another Chance '88
The Campus Corpse '77
Deadly Blessing '81
Flight of the Grey Wolf '76

Huckleberry Finn '74
Mary and Joseph: A Story of Faith '79
Pumpkinhead '88
Tom Sawyer '73

Leslie Easterbrook
Police Academy '84
Police Academy 3: Back in Training '86
Police Academy 5: Assignment Miami Beach '88
Police Academy 6: City Under Siege '89
Private Resort '84
The Taking of Flight 847: The Uli Derickson Story '88

George Eastman
After the Fall of New York '85
Belle Starr '79
Blastfighter '85
Bloody Avenger '80s
Call of the Wild '72
Detective School Dropouts '85
Grim Reaper '81
Hands of Steel '83
Ironmaster '83
Kiss Me, Kill Me '69

Rodney Eastman
Deadly Weapon '88
A Nightmare on Elm Street 4: Dream Master '88

Robert Easton
The Giant Spider Invasion '75
When Hell Broke Loose '58
Working Girl '88

Clint Eastwood
Any Which Way You Can '80
The Beguiled '70
Bronco Billy '80
City Heat '84
Coogan's Bluff '68
The Dead Pool '88
Dirty Harry '71
The Eiger Sanction '75
The Enforcer '76
Escapade in Japan '57
Escape from Alcatraz '79
Every Which Way But Loose '78
Firefox '82
A Fistful of Dollars '64
For a Few Dollars More '65
Francis in the Navy '55
The Gauntlet '77
The Good, the Bad and the Ugly '67
Hang 'Em High '67
Heartbreak Ridge '86
High Plains Drifter '73
Honkytonk Man '82
In the Line of Fire '93
Joe Kidd '72
Kelly's Heroes '70
Lafayette Escadrille '58
Magnum Force '73
The Outlaw Josey Wales '76
Paint Your Wagon '69
Pale Rider '85
A Perfect World '93
Pink Cadillac '89
Play Misty for Me '71
Revenge of the Creature '55
The Rookie '90
Sudden Impact '83
Tarantula '55
Thunderbolt & Lightfoot '74
Tightrope '84
Two Mules for Sister Sara '70
Unforgiven '92
Where Eagles Dare '68
White Hunter, Black Heart '90
Wild West '87

Jayne Eastwood
Hostile Takeover '88
Kidnapping of Baby John Doe '88
My Pleasure Is My Business '74
Night Friend '87

Marjorie Eaton
The Atomic Brain '64
The Attic '80
Night Tide '63

Mary Eaton
The Cocoanuts '29
Glorifying the American Girl '30

Shirley Eaton
Around the World Under the Sea '65
Carry On Nurse '59
Doctor at Large '57
Doctor in the House '53
Girl Hunters '63
Goldfinger '64
Kiss and Kill '68
The Naked Truth '58
What a Carve-Up! '62

John Eaves
Fire and Ice '87
Skier's Dream '88

Christine Ebersole
Acceptable Risks '86
Amadeus '84
Dead Again '91
Folks! '92
Ghost Dad '90
Gypsy '93
Mac and Me '88
My Girl 2 '94
Thief of Hearts '84
Tootsie '82

Buddy Ebsen
The Adventures of Tom Sawyer '73
The Andersonville Trial '70
The Bastard '78
Between Heaven and Hell '56
Born to Dance '36
Breakfast at Tiffany's '61
Broadway Melody of 1936 '35
Broadway Melody of 1938 '37
Captain January '36
Davy Crockett and the River Pirates '56
Davy Crockett, King of the Wild Frontier '55
Girl of the Golden West '38
The Interns '62
My Lucky Star '38
The One and Only, Genuine, Original Family Band '68
The President's Plane is Missing '71
Red Garters '54
Silver City Bonanza '51
Sing Your Worries Away '42
Stone Fox '87

Maude Eburne
The Border Legion '40
Courageous Dr. Christian '40
Doughnuts & Society '36
The Guardsman '31
Ladies They Talk About '33
The Ruggles of Red Gap '35
The Vampire Bat '32

Aimee Eccles
The Concrete Jungle '82
Group Marriage '72
Humanoid Defender '85
Little Big Man '70
Lovelines '84

Guy Ecker
Devil Wears White '86
Night Terror '89

James Eckhouse
Blue Heaven '84
The Christmas Wife '88
Leaving Normal '92

Billy Eckstine
Jo Jo Dancer, Your Life is Calling '86
Skirts Ahoy! '52

Helen Jerome Eddy
The Country Kid '23
County Fair '36
Klondike Annie '36
Rebecca of Sunnybrook Farm '17
A Shot in the Dark '35
The Tong Man '19

Nelson Eddy
Balalaika '39
Bitter Sweet '40
The Chocolate Soldier '41
Dancing Lady '33
Girl of the Golden West '38
I Married an Angel '42
Let Freedom Ring '39
Maytime '37
Naughty Marietta '35
New Moon '40

Northwest Outpost '47
The Phantom of the Opera '43
Rosalie '38
Rose Marie '36
Sweethearts '38

Herb Edelman
The Charge of the Model T's '76
Cracking Up '83
A Cry for Love '80
Goin' Coconuts '78
Marathon '80
On the Right Track '81
Special Olympics '78
A Strange and Deadly Occurence '74
Strike Force '81
The Way We Were '73
The Yakuza '75

Barbara Eden
The Amazing Dobermans '76
Chattanooga Choo Choo '84
Five Weeks in a Balloon '62
Flaming Star '60
From the Terrace '60
Harper Valley P.T.A. '78
How to Break Up a Happy Divorce '76
Lethal Charm '90
Quick, Let's Get Married '71
Return of the Rebels '81
Ride the Wild Surf '64
Seven Faces of Dr. Lao '63
The Stranger Within '74
Voyage to the Bottom of the Sea '61
The Woman Hunter '72
The Wonderful World of the Brothers Grimm '62

Jerome Eden
The Defilers '65
2000 Maniacs '64

Mark Eden
The Crimson Cult '68
Seance on a Wet Afternoon '64

Robert Edeson
On the Night Stage '15
Walking Back '26

George Edgely
Common Law Wife '63
Free, White, and 21 '62

Elizabeth Edmonds
Experience Preferred... But Not Essential '83
Scrubbers '82

Beatie Edney
The Dark Angel '91
Diary of a Mad Old Man '88
Highlander '86
In the Name of the Father '93
Mister Johnson '91

Richard Edson
Attack of the 50 Ft. Woman '93
Do the Right Thing '89
Eight Men Out '88
Good Morning, Vietnam '87
Joey Breaker '93
Let It Ride '89
Love, Cheat & Steal '94
Platoon '86
Posse '93
Stranger than Paradise '84
Super Mario Bros. '93
Tougher than Leather '88

Allan Edwall
Brothers Lionheart '85
The Emigrants '72
Fanny and Alexander '83
The New Land '73
The Sacrifice '86

Anthony Edwards
The Client '94
Delta Heat '92
Downtown '89
El Diablo '90
Fast Times at Ridgemont High '82
Going for the Gold: The Bill Johnson Story '85
Gotcha! '85
Hawks '89
Heart Like a Wheel '83
Hometown Boy Makes Good '93
How I Got into College '89

Landslide '92
Miracle Mile '89
Mr. North '88
Pet Sematary 2 '92
Revenge of the Nerds '84
Revenge of the Nerds 2: Nerds in Paradise '87
Summer Heat '87
The Sure Thing '85
Top Gun '86

Barbara Edwards
Another Chance '88
House Party 3 '94
Malibu Express '85

Bill Edwards
First Man into Space '59
Ladies of the Chorus '49
War Lover '62

Bruce Edwards
The Black Widow '47
The Fallen Sparrow '43
Federal Agents vs. Underworld, Inc. '49
Hitler: Dead or Alive '43
The Iron Major '43

Cliff Edwards
Dance Fools Dance '31
Doughboys '30
Girl of the Golden West '38
Gone with the Wind '39
His Girl Friday '40
Laughing Sinners '31
Parlor, Bedroom and Bath '31
Sagebrush Law '43
Saratoga '37
Sidewalks of New York '31
The Sin of Madelon Claudet '31

Gail Edwards
Get Crazy '83
A Perfect Little Murder '90

James Edwards
Home of the Brave '49
Patton '70
Pork Chop Hill '59
The Set-Up '49
The Steel Helmet '51

Jennifer Edwards
All's Fair '89
Heidi '67
The Man Who Loved Women '83
Overexposed '90
Perfect Match '88
Peter Gunn '89
S.O.B. '81
Sunset '88
That's Life! '86

Lance Edwards
Peacemaker '90
A Woman, Her Men and Her Futon '92

Luke Edwards
Guilty by Suspicion '91
Little Big League '94
Mother's Boys '94
Newsies '92
The Wizard '89

Mark Edwards
The Boldest Job in the West '71
Tower of Evil '72

Penny Edwards
Heart of the Rockies '51
North of the Great Divide '50
Trail of Robin Hood '50
Western Double Feature 11 '50
Western Double Feature 15 '50

Ronnie Clair Edwards
A Day for Thanks on Walton's Mountain '82
8 Seconds '94
Future Cop '76

Snitz Edwards
April Fool '26
Battling Butler '26
Seven Chances '25
The Thief of Baghdad '24

Vince Edwards
Andy and the Airwave Rangers '89
Cellar Dweller '87
Death Stalk '74
Desperados '69

The Devil's Brigade '68
The Dirty Dozen: The Deadly Mission '87
Firehouse '72
The Fix '84
The Gumshoe Kid '89
The Killing '56
The Mad Bomber '72
Motorama '91
Original Intent '91
Return to Horror High '87
The Seduction '82
Sno-Line '85
Space Raiders '83
The Three Faces of Eve '57

Walter Edwards
Grit of the Girl Telegrapher/In the Switch Tower '15
Tale of Two Cities/In the Switch Tower '15

Marshall Efron
First Time '82
Is There Sex After Death? '71

Aeryk Egan
Book of Love '91
Keeper of the City '92

Eddie Egan
Badge 373 '73
The French Connection '71
Out of the Darkness '85

Peter Egan
Hennessy '75
Lillie '79
One Brief Summer '70
A Perfect Spy '88

Richard Egan
The Amsterdam Kill '78
Blackbeard the Pirate '52
Demetrius and the Gladiators '54
The Hunters '58
Love Me Tender '56
Mission to Glory '80
One Minute to Zero '52
Pollyanna '60
Seven Cities of Gold '55
Split Second '53
A Summer Place '59
Sweet Creek County War '82
Tension at Table Rock '56
Underwater '55

Will Egan
Glitch! '88
Ninja Academy '90

Julie Ege
Craze '74
Creatures the World Forgot '70
The Freakmaker '73
On Her Majesty's Secret Service '69
Rentadick '72
The 7 Brothers Meet Dracula '73

Samantha Eggar
All the Kind Strangers '74
Battleforce '79
The Brood '79
The Collector '65
Curtains '83
Dark Horse '92
Demonoid, Messenger of Death '81
Doctor Dolittle '67
Doctor in Distress '63
Exterminator '80s
Hot Touch '80s
Light at the Edge of the World '71
Man of Destiny '73
Molly Maguires '70
A Name for Evil '70
Ragin' Cajun '90
Round Numbers '91
The Seven Percent Solution '76
Tales of the Unexpected '91
The Uncanny '78
Unknown Powers '80
Walk, Don't Run '66
Welcome to Blood City '77
Why Shoot the Teacher '79

Nicole Eggert
Blown Away '90s
The Double O Kid '92
The Haunting of Morella '91
Just One of the Girls '93

Martha Eggerth
Charm of La Boheme '36
For Me and My Gal '42

Stan Egi
Come See the Paradise '90
Golden Gate '93
Hiroshima: Out of the Ashes '90
Rising Sun '93

Lisa Eichhorn
Blind Justice '86
Cutter's Way '81
The Europeans '79
King of the Hill '93
Moon 44 '90
Opposing Force '87
The Vanishing '93
Weather in the Streets '84
Wildrose '85
Yanks '79

Christopher Eigeman
Barcelona '94
Metropolitan '90

Jill Eikenberry
Arthur '81
Assault and Matrimony '87
Between the Lines '77
Butch and Sundance: The Early Days '79
Cast the First Stone '89
Chantilly Lace '93
Family Sins '87
Grace Quigley '84
Hide in Plain Sight '80
An Inconvenient Woman '91
L.A. Law '86
The Manhattan Project '86
Orphan Train '79
Rich Kids '79
Rush It '77
Sessions '83

Lisa Eilbacher
The Amazing Spider-Man '77
Beverly Hills Cop '84
Blind Man's Bluff '91
Deadly Intent '88
Deadly Matrimony '92
The Hunt for the Night Stalker '91
Leviathan '89
Live Wire '92
Monte Carlo '86
Never Say Die '90
An Officer and a Gentleman '82
On the Right Track '81
Run for the Roses '78
Ten to Midnight '83
To Race the Wind '80

Sally Eilers
Clearing the Range '31
Coroner Creek '48
Doughboys '30
Roaring Ranch '30
Strange Illusion '45
Trigger Tricks '30

Aron Eisenberg
The Horror Show '89
Playroom '90

Ike Eisenmann
Escape to Witch Mountain '75
Return from Witch Mountain '78

Anthony Eisley
The Doll Squad '73
Dracula vs. Frankenstein '71
Frankie and Johnny '66
Journey to the Center of Time '67
Killer Commandos
Lightning Bolt '67
Monster '78
Mummy & Curse of the Jackal '67
Naked Kiss '64
Navy vs. the Night Monsters '66
Secrets '77
Star! '68
The Tormentors '80s
The Wasp Woman '59
The Witchmaker '69

Anita Ekberg
Abbott and Costello Go to Mars '53
The Alphabet Murders '65

Artists and Models '55
Back from Eternity '56
Blood Alley '55
Boccaccio '70 '62
Call Me Bwana '63
The Cobra '68
Fangs of the Living Dead '68
Four for Texas '63
Gold of the Amazon Women '79
Hollywood or Bust '56
How I Learned to Love Women '60s
Intervista '87
La Dolce Vita '60
The Mongols '60
Northeast of Seoul '72
Paris Holiday '57
S*H*E '79
War and Peace '56
Woman Times Seven '67

Britt Ekland
After the Fox '66
Asylum '72
Beverly Hills Vamp '88
Bobo '67
The Children '90
Cold Heat '90
Dead Wrong '83
Demon Rage '82
Ecstasy '84
Endless Night '71
Erotic Images '85
Fraternity Vacation '85
The Great Wallendas '78
High Velocity '76
The Hostage Tower '80
King Solomon's Treasure '76
The Man with the Golden Gun '74
Marbella '85
The Monster Club '85
Moon in Scorpio '86
The Night They Raided Minsky's '69
Scandal '89
Sex on the Run '78
Slavers '77
Stiletto '69
The Ultimate Thrill '74
What the Peeper Saw '72
The Wicker Man '75

Gosta Ekman
The Adventures of Picasso '80
Faust '26
The Inside Man '84
Intermezzo '36
Swedenhielms '35

Jack Elam
The Apple Dumpling Gang Rides Again '79
Artists and Models '55
The Aurora Encounter '85
Big Bad John '90
Bonanza: The Return '93
The Bushwackers '52
Cannonball Run '81
Cannonball Run 2 '84
Cattle Queen of Montana '54
Creature from Black Lake '76
Dynamite and Gold '88
Firecreek '68
Four for Texas '63
The Girl in Lover's Lane '60
Grayeagle '77
Hannie Caulder '72
Hawken's Breed '87
High Lonesome '50
Huckleberry Finn '74
Kansas City Confidential '52
Lost '83
The Man from Laramie '55
Never a Dull Moment '68
Norseman '78
Once Upon a Time in the West '68
Pardners '56
Pocketful of Miracles '61
Pony Express Rider '76
Rancho Notorious '52
The Rare Breed '66
Rawhide '50
The Ring '52
Rio Lobo '70
The Sacketts '79
Sacred Ground '83
Shadow Force '92
Suburban Commando '91

Elam ▶cont.

Support Your Local Gunfighter '71
Support Your Local Sheriff '69
Uninvited '93
The Villain '79
The Way West '67
Wild Weed '49

Dana Elcar
Adam at 6 A.M. '70
All of Me '84
Blue Skies Again '83
Code of Honor '84
Condorman '81
Dying Room Only '73
Fireball Forward '72
The Fool Killer '65
Forbidden Love '82
A Gunfight '71
Help Wanted: Male '82
Inside Out '91
The Learning Tree '69
The Nude Bomb '80
Soldier Blue '70
Toughlove '85

Ron Eldard
Drop Dead Fred '91
True Love '89

Florence Eldridge
Christopher Columbus '49
Inherit the Wind '60
Les Miserables '35
Mary of Scotland '36

George Eldridge
Mom & Dad '47
Sherlock Holmes and the
   Secret Weapon '42
Sonora Stagecoach '44
Take Me Back to Oklahoma '40

John Eldridge
Bad Men of the Border '45
Dangerous '35
Square Dance Jubilee '51

Erika Eleniak
The Beverly Hillbillies '93
Broken Angel '88
Chasers '94
Under Siege '92

Sandor Eles
And Soon the Darkness '70
The Evil of Frankenstein '64

Taina Elg
The Bacchantes '63
Diane '55
Les Girls '57
The Prodigal '55

Alix Elias
Citizens Band '77
Rock 'n' Roll High School '79

Christine Elise
Boiling Point '93
Child's Play 2 '90

Hector Elizondo
American Gigolo '79
Being Human '94
Beverly Hills Cop 3 '94
Born to Win '71
Chains of Gold '92
Courage '86
Cuba '79
The Dain Curse '78
Diary of the Dead '80s
The Fan '81
Final Approach '91
The Flamingo Kid '84
Forgotten Prisoners '90
Frankie and Johnny '91
Getting Even with Dad '94
Leviathan '89
Necessary Roughness '91
Nothing in Common '86
Out of the Darkness '85
Pocket Money '72
Pretty Woman '90
Private Resort '84
Report to the Commissioner
   '74
Samantha '91
Taking Care of Business '90
The Taking of Pelham One Two
   Three '74

There Goes the Neighborhood
   '92
Valdez is Coming '71
Young Doctors in Love '82

Duke Ellington
Cabin in the Sky '43
Check & Double Check '30
Murder at the Vanities '34

Ramblin' Jack Elliot
Honkytonk Nights '70s
Roadie '80

Bob Elliott
Cabin Boy '94
Quick Change '90
Vengeance '80

Chris Elliott
The Abyss '89
Cabin Boy '94
CB4: The Movie '93
Groundhog Day '93
New York Stories '89

Denholm Elliott
The Apprenticeship of Duddy
   Kravitz '74
Bleak House '85
The Bourne Identity '88
The Boys from Brazil '78
Brimstone & Treacle '82
Codename Kyril '91
Cruel Sea '53
Cuba '79
Deep Cover '88
Defense of the Realm '85
A Doll's House '89
Hanna's War '88
Holy Terror '65
Hotel du Lac '86
The Hound of the Baskervilles
   '77
The Hound of the Baskervilles
   '83
The House that Dripped Blood
   '71
Indiana Jones and the Last
   Crusade '89
It's Not the Size That Counts
   '74
King Rat '65
Maurice '87
The Missionary '82
The Night They Raided
   Minsky's '69
Noises Off '92
One Against the Wind '91
Over Indulgence '87
A Private Function '84
Quest for Love '71
Raiders of the Lost Ark '81
The Razor's Edge '84
A Room with a View '86
Rude Awakening '81
Russian Roulette '75
Saint Jack '79
Scorchers '92
September '88
Stealing Heaven '88
Strange Case of Dr. Jekyll &
   Mr. Hyde '68
To the Devil, A Daughter '76
Too Late the Hero '70
Toy Soldiers '91
Trading Places '83
Transmutations '85
The Two Faces of Evil '82
Vault of Horror '73
Voyage of the Damned '76
The Wicked Lady '83
Zulu Dawn '79

John Elliott
Big Calibre '35
Bulldog Courage '35
Danger Trails '35
Death Rides the Range '40
A Face in the Fog '36
The Gallant Fool '33
Mother and Son '31
The Phantom of the Range '38
Riding On '37
Rogue's Tavern '36
Toll of the Desert '35
The Wizard of Gore '70

Peter Elliott
Missing Link '88
Snake Dancer

Robert Elliott
The Maltese Falcon '31
Murder at Midnight '31

The Return of Casey Jones '34
White Eagle '32

Ross Elliott
Hot Lead '51
Paper Man '71
Tarantula '55

Sam Elliott
The Blue Lightning '86
Butch Cassidy and the
   Sundance Kid '69
Conagher '91
Fatal Beauty '87
Frogs '72
Gettysburg '93
I Will Fight No More Forever '75
The Legacy '79
Lifeguard '75
Mask '85
Molly & Lawless John '72
Murder in Texas '81
Prancer '89
The Quick and the Dead '87
Road House '89
Rush '91
The Sacketts '79
The Shadow Riders '82
Shakedown '88
Sibling Rivalry '90
Tombstone '93
Wild Times '79

Shawn Elliott
Bloodsucking Pharoahs of
   Pittsburgh '90
Crossover Dreams '85
Impulse '90
Short Eyes '79

Stephen Elliott
Arthur '81
Arthur 2: On the Rocks '88
Assassination '87
Beauty and the Beast '83
Betrayal '83
Beverly Hills Cop '84
Can You Hear the Laughter?
   The Story of Freddie Prinze
   '79
Cutter's Way '81
Days of Hell '84
Jacqueline Bouvier Kennedy
   '81
Mrs. R's Daughter '79
Perry Mason: The Case of the
   Lost Love '87
Report to the Commissioner
   '74
Roadhouse 66 '84
Sergeant Matlovich vs. the U.S.
   Air Force '78
Taking Care of Business '90

Wild Bill Elliott
Bordertown Gunfighters '43
Calling Wild Bill Elliott '43
Death Valley Manhunt '43
Man from Thunder River '43
The Showdown '50
Western Double Feature 1: Wild
   Bill & Sunset Carson '40s
Western Double Feature 7: Wild
   Bill & Crabbe '43
Western Double Feature 12 '44

**Desmond Walter
Ellis**
The Great St. Trinian's Train
   Robbery '66
The Hellfire Club '61

Edward Ellis
Fury '36
I Am a Fugitive from a Chain
   Gang '32
The Return of Peter Grimm '35
The Thin Man '34
Wheel of Fortune '41

Frank Ellis
The Big Stampede '32
Whistlin' Dan '32

Patricia Ellis
Back Door to Heaven '39
Block-heads '38
The Case of the Lucky Legs '35
Postal Inspector '36
Three on a Match '32

Robert Ellis
Broadway to Cheyenne '32
Captured in Chinatown '35
Come On Danger! '32

Daring Danger '32
Fighting Fool '32
The Fighting Sheriff '31
White Eagle '32

Robin Ellis
The Curse of King Tut's Tomb
   '80
The Europeans '79
Poldark '75

James Ellison
Fifth Avenue Girl '39
Guns of Justice '50
Hopalong Cassidy '35
I Walked with a Zombie '43
Kentucky Jubilee '51
Last Bullet '50
Last of the Wild Horses '49
Marshal of Heldorado '50
Next Time I Marry '38
Outlaw Fury '50
Rangeland Empire '50
Sudden Death '50
23 1/2 Hours Leave '37
The Undying Monster '42
Vivacious Lady '38
You Can't Fool Your Wife '40

Michael Elphick
Arthur's Hallowed Ground '84
The Element of Crime '84
Let Him Have It '91
Little Dorrit, Film 1: Nobody's
   Fault '88
Little Dorrit, Film 2: Little
   Dorrit's Story '88
Ordeal by Innocence '84

Isobel Elsom
Casanova Brown '44
Escape Me Never '47
The Ghost and Mrs. Muir '47
Love from a Stranger '47
Love is a Many-Splendored
   Thing '55
Monsieur Verdoux '47

Cary Elwes
Another Country '84
Bram Stoker's Dracula '92
The Crush '93
Days of Thunder '90
Glory '89
Hot Shots! '91
Lady Jane '85
Leather Jackets '91
The Princess Bride '87
Robin Hood: Men in Tights '93

Ron Ely
Cry of the Black Wolves '70s
Doc Savage '75
Once Before I Die '65
Slavers '77

Sallee Elyse
Demented '80
Home Sweet Home '80

Hope Emerson
Adam's Rib '50
All Mine to Give '56
Westward the Women '51

Gilbert Emery
Goin' to Town '35
The Lady Refuses '31
The Royal Bed '31
Wife Versus Secretary '36

John Emery
Forever Darling '56
Here Comes Mr. Jordan '41
Kronos '57
A Lawless Street '55
Mademoiselle Fifi '44
Rocketship X-M '50
Ship Ahoy! '43
The Spanish Main '45

David Emge
Dawn of the Dead '78
Hellmaster '92

Robert Emhardt
Die Sister, Die! '74
Shame '61
Underworld, U.S.A. '60

Michael Emil
Adventures in Spying '92
Always '85
Can She Bake a Cherry Pie?
   '83
In the Spirit '90
Insignificance '85

New Year's Day '89
Sitting Ducks '80
Someone to Love '87

Daniel Emilfork
The Devil's Nightmare '71
Lady L '65

Alphonsia Emmanuel
Peter's Friends '92
Under Suspicion '92

Lena Endre
The Best Intentions '92
The Visitors '89

Georgia Engel
The Day the Women Got Even
   '80
The Outside Man '73
Signs of Life '89

Wera Engels
Fugitive Road '34
Hong Kong Nights '35

Marla English
Flesh and the Spur '57
Voodoo Woman '57

Robert Englund
The Adventures of Ford
   Fairlane '90
Buster and Billie '74
Dance Macabre '91
Eaten Alive '76
Fangoria's Weekend of Horrors
   '86
Freddy's Dead: The Final
   Nightmare '91
Mysterious Two '82
A Nightmare on Elm Street '84
A Nightmare on Elm Street 2:
   Freddy's Revenge '85
A Nightmare on Elm Street 3:
   Dream Warriors '87
A Nightmare on Elm Street 4:
   Dream Master '88
A Nightmare on Elm Street 5:
   Dream Child '89
The Phantom of the Opera '89
Slashed Dreams '74
A Star is Born '76
Stay Hungry '76

Rene Enriquez
Ants '77
Bulletproof '88
The Evil That Men Do '84
Hill Street Blues, Vol. 1: Hill
   Street Station '81

Michael Ensign
Born Yesterday '93
House '86
Life Stinks '91

Dieter Eppler
The Slaughter of the Vampires
   '62
The Torture Chamber of Dr.
   Sadism '69

Omar Epps
Daybreak '93
Juice '92
Major League 2 '94
The Program '93

Kathryn Erbe
D2: The Mighty Ducks '94
Rich in Love '92
What About Bob? '91

Richard Erdman
Cry Danger '51
Namu, the Killer Whale '66
Objective, Burma! '45
Stalag 17 '53
The Stooge '51
Tomboy '85

Leif Erickson
Abbott and Costello Meet
   Captain Kidd '52
Abduction '75
Arabian Nights '42
Blonde Savage '47
Conquest '37
D.C. Cab '84
Desert Gold '36
Fastest Gun Alive '56
Force Five '75
A Gathering of Eagles '63
Hill Number One '51
Invaders from Mars '53
Joan of Arc '48
Never Wave at a WAC '52

Night Monster '42
On the Waterfront '54
One Third of a Nation '39
Pardon My Sarong '42
Penitentiary 2 '82
Rocky 3 '82
Roustabout '64
The Showdown '50
The Snake Pit '48
Strait-Jacket '64
Tea and Sympathy '56
Three Secrets '50
Trouble Along the Way '53
Twilight's Last Gleaming '77

Devon Ericson
Can You Hear the Laughter?
  The Story of Freddie Prinze
  '79
The Runaway Barge '75

John Ericson
Bad Day at Black Rock '54
The Bamboo Saucer '68
The Bounty Man '72
Green Fire '55
Hustler Squad '76
Primary Target '89
Rhapsody '54
The Student Prince '54
Zone of the Dead '78

R. Lee Ermey
Body Snatchers '93
Demonstone '89
Endless Descent '90
Fletch Lives '89
French Silk '94
Full Metal Jacket '87
Hexed '93
I'm Dangerous Tonight '90
Kid '90
Mississippi Burning '88
The Siege of Firebase Gloria
  '89
Sommersby '93
The Take '90
The Terror Within 2 '91

Krista Errickson
First Time '82
Jekyll & Hyde...Together Again
  '82
Killer Image '92
Martial Outlaw '93
Mortal Passions '90

Leon Errol
The Flustered Comedy of Leon
  Errol '39
The Great Ziegfeld '36
Higher and Higher '44
Hurry, Charlie, Hurry '41
The Invisible Man's Revenge
  '44
Joe's Bed-Stuy Barbershop:
  We Cut Heads '83
Make a Wish '37
Mexican Spitfire at Sea '42
Mexican Spitfire/Smartest Girl
  in Town '40
Never Give a Sucker an Even
  Break '41
The Noose Hangs High '48
Pop Always Pays '40
Seven Days Ashore/Hurry,
  Charlie, Hurry '44
Two Reelers: Comedy Classics
  2 '46
Two Reelers: Comedy Classics
  5 '38

Patrick Ersgard
Mandroid '93
The Visitors '89

Bill Erwin
Fallen Angels 1 '93
Hard Knox '83
Huckleberry Finn '75

Stuart Erwin
Bachelor Bait '34
Back Door to Heaven '39
The Bride Came C.O.D. '41
Ceiling Zero '35
Chained '34
Going Hollywood '33
The Great Mike '44
Heading for Heaven '47
Hold Your Man '33
It Could Happen to You '39
Killer Dill '47
The Misadventures of Merlin
  Jones '63

Mr. Boggs Steps Out '38
Palooka '34
Small Town Boy '37
Viva Villa! '34

Carl Esmond
The Navy Comes Through '42
Panama Hattie '42
Without Love '45

Jill Esmond
Casanova Brown '44
F.P. 1 '33
Journey for Margaret '42
A Man Called Peter '55
Skin Game '31
State's Attorney '31
The White Cliffs of Dover '44

Bella Esperance
Lady Dragon '92
Lady Dragon 2 '93

Giancarlo Esposito
Amos and Andrew '93
Bob Roberts '92
Do the Right Thing '89
King of New York '90
Malcolm X '92
Mo' Better Blues '90
Night on Earth '91
School Daze '88
Sweet Lorraine '87

Gianni Esposito
Les Miserables '57
Paris Belongs to Us '60

David Essex
Journey of Honor '91
Octaman '71
Silver Dream Racer '83
That'll Be the Day '73

Christine Estabrook
Almost You '85
Presumed Innocent '90
Second Sight '89

Robert Estes
Aces: Iron Eagle 3 '92
Trapper County War '89

Emilio Estevez
Another Stakeout '93
The Breakfast Club '85
D2: The Mighty Ducks '94
Freejack '92
In the Custody of Strangers '82
Judgment Night '93
Maximum Overdrive '86
Men at Work '90
The Mighty Ducks '92
National Lampoon's Loaded
  Weapon 1 '93
Nightbreaker '89
Nightmares '83
The Outsiders '83
Repo Man '83
St. Elmo's Fire '85
Stakeout '87
Tex '82
That Was Then...This Is Now
  '85
Wisdom '87
Young Guns '88
Young Guns 2 '90

Joe Estevez
Armed for Action '92
Dark Rider '91
Dark Universe '93
The Deadly Secret '94
Eye of the Stranger '93
Fatal Justice '90s
In a Moment of Passion '93
L.A. Goddess '92
Lockdown '90
Money to Burn '94
Murder-in-Law '92
Soultaker '90

Ramon Estevez
Blood on the Badge '92
Cadence '89

Renee Estevez
Bulldance '88
Forbidden Sun '89
Intruder '88
Marked for Murder '89
Single White Female '92
Sleepaway Camp 2: Unhappy
  Campers '88

Erik Estrada
Alien Seed '89

Andy and the Airwave Rangers
  '89
Caged Fury '90
The Cross & the Switchblade
  '72
The Dirty Dozen: The Fatal
  Mission '88
The Divine Enforcer '91
Do or Die '91
Gang Justice '94
Guns '90
Honeyboy '82
Hour of the Assassin '86
Jailbreakin' '72
The Last Riders '90
Lightblast '85
The Line '80
The Lost Idol/Shock Troop '80s
The New Centurions '72
Night of the Wilding '90
A Show of Force '90
Spirits '90
Twisted Justice '89

Pat Estrin
Act of Vengeance '74
America First '70
Dennis the Menace: Dinosaur
  Hunter '93

Ruth Etting
Hips, Hips, Hooray '34
Roman Scandals '33

Shari Eubank
Chesty Anderson USN '76
Supervixens '75

Bob Eubanks
The History of White People in
  America '85
Johnny Dangerously '84
Roger & Me '89

**Corey Michael
Eubanks**
Forced to Kill '93
Payback '90

Wesley Eure
C.H.O.M.P.S. '79
Jennifer '78
The Toolbox Murders '78

Art Evans
CB4: The Movie
Die Hard 2: Die Harder '90
The Finishing Touch '92
The In-Laws '79
Jo Jo Dancer, Your Life is
  Calling '86
King '78
The Mighty Quinn '89
Mom '89
Native Son '86
School Daze '88
A Soldier's Story '84
Trespass '92
White of the Eye '88

Clifford Evans
The Courageous Mr. Penn '41
The Curse of the Werewolf '61
The Foreman Went to France
  '42
The Gilded Cage '54
I'll Get You '53
Love on the Dole '41
The Mutiny of the Elsinore '39
One Brief Summer '70
While I Live '47

Dale Evans
Apache Rose '47
Bells of Coronado '50
Bells of Rosarita '45
Bells of San Angelo '47
Cowboy & the Senorita '44
Down Dakota Way '49
The Golden Stallion '49
Helldorado '46
Home in Oklahoma '47
Lights of Old Santa Fe '47
My Pal Trigger '46
Roll on Texas Moon '46
San Fernando Valley '44
Song of Arizona '46
Song of Nevada '44
Sunset in El Dorado '45
Susanna Pass '49
Trigger, Jr. '50
Twilight in the Sierras '50
Under Nevada Skies '46
Utah '45
Western Double Feature 1 '38

Western Double Feature 3:
  Rogers & Allen '50
Western Double Feature 4:
  Rogers & Evans '40s
Western Double Feature 6:
  Rogers & Trigger '50
Western Double Feature 10:
  Roy, Dale, & Trigger '80s
Western Double Feature 18
  '40s
Western Double Feature 19 '45
Western Double Feature 21
  '40s
Western Double Feature 23
Western Double Feature 24
  '40s
Western Double Feature 25
The Yellow Rose of Texas '44

Douglas Evans
The Golden Stallion '49
The Green Hornet '39
North of the Great Divide '50
Sky High '51

Edith Evans
The Chalk Garden '64
Craze '73
Crooks & Coronets '69
David Copperfield '70
A Doll's House '79
Importance of Being Earnest
  '52
The Last Days of Dolwyn '49
Look Back in Anger '58
The Madwoman of Chaillot '69
Nasty Habits '77
The Nun's Story '59
The Queen of Spades '49
Scrooge '70
Tom Jones '63

Evans Evans
Dead Bang '89
The Story of a Love Story '73

Gene Evans
Apache Uprising '66
The Bounty Man '72
Cattle Queen of Montana '54
The Concrete Cowboys '79
Crashout '55
Devil Times Five '74
Donovan's Brain '53
Gentle Savage '73
It Happens Every Spring '49
Mutiny '52
Operation Petticoat '59
The Sad Sack '57
The Shadow Riders '82
Shock Corridor '63
The Steel Helmet '51
Walking Tall '73

Josh Evans
Born on the Fourth of July '89
The Doors '91
Ricochet '91

Linda Evans
Avalanche Express '79
Beach Blanket Bingo '65
Big Valley '68
Confessions of Tom Harris '72
The Gambler Returns: The
  Luck of the Draw '93
Hunter '77
Kenny Rogers as the Gambler,
  Part 2: The Adventure
  Continues '83
The Klansman '74
Mitchell '75
Standing Tall '78
Those Calloways '65
Tom Horn '80

Madge Evans
David Copperfield '35
Dinner at Eight '33
Hallelujah, I'm a Bum '33
Sinners in Paradise '38
Stand Up and Cheer '34
Three Broadway Girls '32
Transatlantic Tunnel '35

Maurice Evans
Androcles and the Lion '52
Beneath the Planet of the Apes
  '70
Invasion of the Body Snatchers
  '69
Planet of the Apes '68
Rosemary's Baby '68
Scrooge '35
The Tempest '63

Terror in the Wax Museum '73
The War Lord '65
Wedding Rehearsal '32

Mike Evans
The House on Skull Mountain
  '74
The Voyage of the Yes '72

Muriel Evans
The House of Secrets '37
King of the Pecos '36
Manhattan Melodrama '34
The New Frontier '35
The Prizefighter and the Lady
  '33
The Throwback '35

Rex Evans
The Matchmaker '58
The Wrong Road '37

Robin Evans
One Dark Night '82
Rage of Honor '87

Terry Evans
Cody '67
Mongrel '83

Troy Evans
Article 99 '92
Kuffs '92

Edith Evanson
Forever Amber '47
The Jade Mask '45
The Magnificent Yankee '50

Judith Evelyn
The Egyptian '54
Rear Window '54

Kimberly Evenson
The Big Bet '85
Kandyland '87
Porky's Revenge '85

Barbara Everest
Gaslight '44
Jane Eyre '44
Phantom Fiend '35
Tony Draws a Horse '51
The Valley of Decision '45

Chad Everett
Airplane 2: The Sequel '82
Fever Pitch '85
Heroes Stand Alone '89
The Impossible Years '68
Intruder Within '81
Jigsaw Murders '89
Johnny Tiger '66
Official Denial '93
Rome Adventure '62
The Rousters '90
The Singing Nun '66

Francine Everett
Dirty Gertie from Harlem U.S.A.
  '46
Tall, Tan and Terrific '46

Kenny Everett
The Best of the Kenny Everett
  Video Show '81
Bloodbath at the House of
  Death '85

Rupert Everett
Another Country '84
The Comfort of Strangers '91
Dance with a Stranger '85
Hearts of Fire '87
Inside Monkey Zetterland '93
The Right Hand Man '87

Tom Everett
Best of the Best '89
Friday the 13th, Part 4: The
  Final Chapter '84
Prison '88

Nancy Everhard
The China Lake Murders '90
Deepstar Six '89
Demonstone '89
Double Revenge '89
This Gun for Hire '90
The Trial of the Incredible Hulk
  '89

Jason Evers
Barracuda '78
Basket Case 2 '90
Claws '77
Fer-De-Lance '74

Greg Evigan
Deepstar Six '89

Evigan ▶*cont.*

Lies Before Kisses '92
Private Road: No Trespassing '87
Stripped to Kill '87

Pat Evison
Starstruck '82
Tim '79

John Ewart
Island Trader '71
Newsfront '78
Prince and the Great Race '83
The Quest '86
Which Way Home '90

Tom Ewell
Adam's Rib '50
Easy Money '83
The Girl Can't Help It '56
A Life of Her Own '50
Lost in Alaska '52
Mr. Music '50
The Seven Year Itch '55
State Fair '62
They Only Kill Their Masters '72

Barbara Ewing
Dracula Has Risen from the Grave '68
Guardian of the Abyss '82

Richard Eyer
Desperate Hours '55
The Invisible Boy '57
The Seventh Voyage of Sinbad '58

Peter Eyre
Diamond's Edge '88
Hedda '75

William Eythe
Colonel Effingham's Raid '45
The Ox-Bow Incident '43
Wilson '44
A Wing and a Prayer '44

Maynard Eziashi
Bopha! '93
Mister Johnson '91
Twenty-One '91

Shelley Fabares
Brian's Song '71
Clambake '67
Girl Happy '65
Great American Traffic Jam '80
Love or Money? '88
Memorial Day '83
Ride the Wild Surf '64
Sky Hei$t '75
Spinout '66

Fabian
Dear Brigitte '65
Five Weeks in a Balloon '62
Kiss Daddy Goodbye '81
Little Laura & Big John '73
The Longest Day '62
Mr. Hobbs Takes a Vacation '62
North to Alaska '60
Ride the Wild Surf '64
Soul Hustler '76

Ava Fabian
Ski School '91
To Die for '89
Welcome Home, Roxy Carmichael '90

Francoise Fabian
Dressmaker '56
Fernandel the Dressmaker '57
The French Woman '79
Happy New Year '74
Love by Appointment '76
My Night at Maud's '69
Reunion '88
Salut l'Artiste '74
That Naughty Girl '58

Joel Fabiani
President's Mistress '78
Reuben, Reuben '83

Nanette Fabray
Alice Through the Looking Glass '66
Amy '81
The Band Wagon '53
The Happy Ending '69

Harper Valley P.T.A. '78
The Man in the Santa Claus Suit '79
Personal Exemptions '88
The Private Lives of Elizabeth & Essex '39

Franco Fabrizi
Besame '87
Ginger & Fred '86
I Vitelloni '53
The Swindle '55
A Woman of Rome '56

Valeria Fabrizi
Beauty on the Beach '60s
Women in Cell Block 7 '77

Robert Factor
Fear '88
Ninja Academy '90

Jeff Fahey
Backfire '88
Body Parts '91
Curiosity Kills '90
Execution of Raymond Graham '85
Firefall '94
The Hit List '93
Impulse '90
Iran: Days of Crisis '91
Iron Maze '91
The Last of the Finest '90
The Lawnmower Man '92
Psycho 3 '86
Quick '93
Silverado '85
Sketch Artist '92
Split Decisions '88
True Blood '89
White Hunter, Black Heart '90
Woman of Desire '93
Wrangler '88
Wyatt Earp '94

Mary-Anne Fahey
Celia: Child Of Terror '89
The Dunera Boys '85
Mutant Hunt '87

Elinor Fair
Kismet '20
Let 'er Go Gallegher '28
Road to Yesterday/The Yankee Clipper '27
Yankee Clipper '27

Jody Fair
The Brain Eaters '58
High School Confidential '58

Bruce Fairbairn
Cyclone '87
Nightstick '87
The Vampire Hookers '78

Douglas Fairbanks, Jr.
Accused '36
Angels Over Broadway '40
Catherine the Great '34
The Corsican Brothers '42
Ghost Story '81
Gunga Din '39
Having Wonderful Time '38
Having Wonderful Time/Carnival Boat '38
The Hostage Tower '80
Joy of Living '38
Little Caesar '30
Mimi '35
Morning Glory '33
Our Modern Maidens '29
Party Girls '29
Prisoner of Zenda '37
The Rage of Paris '38
Scarlet Dawn '32
Sinbad the Sailor '47
When Thief Meets Thief '37
A Woman of Affairs '28
The Young in Heart '38

Douglas Fairbanks, Sr.
American Aristocracy '17
The Americano '17
The Americano/Variety '17
The Black Pirate '26
Camp Classics #1 '50s
Days of Thrills and Laughter '61
Don Q., Son of Zorro '25
Down to Earth '17
Flirting with Fate '16

His Majesty, the American '19
His Picture in the Papers '16
The Iron Mask '29
A Kiss for Mary Pickford '27
The Lamb '15
The Man from Painted Post '17
Mark of Zorro '20
Matrimaniac '16
Mr. Robinson Crusoe '32
Mystery of the Leaping Fish/Chess Fever '25
Private Life of Don Juan '34
Reaching for the Moon '17
Reaching for the Moon '31
Reggie Mixes In '16
Robin Hood '22
The Taming of the Shrew '29
The Thief of Baghdad '24
The Three Musketeers '21
When the Clouds Roll By '19

Craig Fairbrass
Cliffhanger '93
Prime Suspect 2 '93

Morgan Fairchild
Based on an Untrue Story '93
Body Chemistry 3: Point of Seduction '93
Campus Man '87
Cannon Movie Tales: Sleeping Beauty '89
The Concrete Cowboys '79
Deadly Illusion '87
Even Angels Fall '90
Haunting of Sarah Hardy '89
Honeyboy '82
Initiation of Sarah '78
Midnight Cop '88
Mob Boss '90
North and South Book 2 '86
Pee Wee's Big Adventure '85
Phantom of the Mall: Eric's Revenge '89
Red Headed Stranger '87
The Seduction '82
Sleeping Beauty '89
Test Tube Teens from the Year 2000 '93
Writer's Block '91
The Zany Adventures of Robin Hood '84

Virginia Brown Faire
Cricket on the Hearth '23
Sign of the Wolf '30

Heather Fairfield
A Girl of the Limberlost '90
No Secrets '91
The War of the Roses '89

Frankie Faison
City of Hope '91
Coming to America '88
Do the Right Thing '89
Exterminator 2 '84
Freejack '92
Mississippi Burning '88
Sommersby '93

Adam Faith
McVicar '80
Yesterday's Hero '79

Dolores Faith
The Human Duplicators '64
The Phantom Planet '61

Marianne Faithfull
Assault on Agathon '75
The Girl on a Motorcycle '68
Hamlet '91
Madhouse Mansion '74
The Turn of the Screw '92

Eduardo Fajardo
Apocalipsis Joe '65
Stranger in Paso Bravo '73

Lola Falana
The Klansman '74
Lady Cocoa '75
The Liberation of L.B. Jones '70
A Man Called Adam '66

Edie Falco
Laws of Gravity '92
Sweet Lorraine '87
Trust '91

Peter Falk
...All the Marbles '81
Anzio '68
The Balcony '63
Big Trouble '86

The Bloody Brood '59
Brink's Job '78
The Cheap Detective '78
Columbo: Murder By the Book '71
Columbo: Prescription Murder '67
Cookie '89
Faraway, So Close! '93
Great Race '65
Griffin and Phoenix: A Love Story '76
Happy New Year '87
The In-Laws '79
In the Spirit '90
It's a Mad, Mad, Mad, Mad World '63
Luv '67
Mikey & Nicky '76
Murder by Death '76
Pocketful of Miracles '61
Pressure Point '62
The Princess Bride '87
Robin and the Seven Hoods '64
Tune in Tomorrow '90
Vibes '88
Wings of Desire '88
A Woman Under the Influence '74

Mary Fanaro
Demon Queen '80s
Truth or Dare? '86

Al Fann
Frankie and Johnny '91
Parasite '81

Ennio Fantastichini
Open Doors '89
The Station '92

Sergio Fantoni
Atom Age Vampire '61
The Giant of Marathon '60
Hornet's Nest '70
The Prize '63
Von Ryan's Express '65
What Did You Do in the War, Daddy? '66

Stephanie Faracy
Blind Date '87
The Great Outdoors '88
Hocus Pocus '93

Daniel Faraldo
Above the Law '88
Full Fathom Five '90

Debrah Farentino
Bugsy '91
Capone '89
Mortal Sins '90
Son of the Pink Panther '93

James Farentino
The Cradle Will Fall '83
Dead and Buried '81
Ensign Pulver '64
Family Sins '87
The Final Countdown '80
Her Alibi '88
Honor Thy Father and Mother: The True Story of the Menendez Brothers '94
License to Kill '84
Naked Lie '89
The Possessed '77
Psychomania '63
Silent Victory: The Kitty O'Neil Story '79
Sins '87
A Summer to Remember '84
The War Lord '65

Antonio Fargas
Across 110th Street '72
The Ambush Murders '82
The Borrower '89
Busting '74
Car Wash '76
Cornbread, Earl & Me '75
Firestarter '84
Florida Straits '87
Foxy Brown '74
Howling 6: The Freaks '90
Huckleberry Finn '75
I'm Gonna Git You Sucka '88
Milo Milo '60s
Night of the Sharks '89
Nurse '80
Pretty Baby '78
Shakedown '88
Streetwalkin' '85

Betty Faria
Bye Bye Brazil '79
The Story of Fausta '88

Dennis Farina
Another Stakeout '93
Code of Silence '85
Crime Story: The Complete Saga '93
Drug Wars 2: The Cocaine Cartel '92
The Hillside Strangler '89
Jo Jo Dancer, Your Life is Calling '86
Little Big League '94
Mac '93
Manhunter '86
Men of Respect '91
Midnight Run '88
Street Crimes '92
Striking Distance '93
We're Talkin' Serious Money '92

Chris Farley
Airheads '94
Coneheads '93
Wayne's World 2 '93

Frances Farmer
Come and Get It '36
Son of Fury '42
South of Pago Pago '40
Toast of New York '37

Mimsy Farmer
Allonsanfan '73
Autopsy '73
The Black Cat '81
Codename: Wildgeese '84
Devil's Angels '67
More '69
Road to Salina '68
Spencer's Mountain '63

Suzan Farmer
Death in Deep Water '74
Die, Monster, Die! '65
The Graveyard '74

Alberto Farnese
Conqueror & the Empress '64
The Giants of Thessaly '60
Gladiator of Rome '63

Richard Farnsworth
Anne of Green Gables '85
Chase '85
Comes a Horseman '78
The Fire Next Time '93
The Grey Fox '83
Havana '90
Highway to Hell '92
Independence Day '83
Into the Night '85
Lassie '94
Legend of the Lone Ranger '81
Misery '90
The Natural '84
Resurrection '80
Rhinestone '84
Ruckus '81
Space Rage '86
Strange New World '75
Sylvester '85
Texas Across the River '66
Tom Horn '80
The Two Jakes '90
Waltz Across Texas '83
Witchery '88

Franklin Farnum
Battling with Buffalo Bill '31
Hopalong Cassidy '35
Mark of the Spur '32
Powdersmoke Range '35
Prison Train '38
The Scarlet Car '17

William Farnum
Between Men '35
A Connecticut Yankee '31
Custer's Last Stand '36
The Drifter '32
Dubarry '30
Git Along Little Dogies '37
God's Country '46
Gun Cargo '49
Kid Ranger '36
Law of the Sea '38
Lone Star '52
Million Dollar Haul '35
Mr. Robinson Crusoe '32
My Dog Shep '46
Painted Desert '31

Powdersmoke Range '35
Public Cowboy No. 1 '37
Santa Fe Stampede '38
The Silver Streak '34
The Spoilers '14
Ten Nights in a Bar-Room '31
Today I Hang '42
Trail of Robin Hood '50
Two Reelers: Comedy Classics 8 '33
The Vigilantes are Coming '36

Derek Farr
Man on the Run '49
Spellbound '41
Truth About Women '58

Felicia Farr
Charley Varrick '73
Jubal '56
Kiss Me, Stupid! '64
Kotch '71
3:10 to Yuma '57

Jamie Farr
Cannonball Run '81
Cannonball Run 2 '84
Combat Academy '86
Curse 2: The Bite '88
Fearless Tiger '94
For Love or Money '84
Happy Hour '87
M*A*S*H: Goodbye, Farewell & Amen '83
M*A*S*H: The Collector's Edition '72
No Time for Sergeants '58
Return of the Rebels '81
Scrooged '88
Speed Zone '88
Who's Minding the Mint? '67
With Six You Get Eggroll '68

Patricia Farr
Mistaken Identity '36
Tailspin Tommy '34

David Farrar
Beat Girl '60
Black Narcissus '47
Echo Murders '45
Frieda '47
John Paul Jones '59
Let's Make Up '55
Meet Sexton Blake '44
The Obsessed '51
Pearl of the South Pacific '55
Sea Chase '55
The Small Back Room '49
The World Owes Me a Living '47

Charles Farrell
Aggie Appleby, Maker of Men '33
City Girl '30
Just Around the Corner '38
Moonlight Sonata '38
Night and the City '50
Old Ironsides '26

Glenda Farrell
Bureau of Missing Persons '33
City Without Men '43
Disorderly Orderly '64
Gold Diggers of 1935 '35
Heading for Heaven '47
I Am a Fugitive from a Chain Gang '32
Johnny Eager '42
Kissin' Cousins '64
Lady for a Day '33
Little Caesar '30
Mystery of the Wax Museum '33
A Night for Crime '42
Prison Break '38
Talk of the Town '42

Mike Farrell
Damien: The Leper Priest '80
Dark River: A Father's Revenge '90
Escape from Planet Earth '67
The Graduate '67
Lockdown '90
M*A*S*H: Goodbye, Farewell & Amen '83
Memorial Day '83
Prime Suspect '82
Sex and the Single Parent '82
Silent Motive '91
Vanishing Act '88

Sharon Farrell
Arcade '93
It's Alive '74
The Love Machine '71
Marlowe '69
Night of the Comet '84
One Man Force '89
The Premonition '75
Rage '80
The Reivers '69
The Stunt Man '80

Terry Farrell
Back to School '86
Beverly Hills Madam '86
Hellraiser 3: Hell on Earth '92
Off the Mark '87

Timothy Farrell
The Devil's Sleep '51
Gun Girls '56
Jail Bait '54
Test Tube Babies '48

Tommy Farrell
Kissin' Cousins '64
Meet Danny Wilson '52
Pirates of the High Seas '50

Mia Farrow
Alice '90
Another Woman '88
Avalanche '78
Broadway Danny Rose '84
Crimes & Misdemeanors '89
Dandy in Aspic '68
Death on the Nile '78
Full Circle '77
The Great Gatsby '74
Guns at Batasi '64
Hannah and Her Sisters '86
High Heels '72
Hurricane '79
Husbands and Wives '92
A Midsummer Night's Sex Comedy '82
New York Stories '89
The Purple Rose of Cairo '85
Radio Days '87
Rosemary's Baby '68
Secret Ceremony '69
See No Evil '71
September '88
Shadows and Fog '92
Supergirl '84
A Wedding '78
Widow's Peak '94
Zelig '83

Tisa Farrow
And Hope to Die '72
Fingers '78
Grim Reaper '81
Initiation of Sarah '78
The Last Hunter '80
Manhattan '79
Search and Destroy '81
Some Call It Loving '73
Strange Shadows in an Empty Room '74
Winter Kills '79
Zombie '80

Rainer Werner Fassbinder
Fox and His Friends '75
Kamikaze '89 '83

The Fat Boys
Disorderlies '87
Knights of the City '85
Krush Groove '85

Chow Yung Fat
A Better Tomorrow '86
A Better Tomorrow, Part 2 '88

James Faulkner
Albino '76
Conduct Unbecoming '75
Flashpoint Africa '84
The Maid '90

Sally Faulkner
Alien Prey '83
Vampyres '74

Stephanie Faulkner
The Bus Is Coming '72
Death Journey '76
Virus '82

David Faustino
It's a Bundyful Life '92
Perfect Harmony '91

Jon Favreau
P.C.U. '94
Rudy '93

Alan Fawcett
Blindside '88
A Conspiracy of Love '87

Bill Fawcett
Black Hills '48
Check Your Guns '48
The Tioga Kid '48
Wild Country '47

Farrah Fawcett
Between Two Women '86
The Burning Bed '85
Cannonball Run '81
Double Exposure: The Story of Margaret Bourke-White '89
Extremities '86
Logan's Run '76
Murder in Texas '81
Murder on Flight 502 '75
Myra Breckinridge '70
Poor Little Rich Girl: The Barbara Hutton Story '87
The Red Light Sting '84
Saturn 3 '80
See You in the Morning '89
Small Sacrifices '89
Sunburn '79

George Fawcett
Drums of Jeopardy '31
The Flesh and the Devil '27
The Greatest Question '19
The Mad Whirl '25
The Wedding March '28

William Fawcett
Driftin' River '46
Gun Glory '57
Jesse James Meets Frankenstein's Daughter '65
Storm Rider '57

Dorothy Fay
Law of the Texan '38
Trigger Pals '39

Frank Fay
Love Nest '51
Spotlight Scandals '43

Alice Faye
Alexander's Ragtime Band '38
Every Girl Should Have One '78
The Great American Broadcast '41
Hello, Frisco, Hello '43
In Old Chicago '38
Magic of Lassie '78
On the Avenue '37
The Poor Little Rich Girl '36
The Range Feud/Two Fisted Law '31
Rose of Washington Square '39
State Fair '62
Stowaway '36
Tin Pan Alley '40
Week-End In Havana '41

Frank Faylen
Copper Canyon '50
Detective Story '51
The Flustered Comedy of Leon Errol '39
Francis the Talking Mule '49
Gunfight at the O.K. Corral '57
Hangman's Knot '52
It's a Wonderful Life '46
The Lost Weekend '45
The McConnell Story '55
The Nevadan '50
Red Garters '54
Riot in Cell Block 11 '54
The Road to Rio '47
Seventh Cavalry '56
Tanks a Million '41
Waterfront '39

Louise Fazenda
The Bat '26
Doughnuts & Society '36
A Hash House Fraud/The Sultan's Wife '15
The Night Club '25
The Old Maid '39

Ron Fazio
The Toxic Avenger, Part 2 '89
The Toxic Avenger, Part 3: The Last Temptation of Toxie '89

Melinda Fee
Aliens Are Coming '80
Doin' Time '85
Fade to Black '80

Bekim Fehmiu
The Adventurers '70
Battle of the Eagles '81
Ride to Glory '71

Lung Fei
Buddha Assassinator '82
The Cavalier '80s
Kung Fu Strongman
Marvelous Stunts of Kung Fu '83
Mission Kiss and Kill
Return of the Chinese Boxer '74
Shaolin Temple Strikes Back '72
Shaolin Traitor '82
Snake in the Eagle's Shadow 2 '83

Meng Fei
The Dragon Returns
Prodigal Boxer: The Kick of Death '77
The Unbeaten 28 '80s
Venus the Ninja '80s

Alan Feinstein
Bunco '83
The Hunt for the Night Stalker '91
The Hunted Lady '77
Joe Panther '76
The Two Worlds of Jenny Logan '79

Fritz Feld
The Affairs of Annabel '38
At the Circus '39
Bringing Up Baby '38
The Errand Boy '61
Everything Happens at Night '39
Four Jacks and a Jill '41
Get Smart, Again! '89
Herbie Goes Bananas '80
History of the World: Part 1 '81
Iceland '42
Kentucky Jubilee '51
Last Command '28
The Lovable Cheat '49
Mexican Hayride '48
The Noose Hangs High '48
Promises! Promises! '63
World's Greatest Lover '77

Clarence Felder
The Hidden '87
Killing Floor '85

Corey Feldman
Blown Away '90s
The 'Burbs '89
Dream a Little Dream '89
Edge of Honor '91
Friday the 13th, Part 4: The Final Chapter '84
Friday the 13th, Part 5: A New Beginning '85
The Goonies '85
Gremlins '84
License to Drive '88
Lipstick Camera '93
The Lost Boys '87
Meatballs 4 '92
Rock 'n' Roll High School Forever '91
Round Trip to Heaven '92
Stand By Me '86
Stepmonster '92

Marty Feldman
The Adventures of Sherlock Holmes' Smarter Brother '78
The Last Remake of Beau Geste '77
Sex with a Smile '76
Silent Movie '76
Slapstick of Another Kind '84
Think Dirty '70
To See Such Fun '81
Yellowbeard '83
Young Frankenstein '74

Barbara Feldon
Children of Divorce '80
Get Smart, Again! '89
A Guide for the Married Woman '78
No Deposit, No Return '76

Playmates '72
Smile '75

Tovah Feldshuh
The Amazing Howard Hughes '77
Blue Iguana '88
Brewster's Millions '85
Cheaper to Keep Her '80
A Day in October '92
Holocaust '78
Idolmaker '80
The Triangle Factory Fire Scandal '79

Enrique Alvarez Felix
Los Caifanes '87
Narda or The Summer '76

Maria Felix
Camelia
El Penon de las Animas '47
French Can-Can '55
La Diosa Arrodillada '47
La Generala '87

Norman Fell
The Boatniks '70
The Bone Yard '90
Bullitt '68
Charley Varrick '73
Cleopatra Jones & the Casino of Gold '75
Death Stalk '74
The End '78
For the Boys '91
For the Love of It '80
The Graduate '67
Hexed '93
If It's Tuesday, This Must Be Belgium '69
The Killers '64
On the Right Track '81
Paternity '81
Pork Chop Hill '59
The Stone Killer '73
Stripped to Kill '87
Transylvania 6-5000 '85

Federico Fellini
Bellissimo: Images of the Italian Cinema '87
Ciao Federico! Fellini Directs Satyricon '69
The Flowers of St. Francis '50
Intervista '87
The Miracle '48
We All Loved Each Other So Much '77

Julian Fellowes
Baby...Secret of the Lost Legend '85
Damage '92

Edith Fellows
Heart of the Rio Grande '42
In the Mood '87
Music in My Heart '40

Hansjorg Felmy
The Mad Executioners '65
The Monster of London City '64

Verna Felton
The Oklahoman '56
Picnic '55

Freddy Fender
La Pastorela '92
The Milagro Beanfield War '88
She Came to the Valley '77

Edwige Fenech
Blade of the Ripper '84
Phantom of Death '87
The Seducers '70
Sex with a Smile '76

Ku Feng
Crack Shadow Boxers '70s
Incredible Master Beggars '82
Kung Fu Avengers '85
Shaolin Disciple

Tanya Fenmore
Lisa '90
My Stepmother Is an Alien '88

Sherilyn Fenn
Backstreet Dreams '90
Boxing Helena '93
Crime Zone '88
Desire and Hell at Sunset Motel '92
Diary of a Hitman '91
Fatal Instinct '93

Fenn ▶cont.

Just One of the Guys '85
Meridian: Kiss of the Beast '90
Of Mice and Men '92
Ruby '92
Three of Hearts '93
True Blood '89
Twin Peaks '90
Two Moon Junction '88
Wild at Heart '90
The Wild Life '84
The Wraith '87
Zombie High '87

George Fenneman
How to Succeed in Business without Really Trying '67
The Marx Brothers in a Nutshell '90

Frank Fenton
The Golden Stallion '49
Isle of Forgotten Sins '43
Mexican Hayride '48
Naked Hills '56

Lance Fenton
Heathers '89
Night of the Demons '88

Leslie Fenton
F.P. 1 '33
Fugitive Road '34
The House of Secrets '37
Lady Killer '33
Marie Galante '34
Murder at Midnight '31
Public Enemy '31
The Strange Love of Molly Louvain '32

Colm Feore
Beautiful Dreamers '92
Blades of Courage '88
Dr. Bethune '90
Personals '90
32 Short Films About Glenn Gould '93

Tawny Fere
Angel 3: The Final Chapter '88
Night Children '89
Rockula '90

Al Ferguson
Laramie Kid '35
Lightning Raiders '45
Near the Rainbow's End '30
Roamin' Wild '36
Rose Marie '54
Tarzan the Tiger '29
Tentacles of the North '26

J. Don Ferguson
Loveless '83
Running Mates '86

Fernandel
Angele '34
Dressmaker '56
Fernandel the Dressmaker '57
The French Touch '54
Harvest '37
Little World of Don Camillo '51
The Man in the Raincoat '57
Nais '45
Pantaloons '57
Paris Holiday '57
The Sheep Has Five Legs '54
Topaze '51
Well-Digger's Daughter '46

Emilio Fernandez
Bring Me the Head of Alfredo Garcia '74
Duelo en el Dorado
The Wild Bunch '69

Jaime Fernandez
El Forastero Vengador '65
Emiliano Zapata '87
Los Hermanos Centella '65
Samson vs. the Vampire Women '61

Jesus Fernandez
Nazarin '58
Tristana '70

Juan Fernandez
The Amazing Transplant '70
Cat Chaser '90
Crocodile Dundee 2 '88
Kinjite: Forbidden Subjects '89
Liquid Dreams '92

Miguel Fernandez
The Kidnapping of the President '80
Sorry, Wrong Number '89
True Believer '89

Ashley Ferrare
Cyclone '87
Revenge of the Ninja '83

Christina Ferrare
The Impossible Years '68
Mary, Mary, Bloody Mary '76

Rebecca Ferratti
Cheerleader Camp '88
Gor '88
Hard Vice '94
Outlaw of Gor '87
Small Kill '93

Conchata Ferrell
Backfield in Motion '91
Deadly Hero '75
Edward Scissorhands '90
Eye on the Sparrow '91
Family Prayers '91
Goodbye, Miss 4th of July '88
Heartland '81
Heaven and Earth '93
Lost Legacy: A Girl Called Hatter Fox '77
Mystic Pizza '88
Portrait of a White Marriage '88
Rape and Marriage: The Rideout Case '80
Samurai Cowboy '93
To Love Again '80
True Romance '93
Where the River Runs Black '86

Tyra Ferrell
Boyz N the Hood '91
Equinox '93
Jungle Fever '91
Lady Beware '87
Poetic Justice '93
School Daze '88
Ulterior Motives '92
White Men Can't Jump '92

Andrea Ferreol
Control '87
Despair '78
The Last Metro '80
The Sleazy Uncle '89
Stroke of Midnight '90
Sweet Killing '93
Three Brothers '80
The Tin Drum '79
A Zed & Two Noughts '88

Jose Ferrer
The Art of Crime '75
The Being '83
Berlin Tunnel 21 '81
The Big Brawl '80
The Big Bus '76
Blood Tide '82
Bloody Birthday '80
The Caine Mutiny '54
Christopher Columbus '85
Cyrano de Bergerac '50
Deep in My Heart '54
Dune '84
Enter Laughing '67
The Evil That Men Do '84
The Fifth Musketeer '79
George Washington '84
Gideon's Trumpet '80
The Greatest Story Ever Told '65
Hired to Kill '91
Joan of Arc '48
Lawrence of Arabia '62
A Life of Sin '92
A Midsummer Night's Sex Comedy '82
Miss Sadie Thompson '53
Moulin Rouge '52
Natural Enemies '79
Old Explorers '90
Order to Kill '73
Paco '75
Pleasure Palace '80
The Private Files of J. Edgar Hoover '77
Samson and Delilah '84
Seduced '85
The Sentinel '76
Ship of Fools '65
Strange Interlude '90
The Swarm '78

To Be or Not to Be '83
Voyage of the Damned '76
Who Has Seen the Wind? '77
Zoltan...Hound of Dracula '77

Lupita Ferrer
Balboa '82
Children of Sanchez '79

Mel Ferrer
Blood and Roses '61
Born to Be Bad '50
Brannigan '75
City of the Walking Dead '83
Deadly Game '83
Eaten Alive '76
Elena and Her Men '56
Emerald Jungle '80
The Fall of the Roman Empire '64
The Fifth Floor '80
The Great Alligator '81
The Hands of Orlac '60
Hi-Riders '77
Knights of the Round Table '53
Lili '53
The Longest Day '62
Norseman '78
One Shoe Makes It Murder '82
Outrage! '86
Paris When It Sizzles '64
Rancho Notorious '52
Scaramouche '52
Sex and the Single Girl '64
The Tempter '74
The Visitor '80
War and Peace '56

Miguel Ferrer
Another Stakeout '93
Blank Check '93
Deepstar Six '89
Flashpoint '84
The Harvest '92
Hot Shots! Part Deux '93
Lovelines '84
Point of No Return '93
Python Wolf '88
Revenge '90
RoboCop '87
Scam '93
Star Trek 3: The Search for Spock '84
Stephen King's The Stand '94

Martin Ferrero
High Spirits '88
Jurassic Park '93
Planes, Trains & Automobiles '87
Stop! or My Mom Will Shoot '92

Noel Ferrier
Adventures of Eliza Fraser '76
Great Expectations: The Untold Story '87
Return of Captain Invincible '83

Carla Ferrigno
Black Roses '88
Seven Magnificent Gladiators '84

Lou Ferrigno
All's Fair '89
The Cage '89
Death of the Incredible Hulk '90
Desert Warrior '88
Hercules '83
Hercules 2 '85
The Incredible Hulk '77
The Incredible Hulk Returns '88
Liberty & Bash '90
Pumping Iron '76
Seven Magnificent Gladiators '84
Sinbad of the Seven Seas '89
The Trial of the Incredible Hulk '89

Barbara Ferris
Children of the Damned '63
A Chorus of Disapproval '89
Nice Girl Like Me '69

John Ferris
Monique '83
Torpedo Attack '82

David Ferry
Men of Steel '88
Project: Genesis '93
Tales of the Klondike: Race for Number One '87

Gabriel Ferzetti
Angel in a Taxi '59
Basileus Quartet '82
Counter Punch '71
Julia and Julia '87
L'Avventura '60
The Night Porter '74
On Her Majesty's Secret Service '69
The Psychic '78
Quo Vadis '85
Voyage of Terror: The Achille Lauro Affair '90

Stepin Fetchit
Amazing Grace '74
Judge Priest '34
Miracle in Harlem '48
On the Avenue '37
Stand Up and Cheer '34
The Sun Shines Bright '53
Wild Horse '31

Debra Feuer
Homeboy '88
Night Angel '90
Red Flag: The Ultimate Game '81
To Live & Die in L.A. '85

Peggy Feury
The Orphan '79
Witch Who Came from the Sea '76

Norman Feusier
Border Vengeance '35
Diamond Trail '33

Shelby Fiddis
Cheech and Chong: Things Are Tough All Over '82
Cheech and Chong's, The Corsican Brothers '84

John Fiedler
Bad Ronald '74
A Fine Madness '66
Harper Valley P.T.A. '78
Kiss Me, Stupid! '64
A Raisin in the Sun '61
Sharky's Machine '81
Twelve Angry Men '57

Betty Field
Birdman of Alcatraz '62
Bus Stop '56
Butterfield 8 '60
Coogan's Bluff '68
The Great Moment '44
Kings Row '41
Of Mice and Men '39
Peyton Place '57
Picnic '55
The Southerner '45

Chelsea Field
Andre '94
The Dark Half '91
Dust Devil '93
Extreme Justice '93
Harley Davidson and the Marlboro Man '91
Hotel Room '93
The Last Boy Scout '91
Prison '88
Skin Deep '89
Snapdragon '93

Karin Field
Cave of the Living Dead '65
The Mad Butcher '72
Web of the Spider '70

Sally Field
Absence of Malice '81
Back Roads '81
Beyond the Poseidon Adventure '79
The End '78
Forrest Gump '94
Heroes '77
Home for the Holidays '72
Hooper '78
Kiss Me Goodbye '82
Maybe I'll Be Home in the Spring '70
Mrs. Doubtfire '93
Murphy's Romance '85
Norma Rae '79
Not Without My Daughter '90
Places in the Heart '84
Punchline '88
Smokey and the Bandit '77

Smokey and the Bandit, Part 2 '80
Soapdish '91
Stay Hungry '76
Steel Magnolias '89
Surrender '87
Sybil '76
The Way West '67

Shirley Anne Field
Beat Girl '60
The Entertainer '60
Getting It Right '89
Hear My Song '91
House of the Living Dead '73
My Beautiful Laundrette '85
Peeping Tom '63
Shag: The Movie '89
Two by Forsyth '86
War Lover '62

Todd Field
Back to Back '90
Eye of the Eagle 2 '89
Full Fathom Five '90
Gross Anatomy '89
Ruby in Paradise '93

Virginia Field
A Connecticut Yankee in King Arthur's Court '49
Dance, Girl, Dance '40
Mr. Moto's Last Warning '39
Waterloo Bridge '40

Dorothy Fielding
The Abduction of Kari Swenson '87
Fright Night '85
The Preppie Murder '89

Fenella Fielding
Arrivederci, Baby! '66
Carry On Screaming '66

Marjorie Fielding
Conspirator '49
The Franchise Affair '52
The Lavender Hill Mob '51

Charlie Fields
The Beniker Gang '83
Fish Hawk '79

Christopher John Fields
Alien 3 '92
The Gun in Betty Lou's Handbag '92
Indecency '92

Robert Fields
Anna '87
The Sporting Club '72

Stanley Fields
Cimarron '30
Island of Lost Souls '32
Wide Open Faces '38

Tony Fields
Backstreet Dreams '90
Body Beat '88
Trick or Treat '86

W.C. Fields
The Bank Dick '40
The Barber Shop '33
Best of W.C. Fields '33
Comedy Reel, Vol. 1
Comedy Reel, Vol. 2
David Copperfield '35
The Dentist '32
The Fatal Glass of Beer '33
Hollywood Clowns '85
International House '33
It's A Gift '34
It's the Old Army Game '26
Mrs. Wiggs of the Cabbage Patch '42
My Little Chickadee '40
Never Give a Sucker an Even Break '41
Pharmacist '32
Pool Sharks '15
Running Wild '27
Sally of the Sawdust '25
W.C. Fields Comedy Bag '33
W.C. Fields: Flask of Fields '30
You Can't Cheat an Honest Man '39

Ralph Fiennes
A Dangerous Man: Lawrence after Arabia '91
Prime Suspect '92
Schindler's List '93

Harvey Fierstein
Apology '86
Garbo Talks '84
The Harvest '92
Mrs. Doubtfire '93
Tidy Endings '88
Torch Song Trilogy '88

Dennis Fimple
Creature from Black Lake '76
The Evictors '79
The $5.20 an Hour Dream '80
My Heroes Have Always Been
   Cowboys '91
Of Mice and Men '81
Truck Stop Women '74

Jon Finch
And Nothing But the Truth '82
Breaking Glass '80
Death on the Nile '78
The Final Programme '73
Frenzy '72
Game of Seduction '86
Lady Caroline Lamb '73
Lurking Fear '94
Macbeth '71
Unexplained Laughter '89
Witching Time '84

Peter Finch
The Detective '54
Elephant Walk '54
Eureka Stockade '49
Far from the Madding Crowd
   '67
First Men in the Moon '64
The Flight of the Phoenix '65
Kidnapped '60
Make Me an Offer '55
Network '76
No Love for Johnnie '60
The Nun's Story '59
Operation Amsterdam '60
Pursuit of the Graf Spee '57
Raid on Entebbe '77
Red Tent '71
Robbery Under Arms '57
Shattered '72
The Story of Robin Hood & His
   Merrie Men '52
Sunday, Bloody Sunday '71
Train of Events '49
The Warriors '55
Windom's Way '57
Wooden Horse '50

Larry Fine
Classic Comedy Video Sampler
   '49
Comedy Festival #1 '30s
Dancing Lady '33
Gold Raiders '51
Hollywood Party '34
It's a Mad, Mad, Mad, Mad
   World '63
The Lost Stooges '33
Snow White and the Three
   Stooges '61
The Stooges Story '90
Three Stooges Comedy
   Capers: Vol. 1 '40s
Three Stooges Comedy
   Classics '49
Three Stooges: Cookoo
   Cavaliers and Other Nyuks
   '40
Three Stooges Festival '49
Three Stooges: From Nurse to
   Worse and Other Nyuks '45
The Three Stooges: Half-Wit's
   Holiday and Other Nyuks '35
The Three Stooges: Idiots
   Deluxe and Other Nyuks '40
The Three Stooges Meet
   Hercules '61
The Three Stooges: Nutty but
   Nice and Other Nyuks '36
The Three Stooges: They
   Stooge to Conga and Other
   Nyuks '40

Frank Finlay
Arch of Triumph '85
Assault '71
Bouquet of Barbed Wire '76
Casanova '87
Cromwell '70
Cthulhu Mansion '91
The Death of Adolf Hitler '84
Enigma '82
The Four Musketeers '75

Gumshoe '72
In the Secret State
Lifeforce '85
The Loneliness of the Long
   Distance Runner '62
Molly Maguires '70
Murder by Decree '79
The Ploughman's Lunch '83
The Return of the Musketeers
   '89
Return of the Soldier '82
Robbery '67
Stalin '92
A Study in Terror '66
The Thief of Baghdad '78
The Three Musketeers '74
Wild Geese '78

James Finlayson
All Over Town '37
Block-heads '38
Bohemian Girl '36
Bonnie Scotland '35
A Chump at Oxford '40
Clark & McCullough '33
The Devil's Brother '33
Eyes of Turpin Are Upon You!
   '21
The Flying Deuces '39
Laurel & Hardy: Chickens
   Come Home '31
Laurel & Hardy Comedy
   Classics, Vol. 4 '32
Laurel & Hardy Comedy
   Classics, Vol. 5 '31
Laurel & Hardy Comedy
   Classics, Vol. 6 '35
Laurel & Hardy Comedy
   Classics, Vol. 7 '30s
No Man's Law '21
Our Relations '36
Pack Up Your Troubles '32
Pardon Us '31
Pick a Star '37
Saps at Sea '40
Stan Without Ollie, Vol. 3 '23
Stan Without Ollie, Vol. 4 '25
Way Out West '37

Jon Finlayson
A Kink in the Picasso '90
Lonely Hearts '82

Evelyn Finley
Dynamite Canyon '41
Trail Riders '42

William Finley
Phantom of the Paradise '74
The Wedding Party '69

John Finn
Cover-Up '91
Glory '89
Quicksand: No Escape '91

Warren Finnerty
The Brig '64
The Connection '61
Free Grass '69
Panic in Needle Park '75

Albert Finney
Alpha Beta '73
Annie '82
The Dresser '83
The Duellists '77
The Endless Game '89
The Entertainer '60
The Green Man '91
Gumshoe '72
The Image '89
Looker '81
Loophole '80
Miller's Crossing '90
Murder on the Orient Express
   '74
Orphans '87
The Playboys '92
Pope John Paul II '84
Rich in Love '93
Scrooge '70
Shoot the Moon '82
Tom Jones '63
Two for the Road '67
Under the Volcano '84
Wolfen '81

Shirley Jo Finney
Echo Park '86
Wilma '77

Linda Fiorentino
Acting on Impulse '93
After Hours '85

Chain of Desire '93
Gotcha! '85
The Moderns '88
The Neon Empire '89
Queens Logic '91
Shout '91
Strangers '91
Vision Quest '85
Wildfire '88

Ann Firbank
Flame to the Phoenix '85
Lillie '79

Eddie Firestone
Duel '71
The Law and Jake Wade '58
Two for the Seesaw '62

Colin Firth
Another Country '84
Apartment Zero '88
Dutch Girls '87
Femme Fatale '90
Hostages '93
A Month in the Country '87
The Secret Garden '87
Valmont '89

Peter Firth
Born of Fire '87
Burndown '89
Equus '77
Fire and Sword '82
The Hunt for Red October '90
The Incident '89
Innocent Victim '90
Joseph Andrews '77
King Arthur, the Young Warlord
   '75
Letter to Brezhnev '86
Lifeforce '85
Northanger Abbey '80s
Prisoner of Honor '91
Shadowlands '93
Tess '80
Wings of Fame '93

Kai Fischer
The Goalie's Anxiety at the
   Penalty Kick '71
The Hellfire Club '61

Vera Fischer
I Love You '81
Love Strange Love '82
Quilombo '84

Nancy Fish
Death Becomes Her '92
The Exorcist 3 '90
Ghost in the Machine '93

**Laurence "Larry"
Fishburne**
Apocalypse Now '79
Boyz N the Hood '91
Cadence '89
Class Action '91
Decoration Day '90
Deep Cover '92
For Us, the Living '88
Gardens of Stone '87
Hearts of Darkness: A
   Filmmaker's Apocalypse '91
King of New York '90
A Nightmare on Elm Street 3:
   Dream Warriors '87
Quicksilver '86
Red Heat '88
School Daze '88
Searching for Bobby Fischer
   '93
What's Love Got to Do With It?
   '93
Willie & Phil '80

Carrie Fisher
Amazon Women on the Moon
   '87
Appointment with Death '88
The Blues Brothers '80
The 'Burbs '89
Drop Dead Fred '91
The Empire Strikes Back '80
Frankenstein '82
From Here to Maternity '85
From "Star Wars" to "Jedi":
   The Making of a Saga '83
Garbo Talks '84
Hannah and Her Sisters '86
Hollywood Vice Sqaud '86
Loverboy '89
The Man with One Red Shoe
   '85

Mr. Mike's Mondo Video '79
Return of the Jedi '83
Shampoo '75
She's Back '88
Sibling Rivalry '90
Soapdish '91
Star Wars '77
Sweet Revenge '90
This is My Life '92
Thumbelina '82
The Time Guardian '87
Under the Rainbow '81
When Harry Met Sally '89

Cindy Fisher
Hometown U.S.A. '79
Liar's Moon '82

Eddie Fisher
All About Eve '50
Bundle of Joy '56
Butterfield 8 '60

Frances Fisher
Attack of the 50 Ft. Woman '93
Can She Bake a Cherry Pie?
   '83
Cold Sassy Tree '89
Deadly Conspiracy '91
Frame Up '91
Heart '87
Lucy and Desi: Before the
   Laughter '91
Molly and Gina '94
Patty Hearst '88
Praying Mantis '93
Sudie & Simpson '90
Tough Guys Don't Dance '87
Unforgiven '92

Gregory Fisher
The Girl in the Picture '86
1984 '84

Shug Fisher
The Giant Gila Monster '59
Huckleberry Finn '75

Tricia Leigh Fisher
Book of Love '91
C.H.U.D. 2: Bud the Chud '89
Hollywood Chaos '89
Pretty Smart '87

Robert Fiske
Green Archer '40
Mystic Circle Murder '39

Alan Fisler
If Looks Could Kill '86
New York's Finest '87
Student Affairs '88

Rick Fitts
Hanoi Hilton '87
Platoon Leader '87

Peter Fitz
Au Revoir Les Enfants '87
Club Extinction '89

Barry Fitzgerald
And Then There Were None '45
Bringing Up Baby '38
Broth of a Boy '59
The Catered Affair '56
Dawn Patrol '38
Going My Way '44
How Green was My Valley '41
The Long Voyage Home '40
Marie Antoinette '38
The Naked City '48
None But the Lonely Heart '44
The Quiet Man '52
The Saint Strikes Back '39
The Saint Strikes Back:
   Criminal Court '46
The Sea Wolf '41
The Stork Club '45
The Story of Seabiscuit '49
Tarzan's Secret Treasure '41
Union Station '50

Ella Fitzgerald
Pete Kelly's Blues '55
Ride 'Em Cowboy '42

Geraldine Fitzgerald
Arthur '81
Arthur 2: On the Rocks '88
Bloodlink '86
Dark Victory '39
Department Store '35
Diary of the Dead '80s
Dixie: Changing Habits '85
Easy Money '83
Harry and Tonto '74

Kennedy '83
The Last American Hero '73
Lovespell '79
The Mango Tree '77
The Mill on the Floss '37
The Obsessed '51
The Pawnbroker '65
Poltergeist 2: The Other Side
   '86
Rachel, Rachel '68
The Strange Affair of Uncle
   Harry '45
Ten North Frederick '58
Watch on the Rhine '43
Wilson '44
Wuthering Heights '39

Lewis Fitzgerald
A Cry in the Dark '88
Rikky and Pete '88

Tara Fitzgerald
Hear My Song '91
Sirens '93

Walter Fitzgerald
The Adventures of Sadie '55
Great Day '46
San Demetrio, London '47
Treasure Island '50

Ian Fitzgibbon
A Fine Romance '92
Prime Suspect 2 '93

Kate Fitzpatrick
Fantasy Man '84
Night Nurse '77
Return of Captain Invincible '83

Michael Fitzpatrick
Blood Tracks '86
Pay Off '89

Neil Fitzpatrick
A Cry in the Dark '88
Ground Zero '88

Emily Fitzroy
The Bat '26
The Cheerful Fraud '27
Don Quixote '35
The Frontiersman '38
Mockery '27

Paul Fix
The Bad Seed '56
Blood Alley '55
Captive Wild Woman '43
Desert Trail '35
El Dorado '67
Fargo Express '32
The Fighting Sheriff '31
Grayeagle '77
Gun Law '33
Hitler: Dead or Alive '43
Jet Pilot '57
Lafayette Escadrille '58
Mannequin '37
Phantom Patrol '36
Red River '48
Sherlock Holmes and the
   Secret Weapon '42
Somewhere in Sonora '33
South of Santa Fe '42
Star Reporter '39
The Throwback '35
To Kill a Mockingbird '62
Wanda Nevada '79
Zabriskie Point '70

Cash Flagg
Incredibly Strange Creatures
   Who Stopped Living and
   Became Mixed-Up Zombies
   '63
The Thrill Killers '65

Fannie Flagg
Five Easy Pieces '70
My Best Friend Is a Vampire
   '88

Joe Flaherty
Back to the Future, Part 2 '89
Blue Monkey '87
Going Berserk '83
Looking for Miracles '90
One Crazy Summer '86
Really Weird Tales '86
Sesame Street Presents:
   Follow That Bird '85
Speed Zone '88
Stripes '81
Tunnelvision '76
Used Cars '80
Wedding Band '89

Flaherty ▶cont.

Who's Harry Crumb? '89

Lanny Flaherty
The Ballad of the Sad Cafe '91
Sommersby '93

Georges Flament
The 400 Blows '59
La Chienne '31

Fionnula Flanagan
Death Dreams '92
The Ewok Adventure '84
In the Region of Ice '76
James Joyce's Women '85
Mad at the Moon '92
Mary White '77
Money for Nothing '93
Picture of Dorian Gray '74
A Winner Never Quits '86
Young Love, First Love '79
Youngblood '86

Ed Flanders
The Amazing Howard Hughes '77
Citizen Cohn '92
Eleanor & Franklin '76
The Exorcist 3 '90
Mary White '77
The Ninth Configuration '79
The Passing of Evil '70
The Pursuit of D.B. Cooper '81
Sophia Loren: Her Own Story '80
Special Bulletin '83
Things in Their Season '74
Tomorrow's Child '82
Trial of the Catonsville Nine '72
True Confessions '81

Susan Flannery
Anatomy of a Seduction '79
Gumball Rally '76

John Flaus
Blood Money '80
In Too Deep '90

James Flavin
Abbott and Costello Meet the Killer, Boris Karloff '49
Abroad with Two Yanks '44
Blondie Hits the Jackpot '49
Brand of Hate '34
Cloak and Dagger '46
Hollywood Canteen '44
King Kong '33
The Shanghai Cobra '45

Flea
Back to the Future, Part 2 '89
The Chase '93
Dudes '87
Motorama '91
My Own Private Idaho '91

John Fleck
The Comrades of Summer '92
Mutant on the Bounty '89

Susan Fleetwood
The Krays '90
Murder of a Moderate Man '70s
The Sacrifice '86
White Mischief '88

Charles Fleischer
Back to the Future, Part 2 '89
Bad Dreams '88
A Nightmare on Elm Street '84
Straight Talk '92

Eric Fleming
Conquest of Space '55
Fright '56
The Glass Bottom Boat '66
Queen of Outer Space '58

Ian Fleming
Butler's Dilemma '43
Land of Fury '55
Murder at the Baskervilles '37
Norman Conquest '53
Sherlock Holmes: The Silver Blaze '37
The Triumph of Sherlock Holmes '35
When Thief Meets Thief '37

Lone Fleming
It Happened at Nightmare Inn '70
Tombs of the Blind Dead '72

Rhonda Fleming
Abilene Town '46
Adventure Island '47
Bullwhip '58
A Connecticut Yankee in King Arthur's Court '49
Cry Danger '51
The Great Lover '49
Gun Glory '57
Gunfight at the O.K. Corral '57
The Nude Bomb '80
Out of the Past '47
Pony Express '53
Since You Went Away '44
Slightly Scarlet '56
Spellbound '45
The Spiral Staircase '46
Tennessee's Partner '55
While the City Sleeps '56

Susan Fleming
Range Feud '31
The Range Feud/Two Fisted Law '31

Robert Flemyng
Blood Beast Terror '67
The Blue Lamp '49
Cast a Dark Shadow '55
Conspirator '49
The Horrible Dr. Hichcock '62
Kafka '91
The Man Who Never Was '55

Bramwell Fletcher
Daughter of the Dragon '31
Random Harvest '42
The Undying Monster '42
White Cargo '42

Dexter Fletcher
Lionheart '87
The Rachel Papers '89
The Raggedy Rawney '90
Twisted Obsession '90

Dusty Fletcher
Boardinghouse Blues '48
Killer Diller '48

Louise Fletcher
Best of the Best '89
Blind Vision '91
Blue Steel '90
The Boy Who Could Fly '86
Brainstorm '83
The Cheap Detective '78
The Exorcist 2: The Heretic '77
Final Notice '89
Firestarter '84
Flowers in the Attic '87
Invaders from Mars '86
Islands '87
J. Edgar Hoover '87
Lady in Red '79
The Magician of Lublin '79
Mama Dracula '80
Natural Enemies '79
Nightmare on the 13th Floor '90
Nobody's Fool '86
One Flew Over the Cuckoo's Nest '75
Overnight Sensation '83
Return to Two Moon Junction '93
Russian Roulette '75
Shadowzone '90
Strange Behavior '81
Strange Invaders '83
A Summer to Remember '84
Talk to Me '82
Thieves Like Us '74
Two Moon Junction '88

Suzanne Fletcher
Bloodsucking Pharoahs of Pittsburgh '90
Sleepwalk '88

Sam Flint
The Chinese Cat '44
Evelyn Prentice '34
A Face in the Fog '36
The Lawless Nineties '36
Red River Valley '36
Spy Smasher Returns '42

Jay C. Flippen
Devil's Canyon '53
Far Country '55
Firecreek '68
Hellfighters '68
Jet Pilot '57
The Killing '56
The King and Four Queens '56

The Lemon Drop Kid '51
Marie Galante '34
Oklahoma! '55
The Restless Breed '58
Seventh Cavalry '56
They Live by Night '49
The Wild One '54
Winchester '73 '50
A Woman's Secret '49
The Yellow Cab Man '50

Suzanne Flon
One Deadly Summer '83
The Train '65
Un Singe en Hiver '62

Michael Flood
Crazy Fat Ethel II '85
Criminally Insane '75
Death Nurse '87

Florelle
The Crime of Monsieur Lange '36
Liliom '35

Sheila Florence
Cactus '86
A Woman's Tale '92

Holly Floria
Bikini Island '91
Netherworld '91
Presumed Guilty '91
Private Wars '93

George Flower
Across the Great Divide '76
Candy Tangerine Man '75
The Capture of Bigfoot '79
Cheerleader Camp '88
Devil & Leroy Basset '73
Further Adventures of the Wilderness Family, Part 2 '77
In Search of a Golden Sky '84
Mountain Family Robinson '79
Relentless '89
They Live '88

Darlanne Fluegel
Battle Beyond the Stars '80
Bulletproof '88
Concrete Beat '84
Crime Story: The Complete Saga '86
Deadly Stranger '88
Eyes of Laura Mars '78
Freeway '88
The Last Fight '82
Lock Up '89
Once Upon a Time in America '84
Pet Sematary 2 '92
Project: Alien '89
Running Scared '86
Scanner Cop '94
Slaughter of the Innocents '93
To Live & Die in L.A. '85
Tough Guys '86

Joel Fluellen
A Dream for Christmas '73
The Great White Hope '70
The Jackie Robinson Story '50
Man Friday '75

The Flying Karamazov Brothers
Flying Karamazov Brothers Comedy Hour '83
The Jewel of the Nile '85

Errol Flynn
Adventures of Captain Fabian '51
Adventures of Don Juan '49
The Adventures of Robin Hood '38
Against All Flags '52
Assault of the Rebel Girls '59
Captain Blood '35
The Charge of the Light Brigade '36
Dawn Patrol '38
Desperate Journey '42
Dive Bomber '41
Dodge City '39
Edge of Darkness '43
Escape Me Never '47
Gentleman Jim '42
Hollywood Bloopers '50s
It's a Great Feeling '49
Kim '50
The King's Rhapsody '55

Let's Make Up '55
The Master of Ballantrae '53
Northern Pursuit '43
Objective, Burma! '45
The Prince and the Pauper '37
The Private Lives of Elizabeth & Essex '39
San Antonio '45
Santa Fe Trail '40
The Sea Hawk '40
Silver River '48
The Sisters '38
Thank Your Lucky Stars '43
That Forsyte Woman '50
They Died with Their Boots On '41
Virginia City '40
The Warriors '55

Jerome Flynn
Edward II '92
A Summer Story '88

Joe Flynn
The Computer Wore Tennis Shoes '69
Gentle Savage '73
Lover Come Back '61
Million Dollar Duck '71
My Dog, the Thief '69
Now You See Him, Now You Don't '72
Superdad '73

Miriam Flynn
18 Again! '88
National Lampoon's Christmas Vacation '89

Sean Flynn
Dos Postolas Gemelas '65
Mission to Venice '63
Son of Captain Blood '62

Spiros Focas
The Jewel of the Nile '85
Rambo 3 '88
White Palace '90

Nina Foch
An American in Paris '51
Armistead Maupin's Tales of the City '93
Cash McCall '60
Child of Glass '78
Columbo: Prescription Murder '67
Cry of the Werewolf '44
The Dark Past '49
Dixie Lanes '88
Executive Suite '54
Illegal '55
Jennifer '78
Mahogany '75
Morning Glory '93
Return of the Vampire '43
St. Benny the Dip '51
Salty '73
Scaramouche '52
Skin Deep '89
Sliver '93
A Song to Remember '45
Spartacus '60
The Ten Commandments '56

Brenda Fogarty
Deadly Fielddtrip '74
Fairytales '79

Vladimar Fogel
Bed and Sofa '27
The Girl with the Hat Box '27

Ellen Foley
Fatal Attraction '87
Married to the Mob '88

Macka Foley
Las Vegas Weekend '85
WarCat '88

Michael Foley
The Divine Enforcer '91
Karate Cop '93
Prison Planet '92

Megan Follows
Anne of Avonlea '87
Anne of Green Gables '85
Back to Hannibal: The Return of Tom Sawyer and Huckleberry Finn '90
The Chase '91
Hockey Night '84
Silver Bullet '85
Stacking '87
Termini Station '89

A Time of Destiny '88

Bridget Fonda
Aria '88
Bodies, Rest & Motion '93
Camilla '93
Doc Hollywood '91
Frankenstein Unbound '90
The Godfather, Part 3 '90
Iron Maze '91
It Could Happen to You '94
Jacob Have I Loved '88
Leather Jackets '90
Little Buddha '93
Out of the Rain '90
Point of No Return '93
Scandal '89
Shag: The Movie '89
Single White Female '92
Singles '92
Strapless '90
You Can't Hurry Love '88

Henry Fonda
Advise and Consent '62
Ash Wednesday '73
Battle of the Bulge '65
Battleforce '78
The Best Man '64
A Big Hand for the Little Lady '66
Big Street '42
The Boston Strangler '68
The Cheyenne Social Club '70
City on Fire '78
Clarence Darrow '78
The Displaced Person '76
Drums Along the Mohawk '39
Fail-Safe '64
The Farmer Takes a Wife '35
Firecreek '68
Fort Apache '48
The Fugitive '48
Gideon's Trumpet '80
Golden Age of Hollywood '77
The Grapes of Wrath '40
Great Smokey Roadblock '76
Home to Stay '79
How the West was Won '63
I Dream Too Much '35
Immortal Sergeant '43
In Harm's Way '65
Jesse James '39
Jezebel '38
The Lady Eve '41
Last Four Days '77
The Longest Day '62
Mad Miss Manton '38
Madigan '68
The Magnificent Dope '42
Meteor '79
Midway '76
Mister Roberts '55
Moon's Our Home '36
My Darling Clementine '46
My Name is Nobody '74
Night Flight from Moscow '73
Oldest Living Graduate '82
On Golden Pond '81
Once Upon a Time in the West '68
The Ox-Bow Incident '43
The Red Pony '76
Return of Frank James '40
Rollercoaster '77
Roots: The Next Generation '79
The Rounders '65
Sex and the Single Girl '64
Sometimes a Great Notion '71
Spencer's Mountain '63
Stage Struck '57
Summer Solstice '81
The Swarm '78
Tentacles '77
That Certain Woman '37
There was a Crooked Man '70
The Tin Star '57
Too Late the Hero '70
Twelve Angry Men '57
Wanda Nevada '79
War and Peace '56
Warlock '59
The Wrong Man '56
You Only Live Once '37
Young Mr. Lincoln '39
Yours, Mine & Ours '68

Jane Fonda
Agnes of God '85
Any Wednesday '66
Barbarella '68
Barefoot in the Park '67

California Suite '78
Cat Ballou '65
The Chase '66
The China Syndrome '79
Circle of Love '64
Comes a Horseman '78
Coming Home '78
The Dollmaker '84
A Doll's House '73
The Electric Horseman '79
Fun with Dick and Jane '77
The Game is Over '66
Joy House '64
Julia '77
Klute '71
The Morning After '86
9 to 5 '80
Old Gringo '89
On Golden Pond '81
Period of Adjustment '62
Rollover '81
Spirits of the Dead '68
Stanley and Iris '90
Steelyard Blues '73
Tall Story '60
They Shoot Horses, Don't They? '69
Walk on the Wild Side '62

Peter Fonda
Cannonball Run '81
Certain Fury '85
Deadfall '93
Dirty Mary Crazy Larry '74
Easy Rider '69
Fatal Mission '89
Fighting Mad '76
Futureworld '76
Hawken's Breed '87
High Ballin' '78
Hired Hand '71
The Hostage Tower '80
Jungle Heat '84
Killer Force '75
The Last Movie '71
Lilith '64
Mercenary Fighters '88
Molly and Gina '94
92 in the Shade '76
Outlaw Blues '77
Race with the Devil '75
The Rose Garden '89
South Beach '92
Spasms '82
Spirits of the Dead '68
Split Image '82
Tammy and the Doctor '63
The Trip '67
Wanda Nevada '79
The Wild Angels '66

Phil Fondacaro
Dollman vs Demonic Toys '93
Ghoulies 2 '30
Meridian: Kiss of the Beast '90

Benson Fong
Charlie Chan in the Secret Service '44
The Chinese Cat '44
Conquest of Space '55
Deception '46
Girls! Girls! Girls! '62
His Majesty O'Keefe '53
Kung Fu: The Movie '86
Our Man Flint '66
The Purple Heart '44
The Scarlet Clue '45
The Shanghai Cobra '45

Leo Fong
Blind Rage '78
Enforcer from Death Row '78
Killpoint '84
The Last Reunion '80
Low Blow '85
Ninja Nightmare '88
Showdown '93

Joan Fontaine
Annabel Takes a Tour/Maid's Night Out '38
Beyond a Reasonable Doubt '56
The Bigamist '53
Born to Be Bad '50
Casanova's Big Night '54
A Damsel in Distress '37
Decameron Nights '53
Gunga Din '39
Island in the Sun '57
Ivanhoe '52
Jane Eyre '44

Letter from an Unknown Woman '48
Maid's Night Out '38
A Million to One '37
Othello '52
Rebecca '40
September Affair '50
Suspicion '41
Until They Sail '57
Voyage to the Bottom of the Sea '61
The Women '39

Hallie Foote
Courtship '87
1918 '85
On Valentine's Day '86

Horton Foote, Jr.
Blood Red '88
1918 '85
On Valentine's Day '86

Dick Foran
Atomic Submarine '59
Boy Meets Girl '38
Brighty of the Grand Canyon '67
Dangerous '35
Deputy Marshall '50
Earthworm Tractors '36
The Fighting 69th '40
Four Daughters '38
Guest Wife '45
The Mummy's Hand '40
The Mummy's Tomb '42
My Little Chickadee '40
Petrified Forest '36
Private Buckaroo '42
Ride 'Em Cowboy '42
Riders of Death Valley '41
The Sisters '38
Winners of the West '40

Bryan Forbes
The Baby and the Battleship '56
The Colditz Story '55
December Flower
The League of Gentlemen '60
Quatermass 2 '57
A Shot in the Dark '64
Wooden Horse '50

Mary Forbes
The Awful Truth '37
Tender Comrade '43
Vanity Fair '32
You Can't Cheat an Honest Man '39
You Can't Take It with You '38

Harrison Ford
American Graffiti '73
Apocalypse Now '79
Blade Runner '82
Clear and Present Danger '94
The Conversation '74
Dead Heat on a Merry-Go-Round '66
The Empire Strikes Back '80
Force 10 from Navarone '78
Frantic '88
The Frisco Kid '79
From "Star Wars" to "Jedi": The Making of a Saga '83
The Fugitive '93
Getting Straight '70
Great Movie Stunts & the Making of Raiders of the Lost Ark '81
Hanover Street '79
Heroes '77
Indiana Jones and the Last Crusade '89
Indiana Jones and the Temple of Doom '84
The Mosquito Coast '86
Patriot Games '92
Presumed Innocent '90
Raiders of the Lost Ark '81
Regarding Henry '91
Return of the Jedi '83
Star Wars '77
Witness '85
Working Girl '88
Zabriskie Point '70

Maria Ford
Angel of Destruction '94
Deathstalker 4: Clash of the Titans '92
Final Judgement '92
The Haunting of Morella '91
Masque of the Red Death '89
Naked Obsession '91
The Rain Killer '90
Ring of Fire '91

Border Shootout '90
Casablanca Express '89
Cimarron '60
The Courtship of Eddie's Father '62
Day of the Assassin '81
Destroyer '43
Don't Go Near the Water '57
Experiment in Terror '62
Fastest Gun Alive '56
Final Verdict '91
The Four Horsemen of the Apocalypse '62
The Gazebo '59
Gilda '46
The Green Glove '52
Happy Birthday to Me '81
Human Desire '54
Interrupted Melody '55
Is Paris Burning? '68
It Started with a Kiss '59
Jubal '56
The Lady in Question '40
The Loves of Carmen '48
Lust for Gold '49
Man from Colorado '49
Man from the Alamo '53
Midway '76
Pocketful of Miracles '61
Raw Nerve '91
The Rounders '65
The Sacketts '79
Santee '73
Smith! '69
So Ends Our Night '41
A Stolen Life '46
Superman: The Movie '78
The Teahouse of the August Moon '56
Texas '41
3:10 to Yuma '57
Torpedo Run '58
The Violent Men '55
Virus '82
The Visitor '80
The White Tower '50

Harrison Ford
The Average Woman '24
Foolish Wives '22
Hawthorne of the USA '19
The Nervous Wreck '26
The Primitive Lover '16
Shadows '22

Francis Ford
Accomplice '46
Lucky Cisco Kid '40
Man from Monterey '33
The Quiet Man '52
Stagecoach '39

Glenn Ford
Affair in Trinidad '52
Americano '55
Appointment in Honduras '53
Big Heat '53
Blackboard Jungle '55

Ring of Fire 2: Blood and Steel '92
Slumber Party Massacre 3 '90
Stripped to Kill II: Live Girls '89
The Unnamable 2: The Statement of Randolph Carter '92

Mick Ford
How to Get Ahead in Advertising '89
Scum '79

Paul Ford
Advise and Consent '62
The Comedians '67
Lola '69
Lust for Gold '49
The Matchmaker '58
Missouri Traveler '58
The Music Man '62
The Russians are Coming, the Russians are Coming '66
The Teahouse of the August Moon '56
Who's Got the Action? '63

Ross Ford
Blue Canadian Rockies '52
Jungle Patrol '48
Reform School Girl '57

Ruth Ford
The Eyes of the Amaryllis '82
The Lady is Willing '42
The Woman Who Came Back '45

Steven Ford
Body Count '87
When Harry Met Sally '89

Wallace Ford
The Ape Man '43
Back Door to Heaven '39
Blood on the Sun '45
Coroner Creek '48
Crack-Up '46
Dead Reckoning '47
Employees' Entrance '33
Exiled to Shanghai '37
Freaks '32
Get That Man '35
Great Jesse James Raid '49
Harvey '50
The Informer '35
Inside the Law '42
Jericho '38
Last Hurrah '58
A Lawless Street '55
The Lost Patrol '34
Mad About Money '30
The Man from Laramie '55
The Matchmaker '58
Maverick Queen '55
The Mummy's Hand '40
The Mummy's Tomb '42
Mysterious Mr. Wong '35
Night of Terror '33
O.H.M.S. '37
One Frightened Night '35
A Patch of Blue '65
Possessed '31
The Rainmaker '56
Rogue's Tavern '36
The Set-Up '49
Seven Days' Leave '42
Shadow of a Doubt '43
She Couldn't Say No '52
Skyscraper Souls '32
Spellbound '45
Swing It, Sailor! '37
T-Men '47
Warlock '59

Ken Foree
Dawn of the Dead '78
From Beyond '86
Glitz '87
Leatherface: The Texas Chainsaw Massacre 3 '89

Deborah Foreman
April Fool's Day '86
Destroyer '88
The Experts '89
Friends, Lovers & Lunatics '89
Lobster Man from Mars '89
Lunatics: A Love Story '92
My Chauffeur '86
Sundown '91
3:15—The Moment of Truth '86
Valley Girl '83
Waxwork '88

Mark Forest
Colossus of the Arena '60
Goliath and the Dragon '61
Goliath and the Sins of Babylon '64
The Lion of Thebes '64
Mole Men Against the Son of Hercules '61
Son of Samson '62
Terror of Rome Against the Son of Hercules '64

Michael Forest
Atlas '60
The Beast from Haunted Cave '60
Body of Evidence '92
Dirt Gang '71
Mohammed: Messenger of God '77
Ski Troop Attack '60

Carol Forman
The Black Widow '47
Federal Agents vs. Underworld, Inc. '49

Milos Forman
Heartburn '86
New Year's Day '89

Richard Foronjy
DaVinci's War '92
Midnight Run '88
The Morning After '86
Prince of the City '81
The Public Eye '92

Frederic Forrest
The Adventures of Huckleberry Finn '85
Apocalypse Now '79
Best Kept Secrets '88
Calamity Jane '82
Cat Chaser '90
Citizen Cohn '92
The Conversation '74
Dario Argento's Trauma '93
The Deliberate Stranger '86
The Don is Dead '73
Double Exposure: The Story of Margaret Bourke-White '89
Double Obsession '93
Falling Down '93
Gotham '88
Hammett '82
Hearts of Darkness: A Filmmaker's Apocalypse '91
Hidden Fears '93
It's Alive 2: It Lives Again '78
Larry '74
Lassie '89
Missouri Breaks '76
Music Box '89
One from the Heart '82
Permission To Kill '75
Quo Vadis '88
Return '88
The Rose '79
Saigon: Year of the Cat '87
Shadow on the Sun '88
Stacking '87
The Stone Boy '84
Tucker: The Man and His Dream '88
The Two Jakes '90
Valentino Returns '88
Valley Girl '83
When the Legends Die '72
Where Are the Children? '85

Sally Forrest
Son of Sinbad '55
Streets of Sin '49
Vengeance Valley '51

Steve Forrest
Captain America '79
Clown '53
The Deerslayer '78
Flaming Star '60
Gunsmoke: Return to Dodge '87
The Hanged Man '74
The Hatfields & the McCoys '75
Heller in Pink Tights '60
Hotline '82
The Last of the Mohicans '85
Mommie Dearest '81
North Dallas Forty '79
Roughnecks '80
A Rumor of War '80
Sahara '83
Spies Like Us '85

Forrest ▶cont.

The Wild Country '71

William Forrest
I'll See You in My Dreams '51
Jailhouse Rock '57
The Masked Marvel '43

Constance Forslund
Dear Detective '78
River's Edge '87
A Shining Season '79

Robert Forster
Alligator '80
Avalanche '78
The Banker '89
The Black Hole '79
The City '76
Committed '91
The Death Squad '73
Delta Force '86
Diplomatic Immunity '91
The Don is Dead '73
Goliath Awaits '81
Hollywood Harry '86
In Between '92
Journey Through Rosebud '72
Medium Cool '69
Once a Hero '88
Peacemaker '90
Satan's Princess '90
The Stalking Moon '69
Standing Tall '78
Stunts '77
29th Street '91
Vigilante '83
Walking the Edge '83

Rudolph Forster
The Mad Executioners '65
The Return of Dr. Mabuse '61
The Threepenny Opera '31

Bruce Forsyth
Bedknobs and Broomsticks '71
Star! '68

Rosemary Forsyth
Columbo: Murder By the Book '71
A Friendship in Vienna '88
The Gladiator '86
Gray Lady Down '77
My Father's House '75
Shenandoah '65
Texas Across the River '66
The War Lord '65
Whatever Happened to Aunt Alice? '69

Drew Forsythe
Burke & Wills '85
Doctors and Nurses '82
A Test of Love '84
Wrangler '88

Henderson Forsythe
Carolina Skeletons '92
Crisis at Central High '80
Sessions '83
Teamster Boss: The Jackie Presser Story '92

John Forsythe
The Ambassador's Daughter '56
And Justice for All '79
Cruise into Terror '78
Cry Panic '74
Destination Tokyo '43
Escape from Fort Bravo '53
The Happy Ending '69
In Cold Blood '67
Madame X '66
Murder Once Removed '71
Mysterious Two '82
Scrooged '88
Sizzle '81
Sniper '75
Terror on the 40th Floor '74
A Time for Miracles '80
Topaz '69
The Trouble with Harry '55
Users '78

William Forsythe
American Me '92
Career Opportunities '91
Dead Bang '89
Dick Tracy '90
The Gun in Betty Lou's Handbag '92

The Lightship '86
The Long, Hot Summer '86
Out for Justice '91
Patty Hearst '88
Raising Arizona '87
Relentless 3 '93
Savage Dawn '84
Stone Cold '91
Torrents of Spring '90
The Waterdance '91
Weeds '87

Albert Fortell
Nuclear Conspiracy '85
Scandalous '88
Time Troopers '89

Bob Fosse
The Affairs of Dobie Gillis '53
Give a Girl a Break '53
Kiss Me Kate '53
The Little Prince '74
My Sister Eileen '55

Nicole Fosse
All That Jazz '79
A Chorus Line '85

Brigitte Fossey
Blue Country '77
Chanel Solitaire '81
Enigma '82
Forbidden Games '52
Going Places '74
Honor Among Thieves '68
La Boum '81
The Man Who Loved Women '77
Quintet '79
The Wanderer '67

Barry Foster
After Pilkington '87
Beyond the Next Mountain '87
Frenzy '72
Maurice '87
Quiet Day In Belfast '74
Robbery '67
The Whistle Blower '87

Dianne Foster
The Kentuckian '55
The King of the Roaring '20s: The Story of Arnold Rothstein '61
Last Hurrah '58
The Violent Men '55

Frances Foster
Crooklyn '94
Enemy Territory '87

Gloria Foster
City of Hope '91
The House of Dies Drear '88
Leonard Part 6 '87
Man & Boy '71
Nothing But a Man '64
To All My Friends on Shore '71

Helen Foster
Ghost City '32
Linda '29
The Road to Ruin '28
Saddle Buster '32
Young Blood '33

Jodie Foster
The Accused '88
Alice Doesn't Live Here Anymore '74
Backtrack '89
The Blood of Others '84
Bugsy Malone '76
Candleshoe '78
Carny '80
Five Corners '88
Foxes '80
Freaky Friday '76
The Hotel New Hampshire '84
The Little Girl Who Lives Down the Lane '76
Little Man Tate '91
Maverick '94
Mesmerized '84
Napoleon and Samantha '72
O'Hara's Wife '82
One Little Indian '73
Shadows and Fog '92
Siesta '87
The Silence of the Lambs '91
Smile, Jenny, You're Dead '74
Sommersby '93
Stealing Home '88
Svengali '83
Taxi Driver '76

Tom Sawyer '73

Julia Foster
F. Scott Fitzgerald in Hollywood '76
Great McGonagall '75
Half a Sixpence '67
The Loneliness of the Long Distance Runner '62
Thirteenth Reunion '81

Kimberly Foster
Broken Trust '93
It Takes Two '88

Meg Foster
Adam at 6 A.M. '70
Backstab '90
Best of the Best 2 '93
Blind Fury '90
Carny '80
Different Story '78
Diplomatic Immunity '91
The Emerald Forest '85
Futurekick '91
Hidden Fears '93
Immortal Combat '94
James Dean '76
Jezebel's Kiss '90
The Legend of Sleepy Hollow '79
Leviathan '89
Masters of the Universe '87
The Osterman Weekend '83
Project: Shadowchaser '92
Relentless '89
Relentless 2: Dead On '91
Stepfather 3: Make Room for Daddy '89
They Live '88
Things in Their Season '74
Thumb Tripping '72
Ticket to Heaven '81
To Catch a Killer '92
Tripwire '89
The Wind '87

Norman Foster
Journey into Fear '42
Skyscraper Souls '32

Phil Foster
Bang the Drum Slowly '73
Conquest of Space '55
Hail '73

Preston Foster
American Empire '42
Annie Oakley '35
The Big Cat '49
Doctor X '32
Guadalcanal Diary '43
The Harvey Girls '46
I Am a Fugitive from a Chain Gang '32
I Shot Jesse James '49
The Informer '35
Kansas City Confidential '52
Ladies They Talk About '33
Last Days of Pompeii '35
The Last Mile '32
The Marshal's Daughter '53
My Friend Flicka '43
Ramrod '47
Sea Devils '37
Three Desperate Men '50
The Time Travelers '64
The Valley of Decision '45

Byron Foulger
Bells of San Fernando '47
The Devil's Partner '58
Hoppy Serves a Writ '43
The Panther's Claw '42
Prisoner of Zenda '37
Sullivan's Travels '41

Derek Fowlds
Hotel Paradiso '66
Over the Hill '93

Harry Fowler
Fire Maidens from Outer Space '56
Flight from Singapore '62

Douglas Fowley
Bar-20 '43
Battleground '49
Behind Locked Doors '48
Cat Women of the Moon '53
Colt Comrades '43
Desperate '47
From Noon Till Three '76
The Good Guys and the Bad Guys '69

It Could Happen to You '39
Lost Canyon '43
Meet the Mob '42
Mr. Wise Guy '42
North of the Border '46
On the Avenue '37
Poor White Trash '57
Rider from Tucson '50
Scared to Death '47
Shake Hands with Murder '44
Singin' in the Rain '52
Sunset on the Desert '42
Susanna Pass '49
Tanks a Million '41
The White Buffalo '77
Wild Country '47

Bernard Fox
Arnold '73
House of the Dead '80
The Private Eyes '80
Zone of the Dead '78

Colin Fox
Beautiful Dreamers '92
My Pleasure Is My Business '74

Edward Fox
Anastasia: The Mystery of Anna '86
Battle of Britain '69
The Big Sleep '78
The Bounty '84
A Bridge Too Far '77
The Cat and the Canary '79
The Crucifer of Blood '91
The Day of the Jackal '73
A Doll's House '73
The Dresser '83
The Duellists '77
Edward and Mrs. Simpson '80
Force 10 from Navarone '78
Gandhi '82
The Go-Between '71
The Mirror Crack'd '80
Never Say Never Again '83
Portrait of a Lady '67
Road to 1984
Robin Hood '91
Shaka Zulu '83
The Shooting Party '85
Skullduggery '70
Soldier of Orange '78
The Squeeze '77
Wild Geese 2 '85

Huckleberry Fox
The Blue Yonder '86
Konrad '90s
Misunderstood '84
A Winner Never Quits '86

James Fox
Absolute Beginners '86
Afraid of the Dark '92
The Chase '66
Farewell to the King '89
Greystoke: The Legend of Tarzan, Lord of the Apes '84
Heart of Darkness '93
High Season '88
Hostage '92
Isadora '68
King Rat '65
The Mighty Quinn '89
Nancy Astor '82
A Passage to India '84
Patriot Games '92
Performance '70
A Question of Attribution '91
The Remains of the Day '93
The Russia House '90
The Servant '63
Shadow on the Sun '88
Thoroughly Modern Millie '67
Those Magnificent Men in Their Flying Machines '65
The Whistle Blower '87

Kerry Fox
An Angel at My Table '89
The Last Days of Chez Nous '92

Michael J. Fox
Back to the Future '85
Back to the Future, Part 2 '89
Back to the Future, Part 3 '90
Bright Lights, Big City '88
Casualties of War '89
Class of 1984 '82
Doc Hollywood '91
For Love or Money '93

Greedy '94
The Hard Way '91
High School USA '84
Life with Mikey '93
Light of Day '87
Midnight Madness '80
Poison Ivy '85
The Secret of My Success '87
Teen Wolf '85

Peter Fox
Diamond Run '90
A Minor Miracle '83

Sidney Fox
Don Quixote '35
Midnight '34
Murders in the Rue Morgue '32

Virginia Fox
The Blacksmith/The Balloonatic '23
The Blacksmith/The Cops '22

Robert Foxworth
Ants '77
Beyond the Stars '89
The Black Marble '79
Damien: Omen 2 '78
Deathmoon '78
Double Standard '88
Frankenstein '73
The Invisible Strangler '76
Prophecy '79
The Treasure of Matecumbe '76

Redd Foxx
Cotton Comes to Harlem '70
Harlem Nights '89
Norman, Is That You? '76

Eddie Foy, Jr.
Bells are Ringing '60
The Farmer Takes a Wife '53
Four Jacks and a Jill '41
Gidget Goes Hawaiian '61
Lucky Me '54
Pajama Game '57
30 Is a Dangerous Age, Cynthia '68
Wilson '44
Yankee Doodle Dandy '42

Carla Fracci
Life of Verdi '84
Nijinsky '80

Jonathon Frakes
North and South Book 1 '85
Star Trek The Next Generation: Encounter at Farpoint '87

Victor Francen
The Beast with Five Fingers '46
J'Accuse '37
Madame Curie '43
San Antonio '45
The Tuttles of Tahiti '42

Anthony (Tony) Franciosa
Across 110th Street '72
Assault on a Queen '66
Backstreet Dreams '90
Blood Vows: The Story of a Mafia Wife '87
Career '59
Curse of the Black Widow '77
Daughter of Death '82
Death House
Death Wish 2 '82
Double Threat '92
The Drowning Pool '75
A Face in the Crowd '57
Ghost in the Noonday Sun '74
Ghost Writer '82
Kiss My Grits '82
La Cicada '83
The Long, Hot Summer '58
The Naked Maja '59
Period of Adjustment '62
Rio Conchos '64
Side Show '84
Stagecoach '86
This Could Be the Night '57
Unsane '82
Web of the Spider '70
The World is Full of Married Men '80

Alec B. Francis
Beau Brummel '24
Charley's Aunt '25
His Private Secretary '33

Little Church Around the
Corner '23
The Mad Whirl '25
Mata Hari '32
The Wishing Ring '14

Anne Francis
Bad Day at Black Rock '54
Battle Cry '55
Blackboard Jungle '55
Born Again '78
Cry Panic '74
Don't Go Near the Water '57
Fireball Forward '72
Forbidden Planet '56
Funny Girl '68
Haunts of the Very Rich '72
Laguna Heat '87
A Lion is in the Streets '53
Little Vegas '90
Mazes and Monsters '82
Pancho Villa '72
Poor Little Rich Girl: The
Barbara Hutton Story '87
Portrait of Jennie '48
The Rebels '79
Return '88
Summer Holiday '48
Susan Slept Here '54
Wild Women '70

Arlene Francis
Murders in the Rue Morgue '32
One, Two, Three '61
The Thrill of It All! '63

Clive Francis
The Bretts '88
Man Who Had Power Over
Women '72
Poldark '75

Genie Francis
North and South Book 1 '85
North and South Book 2 '86

Ivor Francis
Hard Frame '70
House of the Dead '80
Zone of the Dead '78

Kay Francis
The Cocoanuts '29
In Name Only '39
It's a Date '40
Little Men '40
Vice Squad '31

Noel Francis
Bachelor Apartment '31
Fire Alarm '38
My Pal, The King '32

Robert Francis
The Caine Mutiny '54
The Long Gray Line '55

James Franciscus
The Amazing Dobermans '76
Beneath the Planet of the Apes
'70
Butterfly '82
The Cat o' Nine Tails '71
Good Guys Wear Black '78
The Greek Tycoon '78
Hunter '77
Jacqueline Bouvier Kennedy
'81
Jonathan Livingston Seagull
'73
Killer Fish '79
The Man Inside '76
Marooned '69
Nightkill '80
One of My Wives Is Missing '76
Puzzle '78
Secret Weapons '85
Secrets of Three Hungry Wives
'78
Snow Treasure '67
The Valley of Gwangi '69

Don Francks
The Christmas Wife '88
Drying Up the Streets '76
Fast Company '78
Finian's Rainbow '68
984: Prisoner of the Future '84
Phoenix Team '80

Ramon Franco
Kiss Me a Killer '91
Tour of Duty '87

Jacques Francois
The Barkleys of Broadway '49
The Gift '82

Billy Franey
Ghost Valley '32
Somewhere in Sonora '33

Ben Frank
Don't Answer the Phone '80
Hollywood Vice Sqaud '86
Hollywood Zap '86

Charles Frank
The Chisholms '79
Danielle Steel's Changes '91
A Guide for the Married Woman
'78
LBJ: The Early Years '88
The Right Stuff '83
Snowblind '78
Tarantulas: The Deadly Cargo
'77

Diana Frank
The Glass Jungle '88
Monster High '89
Pale Blood '91

Gary Frank
Deadly Weapon '88
Enemy Territory '87
Enola Gay: The Men, the
Mission, the Atomic Bomb
'80
Getting Up and Going Home
'92
The Night the City Screamed
'80

Horst Frank
Albino '76
Code Name Alpha '67
Desert Commandos '60s
The Grand Duel '73
The Head '59

Joanna Frank
Always '85
The Savage Seven '68
Say Anything '89

Tony Frank
Riverbend '89
Rush '91

Mark Frankel
Leon the Pig Farmer '93
Young Catherine '91

Al Franken
One More Saturday Night '86
Tunnelvision '76

Steve Franken
Ants '77
Freeway '88
Which Way to the Front? '70

Paul Frankeur
Le Gentleman D'Epsom '62
License to Kill '64
The Milky Way '68
Un Singe en Hiver '62

William Frankfather
Born Yesterday '93
Defense Play '88

Bonnie Franklin
Breaking Up Is Hard to Do '79
Portrait of a Rebel: Margaret
Sanger '82
Your Place or Mine '83

David Franklin
Early Frost '84
Rock & Roll Cowboys '92

Diane Franklin
Better Off Dead '85
Last American Virgin '82
Second Time Lucky '84
Terrorvision '86

Gloria Franklin
Drums of Fu Manchu '40
Without Warning '52

Joe Franklin
Ghoul School '91
29th Street '91

John Franklin
The Addams Family '91
Children of the Corn '84

Pamela Franklin
And Soon the Darkness '70
David Copperfield '70
Eleanor & Franklin '76
Flipper's New Adventure '64
Food of the Gods '76
The Horse Without a Head '63
The Legend of Hell House '73

The Night of the Following Day
'64
The Prime of Miss Jean Brodie
'69
Satan's School for Girls '73
Screamer '74
A Tiger Walks '64
The Witching '72

William Franklyn
Quatermass 2 '57
The Satanic Rites of Dracula
'73
Splitting Heirs '93

Chloe Franks
The House that Dripped Blood
'71
Ivanhoe '82

Mary Frann
Fatal Charm '92
I'm Dangerous Tonight '90

Arthur Franz
Abbott & Costello Meet the
Invisible Man '51
Atomic Submarine '59
Beyond a Reasonable Doubt
'56
Bogie: The Last Hero '80
Dream No Evil '75
Flight to Mars '52
Hellcats of the Navy '57
The Human Factor '75
Invaders from Mars '53
Jungle Patrol '48
The Member of the Wedding
'52
Monster on the Campus '59
Sisters of Death '76

Dennis Franz
Blow Out '81
Body Double '84
Die Hard 2: Die Harder '90
Dressed to Kill '80
Kiss Shot '89
The Package '89
Psycho 2 '83

Eduard Franz
The Burning Hills '56
Francis the Talking Mule '49
The Indian Fighter '55
Latin Lovers '53
The Magnificent Yankee '50
One Minute to Zero '52
Outpost in Morocco '49
The Scar '48
Sins of Jezebel '54
The Story of Ruth '60

Bill Fraser
Alias John Preston '56
Little Dorrit, Film 1: Nobody's
Fault '88
Little Dorrit, Film 2: Little
Dorrit's Story '88
Naughty Knights '71
Pirates '86

Brendan Fraser
Airheads '94
Dogfight '91
Encino Man '92
School Ties '92
The Scout '94
Twenty Bucks '93
With Honors '94

Duncan Fraser
Call of the Wild '93
Timecop '94

Elisabeth Fraser
Ask Any Girl '59
Hills of Oklahoma '50
The Man Who Came to Dinner
'41
A Patch of Blue '65
The Tunnel of Love '58
Two for the Seesaw '62
Young at Heart '54

Hugh Fraser
The Bretts '88
The Draughtsman's Contract
'82

John Fraser
Horsemasters '61
Isadora '68
Repulsion '65

Liz Fraser
Adventures of a Taxi Driver '76

The Americanization of Emily
'64
Carry On Cruising '62
Chicago Joe & the Showgirl '90
Two-Way Stretch '60

Phyllis Fraser
Tough to Handle '37
Western Double Feature 3 '36
Winds of the Wasteland '36

Richard Fraser
Bedlam '45
The Cobra Strikes '48
The Private Affairs of Bel Ami
'47
White Pongo '45

Ronald Fraser
The Killing of Sister George '69
Rentadick '72

Sally Fraser
Dangerous Charter '62
Giant from the Unknown '58
It Conquered the World '56
The War of the Colossal Beast
'58

Stuart Fratkin
Dr. Alien '88
Prehystoria '93
Remote '93
Ski School '91

William Frawley
Abbott & Costello Meet the
Invisible Man '51
The Adventures of Huckleberry
Finn '39
Babe Ruth Story '48
Blondie in Society '41
The Bride Came C.O.D. '41
Down to Earth '47
East Side, West Side '49
Fighting Seabees '44
Flame of the Barbary Coast '45
The General Died at Dawn '36
Gentleman Jim '42
Harmony Lane '35
The Inner Circle '46
The Lemon Drop Kid '51
Miracle on 34th Street '47
Monsieur Verdoux '47
One Night in the Tropics '40
Rancho Notorious '52
Rose of Washington Square
'39
Something to Sing About '36
Whistling in Brooklyn '43
Wildcat '42

Jane Frazee
The Gay Ranchero '42
Grand Canyon Trail '48
Last of the Wild Horses '49
On the Old Spanish Trail '47
Springtime in the Sierras '47
Under California Stars '48

Robert Frazer
Dawn Express '42
Death from a Distance '36
The Drake Case '29
Fighting Parson '35
Fighting Pilot '35
Found Alive '34
The Miracle Rider '35
Monte Carlo Nights '34
Mystery Trooper '32
Partners of the Trail '44
Renfrew on the Great White
Trail '38
Saddle Buster '32
Ten Nights in a Bar-Room '31

Rupert Frazer
Back Home '90
Empire of the Sun '87
The Girl in a Swing '89

Sheila Frazier
Firehouse '72
The Hitter '79
Superfly '72
Superfly T.N.T. '73
Three the Hard Way '74

Peter Frechette
The Kindred '87
No Small Affair '84
Paint It Black '89

Blanche Frederici
A Farewell to Arms '32
Night Nurse '31
Sadie Thompson '28

Lynne Frederick
Amazing Mr. Blunden '72
Phase 4 '74
Prisoner of Zenda '79
Schizo '77
Vampire Circus '71
Voyage of the Damned '76

Vicki Frederick
...All the Marbles '81
Body Rock '84
Chopper Chicks in Zombietown
'91
A Chorus Line '85

Alan Freed
Go, Johnny Go! '59
Rock, Rock, Rock '56

Bert Freed
The Cobweb '55
Detective Story '51
Evel Knievel '72
The Gazebo '59
The Halls of Montezuma '50
Men of the Fighting Lady '54
Paths of Glory '57

Al Freeman, Jr.
Assault at West Point: The
Court-Martial of Johnson
Whittaker '94
The Defense Never Rests '90
The Detective '67
Dutchman '67
Ensign Pulver '64
Finian's Rainbow '68
Malcolm X '92
My Sweet Charlie '70
Perry Mason Returns '85
Seven Hours to Judgment '88

Howard Freeman
Air Raid Wardens '43
Double Dynamite '51
House of Horrors '46
Million Dollar Mermaid '52
Scaramouche '52

J.E. Freeman
Aces: Iron Eagle 3 '92
Casualties of Love: The ''Long
Island Lolita'' Story '93
Fallen Angels 2 '93
Hard Traveling '85
It Could Happen to You '94
Memphis '91
Miller's Crossing '90
Mother's Boys '94
Wild at Heart '90

Joan Freeman
Fastest Guitar Alive '68
Panic in the Year Zero! '62
The Rounders '65
Roustabout '64
Tower of London '62

Kathleen Freeman
Disorderly Orderly '64
The Errand Boy '61
Hollywood Chaos '89
In the Mood '87
Innerspace '87
Love is Better Than Ever '52
Malibu Bikini Shop '86
Naked Gun 33 1/3: The Final
Insult '94
The Nutty Professor '63
The Rounders '65
The Willies '90

Mona Freeman
Battle Cry '55
Black Beauty '46
Black Beauty/Courage of Black
Beauty '57
Branded '50
Copper Canyon '50
Dear Wife '49
Jumping Jacks '52
That Brennan Girl '46
The Way Out '56

Morgan Freeman
Blood Money: The Story of
Clinton and Nadine '88
The Bonfire of the Vanities '90
Brubaker '80
Clean and Sober '88
Driving Miss Daisy '89
Execution of Raymond Graham
'85
Eyewitness '81
Glory '89

Freeman ▶cont.

Harry & Son '84
Johnny Handsome '89
Lean on Me '89
Marie '85
The Power of One '92
Robin Hood: Prince of Thieves '91
Roll of Thunder, Hear My Cry '78
Street Smart '87
Teachers '84
That Was Then...This Is Now '85
Unforgiven '92

Paul Freeman
Aces: Iron Eagle 3 '92
A Dangerous Man: Lawrence after Arabia '91
The Dogs of War '81
Eminent Domain '91
Murderers Among Us: The Simon Wiesenthal Story '89
Prisoner of Rio '89
Raiders of the Lost Ark '81
The Sender '82
Shanghai Surprise '86
Unsuitable Job for a Woman '82
Whose Child Am I? '75
Without a Clue '88
A World Apart '88

Tony Freeman
Invincible Gladiators '64
Ocean Drive Weekend '85

Paul Frees
Hunt the Man Down/Smashing the Rackets '50
Suddenly '54

Alice Freindlikh
Rasputin '85
Stalker '79

Stephane Freiss
Does This Mean We're Married? '89
Vagabond '85

Bruce French
Ants '77
Pipe Dreams '76

Charles French
The Crimson Trail '35
Gun Play '36
King of the Rodeo '28
The Live Wire '34
The Man from Hell '34
Man of Action '33
Trail of Terror '35
When a Man Sees Red '34
Where Trails Divide '37

Edwige French
The Next Victim '71
You've Got to Have Heart '77

Valerie French
Jubal '56
The 27 Day '57

Victor French
Charro! '69
Chato's Land '71
Choices '81
The House on Skull Mountain '74
Little House on the Prairie '74
The Other '72
Spencer's Mountain '63

Pierre Fresnay
Cesar '36
Fanny '32
Grand Illusion '37
Le Corbeau '43
The Man Who Knew Too Much '34
Marius '32
Monsieur Vincent '48

Bernard Fresson
French Connection 2 '75
Hiroshima, Mon Amour '59
Honor Among Thieves '68
The Tenant '76

Matt Frewer
Far from Home '89
The Fourth Protocol '87
Honey, I Shrunk the Kids '89

Max Headroom, the Original Story '86
The Positively True Adventures of the Alleged Texas Cheerleader-Murdering Mom '93
Short Time '90
Speed Zone '88
Stephen King's The Stand '94
Supergirl '84
The Taking of Beverly Hills '91
Twenty Bucks '93

Leonard Frey
The Boys in the Band '70
Fiddler on the Roof '71
The Magic Christian '69
Tattoo '81

Sami Frey
Band of Outsiders '64
Black Widow '87
Cesar & Rosalie '72
Cleo from 5 to 7 '61
The Little Drummer Girl '84
Nea '78
Sand and Blood '87
Sweet Movie '75
War & Remembrance, Part 1 '88
War & Remembrance: The Final Chapter, Part 8 '89

Brenda Fricker
Angels in the Outfield '94
The Field '90
Home Alone 2: Lost in New York '92
My Left Foot '89
So I Married an Axe Murderer '93
The Sound and the Silence '93
Utz '93

Jonathan Frid
House of Dark Shadows '70
Seizure '74

Tom Fridley
Summer Camp Nightmare '86
Vietnam War Story 1 '88

Peter Friedman
Blink '93
The Seventh Sign '88
Single White Female '92

John Friedrich
The Final Terror '83
Forever '78
A Rumor of War '80
Wanderers '79

Colin Friels
Class Action '91
Darkman '90
The Gold & Glory '88
Grievous Bodily Harm '89
Ground Zero '88
High Tide '87
Kangaroo '86
Malcolm '86
Monkey Grip '82
Warm Nights on a Slow-Moving Train '87

Philip Friend
Great Day '46
Vulture '67

Willy Fritsch
Congress Dances '31
Spies '28
Woman in the Moon '29

Gert Frobe
Chitty Chitty Bang Bang '68
Dollars '71
The Eternal Waltz '54
Goldfinger '64
I Killed Rasputin '67
Is Paris Burning? '68
The Longest Day '62
The Return of Dr. Mabuse '62
The Serpent's Egg '78
Shadow Man '73
Sidney Sheldon's Bloodline '79
Ten Little Indians '75
Testament of Dr. Mabuse '62
Those Daring Young Men in Their Jaunty Jalopies '69
Those Fantastic Flying Fools '67
Those Magnificent Men in Their Flying Machines '65

The Thousand Eyes of Dr. Mabuse '60
Tonio Kroger '65
Triple Cross '67

Gustav Froehlich
Homecoming '28
Metropolis '26

Ewa Froling
Fanny and Alexander '83
The Ox '91

Milton Frome
Pardners '56
Ride 'Em Cowgirl '41

Lindsay Frost
Dead Heat '88
Monolith '93

Sadie Frost
Bram Stoker's Dracula '92
The Cisco Kid '94
Dark Obsession '90
Paper Marriage '93
Splitting Heirs '93

Terry Frost
Black Hills '48
The Hawk of Powder River '48
The Monster Maker '44
Waterfront '44

Warren Frost
Psycho 4: The Beginning '90
Twin Peaks '90

Taylor Fry
Lone Justice '93
Necessary Parties '88

Brittain Frye
Hide and Go Shriek '87
Slumber Party Massacre 3 '90

Dwight Frye
The Bride of Frankenstein '35
The Crime of Dr. Crespi '35
Dead Men Walk '43
Dracula '31
Drums of Fu Manchu '40
Frankenstein '31
The Ghost of Frankenstein '42
The Invisible Man '33
The Maltese Falcon '31
Sinners in Paradise '38
The Vampire Bat '32
The Worst of Hollywood: Vol. 2 '90

Sean Frye
Deadline Assault '90
E.T.: The Extra-Terrestrial '82

Virgil Frye
Born in America '90
Dr. Heckyl and Mr. Hype '80
Hot Moves '84
Revenge of the Ninja '83
Running Hot '83
Secret of the Ice Cave '89
Up from the Depths '79

Chi Hsiao Fu
Master of Kung Fu '77
The Story of Drunken Master

Gaby Fuchs
Mark of the Devil '69
The Werewolf vs. the Vampire Woman '70

Leo Fuchs
American Matchmaker '40
Avalon '90

Joachim Fuchsberger
The Black Abbot '63
Dead Eyes of London '61
Inn on the River '62
The Last Tomahawk '65
The Mysterious Magician '65
The Strange Countess '61

Alan Fudge
The Children of An Lac '80
Nightmare on the 13th Floor '90

Miguel Angel Fuentes
Fitzcarraldo '82
The Puma Man '80

Athol Fugard
Gandhi '82
The Killing Fields '84

Tatsuya Fuji
The Empire of Passion '76

In the Realm of Passion '80
In the Realm of the Senses '76

Hiroshi Fujioka
Ghostwarrior '86
K2: The Ultimate High '92
Tidal Wave '75

John Fujioka
American Samurai '92
A Conspiracy of Love '87

Dale Fuller
Greed '24
The Marriage Circle '24
The Unchastened Woman '25

Jonathan Fuller
Arcade '93
The Pit & the Pendulum '91

Kurt Fuller
Bingo '91
Calendar Girl '93
Miracle Mile '89
No Holds Barred '89
Wayne's World '92

Lance Fuller
Apache Woman '55
The Bride & the Beast '58
Cattle Queen of Montana '54
Girls in Prison '56
Kentucky Rifle '55
Voodoo Woman '57

Nancy Belle Fuller
Hard Part Begins '80s
Sky Hei$t '75

Penny Fuller
As Summers Die '86
The Beverly Hillbillies '93
Fire and Rain '89
George Washington: The Forging of a Nation '86
License to Kill '84
Lies Before Kisses '91
Lois Gibbs and the Love Canal '82
Miss Rose White '92
A Piano for Mrs. Cimino '82
Your Place or Mine '83

Robert Fuller
The Brain from Planet Arous '57
Donner Pass: The Road to Survival '84
The Gatling Gun '72
Return of the Seven '66
Sinai Commandos '68
Whatever Happened to Aunt Alice? '69

Samuel Fuller
The American Friend '77
La Vie de Boheme '93
Pierrot le Fou '65
Return to Salem's Lot '87
Slapstick of Another Kind '84
State of Things '82
The Young Nurses '73

Fiona Fullerton
The Charmer '89
Shaka Zulu '83
Spymaker: The Secret Life of Ian Fleming '90

Brad Fulton
Journey Beneath the Desert '61
The Undertaker and His Pals '67

Eiji Funakoshi
Being Two Isn't Easy '62
Fires on the Plain '59
Gamera, the Invincible '66
Gamera vs. Guiron '69

Annette Funicello
Babes in Toyland '61
Back to the Beach '87
Beach Blanket Bingo '65
Beach Party '63
Bikini Beach '64
Dr. Goldfoot and the Bikini Machine '66
El Fego Baca: Six-Gun Law '62
Head '68
Horsemasters '61
How to Stuff a Wild Bikini '65
Lots of Luck '85
The Misadventures of Merlin Jones '63
Monkey's Uncle '65
Muscle Beach Party '64

Pajama Party '64
Pee Wee's Playhouse Christmas Special '88
The Shaggy Dog '59

John Furey
Friday the 13th, Part 2 '81
Mutant on the Bounty '89

Edward Furlong
American Heart '92
Brainscan '94
A Home of Our Own '93
Pet Sematary 2 '92
Terminator 2: Judgment Day '91

Yvonne Furneaux
Frankenstein's Great Aunt Tillie '83
The House of the Arrow '53
La Dolce Vita '60
The Lion of Thebes '64
The Master of Ballantrae '53
The Mummy '59
Repulsion '65
The Warriors '55

Betty Furness
Beggars in Ermine '34
The President's Mystery '36
Renegade Ranger/Scarlet River '38
Swing Time '36

Deborra-Lee Furness
The Last of the Finest '90
Shame '87
Voyager '91

Joseph Furst
Diamonds are Forever '71
The Dunera Boys '85

Stephen Furst
The Dream Team '89
Getting Wasted '80
Magic Kid '92
Midnight Madness '80
National Lampoon's Animal House '78
Swim Team '79
The Unseen '80
Up the Creek '84

George Furth
Butch Cassidy and the Sundance Kid '69
Doctor Detroit '83
Norman, Is That You? '76

Ed Fury
Colossus and the Amazon Queen '64
Samson Against the Sheik '62
Ursus in the Valley of the Lions '62
Wild Women of Wongo '59

Marianne Gaba
The Choppers '61
How to Stuff a Wild Bikini '65

Richard Gabai
Assault of the Party Nerds '89
Dinosaur Island '93
Hot Under the Collar '91
Virgin High '90

Martin Gabel
Lady in Cement '68
Smile, Jenny, You're Dead '74
The Thief '52

Scilla Gabel
Colossus of the Arena '60
Mill of the Stone Women '60

Jean Gabin
The Big Grab '63
Duke of the Derby '62
Four Bags Full '56
French Can-Can '55
Grand Illusion '37
La Bete Humaine '38
L'Anne Sainte '78
Le Cas du Dr. Laurent '57
Le Chat '75
Le Gentleman D'Epsom '62
Le Jour Se Leve '39
Le Plaisir '52
Les Miserables '57
The Lower Depths '36
Maria Chapdelaine '34
Melodie en Sous-Sol '63
Napoleon '55
Pepe Le Moko '37
Stormy Waters '41

Un Singe en Hiver '62
Zou Zou '34

Christopher Gable
The Boy Friend '71
The Lair of the White Worm '88
The Music Lovers '71
The Rainbow '89

Clark Gable
Across the Wide Missouri '51
Adventure '45
Any Number Can Play '49
Band of Angels '57
Betrayed '54
Boom Town '40
But Not for Me '59
Chained '34
China Seas '35
Command Decision '48
Comrade X '40
Dance Fools Dance '31
Dancing Lady '33
Forsaking All Others '35
A Free Soul '31
Gone with the Wind '39
Hold Your Man '33
Homecoming '48
Honky Tonk '41
The Hucksters '47
Idiot's Delight '39
It Happened One Night '34
It Started in Naples '60
Key to the City '50
The King and Four Queens '56
Laughing Sinners '31
Lone Star '52
The Lost Stooges '33
Love on the Run '36
The Making of a Legend:
 "Gone With the Wind" '89
Manhattan Melodrama '34
The Misfits '61
Mogambo '53
Mutiny on the Bounty '35
Never Let Me Go '53
Night Nurse '31
1939, The Movies' Vintage
 Year: Trailers on Tape '39
No Man of Her Own '32
Painted Desert '31
Possessed '31
Red Dust '32
Run Silent, Run Deep '58
San Francisco '36
Saratoga '37
Soldier of Fortune '55
Somewhere I'll Find You '42
Strange Cargo '40
Strange Interlude '32
Susan Lenox: Her Fall and Rise
 '31
The Tall Men '55
Teacher's Pet '58
Test Pilot '38
They Met in Bombay '41
To Please a Lady '50
Too Hot to Handle '38
Wife Versus Secretary '36

Eva Gabor
Artists and Models '55
Don't Go Near the Water '57
Gigi '58
It Started with a Kiss '59
The Last Time I Saw Paris '54
My Man Godfrey '57
A New Kind of Love '63
Princess Academy '87
Tales of the Klondike: The
 Scorn of Women '87
Truth About Women '58

Zsa Zsa Gabor
Arrivederci, Baby! '66
Boy's Night Out '62
Death of a Scoundrel '56
Every Girl Should Have One '78
For the First Time '59
Frankenstein's Great Aunt Tillie
 '83
Lili '53
Lovely to Look At '52
Moulin Rouge '52
Movie Maker '86
Pee Wee's Playhouse
 Christmas Special '88
Picture Mommy Dead '66
Queen of Outer Space '58
Touch of Evil '58
We're Not Married '52

Monique Gabrielle
Amazon Women on the Moon
 '87
Bachelor Party '84
Deathstalker 2: Duel of the
 Titans '87
Emmanuelle 5 '87
Evil Toons '90
Hard to Hold '84
Hot Moves '84
Silk 2 '89

Gabriel Gabrio
Harvest '37
Pepe Le Moko '37

Antonio Gades
Blood Wedding '81
Carmen '83
El Amor Brujo '86

Anna Gael
Alien Women '69
Therese & Isabelle '68

Jenny Gago
Old Gringo '89
Sweet 15 '90

Max Gail
Aliens Are Coming '80
Cardiac Arrest '74
D.C. Cab '84
The Game of Love '90
Heartbreakers '84
Judgment in Berlin '88
Night Moves '75
Street Crimes '92
Where Are the Children? '85

Boyd Gaines
Call Me '88
Heartbreak Ridge '86
Piece of Cake '90
The Sure Thing '85

Jim Gaines
Blood Debts '83
Codename: Terminate '90
Commando Invasion '87
Fist of Steel '93

Richard Gaines
The Enchanted Cottage '45
Humoresque '46
The More the Merrier '43

M.C. Gainey
El Diablo '90
Leap of Faith '92

Courtney Gains
Back to the Future '85
The 'Burbs '89
Can't Buy Me Love '87
Children of the Corn '84
Hardbodies '84
Lust in the Dust '85
Memphis Belle '90

Charlotte Gainsbourg
Le Petit Amour '87
The Little Thief '89

Serge Gainsbourg
The Fury of Hercules '61
I Love All of You '83
Samson '61
Too Pretty to Be Honest '72

Janusz Gajos
The Interrogation '82
Trois Couleurs: Blanc '94

Michel Galabru
Belle Epoque '92
The Judge and the Assassin
 '75
La Cage aux Folles '78
La Cage aux Folles 2 '81
La Cage aux Folles 3: The
 Wedding '86
Le Gendarme de Saint-Tropez
 '67
Soldat Duroc...Ca Va Etre Ta
 Fete! '60s
Uranus '91

David Gale
The Brain '88
Bride of Re-Animator '89
The Guyver '91
The Re-Animator '85
Syngenor '90

Eddra Gale
8 1/2 '63

Revenge of the Cheerleaders
 '76

June Gale
It Could Happen to You '39
Rainbow's End '35

Johnny Galecki
Backfield in Motion '91
National Lampoon's Christmas
 Vacation '89

Anna Galiena
Being Human '94
The Hairdresser's Husband '92
Jamon, Jamon '93
Rorret '87

Kelly Galindo
Angels of the City '89
The Malibu Beach Vampires
 '91

Nacho Galindo
Borderline '50
Green Fire '55

Frank Gallacher
Proof '91
Waterfront '83

Megan Gallagher
The Ambulance '90
In a Stranger's Hand '92

Peter Gallagher
The Caine Mutiny Court Martial
 '88
Dreamchild '85
Fallen Angels 1 '93
Fallen Angels 2 '93
High Spirits '88
Idolmaker '80
An Inconvenient Woman '91
Late for Dinner '91
Long Day's Journey into Night
 '88
Malice '93
Mother's Boys '94
The Murder of Mary Phagan
 '87
My Little Girl '87
The Player '92
Private Contentment '83
sex, lies and videotape '89
Short Cuts '93
Skag '79
Summer Lovers '82
Tune in Tomorrow '90
Watch It '93

**Richard "Skeets"
Gallagher**
Bachelor Bait '34
Danger on the Air '38
Hats Off '37
Possessed '31
Riptide '34

Juan Gallardo
El Cristo de los Milagros '80s
Inquisition '76
Los Sheriffs de la Frontera '47

Silvania Gallardo
Out of the Dark '88
Prison Stories: Women on the
 Inside '91

Gina Gallego
Lust in the Dust '85
My Demon Lover '87
Personals '90

Rosina Galli
Escape to Paradise '39
Fisherman's Wharf '39

Zach Galligan
All Tied Up '92
Caroline at Midnight '93
Gremlins '84
Gremlins 2: The New Batch '90
Ice '93
The Lawrenceville Stories '80s
Mortal Passions '90
Psychic '91
Rebel Storm '90
Round Trip to Heaven '92
Warlock: The Armageddon '93
Waxwork '88
Waxwork 2: Lost in Time '91
Zandalee '91

Robert Gallo
Mayhem '87
Sinners '89

Don Galloway
Demon Rage '82
Rough Night in Jericho '67
Snowblind '78
Two Moon Junction '88

Jose Galvez
Benjamin Argumedo '78
Semaforo en Rojo '47

Rita Gam
Distortions '87
The King of Kings '61
Klute '71
Midnight '89
Mohawk '56
Seeds of Evil '76
The Thief '52

Michael Gambon
Clean Slate '94
The Cook, the Thief, His Wife &
 Her Lover '90
Forbidden Passion: The Oscar
 Wilde Movie '87
The Heat of the Day '91
Missing Link '88
Mobsters '91
The Rachel Papers '89
Toys '92
Turtle Diary '86

Robin Gammell
Full Circle '77
Gore Vidal's Lincoln '88
Guilty by Suspicion '91
Missing Pieces '83
Panic in Echo Park '77
Project X '87
Sinatra '92

James Gammon
The Adventures of Huck Finn
 '93
Ballad of Gregorio Cortez '83
Cabin Boy '94
Coupe de Ville '90
Crisscross '92
Deadly Encounter '72
Gore Vidal's Lincoln '88
Hard Traveling '85
Hard Vice '94
I Love You to Death '90
Ironweed '87
Leaving Normal '92
Major League '89
Major League 2 '94
The Milagro Beanfield War '88
Revenge '90
Roe vs. Wade '89
Running Cool '93

Ken Gampu
African Rage '78
American Ninja 4: The
 Annihilation '91
Chain Gang Killings '85
Dingaka '65
Enemy Unseen '91
Kill and Kill Again '81
The Naked Prey '66
Scavengers '87
Soul Patrol '80

James Gandolfini
Angie '94
Money for Nothing '93
Terminal Velocity '94
True Romance '93

Tony Ganios
Continental Divide '81
Porky's '82
Porky's 2: The Next Day '83
Porky's Revenge '85

Richard Gant
The Freshman '90
Jason Goes to Hell: The Final
 Friday '93

Paul Ganus
Crash and Burn '90
The Silencer '92

Bruno Ganz
The American Friend '77
Black and White as Day and
 Night '63
Children of Nature '92
Faraway, So Close! '93
In the White City '83
Knife in the Head '78
The Last Days of Chez Nous
 '92
Strapless '90

Wings of Desire '88

Yehoram Gaon
Dead End Street '83
Operation Thunderbolt '77

Kaz Garas
Final Mission '84
The Last Safari '67
Naked Vengeance '85

Matthew Garber
The Gnome-Mobile '67
The Three Lives of Thomasina
 '63

Terri Garber
North and South Book 1 '85
North and South Book 2 '86

Victor Garber
Life with Mikey '93
Sleepless in Seattle '93

Greta Garbo
Anna Christie '30
Anna Karenina '35
As You Desire Me '32
The Atonement of Gosta
 Berling '24
Camille '36
Conquest '37
The Flesh and the Devil '27
Grand Hotel '32
Joyless Street '25
The Kiss '29
The Love Goddesses '65
Mata Hari '32
The Mysterious Lady '28
Ninotchka '39
The Painted Veil '34
Queen Christina '33
Romance '30
The Single Standard '29
Susan Lenox: Her Fall and Rise
 '31
Two-Faced Woman '41
Wild Orchids '28
A Woman of Affairs '28

Mauricio Garces
The Brainiac '61
Bromas S.A. '87
Despedida de Casada '87
The Living Head '59
Los Hermanos Diablo '65
World of the Vampires '60

Andres Garcia
Dance of Death '68
La Corona de un Campeon '87

Andy Garcia
American Roulette '88
Black Rain '89
Blood Money: The Story of
 Clinton and Nadine '88
Blue Skies Again '83
Dead Again '91
8 Million Ways to Die '85
The Godfather, Part 3 '90
Hero '92
Internal Affairs '90
Jennifer 8 '92
Mean Season '85
A Night in Heaven '83
A Show of Force '90
Stand and Deliver '88
The Untouchables '87
When a Man Loves a Woman
 '94

**Eleazar Garcia
Chelelo**
El Forastero Vengador '65
Frontera Sin Ley
La Carcel de Laredo '84

Darnell Garcia
Blind Rage '78
Enforcer from Death Row '78

Eddie Garcia
Beast of the Yellow Night '70
Woman Hunt '72

Nicole Garcia
Bolero '82
Corrupt '84
Le Cavaleur '78
Mon Oncle D'Amerique '80
Overseas: Three Women with
 Man Trouble '90
Peril '85

Ginette Garcin
Charles et Lucie '79
Cousin, Cousine '76

Vincent Gardenia
Age Old Friends '89
Bang the Drum Slowly '73
Brass '85
Cold Turkey '71
Death Wish '74
Death Wish 2 '82
The Front Page '74
Greased Lightning '77
Home Movies '79
The Hustler '61
Jenny '70
Kennedy '83
The Last Flight of Noah's Ark '80
Little Murders '71
Little Shop of Horrors '86
Lucky Luciano '74
Marciano '79
Moonstruck '87
Movers and Shakers '85
The Odd Squad '86
Parrish '61
Skin Deep '89
The Super '91
Tragedy of Flight 103: The Inside Story '91
Where's Poppa? '70

Reginald Gardiner
Birds & the Bees '56
Born to Dance '36
Captains of the Clouds '42
Christmas in Connecticut '45
A Damsel in Distress '37
Doctor Takes a Wife '40
Everybody Sing '38
The Flying Deuces '39
The Great Dictator '40
The Halls of Montezuma '50
The Horn Blows at Midnight '45
Immortal Sergeant '43
The Man Who Came to Dinner '41
Marie Antoinette '62
Mr. Hobbs Takes a Vacation '62
Sundown '41
Sweet Rosie O'Grady '43
A Yank in the R.A.F. '41

Arthur Gardner
Assassin of Youth '35
Mystic Circle Murder '39

Ava Gardner
The Barefoot Contessa '54
Bhowani Junction '56
The Bible...In the Beginning '66
The Cassandra Crossing '76
City on Fire '78
Earthquake '74
East Side, West Side '49
55 Days at Peking '63
Harem '86
The Hucksters '47
The Kidnapping of the President '80
Knights of the Round Table '53
Life & Times of Judge Roy Bean '72
Lone Star '52
The Long, Hot Summer '86
Mogambo '53
My Forbidden Past '51
The Naked Maja '59
The Night of the Iguana '64
On the Beach '59
One Touch of Venus '48
Permission To Kill '75
Regina '83
Reunion in France '42
The Sentinel '76
Seven Days in May '64
Show Boat '51
The Snows of Kilimanjaro '52
Whistle Stop '46

Joan Gardner
Dark Journey '37
The Man Who Could Work Miracles '37
Private Life of Don Juan '34
The Scarlet Pimpernel '34
Wedding Rehearsal '32

John Garfield
Air Force '43
Body and Soul '47
Destination Tokyo '43
The Fallen Sparrow '43
Force of Evil '49

Four Daughters '38
Gentleman's Agreement '47
Hollywood Canteen '44
Humoresque '46
Juarez '39
The Postman Always Rings Twice '46
The Sea Wolf '41
Thank Your Lucky Stars '43
They Made Me a Criminal '39
Tortilla Flat '41

John David Garfield
Golden Voyage of Sinbad '73
MacKenna's Gold '69
The Other Side of the Mountain '75
Savage Intruder '68
The Stepmother '71
Swimmer '68
That Cold Day in the Park '69
White Line Fever '75

Art Garfunkel
Boxing Helena '93
Carnal Knowledge '71
Catch-22 '70
Monterey Pop '68
Short Fuse '88

Edward Gargan
Belle of the Nineties '34
The Saint Strikes Back '39

William Gargan
Aggie Appleby, Maker of Men '33
The Animal Kingdom '32
Broadway Serenade '39
The Canterville Ghost '44
Cheers for Miss Bishop '41
Devil's Party '49
Dynamite '49
I Wake Up Screaming '41
Milky Way '36
Miss Annie Rooney '42
Rain '32
They Knew What They Wanted '40
Till the End of Time '46
Who Done It? '42
You Only Live Once '37

Gianno Garko
The Avenger '62
Kapo '59
The Mongols '60
The Psychic '78
Saul and David '68
Waterloo '71

John Garko
Five for Hell '69
Gunslinger '70s
Stranger's Gold '71

Beverly Garland
D.O.A. '49
Gamble on Love '86
The Go-Getter '54
Gunfight at Sandoval '59
The Gunslinger '56
It Conquered the World '56
It's My Turn '80
Pretty Poison '68
Roller Boogie '79
Swamp Women '55
The Voyage of the Yes '72
Where the Red Fern Grows '74
The World's Oldest Living Bridesmaid '92

Judy Garland
Andy Hardy Meets Debutante '40
Babes in Arms '39
Babes on Broadway '41
Broadway Melody of 1938 '37
A Child is Waiting '63
The Clock '45
Easter Parade '48
Everybody Sing '38
For Me and My Gal '42
Girl Crazy '43
The Harvey Girls '46
Hollywood Outtakes & Rare Footage '83
I Could Go on Singing '63
In the Good Old Summertime '49
Judgment at Nuremberg '61
Life Begins for Andy Hardy '41
Listen, Darling '38
Little Nellie Kelly '40
Love Finds Andy Hardy '38

Meet Me in St. Louis '44
The Pirate '48
Presenting Lily Mars '43
A Star is Born '54
Strictly G.I. '44
Strike Up the Band '40
Summer Stock '50
That's Entertainment '74
Thoroughbreds Don't Cry '37
Thousands Cheer '43
Till the Clouds Roll By '46
Till the Clouds Roll By/A Star Is Born '46
The Wizard of Oz '39
Words and Music '48
Ziegfeld Follies '46
Ziegfeld Girl '41

Richard Garland
Panic in the Year Zero! '62
The Undead '57

Lee Garlington
Cold Sassy Tree '89
A Killing in a Small Town '90
My Life '93
The Seventh Sign '88

James Garner
The Americanization of Emily '64
Barbarians at the Gate '93
Boy's Night Out '62
Cash McCall '60
The Castaway Cowboy '74
The Children's Hour '61
Darby's Rangers '58
Decoration Day '90
The Distinguished Gentleman '92
Duel at Diablo '66
The Fan '81
Fire in the Sky '93
The Glitter Dome '84
Grand Prix '66
The Great Escape '63
Hour of the Gun '67
How Sweet It Is! '68
A Man Called Sledge '71
Marlowe '69
Maverick '94
Murphy's Romance '85
One Little Indian '73
Sayonara '57
Skin Game '71
Sunset '88
Support Your Local Gunfighter '71
Support Your Local Sheriff '69
Tank '83
They Only Kill Their Masters '72
The Thrill of It All! '63
Up Periscope '59
Victor/Victoria '82
The Wheeler Dealers '63

Peggy Ann Garner
Betrayal '78
The Big Cat '49
The Cat '66
Eight Witnesses '54
Jane Eyre '44
The Keys of the Kingdom '44
The Lovable Cheat '49
A Tree Grows in Brooklyn '45
A Wedding '78

Gale Garnett
The Children '80
Mr. & Mrs. Bridge '91
32 Short Films About Glenn Gould '93

Teri Garr
After Hours '85
The Black Stallion '79
The Black Stallion Returns '83
Close Encounters of the Third Kind '77
The Conversation '74
The Escape Artist '82
First Born '84
Full Moon in Blue Water '88
Head '68
The History of White People in America '85
Honky Tonk Freeway '81
Let It Ride '89
Miracles '86
Mr. Mike's Mondo Video '79
Mr. Mom '83

Mom and Dad Save the World '92
Oh, God! '77
Once Upon a Brothers Grimm '77
One from the Heart '82
Out Cold '89
Pajama Party '64
A Perfect Little Murder '90
Prime Suspect '82
Short Time '90
Steve Martin Live '85
The Sting 2 '83
The Tale of the Frog Prince '83
To Catch a King '84
Tootsie '82
Waiting for the Light '90
Witches' Brew '79
Young Frankenstein '74

Martin Garralaga
Boots of Destiny '37
The Fighter '52
In Old New Mexico '45
South of Monterey '47
Susanna Pass '49

Ivo Garrani
Black Sunday '60
The Day the Sky Exploded '57
The Giant of Marathon '60
Great Leaders of the Bibles '70s
Street People '76
Waterloo '71

Maurice Garrel
La Discrete '90
Un Coeur en Hiver '93

Betty Garrett
My Sister Eileen '55
Neptune's Daughter '49
On the Town '49
Take Me Out to the Ball Game '49
Words and Music '48

Eliza Garrett
Schlock '73
Terraces '77

Hank Garrett
Blood Frenzy '87
The Boys Next Door '85
Rosebud Beach Hotel '85

Leif Garrett
The Banker '89
Cheerleader Camp '88
Kid Vengeance '75
The Outsiders '83
Party Line '88
Peter Lundy and the Medicine Hat Stallion '77
Shaker Run '85
Skateboard '77
Spirit of '76 '91
Thunder Alley '85
Walking Tall: The Final Chapter '77

Patsy Garrett
Benji '74
Dennis the Menace: Dinosaur Hunter '93
For the Love of Benji '77

Roger Garrett
Night of the Cobra Woman '72
The Passing of Evil '70

Barbara Garrick
Armistead Maupin's Tales of the City '93
The Firm '93
Sleepless in Seattle '93

John Garrick
Broken Melody '34
Lily of Killarney '34
Lottery Bride '30
Song O' My Heart '29

David Garrison
Homeboys '92
On the Town '91

Riccardo Garrone
Terror Creatures from the Grave '66
Two Nights with Cleopatra '54

Greer Garson
Adventure '86
Blossoms in the Dust '41
Goodbye, Mr. Chips '39
The Happiest Millionaire '67

Invincible Mr. Disraeli '63
Julia Misbehaves '48
Julius Caesar '53
Little Women '78
Madame Curie '43
The Miniver Story '50
Mrs. Miniver '42
Mrs. Parkington '44
Pride and Prejudice '40
Random Harvest '42
The Singing Nun '66
Sunrise at Campobello '60
That Forsyte Woman '50
The Valley of Decision '45
When Ladies Meet '41

Christopher Gartin
Danielle Steel's Changes '91
Matters of the Heart '90
No Big Deal '83

Elizabeth Garvie
Diana: Her True Story '93
Pride and Prejudice '85

John Garwood
Hell's Angels on Wheels '67
A Taste of Hell '73

Lorraine Gary
The Crash of Flight 401 '78
Jaws '75
Jaws 2 '78
Jaws: The Revenge '87
1941 '79
Pray for the Wildcats '74

Vittorio Gassman
Big Deal on Madonna Street '58
Bitter Rice '49
Catch as Catch Can '68
The Easy Life '63
The Family '87
The Great War '59
Il Sorpasso '63
Immortal Bachelor '80
Lure of the Sila '49
Mambo '55
The Palermo Connection '91
Quintet '79
Rhapsody '54
The Scent of a Woman '75
Sharky's Machine '81
The Sleazy Uncle '89
The Tempest '82
Tiger and the Pussycat '67
12 Plus 1 '70
War and Peace '56
We All Loved Each Other So Much '77
A Wedding '78
Woman Times Seven '67

Lisa Gastoni
The Baby and the Battleship '56
The Great Armored Car Swindle '64
Messalina vs. the Son of Hercules '64
Submission '77
Tharus Son of Attila '87
Wild, Wild Planet '65

Larry Gates
Above and Beyond '53
Death of a Gunfighter '69
Funny Lady '75
The Henderson Monster '80
The Hoodlum Priest '61
The Sand Pebbles '66
Toys in the Attic '63
Underworld, U.S.A. '60

Nancy Gates
The Atomic City '52
Check Your Guns '48
The Great Gildersleeve '43
Master Race '44
Nevada '44
The Search for Bridey Murphy '56
Some Came Running '58
Suddenly '54
Torch Song '53

Marjorie Gateson
Arizona Mahoney '36
Goin' to Town '35

Jill Gatsby
The Ambulance '90
Return to Salem's Lot '87

Jennifer Gatti
Double Exposure '93
Street Knight '93

Valerie Gaunt
The Curse of Frankenstein '57
The Horror of Dracula '58

Dan Gauthier
Shame '92
Son-in-Law '93
Teen Witch '89

Dick Gautier
Get Smart, Again! '89
Glitch! '88
Marathon '80

John Gavin
Back Street '61
Breath of Scandal '60
History of the World: Part 1 '81
House of Shadows '83
Imitation of Life '59
Jennifer '78
The Madwoman of Chaillot '69
Midnight Lace '60
Murder for Sale '70
Psycho '60
Sophia Loren: Her Own Story '80
Spartacus '60
Thoroughly Modern Millie '67
A Time to Love & a Time to Die '58

Cassandra Gaviola
The Black Room '82
Conan the Barbarian '82

William Gaxton
Best Foot Forward '43
The Heat's On '43
It's the Old Army Game '26

Gregory Gay
The Secret Code '42
Seven Doors to Death '44

Ramon Gay
The Curse of the Aztec Mummy '59
Curse of the Aztec Mummy/Robot vs. the Aztec Mummy '59
The Robot vs. the Aztec Mummy '59

Howard Gaye
Dante's Inferno '24
Flirting with Fate '16

Lisa Gaye
Castle of Evil '66
Class of Nuke 'Em High, Part 2: Subhumanoid Meltdown '91
Night of Evil '59
Shake, Rattle and Rock '57
The Sign of Zorro '60
The Toxic Avenger, Part 3: The Last Temptation of Toxie '89

Jackie Gayle
Bert Rigby, You're a Fool '89
Mr. Saturday Night '92
Pepper and His Wacky Taxi '72
Plain Clothes '88
Tin Men '87

Monica Gayle
Nashville Girl '76
Switchblade Sisters '75

Mitch Gaylord
American Anthem '86
American Tiger '89
Animal Instincts '92

George Gaynes
Breaking Up Is Hard to Do '79
Dead Men Don't Wear Plaid '82
It Came Upon a Midnight Clear '84
Micki & Maude '84
Police Academy '84
Police Academy 2: Their First Assignment '85
Police Academy 3: Back in Training '86
Police Academy 4: Citizens on Patrol '87
Police Academy 5: Assignment Miami Beach '88
Police Academy 6: City Under Siege '89
Stepmonster '92
Tootsie '82

Janet Gaynor
The Farmer Takes a Wife '35
A Star is Born '37
Sunrise '27
Till the Clouds Roll By/A Star Is Born '46
The Young in Heart '38

Mitzi Gaynor
Birds & the Bees '56
For Love or Money '63
Les Girls '57
South Pacific '58
There's No Business Like Show Business '54
We're Not Married '52

Eunice Gayson
Carry On Admiral '57
Dr. No '62
From Russia with Love '63

Wendy Gazelle
Hot Pursuit '87
Sammy & Rosie Get Laid '87
Triumph of the Spirit '89
Understudy: The Graveyard Shift 2 '88

Ben Gazzara
Anatomy of a Murder '59
The Bridge at Remagen '69
Control '87
The Death of Richie '76
An Early Frost '85
Fireball Forward '72
High Velocity '76
The Killing of a Chinese Bookie '76
Lies Before Kisses '92
Neptune Factor '73
Opening Night '77
Passionate Thief '60
Pursuit '72
QB VII '74
Question of Honor '80
Quicker Than the Eye '88
Road House '89
Saint Jack '79
Secret Obsession '88
Shattered Silence '71
Sicilian Connection '74
Sidney Sheldon's Bloodline '79
Tales of Ordinary Madness '83
They All Laughed '81
The Trial of Lee Harvey Oswald '77
Voyage of the Damned '76

Michael Gazzo
Black Sunday '77
Cookie '89
Fingers '78
Gangsters '79
The Godfather 1902-1959: The Complete Epic '81
The Godfather, Part 2 '74
Kill Castro '80
King of the Gypsies '78
Love and Bullets '79
The Mercenaries '80

Anthony Geary
Crack House '89
Dangerous Love '87
High Desert Kill '90
The Imposter '84
Kicks '85
Night of the Warrior '91
Pass the Ammo '88
Penitentiary 3 '87
Scorchers '92
UHF '89
You Can't Hurry Love '88

Bud Geary
D-Day on Mars '45
The Topeka Terror '45

Jason Gedrick
Backdraft '91
Crossing the Bridge '92
The Heavenly Kid '85
Iron Eagle '86
Massive Retaliation '85
Promised Land '88
Rooftops '89
Stacking '87
Still Life '89
The Zoo Gang '85

Prunella Gee
Never Say Never Again '83
The Wilby Conspiracy '75
Witching Time '84

Ellen Geer
Babe! '75
Bloody Birthday '80
Hard Traveling '85
Harold and Maude '71
Memory of Us '74
A Shining Season '79
Silence '73

Will Geer
Bandolero! '68
The Billion Dollar Hobo '78
Black Like Me '64
Broken Arrow '50
Brother John '70
Bunco '83
Dear Dead Delilah '72
Executive Action '73
The Hanged Man '74
Hurricane '74
Jeremiah Johnson '72
Lust for Gold '49
Memory of Us '74
Moving Violation '76
My Sister, My Love '78
Napoleon and Samantha '72
The President's Analyst '67
The Reivers '69
Salt of the Earth '54
Silence '73
Thanksgiving Story '73
To Please a Lady '50
Unknown Powers '80
The Waltons: A Thanksgiving Story '73
Winchester '73 '50
A Woman Called Moses '78

Judy Geeson
Adventures of a Taxi Driver '76
Berserk! '67
Carry On England '76
Danger UXB '81
Doomwatch '72
Dynasty of Fear '72
The Executioner '70
Horror Planet '80
It Happened at Nightmare Inn '70
Murder on the Midnight Express '74
Poldark '75
10 Rillington Place '71
To Sir, with Love '67
Twinsanity '70

Sally Geeson
Cry of the Banshee '70
The Oblong Box '69
What's Good for the Goose '93

Martha Gehman
F/X '86
Father of the Bride '91
The Flamingo Kid '84
A Kiss Before Dying '91
Threesome '94

Bob Geldof
Pink Floyd: The Wall '82
The Secret Policeman's Other Ball '82

Daniel Gelin
Iran: Days of Crisis '91
Is Paris Burning? '68
La Ronde '51
Life Is a Long Quiet River '88
Mademoiselle Striptease '57
The Man Who Knew Too Much '56
Murmur of the Heart '71
The Testament of Orpheus '59
A Woman of Rome '56

Larry Gelman
Chatterbox '76
Slumber Party '57 '76

Giuliano Gemma
Battleforce '78
Blood at Sundown '79
Corleone '79
Erik, the Viking '72
Goliath and the Sins of Babylon '64
Master Touch '74
Smugglers '75
Unsane '82
The Warning '80

Laura Gemser
Ator the Fighting Eagle '83
Black Cobra '83
Caged Women '84
Crime Busters '78
Emmanuelle in the Country '78
Emmanuelle on Taboo Island '76
Emmanuelle, the Queen '75
Emmanuelle's Daughter '79
Fury '80s
Love Camp '76
Naked Paradise '78
Women's Prison Massacre '85

Francois-Eric Gendron
Boyfriends & Girlfriends '88
Cloud Waltzing '87

Bryan Genesse
California Casanova '89
Loose Screws '85

Leo Genn
Circus of Fear '67
Green for Danger '47
Henry V '44
Lady Chatterley's Lover '55
The Longest Day '62
Mackintosh Man '73
The Miniver Story '50
Moby Dick '56
The Snake Pit '48
Strange Case of Dr. Jekyll & Mr. Hyde '68
Velvet Touch '48
When Thief Meets Thief '37
Wooden Horse '50

Minnie Gentry
Def by Temptation '90
Georgia, Georgia '72

Roger Gentry
Alien Massacre '67
Horrors of the Red Planet '64

Paul Geoffrey
Excalibur '81
Flame to the Phoenix '85

Stephen Geoffreys
The Chair '87
Fraternity Vacation '85
Fright Night '85
Moon 44 '90
976-EVIL '88

Chief Dan George
Americathon '79
The Bears & I '74
Cancel My Reservation '72
Dan Candy's Law '73
Harry and Tonto '74
Little Big Man '70
The Outlaw Josey Wales '76

Christopher George
AngKor: Cambodia Express '81
Chisum '70
Cruise into Terror '78
Day of the Animals '77
Dixie Dynamite '76
El Dorado '67
Enter the Ninja '81
Exterminator '80
Gates of Hell '83
Graduation Day '81
Grizzly '76
Man on a String '71
Midway '76
Mortuary '81
Pieces '83
Train Robbers '73
Whiskey Mountain '77

Gladys George
The Best Years of Our Lives '46
Detective Story '51
Flamingo Road '49
House Across the Bay '40
Lullaby of Broadway '51
Madame X '37
The Maltese Falcon '41
Marie Antoinette '38
The Roaring Twenties '39

Heinrich George
Jud Suess '40
Kolberg '45

Lynda Day George
Aliens from Spaceship Earth '77
Ants '77
The Barbary Coast '74
Beyond Evil '80
Casino '80

Crime Busters '78

Cruise into Terror '78
Day of the Animals '77
The Junkman '82
Mortuary '81
Panic on the 5:22 '74
Pieces '83
Racquet '79
Roots '77
Young Warriors '83

Maude George
Foolish Wives '22
The Wedding March '28

Rita George
Hollywood Boulevard '76
On the Run '85

Susan George
Bandera Bandits
Die Screaming, Marianne '73
Dirty Mary Crazy Larry '74
Dr. Jekyll and Mr. Hyde '73
Enter the Ninja '81
Fright '71
House Where Evil Dwells '82
Jack the Ripper '88
The Jigsaw Man '84
Kiss My Grits '82
Lightning: The White Stallion '86
Lola '69
The Looking Glass War '69
Mandingo '75
Mission: Monte Carlo '75
Out of Season '75
Pajama Tops '83
A Small Town in Texas '76
Sonny and Jed '73
Straw Dogs '72
Sudden Terror '70
That Summer of White Roses '90
Tintorera...Tiger Shark '78
Tomorrow Never Comes '77
Venom '82

Olga Georges-Picot
Children of Rage '75
The Day of the Jackal '73
The Graveyard '74
Honor Among Thieves '68
The Man Who Haunted Himself '70

Tom Georgeson
A Fish Called Wanda '88
No Surrender '86

Carmelita Geraghty
Flaming Signal '33
My Lady of Whims '25
Night Life in Reno '31
Rogue of the Rio Grande '30

Danny Gerard
Desperate Hours '90
Drop-Out Mother '88

Gil Gerard
Buck Rogers in the 25th Century '79
Final Notice '89
For Love or Money '89
Fury to Freedom: The Life Story of Raul Ries '85
Help Wanted: Male '82
Hooch '76
Killing Stone '78
Soldier's Fortune '91

Steve Geray
Affair in Trinidad '52
The Big Sky '52
Blondie Knows Best '46
In Society '44
Inspector Hornleigh '39
Jesse James Meets Frankenstein's Daughter '65
Ladies of the Chorus '49
The Moon and Sixpence '43
The Seventh Cross '44
Tobor the Great '54

Richard Gere
American Gigolo '79
Beyond the Limit '83
Bloodbrothers '78
Breathless '83
The Cotton Club '84
Days of Heaven '78
Final Analysis '92
Internal Affairs '90
Intersection '93
King David '85
Looking for Mr. Goodbar '77

Gere ▶cont.

Miles from Home '88
Mr. Jones '93
No Mercy '86
An Officer and a Gentleman '82
Power '86
Pretty Woman '90
Report to the Commissioner '74
Rhapsody in August '91
Sommersby '93
Strike Force '75
Yanks '79

Georges Geret
Diary of a Chambermaid '64
A Very Curious Girl '69
Z '69

Gaia Germani
Castle of the Living Dead '64
Your Turn Darling '63

Greg Germann
The Night We Never Met '93
Once Around '91

Charles Gerrard
Down to Earth '17
The Nervous Wreck '26

Daniel Gerroll
Big Business '88
Drop Dead Fred '91
84 Charing Cross Road '86
A Far Off Place '93

Savina Gersak
Beyond the Door 3 '91
Curse 2: The Bite '88
Iron Warrior '87
Sonny Boy '87
War Bus Commando '89

Gina Gershon
City of Hope '91
Cocktail '88
Joey Breaker '93
Love Matters '93
The Player '92
Pretty in Pink '86
Red Heat '88
Sinatra '92
Voodoo Dawn '89

Jeanne Gerson
She Gods of Shark Reef '56
The Touch of Satan '70

Berta Gersten
A Brivele der Mamen '38
Mirele Efros '38

Frank Gerstle
The Atomic Brain '64
Gang Busters '55
Hell on Wheels '67
Submarine Seahawk '59
The Wasp Woman '59

Valeska Gert
An Occurrence at Owl Creek Bridge/Coup de Grace '62
The Threepenny Opera '31

Jami Gertz
Alphabet City '84
Crossroads '86
Don't Tell Her It's Me '90
Endless Love '81
Jersey Girl '92
Less Than Zero '87
Listen to Me '89
The Lost Boys '87
Mischief '85
Quicksilver '86
Renegades '89
Sibling Rivalry '90
Silence Like Glass '90
Sixteen Candles '84
Solarbabies '86

Balthazar Getty
December '91
Lord of the Flies '90
My Heroes Have Always Been Cowboys '91
The Pope Must Diet '91
Where the Day Takes You '92
Young Guns 2 '90

Estelle Getty
Mannequin '87
Mask '85
Stop! or My Mom Will Shoot '92

Tootsie '82

John Getz
Blood Simple '85
Born on the Fourth of July '89
Concrete Beat '84
Curly Sue '91
Don't Tell Mom the Babysitter's Dead '91
The Fly '86
The Fly 2 '89
Kent State '81
Tattoo '81
Thief of Hearts '84

Alice Ghostley
Blue Sunshine '78
Gator '76
The Graduate '67
New Faces of 1952 '54
Not for Publication '84
To Kill a Mockingbird '62
With Six You Get Eggroll '68

Louis Giambalvo
The Ambush Murders '82
Devlin Connection '82
Fade to Black '93
The Jagged Edge '85
Question of Faith '93
Weekend at Bernie's '89

Joseph Gian
Blackout '78
Mad About You '90
Night Stalker '87

Rick Gianasi
Escape from Safehaven '88
Maximum Thrust '87
Mutant Hunt '87
The Occultist '89
Posed For Murder '89
Robot Holocaust '87

Giancarlo Giannini
American Dreamer '84
Bellissimo: Images of the Italian Cinema '87
Blood Feud '79
Blood Red '88
Fever Pitch '85
Goodnight, Michelangelo '89
How Funny Can Sex Be? '76
Immortal Bachelor '80
The Innocent '76
La Grande Bourgeoise '74
Life is Beautiful '79
Love and Anarchy '73
Lovers and Liars '81
New York Stories '89
A Night Full of Rain '78
Once Upon a Crime '92
Saving Grace '86
Seduction of Mimi '72
The Sensual Man '74
Seven Beauties '76
The Sleazy Uncle '89
Swept Away... '75
Time to Kill '89
Where's Piccone '84

Cynthia Gibb
Death Warrant '90
Gypsy '93
Jack's Back '87
Malone '87
Modern Girls '86
Salvador '86
Short Circuit 2 '88
Stardust Memories '80
Youngblood '86

Robyn Gibbes
Gone to Ground '76
Wild Horses '82

Marla Gibbs
The Meteor Man '93
Up Against the Wall '91

Timothy Gibbs
The Kindred '87
Witchboard 2: The Devil's Doorway '93

Rebecca Gibney
Among the Cinders '83
Jigsaw '90

Henry Gibson
The Blues Brothers '80
Brenda Starr '86
For the Love of It '80
The Incredible Shrinking Woman '81
Innerspace '87

Kentucky Fried Movie '77
Kiss Me, Stupid! '64
Long Gone '87
The Long Goodbye '73
Monster in the Closet '86
Nashville '75
Night Visitor '89
Switching Channels '88
Tulips '81
Tune in Tomorrow '90

Hoot Gibson
Arizona Whirlwind '44
Boiling Point '32
Cavalcade of the West '36
Clearing the Range '31
The Concentratin' Kid '30
Courtin' Wildcats '29
Cowboy Counselor '33
Death Valley Rangers '44
Dude Bandit '32
Feud of the West '35
Fighting Parson '35
Frontier Justice '35
Hard Hombre '31
The Horse Soldiers '59
King of the Rodeo '28
Last Outlaw '36
The Law Rides Again '43
Local Badman '32
Lucky Terror '36
Man's Land '32
Marked Trails '44
The Marshal's Daughter '53
Outlaw Trail '44
The Painted Stallion '37
The Phantom Bullet '26
Powdersmoke Range '35
The Prairie King '27
Rainbow's End '35
The Riding Avenger '36
Roaring Ranch '30
Sonora Stagecoach '44
Spirit of the West '32
Spurs '30
Straight Shootin' '17
Sunset Range '35
Swifty '36
Trailing Trouble '30
Trigger Tricks '30
Wild Engine/Mistaken Orders '23
Wild Horse '31

Margaret Gibson
Last Days of Frank & Jesse James '86
Never a Dull Moment '50

Mel Gibson
Air America '90
Attack Force Z '84
Bird on a Wire '90
The Bounty '84
Forever Young '92
Gallipoli '81
Hamlet '90
Lethal Weapon '87
Lethal Weapon 2 '89
Lethal Weapon 3 '92
Mad Max '80
Mad Max: Beyond Thunderdome '85
The Man Without a Face '93
Maverick '94
Mrs. Soffel '84
The River '84
The Road Warrior '82
Summer City '77
Tequila Sunrise '88
Tim '79
The Year of Living Dangerously '82

Mimi Gibson
Courage of Black Beauty '57
The Monster that Challenged the World '57

Thomas Gibson
Armistead Maupin's Tales of the City '93
Barcelona '94
Far and Away '92

Virginia Gibson
Athena '54
Seven Brides for Seven Brothers '54
Tea for Two '50

Wynne Gibson
Aggie Appleby, Maker of Men '33

Motorcycle Squad '37
Night After Night '32

Bond Gideon
Gold of the Amazon Women '79
Stepsisters '85
Storyville '74

Pamela Gidley
Blue Iguana '88
Disturbed '90
Firefall '94
Highway to Hell '92
Liebestraum '91
Permanent Record '88
S.F.W. '94
Thrashin' '86

John Gielgud
Appointment with Death '88
Arthur '81
Arthur 2: On the Rocks '88
Becket '64
Brideshead Revisited '81
Caligula '80
The Charge of the Light Brigade '68
Chariots of Fire '81
Chimes at Midnight '67
The Conductor '80
The Elephant Man '80
11 Harrowhouse '74
The Formula '80
Frankenstein '82
Gandhi '82
Getting It Right '89
The Human Factor '79
The Hunchback of Notre Dame '82
Inside the Third Reich '82
Invitation to the Wedding '73
James Joyce: A Portrait of the Artist as a Young Man '77
Julius Caesar '53
Julius Caesar '70
Les Miserables '78
Lion of the Desert '81
The Loved One '65
A Man for All Seasons '88
Murder by Decree '79
Murder on the Orient Express '74
Plenty '85
The Power of One '92
Priest of Love '81
Probe '72
Prospero's Books '91
Providence '77
QB VII '74
Richard III '55
Romance on the Orient Express '85
Romeo and Juliet '54
Saint Joan '57
Scandalous '84
The Scarlet & the Black '83
Sebastian '67
The Secret Agent '36
Shining Through '92
The Shoes of the Fisherman '68
The Shooting Party '85
Sphinx '81
Strike It Rich '90
Wagner: The Complete Epic '85
Wagner: The Movie '85
War & Remembrance, Part 1 '88
War & Remembrance, Part 2 '89
War & Remembrance: The Final Chapter, Part 8 '89
The Whistle Blower '87
The Wicked Lady '83

Frances Gifford
American Empire '42
Border Vigilantes '41
Our Vines Have Tender Grapes '45
Thrill of a Romance '45

Gloria Gifford
D.C. Cab '84
Vice Versa '88

Roland Gift
Sammy & Rosie Get Laid '87
Scandal '89

Elaine Giftos
Angel '84
Gas-s-s-s! '70

The Student Nurses '70
The Wrestler '73

Sandro Giglio
For the First Time '59
The War of the Worlds '53

Vincent Gil
Body Melt '93
Solo '77

Billy Gilbert
Block-heads '38
Breaking the Ice '38
Comedy Festival #1 '30s
Comedy Festival #2 '30s
Cooking Up Trouble '49
Destry Rides Again '39
The Firefly '37
Ghost Crazy '44
The Great Dictator '40
Happy Landing '38
His Girl Friday '40
Joy of Living '38
Kelly the Second '36
Laurel & Hardy Comedy Classics, Vol. 1 '33
Laurel & Hardy Comedy Classics, Vol. 2 '30
Laurel & Hardy Comedy Classics, Vol. 3 '34
Laurel & Hardy Comedy Classics, Vol. 6 '35
Little Rascals, Book 6 '30s
Maid's Night Out '38
Melody Master '41
Mr. Wise Guy '42
No, No Nanette '40
Peck's Bad Boy with the Circus '38
Seven Sinners '40
Song of the Islands '42
Spotlight Scandals '43
Tin Pan Alley '40
Toast of New York '37
Two Reelers: Comedy Classics 2 '46
Valley of the Sun '42
Week-End In Havana '41

Eugenia Gilbert
Courtin' Wildcats '29
Test of Donald Norton '26

Helen Gilbert
Andy Hardy Gets Spring Fever '39
Death Valley '46
Girls in Prison '56
God's Country '46

John Gilbert
The Big Parade '25
The Busher '19
The Flesh and the Devil '27
He Who Gets Slapped '24
Queen Christina '33
A Woman of Affairs '28

Melissa Gilbert
Blood Vows: The Story of a Mafia Wife '87
Choices '86
The Christmas Coal Mine Miracle '77
Dying to Remember '93
Family Secrets '84
Ice House '89
Little House on the Prairie '74
The Lookalike '90
The Miracle Worker '79
Penalty Phase '86
The Snow Queen '83
Sylvester '85

Sara Gilbert
Poison Ivy '92
Sudie & Simpson '90

Taylor Gilbert
Alone in the T-Shirt Zone '86
Torment '85

Connie Gilchrist
The Half-Breed '51
Here Comes the Groom '51
Houdini '53
A Letter to Three Wives '49
Long John Silver '53
The Misadventures of Merlin Jones '63
Nothing But Trouble '44
Stars in My Crown '50
Ticket to Tomahawk '50
Tortilla Flat '42

Glenn

Richard Gilden
The Black Klansman '66
Lost, Lonely, and Vicious '59
Sandra Giles
Daddy-O '59
Lost, Lonely, and Vicious '59
Jack Gilford
Arthur 2: On the Rocks '88
Catch-22 '70
Caveman '81
Cheaper to Keep Her '80
Cocoon '85
Cocoon: The Return '88
Enter Laughing '67
A Funny Thing Happened on
 the Way to the Forum '66
Harry & Walter Go to New York
 '76
The Incident '67
Max '79
Save the Tiger '73
They Might Be Giants '71
Wholly Moses! '80
Dana Gillespie
The People That Time Forgot
 '77
Scrubbers '82
Anita Gillette
Ants '77
Bob Roberts '92
Brass '85
Marathon '80
Moonstruck '87
David Gilliam
Frogs '72
Gunpowder '84
Sharks' Treasure '75
Terry Gilliam
And Now for Something
 Completely Different '72
Monty Python and the Holy
 Grail '75
Monty Python Live at the
 Hollywood Bowl '82
Monty Python Meets Beyond
 the Fringe
Monty Python's Life of Brian
 '79
Monty Python's Parrot Sketch
 Not Included '90
Monty Python's The Meaning
 of Life '83
Richard Gilliland
Acceptable Risks '86
Challenge of a Lifetime '85
A Day for Thanks on Walton's
 Mountain '82
Embassy '85
Happy Hour '87
A Killing in a Small Town '90
Linda Gillin
Terror at Red Wolf Inn '72
Windows '80
Rebecca Gilling
The Blue Lightning '86
Heaven Tonight '93
The Naked Country '85
Claude Gillingwater
Green Eyes '34
Illicit '31
My Boy '21
Anne Gillis
The Adventures of Tom Sawyer
 '38
Big Town After Dark '47
In Society '44
'Neath Brooklyn Bridge '42
Peck's Bad Boy with the Circus
 '38
Texas Legionnaires '43
James Gillis
Alien Space Avenger '91
Deranged '87
Dracula Sucks '79
Night of the Zombies '81
Kenneth Gilman
Bedroom Eyes '86
Nights in White Satin '87
Scavengers '87
Lowell Gilmore
Days of Glory '43
Johnny Angel '45
King Solomon's Mines '50
Lone Star '52

Picture of Dorian Gray '45
Virginia Gilmore
The Loves of Edgar Allen Poe
 '42
Orchestra Wives '42
Western Union '41
Jack Gilpin
Barcelona '94
Funny Farm '88
Reversal of Fortune '90
Something Wild '86
Marc Gilpin
Computer Wizard '77
Where's Willie? '77
Clarence Gilyard, Jr.
Off the Mark '87
Walker: Texas Ranger: One
 Riot, One Ranger '93
Teresa Gimpera
Black Box Affair '66
Crypt of the Living Dead '73
Feast for the Devil '70s
Macabre '77
Spirit of the Beehive '73
Jack Ging
Dear Detective '78
Die Sister, Die! '74
Mosby's Marauders '66
Play Misty for Me '71
Where the Red Fern Grows '74
Hermione Gingold
The Adventures of Sadie '55
Bell, Book and Candle '58
Butler's Dilemma '43
Garbo Talks '84
Gigi '58
How to Be a Perfect Person in
 Just Three Days '84
A Little Night Music '77
The Music Man '62
The Naked Edge '61
The Pickwick Papers '54
Promise Her Anything '66
Those Fantastic Flying Fools
 '67
Tough Guy '53
Bob Ginnaven
The Day It Came to Earth '77
Hootch Country Boys '75
Allen Ginsberg
Heavy Petting '89
Kerouac '84
Robert Ginty
The Act '84
The Alchemist '81
Bounty Hunters '89
Codename: Vengeance '87
Coming Home '78
Exterminator '80
Exterminator 2 '84
Gold Raiders '84
Harley Davidson and the
 Marlboro Man '91
Lady Dragon '92
Loverboy '89
Madhouse '90
Mission to Kill '85
Out on Bail '89
Programmed to Kill '86
Three Kinds of Heat '87
Vietnam, Texas '90
Warrior of the Lost World '84
White Fire '83
Rocky Giordani
After Dark, My Sweet '90
Cop and a Half '93
Daniela Giordano
The Girl in Room 2A '76
Inquisition '70
Stranger's Gold '71
Florence Giorgetti
The Lacemaker '77
Monique '83
Elenora Giorgi
Beyond Obsession '82
Creepers '85
Inferno '78
Nudo di Donna '83
To Forget Venice '79
Cindy Girard
Operation Dames '59
Raising Cain '92

Joseph Girard
Defenders of the Law '31
Hurricane Express '32
King of the Rodeo '28
Laughing at Danger '24
Mystery of the Hooded
 Horseman '37
Tentacles of the North '26
The Tonto Kid '35
Annie Girardot
Gypsy '75
Jacko & Lise '82
Jupiter's Thigh '81
La Vie Continue '82
Le Cavaleur '78
Love and the Frenchwoman '60
Mussolini & I '85
Rocco and His Brothers '60
Hippolyte Girardot
Barjo '93
Love Without Pity '91
Manon of the Spring '87
Roland Giraud
Mr. Frost '89
Three Men and a Cradle '85
Bernard Giraudeau
Bilitis '77
La Boum '81
Passion of Love '82
Massimo Girotti
The Giants of Thessaly '60
Ossessione '42
Quo Vadis '85
Red Tent '71
Senso '54
Sins of Rome '54
Teorema '68
Torture Chamber of Baron
 Blood '72
Jackie Giroux
The Cross & the Switchblade
 '72
Trick or Treats '82
Annabeth Gish
Coupe de Ville '90
Desert Bloom '86
Hiding Out '87
Mystic Pizza '88
Shag: The Movie '89
When He's Not a Stranger '89
Wyatt Earp '94
Dorothy Gish
The Cardinal '63
Griffith Biograph Program '09
Hearts of the World '18
Home Sweet Home '14
Judith of Bethulia '14
Orphans of the Storm '21
Romola '25
Short Films of D.W. Griffith,
 Vol. 2 '09
Lillian Gish
The Adventures of Huckleberry
 Finn '85
Battle of Elderbush Gulch '13
The Birth of a Nation '15
Broken Blossoms '19
The Cobweb '55
The Comedians '67
Commandos Strike at Dawn '43
Duel in the Sun '46
D.W. Griffith Triple Feature '13
Follow Me, Boys! '66
Great Chase '63
The Greatest Question '19
Griffith Biograph Program '09
Hambone & Hillie '84
Hearts of the World '18
His Double Life '33
Hobson's Choice '83
Home Sweet Home '14
Intolerance '16
Judith of Bethulia '14
The Night of the Hunter '55
Orphans of the Storm '21
Portrait of Jennie '48
Romola '25
Short Films of D.W. Griffith,
 Vol. 2 '09
Sweet Liberty '86
True Heart Susie '19
The Unforgiven '60
Way Down East '20
A Wedding '78
The Whales of August '87
The White Sister '23

The Wind '28
Sheila Gish
A Day in the Death of Joe Egg
 '71
Highlander '86
Robert Gist
Jack the Giant Killer '62
Jigsaw '49
One Minute to Zero '52
Paul Giusti
Dirty Hands '76
Emmanuelle on Taboo Island
 '76
L'Anne Sainte '78
Robin Givens
Beverly Hills Madam '86
Blankman '94
Boomerang '92
The Penthouse '89
A Rage in Harlem '91
The Women of Brewster Place
 '89
George Givot
April In Paris '52
China Gate '57
DuBarry Was a Lady '43
Hollywood Party '34
Leather Burners '43
Thin Ice '37
Paul Michael Glaser
Jealousy '84
Phobia '80
Single Bars, Single Women '84
Wait Till Your Mother Gets
 Home '83
Ned Glass
Fright '56
Kid Galahad '62
The Rebel Set '59
Requiem for a Heavyweight '56
Street Music '81
West Side Story '61
Ron Glass
The Crash of Flight 401 '78
Deep Space '87
Isabel Glasser
Death Ring '93
Forever Young '92
Pure Country '92
Bob Glaudini
The Alchemist '81
Angel City '84
Chameleon '81
Louise Glaum
The Leopard Woman '20
Return of Draw Egan '16
Sex '20
The Three Musketeers '16
Eugene Glazer
Dollman '91
The Substitute '93
Jackie Gleason
All Through the Night '42
Don't Drink the Water '69
How to Commit Marriage '69
The Hustler '61
Izzy & Moe '85
Mr. Billion '77
Mister Halpren & Mister
 Johnson '83
Nothing in Common '86
Orchestra Wives '42
Papa's Delicate Condition '63
Smokey and the Bandit '77
Smokey and the Bandit, Part 2
 '80
Smokey and the Bandit, Part 3
 '83
Soldier in the Rain '63
Springtime in the Rockies '42
The Sting 2 '83
The Toy '82
James Gleason
Arsenic and Old Lace '44
The Bishop's Wife '47
The Clock '45
Crash Dive '43
The Crooked Circle '32
Down to Earth '47
Ex-Mrs. Bradford '36
Falcon Takes Over/Strange
 Bargain '49
Footlight Serenade '42
Forever Female '53

A Free Soul '31
A Guy Named Joe '44
Here Comes Mr. Jordan '41
I'll See You in My Dreams '51
The Jackpot '50
Key to the City '50
The Keys of the Kingdom '44
Last Hurrah '58
Loving You '57
Man or Gun '58
Meet John Doe '41
Miss Grant Takes Richmond
 '49
Movie Stuntmen '53
The Night of the Hunter '55
Suddenly '54
Tanks a Million '41
A Tree Grows in Brooklyn '45
Tycoon '47
We're Not Married '52
What Price Glory? '52
The Yellow Cab Man '50
Joanna Gleason
Crimes & Misdemeanors '89
F/X 2: The Deadly Art of Illusion
 '91
For Richer, For Poorer '92
Heartburn '86
Pat Gleason
Criminal Court '46
I Killed That Man '42
Rogue's Gallery '44
Swing It, Professor '37
Paul Gleason
Boiling Point '93
The Breakfast Club '85
Challenge of a Lifetime '85
Die Hard '88
The Ewoks: Battle for Endor
 '85
Forever, Lulu '87
Fourth Story '90
Ghost Chase '88
He Knows You're Alone '80
Johnny Be Good '88
Maniac Cop 3 '93
Miami Blues '90
Morgan Stewart's Coming
 Home '87
Night Game '89
Private Duty Nurses '71
Rich Girl '91
Running Cool '93
She's Having a Baby '88
Trading Places '83
Wild Cactus '93
Wishman '93
Russell Gleason
All Quiet on the Western Front
 '30
Condemned to Live '35
The Flying Fool '29
I Can't Escape '34
Iain Glen
Fools of Fortune '90
Mountains of the Moon '90
Rosencrantz & Guildenstern
 Are Dead '90
Roy Glenn
Carmen Jones '54
Jungle Drums of Africa '53
Scott Glenn
Angels Hard as They Come '71
Apocalypse Now '79
As Summers Die '86
The Baby Maker '70
Backdraft '91
The Challenge '82
Extreme Justice '93
Fighting Mad '76
The Hunt for Red October '90
Intrigue '90
The Keep '83
Man on Fire '87
Miss Firecracker '89
More American Graffiti '79
My Heroes Have Always Been
 Cowboys '91
Nashville '75
Off Limits '87
Personal Best '82
The Right Stuff '83
The River '84
Shadowhunter '93
She Came to the Valley '77
The Shrieking '73
The Silence of the Lambs '91

▲ 1289 • CAST INDEX

Glenn ►*cont.*

Silverado '85
Slaughter of the Innocents '93
Urban Cowboy '80
Verne Miller '88
Wild Geese 2 '85
Women & Men: In Love There Are No Rules '91

Sharon Gless
The Crash of Flight 401 '78
Hardhat & Legs '80
Hobson's Choice '83
Letting Go '85
Revenge of the Stepford Wives '80
The Star Chamber '83
Tales of the Unexpected '91

Stacey Glick
Brighton Beach Memoirs '86
Three O'Clock High '87

Brian Glover
Alien 3 '92
An American Werewolf in London '81
The Company of Wolves '85
Kafka '91
Leon the Pig Farmer '93
The McGuffin '85

Bruce Glover
Chrome Hearts '70
Diamonds are Forever '71
Ghost Town '88
Hider in the House '90
Killcrazy '89
Stunts '77
Warlock: The Armageddon '93

Crispin Glover
At Close Range '86
Back to the Future '85
Back to the Future, Part 2 '89
The Doors '91
Friday the 13th, Part 4: The Final Chapter '84
Hotel Room '93
Little Noises '91
My Tutor '82
Racing with the Moon '84
River's Edge '87
Rubin & Ed '92
Teachers '84
Twister '89
What's Eating Gilbert Grape '93
Where the Heart Is '90
Wild at Heart '90

Danny Glover
And the Children Shall Lead '85
Angels in the Outfield '94
Bat 21 '88
Bopha! '93
Chu Chu & the Philly Flash '81
The Color Purple '85
Dead Man Out '89
Escape from Alcatraz '79
Flight of the Intruder '90
Grand Canyon '91
Iceman '84
Keeping On '81
Lethal Weapon '87
Lethal Weapon 2 '89
Lethal Weapon 3 '92
Lonesome Dove '89
Mandela '87
Memorial Day '83
Out '88
Places in the Heart '84
Predator 2 '90
Pure Luck '91
A Rage in Harlem '91
A Raisin in the Sun '89
The Saint of Fort Washington '93
Silverado '85
Stand-In '85
To Sleep with Anger '90
Witness '85

John Glover
Annie Hall '77
Apology '86
Assault at West Point: The Court-Martial of Johnson Whittaker '94
The Chocolate War '88
Dead on the Money '91

Drug Wars 2: The Cocaine Cartel '92
An Early Frost '85
Ed and His Dead Mother '93
El Diablo '90
Ernie Kovacs: Between the Laughter '84
The Evil That Men Do '84
52 Pick-Up '86
Gremlins 2: The New Batch '90
A Killing Affair '85
The Last Embrace '79
A Little Sex '82
Masquerade '88
Meet the Hollowheads '89
The Mountain Men '80
Rocket Gibraltar '88
Scrooged '88
Something Special '86
Traveling Man '89

Julian Glover
The Empire Strikes Back '80
For Your Eyes Only '81
The Fourth Protocol '87
Hearts of Fire '87
Indiana Jones and the Last Crusade '89
Ivanhoe '82
Mandela '87
The Secret Garden '87
The Story of Jacob & Joseph '74
Theatre of Death '67
Tom Jones '63
Treasure Island '89
Tusks '89

Kara Glover
The Beat '88
Caribe '88

Carlin Glynn
Blood Red '88
Continental Divide '81
Night Game '89
Sixteen Candles '84
The Trip to Bountiful '85

Mathias Gnaedinger
The Boat is Full '81
Journey of Hope '90

Hiromi Go
MacArthur's Children '85
Samurai Cowboy '93

George Gobel
Better Late Than Never '79
Birds & the Bees '56
Ellie '84
The Fantastic World of D.C. Collins '84
I Married a Woman '56
Rabbit Test '78

Jean-Luc Godard
Cleo from 5 to 7 '61
First Name: Carmen '83
King Lear '87

John Goddard
Naked Youth '59
Storm Rider '57

Mark Goddard
Blue Sunshine '78
The Death Squad '73
Roller Boogie '79
Strange Invaders '83

Paulette Goddard
Diary of a Chambermaid '46
The Ghost Breakers '40
The Great Dictator '40
The Making of a Legend: "Gone With the Wind" '89
Modern Times '36
Pot O' Gold '41
Reap the Wild Wind '42
Second Chorus '40
Sins of Jezebel '54
Time of Indifference '64
Unholy Four '54
The Women '39
The Young in Heart '38

Arthur Godfrey
Angel's Brigade '79
Flatbed Annie and Sweetiepie: Lady Truckers '79
The Glass Bottom Boat '66
Great Bank Hoax '78

Jacques Godin
Being at Home with Claude '92
Double Identity '89

The Man Inside '76
The Victory '88

Alexander Godunov
Die Hard '88
The Money Pit '86
North '94
The Runestone '91
Waxwork 2: Lost in Time '91
Witness '85

Angela Goethals
Heartbreak Hotel '88
Home Alone '90
V.I. Warshawski '91

Michael C. Goetz
Deadly Encounter '72
Village of the Damned '60

Peter Michael Goetz
Beer '85
Father of the Bride '91
King Kong Lives '86
My Girl '91
Tagget '90

John Goff
The Alpha Incident '76
The Capture of Bigfoot '79
Devil & Leroy Basset '73
Getting Over '81
Night Stalker '87
Party Plane '90

Norris Goff
The Bashful Bachelor '42
Dreaming Out Loud '40

Gila Golan
Catch as Catch Can '68
Our Man Flint '66
The Valley of Gwangi '69

Whoopi Goldberg
Best of Comic Relief '86
Burglar '87
Clara's Heart '88
The Color Purple '85
Corrina, Corrina '94
Doctor Duck's Super Secret All-Purpose Sauce '85
Fatal Beauty '87
Ghost '90
Homer and Eddie '89
Jumpin' Jack Flash '86
Kiss Shot '89
The Long Walk Home '89
Made in America '93
Pee Wee's Playhouse Christmas Special '88
The Player '92
Sarafina! '92
Sister Act '92
Sister Act 2: Back in the Habit '93
Soapdish '91
The Telephone '87

Jeff Goldblum
The Adventures of Buckaroo Banzai Across the Eighth Dimension '84
Annie Hall '77
Between the Lines '77
Beyond Therapy '86
The Big Chill '83
Death Wish '74
Deep Cover '92
Earth Girls are Easy '89
Ernie Kovacs: Between the Laughter '84
Fathers and Sons '92
The Favor, the Watch, & the Very Big Fish '91
The Fly '86
Framed '90
Into the Night '85
Invasion of the Body Snatchers '78
Jurassic Park '93
The Legend of Sleepy Hollow '79
Mr. Frost '89
Nashville '75
Rehearsal for Murder '82
The Right Stuff '83
The Sentinel '76
Shooting Elizabeth '92
Silverado '85
Special Delivery '76
Strange Tales/Ray Bradbury Theatre '86
The Tall Guy '89
Thank God It's Friday '78

The Three Little Pigs '84
Threshold '83
Transylvania 6-5000 '85
Twisted Obsession '90
Vibes '88

Annie Golden
Baby Boom '87
Desperately Seeking Susan '85
Forever, Lulu '87
Hair '79
Key Exchange '85
Love at Stake '87
National Lampoon's Class of '86 '86
Streetwalkin' '85

Ricky Paull Goldin
The Blob '88
Hyper-Sapien: People from Another Star '86
Lambada '90
Mirror, Mirror '90

Lelia Goldoni
Bloodbrothers '78
Choices '81
The Disappearance of Aimee '76
Fatal Chase '77
The Spell '77
Theatre of Death '67

Clio Goldsmith
The Gift '82
Heat of Desire '84
Honey '81
La Cicada '83

Jenette Goldstein
Aliens '86
Near Dark '87
The Presidio '88

Bob(cat) Goldthwait
Burglar '87
Hot to Trot! '88
Little Vegas '90
One Crazy Summer '86
Police Academy 3: Back in Training '86
Police Academy 4: Citizens on Patrol '87
Scrooged '88
Shakes the Clown '92

Tony Goldwyn
Gaby: A True Story '87
Ghost '90
Iran: Days of Crisis '91
Kuffs '92
Love Matters '93
The Pelican Brief '93
Taking the Heat '93
Traces of Red '92

Valeria Golino
Clean Slate '94
Hot Shots! '91
Hot Shots! Part Deux '93
The Indian Runner '91
A Joke of Destiny, Lying in Wait Around the Corner Like a Bandit '84
The King's Whore '90
Rain Man '88
Torrents of Spring '90
Year of the Gun '91

Liza Golm
Come Back, Little Sheba '52
The Hoodlum '51

Arlene Golonka
Dr. Alien '88
Foxtrap '85
The Gumshoe Kid '89
The Hoboken Chicken Emergency '84
The In-Laws '79
My Tutor '82

Minna Gombell
Doomed Caravan '41
The Great Waltz '38
I'll See You in My Dreams '51
The Merry Widow '34
Pagan Love Song '50
Second Fiddle '39
The Thin Man '34

Fernando Gomez
Belle Epoque '94
Gulliver '70s
Mama Turns a Hundred '79
Spirit of the Beehive '73
The Stilts '84

Panchito Gomez
Mi Vida Loca '94
Paco '75
Sweet 15 '90

Thomas Gomez
But Not for Me '59
The Conqueror '56
Force of Evil '49
In Society '44
The Magnificent Matador '55
The Merry Widow '52
Pittsburgh '42
Sorrowful Jones '49
Stay Away, Joe '68
Summer and Smoke '61
Trapeze '56

Milton Goncalves
Kiss of the Spider Woman '85
Subway to the Stars '87

Mascha Gonska
Infernal Trio '74
Tea For Three '84

Dacia Gonzales
El Hombre de la Furia '65
La Hifa Sin Padre '87
Los Hermanos Centella '65

Caroline Goodall
Cliffhanger '93
Hook '91
Schindler's List '93
The Silver Stallion: King of the Wild Brumbies '94

Grant Goodeve
Hot Rod '79
Last Cry for Help '79
Take Two '87

Cuba Gooding, Jr.
Boyz N the Hood '91
Coming to America '88
Daybreak '93
A Few Good Men '92
Gladiator '92
Hitz '92
Judgment Night '93
Lightning Jack '94

Michael Goodliffe
The Gorgon '64
A Night to Remember '58
To the Devil, A Daughter '76
Up the Creek '58
The Way Out '56

Dody Goodman
Bedtime Story '63
Cool As Ice '91
Frozen Assets '92
Magic on Love Island '80
Private Resort '84
Splash '84

John Goodman
Always '89
Arachnophobia '90
The Babe '92
Barton Fink '91
The Big Easy '87
Born Yesterday '93
Burglar '87
C.H.U.D. '84
Eddie Macon's Run '83
Everybody's All American '88
The Flintstones '94
King Ralph '91
Maria's Lovers '92
Matinee '92
Punchline '88
Raising Arizona '87
Revenge of the Nerds '84
Sea of Love '89
Stella '89
Survivors '83
True Stories '86
The Wrong Guys '88

Deborah Goodrich
April Fool's Day '86
Remote Control '88
Survival Game '87

Garry Goodrow
Cardiac Arrest '74
The Committee '68
The Connection '61
A Session with the Committee '69

Angela Goodwin
Autopsy '78
Julia and Julia '87

Bill Goodwin
The Atomic Kid '54
Bathing Beauty '44
House of Horrors '46
It's a Great Feeling '49
Jolson Sings Again '49
The Jolson Story '46
Lucky Me '54
Mickey '48
The Stork Club '45
Tea for Two '50

Harold Goodwin
Abbott and Costello Meet the
 Keystone Kops '54
Angels One Five '54
The Cameraman '28
College '27
Suds '20
Tanks a Million '41

Laurel Goodwin
Girls! Girls! Girls! '62
Papa's Delicate Condition '63

Michael Goodwin
Date with an Angel '87
The Dead Pool '88
Deadline Assault '90
Sizzle '81

Allen (Gooritz) Garfield
Beverly Hills Cop 2 '87
Brink's Job '78
Busting '74
The Candidate '72
Club Fed '90
Continental Divide '81
The Conversation '74
The Cotton Club '84
Cry Uncle '71
Desert Bloom '86
Family Prayers '91
Fyre '78
Get Crazy '83
Greetings '68
Hi, Mom! '70
Irreconcilable Differences '84
Jack and His Friends '92
Leave 'Em Laughing '81
Let It Ride '89
Mother, Jugs and Speed '76
Nashville '75
Night Visitor '89
One Trick Pony '80
The Owl and the Pussycat '70
Paco '75
Skateboard '77
Sketches of a Strangler '78
Slither '73
State of Things '82
The Stunt Man '80
The Virginia Hill Story '76

Bernard Gorcey
Blues Busters '50
Bowery Buckaroos '47
Clipped Wings '53
Ghost Chasers '51
Hard-Boiled Mahoney '47
Spook Busters '46

David Gorcey
Blues Busters '50
Bowery Buckaroos '47
Flying Wild '41
Ghost Chasers '51
Hard-Boiled Mahoney '47
Master Minds '49
Mr. Wise Guy '42
Pride of the Bowery '41
Spook Busters '46
Wild Weed '49

Elizabeth Gorcey
Iced '88
Kidco '83

Leo Gorcey
Angels with Dirty Faces '38
Blues Busters '50
Bowery Blitzkrieg '41
Bowery Buckaroos '47
Boys of the City '40
Clipped Wings '53
Dead End '37
Destroyer '43
Flying Wild '41
Follow the Leader '44
Ghost Chasers '51
Hard-Boiled Mahoney '47
Here Come the Marines '52

It's a Mad, Mad, Mad, Mad
 World '63
Kid Dynamite '43
Let's Get Tough '42
Little Tough Guy '38
Mannequin '37
Master Minds '49
Million Dollar Kid '44
Mr. Wise Guy '42
'Neath Brooklyn Bridge '42
Pride of the Bowery '41
Smart Alecks '42
Smugglers' Cove '48
Spook Busters '46
Spooks Run Wild '41
That Gang of Mine '40
They Made Me a Criminal '39

Barry Gordon
Body Slam '87
Pressure Point '62
A Thousand Clowns '65

Ben Gordon
Goof Balls '87
Utilities '83

C. Henry Gordon
Charlie Chan at the Wax
 Museum '40
The Crooked Circle '32
Gabriel Over the White House
 '33
Mata Hari '32
Penthouse '33
Rasputin and the Empress '32
The Strange Love of Molly
 Louvain '32

Colin Gordon
The Body Beneath '70
Burn Witch, Burn! '62
The Key Man '57
One That Got Away '57

Don Gordon
The Beast Within '82
The Borrower '89
Bruce's Fists of Vengeance '84
Bullitt '68
The Education of Sonny
 Carson '74
Mack '73
Slaughter '72
Zero Population Growth '72

Eve Gordon
Avalon '90
Leaving Normal '92
Paradise '91
The Secret Passion of Robert
 Clayton '92
Switched at Birth '91

Gale Gordon
The 'Burbs '89
Here We Go Again! '42
Our Miss Brooks '56
Speedway '68
30-Foot Bride of Candy Rock
 '59

Gavin Gordon
The Bat '59
The Bitter Tea of General Yen
 '33
The Bride of Frankenstein '35
Female '33
His First Command '29
I Killed That Man '42
The Matchmaker '58
Romance '30
Turf Boy '42

Gerald Gordon
Ants '77
Force Five '75
Hell Up in Harlem '73

Glenn Gordon
The Finger Man '55
Fu Manchu '56

James Gordon
The Last of the Mohicans '20
Mark of the Beast
Trailin' '21

Keith Gordon
All That Jazz '79
Back to School '86
Christine '84
Combat Academy '86
Dressed to Kill '80
Home Movies '79
Kent State '81
Legend of Billie Jean '85

Silent Rebellion '82
Single Bars, Single Women '84
Static '87

Leo Gordon
Alienator '89
Bog '84
Devil's Angels '67
The Haunted Palace '63
The Jayhawkers '59
Riot in Cell Block 11 '54
Seventh Cavalry '56
Shame '61
Soldier of Fortune '55
Ten Wanted Men '54

Mary Gordon
The Adventures of Sherlock
 Holmes '39
Boss of Big Town '43
Double Wedding '37
Follow the Leader '44
Little Giant '46
Million Dollar Kid '44
Riot Squad '41
Sherlock Holmes and the
 Secret Weapon '42
Texas Cyclone '32
The Woman in Green '45

Pamela Gordon
Bloodlust: Subspecies 3 '93
Bloodstone: Subspecies 2 '93

Philip Gordon
The Bridge to Nowhere '86
Came a Hot Friday '85

Roy Gordon
Attack of the 50 Foot Woman
 '58
The Great Man Votes '38

Ruth Gordon
Abe Lincoln in Illinois '40
Action in the North Atlantic '43
Any Which Way You Can '80
The Big Bus '76
Don't Go to Sleep '82
Edge of Darkness '43
Every Which Way But Loose
 '78
Harold and Maude '71
Inside Daisy Clover '65
Jimmy the Kid '82
Maxie '85
Mugsy's Girls '85
My Bodyguard '80
The Prince of Central Park '77
Rosemary's Baby '68
The Trouble with Spies '87
Two-Faced Woman '41
Voyage of the Rock Aliens '87
Whatever Happened to Aunt
 Alice? '69
Where's Poppa? '70

Susan Gordon
Picture Mommy Dead '66
Tormented '60

Sandy Gore
Street Hero '84
Wrangler '84

Galyn Gorg
Body Beat '88
Malibu Bikini Shop '86
RoboCop 2 '90

Marius Goring
The Case of the Frightened
 Lady '39
Charlie Boy '81
Exodus '60
Holocaust '78
The Moonraker '58
Night Ambush '57
Paris Express '53
The Red Shoes '48
Spy in Black '39
The Unstoppable Man '59
Zeppelin '71

Cliff Gorman
All That Jazz '79
Angel '84
The Boys in the Band '70
Class of '63 '73
Cops and Robbers '73
Hoffa '92
Night and the City '92
Night of the Juggler '80
Rosebud '75
Strike Force '75
An Unmarried Woman '78

Jonathan Gorman
Gang Justice '94
Street Soldiers '91

Robert Gorman
Leprechaun '93
Mr. Nanny '93

Karen Gorney
The Hard Way '91
Saturday Night Fever '77

Frank Gorshin
Amore! '93
Batman '66
Between Heaven and Hell '56
Beverly Hills Bodysnatchers '89
Body Trouble '92
Dragstrip Girl '57
The Great Impostor '61
Hail Caesar '94
Hollywood Vice Squad '86
Hot Resort '85
Invasion of the Saucer Men '57
The Meteor Man '93
Midnight '89
Sky Hei$t '75
Star Trek Bloopers '69
Studs Lonigan '60
Sweet Justice '92
That Darn Cat '65
Underground Aces '80
Upper Crust '88

Marjoe Gortner
American Ninja 3: Blood Hunt
 '89
Bobbie Jo and the Outlaw '76
Earthquake '74
Fire, Ice and Dynamite '91
Food of the Gods '76
Hellhole '85
Jungle Warriors '84
Marjoe '72
Mausoleum '83
Pray for the Wildcats '74
Sidewinder One '77
Star Crash '78
The Survivalist '87
Viva Knievel '77

David Goss
Hollywood Cop '87
She '83

Louis Gossett, Jr.
Aces: Iron Eagle 3 '92
The Bushbaby '70
Carolina Skeletons '92
The Choirboys '77
Cover-Up '91
Dangerous Relations '93
The Deep '77
Diggstown '92
Don't Look Back: The Story of
 Leroy "Satchel" Paige '81
El Diablo '90
Enemy Mine '85
The Father Clements Story '87
Finders Keepers '84
Firewalker '86
Goodbye, Miss 4th of July '88
The Guardian '84
He Who Walks Alone '78
Iron Eagle '86
Iron Eagle 2 '88
It Rained All Night the Day I
 Left '79
It's Good to Be Alive '74
Jaws 3 '83
J.D.'s Revenge '76
The Josephine Baker Story '90
Keeper of the City '92
The Laughing Policeman '74
The Lazarus Syndrome '79
Little Ladies of the Night '77
Monolith '93
Murder on the Bayou '91
An Officer and a Gentleman '82
The Principal '87
The Punisher '90
A Raisin in the Sun '61
Return to Lonesome Dove '93
The River Niger '76
Roots: The Gift '88
Sadat '83
Skin Game '71
Straight Up '90
Sudie & Simpson '90
Toy Soldiers '91
Travels with My Aunt '72
The White Dawn '75
Zora Is My Name! '90

Roland Got
Across the Pacific '42
G-Men vs. the Black Dragon
 '43

Walter Gotell
The African Queen '51
Basic Training '86
For Your Eyes Only '81
From Russia with Love '63
The Living Daylights '87
Lord Jim '65
Moonraker '79
Sleepaway Camp 2: Unhappy
 Campers '88
The Spy Who Loved Me '77

Michael Gothard
For Your Eyes Only '81
King Arthur, the Young Warlord
 '75
Lifeforce '85
Young Warlord '75

Gilbert Gottfried
The Adventures of Ford
 Fairlane '90
Bad Medicine '85
Problem Child '90
Problem Child 2 '91

Carl Gottlieb
The Committee '68
Jaws '75
A Session with the Committee
 '69

Ferdinand Gottschalk
Ex-Lady '33
Female '33
King Kelly of the U.S.A. '34
Sing Sing Nights '35

Thomas Gottschalk
Driving Me Crazy '91
Ring of the Musketeers '93
Sister Act 2: Back in the Habit
 '93

Jetta Goudal
The Coming of Amos '25
The Road to Yesterday '25
Road to Yesterday/The Yankee
 Clipper '27
White Gold '28

Michael Gough
The Age of Innocence '93
Batman '89
Batman Returns '92
The Crimson Cult '68
Crucible of Horror '69
The Dresser '83
The Fourth Protocol '87
The Go-Between '71
Horror Hospital '73
The Horror of Dracula '58
The Horse's Mouth '58
Last Reunion '55
Out of Africa '85
Oxford Blues '84
Richard III '55
Rob Roy—The Highland Rogue
 '53
Savage Messiah '72
The Shell Seekers '89
The Skull '65
The Small Back Room '49
Strapless '90
The Sword & the Rose '53
They Came from Beyond
 Space '67
Top Secret! '84
Venom '82
What a Carve-Up! '62
Women in Love '70

Elliott Gould
Amore! '93
Beyond Justice '92
Bob & Carol & Ted & Alice '69
A Bridge Too Far '77
Bugsy '91
Busting '74
Capricorn One '78
Casey at the Bat '85
Conspiracy: The Trial of the
 Chicago Eight '87
Dangerous Love '87
Dead Men Don't Die '91
The Devil & Max Devlin '81
Dirty Tricks '81
Escape to Athena '79

Gould ▶cont.

Falling in Love Again '80
Frog '89
Frogs! '90s
Getting Straight '70
Harry & Walter Go to New York '76
Hitz '92
I Love My...Wife '70
I Will, I Will for Now '76
Inside Out '91
Jack & the Beanstalk '83
The Lady Vanishes '79
The Last Flight of Noah's Ark '80
The Lemon Sisters '90
Lethal Obsession '87
Little Murders '71
The Long Goodbye '73
M*A*S*H '70
Matilda '78
Mean Johnny Barrows '75
My Wonderful Life '90
The Naked Face '84
The Night They Raided Minsky's '69
Night Visitor '89
Over the Brooklyn Bridge '83
Quick, Let's Get Married '71
Roboman '75
The Silent Partner '78
S*P*Y*S '74
The Telephone '87
The Touch '71
Vanishing Act '88
Whiffs '75

Harold Gould
Actor: The Paul Muni Story '78
Better Late Than Never '79
Dream Chasers '84
Fourth Wise Man '85
Get Smart, Again! '89
Help Wanted: Male '82
How to Break Up a Happy Divorce '76
Kenny Rogers as the Gambler '80
Kenny Rogers as the Gambler, Part 2: The Adventure Continues '83
Love and Death '75
The One and Only '78
Playing for Keeps '86
The Red Light Sting '84
Romero '89
Seems Like Old Times '80
The Sting '73

Jason Gould
The Big Picture '89
The Prince of Tides '91
Say Anything '89

William Gould
Man from Montana '41
The Phantom '31
Phantom Thunderbolt '33
Rio Rattler '35
Tanks a Million '41

Robert Goulet
Based on an Untrue Story '93
Naked Gun 2 1/2: The Smell of Fear '91
Scrooged '88

Gibson Gowland
Greed '24
Gun Cargo '49
Hell Harbor '30
The Phantom of the Opera '25
The Secret of the Loch '34
Without Honors '32

Harry Goz
Bill '81
Bill: On His Own '83
Mommie Dearest '81
Rappin' '85

Betty Grable
The Beautiful Blonde from Bashful Bend '49
College Swing '38
Day the Bookies Wept '39
Down Argentine Way '40
The Farmer Takes a Wife '53
Follow the Fleet '36
Footlight Serenade '42
The Gay Divorcee '34

Gotta Dance, Gotta Sing '84
Hold 'Em Jail '32
Hollywood Goes to War '54
How to Marry a Millionaire '53
I Wake Up Screaming '41
The Love Goddesses '65
Moon Over Miami '41
Pin-Up Girl '44
Probation '32
Song of the Islands '42
Springtime in the Rockies '42
Strictly G.I. '44
Sweet Rosie O'Grady '43
Tin Pan Alley '40
Whoopee! '30
The Worst of Hollywood: Vol. 3 '90
A Yank in the R.A.F. '41

Nickolas Grace
Diamond's Edge '88
The Green Man '91
Heat and Dust '82
Max Headroom, the Original Story '86
Robin Hood...The Legend: Herne's Son '85
Robin Hood...The Legend: Robin Hood and the Sorcerer '83
Robin Hood...The Legend: The Swords of Wayland '83
Robin Hood...The Legend: The Time of the Wolf '85
Salome's Last Dance '88

Wayne Grace
Fallen Angels 2 '93
Heroes Stand Alone '89

Elizabeth Gracen
Death of the Incredible Hulk '90
Discretion Assured '93
Lower Level '91

Paulo Gracindo
Amor Bandido '79
Earth Entranced '66

Paul Graetz
Bulldog Jack '35
Heart's Desire '37
Mimi '35
Power '34

David Graf
Police Academy 2: Their First Assignment '85
Police Academy 3: Back in Training '86
Police Academy 4: Citizens on Patrol '87
Police Academy 5: Assignment Miami Beach '88
Police Academy 6: City Under Siege '89

Todd Graff
The Abyss '89
City of Hope '91
Dominick & Eugene '88
Five Corners '88
Framed '90
Opportunity Knocks '90
Sweet Lorraine '87
Vietnam War Story 3 '89

Wilton Graff
Bloodlust '59
The Mozart Story '48
The West Point Story '50

Aimee Graham
Amos and Andrew '93
Fallen Angels 1 '93

Bill Graham
Bugsy '91
The Doors '91
Gardens of Stone '87

Fred Graham
Escape from Fort Bravo '53
The Fuller Brush Girl '50
Heart of the Rockies '51
The Last Hunt '56
Trader Tom of the China Seas '54

Gary Graham
The Dirty Dozen: The Deadly Mission '87
The Last Warrior '89
No Place to Hide '81
Robot Jox '89

Gerrit Graham
The Annihilators '85
Cannonball '76
Child's Play 2 '90
C.H.U.D. 2: Bud the Chud '89
Demon Seed '77
Frozen Assets '92
Greetings '68
Hi, Mom! '70
Home Movies '79
It's Alive 3: Island of the Alive '87
The Man with One Red Shoe '85
Martians Go Home! '90
National Lampoon's Class Reunion '82
Night of the Cyclone '90
Phantom of the Paradise '74
Philadelphia Experiment 2 '93
Ratings Game '84
Son of Blob '72
Soup for One '82
Spaceship '81
Special Delivery '76
Terrorvision '86
This Boy's Life '93
Tunnelvision '76
Used Cars '80

Heather Graham
The Ballad of Little Jo '93
Diggstown '92
Drugstore Cowboy '89
Guilty as Charged '92
I Love You to Death '90
O Pioneers! '91
Shout '91
Six Degrees of Separation '93

Morland Graham
Bonnie Prince Charlie '48
Tower of Terror '42

Ronny Graham
New Faces of 1952 '54
Ratings Game '84
World's Greatest Lover '77

Gloria Grahame
Autopsy '70s
The Bad and the Beautiful '52
Big Heat '53
The Big Scam '79
Chilly Scenes of Winter '79
The Cobweb '55
Crossfire '47
Human Desire '54
In a Lonely Place '50
It Happened in Brooklyn '47
It's a Wonderful Life '46
Loners '72
Macao '52
Mama's Dirty Girls '74
The Man Who Never Was '55
Merton of the Movies '47
The Nesting '80
Not as a Stranger '55
Oklahoma! '55
Song of the Thin Man '47
The Todd Killings '71
A Woman's Secret '49

Margot Grahame
Broken Melody '34
Fabulous Joe '47
The Informer '35
The Three Musketeers '35

Alexander Granach
Dracula/Garden of Eden '28
Joan of Paris '42
Kameradschaft '31
Nosferatu '22
The Seventh Cross '44

Daisy Granados
Memories of Underdevelopment '68
Portrait of Teresa '79
A Very Old Man with Enormous Wings '88

Rosario Granados
The Great Madcap '49
La Diosa Arrodillada '49
A Woman Without Love '51

Bjorn Granath
The Ox '91
Pelle the Conqueror '88

Dorothy Granger
Fighting Fool '32

The Flustered Comedy of Leon Errol '39
Killer Dill '47
Two Reelers: Comedy Classics 2 '46
W.C. Fields Comedy Bag '33

Farley Granger
Arnold '73
Behave Yourself! '52
Deathmask '69
Hans Christian Andersen '52
Imagemaker '86
Night Flight from Moscow '73
The North Star '43
The Prowler '81
The Purple Heart '44
Rope '48
Senso '54
The Slasher '74
Small Town Girl '53
Strangers on a Train '51
Sweet Spirits '80s
They Call Me Trinity '72
They Live by Night '49
Very Close Quarters '84
The Widow '76

Stewart Granger
All the Brothers Were Valiant '53
Beau Brummel '54
Bhowani Junction '56
Caesar and Cleopatra '46
Code Name Alpha '67
Convoy '40
Fine Gold
Green Fire '55
Gun Glory '57
Harry Black and the Tiger '58
Hell Hunters '87
King Solomon's Mines '50
The Last Hunt '56
The Last Safari '67
The Man in Grey '45
Man of Evil '48
Moonfleet '55
North to Alaska '60
Prisoner of Zenda '52
Salome '53
Scaramouche '52
Sodom and Gomorrah '62
Target for Killing '66
Thursday's Child '43
Wild Geese '78
Young Bess '53

Nils T. Granlund
Rhythm Parade '43
Take It Big '44

William Grannell
The Abductors '72
Ginger '72

Beth Grant
The Dark Half '91
Love Field '91
Rain Man '88
Speed '94
White Sands '92

Cary Grant
An Affair to Remember '57
Amazing Adventure '37
Arsenic and Old Lace '44
The Awful Truth '37
The Bachelor and the Bobby-Soxer '47
The Bishop's Wife '47
Blonde Venus '32
Bringing Up Baby '38
The Cary Grant Collection '90
Charade '63
Destination Tokyo '43
Every Girl Should Be Married '48
Father Goose '64
The Grass is Greener '61
Gunga Din '39
His Girl Friday '40
Holiday '38
Houseboat '58
The Howards of Virginia '40
I Was a Male War Bride '49
I'm No Angel '33
In Name Only '39
Indiscreet '58
Mr. Blandings Builds His Dream House '48
Mr. Lucky '43
Monkey Business '52
My Favorite Wife '40

Night and Day '46
1939, The Movies' Vintage Year: Trailers on Tape '39
None But the Lonely Heart '44
North by Northwest '59
Notorious '46
Once Upon a Honeymoon '42
Only Angels Have Wings '39
Operation Petticoat '59
Penny Serenade '41
People Will Talk '51
The Philadelphia Story '40
The Pride and the Passion '57
She Done Him Wrong '33
Suspicion '41
Suzy '26
Sylvia Scarlett '35
Talk of the Town '42
That Touch of Mink '62
To Catch a Thief '55
Toast of New York '37
Topper '37
Walk, Don't Run '66

David Marshall Grant
Air America '90
American Flyers '85
Bat 21 '88
End of August '82
Forever Young '92
Happy Birthday, Gemini '80
Sessions '83

Faye Grant
Omen 4: The Awakening '91
Senior Trip '81

Frances Grant
Cavalry '36
Oh Susannah '38
Red River Valley '36

Hugh Grant
The Big Man: Crossing the Line '91
Bitter Moon '92
The Dawning '88
Four Weddings and a Funeral '93
Impromptu '90
The Lair of the White Worm '88
Maurice '87
The Remains of the Day '93
Sirens '94
White Mischief '88

James Grant
The Innocent '93
Prick Up Your Ears '87

Kathryn Grant
Anatomy of a Murder '59
The Seventh Voyage of Sinbad '58

Kirby Grant
Bad Men of the Border '45
Comin' Round the Mountain '51
In Society '44
The Stranger from Pecos '45

Lawrence Grant
Doomsday '28
The Grand Duchess and the Waiter '26
The Mask of Fu Manchu '32
Shanghai Express '32
Son of Frankenstein '39
Speak Easily '32

Lee Grant
Airport '77 '77
The Balcony '63
Big Town '87
A Billion for Boris '90
Buona Sera, Mrs. Campbell '68
Charlie Chan and the Curse of the Dragon Queen '81
Citizen Cohn '92
Damien: Omen 2 '78
Defending Your Life '91
Detective Story '51
For Ladies Only '81
In the Heat of the Night '67
Internecine Project '73
Little Miss Marker '80
Marooned '69
My Sister, My Love '78
Plaza Suite '71
Portnoy's Complaint '72
Shampoo '75
The Spell '77
The Swarm '78
Teachers '84
There was a Crooked Man '70

Valley of the Dolls '67
Visiting Hours '82
Voyage of the Damned '76

Leon Grant
Beat Street '84
Playing for Keeps '86

Richard E. Grant
The Age of Innocence '93
Bram Stoker's Dracula '92
Codename Kyril '91
Henry & June '90
How to Get Ahead in Advertising '89
Hudson Hawk '91
L.A. Story '91
Mountains of the Moon '90
The Player '92
Warlock '91
Withnail and I '87

Rodney Grant
Dances with Wolves '90
Geronimo: An American Legend '93
Son of the Morning Star '91
Wagons East '94

Schuyler Grant
Anne of Avonlea '87
Anne of Green Gables '85

Shelby Grant
Our Man Flint '66
The Witchmaker '69

Allan Granville
Black Terrorist '85
Prey for the Hunter '92

Bonita Granville
Breakfast in Hollywood '46
The Glass Key '42
Guilty of Treason '50
Hitler's Children '43
Lone Ranger '56
Love Laughs at Andy Hardy '46
The Mortal Storm '40
Nancy Drew, Reporter '39
Now, Voyager '42
Quality Street '37
Seven Miles from Alcatraz/ Flight from Glory '43
These Three '36

Charley Grapewin
Ah, Wilderness! '35
Captains Courageous '37
The Good Earth '37
The Grapes of Wrath '40
Hell's House '32
Heroes for Sale '33
Johnny Apollo '40
Libeled Lady '36
Of Human Hearts '38
One Frightened Night '35
Petrified Forest '36
Shopworn Angel '38
They Died with Their Boots On '41
Three Comrades '38
The Wizard of Oz '39

Karen Grassle
The Best Christmas Pageant Ever '86
Cocaine: One Man's Seduction '83
Harry's War '84
Little House on the Prairie '74
President's Mistress '78
Wyatt Earp '94

Ernest Graves
Hercules in New York '70
One Plus One '61

Peter Graves
The Adventurers '70
Airplane! '80
Airplane 2: The Sequel '82
Beginning of the End '57
Beneath the 12-Mile Reef '53
Casey Jones and Fury (Brave Stallion) '57
The Clonus Horror '79
The Court Martial of Billy Mitchell '55
Cruise Missile '78
Encore '82
The Guns and the Fury '83
It Conquered the World '56
Killers from Space '54
The Legend of the Sea Wolf '58
Let's Make Up '55

The Magic Christian '69
Maytime in Mayfair '52
The Night of the Hunter '55
Number One with a Bullet '87
Poor White Trash '57
The President's Plane is Missing '71
The Rebels '79
Red Planet Mars '52
Savannah Smiles '82
Sergeant Ryker '68
Stalag 17 '53
Survival Run '80
Texas Across the River '66
Where Have All the People Gone? '74
The Winds of War '83

Ralph Graves
The Black Coin '36
Dream Street '21
Extra Girl '23
The Greatest Question '19
That Certain Thing '28
Three Texas Steers '39

Robert Graves
Epic That Never Was '65
Test of Donald Norton '26

Rupert Graves
The Children '90
Damage '92
Fortunes of War '87
A Handful of Dust '88
Maurice '87
A Room with a View '86
Where Angels Fear to Tread '91

Fernand Gravet
The Great Waltz '38
La Ronde '51
The Madwoman of Chaillot '69

Carla Gravina
Alfredo, Alfredo '72
And Now My Love '74
Boomerang '76
Salut l'Artiste '74
The Tempter '74

Cesare Gravina
Foolish Wives '22
Merry-Go-Round '23
The Wedding March '28

Billy Gray
By the Light of the Silvery Moon '53
On Moonlight Bay '51
Two for the Seesaw '62
Werewolves on Wheels '71

Charles Gray
Black Werewolf '75
Diamonds are Forever '71
Dreams Lost, Dreams Found '87
An Englishman Abroad '83
The Executioner '70
The House on Garibaldi Street '79
The Jigsaw Man '84
The Man Outside '68
The Mirror Crack'd '80
Murder on the Midnight Express '74
The Seven Percent Solution '76
Shock Treatment '81
Silver Bears '78
You Only Live Twice '67

Coleen Gray
Cry from the Mountain '85
Kansas City Confidential '52
The Killing '56
Kiss of Death '47
The Leech Woman '59
The Phantom Planet '61
Red River '48

David Barry Gray
Cops and Robbersons '94
S.F.W. '94

Dolores Gray
Designing Woman '57
Kismet '55
The Opposite Sex '56

Donald Gray
Flight from Vienna '58
The Four Feathers '39
Island of Desire '52
Murder on the Campus '52

Dorian Gray
Colossus and the Amazon Queen '64
Il Grido '57

Dulcie Gray
Angels One Five '54
The Franchise Affair '52
A Man About the House '47
Mine Own Executioner '47

Erin Gray
Born Beautiful '82
Breaking Home Ties '87
Buck Rogers in the 25th Century '79
Honor Thy Father and Mother: The True Story of the Menendez Brothers '94
Jason Goes to Hell: The Final Friday '93
Official Denial '93
Six Pack '82
The Ultimate Imposter '79

Eve Gray
Department Store '35
Night Birds '31

Gary Gray
The Next Voice You Hear '50
The Painted Hills '51
Rachel and the Stranger '48
Two Weeks with Love '50

Lawrence Gray
A Face in the Fog '36
Love 'Em and Leave 'Em '26

Linda Gray
Accidental Meeting '93
Bonanza: The Return '93
The Grass is Always Greener Over the Septic Tank '78
Kenny Rogers as the Gambler, Part 3: The Legend Continues '87
Shadows Over Shanghai '38
The Two Worlds of Jenny Logan '79
The Wild and the Free '80

Lorna Gray
The Man They Could Not Hang '39
Ridin' Down the Canyon '42

Marc Gray
Flirting '89
Which Way Home '90

Nadia Gray
The Captain's Table '60
La Dolce Vita '60
Maniac '63
Two for the Road '67
Valley of the Eagles '51

Sally Gray
Dangerous Moonlight '41
The Hidden Room '49
I'll Get You '53
Keeper '84
Lady in Distress '39
Saint in London '39
The Saint's Vacation/The Narrow Margin '52

Spalding Gray
Almost You '85
Beaches '88
Clara's Heart '88
Hard Choices '84
Heavy Petting '89
The Image '89
The Killing Fields '84
King of the Hill '93
Monster in a Box '92
The Paper '94
Spalding Gray: Terrors of Pleasure '88
Stars and Bars '88
Straight Talk '92
Swimming to Cambodia '87
True Stories '86
Twenty Bucks '93

Kathryn Grayson
Anchors Aweigh '45
Andy Hardy's Private Secretary '41
The Desert Song '53
It Happened in Brooklyn '47
Kiss Me Kate '53
Lovely to Look At '52
Rio Rita '42

Show Boat '51
That Midnight Kiss '49
Thousands Cheer '43
Till the Clouds Roll By '46
Till the Clouds Roll By/A Star is Born '46
The Toast of New Orleans '50

Jose Greco
Goliath and the Sins of Babylon '64
Ship of Fools '65

Juliette Greco
Elena and Her Men '56
The Green Glove '52
Uncle Tom's Cabin '69

Adolph Green
Follies in Concert '85
Lily in Love '85
My Favorite Year '82
Simon '80

Brian Austin Green
An American Summer '91
Beverly Hills 90210: The Graduation '93
Kid '90

Harry Green
A King in New York '57
The Light of Western Stars '30

Janet-Laine Green
Bullies '86
Cowboys Don't Cry '88
Kidnapping of Baby John Doe '88

Kerri Green
The Goonies '85
Lucas '86
Summer Rental '85
Tainted Blood '93
Three for the Road '87

Marika Green
Emmanuelle '74
Pickpocket '59

Mitzie Green
Little Orphan Annie '32
Lost in Alaska '52
Tom Sawyer '30

Nigel Green
Africa Texas Style '67
Corridors of Blood '58
The Ipcress File '65
Jason and the Argonauts '63
Khartoum '66
Masque of the Red Death/ Premature Burial '65
Mysterious Island '61
Reach for the Sky '56
The Ruling Class '72
The Skull '65
Sword of Sherwood Forest '60
Tobruk '66
Zulu '64

Seth Green
Airborne '93
Arcade '93
The Hotel New Hampshire '84
My Stepmother Is an Alien '88
Radio Days '87
Something Special '86

Esther Greenberg
Lupo '70
Sallah '63

Angela Greene
The Cosmic Man '59
Night of the Blood Beast '58

Daniel Greene
American Tiger '89
Elvira, Mistress of the Dark '88
Hands of Steel '86
The Opponent '89
Pulsebeat '85
Skeleton Coast '89
Weekend Warriors '86

Ellen Greene
Dinner at Eight '89
Fathers and Sons '92
Glory! Glory! '90
Little Shop of Horrors '86
Me and Him '89
Next Stop, Greenwich Village '76
Pump Up the Volume '90
Stepping Out '91
Talk Radio '88
Wagons East '94

Graham Greene
Benefit of the Doubt '93
The Broken Chain '93
Camilla '94
Clearcut '92
Cooperstown '93
Dances with Wolves '90
Huck and the King of Hearts '93
The Last of His Tribe '92
Lost in the Barrens '91
Maverick '94
North '94
Powwow Highway '89
Spirit Rider '93
Thunderheart '92

James Greene
Pals '87
Philadelphia Experiment 2 '93

Joe "Mean Joe" Greene
The Black Six '74
Lady Cocoa '75
Twisted Brain '74

Jon Greene
Alley Cat '84
Swift Justice '88

Lorne Greene
The Alamo: Thirteen Days to Glory '87
Autumn Leaves '56
The Bastard '78
Battlestar Galactica '78
The Buccaneer '58
Earthquake '74
The Errand Boy '61
Klondike Fever '79
Mission Galactica: The Cylon Attack '79
Peyton Place '57
Ride the Wind '66
Roots '77
The Silver Chalice '54
Tidal Wave '75
A Time for Miracles '80
The Trap '59
The Trial of Lee Harvey Oswald '86
Vasectomy: A Delicate Matter '86

Michael Greene
Americana '81
The Clones '73
In the Heat of Passion '91
Johnny Be Good '88
Lost in America '85
Moon Over Parador '88
The Naked Angels '69
The Night Before '88
Nightmare on the 13th Floor '90
Rubin & Ed '92
White of the Eye '88

Michelle Greene
Double Standard '88
I Posed for Playboy '91
Silent Victim '92
The Unborn 2 '94

Peter Greene
Judgment Night '93
Laws of Gravity '92
The Mask '94

Richard Greene
Captain Scarlett '53
The Castle of Fu Manchu '68
Forever Amber '47
The Hound of the Baskervilles '39
Island of the Lost '68
Kiss and Kill '68
The Little Princess '39
My Lucky Star '38
Robin Hood: The Movie '55
Special Effects '85
Stanley and Livingstone '39
Sword of Sherwood Forest '60
Tales from the Crypt '72

Shecky Greene
The Love Machine '71
Lovelines '84
Splash '84

Kate Greenfield
Night Gallery '69
Robinson Crusoe of Clipper Island '36

Raymond Greenleaf
Pier 23 '51
When Gangland Strikes '56

Brad Greenquist
The Bedroom Window '87
Mutants In Paradise '88

Sydney Greenstreet
Across the Pacific '42
Background to Danger '43
The Best of Bogart '43
Casablanca '42
Christmas in Connecticut '45
Conflict '45
Flamingo Road '49
Hollywood Canteen '44
The Hucksters '47
It's a Great Feeling '49
Malaya '49
The Maltese Falcon '41
Passage to Marseilles '44
They Died with Their Boots On '41
Velvet Touch '48

Bruce Greenwood
Adrift '93
Another Chance '88
The Climb '87
The FBI Murders '88
Malibu Bikini Shop '86
Passenger 57 '92
Rio Diablo '93
Servants of Twilight '91
Spy '89
Striker's Mountain '87
Wild Orchid '90

Charlotte Greenwood
Dangerous When Wet '53
Down Argentine Way '40
Glory '56
Moon Over Miami '41
Oklahoma! '55
Parlor, Bedroom and Bath '31
Springtime in the Rockies '42
Two Reelers: Comedy Classics 5 '38

Joan Greenwood
The Detective '54
Frenzy '46
A Girl in a Million '46
The Hound of the Baskervilles '77
Importance of Being Earnest '52
Kind Hearts and Coronets '49
Little Dorrit, Film 1: Nobody's Fault '88
Little Dorrit, Film 2: Little Dorrit's Story '88
The Man in the White Suit '51
Mr. Peek-A-Boo '50
Moonfleet '55
Mysterious Island '61
October Man '48
Stage Struck '57
Tom Jones '63
Whiskey Galore '48

Dabbs Greer
Cash McCall '60
It! The Terror from Beyond Space '58
Rage '72
Rose Marie '54
Roustabout '64
Trouble Along the Way '53
Two Moon Junction '88

Jane Greer
Against All Odds '84
Big Steal '49
Billie '65
Clown '53
Dick Tracy, Detective '45
Dick Tracy, Detective/The Corpse Vanishes '42
George White's Scandals '45
Immediate Family '89
Just Between Friends '86
Man of a Thousand Faces '57
Out of the Past '47
Prisoner of Zenda '52
Sinbad the Sailor '47
Station West '48
They Won't Believe Me '47
Where Love Has Gone '64

Michael Greer
Fortune and Men's Eyes '71
Messiah of Evil '74

Bradley Gregg
Class of 1999 '90
Eye of the Storm '91
Madhouse '90

John Gregg
Heatwave '83
Trouble in Paradise '88

Julie Gregg
From Hell to Borneo '64
The Seekers '79

Virginia Gregg
The Amazing Mr. X '48
Columbo: Prescription Murder '67
D.I. '57
The Hanging Tree '59
Love is a Many-Splendored Thing '55
No Way Back '74
Operation Petticoat '59
Spencer's Mountain '63
Walk in the Spring Rain '70

Rose Gregorio
City of Hope '91
Desperate Characters '71
Five Corners '87
The Last Innocent Man '87
Swimmer '68

Andre Gregory
Always '85
Author! Author! '82
The Bonfire of the Vanities '90
Follies in Concert '85
The Last Temptation of Christ '88
The Linguini Incident '92
The Mosquito Coast '86
My Dinner with Andre '81
Protocol '84
Some Girls '88
Street Smart '87

Celia Gregory
Agatha '79
Children of the Full Moon '84

James Gregory
Al Capone '59
The Ambushers '67
Beneath the Planet of the Apes '70
Captain Newman, M.D. '63
Clambake '67
Great American Traffic Jam '80
Gun Glory '57
The Manchurian Candidate '62
Murderers' Row '66
Nightfall '57
PT 109 '63
Two Weeks in Another Town '62
Wait Till Your Mother Gets Home '83

Mark Gregory
Blue Paradise '86
Escape from the Bronx '85
Thunder Warrior '86
Thunder Warrior 2 '85
Thunder Warrior 3 '88
War Bus Commando '89

Sebastian Gregory
Help Wanted Female '68
Sweet Trash '89

Thea Gregory
Paid to Kill '54
Profile '54

John Gregson
Above Us the Waves '56
Angels One Five '54
The Captain's Table '60
Fright '71
Genevieve '53
Hans Brinker '69
The Lavender Hill Mob '51
Night of the Generals '67
S.O.S. Pacific '60

Stephen Greif
The Dying Truth '91
The Great Riviera Bank Robbery '79

Robert Greig
The Great Ziegfeld '36
Sullivan's Travels '41

Kim Greist
Brazil '85
C.H.U.D. '84

Duplicates '92
Homeward Bound: The Incredible Journey '93
Manhunter '86
Payoff '91
Punchline '88
Throw Momma from the Train '87
Why Me? '90

Joyce Grenfell
The Americanization of Emily '64
The Belles of St. Trinian's '53
Blue Murder at St. Trinian's '56
The Happiest Days of Your Life '50
The Pure Hell of St. Trinian's '61

Googy Gress
Babes in Toyland '86
Bloodhounds of Broadway '89
First Turn On '83
Promised Land '88
Vibes '87

Anne Grey
Kiss of Death '47
No. 17 '32

Denise Grey
Devil in the Flesh '46
La Boum '81
Sputnik '61

Jennifer Grey
American Flyers '85
Bloodhounds of Broadway '89
A Case for Murder '93
The Cotton Club '84
Criminal Justice '90
Dirty Dancing '87
Ferris Bueller's Day Off '86
Reckless '84
Red Dawn '84
Stroke of Midnight '90
Wind '92

Joel Grey
Buffalo Bill & the Indians '76
Cabaret '72
Kafka '91
Man on a String '71
The Music of Chance '93
Queenie '87
Remo Williams: The Adventure Begins '85
The Seven Percent Solution '76

Nan Grey
Danger on the Air '38
Dracula's Daughter '36
The Invisible Man Returns '40
The Tower of London '39

Shirley Grey
Drifting Souls '32
Get That Girl '32
Green Eyes '34
Hurricane Express '32
The Mystery of the Mary Celeste '37
The Riding Tornado '32
Texas Cyclone '32
Uptown New York '32

Virginia Grey
Another Thin Man '39
Bachelor in Paradise '69
Big Store '41
Broadway Serenade '39
Bullfighter & the Lady '50
Crime of Passion '57
House of Horrors '46
Idaho '43
Lady Scarface/The Threat '49
The Last Command '55
Love has Many Faces '65
Madame X '66
Mexican Hayride '48
The Michigan Kid '28
Naked Kiss '64
The Rose Tattoo '55
Slaughter Trail '51
Swamp Fire '46
Sweet Rosie O'Grady '43
Tarzan's New York Adventure '42
Threat '49
Three Desperate Men '50
Unknown Island '48
Whistling in the Dark '41
Who Killed Doc Robbin? '48

Clinton Greyn
The Love Machine '71
Raid on Rommel '71

Bill Gribble
Dogs of Hell '83
The Wild and the Free '80

Harry Gribbon
Ben Turpin: An Eye for an Eye '24
The Cameraman '28
Ride Him, Cowboy '32
Two Reelers: Comedy Classics 1 '33
Two Reelers: Comedy Classics 7 '38

Richard Grieco
Born to Run '93
If Looks Could Kill '91
Mobsters '91
Tomcat: Dangerous Desires '93

Helmut Griem
Children of Rage '75
The Damned '69
Escape '90
La Passante '83
Les Rendez-vous D'Anna '78
Malou '83
McKenzie Break '70

David Alan Grier
Beer '85
Blankman '94
Boomerang '94
I'm Gonna Git You Sucka '88
In the Army Now '94
Loose Cannons '90
Off Limits '87
A Soldier's Story '84

Pam Grier
Above the Law '88
Badge of the Assassin '85
The Big Bird Cage '72
The Big Doll House '71
Bill & Ted's Bogus Journey '91
Bucktown '75
Class of 1999 '90
Coffy '73
Drum '76
Fort Apache, the Bronx '81
Foxy Brown '74
Friday Foster '75
Greased Lightning '77
Naked Warriors '73
On the Edge '86
The Package '89
Scream Blacula Scream '73
Sheba, Baby '75
Something Wicked This Way Comes '83
Stand Alone '85
Tough Enough '83
Twilight People '72
The Vindicator '85

Roosevelt Grier
The Big Push '75
The Glove '78
The Seekers '79
Sophisticated Gents '81
The Treasure of Jamaica Reef '74

Jonathan Gries
Joy Sticks '83
Kill Me Again '89
Pucker Up and Bark Like a Dog '89
Real Genius '85
Swap Meet '79

Joe Grifasi
Bad Medicine '85
Benny & Joon '93
Chances Are '89
City of Hope '91
F/X '86
The Feud '90
Gentleman Bandit '81
Household Saints '93
Ironweed '87
On the Yard '79
Perfect Witness '89
Presumed Innocent '90
Still of the Night '82

Simone Griffeth
Death Race 2000 '75
Delusion '84
Hot Target '85
The Patriot '86

Sixteen '72

Josephine Griffin
The Man Who Never Was '55
Postmark for Danger '56
The Spanish Gardener '57

Lorie Griffin
Aloha Summer '88
Cheerleader Camp '88

Robert Griffin
Crime of Passion '57
I Was a Teenage Werewolf '57
Monster from Green Hell '58

Tony Griffin
Evil Laugh '86
Robin Hood: Men in Tights '93

Andy Griffith
A Face in the Crowd '57
Fatal Vision '84
From Here to Eternity '79
Hearts of the West '75
Murder in Coweta County '83
Murder in Texas '81
No Time for Sergeants '58
Pray for the Wildcats '74
Return to Mayberry '85
Rustler's Rhapsody '85
Savages '74

Corrine Griffith
Dracula/Garden of Eden '28
The Garden of Eden '28

Eva Griffith
Ride a Wild Pony '75
The Turn of the Screw '74

Gordon Griffith
Little Annie Rooney '25
Outlaws of the Range '36

Hugh Griffith
The Abominable Dr. Phibes '71
Ben-Hur '59
The Big Scam '73
The Canterbury Tales '71
The Counterfeit Traitor '62
Craze '73
Cry of the Banshee '70
Diary of Forbidden Dreams '73
Doctor Phibes Rises Again '72
Exodus '60
The Final Programme '73
The Fixer '68
The Last Days of Dolwyn '49
Legend of the Werewolf '75
Lucky Jim '58
Luther '74
Mutiny on the Bounty '62
Oh Dad, Poor Dad (Momma's Hung You in the Closet & I'm Feeling So Sad) '67
Oliver! '68
The Passover Plot '75
The Sleeping Tiger '54
Start the Revolution Without Me '70
Tom Jones '63
Who Slew Auntie Roo? '71
Wuthering Heights '70

James Griffith
The Amazing Transparent Man '60
Bullwhip '58
The Legend of Sleepy Hollow '79
Tribute to a Bad Man '56

Kenneth Griffith
The Assassination Bureau '69
Circus of Horrors '60
The Final Option '82
Koroshi '67
Night of the Laughing Dead '75
Revenge '71

Melanie Griffith
Body Double '84
The Bonfire of the Vanities '90
Born Yesterday '93
Cherry 2000 '85
The Drowning Pool '75
Fear City '85
Harrad Experiment '73
In the Spirit '90
Joyride '77
The Milagro Beanfield War '88
Milk Money '95
Night Moves '75
One on One '77
Pacific Heights '90
Paradise '91

She's in the Army Now '81
Shining Through '92
Smile '75
Something Wild '86
Steel Cowboy '78
Stormy Monday '88
A Stranger Among Us '92
Underground Aces '80
Women & Men: Stories of
    Seduction '90
Working Girl '88

Raymond Griffith
All Quiet on the Western Front
    '30
Hands Up '26
The Night Club '25
Paths to Paradise '25
White Tiger '23

Thomas Ian Griffith
Excessive Force '93
The Karate Kid: Part 3 '89
Ulterior Motives '92

Tom Griffith
The Alien Factor '78
Hawk and Castile
Night Beast '83

Tracy Griffith
All Tied Up '92
Fast Food '89
The Finest Hour '91
The First Power '89
The Good Mother '88
Skeeter '93
Sleepaway Camp 3: Teenage
    Wasteland '89

Linda Griffiths
Lianna '83
Overdrawn at the Memory
    Bank '83
Reno and the Doc '84

Richard Griffiths
Blame It on the Bellboy '92
Guarding Tess '94
Naked Gun 2 1/2: The Smell of
    Fear '91
Shanghai Surprise '86
Whoops Apocalypse '83
Withnail and I '87

Jeff Griggs
Eden '92
Eden 2 '93
Eden 3 '93
Eden 4 '93

Johanna Grika
Vice Academy 3 '91
Visitants '87

Frank Grimes
Crystalstone '88
The Dive '89

Gary Grimes
Cahill: United States Marshal
    '73
Class of '44 '73
Culpepper Cattle Co. '72
Summer of '42 '71

Scott Grimes
Critters '86
Critters 2: The Main Course '88
Frog '89
Frogs! '90s
It Came Upon a Midnight Clear
    '84
Night Life '90

Tammy Grimes
America '86
Mr. North '88
No Big Deal '83
The Runner Stumbles '79

Herbert Grimwood
Romola '25
When the Clouds Roll By '19

Nikolai Grinko
Andrei Rublev '66
Stalker '79

Stephen Grives
Flambards
Horror Planet '80

George Grizzard
Advise and Consent '62
Attica '80
Bachelor Party '84
Caroline? '90
Comes a Horseman '78

The Deliberate Stranger '86
Embassy '85
False Witness '89
From the Terrace '60
Iran: Days of Crisis '91
Oldest Living Graduate '82
Pueblo Affair '73
Seems Like Old Times '80
The Stranger Within '74
Wrong is Right '82

Charles Grodin
Beethoven '92
Beethoven's 2nd '93
Catch-22 '70
Clifford '91
The Couch Trip '87
Dave '93
11 Harrowhouse '74
The Grass is Always Greener
    Over the Septic Tank '78
The Great Muppet Caper '81
Grown Ups '86
Heart and Souls '93
The Heartbreak Kid '72
Heaven Can Wait '78
The Incredible Shrinking
    Woman '81
Ishtar '87
It Runs in the Family '94
It's My Turn '80
Just Me & You '78
King Kong '76
Last Resort '86
The Lonely Guy '84
The Meanest Men in the West
    '76
Midnight Run '88
Movers and Shakers '85
Real Life '79
Rosemary's Baby '68
Seems Like Old Times '80
Sex and the College Girl '64
So I Married an Axe Murderer
    '93
Sunburn '79
Taking Care of Business '90
The Woman in Red '84
You Can't Hurry Love '88

Kathryn Grody
The Lemon Sisters '90
Parents '89
Quick Change '90

David Groh
A Hero Ain't Nothin' But a
    Sandwich '78
Hot Shot '87
Zertigo Diamond Caper '82

Ake Gronberg
Monika '52
Sawdust & Tinsel '53

Herbert Gronemeyer
Das Boot '81
Spring Symphony '86

Sam Groom
The Baby Maker '70
Betrayal '74
Beyond the Bermuda Triangle
    '75
Deadly Eyes '82
Deadly Games '80
Run for the Roses '78

Arye Gross
Boris and Natasha: The Movie
    '92
The Couch Trip '87
Coupe de Ville '90
The Experts '89
For the Boys '91
Hexed '93
House 2: The Second Story '87
A Matter of Degrees '90
A Midnight Clear '92
The Opposite Sex and How to
    Live With Them '93
Shaking the Tree '92
Soul Man '86
Tequila Sunrise '88

Edan Gross
And You Thought Your Parents
    Were Weird! '91
Best of the Best 2 '93

Mary Gross
Baby Boom '87
Best of Eddie Murphy '89
Big Business '88

Bill Murray Live from the
    Second City '70s
Casual Sex? '88
Club Paradise '86
The Couch Trip '87
Feds '88
There Goes the Neighborhood
    '92
Troop Beverly Hills '89

Michael Gross
Alan & Naomi '92
Big Business '88
Cool As Ice '91
The FBI Murders '88
Summer Fantasy '84
Tremors '89

Paul Gross
Armistead Maupin's Tales of
    the City '93
Aspen Extreme '93
Buffalo Jump '90
Northern Extremes '93

Brigitte Grothum
Inn on the River '62
The Strange Countess '61

Deborah Grover
The Christmas Wife '88
Mania '80s

Robert Grubb
Gallipoli '81
Mad Max: Beyond
    Thunderdome '85
Remember Me '85

Gary Grubbs
The Ernest Green Story '93
Foxfire '87
Without Warning: The James
    Brady Story '91

Franz Gruber
Deutschland im Jahre Null '47
Terror Beneath the Sea '66
X from Outer Space '67

Olivier Gruner
Angel Town '89
Nemesis '93

Dominic Guard
Absolution '81
The Go-Between '71
Picnic at Hanging Rock '75

Kit Guard
El Diablo Rides '39
Fighting Champ '33

Harry Guardino
The Adventures of Bullwhip
    Griffin '66
Any Which Way You Can '80
Dirty Harry '71
The Enforcer '76
Fist of Honor '92
The Five Pennies '59
Get Christie Love! '74
Goldengirl '79
Hell is for Heroes '62
Houseboat '58
Lovers and Other Strangers '70
Madigan '68
Matilda '78
The Neon Empire '89
Octaman '71
Pork Chop Hill '59
Rollercoaster '77
St. Ives '76
They Only Kill Their Masters
    '72
Whiffs '75

Irina Gubanova
Private Life '82
War and Peace '68

Blanca Guerra
Danzon '91
Murderer in the Hotel '83
Santa Sangre '90

Evelyn Guerrero
Cheech and Chong: Things Are
    Tough All Over '82
Cheech and Chong's Next
    Movie '80
Cheech and Chong's Nice
    Dreams '81
The Toolbox Murders '78

Franco Guerrero
American Commandos '84
Deathfight '93
The Kick Fighter '91

One Armed Executioner '80
Warriors of the Apocalypse '85

Monica Guerritore
The Endless Game '89
Together? '79

Fausto Guerzoni
The Bicycle Thief '48
Black Orpheus '58

Christopher Guest
Beyond Therapy '86
Billy Crystal: Don't Get Me
    Started '86
A Few Good Men '92
Girlfriends '78
Heartbeeps '81
The Last Word '80
Little Shop of Horrors '86
The Long Riders '80
A Piano for Mrs. Cimino '82
The Princess Bride '87
The Return of Spinal Tap '92
Sticky Fingers '88
This is Spinal Tap '84

Lance Guest
Halloween 2: The Nightmare
    Isn't Over! '81
I Ought to Be in Pictures '82
Jaws: The Revenge '87
Just the Way You Are '84
The Last Starfighter '84
My Father, My Rival '85
Roommate '84
The Wizard of Loneliness '88

Nicholas Guest
Assassin '89
Chrome Soldiers '92
Criminal Act '88
Dollman '97
Forever: A Ghost of a Love
    Story '92
Grand Tour: Disaster in Time
    '92
The Long Riders '80
My Daughter's Keeper '93
National Lampoon's Christmas
    Vacation '89
Nemesis '93
Strange Case of Dr. Jekyll &
    Mr. Hyde '89

Carla Gugino
Son-in-Law '93
This Boy's Life '93

Wandisa Guida
The Devil's Commandment '56
Gladiator of Rome '63

Giovanni Guidelli
Fiorile '93
Where Angels Fear to Tread
    '91

Nancy Guild
Abbott & Costello Meet the
    Invisible Man '51
Black Magic '49

Paul Guilfoyle
Billy Galvin '86
Cadillac Man '90
The Crime of Dr. Crespi '35
Curiosity Kills '90
Dead Ahead: The Exxon Valdez
    Disaster '92
Fallen Angels 2 '93
Final Analysis '92
Follow Me Quietly '49
The Judge '49
Law of the Underworld '38
The Missing Corpse '45
Mother's Boys '94
The Saint Takes Over '40

Robert Guillaume
Death Warrant '90
Fire and Rain '89
The Kid from Left Field '79
The Kid with the Broken Halo
    '82
The Kid with the 200 I.Q. '83
Lean on Me '89
The Meteor Man '93
North and South Book 1 '85
The Penthouse '92
Prince Jack '83
Seems Like Old Times '80
Superfly T.N.T. '73
They Still Call Me Bruce '86
Wanted Dead or Alive '86
You Must Remember This '90s

Ofelia Guillman
El Forastero Vengador '65
Para Servir a Usted '87

Tim Guinee
American Blue Note '89
Chain of Desire '93
The Night We Never Met '93
Once Around '93
Tai-Pan '86
Vietnam War Story 2 '88

Rick Guinn
Buffalo Rider '78
Mountain Charlie '80

Alec Guinness
The Bridge on the River Kwai
    '57
Brother Sun, Sister Moon '73
Captain's Paradise '53
The Comedians '67
Cromwell '70
Damn the Defiant '62
The Detective '54
Doctor Zhivago '65
The Empire Strikes Back '80
The Fall of the Roman Empire
    '64
From "Star Wars" to "Jedi":
    The Making of a Saga '83
Great Expectations '46
A Handful of Dust '88
Hitler: The Last Ten Days '73
The Horse's Mouth '58
Hotel Paradiso '66
Kafka '91
Kind Hearts and Coronets '49
Ladykillers '55
Last Holiday '50
The Lavender Hill Mob '51
Lawrence of Arabia '62
Little Dorrit, Film 1: Nobody's
    Fault '88
Little Dorrit, Film 2: Little
    Dorrit's Story '88
Little Lord Fauntleroy '80
Lovesick '83
Malta Story '53
The Man in the White Suit '51
Monsignor Quixote '91
Murder by Death '76
Oliver Twist '48
A Passage to India '84
The Prisoner '55
The Promoter '52
The Quiller Memorandum '66
Raise the Titanic '80
Scrooge '70
Star Wars '77
The Swan '56
To Paris with Love '55
To See Such Fun '81
Tunes of Glory '60
Tunes of Glory/Horse's Mouth
    '60

Julien Guiomar
Leolo '92
My New Partner '84
Swashbuckler '84

Tom Guiry
Lassie '94
The Sandlot '93

Tito Guizar
The Gay Ranchero '42
On the Old Spanish Trail '47

Clu Gulager
And Now Miguel '66
Chattanooga Choo Choo '84
Force of One '79
The Glass House '72
He Who Walks Alone '78
The Hidden '87
Hit Lady '74
Hunter's Blood '87
I'm Gonna Git You Sucka '88
The Initiation '84
Into the Night '85
Kenny Rogers as the Gambler
    '80
Kenny Rogers as the Gambler,
    Part 2: The Adventure
    Continues '83
The Killers '64
The Killing Device '92
The Last Picture Show '71
Lies '83
McQ '74
My Heroes Have Always Been
    Cowboys '91

Gulager ►cont.

A Nightmare on Elm Street 2:
  Freddy's Revenge '85
The Offspring '87
The Other Side of Midnight '77
A Question of Love '78
Return of the Living Dead '85
Smile, Jenny, You're Dead '74
Snowblind '78
Tapeheads '89
Teen Vamp '88
Touched by Love '80
The Uninvited '88
Willa '79
Winning '69
Wonderland Cove '75

Dorothy Gulliver
The Fighting Marshal '32
The Galloping Ghost '31
Outlaw Justice '32
Shadow of the Eagle '32
Under Montana Skies '30

David Gulpilil
Crocodile Dundee '86
Dark Age '88
The Last Wave '77
Mad Dog Morgan '76

Moses Gunn
Aaron Loves Angela '75
Amazing Grace '74
Amityville 2: The Possession
  '82
Certain Fury '85
Charlotte Forten's Mission:
  Experiment in Freedom '85
Cornbread, Earl & Me '75
Firestarter '84
The Great White Hope '70
Haunts of the Very Rich '72
Heartbreak Ridge '86
The Hot Rock '70
The House of Dies Drear '88
Killing Floor '85
Memphis '91
The NeverEnding Story '84
Perfect Harmony '91
Ragtime '81
Rollerball '75
Shaft '71
Shaft's Big Score '72
Wild Rovers '71
The Women of Brewster Place
  '89

Bob Gunton
Cookie '89
Dead Ahead: The Exxon Valdez
  Disaster '92
Father Hood '93
Glory '89
Judgment '90
Lois Gibbs and the Love Canal
  '82
Lone Justice '93
Mission of the Shark '91
Rollover '81
Sinatra '92
Static '87
Wild Palms '93

Alizia Gur
Beast of Morocco '66
From Russia with Love '63

Sigrid Gurie
The Adventures of Marco Polo
  '38
Algiers '38
Enemy of Women '44
Three Faces West '40

Eric Gurry
Bad Boys '83
Mystery at Fire Island '81
Something Special '86
The Zoo Gang '85

Louis Guss
American Blue Note '89
The Cemetery Club '93
Moonstruck '87
Nitti: The Enforcer '88
Willie & Phil '80

Arlo Guthrie
Alice's Restaurant '69
Roadside Prophets '92
Woodstock '70

Tani Phelps Guthrie
Daughters of Satan '72
The Thirsty Dead '74

Steve Guttenberg
Amazon Women on the Moon
  '87
Bad Medicine '85
The Bedroom Window '87
The Boys from Brazil '78
Can't Stop the Music '80
The Chicken Chronicles '77
Cocoon '85
Cocoon: The Return '88
The Day After '83
Diner '82
Don't Tell Her It's Me '90
High Spirits '88
The Man Who Wasn't There '83
Miracle on Ice '81
Pecos Bill '86
Police Academy '84
Police Academy 2: Their First
  Assignment '85
Police Academy 3: Back in
  Training '86
Police Academy 4: Citizens on
  Patrol '87
Short Circuit '86
Surrender '87
Three Men and a Baby '87
Three Men and a Little Lady '90
To Race the Wind '80

Lucy Gutteridge
The Secret Garden '87
Top Secret! '84
The Trouble with Spies '87
Tusks '89
The Woman He Loved '88

Ronald Guttman
Iran: Days of Crisis '91
Josh and S.A.M. '93

Jasmine Guy
Harlem Nights '89
Runaway '89
School Daze '88

Sheila Guyse
Boy! What a Girl '45
Miracle in Harlem '48
Sepia Cinderella '47

Joe Guzaldo
Bingo '91
Smooth Talker '90

Luis Guzman
Carlito's Way '93
Guilty as Sin '93
The Hard Way '91
Jumpin' at the Boneyard '92
Mr. Wonderful '93
Q & A '90

**Roberto "Flaco"
Guzman**
Arizona '86
La Hifa Sin Padre '87
Marcados por el Destino '87

Teri Guzman
Escape from Cell Block 3 '78
Women Unchained '70s

Edmund Gwenn
The Bigamist '53
Challenge to Lassie '49
Cheers for Miss Bishop '41
The Devil & Miss Jones '41
Doctor Takes a Wife '40
Foreign Correspondent '40
Forever and a Day '43
Green Dolphin Street '47
The Hills of Home '48
If I Were Rich '33
It's a Dog's Life '55
Java Head '35
The Keys of the Kingdom '44
Lassie, Come Home '43
Life with Father '47
Miracle on 34th Street '47
Pride and Prejudice '40
Skin Game '31
The Student Prince '54
Sylvia Scarlett '35
Them! '54
The Trouble with Harry '55
A Woman of Distinction '50

Jack Gwillim
The Bushbaby '70
Flame Over India '60

Sword of Sherwood Forest '60

Michael Gwynn
Jason and the Argonauts '63
The Scars of Dracula '70

Anne Gwynne
Adam at 6 A.M. '70
Black Tower '50
Breakdown '53
Fear '46
House of Frankenstein '44
Killer Dill '47
King of the Bullwhip '51
Meteor Monster '57
Ride 'Em Cowboy '42

Fred Gwynne
The Boy Who Could Fly '86
The Cotton Club '84
Day with Conrad Green '80
Disorganized Crime '89
Fatal Attraction '87
Ironweed '87
The Littlest Angel '69
The Man That Corrupted
  Hadleyburg '80
Munster's Revenge '81
Murder by the Book '87
My Cousin Vinny '92
The Mysterious Stranger '82
Off Beat '86
Pet Sematary '89
Sanctuary of Fear '79
Shadows and Fog '92
Simon '80
Vanishing Act '88

Michael C. Gwynne
Cherry 2000 '88
Harry Tracy '83
The Last of the Finest '90
Payday '72
Seduced '85
Special Delivery '76
The Streets of L.A. '79

Peter Gwynne
The Dove '74
Puzzle '78
Tim '79

Kim Gyngell
Boulevard of Broken Dreams
  '94
Heaven Tonight '93
The Wacky World of Wills &
  Burke '85

Greta Gynt
The Arsenal Stadium Mystery
  '39
Dear Murderer '47
The Hooded Terror '38
The Human Monster '39
Mr. Emmanuel '44
Sexton Blake and the Hooded
  Terror '38

Hugo Haas
Days of Glory '43
The Fighting Kentuckian '49
Holiday in Mexico '46
King Solomon's Mines '50
Merton of the Movies '47
My Girl Tisa '48
Northwest Outpost '47
The Private Affairs of Bel Ami
  '47

Lukas Haas
Alan & Naomi '92
The Lady in White '88
Leap of Faith '92
Music Box '89
Rambling Rose '91
See You in the Morning '89
Shattered Spirits '91
Solarbabies '86
Witness '85
The Wizard of Loneliness '88

Matthias Habich
Coup de Grace '78
An Occurrence at Owl Creek
  Bridge/Coup de Grace '62
The Savage Woman '91
Straight for the Heart '88

Shelley Hack
Annie Hall '77
Blind Fear '89
A Casualty of War '90
The Finishing Touch '92
If Ever I See You Again '78
Kicks '85

King of Comedy '82
Me, Myself & I '92
Single Bars, Single Women '84
The Stepfather '87
Troll '85

George Hackathorne
The Last of the Mohicans '20
Merry-Go-Round '23
The Worldly Madonna '22

Joseph Hacker
Little Treasure '85
The Ultimate Imposter '79

Buddy Hackett
Bud and Lou '78
God's Little Acre '58
It's a Mad, Mad, Mad, Mad
  World '63
Loose Shoes '80
Muscle Beach Party '64
The Music Man '62
Scrooged '88
The Wonderful World of the
  Brothers Grimm '62

Joan Hackett
Class of '63 '73
Dead of Night '77
The Escape Artist '82
Flicks '85
The Group '66
The Last of Sheila '73
The Long Days of Summer '80
One Trick Pony '80
Only When I Laugh '81
The Possessed '77
Reflections of Murder '74
Rivals '72
Support Your Local Sheriff '69
The Terminal Man '74
The Treasure of Matecumbe
  '76
Will Penny '67

Karl Hackett
Border Phantom '37
Cavalry '36
Feud Maker '38
Gun Lords of Stirrup Basin '37
His Brother's Ghost '45
Lightning Raiders '46
Outlaw of the Plains '46
Phantom Ranger '38
The Red Rope '37
Sagebrush Law '43
Songs and Bullets '38
Sonora Stagecoach '44
Take Me Back to Oklahoma '40

Sandy Hackett
Ex-Cop '93
Hamburger...The Motion
  Picture '86

Gene Hackman
All Night Long '81
America at the Movies '76
Another Woman '88
Bat 21 '88
Bite the Bullet '75
Bonnie & Clyde '67
A Bridge Too Far '77
Class Action '91
Company Business '91
The Conversation '74
Doctors' Wives '70
The Domino Principle '77
Downhill Racer '69
Eureka! '81
The Firm '93
The French Connection '71
French Connection 2 '75
Full Moon in Blue Water '88
Geronimo: An American
  Legend '93
Hawaii '66
Hoosiers '86
I Never Sang For My Father '70
Lilith '64
Loose Cannons '90
March or Die '77
Marooned '69
Mississippi Burning '88
Misunderstood '84
Narrow Margin '90
Night Moves '75
No Way Out '87
The Package '89
The Poseidon Adventure '72
Postcards from the Edge '90
Power '86
Prime Cut '72

The Quick and the Dead '94
Reds '81
Riot '69
Scarecrow '73
Split Decisions '88
Superman: The Movie '78
Superman 2 '80
Superman 4: The Quest for
  Peace '87
Target '85
Twice in a Lifetime '85
Uncommon Valor '83
Under Fire '83
Unforgiven '92
Wyatt Earp '94
Zandy's Bride '74

Dayle Haddon
Bedroom Eyes '86
The Cheaters '76
Cyborg '89
Hitchhiker 3 '87
North Dallas Forty '79
Paperback Hero '73
The World's Greatest Athlete
  '73

Ron Haddrick
Great Expectations: The Untold
  Story '87
Quigley Down Under '90

Sara Haden
Andy Hardy Gets Spring Fever
  '39
Andy Hardy Meets Debutante
  '40
Andy Hardy's Double Life '42
Andy Hardy's Private Secretary
  '41
Finishing School '33
The Great Rupert '50
A Life of Her Own '50
Love Laughs at Andy Hardy '46
Mad Love '35
Mr. Ace '46
Our Vines Have Tender Grapes
  '45
The Poor Little Rich Girl '36
The Shop Around the Corner
  '40
Somewhere I'll Find You '42

Reed Hadley
The Bank Dick '40
Baron of Arizona '51
Brain of Blood '71
Dark Corner '46
Doll Face '46
Guadalcanal Diary '43
The Half-Breed '51
Hollywood Stadium Mystery '38
I Shot Jesse James '49
Kansas Pacific '53
Little Big Horn '51
Return of Jesse James '50
Rimfire '49
A Southern Yankee '48
Whistling in the Dark '41
Ziegfeld Girl '41
Zorro's Fighting Legion '39

Molly Hagan
Code of Silence '85
Some Kind of Wonderful '87

Jean Hagen
Adam's Rib '50
Alexander: The Other Side of
  Dawn '77
The Asphalt Jungle '50
The Big Knife '55
Latin Lovers '53
A Life of Her Own '50
Panic in the Year Zero! '62
The Shaggy Dog '59
Singin' in the Rain '52
Sunrise at Campobello '60

Ross Hagen
Alienator '89
Angel '84
Angels' Wild Women '72
Armed Response '86
Avenging Angel '85
Bad Charleston Charlie '73
Blood Games '90
B.O.R.N. '88
Commando Squad '87
The Deadly and the Beautiful
  '73
Dinosaur Island '93
Hellcats '68
Marked for Murder '89

Night Creature '79
Phantom Empire '87
Speedway '68
Star Slammer '87
Warlords '88

Uta Hagen
The Boys from Brazil '78
The Other '72
Reversal of Fortune '90

Julie Hagerty
Airplane! '80
Airplane 2: The Sequel '82
Bad Medicine '85
Beyond Therapy '86
Bloodhounds of Broadway '89
The Day the Women Got Even '80
Goodbye, New York '85
Lost in America '85
A Midsummer Night's Sex Comedy '82
Necessary Parties '88
Noises Off '92
Reversal of Fortune '90
Rude Awakening '89
What About Bob? '91

Dan Haggerty
Abducted '86
The Adventures of Frontier Fremont '75
Angels Die Hard '84
Blood Brothers '77
Bury Me an Angel '71
California Gold Rush '81
The Capture of Grizzly Adams '82
Chance '89
The Channeler '89
The Chilling '89
Deadly Diamonds '91
Desperate Women '78
Elves '89
Ice Pawn '92
The Inheritor '90
King of the Mountain '81
Life & Times of Grizzly Adams '74
Mind Trap '91
Night Wars '88
Repo Jake '90
The Shrieking '73
Soldier's Fortune '91
Spirit of the Eagle '90
Starbird and Sweet William '73
The Tender Warrior '71
Terror Out of the Sky '78
When the North Wind Blows '74

Marvin Hagler
Indio '90
Indio 2: The Revolt '92

Larry Hagman
Antonio '73
The Big Bus '76
Deadly Encounter '72
The Eagle Has Landed '77
Ensign Pulver '64
Fail-Safe '64
The Group '66
Harry and Tonto '74
Hurricane '74
In Harm's Way '65
Intimate Strangers '77
Mother, Jugs and Speed '76
No Place to Run '72
President's Mistress '78
S.O.B. '81
Son of Blob '72
Three in the Cellar '70

Archie Hahn
Glory Years '87
Meatballs 2 '84
Pray TV '80
Protocol '84

Gisela Hahn
Big Boss '77
Mr. Scarface '77

Jess Hahn
The Grand Duel '73
Mama Dracula '80
Mean Frank and Crazy Tony '75
The Night of the Following Day '69
Secret Agent Super Dragon '66
Triple Cross '67

Jessica Hahn
Bikini Summer 2 '92
Thunder & Mud '89

Mang Hai
Buddha Assassinator '82
Hell's Wind Staff '82

Charles Haid
Altered States '80
Children in the Crossfire '84
The Chinatown Murders: Man Against the Mob '92
The Choirboys '77
Cooperstown '93
Cop '88
Deathmoon '78
Fire and Rain '89
The Fire Next Time '93
Freeze Frame '92
The Great Escape 2: The Untold Story '88
Hill Street Blues, Vol. 1: Hill Street Station '81
Night Breed '90
Oliver's Story '78
The Rescue '88
Storyville '92
Twirl '81
Weekend War '88
Who'll Stop the Rain? '78

Ion Haiduc
Bloodlust: Subspecies 3 '93
Bloodstone: Subspecies 2 '93

Sid Haig
The Big Bird Cage '72
The Big Doll House '71
Busting '74
Chrome Hearts '70
Commando Squad '87
The Deadly and the Beautiful '73
The Forbidden Dance '90
Spider Baby '64
Track of the Vampire '66
Warlords '88
Wizards of the Lost Kingdom 2 '89

Kenneth Haigh
The Bitch '79
Cleopatra '63
Teenage Bad Girl '59

Louisa Haigh
Murderers Among Us: The Simon Wiesenthal Story '89
Shipwrecked '91

Marian Hailey
Jenny '70
Lovers and Other Strangers '70

Corey Haim
Blown Away '90s
The Double O Kid '92
Dream a Little Dream '89
Dream Machine '91
Fast Getaway '91
First Born '84
Just One of the Girls '93
License to Drive '88
The Lost Boys '87
Lucas '86
Murphy's Romance '85
Oh, What a Night '92
Prayer of the Rollerboys '91
Secret Admirer '85
Silver Bullet '85
A Time to Live '85
Watchers '88

Patricia Haines
Night Caller from Outer Space '66
The Virgin Witch '70

William Haines
The Girl Said No '37
Little Annie Rooney '25
Show People '28
Way Out West '37

Alan Hale
Action in the North Atlantic '43
Adventures of Don Juan '49
The Adventures of Marco Polo '38
The Adventures of Mark Twain '44
The Adventures of Robin Hood '38
Algiers '38
Captains of the Clouds '42

The Covered Wagon '23
Desperate Journey '42
Destination Tokyo '43
Dick Turpin '25
Dodge City '39
The Fighting 69th '40
The Four Horsemen of the Apocalypse '21
Gentleman Jim '42
The Inspector General '49
It Happened One Night '34
Last Days of Pompeii '35
The Leatherneck '28
Listen, Darling '38
Little Minister '34
The Lost Patrol '34
The Man I Love '46
The Man in the Iron Mask '39
My Girl Tisa '48
Night and Day '46
Of Human Bondage '34
Our Relations '36
Power '28
The Prince and the Pauper '37
The Private Lives of Elizabeth & Essex '39
Pursued '47
Robin Hood '22
Santa Fe Trail '40
The Scarlet Letter '34
The Sea Hawk '40
The Sin of Madelon Claudet '31
South of St. Louis '48
Stars in My Crown '50
Stella Dallas '37
Strawberry Blonde '41
Susan Lenox: Her Fall and Rise '31
Thank Your Lucky Stars '43
They Drive by Night '40
Thin Ice '37
This is the Army '43
To the Shores of Tripoli '42
The Trap '22
Virginia City '40
When Thief Meets Thief '37

Alan Hale, Jr.
All Mine to Give '56
At Sword's Point '51
Big Trees '52
Casey Jones and Fury (Brave Stallion) '57
The Crawling Hand '63
The Fifth Musketeer '79
The Giant Spider Invasion '75
Gilligan's Island: Meet the Crew '64
Hambone & Hillie '84
Hard Drivin' '60
Home Town Story '51
The Indian Fighter '55
It Happens Every Spring '49
Johnny Dangerously '84
The North Avenue Irregulars '79
Rim of the Canyon '49
The Spirit of West Point '47
There was a Crooked Man '70
The Underworld Story '50
Up Periscope '59
The West Point Story '50
Young at Heart '54

Barbara Hale
The Boy with the Green Hair '48
Buckskin '68
The Clay Pigeon '49
The Defense Never Rests '90
The Falcon in Hollywood '44
First Yank into Tokyo '45
Flight of the Grey Wolf '76
The Giant Spider Invasion '75
Going to Town '44
The Jackpot '50
Jolson Sings Again '49
Last of the Comanches '52
A Lion is in the Streets '53
The Oklahoman '56
Perry Mason Returns '85
Perry Mason: The Case of the Lost Love '87
Seventh Cavalry '56
West of the Pecos '45
The Window '49

Binnie Hale
Love from a Stranger '37
The Phantom Light '35

Creighton Hale
Broken Hearts of Broadway '23
The Cat and the Canary '27
The Idol Dancer '20
The Marriage Circle '24
Shop Angel '32
Way Down East '20

Georgina Hale
The Boy Friend '71
Castaway '87
The Gold Rush '25
Gold Rush/Payday '25
Mahler '74

Jean Hale
In Like Flint '67
Psychomania '63
The St. Valentine's Day Massacre '67

Jonathan Hale
Blondie '38
Blondie Has Trouble '40
Blondie in Society '41
Blondie Knows Best '46
Blondie's Blessed Event '42
Bringing Up Baby '38
Call Northside 777 '48
Exiled to Shanghai '37
Hollywood Canteen '44
It's a Great Life '43
The Judge '49
The Saint Strikes Back '39
The Saint Takes Over '40
The Saint's Double Trouble '40
Saratoga '37
Silver River '48

Louise Closser Hale
Devotion '31
Platinum Blonde '31
Shanghai Express '32
Today We Live '33

Monte Hale
Missourians '50
Pioneer Marshal '49
Son of God's Country '48
Trail of Robin Hood '50
The Vanishing Westerner '50
Western Double Feature 2: Wayne & Hale '80s
Western Double Feature 8: Hale & Carradine '40s

Sonnie Hale
Evergreen '34
It's Love Again '36

Jack Haley
Alexander's Ragtime Band '38
George White's Scandals '45
Higher and Higher '44
Moon Over Miami '41
One Body Too Many '44
People Are Funny '46
Pick a Star '37
The Poor Little Rich Girl '36
Rebecca of Sunnybrook Farm '38
Take It Big '44
Treasure of Fear '45
The Wizard of Oz '39

Jackie Earle Haley
The Bad News Bears '76
The Bad News Bears Go to Japan '78
The Bad News Bears in Breaking Training '77
Breaking Away '79
Damnation Alley '77
Dollman '91
Losin' It '82
The Zoo Gang '85

H.B. Halicki
Deadline Auto Theft '83
Gone in 60 Seconds '74
The Junkman '82

Albert Hall
Apocalypse Now '79
Betrayed '88
Hearts of Darkness: A Filmmaker's Apocalypse '91
The Long, Hot Summer '86
Malcolm X '92
Separate But Equal '91
Uncle Tom's Cabin '87

Anthony Michael Hall
The Breakfast Club '85

Edward Scissorhands '90
Hail Caesar '94
Into the Sun '92
Johnny Be Good '88
National Lampoon's Vacation '83
Out of Bounds '86
Six Degrees of Separation '93
Six Pack '82
Sixteen Candles '84
Weird Science '85

Arch Hall, Jr.
The Choppers '61
Deadwood '65
Eegah! '62
Nasty Rabbit '64
The Sadist '63
Wild Guitar '62

Archie Hall
Border Badmen '45
His Brother's Ghost '45

Arsenio Hall
Amazon Women on the Moon '87
Coming to America '88
Harlem Nights '89

Brad Hall
Best of Eddie Murphy '89
Limit Up '89
Worth Winning '89

Charlie Hall
A Chump at Oxford '40
Laurel & Hardy Comedy Classics, Vol. 1 '33
Laurel & Hardy Comedy Classics, Vol. 6 '35

Delores Hall
Leap of Faith '92
Lethal Weapon 3 '92

Ellen Hall
Raiders of the Border '44
Range Law '44

Grayson Hall
Adam at 6 A.M. '70
House of Dark Shadows '70
Night of Dark Shadows '71
The Night of the Iguana '64
Satan in High Heels '62

Henry Hall
The Ape '40
Lightning Raiders '45
Midnight Warning '32
Rainbow Ranch '33

Huntz Hall
Angels with Dirty Faces '38
Auntie Lee's Meat Pies '92
Blues Busters '50
Bowery Blitzkrieg '41
Bowery Buckaroos '47
Clipped Wings '53
Cyclone '87
The Escape Artist '82
Follow the Leader '44
Gas Pump Girls '79
Gentle Giant '67
Ghost Chasers '51
Hard-Boiled Mahoney '47
Here Come the Marines '52
Junior G-Men '40
Junior G-Men of the Air '42
Kid Dynamite '43
Let's Get Tough '42
Little Tough Guy '38
Master Minds '49
Million Dollar Kid '44
Mr. Wise Guy '42
'Neath Brooklyn Bridge '42
Pride of the Bowery '41
Smart Alecks '42
Smugglers' Cove '48
Spook Busters '46
Spooks Run Wild '41
Valentino '77
Zis Boom Bah '42

James Hall
Hell's Angels '30
Hotel Imperial '27
Millie '31

Jerry Hall
Batman '89
Running Out of Luck '86

Jon Hall
Ali Baba and the Forty Thieves '43

Hall ►cont.

Arabian Nights '42
The Beach Girls and the
  Monster '65
Cobra Woman '44
Deputy Marshall '50
Hell Ship Mutiny '57
Hurricane '37
Invisible Agent '42
The Invisible Man's Revenge
  '44
Kit Carson '40
The Last of the Redmen '47
The Lion Man '36
The Prince of Thieves '48
South of Pago Pago '40
The Tuttles of Tahiti '42

Juanita Hall
Flower Drum Song '61
Paradise in Harlem '40
South Pacific '58

Kevin Peter Hall
Harry and the Hendersons '87
Highway to Hell '92
Misfits of Science '85
Predator '87

Lois Hall
Dead Again '91
Kalifornia '93
Pirates of the High Seas '50

Michael Keys Hall
Blackout '88
Flight of Black Angel '91

Philip Baker Hall
Blue Desert '91
The Last Reunion '80
Secret Honor '85
Three O'Clock High '87

Porter Hall
Arizona '40
The Beautiful Blonde from
  Bashful Bend '49
Bulldog Drummond Escapes
  '37
Bulldog Drummond's Peril '38
Bulldog Drummond's Revenge/
  Bulldog Drummond's Peril
  '38
The Case of the Lucky Legs '35
Double Indemnity '44
The General Died at Dawn '36
Going My Way '44
The Great Moment '44
The Half-Breed '51
His Girl Friday '40
Intruder in the Dust '49
Miracle of Morgan's Creek '44
Miracle on 34th Street '47
Mr. Smith Goes to Washington
  '39
Petrified Forest '36
The Plainsman '37
Satan Met a Lady '36
The Story of Louis Pasteur '36
Sullivan's Travels '41
They Shall Have Music '39
The Thin Man '34
Weekend at the Waldorf '45
The Woman of the Town '44

Rich Hall
Million Dollar Mystery '87
Rich Hall's Vanishing America
  '86

Ruth Hall
Between Fighting Men '32
Man from Monterey '33
Monkey Business '31
The Return of Casey Jones '34
Ride Him, Cowboy '32
Strawberry Roan '33

Shannah Hall
Boogey Man 2 '83
The Princess & the Call Girl '84

Thurston Hall
The Black Room '35
Call of the Canyon '42
Crash Dive '43
Each Dawn I Die '39
The Great Gildersleeve '43
I Dood It '43
In Society '44
The Invisible Woman '40
Lady from Nowhere '36

Night Stage to Galveston '52
Rim of the Canyon '49
West of the Pecos '45
You Can't Cheat an Honest
  Man '39

Zooey Hall
Fortune and Men's Eyes '71
I Dismember Mama '74

Lillian Hall-Davies
The Farmer's Wife '28
The Ring '27

Charles Hallahan
Body of Evidence '92
Margin for Murder '81
Pale Rider '85
The Thing '82
True Believer '89
Vision Quest '85
Warlock: The Armageddon '93
Wild Palms '93
A Winner Never Quits '86

John Hallam
Dragonslayer '81
Lifeforce '85
The Offence '73
Under Capricorn '82

Jane Hallaren
Lianna '83
A Night in the Life of Jimmy
  Reardon '88

Tom Hallick
Hangar 18 '80
A Rare Breed '81

John Halliday
Consolation Marriage '31
Finishing School '33
The Philadelphia Story '40

Peter Halliday
Fast Kill '73
Millie '31

Lori Hallier
Blindside '88
The Gunfighters '87
Higher Education '88
My Bloody Valentine '81

William Halligan
Jive Junction '43
Robot Pilot '41
Turf Boy '42

Billy Halop
Angels with Dirty Faces '38
Junior G-Men '40
Junior G-Men of the Air '42
Little Tough Guy '38
Pride of the Bowery '41

Luke Halpin
Flipper '63
Flipper's New Adventure '64
Flipper's Odyssey '66
If It's Tuesday, This Must Be
  Belgium '69
Island of the Lost '68
Matinee '92
Peter Pan '60
Shock Waves '77

Brett Halsey
Atomic Submarine '59
Black Cat '90
The Crash of Flight 401 '78
Dangerous Obsession '88
The Girl in Lover's Lane '60
Jet Over the Atlantic '59
Magnificent Adventurer '76
Return of the Fly '59
Return to Peyton Place '61
Submarine Seahawk '59
Twice-Told Tales '63

Michael Halsey
Dollman '91
Treasure Island '89
Under the Gun '88

Charles Halton
Across the Pacific '42
The Adventurer '17
The Best Years of Our Lives
  '46
Captains of the Clouds '42
Carrie '52
Come and Get It '36
Dance Hall '41
Dead End '37
Dr. Cyclops '40
Doctor Takes a Wife '40
Dodge City '39

Dodsworth '36
Enemy of Women '44
Foreign Correspondent '40
Friendly Persuasion '56
Golden Boy '39
Heaven Can Wait '43
Here Comes the Groom '51
I Am the Law '38
If You Knew Susie '48
In Old California '42
It's a Wonderful Life '46
Jesse James '39
Juarez '39
The Lady is Willing '42
Lady Scarface '41
Look Who's Laughing '41
Mad Miss Manton '38
Mr. & Mrs. Smith '41
My Dear Secretary '49
Nancy Drew, Reporter '39
Pick a Star '37
Prisoner of Zenda '37
Rhapsody in Blue '45
Room Service '38
Saboteur '42
The Saint in New York '38
The Shop Around the Corner
  '40
Sister Kenny '46
The Spoilers '42
A Star is Born '54
Stranger on the Third Floor '40
They Drive by Night '40
The Thin Man Goes Home '44
To Be or Not to Be '42
A Tree Grows in Brooklyn '45
Up in Arms '44
Virginia City '40
The Westerner '40
Wilson '44
The Young in Heart '38
Young Mr. Lincoln '39

Mie Hama
What's Up, Tiger Lily? '66
You Only Live Twice '67

Veronica Hamel
Cannonball '76
The Gathering '77
The Gathering: Part 2 '79
Hill Street Blues, Vol. 1: Hill
  Street Station '81
A New Life '88
Sessions '83
Snowbling '78
Taking Care of Business '90

Jayne Hamil
Vice Academy '88
Vice Academy 2 '90

Mark Hamill
The Big Red One '80
Black Magic Woman '91
Body Bags '93
Britannia Hospital '82
The City '76
Corvette Summer '78
The Empire Strikes Back '80
Eric '73
The Flash 2: Revenge of the
  Trickster '91
The Guyver '91
The Night the Lights Went Out
  in Georgia '81
Return of the Jedi '83
Slipstream '89
Star Wars '77
Time Runner '92

Antony Hamilton
Howling 4: The Original
  Nightmare '88
Mirrors '85
Samson and Delilah '84

Bernie Hamilton
Bucktown '75
Captain Sinbad '63
The Losers '70
Scream Blacula Scream '73
The Young One '61

Carrie Hamilton
Cool World '92
Shag: The Movie '89
Tokyo Pop '88

George Hamilton
Amore! '93
Angel Baby '61
By Love Possessed '61
The Dead Don't Die '75
Doc Hollywood '91

Evel Knievel '72
Express to Terror '79
From Hell to Victory '79
The Godfather, Part 3 '90
The Happy Hooker Goes to
  Washington '77
Home from the Hill '60
Killer on Board '77
Love at First Bite '79
Medusa '74
Monte Carlo '86
Once is Not Enough '75
Once Upon a Crime '92
Poker Alice '87
The Seekers '79
Sextette '78
Togetherness '70
Two Fathers' Justice '85
Two Weeks in Another Town
  '62
Users '78
Viva Maria! '65
Where the Boys Are '60
Zorro, the Gay Blade '81

Hale Hamilton
The Champ '31
Murder at Midnight '31
Susan Lenox: Her Fall and Rise
  '31

Jane Hamilton
Bedroom Eyes 2 '89
Bloodsucking Pharoahs of
  Pittsburgh '90
Cleo/Leo '89
Deranged '87
New York's Finest '87
Slammer Girls '87
Wildest Dreams '90

John Hamilton
Bandit King of Texas '49
Fangs of the Living Dead '68
The Fatal Hour '40
I Killed That Man '42
On the Waterfront '54
Outcasts of the City '58
Phantom Killer '42
The Saint's Double Trouble '40

Josh Hamilton
Alive '93
O Pioneers! '91
With Honors '94

Judd Hamilton
Gun Crazy '69
The Last Horror Film '82
Star Crash '78

Linda Hamilton
Black Moon Rising '86
Children of the Corn '84
King Kong Lives '86
Mr. Destiny '90
Rape and Marriage: The
  Rideout Case '80
Secret Weapons '85
The Stone Boy '84
Tag: The Assassination Game
  '82
The Terminator '84
Terminator 2: Judgment Day
  '91

Margaret Hamilton
The Adventures of Tom Sawyer
  '38
The Anderson Tapes '71
Breaking the Ice '38
Brewster McCloud '70
Broadway Bill '34
City Without Men '43
Comin' Round the Mountain '51
George White's Scandals '45
Guest in the House '45
The Invisible Woman '40
Moon's Our Home '36
My Little Chickadee '40
Nothing Sacred '37
People Will Talk '51
The Red Pony '49
The Sin of Harold Diddlebock
  '47
These Three '36
13 Ghosts '60
The Wizard of Oz '39
You Only Live Once '37

Murray Hamilton
The Amityville Horror '79
Anatomy of a Murder '59
The Boston Strangler '68
The Brotherhood '68

Brubaker '80
Casey's Shadow '78
Darby's Rangers '58
The Drowning Pool '75
The FBI Story '59
The Graduate '67
Houseboat '58
The Hustler '61
If It's Tuesday, This Must Be
  Belgium '69
Jaws '75
Jaws 2 '78
Last Cry for Help '79
The Last Days of Patton '86
Mazes and Monsters '82
1941 '79
No Time for Sergeants '58
No Way to Treat a Lady '68
Papa's Delicate Condition '63
Sergeant Ryker '68
Spirit of St. Louis '57
The Tattered Web '71
Too Scared to Scream '85
The Way We Were '73

Neil Hamilton
America/The Fall of Babylon
  '24
The Animal Kingdom '32
The Devil's Hand '61
Hollywood Stadium Mystery '38
Isn't Life Wonderful '24
King of Texas Rangers '41
Laughing Sinners '31
The Patsy '64
The Saint Strikes Back '39
The Sin of Madelon Claudet '31
Tarzan and His Mate '34
Tarzan, the Ape Man '32
What Price Hollywood? '32
The White Rose '23
X Marks the Spot '42

Patricia Hamilton
Anne of Avonlea '87
Anne of Green Gables '85
The Christmas Wife '88

Richard Hamilton
In Country '89
Sommersby '93

Suzanna Hamilton
Brimstone & Treacle '82
Duel of Hearts '92
1984 '84
Out of Africa '85
Tale of a Vampire '92
Wetherby '85

Tony Hamilton
Fatal Instinct '92
Nocturna '79

Harry Hamlin
Blue Skies Again '83
Clash of the Titans '81
Deceptions '90
Dinner at Eight '89
King of the Mountain '81
L.A. Law '86
Laguna Heat '87
Making Love '82
Maxie '85
Movie, Movie '78
Murder So Sweet '93
Save Me '93
Target: Favorite Son '87
Under Investigation '93

Ben Hammer
Crazy People '90
The Execution of Private Slovik
  '74
Invasion of the Bee Girls '73
Survival Quest '89

John Hammond
The Blue and the Gray '85
Enforcer from Death Row '78
The Prodigal '83

Kay Hammond
Abraham Lincoln '30
Blithe Spirit '45

Nicholas Hammond
The Amazing Spider-Man '77
Chinese Web '78
The Martian Chronicles: Part 1
  '79
The Martian Chronicles: Part 3
  '79
The Sound of Music '65
Spiderman: The Deadly Dust
  '78

Trouble in Paradise '88

Olivia Hamnett
Deadly Possession '88
Earthling '80
The Last Wave '77
Plunge Into Darkness '77

Walter Hampden
The Adventures of Mark Twain '44
Five Fingers '52
The Hunchback of Notre Dame '39
The Prodigal '55
Reap the Wild Wind '42
Sabrina '54

Susan Hampshire
Baffled '72
Cry Terror '74
David Copperfield '70
The Fighting Prince of Donegal '66
Living Free '72
The Story of David '76
Those Daring Young Men in Their Jaunty Jalopies '69
The Three Lives of Thomasina '63

James Hampton
The Amazing Howard Hughes '77
The China Syndrome '79
Condorman '81
Force Five '75
Hangar 18 '80
Hawmps! '76
Teen Wolf '85
World War III '86

Lionel Hampton
The Benny Goodman Story '55
Force of Impulse '60

Paul Hampton
Deadly Exposure '93
Hit! '73
Private Duty Nurses '71
They Came from Within '75

Master Bong Soo Han
Force: Five '81
Kill the Golden Goose '79

John Hancock
Archer: The Fugitive from the Empire '81
The Black Marble '79
In the Custody of Strangers '82
Traxx '89
Why Me? '90

Sheila Hancock
Buster '88
Hawks '89
Three Men and a Little Lady '90

Irene Handl
Adventures of a Private Eye '87
Morgan! '66
The Private Life of Sherlock Holmes '70
Riding High '78
Small Hotel '57
Wonderwall: The Movie '69

James Handy
Arachnophobia '90
Bird '88
Burglar '87
False Arrest '92
K-9 '89
The Preppie Murder '89
The Rocketeer '91

Daryl Haney
Daddy's Boys '87
Lords of the Deep '89

Helen Hanft
Stardust Memories '80
Used People '92

Roger Hanin
Day of Atonement '93
My Other Husband '85
Rocco and His Brothers '60

Larry Hankin
Armed and Dangerous '86
Black Magic Woman '91
Out on a Limb '92

Tom Hanks
Bachelor Party '84
Big '88
The Bonfire of the Vanities '90

The 'Burbs '89
Dragnet '87
Every Time We Say Goodbye '86
Forrest Gump '94
He Knows You're Alone '80
Joe Versus the Volcano '90
A League of Their Own '92
The Man with One Red Shoe '85
Mazes and Monsters '82
The Money Pit '86
Nothing in Common '86
Philadelphia '93
Punchline '88
Sleepless in Seattle '93
Splash '84
Turner and Hooch '89
Volunteers '85

Jenny Hanley
Flesh and Blood Show '73
On Her Majesty's Secret Service '69
The Scars of Dracula '70

Jimmy Hanley
The Blue Lamp '49
Captive Heart '47
Housemaster '38
Room to Let '49
Salute John Citizen '42

Daryl Hannah
At Play in the Fields of the Lord '91
Attack of the 50 Ft. Woman '93
Blade Runner '82
The Clan of the Cave Bear '86
Crazy People '90
The Final Terror '83
The Fury '78
Grumpy Old Men '93
Hard Country '81
High Spirits '88
Legal Eagles '86
The Little Rascals '94
Memoirs of an Invisible Man '92
The Pope of Greenwich Village '84
Reckless '84
Roxanne '87
Splash '84
Steel Magnolias '89
Summer Lovers '82
Wall Street '87

Page Hannah
Creepshow 2 '87
My Man Adam '86
Racing with the Moon '84
Shag: The Movie '89

Gale Hansen
Dead Poets Society '89
The Deadly and the Beautiful '73
Double Vision '92
The Finest Hour '91
Shaking the Tree '92

Gunnar Hansen
The Demon Lover '77
Hollywood Chainsaw Hookers '88
The Texas Chainsaw Massacre '74

Joachim Hansen
Frozen Alive '64
Secret of the Black Trunk '62

Patti Hansen
Hard to Hold '84
They All Laughed '81

Lars Hanson
The Atonement of Gosta Berling '24
The Flesh and the Devil '27
Homecoming '28
Walpurgis Night '41
The Wind '28

Setsuko Hara
Early Summer '51
The Idiot '51
Late Spring '49
No Regrets for Our Youth '46
Tokyo Story '53

Meiko Harada
Akira Kurosawa's Dreams '90
Nomugi Pass '79
Ran '85

Haya Harareet
Ben-Hur '59
Hill 24 Doesn't Answer '55
The Interns '62
Journey Beneath the Desert '61

Clement Harari
Flight of the Eagle '82
Monkeys, Go Home! '66

Ernest Harden
The Final Terror '83
White Mama '80

Marcia Gay Harden
Crush '93
Fever '91
Late for Dinner '91
Miller's Crossing '90
Sinatra '92
Used People '92

Kate Hardie
Conspiracy '89
Mona Lisa '86

Jerry Hardin
Blaze '89
The Firm '93
Hot Spot '90
Wanted Dead or Alive '86
Wolf Lake '79

Melora Hardin
Big Man on Campus '89
Dead Poets Society '89
Iron Eagle '86
Lambada '89
The North Avenue Irregulars '79
The Rocketeer '91

Ty Hardin
Bad Jim '89
Battle of the Bulge '65
Berserk! '67
I Married a Monster from Outer Space '58
Merrill's Marauders '62
One Step to Hell '68
Palm Springs Weekend '63
PT 109 '63
Rooster: Spurs of Death! '83
You're Jinxed, Friend, You've Met Sacramento '70

Ann Harding
The Animal Kingdom '32
Devotion '31
Love from a Stranger '37
The Magnificent Yankee '50
The Man in the Gray Flannel Suit '56
Promise to Murder '56
Two Weeks with Love '50

John Harding
The Impossible Years '68
This Property is Condemned '66

Kay Harding
The Mummy's Curse '44
Scarlet Claw '44

Lyn Harding
The Man Who Lived Again '36
Murder at the Baskervilles '37
The Mutiny of the Elsinore '39
Old Spanish Custom '36
Sherlock Holmes: The Silver Blaze '41
The Speckled Band '31

Kadeem Hardison
Beat Street '84
Def by Temptation '90
Dream Date '93
Gunmen '93
I'm Gonna Git You Sucka '88
Renaissance Man '94
School Daze '88
White Men Can't Jump '92

Cedric Hardwicke
Becky Sharp '35
Beware of Pity '46
Botany Bay '53
Commandos Strike at Dawn '43
A Connecticut Yankee in King Arthur's Court '49
The Desert Fox '51
Diane '55
Five Weeks in a Balloon '62
The Ghost of Frankenstein '42
The Ghoul '34
The Green Glove '52

The Howards of Virginia '40
The Hunchback of Notre Dame '39
I Remember Mama '48
Invisible Agent '42
The Invisible Man Returns '40
The Keys of the Kingdom '44
King Solomon's Mines '37
Les Miserables '35
The Lodger '44
The Magic Fountain '61
Nicholas Nickleby '46
Nine Days a Queen '34
On Borrowed Time '39
Power '34
Richard III '55
Rope '48
Salome '53
Stanley and Livingstone '39
Sundown '41
Suspicion '41
The Ten Commandments '56
Things to Come '36
Tom Brown's School Days '40
Tycoon '47
Valley of the Sun '42
The White Tower '50
Wilson '44
A Wing and a Prayer '44
The Winslow Boy '48

Edward Hardwicke
The Adventures of Sherlock Holmes: Hound of the Baskervilles '89
Shadowlands '93
Sherlock Holmes: The Master Blackmailer '92

Jonathon Hardy
The Devil's Playground '76
Lonely Hearts '82
The Wacky World of Wills & Burke '85

Oliver Hardy
Air Raid Wardens '43
Bakery/Grocery Clerk '21
Bellhop/The Noon Whistle '22
Block-heads '38
Bohemian Girl '36
Bonnie Scotland '35
Bullfighters '45
A Chump at Oxford '40
Comedy Classics '35
Days of Thrills and Laughter '61
The Devil's Brother '33
A Few Moments with Buster Keaton and Laurel and Hardy '63
The Fighting Kentuckian '49
The Flying Deuces '39
Golden Age of Comedy '58
Great Guns '41
Hollywood Clowns '85
Hollywood Party '34
Laurel & Hardy and the Family '33
Laurel & Hardy: Another Fine Mess '30
Laurel & Hardy: At Work '32
Laurel & Hardy: Be Big '31
Laurel & Hardy: Below Zero '30
Laurel & Hardy: Berth Marks '29
Laurel & Hardy: Blotto '30
Laurel & Hardy: Brats '30
Laurel & Hardy: Chickens Come Home '31
Laurel & Hardy Comedy Classics, Vol. 1 '33
Laurel & Hardy Comedy Classics, Vol. 2 '30
Laurel & Hardy Comedy Classics, Vol. 3 '34
Laurel & Hardy Comedy Classics, Vol. 4 '32
Laurel & Hardy Comedy Classics, Vol. 5 '31
Laurel & Hardy Comedy Classics, Vol. 6 '35
Laurel & Hardy Comedy Classics, Vol. 7 '30s
Laurel & Hardy Comedy Classics, Vol. 8 '30s
Laurel & Hardy Comedy Classics, Vol. 9 '30s
Laurel & Hardy: Hog Wild '30
Laurel & Hardy: Laughing Gravy '31
Laurel & Hardy: Men O'War '29

Laurel & Hardy: Night Owls '30
Laurel & Hardy On the Lam '30
Laurel & Hardy: Perfect Day '29
Laurel & Hardy Special
Laurel & Hardy: Stan ''Helps'' Ollie '33
March of the Wooden Soldiers '34
Music Box/Helpmates '32
No Man's Law '21
Nothing But Trouble '44
Our Relations '36
Pack Up Your Troubles '32
Pardon Us '31
Pick a Star '37
Saps at Sea '40
Silent Laugh Makers, No. 1 '15
Silent Laugh Makers, No. 2 '17
Sons of the Desert '33
Swiss Miss '38
Three Ages '23
Utopia '51
Way Out West '37
The Wizard of Oz '25

Robert Hardy
Blat
Dark Places '73
Demons of the Mind '72
Jenny's War '85
Northanger Abbey '80s
The Shooting Party '85
War & Remembrance, Part 1 '88
War & Remembrance: The Final Chapter, Part 8 '89
The Woman He Loved '88

Sam Hardy
Big News '29
Break of Hearts '35
King Kong '33
Powdersmoke Range '35

Sophie Hardy
Erotic Touch of Hot Skin '65
The Mysterious Magician '65

Lumsden Hare
Gunga Din '39
The Lives of a Bengal Lancer '35
Northwest Passage '40
Rose Marie '54
Shadows on the Stairs '41
That Forsyte Woman '50

Robertson Hare
The Adventures of Sadie '55
Murder on the Campus '52
Things Happen at Night '48

Dorian Harewood
Against All Odds '84
The Ambush Murders '82
An American Christmas Carol '79
Beulah Land '80
The Falcon and the Snowman '85
Full Metal Jacket '87
Getting Up and Going Home '92
God Bless the Child '88
Guilty of Innocence '87
The Jesse Owens Story '84
Kiss Shot '89
Pacific Heights '90
Panic in Echo Park '77
Roots: The Next Generation '79
Sparkle '76
Strike Force '81
Tank '83

Mariska Hargitay
Finish Line '89
Ghoulies '85
Hotel Room '93
Welcome to 18 '87

Mickey Hargitay
The Bloody Pit of Horror '65
Lady Frankenstein '72
The Loves of Hercules '60

Doris Hargrave
Last Night at the Alamo '83
The Whole Shootin' Match '79

John Hargreaves
Beyond Reasonable Doubt '80
Careful, He Might Hear You '84
Cry Freedom '87
Deathcheaters '76
Don's Party '76
Great Gold Swindle '84

Hargreaves ►cont.

Killing of Angel Street '81
Little Boy Lost '78
Malcolm '86
My First Wife '84
Sky Pirates '87

Gordon Harker
Champagne '28
The Farmer's Wife '28
Inspector Hornleigh '39
The Phantom Light '35
The Ring '27
Small Hotel '57
Things Happen at Night '48

Susannah Harker
The Crucifer of Blood '91
A Dry White Season '89

John Harkins
Absence of Malice '81
Amityville 3: The Demon '83
Birdy '84
City Killer '87
Rampage '87
Slaves of New York '89
This Gun for Hire '90

Kenneth Harlan
Dawn Express '42
Death Valley Rangers '44
The Ice Flood '26
Law of the Texan '38
Little Church Around the
   Corner '23
A Million to One '37
Paradise Island '30
Phantom Killer '42
The Primitive Lover '16
Renfrew of the Royal Mounted
   '37
Santa Fe Marshal '40
Under Montana Skies '30
The Virginian '23

Otis Harlan
I Can't Escape '34
King Kelly of the U.S.A. '34
Mr. Boggs Steps Out '38
Mountain Justice '30
Outlaws of Sonora '38
Ride Him, Cowboy '32
Telegraph Trail '33

Jean Harlow
Bombshell '33
China Seas '35
City Lights '31
Dinner at Eight '33
The Girl from Missouri '34
Golden Age of Comedy '58
Hell's Angels '30
Hold Your Man '33
Libeled Lady '36
The Love Goddesses '65
Personal Property '37
Platinum Blonde '31
Public Enemy '31
Reckless '35
Red Dust '32
Red Headed Woman '32
Riff Raff '35
Saratoga '37
Suzy '26
Wife Versus Secretary '36

Deborah Harmon
Bachelor Party '84
Prince of Bel Air '87
Used Cars '80

Mark Harmon
After the Promise '87
Beyond the Poseidon
   Adventure '79
Cold Heaven '90
Comes a Horseman '78
The Deliberate Stranger '86
Fourth Story '90
Goliath Awaits '81
Let's Get Harry '87
The Presidio '88
Prince of Bel Air '87
Stealing Home '88
Summer School '87
Sweet Bird of Youth '89
Till There was You '91
Worth Winning '89
Wyatt Earp '94

Renee Harmon
The Executioner, Part 2:
   Frozen Scream '84
Lady Street Fighter '86
Night of Terror '87

Tom Harmon
Harmon of Michigan '41
The Spirit of West Point '47

Elisabeth Harnois
One Magic Christmas '85
Where Are the Children? '85

Christina Harnos
Denial: The Dark Side of
   Passion '91
The Rescue '88

Ralf Harolde
Baby Face Morgan '42
Behind Locked Doors '48
Hook, Line and Sinker '30
I Killed That Man '42
I'm No Angel '33
Night Nurse '31
The Sea Wolf '41

David W. Harper
A Day for Thanks on Walton's
   Mountain '82
The Waltons: A Thanksgiving
   Story '73

Jessica Harper
Big Man on Campus '89
Blue Iguana '88
Eat a Bowl of Tea '89
The Evictors '79
Imagemaker '86
Inserts '76
My Favorite Year '82
Pennies From Heaven '81
Phantom of the Paradise '74
Shock Treatment '81
Stardust Memories '80
Suspiria '77

Robert Harper
Final Analysis '92
Held Hostage '91
Not Quite Human '87
Running Mates '92
The Wrong Man '93

Tess Harper
Amityville 3: The Demon '83
Chiefs '83
Crimes of the Heart '86
Criminal Law '89
Daddy's Dyin'...Who's Got the
   Will? '90
Dark River: A Father's Revenge
   '90
Far North '88
Flashpoint '84
Her Alibi '88
The Man in the Moon '91
My Heroes Have Always Been
   Cowboys '91
My New Gun '92
Reckless Disregard '84
A Summer to Remember '84
Tender Mercies '83

Valerie Harper
Blame It on Rio '84
Chapter Two '79
Don't Go to Sleep '82
Drop-Out Mother '88
The Execution '85
Freebie & the Bean '74
The Last Married Couple in
   America '80
Night Terror '76
The Shadow Box '80
Thursday's Game '74

Cindy Harrel
The Final Terror '83
Model Behavior '82

Woody Harrelson
Cool Blue '88
The Cowboy Way '94
Doc Hollywood '91
Eye of the Demon '87
Indecent Proposal '93
Natural Born Killers '94
White Men Can't Jump '92
Wildcats '86

William Harrigan
Exiled to Shanghai '37
''G'' Men '35
The Invisible Man '33

Laura Harrington
Linda '93
Maximum Overdrive '86
Perfect Witness '89
The Secret '93
Vietnam War Story 3 '89
What's Eating Gilbert Grape '93

Pat Harrington
The Affair '73
Easy Come, Easy Go '67
The President's Analyst '67

Barbara Harris
Dirty Rotten Scoundrels '88
Family Plot '76
Freaky Friday '76
Movie, Movie '78
Nashville '75
Nice Girls Don't Explode '87
The North Avenue Irregulars
   '79
Oh Dad, Poor Dad (Momma's
   Hung You in the Closet & I'm
   Feeling So Sad) '67
Peggy Sue Got Married '86
Plaza Suite '71
The Seduction of Joe Tynan '79
A Thousand Clowns '65

Brad Harris
The Freakmaker '73
The Fury of Hercules '61
Goliath Against the Giants '63
Hercules '83
Island of Lost Girls '73
Jungle Inferno '70s
King of Kong Island '78
The Mad Butcher '72
Rattler Kid '70s
Samson '61
Seven Magnificent Gladiators
   '84

Cynthia Harris
Edward and Mrs. Simpson '80
Izzy & Moe '85
Pancho Barnes '88
Reuben, Reuben '83
Three Men and a Baby '87

Danielle Harris
Halloween 4: The Return of
   Michael Myers '88
Halloween 5: The Revenge of
   Michael Myers '89
The Last Boy Scout '91
Marked for Death '90

David Harris
Badge of the Assassin '85
Undercover '87
Vietnam War Story 1 '88

Ed Harris
The Abyss '89
Alamo Bay '85
Borderline '80
China Moon '91
Code Name: Emerald '85
Coma '78
Creepshow '82
The Firm '93
A Flash of Green '85
Glengarry Glen Ross '92
Jacknife '89
Knightriders '81
The Last Innocent Man '87
Milk Money '94
Needful Things '93
Paris Trout '91
Places in the Heart '84
The Right Stuff '83
Running Mates '92
The Seekers '79
State of Grace '90
Sweet Dreams '85
Swing Shift '84
To Kill a Priest '89
Under Fire '83
Walker '87

Edna Mae Harris
Lying Lips '39
Paradise in Harlem '40

Fox Harris
Alienator '89
Dr. Caligari '89
Repo Man '83
Warlords '88

Jo Ann Harris
Act of Vengeance '74
Deadly Games '80

Julie Harris
America at the Movies '76
The Bell Jar '79
The Christmas Wife '88
The Dark Half '91
A Doll's House '59
East of Eden '54
Forever James Dean '88
Gorillas in the Mist '88
Harper '66
The Haunting '63
The Hiding Place '75
Holy Terror '65
Home for the Holidays '72
Housesitter '92
I Am a Camera '55
James Dean: The First
   American Teenager '76
The Last of Mrs. Lincoln '76
The Member of the Wedding
   '52
The People Next Door '70
Reflections in a Golden Eye '67
Truth About Women '61
Victoria Regina '61
Voyage of the Damned '76
The Woman He Loved '88
You're a Big Boy Now '66

Julius W. Harris
Black Caesar '73
Crimewave '85
Hell Up in Harlem '73
Live and Let Die '73
Missing Pieces '83
Murder on the Bayou '91
Nothing But a Man '64
Prayer of the Rollerboys '91
Shaft's Big Score '72
Superfly '72
The Taking of Pelham One Two
   Three '74

Lara Harris
All Tied Up '92
Blood Red '88
The Fourth War '91
No Man's Land '87

Leigh Anne Harris
I, the Jury '82
Sorceress '82

Lynette Harris
I, the Jury '82
Sorceress '82

Mel Harris
Cameron's Closet '89
Desperate Motives '92
K-9 '89
My Brother's Wife '89
Raising Cain '92
Wanted Dead or Alive '86

M.K. Harris
Genuine Risk '89
Horseplayer '91
Slumber Party Massacre 3 '90

Neil Patrick Harris
Clara's Heart '88
Cold Sassy Tree '89
Purple People Eater '88

Phil Harris
Dreaming Out Loud '40
The Gatling Gun '72
Goodbye, My Lady '56
Melody Cruise '32
The Patsy '64
The Wheeler Dealers '63

Richard Harris
The Bible...In the Beginning '66
Camelot '67
The Cassandra Crossing '76
Cromwell '70
The Deadly Trackers '73
The Field '90
Game for Vultures '86
Golden Rendezvous '77
Gulliver's Travels '77
The Guns of Navarone '61
Hawaii '66
The Hero '71
Highpoint '80
Juggernaut '74
King of the Wind '93
The Last Word '80
Mack the Knife '89
Major Dundee '65
A Man Called Horse '70
Man in the Wilderness '71
Martin's Day '85

Molly Maguires '70
Mutiny on the Bounty '62
99 & 44/100 Dead '74
Orca '77
Patriot Games '92
The Red Desert '64
The Return of a Man Called
   Horse '76
Robin and Marian '76
Silent Tongue '92
Tarzan, the Ape Man '81
This Sporting Life '63
Triumphs of a Man Called
   Horse '83
Unforgiven '92
Wild Geese '78
The Wreck of the Mary Deare
   '59
Wrestling Ernest Hemingway
   '93
Your Ticket Is No Longer Valid
   '84

Robert Harris
Apache Uprising '66
How to Make a Monster '58
Valley of the Dolls '67

Robin Harris
Hard to Die '90
House Party '90
I'm Gonna Git You Sucka '88
Mo' Better Blues '90
Sorority House Massacre 2:
   Nighty Nightmare '92

Rosemary Harris
Beau Brummel '54
The Chisholms '79
Crossing Delancey '88
Heartbreak House '86
The Ploughman's Lunch '83
To the Lighthouse '83

Ross Harris
Scream, Baby, Scream '69
Testament '83

Cathryn Harrison
Blue Fire Lady '78
The Dresser '83
Empire State '87
A Handful of Dust '88

George Harrison
All You Need Is Cash '78
The Compleat Beatles '82
A Hard Day's Night '64
Help! '65
Let It Be '70
Magical Mystery Tour '67
Monty Python's Life of Brian
   '79

Gregory Harrison
Bare Essentials '91
Body Chemistry 2: Voice of a
   Stranger '91
Cadillac Girls '93
Caught in the Act '93
Dangerous Pursuit '89
Duplicates '92
Enola Gay: The Men, the
   Mission, the Atomic Bomb
   '80
For Ladies Only '81
The Gathering '77
The Hasty Heart '86
North Shore '87
Oceans of Fire '86
Razorback '84
Seduced '85
Trilogy of Terror '75

Jenilee Harrison
Curse 3: Blood Sacrifice '90
Prime Target '91
Tank '83

Kathleen Harrison
Cast a Dark Shadow '55
A Christmas Carol '51
A Cry from the Streets '57
The Ghost Train '41
Let's Make Up '55
The Pickwick Papers '54
Trio '50
The Winslow Boy '48

Linda Harrison
Beneath the Planet of the Apes
   '70
Cocoon '85
Planet of the Apes '68

Lottie Harrison
Driftin' River '46
Lost in a Harem '44

Rex Harrison
The Agony and the Ecstasy '65
Anastasia: The Mystery of Anna '96
Anna and the King of Siam '46
Ashanti, Land of No Mercy '79
Blithe Spirit '45
The Citadel '38
Cleopatra '63
Deadly Thief '78
Doctor Dolittle '67
The Fifth Musketeer '79
The Ghost and Mrs. Muir '47
Heartbreak House '86
The Honey Pot '67
I Live in Grosvenor Square '46
King Richard and the Crusaders '54
The Long Dark Hall '51
Major Barbara '41
Men are not Gods '37
Midnight Lace '60
My Fair Lady '64
Night Train to Munich '40
The Prince and the Pauper '78
The Reluctant Debutante '58
Sidewalks of London '40
Storm in a Teacup '37
Time to Die '83
Unfaithfully Yours '48

Richard Harrison
Between God, the Devil & a Winchester '72
Blood Debts '83
The Channeler '89
The Desert Tigers
Fireback '78
Giants of Rome '63
Gladiators 7 '62
Gun Fight at Red Sands '63
Hands of Death '88
His Name was King '85
The Invincible Gladiator '63
Medusa Against the Son of Hercules '62
Messalina vs. the Son of Hercules '62
Ninja Champion '80s
Ninja Commandments '87
Ninja Dragon '80s
Ninja Operation: Licensed to Terminate '87
Ninja Powerforce '90
Ninja Showdown '90
Ninja Squad '80s
Ninja Strike Force '88
Ninja the Protector '80s
Rescue Force '90
Terminal Force '88
Thirty-Six Hours of Hell '77

David Harrod
Armed for Action '92
Blood on the Badge

Kathryn Harrold
Best Legs in the 8th Grade '84
Bogie: The Last Hero '80
Dead Solid Perfect '88
Deadly Desire '91
Heartbreakers '84
The Hunter '80
Into the Night '85
Modern Romance '81
Nightwing '79
The Pursuit of D.B. Cooper '81
Rainbow Drive '90
Raw Deal '86
The Sender '82
Someone to Love '87
Yes, Giorgio '82

John Harron
Midnight Warning '32
The Night Cry '26
West-Bound Limited '23
The White Zombie '32

Robert Harron
The Birth of a Nation '15
The Greatest Question '19
Hearts of the World '18
Home Sweet Home '14
Hoodoo Ann '16
Judith of Bethulia '14

Lisa Harrow
All Creatures Great and Small '74

The Final Conflict '81
The Last Days of Chez Nous '92
Nancy Astor '82
Shaker Run '85
Under Capricorn '82

Deborah Harry
Body Bags '93
Crazy Streets '80s
The Foreigner '78
Forever, Lulu '87
Hairspray '88
Intimate Stranger '91
Mr. Mike's Mondo Video '79
New York Stories '89
Satisfaction '88
Tales from the Darkside: The Movie '90
Union City '81
Videodrome '83

Christina Hart
Games Girls Play '75
Johnny Firecloud '75
The Runaway Barge '75

Christopher Hart
The Addams Family '91
Addams Family Values '93
Lady Terminator '89

Dianne Lee Hart
The Giant Spider Invasion '75
Pom Pom Girls '76

Dolores Hart
King Creole '58
Lonelyhearts '58
Loving You '57
Where the Boys Are '60

John Hart
Blackenstein '73
The Fighting Redhead '50

Kevin Hart
Lone Wolf '88
Mindkiller '87

Linda Hart
Gypsy '93
A Perfect World '93

Neal Hart
Sands of Sacrifice '21
Trigger Tricks '30

Roxanne Hart
Highlander '86
The Last Innocent Man '87
Oh, God! You Devil '84
Old Enough '84
Once Around '91
Pulse '88
Samaritan: The Mitch Snyder Story '86
Special Bulletin '83
Tagget '90
The Tender Age '84
Vengeance '89

Susan Hart
Dr. Goldfoot and the Bikini Machine '66
Pajama Party '64
Ride the Wild Surf '64
The Slime People '63

William S. Hart
The Bargain '15
Between Men '35
Blue Blazes Rawden '18
Disciple '15
The Fugitive: Taking of Luke McVane '15
Hell's Hinges '16
Narrow Trail '17
On the Night Stage '15
Return of Draw Egan '16
Show People '28
Story of William S. Hart/Sad Clowns '20s
Three Word Brand '21
Toll Gate '20
Tumbleweeds '25
Wagon Tracks '19

Douglas Hartier
Invasion Force '90
White Fury '90

Pat Hartigan
King of the Wild Horses '24
Ranson's Folly '26

Mariette Hartley
Encino Man '92
Improper Channels '82

M.A.D.D.: Mothers Against Drunk Driving
Nightmare at 43 Hillcrest '74
1969 '89
No Place to Hide '81
O'Hara's Wife '82
Passion in Paradise '89
Rainy Day '79
The Return of Count Yorga '71
Ride the High Country '62
Silence of the Heart '84

Elizabeth Hartman
The Beguiled '70
The Fixer '68
The Group '66
A Patch of Blue '65
Walking Tall '73
You're a Big Boy Now '66

Lisa Hartman
Bare Essentials '91
Deadly Blessing '81
Full Exposure: The Sex Tape Scandals '89
Just Tell Me You Love Me '80
Magic on Love Island '80
Red Wind '91
The Return of Eliot Ness '91
The Seventeenth Bride '84
The Take '90
Where the Boys Are '84 '84

Phil Hartman
Blind Date '87
CB4: The Movie '93
Cheech and Chong's Next Movie '80
Coneheads '93
Greedy '94
How I Got into College '89
The Pee Wee Herman Show '82
Quick Change '90
Weekend Pass '84

William Hartnell
Appointment with Crime '45
Brighton Rock '47
Immortal Battalion '44
This Sporting Life '63

Rainbow Harvest
Mirror, Mirror '90
Old Enough '84

Don Harvey
American Heart '92
The Beast '88
Casualties of War '89
Eight Men Out '88
Gang Busters '55
Mission of the Shark '91
Prey of the Chameleon '91

Harry Harvey
Code of the Fearless '39
I'm from Arkansas '44
In Old Montana '39
King of the Sierras '38
The Narrow Margin '52
The Reckless Way '36
Ridin' the Trail '40
Tea for Two '50

Laurence Harvey
The Alamo '60
Butterfield 8 '60
Dandy in Aspic '68
Darling '65
Escape to the Sun '72
I Am a Camera '55
Innocents in Paris '53
King Richard and the Crusaders '54
The Magic Christian '69
Man on the Run '49
The Manchurian Candidate '62
Night Watch '72
Of Human Bondage '64
Romeo and Juliet '54
Room at the Top '59
The Silent Enemy '58
Spy with a Cold Nose '66
Summer and Smoke '61
Truth About Women '58
Walk on the Wild Side '62
The Wonderful World of the Brothers Grimm '62

Paul Harvey
April In Paris '52
Arizona '40
Blondie's Blessed Event '42
Call Northside 777 '48

Helldorado '46
Meet Dr. Christian '39
A Southern Yankee '48
23 1/2 Hours Leave '37
The Yellow Cab Man '50

Rodney Harvey
Five Corners '88
Guncrazy '92
My Own Private Idaho '91
Salsa '88

Kazuo Hasegawa
An Actor's Revenge '63
The Crucified Lovers '54
Gate of Hell '54

Peter Haskell
Child's Play 3 '91
Christina '74
The Cracker Factory '79
Legend of Earl Durand '74
Robot Wars '93

O.E. Hasse
Above Us the Waves '56
Betrayed '54
The Big Lift '50
The Elusive Corporal '62
State of Siege '73

Danny Hassel
A Nightmare on Elm Street 4: Dream Master '88
A Nightmare on Elm Street 5: Dream Child '89

David Hasselhoff
Bail Out '90
Cartier Affair '84
The Final Alliance '89
Fire and Rain '89
Revenge of the Cheerleaders '76
Ring of the Musketeers '93
Star Crash '78
Terror at London Bridge '85
Witchery '88

Marilyn Hassett
The Bell Jar '79
Body Count '87
Messenger of Death '88
The Other Side of the Mountain '75
The Other Side of the Mountain, Part 2 '78
Twenty Dollar Star '91
Two Minute Warning '76

Signe Hasso
A Double Life '47
Heaven Can Wait '43
Johnny Angel '45
Journey for Margaret '42
The Seventh Cross '44

Bob Hastings
Harper Valley P.T.A. '78
Munster's Revenge '81
Shadow Force '92
Snowballing '85

Richard Hatch
Battlestar Galactica '78
Charlie Chan and the Curse of the Dragon Queen '81
Deadman's Curve '78
Delta Force Commando 2 '90
Ghetto Blaster '89
The Hatfields & the McCoys '75
Heated Vengeance '87
Mission Galactica: The Cylon Attack '79
Party Line '88
Prisoners of the Lost Universe '84

Mary Hatcher
The Big Wheel '49
Holiday in Havana '49
Tales of Robin Hood '52

Teri Hatcher
All Tied Up '91
The Big Picture '89
Brain Smasher...A Love Story '93
The Cool Surface '92
Dead in the Water '91
Soapdish '91
Straight Talk '92
Tango and Cash '89

Hurd Hatfield
The Boston Strangler '68
Crimes of the Heart '86

Diary of a Chambermaid '46
Dragon Seed '44
El Cid '61
Her Alibi '89
Invincible Mr. Disraeli '63
King David '85
The King of Kings '61
Lamp at Midnight '66
Picture of Dorian Gray '45
Thief '71
The Word '78

Noah Hathaway
The NeverEnding Story '84
Troll '85

Raymond Hatton
Arizona Bound '41
Behind the Front '26
Below the Border '42
Blazing Guns '50
Border Bandits '46
Buffalo Stampede '33
Covered Wagon Days '40
Cowboys from Texas '39
The Crooked Circle '32
Dawn on the Great Divide '42
Day the World Ended '55
Desert Gold '36
Down Texas Way '42
Drifting Souls '32
The Fighting American '24
Flesh and the Spur '57
Forbidden Trails '41
Frontier Horizon '39
Gentleman from Texas '46
Ghost Rider '43
Ghost Town Law '42
Girls in Prison '56
Gunman from Bodie '41
Guns of Justice '50
Hidden Gold '33
The Kansas Terrors '39
Kentucky Jubilee '51
Lady Killer '33
Land of the Lawless '47
Lawmen '44
The Little American '17
Lonely Trail/Three Texas Steers '39
Male and Female '19
Marshal of Heldorado '50
Motorcycle Gang '57
Northwest Trail '46
Partners of the Trail '44
Peck's Bad Boy '21
Raiders of the Border '44
Range Law '44
Reap the Wild Wind '42
Riders of the West '42
Rocky Mountain Rangers '40
Rogue of the Rio Grande '30
Rolling Home '46
Rough Riders' Roundup '39
Rustlers of Red Dog '35
Shake, Rattle and Rock '57
Six Gun Gospel '43
The Stranger from Pecos '45
Sudden Death '50
Terror Trail '33
Texas Kid '43
The Three Musketeers '33
Uptown New York '32
The Vigilantes are Coming '36
The Virginian '23
We're in the Navy Now '27
West of the Law '42
Wyoming Outlaw '39

Rondo Hatton
The Brute Man '46
House of Horrors '46
The Pearl of Death '44

Rutger Hauer
Beyond Justice '92
Blade Runner '82
Blind Fury '90
Blind Side '93
The Blood of Heroes '89
Bloodhounds of Broadway '89
A Breed Apart '84
Buffy the Vampire Slayer '92
Chanel Solitaire '81
Cold Blood '70s
Dandelions '74
Deadlock '91
Escape from Sobibor '87
Eureka! '81
Fatal Error '93
Flesh and Blood '85
Hitcher '86

Hauer ▶cont.

Inside the Third Reich '82
Keetje Tippei '75
Ladyhawke '85
Mysteries '84
Nighthawks '81
The Osterman Weekend '83
Past Midnight '92
Soldier of Orange '78
Spetters '80
Split Second '92
Surviving the Game '94
Turkish Delights '73
Voyage '93
Wanted Dead or Alive '86
The Wilby Conspiracy '75

Angelika Hauff
The Life and Loves of Mozart '59
Tromba, the Tiger Man '52

Ullrich Haupt
Captain Swagger '25
Morocco '30

Fay Hauser
Christmas Lilies of the Field '84
Jimmy the Kid '82
Jo Jo Dancer, Your Life is Calling '86
Marvin & Tige '84

Wings Hauser
The Art of Dying '90
Beastmaster 2: Through the Portal of Time '91
Bedroom Eyes 2 '89
The Carpenter '89
Code of Honor '84
Coldfire '90
Dead Man Walking '88
Deadly Conspiracy '91
Deadly Force '83
Exiled in America '90
Frame Up '91
Homework '82
Hostage '87
In Between '92
Jo Jo Dancer, Your Life is Calling '86
The Killer's Edge '90
L.A. Bounty '89
Living to Die '91
The Long, Hot Summer '86
Marked for Murder '89
Mind, Body & Soul '92
Mutant '83
Nightmare at Noon '87
No Safe Haven '87
Out of Sight, Out of Her Mind '89
Pale Blood '91
Reason to Die '90
The Siege of Firebase Gloria '89
A Soldier's Story '84
Street Asylum '90
Tough Guys Don't Dance '87
Vice Squad '82
Wilding '90
The Wind '87

Richie Havens
Boss' Son '79
Perfect Harmony '90
Street Hunter '90
Woodstock '70

June Haver
Look for the Silver Lining '49
Love Nest '51

Phyllis Haver
The Balloonatic/One Week '23
The Blacksmith/The Balloonatic '23
The Nervous Wreck '26

Nigel Havers
Burke & Wills '85
Chariots of Fire '81
The Charmer '89
Empire of the Sun '87
Farewell to the King '89
The Little Princess '87
A Passage to India '84
The Whistle Blower '87
Who is Killing the Great Chefs of Europe? '78

Thom Haverstock
Fall from Innocence '88
Skullduggery '79

Allen Havey
Checking Out '89
Love or Money? '88

June Havoc
Brewster's Millions '45
Four Jacks and a Jill '41
Gentleman's Agreement '47
Hello, Frisco, Hello '43
Return to Salem's Lot '87
Sing Your Worries Away '42
Timber Queen '44

Robin Hawdon
Alien Women '69
The Love Factor '69
When Dinosaurs Ruled the Earth '70

Ethan Hawke
Alive '93
Dad '89
Dead Poets Society '89
Explorers '85
A Midnight Clear '92
Mystery Date '91
Reality Bites '94
Rich in Love '93
Waterland '92
White Fang '91

Jack Hawkins
The Adventurers '51
Angels One Five '54
Ben-Hur '59
Bonnie Prince Charlie '48
The Bridge on the River Kwai '57
Cruel Sea '53
The Elusive Pimpernel '50
Escape to the Sun '72
The Fallen Idol '49
Guns at Batasi '64
Land of Fury '55
Land of the Pharaohs '55
Lawrence of Arabia '62
The League of Gentlemen '60
Lola '69
Lord Jim '65
Malta Story '53
Mandy '53
Nicholas and Alexandra '71
Phantom Fiend '35
The Prisoner '55
Restless '72
A Shot in the Dark '33
The Small Back Room '49
Tales That Witness Madness '73
The Third Key '57
Those Daring Young Men in Their Jaunty Jalopies '69
Waterloo '71
Young Winston '72
Zulu '64

Jay Hawkins
Mystery Train '89
A Rage in Harlem '91
Two Moon Junction '88

Ronnie Hawkins
Club Med '83
The Last Waltz '78

Monte Hawley
Double Deal '39
Gang War '40
Look Out Sister '48
Miracle in Harlem '48
Mystery in Swing '40
Tall, Tan and Terrific '46

Wanda Hawley
American Pluck '25
Smouldering Fires '25

Goldie Hawn
Best Friends '82
Bird on a Wire '90
Butterflies Are Free '72
Cactus Flower '69
Crisscross '92
Death Becomes Her '92
Deceived '91
Dollars '71
The Duchess and the Dirtwater Fox '76
Foul Play '78
The Girl from Petrovka '74
Housesitter '92

Lovers and Liars '81
The One and Only, Genuine, Original Family Band '68
Overboard '87
Private Benjamin '80
Protocol '84
Seems Like Old Times '80
Shampoo '75
The Sugarland Express '74
Swing Shift '84
There's a Girl in My Soup '70
Wildcats '86

Jill Haworth
Exodus '60
The Freakmaker '73
In Harm's Way '65
Tower of Evil '72

Nigel Hawthorne
Demolition Man '93
Firefox '82
Jenny's War '85
Pope John Paul II '84
S*P*Y*S '74
Tartuffe '90

Charles Hawtrey
Alien Women '69
A Canterbury Tale '44
Carry On at Your Convenience '71
Carry On Cleo '65
Carry On Screaming '66
Room to Let '47
Terronauts '67
The Terrornauts '67

Alexandra Hay
How Come Nobody's On Our Side? '71
The Love Machine '71

Christian Hay
Autopsy '70s
You're Jinxed, Friend, You've Met Sacramento '70

Sessue Hayakawa
The Bridge on the River Kwai '57
The Cheat '15
Daughter of the Dragon '31
The Geisha Boy '58
Green Mansions '59
Hell to Eternity '60
The Swiss Family Robinson '60
Three Came Home '50
Tokyo Joe '49
The Tong Man '19

Marc Hayashi
Chan is Missing '82
White of the Eye '88

Harry Hayden
Double Dynamite '51
Merton of the Movies '47
The Rains Came '39

Linda Hayden
Baby Love '69
The Barcelona Kill '77
The Blood on Satan's Claw '71
The House on Straw Hill '76
Madhouse '74
Taste the Blood of Dracula '70

Russell Hayden
Apache Chief '50
Blazing Guns '50
Border Vigilantes '41
Doomed Caravan '41
Frontier Law '43
The Frontiersman '38
Gambler's Choice '44
Guns of Justice '50
Hopalong Cassidy: Renegade Trail '39
In Old Colorado '41
Knights of the Range '40
Last Bullet '40
Law of the Pampas '39
The Light of Western Stars '40
Lost City of the Jungle '45
Marshal of Heldorado '50
The Mysterious Rider '38
'Neath Canadian Skies '46
North of the Border '46
Outlaw Fury '50
Rangeland Empire '50
Renegade Trail '39
Rolling Home '48
Santa Fe Marshal '40
The Showdown '40
Sudden Death '50

Trail of the Mounties '47
Where the North Begins '47

Sterling Hayden
The Asphalt Jungle '50
Bahama Passage '42
The Blue and the Gray '85
Cobra '71
Crime of Passion '57
Deadly Strangers '82
The Denver & Rio Grande '51
Dr. Strangelove, or: How I Learned to Stop Worrying and Love the Bomb '64
Fighter Attack '53
The Final Programme '73
Flat Top '52
Gas '81
The Godfather '72
The Godfather 1902-1959: The Complete Epic '81
Johnny Guitar '53
Kansas Pacific '53
The Killing '56
King of the Gypsies '78
The Last Command '55
The Long Goodbye '73
9 to 5 '80
1900 '76
Prince Valiant '54
Shotgun '55
Spaghetti Western '69
Suddenly '54
Venom '82
Winter Kills '79

Richard Haydn
Adventure '45
Clarence, the Cross-eyed Lion '65
Forever Amber '47
Jupiter's Darling '55
The Merry Widow '52
Never Let Me Go '53
Please Don't Eat the Daisies '60
Pride of St. Louis '52
The Sound of Music '65
Young Frankenstein '74

Julie Haydon
Come On Danger! '32
It's Pat '94

Helen Haye
The Case of the Frightened Lady '39
Man of Evil '48

Jeff Hayenga
Prince of Pennsylvania '88
The Unborn '91

Allan Hayes
Neon Maniacs '86
Sam's Son '84

Allison Hayes
Attack of the 50 Foot Woman '58
The Crawling Hand '63
Francis Joins the WACs '54
The Gunslinger '56
The Undead '57
The Unearthly '57
Zombies of Moratau '57

Bernadene Hayes
Heroes in Blue '39
Santa Fe Marshal '40
Sweetheart of the Navy '37

George "Gabby" Hayes
Bad Man of Deadwood '41
Badman's Territory '46
Beggars in Ermine '34
Bells of Rosarita '45
Billy the Kid Returns '38
Blue Steel '34
Border Devils '32
The Border Legion '40
Brand of Hate '34
Breed of the Border '33
Broadway to Cheyenne '32
Calling Wild Bill Elliott '43
The Cariboo Trail '50
Cavalier of the West '31
Colorado '40
Come On Rangers '38
Dark Command '40
Death Valley Manhunt '43
Fighting Champ '32
The Frontiersman '38
The Gallant Fool '33

Galloping Romeo '33
Heart of the Golden West '42
Helldorado '46
Home in Oklahoma '47
Hopalong Cassidy '35
Hopalong Cassidy: Renegade Trail '39
House of Mystery '34
In Old Caliente '39
In Old Cheyenne '41
In Old Santa Fe '34
Jesse James at Bay '41
Lawless Frontier '35
The Lawless Nineties '36
Lights of Old Santa Fe '47
Lonely Trail/Three Texas Steers '39
The Lost City '34
Lucky Texan '34
Man from Cheyenne '42
The Man from Hell '34
Man from Hell's Edges '32
Man from Thunder River '43
Man from Utah '34
Melody Ranch '40
Monte Carlo Nights '34
My Pal Trigger '46
Mystery Liner '34
'Neath the Arizona Skies '34
Night Rider '32
The Outlaw Tamer '33
The Phantom Broadcast '33
The Plainsman '37
Randy Rides Alone '34
Ranger and the Lady '40
Renegade Trail '39
The Return of Casey Jones '34
Return of the Bad Men '48
Riders of Destiny '33
Ridin' Down the Canyon '42
Robin Hood of the Pecos '41
Roll on Texas Moon '46
Romance on the Range '42
Rustler's Valley '37
Saga of Death Valley '39
Smokey Smith '36
Song of Arizona '46
Song of the Trail '36
Sons of the Pioneers '42
South of Santa Fe '42
Southward Ho! '39
The Sphinx '33
The Star Packer '34
Sunset in El Dorado '45
Sunset on the Desert '42
Sunset Serenade '42
Tall in the Saddle '44
Texas Buddies '32
Texas Terror '35
The Throwback '35
Trail Street '47
Under Nevada Skies '46
Utah '45
War of the Wildcats '43
West of the Divide '34
Western Double Feature 1 '38
Western Double Feature 2 '33
Western Double Feature 4: Rogers & Evans '40s
Western Double Feature 11 '40
Western Double Feature 16 '46
Without Honors '32
Young Bill Hickok '40
Young Buffalo Bill '40

Gloria Hayes
Judgment Day '88
Witchboard '87

Helen Hayes
Airport '70
Anastasia '56
Arrowsmith '31
Candleshoe '78
Family Upside Down '78
A Farewell to Arms '32
Herbie Rides Again '74
One of Our Dinosaurs Is Missing '75
Riders of the Range '24
The Sin of Madelon Claudet '31
Skin Game '31
Spy in Black '39

Isaac Hayes
Counterforce '87
Dead Aim '87
Deadly Exposure '93
Escape from New York '81
Final Judgement '92
Guilty as Charged '92
I'm Gonna Git You Sucka '88

It Could Happen to You '94
Jailbait: Betrayed By Innocence '86
Nightstick '87
Prime Target '91
Robin Hood: Men in Tights '93
Truck Turner '74

Linda Hayes
Danger on the Air '38
Ridin' Down the Canyon '42
South of Santa Fe '42

Margaret Hayes
Blackboard Jungle '55
In Old Colorado '41
Omar Khayyam '57
Sullivan's Travels '41

Patricia Hayes
A Fish Called Wanda '88
Little Dorrit, Film 1: Nobody's Fault '88
Little Dorrit, Film 2: Little Dorrit's Story '88
The NeverEnding Story '84
Super Bitch '89
The Terrornauts '67
Willow '88

Peter Lind Hayes
The 5000 Fingers of Dr. T '53
Playmates '41
Seven Days' Leave '42
Zis Boom Bah '42

Cyd Hayman
After Julius '78
The Godsend '79

David Hayman
Hope and Glory '87
A Sense of Freedom '78
Sid & Nancy '86

Dick Haymes
Betrayal '74
DuBarry Was a Lady '43
One Touch of Venus '48
St. Benny the Dip '51
State Fair '45

Cal Haynes
Fyre '78
Kemek '88

Linda Haynes
Human Experiments '79
Rolling Thunder '77

Roberta Haynes
The Adventurers '70
The Fighter '52
Hell Ship Mutiny '57
Return to Paradise '53

Jim Haynie
Bitter Harvest '81
From Hollywood to Deadwood '89
Grand Tour: Disaster in Time '92
Hard Traveling '85
Jack's Back '87
Men Don't Leave '89
On the Edge '86
Out '88
Sleepwalkers '92
Too Much Sun '90

Robert Hays
Airplane! '80
Airplane 2: The Sequel '82
California Gold Rush '81
Cat's Eye '85
The Fall of the House of Usher '80
Fifty/Fifty '93
Homeward Bound: The Incredible Journey '93
Honeymoon Academy '90
Hot Chocolate '92
Initiation of Sarah '78
Murder by the Book '87
Running Against Time '90
Scandalous '84
Take This Job & Shove It '81
Touched '82
Trenchcoat '83
Utilities '83

Dennis Haysbert
Love Field '91
Major League '89
Major League 2 '94
Mr. Baseball '92
Navy SEALS '90

Return to Lonesome Dove '93

James Hayter
Beau Brummel '54
Four Sided Triangle '53
The Pickwick Papers '54
Tom Brown's School Days '51
Trio '50

Chad Hayward
The Killing Game '87
Violent Zone '89

David Hayward
Accidental Meeting '93
Delusion '84
Thousand Pieces of Gold '91

Louis Hayward
And Then There Were None '45
Anthony Adverse '36
Black Arrow '48
The Christmas Kid '68
Chuka '67
Dance, Girl, Dance '40
The Man in the Iron Mask '39
Promise to Murder '56
The Saint in New York '38
The Search for Bridey Murphy '56
The Son of Monte Cristo '41
The Strange Woman '46
Terror in the Wax Museum '73

Susan Hayward
Adam Had Four Sons '41
Back Street '61
Beau Geste '39
The Conqueror '56
David and Bathsheba '51
Deadline at Dawn '46
Demetrius and the Gladiators '54
Fighting Seabees '44
The Hairy Ape '44
The Honey Pot '67
House of Strangers '49
I Married a Witch '42
I Want to Live! '58
I'll Cry Tomorrow '55
Jack Frost '43
Jack London '44
Lost Moment '47
The Lusty Men '52
Rawhide '51
Reap the Wild Wind '42
Say Goodbye, Maggie Cole '72
Smash-Up: The Story of a Woman '47
The Snows of Kilimanjaro '52
Soldier of Fortune '55
Stolen Hours '63
They Won't Believe Me '47
Tulsa '49
Valley of the Dolls '67
Where Love Has Gone '64
Young & Willing '42

Chris Haywood
Attack Force Z '84
Burke & Wills '85
Heatwave '83
Malcolm '86
Man of Flowers '84
The Navigator '88
Newsfront '78
Quigley Down Under '90
Razorback '84
Sweet Talker '91
The Tale of Ruby Rose '87
Waterfront '83
A Woman's Tale '92

Rita Hayworth
Affair in Trinidad '52
Angels Over Broadway '40
Blood and Sand '41
Circus World '64
Cover Girl '44
Down to Earth '47
Fire Down Below '57
Gilda '46
Hit the Saddle '37
The Lady from Shanghai '48
The Lady in Question '40
The Love Goddesses '65
The Loves of Carmen '48
Miss Sadie Thompson '53
Music in My Heart '40
Only Angels Have Wings '39
Pal Joey '57
The Poppy is also a Flower '66
Renegade Ranger/Scarlet River '38

Road to Salina '68
Salome '53
Separate Tables '58
Strawberry Blonde '41
Susan and God '40
They Came to Cordura '59
Tonight and Every Night '45
Trouble in Texas '37
You Were Never Lovelier '42
You'll Never Get Rich '41

Jonathan Haze
Apache Woman '55
The Gunslinger '56
It Conquered the World '56
Little Shop of Horrors '60
Poor White Trash '57
Rock All Night '57
Track of the Vampire '66
X: The Man with X-Ray Eyes '63

Noni Hazlehurst
Fran '85
Monkey Grip '82
True Colors '87
Waterfront '83

Murray Head
Sunday, Bloody Sunday '71
White Mischief '88

Glenne Headly
And the Band Played On '93
Dick Tracy '90
Dirty Rotten Scoundrels '88
Doctor Detroit '83
Fandango '85
Getting Even with Dad '94
Grand Isle '92
Hotel Room '93
Making Mr. Right '86
Mortal Thoughts '91
Nadine '87
Ordinary Magic '93
Paperhouse '89
The Purple Rose of Cairo '85
Seize the Day '86
Stars and Bars '88

Anthony Heald
The Ballad of Little Jo '93
The Client '94
The Silence of the Lambs '91
Whispers in the Dark '92

Myron Healey
Cavalry Command '63
Claws '77
Down to Earth '47
Gang Busters '55
Guns Don't Argue '57
Pulse '88
Smoke in the Wind '75
The Unearthly '57
Varan the Unbelievable '61

David Healy
The Sign of Four '83
Supergirl '84

Mary Healy
The 5000 Fingers of Dr. T '53
Second Fiddle '39
Zis Boom Bah '42

Ted Healy
Dancing Lady '33
Hollywood Party '34
Mad Love '35
Reckless '35
Three Stooges Comedy Classics '49

John Heard
After Hours '85
Awakenings '90
Beaches '88
Best Revenge '83
Betrayed '88
Between the Lines '77
Big '88
Blown Away '90
Cat People '82
Chilly Scenes of Winter '79
C.H.U.D. '84
Cutter's Way '81
Dead Ahead: The Exxon Valdez Disaster '92
Deceived '91
The End of Innocence '90
First Love '77
Gladiator '92
Heart Beat '80
Heaven Help Us '85
Home Alone '90

Home Alone 2: Lost in New York '92
Legs '83
Me & Veronica '93
The Milagro Beanfield War '88
Mindwalk: A Film for Passionate Thinkers '91
On the Yard '79
Out on a Limb '87
The Package '89
The Pelican Brief '93
Radio Flyer '92
Rambling Rose '91
The Seventh Sign '88
The Telephone '87
Too Scared to Scream '85
The Trip to Bountiful '85
Violated '84
Waterland '92

Ann Hearn
The Accused '88
Lorenzo's Oil '92

George Hearn
A Piano for Mrs. Cimino '82
Sanctuary of Fear '79
See You in the Morning '89
Sneakers '92
Sweeney Todd: The Demon Barber of Fleet Street '84
The Vanishing '93

Clifford Heatherly
Bitter Sweet '33
Champagne '28
If I Were Rich '33

Joey Heatherton
Bluebeard '72
Cry-Baby '90
The Happy Hooker Goes to Washington '77
Where Love Has Gone '64

Patricia Heaton
Beethoven '92
Memoirs of an Invisible Man '92

David Heavener
Deadly Reactor '89
Eye of the Stranger '93
Kill or Be Killed '93
Killcrazy '89
L.A. Goddess '92
Outlaw Force '87
Prime Target '91
Ragin' Cajun '90
Twisted Justice '89

Anne Heche
The Adventures of Huck Finn '93
O Pioneers! '91
A Simple Twist of Fate '94

Paul Hecht
Mary and Joseph: A Story of Faith '79
The Savage Bees '76

Eileen Heckart
The Bad Seed '56
Bus Stop '56
Butterflies Are Free '72
A Doll's House '59
Heartbreak Ridge '86
The Hiding Place '75
Hot Spell '58
No Way to Treat a Lady '68
Somebody Up There Likes Me '56
Sorrows of Gin '79
Table Settings '84
Up the Down Staircase '67
White Mama '80
Zandy's Bride '74

Dan Hedaya
The Addams Family '91
The Adventures of Buckaroo Banzai Across the Eighth Dimension '84
Based on an Untrue Story '93
Benny & Joon '93
Blood Simple '85
Boiling Point '93
Commando '86
Courage '86
Endangered Species '82
Fallen Angels 2 '93
For Love or Money '93
Four Eyes and Six Guns '93
The Hunger '83
Joe Versus the Volcano '90

Mr. Wonderful '93
Pacific Heights '90
The Prince of Central Park '77
Reckless '84
Rookie of the Year '93
Running Scared '86
Slow Burn '86
A Smoky Mountain Christmas '86
Tightrope '84
Tune in Tomorrow '90
Wise Guys '86

Serene Hedin
Boggy Creek II '83
Hawken's Breed '87

David Hedison
The Art of Crime '75
Enemy Below '57
ffolkes '80
The Fly '58
Kemek '88
Kenny Rogers as the Gambler, Part 2: The Adventure Continues '83
License to Kill '89
Live and Let Die '73
The Naked Face '84
The Power Within '79
Undeclared War '91

Jack Hedley
For Your Eyes Only '81
Goodbye, Mr. Chips '69

Tippi Hedren
The Birds '63
Deadly Spygames '89
Foxfire Light '84
Harrad Experiment '73
In the Cold of the Night '89
Marnie '64
Mr. Kingstreet's War '71
Pacific Heights '90
Satan's Harvest '65

Kyle T. Heffner
Flashdance '83
Mutant on the Bounty '89

Marta Heflin
Come Back to the Five & Dime Jimmy Dean, Jimmy Dean '82
A Star is Born '76

Nora Heflin
Chilly Scenes of Winter '79
Our Time '74

Van Heflin
Airport '70
Back Door to Heaven '39
Battle Cry '55
Cry of Battle '63
East Side, West Side '49
Flight from Glory '37
The Greatest Story Ever Told '65
Green Dolphin Street '47
Johnny Eager '42
Madame Bovary '49
The Man Outside '68
Patterns '56
The Possessed '47
Presenting Lily Mars '43
Prowler '51
The Ruthless Four '70
Santa Fe Trail '40
Seven Miles from Alcatraz/ Flight from Glory '43
Shane '53
The Strange Love of Martha Ivers '46
They Came to Cordura '59
The Three Musketeers '48
3:10 to Yuma '57
Till the Clouds Roll By '46
Till the Clouds Roll By/A Star Is Born '46
A Woman Rebels '36

O.P. Heggie
Anne of Green Gables '34
The Bride of Frankenstein '35
The Count of Monte Cristo '34
Devotion '31
Midnight '34
Peck's Bad Boy '34
Smilin' Through '32

Robert Hegyes
Just Tell Me You Love Me '80
Underground Aces '80

Peter Hehir
Fast Talking '86
I Live with Me Dad '86
Sweet Talker '91

Katherine Heigl
King of the Hill '93
My Father the Hero '93

Elayne Heilveil
The Adventures of Nellie Bly '81
Birds of Prey '72

Brit Helfer
Alley Cat '84
Body Trouble '92

Marg Helgenberger
After Midnight '89
Always '89
Blind Vengeance '90
China Beach '88
The Cowboy Way '94
Death Dreams '92
Desperate Motives '92
Fallen Angels 2 '93
Stephen King's The Tommyknockers '93

Erik Hell
The Passion of Anna '70
Port of Call '48

Richard Hell
Desperately Seeking Susan '85
Geek Maggot Bingo '83
Smithereens '82

Randee Heller
Can You Hear the Laughter? The Story of Freddie Prinze '79
Danielle Steel's Changes '91
Fast Break '79
The Karate Kid '84

Anne Helm
Follow That Dream '61
Nightmare in Wax '69
The Unkissed Bride '66

Levon Helm
Best Revenge '83
Coal Miner's Daughter '80
The Dollmaker '84
End of the Line '88
Man Outside '88
The Right Stuff '83
Smooth Talk '85

Charlotte J. Helmkamp
Frankenhooker '90
Posed For Murder '89

Katherine Helmond
Amore! '93
The Autobiography of Miss Jane Pittman '74
Brazil '85
Family Plot '76
Inside Monkey Zetterland '93
Jack & the Beanstalk '83
The Lady in White '88
Larry '74
Overboard '87
Rosie: The Rosemary Clooney Story '82
Scout's Honor '80
Shadey '87
Time Bandits '81
World War III '86

Tom Helmore
Designing Woman '57
Flipper's New Adventure '64
The Tender Trap '55
This Could Be the Night '57
Trouble Along the Way '53
Vertigo '58

Robert Helpmann
The Mango Tree '77
Patrick '78
Puzzle '78
The Red Shoes '48
The Tales of Hoffmann '51

Sheila Helpmann
The Getting of Wisdom '77
Image of Death '77

David Hemblen
The Adjuster '91
Brainscan '94
Family Viewing '88
The Room '87

Short Circuit 2 '88
Speaking Parts '89

Mark Hembrow
High Tide '87
Out of the Body '88
Return to Snowy River '88

Margaux Hemingway
Deadly Conspiracy '91
Deadly Rivals '92
Double Obsession '93
Inner Sanctum '91
Killer Fish '79
Lipstick '76
Over the Brooklyn Bridge '83
They Call Me Bruce? '82

Mariel Hemingway
Creator '85
Delirious '91
Falling from Grace '92
Into the Badlands '92
Lipstick '76
Manhattan '79
Mean Season '85
Personal Best '82
Star 80 '83
Steal the Sky '88
The Suicide Club '88
Sunset '88
Superman 4: The Quest for Peace '87

David Hemmings
Barbarella '68
Beyond Erotica '79
Beyond Reasonable Doubt '80
Blood Relatives '77
Blow-Up '66
Calamity Jane '82
Camelot '67
The Charge of the Light Brigade '68
Dark Forces '83
The Deadly Game '80s
Deep Red: Hatchet Murders '75
Disappearance '81
Islands in the Stream '77
Juggernaut '74
Just a Gigolo '79
The Key to Rebecca '85
The Love Machine '71
Man, Woman & Child '83
Murder by Decree '79
The Old Curiosity Shop '75
Power Play '81
The Rainbow '89
The Snow Queen '83
The Squeeze '77
Thirst '87
The Turn of the Screw '89

Anouska Hempel
On Her Majesty's Secret Service '69
The Scars of Dracula '70
Tiffany Jones '75

Sherman Hemsley
Camp Cucamonga: How I Spent My Summer Vacation '90
Club Fed '90
Combat Academy '86
Ghost Dance '83
Ghost Fever '87
Love at First Bite '79
Mr. Nanny '93

Richard Hench
Bio Hazard '85
Tomb '86

Bill Henderson
Ace Crawford, Private Eye
City Slickers '91
Clue '85
Get Crazy '83
Movie Maker '86
Murphy's Law '86

Dell Henderson
The Crowd '28
Love Affair '39
Show People '28

Don Henderson
The Ghoul '75
The Island '80

Florence Henderson
The Brady Bunch, Vol. 1 '69
Shakes the Clown '92
Song of Norway '70
A Very Brady Christmas '88

Jo Henderson
Lianna '83
Rachel River '89

Marcia Henderson
Naked Hills '56
Thunder Bay '53

Ty Henderson
The Competition '80
Happy Hour '87

Tony Hendra
Life with Mikey '93
This is Spinal Tap '84

Jimi Hendrix
Dynamite Chicken '70
Monterey Pop '68
Woodstock '70

Wanda Hendrix
The Admiral Was a Lady '50
My Outlaw Brother '51

Gloria Hendry
Bare Knuckles '77
Black Belt Jones '74
Black Caesar '73
Hell Up in Harlem '73
Live and Let Die '73
Slaughter's Big Ripoff '73

Ian Hendry
The Bitch '78
Captain Kronos: Vampire Hunter '74
Children of the Damned '63
Journey to the Far Side of the Sun '69
Killer with Two Faces '74
McKenzie Break '70
The Passenger '75
Repulsion '65
The Saint '68
Tales from the Crypt '72
Theatre of Blood '73

Sonja Henie
Everything Happens at Night '39
Happy Landing '38
Iceland '42
My Lucky Star '38
One in a Million '36
Second Fiddle '39
Sun Valley Serenade '41
Thin Ice '37
Wintertime '43

Marilu Henner
Between the Lines '77
Bloodbrothers '78
Cannonball Run 2 '84
Chains of Gold '92
Grand Larceny
Grown Ups '86
Hammett '82
Johnny Dangerously '84
L.A. Story '91
Ladykillers '88
Love with a Perfect Stranger '86
The Man Who Loved Women '83
Noises Off '92
Perfect '85
Rustler's Rhapsody '85
Stark '85

Eva Henning
Devil's Wanton '49
Three Strange Loves '49

Paul Henreid
Battle Shock '56
Casablanca '42
Deception '46
Deep in My Heart '54
The Four Horsemen of the Apocalypse '62
Goodbye, Mr. Chips '39
Joan of Paris '42
The Madwoman of Chaillot '69
Never So Few '59
Night Train to Munich '40
Now, Voyager '42
The Scar '48
The Spanish Main '45
A Stolen Face '52
Tall Lie '53

Lance Henriksen
Alien 3 '92
Aliens '86
Choke Canyon '86

Color of Night '94
Comrades in Arms '91
Damien: Omen 2 '78
Deadly Intent '88
Delta Heat '92
Dog Day Afternoon '75
Excessive Force '93
Hard Target '93
The Hit List '88
The Horror Show '89
The Jagged Edge '85
Jennifer 8 '92
Johnny Handsome '89
Knights '93
Man's Best Friend '93
Near Dark '87
Nightmares '83
No Escape '94
The Outfit '73
Piranha 2: The Spawning '82
The Pit & the Pendulum '91
Prince of the City '81
Pumpkinhead '88
The Quick and the Dead '94
The Right Stuff '83
Savage Dawn '84
Stone Cold '91
Super Mario Bros. '93
Survival Quest '89
Tales from the Crypt, Vol. 3 '90
The Terminator '84
The Visitor '80

Anders Henrikson
Miss Julie '50
A Woman's Face '38

Buck Henry
Aria '88
Catch-22 '70
Dark Before Dawn '89
Defending Your Life '91
Eating Raoul '82
Gloria '80
The Graduate '67
Grumpy Old Men '93
Is There Sex After Death? '71
Keep the Change '92
The Linguini Incident '92
The Man Who Fell to Earth '76
Old Boyfriends '79
Rude Awakening '89
Short Cuts '93
Steve Martin Live '85
Tune in Tomorrow '90

Charlotte Henry
Bowery Blitzkrieg '41
Charlie Chan at the Opera '36
God's Country and the Man '37
The Mandarin Mystery '37
March of the Wooden Soldiers '34

Greg Henry
Body Double '84
Fair Game '89
Funny Money '82
Hitchhiker 4 '87
Hot Rod '79
Just Before Dawn '80
Kiss of a Killer '93
The Last of Philip Banter '87
Mean Dog Blues '78
The Patriot '86
The Positively True Adventures of the Alleged Texas Cheerleader-Murdering Mom '93

Justin Henry
Kramer vs. Kramer '79
Martin's Day '85
Sixteen Candles '84
Sweet Hearts Dance '88
Tiger Town '83

Lenny Henry
Bernard and the Genie '90s
The Suicide Club '88
Three of a Kind '80s
True Identity '91

Martha Henry
Dancing in the Dark '86
Glory Enough for All: The Discovery of Insulin '92
White Light '90

Mike Henry
Adios Amigo '75
Smokey and the Bandit '77
Smokey and the Bandit, Part 2 '80

Smokey and the Bandit, Part 3 '83

Robert "Buzzy" Henry
Buzzy Rides the Range '40
The Great Mike '44
Turf Boy '42
The Unknown Ranger '36
Western Frontier '35
Wild West '46

Tim Henry
The Dawson Patrol '78
125 Rooms of Comfort '83

William Henry
The Adventures of Mark Twain '44
Canadian Mounties Vs. Atomic Invaders '53
Dance Hall '41
Madame X '37
Marshal of Cedar Rock '53
Movie Stuntmen '53
Tarzan Escapes '36

Pamela Hensley
Buck Rogers in the 25th Century '79
Doc Savage '75
Double Exposure '82
The Nude Bomb '80
The Rebels '79

Nicky Henson
Number 1 of the Secret Service
Psychomania '73

Audrey Hepburn
Always '89
Breakfast at Tiffany's '61
Charade '63
The Children's Hour '61
Funny Face '57
Green Mansions '59
Love in the Afternoon '57
My Fair Lady '64
The Nun's Story '59
Paris When It Sizzles '64
Robin and Marian '76
Roman Holiday '53
Sabrina '54
Sidney Sheldon's Bloodline '79
They All Laughed '81
Two for the Road '67
The Unforgiven '60
Wait Until Dark '67
War and Peace '56

Katharine Hepburn
Adam's Rib '50
The African Queen '51
Alice Adams '35
A Bill of Divorcement '32
Break of Hearts '35
Bringing Up Baby '38
Christopher Strong '33
Desk Set '57
Dragon Seed '44
Grace Quigley '84
Guess Who's Coming to Dinner '67
Hepburn & Tracy '84
Holiday '38
The Lion in Winter '68
Little Minister '34
Little Women '33
Long Day's Journey into Night '62
Love Among the Ruins '75
The Madwoman of Chaillot '69
The Man Upstairs '93
Mary of Scotland '36
Morning Glory '33
Olly Olly Oxen Free '78
On Golden Pond '81
Pat and Mike '52
The Philadelphia Story '40
Quality Street '37
The Rainmaker '56
Rooster Cogburn '75
Spitfire '34
Stage Door '37
Stage Door Canteen '43
State of the Union '48
Suddenly, Last Summer '59
Summertime '55
Sylvia Scarlett '35
Trojan Women '71
Without Love '45
Woman of the Year '42
A Woman Rebels '36

Bernard Hepton
The Charmer '89
Eminent Domain '91
Mansfield Park '85
Shadey '87
Stealing Heaven '88

Charles Herbert
Gun Glory '57
13 Ghosts '60

Holmes Herbert
Bad Boy '39
British Intelligence '40
Daughter of the Dragon '31
Dr. Jekyll and Mr. Hyde '31
The House of Secrets '37
Invisible Agent '42
The Kiss '29
Sherlock Holmes and the
   Secret Weapon '42
Shop Angel '32
Sons of Steel '35
Stanley and Livingstone '39
Through the Breakers '28

Hugh Herbert
The Beautiful Blonde from
   Bashful Bend '49
Bureau of Missing Persons '33
Diplomaniacs '33
Eternally Yours '39
Fashions of 1934 '34
Gold Diggers of 1935 '35
The Great Waltz '38
Hook, Line and Sinker '30
It's a Great Life '43
A Midsummer Night's Dream
   '35
One Rainy Afternoon '36
Sherlock Holmes and the
   Secret Weapon '42
A Song is Born '48
Sweet Adeline '35
The Villain Still Pursued Her '41

Percy Herbert
Call Me Bwana '63
The Fiend '71
Man in the Wilderness '71
Mysterious Island '61

Carla Herd
Deathstalker 3 '89
Wild Zone '89

Richard Herd
Lovely...But Deadly '82
Wolf Lake '79

Eileen Herlie
Angel with the Trumpet '50
Hamlet '48

Roberto Herlitzka
Summer Night '87
Summer Night with Greek
   Profile, Almond Eyes &
   Scent of Basil '87

Jimmy Herman
Dances with Wolves '90
Geronimo '93

Paul Herman
The Last Temptation of Christ
   '88
New York Stories '89
The Squeeze '87

Woody Herman
Sensations of 1945 '44
Wintertime '43

Irm Hermann
Ali: Fear Eats the Soul '74
The Bitter Tears of Petra von
   Kant '72
The Last Five Days '82
The Merchant of Four Seasons
   '71
Mother Kusters Goes to
   Heaven '76

Juano Hernandez
Intruder in the Dust '49
The Mark of the Hawk '57
Sergeant Rutledge '60
Something of Value '57
Stars in My Crown '50
They Call Me Mr. Tibbs! '70

Marcel Herrand
Children of Paradise '44
Les Visiteurs du Soir '42

Mark Herrier
Porky's '82

Porky's 2: The Next Day '83
Sprague '84
Tank '83

Laura Herring
The Forbidden Dance '90
Silent Night, Deadly Night 3:
   Better Watch Out! '89

Edward Herrmann
The Betsy '78
Big Business '88
Born Yesterday '93
Brass Target '78
Compromising Positions '85
The Day of the Dolphin '73
Death Valley '81
Eleanor & Franklin '76
Freedom Road '79
The Great Gatsby '74
The Great Waldo Pepper '75
Harry's War '84
The Lawrenceville Stories '80s
A Little Sex '82
The Lost Boys '87
Love Affair: The Eleanor & Lou
   Gehrig Story '77
The Man with One Red Shoe
   '85
Memorial Day '83
Mrs. Soffel '84
Murrow '86
My Boyfriend's Back '93
The North Avenue Irregulars
   '79
Overboard '87
The Paper Chase '73
Portrait of a Stripper '79
The Private History of a
   Campaign That Failed '87
The Purple Rose of Cairo '85
Reds '81
Sorrows of Gin '79
Sweet Poison '91
Take Down '79

Mark Herron
8 1/2 '63
Girl in Gold Boots '69

Gary Hershberger
Free Ride '86
Paradise Motel '84

Barbara Hershey
Americana '81
Angel on My Shoulder '80
The Baby Maker '70
Beaches '88
Boxcar Bertha '72
Choice of Weapons '76
A Dangerous Woman '93
Defenseless '91
Diamonds '72
The Entity '83
Falling Down '93
Flood! '76
Hannah and Her Sisters '86
Hoosiers '86
A Killing in a Small Town '90
Last Summer '69
The Last Temptation of Christ
   '88
The Liberation of L.B. Jones
   '70
My Wicked, Wicked Ways '84
The Natural '84
The Nightingale '83
Paris Trout '91
Passion Flower '86
The Public Eye '92
The Pursuit of Happiness '70
Return to Lonesome Dove '93
The Right Stuff '83
Shy People '87
Splitting Heirs '93
The Stunt Man '80
Swing Kids '93
Take This Job & Shove It '81
Tin Men '87
Tune in Tomorrow '90
With Six You Get Eggroll '68
A World Apart '88

Jean Hersholt
Alexander's Ragtime Band '38
Break of Hearts '35
Courageous Dr. Christian '40
Dinner at Eight '33
Disciple '15
Dr. Christian Meets the Women
   '40
Grand Hotel '32

Greed '24
Happy Landing '38
Heart's Haven '22
Hearts of Humanity '32
Heidi '37
Hell Harbor '30
The Mask of Fu Manchu '32
Meet Dr. Christian '39
Melody for Three '41
One in a Million '36
The Painted Veil '34
Private Lives '31
Remedy for Riches '40
The Sin of Madelon Claudet '31
Skyscraper Souls '32
Susan Lenox: Her Fall and Rise
   '31
They Meet Again '41

Gerard Herter
Any Gun Can Play '67
Hornet's Nest '70
Last Day of the War '69

Irene Hervey
The Count of Monte Cristo '34
Destry Rides Again '39
Dude Ranger '34
Gangbusters '38
The Girl Said No '37
Mickey '48
Mr. Peabody & the Mermaid '48
Night Monster '42
Play Misty for Me '71

Jason Hervey
Back to School '86
Back to the Future '85

Werner Herzog
Burden of Dreams '82
Man of Flowers '84

David Hess
Avalanche Express '79
House on the Edge of the Park
   '84
Last House on the Left '72
Let It Rock '86

Howard Hesseman
Amazon Women on the Moon
   '87
Americathon '79
The Big Bus '76
Clue '85
The Committee '68
The Diamond Trap '91
Doctor Detroit '83
Flight of the Navigator '86
Great American Traffic Jam '80
Heat '87
Honky Tonk Freeway '81
Inside Out '91
Jackson County Jail '76
Little Miss Millions '93
Loose Shoes '80
Murder in New Hampshire: The
   Pamela Smart Story '91
My Chauffeur '86
One Shoe Makes It Murder '82
Police Academy 2: Their First
   Assignment '85
The Princess Who Never
   Laughed '84
Private Lessons '81
Rubin & Ed '92
Shampoo '75
Silence of the Heart '84
Steelyard Blues '73
The Sunshine Boys '75
Tarantulas: The Deadly Cargo
   '77
This is Spinal Tap '84
Tunnelvision '76
WKRP in Cincinnati, Vol. 1 '78

Catherine Hessling
Charleston '26
Renoir Shorts '27

Charlton Heston
The Agony and the Ecstasy '65
Airport '75 '75
Almost an Angel '90
Antony and Cleopatra '73
Arrowhead '53
The Awakening '80
Ben-Hur '59
Beneath the Planet of the Apes
   '70
Big Country '58
The Buccaneer '58
Call of the Wild '72
Chiefs '83

The Crucifer of Blood '91
Diamond Head '62
Earthquake '74
El Cid '61
Elizabeth, the Queen '68
55 Days at Peking '63
The Four Musketeers '75
Gray Lady Down '77
The Greatest Show on Earth
   '52
The Greatest Story Ever Told
   '65
Julius Caesar '70
Khartoum '66
Major Dundee '65
A Man for All Seasons '88
Midway '76
Mother Lode '82
The Mountain Men '80
Nairobi Affair '88
Naked Jungle '54
Omega Man '71
Planet of the Apes '68
Pony Express '53
Proud Men '87
Ruby Gentry '52
Solar Crisis '92
Soylent Green '73
The Ten Commandments '56
A Thousand Heroes '94
The Three Musketeers '74
Three Violent People '57
Tombstone '93
Touch of Evil '58
Treasure Island '89
True Lies '94
Two Minute Warning '76
The War Lord '65
Will Penny '67
The Wreck of the Mary Deare
   '59

Martin Hewitt
Alien Predators '80
Carnal Crimes '91
Crime Lords '91
Endless Love '81
Killer Party '86
Night Rhythms '92
Out of Control '85
Private War '90
Secret Games '92
Secret Games 2: The Escort
   '93
White Ghost '88
Yellowbeard '83

Sean Hewitt
Big Zapper '73
The Sender '82

David Hewlett
Desire and Hell at Sunset Motel
   '92
The Penthouse '92
Pin '88
Scanners 2: The New Order '91

Weldon Heyburn
The Chinese Cat '44
Criminals Within '41
Panama Patrol '39
Sea Racketeers '37
The Thirteenth Man '37

Louis Jean Heydt
The Big Sleep '46
The Great McGinty '40
Our Vines Have Tender Grapes
   '45
Thirty Seconds Over Tokyo '44
Zombies on Broadway '44

Herbert Heyes
Behind Locked Doors '48
Calling Wild Bill Elliott '43
The Cobra Strikes '48
Teenage '44

Barton Heyman
Billy Galvin '86
He Who Walks Alone '78
Let's Scare Jessica to Death
   '71
Raising Cain '92
Roadside Prophets '92
Static '85
Valdez is Coming '71

Anne Heywood
The Brain '62
Carthage in Flames '60
Doctor at Large '57
I Want What I Want '72

Sadat '83
Scenes from a Murder '72
The Shaming '71
The Very Edge '63

Pat Heywood
Girly '70
Rude Awakening '81
Wish You Were Here '87

William Hickey
Any Man's Death '90
The Boston Strangler '68
Bright Lights, Big City '88
Da '88
Hobo's Christmas '87
Invitation to a Gunfighter '64
Mikey & Nicky '76
Mob Boss '90
My Blue Heaven '90
The Name of the Rose '86
National Lampoon's Christmas
   Vacation '89
One Crazy Summer '86
Pink Cadillac '89
Prizzi's Honor '85
Puppet Master '89
The Runestone '91
Sea of Love '89
Tales from the Crypt, Vol. 3 '90
Tales from the Darkside: The
   Movie '90
Walls of Glass '85

Catherine Hickland
Ghost Town '88
Millions '90
Witchery '88

Darryl Hickman
The Devil on Wheels '47
Fighting Father Dunne '48
Geronimo's Revenge '60
Johnny Shiloh '63
Men of Boys Town '41
Tea and Sympathy '56
Texas John Slaughter:
   Geronimo's Revenge '60

Dwayne Hickman
Cat Ballou '65
Dr. Goldfoot and the Bikini
   Machine '65
High School USA '84
How to Stuff a Wild Bikini '65
My Dog, the Thief '69
The Sun Comes Up '49

Howard Hickman
Bullet Code '40
Civilization '16
Hell-Ship Morgan '36

Catherine Hicks
Better Late Than Never '83
Child's Play '88
Death Valley '81
Fever Pitch '85
Garbo Talks '84
Laguna Heat '87
Like Father, Like Son '87
Marilyn: The Untold Story '80
Peggy Sue Got Married '86
The Razor's Edge '84
Running Against Time '90
Secret Ingredient '92
She's Out of Control '89
Souvenir '88
Spy '89
Star Trek 4: The Voyage Home
   '86

Dan Hicks
Class Action '91
Evil Dead 2: Dead by Dawn '87

Kevin Hicks
Blood Relations '87
Final Notice '89
Higher Education '88

Russell Hicks
Air Raid Wardens '43
The Bank Dick '40
Blind Fools '40
Devil Dogs of the Air '35
Hitler: Dead or Alive '43
Pick a Star '37
Seventh Cavalry '56
Stanley and Livingstone '39
Tarzan's New York Adventure
   '42

Seymour Hicks
Fame is the Spur '47
Scrooge '35

Hicks ►cont.

The Secret of the Loch '34
William T. Hicks
Challenge '74
Day of Judgment '81
Death Screams '83
House of Death '82
Order of the Black Eagle '87
Unmasking the Idol '86
Joan Hickson
The Body in the Library '87
A Day in the Death of Joe Egg '71
Doctor in the House '53
Great Expectations '81
A Murder is Announced '87
A Pocketful of Rye '87
Sachiko Hidari
The Insect Woman '63
She and He '63
Chieko Higashiyama
Early Summer '51
Tokyo Story '53
Anthony Higgins
The Bride '85
Cold Room '84
The Draughtsman's Contract '82
For Love or Money '93
Max, Mon Amour '86
One Against the Wind '91
Quartet '81
Raiders of the Lost Ark '81
She'll Be Wearing Pink Pajamas '84
Sweet Killing '93
Clare Higgins
Bad Behavior '92
Hellbound: Hellraiser 2 '88
Hellraiser '87
Wonderland '88
Joe Higgins
Flipper's New Adventure '64
Milo Milo '60s
Namu, the Killer Whale '66
Michael Higgins
Angel Heart '87
Born Beautiful '82
The Conversation '74
Courtship '87
Crusoe '89
Dead Bang '89
Desperate Characters '71
1918 '85
On Valentine's Day '86
Paul's Case '80
School Ties '92
Jane Higginson
Devil Wears White '86
Silent Night, Deadly Night 5: The Toymaker '91
Jennifer Hilary
Miss A & Miss M '86
One Brief Summer '70
Lise Hilboldt
A Married Man '84
Noon Wine '84
Arthur Hill
The Amateur '82
The Andromeda Strain '71
A Bridge Too Far '77
The Champ '79
Churchill and the Generals '81
Death Be Not Proud '75
Dirty Tricks '81
Futureworld '76
The Guardian '84
Harper '66
Judge Horton and the Scottsboro Boys '76
The Killer Elite '75
Love Leads the Way '84
Making Love '82
One Magic Christmas '85
The Ordeal of Dr. Mudd '80
Petulia '68
The Pursuit of Happiness '71
Return of Frank Cannon '80
Revenge of the Stepford Wives '80
Riel '79
Tales of the Unexpected '91

Tomorrow's Child '82
The Ugly American '63
Benny Hill
Benny Hill's Crazy World '74
Chitty Chitty Bang Bang '68
The Italian Job '69
Those Magnificent Men in Their Flying Machines '65
To See Such Fun '81
Bernard Hill
Bellman and True '88
The Bounty '84
Drowning by Numbers '87
Mountains of the Moon '90
No Surrender '86
Shirley Valentine '89
Craig Hill
Adios, Hombre '68
Animal Called Man '87
Black Box Affair '66
Detective Story '51
What Price Glory? '52
Doris Hill
Galloping Romeo '33
Tangled Destinies '32
Jack Hill
The Brain Eaters '58
Dance of Death '68
The Female Jungle '56
The Sinister Invasion '68
Lauryn Hill
King of the Hill '93
Sister Act 2: Back in the Habit '93
Marianna Hill
The Baby '72
Blood Beach '81
El Condor '70
The Godfather, Part 2 '74
High Plains Drifter '73
The Invisible Strangler '76
The Last Porno Flick '74
Married Too Young '62
Medium Cool '69
Messiah of Evil '74
Paradise, Hawaiian Style '66
Red Line 7000 '65
Roustabout '64
Schizoid '80
Thumb Tripping '72
Mary Hill
The Beast from 20,000 Fathoms '53
Mesa of Lost Women '52
Nellie Hill
Mistaken Identity '41
Murder with Music '45
Richard Hill
Bloodfist 2 '90
Deathstalker '83
Deathstalker 4: Clash of the Titans '92
Devastator '85
Dune Warriors '91
Warrior Queen '87
Steven Hill
Between Two Women '86
Billy Bathgate '91
The Boost '88
A Child is Waiting '63
Eyewitness '81
The Firm '93
Garbo Talks '84
Heartburn '86
It's My Turn '80
Legal Eagles '86
On Valentine's Day '86
Raw Deal '86
Rich and Famous '81
Running on Empty '88
The Slender Thread '65
White Palace '90
Yentl '83

Terence Hill
Ace High '69
All the Way, Boys '73
Boot Hill '69
Crime Busters '78
Go for It '83
March or Die '77
Miami Supercops '85
Mr. Billion '77
My Name is Nobody '74
Odds and Evens '78
Super Fuzz '81
They Call Me Trinity '72
Trinity is Still My Name '75
Wendy Hiller
Anne of Avonlea '87
The Cat and the Canary '79
The Curse of King Tut's Tomb '80
David Copperfield '70
The Elephant Man '80
I Know Where I'm Going '45
The Lonely Passion of Judith Hearne '87
Major Barbara '41
Making Love '82
A Man for All Seasons '66
Murder on the Orient Express '74
Pygmalion '38
Separate Tables '58
Something of Value '57
Toys in the Attic '63
Voyage of the Damned '76
John Hillerman
Assault and Matrimony '87
Audrey Rose '77
Betrayal '78
Blazing Saddles '74
Chinatown '74
History of the World: Part 1 '81
The Last Picture Show '71
Lawman '71
Little Gloria...Happy at Last '84
Marathon '80
The Outside Man '73
Paper Moon '73
The Thief Who Came to Dinner '73
Up the Creek '84
Verna Hillie
House of Mystery '34
Man of the Forest '33
Trail Beyond '34
Candace Hilligoss
Carnival of Souls '62
Curse of the Living Corpse '64
Beverly Hills
Brides of the Beast '68
Knights & Emeralds '87
Gillian Hills
Beat Girl '60
Demons of the Mind '72
Daisy Hilton
Chained for Life '53
Saturday Night Shockers '50
George Hilton
Any Gun Can Play '67
The Battle of El Alamein '68
The Black Pirate '65
Blade of the Ripper '84
Bullet for Sandoval '70
Day of the Maniac '75
Dead for a Dollar '70s
Guns for Dollars '73
The Next Victim '71
The Ruthless Four '70
Sartana's Here...Trade Your Pistol for a Coffin '70
The Scorpion's Tail '71
Lawrence Hilton-Jacobs
Angels of the City '89
The Annihilators '85
Chance '89
Cooley High '75
East L.A. Warriors '89
For the Love of It '80
The Jacksons: An American Dream '92
Killcrazy '89
L.A. Heat '88
L.A. Vice '89
Paramedics '88
Quiet Fire '91

Art Hindle
Desperate Lives '82
Dixie Lanes '88
The Gunfighters '87
Into the Fire '88
Invasion of the Body Snatchers '78
J. Edgar Hoover '87
The Man Who Wasn't There '83
Octagon '80
The Power Within '79
Raw Courage '84
Say Yes! '86
Surrogate '88
Wild Pony '83
The World's Oldest Living Bridesmaid '92
Earl Hindman
The Ballad of the Sad Cafe '91
Murder in Coweta County '83
The Taking of Pelham One Two Three '74
Samuel S. Hinds
Blossoms in the Dust '41
Deluge '33
Destry Rides Again '39
Devil's Party '38
Gabriel Over the White House '33
It's a Date '40
It's a Wonderful Life '46
Man Made Monster '41
Navy Blue and Gold '37
Pardon My Sarong '42
The Raven '35
Ride 'Em Cowboy '42
Scarlet Street '45
Son of Dracula '43
The Strange Affair of Uncle Harry '45
Test Pilot '38
Weekend at the Waldorf '45
You Can't Take It with You '38
Gregory Hines
The Cotton Club '84
Deal of the Century '83
Eubie! '82
Eve of Destruction '90
History of the World: Part 1 '81
Off Limits '87
Puss 'n Boots '84
A Rage in Harlem '91
Renaissance Man '94
Running Scared '86
T Bone N Weasel '90s
Tap '89
White Lie '91
White Nights '85
Wolfen '81
Johnny Hines
A Girl's Folly '17
The Speed Spook '24
Tillie Wakes Up '17
Pat Hingle
The Act '82
Baby Boom '87
Batman '89
Batman Returns '92
Bloody Mama '70
Brewster's Millions '85
Broken Badge '85
Citizen Cohn '92
Elvis: The Movie '79
The Falcon and the Snowman '85
The Gauntlet '77
Going Berserk '83
The Grifters '90
Hang 'Em High '67
Hazel's People '75
In 'n Out '86
Independence '76
Invitation to a Gunfighter '64
Lady from Yesterday '85
LBJ: The Early Years '88
Lightning Jack '94
Manhunt for Claude Dallas '86
Maximum Overdrive '86
Norma Rae '79
Of Mice and Men '81
The Private History of a Campaign That Failed '87
The Quick and the Dead '94
Running Brave '83
Running Scared '79
Running Wild '73
Sudden Impact '83

Tarantulas: The Deadly Cargo '77
The Ugly American '63
Wild Times '79
Darby Hinton
Firecracker '71
Malibu Express '81
The Treasure of Jamaica Reef '74
Akihiko Hirata
Godzilla vs. the Cosmic Monster '74
H-Man '59
The Secret of the Telegian '61
Thora Hird
Conspirator '49
Consuming Passions '88
The Entertainer '60
A Kind of Loving '62
The Nightcomers '72
Rattle of a Simple Man '64
Daniel Hirsch
Sky High '84
Zero Boys '86
Judd Hirsch
Brotherly Love '85
Fury on Wheels '71
The Goodbye People '83
The Great Escape 2: The Untold Story '88
King of the Gypsies '78
Legend of Valentino '75
Marriage is Alive and Well '80
Ordinary People '80
Running on Empty '88
Sooner or Later '78
Teachers '84
Without a Trace '83
Alice Hirson
Blind Date '87
Miss All-American Beauty '82
Patricia Hitchcock
Psycho '60
Strangers on a Train '51
Judith Hoag
Fine Things '90
A Matter of Degrees '90
Switched at Birth '91
Teenage Mutant Ninja Turtles: The Movie '90
Doug Hobart
The Death Curse of Tartu '66
The Professor '58
Rose Hobart
Cass Timberlane '47
Conflict '45
Dr. Jekyll and Mr. Hyde '31
East of Borneo '31
The Farmer's Daughter '47
The Mad Ghoul '43
Susan and God '40
Halliwell Hobbes
Casanova Brown '44
Dr. Jekyll and Mr. Hyde '31
Gaslight '44
Journey for Margaret '42
Sherlock Holmes Faces Death '43
Son of Fury '42
The Undying Monster '42
You Can't Take It with You '38
Peter Hobbs
In the Mood '87
Next One '84
Mara Hobel
Mommie Dearest '81
Sorrows of Gin '79
Valerie Hobson
The Adventures of Tartu '43
The Bride of Frankenstein '35
Clouds Over Europe '39
Drums '38
Great Expectations '46
Interrupted Journey '49
Kind Hearts and Coronets '49
The Promoter '52
The Rocking Horse Winner '49
Spy in Black '39
Train of Events '49
Werewolf of London '35
When Thief Meets Thief '37
Douglas Hodge
Dark Obsession '90
Salome's Last Dance '88

Kate Hodge
The Hidden 2 '94
Leatherface: The Texas
    Chainsaw Massacre 3 '89
Love Kills '91
Rapid Fire '92

Patricia Hodge
Betrayal '83
Diamond's Edge '88
Dust to Dust '85
The Heat of the Day '91
The Shell Seekers '89
Spymaker: The Secret Life of
    Ian Fleming '90
Sunset '88

Eddie Hodges
The Adventures of Huckleberry
    Finn '60
A Hole in the Head '59
Live a Little, Love a Little '68
Summer Magic '63

Tom Hodges
The Baby Doll Murders '92
Vietnam War Story 3 '89

Earle Hodgins
Aces and Eights '36
The Bashful Bachelor '42
Boss of Bullion City '41
Colt Comrades '43
Heroes of the Alamo '37
Hoppy Serves a Writ '43
Inside the Law '42
A Lawman is Born '37
Santa Fe Marshal '40
The Topeka Terror '45

John Hodiak
Across the Wide Missouri '51
Ambush at Tomahawk Gap '53
Battleground '49
Command Decision '48
Conquest of Cochise '53
Dragonfly Squadron '54
The Harvey Girls '46
Homecoming '48
Lifeboat '44
Love from a Stranger '47
Malaya '49
The Miniver Story '50

Dennis Hoey
Anna and the King of Siam '46
David and Bathsheba '51
Golden Earrings '47
House of Fear '45
The Pearl of Death '44
Power '34
Roll on Texas Moon '46
Sherlock Holmes and the
    Secret Weapon '42
Son of Fury '42
Spider Woman '44

Abbie Hoffman
Born on the Fourth of July '89
Heavy Petting '89

Basil Hoffman
Communion '89
The Double O Kid '92
The Ice Runner '93
Lambada '89

David Hoffman
Children in the Crossfire '84
Wolf Lake '79

Dustin Hoffman
Agatha '79
Alfredo, Alfredo '72
All the President's Men '76
Billy Bathgate '91
Death of a Salesman '86
Dick Tracy '90
Family Business '89
The Graduate '67
Hero '91
Hook '91
Ishtar '87
Kramer vs. Kramer '79
Lenny '74
Little Big Man '70
Madigan's Millions '67
Marathon Man '76
Midnight Cowboy '69
Papillon '73
Rain Man '88
Straight Time '78
Straw Dogs '72
Tootsie '82

Gaby Hoffman
Field of Dreams '89
The Man Without a Face '93
Sleepless in Seattle '93
This is My Life '92
Uncle Buck '89

Jane Hoffman
Senior Trip '81
Static '87
Sybil '76
Up the Sandbox '72

Philip S. Hoffman
Joey Breaker '93
Leap of Faith '92
Scent of a Woman '92
When a Man Loves a Woman
    '94

Robert Hoffman
A Black Veil for Lisa '68
Eyes Behind the Stars '72
Joe Panther '76

Thom Hoffman
The 4th Man '79
Lily was Here '89
Orlando '92

Bosco Hogan
In the Name of the Father '93
James Joyce: A Portrait of the
    Artist as a Young Man '77

Hulk Hogan
Mr. Nanny '93
No Holds Barred '89
Suburban Commando '91
Thunder in Paradise '93

Michael Hogan
Clearcut '92
Lost '86
The Peanut Butter Solution '85
Smokescreen '90

Pat Hogan
Davy Crockett, King of the Wild
    Frontier '55
Indian Paint '64
Savage Wilderness '55
Seventh Cavalry '56

Paul Hogan
Almost an Angel '90
Anzacs: The War Down Under
    '85
Crocodile Dundee '86
Crocodile Dundee 2 '88
Lightning Jack '94

Robert Hogan
Gone are the Days '84
Memory of Us '74

Susan Hogan
Phobia '80
Title Shot '81
White Fang '91

Arthur Hohl
Blondie Has Trouble '40
Mystery of the Riverboat '44
Son of Fury '42

David Holbrook
Creepshow 2 '87
Return to Salem's Lot '87

Hal Holbrook
All the President's Men '76
Behind Enemy Lines '85
Capricorn One '78
Creepshow '82
Day One '89
Dress Gray '86
The Firm '93
Fletch Lives '89
The Fog '80
George Washington '84
The Girl from Petrovka '74
Girls Night Out '83
The Great White Hope '70
The Group '66
Julia '77
The Kidnapping of the
    President '80
A Killing in a Small Town '90
Killing of Randy Webster '81
Magnum Force '73
Midway '76
Murder by Natural Causes '79
Natural Enemies '79
North and South Book 1 '85
North and South Book 2 '86
Our Town '77
The People Next Door '70

Pueblo Affair '73
Rituals '79
Sorry, Wrong Number '89
The Star Chamber '83
They Only Kill Their Masters
    '72
The Unholy '88
Wall Street '87
When Hell Was in Session '82
Wild in the Streets '68

Kathryn Holcomb
Our Time '74
Skag '79

Sarah Holcomb
Caddyshack '80
Happy Birthday, Gemini '80

Diane Holden
Black Starlet '74
Grave of the Vampire '72

Fay Holden
Andy Hardy Gets Spring Fever
    '39
Andy Hardy Meets Debutante
    '40
Andy Hardy's Double Life '42
Andy Hardy's Private Secretary
    '41
The Big Hangover '50
Bitter Sweet '40
Blossoms in the Dust '41
Life Begins for Andy Hardy '41
Love Finds Andy Hardy '38
Love Laughs at Andy Hardy '46
Samson and Delilah '50
Ziegfeld Girl '41

Gloria Holden
Behind the Rising Sun '43
Dracula's Daughter '36
Hawaii Calls '38
The Life of Emile Zola '37

Jan Holden
Fire Maidens from Outer Space
    '56
One Brief Summer '70

Marjean Holden
Philadelphia Experiment 2 '93
Stripped to Kill II: Live Girls '89

Rebecca Holden
The Sisterhood '88
Twenty Dollar Star '91

William Holden
Alvarez Kelly '66
Arizona '40
Ashanti, Land of No Mercy '79
Boots Malone '52
Born Yesterday '50
The Bridge on the River Kwai
    '57
The Bridges at Toko-Ri '55
Casino Royale '67
The Counterfeit Traitor '62
Country Girl '54
Damien: Omen 2 '78
Dance Fools Dance '31
The Dark Past '49
Dear Wife '49
The Devil's Brigade '68
Earthling '80
Escape from Fort Bravo '53
Escape to Athena '79
Executive Suite '54
Forever Female '53
Golden Boy '39
The Horse Soldiers '59
The Key '58
Love is a Many-Splendored
    Thing '55
Man from Colorado '49
Miss Grant Takes Richmond
    '49
Moon is Blue '53
Network '76
Our Town '40
Paris When It Sizzles '64
Picnic '55
Rachel and the Stranger '48
Sabrina '54
S.O.B. '81
Stalag 17 '53
Sunset Boulevard '50
Texas '41
The Towering Inferno '74
21 Hours at Munich '76
Union Station '50
When Time Ran Out '80
When Wolves Cry '69

The Wild Bunch '69
Wild Rovers '71
The World of Suzie Wong '60
Young & Willing '42

Geoffrey Holder
Boomerang '92
Doctor Dolittle '67
Everything You Always Wanted
    to Know About Sex (But
    Were Afraid to Ask) '72
Live and Let Die '73
Swashbuckler '76

Hope Holiday
The Apartment '60
The Rounders '65

John Holland
Defenders of the Law '31
Gentleman from Dixie '41
Girl in Black Stockings '57
Hell Harbor '30
House of Errors '42
Morals for Women '31
Up in the Air '40

Steve Holland
Flash Gordon: Vol. 1 '53
Flash Gordon: Vol. 2 '53

Judy Holliday
Adam's Rib '50
Bells are Ringing '60
Born Yesterday '50
Full of Life '56
It Should Happen to You '54
Phffft! '54

Polly Holliday
Gremlins '84
Konrad '90s
Lots of Luck '85
Moon Over Parador '88

Earl Holliman
Alexander: The Other Side of
    Dawn '77
Anzio '68
Armored Command '61
Big Combo '55
The Bridges at Toko-Ri '55
Broken Lance '54
Cry Panic '74
Don't Go Near the Water '57
Forbidden Planet '56
Giant '56
Gunfight at the O.K. Corral '57
Gunsmoke: Return to Dodge
    '87
Hot Spell '58
I Died a Thousand Times '55
I Love You...Goodbye '73
Last Train from Gun Hill '59
The Rainmaker '56
Sharky's Machine '81
Smoke '70
The Solitary Man '82
Sons of Katie Elder '65
Summer and Smoke '61
The Trap '59
Tribes '70

Bridget Hollman
Evils of the Night '85
Slumber Party '57 '76

Stanley Holloway
Brief Encounter '46
Cotton Queen '37
Hamlet '48
Immortal Battalion '44
In Harm's Way '65
The Lavender Hill Mob '51
Lily of Killarney '34
Mrs. Brown, You've Got a
    Lovely Daughter '68
My Fair Lady '64
Nicholas Nickleby '46
No Love for Johnnie '60
Passport to Pimlico '49
The Private Life of Sherlock
    Holmes '70
Salute John Citizen '42
This Happy Breed '47

Sterling Holloway
The Adventures of Huckleberry
    Finn '60
The Beautiful Blonde from
    Bashful Bend '49
Cheers for Miss Bishop '41
Death Valley '46
Disney's Storybook Classics
    '82
Doubting Thomas '35

I Live My Life '35
International House '33
Kentucky Rifle '55
The Lady is Willing '42
Live a Little, Love a Little '68
Melody Master '41
The Merry Widow '34
Robin Hood of Texas '47
Shake, Rattle and Rock '57
Sioux City Sue '46
Super Seal '77
Thunder and Lightning '77
Tomorrow's Children '34
Twilight on the Rio Grande '41
A Walk in the Sun '46
Wildfire '45

Ellen Holly
Cops and Robbers '73
School Daze '88

Lauren Holly
The Adventures of Ford
    Fairlane '90
Band of the Hand '86
Dangerous Heart '93
Dragon: The Bruce Lee Story
    '93

Celeste Holm
All About Eve '50
Bittersweet Love '76
Champagne for Caesar '50
Cinderella '64
Death Cruise '74
Gentleman's Agreement '47
High Society '56
Murder by the Book '87
Road House '48
The Snake Pit '48
The Tender Trap '55
Three Men and a Baby '87
Tom Sawyer '73

Ian Holm
Alien '79
Another Woman '88
The Borrowers '93
Brazil '85
Chariots of Fire '81
Dance with a Stranger '85
Dreamchild '85
The Endless Game '89
The Fixer '68
Greystoke: The Legend of
    Tarzan, Lord of the Apes '84
Hamlet '90
Henry V '89
Holocaust '78
Inside the Third Reich '82
Juggernaut '74
Kafka '91
The Man in the Iron Mask '77
March or Die '77
A Midsummer Night's Dream
    '68
Naked Lunch '91
Return of the Soldier '82
Shout at the Devil '76
Singleton's Pluck '84
S.O.S. Titanic '79
The Thief of Baghdad '78
Time Bandits '81
Wetherby '85
Young Winston '72

Clare Holman
Afraid of the Dark '92
Let Him Have It '91

Harry Holman
Fugitive Road '34
Inside the Law '42
Mexican Spitfire at Sea '42

Rex Holman
The Choppers '61
Panic in the Year Zero! '62

Helen Holmes
Blood and Steel '25
Wild Engine/Mistaken Orders
    '23

Luree Holmes
How to Stuff a Wild Bikini '65
Pajama Party '64

Phillips Holmes
Criminal Code '31
Dinner at Eight '33
General Spanky '36
Housemaster '38
Penthouse '33

Stuart Holmes
My Pal, The King '32
People Will Talk '51

Taylor Holmes
Before Morning '33
Beware, My Lovely '52
Copper Canyon '50
Double Deal '50
Hoodlum Empire '52
Tobor the Great '54

Rosie Holotik
Don't Look in the Basement '73
Encounter with the Unknown '75
Twisted Brain '74

Charlene Holt
El Dorado '67
Man's Favorite Sport? '63
Red Line 7000 '65

Hans Holt
Almost Angels '62
The Mozart Story '48

Jack Holt
Across the Wide Missouri '51
Cat People '42
The Chase '46
Flight to Nowhere '46
Holt of the Secret Service '42
King of the Bullwhip '51
The Little American '17
The Littlest Rebel '35
Loaded Pistols '48
My Pal Trigger '46
Red Desert '50
Renegade Girl '46
San Francisco '36
Task Force '49
They Were Expendable '45
Trail of Robin Hood '50
Western Double Feature 14 '52

Jennifer Holt
Buffalo Bill Rides Again '47
Fighting Vigilantes '47
Frontier '43
Ghost Town Renegades '47
The Hawk of Powder River '48
Outlaw Trail '44
Raiders of Sunset Pass '43
Range Renegades '48
Song of Old Wyoming '45
Stage to Mesa City '48
The Tioga Kid '48
Where the North Begins '47

Patrick Holt
Alias John Preston '56
Flight from Singapore '62
Men of Sherwood Forest '57
Psychomania '73
Suspended Alibi '56
Unholy Four '71
Vulture '70
When Dinosaurs Ruled the Earth '70

Tim Holt
Dynamite Pass '50
Fifth Avenue Girl '39
Gun Smugglers/Hot Lead '51
Gunplay '51
His Kind of Woman '51
Hitler's Children '43
Hot Lead '51
Law West of Tombstone '38
The Magnificent Ambersons '42
The Monster that Challenged the World '57
My Darling Clementine '46
Mysterious Desperado '49
Mysterious Desperado/Rider From Tucson '49
Renegade Ranger/Scarlet River '38
Rider from Tucson '50
Riders of the Range '49
Riders of the Range/Storm Over Wyoming '50
Sagebrush Law '43
Stagecoach '39
Storm Over Wyoming '50
This Stuff'll Kill Ya! '71
Treasure of the Sierra Madre '48
Western Double Feature 14 '52
Wild Frontier '48
The Yesterday Machine '63

Ula Holt
The New Adventures of Tarzan '35
Tarzan and the Green Goddess '38

Mark Holton
Easy Wheels '89
Leprechaun '93
Pee Wee's Big Adventure '85

Sean Holton
Presumed Guilty '91
White Fury '90

Maria Holvoe
The Last Warrior '89
Worth Winning '89

Robert E. Homans
The Concentratin' Kid '30
I Take This Oath '40
Man from Hell's Edges '32
Rogue's Gallery '44
The Scarlet Clue '45
Spurs '30
Trigger Tricks '30
X Marks the Spot '42

David Homb
The Channeler '89
Street Soldiers '91

Skip Homeier
The Burning Hills '56
Cry Vengeance '54
The Gunfighter '50
The Halls of Montezuma '50
Johnny Shiloh '63
Starbird and Sweet William '73
The Tall T '57
Ten Wanted Men '54
The Voyage of the Yes '72

Oscar Homolka
Ball of Fire '41
Boy's Night Out '62
Comrade X '40
The Executioner '70
Funeral in Berlin '66
The House of the Arrow '53
I Remember Mama '48
The Invisible Woman '40
The Key '58
The Madwoman of Chaillot '69
Mooncussers '62
Rhodes '36
Sabotage '36
Seven Sinners '40
The Seven Year Itch '55
Song of Norway '70
Strange Case of Dr. Jekyll & Mr. Hyde '68
War and Peace '56
The White Tower '50
The Wonderful World of the Brothers Grimm '62

James Hong
Bethune '77
Big Trouble in Little China '86
Black Widow '87
Body Trouble '92
The Brotherhood of the Rose '89
Caged Fury '90
Crime Lords '91
Dragonfight '92
The Dynamite Brothers
The Golden Child '86
The Jitters '88
L.A. Goddess '92
Merlin '93
Question of Faith '93
Revenge of the Nerds 2: Nerds in Paradise '87
Shadowzone '90
Talons of the Eagle '92
Tango and Cash '89
Tax Season '90
The Vineyard '89
Wayne's World 2 '93
Yes, Giorgio '82

Kojiro Hongo
Destroy All Planets '68
Gamera vs. Barugon '66
Gamera vs. Gaos '67

Darla Hood
The Bat '59
Bohemian Girl '36
Little Rascals, Book 3 '38
Little Rascals, Book 4 '30s
Little Rascals, Book 5 '30s

Little Rascals, Book 6 '30s
Little Rascals, Book 7 '30s
Little Rascals, Book 8 '30s
Little Rascals, Book 9 '30s
Little Rascals, Book 10 '30s
Little Rascals, Book 11 '38
Little Rascals, Book 12 '37
Little Rascals, Book 14 '30s
Little Rascals, Book 16 '30s
Little Rascals, Book 17 '31
Little Rascals: Choo Choo/ Fishy Tales '32
Little Rascals Christmas Special '79
Little Rascals Collector's Edition, Vol. 1-6
Little Rascals Comedy Classics, Vol. 1
Little Rascals Comedy Classics, Vol. 2
Little Rascals: Fish Hooky/ Spooky Hooky '33
Little Rascals: Honkey Donkey/ Sprucin' Up '34
Little Rascals: Little Sinner/Two Too Young '33
Little Rascals: Mush and Milk/ Three Men in a Tub '33
Little Rascals on Parade '37
Little Rascals: Pups is Pups/ Three Smart Boys '30
Little Rascals: Readin' and Writin'/Mail and Female '31
Little Rascals: Reunion in Rhythm/Mike Fright '37
Little Rascals: Spanky/Feed 'Em and Weep '32
Little Rascals: The Pinch Singer/Framing Youth '36
Little Rascals Two Reelers, Vol. 1 '29
Little Rascals Two Reelers, Vol. 2 '33
Little Rascals Two Reelers, Vol. 3 '36
Little Rascals Two Reelers, Vol. 4 '30
Little Rascals Two Reelers, Vol. 5 '34
Little Rascals Two Reelers, Vol. 6 '36
Little Rascals, Vol. 1 '29
Our Gang Comedies '40s

Don Hood
Absence of Malice '81
Blind Vengeance '90
Marie '85

Jan Hooks
Batman Returns '92
Coneheads '93
A Dangerous Woman '93
Pee Wee's Big Adventure '85

Kevin Hooks
Aaron Loves Angela '75
Can You Hear the Laughter? The Story of Freddie Prinze '79
Innerspace '87
Sounder '72
The White Shadow, Vol. 1 '78

Robert Hooks
Aaron Loves Angela '75
The Execution '85
Fast Walking '82
Heat Wave '90
Passenger 57 '92
Sweet Love, Bitter '67
A Woman Called Moses '78
Words by Heart '84

Peter Hooten
Deadly Mission '78
Dr. Strange '78
Fantasies '73
Slashed Dreams '74
2020 Texas Gladiators '85

William Hootkins
Dust Devil '93
Hear My Song '91
Valentino '77

Phil Hoover
Black Gestapo '75
Policewomen '73

Bob Hope
Bachelor in Paradise '69
Boy, Did I Get a Wrong Number! '66
Call Me Bwana '63

Cancel My Reservation '72
Casanova's Big Night '54
Caught in the Draft '41
College Swing '38
Fancy Pants '50
The Ghost Breakers '40
A Global Affair '63
The Great Lover '49
Here Come the Girls '53
Hollywood Clowns '85
Hollywood Goes to War '54
How to Commit Marriage '69
I'll Take Sweden '65
The Lemon Drop Kid '51
Louisiana Purchase '41
Monsieur Beaucaire '46
My Favorite Blonde '42
My Favorite Brunette '47
Off Limits '53
The Oscar '66
The Paleface '48
Paris Holiday '57
The Princess and the Pirate '44
The Road to Bali '53
The Road to Hong Kong '62
The Road to Lebanon '60
The Road to Morocco '42
The Road to Rio '47
The Road to Singapore '40
The Road to Utopia '46
The Road to Zanzibar '41
The Seven Little Foys '55
Son of Paleface '52
Sorrowful Jones '49
Strictly G.I. '44
They Got Me Covered '43
Two Reelers: Comedy Classics 9 '34

Leslie Hope
The Abduction of Allison Tate '92
The Big Slice '90
Caught in the Act '93
Doppelganger: The Evil Within '90
It Takes Two '88
Kansas '88
Men at Work '90
Prep School '81
Sweet Killing '93
Sword of Gideon '86
Talk Radio '88

Richard Hope
Antonia and Jane '91
Bellman and True '88
A Casualty of War '90
Piece of Cake '90
Singleton's Pluck '84

Vida Hope
Angels One Five '54
Roadhouse Girl '53

Anthony Hopkins
All Creatures Great and Small '74
Arch of Triumph '85
Audrey Rose '77
The Bounty '84
Bram Stoker's Dracula '92
A Bridge Too Far '77
A Change of Seasons '80
Chaplin '92
A Chorus of Disapproval '89
The Dawning '88
Desperate Hours '90
A Doll's House '89
The Efficiency Expert '92
84 Charing Cross Road '86
The Elephant Man '80
Freejack '92
The Girl from Petrovka '74
The Good Father '87
Great Expectations '89
Hamlet '69
Howard's End '92
The Hunchback of Notre Dame '82
The Innocent '93
International Velvet '78
Juggernaut '74
The Lindbergh Kidnapping Case '76
The Lion in Winter '68
The Looking Glass War '69
Magic '78
A Married Man '84
Mussolini & I '85
One Man's War '90
QB VII '74

The Remains of the Day '93
Shadowlands '93
The Silence of the Lambs '91
The Tenth Man '88
The Trial '93
Young Winston '72

Bo Hopkins
American Graffiti '73
The Ballad of Little Jo '93
Big Bad John '90
Blood Ties '92
Bounty Hunters '89
Casino '80
Center of the Web '92
Culpepper Cattle Co. '72
The Day of the Locust '75
The Fifth Floor '80
The Final Alliance '89
The Getaway '72
Inside Monkey Zetterland '93
Kansas City Massacre '75
The Killer Elite '75
The Legend of Wolf Mountain '92
Midnight Express '78
More American Graffiti '79
Mutant '83
Nightmare at Noon '87
The Only Way Home '72
Plutonium Incident '82
Posse '75
President's Target '93
Rodeo Girl '80
The Runaway Barge '75
A Small Town in Texas '76
A Smoky Mountain Christmas '86
Sweet 16 '81
Tentacles '80
Trapper County War '89
What Comes Around '85
White Lightning '73
The Wild Bunch '69

Harold Hopkins
Demonstrator '71
Fantasy Man '84
Monkey Grip '82
Sara Dane '81

Katherine Hopkins
The Capture of Bigfoot '79
Legend of Big Foot '82

Miriam Hopkins
Barbary Coast '35
Becky Sharp '35
Carrie '52
The Chase '66
The Children's Hour '61
Dr. Jekyll and Mr. Hyde '31
Fanny Hill: Memoirs of a Woman of Pleasure '64
The Heiress '49
Men are not Gods '37
The Old Maid '39
Savage Intruder '68
These Three '36
Virginia City '40

Rhonda Leigh Hopkins
Cover Girl Models '75
Summer School Teachers '75
Tidal Wave '75

Telma Hopkins
The Kid with the Broken Halo '82
Trancers '85
Trancers 3: Deth Lives '92
Vital Signs '90

Rolf Hoppe
Mephisto '81
Spring Symphony '86

Dennis Hopper
The American Friend '77
Apocalypse Now '79
Backtrack '89
Black Widow '87
Blood Red '88
Bloodbath
Blue Velvet '86
Boiling Point '93
Chattahoochee '89
Cool Hand Luke '67
Double-Crossed '91
Easy Rider '69
Eye of the Storm '91
Flashback '89
Giant '56

The Glory Stompers '67
Hearts of Darkness: A
Filmmaker's Apocalypse '91
Hoosiers '86
The Indian Runner '91
The Inside Man '84
King of the Mountain '81
The Last Movie '71
Let It Rock '86
Mad Dog Morgan '76
My Science Project '85
Nails '92
Night Tide '63
O.C. and Stiggs '87
The Osterman Weekend '83
Out of the Blue '80
Paris Trout '91
The Pick-Up Artist '87
Planet of Blood '66
Rebel Without a Cause '55
Reborn '78
Red Rock West '93
Riders of the Storm '88
River's Edge '87
Rumble Fish '83
Running Out of Luck '86
Speed '94
Stark '85
Straight to Hell '87
Sunset Heat '92
Super Mario Bros. '93
Superstar: The Life and Times
of Andy Warhol '90
Texas Chainsaw Massacre,
Part 2 '86
Tracks '76
The Trip '67
True Romance '93
Wild Times '79

Hedda Hopper
Annabel Takes a Tour/Maid's
Night Out '38
As You Desire Me '32
Breakfast in Hollywood '46
Dangerous Holiday '37
The Dark Hour '36
Don Juan '26
Doughnuts & Society '36
Dracula's Daughter '36
The Dropkick '27
Hedda Hopper's Hollywood '42
I Live My Life '35
Maid's Night Out '38
One Frightened Night '35
The Racketeer '29
Reap the Wild Wind '42
Skinner's Dress Suit '26
Speak Easily '32
Tarzan's Revenge '38
Vogues of 1938 '37

William Hopper
Conquest of Space '55
The Deadly Mantis '57
Rebel Without a Cause '55
20 Million Miles to Earth '57

Russell Hopton
Death from a Distance '36
The Girl from Missouri '34
Hopalong Cassidy: Renegade
Trail '39
I'm No Angel '33
Last Outlaw '36
Renegade Trail '39
West of the Pecos '45
The World Accuses '34
Zombies on Broadway '44

Barbara Horan
Bayou Romance '86
Malibu Bikini Shop '86

Gerard Horan
Look Back in Anger '89
Much Ado About Nothing '93

Roy Horan
Eagle's Shadow '84
Snuff-Bottle Connection '82
Story of the Dragon '82

Michael Hordern
Anne of the Thousand Days '69
The Baby and the Battleship
'56
A Christmas Carol '51
Cleopatra '63
Dark Obsession '90
Demons of the Mind '72
Dr. Syn, Alias the Scarecrow
'64

A Funny Thing Happened on
the Way to the Forum '66
The Green Man '91
How I Won the War '67
Ivanhoe '82
Joseph Andrews '77
Khartoum '66
Lady Jane '85
Lamp at Midnight '66
Mackintosh Man '73
The Man Who Never Was '55
The Medusa Touch '78
The Missionary '82
The Old Curiosity Shop '75
Oliver Twist '82
The Possession of Joel
Delaney '72
The Promoter '52
The Secret Garden '87
Sink the Bismarck '60
The Spaniard's Curse '58
The Spanish Gardener '57
The Spy Who Came in from the
Cold '65
The Taming of the Shrew '67
Train of Events '49
The Trouble with Spies '87
The Warriors '55
Where Eagles Dare '68
Yellowbeard '83
Young Sherlock Holmes '85

Camilla Horn
Faust '26
The Tempest/The Eagle '27

David Horne
Late Extra '35
Men of Two Worlds '46

Geoffrey Horne
Bonjour Tristesse '57
The Bridge on the River Kwai
'57
Joseph & His Brethren '60

Lena Horne
Broadway Rhythm '44
Cabin in the Sky '43
Death of a Gunfighter '69
Duchess of Idaho '50
The Duke is the Tops '38
I Dood It '43
Panama Hattie '42
Stormy Weather '43
Thousands Cheer '43
Till the Clouds Roll By '46
Till the Clouds Roll By/A Star Is
Born '46
Two Girls and a Sailor '44
The Wiz '78
Words and Music '48
Ziegfeld Follies '46

Penelope Horner
Half a Sixpence '67
Man Who Had Power Over
Women '70

David Horovitch
Paper Marriage '93
Piece of Cake '90

Adam Horovitz
A Kiss Before Dying '91
Lost Angels '89
Roadside Prophets '92

Jane Horrocks
The Dressmaker '89
Getting It Right '89
Life is Sweet '91
Memphis Belle '90
The Witches '90

Michael Horse
Border Shootout '90
Buckeye and Blue '87
Deadly Weapon '88
House of Cards '92
Legend of the Lone Ranger '81
Passenger 57 '92
Twin Peaks '90
Wagons East '94

Anna Maria Horsford
Charlotte Forten's Mission:
Experiment in Freedom '85
Heartburn '86
Presumed Innocent '90
St. Elmo's Fire '85
Street Smart '87
Taken Away '89
Times Square '80

**Edward Everett
Horton**
Arsenic and Old Lace '44
Cold Turkey '71
College Swing '38
Down to Earth '47
Forever and a Day '43
The Front Page '31
The Gay Divorcee '34
Her Husband's Affairs '47
Here Comes Mr. Jordan '41
Holiday '38
I Married an Angel '42
It's a Mad, Mad, Mad, Mad
World '63
Lonely Wives '31
Lost Horizon '37
The Magnificent Dope '42
The Merry Widow '34
Pocketful of Miracles '61
The Private Secretary '35
Reaching for the Moon '31
Sex and the Single Girl '64
Shall We Dance '37
Springtime in the Rockies '42
Sunny '41
Thank Your Lucky Stars '43
Top Hat '35
Ziegfeld Girl '41

Peter Horton
Children of the Corn '84
Side Out '90
Where the River Runs Black
'86

Robert Horton
The Green Slime '68
Men of the Fighting Lady '54

Shizuko Hoshi
Come See the Paradise '90
M. Butterfly '93

Yuriko Hoshi
Ghidrah the Three Headed
Monster '65
Godzilla vs. Mothra '64
Last War '68

Bob Hoskins
Beyond the Limit '83
Brazil '85
The Cotton Club '84
Cry Terror '74
The Dunera Boys '85
The Favor, the Watch, & the
Very Big Fish '92
Heart Condition '90
Hook '91
The Inner Circle '91
Inserts '76
Lassiter '84
The Lonely Passion of Judith
Hearne '87
The Long Good Friday '79
Mermaids '90
Mona Lisa '86
Mussolini & I '85
Passed Away '92
Pink Floyd: The Wall '82
Prayer for the Dying '87
The Raggedy Rawney '90
Shattered '91
Super Mario Bros. '93
Sweet Liberty '86
Who Framed Roger Rabbit? '88
World War II: When Lions
Roared '94
Zulu Dawn '79

Farina Hoskins
Little Rascals, Book 1 '30s
Little Rascals, Book 12 '37
Little Rascals, Book 18 '29
Our Gang '26
Our Gang Comedy Festival '88
Our Gang Comedy Festival 2
'89
The Return of Our Gang '25

Robert Hossein
The Battle of El Alamein '68
Bolero '82
Double Agents '59
Le Repos du Guerrier '62

German Houde
Les Bons Debarras '81
Night Zoo '87

Katherine Houghton
Billy Bathgate '91
Ethan Frome '92

The Eyes of the Amaryllis '82
Guess Who's Coming to Dinner
'67
Mr. North '88
The Night We Never Met '93
Seeds of Evil '76

Ned Hourani
Fist of Steel '93
Triple Impact '92

Billy House
Bedlam '45
Egg and I '47
Joe's Bed-Stuy Barbershop:
We Cut Heads '83
People Will Talk '51

Ron House
Bullshot '83
Footlight Frenzy '84

John Houseman
Another Woman '88
The Babysitter '80
Bright Lights, Big City '88
The Cheap Detective '78
A Christmas Without Snow '80
The Displaced Person '76
The Fog '78
Ghost Story '81
Gideon's Trumpet '80
Gore Vidal's Lincoln '88
Murder by Phone '82
My Bodyguard '80
The Naked Gun: From the Files
of Police Squad '88
Old Boyfriends '79
Our Town '77
The Paper Chase '73
Rollerball '75
St. Ives '76
Seven Days in May '64
Three Days of the Condor '75
Wholly Moses! '80
The Winds of War '83

Jerry Houser
Class of '44 '73
Slap Shot '77
Summer of '42 '71
A Very Brady Christmas '88

Donald Houston
The Bushbaby '70
Crow Hollow '52
Doctor in the House '53
Maniac '63
The Mark '61
The Prince and the Pauper '62
A Study in Terror '66
Tales That Witness Madness
'73

George Houston
Border Roundup '41
Frontier Scout '38
The Great Waltz '38
Let's Sing Again '36
The Lone Rider in Cheyenne
'42
The Lone Rider in Ghost Town
'41
Rangeland Racket '41
Texas Justice '42
Wallaby Jim of the Islands '37

Glyn Houston
Conspiracy '89
River Beat '54

Joff Houston
Ninja: American Warrior '90
Ninja Death Squad '87

Renee Houston
The Belles of St. Trinian's '53
The Horse's Mouth '58
Mania '60
Tunes of Glory/Horse's Mouth
'60

Anders Hove
Bloodlust: Subspecies 3 '93
Bloodstone: Subspecies 2 '93
Subspecies '91

Adrian Hoven
Castle of the Creeping Flesh
'68
Cave of the Living Dead '65
Fox and His Friends '75
Tromba, the Tiger Man '52

Natasha Hovey
Acqua e Sapone '83
Demons '86

**Adam Coleman
Howard**
No Secrets '91
Quiet Cool '86
Slaves of New York '89

Alan Howard
A Casualty of War '90
The Cook, the Thief, His Wife &
Her Lover '90
Strapless '90

Arliss Howard
Crisscross '92
Door to Door '84
Full Metal Jacket '87
Hands of a Stranger '87
Iran: Days of Crisis '91
The Lightship '86
Men Don't Leave '89
Natural Born Killers '94
Plain Clothes '88
The Prodigal '83
Ruby '92
Somebody Has to Shoot the
Picture '90
Tequila Sunrise '88
Till Death Do Us Part '92
Wilder Napalm '93

Arthur Howard
The Happiest Days of Your Life
'50
Paradisio '61
The Reckless Way '36

Bob Howard
Junction 88 '40
Murder with Music '45

Booth Howard
Mystery Liner '34
Oh Susannah '38
Red River Valley '36

Brie Howard
Android '82
The Runnin' Kind '89

Clint Howard
Backdraft '91
B.O.R.N. '88
Carnosaur '93
Cocoon '85
Cotton Candy '82
The Death of Richie '76
Disturbed '90
Eat My Dust '76
End of the Line '88
Evilspeak '82
Far and Away '92
Forced to Kill '93
Freeway '88
Gentle Giant '67
Grand Theft Auto '77
Gung Ho '85
Huckleberry Finn '75
Leprechaun 2 '94
Rock 'n' Roll High School '79
Salty '73
Silent Night, Deadly Night 4:
Initiation '90
The Wild Country '71
The Wraith '87

Curly Howard
Classic Comedy Video Sampler
'49
Comedy Festival #1 '30s
Hollywood Party '34
The Lost Stooges '33
Snow White and the Three
Stooges '61
The Stooges Story '90
Three Stooges Comedy
Capers: Vol. 1 '40s
Three Stooges Comedy
Classics '49
Three Stooges: Cookoo
Cavaliers and Other Nyuks
'40
Three Stooges Festival '49
Three Stooges: From Nurse to
Worse and Other Nyuks '45
The Three Stooges: Half-Wit's
Holiday and Other Nyuks '35
The Three Stooges: Idiots
Deluxe and Other Nyuks '45
The Three Stooges: Nutty but
Nice and Other Nyuks '36
The Three Stooges: They
Stooge to Conga and Other
Nyuks '40

Esther Howard
Klondike Annie '36
Vice Squad '31

Frank Howard
Hard Knox '83
That Was Then...This Is Now '85

John Howard
Bulldog Drummond Comes Back '37
Bulldog Drummond's Peril '38
Bulldog Drummond's Revenge '37
The Club '81
The Fighting Kentuckian '49
The Invisible Woman '40
Lost Horizon '37
Love from a Stranger '47
Make Haste to Live '54
Murderer's Wife
The Philadelphia Story '40
The Undying Monster '42
Young Einstein '89

Joyce Howard
Appointment with Crime '45
The Night Has Eyes '42

Kathleen Howard
Blossoms in the Dust '41
Crash Dive '43
It's A Gift '34

Ken Howard
Country Girl '82
Damien: The Leper Priest '80
Manhunter '74
Murder in New Hampshire: The Pamela Smart Story '91
Pudd'nhead Wilson '87
Rage of Angels '83
Rage of Angels: The Story Continues '86
Second Thoughts '83
1776 '72
Strange Interlude '90
The Thorn Birds '83
Ulterior Motives '92
The White Shadow, Vol. 1 '78

Kevyn Major Howard
Alien Nation '88
Full Metal Jacket '87

Leslie Howard
The Animal Kingdom '32
Devotion '31
The Forty-Ninth Parallel '41
A Free Soul '31
Gone with the Wind '39
Intermezzo '39
The Making of a Legend: "Gone With the Wind" '89
Of Human Bondage '34
Petrified Forest '36
Pimpernel Smith '42
Pygmalion '38
Romeo and Juliet '36
The Scarlet Pimpernel '34
Smilin' Through '32
Spitfire '42
Stand-In '37

Lisa Howard
Rolling Vengeance '87
Sabaka '55

Mary Howard
Abe Lincoln in Illinois '40
All Over Town '37
Billy the Kid '41
The Loves of Edgar Allen Poe '42

Moe Howard
Classic Comedy Video Sampler '49
Comedy Festival #1 '30s
Comedy Reel, Vol. 2
Dancing Lady '33
Dr. Death, Seeker of Souls '73
Gold Raiders '51
Hollywood Party '34
It's a Mad, Mad, Mad, Mad World '63
The Lost Stooges '33
Snow White and the Three Stooges '61
The Stooges Story '90
Swing Parade of 1946 '46
Three Stooges Comedy Capers: Vol. 1 '40s

Three Stooges Comedy Classics '49
Three Stooges: Cookoo Cavaliers and Other Nyuks '40
Three Stooges Festival '49
Three Stooges: From Nurse to Worse and Other Nyuks '45
The Three Stooges: Half-Wit's Holiday and Other Nyuks '35
The Three Stooges: Idiots Deluxe and Other Nyuks '40
The Three Stooges Meet Hercules '61
The Three Stooges: Nutty but Nice and Other Nyuks '39
The Three Stooges: They Stooge to Conga and Other Nyuks '40

Rance Howard
Bloody Trail '72
B.O.R.N. '88
Dark Before Dawn '89
Eat My Dust '76
Far and Away '92
Forced to Kill '93
Huckleberry Finn '75
Where the Lilies Bloom '74
The Wild Country '71

Ron Howard
American Graffiti '73
Bitter Harvest '81
The Courtship of Eddie's Father '62
Door to Door Maniac '61
Eat My Dust '76
Grand Theft Auto '77
Huckleberry Finn '75
I'm a Fool '77
More American Graffiti '79
The Music Man '62
Return to Mayberry '85
Run, Stranger, Run '73
The Shootist '76
Smoke '70
Village of the Giants '65
The Wild Country '71

Ronald Howard
The Naked Edge '61
Night Beat '48
The Queen of Spades '49

Shemp Howard
Africa Screams '49
The Bank Dick '40
Buck Privates '41
Cooking Up Trouble '44
Dancing Lady '33
Ghost Crazy '44
Gold Raiders '51
The Invisible Woman '40
Pittsburgh '42
Private Buckaroo '42
The Stooges Story '90
Three Stooges Comedy Capers: Vol. 1 '40s
Three Stooges Comedy Classics '49
Three Stooges Festival '49

Susan Howard
Moonshine County Express '77
The Power Within '79
Sidewinder One '77

Trevor Howard
Adventures of Eliza Fraser '76
Albino '76
Battle of Britain '69
The Bawdy Adventures of Tom Jones '76
Brief Encounter '46
The Cary Grant Collection '90
Catch Me a Spy '71
Catholics '73
The Charge of the Light Brigade '68
Conduct Unbecoming '75
The Count of Monte Cristo '74
Craze '74
The Dawning '88
Deadly Game '82
A Doll's House '73
Dust '85
11 Harrowhouse '74
Father Goose '64
Flashpoint Africa '84
Foreign Body '86
Gandhi '82
George Washington '84

The Gift Horse '52
The Golden Salamander '51
The Graveyard '74
Green for Danger '47
Hennessy '75
Hurricane '79
I See a Dark Stranger '46
Inside the Third Reich '82
Invincible Mr. Disraeli '63
The Key '58
Lola '82
Meteor '79
The Missionary '82
Morituri '65
Mutiny on the Bounty '62
The Night Visitor '70
The Offence '73
Operation Crossbow '65
The Poppy is also a Flower '66
Roboman '75
Ryan's Daughter '70
Sea Wolves '81
Shaka Zulu '83
Slavers '77
Staying On '80
Stevie '78
Superman: The Movie '78
Sword of the Valiant '83
The Third Man '49
This Lightning Always Strikes Twice '85
Triple Cross '67
The Unholy '88
Von Ryan's Express '65
White Mischief '88
Windwalker '81

Vanessa Howard
Girly '70
Picture of Dorian Gray '74

Clark Howat
Billy Jack '71
Fu Manchu '56
The Giant Claw '57

C. Thomas Howell
Acting on Impulse '93
Breaking the Rules '92
Curiosity Kills '90
E.T.: The Extra-Terrestrial '82
Eyes of the Panther '90
Far Out Man '89
Gettysburg '93
Grandview U.S.A. '84
Hitcher '86
Into the Homeland '87
Jailbait '93
Kid '90
Nickel & Dime '92
The Outsiders '83
Red Dawn '84
The Return of the Musketeers '89
Secret Admirer '85
Side Out '90
Soul Man '86
Tank '83
That Night '93
A Tiger's Tale '87
To Protect and Serve '92

Hoke Howell
Alienator '89
B.O.R.N. '88

Ursula Howells
The Gilded Cage '54
Girly '70

Frankie Howerd
Carry On Doctor '68
Cool Mikado '63
The Great St. Trinian's Train Robbery '66
Naughty Knights '71
Night of the Laughing Dead '75
The Runaway Bus '54

Reed Howes
Confidential '35
Covered Wagon Days '40
Custer's Last Stand '36
Cyclone Cavalier '25
Dead or Alive '41
Feud of the West '35
Fugitive Valley '41
Million Dollar Haul '35
A Million to One '37
Queen of the Jungle '35

Sally Ann Howes
Chitty Chitty Bang Bang '68
Dead of Night '45
Death Ship '80

Nicholas Nickleby '46
Pink Strings and Sealing Wax '45
Thursday's Child '43

Jobyna Howland
Hook, Line and Sinker '30
Topaze '33

Olin Howland
Apache Rose '47
The Blob '58
Earthworm Tractors '36
Girl of the Golden West '38
Nancy Drew, Reporter '39
Satan Met a Lady '36
Storm Rider '57
The Wistful Widow of Wagon Gap '47

Jack Hoxie
Backfire '22
Gun Law '33
Law and Lawless '33
Outlaw Justice '32
Trouble Busters '33
Wild Engine/Mistaken Orders '23

Christina Hoyos
Blood Wedding '81
Carmen '83
El Amor Brujo '86

Arthur Hoyt
The Great McGinty '40
His Private Secretary '33
In the Money '34

John Hoyt
Blackboard Jungle '55
The Conqueror '56
Flesh Gordon '72
Forever Darling '56
Julius Caesar '53
Loan Shark '52
The Lost Continent '51
Sins of Jezebel '54
The Time Travelers '64
Trapped '49
Winter Meeting '48
X: The Man with X-Ray Eyes '63

Chen Hsing
Dual Flying Kicks '82
Duel of Fists '89
Rage of Wind '82

Carter Huang
The Association '80s
Sting of the Dragon Masters '74

John Hubbard
Cowboy & the Senorita '44
Mexican Hayride '48
The Mummy's Tomb '42
Road Show '41

Cork Hubbert
The Ballad of the Sad Cafe '91
Caveman '81

Harold Huber
Charlie Chan in Rio '41
Kelly the Second '36
Klondike Annie '36
Ladies They Talk About '33

Season Hubley
Child in the Night '90
Elvis: The Movie '79
Escape from New York '81
Hardcore '79
The Key to Rebecca '85
Mrs. R's Daughter '79
Prettykill '87
Stepfather 3: Father's Day '92
Total Exposure '91
Vice Squad '82

Whip Hubley
Desire and Hell at Sunset Motel '92
Russkies '87
Top Gun '86

Cooper Huckabee
Cohen and Tate '88
The Curse '87
The Funhouse '81
Getting Wasted '80
Joni '79
Love Field '91
Night Eyes '90

Walter Hudd
Black Limelight '38

Cast a Dark Shadow '55
Elephant Boy '37
Housemaster '38
The Prince and the Pauper '62
Rembrandt '36

David Huddleston
Crime Busters '78
Double Exposure: The Story of Margaret Bourke-White '89
Finnegan Begin Again '84
Frantic '88
Go for It '83
Life with Mikey '93
McQ '74
On the Run '85
Rio Lobo '70
Santa Claus: The Movie '85
The Tracker '88
When the Bough Breaks '86

Michael Huddleston
Bombs Away! '86
Four Friends '81
World's Greatest Lover '77

Ernie Hudson
Airheads '94
The Cowboy Way '94
The Crow '93
The $5.20 an Hour Dream '80
Ghostbusters '84
Ghostbusters 2 '89
Going Berserk '83
The Hand that Rocks the Cradle '92
In the Army Now '94
Joy of Sex '84
Leviathan '89
No Escape '94
Penitentiary 2 '82
Spacehunter: Adventures in the Forbidden Zone '83
Sugar Hill '94
Trapper County War '89
Weeds '87
Wild Palms '93
The Wrong Guys '88

Gary Hudson
Indecent Behavior '93
Martial Outlaw '93
Mind Twister '93
Scanner Cop '94
Sexual Intent '94
Wild Cactus '92

John Hudson
Return to Paradise '53
When Gangland Strikes '56

Rochelle Hudson
Alien Massacre '67
Bachelor Bait '34
Beyond the Rockies '32
Curly Top '35
The Devil's Cargo '48
Les Miserables '35
Mr. Skitch '33
The Night Walker '64
Rebel Without a Cause '55
The Savage Girl '32
Show Them No Mercy '35

Rock Hudson
The Ambassador '84
Avalanche '78
Bend of the River '52
Darling Lili '70
Devlin Connection '82
Embryo '76
A Gathering of Eagles '63
Giant '56
Gun Fury '53
Horizons West '52
Hornet's Nest '70
Ice Station Zebra '68
James Dean: The First American Teenager '76
Lover Come Back '61
Magnificent Obsession '54
Man's Favorite Sport? '63
The Martian Chronicles: Part 1 '79
The Martian Chronicles: Part 2 '79
The Martian Chronicles: Part 3 '79
The Mirror Crack'd '80
Pillow Talk '59
Sea Devils '53
Send Me No Flowers '64
Showdown '73
Something of Value '57

Tobruk '66
The Undefeated '69
The Vegas Strip Wars '84
Winchester '73 '50
World War III '86
Written on the Wind '56

Toni Hudson
Just One of the Guys '85
Prime Risk '84
The Uninvited '88

William Hudson
The Amazing Colossal Man '57
Attack of the 50 Foot Woman '58
Hysterical '83
The Screaming Skull '58

Matthias Hues
Bounty Tracker '93
Fist Fighter '88
Mission of Justice '92
Talons of the Eagle '92
TC 2000 '93

Brent Huff
Armed Response '86
Deadly Passion '85
Falling from Grace '92
Nine Deaths of the Ninja '85
The Perils of Gwendoline '84
Stormquest '87

David Huffman
Blood Beach '81
Firefox '82
F.I.S.T. '78
Ice Castles '79
Last Plane Out '83
St. Helen's, Killer Volcano '82
Tom Edison: The Boy Who Lit Up the World '78
The Winds of Kitty Hawk '78

Billy Hufsey
Magic Kid '92
Off the Wall '82

Daniel Hugh-Kelly
Cujo '83
The Good Son '93
Nowhere to Hide '87

Andrew Hughes
Destroy All Monsters '68
Terror Beneath the Sea '66

Barnard Hughes
The Adventures of Huckleberry Finn '85
Best Friends '82
Cold Turkey '71
Da '88
Day One '89
Doc Hollywood '91
First Monday in October '81
Hobo's Christmas '87
Homeward Bound '80
The Hospital '71
The Incident '89
Little Gloria...Happy at Last '84
The Lost Boys '87
Maxie '85
Midnight Cowboy '69
Oh, God! '77
Rage '72
Sanctuary of Fear '79
Sister Act 2: Back in the Habit '93
Sisters '73
Tron '82
Under the Biltmore Clock '85
Where Are the Children? '85

Brendan Hughes
Howling 6: The Freaks '90
Return to Horror High '87
To Die for '89

Carol Hughes
The Border Legion '40
Desperate Cargo '41
Earthworm Tractors '36
Flash Gordon Conquers the Universe '40
Home in Oklahoma '47
Love Affair '39
The Man from Music Mountain '38
Miracle Kid '42
Renfrew of the Royal Mounted '37
Robot Pilot '41
Silver Stallion '41

Space Soldiers Conquer the Universe '40
Three Men on a Horse '36

Charles Hughes
Call of the Forest '49
The Frontiersman '38

Finola Hughes
Aspen Extreme '93
Nutcracker Sweet '84
Staying Alive '83

Heather Hughes
Blood Freak '72
Flesh Feast '69

Helen Hughes
The Amityville Curse '90
Incubus '82
Kidnapping of Baby John Doe '88
Off Your Rocker '80
The Peanut Butter Solution '85

John Hughes
A Betrayed Man '36
That Sinking Feeling '79

Kay Hughes
Dick Tracy: The Original Serial, Vol. 1 '37
Dick Tracy: The Original Serial, Vol. 2 '37
The Mandarin Mystery '37
Ride, Ranger, Ride '36
The Vigilantes are Coming '36

Lloyd Hughes
Beau Revel '21
Blake of Scotland Yard '36
Dangerous Hours '19
Drums of Jeopardy '31
Ella Cinders '26
A Face in the Fog '36
The Lost World '25
Where East is East '29

Mary Beth Hughes
Charlie Chan in Rio '41
The Great American Broadcast '41
Great Flamarion '45
Holiday Rhythm '50
I Accuse My Parents '45
Inner Sanctum '48
The Lady Confesses '45
Last of the Wild Horses '49
Lucky Cisco Kid '40
Orchestra Wives '42
The Ox-Bow Incident '43
Return of Wildfire '48
Rimfire '49
Square Dance Jubilee '51
Take It Big '44
Timber Queen '44

Miko Hughes
Cops and Robbersons '94
Jack the Bear '93

Wendy Hughes
Alternative '76
Careful, He Might Hear You '84
Dangerous Summer '82
Echoes of Paradise '86
Happy New Year '87
The Heist '89
High Rolling in a Hot Corvette '77
An Indecent Obsession '85
Jock Petersen '74
Kostas '79
Lonely Hearts '82
My Brilliant Career '79
My First Wife '84
Newsfront '78
Puzzle '78
Remember Me '85
Touch & Go '80
Warm Nights on a Slow-Moving Train '87
Wild Orchid 2: Two Shades of Blue '92
A Woman Named Jackie '91

Liu Chia Hui
Challenge of the Masters '89
Master Killer '84

Claude Hulbert
Bulldog Jack '35
The Dummy Talks '43

Tom Hulce
Amadeus '84
Black Rainbow '91

Dominick & Eugene '88
Echo Park '86
Fearless '93
The Inner Circle '91
National Lampoon's Animal House '78
Parenthood '89
The Rise & Rise of Daniel Rocket '86
September 30, 1955 '77
Slamdance '87
Those Lips, Those Eyes '80

Dianne Hull
Aloha, Bobby and Rose '74
The Fifth Floor '80
Girls on the Road '73
The New Adventures of Pippi Longstocking '88

Henry Hull
Boys Town '38
The Buccaneer '58
The Fool Killer '65
The Fountainhead '49
High Sierra '41
Jesse James '39
Lifeboat '44
Master of the World '61
Midnight '34
Objective, Burma! '45
Portrait of Jennie '48
Return of Frank James '40
Return of Jesse James '50
Rimfire '49
Stanley and Livingstone '39
Three Comrades '38
Werewolf of London '35
The Woman of the Town '44

Josephine Hull
Arsenic and Old Lace '44
Harvey '50

Warren Hull
Bowery Blitzkrieg '41
Hawaii Calls '38
Hidden Enemy '40
Star Reporter '39

George Humbert
Hearts of Humanity '32
Music in My Heart '40

Benita Hume
It Happened in New Orleans '36
Lady of the Lake '28
Power '34
Private Life of Don Juan '34
Suzy '26
Tarzan Escapes '36

William Humphreys
Beau Brummel '24
The Unholy Three '25

Barry Humphries
Barry McKenzie Holds His Own '74
The Getting of Wisdom '77
Les Patterson Saves the World '90

Tessa Humphries
Cassandra '87
Out of the Body '88

Robert Hundar
Bronson's Revenge '79
Fighting Fists of Shanghai Joe '65

Pa Hung
Kick of Death: The Prodigal Boxer '80s
Prodigal Boxer: The Kick of Death '73

Samo Hung
The Deadliest Art: The Best of the Martial Arts Films '90
Paper Marriage '88
The Victim

Arthur Hunnicutt
Abroad with Two Yanks '44
Apache Uprising '66
The Big Sky '52
The Bounty Man '72
Broken Arrow '50
Devil's Canyon '53
Distant Drums '51
El Dorado '67
The French Line '54
Harry and Tonto '74
The Lusty Men '52
She Couldn't Say No '52

Stars in My Crown '50
The Tall T '57
Ticket to Tomahawk '50
Wildcat '42

Gayle Hunnicutt
Con Man '92
Dream Lover '85
Flashpoint Africa '84
The Legend of Hell House '73
The Love Machine '71
Marlowe '69
The Martian Chronicles: Part 2 '79
The Martian Chronicles: Part 3 '79
No Comebacks '85
Once in Paris... '79
Return of the Man from U.N.C.L.E. '83
Scorpio '73
Sell Out '76
Shadow Man '75
Spiral Staircase '75
Strange Shadows in an Empty Room '76
Target '85
Turnaround '87
The Wild Angels '66

Bonnie Hunt
Beethoven '92
Beethoven's 2nd '93
Dave '93
Only You '94
Rain Man '88

David Hunt
Date with an Angel '87
The Dead Pool '88

Eleanor Hunt
Whoopee! '30
Yellow Cargo '36

Gareth Hunt
Bloodbath at the House of Death '85
A Chorus of Disapproval '89
Funny Money '82
It Couldn't Happen Here '88
The World is Full of Married Men '80

Helen Hunt
Bill: On His Own '83
Child Bride of Short Creek '81
Code of Honor '84
Dark River: A Father's Revenge '90
Desperate Lives '82
Girls Just Want to Have Fun '85
Into the Badlands '92
Miles from Home '88
Mr. Saturday Night '92
Murder in New Hampshire: The Pamela Smart Story '91
Next of Kin '89
Only You '92
Peggy Sue Got Married '86
Project X '87
Quarterback Princess '85
The Spell '77
Stealing Home '88
Trancers '85
Trancers 2: The Return of Jack Deth '91
Trancers 3: Deth Lives '92
The Waterdance '91

Jimmy Hunt
The Capture '50
Invaders from Mars '53

Linda Hunt
The Bostonians '84
Dune '84
Eleni '85
If Looks Could Kill '91
Kindergarten Cop '90
Popeye '80
The Room '87
She-Devil '89
Silverado '85
Twenty Bucks '93
Waiting for the Moon '87
The Year of Living Dangerously '82

Marsha Hunt
Actors and Sin '52
Blossoms in the Dust '41
Desert Gold '36
Howling 2: Your Sister is a Werewolf '85

Smash-Up: The Story of a Woman '47
Star Reporter '39
Thunder Pass '37
The Valley of Decision '45
Western Double Feature 3 '36

Martita Hunt
The Brides of Dracula '60
Great Expectations '46
The King's Rhapsody '55
Little Ballerina '47
Song Without End '60
The Story of Robin Hood & His Merrie Men '52
The Unsinkable Molly Brown '64
When Knights were Bold '36
The Wonderful World of the Brothers Grimm '62

Bill Hunter
Fever '88
Hard Knocks '80
Heatwave '83
The Hit '85
In Search of Anna '79
An Indecent Obsession '85
The Last Days of Chez Nous '92
Newsfront '78
Rebel '85
Return of Captain Invincible '83
Rikky and Pete '88
Strictly Ballroom '92

Holly Hunter
Always '89
Animal Behavior '89
Broadcast News '87
The Burning '82
Crazy in Love '92
End of the Line '88
The Firm '93
Miss Firecracker '89
Murder on the Bayou '91
Once Around '93
The Piano '93
The Positively True Adventures of the Alleged Texas Cheerleader-Murdering Mom '93
Raising Arizona '87
Roe vs. Wade '89
Svengali '83
Swing Shift '84
Urge to Kill '84

Ian Hunter
The Adventures of Robin Hood '38
Andy Hardy's Private Secretary '41
Billy the Kid '41
Bitter Sweet '40
Broadway Melody of 1940 '40
Broadway Serenade '39
Doctor Blood's Coffin '62
Easy Virtue '27
Flame Over India '60
The Little Princess '39
The Long Voyage Home '40
A Midsummer Night's Dream '35
Order of the Black Eagle '87
The Phantom Light '35
Pursuit of the Graf Spee '57
The Ring '27
The Sisters '38
Smilin' Through '41
Strange Cargo '40
Tarzan Finds a Son '39
That Certain Woman '37
The Tower of London '39
Unmasking the Idol '86
Ziegfeld Girl '41

Jeffrey Hunter
The Christmas Kid '68
The Great Locomotive Chase '56
Hell to Eternity '60
The King of Kings '61
Last Hurrah '58
The Longest Day '62
The Searchers '56
Sergeant Rutledge '60
Seven Cities of Gold '55
A Witch Without a Broom '68

Kaki Hunter
Just the Way You Are '84
Porky's '82

Hunter ▶cont.

Porky's Revenge '85
Roadie '80
Whose Life Is It Anyway? '81
Willie & Phil '80

Kim Hunter
Bad Ronald '74
Beneath the Planet of the Apes '70
Born Innocent '74
Dark August '76
Drop-Out Mother '88
Escape from the Planet of the Apes '71
The Kindred '87
Lamp at Midnight '66
Lilith '64
Planet of the Apes '68
Requiem for a Heavyweight '56
The Seventh Victim '43
A Streetcar Named Desire '51
Swimmer '68
Tender Comrade '43

Ronald Hunter
Adventure of the Action Hunters '87
Jakarta '88
Rage of Angels '83

Stephen Hunter
Bullies '86
Mania '80s

Tab Hunter
The Arousers '70
Battle Cry '55
The Big Push '75
The Burning Hills '56
Cameron's Closet '89
Damn Yankees '58
Grease 2 '82
Grotesque '87
Hostile Guns '67
Island of Desire '52
The Kid from Left Field '79
Lafayette Escadrille '58
The Loved One '65
Lust in the Dust '85
One Step to Hell '68
Out of the Dark '88
Pandemonium '82
Polyester '81
Ride the Wild Surf '64
Sea Chase '55
They Came to Cordura '59

Thomas Hunter
Battle of the Commandos '71
Escape from the KGB '87
Web of Deception '71

Raymond Huntley
I See a Dark Stranger '46
Immortal Battalion '44
The Long Dark Hall '51
The Prisoner '55

Isabelle Huppert
The Bedroom Window '87
Cactus '86
Coup de Torchon '81
Entre-Nous '83
Going Places '74
Heaven's Gate '81
The Judge and the Assassin '75
La Truite '83
La Vengeance d'une Femme '89
The Lacemaker '77
Loulou '80
Madame Bovary '91
My Best Friend's Girl '84
Rosebud '75
Sincerely Charlotte '86
The Story of Women '88
Violette '78

Elizabeth Hurley
Christabel '89
Kill Cruise '90
Passenger 57 '92

Brandon Hurst
Dr. Jekyll and Mr. Hyde '20
House of Mystery '34
Made for Love '26
The Man Who Laughs '27
Murder at Midnight '31
Murders in the Rue Morgue '32

Stanley and Livingstone '39
The Thief of Baghdad '24

Paul Hurst
Alexander's Ragtime Band '38
Bad Lands '39
The Big Stampede '32
Caught in the Draft '41
Girl Rush '44
Gone with the Wind '39
Hold Your Man '33
It Could Happen to You '39
Legion of Missing Men '37
Missourians '50
Mountain Justice '30
My Pal, The King '32
Paradise Island '30
Pioneer Marshal '49
The Sphinx '33
13th Guest '32
The Vanishing Westerner '50

Veronica Hurst
Angels One Five '54
The Gilded Cage '54
Peeping Tom '63
Second Best Secret Agent in the Whole Wide World '65

John Hurt
After Darkness '85
Alien '79
Aria '88
Champions '84
Disappearance '81
East of Elephant Rock '76
The Elephant Man '80
Even Cowgirls Get the Blues '94
The Field '90
Frankenstein Unbound '90
From the Hip '86
The Ghoul '75
Heaven's Gate '81
History of the World: Part 1 '81
The Hit '85
I, Claudius, Vol. 5: Zeus, By Jove!/Hail Who? '80
Island '77
Jake Speed '86
King Ralph '91
Little Sweetheart '90
A Man for All Seasons '66
Midnight Express '78
Monolith '93
The Naked Civil Servant '75
Night Crossing '81
1984 '84
The Osterman Weekend '83
Partners '82
Scandal '89
The Shout '78
Spaceballs '87
Success is the Best Revenge '84
10 Rillington Place '71
White Mischief '88

Mary Beth Hurt
The Age of Innocence '93
Baby Girl Scott '87
A Change of Seasons '80
Chilly Scenes of Winter '79
Compromising Positions '85
D.A.R.Y.L. '85
Defenseless '91
Interiors '78
Light Sleeper '92
My Boyfriend's Back '93
Parents '89
Six Degrees of Separation '93
Slaves of New York '89
The World According to Garp '82

William Hurt
The Accidental Tourist '88
Alice '90
Altered States '80
The Big Chill '83
Body Heat '81
Broadcast News '87
Children of a Lesser God '86
The Doctor '91
Eyewitness '81
Gorky Park '83
I Love You to Death '90
Kiss of the Spider Woman '85
Mr. Wonderful '93
The Plague '92
A Time of Destiny '88
Until The End of The World '91

Ferlin Husky
Hillbillies in a Haunted House '67
Las Vegas Hillbillys '66

Olivia Hussey
The Bastard '78
Black Christmas '75
The Cat and the Canary '79
Death on the Nile '78
Distortions '87
Escape 2000 '81
H-Bomb '71
Ivanhoe '82
The Jeweller's Shop '90
The Man with Bogart's Face '80
Psycho 4: The Beginning '90
Quest of the Delta Knights '93
Ricco '74
Romeo and Juliet '68
Save Me '93
Stephen King's It '90
Undeclared War '91
Virus '82

Ruth Hussey
Another Thin Man '39
Hill Number One '51
Madame X '37
Marine Raiders '43
Mr. Music '50
Northwest Passage '40
The Philadelphia Story '40
Stars and Stripes Forever '52
Susan and God '40
Tender Comrade '43
The Uninvited '44
The Women '39

Anjelica Huston
The Addams Family '91
Addams Family Values '93
Beauty and the Beast '83
The Cowboy & the Ballerina '84
Crimes & Misdemeanors '89
The Dead '87
Enemies, a Love Story '89
Family Pictures '93
Gardens of Stone '87
The Grifters '90
Hamlet '69
A Handful of Dust '88
Ice Pirates '84
The Last Tycoon '76
Lonesome Dove '89
Manhattan Murder Mystery '93
Mr. North '88
The Postman Always Rings Twice '81
Prizzi's Honor '85
This is Spinal Tap '84
The Witches '90

John Huston
Angela '77
Battle for the Planet of the Apes '73
Battleforce '78
The Bible...In the Beginning '66
Breakout '75
The Cardinal '63
Casino Royale '67
Chinatown '74
Fatal Attraction '80
Jaguar Lives '79
Lovesick '83
Man in the Wilderness '71
A Minor Miracle '83
Mr. Corbett's Ghost '90
Myra Breckinridge '70
Ride to Glory '71
Tentacles '77
The Visitor '80
The Wind and the Lion '75
Winter Kills '79
Wise Blood '79
The Word '78

Virginia Huston
The Doolins of Oklahoma '49
Flamingo Road '49
Night Stage to Galveston '52
Nocturne '46

Walter Huston
Abraham Lincoln '30
And Then There Were None '45
Ann Vickers '33
Criminal Code '31
December 7th: The Movie '91
The Devil & Daniel Webster '41
Dodsworth '36

Dragon Seed '44
Duel in the Sun '46
Edge of Darkness '43
Gabriel Over the White House '33
In This Our Life '42
The North Star '43
Of Human Hearts '38
The Outlaw '43
The Prizefighter and the Lady '33
Rain '32
Rhodes '36
The Shanghai Gesture '42
Summer Holiday '48
Transatlantic Tunnel '35
Treasure of the Sierra Madre '48
The Virginian '29
Yankee Doodle Dandy '42

Michael Hutchence
Dogs in Space '87
Frankenstein Unbound '90

Geoffrey Hutchings
Heart of Darkness '93
Wish You Were Here '87

Wheezer Hutchins
Little Rascals, Book 2 '30s
Little Rascals, Book 3 '38
Little Rascals, Book 15 '30s
Little Rascals, Book 18 '29

Will Hutchins
Clambake '67
Lafayette Escadrille '58
Merrill's Marauders '62
The Shooting '66
Slumber Party '57 '76
Spinout '66

Josephine Hutchinson
The Adventures of Huckleberry Finn '60
Cass Timberlane '47
Love is Better Than Ever '52
North by Northwest '59
Son of Frankenstein '39
The Story of Louis Pasteur '36
The Tender Years '47

Ken Hutchison
Deadly Strangers '82
Ladyhawke '85

Betty Hutton
The Greatest Show on Earth '52
Hollywood Clowns '85
Let's Dance '50
Miracle of Morgan's Creek '44
The Perils of Pauline '47
The Stork Club '45

Brian Hutton
Carnival Rock '57
Last Train from Gun Hill '59

Jim Hutton
Bachelor in Paradise '61
Don't Be Afraid of the Dark '73
The Green Berets '68
The Hallelujah Trail '65
Hellfighters '68
The Honeymoon Machine '61
The Horizontal Lieutenant '62
Major Dundee '65
Nightmare at 43 Hillcrest '74
Period of Adjustment '62
Psychic Killer '75
A Time to Love & a Time to Die '58
Walk, Don't Run '66
Where the Boys Are '60
Who's Minding the Mint? '67

Lauren Hutton
American Gigolo '79
Bulldance '88
The Cradle Will Fall '83
Fear '90
Forbidden Sun '89
From Here to Maternity '85
The Gambler '74
Gator '75
Guilty as Charged '92
Lassiter '84
Malone '87
Millions '90
Monte Carlo '86
My Father the Hero '93
Nashville '75

Once Bitten '85
Paper Lion '68
Paternity '81
Scandalous '88
The Snow Queen '83
Starflight One '83
Timestalkers '87
Trade Secrets '90s
Viva Knievel '77
A Wedding '78
Welcome to L.A. '77
Zorro, the Gay Blade '81

Marion Hutton
In Society '44
Love Happy '50

Robert Hutton
Big Bluff '55
Cinderfella '60
Destination Tokyo '43
Hollywood Canteen '44
Naked Youth '59
Outcasts of the City '58
The Persuaders '71
Showdown at Boot Hill '58
Slaughter Trail '51
The Slime People '63
The Steel Helmet '51
They Came from Beyond Space '67
Vulture '67

Timothy Hutton
And Baby Makes Six '79
Daniel '83
The Dark Half '91
Everybody's All American '88
The Falcon and the Snowman '85
Father Figure '80
Friendly Fire '79
Iceman '84
A Long Way Home '81
Made in Heaven '87
Oldest Living Graduate '82
Ordinary People '80
Q & A '90
Strangers '91
Taps '81
The Temp '93
A Time of Destiny '88
Torrents of Spring '90
Turk 182! '85
Young Love, First Love '79

Leila Hyams
The Big House '30
Freaks '32
Island of Lost Souls '32
Red Headed Woman '32
The Ruggles of Red Gap '35
Spite Marriage '29
Yellow Dust '36

Jonathan Hyde
Fellow Traveler '89
An Indecent Obsession '85

Alex Hyde-White
Biggles '85
Echoes in the Darkness '87
The First Olympics: Athens 1896 '84
Indiana Jones and the Last Crusade '89
Ironclads '90
The Phantom of the Opera '89
Pretty Woman '90
The Seekers '79
Silent Victim '92

Wilfrid Hyde-White
Angel with the Trumpet '50
Betrayed '54
Brand New Life '72
The Browning Version '51
Carry On Nurse '59
The Cat and the Canary '79
Damien: The Leper Priest '80
The Demi-Paradise '43
Fanny Hill '83
Flame Over India '60
Ghosts of Berkeley Square '47
The Golden Salamander '51
Heartburn '86
In Search of the Castaways '62
King Solomon's Treasure '76
Last Holiday '50
The Magic Christian '69
My Fair Lady '64
Oh, God! Book 2 '80
The Rebels '79
Scout's Honor '80

Skullduggery '70
Teenage Bad Girl '59
The Third Man '49
The Toy '82
Truth About Women '58
Two-Way Stretch '60
Up the Creek '58
The Vicious Circle '57

Martha Hyer
Abbott and Costello Go to Mars '53
Bikini Beach '64
The Carpetbaggers '64
Catch as Catch Can '68
The Chase '66
Cry Vengeance '54
The Delicate Delinquent '56
First Men in the Moon '64
Francis in the Navy '55
Gun Smugglers/Hot Lead '51
The House of 1000 Dolls '67
Houseboat '58
Ice Palace '60
Lucky Me '54
Mistress of the World '59
My Man Godfrey '57
Night of the Grizzly '66
Paris Holiday '57
Picture Mommy Dead '66
Sabrina '54
Scarlet Spear '54
Some Came Running '58
Sons of Katie Elder '65

Diana Hyland
The Boy in the Plastic Bubble '76
Hercules and the Princess of Troy '65
One Man's Way '63

Scott Hylands
Coming Out Alive '84
Daddy's Gone A-Hunting '69
Fools '70
Savage Hunger '84
Tales of the Klondike: In a Far Country '87
The Winds of Kitty Hawk '78

Jane Hylton
Circus of Horrors '60
Dear Murderer '47
The Manster '59

Phyllis Hyman
The Kill Reflex '89
School Daze '88

Warren Hymer
Baby Face Morgan '42
Confidential '35
Hitler: Dead or Alive '43
Hong Kong Nights '35
In the Money '34
Joy of Living '38
The Lone Star Ranger '39
Lure of the Islands '42
Meet the Mob '42
Mr. Wise Guy '42
The Mysterious Rider '33
Phantom Killer '42
Sea Racketeers '37
Show Them No Mercy '35
Tango '36

Joyce Hyser
Just One of the Guys '85
Wedding Band '89

Chaing I
Return of the Tiger '78
They Shoot Horses, Don't They? '69

Ice Cube
Boyz N the Hood '91
Trespass '92

Ice-T
New Jack City '91
Ricochet '91
Surviving the Game '94
Trespass '92
Who's the Man? '93

Etsuko Ichihara
Black Rain '88
Snow Country '57

Eric Idle
The Adventures of Baron Munchausen '89
All You Need Is Cash '78
And Now for Something Completely Different '72

Jabberwocky '77
Mom and Dad Save the World '92
Monty Python and the Holy Grail '75
Monty Python Live at the Hollywood Bowl '82
Monty Python Meets Beyond the Fringe
Monty Python's Life of Brian '79
Monty Python's Parrot Sketch Not Included '90
Monty Python's The Meaning of Life '83
Nuns on the Run '90
The Pied Piper of Hamelin '84
Splitting Heirs '93
To See Such Fun '81
Too Much Sun '90
Yellowbeard '83

Cinnamon Idles
Kidco '83
Sixteen Candles '84

Hisashi Igawa
Akira Kurosawa's Dreams '90
Ran '85
Rhapsody in August '91

Steve Ihnat
Countdown '68
Hour of the Gun '67
Hunter '73

Ryo Ikebe
Snow Country '57
War in Space '77

Peter Illing
Against the Wind '48
Bhowani Junction '56
The Electronic Monster '57
Eureka Stockade '49

Iman
Heart of Darkness '93
House Party 2: The Pajama Jam '91
The Human Factor '79
L.A. Story '91
Lies of the Twins '91
No Way Out '87
Out of Africa '85
Star Trek 6: The Undiscovered Country '91
Surrender '87

Roger Imhof
Riff Raff '35
Sweetheart of the Navy '37

Ada Ince
Frontier Days '34
Rainbow's End '35

Rafael Inclan
Bellas de Noche
By Hook or Crook '85

Annabella Incontrera
The Assassination Bureau '69
Double Face '70

Frieda Inescort
Beauty for the Asking '39
The Judge Steps Out '49
The Letter '40
Pride and Prejudice '40
Return of the Vampire '43
Shadows on the Stairs '41
Sunny '41
Tarzan Finds a Son '39
The Underworld Story '50

Eddie Infante
Cavalry Command '63
Ethan '71
Warkill '65

Pedro Infante
El Ametralladora '65
El Gavilan Pollero '47

Marty Ingels
How to Seduce a Woman '74
If It's Tuesday, This Must Be Belgium '69
Instant Karma '90
Round Numbers '91

Randi Ingerman
Deadly Rivals '92
Desperate Crimes '93

James Inglehart
Angels Hard as They Come '71

Death Force '78
Fighting Mad '77
Savage! '73

Lloyd Ingraham
Between Men '35
The Caravan Trail '46
Partners of the Trail '44
Peck's Bad Boy '34
Range Law '44
Red River Valley '36
Sons of Steel '35
Trail of Terror '35
Undercover Man '36

Jack Ingram
The Adventures of the Masked Phantom '38
Arizona Roundup '42
Devil Riders '44
Frontier Fugitives '45
Frontier Law '43
Frontier Outlaws '44
Guns of the Law '44
Lost in Alaska '52
The Mysterious Rider '42
Oath of Vengeance '44
Outlaw Roundup '44
Raiders of Sunset Pass '43
Range Law '44
The Rangers Step In '37
Ridin' the Trail '40
Valley of Terror '38
Whistling Bullets '36
Wyoming Outlaw '39

Rex Ingram
The Adventures of Huckleberry Finn '39
Cabin in the Sky '43
Dark Waters '44
Elmer Gantry '60
Green Pastures '36
Moonrise '48
Sahara '43
Talk of the Town '42
Thief of Baghdad '40

Valeri Inkizhinov
Journey to the Lost City '58
Samson and the 7 Miracles of the World '62
Storm Over Asia '28

George Innes
Archer: The Fugitive from the Empire '81
Danger UXB '81
Ivanhoe '82

Neil Innes
All You Need Is Cash '78
Monty Python and the Holy Grail '75

Harold Innocent
Fergie & Andrew: Behind Palace Doors '93
Robin Hood: Prince of Thieves '91

Dan Inosanto
Counter Attack '84
Warrior Within '80

Tino Insana
The Masters of Menace '90
Wedding Band '89

Franco Interlenghi
I Vitelloni '53
Shoeshine '47

Steve Inwood
The Human Shield '92
Hurry Up or I'll Be Thirty '73

Aharon Ipale
Invisible: The Chronicles of Benjamin Knight '93
One Man Out '89
Too Hot to Handle '76
Tragedy of Flight 103: The Inside Story '91

Jill Ireland
Assassination '87
Breakheart Pass '76
Breakout '75
Chino '73
Cold Sweat '74
Death Wish 2 '82
The Family '73
From Noon Till Three '76
Hard Times '75
Love and Bullets '79
The Mechanic '72

Rider on the Rain '70
Robbery Under Arms '57
Someone Behind the Door '71
Villa Rides '68

John Ireland
The Adventurers '70
All the King's Men '49
Arizona Bushwackers '67
Black Tide '56
Bloody Che Contra
Bordello '79
The Bushwackers '52
Challenge of McKenna '83
Crossbar '79
Dead for a Dollar '70s
Delta Fox '77
Diary of a Rebel '84
Dirty Heroes '71
The Doolins of Oklahoma '49
Escape to the Sun '72
The Fall of the Roman Empire '64
Farewell, My Lovely '75
The Fast and the Furious '54
55 Days at Peking '63
Flying from the Hawk '86
The Gangster '47
Glass Tomb '55
Gunfight at the O.K. Corral '57
The Gunslinger '56
The House of Seven Corpses '73
I Shot Jesse James '49
Incubus '82
Joan of Arc '48
Kavik the Wolf Dog '84
Little Big Horn '51
Maniac '77
Marilyn: The Untold Story '80
Martin's Day '85
Messenger of Death '88
Miami Horror '87
Midnight Auto Supply '78
Mission to Glory '80
My Darling Clementine '46
Northeast of Seoul '72
Open Secret '48
Party Girl '58
Perfect Killer '77
Railroaded '47
Red River '48
Return of Jesse James '50
Satan's Cheerleaders '77
A Southern Yankee '48
Spartacus '60
Tales of the Klondike: Race for Number One '87
Taste of Death '77
Thunder Run '86
Tomorrow Never Comes '77
The Treasure of the Amazon '84
Vengeance Valley '51
A Walk in the Sun '46
Wild in the Country '61

Kathy Ireland
Alien from L.A. '87
Amore! '93
Mr. Destiny '90
Mom and Dad Save the World '92
National Lampoon's Loaded Weapon 1 '93
Necessary Roughness '91
Side Out '90

Jeremy Irons
Betrayal '83
Brideshead Revisited '81
A Chorus of Disapproval '89
Damage '92
Dead Ringers '88
The French Lieutenant's Woman '81
The House of the Spirits '93
Kafka '91
Love for Lydia '79
M. Butterfly '93
The Mission '86
Moonlighting '82
Nijinsky '80
Reversal of Fortune '90
Swann in Love '84
Waterland '92
The Wild Duck '84

Michael Ironside
American Nightmare '81
Black Ice '92
Coming Out Alive '84

Common Bonds '91
Cross Country '83
Dead Man's Revenge '93
Deadly Surveillance '91
Extreme Prejudice '87
The Falcon and the Snowman '85
The Family Man '79
Father Hood '93
Forced to Kill '93
Ford: The Man & the Machine '87
Guncrazy '92
Hello Mary Lou: Prom Night 2 '87
Highlander 2: The Quickening
Hostile Takeover '88
Killer Image '92
Mardi Gras for the Devil '93
McBain '91
Mindfield '89
Murder by Night '89
Murder in Space '85
Neon City '91
Nowhere to Hide '87
Payback '90
Point of Impact '93
Save Me '93
Spacehunter: Adventures in the Forbidden Zone '83
Surrogate '88
Sweet Killing '93
Top Gun '86
Total Recall '90
The Vagrant '92
Visiting Hours '82
Watchers '88

Amy Irving
Anastasia: The Mystery of Anna '86
Benefit of the Doubt '93
Carrie '76
The Competition '80
Crossing Delancey '88
The Far Pavilions '84
The Fury '78
Heartbreak House '86
Honeysuckle Rose '80
I'm a Fool '76
James Dean '76
Micki & Maude '84
Rumpelstiltskin '86
A Show of Force '90
The Turn of the Screw '89
Yentl '83

George Irving
The Abe Lincoln of Ninth Avenue '39
Captain January '36
Coquette '29
The Divorcee '30
Maid's Night Out '38
The Mandarin Mystery '37

Penny Irving
Big Zapper '73
House of Whipcord '75

Bill Irwin
Eight Men Out '88
Hot Shots! '91
My Blue Heaven '90
Popeye '80
Scenes from a Mall '91
Stepping Out '91

Boyd Irwin
Madam Satan '30
The Three Musketeers '21

Tom Irwin
Deceived '91
Ladykiller '92
Mr. Jones '93

Chris Isaak
Little Buddha '93
Married to the Mob '88
The Silence of the Lambs '91
Twin Peaks: Fire Walk with Me

Tom Isbell
Behind Enemy Lines '85
A Case of Deadly Force '86

Claudia Islas
Para Servir a Usted '87
Volver, Volver, Volver! '87

Juzo Itami
The Family Game '83
MacArthur's Children '85

Robert Ito
The Adventures of Buckaroo Banzai Across the Eighth Dimension '84
Pray for Death '85
Women of the Prehistoric Planet '66

Yunosuke Ito
The Burmese Harp '56
Ikiru '52

Jose Iturbi
Anchors Aweigh '45
Holiday in Mexico '46
That Midnight Kiss '49
Three Daring Daughters '48
Two Girls and a Sailor '44

Zeljko Ivanek
Echoes in the Darkness '87
Mass Appeal '84
Rachel River '89
School Ties '92
The Sender '82

Rosalind Iven
The Corn is Green '45
Pursuit to Algiers '45

Daniel Ivernel
Diary of a Chambermaid '64
High Heels '72
Manon '50

Robert Ivers
The Delicate Delinquent '56
G.I. Blues '60

Burl Ives
Baker's Hawk '76
Big Country '58
Cat on a Hot Tin Roof '58
Desire Under the Elms '58
East of Eden '54
Ensign Pulver '64
The McMasters '70
Poor Little Rich Girl: The Barbara Hutton Story '87
Roots '77
So Dear to My Heart '49
Station West '48
Summer Magic '63
Those Fantastic Flying Fools '67
Two Moon Junction '88
Uphill All the Way '85

Dana Ivey
The Addams Family '91
Addams Family Values '93
The Adventures of Huck Finn '93
Dirty Rotten Scoundrels '88
Explorers '85
Guilty as Sin '93
Home Alone 2: Lost in New York '92
Postcards from the Edge '90

Judith Ivey
Brighton Beach Memoirs '86
Compromising Positions '85
Decoration Day '90
Dixie: Changing Habits '85
Everybody Wins '90
Frogs! '90s
Harry & Son '84
Hello Again '87
In Country '89
The Lonely Guy '84
The Long, Hot Summer '86
Love Hurts '91
Miles from Home '88
Sister, Sister '87
There Goes the Neighborhood '92
We are the Children '87
The Woman in Red '84

Shima Iwashita
An Autumn Afternoon '62
Double Suicide '69
Gonza the Spearman '86
MacArthur's Children '85
Red Lion '69

Victor Izay
Premonition '71
The Trial of Billy Jack '74

Jackee
Ladybugs '92
The Women of Brewster Place '89

Anne Jackson
The Bell Jar '79
Blinded by the Light '82
Blood Debts '83
The Family Man '79
Folks! '92
Funny About Love '90
Independence '76
Leave 'Em Laughing '81
Lovers and Other Strangers '70
Nasty Habits '77
Out on a Limb '87
Sam's Son '84
Secret Life of an American Wife '68
Tall Story '60
A Woman Called Golda '82

David Jackson
Music Shoppe '82
The Vernonia Incident '89

Eugene Jackson
Red River Valley '36
The Return of Our Gang '25

Freda Jackson
Beware of Pity '46
Bhowani Junction '56
The Brides of Dracula '60
Great Expectations '46
The Valley of Gwangi '69

Glenda Jackson
And Nothing But the Truth '82
Beyond Therapy '86
Business as Usual '88
The Class of Miss MacMichael '78
Hedda '75
Hopscotch '80
House Calls '78
The Incredible Sarah '76
King of the Wind '93
Lost and Found '79
Marat/Sade '66
The Music Lovers '71
Nasty Habits '77
Negatives '68
The Rainbow '89
Return of the Soldier '82
Romantic Englishwoman '75
Sakharov '84
Salome's Last Dance '88
Stevie '78
Strange Interlude '90
Sunday, Bloody Sunday '71
A Touch of Class '73
Triple Echo '77
Turtle Diary '86
Women in Love '70

Gordon Jackson
Against the Wind '48
The Baby and the Battleship '56
Bergonzi Hand '70
Death Goes to School '53
The Fighting Prince of Donegal '66
The Great Escape '63
Gunpowder '84
Hamlet '69
Pink Strings and Sealing Wax '45
The Prime of Miss Jean Brodie '69
Professionals '76
Those Magnificent Men in Their Flying Machines '65
A Town Like Alice '85
Whiskey Galore '48
The Whistle Blower '87

Howard Jackson
Full Contact '93
Furious '83
Out for Blood '93

John M. Jackson
An American Story '92
Career Opportunities '91
Cold Sassy Tree '89
Deadly Matrimony '92
Ginger Ale Afternoon '89
Hitcher '80
Love, Lies and Murder '91
Sudie & Simpson '90
Switched at Birth '91

Kate Jackson
Adrift '93
Death at Love House '75
Death Cruise '74

Death Scream '75
Dirty Tricks '81
Listen to Your Heart '83
Loverboy '89
Making Love '82
Night of Dark Shadows '71
Satan's School for Girls '73
Thunder and Lightning '77

Lamont Jackson
Assault with a Deadly Weapon '82
Class Act '91

Linda Jackson
Black Bikers from Hell '70
The Outlaw Bikers—Gang Wars '70

Mary Jackson
Skinned Alive '90
Terror at Red Wolf Inn '72

Mary Ann Jackson
Little Rascals, Book 1 '30s
Little Rascals, Book 8 '30s
Little Rascals, Book 9 '30s
Little Rascals, Book 10 '30s
Little Rascals, Book 12 '37
Little Rascals, Book 14 '30s
Little Rascals, Book 18 '29

Philip Jackson
Bad Behavior '92
High Hopes '89

Sam Jackson
Dead Man Out '89
Return of Superfly '90

Sammy Jackson
Fastest Guitar Alive '68
None But the Brave '65
Shame, Shame on the Bixby Boys '82

Samuel L. Jackson
Amos and Andrew '93
Assault at West Point: The Court-Martial of Johnson Whittaker '94
Coming to America '88
Def by Temptation '90
Fathers and Sons '92
Goodfellas '90
Hail Caesar '94
Johnny Suede '92
Juice '92
Jumpin' at the Boneyard '92
Jungle Fever '91
Jurassic Park '93
Menace II Society '93
Mo' Better Blues '90
National Lampoon's Loaded Weapon 1 '93
Patriot Games '92
Pulp Fiction '94
School Daze '88
True Romance '93
White Sands '92

Selmer Jackson
The Fighting Sullivans '42
The Thirteenth Man '37

Sherry Jackson
The Adventures of Huckleberry Finn '60
Bare Knuckles '77
Cotter '72
Miracle of Our Lady of Fatima '52
Stingray '78
Trouble Along the Way '53

Stoney Jackson
Knights of the City '85
Roller Boogie '79
Streets of Fire '84
Sweet Perfection '90
Up Against the Wall '91

Victoria Jackson
Baby Boom '87
Based on an Untrue Story '93
Casual Sex? '88
Dream a Little Dream '89
Family Business '89
I Love You to Death '90
The Pick-Up Artist '87
UHF '89

Irene Jacob
Au Revoir Les Enfants '87
The Double Life of Veronique '91
Trois Couleurs: Rouge '94

Derek Jacobi
Blue Blood '73
Cyrano de Bergerac '85
The Day of the Jackal '73
Dead Again '91
Enigma '82
Henry V '89
The Human Factor '79
The Hunchback of Notre Dame '82
I, Claudius, Vol. 1: A Touch of Murder/Family Affairs '91
I, Claudius, Vol. 2: Waiting in the Wings/What Shall We Do With Claudius? '80
I, Claudius, Vol. 3: Poison is Queen/Some Justice '80
I, Claudius, Vol. 4: Queen of Heaven/Reign of Terror '80
I, Claudius, Vol. 5: Zeus, By Jove!/Hail Who? '80
I, Claudius, Vol. 6: Fool's Luck/A God in Colchester '80
I, Claudius, Vol. 7: Old King Log '80
Inside the Third Reich '82
Little Dorrit, Film 1: Nobody's Fault '88
Little Dorrit, Film 2: Little Dorrit's Story '88
The Medusa Touch '78
The Odessa File '74
Philby, Burgess and MacLean: Spy Scandal of the Century '84
The Secret Garden '87
The Tenth Man '88

Lou Jacobi
Amazon Women on the Moon '87
Arthur '81
Avalon '90
Better Late Than Never '79
The Boss' Wife '86
Chu Chu & the Philly Flash '81
Cotton Comes to Harlem '70
The Diary of Anne Frank '59
Everything You Always Wanted to Know About Sex (But Were Afraid to Ask) '72
I Don't Buy Kisses Anymore '92
Little Murders '71
The Magician of Lublin '79
My Favorite Year '82
Next Stop, Greenwich Village '76
Off Your Rocker '80
Roseland '77
Song Without End '60

Andre Jacobs
Curse of the Crystal Eye '93
Emissary '89
Prey for the Hunter '92
Pursuit '90

Manny Jacobs
Battle of the Bullies '85
The Seventh Sign '88

Steve Jacobs
Alice to Nowhere '86
Echoes of Paradise '86
Father '90

Ulla Jacobsson
Fox and His Friends '75
Smiles of a Summer Night '55

Billy Jacoby
Beastmaster '82
Bloody Birthday '80
Dr. Alien '88
Just One of the Guys '85
Party Camp '87

Bobby Jacoby
The Applegates '89
Iron Eagle '86
Night of the Demons 2 '94
Tremors '89
Wizards of the Lost Kingdom 2 '89

Dale Jacoby
Bloodmatch '91
Ring of Fire '91
Ring of Fire 2: Blood and Steel '92

Scott Jacoby
Bad Ronald '74
The Little Girl Who Lives Down the Lane '76

Midnight Auto Supply '78
Return to Horror High '87
Rivals '72
To Die for '89
To Die for 2 '91

Hattie Jacques
Carry On Nurse '59
Carry On 'Round the Bend '72
A Christmas Carol '51
Make Mine Mink '60

Richard Jaeckel
...All the Marbles '81
Awakening of Candra '81
Battleground '49
Black Moon Rising '86
Blood Song '82
Born Innocent '74
Chisum '70
Cold River '81
Come Back, Little Sheba '52
The Dark '79
Day of the Animals '77
Delta Force 2: Operation Stranglehold '90
The Devil's Brigade '68
The Dirty Dozen '67
The Dirty Dozen: The Next Mission '85
The Drowning Pool '75
Firehouse '72
The $5.20 an Hour Dream '80
The Fix '84
Flaming Star '60
The Gallant Hours '60
Ghetto Blaster '89
The Green Slime '68
Grizzly '76
Guadalcanal Diary '43
Herbie Goes Bananas '80
Hoodlum Empire '52
Jaws of Death '76
Jungle Patrol '48
The Kill '73
The King of the Kickboxers '91
Martial Outlaw '93
Once Before I Die '65
Pacific Inferno '85
Pat Garrett & Billy the Kid '73
Platinum High School '60
Sands of Iwo Jima '49
Sometimes a Great Notion '71
Speedtrap '78
Starman '84
Surabaya Conspiracy '75
3:10 to Yuma '57
Twilight's Last Gleaming '77
Ulzana's Raid '72
Walking Tall: Part 2 '75
When Hell Broke Loose '58
A Wing and a Prayer '44

Frederick Jaeger
Nijinsky '80
Slaughterday '77

Chapelle Jaffe
Confidential '86
One Night Stand '77

Sam Jaffe
The Accused '48
The Asphalt Jungle '50
Barbarian and the Geisha '58
Battle Beyond the Stars '80
Bedknobs and Broomsticks '71
Ben-Hur '59
The Day the Earth Stood Still '51
The Dunwich Horror '70
Gideon's Trumpet '80
Gunga Din '39
Lost Horizon '37
Night Gallery '69
On the Line '83
Scarlet Empress '34
13 Rue Madeleine '46

Seth Jaffe
Beverly Hills Bodysnatchers '89
Stark '85

Madhur Jaffrey
Autobiography of a Princess '75
Shakespeare Wallah '65

Saeed Jaffrey
The Courtesans of Bombay '85
The Deceivers '88
Gandhi '82
Hullabaloo Over Georgie & Bonnie's Pictures '78

The Man Who Would Be King '75
Masala '91
My Beautiful Laundrette '85
The Razor's Edge '84
The Wilby Conspiracy '75

Dean Jagger
Alligator '80
Bad Day at Black Rock '54
Billy Rose's Jumbo '62
The C-Man '49
Cash McCall '60
The Denver & Rio Grande '51
Elmer Gantry '60
End of the World '77
Evil Town '87
Executive Suite '54
Exiled to Shanghai '37
Firecreek '79
Game of Death '79
Gideon's Trumpet '80
The Glass House '72
The Hanged Man '74
The Honeymoon Machine '61
Hootch Country Boys '75
I Heard the Owl Call My Name '73
I Live in Grosvenor Square '46
It's a Dog's Life '55
King Creole '58
The Lindbergh Kidnapping Case '76
The North Star '43
The Nun's Story '59
Parrish '61
Proud Rebel '58
Pursued '47
Rawhide '50
Revolt of the Zombies '36
The Robe '53
Sister Kenny '46
The Stranger '73
Twelve O'Clock High '49
Valley of the Sun '42
Vanishing Point '71
Visions of Light '73
Western Union '41
White Christmas '54

Mick Jagger
All You Need Is Cash '78
Burden of Dreams '82
The Compleat Beatles '82
Freejack '92
Gimme Shelter '70
Ned Kelly '70
The Nightingale '83
Performance '70
Running Out of Luck '86
Sympathy for the Devil '70

Henry Jaglom
Always '89
New Year's Day '89
Psych-Out '68
Sitting Ducks '80
Someone to Love '87

Lisa Jakub
Matinee '92
The Phone Call '89
Rambling Rose '91
The Story Lady '93

Anthony James
Columbo: Prescription Murder '67
The Last Days of Dolwyn '49
Slow Burn '90
The Teacher '74
Unforgiven '92

Brion James
Another 48 Hrs. '90
Armed and Dangerous '86
Ballad of Gregorio Cortez '83
Beyond the Silhouette '90
Black Magic '92
Blade Runner '82
A Breed Apart '84
Cabin Boy '94
Crimewave '85
The Dark '94
Dead Man Walking '88
Enemy Mine '85
Flesh and Blood '85
48 Hrs. '82
Future Shock '93
The Horror Show '89
Mom '89
Mutator '90
Nightmare at Noon '87

The Player '92
Red Scorpion '89
Rio Diablo '93
Scanner Cop '94
Southern Comfort '81
Steel Dawn '87
Street Asylum '90
Striking Distance '93
Tango and Cash '89
Time Runner '93
Ultimate Desires '91
Wishman '93

Clifton James
The Bad News Bears in Breaking Training '77
Bank Shot '74
Black Like Me '64
The Bonfire of the Vanities '90
Buster and Billie '74
Carolina Skeletons '92
David and Lisa '62
Eight Men Out '88
The Last Detail '73
Live and Let Die '73
The Man with the Golden Gun '74
Rancho Deluxe '75
Sniper '75
Talk to Me '82
Werewolf of Washington '73
Where Are the Children? '85
Will Penny '68

Dalton James
My Father the Hero '93
The Substitute '93

Etta James
Chuck Berry: Hail! Hail! Rock 'n' Roll '87
Tap '89

Gennie James
Broadcast News '87
The Secret Garden '87
A Smoky Mountain Christmas '86

Geraldine James
If Looks Could Kill '91
The Jewel in the Crown '84
The Tall Guy '89

Gladden James
Paradise Island '30
The Social Secretary '16

Harry James
The Benny Goodman Story '55
Best Foot Forward '43
Private Buckaroo '42
Strictly G.I. '44
Two Girls and a Sailor '44

Hawthorne James
The Five Heartbeats '91
Speed '94

Ida James
The Devil's Daughter '39
Hi-De-Ho '35

Jessica James
I, the Jury '82
Immediate Family '89

John James
The Devil Bat's Daughter '46
Lonesome Trail '55
Man from Thunder River '43
Range Renegades '48
Secret Passions '78

Julie James
Night of the Death Cult '75
Terror Beach '80s

Ken James
Landslide '92
Switching Channels '88

Lee James
Cassandra '87
The Taking of Beverly Hills '91

Michael James
Commando Invasion '87
Warriors of the Apocalypse '85

Ron James
The Boogey Man '80
Ernest Rides Again '93
Swinging Wives '79

Sidney James
Carry On at Your Convenience '71
Carry On Behind '75
Carry On Cleo '65

Carry On Cowboy '66
Carry On Cruising '62
Carry On Dick '75
Carry On 'Round the Bend '72
Glass Tomb '55
Heat Wave '54
The Lavender Hill Mob '51
Norman Conquest '53
Quatermass 2 '57
The Silent Enemy '58
What a Carve-Up! '62

Steve James
American Ninja '85
American Ninja 2: The Confrontation '87
American Ninja 3: Blood Hunt '89
Avenging Force '86
Bloodfist 5: Human Target '93
The Brother from Another Planet '84
Hero and the Terror '88
I'm Gonna Git You Sucka '88
Johnny Be Good '88
McBain '91
The P.O.W. Escape '86
Python Wolf '88
Riverbend '89
Stalking Danger '86
Street Hunter '90
Weekend at Bernie's 2 '93

Walter James
Battling Butler '26
The Idol Dancer '20
The Kid Brother '27
Little Annie Rooney '25

Joyce Jameson
The Balcony '63
The Comedy of Terrors '64
Good Neighbor Sam '64
Hardbodies '84
Pray TV '80
Savage Run '70
Tales of Terror '62

Malcom Jamieson
Meridian: Kiss of the Beast '90
Pictures '80s

Bud Jamison
Charlie Chaplin: Rare Chaplin '15
The Dentist '32
W.C. Fields: Flask of Fields '30

Krystyna Janda
The Conductor '80
The Interrogation '82
Man of Iron '81
Man of Marble '76
Mephisto '81

Conrad Janis
The Buddy Holly Story '78
The Duchess and the Dirtwater Fox '76
Mr. Saturday Night '92
Oh, God! Book 2 '80
Sonny Boy '87

Leon Janney
Charly '68
Police Court '37

Emil Jannings
The Americano/Variety '25
The Blue Angel '30
Faust '26
Fortune's Fool '21
Last Command '28
The Last Laugh '24
Othello '22
Passion '19
Variety '25
Waxworks '24

Horst Janson
Captain Kronos: Vampire Hunter '74
McKenzie Break '70
To Catch a King '84

David Janssen
Birds of Prey '72
City in Fear '80
Darby's Rangers '58
Fer-De-Lance '74
Francis in the Navy '55
Generation '69
Golden Rendezvous '77
The Green Berets '68
Hell to Eternity '60
High Ice '80

The King of the Roaring '20s: The Story of Arnold Rothstein '61
Lafayette Escadrille '58
Macho Callahan '70
Marooned '69
Moon of the Wolf '72
Once Is Not Enough '75
Pioneer Woman '73
Prisoner in the Middle '74
The Shoes of the Fisherman '68
Smile, Jenny, You're Dead '74
S.O.S. Titanic '79
Stalk the Wild Child '76
Swamp Fire '46
Swiss Conspiracy '77
Two Minute Warning '76
The Word '78

Famke Janssen
Fathers and Sons '92
Model by Day '94

Lois January
Border Caballero '36
Bulldog Courage '35
Cocaine Fiends '36
Lightning Bill Crandall '37
The Red Rope '37
The Roamin' Cowboy '37

Claude Jarman, Jr.
Hangman's Knot '52
Intruder in the Dust '49
Rio Grande '50
The Sun Comes Up '49
The Yearling '46

Jim Jarmusch
American Autobahn '84
Leningrad Cowboys Go America '89
Straight to Hell '87

John Jarratt
Dark Age '88
Next of Kin '82
Sound of Love '77
Summer City '77

Catherine Jarrett
A Fine Romance '92
Quicker Than the Eye '88
S.A.S. San Salvador '84

Graham Jarvis
Cold Turkey '71
Doin' Time '85
Draw! '81
Middle Age Crazy '80
Mischief '85
Misery '90
Parents '89
Vanishing Act '88

Martin Jarvis
Buster '88
Taste the Blood of Dracula '70

Harvey Jason
Oklahoma Crude '73
Star! '68

Peter Jason
Alien Nation '88
Arachnophobia '90
Hyper-Sapien: People from Another Star '86
Texas Lightning '81
They Live '88

Rick Jason
Color Me Dead '69
Eagles Attack at Dawn '74
Partners '82
Witch Who Came from the Sea '76

Sybil Jason
The Blue Bird '40
The Little Princess '39

Star Jasper
Jersey Girl '92
True Love '89

Ricky Jay
House of Games '87
Things Change '88

Michael Jayston
Craze '74
Dust to Dust '85
Macbeth '90
A Midsummer Night's Dream '68
Nicholas and Alexandra '71

Gloria Jean
Copacabana '47
The Ladies' Man '61
Never Give a Sucker an Even Break '41

Isabel Jeans
Easy Virtue '27
Elizabeth of Ladymead '48
Gigi '58
Great Day '46
Heavens Above '63
The Magic Christian '69

Ursula Jeans
Cavalcade '33
Dam Busters '55
Dark Journey '37
Flame Over India '60
The Life and Death of Colonel Blimp '43

Herbert Jefferson, Jr.
Detroit 9000 '73
Private Duty Nurses '71
World War III '86

Barbara Jefford
And the Ship Sails On '83
Lust for a Vampire '71
A Midsummer Night's Dream '68
Murders at Lynch Cross '85
Reunion '89
Ulysses '67
When the Whales Came '89
Where Angels Fear to Tread '91

Peter Jeffrey
The Adventures of Baron Munchausen '89
The Fixer '68
The Horsemen '70
Ring of Bright Water '69
Twinsanity '70

Anne Jeffreys
Billy the Kid Trapped '42
Bordertown Gunfighters '43
Calling Wild Bill Elliott '43
Death Valley Manhunt '43
Dick Tracy, Detective '45
Dick Tracy Double Feature #1 '45
Dick Tracy Double Feature #2 '47
Dick Tracy vs. Cueball '46
Dillinger '45
I Married an Angel '42
Man from Thunder River '43
Nevada '44
Return of the Bad Men '48
Riff-Raff '47
Step Lively '44
Those Endearing Young Charms '45
Trail Street '47
X Marks the Spot '42
Zombies on Broadway '44

Chuck Jeffreys
Aftershock '88
Deathfight '93
Hawkeye '88
Honor and Glory '92

Fran Jeffries
Harum Scarum '65
Sex and the Single Girl '64

Herbert Jeffries
Bronze Buckaroo '39
Chrome and Hot Leather '71
Harlem on the Prairie '38
Harlem Rides the Range '39
Two-Gun Man from Harlem '38

Lang Jeffries
Alone Against Rome '62
Mission Stardust '68

Lionel Jeffries
Arrivederci, Baby! '66
The Baby and the Battleship '56
Bananas Boat '78
Bhowani Junction '56
Blue Murder at St. Trinian's '56
Call Me Bwana '63
Camelot '67
Chitty Chitty Bang Bang '68
A Chorus of Disapproval '89
The Colditz Story '55

Jeffries ▶*cont.*

Fanny '61
First Men in the Moon '64
Hour of Decision '57
Letting the Birds Go Free '86
Lola '69
Lust for Life '56
Murder Ahoy '64
Oh Dad, Poor Dad (Momma's Hung You in the Closet & I'm Feeling So Sad) '67
Prisoner of Zenda '79
Spy with a Cold Nose '66
Sudden Terror '70
Those Fantastic Flying Fools '67
Up the Creek '58
The Vicious Circle '57
Who Slew Auntie Roo? '71
The Wrong Arm of the Law '63

Rudolph Jelinek
Fabulous Adventures of Baron Munchausen '61
The Original Fabulous Adventures of Baron Munchausen '61

Anna Jemison
Heatwave '83
My First Wife '84
Smash Palace '82

Allen Jenkins
The Big Wheel '49
Blessed Event '32
Brother Orchid '40
Bureau of Missing Persons '33
Case of the Baby Sitter '47
The Case of the Lucky Legs '35
Dead End '37
Destry Rides Again '39
Dive Bomber '41
Employees' Entrance '33
Falcon Takes Over/Strange Bargain '49
Hat Box Mystery '47
I Am a Fugitive from a Chain Gang '32
Marked Woman '37
Oklahoma Annie '51
Robin and the Seven Hoods '64
Three Men on a Horse '36
Tin Pan Alley '40
Tomorrow at Seven '33

Daniel H. Jenkins
The Caine Mutiny Court Martial '88
Florida Straits '87
O.C. and Stiggs '87

Jackie "Butch" Jenkins
The Human Comedy '43
National Velvet '44
Our Vines Have Tender Grapes '45
Summer Holiday '48

Megs Jenkins
Murder Most Foul '65
Trouble in Store '53

Rebecca Jenkins
Bob Roberts '92
Bye Bye Blues '89
Clearcut '92
Cowboys Don't Cry '88
Family Reunion '88
Till Death Do Us Part '92

Richard Jenkins
Blaze '89
Descending Angel '90
It Could Happen to You '94
On Valentine's Day '86
Rising Son '90
Sea of Love '89
Stealing Home '88
The Tender Age '84
The Witches of Eastwick '87
Wolf '94

Frank Jenks
Blonde Savage '47
Corregidor '43
The Falcon in Hollywood '44
His Girl Friday '40
Kid Sister '45
The Missing Corpse '45
The Navy Comes Through '42

The Phantom of 42nd Street '45
Rogue's Gallery '44
Shake Hands with Murder '44
That Brennan Girl '46
That Girl from Paris '36
Zombies on Broadway '44

Si Jenks
Captain January '36
Fighting Shadows '35
The Outlaw Deputy '35
Rawhide Romance '34

Bruce Jenner
Can't Stop the Music '80
Grambling's White Tiger '81

Lucinda Jenney
American Heart '92
Matinee '92
Rain Man '88
Thelma & Louise '91
Verne Miller '88
Wired '89

Claudia Jennings
Death Sport '78
Fast Company '78
Gator Bait '73
The Great Texas Dynamite Chase '76
Group Marriage '72
Jud '71
The Love Machine '71
Moonshine County Express '77
Sisters of Death '76
The Stepmother '71
Truck Stop Women '74
Unholy Rollers '72

DeWitt Jennings
The Bat Whispers '30
The Big House '30
Criminal Code '31
Kelly the Second '36

Tom Jennings
Night Master '87
Stones of Death '88

Waylon Jennings
Sesame Street Presents: Follow That Bird '85
Stagecoach '86

Rita Jenrette
End of the Line '88
Malibu Bikini Shop '86
Zombie Island Massacre '84

Salome Jens
Angel Baby '61
Diary of Dead '80s
The Fool Killer '65
A Matter of Life and Death '81
Savages '72
Tomorrow's Child '82

Karen Jensen
Battlestar Galactica '78
Deadly Blessing '81
The Salzburg Connection '72

Sasha Jensen
Dazed and Confused '93
Dream Trap '90
A Girl to Kill for '90

Todd Jensen
Cyborg Cop '93
Prey for the Hunter '92

Roy Jenson
Bandits '73
Crossfire '67

Adele Jergens
Abbott & Costello Meet the Invisible Man '51
Armored Car Robbery '50
Big Chase '54
Blues Busters '50
The Cobweb '55
The Dark Past '49
Day the World Ended '55
Down to Earth '47
Falcon's Adventure/Armored Car Robbery '50
Fuller Brush Man '48
Girls in Prison '56
Ladies of the Chorus '49
The Prince of Thieves '48
Radar Secret Service '50
Treasure of Monte Cristo '50

George Jessel
Diary of a Young Comic '79
Valley of the Dolls '67

Michael Jeter
Dead Bang '89
The Fisher King '91
Gypsy '93
Sister Act 2: Back in the Habit '93

Joan Jett
Dubeat-E-O '84
Light of Day '87

Isabel Jewell
The Arousers '70
Blessed Event '32
Ceiling Zero '35
Evelyn Prentice '34
Go West, Young Man '36
Gone with the Wind '39
The Leopard Man '43
Lost Horizon '37
Manhattan Melodrama '34
Marked Woman '37
The Seventh Victim '43
Swing It, Sailor! '37
A Tale of Two Cities '35

Penn Jillette
Miami Vice 2: The Prodigal Son '85
Penn and Teller Get Killed '90
Tough Guys Don't Dance '87

Ann Jillian
The Ann Jillian Story '88
Convicted: A Mother's Story '87
Girls of the White Orchid '85
Gypsy '62
Little White Lies '89
Mae West '83
Mr. Mom '83

Joyce Jillson
Slumber Party '57 '76
Superchick '71

Yolanda Jilot
Diving In '90
JFK: Reckless Youth '93

Jose Luis Jimenez
Spiritism '61
The Vampire '57

Sergio Jimenez
Los Caifanes '87
Los Dos Hermanos '87

Marlene Jobert
Catch Me a Spy '71
Masculine Feminine '66
Rider on the Rain '70
Swashbuckler '84
Ten Days Wonder '72

David Johansen
Car 54, Where Are You? '94
Desire and Hell at Sunset Motel '92
Freejack '92
Let It Ride '89
Married to the Mob '88
Mr. Nanny '93
Scrooged '88
Tales from the Darkside: The Movie '90

Paul Johansson
Martial Law 2: Undercover '91
Midnight Witness '93
Soapdish '91

I.S. Johar
Flame Over India '60
Maya '66

Elton John
Born to Boogie '72
Tommy '75

Gottfried John
Berlin Alexanderplatz '80
The Marriage of Maria Braun '79
Mata Hari '85
Mother Kusters Goes to Heaven '76

Karl John
The Lost One '51
The Mysterious Magician '65

Rosamund John
Fame is the Spur '47
Spitfire '42

Glynis Johns
The Adventures of Tartu '43
All Mine to Give '56

Another Time, Another Place '58
Court Jester '56
Dear Brigitte '65
Encore '52
The Forty-Ninth Parallel '41
Frieda '47
Land of Fury '55
Mary Poppins '64
Mrs. Amworth '77
Nukie '93
Papa's Delicate Condition '63
The Promoter '52
The Ref '93
Rob Roy—The Highland Rogue '53
Shake Hands with the Devil '59
Spragque '84
The Sundowners '60
The Sword & the Rose '53
Under Milk Wood '73
Vault of Horror '73
Zelly & Me '88

Mervyn Johns
Captive Heart '47
A Christmas Carol '51
Counterblast '48
Day of the Triffids '63
Dead of Night '45
The Master of Ballantrae '53
No Love for Johnnie '60
Pink Strings and Sealing Wax '45
Romeo and Juliet '54
San Demetrio, London '47
Tony Draws a Horse '51

Stratford Johns
A Demon in My View '92
Great Expectations '81
The Lair of the White Worm '88
Salome's Last Dance '88
Splitting Heirs '93
The Strange Case of the End of Civilization as We Know It '93

Tracy C. Johns
Mo' Better Blues '90
New Jack City '91

A.J. Johnson
Double Trouble '91
House Party '90

Anne-Marie Johnson
Dream Date '93
Hollywood Shuffle '87
I'm Gonna Git You Sucka '88
Robot Jox '89
True Identity '91

Arnold Johnson
My Demon Lover '87
Putney Swope '69

Arte Johnson
Bud and Lou '78
Bunco '83
The Charge of the Model T's '76
Evil Spirits '91
Evil Toons '90
If Things Were Different '79
Love at First Bite '79
Munchie '92
The Red Raven Kiss-Off '90
Tax Season '90
What Comes Around '85

Ben Johnson
Angels in the Outfield '94
Back to Back '90
Bite the Bullet '75
Bonanza: The Return '93
Breakheart Pass '76
Champions '84
The Chase '91
Cherry 2000 '88
Chisum '70
Dark Before Dawn '89
Dillinger '73
The Getaway '72
Grayeagle '77
Junior Bonner '72
The Last Picture Show '71
Let's Get Harry '87
Major Dundee '65
Mighty Joe Young '49
My Heroes Have Always Been Cowboys '91
One-Eyed Jacks '61
Radio Flyer '92
The Rare Breed '66

Red Dawn '84
Rio Grande '50
Ruckus '81
The Sacketts '79
The Savage Bees '76
The Shadow Riders '82
Shane '53
She Wore a Yellow Ribbon '49
Soggy Bottom U.S.A. '84
The Sugarland Express '74
The Swarm '78
Terror Train '80
Tex '82
Three Godfathers '48
Tomboy & the Champ '58
Town that Dreaded Sundown '76
Train Robbers '73
Trespasses '86
The Undefeated '69
Wagon Master '50
The Wild Bunch '69
Wild Horses '84
Wild Times '79
Will Penny '67

Beverly Johnson
Ashanti, Land of No Mercy '79
The Cover Girl Murders '93

Brad Johnson
Always '89
An American Story '92
Flight of the Intruder '90
The Losers '70
Nam Angels '88
Philadelphia Experiment 2 '93

Candy Johnson
Beach Party '63
Bikini Beach '64
Muscle Beach Party '64
Pajama Party '64

Celia Johnson
Brief Encounter '46
Captain's Paradise '53
The Hostage Tower '80
In Which We Serve '43
Les Miserables '82
The Prime of Miss Jean Brodie '69
Staying On '80
This Happy Breed '47
Unicorn '83

Chic Johnson
All Over Town '37
Country Gentlemen '36

Clark Johnson
Final Round '93
The Finishing Touch '92
Personals '90

Don Johnson
Beulah Land '80
Born Yesterday '93
A Boy and His Dog '75
Cease Fire '85
The City '76
Dead Bang '89
Guilty as Sin '93
Harley Davidson and the Marlboro Man '91
Harrad Experiment '73
Hot Spot '90
Law of the Land '76
The Long, Hot Summer '86
Melanie '82
Miami Vice '84
Miami Vice 2: The Prodigal Son '85
Paradise '91
The Rebels '79
Return to Macon County '75
Revenge of the Stepford Wives '80
Snowblind '78
Soggy Bottom U.S.A. '84
Sweet Hearts Dance '88
Tales of the Unexpected '91
Zachariah '70

Dots Johnson
Paisan '46
Tall, Tan and Terrific '46

Helen Johnson
The Divorcee '30
Sin Takes a Holiday '30
Vice Squad '31

Jill Johnson
Party Plane '90
Wildest Dreams '90

Joey Johnson
Courier of Death '84
Grad Night '81

Kay Johnson
Madam Satan '30
Son of Fury '42

Kelly Johnson
Carry Me Back '82
Goodbye Pork Pie '81
Utu '83

Kurt Johnson
Jane Austen in Manhattan '80
Sole Survivor '84

Kyle Johnson
The Learning Tree '69
Man on the Run '74

Laura Johnson
Beyond Reason '77
Dario Argento's Trauma '93
Deadly Exposure '93
Fatal Instinct '92
Murderous Vision '91
Nick Knight '80s
Opening Night '77
Red Shoe Diaries 2: Double
   Dare '92

Lynn-Holly Johnson
Alien Predators '80
Digging Up Business '91
For Your Eyes Only '81
Ice Castles '79
The Sisterhood '88
The Watcher in the Woods '81
Where the Boys Are '84 '84

Mae Johnson
The Defilers '65
Keep Punching '39

Mel Johnson, Jr.
Eubie! '82
Total Recall '90

Michelle Johnson
Beaks: The Movie '87
Blame It on Rio '84
Blood Ties '92
Body Shot '93
A Chorus Line '85
Death Becomes Her '92
Driving Me Crazy '91
Far and Away '92
Genuine Risk '89
Gung Ho '85
Jigsaw Murders '89
Slipping into Darkness '88
Waxwork '88
Wishful Thinking '92

Noble Johnson
The Ghost Breakers '40
King Kong '33
The Lives of a Bengal Lancer
   '35
The Navigator '24
North of the Great Divide '50

Reggie Johnson
Platoon '86
Seven Hours to Judgment '88

Richard Johnson
The Amorous Adventures of
   Moll Flanders '65
Beyond the Door '75
The Big Scam '79
The Comeback '77
The Crucifer of Blood '91
Diving In '90
Duel of Hearts '92
Fifth Day of Peace '72
The Four Feathers '78
The Great Alligator '81
The Haunting '63
Hennessy '75
Khartoum '66
Lady Jane '85
A Man for All Seasons '88
The Marquise
Never So Few '59
Operation Crossbow '65
Restless '72
Screamers '80
Spymaker: The Secret Life of
   Ian Fleming '90
Tomb of Ligeia '64
Treasure Island '89
Turtle Diary '86
The Witch '66
Zombie '80

Rita Johnson
All Mine to Give '56
Broadway Serenade '39
Edison the Man '40
Here Comes Mr. Jordan '41
Honolulu '39
My Friend Flicka '43
The Naughty Nineties '45
The Perfect Marriage '46
They Won't Believe Me '47

Robin Johnson
Splitz '84
Times Square '80

Russell Johnson
Fatal Chase '77
Gilligan's Island: Meet the Crew
   '64
The Great Skycopter Rescue
   '82
It Came From Outer Space '53
Rock All Night '57
This Island Earth '55

Steve Johnson
Angel of H.E.A.T. '82
Lemora, Lady Dracula '73

Sunny Johnson
Dr. Heckyl and Mr. Hype '80
Flashdance '83
The Red Light Sting '84

Tor Johnson
Abbott and Costello in the
   Foreign Legion '50
The Beast of Yucca Flats '61
Behind Locked Doors '48
Bride of the Monster '56
Carousel '56
Houdini '53
Human Gorilla '48
Night of the Ghouls '59
Plan 9 from Outer Space '56
The Unearthly '57

Van Johnson
Battleground '49
The Big Hangover '50
Brigadoon '54
The Caine Mutiny '54
Command Decision '48
Delta Force Commando 2 '90
The Doomsday Flight '66
Duchess of Idaho '50
Easy to Love '53
Go for Broke! '51
A Guy Named Joe '44
The Human Comedy '43
In the Good Old Summertime
   '49
The Kidnapping of the
   President '80
The Last Time I Saw Paris '54
Madame Curie '43
Men of the Fighting Lady '54
Pied Piper of Hamelin '57
The Purple Rose of Cairo '85
Scorpion with Two Tails '82
State of the Union '48
Thirty Seconds Over Tokyo '44
Three Days to a Kill '91
Three Guys Named Mike '51
Thrill of a Romance '45
Too Many Girls '40
Two Girls and a Sailor '44
Weekend at the Waldorf '45
The White Cliffs of Dover '44
Yours, Mine & Ours '68

**Victoria (Vicki)
Johnson**
Grizzly '76
Starship Invasions '77

Grace Johnston
God Bless the Child '88
One Good Cop '91

J.J. Johnston
Fatal Attraction '87
Mad Dog and Glory '93
Things Change '88

**John Dennis
Johnston**
A Breed Apart '84
Dear Detective '78
Into Thin Air '85
KISS Meets the Phantom of the
   Park '78
Miracle in the Wilderness '91
Pink Cadillac '89

Streets of Fire '84

Margaret Johnston
Burn Witch, Burn! '62
A Man About the House '47
Sebastian '68

Oliver Johnston
A King in New York '57
Tomb of Ligeia '64

I. Stanford Jolley
Ambush Trail '46
The Black Raven '43
Check Your Guns '48
Cyclotrode "X" '46
Frontier Fugitives '45
King of the Rocketmen '49
Lightning Raiders '45
Midnight Limited '40
Outlaw Roundup '44
The Rebel Set '59
Trail of the Silver Spurs '41
Wild Country '47

Al Jolson
Hallelujah, I'm a Bum '33
The Jazz Singer '27
Rhapsody in Blue '45
Rose of Washington Square
   '39

Allan Jones
A Day at the Races '37
Everybody Sing '38
The Firefly '37
A Night at the Opera '35
One Night in the Tropics '40
Rose Marie '36
Show Boat '36
A Swingin' Summer '65

Andras Jones
Far from Home '89
A Nightmare on Elm Street 4:
   Dream Master '88
Sorority Babes in the Slimeball
   Bowl-A-Rama '87

Barry Jones
Demetrius and the Gladiators
   '54
The Glass Slipper '55
Prince Valiant '54
Return to Paradise '53
Uneasy Terms '48

Ben Jones
Deep in the Heart '83
Don't Change My World '83

Buck Jones
Arizona Bound '41
Below the Border '42
Border Law '31
The Crimson Trail '35
Dawn on the Great Divide '42
Down Texas Way '42
The Fighting Sheriff '31
Forbidden Trails '41
Ghost Town Law '42
Gunman from Bodie '41
Law of the Texan '38
The Phantom Rider '37
Range Feud '31
The Range Feud/Two Fisted
   Law '31
Riders of Death Valley '41
Riders of the West '42
Sandflow '37
The Throwback '35
West of the Law '42
When a Man Sees Red '34
White Eagle '32

Carolyn Jones
Big Heat '53
Career '59
Color Me Dead '69
Eaten Alive '76
Halloween with the Addams
   Family '79
A Hole in the Head '59
House of Wax '53
How the West was Won '63
Ice Palace '60
Invasion of the Body Snatchers
   '56
King Creole '58
Last Train from Gun Hill '59
Little Ladies of the Night '77
The Man Who Knew Too Much
   '56
Marjorie Morningstar '58
The Road to Bali '53
The Seven Year Itch '55

The Shaming '71
The Tender Trap '55

Catherine Zeta Jones
Christopher Columbus: The
   Discovery '92
Splitting Heirs '93

Christopher Jones
The Looking Glass War '69
Ryan's Daughter '70
Three in the Attic '68
Wild in the Streets '68

Chuck Jones
Chuck Amuck: The Movie '91
Innerspace '87

Claude Earl Jones
Bride of Re-Animator '89
Evilspeak '82
Impulse '84

Clyde Jones
Crack House '89
Delta Heat '92
Motown's Mustang '86

Darby Jones
I Walked with a Zombie '43
Zombies on Broadway '44

Dean Jones
Any Wednesday '66
Beethoven '92
Blackbeard's Ghost '67
Born Again '78
Fire and Rain '89
Herbie Goes to Monte Carlo '77
The Horse in the Gray Flannel
   Suit '68
Jailhouse Rock '57
The Long Days of Summer '80
The Love Bug '68
Million Dollar Duck '71
Mr. Superinvisible '73
Monkeys, Go Home! '66
Once Upon a Brothers Grimm
   '77
Other People's Money '91
The Shaggy D.A. '76
Snowball Express '72
Tea and Sympathy '56
That Darn Cat '65
Torpedo Run '58
The Ugly Dachshund '65
When Every Day was the
   Fourth of July '78

Dick Jones
The Frontiersman '38
Nancy Drew, Reporter '39
Trail of the Hawk '37

Duane Jones
Beat Street '84
Black Vampire '73
Fright House '89
Night of the Living Dead '68
To Die for '89

Earl Jones
The Displaced Person '76
Lying Lips '39

Eddie Jones
Apprentice to Murder '88
Sneakers '92

Freddie Jones
Accident '67
All Creatures Great and Small
   '74
And the Ship Sails On '83
Assault '71
The Bliss of Mrs. Blossom '68
Consuming Passions '88
Dune '84
The Elephant Man '80
Erik the Viking '89
Firefox '82
Firestarter '84
Hotel Room '93
Juggernaut '74
Krull '83
Romance with a Double Bass
   '74
The Satanic Rites of Dracula
   '73
Twinsanity '70
Wild at Heart '90
Young Sherlock Holmes '85
Zulu Dawn '79

Gemma Jones
The Devils '71
Paperhouse '89

Gillian Jones
Echoes of Paradise '86
Shame '87

Gordon Jones
Arizona Cowboy '49
Flying Tigers '42
The Green Hornet '39
Heart of the Rockies '51
I Take This Oath '40
Let 'Em Have It '35
McLintock! '63
The Monster that Challenged
   the World '57
North of the Great Divide '50
Sea Devils '37
Trail of Robin Hood '50
Trigger, Jr. '50
Up in the Air '40
Western Double Feature 11 '50
The Wistful Widow of Wagon
   Gap '47

Grace Jones
Boomerang '92
Conan the Destroyer '84
Deadly Vengeance '81
Gordon's War '73
Pee Wee's Playhouse
   Christmas Special '88
Siesta '87
Straight to Hell '87
Vamp '86
A View to a Kill '85

Griff Rhys Jones
The Misadventures of Mr. Wilt
   '90
Morons from Outer Space '85

Griffith Jones
The Day Will Dawn '42
The Mill on the Floss '37
The Secret Four '40
The Wicked Lady '45

Harold W. Jones
The Crazies '73
Provoked '89

Henry Jones
Angel Baby '61
Arachnophobia '90
The Bad Seed '56
Balboa '61
The Bramble Bush '60
Butch Cassidy and the
   Sundance Kid '69
Cash McCall '60
Codename: Foxfire '85
Deathtrap '82
The Grifters '90
The Lady Says No '51
Napoleon and Samantha '72
Nowhere to Run '88
Pete 'n' Tillie '72
Stay Away, Joe '68
Support Your Local Gunfighter
   '71
Vertigo '58

James Earl Jones
Aladdin and His Wonderful
   Lamp '84
Allan Quartermain and the Lost
   City of Gold '86
The Ambulance '90
Best of the Best '89
Bingo Long Traveling All-Stars
   & Motor Kings '76
Blood Tide '82
The Bushido Blade '80
By Dawn's Early Light '89
City Limits '85
Clean Slate '94
Clear and Present Danger '94
Coming to America '88
Conan the Barbarian '82
Deadly Hero '75
Dr. Strangelove, or: How I
   Learned to Stop Worrying
   and Love the Bomb '64
End of the Road '70
Excessive Force '93
The Exorcist 2: The Heretic '77
Field of Dreams '89
Gardens of Stone '87
The Great White Hope '70
The Greatest '77
Grim Prairie Tales '89
The Guyana Tragedy: The
   Story of Jim Jones '80
Heat Wave '90
The Hunt for Red October '90

Jones ▶cont.

Ivory Hunters '90
Last Flight Out: A True Story '90
The Last Remake of Beau Geste '77
Lone Star Kid '90s
Matewan '87
The Meteor Man '93
My Little Girl '87
Patriot Games '92
Paul Robeson '70s
Piece of the Action '77
Return of the Jedi '83
The River Niger '76
Roots: The Next Generation '79
The Sandlot '93
Scorchers '92
Sneakers '92
Sommersby '93
Soul Man '86
Star Wars '77
Swashbuckler '76
Three Fugitives '89
The Vegas Strip Wars '84

Janet Jones
American Anthem '86
A Chorus Line '85
The Flamingo Kid '84
Police Academy 5: Assignment Miami Beach '88

Jeffrey Jones
Amadeus '84
Beetlejuice '88
Ed Wood '94
Ferris Bueller's Day Off '86
George Washington: The Forging of a Nation '86
Hanoi Hilton '87
Howard the Duck '86
The Hunt for Red October '90
Kenny Rogers as the Gambler, Part 3: The Legend Continues '87
Mom and Dad Save the World '92
Out on a Limb '92
Stay Tuned '92
Transylvania 6-5000 '85
Valmont '89
Who's Harry Crumb? '89
Without a Clue '88

Jennifer Jones
Beat the Devil '53
Carrie '52
Dawn Rider/Frontier Horizon '39
Dick Tracy '37
Duel in the Sun '46
Frontier Horizon '39
Indiscretion of an American Wife '54
Love is a Many-Splendored Thing '55
Madame Bovary '49
The Man in the Gray Flannel Suit '56
Portrait of Jennie '48
Ruby Gentry '52
Since You Went Away '44
The Song of Bernadette '43
The Towering Inferno '74

Josephine Jacqueline Jones
Black Venus '83
Warrior Queen '87

L.Q. Jones
The Annapolis Story '55
Ballad of Cable Hogue '70
The Beast Within '82
The Brotherhood of Satan '71
Bulletproof '88
Fireball Forward '72
Flaming Star '60
Grizzly Adams: The Legend Continues '90
Iron Angel '64
Lightning Jack '94
Lone Wolf McQuade '83
Manhunter '70
The McMasters '70
Mother, Jugs and Speed '76
Richard Petty Story '72
Ride the High Country '62

River of Death '90
Sacred Ground '83
Standing Tall '78
Stay Away, Joe '68
A Strange and Deadly Occurence '74
Timerider '83
Torpedo Run '58
White Line Fever '75
The Wild Bunch '69

Marcia Mae Jones
The Adventures of Tom Sawyer '38
The Champ '31
The Gang's All Here '41
Lady in the Death House '44
Let's Go Collegiate '41
The Little Princess '39
Old Swimmin' Hole '40
These Three '36
Tomboy '40

Betsy Jones-Moreland
Creature from the Haunted Sea '60
The Last Woman on Earth '61

Morgan Jones
Apache Woman '55
The Bus Is Coming '72
The Giant Claw '57

Nicholas Jones
Black Beauty '94
A Dangerous Man: Lawrence after Arabia '91

Peter Jones
Man of Evil '48
Whoops Apocalypse '83

Rosie Jones
Alice to Nowhere '86
Ganjasaurus Rex '87

Sam Jones
DaVinci's War '92
Driving Force '88
Fist of Honor '92
Flash Gordon '80
Hard Vice '94
In Gold We Trust '91
Jane & the Lost City '87
Lady Dragon 2 '93
Maximum Force '92
My Chauffeur '86
Night Rhythms '92
One Man Force '89
Silent Assassins '88
Under the Gun '88
WhiteForce '88

Shirley Jones
Bedtime Story '63
Beyond the Poseidon Adventure '79
Black Devil Doll from Hell '84
Carousel '56
The Cheyenne Social Club '70
The Children of An Lac '80
The Courtship of Eddie's Father '62
Elmer Gantry '60
The Girls of Huntington House '73
The Happy Ending '69
Last Cry for Help '79
The Music Man '62
Never Steal Anything Small '59
Oklahoma! '55
Silent Night, Lonely Night '69
Tank '83
Two Rode Together '61
Who'll Save Our Children? '82

Simon Jones
Club Paradise '86
Green Card '90
The Making of The Hitchhiker's Guide to the Galaxy '80s
Privates on Parade '84

Terry Jones
And Now for Something Completely Different '72
Erik the Viking '89
Jabberwocky '77
Monty Python and the Holy Grail '75
Monty Python Live at the Hollywood Bowl '82
Monty Python Meets Beyond the Fringe

Monty Python's Life of Brian '79
Monty Python's Parrot Sketch Not Included '90
Monty Python's The Meaning of Life '83
The Secret Policeman's Other Ball '82
Secret Policeman's Private Parts '81

Tommy Lee Jones
The Amazing Howard Hughes '77
Back Roads '81
The Betsy '78
Big Town '87
Black Moon Rising '86
Blown Away '94
Cat on a Hot Tin Roof '84
The Client '94
Coal Miner's Daughter '80
Eliza's Horoscope '70
The Executioner's Song '82
Eyes of Laura Mars '78
Fire Birds '90
The Fugitive '93
Gotham '88
Heaven and Earth '93
House of Cards '93
Jackson County Jail '76
JFK '91
Lonesome Dove '89
Love Story '70
Nate and Hayes '83
Natural Born Killers '94
The Package '89
The Park is Mine '85
The River Rat '84
Rolling Thunder '77
Stormy Monday '88
Under Siege '92
Yuri Nosenko, KGB '86

Richard Jordahl
The Starfighters '63
To the Shores of Hell '65

Bobby Jordan
Angels with Dirty Faces '38
Bowery Blitzkrieg '41
Bowery Buckaroos '47
Boys of the City '40
Flying Wild '41
Hard-Boiled Mahoney '47
Kid Dynamite '43
Let's Get Tough '42
'Neath Brooklyn Bridge '42
Pride of the Bowery '41
Spook Busters '46
Spooks Run Wild '41
That Gang of Mine '40
Young Tom Edison '40

Dorothy Jordan
The Cabin in the Cotton '32
Min & Bill '30
The Searchers '56

James Carroll Jordan
Slashdance '89
Tales of the Unexpected '91

Jim Jordan
Chains '89
Here We Go Again! '42

Leslie Jordan
Frankenstein General Hospital '88
Jason Goes to Hell: The Final Friday '93
Ski Patrol '89

Louis Jordan
Beware '46
Look Out Sister '48
Reet, Petite and Gone '47

Marion Jordan
Here We Go Again! '42
Look Who's Laughing '41

Marsha Jordan
Class Reunion '87
Lady Godiva Rides '68
Saturday Night Sleazies, Vol. 1 '66
Sweet Georgia '72

Nick Jordan
Five for Hell '67
Reactor '85

Richard Jordan
The Big Scam '79
Chato's Land '71

Dune '84
A Flash of Green '85
Gettysburg '93
Heaven is a Playground '91
The Hunt for Red October '90
The Hunt for the Night Stalker '91
Interiors '78
Lawman '71
Les Miserables '78
Logan's Run '76
Mean Season '85
The Men's Club '86
The Murder of Mary Phagan '87
Old Boyfriends '79
Primary Motive '92
Raise the Titanic '80
Romero '89
Rooster Cogburn '75
The Secret of My Success '87
Shout '91
Solarbabies '86
Timebomb '91
Trial of the Catonsville Nine '72
Valdez is Coming '71
Washington Mistress '81
The Yakuza '75

William Jordan
The Buddy Holly Story '78
The Doors '91
I Wanna Hold Your Hand '78
King '78
The Red Fury '70s

Daniel Jordano
Alphabet City '84
Playing for Keeps '86

Victor Jory
The Adventures of Tom Sawyer '38
Bar-20 '43
Border Vigilantes '41
Buckskin Frontier '43
Bulldog Drummond at Bay '37
The Capture '50
The Cariboo Trail '50
Cat Women of the Moon '53
Charlie Chan in Rio '41
Cheyenne Autumn '64
Colt Comrades '43
Death of a Scoundrel '56
Devil Dog: The Hound of Hell '78
Dodge City '39
Each Dawn I Die '39
Frasier the Sensuous Lion '73
The Fugitive Kind '60
Gone with the Wind '39
Green Archer '40
Hell-Ship Morgan '36
Hoppy Serves a Writ '43
The Kansan '43
Knights of the Range '40
Leather Burners '43
The Light of Western Stars '40
The Loves of Carmen '48
Man from the Alamo '53
Manfish '56
A Midsummer Night's Dream '35
The Miracle Worker '62
The Mountain Men '80
Papillon '73
Riders of the Timberline '41
Sabaka '55
Son of Ali Baba '52
South of St. Louis '48
Susannah of the Mounties '39
A Woman's Secret '49

Erland Josephson
After the Rehearsal '84
Brink of Life '57
Control '87
Cries and Whispers '72
Face to Face '76
Fanny and Alexander '83
Good Evening, Mr. Wallenberg '93
Hanussen '88
Hour of the Wolf '68
Meeting Venus '91
Montenegro '81
The Ox '91
The Passion of Anna '70
Prospero's Books '91
The Sacrifice '86
Saving Grace '86
Scenes from a Marriage '73

Sofie '92
To Forget Venice '79
The Unbearable Lightness of Being '88

Larry Joshua
A Midnight Clear '92
Romeo Is Bleeding '93
Sugar Hill '94
Svengali '83

Allyn Joslyn
As Young As You Feel '51
Fastest Gun Alive '56
Heaven Can Wait '43
The Horn Blows at Midnight '45
I Love Melvin '53
I Wake Up Screaming '41
If You Knew Susie '48
Immortal Sergeant '43
Moonrise '48
Only Angels Have Wings '39
The Shining Hour '38
They Won't Forget '37

Louis Jourdan
Beverly Hills Madam '86
The Bride Is Much Too Beautiful '58
Can-Can '60
The Count of Monte Cristo '74
Counterforce '87
Decameron Nights '53
Double Deal '84
Escape to Love '82
The First Olympics: Athens 1896 '84
For the Love of Angela '86
Gigi '58
Grand Larceny
Letter from an Unknown Woman '48
Madame Bovary '49
The Man in the Iron Mask '77
Octopussy '83
The Paradine Case '47
The Return of Swamp Thing '89
Silver Bears '78
Swamp Thing '82
The Swan '56
Three Coins in the Fountain '54
The V.I.P.'s '63
Year of the Comet '92

Louis Jouvet
Bizarre Bizarre '39
Carnival in Flanders '35
Heart of a Nation '43
Jenny Lamour '47
La Marseillaise '37
The Lower Depths '36
Topaze '33
Volpone '39

Milla Jovovich
Chaplin '92
Kuffs '92
The Night Train to Kathmandu '88
Return to the Blue Lagoon '91

Leatrice Joy
Made for Love '26
Old Swimmin' Hole '40

Nicholas Joy
Gentleman's Agreement '47
Native Son '51

Robert Joy
Amityville 3: The Demon '83
Big Shots '87
The Dark Half '91
Desperately Seeking Susan '85
Joshua Then and Now '85
The Lawrenceville Stories '80s
Longtime Companion '90
Millenium '89
Miracle at Moreaux '86
Shadows and Fog '92
She's Back '88
The Suicide Club '88
Sword of Gideon '86

Alice Joyce
Dancing Mothers '26
Song O' My Heart '29

Brenda Joyce
The Enchanted Forest '45
Little Giant '46
The Rains Came '39

Elaine Joyce
Honor Thy Father and Mother:
  The True Story of the
  Menendez Brothers '94
Motel Hell '80

William Joyce
I Eat Your Skin '64
The Young Nurses '73

Yootha Joyce
Die! Die! My Darling! '65
Horrors of Burke & Hare '71

Odette Joyeux
La Ronde '51
Sylvia and the Phantom '45

Michelle Joyner
Cliffhanger '93
Traces of Red '92

Ashley Judd
Natural Born Killers '94
Ruby in Paradise '93

Carolyn Judd
Escape from Cell Block 3 '78
Women Unchained '70s

Edward Judd
The Day the Earth Caught Fire
  '62
First Men in the Moon '64
Flambards
Invasion '65
Island of Terror '66
The Kitchen Toto '87
Murder Motel '74
Stolen Hours '63
Whose Child Am I? '75

Robert Judd
Crossroads '86
Fight for Your Life '79

Charles Judels
Baby Face Morgan '42
Love on the Run '36
Two Reelers: Comedy Classics
  8 '33

Arline Judge
The Crawling Hand '63
Girls in Chains '43
The Lady is Willing '42
Law of the Jungle '42
Mysterious Mr. Wong '35
One in a Million '36
Song of Texas '43
Take It Big '44
Wildcat '42

Raul Julia
The Addams Family '91
Addams Family Values '93
The Alamo: Thirteen Days to
  Glory '87
Compromising Positions '85
Death Scream '75
The Escape Artist '82
Eyes of Laura Mars '78
Florida Straits '87
Frankenstein Unbound '90
Gumball Rally '76
Havana '90
Kiss of the Spider Woman '85
A Life of Sin '92
Mack the Knife '89
Moon Over Parador '88
The Morning After '86
Onassis '88
One from the Heart '82
The Organization '71
Overdrawn at the Memory
  Bank '83
Panic in Needle Park '75
The Penitent '88
The Plague '92
Presumed Innocent '90
Romero '89
The Rookie '90
Strong Medicine '84
Tango Bar '88
The Tempest '82
Tequila Sunrise '88
Trading Hearts '87

Janet Julian
Ghostwarrior '86
Humongous '82
King of New York '90
Smokey Bites the Dust '81

Max Julien
Getting Straight '70
Mack '73

Julissa
Dance of Death '68
El Robo al Tren Correo '47
The Fear Chamber '68
La Mentira '87
Los Caifanes '87

Gordon Jump
Dirkham Detective Agency '83
Making the Grade '84
Ransom Money '88
WKRP in Cincinnati, Vol. 1 '78

Tito Junco
El Hombre Contra el Mundo '87
Invasion of the Vampires '61
A Woman Without Love '51

Victor Junco
Conexion Mexico '87
Gente Violenta '87

Calvin Jung
American Ninja 3: Blood Hunt
  '89
In the Shadow of Kilimanjaro
  '86

Katy Jurado
Arrowhead '53
The Badlanders '58
Barabbas '62
Broken Lance '54
Bullfighter & the Lady '50
Children of Sanchez '79
El Bruto '52
Fearmaker '89
High Noon '52
Once Upon a Scoundrel '73
One-Eyed Jacks '61
Pat Garrett & Billy the Kid '73
Stay Away, Joe '68
Trapeze '56
Under the Volcano '84

Peter Jurasik
Full Exposure: The Sex Tape
  Scandals '89
Peter Gunn '89
Problem Child '90

Curt Jurgens
And God Created Woman '57
The Assassination Bureau '69
Battle of Britain '69
Battle of Neretva '69
Battle of the Commandos '71
Breakthrough '78
Cruise Missile '78
The Devil in Silk '56
Dirty Heroes '71
Enemy Below '57
Ferry to Hong Kong '59
French Intrigue
Goldengirl '79
The Inn of the Sixth Happiness
  '58
The Invincible Six '68
Just a Gigolo '79
The Longest Day '62
Lord Jim '65
The Mephisto Waltz '71
The Miracle of the White
  Stallions '63
The Mozart Story '48
Murder for Sale '70
Nicholas and Alexandra '71
Sleep of Death '79
The Spy Who Loved Me '77
Tamango '59
Target for Killing '66
This Happy Feeling '58
The Three Penny Opera '62
Twist '76
Vault of Horror '73

Deana Jurgens
Code Name: Zebra '84
Tin Man '83

**James Robertson
Justice**
Above Us the Waves '56
Alien Women '69
David and Bathsheba '51
Doctor at Large '57
Doctor at Sea '56
Doctor in Distress '63
Doctor in the House '53
The Lady Says No '51
Land of the Pharaohs '55
Le Repos du Guerrier '62
The Love Factor '69
Murder She Said '62

Rob Roy—The Highland Rogue
  '53
Spirits of the Dead '68
The Sword & the Rose '53
Whiskey Galore '48

Katherine Justice
Captain America 2: Death Too
  Soon '79
Columbo: Prescription Murder
  '67
Five Card Stud '68
Frasier the Sensuous Lion '73
The Stepmother '71

William Justine
The Bride & the Beast '58
Trauma '62

Suzanne Kaaren
The Devil Bat '41
Phantom Ranger '38
Undercover Man '36

Jane Kaczmarek
All's Fair '89
D.O.A. '88
Door to Door '84
Falling in Love '84
The Heavenly Kid '85
Vice Versa '88

Karen Kadler
The Beatniks '60
It Conquered the World '56

Piotr Kadochnikov
Ivan the Terrible, Part 1 '44
Ivan the Terrible, Part 2 '46

Diane Kagan
The Life and Assassination of
  the Kingfish '76
Mr. & Mrs. Bridge '91

Kyoko Kagawa
The Crucified Lovers '54
The Lower Depths '57
Mother '52
Sansho the Bailiff '54

David Kagen
Body Chemistry '90
Conspiracy: The Trial of the
  Chicago Eight '87
Friday the 13th, Part 6: Jason
  Lives '86

Steve Kahan
Lethal Weapon '87
Lethal Weapon 2 '89
Lethal Weapon 3 '92
Warlock: The Armageddon '93

Madeline Kahn
The Adventures of Sherlock
  Holmes' Smarter Brother '78
Betsy's Wedding '90
Blazing Saddles '74
The Cheap Detective '78
City Heat '84
Clue '85
The Dove '68
First Family '80
For Richer or Poorer '92
Happy Birthday, Gemini '80
The Hideaways '73
High Anxiety '77
History of the World: Part 1 '81
Paper Moon '73
Scrambled Feet '83
Simon '80
Slapstick of Another Kind '84
Wanted: The Perfect Guy '90
Wholly Moses! '80
Yellowbeard '83
Young Frankenstein '74

Chia Kai
Dance of Death '84
Empire of the Dragon '80s
Of Cooks and Kung-Fu '80s

Khalil Kain
Juice '92
Renaissance Man '94

Joel Kaiser
Dead Certain '92
Home for Christmas '90

Elizabeth Kaitan
Aftershock '88
Desperate Crimes '93
Roller Blade Warriors: Taken
  By Force '90
Vice Academy 3 '91

Bonita Kalem
Escape from Cell Block 3 '78
Women Unchained '70s

Toni Kalem
Billy Galvin '86
Silent Rage '82

Patricia Kalember
Big Girls Don't Cry...They Get
  Even '92
A Far Off Place '93
Jacob's Ladder '90

Jean-Pierre Kalfon
Condorman '81
The Cry of the Owl '92
Weekend '67

Helena Kallianiotes
Backtrack '89
Five Easy Pieces '70

Alexander Kalyagin
A Slave of Love '78
An Unfinished Piece for a
  Player Piano '77

Danny Kamekona
The Karate Kid: Part 2 '86
Robot Jox '89
Robot Wars '93

Stanley Kamel
Honor Thy Father and Mother:
  The True Story of the
  Menendez Brothers '94
Murder by Numbers '89

Fritz Kampers
Kameradschaft '31
Westfront 1918 '30

Anna Kanakis
After the Fall of New York '85
Warriors of the Wasteland '83

Steve Kanaly
Balboa '82
Double Trouble '91
Driving Me Crazy '91
Eye of the Eagle 3 '91
Fleshburn '84
Headhunter '89

Sean Kanan
The Karate Kid: Part 3 '89
Rich Girl '91

Babe Kane
The Dentist '32
Pharmacist '32
W.C. Fields Comedy Bag '33
W.C. Fields: Flask of Fields '30

Carol Kane
Addams Family Values '93
Annie Hall '77
Baby on Board '92
Burning Rage '84
Carnal Knowledge '71
Casey at the Bat '85
Desperate Characters '71
Dog Day Afternoon '75
Drop-Out Mother '88
Flashback '89
Harry & Walter Go to New York
  '76
Hester Street '75
Jumpin' Jack Flash '86
Keeping On '81
The Last Detail '73
The Lemon Sisters '90
License to Drive '88
My Blue Heaven '90
My Sister, My Love '78
Norman Loves Rose '82
Over the Brooklyn Bridge '83
Pandemonium '82
The Princess Bride '87
Racing with the Moon '84
Rap Master Ronnie '88
Scrooged '88
The Secret Diary of Sigmund
  Freud '84
Sticky Fingers '88
Strong Medicine '84
Ted & Venus '93
Transylvania 6-5000 '85
Valentino '77
Wedding in White '72
When a Stranger Calls '79
When a Stranger Calls Back '93
World's Greatest Lover '77

Marjorie Kane
Border Romance '30
The Great Gabbo '29

Sunny Skies '30

Nobuo Kaneko
The Human Condition: A
  Soldier's Prayer '61
Ikiru '52

John Kani
An African Dream '90
Killing Heat '81
Options '88
Sarafina! '92

Alexis Kanner
Kings and Desperate Men '83
Nightfall '88
Twinsanity '70

Ivar Kants
Gallagher's Travels '87
The Naked Country '85
Plumber '79
Silver City '84

John Kapelos
All's Fair '89
The Boost '88
The Breakfast Club '85
Man Trouble '92
Nothing in Common '86
Roxanne '87

Gabe Kaplan
Fast Break '79
The Hoboken Chicken
  Emergency '84
Nobody's Perfekt '79
Tulips '81

Jonathan Kaplan
Cannonball '76
Hollywood Boulevard '76

Marvin Kaplan
Adam's Rib '50
Angels in the Outfield '51
Fangs '75
The Severed Arm '73

Shashi Kapoor
Bombay Talkie '70
The Deceivers '88
Heat and Dust '82
The Householder '63
Sammy & Rosie Get Laid '87
Shakespeare Wallah '65

Valerie Kaprisky
Breathless '83
Iran: Days of Crisis '91
L'Annee des Meduses '86

Mitzi Kapture
Angel 3: The Final Chapter '88
Liberty & Bash '90
Private Road: No Trespassing
  '87

Ron Karabatsos
Flashdance '83
Hollywood Heartbreak '89
Missing Pieces '83
Rich Girl '91
29th Street '91

James Karen
Billionaire Boys Club '87
The China Syndrome '79
The Closer '91
Cult People '89
Frankenstein Meets the Space
  Monster '65
Girlfriend from Hell '89
Hardbodies '84
Hercules in New York '70
The Jagged Edge '85
Latino '85
Lies Before Kisses '92
Poltergeist '82
Return of the Living Dead '85
Return of the Living Dead 2 '88
Sam's Son '84
The Unborn '91
Vital Signs '90
Wall Street '87
The Willies '90

Anna Karin
Body of Influence '93
Wild Cactus '92

Rita Karin
Age Isn't Everything '91
Enemies, a Love Story '89
He Said, She Said '91
Sophie's Choice '82

Anna Karina
Alphaville '65

Karina ▶cont.

Band of Outsiders '64
Chinese Roulette '86
Cleo from 5 to 7 '61
Les Carabiniers '63
My Life to Live '62
The Nun '66
Pierrot le Fou '65
Regina '83
The Salzburg Connection '72
Ski Bum '75
A Woman is a Woman '60
Vassilli Karis
Animal Called Man '87
SS Girls '78
Olga Karlatos
Purple Rain '84
Zombie '80
John Karlen
American Dream '81
Babycakes '89
Daughters of Darkness '71
Gimme an F '85
House of Dark Shadows '70
Impulse '84
Melvin Purvis: G-Man '74
Native Son '86
Night of Dark Shadows '71
Nightmare on the 13th Floor '84
Racing with the Moon '84
Rosie: The Rosemary Clooney
    Story '82
Surf Ninjas '93
Trilogy of Terror '75
Boris Karloff
Abbott and Costello Meet Dr.
    Jekyll and Mr. Hyde '52
Abbott and Costello Meet the
    Killer, Boris Karloff '49
The Ape '40
Bedlam '45
Before I Hang '40
The Black Cat '34
The Black Room '35
Black Sabbath '64
The Body Snatcher '45
The Bride of Frankenstein '35
British Intelligence '40
Cauldron of Blood '67
Charlie Chan at the Opera '36
The Comedy of Terrors '64
Corridors of Blood '58
Criminal Code '31
The Crimson Cult '68
Dance of Death '88
Dick Tracy Double Feature #2
    '47
Dick Tracy Meets Gruesome
    '47
Die, Monster, Die! '65
Doomed to Die '40
Dynamite Dan '24
The Fatal Hour '40
The Fear Chamber '68
Frankenstein '31
The Ghoul '34
The Haunted Strangler '58
The Horror of It All '91
House of Frankenstein '44
The Invisible Ray '36
Island Monster '53
Isle of the Dead '45
Juggernaut '37
King of the Kongo '29
The Last of the Mohicans '20
The Lost Patrol '34
The Man They Could Not Hang
    '39
The Man Who Lived Again '36
The Mask of Fu Manchu '32
Mr. Wong, Detective '38
Mr. Wong in Chinatown '39
The Mummy '32
Mystery of Mr. Wong '39
The Old Dark House '32
Old Ironsides '26
The Raven '35
The Raven '63
Sabaka '55
Scarface '31
The Secret Life of Walter Mitty
    '47
The Sinister Invasion '68
The Snake People '68
Son of Frankenstein '39

Targets '69
The Terror '63
The Tower of London '39
You'll Find Out '40
John Karlsen
Maciste in Hell '60
Waterfront '83
Oscar Karlweis
Five Fingers '52
Meet Me in Las Vegas '56
Roscoe Karns
The Crooked Circle '32
The Devil's Cargo '48
Frolics on Ice '40
His Girl Friday '40
It Happened One Night '34
Laughing Sinners '31
Night After Night '32
Pleasure '31
They Drive by Night '40
Today We Live '33
Twentieth Century '34
Vigilantes of Boom Town '46
Woman of the Year '42
Sarah Rose Karr
Beethoven '92
Beethoven's 2nd '93
Homewrecker '92
Alex Karras
Against All Odds '84
Babe! '75
Blazing Saddles '74
FM '78
Goldilocks & the Three Bears
    '83
Hootch Country Boys '75
Mad Bull '77
Nobody's Perfekt '79
Paper Lion '68
Victor/Victoria '82
Win, Place, or Steal '72
Buck Kartalian
The Acid Eaters '67
Please Don't Eat My Mother '72
Tcheky Karyo
The Bear '89
Exposure '91
1492: Conquest of Paradise '92
Full Moon in Paris '84
Husbands and Lovers '91
La Femme Nikita '91
Red Shoe Diaries 3: Another
    Woman's Lipstick '93
Sketch Artist '92
Sorceress '88
Toute Une Nuit '82
Lenore Kasdorf
L.A. Bounty '89
Mr. Bill's Real Life Adventures
    '86
Casey Kasem
Escape from Planet Earth '67
Free Grass '69
The Glory Stompers '67
The Incredible Two-Headed
    Transplant '71
Soul Hustler '76
Wild Wheels '75
Gary Kasper
Humanoid Defender '85
Ring of Steel '94
Daphna Kastner
Eating '90
Julia Has Two Lovers '91
Lana in Love '92
Peter Kastner
Frightmare '81
Unfinished Business '89
You're a Big Boy Now '66
Kurt Kasznar
All the Brothers Were Valiant
    '53
Flame of the Islands '55
For the First Time '59
Give a Girl a Break '53
Legend of the Lost '57
Lili '53
Lovely to Look At '52
My Sister Eileen '55
Anna Katarina
The Blood of Heroes '89
Slaves of New York '89

Kurt Katch
Abbott & Costello Meet the
    Mummy '55
Ali Baba and the Forty Thieves
    '43
Background to Danger '43
The Mummy's Curse '44
Bernard Kates
The Babe '92
Seedpeople '92
Rosanne Katon
Bachelor Party '84
Chesty Anderson USN '76
Lunch Wagon '81
The Muthers '76
She Devils in Chains
Zapped! '82
Shintaro Katsu
Zatoichi: Master Ichi and a
    Chest of Gold '64
Zatoichi: The Blind Swordsman
    and the Chess Expert '65
Zatoichi: The Blind Swordsman
    and the Fugitives '68
Zatoichi: The Blind
    Swordsman's Vengeance
    '66
Zatoichi: The Life and Opinion
    of Masseur Ichi '62
Zatoichi vs. Yojimbo '70
Zatoichi: Zatoichi's Flashing
    Sword '64
Andreas Katsulas
Blame It on the Bellboy '92
Communion '89
The Fugitive '93
Next of Kin '89
Someone to Watch Over Me
    '87
William Katt
Baby...Secret of the Lost
    Legend '85
Big Wednesday '78
Butch and Sundance: The Early
    Days '79
Carrie '76
The Defense Never Rests '90
Desperate Motives '92
First Love '77
House '86
House 4: Home Deadly Home
    '91
Last Call '90
Naked Obsession '91
Perry Mason Returns '85
Perry Mason: The Case of the
    Lost Love '87
Pippin '81
Swimsuit: The Movie '89
Thumbelina '89
Wedding Band '89
White Ghost '88
Omri Katz
Adventures in Dinosaur City '92
Hocus Pocus '93
Matinee '92
Yftach Katzur
Atalia '85
Hot Bubblegum '81
Young Love—Lemon Popsicle
    7 '87
Andy Kaufman
Heartbeeps '81
My Breakfast with Blassie '83
David Kaufman
Invisible: The Chronicles of
    Benjamin Knight '93
The Last Prostitute '91
Maurice Kaufman
Die! Die! My Darling! '65
The Hero '71
Next Victim '74
Christine Kaufmann
Bagdad Cafe '88
The Last Days of Pompeii '60
Murders in the Rue Morgue '71
Taras Bulba '62
Welcome to 18 '87
Joseph Kaufmann
Jud '71
Private Duty Nurses '71
Caroline Kava
Born on the Fourth of July '89
Little Nikita '88

John Kavanagh
Bellman and True '88
Cal '84
Widow's Peak '94
Julie Kavner
Alice '90
Awakenings '90
Bad Medicine '85
Hannah and Her Sisters '86
I'll Do Anything '93
Katherine '75
New York Stories '89
Radio Days '87
Revenge of the Stepford Wives
    '80
Shadows and Fog '92
Surrender '87
This is My Life '92
Hiroyuki Kawase
Godzilla vs. Megalon '76
Godzilla vs. the Smog Monster
    '72
Seizaburo Kawazu
A Geisha '53
Yojimbo '61
Yusuke Kawazu
The Cruel Story of Youth '60
The Human Condition: A
    Soldier's Prayer '61
The Human Condition: Road to
    Eternity '59
Dianne Kay
Andy and the Airwave Rangers
    '89
Portrait of a Showgirl '82
Jody Kay
Death Screams '83
House of Death '82
One Armed Executioner '80
Mary Ellen Kay
Colorado Sundown '52
Government Agents vs.
    Phantom Legion '51
Silver City Bonanza '51
Thunder in God's Country '51
Thunder Pass '54
Yuzo Kayama
Red Beard '65
Zero '84
Caren Kaye
Help Wanted: Male '82
Kill Castro '80
The Mercenaries '80
My Tutor '82
Poison Ivy '85
Satan's Princess '90
Celia Kaye
Final Comedown '72
Island of the Blue Dolphins '64
Danny Kaye
Chasing Those Depression
    Blues '35
Court Jester '56
The Five Pennies '59
Hans Christian Andersen '52
Hollywood Clowns '85
The Inspector General '49
It's a Great Feeling '49
Kid from Brooklyn '47
The Madwoman of Chaillot '69
Pinocchio '92
The Secret Life of Walter Mitty
    '47
A Song is Born '48
Up in Arms '44
White Christmas '54
Wonder Man '45
Lila Kaye
Antonia and Jane '91
Dragonworld '94
Nuns on the Run '90
Norman Kaye
Cactus '86
Frenchman's Farm '87
The Killing Beach '92
Lonely Hearts '82
Man of Flowers '84
Warm Nights on a Slow-Moving
    Train '87
Where the Green Ants Dream
    '84
A Woman's Tale '92
Stubby Kaye
The Big Push '75

Cat Ballou '65
Cool Mikado '63
Guys and Dolls '55
Li'l Abner '59
Minsky's Follies '83
The Way West '67
Who Framed Roger Rabbit? '88
Elia Kazan
The Arrangement '69
City for Conquest '40
Lainie Kazan
Beaches '88
The Cemetery Club '93
A Cry for Love '80
Dayton's Devils '68
Delta Force '86
Eternity '89
Harry and the Hendersons '87
I Don't Buy Kisses Anymore '92
The Journey of Natty Gann '85
Lady in Cement '68
Love Affair: The Eleanor & Lou
    Gehrig Story '77
Lust in the Dust '85
My Favorite Year '82
Obsessive Love '84
One from the Heart '82
Out of the Dark '88
Pinocchio '92
Romance of a Horsethief '71
Sunset Limousine '83
29th Street '91
Tim Kazurinsky
Best of Eddie Murphy '89
Bill Murray Live from the
    Second City '70s
A Billion for Boris '90
Continental Divide '81
Dinner at Eight '89
Hot to Trot! '88
Police Academy 3: Back in
    Training '86
Police Academy 4: Citizens on
    Patrol '87
The Princess and the Pea '83
Shakes the Clown '92
Wedding Band '89
James Keach
The Dance Goes On '92
Evil Town '87
The Experts '89
Film House Fever '86
Hurricane '79
The Long Riders '80
Love Letters '83
Moving Violations '85
National Lampoon's Vacation
    '83
Options '88
The Razor's Edge '84
Slashed Dreams '74
Smokey & the Hotwire Gang
    '79
Stand Alone '85
Till Death Do Us Part '72
Wildcats '86
Stacy Keach
All the Kind Strangers '74
Ants '77
Battleforce '78
The Blue and the Gray '85
Body Bags '93
Brewster McCloud '70
Butterfly '82
Cheech and Chong's Nice
    Dreams '81
Cheech and Chong's Up in
    Smoke '79
Class of 1999 '90
Conduct Unbecoming '75
Diary of a Young Comic '79
Dynasty '81
End of the Road '70
False Identity '90
Fat City '72
The Forgotten '89
Gray Lady Down '77
The Heart is a Lonely Hunter
    '68
Killer Inside Me '76
Life & Times of Judge Roy
    Bean '72
The Long Riders '80
Luther '74
Man of Destiny '73
Mission of the Shark '91
Mistral's Daughter '84
The New Centurions '72

The Ninth Configuration '79
Princess Daisy '83
Raw Justice '93
Rio Diablo '93
Road Games '81
A Rumor of War '80
Slave of the Cannibal God '79
The Squeeze '77
Street People '76
Sunset Grill '92
That Championship Season '82
Watched '73

Marie Kean
Danny Boy '84
The Dead '87
The Lonely Passion of Judith Hearne '87

Edward Keane
Heroes in Blue '39
Midnight Limited '40
Rogue's Gallery '44

Kerrie Keane
Distant Thunder '88
Hot Pursuit '84
Incubus '82
Kung Fu: The Movie '86
Malarek '89
Nightstick '87
Obsessed '88

Robert Emmett Keane
Born to Be Wild '38
Fear in the Night '47
Hills of Oklahoma '50
Susanna Pass '49

Fred Keating
I Live My Life '35
Prison Train '38
Tin Pan Alley '40

Larry Keating
Above and Beyond '53
Daddy Long Legs '55
Francis Goes to the Races '51
Give a Girl a Break '53
Gypsy Colt '54
The Incredible Mr. Limpet '64
A Lion is in the Streets '53
Monkey Business '52
When Worlds Collide '51

Buster Keaton
The Adventures of Huckleberry Finn '60
The Balloonatic/One Week '23
Battling Butler '26
Beach Blanket Bingo '65
The Blacksmith/The Balloonatic '23
The Blacksmith/The Cops '22
Boom in the Moon '46
Buster Keaton Festival, Vol. 1 '22
Buster Keaton Festival, Vol. 2 '23
Buster Keaton Festival, Vol. 3 '20
Buster Keaton Rides Again/The Railrodder '65
Buster Keaton: The Golden Years '21
Buster Keaton: The Great Stone Face '68
The Cameraman '28
College '27
Cops/One Week '22
Days of Thrills and Laughter '61
Doughboys '30
A Few Moments with Buster Keaton and Laurel and Hardy '63
Forever and a Day '43
Free and Easy '30
A Funny Thing Happened on the Way to the Forum '66
The General '27
God's Country '46
Great Chase '63
Hollywood Clowns '85
How to Stuff a Wild Bikini '65
In the Good Old Summertime '49
It's a Mad, Mad, Mad, Mad World '63
Li'l Abner '40
Limelight '52
Man in the Silk Hat '83
The Navigator '24

New Moon '40
Old Spanish Custom '36
Our Hospitality '23
Parlor, Bedroom and Bath '31
Railrodder '65
The Saphead '21
Seven Chances '25
Sidewalks of New York '31
Slapstick '30s
Speak Easily '32
Spite Marriage '29
Steamboat Bill, Jr. '28
Story of William S. Hart/Sad Clowns '20s
Sunset Boulevard '50
Three Ages '23
The Villain Still Pursued Her '41
Voice of Hollywood '29
What! No Beer? '33
When Comedy was King '59

Diane Keaton
Annie Hall '77
Baby Boom '87
Crimes of the Heart '86
Father of the Bride '91
The Godfather '72
The Godfather 1902-1959: The Complete Epic '81
The Godfather, Part 2 '74
The Godfather, Part 3 '90
The Good Mother '88
Harry & Walter Go to New York '76
I Will, I Will for Now '76
Interiors '78
The Lemon Sisters '90
The Little Drummer Girl '84
Looking for Mr. Goodbar '77
Love and Death '75
Lovers and Other Strangers '70
Manhattan '79
Manhattan Murder Mystery '93
Mrs. Soffel '84
Play It Again, Sam '72
Radio Days '87
Reds '81
Running Mates '92
Shoot the Moon '82
Sleeper '73

Joe Keaton
The General '27
Our Hospitality '23

Michael Keaton
Batman '89
Batman Returns '92
Beetlejuice '88
Clean and Sober '88
The Dream Team '89
Gung Ho '85
Johnny Dangerously '84
Mr. Mom '83
Much Ado About Nothing '93
My Life '93
Night Shift '82
One Good Cop '91
Pacific Heights '90
The Paper '94
The Squeeze '87
Touch and Go '86

Steven Keats
Badge of the Assassin '85
Black Sunday '77
Eternity '90
The Executioner's Song '82
For Ladies Only '81
Hester Street '75
In Dangerous Company '88
Mysterious Island of Beautiful Women '79
Silent Rage '82
The Spring '89

Hugh Keays-Byrne
Death Train '79
Kangaroo '86
Mad Max '80

Lila Kedrova
Escape to the Sun '72
Le Cavaleur '78
Modigliani '58
Some Girls '88
Sword of the Valiant '83
Tell Me a Riddle '80
Torn Curtain '66
Widow's Nest '77
Zorba the Greek '64

James Kee
Double Standard '88

Shadow Dancing '88
Cornelius Keefe
The Adorable Cheat '28
Death from a Distance '36
Hong Kong Nights '35
Man from Headquarters '28
Mystery Liner '34
The Trigger Trio '37

Howard Keel
Arizona Bushwackers '67
Armored Command '61
Calamity Jane '53
Day of the Triffids '63
Deep in My Heart '54
I Love Melvin '53
Irving Berlin's America '86
Jupiter's Darling '55
Kismet '55
Kiss Me Kate '53
Lovely to Look At '52
Pagan Love Song '50
Rose Marie '54
Seven Brides for Seven Brothers '54
Show Boat '51
Texas Carnival '51
Three Guys Named Mike '51
The War Wagon '67

Ruby Keeler
Dames '34
Flirtation Walk '34
Footlight Parade '33
42nd Street '33
Gold Diggers of 1933 '33
That's Dancing! '85

Geoffrey Keen
Amin: The Rise and Fall '82
Angels One Five '54
Cry, the Beloved Country '51
Doctor in the House '53
Dr. Syn, Alias the Scarecrow '64
For Your Eyes Only '81
The Living Daylights '87
The Man Who Never Was '55
A Matter of WHO '62
Moonraker '79
Number 1 of the Secret Service '77
Postmark for Danger '56
Sacco & Vanzetti '71
Sink the Bismarck '60
The Spy Who Loved Me '77
Taste the Blood of Dracula '70
The Third Key '57

Tom Keene
Arizona Roundup '42
Beyond the Rockies '32
Cheyenne Kid '33
Come On Danger! '32
Desert Gold '36
Drift Fence '36
The Driftin' Kid '41
Dynamite Canyon '41
Ghost Valley '32
The Glory Trail '37
God's Country and the Man '37
Hong Kong Nights '35
Lone Star Law Men '42
Our Daily Bread '34
Renegade Ranger/Scarlet River '38
Riding the Sunset Trail '41
Saddle Buster '32
Trail of Robin Hood '50
Western Mail '42
Where Trails Divide '37
Where Trails End '42

Catherine Keener
Johnny Suede '92
Survival Quest '89

Jack Kehler
Bloodstone '88
Casualties of Love: The "Long Island Lolita" Story '93

Jack Kehoe
Falling Down '93
The Fish that Saved Pittsburgh '79
Law and Disorder '74
On the Nickel '80
Serpico '73
Servants of Twilight '91
The Untouchables '87
A Winner Never Quits '86
Young Guns 2 '90

Andrew Keir
Absolution '81
Cleopatra '63
Daleks—Invasion Earth 2150 A.D. '66
Dragonworld '94
The Fighting Prince of Donegal '66
Lord Jim '65
The Night Visitor '70
Suspended Alibi '56
The Thirty-Nine Steps '79
Zeppelin '71

Harvey Keitel
Alice Doesn't Live Here Anymore '74
Bad Lieutenant '92
Blindside '88
Blue Collar '78
The Border '82
Buffalo Bill & the Indians '76
Bugsy '91
Camorra: The Naples Connection '85
Corrupt '84
Dangerous Game '93
Death Watch '80
The Duellists '77
Eagle's Wing '79
Exposed '83
Falling in Love '84
Fingers '78
The Inquiry '87
The January Man '89
La Nuit de Varennes '82
The Last Temptation of Christ '88
Mean Streets '73
The Men's Club '86
Monkey Trouble '94
Mortal Thoughts '91
Mother, Jugs and Speed '76
Off Beat '86
The Piano '93
The Pick-up Artist '87
Point of No Return '93
Pulp Fiction '94
Reservoir Dogs '92
Rising Sun '93
Saturn 3 '80
Shining Star '75
Sister Act '92
Taxi Driver '76
Thelma & Louise '91
Two Evil Eyes '90
The Two Jakes '90
The Virginia Hill Story '76
Welcome to L.A. '77
Who's That Knocking at My Door? '68

Brian Keith
The Alamo: Thirteen Days to Glory '87
Arrowhead '53
Bull of the West '89
Charlie Chan and the Curse of the Dragon Queen '81
The Chisholms '79
Deadly Companions '61
Death Before Dishonor '87
Dino '57
Escape '90
The Gambler Returns: The Luck of the Draw '93
The Hallelujah Trail '65
Hooper '78
Joe Panther '76
Johnny Shiloh '63
The Loneliest Runner '76
The Longest Drive '76
McKenzie Break '70
Meteor '79
Moon Pilot '62
The Mountain Men '80
Nevada Smith '66
Nightfall '56
The Parent Trap '61
The Rare Breed '66
Reflections in a Golden Eye '67
Run of the Arrow '56
The Russians are Coming, the Russians are Coming '66
Savage Sam '63
Scandalous John '71
The Seekers '79
Sharky's Machine '81
Suppose They Gave a War and Nobody Came? '70
Ten Who Dared '60

Those Calloways '65
A Tiger Walks '64
The Violent Men '55
Welcome Home '89
The Wind and the Lion '75
With Six You Get Eggroll '68
World War III '86
The Yakuza '75
Young Guns '88
The Young Philadelphians '59

David Keith
Back Roads '81
Brubaker '80
Caged Fear '92
The Curse '87
Desperate Motives '92
Firestarter '84
The Further Adventures of Tennessee Buck '88
The Great Santini '80
Gulag '85
Heartbreak Hotel '88
Independence Day '83
Liar's Edge '92
The Lords of Discipline '83
Major League 2 '94
An Officer and a Gentleman '82
Raw Justice '93
The Rose '79
Take This Job & Shove It '81
The Two Jakes '90
White of the Eye '88

Donald Keith
Bare Knees '28
Branded Men '31
Dancing Mothers '26
Free to Love '25
My Lady of Whims '25
Outlaw Justice '32

Ian Keith
The Chinese Cat '44
Corregidor '43
Dick Tracy's Dilemma '47
It Came from Beneath the Sea '55
Man from Thunder River '43
Mary of Scotland '36
The Payoff '43
Queen Christina '33
Scared to Death/Dick Tracy's Dilemma '47
Song of Old Wyoming '45
The Three Musketeers '35
The White Legion '36

Penelope Keith
Madhouse Mansion '74
The Norman Conquests, Part 1: Table Manners '80
The Norman Conquests, Part 2: Living Together '80
The Norman Conquests, Part 3: Round and Round the Garden '80

Robert Keith
Battle Circus '53
Between Heaven and Hell '56
Cimarron '60
Devil's Canyon '53
Drum Beat '54
Here Comes the Groom '51
Love Me or Leave Me '55
Men in War '57
My Man Godfrey '57
Small Town Girl '53
The Wild One '54
Written on the Wind '56
Young at Heart '54

Sheila Keith
The Comeback '77
The Confessional '75
Frightmare '74
House of the Long Shadows '82

Robert Kellard
Drums of Fu Manchu '40
Gentleman from Dixie '41

Cecil Kellaway
The Beast from 20,000 Fathoms '53
Brother Orchid '40
The Cardinal '63
Francis Goes to the Races '51
Getting Straight '70
Guess Who's Coming to Dinner '67
Gunga Din '39
Harvey '50

Kellaway ▶cont.

Interrupted Melody '55
Kim '50
The Letter '40
Maid's Night Out '38
Monsieur Beaucaire '46
The Mummy's Hand '40
Portrait of Jennie '48
The Postman Always Rings Twice '46
The Prodigal '55
Quick, Let's Get Married '71
Spinout '66
Wuthering Heights '39
Young Bess '53
Zotz! '62

Hiram Keller
Ciao Federico! Fellini Directs Satyricon '69
Countryman '83
Fellini Satyricon '69
Lifespan '75

Marthe Keller
The Amateur '82
And Now My Love '74
Black Sunday '77
Bobby Deerfield '77
Dark Eyes '87
The Formula '80
Marathon Man '76
The Nightmare Years '89
Red Kiss '85
Young Catherine '91

Mary Page Keller
Scared Stiff '87
Ulterior Motives '92

Barbara Kellerman
The Chronicles of Narnia '89
Quatermass Conclusion '79

Sally Kellerman
All's Fair '89
April Fools '69
Back to School '86
The Big Bus '76
Boris and Natasha: The Movie '92
The Boston Strangler '68
Brewster McCloud '70
Dempsey '83
Dirkham Detective Agency '83
Doppelganger: The Evil Within '90
Fatal Attraction '80
Foxes '80
Hands of a Stranger '62
It Rained All Night the Day I Left '78
The KGB: The Secret War '86
Last of the Red Hot Lovers '72
A Little Romance '79
Loving Couples '80
Magee and the Lady '78
M*A*S*H '70
Meatballs 3 '87
Moving Violations '85
Rafferty & the Gold Dust Twins '75
A Reflection of Fear '72
Reform School Girl '57
Secret of the Ice Cave '89
Secret Weapons '85
September Gun '83
Serial '80
Slither '73
Someone to Love '87
That's Life! '86
Three for the Road '87
Victim of Beauty '91
Welcome to L.A. '77
You Can't Hurry Love '88

Susan Kellerman
Elvira, Mistress of the Dark '88
Oh, Heavenly Dog! '80
Where the Buffalo Roam '80

Barry Kelley
The Asphalt Jungle '50
Carrie '52
Francis Goes to the Races '51
Jack the Giant Killer '62
Killer Bait '49
Ma and Pa Kettle '49
Too Late for Tears '49
The Well '51

DeForest Kelley
Apache Uprising '66
Bull of the West '89
Fear in the Night '47
Gunfight at the O.K. Corral '57
Illegal '55
The Law and Jake Wade '58
The Man in the Gray Flannel Suit '56
Star Trek: The Motion Picture '80
Star Trek 2: The Wrath of Khan '82
Star Trek 3: The Search for Spock '84
Star Trek 4: The Voyage Home '86
Star Trek 5: The Final Frontier '89
Star Trek 6: The Undiscovered Country '91
Star Trek Bloopers '69
Warlock '59

Sheila Kelley
Breaking In '89
Mortal Passions '90
Passion Fish '92
Pure Luck '91
Singles '92
Soapdish '91

Mike Kellin
At War with the Army '50
The Boston Strangler '68
Freebie & the Bean '74
The Great Impostor '61
Hell is for Heroes '62
The Incident '67
Invitation to a Gunfighter '64
The Last Porno Flick '74
Lonelyhearts '58
The Mountain Road '60
Next Stop, Greenwich Village '76
On the Yard '79
Riot '69
Sleepaway Camp '83
Wackiest Ship in the Army '61

John Kellogg
The Enforcer '51
Hopalong Cassidy: Borrowed Trouble '48
Jacob Have I Loved '88
Violets Are Blue '86

Brian Kelly
Around the World Under the Sea '65
Flipper's New Adventure '64
Flipper's Odyssey '66

Claire Kelly
And Soon the Darkness '70
Ask Any Girl '59
The Badlanders '58
Dressed for Death '74
Georgy Girl '66
A Guide for the Married Man '67
Party Girl '58

David Patrick Kelly
The Adventures of Ford Fairlane '90
Cheap Shots '91
Commando '85
Crooklyn '94
The Crow '93
Dreamscape '84
48 Hrs. '82
The Jigsaw Man '84
Malcolm X '92
The Misfit Brigade '87
Penn and Teller Get Killed '90
Pirates '86
The Warriors '79

Gene Kelly
An American in Paris '51
Anchors Aweigh '45
The Black Hand '50
Brigadoon '54
Cover Girl '44
Deep in My Heart '54
DuBarry Was a Lady '43
For Me and My Gal '42
Forty Carats '73
Inherit the Wind '60
Invitation to the Dance '56
It's Always Fair Weather '55
Les Girls '57
Let's Make Love '60

Marjorie Morningstar '58
North and South Book 1 '85
On the Town '49
The Pirate '48
Singin' in the Rain '52
Sins '85
Summer Stock '50
Take Me Out to the Ball Game '49
That's Dancing! '85
That's Entertainment '74
That's Entertainment, Part 2 '76
Thousands Cheer '43
The Three Musketeers '48
Viva Knievel '77
Words and Music '48
Xanadu '80
Ziegfeld Follies '46

Grace Kelly
The Bridges at Toko-Ri '55
Country Girl '54
Dial "M" for Murder '54
Green Fire '55
High Noon '52
High Society '56
Mogambo '53
Rear Window '54
The Swan '56
To Catch a Thief '55

Jack Kelly
Commandos '73
The Commies are Coming, the Commies are Coming '57
Cult of the Cobra '55
Forbidden Planet '56
The Gambler Returns: The Luck of the Draw '93
Red Nightmare '62
To Hell and Back '55

Jim Kelly
Black Belt Jones '74
Black Eliminator '70s
Black Samurai '77
Enter the Dragon '73
Hot Potato '76
Kill Factor
One Down, Two to Go! '82
Take a Hard Ride '75
Tattoo Connection '78
Three the Hard Way '74

Judy Kelly
Dead of Night '45
House of Mystery '41
Make-Up '37

Kathleen Kelly
The Avenging Hand '43
The Deputy Drummer '35
Heart's Desire '37
The Mutiny of the Elsinore '39

Lew Kelly
Death from a Distance '36
Forlorn River '37
Mistaken Identity '36

Mike Kelly
Heroes Three '84
Sakura Killers '86
To Live and Die in Hong Kong '89

Moira Kelly
Billy Bathgate '91
Chaplin '92
The Cutting Edge '92
Daybreak '93
Love, Lies and Murder '91
Twin Peaks: Fire Walk with Me '92
With Honors '94

Nancy Kelly
The Bad Seed '56
Betrayal from the East '44
Gambler's Choice '44
One Night in the Tropics '40
Stanley and Livingstone '39
To the Shores of Tripoli '42
The Woman Who Came Back '45

Patsy Kelly
Broadway Limited '41
The Cowboy and the Lady '38
Freaky Friday '76
The Girl from Missouri '34
Going Hollywood '33
The Gorilla '39
In Old California '42
Kelly the Second '36
Naked Kiss '64

The North Avenue Irregulars '79
Pick a Star '37
Playmates '41
Please Don't Eat the Daisies '60
Road Show '41
Rosemary's Baby '68
Sing Your Worries Away '42
Swiss Miss '38

Paul Kelly
Adventure Island '47
Bail Out at 43,000 '57
Call Out the Marines '42
Crossfire '47
Devil's Party '38
Fear in the Night '47
Fit for a King '37
Flying Tigers '42
Girl from Calgary '32
Guilty of Treason '50
The Howards of Virginia '40
Navy Blue and Gold '37
The Painted Hills '51
San Antonio '45
The Secret Code '42
Split Second '53
Springfield Rifle '52
Star of Midnight '35
Tarzan's New York Adventure '42
Texas Legionnaires '43
Ziegfeld Girl '41

Paula Kelly
The Andromeda Strain '71
Jo Jo Dancer, Your Life is Calling '86
The Spook Who Sat By the Door '73
Sweet Charity '69
Top of the Heap '72
Uncle Tom's Cabin '87
The Women of Brewster Place '89

Roz Kelly
Curse of the Black Widow '77
New Year's Evil '78

Tommy Kelly
The Adventures of Tom Sawyer '38
Peck's Bad Boy with the Circus '38

Fred Kelsey
Paths to Paradise '25
People's Choice '46

Linda Kelsey
Baby Girl Scott '87
Eleanor & Franklin '76
Picture of Dorian Gray '74

Pert Kelton
Annie Oakley '35
Bachelor Bait '34
The Comic '69
Kelly the Second '36
The Music Man '62

Richard Kelton
Silence '75
The Ultimate Warrior '75

Edward Kemmer
Earth vs. the Spider '58
Giant from the Unknown '58

Warren Kemmerling
Eat My Dust '76
The Execution of Private Slovik '74
Hit! '73
Trauma '62

Brandis Kemp
Goldilocks & the Three Bears '83
South of Reno '87
Surf 2 '84

Elizabeth Kemp
Eating '90
He Knows You're Alone '80
Killing Hour '84

Gary Kemp
The Bodyguard '92
The Krays '90
Paper Marriage '93

Jeremy Kemp
The Belstone Fox '73
Blockhouse '73
Darling Lili '70

Duel of Hearts '92
East of Elephant Rock '76
Feet Foremost '85
Operation Crossbow '65
Prisoner of Honor '91
Prisoner of Zenda '79
Sadat '83
The Seven Percent Solution '76
Top Secret! '84
The Treasure Seekers '79
War & Remembrance, Part 1 '88
War & Remembrance: The Final Chapter, Part 8 '89
When the Whales Came '89
The Winds of War '83

Martin Kemp
Aspen Extreme '93
Fleshtone '94
The Krays '90

Matty Kemp
Law of the Texan '38
Tango '36

Will Kempe
Hit the Dutchman '92
Metropolitan '90
Pledge Night '90

Charles Kemper
The Doolins of Oklahoma '49
Fighting Father Dunne '48
Mr. Music '50
The Nevadan '50
On Dangerous Ground '51
Stars in My Crown '50
Ticket to Tomahawk '50

Rachel Kempson
Captive Heart '47
The Charge of the Light Brigade '68
Georgy Girl '66
Little Lord Fauntleroy '80
Love for Lydia '79
Out of Africa '85
Stealing Heaven '88
The Virgin Soldiers '69

Felicity Kendal
Shakespeare Wallah '65
Valentino '77

Cy Kendall
Billy the Kid '41
Bulldog Edition '36
Girl Rush '44
The Green Hornet '39
Johnny Eager '42
King of the Pecos '36
Outlaw Trail '44
The Saint Takes Over '40
Tarzan's New York Adventure '42

Henry Kendall
Amazing Adventure '37
The Ghost Camera '33
Rich and Strange '32
The Shadow '36

Kay Kendall
Abdulla the Great '56
Doctor in the House '53
Genevieve '53
Les Girls '57
The Reluctant Debutante '58
The Shadow Man '53
Wings of Danger '52

Suzy Kendall
Adventures of a Private Eye '87
Assault '70
The Bird with the Crystal Plumage '70
Circus of Fear '67
Craze '70
Darker than Amber '70
Tales That Witness Madness '73
30 Is a Dangerous Age, Cynthia '68
To Sir, with Love '67
Torso '72

Tony Kendall
The Black Pirate '65
Island of Lost Girls '73
Justicia para los Mexicanos Oil '78
People Who Own the Dark '75
Return of the Evil Dead '75
When the Screaming Stops '73

Alexa Kenin
Honkytonk Man '82
A Piano for Mrs. Cimino '82
Pretty in Pink '86

Arthur Kennedy
Air Force '43
Anzio '68
Barabbas '62
Bend of the River '52
Champion '49
Cheyenne Autumn '64
City for Conquest '40
Crashout '55
Desperate Hours '55
Desperate Journey '42
Elmer Gantry '60
Emmanuelle on Taboo Island '76
Fantastic Voyage '66
Hail, Hero! '69
High Sierra '41
Impulse '55
Killer Bait '49
Lawrence of Arabia '62
The Lusty Men '52
The Man from Laramie '55
Mean Machine '73
A Minute to Pray, A Second to Die '67
Murder She Said '62
My Old Man's Place '71
Nevada Smith '66
Peyton Place '57
The President's Plane is Missing '71
Rancho Notorious '52
Shark! '68
Signs of Life '89
Some Came Running '58
A Summer Place '59
The Tempter '74
They Died with Their Boots On '41
Too Late for Tears '49
The Window '49

Bill Kennedy
Silver City Bonanza '51
Two Lost Worlds '50

Douglas Kennedy
The Amazing Transparent Man '60
The Land Unknown '57
Lone Ranger and the Lost City of Gold '58
South of St. Louis '48

Edgar Kennedy
Air Raid Wardens '43
Blondie in Society '41
Chasing Those Depression Blues '35
Comedy Reel, Vol. 2
Cowboy Millionaire '35
Dr. Christian Meets the Women '40
Double Wedding '37
Duck Soup '33
Frolics on Ice '40
Hillbilly Blitzkrieg '42
Hold 'Em Jail '32
King Kelly of the U.S.A. '34
Laurel & Hardy Comedy Classics, Vol. 5 '31
Laurel & Hardy: Night Owls '30
Laurel & Hardy: Perfect Day '29
Little Orphan Annie '32
Little Rascals, Book 13 '37
Little Rascals, Book 15 '30s
My Dream is Yours '49
Peck's Bad Boy with the Circus '38
Remedy for Riches '40
The Silver Streak '34
The Sin of Harold Diddlebock '47
Snuffy Smith, Yard Bird '42
Twentieth Century '34
Two Reelers: Comedy Classics 1 '33
Two Reelers: Comedy Classics 2 '46
Two Reelers: Comedy Classics 3 '33
Unfaithfully Yours '48
When's Your Birthday? '37

George Kennedy
Airport '70
Airport '75 '75

Airport '77 '77
Archer: The Fugitive from the Empire '81
Bandolero! '68
The Blue Knight '75
Bolero '84
Born to Race '88
The Boston Strangler '68
Brain Dead '89
Brass Target '78
Bull of the West '89
Cahill: United States Marshal '73
Charade '63
Chattanooga Choo Choo '84
The Concorde: Airport '79 '79
Cool Hand Luke '67
Counterforce '87
Creepshow 2 '87
Death on the Nile '78
Death Ship '80
Delta Force '86
Demonwarp '87
The Dirty Dozen '67
The Double McGuffin '79
Driving Me Crazy '91
Earthquake '74
The Eiger Sanction '75
Final Shot: The Hank Gathers Story '92
The Flight of the Phoenix '65
The Good Guys and the Bad Guys '69
The Gunfighters '87
Guns of the Magnificent Seven '69
Hangfire '91
Hired to Kill '91
Hot Wire '70s
The Human Factor '75
In Harm's Way '65
Island of the Blue Dolphins '64
The Jesse Owens Story '84
Just Before Dawn '80
Kenny Rogers as the Gambler, Part 3: The Legend Continues '87
Lonely are the Brave '62
Mean Dog Blues '78
Ministry of Vengeance '89
Mirage '66
Modern Romance '81
The Naked Gun: From the Files of Police Squad '88
Naked Gun 33 1/3: The Final Insult '94
Naked Gun 2 1/2: The Smell of Fear '91
Nightmare at Noon '87
Private Road: No Trespassing '87
Proof of the Man '84
Radioactive Dreams '86
A Rare Breed '81
Savage Dawn '84
Search and Destroy '81
Shenandoah '65
Steel '80
Strait-Jacket '64
The Terror Within '88
Thunderbolt & Lightfoot '74
The Uninvited '88
Virus '82
Wacko '83

Gerald Kennedy
The Mango Tree '77
Puzzle '78

Gerard Kennedy
Body Melt '93
Newsfront '78
Panic Station '82

Graham Kennedy
The Club '81
Don's Party '76
Return of Captain Invincible '83

Jayne Kennedy
Body & Soul '81
Death Force '78
Fighting Mad '77
Group Marriage '72
The Muthers '76
Mysterious Island of Beautiful Women '79

June Kennedy
Bloodlust '59
Earth vs. the Spider '58
Murderer's Wife
Sorority Girl '57

Leon Isaac Kennedy
Body & Soul '81
Death Force '78
Fighting Mad '77
Hollywood Vice Sqaud '86
Lone Wolf McQuade '83
Penitentiary '79
Penitentiary 2 '82
Penitentiary 3 '87
Skeleton Coast '89
Too Scared to Scream '85

Merele Kennedy
Nemesis '93
Night of the Demons 2 '94

Merna Kennedy
The Circus '19
Ghost Valley '32

Mimi Kennedy
Death Becomes Her '92
Immediate Family '89
Pump Up the Volume '90

Sheila Kennedy
Dead Boyz Can't Fly '93
Ellie '84
First Turn On '83

Tom Kennedy
Big News '29
Day the Bookies Wept '39
The Devil's Cargo '48
Hollywood Party '34
Mantrap '26
Marked Money '28

James Kenney
Above Us the Waves '56
Tough Guy '53

Sean Kenney
The Corpse Grinders '71
Savage Abduction '73

Patsy Kensit
Absolute Beginners '86
Bitter Harvest '93
Blame It on the Bellboy '92
Blue Tornado '90
Bullseye! '90
Chicago Joe & the Showgirl '90
A Chorus of Disapproval '89
Does This Mean We're Married? '90
Full Eclipse '93
The Great Gatsby '74
Kill Cruise '90
Lethal Weapon 2 '89
Monty Python and the Holy Grail '75
Silas Marner '85
Timebomb '91
The Turn of the Screw '92
Twenty-One '91

Barbara Kent
Chinatown After Dark '31
The Dropkick '27
Feet First '30
The Flesh and the Devil '27
Indiscreet '31
No Man's Law '21
Oliver Twist '33
Vanity Fair '32

Crauford Kent
Tea for Two '50
Virtue's Revolt '24

Dorothea Kent
Behind the Mask '37
Danger Ahead '40

Elizabeth Kent
Mindwarp '91
Trapped Alive '93

Jean Kent
Bonjour Tristesse '57
The Browning Version '51
The Gay Lady '49
Man of Evil '48
Sleeping Car to Trieste '45

Kenneth Kent
Dangerous Moonlight '41
House of Mystery '41

Marjorie Kent
Blondie Hits the Jackpot '49
Blondie Knows Best '46

Robert Kent
Dimples '36
Gang Bullets '38
The Gladiator '38
The Phantom Creeps '39

The Phantom Rider '46

Doris Kenyon
A Girl's Folly '17
Monsieur Beaucaire '24

Gwen Kenyon
Charlie Chan in the Secret Service '44
The Great Mike '44
In Old New Mexico '45
Meet the Mob '42

Danny Keogh
Kill Slade '89
Playing with Fire '70s

Ken Kercheval
Beretta's Island '92
Calamity Jane '82
California Casanova '89
Corporate Affairs '90
Judge Horton and the Scottsboro Boys '76

Joanna Kerns
An American Summer '90
Broken Badge '85
A Bunny's Tale '85
Cross My Heart '88
The Great Los Angeles Earthquake '91
The Nightman '93
The Preppie Murder '89
Street Justice '89

Bill Kerr
The Coca-Cola Kid '84
Deadline '81
Dusty '85
Gallipoli '81
The Lighthorsemen '87
Miracle Down Under '87
Pirate Movie '82
Razorback '84
Sweet Talker '91
Vigil '84

Deborah Kerr
An Affair to Remember '57
America at the Movies '76
The Arrangement '69
Black Narcissus '47
Bonjour Tristesse '57
Casino Royale '67
The Chalk Garden '64
The Courageous Mr. Penn '41
The Day Will Dawn '42
From Here to Eternity '53
The Grass is Greener '61
Hold the Dream '85
The Hucksters '47
I See a Dark Stranger '46
Julius Caesar '53
The King and I '56
King Solomon's Mines '50
The Life and Death of Colonel Blimp '43
Love on the Dole '41
Major Barbara '41
The Naked Edge '61
The Night of the Iguana '64
Prisoner of Zenda '52
Quo Vadis '51
Separate Tables '58
The Sundowners '60
Tea and Sympathy '56
A Woman of Substance, Episode 1: Nest of Vipers '84
A Woman of Substance, Episode 2: The Secret is Revealed '84
A Woman of Substance, Episode 3: Fighting for the Dream '84
Young Bess '53

E. Katherine Kerr
Children of a Lesser God '86
Power '86
Reuben, Reuben '83
Suspect '87

John Kerr
The Cobweb '55
The Pit and the Pendulum '61
South Pacific '58
Tea and Sympathy '56

Ken Kerr
Beneath the Valley of the Ultra-Vixens '79
Thundering Ninja '80s

Linda Kerridge
Alien from L.A. '87
Down Twisted '87
Fade to Black '80
Mixed Blood '84
Strangers Kiss '83
Surf 2 '84

J.M. Kerrigan
Fastest Gun Alive '56
The Great Man Votes '38
The Informer '35
Song O' My Heart '29

John Kerry
Bad Georgia Road '77
Memorial Valley Massacre '88

Norman Kerry
Bachelor Apartment '31
The Claw '27
The Hunchback of Notre Dame '23
Merry-Go-Round '23
The Phantom of the Opera '25
Tanks a Million '41
The Unknown '27

Brian Kerwin
Code Name: Chaos '90
Getting Wasted '80
Hard Promises '92
Hometown U.S.A. '79
King Kong Lives '86
Love Field '91
Miss All-American Beauty '82
Murphy's Romance '85
Nickel Mountain '85
A Real American Hero '78
Switched at Birth '91
Torch Song Trilogy '88
Wet Gold '84

Lance Kerwin
Children of Divorce '80
Enemy Mine '85
Fourth Wise Man '85
The Loneliest Runner '76
The Mysterious Stranger '82
Reflections of Murder '74
Salem's Lot '79
Shooting '82
Side Show '81
The Snow Queen '83

Maureen Kerwin
The Destructors '74
Reunion '88

Jillian Kesner
Firecracker '81
Roots of Evil '91
Starhops '78

Quin Kessler
She '83
Wishman '93

Sara Kestelman
Lady Jane '85
Lisztomania '75
Zardoz '73

Tsui Siu Keung
The Bloody Tattoo
The Rebellious Reign

Evelyn Keyes
Before I Hang '40
Gone with the Wind '39
Here Comes Mr. Jordan '41
The Jolson Story '46
The Lady in Question '40
The Making of a Legend: "Gone With the Wind" '89
Prowler '51
Return to Salem's Lot '87
The Seven Year Itch '55
Slightly Honorable '40
Wicked Stepmother '89

Irwin Keyes
The Flintstones '94
Frankenstein General Hospital '88

Mark Keyloun
Gimme an F '85
Mike's Murder '84
Separate Vacations '86

The Keystone Cops
Golden Age of Comedy '58
The Knockout/Dough and Dynamite '14

Persis Khambatta
Conduct Unbecoming '75

Khambatta ▶cont.

Deadly Intent '88
First Strike '85
Megaforce '82
Nighthawks '81
Phoenix the Warrior '88
Star Trek: The Motion Picture '80
Warrior of the Lost World '84
The Wilby Conspiracy '75

Arsinee Khanjian
The Adjuster '91
Family Viewing '88
Speaking Parts '89

Guy Kibbee
Babes in Arms '39
Captain Blood '35
Captain January '36
Dames '34
Dixie Jamboree '44
Earthworm Tractors '36
Footlight Parade '33
42nd Street '33
Gold Diggers of 1933 '33
The Horn Blows at Midnight '45
Joy of Living '38
Lady for a Day '33
Laughing Sinners '31
Let Freedom Ring '39
Little Lord Fauntleroy '36
Miss Annie Rooney '42
Mr. Smith Goes to Washington '39
Of Human Hearts '38
Our Town '40
Rain '32
Scarlet Dawn '32
The Strange Love of Molly Louvain '32
Three Comrades '38
Three Godfathers '48
Three Men on a Horse '36
Whistling in Dixie '42

Michael Kidd
It's Always Fair Weather '55
Smile '75

Margot Kidder
The Amityville Horror '79
Black Christmas '75
The Bounty Man '72
The Glitter Dome '84
The Great Waldo Pepper '75
Heartaches '82
Hitchhiker 2 '85
Keeping Track '86
Little Treasure '85
Louisiana '87
Miss Right '81
Mr. Mike's Mondo Video '79
Mob Story '90
92 in the Shade '76
Quackser Fortune Has a Cousin in the Bronx '70
Quiet Day In Belfast '74
The Reincarnation of Peter Proud '75
Shoot the Sun Down '81
Sisters '73
Some Kind of Hero '82
Superman: The Movie '78
Superman 2 '80
Superman 3 '83
Superman 4: The Quest for Peace '87
To Catch a Killer '92
Trenchcoat '83
Vanishing Act '88
Willie & Phil '80

Nicole Kidman
Billy Bathgate '91
BMX Bandits '83
Days of Thunder '90
Dead Calm '89
Far and Away '92
Flirting '89
Malice '93
My Life '93
Night Master '87
Prince and the Great Race '83
Windrider '86

Richard Kiel
Eegah! '62
Flash & Firecat '75
Force 10 from Navarone '78

The Human Duplicators '64
Hysterical '83
The Longest Yard '74
Mad Mission 3 '84
Moonraker '79
Pale Rider '85
The Phantom Planet '61
Roustabout '64
The Silver Streak '76
So Fine '81
The Spy Who Loved Me '77
They Went That-a-Way & That-a-Way '78
Think Big '90
War of the Wizards '81

Sue Kiel
Red Heat '85
Survivor '87

Udo Kier
Andy Warhol's Dracula '74
Andy Warhol's Frankenstein '74
For Love or Money '93
The House on Straw Hill '76
Mark of the Devil '69
My Own Private Idaho '91
Seduction: The Cruel Woman '89
The Stationmaster's Wife '77
Suspiria '77
Zentropa '92

Robbie Kiger
Children of the Corn '84
Table for Five '83
Welcome Home, Roxy Carmichael '90

Susan Kiger
Death Screams '83
H.O.T.S. '79
House of Death '82
The Return '80
Seven '79

Percy Kilbride
The Adventures of Mark Twain '44
Egg and I '47
George Washington Slept Here '42
Ma and Pa Kettle '49
Ma and Pa Kettle at the Fair '52
Ma and Pa Kettle Back On the Farm '51
Ma and Pa Kettle Go to Town '50
Riff-Raff '47
The Southerner '45
State Fair '45
The Woman of the Town '44

Terence Kilburn
A Christmas Carol '38
Fiend Without a Face '58
National Velvet '44
They Shall Have Music '39

Richard Kiley
The Adventures of Huckleberry Finn '85
Angel on My Shoulder '80
The Bad Seed '85
Blackboard Jungle '55
The Canterville Ghost '91
Chameleon Street '89
Endless Love '81
George Washington '84
Jigsaw '71
The Little Prince '74
Looking for Mr. Goodbar '77
Murder Once Removed '71
Pendulum '69
Pickup on South Street '53
Pray TV '81
Separate But Equal '91
The Thorn Birds '83

Victor Kilian
The Adventures of Tom Sawyer '38
Dangerous Passage '44
Dr. Cyclops '40
Lady from Nowhere '36
One Too Many '51
Riff Raff '35
Rimfire '49
Unknown World '51
Young Tom Edison '40

Val Kilmer
The Doors '91
Gore Vidal's Billy the Kid '89

Kill Me Again '89
The Man Who Broke 1,000 Chains '87
The Murders in the Rue Morgue '86
Real Genius '85
The Real McCoy '93
Thunderheart '92
Tombstone '93
Top Gun '86
Top Secret! '84
True Romance '93
Willow '88

Lincoln Kilpatrick
Deadly Force '83
Fortress '93
Prison '88

Patrick Kilpatrick
The Cellar '90
Class of 1999 '90
Death Warrant '90
Roanoak '86
Showdown '93

Bobby Kim
Kill Line '91
Manchurian Avenger '84

Joon Kim
Gang Justice '94
Street Soldiers '91

Charles Kimbrough
The Good Mother '88
Sunday in the Park with George '86
Switching Channels '88

Clinton Kimbrough
Bloody Mama '70
Night Call Nurses '72

Bruce Kimmel
The First Nudie Musical '75
Spaceship '81

Dana Kimmell
Friday the 13th, Part 3 '82
Sweet 16 '81

Kenneth Kimmins
Eleanor: First Lady of the World '82
My Best Friend Is a Vampire '88

Isao Kimura
Black Lizard '68
Stray Dog '49

Aron Kincaid
Creature of Destruction '67
The Proud and the Damned '72

Kevin Kindlan
Heartstopper '92
The Majorettes '87
Revenge of the Living Zombies '88

Adrienne King
Friday the 13th '80
Friday the 13th, Part 2 '81

Alan King
The Anderson Tapes '71
Author! Author! '82
The Bonfire of the Vanities '90
Cat's Eye '85
Enemies, a Love Story '89
How to Pick Up Girls '78
I, the Jury '82
Just Tell Me What You Want '80
Memories of Me '88
Night and the City '92
Pleasure Palace '80

Andrea King
Band of Angels '57
The Beast with Five Fingers '46
Blackenstein '73
House of the Black Death '65
The Lemon Drop Kid '51
The Man I Love '46
Mr. Peabody & the Mermaid '48
Red Planet Mars '52

Atlas King
Incredibly Strange Creatures Who Stopped Living and Became Mixed-Up Zombies '63
The Thrill Killers '65

Brad King
Outlaws of the Desert '41
Riders of the Timberline '41

Twilight on the Trail '41

Charles "Blackie" King
Along the Sundown Trail '42
Ambush Trail '46
Arizona Stagecoach '42
Below the Border '42
Border Badmen '45
Branded Men '31
The Caravan Trail '46
Colorado Serenade '46
Dead or Alive '44
Death Rides the Range '40
Desert Phantom '36
Devil Riders '44
Down the Wyoming Trail '39
Fighting Champ '33
Fighting Parson '35
Frontier Outlaws '44
The Gambling Terror '37
Gangster's Den '45
God's Country and the Man '37
Gun Packer '36
Headin' for the Rio Grande '36
His Brother's Ghost '45
Hittin' the Trail '37
Last of the Warrens '36
The Lawless Nineties '36
A Lawman is Born '37
Lightning Bill Crandall '37
Lucky Terror '36
Mesquite Buckaroo '39
Mystery of the Hooded Horseman '37
Oath of Vengeance '44
Oklahoma Cyclone '30
Outlaw Justice '32
Outlaw of the Plains '46
The Phantom of the Range '38
The Pocatello Kid '31
Prairie Pals '42
Range Law '31
Red River Valley '36
The Red Rope '37
Riders of the Rockies '37
Ridin' the Lone Trail '37
Rip Roarin' Buckaroo '36
Rustler's Hideout '44
Santa Fe Bound '37
Songs and Bullets '38
Texas Kid '43
Three in the Saddle '45
Thunder in the Desert '38
Trail of Terror '35
Trail Riders '42
Trigger Men '41
Trigger Pals '39
Two Gun Man '31
Where Trails End '42
Wild Horse Canyon '39
Wild Horse Phantom '44
Young Blood '33

Charmion King
Anne of Green Gables '85
Who Has Seen the Wind? '77

Damu King
Black Godfather '74
Black Starlet '74
Blackjack '78

Dave King
The Long Good Friday '79
Naughty Knights '71
Revolution '85

Erik King
Casualties of War '89
Joey Breaker '93

George King
Sexton Blake and the Hooded Terror '38
Spitfire '42

Joe King
Alexander's Ragtime Band '38
Shifting Sands '18
Until They Get Me '18
Woman in the Shadows '34

John "Dusty" King
Ace Drummond '36
Arizona Stagecoach '42
Boot Hill Bandits '42
Fugitive Valley '41
Half a Soldier '30
Haunted Ranch '43
Kid's Last Ride '41
Law of the Jungle '42
Midnight Limited '40
Rock River Renegades '42

Saddle Mountain Round-Up '41
Texas to Bataan '42
Thunder River Feud '42
Tonto Basin Outlaws '41
Trail of the Silver Spurs '41
Trail Riders '42
Trailing Double Trouble '40
Tumbledown Ranch in Arizona '41
Two-Fisted Justice '43
Underground Rustlers '41
West of Pinto Basin '40

Leslie King
Cotton Candy '82
Gas Pump Girls '79

Mabel King
Black Vampire '73
Dead Men Don't Die '91
The Wiz '78

Meegan King
Money to Burn '83
Sweater Girls '78

Morgana King
The Godfather '72
The Godfather, Part 2 '74
A Time to Remember '90

Perry King
Andy Warhol's Bad '77
The Choirboys '77
City in Fear '80
Class of 1984 '82
The Cracker Factory '79
A Cry in the Night '93
Danielle Steel's Kaleidoscope '92
Different Story '78
Disaster at Silo 7 '88
The Hasty Heart '86
Jericho Fever '93
Killing Hour '84
Lipstick '76
The Lords of Flatbush '74
Love's Savage Fury '79
Mandingo '75
The Possession of Joel Delaney '72
The Prize Pulitzer '89
Search and Destroy '81
Slaughterhouse Five '72
Switch '91
Wild Party '74

Stephen King
Creepshow '82
Creepshow 2 '87
Pet Sematary '89

Tony King
Gordon's War '73
The Last Hunter '80
Report to the Commissioner '74
Sparkle '76

Walter Woolf King
A Night at the Opera '35
Smart Alecks '42
Swiss Miss '38
Today I Hang '42
Yank in Libya '42

Wright King
Dangerous Charter '62
Invasion of the Bee Girls '73

Zalman King
Blue Sunshine '78
Deadly Fieldtrip '74
Galaxy of Terror '81
The Passover Plot '75
Ski Bum '75
Smile, Jenny, You're Dead '74
Some Call It Loving '73

Walter Kingsford
The Invisible Ray '36
It Could Happen to You '37
The Man in the Iron Mask '39
My Favorite Blonde '42
The Story of Louis Pasteur '36
Velvet Touch '48

Ben Kingsley
Betrayal '83
Bugsy '91
The Children '90
Dave '93
The Fifth Monkey '90
Gandhi '82
Harem '85
Maurice '87

Murderers Among Us: The Simon Wiesenthal Story '89
Pascali's Island '88
Schindler's List '93
Searching for Bobby Fischer '93
Silas Marner '85
Slipstream '89
Sneakers '92
Turtle Diary '86
Without a Clue '88

Danitza Kingsley
Amazons '86
Jack's Back '87
South of Reno '87

Susan Kingsley
The Dollmaker '84
Old Enough '84

Natalie Kingston
All Night Long/Smile Please '24
Baby Face Harry Langdon '26
His First Flame '26
His Private Secretary '33
Tarzan the Tiger '29

Sam Kinison
Back to School '86
It's a Bundyful Life '92

Kathleen Kinmont
The Art of Dying '90
Bride of Re-Animator '89
C.I.A.: Code Name Alexa '92
C.I.A. 2: Target Alexa '94
Final Impact '91
Final Round '93
Fraternity Vacation '85
Hardbodies '84
Night of the Warrior '91
Phoenix the Warrior '88
Roller Blade Warriors: Taken By Force '90
Rush Week '88
SnakeEater 2: The Drug Buster '89
Sweet Justice '92

Roy Kinnear
The Adventures of Sherlock Holmes' Smarter Brother '78
The Four Musketeers '75
Hawk the Slayer '81
Herbie Goes to Monte Carlo '77
The Hound of the Baskervilles '77
Juggernaut '74
A Man for All Seasons '88
Melody '71
Pirates '86
The Return of the Musketeers '89
Taste the Blood of Dracula '70
Willy Wonka & the Chocolate Factory '71
The Zany Adventures of Robin Hood '84

Terry Kinney
Body Snatchers '93
Deadly Matrimony '92
The Firm '93
JFK: Reckless Youth '93
Murder Ordained '87
Talent for the Game '91

Leonid Kinskey
Broadway Limited '41
Down Argentine Way '40
Duck Soup '33
Everything Happens at Night '39
The Great Waltz '38
I Married an Angel '42
Lady for a Night '42
Les Miserables '35
Somewhere I'll Find You '42

Klaus Kinski
Aguirre, the Wrath of God '72
And God Said to Cain '60s
Android '82
The Avenger '60
Beauty and the Beast '83
Buddy Buddy '81
A Bullet for the General '68
Burden of Dreams '82
Circus of Fear '67
Codename: Wildgeese '84
Count Dracula '71
Crawlspace '86
Creature '85

Creature with the Blue Hand '70
Dead Eyes of London '61
Deadly Sanctuary '68
Doctor Zhivago '65
Door with the Seven Locks '62
Double Face '70
Fighting Fists of Shanghai Joe '65
Fistful of Death '67
Fitzcarraldo '82
Five for Hell '67
Five Golden Dragons '67
For a Few Dollars More '65
The French Woman '79
Gangster's Law '86
Heroes in Hell '67
His Name was King '85
The Indian Scarf '63
Inn on the River '62
Jack the Ripper '80
Liberators '77
Lifespan '75
The Little Drummer Girl '84
Night of the Assassin '77
Operation Thunderbolt '77
Primal Impulse '74
Psychopath '68
Rough Justice '87
The Ruthless Four '70
Schizoid '80
The Secret Diary of Sigmund Freud '84
Shoot the Living, Pray for the Dead '71
Slaughter Hotel '71
The Soldier '82
The Squeaker '65
Target for Killing '66
A Time to Love & a Time to Die '58
Timestalkers '87
Twice a Judas '60s
Venom '82
Venus in Furs '70
Web of the Spider '70
Woyzeck '78

Nastassia Kinski
Boarding School '83
Cat People '82
Exposed '83
Faraway, So Close! '93
For Your Love Only '79
Harem '85
The Hotel New Hampshire '84
Magdalene '88
Maria's Lovers '84
Moon in the Gutter '83
One from the Heart '82
Paris, Texas '83
Revolution '85
Spring Symphony '86
Stay As You Are '78
Terminal Velocity '94
Tess '80
To the Devil, A Daughter '76
Torrents of Spring '90
Unfaithfully Yours '84
The Wrong Move '78

Kipper Kids
Forbidden Zone '80
Spirit of '76 '91

Bruce Kirby
Armed and Dangerous '86
Cinderella Liberty '73
Fyre '78
Getting Up and Going Home '92
Throw Momma from the Train '87
The Young Graduates '71

Bruno Kirby
Bert Rigby, You're a Fool '89
Between the Lines '77
Birdy '84
Borderline '80
City Slickers '91
Fallen Angels 2 '93
Flesh and Blood '85
The Freshman '90
The Godfather 1902-1959: The Complete Epic '81
The Godfather, Part 2 '74
Golden Gate '93
Good Morning, Vietnam '87
Harrad Experiment '73
Kiss My Grits '82
Modern Romance '81

Nitti: The Enforcer '88
This is Spinal Tap '84
Tin Men '87
We're No Angels '89
When Harry Met Sally '89

Jay Kirby
Border Patrol '43
Colt Comrades '43
Hoppy Serves a Writ '43
Leather Burners '43
Lost Canyon '43
Sundown Riders '48

Michael Kirby
Another Woman '88
The Girl in Blue '74
Shadows and Fog '92
Swoon '91

Joe Kirk
The Naughty Nineties '45
The Noose Hangs High '48
Smart Alecks '42

Phyllis Kirk
Back from Eternity '56
House of Wax '53
A Life of Her Own '50
River Beat '54
The Sad Sack '57
Three Guys Named Mike '51
Two Weeks with Love '50

Tommy Kirk
The Absent-Minded Professor '61
Babes in Toyland '61
Blood of Ghastly Horror '72
Bon Voyage! '62
Escapade in Florence '62
Horsemasters '61
It's Alive! '68
Mars Needs Women '66
The Misadventures of Merlin Jones '63
Monkey's Uncle '65
Moon Pilot '62
Old Yeller '57
Pajama Party '64
Savage Sam '63
The Shaggy Dog '59
Son of Flubber '63
The Swiss Family Robinson '60
The Unkissed Bride '66
Village of the Giants '65

Donald Kirke
Country Gentlemen '36
A Night for Crime '42
Oh Susannah '38

Sally Kirkland
Anna '87
Best of the Best '89
Big Bad Mama '74
Bite the Bullet '75
Blue '68
Bullseye! '90
Cheatin' Hearts '93
Cinderella Liberty '73
Cold Feet '89
Death Scream '75
Double Jeopardy '92
Double Threat '92
Eye of the Stranger '93
Fatal Games '84
Forever: A Ghost of a Love Story '92
Futz '69
Gunmen '93
Heat Wave '90
High Stakes '89
Hit the Dutchman '92
Hometown U.S.A. '79
In the Heat of Passion '91
JFK '91
Kansas City Massacre '75
Love Letters '83
Paint It Black '89
Pipe Dreams '76
Primary Motive '92
Private Benjamin '80
Revenge '90
A Star is Born '76
Talking Walls '93
The Way We Were '73
White Hot '88
The Young Nurses '73

Jack Kirkwood
Fancy Pants '50
Never a Dull Moment '50

James Kirkwood
My Pal, The King '32
Short Films of D.W. Griffith, Vol. 2 '09

Rudiger Kirschstein
Coup de Grace '78
An Occurrence at Owl Creek Bridge/Coup de Grace '62

Terry Kiser
Into the Sun '92
Making Love '82
Mannequin 2: On the Move '91
The Offspring '87
Starflight One '83
Steel '80
Surf 2 '84
Weekend at Bernie's '89
Weekend at Bernie's 2 '93

Keiko Kishi
Kwaidan '64
The Makioka Sisters '83
Master Mind '73
Qui Etes Vous, Mr. Sorge? '61
Snow Country '57

Kyoko Kishida
The Human Condition: A Soldier's Prayer '61
Woman in the Dunes '64

Charles Kissinger
Asylum of Satan '72
Grizzly '76
Sheba, Baby '75
Three on a Meathook '72

Tawny Kitaen
Bachelor Party '84
Crystal Heart '87
Glory Years '87
Happy Hour '87
Instant Justice '86
The Perils of Gwendoline '84
White Hot '88
Witchboard '87

Michael Kitchen
The Dive '89
Enchanted April '92
Fools of Fortune '90
Out of Africa '85
The Russia House '90

Eartha Kitt
Boomerang '92
Dragonard '88
Erik the Viking '89
Ernest Scared Stupid '91
The Mark of the Hawk '57
Master of Dragonard Hill '89
Naughty Knights '71
New Faces of 1952 '54
The Pink Chiquitas '86

John Kitzmiller
Cave of the Living Dead '65
Dr. No '62
Jungle Master '56
Uncle Tom's Cabin '69

Gerard Klein
Frantic '88
La Passante '83

Robert Klein
The Bell Jar '79
Dangerous Curves '88
Hooper '78
The Marx Brothers in a Nutshell '90
Nobody's Perfekt '79
The Owl and the Pussycat '70
Pajama Tops '83
Poison Ivy '85
The Pursuit of Happiness '70
Rivals '72
A Secret Space '88
Table Settings '84
Tales from the Darkside: The Movie '90
Your Place or Mine '83

Rudolf Klein-Rogge
Crimes of Dr. Mabuse '32
Das Testament des Dr. Mabuse '33
Dr. Mabuse the Gambler '22
Kriemhilde's Revenge '24
Metropolis '26
Spies '28

Henry Kleinbach (Brandon)
The Garden of Allah '36

March of the Wooden Soldiers '34

Kevin Kline
The Big Chill '83
Chaplin '92
Consenting Adults '92
Cry Freedom '87
Dave '93
A Fish Called Wanda '88
Grand Canyon '91
I Love You to Death '90
The January Man '89
The Pirates of Penzance '83
Silverado '85
Soapdish '91
Sophie's Choice '82
Violets Are Blue '86

Heidi Kling
The Mighty Ducks '92
Out on a Limb '92

Jack Klugman
Days of Wine and Roses '62
The Detective '68
Goodbye Columbus '69
I Could Go on Singing '63
Justice '55
One of My Wives Is Missing '76
Twelve Angry Men '57
Two Minute Warning '76

Vincent Klyn
Bloodmatch '91
Cyborg '89
Dollman '91
Nemesis '93
Point Break '91

Skelton Knaggs
Bowery at Midnight/Dick Tracy vs. Cueball '42
Forever Amber '47

Evelyn Knapp
Bulldog Edition '36
Confidential '35
Hawaiian Buckaroo '38
His Private Secretary '33
In Old Santa Fe '34
Mistaken Identity '36
The Perils of Pauline '34
Rawhide '38
The Strange Love of Molly Louvain '32

Robert Knapp
Lady Scarface/The Threat '49
Mesa of Lost Women '52

David Knell
Bitter Harvest '81
Spring Break '83

Rob Knepper
Gas Food Lodging '92
Renegades '89
That's Life! '86
Where the Day Takes You '92
Wild Thing '87
Young Guns 2 '90

Christopher Knight
The Brady Bunch, Vol. 1 '69
Studs Lonigan '60
A Very Brady Christmas '88

Damien Knight
Class Reunion Massacre '77
The Redeemer '77

David Knight
Across the Bridge '57
Demons 2 '87
Who Shot Pat? '92

Esmond Knight
The Arsenal Stadium Mystery '39
Black Narcissus '47
A Canterbury Tale '44
The Element of Crime '84
Hamlet '48
Henry V '44
Peeping Tom '63
The Red Shoes '48
The River '51
Sink the Bismarck '60

Fuzzy Knight
The Adventures of Gallant Bess '48
Bad Men of the Border '45
Blazing Guns '43
Boss of Bullion City '41
Bury Me Not On the Lone Prairie '41

Knight ▶cont.

The Cowboy and the Lady '38
Frontier Law '43
Hills of Oklahoma '50
Man from Montana '41
Marshal of Heldorado '50
The Masked Rider '41
Naked Hills '56
Oklahoma Annie '51
Oregon Trail '39
Pony Post '40
Riders of Pasco Basin '40
Rimfire '49
Song of the Gringo '36
Song of the Trail '36
Take It Big '44
To the Last Man '33

Gladys Knight
Pipe Dreams '76
Twenty Bucks '93

Harlan E. Knight
The Fighting Sheriff '31
Whistlin' Dan '32

Lily Knight
Static '87
An Unremarkable Life '89

Michael E. Knight
Date with an Angel '87
Hexed '93

Sandra Knight
Frankenstein's Daughter '58
The Terror '63
Thunder Road '58
Track of the Vampire '66

Shirley Knight
Beyond the Poseidon
  Adventure '79
Dutchman '67
Endless Love '81
The Group '66
Ice Palace '60
Juggernaut '74
Petulia '68
The Rain People '69
Return to Earth '76
The Sender '82
Sweet Bird of Youth '62
21 Hours at Munich '76

Ted Knight
Caddyshack '80
Countdown '68
Psycho '60

Wayne Knight
Basic Instinct '92
Dead Again '91
Fallen Angels 2 '93
JFK '91
Jurassic Park '93

William Knight
Action U.S.A. '89
The Lost Platoon '89
21 Hours at Munich '76

Wyatt Knight
Porky's '82
Porky's 2: The Next Day '83
Porky's Revenge '85

Andrew Knott
Black Beauty '94
The Secret Garden '93

Don Knotts
The Apple Dumpling Gang '75
The Apple Dumpling Gang
  Rides Again '79
Herbie Goes to Monte Carlo '77
Hot Lead & Cold Feet '78
The Incredible Mr. Limpet '64
No Deposit, No Return '76
No Time for Sergeants '58
The Private Eyes '80
Prize Fighter '79
Return to Mayberry '85
The Shakiest Gun in the West
  '68

Patric Knowles
The Adventures of Robin Hood
  '38
Auntie Mame '58
Band of Angels '57
Beauty for the Asking '39
Big Steal '49
The Charge of the Light
  Brigade '36

Chisum '70
The Devil's Brigade '68
Five Came Back '39
Frankenstein Meets the
  Wolfman '42
Hit the Ice '43
How Green was My Valley '41
Monsieur Beaucaire '46
Mutiny '52
The Sisters '38
Three Came Home '50
Who Done It? '42
The Wolf Man '41

Alexander Knox
Accident '67
Alias John Preston '56
The Chosen '77
Commandos Strike at Dawn '43
Cry of the Innocent '80
Europa '51
Joshua Then and Now '85
The Judge Steps Out '49
Khartoum '66
The Longest Day '62
Nicholas and Alexandra '71
Operation Amsterdam '60
Puppet on a Chain '72
Reach for the Sky '56
The Sea Wolf '41
Shalako '68
Sister Kenny '46
The Sleeping Tiger '54
Tokyo Joe '49
The Vikings '58
Wilson '44
The Wreck of the Mary Deare
  '59

Elyse Knox
Don Winslow of the Coast
  Guard '43
Hit the Ice '43
Joe's Bed-Stuy Barbershop:
  We Cut Heads '83
The Mummy's Tomb '42
Tanks a Million '41

Mickey Knox
Frankenstein Unbound '90
Western Pacific Agent '51

Terence Knox
Children of the Corn 2: The
  Final Sacrifice '92
Circle of Power '83
City Killer '87
Distortions '87
Forever: A Ghost of a Love
  Story '92
Hard Rain-The Tet 1968 '89
Humanoid Defender '85
The Mighty Pawns '87
Murder Ordained '87
Murder So Sweet '93
Rebel Love '85
Snow Kill '90
Tour of Duty '87
Tripwire '89

Peggy Knudsen
The Big Sleep '46
Copper Canyon '50
Humoresque '46
A Stolen Life '46

Gustav Knuth
Heidi '65
Tromba, the Tiger Man '52

Keiju Kobayashi
Godzilla 1985 '85
Tidal Wave '75

Jeff Kober
Alien Nation '90
The Baby Doll Murders '92
China Beach '88
The First Power '89
Keep the Change '92
Lone Justice '93
Out of Bounds '86

Marianne Koch
A Fistful of Dollars '64
Frozen Alive '64
The Monster of London City '64
A Place Called Glory '66

Walter Koenig
Moontrap '89
Star Trek: The Motion Picture
  '80
Star Trek 2: The Wrath of Khan
  '82

Star Trek 3: The Search for
  Spock '84
Star Trek 4: The Voyage Home
  '86
Star Trek 5: The Final Frontier
  '89
Star Trek 6: The Undiscovered
  Country '91
Star Trek Bloopers '69

Michiyo Kogure
A Geisha '53
Shin Heike Monogatari '55

Fred Kohler, Sr.
The Fiddlin' Buckaroo '33
Riders of the Purple Sage '25
Texas Bad Man '32

Fred Kohler, Jr.
Anna Christie '23
Calling Wild Bill Elliott '43
Daniel Boone: Trail Blazer '56
Deluge '33
Fighting Caravans '31
Honor of the Range '34
The Man from Hell '34
Pecos Kid '35
Toll of the Desert '35
Western Mail '42

Susan Kohner
Dino '57
The Gene Krupa Story '59
Imitation of Life '59

Hiroshi Koizumi
Attack of the Mushroom People
  '63
Godzilla vs. Mothra '64

Clarence Kolb
Caught in the Draft '41
His Girl Friday '40
Honolulu '39

Henry Kolker
Baby Face '33
Charlie Chan in Paris '35
Coquette '29
The Cowboy and the Lady '38
The Ghost Walks '34
Mad Love '35
The Mystery Man '35
Rasputin and the Empress '32

Amos Kollek
Double Edge '92
Goodbye, New York '85

Hosei Komatsu
Double Suicide '69
A Taxing Woman's Return '88

Liliana Komorowska
Martial Outlaw '93
Scanners 3: The Takeover '92

Maja Komorowska
Maids of Wilko '79
Year of the Quiet Sun '84

Kam Kong
Kung Fu Powerhouse
Kung Fu Strongman
Shaolin Warrior

Queen Kong
Deathstalker 2: Duel of the
  Titans '87
Slashdance '89

Magda Konopka
Satanik '69
When Dinosaurs Ruled the
  Earth '70

Phyllis Konstam
Murder '30
Skin Game '31

Guich Koock
American Ninja '85
Picasso Trigger '89
Seven '79
Square Dance '87

Milos Kopecky
Fabulous Adventures of Baron
  Munchausen '61
The Original Fabulous
  Adventures of Baron
  Munchausen '61

Bernie Kopell
Combat Academy '86
Get Smart, Again! '89
The Love Boat '70s
The Loved One '65

Karen Kopins
Creator '85
Jake Speed '86
Once Bitten '85

Arnold Korff
Doughboys '30
The Haunted Castle '21

Jon Korkes
The Day of the Dolphin '73
Jaws of Satan '81
Little Murders '71
Syngenor '90

Harvey Korman
Americathon '79
April Fools '69
Based on an Untrue Story '93
Betrayal of the Dove '92
Blazing Saddles '74
Bud and Lou '78
Curse of the Pink Panther '83
Film House Fever '86
Gone are the Days '84
Herbie Goes Bananas '80
High Anxiety '77
History of the World: Part 1 '81
Huckleberry Finn '74
The Longshot '86
Munchies '87

Mary Kornman
The Adventurous Knights '35
Desert Trail '35
Our Gang '26
Our Gang Comedy Festival '88
Our Gang Comedy Festival 2
  '89
Queen of the Jungle '35
The Return of Our Gang '25
Swing It, Professor '37

Charlie Korsmo
Dick Tracy '90
The Doctor '91
Heat Wave '90
Hook '91
Men Don't Leave '89
What About Bob? '91

**Robert F. (Bob)
Kortman**
The Crimson Trail '35
Feud of the West '35
The Fiddlin' Buckaroo '33
Fugitive Valley '41
Guns of the Law '44
Hopalong Cassidy: Renegade
  Trail '39
Island of Lost Souls '32
Law of the Texan '38
The Lone Defender '32
Phantom Thunderbolt '33
Rainbow Ranch '33
The Rangers Step In '37
Robinson Crusoe of Clipper
  Island '36
Sandflow '37
Terror Trail '33
When a Man Sees Red '34

Fritz Kortner
Backstairs '21
The Hands of Orlac '25
Pandora's Box '28
Warning Shadows '23
Woman in Brown '48

Charles Korvin
Berlin Express '48
Ship of Fools '65

Sylva Koscina
Deadly Sanctuary '68
Hercules '58
Hercules Unchained '59
Hornet's Nest '70
Juliet of the Spirits '65
Lisa and the Devil '75
The Secret War of Harry Frigg
  '68
The Slasher '74

Martin Kosleck
All Through the Night '42
The Flesh Eaters '64
Foreign Correspondent '40
House of Horrors '46
The Mummy's Curse '44
Pursuit to Algiers '45

Paul Koslo
The Annihilators '85
Chained Heat 2 '92

Joe Kidd '72
Maniac '77
A Night in the Life of Jimmy
  Reardon '88
Omega Man '71
Project: Shadowchaser '92
Robot Jox '89
Rooster Cogburn '75
Roots: The Next Generation '79
Vanishing Point '71
Xtro 2: The Second Encounter
  '91

David Kossoff
Svengali '55
Unicorn '83

Kane Kosugi
Journey of Honor '91
Pray for Death '85
Revenge of the Ninja '83

Sho Kosugi
Aloha Summer '88
Black Eagle '88
Blind Fury '90
The Deadliest Art: The Best of
  the Martial Arts Films '90
Eagle Claws Champion '80s
Enter the Ninja '81
Journey of Honor '91
Kingfisher the Killer '80s
Master Ninja '78
Nine Deaths of the Ninja '85
Ninja 3: The Domination '84
Phoenix the Ninja '80s
Pray for Death '85
Rage of Honor '87
Revenge of the Ninja '83
Shaolin Temple Strikes Back
  '72

Elias Koteas
The Adjuster '91
Almost an Angel '90
Blood Red '88
Camilla '94
Chain of Desire '93
Cyborg 2 '93
Desperate Hours '90
Friends, Lovers & Lunatics '89
Full Moon in Blue Water '88
Look Who's Talking, Too '90
Malarek '89
Some Kind of Wonderful '87
Teenage Mutant Ninja Turtles:
  The Movie '90
Teenage Mutant Ninja Turtles 3
  '93
Tucker: The Man and His
  Dream '88

Oded Kotler
Hanna K. '83
My Michael '75

Yaphet Kotto
Across 110th Street '72
After the Shock '90
Alien '79
Almost Blue '93
Badge of the Assassin '85
Blue Collar '78
Brubaker '80
Chrome Soldiers '92
Drum '76
Extreme Justice '93
Eye of the Tiger '86
Fighting Back '82
Five Card Stud '68
Freddy's Dead: The Final
  Nightmare '91
Friday Foster '75
Hangfire '91
Harem '86
Housewife '72
Jigsaw Murders '89
Live and Let Die '73
Man & Boy '71
Midnight Run '88
Ministry of Vengeance '89
Monkey Hustle '77
Nothing but a Man '64
The Park is Mine '85
Prettykill '87
Rage '80
Raid on Entebbe '77
Report to the Commissioner
  '74
The Running Man '87
Sharks' Treasure '75
The Star Chamber '83
Terminal Entry '87

Thomas Crown Affair '68
Tripwire '89
Truck Turner '74
Warning Sign '85
A Whisper to a Scream '88

Nancy Kovack
Diary of a Madman '63
Frankie and Johnny '65
Jason and the Argonauts '63

Ernie Kovacs
Bell, Book and Candle '58
Best of Ernie Kovacs '56
North to Alaska '60
Strangers When We Meet '60

Martin Kove
Firehawk '92
Future Shock '93
The Karate Kid '84
The Karate Kid: Part 2 '86
The Karate Kid: Part 3 '89
The Outfit '93
President's Target '93
Project: Shadowchaser '92
Rambo: First Blood, Part 2 '85
Seven '93
Shootfighter: Fight to the Death '93
Steele Justice '87
To Be the Best '93
White Light '90
Wyatt Earp '94

Harley Jane Kozak
All I Want for Christmas '91
The Amy Fisher Story '93
Arachnophobia '90
The Favor '94
Necessary Roughness '91
Parenthood '89
Side Out '90
The Taking of Beverly Hills '91
When Harry Met Sally '89

Linda Kozlowski
Almost an Angel '90
Crocodile Dundee '86
Crocodile Dundee 2 '88
The Neighbor '93
Pass the Ammo '88
Target: Favorite Son '87

Jeroen Krabbe
Code Name: Dancer '87
Crossing Delancey '88
A Flight of Rainbirds '81
The 4th Man '79
The Fugitive '93
Kafka '91
King of the Hill '93
The Living Daylights '87
No Mercy '86
The Prince of Tides '91
The Punisher '90
Robin Hood '91
Scandal '89
Secret Weapon '90
Soldier of Orange '78
Stalin '92
Till There was You '91
Turtle Diary '86
A World Apart '88

Jane Krakowski
No Big Deal '83
Stepping Out '91

Eric Allen Kramer
The Comrades of Summer '92
Quest for the Mighty Sword '90
Robin Hood: Men in Tights '93

Jeffrey Kramer
Halloween 2: The Nightmare Isn't Over! '81
Hollywood Boulevard '76

Robert Krantz
Paradise Motel '84
Winners Take All '87

Brian Krause
December '91
Return to the Blue Lagoon '91
Sleepwalkers '92

Werner Krauss
The Cabinet of Dr. Caligari '19
Joyless Street '25
Jud Suess '40
Othello '22
Secrets of a Soul '25
Shattered '21
Variety '25
Waxworks '24

Connie Kreski
Black Bird '75
The Trackers '71

Kurt Kreuger
Dark Corner '46
Mademoiselle Fifi '44
Unfaithfully Yours '48

Elisabeth Kreuzer
Alice in the Cities '74
The American Friend '77
Basileus Quartet '82
Birgitt Haas Must Be Killed '83
Kings of the Road—In the Course of Time '76
A Man Like Eva '83

David Kriegel
Alive '93
Quest of the Delta Knights '93
Speed '94

Anneline Kriel
Kill and Kill Again '81
Reason to Die '90

Alice Krige
Barfly '87
Chariots of Fire '81
Code Name: Chaos '90
Ghost Story '81
Haunted Summer '88
Iran: Days of Crisis '91
King David '85
Ladykiller '92
Max and Helen '90
See You in the Morning '89
Sleepwalkers '92
A Tale of Two Cities '80

Sylvia Kristel
Because of the Cats '74
The Big Bet '85
Casanova '87
The Concorde: Airport '79 '79
Dracula's Widow '88
Emmanuelle '74
Emmanuelle 4 '84
Emmanuelle, the Joys of a Woman '76
The Fifth Musketeer '79
Game of Seduction '86
Goodbye Emmanuelle '79
Hot Blood '89
Lady Chatterley's Lover '81
Mata Hari '85
Mysteries '84
The Nude Bomb '80
Private Lessons '81
Private School '83
Red Heat '85
Tigers in Lipstick '80

Marta Kristen
Beach Blanket Bingo '65
Gemini Affair '80s
Savage Sam '63
Terminal Island '73

Romano Kristoff
Bruce's Fists of Vengeance '84
Slash '87
Warbus '85

Kris Kristofferson
Act of Passion: The Lost Honor of Kathryn Beck '83
Alice Doesn't Live Here Anymore '74
Another Pair of Aces: Three of a Kind '91
Big Top Pee Wee '88
Blume in Love '73
Bring Me the Head of Alfredo Garcia '74
Cheatin' Hearts '93
Christmas in Connecticut '92
Convoy '78
Flashpoint '84
Freedom Road '79
Heaven's Gate '81
Knights '93
Last Days of Frank & Jesse James '86
The Last Movie '71
Millenium '89
Miracle in the Wilderness '91
Night of the Cyclone '90
Original Intent '91
Pair of Aces '90
Pat Garrett & Billy the Kid '73
Rollover '81
The Sailor Who Fell from Grace with the Sea '76

Semi-Tough '77
Songwriter '84
Stagecoach '86
A Star is Born '76
The Tracker '88
Trouble in Mind '85
Welcome Home '89

Berry Kroeger
Blood Alley '55
Demon Seed '77
Guilty of Treason '50
Gun Crazy '49
The Incredible Two-Headed Transplant '71
Yellowneck '55

Gary Kroeger
Best of Eddie Murphy '89
A Man Called Sarge '90
Secret Ingredient '92

Josef Kroner
Another Way '82
The Shop on Main Street '65

Margareta Krook
The Adventures of Picasso '80
Pay Off '89
Persona '66

Alma Kruger
Craig's Wife '36
Forever Amber '47
The Great Waltz '38

Hardy Kruger
Bachelor of Hearts '58
Barry Lyndon '75
Battle of Neretva '69
Blue Fin '78
A Bridge Too Far '77
The Flight of the Phoenix '65
Hatari! '61
The Inside Man '84
Liana, Jungle Goddess '56
One That Got Away '57
Paper Tiger '74
Red Tent '69
Sundays & Cybele '62
What the Peeper Saw '72
Wild Geese '78
Wrong is Right '82

Otto Kruger
Another Thin Man '39
Black Eyes '39
Cash McCall '60
Chained '34
Corregidor '43
Cover Girl '44
Dracula's Daughter '36
High Noon '52
Hitler's Children '43
Housemaster '38
I Am the Law '38
Murder, My Sweet '44
The Prizefighter and the Lady '33
Saboteur '42
They Won't Forget '37
Treasure Island '34
The Woman Who Came Back '45
Wonder Man '45
The Wonderful World of the Brothers Grimm '62
The Young Philadelphians '59

David Krumholtz
Addams Family Values '93
Life with Mikey '93

Gene Krupa
Ball of Fire '41
The Benny Goodman Story '55
The Glenn Miller Story '54

Olek Krupa
Ivory Hunters '90
Mac '93

Jack Kruschen
Abbott and Costello Go to Mars '53
The Angry Red Planet '59
The Apartment '60
Cape Fear '61
Cheaters '84
Dear Brigitte '65
Devlin Connection '82
Follow That Dream '61
Freebie & the Bean '74
The Ladies' Man '61
The Last Voyage '60
Lover Come Back '61

McLintock! '63
Meet Danny Wilson '52
Money to Burn '83
Mountain Man '77
Reform School Girl '57
Satan's Cheerleaders '77
Soldier of Fortune '55

Ou-Yang Ksiek
Against the Drunken Cat Paws '75
Eighteen Jade Arhats '84

Chen Kuan-Tai
Challenge of the Masters '89
Shaolin Executioner '80s

Alex Kubik
Carnal Crimes '91
Trapped Alive '93

Akira Kubo
Attack of the Mushroom People '63
Destroy All Monsters '68
Snow Country '57
Son of Godzilla '66
Throne of Blood '57
Yog, Monster from Space '71

Bernie Kuby
Death Journey '76
Jornada de Muerte '80s

Yoshiko Kuga
The Cruel Story of Youth '60
The Idiot '51
Shin Heike Monogatari '55

Jarl Kulle
Babette's Feast '87
The Devil's Eye '60
Fanny and Alexander '83
Secrets of Women '52
Smiles of a Summer Night '55

Nancy Kulp
Forever Darling '56
The Patsy '64
The Three Faces of Eve '57

William J. Kulzer
Lust for Freedom '87
Shadows Run Black '84

Yasuka Kurata
King Boxers '80
Kung Fu Powerhouse
Rage of Wind '82

Alwyn Kurts
Earthling '80
The Efficiency Expert '92
Tim '79

Swoosie Kurtz
Against All Odds '84
Baja Oklahoma '88
Bright Lights, Big City '88
Dangerous Liaisons '88
The Image '90
Marriage is Alive and Well '80
The Positively True Adventures of the Alleged Texas Cheerleader-Murdering Mom '93
Reality Bites '94
A Shock to the System '90
Stanley and Iris '90
A Time to Live '85
True Stories '86
Vice Versa '88
Walking Through the Fire '80
Wildcats '86
The World According to Garp '82

Katy Kurtzman
Child of Glass '78
Long Journey Back '78
When Every Day was the Fourth of July '78

Clyde Kusatsu
The Choirboys '77
Dr. Strange '78
Dream Lover '93
Made in America '93

Dylan Kussman
Dead Poets Society '89
Journey of Honor '91
Wild Hearts Can't Be Broken '91

Miyuki Kuwano
The Cruel Story of Youth '60
Equinox Flower '58

Mimi Kuzyk
Blind Justice '86
Family Sins '87
The Kiss '88
Miles to Go '86
Striker's Mountain '87

Nancy Kwan
Arrivederci, Baby! '66
Blade in Hong Kong '85
The Corrupt Ones '67
The Deadly and the Beautiful '73
Dragon: The Bruce Lee Story '93
Flower Drum Song '61
Fowl Play '83
Lt. Robin Crusoe, U.S.N. '66
The McMasters '70
Night Children '89
Night Creature '79
Project: Kill! '77
Stickfighter '89
Walking the Edge '83
The World of Suzie Wong '60

Burt Kwouk
Empire of the Sun '87
The Pink Panther Strikes Again '76
Plenty '85
Revenge of the Pink Panther '78
Son of the Pink Panther '93
Trail of the Pink Panther '82

Sam Kydd
The House in Marsh Road '60
Island of Terror '66

David Kyle
Cruisin' High '92
L.A. Gangs Rising '89

Machiko Kyo
Drifting Weeds '59
Face of Another '66
Gate of Hell '54
Odd Obsession '60
Princess Yang Kwei Fei '55
Rashomon '51
Street of Shame '56
The Teahouse of the August Moon '56
Ugetsu '53

Kay Kyser
Around the World '43
Playmates '41
Thousands Cheer '43
You'll Find Out '40

Jake La Motta
Hangmen '87
The Hustler '61
Mob War '88

Alison La Placa
Fletch '85
Madhouse '90

Rosemary La Planche
The Devil Bat's Daughter '46
Federal Agents vs. Underworld, Inc. '49
Strangler of the Swamp '46

Laura La Plante
The Cat and the Canary '27
Hold Your Man '33
Lonely Wives '31
Skinner's Dress Suit '26
Smouldering Fires '25

Rod La Rocque
Beyond Tomorrow '40
Braveheart '25
Captain Swagger '25
The Coming of Amos '25
Dr. Christian Meets the Women '40
The Hunchback of Notre Dame '39
International Crime '37
Meet John Doe '41
Our Modern Maidens '29
The Shadow Strikes '37
Show People '28
Stand and Deliver '28
The Ten Commandments '23

Rita La Roy
The Mandarin Mystery '37
Sin Takes a Holiday '30

Jack La Rue
Dangerous Holiday '37
Dangerous Passage '44
The Payoff '43

Barbara Laage
The Respectful Prostitute '52
Therese & Isabelle '68

Patti LaBelle
Fire and Rain '89
Sing '89
A Soldier's Story '84
Unnatural Causes '86

Matthew Laborteaux
Aliens Are Coming '80
Deadly Friend '86
Shattered Spirits '91
A Woman Under the Influence '74

Patrick Laborteaux
Heathers '89
Prince of Bel Air '87
3 Ninjas '92

Catherine Lacey
Cottage to Let '41
The Lady Vanishes '38
Pink Strings and Sealing Wax '45

Margaret Lacey
Diamonds are Forever '71
Seance on a Wet Afternoon '64

Ronald Lacey
Disciple of Death '72
Firefox '82
Flesh and Blood '85
The Hound of the Baskervilles '83
Into the Darkness '86
Jailbird Rock '88
Landslide '92
The Lone Runner '88
Making the Grade '84
Next Victim '74
Nijinsky '80
Raiders of the Lost Ark '81
Sahara '83

Stephen Lack
All the Vermeers in New York '91
Dead Ringers '88
Fatal Attraction '80
Perfect Strangers '84
Scanners '81

Frank Lackteen
The Pony Express '25
Red Barry '38
The Sea Wolf '41

Alan Ladd
All the Young Men '60
The Badlanders '58
Botany Bay '53
Branded '50
Captain Caution '41
The Carpetbaggers '64
Citizen Kane '41
Deep Six '58
Drum Beat '54
Duel of Champions '61
Gangs, Inc. '41
The Glass Key '42
Hell on Frisco Bay '55
The Howards of Virginia '40
Joan of Paris '42
The McConnell Story '55
My Favorite Brunette '47
Proud Rebel '58
Shane '53
They Met in Bombay '41
This Gun for Hire '42

Cheryl Ladd
Danielle Steel's Changes '91
Fulfillment '89
The Hasty Heart '86
Lisa '90
Millenium '89
Now and Forever '82
Poison Ivy '92
Purple Hearts '84
Romance on the Orient Express '89
Satan's School for Girls '73
The Treasure of Jamaica Reef '74

David Ladd
Catlow '71

A Dog of Flanders '59
Misty '61
The Treasure of Jamaica Reef '74

Diane Ladd
Alice Doesn't Live Here Anymore '74
All Night Long '81
Black Widow '87
Carnosaur '93
The Cemetery Club '93
Chinatown '74
Code Name: Chaos '90
Desperate Lives '82
Doctor Quinn, Medicine Woman '92
Embryo '76
Father Hood '93
Forever: A Ghost of a Love Story '92
Hold Me, Thrill Me, Kiss Me '93
I Married a Centerfold '84
A Kiss Before Dying '91
The Lookalike '90
National Lampoon's Christmas Vacation '89
Plain Clothes '88
Rambling Rose '91
Rebel Rousers '69
Something Wicked This Way Comes '83
The Wild Angels '66
Wild at Heart '90
Willa '79

John Lafayette
Full Fathom Five '90
White Sands '92

Patricia Laffan
Devil Girl from Mars '54
Quo Vadis '51

Art LaFleur
Forever Young '92
Jack the Bear '93
Live! From Death Row '92
Rampage '87
The Sandlot '93
Trancers '85
Zone Troopers '85

Bernadette LaFont
Catch Me a Spy '71
Le Beau Serge '58
The Perils of Gwendoline '84
Too Pretty to Be Honest '72
A Very Curious Girl '69
Violette '78

Caroline Lagerfelt
Home at Last '88
Iron Eagle '86

Valerie Lagrange
A Man and a Woman '66
Morgan the Pirate '60
Weekend '67

Bert Lahr
Just Around the Corner '38
The Night They Raided Minsky's '69
Rose Marie '54
Ship Ahoy '42
Sing Your Worries Away '42
Two Reelers: Comedy Classics 4 '36
The Wizard of Oz '39

Christine Lahti
And Justice for All '79
Crazy from the Heart '91
The Doctor '91
The Executioner's Song '82
The Fear Inside '92
Funny About Love '90
The Good Fight '92
Gross Anatomy '89
The Henderson Monster '80
Housekeeping '87
Just Between Friends '86
Leaving Normal '92
Miss Firecracker '89
Running on Empty '88
Single Bars, Single Women '84
Stacking '87
Swing Shift '84
Whose Life Is It Anyway? '81

Jimmy Laine
Driller Killer '74
Ms. 45 '81

Alan Lake
Con Man '92
Don't Open Till Christmas '84

Alice Lake
Broken Hearts of Broadway '23
Playing Dead '15

Arthur Lake
Blondie '38
Blondie Has Trouble '40
Blondie Hits the Jackpot '49
Blondie in Society '41
Blondie Knows Best '46
Blondie Takes a Vacation '39
Blondie's Blessed Event '42
Exiled to Shanghai '37
It's a Great Life '43
Silent Laugh Makers, No. 1 '15
The Silver Streak '34
Skinner's Dress Suit '26
23 1/2 Hours Leave '37

Florence Lake
Crash Dive '43
Going to Town '44
Next Time I Marry '38
Quality Street '37
Romance '30
Savage Intruder '68

Ricki Lake
Babycakes '89
Based on an Untrue Story '93
Cabin Boy '94
The Chase '91
Cookie '89
Cry-Baby '90
Hairspray '88
Inside Monkey Zetterland '93
Last Exit to Brooklyn '90
Serial Mom '94
Where the Day Takes You '92
Working Girl '88

Veronica Lake
Flesh Feast '69
The Glass Key '42
I Married a Witch '42
Ramrod '47
Sullivan's Travels '41
This Gun for Hire '42

Hedy Lamarr
Algiers '38
Boom Town '40
Comrade X '40
Copper Canyon '50
Dishonored Lady '47
Ecstasy '33
Experiment Perilous '45
The Love of Three Queens '54
Samson and Delilah '50
The Strange Woman '46
Tortilla Flat '42
White Cargo '42
Ziegfeld Girl '41

Fernando Lamas
The Cheap Detective '78
Dangerous When Wet '53
The Girl Who Had Everything '53
The Merry Widow '52
Murder on Flight 502 '75
100 Rifles '69
Powder Keg '70
Rich, Young and Pretty '51
Rose Marie '54
Violent Ones '68

Lorenzo Lamas
Body Rock '84
Bounty Tracker '93
C.I.A: Code Name Alexa '92
C.I.A. 2: Target Alexa '94
Final Impact '91
Final Round '93
Killing Streets '91
Night of the Warrior '91
SnakeEater '89
SnakeEater 2: The Drug Buster '89
SnakeEater 3: His Law '92
The Swordsman '92
Take Down '79

Debra Lamb
Beverly Hills Vamp '88
B.O.R.N. '88
Evil Spirits '91
The Invisible Maniac '90
Rock & the Money-Hungry Party Girls '89
Stripped to Kill II: Live Girls '89

Gil Lamb
Comedy Festival #2 '30s
Day of the Animals '77

Larry Lamb
Buster '88
Shadey '87
Transmutations '85

Anne Louise Lambert
The Draughtsman's Contract '82
Great Expectations: The Untold Story '87

Christopher Lambert
Fortress '93
Greystoke: The Legend of Tarzan, Lord of the Apes '84
Gunmen '93
Highlander '86
Highlander 2: The Quickening '91
Highlander 3: The Sorcerer '94
Highlander: The Gathering '93
Knight Moves '93
Love Songs '85
Priceless Beauty '90
The Sicilian '87
Subway '85
To Kill a Priest '89
Why Me? '90

Jack Lambert
Dick Tracy's Dilemma '47
Hue and Cry '47
Machine Gun Kelly '58
Montana Belle '52
North of the Great Divide '50
Stars in My Crown '50

Heath Lamberts
Ordinary Magic '93
To Kill a Clown '72

Ellie Lambetti
Girl in Black '56
A Matter of Dignity '57

Karen Lamm
Ants '77
The Hatfields & the McCoys '75

Duncan Lamont
The Evil of Frankenstein '64
The Golden Coach '52
Murder at the Gallop '63

Marten Lamont
Federal Operator 99 '45
Redwood Forest Trail '50
Son of Fury '42

Molly Lamont
The Awful Truth '37
The Devil Bat's Daughter '46
Somewhere I'll Find You '42

Pascal Lamorisse
The Red Balloon '56
Red Balloon/Occurrence at Owl Creek Bridge '62
Voyage en Balloon '59

John Lamotta
One More Chance '90
Revenge of the Ninja '83
We're Talkin' Serious Money '92

Dorothy Lamour
Caught in the Draft '41
Creepshow 2 '87
Dixiana '30
Donovan's Reef '63
The Greatest Show on Earth '52
Hollywood Goes to War '54
Hurricane '37
Johnny Apollo '40
The Love Goddesses '65
My Favorite Brunette '47
Pajama Party '64
The Road to Bali '53
The Road to Hong Kong '62
The Road to Morocco '42
The Road to Rio '47
The Road to Singapore '40
The Road to Utopia '46
The Road to Zanzibar '41
Swing High, Swing Low '37
They Got Me Covered '43

Zohra Lampert
Alan & Naomi '92
Alphabet City '84

American Blue Note '89
The Connection '73
Isle of Secret Passion '85
Izzy & Moe '85
Let's Scare Jessica to Death '71
Opening Night '77
Splendor in the Grass '61
Stanley and Iris '90
Teachers '84

Chus Lampreave
I'm the One You're Looking For '88
Matador '86
What Have I Done to Deserve This? '85

Gunter Lamprecht
Berlin Alexanderplatz '80
Red Kiss '85

Tse Lan
Enter the Panther '79
Two Dragons Fight Against the Tiger

Burt Lancaster
Airport '70
America at the Movies '76
Apache '54
Atlantic City '81
Barnum '86
Birdman of Alcatraz '62
Buffalo Bill & the Indians '76
The Cassandra Crossing '76
A Child is Waiting '63
Come Back, Little Sheba '52
Control '87
Conversation Piece '75
Crimson Pirate '52
Criss Cross '49
The Devil's Disciple '59
Elmer Gantry '60
Executive Action '73
Field of Dreams '89
The Flame & the Arrow '50
From Here to Eternity '53
Go Tell the Spartans '78
Gunfight at the O.K. Corral '57
The Hallelujah Trail '65
His Majesty O'Keefe '53
Island of Dr. Moreau '77
The Jeweller's Shop '90
Jim Thorpe: All American '51
Judgment at Nuremberg '61
The Kentuckian '55
Lawman '71
The List of Adrian Messenger '63
Little Treasure '85
Local Hero '83
Moses '76
1900 '76
On Wings of Eagles '86
The Osterman Weekend '83
The Professionals '66
The Rainmaker '56
Rocket Gibraltar '88
The Rose Tattoo '55
Run Silent, Run Deep '58
The Scalphunters '68
Scorpio '73
Separate But Equal '91
Separate Tables '58
Seven Days in May '64
Sorry, Wrong Number '48
Sweet Smell of Success '57
Swimmer '68
Tough Guys '86
The Train '65
Trapeze '56
Twilight's Last Gleaming '77
Ulzana's Raid '72
The Unforgiven '60
Valdez is Coming '71
Vengeance Valley '51
Vera Cruz '53
Voyage of Terror: The Achille Lauro Affair '90
Zulu Dawn '79

James Lancaster
Gettysburg '93
Leprechaun 2 '94

Stuart Lancaster
Beneath the Valley of the Ultra-Vixens '79
Faster Pussycat! Kill! Kill! '66
Mantis in Lace '68
Mistress of the Apes '79

Elsa Lanchester
Arnold '73
Beachcomber '38
Bell, Book and Candle '58
The Bishop's Wife '47
Blackbeard's Ghost '67
The Bride of Frankenstein '35
David Copperfield '35
Die Laughing '80
Easy Come, Easy Go '67
Forever and a Day '43
The Ghost Goes West '36
The Glass Slipper '55
The Inspector General '49
Lassie, Come Home '43
Murder by Death '76
My Dog, the Thief '69
Naughty Marietta '35
Northwest Outpost '47
Pajama Party '64
The Private Life of Henry VIII '33
The Razor's Edge '46
Rembrandt '36
The Secret Garden '49
Son of Fury '42
The Spiral Staircase '46
Terror in the Wax Museum '73
That Darn Cat '65
Willard '71
Witness for the Prosecution '57

Micheline Lanctot
The Apprenticeship of Duddy Kravitz '74
Blood Relatives '77

Geoffrey Land
Against A Crooked Sky '75
The Female Bunch '69
Hospital of Terror '78

Paul Land
Idolmaker '80
Spring Break '83

Rodolfo Landa
The Criminal Life of Archibaldo de la Cruz '55
Neutron vs. the Amazing Dr. Caronte '61

David Landau
False Faces '32
Gabriel Over the White House '33
Horse Feathers '32
The Purchase Price '32
Street Scene '31

Martin Landau
Access Code '84
Alone in the Dark '82
The Being '83
By Dawn's Early Light '89
Cleopatra '63
Crimes & Misdemeanors '89
Cyclone '87
Death Blow '87
Destination Moonbase Alpha '75
Ed Wood '94
Empire State '87
Eye of the Stranger '93
The Fall of the House of Usher '80
Firehead '90
The Gazebo '59
The Hallelujah Trail '65
Intersection '93
Kung Fu: The Movie '86
The Last Word '80
Legacy of Lies '92
Max and Helen '90
Meteor '79
Mistress '91
The Neon Empire '89
North by Northwest '59
Paint It Black '89
Pork Chop Hill '59
Real Bullets '90
The Return '80
Run If You Can '87
Sliver '93
Space: 1999—Alien Attack '79
Strange Shadows in an Empty Room '76
Sweet Revenge '87
They Call Me Mr. Tibbs! '70
A Town Called Hell '72
Tucker: The Man and His Dream '88
12:01 '93

Dinsdale Landen
Anatomy of Terror '74
Digby, the Biggest Dog in the World '73
Morons from Outer Space '85

David Lander
Betrayal of the Dove '92
Funland '89
The Man with One Red Shoe '85
Steel and Lace '90
The Tell-Tale Heart '62

Audrey Landers
California Casanova '89
A Chorus Line '85
Deadly Twins '85
Getting Even '86
Ghost Writer '89
Tennessee Stallion '78
Underground Aces '80

Harry Landers
The C-Man '49
The Gallant Hours '60
The Indian Fighter '55
Phantom from Space '53

Judy Landers
Armed and Dangerous '86
The Black Marble '79
Club Fed '90
Deadly Twins '85
The Divine Enforcer '91
Dr. Alien '88
Doin' Time '85
Ghost Writer '89
Hellhole '85
Stewardess School '86
Tennessee Stallion '78
The Yum-Yum Girls '78

Steve Landesburg
Blade '72
Final Notice '89
Leader of the Band '87
Mission of the Shark '91

Janet Landgard
Land Raiders '69
Swimmer '68

Gudrun Landgrebe
The Berlin Affair '85
Colonel Redl '84
A Woman in Flames '84

Karl Landgren
The Black Cobra '87
Urban Warriors '75

Sonny Landham
Best of the Best 2 '93
The Dirty Dozen: The Next Mission '85
Fleshburn '84
48 Hrs. '82
Lock Up '89
Predator '87
Taxi Dancers '93
Three Days to a Kill '91

Elissa Landi
After the Thin Man '36
Corregidor '43
The Count of Monte Cristo '34

Marla Landi
Across the Bridge '57
First Man into Space '59

Sal Landi
Back to Back '90
Savage Streets '83

D. W. Landingham
Karate Cop '93
Omega Cop '90

Carole Landis
Cowboys from Texas '39
Dance Hall '41
Daredevils of the Red Circle '39
The Devil Thumbs a Ride/ Having Wonderful Crime '47
Having Wonderful Crime '45
I Wake Up Screaming '41
Moon Over Miami '41
One Million B.C. '40
Orchestra Wives '42
Out of the Blue '47
Road Show '41
Three Texas Steers '39
Topper Returns '41
Wintertime '43

Cullen Landis
The Broken Mask '28
Soul of the Beast '23

Jessie Royce Landis
Bon Voyage! '62
Boy's Night Out '62
Gidget Goes to Rome '63
Goodbye Again '61
It Happens Every Spring '49
My Man Godfrey '57
North by Northwest '59
The Swan '56
To Catch a Thief '55

Laurene Landon
The Ambulance '90
America 3000 '86
Hundra '85
I, the Jury '82
It's Alive 3: Island of the Alive '87
Maniac Cop '88
Maniac Cop 2 '90
Wicked Stepmother '89
Yellow Hair & the Fortress of Gold '84

Michael Landon
The Errand Boy '61
Fight for the Title '57
God's Little Acre '58
High School Confidential '58
I Was a Teenage Werewolf '57
Little House on the Prairie '74
The Loneliest Runner '76
Ride the Wind '66
Sam's Son '84

Karen Landry
Heartbreak Hotel '88
Patti Rocks '88
The Personals '83

David Landsberg
Detective School Dropouts '85
Dutch Treat '86

Valerie Landsburg
Thank God It's Friday '78
The Triangle Factory Fire Scandal '79

Abbe Lane
Americano '55
Twilight Zone: The Movie '83

Allan "Rocky" Lane
Annabel Takes a Tour/Maid's Night Out '38
Bandit King of Texas '49
El Paso Stampede '53
Homesteaders of Paradise Valley '47
Maid's Night Out '38
Marshal of Cedar Rock '53
Night Nurse '31
Night Riders of Montana '50
Oklahoma Badlands '48
Perils of the Darkest Jungle '44
Santa Fe Uprising '46
Silver City Kid '45
Stagecoach to Denver '46
The Topeka Terror '45
Trail of Robin Hood '50
Vigilantes of Boom Town '46
Western Double Feature 4: Rogers & Evans '40s
Wild Frontier '48

Charles Lane
The Affairs of Dobie Gillis '53
Billie '65
Borderline '50
But Not for Me '59
Call Northside 777 '48
Dr. Jekyll and Mr. Hyde '20
The Invisible Woman '40
It's a Date '40
Little Dragons '80
The Mating Game '59
Mr. Smith Goes to Washington '39
Murphy's Romance '85
Posse '93
Romola '25
Sadie Thompson '28
Strange Invaders '83
Twentieth Century '34
The White Sister '23

Diane Lane
Big Town '87
Chaplin '92
Child Bride of Short Creek '81

The Cotton Club '84
Descending Angel '90
Fallen Angels 1 '93
Indian Summer '93
Knight Moves '93
Lady Beware '87
A Little Romance '79
Lonesome Dove '89
Miss All-American Beauty '82
My New Gun '92
National Lampoon Goes to the Movies '81
The Outsiders '83
Priceless Beauty '90
Rumble Fish '83
Six Pack '82
Streets of Fire '84
Touched by Love '80
Vital Signs '90

Kent Lane
Changes '69
Defiant '70

Lola Lane
Buckskin Frontier '43
Burn 'Em Up Barnes '34
Deadline at Dawn '46
Death from a Distance '36
Four Daughters '38
Marked Woman '37
Woman Condemned '33

Lupino Lane
The Deputy Drummer '35
Isn't Life Wonderful '24

Mike Lane
Code Name: Zebra '84
Curse of the Crystal Eye '93
The Harder They Fall '56
A Name for Evil '70
Zebra Force '76

Nathan Lane
Frankie and Johnny '91
He Said, She Said '91
Ironweed '87
Life with Mikey '93

Nora Lane
The Outlaw Deputy '35
Western Frontier '35

Priscilla Lane
Arsenic and Old Lace '44
Four Daughters '38
The Roaring Twenties '39
Saboteur '42
Silver Queen '42

Richard Lane
Arabian Nights '42
Bullfighters '45
Day the Bookies Wept '39
It Could Happen to You '39
The Jackie Robinson Story '50
Mr. Winkle Goes to War '44
Ride 'Em Cowboy '42
Sunny '41
Take Me Out to the Ball Game '49

Rosemary Lane
Four Daughters '38
Harvest Melody '43
Oklahoma Kid '39

Chang Wu Lang
Image of Bruce Lee '70s
Shadow Killers '80

June Lang
Bonnie Scotland '35
Captain January '36
Wee Willie Winkie '37

k.d. lang
Pee Wee's Playhouse Christmas Special '88
Salmonberries '91

Perry Lang
Body & Soul '81
Eight Men Out '88
Girls Next Door '79
Great Ride '78
Greedy Terror '78
Jocks '87
Little Vegas '91
Mortuary Academy '91
O'Hara's Wife '82
A Rumor of War '80
Sahara '83
Spring Break '83

Tag: The Assassination Game '82

Stephen Lang
Another You '91
Band of the Hand '86
Crime Story: The Complete Saga '86
Death of a Salesman '86
Finish Line '89
Gettysburg '93
Guilty as Sin '93
The Hard Way '91
Last Exit to Brooklyn '90
Manhunter '86
Project X '87
Tombstone '93

Glenn Langan
The Amazing Colossal Man '57
Big Chase '54
Hangman's Knot '52
The Snake Pit '48
Treasure of Monte Cristo '50

Harry Langdon
All Night Long/Smile Please '24
Baby Face Harry Langdon '26
Comedy Festival #3 '30s
Ella Cinders '26
Golden Age of Comedy '58
His First Flame '26
House of Errors '42
Mad About Money '30
Silent Laugh Makers, No. 3 '19
Story of William S. Hart/Sad Clowns '20s
Strong Man '26
Two Reelers: Comedy Classics 10 '31
When Comedy was King '59

Lillian Langdon
The Americano '17
Flirting with Fate '16
His Majesty, the American '19
The Lamb '15
Shifting Sands '18

Sue Ane Langdon
The Cheyenne Social Club '70
The Evictors '79
Frankie and Johnny '65
A Guide for the Married Man '67
The Rounders '65
Roustabout '64
Zapped! '82

Carl Lange
Carpet of Horror '64
Creature with the Blue Hand '70
The Torture Chamber of Dr. Sadism '69

Hope Lange
Beulah Land '80
Blue Velvet '86
Bus Stop '56
Cooperstown '93
Death Wish '74
Fer-De-Lance '74
Ford: The Man & the Machine '87
I Am the Cheese '83
I Love You...Goodbye '73
The Love Bug '68
A Nightmare on Elm Street 2: Freddy's Revenge '85
Peyton Place '57
Pleasure Palace '80
Pocketful of Miracles '61
The Prodigal '83
Tune in Tomorrow '90
Wild in the Country '61
The Young Lions '58

Jessica Lange
All That Jazz '79
Cape Fear '91
Cat on a Hot Tin Roof '84
Country '84
Crimes of the Heart '86
Everybody's All American '88
Far North '88
Frances '82
How to Beat the High Cost of Living '80
King Kong '76
Men Don't Leave '89
Music Box '89
Night and the City '92
O Pioneers! '91

Lange ►cont.

The Postman Always Rings
  Twice '81
Sweet Dreams '85
Tootsie '82
Ted Lange
Glitch! '88
The Love Boat '70s
Perfume '91
Terminal Exposure '89
Jack Langedijk
Blind Fear '89
Evil Judgement '85
Frank Langella
And God Created Woman '88
Body of Evidence '92
Brainscan '94
Dave '93
The Deadly Trap '71
Diary of a Mad Housewife '70
Dracula '79
1492: Conquest of Paradise '92
Kurt Vonnegut's Monkey
  House '90s
Masters of the Universe '87
The Men's Club '86
Sphinx '81
Those Lips, Those Eyes '80
True Identity '91
Twelve Chairs '70
Sarah Langenfeld
The Act '82
Bloodlink '86
Gold Raiders '84
**Heather
Langenkamp**
Nickel Mountain '85
A Nightmare on Elm Street '84
A Nightmare on Elm Street 3:
  Dream Warriors '87
Shocker '89
Frances Langford
Born to Dance '36
Deputy Marshall '50
Dixie Jamboree '44
Dreaming Out Loud '40
Girl Rush '44
Too Many Girls '40
Yankee Doodle Dandy '42
Lisa Langlois
Blood Relatives '77
Deadly Eyes '82
Joy of Sex '84
The Man Who Wasn't There '83
Mindfield '89
The Nest '88
Truth or Die '86
Margaret Langrick
American Boyfriends '89
Boxcar Blues '90
Cold Comfort '90
Harry and the Hendersons '87
My American Cousin '85
Thunderground '89
Murray Langston
Digging Up Business '91
Night Patrol '85
Two Top Bananas '87
Uncensored '85
Up Your Alley '89
Wishful Thinking '92
Jeff Langton
Final Impact '91
Maximum Force '92
Paul Langton
The Big Knife '55
The Cosmic Man '59
The Incredible Shrinking Man
  '57
It! The Terror from Beyond
  Space '58
The Snow Creature '54
Thirty Seconds Over Tokyo '44
Kim Lankford
Cameron's Closet '89
Malibu Beach '78
Octagon '80
Frank Lanning
The Lone Defender '32
Stand and Deliver '28
The Unknown '27

Victor Lanoux
Cousin, Cousine '76
Dog Day '83
The French Detective '75
Investigation '79
Louisiana '87
Make Room for Tomorrow '81
National Lampoon's European
  Vacation '85
One Wild Moment '78
Pardon Mon Affaire '76
Scene of the Crime '87
Angela Lansbury
All Fall Down '62
The Amorous Adventures of
  Moll Flanders '65
Bedknobs and Broomsticks '71
Blue Hawaii '61
Breath of Scandal '60
The Company of Wolves '85
Court Jester '56
Death on the Nile '78
The First Olympics: Athens
  1896 '84
Gaslight '44
The Greatest Story Ever Told
  '65
Harlow '65
The Harvey Girls '46
The Indiscreet Mrs. Jarvis
The Lady Vanishes '79
A Lawless Street '55
Little Gloria...Happy at Last '84
The Long, Hot Summer '58
The Manchurian Candidate '62
Mutiny '52
National Velvet '44
Picture of Dorian Gray '45
The Pirates of Penzance '83
The Private Affairs of Bel Ami
  '47
Rage of Angels: The Story
  Continues '86
The Reluctant Debutante '58
Samson and Delilah '50
The Shell Seekers '89
Something for Everyone '70
State of the Union '48
Sweeney Todd: The Demon
  Barber of Fleet Street '84
The Three Musketeers '48
Till the Clouds Roll By/A Star Is
  Born '46
The World of Henry Orient '64
Joi Lansing
Atomic Submarine '59
Big Foot '72
The Brave One '56
Easter Parade '48
The French Line '54
Hillbillies in a Haunted House
  '67
A Hole in the Head '59
Julia Misbehaves '48
The Merry Widow '52
Neptune's Daughter '49
Pier 23 '51
Singin' in the Rain '52
Son of Sinbad '55
Touch of Evil '58
Two Tickets to Broadway '51
Robert Lansing
Bittersweet Love '76
Empire of the Ants '77
The Equalizer: Memories of
  Manon '88
The 4D Man '59
The Grissom Gang '71
Island Claw '80
Namu, the Killer Whale '66
The Nest '88
Scalpel '76
S*H*E '79
Talion '66
The Widow '76
Mario Lanza
Because You're Mine '52
For the First Time '59
The Great Caruso '51
The Seven Hills of Rome '58
That Midnight Kiss '49
The Toast of New Orleans '50
Anthony LaPaglia
Betsy's Wedding '90
Black Magic '92
The Client '94
Criminal Justice '90

He Said, She Said '91
Innocent Blood '92
Keeper of the City '92
Mortal Sins '90
Nitti: The Enforcer '88
One Good Cop '91
So I Married an Axe Murderer
  '93
29th Street '91
Whispers in the Dark '92
Francine Lapensee
Born Killer '89
Demon Wind '90
Hollywood's New Blood '88
Peter Lapis
Death Blow '87
Undeclared War '91
Victor Laplace
Letters from the Park '88
Under the Earth '86
Jane Lapotaire
The Asphyx '72
The Dark Angel '91
Eureka! '81
Murder by Moonlight '91
Piaf '81
John Larch
Bad Ronald '74
Dirty Harry '71
Future Cop '76
Hail, Hero! '69
Play Misty for Me '71
Santee '73
Veronica Lario
Sotto, Sotto '85
Unsane '82
Bryan Larkin
Born on the Fourth of July '89
She-Devil '89
Mary Laroche
Gidget '59
Psychomania '73
Pierre Larquey
Le Corbeau '43
Topaze '51
John Larroquette
Blind Date '87
Cat People '82
Choose Me '84
Convicted '86
Green Ice '81
Heart Beat '80
Madhouse '90
Meatballs 2 '84
Second Sight '89
Star Trek 3: The Search for
  Spock '84
Stripes '81
Summer Rental '85
Tune in Tomorrow '90
Twilight Zone: The Movie '83
Erik Larsen
Trap on Cougar Mountain '72
Young & Free '78
Ham Larsen
Further Adventures of the
  Wilderness Family, Part 2
  '77
Mountain Family Robinson '79
Keith Larsen
Flat Top '52
Mission Batangas '69
Trap on Cougar Mountain '72
Whitewater Sam '78
Bobby Larson
Leather Burners '43
The Underdog '43
Darrell Larson
City Limits '85
The Girls of Huntington House
  '73
Hero '92
The Last Innocent Man '87
Mike's Murder '84
Murder Ordained '87
Red, White & Busted '75
The Student Nurses '70
Eric Larson
Demon Wind '90
'68 '87
The Uninvited '88

Jack Larson
James Dean: The First
  American Teenager '76
Stamp Day for Superman '53
Eva LaRue
The Barbarians '87
Crash and Burn '90
Frank LaRue
Boothill Brigade '37
Border Bandits '46
Devil Riders '44
Gun Lords of Stirrup Basin '37
A Lawman Is Born '37
Lightning Bill Crandall '37
Mesquite Buckaroo '39
Overland Stage Raiders '38
Range Renegades '48
Red River Valley '36
Riders of Pasco Basin '40
Sidewalks of New York '31
Songs and Bullets '38
The Throwback '35
Trigger Pals '39
Jack LaRue
Captains Courageous '37
Dancing Pirate '36
A Farewell to Arms '32
The Fighting Rookie '34
Follow the Leader '44
Gentleman from Dixie '41
Headline Woman '35
The Kennel Murder Case '33
The Law Rides Again '43
Ride the Man Down '53
The Road to Utopia '46
To the Last Man '33
X Marks the Spot '42
Yellow Cargo '36
The Young Nurses '73
Lash LaRue
The Black Lash '52
Border Feud '47
The Caravan Trail '46
Cheyenne Takes Over '47
The Dark Power '85
Fighting Vigilantes '47
Gangs, Inc. '41
Ghost Town Renegades '47
King of the Bullwhip '51
Law of the Lash '47
Master Key '44
Outlaw Country '49
Pair of Aces '90
Return of the Lash '47
Song of Old Wyoming '45
Stage to Mesa City '48
Thundering Trail '51
Western Double Feature 9:
  LaRue & Beery '40s
Wild West '46
Eriq LaSalle
Coming to America '88
Jacob's Ladder '90
Martin LaSalle
La Mansion de la Locura '87
Pickpocket '59
Dieter Laser
The Lost Honor of Katharina
  Blum '77
The Man Inside '90
Kathleen Lasky
Lethal Lolita—Amy Fisher: My
  Story '92
Love & Murder '91
Dagmar Lassander
The Black Cat '81
Dandelions '74
Flatfoot '78
Hatchet for the Honeymoon '70
S.A.S. San Salvador '84
Louise Lasser
Bananas '71
Blood Rage '87
Crimewave '85
Everything You Always Wanted
  to Know About Sex (But
  Were Afraid to Ask) '72
For Ladies Only '81
Frankenhooker '90
Just Me & You '78
Modern Love '90
The Night We Never Met '93
Rude Awakening '89
Sing '89
Slither '73

Surrender '87
Take the Money and Run '69
Sydney Lassick
The Art of Dying '90
The Billion Dollar Hobo '78
Committed '91
Cool As Ice '91
Deep Cover '92
Monaco Forever '83
Money to Burn '94
Night Patrol '85
Out on Bail '89
Shakes the Clown '92
Silent Madness '84
Smooth Talker '90
Sonny Boy '87
Tale of Two Sisters '89
The Unseen '80
Lassie
Lassie: Adventures of Neeka
  '68
Lassie from Lancashire '38
The Painted Hills '51
Lyle Latelle
Dick Tracy, Detective '45
Dick Tracy, Detective/The
  Corpse Vanishes '42
Dick Tracy Double Feature #1
  '45
Dick Tracy Meets Gruesome
  '47
Dick Tracy's Dilemma '47
Anne Latham
Mind Warp '72
Thieves Like Us '74
Louise Latham
Adam at 6 A.M. '70
Crazy from the Heart '91
Dying Room Only '73
Lois Gibbs and the Love Canal
  '82
Love Field '91
Mass Appeal '84
Paradise '91
Pray TV '82
Toughlove '85
White Lightning '73
Hugh Latimer
The Cosmic Monsters '58
Rogue's Yarn '56
Someone at the Door '50
Frank Latimore
Patton '70
Shock! '46
13 Rue Madeleine '46
Ney Latorraca
The Dolphin '87
The Fable of the Beautiful
  Pigeon Fancier '88
Opera do Malandro '87
Matt Lattanzi
Catch Me...If You Can '89
Diving In '90
My Tutor '82
Rich and Famous '81
Roxanne '87
Chester Lauck
The Bashful Bachelor '42
Dreaming Out Loud '40
Philippe Laudenbach
Confidentially Yours '83
Four Adventures of Reinette
  and Mirabelle '89
John Laughlin
Crimes of Passion '84
Footloose '84
The Hills Have Eyes, Part 2 '84
Memphis '91
Midnight Crossing '87
Motorama '91
Sexual Malice '93
Space Rage '86
Tom Laughlin
Billy Jack '71
Born Losers '67
South Pacific '58
Tall Story '60
The Trial of Billy Jack '74
Charles Laughton
Abbott and Costello Meet
  Captain Kidd '52
Advise and Consent '62
Arch of Triumph '48

The Barretts of Wimpole Street '34
Beachcomber '38
The Best of Abbott & Costello Live '54
The Canterville Ghost '44
Captain Kidd '45
Epic That Never Was '65
Forever and a Day '43
Hobson's Choice '53
The Hunchback of Notre Dame '39
Island of Lost Souls '32
Jamaica Inn '39
Les Miserables '35
Man on the Eiffel Tower '48
Mutiny on the Bounty '35
The Old Dark House '32
The Paradine Case '47
The Private Life of Henry VIII '33
Rembrandt '36
The Ruggles of Red Gap '35
Salome '53
Sidewalks of London '40
Spartacus '60
They Knew What They Wanted '40
This Land is Mine '43
The Tuttles of Tahiti '42
Witness for the Prosecution '57
Young Bess '53

S. John Launer
Crime of Passion '57
I Was a Teenage Werewolf '57

Cyndi Lauper
Life with Mikey '93
Vibes '88

Matthew Laurance
Eddie and the Cruisers '83
Eddie and the Cruisers 2: Eddie Lives! '89

Mitchell Laurance
The Hand that Rocks the Cradle '92
The Portrait '93

Carole Laure
Get Out Your Handkerchiefs '78
Heartbreakers '84
Maria Chapdelaine '84
Strange Shadows in an Empty Room '76
Surrogate '88
Sweet Country '87
Sweet Movie '75
Victory '81

Stan Laurel
Air Raid Wardens '43
Bellhop/The Noon Whistle '22
Block-heads '36
Bohemian Girl '36
Bonnie Scotland '35
Bullfighters '45
A Chump at Oxford '40
Days of Thrills and Laughter '61
The Devil's Brother '33
A Few Moments with Buster Keaton and Laurel and Hardy '63
The Flying Deuces '39
Golden Age of Comedy '58
Great Guns '41
Hollywood Clowns '85
Hollywood Party '34
Laurel & Hardy and the Family '33
Laurel & Hardy: Another Fine Mess '30
Laurel & Hardy: At Work '30
Laurel & Hardy: Be Big '31
Laurel & Hardy: Below Zero '30
Laurel & Hardy: Berth Marks '29
Laurel & Hardy: Blotto '30
Laurel & Hardy: Brats '30
Laurel & Hardy: Chickens Come Home '31
Laurel & Hardy Comedy Classics, Vol. 1 '33
Laurel & Hardy Comedy Classics, Vol. 2 '30
Laurel & Hardy Comedy Classics, Vol. 3 '34
Laurel & Hardy Comedy Classics, Vol. 4 '32

Laurel & Hardy Comedy Classics, Vol. 5 '31
Laurel & Hardy Comedy Classics, Vol. 6 '35
Laurel & Hardy Comedy Classics, Vol. 7 '30s
Laurel & Hardy Comedy Classics, Vol. 8 '30s
Laurel & Hardy Comedy Classics, Vol. 9 '30s
Laurel & Hardy: Hog Wild '30
Laurel & Hardy: Laughing Gravy '31
Laurel & Hardy: Men O'War '29
Laurel & Hardy: Night Owls '30
Laurel & Hardy On the Lam '30
Laurel & Hardy: Perfect Day '29
Laurel & Hardy Special
Laurel & Hardy: Stan "Helps" Ollie '33
March of the Wooden Soldiers '34
Music Box/Helpmates '32
Nothing But Trouble '44
Our Relations '36
Pack Up Your Troubles '32
Pardon Us '31
Pick a Star '37
Saps at Sea '40
Silent Laugh Makers, No. 1 '15
Slapstick '30s
Sons of the Desert '33
Stan Without Ollie, Vol. 1 '23
Stan Without Ollie, Vol. 2 '23
Stan Without Ollie, Vol. 3 '23
Stan Without Ollie, Vol. 4 '25
Swiss Miss '38
Utopia '51
Way Out West '37

Rod Lauren
The Crawling Hand '63
Once Before I Die '65

Ashley Laurence
Hellbound: Hellraiser 2 '88
Hellraiser '87
Hellraiser 3: Hell on Earth '92
One Last Run '89

Michael Laurence
A Conspiracy of Love '87
Syngenor '90

James Laurenson
Assault '70
Codename Kyril '91
Heartbreakers '84
Rainbow Drive '90
Rude Awakening '81

Remy Laurent
The Gift '82
La Cage aux Folles '79

Dan Lauria
In the Line of Duty: Ambush in Waco '93
Stakeout '87

Carol Laurie
Dirty Dishes '82
Naked Massacre '80s

Hugh Laurie
Peter's Friends '92
Strapless '90

John Laurie
Bonnie Prince Charlie '48
Dangerous Moonlight '41
Devil Girl from Mars '54
Edge of the World '37
Encore '52
Hamlet '48
Juno and the Paycock '30
Man of Evil '48
Mine Own Executioner '47
No Trace '50
The 39 Steps '35
Trio '50
The World Owes Me a Living '34

Piper Laurie
Appointment with Death '88
Boss' Son '79
Carrie '76
Children of a Lesser God '86
Dangerous Mission '54
Dario Argento's Trauma '93
Days of Wine and Roses '58
Distortions '87
Dream a Little Dream '89
Francis Goes to the Races '51
The Hustler '61

Mae West '84
Other People's Money '91
Return to Oz '85
Rich in Love '93
Rising Son '90
Ruby '77
Skag '79
Son of Ali Baba '52
Storyville '92
The Thorn Birds '83
Tiger Warsaw '87
Tim '79
Toughlove '85
Twin Peaks '90
Until They Sail '57
Wrestling Ernest Hemingway '93

Ed Lauter
The Amateur '82
Big Score '83
Breakheart Pass '76
Cartier Affair '84
The Chicken Chronicles '77
Class of '63 '73
Cujo '83
Death Hunt '81
Death Wish 3 '85
Eureka! '81
Extreme Justice '93
Family Plot '76
Finders Keepers '84
Girls Just Want to Have Fun '85
Goodbye, Miss 4th of July '88
In the Custody of Strangers '82
King Kong '76
Lassiter '84
The Last Days of Patton '86
The Longest Yard '74
Love's Savage Fury '79
Magic '78
Murder So Sweet '93
Nickel Mountain '85
Rage '72
Revenge of the Nerds 2: Nerds in Paradise '87
The Rocketeer '91
School Ties '92
Stephen King's Golden Years '91
Timerider '83
Under Investigation '93
Youngblood '86
Yuri Nosenko, KGB '86

Harry Lauter
Bandit King of Texas '49
Trader Tom of the China Seas '54

Kathrin Lautner
Final Impact '91
The Last Riders '90
Night of the Wilding '90
Spirits '90

Lucille LaVerne
Hearts of Humanity '32
Kentucky Kernels '34
The White Rose '23

Daliah Lavi
Lord Jim '65
The Return of Dr. Mabuse '61
Spy with a Cold Nose '66
Those Fantastic Flying Fools '67
Two Weeks in Another Town '62

Linda Lavin
The $5.20 an Hour Dream '80
Maricela '88
A Matter of Life and Death '81
See You in the Morning '89

John Phillip Law
African Rage '78
Alienator '89
American Commandos '84
Attack Force Z '84
Barbarella '68
The Cassandra Crossing '76
Cold Heat '90
Danger: Diabolik '68
Golden Voyage of Sinbad '73
L.A. Bad '85
The Last Movie '71
The Love Machine '71
Moon in Scorpio '86
Night Train to Terror '84
No Time to Die '84
Overthrow '82

The Russians are Coming, the Russians are Coming '66
Space Mutiny '88
Spiral Staircase '75
Tarzan, the Ape Man '81
Thunder Warrior 3 '88

Phyllida Law
Much Ado About Nothing '93
Peter's Friends '92

Peter Lawford
Advise and Consent '62
Angel's Brigade '79
April Fools '69
Body & Soul '81
Buona Sera, Mrs. Campbell '68
The Canterville Ghost '44
Easter Parade '48
Exodus '60
Fantasy Island '76
Good News '47
Harlow '65
It Happened in Brooklyn '47
It Should Happen to You '54
Julia Misbehaves '48
Little Women '49
The Longest Day '62
A Man Called Adam '66
Mrs. Miniver '42
Mysterious Island of Beautiful Women '79
Never So Few '59
Ocean's 11 '60
On an Island with You '48
The Oscar '66
Picture of Dorian Gray '45
Rosebud '75
Royal Wedding '51
Son of Lassie '45
They Only Kill Their Masters '72
Togetherness '70
The White Cliffs of Dover '44

Stephanie Lawlor
Cherry Hill High '76
Hot T-Shirts '79

Barbara Lawrence
Kronos '57
A Letter to Three Wives '49
Oklahoma! '55
The Street with No Name '48

Bruno Lawrence
The Bridge to Nowhere '86
The Efficiency Expert '92
Grievous Bodily Harm '89
Heart of the Stag '84
An Indecent Obsession '85
The Quiet Earth '85
Rikky and Pete '88
Smash Palace '82
Treasure of the Yankee Zephyr '83
Utu '83

Cary Lawrence
Canvas: The Fine Art of Crime '92
The Dance Goes On '92

Delphi Lawrence
Frozen Alive '64
Murder on Approval '56
Three Steps to Murder '53

Gertrude Lawrence
Men are not Gods '37
Mimi '35
Rembrandt '36

Joey Lawrence
Chains of Gold '92
Pulse '88
Wait Till Your Mother Gets Home '83

John Lawrence
The Asphyx '72
They Live '88

Marc Lawrence
Abbott and Costello in the Foreign Legion '50
The Asphalt Jungle '50
The Black Hand '50
Cataclysm '81
Charlie Chan at the Wax Museum '40
Cloak and Dagger '46
Dream No Evil '75
Frasier the Sensuous Lion '73
Goin' Coconuts '78
I Am the Law '38

Jigsaw '49
King of Kong Island '78
The Man with the Golden Gun '74
The Monster and the Girl '41
'Neath Brooklyn Bridge '42
Night Train to Terror '84
Pigs '73
Ruby '92
Vengeance '37

Martin Lawrence
Boomerang '92
House Party '90
House Party 2: The Pajama Jam '91
Talkin' Dirty After Dark '91
You So Crazy '94

Michael Lawrence
Elizabeth of Ladymead '48
Othello '55

Peter Lee Lawrence
Garringo '69
Manos Torpes '65
Special Forces '68
They Paid with Bullets: Chicago 1929 '70s

Rosina Lawrence
Charlie Chan's Secret '35
General Spanky '36
Pick a Star '37
Way Out West '37

Scott Lawrence
God's Bloody Acre '75
Laurel Avenue '93
Timecop '94

Stephanie Lawrence
Buster '88
The Phantom of the Opera '89

Steve Lawrence
Express to Terror '79
The Lonely Guy '84

Denis Lawson
Local Hero '83
Return of the Jedi '83

Leigh Lawson
Battling for Baby '92
Brother Sun, Sister Moon '73
Charlie Boy '81
Fire and Sword '82
It's Not the Size That Counts '74
Love Among the Ruins '75
Madame Sousatzka '88
Madhouse Mansion '74
O Pioneers! '91
Sword of the Valiant '83
Tears in the Rain '88
Tess '80

Priscilla Lawson
Flash Gordon: Rocketship '36
Girl of the Golden West '38

Richard Lawson
Fist '79
The Forgotten '89
Foxstyle '73
Johnnie Gibson F.B.I. '87
Poltergeist '82
Scream Blacula Scream '73
Streets of Fire '84

Wilfred Lawson
Man of Evil '48
The Night Has Eyes '42
The Prisoner '55
Pygmalion '38
The Terror '38
Tower of Terror '42

Frank Lawton
Cavalcade '33
David Copperfield '35
Devil Doll '36
The Invisible Ray '36
The Mill on the Floss '37
A Night to Remember '58
The Secret Four '40
Skin Game '31
The Winslow Boy '48

Evelyn Laye
Say Hello to Yesterday '71
Theatre of Death '67

John Lazar
Deathstalker 2: Duel of the Titans '87
Every Girl Should Have One '78

Norma Lazarendo
El Cristo de los Milagros '80s
La Corona de un Campeon '87
Night of the Bloody Apes '68
Para Servir a Usted '87

George Lazenby
Black Eliminator '70s
Eyes of the Beholder '92
Happy Anniversary 007: 25 Years of James Bond '87
Hell Hunters '87
Kentucky Fried Movie '77
Kill Factor
Never Too Young to Die '86
On Her Majesty's Secret Service '69
Saint Jack '79

Gene Le Brock
Beyond Darkness '92
Fortress of Amerikka '89
Metamorphosis '90

Kelly Le Brock
Betrayal of the Dove '92
Hard to Kill '89
Weird Science '85
The Woman in Red '84

Bruce Le
Bruce Le's Greatest Revenge '80
Bruce the Superhero '79
Bruce's Deadly Fingers '80
Bruce's Fists of Vengeance '84
Clones of Bruce Lee '80
The Dragon Returns
My Name Called Bruce '80s

Michael Le Clair
Anatomy of a Seduction '79
Leave 'Em Laughing '81

John Le Mesurier
The Adventures of Sherlock Holmes' Smarter Brother '78
The Baby and the Battleship '56
Brideshead Revisited '81
Brothers in Law '57
Dead Lucky '60
Jabberwocky '77
Jack the Ripper '60
A Married Man '84

Ron Lea
Clearcut '92
The Neighbor '93
The Phone Call '89

Tracy Lea
Desperate Teenage Lovedolls '84
Letter to Brezhnev '86

Britt Leach
Baby Boom '87
The Believers '87

Rosemary Leach
The Charmer '89
The Children '90
D.P. '85
Ghost in the Noonday Sun '74
The Hawk '93
A Room with a View '86
The Seventeenth Bride '84
That'll Be the Day '73
Turtle Diary '86

Cloris Leachman
Acorn People '82
The Beverly Hillbillies '93
Brand New Life '72
Butch Cassidy and the Sundance Kid '69
Charley and the Angel '73
Crazy Mama '75
Daisy Miller '74
Death Scream '75
Death Sentence '74
Dillinger '73
Dixie: Changing Habits '85
Dying Room Only '73
Ernie Kovacs: Between the Laughter '84
Fade to Black '93
Fine Things '90
Foolin' Around '80
Haunts of the Very Rich '72
Herbie Goes Bananas '80
High Anxiety '77
History of the World: Part 1 '81
Kiss Me Deadly '55
The Last Picture Show '71

Long Journey Back '78
Lovers and Other Strangers '70
Miss All-American Beauty '82
Mrs. R's Daughter '79
The North Avenue Irregulars '79
Oldest Living Graduate '82
The People Next Door '70
Prancer '89
Run, Stranger, Run '73
Scavenger Hunt '79
Shadow Play '86
Silent Night, Lonely Night '69
Someone I Touched '75
S.O.S. Titanic '79
The Steagle '71
Texasville '90
Thursday's Game '74
Twigs '84
The Victory '88
Walk Like a Man '87
Willa '79
The Woman Who Willed a Miracle '83
Young Frankenstein '74

Michael Learned
All My Sons '86
A Christmas Without Snow '80
Deadly Business '86
Dragon: The Bruce Lee Story '93
Murder in New Hampshire: The Pamela Smart Story '91
Nurse '80
Power '86
Roots: The Gift '88
Thanksgiving Story '73
The Waltons: A Thanksgiving Story '73
The Widow '76

Denis Leary
Gunmen '93
Judgment Night '93
Natural Born Killers '94
The Ref '93
Who's the Man? '93

Timothy Leary
Fatal Skies '90
Roadside Prophets '92
Shocker '89

Rex Lease
Cavalcade of the West '36
Chinatown After Dark '31
The Clutching Hand '36
Cowboy & the Bandit '35
Custer's Last Stand '36
Cyclone on the Saddle '35
Fast Bullets '44
Fighting Caballero '35
Ghost Rider '35
Gun Cargo '49
Haunted Ranch '43
Heroes of the Alamo '37
Inside Information '34
Lost in Alaska '52
The Man from Gun Town '36
The Monster Walks '32
Pals of the Range '35
People's Choice '46
Riding On '37
Roaring Guns '36
Rough Riding Rangers '35
Sign of the Wolf '30
Sunny Skies '30

Jean-Pierre Leaud
Day for Night '73
The 400 Blows '59
The Joy of Knowledge '65
La Vie de Boheme '93
Last Tango in Paris '73
Love on the Run '78
Masculine Feminine '66
Pierrot le Fou '65
Porcile '69
Stolen Kisses '68
The Testament of Orpheus '59
36 Fillete '88
Two English Girls '72
Weekend '67

Ivan Lebedeff
Goin' to Town '35
Love on the Run '36
Walking Back '26

Ginette LeClerc
The Baker's Wife '33
Le Corbeau '43
Man from Nowhere '37

Friedrich Ledebur
Moby Dick '56
The 27 Day '57

Paul Leder
Five Minutes to Love '63
How to Succeed with Girls '64

Francis Lederer
The Ambassador's Daughter '56
The Bridge of San Luis Rey '44
Diary of a Chambermaid '46
Lisbon '56
One Rainy Afternoon '36
Pandora's Box '28
Return of Dracula '58
Romance in Manhattan '34
Stolen Identity '53
Terror is a Man '59
A Woman of Distinction '50

Suzanne Lederer
Judge Horton and the Scottsboro Boys '76
Women of Valor '86

Fernand Ledoux
La Bete Humaine '38
Les Visiteurs du Soir '42
Pattes Blanches '49
Volpone '39

Anna Lee
Bedlam '45
Commandos Strike at Dawn '43
Eleanor & Franklin '76
Flying Tigers '42
Fort Apache '48
The Ghost and Mrs. Muir '47
The Horse Soldiers '59
How Green was My Valley '41
In Like Flint '67
Jack the Giant Killer '62
King Solomon's Mines '37
The Man Who Lived Again '36
Non-Stop New York '37
O.H.M.S. '37
The Passing of the Third Floor Back '36
The Secret Four '40
The Sound of Music '65
What Ever Happened to Baby Jane? '62

Bernard Lee
Across the Bridge '57
The Adventurers '70
The Blue Lamp '49
The Brain '62
The Courtney Affair '47
The Detective '54
Diamonds are Forever '71
Dr. No '62
Elizabeth of Ladymead '48
The Fallen Idol '49
From Russia with Love '63
The Gift Horse '52
Goldfinger '64
Last Holiday '50
Live and Let Die '73
Long Ago Tomorrow '71
The Man with the Golden Gun '74
Moonraker '79
On Her Majesty's Secret Service '69
Rhodes '36
The Spanish Gardener '57
The Spy Who Loved Me '77
The Terror '38
The Third Man '49
Thunderball '65
Whistle Down the Wind '62
You Only Live Twice '67

Billy Lee
Reg'lar Fellers '41
Wagon Wheels '34

Brandon Lee
The Crow '93
Kung Fu: The Movie '86
Laser Mission '90
Rapid Fire '92
Showdown in Little Tokyo '91

Britton Lee
Ironheart '92
The Power of the Ninjitsu '88

Bruce Lee
Bruce Lee: The Legend '84
Chinese Connection '73

The Deadliest Art: The Best of the Martial Arts Films '90
Enter the Dragon '73
Fists of Fury '73
Game of Death '79
Marlowe '69
Real Bruce Lee '77
Return of the Dragon '73

Canada Lee
Body and Soul '47
Cry, the Beloved Country '51
Lifeboat '44

Carl Lee
The Connection '61
Gordon's War '73
Keeping On '81
Superfly '72

Christopher Lee
Airport '77
Albino '76
Alias John Preston '56
Bear Island '80
Beat Girl '60
The Boy Who Left Home to Find Out About the Shivers '81
Captain America 2: Death Too Soon '79
Captain Horatio Hornblower '51
The Castle of Fu Manchu '68
Castle of the Living Dead '64
Circle of Iron '78
Circus of Fear '67
Corridors of Blood '58
Count Dracula '71
The Creeping Flesh '72
The Crimson Cult '68
Crimson Pirate '52
Curse 3: Blood Sacrifice '90
The Curse of Frankenstein '57
Dark Places '73
Desperate Moves '86
Detonator '93
The Devil's Undead '75
Dr. Terror's House of Horrors '65
Double Vision '92
Dracula & Son '76
Dracula Has Risen from the Grave '68
End of the World '77
An Eye for an Eye '81
The Far Pavilions '84
Five Golden Dragons '67
The Four Musketeers '75
The Girl '86
Goliath Awaits '81
The Gorgon '64
Gremlins 2: The New Batch '90
Hamlet '48
The Hands of Orlac '60
Hannie Caulder '72
Hercules in the Haunted World '64
Horror Express '72
Horror Hotel '60
The Horror of Dracula '58
The Hound of the Baskervilles '59
House of the Long Shadows '82
The House that Dripped Blood '71
Howling 2: Your Sister is a Werewolf '85
Island of the Burning Doomed '67
Jaguar Lives '79
Jocks '87
Journey of Honor '91
Keeper '84
Kiss and Kill '68
The Land of Faraway '87
The Longest Day '62
The Magic Christian '69
The Man with the Golden Gun '74
Many Faces of Sherlock Holmes '86
Moulin Rouge '52
The Mummy '59
Murder Story '89
Night Ambush '57
1941 '79
Nothing But the Night '72
The Oblong Box '69
The Private Life of Sherlock Holmes '70

Return from Witch Mountain '78
Return of Captain Invincible '83
The Return of the Musketeers '89
Rosebud Beach Hotel '85
Safari 3000 '82
The Salamander '82
The Satanic Rites of Dracula '73
The Scars of Dracula '70
Scott of the Antarctic '48
Scream and Scream Again '70
Scream of Fear '61
Serial '80
Shaka Zulu '83
Sherlock Holmes and the Deadly Necklace '62
Sherlock Holmes and the Incident at Victoria Falls '91
The Skull '65
Starship Invasions '77
A Tale of Two Cities '58
Taste the Blood of Dracula '70
Theatre of Death '67
The Three Musketeers '74
To the Devil, A Daughter '76
The Torture Chamber of Dr. Sadism '69
Treasure Island '89
Uncle Was a Vampire '59
Valley of the Eagles '51
The Virgin of Nuremberg '65
The Wicker Man '75

Conan Lee
The Eliminators '86
Gymkata '85

DeWitt Lee
Apache Blood '75
The Legend of Jedediah Carver '70s

Dorothy Lee
Cockeyed Cavaliers '34
Half-Shot at Sunrise '30
Hips, Hips, Hooray '34
Hook, Line and Sinker '30

Dragon Lee
Clones of Bruce Lee '80
The Dragon's Showdown '83
Enter Three Dragons '81

Eric Lee
Out for Blood '93
Ring of Fire '91
Shinobi Ninja '84
Weapons of Death '83

Etta Lee
The Thief of Baghdad '24
The Untamable '23

Gypsy Rose Lee
My Lucky Star '38
The Stripper '63
The Trouble with Angels '66

Hwang Jang Lee
Buddha Assassinator '82
Hell's Wind Staff '82
Instant Kung-Fu Man '84
Snuff-Bottle Connection '82
Story of the Dragon '82

Jason Scott Lee
Back to the Future, Part 2 '89
Dragon: The Bruce Lee Story '93
The Lookalike '90
Map of the Human Heart '93

Jimmy Lee
The Four Hands of Death: Wily Match
The Rebellious Reign

Joanna Lee
The Brain Eaters '58
Making the Grade '84
Sam's Son '84

Joie Lee
Bail Jumper '89
Crooklyn '94
Fathers and Sons '92
Mo' Better Blues '90
School Daze '88

Judy Lee
The Bodyguard '76
Queen Boxer '73

Karen Lee
Eye on the Sparrow '91
Roadhouse 66 '84

Lila Lee
The Adorable Cheat '28
Blood and Sand '22
Blood and Sand/Son of the
  Sheik '26
Champagne for Breakfast '35
Country Gentlemen '36
False Faces '32
Hawthorne of the USA '19
I Can't Escape '34
Male and Female '19
Midnight Girl '25
A Nation Aflame '37
Stand Up and Cheer '34
The Unholy Three '30

Margaret Lee
Casanova '70 '65
Circus of Fear '67
Five for Hell '67
Five Golden Dragons '67
How to Kill 400 Duponts '65
Murder for Sale '70
Rogue '76
Secret Agent Super Dragon '66
Slaughter Hotel '71

Mark Lee
The Everlasting Secret Family
  '88
Gallipoli '81

Mary Lee
Nancy Drew, Reporter '39
Ridin' on a Rainbow '41
Song of Nevada '44

Michele Lee
Broadway Bound '92
Bud and Lou '78
The Comic '69
The Fatal Image '90
How to Succeed in Business
  without Really Trying '67
The Love Bug '68

Pinky Lee
Chasing Those Depression
  Blues '35
Lady of Burlesque '43

Robbie Lee
Big Bad Mama '74
Switchblade Sisters '75

Ruta Lee
Escape from Planet Earth '67
First & Ten '85
First & Ten: The Team Scores
  Again '85
Rooster: Spurs of Death! '83
Sweet Bird of Youth '89

Sheryl Lee
Backbeat '94
Jersey Girl '92
Love, Lies and Murder '91
Red Shoe Diaries 4: Auto
  Erotica '93
Twin Peaks '90
Twin Peaks: Fire Walk with Me
  '92
Wild at Heart '90

Spike Lee
Crooklyn '94
Do the Right Thing '89
Jungle Fever '91
Malcolm X '92
Mo' Better Blues '90
School Daze '88
She's Gotta Have It '86

Stephen Lee
Dolls '87
The Pit & the Pendulum '91
Prehysteria '93
Purple Hearts '84
Steel Fisted Dragon '82

Richard Leech
The Moonraker '58
The Third Key '57

Andrea Leeds
Come and Get It '36
The Goldwyn Follies '38
It Could Happen to You '37
The Real Glory '39
Song of the Trail '36
Stage Door '37
They Shall Have Music '39

Lila Leeds
The Show-Off '46
Wild Weed '49

Phil Leeds
Enemies, a Love Story '89
Frankie and Johnny '91
Ghost '90
Haunting of Harrington House
  '82
He Said, She Said '91

Rene Lefevre
The Crime of Monsieur Lange
  '36
Le Million '31
The Slugger's Wife '85

Eva LeGallienne
The Devil's Disciple '59
Resurrection '80

Lance LeGault
French Quarter '78
Kenny Rogers as the Gambler
  '80
Kidnapped '87
Shadow Force '92

Phoebe Legere
The Toxic Avenger, Part 2 '89
The Toxic Avenger, Part 3: The
  Last Temptation of Toxie '89

James LeGros
Bad Girls '94
Drugstore Cowboy '89
Guncrazy '92
Hollywood Heartbreak '89
Leather Jackets '90
My New Gun '92
Nervous Ticks '93
Phantasm II '88
Point Break '91
Singles '92
Where the Day Takes You '92

John Leguizamo
Carlito's Way '93
Casualties of War '89
Die Hard 2: Die Harder '90
Hangin' with the Homeboys '91
Regarding Henry '91
Street Hunter '90
Super Mario Bros. '93
Whispers in the Dark '92

Carla Lehmann
Cottage to Let '41
Fame is the Spur '47

Frederic Lehne
Amityville 4 '89
Billionaire Boys Club '87
Coward of the County '81
Dream Lover '93
Man's Best Friend '93
This Gun for Hire '90

John Lehne
The Disappearance of Aimee
  '76
Griffin and Phoenix: A Love
  Story '76
A Long Way Home '81
Roboman '75

Fritz Leiber
Cry of the Werewolf '44
Equinox '71
The Story of Louis Pasteur '36

Ron Leibman
The Art of Crime '75
Door to Door '84
The Hot Rock '70
Norma Rae '79
Phar Lap '84
A Question of Guilt '78
Rhinestone '84
Romantic Comedy '83
Seven Hours to Judgment '88
Slaughterhouse Five '72
Up the Academy '80
Where's Poppa? '70
Zorro, the Gay Blade '81

Don Leifert
The Alien Factor '78
Deadly Neighbor '91
Fiend '83
Galaxy Invader '85

Barbara Leigh
Boss '74
Junior Bonner '72
Mistress of the Apes '79
Seven '79
Smile, Jenny, You're Dead '74
The Student Nurses '70

Frank Leigh
American Pluck '25
Below the Deadline '29

Barbara Leigh-Hunt
Frenzy '72
Paper Mask '91

Janet Leigh
Angels in the Outfield '51
Bye, Bye, Birdie '63
The Fog '78
Harper '66
The Hills of Home '48
Holiday Affair '49
Houdini '53
Jet Pilot '57
Little Women '49
The Manchurian Candidate '62
My Sister Eileen '55
The Naked Spur '53
Perfect Furlough '59
Pete Kelly's Blues '55
Prince Valiant '54
Psycho '60
Scaramouche '52
That Forsyte Woman '50
Touch of Evil '58
Two Tickets to Broadway '51
The Vikings '58
Words and Music '48

Jennifer Jason Leigh
Angel City '80
Backdraft '91
The Best Little Girl in the World
  '81
The Big Picture '89
Buried Alive '90
Crooked Hearts '91
Easy Money '83
Eyes of a Stranger '81
Fast Times at Ridgemont High
  '82
Flesh and Blood '85
Girls of the White Orchid '85
Grandview U.S.A. '84
Heart of Midnight '89
Hitcher '86
The Hudsucker Proxy '93
Killing of Randy Webster '81
Last Exit to Brooklyn '90
The Men's Club '86
Miami Blues '90
Rush '91
Short Cuts '93
Single White Female '92
Sister, Sister '87
Undercover '87
Wrong is Right '82

Nelson Leigh
Ma Barker's Killer Brood '60
Texas Masquerade '44

Spencer Leigh
The Last of England '87
Smart Money '88

Steven Leigh
China White '91
Deadly Bet '91
To Be the Best '93

Suzanna Leigh
Boeing Boeing '65
The Fiend '71
Lust for a Vampire '71
Paradise, Hawaiian Style '66

Vivien Leigh
Anna Karenina '48
Caesar and Cleopatra '46
Dark Journey '37
Fire Over England '37
Gone with the Wind '39
Hollywood Outtakes & Rare
  Footage '83
The Making of a Legend:
  "Gone With the Wind" '89
1939, The Movies' Vintage
  Year: Trailers on Tape '89
Roman Spring of Mrs. Stone
  '61
Ship of Fools '65
Sidewalks of London '40
Storm in a Teacup '37
A Streetcar Named Desire '51
That Hamilton Woman '41
21 Days '37
Waterloo Bridge '40

Lillian Leighton
The Jack Knife Man '20
Man from Monterey '33

Peck's Bad Boy '21

Margaret Leighton
The Best Man '64
Bonnie Prince Charlie '48
Carrington, V.C. '54
Choice of Weapons '76
The Elusive Pimpernel '50
From Beyond the Grave '73
The Go-Between '71
The Loved One '65
The Madwoman of Chaillot '69
Under Capricorn '49
Waltz of the Toreadors '62
The Winslow Boy '48
X, Y & Zee '72

Roberta Leighton
Barracuda '78
Covergirl '83

Harald Leipnitz
Fight for Gold '86
River of Evil '64

Frederick Leister
Green Grow the Rushes '51
O.H.M.S. '37
Spellbound '41

Donovan Leitch
And God Created Woman '88
The Blob '88
Cutting Class '89
Dark Horse '92
Gas Food Lodging '92
Glory '89
The In Crowd '88

Paul LeMat
Aloha, Bobby and Rose '74
American Graffiti '73
Blind Witness '89
The Burning Bed '85
Citizens Band '77
Death Valley '81
Easy Wheels '89
Firehouse '72
Grave Secrets '89
Hanoi Hilton '87
Into the Homeland '87
Jimmy the Kid '82
Long Time Gone '86
Melvin and Howard '80
More American Graffiti '79
The Night They Saved
  Christmas '87
On Wings of Eagles '86
P.K. and the Kid '85
Private Investigations '87
Puppet Master '89
Strange Invaders '83
Wishman '83

Harvey Lembeck
Beach Blanket Bingo '65
Beach Party '63
Between Heaven and Hell '56
Bikini Beach '64
How to Stuff a Wild Bikini '65
Love with the Proper Stranger
  '63
Pajama Party '64
Stalag 17 '53

Michael Lembeck
The Boys in Company C '77
Conspiracy: The Trial of the
  Chicago Eight '87
Gorp '80
The In-Laws '79
On the Right Track '81

Chris Lemmon
C.O.D. '83
Corporate Affairs '90
Dad '89
Firehead '90
Going Undercover '88
The Happy Hooker Goes
  Hollywood '80
Just Before Dawn '80
Lena's Holiday '91
Swing Shift '84
That's Life! '86
Thunder in Paradise '93
Weekend Warriors '86

Jack Lemmon
Airport '77 '77
The Apartment '60
April Fools '69
Avanti! '72
Bell, Book and Candle '58
Buddy Buddy '81
The China Syndrome '79

Dad '89
Days of Wine and Roses '62
Fire Down Below '57
For Richer, For Poorer '92
The Fortune Cookie '66
The Front Page '74
Glengarry Glen Ross '92
Good Neighbor Sam '64
Great Race '65
Grumpy Old Men '93
How to Murder Your Wife '64
Irma La Douce '63
It Should Happen to You '54
JFK '91
A Life in the Theater '93
Long Day's Journey into Night
  '88
Luv '67
Macaroni '85
Mass Appeal '84
Missing '82
Mister Roberts '55
The Murder of Mary Phagan
  '87
My Sister Eileen '55
The Odd Couple '68
The Out-of-Towners '70
Phffft! '54
Prisoner of Second Avenue '74
Save the Tiger '73
Short Cuts '93
Some Like It Hot '59
That's Life! '86
Tribute '80
Wackiest Ship in the Army '61

Kasi Lemmons
Candyman '92
Hard Target '93
School Daze '88
Vampire's Kiss '88

Michel Lemoine
Planets Against Us '61
The Sensuous Teenager '70

Genevieve Lemon
The Piano '93
Sweetie '89

Mark Lenard
Noon Sunday '71
Star Trek 3: The Search for
  Spock '84
Star Trek 4: The Voyage Home
  '86
Star Trek 6: The Undiscovered
  Country '91

Harry J. Lennix
Bob Roberts '92
The Five Heartbeats '91
Mo' Money '92

Jarrett Lennon
Servants of Twilight '91
Short Cuts '93

John Lennon
Chuck Berry: Hail! Hail! Rock
  'n' Roll '87
The Compleat Beatles '82
A Hard Day's Night '64
Help! '65
How I Won the War '67
Let It Be '70
The Magic Christian '69
Magical Mystery Tour '67

Annie Lennox
Edward II '92
Revolution '85
The Room '87

Jay Leno
Americathon '79
Collision Course '89
Doctor Duck's Super Secret
  All-Purpose Sauce '85
Silver Bears '78

Jack Lenoir
Breakfast in Paris '81
Once in Paris... '79

Lotte Lenya
From Russia with Love '63
Roman Spring of Mrs. Stone
  '61
Semi-Tough '77
The Threepenny Opera '31

Kay Lenz
Death Wish 4: The Crackdown
  '87
Falling from Grace '92
Fast Walking '82

Lenz ▶cont.

Fear '88
Great Scout & Cathouse
   Thursday '76
Headhunter '89
Hitler's Daughter '90
House '86
Initiation of Sarah '78
Mean Dog Blues '78
Moving Violation '76
Murder by Night '89
Physical Evidence '89
Prisoners of the Lost Universe
   '84
Rich Man, Poor Man '76
Sanctuary of Fear '79
Stripped to Kill '87
White Line Fever '75

Rick Lenz
Cactus Flower '69
Little Dragons '80
Scandalous John '71

Melissa Leo
Always '85
Carolina Skeletons '92
Deadtime Stories '86
Silent Witness '85
Streetwalkin' '85
A Time of Destiny '88

Leon
Above the Rim '94
Bad Attitude '93
Cliffhanger '93
Cool Runnings '93
The Five Heartbeats '91

Loles Leon
Don Juan, My Love '90
Tie Me Up! Tie Me Down! '90

Valerie Leon
Alien Women '69
Never Say Never Again '83
The Spy Who Loved Me '77

Lu Leonard
Circuitry Man '90
A Climate for Killing '91
Princess Academy '87
Shadowzone '90

Queenie Leonard
The Lodger '44
The Narrow Margin '52

Robert Sean Leonard
The Age of Innocence '93
Bluffing It '87
Dead Poets Society '89
Married to It '93
Mr. & Mrs. Bridge '91
Much Ado About Nothing '93
My Best Friend Is a Vampire
   '88
Swing Kids '93

Sheldon Leonard
Abbott & Costello Meet the
   Invisible Man '51
Breakdown '53
Brink's Job '78
Captain Kidd '45
City Without Men '43
The Falcon in Hollywood '44
Force of Evil '49
Gambler's Choice '44
Guys and Dolls '55
Harvest Melody '43
It's a Wonderful Life '46
Open Secret '48
The Road to Lebanon '60
Shep Comes Home '49
Sinbad the Sailor '47
Timber Queen '44
To Have & Have Not '44
Tortilla Flat '42
Week-End in Havana '41
Zombies on Broadway '44

Al Leong
Bill & Ted's Excellent
   Adventure '89
Hard Hunted '92

Chauncey Leopardi
Huck and the King of Hearts
   '93
The Sandlot '93

Philippe Leotard
La Balance '82

La Petite Sirene '80
Two English Girls '72

Ted Leplat
American Kickboxer 1 '91
Emissary '89
The Kirlian Witness '78
Swift Justice '88

Ken Lerner
Fallen Angels 1 '93
Fast Getaway '91
Mother's Boys '94
Relentless '89
Unlawful Entry '92

Michael Lerner
Amos and Andrew '93
Anguish '88
Any Man's Death '90
Barton Fink '91
Blank Check '93
Busting '74
The Candidate '72
The Closer '91
Coast to Coast '80
The Comrades of Summer '92
Eight Men Out '88
The Execution '85
F. Scott Fitzgerald in Hollywood
   '76
Firehouse '72
Hands of a Stranger '87
Harlem Nights '89
Maniac Cop 2 '90
National Lampoon's Class
   Reunion '82
Newsies '92
No Escape '94
Omen 4: The Awakening '91
Outlaw Blues '77
The Postman Always Rings
   Twice '81
Reflections of Murder '74
Rita Hayworth: The Love
   Goddess '83
Strange Invaders '83

Phillippe LeRoy
Alone Against Rome '62
Castle of the Living Dead '64
A Married Woman '65
The Night Porter '74
Quo Vadis '85

Ed LeSaint
Range Feud '31
Texas Bad Man '32

Bethel Leslie
Ironweed '87
Long Day's Journey into Night
   '88

Joan Leslie
Born to Be Bad '50
High Sierra '41
Hollywood Canteen '44
Jubilee Trail '54
Love Affair '39
Rhapsody in Blue '45
Sergeant York '41
The Sky's the Limit '43
Thank Your Lucky Stars '43
This is the Army '43
Yankee Doodle Dandy '42

John Leslie
Dracula Sucks '79
It's Called Murder, Baby '82

Nan Leslie
The Bamboo Saucer '68
Desperate '47
The Devil Thumbs a Ride '47
The Devil Thumbs a Ride/
   Having Wonderful Crime '47
Rim of the Canyon '49
Western Double Feature 14 '52

Mimi Lesseos
The American Angels: Baptism
   of Blood '89
Beyond Fear '93
Final Impact '91
Pushed to the Limit '92

Len Lesser
Dubeat-E-O '84
The Ghost of Fletcher Ridge
   '80s
How to Stuff a Wild Bikini '65
Joy Ride to Nowhere '78

Ben Lessy
The Jackie Robinson Story '50
Pajama Party '64

Bruce Lester
Boy Meets Girl '38
British Intelligence '40
Charade '53
Golden Earrings '47
The Letter '40
Shadows on the Stairs '41

Buddy Lester
Big Mouth '67
Cracking Up '83
The Patsy '64

Jeff Lester
In the Cold of the Night '89
Once a Hero '88

Mark Lester
Black Beauty '71
Melody '71
Oliver! '68
The Prince and the Pauper '78
Redneck '73
Sudden Terror '70
What the Peeper Saw '72
Who Slew Auntie Roo? '71

David Letch
Dark of the Night '85
Death Warmed Up '85

Lori Lethin
Bloody Birthday '80
Brotherly Love '85
The Prey '80
Return to Horror High '87

Al Lettieri
The Deadly Trackers '73
The Don is Dead '73
The Getaway '72
The Godfather '72
The Godfather 1902-1959: The
   Complete Epic '81
McQ '74
Mr. Majestyk '74
Pulp '72

Tony Leung
Hard-Boiled '92
The Lover '92

Lynn Levand
Hellbent '90
Kill or Be Killed '93

Oscar Levant
An American in Paris '51
The Band Wagon '53
The Barkleys of Broadway '49
The Cobweb '55
Dance of Life '29
Humoresque '46
Romance on the High Seas '48

Calvin Levels
Adventures in Babysitting '87
A Christmas Without Snow '80
Johnny Suede '92
Live! From Death Row '92
Point of No Return '93

Sam Levene
Action in the North Atlantic '43
Babe Ruth Story '48
Designing Woman '57
A Dream of Kings '69
Golden Boy '39
I Dood It '43
Mad Miss Manton '38
The Purple Heart '44
Shadow of the Thin Man '41
Shopworn Angel '38
Sweet Smell of Success '57
Three Men on a Horse '36
Whistling in Brooklyn '43

Rachel Levin
Gaby: A True Story '87
White Palace '90

Jean Levine
Hollywood in Trouble '87
The Newlydeads '87

Jerry Levine
Born on the Fourth of July '89
Casual Sex? '88
Iron Eagle '86

Ted Levine
Detonator '93
Fulfillment '89
Ironweed '87
The Last Outlaw '93
Love at Large '89
Nowhere to Run '93
The Silence of the Lambs '91

Emile Levisetti
Bix '90
Sexual Response '92

Steve Levitt
Blue Movies '88
Hunk '87
The Incredible Hulk Returns '88

Eugene Levy
Armed and Dangerous '86
Best of Comic Relief '86
The Best of John Candy on
   SCTV '80s
Billy Crystal: Don't Get Me
   Started '86
Club Paradise '86
Going Berserk '83
The Last Polka '84
National Lampoon's Vacation
   '83
Speed Zone '88
Splash '84
Stay Tuned '92

James Lew
Ninja Turf '86
Private Wars '93

Jose Lewgoy
Earth Entranced '66
Fitzcarraldo '82
Kiss of the Spider Woman '85

Al Lewis
Car 54, Where Are You? '94
Comic Cabby '87
Fright House '89
Married to the Mob '88
Munster's Revenge '81
My Grandpa is a Vampire '92
Way He Was '76

Brittney Lewis
Dream Machine '91
Rubin & Ed '92

Charlotte Lewis
Bare Essentials '91
Dial Help '88
Excessive Force '93
The Golden Child '86
Pirates '86
Sketch Artist '92
Storyville '92
Tripwire '89

Diana Lewis
Andy Hardy Meets Debutante
   '40
Fleshpot on 42nd Street '71
Go West '40
Somewhere I'll Find You '42
Whistling in Dixie '42

Fiona Lewis
Blue Blood '73
Dracula '73
Drum '76
Innerspace '87
Lisztomania '75
Strange Behavior '81
Strange Invaders '83
Stunts '77
Tintorera...Tiger Shark '78
Wanda Nevada '79

Forrest Lewis
Escape from Fort Bravo '53
The Monster of Piedras
   Blancas '57

Geoffrey Lewis
Bronco Billy '80
Catch Me...If You Can '89
Culpepper Cattle Co. '72
Disturbed '90
Double Impact '91
Every Which Way But Loose
   '78
The Great Waldo Pepper '75
Heaven's Gate '81
I, the Jury '82
The Lawnmower Man '92
Lust in the Dust '85
Macon County Line '74
The Man Without a Face '93
Matters of the Heart '90
Maverick '94
Maximum Security '87
Night of the Comet '84
Only the Strong '93
Out of the Dark '88
Pancho Barnes '88
Pink Cadillac '89
Point of No Return '93

The Return of a Man Called
   Horse '76
Return of the Man from
   U.N.C.L.E. '83
September Gun '83
Shoot the Sun Down '81
Smile '75
Stitches '85
Thunderbolt & Lightfoot '74
Tilt '79
When Every Day was the
   Fourth of July '78
White Fang 2: The Myth of the
   White Wolf '94
The Wind and the Lion '75
Wishman '93

George Lewis
The Big Sombrero '49
Federal Operator 99 '45
Indian Paint '64
King of the Bullwhip '51
Outlaws of the Desert '41
Perils of the Darkest Jungle '44
The Sign of Zorro '60
Zorro's Black Whip '44

Gilbert Lewis
Candyman '92
The Kid Who Loved Christmas
   '90
Touched '82

Jenifer Lewis
Corrina, Corrina '94
Renaissance Man '94
What's Love Got to Do With It?
   '93

Jenny Lewis
A Friendship in Vienna '88
Runaway Father '91
Troop Beverly Hills '89
The Wizard '89

Jerry Lewis
Artists and Models '55
At War with the Army '50
The Bellboy '60
Best of Comic Relief '86
Big Mouth '67
Boeing Boeing '65
The Caddy '53
Cinderfella '60
Cookie '89
Cracking Up '83
The Delicate Delinquent '56
Disorderly Orderly '64
Don't Raise the Bridge, Lower
   the River '68
The Errand Boy '61
Family Jewels '65
The Geisha Boy '58
Hardly Working '81
Hollywood Clowns '85
Hollywood or Bust '56
It's a Mad, Mad, Mad, Mad
   World '63
Jumping Jacks '52
King of Comedy '82
The Ladies' Man '61
My Friend Irma '49
The Nutty Professor '63
Pardners '56
The Patsy '64
The Road to Bali '53
The Sad Sack '57
Scared Stiff '53
Slapstick of Another Kind '84
The Stooge '51
Trading Hearts '87
Which Way to the Front? '70

Jerry Lee Lewis
Chuck Berry: Hail! Hail! Rock
   'n' Roll '87
High School Confidential '58

Joe Lewis
Force: Five '81
Jaguar Lives '79

Joe E. Lewis
Lady in Cement '68
Private Buckaroo '42

Juliette Lewis
Cape Fear '91
Husbands and Wives '92
Kalifornia '93
Meet the Hollowheads '89
My Stepmother Is an Alien '88
National Lampoon's Christmas
   Vacation '89
Natural Born Killers '94

Romeo Is Bleeding '93
That Night '93
What's Eating Gilbert Grape '93

Louise Lewis
Blood of Dracula '57
I Was a Teenage Werewolf '57

Mitchell Lewis
Billy the Kid '41
Cairo '42
Linda '29
Salome '22
Salome/Queen Elizabeth '23
The Wizard of Oz '39

Phill Lewis
Brother Future '91
City Slickers '91

Ralph Lewis
Dante's Inferno '24
Outside the Law '21
Somewhere in Sonora '33
Sucker Money '34
When the Clouds Roll By '19

Richard Lewis
Diary of a Young Comic '79
Once Upon a Crime '92
Robin Hood: Men in Tights '93
That's Adequate '90
Wagons East '94
The Wrong Guys '88

Robert Lewis
Hello Again '87
Monsieur Verdoux '47
Son of Lassie '45

Ronald Lewis
Bachelor of Hearts '58
Billy Budd '62
Conspiracy of Hearts '60
Friends '71
Paul and Michelle '74
Robbery Under Arms '57
Scream of Fear '61

Sheldon Lewis
The Phantom '31
Tombstone Canyon '35
With Kit Carson Over the Great
   Divide '25

Johan Leysen
Egg '88
Hail Mary '85
The Music Teacher '88

John Leyton
Guns at Batasi '64
Seaside Swingers '65
Von Ryan's Express '65

Thierry Lhermitte
My Best Friend's Girl '84
My New Partner '84
Next Year If All Goes Well '83
Until September '84

Bruce Li
Blind Fists of Bruce '70s
Bruce Li in New Guinea '80
Bruce Li the Invincible '80
Chinese Connection 2 '84
Counter Attack '84
Enter the Panther '79
Enter Three Dragons '81
Fists of Fury 2 '80
Image of Bruce Lee '70s
Iron Dragon Strikes Back '84
Kung Fu Avengers '85
Return of the Tiger '78
Story of the Dragon '82

Chang Li
Enter Three Dragons '81
Fight to the Death '83

Gong Li
Farewell My Concubine '93
Ju Dou '90
Raise the Red Lantern '91
Red Sorghum '87
The Story of Qui Ju '91

Bruce Liang
The Fist, the Kicks, and the
   Evils '81
Showdown at the Equator '83

Ko Shou Liang
Ninja Exterminators '81
Renegade Monk '82
Shaolin Ex-Monk '82

Tan Tao Liang
Dual Flying Kicks '82
Incredible Master Beggars '82

Brian Libby
Platoon Leader '87
Silent Rage '82

Liberace
The Loved One '65
Sincerely Yours '56

Anne Libert
The Demons '74
Virgin Among the Living Dead
   '71

Richard Libertini
All of Me '84
Animal Behavior '89
Big Trouble '86
The Bonfire of the Vanities '90
Deal of the Century '83
Fletch '85
Fletch Lives '89
Fourth Wise Man '85
Going Berserk '83
The In-Laws '79
Popeye '80
Sharky's Machine '81
Soup for One '82
Unfaithfully Yours '84

Jeremy Licht
Father Figure '80
Lois Gibbs and the Love Canal
   '82
Next One '84
The Seekers '79
Twilight Zone: The Movie '83

Mitchell Lichtenstein
Streamers '83
The Wedding Banquet '93

Gabriella Licudi
The Last Safari '67
The Unearthly Stranger '64

G. Gordon Liddy
Adventures in Spying '92
Camp Cucamonga: How I
   Spent My Summer Vacation
   '90
Street Asylum '90
Super Force '90
When Nature Calls '85

Lo Lieh
Born Invincible '76
Bruce's Deadly Fingers '80
The Dragon Returns
The Golden Triangle '80
King Boxer '90
Kung Fu from Beyond the
   Grave
Ninja Massacre '84
The Ninja Pirates '90
The Noble Ninja '90
Shaolin Executioner '80s
Showdown at the Equator '83
The Stranger and the
   Gunfighter '76

Albert Lieven
Beware of Pity '46
Frieda '47
The Life and Death of Colonel
   Blimp '43
The Seventh Veil '46
Sleeping Car to Trieste '45

Tina Lifford
The Ernest Green Story '93
Grand Canyon '91
Paris Trout '91

Marilyn Lightstone
Anne of Green Gables '85
Grand Tour: Disaster in Time
   '92
Lies My Father Told Me '75
Surrogate '88
Wild Pony '83

Tom Ligon
Fury on Wheels '71
Judge Horton and the
   Scottsboro Boys '76

Beatrice Lillie
On Approval '44
Thoroughly Modern Millie '67

Traci Lin
Class of 1999 '90
Fright Night 2 '88
No Secrets '91
Survival Quest '89
A Tiger's Tale '87
Voyager '91

Abbey Lincoln
For Love of Ivy '68
Mo' Better Blues '90
Nothing But a Man '64

Elmo Lincoln
The Adventures of Tarzan '21
Tarzan of the Apes '17
Wyoming Outlaw '39

Lar Park Lincoln
Friday the 13th, Part 7: The
   New Blood '88
Princess Academy '87

Traci Lind
The Handmaid's Tale '90
My Boyfriend's Back '93

Gunnel Lindblom
Hunger '66
The Seventh Seal '56
The Virgin Spring '59

Doris Linden
Hillbilly Blitzkrieg '42
Snuffy Smith, Yard Bird '42

Eric Linden
Ah, Wilderness! '35
Criminals Within '41
Gone with the Wind '39
Let 'Em Have It '35
Sweetheart of the Navy '37

Hal Linden
Father Figure '80
How to Break Up a Happy
   Divorce '76
I Do! I Do! '84
Mr. Inside, Mr. Outside '74
My Wicked, Wicked Ways '84
A New Life '88
Starflight One '83

Jennie Linden
Hedda '75
Women in Love '70

Cec Linder
Deadly Eyes '82
The Devil's Web '74
Goldfinger '64
Heavenly Bodies '84
A Touch of Class '73

Max Linder
Early Cinema Vol. 1 '19
Laugh with Linder! '13
Man in the Silk Hat '15
Man in the Silk Hat '83
Max '22
Pop Goes the Cork '22
Seven Years Bad Luck '20

Viveca Lindfors
Adventures of Don Juan '49
The Ann Jillian Story '88
Bell from Hell '74
The Best Little Girl in the World
   '81
Cauldron of Blood '67
Child of Darkness, Child of
   Light '91
Creepshow '82
Exiled in America '90
The Exorcist 3 '90
For Ladies Only '81
Four in a Jeep '51
Girlfriends '77
The Hand '81
Inside the Third Reich '82
The King of Kings '61
Lady Beware '87
The Linguini Incident '92
Marilyn: The Untold Story '80
Mom, the Wolfman and Me '80
Moonfleet '55
Natural Enemies '79
A Question of Guilt '78
Rachel River '89
Secret Weapons '85
Silent Madness '84
The Story of Ruth '60
The Sure Thing '85
The Way We Were '73
A Wedding '78
Welcome to L.A. '77
Zandalee '91

Peter Lindgren
I Am Curious (Yellow) '67
The New Land '73

Audra Lindley
Best Friends '82
Cannery Row '82

Desert Hearts '86
The Heartbreak Kid '72
Revenge of the Stepford Wives
   '80
The Spellbinder '88
Stamp of a Killer '87
Troop Beverly Hills '89

Delroy Lindo
Blood In...Blood Out: Bound by
   Honor '93
Bright Angel '91
Crooklyn '94
Malcolm X '92
Mr. Jones '93
Mountains of the Moon '90

Olga Lindo
The Hidden Room '49
Things Happen at Night '48

Vincent Lindon
Betty Blue '86
A Man in Love '87

Margaret Lindsay
Baby Face '33
British Intelligence '40
Cass Timberlane '47
Cavalcade '33
Club Havana '46
Dangerous '35
Devil Dogs of the Air '35
''G'' Men '35
Jezebel '38
Lady Killer '33
Please Don't Eat the Daisies
   '60
The Spoilers '42

Robert Lindsay
Bert Rigby, You're a Fool '89
Strike It Rich '90

Stuart Lindsell
Man of Evil '48
Profile '54

Pierre Lindstedt
The Emigrants '72
The New Land '73

Helga Line
Horror Rises from the Tomb
   '72
The Mummy's Revenge '73
Nightmare Castle '65
Pulsebeat '85
The Saga of the Draculas '73
When the Screaming Stops '73

Richard Lineback
Beyond the Next Mountain '87
Speed '94

Chen Pei Ling
The Furious Avenger '76
Golden Sun '80s

Chia Ling
Against the Drunken Cat Paws
   '75
Eighteen Jade Arhats '84
The Great Hunter '75
Ninja Swords of Death '90
Ten Brothers of Shao-lin '80s

**Shangkuan Ling-
Feng**
Fight for Survival '77
Green Dragon Inn '82
Kung Fu Commandos '80
Shaolin Traitor '82

Wendy Lingham
Alien Women '69
Demonstrator '71

Paul Linke
The Fear Inside '92
Motel Hell '80
Parenthood '89
Time Flies When You're Alive
   '89

Art Linkletter
Champagne for Caesar '50
People Are Funny '46

Mark Linn-Baker
Bare Essentials '91
Ghostwriter '84
Manhattan '79
My Favorite Year '82
Noises Off '92

Rex Linn
Cliffhanger '93
Wyatt Earp '94

Laura Linney
Armistead Maupin's Tales of
   the City '93
Blind Spot '93
Dave '93
A Simple Twist of Fate '94

Joanne Linville
From the Dead of Night '89
Scorpio '73
Secrets '77

Larry Linville
Blue Movies '88
Body Waves '92
Earth Girls are Easy '89
M*A*S*H: The Collector's
   Edition '72
Night Partners '83
Rock 'n' Roll High School
   Forever '91
School Spirit '85
The Stepmother '71

Leon M. Lion
Amazing Adventure '37
No. 17 '32

Alberto Lionello
Porcile '69
Till Marriage Do Us Part '74

Therese Liotard
Cloud Waltzing '87
My Father's Glory '91
My Mother's Castle '91
One Sings, the Other Doesn't
   '77

Ray Liotta
Article 99 '92
Corrina, Corrina '94
Dominick & Eugene '88
Field of Dreams '89
Goodfellas '90
The Lonely Lady '83
No Escape '94
Something Wild '86
Unlawful Entry '92
Women & Men: In Love There
   Are No Rules '91

Eugene Lipinski
Going Home '86
Moonlighting '82
Perfectly Normal '91
Riders of the Storm '88

Maureen Lipman
Educating Rita '83
The Little Princess '87

Jonathon Lippe
Blood Voyage '77
Green Eyes '76

Dennis Lipscomb
Eyes of Fire '84
Guilty of Innocence '87
Retribution '88
Sister, Sister '87
Slow Burn '86
Union City '81

Jack Lipson
Cannon Ball/Eyes Have It '15
Flash Gordon: Rocketship '36

Peggy Lipton
Fatal Charm '92
Kinjite: Forbidden Subjects '89
Mosby's Marauders '66
Purple People Eater '88
Twin Peaks '90
Twin Peaks: Fire Walk with Me
   '92

Joe Lisi
Come See the Paradise '90
Traces of Red '92

Virna Lisi
Assault on a Queen '66
Bluebeard '72
Casanova '70 '65
Christopher Columbus '85
How to Murder Your Wife '64
I Love N.Y. '87
La Cicada '83
Miss Right '81
Night Flight from Moscow '73
The Statue '71
When Wolves Cry '69

Leon Lissek
Adventures of Eliza Fraser '76
Blockhouse '73
Bloodmoon '90

Moira Lister
The Limping Man '53
Trouble in Store '53
Uneasy Terms '48

Tiny Lister
Immortal Combat '94
9 1/2 Ninjas '90
No Holds Barred '89
Posse '93
Prison '88

John Litel
Boss of Big Town '43
Cass Timberlane '47
The Fighting 69th '40
The Fuller Brush Girl '50
Invisible Agent '42
Montana Belle '52
Nancy Drew, Reporter '39
Northwest Trail '49
Outpost in Morocco '49
Pitfall '48
San Antonio '45

John Lithgow
The Adventures of Buckaroo
  Banzai Across the Eighth
  Dimension '84
All That Jazz '79
At Play in the Fields of the Lord
  '91
Baby Girl Scott '87
The Big Fix '78
Blow Out '81
Cliffhanger '93
The Day After '83
Distant Thunder '88
Footloose '84
The Glitter Dome '84
Goldilocks & the Three Bears
  '83
Harry and the Hendersons '87
I'm Dancing as Fast as I Can
  '82
Ivory Hunters '90
Love, Cheat & Steal '94
The Manhattan Project '86
Memphis Belle '90
Mesmerized '84
Mom, the Wolfman and Me '80
Obsession '76
Oldest Living Graduate '82
Out Cold '89
The Pelican Brief '93
Raising Cain '92
Rich Kids '79
Ricochet '91
Santa Claus: The Movie '85
Terms of Endearment '83
Traveling Man '89
Twilight Zone: The Movie '83
2010: The Year We Make
  Contact '84
The World According to Garp
  '82
World War II: When Lions
  Roared '94
The Wrong Man '93

Cleavon Little
Blazing Saddles '74
Cotton Comes to Harlem '70
Don't Look Back: The Story of
  Leroy ''Satchel'' Paige '81
Double Exposure '82
E. Nick: A Legend in His Own
  Mind '84
Fletch Lives '89
FM '78
The Gig '85
Gore Vidal's Lincoln '88
Greased Lightning '77
High Risk '76
Homecoming: A Christmas
  Story '71
Jimmy the Kid '82
Murder by Numbers '89
Once Bitten '85
Once Upon a Brothers Grimm
  '77
Perfect Harmony '91
The Salamander '82
Scavenger Hunt '79
Separate But Equal '91
The Sky is Gray '80
Surf 2 '84
Toy Soldiers '84
Vanishing Point '71

Sacheen Little
Feather
Johnny Firecloud '75
Shoot the Sun Down '81

Mark Little
The Wacky World of Wills &
  Burke '85
Waterfront '83

Michelle Little
Appointment with Fear '85
Blood Clan '91
Bluffing It '87
My Demon Lover '87
Radioactive Dreams '86

Little Nell
I Wanna Be a Beauty Queen
  '85
Jubilee '78
The Rocky Horror Picture
  Show '75

Rich Little
Dirty Tricks '81
Happy Hour '87

Little Richard
Down and Out in Beverly Hills
  '86
Pee Wee's Playhouse
  Christmas Special '88
Purple People Eater '88

Eddie Little Sky
Journey Through Rosebud '72
Savage Run '70

Lucien Littlefield
The Bitter Tea of General Yen
  '33
Bulldog Drummond's Revenge
  '37
Charley's Aunt '25
The Gladiator '38
Hillbilly Blitzkrieg '42
Hollywood Stadium Mystery '38
Let's Sing Again '36
The Sheik '21
Strangers of the Evening '32
Susanna Pass '49
Tom Sawyer '30
Tumbleweeds '25
Wide Open Faces '38
Zorro's Black Whip '44

Gary Littlejohn
Angels Hard as They Come '71
Bury Me an Angel '71

Harrison Liu
Black Robe '91
Dr. Bethune '90

John Liu
Instant Kung-Fu Man '84
Kung Fu Commandos '80
Shaolin Ex-Monk '82
Snuff-Bottle Connection '82

Jason Lively
Ghost Chase '88
Maximum Force '92
National Lampoon's European
  Vacation '85
Night of the Creeps '86

Robin Lively
Buckeye and Blue '87
Crazy from the Heart '91
Not Quite Human '87
Not Quite Human 2 '89
Teen Witch '89

Jack Livesey
Never Too Late to Mend '37
The World Owes Me a Living
  '47

Roger Livesey
Drums '38
The Entertainer '60
Green Grow the Rushes '51
I Know Where I'm Going '45
The League of Gentlemen '60
The Life and Death of Colonel
  Blimp '43
The Master of Ballantrae '53
Of Human Bondage '64

Bob Livingston
Blazing Stewardesses '75
The Bold Caballero '36
Come On, Cowboys '37
Covered Wagon Days '40
Cowboys from Texas '39
Death Rides the Plains '44

Ghost Town Gold '36
Heart of the Rockies '37
Heroes of the Hills '38
Hit the Saddle '37
The Kansas Terrors '39
Law of the Saddle '45
Outlaws of Sonora '38
Purple Vigilantes '38
Raiders of Red Gap '43
Riders of the Whistling Skull '37
Roarin' Lead '37
Rocky Mountain Rangers '40
Texas Layover '75
The Vigilantes are Coming '36
Western Double Feature 6:
  Rogers & Trigger '50
Western Double Feature 12 '44
Western Double Feature 13
  '40s

Margaret Livingston
The Lady Refuses '31
Sunrise '27
Through the Breakers '28

Stanley Livingston
Private Parts '72
Smokey & the Hotwire Gang
  '79

Enrique Lizalde
La Mentira '87
Sexo Y Crimen '87

Kari Lizer
Private School '83
Smokey Bites the Dust '81

L.L. Cool J.
The Hard Way '91
Toys '92

Lucien Littlefield
(see above)

Desmond Llewelyn
Diamonds are Forever '71
For Your Eyes Only '81
From Russia with Love '63
Goldfinger '64
License to Kill '89
The Living Daylights '87
The Man with the Golden Gun
  '74
Merlin '93
Moonraker '79
On Her Majesty's Secret
  Service '69
The Spy Who Loved Me '77
Thunderball '65
A View to a Kill '85
You Only Live Twice '67

Christopher Lloyd
The Addams Family '91
Addams Family Values '93
The Adventures of Buckaroo
  Banzai Across the Eighth
  Dimension '84
Angels in the Outfield '94
Back to the Future '85
Back to the Future, Part 2 '89
Back to the Future, Part 3 '90
The Black Marble '79
Camp Nowhere '94
Clue '85
The Cowboy & the Ballerina '84
Dead Ahead: The Exxon Valdez
  Disaster '92
Dennis the Menace '93
The Dream Team '89
Eight Men Out '88
Goin' South '78
Joy of Sex '84
Lady in Red '79
Legend of the Lone Ranger '81
Miracles '86
Mr. Mom '83
National Lampoon Goes to the
  Movies '81
One Flew Over the Cuckoo's
  Nest '75
Pilgrim, Farewell '82
The Postman Always Rings
  Twice '81
September Gun '83
Star Trek 3: The Search for
  Spock '84
Street Hawk '84
Suburban Commando '91
T Bone N Weasel '90s
Three Warriors '77
To Be or Not to Be '83
Track 29 '88
Twenty Bucks '93
Walk Like a Man '87
Who Framed Roger Rabbit? '88

Why Me? '90

Danny Lloyd
The Shining '80
Will: G. Gordon Liddy '82

Doris Lloyd
Disraeli '29
The Drake Case '29
The Invisible Man's Revenge
  '44
Journey for Margaret '42
A Shot in the Dark '35

Emily Lloyd
Chicago Joe & the Showgirl '90
Cookie '89
In Country '89
A River Runs Through It '92
Scorchers '92
Wish You Were Here '87

Harold Lloyd
Days of Thrills and Laughter
  '61
Dr. Jack/For Heaven's Sake '26
Don't Shove/Two Gun Gussie
  '19
Early Cinema Vol. 1 '19
Feet First '30
For Heaven's Sake '26
The Freshman '25
Girl Shy '24
His Royal Slyness/Haunted
  Spooks '20
Hollywood Clowns '85
Hot Water/Safety Last '24
I'm on My Way/The Non-Stop
  Kid '18
The Kid Brother '27
Kings, Queens, Jokers '30s
Milky Way '36
Never Weaken/Why Worry? '23
Sailor-Made Man/Grandma's
  Boy '20s
Silent Laugh Makers, No. 3 '19
The Sin of Harold Diddlebock
  '47
Slapstick '30s
Speedy '28

Harold Lloyd, Jr.
The Flaming Urge '53
Girls' Town '59
Married Too Young '62
Platinum High School '60

Jimmy Lloyd
G.I. Jane '51
The Jolson Story '46
Miss Grant Takes Richmond
  '49
Riders of the Whistling Pines
  '49
Sea Hound '47

John Bedford Lloyd
The Abyss '89
Crossing Delancey '88
Philadelphia '93
Sweet Lorraine '87
Tough Guys Don't Dance '87
Waiting for the Light '90

Kathleen Lloyd
Gangster Wars '81
It's Alive 2: It Lives Again '78
The Jayne Mansfield Story '80
Missouri Breaks '76
Skateboard '77
Take Down '79

Norman Lloyd
Amityville 4 '89
Jaws of Satan '81
Journey of Honor '91
The Nude Bomb '80
Saboteur '42
The Southerner '45

Sue Lloyd
The Bitch '78
Hysteria '64
The Ipcress File '65
Ned Kelly '70
Number 1 of the Secret Service
  '77

Tony LoBianco
The Ann Jillian Story '88
Blood Ties '87
Bloodbrothers '78
Boiling Point '93
City Heat '84
City of Hope '91
F.I.S.T. '78

The French Connection '71
God Told Me To '76
Goldenrod '77
Honeymoon Killers '70
Last Cry for Help '79
Magee and the Lady '78
Marciano '79
Mean Frank and Crazy Tony
  '75
Mr. Inside, Mr. Outside '74
Separate Ways '82
The Seven-Ups '73
The Story of Jacob & Joseph
  '74
Teamster Boss: The Jackie
  Presser Story '92
The Ten Million Dollar Getaway
  '91

Amy Locane
Airheads '94
Cry-Baby '90
Lost Angels '89
No Secrets '91
School Ties '92

David Lochary
Female Trouble '74
Mondo Trasho '69
Multiple Maniacs '70
Pink Flamingos '72

Katherine Locke
People Will Talk '51
Try and Get Me '50

Sondra Locke
Any Which Way You Can '80
Bronco Billy '80
Every Which Way But Loose
  '78
The Gauntlet '77
The Heart is a Lonely Hunter
  '68
The Outlaw Josey Wales '76
Ratboy '86
A Reflection of Fear '72
Rosie: The Rosemary Clooney
  Story '82
Second Coming of Suzanne '80
Seducers '77
Shadow of Chikara '77
Sudden Impact '83
Suzanne '80
Tales of the Unexpected '91
Willard '71

Anne Lockhart
Dark Tower '87
Hambone & Hillie '84
Joyride '77
Savage Hunger '84
Slashed Dreams '74
Troll '85

Calvin Lockhart
The Baron '88
Black Werewolf '75
Coming to America '88
Cotton Comes to Harlem '70
Dark of the Sun '68
Honeybaby '74
Let's Do It Again '75
Predator 2 '90
Three Days in Beirut '83
Uptown Saturday Night '74

Gene Lockhart
Abe Lincoln in Illinois '40
Action in Arabia '44
Algiers '38
The Big Hangover '50
Billy the Kid '41
Blondie '38
Carousel '56
A Christmas Carol '38
Crime and Punishment '35
The Devil & Daniel Webster '41
Earthworm Tractors '36
Edison the Man '40
Face to Face '52
A Girl in Every Port '52
Going My Way '44
Her Husband's Affairs '47
His Girl Friday '40
Hoodlum Empire '52
The Inspector General '49
Madame Bovary '49
The Man in the Gray Flannel
  Suit '56
Meet John Doe '41
Miracle on 34th Street '47
Northern Pursuit '43
Of Human Hearts '38

The Sea Wolf '41
Sinners in Paradise '38
Something to Sing About '36
South of Pago Pago '40
The Strange Woman '46
They Died with Their Boots On '41

June Lockhart
Adam Had Four Sons '41
The Big Picture '89
Butterfly '82
The Capture of Grizzly Adams '82
Curse of the Black Widow '77
Dead Women in Lingerie '90
Deadly Games '80
The Gift of Love '90
Just Tell Me You Love Me '80
Lassie's Great Adventure '62
Meet Me in St. Louis '44
Miss Annie Rooney '42
Rented Lips '88
Sergeant York '41
Son of Lassie '45
Strange Invaders '83
T-Men '47
Troll '85
Walking Through the Fire '80
The White Cliffs of Dover '44
The Yearling '46

Heather Locklear
The Big Slice '90
Body Language '92
City Killer '87
Fade to Black '93
Firestarter '84
Illusions '91
Lethal Charm '90
The Return of Swamp Thing '89
Twirl '81

Loryn Locklin
Catch Me...If You Can '89
Fortress '93
Taking Care of Business '90

Gary Lockwood
Bad Georgia Road '77
Firecreek '68
The Incredible Journey of Dr. Meg Laurel '79
It Happened at the World's Fair '63
The Magic Sword '62
Manhunter '74
Project: Kill! '77
R.P.M.* (*Revolutions Per Minute) '70
Survival Zone '84
Terror in Paradise '68
2001: A Space Odyssey '68
Wild in the Country '61
The Wild Pair '87

Margaret Lockwood
Cast a Dark Shadow '55
Dr. Syn '37
The Lady Vanishes '38
The Man in Grey '45
Night Train to Munich '40
The Stars Look Down '39
Susannah of the Mounties '39
Trouble in the Glen '54
The Wicked Lady '45

Barbara Loden
Iron Cowboy '68
Splendor in the Grass '61

John Loder
Abroad with Two Yanks '44
Brighton Strangler '45
The Brighton Strangler/Before Dawn '47
Dishonored Lady '47
Dr. Syn '37
The Hairy Ape '44
How Green was My Valley '41
Java Head '35
King Solomon's Mines '37
The Man Who Lived Again '36
My Song Goes Round the World '37
Non-Stop New York '37
Passage to Marseilles '44
The Private Life of Henry VIII '33
River of Unrest '37
Sabotage '36
The Silent Passenger '35
Small Hotel '57
Tin Pan Alley '40

Wedding Rehearsal '32
The Woman Who Came Back '45

Kathryn Loder
The Big Doll House '71
Foxy Brown '74

David Lodge
Edge of Sanity '89
The Hellfire Club '61
Killer with Two Faces '74
Two-Way Stretch '60

Jean Lodge
Dick Barton Strikes Back '48
Terror Ship '54

John Lodge
Bulldog Drummond at Bay '37
The Little Colonel '35
River of Unrest '37
Scarlet Empress '34
The Witchmaker '69

Jeanette Loff
Annapolis '28
Fighting Thru '30
King of Jazz '30
Party Girls '29

Marianne Lofgren
June Night '40
Only One Night '42

Arthur Loft
Charlie Chan in the Secret Service '44
Gang Bullets '38
I Am the Law '38
Riders of Pasco Basin '40

Jacqueline Logan
King of Kings '27
King of the Kongo '29
Ships in the Night '28

Phyllis Logan
And a Nightingale Sang '91
Another Time, Another Place '83
The Doctor and the Devils '85
The Inquiry '87
The Kitchen Toto '87
The McGuffin '85

Ricky Dean Logan
Back to the Future, Part 2 '89
Back to the Future, Part 3 '90
Freddy's Dead: The Final Nightmare '91

Robert F. Logan
Across the Great Divide '76
The Adventures of the Wilderness Family '76
Death Ray 2000 '81
Further Adventures of the Wilderness Family, Part 2 '77
Man Outside '88
Mountain Family Robinson '79
Sea Gypsies '78
Snowbeast '77

Susan Logan
Deadly Encounter '78
The Meal '75

Robert Loggia
Afterburn '92
Armed and Dangerous '86
Bad Girls '94
The Believers '87
Big '88
Code Name: Chaos '90
Conspiracy: The Trial of the Chicago Eight '87
Curse of the Pink Panther '83
Echoes in the Darkness '87
El Fego Baca: Six-Gun Law '62
First Love '77
Gaby: A True Story '87
Gladiator '92
The Greatest Story Ever Told '65
Hot Pursuit '87
I Love Trouble '94
Innocent Blood '92
Intrigue '90
The Jagged Edge '85
Lifepod '93
The Lost Missile '58
The Marrying Man '91
Necessary Roughness '91
The Nine Lives of Elfego Baca '58

The Ninth Configuration '79
An Officer and a Gentleman '82
Opportunity Knocks '90
Over the Top '86
Overnight Sensation '83
Prizzi's Honor '85
Psycho 2 '83
Relentless '89
Revenge of the Pink Panther '78
Running Away '89
Scarface '83
S.O.B. '81
Somebody Up There Likes Me '56
Speedtrap '77
Target: Favorite Son '87
That's Life! '86
Trail of the Pink Panther '82
Triumph of the Spirit '89
Wild Palms '93
A Woman Called Golda '82

Marie Lohr
Counterblast '48
Escapade '55
Pygmalion '38
Small Hotel '57

Gina Lollobrigida
Bad Man's River '72
Beat the Devil '53
Buona Sera, Mrs. Campbell '68
Four Ways Out '57
Hotel Paradiso '66
Imperial Venus '71
King, Queen, Knave '72
Never So Few '59
Solomon and Sheba '59
Trapeze '56
Where the Hot Wind Blows '59
A Woman of Rome '56
Young Caruso '51

Herbert Lom
And Now the Screaming Starts '73
Appointment with Crime '45
Asylum '72
Count Dracula '71
Curse of the Pink Panther '83
Dead Zone '83
The Devil's Daughter '91
Dorian Gray '70
Dual Alibi '47
Fire Down Below '57
Flame Over India '60
Gambit '66
Going Bananas '88
The Golden Salamander '51
Hopscotch '80
The Horse Without a Head '63
Hotel Reserve '44
Journey to the Far Side of the Sun '69
King Solomon's Mines '85
The Lady Vanishes '79
Ladykillers '55
The Man with Bogart's Face '80
Mark of the Devil '69
Masque of the Red Death '90
Murders in the Rue Morgue '71
Mysterious Island '61
Night and the City '50
99 Women '69
Paris Express '53
The Pink Panther Strikes Again '76
The Pope Must Diet '91
Return of the Pink Panther '74
Revenge of the Pink Panther '78
River of Death '90
Room 43 '58
The Seventh Veil '46
A Shot in the Dark '64
Skeleton Coast '89
Son of the Pink Panther '93
Spartacus '60
Ten Little Indians '75
Ten Little Indians '89
Third Man on the Mountain '59
Tiara Tahiti '62
Trail of the Pink Panther '82
Uncle Tom's Cabin '69
Villa Rides '68
War and Peace '56
Whoops Apocalypse '83

Carole Lombard
Big News '29

Golden Age of Comedy '58
High Voltage '29
Hollywood Outtakes & Rare Footage '83
In Name Only '39
Lady by Choice '34
Mack & Carole '28
Made for Each Other '39
The Making of a Legend: ''Gone With the Wind'' '89
Mr. & Mrs. Smith '41
My Man Godfrey '36
No Man of Her Own '32
Nothing Sacred '37
Power '28
The Racketeer '29
Swing High, Swing Low '37
These Girls Won't Talk '20s
They Knew What They Wanted '40
To Be or Not to Be '42
Twentieth Century '34

Karina Lombard
The Firm '93
Wide Sargasso Sea '92

Ulli Lommel
Boogey Man 2 '83
Chinese Roulette '86
Effi Briest '74

Tadeusz Lomnicki
A Generation '54
Man of Marble '76

Jason London
Blood Ties '92
Dazed and Confused '93
December '91
The Man in the Moon '91

Julie London
The Girl Can't Help It '56
Man of the West '58
Nabonga '44
The Red House '47
Task Force '49

Lisa London
H.O.T.S. '79
Savage Beach '89

Tom London
Beyond the Rockies '32
Blue Canadian Rockies '52
Brand of Fear '49
Courage of the North '35
Flaming Lead '39
Fugitive Valley '41
The Miracle Rider '35
Outlaw Justice '32
Red Desert '50
Rio Rattler '35
Sunset in El Dorado '45
Toll of the Desert '35
Tribute to a Bad Man '56
Two Gun Man '31
Zorro's Black Whip '44

John Lone
Echoes of Paradise '86
Iceman '84
The Last Emperor '87
M. Butterfly '93
The Moderns '88
The Shadow '94
Shadow of China '91
Year of the Dragon '85

Audrey Long
The Adventures of Gallant Bess '48
Desperate '47
Indian Uprising '51

Jodi Long
Amos and Andrew '93
Patty Hearst '88

Lotus Long
Mr. Wong in Chinatown '39
Mystery of Mr. Wong '39
Phantom of Chinatown '40

Melissa Long
Reactor '85
War of the Robots '78

Nia Long
Boyz N the Hood '91
Made in America '93

Richard Long
Big Valley '68
Criss Cross '48
Cult of the Cobra '55
Death Cruise '74

Egg and I '47
House on Haunted Hill '58
Ma and Pa Kettle '49
Ma and Pa Kettle Back On the Farm '51
Ma and Pa Kettle Go to Town '50
The Stranger '46
Tomorrow is Forever '46

Shelley Long
Caveman '81
The Cracker Factory '79
Don't Tell Her It's Me '90
Frozen Assets '92
Hello Again '87
Irreconcilable Differences '84
Losin' It '82
The Money Pit '86
Night Shift '82
Outrageous Fortune '87
A Small Circle of Friends '80
Troop Beverly Hills '89

Walter Long
Blood and Sand '22
Flaming Lead '39
The Glory Trail '36
The Little American '17
Little Church Around the Corner '23
Man's Country '38
Moran of the Lady Letty '22
Sea Devils '31
The Sheik '21
Silver Stallion '41
Six Shootin' Sheriff '38
Soul-Fire '25
Yankee Clipper '27

John Longden
Alias John Preston '56
Juno and the Paycock '30
Quatermass 2 '57
Tower of Terror '42

Tony Longo
Bloodhounds of Broadway '89
Prehysteria '93
Rapid Fire '92
Remote '93
Suburban Commando '91
Worth Winning '89

Emily Longstreth
The Big Picture '89
Confessions of a Hit Man '94
Private Resort '84
Rising Son '90
Wired to Kill '86

Ray Lonnen
Belfast Assassin '84
Guardian of the Abyss '82

Michael Lonsdale
The Bride Wore Black '68
Enigma '82
Erendira '83
The Holcroft Covenant '85
Is Paris Burning? '68
Les Assassins de L'Ordre '71
Moonraker '79
Murmur of the Heart '71
The Name of the Rose '86
The Remains of the Day '93
Souvenir '88

Richard Loo
Across the Pacific '42
Back to Bataan '45
Betrayal from the East '44
The Bitter Tea of General Yen '33
China Sky '44
The Clay Pigeon '49
First Yank into Tokyo '45
Five Fingers '52
Love is a Many-Splendored Thing '55
Malaya '49
The Man with the Golden Gun '74
Mr. Wong in Chinatown '39
The Purple Heart '44
The Steel Helmet '51

Michael Lookinland
The Brady Bunch, Vol. 1 '69
A Very Brady Christmas '88

Nancy Loomis
Assault on Precinct 13 '76
Halloween '78

Rod Loomis
Bill & Ted's Excellent
Adventure '89
Jack's Back '87
Tanya Lopert
Navajo Joe '67
Tales of Ordinary Madness '83
Kamala Lopez
Born in East L.A. '87
Crazy from the Heart '91
Dollman '91
Exiled in America '90
Margo Lopez
El Libro de Piedra '68
Nazarin '58
Perry Lopez
Chinatown '74
McLintock! '63
Mister Roberts '55
Taras Bulba '62
Sal Lopez
American Me '92
The Fire Next Time '93
Trini Lopez
Antonio '73
The Dirty Dozen '67
The Poppy is also a Flower '66
Isabel Lorca
Lightning: The White Stallion
'86
She's Having a Baby '88
Theodore Lorch
The Last of the Mohicans '20
The Man on the Box '25
Jack Lord
The Court Martial of Billy
Mitchell '55
Dr. No '62
The Doomsday Flight '66
God's Little Acre '58
Man of the West '58
Justine Lord
He Kills Night After Night After
Night '70
Skeezer '82
Marjorie Lord
Boy, Did I Get a Wrong
Number! '66
Johnny Come Lately '43
Sherlock Holmes in
Washington '43
Traci Lords
Cry-Baby '90
Desperate Crimes '93
Fast Food '89
Ice '93
Laser Moon '92
Not of This Earth '88
Raw Nerve '91
Serial Mom '94
Shock 'Em Dead '90
Stephen King's The
Tommyknockers '93
A Time to Die '91
Tony Lorea
The Deadly and the Beautiful
'73
Smokey & the Hotwire Gang
'79
Donna Loren
Bikini Beach '64
Muscle Beach Party '64
Pajama Party '64
Sophia Loren
Angela '77
Arabesque '66
Bellissimo: Images of the Italian
Cinema '87
Black Orchid '59
Blood Feud '79
Boccaccio '70 '62
Brass Target '78
Breath of Scandal '60
The Cassandra Crossing '76
Courage '86
Desire Under the Elms '58
El Cid '61
The Fall of the Roman Empire
'64
Firepower '79
Get Rita
The Gold of Naples '54
Heller in Pink Tights '60

Houseboat '58
It Started in Naples '60
The Key '58
Lady L '65
Lady of the Evening '79
Legend of the Lost '57
Man of La Mancha '72
Marriage Italian Style '64
Operation Crossbow '65
The Pride and the Passion '57
Running Away '89
Sophia Loren: Her Own Story
'80
A Special Day '77
Two Nights with Cleopatra '54
Two Women '61
Yesterday, Today and
Tomorrow '64
Tray Loren
The American Angels: Baptism
of Blood '89
Gator Bait 2: Cajun Justice '88
Rocktober Blood '85
Livio Lorenzon
Gladiators 7 '62
The Invincible Gladiator '63
Pirates of the Coast '61
Lynn Loring
Journey to the Far Side of the
Sun '69
Kansas City Massacre '75
Teala Loring
Delinquent Daughters '44
Hard-Boiled Mahoney '47
James Lorinz
Frankenhooker '90
Punch the Clock '90
Marion Lorne
The Graduate '67
Strangers on a Train '51
George Loros
Apology '86
Shakedown '88
Peter Lorre
All Through the Night '42
Arsenic and Old Lace '44
Background to Danger '43
The Beast with Five Fingers '46
Beat the Devil '53
Casablanca '42
The Chase '46
The Comedy of Terrors '64
Crime and Punishment '35
Five Weeks in a Balloon '62
F.P. 1 Doesn't Answer '33
Hell Ship Mutiny '57
Hollywood Canteen '44
Invisible Agent '42
The Lost One '51
M '31
Mad Love '35
The Maltese Falcon '41
The Man Who Knew Too Much
'34
Mr. Moto's Last Warning '39
Mr. Moto's Last Warning/
Meeting at Midnight '44
My Favorite Brunette '47
Passage to Marseilles '44
The Patsy '64
Postmark for Danger/
Quicksand '56
Promise to Murder '56
Quicksand '50
The Raven '63
The Sad Sack '57
The Secret Agent '36
Silk Stockings '57
Strange Cargo '40
Stranger on the Third Floor '40
Tales of Terror '62
They Met in Bombay '41
20,000 Leagues Under the Sea
'54
Voyage to the Bottom of the
Sea '61
You'll Find Out '40
Joan Lorring
The Corn is Green '45
The Gangster '47
Good Sam '48
Diana Lorys
The Awful Dr. Orlof '62
Fangs of the Living Dead '68
House of Psychotic Women '73
Lightning Bolt '67

Eb Lottimer
Beyond the Call of Duty '92
The Finest Hour '91
Futurekick '91
Lords of the Deep '89
Quake '92
Quicker Than the Eye '88
Streets '90
Stripped to Kill II: Live Girls '89
Alexander Lou
Mafia vs. Ninja '84
Ninja Condors '87
Ninja the Battalion '90
Ninja vs. the Shaolin '84
Super Ninja
Louanne
A Night in the Life of Jimmy
Reardon '88
Oh, God! Book 2 '80
Jackie Loughery
D.I. '57
Pardners '56
Lori Loughlin
Amityville 3: The Demon '83
Back to the Beach '87
The New Kids '85
The Night Before '88
Rad '86
Secret Admirer '85
Bill Louie
The Bodyguard '76
Fist of Fear, Touch of Death '77
Julia Louis-Dreyfus
Best of Eddie Murphy '89
Jack the Bear '93
National Lampoon's Christmas
Vacation '89
North '94
Joe Louis
The Spirit of Youth '37
This is the Army '43
Justin Louis
The Big Slice '90
Hello Mary Lou: Prom Night 2
'87
Willard Louis
Beau Brummel '24
Don Juan '26
Robin Hood '22
Anita Louise
Anthony Adverse '36
Casanova Brown '44
The Gorilla '39
Harmon of Michigan '41
Judge Priest '34
The Little Princess '39
Marie Antoinette '38
Millie '31
Retreat, Hell! '52
The Sisters '38
Square Shoulders '29
The Story of Louis Pasteur '36
That Certain Woman '37
The Villain Still Pursued Her '41
Tina Louise
Armored Command '61
The Day the Women Got Even
'80
Death Scream '75
Dixie Lanes '88
Evils of the Night '85
Gilligan's Island: Meet the Crew
'64
God's Little Acre '58
The Good Guys and the Bad
Guys '69
The Happy Ending '69
Hellriders '84
How to Commit Marriage '69
Johnny Suede '92
Mean Dog Blues '78
Nightmare in Badham County
'76
O.C. and Stiggs '87
The Trap '59
Alan Love
The Apple '80
That Sinking Feeling '79
Bessie Love
Broadway Melody '29
Catlow '71
Intolerance '16
Isadora '68
The King on Main Street '25

The Lost World '25
Morals for Women '31
Mystery of the Leaping Fish/
Chess Fever '25
The Poppy is also a Flower '66
Reggie Mixes In '16
Roman Spring of Mrs. Stone
'61
Soul-Fire '25
Darlene Love
Lethal Weapon '87
Lethal Weapon 2 '89
Lethal Weapon 3 '92
Lucretia Love
Dr. Heckyl and Mr. Hype '80
Naked Warriors '73
Phenomenal and the Treasure
of Tutankamen '70s
The She-Beast '65
Montagu Love
The Adventures of Robin Hood
'38
Bulldog Drummond '29
A Damsel in Distress '37
Don Juan '26
Gunga Din '39
Hands Up '26
His Double Life '33
Inside the Lines '30
Lady for a Night '42
The Mark of Zorro '40
One in a Million '36
The Prince and the Pauper '37
Prisoner of Zenda '37
The Riding Tornado '32
Sherlock Holmes: The Voice of
Terror '42
The Son of Monte Cristo '41
Vanity Fair '32
The Wind '28
Wings Over the Pacific '43
Suzanna Love
The Boogey Man '80
Boogey Man 2 '83
Brainwaves '82
Cocaine Cowboys '79
Devonsville Terror '83
Olivia '83
Victor Love
Final Shot: The Hank Gathers
Story '92
Guilty of Innocence '87
Heaven is a Playground '91
Native Son '86
Alec Lovejoy
Moon Over Harlem '39
Murder on Lenox Avenue '41
Frank Lovejoy
Americano '55
The Finger Man '55
The Hitch-Hiker '53
Home of the Brave '49
House of Wax '53
I'll See You in My Dreams '51
In a Lonely Place '50
Men of the Fighting Lady '54
Retreat, Hell! '52
Shack Out on 101 '55
Strategic Air Command '55
Three Secrets '50
Try and Get Me '50
The Winning Team '52
Raymond Lovell
Appointment with Crime '45
Hotel Reserve '44
King of the Damned '36
Ray Lovelock
Autopsy '78
From Hell to Victory '79
One Russian Summer '73
Dorothy Lovett
Courageous Dr. Christian '40
Dr. Christian Meets the Women
'40
Remedy for Riches '40
They Meet Again '41
Lyle Lovett
The Player '92
Short Cuts '93
Jon Lovitz
Big '88
City Slickers 2: The Legend of
Curly's Gold '94
Jumpin' Jack Flash '86
Last Resort '86

A League of Their Own '92
Mr. Destiny '90
Mom and Dad Save the World
'92
My Stepmother Is an Alien '88
National Lampoon's Loaded
Weapon 1 '93
North '94
Three Amigos '86
Celia Lovsky
I, Mobster '58
Rhapsody '54
Arthur Lowe
The Bawdy Adventures of Tom
Jones '76
If... '69
O Lucky Man! '73
The Ruling Class '72
The Strange Case of the End of
Civilization as We Know It
'93
Sweet William '79
This Sporting Life '63
Chad Lowe
Apprentice to Murder '88
Highway to Hell '92
An Inconvenient Woman '91
Nobody's Perfect '90
Silence of the Heart '84
True Blood '89
Edmund Lowe
Call Out the Marines '42
Chandu the Magician '32
Dillinger '45
Dinner at Eight '33
The Enchanted Forest '45
Every Day's a Holiday '38
The Eyes of Youth '19
Good Sam '48
Heller in Pink Tights '60
I Love You Again '40
The Squeaker '37
Wings of Eagles '57
Patrick Lowe
Primal Rage '90
Slumber Party Massacre 2 '87
Rob Lowe
About Last Night... '86
Bad Influence '90
Class '83
The Dark Backward '91
The Finest Hour '91
The Hotel New Hampshire '84
Illegally Yours '87
Masquerade '88
The Outsiders '83
Oxford Blues '84
St. Elmo's Fire '85
Square Dance '87
Stephen King's The Stand '94
Stroke of Midnight '90
Wayne's World '92
Youngblood '86
Carey Lowell
Club Paradise '86
Dangerously Close '86
Down Twisted '89
The Guardian '90
License to Kill '89
Me and Him '89
Road to Ruin '91
Sleepless in Seattle '93
Curt Lowens
Invisible: The Chronicles of
Benjamin Knight '93
Mandroid '93
A Midnight Clear '92
Werewolf in a Girl's Dormitory
'61
Andrew Lowery
Color of Night '94
JFK: Reckless Youth '93
My Boyfriend's Back '93
School Ties '92
Robert Lowery
Big Town '47
Border Rangers '50
Call of the Forest '49
Dangerous Passage '44
Dark Mountain '44
Dawn on the Great Divide '42
Death Valley '46
Drums Along the Mohawk '39
God's Country '46
Gunfire '50
Highway 13 '48

House of Horrors '46
I Shot Billy the Kid '50
Johnny Reno '66
Lure of the Islands '42
The Mummy's Ghost '44
Murder Over New York '40
Mystery of the Riverboat '44
Navy Way '49
Outlaw Gang '49
Queen of the Amazons '47
Revenge of the Zombies '43
Rhythm Parade '43
The Rise and Fall of Legs
  Diamond '60
Shep Comes Home '49
Trail of the Mounties '47
Train to Tombstone '50
The Undertaker and His Pals
  '67
Western Pacific Agent '51

William E. Lowery
The Lamb '15
Reggie Mixes In '16
Robin Hood '22

Klaus Lowitsch
Despair '78
The Marriage of Maria Braun
  '79

Lynn Lowry
The Crazies '73
Fighting Mad '76
Sugar Cookies '77
They Came from Within '75

Scooter Lowry
Our Gang '26
Our Gang Comedy Festival '88
Our Gang Comedy Festival 2
  '89

Myrna Loy
After the Thin Man '36
Airport '75 '75
The Ambassador's Daughter
  '56
The Animal Kingdom '32
Another Thin Man '39
Ants '77
April Fools '69
Arrowsmith '31
The Bachelor and the Bobby-
  Soxer '47
The Best Years of Our Lives
  '46
Broadway Bill '34
A Connecticut Yankee '31
Consolation Marriage '31
Don Juan '26
Double Wedding '37
The End '78
Evelyn Prentice '34
From the Terrace '60
The Great Ziegfeld '36
I Love You Again '40
The Jazz Singer '27
Just Tell Me What You Want
  '80
Libeled Lady '36
Lonelyhearts '58
Love Crazy '41
Manhattan Melodrama '34
The Mask of Fu Manchu '32
Midnight Lace '60
Mr. Blandings Builds His
  Dream House '48
Penthouse '33
The Prizefighter and the Lady
  '33
The Rains Came '39
The Red Pony '49
Renegade Ranger/Scarlet River
  '38
Rogue of the Rio Grande '30
Shadow of the Thin Man '41
So This is Paris '26
Song of the Thin Man '47
Summer Solstice '81
Test Pilot '38
The Thin Man '34
The Thin Man Goes Home '44
Too Hot to Handle '38
Topaze '33
Vanity Fair '32
Wife Versus Secretary '36

Margarita Lozano
Half of Heaven '86
Kaos '85
The Night of the Shooting Stars
  '82

Viridiana '61

Antonella Lualdi
Mafia la Ley Que Non Perdona
  '79
The Mongols '60

Arthur Lucan
My Son, the Vampire '52
Old Mother Riley's Ghosts '41

Lisa Lucas
Forbidden Love '82
Hadley's Rebellion '84
A House Without a Christmas
  Tree '72

Wilfrid Lucas
A Chump at Oxford '40
Dishonored '31
The Phantom '31
Roaring Speedboats '37

Susan Lucci
Anastasia: The Mystery of
  Anna '86
French Silk '94
Hit Woman: The Double Edge
  '93
Invitation to Hell '84
Lady Mobster '88
Mafia Princess '86
Secret Passions '78

Angela Luce
The Decameron '70
'Tis a Pity She's a Whore '73

Enrique Lucero
The Evil That Men Do '84
Macario '58
Mr. Horn '79
The Woman Hunter '72

Fabrice Luchini
Full Moon in Paris '84
La Discrete '90
Uranus '91

Chip Lucio
Hospital Massacre '81
Primary Target '89

Laurence Luckinbill
The Boys in the Band '70
Cocktail '88
Death Sentence '74
Ike '79
The Lindbergh Kidnapping
  Case '76
Mating Season '81
Messenger of Death '88
The Money '75
Not for Publication '84
Panic on the 5:22 '74
The Promise '78
Star Trek 5: The Final Frontier
  '89
To Heal a Nation '88

William Lucking
Coast to Coast '80
Duplicates '92
Humanoid Defender '85
Kung Fu: The Movie '86
Naked Lie '89
Rescue Me '93

Jack Luden
The Last Outlaw '27
Phantom Gold '38

Charles Ludlum
The Big Easy '87
Imposters '84

Pamela Ludwig
Dead Man Walking '88
Death of an Angel '86
Over the Edge '79
Pale Blood '91
Race for Glory '89
Rush Week '89

Laurette Luez
Ballad of a Gunfighter '64
Fu Manchu '56
Prehistoric Women '50

Lorna Luft
Grease 2 '82
Where the Boys Are '84 '84

Bela Lugosi
Abbott and Costello Meet
  Frankenstein '48
The Ape Man '43
Bela Lugosi Meets a Brooklyn
  Gorilla '52
Bela Lugosi Scrapbook '70s

The Black Cat '34
The Black Dragons '42
The Body Snatcher '45
Bowery at Midnight '42
Bowery at Midnight/Dick Tracy
  vs. Cueball '42
Bride of the Monster '56
Chandu on the Magic Island '34
Chandu the Magician '32
The Corpse Vanishes '42
The Death Kiss '33
The Devil Bat '41
Dick Tracy, Detective/The
  Corpse Vanishes '42
Dracula '31
Frankenstein Meets the
  Wolfman '42
The Ghost of Frankenstein '42
Glen or Glenda '53
The Gorilla '39
The Horror of It All '91
The Human Monster '39
International House '33
The Invisible Ghost '41
The Invisible Ray '36
Island of Lost Souls '32
Mark of the Vampire '35
Midnight Girl '25
Murder by Television '35
Murders in the Rue Morgue '32
My Son, the Vampire '52
The Mystery of the Mary
  Celeste '37
Night Monster '42
Night of Terror '33
Ninotchka '39
One Body Too Many '44
The Phantom Creeps '39
Plan 9 from Outer Space '56
Postal Inspector '36
The Raven '35
Return of Chandu '34
Return of the Ape Man '44
Return of the Vampire '43
The Saint's Double Trouble '40
Saturday Night Serials '40
Scared to Death '47
Scared to Death/Dick Tracy's
  Dilemma '47
Shadow of Chinatown '36
Son of Frankenstein '39
S.O.S. Coast Guard '37
Spooks Run Wild '41
Whispering Shadow '33
The White Zombie '32
The Wolf Man '41
You'll Find Out '40
Zombies on Broadway '44

James Luisi
The Dark Ride '84
Feds '88
Murphy's Law '86
One in a Million: The Ron
  LaFlore Story '78
Stunts '77

Paul Lukas
Berlin Express '48
Deadline at Dawn '46
Dinner at the Ritz '37
Dodsworth '36
Experiment Perilous '45
55 Days at Peking '63
Fun in Acapulco '63
The Ghost Breakers '40
Hitchcock Collection '87
Kim '50
Lady in Distress '39
The Lady Vanishes '38
Little Women '33
Lord Jim '65
The Monster and the Girl '41
The Mutiny of the Elsinore '39
Strange Cargo '40
The Three Musketeers '35
20,000 Leagues Under the Sea
  '54
Vice Squad '31
Watch on the Rhine '43
Whispering City '47

Paul Lukather
Dinosaurus! '60
Hands of a Stranger '62

Benny Luke
La Cage aux Folles '78
La Cage aux Folles 2 '81
La Cage aux Folles 3: The
  Wedding '86

Jorge Luke
El Sabor de la Venganza '65
The Evil That Men Do '84
Foxtrot '76
Shark Hunter '84
Ulzana's Raid '72

Keye Luke
Across the Pacific '42
Alice '90
The Amsterdam Kill '78
Battle Hell '56
Blade in Hong Kong '85
Bowery Blitzkrieg '41
Charlie Chan at the Opera '36
Charlie Chan in Paris '35
Dead Heat '88
The Falcon's Brother '42
The Gang's All Here '41
The Good Earth '37
The Green Hornet '39
Gremlins '84
Kung Fu '72
Kung Fu: The Movie '86
Let's Go Collegiate '41
The Mighty Quinn '89
No, No Nanette '40
Noon Sunday '71
Phantom of Chinatown '40

Wolfgang Lukschy
Dead Eyes of London '61
Frozen Alive '64

Folco Lulli
The Great War '59
Lightning Bolt '67
Variety Lights '51
Wages of Fear '55

Carl Lumbly
The Bedroom Window '87
Brother Future '91
Everybody's All American '88
Judgment in Berlin '88
Pacific Heights '90
South Central '92
To Sleep with Anger '90

Jenny Lumet
Q & A '90
Tougher than Leather '88

Sidney Lumet
One Third of a Nation '39
Running on Empty '88

Joanna Lumley
Curse of the Pink Panther '83
On Her Majesty's Secret
  Service '69
The Satanic Rites of Dracula
  '73
Shirley Valentine '89
Weather in the Streets '84

Barbara Luna
The Concrete Jungle '82
Firecreek '68
The Gatling Gun '72
Gentle Savage '73
The Hanged Man '74

Art Lund
Black Caesar '73
Bucktown '75
The Last American Hero '73

Deanna Lund
Dr. Goldfoot and the Bikini
  Machine '66
Elves '89
Hardly Working '81
Red Wind '91

John Lund
Dakota Incident '56
Duchess of Idaho '50
Latin Lovers '53
My Friend Irma '49
The Perils of Pauline '47
Wackiest Ship in the Army '61

Lucille Lund
The Black Cat '34
Prison Shadows '36

Christine Lunde
Dead End City '88
Masque of the Red Death '90

Dolph Lundgren
Cover-Up '91
I Come in Peace '90
Masters of the Universe '87
The Punisher '90
Red Scorpion '89
Rocky 4 '85

Showdown in Little Tokyo '91
Universal Soldier '92
A View to a Kill '85

William Lundigan
Andy Hardy's Double Life '42
Danger on the Air '38
Dishonored Lady '47
The Fighting 69th '40
Follow Me Quietly '49
Love Nest '51
Pinky '49
State Department File 649 '49
Terror Ship '54
The White Orchid '54
Wives Under Suspicion '38

Vic Lundin
Ma Barker's Killer Brood '60
Robinson Crusoe on Mars '64
Two for the Seesaw '62

Steve Lundquist
Killer Tomatoes Eat France '91
Killer Tomatoes Strike Back '90
Return of the Killer Tomatoes
  '88

Jessica Lundy
Caddyshack 2 '88
Madhouse '90

Huang I Lung
Fists of Dragons '69
Two Dragons Fight Against the
  Tiger

Suma Wah Lung
Kick of Death: The Prodigal
  Boxer '80s
Prodigal Boxer: The Kick of
  Death '73

Ti Lung
A Better Tomorrow '86
Duel of Fists '89
Duel of the Iron Fist '72
Revenge of the Zombies '81

Cherie Lunghi
Excalibur '81
Harem '86
Intrigue '90
King David '85
Letters to an Unknown Lover
  '84
The Mission '86
Oliver Twist '82
Praying Mantis '83
The Sign of Four '83
Tales of the Klondike: The
  Unexpected '87
To Kill a Priest '89

Alfred Lunt
The Guardsman '31
Sally of the Sawdust '25

Roldano Lupi
The Giant of Metropolis '61
The Mongols '60

Ida Lupino
The Adventures of Sherlock
  Holmes '39
Beware, My Lovely '52
The Big Knife '55
The Bigamist '53
Devil's Rain '75
Escape Me Never '47
Food of the Gods '76
Forever and a Day '43
The Ghost Camera '33
High Sierra '41
Hollywood Canteen '44
Junior Bonner '72
Lust for Gold '49
The Man I Love '46
My Boys are Good Boys '78
On Dangerous Ground '51
One Rainy Afternoon '36
Private Hell 36 '54
Road House '48
Sea Devils '37
The Sea Wolf '41
Thank Your Lucky Stars '43
They Drive by Night '40
While the City Sleeps '56

Alberto Lupo
The Agony and the Ecstasy '65
Atom Age Vampire '61
The Bacchantes '63
Coriolanus, Man without a
  Country '64
Django Shoots First '74
The Giant of Marathon '60

Lupo ▶cont.

Herod the Great '60
Patti LuPone
Driving Miss Daisy '89
Family Prayers '91
Fighting Back '82
LBJ: The Early Years '88
1941 '79
Wise Guys '86
Witness '85
Federico Luppi
Funny, Dirty Little War '83
Mayalunta '86
Time for Revenge '82
John Lupton
All the Brothers Were Valiant '53
Diane '55
Escape from Fort Bravo '53
Jesse James Meets Frankenstein's Daughter '65
The Rebel Set '59
Peter Lupus
Escapist '83
More! Police Squad '82
Muscle Beach Party '64
Pulsebeat '85
Think Big '90
John Lurie
Down by Law '86
The Last Temptation of Christ '88
Permanent Vacation '84
Stranger than Paradise '84
Jaques Lussier
Norman's Awesome Experience '88
Pouvoir Intime '87
Franc Luz
Ecstasy '84
Ghost Town '88
The Nest '88
Jimmy Lydon
Back Door to Heaven '39
Life with Father '47
Little Men '40
The Magnificent Yankee '50
Strange Illusion '45
Tom Brown's School Days '40
Reg Lye
Freedom '81
Walk into Hell '57
Dorothy Lyman
Camp Cucamonga: How I Spent My Summer Vacation '90
Ollie Hopnoodle's Haven of Bliss '88
Ruby in Paradise '93
Summer Fantasy '84
Alfred Lynch
Bewitched '85
Blockhouse '73
David Lynch
Twin Peaks: Fire Walk with Me '92
Zelly & Me '88
Helen Lynch
The Return of Grey Wolf '22
Smouldering Fires '25
John Lynch
Cal '84
Edward II '92
Hardware '90
In the Name of the Father '93
Monkey Boy '90
The Railway Station Man '92
The Secret Garden '93
Kate Lynch
Def-Con 4 '85
Lethal Lolita—Amy Fisher: My Story '92
Meatballs '79
Reckless Disregard '84
Summer's Children '84
Kelly Lynch
Cocktail '88
Curly Sue '91
Desperate Hours '90
Drugstore Cowboy '89

For Better and For Worse '92
Osa '85
Road House '89
Three of Hearts '93
Warm Summer Rain '89
Ken Lynch
Jet Attack/Paratroop Command '58
My Pleasure Is My Business '74
Richard Lynch
Aftershock '88
Bad Dreams '88
The Barbarians '87
The Baron '88
Death Sport '78
Delta Fox '77
Double Threat '92
The Forbidden Dance '90
The Formula '80
God Told Me To '76
High Stakes '89
Inside Edge '92
Invasion Force '90
Invasion U.S.A. '85
Little Nikita '88
Lockdown '90
Maximum Force '92
Merlin '93
Nightforce '86
One Man Force '89
The Premonition '75
Savage Dawn '84
Scanner Cop '94
Scarecrow '73
Showdown '93
Sizzle '81
Steel '80
Sword & the Sorcerer '82
Trancers 2: The Return of Jack Deth '91
Paul Lynde
Beach Blanket Bingo '65
Bye, Bye, Birdie '63
The Glass Bottom Boat '66
How Sweet It Is! '68
New Faces of 1952 '54
Rabbit Test '78
Send Me No Flowers '64
Son of Flubber '63
The Villain '79
Carol Lynley
Bad Georgia Road '77
Balboa '82
Blackout '88
Blood Island '68
The Cardinal '63
The Cat and the Canary '79
Cotter '72
Dark Tower '87
Death Stalk '74
Fantasy Island '76
Flood! '76
Four Deuces '75
Howling 6: The Freaks '90
If It's a Man, Hang Up '75
The Light in the Forest '58
The Poseidon Adventure '72
Return to Peyton Place '61
Son of Blob '72
Spirits '90
The Stripper '63
Vigilante '83
Washington Affair '77
Ann Lynn
Baby Love '69
Estate of Insanity '70
Betty Lynn
June Bride '48
Meet Me in Las Vegas '56
Return to Mayberry '85
Texas John Slaughter: Geronimo's Revenge '60
Cheryl Lynn
Emanon '86
Fate '90
Thunder Run '86
Diana Lynn
The Annapolis Story '55
Bedtime for Bonzo '51
Every Girl Should Be Married '48
The Kentuckian '55
Miracle of Morgan's Creek '44
My Friend Irma '49

Emmett Lynn
The Caravan Trail '46
The Fighting Redhead '50
Frontier Outlaws '44
Song of Old Wyoming '45
Fonda Lynn
Deadly Darling '85
Ninja Brothers of Blood '89
Jeffrey Lynn
All This and Heaven Too '40
The Fighting 69th '40
Four Daughters '38
Home Town Story '51
A Letter to Three Wives '49
The Roaring Twenties '39
Tony Rome '67
Mara Lynn
G.I. Jane '51
Leave It to the Marines '51
Prehistoric Women '50
Sky High '51
Peter George Lynn
Mr. Wong in Chinatown '39
Mystery Plane '39
Wolf Call '39
Rebecca Lynn
Sensations '87
Thrilled to Death '88
Ben Lyon
Crimson Romance '34
The Crooked Circle '32
Hell's Angels '30
I Cover the Waterfront '33
Indiscreet '31
Mad About Money '30
Night Nurse '31
Richard Lyon
Anna and the King of Siam '46
The Tender Years '47
Sue Lyon
End of the World '77
Evel Knievel '72
Flim-Flam Man '67
Four Rode Out '69
The Invisible Strangler '76
Lolita '62
The Night of the Iguana '64
Tony Rome '67
Bruce Lyons
Model Behavior '82
The Navigator '88
Robert F. Lyons
American Eagle '90
Black Oak Conspiracy '77
Cease Fire '85
Getting Straight '70
Murphy's Law '86
Platoon Leader '87
The Todd Killings '71
Tzi Ma
Golden Gate '93
Rapid Fire '92
Byron Mabe
The Defilers '65
The Doberman Gang '72
Moms Mabley
Amazing Grace '74
Boardinghouse Blues '48
Killer Diller '48
Bernie Mac
Above the Rim '94
House Party 3 '94
Anne MacAdams
Common Law Wife '63
Don't Look in the Basement '73
James MacArthur
Bedford Incident '65
Cry of Battle '63
Hang 'Em High '67
The Interns '62
Kidnapped '60
The Light in the Forest '58
Mosby's Marauders '66
Spencer's Mountain '63
The Swiss Family Robinson '60
Third Man on the Mountain '59
Marc Macaulay
Cop and a Half '93
Hidden Fears '93
Donald MacBride
Blondie Takes a Vacation '39
Buck Privates Come Home '47

Egg and I '47
The Great Man Votes '38
Holiday Rhythm '50
The Invisible Woman '40
Meet Danny Wilson '52
Murder Over New York '40
A Night to Remember '42
Room Service '38
The Saint's Double Trouble '40
Ralph Macchio
Crossroads '86
Distant Thunder '88
The Karate Kid '84
The Karate Kid: Part 2 '86
The Karate Kid: Part 3 '89
My Cousin Vinny '92
Naked in New York '93
The Outsiders '83
Teachers '84
Too Much Sun '90
Up the Academy '80
Aldo Maccione
Loose in New York '80s
Loves & Times of Scaramouche '76
Too Shy to Try '82
Katherine MacColl
Gates of Hell '83
The House by the Cemetery '83
Seven Doors of Death '82
Simon MacCorkindale
Cabo Blanco '81
Death on the Nile '78
Jaws 3 '83
The Manions of America '81
Obsessive Love '84
Quatermass Conclusion '79
The Riddle of the Sands '79
Robbers of the Sacred Mountain '83
Sword & the Sorcerer '82
Visitor from the Grave '81
Edmund MacDonald
Detour '46
The Lady Confesses '45
Shoot to Kill '47
J. Farrell MacDonald
Gang Bullets '38
Hearts of Humanity '32
I Take This Oath '40
Knights of the Range '40
Phantom Express '32
Phantom Killer '42
Probation '32
Riders of the Timberline '41
Riff Raff '35
Romance in Manhattan '34
Sky High '22
Snuffy Smith, Yard Bird '42
Sunrise '27
Susannah of the Mounties '39
Texas Masquerade '44
13th Guest '32
Jeanette MacDonald
Bitter Sweet '40
Broadway Serenade '39
Cairo '42
The Cat and the Fiddle '34
The Firefly '37
Girl of the Golden West '38
I Married an Angel '42
Lottery Bride '30
Maytime '37
The Merry Widow '34
Naughty Marietta '35
New Moon '40
Rose Marie '36
San Francisco '36
Smilin' Through '41
The Sun Comes Up '49
Sweethearts '38
Three Daring Daughters '48
Kenneth MacDonald
Border Vengeance '35
Six Gun Gospel '43
U-Boat Prisoner '44
Michael MacDonald
Mr. Nice Guy '86
Mystery of the Million Dollar Hockey Puck '80s
Wallace MacDonald
Between Fighting Men '32
Daring Danger '32
Range Feud '31

Red Signals '27
The Riding Tornado '32
Texas Cyclone '32
Two-Fisted Law '32
Wendy MacDonald
Blood Frenzy '87
Broken Trust '93
Dark Side of the Moon '90
Heat Street '87
Mayhem '87
Andie MacDowell
Bad Girls '94
Deception '92
Four Weddings and a Funeral '93
Green Card '90
Greystoke: The Legend of Tarzan, Lord of the Apes '84
Groundhog Day '93
Hudson Hawk '91
The Object of Beauty '91
St. Elmo's Fire '85
sex, lies and videotape '89
Short Cuts '93
Women & Men: In Love There Are No Rules '91
Rita Macedo
The Criminal Life of Archibaldo de la Cruz '55
The Curse of the Crying Woman '61
El Fugitivo '65
Nazarin '58
Moyna MacGill
The Strange Affair of Uncle Harry '45
Three Daring Daughters '48
Niall MacGinnis
Betrayed '54
Curse of the Demon '57
The Day Will Dawn '42
Edge of the World '37
Island of Terror '66
Lust for Life '56
Martin Luther '53
Sword of Sherwood Forest '60
The War Lord '65
Tara MacGowan
The Dawning '88
Las Vegas Serial Killer '86
Secret Places '85
Jack MacGowran
The Brain '62
Cul de Sac '66
The Exorcist '73
The Fearless Vampire Killers '67
King Lear '71
Lord Jim '65
The Quiet Man '52
Start the Revolution Without Me '70
Wonderwall: The Movie '69
Ali MacGraw
Convoy '78
The Getaway '72
Goodbye Columbus '69
Just Tell Me What You Want '80
Love Story '70
Murder Elite '86
Players '79
The Winds of War '83
Stephen Macht
American Dream '81
Amityville 1992: It's About Time '92
Blind Witness '89
The Choirboys '77
Enola Gay: The Men, the Mission, the Atomic Bomb '80
A Friendship in Vienna '88
Galaxina '80
Graveyard Shift '90
Killjoy '81
The Monster Squad '87
Trancers 3: Deth Lives '92
Trancers 4: Jack of Swords '93
Betty Mack
Fighting Texans '33
The Forty-Niners '32
Outlaw Rule '36
Rough Ridin' Rhythm '37
Toll of the Desert '35

Helen Mack
Fargo Express '32
Fit for a King '37
His Girl Friday '40
Melody Cruise '32
Milky Way '36
The Return of Peter Grimm '35
Son of Kong '33
The Wrong Road '37

Kerry Mack
Fair Game '85
Fantasy Man '84
Savage Attraction '83

Wayne Mack
Crypt of Dark Secrets '76
Mardi Gras Massacre '78
Storyville '74

Dorothy Mackaill
Bulldog Drummond at Bay '37
Kept Husbands '31
No Man of Her Own '32
Ranson's Folly '26
Shore Leave '25

Barry Mackay
Evergreen '34
Gangway '37
The Private Secretary '35
Sailing Along '38

Fulton Mackay
Defense of the Realm '85
Local Hero '83
Nothing But the Night '72
Porridge '91
A Sense of Freedom '78

John MacKay
Alligator Eyes '90
Fat Guy Goes Nutzoid '86
The Rejuvenator '88
Simple Men '92
Trust '91

Helen MacKellar
Bad Boy '39
Delinquent Parents '38

Giselle MacKenzie
Music Shoppe '82
One Minute Before Death '88
The Oval Portrait '88

Jan MacKenzie
The American Angels: Baptism of Blood '89
Gator Bait 2: Cajun Justice '88

Patch MacKenzie
Black Eliminator '70s
Defense Play '88
Goodbye, Norma Jean '75
Graduation Day '81
Isle of Secret Passion '85

Jim MacKrell
Just Between Friends '86
Love at the Top '86

Janet MacLachlan
Big Mo '73
Darker than Amber '70
For Us, the Living '88
Murphy's Law '86
Roll of Thunder, Hear My Cry '78
She's in the Army Now '81
Sounder '72

Kyle MacLachlan
Blue Velvet '86
Don't Tell Her It's Me '90
The Doors '91
Dune '84
The Flintstones '94
The Hidden '87
Rich in Love '93
The Trial '93
Twin Peaks '90
Twin Peaks: Fire Walk with Me '92
Where the Day Takes You '92

Shirley MacLaine
All in a Night's Work '61
The Apartment '60
Around the World in 80 Days '56
Artists and Models '55
Ask Any Girl '59
Being There '79
The Bliss of Mrs. Blossom '68
Can-Can '60
Cannonball Run 2 '84
Career '59

A Change of Seasons '80
The Children's Hour '61
Desperate Characters '71
Gambit '66
Golden Age of Hollywood '77
Guarding Tess '94
Hot Spell '58
Irma La Douce '63
Loving Couples '80
Madame Sousatzka '88
The Matchmaker '58
My Geisha '62
Out on a Limb '87
The Possession of Joel Delaney '72
Postcards from the Edge '90
Some Came Running '58
Steel Magnolias '89
Sweet Charity '69
Terms of Endearment '83
That's Dancing! '85
The Trouble with Harry '55
The Turning Point '77
Two for the Seesaw '62
Two Mules for Sister Sara '70
Used People '92
Waiting for the Light '90
Woman Times Seven '67
Wrestling Ernest Hemingway '93

Barton MacLane
All Through the Night '42
Arizona Bushwackers '67
Big Street '42
Black Fury '35
Bombardier '43
Buckskin '68
Bugles in the Afternoon '52
Bullets or Ballots '38
The Case of the Lucky Legs '35
Ceiling Zero '35
Cry of the Werewolf '44
Drums in the Deep South '51
"G" Men '35
The Geisha Boy '58
The Half-Breed '51
Kansas Pacific '53
Let's Dance '50
The Maltese Falcon '41
Man of the Forest '33
Marine Raiders '43
Melody Ranch '40
The Mummy's Ghost '44
Mutiny in the Big House '39
Nabonga '44
Naked in the Sun '57
The Prince and the Pauper '37
Prison Break '38
Silver River '48
Song of Texas '43
The Spanish Main '45
Three Violent People '57
To the Last Man '33
Treasure of Fear '45
Treasure of the Sierra Madre '48
The Underdog '43
Unknown Island '48
Western Union '41
You Only Live Once '37

Mary MacLaren
A Lawman is Born '37
The New Frontier '35

Gavin MacLeod
The Cary Grant Collection '90
Kelly's Heroes '70
The Love Boat '70s
Only with Married Men '74
The Party '68
The Sand Pebbles '66
Scruples '80

Michael MacLiammoir
Othello '52
What's the Matter with Helen? '71

Ellie MacLure
Air Hawk '84
Alvin Purple '73
Heat of the Flame '82

Aline MacMahon
Ah, Wilderness! '35
Back Door to Heaven '39
Dragon Seed '44
The Flame & the Arrow '50
Gold Diggers of 1933 '33
Heroes for Sale '33

I Could Go on Singing '63
I Live My Life '35
The Lady is Willing '42
The Man from Laramie '55
The Search '48

Fred MacMurray
Above Suspicion '43
The Absent-Minded Professor '61
Alice Adams '35
The Apartment '60
At Gunpoint '55
Beyond the Bermuda Triangle '75
Bon Voyage! '62
Borderline '50
The Caine Mutiny '54
Charley and the Angel '73
Dive Bomber '41
Double Indemnity '44
Egg and I '47
Follow Me, Boys! '66
The Happiest Millionaire '67
Kisses for My President '64
The Lady is Willing '42
The Miracle of the Bells '48
My Love For Yours '39
Never a Dull Moment '50
The Shaggy Dog '59
Son of Flubber '63
The Swarm '78
Swing High, Swing Low '37

Robert MacNaughton
E.T.: The Extra-Terrestrial '82
I Am the Cheese '83

Patrick Macnee
Battlestar Galactica '78
The Bloodsuckers '70
Chill Factor '90
A Christmas Carol '51
Cult People '89
Dead of Night '77
Down Under '86
The Elusive Pimpernel '50
The Gambler Returns: The Luck of the Draw '93
The Howling '81
King Solomon's Treasure '76
Les Girls '57
Lobster Man from Mars '89
Masque of the Red Death '89
Rehearsal for Murder '82
Return of the Man from U.N.C.L.E. '83
Sea Wolves '81
Shadey '87
Sherlock Holmes and the Incident at Victoria Falls '91
Sorry, Wrong Number '89
Spaceship '81
Sweet 16 '81
This is Spinal Tap '84
Transformations '88
A View to a Kill '85
Waxwork '88
Young Doctors in Love '82

Peter MacNicol
Addams Family Values '93
American Blue Note '89
The Boy Who Left Home to Find Out About the Shivers '81
Dragonslayer '81
Ghostbusters 2 '89
Hard Promises '92
Heat '87
Housesitter '92
Sophie's Choice '82

Elle Macpherson
Alice '90
Sirens '94

George MacQuarrie
The Idol Dancer '20
The Love Flower '20

Gordon MacRae
By the Light of the Silvery Moon '53
Carousel '56
Danger in the Skies '79
The Desert Song '53
Look for the Silver Lining '49
Oklahoma! '55
On Moonlight Bay '51
Tea for Two '50
The West Point Story '50

Heather MacRae
Bang the Drum Slowly '73

The Connection '73
Secrets of Three Hungry Wives '78

Meredith MacRae
Bikini Beach '64
Husbands, Wives, Money, and Murder '86
Sketches of a Strangler '78
Vultures '84

Michael MacRae
Dear Detective '78
Great Ride '78
Greedy Terror '78
Isle of Secret Passion '85
Madhouse '87

George Macready
Black Arrow '48
Coroner Creek '48
Detective Story '51
The Doolins of Oklahoma '49
Down to Earth '47
Gilda '46
Great Race '65
The Green Glove '52
The Human Duplicators '64
I Beheld His Glory '53
Julius Caesar '53
Knock on Any Door '49
The Nevadan '50
Paths of Glory '57
The Return of Count Yorga '71
The Seventh Cross '44
The Stranger Wore a Gun '53
Taras Bulba '62
Tora! Tora! Tora! '70
Two Weeks in Another Town '62
Vera Cruz '53
Where Love Has Gone '64

Bill Macy
Bad Medicine '85
Casey at the Bat '85
Diary of a Young Comic '79
The Doctor '91
The Jerk '79
The Late Show '77
Me, Myself & I '92
Movers and Shakers '85
My Favorite Year '82
Oh! Calcutta! '72
Serial '80
Sibling Rivalry '90

William H. Macy
Being Human '94
Benny & Joon '93
Homicide '91
A Private Matter '92
Searching for Bobby Fischer '93
Twenty Bucks '93

Ciaran Madden
Fortunes of War '87
A Married Man '84

Victor Maddern
Blood of the Vampire '58
I'm All Right Jack '59

Amy Madigan
Alamo Bay '85
The Ambush Murders '85
The Dark Half '91
Field of Dreams '89
Love Child '82
Love Letters '83
Nowhere to Hide '87
Places in the Heart '84
Prince of Pennsylvania '88
The Revolt of Mother '88
Roe vs. Wade '89
Streets of Fire '84
Twice in a Lifetime '85
Uncle Buck '89

Guy Madison
Apaches Last Battle '64
Bang Bang Kid '67
Bullwhip '58
Cold Steel for Tortuga '65
Computer Wizard '77
Conqueror & the Empress '64
Drums in the Deep South '51
Executioner of Venice '63
Five Giants from Texas '66
Hell Commandos '69
Jet Over the Atlantic '59
Place in Hell '65
Savage Wilderness '55
Since You Went Away '44

The Snake Hunter Strangler '66
Special Forces '68
Superargo '67
Till the End of Time '46
Where's Willie? '77

Noel Madison
Cocaine Fiends '36
Gangway '37
The House of Secrets '37
A Nation Aflame '37
Sailing Along '38

Rock Madison
Creature of the Walking Dead '60
Man Beast '55

Madonna
Bloodhounds of Broadway '89
Body of Evidence '92
Certain Sacrifice '80
Dangerous Game '93
Desperately Seeking Susan '85
Dick Tracy '90
A League of Their Own '92
Shadows and Fog '92
Shanghai Surprise '86
Truth or Dare '91
Who's That Girl? '87

Michael Madsen
Almost Blue '93
Dead Connection '94
The Doors '91
The End of Innocence '90
Fatal Instinct '92
Free Willy '93
The Getaway '93
A House In The Hills '93
Inside Edge '92
Kill Me Again '89
Money for Nothing '93
The Natural '84
Racing with the Moon '84
Reservoir Dogs '92
Shadows in the Storm '88
Straight Talk '92
Thelma & Louise '91
Trouble Bound '92
Wyatt Earp '94

Virginia Madsen
Becoming Colette '92
Candyman '92
Caroline at Midnight '93
Creator '85
Dune '84
Electric Dreams '84
Fire with Fire '86
Gotham '88
The Hearst and Davies Affair '85
The Heart of Dixie '89
Highlander 2: The Quickening '91
Hot Spot '90
Hot to Trot! '88
Ironclads '90
Linda '93
Long Gone '87
Love Kills '91
Mr. North '88
Modern Girls '86
Slamdance '87
Third Degree Burn '89
Victim of Love '91
Zombie High '87

Macha Magal
S.S. Experiment Camp 2 '86
SS Girls '78

Patrick Magee
And Now the Screaming Starts '73
Anzio '68
Asylum '72
Barry Lyndon '75
The Black Cat '81
Chariots of Fire '81
A Clockwork Orange '71
Cromwell '70
Dementia 13 '63
Demons of the Mind '72
Die, Monster, Die! '65
The Fiend '71
The Final Programme '73
A Killer in Every Corner '74
King Lear '71
Luther '74
Marat/Sade '66
Masque of the Red Death '65

Magee ▶cont.

Masque of the Red Death/
   Premature Burial '65
The Monster Club '85
Portrait in Terror '66
Rough Cut '80
Seance on a Wet Afternoon '64
The Skull '65
Sleep of Death '79
Telefon '77
Trojan Women '71
Young Winston '72

Brandon Maggart
Dressed to Kill '80
Running Mates '92
Terror in Toyland '85
The World According to Garp
   '82

Anna Magnani
Amore '48
Bellissima '51
Bellissimo: Images of the Italian
   Cinema '87
The Fugitive Kind '60
The Golden Coach '52
The Miracle '48
Open City '45
Passionate Thief '60
Peddlin' in Society '47
The Rose Tattoo '55

Ann Magnuson
Cabin Boy '94
Checking Out '89
Desperately Seeking Susan '85
Heavy Petting '89
The Hunger '83
Love at Large '89
Making Mr. Right '86
A Night in the Life of Jimmy
   Reardon '88
Perfect Strangers '84
Sleepwalk '88
Tequila Sunrise '88

Gerard Maguire
Demonstrator '71
Prisoner Cell Block H '80

Valerie Mahaffey
Mr. Bill's Real Life Adventures
   '86
The Rise & Rise of Daniel
   Rocket '86
They Watch '93
Women of Valor '86

George Maharis
The Crash of Flight 401 '78
Desperados '69
Exodus '60
Land Raiders '69
Last Day of the War '69
Murder on Flight 502 '75
Return to Fantasy Island '77
Sword & the Sorcerer '82

Bill Maher
Cannibal Women in the
   Avocado Jungle of Death '89
House 2: The Second Story '87
Pizza Man '91

Joseph Maher
The Evil That Men Do '84
Funny Farm '88
My Stepmother Is an Alien '88
Sister Act '92
Under the Rainbow '81

Grace Mahlaba
Being Human '94
Bopha! '93

Bruce Mahler
Funland '89
Police Academy 6: City Under
   Siege '89

Jock Mahoney
Bad Bunch '76
Cow Town '50
The Glory Stompers '67
The Land Unknown '57
The Nevadan '50
Range Rider '52
Rim of the Canyon '49
A Time to Love & a Time to Die
   '58

John Mahoney
Article 99 '92

Barton Fink '91
Betrayed '88
Dinner at Eight '89
Eight Men Out '88
Frantic '88
The Hudsucker Proxy '93
The Image '93
In the Line of Fire '93
Love Hurts '91
The Manhattan Project '86
Moonstruck '87
Reality Bites '94
The Russia House '90
Say Anything '89
The Secret Passion of Robert
   Clayton '93
Striking Distance '93
Suspect '87
The Ten Million Dollar Getaway
   '91
Tin Men '87
Trapped in Silence '86

Tim Maier
Raw Courage '84
Turnaround '87

Marjorie Main
The Belle of New York '52
Dark Command '40
Dead End '37
Egg and I '47
Friendly Persuasion '56
The Harvey Girls '46
Heaven Can Wait '43
Honky Tonk '41
Johnny Come Lately '43
Little Tough Guy '38
The Long, Long Trailer '54
Ma and Pa Kettle '49
Ma and Pa Kettle at the Fair '52
Ma and Pa Kettle Back On the
   Farm '51
Ma and Pa Kettle Go to Town
   '50
Rose Marie '54
The Show-Off '46
Stella Dallas '37
Summer Stock '50
Susan and God '40
They Shall Have Music '39
The Wistful Widow of Wagon
   Gap '47
A Woman's Face '41
The Women '39
The Wrong Road '37

Valerie Mairesse
Investigation '79
One Sings, the Other Doesn't
   '77
The Sacrifice '86

Marne Maitland
Bhowani Junction '56
The Bushbaby '70
Fellini's Roma '72

Tina Majorino
Andre '94
Corrina, Corrina '94
When a Man Loves a Woman
   '94

Lee Majors
The Agency '81
Big Valley '94
The Bionic Woman '75
Chinatown Connection '90
The Cover Girl Murders '93
The Cowboy & the Ballerina '84
Francis Gary Powers: The True
   Story of the U-2 Spy '76
High Noon: Part 2 '80
Keaton's Cop '90
Killer Fish '79
Last Chase '81
Norseman '78
Scrooged '88
A Smoky Mountain Christmas
   '86
Starflight One '83
Steel '80
Will Penny '67

Chris Makepeace
Aloha Summer '88
Captive Hearts '87
Last Chase '81
Mazes and Monsters '82
My Bodyguard '80
The Mysterious Stranger '82
Savage Hunger '84
The Terry Fox Story '83

Undergrads '85
Vamp '86

Wendy Makkena
Camp Nowhere '94
Sister Act '92
Sister Act 2: Back in the Habit
   '93

Mako
Armed Response '86
The Big Brawl '80
Conan the Barbarian '82
Conan the Destroyer '84
An Eye for an Eye '81
Fatal Mission '89
Hiroshima: Out of the Ashes
   '90
The Island at the Top of the
   World '74
The Killer Elite '75
Kung Fu: The Movie '86
My Samurai '92
The Nightingale '83
Pacific Heights '90
The P.O.W. Escape '86
Rising Sun '93
The Sand Pebbles '66
Sidekicks '93
The Streets of San Francisco
   '72
Taking Care of Business '90
Tucker: The Man and His
   Dream '88
Under the Rainbow '81
An Unremarkable Life '89
The Wash '88

Mala
Hawk of the Wilderness '38
Robinson Crusoe of Clipper
   Island '36
Robinson Crusoe of Mystery
   Island '36
The Tuttles of Tahiti '42

Patrick Malahide
Comfort and Joy '84
The Franchise Affair
A Month in the Country '87

Christophe MaLavoy
The Cry of the Owl '92
Madame Bovary '91
Peril '85

Karl Malden
The Adventures of Bullwhip
   Griffin '66
All Fall Down '62
Baby Doll '56
Beyond the Poseidon
   Adventure '79
Billy Galvin '86
Birdman of Alcatraz '62
Blue '68
The Cat o' Nine Tails '71
Cheyenne Autumn '64
The Cincinnati Kid '65
Diplomatic Courier '52
Fatal Vision '84
Fear Strikes Out '57
The Great Impostor '61
The Gunfighter '50
Gypsy '62
The Halls of Montezuma '50
The Hanging Tree '59
Hot Millions '67
Hotel '67
How the West was Won '63
I Confess '53
Kiss of Death '47
Meteor '79
Miracle on Ice '81
Murderers' Row '66
Nevada Smith '66
Nuts '87
On the Waterfront '54
One-Eyed Jacks '61
Parrish '61
Patton '70
Pollyanna '60
Ricco '74
Ruby Gentry '52
Skag '79
The Sting 2 '83
A Streetcar Named Desire '51
The Streets of San Francisco
   '72
They Knew What They Wanted
   '40
13 Rue Madeleine '46
Urge to Kill '84

Wild Rovers '71

Ruth Maleczech
Anna '87
The Ballad of Little Jo '93
In the Soup '92

Arthur Malet
Beastmaster 2: Through the
   Portal of Time '91
Hook '91

Laurent Malet
Blood Relatives '77
Invitation au Voyage '82
Jacko & Lise '82
Querelle '83
Sword of Gideon '86

Art Malik
City of Joy '92
Harem '86
The Jewel in the Crown '84
The Killing Beach '92
The Living Daylights '87
Transmutations '85
True Lies '94
Year of the Comet '92

Judith Malina
The Addams Family '91
Emergency '68
Enemies, a Love Story '89
Household Saints '93
Signals Through the Flames '83

Ross Malinger
Eve of Destruction '90
Late for Dinner '91
Sleepless in Seattle '93

John Malkovich
American Dream '81
Dangerous Liaisons '88
Death of a Salesman '86
Eleni '85
Empire of the Sun '87
The Glass Menagerie '87
Heart of Darkness '93
In the Line of Fire '93
Jennifer 8 '92
The Killing Fields '84
Making Mr. Right '86
Miles from Home '88
The Object of Beauty '91
Of Mice and Men '92
Places in the Heart '84
Queens Logic '91
Rocket to the Moon '86
Shadows and Fog '92
The Sheltering Sky '90
True West '86

Miles Malleson
Brothers in Law '57
Captain's Paradise '53
A Christmas Carol '51
Dead of Night '45
The Golden Salamander '51
The King's Rhapsody '55
Nine Days a Queen '34
Train of Events '49

**Patricia "Boots"
Mallory**
Carnival Lady '33
Powdersmoke Range '35
Sing Sing Nights '35
Wolf Dog '33

Jan Malmsjo
Fanny and Alexander '83
Scenes from a Marriage '73

Birger Malmsten
Night Is My Future '47
The Silence '63
Summer Interlude '50
Three Strange Loves '49

Dorothy Malone
Abduction '75
Artists and Models '55
At Gunpoint '55
Basic Instinct '92
Battle Cry '55
Beach Party '63
The Big Sleep '46
The Bushwackers '52
Day Time Ended '80
The Fast and the Furious '54
The Last Voyage '60
Man of a Thousand Faces '57
The Man Who Would Not Die
   '75
The Nevadan '50

Night and Day '46
Off Your Rocker '80
Rest In Pieces '87
Scared Stiff '53
Sincerely Yours '56
South of St. Louis '48
Tension at Table Rock '56
Torpedo Alley '53
Warlock '59
Winter Kills '79
Written on the Wind '56
Young at Heart '54

Mollie Malone
Battling Bunyon '24
Straight Shootin' '17

Patrick Malone
Grand Canyon '91
Rock 'n' Roll High School
   Forever '91

Michael Maloney
Henry V '89
Sharma & Beyond '84
Truly, Madly, Deeply '91

Biff Manard
Trancers 2: The Return of Jack
   Deth '91
Zone Troopers '85

**Ray "Boom Boom"
Mancini**
Backstreet Dreams '90
The Dirty Dozen: The Fatal
   Mission '88
Oceans of Fire '86
Timebomb '91
Wishful Thinking '92

Nick Mancuso
Blame It on the Night '84
Death of an Angel '86
Death Ship '80
Double Identity '89
Embassy '85
Fatal Exposure '91
Half a Lifetime '86
Heartbreakers '84
The House on Garibaldi Street
   '79
Legend of Walks Far Woman
   '82
Lena's Holiday '90
Lies Before Kisses '92
Maria Chapdelaine '84
Mother Lode '82
Nightwing '79
Rapid Fire '92
Tell Me That You Love Me '84
Ticket to Heaven '81
Wild Palms '93

Robert Mandan
In Love with an Older Woman
   '82
Perry Mason: The Case of the
   Lost Love '87
Return of the Rebels '81
Zapped! '82

Howie Mandel
Best of Comic Relief '86
Camilla '94
A Fine Mess '86
Gas '81
Little Monsters '89
The Princess Who Never
   Laughed '84
Walk Like a Man '87

Miles Mander
Brighton Strangler '45
The Brighton Strangler/Before
   Dawn '45
Don Quixote '35
Guadalcanal Diary '43
The Little Princess '39
Mad Miss Manton '38
Murder '30
Murder, My Sweet '44
The Pearl of Death '44
Primrose Path '40
The Private Life of Henry VIII
   '33
Return of the Vampire '43
Scarlet Claw '44
Shadows on the Stairs '41
Stanley and Livingstone '39
The Three Musketeers '35
The Three Musketeers '48
The Tower of London '39
Wuthering Heights '39

Barbara Mandrell
Burning Rage '84
The Concrete Cowboys '79

Costas Mandylor
The Doors '91
Mobsters '91
Soapdish '91
Triumph of the Spirit '89

Larry Manetti
C.I.A. 2: Target Alexa '94
The Take '90

Nino Manfredi
Alberto Express '92
Cafe Express '83
Down & Dirty '76
Head of the Family '71
In the Name of the Pope-King '85
Nudo di Donna '83
Spaghetti House '82
We All Loved Each Other So Much '77

Silvana Mangano
Barabbas '62
Bitter Rice '49
Conversation Piece '75
Dark Eyes '87
Death in Venice '71
The Decameron '70
Dune '84
The Gold of Naples '54
The Great War '59
Lure of the Sila '49
Mambo '55
Oedipus Rex '67
Teorema '68
Ulysses '55

Karin Mani
Alley Cat '84
Avenging Angel '85

Cindy Manion
Preppies '82
The Toxic Avenger '86

Hank Mann
City Lights '31
Spite Marriage '29

Leonard Mann
Corrupt '84
Night School '81

Terrence Mann
A Chorus Line '85
Critters '86
Critters 2: The Main Course '88
Critters 4 '91
The Ten Million Dollar Getaway '91

Tracey Mann
Fast Talking '86
Hard Knocks '80

David Manners
A Bill of Divorcement '32
The Black Cat '34
The Death Kiss '33
Dracula '31
The Mummy '32
They Call It Sin '32
Three Broadway Girls '32

Sheila Manners
Desert Phantom '36
Lawless Range '35
Westward Ho '35

Lucie Mannheim
High Command '37
Hotel Reserve '44
The 39 Steps '35

Ettore Manni
Angel in a Taxi '59
The Battle of Austerlitz '60
The Battle of El Alamein '68
City of Women '81
Giants of Rome '63
Hercules and the Captive Women '63
Heroes in Hell '67
Mademoiselle '66
Street People '76
Two Nights with Cleopatra '54

Marilyn Manning
Eegah! '62
The Sadist '63
What's Up Front '63

Dinah Manoff
Backfire '88

Bloodhounds of Broadway '89
Child's Play '88
For Ladies Only '81
I Ought to Be in Pictures '82
Ordinary People '80
The Possessed '77
Table Settings '84
Welcome Home, Roxy Carmichael '90

Silvia Manriquez
Conexion Mexico '87
Emilio Varela vs. Camelia La Texana '87

Jayne Mansfield
Dog Eat Dog '64
The Female Jungle '56
The Girl Can't Help It '56
Hell on Frisco Bay '55
Illegal '55
It Takes a Thief '59
Las Vegas Hillbillys '66
The Loves of Hercules '60
Panic Button '62
Pete Kelly's Blues '55
Promises! Promises! '63
Single Room Furnished '68
Underwater '55
Wild, Wild World of Jayne Mansfield '68

Leonor Manso
Far Away and Long Ago '74
House of Shadows '83
Made in Argentina '86

Alan Manson
Let's Scare Jessica to Death '71
Whiffs '75

Paul Mantee
Lurking Fear '94
Robinson Crusoe on Mars '64

Joe Mantegna
Airheads '94
Alice '90
Baby's Day Out '94
Body of Evidence '92
Bugsy '91
Compromising Positions '85
The Comrades of Summer '92
Critical Condition '86
Elvis: The Movie '79
Fallen Angels 2 '93
Family Prayers '91
The Godfather, Part 3 '90
Homicide '91
House of Games '87
The Money Pit '86
Off Beat '86
Queens Logic '91
Searching for Bobby Fischer '93
Second Thoughts '83
State of Emergency '94
Suspect '87
Things Change '88
Three Amigos '86
Wait Until Spring, Bandini '90
Weeds '87

Michael Mantell
City of Hope '91
The Night We Never Met '93

Randolph Mantooth
The Seekers '79
Terror at London Bridge '85

Leslie Manville
Grown Ups '80
High Hopes '89
High Season '88

Linda Manz
Days of Heaven '78
Orphan Train '79
Out of the Blue '80
The Snow Queen '83
Wanderers '79

Eduardo Manzano
El Aviso Inoportuno '87
Hijazo de Mi Vidaza '70s

Angela Mao
The Association '80s
The Deadliest Art: The Best of the Martial Arts Films '90
The Fate of Lee Khan '73
Return of the Tiger '78
Sting of the Dragon Masters '74
When Taekwondo Strikes '83

Adele Mara
Bells of Rosarita '45
The Inner Circle '46
Night Time in Nevada '48
Robin Hood of Texas '47
Twilight on the Rio Grande '41

Mary Mara
Love Potion #9 '92
Mr. Saturday Night '92

Steve Marachuk
Hot Target '85
Piranha 2: The Spawning '82
The Spawning '82
Waikiki '80

Jean Marais
The Battle of Austerlitz '60
Beauty and the Beast '46
Donkey Skin '70
Dos Cruces en Danger Pass '71
Elena and Her Men '56
Eternal Return '43
Girl in His Pocket '62
Orpheus '49
The Rape of the Sabines '61
The Testament of Orpheus '59
White Nights '57

Cindy Maranne
Provoked '89
Slashdance '89

Marcel Marceau
Barbarella '68
Silent Movie '76

Sophie Marceau
La Boum '81
Police '85

Fredric March
The Adventures of Mark Twain '44
Alexander the Great '55
Anna Karenina '35
Anthony Adverse '36
The Barretts of Wimpole Street '34
The Best Years of Our Lives '46
The Bridges at Toko-Ri '55
A Christmas Carol '54
Christopher Columbus '49
Desperate Hours '55
Dr. Jekyll and Mr. Hyde '31
Executive Suite '54
Hombre '67
I Married a Witch '42
Inherit the Wind '60
Les Miserables '35
The Man in the Gray Flannel Suit '56
Mary of Scotland '36
Nothing Sacred '37
Seven Days in May '64
Smilin' Through '32
So Ends Our Night '41
A Star is Born '37
Susan and God '40
Till the Clouds Roll By/A Star Is Born '46

Jane March
Color of Night '94
The Lover '92

Corinne Marchand
Bandits '86
Borsalino '70
Cleo from 5 to 7 '61

Guy Marchand
Coup de Torchon '81
Cousin, Cousine '76
Entre-Nous '83
Heat of Desire '84
Loulou '80
May Wine '90
Petit Con '84

Nancy Marchand
The Bostonians '84
Brain Donors '92
The Hospital '71
Killjoy '81
Marty '53
The Naked Gun: From the Files of Police Squad '88
North and South Book 2 '86
Regarding Henry '91

Ron Marchini
Death Machines '76

Forgotten Warrior '86
Karate Cop '93
Omega Cop '90
Return Fire '91
Wolf '86

David Marciano
Hellbent '90
Kiss Shot '89

Ted Marcoux
Ghost in the Machine '93
The Nightman '93

Andrea Marcovicci
The Concorde: Airport '79 '79
The Devil's Web '74
The Front '76
The Hand '81
Jack the Bear '93
Kings and Desperate Men '83
Packin' It In '83
Someone to Love '87
Spacehunter: Adventures in the Forbidden Zone '83
Spraggue '84
The Stuff '85

James Marcus
The Broken Mask '28
A Clockwork Orange '71
The Eagle '25
The Lone Avenger '33
Sadie Thompson '28

Richard Marcus
Cannibal Campout '88
Deadly Friend '86
Enemy Mine '85

Tom Mardirosian
The Dark Half '91
Presumed Innocent '90

Arthur Margetson
Juggernaut '37
The Mystery of the Mary Celeste '37
Sherlock Holmes Faces Death '43

Margo
Behind the Rising Sun '43
I'll Cry Tomorrow '55
The Leopard Man '43
Lost Horizon '37
Viva Zapata! '52
Who's Got the Action? '63
Winterset '36

Janet Margolin
Annie Hall '77
Buona Sera, Mrs. Campbell '68
David and Lisa '62
Distant Thunder '88
Enter Laughing '67
The Game of Love '90
The Last Embrace '79
Morituri '65
Planet Earth '74
Plutonium Incident '82
Pray for the Wildcats '74
Take the Money and Run '69
The Triangle Factory Fire Scandal '79

Stuart Margolin
The Big Bus '76
Bye Bye Blues '89
Class '83
Days of Heaven '78
Death Wish '74
A Fine Mess '86
Futureworld '76
The Glitter Dome '84
Guilty by Suspicion '91
Iron Eagle 2 '88
Kelly's Heroes '70
Running Hot '83
S.O.B. '81
Women of the Prehistoric Planet '66

Miriam Margolyes
The Age of Innocence '93
The Butcher's Wife '91
Ed and His Dead Mother '93
I Love You to Death '89
Little Dorrit, Film 1: Nobody's Fault '88
Little Dorrit, Film 2: Little Dorrit's Story '88
Orpheus Descending '91
Pacific Heights '90
Stalin '92

Michael Margotta
The Blue Knight '75
Can She Bake a Cherry Pie? '83

David Margulies
Dressed to Kill '80
Family Prayers '91
Funny About Love '90
Ghostbusters 2 '89
9 1/2 Weeks '86
Out on a Limb '92
Running on Empty '88

Angelica Maria
Somos Novios '68
To Kill a Stranger '70s

Jeanne Marie
If Looks Could Kill '86
Young Nurses in Love '89

Jean-Pierre Marielle
Coup de Torchon '81
Menage '86
One Wild Moment '78
Tous les Matins du Monde '92
Uranus '91

Marietto
Angel in a Taxi '59
It Started in Naples '60

Gloria Marin
Bromas S.A. '87
El Gendarme Desconocido '41
Historia de un Gran Amor '57

Jacques Marin
Darling Lili '70
The Island at the Top of the World '74
The Night of the Following Day '69

Richard "Cheech" Marin
Born in East L.A. '87
Cheech and Chong: Still Smokin' '83
Cheech and Chong: Things Are Tough All Over '82
Cheech and Chong's Next Movie '80
Cheech and Chong's Nice Dreams '81
Cheech and Chong's, The Corsican Brothers '84
Cheech and Chong's Up in Smoke '79
The Cisco Kid '94
Echo Park '86
Far Out Man '89
Fatal Beauty '87
La Pastorela '92
Ring of the Musketeers '93
Rude Awakening '89
The Shrimp on the Barbie '90
Yellowbeard '83

Rikki Marin
Cheech and Chong: Things Are Tough All Over '82
Cheech and Chong's, The Corsican Brothers '84

Ed Marinaro
Born Beautiful '82
Dead Aim '87
The Diamond Trap '91
The Game of Love '90
Hill Street Blues, Vol. 1: Hill Street Station '81
Lethal Lolita—Amy Fisher: My Story '92
Policewoman Centerfold '83
Queens Logic '91

Kenny Marino
Alphabet City '84
Prince of the City '81

Beth Marion
Between Men '35
Phantom Gold '38
The Phantom of the Range '38
Rip Roarin' Buckaroo '36
Trail of Terror '35

George F. Marion, Sr.
Anna Christie '23
Anna Christie '30
The Big House '30
Death from a Distance '36
Hook, Line and Sinker '30

Mona Maris
The Falcon in Mexico '44
Heartbeat '46
I Married an Angel '42
Love on the Run '36

Kensaku Marita
Renegade Ninja '83
War in Space '77

Sari Maritza
Crimson Romance '34
Greek Street '30
International House '33

Robert Marius
The 13th Mission '91
Triple Impact '92

Jane Marken
Crazy for Love '52
A Day in the Country '46
Dedee d'Anvers '49

Enid Markey
Civilization '16
The Fugitive: Taking of Luke McVane '15
Tarzan of the Apes '17

Kika Markham
Deep Cover '88
Miss A & Miss M '86
Two English Girls '72

Monte Markham
Counter Measures '80s
Defense Play '88
Ginger in the Morning '73
Guns of the Magnificent Seven '69
Hotline '82
Hustling '75
Judgment Day '88
Off the Wall '82
Shame, Shame on the Bixby Boys '82

Ted Markland
Angels from Hell '68
Merlin '93
Wanda Nevada '79

Stephen Markle
984: Prisoner of the Future '84
Perfect Timing '84

Margaret Markov
Hot Box '72
Naked Warriors '73
Run, Angel, Run! '69

Olivera Markovic
Fury is a Woman '61
Tito and Me '92

Alfred Marks
Antonia and Jane '91
Mission: Monte Carlo '75
Scream and Scream Again '70
Valentino '77

Winnie Markus
The Devil in Silk '56
The Mozart Story '48

Arnold Marle
Men of Two Worlds '46
The Snake Woman '61

John Marley
Deathdream '72
Framed '75
The Glitter Dome '84
The Godfather '72
The Godfather 1902-1959: The Complete Epic '81
The Greatest '77
Hooper '78
It's Alive 2: It Lives Again '78
Jory '72
Kid Vengeance '75
Love Story '70
A Man Called Sledge '71
On the Edge '86
Robbers of the Sacred Mountain '83
Threshold '83
Utilities '83

Carla Marlier
The Avenger '62
The Big Grab '63
Spirits of the Dead '68
Zazie dans le Metro '61

Hugh Marlowe
All About Eve '50
Birdman of Alcatraz '62

Bugles in the Afternoon '52
Casanova's Big Night '54
Castle of Evil '66
The Day the Earth Stood Still '51
Earth vs. the Flying Saucers '56
Elmer Gantry '60
Illegal '55
Monkey Business '52
Night and the City '50
Rawhide '50
Twelve O'Clock High '49

June Marlowe
Don Juan '26
The Lone Defender '32
The Night Cry '26
Pardon Us '31

Linda Marlowe
Big Zapper '73
The Green Man '91
He Kills Night After Night After Night '70
Mr. Love '86
Night Slasher '84

Florence Marly
Dr. Death, Seeker of Souls '73
Planet of Blood '66
Tokyo Joe '49

Percy Marmont
Four Sided Triangle '53
Lady of the Lake '28
Lisbon '56
Mantrap '26
Rich and Strange '32
Young and Innocent '37

Kelli Maroney
Fast Times at Ridgemont High '82
Night of the Comet '84
Servants of Twilight '91
Slayground '84
Zero Boys '86

Carl Marotte
Breaking All the Rules '85
Pick-Up Summer '79
Workin' for Peanuts '85

Christian Marquand
And God Created Woman '57
The Corrupt Ones '67
End of Desire '62

Maria Elena Marques
Across the Wide Missouri '51
Ambush at Tomahawk Gap '53
The Pearl '48

Margaret Marquis
Brand of the Outlaws '36
Last of the Warrens '36

Eddie Marr
Hollywood Canteen '44
I Was a Teenage Werewolf '57

Moore Marriot
The Flying Scotsman '29
Oh, Mr. Porter '37

Sylvia Marriott
Crimes at the Dark House '39
Two English Girls '72

Kenneth Mars
The Apple Dumpling Gang Rides Again '79
Beer '85
Butch Cassidy and the Sundance Kid '69
Desperate Characters '71
Fletch '85
For Keeps '88
Get Smart, Again! '89
Goin' Coconuts '78
Illegally Yours '87
Misfits of Science '85
Night Moves '75
Parallax View '74
The Producers '68
Protocol '84
Radio Days '87
Rented Lips '88
Shadows and Fog '92
What's Up, Doc? '72
Young Frankenstein '74

Maurice Marsac
Clarence, the Cross-eyed Lion '65
Tarzan and the Trappers '58
Werewolf in a Girl's Dormitory '61

Branford Marsalis
School Daze '88
Throw Momma from the Train '87

Carol Marsh
Alice in Wonderland '50
Brighton Rock '47
A Christmas Carol '51
The Horror of Dracula '58

Garry Marsh
Department Store '35
A Girl in a Million '46
Just William's Luck '47
Pink Strings and Sealing Wax '45
Someone at the Door '50

Jean Marsh
The Changeling '80
Frenzy '72
Goliath Awaits '81
Horsemasters '61
Return to Oz '85
The Unearthly Stranger '64
Willow '88

Joan Marsh
Champagne for Breakfast '35
Follow the Leader '44
High Gear '33
Manhunt in the African Jungle '54

Mae Marsh
The Birth of a Nation '15
D.W. Griffith Triple Feature '13
The Fighting Sullivans '42
From the Terrace '60
The Gunfighter '50
Home Sweet Home '14
Hoodoo Ann '16
How Green was My Valley '41
Intolerance '16
Judith of Bethulia '14
The Quiet Man '52
Sergeant Rutledge '60
Short Films of D.W. Griffith, Vol. 2 '09
Story of the Silent Serials Girls in Danger
The Tall Men '55
Three Godfathers '48
While the City Sleeps '56
The White Rose '23

Marian Marsh
The Black Room '35
Crime and Punishment '35
Gentleman from Dixie '41
House of Errors '42
Svengali '31
When's Your Birthday? '37
Youth on Parole '37

Matthew Marsh
An Affair in Mind '89
In the Secret State

Michele Marsh
Deadly Alliance '78
Evil Town '87

Alan Marshal
After the Thin Man '36
Conquest '37
House on Haunted Hill '58
The Howards of Virginia '40
The Hunchback of Notre Dame '39
Lydia '41
Tom, Dick, and Harry '41
The White Cliffs of Dover '44

Brenda Marshall
Background to Danger '43
Captains of the Clouds '42
The Sea Hawk '40

Bryan Marshall
Because of the Cats '74
The Long Good Friday '79
Return to Snowy River '88

Dodie Marshall
Easy Come, Easy Go '67
Spinout '66

E.G. Marshall
Abduction of St. Anne '75
The Bridge at Remagen '69
Broken Lance '54
The Buccaneer '58
The Caine Mutiny '54
Call Northside 777 '48
Cash McCall '60

The Chase '66
Consenting Adults '92
Creepshow '82
Eleanor: First Lady of the World '82
Interiors '78
Ironclads '90
Is Paris Burning? '68
Kennedy '83
The Lazarus Syndrome '79
The Left Hand of God '55
The Littlest Angel '69
The Mountain '56
My Chauffeur '86
National Lampoon's Christmas Vacation '89
The Poppy is also a Flower '66
Power '86
Pursuit '72
The Pursuit of Happiness '70
Russian Roulette '93
Saigon: Year of the Cat '87
The Silver Chalice '54
Stephen King's The Tommyknockers '93
Superman 2 '80
13 Rue Madeleine '46
Tora! Tora! Tora! '70
Twelve Angry Men '57

Garry Marshall
A League of Their Own '92
Lost in America '85
Soapdish '91

Herbert Marshall
Blonde Venus '32
Captain Blackjack '51
Crack-Up '46
Duel in the Sun '46
The Enchanted Cottage '45
The Fly '58
Foreign Correspondent '40
Forever and a Day '43
The Letter '40
The Little Foxes '41
The Moon and Sixpence '43
Murder '30
The Painted Veil '34
The Razor's Edge '46
Riptide '34
The Secret Garden '49
Stage Struck '36
The Underworld Story '50
The Virgin Queen '55
When Ladies Meet '41
A Woman Rebels '36

James Marshall
A Few Good Men '92
Gladiator '92
Twin Peaks: Fire Walk with Me '92

Ken Marshall
Double Exposure: The Story of Margaret Bourke-White '89
Feds '88
Krull '83
Tilt '78

Marion Marshall
I Was a Male War Bride '49
The Stooge '51

Paula Marshall
Hellraiser 3: Hell on Earth '92
Warlock: The Armageddon '93

Penny Marshall
Challenge of a Lifetime '85
How Come Nobody's On Our Side? '73
Movers and Shakers '85

Peter Marshall
A Guide for the Married Woman '78
Return of Jesse James '50

Sarah Marshall
French Silk '94
The People vs. Jean Harris '81

Trudy Marshall
Crash Dive '43
The Fighting Sullivans '42
Joe's Bed-Stuy Barbershop: We Cut Heads '83
Married Too Young '62

Tully Marshall
Behind Prison Walls '43
Big Trail '30
Broken Hearts of Broadway '23
The Cabin in the Cotton '32

The Cat and the Canary '27
Fighting Caravans '31
Hawthorne of the USA '19
He Who Gets Slapped '24
Let's Go! '23
Mr. Boggs Steps Out '38
Night of Terror '33
Queen Kelly '29
Smouldering Fires '25
Strangers of the Evening '32
Tom Sawyer '30
Two-Fisted Law '32
What Happened to Rosa? '21

William Marshall
Blacula '72
The Boston Strangler '68
Demetrius and the Gladiators '54
The Great Skycopter Rescue '82
Scream Blacula Scream '73
State Fair '45
That Brennan Girl '46
Twilight's Last Gleaming '77
Vasectomy: A Delicate Matter '86

Zena Marshall
Dr. No '62
Terronauts '67
The Terrornauts '67

Christina Marsillach
Every Time We Say Goodbye '86
Terror at the Opera '88

Tony Marsina
Last Mercenary '84
Tornado '83

Lynn Marta
Joe Kidd '72
Richard Petty Story '72

Arlene Martel
Angels from Hell '68
Demon with a Glass Hand '64

June Martel
Arizona Mahoney '36
Forlorn River '37
Santa Fe Stampede '38

K.C. Martel
E.T.: The Extra-Terrestrial '82
Munster's Revenge '81

Chris Martell
Flesh Feast '69
Gruesome Twosome '67
Scream, Baby, Scream '69

Donna Martell
Abbott and Costello Meet the Killer, Boris Karloff '49
Give a Girl a Break '53
Project Moon Base '53
Ten Wanted Men '54

Peter Martell
Mission Phantom '79
Planet on the Prowl '65

Frank Marth
Fright '56
Showdown '93

Ana Martin
Fin de Fiesta '71
Siempre Hay una Primera Vez '87
Tacos al Carbon '87

Andrea Martin
All I Want for Christmas '91
Boris and Natasha: The Movie '92
Club Paradise '86
Gypsy '93
Rude Awakening '89
Soup for One '82
Stepping Out '91
Too Much Sun '90
Worth Winning '89

Chris-Pin Martin
Lucky Cisco Kid '40
South of Santa Fe '32
Stagecoach '39

Christopher Martin
Class Act '91
House Party '90
House Party 2: The Pajama Jam '91
House Party 3 '94

Damon Martin
Amityville 1992: It's About Time '92
Ghoulies 2 '88

Dean Martin
Airport '70
All in a Night's Work '61
The Ambushers '67
Artists and Models '55
At War with the Army '50
Bandolero! '68
Bells are Ringing '60
The Caddy '53
Cannonball Run '81
Cannonball Run 2 '84
Career '59
Five Card Stud '68
Four for Texas '63
Hollywood Clowns '85
Hollywood or Bust '56
Jumping Jacks '52
Kiss Me, Stupid! '64
Murderers' Row '66
My Friend Irma '49
Ocean's 11 '60
Pardners '56
Rio Bravo '59
The Road to Bali '53
Robin and the Seven Hoods '64
Rough Night in Jericho '67
Scared Stiff '53
Showdown '73
Some Came Running '58
Sons of Katie Elder '65
The Stooge '53
Texas Across the River '66
That's Dancing! '85
Toys in the Attic '63
Who's Got the Action? '63
The Young Lions '58

Dean Paul Martin
Backfire '88
Misfits of Science '85
Players '79

Dewey Martin
The Big Sky '52
Desperate Hours '55
Flight to Fury '66
Land of the Pharaohs '55
Men of the Fighting Lady '54
Savage Sam '63
Seven Alone '75
The Thing '51

Diana Martin
Hyena of London '62
Minnesota Clay '65

Dick Martin
Carbon Copy '81
The Glass Bottom Boat '66

D'Urville Martin
Big Score '83
Blind Rage '78
Boss '74
Death Journey '76
Final Comedown '72
Sheba, Baby '75

George Martin
Blood at Sundown
The Compleat Beatles '82
Crossing Delancey '88
Falling in Love '84
Psychopath '68

Helen Martin
Doc Hollywood '91
A Hero Ain't Nothin' But a Sandwich '78
Hollywood Shuffle '87
House Party 2: The Pajama Jam '91
Night Angel '90

Jared Martin
Karate Warrior
The New Gladiators '87
Quiet Cool '86
The Sea Serpent '85

John Martin
Black Roses '88
Dark Before Dawn '89
Fire in the Night '85
The Tell-Tale Heart '62

Kellie Martin
Matinee '92
Troop Beverly Hills '89

Kiel Martin
Child Bride of Short Creek '81
Convicted: A Mother's Story '87
Hill Street Blues, Vol. 1: Hill Street Station '81
Panic in Needle Park '75

Marion Martin
The Great Mike '44
The Man in the Iron Mask '39
Mexican Spitfire at Sea '42
Sinners in Paradise '38

Mary Martin
Irving Berlin's America '86
Night and Day '46
Peter Pan '60

Mel Martin
Love for Lydia '79
White Hunter, Black Heart '90

Millicent Martin
Alfie '66
Horsemasters '61
Those Magnificent Men in Their Flying Machines '65

Nan Martin
For Love of Ivy '68
Goodbye Columbus '69
Matters of the Heart '90
Proud Men '87
Toys in the Attic '63
The Young Nurses '73

Pamela Sue Martin
Buster and Billie '74
A Cry in the Wild '90
Eye of the Demon '87
Flicks '85
The Girls of Huntington House '73
Lady in Red '79
Our Time '74
Torchlight '85

Pepper Martin
Angels from Hell '68
Evil Altar '89
Scream '83

Richard Martin
Dynamite Pass '50
Gun Smugglers/Hot Lead '51
Gunplay '51
Mysterious Desperado '49
Mysterious Desperado/Rider From Tucson '49
Nevada '44
Rider from Tucson '50
Riders of the Range '49
Riders of the Range/Storm Over Wyoming '50
Storm Over Wyoming '50
Tender Comrade '43
West of the Pecos '45

Ross Martin
Conquest of Space '55
Dying Room Only '73
Experiment in Terror '62
Geronimo '93
More Wild, Wild West '80
The Seekers '79
Wild & Wooly '78
Wild, Wild West Revisited '79

Steve Martin
All of Me '84
Dead Men Don't Wear Plaid '82
Dirty Rotten Scoundrels '88
Father of the Bride '91
Grand Canyon '91
Housesitter '92
The Jerk '79
L.A. Story '91
Leap of Faith '92
Little Shop of Horrors '86
The Lonely Guy '84
The Man with Two Brains '83
Movers and Shakers '85
My Blue Heaven '90
Parenthood '89
Pennies From Heaven '81
Planes, Trains & Automobiles '87
Roxanne '87
Sgt. Pepper's Lonely Hearts Club Band '78
A Simple Twist of Fate '94
Steve Martin Live '85
Three Amigos '86

Strother Martin
Ballad of Cable Hogue '70
Better Late Than Never '79
The Brotherhood of Satan '71
Butch Cassidy and the Sundance Kid '69
The Champ '79
Cheech and Chong's Up in Smoke '79
Cool Hand Luke '67
Hannie Caulder '72
Hard Times '75
The Horse Soldiers '59
Hot Wire '70s
Invitation to a Gunfighter '64
Kiss Me Deadly '55
Love and Bullets '79
The Man Who Shot Liberty Valance '62
McLintock! '63
Nightwing '79
Pocket Money '72
Rooster Cogburn '75
Slap Shot '77
Steel Cowboy '78
The Villain '79
The Wild Bunch '69

Tony Martin
Big Store '41
Easy to Love '53
Here Come the Girls '53
Hit the Deck '55
Music in My Heart '40
Till the Clouds Roll By '46
Till the Clouds Roll By/A Star Is Born '46
Two Tickets to Broadway '51
Ziegfeld Girl '41

Vera Martin
Loyalties '86
The Noose Hangs High '48

Vince Martin
Breaking Loose '90
Night Master '87

W.T. Martin
Hardhat & Legs '80
High Stakes '89

Elsa Martinelli
Belle Starr '79
Blood and Roses '61
Hatari '62
The Indian Fighter '55
Madigan's Millions '67
Maroc 7 '67
Oldest Profession '67
Once Upon a Crime '92
10th Victim '65
The Trial '63
The V.I.P.'s '63
Woman Times Seven '67

A. Martinez
Born in East L.A. '87
The Cowboys '72
The Hunt for the Night Stalker '91
Joe Panther '76
Once Upon a Scoundrel '73
Powwow Highway '89
She-Devil '89
Starbird and Sweet William '73

Adalberto "Resortes" Martinez
El Aviador Fenomeno '47
La Marchanta '73
Soy un Golfo '65

Al Martino
The Godfather '72
The Godfather, Part 3 '90

Orlando Martins
Call Me Bwana '63
Men of Two Worlds '46
Simba '55

Lee Marvin
Avalanche Express '79
Bad Day at Black Rock '54
Big Heat '53
The Big Red One '80
The Caine Mutiny '54
Cat Ballou '65
The Comancheros '61
Death Hunt '81
Delta Force '86
The Dirty Dozen '67
The Dirty Dozen: The Next Mission '85

Dog Day '83
Donovan's Reef '63
Gorky Park '83
Great Scout & Cathouse Thursday '76
Gun Fury '53
Hangman's Knot '52
Hell in the Pacific '69
I Died a Thousand Times '55
The Killers '64
The Klansman '74
The Man Who Shot Liberty Valance '62
The Meanest Men in the West '76
Missouri Traveler '58
Monte Walsh '70
Paint Your Wagon '69
Pete Kelly's Blues '55
Pocket Money '72
Point Blank '67
Prime Cut '72
The Professionals '66
Raintree County '57
Sergeant Ryker '68
Shack Out on 101 '55
Ship of Fools '65
Shout at the Devil '76
The Stranger Wore a Gun '53
Union Station '50
The Wild One '54

Alan Marx
For Auld Lang Syne: The Marx Brothers '32
Gore-Met Zombie Chef From Hell '87

Chico Marx
Animal Crackers '30
At the Circus '39
Big Store '41
The Cocoanuts '29
A Day at the Races '37
Duck Soup '33
For Auld Lang Syne: The Marx Brothers '32
Go West '40
Hollywood Clowns '85
Horse Feathers '32
Love Happy '50
The Marx Brothers in a Nutshell '90
Monkey Business '31
A Night at the Opera '35
A Night in Casablanca '46
Room Service '38

Groucho Marx
Animal Crackers '30
At the Circus '39
Big Store '41
The Cocoanuts '29
Copacabana '47
A Day at the Races '37
Double Dynamite '51
Duck Soup '33
For Auld Lang Syne: The Marx Brothers '32
A Girl in Every Port '52
Go West '40
Hollywood Clowns '85
Horse Feathers '32
Love Happy '50
The Marx Brothers in a Nutshell '90
Monkey Business '31
A Night at the Opera '35
A Night in Casablanca '46
Room Service '38

Harpo Marx
Animal Crackers '30
At the Circus '39
Big Store '41
The Cocoanuts '29
A Day at the Races '37
Duck Soup '33
For Auld Lang Syne: The Marx Brothers '32
Go West '40
Hollywood Clowns '85
Hollywood Goes to War '54
Horse Feathers '32
Love Happy '50
The Marx Brothers in a Nutshell '90
Monkey Business '31
A Night at the Opera '35
A Night in Casablanca '46
Room Service '38
Strictly G.I. '44

Zeppo Marx
Animal Crackers '30
The Cocoanuts '29
Duck Soup '33
Horse Feathers '32
The Marx Brothers in a Nutshell '90
Monkey Business '31

Ron Masak
Harper Valley P.T.A. '78
Man from Clover Grove '78

Mil Mascaras
Frontera Sin Ley
Los Vampiros de Coyacan '87

Giulietta Masina
Europa '51 '52
Ginger & Fred '86
Juliet of the Spirits '65
La Strada '54
The Madwoman of Chaillot '69
Nights of Cabiria '57
The Swindle '55
Variety Lights '51
The White Sheik '52

Connie Mason
Blood Feast '63
2000 Maniacs '64

Eric Mason
Black Starlet '75
Kiss of the Tarantula '75

Hilary Mason
Dolls '87
Don't Look Now '73
Meridian: Kiss of the Beast '90
Robot Jox '89

Jackie Mason
Caddyshack 2 '88
History of the World: Part 1 '81
The Jerk '79

James Mason
Arizona Mahoney '36
The Concentratin' Kid '30
For Heaven's Sake '26
Hopalong Cassidy '35
The Plainsman '37

James Mason
The Assisi Underground '84
Autobiography of a Princess '75
Bad Man's River '72
The Blue Max '66
Border Law '31
Botany Bay '53
The Boys from Brazil '78
Caught '49
Charade '53
Cold Sweat '74
Cross of Iron '76
Dangerous Summer '82
The Desert Fox '51
The Desert Rats '53
The Destructors '74
East Side, West Side '49
11 Harrowhouse '74
Evil Under the Sun '82
Face to Face '52
The Fall of the Roman Empire '64
ffolkes '80
Fire Over England '37
Five Fingers '52
Forever Darling '56
George Washington '84
Georgy Girl '66
Heaven Can Wait '78
High Command '37
Hotel Reserve '44
I Met a Murderer '39
Inside Out '75
Island in the Sun '57
Ivanhoe '82
Jesus of Nazareth '77
Journey to the Center of the Earth '59
Julius Caesar '53
Kidnap Syndicate '76
The Last of Sheila '73
Late Extra '35
Lolita '62
Lord Jim '65
Mackintosh Man '73
Madame Bovary '49
The Man in Grey '45
Man of Evil '45
Mandingo '75
The Mill on the Floss '37

Mason ▶cont.

Murder by Decree '79
The Night Has Eyes '42
North by Northwest '59
Odd Man Out '47
Prince Valiant '54
Prisoner of Zenda '52
Reckless Moment '49
Salem's Lot '79
The Seventh Veil '46
The Shooting Party '85
Sidney Sheldon's Bloodline '79
A Star is Born '54
Street War '70s
Tiara Tahiti '62
20,000 Leagues Under the Sea '54
The Verdict '82
Voyage of the Damned '76
Water Babies '79
The Wicked Lady '45
Yellowbeard '83
Yin & Yang of Mr. Go '71

Leroy Mason
Black Gold '36
Daughter of Don Q '46
The Mystery Man '35
Outlaw Express '38
The Painted Stallion '37
Phantom of the Air '33
The Phantom Rider '46
Rocky Mountain Rangers '40
Santa Fe Stampede '38
Silver Stallion '41
Western Mail '42
When a Man Sees Red '34
Wyoming Outlaw '39

Marsha Mason
Audrey Rose '77
Blume in Love '73
Chapter Two '79
The Cheap Detective '78
Cinderella Liberty '73
Dinner at Eight '89
Drop Dead Fred '91
The Goodbye Girl '77
Heartbreak Ridge '86
The Image '89
Lois Gibbs and the Love Canal '82
Max Dugan Returns '83
Only When I Laugh '81
Promises in the Dark '79
Stella '89
Trapped in Silence '86

Pamela Mason
Charade '53
Door to Door Maniac '61
Navy vs. the Night Monsters '66

Tom Mason
Aliens Are Coming '80
The Amy Fisher Story '93
Apocalypse Now '79
Kicks '85
Men Don't Leave '89
Mississippi Burning '88
Walking Through the Fire '80

Lea Massari
Allonsanfan '73
Christ Stopped at Eboli '79
L'Avventura '60
Les Rendez-vous D'Anna '78
Murmur of the Heart '71
The Story of a Love Story '73
The Things of Life '70
Vengeance '86

Michael Massee
The Crow '93
My Father is Coming '91

Osa Massen
Background to Danger '43
Cry of the Werewolf '44
Iceland '42
Master Race '44
Outcasts of the City '58
Rocketship X-M '50
A Woman's Face '41

Anna Massey
Anna Karenina '85
Another Country '84
A Doll's House '89
Foreign Body '86
Frenzy '72

Hotel du Lac '86
Impromptu '91
The Little Drummer Girl '84
Mansfield Park '85
The McGuffin '85
Mountains of the Moon '90
Peeping Tom '63
Sweet William '79
A Tale of Two Cities '91
The Tall Guy '89
Vault of Horror '73

Daniel Massey
The Cat and the Canary '79
The Entertainer '60
In the Name of the Father '93
The Incredible Sarah '76
Intimate Contact '87
Love with a Perfect Stranger '86
Scandal '89
Stalin '92
Star! '68
Vault of Horror '73
Victory '81

Edith Massey
Desperate Living '77
Female Trouble '74
Multiple Maniacs '70
Pink Flamingos '72
Polyester '81

Ilona Massey
Balalaika '39
Holiday in Mexico '46
Invisible Agent '42
Love Happy '50
Melody Master '41
Northwest Outpost '47
Rosalie '38

Raymond Massey
Abe Lincoln in Illinois '40
Action in the North Atlantic '43
Arsenic and Old Lace '44
Battle Cry '55
Black Limelight '38
Chain Lightning '50
David and Bathsheba '51
The Desert Song '53
Desperate Journey '42
Dreaming Lips '37
Drums '38
East of Eden '54
Fire Over England '37
The Forty-Ninth Parallel '41
The Fountainhead '49
The Great Impostor '61
How the West was Won '63
Hurricane '37
MacKenna's Gold '69
The Naked and the Dead '58
The Old Dark House '32
Omar Khayyam '57
The Possessed '47
The President's Plane is Missing '71
Prisoner of Zenda '37
Reap the Wild Wind '42
Santa Fe Trail '40
The Scarlet Pimpernel '34
The Speckled Band '31
Things to Come '36
Under the Red Robe '36

Ben Masters
All That Jazz '79
Celebrity '85
The Deliberate Stranger '86
Dream Lover '85
Key Exchange '85
Making Mr. Right '86
Mandingo '75
Running Mates '92
The Shadow Box '80

Chase Masterson
In a Moment of Passion '93
Married People, Single Sex '93

Fay Masterson
Cops and Robbersons '93
The Man Without a Face '93
The Power of One '92

Mary Stuart Masterson
At Close Range '86
Bad Girls '94
Benny & Joon '93
Chances are '85
Fried Green Tomatoes '91
Funny About Love '90

Gardens of Stone '87
Heaven Help Us '85
Immediate Family '89
Mad at the Moon '92
Married to It '93
Mr. North '88
My Little Girl '87
Some Kind of Wonderful '87

Mary Elizabeth Mastrantonio
The Abyss '89
Class Action '91
The Color of Money '86
Consenting Adults '92
Fools of Fortune '90
The January Man '89
Robin Hood: Prince of Thieves '91
Scarface '83
Slamdance '87
White Sands '92

Marcello Mastroianni
Allonsanfan '73
Bellissimo: Images of the Italian Cinema '87
Beyond Obsession '82
Big Deal on Madonna Street '58
Blood Feud '79
Casanova '70 '65
City of Women '81
Dark Eyes '87
Diary of Forbidden Dreams '73
Divine Nymph '71
Divorce—Italian Style '62
8 1/2 '63
Everybody's Fine '90
A Fine Romance '91
Gabriela '84
Get Rita
Ginger & Fred '86
Henry IV '85
Il Bell'Antonio '60
Intervista '87
La Dolce Vita '60
La Nuit de Varennes '82
Lady of the Evening '79
Lunatics & Lovers '76
Macaroni '85
Marriage Italian Style '64
Massacre in Rome '73
The Poppy is also a Flower '66
Salut l'Artiste '74
Shoot Loud, Louder, I Don't Understand! '66
A Slightly Pregnant Man '79
A Special Day '77
Stay As You Are '78
10th Victim '65
Used People '92
A Very Private Affair '62
We All Loved Each Other So Much '77
Where the Hot Wind Blows '59
White Nights '57
Wifemistress '79
Yesterday, Today and Tomorrow '64

Richard Masur
Adam '83
And the Band Played On '93
The Believers '87
Betrayal '78
The Burning Bed '85
Cast the First Stone '89
East of Eden '80
Embassy '85
Encino Man '92
Fallen Angel '81
Far from Home '89
Flashback '89
The George McKenna Story '86
Heartburn '86
Heaven's Gate '81
Hiroshima Maiden '88
License to Drive '88
The Man Without a Face '93
Mean Season '85
My Girl '91
My Girl 2 '94
My Science Project '85
Nightmares '83
Rent-A-Cop '88
Risky Business '83
Semi-Tough '77
Shoot to Kill '88
Six Degrees of Separation '93
Stephen King's It '90

The Thing '82
Third Degree Burn '89
Timerider '83
Under Fire '83
Walker '87
Walking Through the Fire '80
When the Bough Breaks '86
Who'll Stop the Rain? '78
Wild Horses '84

Julian Mateos
Four Rode Out '69
Hellbenders '67
Kashmiri Run '69

Aubrey Mather
Adventures of Don Juan '49
Hello, Frisco, Hello '43
House of Fear '45
Jane Eyre '44
The Lodger '44
Mrs. Miniver '42
The Silent Passenger '35
That Forsyte Woman '50
The Undying Monster '42

Jerry Mathers
Back to the Beach '87
Down the Drain '90
Men of the Fighting Lady '54
The Trouble with Harry '55

Marissa Mathes
How to Succeed with Girls '64
Track of the Vampire '66

Judy Matheson
The House that Vanished '73
Twins of Evil '71

Michelle Matheson
Howling 6: The Freaks '90
Test Tube Teens from the Year 2000 '93
Threesome '94

Tim Matheson
The Apple Dumpling Gang Rides Again '79
Best Legs in the 8th Grade '84
Blind Justice '86
Buried Alive '90
The Captive: The Longest Drive 2 '76
Dreamer '79
Drop Dead Fred '91
Eye of the Demon '87
Fallen Angels 1 '93
Fletch '85
How to Commit Marriage '69
Impulse '84
Listen to Your Heart '83
A Little Sex '82
Little White Lies '89
The Longest Drive '76
Magnum Force '73
Mary White '77
National Lampoon's Animal House '78
1941 '79
Quicksand: No Escape '91
The Runaway Barge '75
Solar Crisis '92
Sometimes They Come Back '91
Speed Zone '88
To Be or Not to Be '83
Trial and Error '92
Up the Creek '84
Yours, Mine & Ours '68

Carole Mathews
Shark River '53
Strange Awakening '58
Swamp Women '55

George Mathews
Last of the Comanches '52
The Man with the Golden Arm '55

Kerwin Mathews
Battle Beneath the Earth '68
The Devil at 4 O'Clock '61
Jack the Giant Killer '62
Killer Likes Candy '78
Maniac '63
Nightmare in Blood '75
Octaman '71
The Seventh Voyage of Sinbad '58
The Three Worlds of Gulliver '59
Waltz King '63

Thom Mathews
Alien from L.A. '87
Bloodmatch '91
Down Twisted '89
Friday the 13th, Part 6: Jason Lives '86
Midnight Cabaret '90
Return of the Living Dead 2 '88

Samantha Mathis
The Music of Chance '93
Pump Up the Volume '90
Super Mario Bros. '93
The Thing Called Love '93
This is My Life '92

Jacques Mathou
Betty Blue '86
The Hairdresser's Husband '92
Year of the Comet '92

Marlee Matlin
Bridge to Silence '89
Children of a Lesser God '86
Hear No Evil '92
The Linguini Incident '92
Walker '87

John Matshikiza
Dust '85
Dust Devil '93
Mandela '87

Yusaku Matsuda
Black Rain '89
The Family Game '83
Murder in the Doll House '79

Eva Mattes
The Bitter Tears of Petra von Kant '72
Celeste '81
David '79
A Man Like Eva '83
Stroszek '77
Woyzeck '78

Walter Matthau
Atomic Attack '50
The Bad News Bears '76
Buddy Buddy '81
Cactus Flower '69
California Suite '78
Casey's Shadow '78
Charade '63
Charley Varrick '73
The Couch Trip '87
Dennis the Menace '93
Earthquake '74
Ensign Pulver '64
A Face in the Crowd '57
Fail-Safe '64
First Monday in October '81
The Fortune Cookie '66
The Front Page '74
Grumpy Old Men '93
A Guide for the Married Man '67
Hello, Dolly! '69
Hopscotch '80
House Calls '78
I Ought to Be in Pictures '82
The Incident '89
The Indian Fighter '55
JFK '91
The Kentuckian '55
King Creole '58
Kotch '71
The Laughing Policeman '74
Little Miss Marker '80
Lonely are the Brave '62
Mirage '66
Movers and Shakers '85
A New Leaf '71
The Odd Couple '68
Pete 'n' Tillie '72
Pirates '86
Plaza Suite '71
Secret Life of an American Wife '68
Strangers When We Meet '60
The Sunshine Boys '75
Survivors '83
The Taking of Pelham One Two Three '74
Who's Got the Action? '63

A.E. Matthews
Carry On Admiral '57
The Iron Duke '34
Made in Heaven '52

Brian Matthews
The Burning '82
Red Nights '87

Dakin Matthews
Child's Play 3 '91
In a Stranger's Hand '92
My Brother's Wife '89
Naked Lie '89
Nuts '87
Revolver '92
The Temp '93

Francis Matthews
Bhowani Junction '56
Corridors of Blood '58
The Hellfire Club '61
The McGuffin '85
Murder Ahoy '64
Small Hotel '57

Fritz Matthews
Born Killer '89
Deadly Prey '87
Hell on the Battleground '88

Jessie Matthews
Candles at Nine '44
Evergreen '34
Forever and a Day '43
Gangway '37
The Hound of the Baskervilles '77
It's Love Again '36
Sailing Along '38

Lester Matthews
The Invisible Man's Revenge '44
King Richard and the Crusaders '54
The Raven '35
Werewolf of London '35

Robin Mattson
Bonnie's Kids '73
Candy Stripe Nurses '74
Captain America '79
Hot Rod '79
In Between '92
Namu, the Killer Whale '66
Return to Macon County '75
Take Two '87
Wolf Lake '79

Victor Mature
After the Fox '66
Androcles and the Lion '52
Betrayed '54
Captain Caution '40
Dangerous Mission '54
Demetrius and the Gladiators '54
Easy Living '49
The Egyptian '54
Footlight Serenade '42
I Wake Up Screaming '41
Kiss of Death '47
The Las Vegas Story '52
The Long Haul '57
Million Dollar Mermaid '52
My Darling Clementine '46
No, No Nanette '40
One Million B.C. '40
The Robe '53
Samson and Delilah '50
Samson and Delilah '84
Savage Wilderness '55
Seven Days' Leave '42
The Shanghai Gesture '42
Song of the Islands '42

John Matuszak
Caveman '81
Down the Drain '89
Ghost Writer '89
The Goonies '85
Ice Pirates '84
My Darlin' Clementine '86
North Dallas Forty '79
One Man Force '89
Semi-Tough '77

Johanna Matz
The Life and Loves of Mozart '59
Party Girls for Sale '54
They Were So Young '55

Joan Maude
Power '34
The Temptress '49

Monica Maughan
Cactus '86
Prisoner Cell Block H '80
A Woman's Tale '92

Sarah Maur-Thorp
Edge of Sanity '89

River of Death '90
Ten Little Indians '89

Carmen Maura
Ay, Carmela! '90
Between Heaven and Earth '93
Dark Habits '84
Law of Desire '86
Matador '86
Pepi, Luci, Bom and Other Girls on the Heap '80
What Have I Done to Deserve This? '85
Women on the Verge of a Nervous Breakdown '88

Joshua Maurer
Taken Away '89
Tour of Duty '87

Nicole Maurey
Day of the Triffids '63
The Jayhawkers '59
Rogue's Yarn '56

Claire Maurier
Back to the Wall '56
The 400 Blows '59
La Cage aux Folles '78
Sweet Ecstasy '62

Gerda Maurus
Spies '28
Woman in the Moon '29

Edwin Maxwell
Behind Prison Walls '43
Mystery Liner '34
Night of Terror '33
Swamp Fire '46
The Taming of the Shrew '29
Waterfront '44
Way Down South '39
Woman in Brown '48

Frank Maxwell
The Haunted Palace '63
Lonelyhearts '58
Shame '61

John Maxwell
Boss of Big Town '43
Honky Tonk '41
The Payoff '43
Prowler '51

Lois Maxwell
Diamonds are Forever '71
Dr. No '62
Eternal Evil '87
For Your Eyes Only '81
From Russia with Love '63
Goldfinger '64
Live and Let Die '73
The Man with the Golden Gun '74
Moonraker '79
On Her Majesty's Secret Service '69
The Spy Who Loved Me '77
Thunderball '65
The Unstoppable Man '59
A View to a Kill '85
You Only Live Twice '67

Marilyn Maxwell
Arizona Bushwackers '67
Champion '49
Key to the City '50
The Lemon Drop Kid '51
Lost in a Harem '44
Off Limits '53
The Show-Off '46
Summer Holiday '48
Wild Women '51

Paul Maxwell
Cloud Waltzing '87
Going Home '86

Roberta Maxwell
Lois Gibbs and the Love Canal '82
Philadelphia '93
Psycho 3 '86

Deborah May
Caged Fear '92
Johnny Be Good '88
Rage of Angels '83

Donald May
Bogie: The Last Hero '80
Kisses for My President '64

Elaine May
California Suite '78
Enter Laughing '67
In the Spirit '90

Luv '67
A New Leaf '71

Jack May
He Kills Night After Night After Night '70
Night Slasher '84

Jodhi May
Eminent Domain '91
The Last of the Mohicans '92
Max and Helen '90
A World Apart '88

Mathilda May
Becoming Colette '92
The Cry of the Owl '92
Letters to an Unknown Lover '84
Lifeforce '85

Rik Mayall
Drop Dead Fred '91
Little Noises '91
Whoops Apocalypse '83
The Young Ones '88

Anthony Mayans
Heat of the Flame '82
Sex is Crazy '79
Zombie Lake '84

Eddie Mayehoff
Artists and Models '55
How to Murder Your Wife '64
The Stooge '51

Chip Mayer
Our Family Business '81
Survivor '87

Ray Mayer
Special Investigator '36
Swing It, Sailor! '37

Peter Mayhew
The Empire Strikes Back '80
Return of the Jedi '83

Ken Maynard
Arizona Terror '31
Arizona Whirlwind '44
Between Fighting Men '32
Boots of Destiny '37
Branded Men '31
Come On Tarzan '32
Death Rides the Range '40
Death Valley Rangers '44
Desert Guns/Six-Shootin' Sheriff '36
Drum Taps '33
Dynamite Ranch '32
False Faces '32
Fargo Express '32
The Fiddlin' Buckaroo '33
$50,000 Reward '25
Fightin' Ranch '30
The Fighting Legion '30
Fighting Thru '30
Flaming Lead '39
Harmony Trail '44
Hell Fire Austin '32
Honor of the Range '34
In Old Santa Fe '34
The Law Rides Again '43
Lightning Strikes West '40
The Lone Avenger '33
Mountain Justice '30
Mystery Mountain '34
Phantom Rancher '39
Phantom Thunderbolt '33
The Pocatello Kid '31
Range Law '31
Six Shootin' Sheriff '38
Strawberry Roan '33
Sunset Trail '32
Texas Gunfighter '32
Tombstone Canyon '35
Trail Drive '35
Two Gun Man '31
Voice of Hollywood '29
Western Frontier '35
Whirlwind Horseman '38
Whistlin' Dan '32

Kermit Maynard
Along the Sundown Trail '42
Ambush Trail '46
Arizona Stagecoach '42
Billy the Kid '41
The Black Lash '52
Bury Me Not On the Lone Prairie '41
Devil Riders '44
Drum Taps '33
The Fighting Trooper '34

Frontier Outlaws '44
Galloping Dynamite '37
Gangster's Den '45
His Fighting Blood '35
Man from Montana '41
The Mysterious Rider '42
'Neath Canadian Skies '46
Outlaw Justice '32
Phantom Patrol '36
Pony Post '40
Prairie Pals '42
Riders of Pasco Basin '40
Roaring Six Guns '37
Rough Ridin' Rhythm '37
The Showdown '40
Song of the Trail '36
The Stranger from Pecos '45
Texas Kid '43
Trail of Robin Hood '50
Valley of Terror '38
Whistling Bullets '36

Mimi Maynard
Adventures in Dinosaur City '92
False Identity '90

Ferdinand "Ferdy" Mayne
The Adventurers '70
Benefit of the Doubt '93
Captain's Paradise '53
The Fearless Vampire Killers '67
A Friendship in Vienna '88
Frightmare '81
Hawk the Slayer '81
Howling 2: Your Sister is a Werewolf '85
Magdalene '88
Masters of Venus '59
Night Train to Terror '84
River of Diamonds '90
Roadhouse Girl '53
The Secret Diary of Sigmund Freud '84
The Temptress '49
The Vampire Happening '71
The Vampire Lovers '70
White Fire '53

Alfredo Mayo
Bell from Hell '74
The Hunt '67

Frank Mayo
Doughboys '30
Hell's Headquarters '32
Tim Tyler's Luck '37

Virginia Mayo
Along the Great Divide '51
The Best Years of Our Lives '46
Captain Horatio Hornblower '51
Castle of Evil '66
Devil's Canyon '53
Evil Spirits '91
The Flame & the Arrow '50
French Quarter '78
Great Day in the Morning '56
The Haunted '79
Jack London '44
Jet Over the Atlantic '59
Kid from Brooklyn '46
King Richard and the Crusaders '54
Out of the Blue '47
Pearl of the South Pacific '55
The Princess and the Pirate '44
The Secret Life of Walter Mitty '47
Seven Days Ashore/Hurry, Charlie, Hurry '44
The Silver Chalice '54
A Song is Born '48
The West Point Story '50
White Heat '49
Wonder Man '45

Gale Mayron
Almost Blue '93
The Feud '90
Heart of Midnight '89

Melanie Mayron
The Best Little Girl in the World '81
The Boss' Wife '86
Car Wash '76
Checking Out '89
Girlfriends '78
Heartbeeps '81
Missing '82
My Blue Heaven '90

Playing for Time '80
Sticky Fingers '88
Wanted: The Perfect Guy '90
You Light Up My Life '77

Bob Maza
The Fringe Dwellers '86
Ground Zero '88

Debi Mazar
Beethoven's 2nd '93
Inside Monkey Zetterland '93
Little Man Tate '91
Money for Nothing '93

Mike Mazurki
The Adventures of Huckleberry Finn '78
Behind the Rising Sun '43
Blood Alley '55
The Canterville Ghost '44
Challenge To Be Free '76
Cheyenne Autumn '64
Dick Tracy, Detective '45
Dick Tracy, Detective/The Corpse Vanishes '42
Doin' Time '85
Donovan's Reef '63
The Errand Boy '61
Hell Ship Mutiny '57
The Incredible Rocky Mountain Race '77
Killer Dill '47
Murder, My Sweet '44
Neptune's Daughter '49
Night and the City '50
The Noose Hangs High '48
The Shanghai Gesture '42
Sinbad the Sailor '47
Some Like It Hot '59

Paul Mazursky
Alex in Wonderland '70
Enemies, a Love Story '89
History of the World: Part 1 '81
Into the Night '85
A Man, a Woman, and a Bank '79
Man Trouble '92
Punchline '88
Scenes from the Class Struggle in Beverly Hills '89
A Star is Born '76

Joseph Mazzello
Jersey Girl '92
Jurassic Park '93
Radio Flyer '92
Shadowlands '93

Des McAleer
Four Days in July '84
Hidden Agenda '90

Ray McAnally
Cal '84
Danny Boy '84
Empire State '87
The Fourth Protocol '87
The Mission '86
My Left Foot '89
No Surrender '86
A Perfect Spy '88
Taffin '88
A Very British Coup '90s
We're No Angels '89

Marianne McAndrew
The Bat People '74
Hello, Dolly! '69

Alex McArthur
Drug Wars 2: The Cocaine Cartel '92
Race for Glory '89
Rampage '87
Silent Witness '85
Urge to Kill '84

Hugh McArthur
Camp Double Feature '39
Marihuana '36
Panama Patrol '39

May McAvoy
Ben-Hur '26
Gun Glory '57
The Jazz Singer '27
Lady Windermere's Fan '26

Diane McBain
Deathhead Virgin '74
Donner-Pass: The Road to Survival '84
Flying from the Hawk '86
Monster '78
Parrish '61

McBain ►cont.

Spinout '66
Temporada Salvaje '87

Jon McBride
Blades '89
Cannibal Campout '88
Woodchipper Massacre '89

Michelle McBride
Masque of the Red Death '90
Subspecies '91

Ruth McCabe
My Left Foot '89
The Snapper '93

Frances Lee McCain
Broken Badge '85
Gremlins '84
The Lookalike '90
Question of Faith '93
Real Life '79
Tex '82
Two of a Kind '82

William McCall
Outlaws of the Range '36
Rounding Up the Law '22
Trailing Trouble '18

Irish McCalla
Hands of a Stranger '62
She Demons '58

Holt McCallany
Alien 3 '92
Creepshow 2 '87

Lon McCallister
The Big Cat '49
The Red House '47
Stage Door Canteen '43
The Story of Seabiscuit '49

David McCallum
Around the World Under the Sea '65
Behind Enemy Lines '85
Billy Budd '62
The Great Escape '63
The Haunting of Morella '91
Hear My Song '91
King Solomon's Treasure '76
Kingfisher Caper '76
A Night to Remember '58
Return of the Man from U.N.C.L.E. '83
Robbery Under Arms '57
She Waits '71
Terminal Choice '85
The Watcher in the Woods '81
The Wind '87

John McCallum
Devil on Horseback '54
Valley of the Eagles '51

Macon McCalman
Doc Hollywood '91
Fleshburn '84
The Ultimate Imposter '79

Mercedes McCambridge
All the King's Men '49
Angel Baby '61
Cimarron '60
The Concorde: Airport '79 '79
Deadly Sanctuary '68
Echoes '83
Giant '56
The Girls of Huntington House '73
Johnny Guitar '53
99 Women '69
The President's Plane is Missing '71
The Sacketts '79
Sixteen '72
Suddenly, Last Summer '59
Tender Is the Night '55

Chuck McCann
Cameron's Closet '89
C.H.O.M.P.S. '79
Foul Play '78
The Heart is a Lonely Hunter '68
If Things Were Different '79
The Projectionist '71
Rosebud Beach Hotel '85
Storyville '92
That's Adequate '90

Thrashin' '86

Donal McCann
Cal '84
Danny Boy '84
The Dead '87
Hard Way '80
The Miracle '91
Out of Africa '85
Screamer '74

Sean McCann
The Air Up There '94
Guilty as Sin '93
Mindfield '89
Run '91
Trial and Error '92
Unnatural Causes '86

Fred McCarren
How to Pick Up Girls '78
Marriage is Alive and Well '80
Red Flag: The Ultimate Game '81

Andrew McCarthy
The Beniker Gang '83
Class '83
Club Extinction '89
Fresh Horses '88
Heaven Help Us '85
The Joy Luck Club '93
Kansas '88
Less Than Zero '87
Mannequin '87
Only You '92
Pretty in Pink '86
St. Elmo's Fire '85
Waiting for the Moon '87
Weekend at Bernie's '89
Weekend at Bernie's 2 '93
Year of the Gun '91

Frank McCarthy
A Case of Deadly Force '86
Dead Men Don't Wear Plaid '82

Kevin McCarthy
Ace High '68
The Annapolis Story '55
The Best Man '64
A Big Hand for the Little Lady '66
Buffalo Bill & the Indians '76
Dan Candy's Law '73
Dark Tower '87
Dead on the Money '91
Dead Right '68
The Distinguished Gentleman '92
Duplicates '92
Eve of Destruction '91
Fast Food '89
Final Approach '91
For Love or Money '88
A Gathering of Eagles '63
Ghoulies 3: Ghoulies Go to College '91
Hero at Large '80
Hostage '92
Hotel '67
The Howling '81
Innerspace '87
Invasion of the Body Snatchers '56
Invasion of the Body Snatchers '78
Invitation to Hell '84
LBJ: The Early Years '88
Love or Money? '88
The Midnight Hour '86
Mirage '66
My Tutor '82
Order to Kill '73
Piranha '78
Poor Little Rich Girl: The Barbara Hutton Story '87
Ratings Game '84
The Rose and the Jackal '90
Rosie: The Rosemary Clooney Story '82
The Sleeping Car '90
Texas Guns '90
Those Lips, Those Eyes '80
Twilight Zone: The Movie '83
UHF '89

Lin McCarthy
D.I. '57
Yellowneck '55

Nobu McCarthy
The Geisha Boy '58
The Karate Kid: Part 2 '86
Pacific Heights '90

The Wash '88

Sheila McCarthy
Beautiful Dreamers '92
Beethoven Lives Upstairs '92
Bright Angel '91
Die Hard 2: Die Harder '90
Friends, Lovers & Lunatics '89
George's Island '91
I've Heard the Mermaids Singing '87
Pacific Heights '90
Paradise '91
A Private Matter '92
Stepping Out '91

Paul McCartney
The Compleat Beatles '82
Give My Regards to Broad Street '84
A Hard Day's Night '64
Help! '65
Let It Be '70
Magical Mystery Tour '67

Patti McCarty
Devil Riders '44
Fighting Valley '43
Outlaw of the Plains '46

Rod McCary
A Girl to Kill for '90
Night of the Demons 2 '94
No Drums, No Bugles '71
Rebel Storm '90

Constance McCashin
Love on the Run '85
Nightmare at Bittercreek '91
Obsessive Love '84
Special Olympics '78
The Two Worlds of Jenny Logan '79

Charles McCaughan
Impulse '90
Slaves of New York '89

Rue McClanahan
After the Shock '90
Baby of the Bride '91
Five Minutes to Love '63
Hollywood After Dark '65
How to Succeed with Girls '64
The Little Match Girl '87
Modern Love '90
Sergeant Matlovich vs. the U.S. Air Force '78

Sean McClory
Charade '53
Diane '55
Fools of Fortune '90
The King's Thief '55
My Chauffeur '86
The Quiet Man '52
Roller Boogie '79

Leigh McCloskey
Accidental Meeting '93
Alexander: The Other Side of Dawn '77
Cameron's Closet '89
Dirty Laundry '87
Double Revenge '89
Fraternity Vacation '85
Hamburger...The Motion Picture '86
Hearts & Armour '83
Inferno '78
Just One of the Guys '85

Doug McClure
At the Earth's Core '76
Bananas Boat '78
Battling for Baby '92
Bull of the West '89
Dark Before Dawn '89
Enemy Below '57
52 Pick-Up '86
Fight for Gold '86
Firebird 2015 A.D. '81
The Gambler Returns: The Luck of the Draw '91
Hell Hounds of Alaska '70s
House Where Evil Dwells '82
Humanoids from the Deep '80
The Land That Time Forgot '75
Omega Syndrome '87
The People That Time Forgot '77
Playmates '72
Prime Suspect '88
The Rebels '79
Shenandoah '65
Tapeheads '89

The Unforgiven '60
Wild & Wooly '78

Marc McClure
After Midnight '89
Back to the Future '85
Back to the Future, Part 3 '90
Grim Prairie Tales '89
I Wanna Hold Your Hand '78
Pandemonium '82
Perfect Match '88
Strange Behavior '81
Supergirl '84
Superman: The Movie '78
Superman 2 '80
Superman 3 '83
Superman 4: The Quest for Peace '87

Molly McClure
Daddy's Dyin'...Who's Got the Will? '91
Pure Country '92

Edie McClurg
Airborne '93
Back to School '86
Carrie '76
Cheech and Chong's Next Movie '80
Cheech and Chong's, The Corsican Brothers '84
Eating Raoul '82
Elvira, Mistress of the Dark '88
Ferris Bueller's Day Off '86
Mr. Mom '83
Pandemonium '82
Planes, Trains & Automobiles '87
A River Runs Through It '92
She's Having a Baby '88

Warren McCollum
Boy's Reformatory '39
The Great Commandment '41
Reefer Madness '38

Heather McComb
New York Stories '89
Stay Tuned '92

John McConnell
Delta Heat '92
King of the Hill '93

Marilyn McCoo
The Fantastic World of D.C. Collins '84
My Mom's a Werewolf '89

Kent McCord
Accidental Meeting '93
For Heaven's Sake '79
Illicit Behavior '91
Nashville Beat '89
Predator 2 '90
Return of the Living Dead 3 '93

Patty McCormack
The Adventures of Huckleberry Finn '60
All Mine to Give '56
The Bad Seed '56
Invitation to Hell '84
Saturday the 14th Strikes Back '88

Maureen McCormick
The Brady Bunch, Vol. 1 '69
Idolmaker '80
Moonshine County Express '77
Pony Express Rider '76
Take Down '79
Texas Lightning '81
A Very Brady Christmas '88

Michelle McCormick
Fatal Pulse '92
Showdown '93

Myron McCormick
The Hustler '61
Jigsaw '49
No Time for Sergeants '58
Not as a Stranger '55
One Third of a Nation '39
A Public Affair '62

Pat McCormick
Bombs Away! '86
Chinatown Connection '90
Doin' Time '85
E. Nick: A Legend in His Own Mind '84
If You Don't Stop It...You'll Go Blind '77
The Princess and the Pea '83

Rented Lips '88
Smokey and the Bandit '77
Smokey and the Bandit, Part 2 '80
Smokey and the Bandit, Part 3 '83
Under the Rainbow '81
A Wedding '78

Emer McCourt
London Kills Me '91
Riff Raff '92

Malachy McCourt
JFK: Reckless Youth '93
Manny's Orphans '78

Alec McCowen
The Age of Innocence '93
Cry Freedom '87
A Dedicated Man '86
Forever Young '85
Frenzy '72
Hanover Street '79
Henry V '89
Maria's Child '93
A Night to Remember '58
Personal Services '87
The Silent Enemy '58
Stevie '78
Travels with My Aunt '72

Matt McCoy
The Cool Surface '92
Dead On '93
Deepstar Six '89
Eyes of the Beholder '92
Fraternity Vacation '85
The Hand that Rocks the Cradle '92
Police Academy 5: Assignment Miami Beach '88
Police Academy 6: City Under Siege '89
Samurai Cowboy '93

Tim McCoy
Aces and Eights '36
Arizona Bound '41
Arizona Gangbusters '40
Below the Border '42
Border Caballero '36
Bulldog Courage '35
Daring Danger '32
Dawn on the Great Divide '42
Down Texas Way '42
Fighting Fool '32
The Fighting Marshal '32
Fighting Renegade '39
Fighting Shadows '35
Forbidden Trails '41
Ghost Patrol '36
Ghost Town Law '42
Gun Code '40
Gunman from Bodie '41
Lightnin' Carson Rides Again '38
Lion's Den '36
The Man from Gun Town '36
Man of Action '33
The Outlaw Deputy '35
Outlaw's Paradise '39
Phantom Ranger '38
The Range Feud/Two Fisted Law '31
The Revenge Rider '35
Riders of the West '42
The Riding Tornado '32
Roaring Guns '36
Run of the Arrow '56
Straight Shooter '40
Texas Cyclone '32
Texas Wildcats '39
The Traitor '36
Two-Fisted Law '32
West of the Law '42

Paul McCrane
Fame '80
The Portrait '93
Purple Hearts '84
RoboCop '87

Jody McCrea
Beach Blanket Bingo '65
Beach Party '63
Bikini Beach '64
Force of Impulse '60
The Glory Stompers '67
How to Stuff a Wild Bikini '65
Muscle Beach Party '64
Pajama Party '64

Joel McCrea
Barbary Coast '35

Bird of Paradise '32
Buffalo Bill '44
Come and Get It '36
Dead End '37
Foreign Correspondent '40
Four Faces West '48
The Great Moment '44
Kept Husbands '31
Lafayette Escadrille '58
The More the Merrier '43
The Most Dangerous Game '32
The Oklahoman '56
Our Little Girl '35
The Palm Beach Story '42
Primrose Path '40
Ramrod '47
Ride the High Country '62
South of St. Louis '48
Stars in My Crown '50
Sullivan's Travels '41
These Three '36
They Shall Have Music '39

Ian McCulloch
Alien Contamination '81
Doctor Butcher M.D. '80
Witching Time '84
Zombie '80

Kyle McCulloch
Careful '94
Tales from the Gimli Hospital '88

Julie McCullough
Big Bad Mama 2 '87
Round Trip to Heaven '92

Philo McCullough
Captured in Chinatown '35
Inside Information '34
Ridin' Thru '35
Tarzan the Fearless '33

Natalie McCurray
Dead End Drive-In '86
Glass '90
Stones of Death '88

Bill McCutcheon
Family Business '89
Mr. Destiny '90
Tune in Tomorrow '90

Hattie McDaniel
Alice Adams '35
Blonde Venus '32
The Bride Walks Out '36
Carefree '38
George Washington Slept Here '42
Gone with the Wind '39
The Great Lie '41
Harmony Lane '35
In This Our Life '42
Johnny Come Lately '43
Libeled Lady '36
The Little Colonel '35
Mad Miss Manton '38
The Making of a Legend: "Gone With the Wind" '89
Mickey '48
Saratoga '37
Shopworn Angel '38
Show Boat '36
Since You Went Away '44
They Died with Their Boots On '41

Dylan McDermott
Blue Iguana '88
The Cowboy Way '94
The Fear Inside '92
Hamburger Hill '87
Hardware '90
In the Line of Fire '93
Into the Badlands '92
Jersey Girl '92
The Neon Empire '89
Steel Magnolias '89
Twister '89
Where Sleeping Dogs Lie '91

Hugh McDermott
Devil Girl from Mars '54
The Seventh Veil '46

Ruth McDevitt
Change of Habit '69
Homebodies '74
The Shakiest Gun in the West '68

Christopher McDonald
Benefit of the Doubt '93

The Boys Next Door '85
Breakin' '84
Bums '93
Chances Are '89
Chattanooga Choo Choo '84
Conflict of Interest '92
Fatal Exposure '91
Fatal Instinct '93
Grumpy Old Men '93
Monkey Trouble '94
Paramedics '88
Playroom '90
Red Wind '91
Thelma & Louise '91
Wild Orchid 2: Two Shades of Blue '91

Francis McDonald
Bad Men of the Border '45
Battling Butler '26
The Confession '20
Hidden Valley '32
Morocco '30
Mystery Man '44
Mystery of the Riverboat '44
The Sea Wolf '41
Terror Trail '33
Texas Buddies '32
Texas Masquerade '44
Zorro's Black Whip '44

Garry McDonald
Ghosts Can Do It '90
Pirate Movie '82
The Wacky World of Wills & Burke '85

Kenneth McDonald
The Coast Patrol '25
Dynamite Dan '24

Marie McDonald
The Geisha Boy '58
Guest in the House '45
Promises! Promises! '63
Tell It to the Judge '49

Mary Ann McDonald
Far Cry from Home '70s
Love at First Sight '76

Steve McDonald
Desperate Teenage Lovedolls '84
Spirit of '76 '91

Mary McDonnell
Blue Chips '94
Dances with Wolves '90
Grand Canyon '91
Matewan '87
Passion Fish '92
Sneakers '92
Tiger Warsaw '87

Mary McDonough
Children's Carol '80
A Day for Thanks on Walton's Mountain '82
Mom '89
Snowballing '85
The Waltons: A Thanksgiving Story '73

Frances McDormand
Blood Simple '85
The Butcher's Wife '91
Chattahoochee '89
Crazy in Love '92
Darkman '90
Hidden Agenda '90
Mississippi Burning '88
Passed Away '92
Raising Arizona '87
Short Cuts '93

Betty McDowall
Ballad in Blue '66
Dead Lucky '60
Jack the Ripper '60
Time Lock '57

Roddy McDowall
The Adventures of Bullwhip Griffin '67
Arnold '73
Battle for the Planet of the Apes '73
Bedknobs and Broomsticks '71
The Big Picture '89
Carmilla '89
The Cat from Outer Space '78
Charlie Chan and the Curse of the Dragon Queen '81
Circle of Iron '78
Class of 1984 '82

Cleopatra '63
Conquest of the Planet of the Apes '72
Cutting Class '89
Dead of Winter '87
Deadly Game '91
Dirty Mary Crazy Larry '74
Doin' Time on Planet Earth '88
Double Trouble '91
Embryo '76
Escape from the Planet of the Apes '71
Everybody's Dancin' '50
Evil Under the Sun '82
Five Card Stud '68
Flood! '76
Fright Night '85
Fright Night 2 '88
Funny Lady '75
The Greatest Story Ever Told '65
Heads '93
Hill Number One '51
Holiday in Mexico '46
How Green was My Valley '41
An Inconvenient Woman '91
Inside Daisy Clover '65
The Keys of the Kingdom '44
Laserblast '78
Lassie, Come Home '43
The Legend of Hell House '73
Life & Times of Judge Roy Bean '72
The Longest Day '62
The Loved One '65
Macbeth '48
Mae West '84
The Martian Chronicles: Part 2 '79
The Martian Chronicles: Part 3 '79
Mean Johnny Barrows '75
Midnight Lace '60
My Friend Flicka '43
Night Gallery '69
Overboard '87
Planet of the Apes '68
The Poseidon Adventure '72
Rabbit Test '78
Scavenger Hunt '79
Shakma '89
Son of Fury '42
The Tempest '63
That Darn Cat '65
The Thief of Baghdad '78
The White Cliffs of Dover '44
The Zany Adventures of Robin Hood '84

Claire McDowell
Ben-Hur '26
The Big Parade '25
Short Films of D.W. Griffith, Vol. 1 '12
West-Bound Limited '23

Malcolm McDowell
Blue Thunder '83
Bopha! '93
Britannia Hospital '82
Buy & Cell '89
Caligula '80
The Caller '87
Cat People '82
Chain of Desire '93
Class of 1999 '90
A Clockwork Orange '71
Cross Creek '83
Disturbed '90
Get Crazy '83
Gulag '85
If... '69
Jezebel's Kiss '90
The Light in the Jungle '91
Little Red Riding Hood '83
Long Ago Tomorrow '71
Look Back in Anger '80
Merlin and the Sword '85
Milk Money '94
Monte Carlo '86
Moon 44 '90
O Lucky Man! '73
Sunset '88
Time After Time '79
Voyage of the Damned '76

Nelson McDowell
Desert Phantom '36
Feud of the West '36
The Last of the Mohicans '20
Mason of the Mounted '32
Texas Jack '35

James McEachin
The Dead Don't Die '75
Double Exposure '93
The Groundstar Conspiracy '72
He Who Walks Alone '78
Honeyboy '82

Ellen McElduff
Imposters '84
Working Girls '87

John McEnery
Bartleby '70
Black Beauty '94
Codename Kyril '91
Gulag '85
The Land That Time Forgot '75
One Russian Summer '73
Pope John Paul II '84

Peter McEnery
Entertaining Mr. Sloane '70
The Fighting Prince of Donegal '66
The Game is Over '66
I Killed Rasputin '67
The Moon-Spinners '64
Negatives '68
Pictures '80s
Tales That Witness Madness '73
Victim '62

Annie McEnroe
Cop '88
The Hand '81
Howling 2: Your Sister is a Werewolf '85
Purple Hearts '84
Running Scared '79
True Stories '86
Warlords of the 21st Century '82

Reba McEntire
The Gambler Returns: The Luck of the Draw '93
North '94
Tremors '89

Geraldine McEwan
Foreign Body '86
Robin Hood: Prince of Thieves '91

Gates McFadden
Star Trek the Next Generation: Encounter at Farpoint '87
Taking Care of Business '90

George "Spanky" McFarland
The Aurora Encounter '85
General Spanky '36
Kentucky Kernels '34
Little Rascals, Book 1 '30s
Little Rascals, Book 2 '30s
Little Rascals, Book 3 '38
Little Rascals, Book 4 '30s
Little Rascals, Book 5 '48
Little Rascals, Book 6 '30s
Little Rascals, Book 7 '30s
Little Rascals, Book 8 '30s
Little Rascals, Book 9 '30s
Little Rascals, Book 10 '30s
Little Rascals, Book 11 '38
Little Rascals, Book 12 '37
Little Rascals, Book 13 '37
Little Rascals, Book 14 '30s
Little Rascals, Book 15 '30s
Little Rascals, Book 16 '30s
Little Rascals, Book 17 '31
Little Rascals: Choo Choo/ Fishy Tales '32
Little Rascals Collector's Edition, Vol. 1-6
Little Rascals Comedy Classics, Vol. 1
Little Rascals Comedy Classics, Vol. 2
Little Rascals: Fish Hooky/ Spooky Hooky '33
Little Rascals: Honkey Donkey/ Sprucin' Up '34
Little Rascals: Little Sinner/Two Too Young '35
Little Rascals: Mush and Milk/ Three Men in a Tub '33
Little Rascals on Parade '37
Little Rascals: Pups is Pups/ Three Smart Boys '30
Little Rascals: Readin' and Writin'/Mail and Female '31

Little Rascals: Reunion in Rhythm/Mike Fright '37
Little Rascals: Spanky/Feed 'Em and Weep '32
Little Rascals: The Pinch Singer/Framing Youth '36
Little Rascals Two Reelers, Vol. 1 '29
Little Rascals Two Reelers, Vol. 2 '33
Little Rascals Two Reelers, Vol. 3 '36
Little Rascals Two Reelers, Vol. 4 '30
Little Rascals Two Reelers, Vol. 5 '34
Little Rascals Two Reelers, Vol. 6 '36
Little Rascals, Vol. 1 '29
Little Rascals, Vol. 2 '30
Our Gang Comedies '40s
Peck's Bad Boy with the Circus '38

William F. McGaha
Iron Horsemen '71
The Speed Lovers '68

Mark McGann
John & Yoko: A Love Story '85
Let Him Have It '91

Paul McGann
Afraid of the Dark '92
Alien 3 '92
Dealers '89
Innocent Victim '90
Paper Mask '91
The Rainbow '89
Withnail and I '87

Darren McGavin
Airport '77 '77
The Baron and the Kid '84
Blood & Concrete: A Love Story '90
By Dawn's Early Light '89
Captain America '89
Child in the Night '90
A Christmas Story '83
The Court Martial of Billy Mitchell '55
Dead Heat '88
The Delicate Delinquent '56
Firebird 2015 A.D. '81
Hangar 18 '80
Hitchhiker 2 '85
Ike '79
The Man with the Golden Arm '55
The Martian Chronicles: Part 1 '79
The Martian Chronicles: Part 2 '79
The Martian Chronicles: Part 3 '79
Mission Mars '67
My Wicked, Wicked Ways '84
The Natural '84
The Night Stalker: Two Tales of Terror '74
No Deposit, No Return '76
Perfect Harmony '91
Power, Passion & Murder '83
Queen for a Day '51
Raw Deal '86
Richard Petty Story '72
Say Goodbye, Maggie Cole '72
Sunset '88
Tribes '70
Turk 182! '85
Waikiki '80
Zero to Sixty '78

Vonetta McGee
The Big Bust Out '73
Blacula '72
Brother Future '91
The Eiger Sanction '75
Repo Man '83
To Sleep with Anger '90
You Must Remember This '90s

Johnny Rae McGhee
Love Field '92
Project X '87

William Bill McGhee
Don't Look in the Basement '73
1918 '85

Bruce McGill
Ballad of Gregorio Cortez '83
Charlotte Forten's Mission: Experiment in Freedom '85

McGill ►cont.

Citizens Band '77
End of the Line '88
The Hand '81
Into the Night '85
The Last Boy Scout '91
The Last Innocent Man '87
Little Vegas '90
My Cousin Vinny '92
National Lampoon's Animal House '78
No Mercy '86
Out Cold '89
Silkwood '83
Timecop '94
Tough Enough '83
Whale for the Killing '81
Wildcats '86

Everett McGill
Brubaker '80
Dune '84
Field of Honor '86
Heartbreak Ridge '86
Iguana '89
Jezebel's Kiss '90
License to Kill '89
The People Under the Stairs '91
Quest for Fire '82
Silver Bullet '85
Twin Peaks '90
Union City '81

Kelly McGillis
The Accused '88
The Babe '92
Cat Chaser '90
Code of Honor '84
Grand Isle '92
The House on Carroll Street '88
Made in Heaven '87
North '94
Reuben, Reuben '83
Top Gun '86
Unsettled Land '88
Winter People '89
Witness '85

John C. McGinley
Article 99 '92
Car 54, Where Are You? '94
Fat Man and Little Boy '89
Hear No Evil '93
Highlander 2: The Quickening '91
The Last Outlaw '93
Little Noises '91
Lost Angels '89
A Midnight Clear '92
Mother's Boys '94
On Deadly Ground '94
Platoon '86
Point Break '91
Prisoners of Inertia '89
Suffering Bastards '90
Surviving the Game '94
Talk Radio '88
Wagons East '94
Wall Street '87
Watch It '93

Ted McGinley
Blue Tornado '90
It's a Bundyful Life '92
Linda '93
Physical Evidence '89
Revenge of the Nerds '84
Revenge of the Nerds 3: The Next Generation '92

Scott McGinnis
Joy Sticks '83
Making the Grade '84
Odd Jobs '85
You Can't Hurry Love '88

John McGiver
The Adventures of Tom Sawyer '73
Bachelor in Paradise '69
Breakfast at Tiffany's '61
The Gazebo '59
The Glass Bottom Boat '66
A Global Affair '63
Lawman '71
Love in the Afternoon '57
The Man in the Raincoat '57
The Manchurian Candidate '62
Man's Favorite Sport? '63

Midnight Cowboy '69
Mr. Hobbs Takes a Vacation '62
Period of Adjustment '62
Who's Got the Action? '63

Frank McGlynn
Custer's Last Stand '36
Hopalong Cassidy '35
Rogue's Gallery '44

Patrick McGoohan
Baby...Secret of the Lost Legend '85
Brass Target '78
Dr. Syn, Alias the Scarecrow '64
Escape from Alcatraz '79
Hard Way '80
I Am a Camera '55
Ice Station Zebra '68
Jamaica Inn '82
Kings and Desperate Men '83
Koroshi '67
The Man in the Iron Mask '77
Scanners '81
The Silver Streak '76
The Three Lives of Thomasina '63
Three Sovereigns for Sarah '85

Barry McGovern
Joe Versus the Volcano '90
Riders to the Sea '88

Elizabeth McGovern
The Bedroom Window '87
The Favor '94
The Handmaid's Tale '90
Johnny Handsome '89
King of the Hill '93
Lovesick '83
Me & Veronica '93
Native Son '86
Once Upon a Time in America '84
Ordinary People '80
Racing with the Moon '84
Ragtime '81
She's Having a Baby '88
A Shock to the System '90
Snow White and the Seven Dwarfs '83
Tune in Tomorrow '90
Women & Men: Stories of Seduction '90

J.P. McGowan
Heart of the Rockies '37
Hit the Saddle '37
The Outlaw Tamer '33
Red Signals '27
Somewhere in Sonora '33

Walter McGrail
Code of the Fearless '39
The Green Hornet '39
The Lone Star Ranger '39
Night Nurse '31

Charles McGraw
Armored Car Robbery '50
A Boy and His Dog '75
The Bridges at Toko-Ri '55
Cimarron '60
The Defiant Ones '58
Falcon's Adventure/Armored Car Robbery '50
His Kind of Woman '51
The Horizontal Lieutenant '62
Lady Scarface/The Threat '49
Ma and Pa Kettle Go to Town '50
The Mad Ghoul '43
The Narrow Margin '52
One Minute to Zero '52
Pendulum '69
The Saint's Vacation/The Narrow Margin '52
Spartacus '60
T-Men '47
Tell Them Willie Boy Is Here '69
Threat '49
Twilight's Last Gleaming '77

Angela Punch McGregor
Double Deal '84
The Efficiency Expert '92
The Island '80
Newsfront '78
Survivor '80
A Test of Love '84
We of the Never Never '82

Kenneth John McGregor
Primal Scream '87
The Ten Million Dollar Getaway '91

Malcolm McGregor
The Reckless Way '36
Smouldering Fires '25
The Untamable '23

Biff McGuire
Child of Glass '78
Deadline Assault '90
Justice '55

Don McGuire
Double Dynamite '51
Fuller Brush Man '48
The Man I Love '46

Dorothy McGuire
Amos '85
Caroline? '90
The Enchanted Cottage '45
Friendly Persuasion '56
Gentleman's Agreement '47
The Greatest Story Ever Told '65
The Incredible Journey of Dr. Meg Laurel '79
Little Women '78
Make Haste to Live '54
Old Yeller '57
Rich Man, Poor Man '76
The Runaways '75
She Waits '71
The Spiral Staircase '46
Summer Magic '63
A Summer Place '59
The Swiss Family Robinson '60
Three Coins in the Fountain '54
Till the End of Time '46
A Tree Grows in Brooklyn '45

John McGuire
Outlaw Rule '36
Stranger on the Third Floor '40

Kathryn McGuire
Lost Zeppelin '29
Midnight Faces '26
The Navigator '24

Michael McGuire
Bird '88
Blinded by the Light '82
Home to Stay '79
Larry '74
The Long Days of Summer '80
The Ordeal of Dr. Mudd '80
Report to the Commissioner '74
Sanctuary of Fear '79

Stephen McHattie
Belizaire the Cajun '86
Beverly Hills Cop 3 '94
Bloodhounds of Broadway '89
Call Me '88
Caribe '87
The Dark '94
Death Valley '81
Erik '90
Geronimo: An American Legend '93
James Dean '76
Mary and Joseph: A Story of Faith '79
Moving Violation '76
One Man Out '89
The People Next Door '70
Roughnecks '80
Salvation! '87
Search for the Gods '75
Sticky Fingers '88
Tomorrow Never Comes '77

Frank McHugh
All Through the Night '42
Boy Meets Girl '38
Bullets or Ballots '38
City for Conquest '40
Corsair '31
Devil Dogs of the Air '35
Dodge City '39
Easy Come, Easy Go '67
Ex-Lady '33
Fashions of 1934 '34
The Fighting 69th '40
Going My Way '44
Gold Diggers of 1935 '35
I Love You Again '40
Last Hurrah '58

A Lion is in the Streets '53
Marine Raiders '49
Mighty Joe Young '49
Millie '31
Miss Grant Takes Richmond '49
The Roaring Twenties '39
State Fair '45
The Strange Love of Molly Louvain '32
Telegraph Trail '33
There's No Business Like Show Business '54
Three Men on a Horse '36
A Tiger Walks '64
Tomorrow at Seven '33
Velvet Touch '48
Virginia City '40

David McIlwraith
Happy Birthday, Gemini '80
Millennium '89
The Vindicator '85

John McIntire
American Dream '81
Apache '54
As Summers Die '86
The Asphalt Jungle '50
Call Northside 777 '48
Cloak & Dagger '84
Elmer Gantry '60
Far Country '55
Flaming Star '60
Francis the Talking Mule '49
Herbie Rides Again '74
Honkytonk Man '82
Horizons West '52
The Kentuckian '55
The Light in the Forest '58
A Lion is in the Streets '53
The Mark of the Hawk '57
Mrs. R's Daughter '79
Psycho '60
Rooster Cogburn '75
Rough Night in Jericho '67
Summer and Smoke '61
The Tin Star '57
Two Rode Together '61
Walk Softly, Stranger '50
Westward the Women '51
Winchester '73 '50

Tim McIntire
Aloha, Bobby and Rose '74
The Choirboys '77
Fast Walking '82
Gumball Rally '76
Sacred Ground '83
The Sterile Cuckoo '69

Burr McIntosh
The Adorable Cheat '28
The Average Woman '24
That Certain Thing '28

Christine McIntyre
Gentleman from Texas '46
Land of the Lawless '47
Partners of the Trail '44
The Stranger from Pecos '45

Marvin J. McIntyre
Fandango '85
Wilder Napalm '93

John McKay
Assault of the Rebel Girls '59
Rocket Attack U.S.A. '58

Wanda McKay
The Black Raven '43
Bowery at Midnight '42
Corregidor '43
Jungle Goddess '49
The Monster Maker '44
Raiders of Ghost City '44
Texas Justice '42
There Goes Kelly '45
Twilight on the Trail '41

Michael McKean
Airheads '94
The Big Picture '89
Book of Love '91
Clue '85
Coneheads '93
Daniel and the Towers '90s
D.A.R.Y.L. '85
Earth Girls are Easy '89
Flashback '89
Hider in the House '90
Light of Day '87
Man Trouble '92

Memoirs of an Invisible Man '92
Planes, Trains & Automobiles '87
Portrait of a White Marriage '88
The Return of Spinal Tap '92
Short Circuit 2 '88
This is Spinal Tap '84
Used Cars '80
Young Doctors in Love '82

Donna McKechnie
Breakin' Through '84
Twirl '81

Lafe McKee
The Big Stampede '32
Boss Cowboy '35
Covered Wagon Trails '40
Deadwood Pass '33
Fighting Champ '33
Jaws of Justice '33
Last of the Warrens '36
Law of the Wild '34
Lightning Range '33
Man from Monterey '33
Man from Utah '34
Melody of the Plains '37
The Miracle Rider '35
Mystery of the Hooded Horseman '37
Near the Rainbow's End '30
The Pocatello Kid '31
Range Law '31
The Rangers Step In '37
Rawhide Romance '34
The Revenge Rider '35
Riders of Pasco Basin '40
Ridin' Thru '35
The Riding Tornado '32
Rustlers of Red Dog '35
Santa Fe Bound '37
Telegraph Trail '33
Terror Trail '33
Two Gun Man '31
Under Montana Skies '30

Lonette McKee
Brewster's Millions '85
The Cotton Club '84
Cuba '79
Detroit 9000 '73
Gardens of Stone '87
Jungle Fever '91
Malcolm X '92
Round Midnight '86
Sparkle '76
Which Way Is Up? '77
The Women of Brewster Place '89

Raymond McKee
Campus Knights '29
Down to the Sea in Ships '22
Free to Love '25

Ian McKellan
And the Band Played On '93
The Ballad of Little Jo '93
Plenty '85
Priest of Love '81
Scandal '89
The Scarlet Pimpernel '82
The Shadow '93
Six Degrees of Separation '93
Windmills of the Gods '88

Danica McKellar
Camp Cucamonga: How I Spent My Summer Vacation '90
Sidekicks '93

Don McKellar
The Adjuster '91
Highway 61 '91
Roadkill '89

Siobhan McKenna
The Adventurers '51
Doctor Zhivago '65
The King of Kings '61
Of Human Bondage '64
Playboy of the Western World '62

T.P. McKenna
All Creatures Great and Small '74
Beast in the Cellar '70
Bleak House '85
The Charge of the Light Brigade '68
The Doctor and the Devils '85

James Joyce: A Portrait of the Artist as a Young Man '77
Next Victim '74
Red Scorpion '89
Straw Dogs '72
Ulysses '67
Valmont '89

Virginia McKenna
Born Free '66
Carve Her Name with Pride '58
The Chosen '77
Christian the Lion '76
Cruel Sea '53
Disappearance '81
Duel of Hearts '92
The First Olympics: Athens 1896 '84
The Gathering Storm '74
Ring of Bright Water '69
Simba '55
The Smallest Show on Earth '57
Waterloo '71
The Wreck of the Mary Deare '59

Fay McKenzie
Boss Cowboy '35
Death Rides the Range '40
Down Mexico Way '41
Heart of the Rio Grande '42

Richard McKenzie
Corvette Summer '78
In Love and War '91

Tim McKenzie
Gallipoli '81
The Lighthorsemen '87
The 13th Floor '88

Doug McKeon
Breaking Home Ties '87
Desperate Lives '82
Heart of a Champion: The Ray Mancini Story '85
Mischief '85
Night Crossing '81
On Golden Pond '81
Turnaround '87
Where the Red Fern Grows: Part 2 '92

Nancy McKeon
High School USA '84
The Lightning Incident '91
Poison Ivy '85
Where the Day Takes You '92

Philip McKeon
Red Surf '90
Return to Horror High '87

Leo McKern
The Adventures of Sherlock Holmes' Smarter Brother '78
The Amorous Adventures of Moll Flanders '65
The Blue Lagoon '80
Candleshoe '78
The Day the Earth Caught Fire '62
Doctor in Distress '63
The French Lieutenant's Woman '81
Help! '65
The Horse Without a Head '63
The House on Garibaldi Street '79
Ladyhawke '85
Massacre in Rome '73
Monsignor Quixote '91
The Mouse That Roared '59
Rumpole of the Bailey: Rumpole's Return '90
Ryan's Daughter '70
The Shoes of the Fisherman '68
Travelling North '87

Robert McKim
The Bat '26
Disciple '15
Heart's Haven '22
Hell's Hinges '16
Wagon Tracks '19

Bill McKinney
Against All Odds '84
Bronco Billy '80
Cannonball '76
The China Lake Murders '90
City Slickers 2: The Legend of Curly's Gold '94
Deliverance '72

The Gauntlet '77
Heart Like a Wheel '83
The Outlaw Josey Wales '76
Parallax View '74
St. Helen's, Killer Volcano '82
She-Freak '67
The Shootist '76
Tex '82

Nina Mae McKinney
The Devil's Daughter '39
Hallelujah! '29
Pinky '49

Ray McKinnon
Indecency '92
Paris Trout '91
A Perfect World '93

Victor McLaglen
Broadway Limited '41
Call Out the Marines '42
Devil's Party '38
Dishonored '31
Forever and a Day '43
Fort Apache '48
Gunga Din '39
The Informer '35
Klondike Annie '36
Laughing at Life '33
Let Freedom Ring '39
The Lost Patrol '34
Murder at the Vanities '34
Prince Valiant '54
The Princess and the Pirate '44
The Quiet Man '52
Rio Grande '50
Sea Devils '37
She Wore a Yellow Ribbon '49
South of Pago Pago '40
Trouble in the Glen '54
The Unholy Three '25
Wee Willie Winkie '37
Whistle Stop '46

Hollis McLaren
Atlantic City '81
Lost and Found '79
Outrageous! '77
Vengeance Is Mine '84

Ron McLarty
Enormous Changes '83
The Feud '90
Tiger Town '83
Trumps '88

Bill McLaughlin
Comic Cabby '87
Naked Vengeance '85
Silk '86

Gibb McLaughlin
Bulldog Jack '35
Inspector Hornleigh '39
Mr. Reeder in Room 13 '38
The Old Curiosity Shop '35
Power '34

David McLean
Death Sport '78
Hughes & Harlow: Angels in Hell '77
The Strangler '64

Catherine McLeod
I've Always Loved You '46
Sword of Venus '53

Kenneth McLeod
Judgment Day '88
Out for Blood '93
Showdown '93

Allyn Ann McLerie
And Baby Makes Six '79
Calamity Jane '53
Death Scream '75
The Desert Song '53
A Shining Season '79
Someone I Touched '75
They Shoot Horses, Don't They? '69

John McLiam
The Ambush Murders '82
The Five of Me '81
Freedom Road '79
Showdown '73
Split Decisions '88

Rachel McLish
Aces: Iron Eagle 3 '92
Pumping Iron 2: The Women '85

Ed McMahon
Fun with Dick and Jane '77

Great American Traffic Jam '80
The Incident '67
The Kid from Left Field '79
Slaughter's Big Ripoff '73

Horace McMahon
Abbott and Costello Go to Mars '53
The Delicate Delinquent '56
Detective Story '51
Melody Ranch '40
My Sister Eileen '55
The Wrong Road '37

Michael McManus
Captain America '79
Funland '87
Mr. Bill's Real Life Adventures '86
Speaking Parts '89

John McMartin
Day One '89
Dream Lover '85
Gore Vidal's Lincoln '88
Legal Eagles '86
Little Sweetheart '90
Murrow '86
Native Son '86
Private Contentment '83
Roots: The Gift '88
Separate But Equal '91
A Shock to the System '90
Sweet Charity '69

Kenneth McMillan
Acceptable Risks '86
Armed and Dangerous '86
Bloodbrothers '78
Blue Skies Again '83
Borderline '80
Carny '80
Cat's Eye '85
Chilly Scenes of Winter '79
Concrete Beat '84
Dixie: Changing Habits '85
Dune '84
Eyewitness '81
Heartbeeps '81
Hide in Plain Sight '80
In the Custody of Strangers '82
Johnny We Hardly Knew Ye '77
Killing Hour '84
Malone '87
Partners '82
The Pope of Greenwich Village '84
Protocol '84
Ragtime '81
Reckless '84
Runaway Train '85
Salem's Lot '79
The Taking of Pelham One Two Three '74
Three Fugitives '89
True Confessions '81
Whose Life Is It Anyway? '81

W.G. McMillan
The Crazies '73
The Sister-in-Law '74

Sam McMurray
Getting Even with Dad '94
L.A. Story '91
Stone Cold '91

Pamela McMyler
The $5.20 an Hour Dream '80
The Stick-Up '77

Barbara McNair
Change of Habit '69
Dead Right '68
The Organization '71
Stiletto '69
They Call Me Mr. Tibbs! '70
Venus in Furs '70

Kevin McNally
The Berlin Affair '85
Cry Freedom '87

Stephen McNally
Air Raid Wardens '43
A Bullet Is Waiting '54
Criss Cross '48
Dear Detective '78
Devil's Canyon '53
Diplomatic Courier '52
For Me and My Gal '42
Hi-Riders '78
Make Haste to Live '54
Split Second '53
Thirty Seconds Over Tokyo '44
Tribute to a Bad Man '56

Winchester '73 '50

Brian McNamara
Arachnophobia '90
Billionaire Boys Club '87
Detective Sadie & Son '84
Mystery Date '91
Short Circuit '86

Ed McNamara
Johnny Come Lately '43
Tramp at the Door '87

Julianne McNamara
Class of Fear '91
Saturday the 14th Strikes Back '88

Maggie McNamara
The Cardinal '63
Moon is Blue '53
Three Coins in the Fountain '54

William McNamara
The Beat '88
Chasers '94
Stealing Home '88
Surviving the Game '94
Terror at the Opera '88
Texasville '90
Wildflower '91

Julia McNeal
The Refrigerator '93
The Unbelievable Truth '90

Howard McNear
The Errand Boy '61
Escape from Fort Bravo '53
Follow That Dream '61
Fun in Acapulco '63
Kiss Me, Stupid! '64

Ian McNeice
The Lonely Passion of Judith Hearne '87
No Escape '94
The Russia House '90
Valmont '89
Year of the Comet '92

Claudia McNeil
Cry Panic '74
A Raisin in the Sun '61
Roll of Thunder, Hear My Cry '78

Kathy McNeil
Beach House '82
The House on Sorority Row '83

Jimmy McNichol
Blinded by the Light '82
Escape from El Diablo '83
Night Warning '82
Smokey Bites the Dust '81

Kristy McNichol
Baby of the Bride '91
Blinded by the Light '82
Dream Lover '85
The End '78
The Forgotten One '89
Just the Way You Are '84
Little Darlings '80
My Old Man '79
The Night the Lights Went Out in Georgia '81
Only When I Laugh '81
Pirate Movie '82
The Summer of My German Soldier '78
Two Moon Junction '88
Women of Valor '86
You Can't Hurry Love '88

Sandy McPeak
Eye on the Sparrow '91
The Flight '89
Inside Out '91
My Mother's Secret Life '84
Ode to Billy Joe '76
The Taking of Flight 847: The Uli Derickson Story '88
Tarantulas: The Deadly Cargo '77

Murdock McQuarrie
Daring Danger '32
Ghost Town Riders '38
Laramie Kid '35
Man from Montana '41
The New Frontier '35
The Tonto Kid '35

Butterfly McQueen
The Adventures of Huckleberry Finn '85
Amazing Grace '74

Duel in the Sun '46
Gone with the Wind '39
I Dood It '43
Killer Diller '48
The Making of a Legend: "Gone With the Wind" '89
The Mosquito Coast '86

Chad McQueen
Death Ring '93
Fever Pitch '85
Firepower '93
The Karate Kid '84
Martial Law '90
Money to Burn '94
Nightforce '86
Sexual Malice '93
Skateboard '77
Where the Red Fern Grows: Part 2 '92

Steve McQueen
Baby, the Rain Must Fall '64
The Blob '58
Bruce Lee: The Legend '84
Bullitt '68
The Cincinnati Kid '65
The Defender '57
The Getaway '72
The Great Escape '63
Hell is for Heroes '62
The Honeymoon Machine '61
The Hunter '80
Junior Bonner '72
Le Mans '71
Love with the Proper Stranger '63
The Magnificent Seven '60
Nevada Smith '66
Never Love a Stranger '58
Never So Few '59
Papillon '73
The Reivers '69
The Sand Pebbles '66
Soldier in the Rain '63
Somebody Up There Likes Me '56
Thomas Crown Affair '68
Tom Horn '80
The Towering Inferno '74
War Lover '62
Wild West '87

Elizabeth McRae
The Conversation '74
The Incredible Mr. Limpet '64

Frank McRae
*batteries not included '87
Cannery Row '82
Farewell to the King '89
Last Action Hero '93
License to Kill '89
Lightning Jack '94
Lock Up '89
Sketch Artist '92

Leslie McRae
Blood Orgy of the She-Devils '74
Girl in Gold Boots '69

Gerald McRaney
American Justice '86
Blind Vengeance '90
City Killer '87
Dynamite and Gold '88
The Haunting Passion '83
Hobo's Christmas '87
Mind Warp '71
Murder by Moonlight '91
The NeverEnding Story '84
Night of Bloody Horror '76

Ian McShane
Code Name: Diamond Head '77
Con Man '92
Exposed '83
The Fifth Musketeer '79
Grand Larceny
The Great Escape 2: The Untold Story '88
The Great Riviera Bank Robbery '79
If It's Tuesday, This Must Be Belgium '69
Journey into Fear '74
The Last of Sheila '73
The Murders in the Rue Morgue '86
Ordeal by Innocence '84
The Terrorists '75
Too Scared to Scream '85
Torchlight '85

McShane ►cont.

War & Remembrance, Part 1 '88
War & Remembrance: The Final Chapter, Part 8 '89
Yesterday's Hero '79
Young Charlie Chaplin '88

Gerard McSorley
In the Name of the Father '93
Widow's Peak '94

Bud McTaggart
Billy the Kid Trapped '42
Meet the Mob '42

Patrick McVey
Desperate Characters '71
Top of the Heap '72

Paul McVey
Buried Alive '39
Phantom of Chinatown '40

Margaret McWade
The Confession '20
Mr. Deeds Goes to Town '36

Robert McWade
Feet First '30
Healer '36
Kept Husbands '31

Jillian McWhirter
After Midnight '89
Beyond the Call of Duty '92
Dune Warriors '91

Caroline McWilliams
Into Thin Air '85
Mermaids '90
Pigeon Feathers '90
Rage '80
Shattered Vows '84
Switched at Birth '91

Courtland Mead
Dragonworld '94
The Little Rascals '94

Jayne Meadows
City Slickers '91
David and Bathsheba '51
James Dean '76
Lady in the Lake '46
Miss All-American Beauty '82
Murder by Numbers '89
Norman, Is That You? '76
Ratings Game '84
Song of the Thin Man '47

Joyce Meadows
The Brain from Planet Arous '57
Flesh and the Spur '57
The Girl in Lover's Lane '60
Zebra in the Kitchen '65

Stephen Meadows
A Cry in the Wild '90
The End of Innocence '90
Sunstroke '92

Karen Meagher
Experience Preferred... But Not Essential '83
Threads '85

Ray Meagher
Bootleg '89
Dark Age '88

Colm Meaney
The Commitments '91
Far and Away '92
Into the West '92
The Last of the Mohicans '92
The Snapper '93

Russell Means
The Last of the Mohicans '92
Natural Born Killers '94
Wagons East '94

Anne Meara
Awakenings '90
Fame '80
The Longshot '86
Lovers and Other Strangers '70
My Little Girl '87
Nasty Habits '77
The Out-of-Towners '70
That's Adequate '90

Meatloaf
Americathon '79
Leap of Faith '92

Motorama '91
Roadie '80
The Rocky Horror Picture Show '75
The Squeeze '87

Karen Medak
A Girl to Kill for '90
Treacherous Crossing '92

Kay Medford
Butterfield 8 '60
Funny Girl '68
Lola '69
The Rat Race '60
Windows '80

Ofelia Medina
Frida '84
Patsy, Mi Amor '87

Patricia Medina
Abbott and Costello in the Foreign Legion '50
The Big Push '75
Botany Bay '53
The Day Will Dawn '42
Dinner at the Ritz '37
Francis the Talking Mule '49
Hotel Reserve '44
The Jackpot '50
The Killing of Sister George '69
Mr. Arkadin '55
Snow White and the Three Stooges '61
Spitfire '42
The Three Musketeers '48

Michael Medwin
Above Us the Waves '56
The Courtney Affair '47
Four in a Jeep '51
The Gay Lady '49
The Jigsaw Man '84
Rattle of a Simple Man '64
Someone at the Door '50

Lew Meehan
Backfire '22
Feud Maker '38
Feud of the West '36
Melody of the Plains '37
Ridin' the Lone Trail '37
Ridin' Thru '35
Texas Jack '35
Thunder in the Desert '38
Whistlin' Dan '32

Donald Meek
The Adventures of Tom Sawyer '38
Air Raid Wardens '43
Barbary Coast '35
Bathing Beauty '44
Blondie Takes a Vacation '39
Colonel Effingham's Raid '45
DuBarry Was a Lady '43
Fabulous Joe '47
The Informer '35
Little Miss Broadway '38
Magic Town '47
The Merry Widow '34
Mrs. Wiggs of the Cabbage Patch '42
My Little Chickadee '40
One Rainy Afternoon '36
Return of Frank James '40
The Return of Peter Grimm '35
Stagecoach '39
State Fair '45
They Got Me Covered '43
The Thin Man Goes Home '44
Three Legionnaires '37
Toast of New York '37
Tortilla Flat '42
Two Girls and a Sailor '44
A Woman's Face '41
You Can't Take It with You '38
Young Mr. Lincoln '39

Jeffrey Meek
Heart Condition '90
Night of the Cyclone '90
Winter People '89

George Meeker
Apache Rose '47
Danger on the Air '38
The Invisible Monster '50
Murder by Television '35
Night of Terror '33
Omoo Omoo, the Shark God '49
People's Choice '46
Seven Doors to Death '44

Tango '36
Twilight in the Sierras '50

Ralph Meeker
The Alpha Incident '76
The Anderson Tapes '71
Battle Shock '56
Birds of Prey '72
Brannigan '75
Cry Panic '74
The Dead Don't Die '75
The Detective '68
The Dirty Dozen '67
Food of the Gods '76
Four in a Jeep '51
Gentle Giant '67
Hi-Riders '77
Johnny Firecloud '75
Kiss Me Deadly '55
Mind Snatchers '72
My Boys are Good Boys '78
Paths of Glory '57
Run of the Arrow '56
The St. Valentine's Day Massacre '67
Winter Kills '79

Don Megowan
The Creation of the Humanoids '62
The Devil's Brigade '68
The Jayhawkers '59
A Lawless Street '55

Blanche Mehaffey
Battling Orioles '24
Devil Monster '46
Sunrise Trail '31

Thomas Meighan
The Forbidden City '18
Male and Female '19
Peck's Bad Boy '21
Peck's Bad Boy '34

John Meillon
Billy Budd '62
The Blue Lightning '86
The Cars That Ate Paris '74
Crocodile Dundee '86
Crocodile Dundee 2 '88
The Dunera Boys '85
Fourth Wish '75
Frenchman's Farm '87
Inn of the Damned '74
Ride a Wild Pony '75

Gunter Meisner
Between Wars '74
In a Glass Cage '86
Magdalene '88

Karl Meixner
Crimes of Dr. Mabuse '32
Das Testament des Dr. Mabuse '33

Miguel Aceves Mejia
El Ciclon '47
Los Apuros de Dos Gallos '69
Viva Chihuahua (Long Live Chihuahua) '47

Alfonso Mejias
Los Olvidados '50
Rio Hondo '47

Isabelle Mejias
The Bay Boy '85
Daughter of Death '82
Fall from Innocence '88
Higher Education '88
Meatballs 3 '87
Scanners 2: The New Order '91
Unfinished Business '89

Mariangela Melato
By the Blood of Others '73
Dancers '87
Love and Anarchy '73
Seduction of Mimi '72
So Fine '81
Summer Night '87
Summer Night with Greek Profile, Almond Eyes & Scent of Basil '87
Swept Away... '75
To Forget Venice '79

Wendel Meldrum
Beautiful Dreamers '92
City Boy '93

Jack Melford
Department Store '35
When Thief Meets Thief '37

Marisa Mell
Danger: Diabolik '68
Hostages '79
Mad Dog '84
Secret Agent Super Dragon '66

Frank Melton
The Glory Trail '36
Stand Up and Cheer '34
Tanks a Million '41

Sid Melton
Hit! '73
Leave It to the Marines '51
The Lost Continent '51
Sky High '51
The Steel Helmet '51
Stop That Cab '51

Sam Melville
Roughnecks '80
Twice Dead '88

Murray Melvin
The Bawdy Adventures of Tom Jones '76
The Devils '71
The Fixer '68
Madhouse Mansion '74
A Taste of Honey '61

George Memmoli
Hot Potato '76
Mean Streets '73

Ben Mendelsohn
The Efficiency Expert '92
Quigley Down Under '90
Sirens '94
The Year My Voice Broke '87

David Mendenhall
Going Bananas '88
Over the Top '86
Secret of the Ice Cave '89
Space Raiders '83
Streets '90
Witchfire '86

Mauro Mendonca
Calacan '79
Dona Flor and Her Two Husbands '78
Love Strange Love '82

Victor Manuel Mendoza
The Proud Ones '53
Susana '51

John Mengatti
Knights of the City '85
Meatballs 2 '84

Adolphe Menjou
Across the Wide Missouri '51
The Ambassador's Daughter '56
Are Parents People? '25
Bundle of Joy '56
A Farewell to Arms '32
The Front Page '31
Gold Diggers of 1935 '35
Golden Boy '39
The Goldwyn Follies '38
The Grand Duchess and the Waiter '26
Heartbeat '46
Hi Diddle Diddle '43
The Hucksters '47
I Married a Woman '56
The King on Main Street '25
Letter of Introduction '38
Little Miss Marker '34
The Marriage Circle '24
Milky Way '36
Morning Glory '33
Morocco '30
My Dream is Yours '49
One in a Million '36
Paths of Glory '57
Pollyanna '60
Road Show '41
The Sheik '21
The Sorrows of Satan '26
Stage Door '37
A Star is Born '37
State of the Union '48
Step Lively '44
The Swan '56
Sweet Rosie O'Grady '43
Till the Clouds Roll By/A Star Is Born '46
To Please a Lady '50
Woman of Paris/Sunnyside '23

You Were Never Lovelier '42

Heather Menzies
Captain America '79
Piranha '78
Red, White & Busted '75
The Sound of Music '65

Doro Merande
The Gazebo '59
Kiss Me, Stupid! '64
The Man with the Golden Arm '55
The Russians are Coming, the Russians are Coming '66
The Seven Year Itch '55

Beryl Mercer
All Quiet on the Western Front '30
Cavalcade '33
Jane Eyre '34
Smilin' Through '32

Frances Mercer
Beauty for the Asking '39
Hunt the Man Down/Smashing the Rackets '50

Vivien Merchant
Accident '67
Alfie '66
Frenzy '72
The Offence '73
Under Milk Wood '73

Michele Mercier
Black Sabbath '64
Call of the Wild '72
Casanova '70 '65
A Global Affair '63
Oldest Profession '67
Shoot the Piano Player '62
Web of the Spider '70

Melina Mercouri
A Dream of Passion '78
Nasty Habits '77
Never on Sunday '60
Once is Not Enough '75
Phaedra '61
Stella '55
Topkapi '64
Where the Hot Wind Blows '59

Monique Mercure
Naked Lunch '91
The Odyssey of the Pacific '82
Tramp at the Door '87

Burgess Meredith
Advise and Consent '62
Batman '66
A Big Hand for the Little Lady '66
Burnt Offerings '76
The Cardinal '63
Clash of the Titans '81
The Day of the Locust '75
Diary of a Chambermaid '46
Final Assignment '80
Foul Play '78
Full Moon in Blue Water '88
Golden Rendezvous '77
Great Bank Hoax '78
Grumpy Old Men '93
The Hindenburg '75
Idiot's Delight '39
In Harm's Way '65
Johnny We Hardly Knew Ye '77
King Lear '87
Last Chase '81
MacKenna's Gold '69
Madame X '66
Magic '78
Man on the Eiffel Tower '48
The Manitou '78
Mine Own Executioner '47
Mr. Corbett's Ghost '90
92 in the Shade '76
Oddball Hall '91
Of Mice and Men '39
Outrage! '86
Probe '72
Rocky '76
Rocky 2 '79
Rocky 3 '82
Rocky 5 '90
Santa Claus: The Movie '85
Second Chorus '40
The Sentinel '76
Son of Blob '72
State of Grace '90
Stay Away, Joe '68
That Uncertain Feeling '41

There was a Crooked Man '70
Thumbelina '82
Tom, Dick, and Harry '41
Torture Garden '67
True Confessions '81
Twilight Zone: The Movie '83
Wet Gold '84
When Time Ran Out '80
Winterset '36
Yin & Yang of Mr. Go '71

Don Meredith
Express to Terror '79
The Night the City Screamed '80
Sky Hei$t '75
Terror on the 40th Floor '74

Iris Meredith
Green Archer '40
A Lawman is Born '37
Mystery of the Hooded Horseman '37

Judi Meredith
Jack the Giant Killer '62
Planet of Blood '66

Madge Meredith
Falcon's Adventure/Armored Car Robbery '50
Trail Street '47

Luc Merenda
The Cheaters '76
Could It Happen Here? '80s
Le Mans '71
Violent Professionals '82

Jalal Merhi
Fearless Tiger '94
Talons of the Eagle '92
TC 2000 '93
Tiger Claws '91

Macha Meril
Chinese Roulette '86
A Married Woman '65
Meeting Venus '91
Vagabond '85

Philip Merivale
Lady for a Night '42
Nothing But Trouble '44
Sister Kenny '46

Lee Meriwether
Batman '66
Brothers O'Toole '73
The 4D Man '59
Namu, the Killer Whale '66
The Undefeated '69

Una Merkel
Abraham Lincoln '30
The Bank Dick '40
The Bat Whispers '30
Bombshell '33
Born to Dance '36
Broadway Melody of 1936 '35
Destry Rides Again '39
Evelyn Prentice '34
42nd Street '33
The Girl Most Likely '57
I Love Melvin '53
It's a Joke, Son! '47
The Kentuckian '55
The Maltese Falcon '31
The Mating Game '59
The Merry Widow '34
The Merry Widow '52
On Borrowed Time '39
The Parent Trap '61
Private Lives '31
Red Headed Woman '32
Rich, Young and Pretty '51
Riff Raff '35
The Road to Zanzibar '41
Saratoga '37
Spinout '66
Summer and Smoke '61
Summer Magic '63
They Call It Sin '32
A Tiger Walks '64

Jan Merlin
Silk 2 '89
Twilight People '72

Joanna Merlin
Baby It's You '82
Class Action '91
Fame '80
Mystic Pizza '88

Ethel Merman
Airplane! '80

Alexander's Ragtime Band '38
Happy Landing '38
It's a Mad, Mad, Mad, Mad World '63
Kid Millions '34
There's No Business Like Show Business '54

Mary Merrall
Nicholas Nickleby '46
The Obsessed '51
Pink Strings and Sealing Wax '45

Charlotte Merriam
Night Nurse '31
One-Punch O'Day '26

Lynn Merrick
California Joe '43
Down to Earth '47
The Sombrero Kid '42
Western Double Feature 15 '50

Dina Merrill
Anna to the Infinite Power '84
Butterfield 8 '60
Caddyshack 2 '88
The Cary Grant Collection '90
The Courtship of Eddie's Father '62
Deadly Encounter '78
Desk Set '57
Fear '90
The Greatest '77
Hot Pursuit '84
I'll Take Sweden '65
The Meal '75
Operation Petticoat '59
The Player '92
Running Wild '73
The Sundowners '60
Tenth Month '79
Twisted '86
A Wedding '78

Gary Merrill
All About Eve '50
Around the World Under the Sea '65
Clambake '67
The Great Impostor '61
Huckleberry Finn '74
The Incident '67
Missouri Traveler '58
Mysterious Island '61
Phone Call from a Stranger '52
Pueblo Affair '73
The Seekers '79
Twelve O'Clock High '49

Theresa Merritt
All That Jazz '79
The Serpent and the Rainbow '87
Voodoo Dawn '89

Jane Merrow
The Appointment '82
Hands of the Ripper '71
Island of the Burning Doomed '67
The Lion in Winter '68

John Merton
Boot Hill Bandits '42
Border Bandits '46
Code of the Fearless '39
Covered Wagon Days '40
Cowboy Commandos '43
Devil Riders '44
Fighting Valley '43
Gang Bullets '38
The Gun Ranger '34
Hopalong Cassidy: Renegade Trail '39
In Old Montana '39
The Mysterious Rider '42
Phantom Ranger '38
Prairie Pals '42
The Rangers Step In '37
Roaring Six Guns '37
Rustler's Hideout '44
Two-Gun Troubador '37
Valley of Terror '38
Wild Horse Phantom '44

William Mervyn
Murder Ahoy '64
Railway Children '70

Gertrude Messinger
Aces Wild '37
The Adventurous Knights '35
Fighting Pilot '35
Hidden Valley '32

Miracle Kid '42
Roaring Roads '35
Rustler's Paradise '35
Social Error '35

Laurie Metcalf
Blink '93
A Dangerous Woman '93
Desperately Seeking Susan '85
Execution of Raymond Graham '85
Internal Affairs '90
JFK '91
Making Mr. Right '86
Miles from Home '88
Mistress '91
Pacific Heights '90
Stars and Bars '88
Uncle Buck '89

Mark Metcalf
Dead Ahead: The Exxon Valdez Disaster '92
The Final Terror '83
Mr. North '88
National Lampoon's Animal House '78
One Crazy Summer '86

Mayo Methot
Corsair '31
Goodbye Love '34
Marked Woman '37

Art Metrano
Beverly Hills Bodysnatchers '89
Breathless '83
Going Ape! '81
The Heartbreak Kid '72
How to Beat the High Cost of Living '80
Malibu Express '85
Police Academy 2: Their First Assignment '85
Police Academy 3: Back in Training '86
Prisoner in the Middle '74
Rocket Attack U.S.A. '58
Seven '79
Slaughter's Big Ripoff '73
They Only Kill Their Masters '72

Nancy Mette
Key Exchange '85
Meet the Hollowheads '89

Jim Metzler
Circuitry Man '90
Delusion '91
Four Friends '81
French Silk '94
Hot to Trot! '88
Love Kills '91
Murder by Night '89
976-EVIL '88
Old Gringo '89
On Wings of Eagles '86
One False Move '91
River's Edge '87
Squeeze Play '79
Tex '82

Paul Meurisse
Diabolique '55
Gypsy '62
The Monocle '64
Picnic on the Grass '59

Emile Meyer
Riot in Cell Block 11 '54
Shane '53

Torben Meyer
The Matchmaker '58
Sullivan's Travels '41
Thin Ice '37

Ari Meyers
Dark Horse '92
License to Kill '84
Shakma '89
Think Big '90

Michelle Meyrink
Joy of Sex '84
Nice Girls Don't Explode '87
One Magic Christmas '85
Permanent Record '88
Real Genius '85
Revenge of the Nerds '84

Vittorio Mezzogiorno
Cafe Express '83
Car Crash
L'Homme Blesse '83
Moon in the Gutter '83

Three Brothers '80

Cora Miao
Dim Sum: A Little Bit of Heart '85
Eat a Bowl of Tea '89

Nora Miao
Bruce's Deadly Fingers '80
Return of the Dragon '73
Showdown at the Equator '83
Young Dragon '77

Gertrude Michael
Behind Prison Walls '43
Cleopatra '34
Flamingo Road '49
I'm No Angel '33

Ralph Michael
Dead of Night '45
Diary of a Mad Old Man '88
Johnny Frenchman '46
Murder Most Foul '65
San Demetrio, London '47

Dario Michaelis
The Day the Sky Exploded '57
The Devil's Commandment '56

Corinne Michaels
Consenting Adult '85
Laboratory '80

Marc Michel
Lola '61
Umbrellas of Cherbourg '64

Marcella Michelangeli
Could It Happen Here? '80s
Padre Padrone '77

Keith Michell
The Deceivers '88
The Hellfire Club '61
Ruddigore '70s
Six Wives of Henry VIII '70s
Soldier in Love '67
The Story of David '76
The Story of Jacob & Joseph '74

Anne Michelle
French Quarter '78
The Haunted '79
House of Whipcord '75
Mistress Pamela '74
The Virgin Witch '70

Janee Michelle
The House on Skull Mountain '74
Scream Blacula Scream '73

Shelley Michelle
Bikini Summer '91
Married People, Single Sex '93
Sunset Strip '91

Maria Michi
Open City '45
Paisan '46
Redneck '73

Frank Middlemass
The Bretts '88
The Island '80
Oliver Twist '85
One Against the Wind '91

Charles Middleton
Dick Tracy Returns '38
Duck Soup '33
Flash Gordon Conquers the Universe '40
Flash Gordon: Mars Attacks the World '38
Flash Gordon: Rocketship '36
Hopalong Cassidy '35
The Miracle Rider '35
Mystery Ranch '34
Northwest Trail '46
Oklahoma Kid '39
Rocketship '36
Space Soldiers Conquer the Universe '40
Spook Busters '46
The Strange Love of Molly Louvain '32
Strangler of the Swamp '46
Western Union '41
Wyoming Outlaw '39
Yodelin' Kid From Pine Ridge '37

Guy Middleton
Dangerous Moonlight '41

Three Brothers '80
The Happiest Days of Your Life '50
A Man About the House '47

Noelle Middleton
Carrington, V.C. '54
The Vicious Circle '57

Ray Middleton
A Christmas Carol '54
I Dream of Jeannie '52
Jubilee Trail '54
Lady for a Night '42
Lady from Louisiana '42

Robert Middleton
Career '59
Court Jester '56
Desperate Hours '55
Harrad Experiment '73
The Law and Jake Wade '58

Dale Midkiff
Blackmail '91
Elvis and Me '88
Love Potion #9 '92
Nightmare Weekend '86
Pet Sematary '89
Streetwalkin' '85

Bette Midler
Beaches '88
Big Business '88
Divine Madness '80
Down and Out in Beverly Hills '86
For the Boys '91
Gypsy '93
Hawaii '66
Hocus Pocus '93
Jinxed '82
Outrageous Fortune '87
The Rose '79
Ruthless People '86
Scenes from a Mall '91
Stella '89
Thorn '73

Anne-Marie Mieville
Comment Ca Va? '76
Here and Elsewhere '70s

Toshiro Mifune
The Bad Sleep Well '60
The Battle of the Japan Sea '70
The Challenge '82
Drunken Angel '48
The Gambling Samurai '60
Grand Prix '66
Hell in the Pacific '69
The Hidden Fortress '58
High & Low '62
I Live in Fear '55
The Idiot '51
Journey of Honor '91
Life of Oharu '52
Love and Faith '78
The Lower Depths '57
Midway '76
1941 '79
Paper Tiger '74
Proof of the Man '84
Rashomon '51
Red Beard '65
Red Lion '69
Red Sun '71
Rikisha-Man '58
Saga of the Vagabond '59
Samurai 1: Musashi Miyamoto '55
Samurai 2: Duel at Ichijoji Temple '55
Samurai 3: Duel at Ganryu Island '56
Sanjuro '62
Seven Samurai '54
Shadow of the Wolf '92
Shogun '80
Stray Dog '49
Sword of Doom '67
Throne of Blood '57
Winter Kills '79
Yojimbo '61
Zatoichi vs. Yojimbo '70

Julia Migenes-Johnson
Berlin Blues '89
Mack the Knife '89

Tatsuya Mihashi
The Burmese Harp '56
High & Low '62
None But the Brave '65
Tora! Tora! Tora! '70

Mihashi ▶*cont.*

What's Up, Tiger Lily? '66
Nikita Mikhalkov
Close to Eden '90
An Unfinished Piece for a
Player Piano '77
Norihei Miki
Black Rain '88
Himatsuri '85
Rentaro Mikuni
The Burmese Harp '56
The Go-Masters '82
Kwaidan '64
Nomugi Pass '79
Rikyu '90
Swords of Death '71
A Taxing Woman's Return '88
Lita Milan
I, Mobster '58
The Left-Handed Gun '58
Naked in the Sun '57
Never Love a Stranger '58
Poor White Trash '57
Alyssa Milano
Casualties of Love: The ''Long
Island Lolita'' Story '93
Commando '85
Conflict of Interest '92
Little Sister '92
Old Enough '84
Where the Day Takes You '92
Adolph Milar
The Michigan Kid '28
The Savage Girl '32
Bernard Miles
Fame is the Spur '47
Great Expectations '46
In Which We Serve '43
The Man Who Knew Too Much
'56
Never Let Me Go '53
Nicholas Nickleby '46
Sapphire '59
The Smallest Show on Earth
'57
Betty Miles
The Driftin' Kid '41
The Law Rides Again '43
Lone Star Law Men '42
Riding the Sunset Trail '41
Sonora Stagecoach '44
Joanna Miles
Blackout '88
Born Innocent '74
Bug '75
Cooperstown '93
The Orphan '79
Sound of Murder '82
The Ultimate Warrior '75
Kevin Miles
The Cars That Ate Paris '74
Endplay '78
Lillian Miles
Get That Man '35
Reefer Madness '38
Rosalind Miles
The Black Six '74
The Manhandlers '73
Shaft's Big Score '72
Sarah Miles
The Big Sleep '78
Blow-Up '66
Dynasty '82
Harem '82
Hope and Glory '87
Lady Caroline Lamb '73
Man Who Loved Cat Dancing
'73
Ordeal by Innocence '84
Queenie '87
Ryan's Daughter '70
The Sailor Who Fell from Grace
with the Sea '76
The Servant '63
Steaming '86
Those Magnificent Men in Their
Flying Machines '65
Venom '82
White Mischief '88
Sherry Miles
The Todd Killings '71

The Velvet Vampire '71
Sylvia Miles
Cannon Movie Tales: Sleeping
Beauty '89
Crossing Delancey '88
Deadly Thief '78
Evil Under the Sun '82
Farewell, My Lovely '75
The Funhouse '81
Heat '72
The Last Movie '71
Midnight Cowboy '69
No Big Deal '83
Parrish '61
Psychomania '63
The Sentinel '76
She-Devil '89
Sleeping Beauty '89
Spike of Bensonhurst '88
Superstar: The Life and Times
of Andy Warhol '90
Who Killed Mary What's 'Er
Name? '71
Zero to Sixty '78
Vera Miles
And I Alone Survived '78
Autumn Leaves '56
Back Street '61
Baffled '72
Brainwaves '82
The Castaway Cowboy '74
The FBI Story '59
Fire '77
Follow Me, Boys! '66
Gentle Giant '67
Hellfighters '68
The Initiation '84
Into the Night '85
Jigsaw '71
Judge Horton and the
Scottsboro Boys '76
The Man Who Shot Liberty
Valance '62
Mazes and Monsters '82
Mission Batangas '69
Molly & Lawless John '72
One Little Indian '73
Our Family Business '81
Psycho '60
Psycho 2 '83
Roughnecks '80
Run for the Roses '78
The Searchers '56
Sergeant Ryker '68
A Strange and Deadly
Occurence '74
Those Calloways '65
A Tiger Walks '64
Twilight's Last Gleaming '77
The Wrong Man '56
Kim Milford
Corvette Summer '78
Laserblast '78
Penelope Milford
Bloodlink '86
The Burning Bed '85
Cold Justice '89
Coming Home '78
The Golden Seal '83
Heathers '89
The Last Word '80
Oldest Living Graduate '82
Rosie: The Rosemary Clooney
Story '82
Seizure: The Story of Kathy
Morris '82
Take This Job & Shove It '81
Tomas Milian
Almost Human '79
Blood and Guns '79
Boccaccio '70 '62
Cat Chaser '90
Cop in Blue Jeans '78
Counter Punch '71
The Cowboy Way '94
Havana '90
JFK '91
Nails '92
Revenge '90
Salome '85
Sonny and Jed '73
Time of Indifference '64
Frank Military
Dead Bang '89
Everybody Wins '90
John Miljan
Arizona Mahoney '36

Belle of the Nineties '34
Boss of Big Town '43
Charlie Chan in Paris '35
The Fallen Sparrow '43
The Ghost Walks '34
I Accuse My Parents '45
Possessed '31
Queen of the Amazons '47
Riot Squad '41
Susan Lenox: Her Fall and Rise
'31
The Unchastened Woman '25
The Unholy Three '30
What! No Beer? '33
Yankee Clipper '27
Hugh Millais
The Dogs of War '81
McCabe & Mrs. Miller '71
Robyn Millan
Murder Motel '74
Murph the Surf '75
The Witchmaker '69
Ray Milland
The Attic '80
Beau Geste '39
Blackout '78
Blonde Crazy '31
Bugles in the Afternoon '52
Bulldog Drummond Escapes
'37
Copper Canyon '50
Cruise into Terror '78
The Dead Don't Die '75
Dial ''M'' for Murder '54
Doctor Takes a Wife '40
Embassy '72
Escape to Witch Mountain '75
Everything Happens at Night
'39
The Flying Scotsman '29
Forever and a Day '43
Frogs '72
Game for Vultures '86
Golden Earrings '47
Hollywood Come Home '62
It Happens Every Spring '49
The Last Tycoon '76
A Life of Her Own '50
Lisbon '56
The Lost Weekend '45
Love Story '70
A Man Alone '55
Masks of Death '86
Masque of the Red Death/
Premature Burial '65
Night of the Laughing Dead '75
Oil '78
Oliver's Story '78
Our Family Business '81
Panic in the Year Zero! '62
Premature Burial '62
Quick, Let's Get Married '71
Reap the Wild Wind '42
Rich Man, Poor Man '76
The Sea Serpent '85
Slavers '77
Starflight One '83
Survival Run '80
Terror in the Wax Museum '73
The Thief '52
The Uncanny '78
The Uninvited '44
A Woman of Distinction '50
X: The Man with X-Ray Eyes
'63
Gregory Millar
Lethal Weapon 3 '92
Uncaged '91
Allan Miller
Obsessive Love '84
Warlock '91
Ann Miller
Deep in My Heart '54
Easter Parade '48
Having Wonderful Time/
Carnival Boat '38
Hit the Deck '55
Kiss Me Kate '53
Lovely to Look At '52
Melody Ranch '40
On the Town '49
The Opposite Sex '56
Room Service '38
Small Town Girl '53
Texas Carnival '51
Too Many Girls '40
Watch the Birdie '50

You Can't Take It with You '38
Aubree Miller
The Ewok Adventure '84
The Ewoks: Battle for Endor
'85
Barry Miller
Fame '80
The Last Temptation of Christ
'88
Love at Large '89
Peggy Sue Got Married '86
The Pickle '93
Roommate '84
Saturday Night Fever '77
Carl Miller
Great K & A Train Robbery '26
Woman of Paris/Sunnyside '23
Charles Miller
Call Northside 777 '48
Phantom of Chinatown '40
Project: Nightmare
Cheryl Miller
Clarence, the Cross-eyed Lion
'65
Dr. Death, Seeker of Souls '73
Man from Clover Grove '78
Mountain Man '77
Dennis Miller
The Everlasting Secret Family
'88
Madhouse '90
The Quest '86
Denny Miller
Buck and the Preacher '72
The Party '68
Dick Miller
After Hours '85
Amityville 1992: It's About Time
'92
Big Bad Mama '74
Body Waves '92
A Bucket of Blood '59
Candy Stripe Nurses '74
Carnival Rock '57
Chopping Mall '86
Dr. Heckyl and Mr. Hype '80
Evil Toons '90
Explorers '85
Fallen Angels 1 '93
Fallen Angels 2 '93
Far from Home '89
Gremlins '84
The Gunslinger '56
Heart Like a Wheel '83
Hollywood Boulevard '76
The Howling '81
Innerspace '87
It Conquered the World '56
Lies '83
Little Shop of Horrors '60
Matinee '92
Motorama '91
New York, New York '77
Night Call Nurses '72
Night of the Creeps '86
Piranha '78
Project X '87
Quake '92
Rock All Night '57
Rock 'n' Roll High School '79
Sorority Girl '57
Starhops '78
The Terminator '84
The Trip '67
Truck Turner '74
Under the Boardwalk '89
Unlawful Entry '92
X: The Man with X-Ray Eyes
'63
The Young Nurses '73
Eve Miller
April In Paris '52
Big Trees '52
Kansas Pacific '53
The Winning Team '52
F.E. Miller
Bronze Buckaroo '39
Harlem on the Prairie '38
Harlem Rides the Range '39
Mystery in Swing '40
Yes, Sir, Mr. Bones '51
Glenn Miller
Orchestra Wives '42
Sun Valley Serenade '41

Jason Miller
The Best Little Girl in the World
'81
The Dain Curse '78
The Exorcist '73
The Exorcist 3 '90
F. Scott Fitzgerald in Hollywood
'76
The Henderson Monster '80
A Home of Our Own '75
Light of Day '87
Marilyn: The Untold Story '80
Monsignor '82
The Ninth Configuration '79
Rudy '93
Small Kill '93
That Championship Season '82
Toy Soldiers '84
Vengeance '86
Jean Miller
Silent Night, Deadly Night 2 '87
Speak of the Devil '90
Jeremy Miller
Emanon '86
The Willies '90
John Miller
The Brave Bunch '70
Hero Bunker '71
Joshua Miller
And You Thought Your Parents
Were Weird! '91
Class of 1999 '90
Near Dark '87
River's Edge '87
Teen Witch '89
Kathleen Miller
Fighting Mad '76
Strange New World '75
Kenny Miller
Bloodstalkers '76
Surf Party '64
Kristine Miller
High Lonesome '50
Jungle Patrol '48
Killer Bait '49
Too Late for Tears '49
Larry Miller
Corrina, Corrina '94
Dream Lover '93
The Favor '94
Frozen Assets '92
Pretty Woman '90
Suburban Commando '91
Undercover Blues '93
Linda Miller
Alice Sweet Alice '76
Elvis and Me '88
One Summer Love '76
Lorraine Miller
Ambush Trail '46
Border Badmen '45
Frontier Fugitives '45
Lonesome Trail '55
White Gorilla '47
Mark Miller
Ginger in the Morning '73
Love Field '91
Savannah Smiles '82
Mark Thomas Miller
Blue De Ville '86
Misfits of Science '85
Mom '89
Martin Miller
Bergonzi Hand '70
Frenzy '46
Hotel Reserve '44
Man on the Run '49
Marvin Miller
Dead Reckoning '47
Kiss Daddy Goodbye '81
Off Limits '53
Red Planet Mars '52
Patsy Ruth Miller
Headwinds '28
The Hunchback of Notre Dame
'23
Lonely Wives '31
The Sheik '21
So This is Paris '26
Penelope Ann Miller
Adventures in Babysitting '87
Awakenings '90
Big Top Pee Wee '88

Biloxi Blues '88
Carlito's Way '93
Chaplin '92
Dead Bang '89
Downtown '89
The Freshman '90
The Gun in Betty Lou's Handbag '92
Kindergarten Cop '90
Miles from Home '88
Other People's Money '91
The Shadow '94
Year of the Comet '92

Rebecca Miller
Consenting Adults '92
The Murder of Mary Phagan '87
The Pickle '93
Wind '92

Sidney Miller
Boys Town '38
Men of Boys Town '41
There Goes Kelly '45

Stephen E. Miller
Home is Where the Hart is '88
Jane Doe '83

Walter Miller
Blessed Event '32
The Galloping Ghost '31
Ghost Patrol '36
The Lone Defender '32
Rustlers of Red Dog '35
Shadow of the Eagle '32
Tailspin Tommy '34

Andra Millian
Nightfall '88
Stacy's Knights '83

James Millican
The Adventures of Gallant Bess '48
Man from Colorado '49
Rimfire '49
The Winning Team '52

Spike Milligan
The Case of the Mukkinese Battle Horn '56
Digby, the Biggest Dog in the World '73
Down Among the Z Men '52
Ghost in the Noonday Sun '74
Goon Movie '53
Great McGonagall '75
The Hound of the Baskervilles '77
The Magic Christian '69
Rentadick '72
To See Such Fun '81

Alley Mills
Rape and Marriage: The Rideout Case '80
Tainted Blood '93

Brooke Mills
The Big Doll House '71
Dream No Evil '75
The Student Teachers '73

Danny Mills
Female Trouble '74
Pink Flamingos '72

Donna Mills
Beyond the Bermuda Triangle '75
Bunco '83
Curse of the Black Widow '77
False Arrest '92
Fire '77
Haunts of the Very Rich '72
The Hunted Lady '77
The Incident '67
Killer with Two Faces '74
Murph the Surf '75
One Deadly Owner '74
Play Misty for Me '71
Runaway Father '91
Waikiki '80
The World's Oldest Living Bridesmaid '92

Hayley Mills
Appointment with Death '88
Back Home '90
Bananas Boat '78
The Chalk Garden '64
Deadly Strangers '82
Endless Night '71
The Flame Trees of Thika '80s
In Search of the Castaways '62
Kingfisher Caper '76
The Moon-Spinners '64
The Parent Trap '61
Pollyanna '60
Summer Magic '63
That Darn Cat '65
Tiger Bay '59
The Trouble with Angels '66
Whistle Down the Wind '62

John Mills
Above Us the Waves '56
Africa Texas Style '67
The Baby and the Battleship '56
The Big Sleep '78
A Black Veil for Lisa '68
The Chalk Garden '64
Choice of Weapons '76
Chuka '67
The Colditz Story '55
Cottage to Let '41
Dr. Strange '78
Escapade '55
Frankenstein '93
Gandhi '82
The Ghost Camera '33
Goodbye, Mr. Chips '39
Great Expectations '46
Hobson's Choice '53
The Human Factor '75
In Which We Serve '43
King Rat '65
Lady Caroline Lamb '73
Masks of Death '86
Nine Days a Queen '34
October Man '48
O.H.M.S. '37
Oklahoma Crude '73
Operation Crossbow '65
Quatermass Conclusion '79
Ryan's Daughter '70
Sahara '83
Scott of the Antarctic '48
The Swiss Family Robinson '60
A Tale of Two Cities '91
The Thirty-Nine Steps '79
This Happy Breed '47
Tiara Tahiti '62
Tiger Bay '59
Tunes of Glory '60
Tunes of Glory/Horse's Mouth '60
The Vicious Circle '57
War and Peace '56
We Dive at Dawn '43
Who's That Girl? '87
The Wrong Box '66
Young Winston '72
Zulu Dawn '79

Juliet Mills
Alexander: The Other Side of Dawn '77
Avanti! '72
Barnaby and Me '77
Beyond the Door '75
The Cracker Factory '79
Jonathan Livingston Seagull '73
October Man '48
QB VII '74
The Rare Breed '66

Martin Milner
Columbo: Murder By the Book '71
Flood! '76
Francis in the Navy '55
The Halls of Montezuma '50
Hurricane '74
Life with Father '47
Mister Roberts '55
Nashville Beat '89
Pete Kelly's Blues '55
The Seekers '79
Sweet Smell of Success '57
13 Ghosts '60
Valley of the Dolls '67
Zebra in the Kitchen '65

Sandra Milo
Bang Bang Kid '67
Dead for a Dollar '70s
8 1/2 '63
Generale Della Rovere '60
Herod the Great '60
Vanina Vanini '61

Nadia Milton
El Hombre Contra el Mundo '87
Los Dos Hermanos '87
Sin Salida '87

Tacos al Carbon '87

Yvette Mimieux
The Black Hole '79
Caper of the Golden Bulls '67
Circle of Power '83
Dark of the Sun '68
Devil Dog: The Hound of Hell '78
Diamond Head '62
Forbidden Love '82
The Four Horsemen of the Apocalypse '62
Hit Lady '74
Jackson County Jail '76
Journey into Fear '74
Legend of Valentino '75
Monkeys, Go Home! '66
Neptune Factor '73
Night Partners '83
Obsessive Love '84
Outside Chance '78
Platinum High School '60
Snowbeast '77
Three in the Attic '68
The Time Machine '60
Toys in the Attic '63
Where the Boys Are '60
The Wonderful World of the Brothers Grimm '62

Ester Minciotti
Full of Life '56
Marty '55

Sal Mineo
Cheyenne Autumn '64
Dino '57
Escape from the Planet of the Apes '71
Exodus '60
The Gene Krupa Story '59
Giant '56
James Dean: The First American Teenager '76
The Longest Day '62
Rebel Without a Cause '55
Rock, Pretty Baby '56
Somebody Up There Likes Me '56
Tonka '58

Jan Miner
Lenny '74
Mermaids '90
Willie & Phil '80

Liza Minnelli
Arthur '81
Arthur 2: On the Rocks '88
Cabaret '72
Hedda Hopper's Hollywood '42
In the Good Old Summertime '49
King of Comedy '82
A Matter of Time '76
New York, New York '77
The Princess and the Pea '83
Rent-A-Cop '88
Silent Movie '76
Stepping Out '91
The Sterile Cuckoo '69
That's Dancing! '85
A Time to Live '85

Bob Minos
Black Eliminator '70s
Delinquent School Girls '84

Kelly Jo Minter
Miracle Mile '89
A Nightmare on Elm Street 5: Dream Child '89
Pilot '84
Popcorn '89

Miou-Miou
Dog Day '83
Entre-Nous '83
Going Places '74
Jonah Who Will Be 25 in the Year 2000 '76
Josepha '82
La Lectrice '88
May Fools '90
Menage '86
My Other Husband '85
No Problem '70s
Roads to the South '77
This Sweet Sickness '77

Brigitte Mira
Ali: Fear Eats the Soul '74
Berlin Alexanderplatz '80
Chinese Roulette '86

Every Man for Himself & God Against All '75
Mother Kusters Goes to Heaven '76

Irene Miracle
In the Shadow of Kilimanjaro '86
Inferno '78
The Last of Philip Banter '87
Puppet Master '89

Evan Mirand
Brotherhood of Justice '86
My Best Friend Is a Vampire '88
Weekend War '88

Carmen Miranda
Copacabana '47
A Date with Judy '48
Doll Face '46
Down Argentine Way '40
Gotta Dance, Gotta Sing '84
Hollywood Goes to War '54
Nancy Goes to Rio '50
Scared Stiff '53
Springtime in the Rockies '42
Week-End In Havana '41

Isa Miranda
Dog Eat Dog '64
Just Another Pretty Face '58
La Ronde '51
La Signora di Tutti '34
The Night Porter '74
Seven Deadly Sins '53
Twitch of the Death Nerve '71

Robert Miranda
Chips, the War Dog '90
Lost in Yonkers '93
Sister Act '92
What's Love Got to Do With It? '93

Soledad Miranda
Count Dracula '71
Sound of Horror '64

Helen Mirren
Cal '84
Caligula '80
The Comfort of Strangers '91
Coming Through '90
The Cook, the Thief, His Wife & Her Lover '90
Dr. Bethune '90
Excalibur '81
The Fiendish Plot of Dr. Fu Manchu '80
The Gospel According to Vic '87
The Hawk '93
Hussy '80
The Little Mermaid '84
The Long Good Friday '79
A Midsummer Night's Dream '68
The Mosquito Coast '86
O Lucky Man! '73
Pascali's Island '88
Priest of Love '81
Prime Suspect '92
Prime Suspect 2 '93
Red King, White Knight '89
Savage Messiah '72
S.O.S. Titanic '79
2010: The Year We Make Contact '84
When the Whales Came '89
Where Angels Fear to Tread '91
White Nights '85

Karen Mistal
Cannibal Women in the Avocado Jungle of Death '89
Return of the Killer Tomatoes '88

Mr. T
D.C. Cab '84
Penitentiary 2 '82
Rocky 3 '82
Straight Line '88

Jorge Mistral
Camelia
La Justicia Tiene Doce Anos '87
Wuthering Heights '53

Belle Mitchell
Crazed '82
Slipping into Darkness '88

Cameron Mitchell
Action U.S.A. '89
The Adventures of Gallant Bess '48
All Mine to Give '56
The Andersonville Trial '70
Autopsy of a Ghost '67
The Bastard '78
Blood and Black Lace '64
Bloodlink '86
Buck and the Preacher '72
Carousel '56
Cataclysm '81
Code of Honor '88
Codename: Vengeance '87
Conquest of the Normans '62
Crossing the Line '90
Cult People '89
Deadly Prey '87
The Demon '81
Desiree '54
Dog Eat Dog '64
Easy Kill '89
El Sabor de la Venganza '65
Enforcer from Death Row '78
Escapade in Japan '57
Flight to Mars '52
Flood! '76
Frankenstein Island '81
Go for the Gold '84
The Guns and the Fury '83
The Hanged Man '74
Haunts '77
Hollywood Cop '87
Hombre '67
Homecoming '48
How to Marry a Millionaire '53
The Invaders '63
It's Called Murder, Baby '82
Kill Squad '81
Killer Commandos
Killers '88
Killpoint '84
The Klansman '74
Last Gun '64
The Last Reunion '80
The Longest Drive '76
Love Me or Leave Me '55
Low Blow '85
Medusa '74
Memorial Valley Massacre '88
The Messenger '87
Minnesota Clay '65
Mission to Kill '85
My Favorite Year '82
Night Train to Terror '84
Nightforce '86
Nightmare in Wax '69
The Offspring '87
The Ox-Bow Incident '55
Prince Jack '83
Rage to Kill '88
Raw Force '81
Rebel Rousers '69
Return to Fantasy Island '77
Ride in the Whirlwind '67
Scalp Merchant '77
Silent Scream '80
Slaughter '72
Slavers '77
Space Mutiny '88
The Stranger '73
Supersonic Man '78
The Swarm '78
Swift Justice '88
The Tall Men '55
Tension at Table Rock '56
Terror in Beverly Hills '90
Texas Detour '77
Texas Lightning '81
They Were Expendable '45
Thief '71
Tomb '86
The Toolbox Murders '78
Trapped Alive '93
The Unstoppable Man '59
Viking Massacre '70s
Viva Knievel '77

Chuck "Porky" Mitchell
Ghost Chase '88
Goodbye Cruel World '82
Hollywood Zap '86
Porky's Revenge '85
Swift Justice '88

Donna Mitchell
The Portrait '93
Psycho 4: The Beginning '90

Duke Mitchell
Bela Lugosi Meets a Brooklyn Gorilla '52
The Executioner '78

Eric Mitchell
The Foreigner '78
Rome '78 '78
Underground U.S.A. '84

Gordon Mitchell
Battle of Valiant '63
Beyond the Law '68
The Big Bust Out '73
Commando Invasion '87
Erik, the Viking '72
Fighting Fists of Shanghai Joe '65
Frankenstein '80 '79
The Giant of Metropolis '61
Linchamiento '68
Mafia la Ley Que Non Perdona '79
Mines of Kilimanjaro '87
Operation Orient
Rush '84
Slaughterday '77
Suicide Patrol '70s
Vulcan God of Fire

Grant Mitchell
Cairo '42
Conflict '45
Gold Diggers of 1935 '35
The Grapes of Wrath '40
The Great Lie '41
Heroes for Sale '33
In Person '35
Laura '44
The Man Who Came to Dinner '41
No Man of Her Own '32
Three on a Match '32

Heather Mitchell
The Everlasting Secret Family '88
Proof '91

Keith Mitchell
Bergonzi Hand '70
The Executioner '70
Memorial Day '83
Tenth Month '79

Laurie Mitchell
Missile to the Moon '59
Queen of Outer Space '58

Mary Mitchell
Panic in the Year Zero! '62
A Swingin' Summer '65
Toga Party '79

Millard Mitchell
A Double Life '47
The Gunfighter '50
Here Come the Girls '53
The Naked Spur '53
Singin' in the Rain '52
Twelve O'Clock High '49
Winchester '73 '50

Red Mitchell
8 Seconds '94
Forever Evil '87

Sasha Mitchell
Class of 1999 2: The Substitute '93
Kickboxer 2: The Road Back '90
Kickboxer 3: The Art of War '92
Spike of Bensonhurst '88

Scoey Mitchell
Jo Jo Dancer, Your Life is Calling '86
The Voyage of the Yes '72

Steve Mitchell
The Sibling '72
Submarine Seahawk '59

Thomas Mitchell
Adventure '45
Angels Over Broadway '40
Bataan '43
The Big Wheel '49
Buffalo Bill '44
By Love Possessed '61
Dark Mirror '46
Dark Waters '44
The Fighting Sullivans '42
Gone with the Wind '39
High Noon '52

The Hunchback of Notre Dame '39
Immortal Sergeant '43
It's a Wonderful Life '46
Joan of Paris '42
The Keys of the Kingdom '44
The Long Voyage Home '40
Lost Horizon '37
The Making of a Legend: "Gone With the Wind" '89
Mr. Smith Goes to Washington '39
Only Angels Have Wings '39
Our Town '40
The Outlaw '43
Pocketful of Miracles '61
Silver River '48
Song of the Islands '42
Stagecoach '39
While the City Sleeps '56
Wilson '44

Warren Mitchell
Arrivederci, Baby! '66
The Assassination Bureau '69
Bananas Boat '78
The Crawling Eye '58
The Dunera Boys '85
Foreign Body '86
Knights & Emeralds '87
Norman Loves Rose '82
The Unearthly Stranger '64
Waterfront '83

Yvonne Mitchell
Conspiracy of Hearts '60
Crucible of Horror '69
Demons of the Mind '72
Escapade '55
The Incredible Sarah '76
Johnny Nobody '61
The Queen of Spades '49
Sapphire '59
Tiger Bay '59

Ilan Mitchell-Smith
The Chocolate War '88
How to Be a Perfect Person in Just Three Days '84
Identity Crisis '90
Journey to the Center of the Earth '88
Weird Science '85

Bentley Mitchum
Deadly Exposure '93
Demonic Toys '91
Ruby in Paradise '93

Chris Mitchum
Aftershock '88
American Commandos '84
Angel of Death '86
Big Foot '72
Big Jake '71
Day Time Ended '80
Death Feud '89
Desperate Target '80
The Executioner, Part 2: Frozen Scream '84
H-Bomb '71
Mean Machine '73
My Champion '84
No Time to Die '78
One Man Jury '78
Ricco '74
Rio Lobo '70
A Rumor of War '80
Stingray '78
Tombstone '93

Jim Mitchum
Blackout '78
Code Name: Zebra '84
Girls' Town '59
Hollywood Cop '87
In Harm's Way '65
The Invincible Six '68
Maniac '77
Marked for Murder '88
Mercenary Fighters '88
Monster '78
Ride the Wild Surf '64
Thunder Road '58

John Mitchum
Big Foot '72
Bloody Trail '72
The Devil's Sleep '51
The Enforcer '76
Escapes '86

Robert Mitchum
The Agency '81
The Ambassador '84

The Amsterdam Kill '78
Anzio '68
Bar-20 '43
The Big Sleep '78
Big Steal '49
Blood on the Moon '48
Breakthrough '78
The Brotherhood of the Rose '89
Cape Fear '61
Colt Comrades '43
Crossfire '47
El Dorado '67
Enemy Below '57
False Colors '43
Farewell, My Lovely '75
Fire Down Below '57
Five Card Stud '68
Girl Rush '44
The Good Guys and the Bad Guys '69
The Grass is Greener '61
Gung Ho! '43
The Hearst and Davies Affair '85
His Kind of Woman '51
Holiday Affair '49
Hollywood Home Movies '87
Home from the Hill '60
Hopalong Cassidy: Riders of the Deadline '43
Hoppy Serves a Writ '43
The Human Comedy '43
The Hunters '58
The Last Tycoon '76
Leather Burners '43
The List of Adrian Messenger '63
The Longest Day '62
The Lusty Men '52
Macao '52
Maria's Lovers '84
Matilda '78
Midway '76
Mr. North '88
My Forbidden Past '51
Nevada '44
The Night of the Hunter '55
Nightkill '80
North and South Book 1 '85
Not as a Stranger '55
One Minute to Zero '52
One Shoe Makes It Murder '82
Out of the Past '47
Pursued '48
Rachel and the Stranger '48
The Racket '51
The Red Pony '49
River of No Return '54
Ryan's Daughter '70
Scrooged '88
Second Chance '53
Secret Ceremony '69
She Couldn't Say No '52
The Sundowners '60
That Championship Season '82
Thirty Seconds Over Tokyo '44
Thompson's Last Run '90
Thunder Road '58
Till the End of Time '46
Two for the Seesaw '62
Villa Rides '68
War & Remembrance, Part 1 '88
War & Remembrance, Part 2 '89
War & Remembrance, Part 3 '88
War & Remembrance, Part 4 '88
War & Remembrance, Part 5 '88
War & Remembrance, Part 6 '88
War & Remembrance, Part 7 '88
War & Remembrance: The Final Chapter, Part 8 '89
War & Remembrance: The Final Chapter, Part 9 '89
War & Remembrance: The Final Chapter, Part 10 '89
War & Remembrance: The Final Chapter, Part 11 '89
War & Remembrance: The Final Chapter, Part 12 '89
The Way West '67
West of the Pecos '45
The Winds of War '83
Woman of Desire '93

The Yakuza '75

Art Mix
Border Devils '32
Mason of the Mounted '32
Powdersmoke Range '35
Rustlers of Red Dog '35
Way of the West '35
Yodelin' Kid From Pine Ridge '37

Ruth Mix
The Black Coin '36
Custer's Last Stand '36
The Riding Avenger '36
The Tonto Kid '35

Tom Mix
Child of the Prairie '18
Dick Turpin '25
Early Cinema Vol. 1 '19
Great K & A Train Robbery '26
Heart of Texas Ryan '16
Hidden Gold '33
In the Days of the Thundering Herd & the Law & the Outlaw '14
Justice Rides Again '30s
The Miracle Rider '35
My Pal, The King '32
Riders of the Purple Sage '25
Sky High '22
Terror Trail '33
Texas Bad Man '32
Tom Mix Compilation 1 '16
Tom Mix Compilation 2 '16
Trailin' '21

Seiji Miyaguchi
Early Summer '51
The Human Condition: No Greater Love '58
Seven Samurai '54

Nobuko Miyamoto
The Funeral '84
Tampopo '86
A Taxing Woman '87
A Taxing Woman's Return '88

Kim Miyori
The Big Picture '89
Hiroshima: Out of the Ashes '90
John & Yoko: A Love Story '85
The Punisher '90
When the Bough Breaks '86

Eiko Miyoshi
I Live in Fear '55
Snow Country '57

Mary Ann Mobley
Crazy Horse and Custer: "The Untold Story" '90
Girl Happy '65
Harum Scarum '65
My Dog, the Thief '69

Roger Mobley
Emil and the Detective '64
Jack the Giant Killer '62

Carlos Lopez Moctezuma
The Curse of the Crying Woman '61
El Aviso Inoportuno '87
El Gendarme Desconocido '41
Lagrimas de Amor '87
Night of the Bloody Apes '68
The Proud Ones '80

Jayne Modean
Spring Break '83
Street Hawk '84

Matthew Modine
And the Band Played On '93
Baby It's You '82
Birdy '84
Equinox '93
Full Metal Jacket '87
The Gamble '88
Gross Anatomy '89
The Hotel New Hampshire '84
Married to the Mob '88
Memphis Belle '90
Mrs. Soffel '84
Orphans '87
Pacific Heights '90
Private School '83
Short Cuts '93
Streamers '83
Vision Quest '85
Wind '92

Gaston Modot
Grand Illusion '37
L'Age D'Or '30
The Rules of the Game '39
Under the Roofs of Paris '29

Enrica Maria Modugno
Kaos '85
The Story of Boys & Girls '91

Donald Moffatt
Alamo Bay '85
Armistead Maupin's Tales of the City '93
The Best of Times '86
The Bonfire of the Vanities '90
The Bourne Identity '88
Class Action '91
Clear and Present Danger '94
Danielle Steel's Kaleidoscope '92
Far North '88
The Great Northfield Minnesota Raid '72
Housesitter '92
Jacqueline Bouvier Kennedy '81
License to Kill '84
The Long Days of Summer '80
Love, Cheat & Steal '94
Mary White '77
Mrs. R's Daughter '79
Music Box '89
Necessary Parties '88
On the Nickel '80
Promises in the Dark '79
Rachel, Rachel '68
Regarding Henry '91
The Right Stuff '83
Showdown '73
Strangers: The Story of a Mother and Daughter '79
Teamster Boss: The Jackie Presser Story '92
The Thing '82
The Unbearable Lightness of Being '88
When the Time Comes '91
Winter Kills '79

D.W. Moffett
Black Widow '87
An Early Frost '85
Falling Down '93
Fine Things '90
Lisa '90
The Misfit Brigade '87

Gregory Moffett
Let's Dance '50
Robot Monster '53

Michelle Moffett
Deathstalker 4: Clash of the Titans '92
Hired to Kill '91
Wild Cactus '92

Carl Mohner
Cave of the Living Dead '65
It Takes a Thief '59
Rififi '54
Sink the Bismarck '60
Wanted: Babysitter '75

Gerald Mohr
The Angry Red Planet '59
Detective Story '51
Hunt the Man Down '50
Hunt the Man Down/Smashing the Rackets '50
Love Affair '39
The Monster and the Girl '41
The Ring '52
Sirocco '51
Son of Ali Baba '52
Terror in the Haunted House '58

Zia Mohyeddi
Bombay Talkie '70
We are the Children '87

Richard Moir
Heatwave '83
In Search of Anna '79
An Indecent Obsession '85
Panic Station '72
Remember Me '85
Wrangler '88

Jose Mojica Marins
At Midnight, I'll Take Your Soul '63

Awakenings of the Beast '68
Hallucinations of a Deranged
Mind '70
Strange World of Coffin Joe '68

Zakes Mokae
Body Parts '91
The Comedians '67
Cry Freedom '87
Dad '89
A Dry White Season '89
Dust Devil '93
Gross Anatomy '89
A Rage in Harlem '91
The Serpent and the Rainbow
'87
A World of Strangers '62

Karin Molander
Thomas Graal's Best Film '17
Thomas Graal's First Child '18

Alfred Molina
American Friends '91
Blat
Enchanted April '92
Ladyhawke '85
Letter to Brezhnev '86
Maverick '94
Not Without My Daughter '90
Prick Up Your Ears '87
Raiders of the Lost Ark '81
The Trial '93
White Fang 2: The Myth of the
White Wolf '94

Angela Molina
Camorra: The Naples
Connection '85
Demons in the Garden '82
The Eyes, the Mouth '83
1492: Conquest of Paradise '92
Half of Heaven '86
That Obscure Object of Desire
'77

Charles Moll
Cataclysm '81
Combat Academy '86
Night Train to Terror '84

Georgia Moll
Contempt '64
Thief of Baghdad '61
What a Way to Die '70

Richard Moll
Dream Date '93
Driving Me Crazy '91
Dungeonmaster '85
The Flintstones '94
Hard Country '81
Highlander: The Gathering '93
House '86
Metalstorm '83
Savage Journey '83
Sidekicks '93
Survivor '87
Sword & the Sorcerer '82
Think Big '90
Wicked Stepmother '89

Patrick Molloy
Phantom Brother '88
Plutonium Baby '87

Dan Monahan
Porky's '82
Porky's 2: The Next Day '83
Porky's Revenge '85

Jorge Mondragon
The New Invisible Man '58
Spiritism '61

Richard Monette
Big Zapper '73
Dancing in the Dark '86
Far Cry from Home '70s
Hello Mary Lou: Prom Night 2
'87
Higher Education '88
Murder by Night '89

Yvonne Monlaur
The Brides of Dracula '60
Circus of Horrors '60
License to Kill '64

Lawrence Monoson
Dangerous Love '87
Gaby: A True Story '87
Last American Virgin '82
Mask '85

Marilyn Monroe
All About Eve '50
As Young As You Feel '51

The Asphalt Jungle '50
Bus Stop '56
Clash by Night '52
Don't Bother to Knock '52
Gentlemen Prefer Blondes '53
Hollywood Home Movies '87
Hollywood Outtakes & Rare
Footage '83
Home Town Story '51
How to Marry a Millionaire '53
Ladies of the Chorus '49
Let's Make it Legal '51
Let's Make Love '60
The Love Goddesses '65
Love Happy '50
Love Nest '51
The Misfits '61
Monkey Business '52
Niagara '53
The Prince and the Showgirl
'57
River of No Return '54
The Seven Year Itch '55
Some Like It Hot '59
There's No Business Like
Show Business '54
We're Not Married '52

Lee Montague
Brother Sun, Sister Moon '73
Madame Sousatzka '88
Mahler '74

Monte Montague
Courtin' Wildcats '29
King of the Rodeo '28
Radio Patrol '37
Trigger Tricks '30

Ricardo Montalban
Across the Wide Missouri '51
Alice Through the Looking
Glass '66
Battleground '49
Black Water Gold '69
Blue '68
Cannonball Run 2 '84
Cheyenne Autumn '64
Conquest of the Planet of the
Apes '72
Escape from the Planet of the
Apes '71
Fantasy Island '76
Fireball Forward '72
Iron Cowboy '68
Joe Panther '76
Latin Lovers '53
Madame X '66
Mission to Glory '80
The Naked Gun: From the Files
of Police Squad '88
Neptune's Daughter '49
Nosotros '44
On an Island with You '48
Pirate Warrior '64
Return to Fantasy Island '77
Ride to Glory '71
Sayonara '57
The Singing Nun '66
Star Trek 2: The Wrath of Khan
'82
Sweet Charity '69
Train Robbers '73
Two Weeks with Love '50

Karla Montana
La Pastorela '91
Sweet 15 '90

Monte Montana
Circle of Death '36
Down Dakota Way '49

Yves Montand
Cesar & Rosalie '72
Choice of Arms '83
Delusions of Grandeur '76
Goodbye Again '61
Grand Prix '66
Is Paris Burning? '68
Jean de Florette '87
Let's Make Love '60
Lovers Like Us '75
Manon of the Spring '87
My Geisha '62
Napoleon '55
On a Clear Day You Can See
Forever '70
Roads to the South '78
State of Siege '73
Vincent, Francois, Paul and the
Others '75
Wages of Fear '55

Where the Hot Wind Blows '59
Z '69

Carmen Montejo
El Rey '87
Ni Chana Ni Juana '87
The Vampire '57

Lisa Montell
The Nine Lives of Elfego Baca
'58
She Gods of Shark Reef '56

Sasha Montenegro
Bellas de Noche
Los Vampiros de Coyacan '87
Passion for Power '85

Rosenda Monteros
Cauldron of Blood '67
Tiara Tahiti '62
The White Orchid '54

Enrico Montesano
Lobster for Breakfast '82
Sotto, Sotto '85

Maria Montez
Ali Baba and the Forty Thieves
'43
Arabian Nights '42
Boss of Bullion City '41
Cobra Woman '44

**Belinda J.
Montgomery**
Blackout '78
The Man from Atlantis '77
Silent Madness '84
Stone Cold Dead '80
Stone Fox '87
Tell Me That You Love Me '84
The Todd Killings '71

**Douglass
Montgomery**
Harmony Lane '35
Little Women '33

**Elizabeth
Montgomery**
Amos '85
The Court Martial of Billy
Mitchell '55
Deadline Assault '90
Missing Pieces '83

George Montgomery
Battle of the Bulge '65
Bomb at 10:10 '67
From Hell to Borneo '64
Hallucination '67
Hostile Guns '67
Indian Uprising '51
Orchestra Wives '42
Rough Riders' Roundup '39
Samar '62
Satan's Harvest '65
The Steel Claw '61
Sword of Monte Cristo '51
The Texas Rangers '51
Warkill '65

Julia Montgomery
Girls Night Out '83
The Kindred '87
Revenge of the Nerds '84
Revenge of the Nerds 3: The
Next Generation '92
Savage Justice '88
South of Reno '87
Stewardess School '86
Up the Creek '84

Lee Montgomery
Ben '72
Girls Just Want to Have Fun '85
Into the Fire '88
The Midnight Hour '86
Mutant '83
Pete 'n' Tillie '72
Prime Risk '84
Savage is Loose '74

Robert Montgomery
The Big House '30
The Divorcee '30
Eye Witness '49
Forsaking All Others '35
Free and Easy '30
Here Comes Mr. Jordan '41
Hide-Out '34
June Bride '48
Lady in the Lake '46
The Last of Mrs. Cheyney '37
The Lost Stooges '33

Mr. & Mrs. Smith '41
Private Lives '31
Riptide '34
They Were Expendable '45

Silvia Monti
The Brain '69
Sicilian Connection '74

**Anna Maria
Monticelli**
The Empty Beach '85
Nomads '86

Sara Montiel
Besame '87
Cada Noche un Amor '75
La Bella Lola '87
La Violetera '71

Luigi Montini
Mediterraneo '91
Satanik '69

Alex Montoya
Escape from Fort Bravo '53
West to Glory '47

Michael Monty
Slash '87
The 13th Mission '91

Jim Moody
Bad Boys '83
Who's the Man? '93

King Moody
Five Minutes to Love '63
Get Smart, Again! '89

Lynne Moody
A Fight for Jenny '90
Last Light '93
Nightmare in Badham County
'76
Roots: The Next Generation '79
Scream Blacula Scream '73
Some Kind of Hero '82
Wait Till Your Mother Gets
Home '83

Ralph Moody
The Last Hunt '56
The Road to Bali '53

Ron Moody
David Copperfield '70
Dog Pound Shuffle '75
Dominique is Dead '79
Legend of the Werewolf '75
Murder Most Foul '65
Oliver! '68
Twelve Chairs '70
Unidentified Flying Oddball '79
Wrong is Right '82

Keith Moon
Monterey Pop '68
Sextette '78
That'll Be the Day '73
Tommy '75
Woodstock '70

Alvy Moore
A Boy and His Dog '75
The Brotherhood of Satan '71
Designing Woman '57
Intruder '88
Scream '88
Smokey & the Hotwire Gang
'79
The Specialist '75
They're Playing with Fire '84
Three Nuts in Search of a Bolt
'64
The Wild One '54
The Witchmaker '69

Archie Moore
The Adventures of Huckleberry
Finn '60
Breakheart Pass '76
The Carpetbaggers '64
My Sweet Charlie '70

Ben Moore
Moonshine Mountain '64
2000 Maniacs '64

Candy Moore
Lunch Wagon '81
Tomboy & the Champ '58

Christine Moore
Lurkers '88
Prime Evil '88
Thrilled to Death '88

Clayton Moore
The Adventures of Frank and
Jesse James '48
The Black Dragons '42
Cyclotrode "X" '46
Far Frontier '48
G-Men Never Forget '48
Jesse James Rides Again '47
Jungle Drums of Africa '53
Justice of the West '61
Lone Ranger '56
Lone Ranger and the Lost City
of Gold '58
Nyoka and the Tigermen '42
Radar Men from the Moon '52
The Son of Monte Cristo '41

Colleen Moore
Broken Hearts of Broadway '23
The Busher '19
Ella Cinders '26
The Scarlet Letter '34
The Sky Pilot '21
These Girls Won't Talk '20s

Constance Moore
Buck Rogers Conquers the
Universe '39
Delightfully Dangerous '45
Destination Saturn '39
Wives Under Suspicion '38
You Can't Cheat an Honest
Man '39

**Deborah Maria
Moore**
Chaplin '92
Into the Sun '92

Demi Moore
About Last Night... '86
Blame It on Rio '84
The Butcher's Wife '91
Choices '81
A Few Good Men '92
Ghost '90
Indecent Proposal '93
Mortal Thoughts '91
No Small Affair '84
Nothing But Trouble '91
One Crazy Summer '86
Parasite '81
St. Elmo's Fire '85
The Seventh Sign '88
Tales from the Crypt, Vol. 3 '90
We're No Angels '89
Wisdom '87

Dennis Moore
Across the Plains '39
Arizona Bound '41
Black Market Rustlers '43
Border Roundup '41
Colorado Serenade '46
Cowboy Commandos '43
D-Day on Mars '45
Driftin' River '46
East Side Kids '40
East Side Kids/The Lost City
'35
Fast Talking '86
Frontier Law '43
King of the Bullwhip '51
Land of Hunted Men '43
Master Key '44
The Mummy's Curse '44
Mutiny in the Big House '39
The Purple Monster Strikes '45
Raiders of Ghost City '44
Range Renegades '48
Rocky Mountain Rangers '40
Spooks Run Wild '41
Sylvia Scarlett '35
Texas Justice '42
The Tioga Kid '48
Tribute to a Bad Man '56
Wild Horse Canyon '39

Dickie Moore
Blonde Venus '32
Gabriel Over the White House
'33
The Gladiator '38
Heaven Can Wait '43
Jive Junction '43
Little Rascals, Book 7 '30s
Little Red Schoolhouse '36
Miss Annie Rooney '42
Oliver Twist '33
Out of the Past '47
Sergeant York '41
The World Accuses '35

Dudley Moore
Arthur '81
Arthur 2: On the Rocks '88
Bedazzled '68
Best Defense '84
Blame It on the Bellboy '92
Crazy People '90
Foul Play '78
The Hound of the Baskervilles '77
Like Father, Like Son '87
Lovesick '83
Micki & Maude '84
Romantic Comedy '83
Santa Claus: The Movie '85
Six Weeks '82
10 '79
30 Is a Dangerous Age, Cynthia '68
Those Daring Young Men in Their Jaunty Jalopies '69
Unfaithfully Yours '84
Wholly Moses! '80
The Wrong Box '66

Duke Moore
Night of the Ghouls '59
The Sinister Urge '60

Erin O'Brien Moore
Destination Moon '50
Our Little Girl '35

Frank Moore
Kings and Desperate Men '83
Rabid '77

Gar Moore
Abbott and Costello Meet the Killer, Boris Karloff '49
Paisan '46
The Underworld Story '50

Jeanie Moore
Dream Trap '90
The Final Alliance '89
Vampire at Midnight '88

Joanna Moore
Countdown '68
The Dunwich Horror '70
Follow That Dream '61
Iron Horsemen '71
Monster on the Campus '59
Never a Dull Moment '68
Scout's Honor '80
Son of Flubber '63
Touch of Evil '58

Juanita Moore
A Dream for Christmas '73
Foxstyle '73
Imitation of Life '59
The Singing Nun '66

Julianne Moore
Benny & Joon '93
Body of Evidence '92
Cast a Deadly Spell '91
The Fugitive '93
The Gun in Betty Lou's Handbag '92
The Hand that Rocks the Cradle '92
Short Cuts '93
Tales from the Darkside: The Movie '90

Kieron Moore
Anna Karenina '48
David and Bathsheba '51
Day of the Triffids '63
Doctor Blood's Coffin '62
The Key '58
A Man About the House '47
Mine Own Executioner '47

Mary Tyler Moore
Change of Habit '69
Finnegan Begin Again '84
Gore Vidal's Lincoln '88
Just Between Friends '86
Ordinary People '80
Six Weeks '82
Thoroughly Modern Millie '67

Matt Moore
An Affair to Remember '57
Consolation Marriage '31
Coquette '29
Deluge '33
Pride of the Clan '18
That Forsyte Woman '50
Traffic in Souls '13
20,000 Leagues Under the Sea '16

The Unholy Three '25
White Tiger '23
Melissa Moore
Hard to Die '90
The Invisible Maniac '90
The Killing Zone '90
Scream Dream '89
Sorority House Massacre 2: Nighty Nightmare '92
Vampire Cop '90
Norma Moore
Fear Strikes Out '57
Poor White Trash 2 '75
Owen Moore
As You Desire Me '32
Married? '27
She Done Him Wrong '33
Pauline Moore
The Three Musketeers '39
Young Buffalo Bill '40
R.J. Moore
Fit to Kill '93
Hard Hunted '92
Roger Moore
Bed & Breakfast '92
Bullseye! '90
Cannonball Run '81
Diane '55
Escape to Athena '79
ffolkes '80
Fiction Makers '67
Fire, Ice and Dynamite '91
Five Miles to Midnight '80
For Your Eyes Only '81
Happy Anniversary 007: 25 Years of James Bond '87
Interrupted Melody '55
The King's Thief '55
The Last Time I Saw Paris '54
Live and Let Die '73
The Man Who Haunted Himself '70
The Man with the Golden Gun '74
Mission: Monte Carlo '75
Moonraker '79
The Naked Face '84
Octopussy '83
Overture '75
Panama Hattie '42
The Persuaders '71
The Rape of the Sabines '61
The Saint '68
Sea Wolves '81
Shout at the Devil '76
The Spy Who Loved Me '77
Street People '76
That Lucky Touch '75
Vendetta for the Saint '68
A View to a Kill '85
Wild Geese '78
Rudy Ray Moore
Avenging Disco Godfather '76
Devil's Son-in-Law '77
Dolemite '75
Dolemite 2: Human Tornado '76
Monkey Hustle '77
Stephen Moore
Clockwise '86
Under Suspicion '92
Terry Moore
Beneath the 12-Mile Reef '53
Between Heaven and Hell '56
Beverly Hills Brats '89
Come Back, Little Sheba '52
Daddy Long Legs '55
Death Blow '87
Gaslight '44
The Great Rupert '50
Hellhole '85
Kill Factor
Mighty Joe Young '49
Peyton Place '57
Platinum High School '60
Postmark for Danger '56
Postmark for Danger/ Quicksand '56
Shack Out on 101 '55
Since You Went Away '44
Victor Moore
The Heat's On '43
Louisiana Purchase '41
The Seven Year Itch '55
Swing Time '36
We're Not Married '52
Ziegfeld Follies '46

Agnes Moorehead
Adventures of Captain Fabian '51
Alice Through the Looking Glass '66
Bachelor in Paradise '69
The Bat '59
Big Street '42
Captain Blackjack '51
Citizen Kane '41
The Conqueror '56
Dark Passage '47
Dear Dead Delilah '72
Dragon Seed '44
How the West was Won '63
Hush, Hush, Sweet Charlotte '65
Jane Eyre '44
Johnny Belinda '48
Journey into Fear '42
The Left Hand of God '55
Lost Moment '47
The Magnificent Ambersons '42
Magnificent Obsession '54
Main Street to Broadway '53
Meet Me in Las Vegas '56
Mrs. Parkington '44
The Opposite Sex '56
Our Vines Have Tender Grapes '45
Pardners '56
Pollyanna '60
Raintree County '57
The Seventh Cross '44
Show Boat '51
Since You Went Away '44
The Singing Nun '66
Station West '48
The Stratton Story '49
Summer Holiday '48
The Twilight Zone '61
What's the Matter with Helen? '71
Natalie Moorhead
Dancing Man '33
Hook, Line and Sinker '30
Illicit '31
The King Murder Case '32
Morals for Women '31
Murder on the High Seas '32
The Thin Man '34
Norma Mora
Samson in the Wax Museum '63
Viva Chihuahua (Long Live Chihuahua) '47
Esai Morales
Bad Boys '83
Bloodhounds of Broadway '89
Freejack '92
Great Love Experiment '84
In the Army Now '94
L.A. Bad '85
La Bamba '87
On Wings of Eagles '86
The Principal '87
Dolores Moran
The Horn Blows at Midnight '45
The Man I Love '46
To Have & Have Not '44
Erin Moran
Galaxy of Terror '81
How Sweet It Is! '68
Twirl '81
Watermelon Man '70
Frank Moran
Return of the Ape Man '44
Ships in the Night '28
Jackie Moran
The Adventures of Tom Sawyer '38
Buck Rogers Conquers the Universe '39
The Gang's All Here '41
Let's Go Collegiate '41
Old Swimmin' Hole '40
There Goes Kelly '45
Tomboy '40
Lee Moran
High Gear '33
My Lady of Whims '25
Pardon My Gun '30
The Tomboy '24
Peggy Moran
The Mummy's Hand '40

One Night in the Tropics '40
Polly Moran
Adam's Rib '50
Hollywood Party '34
Kings, Queens, Jokers '30s
Rick Moranis
The Best of John Candy on SCTV '80s
Brewster's Millions '85
Club Paradise '86
The Flintstones '94
Ghostbusters '84
Ghostbusters 2 '89
Head Office '86
Hockey Night '84
Honey, I Blew Up the Kid '92
Honey, I Shrunk the Kids '89
The Last Polka '84
Little Shop of Horrors '86
My Blue Heaven '90
Parenthood '89
Spaceballs '87
Splitting Heirs '93
Strange Brew '83
Streets of Fire '84
The Wild Life '84
Richard Morant
John & Yoko: A Love Story '85
Mahler '74
Poldark '75
Milburn Morante
Between Men '35
Ghost Rider '43
Sherlock's Rivals & Where's My Wife '27
Wolf Blood '25
Kenneth More
The Adventures of Sadie '55
Battle of Britain '69
Dark of the Sun '68
Doctor in the House '53
Flame Over India '60
Genevieve '53
Leopard in the Snow '78
The Longest Day '62
Man on the Run '49
Never Let Me Go '53
A Night to Remember '58
Reach for the Sky '56
Scott of the Antarctic '48
Scrooge '70
Sink the Bismarck '60
A Tale of Two Cities '80
Unidentified Flying Oddball '79
Where Time Began '77
Jeanne Moreau
Alberto Express '92
Alex in Wonderland '70
Back to the Wall '56
The Bride Wore Black '68
Chimes at Midnight '67
Dangerous Liaisons '59
Diary of a Chambermaid '64
The 400 Blows '59
Frantic '58
Going Places '74
Heat of Desire '84
Jules and Jim '62
La Femme Nikita '91
La Truite '83
The Last Tycoon '76
The Little Theatre of Jean Renoir '71
The Lovers '59
Lumiere '76
Mademoiselle '66
Map of the Human Heart '93
Mr. Klein '75
Monte Walsh '70
Oldest Profession '67
Querelle '83
The Train '65
The Trial '63
Until The End of The World '91
Viva Maria! '65
Your Ticket Is No Longer Valid '84
Mantan Moreland
Charlie Chan in the Secret Service '44
The Chinese Cat '44
Cosmo Jones, Crime Smasher '43
Footlight Serenade '42
Frontier Scout '38
The Gang's All Here '41
Harlem on the Prairie '38

The Jade Mask '45
Juke Joint '47
King of the Zombies '41
Law of the Jungle '42
Let's Go Collegiate '41
Meeting at Midnight '44
Mr. Moto's Last Warning/ Meeting at Midnight '44
Next Time I Marry '38
Phantom Killer '42
Pin-Up Girl '44
Revenge of the Zombies '43
The Scarlet Clue '45
The Shanghai Cobra '45
Spider Baby '64
The Spirit of Youth '37
Tall, Tan and Terrific '46
Two-Gun Man from Harlem '38
Up in the Air '40
The Young Nurses '73
Andre Morell
The Baby and the Battleship '56
The Bridge on the River Kwai '57
Dark of the Sun '68
The Hound of the Baskervilles '59
The Man Who Never Was '55
A Stolen Face '52
10 Rillington Place '71
Antonio Moreno
Creature from the Black Lagoon '54
Gaiety '43
It '27
Rose of Rio Grande '38
The Searchers '56
Valley of the Sun '42
Jose Elias Moreno
Night of the Bloody Apes '68
Santa Claus '59
Rita Moreno
Age Isn't Everything '91
Anatomy of a Seduction '79
Boss' Son '79
Carnal Knowledge '71
Cry of Battle '63
The Four Seasons '81
Happy Birthday, Gemini '80
The King and I '56
Marlowe '69
The Night of the Following Day '69
Pagan Love Song '50
Popi '69
Portrait of a Showgirl '82
The Ring '52
The Ritz '76
Seven Cities of Gold '55
Singin' in the Rain '52
Summer and Smoke '61
The Toast of New Orleans '50
West Side Story '61
George Morfogen
Deadly Business '86
Deadly Matrimony '93
Twenty Bucks '93
Yuri Nosenko, KGB '86
Debbie Morgan
Guilty of Innocence '87
The Jesse Owens Story '84
Monkey Hustle '77
Dennis (Stanley Morner) Morgan
Captains of the Clouds '42
Christmas in Connecticut '45
The Fighting 69th '40
The Great Ziegfeld '36
I Conquer the Sea '36
In This Our Life '42
It's a Great Feeling '49
Kitty Foyle '40
Pearl of the South Pacific '55
Thank Your Lucky Stars '43
Waterfront '39
Frank Morgan
Any Number Can Play '49
Balalaika '39
Boom Town '40
Broadway Melody of 1940 '40
Broadway Serenade '39
Casanova Brown '44
The Cat and the Fiddle '34
Courage of Lassie '46
Dancing Pirate '36

Dimples '36
The Great Ziegfeld '36
Hallelujah, I'm a Bum '33
Honky Tonk '41
The Human Comedy '43
I Live My Life '35
Key to the City '50
The Last of Mrs. Cheyney '37
The Mortal Storm '40
Naughty Marietta '35
Rosalie '38
Saratoga '37
The Shop Around the Corner '40
The Stratton Story '49
Summer Holiday '48
Sweethearts '38
Thousands Cheer '43
The Three Musketeers '48
Tortilla Flat '42
White Cargo '42
The White Cliffs of Dover '44
The Wizard of Oz '39

Harry Morgan
The Apple Dumpling Gang '75
The Apple Dumpling Gang Rides Again '79
The Barefoot Executive '71
The Bastard '78
Bend of the River '52
Better Late Than Never '79
Boots Malone '52
The Cat from Outer Space '78
Charley and the Angel '73
Dragnet '87
Falcon Takes Over/Strange Bargain '49
Far Country '55
Flim-Flam Man '67
Frankie and Johnny '65
The Gangster '47
The Glenn Miller Story '54
The Incident '89
M*A*S*H: Goodbye, Farewell & Amen '83
Moonrise '48
The Mountain Road '60
Orchestra Wives '42
The Ox-Bow Incident '43
Roots: The Next Generation '79
Roughnecks '80
Scandalous John '71
Scout's Honor '80
The Shootist '76
Snowball Express '72
State Fair '45
Support Your Local Gunfighter '71
Support Your Local Sheriff '69
Torch Song '53
The Well '51
What Did You Do in the War, Daddy? '66
Wild, Wild West Revisited '79
A Wing and a Prayer '44

Helen Morgan
Applause '29
Frankie and Johnny '36
Marie Galante '34
Show Boat '36

Henry Morgan
Crash Dive '43
High Noon '52
Holiday Affair '49
How the West was Won '63
It Started with a Kiss '59
The Showdown '50
The Teahouse of the August Moon '56
To the Shores of Tripoli '42

Jaye P. Morgan
Loose Shoes '80
Night Patrol '85

Melissa Morgan
Deadwood '65
Nasty Rabbit '64

Michael Morgan
Heart of a Nation '43
Homework '82

Michele Morgan
Bluebeard '63
Cat and Mouse '78
The Chase '46
Everybody's Fine '90
The Fallen Idol '49
Higher and Higher '44
Joan of Paris '42

La Symphonie Pastorale '46
The Lost Command '66
Passage to Marseilles '44
The Proud Ones '53
Stormy Waters '41

Nancy Morgan
Americathon '79
Grand Theft Auto '77
The Nest '88
Pray TV '80

Ralph Morgan
Condemned to Live '35
The Creeper '48
Dick Tracy vs. Crime Inc. '41
Enemy of Women '44
General Spanky '36
Heart of the Rockies '51
The Kennel Murder Case '33
Mannequin '37
The Monster Maker '44
Night Monster '42
Rasputin and the Empress '32
Shadows Over Shanghai '38
Song of the Thin Man '47
Strange Interlude '32
Transatlantic Merry-Go-Round '34
Way Down South '39
Yellowstone '36

Richard Morgan
Innocent Prey '88
The Wicked '89

Shelley Taylor Morgan
Malibu Express '85
My Tutor '82

Stafford Morgan
The Alpha Incident '76
The Capture of Bigfoot '79
Legend of Big Foot '82

Terence Morgan
The Lifetaker '89
The Love of Three Queens '54
Svengali '55

Masayuki Mori
The Bad Sleep Well '60
The Idiot '51
Princess Yang Kwei Fei '55
Rashomon '51
Ugetsu '53
When a Woman Ascends the Stairs '60

Toschia Mori
The Bitter Tea of General Yen '33
The Secrets of Wu Sin '32

Pat Moriarity
Kings Row '41
Mutiny in the Big House '39

Cathy Moriarty
Another Stakeout '93
Burndown '89
The Gun in Betty Lou's Handbag '92
Kindergarten Cop '90
The Mambo Kings '92
Matinee '92
Me and the Kid '93
Neighbors '81
Raging Bull '80
Soapdish '91
White of the Eye '88

Michael Moriarty
Bang the Drum Slowly '73
Bloodlink '86
Dark Tower '87
Full Fathom Five '90
Hanoi Hilton '87
Holocaust '78
It's Alive 3: Island of the Alive '87
The Last Detail '73
My Old Man's Place '71
Nitti: The Enforcer '88
Odd Birds '85
Pale Rider '85
Q (The Winged Serpent) '82
Reborn '78
Report to the Commissioner '74
Return to Salem's Lot '87
Secret of the Ice Cave '89
Shoot It Black, Shoot It Blue '74
Sound of Murder '82

The Stuff '85
Tailspin: Behind the Korean Airline Tragedy '89
Troll '85
Who'll Stop the Rain? '78
Windmills of the Gods '88
The Winds of Kitty Hawk '78

Philippe Morier-Genoud
Au Revoir Les Enfants '87
Confidentially Yours '83
Cyrano de Bergerac '90

Patricia Morison
Dressed to Kill '46
The Fallen Sparrow '43
The Prince of Thieves '48
Queen of the Amazons '47
Return of Wildfire '48
Song of the Thin Man '47
Song Without End '60
Without Love '45

Noriyuki "Pat" Morita
Amos '85
Auntie Lee's Meat Pies '92
Babes in Toyland '86
Cancel My Reservation '72
Captive Hearts '87
Collision Course '89
Do or Die '91
Even Cowgirls Get the Blues '94
For the Love of It '80
Hiroshima: Out of the Ashes '90
Honeymoon in Vegas '92
The Karate Kid '84
The Karate Kid: Part 2 '86
The Karate Kid: Part 3 '89
Lena's Holiday '90
Miracle Beach '92
The Next Karate Kid '94
Night Patrol '85
North '94
Slapstick of Another Kind '84
Thoroughly Modern Millie '67
The Vegas Strip Wars '84
When Time Ran Out '80

Louisa Moritz
Chained Heat '83
Last American Virgin '82
New Year's Evil '78
One Flew Over the Cuckoo's Nest '75
True Confessions '81

Henning Moritzen
Cries and Whispers '72
Memories of a Marriage '90
Sofie '92

Karen Morley
Beloved Enemy '36
Dinner at Eight '33
Gabriel Over the White House '33
Healer '36
The Littlest Rebel '35
The Mask of Fu Manchu '32
Mata Hari '32
Our Daily Bread '34
Scarface '31
The Sin of Madelon Claudet '31

Robert Morley
The African Queen '51
The Alphabet Murders '65
The Battle of the Sexes '60
Beat the Devil '53
Beau Brummel '54
Cromwell '70
Curtain Up '53
Deadly Game '82
The Foreman Went to France '42
Ghosts of Berkeley Square '47
High Road to China '83
Hot Millions '68
The Human Factor '79
I Live in Grosvenor Square '46
Istanbul '57
Joseph & His Brethren '60
Little Dorrit, Film 1: Nobody's Fault '88
Little Dorrit, Film 2: Little Dorrit's Story '88
Lola '69
Loophole '83
The Loved One '65

Major Barbara '41
Marie Antoinette '38
Murder at the Gallop '63
Of Human Bondage '64
Oh, Heavenly Dog! '80
Scavenger Hunt '79
Second Time Lucky '84
The Small Back Room '49
Song of Norway '70
A Study in Terror '66
Theatre of Blood '73
Those Magnificent Men in Their Flying Machines '65
Topkapi '64
The Trouble with Spies '87
War & Remembrance, Part 1 '88
War & Remembrance: The Final Chapter, Part 8 '89
Who is Killing the Great Chefs of Europe? '78
The Wind '87
Woman Times Seven '67

Alicia Moro
Exterminators of the Year 3000 '83
Hot Blood '89

Mike Moroff
Angel Town '89
The Cage '89

Priscilla Morrill
The People vs. Jean Harris '81
Right of Way '84

Anita Morris
Absolute Beginners '86
Aria '88
Bloodhounds of Broadway '89
Blue City '86
18 Again! '88
The Hotel New Hampshire '84
Little Miss Millions '93
Maria's Lovers '84
Martians Go Home! '90
Ruthless People '86
Sinful Life '89
A Smoky Mountain Christmas '86

Aubrey Morris
A Clockwork Orange '71
Lifeforce '85
Night Caller from Outer Space '66

Barboura Morris
Atlas '60
A Bucket of Blood '59
Machine Gun Kelly '58
The Wasp Woman '59

Chester Morris
The Bat Whispers '30
The Big House '30
Corsair '31
The Divorcee '30
Five Came Back '39
Flight from Glory '37
Frankie and Johnny '36
Gambler's Choice '44
The Great White Hope '70
Hunt the Man Down/Smashing the Rackets '50
Law of the Underworld '38
Red Headed Woman '32
Seven Miles from Alcatraz/Flight from Glory '43
Tomorrow at Seven '33

Colleen Morris
Crossing the Line '90
Prehysteria '93

Garrett Morris
Almost Blue '93
The Anderson Tapes '71
Cooley High '75
Husbands, Wives, Money, and Murder '86
Motorama '91
Severed Ties '92
The Stuff '85
The Underachievers '88

Greg Morris
The Doomsday Flight '66
Vegas '78

Haviland Morris
For Love or Money '88
Love or Money? '88
Sixteen Candles '84
Who's That Girl? '87

Howard Morris
End of the Line '88
High Anxiety '77
History of the World: Part 1 '81
Life Stinks '91
Munster's Revenge '81
The Nutty Professor '63
Portrait of a Showgirl '82
Splash '84

Jane Morris
Frankie and Johnny '91
Nothing in Common '86
Pretty Woman '90

Judy Morris
Best Enemies '86
Between Wars '74
Cass '78
In Search of Anna '79
Phar Lap '84
Plumber '79
Razorback '84

Kirk Morris
Devil of the Desert Against the Son of Hercules '62
Maciste in Hell '60
Terror of the Steppes '64
Triumph of the Son of Hercules '63

Mary Morris
Pimpernel Smith '42
Train of Events '49

Wayne Morris
The Bushwackers '52
Kid Galahad '37
Paths of Glory '57
Plunder Road '57
Task Force '49

Kenny Morrison
NeverEnding Story 2: The Next Chapter '91
The Quick and the Dead '87

Peter Morrison
Trailing Trouble '30
Trigger Tricks '30

Sammy Morrison
Flying Wild '41
Follow the Leader '44
Let's Get Tough '42
'Neath Brooklyn Bridge '42
Spooks Run Wild '41

Shelly Morrison
Castle of Evil '66
Devil Times Five '74

Jeff Morrow
The Creature Walks Among Us '56
The Giant Claw '57
Hour of Decision '57
Kronos '57
Octaman '71
Pardners '56
The Robe '53
The Story of Ruth '60
This Island Earth '55

Jo Morrow
Dr. Death, Seeker of Souls '73
13 Ghosts '60
The Three Worlds of Gulliver '60

Susan Morrow
Canadian Mounties Vs. Atomic Invaders '53
Cat Women of the Moon '53

Vic Morrow
The Adventures of Tom Sawyer '73
B.A.D. Cats '80
The Bad News Bears '76
Blackboard Jungle '55
Cimarron '60
Curse of the Black Widow '77
Death Stalk '74
Dirty Mary Crazy Larry '74
The Evictors '79
Express to Terror '79
Funeral for an Assassin '77
The Glass House '72
God's Little Acre '58
Humanoids from the Deep '80
King Creole '58
Men in War '57
1990: The Bronx Warriors '83
The Seekers '79

Morrow ▶cont.

The Treasure of Matecumbe '76
Tribute to a Bad Man '56
Twilight Zone: The Movie '83
Wanted: Babysitter '75
Wild & Wooly '78

Barry Morse
Asylum '72
Destination Moonbase Alpha '75
Glory! Glory! '90
Love at First Sight '76
The Martian Chronicles: Part 2 '79
The Martian Chronicles: Part 3 '79
No Trace '50
Power Play '81
Sadat '83
Space: 1999—Alien Attack '79
A Tale of Two Cities '80
Welcome to Blood City '77
Whoops Apocalypse '83

David Morse
The Brotherhood of the Rose '89
Dead Ahead: The Exxon Valdez Disaster '92
Desperate Hours '90
The Getaway '93
The Good Son '93
The Indian Runner '91
Inside Moves '80
Prototype '83
Shattered Vows '84

Helen Morse
Agatha '79
Caddie '81
Far East '85
Iris '89
Picnic at Hanging Rock '75
A Town Like Alice '85

Robert Morse
The Boatniks '70
Cannon Movie Tales: The Emperor's New Clothes '89
A Guide for the Married Man '67
How to Succeed in Business without Really Trying '67
The Loved One '65
The Matchmaker '58
Oh Dad, Poor Dad (Momma's Hung You in the Closet & I'm Feeling So Sad) '67
Where Were You When the Lights Went Out? '68
Wild Palms '93

Glen Morshower
Drive-In '76
84 Charlie Mopic '89

Viggo Mortensen
Boiling Point '93
Carlito's Way '93
Deception '92
The Indian Runner '91
Prison '88
The Reflecting Skin '91
Salvation! '87

Clive Morton
A Matter of WHO '62
The Moonraker '58

Joe Morton
Alone in the Neon Jungle '87
The Brother from Another Planet '84
City of Hope '91
Crossroads '86
Forever Young '92
The Good Mother '88
The Inkwell '94
Legacy of Lies '92
Of Mice and Men '92
Speed '94
Tap '89
Terminator 2: Judgment Day '91
Trouble in Mind '86
Zelly & Me '88

Gastone Moschin
The Conformist '71

A Joke of Destiny, Lying in Wait Around the Corner Like a Bandit '84
Mr. Superinvisible '73

Maurice Moscovich
Everything Happens at Night '39
The Great Commandment '41
The Great Dictator '40
Love Affair '39

David Moscow
Big '88
Newsies '92

Bill Moseley
Crash and Burn '90
Fair Game '89
Osa '85
Silent Night, Deadly Night 3: Better Watch Out! '89

David Moses
Daring Dobermans '73
Scared to Death '80

Harry Moses
Sweater Girls '78
The Van '77

Marian Moses
Buona Sera, Mrs. Campbell '68
Dead Heat on a Merry-Go-Round '66

Mark Moses
Dead Men Don't Die '91
Hollywood Heartbreak '89
The Tracker '88

William R. Moses
Alien from L.A. '87
Double Exposure '93
Mystic Pizza '88

Ivan Mosjoukine
Early Russian Cinema, Vol. 5: Chardynin's Pushkin '17
Early Russian Cinema, Vol. 10: The End of an Era '17

Roger E. Mosley
Attica '80
Darktown Strutters '74
The Greatest '77
Heart Condition '90
I Know Why the Caged Bird Sings '79
The Jericho Mile '79
Mack '73
Pray TV '80
The River Niger '76
Steel '80
Unlawful Entry '92

Arnold Moss
The Fool Killer '65
The Loves of Carmen '48
Reign of Terror '49
The 27 Day '57
Viva Zapata! '52

Ron Moss
Hard Ticket to Hawaii '87
Hearts & Armour '83

Stewart Moss
The Bat People '74
Dr. Death, Seeker of Souls '73

Josh Mostel
Almost You '85
Animal Behavior '89
The Chase '93
City of Hope '91
City Slickers '91
City Slickers 2: The Legend of Curly's Gold '94
Compromising Positions '85
Deadly Hero '75
Harry and Tonto '74
Heavy Petting '89
Jesus Christ, Superstar '73
The King of Marvin Gardens '72
Little Man Tate '91
The Money Pit '86
Radio Days '87
Sophie's Choice '82
Star 80 '83
Stoogemania '85
Wall Street '87
Windy City '84

Zero Mostel
DuBarry Was a Lady '43
The Enforcer '51
Foreplay '75

The Front '76
A Funny Thing Happened on the Way to the Forum '66
The Hot Rock '70
Journey into Fear '74
Marco '73
Master Mind '73
Once Upon a Scoundrel '73
Panic in the Streets '50
The Producers '68
Sirocco '51

Zeze Motta
Quilombo '84
Xica '76

John Moulder-Brown
Deep End '70
First Love '70
Killing Heat '84
King, Queen, Knave '72
Rumpelstiltskin '86
Vampire Circus '71

Movita
Mutiny on the Bounty '35
Panic in Echo Park '77
Rose of Rio Grande '38
Tower of Terror '42
Wolf Call '39

Alan Mowbray
Abbott and Costello Meet the Killer, Boris Karloff '49
The Girl from Missouri '34
I Wake Up Screaming '41
In Person '35
It Happened in New Orleans '36
The King and I '56
The King's Thief '55
The Lovable Cheat '49
The Man Who Knew Too Much '56
Mary of Scotland '36
Merton of the Movies '47
Music in My Heart '40
My Dear Secretary '49
My Man Godfrey '36
On the Avenue '37
Panama Hattie '42
The Phantom of 42nd Street '45
The Prince of Thieves '48
So This is Washington '43
Stand-In '37
A Study in Scarlet '33
That Hamilton Woman '41
That Uncertain Feeling '41
Topper Takes a Trip '39
The Villain Still Pursued Her '41
Vogues of 1938 '37
Way Down South '39

Jack Mower
The Fiddlin' Buckaroo '33
Mystery Squadron '33
Ships in the Night '28

Patrick Mower
The Bloodsuckers '70
Carry On England '76
Catch Me a Spy '71
Cry of the Banshee '70

Armin Mueller-Stahl
Angry Harvest '85
Avalon '90
Colonel Redl '84
Forget Mozart '85
The House of the Spirits '93
Kafka '91
Lethal Obsession '87
A Love in Germany '84
Midnight Cop '88
Music Box '89
Night on Earth '91
The Power of One '92
Utz '93

Gavin Muir
Abbott & Costello Meet the Invisible Man '51
House of Fear '45
Mary of Scotland '36
Night Tide '63
Sherlock Holmes Faces Death '43

Diana Muldaur
Beyond Reason '77
McQ '74
The Other '72
Planet Earth '74
Return of Frank Cannon '80

Kate Mulgrew
Camp Nowhere '94
Danielle Steel's ''Daddy'' '92
Lovespell '79
The Manions of America '81
Remo Williams: The Adventure Begins '85
Roots: The Gift '88
Round Numbers '91
A Stranger is Watching '82
Throw Momma from the Train '87
A Time for Miracles '80
The Word '78

Jack Mulhall
Burn 'Em Up Barnes '34
The Clutching Hand '36
Custer's Last Stand '36
Dawn Express '42
Desperate Cargo '41
A Face in the Fog '36
Hell's Headquarters '32
I Killed That Man '42
Mr. Wise Guy '42
Murder on the High Seas '32
Mystery Squadron '33
'Neath Canadian Skies '46
North of the Border '46
Outlaws of Sonora '38
Radio Patrol '37
Rogue's Tavern '36
Skull & Crown '38
Tim Tyler's Luck '37

Edward Mulhare
Hill 24 Doesn't Answer '55
Megaforce '82
Our Man Flint '66
Von Ryan's Express '65

Chris Mulkey
Bound and Gagged: A Love Story '93
Deadbolt '92
Gas Food Lodging '92
Ghost in the Machine '93
Heartbreak Hotel '88
In Dangerous Company '88
Jack's Back '87
K-9000 '89
Patti Rocks '88
Rainbow Drive '90
Roe vs. Wade '89
Runaway Father '91
The Silencer '92
Tricks of the Trade '88
Write to Kill '91

Martin Mull
Bad Manners '84
The Boss' Wife '86
Clue '85
Cutting Class '89
Dance with Death '89
Far Out Man '89
Flicks '85
FM '78
The History of White People in America '85
The History of White People in America: Vol. 2 '85
Home is Where the Hart is '88
Lots of Luck '85
Miracle Beach '92
Mr. Mom '83
My Bodyguard '80
O.C. and Stiggs '87
Portrait of a White Marriage '88
Rented Lips '88
Serial '80
Ski Patrol '89
Take This Job & Shove It '81
Think Big '90

Jack Mullaney
George! '72
The Honeymoon Machine '61
Spinout '66
Tickle Me '65

Greg Mullavey
Body Count '87
Chrome Hearts '70
Deadly Conspiracy '91
Husbands, Wives, Money, and Murder '86
I Dismember Mama '74
The Love Machine '71
Not Quite Human 2 '89

Patty Mullen
Doom Asylum '88

Frankenhooker '90

Harrison Muller
The Final Executioner '83
Miami Cops '89
She '83
2020 Texas Gladiators '85
Violent Breed '83

Paul Muller
The Black Devils of Kali '55
The Devil's Commandment '56
Fangs of the Living Dead '68
Four Ways Out '57
Goliath and the Sins of Babylon '64
Lady Frankenstein '72
Naked Warriors '73
Nightmare Castle '65
Two Nights with Cleopatra '54
Virgin Among the Living Dead '71

Richard Mulligan
Babes in Toyland '86
The Big Bus '76
Doin' Time '85
A Fine Mess '86
Gore Vidal's Lincoln '88
The Group '66
The Heavenly Kid '85
The Hideaways '73
Little Big Man '70
Meatballs 2 '84
Micki & Maude '84
Poker Alice '87
Pueblo Affair '73
Scavenger Hunt '79
S.O.B. '81
Teachers '84

Rod Mullinar
Breakfast in Paris '81
Dead Calm '89
Echoes of Paradise '86
Patrick '78

Dermot Mulroney
Bad Girls '94
Bright Angel '91
Career Opportunities '91
Family Pictures '93
The Last Outlaw '93
Longtime Companion '90
Point of No Return '93
Samantha '92
Silent Tongue '92
Staying Together '89
Sunset '88
Survival Quest '89
The Thing Called Love '93
Where the Day Takes You '92
Young Guns '88

Kieran Mulroney
Career Opportunities '91
Nowhere to Run '88

Danny Mummert
Blondie Has Trouble '40
Blondie Hits the Jackpot '49
Blondie in Society '41
Blondie Knows Best '46
Blondie Takes a Vacation '39
Blondie's Blessed Event '42
It's a Great Life '43

Billy Mumy
Bless the Beasts and Children '71
Dear Brigitte '65
Sammy, the Way-Out Seal '62
Twilight Zone: The Movie '83

Herbert Mundin
The Adventures of Robin Hood '38
Cavalcade '33
Mutiny on the Bounty '35

Ian Mune
Dangerous Orphans '86
Sleeping Dogs '82

Paul Muni
Angel on My Shoulder '46
Black Fury '35
Commandos Strike at Dawn '43
The Good Earth '37
I Am a Fugitive from a Chain Gang '32
Juarez '39
The Last Angry Man '59
The Life of Emile Zola '37
Scarface '32
A Song to Remember '45

Stage Door Canteen '43
The Story of Louis Pasteur '36

Pep Munne
Barcelona '94
Where Time Began '77

Caroline Munro
The Abominable Dr. Phibes '71
At the Earth's Core '76
Black Cat '90
Captain Kronos: Vampire Hunter '74
Don't Open Till Christmas '84
Golden Voyage of Sinbad '73
Gun Crazy '69
I Don't Want to Be Born '75
The Last Horror Film '82
Maniac '80
Slaughter High '86
The Spy Who Loved Me '77
Star Crash '78

Janet Munro
The Crawling Eye '58
Darby O'Gill & the Little People '59
The Day the Earth Caught Fire '62
Horsemasters '61
Small Hotel '57
The Swiss Family Robinson '60
Third Man on the Mountain '59
The Young and the Guilty '58

Neil Munro
Beethoven Lives Upstairs '92
Confidential '86
Dancing in the Dark '86
Gate 2 '92

Jules Munshin
Easter Parade '48
Take Me Out to the Ball Game '49
That Midnight Kiss '49

Ona Munson
Dakota '45
Gone with the Wind '39
Idaho '43
Lady from Louisiana '42
The Making of a Legend: "Gone With the Wind" '89
The Red House '47
The Shanghai Gesture '42

Jim Henson's Muppets
The Great Muppet Caper '81
The Muppet Movie '79
The Muppets Take Manhattan '84
Sesame Street Presents: Follow That Bird '85

Jean Murat
Carnival in Flanders '35
Rich, Young and Pretty '51

Noe Murayama
El Robo al Tren Correo '47
La Fuga del Rojo '87
La Venganza del Rojo '87

Vince Murdocco
L.A. Wars '94
Ring of Fire '91
Ring of Fire 2: Blood and Steel '92

George Murdock
Breaker! Breaker! '77
Firepower '93
Grand Tour: Disaster in Time '92
In Love with an Older Woman '82
Strange Case of Dr. Jekyll & Mr. Hyde '89

Christopher Murney
Barton Fink '91
The Last Dragon '85
Maximum Overdrive '86
Murder by the Book '87
The Ten Million Dollar Getaway '91

Peter Murnik
Body Parts '91
Golden Gate '93

Audie Murphy
Arizona Raiders '65
The Red Badge of Courage '51
To Hell and Back '55
The Unforgiven '60

Barri Murphy
Action U.S.A. '89
Armed for Action '92

Ben Murphy
The Chisholms '79
The Cradle Will Fall '83
Riding with Death '76
Time Walker '82
The Winds of War '83

Eddie Murphy
Another 48 Hrs. '90
Best Defense '84
Best of Eddie Murphy '89
Beverly Hills Cop '84
Beverly Hills Cop 2 '87
Beverly Hills Cop 3 '94
Boomerang '92
Coming to America '88
The Distinguished Gentleman '92
Eddie Murphy "Delirious" '83
Eddie Murphy: Raw '87
48 Hrs. '82
The Golden Child '86
Harlem Nights '89
Trading Places '83

George Murphy
Bataan '43
Battleground '49
Broadway Melody of 1938 '37
Broadway Melody of 1940 '40
Broadway Rhythm '44
The Devil Thumbs a Ride/ Having Wonderful Crime '42
For Me and My Gal '42
A Girl, a Guy and a Gob '41
Having Wonderful Crime '45
Kid Millions '34
Letter of Introduction '38
Little Miss Broadway '38
Little Nellie Kelly '40
The Navy Comes Through '42
Show Business '44
Step Lively '44
This is the Army '43
Tom, Dick, and Harry '41

Horace Murphy
Boothill Brigade '37
Border Phantom '37
Down the Wyoming Trail '39
Last of the Warrens '36
Undercover Man '36
Wide Open Faces '38

Jimmy Murphy
Jet Attack/Paratroop Command '58
Platinum High School '60

Mary Murphy
Carrie '52
Desperate Hours '55
The Electronic Monster '57
Houdini '53
Main Street to Broadway '53
A Man Alone '55
Maverick Queen '55
The Wild One '54

Maurice Murphy
Abe Lincoln in Illinois '40
Delinquent Parents '38
Found Alive '34
Tailspin Tommy '34

Michael Murphy
The Autobiography of Miss Jane Pittman '74
Batman Returns '92
Brewster McCloud '70
The Caine Mutiny Court Martial '88
The Class of Miss MacMichael '78
Clean Slate '94
Cloak & Dagger '84
Count Yorga, Vampire '70
Countdown '68
Dead Ahead: The Exxon Valdez Disaster '92
Double Trouble '92
Folks! '92
The Front '76
Great Bank Hoax '78
Hot Money '79
Manhattan '79
McCabe & Mrs. Miller '71
Mesmerized '84
Nashville '75
O Youth and Beauty '79

Phase 4 '74
Salvador '86
Shocker '89
Strange Behavior '81
Tailspin: Behind the Korean Airline Tragedy '89
Talk to Me '82
Tanner '88 '88
That Cold Day in the Park '69
The Thief Who Came to Dinner '73
An Unmarried Woman '78
The Year of Living Dangerously '82

M.R. Murphy
In Deadly Heat '87
Stuff Stephanie in the Incinerator '89

Rosemary Murphy
Any Wednesday '66
The Attic '80
Ben '72
Eleanor & Franklin '76
For the Boys '91
Julia '77
To Kill a Mockingbird '62
Walking Tall '73
A Woman Named Jackie '91

Timothy Patrick Murphy
Doin' Time on Planet Earth '88
Sam's Son '84
The Seekers '79

Barbara Murray
The Bretts '88
A Cry from the Streets '57
Death Goes to School '53
Tony Draws a Horse '51

Bill Murray
Bill Murray Live from the Second City '70s
Caddyshack '80
Ed Wood '94
Ghostbusters '84
Ghostbusters 2 '89
Groundhog Day '93
Little Shop of Horrors '86
Loose Shoes '80
Mad Dog and Glory '93
Meatballs '79
Mr. Mike's Mondo Video '79
Quick Change '90
The Razor's Edge '84
Scrooged '88
Stripes '81
Tootsie '82
What About Bob? '91
Where the Buffalo Roam '80

Don Murray
Advise and Consent '62
Baby, the Rain Must Fall '64
Bus Stop '56
Confessions of Tom Harris '72
Conquest of the Planet of the Apes '72
Cotter '72
Deadly Hero '75
Endless Love '81
Ghosts Can't Do It '90
The Hoodlum Priest '61
I Am the Cheese '83
If Things Were Different '79
Justin Morgan Had a Horse '81
Kickboxer the Champion '91
License to Kill '84
Made in Heaven '87
Mistress '87
One Man's Way '63
Peggy Sue Got Married '86
Quarterback Princess '85
Radioactive Dreams '86
Rainbow '78
Return of the Rebels '81
Scorpion '86
Shake Hands with the Devil '59
Something in Common '86
Sweet Love, Bitter '67

Guillermo Murray
El Cuarto Chino '71
World of the Vampires '60

James Murray
Baby Face '33
The Crowd '28
High Gear '33
Skull & Crown '38

Joel Murray
Elvis Stories '89
One Crazy Summer '86

Ken Murray
Follow Me, Boys! '66
Hollywood My Hometown
The Man Who Shot Liberty Valance '62
The Marshal's Daughter '53

Stephen Murray
Alice in Wonderland '50
Four Sided Triangle '53

Tom Murray
The Gold Rush '25
Stuckey's Last Stand '78

Lionel Murton
Carry On Admiral '57
Meet the Navy '46

Tony Musante
The Bird with the Crystal Plumage '70
Breaking Up is Hard to Do '79
Collector's Item '89
The Detective '68
Fatal Chase '77
The Grissom Gang '71
High Ice '80
The Incident '67
The Pope of Greenwich Village '84

Clarence Muse
The Black Stallion '79
Broken Strings '40
A Dream for Christmas '73
Gentleman from Dixie '41
Prison Train '38
That Gang of Mine '40
Way Down South '39

Ornella Muti
Casanova '87
Flash Gordon '80
Hitchhiker 3 '87
Leonor '75
Life is Beautiful '79
Once Upon a Crime '92
Oscar '91
Summer Affair '79
Swann in Love '84
Tales of Ordinary Madness '83
Wait Until Spring, Bandini '90

Klaus Mutter
Clash of the Ninja '86
Thundering Ninja '80s

Carmel Myers
Beau Brummel '24
Ben-Hur '26
Chinatown After Dark '31
Pleasure '31

Harry Myers
City Lights '31
Convicted '32
The Marriage Circle '24
The Savage Girl '32

Kim Myers
A Nightmare on Elm Street 2: Freddy's Revenge '85
White Palace '90

Mike Myers
So I Married an Axe Murderer '93
Wayne's World '92
Wayne's World 2 '93

Susan Myers
Desperate Women '78
The Spell '77

Bruce Myles
A Cry in the Dark '88
Sweet Talker '91
A Woman's Tale '92

Jim Nabors
The Best Little Whorehouse in Texas '82
Cannonball Run 2 '84
Return to Mayberry '85
Stroker Ace '83

Mikola Nademsy
Earth '30
Zvenigora '28

George Nader
Away All Boats '56
Beyond Atlantis '73
Carnival Story '54

The House of 1000 Dolls '67
The Human Duplicators '64
Robot Monster '53
Sins of Jezebel '54

Michael Nader
The Finishing Touch '92
The Flash '90
Lady Mobster '88
Nick Knight '80s

Anne Nagel
Dawn Express '42
Don Winslow of the Navy '43
Gang Bullets '38
The Green Hornet '39
The Mad Monster '42
Man Made Monster '41
The Secret Code '42
The Spirit of West Point '47
Three Legionnaires '37
Winners of the West '40

Conrad Nagel
Ann Vickers '33
The Divorcee '30
Dubarry '30
The Kiss '29
The Michigan Kid '28
The Mysterious Lady '28
Woman in Brown '48
Yellow Cargo '36

Alan Naggar
Cleo/Leo '89
New York's Finest '87

Mayumi Nagisa
Tattooed Hit Man '76
Zatoichi: Zatoichi's Flashing Sword '

Ajay Naidu
Touch and Go '86
Where the River Runs Black '

Jimmy Nail
Crusoe '89
Morons from Outer Space '85

Joanne Nail
Switchblade Sisters '75
The Visitor '

J. Carroll Naish
Across the Wide Missouri '51
The Beast with Five Fingers '46
Beau Geste '39
Behind the Rising Sun '43
Beneath the 12-Mile Reef '53
Black Fury '35
The Black Hand '50
Blood and Sand '41
Captain Blood '35
The Charge of the Light Brigade '36
Clash by Night '52
Confidential '35
The Corsican Brothers '42
The Denver & Rio Grande '51
Down Argentine Way '40
Dracula vs. Frankenstein '71
Dragon Seed '44
Fighter Attack '53
Force of Impulse '60
The Fugitive '48
Hit the Deck '55
House of Frankenstein '44
Humoresque '46
The Last Command '55
The Lives of a Bengal Lancer '35
The Monster Maker '44
Mystery Squadron '33
Rage at Dawn '55
Rio Grande '50
The Royal Bed '31
Sahara '43
Sea Racketeers '37
The Southerner '45
Special Investigator '36
That Midnight Kiss '49
This Could Be the Night '57
The Toast of New Orleans '50
Waterfront '33
The World Gone Mad '33

Laurence Naismith
Amazing Mr. Blunden '72
The Bushbaby '70
Carrington, V.C. '54
Diamonds are Forever '71
Greyfriars Bobby '61
Jason and the Argonauts '63
The Man Who Never Was '55

Naismith ▶*cont.*

Mission: Monte Carlo '75
A Night to Remember '58
The Prince and the Pauper '62
Quest for Love '71
Robbery Under Arms '57
Room to Let '49
Sink the Bismarck '60
Third Man on the Mountain '59
Train of Events '49
The Valley of Gwangi '69
Village of the Damned '60
The World of Suzie Wong '60

Kathy Najimy
Hocus Pocus '93
Sister Act '92
Sister Act 2: Back in the Habit '93
Soapdish '91

Tatsuya Nakadai
Face of Another '66
High & Low '62
The Human Condition: A Soldier's Prayer '61
The Human Condition: No Greater Love '58
The Human Condition: Road to Eternity '59
Hunter in the Dark '80
Kagemusha '80
Kojiro '67
Kwaidan '64
Phoenix '78
Ran '85
Sanjuro '62
Sword of Doom '67
Today We Kill, Tomorrow We Die '71
When a Woman Ascends the Stairs '60
The Wolves '82

Ganjiro Nakamura
An Actor's Revenge '63
Drifting Weeds '59
The Lower Depths '57
Odd Obsession '60

Reggie Nalder
The Day and the Hour '63
Dracula Sucks '79
Mark of the Devil '69
Mark of the Devil 2 '72
Salem's Lot '79
Zoltan...Hound of Dracula '77

Nita Naldi
Blood and Sand '22
Cobra '25
Dr. Jekyll and Mr. Hyde '20
The Man from Beyond '22
The Ten Commandments '23
You Can't Fool Your Wife '40

Joe Namath
Avalanche Express '79
Chattanooga Choo Choo '84
Chrome Hearts '70
Marriage is Alive and Well '80

Jack Nance
Barfly '87
Blue Velvet '86
Dune '84
Eraserhead '78
Ghoulies '85
Hot Spot '90
Meatballs 4 '92
Motorama '91
Twin Peaks '90

Chieko Naniwa
A Geisha '53
Snow Country '57

Erica Nann
Legion of Iron '90
Mind Twister '93

Neriah Napaul
The Bikini Car Wash Company '90
The Bikini Car Wash Company 2 '92

Alan Napier
Across the Wide Missouri '51
Action in Arabia '44
Cat People '42
Challenge to Lassie '49
Forever Amber '47

The Hairy Ape '44
House of Horrors '46
The Loved One '65
Mademoiselle Fifi '44
Master Minds '49
The Mole People '56
The Secret Four '40
Until They Sail '57
Wild in the Country '61

Charles Napier
Center of the Web '92
Citizens Band '77
Deep Space '87
Dragonfight '92
Ernest Goes to Jail '90
Eyes of the Beholder '92
Future Zone '90
The Grifters '90
The Hit List '93
In Search of a Golden Sky '84
The Incredible Hulk Returns '88
Indio 2: The Revolt '92
Instant Justice '86
Kidnapped '87
The Last Embrace '79
Married to the Mob '88
Miami Blues '90
Night Stalker '87
One Man Force '89
Rambo: First Blood, Part 2 '85
Raw Justice '93
The Silence of the Lambs '91
Skeeter '93
Soldier's Fortune '91
Supervixens '75
Treacherous Crossing '92

Marshall Napier
The Navigator '88
Starlight Hotel '90

Toni Naples
Deathstalker 2: Duel of the Titans '87
Dinosaur Island '93

Tom Nardini
Africa Texas Style '67
Self-Defense '88

Paul Naschy
Count Dracula's Great Love '72
The Craving '80
Curse of the Devil '73
The Devil's Possessed '74
Dr. Jekyll and the Wolfman '71
Dr. Jekyll vs. the Werewolf '71
Dracula vs. Frankenstein '69
Dracula's Great Love '72
Exorcism '74
The Fury of the Wolfman '70
The Hanging Woman '72
Horror Rises from the Tomb '72
House of Psychotic Women '73
Human Beasts '80
Inquisition '76
The Mummy's Revenge '73
Night of the Howling Beast '75
People Who Own the Dark '75
The Rue Morgue Massacres '73
Vengeance of the Zombies '72
The Werewolf vs. the Vampire Woman '70

Chris Nash
Mischief '85
Silent Witness '85

Marilyn Nash
Monsieur Verdoux '47
The Rains Came '39
Unknown World '51

Noreen Nash
The Devil on Wheels '47
Phantom from Space '53
The Red Stallion '47
The Tender Years '47
Western Double Feature 14 '52

Marie-Jose Nat
Embassy '72
Les Violons du Bal '74
Love and the Frenchwoman '60

Francesca "Kitten" Natavidad
Beneath the Valley of the Ultra-Vixens '79
Doin' Time '85
My Tutor '82
Takin' It All Off '87

The Wild Life '84

Adam Nathan
I Was a Teenage TV Terrorist '87
Parting Glances '86

Stephen Nathan
The First Nudie Musical '75
1776 '72

Zoe Nathenson
Mona Lisa '86
The Raggedy Rawney '90
Those Glory, Glory Days '83

Yosuke Natsuki
Dagora, the Space Monster '65
Ghidrah the Three Headed Monster '65

Masako Natsume
Antarctica '84
The Imperial Japanese Empire '85
MacArthur's Children '85

Mildred Natwick
Against All Flags '52
Barefoot in the Park '67
Court Jester '56
Daisy Miller '74
Dangerous Liaisons '88
The Enchanted Cottage '45
A House Without a Christmas Tree '72
If It's Tuesday, This Must Be Belgium '69
Kiss Me Goodbye '82
The Long Voyage Home '40
The Quiet Man '52
She Wore a Yellow Ribbon '49
Tammy and the Bachelor '57
Three Godfathers '48
The Trouble with Harry '55
Yolanda and the Thief '45

David Naughton
An American Werewolf in London '81
Amityville: A New Generation '93
Body Bags '93
Boy in Blue '86
Getting Physical '84
Hot Dog...The Movie! '83
Kidnapped '87
Midnight Madness '80
Not for Publication '84
Overexposed '90
Private Affairs '89
Separate Vacations '86
Separate Ways '81
The Sleeping Car '90
Steel and Lace '90
Wild Cactus '92

James Naughton
Blown Away '93
Cat's Eye '85
The Glass Menagerie '87
The Good Mother '88
The Paper Chase '73
Second Wind '90
A Stranger is Watching '82

Cliff Nazarro
Hillbilly Blitzkrieg '42
In Old Colorado '41
'Neath Canadian Skies '46
Rhythm Parade '43
Singing Buckaroo '37

Alla Nazimova
Blood and Sand '41
The Bridge of San Luis Rey '44
Salome '23
Salome/Queen Elizabeth '23
Since You Went Away '44

Amadeo Nazzari
Journey Beneath the Desert '61
Lure of the Sila '49
The Naked Maja '59
Nefertiti, Queen of the Nile '64
Nights of Cabiria '57

Anna Neagle
Bitter Sweet '33
The Courtney Affair '47
Elizabeth of Ladymead '48
Forever and a Day '43
I Live in Grosvenor Square '46
The King's Rhapsody '55
Let's Make Up '55
London Melody '37
Maytime in Mayfair '52

No, No Nanette '40
Nurse Edith Cavell '39
Sunny '41
Teenage Bad Girl '59

Billie Neal
Consenting Adults '92
Down by Law '86
Mortal Thoughts '91

Edwin Neal
Future Kill '85
Neurotic Cabaret '90
The Texas Chainsaw Massacre '74

Ella Neal
Doctor Satan's Robot '40
Mysterious Doctor Satan '40

Patricia Neal
All Quiet on the Western Front '79
The Bastard '78
Breakfast at Tiffany's '61
Caroline? '90
The Day the Earth Stood Still '51
Diplomatic Courier '52
Eric '75
A Face in the Crowd '57
The Fountainhead '49
Ghost Story '81
Heidi '93
Homecoming: A Christmas Story '71
Hud '63
In Harm's Way '65
Love Affair: The Eleanor & Lou Gehrig Story '77
Love Leads the Way '84
Run, Stranger, Run '73
Shattered Vows '84
The Stranger from Venus '54
Things in Their Season '74
Three Secrets '50
An Unremarkable Life '89
Widow's Nest '77

Peggy Neal
Terror Beneath the Sea '66
X from Outer Space '67

Tom Neal
Andy Hardy Meets Debutante '40
Apache Chief '50
Behind the Rising Sun '43
Bowery at Midnight '42
The Brute Man '46
Case of the Baby Sitter '47
Club Havana '46
Courageous Dr. Christian '40
Danger Zone '51
Detour '46
Fingerprints Don't Lie '51
First Yank into Tokyo '45
G.I. Jane '51
Great Jesse James Raid '49
Hat Box Mystery '47
I Shot Billy the Kid '50
King of the Bullwhip '51
Miracle Kid '42
My Dog Shep '46
Radar Secret Service '50
Red Desert '51
Stop That Cab '51
Trail of the Mounties '47
Train to Tombstone '50
Varieties on Parade '52

Kevin Nealon
All I Want for Christmas '91
Roxanne '87

Christopher Neame
Bloodstone '88
Boris and Natasha: The Movie '92
D.O.A. '88
Edge of Honor '91
Steel Dawn '87
Still Not Quite Human '92
Street Knight '93
Suburban Commando '91

Vaclav Neckar
Closely Watched Trains '66
Larks on a String '68

Ted Neeley
Hard Country '81
Jesus Christ, Superstar '73
Of Mice and Men '81
Shadow of Chikara '77

Liam Neeson
The Big Man: Crossing the Line '91
The Bounty '84
Darkman '90
The Dead Pool '88
Deception '92
Duet for One '86
Ethan Frome '92
Excalibur '81
The Good Mother '88
High Spirits '88
Husbands and Wives '92
Krull '83
Leap of Faith '92
The Mission '86
Next of Kin '89
Prayer for the Dying '87
Satisfaction '88
Schindler's List '93
Shining Through '92
Suspect '87
Under Suspicion '92

Hildegarde Neff
Antony and Cleopatra '73
Bluebeard '63
Diplomatic Courier '52
The Snows of Kilimanjaro '52
Svengali '55
The Three Penny Opera '62
Unnatural '52

Natalia Negoda
Back in the USSR '92
The Comrades of Summer '92
Little Vera '88

Francois Negret
Au Revoir Les Enfants '87
Night and Day '91

George Negrete
El Penon de las Animas '47
Fiesta '47
Historia de un Gran Amor '57

Pola Negri
Gypsy Blood '18
Hi Diddle Diddle '43
Hotel Imperial '27
The Moon-Spinners '64
One Arabian Night '21
Passion '19

Mary Joan Negro
The Family Man '79
No Big Deal '83

Taylor Negron
Bad Medicine '85
Better Off Dead '85
Easy Money '83
The Last Boy Scout '91
Nothing But Trouble '91
Punchline '88

David Neidorf
Hoosiers '86
Undercover '87

Hildegarde Neil
The Man Who Haunted Himself '70
A Touch of Class '73

Noel Neill
The Adventures of Frank and Jesse James '48
The Stork Club '45
Superman: The Serial, Vol. 1 '48

Sam Neill
Attack Force Z '84
The Blood of Others '84
A Cry in the Dark '88
Dead Calm '89
Enigma '82
Family Pictures '93
Fever '91
The Final Conflict '81
For Love Alone '86
The Good Wife '86
Hostage '92
The Hunt for Red October '90
Ivanhoe '82
Jurassic Park '93
Memoirs of an Invisible Man '92
My Brilliant Career '79
One Against the Wind '91
The Piano '93
Plenty '85
Possession '81
Question of Faith '93

Reilly: Ace of Spies '87
Sirens '94
Sleeping Dogs '82
Until The End of The World '91

Stacey Nelkin
Children of Divorce '80
Halloween 3: Season of the
    Witch '82
The Triangle Factory Fire
    Scandal '79
Up the Academy '80

Nathalie Nell
Echoes '83
Rape of Love '79

Kate Nelligan
Bethune '77
Control '87
The Count of Monte Cristo '74
Crossover '82
Diamond Fleece '92
Dracula '79
Eleni '85
Eye of the Needle '81
Fatal Instinct '93
Frankie and Johnny '91
Love and Hate: A Marriage
    Made in Hell '90
The Prince of Tides '91
Romantic Englishwoman '75
Shadows and Fog '92
Terror Stalks the Class
    Reunion '93
Without a Trace '83
Wolf '94

Ann Nelson
Ghosts That Still Walk '77
My Girl '91

Barry Nelson
Airport '70
The Human Comedy '43
Island Claw '80
Johnny Eager '42
Pete 'n' Tillie '72
Shadow of the Thin Man '41
The Shining '80

Bob Nelson
Brain Donors '92
Miracles '86
Ryder P.I. '88
Sorceress '82

Bobby Nelson
Boothill Brigade '37
Cowboy & the Bandit '35
Cyclone of the Saddle '35
The Red Rope '37
Roaring Ranch '30
Way of the West '35

Craig Richard Nelson
The Grass is Always Greener
    Over the Septic Tank '78
My Bodyguard '80
The Paper Chase '73

Craig T. Nelson
Action Jackson '88
All the Right Moves '83
And Justice for All '79
Call to Glory '84
Cannon Movie Tales: Red
    Riding Hood '89
The Fire Next Time '93
The Josephine Baker Story '90
The Killing Fields '84
Man, Woman & Child '83
Me and Him '89
Murder in Texas '81
Murderers Among Us: The
    Simon Wiesenthal Story '89
The Osterman Weekend '83
Poltergeist '82
Poltergeist 2: The Other Side
    '86
Private Benjamin '80
Rachel River '89
Rage '80
Red Riding Hood '88
Silkwood '83
Stir Crazy '80
Troop Beverly Hills '89
Turner and Hooch '89

David Nelson
Cry-Baby '90
High School USA '84
Peyton Place '57

Ed Nelson
Anatomy of a Seduction '79

The Bone Yard '90
Brenda Starr '86
A Bucket of Blood '59
Deadly Weapon '88
The Devil's Partner '58
Enola Gay: The Men, the
    Mission, the Atomic Bomb
    '80
For the Love of Benji '77
Invasion of the Saucer Men '57
Night of the Blood Beast '58
Return of Frank Cannon '80
Shining Star '75
Soldier in the Rain '63
T-Bird Gang '59

Gene Nelson
The Atomic Man '56
Lullaby of Broadway '51
Oklahoma! '55
Tea for Two '50
The Way Out '56
The West Point Story '50

**Harriet Hilliard
Nelson**
Follow the Fleet '36
The Kid with the 200 I.Q. '83
Take It Big '44

Herbert Nelson
Future Cop '76
When the North Wind Blows '74

John Allen Nelson
Deathstalker 3 '89
Hunk '87
Killer Klowns from Outer Space
    '88
Saigon Commandos '88

Judd Nelson
Airheads '94
Billionaire Boys Club '87
Blindfold: Acts of Obsession
    '94
Blue City '86
The Breakfast Club '85
Caroline at Midnight '93
Conflict of Interest '92
The Dark Backward '91
Entangled '93
Every Breath '93
Fandango '85
Far Out Man '89
From the Hip '86
Hail Caesar '94
Hiroshima: Out of the Ashes
    '90
Making the Grade '84
New Jack City '91
Primary Motive '92
Relentless '89
St. Elmo's Fire '85

Lloyd Nelson
Curse of the Stone Hand '64
The Incredible Petrified World
    '58
Man Beast '55
The Wild World of Batwoman
    '66

Lori Nelson
Day the World Ended '55
Hot Rod Girl '56
I Died a Thousand Times '55
Ma and Pa Kettle at the Fair '52
Mohawk '56
Pardners '56
Pied Piper of Hamelin '57
Revenge of the Creature '55

Margaret Nelson
Picnic at Hanging Rock '75
Scalp Merchant '77

Ozzie Nelson
Adventures of Ozzie & Harriet
    '50s
Big Street '42
The Impossible Years '68
People Are Funny '46
Take It Big '44

Peter Nelson
Crime Zone '88
The Expendables '89
Eye of the Eagle 3 '91
Silk 2 '89
Sounds of Silence '91

Ricky Nelson
Rio Bravo '59
Wackiest Ship in the Army '61

Ruth Nelson
A Christmas Without Snow '80
The Haunting Passion '83
Humoresque '46
Wilson '44

Tracy Nelson
Down and Out in Beverly Hills
    '86
The Game of Love '90
Maria's Lovers '84
Yours, Mine & Ours '68

Willie Nelson
Amazons '86
Another Pair of Aces: Three of
    a Kind '91
Baja Oklahoma '87
Barbarosa '82
Coming Out of the Ice '82
Dynamite and Gold '88
The Electric Horseman '79
Hell's Angels Forever '83
Honeysuckle Rose '80
Last Days of Frank & Jesse
    James '86
Pair of Aces '90
Red Headed Stranger '87
Songwriter '84
Stagecoach '86
Texas Guns '90
Thief '81

**Corin "Corky"
Nemec**
Solar Crisis '92
Stephen King's The Stand '94
Tucker: The Man and His
    Dream '88

**Rosalba (Sara Bay)
Neri**
The Castle of Fu Manchu '68
Conquest of Mycene '63
Devil's Wedding Night '73
Lady Frankenstein '72
Naked Warriors '73
The Seducers '70
Slaughter Hotel '71

Franco Nero
Battle of Neretva '69
The Bible...In the Beginning '66
Blood Brothers '74
Camelot '67
Challenge to White Fang '86
Confessions of a Police
    Captain '72
Day of the Cobra '84
Devil's Crude '71
Die Hard 2: Die Harder '90
Django '68
Enter the Ninja '81
Falcon '74
Fifth Day of Peace '72
Force 10 from Navarone '78
The Girl '86
High Crime '73
Last Four Days '77
Legend of Valentino '75
Magdalene '88
The Man with Bogart's Face
    '80
Querelle '83
Redneck '73
Ring of Death '72
The Salamander '82
Sardinia Kidnapped '75
Shark Hunter '84
Spaghetti Western '69
Street Law '79
Submission '77
Sweet Country '87
Tristana '70
21 Hours at Munich '76
The Virgin and the Gypsy '70
Wagner: The Movie '85
Wild, Wild Planet '65
Windmills of the Gods '88
Young Catherine '91

Toni Nero
No Dead Heroes '87
Silent Night, Deadly Night '84

Cathleen Nesbitt
An Affair to Remember '57
Desiree '54
Man of Evil '48
Men of Two Worlds '46
Nicholas Nickleby '46
The Passing of the Third Floor
    Back '36

Promise Her Anything '66
Separate Tables '58

Derren Nesbitt
Funny Money '82
Horrors of Burke & Hare '71

Michael Nesmith
Doctor Duck's Super Secret
    All-Purpose Sauce '85
Head '68

Lois Nettleton
The Bamboo Saucer '68
The Best Little Whorehouse in
    Texas '82
Brass '85
Butterfly '82
Deadly Blessing '81
The Good Guys and the Bad
    Guys '69
Manhunt for Claude Dallas '86
Period of Adjustment '62
Soggy Bottom U.S.A. '84

Jenny Neumann
Delos Adventure '86
Hell Night '81
Mistress of the Apes '79
Stage Fright '83
Swim Team '79

Bebe Neuwirth
Bugsy '91
Green Card '90
Malice '93
The Paint Job '93
Say Anything '89
Wild Palms '93

John Neville
The Adventures of Baron
    Munchausen '89
Baby's Day Out '94
Billy Budd '62
A Study in Terror '66
The Unearthly Stranger '64

Robyn Nevin
Careful, He Might Hear You '84
Fourth Wish '75
The Irishman '78

Claudette Nevins
Child of Darkness, Child of
    Light '91
The Mask '61
The Possessed '77
Sleeping with the Enemy '91
Take Your Best Shot '82

Derek Newark
Bellman and True '88
The Offence '73

George Newbern
Adventures in Babysitting '87
Doppelganger: The Evil Within
    '90
Father of the Bride '91
It Takes Two '88
My Little Girl '87
Paramedics '88
Switching Channels '88

Anthony Newcastle
Captive Planet '78
Metallica '85

William Newell
Doctor Satan's Robot '40
Escape from Fort Bravo '53
The Invisible Killer '40
The Mandarin Mystery '37

Bob Newhart
Catch-22 '70
Cold Turkey '71
First Family '80
Hell is for Heroes '62
Hot Millions '68
Little Miss Marker '80
Marathon '80
On a Clear Day You Can See
    Forever '70
Thursday's Game '74

James Newill
Boss of Rawhide '44
Danger Ahead '40
Fighting Mad '39
Fighting Valley '43
The Great American Broadcast
    '41
Guns of the Law '44
Murder on the Yukon '40
Outlaw Roundup '44
Rangers Take Over '43

Renfrew of the Royal Mounted
    '37
Renfrew on the Great White
    Trail '38
Sky Bandits '40
Yukon Flight '40

Anthony Newlands
Circus of Fear '67
Scream and Scream Again '70

Anthony Newley
Above Us the Waves '56
Blade in Hong Kong '85
Boris and Natasha: The Movie
    '92
Doctor Dolittle '67
Fire Down Below '57
The Garbage Pail Kids Movie
    '87
Let's Get Married '63
Little Ballerina '47
The Old Curiosity Shop '75
Oliver Twist '48
Outrage! '86
Stagecoach '86

Barry Newman
Amy '81
City on Fire '78
Deadline '81
Fatal Vision '84
Having It All '82
The Salzburg Connection '72
Vanishing Point '71

Laraine Newman
Coneheads '93
Her Life as a Man '83
Invaders from Mars '86
Mr. Mike's Mondo Video '79
Perfect '85
Problem Child 2 '91
Revenge of the Red Baron '93
Tunnelvision '76
Wholly Moses! '80
Witchboard 2: The Devil's
    Doorway '93

Nanette Newman
Long Ago Tomorrow '71
The Madwoman of Chaillot '69
The Wrong Arm of the Law '63

Paul Newman
Absence of Malice '81
Bang the Drum Slowly '56
Blaze '89
Buffalo Bill & the Indians '76
Butch Cassidy and the
    Sundance Kid '69
Cat on a Hot Tin Roof '58
The Color of Money '86
Cool Hand Luke '67
The Drowning Pool '75
Exodus '60
Fat Man and Little Boy '89
Fort Apache, the Bronx '81
From the Terrace '60
Harper '66
Harry & Son '84
Hombre '67
Hud '63
The Hudsucker Proxy '93
The Hustler '61
Lady L '65
The Left-Handed Gun '58
Life & Times of Judge Roy
    Bean '72
The Long, Hot Summer '58
Mackintosh Man '73
Mr. & Mrs. Bridge '91
A New Kind of Love '63
Paris Blues '61
Pocket Money '72
The Prize '63
Quintet '79
The Secret War of Harry Frigg
    '68
Silent Movie '76
The Silver Chalice '54
Slap Shot '77
Somebody Up There Likes Me
    '56
Sometimes a Great Notion '71
The Sting '73
Sweet Bird of Youth '62
Torn Curtain '66
The Towering Inferno '74
Until They Sail '57
The Verdict '82
When Time Ran Out '80
Winning '69

Newman ▶cont.

The Young Philadelphians '59
Phyllis Newman
Follies in Concert '85
Picnic '55
A Secret Space '88
Stephen D. Newman
Sophie's Choice '82
Yuri Nosenko, KGB '86
Julie Newmar
Deep Space '87
Ecstasy '84
Evils of the Night '85
For Love or Money '63
Hysterical '83
Li'l Abner '59
MacKenna's Gold '69
Nudity Required '90
Robo-Chic '89
Seven Brides for Seven Brothers '54
Streetwalkin' '85
Terraces '77
John Haymes Newton
Alive '93
Desert Kickboxer '92
Olivia Newton-John
Grease '78
Two of a Kind '83
Xanadu '80
Margit Evelyn Newton
The Last Hunter '80
Night of the Zombies '83
Robert Newton
Androcles and the Lion '52
Around the World in 80 Days '56
Beachcomber '38
Blackbeard the Pirate '52
The Desert Rats '53
Epic That Never Was '65
Henry V '44
The Hidden Room '49
Jamaica Inn '39
Long John Silver '53
Odd Man Out '47
Oliver Twist '48
This Happy Breed '47
Tom Brown's School Days '51
Treasure Island '50
21 Days '37
Theodore Newton
Ace of Aces '33
The Sphinx '33
Wayne Newton
The Adventures of Ford Fairlane '90
Best of the Best 2 '93
The Dark Backward '91
License to Kill '89
Richard Ney
The Lovable Cheat '49
Mrs. Miniver '42
Premature Burial '62
Haing S. Ngor
Ambition '91
Heaven and Earth '93
In Love and War '91
The Iron Triangle '89
The Killing Fields '84
Last Flight Out: A True Story '90
My Life '93
Vietnam, Texas '90
Dustin Nguyen
Heaven and Earth '93
No Escape, No Return '93
Rapid Fire '92
3 Ninjas Kick Back '94
Michelle Nicastro
Bad Guys '86
Body Rock '84
When Harry Met Sally '89
Maurizio Nichetti
Allegro Non Troppo '76
The Icicle Thief '89
Volere Volare '92
Angela Nicholas
Alien Space Avenger '91

Galactic Gigolo '87
Denise Nicholas
And the Children Shall Lead '85
Blacula '72
Ghost Dad '90
Let's Do It Again '75
Piece of the Action '77
Sophisticated Gents '81
Harold Nicholas
Fass Black '77
The Five Heartbeats '91
Tap '89
Paul Nicholas
Alice '86
Invitation to the Wedding '73
Lisztomania '75
Nutcracker Sweet '84
The World is Full of Married Men '80
Yesterday's Hero '79
Thomas Ian Nicholas
The Fear Inside '92
Rookie of the Year '93
Anthony Nicholls
Burn Witch, Burn! '62
The Franchise Affair '52
Phoebe Nicholls
Deep Cover '88
Heart of Darkness '93
Maurice '87
Barbara Nichols
Beyond a Reasonable Doubt '56
The Human Duplicators '64
The King and Four Queens '56
Manfish '56
Scarface Mob '62
Sweet Smell of Success '57
Britt Nichols
The Demons '74
Virgin Among the Living Dead '71
Conrad Nichols
Days of Hell '84
A Man Called Rage '84
Rush '84
George Nichols
The Country Kid '23
The Eagle '25
Finishing School '33
The Greatest Question '19
White Gold '28
Nichelle Nichols
Say Goodbye, Maggie Cole '72
Star Trek: The Motion Picture '80
Star Trek 2: The Wrath of Khan '82
Star Trek 3: The Search for Spock '84
Star Trek 4: The Voyage Home '86
Star Trek 5: The Final Frontier '89
Star Trek 6: The Undiscovered Country '91
Star Trek Bloopers '69
The Supernaturals '86
Truck Turner '74
Stephen Nichols
Soapdish '91
Witchboard '87
Taylor Nichols
Barcelona '94
Metropolitan '90
Jack Nicholson
Batman '89
The Border '82
Broadcast News '87
Carnal Knowledge '71
Chinatown '74
Easy Rider '69
Ensign Pulver '64
A Few Good Men '92
Five Easy Pieces '70
Flight to Fury '66
Goin' South '78
Heartburn '86
Hell's Angels on Wheels '67
Hoffa '92
Ironweed '87
The King of Marvin Gardens '72
The Last Detail '73

The Last Tycoon '76
Little Shop of Horrors '60
Man Trouble '92
Missouri Breaks '92
On a Clear Day You Can See Forever '70
One Flew Over the Cuckoo's Nest '75
The Passenger '75
The Postman Always Rings Twice '81
Prizzi's Honor '85
Psych-Out '68
The Raven '63
Rebel Rousers '69
Reds '81
Ride in the Whirlwind '67
The Shining '80
The Shooting '66
Studs Lonigan '60
Terms of Endearment '83
The Terror '63
Tommy '75
The Two Jakes '90
The Wild Ride '60
The Witches of Eastwick '87
Wolf '94
Nick Nicholson
Fist of Steel '93
Triple Impact '92
Denise Nickerson
Smile '75
Willy Wonka & the Chocolate Factory '71
Zero to Sixty '78
Julia Nickson-Soul
Amityville: A New Generation '93
China Cry '91
Glitch! '88
K2: The Ultimate High '92
Rambo: First Blood, Part 2 '85
Sidekicks '93
Alex Nicol
A*P*E* '76
Black Glove '54
Brandy Sheriff '78
The Gilded Cage '54
Great Day in the Morning '56
Heat Wave '54
The Man from Laramie '55
A Matter of WHO '62
Meet Danny Wilson '52
The Screaming Skull '58
Stranger in Town '57
Daria Nicolodi
Beyond the Door 2 '79
Creepers '85
Deep Red: Hatchet Murders '75
Macaroni '85
Terror at the Opera '88
Unsane '82
Brigitte Nielsen
Beverly Hills Cop 2 '87
Bye Bye Baby '88
Chained Heat 2 '92
Cobra '86
Domino '88
The Double O Kid '92
Mission of Justice '92
Murder by Moonlight '91
Red Sonja '85
Rocky 4 '85
Hans Nielsen
The Monster of London City '64
Sherlock Holmes and the Deadly Necklace '62
Karen Nielsen
Assault of the Killer Bimbos '87
Cemetery High '89
Leslie Nielsen
Airplane! '80
All I Want for Christmas '91
The Amsterdam Kill '78
Blade in Hong Kong '85
City on Fire '78
Creepshow '82
Dangerous Curves '88
Day of the Animals '77
Dayton's Devils '68
Forbidden Planet '56
Four Rode Out '69
Foxfire Light '84
Harlow '65
Home is Where the Hart is '88
How to Commit Marriage '69

More! Police Squad '82
The Naked Gun: From the Files of Police Squad '88
Naked Gun 33 1/3: The Final Insult '94
Naked Gun 2 1/2: The Smell of Fear '91
Nightstick '87
Nuts '87
The Opposite Sex '56
The Patriot '86
Police Squad! Help Wanted! '82
Project: Kill! '77
Prom Night '80
Reckless Disregard '84
Repossessed '90
Resurrection of Zachary Wheeler '71
Riel '79
Snatched '72
Soul Man '86
Spaceship '81
Striker's Mountain '87
Surf Ninjas '93
Tammy and the Bachelor '57
Viva Knievel '77
Wrong is Right '82
Lisa Niemi
Steel Dawn '87
Super Force '90
Jane Nigh
Motor Patrol '50
Operation Haylift '50
Bill Nighy
Antonia and Jane '91
The Phantom of the Opera '89
Jan Niklas
Anastasia: The Mystery of Anna '86
Club Extinction '89
Colonel Redl '84
The Rose Garden '89
To the Camp & Back '85
Anna Q. Nilsson
Fighting Father Dunne '48
Grit of the Girl Telegrapher/In the Switch Tower '15
Riders of the Timberline '41
Toll Gate '20
Inger Nilsson
Pippi Goes on Board '75
Pippi in the South Seas '74
Pippi Longstocking '73
Maj-Britt Nilsson
Secrets of Women '52
Summer Interlude '50
Rob Nilsson
Heat and Sunlight '87
Northern Lights '79
Leonard Nimoy
Aladdin and His Wonderful Lamp '84
Baffled! '72
The Balcony '63
The Brain Eaters '58
Catlow '71
Invasion of the Body Snatchers '78
Never Forget '91
Seizure: The Story of Kathy Morris '82
Star Trek: The Motion Picture '80
Star Trek 2: The Wrath of Khan '82
Star Trek 3: The Search for Spock '84
Star Trek 4: The Voyage Home '86
Star Trek 5: The Final Frontier '89
Star Trek 6: The Undiscovered Country '91
Star Trek Bloopers '69
A Woman Called Golda '82
Zombies of the Stratosphere '52
Annabelle Ninchi
La Dolce Vita '60
Time Out for Love '61
Yvette Nipar
Doctor Mordrid: Master of the Unknown '92
Run If You Can '87
Ski Patrol '89

John Nishio
Dim Sum: A Little Bit of Heart '85
Overkill '86
Greta Nissen
Ambassador Bill '31
Melody Cruise '32
David Niven
Around the World in 80 Days '56
Ask Any Girl '59
Bachelor Mother '39
Barbary Coast '35
Bedtime Story '63
Beloved Enemy '36
Better Late Than Never '83
The Big Scam '79
Birds & the Bees '56
The Bishop's Wife '47
Bonjour Tristesse '57
Bonnie Prince Charlie '48
The Brain '69
Candleshoe '78
Carrington, V.C. '54
Casino Royale '67
The Charge of the Light Brigade '36
Curse of the Pink Panther '83
Dawn Patrol '38
Death on the Nile '78
Dinner at the Ritz '37
Dodsworth '36
The Elusive Pimpernel '50
Escape to Athena '79
Eternally Yours '39
55 Days at Peking '63
The Guns of Navarone '61
Happy Go Lovely '51
Immortal Battalion '44
The Impossible Years '68
King, Queen, Knave '72
The King's Thief '55
Lady L '65
The Lady Says No '51
Moon is Blue '53
Murder by Death '76
My Man Godfrey '57
No Deposit, No Return '76
Paper Tiger '74
The Perfect Marriage '46
The Pink Panther '64
Please Don't Eat the Daisies '60
Prisoner of Zenda '37
The Real Glory '39
Rose Marie '36
Rough Cut '80
Sea Wolves '81
Separate Tables '58
Spitfire '42
The Statue '71
The Toast of New Orleans '50
Trail of the Pink Panther '82
Wuthering Heights '39
Kip Niven
Magnum Force '73
New Year's Evil '78
Allan Nixon
Mesa of Lost Women '52
Prehistoric Women '50
Cynthia Nixon
Amadeus '84
Let It Ride '89
The Manhattan Project '86
Tanner '88 '88
Marion Nixon
Hands Up '26
The Reckless Way '36
Spangles '26
Tango '36
Mojo Nixon
Elvis Stories '89
Rock 'n' Roll High School Forever '91
Super Mario Bros. '93
James Noble
Chances Are '89
Dempsey '83
One Summer Love '76
Roboman '75
When the Bough Breaks '86
The Woman Who Willed a Miracle '83
Nancy Lee Noble
The Girl, the Body and the Pill '67

Just for the Hell of It '68
She-Devils on Wheels '68

Ray Noble
A Damsel in Distress '37
Here We Go Again! '42

Trisha Noble
Deadline '81
The Private Eyes '80

Magali Noel
Amarcord '74
The Eighties '83
Elena and Her Men '56
La Dolce Vita '60
Les Rendez-vous D'Anna '78

Noelia Noel
Night of the Bloody Apes '68
Sputnik '61

Natalija Nogulich
Hoffa '92
Homicide '91
Sister, Sister '87

Philippe Noiret
The Assassination Bureau '69
Birgitt Haas Must Be Killed '83
Cinema Paradiso '88
The Clockmaker '76
Coup de Torchon '81
The Family '87
The Holes '72
The Judge and the Assassin '75
Jupiter's Thigh '81
Justine '69
Lady L '65
Le Secret '74
Life and Nothing But '89
Murphy's War '71
My New Partner '84
Next Summer '84
Night Flight from Moscow '73
Night of the Generals '67
Old Gun '76
The Palermo Connection '91
The Purple Taxi '77
The Return of the Musketeers '89
Three Brothers '80
Topaz '69
Uranus '91
Who is Killing the Great Chefs of Europe? '78
Woman Times Seven '67
Zazie dans le Metro '61

Bob Nolan
Heart of the Golden West '42
Lights of Old Santa Fe '47
Song of Arizona '46
Sunset on the Desert '42

Doris Nolan
Follies Girl '43
Holiday '38

Jeanette Nolan
Babe! '75
Cloak & Dagger '84
Hangman's Knot '52
A Lawless Street '55
Macbeth '48
The Man Who Shot Liberty Valance '62
Seventh Cavalry '56
Street Justice '89
Tribute to a Bad Man '56

John Nolan
In the Steps of a Dead Man '74
The Terror '79

Lloyd Nolan
Abduction of St. Anne '75
Airport '70
Bataan '43
Circus World '64
Earthquake '74
Easy Living '49
Every Day's a Holiday '38
''G'' Men '35
Galyon '77
Girl Hunters '63
Guadalcanal Diary '43
Hannah and Her Sisters '86
House Across the Bay '40
Ice Station Zebra '68
It Came Upon a Midnight Clear '84
Johnny Apollo '40
Lady in the Lake '46
The Last Hunt '56

The Lemon Drop Kid '51
My Boys are Good Boys '78
Peyton Place '57
Prince Jack '83
Sergeant Ryker '68
The Street with No Name '48
The Sun Comes Up '49
A Tree Grows in Brooklyn '45

Tom Nolan
School Spirit '85
Voyage of the Rock Aliens '87

Nick Nolte
Another 48 Hrs. '90
Blue Chips '94
Cannery Row '82
Cape Fear '91
Death Sentence '74
The Deep '77
Down and Out in Beverly Hills '86
Everybody Wins '90
Extreme Prejudice '87
Farewell to the King '89
48 Hrs. '82
Grace Quigley '84
Heart Beat '80
I Love Trouble '94
I'll Do Anything '93
Lorenzo's Oil '92
New York Stories '89
North Dallas Forty '79
The Prince of Tides '91
Q & A '90
Return to Macon County '75
Rich Man, Poor Man '76
The Runaway Barge '75
Teachers '84
Three Fugitives '89
Under Fire '83
Weeds '87
Who'll Stop the Rain? '78

Tommy Noonan
Adam's Rib '50
The Ambassador's Daughter '56
Gentlemen Prefer Blondes '53
The Girl Most Likely '57
Jungle Patrol '48
Last Action Hero '93
The Man with One Red Shoe '85
Manhunter '86
The Monster Squad '87
Mystery Train '89
Promises! Promises! '63
Return of Jesse James '50
RoboCop 2 '90
A Star is Born '54
Three Nuts in Search of a Bolt '64
Wolfen '81

Ghita Norby
The Best Intentions '92
Memories of a Marriage '90
Sofie '92
The Wolf at the Door '87

Christine Norden
Mine Own Executioner '47
Night Beat '89

Zack Norman
America '86
Cadillac Man '90
Romancing the Stone '84
Sitting Ducks '80

Mabel Normand
Charlie Chaplin...Our Hero! '15
Charlie Chaplin's Keystone Comedies #1 '14
Charlie Chaplin's Keystone Comedies #2 '14
Charlie Chaplin's Keystone Comedies #3 '14
Charlie Chaplin's Keystone Comedies #4 '14
Early Cinema Vol. 1 '19
Extra Girl '23
Fatty and Mabel Adrift/Mabel, Fatty and the Law '16
Kid's Auto Race/Mabel's Married Life '15
The Knockout/Dough and Dynamite '14
Laughfest '10s
Mabel & Fatty '16
Mack Sennett Comedies: Vol. 2 '16
Mickey '17

Tillie's Punctured Romance '14
What Happened to Rosa? '21

Chuck Norris
Braddock: Missing in Action 3 '88
Breaker! Breaker! '77
Code of Silence '85
Delta Force '86
Delta Force 2: Operation Stranglehold '90
An Eye for an Eye '81
Firewalker '86
Force of One '79
Forced Vengeance '82
Game of Death '79
Good Guys Wear Black '78
Hero and the Terror '88
The Hitman '91
Invasion U.S.A. '85
Lone Wolf McQuade '83
Missing in Action '84
Missing in Action 2: The Beginning '85
Octagon '80
Return of the Dragon '73
Sidekicks '93
Silent Rage '82
Slaughter in San Francisco '81
The Student Teachers '73
Walker: Texas Ranger: One Riot, One Ranger '93
Warrior Within '80

Dean Norris
Hard to Kill '89
The Lawnmower Man '92

Edward Norris
Heartaches '47
The Lady in Question '40
The Man with Two Lives '42
Road Show '41
Show Them No Mercy '35
They Won't Forget '37
Wings Over the Pacific '43

Mike Norris
Born American '86
Death Ring '93
Delta Force 3: The Killing Game '91
Survival Game '87

Alan North
Billy Galvin '86
Crazy People '90
Highlander '86
Lean on Me '89
More! Police Squad '82
Police Squad! Help Wanted! '82
Rachel River '89

Heather North
The Barefoot Executive '71
Git! '65

Jay North
Maya '66
Scout's Honor '80
The Teacher '74
Zebra in the Kitchen '65

Noelle North
Slumber Party '57 '76
Sweater Girls '78

Sheree North
Breakout '75
Charley Varrick '73
Defenseless '91
Lawman '71
Legs '83
Maniac Cop '88
Marilyn: The Untold Story '80
Most Wanted '76
Only Once in a Lifetime '83
The Organization '71
Portrait of a Stripper '79
The Shootist '76
Snatched '72
Telefon '77
The Trouble with Girls (and How To Get Into It) '69

Ted North
Charlie Chan in Rio '41
The Devil Thumbs a Ride '47

Alex Norton
Comfort and Joy '84
Gregory's Girl '80
Hidden City '87
A Sense of Freedom '78

Barry Norton
Devil Monster '46

Dishonored '31
Dracula (Spanish Version) '31

Edgar Norton
Dr. Jekyll and Mr. Hyde '31
Son of Frankenstein '39

Jack Norton
The Bank Dick '40
Finishing School '33
Two Reelers: Comedy Classics 1 '33

Jim Norton
Hidden Agenda '90
Memoirs of an Invisible Man '92
Midnight's Child '93

Ken Norton
Drum '76
Kiss and Be Killed '91
Mandingo '75
Oceans of Fire '86

Richard Norton
China O'Brien '88
China O'Brien 2 '89
Crossfire '89
Deathfight '93
Equalizer 2000 '86
Gymkata '85
Ironheart '92
The Kick Fighter '91
Lady Dragon '92
Rage and Honor '92
Rage and Honor 2: Hostile Takeover '93
Raiders of the Sun '92

Judy Norton-Taylor
Children's Carol '80
A Day for Thanks on Walton's Mountain '82
The Waltons: A Thanksgiving Story '73

Terry Norton
American Kickboxer 1 '91
Emissary '89

Jack Noseworthy
Alive '93
S.F.W. '94

Christopher Noth
Baby Boom '87
Jakarta '88

Michael Nouri
Between Two Women '86
Black Ice '92
Danielle Steel's Changes '91
DaVinci's War '92
Flashdance '83
Gangster Wars '81
The Hidden '87
The Hidden 2 '94
Imagemaker '86
Little Vegas '90
No Escape, No Return '93
Project: Alien '89
Psychic '91
Rage of Angels: The Story Continues '86
Spraggue '84
Thieves of Fortune '89
Total Exposure '91

Eva Novak
Laughing at Danger '24
Red Signals '27
Sky High '22
Trailin' '21

Kim Novak
The Amorous Adventures of Moll Flanders '65
Bell, Book and Candle '58
Boy's Night Out '62
The Children '90
The Eddy Duchin Story '56
The French Line '54
Just a Gigolo '79
Kiss Me, Stupid! '64
Liebestraum '91
The Man with the Golden Arm '55
The Mirror Crack'd '80
Of Human Bondage '64
Pal Joey '57
Phffft! '54
Picnic '55
Strangers When We Meet '60
Tales That Witness Madness '73
Vertigo '58

The White Buffalo '77

Mel Novak
Cat in the Cage '68
Lovely...But Deadly '82

Ramon Novarro
Ben-Hur '26
Big Steal '49
The Cat and the Fiddle '34
Eyes of Turpin Are Upon You! '21
Heller in Pink Tights '60
Mata Hari '32
The Student Prince in Old Heidelberg '27

Don Novello
The Godfather, Part 3 '90
La Pastorela '92
New York Stories '89
Spirit of '76 '91
Tucker: The Man and His Dream '88

Ivor Novello
The Lodger '26
Phantom Fiend '35
The White Rose '23

Jay Novello
The Border Legion '40
Harum Scarum '65
Miracle of Our Lady of Fatima '52
The Prodigal '55
Robin Hood of the Pecos '41
Sabaka '55
What Did You Do in the War, Daddy? '66

Philomena Nowlin
Ebony Dreams '80
Miss Melody Jones '73

Zachi Noy
Hot Bubblegum '81
Private Manoeuvres '83
Young Love—Lemon Popsicle 7 '87

Bruce Nozick
Hit the Dutchman '92
Killer Instinct '92

Winston Ntshona
A Dry White Season '89
Night of the Cyclone '90

Danny Nucci
Book of Love '91
The Children of Times Square '86

Eddie Nugent
Doughnuts & Society '36
Kentucky Blue Streak '35
Night Nurse '31
Prison Shadows '36

Elliott Nugent
Romance '30
The Unholy Three '30

Bill Nunn
Canadian Bacon '94
Def by Temptation '90
Do the Right Thing '89
Mo' Better Blues '90
New Jack City '91
Regarding Henry '91
Save Me '93
School Daze '88
Sister Act '92
White Lie '91

Teri Nunn
Follow That Car '80
Thank God It's Friday '78

Rudolf Nureyev
Exposed '83
Valentino '77

Loredana Nusciak
Django '68
Gladiators 7 '62

Mike Nussbaum
House of Games '87
Things Change '88

Mayf Nutter
The $5.20 an Hour Dream '80
Hunter's Blood '87

France Nuyen
Black Water Gold '69
China Cry '91
Code Name: Diamond Head '77
Diamond Head '62

Nuyen ▶cont.

The Joy Luck Club '93
Return to Fantasy Island '77
South Pacific '58

N!xau
The Gods Must Be Crazy '84
The Gods Must Be Crazy 2 '89

Carrie Nye
Creepshow '82
The Group '66
Hello Again '87

Carroll Nye
Gone with the Wind '39
Lottery Bride '30

Louis Nye
The Charge of the Model T's '76
Harper Valley P.T.A. '78
O.C. and Stiggs '87
The Wheeler Dealers '63

Lena Nyman
The Adventures of Picasso '80
Autumn Sonata '78
I Am Curious (Yellow) '67

Jack Oakie
The Affairs of Annabel '38
Annabel Takes a Tour/Maid's Night Out '38
The Great American Broadcast '41
The Great Dictator '40
Hello, Frisco, Hello '43
Iceland '42
Little Men '40
Lover Come Back '61
Murder at the Vanities '34
The Rat Race '60
Song of the Islands '42
That Girl from Paris '36
Tin Pan Alley '40
Toast of New York '37
Uptown New York '32
Wintertime '43

Simon Oakland
Bullitt '68
Chato's Land '71
Follow That Dream '61
I Want to Live! '58
The Night Stalker: Two Tales of Terror '74
On a Clear Day You Can See Forever '70
Psycho '60
The Rise and Fall of Legs Diamond '60
The Sand Pebbles '66
Tony Rome '67
West Side Story '61

Wheeler Oakman
Aces and Eights '36
The Broken Mask '28
Death from a Distance '36
Frontier Days '34
Ghost Patrol '36
In Old Santa Fe '34
The Lost Jungle '34
The Man from Gun Town '36
Man of Action '33
Meet the Mob '42
Outside the Law '21
Peck's Bad Boy '21
The Riding Tornado '32
Roaring Guns '36
Roaring Ranch '30
Slaves in Bondage '37
Song of the Trail '36
The Spoilers '14
Teenage '44
Texas Cyclone '32
Two-Fisted Law '32
Wolf Call '39

Simon Oates
Doomwatch '72
Terrornauts '67
The Terrornauts '67

Warren Oates
And Baby Makes Six '79
Badlands '74
The Blue and the Gray '85
Blue Thunder '83
The Border '82
Bring Me the Head of Alfredo Garcia '74

Brink's Job '78
Cockfighter '74
Crooks & Coronets '69
Dillinger '73
Dixie Dynamite '76
Drum '76
East of Eden '80
Gunfire '78
Hired Hand '71
In the Heat of the Night '67
My Old Man '79
1941 '79
92 in the Shade '76
Prime Time '80
Race with the Devil '75
Return of the Seven '66
Ride the High Country '62
The Shooting '66
Sleeping Dogs '82
Stripes '81
There was a Crooked Man '70
The Thief Who Came to Dinner '73
Tom Sawyer '73
Tough Enough '83
The White Dawn '75
The Wild Bunch '69

Philip Ober
Come Back, Little Sheba '52
Escapade in Japan '57
From Here to Eternity '53
The Magnificent Yankee '50
The Mating Game '59
Never a Dull Moment '50
North by Northwest '59

Merle Oberon
Beloved Enemy '36
Berlin Express '48
Broken Melody '34
The Cowboy and the Lady '38
Dark Waters '44
Deep in My Heart '54
Desiree '54
The Divorce of Lady X '38
Epic That Never Was '65
Forever and a Day '43
Hotel '67
Interval '73
The Lion Has Wings '40
The Lodger '44
Lydia '41
The Oscar '66
Private Life of Don Juan '34
The Private Life of Henry VIII '33
The Scarlet Pimpernel '34
A Song to Remember '45
Stage Door Canteen '43
That Uncertain Feeling '41
These Three '36
Wedding Rehearsal '32
Wuthering Heights '39

Anna Obregon
Bolero '84
Car Crash
Treasure of the Four Crowns '82

Rodrigo Obregon
Enemy Gold '93
Fit to Kill '94
Hard Hunted '92
L.A. Wars '94
Savage Beach '89
Tides of War '90

Hugh O'Brian
Africa Texas Style '67
Broken Lance '54
Cruise into Terror '78
Doin' Time on Planet Earth '88
Fantasy Island '76
The Gambler Returns: The Luck of the Draw '93
In Harm's Way '65
Killer Force '75
Little Big Horn '51
Love has Many Faces '65
Man from the Alamo '53
Murder on Flight 502 '75
Probe '72
Return of Jesse James '50
Rocketship X-M '50
The Seekers '79
The Shootist '76
Son of Ali Baba '52
There's No Business Like Show Business '54
Twins '88
Vengeance Valley '51

Wild Women '70

Austin O'Brien
Last Action Hero '93
My Girl 2 '94
Prehysteria '93

Dave O'Brien
The Black Coin '36
Boss of Rawhide '44
Bowery at Midnight '42
Buzzy Rides the Range '40
Camp Double Feature '39
Danger Ahead '40
Daughter of the Tong '39
Dead or Alive '41
The Devil Bat '41
Enemy of the Law '45
Fighting Valley '43
Frontier Fugitives '45
Gangsters of the Frontier '44
Guns of the Law '44
King of the Stallions '42
Law of the Texan '38
Lightning Bill Crandall '37
Lion's Den '36
Marked for Murder '45
Murder on the Yukon '40
The Phantom of 42nd Street '45
Rangers Take Over '43
Reefer Madness '38
Sky Bandits '40
Spooks Run Wild '41
That Gang of Mine '40
Three in the Saddle '45
Water Rustlers '39
Yukon Flight '40

Donald O'Brien
Doctor Butcher M.D. '80
Quest for the Mighty Sword '90
Trap Them & Kill Them '84

Edmond O'Brien
The Admiral Was a Lady '50
The Barefoot Contessa '54
The Bigamist '53
Birdman of Alcatraz '62
D-Day, the Sixth of June '56
The Denver & Rio Grande '51
D.O.A. '49
The Doomsday Flight '66
A Double Life '47
Dream No Evil '75
Fantastic Voyage '66
A Girl, a Guy and a Gob '41
The Girl Can't Help It '56
The Great Impostor '61
The Hitch-Hiker '53
The Hunchback of Notre Dame '39
Jigsaw '71
Julius Caesar '53
The Last Voyage '60
The Longest Day '62
Lucky Luciano '74
The Man Who Shot Liberty Valance '62
Moon Pilot '62
99 & 44/100 Dead '74
Pete Kelly's Blues '55
Rio Conchos '64
Seven Days in May '64
Stopover Tokyo '57
They Only Kill Their Masters '72
Up Periscope '59
White Heat '49
The Wild Bunch '69

George O'Brien
Bullet Code '40
Cheyenne Autumn '64
Cowboy Millionaire '35
Daniel Boone '34
Don Amigo/Stage to Chino '40s
Dude Ranger '34
Gold Raiders '51
Legion of the Lawless '40
The Lone Star Ranger '39
Mystery Ranch '34
Painted Desert '31
Racketeers of the Range '39
Renegade Ranger/Scarlet River '38
She Wore a Yellow Ribbon '49
Sunrise '27
Thunder Mountain '35
Windjammer '31

Joan O'Brien
It Happened at the World's Fair '63
Operation Petticoat '59
Samar '62

Margaret O'Brien
Amy '81
The Canterville Ghost '44
Glory '56
Heller in Pink Tights '60
Jane Eyre '44
Journey for Margaret '42
Little Women '49
Meet Me in St. Louis '44
Our Vines Have Tender Grapes '45
The Secret Garden '49
Thousands Cheer '43

Maria O'Brien
In a Stranger's Hand '92
Promised a Miracle '88

Pat O'Brien
Airborne '93
Angels with Dirty Faces '38
Bombardier '43
Bombshell '33
Boy Meets Girl '38
The Boy with the Green Hair '48
Bureau of Missing Persons '33
Ceiling Zero '35
Consolation Marriage '31
Crack-Up '46
Devil Dogs of the Air '35
The Devil Thumbs a Ride/Having Wonderful Crime '47
Doomed Caravan '41
The End '78
Fighting Father Dunne '48
The Fighting 69th '40
Flirtation Walk '34
The Front Page '31
Having Wonderful Crime '45
Hawaiian Buckaroo '38
Hell's House '32
The Iron Major '43
Jubilee Trail '54
Knute Rockne: All American '40
Last Hurrah '58
Marine Raiders '43
The Navy Comes Through '42
Ragtime '81
Riff-Raff '36
Scout's Honor '80
Slightly Honorable '40
Some Like It Hot '59
Tim Tyler's Luck '37
The World Gone Mad '33

Peter O'Brien
Angel of Fury '93
The Grand Duel '73
A Kink in the Picasso '90

Richard O'Brien
Robin Hood...The Legend: The Time of the Wolf '85
The Rocky Horror Picture Show '75
Shock Treatment '81

Tom O'Brien
The Accused '88
The Big Easy '87
The Big Parade '25
The Phantom '31

Virginia O'Brien
Big Store '41
DuBarry Was a Lady '43
The Harvey Girls '46
Lady Be Good '41
Merton of the Movies '47
Panama Hattie '42
Ship Ahoy '42
The Show-Off '46
Thousands Cheer '43
Till the Clouds Roll By '46
Till the Clouds Roll By/A Star Is Born '44
Two Girls and a Sailor '44

Jeffrey Obrow
The Kindred '87
The Power '80

Pat O'Bryan
976-EVIL '88
976-EVIL 2: The Astral Factor '91
Relentless '89

Andrea Occhipinti
A Blade in the Dark '83
Bolero '84
Conquest '83
Control '87
El Barbaro '84
The Family '87
Running Away '89

Manuel Lopez Ochoa
Crossfire '67
El Tesoro de Chucho el Roto '47
Los Tres Calaveras '64

Uwe Ochsenknecht
Fire, Ice and Dynamite '91
Men... '85

Arthur O'Connell
Anatomy of a Murder '59
Ben '72
Blondie's Blessed Event '42
Bus Stop '56
Cimarron '60
Citizen Kane '41
Fantastic Voyage '66
Follow That Dream '61
Gidget '59
The Great Impostor '61
The Hiding Place '75
Huckleberry Finn '74
Kissin' Cousins '64
The Last Valley '71
Law of the Jungle '42
The Man in the Gray Flannel Suit '56
Man of the West '58
Misty '61
Monkey's Uncle '65
Open Secret '48
Operation Petticoat '59
Picnic '55
Pocketful of Miracles '61
Seven Faces of Dr. Lao '63
There was a Crooked Man '70
They Only Kill Their Masters '72

Deidre O'Connell
Cool World '92
Falling from Grace '92
Fearless '93
Pastime '91
Straight Talk '92

Jerry O'Connell
Calendar Girl '93
Ollie Hopnoodle's Haven of Bliss '88
Stand By Me '86

Carroll O'Connor
Brass '85
Cleopatra '63
Convicted '86
Death of a Gunfighter '69
The Devil's Brigade '68
Doctors' Wives '70
The Father Clements Story '87
For Love of Ivy '68
Hawaii '66
In Harm's Way '65
Johnny Frenchman '46
Kelly's Heroes '70
Law and Disorder '74
Lonely are the Brave '62
Marlowe '69
Parrish '61
Point Blank '67
Waterhole #3 '67
What Did You Do in the War, Daddy? '66

Derrick O'Connor
Dealers '89
Hope and Glory '87
Lethal Weapon 2 '89

Donald O'Connor
Beau Geste '39
Francis Goes to the Races '51
Francis in the Navy '55
Francis Joins the WACs '54
Francis the Talking Mule '49
I Love Melvin '53
Pandemonium '82
Private Buckaroo '42
Ragtime '81
Singin' in the Rain '52
There's No Business Like Show Business '54
A Time to Remember '90
The Wonders of Aladdin '61

Glynnis O'Connor
The Boy in the Plastic Bubble '76
California Dreaming '79
A Conspiracy of Love '87
The Dark Side of Love '79
The Deliberate Stranger '86
Johnny Dangerously '84
Kid Vengeance '75
Melanie '82
Night Crossing '81
Ode to Billy Joe '76
Our Town '77
Someone I Touched '75
Those Lips, Those Eyes '80
To Heal a Nation '88

Kevin J. O'Connor
Bogie: The Last Hero '80
The Caine Mutiny Court Martial '88
Canadian Bacon '94
Candy Mountain '87
Color of Night '94
Equinox '93
Hero '92
Let's Scare Jessica to Death '71
Love at Large '89
The Moderns '88
No Escape '94
Peggy Sue Got Married '86
Signs of Life '89
Steel Magnolias '89

Tim O'Connor
Across 110th Street '72
The Groundstar Conspiracy '72
Manhunter '74
Naked Gun 2 1/2: The Smell of Fear '91

Una O'Connor
The Adventures of Robin Hood '38
The Barretts of Wimpole Street '34
The Bride of Frankenstein '35
The Canterville Ghost '44
Cavalcade '33
Chained '34
Christmas in Connecticut '45
David Copperfield '35
Fighting Father Dunne '48
Hopalong Cassidy: Unexpected Guest '47
The Informer '35
The Invisible Man '33
Personal Property '37
The Sea Hawk '40
Strawberry Blonde '41
This Land is Mine '43
Witness for the Prosecution '57

Hugh O'Conor
Da '88
My Left Foot '89

Nell O'Day
Bury Me Not On the Lone Prairie '41
Man from Montana '41
The Masked Rider '41
Pony Post '40

Denis O'Dea
Captain Horatio Hornblower '51
The Long Dark Hall '51
Treasure Island '50
Under Capricorn '49

Georgia O'Dell
Big Calibre '35
Cannon Ball/Eyes Have It '15

Christophe Odent
First Name: Carmen '83
Nouvelle Vague '90

Cathy O'Donnell
The Amazing Mr. X '48
Ben-Hur '59
Detective Story '51
The Love of Three Queens '54
The Man from Laramie '55
The Miniver Story '50
Terror in the Haunted House '58
They Live by Night '49

Chris O'Donnell
Fried Green Tomatoes '91
Men Don't Leave '89
Scent of a Woman '92
School Ties '92

Rosie O'Donnell
Another Stakeout '93
Car 54, Where Are You? '94
The Flintstones '94
A League of Their Own '92
Sleepless in Seattle '93

Michael O'Donoghue
Mr. Mike's Mondo Video '79
The Suicide Club '88

Martha O'Driscoll
Criminal Court '46
The Fallen Sparrow '43
Here Come the Co-Eds '45
House of Dracula '45
Reap the Wild Wind '42
Young & Willing '42

Bernadette O'Farrell
The Happiest Days of Your Life '50
Robin Hood: The Movie '55
Scotland Yard Inspector '52

Damian O'Flynn
Crack-Up '46
Daniel Boone: Trail Blazer '56
The Devil on Wheels '47
X Marks the Spot '42

Ken Ogata
The Ballad of Narayama '83
Eijanaika '81
Mishima: A Life in Four Chapters '85
Vengeance Is Mine '79
Virus '82

Mayumi Ogawa
The Go-Masters '82
Zatoichi: The Blind Swordsman's Vengeance '66

Bulle Ogier
Candy Mountain '87
The Discreet Charm of the Bourgeoisie '72
Tricheurs '84

Ian Ogilvy
And Now the Screaming Starts '73
Anna Karenina '85
The Conqueror Worm '68
Death Becomes Her '92
From Beyond the Grave '73
Invasion of Privacy '92
The Invincible Six '68
The She-Beast '65
Wuthering Heights '70

Gail O'Grady
Blackout '88
Nobody's Perfect '90
Spellcaster '91

Soon-Teck Oh
East of Eden '80
A Home of Our Own '93
The Man with the Golden Gun '74
Missing in Action 2: The Beginning '85

Jack O'Halloran
The Baltimore Bullet '80
Farewell, My Lovely '75
Hero and the Terror '88
King Kong '76
Superman: The Movie '78
Superman 2 '80

Claudia Ohana
Erendira '83
The Fable of the Beautiful Pigeon Fancier '88
Luzia '88
Opera do Malandro '87
Priceless Beauty '90

George O'Hanlon, Jr.
Our Time '74
Where Have All the People Gone? '74

Catherine O'Hara
After Hours '85
Beetlejuice '88
The Best of John Candy on SCTV '80s
Betsy's Wedding '90
Dick Tracy '90
Heartburn '86

Home Alone '90
Home Alone 2: Lost in New York '92
The Last Polka '84
Little Vegas '90
Nothing Personal '80
The Paper '94
Really Weird Tales '86
A Simple Twist of Fate '94
There Goes the Neighborhood '92
Wyatt Earp '94

David O'Hara
Maria's Child '93
WarCat '88

Jenny O'Hara
Angie '94
Career Opportunities '91
Last Song '80

Maureen O'Hara
Against All Flags '52
At Sword's Point '51
Big Jake '71
Buffalo Bill '44
Dance, Girl, Dance '40
Deadly Companions '61
The Fallen Sparrow '43
How Green was My Valley '41
The Hunchback of Notre Dame '39
Immortal Sergeant '43
Jamaica Inn '39
Lisbon '56
The Long Gray Line '55
The Magnificent Matador '55
McLintock! '63
Miracle on 34th Street '47
Mr. Hobbs Takes a Vacation '62
Only the Lonely '91
The Parent Trap '61
The Quiet Man '52
The Rare Breed '66
The Red Pony '76
Rio Grande '50
Sinbad the Sailor '47
The Spanish Main '45
Spencer's Mountain '63
This Land is Mine '43
To the Shores of Tripoli '42
Wings of Eagles '57
A Woman's Secret '49

Dan O'Herlihy
Actors and Sin '52
At Sword's Point '51
The Dead '87
Death Ray 2000 '81
Fail-Safe '64
Halloween 3: Season of the Witch '82
The King of the Roaring '20s: The Story of Arnold Rothstein '61
The Last Starfighter '84
Love, Cheat & Steal '94
MacArthur '77
Macbeth '48
Nancy Astor '82
No Comebacks '85
Odd Man Out '47
The People '71
RoboCop '87
RoboCop 2 '90
Sword of Venus '53
The Tamarind Seed '74
Two by Forsyth '86
The Virgin Queen '55
A Waltz Through the Hills '88
Waterloo '71

Gavan O'Herlihy
Space Riders '83
Tailspin: Behind the Korean Airline Tragedy '89
Willow '88

Carol Ohmart
House on Haunted Hill '58
Naked Youth '59
One Man's Way '63
Spider Baby '64

Eiji Okada
Hiroshima, Mon Amour '59
Mother '52
She and He '63
The Ugly American '63
Woman in the Dunes '64
X from Outer Space '67

Dennis O'Keefe
Abroad with Two Yanks '44
Brewster's Millions '45
Broadway Limited '41
Cimarron '31
Dishonored Lady '47
Doll Face '45
Fighting Seabees '44
Great Dan Patch '49
Hi Diddle Diddle '43
Lady Scarface '41
Lady Scarface/The Threat '49
The Leopard Man '43
Libeled Lady '36
The Naked Flame '68
Pop Always Pays '40
Sensations of 1945 '44
T-Men '47
Topper Returns '41
Unforgotten Crime '41
You'll Find Out '40

Michael O'Keefe
Bridge to Silence '89
Caddyshack '80
The Dark Secret of Harvest Home '78
Disaster at Silo 7 '88
Fear '90
Finders Keepers '84
Gray Lady Down '77
The Great Santini '80
Hitchhiker 4 '87
Ironweed '87
Me & Veronica '93
Nate and Hayes '83
Out of the Rain '90
A Rumor of War '80
The Slugger's Wife '85
Split Image '82
The Whoopee Boys '86

Miles O'Keeffe
Ator the Fighting Eagle '83
Blade Master '84
Campus Man '87
Cartel '90
The Colombian Connection '91
The Drifter '88
Iron Warrior '87
King's Ransom '91
Liberty & Bash '90
The Lone Runner '88
Relentless 2: Dead On '91
S.A.S. San Salvador '84
Shoot '92
Sword of the Valiant '83
Tarzan, the Ape Man '81
Waxwork '88

Don O'Kelly
Frontier Uprising '61
The Hostage '67

Tim O'Kelly
The Passing of Evil '70
Targets '69

Yuji Okumoto
Aloha Summer '88
Bloodfist 5: Human Target '93
The Karate Kid: Part 2 '86
Nemesis '93
Robot Wars '93
True Believer '89

Warner Oland
Charlie Chan at the Opera '36
Charlie Chan in Paris '35
Charlie Chan's Secret '35
Daughter of the Dragon '31
Dishonored '31
Don Juan '26
Drums of Jeopardy '31
The Fighting American '24
The Jazz Singer '27
The Painted Veil '34
Riders of the Purple Sage '25
Shanghai Express '32
Stand and Deliver '28
Werewolf of London '35

Ken Olandt
April Fool's Day '86
Leprechaun '93
Super Force '90

Daniel Olbrychski
Colonel Wolodyjowski '69
La Truite '83
Land of Promise '74
Maids of Wilko '79
Rosa Luxemburg '86
The Structure of Crystals '69

The Tin Drum '79
The Unbearable Lightness of Being '88

Eric Oldfield
Air Hawk '84
Gone to Ground '76
Island Trader '71
Stones of Death '88

William Oldham
Matewan '87
Thousand Pieces of Gold '91

Gary Oldman
Bram Stoker's Dracula '92
Chattahoochee '89
Criminal Law '89
Fallen Angels 2 '93
JFK '91
Prick Up Your Ears '87
Romeo Is Bleeding '93
Rosencrantz & Guildenstern Are Dead '90
Sid & Nancy '86
State of Grace '90
Track 29 '88
True Romance '93
We Think the World of You '88

Sven Ole-Thorsen
Abraxas: Guardian of the Universe '90
Dragon: The Bruce Lee Story '93

William O'Leary
Flight of Black Angel '91
Hot Shots! '91
In the Line of Duty: Ambush in Waco '93
Nice Girls Don't Explode '87

Ken Olin
The Game of Love '90
Queens Logic '91

Lena Olin
After the Rehearsal '84
Enemies, a Love Story '89
Havana '90
Mr. Jones '93
Romeo Is Bleeding '93
The Unbearable Lightness of Being '88

Barret Oliver
Cocoon '85
Cocoon: The Return '88
D.A.R.Y.L. '85
Frankenweenie '84
The NeverEnding Story '84
The Secret Garden '87

Charles Oliver
The Avenging Hand '43
Midnight at the Wax Museum '36

David Oliver
Defense Play '88
Postal Inspector '36

Edna May Oliver
Ann Vickers '33
Cimarron '30
David Copperfield '35
Drums Along the Mohawk '39
Half-Shot at Sunrise '30
Hold 'Em Jail '32
Little Miss Broadway '38
Little Women '33
Lucky Devil '25
Nurse Edith Cavell '39
Pride and Prejudice '40
Romeo and Juliet '36
Rosalie '38
Second Fiddle '39
The Story of Vernon and Irene Castle '39
A Tale of Two Cities '35

Gordon Oliver
Blondie '38
Follies Girl '43
Seven Days Ashore/Hurry, Charlie, Hurry '44
The Spiral Staircase '46
Youth on Parole '37

Michael Oliver
Problem Child '90
Problem Child 2 '91

Rochelle Oliver
Courtship '87
1918 '85
On Valentine's Day '86

Oliver ►cont.

Scent of a Woman '92
An Unremarkable Life '89

Stephen Oliver
Angels from Hell '68
Cycle Psycho
Motor Psycho '65
Savage Abduction '73
Werewolves on Wheels '71

Susan Oliver
Butterfield 8 '60
Disorderly Orderly '64
The Gene Krupa Story '59
Ginger in the Morning '73
Guns of Diablo '64
Hardly Working '81
Tomorrow's Child '82
Widow's Nest '77

Robert Oliveri
Edward Scissorhands '90
Honey, I Blew Up the Kid '92
Honey, I Shrunk the Kids '89

Ramiro Oliveros
Esposa y Amante '70s
Hundra '85

Laurence Olivier
As You Like It '36
Battle of Britain '69
The Betsy '78
The Bounty '84
The Boys from Brazil '78
Brideshead Revisited '81
A Bridge Too Far '77
Carrie '52
Clash of the Titans '81
Clouds Over Europe '39
David Copperfield '70
The Demi-Paradise '43
The Devil's Disciple '59
The Divorce of Lady X '38
Dracula '79
Ebony Tower '86
The Entertainer '60
Fire Over England '37
The Forty-Ninth Parallel '41
Hamlet '48
Henry V '44
I Stand Condemned '36
The Jazz Singer '80
Jesus of Nazareth '77
The Jigsaw Man '84
Khartoum '66
Lady Caroline Lamb '73
A Little Romance '79
Love Among the Ruins '75
The Making of a Legend:
    "Gone With the Wind" '89
Marathon Man '76
The Merchant of Venice '73
Mister Halpren & Mister
    Johnson '83
Nicholas and Alexandra '71
Peter the Great '86
Pride and Prejudice '40
The Prince and the Showgirl
    '57
Rebecca '40
Richard III '55
The Seven Percent Solution '76
The Shoes of the Fisherman
    '68
Sleuth '72
Spartacus '60
That Hamilton Woman '41
21 Days '37
A Voyage' Round My Father
    '89
Wagner: The Complete Epic '85
Wagner: The Movie '85
Wild Geese 2 '85
Wuthering Heights '39

Paul Olivier
A Nous la Liberte '31
Le Million '31

Silvio Oliviero
Graveyard Shift '87
Psycho Girls '86
Understudy: The Graveyard
    Shift 2 '88
A Whisper to a Scream '88

Walter Olkewicz
Can I Do It...Till I Need
    Glasses? '77
The Client '94

Alberto Olmedo
Departamento Compartido '85
Expertos en Pinchazos '79
Naked Is Better '73

Edward James Olmos
Aloha, Bobby and Rose '74
American Me '92
Ballad of Gregorio Cortez '83
Blade Runner '82
Miami Vice 2: The Prodigal Son
    '85
Saving Grace '86
Stand and Deliver '88
Talent for the Game '91
Triumph of the Spirit '89
Virus '82
Wolfen '81
Zoot Suit '81

Gertrude Olmsted
California Straight Ahead '25
The Cheerful Fraud '27
Cobra '25
The Monster '25
Sweet Adeline '26

Gerald S. O'Loughlin
The Crash of Flight 401 '78
Desperate Characters '71
Ensign Pulver '64
A Matter of Life and Death '81
Pleasure Palace '80
Quicksilver '86

Larry Olsen
Curley '47
Who Killed Doc Robbin' '48

Merlin Olsen
The Juggler of Notre Dame '84
Mitchell '75
The Undefeated '69

Moroni Olsen
Ali Baba and the Forty Thieves
    '43
Allegheny Uprising '39
Buffalo Bill '44
Call Northside 777 '48
Father of the Bride '50
Father's Little Dividend '51
The Glass Key '42
Mary of Scotland '36
Notorious '46
The Possessed '47
Reunion in France '42
Rose of Washington Square
    '39
Susannah of the Mounties '39
Task Force '49
The Three Musketeers '35
Yellow Dust '36

Ole Olsen
All Over Town '37
Country Gentlemen '36

James Olson
Amityville 2: The Possession
    '82
The Andromeda Strain '71
Commando '85
The Groundstar Conspiracy '72
My Sister, My Love '78
Paper Man '71
Rachel, Rachel '68
Rachel River '89
Ragtime '81
Someone I Touched '75
The Spell '77
Strange New World '75

Nancy Olson
The Absent-Minded Professor
    '61
Big Jim McLain '52
Making Love '82
Mr. Music '50
Pollyanna '60
Snowball Express '72
Son of Flubber '63
Sunset Boulevard '50
Union Station '50

J. Pat O'Malley
Courage of Black Beauty '57
Lassie, Come Home '43
A Small Killing '81
Star! '68

Pat O'Malley
Evelyn Prentice '34
The Fighting American '24
Fighting Marines '36
The Fighting Marshal '32

The Miracle Rider '35
The Perils of Pauline '34
Spangles '26
Stunt Pilot '39
The Virginian '23

Kate O'Mara
The Horror of Frankenstein '70
Nativity '78
The Vampire Lovers '70
Whose Child Am I? '75

Mollie O'Mara
Escape from Safehaven '88
Girls School Screamers '86

Judd Omen
Dollman '91
Pee Wee's Big Adventure '85

Anny Ondra
Blackmail '29
The Manxman '29

Griffin O'Neal
April Fool's Day '86
The Children of Times Square
    '86
The Escape Artist '82
Ghoulies 3: Ghoulies Go to
    College '91
Hadley's Rebellion '84
Night Children '89
The Wraith '87

Patrick O'Neal
Alice '90
Alvarez Kelly '66
The Defense Never Rests '90
El Condor '70
A Fine Madness '66
For the Boys '91
From the Terrace '60
In Harm's Way '65
Independence '76
King Rat '65
Make Me an Offer '80
New York Stories '89
Perry Mason Returns '85
Q & A '90
Secret Life of an American Wife
    '68
Silent Night, Bloody Night '73
Spraggue '84
Stiletto '69
Under Siege '92
The Way We Were '73
Where Were You When the
    Lights Went Out? '68

Ron O'Neal
As Summers Die '86
Freedom Road '79
Hero and the Terror '88
The Hitter '79
Mercenary Fighters '88
Red Dawn '84
St. Helen's, Killer Volcano '82
Sophisticated Gents '81
Superfly '72
Superfly T.N.T. '73
Up Against the Wall '91

Ryan O'Neal
Barry Lyndon '75
A Bridge Too Far '77
Chances Are '89
The Driver '78
Fever Pitch '85
Green Ice '81
Irreconcilable Differences '84
Love Story '70
The Main Event '79
The Man Upstairs '93
Oliver's Story '78
Paper Moon '73
Partners '82
Small Sacrifices '89
So Fine '81
The Thief Who Came to Dinner
    '73
Tough Guys Don't Dance '87
What's Up, Doc? '72
Wild Rovers '71

Tatum O'Neal
The Bad News Bears '76
Certain Fury '85
Circle of Two '80
Goldilocks & the Three Bears
    '83
International Velvet '78
Little Darlings '80
Little Noises '91
Paper Moon '73

Barbara O'Neil
All This and Heaven Too '40
Flame of the Islands '55
Gone with the Wind '39
I Am the Law '38
I Remember Mama '48
Secret Beyond the Door '48
The Tower of London '39

Sally O'Neil
Battling Butler '26
Sixteen Fathoms Deep '34

Angela O'Neill
Enemy Unseen '91
River of Diamonds '90
Sorority House Massacre '86

Chris O'Neill
Backbeat '94
James Joyce's Women '85

Dick O'Neill
Dark Justice '91
Gamera, the Invincible '66
Hail '73
The Mosquito Coast '86
Pretty Poison '68
She's Out of Control '89
The Taking of Pelham One Two
    Three '74

Ed O'Neill
The Adventures of Ford
    Fairlane '90
Blue Chips '94
The Day the Women Got Even
    '80
Deliverance '72
Disorganized Crime '89
Dutch '91
It's a Bundyful Life '92
K-9 '89
Sibling Rivalry '90
Wayne's World '92
Wayne's World 2 '93
When Your Lover Leaves '83

Henry O'Neill
Air Raid Wardens '43
Billy the Kid '41
Black Fury '35
The Fighting 69th '40
Holiday Affair '49
Honky Tonk '41
Johnny Eager '42
Lady Killer '33
Men of Boys Town '41
Nothing But Trouble '44
Shadow of the Thin Man '41
Whistling in Brooklyn '43
White Cargo '42

Jennifer O'Neill
Chase '85
Cloud Dancer '80
Committed '91
The Cover Girl Murders '93
Discretion Assured '93
Force of One '79
Full Exposure: The Sex Tape
    Scandals '89
I Love N.Y. '87
The Innocent '76
Invasion of Privacy '92
Lady Ice '73
Love's Savage Fury '79
Perfect Family '92
Personals '90
The Psychic '78
The Reincarnation of Peter
    Proud '75
Rio Lobo '70
Scanners '81
Steel '80
Summer of '42 '71
Whiffs '75

Maire O'Neill
Great Day '46
Juno and the Paycock '30

Michael O'Neill
Gore-Met Zombie Chef From
    Hell '87
The Gun in Betty Lou's
    Handbag '92

Nance O'Neill
Cimarron '31
The Royal Bed '31

Remy O'Neill
Hollywood Hot Tubs 2:
    Educating Crystal '89
To Die for 2 '91

Yoko Ono
Let It Be '70
The Magic Christian '69

Peter Onorati
Camp Nowhere '94
Fire Birds '90

Michael Ontkean
The Allnighter '87
The Blood of Others '84
Bye Bye Blues '89
Clara's Heart '88
Cold Front '89
Girls on the Road '73
Just the Way You Are '84
Legacy of Lies '92
Maid to Order '87
Making Love '82
Peacekillers '71
Postcards from the Edge '90
Slap Shot '77
Street Justice '89
Twin Peaks '90
Where the Eagle Flies '72
Willie & Phil '80
The Witching '72

David Opatoshu
Conspiracy of Terror '75
Exodus '60
The Fixer '68
Forty Days of Musa Dagh '85
The Light Ahead '39
Romance of a Horsethief '71
Torn Curtain '66
Who'll Stop the Rain? '78

Alan Oppenheimer
The Bionic Woman '75
Child of Darkness, Child of
    Light '93
The Groundstar Conspiracy '72
Invisible: The Chronicles of
    Benjamin Knight '93
A Pleasure Doing Business '79
Star! '68
Trancers 4: Jack of Swords '93

Don Opper
Android '82
Critters 2: The Main Course '88
Critters 3 '91
Critters 4 '91
The Forgotten '89

Terry O'Quinn
Amityville: A New Generation
    '93
Black Widow '87
Blind Fury '90
Company Business '91
The Cutting Edge '92
The Forgotten One '89
The Good Fight '92
Heaven's Gate '81
Lipstick Camera '93
Mahler '74
Mischief '85
Mrs. Soffel '84
My Samurai '92
Pin '88
Places in the Heart '84
Prisoners of the Sun '91
The Rocketeer '91
Roe vs. Wade '89
Son of the Morning Star '91
SpaceCamp '86
The Stepfather '87
Stepfather 2: Make Room for
    Daddy '89
Tombstone '93
When the Time Comes '91
Wildcard '92
Women of Valor '86
Young Guns '88

Jerry Orbach
Brewster's Millions '85
Broadway Bound '92
California Casanova '89
Crimes & Misdemeanors '89
Dead Women in Lingerie '90
Delirious '91
Delusion '91
Dirty Dancing '87
F/X '86
Foreplay '75
I Love N.Y. '87
Imagemaker '86
Last Exit to Brooklyn '90
Mr. Saturday Night '92
Out for Justice '91
Out on a Limb '87

Prince of the City '81
Someone to Watch Over Me '87
Straight Talk '92
24 Hours in a Woman's Life '61
Underground Aces '80
Universal Soldier '92

Roy Orbison
Chuck Berry: Hail! Hail! Rock 'n' Roll '87
Fastest Guitar Alive '68
Roadie '80

Cyril O'Reilly
The Cool Surface '92
Dance of the Damned '88
Navy SEALS '90
On Wings of Eagles '86
Philadelphia Experiment 2 '93
Porky's '82
Porky's 2: The Next Day '83
Purple Hearts '84

Liana Orfei
The Avenger '62
Casanova '70 '65
The Giant of Metropolis '61
Mill of the Stone Women '60
Nefertiti, Queen of the Nile '64
Pirate Warrior '64
Pirates of the Coast '61

Julia Ormond
Stalin '92
Young Catherine '91

Ed O'Ross
Another 48 Hrs. '90
The Hidden '87
Play Nice '92
Red Heat '88
Tailspin: Behind the Korean Airline Tragedy '89
Universal Soldier '92

Heather O'Rourke
Poltergeist '82
Poltergeist 2: The Other Side '86
Poltergeist 3 '88

Marina Orsini
Battle of the Worlds '61
Eddie and the Cruisers 2: Eddie Lives! '89

Umberto Orsini
Cesar & Rosalie '72
Emmanuelle, the Joys of a Woman '76
Mademoiselle '66
The Outside Man '73

Humberto Ortiz
Arcade '93
Dollman '91

Andrew Osborn
Spaceways '53
Three Stops to Murder '53

Lyn Osborn
The Amazing Colossal Man '57
Invasion of the Saucer Men '57

Ted Osborn
Buried Alive '39
Charlie Chan at the Wax Museum '40

Bud Osborne
Across the Plains '39
Border Badmen '45
Border Bandits '46
The Caravan Trail '46
The Crimson Trail '35
Dead or Alive '41
Deadwood Pass '33
Death Rides the Range '40
Diamond Trail '33
The Fighting Stallion '26
Gun Glory '57
His Brother's Ghost '45
Mark of the Spur '32
The Outlaw Deputy '35
Outlaw of the Plains '46
Range Law '44
Ridin' Thru '35
The Riding Tornado '32
Rustler's Hideout '44
Rustlers of Red Dog '35
Six Gun Gospel '43
Tribute to a Bad Man '56
When a Man Rides Alone '33
Where Trails Divide '37
Wild Horse Phantom '44

Wild West '46

Vivienne Osborne
Captain Caution '40
Let's Sing Again '36
The Phantom Broadcast '33
Primrose Path '40
Tomorrow at Seven '33

Ozzy Osbourne
Decline of Western Civilization 2: The Metal Years '88
Trick or Treat '86

Henry Oscar
Black Limelight '38
The Courageous Mr. Penn '41
The Greed of William Hart '48
Postmark for Danger '56
The Spaniard's Curse '58
The Terror '38

Per Oscarsson
Blockhouse '73
Dandy in Aspic '68
The Doll '62
Endless Night '71
House of Angels '92
Hunger '66
The Last Valley '71
The New Land '73
The Night Visitor '70
Secrets '71
Sleep of Death '79

Brian O'Shaughnessy
Claws '85
Mr. Kingstreet's War '71

Kevin O'Shea
The Purple Heart '44
A Wing and a Prayer '44

Michael O'Shea
The Big Wheel '49
Jack Frost '97
Jack London '44
Lady of Burlesque '43
Lady Scarface/The Threat '49
The Last of the Redmen '47
Parole, Inc. '49
Threat '49
The Underworld Story '50

Milo O'Shea
Barbarella '68
Danger in the Skies '79
The Dream Team '89
Loot...Give Me Money, Honey! '70
No Comebacks '85
Once a Hero '88
Only the Lonely '91
Opportunity Knocks '90
Paddy '70
Peter Lundy and the Medicine Hat Stallion '77
The Playboys '92
Portrait of a Rebel: Margaret Sanger '82
The Purple Rose of Cairo '85
Romeo and Juliet '68
Sacco & Vanzetti '71
Theatre of Blood '73
A Time for Miracles '80
Two by Forsyth '86
Ulysses '67
The Verdict '82

K.T. Oslin
Murder So Sweet '93
The Thing Called Love '93

Cliff Osmond
The Adventures of Nellie Bly '81
The Fortune Cookie '66
Hangar 18 '80
In Search of a Golden Sky '84
Invasion of the Bee Girls '73
Joe Panther '76
Kiss Me, Stupid! '64
Mountain Man '77
Sharks' Treasure '75
Sweet Sugar '72

Marie Osmond
The Gift of Love '90
Goin' Coconuts '78

Jeffery Osterhage
Buckeye and Blue '87
Dark Before Dawn '89
Masque of the Red Death '89
The Sacketts '79
Sex Crimes '92
The Shadow Riders '82

South of Reno '87

Bibi Osterwald
Bank Shot '74
Parrish '61

William Ostrander
Mike's Murder '84
Red Heat '85

Maureen O'Sullivan
Anna Karenina '35
The Barretts of Wimpole Street '34
A Connecticut Yankee '31
David Copperfield '35
A Day at the Races '37
Devil Doll '36
Hannah and Her Sisters '86
Hide-Out '34
Peggy Sue Got Married '86
Pride and Prejudice '40
Skyscraper Souls '32
Song O' My Heart '29
Stranded '87
Strange Interlude '32
The Tall T '57
Tarzan and His Mate '34
Tarzan Escapes '36
Tarzan Finds a Son '39
Tarzan, the Ape Man '32
Tarzan's New York Adventure '42
Tarzan's Secret Treasure '41
The Thin Man '34
Too Scared to Scream '85

Shoji Otake
The Funeral '84
Tampopo '86

Annette O'Toole
Best Legs in the 8th Grade '84
Bridge to Terabithia '85
Cat People '82
Cross My Heart '88
Foolin' Around '80
48 Hrs. '82
A Girl of the Limberlost '90
King of the Gypsies '78
Kiss of a Killer '93
Love at Large '90
Love Matters '93
One on One '77
Smile '75
Stephen King's It '90
Superman 3 '83
White Lie '91

Peter O'Toole
Becket '64
The Bible...In the Beginning '66
Caligula '80
Casino Royale '67
Club Paradise '86
Creator '85
The Dark Angel '91
Foxtrot '76
Goodbye, Mr. Chips '69
High Spirits '88
Kidnapped '60
King Ralph '91
The Last Emperor '87
Lawrence of Arabia '62
The Lion in Winter '68
Lord Jim '65
Man Friday '75
Man of La Mancha '72
Masada '81
Murphy's War '71
My Favorite Year '82
Night of the Generals '67
Power Play '81
Rosebud '75
The Ruling Class '72
The Seventh Coin '92
Strange Tales/Ray Bradbury Theatre '86
The Stunt Man '80
Supergirl '84
Svengali '83
Under Milk Wood '73
What's New Pussycat? '65
Wings of Fame '93
Zulu Dawn '79

Nobuko Otowa
The Island '61
Last War '68
Onibaba '64

John Ottavino
Bob Roberts '92
Malcolm X '92

Barry Otto
Bliss '85
Howling 3: The Marsupials '87
Strictly Ballroom '92

Miranda Otto
The Last Days of Chez Nous '92
The 13th Floor '88

Gerard Oury
Back to the Wall '56
The Love of Three Queens '54
The Prize '63

Maria Ouspenskaya
Beyond Tomorrow '40
Conquest '37
Dance, Girl, Dance '40
Dodsworth '36
Frankenstein Meets the Wolfman '43
Kings Row '41
Love Affair '39
The Rains Came '39
The Shanghai Gesture '42
Waterloo Bridge '40
The Wolf Man '41

Peter Outerbridge
Cool Runnings '93
Victim of Beauty '91

Park Overall
Biloxi Blues '88
The Gambler Returns: The Luck of the Draw '93
House of Cards '92
Kindergarten Cop '90
Lost Angels '89
Mississippi Burning '88
Tainted '87
Undercover Blues '93
The Vanishing '93

Lynne Overman
Caught in the Draft '41
Edison the Man '40
Little Miss Marker '34
Midnight '34
Reap the Wild Wind '42

Frank Overton
Desire Under the Elms '58
To Kill a Mockingbird '62

Rick Overton
Beverly Hills Cop '84
Blind Fury '90
Earth Girls are Easy '89
Million Dollar Mystery '87
Odd Jobs '85
Sinful Life '89
Traxx '87

Bill Owen
The Comeback '77
The Gay Lady '49
Georgy Girl '66
The Hellfire Club '61
Singleton's Pluck '84

Clive Owen
Close My Eyes '91
Lorna Doone '90

Garry Owen
Dark Mirror '46
Hold Your Man '33

Michael Owen
Dick Tracy vs. Crime Inc. '41
Youth Aflame '59

Reginald Owen
Above Suspicion '43
Anna Karenina '35
The Bride Wore Red '37
Cairo '42
The Canterville Ghost '44
Captain Kidd '45
Challenge to Lassie '49
A Christmas Carol '38
Conquest '37
Diary of a Chambermaid '46
Everybody Sing '38
Fashions of 1934 '34
Ghost City '32
The Great Ziegfeld '36
I Married an Angel '42
Julia Misbehaves '48
Love on the Run '36
Madame Curie '43
Madame X '37
The Miniver Story '50
Mrs. Miniver '42
Monsieur Beaucaire '46

National Velvet '44
Of Human Bondage '34
Personal Property '37
The Pirate '48
Queen Christina '33
Random Harvest '42
The Real Glory '39
Red Garters '54
Reunion in France '42
Rosalie '38
Rose Marie '36
Somewhere I'll Find You '42
A Study in Scarlet '33
A Tale of Two Cities '35
Tarzan's Secret Treasure '41
They Met in Bombay '41
The Three Musketeers '48
The Thrill of It All! '63
The Valley of Decision '45
White Cargo '42
Woman of the Year '42
A Woman's Face '41

Seena Owen
Intolerance '16
The Lamb '15
Queen Kelly '29

Gary Owens
Digging Up Business '91
I'm Gonna Git You Sucka '88
Killcrazy '89

Patricia Owens
The Fly '58
The Happiest Days of Your Life '50
Hell to Eternity '60
The Law and Jake Wade '58
Sayonara '57

Earl Owensby
Challenge '74
Death Driver '78
Dogs of Hell '83
Manhunter '83
The Rutherford County Line '87
The Wolfman '82

Monroe Owsley
Ex-Lady '33
Goin' to Town '35

Catherine Oxenberg
Charles & Diana: A Palace Divided '93
K-9000 '89
The Lair of the White Worm '88
Overexposed '90
Rubdown '93
Sexual Response '92
Swimsuit: The Movie '89

David Oxley
House of the Living Dead '73
Night Ambush '57

Moishe Oysher
The Cantor's Son '37
The Singing Blacksmith '38

Frank Oz
An American Werewolf in London '81
The Empire Strikes Back '80
Spies Like Us '85

Eitaro Ozawa
The Human Condition: No Greater Love '58
Sandakan No. 8 '74

Sakae Ozawa
The Crucified Lovers '54
Princess Yang Kwei Fei '55
Ugetsu '53

Shoichi Ozawa
The Ballad of Narayama '83
Black Rain '88
The Pornographers '66

Madeleine Ozeray
Crime and Punishment '35
Liliom '35

Jack Paar
Easy Living '49
Love Nest '51
Walk Softly, Stranger '50

Judy Pace
Brian's Song '71
Cotton Comes to Harlem '70
Frogs '72
Three in the Cellar '70

Tom Pace
The Astro-Zombies '67

Pace ▶cont.

Blood Orgy of the She-Devils
'74
Girl in Gold Boots '69

Al Pacino
America at the Movies '76
And Justice for All '79
Author! Author! '82
Bobby Deerfield '77
Carlito's Way '93
Cruising '80
Dick Tracy '90
Dog Day Afternoon '75
Frankie and Johnny '91
Glengarry Glen Ross '92
The Godfather '72
The Godfather 1902-1959: The
    Complete Epic '81
The Godfather, Part 2 '74
The Godfather, Part 3 '90
Panic in Needle Park '75
Revolution '85
Scarecrow '73
Scarface '83
Scent of a Woman '92
Sea of Love '89
Serpico '73

Charles Lloyd Pack
River Beat '54
Stranger in Town '57

David Packer
The Runnin' Kind '89
Silent Motive '91
Trust Me '89
You Can't Hurry Love '88

Joanna Pacula
Black Ice '92
Death Before Dishonor '87
Deep Red '94
Escape from Sobibor '87
Every Breath '93
Eyes of the Beholder '92
Gorky Park '83
Husbands and Lovers '91
The Kiss '88
Marked for Death '90
Not Quite Paradise '86
Options '88
Sweet Lies '88
Tombstone '93
Under Investigation '93
Warlock: The Armageddon '93

Sarah Padden
Cross Examination '32
Exiled to Shanghai '37
Girl Rush '44
In Old Colorado '41
The Mad Monster '42
Range Law '44
Reg'lar Fellers '41
Riders of the West '42
Snuffy Smith, Yard Bird '42
Song of Old Wyoming '45
Three Comrades '38
Tomorrow's Children '34
Wild West '46

Hugh Paddick
The Killing of Sister George '69
Naughty Knights '71

Robert Padilla
The Great Gundown '75
Twisted Nightmare '87

Lea Padovani
Modigliani '58
The Naked Maja '59

Anita Page
After Midnight '33
Broadway Melody '29
Free and Easy '30
Jungle Bride '33
Our Dancing Daughters '28
Our Modern Maidens '29
Sidewalks of New York '31
Skyscraper Souls '32

Bradley Page
The Affairs of Annabel '38
Champagne for Breakfast '35
Mistaken Identity '36

Dorothy Page
Ride 'Em Cowgirl '41
Water Rustlers '39

Gale Page
Four Daughters '38
Knute Rockne: All American '40
They Drive by Night '40

Genevieve Page
Buffet Froid '79
The Day and the Hour '63
El Cid '61
Girl in His Pocket '62
Gun Crazy '69
The Private Life of Sherlock
    Holmes '70
Song Without End '60

Geraldine Page
ABC Stage 67: Truman
    Capote's A Christmas
    Memory '66
The Adventures of Huckleberry
    Finn '85
Barefoot in Athens '66
The Beguiled '70
The Bride '84
The Day of the Locust '75
The Dollmaker '84
The Happiest Millionaire '67
Harry's War '84
Hazel's People '75
Honky Tonk Freeway '81
I'm Dancing as Fast as I Can
    '82
Interiors '78
Loving '84
My Little Girl '87
Nasty Habits '77
Native Son '86
Pete 'n' Tillie '72
The Pope of Greenwich Village
    '84
Riders to the Sea '88
Summer and Smoke '61
Sweet Bird of Youth '62
Toys in the Attic '63
The Trip to Bountiful '85
Walls of Glass '85
Whatever Happened to Aunt
    Alice? '69
White Nights '85
You're a Big Boy Now '66

Harrison Page
Carnosaur '93
Lionheart '90

Joy Page
Conquest of Cochise '53
Fighter Attack '53

LaWanda Page
B.A.D. Cats '80
Mausoleum '83
Shakes the Clown '92
Zapped! '82

Patti Page
Boy's Night Out '62
Elmer Gantry '60

Alfred Paget
America/The Fall of Babylon
    '24
The Babylon Story from
    "Intolerance" '16
Intolerance '16
The Lamb '15

Debra Paget
Broken Arrow '50
Demetrius and the Gladiators
    '54
From the Earth to the Moon '58
The Haunted Palace '63
House of Strangers '49
Journey to the Lost City '58
The Last Hunt '56
Love Me Tender '56
The Mercenaries '65
Omar Khayyam '57
Prince Valiant '54
Stars and Stripes Forever '52
Tales of Terror '62
The Ten Commandments '56

Nicola Pagetti
Oliver's Story '78
Privates on Parade '84

Marcel Pagliero
Dedee d'Anvers '49
Open City '45

Janis Paige
Angel on My Shoulder '80
Bachelor in Paradise '69
Hero '92

Hollywood Canteen '44
Love at the Top '86
Magic on Love Island '80
Please Don't Eat the Daisies
    '60
Romance on the High Seas '48
Silk Stockings '57
Winter Meeting '48

Mabel Paige
Nocturne '46
The Scar '48

Robert Paige
Abbott and Costello Go to Mars
    '53
The Green Promise '49
The Monster and the Girl '41
Pardon My Sarong '42
The Red Stallion '47
Son of Dracula '43

Didier Pain
My Father's Glory '91
My Mother's Castle '91

Heidi Paine
Alien Seed '89
Lethal Games '90
New York's Finest '87
Wildest Dreams '90

Nestor Paiva
Ballad of a Gunfighter '64
Creature from the Black
    Lagoon '54
Double Dynamite '51
The Falcon in Mexico '44
Fear '46
Five Fingers '52
Follow Me Quietly '49
Frontier Uprising '61
Jesse James Meets
    Frankenstein's Daughter '65
The Mole People '56
The Nine Lives of Elfego Baca
    '58
Outcasts of the City '58
Prison Train '38
The Purple Heart '44
Revenge of the Creature '55
Shoot to Kill '47
Tarantula '55

Holly Palance
The Best of Times '86
Cast the First Stone '89
The Omen '76
Tuxedo Warrior '82

Jack Palance
Alice Through the Looking
    Glass '66
Alone in the Dark '82
Angel's Brigade '79
Arrowhead '53
Bagdad Cafe '88
Barabbas '62
Batman '89
The Battle of Austerlitz '60
Battle of the Commandos '71
Big Boss '77
The Big Knife '55
Black Cobra '83
Bloody Avenger '80s
Chato's Land '71
City Slickers '91
City Slickers 2: The Legend of
    Curly's Gold '94
Cocaine Cowboys '79
Contempt '64
Cop in Blue Jeans '76
Cops and Robbersons '94
Craze '74
Cyborg 2 '93
Deadly Sanctuary '68
Desperados '69
Dr. Jekyll and Mr. Hyde '68
Dracula '73
Four Deuces '75
God's Gun '75
Gor '88
Great Adventure '75
The Halls of Montezuma '50
The Hatfields & the McCoys '75
Hawk the Slayer '81
Hell's Brigade: The Final
    Assault '80
The Horsemen '70
I Died a Thousand Times '55
Keep the Change '92
The Last Contract '86
The Last Ride of the Dalton
    Gang '79

Lonely Man '57
The McMasters '70
Mr. Scarface '77
The Mongols '60
Monte Walsh '70
Oklahoma Crude '73
One Man Jury '78
Outlaw of Gor '87
Panic in the Streets '50
Portrait of a Hitman '77
The Professionals '66
Requiem for a Heavyweight '56
Rulers of the City '71
Second Chance '53
The Sensuous Nurse '76
Shane '53
The Silver Chalice '54
Solar Crisis '92
Sting of the West '76
Strange Case of Dr. Jekyll &
    Mr. Hyde '68
Tango and Cash '89
Torture Garden '67
Unknown Powers '80
Welcome to Blood City '77
Young Guns '88

Ron Palillo
Committed '91
Doin' Time '85
Hellgate '89
SnakeEater '89

Michael Palin
American Friends '91
And Now for Something
    Completely Different '72
Brazil '85
A Fish Called Wanda '88
Jabberwocky '77
John Cleese on How to Irritate
    People '68
The Missionary '82
Monty Python and the Holy
    Grail '75
Monty Python Live at the
    Hollywood Bowl '82
Monty Python Meets Beyond
    the Fringe
Monty Python's Life of Brian
    '79
Monty Python's Parrot Sketch
    Not Included '90
Monty Python's The Meaning
    of Life '83
A Private Function '84
The Secret Policeman's Other
    Ball '82
Secret Policeman's Private
    Parts '81
Time Bandits '81

Anita Pallenberg
Barbarella '68
Performance '70

Eugene Pallette
The Adventures of Robin Hood
    '38
Big Street '42
The Birth of a Nation '15
The Bride Came C.O.D. '41
The Ghost Goes West '36
Heaven Can Wait '43
Intolerance '16
The Kennel Murder Case '33
The Lady Eve '41
Mantrap '26
The Mark of Zorro '40
Mr. Smith Goes to Washington
    '39
My Man Godfrey '36
Pin-Up Girl '44
Sensations of 1945 '44
Shanghai Express '32
Silver Queen '42
Stowaway '36
Strangers of the Evening '32
The Three Musketeers '21
Topper '37
The Virginian '29
Young Tom Edison '40

Gabriella Pallotti
Hero of Rome '63
Il Grido '57
The Mongols '60
The Roof '56

Ulf Palme
Dreams '55
Miss Julie '50

Betsy Palmer
Friday the 13th '80
Friday the 13th, Part 2 '81
The Last Angry Man '59
The Long Gray Line '55
Mister Roberts '55
Still Not Quite Human '92
The Tin Star '57

Geoffrey Palmer
Christabel '89
A Fish Called Wanda '88
A Question of Attribution '91

Gregg Palmer
The Creature Walks Among Us
    '56
The Rebel Set '59
Zombies of Moratau '57

Lilli Palmer
Adorable Julia '62
The Amorous Adventures of
    Moll Flanders '65
Beware of Pity '46
Body and Soul '47
The Boys from Brazil '78
But Not for Me '59
Chamber of Horrors '40
Cloak and Dagger '46
Conspiracy of Hearts '60
The Counterfeit Traitor '62
The Devil in Silk '56
The Holcroft Covenant '85
The Long Dark Hall '51
The Miracle of the White
    Stallions '63
Modigliani '58
Murders in the Rue Morgue '71
My Girl Tisa '48
Sebastian '68
The Secret Agent '36
What the Peeper Saw '72

Maria Palmer
By the Light of the Silvery
    Moon '53
Days of Glory '43
Outcasts of the City '58

Shirley Palmer
Campus Knights '29
Somewhere in Sonora '33

Chazz Palminteri
A Bronx Tale '93
There Goes the Neighborhood
    '92

Carlos Palomino
Die Watching '93
Geronimo: An American
    Legend '93
My Samurai '92
Nasty Hero '89
Strangers Kiss '83

Gwyneth Paltrow
Flesh and Bone '93
Hook '91

Lucianna Paluzzi
A Black Veil for Lisa '68
Carlton Browne of the F.O. '59
Chuka '67
Conexion Oriental '70
The Green Slime '68
Journey to the Lost City '58
The Klansman '74
Manhunt '73
Medusa '74
Muscle Beach Party '64
99 Women '69
One-Eyed Soldiers '67
Return to Peyton Place '61
Thunderball '65

Yang Pan Pan
Duel of the Seven Tigers '79
Return of the Scorpion '80
The Story of Drunken Master

Alessandra Panaro
The Bacchantes '63
Executioner of Venice '63

Richard Panebianco
China Girl '87
Dogfight '91

Tien Pang
Ninja Swords of Death '90
The Samurai
To Subdue the Evil

Franklin Pangborn
All Over Town '37
The Bank Dick '40

Call Out the Marines '42
Carefree '38
Christmas in July '40
Comedy Reel, Vol. 2
Dangerous Holiday '37
Doughnuts & Society '36
Fifth Avenue Girl '39
Flying Down to Rio '33
A Girl, a Guy and a Gob '41
The Great Moment '44
Hail the Conquering Hero '44
Hats Off '37
Just Around the Corner '38
King Kelly of the U.S.A. '34
The Mandarin Mystery '37
My Man Godfrey '36
Never Give a Sucker an Even Break '41
The Palm Beach Story '42
Romance on the High Seas '48
The Sin of Harold Diddlebock '47
A Star is Born '37
Sullivan's Travels '41
Tango '36
Till the Clouds Roll By/A Star Is Born '46
Topper Takes a Trip '39
Two Reelers: Comedy Classics 10 '31
Two Weeks to Live '43
Vivacious Lady '38

Stuart Pankin
Arachnophobia '90
Betrayal of the Dove '92
Dirt Bike Kid '86
Fatal Attraction '87
Life Stinks '91
Love at Stake '87
Mannequin 2: On the Move '91
Second Sight '89
That's Adequate '90
The Vagrant '92

John Pankow
Johnny Be Good '88
Monkey Shines '88
Mortal Thoughts '91
A Stranger Among Us '92
Talk Radio '88
To Live & Die in L.A. '85
Year of the Gun '91

Joe Pantoliano
Baby's Day Out '94
Calendar Girl '93
Dangerous Heart '93
Downtown '89
Eddie and the Cruisers '83
El Diablo '90
Empire of the Sun '87
The Final Terror '83
The Fugitive '93
The Goonies '85
Idolmaker '80
The In Crowd '88
La Bamba '87
The Last of the Finest '90
Me and the Kid '93
Mean Season '85
Midnight Run '88
Nightbreaker '89
Risky Business '83
Running Scared '86
Scenes from the Goldmine '87
Short Time '90
The Squeeze '87
Tales from the Crypt '89
Three of Hearts '93
Used People '92
Zandalee '91

Irene Papas
Anne of the Thousand Days '69
The Assisi Underground '84
The Brotherhood '68
Christ Stopped at Eboli '79
A Dream of Kings '69
Erendira '83
The Guns of Navarone '61
High Season '88
Into the Night '85
Iphigenia '77
Lion of the Desert '81
Mohammed: Messenger of God '77
Moses '76
1931: Once Upon a Time in New York '72
Sidney Sheldon's Bloodline '79
Sweet Country '87

Tribute to a Bad Man '56
Trojan Women '71
Z '69
Zorba the Greek '64

Laslo Papas
Bloodshed '83
Crazed '82
Slipping into Darkness '88

Ike Pappas
Moon Over Parador '88
The Package '89

John Paragon
Eating Raoul '82
The Pee Wee Herman Show '82
Uncensored '85

Kiri Paramore
Flirting '89
The Last Days of Chez Nous '92

Michael Pare
Blink of an Eye '92
The Closer '91
Dragonfight '92
Eddie and the Cruisers '83
Eddie and the Cruisers 2: Eddie Lives! '89
Instant Justice '86
Into the Sun '92
Killing Streets '91
The Last Hour '91
Moon 44 '90
The Philadelphia Experiment '84
Point of Impact '93
Space Rage '86
Streets of Fire '84
Sunset Heat '92
Women's Club '87
World Gone Wild '88

Marisa Paredes
Dark Habits '84
High Heels '91
In a Glass Cage '86

Mila Parely
Beauty and the Beast '46
The Rules of the Game '39
Three Stops to Murder '53

Judy Parfitt
The Charmer '89
Dark Obsession '90
Getting It Right '89
Hamlet '91
The Jewel in the Crown '84
Maurice '87
Midnight's Child '93
Office Romances '86

Anne Parillaud
Innocent Blood '92
La Femme Nikita '91
Map of the Human Heart '93

Jerry Paris
D-Day, the Sixth of June '56
Marty '55
The Wild One '54

Reg Park
Hercules and the Captive Women '63
Hercules in the Haunted World '64
Hercules, Prisoner of Evil '64

Cecil Parker
The Brain '62
Caesar and Cleopatra '46
Court Jester '56
Dangerous Moonlight '41
The Detective '54
Heavens Above '63
Housemaster '38
Lady L '65
The Lady Vanishes '38
Ladykillers '55
The Man Who Lived Again '36
The Pure Hell of St. Trinian's '61
The Stars Look Down '39
Storm in a Teacup '37
A Study in Terror '66
A Tale of Two Cities '58
Tony Draws a Horse '51
Under Capricorn '49
The Wreck of the Mary Deare '59

Cecilia Parker
Ah, Wilderness! '35
Andy Hardy Gets Spring Fever '39
Andy Hardy Meets Debutante '40
Andy Hardy's Double Life '42
Honor of the Range '34
The Lost Jungle '34
Love Finds Andy Hardy '38
Mystery Ranch '34
Naughty Marietta '35
Rainbow Ranch '33
Riders of Destiny '33
Roll Along Cowboy '37
Sweetheart of the Navy '37
Tombstone Canyon '35

Corey Parker
Big Man on Campus '89
Biloxi Blues '88
Broadway Bound '92
How I Got into College '89
I'm Dangerous Tonight '90
The Lost Language of Cranes '92
White Palace '90

Ed Parker
God's Country and the Man '37
Kill the Golden Goose '79
The Secret Code '42

Eleanor Parker
Above and Beyond '53
The Bastard '78
Chain Lightning '50
Dead on the Money '91
Detective Story '51
Escape from Fort Bravo '53
Escape Me Never '47
Fantasy Island '76
Hans Brinker '69
A Hole in the Head '59
Hollywood Canteen '44
Home for the Holidays '72
Home from the Hill '60
Interrupted Melody '55
It's a Great Feeling '49
The King and Four Queens '56
The Man with the Golden Arm '55
Maybe I'll Be Home in the Spring '70
Naked Jungle '54
The Oscar '66
Panic Button '62
Return to Peyton Place '61
Scaramouche '52
She's Dressed to Kill '79
The Sound of Music '65
Three Secrets '50
Tiger and the Pussycat '67

Fess Parker
Davy Crockett and the River Pirates '56
Davy Crockett, King of the Wild Frontier '55
The Great Locomotive Chase '56
Hell is for Heroes '62
The Jayhawkers '59
The Light in the Forest '58
Old Yeller '57
Them! '54
Westward Ho, the Wagons! '56

Fred Parker
Cord & Dischords/Naughty Nurse '74
Roamin' Wild '36

Jameson Parker
American Justice '86
Anatomy of a Seduction '79
Callie and Son '81
Curse of the Crystal Eye '93
The Gathering: Part 2 '79
Prince of Darkness '87
A Small Circle of Friends '80
Spy '89

Jean Parker
Apache Uprising '66
Beyond Tomorrow '40
Bluebeard '44
Flying Blind '41
The Flying Deuces '39
Gabriel Over the White House '33
The Ghost Goes West '36
The Gunfighter '50
Knights of the Range '40

Lady for a Day '33
Lady in the Death House '44
A Lawless Street '55
Little Women '33
Navy Way '44
One Body Too Many '44
Rasputin and the Empress '32
Rolling Home '48

Kim Parker
Fiend Without a Face '58
Fire Maidens from Outer Space '56

Lara Parker
Foxfire Light '84
Hi, Mom! '70
Night of Dark Shadows '71
Race with the Devil '75
The Solitary Man '82

Mary-Louise Parker
The Client '94
Fried Green Tomatoes '91
Grand Canyon '91
Longtime Companion '90
Mr. Wonderful '93
Naked in New York '93
Signs of Life '89

Michael Parker
Kill Line '91
My Own Private Idaho '91

Monica Parker
Coming Out Alive '84
Improper Channels '82

Nathaniel Parker
Piece of Cake '90
Wide Sargasso Sea '92

Noelle Parker
Ernest Saves Christmas '88
Lethal Lolita—Amy Fisher: My Story '92
Twisted '86

Norman Parker
Killing Hour '84
Question of Faith '93

Sachi Parker
The Dancing Princesses '84
Peggy Sue Got Married '86
Riders to the Sea '88
Welcome Home, Roxy Carmichael '90

Sarah Jessica Parker
Almost Royal Family '84
Ed Wood '94
First Born '84
Flight of the Navigator '86
Footloose '84
Girls Just Want to Have Fun '85
Going for the Gold: The Bill Johnson Story '85
Hocus Pocus '93
Honeymoon in Vegas '92
L.A. Story '91
Somewhere Tomorrow '85
Striking Distance '93

Sunshine Parker
Cannery Row '82
Spittin' Image '83

Suzy Parker
Funny Face '57
The Interns '62
Ten North Frederick '58

Willard Parker
Bandit Queen '51
Great Jesse James Raid '49
Hunt the Man Down/Smashing the Rackets '50

Barbara Parkins
Asylum '72
Bear Island '80
Breakfast in Paris '81
Calendar Girl Murders '84
Christina '74
The Deadly Trap '71
Law of the Land '76
The Mephisto Waltz '71
Puppet on a Chain '72
Shout at the Devil '76
Snatched '72
To Catch a King '84
Valley of the Dolls '67

Bert Parks
The Freshman '90
Shining Star '75

Larry Parks
Destroyer '43
Down to Earth '47
Harmon of Michigan '41
Her Husband's Affairs '47
Jolson Sings Again '49
The Jolson Story '46
Love is Better Than Ever '52
You Were Never Lovelier '42

Michael Parks
Arizona Heat '87
Breakthrough '78
Chase '85
The China Lake Murders '90
Club Life '86
Death Wish 5: The Face of Death '94
The Evictors '79
ffolkes '80
French Quarter Undercover '85
Gore Vidal's Billy the Kid '89
Hard Country '81
The Hitman '91
Midnight Auto Supply '78
Night Cries '78
The Private Files of J. Edgar Hoover '77
The Return of Josey Wales '86
The Savage Bees '76
Savannah Smiles '82
Sidewinder One '77
Stamp of a Killer '87
Storyville '92
Welcome to Spring Break '88

Trina Parks
Darktown Strutters '74
Diamonds are Forever '71
The Muthers '76

Dita Parlo
Grand Illusion '37
Homecoming '28
L'Atalante '34

Emory Parnell
Casanova Brown '44
Lost in Alaska '52
Ma and Pa Kettle at the Fair '52
Ma and Pa Kettle Back On the Farm '51
Man of the West '58
Miracle of Morgan's Creek '44
Pardners '56
The Show-Off '46
Trail of Robin Hood '50

Helen Parrish
Big Trail '30
Little Tough Guy '38
Overland Mail '41
Sunset Serenade '42
X Marks the Spot '42
You'll Find Out '40

Julie Parrish
The Doberman Gang '72
Paradise, Hawaiian Style '66

Leslie Parrish
For Love or Money '63
The Giant Spider Invasion '75
The Invisible Strangler '76
Li'l Abner '59
The Manchurian Candidate '62
Sex and the Single Girl '64

Steve Parrish
Midnight '89
Scanners 3: The Takeover '92

David Parry
Auntie Lee's Meat Pies '92
Dr. Caligari '89
The Lost Platoon '89

Nastasha Parry
Crow Hollow '52
Haunted: The Ferryman '74

Tom Parsekian
Club Life '86
Hot Resort '85

Frederick Parslow
The Last Wave '77
Wrangler '88

Estelle Parsons
Bonnie & Clyde '67
Come Along with Me '84
Dick Tracy '90
Don't Drink the Water '69
For Pete's Sake '74
Foreplay '75
Gentleman Bandit '81

Parsons ▶cont.

I Never Sang For My Father '70
A Private Matter '92
Rachel, Rachel '68
Watermelon Man '70

Nancy Parsons
Ladybugs '92
Motel Hell '80
Porky's Revenge '85
Wishman '93

Percy Parsons
Dangerous Moonlight '41
Power '34
Rhodes '36

Dolly Parton
The Best Little Whorehouse in Texas '82
9 to 5 '80
Rhinestone '84
A Smoky Mountain Christmas '86
Steel Magnolias '89
Straight Talk '92

Christine Pascal
The Best Way '82
The Clockmaker '76
Le Grand Chemin '87
Maids of Wilko '79
Sincerely Charlotte '86
Spoiled Children '77

Mary Ann Pascal
Lethal Lolita—Amy Fisher: My Story '92
Writer's Block '91

Olivia Pascal
Bloody Moon '83
C.O.D. '83

Isabelle Pasco
High Frequency '88
Prospero's Books '91

Richard Pasco
The Gorgon '64
Sword of Sherwood Forest '60

Adrian Pasdar
Carlito's Way '93
Cookie '89
Grand Isle '92
The Lost Capone '90
Made in USA '88
Near Dark '87
Streets of Gold '86
Top Gun '86
Torn Apart '89
Vital Signs '90

Pier Paolo Pasolini
Bellissimo: Images of the Italian Cinema '87
The Canterbury Tales '71
The Decameron '70
Oedipus Rex '67

Cyndi Pass
Bikini Island '91
Deadbolt '92
Desperate Motives '92
Mission of Justice '92
Scanner Cop '94

Robert Pastorelli
Dances with Wolves '90
Folks! '92
The Paint Job '93
Sister Act 2: Back in the Habit '93
Striking Distance '93

Willie Pastrano
Alligator Alley '72
Wild Rebels '71

Michael Pataki
The Amazing Spider-Man '77
American Anthem '86
The Baby '74
The Bat People '74
Dead and Buried '81
Delinquent School Girls '84
Dirt Gang '71
Grave of the Vampire '72
Halloween 4: The Return of Michael Myers '88
The Last Porno Flick '74
The Last Word '80
On the Edge: The Survival of Dana '79

One More Chance '90
Rocky 4 '85
The Underachievers '88
When Every Day was the Fourth of July '78
Zoltan...Hound of Dracula '77

Wally Patch
Calling Paul Temple '48
Cottage to Let '41
Don Quixote '35
Inspector Hornleigh '39

Michael Pate
Face to Face '52
Five Fingers '52
Green Mansions '59
Houdini '53
Howling 3: The Marsupials '87
Julius Caesar '53
King Richard and the Crusaders '54
A Lawless Street '55
McLintock! '63
The Oklahoman '56
Return of Captain Invincible '83
Seventh Cavalry '56
The Singing Nun '66
Tower of London '62

Bill Paterson
The Adventures of Baron Munchausen '89
Chaplin '92
Comfort and Joy '84
Coming Up Roses '87
Defense of the Realm '85
Dutch Girls '87
Hidden City '87
The Killing Fields '84
The Object of Beauty '91
The Ploughman's Lunch '83
A Private Function '84
The Rachel Papers '89
Traffik '90
Truly, Madly, Deeply '91
The Witches '90

Mandy Patinkin
Alien Nation '88
The Big Fix '78
Daniel '83
Dick Tracy '90
The Doctor '91
Follies in Concert '85
French Postcards '79
Impromptu '91
The House on Carroll Street '88
The Last Embrace '79
Maxie '85
The Music of Chance '93
Night of the Juggler '80
The Princess Bride '87
Ragtime '81
Sunday in the Park with George '86
True Colors '91
Yentl '83

Laurie Paton
The Amy Fisher Story '93
Norman's Awesome Experience '88

Jason Patric
After Dark, My Sweet '90
The Beast '88
Denial: The Dark Side of Passion '91
Frankenstein Unbound '90
Geronimo: An American Legend '93
The Lost Boys '87
Rush '91
Solarbabies '86
Toughlove '85

Dennis Patrick
The Air Up There '94
Choices '81
Dear Dead Delilah '72
Joe '70
The Time Travelers '64

Dorothy Patrick
Follow Me Quietly '49
Thunder Pass '54
Torch Song '53

Gail Patrick
Badmen of Nevada '33
Brewster's Millions '45
Doctor Takes a Wife '40
Love Crazy '41
My Favorite Wife '40

My Man Godfrey '36
The Mysterious Rider '33
The Phantom Broadcast '33
Stage Door '37
To the Last Man '33
Wagon Wheels '34
Wives Under Suspicion '38

Gregory Patrick
Sexpot '88
A Woman Obsessed '88

Lee Patrick
Black Bird '75
Fisherman's Wharf '39
The Fuller Brush Girl '50
Gambler's Choice '44
In This Our Life '42
Inner Sanctum '48
Law of the Underworld '38
The Maltese Falcon '41
Mrs. Parkington '44
Pillow Talk '59
Seven Faces of Dr. Lao '63
Somewhere I'll Find You '42
Summer and Smoke '61
Vertigo '58

Nigel Patrick
Battle of Britain '69
The Browning Version '51
Encore '52
The Executioner '70
Johnny Nobody '61
The League of Gentlemen '60
Mackintosh Man '73
The Pickwick Papers '54
Raintree County '57
Sapphire '59
Trio '50
The Virgin Soldiers '69

Robert Patrick
Behind Enemy Lines '85
Body Shot '93
The Cool Surface '92
Die Hard 2: Die Harder '90
Eye of the Eagle '87
Fire in the Sky '93
Future Hunters '88
Terminator 2: Judgment Day '91

Luanna Patten
Follow Me, Boys! '66
Johnny Tremain & the Sons of Liberty '58
Rock, Pretty Baby '56
So Dear to My Heart '49

Elizabeth Patterson
A Bill of Divorcement '32
Go West, Young Man '36
Hide-Out '34
Hold Your Man '33
Intruder in the Dust '49
No Man of Her Own '32
The Sky's the Limit '43

Jay Patterson
D.O.A. '88
Double Exposure: The Story of Margaret Bourke-White '89
Heaven Help Us '85
McBain '91
Nadine '87
Street Smart '87

Lee Patterson
Above Us the Waves '56
Chato's Land '71
He Lives: The Search for the Evil One '88
Jack the Ripper '60
The Key Man '57
The Spaniard's Curse '58
Time Lock '57

Neva Patterson
An Affair to Remember '57
David and Lisa '62
Desk Set '57
The Runaways '75
Women of Valor '86

Pat Patterson
The Body Shop '72
Gas-s-s-s! '70
Moonshine Mountain '64

Rocky Patterson
Armed for Action '92
Blood on the Badge
Nail Gun Massacre '86

Shirley Patterson
Black Hills '48

Driftin' River '46
Texas Kid '43

Bill Patton
Fangs of Fate '25
Rustlers of Red Dog '35

Mark Patton
Anna to the Infinite Power '84
A Nightmare on Elm Street 2: Freddy's Revenge '85

Will Patton
Belizaire the Cajun '86
Chinese Boxes '84
The Client '94
Cold Heaven '92
Deadly Desire '91
Everybody Wins '90
In the Soup '92
Murder on the Bayou '91
No Way Out '87
The Paint Job '93
The Rapture '91
Romeo Is Bleeding '93
A Shock to the System '90
Signs of Life '89
Stars and Bars '88
Variety '83
Wildfire '88

Adrian Paul
The Cover Girl Murders '93
Highlander: The Gathering '93
Masque of the Red Death '89

Alexandra Paul
American Flyers '85
American Nightmare '81
Christine '84
Detonator '93
8 Million Ways to Die '85
Getting Physical '84
In Between '92
Just the Way You Are '84
Millions '90
Prey of the Chameleon '91
Sunset Grill '92

David Paul
The Barbarians '87
Double Trouble '91
Ghost Writer '89
Think Big '90

Don Michael Paul
Alien from L.A. '87
Aloha Summer '88
Brotherhood of Justice '86
The Heart of Dixie '89
Lovelines '87
Rich Girl '91
Robot Wars '93
Rolling Vengeance '87
Winners Take All '87

Peter Paul
The Barbarians '87
Double Trouble '91
Ghost Writer '89
Think Big '90

Richard Paul
Bloodfist 3: Forced to Fight '92
Not for Publication '84
Pass the Ammo '88
Princess Academy '87

Stuart Paul
Emanon '86
Fate '90

Scott Paulin
Captain America '89
Deceit '93
From Hollywood to Deadwood '89
Grim Prairie Tales '89
Knights '93
The Last of Philip Banter '87
Pump Up the Volume '90
The Right Stuff '83
A Soldier's Story '84
Teen Wolf '85
To Heal a Nation '88
Tricks of the Trade '88
Turner and Hooch '89
Weekend War '88

Pat Paulsen
Auntie Lee's Meat Pies '92
Ellie '84
Foreplay '75
Harper Valley P.T.A. '78
Night Patrol '85
They Still Call Me Bruce '86

Where Were You When the Lights Went Out? '68

Rob Paulsen
Eyes of Fire '84
Perfect Match '88

Marisa Pavan
Diane '55
Drum Beat '54
John Paul Jones '59
The Man in the Gray Flannel Suit '56
The Rose Tattoo '55
Solomon and Sheba '59
What Price Glory? '52

Muriel Pavlow
Doctor at Large '57
Doctor in the House '53
Malta Story '53

Lennox Pawle
David Copperfield '35
Sylvia Scarlett '35

Katina Paxinou
Inheritance '47
Rocco and His Brothers '60

Bill Paxton
Aliens '86
Back to Back '90
Boxing Helena '93
Brain Dead '89
The Dark Backward '91
Future Shock '93
Impulse '84
Indian Summer '93
The Last of the Finest '90
Monolith '93
Navy SEALS '90
Near Dark '87
Next of Kin '89
One False Move '91
Pass the Ammo '88
Predator 2 '90
Slipstream '89
Streets of Fire '84
The Terminator '84
Tombstone '93
Trespass '92
True Lies '94
The Vagrant '92
Weird Science '85

Johnny Paycheck
Hell's Angels Forever '83
Sweet Country Road '81

David Paymer
City Slickers '91
City Slickers 2: The Legend of Curly's Gold '94
Crazy People '90
Heart and Souls '93
Mr. Saturday Night '92
No Way Out '87
Searching for Bobby Fischer '93

Allen Payne
CB4: The Movie '93
New Jack City '91

Bruce Payne
The Cisco Kid '94
Full Eclipse '93
Passenger 57 '92
Wonderland '89

Bruce Martyn Payne
Howling 6: The Freaks '90
Pyrates '91
Switch '91

John Payne
Bail Out at 43,000 '57
College Swing '38
Dodsworth '36
Footlight Serenade '42
The Great American Broadcast '41
Hats Off '37
Hello, Frisco, Hello '43
Iceland '42
Kansas City Confidential '52
Miracle on 34th Street '47
The Razor's Edge '46
Silver Lode '54
Slightly Scarlet '56
Springtime in the Rockies '42
Sun Valley Serenade '41
Tennessee's Partner '55
Tin Pan Alley '40
To the Shores of Tripoli '42
Week-End In Havana '41

Laurence Payne
The Crawling Eye '58
One Deadly Owner '74
The Tell-Tale Heart '62
Train of Events '49
Vampire Circus '71

Sally Payne
Jesse James at Bay '41
Man from Cheyenne '42
Romance on the Range '42

Amanda Pays
Cold Room '84
Dead on the Money '91
Exposure '91
The Flash '90
The Flash 2: Revenge of the Trickster '91
The Kindred '87
Leviathan '89
Max Headroom, the Original Story '86
Off Limits '87
Oxford Blues '84

Blanche Payson
Laurel & Hardy Comedy Classics, Vol. 5 '31
Stan Without Ollie, Vol. 4 '25

Barbara Payton
Bride of the Gorilla '51
Drums in the Deep South '51
Four Sided Triangle '53
Great Jesse James Raid '49
Kiss Tomorrow Goodbye '50
Only the Valiant '50
Trapped '49

Mary Peach
Ballad in Blue '66
A Gathering of Eagles '63
No Love for Johnnie '60

E. J. Peaker
The Banker '89
Hello, Dolly! '69

Adele Pearce
Pop Always Pays '40
Wyoming Outlaw '39

Alice Pearce
The Belle of New York '52
Dear Brigitte '65
The Glass Bottom Boat '66

Guy Pearce
Heaven Tonight '93
The Hunting '92

Jacqueline Pearce
Don't Raise the Bridge, Lower the River '68
White Mischief '88

Joanne Pearce
Morons from Outer Space '85
Whoops Apocalypse '83

Mary Vivian Pearce
Desperate Living '77
Female Trouble '74
Mondo Trasho '69
Multiple Maniacs '70
Pink Flamingos '72

Patricia Pearcy
Delusion '84
Squirm '76

Richard Pearson
Pirates '86
Thirteenth Reunion '81

Virginia Pearson
The Taxi Mystery '26
The Wizard of Oz '25

Harold Peary
Clambake '67
The Great Gildersleeve '43
Here We Go Again! '42
Look Who's Laughing '41
Seven Days' Leave '42

Sierra Pecheur
Bronco Billy '80
Kalifornia '93

Bob Peck
After Pilkington '88
Edge of Darkness '86
Jurassic Park '93
The Kitchen Toto '87
Slipstream '89

Cecilia Peck
Ambition '91

My Best Friend Is a Vampire '88
The Portrait '93
Torn Apart '89
Wall Street '87

Gregory Peck
Amazing Grace & Chuck '87
Arabesque '66
Behold a Pale Horse '64
Big Country '58
The Blue and the Gray '85
The Boys from Brazil '78
The Bravados '58
Cape Fear '61
Captain Horatio Hornblower '51
Captain Newman, M.D. '63
David and Bathsheba '51
Days of Glory '43
Designing Woman '57
Duel in the Sun '46
Gentleman's Agreement '47
The Gunfighter '50
The Guns of Navarone '61
Hollywood Home Movies '87
How the West was Won '63
The Keys of the Kingdom '44
MacArthur '77
MacKenna's Gold '69
The Man in the Gray Flannel Suit '56
Marooned '69
Mirage '66
Moby Dick '56
Old Gringo '89
The Omen '76
On the Beach '59
Only the Valiant '50
Other People's Money '91
The Paradine Case '47
Pork Chop Hill '59
The Portrait '93
Roman Holiday '53
The Scarlet & the Black '83
Sea Wolves '81
The Snows of Kilimanjaro '52
Spellbound '45
The Stalking Moon '69
To Kill a Mockingbird '62
Twelve O'Clock High '49
The Valley of Decision '45
The Yearling '46

J. Eddie Peck
Curse 2: The Bite '88
Dangerously Close '86
Lambada '89

Tony Peck
Brenda Starr '86
Fit to Kill '93
Hard Hunted '92
Inside Edge '92
The Magic Bubble '93
Poor Little Rich Girl: The Barbara Hutton Story '87

Sam Peckinpah
Gunfire '78
The Visitor '80

Chris Pederson
Point Break '91
Suburbia '83

Nia Peeples
Deepstar Six '89
I Don't Buy Kisses Anymore '92
Music Shoppe '82
North Shore '87
Return to Lonesome Dove '93
Swimsuit: The Movie '89

Joan Peers
Applause '29
The Tip-Off '31

Lisa Peers
Glass '90
Solo '77

Pele
Hot Shot '86
Victory '81

Lisa Pelikan
The Best Little Girl in the World '81
Ghoulies '85
Into the Badlands '92
Jennifer '78
Julia '77
Lionheart '90
Return to the Blue Lagoon '91
Swing Shift '84

Raymond Pellegrin
Imperial Venus '71
Napoleon '55
Street War '70s
A Woman of Rome '56

Pilar Pellicer
La Choca '73
La Trinchera '87

Pina Pellicer
Macario '58
One-Eyed Jacks '61

Matti Pellonpaa
Ariel '89
La Vie de Boheme '93
Leningrad Cowboys Go America '89
Night on Earth '91

Ana Louisa Peluffo
Despedida de Casada '87
Lagrimas de Amor '87
The Living Head '59
The New Invisible Man '58
Siempre Hay una Primera Vez '87

Ron Pember
Bullshot '83
Footlight Frenzy '84

George Pembroke
The Black Dragons '42
Buried Alive '39
Dawn Express '42
I Killed That Man '42

Elizabeth Pena
*batteries not included '87
Blue Steel '90
Crossover Dreams '85
Down and Out in Beverly Hills '86
El Super '79
Jacob's Ladder '90
La Bamba '87
They All Laughed '81
Thief '81
Times Square '80
Vibes '87
The Waterdance '91

Julio Pena
Satanik '68
The Werewolf vs. the Vampire Woman '70

Austin Pendleton
The Ballad of the Sad Cafe '91
Four Eyes and Six Guns '93
The Front Page '74
Guarding Tess '94
Hello Again '87
Mr. & Mrs. Bridge '91
Mr. Nanny '93
My Boyfriend's Back '93
My Cousin Vinny '92
Petulia '68
Short Circuit '86
Simon '80
Starting Over '79
Talk to Me '82
The Thief Who Came to Dinner '73
What's Up, Doc? '72

Nat Pendleton
At the Circus '39
Blonde Crazy '31
Buck Privates Come Home '47
Gangway '37
The Great Ziegfeld '36
Hell Fire Austin '32
Horse Feathers '32
Manhattan Melodrama '34
Northwest Passage '40
Penthouse '33
Reckless '35
Scared to Death '47
Shopworn Angel '38
The Thin Man '34

Thaao Penghlis
Les Patterson Saves the World '90
The Lookalike '90

Susan Penhaligon
Bouquet of Barbed Wire '76
The Confessional '75
The Land That Time Forgot '75
Leopard in the Snow '78
Nasty Habits '77
Patrick '78

Soldier of Orange '78

Bruce Penhall
Do or Die '91
Enemy Gold '93
Fit to Kill '93
Hard Hunted '92
Picasso Trigger '89
Savage Beach '89

Christopher Penn
All the Right Moves '83
At Close Range '86
Beethoven's 2nd '93
Best of the Best '89
Best of the Best 2 '93
Footloose '84
Futurekick '91
Josh and S.A.M. '93
Leather Jackets '90
Made in USA '88
Mobsters '91
The Music of Chance '93
Pale Rider '85
The Pickle '93
Reservoir Dogs '92
Rumble Fish '83
Short Cuts '93
True Romance '93
The Wild Life '84

Leonard Penn
Girl of the Golden West '38
Streets of Sin '49

Matthew Penn
Delta Force 3: The Killing Game '91
Playing for Keeps '86

Sean Penn
At Close Range '86
Bad Boys '83
Carlito's Way '93
Casualties of War '89
Colors '88
Crackers '84
The Falcon and the Snowman '85
Fast Times at Ridgemont High '82
Judgment in Berlin '88
Killing of Randy Webster '81
Racing with the Moon '84
Shanghai Surprise '86
State of Grace '90
Taps '81
We're No Angels '89

Alan Penney
Around the World in 80 Ways '86
Gone to Ground '76

Jack Pennick
Lady from Louisiana '42
Mister Roberts '55
Stagecoach '39

Joe Penny
Blood Vows: The Story of a Mafia Wife '87
Bloody Birthday '80
Deathmoon '78
Gangster Wars '81
Lifepod '80

Sydney Penny
Bernadette '90
Child of Darkness, Child of Light '91
Hyper-Sapien: People from Another Star '86
News at Eleven '86
Pale Rider '85
Running Away '89

George Peppard
Bang the Drum Slowly '56
Battle Beyond the Stars '80
The Blue Max '66
Breakfast at Tiffany's '61
The Carpetbaggers '64
The Chinatown Murders: Man Against the Mob '92
Damnation Alley '77
The Executioner '70
From Hell to Victory '79
The Groundstar Conspiracy '72
Home from the Hill '60
How the West was Won '63
Newman's Law '74
Night of the Fox '90
Operation Crossbow '65
Pendulum '69
Pork Chop Hill '59

Rough Night in Jericho '67
Silence Like Glass '90
Target Eagle '84
The Tigress '93
Tobruk '66
Torn Between Two Lovers '79
Treasure of the Yankee Zephyr '83
Your Ticket Is No Longer Valid '84

Barbara Pepper
Girls in Chains '43
Hollywood Stadium Mystery '38
Kiss Me, Stupid! '64
Last Outlaw '36
Our Daily Bread '34
Rogue's Tavern '36
Wide Open Faces '38

Marilia Pera
Mixed Blood '84
Pixote '81

Eileen Percy
Down to Earth '17
Let's Go! '23
The Man from Painted Post '17
Reaching for the Moon '17

Esme Percy
Accused '36
Bitter Sweet '33
Old Spanish Custom '36
21 Days '37

Jose Perez
Courage '86
Miami Blues '90
One Shoe Makes It Murder '82
Short Eyes '79

Rosie Perez
Criminal Justice '90
Do the Right Thing '89
Fearless '93
It Could Happen to You '94
Night on Earth '91
Untamed Heart '93
White Men Can't Jump '92

Vincent Perez
Cyrano de Bergerac '90
Indochine '92

Francois Perier
Gervaise '51
Godson '72
Orpheus '49
Stavisky '74
Sylvia and the Phantom '45
Tartuffe '51
The Testament of Orpheus '59
Z '69

Anthony Perkins
The Black Hole '79
Catch-22 '70
Crimes of Passion '84
A Demon in My View '91
Desire Under the Elms '58
Destroyer '88
The Double Negative '80
Edge of Sanity '89
Fear Strikes Out '57
ffolkes '80
The Fool Killer '65
Friendly Persuasion '56
Glory Boys '84
Goodbye Again '61
Green Mansions '59
I'm Dangerous Tonight '90
Is Paris Burning? '68
Les Miserables '78
Life & Times of Judge Roy Bean '72
Lonely Man '57
Mahogany '75
The Matchmaker '58
Murder on the Orient Express '74
On the Beach '59
Phaedra '61
Pretty Poison '68
Psycho '60
Psycho 2 '83
Psycho 3 '86
Psycho 4: The Beginning '90
Ravishing Idiot '64
The Sins of Dorian Gray '82
Someone Behind the Door '71
Tall Story '60
Ten Days Wonder '72
The Tin Star '57
The Trial '63

Perkins ▶cont.

Twice a Woman '79
Winter Kills '79

Carl Perkins
Into the Night '85
The Real Patsy Cline '90

Elizabeth Perkins
About Last Night... '86
Avalon '90
Big '88
The Doctor '91
Enid is Sleeping '90
The Flintstones '94
From the Hip '86
He Said, She Said '91
Indian Summer '93
Love at Large '89
Sweet Hearts Dance '88

Millie Perkins
At Close Range '86
Cockfighter '74
The Diary of Anne Frank '59
Ensign Pulver '64
The Haunting Passion '83
License to Kill '84
Pistol: The Birth of a Legend '90
Ride in the Whirlwind '67
Shattered Vows '84
The Shooting '66
Table for Five '83
Two Moon Junction '88
Wall Street '87
Wild in the Country '61
Wild in the Streets '68
Witch Who Came from the Sea '76

Osgood Perkins
Love 'Em and Leave 'Em '26
Scarface '31
Six Degrees of Separation '93

Max Perlich
Born Yesterday '93
The Butcher's Wife '91
Cliffhanger '93
Drugstore Cowboy '89
Ferris Bueller's Day Off '86
Maverick '94
Rush '91

Rhea Perlman
Amazing Stories '85
Canadian Bacon '94
Class Act '91
Enid is Sleeping '90
Intimate Strangers '77
Ratings Game '84
Stamp of a Killer '87
Ted & Venus '93
There Goes the Neighborhood '92

Ron Perlman
The Adventures of Huck Finn '93
Blind Man's Bluff '91
Double Exposure '93
Ice Pirates '84
The Name of the Rose '86
Quest for Fire '82
Romeo Is Bleeding '93
Sleepwalkers '92

Gigi Perreau
Dance with Me, Henry '56
Girls' Town '59
Hell on Wheels '67
Journey to the Center of Time '67
The Man in the Gray Flannel Suit '56
Never a Dull Moment '50

Paul Perri
Delta Force 2: Operation Stranglehold '90
Hit & Run '82

Mireille Perrier
Boy Meets Girl '84
Chocolat '89
Love Without Pity '91
Toto le Heros '91

Jack Perrin
Apache Kid's Escape '30
Bandit Queen '51
The Court Martial of Billy Mitchell '55
Gun Grit '36
Hell Fire Austin '32
I Shot Billy the Kid '50
Midnight Faces '26
New Moon '40
The North Star '43
Rawhide Mail '30s
The Story of Vernon and Irene Castle '39
Sunrise at Campobello '60
Ten Wanted Men '54
Texas Jack '35
Them! '54
West of Pinto Basin '40
When Gangland Strikes '56

Jacques Perrin
Black and White in Color '76
Cinema Paradiso '88
The Desert of the Tartars '76
Donkey Skin '70
Dos Cruces en Danger Pass '71
Flight of the Innocent '93
Le Crabe Tambour '77
State of Siege '73
The 317th Platoon '65
Z '69

Valerie Perrine
The Agency '81
Boiling Point '93
The Border '82
Bright Angel '91
Can't Stop the Music '80
The Electric Horseman '79
The Last American Hero '73
Lenny '74
The Magician of Lublin '79
Maid to Order '87
Mr. Billion '77
Slaughterhouse Five '72
Superman: The Movie '78
Superman 2 '80
Sweet Bird of Youth '89
The Three Little Pigs '84
Water '85
When Your Lover Leaves '83

Leslie Perrins
Man on the Run '49
Nine Days a Queen '34
The Silent Passenger '35

Francoise Perrot
Life and Nothing But '89
My Best Friend's Girl '84
Women's Prison Massacre '85

Felton Perry
Checking Out '89
Night Call Nurses '72
RoboCop '87
RoboCop 2 '90
RoboCop 3 '91
Sudden Death '77
Walking Tall '73

John Bennett Perry
The Last Fling '86
A Matter of Life and Death '81
Only When I Laugh '81

Luke Perry
Beverly Hills 90210: The Graduation '93
Buffy the Vampire Slayer '92
8 Seconds '94
Sweet Trash '89
Terminal Bliss '91

Matthew L. Perry
A Night in the Life of Jimmy Reardon '88
The Whole Shootin' Match '79

Rod Perry
Black Gestapo '75
Black Godfather '74

Roger Perry
The Cat '66
Conspiracy of Terror '75
Count Yorga, Vampire '70
The Return of Count Yorga '71
Roller Boogie '79

Maria Perschy
The Castle of Fu Manchu '68
Exorcism '74
Horror of the Zombies '74
House of Psychotic Women '73
Last Day of the War '69
The Mad Executioners '65

Man's Favorite Sport? '63
No Survivors, Please '63
People Who Own the Dark '75
The Rue Morgue Massacres '73
633 Squadron '64
A Witch Without a Broom '68

Lisa Jane Persky
The Big Easy '87
Breathless '83
Coneheads '93
The Cotton Club '84
Great Balls of Fire '89
The Great Santini '80
The Last of the Finest '90
Peggy Sue Got Married '86
Shattered Vows '91
The Sure Thing '85
Vital Signs '90
When Harry Met Sally '89

Nehemiah Persoff
Al Capone '59
The Badlanders '58
The Comancheros '61
Deadly Harvest '72
Eric '75
Francis Gary Powers: The True Story of the U-2 Spy '76
A Global Affair '63
Green Mansions '59
The Henderson Monster '80
Killing Stone '78
The Last Temptation of Christ '88
On the Waterfront '54
The People Next Door '70
The Rebels '79
Sadat '83
Some Like It Hot '59
The Stranger Within '74
Twins '88
Voyage of the Damned '76
The Wrong Man '56
Yentl '83

Essy Persson
Cry of the Banshee '70
Mission Stardust '68
Therese & Isabelle '68

Jon Pertwee
Carry On Screaming '66
The House that Dripped Blood '71

Frank Pesce
The Pamela Principle '91
29th Street '91

Joe Pesci
Betsy's Wedding '90
Easy Money '83
Eureka! '81
Family Enforcer '76
Goodfellas '90
Home Alone '90
Home Alone 2: Lost in New York '92
I'm Dancing as Fast as I Can '82
JFK '91
Jimmy Hollywood '94
Lethal Weapon 2 '89
Lethal Weapon 3 '92
Man on Fire '87
My Cousin Vinny '92
Once Upon a Time in America '84
The Public Eye '92
Raging Bull '80
Ruby's Dream '91
The Super '91
With Honors '94

Lisa Pescia
Body Chemistry '90
Body Chemistry 2: Voice of a Stranger '91

Donna Pescow
Glory Years '87
Policewoman Centerfold '83
Saturday Night Fever '77

Bernadette Peters
Alice '90
Annie '82
Heartbeeps '81
Impromptu '90
The Jerk '79
The Longest Yard '74
The Martian Chronicles: Part 2 '79
The Martian Chronicles: Part 3 '79
Pennies From Heaven '81
Pink Cadillac '89
Silent Movie '76
Slaves of New York '89
Sleeping Beauty '83
Sunday in the Park with George '86
Tulips '81

Brock Peters
Ace High '68
The Adventures of Huckleberry Finn '78
Alligator 2: The Mutation '90
Carmen Jones '54
Daring Game '68
Framed '75
The Incident '67
The McMasters '70
The Pawnbroker '65
The Secret '93
Slaughter's Big Ripoff '73
Soylent Green '73
Star Trek 6: The Undiscovered Country '91
To Heal a Nation '88
To Kill a Mockingbird '62

Clarke Peters
A Casualty of War '90
Mona Lisa '86

House Peters
Headwinds '28
Human Hearts '22
Outlaw Country '49
Red Planet Mars '52

Jean Peters
Apache '54
As Young As You Feel '51
Broken Lance '54
It Happens Every Spring '49
A Man Called Peter '55
Niagara '53
Pickup on South Street '53
Three Coins in the Fountain '54
Viva Zapata! '52

Luan Peters
Con Man '92
Flesh and Blood Show '73
Land of the Minotaur '77
Man of Violence '71
Not Tonight Darling '72
Twins of Evil '71

Molly Peters
Target for Killing '66
Thunderball '65

Ralph Peters
Death Rides the Range '40
Man's Country '38
Meeting at Midnight '44
Rough Ridin' Rhythm '37

Susan Peters
Andy Hardy's Double Life '42
Random Harvest '42

Werner Peters
The Corrupt Ones '67
The Counterfeit Traitor '62
Curse of the Yellow Snake '63
The Phantom of Soho '64

Chris Petersen
Little Dragons '80
Ninja Masters of Death '85
Vampire Raiders—Ninja Queen '89
When Every Day was the Fourth of July '78

Pat Petersen
Cold River '81
Little Dragons '80

William L. Petersen
Amazing Grace & Chuck '87
Cousins '89
Deadly Currents '93
Hard Promises '92
Keep the Change '92
Long Gone '87
Manhunter '86
Passed Away '92
Return to Lonesome Dove '93
To Live & Die in L.A. '85
Young Guns 2 '90

Amanda Peterson
Can't Buy Me Love '87
Explorers '85

Fatal Charm '92
I Posed for Playboy '91
The Lawless Land '88
Listen to Me '89

Cassandra Peterson
Balboa '82
Echo Park '86
Elvira, Mistress of the Dark '88
Pee Wee's Big Adventure '85
Uncensored '85
Working Girls '75

Dorothy Peterson
I'm No Angel '33
Peck's Bad Boy '34

Stewart Peterson
Against A Crooked Sky '75
Pony Express Rider '76
Seven Alone '75
Where the Red Fern Grows '74

Edward Petherbridge
Lovers of Their Time '85
Strange Interlude '90

Victor Petit
Night of the Death Cult '75
Street Warriors '87
Terror Beach '80s

Gio Petre
The Doll '62
Gorilla '56

Hay Petrie
A Canterbury Tale '44
Crimes at the Dark House '39
Great Expectations '46
The Old Curiosity Shop '35
Spellbound '41
Spy in Black '39
21 Days '37

Joanna Pettet
Blue '68
Casino Royale '67
Cry of the Innocent '80
Double Exposure '82
The Evil '78
The Group '66
A Killer in Every Corner '74
Night of the Generals '67
Pioneer Woman '73
Return of Frank Cannon '80
Robbery '67
Sweet Country '87
Terror in Paradise

Lori Petty
Cadillac Man '90
Free Willy '93
In the Army Now '94
A League of Their Own '92
Point Break '91

Angelique Pettyjohn
Bio Hazard '85
Confessions of Tom Harris '72
G.I. Executioner '71
The Lost Empire '83
Repo Man '83
Revenge of Doctor X '80s
The Wizard of Speed and Time '88

Joseph Pevney
Nocturne '46
The Street with No Name '48

Penny Peyser
The Frisco Kid '79
The In-Laws '79
Messenger of Death '88

Dedee Pfeiffer
Brothers in Arms '88
A Climate for Killing '91
Double Exposure '93
Falling Down '93
The Horror Show '89
King's Ransom '91
The Midnight Hour '86
Red Surf '90
Running Cool '93
Shoot '92
Toughlove '85

Michelle Pfeiffer
The Age of Innocence '93
Amazon Women on the Moon '87
B.A.D. Cats '80
Batman Returns '92
Callie and Son '81

Charlie Chan and the Curse of
    the Dragon Queen '81
Dangerous Liaisons '88
The Fabulous Baker Boys '89
Falling in Love Again '80
Frankie and Johnny '91
Grease 2 '82
Into the Night '85
Ladyhawke '85
Love Field '91
Married to the Mob '88
Power, Passion & Murder '83
The Russia House '90
Scarface '83
The Solitary Man '82
Sweet Liberty '86
Tequila Sunrise '88
The Witches of Eastwick '87
Wolf '94

JoAnn Pflug
Catlow '71
The Day the Women Got Even
    '80
M*A*S*H '70

Joe Phelan
Fatal Pulse '88
South of Reno '87
Terminal Exposure '89
Zero Boys '86

Shawn Phelan
Breaking the Rules '92
Caroline? '90

Peter Phelps
Breaking Loose '90
The Lighthorsemen '87
Merlin '93
Rock & Roll Cowboys '92
Starlight Hotel '90

John Philbin
Martians Go Home! '90
North Shore '87
Point Break '91
Shy People '87

Mary Philbin
Human Hearts '22
The Man Who Laughs '27
Merry-Go-Round '23
The Phantom of the Opera '25

James Philbrook
Finger on the Trigger '65
Last Day of the War '69
Sound of Horror '64

Robert Philip
Adios Amigo '75
Children Shouldn't Play with
    Dead Things '72

Gerard Philippe
Dangerous Liaisons '60
Devil in the Flesh '46
Fever Mounts at El Pao '59
La Chartreuse de Parme '48
La Ronde '51
Modigliani '58
The Proud Ones '53
The Red and the Black '57

Bobbie Philips
Hail Caesar '94
TC 2000 '93

Mary Philips
A Farewell to Arms '32
Prince Valiant '54

Barney Phillips
I Was a Teenage Werewolf '57
Savage Run '70

Chynna Phillips
Caddyshack 2 '88
Goodbye, Miss 4th of July '88
The Invisible Kid '88
The Prize Pulitzer '89
Say Anything '89

Eddie Phillips
Phantom Patrol '36
Probation '32
The Throwback '35

Ethan Phillips
Bloodhounds of Broadway '89
Green Card '90
Lean on Me '89

Julianne Phillips
Fletch Lives '89
Getting Up and Going Home
    '92
Seven Hours to Judgment '88

Skin Deep '89
Summer Fantasy '84
Sweet Lies '88

Lee Phillips
The Hunters '58
Peyton Place '57
Psychomania '63

Leslie Phillips
Empire of the Sun '87
The Limping Man '53
Maroc 7 '67
Mountains of the Moon '90
Scandal '89
The Smallest Show on Earth
    '57
Train of Events '49

**Lou Diamond
Phillips**
Ambition '91
Dakota '88
The Dark Wind '91
Disorganized Crime '89
Extreme Justice '93
The First Power '89
Harley '90
La Bamba '87
Renegades '89
Shadow of the Wolf '92
A Show of Force '90
Stand and Deliver '88
Trespasses '86
Young Guns '88
Young Guns 2 '90

MacKenzie Phillips
American Graffiti '73
Eleanor & Franklin '76
Love Child '82
Miles to Go Before I Sleep '74
More American Graffiti '79
Rafferty & the Gold Dust Twins
    '75

Michelle Phillips
American Anthem '86
Assault and Matrimony '87
The Death Squad '73
Dillinger '73
Let It Ride '89
Rubdown '93
Scissors '91
Secrets of a Married Man '84
Sidney Sheldon's Bloodline '79
Valentino '77

Samantha Phillips
Deceit '93
Sexual Malice '93

Sian Phillips
The Age of Innocence '93
The Carpathian Eagle '81
Clash of the Titans '81
The Doctor and the Devils '85
Dune '84
The Ewoks: Battle for Endor
    '85
Goodbye, Mr. Chips '69
Heidi '93
I, Claudius, Vol. 1: A Touch of
    Murder/Family Affairs '91
I, Claudius, Vol. 2: Waiting in
    the Wings/What Shall We Do
    With Claudius? '80
I, Claudius, Vol. 3: Poison is
    Queen/Some Justice '80
I, Claudius, Vol. 4: Queen of
    Heaven/Reign of Terror '80
Murphy's War '71
Nijinsky '80
Valmont '89

Wendy Phillips
Bugsy '91
Death Be Not Proud '75
Midnight Run '88

Max Phipps
The Blue Lightning '86
Dark Age '88
Nate and Hayes '83
Return of Captain Invincible '83
Sky Pirates '87

Nicholas Phipps
Captain's Paradise '53
Elizabeth of Ladymead '48
Maytime in Mayfair '52

William Phipps
Cavalry Command '63
The Vanishing Westerner '50

**Leaf (Joaquin Rafael)
Phoenix**
Parenthood '89
Russkies '87
SpaceCamp '86

River Phoenix
Dogfight '91
Explorers '85
I Love You to Death '90
Indiana Jones and the Last
    Crusade '89
Little Nikita '88
The Mosquito Coast '86
My Own Private Idaho '91
A Night in the Life of Jimmy
    Reardon '88
Running on Empty '88
Silent Tongue '92
Sneakers '92
Stand By Me '86
The Thing Called Love '93

Maurice Pialat
A Nos Amours '84
Under Satan's Sun '87

Jean Piat
Tower of Screaming Virgins '64
The Would-Be Gentleman '58

Ben Piazza
The Children of An Lac '80
Clean and Sober '88
Consenting Adult '85
A Dangerous Age '57
The Five of Me '81
Guilty by Suspicion '91
The Hanging Tree '59
Scene of the Crime '85

Tony Pica
House of Psychotic Women '73
Yesterday, Today and
    Tomorrow '64

Robert Picardo
Back to School '86
China Beach '88
Explorers '85
Frame Up '91
The Howling '81
Innerspace '87
Jack's Back '87
Matinee '92
Motorama '91
976-EVIL '88
Wagons East '94

Michel Piccoli
Atlantic City '81
Beyond Obsession '82
Contempt '64
Danger: Diabolik '68
Dangerous Moves '84
The Day and the Hour '63
Diary of a Chambermaid '64
The Discreet Charm of the
    Bourgeoisie '72
The Game is Over '66
Infernal Trio '74
La Belle Noiseuse '90
La Passante '83
La Puritaine '86
Lady L '65
Le Doulos '61
Leonor '75
L'Etat Sauvage '78
Mado '76
May Fools '90
The Milky Way '68
Peril '85
Phantom of Liberty '68
Prize of Peril '84
Spoiled Children '77
Success is the Best Revenge
    '84
Ten Days Wonder '72
The Things of Life '70
Topaz '69
Vincent, Francois, Paul and the
    Others '74
Wedding in Blood '74

Paul Picerni
Fearmaker '89
The Scalphunters '68

Irving Pichel
Dick Tracy '37
Dracula's Daughter '36
General Spanky '36
Oliver Twist '33
Torture Ship '39

Sorrels Pickard
Hardbodies '84
Running Hot '83

Slim Pickens
The Apple Dumpling Gang '75
Babe! '83
Ballad of Cable Hogue '70
Beyond the Poseidon
    Adventure '79
Charlie and the Great Balloon
    Chase '82
Colorado Sundown '52
The Cowboys '72
Crazy Horse and Custer: "The
    Untold Story" '90
Dr. Strangelove, or: How I
    Learned to Stop Worrying
    and Love the Bomb '64
Flim-Flam Man '67
The Getaway '72
Ginger in the Morning '73
Hawmps! '76
Honeysuckle Rose '80
The Howling '81
In Harm's Way '65
Iron Horsemen '71
Legend of Earl Durand '74
'Major Dundee '65
Mr. Billion '77
Never a Dull Moment '68
1941 '79
One-Eyed Jacks '61
Pat Garrett & Billy the Kid '73
Pink Motel '82
Pony Express Rider '76
Poor Pretty Eddie '75
Rancho Deluxe '75
Ride to Glory '71
Rough Night in Jericho '67
Shadow of Chikara '78
Story of a Cowboy Angel '81
The Swarm '78
Sweet Creek County War '82
Talion '66
Tom Horn '80
The White Buffalo '77
White Line Fever '75

Sarah Pickering
Little Dorrit, Film 1: Nobody's
    Fault '88
Little Dorrit, Film 2: Little
    Dorrit's Story '88

Blake Pickett
Dark Universe '93
HauntedWeen '91

Cindy Pickett
Call to Glory '84
Circle of Power '83
Crooked Hearts '91
Deepstar Six '89
Echoes in the Darkness '87
Ferris Bueller's Day Off '86
The Goodbye Bird '93
Hot to Trot! '88
Hysterical '83
Margin for Murder '81
The Men's Club '86
Night Games '80
Original Intent '91
Sleepwalkers '92
Son-in-Law '93
Wildcard '92

Mary Pickford
Coquette '29
D.W. Griffith Triple Feature '13
Griffith Biograph Program '09
A Kiss for Mary Pickford '27
The Little American '17
Little Annie Rooney '25
My Best Girl '27
Pollyanna '20
A Poor Little Rich Girl '17
Pride of the Clan '18
Rebecca of Sunnybrook Farm
    '17
Short Films of D.W. Griffith,
    Vol. 1 '12
Sparrows '26
Stella Maris '18
Suds '20
The Taming of the Shrew '29

Vivian Pickles
Candleshoe '78
Harold and Maude '71

Ronald Pickup
The Attic: The Hiding of Anne
    Frank '88

Dr. Bethune '90
Eleni '85
Fortunes of War '87
Ivanhoe '82
Journey of Honor '91
Life of Verdi '84
The Mission '86
My Friend Walter '93
Nijinsky '80

Molly Picon
Cannonball Run '81
Come Blow Your Horn '63
East and West '23
Fiddler on the Roof '71
For Pete's Sake '74
Mamele '38
Murder on Flight 502 '75
Yidl Mitn Fidl '36

Rebecca Pidgeon
The Dawning '88
Homicide '91

Walter Pidgeon
Advise and Consent '62
The Bad and the Beautiful '52
Big Red '62
Blossoms in the Dust '41
Cinderella '64
Command Decision '48
Dark Command '40
Deep in My Heart '54
Executive Suite '54
Forbidden Planet '56
Funny Girl '68
Girl of the Golden West '38
Hit the Deck '55
Holiday in Mexico '46
House Across the Bay '40
How Green was My Valley '41
It's a Date '40
Julia Misbehaves '48
The Last Time I Saw Paris '54
The Lindbergh Kidnapping
    Case '76
Listen, Darling '38
Madame Curie '43
Men of the Fighting Lady '54
Million Dollar Mermaid '52
The Miniver Story '50
Mrs. Miniver '42
Mrs. Parkington '44
Murder on Flight 502 '75
Neptune Factor '73
Saratoga '37
Sextette '78
Shopworn Angel '38
That Forsyte Woman '50
Too Hot to Handle '38
Two Minute Warning '76
Voyage to the Bottom of the
    Sea '61
Weekend at the Waldorf '45
White Cargo '42

Claude Pieplu
The Best Way '82
This Sweet Sickness '77
Wedding in Blood '74

Charles B. Pierce
Boggy Creek II '83
Grayeagle '77

Stack Pierce
Enemy Unseen '91
Murphy's Fault '88
Night Call Nurses '72
A Rage in Harlem '91
24 Hours to Midnight '92

Alexandra Pigg
Chicago Joe & the Showgirl '90
Letter to Brezhnev '86
Smart Money '88
Strapless '90

Tim Pigott-Smith
The Hunchback of Notre Dame
    '82
The Jewel in the Crown '84
The Remains of the Day '93

Joseph Pilato
Day of the Dead '85
Married People, Single Sex '93

Nova Pilbeam
Counterblast '48
The Man Who Knew Too Much
    '34
Nine Days a Queen '34
Young and Innocent '37

Daniel Pilon
Brannigan '75
In Trouble '67
Obsessed '88
The Red Half-Breed '70
Snowballin' '85
Starship Invasions '77

Donald Pilon
Keeping Track '86
Left for Dead '78
The Pyx '73

Silvia Pinal
The Exterminating Angel '62
Los Cacos '87
Viridiana '61

Bronson Pinchot
After Hours '85
Beverly Hills Cop '84
Beverly Hills Cop 3 '94
Blame It on the Bellboy '92
The Flamingo Kid '84
Hot Resort '85
Risky Business '83
Second Sight '89
True Romance '93

Larry Pine
Anna '87
Hullabaloo Over Georgie & Bonnie's Pictures '78
Plain Clothes '88

Phillip Pine
The Lost Missile '58
Money to Burn '83
The Phantom from 10,000 Leagues '56
Pot, Parents, and Police '71

Robert Pine
Are You Lonesome Tonight '92
Empire of the Ants '77
Enola Gay: The Men, the Mission, the Atomic Bomb '80
Mysterious Two '82

Miguel Pinero
Almost You '85
Alphabet City '84
Short Eyes '79

Wang Ping
Duel of the Iron Fist '72
King Boxer '90

Jada Pinkett
The Inkwell '94
Low Down Dirty Shame '94

Dominique Pinon
Alberto Express '92
Delicatessen '92
Diva '82
Moon in the Gutter '83

Gordon Pinsent
Blood Clan '91
Colossus: The Forbin Project '70
John and the Missus '87
Newman's Law '74

Leah K. Pinsent
April Fool's Day '86
The Bay Boy '85
Brutal Glory '89
Double Identity '89

Danny Pintauro
The Beniker Gang '83
Cujo '83

The Pioneers
Song of Arizona '46
Under California Stars '48
Western Double Feature 5: Rogers & Autry '37

Frederick Piper
The Blue Lamp '49
Hue and Cry '47
Johnny Frenchman '46
Oh, Mr. Porter '37
San Demetrio, London '47

Kelly Piper
Maniac '80
Rawhide Rex '87

Roddy Piper
Back in Action '94
Body Slam '87
Buy & Cell '89
Hell Comes to Frogtown '88
Immortal Combat '94

They Live '88

Joe Piscopo
Best of Eddie Murphy '89
Dead Heat '88
Huck and the King of Hearts '93
Johnny Dangerously '84
Sidekicks '93
Wise Guys '86

Marie-France Pisier
Chanel Solitaire '81
Cousin, Cousine '76
French Postcards '79
Hot Touch '80s
Love on the Run '78
Miss Right '81
Nous N'Irons Plus au Bois '69
The Other Side of Midnight '77
Prize of Peril '83
We Will Not Enter the Forest '79

Luigi Pistilli
The Good, the Bad and the Ugly '67
The Scorpion's Tail '71
Twitch of the Death Nerve '71

Kimberly Pistone
Blue De Ville '86
WhiteForce '88

Mario Pisu
Juliet of the Spirits '65
The Sensuous Nurse '76

Maria Pitillo
Cooperstown '93
The Lost Capone '90
Spike of Bensonhurst '88

Sacha Pitoeff
Inferno '78
Last Year at Marienbad '61

Anne Pitoniak
Agnes of God '85
The Ballad of the Sad Cafe '91
Best Seller '87
House of Cards '92
Old Enough '84
Old Gringo '89
Sister, Sister '87
The Wizard of Loneliness '88

Brad Pitt
Across the Tracks '89
Cool World '92
Cutting Class '89
The Favor '92
Johnny Suede '92
Kalifornia '93
A River Runs Through It '92
Thelma & Louise '91
True Romance '93

Charles Pitt
Monaco Forever '83
Moving Target '89

Ingrid Pitt
The Final Option '82
Hanna's War '88
The House that Dripped Blood '71
Sound of Horror '64
Transmutations '88
The Vampire Lovers '70
Where Eagles Dare '68
The Wicker Man '75

Carl Pitti
Billy the Kid '41
Gun Glory '57
Tribute to a Bad Man '56

Tom Pittman
Verboten! '59
The Zodiac Killer '71

ZaSu Pitts
Aggie Appleby, Maker of Men '33
The Bashful Bachelor '42
Breakfast in Hollywood '46
Broadway Limited '41
The Crooked Circle '32
Dames '34
The Denver & Rio Grande '51
Eternally Yours '39
Francis Joins the WACs '54
Francis the Talking Mule '49
Greed '24
The Guardsman '31
It's a Mad, Mad, Mad, Mad World '63

Life with Father '47
Lottery Bride '30
Meet the Mob '42
Mexican Spitfire at Sea '42
Mrs. Wiggs of the Cabbage Patch '42
Mr. Skitch '33
No, No Nanette '40
Nurse Edith Cavell '39
The Perfect Marriage '46
Risky Business '28
The Ruggles of Red Gap '35
Sin Takes a Holiday '30
Strangers of the Evening '32
Sunny Side Up '28
This Could Be the Night '57
The Thrill of It All! '63
Way Out West '37
The Wedding March '28

Jeremy Piven
Car 54, Where Are You? '94
Judgment Night '93
P.C.U. '94
Singles '92
12:01 '93

Mary Kay Place
The Big Chill '83
Bright Angel '91
Captain Ron '92
Crazy from the Heart '91
Explorers '85
For Love or Money '84
The Girl Who Spelled Freedom '86
The History of White People in America '85
Modern Problems '81
A New Life '88
New York, New York '77
Portrait of a White Marriage '88
Private Benjamin '80
Samantha '92
Smooth Talk '85
Starting Over '79
Waltz Across Texas '83

Michele Placido
Big Business '88
Drug Wars 2: The Cocaine Cartel '92
Ernesto '79
Forever Mary '89
Private Affairs '89
The Sicilian Connection '85
Summer Night '87
Summer Night with Greek Profile, Almond Eyes & Scent of Basil '87
Three Brothers '80
Till Marriage Do Us Part '74

Tony Plana
Born in East L.A. '87
Havana '90
The Hillside Strangler '89
JFK '91
Latino '85
One Good Cop '91
Romero '89
Sweet 15 '90
Why Me? '90

Nigel Planer
Supergrass '87
The Young Ones '88

Scott Plank
Dying to Remember '93
The In Crowd '88
Pastime '91
Red Shoe Diaries 4: Auto Erotica '93

Dana Plato
Beyond the Bermuda Triangle '75
High School USA '84
Return to Boggy Creek '77

Edward Platt
Atlantis, the Lost Continent '61
Designing Woman '57
North by Northwest '59
The Rebel Set '59
Rebel Without a Cause '55
Rock, Pretty Baby '56
Written on the Wind '56

Louise Platt
Captain Caution '40
Stagecoach '39

Marc Platt
Down to Earth '47

Tonight and Every Night '45

Oliver Platt
Beethoven '92
Benny & Joon '93
Diggstown '92
Flatliners '90
Indecent Proposal '93
The Temp '93
The Three Musketeers '93
Working Girl '88

Angela Pleasence
The Favor, the Watch, & the Very Big Fish
The Godsend '79
Six Wives of Henry VIII '70s
Stealing Heaven '88

Donald Pleasence
All Quiet on the Western Front '79
Alone in the Dark '82
The Ambassador '84
American Tiger '89
Arch of Triumph '85
Barry McKenzie Holds His Own '74
The Bastard '78
Better Late Than Never '79
The Black Arrow '84
The Black Windmill '74
Blood Relatives '77
A Breed Apart '84
Buried Alive '89
Casablanca Express '89
Choice of Weapons '76
Circus of Horrors '60
The Count of Monte Cristo '74
Creepers '85
Cul de Sac '66
Deep Cover '88
Devonsville Terror '83
Dr. Jekyll and Mr. Hyde '73
Dracula '79
The Eagle Has Landed '77
Escape from New York '81
Escape to Witch Mountain '75
Fantastic Voyage '66
Frankenstein's Great Aunt Tillie '83
The Freakmaker '73
From Beyond the Grave '73
Gold of the Amazon Women '79
Goldenrod '77
The Great Escape '63
The Great Escape 2: The Untold Story '88
The Greatest Story Ever Told '65
Ground Zero '88
The Hallelujah Trail '65
Halloween '78
Halloween 2: The Nightmare Isn't Over! '81
Halloween 4: The Return of Michael Myers '88
Halloween 5: The Revenge of Michael Myers '89
The Hands of Orlac '60
Hanna's War '88
Hearts of the West '75
Horsemasters '61
House of the Damned
The House of Usher '88
I Don't Want to Be Born '75
Into the Darkness '86
Jaguar Lives '79
Journey into Fear '74
Land of the Minotaur '77
The Last Tycoon '76
The Madwoman of Chaillot '69
Mania '60
Mansfield Park '85
Millions '91
The Monster Club '85
Night Creature '79
Night of the Generals '67
No Love for Johnnie '60
Nothing Underneath '85
Oh, God! '77
Operation 'Nam '85
The Passover Plot '75
Phantom of Death '87
Power Play '81
Prince of Darkness '87
The Puma Man '80
The Rainbow Gang '73
River of Death '90
The Room '87

Sgt. Pepper's Lonely Hearts Club Band '78
Shadows and Fog '92
The Shaming '71
Soldier Blue '70
Specters '87
A Tale of Two Cities '58
Tales That Witness Madness '73
Telefon '77
Ten Little Indians '89
THX 1138 '71
To Kill a Stranger '70s
Tomorrow Never Comes '77
The Treasure of the Amazon '84
Treasure of the Yankee Zephyr '83
The Uncanny '78
Warrior of the Lost World '84
Warrior Queen '87
Wedding in White '72
What a Carve-Up! '62
Will Penny '67
You Only Live Twice '67

John Pleshette
Burning Rage '84
Eye of the Stranger '93
The Kid with the Broken Halo '82
Lies of the Twins '91
The Trial of Lee Harvey Oswald '77

Suzanne Pleshette
The Adventures of Bullwhip Griffin '66
Alone in the Neon Jungle '87
Battling for Baby '92
The Birds '63
Blackbeard's Ghost '67
Dixie: Changing Habits '85
For Love or Money '84
The Geisha Boy '58
Hard Frame '70
Help Wanted: Male '82
Hot Stuff '80
If It's Tuesday, This Must Be Belgium '69
If Things Were Different '79
Kojak: The Belarus File '85
Legend of Valentino '75
Nevada Smith '66
Oh, God! Book 2 '80
One Cooks, the Other Doesn't '83
The Queen of Mean '90
Rome Adventure '62
The Shaggy D.A. '76
Support Your Local Gunfighter '71
Suppose They Gave a War and Nobody Came? '70
The Ugly Dachshund '65

George Plimpton
Easy Wheels '89
Little Man Tate '91
Reds '81
Rio Lobo '70
Volunteers '85

Martha Plimpton
Another Woman '88
Chantilly Lace '93
Daybreak '93
The Goonies '85
Inside Monkey Zetterland '93
Josh and S.A.M. '93
The Mosquito Coast '86
Parenthood '89
The River Rat '84
Rollover '81
Running on Empty '88
Samantha '92
Shy People '87
Silence Like Glass '90
Stanley and Iris '90
Stars and Bars '88

Melinda Plowman
Billy the Kid Versus Dracula '66
Home Town Story '51

Joan Plowright
And a Nightingale Sang '91
Avalon '90
Brimstone & Treacle '82
Britannia Hospital '82
A Dedicated Man '86
Dennis the Menace '93
The Dressmaker '89

Drowning by Numbers '87
Enchanted April '92
The Entertainer '60
Equus '77
I Love You to Death '90
The Merchant of Venice '73
Revolution '85
School for Scandal '65
Stalin '92
Widow's Peak '94

Eve Plumb
Alexander: The Other Side of Dawn '77
The Brady Bunch, Vol. 1 '69
Force of Evil '77
I'm Gonna Git You Sucka '88
Little Women '78
Secrets of Three Hungry Wives '78
A Very Brady Christmas '88

Amanda Plummer
Courtship '87
Daniel '83
The Dollmaker '84
The Fisher King '91
Freejack '92
Gryphon '88
The Hotel New Hampshire '84
Joe Versus the Volcano '90
Last Light '93
Made in Heaven '87
Miss Rose White '92
Needful Things '93
Prisoners of Inertia '89
Pulp Fiction '94
Riders to the Sea '88
So I Married an Axe Murderer '93
Static '87
The World According to Garp '82

Christopher Plummer
The Amateur '82
The Assignment '78
Battle of Britain '69
The Boss' Wife '86
Boy in Blue '86
Conduct Unbecoming '75
The Day that Shook the World '78
Disappearance '81
A Doll's House '59
Dragnet '87
Dreamscape '84
Eyewitness '81
The Fall of the Roman Empire '64
Firehead '90
Hanover Street '79
Highpoint '80
I Love N.Y. '87
Inside Daisy Clover '65
International Velvet '78
Liar's Edge '92
Lily in Love '85
Little Gloria...Happy at Last '84
The Man Who Would Be King '75
Many Faces of Sherlock Holmes '86
Mindfield '89
Murder by Decree '79
Night of the Generals '67
Ordeal by Innocence '84
Prototype '83
The Pyx '73
Red Blooded American Girl '90
Return of the Pink Panther '74
Riel '79
The Scarlet & the Black '83
The Shadow Box '80
Shadow Dancing '88
Sherlock Holmes: The Silver Blaze '77
The Silent Partner '78
Somewhere in Time '80
The Sound of Music '65
Souvenir '88
Spiral Staircase '75
Stage Struck '57
Star Crash '78
Star Trek 6: The Undiscovered Country '91
The Thorn Birds '83
Triple Cross '67
Waterloo '71
Where the Heart Is '90

Wolf '94
Young Catherine '91

Glenn Plummer
Menace II Society '93
Pastime '91
South Central '92
Speed '94

Werner Pochat
Flatfoot '78
Laser Mission '90
Thunder Warrior 3 '88

Rick Podell
Lunch Wagon '81
World Gone Wild '88

Rossana Podesta
Alone Against Rome '62
Horno Eroticus/Man of the Year '71
The Sensual Man '74
Sodom and Gomorrah '62
Ulysses '55
The Virgin of Nuremberg '65

Ken Pogue
The Amy Fisher Story '93
Blind Man's Bluff '91
Crazy Moon '87
Dead of Winter '87
The Grey Fox '83
The Hitman '91
Keeping Track '86
Miracle at Moreaux '86
Run '91
Still Not Quite Human '92

Eric Pohlmann
The Belles of St. Trinian's '53
Blackout '50
Glass Tomb '55
Moulin Rouge '52
Terror Street '54
Three Stops to Murder '53
Tiffany Jones '75

Larry Poindexter
American Ninja 2: The Confrontation '87
Blue Movies '88

Priscilla Pointer
Archer: The Fugitive from the Empire '81
The Competition '80
Disturbed '90
The Falcon and the Snowman '85
Honeysuckle Rose '80
The Magic Bubble '93
Mysterious Two '82
A Nightmare on Elm Street 3: Dream Warriors '87
Rumpelstiltskin '86

Jean Poiret
The Elegant Criminal '92
The Last Metro '80

Sidney Poitier
All the Young Men '60
Band of Angels '57
Bedford Incident '65
Blackboard Jungle '55
Brother John '70
Buck and the Preacher '72
Cry, the Beloved Country '51
The Defiant Ones '58
Duel at Diablo '66
For Love of Ivy '68
Goodbye, My Lady '56
The Greatest Story Ever Told '65
Guess Who's Coming to Dinner '67
In the Heat of the Night '67
Let's Do It Again '75
Lilies of the Field '63
Little Nikita '88
The Mark of the Hawk '57
The Organization '71
Paris Blues '61
A Patch of Blue '65
Piece of the Action '77
Pressure Point '62
A Raisin in the Sun '61
Separate But Equal '91
Shoot to Kill '88
The Slender Thread '65
Sneakers '92
Something of Value '57
They Call Me Mr. Tibbs! '70
To Sir, with Love '67
Uptown Saturday Night '74

The Wilby Conspiracy '75

Roman Polanski
Back in the USSR '92
Ciao Federico! Fellini Directs Satyricon '69
Diary of Forbidden Dreams '73
The Fearless Vampire Killers '67
A Generation '54
The Magic Christian '69
The Tenant '76

Jon Polito
Barton Fink '91
Blankman '94
The Crow '93
Deadly Business '86
The Equalizer: Memories of Manon '89
Fallen Angels 2 '93
Fire with Fire '86
The Freshman '90
Highlander '91
Leather Jackets '90
Miller's Crossing '90

Lina Polito
All Screwed Up '74
Blood Brothers '74

Oscar Polk
Gone with the Wind '39
Green Pastures '36

Ben Pollack
The Benny Goodman Story '55
The Glenn Miller Story '54

Sydney Pollack
Death Becomes Her '92
Husbands and Wives '92
The Player '92
Tootsie '82

Cheryl Pollak
Crossing the Bridge '92
My Best Friend Is a Vampire '88
Night Life '90
Pump Up the Volume '90
Swimsuit: The Movie '89

Kevin Pollak
Another You '91
Avalon '90
Canadian Bacon '94
Clean Slate '94
A Few Good Men '92
Grumpy Old Men '93
Indian Summer '93
L.A. Story '91
The Opposite Sex and How to Live With Them '93
Ricochet '91
Wayne's World 2 '93
Willow '88

Tracy Pollan
The Abduction of Kari Swenson '87
Baby It's You '82
Bright Lights, Big City '88
Fine Things '90
Great Love Experiment '84
Promised Land '88
A Stranger Among Us '92
The Tender Age '84

Daphne Pollard
Bonnie Scotland '35
Laurel & Hardy Comedy Classics, Vol. 7 '30s
Our Relations '36

Michael J. Pollard
America '86
American Gothic '88
The Arrival '90
The Art of Dying '90
Between the Lines '77
Bonnie & Clyde '67
Dick Tracy '90
Enter Laughing '67
Fast Food '89
Heated Vengeance '87
I Come in Peace '90
Legend of Frenchie King '71
Melvin and Howard '80
Motorama '91
Next of Kin '89
Night Visitor '89
The Patriot '86
Riders of the Storm '88
Roxanne '87
Scrooged '88

Season of Fear '89
Skeeter '93
Sleepaway Camp 3: Teenage Wasteland '89
Split Second '92
Tango and Cash '89
Vengeance Is Mine '84
Why Me? '90
The Wild Angels '66

Snub Pollard
Arizona Days '37
Comedy Classics '35
Don't Shove/Two Gun Gussie '19
The Errand Boy '61
I'm on My Way/The Non-Stop Kid '19
Laughfest '10s
A Nation Aflame '37
Riders of the Rockies '37
Silent Laugh Makers, No. 3 '19
The White Legion '36

Sarah Polley
The Adventures of Baron Munchausen '89
Lantern Hill '90
Tales from Avonlea, Vol. 1: The Journey Begins '90

Eileen Pollock
Far and Away '92
Four Days in July '84

Teri Polo
Aspen Extreme '93
Born to Ride '91
Golden Gate '93
Mystery Date '91
Passed Away '92
Quick '93

John Polson
Dangerous Game '90
Sirens '94

Lily Pons
I Dream Too Much '35
That Girl from Paris '36

Yvan Ponton
Men of Steel '88
Pouvoir Intime '87
Scanners 2: The New Order '91

Johnny Popwell
Challenge '74
Manhunter '83

Jorge Porcel
Carlito's Way '93
Expertos en Pinchazos '79
Fotografo de Senoras '85
Naked Is Better '73

Paulina Porizkova
Anna '87
Her Alibi '88
Portfolio '88

Louise Portal
The Decline of the American Empire '86
The Klutz '73

Don Porter
Bachelor in Paradise '69
Buck Privates Come Home '47
The Candidate '72
The Christmas Coal Mine Miracle '77
Live a Little, Love a Little '68
Night Monster '42
Our Miss Brooks '56
The Racket '51
Who Done It? '42

Eric Porter
Antony and Cleopatra '73
The Belstone Fox '73
Churchill and the Generals '81
The Fall of the Roman Empire '64
Hands of the Ripper '71
Hennessy '75
Little Lord Fauntleroy '80
Macbeth '83
Oliver Twist '85
The Thirty-Nine Steps '79

Jean Porter
Bathing Beauty '44
G.I. Jane '51
Kentucky Jubilee '51

Robert Porter
Deadly Fieldtrip '74
The Jesus Trip '71

Eric Portman
Bedford Incident '65
A Canterbury Tale '44
The Colditz Story '55
The Crimes of Stephen Hawke '36
Dear Murderer '47
The Forty-Ninth Parallel '41
Great Day '46
Men of Two Worlds '46
Moonlight Sonata '38
Murder in the Old Red Barn '36
The Naked Edge '61
One of Our Aircraft Is Missing '41
Saturday Night Shockers, Vol. 2 '58
We Dive at Dawn '43

Richard Portnow
Barton Fink '91
In Dangerous Company '88
Kindergarten Cop '90
Meet the Hollowheads '89
Say Anything '89
S.F.W. '94
Sister Act '92

Markie Post
Glitz '88
Scene of the Crime '85
Tricks of the Trade '88
TripleCross '85

Saskia Post
Dogs in Space '87
One Night Stand '84

William Post, Jr.
Call Northside 777 '48
Sherlock Holmes and the Secret Weapon '42
Ship Ahoy '42

Peter Postlethwaite
Distant Voices, Still Lives '88
The Dressmaker '89
In the Name of the Father '93
Split Second '92
To Kill a Priest '89
Waterland '92

Laurens C. Postma
Heroes Three '84
To Live and Die in Hong Kong '89

Tom Poston
Carbon Copy '81
Cold Turkey '71
A Perfect Little Murder '90
Soldier in the Rain '63
The Tempest '63
Up the Academy '80
Zotz! '62

Victor Potel
Anna Christie '23
Captain Swagger '25
Doughboys '30
Miracle of Morgan's Creek '44
Paradise Island '30
Thunder Over Texas '34

Madeleine Potter
Bloodhounds of Broadway '89
The Bostonians '84
Hello Again '87
Slaves of New York '89
The Suicide Club '88
Two Evil Eyes '90

Martin Potter
Ciao Federico! Fellini Directs Satyricon '69
Fellini Satyricon '69
Gunpowder '84
The Only Way '70
Twinsanity '70

Annie Potts
Bayou Romance '86
Breaking the Rules '92
Corvette Summer '78
Crimes of Passion '84
Flatbed Annie and Sweetiepie: Lady Truckers '79
Ghostbusters '84
Ghostbusters 2 '89
Heartaches '82
It Came Upon a Midnight Clear '84
Jumpin' Jack Flash '86
King of the Gypsies '78
Pass the Ammo '88
Pretty in Pink '86

Potts ▶cont.

Texasville '90
Who's Harry Crumb? '89

Cliff Potts
The Groundstar Conspiracy '72
The Last Ride of the Dalton
  Gang '79
Little Women '78
Sahara '83
Silent Running '71

Ely Pouget
Cool Blue '88
Endless Descent '90
Silent Victim '92

Georges Poujouly
Forbidden Games '52
Frantic '58

CCH Pounder
Bagdad Cafe '88
Benny & Joon '93
The Disappearance of Christina
  '93
The Ernest Green Story '93
Lifepod '93
Prizzi's Honor '85
Psycho 4: The Beginning '90
Question of Faith '93
Return to Lonesome Dove '93
RoboCop 3 '91
Sliver '93

Jason Rai Pow
Black Dragon '74
Black Dragon's Revenge '75

Brittney Powell
Airborne '93
Dragonworld '94
To Be the Best '93

Dick Powell
The Bad and the Beautiful '52
Blessed Event '32
Christmas in July '40
Cornered '45
Cry Danger '51
Dames '34
Flirtation Walk '34
Footlight Parade '33
42nd Street '33
Gold Diggers of 1933 '33
Gold Diggers of 1935 '35
In the Navy '41
A Midsummer Night's Dream
  '35
Murder, My Sweet '44
On the Avenue '37
Pitfall '48
Station West '48
Susan Slept Here '54

Eleanor Powell
Born to Dance '36
Broadway Melody of 1936 '35
Broadway Melody of 1938 '37
Broadway Melody of 1940 '40
Duchess of Idaho '50
Honolulu '39
I Dood It '43
Lady Be Good '41
Rosalie '38
Sensations of 1945 '44
Ship Ahoy '42
Thousands Cheer '43

Jane Powell
Athena '54
A Date with Judy '48
Deep in My Heart '54
Delightfully Dangerous '45
Enchanted Island '58
The Girl Most Likely '57
Hit the Deck '55
Holiday in Mexico '46
Nancy Goes to Rio '50
Rich, Young and Pretty '51
Royal Wedding '51
Seven Brides for Seven
  Brothers '54
Small Town Girl '53
Three Daring Daughters '48
Two Weeks with Love '50

Lee Powell
Along the Sundown Trail '42
Fighting Devil Dogs '38
The Lone Ranger '38
Prairie Pals '42
Trigger Pals '39

Tumbleweed Trail '42

Michael Powell
Edge of the World '37
Thief of Baghdad '40

Robert Powell
The Asphyx '72
Dark Forces '83
The Four Feathers '78
Frankenstein '82
The Hunchback of Notre Dame
  '82
Jane Austen in Manhattan '80
Jesus of Nazareth '77
The Jigsaw Man '84
Jude the Obscure '71
Mahler '74
Secrets '71
Shaka Zulu '83
Survivor '80
The Thirty-Nine Steps '79
Tommy '75
What Waits Below '83

William Powell
After the Thin Man '36
Another Thin Man '39
Double Wedding '37
Evelyn Prentice '34
Ex-Mrs. Bradford '36
Fashions of 1934 '34
Feel My Pulse '28
The Girl Who Had Everything
  '53
The Great Ziegfeld '36
How to Marry a Millionaire '53
I Love You Again '40
The Kennel Murder Case '33
Last Command '28
The Last of Mrs. Cheyney '37
Libeled Lady '36
Life with Father '47
Love Crazy '41
Manhattan Melodrama '34
Mister Roberts '55
My Man Godfrey '36
Reckless '35
The Senator was Indiscreet '47
Shadow of the Thin Man '41
Song of the Thin Man '47
Star of Midnight '35
The Thin Man '34
The Thin Man Goes Home '44
Ziegfeld Follies '46

Taryn Power
The Count of Monte Cristo '74
Maria '71
Sinbad and the Eye of the Tiger
  '77
Tracks '77

Tyrone Power, Sr.
Big Trail '30
Dream Street '21
Red Kimono '25
Test of Donald Norton '26

Tyrone Power
Alexander's Ragtime Band '38
Blood and Sand '41
Crash Dive '43
Diplomatic Courier '52
The Eddy Duchin Story '56
In Old Chicago '38
Jesse James '39
Johnny Apollo '40
The Long Gray Line '55
Marie Antoinette '38
The Mark of Zorro '40
The Rains Came '39
Rawhide '50
The Razor's Edge '46
Rose of Washington Square
  '39
Second Fiddle '39
Son of Fury '42
Thin Ice '37
Witness for the Prosecution '57
A Yank in the R.A.F. '41

Tyrone Power, Jr.
California Casanova '89
Cocoon '85
Shag: The Movie '89

Alexandra Powers
Cast a Deadly Spell '91
Dangerous Pursuit '89
Mask '85
The Seventh Coin '92
Sonny Boy '87

Beverly Powers
Kissin' Cousins '64
Sixteen '72

Lucille Powers
Texas Bad Man '32
Two Gun Man '31

Mala Powers
City That Never Sleeps '53
Cyrano de Bergerac '50
Daddy's Gone A-Hunting '69
Escape from Planet Earth '67
Rage at Dawn '55
Storm Rider '57

Stefanie Powers
The Boatniks '70
Die! Die! My Darling! '65
Escape to Athena '79
Experiment in Terror '62
Family Secrets '84
Gone with the West '72
Herbie Rides Again '74
The Interns '62
The Invisible Strangler '76
Little Moon & Jud McGraw '78
Love has Many Faces '65
The Man Inside '76
Manhunter '74
McLintock! '63
Mistral's Daughter '84
No Place to Run '72
Palm Springs Weekend '63
Paper Man '71
Return to Earth '76
Shadow on the Sun '88
Sky Hei$t '75

Tom Powers
Destination Moon '50
Double Indemnity '44
Lucky Me '54
Mexican Hayride '48
The Nevadan '50
Station West '48

Vicki Powers
Deadly Encounter '78
The Meal '75

Leon Pownall
Love and Hate: A Marriage
  Made in Hell '90
Termini Station '89

Clare Powney
The Girl '86
Operation Julie '85

Lilia Prado
El Gavilan Pollero '47
The Illusion Travels by
  Streetcar '53
Mexican Bus Ride '51
Wuthering Heights '53

Michael Praed
Nightflyers '87
Robin Hood...The Legend:
  Robin Hood and the
  Sorcerer '83
Robin Hood...The Legend: The
  Swords of Wayland '83
To Die for 2 '91
Writer's Block '91

Joan Prather
The Deerslayer '78
Smile '75

Wolfgang Preiss
Cave of the Living Dead '65
Club Extinction '89
The Invisible Dr. Mabuse '62
The Mad Executioners '65
Mill of the Stone Women '60
Mistress of the World '59
Raid on Rommel '71
The Return of Dr. Mabuse '61
Testament of Dr. Mabuse '62
The Thousand Eyes of Dr.
  Mabuse '60
The Train '65

June Preisser
Babes in Arms '39
Strike Up the Band '40

Albert Prejean
The Crazy Ray '22
Italian Straw Hat '27
Princess Tam Tam '35
Under the Roofs of Paris '29

Otto Preminger
Stalag 17 '53
They Got Me Covered '43

Luis Prendes
Alien Predators '80
The Christmas Kid '68
Ursus in the Valley of the Lions
  '62

Paula Prentiss
Bachelor in Paradise '69
The Black Marble '79
Born to Win '71
Buddy Buddy '81
Catch-22 '70
The Honeymoon Machine '61
The Horizontal Lieutenant '62
In Harm's Way '65
Last of the Red Hot Lovers '72
M.A.D.D.: Mothers Against
  Drunk Driving '83
Man's Favorite Sport? '63
No Room to Run '78
Packin' It In '83
Parallax View '74
Saturday the 14th '81
What's New Pussycat? '65
Where the Boys Are '60
The World of Henry Orient '64

Robert Prescott
Bachelor Party '84
Blue De Ville '86

Micheline Presle
Adventures of Captain Fabian
  '51
The Bride Is Much Too
  Beautiful '58
Devil in the Flesh '46
The French Way '40
The King of Hearts '66
Legend of Frenchie King '71
Mistress of the World '59
The Nun '66
The Prize '63
Time Out for Love '61

Elvis Presley
Blue Hawaii '62
Change of Habit '69
Charro! '69
Clambake '67
Double Trouble '67
Easy Come, Easy Go '67
Elvis in the Movies '90
Elvis Memories '85
Elvis on Tour '72
Elvis: One Night with You '68
Elvis: Rare Moments with the
  King '90
Elvis: The Lost Performances
  '92
Flaming Star '60
Follow That Dream '61
Frankie and Johnny '65
Fun in Acapulco '63
G.I. Blues '60
Girl Happy '65
Girls! Girls! Girls! '62
Harum Scarum '65
It Happened at the World's Fair
  '63
Jailhouse Rock '57
Kid Galahad '62
King Creole '58
Kissin' Cousins '64
Live a Little, Love a Little '68
Love Me Tender '56
Loving You '57
Paradise, Hawaiian Style '66
Roustabout '64
Speedway '68
Spinout '66
Stay Away, Joe '68
This is Elvis '81
Tickle Me '65
The Trouble with Girls (and
  How to Get Into It) '69
Viva Las Vegas '63
Wild in the Country '61

Priscilla Presley
The Adventures of Ford
  Fairlane '90
Elvis Memories '85
The Naked Gun: From the Files
  of Police Squad '88
Naked Gun 33 1/3: The Final
  Insult '94
Naked Gun 2 1/2: The Smell of
  Fear '91

Harve Presnell
Paint Your Wagon '69

The Unsinkable Molly Brown
  '64

Emeric Pressburger
The Red Shoes '48
The Small Back Room '49

Lawrence Pressman
The Deliberate Stranger '86
Fire and Rain '89
For Love or Money '84
The Gathering '77
The Gathering: Part 2 '79
Hanoi Hilton '87
The Hellstrom Chronicle '71
On Wings of Eagles '86
Rehearsal for Murder '82
Rich Man, Poor Man '76
The Trial of Lee Harvey Oswald
  '77
White Hot: The Mysterious
  Murder of Thelma Todd '91
The Winds of War '83

Jason Presson
Explorers '85
The Lady in White '88
Saturday the 14th Strikes Back
  '88
The Stone Boy '84

Billy Preston
Blame It on the Night '84
The Compleat Beatles '82
Let It Be '70
Motown's Mustang '86
Wired '89

Cyndy Preston
The Brain '88
The Darkside '87
Pin '88
Prom Night 3: The Last Kiss '89

J.A. Preston
A Few Good Men '92
Fire Birds '90
The Spook Who Sat By the
  Door '73

Kelly Preston
Amazon Women on the Moon
  '87
Christine '84
The Experts '89
52 Pick-Up '86
Love at Stake '87
Metalstorm '83
Mischief '85
Only You '92
The Perfect Bride '91
Run '91
Secret Admirer '85
SpaceCamp '86
The Spellbinder '88
Tales from the Crypt, Vol. 3 '90
A Tiger's Tale '87
Twins '88

Mike Preston
Blade in Hong Kong '85
Hot Pursuit '84
Metalstorm '83
Surabaya Conspiracy '75

Robert Preston
Beau Geste '39
Best of the Badmen '50
Blood on the Moon '48
The Chisholms '79
Face to Face '52
Finnegan Begin Again '84
How the West was Won '63
Junior Bonner '72
The Last Starfighter '84
Mame '74
The Man That Corrupted
  Hadleyburg '80
The Music Man '62
My Father's House '75
My Outlaw Brother '51
Outrage! '86
Reap the Wild Wind '42
Rehearsal for Murder '82
Savage Wilderness '55
Semi-Tough '77
September Gun '83
S.O.B. '81
This Gun for Hire '42
Tulsa '49
Victor/Victoria '82
Wake Island '42

Wayde Preston
Smokey & the Judge '80

Today We Kill, Tomorrow We
Die '71

Francoise Prevost
Paris Belongs to Us '60
Spirits of the Dead '68
Time Out for Love '61

Marie Prevost
Eyes of Turpin Are Upon You!
'21
The Flying Fool '29
The Marriage Circle '24
Party Girls '29
The Sin of Madelon Claudet '31
Tango '36
Yankee Doodle in Berlin '19

Alan Price
O Lucky Man! '73
Oh, Alfie '75

Dennis Price
The Adventurers '51
A Canterbury Tale '44
Cool Mikado '63
Dear Murderer '47
Echo Murders '45
Horror Hospital '73
The Horror of Frankenstein '70
Kind Hearts and Coronets '49
Murder Most Foul '65
The Naked Truth '58
No Love for Johnnie '60
Pulp '72
The Screaming Dead '72
Theatre of Blood '73
Tunes of Glory '60
Twins of Evil '71
Venus in Furs '70
Victim '62
The V.I.P.'s '63
What a Carve-Up! '62
The Wrong Arm of the Law '63

Hal Price
Across the Plains '39
Cavalry '36
Desert Phantom '36
Man from Texas '39
Melody of the Plains '37
Rustler's Hideout '44
Trigger Men '41
Where Trails Divide '37

Marc Price
Killer Tomatoes Eat France '91
The Rescue '88
Trick or Treat '86

Nancy Price
The Speckled Band '31
The Three Weird Sisters '48

Stanley Price
The Driftin' Kid '41
Dynamite Canyon '41
The Invisible Monster '50
Rangeland Empire '50
Sudden Death '50

Vincent Price
The Abominable Dr. Phibes '71
Adventures of Captain Fabian
'51
Backtrack '89
Baron of Arizona '51
The Bat '89
Bloodbath at the House of
Death '85
The Boy Who Left Home to
Find Out About the Shivers
'81
Casanova's Big Night '54
Champagne for Caesar '50
The Comedy of Terrors '64
The Conqueror Worm '68
Cry of the Banshee '70
Dangerous Mission '54
Dead Heat '88
Diary of a Madman '63
Dr. Goldfoot and the Bikini
Machine '66
Doctor Phibes Rises Again '72
Edward Scissorhands '90
Escapes '86
The Fall of the House of Usher
'60
The Fly '58
The Haunted Palace '63
His Kind of Woman '51
The Horror of It All '91
The House of 1000 Dolls '67
House of the Long Shadows
'82

House of Wax '53
House on Haunted Hill '58
The Invisible Man Returns '40
It's Not the Size That Counts
'74
Journey into Fear '74
The Keys of the Kingdom '44
The Las Vegas Story '52
The Last Man on Earth '64
Laura '44
Madhouse '74
Masque of the Red Death '65
Masque of the Red Death/
Premature Burial '65
Master of the World '61
The Monster Club '85
Nefertiti, Queen of the Nile '64
The Oblong Box '69
The Offspring '87
Pirate Warrior '64
The Pit and the Pendulum '61
The Private Lives of Elizabeth &
Essex '39
The Raven '63
Return of the Fly '59
Ruddigore '70s
Scavenger Hunt '79
Scream and Scream Again '70
Shock! '46
Snow White and the Seven
Dwarfs '83
Son of Sinbad '55
The Song of Bernadette '43
Tales of Terror '62
The Ten Commandments '56
Theatre of Blood '73
The Three Musketeers '48
Tomb of Ligeia '64
The Tower of London '39
Tower of London '62
The Trouble with Girls (and
How To Get Into It) '69
Twice-Told Tales '63
The Whales of August '87
While the City Sleeps '56
Wilson '44

Robert Prichard
Alien Space Avenger '91
The Toxic Avenger '86

Dan Priest
Black Like Me '64
Rattlers '76

Martin Priest
Nothing But a Man '64
The Plot Against Harry '69
Zebrahead '92

Pat Priest
Easy Come, Easy Go '67
The Incredible Two-Headed
Transplant '71
Some Call It Loving '73

Jason Priestly
Beverly Hills 90210: The
Graduation '93
The Boy Who Could Fly '86
Calendar Girl '93
Nowhere to Run '88
Tombstone '93

Suzy Prim
Heart of a Nation '43
The Lower Depths '36

Barry Primus
Absence of Malice '81
Autopsy '78
Big Business '88
Brotherly Love '85
Cannibal Women in the
Avocado Jungle of Death '89
Denial: The Dark Side of
Passion '91
Down and Out in Beverly Hills
'86
Guilty by Suspicion '91
Heartland '81
New York, New York '77
Night and the City '92
Night Games '80
Shooting '82
The Stranger '87
Talking Walls '85
Torn Apart '89

Prince
Graffiti Bridge '90
Purple Rain '84
Under the Cherry Moon '86

Faith Prince
Dave '93
The Last Dragon '85
My Father the Hero '93

Jonathan Prince
Pray TV '82
Private School '83

William Prince
City in Fear '80
Cyrano de Bergerac '50
Dead Reckoning '47
Destination Tokyo '43
Johnny We Hardly Knew Ye '77
Justice '55
Lust for Gold '49
Nuts '87
Objective, Burma! '45
The Portrait '93
The Promise '78
Second Sight '89
Spies Like Us '85
Spontaneous Combustion '89
The Taking of Beverly Hills '91
Vice Versa '88

Victoria Principal
Blind Witness '89
Earthquake '74
Fantasy Island '77
I Will, I Will for Now '76
Life & Times of Judge Roy
Bean '72
Mistress '87
Naked Lie '89
Pleasure Palace '80

Andrew Prine
Amityville 2: The Possession
'82
And the Children Shall Lead '85
Bandolero! '68
Barn of the Naked Dead '73
Callie and Son '81
The Centerfold Girls '74
Chill Factor '90
The Christmas Coal Mine
Miracle '77
Crypt of the Living Dead '73
Deadly Exposure '93
The Devil's Brigade '68
Donner Pass: The Road to
Survival '84
The Eliminators '86
The Evil '78
Generation '69
Gettysburg '93
Grizzly '76
The Last of the Mohicans '85
The Miracle Worker '62
Mission of the Shark '91
One Little Indian '73
Riding with Death '76
Simon, King of the Witches '71
A Small Killing '81
Texas Across the River '66
They're Playing with Fire '84
Town that Dreaded Sundown
'76

Aileen Pringle
Convicted '32
Jane Eyre '34
Murder at Midnight '31
Sons of Steel '35

Bryan Pringle
Getting It Right '89
Haunted Honeymoon '86

Sandra Prinsloo
African Rage '78
Claws '85
The Gods Must Be Crazy '84
The Outcast '84

Ted Prior
Born Killer '89
Center of the Web '92
Deadly Prey '87
Final Sanction '89
Future Zone '90
Hardcase and Fist '89
Hell on the Battleground '88
Jungle Assault '89
Killer Workout '86
Killzone '85
Raw Nerve '91
Sledgehammer '83

Michael Pritchard
Lightblast '85
Massive Retaliation '85

Lucien Prival
Hell's Angels '30
Panama Menace '41
Party Girls '29

Juergen Prochnow
Beverly Hills Cop 2 '87
Body of Evidence '92
The Cop & the Girl '86
Das Boot '81
A Dry White Season '89
Dune '84
The Fire Next Time '93
Forbidden '85
The Fourth War '90
Hurricane Smith '92
Interceptor '92
The Keep '83
Kill Cruise '90
Killing Cars '85
The Lost Honor of Katharina
Blum '75
The Man Inside '90
My Sweet Victim '85
Robin Hood '91
The Seventh Sign '88

Phil Proctor
Firesign Theatre Presents Nick
Danger in the Case of the
Missing Yolks '83
J-Men Forever! '79

Melissa Prophet
Better Late Than Never '83
Invasion U.S.A. '85
Van Nuys Blvd. '79

Robert Prosky
Age Isn't Everything '91
Big Shots '87
Broadcast News '87
Christine '84
Far and Away '92
From the Dead of Night '89
Funny About Love '90
Green Card '90
Hit Woman: The Double Edge
'93
Hoffa '92
Into Thin Air '85
The Keep '83
Last Action Hero '93
The Lords of Discipline '83
Mrs. Doubtfire '93
The Murder of Mary Phagan
'87
The Natural '84
Rudy '93
Teamster Boss: The Jackie
Presser Story '92
Thief '81
Things Change '88
World War III '86

Jed Prouty
Broadway Melody '29
Danger on the Air '38
Ella Cinders '26
Remedy for Riches '40
Small Town Boy '37
Two Reelers: Comedy Classics
3 '33

David Proval
Innocent Blood '92
Mean Streets '73
Romeo Is Bleeding '93
Vice Versa '88

Dorothy Provine
Good Neighbor Sam '64
It's a Mad, Mad, Mad, Mad
World '63
Never a Dull Moment '68
That Darn Cat '65
30-Foot Bride of Candy Rock
'59
Who's Minding the Mint? '67

Jon Provost
All Mine to Give '56
Escapade in Japan '57
Lassie's Great Adventure '62
This Property is Condemned
'66

David Prowse
A Clockwork Orange '71
The Empire Strikes Back '80
Frankenstein and the Monster
from Hell '74
From "Star Wars" to "Jedi":
The Making of a Saga '83
The Horror of Frankenstein '70

Return of the Jedi '83
Star Wars '77
Vampire Circus '71

Juliet Prowse
Can-Can '60
Dingaka '65
G.I. Blues '60

Harold Pruett
Spellcaster '91
Summer Camp Nightmare '86

Jonathan Pryce
The Adventures of Baron
Munchausen '89
The Age of Innocence '93
Barbarians at the Gate '93
Brazil '85
Breaking Glass '80
Consuming Passions '88
The Doctor and the Devils '85
Glengarry Glen Ross '92
Haunted Honeymoon '86
Jumpin' Jack Flash '86
Loophole '83
Man on Fire '87
The Ploughman's Lunch '83
Praying Mantis '83
The Rachel Papers '89
Something Wicked This Way
Comes '83

Nicholas Pryor
Brain Dead '89
East of Eden '80
The Falcon and the Snowman
'85
The Fish that Saved Pittsburgh
'79
The $5.20 an Hour Dream '80
Force Five '75
Gumball Rally '76
Hail Caesar '94
The Happy Hooker '75
Hoffa '92
Into Thin Air '85
Last Song '80
The Life and Assassination of
the Kingfish '76
Morgan Stewart's Coming
Home '87
Night Terror '76
Nightbreaker '89
Pacific Heights '90
Risky Business '83
Smile '75

Richard Pryor
Adios Amigo '75
Another You '91
Bingo Long Traveling All-Stars
& Motor Kings '76
Black Brigade '69
Blue Collar '78
Brewster's Millions '85
Bustin' Loose '81
California Suite '78
Car Wash '76
Critical Condition '86
Dynamite Chicken '70
Greased Lightning '77
Harlem Nights '89
Hit! '73
Jo Jo Dancer, Your Life is
Calling '86
Lady Sings the Blues '72
Mack '73
Moving '88
See No Evil, Hear No Evil '89
The Silver Streak '76
Some Call It Loving '73
Some Kind of Hero '82
Stir Crazy '80
Superman 3 '83
The Toy '82
Uptown Saturday Night '74
Which Way Is Up? '77
Wholly Moses! '80
Wild in the Streets '68
The Wiz '78

Roger Pryor
Belle of the Nineties '34
Headline Woman '35
Identity Unknown '45
Kid Sister '45
Lady by Choice '34
The Man They Could Not Hang
'39
Meet the Mob '42
Panama Menace '41

Wojciech Pszoniak
Angry Harvest '85
Danton '82
Land of Promise '74

Tito Puente
The Mambo Kings '92
Radio Days '87

Willard Pugh
Ambition '91
CB4: The Movie '93
The Color Purple '85
Native Son '86
A Rage in Harlem '91

Frank Puglia
Ali Baba and the Forty Thieves '43
Billy the Kid '41
The Black Hand '50
Bulldog Drummond's Revenge '37
The Fatal Hour '40
Romola '25
20 Million Miles to Earth '57
Viva Villa! '34
Without Reservations '46

Aldo Puglisi
Marriage Italian Style '64
Seduced and Abandoned '64

Bill Pullman
The Accidental Tourist '88
Brain Dead '89
Bright Angel '91
Cold Feet '89
Crazy in Love '92
The Favor '94
Going Under '91
A League of Their Own '92
Liebestraum '91
Malice '93
Nervous Ticks '93
Newsies '92
Rocket Gibraltar '88
Ruthless People '86
The Serpent and the Rainbow '87
Sibling Rivalry '90
Singles '92
Sleepless in Seattle '93
Sommersby '93
Spaceballs '87
Wyatt Earp '94

Lilo (Liselotte) Pulver
A Global Affair '63
The Nun '66
A Time to Love & a Time to Die '58

Kong Pun
Ninja Swords of Death '90
Samurai Blood, Samurai Guts
Soul of Samurai

Dick Purcell
The Abe Lincoln of Ninth Avenue '39
Captain America '44
Heroes in Blue '39
Irish Luck '39
King of the Zombies '41
Phantom Killer '42
Timber Queen '44
Tough Kid '39
X Marks the Spot '42

James Purcell
Playroom '90
White Light '90

Lee Purcell
Adam at 6 A.M. '70
The Amazing Howard Hughes '77
Big Wednesday '78
Eddie Macon's Run '83
Homework '82
The Incredible Hulk Returns '88
Jailbait: Betrayed By Innocence '86
Kenny Rogers as the Gambler '80
Killing at Hell's Gate '81
Mr. Majestyk '74
Space Rage '86
Stir Crazy '80
To Heal a Nation '88
The Witching '72

Noel Purcell
Encore '52
Land of Fury '55
Lust for Life '56

Reginald Purdell
Brighton Rock '47
Candles at Nine '44
The Old Curiosity Shop '35

Edmund Purdom
After the Fall of New York '85
Athena '54
Ator the Fighting Eagle '83
Big Boss '77
Dr. Frankenstein's Castle of Freaks '74
Don't Open Till Christmas '84
The Egyptian '54
Herod the Great '60
The King's Thief '55
Mr. Scarface '77
Nefertiti, Queen of the Nile '64
The Prodigal '55
Rulers of the City '71
The Student Prince '54

Carolyn Purdy-Gordon
Dolls '87
From Beyond '86

Om Puri
City of Joy '92
Wolf '94

Linda Purl
Accidental Meeting '93
The Adventures of Nellie Bly '81
Body Language '92
Crazy Mama '75
Eleanor & Franklin '76
The Flame is Love '79
High Country '81
Last Cry for Help '79
Little Ladies of the Night '77
The Manions of America '81
The Night the City Screamed '80
Outrage! '86
Spies, Lies and Naked Thighs '91
Viper '88
Visiting Hours '82
Web of Deceit '90

Edna Purviance
Burlesque of Carmen '16
The Champion/His New Job '15
Chaplin Essanay Book 1 '15
The Chaplin Revue '58
Charlie Chaplin Cavalcade, Mutual Studios Shorts '16
Charlie Chaplin Festival '17
Charlie Chaplin: Night at the Show '15
Charlie Chaplin: Rare Chaplin '15
Charlie Chaplin: The Early Years, Vol. 1 '17
Charlie Chaplin: The Early Years, Vol. 2 '17
Charlie Chaplin: The Early Years, Vol. 3 '16
Charlie Chaplin: The Early Years, Vol. 4 '16
Charlie Chaplin...Our Hero! '15
Count/Adventurer '17
The Cure '17
The Fireman '16
The Floorwalker/By the Sea '15
His Prehistoric Past/The Bank '15
The Kid '21
The Kid/Idle Class '21
Rink/Immigrant '10s
Three Charlies and One Phoney! '18
Tramp & a Woman '15
Triple Trouble/Easy Street '18
The Vagabond '16
Woman of Paris/Sunnyside '23
Work/Police '16

John Putch
Curfew '88
Fallen Angels 2 '93
Impure Thoughts '86

Denver Pyle
The Adventures of Frontier Fremont '75
Dynamite Pass '50

Geronimo '62
Hawmps! '76
Hills of Utah '51
The Legend of Hillbilly John '73
Legend of the Northwest '78
Life & Times of Grizzly Adams '74
Mountain Man '77
Murder or Mercy '74
Naked Hills '56
Oklahoma Annie '51
Rim of the Canyon '49
The Rounders '65
Seventh Cavalry '56
Too Late for Tears '49

John Quade
And You Thought Your Parents Were Weird! '91
Dirkham Detective Agency '83
Fury to Freedom: The Life Story of Raul Ries '85
Night Terror '76
Peter Lundy and the Medicine Hat Stallion '77
Tigershark '87
The Tracker '88

Stephen Quadros
Auntie Lee's Meat Pies '92
C.I.A.: Code Name Alexa '92
Shock 'Em Dead '90

Dennis Quaid
All Night Long '81
The Big Easy '87
Bill '81
Bill: On His Own '83
Breaking Away '79
Caveman '81
Come See the Paradise '90
D.O.A. '88
Dreamscape '84
Enemy Mine '85
Everybody's All American '88
Flesh and Bone '93
Gorp '80
Great Balls of Fire '89
Innerspace '87
Jaws 3 '83
Johnny Belinda '82
The Long Riders '80
The Night the Lights Went Out in Georgia '81
Postcards from the Edge '90
The Right Stuff '83
The Seniors '78
September 30, 1955 '77
Suspect '87
Tough Enough '83
Undercover Blues '93
Wilder Napalm '93
Wyatt Earp '94

Randy Quaid
The Apprenticeship of Duddy Kravitz '74
Bloodhounds of Broadway '89
Bound for Glory '76
Breakout '75
Caddyshack 2 '88
The Choirboys '77
Days of Thunder '90
Dead Solid Perfect '88
Fool for Love '86
Foxes '80
Frankenstein '93
Freaked '93
The Guyana Tragedy: The Story of Jim Jones '80
Heartbeeps '81
Inside the Third Reich '82
The Last Detail '73
The Last Picture Show '71
The Last Ride of the Dalton Gang '79
LBJ: The Early Years '88
The Long Riders '80
Martians Go Home! '90
Midnight Express '78
Missouri Breaks '76
Moving '88
National Lampoon's Christmas Vacation '89
National Lampoon's Vacation '83
No Man's Land '87
Of Mice and Men '81
Out Cold '89
The Paper '94
Paper Moon '73
Parents '89

Quick Change '90
The Slugger's Wife '85
A Streetcar Named Desire '84
Sweet Country '87
Texasville '90
Three Warriors '77
To Race the Wind '80
What's Up, Doc? '72
The Wild Life '84
The Wraith '87

John Qualen
Adventure '45
Angels Over Broadway '40
At Gunpoint '55
Black Fury '35
Captain Kidd '45
Casablanca '42
Charlie Chan in Paris '35
Cheyenne Autumn '64
Dark Waters '44
The Devil & Daniel Webster '41
The Fugitive '48
The Grapes of Wrath '40
His Girl Friday '40
I'll Take Sweden '65
The Jungle Book '42
Knute Rockne: All American '40
The Long Voyage Home '40
The Man Who Shot Liberty Valance '62
Our Daily Bread '34
Passion '54
A Patch of Blue '65
The Scar '48
Sea Chase '55
The Searchers '56
Seven Faces of Dr. Lao '63
Those Calloways '65
Tortilla Flat '42

Jonathan Ke Quan
Breathing Fire '91
The Goonies '85

Robert Quarry
Alienator '89
Commando Squad '87
Count Yorga, Vampire '70
Cyclone '87
Doctor Phibes Rises Again '72
Evil Spirits '91
Madhouse '74
Phantom Empire '87
The Return of Count Yorga '71
Soldier of Fortune '55
Spirits '90
Teenage Exorcist '93
Warlords '88

Anna Quayle
Arrivederci, Baby! '66
Chitty Chitty Bang Bang '68
Mistress Pamela '74
Naughty Knights '71

Anthony Quayle
Anne of the Thousand Days '69
Barefoot in Athens '66
The Bourne Identity '88
Buster '88
The Chosen '77
Damn the Defiant '62
The Eagle Has Landed '77
The Endless Game '89
Everything You Always Wanted to Know About Sex (But Were Afraid to Ask) '72
The Fall of the Roman Empire '64
The Guns of Navarone '61
Hamlet '48
It Takes a Thief '59
The Key to Rebecca '85
Lawrence of Arabia '62
MacKenna's Gold '69
Magdalene '81
Masada '81
Misunderstood '87
Moses '76
Murder by Decree '79
Operation Crossbow '65
Pursuit of the Graf Spee '57
QB VII '74
The Story of David '76
A Study in Terror '66
The Tamarind Seed '74
21 Hours at Munich '76
The Wrong Man '56

Queen Latifah
House Party 2: The Pajama Jam '91

Quick Change '90
The Slugger's Wife '85

My Life '93

Valerie Quennessen
Conan the Barbarian '82
French Postcards '79
Summer Lovers '82

Mae Questel
National Lampoon's Christmas Vacation '89
New York Stories '89

Diana Quick
Brideshead Revisited '81
The Duellists '77
The Misadventures of Mr. Wilt '90
Ordeal by Innocence '84

Charles Quigley
Charlie Chan's Secret '35
Cyclotrode "X" '46
Daredevils of the Red Circle '38
Heroes in Blue '39
Lady from Nowhere '36
Saddle Buster '32
A Woman's Face '41

Linnea Quigley
Assault of the Party Nerds '89
The Black Room '82
Creepozoids '87
Deadly Embrace '88
Hollywood Chainsaw Hookers '88
Night of the Demons '88
Nightmare Sisters '87
Return of the Living Dead '85
Savage Streets '84
Sorority Babes in the Slimeball Bowl-A-Rama '87
Vice Academy '88
Vice Academy 2 '90
Virgin High '90
WitchTrap '89

Rita Quigley
Riot Squad '41
Susan and God '40

Tim Quill
Army of Darkness '92
Hamburger Hill '87
Hiding Out '87
Listen to Me '89
Staying Together '89
Thou Shalt Not Kill...Except '87

Eddie Quillan
Dark Mountain '44
The Grapes of Wrath '40
Here Comes Kelly '43
The Mandarin Mystery '37
Mutiny on the Bounty '35
Mystery of the Riverboat '44
The Tip-Off '31
Young Mr. Lincoln '39

Marie Quillen
Campus Knights '29
Saddle Buster '32

Denis Quilley
A Dangerous Man: Lawrence after Arabia '91
Foreign Body '86
Mister Johnson '91
Murder of a Moderate Man '70s
Privates on Parade '84
The Shell Seekers '89

Barry Quin
Prisoner Cell Block H '80
Sara Dane '81

Richard Quine
Babes on Broadway '41
For Me and My Gal '42

Kathleen Quinlan
Airport '77 '77
American Graffiti '73
An American Story '92
Blackout '91
Clara's Heart '88
The Doors '91
Dreams Lost, Dreams Found '87
Hanky Panky '82
I Never Promised You a Rose Garden '77
Independence Day '83
Last Light '93
The Last Winter '84
Lifeguard '75
Man Outside '78
The Promise '78

The Runner Stumbles '79
She's in the Army Now '81
Strays '91
Sunset '88
Trapped '89
Twilight Zone: The Movie '83
Warning Sign '85
Where Have All the People Gone? '74
Wild Thing '87

Aidan Quinn
All My Sons '86
At Play in the Fields of the Lord '91
Avalon '90
Benny & Joon '93
Blink '93
Crusoe '89
Desperately Seeking Susan '85
An Early Frost '85
The Handmaid's Tale '90
The Lemon Sisters '91
Lies of the Twins '91
The Mission '86
Perfect Witness '89
The Playboys '92
A Private Matter '92
Reckless '84
Stakeout '87

Anthony Quinn
Across 110th Street '72
African Rage '78
Against All Flags '52
Back to Bataan '45
Barabbas '62
Behold a Pale Horse '64
Black Orchid '59
Blood and Sand '41
Blowing Wild '54
Buffalo Bill '44
Children of Sanchez '79
China Sky '44
City for Conquest '40
The Con Artists '80
The Destructors '74
The Don is Dead '73
A Dream of Kings '69
The Ghost Breakers '40
Ghosts Can't Do It '90
The Greek Tycoon '78
Guadalcanal Diary '43
The Guns of Navarone '61
Heller in Pink Tights '60
High Risk '76
Hot Spell '58
The Inheritance '76
Jesus of Nazareth '77
Jungle Fever '91
La Strada '54
Last Action Hero '93
Last Train from Gun Hill '59
Lawrence of Arabia '62
Lion of the Desert '81
The Lost Command '66
Lust for Life '56
The Magnificent Matador '55
A Man of Passion '90s
Mobsters '91
Mohammed: Messenger of God '77
Onassis '88
Only the Lonely '91
The Ox-Bow Incident '43
The Plainsman '37
Regina '83
Revenge '90
The Road to Morocco '42
The Road to Singapore '40
R.P.M.* (*Revolutions Per Minute) '70
The Salamander '82
Seven Cities of Gold '55
The Shoes of the Fisherman '68
Sinbad the Sailor '47
The Switch '89
They Died with Their Boots On '41
Tycoon '47
Ulysses '55
Viva Zapata! '52
Walk in the Spring Rain '70
Warlock '59
Zorba the Greek '64

Bill Quinn
Big Calibre '35
Bustin' Loose '81
Dead and Buried '81
Twilight Zone: The Movie '83

Daniel Quinn
Conagher '91
Scanner Cop '94

Francesco Quinn
Dead Certain '92
Deadly Rivals '92
Indio '90
Platoon '86
Priceless Beauty '90
Quo Vadis '85

James W. Quinn
Witchboard '87
WitchTrap '89

J.C. Quinn
The Abyss '89
All-American Murder '91
The Babe '92
Barfly '87
Crisscross '92
Megaville '91
Prayer of the Rollerboys '91
Priceless Beauty '90
Turner and Hooch '89
Twisted '86
Violated '84

Louis Quinn
Superchick '73
Unholy Rollers '72

Martha Quinn
Bad Channels '92
Chopper Chicks in Zombietown '91
Motorama '91

Pat Quinn
Alice's Restaurant '69
Clean and Sober '88
Zachariah '70

Patricia Quinn
Shock Treatment '81
Witching Time '84

Adolfo "Shabba Doo" Quinones
Breakin' 2: Electric Boogaloo '84
Lambada '89

Beulah Quo
The Children of An Lac '80
Girls! Girls! Girls! '62

Kurt Raab
Angry Harvest '85
Fox and His Friends '75
Mussolini & I '85
Parker '84
The Stationmaster's Wife '77
Tricheurs '84
Why Does Herr R. Run Amok? '69

Francesco Rabal
Bloody Che Contra
Camorra: The Naples Connection '85
City of the Walking Dead '83
Diary of a Rebel '84
The Eclipse '66
El Muerto '75
Exorcism's Daughter '74
The Holy Innocents '84
Nazarin '58
The Nun '66
Padre Nuestro '85
Reborn '78
Sorcerer '77
Stay As You Are '78
The Stilts '84
Tie Me Up! Tie Me Down! '90
A Time of Destiny '88
Viridiana '61

Francine Racette
Au Revoir Les Enfants '87
Lumiere '76

Alan Rachins
Always '85
Heart Condition '90
L.A. Law '86
Mistress '87

Victoria Racimo
Ernest Goes to Camp '87
G.I. Executioner '71
Green Eyes '76
Prophecy '79
Roanoak '86
Search for the Gods '75

White Fang 2: The Myth of the White Wolf '94

Basil Radford
Captive Heart '47
Dead of Night '45
The Lady Vanishes '38
Passport to Pimlico '49
Whiskey Galore '48
The Winslow Boy '48

Gilda Radner
All You Need Is Cash '78
First Family '80
Hanky Panky '82
Haunted Honeymoon '86
Mr. Mike's Mondo Video '79
Movers and Shakers '85
The Woman in Red '84

Jerzy Radziwilowicz
Man of Iron '81
Man of Marble '76
No End '84

Charlotte Rae
Bananas '71
The Hot Rock '70
Jenny '70
Queen of the Stardust Ballroom '75
Sidewinder One '77
The Triangle Factory Fire Scandal '79
Words by Heart '84
The Worst Witch '86

Chips Rafferty
The Desert Rats '53
Double Trouble '67
Eureka Stockade '49
Forty Thousand Horsemen '41
Overlanders '46
Skullduggery '70
The Sundowners '60
Wackiest Ship in the Army '61
Walk into Hell '57

Frances Rafferty
Abbott and Costello in Hollywood '45
Curley '47
Mrs. Parkington '44
Money Madness '47

Deborah Raffin
Claudia '85
Death Wish 3 '85
The Dove '74
For the Love of It '80
Forty Carats '73
God Told Me To '76
Hanging on a Star '78
How to Pick Up Girls '78
Jungle Heat '84
Killing at Hell's Gate '81
Maniac '77
Morning Glory '93
Night of the Fox '90
Nightmare in Badham County '76
Once is Not Enough '75
Scanners 2: The New Order '91
Snowblind '78
Touched by Love '80
Willa '79

George Raft
Background to Danger '43
The Best of Abbott & Costello Live '54
Casino Royale '67
Each Dawn I Die '39
Five Golden Dragons '67
House Across the Bay '40
I'll Get You '53
Jet Over the Atlantic '59
Johnny Angel '45
Loan Shark '52
Man from Cairo '54
Mr. Ace '46
Night After Night '32
Nocturne '46
Outpost in Morocco '49
Scarface '31
Sextette '78
Some Like It Hot '59
They Drive by Night '40
Whistle Stop '46

Rags Ragland
The Canterville Ghost '44
DuBarry Was a Lady '43
Panama Hattie '42
Whistling in Brooklyn '43

Whistling in Dixie '42
Whistling in the Dark '41

William Ragsdale
Fright Night '85
Fright Night 2 '88
Mannequin 2: On the Move '91

Umberto Raho
Aladdin '86
The Night Evelyn Came Out of the Grave '71
Satanik '69

Steve Railsback
Alligator 2: The Mutation '90
Angela '77
Armed and Dangerous '86
Assassin '89
Blue Monkey '87
Calendar Girl '93
Deadly Games '80
Deadly Intent '88
Distortions '87
Escape 2000 '81
Forever: A Ghost of a Love Story '92
The Forgotten '89
From Here to Eternity '79
The Golden Seal '83
Helter Skelter '76
Lifeforce '85
Nukie '93
Private Wars '93
Quake '93
Save Me '93
Scenes from the Goldmine '87
Scissors '91
The Stunt Man '80
Sunstroke '92
The Survivalist '87
Torchlight '85
Trick or Treats '82
The Wind '87

Sam Raimi
Indian Summer '93
Thou Shalt Not Kill...Except '87

Theodore Raimi
Army of Darkness '92
Clear and Present Danger '94
Evil Dead 2: Dead by Dawn '87
The Finishing Touch '92
Lunatics: A Love Story '92
Shocker '89

Raimu
The Baker's Wife '33
Cesar '36
Fanny '32
Heart of a Nation '43
Marius '31
Well-Digger's Daughter '46

Luise Rainer
The Good Earth '37
The Great Waltz '38
The Great Ziegfeld '36
Tiefland '44

Christina Raines
The Duellists '77
Nashville '75
Nightmares '83
North Shore '87
Quo Vadis '85
Russian Roulette '75
The Sentinel '76
The Shrieking '73
Silver Dream Racer '83
Stacey '73
Touched by Love '80

Ella Raines
Hail the Conquering Hero '44
Impact '49
Ride the Man Down '53
The Senator was Indiscreet '45
The Strange Affair of Uncle Harry '45
Tall in the Saddle '44

Ford Rainey
Babe! '75
Bed & Breakfast '92
The Cellar '90
Mountain Man '77
My Sweet Charlie '70
Sixteen '72
Strange New World '75
Strangers: The Story of a Mother and Daughter '79

Claude Rains
The Adventures of Robin Hood '38
Angel on My Shoulder '46
Anthony Adverse '36
Battle of the Worlds '61
Caesar and Cleopatra '46
Casablanca '42
Deception '46
The Evil Mind '34
Forever and a Day '43
Four Daughters '38
The Greatest Story Ever Told '65
Here Comes Mr. Jordan '41
The Invisible Man '33
Juarez '39
Kings Row '41
Lawrence of Arabia '62
Lisbon '56
Mr. Skeffington '44
Mr. Smith Goes to Washington '39
Notorious '46
Now, Voyager '42
Paris Express '53
Passage to Marseilles '44
The Phantom of the Opera '43
Pied Piper of Hamelin '57
The Prince and the Pauper '37
The Sea Hawk '40
They Made Me a Criminal '39
They Won't Forget '37
The White Tower '50
The Wolf Man '41

Tommy Rall
Dancers '87
Kiss Me Kate '53
My Sister Eileen '55
Seven Brides for Seven Brothers '54

Giovanna Ralli
Caper of the Golden Bulls '67
Sex with a Smile '76
What Did You Do in the War, Daddy? '66

Jessie Ralph
After the Thin Man '36
The Bank Dick '40
The Blue Bird '40
Double Wedding '37
Drums Along the Mohawk '39
Evelyn Prentice '34
I Live My Life '35
The Last of Mrs. Cheyney '37
Les Miserables '35
Little Lord Fauntleroy '36
One Night of Love '34
San Francisco '36
They Met in Bombay '41
Yellow Dust '36

Sheryl Lee Ralph
Codename: Foxfire '85
The Distinguished Gentleman '92
The Mighty Quinn '89
Mistress '91
Sister Act 2: Back in the Habit '93
To Sleep with Anger '90

Esther Ralston
$50,000 Reward '25
Lonely Wives '31
Lucky Devil '25
Old Ironsides '26
Oliver Twist '22
Shadows of the Orient '37
Tin Pan Alley '40
To the Last Man '33
We're in the Legion Now '37

Jobyna Ralston
Dr. Jack/For Heaven's Sake '26
For Heaven's Sake '26
The Freshman '25
Girl Shy '24
The Kid Brother '27

Vera Ralston
Dakota '45
The Fighting Kentuckian '49
Hoodlum Empire '52
Jubilee Trail '54

Enrique Rambal
The Exterminating Angel '62
The Man and the Monster '65
Para Servir a Usted '87
Sexo Y Crimen '87

Marjorie Rambeau
Forever Female '53
Laughing Sinners '31
A Man Called Peter '55
Man of a Thousand Faces '57
Min & Bill '30
Primrose Path '40
The Rains Came '39
Santa Fe Marshal '40
Torch Song '53

Dack Rambo
Hit Lady '74
River of Diamonds '90
The Spring '89
Ultra Warrior '90s
Waikiki '80

Henry Ramer
The Big Slice '90
Hockey Night '84
My Pleasure Is My Business '74
Reno and the Doc '84
Starship Invasions '77

Carlos Ramirez
Anchors Aweigh '45
Bathing Beauty '44
Two Girls and a Sailor '44

Frank Ramirez
Miracle in Rome '88
Smith! '69

Harold Ramis
Baby Boom '87
Best of Comic Relief '86
The Best of John Candy on SCTV '80s
Ghostbusters '84
Ghostbusters 2 '89
Stealing Home '88
Stripes '81

Rudy Ramos
Colors '88
Open House '86
Quicksilver '86

Charlotte Rampling
Angel Heart '87
Caravan to Vaccares '74
The Damned '69
D.O.A. '88
Farewell, My Lovely '75
Foxtrot '76
Georgy Girl '66
Mascara '87
Max, Mon Amour '86
The Night Porter '74
Orca '77
The Purple Taxi '77
Sardinia Kidnapped '75
Ski Bum '75
Stardust Memories '80
'Tis a Pity She's a Whore '73
The Verdict '82
Zardoz '73

Remak Ramsay
The Dining Room '86
Mr. & Mrs. Bridge '91

Anne Ramsey
Another Chance '88
The Black Marble '79
The Boy in the Plastic Bubble '76
Deadly Friend '86
Dr. Hackenstein '88
Goin' South '78
The Goonies '85
Marilyn: The Untold Story '80
Meet the Hollowheads '89
A Small Killing '81
Throw Momma from the Train '87
Weeds '87
White Mama '80

Logan Ramsey
Confessions of Tom Harris '72
Conspiracy of Terror '75
Dr. Hackenstein '88
Fury on Wheels '71
The Hoodlum Priest '61
Say Yes! '86

Marion Ramsey
Police Academy 3: Back in Training '86
Police Academy 5: Assignment Miami Beach '88
Police Academy 6: City Under Siege '89

Nick Ramus
Geronimo '93
Journey to Spirit Island '92

John Rand
Charlie Chaplin: The Early Years, Vol. 1 '17
Charlie Chaplin: The Early Years, Vol. 2 '17

Addison Randall
Chance '89
Deadly Breed '89
Hollow Gate '88

Ethan Randall
All I Want for Christmas '91
Dutch '91
A Far Off Place '93

Jack Randall
Across the Plains '39
Covered Wagon Trails '40
Gun Packer '38
Gunsmoke Trail '38
Man's Country '38
Wild Horse Canyon '39

Lexi Randall
Heidi '93
Sarah, Plain and Tall '91
Skylark '93

Meg Randall
Ma and Pa Kettle '49
Ma and Pa Kettle Back On the Farm '51
Ma and Pa Kettle Go to Town '50

Monica Randall
Commando Attack '67
Five Giants from Texas '66
Witches' Mountain '71

Tony Randall
The Adventures of Huckleberry Finn '60
The Alphabet Murders '65
Boy's Night Out '62
Everything You Always Wanted to Know About Sex (But Were Afraid to Ask) '72
Fatal Instinct '93
Foolin' Around '80
King of Comedy '82
Let's Make Love '60
The Littlest Angel '69
Lover Come Back '61
The Mating Game '59
Pillow Talk '59
Scavenger Hunt '79
Send Me No Flowers '64
Seven Faces of Dr. Lao '63
That's Adequate '89

Ron Randell
Girl in Black Stockings '57
The Loves of Carmen '48
Omoo Omoo, the Shark God '49

Theresa Randle
Beverly Hills Cop 3 '94
CB4: The Movie '93
Malcolm X '92
Sugar Hill '94

Anders Randolf
The Idol Dancer '20
The Kiss '29
The Love Flower '20
Ranson's Folly '26

Jane Randolph
Abbott and Costello Meet Frankenstein '48
Cat People '42
Curse of the Cat People '44
The Falcon's Brother '42
Open Secret '48

John Randolph
The Adventures of Nellie Bly '81
As Summers Die '86
Iron Maze '91
King Kong '76
Lovely...But Deadly '82
National Lampoon's Christmas Vacation '89
Pretty Poison '68
Prizzi's Honor '85
The Runaways '75
Secrets '77
Serpico '73
There was a Crooked Man '70

The Winds of Kitty Hawk '78
The Wizard of Loneliness '88

Ty Randolph
Deadly Embrace '88
Nudity Required '90

Robert Random
Danger Zone 2 '89
Danger Zone 3: Steel Horse War '90

Salvo Randone
Fellini Satyricon '69
Spirits of the Dead '68
10th Victim '65

Dan Ranger
Cop-Out '91
The Last Ride '91

Arthur Rankin
Below the Deadline '29
Fighting Fool '32
Terror Trail '33
Walking Back '26

Tim Ransom
The Dressmaker '89
Vital Signs '90

Prunella Ransome
Far from the Madding Crowd '67
Man in the Wilderness '71

Anthony Rapp
Adventures in Babysitting '87
Dazed and Confused '93
Far from Home '89
School Ties '92
Six Degrees of Separation '93

David Rappaport
The Bride '85
Mysteries '84
Peter Gunn '89

Michael Rappaport
Money for Nothing '93
The Scout '94
True Romance '93
Zebrahead '92

Eva Ras
The Love Affair, or The Case of the Missing Switchboard Operator '67
Man is Not a Bird '65

David Rasche
Bingo '91
Delirious '91
An Innocent Man '89
Manhattan '79
The Masters of Menace '90
Native Son '86
Sanctuary of Fear '79
Silhouette '91
Twenty Bucks '93
Wedding Band '89
Wicked Stepmother '89

Phylicia Rashad
False Witness '89
Uncle Tom's Cabin '87

Fritz Rasp
Diary of a Lost Girl '29
Metropolis '26
Spies '28
The Threepenny Opera '31

Ivan Rassimov
Beyond the Door 2 '79
Man from Deep River '77
The Next Victim '71

Thalmus Rasulala
Adios Amigo '75
Blacula '72
Blind Vengeance '90
Born American '86
Bucktown '75
Bulletproof '88
Friday Foster '75
Mom and Dad Save the World '92
New Jack City '91
The Package '89
Sophisticated Gents '81

Sandy Ratcliff
Family Life '71
Yesterday's Hero '79

Basil Rathbone
Above Suspicion '43
The Adventures of Marco Polo '38

The Adventures of Robin Hood '38
The Adventures of Sherlock Holmes '39
Anna Karenina '35
Autopsy of a Ghost '67
Bathing Beauty '44
Captain Blood '35
Casanova's Big Night '54
A Christmas Carol '54
The Comedy of Terrors '64
Court Jester '56
David Copperfield '35
Dawn Patrol '38
Dressed to Kill '46
The Garden of Allah '36
Heartbeat '46
Hillbillies in a Haunted House '67
The Hound of the Baskervilles '39
House of Fear '45
Last Days of Pompeii '35
Last Hurrah '58
Love from a Stranger '37
The Magic Sword '62
Make a Wish '37
Many Faces of Sherlock Holmes '86
The Mark of Zorro '40
The Pearl of Death '44
Planet of Blood '66
Pursuit to Algiers '45
Romeo and Juliet '36
Scarlet Claw '44
Sherlock Holmes and the Secret Weapon '42
Sherlock Holmes Faces Death '43
Sherlock Holmes in Washington '43
Sherlock Holmes: The Voice of Terror '42
Sin Takes a Holiday '30
Son of Frankenstein '39
Spider Woman '44
A Tale of Two Cities '35
Tales of Terror '62
Terror by Night '46
Terror by Night/Meeting at Midnight '46
The Tower of London '39
Victoria Regina '61
Voyage to the Prehistoric Planet '65
We're No Angels '55
The Woman in Green '45

Gregory Ratoff
Abdulla the Great '56
All About Eve '50
Exodus '60
I'm No Angel '33
Skyscraper Souls '32

Devin Ratray
Home Alone '90
Home Alone 2: Lost in New York '92
Spy Trap '92

Heather Rattray
Across the Great Divide '76
Basket Case 2 '90
Further Adventures of the Wilderness Family, Part 2 '77
Mountain Family Robinson '79
Sea Gypsies '78

John Ratzenberger
The Bitch '78
Camp Cucamonga: How I Spent My Summer Vacation '90
Combat Academy '86
The Empire Strikes Back '80
House 2: The Second Story '87
Timestalkers '87
Twilight's Last Gleaming '77

Andrea Rau
Beyond Erotica '74
Daughters of Darkness '71

Alida Rauffe
Cesar '36
Fanny '32

Mike Raven
Crucible of Terror '72
Disciple of Death '72

Herbert Rawlinson
Blake of Scotland Yard '36

Blind Fools '40
Colt Comrades '43
Confidential '35
Gentleman from Dixie '41
I Killed That Man '42
Jail Bait '54
Lost Canyon '43
Nabonga '44
The Panther's Claw '42
Riot Squad '41
Robinson Crusoe of Clipper Island '36
Robinson Crusoe of Mystery Island '36
Shake Hands with Murder '44
Show Them No Mercy '35
Smart Alecks '42
The Tomboy '24

Aldo Ray
And Hope to Die '72
Bad Bunch '76
Battle Cry '55
Black Eliminator '70s
Blood Red '88
Bog '84
The Centerfold Girls '74
Dark Sanity '82
Dead Heat on a Merry-Go-Round '66
The Dynamite Brothers '74
Evils of the Night '85
The Executioner, Part 2: Frozen Scream '84
Frankenstein's Great Aunt Tillie '83
The Glove '79
God's Little Acre '58
Gone with the West '72
The Great Skycopter Rescue '82
The Green Berets '68
The Haunted '79
Haunts '77
Hollywood Cop '87
Human Experiments '79
Inside Out '75
Johnny Nobody '61
Kill Factor
Little Moon & Jud McGraw '78
The Lucifer Complex '78
The Man Who Would Not Die '75
Men in War '57
Miss Sadie Thompson '53
Mission to Glory '80
Mongrel '83
The Naked and the Dead '58
Nightfall
Nightstalker '79
Pat and Mike '52
Psychic Killer '75
Seven Alone '75
Shock 'Em Dead '90
Shooters '89
Star Slammer '87
Swift Justice '88
Terror on Alcatraz '86
To Kill a Stranger '70s
Vultures '85
We're No Angels '55
What Did You Do in the War, Daddy? '66

Andrew Ray
Escapade '55
Mission Phantom '79
Tarzana, the Wild Girl '70
The Young and the Guilty '58

Charles Ray
The Busher '19
Clodhopper '17
Dracula/Garden of Eden '28
The Garden of Eden '28
Homer Comes Home '20
Sweet Adeline '26

James Ray
Mass Appeal '84
Return Engagement '78
She's Having a Baby '88

Leah Ray
One in a Million '36
Two Reelers: Comedy Classics 9 '34

Nicholas Ray
The American Friend '77
Hair '79
James Dean: The First American Teenager '76

Lightning Over Water '80

Rene Ray
Housemaster '38
The Passing of the Third Floor
  Back '36
The Vicious Circle '57

Martha Raye
Billy Rose's Jumbo '62
College Swing '38
The Concorde: Airport '79 '79
Keep 'Em Flying '41
Monsieur Verdoux '47
Pin-Up Girl '44
Pippin '81

Bill Raymond
City of Hope '91
The Crow '93
The Man Who Envied Women
  '85
My New Gun '92
Sudden Death '77

Candy Raymond
Don's Party '76
Freedom '81
Money Movers '78
Monkey Grip '82

Cyril Raymond
Angels One Five '54
Brief Encounter '46
Men of Two Worlds '46
The Shadow '36
Spy in Black '39

Gary Raymond
Jason and the Argonauts '63
Look Back in Anger '58
The Moonraker '58
Playboy of the Western World
  '62

Gene Raymond
The Best Man '64
The Bride Walks Out '36
Ex-Lady '33
Flying Down to Rio '33
Hit the Deck '55
Mexican Spitfire/Smartest Girl
  in Town '40
Mr. & Mrs. Smith '41
Plunder Road '57
Red Dust '32
Sadie McKee '34
Smilin' Through '41
That Girl from Paris '36
Transatlantic Merry-Go-Round
  '34

Jack Raymond
Last Command '28
Shake Hands with Murder '44

Lina Raymond
The Gypsy Warriors '78
The Key to Rebecca '85

Paula Raymond
Adam's Rib '50
The Beast from 20,000
  Fathoms '53
Blood of Dracula's Castle '69
City That Never Sleeps '53
Duchess of Idaho '50
King Richard and the
  Crusaders '54
Texas Carnival '51

Richard Raymond
Days of Hell '84
Rats '83

Robin Raymond
Girls in Chains '43
High School Confidential '58
Rogue's Gallery '44

Peggy Rea
Children's Carol '70
In Country '89
Love Field '91
Made in America '93

Stephen Rea
Angie '94
Bad Behavior '92
The Company of Wolves '85
The Crying Game '92
Danny Boy '84
The Doctor and the Devils '85
Four Days in July '84
Life is Sweet '91
Loose Connections '87

James Read
Beaches '88

The Initiation '84
Love Crimes '92
North and South Book 1 '85
North and South Book 2 '86
Poor Little Rich Girl: The
  Barbara Hutton Story '87
Remington Steele, Vol. 1:
  License to Steele '82
Web of Deceit '90

Ronald Reagan
Bedtime for Bonzo '51
Boy Meets Girl '38
Cattle Queen of Montana '54
Dark Victory '39
Desperate Journey '42
Hellcats of the Navy '57
Hollywood Bloopers '50s
Hollywood Outtakes & Rare
  Footage '83
It's a Great Feeling '49
The Jungle Trap
The Killers '64
Kings Row '41
Knute Rockne: All American '40
Santa Fe Trail '40
Tennessee's Partner '55
This is the Army '43
The Winning Team '52

Rex Reason
Band of Angels '57
The Creature Walks Among Us
  '56
This Island Earth '55

Sady Rebbot
Friends '71
My Life to Live '62

James Rebhorn
Carlito's Way '93
Deadly Business '86
8 Seconds '94
I Love Trouble '94
JFK: Reckless Youth '93
Lorenzo's Oil '92
Scent of a Woman '92
Skylark '93
White Sands '92
Will: G. Gordon Liddy '82

Winston Reckert
Agnes of God '85
Glory! Glory! '90
The World's Oldest Living
  Bridesmaid '92

Mary-Robin Redd
The Group '66
Mirrors '78

Helen Reddy
Airport '75 '75
Pete's Dragon '77

Quinn Redeker
Coast to Coast '80
The Three Stooges Meet
  Hercules '61

Dennis Redfield
The Annihilators '85
Private Duty Nurses '71
Pulse '88

William Redfield
The Connection '61
Conquest of Space '55
Death Wish '74
Fantastic Voyage '66
For Pete's Sake '74
The Hot Rock '70
Morituri '65
A New Leaf '71
One Flew Over the Cuckoo's
  Nest '75

Robert Redford
All the President's Men '76
Barefoot in the Park '67
A Bridge Too Far '77
Brubaker '80
Butch Cassidy and the
  Sundance Kid '69
The Candidate '72
The Chase '66
Downhill Racer '69
The Electric Horseman '79
The Great Gatsby '74
The Great Waldo Pepper '75
Havana '90
The Hot Rock '70
Indecent Proposal '93
Inside Daisy Clover '65
Jeremiah Johnson '72

Legal Eagles '86
The Natural '84
Out of Africa '85
Sneakers '92
The Sting '73
Tell Them Willie Boy Is Here '69
This Property is Condemned
  '66
Three Days of the Condor '75
The Twilight Zone '61
The Way We Were '73

Rockets Redglare
Cookie '89
Down by Law '86
In the Soup '92
Mystery Train '89
Salvation! '87
Shakedown '88

Corin Redgrave
Between Wars '74
The Charge of the Light
  Brigade '68
Excalibur '81
Four Weddings and a Funeral
  '93
In the Name of the Father '93

Jemma Redgrave
Diana: Her True Story '93
Howard's End '92

Lynn Redgrave
The Bad Seed '85
The Big Bus '76
Everything You Always Wanted
  to Know About Sex (But
  Were Afraid to Ask) '72
Georgy Girl '66
Getting It Right '89
The Happy Hooker '75
Midnight '89
Morgan Stewart's Coming
  Home '87
Rehearsal for Murder '82
Shooting '82
Sooner or Later '78
To Love Again '80
Tom Jones '63
The Turn of the Screw '74
The Virgin Soldiers '69
Walking on Air '87

Michael Redgrave
Battle of Britain '69
The Browning Version '51
Captive Heart '47
Dam Busters '55
Dead of Night '45
Dr. Jekyll and Mr. Hyde '73
Fame is the Spur '47
The Go-Between '71
Goodbye, Mr. Chips '69
Heidi '67
Hitchcock Collection '87
Importance of Being Earnest
  '52
Kipps '41
Lady in Distress '39
The Lady Vanishes '38
The Loneliness of the Long
  Distance Runner '62
Mr. Arkadin '55
Nicholas and Alexandra '71
The Sea Shall Not Have Them
  '55
Secret Beyond the Door '48
Shake Hands with the Devil '59
The Stars Look Down '39
Twinsanity '70
The Wreck of the Mary Deare
  '59

Vanessa Redgrave
Agatha '79
The Ballad of the Sad Cafe '91
Bear Island '80
Blow-Up '66
The Bostonians '84
Camelot '67
The Charge of the Light
  Brigade '68
Consuming Passions '88
The Devils '71
The House of the Spirits '93
Howard's End '92
Isadora '68
Julia '77
A Man for All Seasons '66
A Man for All Seasons '88
Morgan! '66
Mother's Boys '94

Murder on the Orient Express
  '74
Orpheus Descending '91
Out of Season '75
Peter the Great '86
Playing for Time '80
Prick Up Your Ears '87
The Seven Percent Solution '76
Snow White and the Seven
  Dwarfs '83
Steaming '86
They Watch '93
Three Sovereigns for Sarah '85
Trojan Women '71
Wagner: The Complete Epic '85
Wagner: The Movie '85
Wetherby '85
Yanks '79
Young Catherine '91

Juli Reding
Mission in Morocco '59
Tormented '60

Joyce Redman
A Different Kind of Love '85
Tom Jones '63

Liam Redmond
Devil on Horseback '54
The Last Safari '67

Joe Redner
Clash of the Ninja '86
Thundering Ninja '80s

Alan Reed
Actors and Sin '74
Days of Glory '43
The Postman Always Rings
  Twice '46

Alan Reed, Jr.
Peyton Place '57
Rock, Pretty Baby '56

Alyson Reed
A Chorus Line '85
Skin Deep '89

Donna Reed
The Benny Goodman Story '55
The Caddy '53
From Here to Eternity '53
Green Dolphin Street '47
Gun Fury '53
Hangman's Knot '52
The Human Comedy '43
It's a Wonderful Life '46
The Last Time I Saw Paris '54
Picture of Dorian Gray '45
Shadow of the Thin Man '41
They Were Expendable '45
Thousands Cheer '43
Trouble Along the Way '53

George Reed
Green Pastures '36
Strange Illusion '45

James Reed
Eight Men Out '88
Tarzana, the Wild Girl '72

Jerry Reed
Bat 21 '88
The Concrete Cowboys '79
Gator '76
High Ballin' '78
Hot Stuff '80
Smokey and the Bandit '77
Smokey and the Bandit, Part 2
  '80
Smokey and the Bandit, Part 3
  '83
Survivors '83
What Comes Around '85

Lady Reed
Avenging Disco Godfather '76
Dolemite 2: Human Tornado '76

Lou Reed
Faraway, So Close! '93
Get Crazy '83
One Trick Pony '80

Maxwell Reed
Blackout '50
Dear Murderer '47
Night Beat '48
Roadhouse Girl '53
Sea Devils '53

Oliver Reed
The Adventures of Baron
  Munchausen '89
The Assassination Bureau '69
Beat Girl '60

The Big Sleep '78
The Black Arrow '84
Blood Island '68
Blue Blood '73
The Brood '79
Burnt Offerings '76
Captive '87
Captive Rage '88
Castaway '87
Christopher Columbus '85
The Class of Miss MacMichael
  '78
Condorman '81
The Curse of the Werewolf '61
Dante's Inferno: Life of Dante
  Gabriel Rossetti '69
The Devils '71
Dr. Heckyl and Mr. Hype '80
Dragonard '88
Fanny Hill '83
The Four Musketeers '75
Gor '88
Great Scout & Cathouse
  Thursday '76
Hired to Kill '91
The House of Usher '88
Lion of the Desert '81
Maniac '77
Master of Dragonard Hill '89
The Misfit Brigade '87
No Love for Johnnie '60
Oliver! '68
One Russian Summer '73
The Pit & the Pendulum '91
The Prince and the Pauper '78
Prisoner of Honor '91
Rage to Kill '88
The Return of the Musketeers
  '89
Return to Lonesome Dove '93
The Revenger '90
Sell Out '76
Severed Ties '92
Skeleton Coast '89
Spasms '82
The Sting 2 '83
Sword of Sherwood Forest '60
Ten Little Indians '75
The Three Musketeers '74
Tommy '75
Tomorrow Never Comes '77
Trap '66
Treasure Island '89
Triple Echo '77
Two of a Kind '83
Venom '82
Women in Love '70
Zero Population Growth '72

Pamela Reed
The Best of Times '86
Cadillac Man '90
Caroline? '90
Chattahoochee '90
The Clan of the Cave Bear '86
Eyewitness '81
The Goodbye People '83
Kindergarten Cop '90
The Long Riders '80
Melvin and Howard '80
Passed Away '92
Rachel River '89
The Right Stuff '83
Tanner '88 '88
Young Doctors in Love '82

Penelope Reed
Amazons '86
Hired to Kill '91

Philip Reed
Bandit Queen '51
Big Town '47
Big Town After Dark '47
Female '33
Klondike Annie '36
Madame X '37
Song of the Thin Man '47
Underworld Scandal '47
Unknown Island '48

Robert Reed
Bloodlust '59
The Boy in the Plastic Bubble
  '76
The Brady Bunch, Vol. 1 '69
Bud and Lou '78
Casino '80
Death of a Centerfold '81
Haunts of the Very Rich '72
The Hunted Lady '77
The Love Bug '68

Reed ►cont.

Love's Savage Fury '79
Nightmare in Badham County '76
No Prince for My Cinderella '78
Nurse '80
Prime Target '91
Rich Man, Poor Man '76
The Seekers '79
Snatched '72
Star! '68
A Very Brady Christmas '88

Shanna Reed
The Banker '89
Legs '83

Suzanne Reed
Beyond the Bermuda Triangle '75
Up from the Depths '79

Tracy Reed
No Way Back '74
Piece of the Action '77

Walter Reed
Government Agents vs. Phantom Legion '51
How to Make a Monster '58
Macumba Love '60
Seven Days' Leave '42

Harry Reems
Deadly Weapons '70
R.S.V.P. '84

Angharad Rees
Hands of the Ripper '71
Poldark '75

Donough Rees
Crush '93
Starship '87

Roger Rees
Charles & Diana: A Palace Divided '93
Ebony Tower '86
If Looks Could Kill '91
Mountains of the Moon '90
Robin Hood: Men in Tights '93
Star 80 '83
Stop! or My Mom Will Shoot '92

Della Reese
Harlem Nights '89
The Kid Who Loved Christmas '90
Nightmare in Badham County '76
Psychic Killer '75
The Voyage of the Yes '72

Christopher Reeve
Anna Karenina '85
The Aviator '85
The Bostonians '84
Death Dreams '92
Deathtrap '82
Gray Lady Down '77
The Great Escape 2: The Untold Story '88
Monsignor '82
Morning Glory '93
Mortal Sins '92
Noises Off '92
The Remains of the Day '93
The Rose and the Jackal '90
The Sea Wolf '93
Sleeping Beauty '83
Somewhere in Time '80
Street Smart '87
Superman: The Movie '78
Superman 2 '80
Superman 3 '83
Superman 4: The Quest for Peace '87
Switching Channels '88

George Reeves
Bar-20 '43
Blood and Sand '41
Border Patrol '43
Bugles in the Afternoon '52
Colt Comrades '43
The Fighting 69th '40
Forever Female '53
From Here to Eternity '53
Gone with the Wind '39
The Great Lover '49
Hoppy Serves a Writ '43
Jungle Goddess '49

Leather Burners '43
Lydia '41
The Making of a Legend: "Gone With the Wind" '89
Rancho Notorious '52
Stamp Day for Superman '53
Strawberry Blonde '41
Superman & the Mole Men '51
Thunder in the Pines '49
Westward Ho, the Wagons! '56

Keanu Reeves
Act of Vengeance '86
Babes in Toyland '86
Bill & Ted's Bogus Journey '91
Bill & Ted's Excellent Adventure '89
Bram Stoker's Dracula '92
Brotherhood of Justice '86
Dangerous Liaisons '88
Dream to Believe '85
Even Cowgirls Get the Blues '94
I Love You to Death '90
Little Buddha '93
Much Ado About Nothing '93
My Own Private Idaho '91
The Night Before '88
Parenthood '89
Permanent Record '88
Point Break '91
Prince of Pennsylvania '88
River's Edge '87
Speed '94
Tune in Tomorrow '90
Youngblood '86

Lisa Reeves
The Chicken Chronicles '77
Pom Pom Girls '76
Snowblind '78

Saskia Reeves
Antonia and Jane '91
Close My Eyes '91

Scott Reeves
Edge of Honor '91
Friday the 13th, Part 8: Jason Takes Manhattan '89

Steve Reeves
Athena '54
The Avenger '62
The Giant of Marathon '60
Goliath and the Barbarians '60
Hercules '58
Hercules Unchained '59
Jail Bait '54
The Last Days of Pompeii '60
Morgan the Pirate '60
Pirates of the Seven Seas '62
Thief of Baghdad '61

Joe Regalbuto
Invitation to Hell '84
Lassiter '84
Missing '82
The Queen of Mean '90
Writer's Block '91

Mary Regan
Fever '88
Heart of the Stag '84
Midnight Dancer '87
Sylvia '86

Phil Regan
Manhattan Merry-Go-Round '37
Sweet Rosie O'Grady '43
Swing Parade of 1946 '46

George Regas
Hell-Ship Morgan '36
The Rains Came '39
Sixteen Fathoms Deep '34

Duncan Regehr
The Banker '89
Gore Vidal's Billy the Kid '89
The Monster Squad '87
My Wicked, Wicked Ways '84

Benoit Regent
Club Extinction '89
Trois Couleurs: Bleu '93

Serge Reggiani
Cat and Mouse '78
La Ronde '51
Le Doulos '61
Les Miserables '57
Manon '50

Nadja Regin
From Russia with Love '63

Goldfinger '64

Paul Regina
Adam '83
A Long Way Home '81

Regine
Marry Me, Marry Me '69
My New Partner '84
The Seven Percent Solution '76

Frank Reicher
King Kong '33
Scarlet Dawn '32

Wolfgang Reichmann
Beethoven's Nephew '88
The Nun '66
Woyzeck '78

Beryl Reid
The Assassination Bureau '69
Beast in the Cellar '70
The Belles of St. Trinian's '53
Carry On Emmanuelle '78
The Doctor and the Devils '85
Doctor Phibes Rises Again '72
Duel of Hearts '91
Entertaining Mr. Sloane '70
Joseph Andrews '77
The Killing of Sister George '69
Psychomania '73
Star! '68

Carl Benton Reid
The Bramble Bush '60
The Egyptian '54
Escape from Fort Bravo '53
The Fuller Brush Girl '50
In a Lonely Place '50
Indian Uprising '51
Pressure Point '62
The Trap '59

Christopher Reid
Class Act '91
House Party '90
House Party 2: The Pajama Jam '91
House Party 3 '94

Elliott Reid
Follow Me, Boys! '66
Gentlemen Prefer Blondes '53
The Thrill of It All! '63

Fiona Reid
Accident '83
Beethoven Lives Upstairs '92
Heaven on Earth '89
Mark Twain and Me '91

Kate Reid
The Andromeda Strain '71
Atlantic City '81
The Blood of Others '84
Bye Bye Blues '89
Circle of Two '80
Control '87
Crossbar '79
Death of a Salesman '86
Death Ship '80
Deceived '91
The Double Negative '80
Execution of Raymond Graham '85
Fire with Fire '86
Heaven Help Us '85
Highpoint '80
Holy Terror '65
Invincible Mr. Disraeli '80
One Plus One '61
The Rainbow Gang '73
Signs of Life '89
Teamster Boss: The Jackie Presser Story '92
This Property is Condemned '66
Ugly Little Boy '77

Tim Reid
Dead Bang '89
The Fourth War '90
Stephen King's It '90
WKRP in Cincinnati, Vol. 1 '78
You Must Remember This '90s

Wallace Reid
The Birth of a Nation '15
Hawthorne of the USA '19
The Roaring Road '19

Charles Nelson Reilly
Body Slam '87
Cannonball Run 2 '84

Hugh Reilly
Chuka '67
Lassie's Great Adventure '62

John Reilly
Casualties of War '89
Fallen Angels 1 '93
Hoffa '92
Missing Pieces '83
Out on a Limb '92
State of Grace '90
We're No Angels '89
What's Eating Gilbert Grape '93

Luke Reilly
Bye Bye Blues '89
Zebrahead '92

Tom Reilly
Kiss and Be Killed '91
Mirror Images 2 '93

Carl Reiner
Best of Comic Relief '86
Dead Men Don't Wear Plaid '82
The End '78
The Gazebo '59
Generation '69
Gidget Goes Hawaiian '61
It's a Mad, Mad, Mad, Mad World '63
Pinocchio '83
The Russians are Coming, the Russians are Coming '66
Spirit of '76 '91
The Thrill of It All! '63

Rob Reiner
Billy Crystal: Don't Get Me Started '86
Enter Laughing '67
How Come Nobody's On Our Side? '71
Johnny Appleseed '86
Postcards from the Edge '90
Sleepless in Seattle '93
Spirit of '76 '91
This is Spinal Tap '84
Throw Momma from the Train '87
Thursday's Game '74
Where's Poppa? '70

Tracy Reiner
Frankie and Johnny '91
A League of Their Own '92
Masque of the Red Death '89
New Year's Day '89
Nothing in Common '86

Judge Reinhold
Baby on Board '92
Beverly Hills Cop '84
Beverly Hills Cop 2 '87
Beverly Hills Cop 3 '94
Black Magic '92
Daddy's Dyin'...Who's Got the Will? '90
Enid is Sleeping '90
Fast Times at Ridgemont High '82
Four Eyes and Six Guns '93
Gremlins '84
Head Office '86
The Lords of Discipline '83
Near Misses '91
Off Beat '86
On the Edge: The Survival of Dana '79
Pandemonium '82
Promised a Miracle '88
Roadhouse 66 '84
Rosalie Goes Shopping '89
Running Scared '79
Ruthless People '86
A Soldier's Tale '91
Stripes '81
Vice Versa '88
Zandalee '91

Ann Reinking
All That Jazz '79
Annie '82
Micki & Maude '84

Paul Reiser
Aliens '86
Beverly Hills Cop '84
Beverly Hills Cop 2 '87
Crazy People '90
Cross My Heart '88
Diner '82
Family Prayers '91
From Here to Maternity '85
The Marrying Man '91

Odd Jobs '85
Sunset Limousine '83

Winston Rekert
Dead Wrong '83
Eternal Evil '87
Heartaches '82
Toby McTeague '87

Maria Therese Relin
Quo Vadis '85
Secret Places '85

James Remar
Blink '93
The Clan of the Cave Bear '86
Confessions of a Hit Man '94
The Cotton Club '84
Deadlock '91
The Dream Team '89
Drugstore Cowboy '89
Fatal Charm '92
Fatal Instinct '93
48 Hrs. '82
Indecency '92
Quiet Cool '86
Renaissance Man '94
Rent-A-Cop '88
Silence Like Glass '90
Tales from the Darkside: The Movie '90
The Tigress '93
The Warriors '79
White Fang '91
Windwalker '81

Erika Remberg
Cave of the Living Dead '65
Circus of Horrors '60

Lee Remick
Anatomy of a Murder '59
Baby, the Rain Must Fall '64
Breaking Up '78
Bridge to Silence '89
The Competition '80
Days of Wine and Roses '62
The Detective '68
The Europeans '79
Experiment in Terror '62
A Face in the Crowd '57
Follies in Concert '80
The Hallelujah Trail '65
Hennessy '75
Hustling '75
I Do! I Do! '84
Ike '79
Jesse '88
The Long, Hot Summer '58
Loot...Give Me Money, Honey! '70
The Medusa Touch '78
Mistral's Daughter '84
No Way to Treat a Lady '68
The Omen '76
QB VII '74
The Snow Queen '83
Sometimes a Great Notion '71
Telefon '77
The Tempest '79
Torn Between Two Lovers '79
Touch Me Not '74
Toughlove '85
Tribute '80
The Vision '87
The Wheeler Dealers '63

Bert Remsen
Burning Rage '84
Code of Silence '85
Curfew '88
Daddy's Dyin'...Who's Got the Will? '90
The Death Squad '73
Evil Spirits '91
Eye of the Tiger '86
I Married a Centerfold '84
Joni '79
Lies '83
M.A.D.D.: Mothers Against Drunk Driving '83
McCabe & Mrs. Miller '71
Miss Firecracker '89
Nashville '75
Only the Lonely '91
Payback '90
Peacemaker '90
Policewoman Centerfold '83
Pork Chop Hill '59
South of Reno '87
Sweet Hostage '75
Tai-Pan '86

Tarantulas: The Deadly Cargo
  '77
Terrorvision '86
Thieves Like Us '74

Kerry Remsen
Ghoulies 2 '88
Pumpkinhead '88

Albert Remy
Children of Paradise '44
The 400 Blows '59
Shoot the Piano Player '62
The Train '65

Ronald Remy
Revenge of Doctor X '80s
The Vampire People '66

Duncan Renaldo
Border Patrol '43
The Capture '50
Covered Wagon Days '40
Cowboys from Texas '39
Don Amigo/Stage to Chino '40s
Down Mexico Way '41
Guns of Fury '45
In Old New Mexico '45
The Kansas Terrors '39
Manhunt in the African Jungle
  '54
Outlaws of the Desert '41
The Painted Stallion '37
Panama Menace '41
Perils of the Darkest Jungle '44
Roaring Speedboats '37
Rocky Mountain Rangers '40
Rose of Rio Grande '38
Rough Riders' Roundup '39
South of the Rio Grande '45
Tiger Fangs '43
Trader Horn '31
Western Double Feature 12 '44
Zorro Rides Again '37

Simone Renant
Dangerous Liaisons '60
Jenny Lamour '47
That Man from Rio '64

Madeleine Renaud
Maria Chapdelaine '34
Stormy Waters '41

Liz Renay
Blackenstein '73
Desperate Living '77
The Thrill Killers '65

Patrick Renna
The Sandlot '93
Son-in-Law '93

Deborah Rennard
Land of Doom '84
Lionheart '90

Michael Rennie
The Battle of El Alamein '68
Commando Attack '67
The Day the Earth Stood Still
  '51
Demetrius and the Gladiators
  '54
Desiree '54
The Devil's Brigade '68
Die Screaming, Marianne '73
Dracula vs. Frankenstein '69
Five Fingers '52
Hotel '67
Mambo '55
Omar Khayyam '57
Phone Call from a Stranger '52
The Robe '53
Seven Cities of Gold '55
Soldier of Fortune '55
Surabaya Conspiracy '75
Third Man on the Mountain '59
Tower of Terror '42
Trio '50
Uneasy Terms '48
The Wicked Lady '45

Jean Reno
The Big Blue '88
La Femme Nikita '91
Le Dernier Combat '84

John Reno
Bloodspell '87
Mirror of Death '87

Kelly Reno
The Black Stallion '79
The Black Stallion Returns '83
Brady's Escape '84

Jean Renoir
The Little Theatre of Jean
  Renoir '71
The Rules of the Game '39

Pierre Renoir
Children of Paradise '44
La Marseillaise '37
Madame Bovary '34

Eva Renzi
The Bird with the Crystal
  Plumage '70
Funeral in Berlin '66
Night of the Assassin '77

Maggie Renzi
The Brother from Another
  Planet '84
City of Hope '91
Eight Men Out '88
Passion Fish '92

Tommy Rettig
The Cobweb '55
The 5000 Fingers of Dr. T '53
River of No Return '54

**Paul (Pee Wee
Herman) Reubens**
Back to the Beach '87
Batman Returns '92
Big Top Pee Wee '88
Buffy the Vampire Slayer '92
Cheech and Chong's Next
  Movie '80
Cheech and Chong's Nice
  Dreams '81
Meatballs 2 '84
Pandemonium '82
The Pee Wee Herman Show
  '82
Pee Wee's Big Adventure '85
Pee Wee's Playhouse
  Christmas Special '88
Pee Wee's Playhouse Festival
  of Fun '88
Pinocchio '83

Anne Revere
Body and Soul '47
Falcon Takes Over/Strange
  Bargain '49
Forever Amber '47
Gentleman's Agreement '47
The Howards of Virginia '40
The Keys of the Kingdom '44
National Velvet '44
A Place in the Sun '51
Secret Beyond the Door '48
The Song of Bernadette '43
The Thin Man Goes Home '44

Dorothy Revier
Dance of Life '29
The Dropkick '27
Green Eyes '34
The King Murder Case '32
The Secrets of Wu Sin '32
When a Man Sees Red '34

Clive Revill
The Assassination Bureau '69
Avanti! '72
The Black Windmill '74
Cannon Movie Tales: The
  Emperor's New Clothes '89
The Empire Strikes Back '80
Escape to the Sun '72
A Fine Madness '66
George Washington '84
Ghost in the Noonday Sun '74
The Legend of Hell House '73
Mack the Knife '89
Matilda '78
One of Our Dinosaurs Is
  Missing '75
The Private Life of Sherlock
  Holmes '70
Rumpelstiltskin '86
The Sea Wolf '93

Rex
King of the Wild Horses '24
Robinson Crusoe of Mystery
  Island '36

Alejandro Rey
Fun in Acapulco '63
Moscow on the Hudson '84
The Ninth Configuration '79
Rita Hayworth: The Love
  Goddess '83
Solomon and Sheba '59
The Stepmother '71

Bruno Rey
Sorceress '82
Volver, Volver, Volver! '87

Fernando Rey
The Adventurers '70
Angel of Death '86
Antony and Cleopatra '73
The Assignment '78
Attack of the Robots '66
Autopsy '70s
Cabo Blanco '81
The Castilian '63
Chimes at Midnight '67
Cold Eyes of Fear '70s
The Discreet Charm of the
  Bourgeoisie '72
1492: Conquest of Paradise '92
The French Connection '71
French Connection 2 '75
Goliath Against the Giants '63
Great Leaders of the Bibles
  '70s
Guns of the Magnificent Seven
  '69
High Crime '73
The Hit '85
Honey '81
Insanity '82
La Grande Bourgeoise '74
Monsignor '82
Moon Over Parador '88
Navajo Joe '67
Padre Nuestro '85
Pantaloons '57
Quintet '79
Saving Grace '86
Seven Beauties '76
That Obscure Object of Desire
  '77
A Town Called Hell '72
Tristana '70
The Tunnel '89
Violent Blood Bath
Viridiana '61

Mony Rey
Mademoiselle '66
Not Without My Daughter '90

Ernie Reyes, Jr.
Surf Ninjas '93
Teenage Mutant Ninja Turtles
  2: The Secret of the Ooze
  '91

Julian Reyes
Mi Vida Loca '94
Point Break '91

Kamar Reyes
Coldfire '90
East L.A. Warriors '89

Janine Reynaud
Castle of the Creeping Flesh
  '68
The Scorpion's Tail '71
The Sensuous Teenager '70

Burt Reynolds
Angel Baby '61
Armored Command '61
Best Friends '82
The Best Little Whorehouse in
  Texas '82
Breaking In '89
Cannonball Run '81
Cannonball Run 2 '84
City Heat '84
Cop and a Half '93
Deliverance '72
The End '78
Everything You Always Wanted
  to Know About Sex (But
  Were Afraid to Ask) '72
Fuzz '72
Gator '76
Hard Frame '70
Heat '87
Hooper '78
Hustle '75
Iron Cowboy '68
The Longest Yard '74
Malone '87
Man Who Loved Cat Dancing
  '73
The Man Who Loved Women
  '83
Modern Love '90
Navajo Joe '67
100 Rifles '69

Operation C.I.A. '65
Paternity '81
Physical Evidence '89
Rent-A-Cop '88
Rough Cut '80
Savage Run '70
Semi-Tough '77
Shamus '73
Shark! '68
Sharky's Machine '81
Silent Movie '76
Skullduggery '70
Smokey and the Bandit '77
Smokey and the Bandit, Part 2
  '80
Smokey and the Bandit, Part 3
  '83
Starting Over '79
Stick '85
Stroker Ace '83
Switching Channels '88
Uphill All the Way '85
White Lightning '73

Craig Reynolds
I Take This Oath '40
Nevada '44

Debbie Reynolds
The Affairs of Dobie Gillis '53
Athena '54
Battling for Baby '92
Bundle of Joy '56
The Catered Affair '56
Detective Sadie & Son '84
The Gazebo '59
Give a Girl a Break '53
Heaven and Earth '93
Hit the Deck '55
How Sweet It Is! '68
How the West was Won '63
I Love Melvin '53
It Started with a Kiss '59
The Mating Game '59
The Rat Race '60
Singin' in the Rain '52
The Singing Nun '66
Skirts Ahoy! '52
Susan Slept Here '54
Tammy and the Bachelor '57
The Tender Trap '55
This Happy Feeling '58
Three Little Words '50
Two Weeks with Love '50
The Unsinkable Molly Brown
  '64
What's the Matter with Helen?
  '71

Gene Reynolds
Andy Hardy's Private Secretary
  '41
Boys Town '38
Country Girl '54
In Old Chicago '38
Jungle Patrol '48
Life Begins for Andy Hardy '41
Love Finds Andy Hardy '38
They Shall Have Music '39
The Tuttles of Tahiti '42

Marjorie Reynolds
The Abe Lincoln of Ninth
  Avenue '39
Doomed to Die '40
The Fatal Hour '40
Gone with the Wind '39
Holiday Inn '42
Home Town Story '51
Man's Country '38
Midnight Limited '40
Mr. Wong in Chinatown '39
Monsieur Beaucaire '46
Mystery Plane '39
Racketeers of the Range '39
Robin Hood of the Pecos '41
Six Shootin' Sheriff '38
Stunt Pilot '39
The Time of Their Lives '46
Up in the Air '40
Western Trails '38

Peter Reynolds
Devil Girl from Mars '54
The Great Armored Car
  Swindle '64
It Takes a Thief '37

Vera Reynolds
The Monster Walks '32
The Night Club '25
Risky Business '28
The Road to Yesterday '25

Road to Yesterday/The Yankee
  Clipper '27
Sunny Side Up '28
Tangled Destinies '32

William Reynolds
Carrie '52
Cult of the Cobra '55
The Land Unknown '57
Son of Ali Baba '52

David Reynoso
Invasion of the Vampires '61
La Trinchera '87
Orlak, the Hell of Frankenstein
  '60

Ving Rhames
Dave '93
Homicide '91
Jacob's Ladder '90
The Long Walk Home '89
Patty Hearst '88
The People Under the Stairs
  '91
Pulp Fiction '94
Rising Son '90
The Saint of Fort Washington
  '93

Phillip Rhee
Best of the Best '89
Best of the Best 2 '93
Ninja Turf '86
Silent Assassins '88

Simon Rhee
Best of the Best '89
Best of the Best 2 '93
Furious '83

Barbara Rhoades
The Choirboys '77
Conspiracy of Terror '75
The Day the Women Got Even
  '80
The Goodbye Girl '77
Hunter '77
Scream Blacula Scream '73
Serial '80
Sex and the Single Parent '82
The Shakiest Gun in the West
  '68
Up the Sandbox '72

Bobby Rhodes
Demons 2 '87
Endgame '85
The Last Hunter '80

Cynthia Rhodes
Curse of the Crystal Eye '93
Dirty Dancing '87
Flashdance '83
Runaway '84
Staying Alive '83

Donnelly Rhodes
After the Promise '87
Dirty Work '92
Goldenrod '77
Hard Part Begins '80s
The Penthouse '92
Showdown at Williams Creek
  '91

Erik Rhodes
Charlie Chan in Paris '35
The Gay Divorcee '34
Special Investigator '36
Top Hat '35

Hari Rhodes
Coma '78
Conquest of the Planet of the
  Apes '72
Detroit 9000 '73
A Dream for Christmas '73
Shock Corridor '63
A Woman Called Moses '78

Marjorie Rhodes
Decameron Nights '53
Great Day '46

John Rhys-Davies
Best Revenge '83
Canvas: The Fine Art of Crime
  '92
Cyborg Cop '93
The Double O Kid '92
Great Expectations '89
In the Shadow of Kilimanjaro
  '86
Indiana Jones and the Last
  Crusade '89
Ivanhoe '82

Rhys-Davies ▶cont.

Journey of Honor '91
King Solomon's Mines '85
The Little Match Girl '87
The Living Daylights '87
The Lost World '92
Nairobi Affair '88
Nativity '78
Raiders of the Lost Ark '81
Rebel Storm '90
Return to the Lost World '93
Ring of the Musketeers '93
Sadat '83
Sahara '83
Secret Weapon '90
The Seventh Coin '92
Shogun '80
Sphinx '81
Sunset Grill '92
Sword of the Valiant '83
The Trial of the Incredible Hulk '89
Tusks '89
The Unnamable 2: The Statement of Randolph Carter '92
Victor/Victoria '82
War & Remembrance, Part 1 '88
War & Remembrance: The Final Chapter, Part 8 '89

Paul Rhys
Becoming Colette '92
Chaplin '92
Vincent & Theo '90

Candice Rialson
Candy Stripe Nurses '74
Chatterbox '76
Hollywood Boulevard '76
Mama's Dirty Girls '74
Moonshine County Express '77
Summer School Teachers '75

Alfonso Ribeiro
The Mighty Pawns '87
Ticks '93

Christina Ricci
The Addams Family '91
Addams Family Values '93
The Cemetery Club '93
The Hard Way '91
Mermaids '90

Bill Rice
Doomed Love '83
Landlord Blues '87
Vortex '81

Florence Rice
At the Circus '39
Boss of Big Town '43
Double Wedding '37
The Ghost and the Guest '43
Navy Blue and Gold '37
Sweethearts '38

Frank Rice
Border Law '31
Dynamite Dan '24
The Fiddlin' Buckaroo '33
The Fighting Legion '30
Phantom Thunderbolt '33
Red Signals '27
Somewhere in Sonora '33

Joan Rice
His Majesty O'Keefe '53
The Story of Robin Hood & His Merrie Men '52

Adam Rich
The Devil & Max Devlin '81
Zertigo Diamond Caper '82

Allen Rich
Archer: The Fugitive from the Empire '81
Matters of the Heart '90
The Seekers '79

Christopher Rich
The Joy Luck Club '93
Prisoners of Inertia '89

Claude Rich
The Bride Wore Black '68
The Elusive Corporal '62
Is Paris Burning? '68
Le Crabe Tambour '77
Maria Chapdelaine '84

Eli Rich
Deadly Diamonds '91
Murderlust '86
Nudity Required '90

Irene Rich
Angel and the Badman '47
Beau Brummel '24
The Champ '31
Held for Murder '32
The Lady in Question '40
The Mortal Storm '40
The Trap '22

Jean Richard
Elena and Her Men '56
Seven Deadly Sins '53

Jean-Louis Richard
It Means That to Me '63
The Last Metro '80

Pierre Richard
The Daydreamer '75
Johnny Frenchman '46
La Chevre '81
Les Comperes '83
Return of the Tall Blond Man With One Black Shoe '74
Suicide Patrol '70s
The Tall Blond Man with One Black Shoe '72
Too Shy to Try '82

Addison Richards
Bad Lands '39
Bells of Rosarita '45
Betrayal from the East '44
Call Northside 777 '48
Criminal Court '46
The Fighting Sullivans '42
The Man with Two Lives '42
Our Daily Bread '34
Ridin' Down the Canyon '42
A Southern Yankee '48

Ann Richards
Badman's Territory '46
Breakdown '53
Lost Honeymoon '47
Love from a Stranger '47
Sorry, Wrong Number '48

Ariana Richards
Grand Tour: Disaster in Time '92
Jurassic Park '93
Prancer '89
Spaced Invaders '90
Switched at Birth '91

Beah Richards
Acceptable Risks '86
As Summers Die '86
A Christmas Without Snow '80
A Dream for Christmas '73
Drugstore Cowboy '89
Gone are the Days '63
Inside Out '91
The Miracle Worker '62
Roots: The Next Generation '79

Evan Richards
Down and Out in Beverly Hills '86
Dream Machine '91
Rock 'n' Roll High School Forever '91
Society '92

Jeff Richards
Angels in the Outfield '51
It's a Dog's Life '51
Seven Brides for Seven Brothers '54

Keith Richards
Chuck Berry: Hail! Hail! Rock 'n' Roll '87
Gimme Shelter '70

Kim Richards
Assault on Precinct 13 '76
Devil Dog: The Hound of Hell '78
Escape '90
Escape to Witch Mountain '75
Meatballs 2 '84
Return from Witch Mountain '78
Tuff Turf '85

Lisa Richards
Eating '90
The Prince of Central Park '77
Return '88

Michael Richards
Airheads '94
Coneheads '93
Problem Child '90
UHF '89
Whoops Apocalypse '88

Tom Richards
The Cursed Mountain Mystery '93
Dawn! '83
Plunge Into Darkness '77

Ian Richardson
Brazil '85
Burning Secret '89
Cry Freedom '87
Foreign Affairs '93
The Fourth Protocol '87
The Hound of the Baskervilles '83
M. Butterfly '93
Marat/Sade '66
A Midsummer Night's Dream '68
Monsignor Quixote '91
The Sign of Four '83
Whoops Apocalypse '83
Year of the Comet '92

Jack Richardson
Dynamite Dan '24
Marked Money '28
Toll Gate '20
Trigger Tricks '30

Jay Richardson
Alienator '89
Bad Girls from Mars '90
The Channeler '89
Death Row Diner '88
Hollywood Chainsaw Hookers '88
Mind, Body & Soul '92
The Newlydeads '87
Original Intent '91
Sins of Desire '92
Slashdance '89
Teenage Exorcist '90
Vice Academy 2 '90
Vice Academy 3 '91

Joely Richardson
Drowning by Numbers '87
I'll Do Anything '93
King Ralph '91
Shining Through '92
Wetherby '85

John Richardson
Black Sunday '60
Cosmos: War of the Planets '80
Eyeball '78
Frankenstein '80 '79
Torso '73

Lee Richardson
The Believers '87
The Fly 2 '89
Prizzi's Honor '85
Q & A '90
Skylark '93
A Stranger Among Us '92
Sweet Lorraine '87
Tiger Warsaw '87

Miranda Richardson
After Pilkington '88
The Bachelor '93
The Crying Game '92
Damage '92
Dance with a Stranger '85
Empire of the Sun '87
Enchanted April '92
Transmutations '85
Twisted Obsession '90

Natasha Richardson
The Comfort of Strangers '91
Fat Man and Little Boy '89
The Favor, the Watch, & the Very Big Fish '92
Gothic '87
The Handmaid's Tale '90
Hostages '93
A Month in the Country '87
Past Midnight '92
Patty Hearst '88
Widow's Peak '94

Ralph Richardson
Amazing Adventure '37
Anna Karenina '48
Battle of Britain '69
Bulldog Jack '35
The Citadel '38
Clouds Over Europe '39
The Day Will Dawn '42
The Divorce of Lady X '38
Doctor Zhivago '65
A Doll's House '89
Dragonslayer '81
Early Days '81
Exodus '60
The Fallen Idol '49
The Four Feathers '39
The Ghoul '34
Give My Regards to Broad Street '84
Greystoke: The Legend of Tarzan, Lord of the Apes '84
The Heiress '49
Invitation to the Wedding '73
Java Head '35
Khartoum '66
Lady Caroline Lamb '73
The Lion Has Wings '40
Long Day's Journey into Night '62
The Looking Glass War '69
The Man in the Iron Mask '77
The Man Who Could Work Miracles '37
O Lucky Man! '73
Richard III '55
Tales from the Crypt '72
Things to Come '36
Thunder in the City '37
Time Bandits '81
Wagner: The Complete Epic '85
Who Slew Auntie Roo? '71
The Wrong Box '66

Regina Richardson
Nine Deaths of the Ninja '85
Tightrope '84

Salli Richardson
How U Like Me Now? '92
Low Down Dirty Shame '94
Posse '93
Up Against the Wall '91

Sy Richardson
Backtrack '89
Dead Man Walking '88
Fairytales '79
Repo Man '83
Ring of Fire 2: Blood and Steel '92
Straight to Hell '87
Street Asylum '90
They Live '88

Peter Mark Richman
City Killer '87
Dempsey '83
Friday the 13th, Part 8: Jason Takes Manhattan '89
Judgment Day '88
Naked Gun 2 1/2: The Smell of Fear '91
PSI Factor '80

Anthony Richmond
Devil Girl from Mars '54
One Wish Too Many '55

Branscombe Richmond
Christopher Columbus: The Discovery '92
DaVinci's War '92
Inside Edge '92
Jericho Fever '93
The Taking of Beverly Hills '91

Fiona Richmond
Eat the Rich '87
The House on Straw Hill '76

Kane Richmond
The Adventures of Rex & Rinty '35
Anything for a Thrill '37
Behind the Mask '37
Cavalier of the West '31
Confidential '35
Devil Diamond '37
East Side Kids/The Lost City '35
Haunted Harbor '44
The Lost City '34
Motorcycle Squad '37
The Reckless Way '36
Spy Smasher Returns '42
Tough to Handle '37

Warner Richmond
Big News '29

Colorado Serenade '46
Doomed at Sundown '37
Headin' for the Rio Grande '36
A Lawman is Born '37
The Lost Jungle '34
The New Frontier '35
Rainbow's End '35
Song of the Gringo '36
The Speed Spook '24
Where Trails Divide '37
Wild Horse Canyon '39
Wild West '46

Deborah Richter
The Banker '89
Cyborg '89
Hot Moves '84
Promised Land '88
The Rebels '79
Square Dance '87
Swap Meet '79
Twirl '81

Jason James Richter
Cops and Robbersons '94
Free Willy '93

Paul Richter
Dr. Mabuse the Gambler '22
Kriemhilde's Revenge '24
Siegfried '24

Tony Rickards
Castaway '87
Great Gold Swindle '84
Robbery '85
Waterfront '83

Don Rickles
Beach Blanket Bingo '65
Bikini Beach '64
Enter Laughing '67
For the Love of It '80
Innocent Blood '92
Keaton's Cop '90
Kelly's Heroes '70
Muscle Beach Party '64
The Rat Race '60
Run Silent, Run Deep '58
Two Top Bananas '87
X: The Man with X-Ray Eyes '63

Alan Rickman
Bob Roberts '92
Close My Eyes '91
Closet Land '91
Die Hard '88
Fallen Angels 1 '93
The January Man '89
Quigley Down Under '90
Robin Hood: Prince of Thieves '91
Truly, Madly, Deeply '91

Allen Rickman
I Was a Teenage Zombie '87
Shock! Shock! Shock! '87

John Ridgely
Air Force '43
Arsenic and Old Lace '44
The Big Sleep '46
Destination Tokyo '43
The Man I Love '46
The Possessed '47
Task Force '49

Robert Ridgely
Philadelphia '93
Rosie: The Rosemary Clooney Story '82
Who Am I This Time? '82

Stanley Ridges
Each Dawn I Die '39
The Lady is Willing '42
Master Race '44
Mr. Ace '46
The Possessed '47
The Sea Wolf '41
Sergeant York '41
Task Force '49
Wilson '44

Leni Riefenstahl
The Blue Light '32
Sacred Mountain/White Flame '31
Tiefland '44

Peter Riegert
Americathon '79
Barbarians at the Gate '93
Chilly Scenes of Winter '79
Crossing Delancey '88
Gypsy '93

Local Hero '83
A Man in Love '87
The Mask '94
National Lampoon Goes to the Movies '81
National Lampoon's Animal House '78
News at Eleven '86
The Object of Beauty '91
Oscar '91
Passed Away '92
The Runestone '91
A Shock to the System '90
The Stranger '87
That's Adequate '90
Utz '93

Richard Riehle
Body of Evidence '92
A Dangerous Woman '93
Hero '92
Lightning Jack '94
Of Mice and Men '92
The Public Eye '92

Ron Rifkin
Courage '86
Manhattan Murder Mystery '93
Mrs. R's Daughter '79
Silent Running '71
Wolf '94

Jorge Rigaud
Black Box Affair '66
The Castilian '63
Dos Postolas Gemelas '65
Quatorze Juliet '32

Edward Rigby
Convoy '40
The Happiest Days of Your Life '50

Diana Rigg
The Assassination Bureau '69
Bleak House '85
Cannon Movie Tales: Snow White '89
Evil Under the Sun '82
The Great Muppet Caper '81
The Hospital '71
In This House of Brede '75
Julius Caesar '70
A Little Night Music '77
The Marquise
A Midsummer Night's Dream '68
On Her Majesty's Secret Service '69
Running Delilah '93
Theatre of Blood '73
Unexplained Laughter '89
The Worst Witch '86

Rebecca Rigg
Doctors and Nurses '82
The Efficiency Expert '92
Fortress '85
The Hunting '92

Brad Rijn
Perfect Strangers '84
Special Effects '85

Robin Riker
Alligator '80
Body Chemistry 2: Voice of a Stranger '91
Stepmonster '92

Elaine Riley
Clipped Wings '53
Hopalong Cassidy: Borrowed Trouble '48
Hopalong Cassidy: The Devil's Playground '46
Rider from Tucson '50

Jack Riley
McCabe & Mrs. Miller '71
Night Patrol '85
Portrait of a White Marriage '88

Jeannine Riley
Big Mouth '67
The Comic '69
Electra Glide in Blue '73
Wackiest Wagon Train in the West '77

Larry Riley
Crackers '84
Dead Solid Perfect '88
A Soldier's Story '84

Michael Riley
Perfectly Normal '91

Walter Rilla
Black Eyes '39
Frozen Alive '64
The Gamma People '56
The Golden Salamander '51
House of Mystery '41
Mr. Emmanuel '44

Shane Rimmer
Crusoe '89
Dreamchild '85
Out of Africa '85
The People That Time Forgot '77
S*P*Y*S '74

Molly Ringwald
Betsy's Wedding '90
The Breakfast Club '85
Face the Music '92
For Keeps '88
Fresh Horses '88
Johnny Appleseed '86
King Lear '87
Packin' It In '83
The Pick-Up Artist '87
P.K. and the Kid '85
Pretty in Pink '86
Sixteen Candles '84
Spacehunter: Adventures in the Forbidden Zone '83
Stephen King's The Stand '94
Strike It Rich '90
The Tempest '82
Women & Men: Stories of Seduction '90

David Rintoul
Legend of the Werewolf '75
Pride and Prejudice '85

Nicole Rio
Sorority House Massacre '86
Visitants '87
Zero Boys '86

Marjorie Riordan
The Hoodlum '51
Pursuit to Algiers '45
South of Monterey '47
Stage Door Canteen '43

Michael Ripper
The Curse of the Werewolf '61
Dead Lucky '60
Dracula Has Risen from the Grave '68
Eye Witness '49
Girly '70
No Surrender '86
Quatermass 2 '57
The Scars of Dracula '70
Where the Bullets Fly '66

Leon Rippy
Eye of the Storm '91
Hot Spot '90
Jesse '88
Kuffs '92
Moon 44 '90
Track 29 '88

Elisabeth Risdon
Crime and Punishment '35
Down Dakota Way '49
The Great Man Votes '38
Guilty of Treason '50
Hills of Oklahoma '50
The Lady is Willing '42
Mannequin '37
Mexican Spitfire at Sea '42
Reap the Wild Wind '42
Scaramouche '52

Miriam Riselle
The Singing Blacksmith '38
Tevye '39

Robbie Rist
He is My Brother '75
Iron Eagle '86

Cyril Ritchard
Blackmail '29
Half a Sixpence '67
Hans Brinker '69
Peter Pan '60

Clint Ritchie
Against A Crooked Sky '75
Peacekillers '71
The St. Valentine's Day Massacre '67

June Ritchie
A Kind of Loving '62

The Three Penny Opera '62

Martin Ritt
Conrack '74
The Slugger's Wife '85

John Ritter
Americathon '79
The Barefoot Executive '71
Comeback Kid '80
Hero at Large '80
In Love with an Older Woman '82
The Last Fling '86
Letting Go '85
My Brother's Wife '89
Noises Off '92
North '94
The Other '72
Pray TV '82
Problem Child '90
Problem Child 2 '91
Real Men '87
Scandalous John '71
Skin Deep '89
A Smoky Mountain Christmas '86
Stay Tuned '92
Stephen King's It '90
The Stone Killer '73
Sunset Limousine '83
They All Laughed '81
Tricks of the Trade '88
Unnatural Causes '86
Wholly Moses! '80

Tex Ritter
Arizona Days '37
Cowboys of the Saturday Matinee '84
Dead or Alive '41
Down the Wyoming Trail '39
Enemy of the Law '45
Frontier Fugitives '45
Gangsters of the Frontier '44
The Girl from Tobacco Row '66
Headin' for the Rio Grande '36
Hittin' the Trail '37
Holiday Rhythm '50
Man from Texas '39
Marked for Murder '45
The Marshal's Daughter '53
Mystery of the Hooded Horseman '37
The Pioneers '41
Riders of the Rockies '37
Roll, Wagons, Roll '39
Rollin' Plains '38
Sing, Cowboy, Sing '37
Song of the Gringo '36
Take Me Back to Oklahoma '40
Tex Rides with the Boy Scouts '37
Three in the Saddle '45
Trouble in Texas '37
Utah Trail '38

Thelma Ritter
All About Eve '50
As Young As You Feel '51
Birdman of Alcatraz '62
Boeing Boeing '65
Daddy Long Legs '55
The Farmer Takes a Wife '53
For Love or Money '63
A Hole in the Head '59
How the West was Won '63
The Incident '67
A Letter to Three Wives '49
Miracle on 34th Street '47
The Misfits '61
A New Kind of Love '63
Pickup on South Street '53
Pillow Talk '59
Rear Window '54

The Ritz Brothers
The Goldwyn Follies '38
The Gorilla '39
On the Avenue '37
One in a Million '36
The Three Musketeers '39

Harry Ritz
Silent Movie '76
Texas Layover '75

Emmanuelle Riva
Hiroshima, Mon Amour '59
Kapo '59
Leon Morin, Priest '61

Carlos Rivas
The Black Scorpion '57
El Cuarto Chino '71

The King and I '56

Amparo Rivelles
Anita de Montemar '60s
El Fugitivo '65
Remolina de Pasiones '87

Chita Rivera
Mayflower Madam '87
Once Upon a Brothers Grimm '77
Pippin '81
Sweet Charity '69

George Rivero
Bordello '79
Counterforce '87
Fist Fighter '88
Target Eagle '84

Jorge Rivero
Bellas de Noche
Conquest '83
Day of the Assassin '81
El Hombre Contra el Mundo '87
Ice '93
La Montana del Diablo '87
Los Caciques '87
Los Dos Hermanos '87
Priest of Love '81
Rio Lobo '70
Sin of Adam & Eve '72
Sin Salida '87
Soldier Blue '70
Volver, Volver, Volver! '87

Julian Rivero
Arizona Gangbusters '40
Beyond the Rockies '32
Death Rides the Range '40
Heroes of the Alamo '37
Man from Hell's Edges '32
Phantom Patrol '36
Ridin' the Lone Trail '37

Joan Rivers
Les Patterson Saves the World '90
Pee Wee's Playhouse Christmas Special '88
Spaceballs '87

Victor Rivers
Black Magic Woman '91
Blood In...Blood Out: Bound by Honor '93

George Riviere
Castle of Blood '64
Journey Beneath the Desert '61
The Virgin of Nuremberg '65

Marie Riviere
Four Adventures of Reinette and Mirabelle '89
Summer '86

Gianni Rizzo
Desert Commandos '60s
Mission Stardust '68

Bert Roach
The Crowd '28
The Great Waltz '38
Smouldering Fires '25

Adam Roarke
Beach Girls '82
Dirty Mary Crazy Larry '74
Four Deuces '75
Frogs '72
Hell's Angels on Wheels '67
How Come Nobody's On Our Side? '73
Hughes & Harlow: Angels in Hell '77
The Losers '70
The Savage Seven '68
The Stunt Man '80
This is a Hijack '75
Trespasses '86
Women of the Prehistoric Planet '66

Jason Robards, Sr.
Bedlam '45
Crimson Romance '34
Desperate '47
The Fatal Hour '40
Fighting Marines '35
Mademoiselle Fifi '44
The Miracle Rider '35
Return of the Bad Men '48
Riff-Raff '47
Rimfire '49
Stunt Pilot '39
Sweetheart of the Navy '37

Trail Street '47
Wayne Murder Case '38
White Eagle '32

Jason Robards, Jr.
The Adventures of Huck Finn '93
All the President's Men '76
Any Wednesday '66
Ballad of Cable Hogue '70
A Big Hand for the Little Lady '66
Black Rainbow '91
A Boy and His Dog '75
Breaking Home Ties '87
Bright Lights, Big City '88
Burden of Dreams '82
By Love Possessed '61
Cabo Blanco '81
A Christmas to Remember '78
The Christmas Wife '88
Comes a Horseman '78
The Day After '83
A Doll's House '59
Dream a Little Dream '89
Final Warning '90
Fools '70
The Good Mother '88
Heidi '93
Hour of the Gun '67
A House Without a Christmas Tree '72
Hurricane '79
An Inconvenient Woman '91
Isadora '68
Johnny Got His Gun '71
Julia '77
Julius Caesar '70
Laguna Heat '87
Legend of the Lone Ranger '81
Little Big League '94
Long Day's Journey into Night '62
The Long, Hot Summer '86
Mark Twain and Me '91
Max Dugan Returns '83
Melvin and Howard '80
Mr. Sycamore '74
Murders in the Rue Morgue '71
The Night They Raided Minsky's '69
Once Upon a Time in the West '68
The Paper '94
Parenthood '89
Philadelphia '93
Quick Change '90
Raise the Titanic '80
Reunion '88
The St. Valentine's Day Massacre '67
Sakharov '84
Something Wicked This Way Comes '83
Square Dance '87
Storyville '92
A Thousand Clowns '65
Tora! Tora! Tora! '70
The Trial '93
You Can't Take It with You '84

Sam Robards
The Ballad of Little Jo '93
Casualties of War '89
Fandango '85
Into Thin Air '85
Not Quite Paradise '86
Pancho Barnes '88
The Tempest '82

Brian Robbins
Cellar Dweller '87
C.H.U.D. 2: Bud the Chud '89

Gale Robbins
The Barkleys of Broadway '49
The Belle of New York '52
The Fuller Brush Girl '50
My Girl Tisa '48
Parasite '81
Three Little Words '50

Marty Robbins
Ballad of a Gunfighter '64
Hell on Wheels '67
Road to Nashville '67

Oliver Robbins
Poltergeist '82
Poltergeist 2: The Other Side '86

Skeeter Bill Robbins
Fighting Parson '35**

Robbins ▶cont.

Hard Hombre '31
Man's Land '32

Tim Robbins
Bob Roberts '92
Bull Durham '88
Cadillac Man '90
Erik the Viking '89
Five Corners '88
Fraternity Vacation '85
Howard the Duck '86
The Hudsucker Proxy '93
Jacob's Ladder '90
Jungle Fever '91
Miss Firecracker '89
No Small Affair '84
The Player '92
Short Cuts '93
The Sure Thing '85
Tapeheads '89
Top Gun '86
Toy Soldiers '84

Richard Rober
Call Northside 777 '48
Jet Pilot '57
Task Force '49
The Well '51

Allene Roberts
The Hoodlum '51
The Red House '47
Union Station '50

Arthur Roberts
Deadly Vengeance '81
Illegal Entry: Formula for Fear '93
Not of This Earth '88
Revenge of the Ninja '83

Christian Roberts
The Adventurers '70
Desperados '69
To Sir, with Love '67

Conrad Roberts
The Mosquito Coast '86
The Serpent and the Rainbow '87

Des Roberts
Black Bikers from Hell '70
The Outlaw Bikers—Gang Wars '70

Doris Roberts
The Fig Tree '87
Hester Street '75
Honeymoon Killers '70
National Lampoon's Christmas Vacation '89
The Night We Never Met '93
Ordinary Heroes '85
Simple Justice '89
The Taking of Pelham One Two Three '74
Used People '92

Edith Roberts
Man from Headquarters '28
The Taxi Mystery '26

Eric Roberts
The Ambulance '90
Best of the Best '89
Best of the Best 2 '93
Blood Red '88
By the Sword '91
The Coca-Cola Kid '84
Descending Angel '90
A Family Matter '91
Final Analysis '92
Firefall '94
King of the Gypsies '78
Lonely Hearts '91
The Lost Capone '90
Love, Cheat & Steal '94
Nobody's Fool '86
Paul's Case '80
The Pope of Greenwich Village '84
Raggedy Man '81
Rude Awakening '89
Runaway Train '85
Slow Burn '89
Star 80 '83
To Heal a Nation '88
Voyage '93

Florence Roberts
Harmony Lane '35

Kept Husbands '31
Sons of Steel '35

Francesca Roberts
The Heart of Dixie '89
Prison Stories: Women on the Inside '91

Jay Roberts, Jr.
Aftershock '88
Warlords 3000 '93
White Phantom: Enemy of Darkness '87

Julia Roberts
Baja Oklahoma '87
Blood Red '88
Dying Young '91
Flatliners '90
Hook '91
I Love Trouble '94
Mystic Pizza '88
The Pelican Brief '93
Pretty Woman '90
Satisfaction '88
Sleeping with the Enemy '91
Steel Magnolias '89

Ken Roberts
Fatal Pulse '88
The Great Land of Small '86

Lynn (Mary Hart) Roberts
Billy the Kid Returns '38
Dynamite Pass '50
Eyes of Texas '48
Frolics on Ice '40
Heart of the Rockies '37
Hollywood Stadium Mystery '38
Hunt the Man Down '50
Hunt the Man Down/Smashing the Rackets '50
In Old Caliente '39
Robin Hood of Texas '47
Rough Riders' Roundup '39
Shine on, Harvest Moon '38
Sioux City Sue '46

Mariwin Roberts
Enforcer from Death Row '78
Jokes My Folks Never Told Me '77

Michael D. Roberts
Heartbreaker '83
Ice Pirates '84
Live! From Death Row '92
Rain Man '88

Pascale Roberts
Friends '71
Le Grand Chemin '87
The Peking Blond '68

Pernell Roberts
The Errand Boy '61
Four Rode Out '69
High Noon: Part 2 '80
Hot Rod '79
Kashmiri Run '69
Magic of Lassie '78
The Night Train to Kathmandu '88
Paco '75
Ride Lonesome '59
Sniper '75

Rachel Roberts
Alpha Beta '73
Baffled '72
The Belstone Fox '73
Charlie Chan and the Curse of the Dragon Queen '81
Doctors' Wives '70
Foul Play '78
The Hostage Tower '80
Murder on the Orient Express '74
O Lucky Man! '73
Picnic at Hanging Rock '75
Sorrows of Gin '79
This Sporting Life '63
When a Stranger Calls '79
Wild Rovers '71
Yanks '79

Ray Roberts
Alien Dead '85
Force of Evil '49

Roy Roberts
Borderline '50
The Enforcer '51
The Fighting Sullivans '42
Guadalcanal Diary '43

He Walked by Night '48
I'll Take Sweden '65
The King and Four Queens '56
Second Chance '53

Tanya Roberts
Almost Pregnant '91
Beastmaster '82
Body Slam '87
California Dreaming '79
Fingers '78
Forced Entry '75
Hearts & Armour '83
Inner Sanctum '91
Legal Tender '90
Night Eyes '90
Purgatory '89
Racquet '79
Sheena '84
Sins of Desire '92
Tourist Trap '79
A View to a Kill '85
The Yum-Yum Girls '78

Theodore Roberts
The Roaring Road '19
Suds '20
The Ten Commandments '23

Tony Roberts
Amityville 3: The Demon '83
Annie Hall '77
18 Again! '88
Hannah and Her Sisters '86
If Things Were Different '79
Just Tell Me What You Want '80
Key Exchange '85
The Lindbergh Kidnapping Case '76
Lovers Like Us '75
A Midsummer Night's Sex Comedy '82
Million Dollar Duck '71
Packin' It In '83
Play It Again, Sam '72
Popcorn '89
Question of Honor '80
Radio Days '87
Seize the Day '86
Serpico '73
Star Spangled Girl '71
Stardust Memories '80
Switch '91
The Taking of Pelham One Two Three '74

Tracey Roberts
Actors and Sin '52
The Prodigal '55
Queen for a Day '51

Wink Roberts
The Day It Came to Earth '77
The First Time '69

Cliff Robertson
All in a Night's Work '61
Autumn Leaves '56
The Best Man '64
Brainstorm '83
Charly '68
Class '83
Danger in the Skies '79
Days of Wine and Roses '58
Dead Reckoning '89
The Devil's Brigade '68
Dominique is Dead '79
Ford: The Man & the Machine '87
Gidget '59
The Girl Most Likely '57
The Great Northfield Minnesota Raid '72
The Honey Pot '67
The Interns '62
The Key to Rebecca '85
Love has Many Faces '65
Malone '87
Midway '76
My Father's House '75
The Naked and the Dead '58
Obsession '76
Out of Season '75
Picnic '55
PT 109 '63
Return to Earth '76
Shaker Run '85
Shoot '85
633 Squadron '64
Star 80 '83
Three Days of the Condor '75
Too Late the Hero '70

Two of a Kind '82
Underworld, U.S.A. '60
Wild Hearts Can't Be Broken '91
Wind '92

Dale Robertson
Conexion Oriental '70
Dakota Incident '56
Devil's Canyon '53
The Farmer Takes a Wife '53
Kansas City Massacre '75
The Last Ride of the Dalton Gang '79
Melvin Purvis: G-Man '74
One-Eyed Soldiers '67
Son of Sinbad '55

Jenny Robertson
Bull Durham '88
Jacob Have I Loved '88
The Nightman '93

Paul Robeson
Body and Soul '24
Emperor Jones '33
Emperor Jones/Paul Robeson: Tribute to an Artist '33
Jericho '38
King Solomon's Mines '37
Sanders of the River '35
Show Boat '36
Song of Freedom '38

George Robey
Don Quixote '35
Henry V '44

Kim Robillard
Chrome Soldiers '92
Rain Man '88

Laila Robins
An Innocent Man '89
Planes, Trains & Automobiles '87
Welcome Home, Roxy Carmichael '90

Andrew (Andy) Robinson
Charley Varrick '73
Child's Play 3 '91
Cobra '86
Dirty Harry '71
Fatal Charm '92
Hellraiser '87
Into the Badlands '92
Mask '85
Not My Kid '85
Prime Target '91
Shoot to Kill '88
Someone I Touched '75
Trancers 3: Deth Lives '92

Ann Robinson
Dragnet '54
Midnight Movie Massacre '88
The War of the Worlds '53

Bill Robinson
Dixiana '30
Just Around the Corner '38
The Little Colonel '35
The Littlest Rebel '35
Rebecca of Sunnybrook Farm '38
Stormy Weather '43

Charles Robinson
Black Gestapo '75
The Brotherhood of Satan '71
Daring Dobermans '73
Fatal Chase '77

Chris Robinson
Ace of Hearts '85
Amy '81
Darker than Amber '70
Savannah Smiles '82
Stanley '72
Sunshine Run '79
Thunder County '74
Viper '88
Women's Prison Escape

Claudia Robinson
Back in the USSR '92
Wide Sargasso Sea '92

Dar Robinson
Cyclone '87
Stick '85

Edward G. Robinson
Actors and Sin '52
Barbary Coast '35
Brother Orchid '40

Bullets or Ballots '38
Cheyenne Autumn '64
The Cincinnati Kid '65
Destroyer '43
Double Indemnity '44
Good Neighbor Sam '64
Hell on Frisco Bay '55
A Hole in the Head '59
House of Strangers '49
I Am the Law '38
Illegal '55
It's a Great Feeling '49
Key Largo '48
Kid Galahad '37
Kings, Queens, Jokers '30s
Little Caesar '30
MacKenna's Gold '69
Mr. Winkle Goes to War '44
My Geisha '62
Never a Dull Moment '68
Our Vines Have Tender Grapes '45
The Peking Blond '68
The Prize '63
The Red House '47
Scarlet Street '45
The Sea Wolf '41
Seven Thieves '60
Some Like It Hot '59
Song of Norway '70
Soylent Green '73
The Stranger '46
Thunder in the City '37
Two Weeks in Another Town '62
The Violent Men '55

Frances Robinson
Red Barry '38
Riders of Pasco Basin '40
Smilin' Through '41
Tim Tyler's Luck '37

Jay Robinson
Demetrius and the Gladiators '54
Dying to Remember '93
Everything You Always Wanted to Know About Sex (But Were Afraid to Ask) '72
Malibu Bikini Shop '86
My Man Godfrey '57
Partners '82
The Robe '53
Sinatra '92
This is a Hijack '75
Three the Hard Way '74
Transylvania Twist '89
The Virgin Queen '55

Joe Robinson
Diamonds are Forever '71
The Invaders '63
Thor and the Amazon Women '60
Tor '64

Leon Robinson
Band of the Hand '86
The Father Clements Story '87
Streetwalkin' '85

Madeleine Robinson
Camille Claudel '89
Mission to Venice '63

German Robles
Genie of Darkness '60
The Living Head '59
Los Vampiros de Coyacan '87
The Monster Demolisher '60
Semaforo en Rojo '47
The Vampire '57
The Vampire's Coffin '58

Flora Robson
Bahama Passage '42
Beast in the Cellar '70
Black Narcissus '47
Blood Island '68
Caesar and Cleopatra '46
Catherine the Great '34
Epic That Never Was '65
55 Days at Peking '63
Fire Over England '37
Frieda '47
Great Day '46
Guns at Batasi '64
Les Miserables '78
The Lion Has Wings '40
Malta Story '53
Murder at the Gallop '63
Restless '72
Romeo and Juliet '54

The Sea Hawk '40
A Tale of Two Cities '80
Those Magnificent Men in Their
    Flying Machines '65
Wuthering Heights '39

Greer Robson
Smash Palace '82
Starlight Hotel '90

May Robson
The Adventures of Tom Sawyer
    '38
Anna Karenina '35
Bringing Up Baby '38
Dinner at Eight '33
Four Daughters '38
It Happened in New Orleans '36
Joan of Paris '42
Lady by Choice '34
Lady for a Day '33
Little Orphan Annie '32
Nurse Edith Cavell '39
Playmates '41
Reckless '35
Red Headed Woman '32
A Star is Born '37
Strange Interlude '32
Wife Versus Secretary '36

Wayne Robson
And Then You Die '88
Bye Bye Blues '89
The Grey Fox '83
Love & Murder '91
Mania '80s

Patricia Roc
Captain Blackjack '51
Johnny Frenchman '46
Man on the Eiffel Tower '48
The Wicked Lady '45

Pascale Rocard
Field of Honor '87
Police '85

Daniela Rocca
Divorce—Italian Style '62
The Giant of Marathon '60

Alex Rocco
Badge of the Assassin '85
Blood Mania '70
The Blue Knight '75
Bonnie's Kids '73
Boris and Natasha: The Movie
    '92
Detroit 9000 '73
Dream a Little Dream '89
The Entity '83
The Godfather '72
The Godfather 1902-1959: The
    Complete Epic '81
Gotcha! '85
The Grass is Always Greener
    Over the Septic Tank '78
Herbie Goes Bananas '80
Hustling '75
The Lady in White '88
Motor Psycho '65
A Perfect Little Murder '90
P.K. and the Kid '85
The Pope Must Diet '91
A Question of Guilt '78
Rabbit Test '78
Return to Horror High '87
Scenes from the Goldmine '87
Slither '73
Stanley '72
The Stunt Man '80
Three the Hard Way '74
Wild Riders '71
Wired '89

Eugene Roche
Corvette Summer '78
Cotton Comes to Harlem '70
Eternity '90
Foul Play '78
The Late Show '77
Newman's Law '74
Oh, God! You Devil '84
The Possessed '77
Rape and Marriage: The
    Rideout Case '80
Slaughterhouse Five '72
They Might Be Giants '71
W '74
When a Man Loves a Woman
    '94
The Winds of Kitty Hawk '78

Suzzy Roche
Almost You '85

Crossing Delancey '88

Jean Rochefort
Birgitt Haas Must Be Killed '83
The Clockmaker '76
Dirty Hands '76
The Hairdresser's Husband '92
I Sent a Letter to My Love '81
Le Cavaleur '78
Le Complot '73
Le Crabe Tambour '77
Mean Frank and Crazy Tony
    '75
My Wonderful Life '90
Pardon Mon Affaire '76
Pardon Mon Affaire, Too! '77
Return of the Tall Blond Man
    With One Black Shoe '74
Salut l'Artiste '73
The Tall Blond Man with One
    Black Shoe '72
Till Marriage Do Us Part '74
Who is Killing the Great Chefs
    of Europe? '78

Claire Rochelle
Boothill Brigade '37
Code of the Fearless '39
Guns in the Dark '37
Harvest Melody '43
Ridin' the Lone Trail '37
Shake Hands with Murder '44
Texas Justice '42
Two-Gun Troubador '37

Chris Rock
Boomerang '92
CB4: The Movie '93
Coneheads '93
I'm Gonna Git You Sucka '88
New Jack City '91

Charles Rocket
Dances with Wolves '90
Delirious '91
Down Twisted '89
Earth Girls are Easy '89
Fraternity Vacation '85
Hocus Pocus '93
How I Got into College '89
It's Pat '94
Miracles '86
Wild Palms '93

Jack Rockwell
Brand of the Outlaws '36
The Fiddlin' Buckaroo '33
Hopalong Cassidy: Renegade
    Trail '39
The Man from Hell '34
Outlaw Rule '36
Raiders of Sunset Pass '43
The Rangers Step In '37
Renegade Trail '39
The Tonto Kid '35
Tumbleweed Trail '42
Twilight on the Trail '41

Robert Rockwell
Lassie: Adventures of Neeka
    '68
The Red Menace '49

Sam Rockwell
Clown House '88
Jack and His Friends '92

Ziva Rodann
The Giants of Thessaly '60
Last Train from Gun Hill '59
Macumba Love '60
Samar '62

Marcia Rodd
Citizens Band '77
How to Break Up a Happy
    Divorce '76
Keeping On '81
Little Murders '71

Ebbe Rode
Babette's Feast '87
Gertrud '64
Topsy Turvy '84

Anton Rodgers
Dirty Rotten Scoundrels '88
Impromptu '90
Lillie '79
Pictures '80s

**Dagoberto
Rodriguez**
Los Hermanos Centella '65
Mision Suicida '87

Estelita Rodriguez
The Gay Ranchero '42
The Golden Stallion '49
Susanna Pass '49
Twilight in the Sierras '50

Marco Rodriguez
The Crow '93
Internal Affairs '90
The Rookie '90

Paul Rodriguez
Born in East L.A. '87
La Pastorela '92
Made in America '93
Miracles '86
Quicksilver '86
The Whoopee Boys '86

Norman Rodway
The Bretts '88
Chimes at Midnight '67
Coming Through '90

Daniel Roebuck
Cave Girl '85
Disorganized Crime '89
Dudes '87
The Fugitive '93
The Killing Mind '90
Miles from Home '88
River's Edge '87
Terror Eyes '87

William Roerick
The Love Machine '71
A Separate Peace '73
The Wasp Woman '59

Maurice Roeves
The Big Man: Crossing the Line
    '91
Danger UXB '81
Hidden Agenda '90
The Last of the Mohicans '92
Ulysses '67

Michael Rogan
Doom Asylum '88
Punch the Clock '90

Bill Rogers
The Girl, the Body and the Pill
    '67
Shanty Tramp '67

**Charles "Buddy"
Rogers**
Mexican Spitfire at Sea '42
My Best Girl '27
Wings '27

Ginger Rogers
Bachelor Mother '39
The Barkleys of Broadway '49
Carefree '38
Cinderella '64
Fifth Avenue Girl '39
Finishing School '33
Flying Down to Rio '33
Follow the Fleet '36
Forever Female '53
42nd Street '33
The Gay Divorcee '34
Gold Diggers of 1933 '33
Gotta Dance, Gotta Sing '84
Having Wonderful Time '38
Having Wonderful Time/
    Carnival Boat '38
Heartbeat '46
In Person '35
Irving Berlin's America '86
Kitty Foyle '40
Lucky Partners '40
Monkey Business '52
Once Upon a Honeymoon '42
Primrose Path '40
Quick, Let's Get Married '71
Roberta '35
Romance in Manhattan '34
Shall We Dance '37
Shriek in the Night '33
Stage Door '37
Star of Midnight '35
The Story of Vernon and Irene
    Castle '39
Swing Time '36
Tender Comrade '43
That's Dancing! '85
13th Guest '32
The Tip-Off '31
Tom, Dick, and Harry '41
Top Hat '35
Vivacious Lady '38
Weekend at the Waldorf '45

We're Not Married '52

Ivan Rogers
Ballbuster
Crazed Cop '88
Slow Burn '90
Two Wrongs Make a Right '89

Jean Rogers
Ace Drummond '36
Flash Gordon: Mars Attacks
    the World '38
Flash Gordon: Rocketship '36
Rocketship '36
Whistling in Brooklyn '43

Jimmy Rogers
False Colors '43
Hopalong Cassidy: Riders of
    the Deadline '43
Mystery Man '44
Texas Masquerade '44

Kenny Rogers
Coward of the County '81
The Gambler Returns: The
    Luck of the Draw '93
Kenny Rogers as the Gambler
    '80
Kenny Rogers as the Gambler,
    Part 2: The Adventure
    Continues '83
Kenny Rogers as the Gambler,
    Part 3: The Legend
    Continues '87
Rio Diablo '93
Six Pack '82
Wild Horses '84

Mimi Rogers
Blue Skies Again '83
Dark Horse '92
Deadlock '91
Desperate Hours '90
The Doors '91
Embassy '85
Fourth Story '90
Gung Ho '85
Hider in the House '90
Ladykiller '92
The Mighty Quinn '89
Monkey Trouble '94
The Palermo Connection '91
The Rapture '91
The Rousters '90
Shooting Elizabeth '92
Someone to Watch Over Me
    '87
Street Smart '87
White Sands '92

Paul Rogers
Beau Brummel '54
Billy Budd '62
The Mark '61
A Midsummer Night's Dream
    '68
Stolen Hours '63
Svengali '55
The Tenth Man '88

Roxanne Rogers
Punk Vacation '90
Slow Moves '84

Roy Rogers
Apache Rose '47
Arizona Kid '39
Bad Man of Deadwood '41
Bells of Coronado '50
Bells of Rosarita '45
Bells of San Angelo '47
Billy the Kid Returns '38
The Border Legion '40
Carson City Kid '40
Colorado '40
Come On Rangers '38
Cowboy & the Senorita '44
Cowboys of the Saturday
    Matinee '84
Dark Command '40
Down Dakota Way '49
Eyes of Texas '48
Far Frontier '48
Frontier Pony Express '39
The Gay Ranchero '42
The Golden Stallion '49
Grand Canyon Trail '48
Hands Across the Border '43
Heart of the Golden West '42
Heart of the Rockies '51
Helldorado '46
Home in Oklahoma '47
Idaho '43
In Old Caliente '39

In Old Cheyenne '41
Jesse James at Bay '41
King of the Cowboys '43
Lights of Old Santa Fe '47
Man from Cheyenne '42
My Pal Trigger '46
Nevada City '41
Night Time in Nevada '48
North of the Great Divide '50
Old Barn Dance '38
Old Corral '36
On the Old Spanish Trail '47
Ranger and the Lady '40
Ridin' Down the Canyon '42
Robin Hood of the Pecos '41
Roll on Texas Moon '46
Romance on the Range '42
Rough Riders' Roundup '39
Saga of Death Valley '39
Salute to the "King of the
    Cowboys," Roy Rogers '70s
San Fernando Valley '44
Sheriff of Tombstone '41
Shine on, Harvest Moon '38
Silver Spurs '43
Son of Paleface '52
Song of Arizona '46
Song of Nevada '44
Song of Texas '43
Sons of the Pioneers '42
South of Santa Fe '42
Southward Ho! '39
Springtime in the Sierras '47
Sunset in El Dorado '45
Sunset on the Desert '42
Sunset Serenade '42
Susanna Pass '49
Texas Legionnaires '43
Trail of Robin Hood '50
Trigger, Jr. '50
Twilight in the Sierras '50
Under California Stars '48
Under Nevada Skies '46
Under Western Stars '45
Utah '45
Wall Street Cowboy '39
Western Double Feature 1 '38
Western Double Feature 3:
    Rogers & Allen '50
Western Double Feature 4 '37
Western Double Feature 4:
    Rogers & Evans '40s
Western Double Feature 5:
    Rogers & Autry '37
Western Double Feature 6:
    Rogers & Trigger '40s
Western Double Feature 8:
    Hale & Carradine '40s
Western Double Feature 10:
    Roy, Dale, & Trigger '80s
Western Double Feature 11 '50
Western Double Feature 15 '50
Western Double Feature 16 '46
Western Double Feature 17
    '40s
Western Double Feature 18
    '40s
Western Double Feature 19 '45
Western Double Feature 20
Western Double Feature 21
    '40s
Western Double Feature 22
    '40s
Western Double Feature 23
Western Double Feature 24
    '40s
Western Double Feature 25
The Yellow Rose of Texas '44
Young Bill Hickok '40
Young Buffalo Bill '40

Steve Rogers
Trident Force '88
Triple Impact '92

Tristan Rogers
Flesh and Blood Show '73
Night Eyes 3 '93

Wayne Rogers
Chiefs '83
Cool Hand Luke '67
Drop-Out Mother '88
The Gig '85
The Girl Who Spelled Freedom
    '86
The Goodbye Bird '93
Hot Touch '80s
The Killing Time '87
Lady from Yesterday '85
M*A*S*H: The Collector's
    Edition '72

Rogers ▶cont.

Once in Paris... '79
Passion in Paradise '89
Pocket Money '72

Will Rogers
Ambassador Bill '31
A Connecticut Yankee '31
Doubting Thomas '35
Going to Congress/Don't Park There '24
Golden Age of Comedy '58
Judge Priest '34
Mack Sennett Comedies: Vol. 2 '16
Mr. Skitch '33

Maria Rohm
Count Dracula '71
The House of 1000 Dolls '67
Kiss and Kill '68
Venus in Furs '70

Clayton Rohner
April Fool's Day '86
Bat 21 '88
Caroline at Midnight '93
I, Madman '89
Just One of the Guys '85
Private Investigations '87

Alberto Rojas
Esta Noche Cena Pancho '87
The Neighborhood Thief '83
Stallion '88

Gustavo Rojo
The Christmas Kid '68
It Started with a Kiss '59
No Survivors, Please '63
A Witch Without a Broom '68

Helena Rojo
Aguirre, the Wrath of God '72
Mary, Mary, Bloody Mary '76
Siempre Hay una Primera Vez '87

Maria Rojo
Candy Stripe Nurses '74
Danzon '91

Rueben Rojo
Cauldron of Blood '67
Samson in the Wax Museum '63

Gilbert Roland
Any Gun Can Play '67
The Bad and the Beautiful '52
Barbarosa '82
Beneath the 12-Mile Reef '53
Between God, the Devil & a Winchester '72
Bullfighter & the Lady '50
Cabo Blanco '81
Captain Kidd '45
Cheyenne Autumn '64
The French Line '54
Go Kill and Come Back '68
Islands in the Stream '77
Malaya '49
Miracle of Our Lady of Fatima '52
The Poppy is also a Flower '66
The Racers '55
Ridin' the California Trail '47
Running Wild '35
The Ruthless Four '70
The Sacketts '79
Samar '62
The Sea Hawk '40
She Done Him Wrong '33
South of Monterey '47
Three Violent People '57
Thunder Bay '53
Thunder Pass '37
Treasure of Pancho Villa '55
Underwater '55

Gylian Roland
Barn of the Naked Dead '73
Deadly Lullaby '92

Tutta Rolf
Dollar '38
Swedenhielms '35

Guy Rolfe
The Alphabet Murders '65
And Now the Screaming Starts '73
The Dark Angel '91
Dolls '87

Puppet Master 3: Toulon's Revenge '91
Puppet Master 4 '93
Young Bess '53

Esther Rolle
Age Old Friends '89
Driving Miss Daisy '89
House of Cards '92
I Know Why the Caged Bird Sings '79
The Kid Who Loved Christmas '90
The Mighty Quinn '89
P.K. and the Kid '85
A Raisin in the Sun '89
The Summer of My German Soldier '78
To Dance with the White Dog '93

Howard E. Rollins, Jr.
The Children of Times Square '86
For Us, the Living '88
The House of Dies Drear '88
Johnnie Gibson F.B.I. '87
King '78
The Member of the Wedding '83
Ragtime '81
A Soldier's Story '84

Mark Rolston
Body of Evidence '92
The Comrades of Summer '92
Prancer '89
Scanner Cop '94
Sinful Life '89
Survival Quest '89
Weeds '87

Yvonne Romain
The Curse of the Werewolf '61
Double Trouble '67

Candice Roman
The Big Bird Cage '72
Unholy Rollers '72

Leticia Roman
Fanny Hill: Memoirs of a Woman of Pleasure '64
G.I. Blues '60

Ruth Roman
The Baby '72
Beyond the Forest '49
Blowing Wild '54
Champion '49
Day of the Animals '77
Echoes '83
Far Country '55
Good Sam '48
Great Day in the Morning '56
Impulse '74
The Killing Kind '73
Love has Many Faces '65
The Sacketts '79
Since You Went Away '44
Strangers on a Train '51
Three Secrets '50
The Window '49

Viviane Romance
The Big Grab '63
Melodie en Sous-Sol '63
Panique '47
Princess Tam Tam '35

Beatrice Romand
Claire's Knee '71
Four Adventures of Reinette and Mirabelle '89
House of the Yellow Carpet '84
Le Beau Mariage '82
Summer '86

Andy Romano
Afterburn '92
Get Christie Love! '74
Unlawful Entry '92

Maria Romano
Caged Women '84
Thor el Conquistador '86

Anna Romantowska
The Interrogation '82
A Woman and a Woman '80

Richard Romanus
Cops and Robbersons '94
The Couch Trip '87
Hollywood Heartbreak '89
Mean Streets '73

Murphy's Law '86
Night Terror '76
Point of No Return '93
Protocol '84
Sitting Ducks '80
Strangers Kiss '83
To Protect and Serve '92

Robert Romanus
Bad Medicine '85
Fast Times at Ridgemont High '82
Pulse '88

Lina Romay
Adventure '45
Ilsa, the Wicked Warden '78
Love Laughs at Andy Hardy '46
The Loves of Irina '80s
The Perverse Countess '73
Sex is Crazy '79

Sindi Rome
Knock Outs '92
Swift Justice '88

Sydne Rome
Diary of Forbidden Dreams '73
Just a Gigolo '79
Order to Kill '73
The Puma Man '80
That Lucky Touch '75
Twist '76
Wanted: Babysitter '75

Rachel Romen
The Girl from Tobacco Row '66
Ransom Money '88

Cesar Romero
Americano '55
Batman '66
The Beautiful Blonde from Bashful Bend '49
The Big Push '75
The Castilian '63
The Computer Wore Tennis Shoes '69
Crooks & Coronets '69
Dance Hall '41
Donovan's Reef '63
FBI Girl '52
The Great American Broadcast '41
Gun Crazy '69
Happy Go Lovely '51
Happy Landing '38
Hot Millions '68
Judgment Day '88
Julia Misbehaves '48
Jungle '52
The Little Princess '39
The Lost Continent '51
Lucky Cisco Kid '40
Lust in the Dust '85
Madigan's Millions '67
Mission to Glory '80
Mortuary Academy '91
My Lucky Star '38
Now You See Him, Now You Don't '72
Orchestra Wives '42
The Proud and the Damned '72
The Racers '55
Scotland Yard Inspector '52
The Shadow Man '53
Show Them No Mercy '35
Simple Justice '89
The Spectre of Edgar Allen Poe '73
Springtime in the Rockies '42
The Thin Man '34
Vera Cruz '53
Wee Willie Winkie '37
Week-End In Havana '41
Wintertime '43

Chanda Romero
The Last Reunion '80
Olongapo: The American Dream '89

Joanelle Romero
Lost Legacy: A Girl Called Hatter Fox '77
Miracle in the Wilderness '91

Ned Romero
Children of the Corn 2: The Final Sacrifice '92
The Deerslayer '78
House 4: Home Deadly Home '91
I Will Fight No More Forever '75
The Last of the Mohicans '85

Maurice Ronet
Beau Pere '81
Besame '87
The Deadly Trap '71
The Fire Within '64
Frantic '58
How Sweet It Is! '68
L'Odeur des Fauves '66
The Lost Command '66
Scandal Man '67
Sidney Sheldon's Bloodline '79
Sphinx '81
Swimming Pool '70
Time Out for Love '61
Without Warning '52
The Women '69

Linda Ronstadt
Chuck Berry: Hail! Hail! Rock 'n' Roll '87
FM '78
La Pastorela '92
The Pirates of Penzance '83

Michael Rooker
Afterburn '92
Cliffhanger '93
The Dark Half '91
Days of Thunder '90
Eight Men Out '88
Henry: Portrait of a Serial Killer '90
JFK '91
Light of Day '87
Mississippi Burning '88
Music Box '89
Sea of Love '89
Tombstone '93

Mickey Rooney
Ace of Hearts '85
The Adventures of Huckleberry Finn '39
Ah, Wilderness! '35
Andy Hardy Gets Spring Fever '39
Andy Hardy Meets Debutante '40
Andy Hardy's Double Life '42
Andy Hardy's Private Secretary '41
The Atomic Kid '54
Babes in Arms '39
Babes on Broadway '41
The Big Wheel '49
Bill '81
Bill: On His Own '83
The Black Stallion '79
Boys Town '38
Breakfast at Tiffany's '61
The Bridges at Toko-Ri '55
Captains Courageous '37
The Comic '69
The Dark Side of Love '79
The Domino Principle '77
Erik the Viking '89
Find the Lady '75
The Gambler Returns: The Luck of the Draw '93
Girl Crazy '43
Healer '36
Hide-Out '34
Home for Christmas '90
How to Stuff a Wild Bikini '65
The Human Comedy '43
It Came Upon a Midnight Clear '84
It's a Mad, Mad, Mad, Mad World '63
The King of the Roaring '20s: The Story of Arnold Rothstein '61
Leave 'Em Laughing '81
The Legend of Wolf Mountain '92
Life Begins for Andy Hardy '41
Lightning: The White Stallion '86
Little Lord Fauntleroy '36
Love Finds Andy Hardy '38
Love Laughs at Andy Hardy '46
Magic of Lassie '78
Manhattan Melodrama '34
Manipulator '71
Maximum Force '92
Men of Boys Town '41
Mickey the Great '39
A Midsummer Night's Dream '35
My Heroes Have Always Been Cowboys '91

My Outlaw Brother '51
My Pal, The King '32
National Velvet '44
The Odyssey of the Pacific '82
Off Limits '53
Pete's Dragon '77
Platinum High School '60
Postmark for Danger/ Quicksand '56
Pulp '72
Quicksand '50
Rachel's Man '75
Revenge of the Red Baron '93
Riff Raff '35
Senior Trip '81
Silent Night, Deadly Night 5: The Toymaker '91
Strike Up the Band '40
Summer Holiday '48
Thoroughbreds Don't Cry '37
Thousands Cheer '43
Thunder County '74
Women's Prison Escape '78
Words and Music '48
Young Tom Edison '40

Buddy Roosevelt
Boss Cowboy '35
Circle Canyon '33
Lightning Range '33
Powdersmoke Range '35
Range Riders '35
Tribute to a Bad Man '56

Stephen Root
Bed & Breakfast '92
Monkey Shines '88

Hayden Rorke
Francis Goes to the Races '51
The Night Walker '64
Spencer's Mountain '63

Tony Rosato
Busted Up '86
City of Shadows '86
The Good Fight '92
Hog Wild '80
Switching Channels '88

Francoise Rosay
Bizarre Bizarre '39
Carnival in Flanders '35
Johnny Frenchman '46
The Pedestrian '73
September Affair '50
Seven Deadly Sins '53

Gabrielle Rose
The Adjuster '91
Family Viewing '88
Speaking Parts '89
Timecop '94

George Rose
The Devil's Disciple '59
The Hideaways '73
Jack the Ripper '60
Mania '60
A New Leaf '71
A Night to Remember '58
The Pirates of Penzance '83
You Can't Take It with You '84

Jamie Rose
Chopper Chicks in Zombietown '91
Heartbreakers '84
In Love with an Older Woman '82
Playroom '90
Rebel Love '85
Tightrope '84
To Die Standing '91
Twirl '81

Laurie Rose
Blood Voyage '77
Hot Box '72
Woman Hunt '72
Working Girls '75

Rose Marie
Bruce's Deadly Fingers '80
Cheaper to Keep Her '80
Dead Heat on a Merry-Go-Round '66
Ghetto Blaster '89
Man from Clover Grove '78
Memory of Us '74
Witchboard '87

Sherrie Rose
Double Threat '92
Martial Law 2: Undercover '91
Maximum Force '92

Alan Rosenberg
After Midnight '89
Happy Birthday, Gemini '80
Impulse '90
In a Stranger's Hand '92
White of the Eye '88

Michael Rosenberg
His Wife's Lover '31
Mirele Efros '38
The Two Sisters '37

Maxie "Slapsie" Rosenbloom
Abbott and Costello Meet the Keystone Kops '54
Cooking Up Trouble '44
Each Dawn I Die '39
Ghost Crazy '44
Here Comes Kelly '43
Hollywood or Bust '56
I Married a Monster from Outer Space '58
Kelly the Second '36
Louisiana Purchase '41
To the Shores of Tripoli '42

Rosette
Pauline at the Beach '83
Summer '86

Annie Ross
Basket Case 2 '90
Basket Case 3: The Progeny '92
Dressed for Death '74
Funny Money '82
Pump Up the Volume '90
Short Cuts '93
Superman 3 '83
Yanks '79

Betsy King Ross
Fighting with Kit Carson '33
The Phantom Empire '35

Beverly Ross
Bloodshed '83
Crazed '82
Slipping into Darkness '88

Chelcie Ross
Amos and Andrew '93
Basic Instinct '92
Bill & Ted's Bogus Journey '91
Keep My Grave Open '80
Legacy of Lies '92
Rudy '93

Diana Ross
Lady Sings the Blues '72
Mahogany '75
The Wiz '78

Gene Ross
Don't Look in the Basement '73
Don't Open the Door! '74
Encounter with the Unknown '75
Keep My Grave Open '80
Poor White Trash 2 '75

Herbert Ross
Goodbye, Mr. Chips '69
Play It Again, Sam '72

Katharine Ross
The Betsy '78
Butch Cassidy and the Sundance Kid '69
A Climate for Killing '91
Conagher '91
The Final Countdown '80
Fools '70
The Graduate '67
Hellfighters '68
The Legacy '79
Murder by Natural Causes '79
Murder in Texas '81
Pigs '73
Red Headed Stranger '87
Rodeo Girl '80
The Shadow Riders '82
Shenandoah '65
The Singing Nun '66
The Swarm '78
Tell Them Willie Boy Is Here '69
They Only Kill Their Masters '72
Voyage of the Damned '76
Wrong is Right '82

Kimberly Ross
The Last Starfighter '84
Nightmare at Noon '87
Pumpkinhead '88

Marion Ross
Forever Female '53
Grand Theft Auto '77
On the Edge: The Survival of Dana '79

Merrie Lynn Ross
Class of 1984 '82
The Lucifer Complex '78
Way He Was '76

Shavar Ross
Friday the 13th, Part 5: A New Beginning '85
The House of Dies Drear '88

Shirley Ross
Mindkiller '87
Night Vision '87

Ted Ross
Arthur 2: On the Rocks '88
Stealing Home '88
The Wiz '78

Isabella Rossellini
Blue Velvet '86
Cannon Movie Tales: Red Riding Hood '89
Cousins '89
Death Becomes Her '92
Fallen Angels 1 '93
Fearless '93
The Innocent '93
Ivory Hunters '90
Lies of the Twins '91
A Matter of Time '76
Red Riding Hood '88
Siesta '87
Tough Guys Don't Dance '87
White Nights '85
Wild at Heart '90
Wyatt Earp '94
Zelly & Me '88

Leo Rossi
The Accused '88
Fast Getaway '91
Heart Like a Wheel '83
The Hit List '88
Maniac Cop 2 '90
Raw Justice '93
Relentless '89
Relentless 2: Dead On '91
Relentless 3 '93
River's Edge '87
We're Talkin' Serious Money '92
Where the Day Takes You '92

Giacomo "Jack" Rossi-Stuart
The Avenger '62
Gun Fight at Red Sands '63
Hornet's Nest '70
Kill, Baby, Kill '66
The Last Man on Earth '64
Macabre '77
The Night Evelyn Came Out of the Grave '71
Planet on the Prowl '65

Norman Rossington
The Charge of the Light Brigade '68
Man in the Wilderness '71
Negatives '68

Leonard Rossiter
Britannia Hospital '82
Fall and Rise of Reginald Perrin 1 '78
Fall and Rise of Reginald Perrin 2 '78
The Pink Panther Strikes Again '76
Water '85

Angelo Rossitto
Brain of Blood '71
The Corpse Vanishes '42
Dracula vs. Frankenstein '71
Invasion of the Saucer Men '57
Mad Max: Beyond Thunderdome '85
Mesa of Lost Women '52
The Offspring '87

Rick Rossovich
The Gambler Returns: The Luck of the Draw '93
Let's Get Harry '87
The Lords of Discipline '83
The Morning After '86
Navy SEALS '90

Paint It Black '89
Roxanne '87
Secret Ingredient '92
The Spellbinder '88
Streets of Fire '84
Tales from the Crypt, Vol. 3 '90
The Terminator '84
Top Gun '86
Tropical Heat '93
Warning Sign '85

Andrea Roth
The Club '94
The Good Fight '92
Seedpeople '92

Celia Roth
Labyrinth of Passion '82
The Stranger '87

Gene Roth
Attack of the Giant Leeches '59
Earth vs. the Spider '58
Pirates of the High Seas '50

Lillian Roth
Animal Crackers '30
Ladies They Talk About '33
Madam Satan '30

Louis Roth
Clash of the Ninja '86
Ninja Connection '90

Tim Roth
Bodies, Rest & Motion '93
The Cook, the Thief, His Wife & Her Lover '90
Heart of Darkness '93
The Hit '85
Jumpin' at the Boneyard '92
Pulp Fiction '94
Reservoir Dogs '92
Rosencrantz & Guildenstern Are Dead '90
To Kill a Priest '89
Vincent & Theo '90
A World Apart '88

Cynthia Rothrock
Angel of Fury '92
China O'Brien '88
China O'Brien 2 '89
The Deadliest Art: The Best of the Martial Arts Films '90
Fast Getaway '91
Honor and Glory '92
Lady Dragon '92
Lady Dragon 2 '93
Martial Law '90
Martial Law 2: Undercover '91
No Retreat, No Surrender 2 '89
Rage and Honor '92
Rage and Honor 2: Hostile Takeover '91
Tiger Claws '91
24 Hours to Midnight '92

Yella Rottlaender
Alice in the Cities '74
The Scarlet Letter '73

Brigitte Rouan
Olivier, Olivier '92
Overseas: Three Women with Man Trouble '90

Richard Roundtree
Amityville: A New Generation '93
Angel 3: The Final Chapter '88
Bad Jim '89
The Banker '89
The Baron and the Kid '84
Big Score '83
Bloodfist 3: Forced to Fight '93
Body of Influence '93
Bonanza: The Return '93
Christmas in Connecticut '92
City Heat '84
Crack House '89
Day of the Assassin '81
Deadly Rivals '92
Diamonds '72
Earthquake '74
Embassy '72
Escape to Athena '79
An Eye for an Eye '81
Firehouse '72
Game for Vultures '86
Getting Even '92
Gypsy Angels '94
Jocks '87
Killpoint '84
The Last Contract '86
Man Friday '75

Maniac Cop '88
Miami Cops '89
Mind Twister '93
Night Visitor '89
One Down, Two to Go! '82
Opposing Force '87
Party Line '88
Portrait of a Hitman '77
Q (The Winged Serpent) '82
Shaft '71
Shaft's Big Score '72
A Time to Die '91
Young Warriors '83

Robert Rounseville
Carousel '56
The Tales of Hoffmann '51

Mickey Rourke
Angel Heart '87
Barfly '87
Body Heat '81
City in Fear '80
Desperate Hours '90
Diner '82
Eureka! '81
Fade to Black '80
Francesco '93
Harley Davidson and the Marlboro Man '91
Heaven's Gate '81
Homeboy '88
Johnny Handsome '89
The Last Outlaw '93
9 1/2 Weeks '86
1941 '79
The Pope of Greenwich Village '84
Prayer for the Dying '87
Rape and Marriage: The Rideout Case '80
Rumble Fish '83
White Sands '92
Wild Orchid '90
Year of the Dragon '85

Graham Rouse
Ride a Wild Pony '75
Weekend of Shadows '77

Myriem Roussel
First Name: Carmen '83
Hail Mary '85
Sacrilege '86

Nathalie Roussel
My Father's Glory '91
My Mother's Castle '91

Alison Routledge
The Bridge to Nowhere '86
The Quiet Earth '85

Catherine Rouvel
Black and White in Color '76
Borsalino '70
La Rupture '70
Les Assassins de L'Ordre '71
Picnic on the Grass '59
Sand and Blood '87

Misty Rowe
Goodbye, Norma Jean '75
Goodnight, Sweet Marilyn '89
Hitchhikers '72
Loose Shoes '80
The Man with Bogart's Face '80
Meatballs 2 '84
A Pleasure Doing Business '79

Nevan Rowe
Nutcase '83
Sleeping Dogs '82

Nicholas Rowe
The Lawrenceville Stories '80s
Young Sherlock Holmes '85

Steve Rowland
Gun Glory '57
Naked Youth '59

Gena Rowlands
Another Woman '88
Brink's Job '78
A Child is Waiting '63
Crazy in Love '92
An Early Frost '85
Gloria '80
Light of Day '87
Lonely are the Brave '62
Love Streams '84
Montana '90
Night on Earth '91
Once Around '91
Opening Night '77

A Question of Love '78
Rapunzel '82
Strangers: The Story of a Mother and Daughter '79
The Tempest '82
Tony Rome '67
Two Minute Warning '76
A Woman Under the Influence '74

Polly Rowles
Power '86
Springtime in the Rockies '37

Lionel Royce
My Favorite Blonde '42
Panama Menace '41
The Road to Zanzibar '41
White Pongo '45

Roselyn Royce
Malibu Hot Summer '81
Retrievers '82
Sizzle Beach U.S.A. '86

Virginia Roye
Pace That Kills '28
The Road to Ruin '28

Selena Royle
The Big Hangover '50
Cass Timberlane '47
Courage of Lassie '46
A Date with Judy '48
The Fighting Sullivans '42
The Harvey Girls '46
Mrs. Parkington '44
Moonrise '48
My Dream is Yours '49
Robot Monster '53
Summer Holiday '48

William Royle
Mr. Wong in Chinatown '39
Mutiny in the Big House '39
The Rains Came '39

Gregory Rozakis
Abduction '75
Five Corners '88

Katt Shea Ruben
Barbarian Queen '85
Devastator '85
Hollywood Hot Tubs '84
Preppies '82

Alma Rubens
The Americano '17
Mystery of the Leaping Fish/ Chess Fever '25
She Goes to War '29

Jan Rubes
The Amityville Curse '90
Blind Fear '89
Blood Relations '87
Charlie Grant's War '80
Class Action '91
Courage Mountain '89
Dead of Winter '87
Deceived '91
Descending Angel '90
D2: The Mighty Ducks '94
The Kiss '88

Benny Rubin
The Bashful Bachelor '42
Mr. Wise Guy '42
The Noose Hangs High '48
Sunny '41
Sunny Skies '30
The Tender Trap '55
Torch Song '53
Two Reelers: Comedy Classics 7 '38
Zis Boom Bah '42

Jennifer Rubin
Bad Dreams '88
Bitter Harvest '93
Blueberry Hill '88
The Crush '93
Delusion '91
The Fear Inside '92
Permanent Record '88
Victim of Beauty '91
A Woman, Her Men and Her Futon '92

Saul Rubinek
Against All Odds '84
The Agency '81
And the Band Played On '93
The Bonfire of the Vanities '90
Death Ship '80
Getting Even with Dad '94

Rubinek ►cont.

Half a Lifetime '86
Highpoint '80
I Love Trouble '94
Man Trouble '92
Obsessed '88
Outside Chance of Maximillian
   Glick '88
Soup for One '82
Ticket to Heaven '81
True Romance '93
Undercover Blues '93
Unforgiven '92
Wall Street '87
Young Doctors in Love '82

Giulia Rubini
Adios, Hombre '68
Journey Beneath the Desert '61
Stranger in Paso Bravo '73

John Rubinstein
Another Stakeout '93
Defiant '70
Getting Straight '70
Happily Ever After '82
Killjoy '81
Shadow on the Sun '88
She's Dressed to Kill '79
Someone to Watch Over Me
   '87
The Trouble with Girls (and
   How To Get Into It) '69
Zachariah '70

Zelda Rubinstein
Anguish '88
Poltergeist '82
Poltergeist 2: The Other Side
   '86
Poltergeist 3 '88
Sixteen Candles '84
Teen Witch '89
Under the Rainbow '81

Alan Ruck
Ferris Bueller's Day Off '86
Hard Knox '83
Speed '94
Three for the Road '87
Three Fugitives '89
Young Guns 2 '90

Paul Rudd
Beulah Land '80
Johnny We Hardly Knew Ye '77
Last Song '80

Michael Rudder
Blindside '88
Buying Time '89

Herbert Rudley
Abe Lincoln in Illinois '40
Artists and Models '55
The Jayhawkers '59
Rhapsody in Blue '45
The Scar '48
The Seventh Cross '44

Joshua Rudoy
Flatliners '90
Harry and the Hendersons '87

Reed Rudy
Free Ride '86
Zapped Again '89

Mercedes Ruehl
Another You '91
Big '88
Crazy People '90
84 Charing Cross Road '86
The Fisher King '91
Heartburn '86
Last Action Hero '93
Leader of the Band '87
Lost in Yonkers '93
Married to the Mob '88
Radio Days '87
Slaves of New York '89

Heinz Ruehmann
The Captain from Koepenick
   '56
Ship of Fools '65

Leonora Ruffo
Goliath and the Dragon '61
Hercules in the Haunted World
   '64

Rufus
Erendira '83

Jonah Who Will Be 25 in the
   Year 2000 '76

Charlie Ruggles
All in a Night's Work '61
Balalaika '39
Breaking the Ice '38
Bringing Up Baby '38
Follow Me, Boys! '66
Goodbye Love '34
The Invisible Woman '40
Look for the Silver Lining '49
The Lovable Cheat '49
Melody Cruise '32
Papa's Delicate Condition '63
The Parent Trap '61
The Perfect Marriage '46
Ramrod '47
The Ruggles of Red Gap '35
Son of Flubber '63
A Stolen Life '46
The Ugly Dachshund '65

Vyto Ruginis
Clean Slate '94
Descending Angel '90

Barbara Ruick
The Affairs of Dobie Gillis '53
Carousel '56

Janice Rule
Alvarez Kelly '66
The Ambushers '67
American Flyers '85
Battle Shock '56
The Chase '66
Doctors' Wives '70
Gumshoe '72
Invitation to a Gunfighter '64
L.A. Bad '85
Missing '82
Swimmer '68
The Word '78

Sig Rumann
Bitter Sweet '40
The Bold Caballero '36
Comrade X '40
A Day at the Races '37
The Errand Boy '61
The Great Waltz '38
Houdini '53
House of Frankenstein '44
Love Crazy '41
Marie Galante '34
A Night at the Opera '35
A Night in Casablanca '46
Ninotchka '39
Nothing Sacred '37
On the Avenue '37
Only Angels Have Wings '39
Stalag 17 '53
Sweet Rosie O'Grady '43
That Uncertain Feeling '41
Thin Ice '37
To Be or Not to Be '42
Wings of Eagles '57

Jenny Runacre
The Canterbury Tales '71
The Final Programme '73
Hussy '80
Jubilee '78
The Passenger '75

Jennifer Runyon
Blue De Ville '86
Carnosaur '93
18 Again! '88
The Falcon and the Snowman
   '85
The In Crowd '88
A Man Called Sarge '90
To All a Goodnight '80
Up the Creek '84
A Very Brady Christmas '88

Ying Ruocheng
The Last Emperor '87
Little Buddha '93

Al Ruscio
The Cage '89
Deadly Force '83
Romero '89

Elizabeth Ruscio
Hider in the House '89
The Positively True Adventures
   of the Alleged Texas
   Cheerleader-Murdering
   Mom '93

Barbara Rush
The Bramble Bush '60

Come Blow Your Horn '63
First Legion '51
Harry Black and the Tiger '58
Hombre '67
It Came From Outer Space '53
Magnificent Obsession '54
Moon of the Wolf '72
Portrait of Grandpa Doc '77
Robin and the Seven Hoods '64
The Seekers '79
Strangers When We Meet '60
Superdad '73
Web of Deceit '90
When Worlds Collide '51
The Young Lions '58
The Young Philadelphians '59

Deborah Rush
Family Business '89
Parents '89
The Purple Rose of Cairo '85

Jared Rushton
Big '88
A Cry in the Wild '90
Honey, I Shrunk the Kids '89
The Lady in White '88
Pet Sematary 2 '92

Joseph Ruskin
Captain America '79
Firepower '93
The Gypsy Warriors '78
Prizzi's Honor '85

Robert Rusler
Final Embrace '90
The Game of Love '90
Shag: The Movie '89
Sometimes They Come Back
   '91
Thrashin' '86
Vamp '86

William Russ
Aspen Extreme '93
Beer '85
Crazy from the Heart '91
Dead of Winter '87
Disorganized Crime '89
The Long, Hot Summer '86
Pastime '91
The Right Stuff '83
Traces of Red '92
The Unholy '88
Wanted Dead or Alive '86

Jorge Russek
Emilio Varela vs. Camelia La
   Texana '87
La Hija del General '84
Miracles '86

Andy Russell
Copacabana '47
The Stork Club '45

Betsy Russell
Amore! '93
Avenging Angel '85
Cheerleader Camp '88
Delta Heat '92
Out of Control '85
Private School '83
The Prize Pulitzer '89
Tomboy '85
Trapper County War '89

Bing Russell
Billy the Kid Versus Dracula '66
Elvis: The Movie '79
Stakeout '62
Suicide Battalion/Hell Squad
   '58

Elizabeth Russell
Cat People '42
The Corpse Vanishes '42
Curse of the Cat People '44
Meet the Mob '42

Gail Russell
Angel and the Badman '47
Great Dan Patch '49
Moonrise '48
The Uninvited '44
Wake of the Red Witch '49

Jane Russell
Born Losers '67
Darker than Amber '70
Double Dynamite '51
The French Line '54
Gentlemen Prefer Blondes '53
His Kind of Woman '51
Johnny Reno '66
The Las Vegas Story '52

Macao '52
Montana Belle '52
The Outlaw '43
The Paleface '48
The Road to Bali '53
Son of Paleface '52
The Tall Men '55
Underwater '55

John Russell
Apache Uprising '66
Blood Legacy '73
The Blue Bird '40
Buckskin '68
The Changeling '80
Forever Amber '47
Hoodlum Empire '52
Hostile Guns '67
Jubilee Trail '54
Noon Sunday '71
Oklahoma Annie '51
Pale Rider '85
Rio Bravo '59
Runaways '84
Smoke in the Wind '75
The Sun Shines Bright '53
Under the Gun '88

Karen Russell
Dead Certain '92
Easy Wheels '89
Lethal Games '90
Vice Academy '88
Wilding '90

Kurt Russell
Amber Waves '82
Backdraft '91
The Barefoot Executive '71
The Best of Times '86
Big Trouble in Little China '86
Captain Ron '92
The Captive: The Longest Drive
   2 '76
Charley and the Angel '73
The Christmas Coal Mine
   Miracle '77
The Computer Wore Tennis
   Shoes '69
Elvis: The Movie '79
Escape from New York '81
Follow Me, Boys! '66
Guns of Diablo '64
The Horse in the Gray Flannel
   Suit '68
It Happened at the World's Fair
   '63
The Longest Drive '76
Mean Season '85
Mosby's Marauders '66
Now You See Him, Now You
   Don't '72
The One and Only, Genuine,
   Original Family Band '68
Overboard '87
Search for the Gods '75
Silkwood '83
Sniper '75
Superdad '73
Swing Shift '84
Tango and Cash '89
Tequila Sunrise '88
The Thing '82
Tombstone '93
Unlawful Entry '92
Used Cars '80
Winter People '89

Nipsey Russell
Car 54, Where Are You? '94
The Wiz '78

Reb Russell
Arizona Badman '42
Border Vengeance '35
The Man from Hell '34
Outlaw Rule '36

Rosalind Russell
Auntie Mame '58
China Seas '35
The Citadel '38
Craig's Wife '36
Evelyn Prentice '34
Forsaking All Others '35
Gypsy '62
His Girl Friday '40
Hollywood Bloopers '51
Never Wave at a WAC '52
Oh Dad, Poor Dad (Momma's
   Hung You in the Closet & I'm
   Feeling So Sad) '67
Picnic '55

Reckless '35
Sister Kenny '46
Tell It to the Judge '49
They Met in Bombay '41
The Trouble with Angels '66
Velvet Touch '48
Where Angels Go, Trouble
   Follows '68
A Woman of Distinction '50
The Women '39

Theresa Russell
Aria '88
Being Human '94
Black Widow '87
Cold Heaven '92
Eureka! '81
Impulse '90
Insignificance '85
Kafka '91
The Last Tycoon '76
Physical Evidence '89
The Razor's Edge '84
Straight Time '78
Track 29 '88
Whore '91

William Russell
Above Us the Waves '56
Anna Christie '23

James Russo
Bad Girls '94
Beverly Hills Cop '84
Blue Iguana '88
China Girl '87
Cold Heaven '92
Dangerous Game '93
Dario Argento's Trauma '93
Extremities '86
Fast Times at Ridgemont High
   '82
Freeway '88
Illicit Behavior '91
Intimate Stranger '91
A Kiss Before Dying '91
My Own Private Idaho '91
Vortex '81
We're No Angels '89

Michael Russo
Demonic Toys '91
Nitti: The Enforcer '88

Rene Russo
Freejack '92
In the Line of Fire '93
Lethal Weapon 3 '92
Major League '89
Mr. Destiny '90
One Good Cop '91

Richard Rust
Double Revenge '89
The Great Gundown '75
The Naked Angels '69
The Student Nurses '70

Babe Ruth
Heading Home '24
The Pride of the Yankees '42

Mary Ruth
Gentleman from Dixie '41
Riot Squad '41

Ann Rutherford
Adventures of Don Juan '49
Andy Hardy Gets Spring Fever
   '39
Andy Hardy Meets Debutante
   '40
Andy Hardy's Double Life '42
A Christmas Carol '38
Doughnuts & Society '36
Fighting Marines '36
Ghost City '32
Gone with the Wind '39
The Lawless Nineties '36
Life Begins for Andy Hardy '41
Love Finds Andy Hardy '38
The Making of a Legend:
   ''Gone With the Wind'' '89
Melody Trail '35
Of Human Hearts '38
Operation Haylift '50
Orchestra Wives '42
Pride and Prejudice '40
The Secret Life of Walter Mitty
   '47
They Only Kill Their Masters
   '72
Whistling in Brooklyn '43
Whistling in Dixie '42
Whistling in the Dark '41

Margaret Rutherford
Blithe Spirit '45
Chimes at Midnight '67
Curtain Up '53
The Demi-Paradise '43
The Happiest Days of Your Life '50
Importance of Being Earnest '52
Innocents in Paris '53
Murder Ahoy '64
Murder at the Gallop '63
Murder Most Foul '65
Murder She Said '62
Passport to Pimlico '49
The Runaway Bus '54
The Smallest Show on Earth '57
To See Such Fun '81
Trouble in Store '53
The V.I.P.'s '63

Susan Ruttan
Bad Dreams '88
Bad Manners '84
Chances Are '89
Deadly Matrimony '92
Eye of the Demon '87
Fire and Rain '89
Funny About Love '90
L.A. Law '86
A Perfect Little Murder '90
Sweet 15 '90

Barbara Rutting
The Phantom of Soho '64
River of Evil '64
The Squeaker '65

Wolf Ruvinskis
Neutron and the Black Mask '61
Neutron vs. the Amazing Dr. Caronte '61
Neutron vs. the Death Robots '62
Neutron vs. the Maniac '62
Vivo o Muerto '87

Basil Ruysdael
Broken Arrow '50
Carrie '52
Davy Crockett, King of the Wild Frontier '55
High Lonesome '50
People Will Talk '51

Anne Ryan
All the Lovin' Kinfolk '89
Three O'Clock High '87

Eddie Ryan
Breakfast in Hollywood '46
The Fighting Sullivans '42
Hollywood Varieties '50

Eileen Ryan
At Close Range '86
Benny & Joon '93
Winter People '89

Fran Ryan
Chances Are '89
Eyes of Fire '84
Gunsmoke: Return to Dodge '87
Johnny Belinda '82
Pale Rider '85
Private School '83
Quiet Cool '86

James Ryan
Go for the Gold '84
Kill and Kill Again '81
Kill or Be Killed '80
Pursuit '90
Rage to Kill '88
Space Mutiny '88

John P. Ryan
Avenging Force '86
Best of the Best '89
Breathless '83
C.I.A. 2: Target Alexa '94
City of Shadows '86
Class of 1999 '90
Cops and Robbers '73
Death Scream '75
Death Wish 4: The Crackdown '87
Delta Force 2: Operation Stranglehold '90
Delta Force 3: The Killing Game '91
Eternity '90

Hoffa '92
It's Alive '74
It's Alive 2: It Lives Again '78
Paramedics '88
The Postman Always Rings Twice '81
Rent-A-Cop '88
The Right Stuff '83
Runaway Train '85
Shamus '73
Star Time '92
Three O'Clock High '87

Kathleen Ryan
Odd Man Out '47
Try and Get Me '50

Meg Ryan
Amityville 3: The Demon '83
Armed and Dangerous '86
D.O.A. '88
The Doors '91
Flesh and Bone '93
Innerspace '87
Joe Versus the Volcano '90
Prelude to a Kiss '92
The Presidio '88
Promised Land '88
Rich and Famous '81
Sleepless in Seattle '93
Top Gun '86
When a Man Loves a Woman '94
When Harry Met Sally '89

Mitchell Ryan
Aces: Iron Eagle 3 '92
Angel City '80
The Choice '81
The Christmas Coal Mine Miracle '77
Death of a Centerfold '81
Dirty Work '92
Double Exposure: The Story of Margaret Bourke-White '89
Electra Glide in Blue '73
The Five of Me '81
High Plains Drifter '73
Hot Shots! Part Deux '93
Judgment '90
Lethal Weapon '87
Magnum Force '73
Monte Walsh '70
My Old Man's Place '71
Of Mice and Men '81
The Opposite Sex and How to Live With Them '93
Peter Lundy and the Medicine Hat Stallion '77
Sergeant Matlovich vs. the U.S. Air Force '78
Winter People '89

Peggy Ryan
Here Come the Co-Eds '45
Miss Annie Rooney '42

R.L. Ryan
Eat and Run '86
Street Trash '87

Robert Ryan
And Hope to Die '72
Anzio '68
Back from Eternity '56
Bad Day at Black Rock '54
Battle of the Bulge '65
Behind the Rising Sun '43
Berlin Express '48
Best of the Badmen '50
Beware, My Lovely '52
Billy Budd '62
Bombardier '43
Born to Be Bad '50
The Boy with the Green Hair '48
Caught '49
Clash by Night '52
Crossfire '47
The Dirty Dozen '67
Escape to Burma '55
Executive Action '73
Flying Leathernecks '51
God's Little Acre '58
Horizons West '52
Hour of the Gun '67
Ice Palace '60
The Iron Major '43
The King of Kings '61
Lawman '71
Lonelyhearts '58
The Longest Day '62
The Love Machine '71

Marine Raiders '43
Men in War '57
A Minute to Pray, A Second to Die '67
The Naked Spur '53
On Dangerous Ground '51
The Professionals '66
The Racket '51
Return of the Bad Men '48
The Set-Up '49
The Sky's the Limit '43
The Tall Men '55
Tender Comrade '43
Trail Street '47
The Wild Bunch '69

Sheila Ryan
The Cobra Strikes '48
Fingerprints Don't Lie '51
Gold Raiders '51
Great Guns '41
Heartaches '47
Mask of the Dragon '51
On Top of Old Smoky '53
Railroaded '47
Ringside '49
Western Pacific Agent '51

Tim Ryan
China Beach '88
Harmon of Michigan '41
Here Come the Marines '52
The Lightning Incident '91
The Runestone '91

Georg Rydeberg
Dollar '38
Walpurgis Night '41
A Woman's Face '38

Christopher Rydell
Blood and Sand '89
By the Sword '93
Dario Argento's Trauma '93
Flesh and Bone '93
For the Boys '91
Gotcha! '85
How I Got into College '89
Side Out '90

Derek Rydell
Night Visitor '89
Phantom of the Mall: Eric's Revenge '89
Popcorn '89

Mark Rydell
Havana '90
The Long Goodbye '73
Punchline '88

Alfred Ryder
Bogie: The Last Hero '80
Probe '72
T-Men '47

Red Ryder
Western Double Feature 13 '40s
Western Double Feature 21 '40s

Winona Ryder
The Age of Innocence '93
Beetlejuice '88
Bram Stoker's Dracula '92
Edward Scissorhands '90
Great Balls of Fire '89
Heathers '89
The House of the Spirits '93
Lucas '86
Mermaids '90
Night on Earth '91
1969 '89
Reality Bites '94
Square Dance '87
Welcome Home, Roxy Carmichael '90

Patrick Ryecart
The Bretts '88
Heart of Darkness '93
Jenny's War '85
Silas Marner '85
True Colors '87
Twenty-One '91

Chishu Ryu
Akira Kurosawa's Dreams '90
An Autumn Afternoon '62
Early Summer '51
Equinox Flower '58
The Human Condition: A Soldier's Prayer '61
Late Spring '49
Tokyo Story '53

Twenty-Four Eyes '54

Bruno S
Every Man for Himself & God Against All '75
Stroszek '77

Antonio Sabato
Beyond the Law '68
Black Lemons '80s
Crimebusters '79
New Mafia Boss '72
Thundersquad '78
War of the Robots '78

Bo Sabato
L.A. Crackdown 2 '88
Neon Maniacs '86

Sabu
Arabian Nights '42
Black Narcissus '47
Cobra Woman '44
Drums '38
Elephant Boy '37
The Jungle Book '42
Jungle Hell '55
Mistress of the World '59
Pardon My Trunk '52
Savage Drums '51
Thief of Baghdad '40
A Tiger Walks '64
The Treasure of Bengal '53

Robert Sacchi
Cold Feet '89
The Man with Bogart's Face '80

Orlando Sacha
Crime Zone '88
To Die Standing '91

Adrienne Sachs
In the Cold of the Night '89
Two to Tango '88

Michael Sacks
Slaughterhouse Five '72
The Sugarland Express '74

Keiji Sada
An Autumn Afternoon '62
The Human Condition: No Greater Love '58
The Human Condition: Road to Eternity '59

William Sadler
Bill & Ted's Bogus Journey '91
Die Hard 2: Die Harder '90
Freaked '93
Hard to Kill '89
Hot Spot '90
Project X '87
Rush '91
Tagget '90
Tales from the Crypt '89
Trespass '92

Elizabeth Sagal
Flashdance '83
Skinheads: The Second Coming of Hate '88

Katey Sagal
The Good Mother '88
It's a Bundyful Life '92

Jonathan Sagalle
Drifting '82
Schindler's List '93

Marianne Sagebrecht
Bagdad Cafe '88
Dust Devil '93
Moon Over Parador '88
Rosalie Goes Shopping '89
Sugarbaby '85
The War of the Roses '89

Ray Sager
Blast-Off Girls '67
Just for the Hell of It '68
This Stuff'll Kill Ya! '71
The Wizard of Gore '70

Ken Sagoes
Death by Dialogue '88
A Nightmare on Elm Street 4: Dream Master '88

Elena Sahagun
Teenage Exorcist '93
Uncaged '91

Kenji Sahara
Attack of the Mushroom People '63
Destroy All Monsters '68

Godzilla's Revenge '69
H-Man '59
The Mysterians '58
Rodan '56

Lili St. Cyr
The Naked and the Dead '58
Son of Sinbad '55

Eva Marie Saint
All Fall Down '62
The Best Little Girl in the World '81
Breaking Home Ties '87
Cancel My Reservation '72
A Christmas to Remember '78
The Curse of King Tut's Tomb '80
Exodus '60
Fatal Vision '84
Grand Prix '66
Jane Doe '83
Kiss of a Killer '93
The Last Days of Patton '86
Love Leads the Way '84
North by Northwest '59
Nothing in Common '86
On the Waterfront '54
Prudential Family Playhouse '50
Raintree County '57
The Russians are Coming, the Russians are Coming '66
The Sandpiper '65
The Stalking Moon '69
Voyage of Terror: The Achille Lauro Affair '90
When Hell Was in Session '82

Michael St. Gerard
Great Balls of Fire '89
Hairspray '88
Senior Week '88
Star Time '92

Raymond St. Jacques
The Comedians '67
Cotton Comes to Harlem '70
Dead Right '68
The Evil That Men Do '84
Final Comedown '72
Glory '89
The Green Berets '68
Kill Castro '80
The Mercenaries '80
The Private Files of J. Edgar Hoover '77
Search for the Gods '75
Sophisticated Gents '81
They Live '88
Timebomb '91
Voodoo Dawn '89
The Wild Pair '87

Susan St. James
Carbon Copy '81
Desperate Women '78
Don't Cry, It's Only Thunder '82
How to Beat the High Cost of Living '80
Love at First Bite '79
Night Cries '78
Outlaw Blues '77
Sex and the Single Parent '82
S.O.S. Titanic '79
Where Angels Go, Trouble Follows '68

Al "Fuzzy" St. John
Billy the Kid Trapped '42
The Black Lash '52
Border Feud '47
Border Roundup '41
Cheyenne Takes Over '47
Dance of Life '29
Dead Men Walk '43
Death Rides the Plains '44
Devil Riders '44
A Face in the Fog '36
Fatty and Mabel Adrift/Mabel, Fatty and the Law '16
Fighting Vigilantes '47
Frontier Outlaws '44
Gangster's Den '45
Ghost Town Renegades '47
Gunsmoke Trail '38
His Brother's Ghost '45
His Private Secretary '33
King of the Bullwhip '51
Law and Order '42
Law of the Lash '47
Lightning Raiders '45

St. John ▶cont.

The Lone Rider in Cheyenne '42
The Lone Rider in Ghost Town '41
Mabel & Fatty '16
Melody of the Plains '37
The Mysterious Rider '42
Oath of Vengeance '44
Oklahoma Cyclone '30
Outlaw Country '49
Outlaw of the Plains '46
Prairie Pals '42
Raiders of Red Gap '43
Rangeland Racket '41
Ranger's Roundup '38
Return of the Lash '47
Riders of Destiny '33
The Roamin' Cowboy '37
Rustler's Hideout '44
Shadows of Death '45
She Goes to War '29
Silent Movies...Just For the Fun of It! '26
Songs and Bullets '38
Stage to Mesa City '48
Texas Justice '42
Thundering Trail '51
Trigger Men '41
Trigger Pals '39
West of Nevada '36
Wild Horse Phantom '44

Betta St. John
Alias John Preston '56
All the Brothers Were Valiant '53
Corridors of Blood '58
Horror Hotel '60
The Student Prince '54

Howard St. John
I Died a Thousand Times '55
Illegal '55
Li'l Abner '59
Lover Come Back '61
The Tender Trap '55

Jill St. John
The Act '82
Come Blow Your Horn '63
The Concrete Jungle '82
Diamonds are Forever '71
The Oscar '66
Roman Spring of Mrs. Stone '61
Tony Rome '67

Michelle St. John
Geronimo '93
Spirit Rider '93
Where the Spirit Lives '89

John St. Polis
Coquette '29
Death from a Distance '36
Party Girls '29
Phantom Ranger '38
Rocky Mountain Rangers '40
Terror Trail '33
The Unknown '27
The Untamable '23

Marin Sais
The Fighting Redhead '50
Frontier Outlaws '44
Lightning Raiders '45

Frankie Sakai
Last War '68
Master Mind '73
Mothra '62

S.Z. Sakall
Ball of Fire '41
Casablanca '42
Christmas in Connecticut '45
The Devil & Miss Jones '41
Hollywood Canteen '44
In the Good Old Summertime '49
It's a Date '40
Look for the Silver Lining '49
Lullaby of Broadway '51
My Dream is Yours '49
Romance on the High Seas '48
San Antonio '45
Small Town Girl '53
The Student Prince '54
Tea for Two '50
Wintertime '43
Wonder Man '45

Sumiko Sakamota
The Ballad of Narayama '83
The Pornographers '66

Ryuichi Sakamoto
The Last Emperor '87
Merry Christmas, Mr. Lawrence '83

Amy Sakasitz
Dennis the Menace '93
A Home of Our Own '93

Harold Sakata
Black Eliminator '70s
Goin' Coconuts '78
Goldfinger '64
Impulse '74
Jaws of Death '76
Kill Factor
The Wrestler '73

Gene Saks
A Fine Romance '92
The One and Only '78
Prisoner of Second Avenue '74
A Thousand Clowns '65

Renato Sala
Full Metal Ninja '89
Ninja of the Magnificence '89

Abel Salazar
The Brainiac '61
The Curse of the Crying Woman '61
The Living Head '59
Los Hermanos Diablo '65
Los Tres Amores de Losa '47
The Man and the Monster '65
The Vampire '57
The Vampire's Coffin '58

Theresa Saldana
Angel Town '89
Defiance '80
Double Revenge '89
The Evil That Men Do '84
I Wanna Hold Your Hand '78
The Night Before '88
Raging Bull '80

Chic Sale
The Fighting Westerner '35
Treasure Island '34
Two Reelers: Comedy Classics 9 '34

Kario Salem
1492: Conquest of Paradise '92
Triumph of the Spirit '89

Pamela Salem
After Darkness '85
Never Say Never Again '83
Salome '85

Meredith Salenger
Dream a Little Dream '89
Edge of Honor '91
The Journey of Natty Gann '85
The Kiss '88
A Night in the Life of Jimmy Reardon '88

Carmen Salinas
Danzon '91
Esta Noche Cena Pancho '87

Diane Salinger
The Butcher's Wife '91
Creature '85
The Magic Bubble '93
The Morning After '86
Pee Wee's Big Adventure '85

Matt Salinger
Captain America '89
Firehawk '92
Manhunt for Claude Dallas '86
Options '88
Power '86

Pascale Salkin
Akermania, Vol. 1 '92
The Eighties '83
Window Shopping '86

Albert Salmi
The Ambushers '67
Bang the Drum Slowly '56
Black Oak Conspiracy '77
Born American '86
The Bravados '58
Breaking In '89
Dragonslayer '81
Empire of the Ants '77
Gore Vidal's Billy the Kid '89

The Guns and the Fury '83
Hard to Hold '84
Hour of the Gun '67
Jesse '88
Kill Castro '80
Lawman '71
Love Child '82
The Meanest Men in the West '76
Menace on the Mountain '70
The Mercenaries '80
Moonshine County Express '77
St. Helen's, Killer Volcano '82
Steel '80
Superstition '82
Sweet Creek County War '82
The Unforgiven '60
Viva Knievel '77

Jennifer Salt
Hi, Mom! '70
Out of the Darkness '85
Play It Again, Sam '72

Renato Salvatori
Burn! '70
La Cicada '83
Rocco and His Brothers '60
State of Siege '73

Aldo Sambrel
Hot Blood '89
Navajo Joe '67
Voodoo Black Exorcist '89

Emma Samms
Delirious '91
Goliath Awaits '81
Illusions '91
The Shrimp on the Barbie '90

Robert Sampson
The Arrival '90
Dark Side of the Moon '90
Ethan '71
Gates of Hell '83
The Grass is Always Greener Over the Septic Tank '78
The Re-Animator '85
Robot Jox '89

Will Sampson
Buffalo Bill & the Indians '76
Fish Hawk '79
From Here to Eternity '79
The Hunted Lady '77
Insignificance '85
One Flew Over the Cuckoo's Nest '75
Orca '77
Poltergeist 2: The Other Side '86
Roanoak '86
Standing Tall '78
Vegas '78
The White Buffalo '77

Joanne Samuel
Alison's Birthday '79
Gallagher's Travels '87
Mad Max '80
Queen of the Road '84

Laura San Giacomo
Miles from Home '88
Once Around '91
Pretty Woman '90
Quigley Down Under '90
sex, lies and videotape '89
Stephen King's The Stand '94
Under Suspicion '92
Vital Signs '90

Olga San Juan
The Beautiful Blonde from Bashful Bend '49
One Touch of Venus '48

Maria Eugenia San Martin
Bring Me the Vampire '61
El Aviador Fenomeno '47
El Zorro Vengador '47

Blanca Sanchez
La Mentira '81
Los Jinetes de la Bruja '76

Jaime Sanchez
The Pawnbroker '64
The Wild Bunch '69

Pedro Sanchez
Any Gun Can Play '67
Night and the City '92
White Fang and the Hunter '85

Fernando Sancho
Blood at Sundown
Duel in the Eclipse
Voodoo Black Exorcist '89

Paul Sand
Can't Stop the Music '80
Frozen Assets '92
Getting Up and Going Home '92
Great Bank Hoax '78
The Last Fling '86
The Legend of Sleepy Hollow '79
Once Upon a Brothers Grimm '77
Teen Wolf Too '87
Wholly Moses! '80

Dominique Sanda
Cabo Blanco '81
The Conformist '71
Damnation Alley '77
First Love '70
The Garden of the Finzi-Continis '71
The Inheritance '76
Mackintosh Man '73
1900 '76
Steppenwolf '74
The Story of a Love Story '73
Voyage of Terror: The Achille Lauro Affair '90

Walter Sande
Don Winslow of the Navy '43
I'll Take Sweden '65
Nocturne '46
Rim of the Canyon '49

Otto Sander
Faraway, So Close! '93
Rosa Luxemburg '86
Wings of Desire '88

John Sanderford
The Alchemist '81
Leprechaun '93

George Sanders
Action in Arabia '44
All About Eve '50
Allegheny Uprising '39
The Amorous Adventures of Moll Flanders '65
Bitter Sweet '40
Captain Blackjack '51
Death of a Scoundrel '56
Doomwatch '72
Endless Night '71
Falcon Takes Over/Strange Bargain '49
The Falcon's Brother '42
Foreign Correspondent '40
Forever Amber '47
From the Earth to the Moon '58
The Ghost and Mrs. Muir '47
In Search of the Castaways '62
Invasion of the Body Stealers '69
Ivanhoe '52
Jupiter's Darling '55
King Richard and the Crusaders '54
The King's Thief '55
The Last Voyage '60
The Lodger '44
Mr. Moto's Last Warning '39
The Moon and Sixpence '43
Moonfleet '55
Nurse Edith Cavell '39
One Step to Hell '68
Outcasts of the City '58
Picture of Dorian Gray '45
The Private Affairs of Bel Ami '47
Psychomania '73
The Quiller Memorandum '66
Rebecca '40
Saint in London '39
The Saint Strikes Back '39
The Saint Strikes Back: Criminal Court '46
The Saint Takes Over '40
The Saint's Double Trouble '40
Samson and Delilah '50
A Shot in the Dark '64
Solomon and Sheba '59
Son of Fury '42
The Son of Monte Cristo '41
The Strange Affair of Uncle Harry '45
The Strange Woman '46

Sundown '41
This Land is Mine '43
Village of the Damned '60
Voyage to Italy '53
While the City Sleeps '56

Henry Sanders
Boss' Son '79
Deadly Sunday '82

Hugh Sanders
The Fighter '52
The Magnificent Yankee '50
Pride of St. Louis '52

Jay O. Sanders
Angels in the Outfield '94
Hostages '93
JFK '91
Meeting Venus '91
Mr. Destiny '90
My Boyfriend's Back '93
V.I. Warshawski '91

Richard Sanders
Neon City '91
WKRP in Cincinnati, Vol. 1 '78

Martyn Sanderson
An Angel at My Table '89
Beyond Reasonable Doubt '80
Solo '77

William Sanderson
Ballad of Gregorio Cortez '83
Circle Man '89
City Heat '84
Fight for Your Life '79
Last Man Standing '87
Mirror, Mirror '90
Raggedy Man '81
Return to Lonesome Dove '93
Wagons East '94

Tiny Sandford
Laurel & Hardy Comedy Classics, Vol. 2 '30
Laurel & Hardy Comedy Classics, Vol. 3 '34

Adam Sandler
Airheads '94
Coneheads '93
Shakes the Clown '92

Debra Sandlund
Murder by Numbers '89
Tough Guys Don't Dance '87
Victimless Crimes '90

Steve Sandor
The Only Way Home '72
Stryker '83

Miguel Sandoval
Clear and Present Danger '94
El Diablo '90
Lone Justice '93
Walker '87
White Sands '92

Stefania Sandrelli
Alfredo, Alfredo '72
The Conformist '71
The Family '87
Jamon, Jamon '93
1900 '76
Partner '68
Seduced and Abandoned '64
The Sleazy Uncle '89
We All Loved Each Other So Much '77

Diana Sands
Doctors' Wives '70
Georgia, Georgia '72
Honeybaby '74
A Raisin in the Sun '61
Three Days in Beirut '83

Julian Sands
After Darkness '85
Arachnophobia '90
Boxing Helena '93
Crazy in Love '92
The Doctor and the Devils '85
Gothic '87
Grand Isle '92
Harem '86
Husbands and Lovers '91
Impromptu '90
The Killing Fields '84
Murder by Moonlight '91
Naked Lunch '91
Oxford Blues '84
Privates on Parade '84
The Room '87
A Room with a View '86

Siesta '87
Tale of a Vampire '92
The Turn of the Screw '92
Vibes '88
Warlock '91
Warlock: The Armageddon '93

Tommy Sands
Babes in Toyland '61
None But the Brave '65

Gary Sandy
Hail '73
Troll '85
WKRP in Cincinnati, Vol. 1 '78

Erskine Sanford
Citizen Kane '41
Crack-Up '46
The Lady from Shanghai '48
The Magnificent Ambersons '42

Isabel Sanford
Desperate Moves '86
Love at First Bite '79

Ralph Sanford
A Night for Crime '42
There Goes Kelly '45

Saundra Santiago
Beat Street '84
Miami Vice '84

Santo
Invasion of the Zombies '61
Mision Suicida '87
Samson in the Wax Museum '63
Samson vs. the Vampire Women '61

Espartaco Santoni
The Castilian '63
Exorcism's Daughter '74

Reni Santoni
Anzio '68
Bad Boys '83
Cobra '86
Dead Men Don't Wear Plaid '82
Dirty Harry '71
Enter Laughing '67
Guns of the Magnificent Seven '69
The Package '89
The Student Nurses '70

Gaston Santos
Black Pit of Dr. M '47
The Living Coffin '58
Swamp of the Lost Monster '65

Joe Santos
Deadly Desire '91
Fear City '85
Mo' Money '92
Revenge '90
Shaft's Big Score '72
Sinatra '92
Zandy's Bride '74

Thomas Santschi
Paradise Island '30
Paths to Paradise '25
Phantom of the West '31
The Spoilers '14
Ten Nights in a Bar-Room '31

Michael Sanville
Dreams Come True '84
First Turn On '83

Jorge Sanz
Belle Epoque '92
Lovers: A True Story '90

Mia Sara
Any Man's Death '90
Apprentice to Murder '88
By the Sword '93
Call of the Wild '93
Caroline at Midnight '93
A Climate for Killing '91
Ferris Bueller's Day Off '86
Legend '86
Queenie '87
Shadows in the Storm '88
A Stranger Among Us '92
Timecop '94

Richard Sarafian
Bugsy '91
Ruby '92

Chris Sarandon
Child's Play '88
Collision Course '89
Cuba '79

Dark Tide '93
Dog Day Afternoon '75
Forced March '90
Fright Night '85
Goodbye, Miss 4th of July '88
Lipstick '76
Mayflower Madam '87
The Osterman Weekend '83
The Princess Bride '87
Protocol '84
The Resurrected '91
The Sentinel '76
Slaves of New York '89
Tailspin: Behind the Korean Airline Tragedy '89
A Tale of Two Cities '80
Whispers '89

Susan Sarandon
Atlantic City '81
Beauty and the Beast '83
The Buddy System '83
Bull Durham '88
The Client '94
Compromising Positions '85
A Dry White Season '89
The Front Page '74
Great Smokey Roadblock '76
The Great Waldo Pepper '75
The Hunger '83
The January Man '89
Joe '70
King of the Gypsies '78
Light Sleeper '92
Lorenzo's Oil '92
Loving Couples '80
Mussolini & I '85
One Summer Love '76
The Other Side of Midnight '77
Pretty Baby '78
The Rocky Horror Picture Show '79
Something Short of Paradise '79
Sweet Hearts Dance '88
The Tempest '82
Thelma & Louise '91
White Palace '90
Who Am I This Time? '82
The Witches of Eastwick '87
Women of Valor '86

Martine Sarcey
One Wild Moment '78
Pardon Mon Affaire '76

Fernand Sardou
The Little Theatre of Jean Renoir '71
Picnic on the Grass '59

Leilani Sarelle Ferrer
Barbarians at the Gate '93
Basic Instinct '92
The Harvest '92
Neon Maniacs '86
Shag: The Movie '89

Dick Sargent
Billie '65
Body Count '87
The Clonus Horror '79
Fantasy Island '76
Frame Up '79
Hardcore '79
Live a Little, Love a Little '68
Melvin Purvis: G-Man '74
Murder by Numbers '89
Teen Witch '89
That Touch of Mink '62
Twenty Dollar Star '91

Richard Sargent
For Love or Money '63
Tanya's Island '81

Michael Sarne
Cult People '89
Head Over Heels '67
Seaside Swingers '65

Michael Sarrazin
Beulah Land '80
Captive Hearts '87
The Doomsday Flight '66
The Double Negative '80
Fighting Back '82
Flim-Flam Man '67
For Pete's Sake '74
The Groundstar Conspiracy '72
Gumball Rally '76
Joshua Then and Now '85
Keeping Track '86

Lena's Holiday '90
Loves & Times of Scaramouche '76
Malarek '89
Mascara '87
The Phone Call '89
The Pursuit of Happiness '70
The Reincarnation of Peter Proud '75
The Seduction '82
Sometimes a Great Notion '71
They Shoot Horses, Don't They? '69
The Train Killer '83

Gailard Sartain
Blaze '89
Equinox '93
Ernest Goes to Camp '87
Ernest Goes to Jail '90
Fried Green Tomatoes '91
Getting Even with Dad '94
The Grifters '90
Guilty by Suspicion '91
Hard Country '81
Leader of the Band '87
Mississippi Burning '88
The Real McCoy '93
Roadie '80
Stop! or My Mom Will Shoot '92
Wagons East '94
Walker: Texas Ranger: One Riot, One Ranger '93
Wishman '93

Katsuhiko Sasakai
Godzilla vs. Megalon '76
Terror of Mechagodzilla '78

Jacqueline Sassard
Accident '67
Les Biches '68
Pirates of the Seven Seas '62

Catya Sassoon
Bloodfist 4: Die Trying '92
Dance with Death '91
Tuff Turf '85

Lina Sastri
Goodnight, Michelangelo '89
The Inquiry '87
Where's Piccone '84

Tura Satana
The Astro-Zombies '67
The Doll Squad '73
Faster Pussycat! Kill! Kill! '66

Kei Sato
Onibaba '64
Zatoichi: The Blind Swordsman's Vengeance '66

Ann Savage
Detour '46
The More the Merrier '43
Pier 23 '51
Renegade Girl '46
Treasure of Fear '45

Ben Savage
Big Girls Don't Cry...They Get Even '92
Little Monsters '89
Wild Palms '93

Fred Savage
The Boy Who Could Fly '86
Convicted: A Mother's Story '87
Little Monsters '89
The Princess Bride '87
Vice Versa '88
The Wizard '89

John Savage
All the Kind Strangers '74
The Amateur '82
Any Man's Death '90
Bad Company '72
The Beat '88
Brady's Escape '87
Caribe '87
C.I.A. 2: Target Alexa '94
Coming Out of the Ice '82
Daybreak '93
The Deer Hunter '78
Do the Right Thing '89
Eric '73
The Godfather, Part 3 '90
Hair '79
Hotel Colonial '88
The Hunting '92
Inside Moves '80

The Killing Kind '73
Killing Obsession '94
Maria's Lovers '84
Nairobi Affair '88
The Onion Field '79
Primary Motive '92
Salvador '86
Silent Witness '85
The Sister-in-Law '74
Soldier's Revenge '70s
Steelyard Blues '73
The Tender Age '84

Rick Savage
Ex-Cop '93
Sensations '87

Dany Saval
Boeing Boeing '65
Moon Pilot '62

Telly Savalas
The Assassination Bureau '69
Bandera Bandits
Battle of the Bulge '65
Beyond Reason '77
Beyond the Poseidon Adventure '79
Birdman of Alcatraz '62
Buona Sera, Mrs. Campbell '68
Cannonball Run 2 '84
Cape Fear '61
Capricorn One '78
Cartier Affair '84
Crooks & Coronets '69
The Dirty Dozen '67
The Dirty Dozen: The Deadly Mission '87
The Dirty Dozen: The Fatal Mission '88
Escape to Athena '79
Fake Out '82
The Family '73
The Greatest Story Ever Told '65
The Hollywood Detective '89
Horror Express '72
Inside Out '75
The Interns '62
Kelly's Heroes '70
Killer Force '75
Kojak: The Belarus File '85
Land Raiders '69
Lisa and the Devil '75
MacKenna's Gold '69
Mind Twister '93
New Mafia Boss '72
On Her Majesty's Secret Service '69
Pancho Villa '72
A Reason to Live, A Reason to Die '73
Redneck '73
The Scalphunters '68
Scenes from a Murder '72
Silent Rebellion '82
The Slender Thread '65
Sonny and Jed '73
A Town Called Hell '72

Doug Savant
Maniac Cop 3 '93
Masquerade '88
Paint It Black '89
Red Surf '90
Shaking the Tree '92

Lyudmila Savelyeva
The Seagull '71
War and Peace '68

John Savident
Brain Donors '92
Mountains of the Moon '90

Tom Savini
Creepshow 2 '87
Heartstopper '92
Knightriders '81
Maniac '80

Joseph Sawyer
Ace of Aces '33
As You Were '51
The Border Legion '40
Comin' Round the Mountain '51
Fighting Father Dunne '48
Indian Uprising '51
The Informer '35
The Killing '56
Lucky Cisco Kid '40
Melody Ranch '40
Mr. Walkie Talkie '52
The Naughty Nineties '45
Special Investigator '36

Tanks a Million '41

John Saxon
Aftershock '88
Animal Instincts '92
The Appaloosa '66
The Arrival '90
The Baby Doll Murders '92
Battle Beyond the Stars '80
The Bees '78
Beverly Hills Cop 3 '94
Beyond Evil '80
Big Score '83
Black Christmas '75
Blackmail '91
Blood Beach '81
Blood Salvage '90
The Cardinal '63
Criminal Act '90
Crossing the Line '90
Deadly Conspiracy '91
Deadly Thief '78
Death House
Death of a Gunfighter '69
The Doomsday Flight '66
The Electric Horseman '79
Enter the Dragon '73
Fast Company '78
Fever Pitch '85
The Final Alliance '89
The Glove '78
Half Slave, Half Free '85
Hands of Steel '86
Hellmaster '92
Invasion of the Flesh Hunters '82
Joe Kidd '72
Killing Obsession '94
Maximum Force '92
Mr. Hobbs Takes a Vacation '62
Mr. Kingstreet's War '71
Mitchell '75
Moonshine County Express '77
My Mom's a Werewolf '89
Night Caller from Outer Space '66
A Nightmare on Elm Street '84
A Nightmare on Elm Street 3: Dream Warriors '87
No Escape, No Return '93
Payoff '91
Planet Earth '74
Planet of Blood '66
Prisoners of the Lost Universe '84
Raid on Entebbe '77
The Reluctant Debutante '58
Rock, Pretty Baby '56
Running Scared '79
Scorpion with Two Tails '82
Snatched '72
Strange New World '75
Strange Shadows in an Empty Room '76
This Happy Feeling '58
The Unforgiven '60
Unsane '82
Welcome to Spring Break '88
Wrong is Right '82

Glen Saxson
Django Shoots First '74
Linchamiento '68

Philip Sayer
Green Horizon '83
Slayground '84
Xtro '83

Alexei Sayle
Deadly Currents '93
Siesta '87
Whoops Apocalypse '83
The Young Ones '88

John Sayles
City of Hope '91
Eight Men Out '88
Hard Choices '84
Little Vegas '90
Matinee '92
Straight Talk '92
Unnatural Causes '86

Syd Saylor
Ambush Trail '46
Arizona Days '37
Forlorn River '37
Harvest Melody '43
Headin' for the Rio Grande '36
Kelly the Second '36
The Light of Western Stars '30

Saylor ►cont.

The Lost Jungle '34
Prison Shadows '36
Sea Racketeers '37
When a Man Sees Red '34

Raphael Sbarge
Back to Hannibal: The Return
   of Tom Sawyer and
   Huckleberry Finn '90
Billionaire Boys Club '87
Carnosaur '93
The Hidden 2 '94
Murder 101 '91
My Man Adam '86
My Science Project '85
Risky Business '83

Mattia Sbragia
Dial Help '89
Year of the Gun '91

Greta Scacchi
Burke & Wills '85
The Coca-Cola Kid '84
Defense of the Realm '85
Desire '93
Ebony Tower '86
Fires Within '91
Good Morning, Babylon '87
Heat and Dust '82
The Killing Beach '92
A Man in Love '87
The Player '92
Presumed Innocent '90
Shattered '91
Waterfront '83
White Mischief '88

Gia Scala
Don't Go Near the Water '57
The Tunnel of Love '58

Prunella Scales
A Chorus of Disapproval '89
Consuming Passions '88
Howard's End '92
The Lonely Passion of Judith
   Hearne '87
My Friend Walter '93
A Question of Attribution '91
The Wicked Lady '83
Wolf '94

Jack Scalia
After the Shock '90
The Amazons '84
Amore! '93
Casualties of Love: The "Long
   Island Lolita" Story '93
Deadly Desire '91
Devlin Connection '82
Endless Descent '90
Fear City '85
Illicit Behavior '91
Runaway Father '91

Carlo Scandiuzzi
Red Snow '91
Shredder Orpheus '89

Kevin Scannell
Backfield in Motion '91
Shoot to Kill '88

Michelle Scarabelli
Age Old Friends '89
Deadbolt '92
Perfect Timing '84
SnakeEater 2: The Drug Buster
   '89

Don Scardino
He Knows You're Alone '80
Squirm '76

Alan Scarfe
The Bay Boy '85
Cathy's Curse '77
The Deserters '80s
Heart of Darkness '93
Iron Eagle 2 '88
Jericho Fever '93
Joshua Then and Now '85
Keeping Track '86
Python Wolf '88

Renato Scarpa
The Icicle Thief '89
Volere Volare '92

Diana Scarwid
After the Promise '87
Brenda Starr '86
A Bunny's Tale '85

Desperate Lives '82
Extremities '86
Forever '78
Inside Moves '80
JFK: Reckless Youth '93
The Ladies Club '86
Mommie Dearest '81
The Possessed '77
Pretty Baby '78
Psycho 3 '86
Rumble Fish '83
Silkwood '83
Strange Invaders '83

Wendy Schaal
Creature '85
Going Under '91
Innerspace '87
When the Time Comes '91
Where the Boys Are '84 '84

Sam Schacht
Heart of Midnight '89
A Secret Space '88

Laura Schaefer
Catacombs '89
Curse 4: The Ultimate Sacrifice
   '92
Ghost Town '88 •

Rebecca Schaeffer
The End of Innocence '90
Scenes from the Class Struggle
   in Beverly Hills '89
Voyage of Terror: The Achille
   Lauro Affair '90

Natalie Schafer
Caught '49
Forever Darling '56
Gilligan's Island: Meet the Crew
   '64
The Time of Your Life '48

William Schallert
The Computer Wore Tennis
   Shoes '69
Death Sentence '74
Held Hostage '91
House Party 2: The Pajama
   Jam '91
The Incident '89
Innerspace '87
Man on a String '71
Speedway '68
Sword of Venus '53
Trial of the Catonsville Nine '72
Twilight Zone: The Movie '83
War & Remembrance, Part 1
   '88
War & Remembrance: The
   Final Chapter, Part 8 '89

Sabrina Scharf
Hell's Angels on Wheels '67
Hunter '73

Roy Scheider
All That Jazz '79
Blue Thunder '83
Cohen and Tate '88
Curse of the Living Corpse '64
52 Pick-Up '86
The Fourth War '90
The French Connection '71
Jaws '75
Jaws 2 '78
Klute '71
The Last Embrace '79
Listen to Me '89
Marathon Man '76
The Men's Club '86
Naked Lunch '91
Night Game '89
The Outside Man '73
Paper Lion '68
Romeo Is Bleeding '93
The Russia House '90
The Seven-Ups '73
Somebody Has to Shoot the
   Picture '90
Sorcerer '77
Stiletto '69
Still of the Night '82
Tiger Town '83
2010: The Year We Make
   Contact '84

Carl Schell
Quick, Let's Get Married '71
Werewolf in a Girl's Dormitory
   '61

Catherine Schell
Gulliver's Travels '77

On Her Majesty's Secret
   Service '69
On the Third Day '83
Return of the Pink Panther '74

Maria Schell
Angel with the Trumpet '50
The Brothers Karamazov '58
Christmas Lilies of the Field '84
Cimarron '60
End of Desire '62
Gervaise '56
The Hanging Tree '59
Inside the Third Reich '82
Just a Gigolo '79
La Passante '83
The Mark '61
Napoleon '55
99 Women '69
The Odessa File '74
Samson and Delilah '84
Twist '76
Voyage of the Damned '76
White Nights '57

Maximilian Schell
The Assisi Underground '84
Avalanche Express '79
The Black Hole '79
The Castle '68
Cross of Iron '76
The Day that Shook the World
   '78
A Far Off Place '93
First Love '70
The Freshman '90
Heidi '67
Judgment at Nuremberg '61
Julia '77
Miss Rose White '92
The Odessa File '74
The Pedestrian '73
Peter the Great '86
Players '79
The Rose Garden '89
St. Ives '76
Simon Bolivar '69
Stalin '92
Together? '79
Topkapi '64
Young Catherine '91
The Young Lions '58

August Schellenberg
Black Robe '91
Confidential '86
Free Willy '93
Geronimo '93
Iron Will '93
Mark of Cain '84
Striker's Mountain '87
Tramp at the Door '87

Robert Schenkkan
Act of Vengeance '86
The Manhattan Project '86
Sanctuary of Fear '79

Rosanna Schiaffino
Arrivederci, Baby! '66
Code Name Alpha '67
Simon Bolivar '69
Two Weeks in Another Town
   '62
The Witch '66

Vincent Schiavelli
The Adventures of Buckaroo
   Banzai Across the Eighth
   Dimension '84
Amadeus '84
Batman Returns '92
Better Off Dead '85
Cold Feet '89
Fast Times at Ridgemont High
   '82
Ghost '90
Lurking Fear '94
Miracle Beach '92
One Flew Over the Cuckoo's
   Nest '75
Playroom '90
The Return '80
Valmont '89
Waiting for the Light '90

Joseph Schildkraut
Cleopatra '34
The Diary of Anne Frank '59
Flame of the Barbary Coast '45
The Garden of Allah '36
King of Kings '27
The Life of Emile Zola '37
The Man in the Iron Mask '39

Marie Antoinette '38
Monsieur Beaucaire '46
Orphans of the Storm '21
The Rains Came '39
The Road to Yesterday '25
Road to Yesterday/The Yankee
   Clipper '27
The Shop Around the Corner
   '40
The Three Musketeers '39
Viva Villa! '34
Wandering Jew '20

Gus Schilling
Citizen Kane '41
The Lady from Shanghai '48

Vivian Schilling
Future Shock '93
In a Moment of Passion '93
The Legend of Wolf Mountain
   '92
Project: Eliminator '91
Soultaker '90
Terror Eyes '87

Tom Schioler
Maniac Warriors '90s
Storm '87

Sharon Schlarth
Dead as a Doorman '85
Eat and Run '86

Charlie Schlatter
All-American Murder '91
Bright Lights, Big City '88
18 Again! '88
Heartbreak Hotel '88
Sunset Heat '92

Walter Schmidinger
From the Life of the
   Marionettes '80
Hanussen '88

Lisa Schmidt
Assault of the Killer Bimbos '87
Cemetery High '89

Marlene Schmidt
Scorchy '76
The Stepmother '71

**Christianne
Schmidtmer**
The Big Doll House '71
Boeing Boeing '65
The Giant Spider Invasion '75

Sybille Schmitz
Diary of a Lost Girl '29
F.P. 1 Doesn't Answer '33
Vampyr '31

Stefan Schnabel
Anna '87
Houdini '53
The 27 Day '57
Two Weeks in Another Town
   '62

Monika Schnarre
The Death Merchant '91
Fearless Tiger '94
Waxwork 2: Lost in Time '91

Bonnie Schneider
Mama Dracula '80
Murderlust '86

Dan Schneider
Better Off Dead '85
The Big Picture '89
Happy Together '89

Helmut Schneider
Captain Sinbad '63
Fifth Day of Peace '72

John Schneider
Christmas Comes to Willow
   Creek '87
Cocaine Wars '86
The Curse '87
Eddie Macon's Run '83
Ministry of Vengeance '89
Speed Zone '89
Stagecoach '86

Maria Schneider
Crime of Honor '85
Last Tango in Paris '73
Les Nuits Fauves '92
Mama Dracula '80
The Passenger '75
Wanted: Babysitter '75

Rob Schneider
The Beverly Hillbillies '93

Home Alone 2: Lost in New
   York '92
Surf Ninjas '93

Romy Schneider
Assassination of Trotsky '72
Boccaccio '70 '62
Cesar & Rosalie '72
Death Watch '80
Dirty Hands '76
Good Neighbor Sam '64
The Hero '71
Infernal Trio '74
La Passante '83
The Last Train '74
Mado '76
Old Gun '76
Sidney Sheldon's Bloodline '79
A Simple Story '79
Swimming Pool '70
The Things of Life '70
The Trial '63
Triple Cross '67
What's New Pussycat? '65

Andrea Schober
Chinese Roulette '86
The Merchant of Four Seasons
   '71

Michael Schoeffling
Belizaire the Cajun '86
Let's Get Harry '87
Longtime Companion '90
Mermaids '90
Sixteen Candles '84
Sylvester '85
Vision Quest '85
Wild Hearts Can't Be Broken
   '91

Jill Schoelen
Adventures in Spying '92
Babes in Toyland '86
Billionaire Boys Club '87
Curse 2: The Bite '88
Cutting Class '89
D.C. Cab '84
Hot Moves '84
The Phantom of the Opera '89
Popcorn '89
Rich Girl '91
The Stepfather '87
That Was Then...This Is Now
   '85
Thunder Alley '85
When a Stranger Calls Back '93

Ingrid Schoeller
Psychopath '68
They Paid with Bullets: Chicago
   1929 '70s

Margareta Schoen
Kriemhilde's Revenge '24
Siegfried '24

Ingeborg Schoener
Cold Steel for Tortuga '65
Mark of the Devil '69
Mr. Superinvisible '73

Dietmar Schoenherr
Journey of Hope '90
The Monster of London City '64

Annabel Schofield
Dragonard '88
Solar Crisis '92

Jason Schombing
3 Ninjas Kick Back '94
Timecop '94

Bob Schott
Future Hunters '88
Out for Blood '93

Lisa Schrage
China White '91
Food of the Gods: Part 2 '88
Hello Mary Lou: Prom Night 2
   '87

Max Schreck
Dracula/Garden of Eden '28
Nosferatu '22

Avery Schreiber
Galaxina '80
Hunk '87
Saturday the 14th Strikes Back
   '88
Silent Scream '80

Rick Schroder
Across the Tracks '89
Call of the Wild '93
The Champ '79

Earthling '80
Hansel and Gretel '82
The Last Flight of Noah's Ark '80
Little Lord Fauntleroy '80
Lonesome Dove '89
Return to Lonesome Dove '93
Two Kinds of Love '85

Karin Schubert
Cold Eyes of Fear '70s
Delusions of Grandeur '76
Till Marriage Do Us Part '74

John Schuck
Blade '72
Brewster McCloud '70
Butch and Sundance: The Early Days '79
Finders Keepers '84
Hammersmith is Out '72
M*A*S*H '70
McCabe & Mrs. Miller '71
My Mom's a Werewolf '89
The New Adventures of Pippi Longstocking '88
Second Sight '89
Star Trek 6: The Undiscovered Country '91
Thieves Like Us '74

Dwight Schultz
Alone in the Dark '82
Fat Man and Little Boy '89
The Long Walk Home '89
The Temp '93
When Your Lover Leaves '83

Reinhold Schunzel
Fortune's Fool '21
Golden Earrings '47
Notorious '46
The Threepenny Opera '31
Woman in Brown '48

Maurice Schwartz
Salome '53
Tevye '39
Uncle Moses '32

Scott Schwartz
Kidco '83
A Time to Live '85

Arnold Schwarzenegger
Commando '85
Conan the Barbarian '82
Conan the Destroyer '84
Hercules in New York '70
The Jayne Mansfield Story '80
Kindergarten Cop '90
Last Action Hero '93
Predator '87
Pumping Iron '76
Raw Deal '86
Red Heat '88
Red Sonja '85
The Running Man '87
Stay Hungry '76
The Terminator '84
Terminator 2: Judgment Day '91
Total Recall '90
True Lies '94
Twins '88
The Villain '79

Eric Schweig
The Broken Chain '93
The Last of the Mohicans '92

Hanna Schygulla
Barnum '86
Berlin Alexanderplatz '80
The Bitter Tears of Petra von Kant '72
Casanova '87
Dead Again '91
Delta Force '86
Effi Briest '74
Forever, Lulu '87
Gods of the Plague '69
La Nuit de Varennes '82
A Love in Germany '84
The Marriage of Maria Braun '79
The Merchant of Four Seasons '71
Sheer Madness '84
The Summer of Miss Forbes '88
Why Does Herr R. Run Amok? '69
The Wrong Move '78

Annabella Sciorra
Cadillac Man '90
The Hand that Rocks the Cradle '92
The Hard Way '91
Internal Affairs '90
Jungle Fever '91
Mr. Wonderful '93
The Night We Never Met '93
Prison Stories: Women on the Inside '91
Reversal of Fortune '90
Romeo Is Bleeding '93
True Love '89
Whispers in the Dark '92

Edith Scob
The Burning Court '62
The Horror Chamber of Dr. Faustus '62
The Milky Way '68

Dean Scofield
Eden 3 '93
Eden 4 '93

Paul Scofield
Anna Karenina '85
The Attic: The Hiding of Anne Frank '88
Bartleby '70
Carve Her Name with Pride '58
Hamlet '90
Henry V '89
King Lear '71
A Man for All Seasons '66
Mr. Corbett's Ghost '90
Scorpio '73
The Train '65
Utz '93
When the Whales Came '89

Tracy Scoggins
Alien Intruder '93
Beyond the Silhouette '90
Dead On '93
Demonic Toys '91
Dollman vs Demonic Toys '93
The Gumshoe Kid '89
In Dangerous Company '88
One Last Run '89
Play Murder for Me '91
The Red Raven Kiss-Off '90
Timebomb '91
Toy Soldiers '84
Twirl '81
Ultimate Desires '91
Watchers 2 '90

Peter Scolari
Camp Nowhere '94
Corporate Affairs '90
Fallen Angels 2 '93
Mr. Bill's Real Life Adventures '86
Perfect Harmony '91
Rosebud Beach Hotel '85
Ticks '93

Zvee Scooler
Trumps '88
Uncle Moses '32

Martin Scorsese
Akira Kurosawa's Dreams '90
Guilty by Suspicion '91
Round Midnight '86

Nicolette Scorsese
Aspen Extreme '93
Boxing Helena '93

Alex Scott
The Abominable Dr. Phibes '71
The Asphyx '72
Next of Kin '82
The Persuaders '71
Peter's Friends '92

Bainbridge Scott
Death Chase '87
Hell Squad '85

Brenda Scott
Johnny Tiger '66
Simon, King of the Witches '71

Campbell Scott
Dead Again '91
Dying Young '91
The Ghost of Fletcher Ridge '80s
The Innocent '93
Longtime Companion '90
The Sheltering Sky '90
Singles '92

Carey Scott
Diving In '90
Making the Grade '84

Debralee Scott
Deathmoon '78
Just Tell Me You Love Me '80
Our Time '74
Police Academy '84

Donovan Scott
Goldilocks & the Three Bears '83
Savannah Smiles '82
Sheena '84

Eric Scott
Children's Carol '80
A Day for Thanks on Walton's Mountain '82
The Waltons: A Thanksgiving Story '73

Fred Scott
Code of the Fearless '39
In Old Montana '39
Melody of the Plains '37
Ranger's Roundup '38
Ridin' the Trail '40
The Roamin' Cowboy '37
Singing Buckaroo '37
Songs and Bullets '38
Two-Gun Troubador '37

Geoffrey Scott
First & Ten '85
First & Ten: The Team Scores Again '85
The Morning After '86

George C. Scott
Anatomy of a Murder '59
Bank Shot '74
The Bible...In the Beginning '66
The Changeling '80
Choices '86
The Day of the Dolphin '73
Deadly Currents '93
Descending Angel '90
Dr. Strangelove, or: How I Learned to Stop Worrying and Love the Bomb '64
The Exorcist 3 '90
Firestarter '84
Flim-Flam Man '67
The Formula '80
The Hanging Tree '59
Hardcore '79
The Hindenburg '75
The Hospital '71
The Hustler '61
Islands in the Stream '77
The Last Days of Patton '86
The List of Adrian Messenger '63
Malice '93
Movie, Movie '78
The Murders in the Rue Morgue '86
The New Centurions '72
Oklahoma Crude '73
Oliver Twist '82
Pals '87
Patton '70
Petulia '68
The Prince and the Pauper '78
Rage '72
Savage is Loose '74
Taps '81
They Might Be Giants '71

Gordon Scott
Conquest of Mycene '63
Coriolanus, Man without a Country '64
Death Ray
Gladiator of Rome '63
Hercules and the Princess of Troy '65
Hero of Rome '63
Marauder '65
Samson and the 7 Miracles of the World '62
Tarzan and the Trappers '58
Tramplers '66
Tyrant of Lydia Against the Son of Hercules '63

Janet Scott
Day of the Triffids '63
The Devil's Disciple '59

Jay Scott
All the Lovin' Kinfolk '89
The Cut Throats '69

Grave of the Vampire '72

John Scott
Horror of Party Beach '64
The Tell-Tale Heart '62

Kathryn Leigh Scott
House of Dark Shadows '70
The Last Days of Patton '86
Murrow '86
Visitor from the Grave '81
Witches' Brew '79

Ken Scott
Showdown '93
Stopover Tokyo '57

Kimberly Scott
The Abyss '89
Flatliners '90

Larry B. Scott
The Children of Times Square '86
A Hero Ain't Nothin' But a Sandwich '78
Iron Eagle '86
My Man Adam '86
Revenge of the Nerds '84
Revenge of the Nerds 2: Nerds in Paradise '87
SnakeEater 2: The Drug Buster '89
SpaceCamp '86
Super Force '90
That Was Then...This Is Now '85

Lizabeth Scott
Dead Reckoning '47
Easy Living '49
Killer Bait '49
Loving You '57
Pitfall '48
Pulp '72
The Racket '51
Scared Stiff '53
Silver Lode '54
A Stolen Face '52
The Strange Love of Martha Ivers '46
Too Late for Tears '49

Margaretta Scott
Action for Slander '38
Calling Paul Temple '48
Counterblast '48
Man of Evil '48

Martha Scott
Adam '83
Ben-Hur '59
Cheers for Miss Bishop '41
Desperate Hours '55
Falcon Takes Over/Strange Bargain '49
Father Figure '80
Hi Diddle Diddle '43
The Howards of Virginia '40
Our Town '40
Sayonara '57
The Ten Commandments '56
The Turning Point '77
War of the Wildcats '43

Pippa Scott
Bad Ronald '74
Cold Turkey '71
Petulia '68

Randolph Scott
Abilene Town '46
Badman's Territory '46
Bombardier '43
Buffalo Stampede '33
Captain Kidd '45
The Cariboo Trail '50
China Sky '44
Coroner Creek '48
The Doolins of Oklahoma '49
The Fighting Westerner '35
Follow the Fleet '36
Go West, Young Man '36
Gung Ho! '43
Hangman's Knot '52
Heritage of the Desert '33
Jesse James '39
The Last of the Mohicans '36
A Lawless Street '55
Man of the Forest '33
My Favorite Wife '40
The Nevadan '50
Pittsburgh '42
Rage at Dawn '55
Rebecca of Sunnybrook Farm '38

Return of the Bad Men '48
Ride Lonesome '59
Ride the High Country '62
Roberta '35
Seventh Cavalry '56
The Spoilers '42
The Stranger Wore a Gun '53
Susannah of the Mounties '39
The Tall T '57
Ten Wanted Men '54
To the Last Man '33
To the Shores of Tripoli '42
Trail Street '47
Virginia City '40
Wagon Wheels '34
Western Union '41
When the West Was Young '32

Susan Scott
Day of the Maniac '77
The Slasher '74
Student Confidential '87
Trap Them & Kill Them '84

Timothy Scott
Fried Green Tomatoes '91
Inside Out '91
Lone Justice '93
Love Me Deadly '76
Return to Lonesome Dove '93

Zachary Scott
Appointment in Honduras '53
Born to Be Bad '50
Cass Timberlane '47
Flame of the Islands '55
Flamingo Road '49
Let's Make it Legal '51
Mildred Pierce '45
Shotgun '55
South of St. Louis '48
The Southerner '45
Wings of Danger '52
The Young One '61

Kristin Scott Thomas
The Bachelor '93
Bitter Moon '92
The Endless Game '89
Four Weddings and a Funeral '93
Framed '90
A Handful of Dust '88
Spymaker: The Secret Life of Ian Fleming '90
The Tenth Man '88
Under the Cherry Moon '86
Weep No More My Lady '93

Vito Scotti
Caper of the Golden Bulls '67
I Wonder Who's Killing Her Now? '76
Two Weeks in Another Town '62
Von Ryan's Express '65
What Did You Do in the War, Daddy? '66

Alexander Scourby
Affair in Trinidad '52
Big Heat '53

Angus Scrimm
The Lost Empire '83
Mindwarp '91
Phantasm '79
Phantasm II '88
Subspecies '91
Transylvania Twist '89

Susan Seaforth Hayes
Billie '65
Dream Machine '91

Steven Seagal
Above the Law '88
Hard to Kill '89
Marked for Death '90
On Deadly Ground '94
Out for Justice '91
Under Siege '92

Jenny Seagrove
Appointment with Death '88
Bullseye! '90
A Chorus of Disapproval '89
Deadly Game '91
The Guardian '90
Hold the Dream '85
Local Hero '83
Nate and Hayes '83
Sherlock Holmes and the Incident at Victoria Falls '91

Seagrove ►*cont.*

A Woman of Substance, Episode 1: Nest of Vipers '84
A Woman of Substance, Episode 2: The Secret is Revealed '84
A Woman of Substance, Episode 3: Fighting for the Dream '84

Douglas Seale
Ernest Saves Christmas '88
Mr. Destiny '90

Franklyn Seales
The Onion Field '79
Southern Comfort '81

Jackie Searl
Hearts of Humanity '32
High Gear '33
Peck's Bad Boy '34
The Return of Casey Jones '34
Topaze '33

Heather Sears
Estate of Insanity '64
Room at the Top '59

James Seay
The Amazing Colossal Man '57
Beginning of the End '57
Heartaches '47
In Old Colorado '41
Phantom from Space '53
Ridin' Down the Canyon '42
Turf Boy '42

Dorothy Sebastian
His First Command '29
Our Dancing Daughters '28
Rough Riders' Roundup '39
The Single Standard '29
Spite Marriage '29
They Never Come Back '32
Two Reelers: Comedy Classics 8 '33
A Woman of Affairs '28

Tracy Sebastian
On the Air Live with Captain Midnight '79
Running Cool '93

Jean Seberg
Airport '70
Bonjour Tristesse '57
Breathless '59
A Fine Madness '66
Lilith '64
Macho Callahan '70
The Mouse That Roared '59
Paint Your Wagon '69
Pendulum '69
Saint Joan '57
Time Out for Love '61

Harry Secombe
Down Among the Z Men '52
Goon Movie '53
Song of Norway '70

Kyle Secor
City Slickers '91
Delusion '91
The Heart of Dixie '89
Silent Victim '92
Sleeping with the Enemy '91
Untamed Heart '93

Margaret Seddon
Little Church Around the Corner '23
Mr. Deeds Goes to Town '36
The Return of Casey Jones '34
Smilin' Through '32

Kyra Sedgwick
Born on the Fourth of July '89
Family Pictures '93
Heart and Souls '93
Kansas '88
Miss Rose White '92
Mr. & Mrs. Bridge '91
Pyrates '91
Singles '92
Tai-Pan '86
War & Love '84
Women & Men: In Love There Are No Rules '91

Robert Sedgwick
Morgan Stewart's Coming Home '87

Nasty Hero '89
Tune in Tomorrow '90

George Segal
All's Fair '89
Black Bird '75
Blume in Love '73
Born to Win '71
The Bridge at Remagen '69
Carbon Copy '81
Cold Room '84
Deadly Game '82
The Duchess and the Dirtwater Fox '76
The Endless Game '89
For the Boys '91
Fun with Dick and Jane '77
The Hot Rock '72
Invitation to a Gunfighter '64
Killing 'em Softly '85
King Rat '65
The Last Married Couple in America '80
Look Who's Talking '89
Look Who's Talking Now '93
Lost and Found '79
The Lost Command '66
Me, Myself & I '92
No Way to Treat a Lady '68
Not My Kid '85
The Owl and the Pussycat '70
The Quiller Memorandum '66
Rollercoaster '77
Russian Roulette '75
The St. Valentine's Day Massacre '67
Ship of Fools '65
Stick '85
Taking the Heat '93
The Terminal Man '74
A Touch of Class '73
Where's Poppa? '70
Who is Killing the Great Chefs of Europe? '78
Who's Afraid of Virginia Woolf? '66
The Zany Adventures of Robin Hood '84

Zohra Segal
The Courtesans of Bombay '85
Masala '91

Jonathan Segall
Hot Bubblegum '81
Young Love—Lemon Popsicle 7 '87

Pamela Segall
After Midnight '89
Bad Manners '84
Gate 2 '92
Say Anything '89
Something Special '86

Emmanuelle Seigner
Bitter Moon '92
Frantic '88

Louis Seigner
The Eclipse '66
Seven Deadly Sins '53
This Special Friendship '67
The Would-Be Gentleman '58

John Seitz
Five Corners '88
Forced March '90
Hard Choices '84
Out of the Rain '90
The Prowler '81

Johnny Sekka
Khartoum '66
The Last Safari '67
Mohammed: Messenger of God '77

David Selby
Dying Young '91
The Girl in Blue '74
Grave Secrets: The Legacy of Hilltop Drive '92
Intersection '93
Night of Dark Shadows '71
Rich and Famous '81
Rich Kids '79
Up the Sandbox '72

Nicholas Selby
Macbeth '71
A Midsummer Night's Dream '68

Sarah Selby
An Affair to Remember '57

Huckleberry Finn '75

Elizabeth Sellars
The Chalk Garden '64
Desiree '54
Never Let Go '60
A Voyage' Round My Father '89

Connie Sellecca
The Brotherhood of the Rose '89
Captain America 2: Death Too Soon '79
The Last Fling '86
She's Dressed to Kill '79

Tom Selleck
Bunco '83
Christopher Columbus: The Discovery '92
Coma '78
The Concrete Cowboys '79
Daughters of Satan '72
Folks! '92
The Gypsy Warriors '78
Her Alibi '88
High Road to China '83
An Innocent Man '89
Lassiter '84
Midway '76
Mr. Baseball '92
Most Wanted '76
Myra Breckinridge '70
Quigley Down Under '90
Runaway '84
The Sacketts '79
The Shadow Riders '82
Terminal Island '73
Three Men and a Baby '87
Three Men and a Little Lady '90
Washington Affair '77

Peter Sellers
After the Fox '66
America at the Movies '76
The Battle of the Sexes '60
Being There '79
Blockhouse '73
Bobo '67
Carlton Browne of the F.O. '59
The Case of the Mukkinese Battle Horn '56
Casino Royale '67
Dr. Strangelove, or: How I Learned to Stop Worrying and Love the Bomb '64
Down Among the Z Men '52
The Fiendish Plot of Dr. Fu Manchu '80
Ghost in the Noonday Sun '74
Goon Movie '53
Great McGonagall '75
Heavens Above '63
I Love You, Alice B. Toklas '68
I'm All Right Jack '59
King Lear '87
Ladykillers '55
Lolita '62
The Magic Christian '69
The Mouse That Roared '59
Murder by Death '76
The Naked Truth '58
Never Let Go '60
Only Two Can Play '62
The Party '68
The Pink Panther '64
The Pink Panther Strikes Again '76
Prisoner of Zenda '79
Return of the Pink Panther '74
Revenge of the Pink Panther '78
The Road to Hong Kong '62
A Shot in the Dark '64
The Smallest Show on Earth '57
There's a Girl in My Soup '70
To See Such Fun '81
Tom Thumb '58
Trail of the Pink Panther '82
Two-Way Stretch '60
Up the Creek '58
Waltz of the Toreadors '62
What's New Pussycat? '65
Woman Times Seven '67
The World of Henry Orient '64
The Wrong Arm of the Law '63
The Wrong Box '66

Charles Sellon
Behind Office Doors '31
The Monster '25

The Prairie King '27
Ride Him, Cowboy '32

Milton Selzer
Miss Rose White '92
The Triangle Factory Fire Scandal '79

Harry Semels
Ghost Valley '32
Texas Buddies '32

Larry Semon
Bakery/Grocery Clerk '21
Sawmill/The Dome Doctor '22
The Wizard of Oz '25

Aparna Sen
Bombay Talkie '70
Hullabaloo Over Georgie & Bonnie's Pictures '78

Joe Seneca
The Blob '88
Crossroads '86
Half Slave, Half Free '85
Mississippi Masala '92
Mo' Better Blues '90
Murder on the Bayou '91
The Saint of Fort Washington '93
Samaritan: The Mitch Snyder Story '86
School Daze '88
Wilma '77

Mack Sennett
Abbott and Costello Meet the Keystone Kops '54
Charlie Chaplin...Our Hero! '15
Charlie Chaplin's Keystone Comedies #2 '14
Man in the Silk Hat '83

Massimo Serato
Battle of Valiant '63
The Love of Three Queens '54
The Naked Maja '59
10th Victim '65
Tyrant of Lydia Against the Son of Hercules '63
Wild, Wild Planet '65

Serena
Dracula Sucks '79
Jive Turkey '76

Assumpta Serna
Chain of Desire '93
Matador '86
Revolver '92
Wild Orchid '90

Pepe Serna
The Adventures of Buckaroo Banzai Across the Eighth Dimension '84
American Me '92
Bad Jim '89
Ballad of Gregorio Cortez '83
Fandango '85
The Forgotten '89
The Rookie '90
Sniper '75
The Student Nurses '70

Jacques Sernas
Blue Country '77
55 Days at Peking '63
The Golden Salamander '51
Hornet's Nest '70
La Dolce Vita '60
Superfly T.N.T. '73

Ray Serra
Alphabet City '84
Hardhat & Legs '80
Hooch '76

Raymond Serra
Splitz '84
Sugar Hill '94

Julieta Serrano
Dark Habits '84
Matador '86
Tie Me Up! Tie Me Down! '90
Women on the Verge of a Nervous Breakdown '88

Nestor Serrano
Brenda Starr '86
Hangin' with the Homeboys '91

Michel Serrault
The Associate '82
Buffet Froid '79
Diabolique '55
La Cage aux Folles '78

La Cage aux Folles 2 '81
La Cage aux Folles 3: The Wedding '86

Jean Servais
The Devil's Nightmare '71
Fever Mounts at El Pao '59
The Liars '64
Murder at 45 R.P.M. '65
Rififi '54
Tamango '59
That Man from Rio '64

Almira Sessions
Diary of a Chambermaid '46
The Heat's On '43
Miracle of Morgan's Creek '44
Oklahoma Annie '51

Roshan Seth
Gandhi '82
Little Dorrit, Film 1: Nobody's Fault '88
Little Dorrit, Film 2: Little Dorrit's Story '88
London Kills Me '91
Mississippi Masala '92
Mountains of the Moon '90
My Beautiful Laundrette '85
Not Without My Daughter '90
Stalin '92

Bruce Seton
The Blue Lamp '49
Demon Barber of Fleet Street '36
Gorgo '61
Love from a Stranger '37

Gerard Sety
Modigliani '58
Van Gogh '92

Joan Severance
Almost Pregnant '91
Another Pair of Aces: Three of a Kind '91
Illicit Behavior '91
Lake Consequence '92
No Holds Barred '89
Red Shoe Diaries 2: Double Dare '92
The Runestone '91
See No Evil, Hear No Evil '89
Write to Kill '91

William Severn
Journey for Margaret '42
Son of Lassie '45

Carmen Sevilla
The Boldest Job in the West '71
Pantaloons '57

Billie Seward
Branded a Coward '35
The Man from Gun Town '36
The Revenge Rider '35

Andrzej Seweryn
The Conductor '80
Land of Promise '74

Athene Seyler
The Franchise Affair '52
Private Life of Don Juan '34
Sailing Along '38

Anne Seymour
All the King's Men '49
Gemini Affair '80s
Portrait of Grandpa Doc '77

Carolyn Seymour
The Assignment '78
The Bitch '78
Gumshoe '72
Midnight Cabaret '90

Dan Seymour
Abbott & Costello Meet the Mummy '55
Hard-Boiled Mahoney '47
A Night in Casablanca '46
Return of the Fly '59
To Have & Have Not '44

Jane Seymour
Are You Lonesome Tonight '92
Battlestar Galactica '78
Doctor Quinn, Medicine Woman '92
East of Eden '80
The Four Feathers '77
The Haunting Passion '83
Head Office '86
Heidi '93
Jack the Ripper '88

Jamaica Inn '82
Killer on Board '77
Lassiter '84
Live and Let Die '73
Matters of the Heart '90
Oh, Heavenly Dog! '80
Onassis '88
The Only Way '70
Praying Mantis '93
The Scarlet Pimpernel '82
Sinbad and the Eye of the Tiger '77
Somewhere in Time '80
The Story of David '76
Sunstroke '92
The Tunnel '89
War & Remembrance, Part 1 '88
War & Remembrance, Part 2 '89
War & Remembrance, Part 3 '88
War & Remembrance, Part 4 '88
War & Remembrance, Part 5 '88
War & Remembrance, Part 6 '88
War & Remembrance, Part 7 '88
War & Remembrance: The Final Chapter, Part 8 '89
War & Remembrance: The Final Chapter, Part 9 '89
War & Remembrance: The Final Chapter, Part 10 '89
War & Remembrance: The Final Chapter, Part 11 '89
War & Remembrance: The Final Chapter, Part 12 '89
The Woman He Loved '88
Young Winston '72

Ralph Seymour
Killer Party '86
Meatballs 2 '84
Rain Man '88

Delphine Seyrig
Accident '67
The Black Windmill '74
Daughters of Darkness '71
The Discreet Charm of the Bourgeoisie '72
A Doll's House '73
Donkey Skin '70
Dos Cruces en Danger Pass '71
Grain of Sand '84
I Sent a Letter to My Love '81
Last Year at Marienbad '61
The Milky Way '68
Muriel '63
Stolen Kisses '68
Window Shopping '86

Sha-Na-Na
Dynamite Chicken '70
Grease '78

Ted Shackleford
Baby of the Bride '91
Dying to Remember '93
Summer Fantasy '84
Sweet Revenge '87

Glenn Shadix
The Applegates '89
Bingo '91
Heathers '89
Nightlife '90

Bobby Ray Shafer
Psycho Cop '88
Psycho Cop 2 '94

Jamal Shah
K2: The Ultimate High '92
Traffik '90

Tupac Shakur
Above the Rim '94
Juice '92
Poetic Justice '93

Tony Shalhoub
Barton Fink '91
Honeymoon in Vegas '92

Chuck Shamata
Death Weekend '76
Joshua Then and Now '85
Mafia Princess '86
Night Friend '87
Princes in Exile '90
Unfinished Business '89

Chang Shan
Empire of the Dragon '80s
Shaolin Temple Strikes Back '72

Michael Shaner
Bloodfist '89
Crime Zone '88

Amelia Shankley
Dreamchild '85
The Little Princess '87

Don Shanks
Halloween 5: The Revenge of Michael Myers '89
The Last of the Mohicans '85
The Legend of Wolf Mountain '92
Life & Times of Grizzly Adams '74
Mountain Man '77
Spirit of the Eagle '90

Al Shannon
The Drifter '88
Out of the Rain '90

Frank Shannon
Flash Gordon Conquers the Universe '40
Flash Gordon: Rocketship '36

Harry Shannon
Citizen Kane '41
Cow Town '50
Fighting Father Dunne '48
Idaho '43
The Jackie Robinson Story '50
The Lady is Willing '42
Man or Gun '58
Song of Texas '43
Summer and Smoke '61
The Underworld Story '50
Written on the Wind '56
The Yellow Rose of Texas '44

Michael J. Shannon
Afterward '85
Future Cop '76
Smart-Aleck Kill '85

Peggy Shannon
The Case of the Lucky Legs '35
Deluge '33
False Faces '32

Omar Sharif
Anastasia: The Mystery of Anna '86
Ashanti, Land of No Mercy '79
The Baltimore Bullet '80
Behold a Pale Horse '64
Beyond Justice '92
Crime & Passion '75
Doctor Zhivago '65
The Fall of the Roman Empire '64
The Far Pavilions '84
Funny Girl '68
Funny Lady '75
Grand Larceny
Green Ice '81
Harem '86
The Horsemen '70
Juggernaut '74
The Last Valley '71
Lawrence of Arabia '62
MacKenna's Gold '69
Night of the Generals '67
Oh, Heavenly Dog! '80
Peter the Great '80
Pleasure Palace '80
Sidney Sheldon's Bloodline '79
The Tamarind Seed '74
Top Secret! '84

David Shark
Dark Rider '91
Invasion Force '90
The Legend of Wolf Mountain '92
Soultaker '90

Ray Sharkey
Act of Piracy '89
Behind Enemy Lines '85
Body Rock '84
Caged Fear '92
Capone '89
Chrome Soldiers '92
Cop and a Half '93
Dubeat-E-O '84
Heart Beat '80
Hellhole '85
Idolmaker '80

The Neon Empire '89
No Mercy '86
Private Investigations '87
The Rain Killer '90
Regina '83
Relentless 2: Dead On '91
Round Trip to Heaven '92
Scenes from the Class Struggle in Beverly Hills '89
Some Kind of Hero '82
The Take '90
Who'll Stop the Rain? '78
Willie & Phil '80
Wired '89
Wise Guys '86
Zebrahead '92

Lesley Sharp
Naked '93
The Rachel Papers '89
Rita, Sue & Bob Too '87

Cornelia Sharpe
The Arab Conspiracy '76
Busting '74
The Reincarnation of Peter Proud '75
Serpico '73
S*H*E '79
Venom '82

David Sharpe
The Adventurous Knights '35
Colorado Serenade '46
Covered Wagon Trails '40
Doomed at Sundown '37
Gun Grit '36
Haunted Ranch '43
Melody of the Plains '37
Roaring Roads '35
Silver Stallion '41
Social Error '35
Texas to Bataan '42
Trail Riders '42
Two-Fisted Justice '43
Where Trails Divide '37

Melanie Shatner
Cthulhu Mansion '91
Syngenor '90

William Shatner
Airplane 2: The Sequel '82
The Andersonville Trial '70
The Babysitter '80
The Barbary Coast '74
The Bastard '78
Big Bad Mama '74
Bill & Ted's Bogus Journey '91
Broken Angel '88
The Brothers Karamazov '58
The Crash of Flight 401 '78
The Defender '57
Devil's Rain '75
Impulse '74
Judgment at Nuremberg '61
The Kidnapping of the President '80
Kingdom of the Spiders '77
Little Women '78
National Lampoon's Loaded Weapon 1 '93
The People '71
Pioneer Woman '73
Pray for the Wildcats '74
Riel '79
Secrets of a Married Man '84
Shame '61
Star Trek: The Motion Picture '80
Star Trek 2: The Wrath of Khan '82
Star Trek 3: The Search for Spock '84
Star Trek 4: The Voyage Home '86
Star Trek 5: The Final Frontier '89
Star Trek 6: The Undiscovered Country '91
Star Trek Bloopers '69
Third Walker '79
Visiting Hours '82
Whale of a Tale '76
White Comanche '67

Shari Shattuck
Arena '88
Body Chemistry 3: Point of Seduction '93
Dead On '93
Desert Warrior '88
Hot Child in the City '87

Mad About You '90
Naked Cage '86
Out for Blood '93
The Spring '89
Tainted '88
The Uninvited '88

Grant Shaud
The Distinguished Gentleman '92
Wall Street '87

Mickey Shaughnessy
The Adventures of Huckleberry Finn '60
Conquest of Space '55
Designing Woman '57
From Here to Eternity '53
A Global Affair '63
Jailhouse Rock '57
The King of the Roaring '20s: The Story of Arnold Rothstein '61
Last of the Comanches '52
My Dog, the Thief '69
Pocketful of Miracles '61
Primal Scream '87

Helen Shaver
The Amityville Horror '79
The Believers '87
Best Defense '84
The Color of Money '86
Coming Out Alive '84
Desert Hearts '86
Dr. Bethune '90
Gas '81
Harry Tracy '83
High Ballin' '78
In Praise of Older Women '78
Innocent Victim '90
Lost '86
Morning Glory '93
Murder So Sweet '93
Off Your Rocker '80
The Osterman Weekend '83
Outrageous! '77
Pair of Aces '90
The Park is Mine '85
Shoot '85
Starship Invasions '77
That Night '93
Trial and Error '92
The War Boy '85
Who Has Seen the Wind? '77
Zebrahead '92

Anabel Shaw
Gun Crazy '49
Shock! '46

Bobbi Shaw
Beach Blanket Bingo '65
How to Stuff a Wild Bikini '65
Pajama Party '64

Crystal Shaw
Hardbodies '84
Laser Moon '92

Fiona Shaw
London Kills Me '91
Maria's Child '93
Mountains of the Moon '90
My Left Foot '89
Super Mario Bros. '93
Three Men and a Little Lady '90
Undercover Blues '93

Huang Hsing Shaw
Renegade Monk '82
Shaolin Ex-Monk '82

Martin Shaw
Golden Voyage of Sinbad '73
The Hound of the Baskervilles '83
Intrigue '90
Macbeth '71
Professionals '76

Montague Shaw
Holt of the Secret Service '42
The Rains Came '39
Square Shoulders '29

Reta Shaw
All Mine to Give '56
Pajama Game '57
Picnic '55

Robert Shaw
Adam Had Four Sons '41
Avalanche Express '79
Battle of Britain '79
Battle of the Bulge '65
Black Sunday '77

The Deep '77
Diamonds '77
Force 10 from Navarone '78
From Russia with Love '63
Jaws '75
A Man for All Seasons '66
A Reflection of Fear '72
Robin and Marian '76
The Sting '73
Swashbuckler '76
The Taking of Pelham One Two Three '74
A Town Called Hell '72
Young Winston '72

Sebastian Shaw
Department Store '35
High Season '88
A Midsummer Night's Dream '68
Reilly: Ace of Spies '87
Spy in Black '39
The Squeaker '37

Stan Shaw
Billionaire Boys Club '87
Bingo Long Traveling All-Stars & Motor Kings '76
Body of Evidence '92
The Boys in Company C '77
Busted Up '86
The Court Martial of Jackie Robinson '90
Dirkham Detective Agency '83
D.P. '85
Fear '90
Fried Green Tomatoes '91
The Gladiator '86
Lifepod '93
Roots: The Next Generation '79
Runaway '84
Samaritan: The Mitch Snyder Story '86
Tough Enough '83

Susan Shaw
Blonde Blackmailer '58
Fire Maidens from Outer Space '56
The Junkman '82
Train of Events '49

Susan Damante Shaw
The Adventures of the Wilderness Family '76
Further Adventures of the Wilderness Family, Part 2 '77
Image of Passion '86
Mountain Family Robinson '79
The Student Teachers '73

Vinessa Shaw
Fallen Angels 2 '93
Hocus Pocus '93
Ladybugs '92

Joan Shawlee
The Apartment '60
Buck Privates Come Home '47
Francis Joins the WACs '54
House of Horrors '46
Prehistoric Women '50
Some Like It Hot '59

Dick Shawn
Angel '84
Beer '85
Check Is in the Mail '85
The Emperor's New Clothes '84
Goodbye Cruel World '82
The Happy Ending '69
It's a Mad, Mad, Mad, Mad World '63
Love at First Bite '79
Maid to Order '87
The Producers '68
Rented Lips '88
The Secret Diary of Sigmund Freud '84
What Did You Do in the War, Daddy? '66
Young Warriors '83

Wallace Shawn
All That Jazz '79
The Bedroom Window '87
The Bostonians '84
The Cemetery Club '93
Crackers '84
Deal of the Century '83
The Double O Kid '93
First Time '82
Heaven Help Us '85

Shawn ▶cont.
The Hotel New Hampshire '84
How to Be a Perfect Person in Just Three Days '84
A Little Sex '82
The Magic Bubble '93
Manhattan '79
Micki & Maude '84
The Moderns '88
Mom and Dad Save the World '92
My Dinner with Andre '81
Nice Girls Don't Explode '87
Nickel & Dime '92
Prick Up Your Ears '87
The Princess Bride '87
Radio Days '87
Scenes from the Class Struggle in Beverly Hills '89
Shadows and Fog '92
She's Out of Control '89
Simon '80
Strange Invaders '83
Strong Medicine '84
We're No Angels '89

Robert Shayne
Behind the Mask '41
Christmas in Connecticut '45
The Giant Claw '57
Marshal of Cedar Rock '53
Rhapsody in Blue '45
The Spirit of West Point '47
Stamp Day for Superman '53

Tamara Shayne
The Jolson Story '46
Somewhere I'll Find You '42

Gloria Shea
Dude Bandit '32
The Fiddlin' Buckaroo '33
Last Days of Pompeii '35
Phantom of the Air '33

John Shea
A Case of Deadly Force '86
The Dining Room '86
Freejack '92
Honey, I Blew Up the Kid '92
Honeymoon '87
Hussy '80
The Impossible Spy '87
Kennedy '83
Ladykiller '92
Missing '82
Nativity '78
A New Life '88
Small Sacrifices '89
Stealing Home '88
Unsettled Land '88
Windy City '84

Al Shear
The Great Waltz '38
It Could Happen to You '37
San Francisco '36
Tim Tyler's Luck '37
Ziegfeld Girl '41

Harry Shearer
The Fisher King '91
One Trick Pony '80
Portrait of a White Marriage '88
Pure Luck '91
The Return of Spinal Tap '92
The Right Stuff '83
This is Spinal Tap '84

Moira Shearer
Peeping Tom '63
The Red Shoes '48
The Tales of Hoffmann '51

Norma Shearer
The Barretts of Wimpole Street '34
The Divorcee '30
A Free Soul '31
He Who Gets Slapped '24
Idiot's Delight '39
Marie Antoinette '38
Private Lives '31
Riptide '34
Romeo and Juliet '36
Smilin' Through '32
Strange Interlude '32
The Student Prince in Old Heidelberg '27
Two Reelers: Comedy Classics 10 '31
The Women '39

Alan Shearman
Bullshot '83
Footlight Frenzy '84

Ally Sheedy
Bad Boys '83
The Best Little Girl in the World '81
Betsy's Wedding '90
Blue City '86
The Breakfast Club '85
Chantilly Lace '93
Fear '90
The Heart of Dixie '89
The Lost Capone '90
Maid to Order '87
Man's Best Friend '93
Only the Lonely '91
Oxford Blues '84
Red Shoe Diaries 4: Auto Erotica '93
St. Elmo's Fire '85
Short Circuit '86
Twice in a Lifetime '85
WarGames '83
We are the Children '87

Charlie Sheen
The Boys Next Door '85
Cadence '89
The Chase '93
Courage Mountain '89
Deadfall '93
Eight Men Out '88
Ferris Bueller's Day Off '86
Hot Shots! '91
Hot Shots! Part Deux '93
Lucas '86
Major League '89
Major League 2 '94
Men at Work '90
Navy SEALS '90
No Man's Land '87
Platoon '86
Red Dawn '84
The Rookie '90
Silence of the Heart '84
Terminal Velocity '94
Three for the Road '87
The Three Musketeers '93
Wall Street '87
The Wraith '87
Young Guns '88

Martin Sheen
The Andersonville Trial '70
Apocalypse Now '79
Badlands '74
The Believers '87
Beverly Hills Brats '89
Beyond the Stars '89
Blind Ambition '82
Cadence '89
The Cassandra Crossing '76
Catch-22 '70
Catholics '73
Cold Front '89
Consenting Adult '85
Conspiracy: The Trial of the Chicago Eight '87
Da '88
Dead Zone '83
Eagle's Wing '79
Enigma '82
The Execution of Private Slovik '74
The Final Countdown '80
Firestarter '84
Fourth Wise Man '85
Gandhi '82
Gettysburg '93
The Guardian '84
Hear No Evil '93
Hearts of Darkness: A Filmmaker's Apocalypse '91
In the Custody of Strangers '82
In the King of Prussia '83
The Incident '67
Judgment in Berlin '88
Kennedy '83
Legend of Earl Durand '74
The Little Girl Who Lives Down the Lane '76
Loophole '83
The Maid '90
Man, Woman & Child '83
Missiles of October '74
News at Eleven '86
Nightbreaker '89
No Drums, No Bugles '71
Out of the Darkness '85

Pursuit '72
Rage '72
Samaritan: The Mitch Snyder Story '86
Shattered Spirits '91
Siesta '87
Sweet Hostage '75
That Championship Season '82
Wall Street '87
When the Line Goes Through '71
Where the Eagle Flies '72

Chad Sheets
Dirt Bike Kid '86
Lone Star Kid '90s

Craig Sheffer
Babycakes '89
Blue Desert '91
Eye of the Storm '91
Fire in the Sky '93
Fire with Fire '86
Instant Karma '90
Night Breed '90
The Program '93
A River Runs Through It '92
Some Kind of Wonderful '87
Split Decisions '88
That Was Then...This Is Now '85
Voyage of the Rock Aliens '87

Johnny Sheffield
Tarzan Finds a Son '39
Tarzan's New York Adventure '42
Tarzan's Secret Treasure '41

Maceo B. Sheffield
Gang War '40
Harlem on the Prairie '38
Look Out Sister '48

Sheila E
The Adventures of Ford Fairlane '90
Krush Groove '85

Gene Sheldon
The Sign of Zorro '60
Toby Tyler '59

Tom Shell
Dinosaur Island '93
Surf Nazis Must Die '87
Teenage Exorcist '93

Stephen Shellan
Casual Sex? '88
Damned River '89
Gimme an F '85
Model by Day '94
Murder One '88
A River Runs Through It '92
The Stepfather '87
Still Life '92
Talking Walls '85
Victim of Beauty '91

Barbara Shelley
Blood of the Vampire '58
Cat Girl '57
The Dark Angel '91
The Gorgon '64
Madhouse Mansion '74
Village of the Damned '60

Adrienne Shelly
Big Girls Don't Cry...They Get Even '92
Hexed '93
Hold Me, Thrill Me, Kiss Me '93
Trust '91
The Unbelievable Truth '90

Deborah Shelton
Blind Vision '91
Body Double '84
Hunk '87
Mysterious Island of Beautiful Women '79
Perfect Victims '87
Sins of the Night '93

John Shelton
Ghost City '32
The Time of Their Lives '46

Joy Shelton
Impulse '55
Norman Conquest '53
Uneasy Terms '48

Maria Shelton
Escape to Paradise '39
The Phantom Rider '37

Reid Shelton
Breakin' Through '84
First & Ten '85
First & Ten: The Team Scores Again '85

Paul Shenar
The Bedroom Window '87
Best Seller '87
The Big Blue '88
Brass '85
Deadly Force '83
Dream Lover '85
Man on Fire '87
Raw Deal '86
Scarface '83
The Tragedy of King Richard II '82

Hilary Shepard
Peacemaker '90
Scanner Cop '94

Jewel Shepard
Hollywood Hot Tubs '84
Hollywood Hot Tubs 2: Educating Crystal '89
My Tutor '82
Return of the Living Dead '85
Scenes from the Goldmine '87

Patty Shepard
Crypt of the Living Dead '73
Curse of the Devil '73
Dracula vs. Frankenstein '69
El Monte de las Brujas '70s
The Stranger and the Gunfighter '76
Surprise Attack '70s
The Werewolf vs. the Vampire Woman '70
Witches' Mountain '71

Sam Shepard
Baby Boom '87
Bright Angel '91
Country '84
Crimes of the Heart '86
Days of Heaven '78
Defenseless '91
Fool for Love '86
Frances '82
The Pelican Brief '93
Raggedy Man '81
Resurrection '80
The Right Stuff '83
Steel Magnolias '89
Thunderheart '92
Voyager '91

Cybill Shepherd
Alice '90
Chances Are '89
Daisy Miller '74
Elvis Memories '85
A Guide for the Married Woman '78
The Heartbreak Kid '72
The Lady Vanishes '79
The Last Picture Show '71
The Long, Hot Summer '86
Married to It '93
Memphis '91
Moonlighting '85
Once Upon a Crime '92
The Return '80
Secrets of a Married Man '84
Seduced '85
Silver Bears '78
Special Delivery '76
Taxi Driver '76
Texasville '90
Which Way Home '90

Elizabeth Shepherd
The Double Negative '80
Invitation to the Wedding '73
Phoenix Team '80
Tomb of Ligeia '64

Jack Shepherd
Escape from Sobibor '87
Murderers Among Us: The Simon Wiesenthal Story '89
No Escape '91
Twenty-One '91
The Virgin Soldiers '69

John Shepherd
Banzai Runner '86
Friday the 13th, Part 5: A New Beginning '85
Thunder Run '86

Simon Shepherd
Fire, Ice and Dynamite '91
Murder on Line One '90

Michael Shepley
Housemaster '38
Mine Own Executioner '47
The Private Secretary '35
A Shot in the Dark '33

Delia Sheppard
Animal Instincts '92
Dead Boyz Can't Fly '93
Mirror Images '91
Night Rhythms '92
Roots of Evil '91
Secret Games '92
Sins of Desire '92
Witchcraft 2: The Temptress '90

Paula Sheppard
Alice Sweet Alice '76
Liquid Sky '83

Anthony Sher
Erik the Viking '89
Shadey '87
Tartuffe '90

Ann Sheridan
Angels with Dirty Faces '38
Appointment in Honduras '53
City for Conquest '40
Dodge City '39
Edge of Darkness '43
The Fighting Westerner '35
George Washington Slept Here '42
Good Sam '48
I Was a Male War Bride '49
Kings Row '41
Letter of Introduction '38
The Man Who Came to Dinner '41
The Opposite Sex '56
Silver River '48
Thank Your Lucky Stars '43
They Drive by Night '40
They Made Me a Criminal '39

Dinah Sheridan
Blackout '50
Calling Paul Temple '48
Genevieve '53
No Trace '50
Railway Children '70
Salute John Citizen '42
Thirteenth Reunion '81

Jamey Sheridan
All I Want for Christmas '91
Quick Change '90
Stanley and Iris '90
Stephen King's The Stand '94
A Stranger Among Us '92
Talent for the Game '91
Whispers in the Dark '92

Margaret Sheridan
One Minute to Zero '52
The Thing '51

Nicolette Sheridan
Deceptions '90
Noises Off '92
The Sure Thing '85

Ellen Sherman
Dr. Tarr's Torture Dungeon '75
La Mansion de la Locura '87

Lowell Sherman
Bachelor Apartment '31
False Faces '32
The Garden of Eden '28
Monsieur Beaucaire '24
The Royal Bed '31
Three Broadway Girls '32
Way Down East '20
What Price Hollywood? '32

David Sherwood
Curse of the Crystal Eye '93
River of Diamonds '90

Madeline Sherwood
Parrish '61
Pendulum '69
Sweet Bird of Youth '62
Teachers '84

Robin Sherwood
Love Butcher '82
Tourist Trap '79

Vladek Sheybal
The Boy Friend '71

Scorpio '73
S*P*Y*S '74

Arthur Shields
The Corn is Green '45
The Daughter of Dr. Jekyll '57
Drums Along the Mohawk '39
Enchanted Island '58
The Fabulous Dorseys '47
Fighting Father Dunne '48
Gentleman Jim '42
How Green was My Valley '41
The Keys of the Kingdom '44
The King and Four Queens '56
The Quiet Man '52
The River '51
The White Cliffs of Dover '44

Brooke Shields
Alice Sweet Alice '76
Backstreet Dreams '90
The Blue Lagoon '80
Brenda Starr '86
The Diamond Trap '91
Endless Love '81
Freaked '93
King of the Gypsies '78
Pretty Baby '78
The Prince of Central Park '77
Sahara '83
Speed Zone '88
Tilt '78
Wanda Nevada '79
Wet Gold '84

Nicholas Shields
Liar's Edge '92
Lost in the Barrens '91
Princes in Exile '90

James Shigeta
The Cage '93
China Cry '91
Die Hard '88
Enola Gay: The Men, the
  Mission, the Atomic Bomb
  '80
Flower Drum Song '61
Paradise, Hawaiian Style '66
Tomorrow's Child '82

Marion Shilling
Captured in Chinatown '35
Cavalcade of the West '36
Gun Play '36
I'll Name the Murderer '36
Inside Information '34
Man's Land '32
Rio Rattler '35
Shop Angel '32
A Shot in the Dark '35
Thunder Over Texas '34

Shmuel Shilo
Double Edge '92
Goodbye, New York '85
Noa at Seventeen '82

Yoseph Shiloah
I Love You Rosa '72
Private Manoeuvres '83

Joseph Shiloal
Eagles Attack at Dawn '74
The Lion of Africa '87

Yoko Shimada
My Champion '84
Shogun '80

Joanna Shimkus
Les Aventuriers '77
Six in Paris '68
The Virgin and the Gypsy '70

Sab Shimono
Come See the Paradise '90
Gung Ho '85
Hiroshima: Out of the Ashes
  '90
Presumed Innocent '90
Teenage Mutant Ninja Turtles 3
  '93
3 Ninjas Kick Back '94
The Wash '88

Takashi Shimura
The Bad Sleep Well '60
Drunken Angel '48
Godzilla, King of the Monsters
  '56
I Live in Fear '55
The Idiot '51
Ikiru '52
Kwaidan '64
Love and Faith '78
The Mysterians '58

Rashomon '51
Sanshiro Sugata '43
Seven Samurai '54
Stray Dog '49
Throne of Blood '57

Eitaro Shindo
The Crucified Lovers '54
A Geisha '53
Sansho the Bailiff '54

Chen Shing
The Amsterdam Connection
  '70s
Snake in the Eagle's Shadow 2
  '83
The Two Great Cavaliers '73

Sue Shiomi
Dragon Princess '70s
Shogun's Ninja '83
The Street Fighter's Last
  Revenge '79

Toshi Shioya
Mr. Baseball '92
Prisoners of the Sun '91

John Wesley Shipp
Baby of the Bride '91
The Flash '90
The Flash 2: Revenge of the
  Trickster '91
NeverEnding Story 2: The Next
  Chapter '91

Yumi Shirakawa
H-Man '59
The Mysterians '58
Rodan '56
The Secret of the Telegian '61

Talia Shire
Bed & Breakfast '92
Blood Vows: The Story of a
  Mafia Wife '87
Chantilly Lace '93
Cold Heaven '92
For Richer, For Poorer '92
Gas-s-s-s! '70
The Godfather '72
The Godfather 1902-1959: The
  Complete Epic '81
The Godfather, Part 2 '74
The Godfather, Part 3 '90
Hyper-Sapien: People from
  Another Star '86
Lionheart '87
Mark Twain and Me '91
Murderer's Keep '88
New York Stories '89
Old Boyfriends '79
Prophecy '79
Rad '86
Rich Man, Poor Man '76
Rip van Winkle '85
Rocky '76
Rocky 2 '79
Rocky 3 '82
Rocky 4 '85
Rocky 5 '90
Windows '80

Bill Shirk
Ballbuster
Escapist '83

Anne Shirley
Anne of Green Gables '34
Bombardier '43
The Devil & Daniel Webster '41
Four Jacks and a Jill '41
Law of the Underworld '38
Murder, My Sweet '44
Rasputin and the Empress '32
Stella Dallas '37

Bill Shirley
Abbott and Costello Meet
  Captain Kidd '52
I Dream of Jeannie '52

Cathie Shirriff
Covergirl '83
Star Trek 3: The Search for
  Spock '84

William Shockley
Dream Lover '93
Howling 5: The Rebirth '89

Dan Shor
Bill & Ted's Excellent
  Adventure '89
Daddy's Boys '87
Mesmerized '84
Mike's Murder '84

Red Rock West '93
A Rumor of War '80
Strange Behavior '81
Strangers Kiss '83
Tron '82

Dinah Shore
Fun & Fancy Free '47
Hollywood Goes to War '54
Oh, God! '77
Pee Wee's Playhouse
  Christmas Special '88
Thank Your Lucky Stars '43
Till the Clouds Roll By '46
Till the Clouds Roll By/A Star Is
  Born '46
Up in Arms '44

Pauly Shore
Dream Date '93
Encino Man '92
In the Army Now '94
Son-in-Law '93

Bobby Short
For Love or Money '93
Hardhat & Legs '80

Dorothy Short
Brothers of the West '37
Camp Double Feature '39
Daughter of the Tong '39
Pony Post '40
Reefer Madness '38
Savage Fury '33
Trail of the Silver Spurs '41
Wild Horse Canyon '39

Martin Short
Best of Comic Relief '86
The Best of John Candy on
  SCTV '80s
The Big Picture '89
Captain Ron '92
Clifford '93
Cross My Heart '88
The Family Man '79
Father of the Bride '91
Innerspace '87
Johnny Appleseed '86
Lost and Found '79
Pure Luck '91
Really Weird Tales '86
Sunset Limousine '83
Three Amigos '86
Three Fugitives '89

Grant Show
Treacherous Crossing '92
A Woman, Her Men and Her
  Futon '92

Max Showalter
Racing with the Moon '84
Sixteen Candles '84

Kathy Shower
Bedroom Eyes 2 '89
Commando Squad '87
Frankenstein General Hospital
  '88
The Further Adventures of
  Tennessee Buck '88
L.A. Goddess '92
Out on Bail '89
Robo-Chic '89
Sexual Malice '93
Wild Cactus '93

John Shrapnel
How to Get Ahead in
  Advertising '89
Tragedy of Flight 103: The
  Inside Story '91

Kin Shriner
Angel 3: The Final Chapter '88
Escape '90
Obsessive Love '84
Vendetta '85

Elisabeth Shue
Adventures in Babysitting '87
Back to the Future, Part 2 '89
Back to the Future, Part 3 '90
Call to Glory '84
Cocktail '88
Heart and Souls '93
The Karate Kid '84
Link '86
The Marrying Man '91
Soapdish '91
Twenty Bucks '93

Lee Shue
Samurai Blood, Samurai Guts
Samurai Sword of Justice

Richard B. Shull
The Big Bus '76
Cockfighter '74
Dreamer '79
Hail '73
Housesitter '92
The Pack '77
Slither '73
Splash '84
Unfaithfully Yours '84

Antonina Shuranova
Tchaikovsky '71
An Unfinished Piece for a
  Player Piano '77
War and Peace '68

Sabrina Siani
Ator the Fighting Eagle '83
Conquest '83
Throne of Fire '82

Sylvia Sidney
Beetlejuice '88
Blood on the Sun '45
Come Along with Me '84
Corrupt '84
Damien: Omen 2 '78
Dead End '37
Death at Love House '75
An Early Frost '85
Finnegan Begin Again '84
Fury '36
God Told Me To '76
Hammett '82
Having It All '82
I Never Promised You a Rose
  Garden '77
Love from a Stranger '47
Mr. Ace '46
One Third of a Nation '39
Pals '87
Raid on Entebbe '77
Sabotage '36
The Shadow Box '80
A Small Killing '81
Snowbeast '77
Street Scene '31
Summer Wishes, Winter
  Dreams '73
Used People '92
You Only Live Once '37

Charles Siebert
Blue Sunshine '78
A Cry for Love '80
Tarantulas: The Deadly Cargo
  '77

Jim Siedow
The Texas Chainsaw Massacre
  '74
Texas Chainsaw Massacre,
  Part 2 '86

Don Siegel
Invasion of the Body Snatchers
  '56
Invasion of the Body Snatchers
  '78

George Siegmann
Anna Christie '23
Hotel Imperial '27
The Man Who Laughs '27
Oliver Twist '22
The Three Musketeers '21

Casey Siemaszko
Amazing Stories '85
Back to the Future '85
Back to the Future, Part 2 '89
The Big Slice '90
Biloxi Blues '88
Breaking In '89
The Chase '91
Class '83
Gardens of Stone '87
Milk Money '94
Miracle of the Heart: A Boys
  Town Story '86
Near Misses '92
Of Mice and Men '92
Secret Admirer '85
Stand By Me '86
Three O'Clock High '87
Young Guns '88

Nina Siemaszko
Airheads '94
Bed & Breakfast '92
Red Shoe Diaries 3: Another
  Woman's Lipstick '93
The Saint of Fort Washington
  '93

Sinatra '92
Tucker: The Man and His
  Dream '88
Wild Orchid 2: Two Shades of
  Blue '92

Gregory Sierra
The Clones '73
Code Name: Dancer '87
Deep Cover '92
Dynamite and Gold '88
Honey, I Blew Up the Kid '92
Hot Shots! Part Deux '93
Let's Get Harry '87
Mean Dog Blues '78
Miami Vice '84
Pocket Money '72
The Thief Who Came to Dinner
  '73

Tom Signorelli
Crossover Dreams '85
The Last Porno Flick '74

Simone Signoret
Against the Wind '48
The Day and the Hour '63
Dedee d'Anvers '49
Diabolique '55
I Sent a Letter to My Love '81
Is Paris Burning? '68
La Ronde '51
Le Chat '75
Madame Rosa '77
Room at the Top '59
Ship of Fools '65
Widow Couderc '74

Caroline Sihol
Confidentially Yours '83
Tous les Matins du Monde '92

Cynthia Sikes
Goodbye Cruel World '82
Love Hurts '91
The Man Who Loved Women
  '83
Oceans of Fire '86

James B. Sikking
Black Force 2 '78
The Brotherhood of the Rose
  '89
Charro! '69
The Competition '80
Daddy's Gone A-Hunting '69
Dress Gray '86
The Electric Horseman '79
Final Approach '91
Hill Street Blues, Vol. 1: Hill
  Street Station '81
Man on the Run '74
Morons from Outer Space '85
Narrow Margin '90
The New Centurions '72
The Night God Screamed '80s
Ollie Hopnoodle's Haven of
  Bliss '88
Ordinary People '80
Outland '81
The Pelican Brief '93
Point Blank '67
Scorpio '73
The Star Chamber '83
Star Trek 3: The Search for
  Spock '84
The Stranger '64
The Terminal Man '74
Up the Creek '84
Von Ryan's Express '65

Tusse Silberg
The Company of Wolves '85
Hidden City '87

Vira Silenti
Atlas in the Land of the Cyclops
  '61
Maciste in Hell '60
Son of Samson '62

David Silva
El Aviador Fenomeno '47
Senora Tentacion '49
Sisters of Satan '75

Geno Silva
Drug Wars 2: The Cocaine
  Cartel '92
Geronimo '93
Night Eyes 2 '91

Henry Silva
Above the Law '88
Alligator '80
Almost Human '79

Silva ▶cont.

The Bravados '58
Buck Rogers in the 25th
　Century '79
Bulletproof '88
Chained Heat '83
Cinderfella '60
Code of Silence '85
The Colombian Connection '91
Crimebusters '79
Cry of a Prostitute: Love Kills
　'72
Day of the Assassin '81
Deadly Sting '82
The Desperados '80s
Escape from the Bronx '85
A Gathering of Eagles '63
Green Mansions '59
The Harvest '92
Hired to Kill '73
Hit Men '73
The Jayhawkers '59
Killer '70s
Killing in the Sun
The Law and Jake Wade '58
Love and Bullets '79
Lust in the Dust '85
Man & Boy '71
The Manchurian Candidate '62
Manhunt '73
Megaforce '82
Never a Dull Moment '68
Sharky's Machine '81
Shoot '85
The Tall T '57
Thirst '87
Three Days to a Kill '91
Violent Breed '83
Wrong is Right '82

Maria Silva
Curse of the Devil '73
The Mummy's Revenge '73

Simone Silva
Big Deadly Game '54
The Shadow Man '53

Trinidad Silva
Colors '88
Crackers '84
The Night Before '88

Fawn Silver
Orgy of the Dead '65
Terror in the Jungle '68

Joe Silver
Almost You '85
The Apprenticeship of Duddy
　Kravitz '74
The Gig '85
Mr. Nice Guy '86
Rabid '77
Switching Channels '88
They Came from Within '75

Ron Silver
Best Friends '82
Betrayal '83
Billionaire Boys Club '87
Blind Side '93
Blue Steel '90
Eat and Run '86
Enemies, a Love Story '89
The Entity '83
A Father's Revenge '88
Fellow Traveler '89
Forgotten Prisoners '90
Garbo Talks '84
The Goodbye People '83
Lifepod '93
Live Wire '92
Lovesick '83
Married to It '93
Mr. Saturday Night '92
Oh, God! You Devil '84
Reversal of Fortune '90
Romancing the Stone '84
Semi-Tough '77
Silent Rage '82
Silkwood '83
Timecop '94
Tunnelvision '76

Veronique Silver
Toute Une Nuit '82
The Woman Next Door '81

Frank Silvera
Death Tide '58
The Fighter '52

Killer's Kiss '55
Miracle of Our Lady of Fatima
　'52
Toys in the Attic '63
Valdez is Coming '71
White Mane '52

Jay Silverheels
Broken Arrow '50
Indian Paint
Justice of the West '61
Lone Ranger '56
Lone Ranger and the Lost City
　of Gold '58
Lust for Gold '49
Man Who Loved Cat Dancing
　'73
Santee '73

Jonathan Silverman
Age Isn't Everything '91
Breaking the Rules '92
Brighton Beach Memoirs '86
Broadway Bound '92
Caddyshack 2 '88
Challenge of a Lifetime '85
Class Action '91
Death Becomes Her '92
For Richer, For Poorer '92
Little Big League '94
Little Sister '92
Stealing Home '88
Traveling Man '89
12:01 '93
Weekend at Bernie's '89
Weekend at Bernie's 2 '93

Phil Silvers
All Through the Night '42
The Boatniks '70
Buona Sera, Mrs. Campbell '68
The Cheap Detective '78
The Chicken Chronicles '77
Cover Girl '44
Follow That Camel '67
Footlight Serenade '42
A Funny Thing Happened on
　the Way to the Forum '66
The Happy Hooker Goes
　Hollywood '80
Hey Abbott! '78
It's a Mad, Mad, Mad, Mad
　World '63
Lady Be Good '41
Lady Takes a Chance '43
Lucky Me '54
Racquet '79
Summer Stock '50
Tom, Dick, and Harry '41

Sid Silvers
Born to Dance '36
Broadway Melody of 1936 '35

Armando Silvestre
Esta Noche Cena Pancho '87
Gente Violenta '87
Geronimo '62
The Killing Zone '90
La Choca '73
The Last Riders '90
Neutron and the Black Mask
　'61
Neutron vs. the Amazing Dr.
　Caronte '61
Neutron vs. the Death Robots
　'62
Night of the Bloody Apes '68
Temporada Salvaje '87
The White Orchid '54
Wrestling Women vs. the Aztec
　Ape '62
Wrestling Women vs. the Aztec
　Mummy '59

Flor Silvestre
Benjamin Argumedo '78
El Ciclon '47
Vivo o Muerto '87

Soledad Silveyra
Don Segundo Sombra '69
El Profesor Hippie '69

Alastair Sim
The Belles of St. Trinian's '53
Blue Murder at St. Trinian's '56
A Christmas Carol '51
Cottage to Let '41
Escapade '55
Gangway '37
Green for Danger '47
The Happiest Days of Your Life
　'50
Hue and Cry '47

Innocents in Paris '53
Inspector Hornleigh '39
Late Extra '35
The Littlest Horse Thieves '76
The Private Secretary '35
The Ruling Class '72
Stage Fright '50
The Terror '38

Gerald Sim
Dr. Jekyll and Sister Hyde '71
Long Ago Tomorrow '71

Sheila Sim
A Canterbury Tale '44
Great Day '46

Gene Simmons
Decline of Western Civilization
　2: The Metal Years '88
KISS Meets the Phantom of the
　Park '78
Never Too Young to Die '86
Red Surf '90
Runaway '84
Trick or Treat '86
Wanted Dead or Alive '86

Jean Simmons
Androcles and the Lion '52
Big Country '58
Black Narcissus '47
A Bullet Is Waiting '54
The Dain Curse '78
The Dawning '88
December Flower
Desiree '54
Dominique is Dead '79
The Egyptian '54
Elmer Gantry '60
Going Undercover '88
The Grass is Greener '61
Great Expectations '46
Great Expectations '89
Guys and Dolls '55
Hamlet '48
The Happy Ending '69
Heidi '67
Inheritance '47
Mr. Emmanuel '44
Mr. Sycamore '74
Moment in Time '84
North and South Book 1 '85
North and South Book 2 '86
Perry Mason: The Case of the
　Lost Love '87
The Robe '53
Rough Night in Jericho '67
Say Hello to Yesterday '71
She Couldn't Say No '52
A Small Killing '81
Soldier in Love '67
Spartacus '60
This Could Be the Night '57
The Thorn Birds '83
Trio '50
Until They Sail '57
Young Bess '53

Pat Simmons
The Giant Gila Monster '59
My Science Project '85

Ginny Simms
Around the World '43
Broadway Rhythm '44
Hit the Ice '43
Night and Day '46
Playmates '41
Seven Days' Leave '42

Larry Simms
Blondie '38
Blondie Has Trouble '40
Blondie Hits the Jackpot '49
Blondie in Society '41
Blondie Knows Best '46
Blondie Takes a Vacation '39
Blondie's Blessed Event '42
It's a Great Life '43

Michel Simon
Bizarre Bizarre '39
Boudu Saved from Drowning
　'32
Circonstances Attenuantes '36
Fabiola '48
The Head '59
La Chienne '31
L'Atalante '34
Panique '47
The Train '65
The Two of Us '68

Paul Simon
All You Need Is Cash '78
Annie Hall '77
Monterey Pop '68
One Trick Pony '80
Steve Martin Live '85

Robert Simon
The Catered Affair '56
The Court Martial of Billy
　Mitchell '55
The Nine Lives of Elfego Baca
　'58

Robert F. Simon
Chinese Web '78
Spiderman: The Deadly Dust
　'78

Simone Simon
Cat People '42
Curse of the Cat People '44
The Devil & Daniel Webster '41
La Bete Humaine '38
La Ronde '51
Le Plaisir '52
Mademoiselle Fifi '44

Simone
Assault of the Killer Bimbos '87
Cemetery High '89

O.J. Simpson
Capricorn One '78
The Cassandra Crossing '76
C.I.A.: Code Name Alexa '92
Firepower '79
Hambone & Hillie '84
The Klansman '74
The Naked Gun: From the Files
　of Police Squad '88
Naked Gun 33 1/3: The Final
　Insult '94
Naked Gun 2 1/2: The Smell of
　Fear '91
Roots '77
The Towering Inferno '74

Russell Simpson
Abraham Lincoln '30
Border Patrol '43
The Grapes of Wrath '40
The Horse Soldiers '59
Human Hearts '22
The Lone Star Ranger '39
Ma and Pa Kettle at the Fair '52
Peg O' My Heart '22
The Riding Tornado '32
Sixteen Fathoms Deep '48
The Sun Shines Bright '53
Texas Masquerade '44
Three Faces West '40
The Virginian '23

Joan Sims
Carry On Admiral '57
Carry On at Your Convenience
　'71
Carry On Behind '75
Carry On Cleo '65
Carry On Dick '75
Carry On Screaming '66
One of Our Dinosaurs Is
　Missing '75

Mike Sims
The Bus Is Coming '72
Ghetto Revenge

Robin Sims
The Channeler '89
Shooters '89

Frank Sinatra
Anchors Aweigh '45
Assault on a Queen '66
Can-Can '60
Cannonball Run 2 '84
Cast a Giant Shadow '66
Come Blow Your Horn '63
The Detective '68
The Devil at 4 O'Clock '61
Double Dynamite '51
The First Deadly Sin '80
Four for Texas '63
From Here to Eternity '53
Guys and Dolls '55
High Society '56
Higher and Higher '44
A Hole in the Head '59
Hollywood Goes to War '54
It Happened in Brooklyn '47
Kings Go Forth '58
Lady in Cement '68

The List of Adrian Messenger
　'63
The Man with the Golden Arm
　'55
The Manchurian Candidate '62
Meet Danny Wilson '52
The Miracle of the Bells '48
Never So Few '59
None But the Brave '65
Not as a Stranger '55
Ocean's 11 '60
On the Town '49
The Oscar '66
Pal Joey '57
Paris When It Sizzles '64
The Pride and the Passion '57
Robin and the Seven Hoods '64
Some Came Running '58
Step Lively '44
Strictly G.I. '44
Suddenly '54
Take Me Out to the Ball Game
　'49
The Tender Trap '55
That's Entertainment '74
Till the Clouds Roll By '46
Till the Clouds Roll By/A Star is
　Born '46
Tony Rome '67
Von Ryan's Express '65
Young at Heart '54

Frank Sinatra, Jr.
Code Name: Zebra '84
Cool World '92
A Man Called Adam '66
Pepper and His Wacky Taxi '72

Nancy Sinatra
Speedway '68
The Wild Angels '66

Sinbad
Coneheads '93
Necessary Roughness '91

Gordon John Sinclair
Erik the Viking '89
Gregory's Girl '80

Hugh Sinclair
The Gay Lady '49
No Trace '50
The Rocking Horse Winner '49
The Saint's Vacation/The
　Narrow Margin '52
The Secret Four '40

Madge Sinclair
Almos' a Man '78
Coming to America '88
Conrack '74
Convoy '78
Cornbread, Earl & Me '75
The End of Innocence '90
One in a Million: The Ron
　LaFlore Story '78

Donald Sinden
Above Us the Waves '56
The Captain's Table '60
The Children '90
Doctor at Large '57
Doctor in the House '53
The Island at the Top of the
　World '74
Rentadick '72
Simba '55

Jeremy Sinden
Danger UXB '81
Fortunes of War '87
The Innocent '93

Chen Sing
Bruce Li in New Guinea '80
Bruce Li the Invincible '80
Invincible '80
Shaolin Vengence '82
Shaolin Warrior

Linda Singer
Junior '86
Zombie Nightmare '86

Lori Singer
Born Beautiful '82
Equinox '93
The Falcon and the Snowman
　'85
Footloose '84
Made in USA '88
The Man with One Red Shoe
　'85
Short Cuts '93
Storm and Sorrow '90

Summer Heat '87
Sunset Grill '92
Trouble in Mind '86
Warlock '91

Marc Singer
Beastmaster '82
Beastmaster 2: Through the Portal of Time '91
The Berlin Conspiracy '91
Beyond the Silhouette '90
Body Chemistry '90
Born to Race '88
Dead Space '90
Deadly Game '91
For Ladies Only '81
Go Tell the Spartans '78
Her Life as a Man '83
High Desert Kill '90
If You Could See What I Hear '82
In the Cold of the Night '89
A Man Called Sarge '90
The Red Raven Kiss-Off '90
Roots: The Next Generation '79
Sergeant Matlovich vs. the U.S. Air Force '78
Sweet Justice '92
Things in Their Season '74
The Two Worlds of Jenny Logan '79
Ultimate Desires '91
Watchers 2 '90

Joseph Singleton
The Mad Whirl '25
Reggie Mixes In '16
Toll Gate '20

Penny Singleton
Blondie '38
Blondie Has Trouble '40
Blondie Hits the Jackpot '49
Blondie in Society '41
Blondie Knows Best '46
Blondie Takes a Vacation '39
Blondie's Blessed Event '42
Boy Meets Girl '38
It's a Great Life '43
Vogues of 1938 '37

Gary Sinise
Forrest Gump '94
Jack the Bear '93
A Midnight Clear '92
Of Mice and Men '92
Stephen King's The Stand '94
True West '86

Sir Lancelot
I Walked with a Zombie '43
Zombies on Broadway '44

G. Anthony Sirico
Backtrack '89
Cookie '89

Marina Sirtis
Blind Date '84
Death Wish 3 '85
Star Trek the Next Generation: Encounter at Farpoint '87

Noble Sissle
Junction 88 '40
Murder with Music '45

Rocco Sisto
Innocent Blood '92
Red Riding Hood '88
Truth or Die '86

Frank Sivero
Cop and a Half '93
Fist of Honor '92
Goodfellas '90

Tom Sizemore
An American Story '92
Blue Steel '90
Flight of the Intruder '90
Harley Davidson and the Marlboro Man '91
Heart and Souls '93
A Matter of Degrees '90
Natural Born Killers '94
Passenger 57 '92
Striking Distance '93
Watch It '93
Where Sleeping Dogs Lie '91
Wyatt Earp '94

Gunnar Sjoberg
Brink of Life '57
June Night '40

Victor Sjostrom
The Outlaw and His Wife '17
Thomas Graal's Best Film '17
Thomas Graal's First Child '18
Walpurgis Night '41
Wild Strawberries '57

George Skaff
Frogs '72
The Incredible Petrified World '58
Man Beast '55

Jimmie F. Skaggs
Ghost Town '88
The Lost Capone '90
Puppet Master '89
Thousand Pieces of Gold '91

Lilia Skala
Charly '68
Deadly Hero '75
Flashdance '83
Heartland '81
House of Games '87
Lilies of the Field '63
Probe '72

Stellan Skarsgard
Good Evening, Mr. Wallenberg '93
Noon Wine '84
The Ox '91
The Unbearable Lightness of Being '88
Wind '92

Jackie Skarvellis
The Body Beneath '70
The Rats are Coming! The Werewolves are Here! '72

Red Skelton
Bathing Beauty '44
Clown '53
DuBarry Was a Lady '43
Fuller Brush Man '48
Having Wonderful Time '38
Having Wonderful Time/Carnival Boat '38
Hollywood Clowns '85
Hollywood Goes to War '54
I Dood It '43
Lady Be Good '41
Lovely to Look At '52
Merton of the Movies '47
Neptune's Daughter '49
Panama Hattie '42
Ship Ahoy '42
The Show-Off '46
A Southern Yankee '48
Texas Carnival '51
Those Magnificent Men in Their Flying Machines '65
Thousands Cheer '43
Three Little Words '50
Watch the Birdie '50
Whistling in Brooklyn '43
Whistling in Dixie '42
Whistling in the Dark '41
The Yellow Cab Man '50
Ziegfeld Follies '46

Tom Skerritt
Alien '79
Big Bad Mama '74
Big Man on Campus '89
Big Town '87
Calendar Girl Murders '84
Cheech and Chong's Up in Smoke '78
Child in the Night '90
The China Lake Murders '90
Dangerous Summer '82
Dead Zone '83
Devil's Rain '75
Fighting Back '82
Fuzz '72
Getting Up and Going Home '92
The Heist '89
Hitchhiker 3 '87
Ice Castles '79
Knight Moves '93
Maid to Order '87
M*A*S*H '70
Miles to Go '86
Nightmare at Bittercreek '91
Opposing Force '87
Poison Ivy '92
Poker Alice '87
Poltergeist 3 '88
Red King, White Knight '89
A River Runs Through It '92

The Rookie '90
Silence of the North '81
SpaceCamp '86
Steel Magnolias '89
Thieves Like Us '74
Top Gun '86
The Turning Point '77
Wild Orchid 2: Two Shades of Blue '92
Wild Rovers '71
Wisdom '87

Anita Skinner
Girlfriends '78
Sole Survivor '84

Claire Skinner
Life is Sweet '91
Naked '93

Alison Skipworth
Dangerous '35
Doubting Thomas '35
Dubarry '31
Night After Night '32
Satan Met a Lady '36
Wide Open Faces '38

Jerzy Skolimowski
Big Shots '87
White Nights '85

Ione Skye
Carmilla '89
Gas Food Lodging '92
Guncrazy '92
Mindwalk: A Film for Passionate Thinkers '91
A Night in the Life of Jimmy Reardon '88
The Rachel Papers '89
River's Edge '87
Samantha '92
Say Anything '89
Stranded '87

Max Elliott Slade
3 Ninjas '92
3 Ninjas Kick Back '94

Jeremy Slate
Alligator Alley '72
Born Losers '67
The Centerfold Girls '74
Dead Pit '89
The Devil's Brigade '68
Dream Machine '91
G.I. Blues '60
Girls! Girls! Girls! '62
Goodnight, Sweet Marilyn '89
Hell's Angels '69 '69
The Hooked Generation '69
I'll Take Sweden '65
The Lawnmower Man '92
Mr. Horn '79

Christian Slater
Beyond the Stars '89
Gleaming the Cube '89
Heathers '89
Jimmy Hollywood '94
Kuffs '92
Legend of Billie Jean '85
Mobsters '91
The Name of the Rose '86
Pump Up the Volume '90
Robin Hood: Prince of Thieves '91
Tales from the Darkside: The Movie '90
True Romance '93
Tucker: The Man and His Dream '88
Twisted '86
Untamed Heart '93
Where the Day Takes You '92
The Wizard '89
Young Guns 2 '90

Helen Slater
Betrayal of the Dove '92
Chantilly Lace '93
City Slickers '91
Happy Together '89
A House In The Hills '93
Lassie '94
Legend of Billie Jean '85
Ruthless People '86
The Secret of My Success '87
Sticky Fingers '88
Supergirl '84
12:01 '93

Tod Slaughter
Crimes at the Dark House '39

The Crimes of Stephen Hawke '36
Demon Barber of Fleet Street '36
The Face at the Window '39
The Greed of William Hart '48
The Hooded Terror '38
Murder in the Old Red Barn '36
Never Too Late to Mend '37
Saturday Night Shockers, Vol. 2 '58
Sexton Blake and the Hooded Terror '38
Ticket of Leave Man '37

Darla Slavens
Married People, Single Sex '93
Red Snow '91

Walter Slezak
Abbott and Costello in the Foreign Legion '50
Bedtime for Bonzo '51
Black Beauty '71
Born to Kill '47
Caper of the Golden Bulls '67
Cornered '45
Emil and the Detective '64
The Fallen Sparrow '43
The Inspector General '49
Lifeboat '44
Once Upon a Honeymoon '42
People Will Talk '51
The Pirate '48
The Princess and the Pirate '44
Riff-Raff '47
Salome, Where She Danced '45
Sinbad the Sailor '47
The Spanish Main '45
Step Lively '44
This Land is Mine '43
Treasure Island '34
The Wonderful World of the Brothers Grimm '62
The Yellow Cab Man '50

Everett Sloane
The Big Knife '55
Citizen Kane '41
Disorderly Orderly '64
The Enforcer '51
Hercules and the Princess of Troy '65
Home from the Hill '60
The Lady from Shanghai '48
Lust for Life '56
Marjorie Morningstar '58
The Men '50
The Patsy '64
Patterns '56
Sirocco '51
Somebody Up There Likes Me '56

James Sloyan
Amos '85
Billionaire Boys Club '87
Callie and Son '81
Danielle Steel's Changes '91
Deadline Assault '90
The Disappearance of Aimee '76
Prime Suspect '82

Errol Slue
Baby on Board '92
Murder One '88

Jean Smart
A Fight for Jenny '90
Fire with Fire '86
Homeward Bound: The Incredible Journey '93
Maximum Security '87
Mistress '91
Project X '87

Richard Smedley
The Abductors '72
A Place Called Today '72

Ron Smerczak
Hunted '88
Return of the Family Man '89

Yakov Smirnoff
The Adventures of Buckaroo Banzai Across the Eighth Dimension '84
Heartburn '86
Up Your Alley '89

Alexis Smith
The Adventures of Mark Twain '44
The Age of Innocence '93

Any Number Can Play '49
Casey's Shadow '78
Conflict '45
Dive Bomber '41
Dress Gray '86
Gentleman Jim '42
Here Comes the Groom '51
Hollywood Canteen '44
The Horn Blows at Midnight '45
La Truite '83
The Little Girl Who Lives Down the Lane '76
Night and Day '46
Once is Not Enough '75
Rhapsody in Blue '45
San Antonio '45
The Sleeping Tiger '54
South of St. Louis '48
Split Second '53
This Happy Feeling '58
Tough Guys '86
The Two Mrs. Carrolls '47
The Young Philadelphians '59

Anna Deavere Smith
Dave '93
Philadelphia '93

Art Smith
Caught '49
In a Lonely Place '50
Letter from an Unknown Woman '48
Mr. Peabody & the Mermaid '48
The Next Voice You Hear '50
The Painted Hills '51

Bill Smith
Atlantis, the Lost Continent '61
Spirit of the Eagle '90

Brooke Smith
The Night We Never Met '93
The Silence of the Lambs '91

Bubba Smith
Fist of Honor '92
My Samurai '92
Police Academy '84
Police Academy 2: Their First Assignment '85
Police Academy 3: Back in Training '86
Police Academy 4: Citizens on Patrol '87
Police Academy 5: Assignment Miami Beach '88
Police Academy 6: City Under Siege '89
The Wild Pair '87

Sir C. Aubrey Smith
The Adventures of Mark Twain '44
And Then There Were None '45
Another Thin Man '39
Balalaika '39
Beyond Tomorrow '40
Bombshell '33
The Charge of the Light Brigade '36
China Seas '35
Cleopatra '34
Eternally Yours '39
Five Came Back '39
Forever and a Day '43
The Four Feathers '39
The Garden of Allah '36
Hurricane '37
Little Lord Fauntleroy '36
The Lives of a Bengal Lancer '35
Madame Curie '43
Prisoner of Zenda '37
Queen Christina '33
Rebecca '40
Scarlet Empress '34
Sensations of 1945 '44
Thoroughbreds Don't Cry '37
Trader Horn '31
Transatlantic Tunnel '35
Waterloo Bridge '40
Wee Willie Winkie '37
The White Cliffs of Dover '44

Cedric Smith
Love and Hate: A Marriage Made in Hell '90
The Penthouse '92

Charles Martin Smith
American Graffiti '73
And the Band Played On '93
The Buddy Holly Story '78
The Campus Corpse '77

Smith ►cont.

Cotton Candy '82
Culpepper Cattle Co. '72
Deep Cover '92
The Experts '89
Fifty/Fifty '93
Fuzz '72
Herbie Goes Bananas '80
Hot Spot '90
Law of the Land
More American Graffiti '79
Never Cry Wolf '83
No Deposit, No Return '76
Pat Garrett & Billy the Kid '73
Rafferty & the Gold Dust Twins '75
Starman '84
Strange Tales/Ray Bradbury Theatre '86
The Untouchables '87

Cheryl "Rainbeaux" Smith
Caged Heat '74
Cheech and Chong's Up in Smoke '79
Drum '76
Farewell, My Lovely '75
Incredible Melting Man '77
Independence Day '83
Laserblast '78
Lemora, Lady Dracula '73
Melvin and Howard '80
Parasite '81
Pom Pom Girls '76
Revenge of the Cheerleaders '76
Slumber Party '57 '76
The Swinging Cheerleaders '74
Vice Squad '82

Connie Smith
Hell on Wheels '67
Road to Nashville '67
Room to Let '49
Treasure of the Golden Condor '53

Cotter Smith
Broken Badge '85
A Bunny's Tale '85
Cameron's Closet '89
K-9 '89
Lady Beware '87
The Last Prostitute '91
Midnight's Child '93

Cynthia Smith
Benji '74
For the Love of Benji '77

David Anthony Smith
Judgment Day '88
Terror in Paradise

Garnett Smith
Laboratory '80
Whitcomb's War '88

Geraldine Smith
Flesh '68
Mixed Blood '84
Spike of Bensonhurst '88

Howard Smith
Call Northside 777 '48
State of the Union '48

Jaclyn Smith
The Adventurers '70
The Bourne Identity '88
Danielle Steel's Kaleidoscope '92
Deja Vu '84
George Washington '84
Goodbye Columbus '69
Jacqueline Bouvier Kennedy '81
Lies Before Kisses '92
The Night They Saved Christmas '87
Nightkill '80
Probe '72
Rage of Angels '83
Rage of Angels: The Story Continues '86
Users '78
Windmills of the Gods '88

John W. Smith
Hot Rod Girl '56
Star Crystal '85

Kate Smith
Irving Berlin's America '86
This is the Army '43

Kent Smith
The Affair '73
Back Door to Heaven '39
The Badlanders '58
The Balcony '63
Cat People '42
Curse of the Cat People '44
Die Sister, Die! '74
Magic Town '47
Party Girl '58
Pete 'n' Tillie '72
Probe '72
The Spiral Staircase '46
Strangers When We Meet '60

Kurtwood Smith
Boxing Helena '93
Company Business '91
The Crush '93
Dead Poets Society '89
Fortress '93
The Heart of Dixie '89
The Nightmare Years '89
Quick Change '90
Rambo 3 '88
RoboCop '87
Shadows and Fog '92
Star Trek 6: The Undiscovered Country '91
True Believer '89

Lane Smith
Air America '90
Blind Vengeance '90
The Displaced Person '76
The Distinguished Gentleman '92
Dress Gray '86
Duplicates '92
False Arrest '92
The Mighty Ducks '92
My Cousin Vinny '92
Night Game '89
Prime Suspect '82
Prison '88
The Scout '94
The Solitary Man '82
Son-in-Law '93
Weeds '87

Lewis Smith
The Adventures of Buckaroo Banzai Across the Eighth Dimension '84
Diary of a Hitman '91
The Final Terror '83
Fulfillment '89
The Heavenly Kid '85
North and South Book 2 '86

Liz Smith
Apartment Zero '88
A Private Function '84
We Think the World of You '88

Lois Smith
Black Widow '87
Falling Down '93
Five Easy Pieces '70
Fried Green Tomatoes '91
Green Card '90
Hard Promises '92
Keep the Change '92
Reckless '84
Reuben, Reuben '83
Skylark '93
Switched at Birth '91
Twisted '86

Madeleine Smith
Frankenstein and the Monster from Hell '74
Live and Let Die '73
The Vampire Lovers '70

Madolyn Smith
All of Me '84
The Caller '87
Ernie Kovacs: Between the Laughter '84
Final Approach '91
Funny Farm '88
Pray TV '82
Rehearsal for Murder '82
The Rose and the Jackal '90
Sadat '83
The Super '91
2010: The Year We Make Contact '84
Urban Cowboy '80

Dame Maggie Smith
Better Late Than Never '83
California Suite '78
Clash of the Titans '81
Death on the Nile '78
Evil Under the Sun '82
The Honey Pot '67
Hook '91
Hot Millions '68
Lily in Love '85
The Lonely Passion of Judith Hearne '87
The Missionary '82
Mrs. Silly '85
Murder by Death '76
The Prime of Miss Jean Brodie '69
A Private Function '84
Quartet '81
A Room with a View '86
The Secret Garden '93
Sister Act '92
Sister Act 2: Back in the Habit '93
Travels with My Aunt '72
The V.I.P.'s '63

Mel Smith
Brain Donors '92
The Misadventures of Mr. Wilt '90
Morons from Outer Space '85
The Princess Bride '87
Slayground '84

Melanie Smith
The Baby Doll Murders '92
Trancers 3: Deth Lives '92

Oliver Smith
Hellbound: Hellraiser 2 '88
Hellraiser '87

Patricia Smith
Save the Tiger '73
Spirit of St. Louis '57

Paul Smith
Caged Fury '90
Crimewave '85
Crossing the Line '90
Death Chase '87
Desert Kickboxer '92
Dune '84
The Fire in the Stone '85
Gor '87
Haunted Honeymoon '86
Jungle Warriors '84
Madron '74
Maverick '94
Midnight Express '78
Mortuary '81
Outlaw Force '87
Pieces '83
Platypus Cove '86
Popeye '80
Raiders in Action '71
Red Sonja '85
Return of the Tiger '78
The Salamander '82
Sno-Line '85
Sonny Boy '87

Rex Smith
The Pirates of Penzance '83
Snow White and the Seven Dwarfs '83
Sooner or Later '78
Street Hawk '84
Transformations '88
The Trial of the Incredible Hulk '89

Roger Smith
Auntie Mame '58
Man of a Thousand Faces '57

Savannah Smith
Code of Honor '84
Everybody's All American '88
The Long Riders '80

Shawn Smith
It! The Terror from Beyond Space '58
The Land Unknown '57
The River Rat '84

Shawnee Smith
The Blob '88
Desperate Hours '90
Stephen King's The Stand '94
Summer School '87
Who's Harry Crumb? '89

Shelley Smith
The Fantastic World of D.C. Collins '84
National Lampoon's Class Reunion '82
The Night the City Screamed '80

Stuart Smith
Ninja Destroyer '70s
Ninja Hunt '80s

Will Smith
Made in America '93
Six Degrees of Separation '93
Where the Day Takes You '92

William Smith
Action U.S.A. '89
Angels Die Hard '84
Blackjack '78
B.O.R.N. '88
Boss '74
Chrome and Hot Leather '71
Chrome Hearts '70
Commando Squad '87
Conan the Barbarian '82
Darker than Amber '70
Deadly Breed '89
The Deadly Trackers '73
East L.A. Warriors '89
Emperor of the Bronx '89
Evil Altar '89
Eye of the Tiger '86
Fast Company '88
Fever Pitch '85
The Frisco Kid '79
Gentle Savage '73
Grave of the Vampire '72
Hell on the Battleground '89
Hollywood Man '76
Invasion of the Bee Girls '73
Jungle Assault '89
L.A. Vice '89
The Last Riders '90
The Losers '70
Maniac Cop '88
Mean Season '85
Memorial Valley Massacre '88
Moon in Scorpio '86
Platoon Leader '87
The Rebels '79
Red Dawn '84
Run, Angel, Run! '69
Scorchy '76
Seven '79
Slow Burn '90
A Taste of Hell '73
Terror in Beverly Hills '90
Twilight's Last Gleaming '77
The Ultimate Warrior '75

Yeardley Smith
City Slickers '91
Ginger Ale Afternoon '89
Heaven Help Us '85
Legend of Billie Jean '85
Maximum Overdrive '86

Jan Smithers
Mr. Nice Guy '86
Where the Lilies Bloom '74
WKRP in Cincinnati, Vol. 1 '78

William Smithers
Death Sport '78
Scorpio '73

Bill Smitrovich
Crazy People '90
Crime Story: The Complete Saga '86
A Killing Affair '85
Renegades '89

Jimmy Smits
The Believers '87
The Cisco Kid '94
Fires Within '91
Glitz '88
L.A. Law '86
Old Gringo '89
Running Scared '86
Stamp of a Killer '87
Stephen King's The Tommyknockers '93
Switch '91
Vital Signs '90

Sonja Smits
Hitchhiker 4 '87
The Pit '81
That's My Baby! '88
Videodrome '83
War Brides '80s

Dick Smothers
Rap Master Ronnie '88
Speed Zone '88
Tales of the Unexpected '91

Tom Smothers
Alice Through the Looking Glass '66
Pandemonium '82
A Pleasure Doing Business '79
Rap Master Ronnie '88
Serial '80
Silver Bears '78
Speed Zone '88

Ann Smyrner
Beyond the Law '68
The House of 1000 Dolls '67

Wesley Snipes
Boiling Point '93
Demolition Man '93
Jungle Fever '91
King of New York '90
Major League '89
Mo' Better Blues '90
New Jack City '91
Passenger 57 '92
Rising Sun '93
Streets of Gold '86
Sugar Hill '94
Vietnam War Story 2 '88
The Waterdance '91
White Men Can't Jump '92
Wildcats '86

Carrie Snodgress
Across the Tracks '89
The Attic '80
The Ballad of Little Jo '93
Blueberry Hill '88
Chill Factor '90
Diary of a Mad Housewife '70
8 Seconds '94
The Fury '78
L.A. Bad '85
Mission of the Shark '91
Murphy's Law '86
Nadia '84
A Night in Heaven '83
Pale Rider '85
The Rose and the Jackal '90
Silent Night, Lonely Night '69
The Solitary Man '82
Trick or Treats '82

Victoria Snow
Buffalo Jump '90
Love and Hate: A Marriage Made in Hell '90

Arlen Dean Snyder
Deadly Force '83
Dear Detective '79
Heartbreak Ridge '86
Marked for Death '90
Night Partners '83
No Place to Hide '81
Red Flag: The Ultimate Game '81
Running Cool '93
Scalpel '76
Wheels of Terror '90
Yanks '79
Young Love, First Love '79

Drew Snyder
Blindfold: Acts of Obsession '94
Dance with Death '91
Firestarter '84
Izzy & Moe '85
Night School '81
Project: Eliminator '91

Suzanne Snyder
Killer Klowns from Outer Space '88
The Night Before '88
Prettykill '87
Retribution '88

Barry Sobel
Doc Hollywood '91
Martians Go Home! '90
Punchline '88

Maria Socas
Deathstalker 2: Duel of the Titans '87
The Warrior & the Sorceress '84

Kristina Söderbaum
Jud Suess '40
Kolberg '45

Abraham Sofaer
Bhowani Junction '56
Calling Paul Temple '48
Captain Sinbad '63
Demon with a Glass Hand '64
Dual Alibi '47
Elephant Walk '54
Naked Jungle '54
Quo Vadis '51

Hans Sohnker
For the First Time '59
The Phantom of Soho '64
Sherlock Holmes and the
    Deadly Necklace '62

Marilyn Sokol
The Goodbye Girl '77
Something Short of Paradise
    '79

Vladimir Sokoloff
Baron of Arizona '51
Beyond the Time Barrier '60
Cloak and Dagger '46
Comrade X '40
Conquest '37
I Was a Teenage Werewolf '57
The Lower Depths '36
The Road to Morocco '42
Taras Bulba '62

Miguel Angel Sola
Funny, Dirty Little War '83
Mayalunta '86

Silvia Solar
As If It Were Raining '63
Finger on the Trigger '65
The Gentleman Killer '78
Night of the Howling Beast '75

Andres Soler
El Bruto '52
El Ceniciento '47
Orlak, the Hell of Frankenstein
    '60

Fernando Soler
Anita de Montemar '60s
The Great Madcap '49
Susana '51

Paul Soles
Beethoven Lives Upstairs '92
The Gunrunner '84

P.J. Soles
Alienator '89
B.O.R.N. '88
Halloween '78
Innocent Prey '88
The Possessed '77
Rock 'n' Roll High School '79
Saigon Commandos '88
Soldier's Fortune '91
Stripes '81

Javier Solis
El Hombre de la Furia '65
Los Tres Calaveras '64

Bruce Solomon
Children Shouldn't Play with
    Dead Things '72
Foul Play '78

Charles Solomon
The Channeler '89
Witchcraft 2: The Temptress
    '90
Witchcraft 3: The Kiss of Death
    '90
Witchcraft 4: Virgin Heart '92

Anatoli Solonitzin
Andrei Rublev '66
Stalker '80

Elena Solovei
Oblomov '81
A Slave of Love '78
An Unfinished Piece for a
    Player Piano '77

Yanti Somer
Cosmos: War of the Planets '80
Reactor '85

Kristi Somers
Hardbodies '84
Tomboy '85

Suzanne Somers
American Graffiti '73
Ants '77
Happily Ever After '82
Nothing Personal '80
Sky Hei$t '75

Yesterday's Hero '79

Julie Sommars
Herbie Goes to Monte Carlo '77
I'm the Girl He Wants to Kill '74
Sex and the Single Parent '82

Elke Sommer
Adventures Beyond Belief '87
Anastasia: The Mystery of
    Anna '86
The Big Scam '79
Boy, Did I Get a Wrong
    Number! '66
Carry On Behind '75
The Corrupt Ones '67
The Double McGuffin '79
Fantastic Seven '82
Inside the Third Reich '82
The Invincible Six '68
The Invisible Strangler '76
It's Not the Size That Counts
    '74
Jenny's War '85
Left for Dead '78
Lily in Love '85
Lisa and the Devil '75
No One Cries Forever '85
One Away '80
The Oscar '66
Prisoner of Zenda '79
The Prize '63
Probe '72
Severed Ties '92
A Shot in the Dark '64
Sweet Ecstasy '62
Ten Little Indians '75
Torture Chamber of Baron
    Blood '72
The Treasure Seekers '79
Zeppelin '71

Josef Sommer
Absence of Malice '81
An American Story '92
Bloodhounds of Broadway '89
Bridge to Silence '89
Chances are '89
Dracula's Widow '88
Execution of Raymond Graham
    '85
Forced March '90
Hide in Plain Sight '80
Hostages '93
Iceman '84
Independence Day '83
Malice '93
The Mighty Ducks '92
Reds '81
Rollover '81
The Rosary Murders '87
Shadows and Fog '92
Silkwood '83
Still of the Night '82
Target '85
Witness '85
A Woman Named Jackie '91
Yuri Nosenko, KGB '86

Helga Sommerfeld
Code Name Alpha '67
The Phantom of Soho '64

Gale Sondergaard
Anna and the King of Siam '46
Anthony Adverse '36
The Blue Bird '40
East Side, West Side '49
Echoes '83
The Invisible Man's Revenge
    '44
Isle of Forgotten Sins '43
Juarez '39
The Letter '40
The Life of Emile Zola '37
The Mark of Zorro '40
My Favorite Blonde '42
A Night to Remember '42
The Return of a Man Called
    Horse '76
The Road to Rio '47
Savage Intruder '68
Spider Woman '44
The Time of Their Lives '46

Jack Soo
Flower Drum Song '61
Return from Witch Mountain
    '78

Michael Sopkiw
After the Fall of New York '85
Blastfighter '85

Massacre in Dinosaur Valley
    '85

Agnes Soral
Killing Cars '85
One Wild Moment '78
Tchao Pantin '84

Alberto Sordi
The Great War '59
I Vitelloni '53
Those Magnificent Men in Their
    Flying Machines '65
Two Nights with Cleopatra '54
The White Sheik '52

Louise Sorel
Get Christie Love! '74
Mazes and Monsters '82
Plaza Suite '71
The President's Plane is
    Missing '71
When Every Day was the
    Fourth of July '78

Ted Sorel
Basket Case 2 '90
From Beyond '86

Linda Sorensen
Family Reunion '81
Joshua Then and Now '85
Kavik the Wolf Dog '84
Stone Cold Dead '80

Charo Soriano
Dracula's Great Love '72
The Garden of Delights '70
Orgy of the Vampires '73

Arleen Sorkin
From Here to Maternity '85
I Don't Buy Kisses Anymore '92
It's Pat '94

Mira Sorvino
Amongst Friends '93
Barcelona '94

Paul Sorvino
Age Isn't Everything '91
Almost Partners '87
Bloodbrothers '78
Brink's Job '78
Chiefs '83
Cruising '80
Cry Uncle '71
The Day of the Dolphin '73
Dick Tracy '90
A Fine Mess '86
Fury on Wheels '71
The Gambler '74
Goodfellas '90
I, the Jury '82
I Will, I Will for Now '76
Jailbait: Betrayed By Innocence
    '86
Lost and Found '79
Melanie '82
My Mother's Secret Life '84
Off the Wall '82
Oh, God! '77
Panic in Needle Park '75
Question of Honor '80
Reds '81
The Rocketeer '91
The Stuff '85
Tell Me Where It Hurts '74
That Championship Season '82
A Touch of Class '73
Turk 182! '85
Vasectomy: A Delicate Matter
    '86
Very Close Quarters '84

Ann Sothern
The Best Man '64
Brother Orchid '40
Crazy Mama '75
Hell-Ship Morgan '36
The Judge Steps Out '49
Kid Millions '34
The Killing Kind '73
Lady Be Good '41
Lady in a Cage '64
A Letter to Three Wives '49
Little Dragons '80
The Manitou '78
Mexican Spitfire/Smartest Girl
    in Town '40
Nancy Goes to Rio '50
Panama Hattie '42
The Whales of August '87
Words and Music '48

Fernando Soto
Boom in the Moon '46
El Hombre de la Furia '65
The Illusion Travels by
    Streetcar '53
Invasion of the Vampires '61

Hugo Soto
Man Facing Southeast '86
Times to Come '81

Talisa Soto
Hostage '92
License to Kill '89
The Mambo Kings '92
Prison Stories: Women on the
    Inside '91
Silhouette '91
Spike of Bensonhurst '88

David Soul
Appointment with Death '88
Dog Pound Shuffle '75
The FBI Murders '88
Grave Secrets: The Legacy of
    Hilltop Drive '92
Hanoi Hilton '87
Homeward Bound '80
In the Cold of the Night '89
The Key to Rebecca '85
Little Ladies of the Night '77
Magnum Force '73
The Manions of America '81
Rage '80
Salem's Lot '79
The Stick-Up '77
Through Naked Eyes '87
Tides of War '90
World War III '86

Renee Soutendijk
Cold Room '84
Eve of Destruction '90
Forced March '90
The 4th Man '79
Grave Secrets '89
Inside the Third Reich '82
Keeper of the City '92
Murderers Among Us: The
    Simon Wiesenthal Story '89
Out of Order '84
Second Victory '87
Spetters '80

Charles Southwood
Guns for Dollars '73
Sartana's Here...Trade Your
    Pistol for a Coffin '70

Ben Soutten
The Crimes of Stephen Hawke
    '36
The Mutiny of the Elsinore '39

Catherine Spaak
The Cat o' Nine Tails '71
Circle of Love '64
Counter Punch '71
The Easy Life '63
Empty Canvas '64
Honey '67
Hotel '67

Arthur Space
Canadian Mounties Vs. Atomic
    Invaders '53
Miss Grant Takes Richmond
    '49
Riot Squad '41
A Southern Yankee '48
Terror at Red Wolf Inn '72
The Vanishing Westerner '50

Sissy Spacek
Badlands '74
Carrie '76
Coal Miner's Daughter '80
Crimes of the Heart '86
Ginger in the Morning '73
The Girls of Huntington House
    '73
Hard Promises '92
Heart Beat '80
JFK '91
Katherine '75
The Long Walk Home '89
The Man with Two Brains '83
Marie '85
Missing '82
'night, Mother '86
Prime Cut '72
A Private Matter '92
Raggedy Man '81
The River '84
Violets Are Blue '86

Welcome to L.A. '77

Kevin Spacey
Consenting Adults '92
Dad '89
Glengarry Glen Ross '92
Henry & June '90
Iron Will '93
Long Day's Journey into Night
    '88
The Murder of Mary Phagan
    '87
The Ref '93
Rocket Gibraltar '88
Working Girl '88

David Spade
Coneheads '93
P.C.U. '94

James Spader
Baby Boom '87
Bad Influence '90
Dream Lover '93
Endless Love '81
Family Secrets '84
Jack's Back '87
Less Than Zero '87
Mannequin '87
The Music of Chance '93
The New Kids '85
Pretty in Pink '86
The Rachel Papers '89
sex, lies and videotape '89
Storyville '92
True Colors '91
Tuff Turf '85
Wall Street '87
White Palace '90
Wolf '94

Fay Spain
Al Capone '59
Dragstrip Girl '57
Flight to Fury '66
The Godfather, Part 2 '74
Hercules and the Captive
    Women '63

Timothy Spall
Crusoe '89
Dutch Girls '87
Gothic '87
Life is Sweet '91
The Sheltering Sky '90
White Hunter, Black Heart '90

Joe Spano
American Graffiti '73
Brotherhood of Justice '86
Brujo Luna
Cast the First Stone '89
Disaster at Silo 7 '88
The Dunera Boys '85
Fever '91
Hill Street Blues, Vol. 1: Hill
    Street Station '81
Northern Lights '79
Terminal Choice '85
Warlock Moon '73

Vincent Spano
Afterburn '92
Alive '93
Alphabet City '84
And God Created Woman '88
Baby It's You '82
The Black Stallion Returns '83
Blood Ties '87
City of Hope '91
Creator '85
The Double McGuffin '79
Good Morning, Babylon '87
High Frequency '88
Indian Summer '93
Maria's Lovers '84
Over the Edge '79
Rumble Fish '83
Senior Trip '81

Adrian Sparks
My Stepmother Is an Alien '88
Roanoak '86

Ned Sparks
The Bride Walks Out '36
Corsair '31
42nd Street '33
Going Hollywood '33
Gold Diggers of 1933 '33
Hawaii Calls '38
Kept Husbands '31
Lady for a Day '33
Marie Galante '34
One in a Million '36

Sparks ▶cont.

Sweet Adeline '35
Camilla Sparv
Dead Heat on a Merry-Go-Round '66
Downhill Racer '69
Survival Zone '84
Jeff Speakman
The Perfect Weapon '91
Street Knight '93
Carol Speed
Avenging Disco Godfather '76
The Big Bird Cage '72
Bummer '73
Mack '73
Savage! '73
Hermann Speelmanns
Baron Munchausen '43
F.P. 1 Doesn't Answer '33
Martin Speer
The Dark Ride '84
The Hills Have Eyes '77
Dona Speir
Do or Die '91
Fit to Kill '93
Guns '90
Hard Hunted '92
Hard Ticket to Hawaii '87
Picasso Trigger '89
Savage Beach '89
George Spell
All God's Children '80
A Dream for Christmas '73
Man & Boy '71
Georgina Spelvin
Honkytonk Nights '70s
I Spit on Your Corpse '74
Police Academy '84
Bruce Spence
...Almost '90
Mad Max: Beyond Thunderdome '85
Midnite Spares '85
Rikky and Pete '88
The Road Warrior '82
The Shrimp on the Barbie '90
Sweet Talker '91
Where the Green Ants Dream '84
Peter Spence
Crazy Moon '87
Unfinished Business '89
Bud Spencer
Ace High '68
Aladdin '86
All the Way, Boys '73
Beyond the Law '68
Boot Hill '69
Crime Busters '78
Flatfoot '78
Go for It '83
Miami Supercops '85
Odds and Evens '78
A Reason to Live, A Reason to Die '73
They Call Me Trinity '72
Today We Kill, Tomorrow We Die '71
Trinity is Still My Name '75
Douglas Spencer
River of No Return '54
Trouble Along the Way '53
John Spencer
Black Rain '89
Echoes '83
Presumed Innocent '90
Simple Justice '89
Volker Spengler
Chinese Roulette '86
Despair '78
The Stationmaster's Wife '77
Veronika Voss '82
Jeremy Spenser
Devil on Horseback '54
Escapade '55
Wendie Jo Sperber
Bachelor Party '84
Back to the Future '85
Back to the Future, Part 3 '90

First Time '82
I Wanna Hold Your Hand '78
Moving Violations '85
Stewardess School '86
Scott Spiegel
The Dead Next Door '89
Skinned Alive '89
David Spielberg
Alice '90
The Best Little Girl in the World '81
Force Five '75
The Henderson Monster '80
Policewoman Centerfold '83
Prime Time '80
Sergeant Matlovich vs. the U.S. Air Force '78
The Stranger '87
Riva Spier
Ghost Keeper '80
Syngenor '90
Jacques Spiesser
Baxter '90
Black and White in Color '76
La Truite '83
Grazia Maria Spina
Revolt of the Barbarians '64
Tiger of the Seven Seas '62
Joe Spinell
Big Score '83
Cops and Robbers '73
The Godfather 1902-1959: The Complete Epic '81
The Godfather, Part 2 '74
Hollywood Harry '86
The Last Fight '82
The Last Horror Film '82
Little Dragons '80
Maniac '80
Nighthawks '81
One Man Jury '78
Operation War Zone '89
The Pick-Up Artist '87
Rapid Fire '89
Star Crash '78
Walking the Edge '83
Winter Kills '79
Brent Spiner
Crazy from the Heart '91
Family Sins '87
Star Trek the Next Generation: Encounter at Farpoint '87
Victor Spinetti
Magical Mystery Tour '67
Return of the Pink Panther '74
Start the Revolution Without Me '70
G.D. Spradlin
And I Alone Survived '78
Apocalypse Now '79
Call to Glory '84
Canadian Bacon '94
Carolina Skeletons '92
The Formula '80
The Godfather 1902-1959: The Complete Epic '81
The Godfather, Part 2 '74
The Jayne Mansfield Story '80
The Lords of Discipline '83
North Dallas Forty '79
One on One '77
The Only Way Home '72
Tank '83
The War of the Roses '89
Wrong is Right '82
Zabriskie Point '70
Charlie Spradling
Angel of Destruction '94
Bad Channels '92
Puppet Master 2 '91
To Sleep with a Vampire '92
Rick Springfield
Dead Reckoning '89
Hard to Hold '84
Nick Knight '80s
Silent Motive '91
Pamela Springsteen
Dixie Lanes '88
Fast Times at Ridgemont High '82
The Gumshoe Kid '89
My Science Project '85
Reckless '84
Sleepaway Camp 2: Unhappy Campers '88

Sleepaway Camp 3: Teenage Wasteland '89
Ronald Squire
Action for Slander '38
Encore '52
Robert Stack
Airplane! '80
Big Trouble '86
Bullfighter & the Lady '50
Caddyshack 2 '88
Conquest of Cochise '53
The Corrupt Ones '67
Dangerous Curves '88
A Date with Judy '48
George Washington '84
Great Day in the Morning '56
Is Paris Burning? '68
Joe Versus the Volcano '90
John Paul Jones '59
The Last Voyage '60
Mr. Music '50
The Mortal Storm '40
Most Wanted '76
Murder on Flight 502 '75
My Outlaw Brother '51
1941 '79
Plain Clothes '88
The Return of Eliot Ness '91
Sabre Jet '53
Scarface Mob '62
A Strange and Deadly Occurence '74
Strike Force '81
To Be or Not to Be '42
Uncommon Valor '83
Written on the Wind '56
James Stacy
The Dark Side of Love '79
Double Exposure '82
Matters of the Heart '90
Paper Man '71
Posse '75
Something Wicked This Way Comes '83
A Swingin' Summer '65
Lewis J. Stadlen
Between the Lines '77
Savages '72
Windy City '84
Ann Stafford
Keep My Grave Open '80
Poor White Trash 2 '75
Frederick Stafford
The Battle of El Alamein '68
Topaz '69
Jim Stafford
E.S.P. '83
Kid Colter '85
Jon Stafford
Crossing the Line '90
Spitfire '42
Richard Stahl
Private School '83
The Student Nurses '70
Brent Stait
Born to Run '93
Call of the Wild '93
James Staley
American Dreamer '84
Protocol '84
Robot Wars '93
Frank Stallone
Barfly '87
Death Blow '87
Death Feud '89
Easy Kill '89
Fear '88
Heart of Midnight '89
Hudson Hawk '91
Lethal Games '90
Masque of the Red Death '90
Midnight Cop '88
Order of the Eagle '89
Outlaw Force '87
The Pink Chiquitas '86
Prime Suspect '88
Take Two '87
Ten Little Indians '89
Terror in Beverly Hills '90
Sylvester Stallone
Cannonball '76
Cliffhanger '93
Cobra '86
Death Race 2000 '75

Demolition Man '93
Farewell, My Lovely '75
First Blood '82
F.I.S.T. '78
The Italian Stallion '73
Lock Up '89
The Lords of Flatbush '74
Nighthawks '81
Oscar '91
Over the Top '86
Paradise Alley '78
Prisoner of Second Avenue '74
Rambo: First Blood, Part 2 '85
Rambo 3 '88
Rebel '73
Rhinestone '84
Rocky '76
Rocky 2 '79
Rocky 3 '82
Rocky 4 '85
Rocky 5 '90
Stop! or My Mom Will Shoot '92
Tango and Cash '89
Victory '81
Anne Stallybrass
Diana: Her True Story '93
Six Wives of Henry VIII '70s
John Stamos
Born to Ride '91
The Disappearance of Christina '93
Never Too Young to Die '86
Terence Stamp
Alamut Ambush '86
Alien Nation '88
Billy Budd '62
Blue '68
Cold War Killers '86
The Collector '65
Deadly Recruits '86
Divine Nymph '71
Far from the Madding Crowd '67
Genuine Risk '89
The Hit '85
Insanity '83
Iron Cowboy '68
Legal Eagles '86
Link '86
Meetings with Remarkable Men '79
The Real McCoy '93
The Sicilian '87
Spirits of the Dead '68
Superman: The Movie '78
Superman 2 '80
Teorema '68
The Thief of Baghdad '78
Together? '79
Vatican Conspiracy '81
Wall Street '87
Young Guns '88
Wadeck Stanczak
Rendez-vous '85
Scene of the Crime '87
Lionel Stander
Beyond the Law '68
Black Bird '75
Black Hand '76
Boot Hill '69
Call Northside 777 '48
The Cassandra Crossing '76
Cookie '89
Cul de Sac '66
Dandy in Aspic '68
Guadalcanal Diary '43
The Heist '88
I Live My Life '35
The Loved One '65
Mr. Deeds Goes to Town '36
New York, New York '77
1931: Once Upon a Time in New York '72
Once Upon a Time in the West '68
Promise Her Anything '66
Pulp '72
St. Benny the Dip '51
The Sensual Man '74
The Sin of Harold Diddlebock '47
Spectre of the Rose '46
The Squeeze '80
A Star is Born '37
Sting of the West '76
Till the Clouds Roll By/A Star Is Born '46
Treasure Island '72

Unfaithfully Yours '48
Wicked Stepmother '89
Guy Standing
Bulldog Drummond Comes Back '37
Bulldog Drummond Escapes '37
I'd Give My Life '36
The Lives of a Bengal Lancer '35
John Standing
Chaplin '92
The Endless Game '89
The Legacy '79
Nightflyers '87
To Catch a King '84
Walk, Don't Run '66
Arnold Stang
Dennis the Menace '93
Ghost Dad '90
Hercules in New York '70
The Man with the Golden Arm '55
Seven Days' Leave '42
The Wonderful World of the Brothers Grimm '62
Florence Stanley
A Perfect Little Murder '90
Trouble Bound '92
Forrest Stanley
Bare Knees '28
Outlaws of the Desert '41
Helene Stanley
Bandit King of Texas '49
The Snows of Kilimanjaro '52
Kim Stanley
Frances '82
The Goddess '58
The Right Stuff '83
Seance on a Wet Afternoon '64
Louise Stanley
Danger on the Air '38
Gun Lords of Stirrup Basin '37
Gun Packer '38
Pinto Canyon '40
Riders of the Rockies '37
Sky Bandits '40
Thunder in the Desert '38
Paul Stanley
I Heard the Owl Call My Name '73
KISS Meets the Phantom of the Park '78
Rebecca Stanley
Body Double '84
Eyes of Fire '84
Don Stannard
Dick Barton, Special Agent '48
Dick Barton Strikes Back '48
The Temptress '49
Claire Stansfield
Best of the Best 2 '93
The Swordsman '92
Harry Dean Stanton
The Adventures of Huckleberry Finn '60
Alien '79
The Black Marble '79
Christine '84
Cockfighter '74
Cool Hand Luke '67
Death Watch '80
Dillinger '73
Dream a Little Dream '89
Escape from New York '81
Farewell, My Lovely '75
Flatbed Annie and Sweetiepie: Lady Truckers '79
Fool for Love '86
The Fourth War '90
The Godfather 1902-1959: The Complete Epic '81
The Godfather, Part 2 '74
The Hostage '67
Hostages '93
Hotel Room '93
Kelly's Heroes '70
The Last Temptation of Christ '88
Man Trouble '92
Missouri Breaks '76
Mr. North '88
92 in the Shade '76
Oldest Living Graduate '82

One from the Heart '82
One Magic Christmas '85
Paris, Texas '83
Pat Garrett & Billy the Kid '73
Payoff '91
Pretty in Pink '86
Private Benjamin '80
Proud Rebel '58
Rafferty & the Gold Dust Twins '75
Rancho Deluxe '75
Rebel Rousers '69
Red Dawn '84
Repo Man '83
Ride in the Whirlwind '67
Rip van Winkle '85
The Rose '79
Slamdance '87
Stars and Bars '88
Straight Time '78
Twister '89
Uforia '81
Where the Lilies Bloom '74
Wild at Heart '90
Wise Blood '79
Young Doctors in Love '82
Zandy's Bride '74

John Stanton
Bellamy '80
Day of the Panther '88
Dusty '85
Great Expectations: The Untold Story '87
The Naked Country '85
Rent-A-Cop '88
Tai-Pan '86

Paul Stanton
Stanley and Livingstone '39
Whistling in the Dark '41

Robert Stanton
Bob Roberts '92
Dennis the Menace '93

Barbara Stanwyck
Annie Oakley '35
Baby Face '33
Ball of Fire '41
Big Valley '68
The Bitter Tea of General Yen '33
Blowing Wild '54
The Bride Walks Out '36
Cattle Queen of Montana '54
Christmas in Connecticut '45
Clash by Night '52
Crime of Passion '57
Double Indemnity '44
East Side, West Side '49
Escape to Burma '55
Executive Suite '54
Golden Boy '39
Hollywood Bloopers '50s
Hollywood Canteen '44
Illicit '31
Ladies They Talk About '33
The Lady Eve '41
Lady of Burlesque '43
Mad Miss Manton '38
Maverick Queen '55
Meet John Doe '41
Night Nurse '31
The Night Walker '64
The Purchase Price '32
Roustabout '64
Sorry, Wrong Number '48
Stella Dallas '37
The Strange Love of Martha Ivers '46
The Thorn Birds '83
To Please a Lady '50
The Two Mrs. Carrolls '47
The Violent Men '55
Walk on the Wild Side '62

Huub Stapel
Amsterdamned '88
The Attic: The Hiding of Anne Frank '87
The Lift '85

Jean Stapleton
Bells are Ringing '60
The Buddy System '83
Cinderella '84
Cold Turkey '71
Damn Yankees '58
Eleanor: First Lady of the World '82
Grown Ups '86
Jack & the Beanstalk '83

Klute '71
Up the Down Staircase '67

Maureen Stapleton
Airport '70
Bye, Bye, Birdie '63
Cocoon '85
Cocoon: The Return '88
Doin' Time on Planet Earth '88
Family Secrets '84
The Fan '81
The Fugitive Kind '60
The Gathering '77
The Gathering: Part 2 '79
Heartburn '86
Interiors '78
Johnny Dangerously '84
Little Gloria...Happy at Last '84
Lonelyhearts '58
Lost and Found '79
Made in Heaven '87
Miss Rose White '92
The Money Pit '86
Nuts '87
On the Right Track '81
Passed Away '92
Plaza Suite '71
Queen of the Stardust Ballroom '75
Reds '81
The Runner Stumbles '79
Sweet Lorraine '87
Tell Me Where It Hurts '74

Don Stark
Bloodfist 5: Human Target '93
Evilspeak '82

Graham Stark
Adventures Beyond Belief '87
Blind Date '87

Jonathan Stark
Fright Night '85
House 2: The Second Story '87
Project X '87

Koo Stark
Electric Dreams '84
Emily '77

Anthony Starke
Repossessed '90
Return of the Killer Tomatoes '88

Pauline Starke
Dante's Inferno '24
Little Church Around the Corner '23
Until They Get Me '18

Mike Starr
Billy Bathgate '91
The Bodyguard '92
Goodfellas '90
Mad Dog and Glory '93
Mardi Gras for the Devil '93
Nasty Hero '89

Ringo Starr
Born to Boogie '72
Caveman '81
The Compleat Beatles '82
Give My Regards to Broad Street '84
A Hard Day's Night '64
Help! '65
Let It Be '70
Lisztomania '75
The Magic Christian '69
Magical Mystery Tour '67
Princess Daisy '83
Sextette '78
That'll Be the Day '73
200 Motels '71

Charles Starrett
Dangerous Appointment '34
Green Eyes '34
Jungle Bride '33
Make a Million '35
The Mask of Fu Manchu '32
Mr. Skitch '33
The Return of Casey Jones '34
A Shot in the Dark '35
The Silver Streak '34
Sons of Steel '35

Jack Starrett
Angels from Hell '68
Brothers in Arms '88
Death Chase '87
First Blood '82
Mr. Horn '79
Nightwish '89

Imelda Staunton
Antonia and Jane '91
Much Ado About Nothing '93
Peter's Friends '92

Mary Stavin
House '85
Open House '86
The Opponent '89

Eddie Stazak
Day of the Panther '88
Fists of Blood '87

Alison Steadman
Abigail's Party '77
The Adventures of Baron Munchausen '89
Blame It on the Bellboy '92
Champions '84
Clockwise '86
Coming Through '90
Kipperbang '82
Life is Sweet '91
The Misadventures of Mr. Wilt '90
Nuts in May '76
Shirley Valentine '89
Tartuffe '90

John Steadman
The Hills Have Eyes '77
Poco '77

Red Steagall
Benji the Hunted '87
Dark Before Dawn '89

Michael Stearns
Chain Gang Women '72
Chrome and Hot Leather '71

Myrtle Stedman
In the Days of the Thundering Herd & the Law & the Outlaw '14
The Mad Whirl '25
Sex '20

Ted Steedman
Bill & Ted's Excellent Adventure '89

Alan Steel
The Fury of Hercules '61
Hercules Against the Moon Men '64
Samson '61
Samson and His Mighty Challenge '64

Amy Steel
April Fool's Day '86
Friday the 13th, Part 2 '81
Walk Like a Man '87

Anthony Steel
48 Hours to Live '60
Harry Black and the Tiger '58
I'm the Girl He Wants to Kill '74
Malta Story '53
Massacre in Rome '73
The Master of Ballantrae '53
Perfect Crime '90
The Story of O '75
Tiger of the Seven Seas '62
Wooden Horse '50

Barbara Steele
An Angel for Satan '66
Black Sunday '60
Caged Heat '74
Castle of Blood '64
The Crimson Cult '68
8 1/2 '63
The Ghost '63
The Horrible Dr. Hichcock '62
La Dolce Vita '60
The Monocle '64
Nightmare Castle '65
Piranha '78
The Pit and the Pendulum '61
Pretty Baby '78
The She-Beast '65
Silent Scream '80
Terror Creatures from the Grave '66
They Came from Within '75
The Winds of War '83

Bob Steele
Alias John Law '35
Ambush Trail '46
Arizona Gunfighter '37
Arizona Whirlwind '44
Atomic Submarine '59
Battling Outlaws '40s

Big Calibre '35
The Big Sleep '46
Billy the Kid in Texas '40
Border Phantom '37
Brand of Hate '34
Brand of the Outlaws '36
Breed of the Border '33
Cavalry '36
City for Conquest '40
Death Valley Rangers '44
Demon for Trouble '34
Doomed at Sundown '37
Durango Valley Raiders '38
El Diablo Rides '39
The Enforcer '51
Feud Maker '38
Fighting Champ '33
The Gallant Fool '33
Galloping Romeo '33
Giant from the Unknown '58
Gun Lords of Stirrup Basin '37
The Gun Ranger '34
Hidden Valley '32
Kid Courageous '35
Kid Ranger '36
Last of the Warrens '36
The Law Rides '36
Lightning Bill Crandall '37
Man from Hell's Edges '32
Marked Trails '44
Mesquite Buckaroo '39
Mystery Squadron '33
Near the Rainbow's End '30
No Man's Range '35
Northwest Trail '46
Of Mice and Men '39
Oklahoma Cyclone '30
Outlaw Trail '44
Pardners '56
Paroled to Die '38
Pinto Canyon '40
Pork Chop Hill '59
Powdersmoke Range '35
The Red Rope '37
Rider of the Law '35
Riders of the Desert '32
Ridin' the Lone Trail '37
Rio Bravo '59
Rio Grande Raiders '46
Smokey Smith '36
Sonora Stagecoach '44
South of Santa Fe '32
Sundown Saunders '36
Sunrise Trail '31
Texas Buddies '32
Texas Trouble '30s
Thunder in the Desert '38
Tombstone Terror '34
Trail of Terror '35
Trails West '40s
Trigger Men '41
Twilight on the Rio Grande '41
Western Double Feature 6: Rogers & Trigger '50
Western Justice '35
Wildfire '45
Young Blood '33

Jadrien Steele
The Mosquito Coast '86
The Secret Garden '87

Karen Steele
Bail Out at 43,000 '57
Marty '55
Ride Lonesome '59
The Rise and Fall of Legs Diamond '60
Trap on Cougar Mountain '72

Marjorie Steele
Face to Face '52
Tough Assignment '49

Pippa Steele
Lust for a Vampire '71
The Vampire Lovers '70

Tommy Steele
Finian's Rainbow '68
G-Men Never Forget '48
Half a Sixpence '67
The Happiest Millionaire '67

Jessica Steen
John and the Missus '87
Sing '89
Still Life '90

Mary Steenburgen
The Attic: The Hiding of Anne Frank '87
Back to the Future, Part 3 '90
The Butcher's Wife '91

Clifford '92
Cross Creek '83
Dead of Winter '87
End of the Line '88
Goin' South '78
It Runs In the Family '94
Little Red Riding Hood '83
Melvin and Howard '80
A Midsummer Night's Sex Comedy '82
Miss Firecracker '89
One Magic Christmas '85
Parenthood '89
Philadelphia '93
Ragtime '81
Romantic Comedy '83
Time After Time '79
The Whales of August '87
What's Eating Gilbert Grape '93

Anthony Steffen
An Angel for Satan '66
Escape from Hell '89
Garringo '69
The Gentleman Killer '78
The Last Tomahawk '65
The Night Evelyn Came Out of the Grave '71
On the Edge '82
Savage Island '85
Stranger in Paso Bravo '73

Bernice Stegers
City of Women '81
Frozen Terror '80
The Girl '86
Xtro '83

Rod Steiger
Across the Bridge '57
Al Capone '59
American Gothic '88
The Amityville Horror '79
Back from Eternity '56
The Ballad of the Sad Cafe '91
The Big Knife '55
Breakthrough '78
Catch the Heat '87
The Court Martial of Billy Mitchell '55
Dirty Hands '76
Doctor Zhivago '65
F.I.S.T. '78
A Fistful of Dynamite '72
Glory Boys '84
Guilty as Charged '92
The Harder They Fall '56
Hennessy '75
The Illustrated Man '69
In the Heat of the Night '67
The January Man '89
Jubal '56
The Kindred '87
Klondike Fever '79
The Last Contract '86
Last Four Days '77
Lion of the Desert '81
The Longest Day '62
Love and Bullets '79
The Loved One '65
Lucky Luciano '74
The Mark '61
Marty '53
The Naked Face '84
The Neighbor '93
No Way to Treat a Lady '68
Oklahoma! '55
On the Waterfront '54
Passion in Paradise '89
The Pawnbroker '65
Portrait of a Hitman '77
Run of the Arrow '56
Seven Thieves '60
Sinatra '92
Sword of Gideon '86
That Summer of White Roses '90
Time of Indifference '64
Unholy Wife '57
Waterloo '71
Wolf Lake '79

Margaret Sophie Stein
Enemies, a Love Story '89
Sarah, Plain and Tall '91
Skylark '93

David Steinberg
The End '78
The Marx Brothers in a Nutshell '90

Steinberg ▶cont.

Something Short of Paradise '79

John Steiner
Ark of the Sun God '82
Beyond the Door 2 '79
Blood and Guns '79
Dagger Eyes '80s
Hunters of the Golden Cobra '82
The Last Hunter '80
The Lone Runner '88
Massacre in Rome '73
Operation 'Nam '85
Sinbad of the Seven Seas '89
Yor, the Hunter from the Future '83

Sherry Steiner
Asylum of Satan '72
Heaven Help Us '85
Three on a Meathook '72

Robert J. Steinmiller, Jr.
Bingo '91
Jack the Bear '93
The Ref '93

William Steis
Demon of Paradise '87
Equalizer 2000 '86
Eye of the Eagle '87
Raiders of the Sun '92

Anna Sten
The Girl with the Hat Box '27
So Ends Our Night '41
Soldier of Fortune '55

Yutte Stensgaard
Alien Women '69
The Love Factor '69
Lust for a Vampire '71
Scream and Scream Again '70

Karel Stepanek
Counterblast '48
Never Let Me Go '53
Second Best Secret Agent in the Whole Wide World '65
Sink the Bismarck '60

Daniel Stephen
2020 Texas Gladiators '85
Warbus '85

Susan Stephen
Heat Wave '54
A Stolen Face '52
White Huntress '57

Harvey Stephens
Abe Lincoln in Illinois '40
Evelyn Prentice '34
Forlorn River '37
The Lady is Willing '42
Let 'Em Have It '35
Oklahoma Kid '39

James Stephens
First Monday in October '81
Mysterious Two '82
Pancho Barnes '88

Robert Stephens
Afraid of the Dark '92
American Roulette '88
The Asphyx '72
The Bonfire of the Vanities '90
Chaplin '92
The Children '90
Empire of the Sun '87
Fortunes of War '87
Henry V '89
High Season '88
Luther '74
Morgan! '66
The Prime of Miss Jean Brodie '69
The Private Life of Sherlock Holmes '70
Searching for Bobby Fischer '93
A Taste of Honey '61
Travels with My Aunt '72
Wonderland '88

Henry Stephenson
The Animal Kingdom '32
A Bill of Divorcement '32
Challenge to Lassie '49
The Charge of the Light Brigade '36
Conquest '37
Down Argentine Way '40
Heartbeat '46
It's a Date '40
Lady from Louisiana '42
Marie Antoinette '38
Mr. Lucky '43
Mutiny on the Bounty '35
The Old Maid '39
Oliver Twist '48
The Prince and the Pauper '37
Red Headed Woman '32
Tarzan Finds a Son '39
Tomorrow at Seven '33

James Stephenson
Beau Geste '39
Boy Meets Girl '38
The Letter '40
The Sea Hawk '40

Mark Kinsey Stephenson
The Unnamable '88
The Unnamable 2: The Statement of Randolph Carter '92

Michael Stephenson
Beyond Darkness '92
Troll 2 '92

Pamela Stephenson
Bloodbath at the House of Death '85
The Comeback '77
Finders Keepers '84
Ghosts Can Do It '90
History of the World: Part 1 '81
Les Patterson Saves the World '90
Scandalous '84

Ford Sterling
Desperate Scoundrel/The Pride of Pikeville '22
He Who Gets Slapped '24
Headline Woman '35
Mack Sennett Comedies: Vol. 1 '21
Yankee Doodle in Berlin '19

Jan Sterling
The Dark Side of Love '79
First Monday in October '81
The Harder They Fall '56
High School Confidential '58
The Incident '67
Pony Express '53
Split Second '53
Union Station '50

Robert Sterling
A Global Affair '63
Johnny Eager '42
Return to Peyton Place '61
Somewhere I'll Find You '42
Two-Faced Woman '41
Voyage to the Bottom of the Sea '61

Tisha Sterling
Betrayal '74
Coogan's Bluff '68
Defiant '70
Killer Inside Me '76
Powder Keg '70
Snatched '72

Daniel Stern
Blue Thunder '83
Born in East L.A. '87
The Boss' Wife '86
Breaking Away '79
C.H.U.D. '84
City Slickers '91
City Slickers 2: The Legend of Curly's Gold '94
Coupe de Ville '90
The Court Martial of Jackie Robinson '90
Diner '82
D.O.A. '88
Frankenweenie '84
Friends, Lovers & Lunatics '89
Get Crazy '83
Hannah and Her Sisters '86
Home Alone '90
Home Alone 2: Lost in New York '92
I'm Dancing as Fast as I Can '82
It's My Turn '80

Key Exchange '85
Leviathan '89
Little Monsters '89
The Milagro Beanfield War '88
My Blue Heaven '90
One Trick Pony '80
Rookie of the Year '93
Stardust Memories '80
Starting Over '79
Weekend War '88

Tom Stern
Angels from Hell '68
The Devil's Brigade '68
Hell's Angels '69 '69

Wes Stern
The First Time '69
Three in the Cellar '70

Frances Sternhagen
Bright Lights, Big City '88
Communion '89
The Dining Room '86
Doc Hollywood '91
Independence Day '83
The Man That Corrupted Hadleyburg '80
Misery '90
Mother & Daughter: A Loving War '80
Outland '81
Prototype '83
Raising Cain '92
Romantic Comedy '83
See You in the Morning '89
Sibling Rivalry '90
Starting Over '79
Stephen King's Golden Years '91

Robyn Stevan
Bye Bye Blues '89
Stepping Out '91

Jean-Francois Stevenin
Olivier, Olivier '92
Small Change '76

Andrew Stevens
The Bastard '78
Body Chemistry 3: Point of Seduction '93
The Boys in Company C '77
Counterforce '87
Day of the Animals '77
Deadly Innocence '88
Deadly Rivals '92
Death Hunt '81
Double Threat '92
Down the Drain '89
Eyewitness to Murder '93
Fine Gold
Forbidden Love '82
The Fury '78
Las Vegas Lady '76
Massacre at Central High '76
Miracle on Ice '81
Munchie '92
Night Eyes '90
Night Eyes 2 '91
Night Eyes 3 '93
The Ranch '88
The Rebels '79
Red Blooded American Girl '90
Scared Stiff '87
Scorned '93
Secrets '77
The Seduction '82
Ten to Midnight '83
The Terror Within '88
The Terror Within 2 '91
Tusks '89

Brinke Stevens
Bad Girls from Mars '90
Grandma's House '88
Haunting Fear '91
Nightmare Sisters '87
Slave Girls from Beyond Infinity '87
The Slumber Party Massacre '82
Sorority Babes in the Slimeball Bowl-A-Rama '87
Spirits '90
Teenage Exorcist '93
Transylvania Twist '89
Warlords '88

Charles Stevens
Border Bandits '46
Buffalo Bill Rides Again '47

The Three Musketeers '21

Connie Stevens
Back to the Beach '87
The Grissom Gang '71
The Littlest Angel '69
Love's Savage Fury '79
Palm Springs Weekend '63
Parrish '61
Playmates '72
Scorchy '76
Scruples '80
Side Show '84
Tapeheads '89

Craig Stevens
Abbott and Costello Meet Dr. Jekyll and Mr. Hyde '52
Blues Busters '50
The Deadly Mantis '57
Dive Bomber '41
Drums in the Deep South '51
The French Line '54
Humoresque '46
La Truite '83
The Man I Love '46
Phone Call from a Stranger '52
Secrets of Three Hungry Wives '78
Since You Went Away '44
S.O.B. '81

Fisher Stevens
The Flamingo Kid '84
The Marrying Man '91
My Science Project '85
Mystery Date '91
Only You '94
Reversal of Fortune '90
Short Circuit '86
Short Circuit 2 '88
Super Mario Bros. '93

Inger Stevens
The Buccaneer '58
A Dream of Kings '69
Firecreek '68
Five Card Stud '68
A Guide for the Married Man '67
Hang 'Em High '67
Madigan '68
Savage Run '70

K.T. Stevens
Jungle Hell '55
Missile to the Moon '59
Port of New York '49
They're Playing with Fire '84

Mark Stevens
Cry Vengeance '54
Dark Corner '46
Frozen Alive '64
Mutiny '52
Objective, Burma! '45
The Snake Pit '48
The Street with No Name '48
Torpedo Alley '53

Morgan Stevens
Survival Zone '84
Up River '79

Onslow Stevens
Angel on My Shoulder '46
The Creeper '48
Fangs of the Wild '54
Flight from Glory '37
Hands Across the Border '43
House of Dracula '45
I Can't Escape '34
A Lion is in the Streets '53
The Monster and the Girl '41
One Too Many '51
Seven Miles from Alcatraz/ Flight from Glory '43
Them! '54
The Three Musketeers '35
Tribute to a Bad Man '56
Yellow Dust '36

Paul Stevens
Exodus '60
Get Christie Love! '74
Hercules and the Princess of Troy '65
The Mask '61

Rise Stevens
The Chocolate Soldier '41
Going My Way '44

Stella Stevens
Adventures Beyond Belief '87
The Amazons '84

Arnold '73
Ballad of Cable Hogue '70
Chained Heat '83
Cleopatra Jones & the Casino of Gold '75
The Courtship of Eddie's Father '62
Cruise into Terror '78
Down the Drain '89
Exiled in America '90
Express to Terror '79
Eye of the Stranger '93
Girls! Girls! Girls! '62
Las Vegas Lady '76
Last Call '90
Li'l Abner '59
The Longshot '86
Make Me an Offer '80
The Manitou '78
Molly and Gina '94
Mom '89
Monster in the Closet '86
The Nutty Professor '63
Power, Passion & Murder '83
Slaughter '72
The Terror Within 2 '91
A Town Called Hell '72
Twirl '81
Wacko '83
Where Angels Go, Trouble Follows '68

Warren Stevens
Forbidden Planet '56
Man or Gun '58
Shark River '53

Cynthia Stevenson
The Player '92
Watch It '93

Juliet Stevenson
Drowning by Numbers '87
The Trial '93
Truly, Madly, Deeply '91

McLean Stevenson
The Cat from Outer Space '78
M*A*S*H: The Collector's Edition '72
Win, Place, or Steal '72

Parker Stevenson
Are You Lonesome Tonight '92
Lifeguard '75
North and South Book 2 '86
Official Denial '93
Our Time '74
A Separate Peace '73
Shooting Stars '85
Stitches '85
Stroker Ace '83

Robert Stevenson
Fangs of the Wild '54
One of Our Dinosaurs Is Missing '75

Venetia Stevenson
Darby's Rangers '58
Horror Hotel '60

Joe Stewardson
City of Blood '88
Flatfoot '78
Follow That Rainbow '66

Alexandra Stewart
The Agency '81
Because of the Cats '74
Day for Night '73
The Destructors '74
Exodus '60
In Praise of Older Women '78
Kemek '88
Last Chase '81
Zeppelin '71

Athole Stewart
Accused '36
The Speckled Band '31

Byron Stewart
Grambling's White Tiger '81
How U Like Me Now? '92
The White Shadow, Vol. 1 '78

Catherine Mary Stewart
The Apple '80
Cafe Romeo '91
Dudes '87
The Last Starfighter '84
Mischief '85
Murder by the Book '87
Night of the Comet '84

Nightflyers '87
Nighthawks '81
Passion in Paradise '89
Perfect Harmony '91
Psychic '91
Samurai Cowboy '93
Scenes from the Goldmine '87
The Sea Wolf '93
Sins '85
Weekend at Bernie's '89
World Gone Wild '88

Charlotte Stewart
Eraserhead '78
Tremors '89

Don Stewart
The Doomsday Flight '66
Lost '83

Elaine Stewart
Riders of the Timberline '41
The Rise and Fall of Legs
    Diamond '60

Eleanor Stewart
Arizona Days '37
Flaming Lead '39
The Gun Ranger '34
Headin' for the Rio Grande '36
Mystery Man '44
The Rangers Step In '37
Where Trails Divide '37

Evelyn Stewart
Adios Gringo '65
Blood for a Silver Dollar '66
Django Shoots First '74
Murder Mansion '70
The Psychic '78
The Scorpion's Tail '71

Frank Stewart
Cemetery High '89
Galactic Gigolo '87
Psychos in Love '87
Sensations '87
Sexpot '88

James Stewart
After the Thin Man '36
Airport '77 '77
Anatomy of a Murder '59
Bandolero! '68
Bell, Book and Candle '58
Bend of the River '52
The Big Sleep '78
Born to Dance '36
Broken Arrow '50
Call Northside 777 '48
The Cheyenne Social Club '70
Dear Brigitte '65
Destry Rides Again '39
Far Country '55
The FBI Story '59
Firecreek '68
The Flight of the Phoenix '65
The Glenn Miller Story '54
The Gorgeous Hussy '36
The Greatest Show on Earth
    '52
Green Horizon '83
Harvey '50
Hollywood Bloopers '50s
How the West was Won '63
It's a Wonderful Life '46
The Jackpot '50
Made for Each Other '39
Magic of Lassie '78
Magic Town '47
Malaya '49
The Man from Laramie '55
The Man Who Knew Too Much
    '56
The Man Who Shot Liberty
    Valance '62
Mr. Hobbs Takes a Vacation
    '62
Mr. Smith Goes to Washington
    '39
The Mortal Storm '40
The Mountain Road '60
The Naked Spur '53
Navy Blue and Gold '37
North and South Book 2 '86
Of Human Hearts '38
The Philadelphia Story '40
Pot O' Gold '41
The Rare Breed '66
Rear Window '54
Right of Way '84
Rope '48
Rose Marie '36
Shenandoah '65

The Shootist '76
The Shop Around the Corner
    '40
Shopworn Angel '38
Spirit of St. Louis '57
Strategic Air Command '55
The Stratton Story '49
Thunder Bay '53
Two Rode Together '61
Vertigo '58
Vivacious Lady '38
Wife Versus Secretary '36
Winchester '73 '50
You Can't Take It with You '38
Ziegfeld Girl '41

John Stewart
Boots Malone '52
Last of the Comanches '52

Melvin Stewart
Scorpio '73
A Session with the Committee
    '69

Patrick Stewart
Code Name: Emerald '85
Detonator '93
The Doctor and the Devils '85
Excalibur '81
Gunmen '93
Hedda '75
L.A. Story '91
Lady Jane '85
Lifeforce '85
Star Trek the Next Generation:
    Encounter at Farpoint '87

Paul Stewart
Bite the Bullet '75
Citizen Kane '41
The Cobweb '55
Easy Living '49
How to Commit Marriage '69
The Joe Louis Story '53
King Creole '58
Kiss Me Deadly '55
Mr. Lucky '43
Murph the Surf '75
Opening Night '77
Seduced '85
The Tempest '82
Twelve O'Clock High '49
Walk Softly, Stranger '50

Peggy Stewart
The Black Lash '52
The Fighting Redhead '50
The Phantom Rider '46
Rough Riders of Cheyenne '45
Son of Zorro '47
Stagecoach to Denver '46
The Vampire's Ghost '45
Vigilantes of Boom Town '46

Richard Stewart
Terror Ship '54
Watch Me When I Kill '81

Roy Stewart
Live and Let Die '73
Sparrows '26
With Kit Carson Over the Great
    Divide '25

Sophie Stewart
Devil Girl from Mars '54
Murder in the Old Red Barn '36

Trish Stewart
Breaking Up Is Hard to Do '79
Wild Times '79

Phyllis Stickney
The Inkwell '94
Talkin' Dirty After Dark '91
What's Love Got to Do With It?
    '93

David Ogden Stiers
The Accidental Tourist '88
Another Woman '88
The Bad Seed '85
Better Off Dead '85
Breaking Up Is Hard to Do '79
Creator '85
Damien: The Leper Priest '80
Day One '89
Doc Hollywood '91
Final Notice '89
The First Olympics: Athens
    1896 '84
Harry's War '84
The Innocents Abroad '84
Iron Will '93
J. Edgar Hoover '87

The Kissing Place '90
The Last of His Tribe '92
The Man with One Red Shoe
    '85
M*A*S*H: Goodbye, Farewell &
    Amen '83
North and South Book 1 '85
Oh, God! '77
Oldest Living Graduate '82
Perry Mason: The Case of the
    Lost Love '87
Sergeant Matlovich vs. the U.S.
    Air Force '78

Hugo Stiglitz
City of the Walking Dead '83
Counterforce '87
Fantastic Balloon Voyage '80s
Night of a Thousand Cats '72
Robinson Crusoe & the Tiger
    '72

Robin Stille
American Ninja 4: The
    Annihilation '91
The Slumber Party Massacre
    '82

Ben Stiller
Elvis Stories '89
Empire of the Sun '87
Fresh Horses '88
Next of Kin '89
Reality Bites '94
Stella '89

Jerry Stiller
Hairspray '88
Hot Pursuit '87
Little Vegas '90
The McGuffin '85
Nadine '87
Nasty Habits '77
The Pickle '93
The Ritz '76
Seize the Day '86
The Taking of Pelham One Two
    Three '74
That's Adequate '90
Those Lips, Those Eyes '80
Women & Men: In Love There
    Are No Rules '91

Sting
The Adventures of Baron
    Munchausen '89
The Bride '85
Brimstone & Treacle '82
Dune '84
Julia and Julia '87
Plenty '85
Quadrophenia '79
The Secret Policeman's Other
    Ball '82
Stormy Monday '88

Linda Stirling
Cyclotrode "X" '46
D-Day on Mars '45
Jesse James Rides Again '47
Manhunt of Mystery Island '45
Perils of the Darkest Jungle '44
The Purple Monster Strikes '45
Rio Grande Raiders '46
The Topeka Terror '45
Zorro's Black Whip '44

Barbara Stock
Long Time Gone '86
Verne Miller '88

Nigel Stock
Brighton Rock '47
The Lion in Winter '68
The Silent Enemy '58

Amy Stock-Poynton
Bill & Ted's Bogus Journey '91
Bill & Ted's Excellent
    Adventure '89

Carl Stockade
The Americano '17
Condemned to Live '35

Carl Stockdale
The Crimson Trail '35
Get That Girl '32
The Greatest Question '19

Dean Stockwell
Alsino and the Condor '82
Anchors Aweigh '45
Backtrack '89
Banzai Runner '86
Beverly Hills Cop 2 '87
Blue Iguana '88

Blue Velvet '86
Bonanza: The Return '93
The Boy with the Green Hair
    '48
Buying Time '89
Dune '84
The Dunwich Horror '70
Gardens of Stone '87
Gentleman's Agreement '47
Kenny Rogers as the Gambler,
    Part 3: The Legend
    Continues '87
Kim '50
Legend of Billie Jean '85
Limit Up '89
Loners '72
Long Day's Journey into Night
    '62
Married to the Mob '88
One Away '80
Palais Royale '88
Paper Man '71
Paris, Texas '83
The Player '92
Psych-Out '68
The Secret Garden '49
Shame '92
She Came to the Valley '77
Smokescreen '90
Son of the Morning Star '91
Song of the Thin Man '47
Stars in My Crown '50
Stickfighter '89
The Time Guardian '87
To Kill a Stranger '70s
To Live & Die in L.A. '85
Tracks '76
Tucker: The Man and His
    Dream '88
Werewolf of Washington '73
Win, Place, or Steal '72
Wrong is Right '82

Guy Stockwell
And Now Miguel '66
The Gatling Gun '72
Grotesque '87
It's Alive '74
Santa Sangre '90
Tobruk '66
The War Lord '65

John Stockwell
Billionaire Boys Club '87
Born to Ride '91
Christine '84
City Limits '85
Dangerously Close '86
Eyes of the Panther '90
Losin' It '82
My Science Project '85
Quarterback Princess '85
Radioactive Dreams '86
Top Gun '86

Malcolm Stoddard
The Assassination Run '84
The Godsend '79

Austin Stoker
Assault on Precinct 13 '76
Sheba, Baby '75
Twisted Brain '74
The Uninvited '88

Barry Stokes
Alien Prey '83
Spaced Out '80

Susan Stokey
Phantom Empire '87
The Power '80

Mink Stole
Cry-Baby '90
Desperate Living '77
Female Trouble '74
Liquid Dreams '92
Mondo Trasho '69
Multiple Maniacs '70
Pink Flamingos '72
Polyester '81
Serial Mom '94

Shirley Stoler
The Deer Hunter '78
The Displaced Person '76
Honeymoon Killers '70
Malcolm X '92
Seven Beauties '76
Shakedown '88
Splitz '84

Eric Stoltz
Bodies, Rest & Motion '93

Code Name: Emerald '85
Fast Times at Ridgemont High
    '82
The Fly 2 '89
Foreign Affairs '93
The Grass is Always Greener
    Over the Septic Tank '78
Haunted Summer '88
Lionheart '87
Mask '85
Memphis Belle '90
Naked in New York '93
The New Kids '85
Pulp Fiction '94
Running Hot '83
Say Anything '89
The Seekers '79
Sister, Sister '87
Some Kind of Wonderful '87
Surf 2 '84
The Waterdance '91
The Wild Life '84

Lena Stolze
The Last Five Days '82
The Nasty Girl '90
The White Rose '83

Christopher Stone
The Annihilators '85
Cujo '83
Dying to Remember '93
The Howling '81
The Junkman '82
Love Me Deadly '76
The Passing of Evil '70
Prisoner in the Middle '74

Danton Stone
Crazy People '90
He Said, She Said '91
Once Around '91

George E. Stone
Broadway Limited '41
Cimarron '30
42nd Street '33
Jungle Hell '55
The Last Mile '32
Medicine Man '30
Road Show '41
Timber Queen '44
Unforgotten Crime '41
The Vampire Bat '32
Viva Villa! '34

Harold J. Stone
Big Mouth '67
Girl Happy '65
The Invisible Boy '57
Legend of Valentino '75
Mitchell '75
X: The Man with X-Ray Eyes
    '63

Lewis Stone
All the Brothers Were Valiant
    '53
Andy Hardy Gets Spring Fever
    '39
Andy Hardy Meets Debutante
    '40
Andy Hardy's Double Life '42
Andy Hardy's Private Secretary
    '41
Angels in the Outfield '51
Any Number Can Play '49
Beau Revel '21
The Big House '30
Bureau of Missing Persons '33
China Seas '35
David Copperfield '35
The Girl from Missouri '34
Grand Hotel '32
Key to the City '50
Life Begins for Andy Hardy '41
The Lost World '25
Love Finds Andy Hardy '38
Love Laughs at Andy Hardy '46
The Mask of Fu Manchu '32
Mata Hari '32
Nomads of the North '20
Prisoner of Zenda '52
Queen Christina '33
Red Headed Woman '32
Romance '30
Scaramouche '52
The Sin of Madelon Claudet '31
Stars in My Crown '50
State of the Union '48
The Sun Comes Up '49
Suzy '36
Treasure Island '34

Stone ▶cont.

Wild Orchids '28
A Woman of Affairs '28

Mike Stone
Tigershark '87
Warrior Within '80

Milburn Stone
Arrowhead '53
The Atomic City '52
Branded '50
Captive Wild Woman '43
Colorado '40
Fighting Mad '39
Heading for Heaven '47
The Judge '49
Killer Dill '47
The Mad Ghoul '43
Master Key '44
Mr. Boggs Steps Out '38
Mystery Plane '39
Pickup on South Street '53
The Port of Missing Girls '38
Sherlock Holmes Faces Death '43
Sinners in Paradise '38
Stunt Pilot '39
The Sun Shines Bright '53
Swing It, Professor '37
The Thirteenth Man '37

Oliver Stone
Midnight Express '78
Scarface '83

Paula Stone
Convicts at Large '38
Hopalong Cassidy '35
Swing It, Professor '37

Philip Stone
Monsignor Quixote '91
The Unearthly Stranger '64

Sharon Stone
Above the Law '88
Action Jackson '88
Allan Quartermain and the Lost City of Gold '86
Basic Instinct '92
Beyond the Stars '89
Blood and Sand '89
Calendar Girl Murders '84
Cold Steel '87
Deadly Blessing '81
Diary of a Hitman '91
He Said, She Said '91
Intersection '93
Irreconcilable Differences '84
King Solomon's Mines '85
Police Academy 4: Citizens on Patrol '87
The Quick and the Dead '94
Scissors '91
Sliver '93
Tears in the Rain '88
Total Recall '90
The Vegas Strip Wars '84
War & Remembrance, Part 1 '88
War & Remembrance: The Final Chapter, Part 8 '89
Where Sleeping Dogs Lie '91
Year of the Gun '91

Sherri Stoner
Impulse '84
Lovelines '84
Reform School Girls '86

Paolo Stoppa
The Gold of Naples '54
Miracle in Milan '51
Seven Deadly Sins '53
Where the Hot Wind Blows '59

Larry Storch
Adventures Beyond Belief '87
The Adventures of Huckleberry Finn '78
Better Late Than Never '79
Captain Newman, M.D. '63
Hard Frame '70
I Don't Buy Kisses Anymore '92
The Incredible Rocky Mountain Race '77
Sex and the Single Girl '64
S.O.B. '81
Sweet 16 '81
The Woman Hunter '72

June Storey
Dance Hall '41
The Strange Woman '46

Adam Storke
Death Becomes Her '92
Highway to Hell '92
Lifepod '93
Mystic Pizza '88
Stephen King's The Stand '94

Gale Storm
Let's Go Collegiate '41
Lure of the Islands '42
Man from Cheyenne '42
Revenge of the Zombies '43
Rhythm Parade '43
Smart Alecks '42
Swing Parade of 1946 '46
The Texas Rangers '51
The Underworld Story '50

James Storm
Ants '77
Night of Dark Shadows '71

Ludwig Stossel
Cloak and Dagger '46
G.I. Blues '60
House of Dracula '45
Pittsburgh '42

George Stover
Deadly Neighbor '91
Fiend '83

Madeleine Stowe
The Amazons '84
Another Stakeout '93
Bad Girls '94
Blink '93
China Moon '91
Closet Land '90
Gangster Wars '81
The Last of the Mohicans '92
Nativity '78
Revenge '90
Short Cuts '93
Stakeout '87
Tropical Snow '88
The Two Jakes '90
Unlawful Entry '92
Worth Winning '89

Beatrice Straight
The Dain Curse '78
Deceived '91
Endless Love '81
The Formula '80
Killer on Board '77
Network '76
The Nun's Story '59
Patterns '56
Poltergeist '82
Power '86
The Princess and the Pea '83
The Promise '78
Robert Kennedy and His Times '90
Sidney Sheldon's Bloodline '79
Two of a Kind '83

Julie Strain
Enemy Gold '93
Fit to Kill '93
Mirror Images '91
Money to Burn '94
Night Rhythms '92
Psycho Cop 2 '94
The Unnamable 2: The Statement of Randolph Carter '92
Witchcraft 4: Virgin Heart '92

Harry Strang
The Fighting Sullivans '42
Phantom Ranger '38

Glenn Strange
Abbott and Costello Meet Frankenstein '48
Across the Plains '39
Billy the Kid Trapped '42
The Black Raven '43
Boot Hill Bandits '42
Border Law '31
Border Vengeance '35
Comin' 'Round the Mountain '51
Covered Wagon Trails '40
The Driftin' Kid '41
Fugitive Valley '41
Ghost Town Riders '38
Gun Packer '38
Hard Hombre '31
House of Dracula '45

House of Frankenstein '44
Jailhouse Rock '57
Law of the Pampas '39
The Mad Monster '42
Master Minds '49
Sonora Stagecoach '44
Sunset on the Desert '42
The Wistful Widow of Wagon Gap '47

Lee Strasberg
And Justice for All '79
The Cassandra Crossing '76
The Godfather 1902-1959: The Complete Epic '81
The Godfather, Part 2 '74
Going in Style '79

Susan Strasberg
Bloody Birthday '80
The Brotherhood '68
The Cobweb '55
Delta Force '86
Frankenstein '73
In Praise of Older Women '78
Kapo '61
The Legend of Hillbilly John '73
The Light in the Jungle '91
The Manitou '78
Mazes and Monsters '82
Picnic '55
Prime Suspect '88
Psych-Out '68
Rollercoaster '77
The Runnin' Kind '89
Scream of Fear '61
The Sibling '72
Stage Struck '57
Sweet 16 '81
The Trip '67

Marcia Strassman
And You Thought Your Parents Were Weird! '91
Another Stakeout '93
The Aviator '85
Changes '69
Fast Getaway '91
Honey, I Blew Up the Kid '92
Honey, I Shrunk the Kids '89
Soup for One '82

David Strathairn
At Close Range '86
Big Girls Don't Cry...They Get Even '92
Bob Roberts '92
The Brother from Another Planet '84
City of Hope '91
A Dangerous Woman '93
Day One '89
Dominick & Eugene '88
Eight Men Out '88
Enormous Changes '83
The Feud '90
The Firm '93
Heat Wave '90
Iceman '84
Judgment '90
A League of Their Own '92
Lost in Yonkers '93
Matewan '87
Memphis Belle '90
O Pioneers! '91
Passion Fish '92
Return of the Secaucus 7 '80
Silkwood '83
Sneakers '92
Son of the Morning Star '91
Without Warning: The James Brady Story '91

Dorothy Stratten
Autumn Born '79
Galaxina '80
They All Laughed '81

Charles Stratton
Munchies '87
Summer Camp Nightmare '86

Peter Strauss
Angel on My Shoulder '80
The Brotherhood of the Rose '89
Flight of Black Angel '91
Hail, Hero! '69
The Jericho Mile '79
The Last Tycoon '76
Man of Legend '71
Masada '81
Penalty Phase '86
Peter Gunn '89

Proud Men '87
Rich Man, Poor Man '76
Soldier Blue '70
Spacehunter: Adventures in the Forbidden Zone '83
Trial of the Catonsville Nine '72
Whale for the Killing '81

Robert Strauss
The Atomic Kid '54
The Bridges at Toko-Ri '55
Family Jewels '65
The 4D Man '59
Frankie and Johnny '65
Girls! Girls! Girls! '62
Here Come the Girls '53
I, Mobster '58
Jumping Jacks '52
The Man with the Golden Arm '55
The Seven Year Itch '55
Stalag 17 '53

Meryl Streep
A Cry in the Dark '88
Death Becomes Her '92
The Deer Hunter '78
Defending Your Life '91
Falling in Love '84
The French Lieutenant's Woman '81
Heartburn '86
Holocaust '78
The House of the Spirits '93
Ironweed '87
Julia '77
Kramer vs. Kramer '79
Manhattan '79
Out of Africa '85
Plenty '85
Postcards from the Edge '90
The Seduction of Joe Tynan '79
She-Devil '89
Silkwood '83
Sophie's Choice '82
Still of the Night '82

Elliot Street
Harrad Experiment '73
Melvin Purvis: G-Man '74
Paper Man '71

Barbra Streisand
All Night Long '81
For Pete's Sake '74
Funny Girl '68
Funny Lady '75
Hello, Dolly! '69
The Main Event '79
Nuts '87
On a Clear Day You Can See Forever '70
The Owl and the Pussycat '70
The Prince of Tides '91
A Star is Born '76
Up the Sandbox '72
The Way We Were '73
What's Up, Doc? '72
Yentl '83

Melissa Stribling
Crow Hollow '52
The Horror of Dracula '58

Connie Strickland
Act of Vengeance '74
Bummer! '73

Gail Strickland
Eleanor: First Lady of the World '82
The Gathering '77
The Gathering: Part 2 '79
Hyper-Sapien: People from Another Star '86
Lies '83
The Man in the Moon '91
A Matter of Life and Death '81
One on One '77
Oxford Blues '84
Protocol '84
Rape and Marriage: The Rideout Case '80
Snowblind '78
Three of Hearts '93
Who'll Stop the Rain? '78

Anita Strindberg
The Scorpion's Tail '71
The Tempter '74
Women in Cell Block 7 '77

Elaine Stritch
Follies in Concert '85
Perfect Furlough '59

Providence '77
September '88
Three Violent People '57

Woody Strode
Boot Hill '69
The Final Executioner '83
The Gatling Gun '72
Hired to Kill '73
Hit Men '73
Jaguar Lives '79
Jungle Warriors '84
Kill Castro '80
Kingdom of the Spiders '77
The Last Voyage '60
Loaded Guns '75
Lust in the Dust '85
The Man Who Shot Liberty Valance '62
Manhunt '73
The Mercenaries '80
Murder on the Bayou '91
Oil '78
Once Upon a Time in the West '68
Pork Chop Hill '59
The Professionals '66
Ride to Glory '71
Scream '81
Sergeant Rutledge '60
Shalako '68
Spartacus '60
Storyville '92
Super Brother '90
Violent Breed '83

Michael Strong
Patton '70
Point Blank '67
Queen of the Stardust Ballroom '75

Don Stroud
The Amityville Horror '79
Armed and Dangerous '86
Bloody Mama '70
The Buddy Holly Story '78
The Choirboys '77
Coogan's Bluff '68
Death Weekend '76
The Divine Enforcer '91
Down the Drain '89
Explosion '69
Express to Terror '79
Hollywood Man '76
Joe Kidd '72
Killer Inside Me '76
The King of the Kickboxers '91
Madigan '68
Murph the Surf '75
The Night the Lights Went Out in Georgia '81
Prime Target '91
Search and Destroy '81
Slaughter's Big Ripoff '73
Sudden Death '77
Sweet 16 '81
Twisted Justice '89
Two to Tango '88

Sheppard Strudwick
All the King's Men '49
Beyond a Reasonable Doubt '56
Cops and Robbers '73
Let's Dance '50
The Loves of Edgar Allen Poe '42
Psychomania '63
The Red Pony '49
Three Husbands '50

Joe Strummer
Mystery Train '89
Straight to Hell '87

Sally Struthers
Five Easy Pieces '70
The Getaway '72
A Gun in the House '81
Intimate Strangers '77

Carel Struycken
The Addams Family '91
Addams Family Values '93
The Ewoks: Battle for Endor '85
Servants of Twilight '91
The Witches of Eastwick '87

Cassie Stuart
Dolls '87
Hidden City '87

Gloria Stuart
Enemy of Women '44
Gold Diggers of 1935 '35
The Invisible Man '33
It Could Happen to You '39
My Favorite Year '82
The Old Dark House '32
The Poor Little Rich Girl '36
Rebecca of Sunnybrook Farm '38
Roman Scandals '33
The Three Musketeers '39
The Two Worlds of Jenny Logan '79

James R. Stuart
Reactor '85
War of the Robots '78

John Stuart
Alias John Preston '56
Candles at Nine '44
The Gilded Cage '54
Man on the Run '49
No. 17 '32
Old Mother Riley's Ghosts '41
The Temptress '49

Maxine Stuart
Coast to Coast '80
The Rousters '90

Randy Stuart
I Was a Male War Bride '49
The Incredible Shrinking Man '57

Imogen Stubbs
Erik the Viking '89
Fellow Traveler '89
A Summer Story '88
True Colors '91

Stephen Stucker
Airplane! '80
Airplane 2: The Sequel '82
Delinquent School Girls '84

Wes Studi
The Broken Chain '93
Dances with Wolves '90
The Doors '91
Geronimo: An American Legend '93
The Last of the Mohicans '92

Jerzy Stuhr
Deja Vu '89
Trois Couleurs: Blanc '94

Johnny Stumper
Covert Action '88
Mob War '88

Hector Suarez
Despedida de Casada '87
Diamante, Oro y Amor '87
Fin de Fiesta '79
Passion for Power '85

Jose Suarez
Carthage in Flames '60
Maria '71

David Suchet
Crime of Honor '85
Don't Hang Up '90
The Falcon and the Snowman '85
Gulag '85
Harry and the Hendersons '87
Iron Eagle '86
The Last Innocent Man '87
Murrow '86
To Kill a Priest '89
When the Whales Came '89
A World Apart '88

Ichiro Sugai
Early Summer '51
Sansho the Bailiff '54

Haruko Sugimura
Drifting Weeds '59
Early Summer '51
Late Chrysanthemums '54
Late Spring '49
Tokyo Story '53

Barbara Sukowa
Berlin Alexanderplatz '80
Deadly Game '83
M. Butterfly '93
Rosa Luxemburg '86
The Sicilian '87
Voyager '91
Zentropa '92

Margaret Sullavan
Moon's Our Home '36
The Mortal Storm '40
The Shining Hour '38
The Shop Around the Corner '40
Shopworn Angel '38
So Ends Our Night '41
Three Comrades '38

Barry Sullivan
Another Time, Another Place '58
Any Number Can Play '49
The Bad and the Beautiful '52
The Bastard '78
Buckskin '68
Casino '80
Cause for Alarm '51
Earthquake '74
The Gangster '47
A Gathering of Eagles '63
The Human Factor '75
Hurricane '74
Kung Fu '72
The Legend of the Sea Wolf '58
A Life of Her Own '50
Maverick Queen '55
Nancy Goes to Rio '50
Night Gallery '69
No Room to Run '78
Oh, God! '77
Planet of the Vampires '65
Shark! '68
Skirts Ahoy! '52
Strategic Air Command '55
Take a Hard Ride '75
Tell Them Willie Boy Is Here '69
Texas Lady '56
Three Guys Named Mike '51
Washington Affair '77
The Woman of the Town '44
Yuma '70

Billy Sullivan
One-Punch O'Day '26
Stamp of a Killer '87

Brad Sullivan
Funny Farm '88
Guilty by Suspicion '91
Orpheus Descending '91
The Prince of Tides '91
Sister Act 2: Back in the Habit '93

Don Sullivan
The Giant Gila Monster '59
The Rebel Set '59
Teenage Zombies '58

Ed Sullivan
Bye, Bye, Birdie '63
A Few Moments with Buster Keaton and Laurel and Hardy '63

Francis L. Sullivan
Action for Slander '38
Behave Yourself! '52
Butler's Dilemma '43
Caesar and Cleopatra '46
Christopher Columbus '49
The Day Will Dawn '42
Great Expectations '46
Night and the City '50
Non-Stop New York '37
Oliver Twist '48
Pimpernel Smith '42
Power '34
The Prodigal '55
The Secret Four '40
Spy of Napoleon '36
21 Days '37

Susan Sullivan
City in Fear '80
The Dark Ride '84
Deadman's Curve '78
The Incredible Hulk '77
Marriage is Alive and Well '80
The Ordeal of Dr. Mudd '80
Rage of Angels: The Story Continues '86

Frank Sully
Inside the Law '42
The Tender Trap '55

Diane Summerfield
Black Godfather '74
Blackjack '78

Eleanor Summerfield
Black Glove '54

Man on the Run '49

Roy Summerset
Cold Heat '90
Overkill '86

Slim Summerville
All Quiet on the Western Front '30
The Beloved Rogue '27
Captain January '36
Charlie Chaplin's Keystone Comedies #4 '14
The Farmer Takes a Wife '35
I'm from Arkansas '44
King of the Rodeo '28
Rebecca of Sunnybrook Farm '38
Under Montana Skies '30
Western Union '41

Bart Sumner
Video Violence '87
Video Violence Part 2...The Exploitation! '87

Clinton Sundberg
As Young As You Feel '51
The Belle of New York '52
In the Good Old Summertime '49
Main Street to Broadway '53
Mr. Peabody & the Mermaid '48
Two Weeks with Love '50

Bjorn Sundquist
The Dive '89
Shipwrecked '90

Gerry Sundquist
Don't Open Till Christmas '84
Great Expectations '81

Nicolas Surovy
The Act '82
Anastasia: The Mystery of Anna '86
Forever Young '92
Stark '85
12:01 '93

Todd Susman
Only the Strong '93
Star Spangled Girl '71

Donald Sutherland
Alex in Wonderland '70
Apprentice to Murder '88
Backdraft '91
Bear Island '80
Bedford Incident '65
Benefit of the Doubt '93
Bethune '77
Blood Relatives '77
Buffy the Vampire Slayer '92
Castle of the Living Dead '64
Crackers '84
Dan Candy's Law '73
The Day of the Locust '75
Die! Die! My Darling! '65
The Dirty Dozen '67
Disappearance '81
Dr. Bethune '90
Dr. Terror's House of Horrors '65
Don't Look Now '73
A Dry White Season '89
The Eagle Has Landed '77
Eminent Domain '91
Eye of the Needle '81
Gas '81
The Great Train Robbery '79
Heaven Help Us '85
Invasion of the Body Snatchers '78
JFK '91
Johnny Got His Gun '71
Kelly's Heroes '70
Kentucky Fried Movie '77
Klute '71
Lady Ice '73
Little Murders '71
Lock Up '89
Lost Angels '89
A Man, a Woman, and a Bank '79
M*A*S*H '70
Max Dugan Returns '83
Murder by Decree '79
National Lampoon's Animal House '78
1900 '76
Nothing Personal '80
Ordeal by Innocence '84
Ordinary People '80

Quicksand: No Escape '91
The Railway Station Man '92
Revolution '85
The Rosary Murders '87
Sebastian '68
Shadow of the Wolf '93
Six Degrees of Separation '93
S*P*Y*S '74
Start the Revolution Without Me '70
Steelyard Blues '73
Threshold '83
The Trouble with Spies '87
The Wolf at the Door '87

Kiefer Sutherland
Amazing Stories '85
Article 99 '92
At Close Range '86
The Bay Boy '85
Bright Lights, Big City '88
Brotherhood of Justice '86
Chicago Joe & the Showgirl '90
The Cowboy Way '94
Crazy Moon '87
A Few Good Men '92
Flashback '89
Flatliners '90
The Killing Time '87
Last Light '93
The Lost Boys '87
Max Dugan Returns '83
1969 '88
Promised Land '88
Renegades '89
Stand By Me '86
The Three Musketeers '93
Trapped in Silence '86
Twin Peaks: Fire Walk with Me '92
The Vanishing '93
Young Guns '88
Young Guns 2 '90

James Sutorius
My Mother's Secret Life '84
On Wings of Eagles '86
Prototype '83
A Question of Love '78
Windy City '84

Dolores Sutton
F. Scott Fitzgerald in Hollywood '76
Where Angels Go, Trouble Follows '68

Dudley Sutton
The Devils '71
Edward II '92
Leather Boys '63
Orlando '92

Grady Sutton
The Bank Dick '40
The Bashful Bachelor '42
Dangerous Holiday '37
Going to Town '44
The More the Merrier '43
Paradise, Hawaiian Style '66
Pharmacist '32
Two Reelers: Comedy Classics 4 '36

John Sutton
Arrest Bulldog Drummond '38
The Bat '59
David and Bathsheba '51
The Invisible Man Returns '40
Jane Eyre '44
Mickey '48
Return of the Fly '59
Second Woman '51
The Tower of London '39
A Yank in the R.A.F. '41

Janet Suzman
And the Ship Sails On '83
The Black Windmill '74
Bright Smiler '85
A Day in the Death of Joe Egg '71
The Draughtsman's Contract '82
A Dry White Season '89
The House on Garibaldi Street '79
Leon the Pig Farmer '93
Macbeth '73
Nicholas and Alexandra '71
Nijinsky '80
Nuns on the Run '90
Priest of Love '81
Voyage of the Damned '76

The Zany Adventures of Robin Hood '84

Semyon Svashenko
Arsenal '29
Earth '30
Zvenigora '28

Bo Svenson
Andy and the Airwave Rangers '89
Beyond the Door 3 '91
Big Mo '73
Choke Canyon '86
Curse 2: The Bite '88
Deadly Impact '84
Deadly Mission '70
Deep Space '87
Delta Force '86
Delta Force Commando '87
The Dirty Dozen: The Deadly Mission '87
Frankenstein '73
Gold of the Amazon Women '79
The Great Waldo Pepper '75
Heartbreak Ridge '86
Jealousy '84
The Kill Reflex '89
The Last Contract '86
The Manhunt '86
Night Warning '82
North Dallas Forty '79
Portrait of a Hitman '77
Primal Rage '90
Snowbeast '77
Special Delivery '76
Steele's Law '91
Three Days to Kill '91
Thunder Warrior '85
Thunder Warrior 2 '85
Tides of War '90
Virus '82
Walking Tall: Part 2 '75
Walking Tall: The Final Chapter '77
White Phantom: Enemy of Darkness '87
Wizards of the Lost Kingdom '85

Mack Swain
The Beloved Rogue '27
The Champion/His New Job '15
The Chaplin Revue '58
Charlie Chaplin's Keystone Comedies #1 '14
Charlie Chaplin's Keystone Comedies #2 '14
Charlie Chaplin's Keystone Comedies #3 '14
Charlie Chaplin's Keystone Comedies #4 '14
Early Cinema Vol. 1 '19
The Gold Rush '25
Gold Rush/Payday '25
Hands Up '26
His Prehistoric Past/The Bank '15
Kid's Auto Race/Mabel's Married Life '15
The Lizzies of Mack Sennett '15
The Nervous Wreck '26
Rink/Immigrant '10s
Three Charlies and One Phoney! '18
Tillie's Punctured Romance '14
Two Reelers: Comedy Classics 8 '33

Darwyn Swalve
Deadly Reactor '89
Take Two '87

Hilary Swank
Buffy the Vampire Slayer '92
The Next Karate Kid '94

Gary Swanson
Coldfire '90
TripleCross '85
Vice Squad '82
Witchfire '86

Gloria Swanson
Airport '75 '75
The Champion/His New Job '15
A Hash House Fraud/The Sultan's Wife '15
Hedda Hopper's Hollywood '42
Indiscreet '31
The Love Goddesses '65
Male and Female '19

Swanson ▶cont.

Queen Kelly '29
Sadie Thompson '28
Shifting Sands '18
Story of the Silent Serials Girls in Danger
Sunset Boulevard '50
Teddy at the Throttle '16
Teddy at the Throttle/Speeding Along '17
Three for Bedroom C '52

Kristy Swanson
Buffy the Vampire Slayer '92
The Chase '93
Deadly Friend '86
Diving In '90
Dream Trap '90
Flowers in the Attic '87
Highway to Hell '92
Hot Shots! '91
Mannequin 2: On the Move '91
The Program '93

Maureen Swanson
Robbery Under Arms '57
The Spanish Gardener '57

Don Swayze
Body of Influence '93
Broken Trust '93
Death Blow '87
Death Ring '93
Driving Force '88
Edge of Honor '91
Eye of the Stranger '93
Forced to Kill '93
Money to Burn '94
Payback '90
Sexual Malice '93
Shy People '87
The Tracker '88
Trapper County War '89

Patrick Swayze
City of Joy '92
Dirty Dancing '87
Father Hood '93
Ghost '90
Grandview U.S.A. '84
Next of Kin '89
North and South Book 1 '85
North and South Book 2 '86
The Outsiders '83
Point Break '91
Red Dawn '84
Return of the Rebels '81
Road House '89
Steel Dawn '87
Tiger Warsaw '87
Uncommon Valor '83
Youngblood '86

Bob Sweeney
A Christmas Carol '54
Toby Tyler '59

D.B. Sweeney
Blue Desert '91
The Cutting Edge '92
A Day in October '92
Eight Men Out '88
Fire in the Sky '93
Fire with Fire '86
Gardens of Stone '87
Hear No Evil '93
Heaven is a Playground '91
Leather Jackets '90
Lonesome Dove '89
Memphis Belle '90
Miss Rose White '91
No Man's Land '87

Joseph Sweeney
The Man in the Gray Flannel Suit '56
Twelve Angry Men '57

Julia Sweeney
Coneheads '93
Honey, I Blew Up the Kid '92
It's Pat '94

Blanche Sweet
Anna Christie '23
Avenging Conscience '14
D.W. Griffith Triple Feature '13
Griffith Biograph Program '09
Home Sweet Home '14
Judith of Bethulia '14
Short Films of D.W. Griffith, Vol. 1 '12

Dolph Sweet
Acorn People '82
Amazing Grace '74
Cops and Robbers '73
Deathmoon '78
Finian's Rainbow '68
Jacqueline Bouvier Kennedy '81
Reds '81

Gary Sweet
Fever '88
An Indecent Obsession '85
Stage Fright '83

Rod Sweitzer
The Invisible Maniac '90
The Malibu Beach Vampires '91

Inga Swenson
The Miracle Worker '62
North and South Book 1 '85

Karl Swenson
Brighty of the Grand Canyon '67
The Gallant Hours '60
The Hanging Tree '59

Tommy Swerdlow
Child's Play '88
Hamburger Hill '87

Josef Swickard
Custer's Last Stand '36
Dante's Inferno '24
The Four Horsemen of the Apocalypse '21
The Lone Defender '32
The Night Patrol '26
The Wizard of Oz '25

Nora Swinburne
Betrayed '54
Man of Evil '48
Quo Vadis '51
The River '51
Strange Awakening '58

Tilda Swinton
Caravaggio '86
Edward II '92
The Last of England '87
Orlando '92

Loretta Swit
Beer '85
The Execution '85
First Affair '83
Freebie & the Bean '74
M*A*S*H: Goodbye, Farewell & Amen '83
M*A*S*H: The Collector's Edition '72
Miracle at Moreaux '86
Race with the Devil '75
S.O.B. '81
Whoops Apocalypse '88

Carl "Alfalfa" Switzer
Cause for Alarm '51
General Spanky '36
The Great Mike '44
Little Rascals, Book 1 '30s
Little Rascals, Book 2 '30s
Little Rascals, Book 3 '38
Little Rascals, Book 4 '30s
Little Rascals, Book 5 '30s
Little Rascals, Book 6 '30s
Little Rascals, Book 7 '30s
Little Rascals, Book 8 '30s
Little Rascals, Book 9 '30s
Little Rascals, Book 10 '30s
Little Rascals, Book 11 '38
Little Rascals, Book 12 '37
Little Rascals, Book 13 '37
Little Rascals, Book 14 '30s
Little Rascals, Book 15 '30s
Little Rascals, Book 16 '30s
Little Rascals: Choo Choo/Fishy Tales
Little Rascals Collector's Edition, Vol. 1-6
Little Rascals Comedy Classics, Vol. 1
Little Rascals Comedy Classics, Vol. 2
Little Rascals: Fish Hooky/Spooky Hooky '33
Little Rascals: Honkey Donkey/Sprucin' Up '34
Little Rascals: Little Sinner/Two Too Young '35

Little Rascals: Mush and Milk/Three Men in a Tub '33
Little Rascals on Parade '37
Little Rascals: Pups is Pups/Three Smart Boys '30
Little Rascals: Readin' and Writin'/Mail and Female '31
Little Rascals: Reunion in Rhythm/Mike Fright '37
Little Rascals: Spanky/Feed 'Em and Weep '36
Little Rascals: The Pinch Singer/Framing Youth '36
Little Rascals Two Reelers, Vol. 1 '29
Little Rascals Two Reelers, Vol. 2 '33
Little Rascals Two Reelers, Vol. 3 '36
Little Rascals Two Reelers, Vol. 4 '30
Little Rascals Two Reelers, Vol. 5 '34
Little Rascals Two Reelers, Vol. 6 '36
Little Rascals, Vol. 1 '29
Little Rascals, Vol. 2 '30
Motorcycle Gang '57
Our Gang Comedies '40s
Pat and Mike '52
Redwood Forest Trail '50
Reg'lar Fellers '41

Ken Swofford
All God's Children '80
Black Roses '88
Bless the Beasts and Children '71
Sky Hei$t '75
The Taking of Beverly Hills '91

Topo Swope
The Hot Rock '70
My Old Man's Place '71

Tracy Brooks Swope
The Big Picture '89
The Power of One '92

Basil Sydney
Accused '36
Angel with the Trumpet '50
Dam Busters '55
The Devil's Disciple '59
Hamlet '48
The Hands of Orlac '60
John Paul Jones '59
Rhodes '36
Salome '53
The Secret Four '40
The Three Worlds of Gulliver '59
Treasure Island '50

Brenda Sykes
Cleopatra Jones '73
Honky '71
Mandingo '75

Eric Sykes
Heavens Above '63
Those Daring Young Men in Their Jaunty Jalopies '69

Harold Sylvester
Fast Break '79
Innerspace '87
Uncommon Valor '83

William Sylvester
Beast of Morocco '66
Devil Doll '64
Gorgo '61
Postmark for Danger '56
2001: A Space Odyssey '68
Unholy Four '54

Robert Symonds
Ice Pirates '84
Mandroid '93
Rumpelstiltskin '86

Sylvia Syms
Bachelor of Hearts '58
A Chorus of Disapproval '89
Conspiracy of Hearts '60
Desperados '69
Ferry to Hong Kong '59
Fiction Makers '67
Intimate Contact '87
The Moonraker '58
Murders at Lynch Cross '85
Nancy Astor '82
Shining Through '92
Shirley Valentine '89
The Tamarind Seed '74

Teenage Bad Girl '59
Victim '62
The World of Suzie Wong '60

Clancy Syrko
Black Bikers from Hell '70
The Outlaw Bikers—Gang Wars '70

Laszlo Szabo
Bad Guys '79
Nice Neighbor '79

Grazyna Szapolowska
Another Way '82
No End '84

Keith Szarabajka
Andre '94
Billy Galvin '86
The Equalizer: Memories of Manon '88
Marie '85
The Misfit Brigade '87
Nightlife '90
A Perfect World '93
Protocol '82
Stephen King's Golden Years '91

Oleg Tabakov
Oblomov '81
An Unfinished Piece for a Player Piano '77

Eron Tabor
I Spit on Your Grave '77
Krush Groove '85

Kristopher Tabori
The Glass House '72
Rappaccini's Daughter '80

Sydney Tafler
The Adventurers '70
Fire Maidens from Outer Space '56
The Way Out '56

Cary-Hiroyuki Tagawa
American Me '92
The Last Warrior '89
Nemesis '93
Rising Sun '93
Showdown in Little Tokyo '91

Rita Taggart
Coupe de Ville '90
The Horror Show '89
Torchlight '85
Weeds '87

Sharon Taggart
Harrad Experiment '73
The Last Picture Show '71

Sharmila Tagore
Devi '60
Mississippi Masala '92
The World of Apu '59

Taj Mahal
Bill & Ted's Bogus Journey '91
Sounder '72

Miiko Taka
A Global Affair '63
Walk, Don't Run '66

Ken Takakura
Antarctica '84
Black Rain '89
Mr. Baseball '92
Station '81
The Yakuza '75

Hideko Takamine
Mistress '53
Twenty-Four Eyes '54
When a Woman Ascends the Stairs '60

Akira Takarada
Godzilla vs. Mothra '64
Half Human '58
Last War '68

Tadao Takashima
King Kong Versus Godzilla '63
Son of Godzilla '66

George Takei
The Green Berets '68
Ice Palace '60
Prisoners of the Sun '91
Red Line 7000 '65
Star Trek: The Motion Picture '80

Star Trek 2: The Wrath of Khan '82
Star Trek 3: The Search for Spock '84
Star Trek 4: The Voyage Home '86
Star Trek 5: The Final Frontier '89
Star Trek 6: The Undiscovered Country '91
Star Trek Bloopers '69

Osamu Takizawa
Fires on the Plain '59
Zatoichi vs. Yojimbo '70

Helen Talbot
California Joe '43
Federal Operator 99 '45
King of the Forest Rangers '46

Lyle Talbot
Border Rangers '50
The Case of the Lucky Legs '35
Clipped Wings '53
The Devil's Cargo '48
Gambler's Choice '44
Glen or Glenda '53
Go West, Young Man '36
Gold Raiders '51
High School Confidential '58
Highway 13 '48
Jail Bait '54
Ladies They Talk About '33
Mesa of Lost Women '52
Mystery of the Riverboat '44
A Night for Crime '42
North of the Border '46
One Body Too Many '44
One Night of Love '34
One Too Many '51
Our Little Girl '35
Parole, Inc. '49
Plan 9 from Outer Space '56
The Purchase Price '32
Second Fiddle '39
Sensations of 1945 '44
Shriek in the Night '33
Song of Arizona '46
Sunrise at Campobello '60
13th Guest '32
Three Legionnaires '37
Three on a Match '32
Thunder in the Pines '49
Torture Ship '39
Trader Tom of the China Seas '54
Up in Arms '44
Vengeance '37
Wild Weed '49

Nita Talbot
Amityville 1992: It's About Time '92
Chained Heat '83
The Concrete Jungle '82
Fraternity Vacation '85
Frightmare '81
Girl Happy '65
I Married a Woman '56
Night Shift '82
Puppet Master 2 '91
Sweet Creek County War '82
Take Two '87
Who's Got the Action? '63

Gloria Talbott
Arizona Raiders '65
Cyclops '56
The Daughter of Dr. Jekyll '57
Girls' Town '59
I Married a Monster from Outer Space '58
The Oklahoman '56

Michael Talbott
Miami Vice '84
Racing with the Moon '84

Hal Taliaferro
Border Vigilantes '41
Frontier Law '43
Hoppy Serves a Writ '43
Leather Burners '43
Phantom Gold '38
The Rangers Step In '37
Riders of the Timberline '41
The Unknown Ranger '36

Patricia Tallman
Army of Darkness '92
Night of the Living Dead '90

Constance Talmadge
America/The Fall of Babylon '24
The Babylon Story from "Intolerance" '16
Intolerance '16
Matrimaniac '16
The Primitive Lover '16

Norma Talmadge
Dubarry '30
The Forbidden City '18
The Social Secretary '16
Tale of Two Cities/In the Switch Tower '15

Richard Talmadge
Fighting Pilot '35
Get That Girl '32
Laughing at Danger '24
Let's Go! '23
The Live Wire '34
The Night Patrol '26
Speed Reporter '36

William Talman
Armored Car Robbery '50
Crashout '55
Falcon's Adventure/Armored Car Robbery '50
The Hitch-Hiker '53
One Minute to Zero '52

Tetsuro Tamba
Hunter in the Dark '80
The Imperial Japanese Empire '85
One-Eyed Swordsman '63
A Taxing Woman's Return '88
Tokyo Pop '88
You Only Live Twice '67
Zero '84

Russ Tamblyn
Aftershock '88
B.O.R.N. '88
Cabin Boy '94
Cimarron '60
Commando Squad '87
Cyclone '87
Don't Go Near the Water '57
Dracula vs. Frankenstein '71
Fastest Gun Alive '56
Father of the Bride '50
Father's Little Dividend '51
The Female Bunch '69
Free Grass '69
Gun Crazy '49
The Haunting '63
High School Confidential '58
Hit the Deck '55
How the West was Won '63
The Last Hunt '56
The Last Movie '71
Necromancer: Satan's Servant '88
Peyton Place '57
Phantom Empire '87
Retreat, Hell! '52
Running Mates '92
Satan's Sadists '69
Seven Brides for Seven Brothers '54
Tom Thumb '58
Twin Peaks '90
War of the Gargantuas '70
West Side Story '61
The Winning Team '52
The Wonderful World of the Brothers Grimm '62

Jeffrey Tambor
Article 99 '92
Brenda Starr '86
City Slickers '91
Crossing the Bridge '92
Desert Hearts '86
A Gun in the House '81
Life Stinks '91
Lisa '90
The Man Who Wasn't There '83
Mr. Mom '83
Pastime '91
A Perfect Little Murder '83
Sadat '83
Take Your Best Shot '82
Tales from the Crypt, Vol. 3 '90
Three O'Clock High '87

Jenny Tamburi
Bloody Avenger '80s
Women in Cell Block 7 '77

Zoe Tamerlis
Ms. 45 '81
Special Effects '85

Akim Tamiroff
Alphaville '65
Anastasia '56
The Bacchantes '63
Battle Hell '56
Black Magic '49
The Bridge of San Luis Rey '44
The Corsican Brothers '42
Deadly Sanctuary '68
Dragon Seed '44
The Gangster '47
The General Died at Dawn '36
The Great McGinty '40
Hotel Paradiso '66
Lt. Robin Crusoe, U.S.N. '66
The Lives of a Bengal Lancer '35
Lord Jim '65
The Merry Widow '34
Miracle of Morgan's Creek '44
Mr. Arkadin '55
My Girl Tisa '48
Outpost in Morocco '49
Panic Button '62
The Story of Louis Pasteur '36
Topkapi '64
Tortilla Flat '42
Touch of Evil '58
The Trial '63
Vulture '67

Jiro Tamiya
Professional Killers 1 '73
Sword of Fury II '73

Mary Tamm
The Assassination Run '84
The Odessa File '74
Tales That Witness Madness '73

Takahiro Tamura
The Empire of Passion '76
In the Realm of Passion '80
The Silk Road '92

Tin Tan
El Ceniciento '47
Musico, Poeta y Loco '47

Haruo Tanaka
The Pornographers '66
Snow Country '57

Kinuyo Tanaka
Equinox Flower '58
Life of Oharu '52
Mother '52
Sandakan No. 8 '74
Sansho the Bailiff '54
Ugetsu '53
Utamaro and His Five Women '46

Toru Tanaka
Tax Season '90
3 Ninjas '92

Jessica Tandy
*batteries not included '87
Best Friends '82
The Birds '63
The Bostonians '84
Camilla '94
Cocoon '85
Cocoon: The Return '88
The Desert Fox '51
Driving Miss Daisy '89
Forever Amber '47
Foxfire '87
Fried Green Tomatoes '91
Gin Game '84
The House on Carroll Street '88
The Light in the Forest '58
September Affair '50
The Seventh Cross '44
Still of the Night '82
The Story Lady '93
To Dance with the White Dog '93
Used People '92
The Valley of Decision '45
The World According to Garp '82

Mark Tandy
Maurice '87
The Railway Station Man '92

Alan Tang
The Bloody Fight '70s
The Dynamite Brothers

Yoko Tani
First Spaceship on Venus '60
Invasion '66
Koroshi '67
Samson and the 7 Miracles of the World '62

William Tannen
Jupiter's Darling '55
Whistling in the Dark '41

Warhawk Tanzania
Black Force '75
Gang Wars '75

Wang Tao
The Hot, the Cool, and the Vicious '80s
Snake in the Eagle's Shadow 2 '83
Ten Brothers of Shao-lin '80s
Two Assassins in the Dark '80s

Rockne Tarkington
Black Starlet '74
Clarence, the Cross-eyed Lion '65
Trained to Kill, U.S.A. '83
Zebra Force '76

Ignacio Lopez Tarso
El Gallo de Oro '65
La Trinchera '87
Macario '58
Nazarin '58

Lilyan Tashman
Millie '31
Riptide '34
Scarlet Dawn '32
So This is Paris '26

Coralina Cataldi Tassoni
Demons 2 '87
Evil Clutch '89
Terror at the Opera '88

Larenz Tate
The Inkwell '94
Menace II Society '93

Laura Tate
Dead Space '90
Subspecies '91

Nick Tate
A Cry in the Dark '88
The Devil's Playground '76
Space: 1999—Alien Attack '79

Reginald Tate
Immortal Battalion '44
The King's Rhapsody '55

Sharon Tate
Ciao Federico! Fellini Directs Satyricon '70
The Fearless Vampire Killers '67
12 Plus 1 '70
Valley of the Dolls '67

Jacques Tati
Jour de Fete '48
Mr. Hulot's Holiday '53
Mon Oncle '58
Parade '74
Playtime '67
Sylvia and the Phantom '45

Sven-Bertil Taube
Codename Kyril '91
Puppet on a Chain '72

Nils Tavernier
Beatrice '88
The Story of Women '88

Vic Tayback
Alice Doesn't Live Here Anymore '74
Beverly Hills Bodysnatchers '89
The Cheap Detective '78
The Choirboys '77
Criminal Act '88
Door to Door Maniac '61
Great American Traffic Jam '80
Horseplayer '91
Lepke '75
Murderer's Keep '88
Mysterious Two '82
The Night the City Screamed '80
Portrait of a Stripper '79
Rage '80
Special Delivery '76
Tut & Tuttle '82

The Underachievers '88
Weekend Warriors '86
With Six You Get Eggroll '68

Benedict Taylor
The Black Arrow '84
Charles & Diana: A Palace Divided '93
Duel of Hearts '92
Every Time We Say Goodbye '86
The Far Pavilions '84
A Perfect Spy '88

Buck Taylor
And Now Miguel '66
Conagher '91
Gunsmoke: Return to Dodge '87
Pony Express Rider '76
Tombstone '93

Delores Taylor
Billy Jack '71
The Trial of Billy Jack '74

Don Taylor
Battleground '49
Father of the Bride '50
Father's Little Dividend '51
I'll Cry Tomorrow '55
Men of Sherwood Forest '57
The Naked City '48
Song of the Thin Man '47
Stalag 17 '53

Dub Taylor
Back to the Future, Part 3 '90
Brand of Fear '49
Conagher '91
Creature from Black Lake '76
Falling from Grace '92
Flash & Firecat '75
Gator '76
The Getaway '72
A Man Called Horse '70
Moonshine County Express '77
My Heroes Have Always Been Cowboys '91
On the Run '85
Parrish '61
Pony Express Rider '76
Poor Pretty Eddie '73
Range Renegades '48
Soggy Bottom U.S.A. '84
Spencer's Mountain '63
Support Your Local Gunfighter '71
Texas Guns '90
This is a Hijack '75
The Wild Bunch '69
You Can't Take It with You '38

Elizabeth Taylor
Ash Wednesday '73
Beau Brummel '54
Between Friends '83
The Big Hangover '50
Butterfield 8 '60
Cat on a Hot Tin Roof '58
Cleopatra '63
The Comedians '67
Conspirator '49
Courage of Lassie '46
A Date with Judy '48
Divorce His, Divorce Hers '72
Doctor Faustus '68
Driver's Seat '73
Elephant Walk '54
Father of the Bride '50
Father's Little Dividend '51
The Flintstones '94
Giant '56
The Girl Who Had Everything '53
Hammersmith is Out '72
Ivanhoe '52
James Dean: The First American Teenager '76
Jane Eyre '44
Julia Misbehaves '48
Lassie, Come Home '43
The Last Time I Saw Paris '54
Life with Father '47
A Little Night Music '77
Little Women '49
The Love Goddesses '65
Love is Better Than Ever '52
The Mirror Crack'd '80
National Velvet '44
Night Watch '72
North and South Book 1 '85
A Place in the Sun '51

Poker Alice '87
Raintree County '57
Reflections in a Golden Eye '67
Return Engagement '78
Rhapsody '54
The Rumor Mill '86
The Sandpiper '65
Secret Ceremony '69
Suddenly, Last Summer '59
Sweet Bird of Youth '89
The Taming of the Shrew '67
Under Milk Wood '73
The V.I.P.'s '63
The White Cliffs of Dover '44
Who's Afraid of Virginia Woolf? '66
Winter Kills '79
X, Y & Zee '72

Estelle Taylor
Cimarron '30
Don Juan '26
The Southerner '45
Street Scene '31
Where East is East '29

Forrest Taylor
Arizona Gangbusters '40
Colorado Serenade '46
Driftin' River '46
A Face in the Fog '36
Ghost Town Riders '38
Lightnin' Carson Rides Again '38
Mystery Man '44
Outlaw's Paradise '39
The Phantom of the Range '38
Prison Shadows '36
The Red Rope '37
Riders of Destiny '33
The Roamin' Cowboy '37
Shake Hands with Murder '44
Sons of the Pioneers '42
Trail of Terror '35
Trail Riders '42
Trigger Men '41

Grant Taylor
Forty Thousand Horsemen '41
His Majesty O'Keefe '53
Long John Silver '53

Holland Taylor
Alice '90
Cop and a Half '93
The Favor '94
The Jewel of the Nile '85
She's Having a Baby '88

Jack Taylor
Dr. Jekyll and the Wolfman '71
Dr. Jekyll vs. the Werewolf '71
Horror of the Zombies '74
Icebox Murders '80s
The Loves of Irina '80s
The Mummy's Revenge '73
Night of the Sorcerers '70
Orgy of the Vampires '73
Where Time Began '77

Jana Taylor
Dreamscape '84
Hell's Angels on Wheels '67

Joan Taylor
Apache Woman '55
Earth vs. the Flying Saucers '56
Girls in Prison '56
Omar Khayyam '57
Rose Marie '54
20 Million Miles to Earth '57

John Taylor
Foxstyle '73
The Seventh Sign '88

Kent Taylor
Angels' Wild Women '72
Badmen of Nevada '33
Blood of Ghastly Horror '72
Brain of Blood '71
Brides of the Beast '68
The Crawling Hand '63
Escape to Paradise '39
Five Came Back '39
Gangbusters '38
I Spit on Your Corpse '74
I'm No Angel '33
The Mysterious Rider '38
The Phantom from 10,000 Leagues '56
Satan's Sadists '69
Slightly Scarlet '56
Western Pacific Agent '51

▲ 1413 • CAST INDEX

Kit Taylor
Cassandra '87
Innocent Prey '88
Long John Silver '53

Lili Taylor
Bright Angel '91
Dogfight '91
Household Saints '93
Mystic Pizza '88
Rudy '93
Say Anything '89
Short Cuts '93
Watch It '93

Marjorie Taylor
The Crimes of Stephen Hawke '36
The Face at the Window '39
Never Too Late to Mend '37
Ticket of Leave Man '37

Meshach Taylor
Class Act '91
Explorers '85
House of Games '87
Inside Out '91
Mannequin '87
Mannequin 2: On the Move '91
Ultra Warrior '90s

Noah Taylor
Flirting '89
The Year My Voice Broke '87

Ray Taylor
Man from Montana '41
Robinson Crusoe of Mystery Island '36

Renee Taylor
Delirious '91
The End of Innocence '90
The Errand Boy '61
Forever: A Ghost of a Love Story '92
Last of the Red Hot Lovers '72
That's Adequate '90
White Palace '90

Rip Taylor
Cheech and Chong: Things Are Tough All Over '82
Indecent Proposal '93
Minsky's Follies '83

Robert Taylor
Above and Beyond '53
All the Brothers Were Valiant '53
Bataan '43
Billy the Kid '41
Broadway Melody of 1936 '35
Broadway Melody of 1938 '35
Camille '36
Conspirator '49
D-Day, the Sixth of June '56
The Gorgeous Hussy '36
The Hot Line '69
I Love Melvin '53
Ivanhoe '52
Johnny Eager '42
Johnny Tiger '66
Knights of the Round Table '53
The Last Hunt '56
The Law and Jake Wade '58
The Miracle of the White Stallions '63
The Night Walker '64
Party Girl '58
Personal Property '37
Quo Vadis '51
Three Comrades '38
Waterloo Bridge '40
Westward the Women '51
When Ladies Meet '41

Rod Taylor
Ask Any Girl '59
The Birds '63
The Catered Affair '56
Chuka '67
Colossus and the Amazon Queen '64
Cry of the Innocent '80
Dark of the Sun '68
Darker than Amber '70
The Deadly Trackers '73
A Gathering of Eagles '63
Germicide '74
Giant '56
The Glass Bottom Boat '66
Hell River '75
Hotel '67

Jacqueline Bouvier Kennedy '81
Long John Silver '53
Man Who Had Power Over Women '70
Marbella '85
Nowhere to Hide
Powder Keg '70
Raintree County '57
Separate Tables '58
The Time Machine '60
Time to Die '83
Train Robbers '73
The Treasure Seekers '79
The V.I.P.'s '63
Zabriskie Point '70

Tammy Taylor
Lovelines '84
Meatballs 2 '84

Vaughn Taylor
Francis Goes to the Races '51
Jailhouse Rock '57
Meet Danny Wilson '52

Wally Taylor
Hidden Fears '93
Shaft's Big Score '72

Zack Taylor
Group Marriage '72
The Young Nurses '73

Leigh Taylor-Young
Accidents '89
The Adventurers '70
Can't Stop the Music '80
Devlin Connection '82
Honeymoon Academy '90
The Horsemen
I Love You, Alice B. Toklas '68
The Jagged Edge '85
Looker '81
Marathon '80
Secret Admirer '85
Soylent Green '73

Ludmila Tcherina
The Red Shoes '48
Sins of Rome '54

Phil Tead
Fangs of the Wild '54
Music in My Heart '40

Anthony Teague
How to Succeed in Business without Really Trying '67
The Trouble with Girls (and How To Get Into It) '69

Marshall Teague
Road House '89
The Shadow Riders '82
Super Force '90

Ray Teal
Ambush at Tomahawk Gap '53
Band of Angels '57
Carrie '52
Distant Drums '51
Hollywood Canteen '44
Jumping Jacks '52
Lucky Me '54
Montana Belle '52

Owen Teale
The Hawk '93
Robin Hood '91

Conway Tearle
Dancing Mothers '26
Desert Guns/Six-Shootin' Sheriff '36
Headline Woman '35
Held for Murder '32
Hurricane Express '32
The King Murder Case '32
Klondike Annie '36
Lost Zeppelin '29
Morals for Women '31
Pleasure '31
Sing Sing Nights '35
Stella Maris '18
Vanity Fair '32

Godfrey Tearle
One of Our Aircraft Is Missing '41
The 39 Steps '35

Verree Teasdale
Goodbye Love '34
Milky Way '36
Skyscraper Souls '32

Irene Tedrow
Special Olympics '78

The Two Worlds of Jenny Logan '79

Maureen Teefy
Fame '80
Legs '83
Star Time '92
Supergirl '84

Blair Tefkin
Dream Lover '93
Sinful Life '89

Aaron Teich
Bloodspell '87
Darkroom '90

Shirley Temple
Baby, Take a Bow '34
The Bachelor and the Bobby-Soxer '47
The Blue Bird '40
Bright Eyes '34
Captain January '36
Comedy Festival #3 '30s
Curly Top '35
Dimples '36
Fort Apache '48
Gotta Dance, Gotta Sing '84
Heidi '37
Just Around the Corner '38
Kid 'n' Hollywood and Polly Tix in Washington '33
The Little Colonel '35
Little Miss Broadway '38
Little Miss Marker '34
The Little Princess '39
The Littlest Rebel '35
Miss Annie Rooney '42
Our Little Girl '35
The Poor Little Rich Girl '36
Rebecca of Sunnybrook Farm '38
Shirley Temple Festival '33
Since You Went Away '44
Stand Up and Cheer '34
The Story of Seabiscuit '49
Stowaway '36
Susannah of the Mounties '39
To the Last Man '33
Wee Willie Winkie '37

Victoria Tennant
All of Me '84
Best Seller '87
Chiefs '83
Dempsey '83
The Dogs of War '81
Flowers in the Attic '87
The Handmaid's Tale '90
The Holcroft Covenant '85
Horror Planet '81
L.A. Story '91
Little Lord Fauntleroy '80
Strangers Kiss '83
War & Remembrance, Part 1 '88
War & Remembrance, Part 2 '89
War & Remembrance, Part 3 '88
War & Remembrance, Part 4 '88
War & Remembrance, Part 5 '88
War & Remembrance, Part 6 '88
War & Remembrance, Part 7 '88
War & Remembrance: The Final Chapter, Part 8 '89
War & Remembrance: The Final Chapter, Part 9 '89
War & Remembrance: The Final Chapter, Part 10 '89
War & Remembrance: The Final Chapter, Part 11 '89
War & Remembrance: The Final Chapter, Part 12 '89
Whispers '89
The Winds of War '83

Jon Tenney
Lassie '94
Tombstone '93
Watch It '93

William Tepper
Bachelor Party '84
Miss Right '81

Johanna Ter Steege
Meeting Venus '91
The Vanishing '88
Vincent & Theo '90

Akira Terao
Akira Kurosawa's Dreams '90
Ran '85

Max Terhune
Arizona Stagecoach '42
Black Market Rustlers '43
Boot Hill Bandits '42
Cowboy Commandos '43
Fugitive Valley '41
Ghost Town Gold '36
Haunted Ranch '43
Heart of the Rockies '37
Heroes of the Hills '38
Hit the Saddle '37
Kid's Last Ride '41
Land of Hunted Men '41
Outlaws of Sonora '38
Overland Stage Raiders '38
Pals of the Saddle '38
Purple Vigilantes '38
Range Busters '40
Ride, Ranger, Ride '36
Riders of the Whistling Skull '37
Roarin' Lead '37
Saddle Mountain Round-Up '41
Santa Fe Stampede '38
Texas to Bataan '42
Three Texas Steers '39
Thunder River Feud '42
Tonto Basin Outlaws '41
Trail of the Silver Spurs '41
Trail Riders '42
Trailing Double Trouble '40
The Trigger Trio '37
Tumbledown Ranch in Arizona '41
Two-Fisted Justice '43
Underground Rustlers '41
West of Pinto Basin '40

Studs Terkel
Eight Men Out '88
Long Shadows '86

John Terlesky
The Allnighter '87
Battling for Baby '92
Chopping Mall '86
Damned River '89
Deathstalker 2: Duel of the Titans '87
When He's Not a Stranger '89

Leonard Termo
Midnight Cabaret '90
Year of the Dragon '85

Steven Terrell
Dragstrip Girl '57
Invasion of the Saucer Men '57
Motorcycle Gang '57

Bob Terry
Brothers of the West '37
Danger Ahead '40
Down the Wyoming Trail '39
Outlaw's Paradise '39

Don Terry
Border Romance '30
Don Winslow of the Coast Guard '43
Don Winslow of the Navy '43

Harry Terry
Broken Melody '34
The Face at the Window '39

John Terry
A Dangerous Woman '93
Hawk the Slayer '81
In Country '89
Iron Will '93
A Killing in a Small Town '90
Of Mice and Men '92
The Resurrected '91
Silhouette '91

Nigel Terry
Caravaggio '86
Christopher Columbus: The Discovery '92
Deja Vu '84
Edward II '92
Excalibur '81
The Lion in Winter '68
Sylvia '86

Phillip Terry
George White's Scandals '45
The Leech Woman '59
The Lost Weekend '45
The Monster and the Girl '41

Ruth Terry
Alexander's Ragtime Band '38
Call of the Canyon '42
Hands Across the Border '43
Heart of the Golden West '42
Texas Legionnaires '43

Sheila Terry
Haunted Gold '32
Lawless Frontier '35
'Neath the Arizona Skies '34
Scarlet Dawn '32
The Sphinx '33

Terry-Thomas
The Abominable Dr. Phibes '71
The Bawdy Adventures of Tom Jones '76
Blue Murder at St. Trinian's '56
Brothers in Law '57
Carlton Browne of the F.O. '59
Danger: Diabolik '68
Doctor Phibes Rises Again '72
Don't Raise the Bridge, Lower the River '68
How Sweet It Is! '68
How to Kill 400 Duponts '65
How to Murder Your Wife '64
I'm All Right Jack '59
It's a Mad, Mad, Mad, Mad World '63
La Grande Vadrouille '66
Lucky Jim '58
Make Mine Mink '60
A Matter of WHO '62
The Naked Truth '58
Those Daring Young Men in Their Jaunty Jalopies '69
Those Fantastic Flying Fools '67
Those Magnificent Men in Their Flying Machines '65
Tom Thumb '58
Too Many Crooks '59
12 Plus 1 '70
Vault of Horror '73
Where Were You When the Lights Went Out? '68
The Wonderful World of the Brothers Grimm '62

Laurent Terzieff
A Coeur Joie '67
Head Over Heels '67
Kapo '59
The Milky Way '68
Red Kiss '85
Vanina Vanini '61

Robert Tessier
Avenging Angel '85
Born Losers '67
The Fix '84
Future Force '89
The Glory Stompers '67
The Last of the Mohicans '85
The Lost Empire '83
Nightwish '89
No Safe Haven '87
Star Crash '78
Sword & the Sorcerer '82
The Velvet Vampire '71
The Villain '79

Fabio Testi
The Ambassador '84
Contraband '86
The Garden of the Finzi-Continis '71
Gunfire '78
The Inheritance '76
Mussolini & I '85
Stateline Motel '75
'Tis a Pity She's a Whore '73
The Uranium Conspiracy '78

Lauren Tewes
Camp Cucamonga: How I Spent My Summer Vacation '90
The China Lake Murders '90
Eyes of a Stranger '81
The Love Boat '70s
Magic Kid '92

Eric Thal
The Gun in Betty Lou's Handbag '92
Six Degrees of Separation '93
A Stranger Among Us '92

Katharina Thalbach
Good Evening, Mr. Wallenberg '93

The Tin Drum '79

Byron Thames
Blame It on the Night '84
84 Charlie Mopic '89
Seven Minutes in Heaven '86

Heather Thatcher
The Moon and Sixpence '43
Son of Fury '42
The Undying Monster '42

Torin Thatcher
Affair in Trinidad '52
Band of Angels '57
Crimson Pirate '52
Darby's Rangers '58
The Desert Rats '53
Diane '55
From Hell to Borneo '64
Great Expectations '46
Holy Terror '65
Houdini '53
Jack the Giant Killer '62
Love is a Many-Splendored
   Thing '55
The Seventh Voyage of Sinbad
   '58
The Snows of Kilimanjaro '52

John Thaw
Business as Usual '88
Chaplin '92
Cry Freedom '87
Killing Heat '84
A Year in Provence '89

Phyllis Thaxter
Jim Thorpe: All American '51
Springfield Rifle '52
Superman: The Movie '78
Thirty Seconds Over Tokyo '44
Three Sovereigns for Sarah '85
Weekend at the Waldorf '45

Brynn Thayer
The Game of Love '90
Hero and the Terror '88
The Tracker '88

Max Thayer
The Dolls '83
No Dead Heroes '87
No Retreat, No Surrender 2 '89
Retrievers '82

Tina Thayer
Jive Junction '43
The Payoff '43

Rosemary Theby
The Fatal Glass of Beer '33
W.C. Fields: Flask of Fields '30

Brother Theodore
The 'Burbs '89
The Invisible Kid '88
That's Adequate '90

Ernest Thesiger
Beware of Pity '46
The Bride of Frankenstein '35
A Christmas Carol '51
The Ghoul '34
Henry V '44
The Old Dark House '32
The Robe '53

David Thewlis
Black Beauty '94
Life is Sweet '91
Naked '93

Debi Thibeault
Assault of the Killer Bimbos '87
Cemetery High '89
Galactic Gigolo '87
Psychos in Love '87

Alan Thicke
Betrayal of the Dove '92
Club Med '83
Not Quite Human '87
Not Quite Human 2 '89
Obsessed '88
Rubdown '93
Scene of the Crime '85
Stepmonster '92
Still Not Quite Human '92

Lynne Thigpen
Article 99 '92
Impulse '90
Lean on Me '89
Naked in New York '93
The Paper '94
Separate But Equal '91
Streets of Fire '84

Roy Thinnes
Code Name: Diamond Head '77
From Here to Eternity '79
The Hindenburg '75
Journey to the Far Side of the
   Sun '69
Rush Week '88
Satan's School for Girls '73
Secrets '77
Sizzle '81

Betty Thomas
Hill Street Blues, Vol. 1: Hill
   Street Station '81
Homework '82
Troop Beverly Hills '89
When Your Lover Leaves '83

**Billie "Buckwheat"
Thomas**
General Spanky '36
Our Gang Comedies '40s

Damien Thomas
Mohammed: Messenger of God
   '77
Pirates '86
Shogun '80
Twins of Evil '71

Danny Thomas
I'll See You in My Dreams '51
The Road to Lebanon '60
Side By Side '88

Dave Thomas
Boris and Natasha: The Movie
   '92
Cold Sweat '93
Coneheads '93
Love at Stake '87
Moving '88
My Man Adam '86
Sesame Street Presents:
   Follow That Bird '85
Strange Brew '83
Stripes '81

**Frank M. Thomas,
Sr.**
Law of the Underworld '36
Sunset on the Desert '42

Frankie Thomas, Jr.
Boys Town '38
Nancy Drew, Reporter '39
Tim Tyler's Luck '37

Gareth Thomas
Super Bitch '89
Visitor from the Grave '81

Heather Thomas
Cyclone '87
The Dirty Dozen: The Fatal
   Mission '87
Ford: The Man & the Machine
   '87
Hidden Obsession '92
Red Blooded American Girl '90
Zapped! '82

Henry Thomas
Cloak & Dagger '84
E.T.: The Extra-Terrestrial '82
Fire in the Sky '93
Misunderstood '88
Murder One '88
Psycho 4: The Beginning '90
The Quest '86
Raggedy Man '81
A Taste for Killing '92
Valmont '89

Jameson Thomas
Beggars in Ermine '34
Convicted '32
The Farmer's Wife '28
Jane Eyre '34
Night Birds '31
Night Life in Reno '31
Sing Sing Nights '35

Jay Thomas
The Gig '85
Little Vegas '90
Straight Talk '92

Marlo Thomas
Act of Passion: The Lost Honor
   of Kathryn Beck '83
Consenting Adult '85
Held Hostage '90
In the Spirit '90
Jenny '70

**Philip Michael
Thomas**
Death Drug '83
False Witness '89
A Fight for Jenny '90
Homeboy '80s
Miami Vice '84
Miami Vice 2: The Prodigal Son
   '85
Sparkle '76
Stigma '73
Streetfight '75
The Wizard of Speed and Time
   '88

Richard Thomas
All Quiet on the Western Front
   '79
Andy and the Airwave Rangers
   '89
Battle Beyond the Stars '80
Berlin Tunnel 21 '81
Cactus in the Snow '72
A Doll's House '59
Glory! Glory! '90
Hobson's Choice '83
Homecoming: A Christmas
   Story '71
Johnny Belinda '82
Last Summer '69
Linda '93
Mission of the Shark '91
Roots: The Next Generation '79
September 30, 1955 '77
Stephen King's It '90
Thanksgiving Story '73
A Thousand Heroes '94
The Todd Killings '71
The Waltons: A Thanksgiving
   Story '73
Winning '69

Robin Thomas
About Last Night... '86
From the Dead of Night '89
Memories of Murder '90
Personals '90
Summer School '87

Ron Thomas
The Big Bet '85
Night Screams '87

Tim Thomerson
Air America '90
Cherry 2000 '88
The Cisco Kid '94
Die Watching '93
Dollman '91
Dollman vs Demonic Toys '93
Fade to Black '80
Fleshtone '94
Glory Years '87
The Harvest '92
Intimate Stranger '91
Iron Eagle '86
Jekyll & Hyde...Together Again
   '82
The Legend of Sleepy Hollow
   '86
Metalstorm '83
Near Dark '87
Nemesis '93
Rhinestone '84
Terraces '77
A Tiger's Tale '87
Trancers '85
Trancers 2: The Return of Jack
   Deth '91
Trancers 3: Deth Lives '92
Trancers 4: Jack of Swords '93
Uncommon Valor '83
Vietnam, Texas '90
Volunteers '85
Who's Harry Crumb? '89
The Wrong Guys '88
Zone Troopers '85

Brian Thompson
Commando Squad '87
Doctor Mordrid: Master of the
   Unknown '92
Hired to Kill '90
Lionheart '90
Moon 44 '90
Rage and Honor '92

Derek Thompson
Belfast Assassin '82
The Long Good Friday '79

Emma Thompson
Dead Again '91
Fortunes of War '87
Henry V '89
Howard's End '92
Impromptu '90
In the Name of the Father '93
Look Back in Anger '89
Much Ado About Nothing '93
Peter's Friends '92
The Remains of the Day '93
The Tall Guy '89

**Fred Dalton
Thompson**
Aces: Iron Eagle 3 '92
Baby's Day Out '94
Barbarians at the Gate '93
Born Yesterday '93
Cape Fear '91
Class Action '91
Curly Sue '91
Days of Thunder '90
Die Hard 2: Die Harder '90
Feds '88
The Hunt for Red October '90
In the Line of Fire '93
Keep the Change '92
Marie '85
No Way Out '87
Thunderheart '92

Hal Thompson
Animal Crackers '30
Lassie from Lancashire '38

Jack Thompson
Bad Blood '87
Breaker Morant '80
Burke & Wills '85
Caddie '81
The Club '81
Deception '92
Earthling '80
A Far Off Place '93
Flesh and Blood '85
Ground Zero '88
Jock Petersen '74
The Killing Beach '92
The Man from Snowy River '82
Merry Christmas, Mr. Lawrence
   '83
Shadow on the Sun '88
Sunday Too Far Away '74
Trouble in Paradise '88
Waterfront '83
Wind '92

Kay Thompson
Funny Face '57
Manhattan Merry-Go-Round
   '37

Lea Thompson
All the Right Moves '83
Article 99 '92
Back to the Future '85
Back to the Future, Part 2 '89
Back to the Future, Part 3 '90
The Beverly Hillbillies '93
Casual Sex? '88
Dennis the Menace '93
Going Undercover '88
Howard the Duck '86
Jaws 3 '83
Montana '90
Nightbreaker '89
Red Dawn '84
Some Kind of Wonderful '87
SpaceCamp '86
The Wild Life '84
The Wizard of Loneliness '88

Marshall Thompson
Battleground '49
Bog '84
The Caddy '53
Clarence, the Cross-eyed Lion
   '65
The Clock '45
Crashout '55
Cult of the Cobra '55
East of Kilimanjaro '59
Fiend Without a Face '58
First Man into Space '59
George! '70
It! The Terror from Beyond
   Space '58
Mighty Jungle '64
The Purple Heart '44
The Show-Off '46
They Were Expendable '45
To Hell and Back '55
To the Shores of Hell '65
The Turning Point '77

Words and Music '48

Rex Thompson
All Mine to Give '56
The Eddy Duchin Story '56
The King and I '56
Young Bess '53

Sada Thompson
The Adventures of Huckleberry
   Finn '85
Desperate Characters '71
Our Town '77

Victoria Thompson
Harrad Experiment '73
Harrad Summer '74

Anna Thomson
The Crow '93
Unforgiven '92

Kenneth Thomson
Broadway Melody '29
Held for Murder '32
Hopalong Cassidy '35
In Old Santa Fe '34
White Gold '28

Kim Thomson
Murder 101 '91
Stealing Heaven '88
The Tall Guy '89

R.H. Thomson
And Then You Die '88
Charlie Grant's War '80
Ford: The Man & the Machine
   '87
Glory Enough for All: The
   Discovery of Insulin '92
Heaven on Earth '89
If You Could See What I Hear
   '82
Love and Hate: A Marriage
   Made in Hell '91
Mark Twain and Me '91
Surfacing '84
Ticket to Heaven '81

Scott Thomson
Fast Times at Ridgemont High
   '82
Ghoulies '85

Jon Mikl Thor
Rock 'n' Roll Nightmare '85
Zombie Nightmare '86

Frankie Thorn
Bad Lieutenant '92
Liquid Dreams '92

Sybil Thorndike
Major Barbara '41
Nicholas Nickleby '46
Nine Days a Queen '34
The Prince and the Showgirl
   '57
Shake Hands with the Devil '59
Stage Fright '50

Dyanne Thorne
Hellhole '85
Ilsa, Harem Keeper of the Oil
   Sheiks '76
Ilsa, She-Wolf of the SS '74
Ilsa, the Tigress of Siberia '79
Ilsa, the Wicked Warden '78
Point of Terror '71

**Courtney Thorne-
Smith**
Lucas '86
Revenge of the Nerds 2: Nerds
   in Paradise '87
Side Out '90
Summer School '87
Welcome to 18 '87

Billy Bob Thornton
Indecent Proposal '93
One False Move '91
Tombstone '93

Noley Thornton
Fine Things '90
Heidi '93

Sigrid Thornton
All the Rivers Run '84
Best Enemies '86
Great Expectations: The Untold
   Story '87
The Lighthorsemen '87
The Man from Snowy River '82
Nevil Shute's The Far Country
   '85
The Night After Halloween '83

Thornton ▶cont.

Over the Hill '93
Return to Snowy River '88
Slate, Wyn & Me '87
Street Hero '84
Jim Thorpe
My Pal, The King '32
White Eagle '32
William Thourlby
Castle of Evil '66
Creeping Terror '64
David Threlfall
A Casualty of War '90
Diana: Her True Story '93
The Russia House '90
When the Whales Came '89
Frank Thring
Alvin Rides Again '74
Howling 3: The Marsupials '87
Mad Max: Beyond
  Thunderdome '85
Ingrid Thulin
After the Rehearsal '84
Brink of Life '57
The Cassandra Crossing '76
Control '87
Cries and Whispers '72
The Damned '69
Hour of the Wolf '68
The Magician '58
Moses '76
Paralyzed '70s
The Silence '63
Wild Strawberries '57
The Winter Light '62
Chief Thundercloud
Call of the Forest '49
King of the Stallions '42
Outlaw Trail '44
The Phantom Rider '46
Ride, Ranger, Ride '36
Rustlers of Red Dog '35
Sonora Stagecoach '44
Bill Thurman
Creature from Black Lake '76
Curse of the Swamp Creature
  '66
Gator Bait '73
It's Alive! '68
Mountaintop Motel Massacre
  '86
Slumber Party '57 '76
Uma Thurman
The Adventures of Baron
  Munchausen '89
Dangerous Liaisons '88
Even Cowgirls Get the Blues
  '94
Final Analysis '92
Henry & June '90
Jennifer 8 '92
Johnny Be Good '88
Kiss Daddy Goodnight '87
Mad Dog and Glory '93
Pulp Fiction '94
Robin Hood '91
Where the Heart Is '90
Carol Thurston
Apache Chief '50
China Sky '44
Swamp Fire '46
Gerard Tichy
Gladiators 7 '62
The Hanging Woman '72
Hatchet for the Honeymoon '70
The Hot Line '69
Ricco '74
Rachel Ticotin
F/X 2: The Deadly Art of Illusion
  '91
Falling Down '93
Fort Apache, the Bronx '81
Keep the Change '92
Natural Born Killers '94
One Good Cop '91
Prison Stories: Women on the
  Inside '91
Spies, Lies and Naked Thighs
  '91
Total Recall '90
When the Bough Breaks '86
Where the Day Takes You '92

Gene Tierney
Advise and Consent '62
The Egyptian '54
The Ghost and Mrs. Muir '47
Heaven Can Wait '43
Laura '44
The Left Hand of God '55
Never Let Me Go '53
Night and the City '50
The Razor's Edge '46
Return of Frank James '40
Scruples '80
The Shanghai Gesture '42
Son of Fury '42
Sundown '41
Toys in the Attic '63
Lawrence Tierney
Abduction '75
Back to Bataan '45
Best of the Badmen '50
Born to Kill '47
The Bushwackers '52
Casualties of Love: The "Long
  Island Lolita" Story '93
City of Hope '91
The Death Merchant '91
The Devil Thumbs a Ride '47
The Devil Thumbs a Ride/
  Having Wonderful Crime '47
Dillinger '45
The Female Jungle '56
The Greatest Show on Earth
  '52
The Hoodlum '51
Midnight '81
Murphy's Law '86
Never Pick Up a Stranger '79
The Offspring '87
Prizzi's Honor '85
The Prowler '81
Reservoir Dogs '92
Those Endearing Young
  Charms '45
Tough Guys Don't Dance '87
Why Me? '90
Maura Tierney
Dead Women in Lingerie '90
The Temp '93
White Sands '92
Pamela Tiffin
The Hallelujah Trail '65
State Fair '62
Summer and Smoke '61
Viva Max '69
Marie Tifo
Les Bons Debarras '81
Pouvoir Intime '87
Kevin Tighe
Another 48 Hrs. '90
Bright Angel '91
Caught in the Act '93
City of Hope '91
Eight Men Out '88
Geronimo: An American
  Legend '93
K-9 '89
Lost Angels '89
Matewan '87
Newsies '92
Road House '89
School Ties '92
Tales from the Crypt, Vol. 3 '90
What's Eating Gilbert Grape '93
Zeffie Tilbury
The Grapes of Wrath '40
The Single Standard '29
Nadja Tiller
The Burning Court '62
Tonio Kroger '65
Wanted: Babysitter '75
Mel Tillis
Uphill All the Way '85
The Villain '79
Grant Tilly
Beyond Reasonable Doubt '80
Carry Me Back '82
Treasure of the Yankee Zephyr
  '83
Jennifer Tilly
The Fabulous Baker Boys '89
Far from Home '89
The Getaway '93
Heads '93
He's My Girl '87
High Spirits '88

Inside Out '91
Let It Ride '89
Made in America '93
Moving Violations '85
No Small Affair '84
Remote Control '88
Rented Lips '88
Scorchers '91
Shadow of the Wolf '92
Meg Tilly
Agnes of God '85
The Big Chill '83
Body Snatchers '93
Carmilla '89
Fallen Angels 2 '93
The Girl in a Swing '89
Impulse '84
Leaving Normal '92
Masquerade '88
Off Beat '86
One Dark Night '82
Psycho 2 '83
Tex '82
The Two Jakes '90
Valmont '89
Charlene Tilton
Border Shootout '90
Center of the Web '92
Deadly Bet '91
Diary of a Teenage Hitchhiker
  '82
The Fall of the House of Usher
  '80
Problem Child 2 '91
Ragin' Cajun '90
Sweater Girls '78
Martha Tilton
The Benny Goodman Story '55
Sunny '41
Charles Tingwell
All the Rivers Run '84
A Cry in the Dark '88
The Desert Rats '53
Endplay '75
Gone to Ground '76
Malcolm '86
Miracle Down Under '87
Money Movers '78
Murder Ahoy '64
Murder at the Gallop '63
Murder Most Foul '65
Murder She Said '62
Windrider '86
Gabriele Tinti
Caged Women '84
Delusions of Grandeur '76
Emmanuelle's Daughter '79
Journey Beneath the Desert '61
Love Camp '76
Trap Them & Kill Them '84
Web of Deception '71
Kenneth Tobey
The Beast from 20,000
  Fathoms '53
The Bigamist '53
Davy Crockett, King of the Wild
  Frontier '55
Freeway '88
The Great Locomotive Chase
  '56
Gunfight at the O.K. Corral '57
Honey, I Blew Up the Kid '92
I Was a Male War Bride '49
Innerspace '87
It Came from Beneath the Sea
  '55
The Lost Empire '83
The Man in the Gray Flannel
  Suit '56
Rage '72
The Search for Bridey Murphy
  '56
Single White Female '92
Strange Invaders '83
The Thing '51
Wings of Eagles '57
George Tobias
Air Force '43
The Bride Came C.O.D. '41
Captains of the Clouds '42
City for Conquest '40
The Hunchback of Notre Dame
  '39
The Judge Steps Out '49
Music in My Heart '40
A New Kind of Love '63
Objective, Burma! '45

Passage to Marseilles '44
Rawhide '50
Sergeant York '41
The Set-Up '49
The Seven Little Foys '55
Silk Stockings '57
Sinbad the Sailor '47
Strawberry Blonde '41
This is the Army '43
Yankee Doodle Dandy '42
Oliver Tobias
The Big Scam '79
King Arthur, the Young Warlord
  '75
Mata Hari '85
Operation 'Nam '85
Romance of a Horsethief '71
The Stud '78
'Tis a Pity She's a Whore '73
The Wicked Lady '83
Young Warlord '75
Dan Tobin
Black Limelight '38
The Last Angry Man '59
Velvet Touch '48
Woman of the Year '42
Vivian Tobin
The Flustered Comedy of Leon
  Errol '39
The World Accuses '35
Stephen Tobolowsky
Basic Instinct '92
Bird on a Wire '90
Breaking In '89
Calendar Girl '93
Deadlock '91
Funny About Love '90
Great Balls of Fire '89
Groundhog Day '93
Hero '92
Josh and S.A.M. '93
Keep My Grave Open '80
Memoirs of an Invisible Man '92
Mississippi Burning '88
Roe vs. Wade '89
Single White Female '92
Sneakers '92
Spaceballs '87
Tagget '90
Thelma & Louise '91
Where the Day Takes You '92
Brian Tochi
Revenge of the Nerds '84
Stitches '85
Ann Todd
Action for Slander '38
The Fiend '71
How Green was My Valley '41
The Human Factor '79
Intermezzo '39
Madeleine '50
The Paradine Case '47
Scream of Fear '61
The Seventh Veil '46
Son of Captain Blood '62
Three Daring Daughters '48
Beverly Todd
Brother John '70
Clara's Heart '88
Don't Look Back: The Story of
  Leroy "Satchel" Paige '81
The Ladies' Club '86
Lean on Me '89
James Todd
High School Confidential '58
Trapped '49
Lisa Todd
Blood Hook '86
Imposters '84
Woman Hunt '72
Mabel Todd
The Cowboy and the Lady '38
The Ghost and the Guest '43
Richard Todd
Battle Hell '56
The Big Sleep '78
Bloodbath
D-Day, the Sixth of June '56
Dam Busters '55
Dorian Gray '70
House of the Long Shadows
  '82
Interrupted Journey '49
The Longest Day '62

A Man Called Peter '55
Never Let Go '60
Number 1 of the Secret Service
  '77
Rob Roy—The Highland Rogue
  '53
Saint Joan '57
The Story of Robin Hood & His
  Merrie Men '52
Subterfuge '68
The Sword & the Rose '53
The Very Edge '63
The Virgin Queen '55
Russell Todd
Border Shootout '90
One Last Run '89
Thelma Todd
Bohemian Girl '36
Cockeyed Cavaliers '34
Corsair '31
The Devil's Brother '33
Hips, Hips, Hooray '34
Horse Feathers '32
Laurel & Hardy Comedy
  Classics, Vol. 4 '32
The Maltese Falcon '31
Monkey Business '31
Palooka '34
Speak Easily '32
Swiss Miss '38
Way Out West '37
Tony Todd
Candyman '92
Criminal Justice '90
The Crow '93
Excessive Force '93
Ivory Hunters '90
Keeper of the City '92
Night of the Living Dead '90
Voodoo Dawn '89
Ugo Tognazzi
Head of the Family '71
A Joke of Destiny, Lying in Wait
  Around the Corner Like a
  Bandit '84
La Cage aux Folles '78
La Cage aux Folles 2 '81
La Cage aux Folles 3: The
  Wedding '86
Love in the City '53
L'Udienza '71
Porcile '71
The Tragedy of a Ridiculous
  Man '81
Niall Toibin
Eat the Peach '86
Lovespell '79
Marilyn Tokuda
The Cage '89
Farewell to the King '89
The Jitters '88
My Tutor '82
Henriette Tol
Broken Mirrors '85
Question of Silence '83
Michael Tolan
Half Slave, Half Free '85
Night Terror '77
Presumed Innocent '90
Sidney Toler
Adventures of Smilin' Jack '43
Blonde Venus '32
Castle in the Desert '42
Champagne for Breakfast '35
Charlie Chan at the Wax
  Museum '40
Charlie Chan in Rio '41
Charlie Chan in the Secret
  Service '44
The Chinese Cat '44
Double Wedding '37
Isle of Forgotten Sins '43
The Jade Mask '45
Law of the Pampas '39
Meeting at Midnight '44
Mr. Moto's Last Warning/
  Meeting at Midnight '44
Murder Over New York '40
The Mysterious Rider '38
A Night to Remember '42
Our Relations '36
The Scarlet Clue '45
The Shanghai Cobra '45
Speak Easily '32
Spitfire '34

Terror by Night/Meeting at Midnight '46
Wide Open Faces '38

John Toles-Bey
Leap of Faith '92
A Rage in Harlem '91
Weeds '87

James Tolkan
Back to the Future '85
Back to the Future, Part 2 '89
Back to the Future, Part 3 '90
Bloodfist 4: Die Trying '92
Boiling Point '93
Dick Tracy '90
Family Business '89
The Hillside Strangler '89
Ministry of Vengeance '89
Off Beat '86
Opportunity Knocks '90
Problem Child 2 '91
Question of Faith '93
Second Sight '89
Sketch Artist '92
Split Decisions '88
Viper '88
Weekend War '88

Marilu Tolo
Confessions of a Police Captain '72
Killer Likes Candy '78
Marriage Italian Style '64
Messalina vs. the Son of Hercules '64
Sleep of Death '79
Terror of Rome Against the Son of Hercules '64

David Tom
Stay Tuned '92
Swing Kids '93

Lauren Tom
The Joy Luck Club '93
Mr. Jones '93
When a Man Loves a Woman '94

Nicholle Tom
Beethoven '92
Beethoven's 2nd '93

Jeana Tomasina
Beach Girls '82
Up the Creek '84

Concetta Tomei
China Beach '88
Don't Tell Mom the Babysitter's Dead '91
The Goodbye Bird '93
In Love and War '91

Marisa Tomei
Chaplin '92
Equinox '93
My Cousin Vinny '92
Only You '94
The Paper '94
Untamed Heart '93
Zandalee '91

Frances Tomelty
Bellman and True '88
Blue Money '84
Bullshot '83
The Field '90
Footlight Frenzy '84
A Perfect Spy '88

Joseph Tomelty
The Atomic Man '56
Devil Girl from Mars '54

Akihiro Tomikawa
Baby Cart 1: Lend a Child...Lend an Arm '72
Baby Cart 4: Heart of a Parent...Heart of a Child '72
Baby Cart at the River Styx '72
Baby Cart to Hades '72

Tamlyn Tomita
Come See the Paradise '90
Hiroshima Maiden '88
Hiroshima: Out of the Ashes '90
The Joy Luck Club '93
The Karate Kid: Part 2 '86
Vietnam, Texas '90

Lily Tomlin
All of Me '84
And the Band Played On '93
The Beverly Hillbillies '93
Big Business '88

The Incredible Shrinking Woman '81
The Late Show '77
Nashville '75
9 to 5 '80
Search for Signs of Intelligent Life in the Universe '91
Shadows and Fog '92
Short Cuts '93

David Tomlinson
Bedknobs and Broomsticks '71
Carry On Admiral '57
Fame is the Spur '47
The Fiendish Plot of Dr. Fu Manchu '80
Made in Heaven '52
Mary Poppins '64
Pimpernel Smith '42
Sleeping Car to Trieste '45
Tom Jones '63
Up the Creek '58
Water Babies '79
Wombling Free '77
Wooden Horse '50

Angel Tompkins
The Bees '78
Crack House '89
The Don is Dead '73
I Love My...Wife '70
Murphy's Law '86
Naked Cage '86
Prime Cut '72
Probe '72
Relentless '89
The Teacher '74
A Tiger's Tale '87
Walking Tall: Part 2 '75

Kate Toncray
The Country Kid '23
The Lamb '15

Franchot Tone
Advise and Consent '62
Bombshell '33
The Bride Wore Red '37
Dancing Lady '33
Dangerous '35
Dark Waters '44
Every Girl Should Be Married '48
Gabriel Over the White House '33
The Girl from Missouri '34
The Gorgeous Hussy '36
Her Husband's Affairs '47
Here Comes the Groom '51
In Harm's Way '65
Jigsaw '49
The Lives of a Bengal Lancer '35
Lost Honeymoon '47
Love on the Run '36
Man on the Eiffel Tower '48
Mutiny on the Bounty '35
Quality Street '37
Reckless '35
Sadie McKee '34
Suzy '26
Three Comrades '38
Today We Live '33

Tone Loc
Ace Ventura: Pet Detective '93
The Adventures of Ford Fairlane '90
Blank Check '93
Posse '93
Surf Ninjas '93

Eijiro Tono
The Human Condition: No Greater Love '58
Yojimbo '61

Taiji Tonoyama
The Island '61
Tokyo Pop '88

Regis Toomey
The Adventures of the Flying Cadets '44
Arizona '40
Betrayal from the East '44
Beyond the Forest '49
The Big Sleep '46
The Bishop's Wife '47
Bulldog Edition '36
Change of Habit '69
Dark Mountain '44
Destroyer '43
Dive Bomber '41
Dynamite Pass '50

"G" Men '35
Great Day in the Morning '56
Laughing at Life '33
The Light of Western Stars '30
Magic Town '47
Meet John Doe '41
Never Wave at a WAC '52
The Phantom Creeps '39
Raiders of Ghost City '44
Shadows of the Orient '37
Skull & Crown '38
Spellbound '45
Strange Illusion '45
They Died with Their Boots On '41
They Never Come Back '32
Warlock '59
Wayne Murder Case '38

Gordon Tootoosis
Call of the Wild '92
Dan Candy's Law '73
Spirit Rider '93
Stone Fox '87

Chaim Topol
Cast a Giant Shadow '66
Fiddler on the Roof '71
Flash Gordon '80
For Your Eyes Only '81
Gun Crazy '69
The House on Garibaldi Street '79
Queenie '87
Sallah '63
War & Remembrance, Part 1 '88
War & Remembrance, The Final Chapter, Part 8 '89
The Winds of War '83

Peta Toppano
Echoes of Paradise '86
Which Way Home '90

Sarah Torgov
American Gothic '88
Drying Up the Streets '76
If You Could See What I Hear '82

Mel Torme
Girls' Town '59
Good News '47
A Man Called Adam '66
Words and Music '48

Rip Torn
Airplane 2: The Sequel '82
Another Pair of Aces: Three of a Kind '91
Baby Doll '56
Beastmaster '82
Beautiful Dreamers '92
Beer '85
Betrayal '78
The Birch Interval '78
Blind Ambition '82
By Dawn's Early Light '89
Canadian Bacon '94
Cat on a Hot Tin Roof '84
The Cincinnati Kid '65
City Heat '84
Cold Feet '89
Coma '78
Cotter '72
Cross Creek '83
Dead Ahead: The Exxon Valdez Disaster '92
Defending Your Life '91
Dolly Dearest '92
The Execution '85
Extreme Prejudice '87
Flashpoint '84
Hard Promises '92
Heartland '81
The Hit List '88
J. Edgar Hoover '87
Jinxed '82
The King of Kings '61
Laguna Heat '87
The Man Who Fell to Earth '76
Manhunt for Claude Dallas '86
Misunderstood '84
Nadine '87
Nasty Habits '77
One Trick Pony '80
Pair of Aces '90
Payday '72
Pork Chop Hill '59
The President's Plane is Missing '71

The Private Files of J. Edgar Hoover '77
Rape and Marriage: The Rideout Case '80
RoboCop 3 '91
The Seduction of Joe Tynan '79
A Shining Season '79
Silence Like Glass '90
Slaughter '72
Songwriter '84
Steel Cowboy '78
A Stranger is Watching '82
Summer Rental '85
Sweet Bird of Youth '62
Sweet Bird of Youth '89
Tropic of Cancer '70
24 Hours in a Woman's Life '61
You're a Big Boy Now '66

Regina Torne
El Cuarto Chino '71
Like Water for Chocolate '93
Los Asesinos '68

Mari Torocsik
The Bachelor '93
Love '71

David Torrence
Disraeli '29
Jane Eyre '34
The Mask of Fu Manchu '32

Ernest Torrence
The Covered Wagon '23
Fighting Caravans '31
The Hunchback of Notre Dame '23
I Cover the Waterfront '33
King of Kings '27
Mantrap '26
The Pony Express '25
Steamboat Bill, Jr. '28
Tol'able David '21

Ana Torrent
Blood and Sand '89
Cria '76
The Nest '80
Spirit of the Beehive '73

Liz Torres
America '86
Bloodfist 4: Die Trying '92
Lena's Holiday '90

Raquel Torres
Duck Soup '33
White Shadows in the South Seas '28

Jose Torvay
Borderline '50
Green Fire '55
The Hitch-Hiker '53
My Outlaw Brother '51

Leslie Toth
Buying Time '89
Unfinished Business '89

Toto
Bellissimo: Images of the Italian Cinema '87
Big Deal on Madonna Street '58
The Gold of Naples '54
The Hawks & the Sparrows '67
Passionate Thief '60

Merle Tottenham
Cavalcade '33
Room to Let '49

Audrey Totter
Any Number Can Play '49
The Carpetbaggers '64
FBI Girl '51
Jet Attack/Paratroop Command '58
Lady in the Lake '46
Man or Gun '58
Murderer's Wife
The Postman Always Rings Twice '46
The Set-Up '49

George Touliatos
Firebird 2015 A.D. '81
Robbers of the Sacred Mountain '83

Tamara Toumanova
Days of Glory '43
Invitation to the Dance '56

Sheila Tousey
Silent Tongue '92
Slaughter of the Innocents '93

Thunderheart '92

Lorraine Toussaint
Breaking In '89
A Case of Deadly Force '86
Mother's Boys '94
Point of No Return '93

Roland Toutain
Liliom '35
The Rules of the Game '39

Lupita Tova
Border Law '31
Dracula (Spanish Version) '31
Old Spanish Custom '36

Constance Towers
Naked Kiss '64
On Wings of Eagles '86
Sergeant Rutledge '60
Shock Corridor '63
Sylvester '85

Tom Towles
Blood In...Blood Out: Bound by Honor '93
The Borrower '89
Henry: Portrait of a Serial Killer '90
Mad Dog and Glory '93
Night of the Living Dead '90
The Pit & the Pendulum '91

Aline Towne
Don Daredevil Rides Again '51
The Invisible Monster '50
Radar Men from the Moon '52
Trader Tom of the China Seas '54
The Vanishing Westerner '50
Zombies of the Stratosphere '52

Robert Towne
The Pick-Up Artist '87
Villa Rides '68

Jill Townsend
Oh, Alfie '75
Poldark '75

Patrice Townsend
Always '85
Sitting Ducks '80

Robert Townsend
American Flyers '85
The Five Heartbeats '91
Hollywood Shuffle '87
The Meteor Man '93
The Mighty Quinn '89
Odd Jobs '85
Ratboy '86
A Soldier's Story '84
Streets of Fire '84
That's Adequate '90

Pete Townshend
Monterey Pop '68
Pete Townshend: White City '85
The Secret Policeman's Other Ball '82
Secret Policeman's Private Parts '81
Tommy '75
Woodstock '70

Fausto Tozzi
East of Kilimanjaro '59
The Return of Dr. Mabuse '61
Sicilian Connection '74

Ian Tracey
The Comrades of Summer '92
Timecop '94

Emerson Tracy
Champagne for Breakfast '35
A Star is Born '54

Lee Tracy
The Best Man '64
Betrayal from the East '44
Blessed Event '32
Bombshell '33
Dinner at Eight '33
Doctor X '32
The Payoff '43
The Strange Love of Molly Louvain '32

Spencer Tracy
Adam's Rib '50
Bad Day at Black Rock '54
Boom Town '40
Boys Town '38
Broken Lance '54

Tracy ►*cont.*

Captains Courageous '37
Cass Timberlane '47
Desk Set '57
The Devil at 4 O'Clock '61
Dr. Jekyll and Mr. Hyde '41
Edison the Man '40
Father of the Bride '50
Father's Little Dividend '51
Fury '36
Guess Who's Coming to Dinner '67
A Guy Named Joe '44
Hepburn & Tracy '84
How the West was Won '63
Inherit the Wind '60
It's a Mad, Mad, Mad, Mad World '63
Judgment at Nuremberg '61
Last Hurrah '58
Libeled Lady '36
Malaya '49
Mannequin '37
Marie Galante '34
Men of Boys Town '41
The Mountain '56
Northwest Passage '40
Pat and Mike '52
Riff Raff '35
San Francisco '36
The Seventh Cross '44
Stanley and Livingstone '39
State of the Union '48
Test Pilot '38
Thirty Seconds Over Tokyo '44
Tortilla Flat '42
Without Love '45
Woman of the Year '42

William Tracy
Angels with Dirty Faces '38
As You Were '51
George Washington Slept Here '42
Mr. Walkie Talkie '52
Strike Up the Band '40
Tanks a Million '41
To the Shores of Tripoli '42

Mary Ellen Trainor
Die Hard '88
Fire Birds '90
The Goonies '85
Grand Canyon '91
Lethal Weapon 2 '89
Ricochet '91
Tales from the Crypt '89

Cordula Trantow
The Castle '68
Hitler '62

Helen Traubel
Deep in My Heart '54
The Ladies' Man '61

Daniel J. Travanti
Adam '83
A Case of Libel '83
Fellow Traveler '89
Hill Street Blues, Vol. 1: Hill Street Station '81
Megaville '91
Midnight Crossing '87
Millenium '89
Murrow '86
St. Ives '76
Tagget '90
Weep No More My Lady '93

Bill Travers
Bhowani Junction '56
Born Free '66
The Browning Version '51
Christian the Lion '76
Duel at Diablo '66
The First Olympics: Athens 1896 '84
Gorgo '61
A Midsummer Night's Dream '68
Ring of Bright Water '69
Romeo and Juliet '54
The Smallest Show on Earth '57
Trio '50

Henry Travers
Ball of Fire '41
The Bells of St. Mary's '45
Dark Victory '39

Dodge City '39
Dragon Seed '44
Edison the Man '40
A Girl, a Guy and a Gob '41
High Sierra '41
It's a Wonderful Life '46
Madame Curie '43
Mrs. Miniver '42
The Naughty Nineties '45
On Borrowed Time '39
Primrose Path '40
The Rains Came '39
Random Harvest '42
Shadow of a Doubt '43
The Sisters '38
Stanley and Livingstone '39
Thrill of a Romance '45
The Yearling '46

Linden Travers
The Lady Vanishes '38
The Terror '38

Susan Travers
The Abominable Dr. Phibes '71
Peeping Tom '63
The Snake Woman '61

June Travis
Ceiling Zero '35
Earthworm Tractors '36
Exiled to Shanghai '37
The Gladiator '38
Monster a Go-Go! '65

Nancy Travis
Air America '90
Chaplin '92
Fallen Angels 1 '93
Greedy '94
Harem '85
Internal Affairs '90
Loose Cannons '90
Married to the Mob '88
Passed Away '92
So I Married an Axe Murderer '93
Three Men and a Baby '87
Three Men and a Little Lady '90
The Vanishing '93

Richard Travis
Big Town After Dark '47
Danger Zone '51
Fingerprints Don't Lie '51
The Man Who Came to Dinner '41
Mask of the Dragon '51
Mesa of Lost Women '52
Missile to the Moon '59
One Too Many '51
Roaring City '51
Sky Liner '49

Stacy Travis
Dr. Hackenstein '88
Dracula Rising '93
Hardware '90
Only the Strong '93

Joey Travolta
American Born '89
Car Crash
DaVinci's War '92
Ghost Writer '89
The Prodigal '83
Rosie: The Rosemary Clooney Story '82
Sinners '89
Sunnyside '79
Wilding '90

John Travolta
Blow Out '81
The Boy in the Plastic Bubble '76
Carrie '76
Chains of Gold '92
Devil's Rain '75
Dumb Waiter '87
The Experts '89
Grease '78
Look Who's Talking '89
Look Who's Talking Now '93
Look Who's Talking, Too '90
Perfect '85
Pulp Fiction '94
Saturday Night Fever '77
Shout '91
Staying Alive '83
Two of a Kind '83
Urban Cowboy '80

Arthur Treacher
Curly Top '35

David Copperfield '35
Delightfully Dangerous '45
Heidi '37
I Live My Life '35
In Society '44
The Little Princess '39
A Midsummer Night's Dream '35
My Lucky Star '38
National Velvet '44
Satan Met a Lady '36
Stowaway '36
Thin Ice '37

Terri Treas
Deathstalker 3 '89
House 4: Home Deadly Home '91
The Nest '88
Rage and Honor '92
The Terror Within '88

Robert Trebor
52 Pick-Up '86
Out of the Darkness '85

Dorothy Tree
Abe Lincoln in Illinois '40
Hitler: Dead or Alive '43
Mystery of Mr. Wong '39

Mary Treen
Casanova Brown '44
Clipped Wings '53
Hands Across the Border '43
I Married a Monster from Outer Space '58
It's a Wonderful Life '46
Paradise, Hawaiian Style '66
The Sad Sack '57
Swing It, Sailor! '37

Les Tremayne
The Angry Red Planet '59
Creature of Destruction '67
Fangs '75
The Gallant Hours '60
I Love Melvin '53
A Man Called Peter '55
The Monolith Monsters '57
The Monster of Piedras Blancas '57
The Slime People '63
The War of the Worlds '53

Johanne-Marie Tremblay
Jesus of Montreal '89
Straight for the Heart '88

John Trent
Mystery Plane '39
Stunt Pilot '39

Adam Trese
The Good Fight '92
Laws of Gravity '92

Frederick Treves
Flame to the Phoenix '85
Paper Mask '91

Roger Treville
The Green Glove '52
Mr. Peek-A-Boo '50

Vic Trevino
Born in East L.A. '87
Firehawk '92

Austin Trevor
Broken Melody '34
Mimi '35
The Silent Passenger '35

Claire Trevor
Allegheny Uprising '39
Babe Ruth Story '48
Baby, Take a Bow '34
Best of the Badmen '50
Borderline '50
Born to Kill '47
Breaking Home Ties '87
Crack-Up '46
Dark Command '40
Dead End '37
Honky Tonk '41
Hoodlum Empire '52
How to Murder Your Wife '64
Johnny Angel '45
Key Largo '48
Kiss Me Goodbye '82
Man Without a Star '55
Marjorie Morningstar '58
The Mountain '56
Murder, My Sweet '44
Stagecoach '39

The Stranger Wore a Gun '53
The Stripper '63
Texas '41
Two Weeks in Another Town '62
Velvet Touch '48
The Woman of the Town '44

Jack Trevor
Champagne '28
Secrets of a Soul '25

Ivan Triesault
The Amazing Transparent Man '60
Cry of the Werewolf '44
Five Fingers '52
Golden Earrings '47
Jet Pilot '57

Leopoldo Trieste
Cinema Paradiso '88
Divorce—Italian Style '62
Henry IV '85
I Vitelloni '53
Quo Vadis '85
The White Sheik '52

Trigger
Under Western Stars '45
Western Double Feature 6: Rogers & Trigger '50
Western Double Feature 10: Roy, Dale, & Trigger '80s
Western Double Feature 15 '50
Western Double Feature 19 '45

Sarah Trigger
Bill & Ted's Bogus Journey '91
Deadfall '93
El Diablo '90
Kid '90
Paradise '91
P.C.U. '94
Pet Sematary 2 '92
Sleepless in Seattle '93

Jerry Trimble
Breathing Fire '91
Full Contact '93

Jean-Louis Trintignant
Act of Aggression '73
And God Created Woman '57
And Hope to Die '72
Confidentially Yours '83
The Conformist '71
Dangerous Liaisons '60
The Easy Life '63
I Love All of You '83
Il Sorpasso '63
Intruder '77
Is Paris Burning? '68
Journey Beneath the Desert '61
The Last Train '74
Le Secret '74
Les Biches '68
Les Violons du Bal '74
A Man and a Woman '66
A Man and a Woman: 20 Years Later '86
My Night at Maud's '69
Next Summer '84
The Outside Man '73
Passion of Love '82
Rendez-vous '85
Trois Couleurs: Rouge '94
Under Fire '83
Z '69

Marie Trintignant
Alberto Express '92
Next Summer '84
The Story of Women '88

Louis Tripp
The Gate '87
Gate 2 '92

Jeanne Tripplehorn
Basic Instinct '92
The Firm '93
The Night We Never Met '93

Elisabeth Trissenaar
Angry Harvest '85
Berlin Alexanderplatz '80
A Love in Germany '84
The Stationmaster's Wife '77

Dorothy Tristan
Down and Out in Beverly Hills '86
End of the Road '70

Griffin and Phoenix: A Love Story '76

Laura Trotter
City of the Walking Dead '83
Miami Horror '87
Rush '84

Patrick Troughton
The Franchise Affair '52
The Gorgon '64
The Moonraker '58
The Scars of Dracula '70

Charles Trowbridge
The Fatal Hour '40
Gang Bullets '38
Libeled Lady '36
The Mummy's Hand '40
Sea Racketeers '37

Phillip Troy
Ice '93
To Be the Best '93

Isabelle Truchon
Backstab '90
Deadbolt '92

Jim True
The Hudsucker Proxy '93
Singles '92

Ernest Truex
The Adventures of Marco Polo '38
All Mine to Give '56
Club Havana '46
His Girl Friday '40

Francois Truffaut
Close Encounters of the Third Kind '77
Day for Night '73
The 400 Blows '59
The Green Room '78

Raoul Trujillo
The Adjuster '91
Scanners 2: The New Order '91

Valentin Trujillo
La Virgen de Guadalupe '87
Scanners 2: The New Order '91
Simon Blanco '87

Ralph Truman
Henry V '44
The Man Who Knew Too Much '56
The Silent Passenger '35
The Spaniard's Curse '58
Treasure Island '50

Natalie Trundy
Battle for the Planet of the Apes '73
Beneath the Planet of the Apes '70
Conquest of the Planet of the Apes '72
Escape from the Planet of the Apes '71
Huckleberry Finn '74

Glenn Tryon
Battling Orioles '24
Tangled Destinies '32

Tom Tryon
The Cardinal '63
Color Me Dead '69
Geronimo's Revenge '60
Gunfight at Sandoval '59
I Married a Monster from Outer Space '58
In Harm's Way '65
The Longest Day '62
Moon Pilot '62
The Story of Ruth '60
Texas John Slaughter: Geronimo's Revenge '60
Texas John Slaughter: Stampede at Bitter Creek '62
Three Violent People '57
Unholy Wife '57

Ludmila Tselikovskaya
Ivan the Terrible, Part 1 '44
Ivan the Terrible, Part 2 '46

Irene Tsu
How to Stuff a Wild Bikini '65
Paradise, Hawaiian Style '66
Women of the Prehistoric Planet '66

Yoshio Tsuchiya
Attack of the Mushroom People '63
Destroy All Monsters '68
Red Beard '65
Yog, Monster from Space '71

Masahiko Tsugawa
Heaven & Earth '90
The Sun's Burial '60
A Taxing Woman's Return '88

Koji Tsurata
Samurai 3: Duel at Ganryu Island '56
The Secret of the Telegian '61

Barry Tubb
Billionaire Boys Club '87
Consenting Adult '85
Guilty by Suspicion '91
Mask '85
Return to Lonesome Dove '93
Top Gun '86
Valentino Returns '88
Warm Summer Rain '89

William Tubbs
Paisan '46
Wages of Fear '55

Maria Tucci
Enormous Changes '83
Touch and Go '86
Trumps '82

Stanley Tucci
Beethoven '92
Billy Bathgate '91
Fear, Anxiety and Depression '89
In the Soup '92
It Could Happen to You '94
Men of Respect '91
Monkey Shines '88
The Pelican Brief '93
Prelude to a Kiss '92
The Public Eye '92
Undercover Blues '93

Forrest Tucker
The Adventures of Huckleberry Finn '78
Auntie Mame '58
The Big Cat '49
Bugles in the Afternoon '52
Cancel My Reservation '72
Chisum '70
Coroner Creek '48
The Cosmic Monsters '58
The Crawling Eye '58
The Finger Man '55
Hellfire '49
Hoodlum Empire '52
The Incredible Rocky Mountain Race '77
Jubilee Trail '54
Montana Belle '52
The Nevadan '50
Outtakes '85
Pony Express '53
Rage at Dawn '55
A Rare Breed '81
A Real American Hero '78
The Rebels '79
Robot Pilot '41
Sands of Iwo Jima '49
Three Violent People '57
Thunder Run '86
Timestalkers '87
Trouble in the Glen '54
Wackiest Wagon Train in the West '77
Walking Tall: The Final Chapter '77
The Westerner '40
The Yearling '46

Martin Tucker
Death Screams '83
House of Death '82

Michael Tucker
Assault and Matrimony '89
Checking Out '89
Day One '89
Diner '82
D2: The Mighty Ducks '94
Eyes of Laura Mars '78
For Love or Money '93
L.A. Law '86
The Purple Rose of Cairo '85
Radio Days '87
Spy '89
Tin Men '87

Richard Tucker
The Bat Whispers '30
Captain Swagger '25
Convicted '32
Delinquent Parents '38
King of the Kongo '29
The Worldly Madonna '22

Rocky Tucker
Lunatic '91
Steps from Hell '92

Sophie Tucker
Broadway Melody of 1938 '37
Sensations of 1945 '44
Thoroughbreds Don't Cry '37

Tanya Tucker
Follow That Car '80
Hard Country '81
The Rebels '79

Sonny Tufts
Cat Women of the Moon '53
Easy Living '49
The Gift Horse '52
Serpent Island '54
The Seven Year Itch '55

Tom Tully
Adventure '45
The Caine Mutiny '54
Coogan's Bluff '68
Destination Tokyo '43
June Bride '48
Lady in the Lake '46
Love is Better Than Ever '52
Love Me or Leave Me '55
Northern Pursuit '43
Soldier of Fortune '55
Ten North Frederick '58
Texas Carnival '51
Till the End of Time '46
Trouble Along the Way '53

Tommy Tune
The Boy Friend '71
Hello, Dolly! '69

Robin Tunney
Encino Man '92
JFK: Reckless Youth '93

Paige Turco
Teenage Mutant Ninja Turtles 2: The Secret of the Ooze '91
Teenage Mutant Ninja Turtles 3 '93

Ann Turkel
The Cassandra Crossing '76
Death Ray 2000 '81
Deep Space '87
Golden Rendezvous '77
Humanoids from the Deep '80
The Last Contract '86
99 & 44/100 Dead '74
Paper Lion '68
Portrait of a Hitman '77

Joe Turkel
Blade Runner '82
Cycle Psycho
Dark Side of the Moon '90
The Desperados '80s
The Shining '80

Glynn Turman
The Blue Knight '75
Charlotte Forten's Mission: Experiment in Freedom '85
Cooley High '75
Deep Cover '92
A Hero Ain't Nothin' But a Sandwich '78
J.D.'s Revenge '76
Penitentiary 2 '82
The River Niger '76
Secrets of a Married Man '84

John Turnbull
The Happiest Days of Your Life '50
Make-Up '37
Man of Evil '48
The Passing of the Third Floor Back '36

Elizabeth Turner
Invasion of the Flesh Hunters '82
Truck Stop

Florence Turner
Pace That Kills '28
Tale of Two Cities/In the Switch Tower '15

Walking Back '26

George Turner
Son of Zorro '47
Vigilantes of Boom Town '46

Janine Turner
The Ambulance '90
Cliffhanger '93
Knights of the City '85
Monkey Shines '88
Steel Magnolias '89

Jim Turner
Kid Colter '85
My Samurai '92

Kathleen Turner
The Accidental Tourist '88
Body Heat '81
A Breed Apart '84
Crimes of Passion '84
House of Cards '92
The Jewel of the Nile '85
Julia and Julia '87
The Man with Two Brains '83
Naked in New York '93
Peggy Sue Got Married '86
Prizzi's Honor '85
Romancing the Stone '84
Serial Mom '94
Switching Channels '88
Undercover Blues '93
V.I. Warshawski '91
The War of the Roses '89

Lana Turner
Another Time, Another Place '58
Bachelor in Paradise '69
The Bad and the Beautiful '52
Betrayed '54
Bittersweet Love '76
By Love Possessed '61
Cass Timberlane '47
Diane '55
Dr. Jekyll and Mr. Hyde '41
The Graveyard '74
Green Dolphin Street '47
Homecoming '48
Honky Tonk '41
Imitation of Life '59
Johnny Eager '42
Latin Lovers '53
A Life of Her Own '50
Love Finds Andy Hardy '38
Love has Many Faces '65
Madame X '66
The Making of a Legend: "Gone With the Wind" '89
The Merry Widow '52
Peyton Place '57
The Postman Always Rings Twice '46
The Prodigal '55
Sea Chase '55
Somewhere I'll Find You '42
They Won't Forget '37
The Three Musketeers '48
Weekend at the Waldorf '45
Who's Got the Action? '63
Witches' Brew '79
Ziegfeld Girl '41

Tina Turner
Mad Max: Beyond Thunderdome '85
Tommy '75

Ben Turpin
Ben Turpin: An Eye for an Eye '24
Burlesque of Carmen '16
Cannon Ball/Eyes Have It '15
The Champion/His New Job '15
Chaplin Essanay Book 1 '15
Charlie Chase and Ben Turpin '21
Chasing Those Depression Blues '35
Desperate Scoundrel/The Pride of Pikeville '22
Eyes of Turpin Are Upon You! '21
Golden Age of Comedy '58
Laughfest '10s
Laurel & Hardy Comedy Classics, Vol. 6 '35
Law of the Wild '34
Mack Sennett Comedies: Vol. 1 '21
Saps at Sea '40
Silent Laugh Makers, No. 1 '15
Slapstick '30s

When Comedy was King '59
Yankee Doodle in Berlin '19

Aida Turturro
Angie '94
Jersey Girl '92
True Love '89

John Turturro
Backtrack '89
Barton Fink '91
Being Human '94
Brain Donors '92
The Color of Money '86
Desperately Seeking Susan '85
Do the Right Thing '89
Fearless '93
Five Corners '88
Gung Ho '85
Hannah and Her Sisters '86
Jungle Fever '91
Mac '93
Men of Respect '91
Miller's Crossing '90
Mo' Better Blues '90
Off Beat '86
The Sicilian '87
State of Grace '90
To Live & Die in L.A. '85

Nicholas Turturro
Mac '93
Mo' Better Blues '90

Rita Tushingham
Doctor Zhivago '65
Dream to Believe '85
Dressed for Death '74
Green Eyes '76
The Housekeeper '86
The Human Factor '75
The Knack '65
Leather Boys '63
Loose in New York '80s
Mysteries '84
Paper Marriage '93
Rachel's Man '75
Slaughterday '77
Spaghetti House '82
A Taste of Honey '61
Trap '66

Dorothy Tutin
Savage Messiah '72
The Shooting Party '85
Sister Dora '77
Six Wives of Henry VIII '70s
A Tale of Two Cities '58

Lurene Tuttle
The Affairs of Dobie Gillis '53
Don't Bother to Knock '52
The Fortune Cookie '66
The Glass Slipper '55
Homecoming '48
Ma Barker's Killer Brood '60
White Mama '80

Shannon Tweed
Cannibal Women in the Avocado Jungle of Death '89
Codename: Vengeance '87
Cold Sweat '93
The Firing Line '91
Hard Vice '94
Hitchhiker 4 '87
Hot Dog...The Movie! '83
In the Cold of the Night '89
Indecent Behavior '93
Last Call '90
The Last Fling '86
The Last Hour '91
Lethal Woman '88
Liar's Edge '92
Meatballs 3 '87
Model by Day '94
Night Eyes 2 '91
Night Eyes 3 '93
Night Visitor '89
Of Unknown Origin '83
Scorned '93
Sexual Response '92
Surrogate '88
Twisted Justice '89

Terry Tweed
Night Rhythms '92
The Reincarnate '71

Helen Twelvetrees
Millie '31
Painted Desert '31
State's Attorney '31

Twiggy
Body Bags '93

The Boy Friend '71
Butterfly Ball '76
Club Paradise '86
The Diamond Trap '91
The Doctor and the Devils '85
Istanbul '90
The Little Match Girl '87
Madame Sousatzka '88
W '74
Young Charlie Chaplin '88

Anne Twomey
Behind Enemy Lines '85
Deadly Friend '86
Last Rites '88
Orpheus Descending '91
The Scout '94

Tom Tyler
The Adventures of Captain Marvel '41
Battling with Buffalo Bill '31
Brothers of the West '37
Cheyenne Rides Again '38
Coyote Trails '35
Deadwood Pass '33
Fast Bullets '44
Feud of the Trail '37
The Forty-Niners '32
Guns of Justice '50
Laramie Kid '35
Last Outlaw '36
The Mummy's Hand '40
Phantom of the Air '33
The Phantom of the Range '38
Phantom of the West '31
Pinto Rustlers '36
Powdersmoke Range '35
Riders of the Timberline '41
Ridin' Thru '35
Riding On '37
Rio Rattler '35
Rip Roarin' Buckaroo '36
Roamin' Wild '36
Santa Fe Bound '37
Silent Code '35
Silent Valley '35
Stagecoach '39
Two Fisted Justice '31
Valley of the Sun '42
When a Man Rides Alone '33

George Tyne
Call Northside 777 '48
Open Secret '48

Charles Tyner
Harold and Maude '71
Planes, Trains & Automobiles '87
Pulse '88

Susan Tyrrell
Andy Warhol's Bad '77
Angel '84
Another Man, Another Chance '77
Avenging Angel '85
Big Top Pee Wee '88
Cry-Baby '90
Far from Home '89
Fast Walking '82
Fat City '72
Flesh and Blood '85
Forbidden Zone '80
Islands in the Stream '77
Killer Inside Me '76
Lady of the House '78
Liar's Moon '82
Loose Shoes '80
Motorama '91
Night Warning '82
The Offspring '87
Poker Alice '87
Rockula '90
September 30, 1955 '77
Tales of Ordinary Madness '83
Tapeheads '89
Thompson's Last Run '90
The Underachievers '88
Windmills of the Gods '88
Zandy's Bride '74

Cathy Tyson
Business as Usual '88
The Lost Language of Cranes '92
Mona Lisa '86
The Serpent and the Rainbow '87

Cicely Tyson
Acceptable Risks '86

Tyson ▶*cont.*

The Autobiography of Miss
  Jane Pittman '74
Bustin' Loose '81
The Concorde: Airport '79 '79
Duplicates '92
Fried Green Tomatoes '91
The Heart is a Lonely Hunter
  '68
Heat Wave '90
A Hero Ain't Nothin' But a
  Sandwich '78
The Kid Who Loved Christmas
  '90
King '78
A Man Called Adam '66
The River Niger '76
Roots '77
Samaritan: The Mitch Snyder
  Story '86
Sounder '72
Wilma '77
A Woman Called Moses '78
The Women of Brewster Place
  '89

Richard Tyson
The Babe '92
Dark Tide '93
Kindergarten Cop '90
Red Shoe Diaries 3: Another
  Woman's Lipstick '93
Three O'Clock High '87
Two Moon Junction '88

Margaret Tyzack
The King's Whore '90
Mr. Love '86
Quatermass Conclusion '79

Fabiana Udenio
Bride of Re-Animator '89
Hardbodies 2 '86

Claudia Udy
Captive Rage '88
Out of Control '85
The Pink Chiquitas '86

Bob Uecker
Major League '89
Major League 2 '94

Leslie Uggams
Poor Pretty Eddie '73
Sizzle '81
Sugar Hill '94
Two Weeks in Another Town
  '62

Gisela Uhlen
The Indian Scarf '63
The Marriage of Maria Braun
  '79
Toto le Heros '91

Tracey Ullman
Give My Regards to Broad
  Street '84
Household Saints '93
I Love You to Death '90
I'll Do Anything '93
Plenty '85
Robin Hood: Men in Tights '93
Three of a Kind '80s

Liv Ullmann
Autumn Sonata '78
The Bay Boy '85
A Bridge Too Far '77
Cold Sweat '74
Cries and Whispers '72
Dangerous Moves '84
The Emigrants '72
Face to Face '76
Forty Carats '73
Gaby: A True Story '87
Hour of the Wolf '68
Leonor '75
Mindwalk: A Film for
  Passionate Thinkers '91
The New Land '73
The Night Visitor '70
The Ox '91
The Passion of Anna '70
Persona '66
Richard's Things '80
The Rose Garden '89
Scenes from a Marriage '73
The Serpent's Egg '78
The Shame '68
The Wild Duck '84

Zandy's Bride '74

Lenore Ulric
Camille '36
Northwest Outpost '47

Mikhail Ulyanov
Private Life '82
The Theme '79

Margaret Umbers
The Bridge to Nowhere '86
Death Warmed Up '85

Miyoshi Umeki
Flower Drum Song '61
The Horizontal Lieutenant '62
Sayonara '57

Yoko Umemura
Sisters of Gion '36
The Story of the Late
  Chrysanthemum '39

Edward Underdown
Inspector Hornleigh '39
Man on the Run '49
The Shadow Man '53

Blair Underwood
Dangerous Relations '93
Heat Wave '90
Krush Groove '85
Posse '93

Jay Underwood
The Boy Who Could Fly '86
Desert Bloom '86
The Gumshoe Kid '89
The Invisible Kid '88
Not Quite Human '87
Not Quite Human 2 '89
Promised Land '88
Still Not Quite Human '92
To Die for 2 '91
Uncle Buck '89

Deborah Unger
Highlander 3: The Sorcerer '94
Hotel Room '93
Prisoners of the Sun '91
Till There was You '91
Whispers in the Dark '92

Mary Ure
Look Back in Anger '58
A Reflection of Fear '72
Where Eagles Dare '68
Windom's Way '57

Fabio Urena
The Bronx War '90
Return of the Living Dead 3 '93

Robert Urich
Blind Man's Bluff '91
Bunco '83
Endangered Species '82
Hit Woman: The Double Edge
  '93
Ice Pirates '84
In a Stranger's Hand '92
Invitation to Hell '84
Killing at Hell's Gate '81
Lonesome Dove '89
Magnum Force '73
Mistral's Daughter '84
Murder by Night '89
A Perfect Little Murder '90
Revolver '92
The Shadow Box '80
Take Your Best Shot '82
Turk 182! '85
Vegas '78

Robert Urquhart
Children of the Full Moon '84
The Curse of Frankenstein '57
The House of the Arrow '53
The Kitchen Toto '87
Playing Away '87
Sharma & Beyond '84
White Huntress '57

**Benny "The Jet"
Urquidez**
Bloodmatch '91
Down the Drain '89
The Kick Fighter '91

Susan Ursitti
Defense Play '88
Teen Wolf '85

Peter Ustinov
Appointment with Death '88
Ashanti, Land of No Mercy '79
Barefoot in Athens '66
Beau Brummel '54

Billy Budd '62
Blackbeard's Ghost '67
Charlie Chan and the Curse of
  the Dragon Queen '81
The Comedians '67
Death on the Nile '78
The Egyptian '54
Evil Under the Sun '82
Hammersmith is Out '72
Hot Millions '68
Immortal Battalion '44
The Last Remake of Beau
  Geste '77
Logan's Run '76
Lola Montes '55
Lorenzo's Oil '92
The Man Who Wagged His Tail
  '57
One of Our Aircraft Is Missing
  '41
One of Our Dinosaurs Is
  Missing '75
The Purple Taxi '77
Quo Vadis '51
Spartacus '60
The Sundowners '60
The Thief of Baghdad '78
Topkapi '64
The Treasure of Matecumbe
  '76
Viva Max '69
We're No Angels '55

Kari Vaananen
Amazon '90
La Vie de Boheme '93
Leningrad Cowboys Go
  America '89
Night on Earth '91

Brenda Vaccaro
Airport '77 '77
Capricorn One '78
Cookie '89
Dear Detective '78
Death Weekend '76
The First Deadly Sin '80
The Guyana Tragedy: The
  Story of Jim Jones '80
Heart of Midnight '89
Honor Thy Father '73
I Love My...Wife '70
Lethal Games '90
A Long Way Home '81
Masque of the Red Death '90
Midnight Cowboy '69
Once is Not Enough '75
Pride of Jesse Hallum '81
Summertree '71
Supergirl '84
Ten Little Indians '89
Water '85
Zorro, the Gay Blade '81

Annette Vadim
Blood and Roses '61
Dangerous Liaisons '60

Roger Vadim
Edie in Ciao! Manhattan '72
Into the Night '85

Dan Vadis
Bronco Billy '80
Seven Magnificent Gladiators
  '84
Sons of Hercules in the Land of
  Darkness '55

Lester Vail
Consolation Marriage '31
Dance Fools Dance '31

Charlotte Valandrey
Orlando '92
Red Kiss '85

Brigitta Valberg
The Shame '68
The Virgin Spring '59

German Valdes
Duelo en el Dorado
Viva Chihuahua (Long Live
  Chihuahua) '47

Virginia Vale
Bullet Code '40
The Flustered Comedy of Leon
  Errol '39
Legion of the Lawless '40
Panama Menace '41

Anthony Valentine
The Carpathian Eagle '81

Robin Hood...The Legend:
  Robin Hood and the
  Sorcerer '83

Karen Valentine
Children in the Crossfire '84
Hot Lead & Cold Feet '78
Jane Doe '83
The North Avenue Irregulars
  '79
Return to Fantasy Island '77
Skeezer '82

Scott Valentine
After the Shock '90
Dangerous Pursuit '89
Deadtime Stories '86
Double Obsession '93
Homicidal Impulse '92
My Demon Lover '87
The Secret Passion of Robert
  Clayton '92
To Sleep with a Vampire '92
The Unborn 2 '94
Write to Kill '91

Rudolph Valentino
Blood and Sand '22
Blood and Sand/Son of the
  Sheik '26
Cobra '25
The Eagle '25
The Eyes of Youth '19
The Four Horsemen of the
  Apocalypse '21
Monsieur Beaucaire '24
Moran of the Lady Letty '22
The Sheik '21
Son of the Sheik '26
The Tempest/The Eagle '27

Tasia Valenza
Crackers '84
The Hillside Strangler '89
Rappin' '85

Jeanne Valeri
Dangerous Liaisons '60
Desert Commandos '60s

Frederick Valk
Dangerous Moonlight '41
Dead of Night '45
Frenzy '46
Hotel Reserve '44

Kitty Vallacher
Grave of the Vampire '72
The Legend of Frank Woods
  '77

Marcel Vallee
The Crazy Ray '22
Topaze '33

Rudy Vallee
The Admiral Was a Lady '50
The Bachelor and the Bobby-
  Soxer '47
The Beautiful Blonde from
  Bashful Bend '49
Glorifying the American Girl '30
How to Succeed in Business
  without Really Trying '67
I Remember Mama '48
International House '33
Live a Little, Love a Little '68
My Dear Secretary '49
The Palm Beach Story '42
People Are Funny '46
Second Fiddle '39
The Sin of Harold Diddlebock
  '47
Slashed Dreams '74
Unfaithfully Yours '48
Vagabond Lover '29

Alida Valli
Beyond Erotica '79
The Cassandra Crossing '76
The Castilian '63
The Horror Chamber of Dr.
  Faustus '59
Il Grido '57
The Miracle of the Bells '48
1900 '76
Oedipus Rex '67
The Paradine Case '47
Senso '54
The Spider's Stratagem '70
Suspiria '77
The Tempter '74
The Third Man '49
Walk Softly, Stranger '50
We the Living '42

Frankie Valli
Dirty Laundry '87
Eternity '90
Modern Love '90

Romolo Valli
Bobby Deerfield '77
A Fistful of Dynamite '72
The Garden of the Finzi-
  Continis '71

Virginia Valli
Lost Zeppelin '29
Night Life in Reno '31
The Shock '23

Rick Vallin
Corregidor '43
King of the Stallions '42
The Last of the Redmen '47
The Panther's Claw '42

Raf Vallone
An Almost Perfect Affair '79
Bitter Rice '49
Christopher Columbus '85
El Cid '61
The Girl in Room 2A '76
The Godfather, Part 3 '90
The Greek Tycoon '78
A Gunfight '71
Harlow '65
Honor Thy Father '73
The Human Factor '75
The Italian Job '69
La Violetera '71
Lion of the Desert '81
Nevada Smith '66
The Other Side of Midnight '77
Phaedra '61
Ricco '74
Rosebud '75
The Scarlet & the Black '83
That Lucky Touch '75
Time to Die '83
Two Women '61

**Willeke Van
Ammelrooy**
Fatal Error '83
The Lift '85

Lee Van Atta
Dick Tracy: The Original Serial,
  Vol. 1 '37
Dick Tracy: The Original Serial,
  Vol. 2 '37

Lewis Van Bergen
Bugsy '91
False Arrest '92
Overthrow '82
Rage of Honor '87
South of Reno '87
Street Knight '93

Bobby Van
The Affairs of Dobie Gillis '53
Escape from Planet Earth '67
Kiss Me Kate '53
Navy vs. the Night Monsters
  '66
Small Town Girl '53

Lee Van Cleef
Armed Response '86
Bad Man's River '72
The Beast from 20,000
  Fathoms '53
Beyond the Law '68
Big Combo '55
The Bravados '58
Captain Apache '71
China Gate '57
Codename: Wildgeese '84
Commandos '73
The Conqueror '56
El Condor '70
Escape from Death Row '76
Escape from New York '81
Fatal Chase '77
For a Few Dollars More '65
God's Gun '73
The Good, the Bad and the
  Ugly '67
The Grand Duel '73
Gunfight at the O.K. Corral '57
Gypsy Colt '54
Hard Way '80
The Heist '88
High Noon '52
It Conquered the World '56
Jungle Raiders '85
Kansas City Confidential '52

Kid Vengeance '75
A Man Alone '55
The Man Who Shot Liberty Valance '62
Master Ninja '78
Mean Frank and Crazy Tony '75
New Mafia Boss '72
Octagon '80
Pardners '56
Perfect Killer '77
Ride Lonesome '59
The Rip Off '78
Speed Zone '88
The Squeeze '80
The Stranger and the Gunfighter '76
Take a Hard Ride '75
Thieves of Fortune '89
The Tin Star '57
Tribute to a Bad Man '56
The Young Lions '58

Ron Van Cliff
Black Dragon '74
Black Dragon's Revenge '75
Fight to the Death '83
Fist of Fear, Touch of Death '77
Way of the Black Dragon '81

Jean-Claude Van Damme
Black Eagle '88
Bloodsport '88
Cyborg '89
Death Warrant '90
Double Impact '91
Hard Target '93
Kickboxer '89
Lionheart '90
Monaco Forever '83
No Retreat, No Surrender '86
Nowhere to Run '93
Timecop '94
Universal Soldier '92

Monique Van De Ven
Amsterdamned '88
The Assault '86
Keetje Tippei '75
The Man Inside '89
Paint It Black '89
Turkish Delights '73

Sylvie van den Elsen
La Vie de Boheme '93
L'Argent '83

Nadine Van Der Velde
After Midnight '89
Critters '86
Munchies '87
Shadow Dancing '88

Diana Van Der Vlis
Girl in Black Stockings '57
Lovespell '79
X: The Man with X-Ray Eyes '63

Trish Van Devere
All God's Children '80
The Changeling '80
The Day of the Dolphin '73
Deadly Currents '93
The Hearse '80
Hollywood Vice Sqaud '86
Messenger of Death '88
Movie, Movie '78
Savage is Loose '74
Stalk the Wild Child '76
Uphill All the Way '85
Where's Poppa? '70

Mamie Van Doren
Francis Joins the WACs '54
Girl in Black Stockings '57
Girls' Town '59
High School Confidential '58
Las Vegas Hillbillys '66
Navy vs. the Night Monsters '66
Teacher's Pet '58
Three Nuts in Search of a Bolt '64
Voyage to the Planet of Prehistoric Women '68

Granville Van Dusen
Breaking Up '78
Hotline '82
The Rose and the Jackal '90
War Between the Tates '76

The Wild and the Free '80

Barry Van Dyke
Ants '77
Foxfire Light '84

Conny Van Dyke
Framed '75
Hell's Angels '69 '69

Dick Van Dyke
Bye, Bye, Birdie '63
Chitty Chitty Bang Bang '68
Cold Turkey '71
The Comic '69
Country Girl '82
Dick Tracy '90
Lt. Robin Crusoe, U.S.N. '66
Mary Poppins '64
Never a Dull Moment '68
The Runner Stumbles '79

Jerry Van Dyke
The Courtship of Eddie's Father '62
Death Blow '87
McLintock! '63
Run If You Can '87

Peter Van Eyck
The Brain '62
Dr. Mabuse vs. Scotland Yard '64
The Spy Who Came in from the Cold '65
The Thousand Eyes of Dr. Mabuse '60
Wages of Fear '55

John Van Eyssen
Four Sided Triangle '53
The Horror of Dracula '58
Men of Sherwood Forest '57
Quatermass 2 '57

Jo Van Fleet
Cool Hand Luke '67
East of Eden '54
Gunfight at the O.K. Corral '57
I Love You, Alice B. Toklas '68
I'll Cry Tomorrow '55
The King and Four Queens '56
The Rose Tattoo '55
Satan's School for Girls '73
The Tenant '76

Kevin Van Hentenryck
Basket Case '82
Basket Case 2 '90
Basket Case 3: The Progeny '92

Merete Van Kamp
Lethal Woman '88
Princess Daisy '83

Peter Van Norden
The Accused '88
Casualties of Love: The "Long Island Lolita" Story '93
Scandal in a Small Town '88

Nina Van Pallandt
Assault on Agathon '75
Cutter's Way '81
Diary of a Young Comic '79
Jungle Warriors '84
The Long Goodbye '73
Quintet '79
Sword & Sorcerer '82
A Wedding '78

Dick Van Patten
Body Trouble '92
Charly '68
Diary of a Teenage Hitchhiker '82
Final Embrace '92
Freaky Friday '76
Gus '76
High Anxiety '77
The Hoboken Chicken Emergency '84
Joe Kidd '72
The Midnight Hour '86
The New Adventures of Pippi Longstocking '88
Psychomania '63
Robin Hood: Men in Tights '93
Son of Blob '72
Spaceballs '87
Superdad '73
Westworld '73
Zachariah '70

James Van Patten
The Dirty Dozen: The Deadly Mission '87
Nightforce '86
Roller Boogie '79
Tennessee Stallion '78
Twisted Justice '89
Young Warriors '83

Joyce Van Patten
The Bad News Bears '76
Billy Galvin '86
Crawlspace '86
Eleanor: First Lady of the World '82
The Falcon and the Snowman '85
Housewife '72
I Love You, Alice B. Toklas '68
Mame '74
Monkey Shines '88
The Rumor Mill '86
St. Elmo's Fire '85
The Stranger Within '74
Thumb Tripping '72
The Trouble with Girls (and How To Get Into It) '69
Trust Me '89

Nels Van Patten
Grotesque '87
Mirror Images '91
One Last Run '89
Summer School '87

Timothy Van Patten
Catacombs '89
Class of 1984 '82
Curse 4: The Ultimate Sacrifice '92
Dress Gray '86
Escape from El Diablo '83
Master Ninja '78
The White Shadow, Vol. 1 '78
The Wrong Guys '88
Zone Troopers '85

Vincent Van Patten
Charley and the Angel '73
Chino '75
The Dirty Dozen: The Deadly Mission '87
Hell Night '81
Payback '90
Rock 'n' Roll High School '79
Rooster: Spurs of Death! '83
Survival Run '80
The Victory '88

Mario Van Peebles
Delivery Boys '84
Exterminator 2 '84
Full Eclipse '93
Gunmen '93
Heartbreak Ridge '86
Highlander 3: The Sorcerer '94
Hot Shot '86
Identity Crisis '90
Jaws: The Revenge '87
New Jack City '91
Posse '93
Rappin' '85
South Bronx Heroes '85

Melvin Van Peebles
Boomerang '92
O.C. and Stiggs '87
Sophisticated Gents '81
Sweet Sweetback's Baadasssss Song '71

Edward Van Sloan
Before I Hang '40
Danger on the Air '38
The Death Kiss '33
Deluge '33
Dracula '31
Dracula's Daughter '36
Frankenstein '31
Manhattan Melodrama '34
The Mask of Dijon '46
The Mummy '32
A Shot in the Dark '35

Deborah Van Valkenburgh
A Bunny's Tale '85
Erik '90
Going for the Gold: The Bill Johnson Story '85
King of the Mountain '81
One Man Out '89
Phantom of the Ritz '88
Python Wolf '88

Rampage '87
Streets of Fire '84
The Warriors '79

Monique Van Vooren
Andy Warhol's Frankenstein '74
Ash Wednesday '73
Sugar Cookies '77

Philip Van Zandt
Citizen Kane '41
Clipped Wings '53
Ghost Chasers '51
Sherlock Holmes and the Secret Weapon '42
Woman in Brown '48

Joan VanArk
Frogs '72
Red Flag: The Ultimate Game '81
Tainted Blood '93

Courtney B. Vance
The Adventures of Huck Finn '93
Hamburger Hill '87
The Hunt for Red October '90

Danitra Vance
Jumpin' at the Boneyard '92
Limit Up '89
Little Man Tate '91
Sticky Fingers '88
The War of the Roses '89

Jim Vance
Blood Cult '85
How to Make a Doll '68
Young Eagles '34

Joe Vance
Deadly Breed '89
L.A. Crackdown 2 '88

Tito Vandis
Never on Sunday '60
Once Upon a Scoundrel '73
Piece of the Action '77

Pierre Vaneck
Is Paris Burning? '68
Sweet Country '87

Charles Vanel
Diabolique '55
Three Brothers '80
To Catch a Thief '55
Wages of Fear '55

Vanilla Ice
Cool As Ice '91
Teenage Mutant Ninja Turtles 2: The Secret of the Ooze '91

Vanity
Action Jackson '88
DaVinci's War '92
Deadly Illusion '87
52 Pick-Up '86
Highlander: The Gathering '93
The Last Dragon '85
Memories of Murder '90
Neon City '91
Never Too Young to Die '86
South Beach '92
Tanya's Island '81
Terror Train '80

Renato Vanni
The Lady in White '88
Wait Until Spring, Bandini '90
Westward the Women '51

Luigi Vannucchi
Lovers Like Us '75
Red Tent '69

Victor Varconi
Dancing Pirate '36
King of Kings '27
My Favorite Blonde '42

Evelyn Varden
Athena '54
The Bad Seed '56
The Night of the Hunter '55

Norma Varden
Fancy Pants '50
Forever Amber '47
Jupiter's Darling '55
National Velvet '44
The Sound of Music '65
The White Cliffs of Dover '44

Antonio Vargas
Strictly Ballroom '92

Whore '91

Jacob Vargas
Gas Food Lodging '92
Mi Vida Loca '94

Valentina Vargas
Dirty Games '93
The Tigress '93

Beatrice Varley
Death Goes to School '53
Great Day '46

Jim Varney
The Beverly Hillbillies '93
Dr. Otto & the Riddle of the Gloom Beam '86
Ernest Goes to Camp '87
Ernest Goes to Jail '90
Ernest Rides Again '93
Ernest Saves Christmas '88
Ernest Scared Stupid '91
Fast Food '89
The Rousters '90
Wilder Napalm '93

Diane Varsi
Bloody Mama '70
I Never Promised You a Rose Garden '77
Johnny Got His Gun '71
The People '71
Peyton Place '57
Sweet Love, Bitter '67
Ten North Frederick '58
Wild in the Streets '68

Roberta Vasquez
Do or Die '91
Easy Wheels '89
Fit to Kill '93
Hard Hunted '92
Picasso Trigger '89
The Rookie '90
Street Asylum '90

Robert Vattier
The Baker's Wife '33
Letters from My Windmill '54

Paris Vaughan
Buffy the Vampire Slayer '92
Heat Wave '90

Peter Vaughan
Bleak House '85
Blockhouse '73
Brazil '85
Codename Kyril '91
Coming Out of the Ice '82
Die! Die! My Darling! '65
Forbidden '85
Haunted Honeymoon '86
Heart of Darkness '93
Mackintosh Man '73
The Man Outside '68
Mountains of the Moon '90
Porridge '91
Prisoner of Honor '91
The Razor's Edge '84
The Remains of the Day '93
Savage Messiah '72
Straw Dogs '72
Time Bandits '81
Valentino '77

Alberta Vaughn
All Night Long/Smile Please '24
Daring Danger '32
The Dropkick '27
Laramie Kid '35
The Live Wire '34
Randy Rides Alone '34
Wild Horse '31

Heidi Vaughn
Heaven's Heroes '88
Trained to Kill, U.S.A. '83

Ned Vaughn
Chips, the War Dog '90
Wind '92

Robert Vaughn
Battle Beyond the Stars '80
Black Moon Rising '86
Blind Vision '91
Blue Jeans and Dynamite '80s
Brass Target '78
The Bridge at Remagen '69
Brutal Glory '89
Bullitt '68
Buried Alive '89
Captive Rage '88
C.H.U.D. 2: Bud the Chud '89
City in Fear '80

Vaughn ►cont.

Delta Force '86
Emissary '89
Going Under '91
Hangar 18 '80
Hitchhiker 4 '87
Hour of the Assassin '86
Inside the Third Reich '82
Julius Caesar '70
Kill Castro '80
The Last Bastion '84
The Lucifer Complex '78
The Magnificent Seven '60
The Mercenaries '80
Murrow '86
Nightstick '87
Nobody's Perfect '90
Prince of Bel Air '87
Question of Honor '80
The Rebels '79
Return of the Man from
 U.N.C.L.E. '83
River of Death '90
The Shaming '71
Skeleton Coast '89
S.O.B. '81
Starship Invasions '77
The Statue '71
Superman 3 '83
Teenage Caveman '58
That's Adequate '90
The Towering Inferno '74
Transylvania Twist '89
Virus '82
Wanted: Babysitter '75
The Woman Hunter '72
The Young Philadelphians '59

Ron Vawter
Internal Affairs '90
King of the Hill '93
Philadelphia '93
sex, lies and videotape '89
Sudden Death '77
Swoon '91

Bruno Ve Sota
Attack of the Giant Leeches '59
The Choppers '61
Creature of the Walking Dead
 '60
Daughter of Horror '55
The Gunslinger '56
The Wasp Woman '59

Isela Vega
Barbarosa '82
Bordello '79
Bring Me the Head of Alfredo
 Garcia '74
Drum '76
El Sabor de la Venganza '65
Fin de Fiesta '71
Joshua '76
Temporada Salvaje '87

Conrad Veidt
Above Suspicion '43
All Through the Night '42
The Beloved Rogue '27
The Cabinet of Dr. Caligari '19
Casablanca '42
Congress Dances '31
Dark Journey '37
F.P. 1 '33
The Hands of Orlac '25
King of the Damned '36
The Man Who Laughs '27
The Passing of the Third Floor
 Back '34
Power '34
Spy in Black '39
Thief of Baghdad '40
Under the Red Robe '36
Waxworks '24
Whistling in the Dark '41
A Woman's Face '41

**Reginald Vel
Johnson**
Die Hard '88
Die Hard 2: Die Harder '90
Posse '93

Lorena Velasquez
Mision Suicida '87
Samson vs. the Vampire
 Women '61
Wrestling Women vs. the Aztec
 Ape '62

Wrestling Women vs. the Aztec
 Mummy '59

Pilar Velasquez
Ace of Hearts '85
Manos Torpes '65

Teresa Velasquez
Dos Esposas en Mi Cama '87
Night of a Thousand Cats '72

Eddie Velez
Doin' Time '85
Romero '89
Rooftops '89
Split Decisions '88
Women's Club '87

Lupe Velez
Hell Harbor '30
Hollywood Party '34
Mad About Money '30
Mexican Spitfire at Sea '42
Mexican Spitfire/Smartest Girl
 in Town '40
Palooka '34
Playmates '41
Stand and Deliver '28
Where East is East '29

Evelyn Venable
Alice Adams '35
The Frontiersman '38
Harmony Lane '35
Hollywood Stadium Mystery '38
The Little Colonel '35
Lucky Cisco Kid '40
Mrs. Wiggs of the Cabbage
 Patch '42

Chick Vennera
Double Threat '92
Kidnapped '87
Last Rites '88
The Milagro Beanfield War '88
The Terror Within 2 '91
Thank God It's Friday '78
Yanks '79

Diane Venora
Bird '88
The Cotton Club '84
F/X '86
Ironweed '87
Terminal Choice '85
Wolfen '81

Wanda Ventham
Blood Beast Terror '67
Captain Kronos: Vampire
 Hunter '74

Clyde Ventura
Bury Me an Angel '71
Gator Bait '73

Jesse Ventura
Abraxas: Guardian of the
 Universe '90
Boxcar Blues '90
Predator '87
Repossessed '90
Ricochet '91
The Running Man '87
Thunderground '89

Lino Ventura
The French Detective '75
Happy New Year '74
Jailbird's Vacation '65
Les Aventuriers '77
Les Grandes Gueules '65
The Medusa Touch '78
Mistress of the World '59
Modigliani '58
Pain in the A— '77
The Slap '76
Sword of Gideon '86
The Three Penny Opera '62

Richard Venture
The Effect of Gamma Rays on
 Man-in-the-Moon Marigolds
 '73
Missing '82
Scent of a Woman '92
Street Hawk '84

Massimo Venturiello
My Wonderful Life '90
Rorret '87

Billy Vera
The Doors '91
Finish Line '89

Victoria Vera
A Man of Passion '90s
Monster Dog '82

Vera-Ellen
The Belle of New York '52
Happy Go Lovely '51
Love Happy '50
On the Town '49
Three Little Words '50
White Christmas '54
Wonder Man '45
Words and Music '48

Gwen Verdon
Alice '90
Cocoon '85
Cocoon: The Return '88
The Cotton Club '84
Damn Yankees '58
Legs '83
Nadine '87

Maribel Verdu
Belle Epoque '92
Lovers: A True Story '90

Elena Verdugo
The Big Sombrero '49
Boss' Son '79
Cyrano de Bergerac '50
House of Frankenstein '44
Little Giant '46
The Moon and Sixpence '43

Ben Vereen
All That Jazz '79
Breakin' Through '84
Buy & Cell '89
Funny Lady '75
Gas-s-s-s! '70
Intruders '92
The Jesse Owens Story '84
The Kid Who Loved Christmas
 '90
Pippin '81
Puss 'n Boots '84
Roots '77
The Zoo Gang '85

Tom Verica
Die Hard 2: Die Harder '90
800 Leagues Down the
 Amazon '90s

Bernard Verley
Chloe in the Afternoon '72
The Milky Way '68

Karen Verne
All Through the Night '42
Kings Row '41
The Seventh Cross '44
Sherlock Holmes and the
 Secret Weapon '42

Guy Verney
Fame in the Spur '47
Martin Luther '53

Anne Vernon
Therese & Isabelle '68
Umbrellas of Cherbourg '64

Bobby Vernon
A Hash House Fraud/The
 Sultan's Wife '15
Teddy at the Throttle '16
Teddy at the Throttle/Speeding
 Along '17

Glenn Vernon
Bedlam '45
Hollywood Varieties '50

Howard Vernon
The Awful Dr. Orlof '62
Castle of the Creeping Flesh
 '68
The Diabolical Dr. Z '65
Dr. Orloff's Invisible Horror '72
The Invisible Dead
The Perverse Countess '73
Revenge in the House of Usher
 '82
The Screaming Dead '72
Triple Cross '67
Virgin Among the Living Dead
 '71
Zombie Lake '84

John Vernon
Angela '77
Bail Out '90
The Barbary Coast '74
The Black Windmill '74
The Blood of Others '84
Blue Monkey '87
Brannigan '75
Chained Heat '83
Charley Varrick '73

Curtains '83
Deadly Stranger '88
Dirty Harry '71
Dixie Lanes '88
Doin' Time '85
Ernest Goes to Camp '87
Fraternity Vacation '85
Golden Rendezvous '77
Herbie Goes Bananas '80
Hunter '73
I'm Gonna Git You Sucka '88
Journey '77
Jungle Warriors '84
Justine '69
Killer Klowns from Outer Space
 '88
Mob Story '90
National Lampoon's Animal
 House '78
Nightstick '87
The Outlaw Josey Wales '76
Savage Streets '83
Tell Them Willie Boy Is Here '69
Terminal Exposure '89
The Virginia Hill Story '76
W '74
War Bus Commando '89

Kate Vernon
Alphabet City '84
Hostile Takeover '88
The Last of Philip Banter '87
Malcolm X '92
Mob Story '90
Roadhouse 66 '84

Richard Vernon
The Human Factor '79
The Satanic Rites of Dracula
 '73

Wally Vernon
Broadway Serenade '39
Gunfire '50
Happy Landing '38
Square Dance Jubilee '51

Christine Veronica
Love Notes '88
Party Incorporated '89

Cec Verrell
Eye of the Eagle '87
Mad at the Moon '92
Silk '86
Three of Hearts '93

Odile Versois
Cartouche '62
Le Crabe Tambour '77
To Paris with Love '55

Veruschka
Blow-Up '66
The Bride '85

Victoria Vetri
Group Marriage '72
Invasion of the Bee Girls '73
When Dinosaurs Ruled the
 Earth '70

Carmen Vicarte
La Montana del Diablo '87
Los Caciques '87

Martha Vickers
Big Bluff '55
The Big Sleep '46
The Man I Love '46

Yvette Vickers
Attack of the Giant Leeches '59
Beach Party '63
Evil Spirits '91

Charles Victor
Motor Patrol '50
San Demetrio, London '47
Seven Days' Leave '42

Henry Victor
The Beloved Rogue '27
King of the Zombies '41
Sherlock Holmes and the
 Secret Weapon '42

Katherine Victor
Curse of the Stone Hand '64
House of the Black Death '65
Mesa of Lost Women '52
Teenage Zombies '58
The Wild World of Batwoman
 '66

Gil Vidal
Night of the Howling Beast '75
Rape '80s

Gore Vidal
Bob Roberts '92
With Honors '94

Henri Vidal
Fabiola '48
Just Another Pretty Face '58
Sois Belle et Tais-Toi '58
Voulez-Vous Danser Avec Moi?
 '59

Steven Vidler
The Dunera Boys '85
Encounter at Raven's Gate '88
The Good Wife '86
Three's Trouble '85
Wrangler '88

Florence Vidor
Are Parents People? '25
Beau Revel '21
The Coming of Amos '25
Doomsday '28
The Grand Duchess and the
 Waiter '26
The Marriage Circle '24
The Virginian '23

Asia Vieira
The Good Mother '88
Omen 4: The Awakening '91

Abe Vigoda
The Cheap Detective '78
Fist of Honor '92
The Godfather '72
The Godfather 1902-1959: The
 Complete Epic '81
The Godfather, Part 2 '74
Great American Traffic Jam '80
How to Pick Up Girls '78
Joe Versus the Volcano '90
Keaton's Cop '90
Look Who's Talking '89
Newman's Law '74
North '94
Plain Clothes '88
Prancer '89
Sugar Hill '94
Vasectomy: A Delicate Matter
 '86

Robert Viharo
Bare Knuckles '77
Coldfire '90
Happy Birthday, Gemini '80
Hide in Plain Sight '80
Kid from Not-So-Big '78
Night Stalker '87
Romero '89
Valley of the Dolls '67

Henri Vilbert
Ali Baba and the 40 Thieves '54
Manon '50

Lucha Villa
El Fugitivo '65
El Gallo de Oro '65
Guitarras Lloren Guitarras '47
La Marchanta '73
Los Tres Calaveras '64

Frank Villard
La Bella Lola '87
La Violetera '71
Seven Deadly Sins '53

Tom Villard
My Girl '91
One Crazy Summer '86
Popcorn '91
Swimsuit: The Movie '89
The Trouble with Dick '88
Weekend Warriors '86

Daniel Villarreal
American Me '92
Speed '94

Astrid Villaume
Famous Five Get Into Trouble
 '87
Pelle the Conqueror '88

Herve Villechaize
Forbidden Zone '80
The Man with the Golden Gun
 '74
The One and Only '78
Return to Fantasy Island '77
Rumpelstiltskin '82
Seizure '74
Two Moon Junction '88

James Villemaire
Gate 2 '92
Matinee '92

Jacques Villeret
Bolero '82
Edith & Marcel '83
The Favor, the Watch, & the Very Big Fish '92
Robert et Robert '79

James Villers
Fortunes of War '87
The Marquise
Mrs. Silly '85
Mountains of the Moon '90
Nice Girl Like Me '69
Repulsion '65
The Scarlet Pimpernel '82

Pruitt Taylor Vince
City Slickers 2: The Legend of Curly's Gold '94
Come See the Paradise '90
Jacob's Ladder '90
Mississippi Burning '88
Shy People '87

Alex Vincent
Child's Play '88
Child's Play 2 '90
Wait Until Spring, Bandini '90

Frank Vincent
Goodfellas '90
Jungle Fever '91
Raging Bull '80
Street Hunter '90

Jan-Michael Vincent
Alienator '89
Animal Instincts '92
Bandits '73
Beyond the Call of Duty '92
Big Wednesday '78
Bite the Bullet '75
Born in East L.A. '87
Buster and Billie '74
Crossfire '67
Damnation Alley '77
Deadly Embrace '88
Defiance '79
Demonstone '89
Dirty Games '93
The Divine Enforcer '91
Enemy Territory '87
Hangfire '91
Hard Country '81
Haunting Fear '91
Hidden Obsession '92
The Hit List '88
Hooper '78
In Gold We Trust '91
Indecent Behavior '93
Last Plane Out '83
The Mechanic '72
Midnight Witness '93
Raw Nerve '91
The Return '80
Sins of Desire '92
Tribes '70
The Undefeated '69
White Line Fever '75
The Winds of War '83
The World's Greatest Athlete '73
Xtro 2: The Second Encounter '91

June Vincent
Clipped Wings '53
Colorado Sundown '52
The Creeper '48
Here Come the Co-Eds '45

Russ Vincent
Heading for Heaven '47
Twilight in the Sierras '50

Lee Ving
Clue '85
Dudes '87
Flashdance '83
Grave Secrets '89
Scenes from the Goldmine '87
Streets of Fire '84
The Wild Life '84

Helen Vinson
Broadway Bill '34
I Am a Fugitive from a Chain Gang '32
King of the Damned '36
They Call It Sin '32
The Thin Man Goes Home '44
Transatlantic Tunnel '35
Vogues of 1938 '37

Alan Vint
Ballad of Gregorio Cortez '83
Macon County Line '74
The McMasters '70
Panic in Needle Park '75
Sniper '75
Unholy Rollers '72

Bill Vint
Marilyn: The Untold Story '80
Summertree '71

Jesse Vint
Black Oak Conspiracy '77
Bobbie Jo and the Outlaw '76
Death Sport '78
Dempsey '83
Forbidden World '82
I Come in Peace '90
Macon County Line '74
Merchants of War '90
On the Line '83
Pigs '73

Gustav Vintas
And You Thought Your Parents Were Weird! '91
Drug Wars 2: The Cocaine Cartel '92
Midnight '89
Tales from the Crypt '89
Vampire at Midnight '88
Welcome Back Mr. Fox '83

Bobby Vinton
Big Jake '71
Surf Party '64
Train Robbers '73

Michael Visaroff
Charlie Chan at the Wax Museum '40
Last Command '28

Sal Viscuso
Spaceballs '87
The Taking of Pelham One Two Three '74

Alex Vitale
Beyond the Door 3 '91
Urban Warriors '75

Joseph Vitale
The Stranger Wore a Gun '53
Zombies on Broadway '44

Keith Vitali
American Kickboxer 1 '91
No Retreat, No Surrender 3: Blood Brothers '91
Revenge of the Ninja '83

Ray Vitte
Grambling's White Tiger '81
Sky Hei$t '75

Monica Vitti
An Almost Perfect Affair '79
Bellissimo: Images of the Italian Cinema '87
Blonde in Black Leather '77
The Eclipse '66
Immortal Bachelor '80
L'Avventura '60
Phantom of Liberty '68
The Red Desert '64
Tigers in Lipstick '80

Viva
Edie in Ciao! Manhattan '72
Forbidden Zone '80
Play It Again, Sam '72
State of Things '82

Sal Viviano
Black Roses '88
The Jitters '88

Floyd Vivino
Crazy People '90
Good Morning, Vietnam '87

Marina Vlady
Chimes at Midnight '67
Double Agents '59

Emmett Vogan
Down Dakota Way '49
The Lady Confesses '45
Robot Pilot '41

Darlene Vogel
Back to the Future, Part 2 '89
Ring of Steel '94

Jack Vogel
Lock 'n' Load '90
Presumed Guilty '91

Nikolas Vogel
Dangerous Liaisons '60
The Inheritors '85

Ruediger Vogler
Alice in the Cities '74
Faraway, So Close! '93
Kings of the Road—In the Course of Time '76
Until The End of The World '91
The Wrong Move '78

Joan Vohs
As You Were '51
Cry Vengeance '54

Jon Voight
Catch-22 '70
The Champ '79
Coming Home '78
Conrack '74
Deliverance '72
Desert Bloom '86
Eternity '89
Final Warning '90
Hour of the Gun '67
The Last of His Tribe '92
Lookin' to Get Out '82
Midnight Cowboy '69
The Odessa File '74
Return to Lonesome Dove '93
Runaway Train '85
Table for Five '83

Vicki Volante
Angels' Wild Women '72
Blood of Dracula's Castle '69
Brain of Blood '71
Horror of the Blood Monsters '70

Gian Marie Volonte
A Bullet for the General '68
Christ Stopped at Eboli '79
A Fistful of Dollars '64
For a Few Dollars More '65
Journey Beneath the Desert '61
Lucky Luciano '74
Open Doors '89
Sacco & Vanzetti '71
The Witch '67

Phillipe Volter
Cyrano de Bergerac '90
The Double Life of Veronique '91
The Music Teacher '88

William von Brinken
Hidden Enemy '40
International Crime '37
King Kelly of the U.S.A. '34

Lenny Von Dohlen
Billy Galvin '86
Blind Vision '91
Dracula's Widow '88
Electric Dreams '84
Eyes of the Beholder '92
Leaving Normal '92
Love Kills '91
Under the Biltmore Clock '85

Theodore von Eltz
Confidential '35
Drifting Souls '32
High Gear '33
No Man's Law '21
Strangers of the Evening '32

Rik von Nutter
Assignment Outer Space '61
Tharus Son of Attila '87
Thunderball '65

Joel von Ornsteiner
Robot Holocaust '87
Slashdance '89

Heidi von Palleske
Blind Fear '89
Dead Ringers '88
White Light '90

Gustav von Seyffertitz
Dishonored '31
Don Juan '26
Down to Earth '17
The Mysterious Lady '28
Mystery Liner '34
Rasputin and the Empress '32
Sparrows '26

Erich von Stroheim
As You Desire Me '32
The Birth of a Nation '15

Blind Husbands '19
The Crime of Dr. Crespi '35
Crimson Romance '34
Foolish Wives '22
Fugitive Road '34
Grand Illusion '37
Great Flamarion '45
The Great Gabbo '29
Heart of Humanity '18
Hearts of the World '18
Intolerance '16
Lost Squadron '32
The Mask of Dijon '46
Napoleon '55
The North Star '43
So Ends Our Night '41
Sunset Boulevard '50
Unnatural '52
The Wedding March '28
The Worst of Hollywood: Vol. 2 '90

Max von Sydow
Awakenings '90
The Bachelor '93
The Best Intentions '92
Brass Target '78
Brink of Life '57
Christopher Columbus '85
Code Name: Emerald '85
Conan the Barbarian '84
Death Watch '80
Dreamscape '84
Duet for One '86
Dune '84
Embassy '72
The Emigrants '72
The Exorcist '73
The Exorcist 2: The Heretic '77
Father '90
Flash Gordon '80
Flight of the Eagle '82
Foxtrot '76
The Greatest Story Ever Told '65
Hannah and Her Sisters '86
Hawaii '66
Hiroshima: Out of the Ashes '90
Hour of the Wolf '68
Hurricane '79
A Kiss Before Dying '91
Kojak: The Belarus File '85
The Magician '58
March or Die '77
Needful Things '93
Never Say Never Again '83
The New Land '73
The Night Visitor '70
The Ox '91
The Passion of Anna '70
Pelle the Conqueror '88
The Quiller Memorandum '66
Quo Vadis '85
Red King, White Knight '89
Samson and Delilah '84
Second Victory '87
The Seventh Seal '56
The Shame '68
Steppenwolf '74
Strange Brew '83
Target Eagle '84
Three Days of the Condor '75
Through a Glass Darkly '61
The Touch '71
The Ultimate Warrior '75
Until The End of The World '91
Victory '81
The Virgin Spring '59
Voyage of the Damned '76
Wild Strawberries '57
The Winter Light '62
The Wolf at the Door '87

Margarethe von Trotta
Coup de Grace '78
An Occurrence at Owl Creek Bridge/Coup de Grace '62

Gustav von Wagenheim
Nosferatu '22
Woman in the Moon '29

Harry von Zell
Son of Paleface '52
The Strange Affair of Uncle Harry '45

Danielle von Zernaeck
Dangerous Curves '88
La Bamba '87
My Science Project '85
Under the Boardwalk '89

Zandor Vorkov
Brain of Blood '71
Dracula vs. Frankenstein '71

George Voskovec
The Boston Strangler '68
The Bravados '58
Twelve Angry Men '57
The 27 Day '57

Arnold Vosloo
The Finishing Touch '92
Hard Target '93
Living to Die '91
Reason to Die '90
Red Shoe Diaries 2: Double Dare '92
The Rutanga Tapes '90

Yorgo Voyagis
The Adventurers '70
The Bourne Identity '88
Courage Mountain '89
Frantic '88
The Little Drummer Girl '84

Vlasta Vrana
Deadly Surveillance '91
Keeping Track '86
Scanners 2: The New Order '91

Ron Vreeken
Deathfight '93
Rage and Honor 2: Hostile Takeover '93

Murvyn Vye
Al Capone '59
A Connecticut Yankee in King Arthur's Court '49
Green Fire '55
Pickup on South Street '53
River of No Return '54
The Road to Bali '53

Steven Waddington
Edward II '92
1492: Conquest of Paradise '92
The Last of the Mohicans '92

Russell Wade
The Body Snatcher '45
The Iron Major '43
Shoot to Kill '47
Sundown Riders '48

Stuart Wade
Meteor Monster '57
Monster from the Ocean Floor '54

Henry Wadsworth
Applause '29
Ceiling Zero '35
Evelyn Prentice '34

Michael Wager
Exodus '60
Hill 24 Doesn't Answer '55
Jane Austen in Manhattan '80

Lyle Waggoner
Dead Women in Lingerie '90
Journey to the Center of Time '67
Love Me Deadly '76
Mind Trap '91
Robo-Chic '89
Surf 2 '84
Women of the Prehistoric Planet '66

Chuck Wagner
America 3000 '86
The Sisterhood '88

Fernando Wagner
The Pearl '48
Virgin Sacrifice '59

Jack Wagner
Jive Junction '43
Play Murder for Me '91
Swimsuit: The Movie '89

Lindsay Wagner
The Bionic Woman '75
Callie and Son '81
Convicted '86
The Flight '89
From the Dead of Night '89
High Risk '76

Wagner ▶cont.

The Incredible Journey of Dr. Meg Laurel '79
Martin's Day '85
Nighthawks '81
Nightmare at Bittercreek '91
The Paper Chase '73
Princess Daisy '83
Ricochet '91
Scruples '80
Second Wind '90
The Taking of Flight 847: The Uli Derickson Story '88
Treacherous Crossing '92
Two Kinds of Love '85
The Two Worlds of Jenny Logan '79

Natasha Gregson Wagner
Buffy the Vampire Slayer '92
Fathers and Sons '92
Molly and Gina '94
The Substitute '93
Tainted Blood '93

Robert Wagner
Abduction of St. Anne '75
The Affair '73
Beneath the 12-Mile Reef '53
Between Heaven and Hell '60
Broken Lance '54
The Concorde: Airport '79 '79
Curse of the Pink Panther '83
Death at Love House '75
Delirious '91
Dragon: The Bruce Lee Story '93
False Arrest '92
The Halls of Montezuma '50
Harper '66
The Hunters '58
I Am the Cheese '83
Indiscreet '88
Let's Make it Legal '51
The Longest Day '62
Madame Sin '71
Midway '76
The Mountain '56
The Ox-Bow Incident '55
The Pink Panther '64
Prince Valiant '54
Stars and Stripes Forever '52
Stopover Tokyo '57
The Streets of San Francisco '72
This Gun for Hire '90
To Catch a King '84
The Towering Inferno '74
Trail of the Pink Panther '82
War Lover '62
What Price Glory? '52
Windmills of the Gods '88
Winning '69

Thomas Wagner
Dead On '93
The Drifter '88

Ken Wahl
The Dirty Dozen: The Next Mission '85
The Favor '94
Fort Apache, the Bronx '81
The Gladiator '86
Jinxed '82
Omega Syndrome '87
Purple Hearts '84
Running Scared '79
The Soldier '82
The Taking of Beverly Hills '91
Treasure of the Yankee Zephyr '83
Wanderers '79

"Marky" Mark Wahlberg
Renaissance Man '94
The Substitute '93

Chan Wai
Bruce's Deadly Fingers '80
Cold Blooded Murder
Shaolin Warrior

Edward Wain
Creature from the Haunted Sea '60
The Last Woman on Earth '61

James Wainwright
Jigsaw '71
Joe Kidd '72
The President's Plane is Missing '71
Warlords of the 21st Century '82
A Woman Called Moses '78

Loudon Wainwright, III
Jacknife '89
The Slugger's Wife '85

Ralph Waite
Angel City '80
The Bodyguard '92
Chato's Land '71
Cliffhanger '93
Cool Hand Luke '67
Crash and Burn '90
A Day for Thanks on Walton's Mountain '80
Five Easy Pieces '70
Gentleman Bandit '81
Girls on the Road '73
The Grissom Gang '71
Lawman '71
On the Nickel '80
Red Alert '77
The Sporting Club '72
The Stone Killer '73
Thanksgiving Story '73
The Waltons: A Thanksgiving Story '73

Thomas G. Waites
And Justice for All '79
The Clan of the Cave Bear '86
McBain '91
On the Yard '79
The Thing '82
Verne Miller '88
The Warriors '79

Tom Waits
At Play in the Fields of the Lord '91
Bram Stoker's Dracula '92
Candy Mountain '87
Cold Feet '89
The Cotton Club '84
Down by Law '86
Ironweed '87
The Outsiders '83
Queens Logic '91
Rumble Fish '83
Shakedown '88
Short Cuts '93

Akiko Wakabayashi
What's Up, Tiger Lily? '66
You Only Live Twice '67

Ayako Wakao
An Actor's Revenge '63
Drifting Weeds '59
A Geisha '53

Tomisaburo Wakayama
Baby Cart 1: Lend a Child...Lend an Arm '72
Baby Cart 4: Heart of a Parent...Heart of a Child '72
Baby Cart at the River Styx '72
Baby Cart to Hades '72
The Bad News Bears Go to Japan '78
Phoenix '78
Shogun Assassin '80

Deborah Wakeham
Covergirl '83
House of the Rising Sun '87
Middle Age Crazy '80

Jimmy Wakely
Brand of Fear '49
Lonesome Trail '55
Range Renegades '48
Silver Star '55

Anton Walbrook
Dangerous Moonlight '41
The Forty-Ninth Parallel '41
Gaslight '39
La Ronde '51
The Life and Death of Colonel Blimp '43
Lola Montes '55
The Queen of Spades '49
The Red Shoes '48
Saint Joan '57

Raymond Walburn
Born to Dance '36
Christmas in July '40
The Count of Monte Cristo '34
Hail the Conquering Hero '44
It Could Happen to You '39
Key to the City '50
Lady by Choice '34
Let Freedom Ring '39
Louisiana Purchase '41
Mr. Deeds Goes to Town '36
Thin Ice '37

Gregory Walcott
Jet Attack/Paratroop Command '58
Joe Kidd '72
Plan 9 from Outer Space '56
Prime Cut '72
Texas Lady '56

Lynette Walden
Almost Blue '93
The Silencer '92

Robert Walden
Bloody Mama '70
Blue Sunshine '78
Enola Gay: The Men, the Mission, the Atomic Bomb '80
Everything You Always Wanted to Know About Sex (But Were Afraid to Ask) '72
Kansas City Massacre '75
Larry '74
Memorial Day '83
Murderer's Keep '88
Our Time '74
Perry Mason: The Case of the Lost Love '87

Ethel Wales
Border Vigilantes '41
The Gladiator '38
Made for Love '26
Under Montana Skies '30

Wally Wales
Danger Trails '35
Deadwood Pass '33
Desert of the Lost '27
Gun Play '36
Lone Bandit '33
The Miracle Rider '35
Powdersmoke Range '35
Rustlers of Red Dog '35
Sagebrush Trail '33
The Trigger Trio '37
Way of the West '35

Christopher Walken
All-American Murder '91
The Anderson Tapes '71
Annie Hall '77
At Close Range '86
Batman Returns '92
Biloxi Blues '88
Brainstorm '83
The Comfort of Strangers '91
Communion '89
Day of Atonement '93
Dead Zone '83
Deadline '87
The Deer Hunter '78
The Dogs of War '81
Heaven's Gate '81
Homeboy '90
King of New York '90
The Last Embrace '79
McBain '91
The Milagro Beanfield War '88
Mind Snatchers '72
Next Stop, Greenwich Village '76
Pennies From Heaven '81
Pulp Fiction '94
Roseland '77
Sarah, Plain and Tall '91
Scam '93
Shoot the Sun Down '81
Skylark '93
True Romance '93
A View to a Kill '85
Wayne's World 2 '93
Who Am I This Time? '82

Ally Walker
The Seventh Coin '92
Singles '92
Universal Soldier '92

Arnetia Walker
Love Crimes '92

Scenes from the Class Struggle in Beverly Hills '89
The Wizard of Speed and Time '88

Bill Walker
The Mask '61
No Time for Romance '48

Cheryl Walker
Identity Unknown '45
Stage Door Canteen '43

Clint Walker
Baker's Hawk '76
The Bounty Man '72
Deadly Harvest '72
The Dirty Dozen '67
The Gambler Returns: The Luck of the Draw '93
Maya '66
Mysterious Island of Beautiful Women '79
Night of the Grizzly '66
None But the Brave '65
Pancho Villa '72
Snowbeast '77
The White Buffalo '77
Yuma '70

Eric Walker
And You Thought Your Parents Were Weird! '91
The Ewok Adventure '84
The Ewoks: Battle for Endor '85

Fiona Walker
The Asphyx '72
Jude the Obscure '71

Helen Walker
Abroad with Two Yanks '44
Big Combo '55
Brewster's Millions '45
Call Northside 777 '48
People Are Funny '46

Jimmie Walker
B.A.D. Cats '80
The Concorde: Airport '79 '79
Doin' '85
Going Bananas '88
Let's Do It Again '75
My African Adventure '87
Water '85

Kathryn Walker
Blade '72
Dangerous Game '90
The Murder of Mary Phagan '87
Neighbors '81
O Youth and Beauty '79
Private Contentment '83
Rich Kids '79
Special Bulletin '83
Uncle Tom's Cabin '87
Whale for the Killing '81
The Winds of Kitty Hawk '78

Kim Walker
Deadly Weapon '90
Heathers '89

Nancy Walker
Best Foot Forward '43
Broadway Rhythm '44
Death Scream '75
Forty Carats '73
Girl Crazy '43
Lucky Me '54
Murder by Death '76
Thursday's Game '74

Polly Walker
A Dangerous Man: Lawrence after Arabia '91
Enchanted April '92
Lorna Doone '90
Patriot Games '92
Sliver '93
The Trial '93

Ray Walker
Bulldog Edition '36
The Dark Hour '36
Goodbye Love '34
House of Errors '42
Rogue's Gallery '44

Robert Walker
Bataan '43
The Clock '45
The Crimson Trail '35
Madame Curie '43
One Touch of Venus '48

Since You Went Away '44
Strangers on a Train '51
Thirty Seconds Over Tokyo '44
Till the Clouds Roll By '46
Till the Clouds Roll By/A Star is Born '46
Vengeance Valley '51

Robert Walker, Jr.
AngKor: Cambodia Express '81
Devonsville Terror '83
Easy Rider '69
Ensign Pulver '64
Evil Town '87
Hambone & Hillie '84
Olivia '83
Road to Salina '68
The Savage Seven '68
The Shrieking '73
Son of Blob '72
The Spectre of Edgar Allen Poe '73
The War Wagon '67

Sarah Walker
Housekeeping '87
Man of Flowers '84

Terry Walker
Delinquent Parents '38
Renfrew on the Great White Trail '38
Take Me Back to Oklahoma '40
23 1/2 Hours Leave '37

Tippy Walker
The Jesus Trip '71
The World of Henry Orient '64

Max Wall
Jabberwocky '77
A Killer in Every Corner '74
Little Dorrit, Film 1: Nobody's Fault '88
Little Dorrit, Film 2: Little Dorrit's Story '88
Strike It Rich '90
We Think the World of You '88

Basil Wallace
Deadlock '91
Marked for Death '90
Return of the Living Dead 3 '93

Beryl Wallace
Rough Ridin' Rhythm '37
Sunset on the Desert '42

Bill Wallace
Force of One '79
Manchurian Avenger '84
Ninja Turf '86

David Wallace
The Babysitter '80
Humongous '82
Mazes and Monsters '82
Money to Burn '83

George Wallace
Defending Your Life '91
Diggstown '92
Forbidden Planet '56
Radar Men from the Moon '52
A Rage in Harlem '91

Jack Wallace
The Bear '89
Things Change '88

Jean Wallace
Big Combo '55
Jigsaw '49
Native Son '51
Sword of Lancelot '63

Marcia Wallace
My Mom's a Werewolf '89
Pray TV '80

Morgan Wallace
Confidential '35
Delinquent Parents '38
Gang Bullets '38
Honky Tonk '41
The House of Secrets '37
In Old Colorado '41
Star Reporter '39

Dee Wallace Stone
Alligator 2: The Mutation '90
Club Life '86
Critters '86
Cujo '83
Discretion Assured '93
E.T.: The Extra-Terrestrial '82
The Five of Me '81
The Hills Have Eyes '77
The Howling '81

Huck and the King of Hearts '93
I'm Dangerous Tonight '90
Jimmy the Kid '82
Miracle Down Under '87
Popcorn '89
Rescue Me '93
Secret Admirer '85
Shadow Play '86
Skeezer '82
10 '79
Wait Till Your Mother Gets Home '83
Whale for the Killing '81

Eli Wallach
Ace High '68
Article 99 '92
Baby Doll '56
The Brain '69
Christopher Columbus '85
Cinderella Liberty '73
Circle of Iron '78
The Deep '77
The Domino Principle '77
Embassy '85
The Executioner's Song '82
A Family Matter '91
Girlfriends '78
The Godfather, Part 3 '90
The Good, the Bad and the Ugly '67
How the West was Won '63
The Hunter '80
The Impossible Spy '87
Independence '76
Kisses for My President '64
Legacy of Lies '92
Lord Jim '65
MacKenna's Gold '69
The Magnificent Seven '60
The Misfits '61
Mistress '91
The Moon-Spinners '64
Movie, Movie '78
Nasty Habits '77
Night and the City '92
Nuts '87
The People Next Door '70
The Poppy is also a Flower '66
Pride of Jesse Hallum '81
Rocket to the Moon '86
Romance of a Horsethief '71
The Salamander '82
Sam's Son '84
Seven Thieves '60
Something in Common '86
Stateline Motel '75
Teamster Boss: The Jackie Presser Story '92
Tough Guys '86
The Two Jakes '90
Winter Kills '79

Sigurd Wallen
The Count of the Old Town '34
Swedenhielms '35

Eddy Waller
Bandit King of Texas '49
El Paso Stampede '53
Marshal of Cedar Rock '53

Deborah Walley
Beach Blanket Bingo '65
Benji '74
Bon Voyage! '62
Dr. Goldfoot and the Bikini Machine '66
Gidget Goes Hawaiian '61
The Severed Arm '73
Spinout '66
Summer Magic '63

William Walling
Great K & A Train Robbery '26
Range Feud '31

Shani Wallis
Arnold '73
Oliver! '68
Round Numbers '91

Tom Walls
Johnny Frenchman '46
Maytime in Mayfair '52
While I Live '47

Jon Walmsley
Children's Carol '80
A Day for Thanks on Walton's Mountain '82
The Waltons: A Thanksgiving Story '73

Dermot Walsh
Ghost Ship '53
The Great Armored Car Swindle '64
Mania '60
Murder on the Campus '52
The Tell-Tale Heart '62

George Walsh
American Pluck '25
The Broadway Drifter '27
The Live Wire '34
Test of Donald Norton '26

Gwynyth Walsh
Blue Monkey '87
The Challengers '93
The Crush '93

Johnny Walsh
Body Parts '91
Wild Women of Wongo '59

J.T. Walsh
Backdraft '91
The Big Picture '89
Blue Chips '94
The Client '94
Crazy People '90
Dad '89
Defenseless '91
A Few Good Men '92
Good Morning, Vietnam '87
The Grifters '90
Hard Choices '84
Hoffa '92
House of Games '87
Iron Maze '91
Morning Glory '93
Narrow Margin '90
Needful Things '93
Power '86
Red Rock West '93
The Russia House '90
Sniper '92
Tequila Sunrise '88
Things Change '88
Tin Men '87
Why Me? '90
Wired '89

Kay Walsh
Cast a Dark Shadow '55
Encore '52
Greyfriars Bobby '61
The Horse's Mouth '58
In Which We Serve '43
Last Holiday '50
October Man '48
Oliver Twist '48
Stage Fright '50
This Happy Breed '47
Tunes of Glory '60
Tunes of Glory/Horse's Mouth '60
Young Bess '53

Ken Walsh
Dead Ahead: The Exxon Valdez Disaster '92
Love and Hate: A Marriage Made in Hell '90
Love, Lies and Murder '91
Reno and the Doc '84

M. Emmet Walsh
The Abduction of Kari Swenson '87
Back to School '86
The Best of Times '86
Bitter Harvest '93
Blade Runner '82
Blood Simple '85
Boxcar Blues '90
The Brotherhood of the Rose '89
Brubaker '80
Camp Nowhere '94
Cannery Row '82
Catch Me...If You Can '89
Chattahoochee '89
Clean and Sober '88
Critters '86
Dear Detective '78
The Deliberate Stranger '86
East of Eden '80
Equinox '93
Fast Walking '82
Fletch '85
Four Eyes and Six Guns '93
Fourth Story '91
Grandview U.S.A. '84
Harry and the Hendersons '87
Killer Image '92

The Mighty Quinn '89
The Milagro Beanfield War '88
Missing in Action '84
Murder Ordained '87
The Music of Chance '93
Narrow Margin '90
Night Partners '83
Ordinary People '80
The Pope of Greenwich Village '84
Raising Arizona '87
Raw Courage '84
Red Scorpion '89
Reds '81
Rich Hall's Vanishing America '86
Scandalous '84
Stiletto '69
Straight Time '78
Sunset '88
They Might Be Giants '71
Thunderground '89
War Party '90
White Sands '92
Wildcard '92
Wildcats '86
Wilder Napalm '93

Percy Walsh
The Golden Salamander '51
King of the Damned '36

Raoul Walsh
Background to Danger '43
The Birth of a Nation '15
Sadie Thompson '28

Sydney Walsh
Homewrecker '92
Point Break '91
Three Men and a Little Lady '90
To Die for '89

Ray Walston
Amos '85
The Apartment '60
Blood Relations '87
Blood Salvage '90
Damn Yankees '58
The Fall of the House of Usher '80
Fast Times at Ridgemont High '82
Fine Gold
For Love or Money '84
From the Hip '86
Galaxy of Terror '81
The Happy Hooker Goes to Washington '77
Johnny Dangerously '84
The Kid with the Broken Halo '82
Kiss Me, Stupid! '64
A Man of Passion '90s
O.C. and Stiggs '87
Of Mice and Men '92
O'Hara's Wife '82
Paramedics '88
Popcorn '89
Popeye '80
Private School '83
Saturday the 14th Strikes Back '88
The Silver Streak '76
Ski Patrol '89
South Pacific '58
Stephen King's The Stand '94
The Sting '73
Tall Story '60

Harriet Walter
The Good Father '87
May Fools '90

Jessica Walter
Dr. Strange '78
The Execution '85
The Flamingo Kid '84
Ghost in the Machine '93
Going Ape! '81
Goldengirl '79
The Group '66
Home for the Holidays '72
Hurricane '74
Miracle on Ice '81
P.C.U. '94
Play Misty for Me '71
Secrets of Three Hungry Wives '78
She's Dressed to Kill '79
Tapeheads '89
Wild & Wooly '78

Tracey Walter
Married to the Mob '88
Philadelphia '93

Tracy Walter
At Close Range '86
Batman '89
City Slickers '91
Delusion '91
Liquid Dreams '92
Mad Bull '77
Mortuary Academy '91
Out of the Dark '88
Raggedy Man '81
Repo Man '83
Something Wild '86
Timerider '83
The Two Jakes '90
Under the Boardwalk '89
Young Guns 2 '90

Julie Walters
Buster '88
Car Trouble '86
Educating Rita '83
Happy Since I Met You '89
Mack the Knife '89
Personal Services '87
Prick Up Your Ears '87
She'll Be Wearing Pink Pajamas '84
Stepping Out '91

Laurie Walters
Brujo Luna
Harrad Experiment '73
Harrad Summer '74
The Taking of Flight 847: The Uli Derickson Story '88
Warlock Moon '73

Luana Walters
Aces and Eights '36
Arizona Bound '41
Assassin of Youth '35
The Corpse Vanishes '42
Dick Tracy, Detective/The Corpse Vanishes '42
Fighting Texans '33
Inside the Law '42
Kid's Last Ride '41
Speed Reporter '36

Melora Walters
America's Deadliest Home Video '92
Twenty Bucks '93

Susan Walters
Elvis and Me '88
Shoot to Kill '47

Thorley Walters
The Adventures of Sherlock Holmes' Smarter Brother '78
Bartleby '70
Blue Murder at St. Trinian's '56
In the Secret State
The Little Drummer Girl '84
Murder She Said '62
The People That Time Forgot '77
The Pure Hell of St. Trinian's '61
Sherlock Holmes and the Deadly Necklace '62
Sherlock Holmes: The Silver Blaze '77
The Sign of Four '83
Vampire Circus '71

Henry B. Walthall
Abraham Lincoln '30
Avenging Conscience '14
Beggars in Ermine '34
The Birth of a Nation '15
The Cabin in the Cotton '32
Chandu the Magician '32
The Confession '20
Flaming Signal '33
Home Sweet Home '14
Judge Priest '34
Judith of Bethulia '14
Last Outlaw '36
Laughing at Life '33
The Phantom in the House '29
Police Court '37
The Raven '15
Ride Him, Cowboy '32
The Scarlet Letter '34
Short Films of D.W. Griffith, Vol. 2 '09
Somewhere in Sonora '33
Strange Interlude '32

A Tale of Two Cities '35
Viva Villa! '34
With Kit Carson Over the Great Divide '25

Douglas Walton
Bad Lands '39
The Bride of Frankenstein '35
I Conquer the Sea '36
Mary of Scotland '36
Wallaby Jim of the Islands '37

John Walton
Kangaroo '86
The Lighthorsemen '87

Lisa Waltz
Brighton Beach Memoirs '86
Pet Sematary 2 '92

Sam Wanamaker
The Aviator '85
Baby Boom '87
The Competition '80
Detective Sadie & Son '84
Embassy '85
From Hell to Victory '79
Ghostwriter '84
Guilty by Suspicion '91
Irreconcilable Differences '84
Judgment in Berlin '88
My Girl Tisa '48
Our Family Business '81
Private Benjamin '80
Pure Luck '91
Raw Deal '86
Running Against Time '90
Secret Ingredient '92
Sell Out '76
The Shell Seekers '89
Spiral Staircase '75
The Spy Who Came in from the Cold '65
Superman 4: The Quest for Peace '87
Taras Bulba '62
Those Magnificent Men in Their Flying Machines '65
Voyage of the Damned '76

Zoe Wanamaker
Poor Little Rich Girl: The Barbara Hutton Story '87
Prime Suspect '92
The Raggedy Rawney '90
Tales of the Unexpected '91

Peter Wang
Chan is Missing '82
A Great Wall '86

David Warbeck
Ark of the Sun God '82
The Black Cat '81
Formula for a Murder '85
Hunters of the Golden Cobra '82
The Last Hunter '80
Miami Horror '87
Panic '83
Seven Doors of Death '82
Tiger Joe '85
Twins of Evil '71

John Warburton
Cavalcade '33
Nothing But Trouble '44
Secret File of Hollywood '62
The White Cliffs of Dover '44

Burt Ward
Batman '66
Killcrazy '89
Robo-Chic '89
Smooth Talker '90
Virgin High '90

Fred Ward
Backtrack '89
Big Business '88
Cast a Deadly Spell '91
Equinox '93
Escape from Alcatraz '79
Florida Straits '87
Four Eyes and Six Guns '93
Henry & June '90
Miami Blues '90
Naked Gun 33 1/3: The Final Insult '94
Noon Wine '84
Off Limits '87
The Player '92
Prince of Pennsylvania '88
Remo Williams: The Adventure Begins '85
The Right Stuff '83

Ward ►cont.

Secret Admirer '85
Short Cuts '93
Silkwood '83
Southern Comfort '81
Swing Shift '84
Thunderheart '92
Timerider '83
Tremors '89
Uforia '81
Uncommon Valor '83

John Ward
Holt of the Secret Service '42
Ridin' the Trail '40
Robinson Crusoe of Clipper Island '36

Jonathan Ward
Mac and Me '88
White Water Summer '87

Larry Ward
Deathhead Virgin '74
Macabre '77

Lyman Ward
Creature '85
Mikey '92
Perfect Victims '87
Sleepwalkers '92
The Taking of Beverly Hills '91

Mary B. Ward
Hangin' with the Homeboys '91
Surviving Desire '91

Megan Ward
Amityville 1992: It's About Time '92
Arcade '93
Encino Man '92
Freaked '93
P.C.U. '94
Trancers 2: The Return of Jack Deth '91
Trancers 3: Deth Lives '92

Penelope Dudley Ward
The Case of the Frightened Lady '39
The Citadel '38
The Demi-Paradise '43
I Stand Condemned '36

Rachel Ward
After Dark, My Sweet '90
Against All Odds '84
Black Magic '92
Christopher Columbus: The Discovery '92
Dead Men Don't Wear Plaid '82
Double Jeopardy '92
The Final Terror '83
Fortress '85
The Good Wife '86
Hotel Colonial '88
How to Get Ahead in Advertising '89
Night School '81
Sharky's Machine '81
The Thorn Birds '83
Wide Sargasso Sea '92

Richard Ward
Across 110th Street '72
Mandingo '75

Robin Ward
Mark of Cain '84
Thrillkill '84
When Angels Fly '82

Roger Ward
Mad Max '80
Quigley Down Under '90

Sandy Ward
Blue Desert '91
Delta Force 3: The Killing Game '91
Tank '83
The Velvet Vampire '71

Sela Ward
Child of Darkness, Child of Light '91
Double Jeopardy '92
The Fugitive '93
Haunting of Sarah Hardy '89
Hello Again '87
Nothing in Common '86
Rainbow Drive '90

Steele Justice '87

Simon Ward
All Creatures Great and Small '74
Children of Rage '75
The Chosen '77
Deadly Strangers '82
Dominique is Dead '79
Dracula '73
The Four Feathers '78
The Four Musketeers '75
Hitler: The Last Ten Days '73
If... '69
The Monster Club '85
Supergirl '84
The Three Musketeers '74
Young Winston '72
Zulu Dawn '79

Sophie Ward
Casanova '87
A Demon in My View '92
Little Dorrit, Film 1: Nobody's Fault '88
Little Dorrit, Film 2: Little Dorrit's Story '88
The Shell Seekers '89
A Summer Story '88
Young Sherlock Holmes '85

Wally Ward
The Chocolate War '88
The Invisible Kid '88
Thunder Run '86

Anthony Warde
The Black Widow '47
King of the Forest Rangers '46
There Goes Kelly '45

Jack Warden
And Justice for All '79
The Apprenticeship of Duddy Kravitz '74
The Aviator '85
Being There '79
Beyond the Poseidon Adventure '79
Brian's Song '71
Carbon Copy '81
The Champ '79
Chu Chu & the Philly Flash '81
Crackers '84
Darby's Rangers '58
Dead Solid Perfect '88
Death on the Nile '78
Donovan's Reef '63
Dreamer '79
Everybody Wins '90
From Here to Eternity '53
Guilty as Sin '93
Heaven Can Wait '78
Hobson's Choice '83
Judgment '90
Justice '55
Man on a String '71
Man Who Loved Cat Dancing '73
Night and the City '92
Passed Away '92
The Presidio '88
Problem Child '90
Problem Child 2 '91
Raid on Entebbe '77
Robert Kennedy and His Times '90
Run Silent, Run Deep '58
September '88
Shampoo '75
So Fine '81
The Sporting Club '72
Summertree '71
Twelve Angry Men '57
Used Cars '80
The Verdict '82
The White Buffalo '77

Herta Ware
Cocoon '85
Crazy in Love '92
Dakota '88

Irene Ware
Chandu the Magician '32
The Dark Hour '36
Federal Agent '36
King Kelly of the U.S.A. '34
The Raven '35

Chris Warfield
Dangerous Charter '62
Diary of a Madman '63

Emily Warfield
Bonanza: The Return '93
Calendar Girl '93
The Man in the Moon '91
Pair of Aces '90

Marsha Warfield
D.C. Cab '84
Mask '85

William Warfield
Old Explorers '90
Show Boat '51

Andy Warhol
Cocaine Cowboys '79
Driver's Seat '73

Todd Waring
Love & Murder '91
Sinatra '92

Billy Warlock
Honor Thy Father and Mother: The True Story of the Menendez Brothers '94
Hot Shot '86
Society '92
Swimsuit: The Movie '89

Gordon Warnecke
London Kills Me '91
My Beautiful Laundrette '85

David Warner
Ballad of Cable Hogue '70
Blue Tornado '90
Body Bags '93
Cast a Deadly Spell '91
Code Name: Chaos '90
The Company of Wolves '85
The Concorde: Airport '79 '79
Cross of Iron '76
Disappearance '81
A Doll's House '73
The Fixer '68
Frankenstein '82
From Beyond the Grave '73
Grave Secrets '89
Hanna's War '88
Holocaust '78
Hostile Takeover '88
The Island '80
The Lost World '92
Magdalene '88
The Man with Two Brains '83
Masada '81
A Midsummer Night's Dream '68
Mr. North '88
Morgan! '66
Mortal Passions '90
My Best Friend Is a Vampire '88
Nightwing '79
The Old Curiosity Shop '75
The Omen '76
Providence '77
Quest of the Delta Knights '93
Return to the Lost World '93
Silver Bears '78
S.O.S. Titanic '79
Spymaker: The Secret Life of Ian Fleming '90
Star Trek 5: The Final Frontier '89
Star Trek 6: The Undiscovered Country '91
Straw Dogs '72
Teenage Mutant Ninja Turtles 2: The Secret of the Ooze '91
The Thirty-Nine Steps '79
Time After Time '79
Time Bandits '81
Tom Jones '63
Tripwire '89
Tron '82
The Unnamable 2: The Statement of Randolph Carter '92
Waxwork '88
Wild Palms '93

H.B. Warner
Action in Arabia '44
The Adventures of Marco Polo '38
Arrest Bulldog Drummond '38
Boss of Big Town '43
Bulldog Drummond in Africa/Arrest Bulldog Drummond '38
Bulldog Drummond's Bride '39

Bulldog Drummond's Secret Police '39
The Corsican Brothers '42
Cross Examination '32
The Devil & Daniel Webster '41
Enemy of Women '44
Hitler's Children '43
It's a Wonderful Life '46
The Judge Steps Out '49
King of Kings '27
Let Freedom Ring '39
Lost Horizon '37
Mr. Deeds Goes to Town '36
Mr. Smith Goes to Washington '39
The Rains Came '39
Rogue's Gallery '44
A Tale of Two Cities '35
The Ten Commandments '56
Topper Returns '41
Yank in Libya '42
You Can't Take It with You '38

Jack Warner
Against the Wind '48
The Blue Lamp '49
Captive Heart '47
A Christmas Carol '51
Dear Murderer '47
The Dummy Talks '43
Hue and Cry '47
The Quatermass Experiment '56
Train of Events '49
Valley of the Eagles '51

Julie Warner
Doc Hollywood '91
Indian Summer '93
Mr. Saturday Night '92

E. Allen Warren
Abraham Lincoln '30
Get That Man '35
Medicine Man '30
Tarzan the Fearless '33

Jennifer Warren
The Amazons '84
Angel City '80
Another Man, Another Chance '77
The Choice '81
Ice Castles '79
Intruder Within '81
Mutant '83
Night Moves '75
Slap Shot '77
Steel Cowboy '78
The Swap '71

Lesley Ann Warren
Apology '86
Baja Oklahoma '87
Betrayal '83
Beulah Land '80
Burglar '87
Choose Me '84
Cinderella '64
Clue '85
Color of Night '94
Cop '88
The Dancing Princesses '84
A Fight for Jenny '90
The Happiest Millionaire '67
Harry & Walter Go to New York '76
Legend of Valentino '75
Life Stinks '91
A Night in Heaven '83
The One and Only, Genuine, Original Family Band '68
Portrait of a Showgirl '82
Portrait of a Stripper '79
Pure Country '92
Songwriter '84
Treasure of the Yankee Zephyr '83
Victor/Victoria '82
Where the Eagle Flies '72
Worth Winning '89

Michael Warren
Heaven is a Playground '91
Hill Street Blues, Vol. 1: Hill Street Station '81
The Kid Who Loved Christmas '90
Norman, Is That You? '76
Storyville '92

Harold Warrender
Conspirator '49
Mimi '35

Ruth Warrick
China Sky '44
Citizen Kane '41
The Corsican Brothers '42
Deathmask '69
Great Dan Patch '49
Guest in the House '45
The Iron Major '43
Let's Dance '50
Mr. Winkle Goes to War '44
One Too Many '51
Three Husbands '50

David Warrilow
Barton Fink '91
Strong Medicine '84

James Warwick
The Affair of the Pink Pearl '84
The Case of the Missing Lady '83
The Clergyman's Daughter '84
The Crackler '84
Finessing the King '84
The House of Lurking Death '84
The Man in the Mist '83
The Secret Adversary '83
The Unbreakable Alibi '83

John Warwick
The Face at the Window '39
Ticket of Leave Man '37
While I Live '47

Robert Warwick
The Awful Truth '37
The Bold Caballero '36
Bulldog Edition '36
A Girl's Folly '17
Hopalong Cassidy '35
It Started with a Kiss '59
The Royal Bed '31
The Secrets of Wu Sin '32
A Shot in the Dark '35
Sullivan's Travels '41
The Trigger Trio '37
Two Reelers: Comedy Classics 9 '34
Whispering Shadow '33
A Woman's Face '41

Mona Washbourne
The Brides of Dracula '60
Brideshead Revisited '81
Cast a Dark Shadow '55
The Collector '65
December Flower '
Driver's Seat '73
If... '69
Mrs. Brown, You've Got a Lovely Daughter '68
My Fair Lady '64
O Lucky Man! '73
Stevie '78
Stranger in Town '57

Beverly Washburn
Old Yeller '57
When the Line Goes Through '71

Bryant Washburn
Drifting Souls '32
Kept Husbands '31
The Throwback '35
The Wizard of Oz '25

Rick Washburne
Comrades in Arms '91
Covert Action '88
Hangmen '87
The Outfit '93

Denzel Washington
Carbon Copy '81
Cry Freedom '87
The George McKenna Story '86
Glory '89
Heart Condition '90
License to Kill '84
Malcolm X '92
The Mighty Quinn '89
Mississippi Masala '92
Mo' Better Blues '90
Much Ado About Nothing '93
The Pelican Brief '93
Philadelphia '93
Power '86
Ricochet '91
A Soldier's Story '84

Gene Washington
The Black Six '74
Lady Cocoa '75

Shirley Washington
Darktown Strutters '74
The Deadly and the Beautiful '73

Ted Wass
Curse of the Pink Panther '83
Fine Gold
The Longshot '86
Oh, God! You Devil '84
Pancho Barnes '88
Sheena '84
The Triangle Factory Fire Scandal '79
TripleCross '85

Craig Wasson
Body Double '84
The Boys in Company C '77
Carny '80
Four Friends '81
Ghost Story '81
Go Tell the Spartans '78
The Innocents Abroad '84
Malcolm X '92
The Men's Club '86
Midnight Fear '90
A Nightmare on Elm Street 3: Dream Warriors '87
Schizoid '80
Second Thoughts '83
Skag '79
Strapped '93

Gedde Watanabe
Gung Ho '85
Sixteen Candles '84
The Spring '89
Vamp '86
Volunteers '85

Ken Watanabe
Bruce's Fists of Vengeance '84
Commando Invasion '87
Karate Warrior
MacArthur's Children '85
Tampopo '86

Tsunehiko Watase
Heaven & Earth '90
The Silk Road '92
Tattooed Hit Man '76

Nick Wateres
The Big Hurt '87
The Lighthorsemen '87

Dennis Waterman
Cold Justice '89
Fright '71
Man in the Wilderness '71
The Scars of Dracula '70

Felicity Waterman
Lena's Holiday '90
Miracle Beach '92

Willard Waterman
Hail '73
Hollywood or Bust '56

Cheryl Waters
Didn't You Hear? '83
Image of Death '77
Macon County Line '74

Ethel Waters
Cabin in the Sky '43
Cairo '42
The Member of the Wedding '52
Pinky '49
Stage Door Canteen '43

Harry Waters, Jr.
Back to the Future '85
Back to the Future, Part 2 '89

John Waters
Alice to Nowhere '86
All the Rivers Run '84
Attack Force Z '84
Boulevard of Broken Dreams '94
Breaker Morant '80
Cass '78
Demolition '77
Endplay '75
The Getting of Wisdom '77
Grievous Bodily Harm '89
Heaven Tonight '93
Miracle Down Under '87
Scalp Merchant '77
Three's Trouble '85
True Colors '87
Weekend of Shadows '77
Which Way Home '90

Sam Waterston
Assault at West Point: The Court-Martial of Johnson Whittaker '94
The Boy Who Loved Trolls '84
Capricorn One '78
Crimes & Misdemeanors '89
Dempsey '83
Eagle's Wing '79
Finnegan Begin Again '84
Friendly Fire '79
Generation '69
Gore Vidal's Lincoln '88
The Great Gatsby '74
Hannah and Her Sisters '86
Heaven's Gate '81
Hopscotch '80
Interiors '78
Journey into Fear '74
Just Between Friends '86
The Killing Fields '84
Lantern Hill '90
The Man in the Moon '91
Mindwalk: A Film for Passionate Thinkers '91
The Nightmare Years '89
Rancho Deluxe '75
Reflections of Murder '74
Savages '72
September '88
Serial Mom '94
Sweet William '79
Trade Secrets '90s
Warning Sign '85
Welcome Home '89
Who Killed Mary What's 'Er Name? '71

Gwen Watford
The Fall of the House of Usher '82
Taste the Blood of Dracula '70

Ian Watkin
Beyond Reasonable Doubt '80
Dead Alive '93
Nutcase '83

Pierre Watkin
Country Gentlemen '36
The Great Mike '44
Little Giant '46
The Magnificent Dope '42
Redwood Forest Trail '50
The Road to Singapore '40
The Stranger Wore a Gun '53
Superman: The Serial, Vol. 1 '48
Swamp Fire '46

Joanne Watkins
The Big Sweat '90
Cold Heat '90

Jack Watling
The Courtney Affair '47
Under Capricorn '49

Alberta Watson
Best Revenge '83
The Hitman '91
The Keep '83
White of the Eye '88
Women of Valor '86

Bob Watson
In Hot Pursuit '82
Tough Enough '83

Bobby Watson
The Band Wagon '53
Captains Courageous '37
Hitler: Dead or Alive '43
Show Boat '36

Bobs Watson
Dreaming Out Loud '40
In Old Chicago '38
On Borrowed Time '39

Jack Watson
The Devil's Brigade '68
King Arthur, the Young Warlord '75
McKenzie Break '70
Night Caller from Outer Space '66
Peeping Tom '63
Tower of Evil '72
Young Warlord '75

James A. Watson, Jr.
Killings at Outpost Zeta '80
Sex Through a Window '72

Lucile Watson
The Great Lie '41
Julia Misbehaves '48
Let's Dance '50
Made for Each Other '39
Mr. & Mrs. Smith '41
The Thin Man Goes Home '44
Tomorrow is Forever '46
Waterloo Bridge '40
The Women '39

Mills Watson
Heated Vengeance '87
Kansas City Massacre '75

Minor Watson
Abe Lincoln in Illinois '40
The Ambassador's Daughter '56
As Young As You Feel '51
Beyond the Forest '49
Charlie Chan in Paris '35
Crash Dive '43
Face to Face '52
Guadalcanal Diary '43
The Jackie Robinson Story '50
Navy Blue and Gold '37
A Southern Yankee '48
That Certain Woman '37
To the Shores of Tripoli '42
Western Union '41
Woman of the Year '42

Tom Watson
Another Time, Another Place '83
Prime Suspect 2 '93

Vernee Watson
Death Drug '83
Norman, Is That You? '76

William Watson
Force of Evil '77
Girl on a Chain Gang '65

Woody Watson
All-American Murder '91
The Last Prostitute '91
Skylark '93

Wylie Watson
Brighton Rock '47
A Girl in a Million '46
The Sundowners '60
Things Happen at Night '48
The 39 Steps '35

Richard Wattis
Doctor in the House '53
The Happiest Days of Your Life '50
My Son, the Vampire '52
Norman Conquest '53
Three Stops to Murder '53

Victoria Wauchope
Bluffing It '87
Cop '88
Love and Hate: A Marriage Made in Hell '90

Al Waxman
Class of 1984 '82
Clown Murders '83
Collision Course '89
The Double Negative '80
The Hitman '91
Malarek '89
Meatballs 3 '87
Millenium '89
Mob Story '90
Switching Channels '88
Teamster Boss: The Jackie Presser Story '92
Wild Horse Hank '79

Eileen Way
Queen of Hearts '89
Three Stops to Murder '53

Damon Wayans
Beverly Hills Cop '84
Blankman '94
Earth Girls are Easy '89
Hollywood Shuffle '87
I'm Gonna Git You Sucka '88
The Last Boy Scout '91
Mo' Money '92
Punchline '88
Roxanne '87

Keenan Ivory Wayans
Hollywood Shuffle '87
I'm Gonna Git You Sucka '88
Low Down Dirty Shame '94

Marlon Wayans
Above the Rim '94
Mo' Money '92

Carol Wayne
Heartbreakers '84
The Party '68
Surf 2 '84
Two Top Bananas '87

David Wayne
Adam's Rib '50
An American Christmas Carol '79
The Andromeda Strain '71
The Apple Dumpling Gang '75
As Young As You Feel '51
Finders Keepers '84
The Gift of Love '90
How to Marry a Millionaire '53
Huckleberry Finn '74
Lamp at Midnight '66
The Last Angry Man '59
Naked Hills '56
Poker Alice '87
Portrait of Jennie '48
The Sad Sack '57
The Survivalist '87
The Tender Trap '55
The Three Faces of Eve '57
We're Not Married '52

John Wayne
The Alamo '60
Allegheny Uprising '39
America at the Movies '76
Angel and the Badman '47
Baby Face '33
Back to Bataan '45
Barbarian and the Geisha '58
Beneath Arizona Skies/ Paradise Canyon '35
Big Jake '71
Big Jim McLain '52
The Big Stampede '32
Big Trail '30
Blood Alley '55
Blue Steel '34
Brannigan '75
Cahill: United States Marshal '73
Cast a Giant Shadow '66
Chisum '70
Circus World '64
The Comancheros '61
The Conqueror '56
The Cowboys '72
Dakota '45
Dark Command '40
Dawn Rider '35
Dawn Rider/Frontier Horizon '39
Desert Trail '35
Donovan's Reef '63
Duke: The Films of John Wayne '89
El Dorado '67
The Fighting Kentuckian '49
Fighting Seabees '44
Flame of the Barbary Coast '45
Flying Leathernecks '51
Flying Tigers '42
Fort Apache '48
Frontier Horizon '39
The Greatest Story Ever Told '65
The Green Berets '68
Hatari '62
Haunted Gold '32
Hellfighters '69
Helltown '38
His Private Secretary '33
Hollywood Home Movies '87
The Horse Soldiers '59
How the West was Won '63
Hurricane Express '32
In Harm's Way '65
In Old California '42
Jet Pilot '57
John Wayne Anthology: Star Packer/Lawless Range '34
King of the Pecos '36
Lady for a Night '42
Lady from Louisiana '42
Lady Takes a Chance '43
Lawless Frontier '35
The Lawless Nineties '36
Lawless Range '35
Legend of the Lost '57
Lonely Trail/Three Texas Steers '39

The Long Voyage Home '40
The Longest Day '62
Lucky Texan '34
Man from Monterey '33
Man from Utah '34
The Man Who Shot Liberty Valance '62
McLintock! '63
McQ '74
'Neath the Arizona Skies '34
The New Frontier '35
North to Alaska '60
Overland Stage Raiders '38
Pals of the Saddle '38
Paradise Canyon '35
Pittsburgh '42
The Quiet Man '52
Randy Rides Alone '34
Range Feud '31
The Range Feud/Two Fisted Law '31
Reap the Wild Wind '42
Red River '48
Reunion in France '42
Ride Him, Cowboy '32
Riders of Destiny '33
Rio Bravo '59
Rio Grande '50
Rio Lobo '70
Rooster Cogburn '75
Sagebrush Trail '33
Sands of Iwo Jima '49
Santa Fe Stampede '38
Sea Chase '55
The Searchers '56
Seven Sinners '40
Shadow of the Eagle '32
She Wore a Yellow Ribbon '49
The Shootist '76
Somewhere in Sonora '33
Sons of Katie Elder '65
The Spoilers '42
Stagecoach '39
The Star Packer '34
Tall in the Saddle '44
Telegraph Trail '33
Texas Cyclone '32
Texas Terror '35
They Were Expendable '45
Three Faces West '40
Three Godfathers '48
The Three Musketeers '33
Three Texas Steers '39
Trail Beyond '34
Train Robbers '73
Trouble Along the Way '53
True Grit '69
Two-Fisted Law '32
Tycoon '47
The Undefeated '69
Wake of the Red Witch '49
War of the Wildcats '43
The War Wagon '67
West of the Divide '34
Western Double Feature 2 '33
Western Double Feature 2: Wayne & Hale '80s
Western Double Feature 3 '36
Western Double Feature 5 '35
Westward Ho '35
Wheel of Fortune '41
Wild West '87
Winds of the Wasteland '36
Wings of Eagles '57
Without Reservations '46
Wyoming Outlaw '39

John Ethan Wayne
Escape from El Diablo '83
The Manhunt '86
Scream '83

Michael Wayne
Alley Cat '84
Rapid Fire '89

Naunton Wayne
Dead of Night '45
A Girl in a Million '46
The Hidden Room '49
The Lady Vanishes '38
Passport to Pimlico '49

Nina Wayne
The Comic '69
Dead Heat on a Merry-Go-Round '66

Patricia Wayne
Eye Witness '49
The Long Dark Hall '51

Patrick Wayne
The Bears & I '74
Beyond Atlantis '73
Big Jake '71
Chill Factor '90
The Gatling Gun '72
Her Alibi '88
McLintock! '63
Mister Roberts '55
The People That Time Forgot '77
Revenge '86
Ride to Glory '71
Rustler's Rhapsody '85
The Searchers '56
Shenandoah '65
Sinbad and the Eye of the Tiger '77
Talion '66
Texas Detour '77
Young Guns '88

Shawn Weatherly
Amityville 1992: It's About Time '92
Mind Games '89
Party Line '88
Police Academy 3: Back in Training '86
Shadowzone '90
Thieves of Fortune '89

Carl Weathers
Action Jackson '88
Death Hunt '81
Force 10 from Navarone '78
Fortune Dane '86
Friday Foster '75
Hurricane Smith '92
Predator '87
Rocky '76
Rocky 2 '79
Rocky 3 '82
Rocky 4 '85
Semi-Tough '77

Dennis Weaver
Amber Waves '82
The Best Christmas Pageant Ever '86
Bluffing It '87
Cocaine: One Man's Seduction '83
Disaster at Silo 7 '88
Don't Go to Sleep '82
Duel '71
Duel at Diablo '66
The Gallant Hours '60
Gentle Giant '67
Going for the Gold: The Bill Johnson Story '85
Horizons West '52
Intimate Strangers '77
A Man Called Sledge '71
Mission Batangas '69
The Ordeal of Dr. Mudd '80
Touch of Evil '58
What's the Matter with Helen? '71
A Winner Never Quits '86

Doodles Weaver
The Errand Boy '61
The Ladies' Man '61
Road to Nashville '67
Way He Was '76

Fritz Weaver
The Big Fix '78
Black Sunday '77
Blind Spot '93
Creepshow '82
The Day of the Dolphin '73
Demon Seed '77
Fail-Safe '64
The Hearst and Davies Affair '85
Holocaust '78
Hunter '73
Ironclads '90
Jaws of Satan '81
Marathon Man '76
The Martian Chronicles: Part 2 '79
The Martian Chronicles: Part 3 '79
Power '86
Walk in the Spring Rain '70

Jacki Weaver
Alvin Purple '73
Picnic at Hanging Rock '75
Squizzy Taylor '84

Three's Trouble '85

Marjorie Weaver
The Gentleman from California '37
Murder Over New York '40
Young Mr. Lincoln '39

Sigourney Weaver
Alien '79
Alien 3 '92
Aliens '86
Annie Hall '77
Dave '93
Deal of the Century '83
Eyewitness '81
1492: Conquest of Paradise '92
Ghostbusters '84
Ghostbusters 2 '89
Gorillas in the Mist '88
Half Moon Street '86
Madman '79
One Woman or Two '85
Sorrows of Gin '79
Working Girl '88
The Year of Living Dangerously '82

Hugo Weaving
For Love Alone '86
Frauds '91
Proof '91
The Right Hand Man '87

Alan Webb
Challenge to Lassie '49
Deadly Game '82
Entertaining Mr. Sloane '70
The Great Train Robbery '79
King Lear '71

Chloe Webb
Armistead Maupin's Tales of the City '93
The Belly of an Architect '91
China Beach '88
A Dangerous Woman '93
Heart Condition '90
Queens Logic '91
Sid & Nancy '86
Twins '88

Clifton Webb
Dark Corner '46
Laura '44
The Man Who Never Was '55
The Razor's Edge '46
Stars and Stripes Forever '52
Three Coins in the Fountain '54

Greg Webb
Puppet Master 2 '91
Running Mates '86

Jack Webb
The Commies are Coming, the Commies are Coming '57
D.I. '57
Dragnet '54
The Halls of Montezuma '50
He Walked by Night '48
The Men '50
Pete Kelly's Blues '55
Red Nightmare '62
Sunset Boulevard '50

Richard Webb
Attack of the Mayan Mummy '63
Distant Drums '51
Git! '65
Hell Raiders '68
The Invisible Monster '50

Diane Webber
The Mermaids of Tiburon '62
Sinthia: The Devil's Doll '70

Robert Webber
Assassin '86
Bring Me the Head of Alfredo Garcia '74
Casey's Shadow '78
The Choirboys '77
Dead Heat on a Merry-Go-Round '66
Death Stalk '74
Dollars '71
Don't Go to Sleep '82
The Final Option '82
The Great White Hope '70
Hysteria '64
Nuts '87
Private Benjamin '80
Revenge of the Pink Panther '78

The Sandpiper '65
S.O.B. '81
Soldat Duroc...Ca Va Etre Ta Fete! '60s
Starflight One '83
The Streets of L.A. '79
The Stripper '63
10 '79
Thief '71
Twelve Angry Men '57
Wild Geese 2 '85
Wrong is Right '82

Timothy Webber
The Grey Fox '83
That's My Baby! '88
Toby McTeague '87

Jacques Weber
Cyrano de Bergerac '90
The Elegant Criminal '92

Steven Weber
Single White Female '92
The Temp '93

Ann Wedgeworth
Bang the Drum Slowly '73
The Birch Interval '78
Bogie: The Last Hero '80
The Catamount Killing '74
Citizens Band '77
Cooperstown '93
Far North '88
Green Card '90
Hard Promises '92
Killjoy '81
Law and Disorder '74
Made in Heaven '87
Miss Firecracker '89
My Science Project '85
No Small Affair '84
One Summer Love '76
Scarecrow '73
Soggy Bottom U.S.A. '84
Steel Magnolias '89
Sweet Dreams '85
A Tiger's Tale '87

Barbara Weeks
Hell's Headquarters '32
The Violent Years '56
White Eagle '32

Jimmie Ray Weeks
The Abyss '89
Apology '86
Frantic '88

Paul Wegener
The Golem '20
Kolberg '45
One Arabian Night '21
Student of Prague '13

Lam Men Wei
Duel of the Seven Tigers '80
Return of the Scorpion '80

Tang Wei
The Cavalier '80s
Dynasty '77

Virginia Weidler
All This and Heaven Too '40
Babes on Broadway '41
Best Foot Forward '43
The Great Man Votes '38
The Philadelphia Story '40
Too Hot to Handle '38
Young Tom Edison '40

Teri Weigel
The Banker '89
Cheerleader Camp '88
Glitch! '88
Marked for Death '90
Predator 2 '90
Return of the Killer Tomatoes '88
Savage Beach '89

Cindy Weintraub
Humanoids from the Deep '80
The Prowler '81

Heidelinde Weis
The Man Outside '68
Something for Everyone '70

Robin Weisman
Three Men and a Little Lady '90
Thunder in Paradise '93

Florence Weiss
The Cantor's Son '37
Overture to Glory '40
The Singing Blacksmith '38

Shaun Weiss
D2: The Mighty Ducks '94
The Mighty Ducks '92

Norbert Weisser
Arcade '93
Deceit '93
Midnight Cabaret '90
Secret of the Ice Cave '89
Sweet Lies '88

Jeffrey Weissman
Back to the Future, Part 2 '89
Back to the Future, Part 3 '90

Johnny Weissmuller
Swamp Fire '46
Tarzan and His Mate '34
Tarzan Escapes '36
Tarzan Finds a Son '39
Tarzan, the Ape Man '32
Tarzan's New York Adventure '42
Tarzan's Secret Treasure '41

Bruce Weitz
Death of a Centerfold '81
Hill Street Blues, Vol. 1: Hill Street Station '81
Molly and Gina '94
The Queen of Mean '90
Rainbow Drive '90

Raquel Welch
Bandolero! '68
Bedazzled '68
Bluebeard '72
Fantastic Voyage '66
The Four Musketeers '75
Fuzz '72
Hannie Caulder '72
Lady in Cement '68
The Last of Sheila '73
Legend of Walks Far Woman '82
The Magic Christian '69
Mother, Jugs and Speed '76
Myra Breckinridge '70
Naked Gun 33 1/3: The Final Insult '94
Oldest Profession '67
100 Rifles '69
The Prince and the Pauper '78
Restless '72
Roustabout '64
Scandal in a Small Town '88
Shoot Loud, Louder, I Don't Understand! '66
Stuntwoman '81
A Swingin' Summer '65
Tainted Blood '93
The Three Musketeers '74
Trouble in Paradise '88
Wild Party '74

Tahnee Welch
Cocoon '85
Cocoon: The Return '88
Lethal Obsession '87
Sleeping Beauty '89

Tuesday Weld
Author! Author! '82
The Cincinnati Kid '65
F. Scott Fitzgerald in Hollywood '76
Falling Down '93
The Five Pennies '59
Heartbreak Hotel '88
I'll Take Sweden '65
Looking for Mr. Goodbar '77
Mistress '91
Mother & Daughter: A Loving War '80
Once Upon a Time in America '84
Pretty Poison '68
A Question of Guilt '78
Reflections of Murder '74
Return to Peyton Place '61
Rock, Rock, Rock '56
Serial '80
Soldier in the Rain '63
Something in Common '86
Thief '81
Who'll Stop the Rain? '78
Wild in the Country '61

Mary Louise Weller
Forced Vengeance '82
National Lampoon's Animal House '78

Peter Weller
The Adventures of Buckaroo Banzai Across the Eighth Dimension '84
Apology '86
Butch and Sundance: The Early Days '79
Cat Chaser '90
The Dancing Princesses '84
Fifty/Fifty '93
First Born '84
A Killing Affair '85
Leviathan '89
Naked Lunch '91
Of Unknown Origin '83
Rainbow Drive '90
Road to Ruin '91
RoboCop '87
RoboCop 2 '90
Shakedown '88
Shoot Moon '82
Sunset Grill '92
The Tunnel '89
Two Kinds of Love '85
Women & Men: Stories of Seduction '90

Gwen Welles
Desert Hearts '86
Eating '90
Hit! '73
The Men's Club '86
Nashville '75
New Year's Day '89
Sticky Fingers '88

Mel Welles
Abbott & Costello Meet the Mummy '55
Commando Squad '87
Dr. Heckyl and Mr. Hype '80
Joy Ride to Nowhere '78
Little Shop of Horrors '60
Rented Lips '88
The She-Beast '65
The Undead '57
Wizards of the Lost Kingdom 2 '89

Orson Welles
America at the Movies '76
The Battle of Austerlitz '60
Battle of Neretva '69
Black Magic '49
Blood and Guns '79
Butterfly '82
Casino Royale '67
Catch-22 '70
Chimes at Midnight '67
Citizen Kane '41
Ferry to Hong Kong '59
Hot Money '79
Inspiration of Mr. Budd '75
Is Paris Burning? '68
Jane Eyre '44
Journey into Fear '42
The Lady from Shanghai '48
The Long, Hot Summer '58
Macbeth '48
A Man for All Seasons '66
Mr. Arkadin '55
Moby Dick '56
Napoleon '55
Othello '52
Slapstick of Another Kind '84
Someone to Love '87
Start the Revolution Without Me '70
The Stranger '46
Ten Days Wonder '72
Ten Little Indians '75
The Third Man '49
Tomorrow is Forever '46
Touch of Evil '58
Treasure Island '72
The Trial '63
Trouble in the Glen '54
12 Plus 1 '70
The V.I.P.'s '63
Voyage of the Damned '76
Waterloo '71
The Witching '72

William Wellman, Jr.
Born Losers '67
Curfew '88
High School Confidential '58
Lafayette Escadrille '58
Macumba Love '60
The Prodigal Planet '83
A Swingin' Summer '65
The Trial of Billy Jack '74

Carole Wells
Funny Lady '75
The House of Seven Corpses
'73

Dawn Wells
Gilligan's Island: Meet the Crew
'64
Return to Boggy Creek '77
Town that Dreaded Sundown
'76

Dolores Wells
Beach Party '63
Bikini Beach '64
Muscle Beach Party '64
The Time Travelers '64

Jacqueline Wells
The Black Cat '34
Bohemian Girl '36
The Kansas Terrors '39
Laurel & Hardy Comedy
Classics, Vol. 4 '32
Riders of the Range/Storm
Over Wyoming '50
Tarzan the Fearless '33
Torture Ship '39

Vernon Wells
American Eagle '90
Circle of Fear '89
Circuitry Man '90
Commando '85
Crossing the Line '90
Enemy Unseen '91
Innerspace '87
Last Man Standing '87
The Losers '70
Nam Angels '88
The Road Warrior '82
Sexual Response '92
The Shrimp on the Barbie '90
Undeclared War '91

Kenneth Welsh
Adrift '93
And Then You Die '88
Another Woman '88
The Big Slice '90
The Climb '87
Crocodile Dundee 2 '88
Death Wish 5: The Face of
Death '94
The Good Fight '92
Lost '86
Loyalties '86
Of Unknown Origin '83
Perfectly Normal '91
Screwball Academy '86
Timecop '94
The War Boy '85

Margaret Welsh
American Heart '92
Mr. & Mrs. Bridge '91

William Welsh
Traffic in Souls '13
20,000 Leagues Under the Sea
'16

Ariadne Welter
The Brainiac '61
The Criminal Life of Archibaldo
de la Cruz '55
The Devil's Hand '61
The Vampire '57
The Vampire's Coffin '58

Lara Wendell
Ghosthouse '88
Intervista '87

Wim Wenders
The American Friend '77
Lightning Over Water '80

George Wendt
Bill Murray Live from the
Second City '70s
Dreamscape '84
Fletch '85
Forever Young '92
Guilty by Suspicion '91
Gung Ho '85
House '86
The Masters of Menace '90
Never Say Die '90
No Small Affair '84
Plain Clothes '88
Thief of Hearts '84

John Wengraf
Five Fingers '52
U-Boat Prisoner '44

Martha Wentworth
Jupiter's Darling '55
Stagecoach to Denver '46
The Stranger '46
Vigilantes of Boom Town '46

Jan Werich
Fabulous Adventures of Baron
Munchausen '61
The Original Fabulous
Adventures of Baron
Munchausen '61

Oskar Werner
Angel with the Trumpet '50
Fahrenheit 451 '66
Jules and Jim '62
The Life and Loves of Mozart
'59
Lola Montes '55
Ship of Fools '65
The Shoes of the Fisherman
'68
The Spy Who Came in from the
Cold '65
Voyage of the Damned '76

Otto Wernicke
Crimes of Dr. Mabuse '32
Das Testament des Dr. Mabuse
'33

Massimo Wertmuller
Sotto, Sotto '85
Summer Night '87

Dick Wessel
Bowery at Midnight/Dick Tracy
vs. Cueball '42
Tanks a Million '41
X Marks the Spot '42

Dick Wesson
The Desert Song '53
Destination Moon '50
The Errand Boy '61
Jim Thorpe: All American '51

Adam West
Batman '66
Doin' Time on Planet Earth '88
For the Love of It '80
Geronimo '62
The Happy Hooker Goes
Hollywood '80
Hell River '75
Hellriders '84
Hooper '78
Mad About You '90
Maxim Xul '91
Night of the Kickfighters '91
Omega Cop '90
One Dark Night '82
Return Fire '91
Robinson Crusoe on Mars '64
The Specialist '75
Young Lady Chatterly 2 '85
Zombie Nightmare '86

Charles West
D.W. Griffith Triple Feature '13
Short Films of D.W. Griffith,
Vol. 1 '12

Dottie West
The Aurora Encounter '85
The Real Patsy Cline '90

Jeremy West
Catacombs '89
Curse 4: The Ultimate Sacrifice
'92

Mae West
Belle of the Nineties '34
Every Day's a Holiday '38
Go West, Young Man '36
Goin' to Town '35
The Heat's On '43
I'm No Angel '33
Klondike Annie '36
The Love Goddesses '65
My Little Chickadee '40
Myra Breckinridge '70
Night After Night '32
Sextette '78
She Done Him Wrong '33

Martin West
Assault on Precinct 13 '76
A Swingin' Summer '65

Red West
Grizzly Adams: The Legend
Continues '90
Hard Knox '83
Proud Men '87

Will: G. Gordon Liddy '82
Sam West
Howard's End '92
Reunion '88

Sonny West
Hellcats '68
Outlaw Riders '72

Timothy West
Agatha '79
Churchill and the Generals '81
Cry Freedom '87
Death by Prescription '80s
Hedda '75
The Last Bastion '84
Oliver Twist '82
Rough Cut '80
Tragedy of Flight 103: The
Inside Story '91

Helen Westcott
Abbott and Costello Meet Dr.
Jekyll and Mr. Hyde '52
The Gunfighter '50
The Invisible Avenger '58
Thunder Over Texas '34

Hakan Westergren
Dollar '38
Swedenhielms '35

**Floyd "Red Crow"
Westerman**
The Broken Chain '93
Clearcut '92
Dances with Wolves '90
Walker: Texas Ranger: One
Riot, One Ranger '93

Dr. Ruth Westheimer
Forever, Lulu '87
One Woman or Two '85

Helen Westley
Alexander's Ragtime Band '38
All This and Heaven Too '40
Dimples '36
Heidi '37
Lady from Louisiana '42
Rebecca of Sunnybrook Farm
'38
Stowaway '36
Sunny '41

Nydia Westman
Bulldog Drummond's Revenge
'37
The Chocolate Soldier '41
One Night of Love '34
Velvet Touch '48

James Westmoreland
Don't Answer the Phone '80
Stacey '73

Celia Weston
Little Man Tate '91
Lost Angels '89

Doris Weston
Born to Be Wild '38
Delinquent Parents '38

Jack Weston
Cactus Flower '69
The Cincinnati Kid '65
Cuba '79
Dirty Dancing '87
The Four Seasons '81
Fuzz '72
Gator '76
High Road to China '83
The Honeymoon Machine '61
The Incredible Mr. Limpet '64
The Longshot '86
Marco '73
Mirage '66
A New Leaf '71
Palm Springs Weekend '63
Please Don't Eat the Daisies
'60
Rad '86
The Ritz '76
Short Circuit 2 '88
Thomas Crown Affair '68
Wait Until Dark '67

Jeff Weston
Demonic Toys '91
Puppet Master 2 '91

Virginia Wetherell
The Big Switch '70
The Crimson Cult '68
Demons of the Mind '72
Disciple of Death '72

Patricia Wettig
City Slickers '91
City Slickers 2: The Legend of
Curly's Gold '94
Guilty by Suspicion '91
Me & Veronica '93
Silent Motive '91

Marius Weyers
African Rage '78
Bopha! '93
Deepstar Six '89
Farewell to the King '89
The Gods Must Be Crazy '84
Happy Together '89
The Power of One '92

Michael Whalen
Dawn Express '42
G.I. Jane '51
Highway 13 '48
King of the Bullwhip '51
Missile to the Moon '59
Omoo Omoo, the Shark God
'49
The Phantom from 10,000
Leagues '56
The Poor Little Rich Girl '36
Thunder in the Pines '49
Wee Willie Winkie '37

Frank Whaley
Back in the USSR '92
Born on the Fourth of July '89
Career Opportunities '91
The Doors '91
Field of Dreams '89
The Freshman '90
Hoffa '92
Ironweed '87
Little Monsters '89
A Midnight Clear '92
Swing Kids '93
To Dance with the White Dog
'93

Justin Whalin
Child's Play 3 '91
The Fire Next Time '93
Perfect Harmony '91

**Joanne Whalley-
Kilmer**
The Big Man: Crossing the Line
'91
Dance with a Stranger '85
Edge of Darkness '86
The Good Father '87
Kill Me Again '89
Mother's Boys '94
Navy SEALS '90
No Surrender '86
Scandal '89
Shattered '91
Storyville '92
To Kill a Priest '89
Willow '88

Liem Whatley
Heaven and Earth '93
The Iron Triangle '89

Alan Wheatley
Appointment with Crime '45
Brighton Rock '47
Calling Paul Temple '48
Counterblast '48
The Limping Man '53
Robin Hood: The Movie '55

Wil Wheaton
The Buddy System '83
The Curse '87
December '91
The Last Prostitute '91
The Last Starfighter '84
Long Time Gone '86
Stand By Me '86
Star Trek the Next Generation:
Encounter at Farpoint '87
Toy Soldiers '91

Bert Wheeler
Cockeyed Cavaliers '34
Diplomaniacs '33
Dixiana '30
Half-Shot at Sunrise '30
Hips, Hips, Hooray '34
Hold 'Em Jail '32
Hook, Line and Sinker '30
Kentucky Kernels '34

Dave Wheeler
Ninja Commandments '87
Ninja Squad '80s

John Wheeler
Bad Georgia Road '77
Lucy and Desi: Before the
Laughter '91

**Dana Wheeler-
Nicholson**
Circuitry Man '90
Fletch '85
Mrs. Soffel '84
The Night We Never Met '93
Tombstone '93

Arleen Whelan
Castle in the Desert '42
Never Wave at a WAC '52
Ramrod '47
The Sun Shines Bright '53
Young Mr. Lincoln '39

Lisa Whelchel
The Double McGuffin '79
Twirl '81
Where the Red Fern Grows:
Part 2 '92

Manning Whiley
The Dummy Talks '43
Meet Sexton Blake '44

Barbara Whinnery
Crawlspace '86
Hot to Trot! '88

Shannon Whirry
Animal Instincts '92
Body of Influence '93
Mirror Images 2 '93

**Charles "Slim"
Whitaker**
Border Vengeance '35
Bullet Code '40
Cheyenne Rides Again '38
Deadwood Pass '33
Desert of the Lost '27
The Fiddlin' Buckaroo '33
Ghost Valley '32
The Man from Hell '34
Man from Monterey '33
Melody of the Plains '37
The Mysterious Rider '42
Outlaw of the Plains '46
Phantom Gold '38
Saddle Buster '32
Santa Fe Bound '37

Christina Whitaker
Naked Cage '86
Vampire at Midnight '88

Forest Whitaker
Article 99 '92
Bird '88
Bloodsport '88
Blown Away '94
Body Snatchers '93
The Color of Money '86
Consenting Adults '92
Criminal Justice '90
The Crying Game '92
Diary of a Hitman '91
Downtown '89
Fast Times at Ridgemont High
'82
Good Morning, Vietnam '87
Johnny Handsome '89
Last Light '93
Platoon '86
A Rage in Harlem '91
Stakeout '87

Johnny Whitaker
The Littlest Angel '69
Napoleon and Samantha '72
Tom Sawyer '73

Alice White
Annabel Takes a Tour/Maid's
Night Out '38
Employees' Entrance '33
Flamingo Road '49
Murder at Midnight '31

Bernie White
The Abduction of Allison Tate
'92
Body Count '87
The Ghost of Fletcher Ridge
'80s
Killing Obsession '94
Twenty Dollar Star '91

Carol White
Daddy's Gone A-Hunting '69
The Fixer '68

White ▶cont.

Man Who Had Power Over
  Women '70
A Matter of WHO '62
Never Let Go '60
Some Call It Loving '73
The Squeeze '77

Dan White
The Last Hunt '56
Outlaw Country '49

David White
The Amazing Spider-Man '77
The Tender Trap '55

Diz White
Bullshot '83
Footlight Frenzy '84

Harriet White
The Ghost '63
Paisan '46

Jacqueline White
Air Raid Wardens '43
The Capture '50
The Narrow Margin '52
Return of the Bad Men '48
The Saint's Vacation/The
  Narrow Margin '52
The Show-Off '46

Jesse White
Bedtime for Bonzo '51
Bless the Beasts and Children
  '71
Designing Woman '57
Forever Female '53
Francis Goes to the Races '51
Harvey '50
Matinee '92
Million Dollar Mermaid '52
Monster in the Closet '86
Music Shoppe '82
Pajama Party '64
The Rise and Fall of Legs
  Diamond '60
Togetherness '70
Tomboy & the Champ '58

Lee White
Lonesome Trail '55
Red Rock Outlaw '47

Ron White
Cowboys Don't Cry '88
Guilty as Sin '93
Love & Murder '91

Slappy White
Amazing Grace '74
Mr. Saturday Night '92

Vanna White
Graduation Day '81
Gypsy Angels '94

O.Z. Whitehead
Beware, My Lovely '52
The Grapes of Wrath '40
Road House '48

Paxton Whitehead
The Adventures of Huck Finn
  '93
Baby Boom '87
Back to School '86
Boris and Natasha: The Movie
  '92
Child of Darkness, Child of
  Light '91
Chips, the War Dog '90
My Boyfriend's Back '93

Billie Whitelaw
The Dressmaker '89
Duel of Hearts '92
Frenzy '72
Gumshoe '72
The Krays '90
Leopard in the Snow '78
Lorna Doone '90
Make Mine Mink '60
Mania '85
Maurice '87
Murder Elite '86
Night Watch '72
No Love for Johnnie '60
The Omen '76
The Secret Garden '87
Shadey '87
Slayground '84
Small Hotel '57

Start the Revolution Without
  Me '70
Strange Case of Dr. Jekyll &
  Mr. Hyde '68
A Tale of Two Cities '80
Unsuitable Job for a Woman
  '82
Water Babies '79

Jon Whiteley
Moonfleet '55
The Spanish Gardener '57

Paul Whiteman
The Fabulous Dorseys '47
King of Jazz '30
Strike Up the Band '40

Lynn Whitfield
Doctor Detroit '83
The George McKenna Story '86
Jaws: The Revenge '87
Johnnie Gibson F.B.I. '87
The Josephine Baker Story '90
The Slugger's Wife '85
State of Emergency '94
Taking the Heat '93

Mitchell Whitfield
Dogfight '91
My Cousin Vinny '92

Bradley Whitford
The Client '94
Dead as a Doorman '85
My Life '93
A Perfect World '93
Philadelphia '93
Scent of a Woman '92
Vital Signs '90

Peter Whitford
Dead End Drive-In '86
Strictly Ballroom '92
Warm Nights on a Slow-Moving
  Train '87

Leonard Whiting
Rachel's Man '75
Romeo and Juliet '68
Say Hello to Yesterday '71

Margaret Whiting
Sinbad and the Eye of the Tiger
  '77
Trespasser '85

Ray Whitley
Hittin' the Trail '37
Racketeers of the Range '39
Renegade Ranger/Scarlet River
  '38

Lloyd Whitlock
Diamond Trail '33
The Michigan Kid '28
The Prairie Pirate '25
Tangled Destinies '32
West of the Divide '34

Jill Whitlow
Adventures Beyond Belief '87
Ghost Chase '88
Night of the Creeps '86
Thunder Run '86
Twice Dead '88

Kari Whitman
Chained Heat 2 '92
Forced to Kill '93
Phantom of the Mall: Eric's
  Revenge '89

Stuart Whitman
Butterfly '82
Call Him Mr. Shatter '74
Captain Apache '71
The Comancheros '61
Crazy Mama '75
Darby's Rangers '58
The Day and the Hour '63
Deadly Reactor '89
Delta Fox '77
Demonoid, Messenger of
  Death '81
Eaten Alive '76
First Strike '85
Fury '80s
Hostages '79
The Invincible Six '68
Kill Castro '80
Las Vegas Lady '76
The Longest Day '62
Maniac '77
The Mark '61
Mean Johnny Barrows '75
The Mercenaries '80

Mob Boss '90
The Monster Club '85
Moving Target '89
Oil '78
Omega Cop '90
Private Wars '93
Rio Conchos '64
Ruby '77
Run for the Roses '78
The Seekers '79
Silver Lode '54
Smooth Talker '90
The Story of Ruth '60
Strange Shadows in an Empty
  Room '76
Ten North Frederick '58
Those Magnificent Men in Their
  Flying Machines '65
The Treasure of the Amazon
  '84
The Treasure Seekers '79
Vultures '84
The White Buffalo '77
The Woman Hunter '72

James Whitmore
Above and Beyond '53
All My Sons '48
All the Brothers Were Valiant
  '53
The Asphalt Jungle '50
Battle Cry '55
Battleground '49
Because You're Mine '52
Black Like Me '64
Chato's Land '71
Chuka '67
Deep Six '58
Don't Cry, It's Only Thunder '82
The Eddy Duchin Story '56
The First Deadly Sin '80
The Girl Who Had Everything
  '53
Give 'Em Hell, Harry! '75
Glory! Glory! '90
Guns of the Magnificent Seven
  '69
Harrad Experiment '73
High Crime '73
I Will Fight No More Forever '75
Kiss Me Kate '53
Madigan '68
The McConnell Story '55
The Next Voice You Hear '50
Nuts '87
Oklahoma! '55
Old Explorers '90
Planet of the Apes '68
Rage '80
Savage Wilderness '55
The Serpent's Egg '78
Target: Favorite Son '87
Them! '54
Tora! Tora! Tora! '70
Waterhole #3 '67
Where the Red Fern Grows '74
The Word '78

James Whitmore, Jr.
The Five of Me '81
The Gypsy Warriors '78
The Long Riders '80
Tricks of the Trade '88

Grace Lee Whitney
Star Trek 3: The Search for
  Spock '84
Star Trek 6: The Undiscovered
  Country '91

Peter Whitney
All the Brothers Were Valiant
  '53
Destination Tokyo '43
Rio Rita '42
Savage Wilderness '55
Valley of the Sun '42
Whistling in Dixie '42

Marguerite Whitten
Mystery in Swing '40
Two-Gun Man from Harlem '38

Margaret Whitton
The Best of Times '86
Big Girls Don't Cry...They Get
  Even '92
Ironweed '87
Little Monsters '89
Major League '89
Major League 2 '94
The Man Without a Face '93
9 1/2 Weeks '86

The Secret of My Success '87

May Whitty
Conquest '37
Crash Dive '43
Gaslight '44
The Lady Vanishes '38
Lassie, Come Home '43
Madame Curie '43
Mrs. Miniver '42
Suspicion '41
The White Cliffs of Dover '44

James Whitworth
Black Bikers from Hell '70
The Hills Have Eyes '77
Planet of the Dinosaurs '80
357 Magnum '79

Richard Whorf
Chain Lightning '50
Midnight '34
Yankee Doodle Dandy '42

Anna Wiazemsky
Porcile '69
Teorema '68

Mary Wickes
Almost Partners '87
Blondie's Blessed Event '42
By the Light of the Silvery
  Moon '53
The Canterville Ghost '91
Dance with Me, Henry '56
How to Murder Your Wife '64
I'll See You in My Dreams '51
June Bride '48
The Man Who Came to Dinner
  '41
On Moonlight Bay '51
Postcards from the Edge '90
Private Buckaroo '42
Sister Act '92
Sister Act 2: Back in the Habit
  '93
Where Angels Go, Trouble
  Follows '68
Who Done It? '42

Bernhard Wicki
Crime & Passion '75
The Eternal Waltz '54

Kathleen Widdoes
The Group '66
Mafia Princess '86
The Mephisto Waltz '71
Petulia '68
Savages '72

Richard Widmark
Against All Odds '84
The Alamo '60
All God's Children '80
Alvarez Kelly '66
Bear Island '80
Bedford Incident '65
Blackout '85
Broken Lance '54
Cheyenne Autumn '64
The Cobweb '55
Cold Sassy Tree '89
Coma '78
Death of a Gunfighter '69
The Domino Principle '77
Don't Bother to Knock '52
The Final Option '80
Gun Crazy '69
The Halls of Montezuma '50
Hanky Panky '82
How the West was Won '63
Judgment at Nuremberg '61
Kiss of Death '47
The Law and Jake Wade '58
Madigan '68
Mr. Horn '79
Murder on the Bayou '91
Murder on the Orient Express
  '74
National Lampoon Goes to the
  Movies '81
Night and the City '50
Panic in the Streets '50
Pickup on South Street '53
Road House '48
Rollercoaster '77
Saint Joan '57
Sell Out '76
The Street with No Name '48
The Swarm '78
Texas Guns '90
To the Devil, A Daughter '76
The Trap '59
True Colors '91

The Tunnel of Love '58
Twilight's Last Gleaming '77
Two Rode Together '61
Warlock '59
The Way West '67
Whale for the Killing '81
When the Legends Die '72

Lynda Wiesmeier
Preppies '82
R.S.V.P. '84
Wheels of Fire '84

Dianne Wiest
Bright Lights, Big City '88
Cookie '89
Cops and Robbersons '94
Edward Scissorhands '90
Falling in Love '84
Footloose '84
Hannah and Her Sisters '86
Independence Day '83
It's My Turn '80
Little Man Tate '91
The Lost Boys '87
Parenthood '89
The Purple Rose of Cairo '85
Radio Days '87
The Scout '94
September '88

Naima Wifstrand
The Magician '58
Night Is My Future '47

Chris Wiggins
The Bay Boy '85
Ford: The Man & the Machine
  '87
Kavik the Wolf Dog '84
King of the Grizzlies '69
Mark Twain and Me '91
Why Shoot the Teacher '79

Robert Wightman
A Day for Thanks on Walton's
  Mountain '82
Opposing Force '87
Stepfather 3: Father's Day '92

James Wilby
Conspiracy '89
Dreamchild '85
A Handful of Dust '88
Howard's End '92
Maurice '87
A Summer Story '88
A Tale of Two Cities '91

Frank Wilcox
Abbott and Costello Meet the
  Keystone Kops '54
Infamous Crimes '47
Seventh Cavalry '56

Larry Wilcox
The Dirty Dozen: The Next
  Mission '85
The Last Ride of the Dalton
  Gang '79
Mission Manila '87
Sky Hei$t '75

Lisa Wilcox
A Nightmare on Elm Street 4:
  Dream Master '88
A Nightmare on Elm Street 5:
  Dream Child '89

Mary Wilcox
Beast of the Yellow Night '70
Love Me Deadly '76

Robert Wilcox
Blondie Takes a Vacation '39
Buried Alive '39
Doctor Satan's Robot '40
Dreaming Out Loud '40
The Man They Could Not Hang
  '39
Mysterious Doctor Satan '40

Shannon Wilcox
Hollywood Harry '86
When Your Lover Leaves '83

Toyah Wilcox
Ebony Tower '86
Jubilee '78
Murder: Ultimate Grounds for
  Divorce '85

Collin Wilcox-Horne
The Baby Maker '70
Fury on Wheels '71

Henry Wilcoxon
Cleopatra '34

A Connecticut Yankee in King Arthur's Court '49
The Corsican Brothers '42
Enola Gay: The Men, the Mission, the Atomic Bomb '80
Escape from Planet Earth '67
Jericho '38
The Last of the Mohicans '36
Man in the Wilderness '71
Mrs. Miniver '42
Pony Express Rider '76
The President's Mystery '36
Samson and Delilah '50
Scaramouche '52
Tarzan Finds a Son '39
The Ten Commandments '56
That Hamilton Woman '41
The Two Worlds of Jenny Logan '79
The War Lord '65
When Every Day was the Fourth of July '78

Jack Wild
Melody '71
Oliver! '68
Robin Hood: Prince of Thieves '91

Andrew Wilde
Murder on Line One '90
1984 '84
Pete Townshend: White City '85

Cornel Wilde
At Sword's Point '51
Big Combo '55
The Comic '69
The Fifth Musketeer '79
Forever Amber '47
The Greatest Show on Earth '52
High Sierra '41
The Naked Prey '66
Norseman '78
Omar Khayyam '57
Passion '54
Road House '48
Sharks' Treasure '75
A Song to Remember '45
Sword of Lancelot '63
Treasure of the Golden Condor '53
Wintertime '43

Gene Wilder
The Adventures of Sherlock Holmes' Smarter Brother '78
Another You '91
Blazing Saddles '74
Everything You Always Wanted to Know About Sex (But Were Afraid to Ask) '72
The Frisco Kid '79
Funny About Love '90
Hanky Panky '82
Haunted Honeymoon '86
The Little Prince '74
The Producers '68
Quackser Fortune Has a Cousin in the Bronx '70
See No Evil, Hear No Evil '89
The Silver Streak '76
Start the Revolution Without Me '70
Stir Crazy '80
Thursday's Game '74
Willy Wonka & the Chocolate Factory '71
The Woman in Red '84
World's Greatest Lover '77
Young Frankenstein '74

James Wilder
Murder One '88
Prey of the Chameleon '91
Scorchers '92
Zombie High '87

Yvonne Wilder
Bloodbrothers '78
Honeyboy '82
The Return of Count Yorga '71

Michael Wilding
Convoy '40
Cottage to Let '41
The Courtney Affair '47
The Egyptian '54
The Glass Slipper '55
Kipps '41
Late Extra '35

Maytime in Mayfair '52
The Naked Edge '61
Stage Fright '50
Torch Song '53
Under Capricorn '49
Waterloo '71
The World of Suzie Wong '60

John Wildman
American Boyfriends '89
Lethal Pursuit '88
My American Cousin '85
Sorority Babes in the Slimeball Bowl-A-Rama '87

Valerie Wildman
Inner Sanctum '91
Neon City '91

Dawn Wildsmith
Alienator '89
Cyclone '87
Evil Spawn '87
Phantom Empire '87
Surf Nazis Must Die '87
Terminal Force '88
Warlords '88

Mike Wiles
Cole Justice '89
Terror at Tenkiller '86

Jan Wiley
Dawn on the Great Divide '42
Jive Junction '43
Master Key '44
Rhythm Parade '43
There Goes Kelly '45
Tonto Basin Outlaws '41
The Underdog '43

John Wilford
Ninja: American Warrior '90
Ninja Death Squad '87

Kathleen Wilhoite
Angel Heart '87
Bad Influence '90
Campus Man '87
Everybody Wins '90
Getting Even with Dad '94
Lorenzo's Oil '92
The Morning After '86
Murphy's Law '86
Private School '83
Undercover '87
Witchboard '87

Robert J. Wilke
High Noon '52
20,000 Leagues Under the Sea '54

Jose Wilker
Bye Bye Brazil '79
Dona Flor and Her Two Husbands '78
Medicine Man '92
Xica '76

Guy Wilkerson
Comin' Round the Mountain '51
Dead or Alive '41
Fighting Valley '43
Frontier Fugitives '45
Guns of the Law '44
Man of the West '58
Marked for Murder '45
Outlaw Roundup '44

Donna Wilkes
Angel '84
Blood Song '82
Fyre '78
Grotesque '87
Hard Knocks

Elaine Wilkes
Killer Party '86
Roommate '84

Barbara Wilkin
The Flesh Eaters '64
Six in Paris '68

June Wilkinson
The Bellboy and the Playgirls '62
The Florida Connection '74
Frankenstein's Great Aunt Tillie '83
Macumba Love '60
Sno-Line '85
Vasectomy: A Delicate Matter '86

Tom Wilkinson
Paper Mask '91
Prime Suspect '92

Sylvia '86

Fred Willard
Americathon '79
Chesty Anderson USN '76
The History of White People in America '85
How to Beat the High Cost of Living '80
Lots of Luck '85
Moving Violations '85
Portrait of a White Marriage '88
Roxanne '87
Salem's Lot '79
Second City Insanity '81

Warren William
Arizona '40
Black Tower '50
The Case of the Lucky Legs '35
Cleopatra '34
Employees' Entrance '33
Fear '46
The Firefly '37
Go West, Young Man '36
Gold Diggers of 1933 '33
Lady for a Day '33
Madame X '37
The Man in the Iron Mask '39
The Private Affairs of Bel Ami '47
Satan Met a Lady '36
Skyscraper Souls '32
Strange Illusion '45
Three on a Match '32
Wives Under Suspicion '38
The Wolf Man '41

Adam Williams
The Badlanders '58
Fear Strikes Out '57
North by Northwest '59
Queen for a Day '51
Without Warning '52

Allen Williams
Scorpion '86
The Two Worlds of Jenny Logan '79

Barbara Williams
City of Hope '91
Indecency '92
Jo Jo Dancer, Your Life is Calling '86
Oh, What a Night '92
Peter Gunn '89
Tell Me That You Love Me '84
Thief of Hearts '84
Tiger Warsaw '87
Watchers '88

Barry Williams
The Brady Bunch, Vol. 1 '69
A Very Brady Christmas '88

Bill Williams
Buckskin '68
The Cariboo Trail '50
The Clay Pigeon '49
Deadline at Dawn '46
Flight of the Grey Wolf '76
The Giant Spider Invasion '75
Operation Haylift '50
Son of Paleface '52
Storm Rider '57
The Stratton Story '49
Till the End of Time '46
Torpedo Alley '53
A Woman's Secret '49

Billy Dee Williams
Alien Intruder '93
Batman '89
Bingo Long Traveling All-Stars & Motor Kings '76
Black Brigade '69
Brian's Song '71
Chiefs '83
Children of Divorce '80
Christmas Lilies of the Field '84
Courage '86
Deadly Illusion '87
Driving Me Crazy '91
The Empire Strikes Back '80
Fear City '85
Final Comedown '72
From "Star Wars" to "Jedi": The Making of a Saga '83
Giant Steps
The Glass House '72
Hit! '73
The Hostage Tower '80
The Imposter '84

The Jacksons: An American Dream '92
Lady Sings the Blues '72
Mahogany '75
Marvin & Tige '84
Nighthawks '81
Number One with a Bullet '87
Oceans of Fire '86
The Out-of-Towners '70
Return of the Jedi '83
Shooting Stars '85

Billy "Sly" Williams
Mission of Justice '92
Voodoo Dawn '89

Cara Williams
The Defiant Ones '58
Meet Me in Las Vegas '56
Never Steal Anything Small '59
The White Buffalo '77

Caroline Williams
Stepfather 2: Make Room for Daddy '89
Texas Chainsaw Massacre, Part 2 '86

Charles Williams
Born to Be Wild '38
Hollywood Stadium Mystery '38

Chuck Williams
Dark Rider '91
Soultaker '90

Cindy Williams
American Graffiti '73
Big Man on Campus '89
Bingo '91
The Conversation '74
The First Nudie Musical '75
Gas-s-s-s! '70
The Killing Kind '73
More American Graffiti '79
Rude Awakening '89
Spaceship '81
Travels with My Aunt '72
Tricks of the Trade '88
Uforia '81

Clara Williams
Hell's Hinges '16
Italian '15

Clarence Williams, III
Dangerous Relations '93
Deep Cover '92
52 Pick-Up '86
The House of Dies Drear '88
I'm Gonna Git You Sucka '88
The Last Innocent Man '87
Maniac Cop 2 '90
My Heroes Have Always Been Cowboys '91
Perfect Victims '87
Purple Rain '84
Sugar Hill '94
Tough Guys Don't Dance '87

Cynda Williams
Armistead Maupin's Tales of the City '93
Mo' Better Blues '90
One False Move '91

Dick Anthony Williams
An Almost Perfect Affair '79
Edward Scissorhands '90
For Us, the Living '88
Keeping On '81
Mo' Better Blues '90
The Night the City Screamed '80
Sophisticated Gents '81
Tap '89
A Woman Called Moses '78

D.J. Williams
The Courageous Mr. Penn '41
The Crimes of Stephen Hawke '36
Murder in the Old Red Barn '36

Edy Williams
Bad Girls from Mars '90
Bad Manners '84
Beyond the Valley of the Dolls '70
Hellhole '85
Hollywood Hot Tubs '84
Mankillers '87
Rented Lips '88

Secret Life of an American Wife '68

Emlyn Williams
The Citadel '38
Deadly Game '82
Epic That Never Was '65
The Iron Duke '34
The Last Days of Dolwyn '49
The Stars Look Down '39
The Wreck of the Mary Deare '59

Esther Williams
Andy Hardy's Double Life '42
Bathing Beauty '44
Dangerous When Wet '53
Duchess of Idaho '50
Easy to Love '53
A Guy Named Joe '44
Jupiter's Darling '55
Million Dollar Mermaid '52
Neptune's Daughter '49
On an Island with You '48
Pagan Love Song '50
Skirts Ahoy! '52
Take Me Out to the Ball Game '49
Texas Carnival '51
That's Entertainment '74
Thrill of a Romance '45
Ziegfeld Follies '46

Grant Williams
Brain of Blood '71
Escape from Planet Earth '67
The Incredible Shrinking Man '57
The Leech Woman '59
The Monolith Monsters '57
Written on the Wind '56

Guinn Williams
Bad Lands '39
Billy the Kid '41
Danger Trails '35
Dangerous Holiday '37
Feud of the Trail '37
The Fighting 69th '40
Gun Play '36
Hands Across the Border '43
Heritage of the Desert '33
Hidden Guns '56
Kelly the Second '36
Lure of the Islands '42
Mr. Wise Guy '42
Mystery Squadron '33
Nevada '44
The Phantom '31
The Phantom Broadcast '33
Powdersmoke Range '35
Rounding Up the Law '22
Springfield Rifle '52
The Vigilantes are Coming '36
Virginia City '40
When the West Was Young '32
Wolfheart's Revenge '25

Guy Williams
Captain Sinbad '63
I Was a Teenage Werewolf '57
The Prince and the Pauper '62
Savage Wilderness '55
The Secret of El Zorro '57
The Sign of Zorro '60

Hal Williams
Don't Look Back: The Story of Leroy "Satchel" Paige '81
On the Nickel '80

Hugh Williams
Bitter Sweet '33
The Day Will Dawn '42
Elizabeth of Ladymead '48
A Girl in a Million '46
The Human Monster '39
Inspector Hornleigh '39
Khartoum '66
One of Our Aircraft Is Missing '41
Wuthering Heights '39

Ian Patrick Williams
Bad Channels '92
Bloodmoon '90
Dolls '87

Jason Williams
Cheerleaders' Wild Weekend '85
Copkillers '77
Danger Zone '87
Danger Zone 2 '89

Williams ►cont.

Danger Zone 3: Steel Horse War '90
Flesh Gordon '72
Vampire at Midnight '88

Jim Williams
Ex-Cop '93
The Executioner '78
Island of Blood '58
Living to Die '91
The Newlydeads '87

JoBeth Williams
Adam '83
American Dreamer '84
The Big Chill '83
Chantilly Lace '93
Child in the Night '90
The Day After '83
Desert Bloom '86
The Dogs of War '81
Dutch '91
Endangered Species '82
Kramer vs. Kramer '79
Me, Myself & I '92
Memories of Me '88
Murder Ordained '87
Poltergeist '82
Poltergeist 2: The Other Side '86
Sex, Love and Cold Hard Cash '93
Stir Crazy '80
Stop! or My Mom Will Shoot '92
Switch '91
Teachers '84
Victim of Love '91
Welcome Home '89
Wyatt Earp '94

John Williams
D-Day, the Sixth of June '56
Dear Brigitte '65
Dial ''M'' for Murder '54
Double Trouble '67
Island in the Sun '57
Sabrina '54
The Secret War of Harry Frigg '68
To Catch a Thief '55
24 Hours in a Woman's Life '61
Witness for the Prosecution '57
The Young Philadelphians '59

Kelli Williams
Lifepod '93
Zapped Again '89

Kenneth Williams
Carry On at Your Convenience '71
Carry On Behind '75
Carry On Cleo '65
Carry On Cowboy '66
Carry On Cruising '62
Carry On Doctor '68
Carry On Emmanuelle '78
Carry On 'Round the Bend '72
Carry On Screaming '66
Follow That Camel '67

Kimberly Williams
Father of the Bride '91
Indian Summer '93

Michael Williams
Educating Rita '83
Marat/Sade '66
Murder by Night '89

Paul Williams
Battle for the Planet of the Apes '73
Best Enemies '86
The Cheap Detective '78
Chill Factor '90
The Doors '91
Frog '89
Frogs! '90s
The Night They Saved Christmas '87
Phantom of the Paradise '74
Smokey and the Bandit '77
Smokey and the Bandit, Part 2 '80
Smokey and the Bandit, Part 3 '83
Stone Cold Dead '80
Zombie High '87

Peter Williams
Destroy All Planets '68
Robin Hood...The Legend: Robin Hood and the Sorcerer '83

Rhys Williams
The Corn is Green '45
Fastest Gun Alive '56
How Green was My Valley '41
Kiss Tomorrow Goodbye '50
Mrs. Miniver '42
The Restless Breed '58
The Showdown '50
Skullduggery '70

Robert Williams
Devotion '31
The Lady Says No '51
Platinum Blonde '31
Revenge of the Creature '55
U-Boat Prisoner '44

Robin Williams
Awakenings '90
Being Human '94
Best of Comic Relief '86
The Best of Times '86
Cadillac Man '90
Can I Do It...Till I Need Glasses? '77
Club Paradise '86
Dead Poets Society '89
An Evening with Robin Williams '83
The Fisher King '91
Good Morning, Vietnam '87
Hook '91
Mrs. Doubtfire '93
Moscow on the Hudson '84
Popeye '80
Seize the Day '86
Survivors '83
The Tale of the Frog Prince '83
Toys '92
The World According to Garp '82

Roger Williams
Aces Wild '37
Cheyenne Rides Again '38
Code of the Fearless '39
Feud Maker '38
Gun Grit '36
Heroes of the Alamo '37
Phantom Patrol '36
The Roamin' Cowboy '37
Toll of the Desert '35
Valley of Terror '38

Samm-Art Williams
The Adventures of Huckleberry Finn '85
A Rage in Harlem '91

Spencer Williams, Jr.
Blood of Jesus '41
Bronze Buckaroo '39
Cord & Dischords/Naughty Nurse '42
Dirty Gertie from Harlem U.S.A. '46
Go Down Death '41
Harlem Rides the Range '39
Juke Joint '47
Son of Ingagi '40

Steven Williams
Jason Goes to Hell: The Final Friday '93
Missing in Action 2: The Beginning '85
Revolver '92
Silent Witness '85

Treat Williams
Dead Heat '88
Deadly Hero '75
Deadly Matrimony '92
Dempsey '83
The Eagle Has Landed '77
Echoes in the Darkness '87
Final Verdict '91
Flashpoint '84
Hair '79
The Heart of Dixie '89
J. Edgar Hoover '87
The Little Mermaid '84
Max and Helen '90
The Men's Club '86
Night of the Sharks '89
1941 '79
Once Upon a Time in America '84

Prince of the City '81
The Pursuit of D.B. Cooper '81
The Ritz '76
Smooth Talk '85
A Streetcar Named Desire '84
Sweet Lies '88
Third Degree Burn '89
Third Solution '89
Till Death Do Us Part '92

Vanessa Williams
Another You '91
Candyman '92
Full Exposure: The Sex Tape Scandals '89
Harley Davidson and the Marlboro Man '91
The Jacksons: An American Dream '92
The Kid Who Loved Christmas '90
New Jack City '91
The Pick-Up Artist '87
Under the Gun '88

Clayton Williamson
Clowning Around '92
Clowning Around 2 '93

Fred Williamson
Adios Amigo '75
Big Score '83
Black Caesar '73
The Black Cobra '87
Black Cobra 2 '89
Black Cobra 3: The Manila Connection '90
Blind Rage '78
Boss '74
Bucktown '75
Deadly Impact '84
Deadly Intent '88
Deadly Mission '78
Death Journey '76
Delta Force Commando '87
Delta Force Commando 2 '90
Express to Terror '79
Fear in the City '81
Fist of Fear, Touch of Death '77
Foxtrap '85
Hell Up in Harlem '73
Johnny Barrows, El Malo '70s
Jornada de Muerte '80s
Joshua '76
The Kill Reflex '89
The Last Fight '82
M*A*S*H '70
Mean Johnny Barrows '75
The Messenger '87
Mister Mean '77
The New Gladiators '87
New York Ripper '82
1990: The Bronx Warriors '83
No Way Back '82
One Down, Two to Go! '82
South Beach '92
Steele's Law '91
Take a Hard Ride '75
Three Days to a Kill '91
Three the Hard Way '74
Warriors of the Wasteland '83
White Fire '83

Mykel T. Williamson
The First Power '89
Miracle Mile '89
Streets of Fire '84

Nicol Williamson
Black Widow '87
The Cheap Detective '78
Christopher Columbus '85
Excalibur '81
The Exorcist 3 '90
Hamlet '69
The Human Factor '79
I'm Dancing as Fast as I Can '82
Passion Flower '86
Return to Oz '85
The Seven Percent Solution '76
Venom '82
The Wilby Conspiracy '75
The Word '78

Noble Willingham
Article 99 '92
Big Bad Mama '74
Blind Fury '90
Career Opportunities '91
City Slickers '91
City Slickers 2: The Legend of Curly's Gold '94

Coward of the County '81
Good Morning, Vietnam '87
Kenny Rogers as the Gambler '80
The Last Boy Scout '91
My Sweet Charlie '70
Pastime '91

Bruce Willis
Billy Bathgate '91
Blind Date '87
The Bonfire of the Vanities '90
Color of Night '94
Death Becomes Her '92
Die Hard '88
Die Hard 2: Die Harder '90
Hudson Hawk '91
In Country '89
The Last Boy Scout '91
Moonlighting '85
Mortal Thoughts '91
North '94
Pulp Fiction '94
Striking Distance '93
Sunset '88
That's Adequate '90

Matt Willis
Behind Prison Walls '43
Blonde Savage '47
The Noose Hangs High '48
Return of the Vampire '43

Noel Willman
Beau Brummel '54
21 Hours at Munich '76
The Warriors '55

Chill Wills
The Alamo '60
Allegheny Uprising '39
Billy the Kid '41
Boom Town '40
City That Never Sleeps '53
Deadly Companions '61
Francis Joins the WACs '54
Giant '56
Gun Glory '57
The Harvey Girls '46
Heartaches '47
High Lonesome '50
Honky Tonk '41
Kentucky Rifle '55
Man from the Alamo '53
McLintock! '63
Mr. Billion '77
Pat Garrett & Billy the Kid '73
Poco '77
Racketeers of the Range '39
Ride the Man Down '53
Rio Grande '50
The Rounders '65
Small Town Girl '53
Tarzan's New York Adventure '42
Tulsa '49
Western Union '41
The Wheeler Dealers '63
The Yearling '46

Maury Wills
The Black Six '74
The Sandlot '93

Douglas Wilmer
The Adventures of Sherlock Holmes' Smarter Brother '78
Golden Voyage of Sinbad '73
The Incredible Sarah '76
Men of Sherwood Forest '57

Andre Wilms
La Vie de Boheme '92
Life Is a Long Quiet River '88
Monsieur Hire '89

Ajita Wilson
Escape from Hell '89
Savage Island '85

Barbara Wilson
Invasion of the Animal People '62
Lost, Lonely, and Vicious '59

Dana Wilson
The Body Vanished '39
Wild Women '53

David Wilson
Hometown U.S.A. '79
The Inside Man '84

Don ''The Dragon'' Wilson
Bloodfist '89

Bloodfist 2 '90
Bloodfist 3: Forced to Fight '92
Bloodfist 4: Die Trying '92
Bloodfist 5: Human Target '93
The Chase '46
Dirty Gertie from Harlem U.S.A. '46
Futurekick '91
Magic Kid '92
Niagara '52
Out for Blood '93
Ring of Fire '91
Ring of Fire 2: Blood and Steel '92

Dooley Wilson
Casablanca '42
Seven Days Ashore/Hurry, Charlie, Hurry '44
Stormy Weather '43

Dorothy Wilson
The Brighton Strangler/Before Dawn '45
Dangerous Appointment '34
Last Days of Pompeii '35

Earl Wilson
Beach Blanket Bingo '65
Copacabana '47

Elizabeth Wilson
The Addams Family '91
The Believers '87
A Conspiracy of Love '87
Grace Quigley '84
The Graduate '67
Jenny '70
Little Murders '71
Miles to Go Before I Sleep '74
Patterns '56
Prisoner of Second Avenue '74
Regarding Henry '91
Sanctuary of Fear '79
Skylark '93
The Tunnel of Love '58
Where Are the Children? '85
You Can't Take It with You '84

Flip Wilson
Cancel My Reservation '72
The Fish that Saved Pittsburgh '79
Uptown Saturday Night '74

Frank Wilson
Beware '46
The Club '81
Emperor Jones '33
Emperor Jones/Paul Robeson: Tribute to an Artist '33
Girl from Chicago '32
Green Pastures '36
Maniac Warriors '90s
Paradise in Harlem '40
Ultimate Desires '91

George Wilson
Make Room for Tomorrow '81
Nudo di Donna '83

Lambert Wilson
The Belly of an Architect '91
The Blood of Others '84
Five Days One Summer '82
Frankenstein '93
Red Kiss '85
Rendez-vous '85
Sahara '83

Lewis Wilson
The Body Vanished '39
Wild Women '53

Lois Wilson
Bright Eyes '34
The Covered Wagon '23
Drifting Souls '32
Female '33
In the Money '34
Laughing at Life '33
Monsieur Beaucaire '24
The Secrets of Wu Sin '32

Marie Wilson
Boy Meets Girl '38
Fabulous Joe '47
Flying Blind '41
A Girl in Every Port '52
March of the Wooden Soldiers '34
Mr. Hobbs Takes a Vacation '62
My Friend Irma '49
Never Wave at a WAC '52

The Private Affairs of Bel Ami '47
Satan Met a Lady '36
Waterfront '39

Mary Louise Wilson
The Adventures of Huck Finn '93
Cheap Shots '91
Green Card '90

Paul Wilson
Devonsville Terror '83
My Best Friend Is a Vampire '88

Perry Wilson
Fear Strikes Out '57
The Matchmaker '58

Rita Wilson
The Day It Came to Earth '77
Sleepless in Seattle '93
Volunteers '85

Robert Wilson
Day of Triumph '54
I Beheld His Glory '53

Roger Wilson
Overthrow '82
Porky's '82
Porky's 2: The Next Day '83
Second Time Lucky '84
Thunder Alley '85

Scott Wilson
The Aviator '85
Blue City '86
The Exorcist 3 '90
Femme Fatale '90
Flesh and Bone '93
The Grissom Gang '71
In Cold Blood '67
Jesse '88
Johnny Handsome '89
Malone '87
The New Centurions '72
The Ninth Configuration '79
On the Line '83
The Passover Plot '75
Pure Luck '91
The Right Stuff '83
The Tracker '88
Year of the Quiet Sun '84

Sheree J. Wilson
Crimewave '85
Fraternity Vacation '85
News at Eleven '86
Walker, Texas Ranger: One Riot, One Ranger '93

Stuart Wilson
The Age of Innocence '93
The Highest Honor '84
Lethal Weapon 3 '92
No Escape '94
Romance on the Orient Express '89
Running Blind '70s
Secret Weapon '90
Teenage Mutant Ninja Turtles 3 '93

Teddy Wilson
The Ambush Murders '82
The Benny Goodman Story '55
Cotton Comes to Harlem '70
Kiss Shot '89
Life Stinks '91
The Mighty Pawns '87

Thomas F. Wilson
April Fool's Day '86
Back to the Future '85
Back to the Future, Part 2 '89
Back to the Future, Part 3 '90

Tom Wilson
The Americano '17
Battling Butler '26
California Straight Ahead '25

Trey Wilson
Bull Durham '88
End of the Line '88
Great Balls of Fire '89
Married to the Mob '88
Miss Firecracker '89
Raising Arizona '87
Twins '88
The Vampire Hookers '78
Welcome Home '89

Penelope Wilton
Blame It on the Bellboy '92
The Borrowers '93

Clockwise '86
Cry Freedom '87
Singleton's Pluck '84

Brian Wimmer
China Beach '88
Dangerous Pursuit '89
Kiss of a Killer '93
Late for Dinner '91
Lipstick Camera '93
The World's Oldest Living Bridesmaid '92

Jeff Wincott
Deadly Bet '91
Martial Law 2: Undercover '91
Martial Outlaw '93
Mission of Justice '92

Michael Wincott
The Crow '93
The Doors '91
1492: Conquest of Paradise '92
Robin Hood: Prince of Thieves '91
Romeo Is Bleeding '93
Talk Radio '88
The Three Musketeers '93
Tragedy of Flight 103: The Inside Story '91
Wild Horse Hank '79

William Windom
Abduction of St. Anne '75
Attack of the 50 Ft. Woman '93
Back to Hannibal: The Return of Tom Sawyer and Huckleberry Finn '90
Brewster McCloud '70
Columbo: Prescription Murder '67
Committed '91
Dennis the Menace: Dinosaur Hunter '93
Desperate Lives '82
The Detective '68
Escape from the Planet of the Apes '71
For Love or Money '63
Funland '89
The Girls of Huntington House '73
Grandview U.S.A. '84
Last Plane Out '83
Leave 'Em Laughing '81
Mean Dog Blues '78
The Mephisto Waltz '71
One Man's Way '63
Planes, Trains & Automobiles '87
Pursuit '72
She's Having a Baby '88
Sommersby '93
Street Justice '89
To Kill a Mockingbird '62

Claire Windsor
The Blot '21
The Claw '27
Too Wise Wives '21

Marie Windsor
Abbott & Costello Meet the Mummy '55
Bedtime Story '63
Cahill: United States Marshal '73
Cat Women of the Moon '53
City That Never Sleeps '53
Commando Squad '87
Double Deal '50
The Fighting Kentuckian '49
Force of Evil '49
Girl in Black Stockings '57
Hellfire '48
Jungle '52
The Killing '56
Little Big Horn '51
The Narrow Margin '52
Outlaw Women '52
Outpost in Morocco '49
The Saint's Vacation/The Narrow Margin '52
Salem's Lot '79
The Showdown '50
Silver Star '55
Smart Alecks '42
Swamp Women '55
Tall Texan '53
Trouble Along the Way '53
Unholy Wife '57
Wild Women '70

Romy Windsor
Big Bad John '90
The House of Usher '88
Howling 4: The Original Nightmare '88

Paul Winfield
Angel City '80
Back to Hannibal: The Return of Tom Sawyer and Huckleberry Finn '90
Big Shots '87
Blue City '86
Brother John '70
Carbon Copy '81
Cliffhanger '93
Conrack '74
Damnation Alley '77
Death Before Dishonor '87
Dennis the Menace '93
For Us, the Living '88
Gordon's War '73
The Greatest '77
Green Eyes '76
Guilty of Innocence '87
A Hero Ain't Nothin' But a Sandwich '78
High Velocity '76
Huckleberry Finn '74
It's Good to Be Alive '74
King '78
The Mighty Pawns '87
Mike's Murder '84
Nowhere to Hide
Presumed Innocent '90
Roots: The Next Generation '79
R.P.M.* (*Revolutions Per Minute) '70
The Serpent and the Rainbow '87
Sophisticated Gents '81
Sounder '72
Star Trek 2: The Wrath of Khan '82
The Terminator '84
Twilight's Last Gleaming '77
The Women of Brewster Place '89

Oprah Winfrey
The Color Purple '85
Native Son '86
Pee Wee's Playhouse Christmas Special '88
The Women of Brewster Place '89

Leslie Wing
The Cowboy & the Ballerina '84
Dungeonmaster '85
Retribution '88

Debra Winger
Betrayed '88
Black Widow '87
Cannery Row '82
A Dangerous Woman '93
Everybody Wins '90
French Postcards '79
Leap of Faith '92
Legal Eagles '86
Mike's Murder '84
An Officer and a Gentleman '82
Shadowlands '93
The Sheltering Sky '90
Slumber Party '57 '76
Special Olympics '78
Terms of Endearment '83
Thank God It's Friday '78
Urban Cowboy '80
Wilder Napalm '93

Angela Winkler
Danton '82
Knife in the Head '78
The Lost Honor of Katharina Blum '75
Sheer Madness '84
The Tin Drum '79

Henry Winkler
An American Christmas Carol '79
Heroes '77
Katherine '75
The Lords of Flatbush '74
Night Shift '82
The One and Only '78

Kitty Winn
The Exorcist '73
The Exorcist 2: The Heretic '77
Man on a String '71
Miles to Go Before I Sleep '74

Mirrors '78
Panic in Needle Park '75
They Might Be Giants '71

Vic Winner
Horror Rises from the Tomb '72
The Rue Morgue Massacres '73

Lucyna Winnicka
First Spaceship on Venus '60
25 Fireman's Street '73

Charles Winninger
Babes in Arms '39
Beyond Tomorrow '40
Broadway Rhythm '44
Destry Rides Again '39
Every Day's a Holiday '38
Lady Takes a Chance '43
Little Nellie Kelly '40
Night Nurse '31
Nothing Sacred '37
Show Boat '36
The Sin of Madelon Claudet '31
State Fair '45
The Sun Shines Bright '53
Torpedo Alley '53
Ziegfeld Girl '41

Mare Winningham
Eye on the Sparrow '91
Fatal Exposure
God Bless the Child '88
Hard Promises '92
Intruders '92
Made in Heaven '87
Miracle Mile '89
Nobody's Fool '86
One Trick Pony '80
St. Elmo's Fire '85
Shy People '87
Single Bars, Single Women '84
Special Olympics '78
The Thorn Birds '83
Threshold '83
Turner and Hooch '89
A Winner Never Quits '86
Wyatt Earp '94

George Winslow
Artists and Models '55
Gentlemen Prefer Blondes '53
Monkey Business '52

Michael Winslow
Alphabet City '84
Buy & Cell '89
Far Out Man '89
Going Under '91
Lovelines '84
Police Academy '84
Police Academy 2: Their First Assignment '85
Police Academy 3: Back in Training '86
Police Academy 4: Citizens on Patrol '87
Police Academy 5: Assignment Miami Beach '88
Police Academy 6: City Under Siege '89
Spaceballs '87
Tag: The Assassination Game '82

Alex Winter
Bill & Ted's Bogus Journey '91
Bill & Ted's Excellent Adventure '89
Death Wish 3 '85
Freaked '93
Haunted Summer '88
Rosalie Goes Shopping '89

Ed Winter
The Buddy System '83
Held Hostage '91
Mother & Daughter: A Loving War '80

Vincent Winter
Almost Angels '62
Gorgo '61
The Horse Without a Head '63
Time Lock '57

Deborah Winters
Blue Sunshine '78
Class of '44 '73
Hail, Hero! '69
Kotch '71
The Outing '87
The People Next Door '70

Tarantulas: The Deadly Cargo '77

Jonathan Winters
The Fish that Saved Pittsburgh '79
The Flintstones '94
It's a Mad, Mad, Mad, Mad World '63
The Longshot '86
The Loved One '65
Moon Over Parador '88
More Wild, Wild West '80
Oh Dad, Poor Dad (Momma's Hung You in the Closet & I'm Feeling So Sad) '67
The Russians are Coming, the Russians are Coming '66
Say Yes! '86
The Shadow '94
Viva Max '69

Roland Winters
Abbott and Costello Meet the Killer, Boris Karloff '49
Blue Hawaii '62
Cash McCall '60
Guilty of Treason '50
Jet Pilot '57
Malaya '49
Riders of the Whistling Skull '37
To Please a Lady '50
The Underworld Story '50
The West Point Story '50

Shelley Winters
Alfie '66
The Balcony '63
Behave Yourself! '52
The Big Knife '55
Bloody Mama '70
Blume in Love '73
Buona Sera, Mrs. Campbell '68
City on Fire '78
Cleopatra Jones '73
Deja Vu '84
Delta Force '86
Diamonds '72
The Diary of Anne Frank '59
A Double Life '47
Ellie '84
Elvis: The Movie '79
Enter Laughing '67
Executive Suite '54
Fanny Hill '83
The Gangster '47
The Greatest Story Ever Told '65
Harper '66
I Am a Camera '55
I Died a Thousand Times '55
Initiation of Sarah '78
Journey into Fear '74
King of the Gypsies '78
Lolita '62
The Magician of Lublin '79
Mambo '55
Meet Danny Wilson '52
Next Stop, Greenwich Village '76
The Night of the Hunter '55
Over the Brooklyn Bridge '83
A Patch of Blue '65
Pete's Dragon '77
Phone Call from a Stranger '52
The Pickle '93
A Place in the Sun '51
Poor Pretty Eddie '73
The Poseidon Adventure '72
Purple People Eater '88
The Scalphunters '68
Shattered '72
S.O.B. '81
Stepping Out '91
The Tenant '76
Tentacles '77
That Lucky Touch '75
Time of Indifference '64
Treasure of Pancho Villa '55
An Unremarkable Life '89
Very Close Quarters '84
The Visitor '80
Weep No More My Lady '93
What's the Matter with Helen? '71
Who Slew Auntie Roo? '71
Wild in the Streets '68
Winchester '73 '50
Witchfire '86

Estelle Winwood
Darby O'Gill & the Little People
'59
The Glass Slipper '55
The Magic Sword '62
The Misfits '61
Murder by Death '76
The Producers '68
Quality Street '37
The Swan '56
This Happy Feeling '58

Billy Wirth
Body Snatchers '93
The Lost Boys '87
Red Shoe Diaries '92
War Party '89

Robert Wisden
Blood Clan '91
Glory Enough for All: The
Discovery of Insulin '92

Norman Wisdom
The Night They Raided
Minsky's '69
Trouble in Store '53
What's Good for the Goose '93

Ray Wise
Bob Roberts '92
The Chase '93
Endless Descent '90
The Journey of Natty Gann '85
Rising Sun '93
RoboCop '87
Season of Fear '89
Sunstroke '92
Swamp Thing '82
The Taking of Flight 847: The
Uli Derickson Story '88
Twin Peaks '90
Twin Peaks: Fire Walk with Me
'92
Write to Kill '91

Joseph Wiseman
Detective Story '51
Dr. No '62
Ghostwriter '84
Jaguar Lives '79
Lady Mobster '88
Lawman '71
The Prodigal '55
Pursuit '72
Seize the Day '86
The Silver Chalice '54
Stiletto '69
The Unforgiven '60
Viva Zapata! '52
Zalmen or the Madness of God
'75

Googie Withers
Accused '36
Action for Slander '38
Dead of Night '45
Devil on Horseback '54
Hotel du Lac '86
The Lady Vanishes '38
Night and the City '50
Northanger Abbey '80s
On Approval '44
One of Our Aircraft Is Missing
'41
Pink Strings and Sealing Wax
'45

Grant Withers
Bells of Coronado '50
Bells of Rosarita '45
Billy the Kid '41
Boy's Reformatory '39
Daughter of the Tong '39
Doomed to Die '40
The Fatal Hour '40
The Fighting Kentuckian '49
Fighting Marines '36
Final Extra '27
Hoodlum Empire '52
Let's Sing Again '36
The Masked Rider '41
Mr. Wong, Detective '38
Mr. Wong in Chinatown '39
Mystery of Mr. Wong '39
Night Time in Nevada '48
Oklahoma Annie '51
Phantom of Chinatown '40
Radio Patrol '37
The Road to Ruin '28
The Secrets of Wu Sin '32
Tailspin Tommy '34
Trigger, Jr. '50
The Yellow Rose of Texas '44

Jane Withers
Bright Eyes '34
Captain Newman, M.D. '63
The Farmer Takes a Wife '35
Giant '56

Cora Witherspoon
The Bank Dick '40
Just Around the Corner '38
Just for You '52
Libeled Lady '36
Marie Antoinette '38
On the Avenue '37
Personal Property '37
Quality Street '37

John Witherspoon
Boomerang '92
Killer Tomatoes Strike Back '90

Reese Witherspoon
A Far Off Place '93
Jack the Bear '93
The Man in the Moon '91
Return to Lonesome Dove '93
S.F.W. '94
Wildflower '91

Glenn Withrow
Dudes '87
Naked Lie '89
Pass the Ammo '88

Michael Witney
Darling Lili '70
The Way West '67

Kathryn Witt
Cocaine Wars '86
Demon of Paradise '87
Philadelphia '93

Karen Witter
Buried Alive '89
Midnight '89
Perfect Match '88
The Vineyard '89

Stefan Wodoslowsky
Mindfield '89
90 Days '86

David Wohl
Armed and Dangerous '86
Chillers '88

Hillary Wolf
Big Girls Don't Cry...They Get
Even '92
Home Alone 2: Lost in New
York '92

Kelly Wolf
A Day in October '92
Graveyard Shift '90
Great Love Experiment '84
Triumph of the Spirit '89

David Wolfe
Five Fingers '52
Salt of the Earth '54

Ian Wolfe
The Barretts of Wimpole Street
'34
Bedlam '45
Diary of a Madman '63
Houdini '53
The Judge Steps Out '49
The Magnificent Yankee '50
Moonfleet '55
Mutiny on the Bounty '35
One Man's Way '63
Zombies on Broadway '44

Jim Wolfe
Chillers '88
Invasion of the Space
Preachers '90

Traci Wolfe
Lethal Weapon '87
Lethal Weapon 2 '89
Lethal Weapon 3 '92

Frank Wolff
Atlas '60
The Awful Dr. Orlof '62
The Beast from Haunted Cave
'60
The King's Rhapsody '55
Ski Troop Attack '60
The Wasp Woman '59
When Women Had Tails '70

Donald Wolfit
Becket '64
Blood of the Vampire '58

**The Charge of the Light
Brigade '68**
The Hands of Orlac '60
Late Extra '35
The Mark '61
Room at the Top '59
The Silent Passenger '35
Svengali '55

Wolfman Jack
American Graffiti '73
The Committee '68
Deadman's Curve '78
Hanging on a Star '78
Midnight '89
Mortuary Academy '91
Motel Hell '80

Louis Wolheim
All Quiet on the Western Front
'30
Danger Lights '30
Square Shoulders '29
The Tempest '28

Sven Wollter
House of Angels '92
The Sacrifice '86

Stevie Wonder
Bikini Beach '64
Muscle Beach Party '64

Anna May Wong
Daughter of the Dragon '31
Java Head '35
Shanghai Express '32
A Study in Scarlet '33
The Thief of Baghdad '24

B.D. Wong
Father of the Bride '91
The Freshman '90
Jurassic Park '93
Mystery Date '91

Carter Wong
Born Invincible '76
Cold Blooded Murder
The Ninja Pirates '90
Shaolin Traitor '82
Story of the Dragon '82

Chung Wong
The Samurai
Samurai Death Bells

Russell Wong
China Cry '91
China Girl '87
China White '91
Eat a Bowl of Tea '89
The Joy Luck Club '93
New Jack City '91
Tai-Pan '86

Victor Wong
Big Trouble in Little China '86
Dim Sum: A Little Bit of Heart
'85
Eat a Bowl of Tea '89
The Golden Child '86
The Ice Runner '93
The Joy Luck Club '93
The Last Emperor '87
Prince of Darkness '87
3 Ninjas '92
3 Ninjas Kick Back '94
Tremors '89

Arthur Wontner
Murder at the Baskervilles '37
Sherlock Holmes: The Silver
Blaze '77
The Terror '38
The Triumph of Sherlock
Holmes '35

Andy Wood
The Annihilators '85
Eye of the Eagle 2 '89
Ghostwarrior '86

Britt Wood
Detour to Danger '45
Knights of the Range '40
The Showdown '40

Clive Wood
The Crucifer of Blood '91
Treasure Island '89

David Wood
If... '69
Tales That Witness Madness
'73

Elijah Wood
The Adventures of Huck Finn
'93
Avalon '90
Child in the Night '90
Forever Young '92
The Good Son '93
North '94
Paradise '91
Radio Flyer '92

G. Wood
Bank Shot '74
M*A*S*H '70

Gary Wood
Hardbodies '84
Martial Outlaw '93

Gordon Wood
The Forty-Niners '32
Mother and Son '31

Harley Wood
Border Phantom '37
Camp Double Feature '39
Marihuana '36
Valley of Terror '38

Janet Wood
Fangs '75
G.I. Executioner '71
Slumber Party '57 '76
Terror at Red Wolf Inn '72

John Wood
Black Eyes '39
Housemaster '38
Jumpin' Jack Flash '86
Ladyhawke '85
Last Days of Pompeii '35
Orlando '93
The Purple Rose of Cairo '85
Shadowlands '93
A Stolen Face '52
WarGames '83
Which Way to the Front? '70

Karen Wood
Loose Screws '85
Scalps '83

Lana Wood
Black Water Gold '69
Captain America 2: Death Too
Soon '79
Demon Rage '82
Diamonds are Forever '71
Free Grass '69
Grayeagle '77
Justin Morgan Had a Horse '81
A Place Called Today '72
A Question of Guilt '78
The Searchers '56

Mary Laura Wood
Hour of Decision '57
Stranger in Town '57

Montgomery Wood
Adios Gringo '65
Blood for a Silver Dollar '66

Natalie Wood
The Affair '73
Bob & Carol & Ted & Alice '69
Brainstorm '83
The Burning Hills '56
Cash McCall '60
The Cracker Factory '79
From Here to Eternity '79
The Ghost and Mrs. Muir '47
Great Race '65
The Green Promise '49
Gypsy '62
Inside Daisy Clover '65
The Jackpot '50
James Dean: The First
American Teenager '76
Just for You '52
Kings Go Forth '58
The Last Married Couple in
America '80
Love with the Proper Stranger
'63
Marjorie Morningstar '58
Meteor '79
Miracle on 34th Street '47
Never a Dull Moment '50
Rebel Without a Cause '55
The Searchers '56
Sex and the Single Girl '64
The Silver Chalice '54
Splendor in the Grass '61
This Property is Condemned
'66

Tomorrow is Forever '46
West Side Story '61
Willie & Phil '80

Peggy Wood
The Sound of Music '65
The Story of Ruth '60

Robert Wood
Belle Starr '79
How to Make a Doll '68
White Fang and the Hunter '85

Thomas Wood
Blood Feast '63
2000 Maniacs '64

Alfre Woodard
The Ambush Murders '82
Blue Chips '94
Bopha! '93
Code of Honor '84
Crooklyn '94
Cross Creek '83
Extremities '86
Freedom Road '79
Grand Canyon '91
The Gun in Betty Lou's
Handbag '92
Heart and Souls '93
Killing Floor '85
Mandela '87
Miss Firecracker '89
Passion Fish '92
Rich in Love '93
Scrooged '88
Sophisticated Gents '81
Unnatural Causes '86
Words by Heart '84

Charlaine Woodard
Crackers '84
God Bless the Child '88
He Said, She Said '91
One Good Cop '91

Joan Woodbury
Bulldog Courage '35
The Chinese Cat '44
Gangs, Inc. '41
Here Comes Kelly '43
I Killed That Man '42
King of the Zombies '41
Northwest Trail '46
Phantom Killer '42
Rogue's Tavern '36
Song of the Gringo '36
The Time Travelers '64

Margo Woode
Bullfighters '45
Iron Angel '64

Pat Woodell
The Big Doll House '71
Twilight People '72

Holly Woodlawn
Is There Sex After Death? '71
Trash '70

Bert Woodruff
Marked Money '28
Paths to Paradise '25
Speedy '28

Kurt Woodruff
Moving Target '89
Party Incorporated '89

Largo Woodruff
Bill '81
Bill: On His Own '83
The Choice '81
Coward of the County '81
The Funhouse '81

Barbara Alyn Woods
Circuitry Man '90
Eden '92
Eden 2 '93
Eden 3 '93
Eden 4 '93

Bill Woods
Maniac '34
The Worst of Hollywood: Vol. 1
'90

Donald Woods
The Beast from 20,000
Fathoms '53
Beauty for the Asking '39
Bells of San Fernando '47
The Bridge of San Luis Rey '44
Corregidor '43
Danger on the Air '38
Door to Door Maniac '61
Enemy of Women '44

Glen or Glenda '53
Kissin' Cousins '64
Mexican Spitfire/Smartest Girl in Town '40
Mr. Music '50
Sea Devils '37
The Story of Louis Pasteur '36
Sweet Adeline '35
A Tale of Two Cities '35
13 Ghosts '60
Watch on the Rhine '43

Edward Woods
Public Enemy '31
Shadows Over Shanghai '38
Tarzan the Fearless '33

Harry Woods
The Adventures of Rex & Rinty '35
Belle of the Nineties '34
Boss of Bullion City '41
Bullet Code '40
Dawn on the Great Divide '42
Dynamite Dan '24
Haunted Gold '32
Hawaiian Buckaroo '38
Last Outlaw '36
The Lawless Nineties '36
Monkey Business '31
Nevada '44
Pardon My Gun '30
Range Feud '31
Riders of the West '42
Rustlers of Red Dog '35
Today I Hang '42
The Unknown Ranger '36
West of the Pecos '45
Winners of the West '40

James Woods
Against All Odds '84
Badge of the Assassin '85
Best Seller '87
The Black Marble '79
The Boost '88
Cat's Eye '85
Chaplin '92
The Choirboys '77
Citizen Cohn '92
Cop '88
Diggstown '92
The Disappearance of Aimee '76
Eyewitness '81
F. Scott Fitzgerald in Hollywood '76
Fallen Angels 1 '93
Fast Walking '82
The Gambler '74
The Getaway '93
The Gift of Love '90
The Hard Way '91
Holocaust '78
Immediate Family '89
In Love and War '91
The Incredible Journey of Dr. Meg Laurel '79
Joshua Then and Now '85
Night Moves '75
Once Upon a Time in America '84
The Onion Field '79
Salvador '86
Split Image '82
Straight Talk '92
True Believer '89
Videodrome '83
The Way We Were '73
Women & Men: Stories of Seduction '90

Michael Woods
Blindfold: Acts of Obsession '94
Haunting of Sarah Hardy '89
Hit Woman: The Double Edge '93
Lady Beware '87
Omen 4: The Awakening '91
War & Remembrance, Part 1 '88
War & Remembrance, Part 2 '89
War & Remembrance, Part 3 '88
War & Remembrance, Part 4 '88
War & Remembrance, Part 5 '88
War & Remembrance, Part 6 '88

War & Remembrance, Part 7 '88
War & Remembrance: The Final Chapter, Part 8 '89
War & Remembrance: The Final Chapter, Part 9 '89
War & Remembrance: The Final Chapter, Part 10 '89
War & Remembrance: The Final Chapter, Part 11 '89
War & Remembrance: The Final Chapter, Part 12 '89

Nan Woods
China Beach '88
One More Saturday Night '86

Robert Woods
Challenge of McKenna '83
Chase '85
The Perverse Countess '73

Kate Woodville
Computer Wizard '77
Posse '75
Sex Through a Window '72
Where's Willie? '77

John Woodvine
And a Nightingale Sang '91
Assault on Agathon '75
Dragonworld '94
Edge of Darkness '86
Glory Enough for All: The Discovery of Insulin '92

Edward Woodward
The Appointment '82
The Bloodsuckers '70
Breaker Morant '80
Champions '84
Codename Kyril '91
The Equalizer: Memories of Manon '88
The Final Option '82
King David '85
Merlin and the Sword '85
Mister Johnson '91
Uncle Tom's Cabin '87
The Wicker Man '75
Young Winston '72

Joanne Woodward
A Big Hand for the Little Lady '66
Blind Spot '93
A Christmas to Remember '78
Crisis at Central High '80
The Drowning Pool '75
The Effect of Gamma Rays on Man-in-the-Moon Marigolds '73
The End '78
A Fine Madness '66
Foreign Affairs '93
From the Terrace '60
The Fugitive Kind '60
The Glass Menagerie '87
Harry & Son '84
The Long, Hot Summer '58
Mr. & Mrs. Bridge '91
A New Kind of Love '63
Paris Blues '61
Philadelphia '93
Rachel, Rachel '68
See How She Runs '78
The Shadow Box '80
The Streets of L.A. '79
The Stripper '63
Summer Wishes, Winter Dreams '73
Sybil '76
They Might Be Giants '71
The Three Faces of Eve '57
Winning '69

Morgan Woodward
Dark Before Dawn '89
Girls Just Want to Have Fun '84
The Killing of a Chinese Bookie '76
The Longest Drive '76
Moonshine County Express '77
Ride in a Pink Car '74
Running Wild '73
Speedtrap '78
Walking Tall: The Final Chapter '77
Which Way Is Up? '77

Tim Woodward
The Dark Angel '91
The Europeans '79
Personal Services '87
Piece of Cake '90

Marjorie Woodworth
Broadway Limited '41
Road Show '41

Norman Wooland
Angel with the Trumpet '50
Saul and David '68
Teenage Bad Girl '59

Susan Wooldridge
Hope and Glory '87
How to Get Ahead in Advertising '89
The Jewel in the Crown '84
Loyalties '86
Twenty-One '91

Sheb Wooley
High Noon '52
Hoosiers '86

Charles Woolf
No Way Back '74
Private Parts '72

Monty Woolley
As Young As You Feel '51
The Bishop's Wife '47
Everybody Sing '38
The Man Who Came to Dinner '41
Night and Day '46
Since You Went Away '44
Three Comrades '38

Robert Woolsey
Cockeyed Cavaliers '34
Diplomaniacs '33
Dixiana '30
Half-Shot at Sunrise '30
Hips, Hips, Hooray '34
Hold 'Em Jail '32
Hook, Line and Sinker '30
Kentucky Kernels '34

Jaimz Woolvett
The Dark '94
Unforgiven '92

Tom Wopat
Burning Rage '84
Christmas Comes to Willow Creek '87

Hank Worden
Ghost Town Riders '38
Red River '48
The Searchers '56

Jimmy Workman
The Addams Family '91
Addams Family Values '93

Frederick Worlock
The Last of the Redmen '47
Strange Cargo '40
The Woman in Green '45

Mary Woronov
Angel of H.E.A.T. '82
Black Widow '87
Challenge of a Lifetime '85
Chopping Mall '86
Club Fed '90
Cover Girl Models '75
Death Race 2000 '75
Eating Raoul '82
Hellhole '85
Hollywood Boulevard '76
Hollywood Man '76
Jackson County Jail '76
Kemek '88
Let It Ride '89
Mortuary Academy '91
Motorama '91
The Movie House Massacre '78
Night of the Comet '84
Nomads '86
The Princess Who Never Laughed '84
Rock 'n' Roll High School '79
Rock 'n' Roll High School Forever '91
Scenes from the Class Struggle in Beverly Hills '89
Silent Night, Bloody Night '73
Sugar Cookies '77
Terrorvision '86
Warlock '91

Barbara Worth
Below the Deadline '29
The Prairie King '27
Racing Luck '35

Constance Worth
Criminals Within '41
Dawn Express '42

G-Men vs. the Black Dragon '43
Kid Sister '45
Windjammer '31

Irene Worth
Deathtrap '82
The Displaced Person '76
Eyewitness '81
Forbidden '85
King Lear '71
Lost in Yonkers '93
Separate Tables '83
The Shell Seekers '89

Lilian Worth
The Fighting Sheriff '31
Tarzan the Tiger '29

Mike Worth
Final Impact '91
Street Crimes '92
To Be the Best '93

Nicholas Worth
Dirty Laundry '87
Doin' Time '85
Fist of Honor '92
The Red Raven Kiss-Off '90

Fay Wray
Adam Had Four Sons '41
Blind Husbands '19
Bulldog Jack '35
The Coast Patrol '25
The Cobweb '55
Crime of Passion '57
Doctor X '32
The Evil Mind '34
Gideon's Trumpet '80
Hell on Frisco Bay '55
King Kong '33
Melody for Three '41
The Most Dangerous Game '32
Mystery of the Wax Museum '33
Rock, Pretty Baby '56
Small Town Girl '53
Tammy and the Bachelor '57
Treasure of the Golden Condor '53
The Vampire Bat '32
Viva Villa! '34
The Wedding March '28
When Knights Were Bold '36
Woman in the Shadows '34

John Wray
All Quiet on the Western Front '30
Green Eyes '34

Clare Wren
Season of Fear '89
Steel and Lace '90

Amy Wright
The Accidental Tourist '88
The Amityville Horror '79
Breaking Away '79
Crossing Delancey '88
Daddy's Dyin'...Who's Got the Will? '91
Deceived '91
The Deer Hunter '78
Final Verdict '91
Girlfriends '78
Hard Promises '92
Inside Moves '80
Love Hurts '91
Miss Firecracker '89
Off Beat '86
Stardust Memories '80
The Telephone '87
To Dance with the White Dog '93
Trapped in Silence '86
Wise Blood '79

Cobina Wright, Jr.
Charlie Chan in Rio '41
Week-End In Havana '41

Jenny Wright
The Chocolate War '88
The Executioner's Song '82
I, Madman '89
The Lawnmower Man '92
Near Dark '87
Out of Bounds '86
St. Elmo's Fire '85
A Shock to the System '90
Twister '89
Valentino Returns '88
The Wild Life '84
Young Guns 2 '90

Ken Wright
Eye of the Eagle 3 '91
Hollywood Boulevard 2 '89
Opposing Force '87

Max Wright
Fraternity Vacation '85
Konrad '90s
Touch and Go '86

Michael Wright
Confessions of a Hit Man '94
The Five Heartbeats '91
The Principal '87
Streamers '83
Sugar Hill '94

Patrick Wright
The Abductors '72
If You Don't Stop It...You'll Go Blind '77

Robin Wright
Denial: The Dark Side of Passion '91
Forrest Gump '94
Hollywood Vice Squad '86
The Playboys '92
The Princess Bride '87
State of Grace '90
Toys '92

Steven Wright
Canadian Bacon '94
Desperately Seeking Susan '85
Men of Respect '91
Natural Born Killers '94
Sledgehammer '83

Teresa Wright
The Best Years of Our Lives '46
Bill: On His Own '83
The Capture '50
Casanova Brown '44
Escapade in Japan '57
The Fig Tree '87
Flood! '92
The Good Mother '88
Hail, Hero! '69
The Happy Ending '69
The Little Foxes '41
The Men '50
Mrs. Miniver '42
The Pride of the Yankees '42
Pursued '47
Roseland '77
The Search for Bridey Murphy '56
Shadow of a Doubt '43
Somewhere in Time '80

Tom Wright
City of Hope '91
Marked for Death '90
Weekend at Bernie's 2 '93

Tony Wright
Broth of a Boy '59
The House in Marsh Road '60
The Spaniard's Curse '58

William Wright
Infamous Crimes '47
The Mask of Dijon '46
Miss Grant Takes Richmond '49
A Night to Remember '42

Maris Wrixon
The Ape '40
British Intelligence '40
Highway 13 '48
Sons of the Pioneers '42
Waterfront '44
White Pongo '45

Vivian Wu
The Guyver '91
Iron & Silk '91
The Joy Luck Club '93
Shadow of China '91
Teenage Mutant Ninja Turtles 3 '93

Robert Wuhl
Batman '89
Blaze '89
The Bodyguard '92
Bull Durham '88
Flashdance '83
Good Morning, Vietnam '87
Mistress '91
Tales from the Crypt '89

Kari Wuhrer
The Adventures of Ford Fairlane '90
Beastmaster 2: Through the Portal of Time '91

Kai Wulff
Firefox '82
Jungle Warriors '84

Shelley Wyant
Home Free All '84
Pilgrim, Farewell '82

Jane Wyatt
The Adventures of Tom Sawyer '73
Amityville 4 '89
Buckskin Frontier '43
Gentleman's Agreement '47
Katherine '75
Lost Horizon '37
Nativity '78
The Navy Comes Through '42
None But the Lonely Heart '44
Pitfall '48
Task Force '49

Margaret Wycherly
Forever Amber '47
Midnight '34
Random Harvest '42
Sergeant York '41
White Heat '49
The Yearling '46

Katya Wyeth
Dressed for Death '74
Twins of Evil '71

Gretchen Wyler
The Devil's Brigade '68
The Marrying Man '91

Jane Wyman
Bon Voyage! '62
Footlight Serenade '42
Here Comes the Groom '51
How to Commit Marriage '69
The Incredible Journey of Dr. Meg Laurel '79
It's a Great Feeling '49
Johnny Belinda '48
Just for You '52
The Lost Weekend '45
Magic Town '47
Magnificent Obsession '54
My Man Godfrey '36
Night and Day '46
Pollyanna '60
Stage Fright '50
Three Guys Named Mike '51
Wide Open Faces '38
The Yearling '46

John Wyman
For Your Eyes Only '81
Tuxedo Warrior '82

Patrick Wymark
The Blood on Satan's Claw '71
The Conqueror Worm '68
Journey to the Far Side of the Sun '69
Repulsion '65
The Skull '65
Where Eagles Dare '68
Woman Times Seven '67

Patrice Wymore
Big Trees '52
I'll See You in My Dreams '51
The King's Rhapsody '55
Tea for Two '50

George Wyner
The Bad News Bears Go to Japan '78
For Richer, For Poorer '92
Spaceballs '87
The Taking of Beverly Hills '91

Peter Wyngarde
Burn Witch, Burn! '62
Double Cross '92

Ed Wynn
The Absent-Minded Professor '61
Babes in Toyland '61
Cinderfella '60
Dear Brigitte '65
The Diary of Anne Frank '59
The Gnome-Mobile '67
The Greatest Story Ever Told '65
Marjorie Morningstar '58

Mary Poppins '64
Requiem for a Heavyweight '56
Those Calloways '65

Keenan Wynn
The Absent-Minded Professor '61
All the Brothers Were Valiant '53
The Americanization of Emily '64
Angels in the Outfield '51
Around the World Under the Sea '65
The Bastard '78
Battle Circus '53
The Belle of New York '52
Best Friends '82
Bikini Beach '64
Call to Glory '84
Cancel My Reservation '72
The Capture of Grizzly Adams '82
The Clock '45
The Clonus Horror '79
Coach '78
The Dark '79
Deep Six '58
The Desperados '80s
Devil's Rain '75
Dr. Strangelove, or: How I Learned to Stop Worrying and Love the Bomb '64
Don't Go Near the Water '57
Finian's Rainbow '68
For Me and My Gal '42
The Glass Slipper '55
Great Race '65
Hard Knocks
He is My Brother '75
Herbie Rides Again '74
High Velocity '76
Hit Lady '74
A Hole in the Head '59
The Hucksters '47
Hyper-Sapien: People from Another Star '86
Internecine Project '73
Just Tell Me What You Want '80
Killer Inside Me '76
The King of the Roaring '20s: The Story of Arnold Rothstein '61
Kiss Me Kate '53
Laserblast '78
Legend of Earl Durand '74
The Long, Long Trailer '54
The Longest Drive '76
The Lucifer Complex '78
MacKenna's Gold '69
The Man in the Gray Flannel Suit '56
The Man Who Would Not Die '75
Manipulator '71
The Mechanic '72
Men of the Fighting Lady '54
Mid Knight Rider '84
Mission to Glory '80
Mom, the Wolfman and Me '80
Monster '78
My Dear Secretary '49
Naked Hills '56
Nashville '75
Neptune's Daughter '49
Once Upon a Time in the West '68
Orca '77
The Patsy '64
Perfect Furlough '59
Phone Call from a Stranger '52
A Piano for Mrs. Cimino '82
Piranha '78
Point Blank '67
Promise Her Anything '66
Requiem for a Heavyweight '56
Royal Wedding '51
Shack Out on 101 '55
The Shaggy D.A. '76
Since You Went Away '44
Smith! '69
Snowball Express '72
Somewhere I'll Find You '42
Son of Flubber '63
Song of the Thin Man '47
Texas Carnival '51
That Midnight Kiss '49
Three Little Words '50
The Three Musketeers '48

A Time to Love & a Time to Die '58
The Treasure Seekers '79
Viva Max '69
The War Wagon '67
Wavelength '83
Weekend at the Waldorf '45
Without Love '45

May Wynn
The Caine Mutiny '54
The Violent Men '55

Dana Wynter
The Connection '73
D-Day, the Sixth of June '56
Dead Right '68
Invasion of the Body Snatchers '56
The List of Adrian Messenger '63
Lovers Like Us '75
Santee '73
Shake Hands with the Devil '59
Sink the Bismarck '60
Something of Value '57

Charlotte Wynters
Harvest Melody '43
Hopalong Cassidy: Renegade Trail '39
Panama Patrol '39
Renegade Trail '39
Sinners in Paradise '38

Diana Wynyard
Cavalcade '33
Gaslight '39
Rasputin and the Empress '32

Amanda Wyss
Better Off Dead '85
Black Magic Woman '91
Bloodfist 4: Die Trying '92
Deadly Innocence '88
Fast Times at Ridgemont High '82
My Mother's Secret Life '84
A Nightmare on Elm Street '84
Powwow Highway '89
Shakma '89
To Die for '89
To Die for 2 '91

Nelson Xavier
At Play in the Fields of the Lord '91
Gabriela '84

Frank Yaconelli
Across the Plains '39
The Barber Shop '33
The Driftin' Kid '41
Escape to Paradise '39
Gun Play '36
Lone Star Law Men '42
Riding the Sunset Trail '41
South of Monterey '47
Western Frontier '39
Western Mail '42
Wild Horse Canyon '39

Jeff Yagher
Lower Level '91
Shag: The Movie '89

Simon Yam
Naked Killer '92
Tongs: An American Nightmare '88

Isuzu Yamada
The Lower Depths '57
Osaka Elegy '36
Sisters of Gion '36
Throne of Blood '57
Yojimbo '61

Fujiko Yamamoto
An Actor's Revenge '63
Being Two Isn't Easy '62
Golden Demon '53

So Yamamura
Barbarian and the Geisha '58
Gung Ho '85
The Human Condition: No Greater Love '58
Princess Yang Kwei Fei '55
Tokyo Story '53

Al Yamanouchi
The Lone Runner '88
2020 Texas Gladiators '85

Tadashi Yamashita
Bronson Lee, Champion '78
Shinobi Ninja '84

Tsutomu Yamazaki
The Funeral '84
Kagemusha '80
Rikyu '90
Tampopo '86
A Taxing Woman '87

Nancy Yan
Born Invincible '76
The Ninja Pirates '90

Oleg Yankovsky
The Mirror '75
The Shooting Party '77

Jean Yanne
Bandits '86
Cobra '71
Hanna K. '83
Indochine '92
Le Boucher '69
Madame Bovary '91
Quicker Than the Eye '88
This Man Must Die '70
Weekend '67
The Wolf at the Door '87

Rossana Yanni
Fangs of the Living Dead '68
The Rue Morgue Massacres '73
White Comanche '67

Celeste Yarnall
Born Yesterday '93
Scorpio '73
The Velvet Vampire '71

Amy Yasbeck
The Mask '94
Problem Child '90
Problem Child 2 '91
Robin Hood: Men in Tights '93

Cassie Yates
Convoy '78
The Evil '78
Father Figure '80
F.I.S.T. '78
FM '78
Of Mice and Men '81
Perry Mason Returns '85
St. Helen's, Killer Volcano '82
Unfaithfully Yours '84

Bolo Yeung
Bloodfight '90
Bloodsport '88
Breathing Fire '91
Fearless Tiger '94
Ironheart '92
Shootfighter: Fight to the Death '93
TC 2000 '93
Tiger Claws '91

Chang Yi
Bells of Death '90
Shaolin Traitor '82
Ten Brothers of Shao-lin '80s
Two Assassins in the Dark '80s

Liu Hao Yi
Kung Fu Terminator
The Young Taoism Fighter

Mao Ying
Dance of Death '84
The Two Great Cavaliers '73

Pai Ying
The Bloody Fight '70s
Dynasty '77
Militant Eagle
Ninja Massacre '84

Richard Yniguez
Boulevard Nights '79
Sniper '75
World War III '86

Erica Yohn
Corrina, Corrina '94
A Streetcar Named Desire '84

Dick York
Inherit the Wind '60
My Sister Eileen '55
They Came to Cordura '59

Francine York
The Centerfold Girls '74
Curse of the Swamp Creature '66
The Doll Squad '73
Flood! '76
Secret File of Hollywood '62
Wild Ones on Wheels '62

Jeff York
Davy Crockett and the River Pirates '56
The Lady Says No '51
Old Yeller '57
Savage Sam '63
Westward Ho, the Wagons! '56
The Yearling '46

Kathleen York
Checking Out '89
Cold Feet '89
Dream Lover '93
Thompson's Last Run '90
Wild Hearts Can't Be Broken '91
Winners Take All '87

Michael York
Accident '67
Cabaret '72
Conduct Unbecoming '75
Discretion Assured '93
Duel of Hearts '92
Final Assignment '80
The Four Musketeers '75
The Heat of the Day '91
Island of Dr. Moreau '77
Justine '69
The Last Remake of Beau Geste '77
Lethal Obsession '87
Logan's Run '76
Midnight Cop '88
Murder on the Orient Express '74
Nevil Shute's The Far Country '85
Night of the Fox '90
Phantom of Death '87
The Return of the Musketeers '89
The Riddle of the Sands '79
Romeo and Juliet '68
Something for Everyone '70
Success is the Best Revenge '84
Sword of Gideon '86
The Taming of the Shrew '67
The Three Musketeers '74
Weather in the Streets '84
Wide Sargasso Sea '92
Zeppelin '71

Susannah York
Adventures of Eliza Fraser '76
Alice '86
American Roulette '88
The Awakening '80
Battle of Britain '69
Conduct Unbecoming '75
Diamond's Edge '88
Falling in Love Again '80
Fate '90
The Killing of Sister George '69
The Land of Faraway '87
Loophole '80
A Man for All Seasons '66
Prettykill '87
Sebastian '68
Second Chance '80
The Shout '78
The Silent Partner '78
Sky Riders '76
A Summer Story '88
Superman: The Movie '78
Superman 2 '80
That Lucky Touch '75
They Shoot Horses, Don't They? '69
Tom Jones '63
Tunes of Glory '60
X, Y & Zee '72
Yellowbeard '83

Yitsuko Yoshimura
The Insect Woman '63
Onibaba '64

Kazuko Yoshiyuki
The Empire of Passion '76
In the Realm of Passion '80

Aden Young
Black Robe '91
Sniper '92

Alan Young
Androcles and the Lion '52
Beverly Hills Cop 3 '94
The Time Machine '60

Artie Young
Bronze Buckaroo '39

Harlem Rides the Range '39

Bruce A. Young
Basic Instinct '92
Blink '93

Burt Young
...All the Marbles '81
Amityville 2: The Possession '82
Back to School '86
Backstreet Dreams '90
Betsy's Wedding '90
Beverly Hills Brats '89
Blood Beach '81
Blood Red '88
Bright Angel '91
Carnival of Blood '71
Chinatown '74
The Choirboys '77
Cinderella Liberty '73
Club Fed '90
Convoy '78
Diving In '90
Excessive Force '93
A Family Matter '91
The Gambler '74
Harry & Walter Go to New York '76
The Killer Elite '75
Last Exit to Brooklyn '90
Lookin' to Get Out '82
Once Upon a Time in America '84
Over the Brooklyn Bridge '84
The Pope of Greenwich Village '84
Rocky '76
Rocky 2 '79
Rocky 3 '82
Rocky 4 '85
Rocky 5 '90
A Summer to Remember '84
Twilight's Last Gleaming '77
Wait Until Spring, Bandini '90

Carleton Young
Armored Command '61
El Diablo Rides '39
The Man Who Shot Liberty Valance '62
Outlaw Express '38
People Will Talk '51
Reefer Madness '38
Sergeant Rutledge '60
Trigger Men '41
20,000 Leagues Under the Sea '54
Up in the Air '40

Chris Young
Book of Love '91
December '91
The Great Outdoors '88
P.C.U. '94
The Runestone '91
Warlock: The Armageddon '93

Clara Kimball Young
Chandu on the Magic Island '34
The Eyes of Youth '19
The Frontiersman '38
I Can't Escape '34
Kept Husbands '31
Mid-Channel '20
Mother and Son '31
Oh Susannah '38
Probation '32
Return of Chandu '34
Rogue's Tavern '36
Trilby '23
The Worldly Madonna '22

Dey Young
Back in the USSR '92
Conflict of Interest '92
Doin' Time '85
Frankie and Johnny '91
Murder 101 '91
Rock 'n' Roll High School '79
Strange Invaders '83

Faron Young
Daniel Boone: Trail Blazer '56
Hidden Guns '56

Gig Young
Air Force '43
Ask Any Girl '59
Blood Island '68
Bring Me the Head of Alfredo Garcia '74
City That Never Sleeps '53
Desk Set '57
Desperate Hours '55

Escape Me Never '47
For Love or Money '63
The Girl Who Had Everything '53
The Hindenburg '75
Hunt the Man Down '50
Hunt the Man Down/Smashing the Rackets '50
Kid Galahad '62
The Killer Elite '75
Lovers and Other Strangers '70
Lust for Gold '49
Only the Valiant '50
Slaughter Trail '51
Teacher's Pet '58
Tell It to the Judge '49
That Touch of Mink '62
They Shoot Horses, Don't They? '69
The Three Musketeers '48
Torch Song '53
The Tunnel of Love '58
Wake of the Red Witch '49
Young at Heart '54

Karen Young
Almost You '85
Birdy '84
Criminal Law '89
Deep in the Heart '83
Drug Wars 2: The Cocaine Cartel '92
Heat '87
Hoffa '92
Jaws: The Revenge '87
Little Sweetheart '90
Maria's Lovers '84
Night Game '89
9 1/2 Weeks '86
The Ten Million Dollar Getaway '91
Torch Song Trilogy '88

Loretta Young
The Accused '48
Along Came Jones '45
Big Business Girl '31
The Bishop's Wife '47
Cause for Alarm '51
Doctor Takes a Wife '40
Employees' Entrance '33
Eternally Yours '39
The Farmer's Daughter '47
Heroes for Sale '33
Key to the City '50
The Loretta Young Show '54
A Night to Remember '42
The Perfect Marriage '46
Platinum Blonde '31
Rachel and the Stranger '48
The Stranger '46
They Call It Sin '32

Nedrick Young
Captain Scarlett '53
Dead Men Walk '43
Gun Crazy '49

Neil Young
Love at Large '89
'68 '87

Noah Young
Don't Shove/Two Gun Gussie '19
For Heaven's Sake '26

Otis Young
Blood Beach '81
The Capture of Bigfoot '79
The Last Detail '73

Paul Young
Another Time, Another Place '83
The Girl in the Picture '86

Polly Ann Young
The Crimson Trail '35
The Invisible Ghost '41
Man from Utah '34
Murder on the Yukon '40
Mystery Plane '39
Road Show '41
Sons of Steel '35
Western Double Feature 5 '35

Ray Young
Blood of Dracula's Castle '69
Blue Sunshine '78

Ric Young
Drachenfutter '87
Dragon: The Bruce Lee Story '93
The Last Emperor '87

Ping Pong '87

Richard Young
Assassin '86
Final Mission '84
Friday the 13th, Part 5: A New Beginning '85
Inferno in Paradise '88
An Innocent Man '89
Love at the Top '86
Night Call Nurses '72
Ninja Masters of Death '85
Saigon Commandos '88

Robert Young
The Bride Walks Out '36
The Bride Wore Red '37
Cairo '42
The Canterville Ghost '44
A Conspiracy of Love '87
Crossfire '47
The Enchanted Cottage '45
The Half-Breed '51
Hollywood Party '34
Honolulu '39
It's Love Again '36
Journey for Margaret '42
Lady Be Good '41
Little Women '78
The Mortal Storm '40
Navy Blue and Gold '37
Northwest Passage '40
Second Woman '51
The Secret Agent '36
The Shining Hour '38
The Sin of Madelon Claudet '31
Spitfire '34
Stowaway '36
Strange Interlude '32
Sweet Rosie O'Grady '43
That Forsyte Woman '50
They Won't Believe Me '47
Those Endearing Young Charms '45
Three Comrades '38
Today We Live '33
Western Union '41

Roland Young
And Then There Were None '45
David Copperfield '35
Forever and a Day '43
The Great Lover '49
The Guardsman '31
His Double Life '33
King Solomon's Mines '37
Let's Dance '50
Madam Satan '30
The Man Who Could Work Miracles '37
No, No Nanette '40
One Rainy Afternoon '36
The Philadelphia Story '40
The Ruggles of Red Gap '35
Sailing Along '38
St. Benny the Dip '51
Topper '37
Topper Returns '41
Topper Takes a Trip '39
Two-Faced Woman '41
Wedding Rehearsal '32
The Young in Heart '38

Sean Young
Ace Ventura: Pet Detective '93
Baby...Secret of the Lost Legend '85
Blade Runner '82
Blue Ice '92
The Boost '88
Cousins '89
Dune '84
Fatal Instinct '93
Fire Birds '90
Forever: A Ghost of a Love Story '92
Hold Me, Thrill Me, Kiss Me '93
Jane Austen in Manhattan '80
A Kiss Before Dying '91
Love Crimes '92
Model by Day '94
No Way Out '87
Once Upon a Crime '92
Sketch Artist '92
Stripes '81
Under the Biltmore Clock '85
Wall Street '87
Young Doctors in Love '82

Stephen Young
Deadline '82
Lifeguard '75
Patton '70

Scorned '93
Who's Harry Crumb? '89

Tony Young
Chrome and Hot Leather '71
Policewomen '73

William Allen Young
Johnnie Gibson F.B.I. '87
Outrage! '86

Jack Youngblood
Python Wolf '88
Stalking Danger '86

Barrie Youngfellow
It Came Upon a Midnight Clear '84
Lady from Yesterday '85
Nightmare in Blood '75

Henny Youngman
Amazon Women on the Moon '87
Goodfellas '90
National Lampoon Goes to the Movies '81
The Unkissed Bride '66

Gail Youngs
Belizaire the Cajun '86
Hockey Night '84
Last Days of Frank & Jesse James '86
Timestalkers '87

Jim Youngs
Hot Shot '86
Nobody's Fool '86
Skeeter '93
You Talkin' to Me? '87

Chief Yowlachie
Bowery Buckaroos '47
King of the Stallions '42
Red River '48
Rose Marie '54
Wild West '46

Jimmy Wang Yu
Fast Fists
Return of the Chinese Boxer '74
Thundering Ninja '80s

Jimmy Yuill
Much Ado About Nothing '93
Paper Mask '91

Ian Yule
Chain Gang Killings '85
City of Blood '88

Joe Yule
Billy the Kid '41
New Moon '40

Harris Yulin
Another Woman '88
Bad Dreams '88
The Believers '87
Candy Mountain '87
Clear and Present Danger '94
Dynasty '82
End of the Road '70
Fatal Beauty '87
Final Analysis '92
Ghostbusters 2 '89
Judgment in Berlin '88
The Last Hit '93
Melvin Purvis: G-Man '74
Night Moves '75
St. Ives '76
Scarface '83
Short Fuse '88
Steel '80
Tailspin: Behind the Korean Airline Tragedy '90
There Goes the Neighborhood '92
Watched '73
When Every Day was the Fourth of July '78

Chow Yun-fat
Hard-Boiled '92
The Killer '90

Johnny Yune
They Call Me Bruce? '82
They Still Call Me Bruce '86

Sen Yung
Betrayal from the East '44
Charlie Chan at the Wax Museum '40
Charlie Chan in Rio '41
Murder Over New York '40

Victor Sen Yung
Across the Pacific '42
Castle in the Desert '42
The Letter '40
She Demons '58
Ticket to Tomahawk '50

Blanche Yurka
At Sword's Point '51
The Bridge of San Luis Rey '44
City for Conquest '40
Cry of the Werewolf '44
Lady for a Night '42
A Night to Remember '42
The Southerner '45
A Tale of Two Cities '35

Zabou
One Woman or Two '85
The Perils of Gwendoline '84

Grace Zabriskie
Ambition '91
The Big Easy '87
Blood Ties '92
Body Rock '84
The Boost '88
Chain of Desire '93
Child's Play 2 '90
Drugstore Cowboy '89
East of Eden '80
Fried Green Tomatoes '91
Galaxy of Terror '81
Hometown Boy Makes Good '93
Intimate Stranger '91
Megaville '91
My Own Private Idaho '91
Nickel Mountain '85
Prison Stories: Women on the Inside '91
Servants of Twilight '91
The Waterdance '91
Wild at Heart '90

Krystyna Zachwatowicz
Maids of Wilko '79
Man of Marble '76

Ramy Zada
After Midnight '89
Dark Justice '91
Two Evil Eyes '90

Arnon Zadok
Beyond the Walls '84
Torn Apart '89
Unsettled Land '88

Pia Zadora
Butterfly '82
Fake Out '82
Hairspray '88
The Lonely Lady '83
Pajama Tops '83
Santa Claus Conquers the Martians '64
Voyage of the Rock Aliens '87

Anita Zagaria
Maria's Child '93
Queen of Hearts '89

Frank Zagarino
Barbarian Queen '85
Blood Warriors '93
Project: Eliminator '91
Project: Shadowchaser '92
The Revenger '90
Striker '88

Roxana Zal
Goodbye, Miss 4th of July '88
River's Edge '87
Shattered Spirits '91
Table for Five '83
Testament '83
Under the Boardwalk '89

Bruno Zamin
Amarcord '74
The Boss Is Served '60s

Del Zamora
Heat Street '87
RoboCop '87

Billy Zane
Back to the Future '85
Back to the Future, Part 2 '89
Betrayal of the Dove '92
Blood & Concrete: A Love Story '90
Brotherhood of Justice '86
Critters '86
Dead Calm '89

Zane ▶*cont.*

Femme Fatale '90
The Hillside Strangler '89
Lake Consequence '92
Megaville '91
Memphis Belle '90
Millions '90
Only You '94
Orlando '92
Posse '93
Running Delilah '93
Sniper '92
Tombstone '93

Lisa Zane
Bad Influence '90
Femme Fatale '90
Freddy's Dead: The Final
  Nightmare '91
Pucker Up and Bark Like a Dog
  '89

Lenore Zann
American Nightmare '81
Mania '80s
One Night Only '84

Angelo Zanolli
Maciste in Hell '60
Son of Samson '62

**Zbigniew
Zapassiewicz**
Baritone '85
Stand Off '89

Carmen Zapata
Boulevard Nights '79
Daniel and the Towers '90s
The Last Porno Flick '74

Dweezil Zappa
Pretty in Pink '86
The Running Man '87

Frank Zappa
Baby Snakes: The Complete
  Version '79
Head '68
200 Motels '71

Moon Zappa
The Boys Next Door '85
Heartstopper '92
Nightmares '83
Spirit of '76 '91

Alfonso Zayas
Esta Noche Cena Pancho '87
The Neighborhood Thief '83

Edmund Zayenda
A Brivele der Mamen '38
Mamele '38

Robert Z'Dar
Beastmaster 2: Through the
  Portal of Time '91
The Big Sweat '90
Dead End City '88
The Divine Enforcer '91
Dragonfight '92
Evil Altar '89
Final Sanction '89
In a Moment of Passion '93
The Killer's Edge '90
The Legend of Wolf Mountain
  '92
Maniac Cop '88
Maniac Cop 2 '90
Maniac Cop 3 '93
Night Stalker '87
Quiet Fire '91
Soultaker '90
Tango and Cash '89
Wild Cactus '92

Rosel Zech
Salmonberries '91
Veronika Voss '82

Michael Zelniker
Bird '88
Glory Enough for All: The
  Discovery of Insulin '92
Naked Lunch '91
Pick-Up Summer '79
The Terry Fox Story '83

Anthony Zerbe
Attica '80
Child of Glass '78
Cool Hand Luke '67
Dead Zone '83

The Equalizer: Memories of
  Manon '88
Farewell, My Lovely '75
KISS Meets the Phantom of the
  Park '78
The Liberation of L.B. Jones
  '70
License to Kill '89
Omega Man '71
Onassis '88
Opposing Force '87
Papillon '73
Parallax View '74
Private Investigations '87
Question of Honor '80
Rooster Cogburn '75
See No Evil, Hear No Evil '89
Soggy Bottom U.S.A. '84
Steel Dawn '87
They Call Me Mr. Tibbs! '70
Who'll Stop the Rain? '78
Will Penny '67

Mai Zetterling
Frieda '47
Hidden Agenda '90
Night Is My Future '47
Only Two Can Play '62
Truth About Women '58
The Witches '90

Monica Zetterlund
The Emigrants '72
The New Land '73

Sonja Ziemann
Made in Heaven '52
A Matter of WHO '62

Madeline Zima
The Hand that Rocks the
  Cradle '92
Mr. Nanny '93

Efrem Zimbalist, Jr.
Airport '75 '75
Band of Angels '57
By Love Possessed '61
Deep Six '58
Family Upside Down '78
The Gathering: Part 2 '79
Hot Shots! '91
House of Strangers '49
Scruples '80
Shooting Stars '85
Terror Out of the Sky '78
Wait Until Dark '67
Who Is the Black Dahlia? '75

Stephanie Zimbalist
The Awakening '80
The Babysitter '80
Caroline? '90
Forever '78
The Gathering '77
Jericho Fever '93
The Killing Mind '90
Long Journey Back '78
Love on the Run '85
Magic of Lassie '78
Personals '90
Remington Steele, Vol. 1:
  License to Steele '82
The Story Lady '93
Tomorrow's Child '82
The Triangle Factory Fire
  Scandal '79

Victoria Zinny
Beyond the Door 3 '91
Viridiana '61

William Zipp
Death Chase '87
Future Force '89
Jungle Assault '89
Mankillers '87

Hanns Zischler
Club Extinction '89
Kings of the Road—In the
  Course of Time '76
Les Rendez-vous D'Anna '78
A Woman in Flames '84

Dan Ziskie
Twisted '86
Zebrahead '92

Adrian Zmed
Bachelor Party '84
Eyewitness to Murder '93
The Final Terror '83
For the Love of It '80
Grease 2 '82

Michael Zorek
Hot Moves '84
Private School '83

Louis Zorich
Cheap Shots '91
City of Hope '91
Death of a Salesman '86
Newman's Law '74

Vera Zorina
The Goldwyn Follies '38
Louisiana Purchase '41

Zouzou
Chloe in the Afternoon '72
S*P*Y*S '74

Rod Zuanic
Fast Talking '86
Mad Max: Beyond
  Thunderdome '85

Olga Zubarry
Desde el Abismo
La Nueva Cigarra '86
Somos Novios '68

George Zucco
The Adventures of Sherlock
  Holmes '39
Arrest Bulldog Drummond '38
The Black Raven '43
The Bride Wore Red '37
Bulldog Drummond in Africa/
  Arrest Bulldog Drummond
  '38
David and Bathsheba '51
Dead Men Walk '43
The Devil Thumbs a Ride/
  Having Wonderful Crime '47
The Firefly '37
Fog Island '45
Having Wonderful Crime '45
House of Frankenstein '44
The Hunchback of Notre Dame
  '39
The Mad Ghoul '43
The Mad Monster '42
Madame Bovary '49
Marie Antoinette '38
The Monster and the Girl '41
The Mummy's Ghost '44
The Mummy's Hand '40
The Mummy's Tomb '42
My Favorite Blonde '42
The Pirate '48
Return of the Ape Man '44
Saratoga '37
Scared to Death '47
Scared to Death/Dick Tracy's
  Dilemma '47
The Seventh Cross '44
Sherlock Holmes in
  Washington '43
Three Comrades '38
A Woman's Face '41

Alex Zuckerman
Freaked '93
Me and the Kid '93

Daphne Zuniga
800 Leagues Down the
  Amazon '90s
Eyes of the Panther '90
The Fly 2 '89
Gross Anatomy '89
The Initiation '84
Last Rites '88
Modern Girls '86
Prey of the Chameleon '91
Quarterback Princess '85
Spaceballs '87
Staying Together '89
The Sure Thing '85
Vision Quest '85

Dianik Zurakowska
Cauldron of Blood '67
Orgy of the Vampires '73

Yoshitaka Zushi
Akira Kurosawa's Dreams '90
Dodes 'ka-den '70

Brad Zutaut
Hardbodies 2 '86
Knock Outs '92
Nudity Required '90

Noam Zylberman
Love and Hate: A Marriage
  Made in Hell '90
Outside Chance of Maximillian
  Glick '88

The **DIRECTOR INDEX** lists the video accomplishments of nearly 6,000 directors, arranged in a straight alphabetical format by last name (names are presented in a first name, last name format, but alphabetization begins with the last name). Every director cited in the main review section is included in the index, presenting a surefire locator for hard-to-find directors and their movies. The **Cast Index** immediately precedes this index. The **Writer** and **Composer Indexes** immediately follow this index.

Paul Aaron
Deadly Force '83
Different Story '78
Force of One '79
Imperial Navy '80s
In Love and War '91
Maxie '85
The Miracle Worker '79

Dodo Abashidze
Ashik Kerib '88

Charles Abbott
The Adventures of the Masked Phantom '38

George Abbott
Damn Yankees '58
Pajama Game '57
Too Many Girls '40

Alan Abel
Is There Sex After Death? '71

Jeanne Abel
Is There Sex After Death? '71

Robert Abel
Elvis on Tour '72

Lewis Abernathy
House 4: Home Deadly Home '91

Derwin Abrahams
Border Vigilantes '41
Northwest Trail '46

Jim Abrahams
Airplane! '80
Big Business '88
Hot Shots! '91
Hot Shots! Part Deux '93
Police Squad! Help Wanted! '82
Ruthless People '86
Top Secret! '84
Welcome Home, Roxy Carmichael '90

Tengiz Abuladze
Repentance '87

Jon Acevski
Freddie as F.R.O.7 '92

Jovan Acin
Hey, Babu Riba '88

Rodney Ackland
Thursday's Child '43

David Acomba
Night Life '90

Catlin Adams
Sticky Fingers '88

Daniel Adams
Primary Motive '92

Doug Adams
Blackout '88

Al Adamson
Angels' Wild Women '72
Black Samurai '77
Blazing Stewardesses '75
Blood of Dracula's Castle '69
Blood of Ghastly Horror '72
Brain of Blood '71
Cinderella 2000 '78
Dracula vs. Frankenstein '71
The Dynamite Brothers '74
The Female Bunch '69
Gun Riders '69
Horror of the Blood Monsters '70
Hospital of Terror '78
I Spit on Your Corpse '74
Jessie's Girls '75
Satan's Sadists '69
Texas Layover '75

Victor Adamson
Boss Cowboy '35
Rawhide Romance '34

Pierre Adidge
Elvis on Tour '72

Joseph Adler
Scream, Baby, Scream '69
Sex and the College Girl '64

Lou Adler
Cheech and Chong's Up in Smoke '79

Percy Adlon
Bagdad Cafe '88
Celeste '81
The Last Five Days '82
Rosalie Goes Shopping '89
Salmonberries '91
Sugarbaby '85

Ed Adlum
Invasion of the Blood Farmers '72

Edvin Adolphson
The Count of the Old Town '34

Frank Agrama
Dawn of the Mummy '82

Joseph Louis Agraz
Treasure of the Moon Goddess '88

Javier Aguirre
Dracula's Great Love '72
The Rue Morgue Massacres '73

Agust Agustsson
Maya '82

Charlie Ahearn
Wild Style '83

Mac Ahlberg
Gangsters '79

Faruque Ahmed
Warlords 3000 '93

Chantal Akerman
Akermania, Vol. 1 '92
The Eighties '83
Je Tu Il Elle '74
Les Rendez-vous D'Anna '78
News from Home '76
Night and Day '91
Toute Une Nuit '82
Window Shopping '86

Moustapha Akkad
Lion of the Desert '81
Mohammed: Messenger of God '77

Benito Alazraki
Invasion of the Zombies '61
Spiritism '61

Rafael Morena Alba
Exorcism's Daughter '74

Jean-Gabriel Albicocco
The Wanderer '67

Hans Albin
No Survivors, Please '63

Carlton J. Albright
Luther the Geek '90

Alan Alda
Betsy's Wedding '90
The Four Seasons '81
A New Life '88
Sweet Liberty '86

Thomas Alderman
The Severed Arm '73

Will Aldis
Stealing Home '88

Adell Aldrich
The Kid from Left Field '79

Robert Aldrich
...All the Marbles '81
Apache '54
Autumn Leaves '56
The Big Knife '55
The Choirboys '77
The Dirty Dozen '67
The Flight of the Phoenix '65
Four for Texas '63
The Frisco Kid '79
The Grissom Gang '71
Hush, Hush, Sweet Charlotte '65
Hustle '75
The Killing of Sister George '69
Kiss Me Deadly '55
The Longest Yard '74
Sodom and Gomorrah '62
Too Late the Hero '70
Twilight's Last Gleaming '77
Ulzana's Raid '72
Vera Cruz '53
What Ever Happened to Baby Jane? '62

Thomas Gutierrez Alea
Death of a Bureaucrat '66
Letters from the Park '88
Memories of Underdevelopment '68

Goffredo Alessandrini
We the Living '42

Ottavio Alessi
The Seducers '70

Bill Alexander
Tartuffe '90

Max Alexander
Flaming Lead '39

Grigori Alexandrov
Que Viva Mexico '32
Ten Days That Shook the World '27

James Algar
The Adventures of Ichabod and Mr. Toad '49
The Legend of Sleepy Hollow '49
Vanishing Prairie '54

Sidney Algier
Wild Horse '31

Dan Algrant
Naked in New York '93

Marcello Aliprandi
Vatican Conspiracy '81

Howard Alk
Janis: A Film '74

Marc Allegret
Fanny '32
Lady Chatterley's Lover '55
The Love of Three Queens '54
Mademoiselle Striptease '57
Sois Belle et Tais-Toi '58
Zou Zou '34

Yves Allegret
Dedee d'Anvers '49
Johnny Apollo '40
The Proud Ones '53
Seven Deadly Sins '53

A.K. Allen
The Ladies Club '86

Corey Allen
The Ann Jillian Story '88
Avalanche '78
Brass '85
Codename: Foxfire '85
The Last Fling '86
The Man in the Santa Claus Suit '79
Return of Frank Cannon '80
Thunder and Lightning '77

David Allen
Dungeonmaster '85
Puppet Master 2 '91

Fred Allen
Beyond the Rockies '32
Ghost Valley '32
The Mysterious Rider '33
Ride Him, Cowboy '32
Saddle Buster '32

Irving Allen
Slaughter Trail '51

Irwin Allen
Beyond the Poseidon Adventure '79
Five Weeks in a Balloon '62
The Swarm '78
The Towering Inferno '74
Voyage to the Bottom of the Sea '61

James Allen
Burndown '89

Jordan Allen
Terminal Bliss '91

Lewis Allen
Another Time, Another Place '58
At Sword's Point '51
Illegal '55
The Perfect Marriage '46
Suddenly '54
Those Endearing Young Charms '45
The Uninvited '44

Patrick Allen
Shootfighter: Fight to the Death '93

Woody Allen
Alice '90
Annie Hall '77
Another Woman '88
Bananas '71
Broadway Danny Rose '84
Crimes & Misdemeanors '89
Everything You Always Wanted to Know About Sex (But Were Afraid to Ask) '72
Hannah and Her Sisters '86
Husbands and Wives '92
Interiors '78
Love and Death '75
Manhattan '79
Manhattan Murder Mystery '93
A Midsummer Night's Sex Comedy '82
New York Stories '89
The Purple Rose of Cairo '85
Radio Days '87
September '88
Shadows and Fog '92
Sleeper '73
Stardust Memories '80
Take the Money and Run '69
What's Up, Tiger Lily? '66
Zelig '83

Roger Allers
The Lion King '94

Michael Almereyda
Twister '89

Pedro Almodovar
Dark Habits '84
High Heels '91
Labyrinth of Passion '82
Law of Desire '86
Matador '86
Pepi, Luci, Bom and Other Girls on the Heap '80
Tie Me Up! Tie Me Down! '90
What Have I Done to Deserve This? '85
Women on the Verge of a Nervous Breakdown '88

Paul Almond
Captive Hearts '87
The Dance Goes On '92
Final Assignment '80
Journey '77
Prep School '81

Rami Alon
Choices '81

John Alonzo
Blinded by the Light '82
Portrait of a Stripper '79

Emmett Alston
Little Ninjas '92
New Year's Evil '78
Nine Deaths of the Ninja '85
Three Way Weekend '81
Tigershark '87

Robert Altman
Aria '88
Beyond Therapy '86
Brewster McCloud '70
Buffalo Bill & the Indians '76
The Caine Mutiny Court Martial '88
Come Back to the Five & Dime Jimmy Dean, Jimmy Dean '82
Countdown '68
Dumb Waiter '87
Fool for Love '86
The Long Goodbye '73
M*A*S*H '70
McCabe & Mrs. Miller '71
Nashville '75
O.C. and Stiggs '87
The Player '92
Popeye '80
Quintet '79
The Room '87
Secret Honor '85
Short Cuts '93
Streamers '83
Tanner '88 '88
That Cold Day in the Park '69
Thieves Like Us '74
Vincent & Theo '90
A Wedding '78

Robert Alton
Merton of the Movies '47
Pagan Love Song '50

Joe Alves
Jaws 3 '83

Denis Amar
L'Addition '85

Suzana Amaral
The Hour of the Star '85

Rod Amateau
The Bushwackers '52
Drive-In '76
The Garbage Pail Kids Movie '87
High School USA '84
Lovelines '84
The Seniors '78
The Statue '71

Gianni Amelio
Open Doors '89

Keita Amemiya
Zeram '91

Pina Amenta
All the Rivers Run '84
Bellamy '92
Heaven Tonight '93
True Colors '87

Lem Amero
R.S.V.P. '84

Jon Amiel
Queen of Hearts '89
Sommersby '93
Tune in Tomorrow '90

Gideon Amir
Accidents '89
The P.O.W. Escape '86

James Amonte
The Alchemist '81

Franco Amurri
Flashback '89
Monkey Trouble '94

Allison Anders
Border Radio '88
Gas Food Lodging '92
Mi Vida Loca '94

Andy Anderson
Positive I.D. '87

Clyde Anderson
Beyond Darkness '92
Monster Dog '82

G.M. Anderson
The First Movie Cowboy '13

John Murray Anderson
King of Jazz '30

Kurt Anderson
Martial Law 2: Undercover '91
Martial Outlaw '93

Lindsay Anderson
Britannia Hospital '82
Glory! Glory! '90
If... '69
In Celebration '75
O Lucky Man! '73
This Sporting Life '63
The Whales of August '87

Michael Anderson, Sr.
Around the World in 80 Days '56
Battle Hell '56
Conduct Unbecoming '75
Dam Busters '55
Doc Savage '75
Dominique is Dead '79
The House of the Arrow '53
Logan's Run '76
The Martian Chronicles: Part 1 '79
The Martian Chronicles: Part 2 '79
The Martian Chronicles: Part 3 '79
Millenium '89
Murder by Phone '82
The Naked Edge '61
Operation Crossbow '65
Orca '77
The Quiller Memorandum '66
Second Time Lucky '84
Separate Vacations '86
Shake Hands with the Devil '59
The Shoes of the Fisherman '68
Sword of Gideon '86
The Wreck of the Mary Deare '59
Young Catherine '91

Michael Anderson, Jr.
The Sea Wolf '93

Robert Anderson
The Young Graduates '71

Steve Anderson
South Central '92

George Andrews
Hero Bunker '71

Stephen M. Andrews
Striker '88

Roger Andrieux
La Petite Sirene '80

Mikel Angel
Love Butcher '82

Edmond Angelo
Breakdown '53

Theo Angelopoulos
Landscape in the Mist '88

Gianfranco Angelucci
Honey '81

Erik Anjou
The Cool Surface '92

Ken Annakin
Across the Bridge '57
Battle of the Bulge '65
Call of the Wild '72
Cheaper to Keep Her '80
The Fifth Musketeer '79
Land of Fury '55
The Longest Day '62
The New Adventures of Pippi Longstocking '88
Paper Tiger '74
Pirate Movie '82
The Story of Robin Hood & His Merrie Men '52
The Swiss Family Robinson '60
The Sword & the Rose '53
Third Man on the Mountain '59
Those Daring Young Men in Their Jaunty Jalopies '69
Those Magnificent Men in Their Flying Machines '65
Trio '50

Jean-Jacques Annaud
The Bear '89
Black and White in Color '76
Hothead '78
The Lover '92
The Name of the Rose '86
Quest for Fire '82

Paul Annett
Black Werewolf '75
Poldark '75
Tales of the Unexpected '91

David Anspaugh
Fresh Horses '88
Hoosiers '86
Rudy '93

Jerzy Antczak
Nights and Days '76

Joseph Anthony
All in a Night's Work '61
Career '59
The Matchmaker '58
The Rainmaker '56
Tomorrow '83

Len Anthony
Fright House '89

Manuel Antin
Don Segundo Sombra '69
Far Away and Long Ago '74

Karl Anton
The Avenger '60

Lou Antonio
Between Friends '83
Breaking Up Is Hard to Do '79
The Gypsy Warriors '78
The Last Prostitute '91
Lies Before Kisses '92
Mayflower Madam '87
Pals '87
A Real American Hero '78
Silent Victory: The Kitty O'Neil Story '79
Someone I Touched '75
A Taste for Killing '92
This Gun for Hire '91

Michelangelo Antonioni
Blow-Up '66
The Eclipse '66
Il Grido '57
L'Avventura '60
Love in the City '53
The Passenger '75
The Red Desert '64
Zabriskie Point '70

Ackyl Anwary
Angel of Fury '93

Daniel Appleby
Bound and Gagged: A Love Story '93

Michael Apted
Agatha '79
Blink '93
Class Action '91
Coal Miner's Daughter '80
Continental Divide '81
Critical Condition '86
First Born '84
Gorillas in the Mist '88
Gorky Park '83
Incident at Oglala: The Leonard Peltier Story '92
Kipperbang '82
Poor Girl, A Ghost Story '74
The Squeeze '77
Thunderheart '92
Triple Echo '77

Manuel Gutierrez Aragon
Demons in the Garden '82
Half of Heaven '86

Gregg Araki
The Living End '92

Vicente Aranda
The Blood Spattered Bride '72
Lovers: A True Story '90

Alfonso Arau
Like Water for Chocolate '93

Denys Arcand
The Decline of the American Empire '86
Jesus of Montreal '89

George Archainbaud
Blue Canadian Rockies '52
False Colors '43
Gene Autry Matinee Double Feature #1 '53
Gene Autry Matinee Double Feature #2 '53
Gene Autry Matinee Double Feature #3 '53
Hopalong Cassidy: Borrowed Trouble '48
Hopalong Cassidy: False Paradise '48
Hopalong Cassidy: Hoppy's Holiday '47
Hopalong Cassidy: Silent Conflict '48
Hopalong Cassidy: Sinister Journey '48
Hopalong Cassidy: The Dead Don't Dream '48
Hopalong Cassidy: The Devil's Playground '46
Hopalong Cassidy: The Marauders '47
Hopalong Cassidy: Unexpected Guest '47
Hoppy Serves a Writ '43
Hunt the Man Down '50
Hunt the Man Down/Smashing the Rackets '50
The Kansan '43
The Lady Refuses '31
Last of the Pony Riders '53
Lost Squadron '32
Mystery Man '44
Night Stage to Galveston '52
On Top of Old Smoky '53
State's Attorney '31
Texas Masquerade '44
Winning of the West '53
The Woman of the Town '44

Emile Ardolino
Chances Are '89
Dirty Dancing '87
George Balanchine's The Nutcracker '93
Gypsy '93
The Rise & Rise of Daniel Rocket '86
Sister Act '92
Three Men and a Little Lady '90

Mats Arehn
The Assignment '78
Istanbul '90

Dario Argento
The Bird with the Crystal Plumage '70
The Cat o' Nine Tails '71
Creepers '85
Dario Argento's Trauma '93
Deep Red: Hatchet Murders '75
Inferno '80
Suspiria '77
Terror at the Opera '88
Two Evil Eyes '90
Unsane '82

Adolfo Aristarain
The Stranger '87
Time for Revenge '82

Alan Arkin
Little Murders '71

Robert Arkless
The Man Who Would Not Die
'75

Allan Arkush
Caddyshack 2 '88
Death Sport '78
Get Crazy '83
Heartbeeps '81
Hollywood Boulevard '76
Rock 'n' Roll High School '79

Leslie Arliss
A Man About the House '47
The Man in Grey '45
The Night Has Eyes '42

George Armitage
Hot Rod '79
Miami Blues '90
Private Duty Nurses '71

Gillian Armstrong
Fires Within '91
High Tide '87
The Last Days of Chez Nous
'92
Mrs. Soffel '84
My Brilliant Career '79
Starstruck '82

Karl Armstrong
Ninja Vengeance '93

Michael Armstrong
Mark of the Devil '69

Moira Armstrong
How Many Miles to Babylon?
'82

Robin B. Armstrong
Pastime '91

Gwen Arner
A Matter of Principle '83
Necessary Parties '88

Eddie Arno
Murder Story '89

Frank Arnold
A Waltz Through the Hills '88

Jack Arnold
Bachelor in Paradise '69
Boss '74
Creature from the Black
Lagoon '54
Games Girls Play '75
A Global Affair '63
High School Confidential '58
The Incredible Shrinking Man
'57
It Came From Outer Space '53
Marilyn: The Untold Story '80
Monster on the Campus '58
The Mouse That Roared '59
Revenge of the Creature '55
Swiss Conspiracy '77
Tarantula '55

Newton Arnold
Bloodsport '88
Hands of a Stranger '62

Fernando Arrabal
The Odyssey of the Pacific '82

Karen Arthur
Bridge to Silence '89
Broken Badge '85
A Bunny's Tale '85
The Disappearance of Christina
'93
The Jacksons: American
Dream '92
Lady Beware '87
My Sister, My Love '78
The Secret '93

Raul Artigot
Witches' Mountain '71

Ami Artzi
Purgatory '89

Dorothy Arzner
The Bride Wore Red '37
Christopher Strong '33
Craig's Wife '36
Dance, Girl, Dance '40

Anthony Ascot
Guns for Dollars '73
Gunslinger '70s

Hal Ashby
Being There '79
Bound for Glory '76
Coming Home '78
8 Million Ways to Die '85
Harold and Maude '71
The Last Detail '73
Lookin' to Get Out '82
Shampoo '75
The Slugger's Wife '85

Ronnie Ashcroft
The Astounding She-Monster
'58

Richard Ashe
Track of the Moonbeast '76

Robert Asher
Make Mine Mink '60

William Asher
Beach Blanket Bingo '65
Beach Party '63
Bikini Beach '64
How to Stuff a Wild Bikini '65
Movers and Shakers '85
Muscle Beach Party '64
Night Warning '82

Melvin Ashford
Mondo Magic '76

Alexander Askoldov
Commissar '68

Samson Aslanian
Torment '85

Anthony Asquith
The Browning Version '51
Carrington, V.C. '54
Cottage to Let '41
The Demi-Paradise '43
I Stand Condemned '36
Importance of Being Earnest
'52
Man of Evil '48
Pygmalion '38
The V.I.P.'s '63
We Dive at Dawn '43
The Winslow Boy '48

Ovidio G. Assonitis
Madhouse '87

Alexandre Astruc
End of Desire '62

Thomas Atcheson
Deadly Diamonds '91

Thomas Atkins
The Silver Streak '34

**Richard
Attenborough**
A Bridge Too Far '77
Chaplin '92
A Chorus Line '85
Cry Freedom '87
Gandhi '82
Magic '78
Shadowlands '93
Young Winston '72

Daniel Attias
Silver Bullet '85

Bobby A. Auarez
One Armed Executioner '80

Pascal Aubier
Death of the Rat '75

**Guillaume Martin
Aucion**
Oh! Calcutta! '72

Michael Audley
The Mark of the Hawk '57

John H. Auer
City That Never Sleeps '53
The Crime of Dr. Crespi '35
Wheel of Fortune '41

Bille August
The Best Intentions '92
The House of the Spirits '93
Pelle the Conqueror '88
Twist & Shout '84

Carlos Aured
Curse of the Devil '73
Horror Rises from the Tomb
'72
House of Psychotic Women '73
The Mummy's Revenge '73

Carl Ausino
Don't Look in the Attic '81

Sam Auster
Screen Test '85

Albert Austin
My Boy '21

Ray Austin
Highlander: The Gathering '93
House of the Living Dead '73
Return of the Man from
U.N.C.L.E. '83
The Virgin Witch '70
The Zany Adventures of Robin
Hood '84

Claude Autant-Lara
Devil in the Flesh '46
Four Bags Full '56
Oldest Profession '67
The Red and the Black '57
Seven Deadly Sins '53
Sylvia and the Phantom '45

Igor Auzins
Death Train '79
High Rolling in a Hot Corvette
'77
Night Nurse '77
We of the Never Never '82

Aram Avakian
Cops and Robbers '73
11 Harrowhouse '74
End of the Road '70

Marcello Avallone
Specters '87

Pupi Avati
Bix '90
Revenge of the Dead '84
The Story of Boys & Girls '91

**Howard (Hikmet)
Avedis**
The Fifth Floor '80
Kidnapped '87
Mortuary '81
Scorchy '76
Separate Ways '82
The Specialist '75
The Stepmother '71
The Teacher '74
Texas Detour '77
They're Playing with Fire '84

Hy Averback
A Guide for the Married Woman
'78
I Love You, Alice B. Toklas '68
She's in the Army Now '81
Suppose They Gave a War and
Nobody Came? '70
Where the Boys Are '84 '84
Where Were You When the
Lights Went Out? '68

Tex Avery
Bugs Bunny Superstar '75

John G. Avildsen
Cry Uncle '71
8 Seconds '94
For Keeps '88

Foreplay '75
The Formula '80
Guess What We Learned in
School Today? '70
Happy New Year '87
Joe '70
The Karate Kid '84
The Karate Kid: Part 2 '86
The Karate Kid: Part 3 '89
Lean on Me '89
Neighbors '81
A Night in Heaven '83
The Power of One '92
Rocky '76
Rocky 5 '90
Save the Tiger '73

Tom Avildsen
Cheech and Chong: Things Are
Tough All Over '82

Meiert Avis
Far from Home '89

Jon Avnet
Fried Green Tomatoes '91

Gabriel Axel
Babette's Feast '87

George Axelrod
Secret Life of an American Wife
'68

Fernando Ayala
El Profesor Hippie '69

Dan Aykroyd
Nothing But Trouble '91

Julian Aymes
Jane Eyre '83

Mario Azzopardi
Deadline '82
Nowhere to Hide '87

Beth B
Salvation! '87
Vortex '81

Scott B
Vortex '81

Hector Babenco
At Play in the Fields of the Lord
'91
Ironweed '87
Kiss of the Spider Woman '85
Pixote '81

Gideon Bachmann
Ciao Federico! Fellini Directs
Satyricon '69

Lloyd Bacon
Action in the North Atlantic '43
Boy Meets Girl '38
Brother Orchid '40
Devil Dogs of the Air '35
The Fighting Sullivans '42
Footlight Parade '33
42nd Street '33
The French Line '54
The Fuller Brush Girl '50
It Happens Every Spring '49
Kept Husbands '31
Knute Rockne: All American '40
Marked Woman '37
Miss Grant Takes Richmond
'49
Oklahoma Kid '39
She Couldn't Say No '52
Silver Queen '42

Peter Bacso
Oh, Bloody Life! '88

Randall Badat
Surf 2 '84

Clarence Badger
Hands Up '26
It '27
Paths to Paradise '25
Teddy at the Throttle '16

Phillip Badger
The Forgotten One '89

John Badham
American Flyers '85
Another Stakeout '93
Bingo Long Traveling All-Stars
& Motor Kings '76
Bird on a Wire '90
Blue Thunder '83
Dracula '79
The Hard Way '91
Point of No Return '93
Reflections of Murder '74
Saturday Night Fever '77
Short Circuit '86
Stakeout '87
WarGames '83
Whose Life Is It Anyway? '81

Reza Badiyi
Blade in Hong Kong '85
Of Mice and Men '81
Policewoman Centerfold '83

Max Baer, Jr.
Hometown U.S.A. '79
Ode to Billy Joe '76

Milton Bagby, Jr.
Rebel Love '85

King Baggott
Tumbleweeds '25

James Bagle
Stones of Death '88

Fax Bahr
Hearts of Darkness: A
Filmmaker's Apocalypse '91

Chuck Bail
Choke Canyon '86
Cleopatra Jones & the Casino
of Gold '75
Gumball Rally '76

John Bailey
China Moon '91
Search for Signs of Intelligent
Life in the Universe '91

Patrick Bailey
Door to Door '84

Richard Bailey
Win, Place, or Steal '72

Whitney Bain
That Darn Sorceress '88

David Baker
Air Hawk '84
Best Enemies '86

Graham Baker
Alien Nation '88
Born to Ride '91
The Final Conflict '81
Impulse '84

Michael Baker
An Affair in Mind '89

Robert S. Baker
Blackout '50
The Hellfire Club '61
Jack the Ripper '60

Roy Ward Baker
And Now the Screaming Starts
'73
Asylum '72
Dr. Jekyll and Sister Hyde '71
Don't Bother to Knock '52
Masks of Death '86
Mission: Monte Carlo '75
The Monster Club '85
A Night to Remember '58
October Man '48
One That Got Away '57
The Scars of Dracula '70
The 7 Brothers Meet Dracula
'73
The Vampire Lovers '70
Vault of Horror '73

Ralph Bakshi
Cool World '92
Fire and Ice '83

Bakshi ▶*cont.*

Fritz the Cat '72
Heavy Traffic '73
Hey Good Lookin' '82
The Lord of the Rings '78
Streetfight '75
Wizards '77

Walter Bal
Jacko & Lise '82

Bob Balaban
My Boyfriend's Back '93
Parents '89

Antony Balch
Horror Hospital '73

Jim Balden
Gamble on Love '86

Ferdinando Baldi
Duel of Champions '61
Treasure of the Four Crowns '82

Armenia Balducci
Together? '79

Richard Balducci
L'Odeur des Fauves '66
Scandal Man '67
Too Pretty to Be Honest '72

Peter Baldwin
The Hoboken Chicken Emergency '84
Lots of Luck '85
A Very Brady Christmas '88

Rafael Baledon
The Man and the Monster '65
Orlak, the Hell of Frankenstein '60
Swamp of the Lost Monster '65

Carroll Ballard
The Black Stallion '79
Never Cry Wolf '83
Nutcracker: The Motion Picture '86
Wind '92

John Ballard
The Orphan '79

Robert E. Balzer
It's Three Strikes, Charlie Brown '86

Anne Bancroft
Fatso '80

Albert Band
Doctor Mordrid: Master of the Unknown '92
Ghoulies 2 '88
I Bury the Living '58
Prehysteria '93
Robot Wars '93
Tramplers '66
Zoltan...Hound of Dracula '77

Charles Band
Crash and Burn '90
Doctor Mordrid: Master of the Unknown '92
Dollman vs Demonic Toys '93
Dungeonmaster '85
Meridian: Kiss of the Beast '90
Metalstorm '83
Parasite '81
Prehysteria '93
Trancers '85
Trancers 2: The Return of Jack Deth '91

Mirra Bank
Enormous Changes '83

Montague Banks
Great Guns '41

Walter Bannert
The Inheritors '85

Yoshimitu Banno
Godzilla vs. the Smog Monster '72

Richard Bansbach
Claws '77

Uri Barbash
Beyond the Walls '84
Unsettled Land '88

Peter Barber-Fleming
Coming Through '90

Joseph Barbera
Jetsons: The Movie '90

Juan Antonio Bardem
Last Day of the War '69

Geoffrey Barkas
Q Ships '28

Clive Barker
Hellraiser '87
Night Breed '90

Reginald Barker
Healer '36
On the Night Stage '15

Christopher Barnard
Conspiracy '89

Boris Barnett
The Girl with the Hat Box '27
The Patriots '33

Ivan Barnett
The Fall of the House of Usher '52

Ken Barnett
Dark Tower '87

Steve Barnett
Emmanuelle 5 '87
Hollywood Boulevard 2 '89
Mindwarp '91
Mission of Justice '92

Allen Baron
Foxfire Light '84

Bruno Barreto
Amor Bandido '79
Dona Flor and Her Two Husbands '78
Gabriela '84
Happily Ever After '86
A Show of Force '90
The Story of Fausta '88

Fabio Barreto
Luzia '88

Lezli-Ann Barrett
Business as Usual '88

Steven Barron
Coneheads '93
Electric Dreams '84
Teenage Mutant Ninja Turtles: The Movie '90

Zelda Barron
Bulldance '88
Forbidden Sun '89
Secret Places '85
Shag: The Movie '89

Christopher Barry
Poldark '75

Ian Barry
Chain Reaction '80
Wrangler '88

Michael Barry
Second Coming of Suzanne '80

Wesley E. Barry
The Creation of the Humanoids '62

Roger J. Barski
Chains '89

Bud Barsky
Wallaby Jim of the Islands '37

Paul Bartel
Cannonball '76
Death Race 2000 '75
Eating Raoul '82
The Longshot '86
Lust in the Dust '85
Not for Publication '84
Paul Bartel's The Secret Cinema '69
Private Parts '72
Scenes from the Class Struggle in Beverly Hills '89
The Secret Cinema

Carl Bartholomew
Cole Justice '89

Charles Bartlett
Sands of Sacrifice '21

Dick Bartlett
Ollie Hopnoodle's Haven of Bliss '88

Hall Bartlett
All the Young Men '60
Changes '69
Children of Sanchez '79
Defiant '70
Jonathan Livingston Seagull '73

Richard Bartlett
Lonesome Trail '55
Rock, Pretty Baby '56

William S. Bartman
O'Hara's Wife '82

Charles T. Barton
Abbott and Costello Meet Frankenstein '48
Abbott and Costello Meet the Killer, Boris Karloff '49
Africa Screams '49
Buck Privates Come Home '47
Dance with Me, Henry '56
Desert Gold '36
Forlorn River '37
Harmon of Michigan '41
Helltown '38
Ma and Pa Kettle at the Fair '52
Mexican Hayride '48
The Noose Hangs High '48
The Shaggy Dog '59
Thunder Pass '37
The Time of Their Lives '46
Toby Tyler '59
Wagon Wheels '34
Western Double Feature 3 '36
The Wistful Widow of Wagon Gap '47

Earl Barton
Deadly Fieldtrip '74

Sean Barton
Curse 3: Blood Sacrifice '90

Hal Barwood
Warning Sign '85

Nick Barwood
Nasty Hero '89

Juliet Bashore
Kamikaze Hearts '91

Richard Baskin
Sing '89

Jules Bass
The Ballad of Paul Bunyan '72
Flight of Dragons '82
The Hobbit '78
The Last Unicorn '82
Mad Monster Party '68
The Return of the King '80
Santa Claus is Coming to Town '70

Saul Bass
Phase 4 '74

Lawrence Bassoff
Hunk '87
Weekend Pass '84

William Bast
James Dean '76

Michal Bat-Adam
Boy Takes Girl '83

Alexei Batalov
The Overcoat '59

Joy Batchelor
Animal Farm '55

Kent Bateman
Headless Eyes '83

Bradley Battersby
Blue Desert '91

Roy Battersby
Mr. Love '85
Winter Flight '84

Giacomo Battiato
Blood Ties '87
Hearts & Armour '83

Evgenii Bauer
Early Russian Cinema, Vol. 6: Class Distinctions '14
Early Russian Cinema, Vol. 7: Evgenii Bauer '15
Early Russian Cinema, Vol. 9: High Society '19
Early Russian Cinema, Vol. 10: The End of an Era '17

L. Frank Baum
His Majesty, the Scarecrow of Oz/The Magic Cloak of Oz '14
Patchwork Girl of Oz '14

Lamberto Bava
A Blade in the Dark '83
Blastfighter '85
Demons '86
Demons 2 '87
Devilfish '84
Frozen Terror '80

Mario Bava
Beyond the Door 2 '79
Black Sabbath '64
Black Sunday '60
Blood and Black Lace '64
Danger: Diabolik '68
Hatchet for the Honeymoon '70
Hercules in the Haunted World '64
The Invaders '63
Kill, Baby, Kill '66
Lisa and the Devil '75
Planet of the Vampires '65
Torture Chamber of Baron Blood '72
Twitch of the Death Nerve '71
The Wonders of Aladdin '61

Craig R. Baxley
Action Jackson '88
Deep Red '94
I Come in Peace '90
Stone Cold '91

John Baxter
Love on the Dole '41
Old Mother Riley's Ghosts '41

Rolf Bayer
Pacific Inferno '85

Stephen Bayly
Coming Up Roses '87
Diamond's Edge '88

Camillo Bazzoni
Black Lemons '80s

David Beaird
It Takes Two '88
My Chauffeur '86
Octavia '82
Party Animal '83
Pass the Ammo '92
Scorchers '92

Rick Beairsto
Close to Home '86

Chris Bearde
Hysterical '83

Alan Beattie
Delusion '84
Stand Alone '85

Warren Beatty
Dick Tracy '90
Reds '81

William Beaudine
The Ape Man '43
Bela Lugosi Meets a Brooklyn Gorilla '52
Billy the Kid Versus Dracula '66
Blues Busters '50
Bowery Buckaroos '47
The Country Kid '23
Follow the Leader '44
Ghost Chasers '51
Hard-Boiled Mahoney '47
Here Come the Marines '52
Here Comes Kelly '43
Infamous Crimes '47
Jesse James Meets Frankenstein's Daughter '65
Little Annie Rooney '25
Miracle Kid '42
Mom & Dad '47
The Panther's Claw '42
Phantom Killer '42
Robot Pilot '41
Smugglers' Cove '48
Sparrows '26
Spook Busters '46
Spotlight Scandals '43
Ten Who Dared '60
Turf Boy '42
Westward Ho, the Wagons! '56

Gabrielle Beaumont
Carmilla '89
Death of a Centerfold '81
The Godsend '79
Gone are the Days '84
He's My Girl '87

Harry Beaumont
Beau Brummel '24
Broadway Melody '29
Dance Fools Dance '31
Laughing Sinners '31
Our Dancing Daughters '28
The Show-Off '46
When's Your Birthday? '37

Gorman Bechard
Assault of the Killer Bimbos '87
Cemetery High '89
Galactic Gigolo '87
Psychos in Love '87

George Beck
Behave Yourself! '52

Josh Beck
Lunatics: A Love Story '92

Martin Beck
Challenge '74
Last Game '80

Reginald Beck
Henry V '44
The Long Dark Hall '51

Harold Becker
The Black Marble '79
The Boost '88
Malice '93
The Onion Field '79
Sea of Love '89
Taps '81
Vision Quest '85

Jacques Becker
Ali Baba and the 40 Thieves '54
Modigliani '58

Jean Becker
One Deadly Summer '83

Terry Becker
The Thirsty Dead '74**

Vernon Becker
A Man with a Maid '73

James Becket
Ulterior Motives '92

Terry Bedford
Slayground '84

Ford Beebe
Ace Drummond '36
The Adventures of Rex & Rinty '35
Buck Rogers Conquers the Universe '39
Destination Saturn '39
Don Winslow of the Coast Guard '43
Don Winslow of the Navy '43
The Invisible Man's Revenge '44
The Last of the Mohicans '32
Laughing at Life '33
The Man from Gun Town '36
The Masked Rider '41
My Dog Shep '46
Night Monster '42
Oregon Trail '39
The Phantom Creeps '39
Radio Patrol '37
Red Barry '38
Riders of Death Valley '41
Shadow of the Eagle '32
Tim Tyler's Luck '37
Winners of the West '40

Greg Beeman
License to Drive '88
Mom and Dad Save the World '92

Tom Beeman
The Legend of Black Thunder Mountain '79

Jean-Jacques Beineix
Betty Blue '86
Diva '82
Moon in the Gutter '83

Arnold Belgard
East of Kilimanjaro '59

Alan J.W. Bell
The Hitchhiker's Guide to the Galaxy '81
The Making of The Hitchhiker's Guide to the Galaxy '80s

Martin Bell
American Heart '92
Streetwise '85

Earl Bellamy
Against A Crooked Sky '75
Desperate Women '78
Fire '77
Flood! '76
Justice of the West '61
Magic on Love Island '80
Seven Alone '75
Sidewinder One '77
Speedtrap '78
The Trackers '71
Walking Tall: Part 2 '75

Donald P. Bellisario
Last Rites '88

Marco Bellochio
Devil in the Flesh '87
The Eyes, the Mouth '83
Henry IV '85

Yannick Bellon
Rape of Love '79

Vera Belmont
Red Kiss '85

Jerry Belson
Jekyll & Hyde...Together Again '82
Surrender '87

Remy Belvaux
Man Bites Dog '91

Maria-Luisa Bemberg
Camila '84
Miss Mary '86

Jacob Ben-Ami
Green Fields '37

Don Bendell
The Instructor '83

Jack Bender
Child's Play 3 '91
In Love with an Older Woman '82
Letting Go '85
The Midnight Hour '86
My Brother's Wife '89
Shattered Vows '84
Side By Side '88
Tricks of the Trade '88
Two Kinds of Love '85

Joel Bender
Gas Pump Girls '79
The Immortalizer '89
Midnight Kiss '93
Rich Girl '91

Laslo Benedek
Assault on Agathon '75
Daring Game '68
Namu, the Killer Whale '66
The Night Visitor '70
Port of New York '49
The Wild One '54

Rodney Bennett
Sense & Sensibility '85

Roberto Benigni
Johnny Stecchino '92

Richard Benjamin
City Heat '84
Downtown '89
Little Nikita '88
Made in America '93
Mermaids '90
Milk Money '94
The Money Pit '86
My Favorite Year '82
My Stepmother Is an Alien '88
Racing with the Moon '84

Richard Benner
Happy Birthday, Gemini '80
Outrageous! '77

Spencer Gordon Bennet
Across the Plains '39
Arizona Bound '41
Atomic Submarine '59
The Black Widow '47
Calling Wild Bill Elliott '43
D-Day on Mars '45
The Fighting Rookie '34
Get That Man '35
Gunman from Bodie '41
King of the Congo '52
Last Frontier '32
Manhunt of Mystery Island '45
Marked Money '28
The Masked Marvel '43
Midnight Warning '32
Perils of the Darkest Jungle '44
Pirates of the High Seas '50
The Purple Monster Strikes '45
The Rangers Step In '37
The Secret Code '42
Submarine Seahawk '59
Superman: The Serial, Vol. 1 '48
The Unknown Ranger '36
Western Double Feature 1: Wild Bill & Sunset Carson '40s
Zorro's Black Whip '44

Bill Bennett
Backlash '86

Compton Bennett
The Gift Horse '52
King Solomon's Mines '50
The Seventh Veil '46

That Forsyte Woman '50

Richard Bennett
Harper Valley P.T.A. '78

Rodney Bennett
Monsignor Quixote '91

Wallace C. Bennett
George! '70

Walter Bennett
Young Love—Lemon Popsicle 7 '87

Leon Benson
Flipper's New Adventure '64

Richard Benson
The Day the Sky Exploded '57
Werewolf in a Girl's Dormitory '61

Robby Benson
Modern Love '90
White Hot '88

Steve Benson
Endgame '85

Thomas Bentley
Murder at the Baskervilles '37
The Old Curiosity Shop '35

Robert Benton
Bad Company '72
Billy Bathgate '91
Kramer vs. Kramer '79
The Late Show '77
Nadine '87
Places in the Heart '84
Still of the Night '82

Yakov Bentsvi
Legion of Iron '90

Obie Benz
Heavy Petting '89

Luc Beraud
Heat of Desire '84

Luca Bercovici
Ghoulies '85
Rockula '90

Geza Beremenyi
The Midas Touch '89

Al Beresford
Screamtime '83

Bruce Beresford
Aria '88
Barry McKenzie Holds His Own '74
Black Robe '91
Breaker Morant '80
The Club '81
Crimes of the Heart '86
Don's Party '76
Driving Miss Daisy '89
The Fringe Dwellers '86
The Getting of Wisdom '77
Her Alibi '88
King David '85
Mister Johnson '91
Money Movers '78
Puberty Blues '81
Rich in Love '93
Tender Mercies '83

Phyllis Berg-Pigorsch
The Islander '88

Ludwig Berger
Thief of Baghdad '40

Pamela Berger
The Imported Bridegroom '89

Andrew Bergman
The Freshman '90
Honeymoon in Vegas '92
It Could Happen to You '94
So Fine '81

Ingmar Bergman
After the Rehearsal '84

Autumn Sonata '78
Brink of Life '57
Cries and Whispers '72
The Devil's Eye '60
Devil's Wanton '49
Dreams '55
Face to Face '76
Fanny and Alexander '83
From the Life of the Marionettes '80
Hour of the Wolf '68
Lesson in Love '54
The Magic Flute '73
The Magician '58
Monika '52
Night Is My Future '47
The Passion of Anna '70
Persona '66
Port of Call '48
Sawdust & Tinsel '53
Scenes from a Marriage '73
Secrets of Women '52
The Serpent's Egg '78
The Seventh Seal '56
The Shame '68
The Silence '63
Smiles of a Summer Night '55
Summer Interlude '50
Three Strange Loves '49
Through a Glass Darkly '61
To Joy '50
The Touch '71
The Virgin Spring '59
Wild Strawberries '57
The Winter Light '62

Robert Bergman
Skull: A Night of Terror '88
A Whisper to a Scream '88

William Berke
Bandit Queen '51
Betrayal from the East '44
Border Rangers '50
Dangerous Passage '44
Dick Tracy, Detective/The Corpse Vanishes '42
The Falcon in Mexico '44
Falcon's Adventure/Armored Car Robbery '50
FBI Girl '49
Gun Grit '36
Gunfire '50
Highway 13 '48
I Shot Billy the Kid '50
Jungle '52
The Lost Missile '58
The Marshal's Daughter '53
Operation Haylift '50
Renegade Girl '46
Roaring City '51
Savage Drums '51
Shoot to Kill '47
Toll of the Desert '35
Treasure of Monte Cristo '50

Busby Berkeley
Babes in Arms '39
Babes on Broadway '41
For Me and My Gal '42
Gold Diggers of 1935 '35
Strike Up the Band '40
Take Me Out to the Ball Game '49
They Made Me a Criminal '39

Abby Berlin
Blondie Knows Best '46
Double Deal '50

Joe Berlinger
Brother's Keeper '92

Harvey Berman
The Wild Ride '60

Monty Berman
The Hellfire Club '61
Jack the Ripper '60

Pandro S. Berman
Romance in Manhattan '34

Ted Berman
The Fox and the Hound '81

Chris Bernard
Letter to Brezhnev '86

John Bernard
Stay Awake '87

Michael Bernard
Nights in White Satin '87

Paul Bernard
Doctor Who: Day of the Daleks '72

Edward L. Bernds
Blondie Hits the Jackpot '49
Clipped Wings '53
Gold Raiders '51
Queen of Outer Space '58
Reform School Girl '57
Return of the Fly '59
Storm Rider '57
The Three Stooges Meet Hercules '61

Joseph Berne
Mirele Efros '38

Peter Berneis
No Survivors, Please '63

Jack Bernhard
Unknown Island '48

Curtis Bernhardt
Beau Brummel '54
Conflict '45
Interrupted Melody '55
Kisses for My President '64
The Merry Widow '52
Miss Sadie Thompson '53
The Possessed '47
Sirocco '51
A Stolen Life '46

Adam Bernstein
It's Pat '94

Armyan Bernstein
Cross My Heart '88
Windy City '84

Walter Bernstein
Little Miss Marker '80
Women & Men: In Love There Are No Rules '91

Claude Berri
I Love All of You '83
Jean de Florette '87
Le Sex Shop '73
Manon of the Spring '87
Marry Me, Marry Me '69
One Wild Moment '78
Tchao Pantin '84
The Two of Us '68
Uranus '91

Bill Berry
Brotherhood of Death '76
Off the Mark '87

John Berry
Angel on My Shoulder '80
The Bad News Bears Go to Japan '78
Honeyboy '82
Maya '66
Pantaloons '59
Tamango '59

Robert Berry
House of Dreams '64

Tom Berry
The Amityville Curse '90
Blind Fear '89

Bernardo Bertolucci
Before the Revolution '65
The Conformist '71
The Grim Reaper '62
The Last Emperor '87
Last Tango in Paris '73
Little Buddha '93
1900 '76
Partner '68
The Sheltering Sky '90
The Spider's Stratagem '70

Bertolucci ▶cont.

The Tragedy of a Ridiculous Man '81

Kenneth Berton
Devil's Gift '84

Jean-Louis Bertucelli
Ramparts of Clay '71

Irvin Berwick
Malibu High '79
The Monster of Piedras Blancas '57
The 7th Commandment '61

Wayne Berwick
Microwave Massacre '83

Michael Berz
Cannon Movie Tales: Snow White '89

James Beshears
Homework '82

Milad Bessada
Quiet Day In Belfast '74

Dan Bessie
Hard Traveling '85

Luc Besson
The Big Blue '88
La Femme Nikita '91
Le Dernier Combat '84
Subway '85

Bruce Best
Queen of the Road '84

Gil Bettman
Crystal Heart '87
Never Too Young to Die '86

Jonathan Betuel
My Science Project '85

Eddie Beverly, Jr.
Ballbuster
Escapist '83

Radha Bharadwaj
Closet Land '90

Andrew Bianchi
Burial Ground '85
Cry of a Prostitute: Love Kills '72

Edward Bianchi
The Fan '81

Herbert Biberman
Master Race '44
Salt of the Earth '54

Robert Bierman
Apology '86
Vampire's Kiss '88

Edward A. Biery
How to Succeed with Girls '64

Kathryn Bigelow
Blue Steel '90
Loveless '83
Near Dark '87
Point Break '91
Wild Palms '93

Joseph Bigwood
Never Pick Up a Stranger '79

David Bilcock
Alvin Rides Again '74

Tony Bill
Crazy People '90
Five Corners '88
A Home of Our Own '93
My Bodyguard '80
The Princess and the Pea '83
Six Weeks '82

Kevin Billington
Light at the Edge of the World '71

Bruce Bilson
Chattanooga Choo Choo '84
The North Avenue Irregulars '79

Danny Bilson
The Wrong Guys '88
Zone Troopers '85

John Binder
Uforia '88

Mike Binder
Blankman '94
Crossing the Bridge '92
Indian Summer '93

Steve Binder
Give 'Em Hell, Harry! '75

William Bindley
Freeze Frame '92

Steve Bing
Every Breath '93

Joe Binney
Killer Diller '48

Josh Binney
Boardinghouse Blues '48
Hi-De-Ho '35

Claude Binyon
Here Come the Girls '53

Dudley Birch
Flight from Singapore '62

Patricia Birch
Grease 2 '82

Dick Bird
Men of Ireland '38

Richard Bird
The Terror '38

Stuart Bird
Home Free All '84

Andrew Birkin
Burning Secret '89
Desire '93

Alan Birkinshaw
The House of Usher '88
Masque of the Red Death '90
Ten Little Indians '89

Fernando Birri
A Very Old Man with Enormous Wings '88

Daniel Birt
Interrupted Journey '49
Robin Hood: The Movie '55
The Three Weird Sisters '48

Sam Bischoff
The Last Mile '32

Terry Bishop
The Unstoppable Man '59

Lauren Bivens
Trespasses '86

Bill Bixby
Another Pair of Aces: Three of a Kind '91
Baby of the Bride '91
The Barbary Coast '74
Death of the Incredible Hulk '90
The Trial of the Incredible Hulk '89

Stig Bjorkman
Georgia, Georgia '72

Herbert Blache
The Saphead '21
The Untamable '23

Noel Black
A Conspiracy of Love '87
Eyes of the Panther '90
The Golden Honeymoon '80
I'm a Fool '77
A Man, a Woman, and a Bank '79

Mirrors '78
Pretty Poison '68
Prime Suspect '82
Private School '83
Quarterback Princess '85

Richard Blackburn
Lemora, Lady Dracula '73

Cullen Blaine
R.O.T.O.R. '88

David Blair
Wax, or the Discovery of Television Among the Bees '93

George Blair
Silver City Bonanza '51

Les Blair
Bad Behavior '92

Mark Blair
Confessions of a Serial Killer '87

Alfonso Corona Blake
Samson in the Wax Museum '63
Samson vs. the Vampire Women '61
World of the Vampires '60

T.C. Blake
Nightflyers '87

Michael Blakemore
Privates on Parade '84

Ken Blancato
Stewardess School '86

John Blanchard
The Last Polka '84

Harrod Blank
In the Land of the Owl Turds '87

Les Blank
Burden of Dreams '82

Alexandro Blasetti
1860 '33
Fabiola '48
The Iron Crown '41

William Peter Blatty
The Exorcist 3 '90
The Ninth Configuration '79

Jeff Bleckner
Brotherly Love '85
When Your Lover Leaves '83
White Water Summer '87

Bertrand Blier
Beau Pere '81
Buffet Froid '79
Get Out Your Handkerchiefs '78
Going Places '74
Menage '86
My Best Friend's Girl '84
Too Beautiful for You '88

Bob Blizz
Vengeance '80

Bruce Block
Princess Academy '87

George J. Bloom, III
Brothers in Arms '88

Jeffrey Bloom
Blood Beach '81
Dog Pound Shuffle '75
Flowers in the Attic '87
Jealousy '84
The Stick-Up '77

George Bloomfield
The Double Negative '80
Nothing Personal '80
Riel '79
To Kill a Clown '72

Philippe Blot
Hot Blood '89

Pavel Blumenfeld
Tereza '61

Mort Blumenstock
Morals for Women '31

Andy Blumenthal
Bloodfist 2 '90

Ralph Blumke
Robby '68

Don Bluth
All Dogs Go to Heaven '89
An American Tail '86
The Land Before Time '88
Rock-a-Doodle '92
The Secret of NIMH '82
Thumbelina '94
A Troll in Central Park '94

John Blystone
Block-heads '38
Dick Turpin '25
Great Guy '36
Our Hospitality '23
Swiss Miss '38
23 1/2 Hours Leave '37

David Blyth
Death Warmed Up '85
My Grandpa is a Vampire '92
Red Blooded American Girl '90

Jeff Blyth
Cheetah '89

Paul Bnarbic
Cold Front '89

Kam Bo
Blind Fists of Bruce '70s

Hart Bochner
P.C.U. '94

Jean Bodon
Hidden Fears '93

Sergei Bodrov
Freedom is Paradise '89

Budd Boetticher
Behind Locked Doors '48
Bullfighter & the Lady '50
Horizons West '52
The Magnificent Matador '55
Man from the Alamo '53
Ride Lonesome '59
The Rise and Fall of Legs Diamond '60
The Tall T '57

Paul Bogart
Broadway Bound '92
Cancel My Reservation '72
Class of '44 '73
A House Without a Christmas Tree '72
Marlowe '69
Oh, God! You Devil '84
Power, Passion & Murder '83
Skin Game '71
Tell Me Where It Hurts '74
Torch Song Trilogy '88

Yurek Bogayevicz
Anna '87
Three of Hearts '93

Peter Bogdanovich
Daisy Miller '74
Illegally Yours '87
The Last Picture Show '71
Mask '85
Noises Off '92
Paper Moon '73
Saint Jack '79
Targets '68
Texasville '90
They All Laughed '81
The Thing Called Love '93
Voyage to the Planet of Prehistoric Women '68
What's Up, Doc? '72

Willy Bogner
Fire and Ice '87
Fire, Ice and Dynamite '91

Michael Derek Bohusz
Uninvited '93

Michel Boisrond
Catherine & Co. '76
That Naughty Girl '58
Voulez-Vous Danser Avec Moi? '59

Yves Boisset
Cobra '71
Dog Day '83
Double Identity '89
Prize of Peril '84
The Purple Taxi '77

Johanne Boisvert
Being at Home with Claude '92

Jerome Boivin
Barjo '93
Baxter '89

Jose Antonio Bolanos
Born in America '90

Richard Boleslawski
The Garden of Allah '36
The Last of Mrs. Cheyney '37
Les Miserables '35
The Painted Veil '34
Rasputin and the Empress '32

Heinrich Boll
Germany in Autumn '78

Mauro Bolognini
Husbands and Lovers '91
Il Bell'Antonio '60
The Inheritance '76
La Grande Bourgeoise '74
Oldest Profession '67

Craig Bolotin
That Night '93

Ben Bolt
Big Town '87

Robert Bolt
Lady Caroline Lamb '73

Jack Bond
It Couldn't Happen Here '88

James Bond, III
Def by Temptation '90

Timothy Bond
Deadly Harvest '72
The Lost World '92
One Night Only '84

Sergei Bondarchuk
War and Peace '68
Waterloo '71

Peter Bonerz
Nobody's Perfekt '79
Police Academy 6: City Under Siege '89

Mike Bonifer
Lipstick Camera '93

Mario Bonnard
The Last Days of Pompeii '60

Lee Bonner
Adventure of the Action Hunters '87

Rene Bonniere
Perfect Timing '84

Miguel Iglesias Bonns
Night of the Howling Beast '75

Andre Bonzel
Man Bites Dog '91

John Boorman
Deliverance '72
The Emerald Forest '85

Excalibur '81
The Exorcist 2: The Heretic '77
Hell in the Pacific '69
Hope and Glory '87
Point Blank '67
Where the Heart Is '90
Zardoz '73

H. Gordon Boos
Red Surf '90

Walter Boos
Train Station Pickups '70s

Jose Luis Borau
On the Line '83

Donald P. Borchers
Grave Secrets '89

Lizzie Borden
Born in Flames '83
Love Crimes '92
Working Girls '87

Bernard Borderie
Your Turn Darling '63

Michael Bordon
The Ghost of Fletcher Ridge '80s

Robert Boris
Buy & Cell '89
Oxford Blues '84
Steele Justice '87

Walerian Borowczyk
Emmanuelle 5 '87

Clay Borris
The Gunfighters '87
Prom Night 4: Deliver Us From Evil '91
Quiet Cool '86

Phillip Borsos
Dr. Bethune '90
The Grey Fox '83
Mean Season '85
One Magic Christmas '85

Michael Bortman
Crooked Hearts '91

Frank Borzage
A Farewell to Arms '32
Flirtation Walk '34
History is Made at Night '37
I've Always Loved You '46
Journey Beneath the Desert '61
Mannequin '37
Moonrise '48
The Mortal Storm '40
The Shining Hour '38
Smilin' Through '41
Song O' My Heart '29
The Spanish Main '45
Stage Door Canteen '43
Strange Cargo '40
Three Comrades '38

Juan Bosch
Exorcism '74

Mark Steven Bosko
Bride of Killer Nerd '91

Fritz Bottger
Horrors of Spider Island '59

John Boulting
Brighton Rock '47
Heavens Above '63
I'm All Right Jack '59
Lucky Jim '58

Roy Boulting
Brothers in Law '57
Carlton Browne of the F.O. '59
Fame is the Spur '47
Heavens Above '63
There's a Girl in My Soup '70

Serge Bourguignon
A Coeur Joie '67
Head Over Heels '67
Sundays & Cybele '62

Robert Bouvier
City in Panic '86

Haim Bouzaglo
Fictitious Marriage '88

John Bowab
Love at the Top '86

Jenny Bowen
Animal Behavior '89
Street Music '81
The Wizard of Loneliness '88

John Bowen
Knock Outs '92
Lethal Games '90

Dallas Bower
Alice in Wonderland '50

Anthony Bowers
Shame, Shame on the Bixby Boys '82

Geoffrey G. Bowers
Danger Zone 2 '89

George Bowers
Body & Soul '81
The Hearse '80
My Tutor '82
Private Resort '84

John R. Bowey
Mutator '90

Rob Bowman
Airborne '93

John Bown
Nudity Required '90

Kenneth Bowser
In a Shallow Grave '88

Muriel Box
Rattle of a Simple Man '64
Truth About Women '58

Daniel Boyd
Chillers '88
Invasion of the Space Preachers '90

Don Boyd
East of Elephant Rock '76
Twenty-One '91

Julianne Boyd
Eubie! '82

Jean Boyer
Circonstances Attenuantes '36
Dressmaker '56
Fernandel the Dressmaker '57
The French Touch '54
Mr. Peek-A-Boo '50

Pat Boyette
Dungeon of Harrow '64

Bruno Bozzetto
Allegro Non Troppo '76
Vip, My Brother Superman '90

Charles Brabant
The Respectful Prostitute '52

Charles Brabin
The Mask of Fu Manchu '32
The Raven '15

Bertram Bracken
The Confession '20

Robert North Bradbury
Alias John Law '35
Between Men '35
Big Calibre '35
Blue Steel '34
Brand of the Outlaws '36
Breed of the Border '33
Cavalry '36
Dawn Rider '35
Dawn Rider/Frontier Horizon '39
Desert Trail '35
Forbidden Trails '41

The Gallant Fool '33
Galloping Romeo '33
God's Country and the Man '37
The Gun Ranger '34
Headin' for the Rio Grande '36
Hidden Valley '32
Hittin' the Trail '37
John Wayne Anthology: Star Packer/Lawless Range '34
Kid Ranger '36
Last of the Warrens '36
Lawless Frontier '35
Lawless Range '35
Lucky Texan '34
Man from Hell's Edges '32
Man from Utah '34
Riders of Destiny '33
Riders of the Rockies '37
Smokey Smith '36
The Star Packer '34
Sundown Saunders '36
Texas Buddies '32
Trail Beyond '34
Trail of Terror '35
Trouble in Texas '37
Valley of the Lawless '36
West of the Divide '34
Western Double Feature 2 '33
Western Double Feature 5 '35
Western Justice '35
Westward Ho '35
Where Trails Divide '37

Samuel Bradford
Teen Vamp '88

Al Bradley
Bloody Avenger '80s
Captive Planet '78
Cosmos: War of the Planets '80
Cross Mission '89
Iron Warrior '87
Metallica '85
Miami Cops '89

David Bradley
They Saved Hitler's Brain '64

John Bradshaw
The Big Slice '90
That's My Baby! '88

Randy Bradshaw
Blades of Courage '88

Carlo L. Bragaglia
The Loves of Hercules '60
The Sword and the Cross '58

John Brahm
Face to Face '52
Guest in the House '45
The Lodger '44
Miracle of Our Lady of Fatima '52
The Undying Monster '42
Wintertime '43

Stan Brakhage
Dog Star Man '64

Marco Brambilla
Demolition Man '93

Bill Brame
Ebony Dreams '80
Jive Turkey '76
Miss Melody Jones '73

Kenneth Branagh
Dead Again '91
Henry V '89
Much Ado About Nothing '93
Peter's Friends '92

Larry Brand
The Drifter '88
Masque of the Red Death '89
Overexposed '90

Timothy Brand
Till Death Do Us Part '72

Richard Brander
Sizzle Beach U.S.A. '86

Marlon Brando
One-Eyed Jacks '61

Clark Brandon
Skeeter '93

Michael Brandon
Queen of the Stardust Ballroom '75

Charlotte Brandstrom
Road to Ruin '91
Sweet Revenge '90

Fred Brannon
Bandit King of Texas '49
Cyclotrode "X" '46
D-Day on Mars '45
Federal Agents vs. Underworld, Inc. '49
G-Men Never Forget '48
The Invisible Monster '50
Jesse James Rides Again '47
Jungle Drums of Africa '53
King of the Rocketmen '49
Lost Planet Airmen '49
Radar Men from the Moon '52
Zombies of the Stratosphere '52

Dominick Brascia
Evil Laugh '86

Enrique Braso
In Memoriam '76

Tinto Brass
Caligula '80

Keefe Brasselle
If You Don't Stop It...You'll Go Blind '77

Michel Brault
A Paper Wedding '89

Joseph Braunstein
Edge of the Axe '89
Rest in Pieces '87

Charles Braverman
Brotherhood of Justice '86
Hit & Run '82
Prince of Bel Air '87

Bob Bravler
Rush Week '88

John Bravman
Zombie Nightmare '86

William Brayne
Cold War Killers '86
Flame to the Phoenix '85

Rossano Brazzi
The Christmas That Almost Wasn't '66

George Breakston
Scarlet Spear '54
White Huntress '57

Gil Brealey
A Test of Love '84

Richard L. Breen
Stopover Tokyo '57

Catherine Breillat
36 Fillete '88

Jacques Brel
Franz '72

Milton Bren
Three for Bedroom C '52

Herbert Brenon
Black Eyes '39
Dancing Mothers '26
Housemaster '38

Alfonso Brescia
White Fang and the Hunter '85

Robert Bresson
Diary of a Country Priest '50
L'Argent '83
A Man Escaped '57
Mouchette '60
Pickpocket '59

Martin Brest
Beverly Hills Cop '84
Going in Style '79
Midnight Run '88
Scent of a Woman '92

Howard Bretherton
Below the Border '42
Boy's Reformatory '39
Dawn on the Great Divide '42
Down Texas Way '42
Ghost Town Law '42
Hidden Enemy '40
Hopalong Cassidy '35
In Old Colorado '41
Ladies They Talk About '33
Midnight Limited '40
Outlaws of the Desert '41
The Prince of Thieves '48
Rhythm Parade '43
Riders of the West '42
The Showdown '40
Star Reporter '39
The Topeka Terror '45
Tough Kid '39
Up in the Air '40
West of the Law '42

Michael E. Briant
Blake's Seven '78
Doctor Who: Death to the Daleks '74
Doctor Who: Revenge of the Cybermen '75
Doctor Who: Robots of Death '77
Doctor Who: The Talons of Weng-Chiang '77

Jules Bricken
Explosion '69

Marshall Brickman
Lovesick '83
The Manhattan Project '86
Simon '80

Paul Brickman
Men Don't Leave '89
Risky Business '83

Alan Bridges
Invasion '65
Out of Season '75
Pudd'nhead Wilson '87
Return of the Soldier '82
The Shooting Party '85

Beau Bridges
Seven Hours to Judgment '88
The Wild Pair '87

James Bridges
The Baby Maker '70
Bright Lights, Big City '88
The China Syndrome '79
Mike's Murder '84
The Paper Chase '73
Perfect '85
September 30, 1955 '77
Urban Cowboy '80

Burt Brinckerhoff
Can You Hear the Laughter? The Story of Freddie Prinze '79
The Cracker Factory '79
The Day the Women Got Even '80
Mother & Daughter: A Loving War '80

Irving Briskin
Texas Cyclone '32

Jean Brismee
The Devil's Nightmare '71

Donald Britlain
Accident '83

Lawrence Britten
Whose Child Am I? '75

Tracy Lynch Britton
Maximum Breakout '91

Deborah Brock
Andy and the Airwave Rangers '89
Rock 'n' Roll High School Forever '91
Slumber Party Massacre 2 '87

John Broderick
Bad Georgia Road '77
The Warrior & the Sorceress '84

Kevin Brodie
Mugsy's Girls '85

Rex Bromfield
Cafe Romeo '91
Home is Where the Hart is '88
Love at First Sight '76
Melanie '82

Douglas Bronco
Danger Zone 3: Steel Horse War '90

Clive Brook
On Approval '44

Peter Brook
King Lear '71
Lord of the Flies '63
The Mahabharata '89
Marat/Sade '66
Meetings with Remarkable Men '79

Ralph Brooke
Bloodlust '59

Howard Brookner
Bloodhounds of Broadway '89

Adam Brooks
Almost You '85
Cannon Movie Tales: Red Riding Hood '89

Albert Brooks
Defending Your Life '91
Lost in America '85
Modern Romance '81
Real Life '79

Bob Brooks
Tattoo '81

James L. Brooks
Broadcast News '87
I'll Do Anything '93
Terms of Endearment '83
Thursday's Game '74

Joseph Brooks
If Ever I See You Again '78
Invitation to the Wedding '73
You Light Up My Life '77

Mel Brooks
Blazing Saddles '74
High Anxiety '77
History of the World: Part 1 '81
Life Stinks '91
The Producers '68
Robin Hood: Men in Tights '93
Silent Movie '76
Spaceballs '87
Twelve Chairs '70
Young Frankenstein '74

Richard Brooks
Battle Circus '53
Bite the Bullet '75
Blackboard Jungle '55
The Brothers Karamazov '58
Cat on a Hot Tin Roof '58
The Catered Affair '56
Dollars '71
Elmer Gantry '60
Fever Pitch '85
The Happy Ending '69
In Cold Blood '67
The Last Hunt '56
The Last Time I Saw Paris '54
Looking for Mr. Goodbar '77
Lord Jim '65
The Professionals '66
Something of Value '57
Sweet Bird of Youth '62

Wrong is Right '82

Robert Brooks
Who Shot Pat? '92

Nick Broomfield
Dark Obsession '90
Monster in a Box '92

Philip Brophy
Body Melt '93

James Broughton
Dreamwood '72

Otto Brower
Clearing the Range '31
Devil Horse '32
Fighting Caravans '31
Hard Hombre '31
I Can't Escape '34
The Light of Western Stars '30
Mystery Mountain '34
The Outlaw Deputy '35
The Phantom Empire '35
Postal Inspector '36
Spirit of the West '32

Arvin Brown
Diary of the Dead '80s

Barry Brown
Cloud Dancer '80
Lonely in America '90

Bruce Brown
The Endless Summer '66
The Endless Summer 2 '94

Clarence Brown
Ah, Wilderness! '35
Angels in the Outfield '51
Anna Christie '30
Anna Karenina '35
Chained '34
Conquest '37
The Eagle '25
Edison the Man '40
The Flesh and the Devil '27
A Free Soul '31
The Gorgeous Hussy '36
The Human Comedy '43
Idiot's Delight '39
Intruder in the Dust '49
The Last of the Mohicans '20
The Light of Faith '22
National Velvet '44
Of Human Hearts '38
Possessed '31
The Rains Came '39
Romance '30
Sadie McKee '34
Smouldering Fires '25
The Tempest/The Eagle '27
They Met in Bombay '41
To Please a Lady '50
The White Cliffs of Dover '44
Wife Versus Secretary '36
A Woman of Affairs '28
The Yearling '46

Edwin Scott Brown
The Prey '80

Ewing Miles Brown
Killers '88
Whale of a Tale '76

Georg Stanford Brown
Alone in the Neon Jungle '87
Grambling's White Tiger '81
Miracle of the Heart: A Boys Town Story '86

Gregory Brown
Dead Man Walking '88
Street Asylum '90

Gwen Brown
Emergency '68

Harry Joe Brown
The Fighting Legion '30
Mountain Justice '30
One-Punch O'Day '26

Karl Brown
Fire Alarm '38
The Port of Missing Girls '38
The White Legion '36

Larry G. Brown
Final Cut '88
Psychopath '73

Melville Brown
Behind Office Doors '31
Champagne for Breakfast '35
Check & Double Check '30
Mad About Money '30

Mitch Brown
Death Shot '73

Robert Brown
Two Wrongs Make a Right '89

William O. Brown
The Witchmaker '69

Cara Brownell
Cave Girls '82

Ricou Browning
Salty '73

Tod Browning
Devil Doll '36
Dracula '31
Freaks '32
Mark of the Vampire '35
Outside the Law '21
The Unholy Three '25
The Unknown '27
West of Zanzibar '28
White Tiger '23

S.F. Brownrigg
Don't Look in the Basement '73
Don't Open the Door! '74
Keep My Grave Open '80
Poor White Trash 2 '75
Thinkin' Big '87

James Bruce
The Suicide Club '88

Clyde Bruckman
Feet First '30
The General '27

Adrian Brunel
Old Spanish Custom '36

Franco Brusati
The Sleazy Uncle '89
To Forget Venice '79

Alf Brustellin
Germany in Autumn '78

Charles Bryant
Salome '22
Salome/Queen Elizabeth '23

James Bryant
The Executioner, Part 2: Frozen Scream '84

Bill Bryden
Aria '88

Zbynek Brynych
Transport from Paradise '65

Larry Buchanan
Creature of Destruction '67
Curse of the Swamp Creature '66
The Eye Creatures '65
Free, White, and 21 '62
Goodbye, Norma Jean '75
Goodnight, Sweet Marilyn '89
Hell Raiders '68
Hughes & Harlow: Angels in Hell '77
It's Alive! '68
The Loch Ness Horror '82
Mars Needs Women '66
Mistress of the Apes '79
Zontar, the Thing from Venus '66

Dimitri Buchowetzki
Othello '22
The Swan '25

Julio Buchs
Bullet for Sandoval '70

Chris Buck
Family Dog: Complete Series '92

Bethel Buckalew
My Boys are Good Boys '78

Allan A. Buckhantz
The Last Contract '86
Portrait of a Hitman '77

Colin Bucksey
Blue Money '84
Curiosity Kills '90
Dealers '89
The McGuffin '85
Midnight's Child '93

Harold Bucquet
The Adventures of Tartu '43
Dr. Kildare's Strange Case '40
On Borrowed Time '39
Without Love '45

Colin Budds
Hurricane Smith '92

John Carl Buechler
Cellar Dweller '87
Dungeonmaster '85
Friday the 13th, Part 7: The New Blood '88
Ghoulies 3: Ghoulies Go to College '91
Troll '85

Peter Bufa
Ghost Dance '83

Richard Bugajski
Clearcut '92
The Interrogation '82
A Woman and a Woman '80

Veljko Bulajic
Battle of Neretva '69
The Day that Shook the World '78

Alan Bunce
Babar: The Movie '88

Mark Buntzman
Exterminator 2 '84

Joyce Bunuel
Dirty Dishes '82

Juan Bunuel
Leonor '75

Luis Bunuel
The Criminal Life of Archibaldo de la Cruz '55
Diary of a Chambermaid '64
The Discreet Charm of the Bourgeoisie '72
El Bruto '52
El: This Strange Passion '52
The Exterminating Angel '62
Fever Mounts at El Pao '59
The Great Madcap '49
The Illusion Travels by Streetcar '53
L'Age D'Or '30
Los Olvidados '50
Mexican Bus Ride '51
The Milky Way '68
Nazarin '58
Phantom of Liberty '68
Simon of the Desert '66
Susana '51
That Obscure Object of Desire '77
Tristana '70
Un Chien Andalou '28
Viridiana '61
A Woman Without Love '51
Wuthering Heights '53
The Young One '61

Jacob Burckhardt
Landlord Blues '87

Bob Burge
Keaton's Cop '90

Robert Burge
Vasectomy: A Delicate Matter '86

Stuart Burge
Julius Caesar '70

Martyn Burke
Clown Murders '83
Last Chase '81
Power Play '81

Terry Burke
Inn of the Damned '74

William Burke
Dick Tracy, Detective '45

Tom Burman
Meet the Hollowheads '89

Charles Burnett
To Sleep with Anger '90

Allan Burns
Just Between Friends '86

Ken Burns
The Civil War, Episode 1: The Cause—1861 '90
The Civil War, Episode 2: A Very Bloody Affair—1862 '90
The Civil War, Episode 3: Forever Free—1862 '90
The Civil War, Episode 4: Simply Murder—1863 '90
The Civil War, Episode 5: The Universe of Battle—1863 '90
The Civil War, Episode 6: Valley of the Shadow of Death—1864 '90
The Civil War, Episode 7: Most Hallowed Ground—1864 '90
The Civil War, Episode 8: War is All Hell—1865 '90
The Civil War, Episode 9: The Better Angels of Our Nature—1865 '90

Robert Burns
Mongrel '83

Jeff Burr
Leatherface: The Texas Chainsaw Massacre 3 '89
The Offspring '87
Puppet Master 4 '93
Stepfather 2: Make Room for Daddy '89

Robert L. Burrill
The Milpitas Monster '75

Geoff Burrowes
Return to Snowy River '88
Run '91

James Burrows
Partners '82

Tim Burstall
Adventures of Eliza Fraser '76
Alvin Purple '73
Attack Force Z '84
Endplay '75
Great Expectations: The Untold Story '74
Jock Petersen '74
Kangaroo '86
The Naked Country '85
Nightmare at Bittercreek '91

David Burton
Fighting Caravans '31
Lady by Choice '34

Richard Burton
Doctor Faustus '68

Tim Burton
Aladdin and His Wonderful Lamp '84
Batman '89
Batman Returns '92
Beetlejuice '88

Ed Wood '94
Edward Scissorhands '90
Frankenweenie '84
Pee Wee's Big Adventure '85

Leszek Burzynski
Trapped Alive '93

Anthony Bushell
Angel with the Trumpet '50
The Long Dark Hall '51

John Bushelman
L.A. Gangs Rising '89

Christel Bushmann
Comeback '83

William H. Bushnell, Jr.
Four Deuces '75

Tom Bussmann
Whoops Apocalypse '83

Adolfo Fernandez Bustamante
Mariachis '49

David Butler
April In Paris '52
Bright Eyes '34
By the Light of the Silvery Moon '53
Calamity Jane '53
Captain January '36
Caught in the Draft '41
A Connecticut Yankee '31
Doubting Thomas '35
It's a Great Feeling '49
King Richard and the Crusaders '54
The Little Colonel '35
The Littlest Rebel '35
Look for the Silver Lining '49
Lullaby of Broadway '51
Playmates '41
The Princess and the Pirate '44
The Road to Morocco '42
San Antonio '45
The Story of Seabiscuit '49
Tea for Two '50
Thank Your Lucky Stars '43
They Got Me Covered '43
You'll Find Out '40

Dick Butler
Glory '56

George Butler
Pumping Iron '76
Pumping Iron 2: The Women '85

Robert Butler
The Barefoot Executive '71
The Computer Wore Tennis Shoes '69
Concrete Beat '84
Hot Lead & Cold Feet '78
James Dean '76
Long Time Gone '86
Moonlighting '85
Night of the Juggler '80
Now You See Him, Now You Don't '72
Out on a Limb '87
A Question of Guilt '78
Scandalous John '71
Star Trek: The Cage '65
Strange New World '75
The Ultimate Thrill '74
Underground Aces '80
Up the Creek '84

Hendel Butoy
The Rescuers Down Under '90

Bernard Buys
Demon Lust

Zane Buzby
Last Resort '86

Edward Buzzell
At the Circus '39
Best Foot Forward '43

Go West '40
Honolulu '39
Neptune's Daughter '49
Ship Ahoy '42
Song of the Thin Man '47
A Woman of Distinction '50

Mark Byers
Criminal Act '88
Digging Up Business '91

Caruth C. Byrd
Hollywood High, Part 2 '81

David Byrne
True Stories '86

John Byrum
Heart Beat '80
Inserts '76
The Razor's Edge '84
The Whoopee Boys '86

James Caan
Hide in Plain Sight '80

Richard Caan
War of the Wizards '81

Christy Cabanne
Annapolis '28
Convicted '32
Dixie Jamboree '44
Flirting with Fate '16
Hearts of Humanity '32
Jane Eyre '34
The Lamb '15
Last Outlaw '36
The Mummy's Hand '40
One Frightened Night '35
Reggie Mixes In '16
The World Gone Mad '33

William Cabanne
The Average Woman '24

Ellen Cabot
Deadly Embrace '88
Test Tube Teens from the Year 2000 '93

Sergio Cabrera
Details of a Duel: A Question of Honor '89

Nick Cacas
Forgotten Warrior '86

Michael Cacoyannis
Girl in Black '56
Iphigenia '77
A Matter of Dignity '57
Stella '55
The Story of Jacob & Joseph '74
Sweet Country '87
Trojan Women '71
Zorba the Greek '64

Michael Caffey
The Hanged Man '74

Edward L. Cahn
Confidential '35
Dragstrip Girl '57
Flesh and the Spur '57
Frontier Uprising '61
Girls in Prison '57
Invasion of the Saucer Men '57
It! The Terror from Beyond Space '58
Jet Attack/Paratroop Command '58
Motorcycle Gang '57
Shake, Rattle and Rock '57
Suicide Battalion/Hell Squad '58
Voodoo Woman '57
Zombies of Moratau '57

Mario Caiano
Adios, Hombre '68

Christopher Cain
Elmer '76
The Next Karate Kid '94
The Principal '87
Pure Country '92

The Stone Boy '84
That Was Then...This Is Now '85
Wheels of Terror '90
Where the River Runs Black '86
Young Guns '88

Thomas Calabrese
Even Angels Fall '90

Stephen Calamari
The Satan Killer '93

Antonio Calenda
One Russian Summer '73

Mark Callan
Hector's Bunyip '86

John Callas
Lone Wolf '88

Simon Callow
The Ballad of the Sad Cafe '91

Marcel Came
Les Assassins de L'Ordre '71

Mario Camerini
Ulysses '55

James Cameron
The Abyss '89
Aliens '86
Piranha 2: The Spawning '82
The Spawning '82
The Terminator '84
Terminator 2: Judgment Day '91
True Lies '94

Ken Cameron
Fast Talking '86
The Good Wife '86
Monkey Grip '82
Wild Thing '87

Ray Cameron
Bloodbath at the House of Death '85

Douglas Camfield
Ivanhoe '82

Donald Cammell
Demon Seed '77
Performance '70
White of the Eye '88

Joe Camp
Benji '74
Benji the Hunted '87
The Double McGuffin '79
For the Love of Benji '77
Hawmps! '76
Oh, Heavenly Dog! '80

Pasquale Festa Campanile
When Women Had Tails '70
When Women Lost Their Tails '75

Colin Campbell
The Spoilers '14

Douglas Campbell
Season of Fear '89
Zapped Again '89

Graeme Campbell
Blood Relations '87
Into the Fire '88
Murder One '88
Still Life '92

Martin Campbell
Cast a Deadly Spell '91
Criminal Law '89
Defenseless '91
Edge of Darkness '86
No Escape '94

Jane Campion
An Angel at My Table '89
The Piano '93
Sweetie '89

Carlo Campogalliani
Goliath and the Barbarians '60
Son of Samson '62
Ursus in the Valley of the Lions '62

Michael Campus
The Education of Sonny Carson '74
Mack '73
The Passover Plot '75
Zero Population Growth '72

Marcel Camus
Black Orpheus '58
Where the Sky Begins '84

Mario Camus
The Holy Innocents '84

Joseph Cane
Oh Susannah '38

Richard Cannistraro
Violated '84

Dyan Cannon
The End of Innocence '90

Yakima Canutt
G-Men Never Forget '48
Oklahoma Badlands '48

Louis Capauno
Executioner of Venice '63

Giorgio Capitani
I Hate Blondes '83
Lobster for Breakfast '82
The Ruthless Four '70

Bernt Capra
Mindwalk: A Film for Passionate Thinkers '91

Frank Capra
Arsenic and Old Lace '44
Battle of China '44
The Battle of Russia '44
The Bitter Tea of General Yen '33
Broadway Bill '34
Here Comes the Groom '51
A Hole in the Head '59
It Happened One Night '34
It's a Wonderful Life '46
Lady for a Day '33
Lost Horizon '37
Meet John Doe '41
Mr. Deeds Goes to Town '36
Mr. Smith Goes to Washington '39
Platinum Blonde '31
Pocketful of Miracles '61
Prelude to War '42
State of the Union '48
Strong Man '26
That Certain Thing '28
You Can't Take It with You '38

Luigi Capuano
Cold Steel for Tortuga '65
Marauder '63
The Snake Hunter Strangler '66
Tiger of the Seven Seas '62

Leo Carax
Boy Meets Girl '84

Dacosta Carayan
The Brave Bunch '70

Costa Carayiannis
Land of the Minotaur '77

Lamar Card
The Clones '73

Hernan Cardenas
Island Claw '80

Jack Cardiff
Dark of the Sun '68
The Freakmaker '73
The Girl on a Motorcycle '68
My Geisha '62

Roger Cardinal
Malarek '89

Rene Cardona, Sr.
Santa Claus '59
Wrestling Women vs. the Aztec Ape '62
Wrestling Women vs. the Aztec Mummy '59

Rene Cardona, Jr.
Beaks: The Movie '87
Night of a Thousand Cats '72
Night of the Bloody Apes '68
Robinson Crusoe & the Tiger '72
Tintorera...Tiger Shark '72
The Treasure of the Amazon '84

J.S. Cardone
A Climate for Killing '91
Shadowzone '90
The Slayer '82
The Slayer/The Scalps '82
Thunder Alley '85

John Cardos
The Dark '79
Day Time Ended '80
The Female Bunch '69
Kingdom of the Spiders '77
Mutant '83
Outlaw of Gor '87
Skeleton Coast '89

Topper Carew
Talkin' Dirty After Dark '91

Gilles Carle
In Trouble '67
Maria Chapdelaine '84
The Red Half-Breed '70

Carlo Carlei
Flight of the Innocent '93

Lewis John Carlino
Class '83
The Great Santini '80
The Sailor Who Fell from Grace with the Sea '76

Henning Carlsen
The Wolf at the Door '87
A World of Strangers '62

Don Carmody
Surrogate '88

Marcel Carne
Bizarre Bizarre '39
Children of Paradise '44
La Merveilleuse Visite '74
Le Jour Se Leve '39
Les Visiteurs du Soir '42

Marc Caro
Delicatessen '92

Glenn Gordon Caron
Clean and Sober '88
Wilder Napalm '93

Horace Carpenter
Arizona Kid '39

John Carpenter
Assault on Precinct 13 '76
Big Trouble in Little China '86
Body Bags '93
Christine '84
Dark Star '74
Elvis: The Movie '79
Escape from New York '81
The Fog '78
Halloween '78
Memoirs of an Invisible Man '92
Prince of Darkness '87
Starman '84
They Live '88
The Thing '82

Stephen Carpenter
Dorm That Dripped Blood '82
The Kindred '87
The Power '80

Fabio Carpi
Basileus Quartet '82

Adrian Carr
Now and Forever '82

Bernard Carr
Curley '47
Fabulous Joe '47

John Carr
Death Wish Club '83

Terry Carr
Welcome to 18 '87

Thomas Carr
Captain Scarlett '53
Dino '57
Guns of Justice '50
Jesse James Rides Again '47
Marshal of Heldorado '50
Pirates of the High Seas '50
Wanted: Dead or Alive '59

David Carradine
Americana '81

Anthony Carras
Fearmaker '89

Enrique Carreras
Somos Novios '68

Michael Carreras
Call Him Mr. Shatter '74
Maniac '63

Rick Carrier
Strangers in the City '62

Larry Carroll
Ghostwarrior '86

Robert Martin Carroll
Sonny Boy '87

Willard Carroll
The Runestone '91

John Paddy Carstairs
Made in Heaven '52
Saint in London '39
Sleeping Car to Trieste '45
Tony Draws a Horse '51
Trouble in Store '53

Michael Cartel
Runaway Nightmare '84

Bruce Carter
Laser Moon '92

John N. Carter
Zombie Island Massacre '84

Karen Carter
The Big Bust Out '73

Peter Carter
High Ballin' '78
Highpoint '80
Intruder Within '81
Kavik the Wolf Dog '84
Klondike Fever '79
Rituals '79

Thomas Carter
Miami Vice '84
Swing Kids '93

Steve Carver
Big Bad Mama '74
Bulletproof '88
Drum '76
An Eye for an Eye '81
Jocks '87
Lone Wolf McQuade '83
Naked Warriors '73
Oceans of Fire '86
River of Death '90
Steel '80

Ron Casden
Campus Man '87

Kimberly Casey
Born Killer '89
Deadly Dancer '90

Richard Casey
Hellbent '90

Horror House on Highway 5 '86

George S. Casorati
Summer Affair '79

Henry Cass
Blood of the Vampire '58
The Hand '60
Last Holiday '50

John Cassavetes
Big Trouble '86
A Child is Waiting '63
Gloria '80
The Killing of a Chinese Bookie '76
Love Streams '84
Opening Night '77
A Woman Under the Influence '74

Richard Cassidy
Bloodshed '83
Crazed '82

Alexander Cassini
Star Time '92

Renato Castellani
Romeo and Juliet '54

Enzo G. Castellari
Any Gun Can Play '67
Cold Eyes of Fear '70s
Day of the Cobra '84
Escape from the Bronx '85
Go Kill and Come Back '68
High Crime '73
Lightblast '85
Loves & Times of Scaramouche '76
1990: The Bronx Warriors '83
Sinbad of the Seven Seas '89
Warriors of the Wasteland '83

Nardo Castillo
The Gunrunner '84

Alien Castle
Desire and Hell at Sunset Motel '92

Nick Castle
The Boy Who Could Fly '86
Dennis the Menace '93
The Last Starfighter '84
Tag: The Assassination Game '82
Tap '89

William Castle
Americano '55
Conquest of Cochise '53
House on Haunted Hill '58
The Law Rides Again '43
The Night Walker '64
Strait-Jacket '64
13 Ghosts '60

William Allen Castleman
Bummer '73
Johnny Firecloud '75

Hoite C. Caston
Dirt Bike Kid '86

Claude Castravelli
Evil Judgement '85

Victor Manuel Castro
Esta Noche Cena Pancho '87

Joe Catalanotto
French Quarter Undercover '85
Terror in the Swamp '85

Gilbert Cates
The Affair '73
Backfire '88
Burning Rage '84
Consenting Adult '85
Goldilocks & the Three Bears '83
Hobson's Choice '83
I Never Sang For My Father '70
The Last Married Couple in America '80

Oh, God! Book 2 '80
One Summer Love '76
The Promise '78
Summer Wishes, Winter Dreams '73
To All My Friends on Shore '71

Don Cato
Dixie Lanes '88

Michael Caton-Jones
Doc Hollywood '91
Memphis Belle '90
Scandal '89
This Boy's Life '93

Michael Caulfield
Gallagher's Travels '87

Alberto Cavalcanti
Dead of Night '45
Nicholas Nickleby '46

Alain Cavalier
Therese '86

Liliana Cavani
The Berlin Affair '85
Beyond Obsession '82
Francesco '89
The Night Porter '74

Vladimir Cech
New Pastures '62

Fernando Cerchio
Nefertiti, Queen of the Nile '64

Norman A. Cerf
Jungle Hell '55

Tonino Cervi
Today We Kill, Tomorrow We Die '71

Gerban Ceth
Counter Measures '80s

Claude Chabrol
The Blood of Others '84
Blood Relatives '77
Bluebeard '63
Club Extinction '89
The Cousins '59
The Cry of the Owl '92
Dirty Hands '76
High Heels '72
The Horse of Pride '80
La Rupture '70
Le Beau Serge '58
Le Boucher '69
Les Biches '68
Madame Bovary '91
A Piece of Pleasure '70
Six in Paris '68
The Story of Women '88
Ten Days Wonder '72
This Man Must Die '70
Twist '78
Violette '78
Wedding in Blood '74

Don Chaffey
Casino '80
C.H.O.M.P.S. '79
Creatures the World Forgot '70
Fourth Wish '75
The Gift of Love '90
The Graveyard '74
Greyfriars Bobby '61
The Horse Without a Head '63
Jason and the Argonauts '63
Magic of Lassie '78
A Matter of WHO '62
Pete's Dragon '77
The Prisoner: Arrival '68
Ride a Wild Pony '75
Secret Agent '64
The Three Lives of Thomasina '63

Karen Chakhnazarov
Jazzman '84

P. Chalong
H-Bomb '71
In Gold We Trust '91

Gower Champion
Bank Shot '74

Gregg Champion
The Cowboy Way '94
Short Time '90

Jackie Chan
The Armour of God '86
Jackie Chan's Police Force '85
New Fist of Fury '85

Philip Chan
Tongs: An American Nightmare '88

Tony Chan
Combination Platter '93

Wallace Chan
Clash of the Ninja '86

Cheung Wo Chang
The Association '80s

Li Chao
Cantonen Iron Kung Fu '70s

Charlie Chaplin
The Adventurer '17
The Best of Chaplin '18
Burlesque of Carmen '16
The Champion/His New Job '15
The Chaplin Revue '58
Charlie Chaplin Cavalcade, Mutual Studios Shorts '16
Charlie Chaplin Centennial Collection '10s
Charlie Chaplin Festival '17
Charlie Chaplin: Night at the Show '15
Charlie Chaplin: Rare Chaplin '15
Charlie Chaplin...Our Hero! '15
Charlie Chaplin's Keystone Comedies #3 '14
Charlie Chaplin's Keystone Comedies #5 '14
The Circus '19
City Lights '31
The Count '16
Count/Adventurer '17
The Cure '17
Easy Street '16
The Fireman '16
The Floorwalker '17
The Floorwalker/By the Sea '15
The Gold Rush '25
The Great Dictator '40
His Prehistoric Past/The Bank '15
The Immigrant '17
The Kid '21
The Kid/Idle Class '21
A King in New York '57
The Knockout/Dough and Dynamite '14
Limelight '52
Modern Times '36
Monsieur Verdoux '47
The Rink '16
Three Charlies and One Phoney! '18
The Vagabond '16
Woman of Paris/Sunnyside '23
Work/Police '16

Sydney Chaplin
The Knockout/Dough and Dynamite '14

Matthew Chapman
Heart of Midnight '89
Hussy '80
Slow Burn '86
Strangers Kiss '83

Michael Chapman
All the Right Moves '83
The Clan of the Cave Bear '86

Robert Chappell
Diamond Run '90

Petr Chardynin
Early Russian Cinema, Vol. 5: Chardynin's Pushkin '13

Erik Charell
Congress Dances '31

Robert Charlton
No Big Deal '83

Henri Charr
Illegal Entry: Formula for Fear '93

Richard Chase
Hell's Angels Forever '83

Etienne Chatiliez
Life Is a Long Quiet River '88
Tatie Danielle '91

Louis Chaudet
Fighting Jack '26
Tentacles of the North '26

Amin Q. Chaudhri
Tiger Warsaw '87
An Unremarkable Life '89

Jaime Chavarri
I'm the One You're Looking For '88

Jeremiah S. Chechik
Benny & Joon '93
National Lampoon's Christmas Vacation '89

Douglas Cheek
C.H.U.D. '84

Ara Chekmayan
Forever James Dean '88

Peter Chelsom
Hear My Song '91

Chen Chen
The Chinatown Kid '78

Yeung Ching Chen
The Two Great Cavaliers '73

Pierre Chenal
Crime and Punishment '35
Man from Nowhere '37
Native Son '51

Tommy Cheng
Ninja: American Warrior '90
Ninja Death Squad '87

Patrice Chereau
L'Homme Blesse '83

John Cherry
Ernest Rides Again '93

John R. Cherry, III
Dr. Otto & the Riddle of the Gloom Beam '86
Ernest Goes to Camp '87
Ernest Goes to Jail '90
Ernest Saves Christmas '88
Ernest Scared Stupid '91

George Cheseboro
Wolf Blood '25

Lionel Chetwynd
Hanoi Hilton '87

Alfred Cheung
Paper Marriage '88

Alton Cheung
Kickboxer the Champion '91

Lu Chia-Liang
Challenge of the Masters '89
Shaolin Executioner '80s

Yvan Chiffre
President's Target '93

Stephen Chiodo
Killer Klowns from Outer Space '88

Marvin J. Chomsky
Anastasia: The Mystery of Anna '86
Attica '80
Billionaire Boys Club '87
The Brotherhood of the Rose '89

The Deliberate Stranger '86
Evel Knievel '72
Fireball Forward '72
Holocaust '78
Inside the Third Reich '82
Little Ladies of the Night '77
Murph the Surf '75
Nairobi Affair '88
Robert Kennedy and His Times '90
The Shaming '71
Tank '83

Thomas Chong
Cheech and Chong: Still Smokin' '83
Cheech and Chong's Next Movie '80
Cheech and Chong's Nice Dreams '81
Cheech and Chong's, The Corsican Brothers '84
Far Out Man '89

Joyce Chopra
The Lemon Sisters '90
Murder in New Hampshire: The Pamela Smart Story '91
Smooth Talk '85

Elie Chouraqui
Love Songs '85
Man on Fire '87

Raymond Chow
When Taekwondo Strikes '83

Nathaniel Christian
California Casanova '89
Club Fed '90

Roger Christian
The Sender '82
Starship '87

Benjamin Christiansen
Mockery '27
Witchcraft Through the Ages '22

Jean Christopher
One-Eyed Soldiers '67

Yeh Yung Chu
Fists of Dragons '69

Byron Ross Chudnow
The Amazing Dobermans '76
Daring Dobermans '73
The Doberman Gang '72

Grigori Chukrai
Ballad of a Soldier '60

Mario Ciano
Fighting Fists of Shanghai Joe '65
Terror of Rome Against the Son of Hercules '64

Gerard Ciccoritti
Graveyard Shift '87
Psycho Girls '86
Understudy: The Graveyard Shift 2 '88

Matt Cimber
The Black Six '74
Butterfly '82
Candy Tangerine Man '75
Fake Out '82
Hundra '85
Lady Cocoa '75
Single Room Furnished '68
Time to Die '83
Witch Who Came from the Sea '76
Yellow Hair & the Fortress of Gold '84

Michael Cimino
The Deer Hunter '78
Desperate Hours '90
Heaven's Gate '81
The Sicilian '87
Thunderbolt & Lightfoot '74
Year of the Dragon '85

Grigorij Ciukhrai
Life is Beautiful '79

Rene Clair
A Nous la Liberte '31
And Then There Were None '45
The Crazy Ray '22
Entr'acte '24
Forever and a Day '43
The Ghost Goes West '36
I Married a Witch '42
Italian Straw Hat '27
Le Million '31
Quatorze Juliet '32
Under the Roofs of Paris '29

Bob Clampett
Bugs Bunny Superstar '75
Looney Looney Looney Bugs Bunny Movie '81

B.D. Clark
Galaxy of Terror '81

Barry Clark
Bimini Code '84

Bob (Benjamin) Clark
Black Christmas '75
Children Shouldn't Play with Dead Things '72
A Christmas Story '83
Deathdream '72
From the Hip '86
It Runs In the Family '94
Loose Cannons '90
Murder by Decree '79
Porky's '82
Porky's 2: The Next Day '83
Rhinestone '84
Tribute '80
Turk 182! '85

Bruce Clark
The Naked Angels '69
Ski Bum '75

Colbert Clark
Fighting with Kit Carson '33
Mystery Squadron '33
Whispering Shadow '33
Wolf Dog '33

Duane Clark
Bitter Harvest '93
Shaking the Tree '92

Greydon Clark
Angel's Brigade '79
Bad Bunch '76
Black Shampoo '76
Dance Macabre '91
Final Justice '84
The Forbidden Dance '90
Hi-Riders '77
Joy Sticks '83
Killer Instinct '92
The Return '80
Russian Roulette '93
Satan's Cheerleaders '77
Skinheads: The Second Coming of Hate '88
The Uninvited '88
Wacko '83

James B. Clark
And Now Miguel '66
A Dog of Flanders '59
Flipper '63
Island of the Blue Dolphins '64
Misty '61
My Side of the Mountain '69

Jim Clark
Madhouse '74
Rentadick '72
Think Dirty '70

Lawrence Gordon Clark
Jamaica Inn '82
Monkey Boy '90
Romance on the Orient Express '89

Les Clark
Sleeping Beauty '59

Matt Clark
Da '88

Richard Clark
Dr. Hackenstein '88

Ron Clark
The Funny Farm '82

Warren Clark
Inside Edge '92

William Clark
The Goodbye Bird '93

Alan Clarke
Rita, Sue & Bob Too '87
Scum '79

James Kenelm Clarke
Funny Money '82
Going Undercover '88
The House on Straw Hill '76

Robert Clarke
Hideous Sun Demon '59

Shirley Clarke
The Connection '61

Stephen Clarkson
Death Goes to School '53

James Clavell
The Last Valley '71
To Sir, with Love '67

Bob Claver
Jaws of Satan '81

William Claxton
Fangs of the Wild '54

Jack Clayton
The Great Gatsby '74
The Lonely Passion of Judith Hearne '87
Room at the Top '59
Something Wicked This Way Comes '83

John Clayton
Summerdog '78

Tom Clegg
Any Man's Death '90
A Casualty of War '90
Children of the Full Moon '84
The Inside Man '84
McVicar '80
Stroke of Midnight '90

John Clein
Keep Punching '39

Brian Clemens
Captain Kronos: Vampire Hunter '74

William Clemens
Nancy Drew, Reporter '39

Dick Clement
Bullshot '83
Catch Me a Spy '71
Porridge '91
Water '85

Rene Clement
And Hope to Die '72
The Day and the Hour '63
The Deadly Trap '71
Forbidden Games '52
Gervaise '56
Is Paris Burning? '68
Joy House '64
Rider on the Rain '70
Wanted: Babysitter '75

Ron Clements
Aladdin '92
The Great Mouse Detective '86
The Little Mermaid '89

Max Cleven
Night Stalker '87

Graeme Clifford
The Boy Who Left Home to Find Out About the Shivers '81
Burke & Wills '85
Deception '92
Frances '82
Gleaming the Cube '89
Little Red Riding Hood '83
The Turn of the Screw '89

Elmer Clifton
Assassin of Youth '35
Captured in Chinatown '35
Custer's Last Stand '36
Cyclone of the Saddle '35
Dead or Alive '41
Down to the Sea in Ships '22
Fighting Caballero '35
Frontier Law '43
Gangsters of the Frontier '44
Guns of the Law '44
The Judge '49
Law of the Texan '38
Let 'er Go Gallegher '28
Marked for Murder '45
Roaring Speedboats '37
Seven Doors to Death '44
Streets of Sin '49
Youth Aflame '59

Paul E. Clinco
Death Magic '92

Eddie Cline
The Bank Dick '40
Cops/One Week '22
Cowboy Millionaire '35
Dude Ranger '34
Hawaii Calls '38
Hook, Line and Sinker '30
My Little Chickadee '40
Never Give a Sucker an Even Break '41
Peck's Bad Boy '34
Peck's Bad Boy with the Circus '38
Private Buckaroo '42
Snuffy Smith, Yard Bird '42
Three Ages '23
The Villain Still Pursued Her '41

Maurice Cloche
Monsieur Vincent '48

Hans Peter Cloos
Germany in Autumn '78

Robert Clouse
The Amsterdam Kill '78
The Big Brawl '80
Black Belt Jones '74
China O'Brien '88
China O'Brien 2 '89
Darker than Amber '70
Deadly Eyes '82
Enter the Dragon '73
Force '81
Game of Death '79
Gymkata '85
Ironheart '92
The Pack '77
The Ultimate Warrior '75

Henri-Georges Clouzot
Diabolique '55
Jenny Lamour '47
Le Corbeau '43
Manon '50
Wages of Fear '55

E.B. Clucher
Crime Busters '78
Go for It '83
The Odd Squad '86
They Call Me Trinity '72
Trinity is Still My Name '75

Rick Cluchey
The Cage '90

Harold Clurman
Deadline at Dawn '46

Craig Clyde
The Legend of Wolf Mountain '92
Little Heroes '91

Franklin Coates
Jesse James Under the Black Flag '21

Lewis (Luigi Cozzi) Coates
Alien Contamination '81
Black Cat '90
Hercules '83
Hercules 2 '85
Star Crash '78

David Cobham
Tales of the Klondike: Race for Number One '87

Glenn Coburn
Bloodsuckers from Outer Space '83

Stacy Cochran
My New Gun '92

Jean Cocteau
Beauty and the Beast '46
The Blood of a Poet '30
Orpheus '49
The Testament of Orpheus '59

Fred Coe
A Thousand Clowns '65

Wayne Coe
Grim Prairie Tales '89

Joel Coen
Barton Fink '91
Blood Simple '85
The Hudsucker Proxy '93
Miller's Crossing '90
Raising Arizona '87

Nevill Coghill
Doctor Faustus '68

Dan Cohen
Madman '79

David Cohen
Hollywood Zap '86

Gary P. Cohen
Video Violence '87
Video Violence Part 2...The Exploitation! '87

Gerry Cohen
It's a Bundyful Life '92

Herman Cohen
Crocodile '81

Howard R. Cohen
Deathstalker 4: Clash of the Titans '92
Saturday the 14th '81
Saturday the 14th Strikes Back '88
Space Raiders '83
Time Trackers '88

Larry Cohen
The Ambulance '90
Black Caesar '73
Deadly Illusion '87
God Told Me To '76
Hell Up in Harlem '73
Housewife '72
It's Alive '74
It's Alive 2: It Lives Again '78
It's Alive 3: Island of the Alive '87
Perfect Strangers '84
The Private Files of J. Edgar Hoover '77
Q (The Winged Serpent) '82
Return to Salem's Lot '87
Special Effects '85
The Stuff '85
Wicked Stepmother '89

Martin B. Cohen
Rebel Rousers '69

Rob Cohen
Dragon: The Bruce Lee Story '93
Scandalous '84
A Small Circle of Friends '80

S.E. Cohen
Martial Law '90

Thomas A. Cohen
Massive Retaliation '85

Randolph Cohlan
Night Shadow '90

Michael Cohn
Interceptor '92

Cyril Coke
Pride and Prejudice '85

Harley Cokliss
Black Moon Rising '86
Malone '87
Warlords of the 21st Century '82

Sidney Cole
Train of Events '49

Tristan De Vere Cole
The Dive '89

John David Coles
The Good Fight '92
Rising Son '90
Signs of Life '89

Duilio Coletti
Lure of the Sila '49

Giuseppe Colizzi
Ace High '68
All the Way, Boys '73
Boot Hill '69

Richard A. Colla
Battlestar Galactica '78
Blind Witness '89
Don't Look Back: The Story of Leroy "Satchel" Paige '81
Fuzz '72
Naked Lie '89
Olly Olly Oxen Free '78
The Prize Pulitzer '89

Jeanne Collachia
Odd Birds '85

Cyril Collard
Les Nuits Fauves '92

Robert Collector
Red Heat '85

James F. Collier
Beyond the Next Mountain '87
China Cry '91
Cry from the Mountain '85
The Hiding Place '75
Joni '79

Bob Collins
The Bronx Executioner '86

Boon Collins
Abducted '86
Spirit of the Eagle '90

Edward Collins
Evil Town '87

Gunther Collins
Jud '71

Lewis Collins
Brand of Hate '34
Gun Law '33
The Man from Hell '34
Sing Sing Nights '35
Trouble Busters '33

Lewis D. Collins
The Adventures of the Flying Cadets '44
The Fighting Redhead '50
Heading for Heaven '47
Jungle Goddess '49
Killer Dill '47
Lost City of the Jungle '45

Master Key '44
Mystery of the Riverboat '44

Robert Collins
Gideon's Trumpet '80
J. Edgar Hoover '87
The Life and Assassination of the Kingfish '76
Mafia Princess '86
Our Family Business '81

Peter Collinson
African Rage '78
Dressed for Death '74
Earthling '80
Fright '71
The House on Garibaldi Street '79
The Italian Job '69
Sell Out '76
Spiral Staircase '75
Ten Little Indians '75
Tomorrow Never Comes '77

Walter Colmes
Accomplice '46
Identity Unknown '45
The Woman Who Came Back '45

Fernando Colombo
Skyline '84

Carl Colpaert
Delusion '91
In the Aftermath: Angels Never Sleep '87

Chris Columbus
Adventures in Babysitting '87
Heartbreak Hotel '88
Home Alone '90
Home Alone 2: Lost in New York '92
Mrs. Doubtfire '93
Only the Lonely '91

Luigi Comencini
Heidi '52
Misunderstood '87
Till Marriage Do Us Part '74

Lance Comfort
The Courageous Mr. Penn '41
The Great Armored Car Swindle '64
Great Day '46
Hotel Reserve '44

Don Como
Aliens from Spaceship Earth '77
Unknown Powers '80

J.C. Compton
Buckeye and Blue '87

Richard Compton
Angels Die Hard '84
Deadman's Curve '78
Macon County Line '74
Maniac '77
Return to Macon County '75
Super Force '90
Wild Times '79

Jeff Conaway
Bikini Summer 2 '92

Bill Condon
Dead in the Water '91
Murder 101 '91
Sister, Sister '87
White Lie '91

John Coney
Sun Ra & His Intergalactic Solar Arkestra: Space is the Place '74

Maurice Conn
Swing It, Professor '37

Nicole Conn
Claire of the Moon '92

W. Merle Connell
The Devil's Sleep '51
Test Tube Babies '48

Marc Connelly
Green Pastures '36

W.A. Conner
Cocaine Fiends '36

Raymond Connon
Swing It, Sailor! '37

Carey Connor
Fall from Innocence '88

Kevin Connor
At the Earth's Core '76
Choice of Weapons '76
Diana: Her True Story '93
From Beyond the Grave '73
Goliath Awaits '81
Great Expectations '89
The Hollywood Detective '89
House Where Evil Dwells '82
Iran: Days of Crisis '91
The Land That Time Forgot '75
The Lion of Africa '87
Motel Hell '80
The People That Time Forgot '77
Sunset Grill '92

Claude Conrad
Birthday Boy '85

Mikel Conrad
The Flying Saucer '50

Patrick Conrad
Mascara '87

Robert Conrad
Bandits '73
Crossfire '67

William Conrad
Side Show '84

Richard Conte
Operation Cross Eagles '69

Therese Conte
Chasing Dreams '81

James A. Contner
The Cover Girl Murders '93
Hitler's Daughter '90
The Return of Eliot Ness '91
The Ten Million Dollar Getaway '91

Bert Convy
Weekend Warriors '86

Gary Conway
Sara Dane '81

Jack Conway
Boom Town '40
Dragon Seed '44
The Girl from Missouri '34
Honky Tonk '41
The Hucksters '47
Julia Misbehaves '48
Let Freedom Ring '39
Libeled Lady '36
Love Crazy '41
Our Modern Maidens '29
Red Headed Woman '32
Saratoga '37
A Tale of Two Cities '35
Tarzan and His Mate '34
Too Hot to Handle '38
The Unholy Three '30
Viva Villa! '34

James L. Conway
Donner Pass: The Road to Survival '84
The Fall of the House of Usher '80
Hangar 18 '80
The Incredible Rocky Mountain Race '77
The Last of the Mohicans '85

Rif Coogan
The Invisible Maniac '90
Psycho Cop 2 '94

Bruce Cook, Jr.
Husbands, Wives, Money, and Murder '86
Nightwish '89

Fielder Cook
A Big Hand for the Little Lady '66
The Hideaways '73
Homecoming: A Christmas Story '71
I Know Why the Caged Bird Sings '79
Judge Horton and the Scottsboro Boys '76
Love Affair: The Eleanor & Lou Gehrig Story '77
Miles to Go Before I Sleep '74
Patterns '56
Seize the Day '86

Phillip Cook
Invader '91
Star Quest '89

Alan Cooke
Nadia '84

Tony Cookson
And You Thought Your Parents Were Weird! '91

Martha Coolidge
Angie '94
Bare Essentials '91
Crazy in Love '92
Joy of Sex '84
Lost in Yonkers '93
Plain Clothes '88
Rambling Rose '91
Real Genius '85
Valley Girl '83

Buddy Cooper
The Mutilator '85

Ellen Cooper
Cave Girls '82

George Cooper
The Shadow '36

Jackie Cooper
Izzy & Moe '85
Leave 'Em Laughing '81
Marathon '80
The Night They Saved Christmas '87
Rainbow '78
Rodeo Girl '80
Rosie: The Rosemary Clooney Story '82
Sex and the Single Parent '82
White Mama '80

Peter H. Cooper
Ordinary Heroes '85

Stuart Cooper
Disappearance '81
The Long, Hot Summer '86
Payoff '91
Rubdown '93

Christopher Coppola
Deadfall '93
Dracula's Widow '88

Francis Ford Coppola
Apocalypse Now '79
Battle Beyond the Sun '63
The Bellboy and the Playgirls '62
Bram Stoker's Dracula '92
The Conversation '74
The Cotton Club '84
Dementia 13 '63
Finian's Rainbow '68
Gardens of Stone '87
The Godfather '72
The Godfather 1902-1959: The Complete Epic '81
The Godfather, Part 2 '74
The Godfather, Part 3 '90
New York Stories '89
One from the Heart '82

The Outsiders '83
Peggy Sue Got Married '86
The Rain People '69
Rip van Winkle '85
Rumble Fish '83
Tonight for Sure '61
Tucker: The Man and His Dream '88
You're a Big Boy Now '66

Gregory Corarito
Delinquent School Girls '84
Wanda, The Sadistic Hypnotist '67

Gerard Corbiau
The Music Teacher '88

Bruno Corbucci
Aladdin '86
Cop in Blue Jeans '78
Miami Supercops '85

Sergio Corbucci
The Con Artists '80
Django '68
Hellbenders '67
Minnesota Clay '65
Navajo Joe '67
Odds and Evens '78
Sonny and Jed '73
Super Fuzz '81

Bill Corcoran
Sherlock Holmes and the Incident at Victoria Falls '91

Nick Corea
Archer: The Fugitive from the Empire '81
The Incredible Hulk Returns '88

Roger Corman
Apache Woman '55
Atlas '60
Bloody Mama '70
A Bucket of Blood '59
Carnival Rock '57
Creature from the Haunted Sea '60
Day the World Ended '55
The Fall of the House of Usher '60
Frankenstein Unbound '90
Gas-s-s-s! '70
The Gunslinger '56
The Haunted Palace '63
I, Mobster '58
It Conquered the World '56
The Last Woman on Earth '61
Little Miss Millions '93
Little Shop of Horrors '60
Machine Gun Kelly '58
Masque of the Red Death '65
Masque of the Red Death/Premature Burial '65
The Pit and the Pendulum '61
Premature Burial '62
The Raven '63
Rock All Night '57
The St. Valentine's Day Massacre '67
Shame '61
She Gods of Shark Reef '56
Sorority Girl '57
Swamp Women '55
Tales of Terror '62
Teenage Caveman '58
The Terror '63
Tomb of Ligeia '64
Tower of London '62
The Trip '67
The Undead '57
The Wasp Woman '59
The Wild Angels '66
X: The Man with X-Ray Eyes '63

Alain Corneau
Choice of Arms '83
Tous les Matins du Monde '92

Henry Cornelius
Genevieve '53
I Am a Camera '55
Passport to Pimlico '49

John Cornell
Almost an Angel '90
Crocodile Dundee 2 '88

Hubert Cornfield
Angel Baby '61
The Night of the Following Day '69
Plunder Road '57
Pressure Point '62

Stephen Cornwell
Killing Streets '91
Philadelphia Experiment 2 '93

Alfonso Corona
Deathstalker 3 '89

Eugene Corr
Desert Bloom '86

Charles Correll
Deadly Desire '91
Writer's Block '91

Richard Correll
Ski Patrol '89

Lloyd Corrigan
Dancing Pirate '36
Daughter of the Dragon '31

Bud Cort
Ted & Venus '93

Michael Cort
Alien Women '69

Frederic Corte
Creature of the Walking Dead '60

Fernando Cortes
Los Tres Calaveras '64

Bill Cosby
Bill Cosby, Himself '81

Don A. Coscarelli
Beastmaster '82
Phantasm '79
Phantasm II '88
Survival Quest '89

George P. Cosmatos
The Cassandra Crossing '76
Cobra '86
Escape to Athena '79
Leviathan '89
Massacre in Rome '73
Of Unknown Origin '83
Rambo: First Blood, Part 2 '85
Restless '72
Tombstone '93

Mario Costa
Gladiator of Rome '63
Rough Justice '87

Mary Costa
Pirate Warrior '64

Constantin Costa-Gavras
Betrayed '88
Hanna K. '83
Missing '82
Music Box '89
State of Siege '73
Z '69

Kevin Costner
Dances with Wolves '90

Peter Cotes
The Young and the Guilty '58

Manny Coto
Cover-Up '91
Dr. Giggles '92
Playroom '90

Vittorio Cottafavi
Goliath and the Dragon '61
Hercules and the Captive Women '63

John Cotter
Mountain Family Robinson '79

Jack Couffer
Living Free '72
Nikki, the Wild Dog of the North '61

Ian Coughlan
Alison's Birthday '79

Bill Couturie
Dear America: Letters Home from Vietnam '88

Hil Covington
Adventures in Spying '92

William J. Cowan
Oliver Twist '33

Noel Coward
In Which We Serve '43

Alex Cox
Repo Man '83
Sid & Nancy '86
Straight to Hell '87
Walker '87

Neil Cox
Once Upon a Midnight Scary '90
Roommate '84

Paul Cox
Cactus '86
Kostas '79
Lonely Hearts '82
Man of Flowers '84
My First Wife '84
Vincent: The Life and Death of Vincent van Gogh '87
A Woman's Tale '92

Arthur Crabtree
Dear Murderer '47
Fiend Without a Face '58

Bill Crain
Kid from Not-So-Big '78
Midnight Fear '90

William Crain
Blacula '72
Dr. Black, Mr. Hyde '76

Massey Cramer
Demon Hunter '88

Ross Cramer
Riding High '78

Barry Crane
Charlotte Forten's Mission: Experiment in Freedom '85

Kenneth Crane
The Manster '59
Monster from Green Hell '58
When Hell Broke Loose '58

Wes Craven
Deadly Blessing '81
Deadly Friend '86
The Hills Have Eyes '77
The Hills Have Eyes, Part 2 '84
Invitation to Hell '84
Last House on the Left '72
A Nightmare on Elm Street '84
The People Under the Stairs '91
The Serpent and the Rainbow '87
Shocker '89
Summer of Fear '78
Swamp Thing '82

Wayne Crawford
Crime Lords '91

Francis Creighton
The Malibu Beach Vampires '91

Lol Creme
The Lunatic '92

Richard Crenna
Better Late Than Never '79

Alfredo B. Crevenna
The New Invisible Man '58

Charles Crichton
Against the Wind '48
The Battle of the Sexes '60
Dead of Night '45
A Fish Called Wanda '88
Hue and Cry '47
The Lavender Hill Mob '51
Train of Events '49

Michael Crichton
Coma '78
The Great Train Robbery '79
Looker '81
Physical Evidence '89
Pursuit '72
Runaway '84
Westworld '73

Donald Crisp
The Navigator '24
Stand and Deliver '28
Sunny Side Up '28

Armando Crispino
Autopsy '78
Commandos '73

George Cristallini
You're Jinxed, Friend, You've Met Sacramento '70

Donald Crombie
Caddie '81
The Irishman '78
Killing of Angel Street '81
Kitty and the Bagman '82

John Cromwell
Abe Lincoln in Illinois '40
Algiers '38
Ann Vickers '33
Anna and the King of Siam '46
Dance of Life '29
Dead Reckoning '47
The Enchanted Cottage '45
The Goddess '58
I Dream Too Much '35
In Name Only '39
Little Lord Fauntleroy '36
Made for Each Other '39
Of Human Bondage '34
Prisoner of Zenda '37
The Racket '51
Since You Went Away '44
So Ends Our Night '41
Son of Fury '42
Spitfire '34
Tom Sawyer '30
Vice Squad '31

George Crone
Get That Girl '32

David Cronenberg
The Brood '79
Dead Ringers '88
Dead Zone '83
Fast Company '78
The Fly '86
M. Butterfly '93
Naked Lunch '91
Rabid '77
Scanners '81
They Came from Within '75
Videodrome '83

Alan Crosland
The Beloved Rogue '27
Don Juan '26
The Jazz Singer '27

William Forest Crouch
Reet, Petite and Gone '47

Avery Crounse
Eyes of Fire '84
The Invisible Kid '88

Dean Crow
Backwoods '87

Cameron Crowe
Say Anything '89
Singles '92

Christopher Crowe
Off Limits '88
Whispers in the Dark '92

Tom Cruise
Fallen Angels 1 '93

James Cruze
The Covered Wagon '23
The Great Gabbo '29
Hawthorne of the USA '19
I Cover the Waterfront '33
Mr. Skitch '33
Old Ironsides '26
The Pony Express '25
The Roaring Road '19
The Wrong Road '37

Billy Crystal
Mr. Saturday Night '92

Alfonso Cuaron
Fallen Angels 1 '93

George Cukor
Adam's Rib '50
Bhowani Junction '56
A Bill of Divorcement '32
Born Yesterday '50
Camille '36
David Copperfield '35
Dinner at Eight '33
A Double Life '47
Gaslight '44
Heller in Pink Tights '60
Holiday '38
It Should Happen to You '54
Justine '69
Les Girls '57
Let's Make Love '60
A Life of Her Own '50
Little Women '33
Love Among the Ruins '75
My Fair Lady '64
Pat and Mike '52
The Philadelphia Story '40
Rich and Famous '81
Romeo and Juliet '36
Song Without End '60
A Star Is Born '54
Susan and God '40
Sylvia Scarlett '35
Travels with My Aunt '72
Two-Faced Woman '41
What Price Hollywood? '32
A Woman's Face '41
The Women '39

Mark Cullingham
Cinderella '84
Dead on the Money '91
Gryphon '88

Bill Cummings
Bad Attitude '93

Howard Cummings
Courtship '87

Irving Cummings
Broken Hearts of Broadway '23
Curly Top '35
Double Dynamite '51
Down Argentine Way '40
Everything Happens at Night '39
Flesh and Blood '22
Just Around the Corner '38
Little Miss Broadway '38
Louisiana Purchase '41
The Poor Little Rich Girl '36
Springtime in the Rockies '42
Sweet Rosie O'Grady '43
Vogues of 1938 '37

James Cummins
The Bone Yard '90

Richard Cunha
Frankenstein's Daughter '58
Giant from the Unknown '58
Missile to the Moon '59
She Demons '58

Curtis Cunningham
Mata Hari '85

Sean S. Cunningham
Deepstar Six '89
Friday the 13th '80
Manny's Orphans '78
The New Kids '85
Spring Break '83
A Stranger is Watching '82

Frederick Curiel
Genie of Darkness '60
The Monster Demolisher '60
Neutron and the Black Mask '61
Neutron vs. the Amazing Dr. Caronte '61
Neutron vs. the Death Robots '62

Pauline Curley
The Walloping Kid '26

William Curran
Love, Cheat & Steal '94

Anthony Currie
The Pink Chiquitas '86

Dan Curtis
Burnt Offerings '76
Curse of the Black Widow '77
Dead of Night '77
Dracula '73
Express to Terror '79
House of Dark Shadows '70
Intruders '92
Kansas City Massacre '75
The Last Ride of the Dalton Gang '79
The Long Days of Summer '80
Me and the Kid '93
Melvin Purvis: G-Man '74
Mrs. R's Daughter '79
Night of Dark Shadows '71
Trilogy of Terror '75
The Turn of the Screw '74
War & Remembrance, Part 1 '88
War & Remembrance, Part 2 '89
War & Remembrance, Part 3 '88
War & Remembrance, Part 4 '88
War & Remembrance, Part 5 '88
War & Remembrance, Part 6 '88
War & Remembrance, Part 7 '88
War & Remembrance: The Final Chapter, Part 8 '89
War & Remembrance: The Final Chapter, Part 9 '89
War & Remembrance: The Final Chapter, Part 10 '89
War & Remembrance: The Final Chapter, Part 11 '89
War & Remembrance: The Final Chapter, Part 12 '89
When Every Day was the Fourth of July '78
The Winds of War '83

Douglas Curtis
The Campus Corpse '77
The Sleeping Car '90

Jack Curtis
The Flesh Eaters '64

Michael Curtiz
The Adventures of Huckleberry Finn '60
The Adventures of Robin Hood '38
Angels with Dirty Faces '38
Black Fury '35
Breath of Scandal '60
The Cabin in the Cotton '32
Captain Blood '35
Captains of the Clouds '42
Casablanca '42
The Charge of the Light Brigade '36
The Comancheros '61

Curtiz

Curtiz ▶cont.

Dive Bomber '41
Doctor X '32
Dodge City '39
The Egyptian '54
Female '33
Flamingo Road '49
Four Daughters '38
I'll See You in My Dreams '51
Jim Thorpe: All American '51
The Kennel Murder Case '33
Kid Galahad '37
King Creole '58
Life with Father '47
Mildred Pierce '45
My Dream is Yours '49
Mystery of the Wax Museum '33
Night and Day '46
Passage to Marseilles '44
The Private Lives of Elizabeth & Essex '39
Proud Rebel '58
Santa Fe Trail '40
The Sea Hawk '40
The Sea Wolf '41
The Strange Love of Molly Louvain '32
This is the Army '43
Trouble Along the Way '53
Virginia City '40
We're No Angels '55
White Christmas '54
Yankee Doodle Dandy '42
Young Man with a Horn '50

Ralph Cushman
Secret File of Hollywood '62

Rudolph Cusumano
Wild Ones on Wheels '62

Paul Czinner
As You Like It '36
Catherine the Great '34
Dreaming Lips '37

Renee Daalder
Massacre at Central High '76

Morton DaCosta
Auntie Mame '58
The Music Man '62

Dimis Dadiras
The Mediterranean in Flames '72

John Dahl
Kill Me Again '89
Red Rock West '93

Bob Dahlin
Monster in the Closet '86

Reno Dakota
American Fabulous '92

Tom Daley
The Outing '87

Salvador Dali
Un Chien Andalou '28

Massimo Dallamano
A Black Veil for Lisa '68
Dorian Gray '70
Super Bitch '89

Neville D'Almedia
Lady on the Bus '78

Robert Dalva
The Black Stallion Returns '83

William Robert Daly
Uncle Tom's Cabin '14

Joe D'Amato
Buried Alive '81
Grim Reaper '81

Damiano Damiani
Amityville 2: The Possession '82
A Bullet for the General '68

Confessions of a Police Captain '72
Empty Canvas '64
The Inquiry '87
The Warning '80
The Witch '66

Charles Damic
Bomb at 10:10 '67

Mel Damski
American Dream '81
Badge of the Assassin '85
For Ladies Only '81
Happy Together '89
Legend of Walks Far Woman '82
Long Journey Back '78
Mischief '85
Murder by Book '87
Wildcard '92
A Winner Never Quits '86
Yellowbeard '83

Anthony D'Andrea
Thrillkill '84

Lawrence Dane
Heavenly Bodies '84

Rod Daniel
Beethoven's 2nd '93
K-9 '89
Like Father, Like Son '87
The Super '91
Teen Wolf '85

Georgi Daniela
Autumn Marathon '79

Godfrey Daniels
Cassie '87

Harold Daniels
House of the Black Death '65
Poor White Trash '57
Sword of Venus '53
Terror in the Haunted House '58

Marc Daniels
Planet Earth '74
Vengeance '89

Tage Danielsson
The Adventures of Picasso '80

Claude D'Anna
Salome '85

Danniel Danniel
Egg '88

Herbert Danska
Sweet Love, Bitter '67

Joe Dante
Amazon Women on the Moon '87
The 'Burbs '89
Explorers '85
Gremlins '84
Gremlins 2: The New Batch '90
Hollywood Boulevard '76
The Howling '81
Innerspace '87
Matinee '92
Piranha '78
Twilight Zone: The Movie '83

Ray Danton
Crypt of the Living Dead '73
Psychic Killer '75
Tales of the Unexpected '91

Phil D'Antoni
The Seven-Ups '73

Frank Darabont
Buried Alive '90

Joan Darling
Check Is in the Mail '85
First Love '77
Hiroshima Maiden '88
Willa '79

David Darlow
Tailspin: Behind the Korean Airline Tragedy '89

Mark D'Aruia
Smoke '93

Julie Dash
Daughters of the Dust '92

Jules Dassin
The Canterville Ghost '44
Circle of Two '80
A Dream of Passion '78
The Naked City '48
Never on Sunday '60
Night and the City '50
Phaedra '61
Reunion in France '42
Rififi '54
Topkapi '64
Where the Hot Wind Blows '59

Tony Zarin Dast
Cat in the Cage '68

Herschel Daugherty
The Light in the Forest '58

Darrell Davenport
Shadow Force '92

Harry Davenport
Tillie Wakes Up '17

Harry Bromley Davenport
Xtro '83
Xtro 2: The Second Encounter '91

Delmer Daves
The Badlanders '58
Broken Arrow '50
Dark Passage '47
Demetrius and the Gladiators '54
Destination Tokyo '43
Drum Beat '54
The Hanging Tree '59
Hollywood Canteen '44
Jubal '56
Kings Go Forth '58
Never Let Me Go '53
Parrish '61
The Red House '47
Rome Adventure '62
Spencer's Mountain '63
A Summer Place '59
Task Force '49
3:10 to Yuma '57
Treasure of the Golden Condor '53

Allan David
The Magic Fountain '61

Hugh David
Jude the Obscure '71

Pierce David
Scanner Cop '94

Boaz Davidson
Dutch Treat '86
Going Bananas '88
Hospital Massacre '81
Last American Virgin '82
Salsa '88

Gordon Davidson
The Trial of Lee Harvey Oswald '77
Trial of the Catonsville Nine '72

John Davidson
The Hanging Woman '72

Martin Davidson
Eddie and the Cruisers '83
Hard Promises '92
The Heart of Dixie '89
Hero at Large '80
Long Gone '87

The Lords of Flatbush '74

John Davies
A Married Man '84
Sherlock Holmes: The Silver Blaze '77

Ray Davies
Return to Waterloo '85

Rupert Davies
Target for Killing '66

Terence Davies
Distant Voices, Still Lives '88
The Long Day Closes '92

Valentine Davies
The Benny Goodman Story '55

Andrew Davis
Above the Law '88
Code of Silence '85
The Final Terror '83
The Fugitive '93
The Package '89

B.J. Davis
White Ghost '88

Beau Davis
Laser Mission '90

Charles Davis
Die Watching '93

Desmond Davis
Clash of the Titans '81
Nice Girl Like Me '69
Ordeal by Innocence '84
The Sign of Four '83

Eddie Davis
Color Me Dead '69

Gary Davis
Conflict of Interest '92

Ossie Davis
Cotton Comes to Harlem '70
Gordon's War '73

Roy Davis
Surabaya Conspiracy '75

Tamra Davis
CB4: The Movie '93
Guncrazy '92

Tito Davison
Maria '71

Norman Dawn
Orphans of the North '40
Tundra '36
Two Lost Worlds '50

Vincent Dawn
Caged Women '84
Rats '83
Strike Commando '87

Anthony M. (Antonio Margheteti) Dawson
Ark of the Sun God '82
Assignment Outer Space '61
Battle of the Worlds '61
Castle of Blood '64
Codename: Wildgeese '84
Death Rage '77
Hercules, Prisoner of Evil '64
Hunters of the Golden Cobra '82
Indio '90
Invasion of the Flesh Hunters '82
Jungle Raiders '85
Killer Fish '79
The Last Hunter '80
Lightning Bolt '67
Mr. Superinvisible '73
Planet on the Prowl '65
The Rip Off '78
Seven Deaths in the Cat's Eye '72
The Squeeze '80
The Stranger and the Gunfighter '76
Take a Hard Ride '75

Tiger Joe '85
Tornado '83
The Virgin of Nuremberg '65
Web of the Spider '70
Wild, Wild Planet '65
Yor, the Hunter from the Future '83

Ernest Day
Green Ice '81
Waltz Across Texas '83

Robert Day
Corridors of Blood '58
Death Stalk '74
First Man into Space '59
The Grass is Always Greener Over the Septic Tank '78
The Haunted Strangler '58
Initiation of Sarah '78
Lady from Yesterday '85
The Man with Bogart's Face '80
Murder by Natural Causes '79
The Quick and the Dead '87
Two-Way Stretch '60
Walking Through the Fire '80
Your Place or Mine '83

Lyman Dayton
Baker's Hawk '76
Dream Machine '91

Rodolfo de Anda
La Carcel de Laredo '84

Jaime de Arminan
The Nest '80

Jacques de Baroncelli
The French Way '40

Jan De Bont
Speed '94

Philippe de Broca
Cartouche '62
Jupiter's Thigh '81
The King of Hearts '66
Le Cavaleur '78
Louisiana '87
Oldest Profession '67
That Man from Rio '64

Pierre de Celles
Pound Puppies and the Legend of Big Paw '88

Ennio de Concini
Hitler: The Last Ten Days '73

Fred de Cordova
Bedtime for Bonzo '51
Frankie and Johnny '65
I'll Take Sweden '65

Paul de Cruccio
Desert Snow '89

Frank de Felitta
Dark Night of the Scarecrow '81
Scissors '91
The Two Worlds of Jenny Logan '79

Eduardo de Filippo
Seven Deadly Sins '53
Shoot Loud, Louder, I Don't Understand! '66

Michael de Gaetano
The Haunted '79
UFO: Target Earth '74

Rolf de Heer
Encounter at Raven's Gate '88

Ate De Jong
Drop Dead Fred '91
A Flight of Rainbirds '81
Highway to Hell '92

Paula de Koenigsberg
Rate It X '86

DIRECTOR INDEX • 1452 ▲

Eloy De La Iglesia
El Diputado '78

Jose Antonio De La Loma
The Barcelona Kill '77
Street Warriors '87
Street Warriors, Part 2 '87

Robert De Lacy
Pardon My Gun '30

Charles De Latour
Impulse '55
The Limping Man '53

Gerardo (Gerry) De Leon
Brides of the Beast '68
Mad Doctor of Blood Island '69
Terror is a Man '59
The Vampire People '66

Marcus De Leon
Kiss Me a Killer '91

Paul de Lussanet
Dear Boys '80
Mysteries '84

Alberto De Martino
Bloodlink '86
The Chosen '77
Dirty Heroes '71
New Mafia Boss '72
The Puma Man '80
Scenes from a Murder '72
Secret Agent 00 '67
The Tempter '74

Pierre De Moro
Hellhole '85
Savannah Smiles '82

Robert De Niro
A Bronx Tale '93

Oswald De Oliveira
Amazon Jail '85

Armando de Ossorio
Fangs of the Living Dead '68
Horror of the Zombies '74
Night of the Death Cult '75
Night of the Sorcerers '70
People Who Own the Dark '75
Return of the Evil Dead '75
Tombs of the Blind Dead '72
When the Screaming Stops '73

Frank De Palma
Private War '90

Guiseppe de Santis
Bitter Rice '49

Vittorio de Seta
Bandits of Orgosolo '61

Vittorio De Sica
After the Fox '66
The Bicycle Thief '48
Boccaccio '70 '62
The Children Are Watching Us '44
The Garden of the Finzi-Continis '71
The Gold of Naples '54
Indiscretion of an American Wife '54
It Happened in the Park '56
Marriage Italian Style '64
Miracle in Milan '51
The Roof '56
Shoeshine '47
Teresa Venerdi '41
Two Women '61
Umberto D '55
Woman Times Seven '67
Yesterday, Today and Tomorrow '64

Tom De Simone
Angel 3: The Final Chapter '88
Chatterbox '76
The Concrete Jungle '82
Hell Night '81

Reform School Girls '86
Terror in the Jungle '68

Andre de Toth
Dark Waters '44
House of Wax '53
The Indian Fighter '55
Last of the Comanches '52
The Mongols '60
Morgan the Pirate '60
Pitfall '48
Ramrod '47
Springfield Rifle '52
The Stranger Wore a Gun '53

Ralph De Vito
Family Enforcer '76

Elmo De Witt
Enemy Unseen '91

Basil Dean
21 Days '37

Charles Deane
Blonde Blackmailer '58

William Dear
Angels in the Outfield '94
Harry and the Hendersons '87
If Looks Could Kill '91
Timerider '83

Basil Dearden
The Assassination Bureau '69
The Blue Lamp '49
Captive Heart '47
Dead of Night '45
Frieda '47
Khartoum '66
The League of Gentlemen '60
The Man Who Haunted Himself '70
Mission: Monte Carlo '75
The Persuaders '71
Sapphire '59
The Smallest Show on Earth '57
Train of Events '49
Victim '62

James Dearden
Cold Room '84
A Kiss Before Dying '91
Pascali's Island '88

Frank Deasy
The Courier '88

John DeBello
Attack of the Killer Tomatoes '77
Happy Hour '87
Killer Tomatoes Eat France '91
Killer Tomatoes Strike Back '90
Return of the Killer Tomatoes '88

Gianfranco DeBosio
Moses '76

Henri Decoin
License to Kill '64

David DeCoteau
Creepozoids '87
Dr. Alien '89
Nightmare Sisters '87
Puppet Master 3: Toulon's Revenge '91
Sorority Babes in the Slimeball Bowl-A-Rama '87

Miles Deem
Jungle Master '56

Allessandro DeGaetano
Bloodbath in Psycho Town '89

Andre Degas
American Autobahn '84

Joseph DeGrasse
The Scarlet Car '17

Philip DeGuere
Dr. Strange '78

Jamil Dehlavi
Born of Fire '87

Mark Deimel
Perfect Match '88

Edward Dein
The Leech Woman '59
Shack Out on 101 '55

Donna Deitch
Desert Hearts '86
Prison Stories: Women on the Inside '91
The Women of Brewster Place '89

Steve DeJarnatt
Cherry 2000 '88
Miracle Mile '89

Fred Dekker
The Monster Squad '87
Night of the Creeps '86
RoboCop 3 '91

Jack Del
The Committee '68
A Session with the Committee '69

Peter Del Monte
Invitation au Voyage '82
Julia and Julia '87

Deborah Del Prete
Simple Justice '89

Roy Del Ruth
Babe Ruth Story '48
Blessed Event '32
Blonde Crazy '31
Born to Dance '36
Broadway Melody of 1936 '35
Broadway Melody of 1938 '37
Broadway Rhythm '44
Bureau of Missing Persons '33
The Chocolate Soldier '41
DuBarry Was a Lady '43
Employees' Entrance '33
Happy Landing '38
Kid Millions '34
Lady Killer '33
The Maltese Falcon '31
My Lucky Star '38
On Moonlight Bay '51
On the Avenue '37
Topper Returns '41
The West Point Story '50

Jean Delannoy
Bernadette '90
Eternal Return '43
Imperial Venus '71
La Symphonie Pastorale '46
Love and the Frenchwoman '60
This Special Friendship '67

Miguel M. Delgado
El Gendarme Desconocido '41

Bill D'Elia
The Feud '90

Francis Delia
Freeway '88

Bert Deling
Dead Easy '82

Jeffrey Dell
Carlton Browne of the F.O. '59

Jeffrey Delman
Deadtime Stories '86

Nathalie Delon
Sweet Lies '88

Robert Deltano
Gun Girls '56

Rudy DeLuca
Transylvania 6-5000 '85

Dom DeLuise
Hot Stuff '80

Michael DeLuise
Almost Pregnant '91

Richard Dembo
Dangerous Moves '84

Eames Demetrios
Mind Trap '91

Tulio Demicheli
Dracula vs. Frankenstein '69
Son of Captain Blood '62

Cecil B. DeMille
The Cheat '15
Cleopatra '34
The Greatest Show on Earth '52
King of Kings '27
Madam Satan '30
Male and Female '19
The Plainsman '37
Reap the Wild Wind '42
The Road to Yesterday '25
Road to Yesterday/The Yankee Clipper '27
Samson and Delilah '50
The Ten Commandments '23
The Ten Commandments '56

Jonathan Demme
Caged Heat '74
Citizens Band '77
Crazy Mama '75
Fighting Mad '76
The Last Embrace '79
Married to the Mob '88
Melvin and Howard '80
Philadelphia '93
The Silence of the Lambs '91
Something Wild '86
Stop Making Sense '84
Swimming to Cambodia '87
Swing Shift '84
Who Am I This Time? '82

Ted Demme
The Ref '93
Who's the Man? '93

Rene Demoulin
Charlie Bravo '80s

Jacques Demy
Donkey Skin '70
Dos Cruces en Danger Pass '71
Lola '61
A Slightly Pregnant Man '79
Umbrellas of Cherbourg '64

Drew Denbaum
Nickel Mountain '85

Reginald Denham
The Silent Passenger '35

Claire Denis
Chocolat '88
No Fear, No Die '90

Jean-Pierre Denis
Field of Honor '87

Charles Dennis
Reno and the Doc '84

Pen Densham
The Kiss '88
The Zoo Gang '85

Ruggero Deodato
The Barbarians '87
Dial Help '88
House on the Edge of the Park '84
The Lone Runner '88
Phantom of Death '87

Brian DePalma
Blow Out '81
Body Double '84
The Bonfire of the Vanities '90
Carlito's Way '93
Carrie '76
Casualties of War '89
Dressed to Kill '80
The Fury '78
Greetings '68
Hi, Mom! '70
Home Movies '79

Obsession '76
Phantom of the Paradise '74
Raising Cain '92
Scarface '83
Sisters '73
The Untouchables '87
The Wedding Party '69
Wise Guys '86

Gerard Depardieu
Tartuffe '84

Jacques Deray
Borsalino '70
The Outside Man '73
Swimming Pool '70

John Derek
Bolero '84
Confessions of Tom Harris '72
Fantasies '73
Ghosts Can't Do It '90
Once Before I Die '65
Tarzan, the Ape Man '81

Dominique Deruddere
Wait Until Spring, Bandini '90

Hugues des Roziers
Blue Jeans '78

Caleb Deschanel
Crusoe '89
The Escape Artist '82

Henri Desfontaines
Salome/Queen Elizabeth '23

James Desmond
Monterey Pop '68

Robert Deubel
Girls Night Out '83

Howard Deutch
Article 99 '92
Getting Even with Dad '94
The Great Outdoors '88
Pretty in Pink '86
Some Kind of Wonderful '87
Tales from the Crypt, Vol. 3 '90

Ross Devenish
Bleak House '85
Over Indulgence '87

Michel DeVille
La Lectrice '88
La Petite Bande '84
Peril '85

Dirk DeVilliers
Kingfisher Caper '76
Snake Dancer

David Devine
Beethoven Lives Upstairs '92

Dennis Devine
Dead Girls '90

Danny DeVito
Amazing Stories '85
Hoffa '92
Ratings Game '84
Throw Momma from the Train '87
The War of the Roses '89

Tom Dewier
Death by Dialogue '88

Peter Dews
The Taming of the Shrew '81

John Dexter
I Want What I Want '72
The Virgin Soldiers '69

Maury Dexter
Surf Party '64

Bernard Deyries
Here Come the Littles: The Movie '85

Fernando Di Leo
Kidnap Syndicate '76
Loaded Guns '75

Di Leo ▶cont.

Manhunt '73
Mr. Scarface '77
Slaughter Hotel '71
Violent Breed '83

Mario Di Leo
The Final Alliance '89

Rino Di Silvestro
Women in Cell Block 7 '77

Jose Diaz Morales
Loyola, the Soldier Saint '52

Tom DiCillo
Johnny Suede '92

Nigel Dick
Dead Connection '94
Deadly Intent '88
Private Investigations '87

Ernest R. Dickerson
Juice '92
Surviving the Game '94

Thorold Dickinson
The Arsenal Stadium Mystery '39
Gaslight '39
High Command '37
Hill 24 Doesn't Answer '55
Men of Two Worlds '46
The Queen of Spades '49

Lance Dickson
Hollywood Heartbreak '89

Marc Didden
Istanbul '85

Samuel Diege
King of the Sierras '38
Ride 'Em Cowgirl '41
Water Rustlers '39

Carlos Diegues
Bye Bye Brazil '79
Quilombo '84
Subway to the Stars '87
Xica '76

Baruch Dienar
They Were Ten '61

William Dieterle
The Accused '48
Boots Malone '52
The Devil & Daniel Webster '41
Elephant Walk '54
Fashions of 1934 '34
Female '33
The Hunchback of Notre Dame '39
Juarez '39
The Life of Emile Zola '37
A Midsummer Night's Dream '35
Mistress of the World '59
Omar Khayyam '57
Portrait of Jennie '48
Quick, Let's Get Married '71
Salome '53
Satan Met a Lady '36
Scarlet Dawn '32
September Affair '50
The Story of Louis Pasteur '36

Eric Dignam
Denial: The Dark Side of Passion '91

Jack Dillon
Suds '20

John Francis Dillon
Millie '31

Steve DiMarco
Back in Action '94

Dennis Dimster
Mikey '92

Pece Dingo
Midnight Cabaret '90

Michael Dinner
Heaven Help Us '85
Hot to Trot! '88
Off Beat '86

Carlo DiPalma
Blonde in Black Leather '77

John Dirlam
Fatal Instinct '92

Mark DiSalle
Kickboxer '89
The Perfect Weapon '91

Denver Dixon
Fighting Cowboy '33

Ivan Dixon
The Spook Who Sat By the Door '73

Ken Dixon
Slave Girls from Beyond Infinity '87

Edward Dmytryk
Alvarez Kelly '66
Anzio '68
Back to Bataan '45
Behind the Rising Sun '43
Bluebeard '72
Broken Lance '54
The Caine Mutiny '54
Captive Wild Woman '43
The Carpetbaggers '64
Cornered '45
Crossfire '47
He is My Brother '75
The Hidden Room '49
Hitler's Children '43
The Human Factor '75
The Left Hand of God '55
Mirage '66
The Mountain '56
Murder, My Sweet '44
Mutiny '52
Raintree County '57
Seven Miles from Alcatraz/Flight from Glory '43
Shalako '68
Soldier of Fortune '55
Tender Comrade '43
Till the End of Time '46
Trail of the Hawk '37
Walk on the Wild Side '62
Warlock '59
Where Love Has Gone '64
The Young Lions '58

Tony B. Dobb
Blue Tornado '90

Frank Q. Dobbs
Uphill All the Way '85

Lawrence Dobkin
Children's Carol '80
Sixteen '72

Kevin Dobson
Demolition '77
Image of Death '77
The Mango Tree '77
Miracle in the Wilderness '91
Squizzy Taylor '84

James Dodson
Deadly Rivals '92
Quest of the Delta Knights '93

Donald M. Dohler
The Alien Factor '78
Deadly Neighbor '91
Fiend '83

Jacques Doillon
La Vengeance d'une Femme '89

Lou Doillon
La Puritaine '86

Martin Dolman
After the Fall of New York '85
American Tiger '89
Hands of Steel '86

Roger Donaldson
The Bounty '84
Cadillac Man '90
Cocktail '88
The Getaway '93
Marie '85
No Way Out '87
Nutcase '83
Sleeping Dogs '82
Smash Palace '82
White Sands '92

Vincent J. Donehue
Lonelyhearts '58
Peter Pan '60
Sunrise at Campobello '60

Stanley Donen
Arabesque '66
Bedazzled '67
Blame It on Rio '84
The Cary Grant Collection '90
Charade '63
Damn Yankees '58
Deep in My Heart '54
Funny Face '57
Give a Girl a Break '53
The Grass is Greener '61
Indiscreet '58
It's Always Fair Weather '55
The Little Prince '74
Love is Better Than Ever '52
Movie, Movie '78
On the Town '49
Pajama Game '57
Royal Wedding '51
Saturn 3 '80
Seven Brides for Seven Brothers '54
Singin' in the Rain '52
Two for the Road '67

Walter Doniger
Mad Bull '77

Dennis Donnelly
The Toolbox Murders '78

Tom Donnelly
Quicksilver '86

Clive Donner
Babes in Toyland '86
Charlie Chan and the Curse of the Dragon Queen '81
Luv '67
Merlin and the Sword '85
The Nude Bomb '80
Oliver Twist '82
The Scarlet Pimpernel '82
Stealing Heaven '88
The Thief of Baghdad '78
To Catch a King '84
What's New Pussycat? '65

Richard Donner
The Goonies '85
Inside Moves '80
Ladyhawke '85
Lethal Weapon '87
Lethal Weapon 2 '89
Lethal Weapon 3 '92
Lola '69
Maverick '94
The Omen '76
Radio Flyer '92
Scrooged '88
Superman: The Movie '78
Tales from the Crypt '89
The Toy '82
Wanted: Dead or Alive '59

Mary Agnes Donoghue
Paradise '91

Jack Donohue
Assault on a Queen '66
Babes in Toyland '61
Lucky Me '54
Watch the Birdie '50
The Yellow Cab Man '50

Martin Donovan
Apartment Zero '88

Death Dreams '92
Mad at the Moon '92
The Substitute '93

Paul Donovan
Def-Con 4 '85
George's Island '91
Norman's Awesome Experience '88
Northern Extremes '93

Tom Donovan
Lovespell '79

Mark Donskoi
My Apprenticeship '39
My Childhood '38
My Universities '40

Lee Doo-yong
Silent Assassins '88

Thomas Doran
Spookies '85

Jacques Dorfman
Shadow of the Wolf '92

Robert Dornhelm
The Children of Theatre Street '77
Cold Feet '89
Echo Park '86
Requiem for Dominic '91

Doris Dorrie
Me and Him '89
Men... '85

Shimon Dotan
The Finest Hour '91

Jean Douchet
Six in Paris '68

Russell S. Doughten, Jr.
The Hostage '67
Whitcomb's War '88

Gordon Douglas
Black Arrow '48
Broadway Limited '41
Call Me Bwana '63
Chuka '67
The Detective '68
Dick Tracy vs. Cueball '46
The Doolins of Oklahoma '49
The Falcon in Hollywood '44
First Yank into Tokyo '45
Follow That Dream '61
Girl Rush '44
The Great Gildersleeve '43
Great Missouri Raid '51
Harlow '65
If You Knew Susie '48
In Like Flint '67
Kiss Tomorrow Goodbye '50
Lady in Cement '68
The McConnell Story '55
The Nevadan '50
Only the Valiant '50
Rio Conchos '64
Robin and the Seven Hoods '64
Saps at Sea '40
Sincerely Yours '56
Skullduggery '70
Slaughter's Big Ripoff '73
Them! '54
They Call Me Mr. Tibbs! '70
Tony Rome '67
Up Periscope '59
Viva Knievel! '77
Young at Heart '54
Zombies on Broadway '44

Kirk Douglas
Posse '75

Neil Douglas
Sinner's Blood '70

Peter Douglas
A Tiger's Tale '87

Lorenzo Doumani
Amore! '93
Mad About You '90

Alexander Dovzhenko
Arsenal '29
Earth '30
Zvenigora '28

Kathleen Dowdey
Blue Heaven '84

Robert Downey
America '86
Greaser's Palace '72
Putney Swope '69
Rented Lips '88
Too Much Sun '90
Up the Academy '80

Michael Drach
Les Violons du Bal '74

Mircea Dragan
Oil '78

Bert L. Dragin
Summer Camp Nightmare '86
Twice Dead '88

Stan Dragoti
Love at First Bite '79
The Man with One Red Shoe '85
Mr. Mom '83
Necessary Roughness '91
She's Out of Control '89

Jim Drake
Based on an Untrue Story '93
Mr. Bill's Real Life Adventures '86
Police Academy 4: Citizens on Patrol '87
Speed Zone '88

Oliver Drake
Battling Marshal '48
Brand of Fear '49
Fighting Valley '43
Mummy & Curse of the Jackal '67
Today I Hang '42

Tom Drake
Keeper '84

Tony Drazan
Zebrahead '92

Arthur Dreifuss
Baby Face Morgan '42
Boss of Big Town '43
Double Deal '39
Mystery in Swing '40
The Payoff '43
Reg'lar Fellers '41

Fred Dresch
My Samurai '92

Jean Dreville
Seven Deadly Sins '53
Sputnik '61

Di Drew
The Right Hand Man '87
Trouble in Paradise '88

Sidney Drew
Playing Dead '15

Carl Theodor Dreyer
Day of Wrath '43
Gertrud '64
Leaves from Satan's Book '19
Master of the House '25
Ordet '55
The Passion of Joan of Arc '28
Vampyr '31

Richard Driscoll
The Comic '85

Sara Driver
Sleepwalk '88

Antonio Drove
The Tunnel '89

David Drury
Defense of the Realm '85

Forever Young '85
Intrigue '90
Split Decisions '88

Mihael Dryhurst
Hard Way '80

Lee Drysdale
Leather Jackets '90

Charles S. Dubin
Cinderella '64
Drop-Out Mother '88
The Gathering: Part 2 '79
The Manions of America '81
Moving Violation '76
Murder Once Removed '71

Jay Dubin
Rap Master Ronnie '88

Jean-Claude Dubois
The Evil Below '87

Arthur Dubs
Vanishing Wilderness '73

Roger Duchonwny
Camp Cucamonga: How I Spent My Summer Vacation '90

Peter Duffell
Experience Preferred... But Not Essential '83
The Far Pavilions '84
The House that Dripped Blood '71
Inside Out '75
Letters to an Unknown Lover '84

Dennis Dugan
Brain Donors '92
Problem Child '90

Michael Dugan
Mausoleum '83
Super Seal '77

George Dugdale
Slaughter High '86

Christian Duguay
Adrift '93
Live Wire '92
Model by Day '94
Scanners 2: The New Order '91
Scanners 3: The Takeover '92

John Duigan
Far East '85
Flirting '89
One Night Stand '84
Romero '89
Sirens '94
Wide Sargasso Sea '92
The Winter of Our Dreams '82
The Year My Voice Broke '87

Bill Duke
The Cemetery Club '93
Deep Cover '92
Johnnie Gibson F.B.I. '87
Maximum Security '87
A Rage in Harlem '91
A Raisin in the Sun '89
Sister Act 2: Back in the Habit '93

Daryl Duke
Griffin and Phoenix: A Love Story '76
I Heard the Owl Call My Name '73
Payday '72
The President's Plane is Missing '71
The Silent Partner '78
Tai-Pan '86
The Thorn Birds '83

William Duke
Killing Floor '85

Germaine Dulac
Smiling Madame Beudet/The Seashell and the Clergyman '28

Georges Dumoulin
Nous N'Irons Plus au Bois '69
We Will Not Enter the Forest '79

Patrick Duncan
84 Charlie Mopic '89
Live! From Death Row '92

Duwayne Dunham
Homeward Bound: The Incredible Journey '93

Scott R. Dunlap
Irish Luck '39

Philip Dunne
Ten North Frederick '58
Wild in the Country '61

E.A. Dupont
The Americano/Variety '25
Variety '25

Michael DuPont
Ethan '71

William Duprey
Uncaged '91

Ciro Duran
Tropical Snow '88

Fernando Duran
La Hora 24 '87

Rudy Durand
Tilt '78

John Durst
One Wish Too Many '55

David E. Durston
I Drink Your Blood '71
Stigma '73

Robert Duvall
Angelo My Love '83

Julien Duvivier
Anna Karenina '48
Captain Blackjack '51
Diabolically Yours '67
The Great Waltz '38
Little World of Don Camillo '51
Lydia '41
The Man in the Raincoat '57
Maria Chapdelaine '34
Panique '47
Pepe Le Moko '37
Poil de Carotte '31

Allan Dwan
Abroad with Two Yanks '44
Around the World '43
Brewster's Millions '45
Cattle Queen of Montana '54
Enchanted Island '58
Escape to Burma '55
The Gorilla '39
Heidi '37
Here We Go Again! '42
Hollywood Party '34
I Dream of Jeannie '52
The Iron Mask '29
Look Who's Laughing '41
Montana Belle '52
Northwest Outpost '47
Passion '54
Pearl of the South Pacific '55
Rebecca of Sunnybrook Farm '38
The Restless Breed '58
Robin Hood '22
Sands of Iwo Jima '49
Silver Lode '54
Slightly Scarlet '56
Tennessee's Partner '55
The Three Musketeers '39

H. Kaye Dyal
Memory of Us '74
Project: Eliminator '91

Robert Dyke
Moontrap '89

Boris Eagle
The Tormentors '80s

B. Reeves Eason
The Adventures of Rex & Rinty '35
The Coast Patrol '25
Fighting Marines '36
The Galloping Ghost '31
Hollywood Mystery '34
The Last of the Mohicans '32
Law of the Wild '34
The Miracle Rider '35
Mystery Mountain '34
North of the Border '46
The Phantom Empire '35
Red River Valley '36
Rimfire '49
Roaring Ranch '30
Test of Donald Norton '26
Trigger Tricks '30
Undersea Kingdom '36
Vanishing Legion '31

Walter B. Eason
Sea Hound '47

Allan Eastman
Crazy Moon '87
Ford: The Man & the Machine '87
The War Boy '85

G.L. Eastman
Metamorphosis '90

Clint Eastwood
Bird '88
Bronco Billy '80
The Eiger Sanction '75
Firefox '82
The Gauntlet '77
Heartbreak Ridge '86
High Plains Drifter '73
Honkytonk Man '82
The Outlaw Josey Wales '76
Pale Rider '85
A Perfect World '93
Play Misty for Me '71
The Rookie '90
Sudden Impact '83
Unforgiven '92
White Hunter, Black Heart '90

Thom Eberhardt
Captain Ron '92
Gross Anatomy '89
The Night Before '88
Night of the Comet '84
Sole Survivor '84
Without a Clue '88

Ghasem Ebrahimian
The Suitors '88

Nicolas Echevarria
Cabeza de Vaca '90

Uli Edel
Body of Evidence '92
Christiane F. '82
Last Exit to Brooklyn '90

Gustaf Edgren
Walpurgis Night '41

Don Edmunds
Bare Knuckles '77
Ilsa, She-Wolf of the SS '74
Tender Loving Care '73
Terror on Tour '83

Blake Edwards
Blind Date '87
Breakfast at Tiffany's '61
The Cary Grant Collection '90
Curse of the Pink Panther '83
Darling Lili '70
Days of Wine and Roses '62
Experiment in Terror '62
A Fine Mess '86
Great Race '65
The Man Who Loved Women '83
Micki & Maude '84
Operation Petticoat '59
The Party '68
Perfect Furlough '59
Peter Gunn '89

The Pink Panther '64
The Pink Panther Strikes Again '76
Return of the Pink Panther '74
Revenge of the Pink Panther '78
A Shot in the Dark '64
Skin Deep '89
S.O.B. '81
Son of the Pink Panther '93
Sunset '88
Switch '91
The Tamarind Seed '74
10 '79
That's Life! '86
This Happy Feeling '58
Trail of the Pink Panther '82
Victor/Victoria '82
What Did You Do in the War, Daddy? '66
Wild Rovers '71

Charles Edwards
The Flaming Teen-Age '56

Don Edwards
Black Cobra 3: The Manila Connection '90

George Edwards
The Attic '80

Harry Edwards
Baby Face Harry Langdon '26

Henry Edwards
The Private Secretary '35
Scrooge '35

Robert Edwards
Thunder in the Pines '49

Christine Edzard
Little Dorrit, Film 1: Nobody's Fault '88
Little Dorrit, Film 2: Little Dorrit's Story '88

Arthur Egeli
Maxim Xul '91

Mark Egerton
The Winds of Jarrah '83

Colin Eggleston
Bellamy '80
Cassandra '87
Innocent Prey '88
Sky Pirates '87
The Wicked '89

Jan Egleson
The Last Hit '93
Roanoke '89
A Shock to the System '90
The Tender Age '84

Oleg Egorov
Osa '85

Atom Egoyan
The Adjuster '91
Family Viewing '88
Next of Kin '84
Speaking Parts '89

Richard Eichberg
Night Birds '31

Franz Eichorn
The Violent Years '56

Rafael Eisenman
Lake Consequence '92
Red Shoe Diaries 3: Another Woman's Lipstick '93

Sergei Eisenstein
Alexander Nevsky '38
The Battleship Potemkin '25
The General Line '29
Ivan the Terrible, Part 1 '44
Ivan the Terrible, Part 2 '46
Que Viva Mexico '32
Strike '24
Ten Days That Shook the World '27

George Elanjian, Jr.
Syngenor '90

Judit Elek
Maria's Day '84

Richard Elfman
Forbidden Zone '80

Jan Eliasberg
Past Midnight '92

Larry Elikann
Charlie and the Great Balloon Chase '82
Disaster at Silo 7 '88
Fever '91
God Bless the Child '88
The Great Los Angeles Earthquake '90
The Great Wallendas '78
Hands of a Stranger '87
Kiss of a Killer '93
One Against the Wind '91
Poison Ivy '85
Spraggue '84
Stamp of a Killer '87
The Story Lady '93

Harrison Ellenshaw
Dead Silence '90

B. Ron Elliott
The Acid Eaters '67

Lang Elliott
Dorf and the First Games of Mount Olympus '87
The Private Eyes '80

Paul Elliotts
Great Adventure '75

Bob Ellis
Warm Nights on a Slow-Moving Train '87

Joseph Ellison
Don't Go in the House '80

Javier Elorrieta
Blood and Sand '89

Maurice Elvey
Beware of Pity '46
The Evil Mind '34
Lily of Killarney '34
The Obsessed '51
Phantom Fiend '35
Transatlantic Tunnel '35

John Emerson
The Americano '17
The Americano/Variety '25
Down to Earth '17
His Picture in the Papers '16
Mystery of the Leaping Fish/Chess Fever '25
Reaching for the Moon '17
The Social Secretary '16

Dick Emery
Yellow Submarine '68

Robert Emery
Ride in a Pink Car '74
Scream Bloody Murder '72

Ian Emes
Knights & Emeralds '87

Roland Emmerich
Ghost Chase '88
Making Contact '86
Moon 44 '90
Universal Soldier '92

Robert Emmett
The Caravan Trail '46
Colorado Serenade '46
Way of the West '35

Robert Enders
Stevie '78

Cy Endfield
Mysterious Island '61
Try and Get Me '50
The Underworld Story '50
Zulu '64

Erich Engel
The Blum Affair '48

David Engelbach
America 3000 '86

Harrison Engle
Indomitable Teddy Roosevelt '83

John English
Arizona Days '37
Captain America '44
Cow Town '50
Daredevils of the Red Circle '38
Death Valley Manhunt '43
Dick Tracy '37
Doctor Satan's Robot '40
Drums of Fu Manchu '40
Fighting Devil Dogs '38
Hills of Utah '51
King of the Texas Rangers '41
Loaded Pistols '48
The Lone Ranger '38
Man from Thunder River '43
Raiders of Sunset Pass '43
Riders of the Whistling Pines '49
Rim of the Canyon '49
Utah '45
Valley of Fire '51
Whistling Bullets '36
Zorro Rides Again '37
Zorro's Fighting Legion '39

George Englund
A Christmas to Remember '78
Dixie: Changing Habits '85
The Ugly American '63
The Vegas Strip Wars '84
Zachariah '70

Robert Englund
976-EVIL '88

Robert Enrico
Jailbird's Vacation '65
Le Secret '74
Les Grandes Gueules '65
An Occurrence at Owl Creek Bridge '62
An Occurrence at Owl Creek Bridge/Coup de Grace '62
Old Gun '76
Red Balloon/Occurrence at Owl Creek Bridge '62

Ray Enright
China Sky '44
Coroner Creek '48
Dames '34
Earthworm Tractors '36
Gung Ho! '43
The Iron Major '43
Man from Cairo '54
Return of the Bad Men '48
South of St. Louis '48
The Spoilers '42
Tomorrow at Seven '33
Trail Street '47

Ildiko Enyedi
My Twentieth Century '90

Nora Ephron
Sleepless in Seattle '93
This is My Life '92

Jean Epstein
La Chute de la Maison Usher '28

Marcelo Epstein
Body Rock '84

Robert Epstein
Common Threads: Stories from the Quilt '89
Times of Harvey Milk '83

Richard Erdman
Brothers O'Toole '73

Victor Erice
Spirit of the Beehive '73

A.E. Erickson
The Lone Star Ranger '39

Gordon Eriksen
The Big Dis '89

Charles Erman
Just Me & You '78

John Erman
Alexander: The Other Side of Dawn '77
The Attic: The Hiding of Anne Frank '88
Carolina Skeletons '92
Child of Glass '78
An Early Frost '85
Eleanor: First Lady of the World '82
Green Eyes '76
My Old Man '79
Stella '90
A Streetcar Named Desire '84
When the Time Comes '91

Frederic Ermler
No Greater Love '43

George Erschbamer
Final Round '93
SnakeEater '89
SnakeEater 2: The Drug Buster '89
SnakeEater 3: His Law '92

Jack Ersgard
Invisible: The Chronicles of Benjamin Knight '93

Joakim Ersgard
Mandroid '93
The Visitors '89

Chester Erskine
Androcles and the Lion '52
Egg and I '47
Frankie and Johnny '36
A Girl in Every Port '52
Midnight '34

Dwain Esper
Maniac '34
Marihuana '36
The Worst of Hollywood: Vol. 1 '90

Jett C. Espirtu
P.O.W. Deathcamp '89

Harry Essex
The Cremators '72
Octaman '71

Emilio Estevez
Men at Work '90
Wisdom '87

Ray Etheridge
The Vernonia Incident '89

Bruce A. Evans
Kuffs '92

David Mickey Evans
The Sandlot '93

John Evans
Black Godfather '74
Blackjack '78

Roger Evans
Jet Benny Show '86

D.S. Everett
Running Brave '83

Valie Export
Invisible Adversaries '77
Menschenfrauen '80
The Practice of Love '84

Richard Eyre
Loose Connections '87
The Ploughman's Lunch '83
Singleton's Pluck '84

John Eyres
Monolith '93
Project: Shadowchaser '92

Christian Faber
Bail Jumper '89

Zoltan Fabri
The Fifth Seal '76

Roberto Faenza
The Bachelor '93
Corrupt '84

Peter Faiman
Crocodile Dundee '86
Dutch '91

William Fairchild
Horsemasters '61
The Silent Enemy '58

Ferdinand Fairfax
Nate and Hayes '83
The Rescue '88
Spymaker: The Secret Life of Ian Fleming '90

Feliks Falk
Hero of the Year '85

Harry Falk
Abduction of St. Anne '75
Beulah Land '80
The Death Squad '73
High Desert Kill '90
The Night the City Screamed '80
Sophisticated Gents '81

Jamaa Fanaka
Black Sister's Revenge '76
Penitentiary '79
Penitentiary 2 '82
Penitentiary 3 '87
Soul Vengeance '75

Jacques Fansten
Cross My Heart '91

James Fargo
Born to Race '88
The Enforcer '76
Every Which Way But Loose '78
Forced Vengeance '82
Game for Vultures '86
Voyage of the Rock Aliens '87

Ernest Farino
Steel and Lace '90

W. Farkas
Prime Risk '84

Donald Farmer
Demon Queen '80s
Scream Dream '89

Anthony Farrar
Sin You Sinners '63

John Farris
Dear Dead Delilah '72

John Farrow
Back from Eternity '56
Botany Bay '53
A Bullet Is Waiting '54
Commandos Strike at Dawn '43
Copper Canyon '50
Five Came Back '39
His Kind of Woman '51
John Paul Jones '59
The Saint Strikes Back '39
The Saint Strikes Back: Criminal Court '46
Sea Chase '55
Unholy Wife '57
Wake Island '42

Andre Farwagi
Boarding School '83

John Fasano
Black Roses '88
The Jitters '88
Rock 'n' Roll Nightmare '85

Rainer Werner Fassbinder
Ali: Fear Eats the Soul '74
The American Soldier '70
Berlin Alexanderplatz '80

The Bitter Tears of Petra von Kant '72
Chinese Roulette '86
Despair '78
Effi Briest '74
Fox and His Friends '75
Germany in Autumn '78
Gods of the Plague '69
The Marriage of Maria Braun '79
The Merchant of Four Seasons '71
Mother Kusters Goes to Heaven '76
Querelle '83
The Stationmaster's Wife '77
The Tin Drum '79
Veronika Voss '82
Why Does Herr R. Run Amok? '69

William C. Faure
Shaka Zulu '83

Neill Fearnley
Black Ice '92

Linda Feferman
Seven Minutes in Heaven '86

Xie Fei
Girl from Hunan '86

Beda Ocampo Feijoo
Under the Earth '86

Felix Feist
Big Trees '52
Deluge '33
The Devil Thumbs a Ride '47
The Devil Thumbs a Ride/Having Wonderful Crime '47
Donovan's Brain '53
George White's Scandals '45
Guilty of Treason '50
Threat '49

Dennis Feldman
Real Men '87

Gene Feldman
Danny '79

John Feldman
Alligator Eyes '90

Marty Feldman
The Last Remake of Beau Geste '77

Federico Fellini
Amarcord '74
And the Ship Sails On '83
Boccaccio '70 '62
City of Women '81
The Clowns '71
8 1/2 '63
Fellini Satyricon '69
Fellini's Roma '72
Ginger & Fred '86
I Vitelloni '53
Intervista '87
Juliet of the Spirits '65
La Dolce Vita '60
La Strada '54
Love in the City '53
Nights of Cabiria '57
Spirits of the Dead '68
The Swindle '55
Variety Lights '51
The White Sheik '52

Georg Fenady
Arnold '73
Terror in the Wax Museum '73

Huang Feng
Sting of the Dragon Masters '74

Michael Fengler
Why Does Herr R. Run Amok? '69

Philip Fently
The Baron '88

Claude Feraldo
Trade Secrets '90s

Rene Feret
The Mystery of Alexina '86

Michael Ferguson
Doctor Who: The Seeds of Death '69
Glory Boys '84

Emilio Fernandez
Flor Silvestre '58
La Choca '73
Maria Candelaria '46
The Pearl '48

Pablo Fero
Me, Myself & I '92

Abel Ferrara
Bad Lieutenant '92
Body Snatchers '93
Cat Chaser '90
China Girl '87
Dangerous Game '93
Driller Killer '74
Fear City '85
The Gladiator '86
King of New York '90
Ms. 45 '81

Romano Ferrara
Planets Against Us '61

Jeff Ferrell
Revenge of the Teenage Vixens from Outer Space '86

Jose Ferrer
Return to Peyton Place '61
State Fair '62

Mel Ferrer
Green Mansions '59

Marco Ferreri
El Cochecito '60
L'Udienza '71
Tales of Ordinary Madness '83

Robert A. Ferretti
Fear '88

Frank Ferrin
Sabaka '55

Stan Ferris
Tulips '81

George Ferron
The Scalawag Bunch '75

Giorgio Ferroni
The Bacchantes '63
Conquest of Mycene '63
Mill of the Stone Women '60

Jacques Feyder
Carnival in Flanders '35
Crainquebille '23
The Kiss '29
Knight Without Armour '37

Leonard Fields
King Kelly of the U.S.A. '34

Michael Fields
Bright Angel '91
Noon Wine '84

Steven Fierberg
Voodoo Dawn '89

Douglas Fifthian
Touch Me Not '74

Mike Figgis
Internal Affairs '90
Liebestraum '91
Mr. Jones '93
Stormy Monday '88
Women & Men: In Love There Are No Rules '91

Charles Finch
Priceless Beauty '90
Where Sleeping Dogs Lie '91

Nigel Finch
The Lost Language of Cranes '92

David Fincher
Alien 3 '92

Michael Findlay
Shriek of the Mutilated '74

Roberta Findlay
Blood Sisters '86
Lurkers '88
The Oracle '85
Prime Evil '88

John P. Finegan
Girls School Screamers '86

B.P. Fineman
Beauty for the Asking '39

Janace Fink
Velvet Smooth '76

Michael Fink
Black Force '75

Ken Finkleman
Airplane 2: The Sequel '82
Head Office '86

Joe Finley
Barbarian Queen 2: The Empress Strikes Back '89

Edward Finney
King of the Stallions '42
Riot Squad '41
Silver Stallion '41

Rex Firlin
The Death of Adolf Hitler '84

Sam Firstenberg
American Ninja '85
American Ninja 2: The Confrontation '87
American Samurai '92
Avenging Force '86
Blood Warriors '93
Breakin' 2: Electric Boogaloo '84
Delta Force 3: The Killing Game '91
My African Adventure '87
Ninja 3: The Domination '84
One More Chance '90
Revenge of the Ninja '83
Riverbend '89

Michael Firth
Heart of the Stag '84
Sylvia '86

Michael Fischa
Crack House '89
Death Spa '87
My Mom's a Werewolf '89

Max Fischer
Entangled '93
Killing 'em Softly '85

David Fisher
Liar's Moon '82
Toy Soldiers '84

Jack Fisher
Torn Apart '89

Mary Ann Fisher
Lords of the Deep '89

Terence Fisher
Blackout '54
The Brides of Dracula '60
The Curse of Frankenstein '57
The Curse of the Werewolf '61
Four Sided Triangle '53
Frankenstein and the Monster from Hell '74
The Gorgon '64
The Horror of Dracula '58
The Hound of the Baskervilles '59
Island of Terror '66
Island of the Burning Doomed '67

Man Bait '52
The Mummy '59
Race for Life '55
Robin Hood: The Movie '55
Sherlock Holmes and the Deadly Necklace '62
Spaceways '53
A Stolen Face '52
Sword of Sherwood Forest '60
Three Stops to Murder '53
Unholy Four '54

Tom Fisher
Cannibal Campout '88

Bill Fishman
Car 54, Where Are You? '94
Tapeheads '89

Jack Fisk
Daddy's Dyin'...Who's Got the Will? '90
Final Verdict '91
Raggedy Man '81
Violets Are Blue '86

Christopher Fitchett
Blood Money '80
Fair Game '85

George Fitzmaurice
As You Desire Me '32
The Last of Mrs. Cheyney '37
Mata Hari '32
Son of the Sheik '26
Suzy '26

James A. Fitzpatrick
Lady of the Lake '28

Robert S. Fiveson
The Clonus Horror '79

Paul Flaherty
Billy Crystal: Midnight Train to Moscow '89
Clifford '91
18 Again! '88
Who's Harry Crumb? '89

Robert Flaherty
Elephant Boy '37
Louisiana Story '48
Man of Aran '34
Moana, a Romance of the Golden Age '26
Tabu: A Story of the South Seas '31

Freddie Fleck
The Magnificent Ambersons '42

Dave Fleischer
Gulliver's Travels '39
Hoppity Goes to Town '41

Max Fleischer
Max Fleischer's Documentary Features '23

Richard Fleischer
Amityville 3: The Demon '83
Armored Car Robbery '50
Ashanti, Land of No Mercy '79
Barabbas '62
Between Heaven and Hell '56
The Boston Strangler '68
The Clay Pigeon '49
Conan the Destroyer '84
Doctor Dolittle '67
The Don is Dead '73
Fantastic Voyage '66
Follow Me Quietly '49
The Incredible Sarah '76
The Jazz Singer '80
Mandingo '75
Million Dollar Mystery '87
Mr. Majestyk '74
The New Centurions '72
The Prince and the Pauper '78
Red Sonja '85
See No Evil '71
Soylent Green '73
10 Rillington Place '71
Tora! Tora! Tora! '70
Tough Enough '83

Trapped '49
20,000 Leagues Under the Sea '54
The Vikings '58

Andrew Fleming
Bad Dreams '88
Threesome '94

Edward Fleming
Topsy Turvy '84

Victor Fleming
Adventure '45
Bombshell '33
Captains Courageous '37
Dr. Jekyll and Mr. Hyde '41
The Farmer Takes a Wife '35
Gone with the Wind '39
A Guy Named Joe '44
Hula '28
Joan of Arc '48
Mantrap '26
Reckless '35
Red Dust '32
Test Pilot '38
Tortilla Flat '42
Treasure Island '34
The Virginian '29
When the Clouds Roll By '19
The Wizard of Oz '39

Gordon Flemyng
Cloud Waltzing '87
Daleks—Invasion Earth 2150 A.D. '66
Doctor Who and the Daleks '65
Philby, Burgess and MacLean: Spy Scandal of the Century '84

Rodman Flender
In the Heat of Passion '91
Leprechaun 2 '94
The Unborn '91

Theodore J. Flicker
Playmates '72
The President's Analyst '67
Soggy Bottom U.S.A. '84
Three in the Cellar '70

James T. Flocker
Ghosts That Still Walk '77
Ground Zero '88
The Secret of Navajo Cave '76

John Florea
Computer Wizard '77
The Invisible Strangler '76
Island of the Lost '68
Where the Eagle Flies '72
Where's Willie? '77

Isaac Florentine
Desert Kickboxer '92

John Flores
Hot Child in the City '87

Robert Florey
The Beast with Five Fingers '46
The Cocoanuts '29
The Desert Song '53
Ex-Lady '33
Murders in the Rue Morgue '32
Outpost in Morocco '49

Aldo Florio
Five Giants from Texas '66

Calvin Floyd
Sleep of Death '79

Drago Floyd
Troll 2 '92

John Flynn
Best Seller '87
Brainscan '94
Defiance '79
Lock Up '89
Marilyn: The Untold Story '80
Nails '92
Rolling Thunder '77
Scam '93
Touched '82

Tom Flynn
Watch It '93

Helmut Foernbacher
What a Way to Die '70

Lawrence Foldes
Curse of the Living Dead '89
The Great Skycopter Rescue '82
Nightforce '80
Young Warriors '83

Peter Foldy
Midnight Witness '93

Peter Foleg
The Unseen '80

James Foley
After Dark, My Sweet '90
At Close Range '86
Glengarry Glen Ross '92
Reckless '84
Who's That Girl? '87

Peter Fonda
Hired Hand '71
Idaho Transfer '73
Wanda Nevada '79

Marcello Fondato
Immortal Bachelor '80

Allen Fong
Just Like Weather '86

Leo Fong
Hawkeye '88
Showdown '93
24 Hours to Midnight '92

Angelino Fons
Marianela '70s

Jorge Fons
Jory '72

Lloyd Fonvielle
Gotham '88

Bryan Forbes
Better Late Than Never '83
International Velvet '78
King Rat '65
Long Ago Tomorrow '71
The Madwoman of Chaillot '69
The Naked Face '84
Seance on a Wet Afternoon '64
Whistle Down the Wind '62
The Wrong Box '66

Francis Ford
Custer's Last Fight '12

Greg Ford
Daffy Duck's Quackbusters '89

John Ford
Arrowsmith '31
Cheyenne Autumn '64
December 7th: The Movie '91
Donovan's Reef '63
Drums Along the Mohawk '39
Fort Apache '48
The Fugitive '48
The Grapes of Wrath '40
The Horse Soldiers '59
How Green was My Valley '41
How the West was Won '63
Hurricane '37
The Informer '35
Judge Priest '34
Last Hurrah '58
The Long Gray Line '55
The Long Voyage Home '40
The Lost Patrol '34
The Man Who Shot Liberty Valance '62
Mary of Scotland '36
Mister Roberts '55
Mogambo '53
My Darling Clementine '46
The Quiet Man '52
Rio Grande '50
The Searchers '56
Sergeant Rutledge '60
She Wore a Yellow Ribbon '49

Stagecoach '39
Straight Shootin' '17
The Sun Shines Bright '53
They Were Expendable '45
Three Godfathers '48
Two Rode Together '61
Wagon Master '50
Wee Willie Winkie '37
What Price Glory? '52
Wings of Eagles '57
Young Mr. Lincoln '39

Philip Ford
The Inner Circle '46
Redwood Forest Trail '50
The Vanishing Westerner '50

Stephen Ford
Dungeonmaster '85

Eugene Forde
Inspector Hornleigh '39

Walter Forde
Bulldog Jack '35
The Ghost Train '41
King of the Damned '36
The Secret Four '40

Richard Foreman
Sudden Death '77

Milos Forman
Amadeus '84
The Firemen's Ball '68
Hair '79
Loves of a Blonde '65
One Flew Over the Cuckoo's Nest '75
Ragtime '81
Valmont '89

Tom Forman
The Fighting American '24
Shadows '22
The Virginian '23

Rolf Forsberg
Beyond the Next Mountain '87

Robert Forster
Hollywood Harry '86

Bill Forsyth
Being Human '94
Breaking In '89
Comfort and Joy '84
Gregory's Girl '80
Housekeeping '87
Local Hero '83
That Sinking Feeling '79

Ed Forsyth
Chesty Anderson USN '76
Inferno in Paradise '88
Superchick '71

Bob Fosse
All That Jazz '79
Cabaret '72
Lenny '74
Star 80 '83
Sweet Charity '69

Giles Foster
Consuming Passions '88
Dutch Girls '87
Hotel du Lac '86
Innocent Victim '90
Silas Marner '85

Jodie Foster
Little Man Tate '91

Lewis R. Foster
Crashout '55
Dakota Incident '56
The Sign of Zorro '60
Tonka '58

Norman Foster
Brighty of the Grand Canyon '67
Davy Crockett and the River Pirates '56
Davy Crockett, King of the Wild Frontier '55
Indian Paint '64

Foster ▶cont.

Journey into Fear '42
Mr. Moto's Last Warning '39
The Nine Lives of Elfego Baca '58
Rachel and the Stranger '48
The Sign of Zorro '60
Tell It to the Judge '49

Claude Fournier
Dan Candy's Law '73
Tales of the Klondike: The Scorn of Women '87

Gene Fowler
I Married a Monster from Outer Space '58
I Was a Teenage Werewolf '57
The Rebel Set '59
Showdown at Boot Hill '58

Robert Fowler
Below the Belt '80

Douglas Fowley
Macumba Love '60

Emerson Fox
Shocking Asia '75

Erika Fox
Dead Women in Lingerie '90

Marilyn Fox
Codename: Icarus '85

Wallace Fox
Bad Men of the Border '45
Bowery at Midnight '42
Bowery Blitzkrieg '41
The Corpse Vanishes '42
Ghost Rider '43
The Great Mike '44
Gun Packer '38
Kid Dynamite '43
Let's Get Tough '42
Million Dollar Kid '44
'Neath Brooklyn Bridge '42
Powdersmoke Range '35
Smart Alecks '42
Yellow Dust '36

William A. Fraker
Legend of the Lone Ranger '81
Monte Walsh '70
A Reflection of Fear '72

Gianni Franciolini
Pardon My Trunk '52

Coleman Francis
The Beast of Yucca Flats '61

Freddie Francis
The Brain '62
Craze '74
The Creeping Flesh '72
The Doctor and the Devils '85
Dr. Terror's House of Horrors '65
Dracula Has Risen from the Grave '68
The Evil of Frankenstein '64
The Ghoul '75
Girly '70
Hysteria '64
Legend of the Werewolf '75
The Skull '65
Tales from the Crypt '72
Tales That Witness Madness '73
They Came from Beyond Space '67
Torture Garden '67
The Vampire Happening '71

Karl Francis
And Nothing But the Truth '82

Pietro Francisci
Hercules '58
Hercules Unchained '59

Jess (Jesus) Franco
Angel of Death '86

Attack of the Robots '66
The Awful Dr. Orlof '62
Bloody Moon '83
The Castle of Fu Manchu '68
Count Dracula '71
Deadly Sanctuary '68
The Diabolical Dr. Z '65
Dr. Orloff's Monster '64
Ilsa, the Wicked Warden '78
The Invisible Dead
Jack the Ripper '80
Kiss and Kill '68
The Loves of Irina '80s
99 Women '69
The Perverse Countess '73
Revenge in the House of Usher '82
The Screaming Dead '72
Sex is Crazy '79
Venus in Furs '70
Virgin Among the Living Dead '71

Richardo Franco
Berlin Blues '89

Georges Franju
The Horror Chamber of Dr. Faustus '59
Judex '64

A.M. Frank
Oasis of the Zombies '82

Carol Frank
Sorority House Massacre '86

Charles Frank
Inheritance '47

Christopher Frank
Josepha '82
L'Annee des Meduses '86

Hubert Frank
The Dolls '83
Melody in Love '78

Melvin Frank
Above and Beyond '53
Buona Sera, Mrs. Campbell '68
Court Jester '56
The Duchess and the Dirtwater Fox '76
The Jayhawkers '59
Li'l Abner '59
Lost and Found '79
Prisoner of Second Avenue '75
A Touch of Class '73
Walk Like a Man '87

Robert Frank
Candy Mountain '87

Cyril Frankel
Devil on Horseback '54
Make Me an Offer '55
Permission To Kill '75
The Very Edge '63

John Frankenheimer
All Fall Down '62
Birdman of Alcatraz '62
Black Sunday '77
The Challenge '82
Days of Wine and Roses '58
Dead Bang '89
52 Pick-Up '86
The Fixer '68
The Fourth War '90
French Connection 2 '75
Grand Prix '66
The Holcroft Covenant '85
The Horsemen '70
The Manchurian Candidate '62
99 & 44/100 Dead '74
Prophecy '79
Seven Days in May '64
The Story of a Love Story '73
The Train '65
Year of the Gun '91

Carl Franklin
Eye of the Eagle 2 '89
Full Fathom Five '90
Laurel Avenue '93
Nowhere to Run '88

One False Move '91

Chester M. Franklin
Vanity Fair '32

Howard Franklin
The Public Eye '92
Quick Change '90

Jimmy Franklin
Ripping Yarns '75

Richard Franklin
Cloak & Dagger '84
F/X 2: The Deadly Art of Illusion '91
Link '86
Patrick '78
Psycho 2 '83
Road Games '81

Roger Franklin
Raiders of Atlantis '83

Sidney Franklin
The Barretts of Wimpole Street '34
The Forbidden City '18
The Good Earth '37
The Guardsman '31
The Primitive Lover '16
Private Lives '31
Smilin' Through '32
Wild Orchids '28

Harry Fraser
Aces Wild '37
Ambush Trail '46
Broadway to Cheyenne '32
Cavalcade of the West '36
Chained for Life '51
Diamond Trail '33
Enemy of the Law '45
Feud of the West '35
Fighting Parson '35
Frontier Fugitives '45
Galloping Dynamite '37
Ghost City '32
Ghost Town '37
Heroes of the Alamo '37
Mason of the Mounted '32
'Neath the Arizona Skies '34
Outlaw Roundup '44
Rainbow Ranch '33
Randy Rides Alone '34
Rustler's Paradise '35
The Savage Girl '32
Six Shootin' Sheriff '38
Three in the Saddle '45
The Tonto Kid '35
Wagon Trail '35
Wild Mustang '35
Wolf Dog '33

James Frawley
Assault and Matrimony '87
The Big Bus '76
Fraternity Vacation '85
Great American Traffic Jam '80
Hansel and Gretel '82
The Muppet Movie '79
Spies, Lies and Naked Thighs '91

Stephen Frears
Dangerous Liaisons '88
The Grifters '90
Gumshoe '72
Hero '92
The Hit '85
My Beautiful Laundrette '85
Prick Up Your Ears '87
Saigon: Year of the Cat '87
Sammy & Rosie Get Laid '87
The Snapper '93

Riccardo (Robert Hampton) Freda
Devil of the Desert Against the Son of Hercules '62
The Devil's Commandment '56
Evil's Commandment '56
The Ghost '63
The Giants of Thessaly '60
The Horrible Dr. Hichcock '62
Les Miserables '52

Maciste in Hell '60
The Mongols '60
Samson and the 7 Miracles of the World '62
Sins of Rome '54

Herb Freed
Beyond Evil '80
Graduation Day '81
Haunts '77
Survival Game '87
Tomboy '85

Mark Freed
Shock 'Em Dead '90

Jerrold Freedman
Best Kept Secrets '88
Borderline '80
Family Sins '87
He Who Walks Alone '78
Legs '83
Native Son '86
Seduced '85
The Streets of L.A. '79
Thompson's Last Run '90

Thornton Freeland
Accused '36
Flying Down to Rio '33
Jericho '38
They Call It Sin '32
Whoopee! '30

Hal Freeman
Blood Frenzy '87

Joan Freeman
Satisfaction '88
Streetwalkin' '85

Morgan Freeman
Bopha! '93

Warwick Freeman
Demonstrator '71

Paul Frees
The Beatniks '60

Hugo Fregonese
Blowing Wild '54
Decameron Nights '53
Dracula vs. Frankenstein '69
Harry Black and the Tiger '58

Friz Freleng
Best of Bugs Bunny & Friends '40
Bugs & Daffy: The Wartime Cartoons '45
Bugs Bunny Superstar '75
Bugs Bunny's 3rd Movie: 1,001 Rabbit Tales '82
Daffy Duck's Movie: Fantastic Island '83
Looney Looney Looney Bugs Bunny Movie '81
Starring Bugs Bunny! '48

Harold French
The Day Will Dawn '42
Encore '52
Paris Express '53
Rob Roy—The Highland Rogue '53
Trio '50

Charles Frend
Cruel Sea '53
The Foreman Went to France '42
Johnny Frenchman '46
San Demetrio, London '47
Scott of the Antarctic '48
The Third Key '57

Robert M. Fresco
Small Kill '93

Karl Freund
Mad Love '35
The Mummy '32

Fridrik Thor Fridriksson
Children of Nature '92

Randall Fried
Heaven is a Playground '91

Rick Friedberg
Off the Wall '82
Pray TV '80

Richard Friedenberg
The Adventures of Frontier Fremont '75
The Deerslayer '78
Life & Times of Grizzly Adams '74

Bud Friedgen
That's Entertainment, Part 3 '93

William Friedkin
Blue Chips '94
The Boys in the Band '70
Brink's Job '78
Cruising '80
Deal of the Century '83
The Exorcist '73
The French Connection '71
The Guardian '90
The Night They Raided Minsky's '69
Python Wolf '88
Rampage '87
Sorcerer '77
Stalking Danger '86
To Live & Die in L.A. '85

Louis Friedlander
Tailspin Tommy '34

Adam Friedman
To Sleep with a Vampire '92

Anthony Friedman
Bartleby '70

David Friedman
The Defilers '65

Jeffrey Friedman
Common Threads: Stories from the Quilt '89

Ken Friedman
Made in USA '88

Richard S. Friedman
Deathmask '69
Doom Asylum '88
Phantom of the Mall: Eric's Revenge '89
Scared Stiff '87

Seymour Friedman
I'll Get You '53
Loan Shark '52

Gunther Fritsch
Stolen Identity '53

Bill Froechlich
Return to Horror High '87

David Frost
Ring of Steel '94

Lee Frost
Chain Gang Women '72
Chrome and Hot Leather '71
Dixie Dynamite '76
Policewomen '73

Mark Frost
Storyville '92

William Fruet
Bedroom Eyes '86
Blue Monkey '87
Death Weekend '76
Funeral Home '82
Killer Party '86
Search and Destroy '81
Spasms '82
Wedding in White '72

E. Max Frye
Amos and Andrew '93

Robert Fuest
The Abominable Dr. Phibes '71
And Soon the Darkness '70
Devil's Rain '75
Doctor Phibes Rises Again '72

The Final Programme '73
Island '77
A Movie Star's Daughter '79
Revenge of the Stepford Wives '80
Wuthering Heights '70

Kinji Fukasaku
Black Lizard '68
The Green Slime '68
Samurai Reincarnation '81
Tora! Tora! Tora! '70
Virus '82

Jun Fukuda
Godzilla on Monster Island '72
Godzilla vs. Megalon '76
Godzilla vs. the Cosmic Monster '74
Godzilla vs. the Sea Monster '66
The Secret of the Telegian '61
Son of Godzilla '66

Lucio Fulci
The Black Cat '81
Challenge to White Fang '86
Conquest '83
Contraband '86
Dangerous Obsession '88
Gates of Hell '83
The House by the Cemetery '83
Manhattan Baby '82
The New Gladiators '87
New York Ripper '82
The Psychic '78
Zombie '80

Fleming Fuller
Prey of the Chameleon '91

Louis Fuller
Seven Doors of Death '82

Samuel Fuller
Baron of Arizona '51
The Big Red One '80
China Gate '57
I Shot Jesse James '49
The Meanest Men in the West '76
Merrill's Marauders '62
Naked Kiss '64
Pickup on South Street '53
Run of the Arrow '56
Shark! '68
Shock Corridor '63
The Steel Helmet '51
Underworld, U.S.A. '60
Verboten! '59

Tex Fuller
Stranded '87

Jill Fullerton-Smith
Alive: 20 Years Later '93

Yueh Fung
Bells of Death '90

Allen Funt
What Do You Say to a Naked Lady? '70

John Furey
Shadow Dancing '88

Sidney J. Furie
The Appaloosa '66
The Boys in Company C '77
Doctor Blood's Coffin '62
The Entity '83
Hit! '73
The Ipcress File '65
Iron Eagle '86
Iron Eagle 2 '88
Lady Sings the Blues '72
Ladybugs '92
Leather Boys '63
Purple Hearts '84
The Snake Woman '61
Superman 4: The Quest for Peace '87
The Taking of Beverly Hills '91

Yasuo Furuhata
Station '81

Richard Gabai
Assault of the Party Nerds '89
Hot Under the Collar '91
Virgin High '90

Martin Gabel
Lost Moment '47

Pal Gabor
Brady's Escape '84

Mitchell Gabourie
Buying Time '89

Radu Gabrea
A Man Like Eva '83
Secret of the Ice Cave '89

Mike Gabriel
The Rescuers Down Under '90

Frederic Gadette
This is Not a Test '62

Robert Gaffney
Frankenstein Meets the Space Monster '65

George Gage
Fleshburn '84

John Gage
Velvet Touch '48

Rene Gainville
The Associate '82
Le Complot '73

Pierre-Dominique Gaisseau
The Sky Above, the Mud Below '61

Richard Galbreath
Night of Evil '62

John Gale
Commando Invasion '87
The Firing Line '91
Slash '89

Ricardo Jacques Gale
Alien Intruder '93

Timothy Galfas
Sunnyside '79

John A. Gallagher
Street Hunter '90

Andy Galler
Bums '93

Fred Gallo
Dead Space '90
Dracula Rising '93
The Finishing Touch '92

George Gallo
29th Street '91

Carmine Gallone
Carthage in Flames '60

Samuel Gallu
The Man Outside '68
Theatre of Death '67

Lee Games
Actors and Sin '52

Abel Gance
The Battle of Austerlitz '60
J'Accuse '37
Napoleon '27
The Torture of Silence '17

Albert C. Gannaway
Daniel Boone: Trail Blazer '56
Hidden Guns '56
Man or Gun '58

David Garcia
Sex Crimes '92

Bud Gardner
Model Behavior '82

Herb Gardner
The Goodbye People '83

Leo Garen
The Shrieking '73

Patrick Garland
A Doll's House '89

Lee Garmes
Angels Over Broadway '40
Dreaming Lips '37

Tay Garnett
Bataan '43
The Big Push '75
Cause for Alarm '51
Challenge To Be Free '76
Cheers for Miss Bishop '41
China Seas '35
A Connecticut Yankee in King Arthur's Court '49
Eternally Yours '39
The Flying Fool '29
Joy of Living '38
Main Street to Broadway '53
Mrs. Parkington '44
One Minute to Zero '52
The Postman Always Rings Twice '46
Seven Sinners '40
Slightly Honorable '40
Stand-In '37
The Valley of Decision '45

Tony Garnett
Deep in the Heart '83

Lila Garrett
Terraces '77

Otis Garrett
Danger on the Air '38

Roy Garrett
Eyes Behind the Stars '72
White Slave '86

Mick Garris
Critters 2: The Main Course '88
Psycho 4: The Beginning '90
Sleepwalkers '92
Stephen King's The Stand '94

Andrew Garroni
Body of Influence '93

Harry Garson
Mid-Channel '20
The Worldly Madonna '22

John Garwood
Violent Zone '89

Jerome Gary
Stripper '86
Traxx '87

Louis Gasnier
Kismet '20
Murder on the Yukon '40
Reefer Madness '38
Topaze '33

Mark Gasper
An Empty Bed '90

Gilbert Gates
Johnny We Hardly Knew Ye '77

Nils Gaup
Pathfinder '87
Shipwrecked '90

Roberto Gavaldon
La Diosa Arrodillada '47
The Littlest Outlaw '54
Macario '58

Eleanor Gaver
Slipping into Darkness '88

Victor Gaviria
Rodrigo D.: No Future '91

Joe Gayton
Warm Summer Rain '89

Armand Gazarian
Game of Survival '89
Prison Planet '92

Gyula Gazdag
A Hungarian Fairy Tale '87
Stand Off '89

Glenn Gebhard
One Last Run '89

Dieter Geissler
Deadly Game '83

Bruce Geller
The Savage Bees '76

Augusto Genina
Prix de Beaute '30

Arnaldo Genoino
Herod the Great '60

John Gentil
Battle of Valiant '63

Giacomo Gentilomo
Hercules Against the Moon Men '64

George W. George
James Dean Story '57

Peter George
Surf Nazis Must Die '87

Maurice Geraghty
Sword of Monte Cristo '51

Haile Gerima
Ashes and Embers '82
Bush Mama '76

Marion Gering
Thunder in the City '37

Pietro Germi
Alfredo, Alfredo '72
Divorce—Italian Style '62
Four Ways Out '57
Seduced and Abandoned '64

Clyde Geronomi
The Adventures of Ichabod and Mr. Toad '49
Alice in Wonderland '51
The Legend of Sleepy Hollow '49
101 Dalmations '61
Sleeping Beauty '59

Peter Gerretsen
Night Friend '87

Theodore Gershuny
Silent Night, Bloody Night '73

Nicolas Gessner
It Rained All Night the Day I Left '78
The Little Girl Who Lives Down the Lane '76
The Peking Blond '68
Quicker Than the Eye '88
Someone Behind the Door '71
12 Plus 1 '70

Steven Gethers
Billy: Portrait of a Street Kid '77
Damien: The Leper Priest '80
The Hillside Strangler '89
Jacqueline Bouvier Kennedy '81
Jenny's War '85

Francis Giacobetti
Emmanuelle 4 '84
Emmanuelle, the Joys of a Woman '76

Alfredo Gianelli
Mother Doesn't Always Know Best '60s

Duncan Gibbins
A Case for Murder '93
Eve of Destruction '90
Fire with Fire '86

Pamela Gibbons
Midnight Dancer '87

Rodney Gibbons
The Neighbor '93

Alan Gibson
The Charmer '89
Martin's Day '85
The Satanic Rites of Dracula '73
Silent Scream '84
Twinsanity '70
The Two Faces of Evil '82
A Woman Called Golda '82

Brian Gibson
Breaking Glass '80
The Josephine Baker Story '90
Murderers Among Us: The Simon Wiesenthal Story '89
Poltergeist 2: The Other Side '86
What's Love Got to Do With It? '93

Hoot Gibson
Spurs '30

Mel Gibson
The Man Without a Face '93

Robert Gibson
Snow: The Movie '83

Tom Gibson
Singing Buckaroo '37

Brian Gilbert
The French Lesson '86
Not Without My Daughter '90
Sharma & Beyond '84
Vice Versa '88

Lewis Gilbert
The Adventurers '70
Alfie '66
Cast a Dark Shadow '55
A Cry from the Streets '57
Damn the Defiant '62
Educating Rita '83
Ferry to Hong Kong '59
Friends '71
Moonraker '79
Not Quite Paradise '86
Paul and Michelle '74
Reach for the Sky '56
The Sea Shall Not Have Them '55
Shirley Valentine '89
Sink the Bismarck '60
The Spy Who Loved Me '77
Stepping Out '91
Tough Guy '53
You Only Live Twice '67

David Giler
Black Bird '75

David Giles
Mansfield Park '85
A Murder is Announced '87

Tom Giles
Journey Through Rosebud '72

Joseph Gilford
Max '79

Mark Gilhuis
Bloody Wednesday '87

Tony Jiti Gill
Murder-in-Law '92

Stuart Gillard
A Man Called Sarge '90
Paradise '82
Teenage Mutant Ninja Turtles 3 '93

Jeff Gillen
Deranged '74

Terry Gilliam
The Adventures of Baron Munchausen '89
Brazil '85
The Fisher King '91
Jabberwocky '77
Monty Python and the Holy Grail '75
Time Bandits '81

Sidney Gilliat
Endless Night '71
The Great St. Trinian's Train Robbery '66
Green for Danger '47
Only Two Can Play '62

John Gilling
The Gamma People '56
The Gilded Cage '54
It Takes a Thief '59
Mania '60
My Son, the Vampire '52
Night Caller from Outer Space '66
No Trace '50
Where the Bullets Fly '66
White Fire '53

Stuart Gilmore
The Half-Breed '51
Hot Lead '51

Frank D. Gilroy
Desperate Characters '71
From Noon Till Three '76
The Gig '85
Once in Paris... '79

Milton Moses Ginsberg
Werewolf of Washington '73

Brad F. Ginter
Flesh Feast '69

Robert Ginty
Bounty Hunters '89
Vietnam, Texas '90

Christian Gion
Here Comes Santa Claus '84

Jose Giovanni
Boomerang '76
Gypsy '75

Buddy Giovnazzo
Combat Shock '84

Bob Giraldi
Club Med '83
Hiding Out '87

Franco Giraldi
A Minute to Pray, A Second to Die '67

Andre Girard
Qui Etes Vous, Mr. Sorge? '61

Bernard Girard
Dead Heat on a Merry-Go-Round '66
Hard Frame '70
Little Moon & Jud McGraw '78
Mind Snatchers '70
A Name for Evil '70

Francois Girard
32 Short Films About Glenn Gould '93

Bernard Giraudeau
Gone with the West '72

William Girdler
Asylum of Satan '72
Day of the Animals '77
Grizzly '76
The Manitou '78
Sheba, Baby '75
Three on a Meathook '72

Francis Girod
The Elegant Criminal '92
Infernal Trio '74
L'Etat Sauvage '78

Marcel Gisler
The Blue Hour '91

Wyndham Gittens
Tim Tyler's Luck '37

Paul Michael Glaser
The Air Up There '94
The Amazons '84
Band of the Hand '86

The Cutting Edge '92
The Running Man '87

Arnold Glassman
Visions of Light: The Art of Cinematography '93

Lesli Linka Glatter
Into the Homeland '87
State of Emergency '94

Michie Gleason
Summer Heat '87

John Glen
Aces: Iron Eagle 3 '92
Christopher Columbus: The Discovery '92
For Your Eyes Only '81
License to Kill '89
The Living Daylights '87
Octopussy '83
A View to a Kill '85

John Glenister
After Julius '78

Bert Glennon
Paradise Island '30
South of Santa Fe '32

Peter Glenville
Becket '64
The Comedians '67
Hotel Paradiso '66
The Prisoner '55
Summer and Smoke '61

James Glickenhaus
Exterminator '80
McBain '91
Protector '85
Shakedown '88
Slaughter of the Innocents '93
The Soldier '82

Paul Glickler
The Cheerleaders '72
Running Scared '79

Arne Glimcher
The Mambo Kings '92

Greg Glionna
Meet the Parents '91

Wolfgang Gluck
'38: Vienna Before the Fall '88

Tom Gniazdowski
Death Collector '89

Constantine S. Gochis
The Redeemer '76

Jean-Luc Godard
Alphaville '65
Aria '88
Band of Outsiders '64
Breathless '59
Comment Ca Va? '76
Contempt '64
First Name: Carmen '83
France/Tour/Detour/Deux/Enfants '78
Godard/Truffaut Shorts '58
Hail Mary '85
Here and Elsewhere '70s
The Joy of Knowledge '65
King Lear '87
Les Carabiniers '63
A Married Woman '65
Masculine Feminine '66
My Life to Live '62
Nouvelle Vague '90
Numero Deux '75
Oldest Profession '67
Pierrot le Fou '65
Scenario du Film Passion '82
Six Fois Deux/Sur et Sous la Communication '76
Six in Paris '68
Soft and Hard '85
Sympathy for the Devil '70
Weekend '67
A Woman is a Woman '60

Gary Goddard
Masters of the Universe '87

Jim Goddard
The Impossible Spy '87
Reilly: Ace of Spies '87
Shanghai Surprise '86
A Tale of Two Cities '80

Peter Godfrey
Christmas in Connecticut '45
Escape Me Never '47
The Two Mrs. Carrolls '47

Jill Godmillow
Waiting for the Moon '87

Alex E. Goiten
Cherry Hill High '76

Menahem Golan
The Apple '80
Delta Force '86
Diamonds '72
Enter the Ninja '81
Escape to the Sun '72
Hanna's War '88
Hit the Dutchman '92
Lepke '75
Lupo '70
Mack the Knife '89
The Magician of Lublin '79
Operation Thunderbolt '77
Over the Brooklyn Bridge '83
Over the Top '86
Silent Victim '92
What's Good for the Goose '93

Greg Gold
House of the Rising Sun '87

Jack Gold
Catholics '73
Escape from Sobibor '87
Little Lord Fauntleroy '80
Man Friday '75
The Medusa Touch '78
Murrow '86
The Naked Civil Servant '75
Praying Mantis '83
Roboman '75
The Rose and the Jackal '90
Sakharov '84
The Tenth Man '88

Myron G. Gold
Frankenstein's Great Aunt Tillie '83

Willis Goldbeck
Between Two Women '86
Love Laughs at Andy Hardy '46

Dan Goldberg
Feds '88

Gary David Goldberg
Dad '89

Mark Goldblatt
Dead Heat '88
The Punisher '90

Dan Golden
Naked Obsession '91

John Golden
Fat Guy Goes Nutzoid '86

Murray Golden
Haunting of Harrington House '82

Sidney Goldin
East and West '23
His Wife's Lover '31
Uncle Moses '32

Paul Golding
Pulse '88

Gary Goldman
Thumbelina '94
A Troll in Central Park '94

Jim Goldman
Desert Warrior '88

Martin Goldman
Dark August '76

Stuart Goldman
Senior Week '88

John Goldschmidt
Crime of Honor '85
She'll Be Wearing Pink Pajamas '84

Allan Goldstein
Common Bonds '91
Death Wish 5: The Face of Death '94
The Dining Room '86
The House of Dies Drear '88
Outside Chance of Maximillian Glick '88
The Phone Call '89
True West '86

Amy Goldstein
The Silencer '92

Scott Goldstein
Ambition '91
Walls of Glass '85

James Goldstone
Brother John '70
Calamity Jane '82
Cry Panic '74
Eric '75
Kent State '81
Rita Hayworth: The Love Goddess '83
Rollercoaster '77
Swashbuckler '76
They Only Kill Their Masters '72
Things in Their Season '74
When Time Ran Out '80
Winning '69

Bob(cat) Goldthwait
Shakes the Clown '92

Steve Gomer
Sweet Lorraine '87

Nick Gomez
Laws of Gravity '92

Vasilii Goncharov
Early Russian Cinema, Vol. 2: Folklore & Legend '12
Early Russian Cinema, Vol. 6: Class Distinctions '14

Regelio A. Gonzalez, Jr.
The Oval Portrait '88

Servando Gonzalez
The Fool Killer '65

Gregory Goodell
Human Experiments '79

Saul Goodkind
Buck Rogers Conquers the Universe '39
The Phantom Creeps '39

Fred Goodwin
Curse 2: The Bite '88

Leslie Goodwins
Day the Bookies Wept '39
Mexican Spitfire at Sea '42
The Mummy's Curse '44
Pop Always Pays '40

Bert I. Gordon
The Amazing Colossal Man '57
Beginning of the End '57
The Big Bet '85
Cyclops '56
Earth vs. the Spider '58
Empire of the Ants '77
Food of the Gods '76
The Mad Bomber '72
The Magic Sword '62
Picture Mommy Dead '66
Satan's Princess '90
Tormented '60
Village of the Giants '65
The War of the Colossal Beast '58
The Witching '72

Bette Gordon
Variety '83

Bryan Gordon
Career Opportunities '91

Keith Gordon
The Chocolate War '88
A Midnight Clear '92
Wild Palms '93

Michael Gordon
Boy's Night Out '62
Cyrano de Bergerac '50
For Love or Money '63
The Impossible Years '68
Pillow Talk '59
Texas Across the River '66

Robert Gordon
The Gatling Gun '72
It Came from Beneath the Sea '55
Revenge of the Red Baron '93

Steve Gordon
Arthur '81

Stuart Gordon
Dolls '87
Fortress '93
From Beyond '86
The Pit & the Pendulum '91
The Re-Animator '85
Robot Jox '89

Berry Gordy
Mahogany '75

Serif Goren
Yol '82

Claude Goretta
The Lacemaker '77

Vladimir Gorikker
The Tsar's Bride '66

Jean-Pierre Gorin
Here and Elsewhere '70s

Charles Gormley
The Gospel According to Vic '87

Michael Gornick
Creepshow 2 '87

Morleen Gorris
Broken Mirrors '85
Question of Silence '83

Ron Gorton, Sr.
Whispers of White '93

Hideo Gosha
Hunter in the Dark '80
The Wolves '82

Jurgen Goslar
Albino '76
Slavers '77

Peter Gothar
Time Stands Still '82

Toshio Goto
Forest of Little Bear '79

Carl Gottlieb
Amazon Women on the Moon '87
Caveman '81

Franz Gottlieb
The Black Abbot '63
Curse of the Yellow Snake '63
The Phantom of Soho '64

Lisa Gottlieb
Just One of the Guys '85

Michael Gottlieb
Mannequin '87
Mr. Nanny '93

Robert Gottschalk
Dangerous Charter '62

Heywood Gould
One Good Cop '91

Alfred Goulding
A Chump at Oxford '40
Dick Barton, Special Agent '48

Edmund Goulding
Dark Victory '39
Dawn Patrol '38
Forever and a Day '43
Grand Hotel '32
The Great Lie '41
The Old Maid '39
The Razor's Edge '46
Reaching for the Moon '31
Riptide '34
That Certain Woman '37
We're Not Married '52

Richard Governor
Ghost Town '88

Bruce Gowers
Eddie Murphy "Delirious" '83

William Grace
Tomb of Torture '65

Marc Gracie
A Kink in the Picasso '90

Roger Graef
Secret Policeman's Private
Parts '81

Tom Graeff
Teenagers from Outer Space
'59

Paul Graetz
Heart of a Nation '43

Anders Grafstrom
The Long Island Four '80

Bob Graham
End of August '82

David C. Graham
The Undertaker and His Pals
'67

S. Edward Graham
Devil Monster '46

William A. Graham
The Amazing Howard Hughes
'77
And I Alone Survived '78
Beyond the Bermuda Triangle
'75
Birds of Prey '72
Calendar Girl Murders '84
Change of Habit '69
Deadly Encounter '72
The Doomsday Flight '66
George Washington: The
Forging of a Nation '86
Get Christie Love! '74
Gore Vidal's Billy the Kid '89
The Guyana Tragedy: The
Story of Jim Jones '80
Harry Tracy '83
Honky '71
Jigsaw '71
Larry '74
Last Days of Frank & Jesse
James '86
M.A.D.D.: Mothers Against
Drunk Driving '83
Mr. Inside, Mr. Outside '74
Montana '90
One in a Million: The Ron
LaFlore Story '78
Orphan Train '79
Proud Men '87
Rage '80
Return to the Blue Lagoon '91
Secrets of a Married Man '84
Thief '71
21 Hours at Munich '76
Waterhole #3 '67
Where the Lilies Bloom '74

**Vladimir
Grammatikov**
The Land of Faraway '87

Richard Grand
Fyre '78

S.A. Grandi
Anything for a Thrill '37

Gilles Grangier
Duke of the Derby '62

**Pierre Granier-
Deferre**
The French Detective '75
Le Chat '75
Widow Couderc '74

Brian Grant
Love Kills '91
Sweet Poison '91

James Edward Grant
Angel and the Badman '47

Lee Grant
Staying Together '89
Tell Me a Riddle '80

Michael Grant
Fatal Attraction '80

Alex Grasshof
Pepper and His Wacky Taxi '72

Jorge Grau
The Legend of Blood Castle '72

Walter Grauman
Are You in the House Alone?
'78
Force Five '75
Lady in a Cage '64
Manhunter '74
Most Wanted '76
Nightmare on the 13th Floor '90
Outrage! '86
Paper Man '71
Pleasure Palace '80
Scene of the Crime '85
633 Squadron '64
The Streets of San Francisco
'72
To Race the Wind '80

Gary Graver
Crossing the Line '90
Evil Spirits '91
Moon in Scorpio '86
Party Camp '87
Roots of Evil '91
Trick or Treats '82

John Gray
An American Story '92
Billy Galvin '86
The Lost Capone '90
When He's Not a Stranger '89

Mike Gray
Wavelength '83

Godfrey Grayson
Dick Barton Strikes Back '48
Room to Let '49

Kjell Grede
Good Evening, Mr. Wallenberg
'93

Janet Greek
The Spellbinder '88

Alfred E. Green
Baby Face '33
Copacabana '47
Dangerous '35
Disraeli '29
Ella Cinders '26
The Fabulous Dorseys '47
Four Faces West '48
The Jackie Robinson Story '50
The Jolson Story '46
Mr. Winkle Goes to War '44
The Narrow Margin '52
South of Pago Pago '40
Thoroughbreds Don't Cry '37

Bruce Seth Green
The Hunt for the Night Stalker

Running Against Time '90

David Green
Buster '88
Car Trouble '86
Code of Honor '87
Fire Birds '90

Guy Green
Diamond Head '62
The Incredible Journey of Dr.
Meg Laurel '79
Luther '74
The Mark '61
Once is Not Enough '75
A Patch of Blue '65
Postmark for Danger '56
Postmark for Danger/
Quicksand '56
River Beat '54
S.O.S. Pacific '60
Strong Medicine '84
Walk in the Spring Rain '70

Joseph Green
The Brain That Wouldn't Die
'63
A Brivele der Mamen '38
Der Purimshpiler '37
Mamele '38
Yidl Mitn Fidl '36

Sparky Green
Savage Hunger '84

Terry Green
Cold Justice '89

Walon Green
The Hellstrom Chronicle '71

Peter Greenaway
The Belly of an Architect '91
The Cook, the Thief, His Wife &
Her Lover '90
The Draughtsman's Contract
'82
Drowning by Numbers '87
Prospero's Books '91
A Zed & Two Noughts '88

**Richard Alan
Greenberg**
Little Monsters '89

Danford B. Greene
The Secret Diary of Sigmund
Freud '84

David Greene
After the Promise '87
Blood Island '68
The Choice '81
The Count of Monte Cristo '74
Fatal Vision '84
Friendly Fire '79
Gray Lady Down '77
The Guardian '84
Hard Country '81
In a Stranger's Hand '92
Madame Sin '71
Miles to Go '86
The Penthouse '92
The People Next Door '70
Prototype '83
Rehearsal for Murder '82
Roots '77
Sebastian '68
Small Sacrifices '89
Take Your Best Shot '82
TripleCross '85
Vanishing Act '88
World War III '86

Herbert Greene
The Cosmic Man '59

Martin Greene
Dark Sanity '82
Undercover Cop '94

Max Greene
Hotel Reserve '44

Gregory Greens
The Sea Serpent '85

Bud Greenspan
Wilma '77

Maggie Greenwald
The Ballad of Little Jo '93
Home Remedy '88

Robert Greenwald
The Burning Bed '85
Flatbed Annie and Sweetiepie:
Lady Truckers '79
Forgotten Prisoners '90
Hear No Evil '93
In the Custody of Strangers '82
Sweet Hearts Dance '88
Xanadu '80

David Greenwalt
Rude Awakening '89
Secret Admirer '85

William Grefe
Alligator Alley '72
The Checkered Flag '63
Impulse '74
Jaws of Death '76
Stanley '72
Whiskey Mountain '77
Wild Rebels '71

Colin Gregg
We Think the World of You '88

Frank Gregory
The Invincible Gladiator '63

Jean Gremillon
Pattes Blanches '49
Stormy Waters '41

Wolf Gremm
Kamikaze '89 '83

Edmond T. Greville
Beat Girl '60
The Hands of Orlac '60
The Liars '64
Princess Tam Tam '35

Sharon Greytak
Hearing Voices '90

Sergio Grieco
Mad Dog '84
Man of Legend '71

Tom Gries
Breakheart Pass '76
Breakout '75
The Connection '73
Fools '70
The Glass House '72
The Greatest '77
Helter Skelter '76
Lady Ice '73
100 Rifles '69
QB VII '74
Will Penny '67

Andrew Grieve
Lorna Doone '90
Suspicion '87

Ken Grieve
Alamut Ambush '86

**Giuseppe Patroni
Griffi**
Collector's Item '89
Divine Nymph '71
Driver's Seat '73
'Tis a Pity She's a Whore '73

Charles B. Griffith
Dr. Heckyl and Mr. Hype '80
Eat My Dust '76
Smokey Bites the Dust '81
Up from the Depths '79
Wizards of the Lost Kingdom 2
'89

D.W. Griffith
Abraham Lincoln '30
Avenging Conscience '14
The Babylon Story from
"Intolerance" '16
Battle of Elderbush Gulch '13
The Birth of a Nation '15

Broken Blossoms '19
Dream Street '21
D.W. Griffith Triple Feature '13
The Greatest Question '19
Griffith Biograph Program '09
Hearts of the World '18
Home Sweet Home '14
The Idol Dancer '20
Intolerance '16
Isn't Life Wonderful '24
Judith of Bethulia '14
The Love Flower '20
Orphans of the Storm '21
Sally of the Sawdust '25
Short Films of D.W. Griffith,
Vol. 1 '12
The Sorrows of Satan '26
True Heart Susie '19
Way Down East '20
The White Rose '23

Edward H. Griffith
The Animal Kingdom '32
Bahama Passage '42
Captain Swagger '25
My Love For Yours '39
The Sky's the Limit '43
Young & Willing '42

Mark Griffiths
A Cry in the Wild '90
Hardbodies '84
Hardbodies 2 '86
Heroes Stand Alone '89
Running Hot '83

Gary Grillo
American Justice '86

Hugo Grimaldi
The Human Duplicators '64

Nick Grinde
Before I Hang '40
Delinquent Parents '38
Hitler: Dead or Alive '43
The Man They Could Not Hang
'39

Brad Grinter
Blood Freak '72

Wallace Grissell
King of the Congo '52

John Grissmer
Blood Rage '87
Scalpel '76

Rajko Grlic
That Summer of White Roses
'90

Ferde Grofe, Jr.
Judgment Day '88
The Proud and the Damned '72
Satan's Harvest '65
Warkill '65

Ulu Grosbard
Falling in Love '84
Straight Time '78
True Confessions '81

Jerry Gross
Girl on a Chain Gang '65
Teenage Mother '67

Larry Gross
3:15—The Moment of Truth '86

Yoram Gross
Camel Boy '84

Douglas Grossman
Hell High '86

Sam Grossman
The Van '77

Charles Grosvenor
Once Upon a Forest '93

Krzysztof Gruber
Greta '86

David Grubin
LBJ: A Biography '91

Karl Grune
The Street '23

Allan Grunewald
Nightmare Castle '65

Enrico Guazzoni
Quo Vadis '12

Nikolai Gubenko
Orphans '83

Robert Guenette
Here's Looking at You, Warner
Bros. '93

James W. Guercio
Electra Glide in Blue '73

Ruy Guerra
Erendira '83
The Fable of the Beautiful
Pigeon Fancier '88
Opera do Malandro '87

Juan Guerreo
Narda or The Summer '76

Romolo Guerrieri
The Final Executioner '83

Mino Guerrini
Mines of Kilimanjaro '87

Christopher Guest
Attack of the 50 Ft. Woman '93
The Big Picture '89

Cliff Guest
Disturbance '89

Robert Guest
Fatal Confinement '64

Val Guest
Carry On Admiral '57
Casino Royale '67
The Day the Earth Caught Fire
'62
Just William's Luck '47
Killer Force '75
Men of Sherwood Forest '57
Quatermass 2 '57
The Quatermass Experiment
'56
The Runaway Bus '54
Up the Creek '58
When Dinosaurs Ruled the
Earth '70

John Guillermin
The Blue Max '66
The Bridge at Remagen '69
Crossover '82
Death on the Nile '78
El Condor '70
Guns at Batasi '64
King Kong '76
King Kong Lives '86
Never Let Go '60
Sheena '83
The Towering Inferno '74
The Tracker '88
Waltz of the Toreadors '62

Fred Guiol
Mr. Walkie Talkie '52
Tanks a Million '41

Sacha Guitry
Napoleon '55

Yilmaz Guney
Baba '73
The Wall '83

Bill Gunn
Black Vampire '73

Gilbert Gunn
The Cosmic Monsters '58

Hrafn Gunnlaugsson
Revenge of the Barbarians '85

Tyrone Guthrie
Oedipus Rex '57

Nathaniel Gutman
Deadline '87

Linda '93

Andre Guttfreund
Femme Fatale '90

Amos Guttman
Drifting '82

Claudio Guzman
Antonio '73
The Hostage Tower '80
Willa '79

Stephen Gyllenhaal
The Abduction of Kari Swenson
'87
Certain Fury '85
A Dangerous Woman '93
A Killing in a Small Town '90
Paris Trout '91
Promised a Miracle '88
Question of Faith '93
Waterland '92

Imre Gyongyossy
The Revolt of Job '84

Charles Haas
Girls' Town '59
Platinum High School '60

Philip Haas
The Music of Chance '93

Herve Hachuel
The Last of Philip Banter '87

Taylor Hackford
Against All Odds '84
Blood In...Blood Out: Bound by
Honor '93
Chuck Berry: Hail! Hail! Rock
'n' Roll '87
Everybody's All American '88
Idolmaker '80
An Officer and a Gentleman '82
White Nights '85

Rolf Haedrich
Among the Cinders '83

Petra Hafter
A Demon in My View '92

Ross Hagen
B.O.R.N. '88
The Glove '78

Mark Haggard
The First Nudie Musical '75

Piers Haggard
Back Home '90
The Blood on Satan's Claw '71
The Fiendish Plot of Dr. Fu
Manchu '80
Four Eyes and Six Guns '93
Fulfillment '89
Quatermass Conclusion '79
A Summer Story '88
Venom '82

Larry Hagman
Son of Blob '72

Stuart Hagmann
The Strawberry Statement '70
Tarantulas: The Deadly Cargo
'77

Steven Hahn
Starchaser: The Legend of Orin
'85

Weng Yao Hai
Crack Shadow Boxers '70s

Charles Haid
Cooperstown '93
Iron Will '93
The Nightman '93

Fred Haines
Steppenwolf '74

Randa Haines
Children of a Lesser God '86
The Doctor '91
Wrestling Ernest Hemingway
'93

Richard W. Haines
Alien Space Avenger '91
Class of Nuke 'Em High '86
Splatter University '84

John Halas
Animal Farm '55

Don Haldane
Nikki, the Wild Dog of the North
'61
The Reincarnate '71

Alan Hale
Braveheart '25
Risky Business '28

Billy Hale
Harem '86
The Murder of Mary Phagan
'87
Red Alert '77
S.O.S. Titanic '79

Sonnie Hale
Gangway '37
Sailing Along '38

William Hale
Murder in Texas '81
One Shoe Makes It Murder '82
Stalk the Wild Child '76

Jack Haley, Jr.
The Love Machine '71
That's Dancing! '85
That's Entertainment '74

H.B. Halicki
Deadline Auto Theft '83
Gone in 60 Seconds '74
The Junkman '82

Alexander Hall
Because You're Mine '52
Doctor Takes a Wife '40
Down to Earth '47
Forever Darling '56
Goin' to Town '35
The Great Lover '49
Here Comes Mr. Jordan '41
I Am the Law '38
Little Miss Marker '34

**Anthony Michael
Hall**
Hail Caesar '94

Godfrey Hall
Honor and Glory '92

Ivan Hall
Funeral for an Assassin '77
Kill and Kill Again '81
Kill or Be Killed '80

Jon Hall
The Beach Girls and the
Monster '65

Kenneth J. Hall
Evil Spawn '87
Ghost Writer '89

Peter Hall
A Midsummer Night's Dream
'68
Orpheus Descending '91

Daniel Haller
Buck Rogers in the 25th
Century '79
Devil's Angels '67
Die, Monster, Die! '65
The Dunwich Horror '70
Follow That Car '80
Margin for Murder '81
Paddy '70

Todd Hallowell
Love or Money? '88

Lasse Hallstrom
My Life as a Dog '85
Once Around '91
What's Eating Gilbert Grape '93

Victor Halperin
Buried Alive '39

I Conquer the Sea '36
Party Girls '29
Revolt of the Zombies '36
Torture Ship '39
The White Zombie '32

Glenda Hambly
Fran '85

Robert Hamer
Dead of Night '45
The Detective '54
Kind Hearts and Coronets '49
Pink Strings and Sealing Wax
'45
To Paris with Love '55

David Hamilton
Bilitis '77

Dean Hamilton
Strike a Pose '93

Guy Hamilton
Battle of Britain '69
The Colditz Story '55
The Devil's Disciple '59
Diamonds are Forever '71
Evil Under the Sun '82
Force 10 from Navarone '78
Funeral in Berlin '66
Goldfinger '64
Live and Let Die '73
The Man with the Golden Gun
'74
The Mirror Crack'd '80
Remo Williams: The Adventure
Begins '85

Strathford Hamilton
Betrayal of the Dove '92
Blueberry Hill '88
Diving In '90

Robert Hammer
Don't Answer the Phone '80

Jason Hammond
The Deadly Secret '94

Peter Hammond
The Dark Angel '91

**Benjamin B.
Hampton**
Heart's Haven '22

Victor Hanbury
The Avenging Hand '43
Hotel Reserve '44

John Hancock
Bang the Drum Slowly '73
California Dreaming '79
Let's Scare Jessica to Death
'71
Prancer '89
Steal the Sky '88
Weeds '87

David Hand
Bambi '42
Snow White and the Seven
Dwarfs '37

Richard Handford
Second Chance '80

Alan Handley
Alice Through the Looking
Glass '66

Ken Handley
Delivery Boys '84

Susumu Hani
She and He '63

Tom Hanks
Fallen Angels 2 '93

William Hanna
Hey There, It's Yogi Bear '64
Jetsons: The Movie '90

Ken Hannam
The Assassination Run '84
Sunday Too Far Away '74

Brian Hannant
The Time Guardian '87

Izhak Hanooka
Red Nights '87

Marion Hansel
Between Heaven and Earth '93
Dust '85

Ed Hansen
The Bikini Car Wash Company
'90
Party Favors '89
Party Plane '90
Takin' It All Off '87

Rolf Hansen
The Devil in Silk '56

Curtis Hanson
The Arousers '70
Bad Influence '90
The Bedroom Window '87
The Children of Times Square
'86
The Hand that Rocks the
Cradle '92
Little Dragons '80
Losin' It '82

David W. Hanson
Night of the Bloody Transplant
'86

John Hanson
Northern Lights '79
Wildrose '85

Tom Hanson
The Zodiac Killer '71

Richard Harbinger
T-Bird Gang '59

Cedric Hardwicke
Forever and a Day '43

Joseph Hardy
Love's Savage Fury '79
Return Engagement '78
To Love Again '80
Users '78

Robin Hardy
The Fantasist '89
The Wicker Man '75

Rod Hardy
Sara Dane '81
Thirst '87
Under Capricorn '82

David Hare
Strapless '90
Wetherby '85

Dean Hargrove
Dear Detective '78

Veit Harlan
Jud Suess '40
Kolberg '45

Renny Harlin
The Adventures of Ford
Fairlane '90
Born American '86
Cliffhanger '93
Die Hard 2: Die Harder '90
A Nightmare on Elm Street 4:
Dream Master '88
Prison '88

John Harlow
Appointment with Crime '45
Candles at Nine '44
Meet Sexton Blake '44
Spellbound '41
While I Live '47

Robert Harmon
Hitcher '86
Nowhere to Run '93

Curtis Harrington
The Dead Don't Die '75
Devil Dog: The Hound of Hell
'78
The Killing Kind '73

Night Tide '63
Planet of Blood '66
Ruby '77
What's the Matter with Helen? '71
Who Slew Auntie Roo? '71

Damien Harris
Deceived '91
The Rachel Papers '89

Denny Harris
Silent Scream '80

Frank Harris
Aftershock '88
Killpoint '84
Low Blow '85
The Patriot '86

Harry Harris
A Day for Thanks on Walton's Mountain '82
The Runaways '75

Jack H. Harris
The Unkissed Bride '66

James B. Harris
Bedford Incident '65
Boiling Point '93
Cop '88
Fast Walking '82
Some Call It Loving '73

Leslie Harris
Just Another Girl on the I.R.T. '93

Richard Harris
The Hero '71

Steven Harris
At Gunpoint '90

Trent Harris
Rubin & Ed '92

Wendell B. Harris, Jr.
Chameleon Street '89

John Harrison
Tales from the Darkside: The Movie '90

John Kent Harrison
Beautiful Dreamers '92
City Boy '93
The Sound and the Silence '93

Jules Harrison
Exterminators of the Year 3000 '83

Ken Harrison
1918 '85
On Valentine's Day '86

Paul Harrison
The House of Seven Corpses '73

Sam Harrison
Sex and Buttered Popcorn '91

Lee Harry
Silent Night, Deadly Night 2 '87
Street Soldiers '91

Bruce Hart
Sooner or Later '78

Christopher Hart
Eat and Run '86

Harvey Hart
Aliens Are Coming '80
Beverly Hills Madam '86
Born Beautiful '82
The City '76
East of Eden '80
Fortune and Men's Eyes '71
Goldenrod '77
High Country '81
Murder or Mercy '74
Panic on the 5:22 '74
Passion in Paradise '89
The Prince of Central Park '77
The Pyx '73

Reckless Disregard '84
Shoot '85
Standing Tall '78
Stone Fox '87
Utilities '83

William S. Hart
Disciple '15
Hell's Hinges '16
Narrow Trail '17
Return of Draw Egan '16

Kenneth Hartford
Hell Squad '85
The Lucifer Complex '78

Robert Hartford-Davis
The Bloodsuckers '70
Estate of Insanity '70
The Fiend '71

Karl Hartl
F.P. 1 Doesn't Answer '33
The Life and Loves of Mozart '59
The Mozart Story '48

Hal Hartley
Simple Men '92
Surviving Desire '91
Trust '91
The Unbelievable Truth '90

Richard Hartley
Kennedy '83

Don Hartman
Every Girl Should Be Married '48
Holiday Affair '49

Anthony Harvey
Dutchman '67
Eagle's Wing '79
Grace Quigley '84
The Lion in Winter '68
Players '79
Richard's Things '80
Svengali '83
They Might Be Giants '71

Gail Harvey
Cold Sweat '93

Herk Harvey
Carnival of Souls '62

Rupert Harvey
Critters 4 '91

Patrick Hasburgh
Aspen Extreme '93

Kohji Hashimoto
Godzilla 1985 '85

Byron Haskin
Armored Command '61
Captain Sinbad '63
Conquest of Space '55
The Denver & Rio Grande '51
From the Earth to the Moon '58
His Majesty O'Keefe '53
Jet Over the Atlantic '59
Killer Bait '49
Long John Silver '53
Naked Jungle '54
Robinson Crusoe on Mars '64
Too Late for Tears '49
Treasure Island '49
The War of the Worlds '53

Masami Hata
Little Nemo: Adventures in Slumberland '92

Masanori Hata
The Adventures of Milo & Otis '89

Henry Hathaway
Call Northside 777 '48
Circus World '64
Dark Corner '46
The Desert Fox '51
Diplomatic Courier '52
Five Card Stud '68

Go West, Young Man '36
Heritage of the Desert '33
How the West was Won '63
Kiss of Death '47
The Last Safari '67
Legend of the Lost '57
The Lives of a Bengal Lancer '35
Man of the Forest '33
Nevada Smith '66
Niagara '52
North to Alaska '60
Of Human Bondage '64
Prince Valiant '54
The Racers '55
Raid on Rommel '71
Rawhide '51
The Real Glory '39
Seven Thieves '60
Sons of Katie Elder '65
Sundown '41
13 Rue Madeleine '46
To the Last Man '33
True Grit '69
When the West Was Young '32
A Wing and a Prayer '44

Bob Hathcock
DuckTales the Movie: Treasure of the Lost Lamp '90

Jeff Hathcock
Night Ripper '86

Maurice Hatton
American Roulette '88

Didier Haudepin
Elsa, Elsa '85

Reinhard Hauff
Knife in the Head '78

Wlodzimierz Haupe
Dr. Judym

Wings Hauser
The Art of Dying '90
Coldfire '90
Living to Die '91

Steve Hawkes
Blood Freak '72

Tara Hawkins Moore
Tusks '89

Don Hawks
Hush Little Baby, Don't You Cry '86

Howard Hawks
Air Force '43
Ball of Fire '41
Barbary Coast '35
The Big Sky '52
The Big Sleep '46
Bringing Up Baby '38
Ceiling Zero '35
Come and Get It '36
Criminal Code '31
El Dorado '67
Gentlemen Prefer Blondes '53
Hatari '62
His Girl Friday '40
I Was a Male War Bride '49
Land of the Pharaohs '55
Man's Favorite Sport? '63
Monkey Business '52
Only Angels Have Wings '39
Red Line 7000 '65
Red River '48
Rio Bravo '59
Rio Lobo '70
Scarface '31
Sergeant York '41
A Song is Born '48
The Thing '51
To Have & Have Not '44
Today We Live '33
Twentieth Century '34

Peter Hawley
Victimless Crimes '90

Rod Hay
Breaking Loose '90

Richard Haydn
Dear Wife '49
Mr. Music '50

Sidney Hayers
Assault '70
Bananas Boat '78
Burn Witch, Burn! '62
Circus of Horrors '60
Deadly Strangers '82
King Arthur, the Young Warlord '75
Revenge '71
The Seekers '79
Trap '66

Bill Hayes
King Kung Fu '87

John Hayes
All the Lovin' Kinfolk '89
The Cut Throats '89
Dream No Evil '75
End of the World '77
Five Minutes to Love '63
Grave of the Vampire '72
Mama's Dirty Girls '74
Shell Shock '80s
Sweet Trash '89
Tomb of the Undead '72

John Patrick Hayes
The Farmer's Other Daughter '65

Robert Hayes
Phoenix the Warrior '88

David Hayman
The Hawk '93

Todd Haynes
Poison '91

Jonathan Heap
Benefit of the Doubt '93

Howard Heard
Shadows Run Black '84

Robert Heath
Hugh Hefner: Once Upon a Time '92

David Heavener
Deadly Reactor '89
Eye of the Stranger '93
Killcrazy '89
Outlaw Force '87
Prime Target '91
Twisted Justice '89

Ben Hecht
Actors and Sin '52
Angels Over Broadway '40
Spectre of the Rose '46

Amy Heckerling
Fast Times at Ridgemont High '82
Johnny Dangerously '84
Look Who's Talking '89
Look Who's Talking, Too '90
National Lampoon's European Vacation '85

Rob Hedden
Friday the 13th, Part 8: Jason Takes Manhattan '89

Trine Hedman
Famous Five Get Into Trouble '87

Avram Heffner
But Where Is Daniel Wax? '74

Richard T. Heffron
Broken Angel '88
Convicted: A Mother's Story '87
Death Scream '75
Foolin' Around '80
Futureworld '76
Guilty of Innocence '87
I, the Jury '82
I Will Fight No More Forever '75
Newman's Law '74

Outlaw Blues '77
Pancho Barnes '88
A Rumor of War '80
Samaritan: The Mitch Snyder Story '86
See How She Runs '78
Tagget '90
Whale for the Killing '81

Chris Hegedus
The War Room '93

Robert Hegyes
E. Nick: A Legend in His Own Mind '84

Yosif Heifitz
Baltic Deputy '37
The Lady with the Dog '59

Ray Heinz
Border Vengeance '35

Stuart Heisler
Along Came Jones '45
The Burning Hills '56
Chain Lightning '50
The Glass Key '42
Hitler '62
I Died a Thousand Times '55
Island of Desire '52
Lone Ranger '56
The Monster and the Girl '41
Smash-Up: The Story of a Woman '47
Tokyo Joe '49
Tulsa '49

Mats Helge
Ninja Mission '84
The Russian Terminator '90

Olle Hellbron
Brothers Lionheart '85
Pippi Goes on Board '75
Pippi in the South Seas '74
Pippi Longstocking '73

Gerome Hellman
Promises in the Dark '79

Monte Hellman
The Beast from Haunted Cave '60
Cockfighter '74
Creature from the Haunted Sea '60
Flight to Fury '66
Gunfire '78
Iguana '89
Ride in the Whirlwind '67
The Shooting '66
Silent Night, Deadly Night 3: Better Watch Out! '89

Oliver Hellman
Beyond the Door '75
Desperate Moves '86
Tentacles '77

Paul Helmick
Hard Drivin' '60

David Helpern
Something Short of Paradise '79

Ralph Hemecker
Dead On '93

David Hemmings
Dark Horse '92
Just a Gigolo '79
The Key to Rebecca '85
Survivor '80
Treasure of the Yankee Zephyr '83

Joseph Henabery
Cobra '25
His Majesty, the American '19
Leather Burners '43
The Man from Painted Post '17

Clark Henderson
Circle of Fear '89
Primary Target '89
Saigon Commandos '88

Warlords from Hell '87

Don Henderson
The Touch of Satan '70
Weekend with the Babysitter '70

John Henderson
The Borrowers '93

Frank Henenlotter
Basket Case '82
Basket Case 2 '90
Basket Case 3: The Progeny '92
Brain Damage '88
Frankenhooker '90

Peter Henkel
Three Bullets for a Long Gun '73

Paul Henreid
Ballad in Blue '66
Battle Shock '56
Tall Lie '53

Buck Henry
First Family '80
Heaven Can Wait '78

Brian Henson
The Muppet Christmas Carol '92

Jim Henson
The Dark Crystal '82
The Great Muppet Caper '81
Labyrinth '86

Stefan Christian Henszelman
Friends Forever '86

Perry Henzell
The Harder They Come '72

Bill Herbert
Warlock Moon '73

Henry Herbert
Emily '77

Martin Herbert
Miami '87
Strange Shadows in an Empty Room '76

Stephen Herek
Bill & Ted's Excellent Adventure '89
Critters '86
Don't Tell Mom the Babysitter's Dead '91
The Mighty Ducks '92
The Three Musketeers '93

Al Herman
Down the Wyoming Trail '39
Gentleman from Dixie '41
Man from Texas '39
Outlaws of the Range '36
Renfrew of the Royal Mounted '37
Renfrew on the Great White Trail '38
Roll, Wagons, Roll '39
Rollin' Plains '38
Take Me Back to Oklahoma '40
Utah Trail '38
Valley of Terror '38
Western Frontier '35
Whispering Shadow '33

Albert Herman
Cowboy & the Bandit '35
Dawn Express '42
Delinquent Daughters '44
Gun Play '36
The Missing Corpse '45
Rogue's Gallery '44
Shake Hands with Murder '44

Jean Herman
Butterfly Affair '71

Honor Among Thieves '68

Mark Herman
Blame It on the Bellboy '92

Victor Herman
My Boy '21

Jaime Humberto Hermosillo
Dona Herlinda & Her Son '86
The Summer of Miss Forbes '88

Miguel Hermoso
Marbella '85

Mario Hernandez
Benjamin Argumedo '78

Denis Heroux
Naked Massacre '80s
The Uncanny '78

Mark Herrier
Popcorn '89

Rowdy Herrington
Gladiator '92
Jack's Back '87
Road House '89
Striking Distance '93

W. Blake Herron
Skin Art '93

Joel Hershman
Hold Me, Thrill Me, Kiss Me '93

Marshall Herskovitz
Jack the Bear '93

Nathan Hertz
Attack of the 50 Foot Woman '58

Michael Herz
First Turn On '83
Stuck on You '84
Sugar Cookies '77
The Toxic Avenger '86
The Toxic Avenger, Part 2 '89
The Toxic Avenger, Part 3: The Last Temptation of Toxie '89
Troma's War '88

John Herzfeld
Casualties of Love: The "Long Island Lolita" Story '93
A Father's Revenge '88
The Preppie Murder '89
Two of a Kind '83

Werner Herzog
Aguirre, the Wrath of God '72
Every Man for Himself & God Against All '75
Fitzcarraldo '82
Heart of Glass '74
Stroszek '77
Where the Green Ants Dream '84
Woyzeck '78

David Hess
To All a Goodnight '80

Jon Hess
Assassin '89
Excessive Force '93
The Lawless Land '88
Watchers '88

Gordon Hessler
Betrayal '74
Cry of the Banshee '70
Embassy '72
Escape from El Diablo '83
The Girl in a Swing '89
Golden Voyage of Sinbad '73
Journey of Honor '91
KISS Meets the Phantom of the Park '78
Medusa '74
The Misfit Brigade '87
Murders in the Rue Morgue '71
The Oblong Box '69
Out on Bail '89
Pray for Death '85

Puzzle '78
Rage of Honor '87
Scream and Scream Again '70
Secrets of Three Hungry Wives '78
Tales of the Unexpected '91

Charlton Heston
Antony and Cleopatra '73
A Man for All Seasons '88
Mother Lode '82

Fraser Heston
The Crucifer of Blood '91
Needful Things '93
Treasure Island '89

Neil Hetherington
Black Terrorist '85

David L. Hewitt
Alien Massacre '67
Horrors of the Red Planet '64
Journey to the Center of Time '67
The Lucifer Complex '78

Jean Hewitt
Blood of Dracula's Castle '69

Pete Hewitt
Bill & Ted's Bogus Journey '91
Wild Palms '93

Rob Hewitt
Verne Miller '88

Douglas Heyes
Powder Keg '70

Laurent Heynemann
Birgitt Haas Must Be Killed '83

Jesse Hibbs
To Hell and Back '55

Winston Hibler
Charlie, the Lonesome Cougar '67

Jochen Hick
Via Appia '92

George Hickenlooper
Hearts of Darkness: A Filmmaker's Apocalypse '91

Bruce Hickey
Necropolis '87

Anthony Hickox
Full Eclipse '93
Hellraiser 3: Hell on Earth '92
Sundown '91
Warlock: The Armageddon '93
Waxwork '88
Waxwork 2: Lost in Time '91

Douglas Hickox
Blackout '85
Brannigan '75
Entertaining Mr. Sloane '70
The Hound of the Baskervilles '83
Mistral's Daughter '84
Sins '85
Sky Riders '76
Theatre of Blood '73
Zulu Dawn '79

Howard Higgin
Hell's House '32
High Voltage '29
Painted Desert '31
The Racketeer '29

Colin Higgins
The Best Little Whorehouse in Texas '82
Foul Play '78
9 to 5 '80

Nat Hiken
Car 54, Where Are You? '61

Bob Hill
Danger Trails '35
A Face in the Fog '36
The Phantom of the Range '38

Rogue's Tavern '36
Whirlwind Horseman '38

Claudio Guerin Hill
Bell from Hell '74

David Hill
Ator the Fighting Eagle '83

George Hill
The Big House '30

George Roy Hill
Butch Cassidy and the Sundance Kid '69
Funny Farm '88
The Great Waldo Pepper '75
Hawaii '66
The Little Drummer Girl '84
A Little Romance '79
Min & Bill '30
Period of Adjustment '62
Slap Shot '77
Slaughterhouse Five '72
The Sting '73
Thoroughly Modern Millie '67
Toys in the Attic '63
The World According to Garp '82
The World of Henry Orient '64

Jack Hill
The Big Bird Cage '72
The Big Doll House '71
Coffy '73
The Fear Chamber '68
Foxy Brown '74
Portrait in Terror '66
Spider Baby '64
The Swinging Cheerleaders '74
Switchblade Sisters '75
Track of the Vampire '66

James Hill
The Belstone Fox '73
Black Beauty '71
Born Free '66
The Corrupt Ones '67
Seaside Swingers '65
A Study in Terror '66
The Wild and the Free '80

Robert F. Hill
Blake of Scotland Yard '36
Cheyenne Rides Again '38
Come On Danger! '32
East Side Kids '40
Feud of the Trail '37
Man's Country '38
Prison Shadows '36
Queen of the Jungle '35
Rip Roarin' Buckaroo '36
The Roamin' Cowboy '37
Tarzan the Fearless '33
Wild Horse Canyon '39

Sinclair Hill
Greek Street '30

Walter Hill
Another 48 Hrs. '90
Brewster's Millions '85
Crossroads '86
The Driver '78
Extreme Prejudice '87
48 Hrs. '82
Geronimo: An American Legend '93
Hard Times '75
Johnny Handsome '89
The Long Riders '80
Red Heat '88
Southern Comfort '81
Streets of Fire '84
Tales from the Crypt '89
Tales from the Crypt, Vol. 3 '90
Trespass '92
The Warriors '79

Arthur Hiller
The Americanization of Emily '64
Author! Author! '82
The Babe '92
The Hospital '71
The In-Laws '79

The Lonely Guy '84
Love Story '70
Making Love '82
Man of La Mancha '72
Married to It '93
The Miracle of the White Stallions '63
Nightwing '79
The Out-of-Towners '70
Outrageous Fortune '87
Plaza Suite '71
Popi '69
Promise Her Anything '66
Romantic Comedy '83
See No Evil, Hear No Evil '89
The Silver Streak '76
Taking Care of Business '90
Teachers '84
Tobruk '66
The Wheeler Dealers '63

Richard Hilliard
Psychomania '63

David Michael Hillman
The Strangeness '85

William B. Hillman
Double Exposure '82
Photographer '75
Ragin' Cajun '90

David Hills
Blade Master '84
Quest for the Mighty Sword '90

Lambert Hillyer
Border Bandits '46
Dracula's Daughter '36
Fighting Fool '32
Gang Bullets '38
Gentleman from Texas '46
Hat Box Mystery '47
The Invisible Ray '36
Land of the Lawless '47
Partners of the Trail '44
Range Law '44
Range Renegades '48
The Shock '23
Six Gun Gospel '43
South of the Rio Grande '45
The Stranger from Pecos '45
Sundown Riders '48
Texas Kid '43
Three Word Brand '21
Toll Gate '20
Wagon Tracks '19
White Eagle '32

Arthur Hilton
Cat Women of the Moon '53
Return of Jesse James '50

Lawrence Hilton-Jacobs
Angels of the City '89
Quiet Fire '91

Charles Hines
The Speed Spook '24

Bill Hinzman
Revenge of the Living Zombies '88

Alexander Gregory Hippolyte
Animal Instincts '92
Carnal Crimes '91
Mirror Images '91
Mirror Images 2 '93
Night Rhythms '92
Secret Games '92
Secret Games 2: The Escort '93

Bettina Hirsch
Munchies '87

Ray Hirschman
Plutonium Baby '87

Leslie Hiscott
Department Store '35

The Triumph of Sherlock
  Holmes '35

Alfred Hitchcock
Aventure Malgache '44
The Birds '63
Blackmail '29
Bon Voyage '44
Champagne '28
Dial ''M'' for Murder '54
Easy Virtue '27
Family Plot '76
The Farmer's Wife '28
Foreign Correspondent '40
Frenzy '72
Hitchcock Classics Collection:
  Trailers on Tape '85
Hitchcock Collection '87
I Confess '53
Jamaica Inn '39
Juno and the Paycock '30
The Lady Vanishes '38
Lifeboat '44
The Lodger '26
The Man Who Knew Too Much
  '34
The Man Who Knew Too Much
  '56
The Manxman '29
Marnie '64
Mr. & Mrs. Smith '41
Murder '30
North by Northwest '59
Notorious '46
No. 17 '32
The Paradine Case '47
Psycho '60
Rear Window '54
Rebecca '40
Rich and Strange '32
The Ring '27
Rope '48
Sabotage '36
Saboteur '42
The Secret Agent '36
Shadow of a Doubt '43
Skin Game '31
Spellbound '45
Stage Fright '50
Strangers on a Train '51
Suspicion '41
The 39 Steps '35
Three by Hitchcock '28
To Catch a Thief '55
Topaz '69
Torn Curtain '66
The Trouble with Harry '55
Under Capricorn '49
Vertigo '58
The Wrong Man '56
Young and Innocent '37

Carl K. Hittleman
Kentucky Rifle '55

Rupert Hitzig
Backstreet Dreams '90
Night Visitor '89

Jack Hively
Four Jacks and a Jill '41
The Saint Takes Over '40
The Saint's Double Trouble '40

Jack B. Hively
The Adventures of Huckleberry
  Finn '78
California Gold Rush '81
Lassie: Adventures of Neeka
  '68
Starbird and Sweet William '73

A.J. Hixon
Little Marines '90

Godfrey Ho
The Blazing Ninja
The Dragon's Showdown '83
Hands of Death '88
Ninja Champion '80s
Ninja Destroyer '70s

Fredric Hobbs
Alabama's Ghost '72

Lyndall Hobbs
Back to the Beach '87

Victoria Hochberg
Jacob Have I Loved '88
Sweet 15 '90

Roberta Hodes
A Secret Space '88

Mike Hodges
Black Rainbow '91
Flash Gordon '80
Florida Straits '87
Missing Pieces '83
Morons from Outer Space '85
Prayer for the Dying '87
Pulp '72
The Terminal Man '74

Jeno Hodl
Deadly Obsession '88

Mark Hoeger
The Little Match Girl '84

Jeremy Hoenack
The Dark Ride '84

Arthur Hoerl
Drums O'Voodoo '34

Michael Hoey
Navy vs. the Night Monsters
  '66

Gray Hof-meyr
The Light in the Jungle '91

Ernest Hofbauer
Code Name Alpha '67

Hermann Hoffman
The Invisible Boy '57
It's a Dog's Life '55

Jerzy Hoffman
Colonel Wolodyjowski '69
Leper '76

Julian Hoffman
The Bloody Brood '59

Michael Hoffman
Promised Land '88
Soapdish '91
Some Girls '88

Peter Hoffman
Valentino Returns '88

Tamar Simon Hoffs
The Allnighter '87

Grey Hofmeyr
Dirty Games '93

Jack Hofsiss
Cat on a Hot Tin Roof '84
Family Secrets '84
I'm Dancing as Fast as I Can
  '82

James Hogan
Arizona Mahoney '36
Arrest Bulldog Drummond '38
The Broken Mask '28
Bulldog Drummond Escapes
  '37
Bulldog Drummond's Bride '39
Bulldog Drummond's Peril '38
Bulldog Drummond's Secret
  Police '39
The Mad Ghoul '43

Michael Hohensee
Mad Wax: The Surf Movie '90

Gregory Holbit
L.A. Law '86
Roe vs. Wade '89

Rod Holcomb
Blind Justice '86
Captain America '79
Cartier Affair '84
Chains of Gold '92
Chase '85
China Beach '88
The Red Light Sting '84

Stark '85
Two Fathers' Justice '85

John Hold
Viking Massacre '70s

Anton Holden
Aroused '66

William Hole, Jr.
The Devil's Hand '61

Adam Holender
Twisted '86

Agnieszka Holland
Angry Harvest '85
Europa, Europa '91
Fever '81
Olivier, Olivier '92
The Secret Garden '93
To Kill a Priest '89

Steve Holland
Better Off Dead '85
How I Got into College '89
One Crazy Summer '86

Todd Holland
The Wizard '89

Tom Holland
Child's Play '88
Fatal Beauty '87
Fright Night '85
The Temp '93

Eli Hollander
Out '88

Allan Holleb
Candy Stripe Nurses '74
School Spirit '85

Doug Holloway
Fast Money '83

Ben Holmes
Maid's Night Out '38
The Saint in New York '38

Fred Holmes
Dakota '88
Harley '90

Jason Holt
Swindle '92
Wager of Love '90

Seth Holt
Scream of Fear '61

Allen Holubar
Heart of Humanity '18

Roger Holzberg
Midnight Crossing '87

Allan Holzman
Forbidden World '82
Grunt! The Wrestling Movie '85
Intimate Stranger '91
Out of Control '85
Programmed to Kill '86

Lau Shing Hon
To Live and Die in Hong Kong
  '89

Inoshiro Honda
Attack of the Mushroom People
  '63
Destroy All Monsters '68
Ghidrah the Three Headed
  Monster '65
Godzilla vs. Monster Zero '68
Godzilla vs. Mothra '64
Godzilla's Revenge '69
Gorath '64
H-Man '59
Half Human '58
Mothra '62
The Mysterians '58
Rodan '56
Varan the Unbelievable '61
Yog, Monster from Space '71

Elliot Hong
Kill the Golden Goose '79
They Call Me Bruce? '82

James Hong
Girls Next Door '79
The Vineyard '89

Ron Honthaner
The House on Skull Mountain
  '74

Randall Hood
Die Sister, Die! '74

Harry Hook
The Kitchen Toto '87
The Last of His Tribe '92
Lord of the Flies '90

Kevin Hooks
Passenger 57 '92
Roots: The Gift '88
Strictly Business '91

Lance Hool
Missing in Action 2: The
  Beginning '85
Steel Dawn '87

Tobe Hooper
Body Bags '93
Eaten Alive '76
The Funhouse '81
I'm Dangerous Tonight '90
Invaders from Mars '86
Lifeforce '85
Poltergeist '82
Salem's Lot '79
Spontaneous Combustion '89
The Texas Chainsaw Massacre
  '74
Texas Chainsaw Massacre,
  Part 2 '86

Claudia Hoover
Double Exposure '93

Harry Hope
Swift Justice '88

Arthur Hopkins
His Double Life '33

John Hopkins
Torment '85

Stephen Hopkins
Blown Away '94
Dangerous Game '90
Judgment Night '93
A Nightmare on Elm Street 5:
  Dream Child '89
Predator 2 '90

Dennis Hopper
Backtrack '89
Chasers '94
Colors '88
Easy Rider '69
Hot Spot '90
The Last Movie '71
Out of the Blue '80

E. Mason Hopper
Held for Murder '32
Hong Kong Nights '35
Shop Angel '32
Square Shoulders '29

Jerry Hopper
The Atomic City '52
Madron '70
Pony Express '53

Russell Hopton
Black Gold '36
Song of the Trail '36

Richard Horian
Student Confidential '87

Andrew Horn
Doomed Love '83

Leonard Horn
Hunter '73

Jeffrey Hornaday
Shout '91

James W. Horne
All Over Town '37
Bohemian Girl '36

Bonnie Scotland '35
College '27
Green Archer '40
Holt of the Secret Service '42
Laughing at Danger '24
Way Out West '37

Harry Horner
Beware, My Lovely '52
New Faces of 1952 '54
Red Planet Mars '52

Peter Horton
Amazon Women on the Moon
  '87

Bob Hoskins
The Raggedy Rawney '90

Dan Hoskins
Chopper Chicks in Zombietown
  '91

Robert Hossein
I Killed Rasputin '67

Joy Houck, Jr.
Creature from Black Lake '76
Mind Warp '72
Night of the Strangler '73

John Hough
American Gothic '88
Biggles '85
The Black Arrow '84
Brass Target '78
Dirty Mary Crazy Larry '74
Duel of Hearts '92
The Dying Truth '91
Escape to Witch Mountain '75
Howling 4: The Original
  Nightmare '88
Incubus '82
The Legend of Hell House '73
Return from Witch Mountain
  '78
Sudden Terror '70
Treasure Island '72
Triumphs of a Man Called
  Horse '83
Twins of Evil '71
The Watcher in the Woods '81

Bobby Houston
Bad Manners '84
Caged Fear '92
Trust Me '89

Clyde Houston
Foxstyle '73

Robert Houston
Shogun Assassin '80

Tony Houston
Outlaw Riders '72

Adrian Hoven
Dandelions '74
Mark of the Devil 2 '72

Cy Howard
Lovers and Other Strangers '70

David Howard
Bullet Code '40
Crimson Romance '34
Daniel Boone '34
Hollywood Stadium Mystery '38
In Old Santa Fe '34
The Lost Jungle '34
Mystery Ranch '34
Renegade Ranger/Scarlet River
  '38

Leslie Howard
Pimpernel Smith '42
Pygmalion '38
Spitfire '42

Paul Howard
Night Terror '89

Ron Howard
Backdraft '91
Cocoon '85
Cotton Candy '82
Far and Away '92
Grand Theft Auto '77

Howard ►*cont.*

Gung Ho '85
Night Shift '82
The Paper '94
Parenthood '89
Splash '84
Willow '88

William K. Howard
Back Door to Heaven '39
Evelyn Prentice '34
Fire Over England '37
Johnny Come Lately '43
White Gold '28

John Howley
Happily Ever After '93

Frank Howson
The Hunting '92

Harry Hoyt
The Lost World '25
The Return of Boston Blackie '27

Talun Hsu
Witchcraft 5: Dance with the Devil '92

VV Dachin Hsu
Pale Blood '91

Hua-Shan
Infra-Man '76

Daniel Hubenbecker
Wardogs '87

Jean-Loup Hubert
Le Grand Chemin '87
Next Year If All Goes Well '83

Faith Hubley
The Cosmic Eye '71

John Huckert
The Passing '88

Reginald Hudlin
Boomerang '92
House Party '90

Gary Hudson
Thunder Run '86

Hugh Hudson
Chariots of Fire '81
Greystoke: The Legend of Tarzan, Lord of the Apes '84
Lost Angels '89
Revolution '85

P.I. Huemer
Kiss Daddy Goodnight '87

Marc Huestis
Men in Love '90

Roy Huggins
Hangman's Knot '52

R. John Hugh
Deadly Encounter '78
The Meal '75
Naked in the Sun '57
Yellowneck '55

Albert Hughes
Menace II Society '93

Allen Hughes
Menace II Society '93

David Hughes
Missing Link '88

Howard Hughes
Hell's Angels '30
The Outlaw '43
Power '28

John Hughes
The Breakfast Club '85
Curly Sue '91
Ferris Bueller's Day Off '86
Planes, Trains & Automobiles '87

She's Having a Baby '88
Sixteen Candles '84
Uncle Buck '89
Weird Science '85

Ken Hughes
Arrivederci, Baby! '66
The Atomic Man '56
Casino Royale '67
Chitty Chitty Bang Bang '68
Cromwell '70
Heat Wave '54
Internecine Project '73
The Long Haul '57
Night School '81
Of Human Bondage '64
Oh, Alfie '75
Sextette '78

Robert C. Hughes
Down the Drain '89
Hunter's Blood '87
Memorial Valley Massacre '88

Terry Hughes
The Butcher's Wife '91
For Love or Money '84
Monty Python Live at the Hollywood Bowl '82
Ripping Yarns '75
Sunset Limousine '83

Ann Hui
Song of the Exile '90

Don Hulette
Breaker! Breaker! '77
Great Ride '78

Steven A. Hull
Devil Wears White '86

Ron Hulme
Fearless Tiger '94

H. Bruce Humberstone
Charlie Chan at the Opera '36
The Crooked Circle '32
Happy Go Lovely '51
Hello, Frisco, Hello '43
I Wake Up Screaming '41
Iceland '42
Lucky Cisco Kid '40
Pin-Up Girl '44
Strangers of the Evening '32
Sun Valley Serenade '41
Tarzan and the Trappers '58
Ten Wanted Men '54
To the Shores of Tripoli '42
Wonder Man '45

Humphrey Humbert
Ghosthouse '88

Chieng Hung
Tough Guy '70s

Tran Anh Hung
The Scent of Green Papaya '93

Jackson Hunsicker
Oddball Hall '91

David Hunt
Triple Impact '92

Edward Hunt
Alien Warrior '85
Bloody Birthday '80
The Brain '88
Starship Invasions '77

Paul Hunt
The Clones '73
The Great Gundown '75
Merlin '93
Twisted Nightmare '87

Peter Hunt
The Adventures of Huckleberry Finn '85
Assassination '87
Death Hunt '81
Gulliver's Travels '77
Hyper-Sapien: People from Another Star '86

It Came Upon a Midnight Clear '84
The Mysterious Stranger '82
On Her Majesty's Secret Service '69
1776 '72
Shout at the Devil '76
Skeezer '82
Smart-Aleck Kill '85
Wild Geese 2 '85

Max (Massimo Pupillo) Hunter
The Bloody Pit of Horror '65

Ross Hunter
Son of Ali Baba '52

T. Hayes Hunter
The Ghoul '34

Tim Hunter
Lies of the Twins '91
Paint It Black '89
River's Edge '87
The Saint of Fort Washington '93
Sylvester '85
Tex '82

Lawrence Huntington
The Franchise Affair '52
Man on the Run '49
Tower of Terror '42
Vulture '67

Caroline Huppert
Sincerely Charlotte '86

Brian Desmond Hurst
Dangerous Moonlight '41
The Gay Lady '49
The Lion Has Wings '40
Malta Story '53
Playboy of the Western World '62
Simba '55

William T. Hurtz
Little Nemo: Adventures in Slumberland '92

Harry Hurwitz
Fleshtone '94
The Projectionist '71
Rosebud Beach Hotel '85
Safari 3000 '82
That's Adequate '90

Waris Hussein
And Baby Makes Six '79
Arch of Triumph '85
Callie and Son '81
Coming Out of the Ice '82
Divorce His, Divorce Hers '72
Doctor Who: An Unearthly Child '63
Edward and Mrs. Simpson '80
The Henderson Monster '80
Intimate Contact '87
Little Gloria...Happy at Last '84
Melody '71
Onassis '88
The Possession of Joel Delaney '72
Princess Daisy '83
Quackser Fortune Has a Cousin in the Bronx '70
The Shell Seekers '89
Switched at Birth '91
When the Bough Breaks '86

Danny Huston
Becoming Colette '92
Mr. North '88

Jimmy Huston
Death Driver '78
Final Exam '81
My Best Friend Is a Vampire '88

John Huston
Across the Pacific '42

The African Queen '51
Annie '82
The Asphalt Jungle '50
Barbarian and the Geisha '58
Beat the Devil '53
The Bible...In the Beginning '66
Casino Royale '67
The Dead '87
Fat City '72
In This Our Life '42
Independence '76
Key Largo '48
Life & Times of Judge Roy Bean '72
The List of Adrian Messenger '63
Mackintosh Man '73
The Maltese Falcon '41
The Man Who Would Be King '75
The Misfits '61
Moby Dick '56
Moulin Rouge '52
The Night of the Iguana '64
Phobia '80
Prizzi's Honor '85
The Red Badge of Courage '51
Reflections in a Golden Eye '67
Treasure of the Sierra Madre '48
Under the Volcano '84
The Unforgiven '60
Victory '81
Wise Blood '79

Zoltan Huszarik
Sinbad '71

Charles Hutchinson
Found Alive '34
Phantom Patrol '36

Harold Huth
Night Beat '47

Brian G. Hutton
The First Deadly Sin '80
High Road to China '83
Kelly's Heroes '70
Night Watch '72
Where Eagles Dare '69
X, Y & Zee '72

Robert Hutton
The Slime People '63

Willard Huyck
Best Defense '84
French Postcards '79
Howard the Duck '86
Messiah of Evil '74

Jacky Hwong
Ninja vs. the Shaolin '84

Nessa Hyams
Leader of the Band '87

Peter Hyams
Busting '74
Capricorn One '78
Death Target '83
Hanover Street '79
Narrow Margin '90
Our Time '74
Outland '81
The Presidio '88
Running Scared '86
The Star Chamber '83
Stay Tuned '92
Timecop '94
2010: The Year We Make Contact '84

Chang Shinn I
Snake in the Eagle's Shadow 2 '83

Juan Ibanez
Dance of Death '68
The Fear Chamber '68
The Sinister Invasion '68

Leon Ichaso
Crossover Dreams '85
El Super '79
Power, Passion & Murder '83

Sugar Hill '94
The Take '90

Kon Ichikawa
An Actor's Revenge '63
Being Two Isn't Easy '62
The Burmese Harp '56
Fires on the Plain '59
The Makioka Sisters '83
Odd Obsession '60
Revenge of a Kabuki Actor '63
Tokyo Olympiad '65

Eric Idle
All You Need Is Cash '78
The Tale of the Frog Prince '83

Miguel Iglesias
The Sword of El Cid '62

Kazuo Ikehiro
Zatoichi: Master Ichi and a Chest of Gold '64
Zatoichi: Zatoichi's Flashing Sword '64

Shohei Imamura
The Ballad of Narayama '83
Black Rain '88
Eijanaika '81
The Insect Woman '63
The Pornographers '66
Vengeance Is Mine '79

Shmuel Imberman
I Don't Give a Damn '88

Markus Imhoof
The Boat is Full '81

Hiroshi Inagaki
Kojiro '67
Rikisha-Man '58
Samurai 1: Musashi Miyamoto '55
Samurai 2: Duel at Ichijoji Temple '55
Samurai 3: Duel at Ganryu Island '56

Thomas Ince
Civilization '16
The Three Musketeers '16

Franco Indovina
Catch as Catch Can '68
Oldest Profession '67

Lloyd Ingraham
American Aristocracy '17
Eyes of Julia Deep '18

Rex Ingram
The Four Horsemen of the Apocalypse '21

Boris Ingster
The Judge Steps Out '49
Stranger on the Third Floor '40

J. Christian Ingvordsen
Comrades in Arms '91
Covert Action '88
Firehouse '87
Hangmen '87
Mob War '88
The Outfit '93
Search and Destroy '88

Markus Innocenti
Murder Story '89

Jerald Intrator
Satan in High Heels '62

John Ireland
The Fast and the Furious '54

O'Dale Ireland
Date Bait '60
High School Caesar '56

John Irvin
Champions '84
The Dogs of War '81
Eminent Domain '91
Firefall '94
Ghost Story '81

Hamburger Hill '87
Haunted: The Ferryman '74
Next of Kin '89
Raw Deal '86
Robin Hood '91
Turtle Diary '86
Widow's Peak '94

Sam Irvin
Guilty as Charged '92

Kevin Irvine
Greenstone '85

David Irving
Cannon Movie Tales: Sleeping
    Beauty '89
Cannon Movie Tales: The
    Emperor's New Clothes '89
C.H.U.D. 2: Bud the Chud '89
Goodbye Cruel World '82
Night of the Cyclone '90
Rumpelstiltskin '82
Rumpelstiltskin '86

Richard Irving
The Art of Crime '75
Columbo: Prescription Murder
    '67
The Jesse Owens Story '84

James Isaac
The Horror Show '89

Ronnie Isaacs
Warriors from Hell '90

Antonio Isasi
Ricco '74
Vengeance '86

Robert Iscove
The Lawrenceville Stories '80s
The Little Mermaid '84
Mission of the Shark '91
Puss 'n Boots '84

Gerald I. Isenberg
Seizure: The Story of Kathy
    Morris '82

Wayne Isham
For Those About to Rock:
    Monsters in Moscow '91

Neal Israel
Americathon '79
Bachelor Party '84
Breaking the Rules '92
Combat Academy '86
Moving Violations '85
Surf Ninjas '93
Tunnelvision '76

Peter Israelson
Side Out '90

Juzo Itami
The Funeral '84
Tampopo '86
A Taxing Woman '87
A Taxing Woman's Return '88

Kenneth Ives
Poldark '75

James Ivory
Autobiography of a Princess
    '75
Bombay Talkie '70
The Bostonians '84
The Courtesans of Bombay '85
The Europeans '79
Heat and Dust '82
The Householder '63
Howard's End '92
Hullabaloo Over Georgie &
    Bonnie's Pictures '78
Jane Austen in Manhattan '80
Maurice '87
Mr. & Mrs. Bridge '91
Quartet '81
The Remains of the Day '93
A Room with a View '86
Roseland '77
Savages '72
Shakespeare Wallah '65
Slaves of New York '89

Wild Party '74

Arnaldo Jabor
I Love You '81

Fred Jackman
King of the Wild Horses '24
No Man's Law '21

David S. Jackson
Detonator '93

Donald G. Jackson
The Demon Lover '77
Roller Blade '85

Douglas Jackson
Whispers '89

George Jackson
House Party 2: The Pajama
    Jam '91

Horace Jackson
The Bus Is Coming '72

Jalil Jackson
Lady Terminator '89

Larry Jackson
Bugs Bunny Superstar '75

Lewis Jackson
Terror in Toyland '85

Mick Jackson
The Bodyguard '92
Chattahoochee '89
Clean Slate '94
L.A. Story '91
Threads '85
Yuri Nosenko, KGB '86

Mike Jackson
Blood Tracks '86

Pat Jackson
Encore '52
King Arthur, the Young Warlord
    '75
What a Carve-Up! '62

Peter Jackson
Bad Taste '88
Dead Alive '93

Philip Jackson
Project: Genesis '93

Wilfred Jackson
Cinderella '50

Harry Jacobs
Rebel High '88

John Jacobs
Rocket to the Moon '86

Nicholas A.E. Jacobs
The Refrigerator '93

Werner Jacobs
Heidi '65

Rick Jacobson
Full Contact '93

Irving Jacoby
Snow Treasure '67

Joseph Jacoby
Great Bank Hoax '78
Hurry Up or I'll Be Thirty '73

Gualtiero Jacopetti
Mondo Cane '63
Mondo Cane 2 '64

Just Jaeckin
Emmanuelle '74
The French Woman '79
Lady Chatterley's Lover '81
The Perils of Gwendoline '84
The Story of O '75

Stanley R. Jaffe
Without a Trace '83

Henry Jaglom
Always '85
Can She Bake a Cherry Pie?
    '83
Eating '90

National Lampoon Goes to the
    Movies '81
New Year's Day '89
Sitting Ducks '80
Someone to Love '87
Tracks '76

Sam Jaimes
Good Grief, Charlie Brown '83
Happy New Year, Charlie
    Brown '82

Patrick Jamain
Honeymoon '87

Alan James
Fargo Express '32
Lucky Terror '36
Phantom Thunderbolt '33
Red Barry '38
When a Man Sees Red '34

Bob James
Alien Seed '89

Jerry Jameson
The Bat People '74
The Cowboy & the Ballerina '84
Dirt Gang '71
Fire and Rain '89
High Noon: Part 2 '80
Hotline '82
Hurricane '74
Killing at Hell's Gate '81
Raise the Titanic '80
Sniper '75
Starflight One '83
Terror on the 40th Floor '74

Miklos Jancso
Hungarian Rhapsody '78
The Red and the White '68
The Round Up '66

Gerhard Janda
Tea For Three '84

Annabel Jankel
D.O.A. '88
Super Mario Bros. '93

Stole Jankovic
Hell River '75

Victor Janos
Last House on Dead End Street
    '77

Christian Jaque
Legend of Frenchie King '71

Derek Jarman
Aria '88
Blue '93
Caravaggio '86
Edward II '92
The Last of England '87
Sebastiane '79

Jim Jarmusch
Down by Law '86
Mystery Train '89
Night on Earth '91
Permanent Vacation '84
Stranger than Paradise '84

Charles Jarrott
The Amateur '82
Boy in Blue '86
Condorman '81
Danielle Steel's Changes '91
The Dove '74
The Last Flight of Noah's Ark
    '80
The Littlest Horse Thieves '76
Lucy and Desi: Before the
    Laughter '91
Night of the Fox '90
The Other Side of Midnight '77
Poor Little Rich Girl: The
    Barbara Hutton Story '87
Strange Case of Dr. Jekyll &
    Mr. Hyde '68
The Woman He Loved '88

Vojtech Jasny
All My Good Countrymen '68
The Great Land of Small '86

Leigh Jason
The Bride Walks Out '36
The Choppers '61
High Gear '33
Lady for a Night '42
Lost Honeymoon '47
Mad Miss Manton '38
Out of the Blue '47
That Girl from Paris '36

Will Jason
Everybody's Dancin' '50

Vadim Jean
Leon the Pig Farmer '93

Roland S. Jefferson
Perfume '91

Tom Jeffrey
The Odd Angry Shot '79
Weekend of Shadows '77

Herbert Jeffries
World of the Depraved '67

Lionel Jeffries
Amazing Mr. Blunden '72
Railway Children '70
Water Babies '79
Wombling Free '77

Andras Jeles
The Little Valentino '79

Bunker Jenkins
Space Ninja: Sword of the
    Space Ark '81

Michael Jenkins
Rebel '85
Sweet Talker '91

Patrick Jenkins
The Gambler & the Lady '52

Astrid Henning Jensen
Boy of Two Worlds '70

Leopold Jessner
Backstairs '21

Alain Jessua
The Killing Game '67

Jean-Marie Jeunet
Delicatessen '92

Norman Jewison
Agnes of God '85
And Justice for All '79
Best Friends '82
The Cincinnati Kid '65
Fiddler on the Roof '71
F.I.S.T. '78
In Country '89
In the Heat of the Night '67
Jesus Christ, Superstar '73
Moonstruck '87
Only You '94
Other People's Money '91
Rollerball '75
The Russians are Coming, the
    Russians are Coming '66
Send Me No Flowers '64
A Soldier's Story '84
Thomas Crown Affair '68
The Thrill of It All! '63

Ruth Prawer Jhabvala
The Courtesans of Bombay '85

Neal Jimenez
The Waterdance '91

Robert Jiras
I Am the Cheese '83

Duan Jishun
The Go-Masters '82

Mike Jittlov
The Wizard of Speed and Time
    '88

Leo Joannon
Utopia '51

Phil Joanou
Fallen Angels 2 '93
Final Analysis '92
State of Grace '90
Three O'Clock High '87
Wild Palms '93

Dickie Jobson
Countryman '83

Alejandro Jodorowsky
Santa Sangre '90

Steve Jodrell
Shame '87

Michael Joens
My Little Pony: The Movie '86

Alfred Joffe
Harem '85

Arthur Joffe
Alberto Express '92

Mark Joffe
The Efficiency Expert '92
Grievous Bodily Harm '89
Night Master '87

Roland Joffe
City of Joy '92
Fat Man and Little Boy '89
The Killing Fields '84
The Mission '86

Sande Johnsen
Teenage Gang Debs '66

Alan Johnson
Solarbabies '86
To Be or Not to Be '83

Emory Johnson
Phantom Express '32

Irvin Johnson
Blood Ring '93
Fist of Steel '93

Jed Johnson
Andy Warhol's Bad '77

John H. Johnson
Curse of the Blue Lights '88

Kenneth Johnson
The Incredible Hulk '77
Senior Trip '81
Short Circuit 2 '88

Lamont Johnson
The Broken Chain '93
Crisis at Central High '80
Ernie Kovacs: Between the
    Laughter '84
Escape '90
The Execution of Private Slovik
    '74
FM '78
Gore Vidal's Lincoln '88
The Groundstar Conspiracy '72
A Gunfight '71
Jack & the Beanstalk '83
The Last American Hero '73
Lipstick '76
McKenzie Break '70
My Sweet Charlie '70
One on One '77
Paul's Case '80
Spacehunter: Adventures in the
    Forbidden Zone '83
The Twilight Zone '61
Unnatural Causes '86

Nunnally Johnson
The Man in the Gray Flannel
    Suit '56
The Three Faces of Eve '57

Patrick Read Johnson
Baby's Day Out '94
Spaced Invaders '90

Raymond K. Johnson
Code of the Fearless '39
Covered Wagon Trails '40

Johnson ▶cont.

Daughter of the Tong '39
I'll Name the Murderer '36
In Old Montana '39
Pinto Canyon '40
The Reckless Way '36
Ridin' the Trail '40

Tucker Johnson
Blood Salvage '90

Jim Johnston
Blue De Ville '86

Joe Johnston
Honey, I Shrunk the Kids '89
The Rocketeer '91

Amy Jones
Love Letters '83
Maid to Order '87
The Slumber Party Massacre '82

Brian Thomas Jones
Escape from Safehaven '88
Ocean Drive Weekend '85
Posed For Murder '89
The Rejuvenator '88

Chuck Jones
Best of Bugs Bunny & Friends '40
Bugs & Daffy: The Wartime Cartoons '45
The Bugs Bunny/Road Runner Movie '79
Bugs Bunny's 3rd Movie: 1,001 Rabbit Tales '82
Looney Looney Looney Bugs Bunny Movie '81
Phantom Tollbooth '69
Starring Bugs Bunny! '48

David Jones
Betrayal '83
The Christmas Wife '88
84 Charing Cross Road '86
Jacknife '89
Look Back in Anger '89
The Trial '93

Donald M. Jones
Deadly Sunday '82
The Forest '83
Lethal Pursuit '88
Love Butcher '82
Murderlust '86
Project: Nightmare
Sweater Girls '78

Eugene S. Jones
High Ice '80

F. Richard Jones
Bulldog Drummond '29
Extra Girl '23

Gary Jones
Stay Tuned for Murder '88

Harmon Jones
As Young As You Feel '51
Bullwhip '58
The Legend of the Sea Wolf '58
Pride of St. Louis '52

James Cellan Jones
Fortunes of War '87

Lee Jones
Invasion of the Girl Snatchers '73

L.Q. Jones
A Boy and His Dog '75

Mark Jones
Leprechaun '93

Terry Jones
Erik the Viking '89
Monty Python and the Holy Grail '75
Monty Python's Life of Brian '79

Monty Python's The Meaning of Life '83
Personal Services '87

Andrew Jordan
Things '80s

Glenn Jordan
Barbarians at the Gate '93
The Buddy System '83
The Displaced Person '76
Dress Gray '86
Echoes in the Darkness '87
The Family Man '79
Frankenstein '73
Jesse '88
Les Miserables '78
Lois Gibbs and the Love Canal '82
Mass Appeal '84
O Pioneers! '91
One of My Wives Is Missing '76
Only When I Laugh '81
Picture of Dorian Gray '74
Sarah, Plain and Tall '91
Something in Common '86
To Dance with the White Dog '93
Toughlove '85

Neil Jordan
The Company of Wolves '85
The Crying Game '92
Danny Boy '84
High Spirits '88
The Miracle '91
Mona Lisa '86
We're No Angels '89

George Joseph
Horror of the Blood Monsters '70

Jon Jost
All the Vermeers in New York '91
Angel City '84
Bell Diamond '81
Chameleon '81
Slow Moves '84
Sure Fire '90

Pierre Jourdan
Phedre '68

Ron Joy
The Desperados '80s

C. Courtney Joyner
Lurking Fear '94
Trancers 3: Deth Lives '92

Rupert Julian
Merry-Go-Round '23
The Phantom of the Opera '25
Walking Back '26
Yankee Clipper '27

Nathan Juran
The Brain from Planet Arous '57
The Deadly Mantis '57
First Men in the Moon '64
Hellcats of the Navy '57
Jack the Giant Killer '62
Land Raiders '69
The Seventh Voyage of Sinbad '58
20 Million Miles to Earth '57

Juan Jose Jusid
Made in Argentina '86

James Robertson Justice
Superstition '82

Paul Justman
Gimme an F '85

Claude Jutra
By Design '82
Mon Oncle Antoine '71
Surfacing '84

Barna Kabay
The Revolt of Job '84

George Kaczender
The Agency '81
Chanel Solitaire '81
The Girl in Blue '74
In Praise of Older Women '78
Prettykill '87
Your Ticket Is No Longer Valid '84

Jan Kadar
Death is Called Engelchen '63
Freedom Road '79
Lies My Father Told Me '75
The Shop on Main Street '65

Ellis Kadison
The Cat '66
Git! '65

Helmut Kaeutner
The Captain from Koepenick '56

Jeremy Paul Kagan
The Big Fix '78
Big Man on Campus '89
By the Sword '93
Conspiracy: The Trial of the Chicago Eight '87
Courage '86
Descending Angel '90
Heroes '77
The Journey of Natty Gann '85
Katherine '75
The Sting 2 '83

Jeff Kahn
Revolution! A Red Comedy '91

Richard C. Kahn
Bronze Buckaroo '39
Harlem Rides the Range '39
Son of Ingagi '40
Two-Gun Man from Harlem '38

Chen Kaige
Farewell My Concubine '93
Life on a String '90
Yellow Earth '89

Connie Kaiserman
My Little Girl '87

Mikhail Kalatozov
The Cranes are Flying '57
Red Tent '69

Tom Kalin
Swoon '91

Max Kalmanowicz
The Children '80
Dreams Come True '84

Steven Kampmann
Stealing Home '88

Yu Kan-Ping
The Outcasts '86

Tony Kandah
L.A. Wars '94

Dennis Kane
French Quarter '78

Joseph Kane
Billy the Kid Returns '38
Boots & Saddles '37
The Border Legion '40
Born to Be Wild '38
Colorado '40
Dakota '45
Fighting Marines '36
Flame of the Barbary Coast '45
Frontier Pony Express '39
Gene Autry Matinee Double Feature #2 '53
Ghost Town Gold '36
Git Along Little Dogies '37
Hands Across the Border '43
Heart of the Golden West '42
Heart of the Rockies '37
Hoodlum Empire '52
Idaho '43
In Old Santa Fe '34
Jesse James at Bay '41
Jubilee Trail '54

King of the Pecos '36
The Lawless Nineties '36
Maverick Queen '55
Melody Trail '35
Old Barn Dance '38
Old Corral '36
Ranger and the Lady '40
Ride, Ranger, Ride '36
Ride the Man Down '53
Ridin' Down the Canyon '42
Robin Hood of the Pecos '41
Rough Riders' Roundup '39
Round-Up Time in Texas '37
Saga of Death Valley '39
Shine on, Harvest Moon '38
Silver Spurs '43
Smoke in the Wind '75
Song of Nevada '44
Song of Texas '43
Sons of the Pioneers '42
South of Santa Fe '42
Springtime in the Rockies '37
Sunset on the Desert '42
Sunset Serenade '42
Texas Legionnaires '43
Western Double Feature 1 '38
Western Double Feature 4 '37
Western Double Feature 20
The Yellow Rose of Texas '44
Yodelin' Kid From Pine Ridge '37
Young Buffalo Bill '40

Rolfe Kanefsky
There's Nothing Out There '90

Shusuke Kaneko
Summer Vacation: 1999 '88

Vitaly Kanevski
Freeze-Die-Come to Life '90

Jeff Kanew
Eddie Macon's Run '83
Gotcha! '85
Natural Enemies '79
Revenge of the Nerds '84
Tough Guys '86
Troop Beverly Hills '89
V.I. Warshawski '91

Charles Kanganis
Chance '89
Deadly Breed '89
No Escape, No Return '93
Sinners '89
3 Ninjas Kick Back '94
A Time to Die '91

Marek Kanievska
Another Country '84
Less Than Zero '87

Garson Kanin
Bachelor Mother '39
The Great Man Votes '38
My Favorite Wife '40
Next Time I Marry '38
They Knew What They Wanted '40
Tom, Dick, and Harry '41

Alexis Kanner
Kings and Desperate Men '83

Hal Kanter
For the Love of It '80
I Married a Woman '56
Loving You '57

Richard Kanter
Wild Riders '71

Ed Kaplan
Chips, the War Dog '90
Walking on Air '87

Jonathan Kaplan
The Accused '88
Bad Girls '94
Fallen Angels 1 '93
Gentleman Bandit '81
Girls of the White Orchid '85
Heart Like a Wheel '83
Immediate Family '89
Love Field '91
Mr. Billion '77

Night Call Nurses '72
Over the Edge '79
Project X '87
The Student Teachers '73
Truck Turner '74
Unlawful Entry '92
White Line Fever '75

Nelly Kaplan
Charles et Lucie '79
Nea '78
A Very Curious Girl '69

Ted Kaplan
Warbus '85

Yuri Karasik
The Seagull '71

Michael Karbelnikoff
Mobsters '91

Leslie Kardos
Small Town Girl '53

Phil Karlson
Behind the Mask '37
Ben '72
The Big Cat '49
Framed '75
Hell to Eternity '60
Hornet's Nest '70
Kansas City Confidential '52
Kid Galahad '62
Ladies of the Chorus '49
Scarface Mob '62
The Shanghai Cobra '45
Swing Parade of 1946 '46
The Texas Rangers '51
There Goes Kelly '45
Walking Tall '73

Janice Karman
The Chipmunk Adventure '87

Bill Karn
Door to Door Maniac '61
Gang Busters '55
Ma Barker's Killer Brood '60

Eric Karson
Angel Town '89
Black Eagle '88
Octagon '80
Opposing Force '87

Y. Kasancki
The Amphibian Man '61

Lawrence Kasdan
The Accidental Tourist '88
The Big Chill '83
Body Heat '81
Grand Canyon '91
I Love You to Death '90
Silverado '85
Wyatt Earp '94

Peter Kassovitz
Make Room for Tomorrow '81

Pierre Kast
Girl in His Pocket '62

Leonard Kastle
Honeymoon Killers '70

Milton Katselas
Butterflies Are Free '72
Forty Carats '73
Report to the Commissioner '74
Strangers: The Story of a Mother and Daughter '79

Gloria Katz
Messiah of Evil '74

Lee H. Katzin
The Bastard '78
Death Ray 2000 '81
The Dirty Dozen: The Deadly Mission '87
The Dirty Dozen: The Fatal Mission '88
Le Mans '71
The Longest Drive '76
The Man from Atlantis '77
The Salzburg Connection '72

Savages '75
Sky Hei$t '75
Space: 1999—Alien Attack '79
The Stranger '73
Terror Out of the Sky '78
The Voyage of the Yes '72
Whatever Happened to Aunt
  Alice? '69
World Gone Wild '88

Jonathan Kaufer
Soup for One '82

Charles Kaufman
Jakarta '88
Mother's Day '80
When Nature Calls '85

George S. Kaufman
The Senator was Indiscreet '47

Jim Kaufman
Backstab '90

Lloyd Samuel Weil Kaufman
First Turn On '83
Squeeze Play '79
Stuck on You '84
The Toxic Avenger '86
The Toxic Avenger, Part 2 '89
The Toxic Avenger, Part 3: The
  Last Temptation of Toxie '89
Troma's War '88
Waitress '81

Philip Kaufman
The Great Northfield Minnesota
  Raid '72
Henry & June '90
Invasion of the Body Snatchers
  '78
The Outlaw Josey Wales '76
The Right Stuff '83
Rising Sun '93
The Unbearable Lightness of
  Being '88
Wanderers '79
The White Dawn '75

Aki Kaurismaki
Ariel '89
La Vie de Boheme '93
Leningrad Cowboys Go
  America '89
The Match Factory Girl '90

Mika Kaurismaki
Amazon '90

Brian Kavanagh
Double Deal '84

Anwar Kawadri
Claudia '85
Nutcracker Sweet '84

Jerzy Kawalerowicz
Pharaoh '66

Gilbert Kay
White Comanche '67

James H. Kay
Seeds of Evil '76

Robert Kaylor
Carny '80
Derby '71
Nobody's Perfect '90

Elia Kazan
The Arrangement '69
Baby Doll '56
East of Eden '54
A Face in the Crowd '57
Gentleman's Agreement '47
The Last Tycoon '76
On the Waterfront '54
Panic in the Streets '50
Pinky '49
Splendor in the Grass '61
A Streetcar Named Desire '51
A Tree Grows in Brooklyn '45
Viva Zapata! '52

Nicholas Kazan
Dream Lover '93

Fran Rubel Kazui
Buffy the Vampire Slayer '92
Tokyo Pop '88

Lo Ke
The Amsterdam Connection
  '70s

James Keach
False Identity '90
The Forgotten '89
Praying Mantis '93
Sunstroke '92

Buster Keaton
The Balloonatic/One Week '23
Battling Butler '26
The Blacksmith/The Balloonatic
  '23
Cops/One Week '22
The General '27
The Navigator '24
Our Hospitality '23
Seven Chances '25
Three Ages '23

Diane Keaton
Heaven '87
Wildflower '91

Zsolt Kedzi-Kovacs
Nice Neighbor '79

Worth Keeter
Dogs of Hell '83
Illicit Behavior '91
L.A. Bounty '89
Lady Grey '82
Order of the Black Eagle '87
Snapdragon '93
Trapper County War '89
Unmasking the Idol '86
The Wolfman '82

Peter Keglevic
The Cop & the Girl '86
Kill Cruise '90

William Keighley
The Bride Came C.O.D. '41
Bullets or Ballots '38
Each Dawn I Die '39
The Fighting 69th '40
"G" Men '35
George Washington Slept Here
  '42
Green Pastures '36
Ladies They Talk About '33
The Man Who Came to Dinner
  '41
The Master of Ballantrae '53
The Prince and the Pauper '37
The Street with No Name '48

George Keil
2069: A Sex Odyssey '78

David Keith
The Curse '87
The Further Adventures of
  Tennessee Buck '88

Harvey Keith
Jezebel's Kiss '90

Frederick King Keller
The Eyes of the Amaryllis '82
Vamping '84

Harry Keller
El Paso Stampede '53
Geronimo's Revenge '60
Marshal of Cedar Rock '53
Tammy and the Doctor '63
Texas John Slaughter:
  Geronimo's Revenge '60
Texas John Slaughter:
  Stampede at Bitter Creek
  '62

Bob Kellett
Naughty Knights '71
Space: 1999 '75

Hugh Kelley
The Cage '91

Roy Kellino
Charade '87
I Met a Murderer '39

Bob Kelljan
Act of Vengeance '74
Black Oak Conspiracy '77
Count Yorga, Vampire '70
The Return of Count Yorga '71
Scream Blacula Scream '73

Barnet Kellman
Key Exchange '85
Straight Talk '92

David Kellogg
Cool As Ice '91

Ray Kellogg
The Giant Gila Monster '59
The Killer Shrews '59

Albert Kelly
Campus Knights '29

Gene Kelly
The Cheyenne Social Club '70
A Guide for the Married Man
  '67
Hello, Dolly! '69
Invitation to the Dance '56
On the Town '49
Singin' in the Rain '52
The Tunnel of Love '58

James Kelly
Beast in the Cellar '70

Nancy Kelly
Thousand Pieces of Gold '91

Patrick Kelly
Beer '85

Peter Kelly
The Dawson Patrol '78

Ron Kelly
King of the Grizzlies '69

Jack Kemp
Miracle in Harlem '48

Ralph Kemplen
The Spaniard's Curse '58

David Kendall
Luggage of the Gods '87

James Kennaway
Tunes of Glory/Horse's Mouth
  '60

Arthur Kennedy
Assault with a Deadly Weapon
  '82

Burt Kennedy
All the Kind Strangers '74
The Concrete Cowboys '79
Dynamite and Gold '88
The Good Guys and the Bad
  Guys '69
Hannie Caulder '72
Killer Inside Me '76
More Wild, Wild West '80
Return of the Seven '66
Ride to Glory '71
The Rounders '65
Suburban Commando '91
Support Your Local Gunfighter
  '71
Support Your Local Sheriff '69
Train Robbers '73
The Trouble with Spies '87
The War Wagon '67
Wild, Wild West Revisited '79
Wolf Lake '79

Ken Kennedy
Grizzly Adams: The Legend
  Continues '90
Iron Angel '64
Mission to Glory '80

Leon Isaac Kennedy
Knights of the City '85

Lou Kennedy
Breathing Fire '91

Michael Kennedy
Caribe '87
One Man Out '89
The Swordsman '92
Talons of the Eagle '92

Tom Kennedy
Time Walker '82

Larry Kent
The Victory '88

Willis Kent
Mad Youth '40

Eric Kenton
Fight for the Title '57

Erle C. Kenton
Bare Knees '28
Escape to Paradise '39
The Ghost of Frankenstein '42
House of Dracula '45
House of Frankenstein '44
Island of Lost Souls '32
Melody for Three '41
Pardon My Sarong '42
Remedy for Riches '40
They Meet Again '41
Who Done It? '42

Patrick Kerby
Ex-Cop '93

James V. Kern
Second Woman '51
Two Tickets to Broadway '51

Russell Kern
Spittin' Image '83

Sarah Kernochan
Marjoe '72

Irvin Kershner
The Empire Strikes Back '80
Eyes of Laura Mars '78
A Fine Madness '66
Flim-Flam Man '67
The Hoodlum Priest '61
Never Say Never Again '83
Raid on Entebbe '77
The Return of a Man Called
  Horse '76
RoboCop 2 '90
S*P*Y*S '74
Traveling Man '89
Up the Sandbox '72

Emmanuel Kervyn
Rabid Grannies '89

Harry Kerwin
Barracuda '78
Cheering Section '73
God's Bloody Acre '75

Alek Keshishian
Truth or Dare '91
With Honors '94

Bruce Kessler
Angels from Hell '68
Cruise into Terror '78
Deathmoon '78
Simon, King of the Witches '71

Kliff Keuhl
Murder Rap '87

Michael Keusch
Huck and the King of Hearts
  '93
Just One of the Girls '93
Lena's Holiday '90
Samurai Cowboy '93

Riffat A. Khan
Feelin' Screwy '90

Michel Khleifi
A Wedding in Galilee '87

Kim Ki-dak
Yongkari Monster of the Deep
  '67

Beeban Kidron
Antonia and Jane '91
Used People '92

Fritz Kiersch
Children of the Corn '84
Gor '88
Into the Sun '92
Tuff Turf '85
Under the Boardwalk '89
Winners Take All '87

Krzysztof Kieslowski
The Double Life of Veronique
  '91
No End '84
Trois Couleurs: Blanc '94
Trois Couleurs: Bleu '93
Trois Couleurs: Rouge '94

Gerard Kikicione
Buried Alive '89
Dragonard '87
Edge of Sanity '89

Jon Killough
Skinned Alive '89

Edward Killy
Don Amigo/Stage to Chino '40s
Nevada '44
West of the Pecos '45

Richard H. Kim
Kill Line '91

Clinton Kimbrough
The Young Nurses '73

Bruce Kimmel
Spaceship '81

Anthony Kimmins
Bonnie Prince Charlie '48
Captain's Paradise '53
Mine Own Executioner '47

John Kincade
Back to Back '90
Terminal Entry '87

Tim Kincaid
Bad Girls Dormitory '84
Mutant Hunt '87
The Occultist '89
Robot Holocaust '87
She's Back '88

Allan Winton King
Silence of the North '81

Allen King
Termini Station '89

Burton King
The Adorable Cheat '28
The Man from Beyond '22

George King
The Case of the Frightened
  Lady '39
Crimes at the Dark House '39
The Crimes of Stephen Hawke
  '36
Demon Barber of Fleet Street
  '36
The Face at the Window '39

Henry King
Alexander's Ragtime Band '38
The Bravados '58
Carousel '56
David and Bathsheba '51
The Gunfighter '50
Hell Harbor '30
In Old Chicago '38
Jesse James '39
Love is a Many-Splendored
  Thing '55
Marie Galante '34
Romola '25
She Goes to War '29
The Snows of Kilimanjaro '52
The Song of Bernadette '43
Stanley and Livingstone '39
Tol'able David '21
Twelve O'Clock High '49
The White Sister '23
Wilson '44
A Yank in the R.A.F. '41

Louis King
Border Law '31
Bulldog Drummond Comes
Back '37
Bulldog Drummond's Revenge
'37
Dangerous Mission '54
Drifting Souls '32
The Fighting Sheriff '31
Sabre Jet '53
Special Investigator '36

Rick King
Forced March '90
Hard Choices '84
Hot Shot '86
Kickboxer 3: The Art of War '92
The Killing Time '87
Prayer of the Rollerboys '91
Quick '93

Stephen King
Maximum Overdrive '86

Zalman King
Red Shoe Diaries '92
Red Shoe Diaries 2: Double
Dare '91
Red Shoe Diaries 3: Another
Woman's Lipstick '93
Red Shoe Diaries 4: Auto
Erotica '93
Two Moon Junction '88
Wild Orchid '90
Wild Orchid 2: Two Shades of
Blue '92
Wildfire '88

Kinghu
The Fate of Lee Khan '73

Alan Kingsberg
Almost Partners '87

Jack Kinney
The Legend of Sleepy Hollow
'49
1001 Arabian Nights '59

Keisuke Kinoshita
Twenty-Four Eyes '54

Teinosuke Kinugasa
Gate of Hell '54

Alex Kirby
The Chronicles of Narnia '89

Robert Kirk
Destroyer '88

David Kirkland
The Tomboy '24

John Kirkland
Curse of the Headless
Horseman '72

Klaus Kirschner
Mozart: A Childhood Chronicle
'76

John Kirsh
Jesus '79

Ephraim Kishon
Sallah '63

Lek Kitiparaporn
AngKor: Cambodia Express '81

Carl Kitt
Up River '79

Robert J. Kizer
Death Ring '93
Godzilla 1985 '85
Hell Comes to Frogtown '88

Alf Kjellin
The Girls of Huntington House
'73
The McMasters '70

Robert Klane
Thank God It's Friday '78
Weekend at Bernie's 2 '93

Damian Klaus
Futurekick '91

Dennis Klein
One More Saturday Night '86

Randal Kleiser
Big Top Pee Wee '88
The Blue Lagoon '80
The Boy in the Plastic Bubble
'76
Flight of the Navigator '86
The Gathering '77
Getting It Right '89
Grandview U.S.A. '84
Grease '78
Honey, I Blew Up the Kid '92
Summer Lovers '82
White Fang '91

Max Kleven
Bail Out '90
Deadly Stranger '88
Ruckus '81

Roland Klick
Let It Rock '86

Elem Klimov
Come and See '85
Rasputin '78

Leon Klimovsky
The Devil's Possessed '74
Dr. Jekyll and the Wolfman '71
Orgy of the Vampires '73
The Saga of the Draculas '72
Vengeance of the Zombies '72
The Werewolf vs. the Vampire
Woman '70

Ben Kline
Lightning Warrior '31

Herbert Kline
The Fighter '52

Tony Klinger
Butterfly Ball '76

Werner Klinger
Secret of the Black Trunk '62

Elmar Klos
Death is Called Engelchen '63
The Shop on Main Street '65

Steven Kloves
The Fabulous Baker Boys '89
Flesh and Bone '93

Alexander Kluge
Germany in Autumn '78

Pavel Klushantsev
Planet Burg '62

Castleton Knight
The Flying Scotsman '29

Robert Knights
The Dawning '88
A Dedicated Man '86
Double Vision '92
Ebony Tower '86
Lovers of Their Time '85

Edwin H. Knopf
The Light of Western Stars '30

Bernard Knowles
Frozen Alive '64
Murder on Approval '56
Norman Conquest '53

Werner Knox
Scalps '83

Philip Ko
Platoon the Warriors '88

Masaki Kobayashi
The Human Condition: A
Soldier's Prayer '61
The Human Condition: No
Greater Love '58
The Human Condition: Road to
Eternity '59
Kwaidan '64

Howard W. Koch
Badge 373 '73
Girl in Black Stockings '57

Philip Koch
Pink Nights '87

Pancho Kohner
Mr. Sycamore '74

Marja Kok
In for Treatment '82

Amos Kollek
Crazy Streets '80s
Double Edge '92
Forever, Lulu '87
Goodbye, New York '85
High Stakes '89

Xavier Koller
Journey of Hope '90

James Komack
Porky's Revenge '85

Sergei Komarov
A Kiss for Mary Pickford '27

**Andrei
Konchalovsky**
Duet for One '86
Homer and Eddie '89
The Inner Circle '91
Maria's Lovers '84
Runaway Train '85
Shy People '87
Tango and Cash '89

Jackie Kong
The Being '83
Blood Diner '87
Night Patrol '85
The Underachievers '88

Joseph Kong
Clones of Bruce Lee '80
Thundering Ninja '80s

Barbara Kopple
Fallen Champ: The Untold
Story of Mike Tyson '93
Harlan County, U.S.A. '76
Keeping On '81

Alexander Korda
Marius '31
Private Life of Don Juan '34
The Private Life of Henry VIII
'33
Rembrandt '36
That Hamilton Woman '41
Wedding Rehearsal '32

Zoltan Korda
Cry, the Beloved Country '51
Drums '38
Elephant Boy '37
The Four Feathers '39
If I Were Rich '33
The Jungle Book '42
Sahara '43
Sanders of the River '35

John Korty
The Autobiography of Miss
Jane Pittman '74
Cast the First Stone '89
A Christmas Without Snow '80
Class of '63 '73
Deadly Business '86
The Ewok Adventure '84
Eye on the Sparrow '91
Forever '78
The Haunting Passion '83
Oliver's Story '78
The People '71
Silence '73
They Watch '93

**Waldemar
Korzenioswsky**
The Chair '87

Grigori Kosintsev
Don Quixote '57

Henry Koster
The Bishop's Wife '47
D-Day, the Sixth of June '56
Dear Brigitte '65

Desiree '54
Flower Drum Song '61
Harvey '50
The Inspector General '49
A Man Called Peter '55
Mr. Hobbs Takes a Vacation
'62
My Man Godfrey '57
The Naked Maja '59
The Rage of Paris '38
The Robe '53
The Singing Nun '66
Stars and Stripes Forever '52
The Story of Ruth '60
The Virgin Queen '55

Tom Kotani
The Bushido Blade '80

Ted Kotcheff
The Apprenticeship of Duddy
Kravitz '74
First Blood '82
Folks! '92
Fun with Dick and Jane '77
Joshua Then and Now '85
North Dallas Forty '79
Red Shoe Diaries 3: Another
Woman's Lipstick '93
Split Image '82
Switching Channels '88
Tiara Tahiti '62
Uncommon Valor '83
Weekend at Bernie's '89
Who is Killing the Great Chefs
of Europe? '78
Winter People '89

Jerzy Kotkowski
In an Old Manor House '84

Jim Kouf
Disorganized Crime '89
Miracles '86

Nikos Koundouros
Young Aphrodites '63

Steven Kovacs
'68 '87

Andras Kovacs
Cold Days '66

Paul Koval
Blue Movies '88

Bernard L. Kowalski
Attack of the Giant Leeches '59
B.A.D. Cats '80
Macho Callahan '70
Marciano '79
Nashville Beat '89
Nativity '78
Night of the Blood Beast '58
Stiletto '69
The Woman Hunter '72

**Soeren Kragh-
Jacobsen**
Emma's Shadow '88

Frank Kramer
Five for Hell '67
God's Gun '75
This Time I'll Make You Rich
'75

Jerry Kramer
Modern Girls '86

Remi Kramer
High Velocity '76

Stanley Kramer
Bless the Beasts and Children
'71
The Defiant Ones '58
The Domino Principle '77
Guess Who's Coming to Dinner
'67
Inherit the Wind '60
It's a Mad, Mad, Mad, Mad
World '63
Judgment at Nuremberg '61
Not as a Stranger '55
Oklahoma Crude '73

On the Beach '59
The Pride and the Passion '57
R.P.M.* (*Revolutions Per
Minute) '70
The Runner Stumbles '79
Ship of Fools '65

Norman Krasna
The Ambassador's Daughter
'56
The Big Hangover '50

Paul Krasny
Back to Hannibal: The Return
of Tom Sawyer and
Huckleberry Finn '90
Christina '74
Drug Wars 2: The Cocaine
Cartel '92
Joe Panther '76
When Hell Was in Session '82

Lee Kresel
Alakazam the Great! '61

Harold F. Kress
The Painted Hills '51

John Krish
Man Who Had Power Over
Women '70
The Unearthly Stranger '64

Srinivas Krishna
Masala '91

Allen Kroeker
Age Old Friends '89
Heaven on Earth '89
Showdown at Williams Creek
'91
Tramp at the Door '87

Bill Krohn
It's All True '93

Frank Krom
To Play or To Die '91

**Jeremy Joe
Kronsberg**
Going Ape! '81

Bill Kroyer
Ferngully: The Last Rain Forest
'92

Michael Krueger
Mindkiller '87
Night Vision '87

Stanley Kubrick
Barry Lyndon '75
A Clockwork Orange '71
Dr. Strangelove, or: How I
Learned to Stop Worrying
and Love the Bomb '64
Full Metal Jacket '87
Killer's Kiss '55
The Killing '56
Lolita '62
Paths of Glory '57
The Shining '80
Spartacus '60
2001: A Space Odyssey '68

Andrew J. Kuehn
Flush '81

Steven Kuether
Demons of Ludlow '75

Lev Kuleshov
The Extraordinary Adventures
of Mr. West in the Land of
the Bolsheviks '24

Lev Kulijanov
Crime and Punishment '70

Buzz Kulik
Babe! '75
Bad Ronald '74
Brian's Song '71
From Here to Eternity '79
The Hunter '80
The Lindbergh Kidnapping
Case '76
Pioneer Woman '73

Rage of Angels '83
Riot '69
Sergeant Ryker '68
Shamus '73
Villa Rides '68
Women of Valor '86

Edward Kull
The New Adventures of Tarzan '35
Tarzan and the Green Goddess '38

Victor Kulle
Illusions '91

Kei Kumai
Love and Faith '78
Sandakan No. 8 '74

Harry Kumel
Daughters of Darkness '71

Joseph Kuo
Born Invincible '76
Dragon's Claw '80s
Shaolin Temple Strikes Back '72
The Unbeaten 28 '80s

Koreyoshi Kurahara
Antarctica '84

Hanif Kureishi
London Kills Me '91

Akira Kurosawa
Akira Kurosawa's Dreams '90
The Bad Sleep Well '60
Dersu Uzala '75
Dodes 'ka-den '70
Drunken Angel '48
The Hidden Fortress '58
High & Low '62
I Live in Fear '55
The Idiot '51
Ikiru '52
Kagemusha '80
The Lower Depths '57
The Men Who Tread on the Tiger's Tail '45
No Regrets for Our Youth '46
Ran '85
Rashomon '51
Red Beard '65
Rhapsody in August '91
Sanjuro '62
Sanshiro Sugata '43
Seven Samurai '54
Stray Dog '49
Throne of Blood '57
Yojimbo '61

Diane Kurys
Entre-Nous '83
A Man in Love '87
Peppermint Soda '77

Donald Kushner
First & Ten '85

Emir Kusturica
Time of the Gypsies '90
When Father was Away on Business '85

Stanley Kwan
Rouge '87

Ken Kwapis
The Beniker Gang '83
He Said, She Said '91
Sesame Street Presents: Follow That Bird '85
Vibes '88

Jeff Kwitny
Beyond the Door 3 '91
Iced '88

Paul Kyriazi
Crazed Cop '88
Death Machines '76
Omega Cop '90

Gregory La Cava
Big News '29
Feel My Pulse '28

Fifth Avenue Girl '39
Gabriel Over the White House '33
His First Command '29
My Man Godfrey '36
Primrose Path '40
Running Wild '27
Stage Door '37

Steven La Rocque
Samantha '92

Jeanne Labrune
Sand and Blood '87

Harry Lachman
Baby, Take a Bow '34
Castle in the Desert '42
Charlie Chan in Rio '41
The Loves of Edgar Allen Poe '42
Murder Over New York '40
Our Relations '36

Georges Lacombe
Seven Deadly Sins '53

Joe Lacy
A Witch Without a Broom '68

Aldo Lado
Paralyzed '70s

Edward Laemmle
Texas Bad Man '32

John Lafia
Blue Iguana '88
Child's Play 2 '90
Man's Best Friend '93

Jean LaFleur
Ilsa, the Tigress of Siberia '79
Mystery of the Million Dollar Hockey Puck '80s

Ron Lagomarsino
Dinner at Eight '89

Craig Lahiff
Deadly Possession '88
Fever '88
Strangers '90

Joseph Lai
Cobra Against Ninja '80s
Ninja Commandments '87
Ninja Hunt '80s
Ninja Operation: Licensed to Terminate '87
Ninja Powerforce '90
Ninja Showdown '87
Ninja Strike Force '88
The Power of the Ninjitsu '88

Harvey Laidman
The Boy Who Loved Trolls '84
Steel Cowboy '78

John Laing
Beyond Reasonable Doubt '80
Dangerous Orphans '86
The Lost Tribe '89

Frank Laloggia
Fear No Evil '80
The Lady in White '88

Rene Laloux
Fantastic Planet '73

Ringo Lam
Undeclared War '91

York Lam
Ninja Connection '90

Fernando Lamas
Violent Ones '68

Lorenzo Lamas
C.I.A. 2: Target Alexa '94

John Lamb
The Mermaids of Tiburon '62

Gregory Lamberson
Slime City '89

Bruce Lambert
Empire of Spiritual Ninja

Ninja Fantasy '86
Ninja Masters of Death '85
Ninja Phantom Heroes '87
Ninja, the Violent Sorcerer '86
Vampire Raiders—Ninja Queen '89

Mary Lambert
Grand Isle '92
Pet Sematary '89
Pet Sematary 2 '92
Siesta '87

John Lamond
Breakfast in Paris '81

Charles Lamont
Abbott and Costello Go to Mars '53
Abbott and Costello in the Foreign Legion '50
Abbott and Costello Meet Captain Kidd '52
Abbott and Costello Meet Dr. Jekyll and Mr. Hyde '52
Abbott & Costello Meet the Invisible Man '51
Abbott and Costello Meet the Keystone Kops '54
Abbott & Costello Meet the Mummy '55
Bulldog Edition '36
Comin' Round the Mountain '51
The Dark Hour '36
Hit the Ice '43
International Crime '37
Ma and Pa Kettle '49
Ma and Pa Kettle Go to Town '50
Panama Patrol '39
Ring of Bright Water '69
Salome, Where She Danced '45
Shadows Over Shanghai '38
A Shot in the Dark '35
Sons of Steel '35
The World Accuses '35

Albert Lamorisse
Circus Angel '65
The Red Balloon '56
Red Balloon/Occurrence at Owl Creek Bridge '56
Red Balloon/White Mane '56
Voyage en Balloon '59
White Mane '52

Burt Lancaster
The Kentuckian '55

Lew Landers
The Adventures of Gallant Bess '48
Annabel Takes a Tour/Maid's Night Out '38
Bad Lands '39
Death Valley '46
Dynamite Pass '50
The Enchanted Forest '45
Flight from Glory '37
I'm from Arkansas '44
Inner Sanctum '48
Law of the Underworld '38
The Mask of Dijon '46
The Raven '35
Return of the Vampire '43
Ridin' on a Rainbow '41
Rustlers of Red Dog '35
Torpedo Alley '53
U-Boat Prisoner '44

James Landis
Deadwood '65
Nasty Rabbit '64
The Sadist '63
Stakeout '62

John Landis
Amazon Women on the Moon '87
An American Werewolf in London '81
Beverly Hills Cop 3 '94
The Blues Brothers '80
Coming to America '88
Innocent Blood '92

Into the Night '85
Kentucky Fried Movie '77
National Lampoon's Animal House '78
Oscar '91
Schlock '73
Spies Like Us '85
Three Amigos '86
Trading Places '83
Twilight Zone: The Movie '83

Michael Landon
It's Good to Be Alive '74
Killing Stone '78
Little House on the Prairie '74
The Loneliest Runner '76
Sam's Son '84

Paul Landres
Flipper's Odyssey '66
Go, Johnny Go! '59
Return of Dracula '58
Square Dance Jubilee '51

Alan Landsburg
Black Water Gold '69

Andrew Lane
Desperate Motives '92
Jake Speed '86
Mortal Passions '90

Charles Lane
True Identity '91

Rocky Lane
All's Fair '89

Eric Laneuville
The Ernest Green Story '93
The George McKenna Story '86
The Mighty Pawns '87

Sidney Lanfield
The Hound of the Baskervilles '39
The Lemon Drop Kid '51
My Favorite Blonde '42
One in a Million '36
Second Fiddle '39
Skirts Ahoy! '52
Sorrowful Jones '49
Station West '48
Thin Ice '37
You'll Never Get Rich '41

Fritz Lang
Beyond a Reasonable Doubt '56
Big Heat '53
Clash by Night '52
Cloak and Dagger '46
Crimes of Dr. Mabuse '32
Das Testament des Dr. Mabuse '33
Dr. Mabuse the Gambler '22
Fury '36
Human Desire '54
Journey to the Lost City '58
Kriemhilde's Revenge '24
Liliom '35
M '31
Metropolis '26
Moonfleet '55
Rancho Notorious '52
Return of Frank James '40
Scarlet Street '45
Secret Beyond the Door '48
Siegfried '24
Spiders '18
Spies '28
The Thousand Eyes of Dr. Mabuse '60
Western Union '41
While the City Sleeps '56
Woman in the Moon '29
You Only Live Once '37

Krzysztof Lang
Paper Marriage '93

Michael Lang
The Gift '82
Holiday Hotel '77

Perry Lang
Little Vegas '90

Richard Lang
A Change of Seasons '80
Christmas Comes to Willow Creek '87
Don't Go to Sleep '82
Fantasy Island '76
Force of Evil '77
The Hunted Lady '77
Kung Fu: The Movie '86
The Mountain Men '80
Night Cries '78
Shooting Stars '85
Strike Force '81
Vegas '78

Rocky Lang
Nervous Ticks '93
Race for Glory '89

Walter Lang
The Blue Bird '40
But Not for Me '59
Can-Can '60
Desk Set '57
The Jackpot '50
The King and I '56
The Little Princess '39
The Magnificent Dope '42
Moon Over Miami '41
Red Kimono '25
Snow White and the Three Stooges '61
Song of the Islands '42
State Fair '45
There's No Business Like Show Business '54
Tin Pan Alley '40
Week-End In Havana '41

Declan Langan
Erotic Images '85

Noel Langley
The Adventures of Sadie '55
The Pickwick Papers '54
The Search for Bridey Murphy '56
Svengali '55

Chris Langman
Moving Targets '87

Murray Langston
Wishful Thinking '92

Simon Langton
Act of Passion: The Lost Honor of Kathryn Beck '83
Anna Karenina '85
Casanova '87
Laguna Heat '87
The Whistle Blower '87

Lawrence Lanoff
Indecent Behavior '93

Anthony M. Lanza
The Glory Stompers '67
The Incredible Two-Headed Transplant '71

James Lapine
Impromptu '90
Life with Mikey '93
Sunday in the Park with George '86

Joseph Larraz
Golden Lady '79
The House that Vanished '73
Vampyres '74

Sheldon Larry
Behind Enemy Lines '85
Terminal Choice '85

Keith Larsen
Mission Batangas '69
Trap on Cougar Mountain '72
Whitewater Sam '78
Young & Free '78

Robert W. Larsen
The Narcotics Story '58

Eric Larson
Sleeping Beauty '59

Larry Larson
Deadly Passion '85

J.A. Laser
Zombie Lake '84

Stan Lathan
Amazing Grace '74
Beat Street '84
The Sky is Gray '80
Uncle Tom's Cabin '87

John Latos
The Voyage of Tanai '75

Steve Latshaw
Dark Universe '93

David Michael Latt
Sorority House Party '92

Alberto Lattuada
Christopher Columbus '85
La Cicada '83
Love in the City '53
Stay As You Are '78
Variety Lights '51

S.H. Lau
Heroes Three '84

Frank Laudner
I See a Dark Stranger '46

Frank Laughlin
The Trial of Billy Jack '74

Michael Laughlin
Mesmerized '84
Strange Behavior '81
Strange Invaders '83

Tom Laughlin
Billy Jack '71
Born Losers '67

Charles Laughton
The Night of the Hunter '55

Frank Launder
The Belles of St. Trinian's '53
Blue Murder at St. Trinian's '56
The Great St. Trinian's Train
    Robbery '66
The Happiest Days of Your Life
    '50
The Pure Hell of St. Trinian's
    '61

Dale Launer
Love Potion #9 '92

S.K. Lauren
When Ladies Meet '41

Fabrizio Laurenti
Witchery '88

George Lauris
Buffalo Rider '78

Fernand Lauterier
Nais '45

Georges Lautner
Icy Breasts '75
La Cage aux Folles 3: The
    Wedding '86
My Other Husband '85
Road to Salina '68

Linda Lautrec
My Breakfast with Blassie '83

Gerard Lauzier
Petit Con '84

Jean-Claude Lauzon
Leolo '92
Night Zoo '87

Arnold Laven
Geronimo '62
The Monster that Challenged
    the World '57
Rough Night in Jericho '67
Without Warning '52

Martin Lavut
Palais Royale '88
Smokescreen '90

Albert Law
Cold Blooded Murder

Clara Law
The Reincarnation of Golden
    Lotus '89

George Law
Torpedo Attack '72

Tom Law
Tax Season '90

Denny Lawrence
Archer's Adventure '85

John Lawrence
Savage Abduction '73

Marc Lawrence
Pigs '73

Quentin Lawrence
The Crawling Eye '58

Ray Lawrence
Bliss '85

J.F. Lawton
Cannibal Women in the
    Avocado Jungle of Death '89
Pizza Man '91

Jennifer Lax
Max '79

Pedro Lazaga
Gladiators 7 '62

Ashley Lazarus
Golden Rendezvous '77

Wilford Leach
The Pirates of Penzance '83
The Wedding Party '69

Philip Leacock
Angel City '80
Baffled '72
The Curse of King Tut's Tomb
    '80
Dying Room Only '73
Escapade '55
Killer on Board '77
Shattered Silence '71
The Spanish Gardener '57
Thanksgiving Story '73
Three Sovereigns for Sarah '85
The Waltons: A Thanksgiving
    Story '73
War Lover '62
Wild & Wooly '78

Anton Leader
Children of the Damned '63

Paul Leaf
Sergeant Matlovich vs. the U.S.
    Air Force '78

Louis Leahman
South of Hell Mountain '70

Larry Leahy
Confessions of a Hit Man '94

David Lean
Blithe Spirit '45
The Bridge on the River Kwai
    '57
Brief Encounter '46
Doctor Zhivago '65
Great Expectations '46
Hobson's Choice '53
In Which We Serve '43
Lawrence of Arabia '62
Madeleine '50
Oliver Twist '48
A Passage to India '84
Ryan's Daughter '70
Summertime '55
This Happy Breed '47

Norman Lear
Cold Turkey '71

Timothy Leary
Cheech and Chong's Nice
    Dreams '81

Maria Lease
Dolly Dearest '92

Don Leaver
Witching Time '84

Reginald LeBorg
Diary of a Madman '63
G.I. Jane '51
Great Jesse James Raid '49
House of the Black Death '65
The Mummy's Ghost '44
The Sibling '72
Sins of Jezebel '54
The White Orchid '54

Jean-Paul LeChanois
Le Cas du Dr. Laurent '57
L'Ecole Buisoniere '57
Les Miserables '57
Passion for Life '48

Patrice Leconte
The Hairdresser's Husband '92
Monsieur Hire '89

Paul Leder
The Abduction of Allison Tate
    '92
A*P*E* '76
The Baby Doll Murders '92
Body Count '87
Deadly Conspiracy '91
Exiled in America '90
Frame Up '91
I Dismember Mama '74
Killing Obsession '94
Molly and Gina '94
Murder by Numbers '89
Sketches of a Strangler '78
Twenty Dollar Star '91
Vultures '84

Charles Lederer
Never Steal Anything Small '59

**David Ross
Lederman**
Daring Danger '32
The Fighting Marshal '32
Hell-Ship Morgan '36
Phantom of the West '31
Racketeers of the Range '39
Range Feud '31
The Range Feud/Two Fisted
    Law '31
The Riding Tornado '32
Shadows on the Stairs '41
Tarzan's Revenge '38
Two-Fisted Law '32

Paul Leduc
Frida '84

Ang Lee
The Wedding Banquet '93

Bruce Lee
Return of the Dragon '73

Charles Lee
Full Metal Ninja '89
Ninja of the Magnificence '89

Damian Lee
Boxcar Blues '90
Food of the Gods: Part 2 '88
Last Man Standing '87
Ski School '91

DeWitt Lee
The Legend of Jedediah Carver
    '70s
Ransom Money '88

Jack Lee
The Captain's Table '60
Robbery Under Arms '57
Wooden Horse '50

Joanna Lee
Children of Divorce '80

Joe Lee
The Courier '88

Norman Lee
Bulldog Drummond at Bay '37

Chamber of Horrors '40

Rowland V. Lee
The Bridge of San Luis Rey '44
Captain Kidd '45
The Count of Monte Cristo '34
Doomsday '28
Love from a Stranger '37
One Rainy Afternoon '36
Son of Frankenstein '39
The Son of Monte Cristo '41
The Three Musketeers '35
Toast of New York '37
The Tower of London '39

Spike Lee
Crooklyn '94
Do the Right Thing '89
Joe's Bed-Stuy Barbershop:
    We Cut Heads '83
Jungle Fever '91
Malcolm X '92
Mo' Better Blues '90
School Daze '88
She's Gotta Have It '86

David Leeds
Shoot the Sun Down '81

Abraham Leff
Where is My Child? '37

Johnny Legend
My Breakfast with Blassie '83

Gary Legon
My Therapist '84

Francosis Legrand
Sex on the Run '78

Ernest Lehman
Portnoy's Complaint '72

Lew Lehman
The Pit '81

Michael Lehmann
Airheads '94
The Applegates '89
Heathers '89
Hudson Hawk '91

Peter Lehner
Megaville '91

Arnold Leibovit
The Puppetoon Movie '87

Neil Leifer
Trading Hearts '87
Yesterday's Hero '79

Mike Leigh
Abigail's Party '77
Four Days in July '84
Grown Ups '80
High Hopes '89
Life is Sweet '91
Naked '93
Nuts in May '76
Who's Who '78

Warren Leight
The Night We Never Met '93

Mitchell Leisen
The Girl Most Likely '57
The Lady is Willing '42
Murder at the Vanities '34
Swing High, Swing Low '37

Erwin Leiser
Mein Kampf '60

Christopher Leitch
Courage Mountain '89
The Hitter '79
Teen Wolf Too '87

David Leland
The Big Man: Crossing the Line
    '91
Checking Out '89
Wish You Were Here '87

Claude Lelouch
And Now My Love '74
Another Man, Another Chance
    '77

**Bandits '86
Bolero '82
Cat and Mouse '78
Edith & Marcel '83
Happy New Year '74
A Man and a Woman '66
A Man and a Woman: 20 Years
    Later '86
Robert et Robert '79

Alan LeMay
High Lonesome '50

James Lemmo
Heart '87
Relentless 3 '93
Tripwire '89
We're Talkin' Serious Money
    '92

Jack Lemmon
Kotch '71

Rusty Lemorande
Journey to the Center of the
    Earth '88

Paul Leni
The Cat and the Canary '27
The Man Who Laughs '27
Waxworks '24

Terry Lennon
Daffy Duck's Quackbusters '89

Miklos Lente
Oddballs '84

Umberto Lenzi
Almost Human '79
Battle of the Commandos '71
Battleforce '78
Bridge to Hell '87
Bruce Lee Fights Back From
    the Grave '76
City of the Walking Dead '83
Emerald Jungle '80
Eyeball '78
From Hell to Victory '79
Man from Deep River '77
Messalina vs. the Son of
    Hercules '64
Paranoia '69
Pirates of the Seven Seas '62

Malcolm Leo
Beach Boys: An American
    Band '85
It Came from Hollywood '82
This is Elvis '81

Arthur Leonard
Boy! What a Girl '45

Brett Leonard
Dead Pit '89
The Lawnmower Man '92

Leo Leonard
Omoo Omoo, the Shark God
    '49

Robert Z. Leonard
Broadway Serenade '39
Clown '53
Dancing Lady '33
The Divorcee '30
Duchess of Idaho '50
The Firefly '37
Girl of the Golden West '38
The Great Ziegfeld '36
In the Good Old Summertime
    '49
The King's Thief '55
Maytime '37
A Mormon Maid '17
Nancy Goes to Rio '50
New Moon '40
Pride and Prejudice '40
Strange Interlude '32
Susan Lenox: Her Fall and Rise
    '31
Weekend at the Waldorf '45
When Ladies Meet '41
Ziegfeld Girl '41

Terry J. Leonard
Death Before Dishonor '87

Jordan Leondopoulos
The Swap '71

John Leone
Great Smokey Roadblock '76

Sergio Leone
A Fistful of Dollars '64
A Fistful of Dynamite '72
For a Few Dollars More '65
The Good, the Bad and the Ugly '67
Once Upon a Time in America '84
Once Upon a Time in the West '68

Po Chich Leong
Ping Pong '87

Antonio Leonuiola
Atlas in the Land of the Cyclops '61
Tor '64

Reymond LePlont
La Balance '82

Carl Lerner
Black Like Me '64

Dan Lerner
Shame '92

Irving Lerner
Cry of Battle '63
Studs Lonigan '60

Joseph Lerner
The C-Man '49

Richard Lerner
Revenge of the Cheerleaders '76

Mervyn LeRoy
Anthony Adverse '36
Any Number Can Play '49
The Bad Seed '56
Blossoms in the Dust '41
The Devil at 4 O'Clock '61
East Side, West Side '49
The FBI Story '59
Gold Diggers of 1933 '33
Gypsy '62
Homecoming '48
I Am a Fugitive from a Chain Gang '32
Johnny Eager '42
Latin Lovers '53
Little Caesar '30
Little Women '49
Lovely to Look At '52
Madame Curie '43
Million Dollar Mermaid '52
Mister Roberts '55
No Time for Sergeants '58
Quo Vadis '51
Random Harvest '42
Rose Marie '54
Sweet Adeline '35
They Won't Forget '37
Thirty Seconds Over Tokyo '44
Three Men on a Horse '36
Three on a Match '32
Waterloo Bridge '40
Without Reservations '46

Bill Lesley
Nail Gun Massacre '86

Michael Lessac
House of Cards '92

Mark L. Lester
Armed and Dangerous '86
Bobbie Jo and the Outlaw '76
Class of 1984 '82
Class of 1999 '90
Commando '85
Firestarter '84
Gold of the Amazon Women '79
Roller Boogie '79
Showdown in Little Tokyo '91
Steel Arena '72

Stunts '77
Truck Stop Women '74

Richard Lester
Butch and Sundance: The Early Days '79
Cuba '79
Finders Keepers '84
The Four Musketeers '75
A Funny Thing Happened on the Way to the Forum '66
A Hard Day's Night '64
Help! '65
How I Won the War '67
Juggernaut '74
The Knack '65
Petulia '68
The Return of the Musketeers '89
The Ritz '76
Robin and Marian '76
Superman 2 '80
Superman 3 '83
The Three Musketeers '74

Sheldon Lettich
Double Impact '91
Lionheart '90
Only the Strong '93

Clarence Fok Yiu Leung
Naked Killer '92

Brian Levant
Beethoven '92
The Flintstones '94
Problem Child 2 '91

Joseph Levering
Defenders of the Law '31
Phantom Gold '38
Sea Devils '31

Michel Levesque
Sweet Sugar '72
Werewolves on Wheels '71

Jay Levey
UHF '89

William A. Levey
Blackenstein '73
Committed '91
The Happy Hooker Goes to Washington '77
Hellgate '89
Lightning: The White Stallion '86
Monaco Forever '83
Slumber Party '57 '76

Alan J. Levi
Blood Song '82
Dead Man's Revenge '93
Last Song '80
Riding with Death '76

Henry Levin
The Ambushers '67
Cry of the Werewolf '44
Desperados '69
The Farmer Takes a Wife '53
Jolson Sings Again '49
Journey to the Center of the Earth '59
Lonely Man '57
Man from Colorado '49
Murderers' Row '66
Run for the Roses '78
Scout's Honor '80
The Warriors '55
Where the Boys Are '60
The Wonderful World of the Brothers Grimm '62
The Wonders of Aladdin '61

Peter Levin
Comeback Kid '80
Rape and Marriage: The Rideout Case '80
Washington Mistress '81

Jack Levine
Ghost Rider '35

Barry Levinson
Avalon '90
Bugsy '91
Diner '82
Good Morning, Vietnam '87
Jimmy Hollywood '94
The Natural '84
Rain Man '88
Tin Men '87
Toys '92
Young Sherlock Holmes '85

Fred Levinson
Hail '73

Israeli Nadav Levitan
Intimate Story '81
The Seventeenth Bride '84

Abe Levitow
Gay Purr-ee '62

Gene Levitt
Magee and the Lady '78

Bob Levy
If You Don't Stop It...You'll Go Blind '77

Edmond Levy
Mom, the Wolfman and Me '80

Eugene Levy
Once Upon a Crime '92

Gerry Levy
Invasion of the Body Stealers '69

I. Robert Levy
Can I Do It...Till I Need Glasses? '77

Jefery Levy
Inside Monkey Zetterland '93
S.F.W. '94

Louis Levy
The Wicked Lady '45

Ralph Levy
Bedtime Story '63

Shuki Levy
Blind Vision '91
Perfect Victims '87

Stephen Lewicki
Certain Sacrifice '80

Albert Lewin
The Moon and Sixpence '43
Picture of Dorian Gray '45
The Private Affairs of Bel Ami '47

Ben Lewin
The Favor, the Watch, & the Very Big Fish '92
Georgia '84

Sam Lewin
The Dunera Boys '85

Al Lewis
Our Miss Brooks '56

Christopher Lewis
Blood Cult '85
The Red Raven Kiss-Off '90
Revenge '86
The Ripper '86

David Lewis
Dangerous Curves '88

Herschell Gordon Lewis
Blast-Off Girls '67
Blood Feast '63
Color Me Blood Red '64
The Girl, the Body and the Pill '67
The Gore-Gore Girls '72
Gruesome Twosome '67
How to Make a Doll '68
Jimmy, the Boy Wonder '66
Just for the Hell of It '68
Monster a Go-Go! '65
Moonshine Mountain '64

Nature's Playmates '62
The Prime Time '60
The Psychic '68
She-Devils on Wheels '68
Something Weird '68
Suburban Roulette '67
This Stuff'll Kill Ya! '71
2000 Maniacs '64
The Wizard of Gore '70

Jay Lewis
The Baby and the Battleship '56

Jerry Lewis
The Bellboy '60
Big Mouth '67
Cracking Up '83
The Errand Boy '61
Family Jewels '65
Hardly Working '81
The Ladies' Man '61
The Nutty Professor '63
The Patsy '64
Which Way to the Front? '70

Joseph H. Lewis
Big Combo '55
Boys of the City '40
Criminals Within '41
Gun Crazy '49
The Invisible Ghost '41
A Lawless Street '55
Pride of the Bowery '41
Retreat, Hell! '52
Seventh Cavalry '56
That Gang of Mine '40

Robert Lewis
Child Bride of Short Creek '81
City Killer '87
Dead Reckoning '89
Desperate Lives '82
Embassy '85
Fallen Angel '81
If Things Were Different '79
Ladykillers '88
Memories of Murder '90
No Room to Run '78
Pray for the Wildcats '74
S*H*E '79
A Summer to Remember '84

Stanley Lewis
Punk Vacation '90

Denis Lewiston
Hot Target '85

Bruce Li
Counter Attack '84

Liu Chia Liang
Master Killer '84

Carlo Liconti
Goodnight, Michelangelo '89

Jeff Lieberman
Blue Sunshine '78
Just Before Dawn '80
Remote Control '88
Squirm '76

Robert Lieberman
All I Want for Christmas '91
Fire in the Sky '93
Table for Five '83
Will: G. Gordon Liddy '82

Mike Light
Flesh Gordon '72

Ralph M. Like
Chinatown After Dark '31

Peter Lilienthal
David '79
The Uprising '81

Walter Lima, Jr.
The Dolphin '87

Fred J. Lincoln
Wild Man '89

Per Lindberg
June Night '40

Mitchell Linden
The American Scream '80s

Maud Linder
Man in the Silk Hat '15

Max Linder
Early Cinema Vol. 1 '19

Lance Lindsay
Real Bullets '90
Star Crystal '85

Michael Lindsay-Hogg
Annie Oakley '85
As Is '85
Brideshead Revisited '81
Let It Be '70
The Little Match Girl '87
Master Harold and the Boys '84
Murder by Moonlight '91
Nasty Habits '77
The Object of Beauty '91
Running Mates '92
Strange Case of Dr. Jekyll & Mr. Hyde '89
Thumbelina '82

Leopold Lindtberg
Four in a Jeep '51
The Last Chance '45

John F. Link
Call of the Forest '49
The Devil's Cargo '48

Ron Link
Zombie High '87

Richard Linklater
Dazed and Confused '93
Slacker '91

Art Linson
Where the Buffalo Roam '80
The Wild Life '84

Aaron Lipstadt
Android '82
City Limits '85
Pair of Aces '90
The Slumber Party Massacre '82

Steven Lisberger
Hot Pursuit '87
Slipstream '89
Tron '82

David Lister
Hunted '85
The Rutanga Tapes '90

Miguel Littin
Alsino and the Condor '82

Dwight Little
Bloodstone '88
Getting Even '86
Halloween 4: The Return of Michael Myers '88
Marked for Death '90
The Phantom of the Opera '89
Rapid Fire '92

Lynne Littman
Testament '83

Anatole Litvak
All This and Heaven Too '40
Anastasia '56
City for Conquest '40
Goodbye Again '61
Mayerling '36
Night of the Generals '67
The Sisters '38
The Snake Pit '48
Sorry, Wrong Number '48

Gerry Lively
Body Moves '90

Jennie Livingston
Paris is Burning '91

Carlo Lizzani
House of the Yellow Carpet '84
Last Four Days '77

Lizzani ▶cont.

Love in the City '53

Julio Ruiz Llaneza
By Hook or Crook '85

Luis Llosa
Crime Zone '88
800 Leagues Down the Amazon '90s
Hour of the Assassin '86
Sniper '92

Frank Lloyd
Blood on the Sun '45
Cavalcade '33
Forever and a Day '43
The Howards of Virginia '40
The Last Command '55
Mutiny on the Bounty '35
Oliver Twist '22

Harold Lloyd
Early Cinema Vol. 1 '19
His Royal Slyness/Haunted Spooks '20
I'm on My Way/The Non-Stop Kid '18

Norman Lloyd
Tales of the Unexpected '91

Ken Loach
Family Life '71
Hidden Agenda '90
Riff Raff '92
Singing the Blues in Red '87

Tony LoBianco
Too Scared to Scream '85

Victor Lobl
Eden '92
Eden 3 '93

Sondra Locke
Impulse '90
Ratboy '86

Roy Lockwood
The Mutiny of the Elsinore '39

Norman Loftis
Small Time '91

Bob Logan
Meatballs 4 '92
Repossessed '90
Up Your Alley '89

Bruce Logan
Vendetta '85

Joshua Logan
Bus Stop '56
Camelot '67
Ensign Pulver '64
Fanny '61
Paint Your Wagon '69
Picnic '55
Sayonara '57
South Pacific '58
Tall Story '60

Stanley Logan
The Falcon's Brother '42

Tom Logan
Dream Trap '90
The Night Brings Charlie '90

Dimitri Logothetis
Body Shot '90
The Closer '91
Pretty Smart '87
Slaughterhouse Rock '88

J. Anthony Loma
Counterforce '87
A Man of Passion '90s
Target Eagle '84

Joseph Loman
The Boldest Job in the West '71
Surprise Attack '70s

Francisco J. Lombardi
La Boca del Lobo '89

Lou Lombardo
P.K. and the Kid '85
Russian Roulette '75

Ulli Lommel
The Big Sweat '90
The Boogey Man '80
Brainwaves '82
Cocaine Cowboys '79
Cold Heat '90
Devonsville Terror '83
Olivia '83
Overkill '86
Strangers in Paradise '86
Warbirds '88

Richard Loncraine
Bellman and True '88
Brimstone & Treacle '82
Deep Cover '88
Full Circle '77
The Missionary '82

Jerry London
Chiefs '83
Father Figure '80
Haunting of Sarah Hardy '89
Kiss Shot '89
Manhunt for Claude Dallas '86
Rent-A-Cop '88
The Scarlet & the Black '83
Shogun '80
Victim of Love '91

Roy London
Diary of a Hitman '91

Richard Long
The Word '78

Stanley Long
Adventures of a Private Eye '87
Adventures of a Taxi Driver '76

Harry S. Longstreet
Sex, Love and Cold Hard Cash '93

Anita Loos
When Ladies Meet '41

Temistocles Lopez
Chain of Desire '93
Exquisite Corpses '88

Del Lord
Vengeance '37

Jean-Claude Lord
Covergirl '83
Eddie and the Cruisers 2: Eddie Lives! '89
Landslide '92
Mindfield '89
Toby McTeague '87
The Vindicator '85
Visiting Hours '82

Ken Loring
Combat Killers '80

Peter Lorre
The Lost One '51

Joseph Losey
Accident '67
Assassination of Trotsky '72
The Boy with the Green Hair '48
A Doll's House '73
The Go-Between '71
La Truite '83
Mr. Klein '75
Prowler '51
Roads to the South '78
Romantic Englishwoman '75
Secret Ceremony '69
The Servant '63
The Sleeping Tiger '54
Steaming '86

Emil Loteanu
The Shooting Party '77

Eb Lottimer
Love Matters '93

Patrick Loubert
125 Rooms of Comfort '83

Pavel Lounguine
Taxi Blues '90

John Lounsbery
The Rescuers '77

Eugene Lourie
The Beast from 20,000 Fathoms '53
Gorgo '61

Eric Louzil
Class of Nuke 'Em High, Part 2: Subhumanoid Meltdown '91
Lust for Freedom '87
Wilding '90

Horace Love
Playing Away '87

Charles Loventhal
First Time '82
My Demon Lover '87

Otto Lovering
Drift Fence '36

Bert Lovitt
Prince Jack '83

Steven Lovy
Circuitry Man '90

Lucas Lowe
American Shaolin: King of the Kickboxers 2 '92
The King of the Kickboxers '91

William Lowe
Slaughter in San Francisco '81

Richard Lowenstein
Dogs in Space '87
Pete Townshend: White City '85

Dick Lowry
Coward of the County '81
The FBI Murders '88
The Gambler Returns: The Luck of the Draw '93
In the Line of Duty: Ambush in Waco '93
The Jayne Mansfield Story '80
Kenny Rogers as the Gambler '80
Kenny Rogers as the Gambler, Part 2: The Adventure Continues '83
Kenny Rogers as the Gambler, Part 3: The Legend Continues '87
Smokey and the Bandit, Part 3 '83
Wet Gold '84
Wild Horses '84

David Loxton
Lathe of Heaven '80

Nanni Loy
Cafe Express '83
Head of the Family '71
Where's Piccone '84

Arthur Lubin
Ali Baba and the Forty Thieves '43
Buck Privates '41
Delightfully Dangerous '45
Escapade in Japan '57
Francis Goes to the Races '51
Francis in the Navy '55
Francis Joins the WACs '54
Francis the Talking Mule '49
Hold That Ghost '41
Impact '49
In the Navy '41
The Incredible Mr. Limpet '64
Keep 'Em Flying '41
The Phantom of the Opera '43
Queen for a Day '51

Ride 'Em Cowboy '42
Thief of Baghdad '61
Yellowstone '36

Ernst Lubitsch
Gypsy Blood '18
Heaven Can Wait '43
Lady Windermere's Fan '26
The Marriage Circle '24
The Merry Widow '34
Ninotchka '39
One Arabian Night '21
Passion '19
The Shop Around the Corner '40
So This is Paris '26
The Student Prince in Old Heidelberg '27
That Uncertain Feeling '41
To Be or Not to Be '42

S. Roy Luby
Arizona Badman '42
Arizona Stagecoach '42
Black Market Rustlers '43
Boot Hill Bandits '42
Border Phantom '37
Cowboy Commandos '43
Desert Phantom '36
Fugitive Valley '41
Kid's Last Ride '41
Outlaw Rule '36
The Red Rope '37
Tonto Basin Outlaws '41
Tough to Handle '37
Trail of the Silver Spurs '41
Tumbledown Ranch in Arizona '41
Underground Rustlers '41

George Lucas
American Graffiti '73
From "Star Wars" to "Jedi": The Making of a Saga '83
Star Wars '77
THX 1138 '71

Leandro Lucchetti
Getting Even '92

Francesco Lucente
Virgin Queen of St. Francis High '88

Maurizio Lucidi
Stateline Motel '75
Street People '76

William Lucking
Humanoid Defender '85

Larry Ludman
Deadly Impact '84
The Manhunt '86
Operation 'Nam '85
Overthrow '82
Thunder Warrior '85
Thunder Warrior 2 '85
Thunder Warrior 3 '88

Edward Ludwig
Big Jim McLain '52
The Big Wheel '49
The Black Scorpion '57
Fighting Seabees '44
Flame of the Islands '55
Wake of the Red Witch '49

Laszlo Lugossy
Flowers of Reverie '84

Baz Luhrmann
Strictly Ballroom '92

Eric Luke
Not Quite Human 2 '89
Still Not Quite Human '92

Sidney Lumet
The Anderson Tapes '71
Daniel '83
Deathtrap '82
Dog Day Afternoon '75
Equus '77
Fail-Safe '64
Family Business '89
The Fugitive Kind '60

Garbo Talks '84
The Group '66
Guilty as Sin '93
Just Tell Me What You Want '80
Long Day's Journey into Night '62
The Morning After '86
Murder on the Orient Express '74
Network '76
The Offence '73
The Pawnbroker '65
Power '86
Prince of the City '81
Q & A '90
Running on Empty '88
Serpico '73
Stage Struck '57
A Stranger Among Us '92
Twelve Angry Men '57
The Verdict '82
The Wiz '78

Auguste Lumiere
The Great Train Robbery: Cinema Begins '03

Bigas Luna
Anguish '88
Jamon, Jamon '93

Ida Lupino
The Bigamist '53
The Hitch-Hiker '53
The Trouble with Angels '66

Michele Lupo
Goliath and the Sins of Babylon '64
Master Touch '74
Mean Frank and Crazy Tony '75

Hamilton Luske
Lady and the Tramp '55
101 Dalmations '61
Peter Pan '53

William Lustig
The Hit List '88
Maniac '80
Maniac Cop '88
Maniac Cop 2 '90
Maniac Cop 3 '93
Relentless '89
Vigilante '83

Salvo Luther
Forget Mozart '85

David Lynch
Blue Velvet '86
Dune '84
The Elephant Man '80
Eraserhead '78
Hotel Room '93
Twin Peaks '90
Twin Peaks '90
Twin Peaks: Fire Walk with Me '92
Wild at Heart '90

Jennifer Lynch
Boxing Helena '93

Paul Lynch
Blindside '88
Bullies '86
Cross Country '83
Humongous '82
Murder by Night '89
Prom Night '80
Victim of Beauty '91

Paul Lynde
Dream to Believe '85

Adrian Lyne
Fatal Attraction '87
Foxes '80
Indecent Proposal '93
Jacob's Ladder '90
9 1/2 Weeks '86

Harry Lynn
Where is My Child? '37

Jonathan Lynn
Clue '85
The Distinguished Gentleman
'92
Greedy '94
My Cousin Vinny '92
Nuns on the Run '90

Francis D. Lyon
Bail Out at 43,000 '57
Castle of Evil '66
Cult of the Cobra '55
The Great Locomotive Chase
'56
The Oklahoman '56
Tomboy & the Champ '58

Dick Maas
Amsterdamned '88
The Lift '85

Byron Mabe
She-Freak '67

Kurt MacCarley
Rock & the Money-Hungry
Party Girls '89
Sexual Intent '94

David MacDonald
The Adventurers '51
Alias John Preston '56
Christopher Columbus '49
Devil Girl from Mars '54
The Moonraker '58
Never Too Late to Mend '37
Small Hotel '57

Peter Macdonald
Mo' Money '92

**Hamilton
MacFadden**
Inside the Law '42
Legion of Missing Men '37
Sea Racketeers '37
Stand Up and Cheer '34

Mike MacFarland
Hanging on a Star '78
Pink Motel '82

Gustav Machaty
Ecstasy '33

Juliusz Machulski
Deja Vu '89

Brice Mack
Jennifer '78
Swap Meet '79

Earle Mack
The Children of Theatre Street
'77

Roy Mack
Hillbilly Blitzkrieg '42

Russell Mack
Lonely Wives '31

Yvonne Mackay
The Silent One '86

**Alexander
MacKendrick**
Ladykillers '55
The Man in the White Suit '51
Mandy '53
Sweet Smell of Success '57
Whiskey Galore '48

John MacKenzie
Act of Vengeance '86
Beyond the Limit '83
The Fourth Protocol '87
The Last of the Finest '90
The Long Good Friday '79
One Brief Summer '70
Ruby '92
A Sense of Freedom '78
Voyage '93

Peter M. MacKenzie
Merchants of War '90

Will MacKenzie
Hobo's Christmas '87

Perfect Harmony '91
Worth Winning '89

Gilles Mackinnon
The Playboys '92
A Simple Twist of Fate '94

Alison Maclean
Crush '93

Stephen MacLean
Around the World in 80 Ways
'86

Ian MacNaughton
Monty Python's Flying Circus
'71

Henry MacRae
King of the Rodeo '28
Tarzan the Tiger '29

William H. Macy
Lip Service '88

John Madden
Ethan Frome '92
Golden Gate '93
Grown Ups '86

Lee Madden
Hell's Angels '69 '69
The Manhandlers '73
Night Creature '79
The Night God Screamed '80s

Guy Maddin
Careful '94
Tales from the Gimli Hospital
'88

Miguel Madrid
Graveyard of Horror '71

Kenneth Madsen
A Day in October '92

Jose Maesso
Order to Kill '73

Kurt Maetzig
First Spaceship on Venus '60

Guy Magar
Retribution '88
Stepfather 3: Father's Day '92

**Constantino
Magnatta**
The Darkside '87

Luigi Magni
In the Name of the Pope-King
'85

Albert Magnoli
American Anthem '86
Atom Age Vampire '61
Born to Run '93
Purple Rain '84
Street Knight '93

Dezso Magyar
King of America '80
No Secrets '91
Rappaccini's Daughter '80

Anthony Maharaj
Crossfire '89
Deathfight '93
The Kick Fighter '91

Barry Mahon
Assault of the Rebel Girls '59
The Beast that Killed Women
'65
Pagan Island '60
Rocket Attack U.S.A. '58
Violent Women '59

Bob Mahoney
Operation Julie '85

Norman Mailer
Tough Guys Don't Dance '87

Maximiliane Mainka
Germany in Autumn '78

**Beate Mainka-
Jellinghaus**
Germany in Autumn '78

George Maitland
Invasion Earth: The Aliens Are
Here! '87

Lech Majewski
Prisoner of Rio '89

Dusan Makavejev
The Coca-Cola Kid '84
Innocence Unprotected '68
The Love Affair, or The Case of
the Missing Switchboard
Operator '67
Man is Not a Bird '65
Montenegro '81
Sweet Movie '75
WR: Mysteries of the Organism
'71

Karoly Makk
Another Way '82
Cat's Play '74
Deadly Game '83
Lily in Love '85
Love '71

Guido Malatesta
Goliath Against the Giants '63

Roberto Malenotti
Slave Trade in the World Today
'64

Terence Malick
Badlands '74
Days of Heaven '78

Louis Malle
Alamo Bay '85
Atlantic City '81
Au Revoir Les Enfants '87
Crackers '84
Damage '92
The Fire Within '64
Frantic '58
The Lovers '59
May Fools '90
Murmur of the Heart '71
My Dinner with Andre '81
Pretty Baby '78
Spirits of the Dead '68
A Very Private Affair '62
Viva Maria! '65

Matthew Mallinson
Fist of Fear, Touch of Death '77

James Mallon
Blood Hook '86

Bruce Malmuth
Foreplay '75
Hard to Kill '89
The Man Who Wasn't There '83
Nighthawks '81
Where Are the Children? '85

William Malone
Creature '85
Scared to Death '80

David Maloney
Doctor Who: The Deadly
Assassin '76
Doctor Who: The War Games
'69

Paul Maloney
I Live with Me Dad '86

David Mamet
Homicide '91
House of Games '87
Things Change '88

Yurii Mamin
Sideburns '91

Oshii Mamoru
Urusei Yatsura Movie 2:
Beautiful Dreamer '92

Rouben Mamoulian
Applause '29

Becky Sharp '35
Blood and Sand '41
Dr. Jekyll and Mr. Hyde '31
Golden Boy '39
The Mark of Zorro '40
Queen Christina '33
Silk Stockings '57
Summer Holiday '48

Janine Manatis
Tales of the Klondike: In a Far
Country '87

Mario Mancini
Frankenstein '80 '79

Kevin Mancuso
2020 Texas Gladiators '85

Jeffrey Mandel
Elves '89

Robert Mandel
Big Shots '87
F/X '86
Independence Day '83
Perfect Witness '89
School Ties '92
Touch and Go '86

Luis Mandoki
Born Yesterday '93
Gaby: A True Story '87
Murderer in the Hotel '83
When a Man Loves a Woman
'94
White Palace '90

Dharan Mandrayar
Ele, My Friend '93

Joseph Manduke
Beatlemania! The Movie '81
Cornbread, Earl & Me '75
The Gumshoe Kid '89
Kid Vengeance '75
Omega Syndrome '87

Gianni Manera
Fear in the City '81

Nino Manfredi
Nudo di Donna '83

Joseph Mangine
Neon Maniacs '86

Francis Mankiewicz
And Then You Die '88
Les Bons Debarras '81
Love and Hate: A Marriage
Made in Hell '90

**Joseph L.
Mankiewicz**
All About Eve '50
The Barefoot Contessa '54
Cleopatra '63
Five Fingers '52
The Ghost and Mrs. Muir '47
Guys and Dolls '55
The Honey Pot '67
House of Strangers '49
Julius Caesar '53
A Letter to Three Wives '49
People Will Talk '51
Sleuth '72
Suddenly, Last Summer '59
There was a Crooked Man '70

Tom Mankiewicz
Delirious '91
Dragnet '87
Taking the Heat '93

Henry Mankiewirk
Hell's Brigade: The Final
Assault '80

Abby Mann
King '78

Anthony Mann
Bend of the River '52
Cimarron '60
Dandy in Aspic '68
Desperate '47
El Cid '61

The Fall of the Roman Empire
'64
Far Country '55
The Glenn Miller Story '54
God's Little Acre '58
Great Flamarion '45
He Walked by Night '48
The Man from Laramie '55
Man of the West '58
Men in War '57
The Naked Spur '53
Railroaded '47
Reign of Terror '49
Savage Wilderness '55
Strategic Air Command '55
T-Men '47
Thunder Bay '53
The Tin Star '57
Winchester '73 '50

Daniel Mann
Big Mo '73
Butterfield 8 '60
Come Back, Little Sheba '52
A Dream of Kings '69
For Love of Ivy '68
Hot Spell '58
I'll Cry Tomorrow '55
Interval '73
Journey into Fear '74
The Last Angry Man '59
The Man Who Broke 1,000
Chains '87
Matilda '78
The Mountain Road '60
Our Man Flint '66
Playing for Time '80
The Rose Tattoo '55
The Teahouse of the August
Moon '56
Who's Got the Action? '63
Willard '71

Delbert Mann
All Quiet on the Western Front
'79
The Birch Interval '78
Breaking Up '78
David Copperfield '70
Desire Under the Elms '58
Francis Gary Powers: The True
Story of the U-2 Spy '76
A Gathering of Eagles '63
Heidi '67
Home to Stay '79
Ironclads '90
The Last Days of Patton '86
Love Leads the Way '84
Lover Come Back '61
Marty '53
Marty '55
The Member of the Wedding
'83
Night Crossing '81
No Place to Run '72
Separate Tables '58
She Waits '71
That Touch of Mink '62
Torn Between Two Lovers '79

Edward Mann
Cauldron of Blood '67
Hallucination '67
Hooch '76

Ferhad Mann
Return to Two Moon Junction
'93

Michael Mann
The Jericho Mile '79
The Keep '83
The Last of the Mohicans '92
Manhunter '86
Thief '81

Kim Manners
K-9000 '89

Michelle Manning
Blue City '86

Peter Manoogian
Arena '88
Demonic Toys '91

Manoogian ▶cont.

Dungeonmaster '85
The Eliminators '86
Enemy Territory '87
Seedpeople '92

Mark Manos
Liquid Dreams '92

Manoussos Manoussakis
The Enchantress '85

Duncan Mansfield
Sweetheart of the Navy '37

Scott Mansfield
Deadly Games '80

Guido Manuli
Volere Volare '92

Ray Manzarek
The Doors: Soft Parade, a Retrospective '69

Robert Marcarelli
I Don't Buy Kisses Anymore '92
Original Intent '91

Terry Marcel
Hawk the Slayer '81
Jane & the Lost City '87
Prisoners of the Lost Universe '84

Siro Marcellini
Gangster's Law '86

Alex March
Firehouse '72
Master Mind '73
Paper Lion '68

Rafael Romero Marchent
Garringo '69

David Marconi
The Harvest '92

Adam Marcus
Jason Goes to Hell: The Final Friday '93

James Marcus
Double Cross '92

Philip Marcus
Terror on Alcatraz '86

Andreas Marfori
Desperate Crimes '93
Evil Clutch '89

Stuart Margolin
The Glitter Dome '84
Paramedics '88
A Shining Season '79

Jeff Margolis
Oscar's Greatest Moments: 1971-1991 '92

Edwin L. Marin
Abilene Town '46
The Cariboo Trail '50
A Christmas Carol '38
The Death Kiss '33
Everybody Sing '38
I'd Give My Life '36
Invisible Agent '42
Johnny Angel '45
Listen, Darling '38
Miss Annie Rooney '42
Mr. Ace '46
Nocturne '46
Show Business '44
A Study in Scarlet '33
Tall in the Saddle '44

Richard "Cheech" Marin
Born in East L.A. '87

Lex Marinos
An Indecent Obsession '85

Remember Me '85

Peter Maris
Delirium '77
Diplomatic Immunity '91
Hangfire '91
Land of Doom '84
Terror Squad '87
True Blood '89
Viper '88

Chris Marker
Le Joli Mai '62
Sans Soleil '82

Russ Marker
The Yesterday Machine '63

Anthony Markes
Bikini Island '91
Last Dance '91

David Markey
Desperate Teenage Lovedolls '84
1991: The Year Punk Broke '92

Monte Markham
Defense Play '88
Neon City '91

Kelly Markin
Tiger Claws '91

Gabriel Markiw
Mob Story '90

Jancarlo Markiw
Mob Story '90

Fletcher Markle
The Incredible Journey '63
Jigsaw '49

Peter Markle
Bat 21 '88
El Diablo '90
Hot Dog...The Movie! '83
Nightbreaker '89
The Personals '83
Wagons East '94
Youngblood '86

Goran Markovic
Tito and Me '92

Murray Markowitz
Left for Dead '78

Robert Markowitz
Afterburn '91
Decoration Day '90
Kojak: The Belarus File '85
A Long Way Home '81
Love, Lies and Murder '91
My Mother's Secret Life '84
Pray TV '82

Arthur Marks
Bonnie's Kids '73
Bucktown '75
Detroit 9000 '73
Friday Foster '75
J.D.'s Revenge '76
Monkey Hustle '77
Togetherness '70

Morley Markson
Off Your Rocker '80

Malcolm Marmorstein
Dead Men Don't Die '91

Richard Marquand
Eye of the Needle '81
Hearts of Fire '87
The Jagged Edge '85
The Legacy '79
Return of the Jedi '83
Until September '84

Jacques Marquette
Meteor Monster '57

Charles Marquis
Tension at Table Rock '56

Leon Marr
Dancing in the Dark '86

Roberto Marrtero
Thirty-Six Hours of Hell '77

David Marsh
Lords of Magick '88

Ray Marsh
The Last Porno Flick '74

Philip Marshak
Cataclysm '81
Dracula Sucks '79

Frank Marshall
Alive '93
Arachnophobia '90

Garry Marshall
Beaches '88
The Flamingo Kid '84
Frankie and Johnny '91
Nothing in Common '86
Overboard '87
Pretty Woman '90
Young Doctors in Love '82

George Marshall
Boy, Did I Get a Wrong Number! '66
Destry Rides Again '39
Fancy Pants '50
The Gazebo '59
The Ghost Breakers '40
The Goldwyn Follies '38
Houdini '53
How the West was Won '63
It Started with a Kiss '59
The Mating Game '59
Monsieur Beaucaire '46
My Friend Irma '49
Never a Dull Moment '50
Off Limits '53
Pack Up Your Troubles '32
Papa's Delicate Condition '63
The Perils of Pauline '47
Pot O' Gold '41
Red Garters '54
The Sad Sack '57
Scared Stiff '53
Show Them No Mercy '35
Texas '41
Valley of the Sun '42
You Can't Cheat an Honest Man '39

Penny Marshall
Awakenings '90
Big '88
Jumpin' Jack Flash '86
A League of Their Own '92
Renaissance Man '94

William Marshall
Adventures of Captain Fabian '51
The Phantom Planet '61

Charles Martin
Death of a Scoundrel '56
My Dear Secretary '49
One Man Jury '78

D'Urville Martin
Dolemite '75
Fass Black '77

Eugenio Martin
It Happened at Nightmare Inn '70
Pancho Villa '72

Frank Martin
Doctor Butcher M.D. '80
Elvis in Hollywood '93

Gene Martin
Bad Man's River '72
Horror Express '72

James Aviles Martin
Flesh Eating Mothers '89

Vince Martin
The Cursed Mountain Mystery '93

Wyre Martin
The Unearthing '93

Arturo Martinez
La Marchanta '73

Chuck Martinez
Nice Girls Don't Explode '87

Rene Martinez, Jr.
The Guy from Harlem '77

Richard Martini
Limit Up '89
You Can't Hurry Love '88

Raymond Martino
American Born '89
DaVinci's War '92

Sergio Martino
Casablanca Express '89
The Cheaters '76
Day of the Maniac '77
The Great Alligator '81
The Next Victim '71
The Opponent '89
The Scorpion's Tail '71
Screamers '80
Sex with a Smile '76
Slave of the Cannibal God '79
Torso '73
Violent Professionals '82

Leslie Martinson
The Atomic Kid '54
Batman '66
The Fantastic World of D.C. Collins '84
Hot Rod Girl '56
The Kid with the Broken Halo '82
The Kid with the 200 I.Q. '83
PT 109 '63
Return to Africa '89

Andrew Marton
Africa Texas Style '67
Around the World Under the Sea '65
Clarence, the Cross-eyed Lion '65
Green Fire '55
Gypsy Colt '54
Men of the Fighting Lady '54

Mike Marvin
Hamburger...The Motion Picture '86
Wishman '93
The Wraith '87

Joseph Mascelli
The Atomic Brain '64

Francesco Maselli
Love in the City '53
Time of Indifference '64

Claudio Masenza
James Dean '85
Marlon Brando '85

Giuseppe Masini
Journey Beneath the Desert '61

Herbert Mason
Lady in Distress '39

Noel Mason
Fighting Pilot '35

Francesco Massaro
Private Affairs '89

Ivana Massetti
Domino '88

Joe Massot
Space Riders '83
Wonderwall: The Movie '69

Quentin Masters
Dangerous Summer '82
PSI Factor '80
The Stud '78
Thumb Tripping '72

Peter Masterson
Blood Red '88
Full Moon in Blue Water '88
Night Game '89

The Trip to Bountiful '85

Nico Mastorakis
Blind Date '84
Glitch! '88
Hired to Kill '91
In the Cold of the Night '89
Next One '84
Nightmare at Noon '87
Ninja Academy '90
Sky High '84
Terminal Exposure '89
The Wind '87
Zero Boys '86

Camillo Mastrocinque
Full Hearts & Empty Pockets '63

Armand Mastroianni
Cameron's Closet '89
Distortions '87
Double Revenge '89
He Knows You're Alone '80
Killing Hour '84
The Supernaturals '86

Toshio Masuda
Tora! Tora! Tora! '70
Zero '84

Orestes Matacena
Tainted '88

Eddy Matalon
Blackout '78
Cathy's Curse '77
Sweet Killing '93

Vivian Matalon
Private Contentment '83

Rudolph Mate
Branded '50
The Dark Past '49
Deep Six '58
D.O.A. '49
For the First Time '59
The Green Glove '52
Second Chance '53
Three Violent People '57
Union Station '50
The Violent Men '55
When Worlds Collide '51

Shue Matsubayashi
Last War '68

Bruno Mattei
Night of the Zombies '83
Seven Magnificent Gladiators '84

Marius Mattei
Moving Target '89

Charles Matthau
Doin' Time on Planet Earth '88

Burny Mattinson
The Great Mouse Detective '86

Frank S. Mattison
With Kit Carson Over the Great Divide '25

Sally Mattison
Slumber Party Massacre 3 '90

Mario Mattoli
Two Nights with Cleopatra '54

Walt Mattox
Scared to Death '47

Arne Mattson
The Doll '62
The Girl '86

Robert Mauri
Invincible Gladiators '64
The Slaughter of the Vampires '62

John Maxwell
The Man I Love '46

Paul Maxwell
Superargo '67

Peter Maxwell
The Highest Honor '84
Platypus Cove '86
Plunge Into Darkness '77
Run, Rebecca, Run '81
Touch & Go '80

Ronald Maxwell
Gettysburg '93

Ronald F. Maxwell
Kidco '83
Little Darlings '80
The Night the Lights Went Out in Georgia '81

Bradford May
Lethal Lolita—Amy Fisher: My Story '92
Mortal Sins '92

Elaine May
The Heartbreak Kid '72
Ishtar '87
Mikey & Nicky '76
A New Leaf '71

Joe May
Homecoming '28
The Invisible Man Returns '40

Paul May
Dr. Mabuse vs. Scotland Yard '64

Russ Mayberry
Challenge of a Lifetime '85
Fer-De-Lance '74
The $5.20 an Hour Dream '80
The Jesus Trip '71
Marriage is Alive and Well '80
A Matter of Life and Death '81
Probe '72
The Rebels '79
Unidentified Flying Oddball '79

Gerald Mayer
The Man Inside '76

Paul Mayersberg
Captive '87
Nightfall '88

Les Mayfield
Encino Man '92

Tony Maylam
The Burning '82
The Riddle of the Sands '79
The Sins of Dorian Gray '82
Split Second '92

Ken Maynard
The Fiddlin' Buckaroo '33
Honor of the Range '34
Strawberry Roan '33

Archie Mayo
The Adventures of Marco Polo '38
Angel on My Shoulder '46
The Case of the Lucky Legs '35
Crash Dive '43
The Great American Broadcast '41
House Across the Bay '40
Illicit '31
Night After Night '32
A Night in Casablanca '46
Orchestra Wives '42
Petrified Forest '36
Svengali '31
They Shall Have Music '39

David Maysles
Gimme Shelter '70

Michael Mazo
Possession: Until Death Do You Part '90
Time Runner '92

Paul Mazursky
Alex in Wonderland '70
Blume in Love '73
Bob & Carol & Ted & Alice '69
Down and Out in Beverly Hills '86

Enemies, a Love Story '89
Harry and Tonto '74
Moon Over Parador '88
Moscow on the Hudson '84
Next Stop, Greenwich Village '76
The Pickle '92
Scenes from a Mall '91
The Tempest '82
An Unmarried Woman '78
Willie & Phil '80

Joseph Mazzuca
Sisters of Death '76

Don McBrearty
American Nightmare '81
Child's Christmas in Wales '88

Jim McBride
The Big Easy '87
Blood Ties '92
Breathless '83
David Holzman's Diary '67
Glen and Randa '71
Great Balls of Fire '89
Hot Times '74
The Wrong Man '93

Jon McBride
Cannibal Campout '88
Woodchipper Massacre '89

Gene McCabe
Follow Me '69

Robert McCahon
Running Wild '73

James McCalmont
Escape from Safehaven '88
Underground Terror '88

Leo McCarey
An Affair to Remember '57
The Awful Truth '37
Belle of the Nineties '34
The Bells of St. Mary's '45
Duck Soup '33
Going My Way '44
Good Sam '48
Indiscreet '31
Love Affair '39
Milky Way '36
Once Upon a Honeymoon '42
The Ruggles of Red Gap '35

Ray McCarey
Devil's Party '38
The Mystery Man '35
You Can't Fool Your Wife '40

John P. McCarthy
Cavalier of the West '31
The Forty-Niners '32
Mother and Son '31
Oklahoma Cyclone '30
The Return of Casey Jones '34
Song of the Gringo '36
Sunrise Trail '31

Michael McCarthy
Crow Hollow '52
Operation Amsterdam '60

Todd McCarthy
Visions of Light: The Art of Cinematography '93

John McCauley
Rattlers '76

Gregory McClatchy
Vampire at Midnight '88

Arn McConnell
Shock! Shock! Shock! '87

Bret McCormick
Blood on the Badge
Tabloid! '88

George McCowan
Frogs '72
Murder on Flight 502 '75
Return to Fantasy Island '77
Savage Run '70

Peter McCubbin
Home for Christmas '90

Jim McCullough
The Aurora Encounter '85
The Charge of the Model T's '76
Mountaintop Motel Massacre '86
Where the Red Fern Grows: Part 2 '92

Bruce McDonald
Highway 61 '91
Roadkill '89

Frank McDonald
Apache Chief '50
Bells of Rosarita '45
The Big Sombrero '49
Gambler's Choice '44
My Pal Trigger '46
One Body Too Many '44
Song of Arizona '46
Sunset in El Dorado '45
Take It Big '44
Thunder Pass '54
Timber Queen '44
Treasure of Fear '45
Twilight on the Rio Grande '41
Under Nevada Skies '46
Wildcat '42

Peter McDonald
Rambo 3 '88

Rodney McDonald
Night Eyes 2 '91

Donald McDougall
Chinese Web '78

Ross McElwee
Sherman's March: An Improbable Search for Love '86
Time Indefinite '93

Bernard McEveety
The Bears & I '74
The Broadway Drifter '27
The Brotherhood of Satan '71
Napoleon and Samantha '72
One Little Indian '73
Roughnecks '80

Vincent McEveety
Amy '81
The Apple Dumpling Gang Rides Again '79
The Castaway Cowboy '74
Charley and the Angel '73
Firecreek '68
Gunsmoke: Return to Dodge '87
Gus '76
Herbie Goes Bananas '80
Herbie Goes to Monte Carlo '77
Million Dollar Duck '71
Smoke '70
Superdad '73
The Treasure of Matecumbe '76

Bruce McFarlane
Kill Slade '89

William F. McGaha
Iron Horsemen '71
The Speed Lovers '68

William McGann
American Empire '42
Dr. Christian Meets the Women '40
In Old California '42

Darren McGavin
Run, Stranger, Run '73

Robert McGinley
Shredder Orpheus '89

Scott McGinnis
Caroline at Midnight '93

Dorrell McGowan
The Showdown '50

J.P. McGowan
Below the Deadline '29
Blood and Steel '25
Deadwood Pass '33
Drum Taps '33
Hurricane Express '32
Lone Bandit '33
Mark of the Spur '32
Near the Rainbow's End '30
The Outlaw Tamer '33
Red Signals '27
Road Agent '26
Rough Ridin' Rhythm '37
When a Man Rides Alone '33

Robert McGowan
Frontier Justice '35
Old Swimmin' Hole '40

Stuart E. McGowan
The Billion Dollar Hobo '78
The Showdown '50

Tom McGowan
Cataclysm '81
Savage Journey '83

Joseph McGrath
The Bliss of Mrs. Blossom '68
Casino Royale '67
Digby, the Biggest Dog in the World '73
Great McGonagall '75
The Magic Christian '69
30 Is a Dangerous Age, Cynthia '68

Sean McGregor
Devil Times Five '74
Gentle Savage '73

Thomas McGuane
92 in the Shade '76

Don McGuire
The Delicate Delinquent '56

Doug McHenry
House Party 2: The Pajama Jam '91

C.T. McIntyre
Border Shootout '90

Thom McIntyre
The Rutherford County Line '87

Cole McKay
The Secret of the Golden Eagle '91

Malcolm McKay
Maria's Child '93

Douglas McKeown
Return of the Aliens: The Deadly Spawn '83

Robert McKimson
Best of Bugs Bunny & Friends '40
Bugs & Daffy: The Wartime Cartoons '45
Bugs Bunny's 3rd Movie: 1,001 Rabbit Tales '82
Starring Bugs Bunny! '48

Duncan McLachlan
The Double O Kid '92
Scavengers '87

Andrew V. McLaglen
Bandolero! '68
The Blue and the Gray '85
Breakthrough '78
Cahill: United States Marshal '73
Chisum '70
The Devil's Brigade '68
The Dirty Dozen: The Next Mission '85
ffolkes '80
Hellfighters '68
McLintock! '63
Mitchell '75
Monkeys, Go Home! '66
On Wings of Eagles '86
The Rare Breed '66

Sahara '83
Sea Wolves '81
The Shadow Riders '82
Shenandoah '65
The Undefeated '69
The Way West '67
Wild Geese '78

Norman McLaren
Scherzo '39

Don McLennan
Hard Knocks '80
Slate, Wyn & Me '87

Norman Z. McLeod
Casanova's Big Night '54
Horse Feathers '32
It's A Gift '34
Kid from Brooklyn '46
Lady Be Good '41
Let's Dance '50
Little Men '40
Monkey Business '31
Never Wave at a WAC '52
The Paleface '48
Panama Hattie '42
The Road to Rio '47
The Secret Life of Walter Mitty '47
Topper '37
Topper Takes a Trip '39

Tom McLoughlin
Date with an Angel '87
The Fire Next Time '93
Friday the 13th, Part 6: Jason Lives '86
One Dark Night '82

Marshall McLuhan
Third Walker '79

Robert McMahon
Night of the Assassin '77

Sean McNamara
Hollywood Chaos '89

Ian McNaughton
And Now for Something Completely Different '72

John McNaughton
The Borrower '90
Henry: Portrait of a Serial Killer '90
Mad Dog and Glory '93
Sex, Drugs, Rock & Roll: Eric Bogosian '91

John McPherson
Dirty Work '92
Fade to Black '93
Strays '91

John McTiernan
Die Hard '88
The Hunt for Red October '90
Last Action Hero '93
Medicine Man '92
Nomads '86
Predator '87

John Meagher
Fantasy Man '84

Peter Medak
The Babysitter '80
Breakin' Through '84
The Changeling '80
The Dancing Princesses '84
A Day in the Death of Joe Egg '71
The Emperor's New Clothes '84
Ghost in the Noonday Sun '74
The Krays '90
Let Him Have It '91
The Men's Club '86
Negatives '68
The Odd Job '78
Pinocchio '83
Romeo Is Bleeding '93
The Ruling Class '72
The Snow Queen '83

Medak ▶cont.

Snow White and the Seven
    Dwarfs '83
Zorro, the Gay Blade '81

Don Medford
The Organization '71
Sizzle '81

Cary Medoway
The Heavenly Kid '85
Paradise Motel '84

**Alexander
Medvedkin**
Happiness '34

Jeanine Meerapfel
Malou '83

Pomme Meffre
Grain of Sand '84

Francis Megahy
The Carpathian Eagle '81
Con Man '92
The Great Riviera Bank
    Robbery '79
Taffin '89

Deepa Mehta
Camilla '94

Ketan Mehta
Spices '86

Zhang Meijun
Dynasty '77

Gus Meins
The Gentleman from California
    '37
Kelly the Second '36
March of the Wooden Soldiers
    '34
Roll Along Cowboy '37

Myron Meise
It's All True '93

Norbert Meisel
The Adultress '77
Night Children '89
Walking the Edge '83

John Mekas
The Brig '64

Andre Melancon
The Dog Who Stopped the War
    '84

Ib Melchior
The Angry Red Planet '59
The Time Travelers '64

Arthur N. Mele
Soldier's Fortune '91

Bill Melendez
Bon Voyage, Charlie Brown '80
A Boy Named Charlie Brown
    '70
A Charlie Brown Celebration
    '84
A Charlie Brown Christmas '65
A Charlie Brown Thanksgiving
    '81
Charlie Brown's All-Stars '66
Good Grief, Charlie Brown '83
Happy New Year, Charlie
    Brown '82
It Was a Short Summer, Charlie
    Brown '69
It's an Adventure, Charlie
    Brown! '83
It's Flashbeagle, Charlie
    Brown/She's a Good Skate,
    Charlie Brown '84
It's Three Strikes, Charlie
    Brown '86
Snoopy, Come Home '72

George Melford
Dracula (Spanish Version) '31
East of Borneo '31

Man of Action '33
Moran of the Lady Letty '22
The Sheik '21

Georges Melies
Early Cinema Vol. 1 '19

**John Cougar
Mellencamp**
Falling from Grace '92

Jean-Pierre Melville
Bob le Flambeur '55
Godson '72
Le Doulos '61
Leon Morin, Priest '61
Les Enfants Terrible '50

Christopher Menaul
A Dangerous Man: Lawrence
    after Arabia '91
Prime Suspect '92

George Mendeluk
Doin' Time '85
The Kidnapping of the
    President '80
Meatballs 3 '87
Stone Cold Dead '80

Lothar Mendes
The Man Who Could Work
    Miracles '37
Moonlight Sonata '38
Power '34

Odorico Mendes
Discretion Assured '93

Fernando Mendez
Black Pit of Dr. M '47
The Living Coffin '58
The Vampire '57
The Vampire's Coffin '58

Ramon Menendez
Money for Nothing '93
Stand and Deliver '88

Chris Menges
Crisscross '92
A World Apart '88

Nina Menkes
Queen of Diamonds '91

Gian-Carlo Menotti
The Medium '51

Barnard Menoud
Scenario du Film Passion '82

Vladimir Menshov
Moscow Does Not Believe in
    Tears '80

Jiri Menzel
Closely Watched Trains '66
Larks on a String '68

**William Cameron
Menzies**
Chandu the Magician '32
Drums in the Deep South '51
Invaders from Mars '53
Things to Come '36

Louis Mercanton
Salome/Queen Elizabeth '23

Antonio Mercero
Don Juan, My Love '90

Ismail Merchant
The Courtesans of Bombay '85

Burgess Meredith
Man on the Eiffel Tower '48
Yin & Yang of Mr. Go '71

James Merendino
Witchcraft 4: Virgin Heart '92

Joseph Merhi
C.I.A.: Code Name Alexa '92
Epitaph '87
Final Impact '91
Fresh Kill '87
The Glass Jungle '88
Heat Street '87

The Killing Game '87
L.A. Crackdown '87
L.A. Crackdown 2 '88
L.A. Heat '88
L.A. Vice '89
The Last Riders '90
Magic Kid '92
Maximum Force '92
Midnight Warrior '89
The Newlydeads '87
Night of the Wilding '90
To Be the Best '93

J.L. Merino
Hell Commandos '69
Scream of the Demon Lover
    '71

Ron Merk
Pinocchio's Storybook
    Adventures '79

Ian Merrick
Black Panther '77

Lawrence Merrick
Black Bikers from Hell '70
The Outlaw Bikers—Gang
    Wars '70

Keith Merrill
Harry's War '84
Take Down '79
Windwalker '81

Matthew Meshekoff
The Opposite Sex and How to
    Live With Them '93

Jason Meshover-Iorg
Legacy of Lies '92

Philip Frank Messina
Spy '89

Marta Meszaros
Adoption '75
The Girl '68
Riddance '73

Alan Metter
Back to School '86
Girls Just Want to Have Fun '85
Moving '88

Alan Metzger
The China Lake Murders '90
Fatal Exposure '91
Red Wind '91

Radley Metzger
The Cat and the Canary '79
The Princess & the Call Girl '84
Therese & Isabelle '68

Andrew Meyer
Night of the Cobra Woman '72
Tidal Wave '75

Kevin Meyer
Invasion of Privacy '92
Under Investigation '93

Nicholas Meyer
Company Business '91
The Day After '83
The Deceivers '88
The Pied Piper of Hamelin '84
Star Trek 2: The Wrath of Khan
    '82
Star Trek 6: The Undiscovered
    Country '91
Time After Time '79
Volunteers '85

Russ Meyer
Beneath the Valley of the Ultra-
    Vixens '79
Beyond the Valley of the Dolls
    '70
Fanny Hill: Memoirs of a
    Woman of Pleasure '64
Faster Pussycat! Kill! Kill! '66
Motor Psycho '65
Supervixens '75

Eric Meza
House Party 3 '94

Richard Michaels
Backfield in Motion '91
Berlin Tunnel 21 '81
Blue Skies Again '83
Heart of a Champion: The Ray
    Mancini Story '85
Homeward Bound '80
Indiscreet '88
One Cooks, the Other Doesn't
    '83
Plutonium Incident '82
The Queen of Mean '90
Sadat '83
Silence of the Heart '84

John E. Michalakis
I Was a Teenage Zombie '87

Oscar Micheaux
Body and Soul '24
Girl from Chicago '32
Lying Lips '39

Dave Michener
The Great Mouse Detective '86

Paulmichel Miekhe
Murderer's Keep '88

Anne-Marie Mieville
France/Tour/Detour/Deux/
    Enfants '78
Scenario du Film Passion '82
Six Fois Deux/Sur et Sous la
    Communication '76
Soft and Hard '85

George Mihalka
Eternal Evil '87
Hostile Takeover '88
My Bloody Valentine '81
Pick-Up Summer '79

**Humberto Martinez
Mijares**
Bestia Nocturna '86

Ted V. Mikels
Aftermath '85
The Astro-Zombies '67
The Black Klansman '66
The Corpse Grinders '71
Cruise Missile '78
The Doll Squad '73
Girl in Gold Boots '69
Hustler Squad '76
10 Violent Women '79
WarCat '88

Elfi Mikesch
Seduction: The Cruel Woman
    '89

Nikita Mikhalkov
Close to Eden '90
Dark Eyes '87
Oblomov '81
A Slave of Love '78
An Unfinished Piece for a
    Player Piano '77

Christopher Miles
Priest of Love '81
That Lucky Touch '75
The Virgin and the Gypsy '70

Lewis Milestone
All Quiet on the Western Front
    '30
Arch of Triumph '48
Edge of Darkness '43
The Front Page '31
The Garden of Eden '28
The General Died at Dawn '36
Hallelujah, I'm a Bum '33
The Halls of Montezuma '50
Lucky Partners '40
Mutiny on the Bounty '62
The North Star '43
Ocean's 11 '60
Of Mice and Men '39
Pork Chop Hill '59
The Purple Heart '44
Rain '32
The Red Pony '49

The Strange Love of Martha
    Ivers '46
A Walk in the Sun '46

John Milius
Big Wednesday '78
Conan the Barbarian '82
Dillinger '73
Farewell to the King '89
Flight of the Intruder '90
Red Dawn '84
The Wind and the Lion '75

Gerry Mill
Second Chance '80

Ray Milland
Lisbon '56
A Man Alone '55
Panic in the Year Zero! '62

Gavin Millar
Dreamchild '85
My Friend Walter '93
Secrets '82
Tidy Endings '88

Stuart Millar
Rooster Cogburn '75
When the Legends Die '72

Claude Miller
The Best Way '82
The Little Thief '89
This Sweet Sickness '77

Dan T. Miller
Screamers '80

David Miller
Back Street '61
Billy the Kid '41
Bittersweet Love '76
Captain Newman, M.D. '63
Diane '55
Executive Action '73
Flying Tigers '42
Hail, Hero! '69
Lonely are the Brave '62
Love Happy '50
Midnight Lace '60
The Opposite Sex '56

George Miller
All the Rivers Run '84
Andre '94
Anzacs: The War Down Under
    '85
The Aviator '85
Frozen Assets '92
Goodbye, Miss 4th of July '88
Les Patterson Saves the World
    '90
The Man from Snowy River '82
NeverEnding Story 2: The Next
    Chapter '91
Nevil Shute's The Far Country
    '85
Over the Hill '93

George Miller
Lorenzo's Oil '92
Mad Max '80
Mad Max: Beyond
    Thunderdome '85
Miracle Down Under '87
The Road Warrior '82
Twilight Zone: The Movie '83
The Witches of Eastwick '87

Harvey Miller
Bad Medicine '85

Ira Miller
Loose Shoes '80

J.C. Miller
No Dead Heroes '87

Jason Miller
That Championship Season '82

Jonathan Miller
Long Day's Journey into Night
    '88

Mark Miller
Sister Dora '77

Michael Miller
Blown Away '90
A Case of Deadly Force '86
Danielle Steel's "Daddy" '92
Jackson County Jail '76
National Lampoon's Class
Reunion '82
Outside Chance '78
Silent Rage '82
Silent Witness '85
Street Girls '75

Neal Miller
Under the Biltmore Clock '85

Randall Miller
Class Act '91

Robert Ellis Miller
Any Wednesday '66
The Baltimore Bullet '80
Bed & Breakfast '92
Brenda Starr '86
The Girl from Petrovka '74
Hawks '89
The Heart is a Lonely Hunter
'68
Her Life as a Man '83
Reuben, Reuben '83

Sharron Miller
The Woman Who Willed a
Miracle '83

Sidney Miller
30-Foot Bride of Candy Rock
'59

Stephen E. Miller
Visions '90

Andy Milligan
The Body Beneath '70
Carnage '84
Fleshpot on 42nd Street '71
The Ghastly Ones '68
Legacy of Horror '78
Man with Two Heads '72
The Naked Witch '64
The Rats are Coming! The
Werewolves are Here! '72
Torture Dungeon '70
The Weirdo '89

Bill Milling
Body Trouble '92
Caged Fury '90
Lauderdale '89

Alec Mills
Bloodmoon '90
Dead Sleep '91

Reginald Mills
Tales of Beatrix Potter '71

Dan Milner
The Phantom from 10,000
Leagues '54

Tom Milo
Kiss and Be Killed '91
Smooth Talker '90

Elia Milonakos
Operation Orient

Robert Milton
Devotion '31

Chai Yang Min
Kick of Death: The Prodigal
Boxer '80s

Michael Miner
Deadly Weapon '88

Steve Miner
Forever Young '92
Friday the 13th, Part 2 '81
Friday the 13th, Part 3 '82
House '86
My Father the Hero '93
Soul Man '86
Warlock '89
Wild Hearts Can't Be Broken
'91

Anthony Minghella
Mr. Wonderful '93
Truly, Madly, Deeply '91

Gianfranco Mingozzi
Bellissimo: Images of the Italian
Cinema '87
Sardinia Kidnapped '75

Joe Minion
Daddy's Boys '87

Rob Minkoff
Honey, I Shrunk the Kids '89
The Lion King '94

Vincente Minnelli
An American in Paris '51
The Bad and the Beautiful '52
The Band Wagon '53
Bells are Ringing '60
Brigadoon '54
Cabin in the Sky '43
The Clock '45
The Cobweb '55
The Courtship of Eddie's
Father '62
Designing Woman '57
Father of the Bride '50
Father's Little Dividend '51
The Four Horsemen of the
Apocalypse '62
Gigi '58
Home from the Hill '60
I Dood It '43
Kismet '55
The Long, Long Trailer '54
Lust for Life '56
Madame Bovary '49
A Matter of Time '76
Meet Me in St. Louis '44
On a Clear Day You Can See
Forever '70
The Pirate '48
The Reluctant Debutante '58
The Sandpiper '65
Some Came Running '58
Tea and Sympathy '56
Two Weeks in Another Town
'62
Yolanda and the Thief '45
Ziegfeld Follies '46

Murray Mintz
Cardiac Arrest '74

Emilio P. Miraglio
Halloween Night '90
The Night Evelyn Came Out of
the Grave '71
Night Eyes '90

Kenji Misumi
Baby Cart 1: Lend a
Child...Lend an Arm '72
Baby Cart at the River Styx '72
Baby Cart to Hades '72
Shogun Assassin '80
Zatoichi: The Blind Swordsman
and the Chess Expert '65
Zatoichi: The Life and Opinion
of Masseur Ichi '62

Bruce Mitchell
Dynamite Dan '24

David Mitchell
City of Shadows '86
Club Med '83
Thunderground '89

Duke Mitchell
The Executioner '78

Eric Mitchell
Underground U.S.A. '84

Frank Mitchell
Blood Voyage '77

George Mitchell
Wolf Blood '25

Oswald Mitchell
The Dummy Talks '43
The Greed of William Hart '48
The Temptress '49

Sollace Mitchell
Call Me '88

Roberto Mitrotti
Little Girl...Big Tease '75

Tom Mix
In the Days of the Thundering
Herd & the Law & the Outlaw
'14

Hayao Miyazaki
My Neighbor Totoro '93

Kenji Mizoguchi
The Crucified Lovers '54
47 Ronin, Part 1 '42
47 Ronin, Part 2 '42
A Geisha '53
Life of Oharu '52
Osaka Elegy '36
Princess Yang Kwei Fei '55
Sansho the Bailiff '54
Shin Heike Monogatari '55
Sisters of Gion '36
The Story of the Late
Chrysanthemum '39
Street of Shame '56
Ugetsu '53
Utamaro and His Five Women
'46

Moshe Mizrahi
Every Time We Say Goodbye
'86
The House on Chelouche
Street '73
I Love You Rosa '72
I Sent a Letter to My Love '81
La Vie Continue '82
Madame Rosa '77
Rachel's Man '75
War & Love '84

Luke Moberly
Little Laura & Big John '73

**Carlos Lopez
Moctezuma**
Mary, Mary, Bloody Mary '76

Richard Moder
The Bionic Woman '75
Lassie: Adventures of Neeka
'68

Phillip Moeller
Break of Hearts '35

Peter Moffatt
Doctor Who: The Five Doctors
'83

John Moffitt
Love at Stake '87

Flavio Mogherini
Lunatics & Lovers '76

Leonide Moguy
Action in Arabia '44
Whistle Stop '46

Hanro Mohr
Hostage '87

Jose Mojica Marins
At Midnight, I'll Take Your Soul
'63
Awakenings of the Beast '68
Hallucinations of a Deranged
Mind '70
Strange World of Coffin Joe '68

Gustaf Molander
Dollar '38
Intermezzo '36
Only One Night '42
Swedenhielms '35
A Woman's Face '38

Jack Molina
The Craving '80

Edouard Molinaro
Back to the Wall '56
Dracula & Son '76
Just the Way You Are '84

La Cage aux Folles '78
La Cage aux Folles 2 '81
Pain in the A— '77
Ravishing Idiot '64

Paul Mones
Fathers and Sons '92

Peter Mones
The Beat '88

Christopher Monger
Waiting for the Light '90

Mario Monicelli
Big Deal on Madonna Street
'58
Casanova '70 '65
The Great War '59
Joyful Laughter '54
Lovers and Liars '81
Passionate Thief '60

Egon Monk
The Oppermann Family '82

Noel Monkman
Typhoon Treasure '39

Phil Monroe
The Bugs Bunny/Road Runner
Movie '79

Carl Monson
Blood Legacy '73
Please Don't Eat My Mother '72

Edward Montagne
They Went That-a-Way & That-
a-Way '78

Guiliano Montaldo
Control '87
Fifth Day of Peace '72
Sacco & Vanzetti '71
Time to Kill '89

Juan Monteczuma
Sisters of Satan '75

Jose Monter
As If It Were Raining '63

Robert Montero
Island Monster '53
Mondo Balardo '64
Tharus Son of Attila '87

Eduardo Montes
Double Obsession '93

Jorge Montesi
Omen 4: The Awakening '91

George Montgomery
From Hell to Borneo '64
Samar '62
The Steel Claw '61

Patrick Montgomery
The Compleat Beatles '82

Robert Montgomery
Eye Witness '49
The Gallant Hours '60
Lady in the Lake '46

Thomas Montgomery
King Kong Versus Godzilla '63

Vincent Monton
Fatal Bond '91
Windrider '86

Martin Mooney
The Phantom of 42nd Street
'45

Charles Philip Moore
Angel of Destruction '94
Dance with Death '91
Demon Wind '90

Michael Moore
Buckskin '68
Fastest Guitar Alive '68
Paradise, Hawaiian Style '66
Talion '66

Michael Moore
Canadian Bacon '94

Roger & Me '89

Richard Moore
Circle of Iron '78

Robert Moore
Chapter Two '79
The Cheap Detective '78
Murder by Death '76

Ronald W. Moore
Future Kill '85

Rudy Ray Moore
Avenging Disco Godfather '76

Simon Moore
Under Suspicion '92

Tom Moore
Fine Things '90
'night, Mother '86
Return to Boggy Creek '77

Jocelyn Moorhouse
Proof '91

Philippe Mora
The Beast Within '82
A Breed Apart '84
Communion '89
Death of a Soldier '85
Howling 2: Your Sister is a
Werewolf '85
Howling 3: The Marsupials '87
Mad Dog Morgan '76
Return of Captain Invincible '83

Andrew Morahan
Highlander 3: The Sorcerer '94

**Christopher
Morahan**
After Pilkington '88
Clockwise '86
The Jewel in the Crown '84
Paper Mask '91

Rick Moranis
Strange Brew '83

Miguel Morayta
Invasion of the Vampires '61

Tony Mordente
Just Tell Me You Love Me '80

Jeanne Moreau
Lumiere '76

Nanni Moretti
Palombella Rossa '89

Robert W. Morgan
Bloodstalkers '76

W.T. Morgan
A Matter of Degrees '90

William M. Morgan
Heart of the Rio Grande '42

Yoshimitsu Morita
The Family Game '83

Louis Morneau
Final Judgement '92
Quake '92
To Die Standing '90

David Burton Morris
Hometown Boy Makes Good
'93
Jersey Girl '92
Patti Rocks '88

Ernest Morris
The Tell-Tale Heart '62

Errol Morris
A Brief History of Time '92
The Dark Wind '91
The Making of "A Brief History
of Time" '92
The Thin Blue Line '88

Howard Morris
Don't Drink the Water '69
Goin' Coconuts '78
Who's Minding the Mint? '67
With Six You Get Eggroll '68

Martin Morris
L.A. Wars '94

Robert Morris
King of Kong Island '78

Bruce Morrison
Shaker Run '85
Tearaway '87

Paul Morrissey
Andy Warhol's Dracula '74
Andy Warhol's Frankenstein '74
Beethoven's Nephew '88
Flesh '68
Heat '72
The Hound of the Baskervilles '77
Mixed Blood '84
Spike of Bensonhurst '88
Trash '70

Vic Morrow
A Man Called Sledge '71

Barry Morse
Ugly Little Boy '77

Hollingsworth Morse
Daughters of Satan '72
Justin Morgan Had a Horse '81

Terry Morse
Bells of San Fernando '47
British Intelligence '40
Fog Island '45
Godzilla, King of the Monsters '56
Unknown World '51
Waterfront '39

Edmund Mortimer
The Prairie Pirate '25

Derek Morton
Wild Horses '82

Rocky Morton
D.O.A. '88
Super Mario Bros. '93

Lawrence Mortorff
Deadly Exposure '93

Ben Moses
Nickel & Dime '92

Gilbert Moses
A Fight for Jenny '90
The Fish that Saved Pittsburgh '79
Runaway '89

Harry Moses
Assault at West Point: The Court-Martial of Johnson Whittaker '94

Han Moshenson
The Wooden Gun '79

Gregory Mosher
A Life in the Theater '93

Elijah Moshinsky
The Green Man '91

George Moskov
Married Too Young '62

Gustavo Mosquera
Times to Come '81

Jon Mostow
Beverly Hills Bodysnatchers '89
Flight of Black Angel '91

Ilya Motyleff
The Cantor's Son '37

W.K. Moward
Let's Go! '23

Malcolm Mowbray
Don't Tell Her It's Me '90
Out Cold '89
A Private Function '84

John Llewellyn Moxey
The Bounty Man '72
Circus of Fear '67
Conspiracy of Terror '75
The Cradle Will Fall '83
Home for the Holidays '72
Horror Hotel '60
Intimate Strangers '77
Killjoy '81
Lady Mobster '88
Mating Season '81
Nightmare in Badham County '76
No Place to Hide '81
Panic in Echo Park '77
The Power Within '79
President's Mistress '78
Sanctuary of Fear '79
The Solitary Man '82
A Strange and Deadly Occurence '74
Through Naked Eyes '87
Where Have All the People Gone? '74

Allan Moyle
The Gun in Betty Lou's Handbag '92
Pump Up the Volume '90
Times Square '80

Russell Mulcahy
Blue Ice '92
Highlander '86
Highlander 2: The Quickening '91
Razorback '84
The Real McCoy '93
Ricochet '91
The Shadow '94

Edward Muller
Escape from Hell '89
Savage Island '85

Robert Mulligan
Baby, the Rain Must Fall '64
Bloodbrothers '78
Clara's Heart '88
Fear Strikes Out '57
The Great Impostor '61
Inside Daisy Clover '65
Kiss Me Goodbye '82
Love with the Proper Stranger '63
The Man in the Moon '91
The Other '72
The Pursuit of Happiness '70
The Rat Race '60
Same Time, Next Year '78
The Stalking Moon '69
Summer of '42 '71
To Kill a Mockingbird '62
Up the Down Staircase '67

Mark Mullin
Cool Blue '88

Claude Mulot
Black Venus '83

Richard W. Munchkin
Dance or Die '87
Deadly Bet '91
Out for Blood '93
Ring of Fire '91
Ring of Fire 2: Blood and Steel '92

Jag Mundhra
Eyewitness to Murder '93
Hack O'Lantern '87
Jigsaw Murders '89
L.A. Goddess '92
Last Call '90
Legal Tender '90
Open House '86
Sexual Malice '93
Tropical Heat '93
Wild Cactus '92

Ian Mune
The Bridge to Nowhere '86

Came a Hot Friday '85

Chris Munger
Black Starlet '74
Kiss of the Tarantula '75

Cynthia Munroe
The Wedding Party '69

Jimmy T. Murakami
Battle Beyond the Stars '80
When the Wind Blows '86

Ryu Murakami
Tokyo Decadence '91

Walter Murch
Return to Oz '85

Fredi M. Murer
Alpine Fire '89

John Murlowski
Amityville: A New Generation '93
Return of the Family Man '89

F.W. Murnau
City Girl '30
Faust '26
The Haunted Castle '21
The Last Laugh '24
Nosferatu '22
Sunrise '27
Tabu: A Story of the South Seas '31

Jim Muro
Street Trash '87

Dudley Murphy
Emperor Jones '33
Emperor Jones/Paul Robeson: Tribute to an Artist '33
One Third of a Nation '39

Eddie Murphy
Harlem Nights '89

Edward Murphy
Heated Vengeance '87
Raw Force '81

Geoff Murphy
Blind Side '93
Freejack '92
Goodbye Pork Pie '81
The Last Outlaw '93
Never Say Die '90
The Quiet Earth '85
Red King, White Knight '89
Utu '83
Young Guns 2 '90

Maurice Murphy
Doctors and Nurses '82
Fatty Finn '84

Ralph Murphy
The Black Devils of Kali '55
Mickey '48
The Spirit of West Point '47

Richard Murphy
Wackiest Ship in the Army '61

Bill Murray
Quick Change '90

Don Murray
The Cross & the Switchblade '72

Katrina Murray
The Secret Garden '84

Robin Murray
Dance '90

Scott Murray
Beyond Innocence '87

William Murray
Primal Scream '87

John Musker
Aladdin '92
The Great Mouse Detective '86
The Little Mermaid '89

Floyd Mutrux
Aloha, Bobby and Rose '74

Frank Myers
Lost, Lonely, and Vicious '59

Zion Myers
Sidewalks of New York '31

Alan Myerson
Police Academy 5: Assignment Miami Beach '88
Private Lessons '81
Steelyard Blues '73

John Myhers
Terror in Beverly Hills '90

Bruce Myles
Ground Zero '88

Arthur Nadel
Clambake '67

Michael Nader
The Great Escape 2: The Untold Story '88

Ivan Nagy
Bad Charleston Charlie '73
Captain America 2: Death Too Soon '79
Deadly Hero '75
A Gun in the House '81
Jane Doe '83

Philippe Nahoun
A Girl on Her Own '76

Mira Nair
Mississippi Masala '92
Salaam Bombay! '88

Sadao Nakajima
Renegade Ninja '83

Takehiro Nakajima
Okoge '93

Novuru Nakamuru
Shiokari Pass '77

Key-Nam Nam
Dragon Force '82

Lisandro Duque Naranjo
Miracle in Rome '88

Don Nardo
In Deadly Heat '87
Stuff Stephanie in the Incinerator '89

James Nares
Rome '78 '78

Silvio Narizzano
Bloodbath
Blue '68
The Body in the Library '87
The Class of Miss MacMichael '78
Die! Die! My Darling! '65
Georgy Girl '66
Loot...Give Me Money, Honey! '70
Redneck '73
24 Hours in a Woman's Life '61
Why Shoot the Teacher '79

Mikio Naruse
Late Chrysanthemums '54
Mother '52
When a Woman Ascends the Stairs '60

Paul Naschy
Human Beasts '80
Inquisition '76

Alan Nathanson
Playing with Fire '70s

Bill Naud
Ricky 1 '88
Whodunit '82

Gregory Nava
El Norte '83

A Time of Destiny '88

Tony Navarro
Widow's Nest '77

Erastheo J. Navda
The Boy God '86

Ray Nazarro
Dog Eat Dog '64
Gunners & Guns '34
Indian Uprising '51
Kansas Pacific '53

Ronald Neame
The Chalk Garden '64
First Monday in October '81
Foreign Body '86
Gambit '66
The Golden Salamander '51
Hopscotch '80
The Horse's Mouth '58
I Could Go on Singing '63
The Man Who Never Was '55
Meteor '79
The Odessa File '74
The Poseidon Adventure '72
The Prime of Miss Jean Brodie '69
The Promoter '52
Scrooge '70
Tunes of Glory '60
Tunes of Glory/Horse's Mouth '60
Windom's Way '57

Hal Needham
Body Slam '87
Cannonball Run '81
Cannonball Run 2 '84
Hooper '78
Megaforce '82
Rad '86
Smokey and the Bandit '77
Smokey and the Bandit, Part 2 '80
Stroker Ace '83
The Villain '79

Victor Neerman
Animal Crackers '30

Thomas L. Neff
Running Mates '86

Alberto Negrin
Mussolini & I '85
Voyage of Terror: The Achille Lauro Affair '90

Jean Negulesco
Daddy Long Legs '55
How to Marry a Millionaire '53
Humoresque '46
The Invincible Six '68
Johnny Belinda '48
Phone Call from a Stranger '52
Road House '48
Three Came Home '50
Three Coins in the Fountain '54

Marshall Neilan
Rebecca of Sunnybrook Farm '17
Stella Maris '18
Vagabond Lover '29

Roy William Neill
The Black Room '35
Dr. Syn '37
Dressed to Kill '46
Frankenstein Meets the Wolfman '42
House of Fear '45
The Pearl of Death '44
Pursuit to Algiers '45
Scarlet Claw '44
Sherlock Holmes and the Secret Weapon '42
Sherlock Holmes Faces Death '43
Sherlock Holmes in Washington '43
Spider Woman '44
Terror by Night '46

Terror by Night/Meeting at
  Midnight '46
The Woman in Green '45

James Neilson
The Adventures of Bullwhip
  Griffin '66
Bon Voyage! '62
Dr. Syn, Alias the Scarecrow
  '64
The First Time '69
Gentle Giant '67
Johnny Shiloh '63
Moon Pilot '62
The Moon-Spinners '64
Mooncussers '62
Summer Magic '63
Where Angels Go, Trouble
  Follows '68

L.E. Neiman
Time Troopers '89

Daniel Neira
Immortal Combat '94

Alvin J. Neitz
Backfire '22
The Phantom '31
The Puma Man '80

Frans Nel
American Kickboxer 1 '91
Lights! Camera! Murder! '89

Art J. Nelson
Creeping Terror '64

David Nelson
Confessions of Tom Harris '72
Last Plane Out '83
A Rare Breed '81

Dusty Nelson
Necromancer: Satan's Servant
  '88
White Phantom: Enemy of
  Darkness '87

Gary Nelson
Allan Quartermain and the Lost
  City of Gold '86
The Baron and the Kid '84
The Black Hole '79
Freaky Friday '76
Get Smart, Again! '89
Jimmy the Kid '82
The Lookalike '90
Molly & Lawless John '72
Murder in Coweta County '83
Pride of Jesse Hallum '81
Revolver '92
Santee '73

Gene Nelson
Harum Scarum '65
Kissin' Cousins '64

Jessie Nelson
Corrina, Corrina '94

Ozzie Nelson
Adventures of Ozzie & Harriet
  '50s

Ralph Nelson
The Cary Grant Collection '90
Charly '68
Christmas Lilies of the Field '84
Duel at Diablo '66
Embryo '76
Father Goose '64
A Hero Ain't Nothin' But a
  Sandwich '78
Lady of the House '78
Lilies of the Field '63
Requiem for a Heavyweight '56
Soldier Blue '70
Soldier in the Rain '63
The Wilby Conspiracy '75

Sam Nelson
Sagebrush Law '43

Jan Nemec
Diamonds of the Night '64
The Report on the Party and
  the Guests '66

Luis Nepomuceno
Stickfighter '89

Efrain Lopez Neris
A Life of Sin '92

Avi Nesher
Doppelganger: The Evil Within
  '90
She '83
Timebomb '91

Michael Nesmith
Doctor Duck's Super Secret
  All-Purpose Sauce '85

Max Neufeld
An Orphan Boy of Vienna '37

Sigmund Neufeld
The Lone Rider in Cheyenne
  '42
The Lone Rider in Ghost Town
  '41

Kurt Neumann
Bad Boy '39
Carnival Story '54
The Fly '58
Kronos '57
Let's Sing Again '36
Make a Wish '37
Mohawk '56
My Pal, The King '32
Return of the Vampire '43
The Ring '52
Rocketship X-M '50
They Were So Young '55
Wide Open Faces '38

Peter Newbrook
The Asphyx '72

Mike Newell
Amazing Grace & Chuck '87
The Awakening '80
Bad Blood '87
Dance with a Stranger '85
Enchanted April '92
Four Weddings and a Funeral
  '93
The Good Father '87
Into the West '92
The Man in the Iron Mask '77

Sam Newfield
Aces and Eights '36
Along the Sundown Trail '42
Arizona Gunfighter '37
The Black Raven '43
Boothill Brigade '37
Border Badmen '45
Border Caballero '36
Border Roundup '41
Branded a Coward '35
Bulldog Courage '35
Dead Men Walk '43
Death Rides the Plains '44
Death Rides the Range '40
Devil Riders '44
Doomed at Sundown '37
Durango Valley Raiders '38
Federal Agent '36
Feud Maker '38
Fighting Mad '39
Fighting Renegade '39
Fingerprints Don't Lie '51
Frontier Days '34
Frontier Outlaws '44
Frontier Scout '38
The Gambling Terror '37
Gangster's Den '45
Ghost Patrol '36
Gun Lords of Stirrup Basin '37
Guns in the Dark '37
Harlem on the Prairie '38
Harvest Melody '43
His Brother's Ghost '45
The Invisible Killer '40
Jungle Siren '42
The Lady Confesses '45
A Lawman is Born '37
Lightnin' Carson Rides Again
  '38
Lightning Bill Crandall '37

Lightning Raiders '45
The Lost Continent '51
The Mad Monster '42
Melody of the Plains '37
The Monster Maker '44
Nabonga '44
Oath of Vengeance '44
Outlaw of the Plains '46
Outlaw Women '52
Outlaw's Paradise '39
Phantom Ranger '38
Prairie Pals '42
Racing Luck '35
Ridin' the Lone Trail '37
Roaring Guns '36
Rustler's Hideout '44
Scotland Yard Inspector '52
Songs and Bullets '38
Terror of Tiny Town '38
Texas Justice '42
Three Desperate Men '50
Thunder in the Desert '38
The Traitor '36
Trigger Men '41
Trigger Pals '39
Tumbleweed Trail '42
Western Pacific Agent '51
White Pongo '45
Wild Horse Phantom '44
Wild Weed '49

John Newland
Don't Be Afraid of the Dark '73
The Legend of Hillbilly John '73
One Step Beyond '59

Anthony Newley
Summertree '71

Martin Newlin
The Crawlers '93

Joseph M. Newman
Great Dan Patch '49
Jungle Patrol '48
The King of the Roaring '20s:
  The Story of Arnold
  Rothstein '61
Love Nest '51
This Island Earth '55

Paul Newman
The Effect of Gamma Rays on
  Man-in-the-Moon Marigolds
  '73
The Glass Menagerie '87
Harry & Son '84
Rachel, Rachel '68
The Shadow Box '80
Sometimes a Great Notion '71

Fred Newmeyer
The Freshman '25
General Spanky '36
Girl Shy '24

Ted Newsom
Dracula: A Cinematic
  Scrapbook '91
Frankenstein: A Cinematic
  Scrapbook '91

Chan Wui Ngai
Way of the Black Dragon '81

Phil Nibbelink
An American Tail: Fievel Goes
  West '91
We're Back! A Dinosaur's Story
  '93

Fred Niblo
Ben-Hur '26
Blood and Sand '22
Dangerous Hours '19
Mark of Zorro '20
Sex '20
The Three Musketeers '21

Maurizio Nichetti
The Icicle Thief '89
Volere Volare '92

Paul Nicholas
Chained Heat '83
Daughter of Death '82
Naked Cage '86

Charles A. Nichols
Charlotte's Web '79

Dudley Nichols
Sister Kenny '46

George Nichols
Anne of Green Gables '34
Finishing School '33
The Return of Peter Grimm '35

Mike Nichols
Biloxi Blues '88
Carnal Knowledge '71
Catch-22 '70
The Day of the Dolphin '73
Gin Game '84
The Graduate '67
Heartburn '86
Postcards from the Edge '90
Regarding Henry '91
Silkwood '83
Who's Afraid of Virginia Woolf?
  '66
Wolf '94
Working Girl '88

Arch Nicholson
Dark Age '88
Fortress '85

Jack Nicholson
Goin' South '78
The Two Jakes '90

Sam Nicholson
It's Three Strikes, Charlie
  Brown '86

Alex Nicol
Point of Terror '71
The Screaming Skull '58

Ted Nicolaou
Bad Channels '92
Bloodlust: Subspecies 3 '93
Bloodstone: Subspecies 2 '93
Dragonworld '94
Dungeonmaster '85
Remote '93
Subspecies '91
Terrorvision '86

John Nicolella
Finish Line '89
Runaway Father '91
Sunset Heat '92

Douglas C. Nicolle
Ladies of the Lotus '87

**Jose Antonio Nieves-
Conde**
Sound of Horror '64

William Nigh
The Abe Lincoln of Ninth
  Avenue '39
The Ape '40
The Black Dragons '42
Border Devils '32
Corregidor '43
Doomed to Die '40
The Fatal Hour '40
Fighting Thru '30
The Ghost and the Guest '43
Headline Woman '35
House of Mystery '34
Mr. Wise Guy '42
Mr. Wong, Detective '38
Mr. Wong in Chinatown '39
Monte Carlo Nights '34
Mysterious Mr. Wong '35
Mystery Liner '34
Mystery of Mr. Wong '39
Rose of Rio Grande '38
South of Monterey '47
The Thirteenth Man '37
The Underdog '43
Without Honors '32

Nazui Nihonmatsu
X from Outer Space '67

Rob Nilsson
Heat and Sunlight '87
Northern Lights '79

On the Edge '86
Signal 7 '83

Leonard Nimoy
Funny About Love '90
The Good Mother '88
Star Trek 3: The Search for
  Spock '84
Star Trek 4: The Voyage Home
  '86
Three Men and a Baby '87

Charles Nizet
Commando Squad '76

Rudolf Noelte
The Castle '68

Tommy Noonan
Three Nuts in Search of a Bolt
  '64

Lindsay Norgard
Homeboys '92

Mabel Normand
Early Cinema Vol. 1 '19

Aaron Norris
Braddock: Missing in Action 3
  '88
Delta Force 2: Operation
  Stranglehold '90
The Hitman '91
Platoon Leader '87
Sidekicks '93

Guy Norris
Rage and Honor 2: Hostile
  Takeover '93

B.W.L. Norton
Baby...Secret of the Lost
  Legend '85
More American Graffiti '79
Three for the Road '87

Bill L. Norton
False Arrest '92
Hard Rain-The Tet 1968 '89
Tour of Duty '87

Max Nosseck
Black Beauty '46
Black Beauty/Courage of Black
  Beauty '57
Brighton Strangler '45
Dillinger '45
The Hoodlum '51

Noel Nosseck
Dreamer '79
Full Exposure: The Sex Tape
  Scandals '89
King of the Mountain '81
Las Vegas Lady '76
Night Partners '83
Return of the Rebels '81
Summer Fantasy '84

Thierry Notz
The Terror Within '88
Watchers 2 '90

Blaine Novak
Short Fuse '88

Maria Novaro
Danzon '91

Phillip Noyce
Blind Fury '90
Clear and Present Danger '94
Dead Calm '89
Echoes of Paradise '86
Heatwave '83
Newsfront '78
Patriot Games '92
Sliver '93

Simon Nuchtern
New York Nights '84
Savage Dawn '84
Silent Madness '84

Elliott Nugent
Just for You '52
My Favorite Brunette '47
My Girl Tisa '48

Nugent ►cont.

My Outlaw Brother '51
Up in Arms '44

Victor Nunez
A Flash of Green '85
Gal Young 'Un '79
Ruby in Paradise '93

Trevor Nunn
Hedda '75
Lady Jane '85

Deland Nuse
The Chilling '89

Raphael Nussbaum
Death Blow '87
Private Road: No Trespassing '87
Sinai Commandos '68

Colin Nutley
House of Angels '92

David Nutter
Cease Fire '85

Bruno Nuytten
Camille Claudel '89

Christian Nyby
Devlin Connection '82
Operation C.I.A. '65
The Thing '51

Sven Nykvist
Gorilla '56
The Ox '91

Ron Nyswaner
Prince of Pennsylvania '88

Joe Oaks
Deadly Twins '85

Dan O'Bannon
The Resurrected '91
Return of the Living Dead '85

Rockne S. O'Bannon
Fear '90

Stefan Oblowsky
Other Hell '85

Arch Oboler
One Plus One '61

Edmund Oboler
Bewitched '85

Jim O'Brien
The Dressmaker '89
Foreign Affairs '93
The Jewel in the Crown '84

John O'Brien
The Big Dis '89

Jeffrey Obrow
Dorm That Dripped Blood '82
The Kindred '87
Servants of Twilight '91

Jack O'Connell
Revolution '69

John O'Conner
Prisoner in the Middle '74

James O'Connolly
Berserk! '67
Crooks & Coronets '69
Tower of Evil '72
The Valley of Gwangi '69
Vendetta for the Saint '68

Frank O'Connor
Free to Love '25
Mystic Circle Murder '39
Spangles '26

Jim O'Connor
Mistress Pamela '74

Pat O'Connor
Cal '84
Fools of Fortune '90

The January Man '89
A Month in the Country '87
Stars and Bars '88

Terry O'Connor
Early Frost '84

William O'Connor
Ten Nights in a Bar-Room '31

David Odell
Martians Go Home! '90

Sias Odendal
Nukie '93

Clifford Odets
None But the Lonely Heart '44

Luciano Odorisio
Sacrilege '86

George Ogilvie
Mad Max: Beyond Thunderdome '85

Gerry O'Hara
The Bitch '78
Leopard in the Snow '78
Maroc 7 '67

Terrence O'Hara
Darkroom '90
The Perfect Bride '91

Michael O'Herlihy
Cry of the Innocent '80
The Fighting Prince of Donegal '66
The Flame is Love '79
Mosby's Marauders '66
The One and Only, Genuine, Original Family Band '68
Peter Lundy and the Medicine Hat Stallion '77
Smith! '69
A Time for Miracles '80

Don Ohlmeyer
The Heroes of Desert Storm '91

Kazuki Ohmori
Godzilla vs. Biollante '89

Tom O'Horgan
Futz '69

Kihachi Okamoto
Red Lion '69
Sword of Doom '67
Zatoichi vs. Yojimbo '70

Steven Okazaki
Living on Tokyo Time '87

Sidney Olcott
The Claw '27
Monsieur Beaucaire '24
Ranson's Folly '26

Enrico Oldoini
Bye Bye Baby '88

Ronan O'Leary
Riders to the Sea '88

Joel Oliansky
The Competition '80

Ken Olin
White Fang 2: The Myth of the White Wolf '94

David Oliver
Cave Girl '85

Richard Oliver
A Girl to Kill for '90

Robert Oliver
Dr. Frankenstein's Castle of Freaks '74

Ron Oliver
Liar's Edge '92
Prom Night 3: The Last Kiss '89

Ruby L. Oliver
Love Your Mama '89

Hector Olivera
Barbarian Queen '85
Cocaine Wars '86
El Muerto '75
Fridays of Eternity '81
Funny, Dirty Little War '83
Play Murder for Me '91
Two to Tango '88
Wizards of the Lost Kingdom '85

Laurence Olivier
Hamlet '48
Henry V '44
The Prince and the Showgirl '57
Richard III '55

Marty Ollstein
Dangerous Love '87

Ermanno Olmi
The Tree of Wooden Clogs '78

Edward James Olmos
American Me '92

William Olsen
Getting It On '83
Return to Eden '89

David O'Malley
Easy Wheels '89
Kid Colter '85
Mountain Man '77

Carlo Ombra
Dracula Blows His Cool '82

Ron O'Neal
Superfly T.N.T. '73
Up Against the Wall '91

Douglas F. Oneans
Sno-Line '85

Robert Vincent O'Neil
Angel '84
Avenging Angel '85
Blood Mania '70
The Deadly and the Beautiful '73
Paco '75

Marcel Ophuls
The Sorrow and the Pity '71

Max Ophuls
Caught '49
The Earrings of Madame De... '54
La Ronde '51
La Signora di Tutti '34
Le Plaisir '52
Letter from an Unknown Woman '48
Lola Montes '55
Reckless Moment '49

Peer J. Oppenheimer
Terror in Paradise

Charlie Ordonez
Forgotten Warrior '86
Wolf '86

Wyott Ordung
Monster from the Ocean Floor '54

Mario Orfini
Fair Game '89

Valery Orgorodnikov
Burglar '87

Dominic Orlando
Knights of the City '85

Susan Orlikoff-Simon
Image of Passion '86

Stuart Orme
The Heist '89

James Ormerod
Frankenstein '82

Next Victim '74

Ron Ormond
The Black Lash '52
The Girl from Tobacco Row '66
King of the Bullwhip '51
Mesa of Lost Women '52
Yes, Sir, Mr. Bones '51

Peter Ormrod
Eat the Peach '86

Alan Ormsby
Deranged '74

Bruce Ornstein
Jack and His Friends '92

Gary Orona
The Bikini Car Wash Company 2 '92
Great Bikini Off-Road Adventure '94

James Orr
Breaking All the Rules '85
Mr. Destiny '90

Valintino Orsini
Smugglers '75

Kenny Ortega
Hocus Pocus '93
Newsies '92

Kent Osborne
Women Unchained '70s

Nagisa Oshima
The Cruel Story of Youth '60
The Empire of Passion '76
In the Realm of Passion '80
In the Realm of the Senses '76
Max, Mon Amour '86
Merry Christmas, Mr. Lawrence '83
The Sun's Burial '60
Violence at Noon '66

Cliff Osmond
The Penitent '88

Sam O'Steen
The Best Little Girl in the World '81
Brand New Life '72
Sparkle '76

Suzanne Osten
The Mozart Brothers '86

Gerd Oswald
Crime of Passion '57
Paris Holiday '57

Richard Oswald
The Lovable Cheat '49
My Song Goes Round the World '34

Dominique Othenin-Girard
After Darkness '85
Halloween 5: The Revenge of Michael Myers '89
Night Angel '90
Omen 4: The Awakening '91

Katsuhiro Otomo
Akira '89

Matteo Ottaviano
Single Room Furnished '68

Henry Otto
Dante's Inferno '24

Filippo Ottoni
Detective School Dropouts '85

Lar Henrik Ottoson
Gorilla '56

Jean-Paul Ouellette
Chinatown Connection '90
The Unnamable '88
The Unnamable 2: The Statement of Randolph Carter '92

Gerard Oury
The Brain '69
Delusions of Grandeur '76
La Grande Vadrouille '66

Cliff Owen
The Bawdy Adventures of Tom Jones '76
The Wrong Arm of the Law '63

Don Owen
Unfinished Business '89

Richard Owens
Killer Likes Candy '78

Earl Owensby
Manhunter '83

Jan Oxenberg
Thank You & Good Night '91

Frank Oz
Dirty Rotten Scoundrels '88
Housesitter '92
Little Shop of Horrors '86
The Muppets Take Manhattan '84
What About Bob? '91

Sakae Ozawa
The Street Fighter's Last Revenge '79

Fedor Ozep
Whispering City '47

Ali Ozgenturk
The Horse '82

Yasujiro Ozu
An Autumn Afternoon '62
Drifting Weeds '59
Early Summer '51
Equinox Flower '58
Late Spring '49
Tokyo Story '53

G.W. Pabst
Diary of a Lost Girl '29
Don Quixote '35
Joyless Street '25
Kameradschaft '31
Pandora's Box '28
Secrets of a Soul '25
The Threepenny Opera '31
Westfront 1918 '30

Frank Packard
In Your Face '77

Calvin Jackson Padget
The Battle of El Alamein '68
Secret Agent Super Dragon '66

Anthony Page
Absolution '81
Alpha Beta '73
Bill '81
Bill: On His Own '83
F. Scott Fitzgerald in Hollywood '76
Final Warning '90
Forbidden '85
Heartbreak House '86
I Never Promised You a Rose Garden '77
Johnny Belinda '82
The Lady Vanishes '79
Missiles of October '74
Monte Carlo '86
The Nightmare Years '89
Pueblo Affair '73
Scandal in a Small Town '88

Teddy Page
Blood Debts '83

Marcel Pagliero
The Respectful Prostitute '52

Marcel Pagnol
Angele '34
The Baker's Wife '33
Cesar '36
Harvest '37
Letters from My Windmill '54

Topaze '51
Well-Digger's Daughter '46

John Paizs
The Big Crimewave '86

Alan J. Pakula
All the President's Men '76
Comes a Horseman '78
Consenting Adults '92
Dream Lover '85
Klute '71
Orphans '87
Parallax View '74
The Pelican Brief '93
Presumed Innocent '90
Rollover '81
See You in the Morning '89
Sophie's Choice '82
Starting Over '79
The Sterile Cuckoo '69

George Pal
Atlantis, the Lost Continent '61
Seven Faces of Dr. Lao '63
The Time Machine '60
Tom Thumb '58
The Wonderful World of the
   Brothers Grimm '62

Laszlo Pal
Journey to Spirit Island '92

Tom Palazzolo
Caligari's Cure '82

Euzhan Palcy
A Dry White Season '89
Sugar Cane Alley '83

Larry Pall
Off Your Rocker '80

Jean Marie Pallardy
Truck Stop

Rospo Pallenberg
Cutting Class '89

Anders Palm
Dead Certain '92
Murder on Line One '90
Unmasked Part 25 '88

Thomas Palmer, Jr.
Forever: A Ghost of a Love
   Story '92

Tony Palmer
The Children '90
Wagner: The Complete Epic '85
Wagner: The Movie '85

Conrad Palmisano
Busted Up '86
Space Rage '86

Bruce Paltrow
A Little Sex '82

Rick Pamplin
Provoked '89

George Pan-Andreas
Crime Killer '85

Norman Panama
Above and Beyond '53
Barnaby and Me '77
Court Jester '56
How to Commit Marriage '69
I Will, I Will for Now '76
The Road to Hong Kong '62
The Trap '59

Gleb Panfilov
The Theme '79

Domenico Paolella
Pirates of the Coast '61

Deno Paoli
The Legend of Frank Woods
   '77

Phedon Papamichael
Sketch Artist '92

Michael Papas
The Lifetaker '89

Giullo Paradisi
Spaghetti House '82
The Visitor '80

Sergei Paradjanov
Ashik Kerib '88
The Color of Pomegranates '69
The Legend of Suram Fortress
   '85
Shadows of Forgotten
   Ancestors '64

John Paragon
Double Trouble '91
Ring of the Musketeers '93

Paul S. Parco
Deadly Alliance '78
Pucker Up and Bark Like a Dog
   '89

Domonic Paris
Dracula's Last Rites '79
Splitz '84

Jerry Paris
Don't Raise the Bridge, Lower
   the River '68
How Sweet It Is! '68
How to Break Up a Happy
   Divorce '76
Make Me an Offer '80
Never a Dull Moment '68
Only with Married Men '74
The Passing of Evil '70
Police Academy 2: Their First
   Assignment '85
Police Academy 3: Back in
   Training '86
Star Spangled Girl '71
Viva Max '69

Richard W. Park
Gang Justice '94

Alan Parker
Angel Heart '87
Birdy '84
Bugsy Malone '76
Come See the Paradise '90
The Commitments '91
Fame '80
Midnight Express '78
Mississippi Burning '88
Pink Floyd: The Wall '82
Shoot the Moon '82

Albert Parker
The Black Pirate '26
Late Extra '35

Ben Parker
The Invisible Avenger '58

Cary Parker
The Girl in the Picture '86

John Parker
Daughter of Horror '55

Norton S. Parker
The Road to Ruin '28

Percy G. Parker
Castle of the Creeping Flesh
   '68

Eric Parkinson
Future Shock '93

Tom Parkinson
Disciple of Death '72

Gordon Parks
Half Slave, Half Free '85
The Learning Tree '69
Shaft '71
Shaft's Big Score '72
Three the Hard Way '74

Gordon Parks, Jr.
Aaron Loves Angela '75
Superfly '72

Hugh Parks
Deadly Innocence '88
Dream Trap '90
King's Ransom '91
Shakma '89

Shoot '92

Michael Parks
The Return of Josey Wales '86

Billy Parolini
Igor & the Lunatics '85

Gianfranco Parolini
The Fury of Hercules '61
Samson '61

John H. Parr
Prey for the Hunter '92
Pursuit '90

Larry Parr
A Soldier's Tale '91

James D. Parriott
Heart Condition '90

Robert Parrish
Bobo '67
Casino Royale '67
Cry Danger '51
The Destructors '74
Fire Down Below '57
Journey to the Far Side of the
   Sun '69
A Town Called Hell '72

James Parrott
Pardon Us '31

Gordon Parry
Innocents in Paris '53
Tom Brown's School Days '51

John Parsons
Watched '73

Gabriel Pascal
Caesar and Cleopatra '46
Major Barbara '41

Pier Paolo Pasolini
Accatone! '61
Arabian Nights '74
The Canterbury Tales '71
The Decameron '70
The Gospel According to St.
   Matthew '64
The Hawks & the Sparrows '67
Love Meetings '64
Medea '70
Notes for an African Orestes
   '70
Oedipus Rex '67
Porcile '69
Salo, or the 120 Days of
   Sodom '75
Teorema '68

Ivan Passer
Born to Win '71
Creator '85
Crime & Passion '75
Cutter's Way '81
Fourth Story '90
Haunted Summer '88
Law and Disorder '74
The Nightingale '83
Silver Bears '78
Stalin '92

Giovanni Pastrone
Cabiria '14
Salammbo '14

Franca Pasut
Flashdance '83

Tom Patchett
Best Legs in the 8th Grade '84

Michael Pate
Tim '79

Raju Patel
In the Shadow of Kilimanjaro
   '86

Sharad Patel
Amin: The Rise and Fall '82

Stuart Paton
20,000 Leagues Under the Sea
   '16

Matthew Patrick
Tainted Blood '93

Michael Patrick
Hider in the House '90

Nigel Patrick
Johnny Nobody '61

Robert Patrick
Road to Nashville '67

John D. Patterson
Deadly Innocence '88
Grave Secrets: The Legacy of
   Hilltop Drive '92
Legend of Earl Durand '74
The Spring '89
Taken Away '89

Pat Patterson
The Body Shop '72

Ray Patterson
The Good, the Bad, and
   Huckleberry Hound '88

Richard Patterson
J-Men Forever! '79

Willi Patterson
Dreams Lost, Dreams Found
   '87

Michael Pattinson
...Almost '90
Ground Zero '88
Moving Out '83

Peter Patzak
Lethal Obsession '87
Midnight Cop '88
Slaughterday '77

Byron Paul
Lt. Robin Crusoe, U.S.N. '66

Steven Paul
Eternity '90
Falling in Love Again '80
Slapstick of Another Kind '84

Stuart Paul
Emanon '86
Fate '90

David Paulsen
Schizoid '80

George Pavlou
Rawhead Rex '87
Transmutations '85

Alain Payet
Helltrain '80

Clark Paylow
Ring of Terror '62

Barry Peak
The Big Hurt '87

Michael Pearce
James Joyce's Women '85

Richard Pearce
Country '84
Dead Man Out '89
Heartland '81
Leap of Faith '92
The Long Walk Home '89
No Mercy '86
Sessions '83
Threshold '83

Robert E. Pearso
Devil & Leroy Basset '73

George Pearson
Midnight at the Wax Museum
   '36
A Shot in the Dark '33

Peter Pearson
Paperback Hero '73
Tales of the Klondike: The
   Unexpected '87

Max Pecas
Erotic Touch of Hot Skin '65
The Sensuous Teenager '70

Sweet Ecstasy '62

Brian Peck
The Willies '90

Ron Peck
Empire State '87

Sam Peckinpah
Ballad of Cable Hogue '70
Bring Me the Head of Alfredo
   Garcia '74
Convoy '78
Cross of Iron '76
Deadly Companions '61
The Getaway '72
Junior Bonner '72
The Killer Elite '75
Major Dundee '65
The Osterman Weekend '83
Pat Garrett & Billy the Kid '73
Ride the High Country '62
Straw Dogs '72
The Wild Bunch '69

Larry Peerce
Ash Wednesday '73
The Bell Jar '79
The Court Martial of Jackie
   Robinson '90
Elvis and Me '88
Goodbye Columbus '69
Hard to Hold '84
The Incident '67
Love Child '82
The Neon Empire '89
The Other Side of the Mountain
   '75
The Other Side of the
   Mountain, Part 2 '78
Queenie '87
A Separate Peace '73
The Sporting Club '72
The Stranger Who Looks Like
   Me '74
Two Minute Warning '76
Wired '89
A Woman Named Jackie '91

Barbara Peeters
Bury Me an Angel '71
Humanoids from the Deep '80
Starhops '78
Summer School Teachers '75

Antonio Pelaez
Crystalstone '88

Anthony Pelissier
Encore '52
The Rocking Horse Winner '49

Scott Pembroke
Medicine Man '30

Nettie Pena
Home Sweet Home '80

Maurice Penczner
I Was a Zombie for the FBI '82

Sze Ma Peng
Venus the Ninja '80s

Chang Peng-I
Shaolin Kung Fu Mystagogue
   '84

Arthur Penn
Alice's Restaurant '69
Bonnie & Clyde '67
The Chase '66
Dead of Winter '87
Four Friends '81
The Left-Handed Gun '58
Little Big Man '70
The Miracle Worker '62
Missouri Breaks '76
Night Moves '75
Penn and Teller Get Killed '90
The Portrait '93
Target '85

Leonard Penn
The Dark Secret of Harvest
   Home '78
Judgment in Berlin '88
A Man Called Adam '66

Sean Penn
The Indian Runner '91

D.A. Pennebaker
Don't Look Back '67
The War Room '93

Eagle Pennell
Ice House '89
Last Night at the Alamo '83
The Whole Shootin' Match '79

David Peoples
The Blood of Heroes '89

Richard Pepin
Fist of Honor '92

Clare Peploe
High Season '88

Mark Peploe
Afraid of the Dark '92

Frank Peregini
Scar of Shame '27

Miguel Pereira
Veronico Cruz '87

Hope Perello
Howling 6: The Freaks '90

Antonio Perez
The 13th Mission '91

Jack Perez
America's Deadliest Home
Video '92

Etienne Perier
The Hot Line '69
Investigation '79
Murder at 45 R.P.M. '65
Zeppelin '71

Anthony Perkins
Lucky Stiff '88
Psycho 3 '86

Harold Perkins
Help Wanted Female '68

Paul Perri
Revenge of the Virgins '62

Frank Perry
ABC Stage 67: Truman
Capote's A Christmas
Memory '66
Compromising Positions '85
David and Lisa '62
Diary of a Mad Housewife '70
Hello Again '87
Last Summer '69
Mommie Dearest '81
Monsignor '82
Rancho Deluxe '75
Skag '79
Swimmer '68

Peter Perry
Cycle Vixens '79

Bill Persky
How to Pick Up Girls '78
Serial '80
Wait Till Your Mother Gets
Home '83

**Francisco J.
Lombardi Pery**
The City and the Dogs '85

P.J. Pesce
Body Waves '92

Brooke L. Peters
Anatomy of a Psycho '61
The Unearthly '57

Charlie Peters
Passed Away '92

Wolfgang Petersen
Das Boot '81
Enemy Mine '85
For Your Love Only '79
In the Line of Fire '93
The NeverEnding Story '84

Shattered '91

Daniel M. Peterson
Girlfriend from Hell '89

Kristine Peterson
Body Chemistry '90
Critters 3 '91
Deadly Dreams '88
Eden 2 '93
Eden 4 '93
Lower Level '91

Christopher Petit
Chinese Boxes '84
Unsuitable Job for a Woman
'82

Elio Petri
10th Victim '65

Dan Petrie, Jr.
In the Army Now '94
Toy Soldiers '91

Daniel Petrie
The Bay Boy '85
The Betsy '78
The Bramble Bush '60
Buster and Billie '74
Cocoon: The Return '88
The Dollmaker '84
Eleanor & Franklin '76
Execution of Raymond Graham
'85
Fort Apache, the Bronx '81
Lassie '94
Lifeguard '75
Mark Twain and Me '91
Moon of the Wolf '72
Mystic Pizza '88
Neptune Factor '73
A Raisin in the Sun '61
Resurrection '80
Rocket Gibraltar '88
Silent Night, Lonely Night '69
Six Pack '82
Spy with a Cold Nose '66
Square Dance '87
Stolen Hours '63
Sybil '76

Donald Petrie
The Favor '94
Grumpy Old Men '93
Opportunity Knocks '90

Boris L. Petroff
Hats Off '37
Outcasts of the City '58

Giulio Petroni
Blood and Guns '79

Vladimir Petrov
The Inspector General '54
Peter the First: Part 1 '37
Peter the First: Part 2 '38

Joseph Pevney
Away All Boats '56
Cash McCall '60
Man of a Thousand Faces '57
Meet Danny Wilson '52
Mysterious Island of Beautiful
Women '79
Night of the Grizzly '66
Tammy and the Bachelor '57
Torpedo Run '58
Who Is the Black Dahlia? '75

John Peyser
The Centerfold Girls '74
Four Rode Out '69
Kashmiri Run '69

Scott Pfeiffer
Firefight '87

Michael Pfleghar
Oldest Profession '67

Will Phelps
North Shore '87

Lee Philips
Barnum '86
Blind Vengeance '90

The Blue Lightning '86
Hardhat & Legs '80
Mae West '82
On the Right Track '81
Samson and Delilah '84
Silent Motive '91
Special Olympics '78
The Spell '77
The Stranger Within '74
Sweet Hostage '75
War Between the Tates '76
Windmills of the Gods '88

Harald Phillipe
Escape from the KGB '87

Bill Phillips
There Goes the Neighborhood
'92

Maurice Phillips
Another You '91
Enid is Sleeping '90
Riders of the Storm '88

Nick Phillips
Crazy Fat Ethel II '85
Criminally Insane '75
Death Nurse '87

Toby Phillips
The Pamela Principle '91

Maurice Pialat
Loulou '80
A Nos Amours '84
Police '85
Under Satan's Sun '87
Van Gogh '92

Picha
Shame of the Jungle '90

Irving Pichel
Colonel Effingham's Raid '45
Dance Hall '41
Day of Triumph '54
Destination Moon '50
The Great Commandment '41
The Great Rupert '50
The Miracle of the Bells '48
Mr. Peabody & the Mermaid '48
The Most Dangerous Game '32
Quicksand '50
They Won't Believe Me '47
Tomorrow is Forever '46

Lupu Pick
Shattered '21

Rex Pickett
From Hollywood to Deadwood
'89

Arthur C. Pierce
Las Vegas Hillbillys '66
Women of the Prehistoric
Planet '66

Charles B. Pierce
Boggy Creek II '83
The Evictors '79
Grayeagle '77
Hawken's Breed '87
Legend of Boggy Creek '75
Norseman '78
Sacred Ground '83
Town that Dreaded Sundown
'76

Arthur Pierson
Home Town Story '51

Carl Pierson
The New Frontier '35

Frank Pierson
Citizen Cohn '92
King of the Gypsies '78
The Looking Glass War '69
Somebody Has to Shoot the
Picture '90
A Star is Born '76

R.E. Pierson
Claws '77

Vivian Pieters
Death in the Shadows

Sam Pillsbury
Into the Badlands '92
Starlight Hotel '90
Zandalee '91

Phillip Pine
Pot, Parents, and Police '71

William H. Pine
Dark Mountain '44
Dynamite '49
Navy Way '44
Swamp Fire '46

Yuen Woo Ping
Eagle's Shadow '84

Sidney Pink
The Christmas Kid '68
Finger on the Trigger '65

Efren C. Pinon
Blind Rage '78

Claude Pinoteau
La Boum '81
The Slap '76

Gordon Pinsent
John and the Missus '87

Seth Pinsker
The Hidden 2 '94

Lucian Pintilie
The Oak '93
Ward Six

Ernie Pintoff
Blade '72
Dynamite Chicken '70
Jaguar Lives '79
Lunch Wagon '81
St. Helen's, Killer Volcano '82
Who Killed Mary What's 'Er
Name? '71

Mario Pinzauti
Mandinga '77

Robert Pirosh
Go for Broke! '51

Massimo Pirri
Could It Happen Here? '80s
Fatal Fix '80

Mark Pirro
Buford's Beach Bunnies '92
Curse of the Queerwolf '87
Deathrow Gameshow '88
A Polish Vampire in Burbank
'80

Vassili Pitchul
Little Vera '88

Glen Pitre
Belizaire the Cajun '86

Arthur Pitt
Sundance and the Kid '76

Walter W. Pitt, III
Welcome Back Mr. Fox '83

Bruce Pittman
Confidential '86
Hello Mary Lou: Prom Night 2
'87
Mark of Cain '84
Where the Spirit Lives '89

**Radoslaw
Piwowarski**
Train to Hollywood '86

Lou Place
Daddy-O '59

Allen Plone
Night Screams '87
Phantom of the Ritz '88
Sweet Justice '92

Bill Plympton
The Tune '91

Amos Poe
Alphabet City '84
The Foreigner '78

Rudiger Poe
Monster High '89

Benoit Poelvoorde
Man Bites Dog '91

Sidney Poitier
Buck and the Preacher '72
Fast Forward '84
Ghost Dad '90
Hanky Panky '82
Let's Do It Again '75
Piece of the Action '77
Stir Crazy '80
Uptown Saturday Night '74

James Polakof
Balboa '82
Demon Rage '82
Midnight Auto Supply '78
Slashed Dreams '74
Swim Team '79
The Vals '85

Roman Polanski
Bitter Moon '92
Chinatown '74
Cul de Sac '66
Diary of Forbidden Dreams '73
Fat and the Lean '61
The Fearless Vampire Killers
'67
Frantic '88
Knife in the Water '62
Macbeth '71
Pirates '86
Repulsion '65
Rosemary's Baby '68
The Tenant '76
Tess '80
Two Men & a Wardrobe '58

Stephen Poliakoff
Close My Eyes '91
Hidden City '87

Gian Polidoro
Loose in New York '80s

Jeff Pollack
Above the Rim '94

Sydney Pollack
Absence of Malice '81
Bobby Deerfield '77
The Electric Horseman '79
The Firm '93
Havana '90
Jeremiah Johnson '72
Out of Africa '85
The Scalphunters '68
The Slender Thread '65
They Shoot Horses, Don't
They? '69
This Property is Condemned
'66
Three Days of the Condor '75
Tootsie '82
The Way We Were '73
The Yakuza '75

Bud Pollard
Beware '46
The Black King '32
Look Out Sister '48
Tall, Tan and Terrific '46

Harry Pollard
California Straight Ahead '25

Jean-Daniel Pollet
Six in Paris '68

Jack Pollexfen
The Indestructible Man '56

George Pollock
Broth of a Boy '59
Murder Ahoy '64
Murder at the Gallop '63
Murder Most Foul '65
Murder She Said '62
Stranger in Town '57

Abraham Polonsky
Force of Evil '49
Romance of a Horsethief '71

Tell Them Willie Boy Is Here '69

Francisco Lara Polop
Murder Mansion '70

Barry Poltermann
The Unearthing '93

Erich Pommer
Beachcomber '38

Gillo Pontecorvo
The Battle of Algiers '66
Burn! '70
Kapo '59

Maurizio Ponzi
Pool Hustlers '83

Lea Pool
The Savage Woman '91
Straight for the Heart '88

Patrick C. Poole
Oklahoma Bound '81

Petru Popescu
Death of an Angel '86

Leo Popkin
Gang War '40
The Well '51

Edwin S. Porter
The Count of Monte Cristo '12
The Great Train Robbery:
    Cinema Begins '03

Eric Porter
Marco Polo, Jr. '72

Rafael Portillo
Broken Trust '93
The Curse of the Aztec Mummy '59
Curse of the Aztec Mummy/
    Robot vs. the Aztec Mummy '59
The Robot vs. the Aztec Mummy '59

Bill Posner
Teenage Strangler '64

Geoffrey Posner
The Young Ones '88

Ted Post
The Baby '72
Beneath the Planet of the Apes '70
Diary of a Teenage Hitchhiker '82
Go Tell the Spartans '78
Good Guys Wear Black '78
Hang 'Em High '67
Harrad Experiment '73
The Human Shield '92
Magnum Force '73
Nightkill '80
Stagecoach '86
Whiffs '75
Yuma '70

George Potter
Seven Sixgunners '87

H.C. Potter
Beloved Enemy '36
The Cowboy and the Lady '38
The Farmer's Daughter '47
The Miniver Story '50
Mr. Blandings Builds His Dream House '48
Mr. Lucky '43
Second Chorus '40
Shopworn Angel '38
The Story of Vernon and Irene Castle '39
The Time of Your Life '48

Sally Potter
Orlando '92

Richard Pottier
The Rape of the Sabines '61

Wallace Potts
Psycho Cop '88

Mansour Pourmand
Zipperface '92

Dick Powell
The Conqueror '56
Enemy Below '57
The Hunters '58
Split Second '53

Frank Powell
A Fool There Was '14

Michael Powell
Black Narcissus '47
A Canterbury Tale '44
Edge of the World '37
The Elusive Pimpernel '50
The Forty-Ninth Parallel '41
I Know Where I'm Going '45
The Life and Death of Colonel Blimp '43
The Lion Has Wings '40
Night Ambush '57
One of Our Aircraft Is Missing '41
Peeping Tom '63
The Phantom Light '35
Pursuit of the Graf Spee '57
The Red Shoes '48
The Small Back Room '49
Spy in Black '39
The Tales of Hoffmann '51

Tristam Powell
American Friends '91
Ghostwriter '84

John Power
Alice to Nowhere '86
All My Sons '86
Charles & Diana: A Palace Divided '93
Father '90
Stephen King's The Tommyknockers '93

Stanley Prager
Bang Bang Kid '67
Car 54, Where Are You? '61
Madigan's Millions '67

Jean-Yves Prate
Regina '83

Michael Preece
Prize Fighter '79

Otto Preminger
Advise and Consent '62
Anatomy of a Murder '59
Bonjour Tristesse '57
The Cardinal '63
Carmen Jones '54
The Court Martial of Billy Mitchell '55
Exodus '60
Forever Amber '47
The Human Factor '79
In Harm's Way '65
Laura '44
The Man with the Golden Arm '55
Moon is Blue '53
River of No Return '54
Rosebud '75
Saint Joan '57

John Prescott
Bootleg '89

Emeric Pressburger
Black Narcissus '47
A Canterbury Tale '44
The Life and Death of Colonel Blimp '43
Night Ambush '57
One of Our Aircraft Is Missing '41
The Tales of Hoffmann '51

Michael Pressman
And the Children Shall Lead '85
The Bad News Bears in Breaking Training '77
Boulevard Nights '79
Doctor Detroit '83

The Great Texas Dynamite Chase '76
The Imposter '84
Quicksand: No Escape '91
Secret Passions '78
Some Kind of Hero '82
Teenage Mutant Ninja Turtles 2: The Secret of the Ooze '91
Those Lips, Those Eyes '80
To Heal a Nation '88

Gaylene Preston
Dark of the Night '85

Ruben Preuss
Blackmail '91
In Dangerous Company '88
Write to Kill '91

Pierre Prevert
Voyage-Suprise '46

Steve Previn
Almost Angels '62
Escapade in Florence '62
Waltz King '63

B. Lawrence Price
Teenage Devil Dolls '53

David F. Price
Children of the Corn 2: The Final Sacrifice '92
To Die for 2 '91

Will Price
Rock, Rock, Rock '56

Joseph Prieto
Savages from Hell '68
Shanty Tramp '67

Barry Primus
Mistress '91

Prince
Graffiti Bridge '90
Under the Cherry Moon '86

Harold Prince
A Little Night Music '77
Something for Everyone '70
Sweeney Todd: The Demon Barber of Fleet Street '84

Jonathan Prince
Camp Nowhere '94

Ian Pringle
Panic Station '82

David A. Prior
Center of the Web '92
Deadly Prey '87
Death Chase '87
Double Threat '92
Final Sanction '89
Future Zone '90
Hell on the Battleground '88
Invasion Force '90
Jungle Assault '89
Killer Workout '86
Killzone '85
Lock 'n' Load '90
The Lost Platoon '89
Mankillers '87
Mardi Gras for the Devil '93
Night Wars '88
Rapid Fire '89
Raw Justice '93
White Fury '90

Vincent J. Privitera
Witchfire '86

Franco Prosperi
Counter Punch '71
Throne of Fire '82
The Wild Beasts '85

Iakov Protazanov
Aelita: Queen of Mars '24
Early Russian Cinema, Vol. 8: Iakov Protazanov '16

A.J. Prowse
Driving Force '88

Andrew Prowse
Demonstone '89

Alex Proyas
The Crow '93

Craig Pryce
The Dark '94
Revenge of the Radioactive Reporter '91

Richard Pryor
Jo Jo Dancer, Your Life is Calling '86

Alexander Ptushko
The Magic Voyage of Sinbad '52
Sword & the Dragon '56

Vsevolod Pudovkin
The End of St. Petersburg '27
Mother '26
Mystery of the Leaping Fish/ Chess Fever '25
Storm Over Asia '28

Luis Puenzo
The Official Story '85
Old Gringo '89
The Plague '92

Evelyn Purcell
Nobody's Fool '86

Joseph Purcell
Delos Adventure '86

Edmund Purdom
Don't Open Till Christmas '84

Manfred Purzer
Girls Riot '88

Dorothy Ann Puzo
Cold Steel '87

Joe Pytka
Let It Ride '89

Albert Pyun
Alien from L.A. '87
Arcade '93
Bloodmatch '91
Brain Smasher...A Love Story '93
Captain America '89
Cyborg '89
Dangerously Close '86
Deceit '93
Dollman '91
Down Twisted '89
Kickboxer 2: The Road Back '91
Knights '93
Nemesis '93
Radioactive Dreams '86
Sword & the Sorcerer '82

Mohy Quandour
The Spectre of Edgar Allen Poe '73

John Quested
Loophole '83

George P. Quigley
Murder with Music '45

Thomas Quillen
Apache Blood '75

Richard Quine
Bell, Book and Candle '58
Full of Life '56
Gun Crazy '69
Hotel '67
How to Murder Your Wife '64
My Sister Eileen '55
Oh Dad, Poor Dad (Momma's Hung You in the Closet & I'm Feeling So Sad) '67
Paris When It Sizzles '64
Prisoner of Zenda '79
Sex and the Single Girl '64
Strangers When We Meet '60
W '74
The World of Suzie Wong '60

Anthony Quinn
The Buccaneer '58

James Quinn
Blind Man's Bluff '91

John Quinn
Cheerleader Camp '88
Total Exposure '91

Gene Quintano
Honeymoon Academy '90
National Lampoon's Loaded Weapon 1 '93
Why Me? '90

Jose Quintero
Medea '59
Roman Spring of Mrs. Stone '61

Byron Quisenberry
Scream '83

Ellis Raab
You Can't Take It with You '84

Arthur Maria Rabenalt
Unnatural '52

Al Raboch
The Crimson Trail '35

Fons Rademakers
The Assault '86
Because of the Cats '74
The Rose Garden '89

Peter Rader
Grandma's House '88
Hired to Kill '91

Michael Radford
Another Time, Another Place '83
1984 '84
White Mischief '88

Robert Radler
Best of the Best '89
Best of the Best 2 '93
Showdown '93

Eric Radomski
Batman: Mask of the Phantasm '93

Michael Raeburn
Killing Heat '84

Bob Rafelson
Black Widow '87
Five Easy Pieces '70
Head '68
The King of Marvin Gardens '72
Man Trouble '92
Mountains of the Moon '90
The Postman Always Rings Twice '81
Stay Hungry '76

Piccio Raffanini
Obsession: A Taste for Fear '89

Kevin Rafferty
The Atomic Cafe '82

Stewart Raffill
Across the Great Divide '76
The Adventures of the Wilderness Family '76
High Risk '76
Ice Pirates '84
Mac and Me '88
Mannequin 2: On the Move '91
The Philadelphia Experiment '84
Sea Gypsies '78
The Tender Warrior '71
When the North Wind Blows '74

Alan Rafkin
The Shakiest Gun in the West '68

Ubaldo Ragona
The Last Man on Earth '64

Ed Ragozzini
Sasquatch '76

Ken Raich
Hollywood Hot Tubs 2:
Educating Crystal '89

Sam Raimi
Army of Darkness '92
Crimewave '85
Darkman '90
Evil Dead '83
Evil Dead 2: Dead by Dawn '87
The Quick and the Dead '94

Yvonne Rainer
The Man Who Envied Women
'85

Alvin Rakoff
City on Fire '78
Death Ship '80
Dirty Tricks '81
The First Olympics: Athens
1896 '76
King Solomon's Treasure '76
Mrs. Amworth '77
Mister Halpren & Mister
Johnson '83
Room 43 '58
Say Hello to Yesterday '71
A Voyage' Round My Father
'89

Alexander Ramati
The Assisi Underground '84

Vittoria Rambaldi
Primal Rage '90

Harold Ramis
Caddyshack '80
Club Paradise '86
Groundhog Day '93
National Lampoon's Vacation
'83
Untamed Heart '93

Patrick Rand
Mom '89

Addison Randall
Chance '89
East L.A. Warriors '89
The Killing Zone '90

Tony Randel
Amityville 1992: It's About Time
'92
Children of the Night '92
Hellbound: Hellraiser 2 '88
Ticks '93

Arthur Rankin, Jr.
The Ballad of Paul Bunyan '72
Flight of Dragons '82
The Hobbit '78
The Return of the King '80
Santa Claus is Coming to Town
'70

Lazlo Ranody
Nobody's Daughter '76

Frederic Raphael
Women & Men: Stories of
Seduction '90

Joel Rapp
The Battle of Blood Island '60

Mark Rappaport
Rock Hudson's Home Movies
'92

**Jean-Paul
Rappeneau**
Cyrano de Bergerac '90
Lovers Like Us '75
Swashbuckler '84

Irving Rapper
The Adventures of Mark Twain
'44
Born Again '78
The Brave One '56
The Corn is Green '45
Deception '46
Forever Female '53
Joseph & His Brethren '60
Marjorie Morningstar '58
Now, Voyager '42
Rhapsody in Blue '45

Steve Rash
The Buddy Holly Story '78
Can't Buy Me Love '87
Queens Logic '91
Rich Hall's Vanishing America
'86
Son-in-Law '93
Under the Rainbow '81

Jay Raskin
I Married a Vampire '87

Daniel Raskov
The Masters of Menace '90
Wedding Band '89

Tina Rathborne
Zelly & Me '88

Gregory Ratoff
Abdulla the Great '56
Adam Had Four Sons '41
Black Magic '49
The Corsican Brothers '42
Footlight Serenade '42
The Heat's On '43
Intermezzo '39
Rose of Washington Square
'39

Jans Rautenbach
No One Cries Forever '85

Max Raven
The Abomination '88

Ousama Rawi
The Housekeeper '86

John Rawlins
Arabian Nights '42
Dick Tracy Meets Gruesome
'47
Dick Tracy's Dilemma '47
Shark River '53
Sherlock Holmes: The Voice of
Terror '42

Albert Ray
Dancing Man '33
Shriek in the Night '33
13th Guest '32
Undercover Man '36

Bernard B. Ray
Broken Strings '40
Buffalo Bill Rides Again '47
House of Errors '42
Movie Stuntmen '53
Rio Rattler '35
Roamin' Wild '36
Speed Reporter '36
Texas Jack '35

Fred Olen Ray
Alien Dead '85
Alienator '89
Armed Response '86
Bad Girls from Mars '90
Beverly Hills Vamp '88
Bio Hazard '85
Commando Squad '87
Cyclone '87
Deep Space '87
Dinosaur Island '93
Evil Toons '90
Haunting Fear '91
Hollywood Chainsaw Hookers
'88
Inner Sanctum '91
Mind Twister '93
Mob Boss '90
Phantom Empire '87
Spirits '90
Star Slammer '87
Terminal Force '88
Tomb '86
Warlords '88

Nicholas Ray
Born to Be Bad '50
55 Days at Peking '63
Flying Leathernecks '51
In a Lonely Place '50
Johnny Guitar '53
The King of Kings '61
Knock on Any Door '49
The Lusty Men '52
On Dangerous Ground '51
Party Girl '58
Rebel Without a Cause '55
They Live by Night '49
A Woman's Secret '49

Satyajit Ray
The Adversary '71
Aparajito '58
Days and Nights in the Forest
'70
Devi '60
Distant Thunder '73
The Home and the World '84
Pather Panchali '54
Two Daughters '61
The World of Apu '59

Michael Raye
Laserblast '78

**Herman C.
Raymaker**
The Night Cry '26

Jack Raymond
The Speckled Band '31

Tom Raymonth
Battle of the Eagles '81

Spiro Razatos
Class of 1999 2: The Substitute
'93
Fast Getaway '91

Bill Rebane
The Alpha Incident '76
The Capture of Bigfoot '79
The Giant Spider Invasion '75

Eric Red
Body Parts '91
Cohen and Tate '88

Robert Redford
The Milagro Beanfield War '88
Ordinary People '80
A River Runs Through It '92

Carol Reed
The Agony and the Ecstasy '65
The Fallen Idol '49
Immortal Battalion '44
The Key '58
Kipps '41
Night Train to Munich '40
Odd Man Out '47
Oliver! '68
The Stars Look Down '39
The Third Man '49
Trapeze '56
Unicorn '83

James Reed
Mission Phantom '79

Jerry Reed
What Comes Around '85

Joel M. Reed
Bloodsucking Freaks '75
G.I. Executioner '71
Night of the Zombies '81

Luther Reed
Dixiana '30

Roland D. Reed
The House of Secrets '37

William Reed
Scorpion '86

Clive Rees
Blockhouse '73
When the Whales Came '89

Jerry Rees
The Marrying Man '91

Geoffrey Reeve
Caravan to Vaccares '74
Puppet on a Chain '72
Souvenir '88

Michael Reeves
The Conqueror Worm '68
The She-Beast '65

Thomas G. Reeves
Angry Joe Bass '76

Patrick Regan
Kiss Daddy Goodbye '81

Godfrey Reggio
Koyaanisqatsi '83
Powaqqatsi: Life in
Transformation '88

Francisco Regueiro
Padre Nuestro '85

Mark Reichart
Union City '81

Alastair Reid
Armistead Maupin's Tales of
the City '93
Baby Love '69
Shattered '72
Teamster Boss: The Jackie
Presser Story '92
Traffik '90

**Dorothy Davenport
Reid**
Linda '29
Sucker Money '34

Max Reid
Wild Thing '87

Tim Reid
The Little Mermaid '78

William Reilly
Men of Respect '91

Carl Reiner
All of Me '84
Bert Rigby, You're a Fool '89
The Comic '69
Dead Men Don't Wear Plaid '82
Enter Laughing '67
Fatal Instinct '93
The Jerk '79
The Man with Two Brains '83
Oh, God! '77
The One and Only '78
Sibling Rivalry '90
Summer Rental '85
Summer School '87
Where's Poppa? '70

Jeff Reiner
Blood & Concrete: A Love
Story '90
Trouble Bound '92

Lucas Reiner
Spirit of '76 '91

Rob Reiner
A Few Good Men '92
Misery '90
North '94
The Princess Bride '87
Stand By Me '86
The Sure Thing '85
This is Spinal Tap '84
When Harry Met Sally '89

Gottfried Reinhardt
Betrayed '54

John Reinhardt
Open Secret '48

Max Reinhardt
A Midsummer Night's Dream
'35

Deborah Reinisch
Caught in the Act '93

Harald Reinl
Fight for Gold '86
Forger of London '61
The Invisible Dr. Mabuse '62
The Return of Dr. Mabuse '61
The Torture Chamber of Dr.
Sadism '69

Irving Reis
The Bachelor and the Bobby-
Soxer '47
Big Street '42
Crack-Up '46
Falcon Takes Over/Strange
Bargain '49
Three Husbands '50

Walter Reisch
Men are not Gods '37

Allen Reisner
All Mine to Give '56

Charles F. Reisner
The Cobra Strikes '48
The Man on the Box '25
Train to Tombstone '50

Karel Reisz
Everybody Wins '90
The French Lieutenant's
Woman '81
The Gambler '74
Isadora '68
Morgan! '66
Sweet Dreams '85
Who'll Stop the Rain? '78

**Wolfgang
Reitherman**
The Jungle Book '67
101 Dalmations '61
The Rescuers '77
Robin Hood '73
Sleeping Beauty '59
The Sword in the Stone '63

Ivan Reitman
Dave '93
Ghostbusters '84
Ghostbusters 2 '89
Kindergarten Cop '90
Legal Eagles '86
Meatballs '79
Stripes '81
Twins '88

Edgar Reitz
Germany in Autumn '78

Norman Rene
Longtime Companion '90
Prelude to a Kiss '92

Jean Renoir
Boudu Saved from Drowning
'32
Charleston '26
The Crime of Monsieur Lange
'36
A Day in the Country '46
Diary of a Chambermaid '46
Elena and Her Men '56
The Elusive Corporal '62
French Can-Can '55
The Golden Coach '52
Grand Illusion '37
La Bete Humaine '38
La Chienne '31
La Marseillaise '37
The Little Theatre of Jean
Renoir '71
The Lower Depths '36
Madame Bovary '34
Picnic on the Grass '59
Renoir Shorts '27
The River '51
The Rules of the Game '39
The Southerner '45
The Testament of Dr. Cordelier
'59
This Land is Mine '43
Toni '34
Tournament '29

Zero for Conduct/Taris/A Propos de Nice '91

Alain Resnais
Hiroshima, Mon Amour '59
Last Year at Marienbad '61
Mon Oncle D'Amerique '80
Muriel '63
Providence '77
Stavisky '74

Adam Resnick
Cabin Boy '94

Robert Resnikoff
The First Power '89

Harry Revier
The Lost City '34

Bernard Revon
The Rascals '81

Buddy Reyes
Night of the Kickfighters '91

Burt Reynolds
The End '78
Gator '76
Sharky's Machine '81
Stick '85

C.D.H. Reynolds
Day of Judgment '81

Christopher Reynolds
Offerings '89

Don Reynolds
His Name was King '85

Gene Reynolds
Truth or Die '86

Kevin Reynolds
The Beast '88
Fandango '85
Robin Hood: Prince of Thieves '91

Lynn F. Reynolds
Riders of the Purple Sage '25
Sky High '22
Trailin' '21

Ursi Reynolds
Ganjasaurus Rex '87

Mark Rezyka
South of Reno '87

Michael Rhodes
Heidi '93
The Killing Mind '90
Matters of the Heart '90

Tonino Ricci
Great Treasure Hunt '70s
Rush '84

Bill Rice
The Vineyard '89

David Rice
Quiet Thunder '87

David Lowell Rich
Choices '86
Chu Chu & the Philly Flash '81
The Concorde: Airport '79 '79
Convicted '86
Enola Gay: The Men, the Mission, the Atomic Bomb '80
Family Upside Down '78
The Hearst and Davies Affair '85
Little Women '78
Madame X '66
Northeast of Seoul '72
Nurse '80
Satan's School for Girls '73

John Rich
Boeing Boeing '65
Clarence Darrow '78
Easy Come, Easy Go '67
Roustabout '64

Matty Rich
The Inkwell '94
Straight Out of Brooklyn '91

Richard Rich
The Fox and the Hound '81

Jef Richard
Berserker '87

Jefferson Richard
In Search of a Golden Sky '84

Pierre Richard
The Daydreamer '75
Too Shy to Try '82

C. Pennington Richards
Hour of Decision '57

Dick Richards
Culpepper Cattle Co. '72
Death Valley '81
Farewell, My Lovely '75
Man, Woman & Child '83
March or Die '77
Rafferty & the Gold Dust Twins '75

Lloyd Richards
Paul Robeson '70s

R.M. Richards
Heat '87

John Richardson
Dusty '85

Peter Richardson
Eat the Rich '87
The Pope Must Diet '91
Supergrass '87

Tony Richardson
The Border '82
The Charge of the Light Brigade '68
The Entertainer '60
Hamlet '69
The Hotel New Hampshire '84
Joseph Andrews '77
The Loneliness of the Long Distance Runner '62
Look Back in Anger '58
The Loved One '65
Mademoiselle '66
Ned Kelly '70
Penalty Phase '86
Shadow on the Sun '88
A Taste of Honey '61
Tom Jones '63
Women & Men: Stories of Seduction '90

William Richert
A Night in the Life of Jimmy Reardon '88
Winter Kills '79

Anthony Richmond
Days of Hell '84
Deja Vu '84
A Man Called Rage '84
Night of the Sharks '89

Ota Richter
Skullduggery '79

W.D. Richter
The Adventures of Buckaroo Banzai Across the Eighth Dimension '84
Late for Dinner '91

James Ricketson
Kiss the Night '87

Tom Rickman
The River Rat '84

Philip Ridley
The Reflecting Skin '91

Leni Riefenstahl
The Blue Light '32
Tiefland '44
Triumph of the Will '34

Charles Riesner
Big Store '41
Lost in a Harem '44
Manhattan Merry-Go-Round '37
Steamboat Bill, Jr. '28

Dean Riesner
Bill and Coo '47

Vladmir Rif
Very Close Quarters '84

J. Riffel
The House on Tombstone Hill '92

Adam Rifkin
The Chase '93
The Dark Backward '91
Never on Tuesday '88

Gennaro Righelli
Peddlin' in Society '47

Eran Riklis
Cup Final '92

Wolf Rilla
Bachelor of Hearts '58
Roadhouse Girl '53
Village of the Damned '60

Carlo Rim
Seven Deadly Sins '53

Alfredo Ringel
The Magic Bubble '93

Deborah Taper Ringel
The Magic Bubble '93

Arthur Ripley
The Chase '46
Thunder Road '58

Frank Ripploh
Taxi zum Klo '81

Arturo Ripstein
Foxtrot '76

Michael Rischa
Delta Heat '92

Dino Risi
The Easy Life '63
How Funny Can Sex Be? '76
Il Sorpasso '63
Love in the City '53
Running Away '89
The Scent of a Woman '75
Tiger and the Pussycat '67

Marco Risi
Forever Mary '89

Michael Rissi
Soultaker '90

Michael Ritchie
An Almost Perfect Affair '79
The Bad News Bears '76
The Candidate '72
Cops and Robbersons '94
The Couch Trip '87
Diggstown '92
Divine Madness '80
Downhill Racer '69
Fletch '85
Fletch Lives '89
The Golden Child '86
The Island '80
The Positively True Adventures of the Alleged Texas Cheerleader-Murdering Mom '93
Prime Cut '72
The Scout '94
Semi-Tough '77
Smile '75
Survivors '83
Wildcats '86

Viktors Ritelis
Crucible of Horror '69

Martin Ritt
Back Roads '81
Black Orchid '59
The Brotherhood '68
Casey's Shadow '78
Conrack '74
Cross Creek '83
The Front '76
The Great White Hope '70
Hombre '67
Hud '63
The Long, Hot Summer '58
Molly Maguires '70
Murphy's Romance '85
Norma Rae '79
Nuts '87
Paris Blues '61
Pete 'n' Tillie '72
Sounder '72
The Spy Who Came in from the Cold '65
Stanley and Iris '90

Giorgio Rivalta
The Avenger '62

Fernando A. Rivero
Nosotros '61

Joan Rivers
Rabbit Test '78

Jacques Rivette
La Belle Noiseuse '90
The Nun '66
Paris Belongs to Us '60

Chris Roach
The 13th Floor '88

Frank Roach
Nomad Riders '81

Hal Roach
Battling Orioles '24
The Devil's Brother '33
One Million B.C. '40
Road Show '41

Hal Roach, Jr.
One Million B.C. '40

Seymour Robbie
Chrome Hearts '70
Marco '73

Jerome Robbins
West Side Story '61

Matthew Robbins
*batteries not included '87
Bingo '91
Corvette Summer '78
Dragonslayer '81
Legend of Billie Jean '85

Tim Robbins
Bob Roberts '92

Mike Robe
Child in the Night '90
Murder Ordained '87
News at Eleven '86
Return to Lonesome Dove '93
Son of the Morning Star '91
Urge to Kill '84

Jim Roberson
Legend of Alfred Packer '80

Syd Roberson
Robin Hood...The Legend: The Time of the Wolf '85

Genevieve Robert
Casual Sex? '88

Yves Robert
My Father's Glory '91
My Mother's Castle '91
Pardon Mon Affaire '76
Pardon Mon Affaire, Too! '77
Return of the Tall Blond Man With One Black Shoe '74
Salut l'Artiste '74
The Tall Blond Man with One Black Shoe '72

Alan Roberts
The Happy Hooker Goes Hollywood '80
Karate Cop '93
Round Trip to Heaven '92
Save Me '93
Young Lady Chatterly 2 '85

Daryll Roberts
How U Like Me Now? '92

Deborah Roberts
Frankenstein General Hospital '88

Edward Roberts
The Adventurous Knights '35

Stephen Roberts
Ex-Mrs. Bradford '36
Star of Midnight '35

Cliff Robertson
Danger in the Skies '79

David Robertson
Firebird 2015 A.D. '81

Doug Robertson
HauntedWeen '91

John S. Robertson
Dr. Jekyll and Mr. Hyde '20
Little Orphan Annie '32
Our Little Girl '35
Shore Leave '25
The Single Standard '29
Soul-Fire '25

Joseph F. Robertson
Auntie Lee's Meat Pies '92

Herb Robins
The Worm Eaters '77

John Robins
Hot Resort '85

Arthur Robinson
Warning Shadows '23

Bruce Robinson
How to Get Ahead in Advertising '89
Jennifer 8 '92
Withnail and I '87

Chris Robinson
Sunshine Run '79
Women's Prison Escape

John Mark Robinson
All Tied Up '92
Kid '90
Roadhouse 66 '84

Lee Robinson
Walk into Hell '57

Phil Alden Robinson
Field of Dreams '89
In the Mood '87
Sneakers '92

Richard Robinson
Bloody Trail '72
Poor Pretty Eddie '73

Armando Robles
The Green Wall '70

Mark Robson
Avalanche Express '79
Bedlam '45
The Bridges at Toko-Ri '55
Champion '49
Daddy's Gone A-Hunting '69
Earthquake '74
From the Terrace '60
The Harder They Fall '56
Home of the Brave '49
The Inn of the Sixth Happiness '58
Isle of the Dead '45
The Lost Command '66
Peyton Place '57
Phffft! '54
The Prize '63
Return to Paradise '53
The Seventh Victim '43

Robson ▶cont.

Valley of the Dolls '67
Von Ryan's Express '65

Marc Rocco
Dream a Little Dream '89
Scenes from the Goldmine '87
Where the Day Takes You '92

Glauce Rocha
Antonio Das Mortes '68
Black God & White Devil '64
Earth Entranced '66

Eric Rochant
The Fifth Monkey '90
Love Without Pity '91

Sean Roche
Chasing Dreams '81

Sheldon Rochlin
Signals Through the Flames '83

Joe Rock
Cotton Queen '37

Alexandre Rockwell
In the Soup '92
Sons '91

Franc Roddam
Aria '88
The Bride '85
K2: The Ultimate High '92
The Lords of Discipline '83
Quadrophenia '79
War Party '89

Serge Rodnunsky
Lovers' Lovers '94

Ismael Rodriguez
Daniel Boone: Trail Blazer '56

Robert Rodriguez
El Mariachi '93

Nicolas Roeg
Aria '88
Castaway '87
Cold Heaven '92
Don't Look Now '73
Eureka! '81
Heart of Darkness '93
Insignificance '85
The Man Who Fell to Earth '76
Performance '70
Sweet Bird of Youth '89
Track 29 '88
The Witches '90

Larry Roemer
Rudolph the Red-Nosed
Reindeer '64

Michael Roemer
Nothing But a Man '64
Pilgrim, Farewell '82
The Plot Against Harry '69

Rick Roessler
Slaughterhouse '87

Koos Roets
Brutal Glory '89

Julian Roffman
The Mask '61

Albert Rogell
The Admiral Was a Lady '50
Cyclone Cavalier '25
Li'l Abner '40
The Tip-Off '31
War of the Wildcats '43

Charles "Buddy" Rogers
The Devil's Brother '33
March of the Wooden Soldiers '34

Maclean Rogers
Calling Paul Temple '48
Down Among the Z Men '52

Cliff Roguemore
Devil's Son-in-Law '77

Eric Rohmer
Boyfriends & Girlfriends '88
Chloe in the Afternoon '72
Claire's Knee '71
Four Adventures of Reinette and Mirabelle '89
Full Moon in Paris '84
Le Beau Mariage '82
My Night at Maud's '69
Pauline at the Beach '83
Six in Paris '68
Summer '86
A Tale of Springtime '92

Sutton Roley
Loners '72
Snatched '72

Bernie Rollins
Getting Over '81

Phil Roman
Be My Valentine, Charlie Brown '75
A Charlie Brown Thanksgiving '81
Good Grief, Charlie Brown '83
It's a Mystery, Charlie Brown '87
It's Magic, Charlie Brown/Charlie Brown's All Star '81
It's Three Strikes, Charlie Brown '86
It's Your First Kiss, Charlie Brown/Someday You'll Find Her, Charlie Brown '77
Life is a Circus, Charlie Brown/You're the Greatest, Charlie Brown '80
She's a Good Skate, Charlie Brown '80
Tom and Jerry: The Movie '93

Mark Romanek
Static '87

Eddie Romero
Beast of the Yellow Night '70
Beyond Atlantis '73
Brides of the Beast '68
Cavalry Command '63
Twilight People '72
WhiteForce '88
Woman Hunt '72

George A. Romero
The Crazies '73
Creepshow '82
The Dark Half '91
Dawn of the Dead '78
Day of the Dead '85
Knightriders '81
Martin '77
Monkey Shines '88
Night of the Living Dead '68
Season of the Witch '73
Two Evil Eyes '90

Joanelle Romero
Powwow Highway '89

Charles R. Rondeau
The Devil's Partner '58
The Girl in Lover's Lane '60

Ronnie Rondell
No Safe Haven '87

Chito Rono
Olongapo: The American Dream '89

Darrell Roodt
City of Blood '88
Father Hood '93
Place of Weeping '86
Sarafina! '92
To the Death '93

Abram Room
Bed and Sofa '27

Wills Root
The Bold Caballero '36

Tom Ropelewski
Look Who's Talking Now '93
Madhouse '90

Faliero Rosati
High Frequency '88

Nello Rosatti
The Sensuous Nurse '76

Bernard Rose
Candyman '92
Chicago Joe & the Showgirl '90
Paperhouse '89

Les Rose
Gas '81
Hog Wild '80
Title Shot '81

Mickey Rose
Student Bodies '81

Pierre Rose
The Klutz '73

Reuben Rose
Screwball Academy '86

Barry Rosen
Gang Wars '75
The Yum-Yum Girls '78

Martin Rosen
The Plague Dogs '82
Stacking '87
Watership Down '78

Phil Rosen
Beggars in Ermine '34
Branded Men '31
Charlie Chan in the Secret Service '44
The Chinese Cat '44
Gangs, Inc. '41
I Killed That Man '42
It Could Happen to You '37
The Jade Mask '45
Man's Land '32
Meeting at Midnight '44
Mistaken Identity '36
The Phantom Broadcast '33
The Phantom in the House '29
Phantom of Chinatown '40
The Pocatello Kid '31
The President's Mystery '36
Return of the Ape Man '44
The Scarlet Clue '45
The Sphinx '33
Spooks Run Wild '41
Tango '36
Two Gun Man '31
Whistlin' Dan '32
Wings Over the Pacific '43
Young Blood '33

Robert L. Rosen
Raw Courage '84

Rick Rosenberg
Distant Thunder '88

Stuart Rosenberg
The Amityville Horror '79
April Fools '69
Brubaker '80
Cool Hand Luke '67
The Drowning Pool '75
The Laughing Policeman '74
Love and Bullets '79
My Heroes Have Always Been Cowboys '91
Pocket Money '72
The Pope of Greenwich Village '84
Voyage of the Damned '76

Tanya Rosenberg
Blood Games '90

Ralph Rosenblum
The Man That Corrupted Hadleyburg '80
Summer Solstice '81

Keva Rosenfeld
Twenty Bucks '93

Scott Rosenfelt
Family Prayers '91

Dan Rosenthal
Sloane '84

Mark Rosenthal
The In Crowd '88

Rick Rosenthal
American Dreamer '84
Bad Boys '83
Devlin '92
Halloween 2: The Nightmare Isn't Over! '81
Russkies '87

Robert J. Rosenthal
Malibu Beach '78
Zapped! '82

Francesco Rosi
Christ Stopped at Eboli '79
Lucky Luciano '74
The Palermo Connection '91
Three Brothers '80

Mark Rosman
The Blue Yonder '86
The House on Sorority Row '83

Milton Rosmer
Murder in the Old Red Barn '36
The Secret of the Loch '34

Frank Ross
The Lady Says No '51

Herbert Ross
California Suite '78
Dancers '87
Footloose '84
Funny Lady '75
The Goodbye Girl '77
Goodbye Love '34
Goodbye, Mr. Chips '69
I Ought to Be in Pictures '82
The Last of Sheila '73
Max Dugan Returns '83
My Blue Heaven '90
Nijinsky '80
The Owl and the Pussycat '70
Pennies From Heaven '81
Play It Again, Sam '72
Protocol '84
The Secret of My Success '87
The Seven Percent Solution '76
Steel Magnolias '89
The Sunshine Boys '75
True Colors '91
The Turning Point '77
Undercover Blues '93

Nat Ross
April Fool '26

Neil Rossati
Tides of War '90

Roberto Rossellini
Amore '48
Augustine of Hippo '72
Blaise Pascal '71
Deutschland im Jahre Null '47
Era Notte a Roma '60
Europa '51 '52
The Flowers of St. Francis '50
Generale Della Rovere '60
Man with a Cross '43
The Messiah '75
The Miracle '48
Open City '45
Paisan '46
The Rise of Louis XIV '66
Seven Deadly Sins '53
Stromboli '50
Vanina Vanini '61
Voyage to Italy '53

Robert Rossen
Alexander the Great '55
All the King's Men '49
Body and Soul '47
The Hustler '61
Island in the Sun '57
Lilith '64
Mambo '55

They Came to Cordura '59

Franco Rossi
Quo Vadis '85

Arthur Rosson
Boots of Destiny '37
The Concentratin' Kid '30
Hidden Gold '33
The Last Outlaw '27
Trailing Trouble '30

Kaspar Rostrup
Memories of a Marriage '90

Bobby Roth
Baja Oklahoma '87
Boss' Son '79
Circle of Power '83
Dead Solid Perfect '88
The Game of Love '90
Heartbreakers '84
Keeper of the City '92
The Man Inside '90
Rainbow Drive '90

Cy Roth
Fire Maidens from Outer Space '56

Joe Roth
Coupe de Ville '90
Revenge of the Nerds 2: Nerds in Paradise '87
Streets of Gold '86

Phillip J. Roth
A.P.E.X. '94
Red Snow '91

Stephanie Rothman
Group Marriage '72
The Student Nurses '70
Terminal Island '73
Track of the Vampire '66
The Velvet Vampire '71
Working Girls '75

William Rotsler
Mantis in Lace '68
Psychedelic Fever '90

Brigitte Rouan
Overseas: Three Women with Man Trouble '90

Jean Rouch
Jaguar '56
Six in Paris '68

Jacques Rouffio
La Passante '83

Russel Rouse
Caper of the Golden Bulls '67
Fastest Gun Alive '56
The Oscar '66
The Thief '52
The Well '51

Gilbert Roussel
Women's Prison Massacre '85

Peter Rowe
Lost '86
Personal Exemptions '88
Take Two '87

Tom Rowe
Get Rita

Roy Rowland
Bugles in the Afternoon '52
The 5000 Fingers of Dr. T '53
Girl Hunters '63
Gun Glory '57
Hit the Deck '55
Meet Me in Las Vegas '56
Our Vines Have Tender Grapes '45
The Seven Hills of Rome '58
Two Weeks with Love '50

William Rowland
Flight to Nowhere '46
Follies Girl '43

Christopher Rowley
Soul Patrol '80

Jean-Claude Roy
Deadly Sting '82

Fanchon Royer
Bell Ringer of Antigua '46

Patricia Rozema
I've Heard the Mermaids
 Singing '87

Janosz Rozsa
Sunday Daughters '80

Michael Rubbo
The Peanut Butter Solution '85

J. Walter Ruben
Ace of Aces '33
Java Head '35
Riff Raff '35

Joseph Ruben
Dreamscape '84
The Good Son '93
Gorp '80
Joyride '77
Pom Pom Girls '76
Sleeping with the Enemy '91
The Stepfather '87
True Believer '89

Katt Shea Ruben
Dance of the Damned '88
Poison Ivy '92
Streets '90
Stripped to Kill '87
Stripped to Kill II: Live Girls '89

Nik Rubenfeld
Alien Private Eye '87

Percival Rubens
Mr. Kingstreet's War '71
Survival Zone '84
Wild Zone '89

Harold Rubie
Island Trader '71

Howard Rubie
Scalp Merchant '77

Bruce Joel Rubin
My Life '93

Joseph Rubin
The Sister-in-Law '74

Rick Rubin
Tougher than Leather '88

Sergio Rubini
The Station '92

Alan Rudolph
Barn of the Naked Dead '73
Choose Me '84
Endangered Species '82
Equinox '93
Love at Large '89
Made in Heaven '87
The Moderns '88
Mortal Thoughts '91
Premonition '71
Roadie '80
Songwriter '84
Trouble in Mind '86
Welcome to L.A. '77

Louis Rudolph
Double Standard '88

Wesley Ruggles
Arizona '40
Cimarron '30
I'm No Angel '33
No Man of Her Own '32
Somewhere I'll Find You '42

Raul Ruiz
The Hypothesis of the Stolen
 Painting '78
On Top of the Whale '82

Craig T. Rumar
Instant Justice '86

Robert Rundle
The Divine Enforcer '91

Katja Rupe
Germany in Autumn '78

Richard Rush
Color of Night '94
Freebie & the Bean '74
Getting Straight '70
Hell's Angels on Wheels '67
Psych-Out '68
The Savage Seven '68
The Stunt Man '80

Chuck Russell
The Blob '88
The Mask '94
A Nightmare on Elm Street 3:
 Dream Warriors '87

Jay Russell
End of the Line '88

Ken Russell
Altered States '80
Aria '88
The Boy Friend '71
Crimes of Passion '84
Dante's Inferno: Life of Dante
 Gabriel Rossetti '69
The Devils '71
Gothic '87
The Lair of the White Worm '88
Lisztomania '75
Mahler '74
The Music Lovers '71
Prisoner of Honor '91
The Rainbow '89
Salome's Last Dance '88
Savage Messiah '72
Tommy '75
Valentino '77
Whore '91
Women & Men: Stories of
 Seduction '90
Women in Love '70

Paddy Russell
Doctor Who: Pyramids of Mars
 '75

Ray Russell
Zotz! '62

William D. Russell
Best of the Badmen '50
The Green Promise '49

Aaron Russo
Rude Awakening '89

John Russo
The Majorettes '87
Midnight '81
Midnight 2: Sex, Death, and
 Videotape '93

Maria Russo
The Naked Maja '59

Mardi Rustam
Evils of the Night '85

Mark Rutland
Prime Suspect '88

Todd Rutt
Shock! Shock! Shock! '87

Frank Ryan
Call Out the Marines '42

Edgar Ryazanov
A Forgotten Tune for the Flute
 '88
Private Life '82

Mark Rydell
Cinderella Liberty '73
The Cowboys '72
For the Boys '91
Harry & Walter Go to New York
 '76
Intersection '93
On Golden Pond '81
The Reivers '69
The River '84
The Rose '79

Stellan Rye
Student of Prague '13

Judy Rymer
Who Killed Baby Azaria? '83

William Sachs
Galaxina '80
Incredible Melting Man '77
The Last Hour '91
South of Hell Mountain '70
Van Nuys Blvd. '79

Alan Sacks
Dubeat-E-O '84

James Sadwith
Bluffing It '87
Sinatra '92

Eddie Saeta
Dr. Death, Seeker of Souls '73

Henri Safran
Norman Loves Rose '82
The Wild Duck '84

Boris Sagal
Angela '77
Girl Happy '65
Guns of Diablo '64
Masada '81
Night Gallery '69
Omega Man '71
The Runaway Barge '75

Leontine Sagan
Maedchen in Uniform '31

Malcolm St. Clair
The Bashful Bachelor '42
Bullfighters '45
The Grand Duchess and the
 Waiter '26

Christopher St. John
Top of the Heap '72

Gene Saks
Barefoot in the Park '67
Brighton Beach Memoirs '86
Cactus Flower '69
Last of the Red Hot Lovers '72
Mame '74
The Odd Couple '68

Henry Sala
Nightmare Weekend '86

Richard Sale
Let's Make it Legal '51
Ticket to Tomahawk '50

Sidney Salkow
City Without Men '43
The Last Man on Earth '64
Twice-Told Tales '63

Mikael Salomon
A Far Off Place '93

Victor Salva
Clown House '88

Jaime Salvador
Boom in the Moon '46

Gabriele Salvatores
Mediterraneo '91

Salvatore Samperi
Ernesto '79
Malicious '74
Submission '77

Edwards Sampson
The Fast and the Furious '54

Barry Samson
Ice Pawn '92
The Ice Runner '93

Stuart Samuels
Visions of Light: The Art of
 Cinematography '93

Fang Mui San
The Amsterdam Connection
 '70s

Denis Sanders
Invasion of the Bee Girls '73
One Man's Way '63

Clifford Sandforth
Murder by Television '35

Jay Sandrich
For Richer, For Poorer '92
Seems Like Old Times '80

Mark Sandrich
Aggie Appleby, Maker of Men
 '33
Carefree '38
Cockeyed Cavaliers '34
Follow the Fleet '36
The Gay Divorcee '34
Hips, Hips, Hooray '34
Holiday Inn '42
Melody Cruise '32
Shall We Dance '37
Top Hat '35
A Woman Rebels '36

Helen Sanford
Angel of H.E.A.T. '82

Luk Pak Sang
Tattoo Connection '78

Jonathan Sanger
Code Name: Emerald '85

Jimmy Sangster
Dynasty of Fear '72
The Horror of Frankenstein '70
Lust for a Vampire '71

Erick Santamaria
Playgirl Killer '66

Alfred Santell
The Hairy Ape '44
Having Wonderful Time '38
Jack London '44
That Brennan Girl '46
Winterset '36

Cirio H. Santiago
Beyond the Call of Duty '92
Caged Fury '80
Cover Girl Models '75
Death Force '78
Demon of Paradise '87
Devastator '85
Dune Warriors '91
Equalizer 2000 '86
The Expendables '89
Eye of the Eagle '87
Eye of the Eagle 3 '91
Field of Fire '92
Fighting Mad '77
Final Mission '84
Firecracker '71
Firehawk '92
Future Hunters '88
The Muthers '76
Naked Vengeance '85
Nam Angels '88
Raiders of the Sun '92
Savage! '73
She Devils in Chains '76
Silk '86
Silk 2 '89
The Sisterhood '88
Stryker '83
TNT Jackson '75
The Vampire Hookers '78
Wheels of Fire '84

Pablo Santiago
South Seas Massacre

Joseph Santley
Call of the Canyon '42
The Cocoanuts '29
Down Mexico Way '41
Harmony Lane '35
Melody Ranch '40
Music in My Heart '40

Damon Santostefano
Severed Ties '92

David Saperstein
Beyond the Stars '89

A Killing Affair '85

Deran Sarafian
Alien Predators '80
Back in the USSR '92
Death Warrant '90
Gunmen '93
Interzone '88
Terminal Velocity '94
To Die for '89

Richard Sarafian
The Arab Conspiracy '76
Eye of the Tiger '86
Gangster Wars '81
Man in the Wilderness '71
Man Who Loved Cat Dancing
 '73
Street Justice '89
Sunburn '79
Vanishing Point '71

Joseph Sargent
Amber Waves '82
Caroline? '90
Coast to Coast '80
Colossus: The Forbin Project
 '70
Day One '89
Goldengirl '79
Hustling '75
The Incident '89
The Invaders '67
Ivory Hunters '90
Jaws: The Revenge '87
MacArthur '77
Man on a String '71
The Manions of America '81
Maybe I'll Be Home in the
 Spring '70
Memorial Day '83
Miss Rose White '92
Never Forget '91
Nightmares '83
Passion Flower '86
Skylark '93
The Taking of Pelham One Two
 Three '74
Tomorrow's Child '82
Tribes '70
White Lightning '73
World War II: When Lions
 Roared '94

Marina Sargenti
Child of Darkness, Child of
 Light '91
Mirror, Mirror '90

Dick Sarin
Family Reunion '88

Vic Sarin
Cold Comfort '90

Maurice Sarli
The Bodyguard '76

Michael Sarne
Myra Breckinridge '70

Jonathan Sarno
The Kirlian Witness '78

Peter Sasdy
The Devil's Undead '75
Doomwatch '72
Hands of the Ripper '71
I Don't Want to Be Born '75
King Arthur, the Young Warlord
 '75
The Lonely Lady '83
Nothing But the Night '72
Rude Awakening '81
Taste the Blood of Dracula '70
Thirteenth Reunion '81
The Two Faces of Evil '82
Young Warlord '75

Barbara Sass
Without Love '80

Oley Sassone
Bloodfist 3: Forced to Fight '92
Final Embrace '92

Ron Satlof
Perry Mason Returns '85
Perry Mason: The Case of the
    Lost Love '87
Spiderman: The Deadly Dust
    '78
Waikiki '80

Buichi Sato
Baby Cart 4: Heart of a
    Parent...Heart of a Child '72

Hajime Sato
Body Snatcher from Hell '69
Terror Beneath the Sea '66

Junya Sato
The Go-Masters '82
The Silk Road '92

Shimako Sato
Tale of a Vampire '92

Carlos Saura
Ay, Carmela! '90
Blood Wedding '81
Carmen '83
Cria '76
El Amor Brujo '86
The Garden of Delights '70
The Hunt '67
Mama Turns a Hundred '79

Claude Sautet
Cesar & Rosalie '72
Mado '76
A Simple Story '79
The Things of Life '70
Un Coeur en Hiver '93
Vincent, Francois, Paul and the
    Others '76

Derek Savage
The Meateater '79

Telly Savalas
Beyond Reason '77

Igor Savchenko
Guerilla Brigade '39

Brian Savegar
The Inheritor '90

Philip Saville
Family Pictures '93
Fellow Traveler '89
Mandela '87
Max and Helen '90
Secrets '71
Shadey '87
Those Glory, Glory Days '83
Wonderland '88

Victor Saville
Conspirator '49
Dark Journey '37
Evergreen '34
Forever and a Day '43
Green Dolphin Street '47
The Iron Duke '34
It's Love Again '36
Kim '50
The Silver Chalice '54
Storm in a Teacup '37
Tonight and Every Night '45

Tom Savini
Night of the Living Dead '90

Nancy Savoca
Dogfight '91
Household Saints '93
True Love '89

Leopoldo Savona
The Mongols '60

Carlos Savrat
The Stilts '84

Stephen Sayadian
Dr. Caligari '89

Eric Sayers
Common Law Wife '63

John Sayles
Baby It's You '82
The Brother from Another
    Planet '84
City of Hope '91
Eight Men Out '88
Lianna '83
Matewan '87
Passion Fish '92
Return of the Secaucus 7 '80

James Sbardellati
Under the Gun '88

Joseph L. Scanlan
Nightstick '87
Spring Fever '81
The World's Oldest Living
    Bridesmaid '92

Don Scardino
Me & Veronica '93

Umberto Scarpelli
The Giant of Metropolis '61

Romano Scavolini
Nightmare '82

Steven Schachter
Getting Up and Going Home
    '92

Armand Schaefer
Exiled to Shanghai '37
Fighting Texans '33
Fighting with Kit Carson '33
Hurricane Express '32
Law of the Wild '34
Lightning Warrior '31
The Lost Jungle '34
The Miracle Rider '35
Outlaw Justice '32
Sagebrush Trail '33
Sixteen Fathoms Deep '34
Terror Trail '33

George Schaefer
Barefoot in Athens '66
Children in the Crossfire '84
Deadly Game '82
Doctors' Wives '70
Elizabeth, the Queen '68
Generation '69
Holy Terror '65
In This House of Brede '75
Invincible Mr. Disraeli '63
Lamp at Midnight '66
Lost Legacy: A Girl Called
    Hatter Fox '77
The Man Upstairs '93
Once Upon a Scoundrel '73
Pendulum '69
The People vs. Jean Harris '81
A Piano for Mrs. Cimino '82
Right of Way '84
Soldier in Love '67
The Tempest '63
Victoria Regina '61
Who'll Save Our Children? '82

Francis Schaeffer
Baby on Board '92
Headhunter '89
Rebel Storm '90

Franky Schaeffer
Wired to Kill '86

Marianne Schafer
Traenen in Florenz '84

Franklin J. Schaffner
The Best Man '64
The Boys from Brazil '78
Islands in the Stream '77
Lionheart '87
Nicholas and Alexandra '71
Our Town '77
Papillon '73
Patton '70
Planet of the Apes '68
Sphinx '81
The Stripper '63
The War Lord '65
Welcome Home '89
Yes, Giorgio '82

Don Schain
The Abductors '72
Ginger '72
Girls are for Loving '73
A Place Called Today '72
Too Hot to Handle '76

Peter Schamoni
Spring Symphony '86

Jerry Schatzberg
Blood Money: The Story of
    Clinton and Nadine '88
Honeysuckle Rose '80
Misunderstood '84
No Small Affair '84
Panic in Needle Park '75
Reunion '88
Scarecrow '73
The Seduction of Joe Tynan '79
Street Smart '87

Hans Scheepmaker
Field of Honor '86

Robert Scheerer
Adam at 6 A.M. '70
Ants '77
Hans Brinker '69
Happily Ever After '82
How to Beat the High Cost of
    Living '80
The World's Greatest Athlete
    '73

Andrew Scheinman
Little Big League '94

Maximilian Schell
First Love '70
The Pedestrian '73

Henning Schellerup
The Adventures of Nellie Bly
    '81
Time Machine '78
Tom Edison: The Boy Who Lit
    Up the World '78

Carl Schenkel
Eye of the Demon '87
Knight Moves '93
The Mighty Quinn '89
Out of Order '84
Silence Like Glass '90
Silhouette '91
Strike Back '80

Fred Schepisi
Barbarosa '82
A Cry in the Dark '88
The Devil's Playground '76
Iceman '84
Mr. Baseball '92
Plenty '85
Roxanne '87
The Russia House '90
Six Degrees of Separation '93

Edgar J. Scherick
Jenny '70

Victor Schertzinger
Clodhopper '17
One Night of Love '34
The Road to Singapore '40
The Road to Zanzibar '41
Something to Sing About '36
Uptown New York '32
What Happened to Rosa? '21

Paul Schibli
The Nutcracker Prince '91

Suzanne Schiffman
Sorceress '88

Lawrence Schiller
Double Exposure: The Story of
    Margaret Bourke-White '89
Double Jeopardy '92
The Executioner's Song '82
Marilyn: The Untold Story '80

Vittorio Schiraldi
Fangs '75

Heinz Schirk
The Wannsee Conference '84

Eric L. Schlagman
Punch the Clock '90

Thomas Schlamme
Crazy from the Heart '91
Miss Firecracker '89
So I Married an Axe Murderer
    '93
Spalding Gray: Terrors of
    Pleasure '88
You So Crazy '94

George Schlatter
Norman, Is That You? '76

John Schlesinger
The Believers '87
Billy Liar '63
Darling '65
The Day of the Locust '75
An Englishman Abroad '83
The Falcon and the Snowman
    '85
Far from the Madding Crowd
    '67
Honky Tonk Freeway '81
The Innocent '93
A Kind of Loving '62
Madame Sousatzka '88
Marathon Man '76
Midnight Cowboy '69
Pacific Heights '90
A Question of Attribution '91
Separate Tables '83
Sunday, Bloody Sunday '71
Yanks '79

Volker Schlondorff
Coup de Grace '78
Death of a Salesman '86
Germany in Autumn '78
The Handmaid's Tale '90
The Lost Honor of Katharina
    Blum '75
Murder on the Bayou '91
An Occurrence at Owl Creek
    Bridge/Coup de Grace '62
Swann in Love '84
The Tin Drum '79
Voyager '91

Julian Schlossberg
Muse Concert: No Nukes '80

**Jay Schlossberg-
Cohen**
Night Train to Terror '84

Rick Schmidt
A Man, a Woman and a Killer
    '76

Thomas J. Schmidt
Girls on the Road '73

David Schmoeller
The Arrival '90
Catacombs '89
Crawlspace '86
Curse 4: The Ultimate Sacrifice
    '92
Netherworld '91
Puppet Master '89
The Seduction '82
Tourist Trap '79

Paul Schneider
Babycakes '89
Honor Thy Father and Mother:
    The True Story of the
    Menendez Brothers '94
Something Special '86

**Robert Allen
Schnitzer**
Kandyland '87
The Premonition '75

Ernest B. Schoedsack
Chang: A Drama of the
    Wilderness '27
Dr. Cyclops '40
King Kong '33
Last Days of Pompeii '35
Mighty Joe Young '49
The Most Dangerous Game '32
Son of Kong '33

**Pierre
Schoendoerffer**
Le Crabe Tambour '77
The 317th Platoon '65

Jan Scholtz
Emissary '89

Skip Schoolnik
Hide and Go Shriek '87

Renen Schorr
Late Summer Blues '87

Dale Schott
The Care Bears Movie 2: A
    New Generation '86

Paul Schrader
American Gigolo '79
Blue Collar '78
Cat People '82
The Comfort of Strangers '91
Hardcore '79
Light of Day '87
Light Sleeper '92
Mishima: A Life in Four
    Chapters '85
Patty Hearst '88

Myrl A. Schreibman
Angel of H.E.A.T. '82
Liberty & Bash '90

William Schreiner
Sinful Life '89

John F. Schreyer
Naked Youth '59

Barbet Schroeder
Barfly '87
Maitresse '76
More '69
Reversal of Fortune '90
Single White Female '92
Tricheurs '84
The Valley Obscured by the
    Clouds '72

Frank C. Schroeder
Pistol: The Birth of a Legend
    '90

Michael Schroeder
Damned River '89
Mortuary Academy '91
Out of the Dark '88
Relentless 2: Dead On '91

Peter Schubert
Germany in Autumn '78

Patrick Schulmann
Et La Tenoresse?...Bordel! '84
Rendez-Moi Ma Peau '81

Carl Schultz
Blue Fin '78
Careful, He Might Hear You '84
Deadly Currents '93
The Seventh Sign '88
Travelling North '87
Which Way Home '90

Michael A. Schultz
Car Wash '76
Carbon Copy '81
Cooley High '75
Disorderlies '87
For Us, the Living '88
Greased Lightning '77
Honeybaby '74
Krush Groove '85
The Last Dragon '85
Livin' Large '91
Scavenger Hunt '79
Sgt. Pepper's Lonely Hearts
    Club Band '78
Three Days in Beirut '83
Timestalkers '87
Which Way Is Up? '77

Bob Schulz
Robbers of the Sacred
　Mountain '83

Douglas Schulze
Hellmaster '92

Joel Schumacher
The Client '94
Cousins '89
D.C. Cab '84
Dying Young '91
Falling Down '93
Flatliners '90
The Incredible Shrinking
　Woman '81
The Lost Boys '87
St. Elmo's Fire '85
The Virginia Hill Story '76

Phillip Schuman
Jailbird Rock '88

Reinhold Schunzel
Balalaika '39
Fortune's Fool '21

Harold Schuster
Black Beauty/Courage of Black
　Beauty '57
Breakfast in Hollywood '46
Courage of Black Beauty '57
Dinner at the Ritz '37
The Finger Man '55
Marine Raiders '43
My Friend Flicka '43
So Dear to My Heart '49
The Tender Years '47

Jan Schutte
Drachenfutter '87

Douglas Schwartz
Peacekillers '71

Jack Schwartz
Tiger Fangs '43

Maurice Schwartz
Tevye '39

**Arnold
Schwarzenegger**
Christmas in Connecticut '92
Tales from the Crypt, Vol. 3 '90

David Scmidlapp
Not Quite Love '88

Ettore Scola
Down & Dirty '76
The Family '87
La Nuit de Varennes '82
Le Bal '82
Macaroni '85
Passion of Love '82
A Special Day '77
We All Loved Each Other So
　Much '77

Martin Scorsese
After Hours '85
The Age of Innocence '93
Alice Doesn't Live Here
　Anymore '74
Boxcar Bertha '72
Cape Fear '91
The Color of Money '86
Goodfellas '90
Italianamerican/The Big Shave
King of Comedy '82
The Last Temptation of Christ
　'88
The Last Waltz '78
Mean Streets '73
New York, New York '77
New York Stories '89
Raging Bull '80
Taxi Driver '76
Who's That Knocking at My
　Door? '68

Cynthia Scott
Strangers in Good Company
　'91

Ewing Scott
Windjammer '31

George C. Scott
The Andersonville Trial '70
Descending Angel '90
Don't Look Back: The Story of
　Leroy "Satchel" Paige '81
Rage '72
Savage is Loose '74

James Scott
Strike It Rich '90

Michael Scott
Dangerous Heart '93
Ladykiller '92

Oz Scott
Bustin' Loose '81

Peter Graham Scott
Subterfuge '68

Ridley Scott
Alien '79
Black Rain '89
Blade Runner '82
The Duellists '77
1492: Conquest of Paradise '92
Legend '86
Someone to Watch Over Me
　'87
Thelma & Louise '91

Robert Scott
The Video Dead '87

Sherman Scott
Billy the Kid Trapped '42
I Take This Oath '40
The Mysterious Rider '42

T.J. Scott
TC 2000 '93

Tony Scott
Beverly Hills Cop 2 '87
Days of Thunder '90
The Hunger '83
The Last Boy Scout '91
Revenge '90
Top Gun '86
True Romance '93

Aubrey Scotto
Uncle Moses '32

Sandra Seacat
In the Spirit '90

Steven Seagal
On Deadly Ground '94

John Seale
Till There was You '91

Francis Searle
A Girl in a Million '46
Profile '54
Someone at the Door '50
Things Happen at Night '48

Fred F. Sears
Ambush at Tomahawk Gap '53
Earth vs. the Flying Saucers '56
The Giant Claw '57
Teenage Crime Wave '55

Victor Sears
Ninja the Battalion '90
Ninja's Extreme Weapons '90

George Seaton
Airport '70
The Big Lift '50
The Counterfeit Traitor '62
Country Girl '54
Miracle on 34th Street '47
Showdown '73
Teacher's Pet '58

Beverly Sebastian
The American Angels: Baptism
　of Blood '89
Delta Fox '77
Gator Bait '73
Gator Bait 2: Cajun Justice '88
Running Cool '93

Ferd Sebastian
The American Angels: Baptism
　of Blood '89
Delta Fox '77
Flash & Firecat '75
Gator Bait '73
Gator Bait 2: Cajun Justice '88
Hitchhikers '72
On the Air Live with Captain
　Midnight '79
Rocktober Blood '85
Running Cool '93

John Sebastian
Voyage to the Prehistoric
　Planet '65

Gregg Sebelious
The Day the Earth Froze '59

David Secter
Feelin' Up '76

Mike Sedan
Married People, Single Sex '93

Edward Sedgwick
Air Raid Wardens '43
The Cameraman '28
Doughboys '30
Fit for a King '37
Free and Easy '30
The Gladiator '38
Ma and Pa Kettle Back On the
　Farm '51
Parlor, Bedroom and Bath '31
Pick a Star '37
Riding on Air '37
A Southern Yankee '48
Speak Easily '32
Spite Marriage '29
What! No Beer? '33

John Sedwick
Dark Shadows '67

Paul Seed
Dead Ahead: The Exxon Valdez
　Disaster '92

Charles Seeling
Rounding Up the Law '22

Steven Seemayer
Miami Vendetta '87

Alex Segal
The Story of David '76

Peter Segal
Naked Gun 33 1/3: The Final
　Insult '94

Arthur Seidelman
Body Language '92
The Caller '87
Children of Rage '75
Dying to Remember '93
Echoes '83
False Witness '89
A Friendship in Vienna '88
Glory Years '87
Hercules in New York '70
Poker Alice '87
Rescue Me '93

Susan Seidelman
Cookie '89
Desperately Seeking Susan '85
Making Mr. Right '86
She-Devil '89
Smithereens '82

Joseph Seiden
Eli Eli '40
God, Man and Devil '49
Paradise in Harlem '40

Lewis Seiler
Charlie Chan in Paris '35
Doll Face '46
Great K & A Train Robbery '26
Guadalcanal Diary '43
Pittsburgh '42
The Winning Team '52

William Seiler
Big Business Girl '31

William A. Seiter
Allegheny Uprising '39
Borderline '50
The Cheerful Fraud '27
Destroyer '43
Dimples '36
Diplomaniacs '33
In Person '35
It's a Date '40
Lady Takes a Chance '43
Little Church Around the
　Corner '23
Little Giant '46
Make Haste to Live '54
Moon's Our Home '36
One Touch of Venus '48
Roberta '35
Room Service '38
Skinner's Dress Suit '26
Sons of the Desert '33
Stowaway '40
Susannah of the Mounties '39
Way Back Home '32
The White Sin '24
You Were Never Lovelier '42

George B. Seitz
Andy Hardy Meets Debutante
　'40
Andy Hardy's Double Life '42
Andy Hardy's Private Secretary
　'41
Danger Lights '30
Drums of Jeopardy '31
The Ice Flood '26
Kit Carson '40
The Last of the Mohicans '36
Life Begins for Andy Hardy '41
Love Finds Andy Hardy '38
Vanishing American '26

Steve Sekely
Behind Prison Walls '43
Blonde Savage '47
Day of the Triffids '63
Revenge of the Zombies '43
The Scar '48
Waterfront '44

Lesley Selander
Arizona Bushwackers '67
Bar-20 '43
Border Patrol '43
Buckskin Frontier '43
Colt Comrades '43
Doomed Caravan '41
Dragonfly Squadron '54
Fighter Attack '53
Flat Top '52
Flight to Mars '52
The Frontiersman '38
Hopalong Cassidy: Renegade
　Trail '39
Hopalong Cassidy: Riders of
　the Deadline '43
Knights of the Range '40
The Light of Western Stars '40
Lone Ranger and the Lost City
　of Gold '58
Lost Canyon '43
The Mysterious Rider '38
The Red Stallion '47
Renegade Trail '39
Rider from Tucson '50
Riders of the Timberline '41
Robin Hood of Texas '47
Sandflow '37
Santa Fe Marshal '40
Shotgun '55
The Vampire's Ghost '45

Jay Noyles Seles
Prisoners of Inertia '89

Henry Selick
The Nightmare Before
　Christmas '93

Jack M. Sell
Deadly Spygames '89
Outtakes '85
The Psychotronic Man '91

Charles E. Sellier
The Annihilators '85

Silent Night, Deadly Night '84

David Selman
Fighting Shadows '35
The Revenge Rider '35

Herbert Selpin
Geheimakte WB1 '42

David Seltzer
Lucas '86
Punchline '88
Shining Through '92

Edgar Selwyn
The Sin of Madelon Claudet '31
Skyscraper Souls '32

Arna Selznick
The Care Bears Movie '84

Larry Semon
Bakery/Grocery Clerk '21
The Wizard of Oz '25

Dominic Sena
Kalifornia '93

Ralph Senensky
Death Cruise '74
A Dream for Christmas '73

Ron Senkowski
Let's Kill All the Lawyers '93

Mack Sennett
Cannonball/Dizzy Heights and
　Daring Hearts '16
Early Cinema Vol. 1 '19
Kid's Auto Race/Mabel's
　Married Life '15
The Lizzies of Mack Sennett
　'15
Mack Sennett Comedies: Vol. 1
　'21
Mack Sennett Comedies: Vol. 2
　'16
Mickey '17
Tillie's Punctured Romance '14

Mario Sequi
The Cobra '68
Tramplers '66

Michael Seresin
Homeboy '88

Yahoo Serious
Young Einstein '89

Coline Serreau
Mama, There's a Man in Your
　Bed '89
Three Men and a Cradle '85

Juan Carlos Sesanzo
Deadly Revenge '83

Alex Sessa
Amazons '86
Stormquest '87

Phillip Setbon
Mr. Frost '89

Javier Seto
The Castilian '63

Vernon Sewell
Blood Beast Terror '67
The Crimson Cult '68
Frenzy '46
Ghost Keeper '80
Ghost Ship '53
Ghosts of Berkeley Square '47
Horrors of Burke & Hare '71
Rogue's Yarn '56
Terror Ship '54
Uneasy Terms '48
The World Owes Me a Living
　'47

Nicholas Sgarro
Fortune Dane '86
The Happy Hooker '75

Michael Shackleton
Survivor '87

Susan Shadburne
Shadow Play '86

Tom Shadyac
Ace Ventura: Pet Detective '93

Matt Shaffen
Tabloid! '88

Josef Shaftel
Naked Hills '56

Krishna Shah
Deadly Thief '78
Hard Rock Zombies '85
Rivals '72
The River Niger '76

Maxwell Shane
Fear in the Night '47

John Patrick Shanley
Joe Versus the Volcano '90

Joy Shannon
Uptown Angel '90

Alan Shapiro
The Crush '93
Tiger Town '83

Ken Shapiro
The Groove Tube '72
Modern Problems '81

Mike Shapiro
Fireballs '90

Paul Shapiro
Heads '93
Hockey Night '84
Miracle at Moreaux '86

Jim Sharman
The Rocky Horror Picture
    Show '75
Shock Treatment '81

Alan Sharp
Little Treasure '85

Don Sharp
Bear Island '80
Dark Places '73
The Four Feathers '78
Guardian of the Abyss '82
Hennessy '75
Hold the Dream '85
Psychomania '73
Tears in the Rain '88
The Thirty-Nine Steps '79
Those Fantastic Flying Fools
    '67
What Waits Below '83
A Woman of Substance,
    Episode 1: Nest of Vipers
    '84
A Woman of Substance,
    Episode 2: The Secret is
    Revealed '84
A Woman of Substance,
    Episode 3: Fighting for the
    Dream '84

Ian Sharp
Codename Kyril '91
The Final Option '82
Robin Hood...The Legend:
    Robin Hood and the
    Sorcerer '83
Secret Weapon '90

Ben Sharpsteen
Dumbo '41
Pinocchio '40

William Shatner
Star Trek 5: The Final Frontier
    '89

Alfred Shaughnessy
Cat Girl '57
Suspended Alibi '56

Melville Shavelson
Cast a Giant Shadow '66
The Five Pennies '59
Houseboat '58
Ike '79
It Started in Naples '60
Legend of Valentino '75
A New Kind of Love '63

The Seven Little Foys '55
Yours, Mine & Ours '68

Chris Shaw
Split '90

Jimmy Shaw
Return of the Tiger '78

Tom Shaw
Courier of Death '84

Robert Shaye
Book of Love '91

Linda Shayne
Purple People Eater '88

Bashar Shbib
Julia Has Two Lovers '91

Jack Shea
Dayton's Devils '68

James K. Shea
Planet of the Dinosaurs '80

Barry Shear
Across 110th Street '72
The Crash of Flight 401 '78
The Deadly Trackers '73
Strike Force '75
The Todd Killings '71
Wild in the Streets '68

Harry Shearer
The History of White People in
    America '85
The History of White People in
    America: Vol. 2 '85
Portrait of a White Marriage '88

Donald Shebib
The Climb '87
Fish Hawk '79
Heartaches '82
Men of Steel '88

Martin Sheen
Cadence '89

Riki Shelach
The Last Winter '84
Mercenary Fighters '88

David Sheldon
Lovely...But Deadly '82

Forrest Sheldon
Between Fighting Men '32
Hell Fire Austin '32

Ron Shelton
Blaze '89
Bull Durham '88
White Men Can't Jump '92

Richard Shepard
Cool Blue '88
The Linguini Incident '92

Sam Shepard
Far North '88
Silent Tongue '92

Gordon Sheppard
Eliza's Horoscope '70

John Sheppard
Higher Education '88

Jack Sher
The Three Worlds of Gulliver
    '59

Jim Sheridan
The Field '90
In the Name of the Father '93
My Left Foot '89

Michael J. Sheridan
That's Entertainment, Part 3 '93

Edwin Sherin
The Father Clements Story '87
My Old Man's Place '71
Valdez is Coming '71

Arthur Sherman
Spy Trap '92

Gary Sherman
After the Shock '90
Dead and Buried '81
Lisa '90
Murderous Vision '91
Mysterious Two '82
Poltergeist 3 '88
Vice Squad '82
Wanted Dead or Alive '86

George Sherman
Against All Flags '52
Big Jake '71
Covered Wagon Days '40
Dawn Rider/Frontier Horizon
    '39
Frontier Horizon '39
The Kansas Terrors '39
The Last of the Redmen '47
Lonely Trail/Three Texas
    Steers '39
Outlaws of Sonora '38
Overland Stage Raiders '38
Pals of the Saddle '38
Panic Button '62
Rocky Mountain Rangers '40
Santa Fe Stampede '38
The Sombrero Kid '42
Three Texas Steers '39
Treasure of Pancho Villa '55
Western Double Feature 2:
    Wayne & Hale '80s
Wyoming Outlaw '39
X Marks the Spot '42

Lowell Sherman
Bachelor Apartment '31
False Faces '32
Morning Glory '33
The Royal Bed '31
She Done Him Wrong '33
Three Broadway Girls '32

Vincent Sherman
Adventures of Don Juan '49
Affair in Trinidad '52
All Through the Night '42
Bogie: The Last Hero '80
Ice Palace '60
Lone Star '52
Mr. Skeffington '44
The Young Philadelphians '59

Amir Shervan
Hollywood Cop '87

Bill Sherwood
Parting Glances '86

John Sherwood
The Creature Walks Among Us
    '56
The Monolith Monsters '57

Frank Shields
Project: Alien '89
Savage Attraction '83

Pat Shields
Frasier the Sensuous Lion '73

Slobodan Shijan
Secret Ingredient '92

Barry Shils
Motorama '91

Koji Shima
Golden Demon '53
Warning from Space '56

Nelson Shin
Transformers: The Movie '86

Kaneto Shindo
The Island '61
Onibaba '64

Masahiro Shinoda
Double Suicide '69
Gonza the Spearman '86
MacArthur's Children '85

Jack Sholder
Alone in the Dark '82
By Dawn's Early Light '89
The Hidden '87

A Nightmare on Elm Street 2:
    Freddy's Revenge '85
Renegades '89
12:01 '93

Lee Sholem
Escape from Planet Earth '67
Hell Ship Mutiny '57
Superman & the Mole Men '51
Tobor the Great '54

Roger Sholes
The Tale of Ruby Rose '87

Lindsay Shonteff
Big Zapper '73
Devil Doll '64
Fast Kill '73
The Killing Edge '86
Number 1 of the Secret Service
    '77
Permissive
Second Best Secret Agent in
    the Whole Wide World '65

Sig Shore
The Act '82
Shining Star '75
Sudden Death '85
The Survivalist '87

Lynn Shores
Charlie Chan at the Wax
    Museum '40
The Glory Trail '36
A Million to One '37

Richard Shorr
Witches' Brew '79

Ko Shu-How
Five Fighters from Shaolin '70s

Irene Shubik
Staying On '80

Herman Shumlin
Watch on the Rhine '43

Charles Shyer
Baby Boom '87
Father of the Bride '91
I Love Trouble '94
Irreconcilable Differences '84

James Shyman
Hollywood's New Blood '88
Slashdance '89

Mussef Sibay
A Woman, Her Men and Her
    Futon '92

Andy Sidaris
Do or Die '91
Fit to Kill '93
Guns '90
Hard Hunted '92
Hard Ticket to Hawaii '87
Malibu Express '85
Picasso Trigger '89
Savage Beach '89
Seven '79
Stacey '73

Drew Sidaris
Enemy Gold '93

George Sidney
Anchors Aweigh '45
Bathing Beauty '44
Bye, Bye, Birdie '63
Cass Timberlane '47
The Eddy Duchin Story '56
Half a Sixpence '67
The Harvey Girls '46
Holiday in Mexico '46
Jupiter's Darling '55
Key to the City '50
Kiss Me Kate '53
Pal Joey '57
Scaramouche '52
Show Boat '51
Thousands Cheer '43
The Three Musketeers '48
Viva Las Vegas '63
Young Bess '53

Scott Sidney
Charley's Aunt '25
The Nervous Wreck '26
Tarzan of the Apes '17

Don Siegel
The Annapolis Story '55
The Beguiled '70
Big Steal '49
The Black Windmill '74
Charley Varrick '73
Coogan's Bluff '68
Death of a Gunfighter '69
Dirty Harry '71
Escape from Alcatraz '79
Flaming Star '60
Hell is for Heroes '62
Invasion of the Body Snatchers
    '56
Jinxed '82
The Killers '64
Madigan '68
Private Hell 36 '54
Riot in Cell Block 11 '54
Rough Cut '80
The Shootist '76
Telefon '77
Two Mules for Sister Sara '70

Robert Siegel
The Line '80

James Signorelli
Easy Money '83
Elvira, Mistress of the Dark '88
Hotel Room '93

Dai Sijie
China, My Sorrow '89

Joel Silberg
Bad Guys '86
Breakin' '84
Catch the Heat '87
Lambada '89
Rappin' '85

Yoel Silberg
Kuni Lemel in Tel Aviv '77

Andrew Silver
Return '88

Joan Micklin Silver
Between the Lines '77
Big Girls Don't Cry...They Get
    Even '92
Chilly Scenes of Winter '79
Crossing Delancey '88
Finnegan Begin Again '84
Hester Street '75
Loverboy '89
Prison Stories: Women on the
    Inside '91
A Private Matter '92

Lynn Silver
Ghost Stories: Graveyard
    Thriller '86

Marisa Silver
He Said, She Said '91
Indecency '92
Old Enough '84
Permanent Record '88
Vital Signs '90

Raphael D. Silver
The Legend of the Wolf Woman
    '77
On the Yard '79

Ron Silver
Lifepod '93

Elliot Silverstein
Cat Ballou '65
Jailbait: Betrayed By Innocence
    '86
A Man Called Horse '70

Dario Silvester
Between God, the Devil & a
    Winchester '72

Lloyd A. Simandl
Beyond the Silhouette '90
Chained Heat 2 '92

Ladies of the Lotus '87
Possession: Until Death Do You Part '90
Ultimate Desires '91

Marc Simenon
By the Blood of Others '73

Lawrence L. Simeone
Blindfold: Acts of Obsession '94
Cop-Out '91
Eyes of the Beholder '92
Presumed Guilty '91

Allen Simmonds
Striker's Mountain '87

Anthony Simmons
Little Sweetheart '90

Sandor Simo
The Train Killer '83

Adam Simon
Body Chemistry 2: Voice of a Stranger '91
Brain Dead '89
Carnosaur '93

Francis Simon
The Chicken Chronicles '77

J.P. Simon
Cthulhu Mansion '91
Endless Descent '90
Pieces '83
Slugs '87
Where Time Began '77

Piquer Simon
Supersonic Man '78

Roger L. Simon
My Man Adam '86

Sylvan Simon
Abbott and Costello in Hollywood '45
Her Husband's Affairs '47
Lust for Gold '49
Rio Rita '42
Son of Lassie '45
Whistling in Brooklyn '43
Whistling in Dixie '42
Whistling in the Dark '41

Yves Simoneau
Memphis '91
Mother's Boys '94
Perfectly Normal '91
Pouvoir Intime '87
Till Death Do Us Part '92

Gregory Simpson
Rogue '76

Michael A. Simpson
Fast Food '89
Funland '89
Impure Thoughts '86
Sleepaway Camp 2: Unhappy Campers '88
Sleepaway Camp 3: Teenage Wasteland '89

Peter Simpson
Prom Night 3: The Last Kiss '89

Frank Sinatra
None But the Brave '65

Andrew Sinclair
Blue Blood '73
Tuxedo Warrior '82
Under Milk Wood '73

Gerald Seth Sindell
H.O.T.S. '79
Teenager '74

Alexander Singer
Captain Apache '71
Love has Many Faces '65

Gail Singer
Wisecracks '93

Stanford Singer
I Was a Teenage TV Terrorist '87

John Singleton
Boyz N the Hood '91
Poetic Justice '93

Ralph S. Singleton
Graveyard Shift '90

Gary Sinise
Miles from Home '88
Of Mice and Men '92

Bernhard Sinkel
Germany in Autumn '78

Bruce Sinofsky
Brother's Keeper '92

Gary Sinyor
Leon the Pig Farmer '93

Robert Siodmak
Bride of the Gorilla '51
Cobra Woman '44
Crimson Pirate '52
Criss Cross '48
Dark Mirror '46
Son of Dracula '43
The Spiral Staircase '46
The Strange Affair of Uncle Harry '45

Douglas Sirk
First Legion '51
Imitation of Life '59
Magnificent Obsession '54
A Time to Love & a Time to Die '58
Written on the Wind '56

Marlon Sirko
Perfect Killer '77

Hal Sitowitz
Last Cry for Help '79

Yuri Sivo
Mortal Sins '90

Alf Sjoberg
Miss Julie '50
Torment '44

John Sjogren
Money to Burn '94

Vilgot Sjoman
I Am Curious (Yellow) '67

Victor Sjostrom
He Who Gets Slapped '24
The Outlaw and His Wife '17
The Phantom Chariot '20
Under the Red Robe '36
The Wind '28

Calvin Skaggs
The Fig Tree '87

Jerzy Skolimowski
Deep End '70
Hands Up '81
King, Queen, Knave '72
The Lightship '86
Moonlighting '82
The Shout '78
Success is the Best Revenge '84
Torrents of Spring '90

Guy Slater
A Pocketful of Rye '87

Bob Slatzer
Big Foot '72
Hellcats '68

John Sledge
The Invisible Avenger '58
New Orleans After Dark '58

Wladyslaw Slesicki
In Desert and Wilderness '73

Paul Sloane
The Coming of Amos '25
Consolation Marriage '31

Rick Sloane
Hobgoblins '80s
Marked for Murder '89
Mind, Body & Soul '92
Vice Academy '88
Vice Academy 2 '90
Vice Academy 3 '91
Visitants '87

Edward Sloman
Lost Zeppelin '29

George Sluizer
Red Desert Penitentiary '83
Utz '93
The Vanishing '88
The Vanishing '93

John Smallcombe
An African Dream '90

Ralph Smart
Curtain Up '53
Robin Hood: The Movie '55

Robert J. Smawley
American Eagle '90
Murphy's Fault '88
River of Diamonds '90

Jack Smight
Airport '75 '75
Airport '77 '77
Damnation Alley '77
Fast Break '79
Harper '66
Holocaust Survivors...Remembrance of Love '83
The Illustrated Man '69
Intimate Power '89
Loving Couples '80
Midway '76
No Way to Treat a Lady '68
Number One with a Bullet '87
Roll of Thunder, Hear My Cry '78
The Secret War of Harry Frigg '68

Bruce Smith
Bebe's Kids '92

Bud Smith
Johnny Be Good '88

Charles Martin Smith
Boris and Natasha: The Movie '92
Fifty/Fifty '93
Trick or Treat '86

Cliff Smith
Radio Patrol '37

Clive A. Smith
Rock & Rule '83

Howard Smith
Marjoe '72

Kent Smith
Forever and a Day '43

Kiki Smith
Cave Girls '82

Mel Smith
The Tall Guy '89

Noel Mason Smith
The Night Patrol '26

Peter Smith
No Surrender '86

Richard Smith
Trident Force '88

Alan Smithee
Appointment with Fear '85
Bloodsucking Pharoahs of Pittsburgh '80s
City in Fear '80
Fatal Charm '92
Ghost Fever '87
Gypsy Angels '94

I Love N.Y. '87
The Indiscreet Mrs. Jarvis
Iron Cowboy '68
Let's Get Harry '87
Morgan Stewart's Coming Home '87
The Shrimp on the Barbie '90
Stitches '85

Stephen Smoke
Final Impact '91
Street Crimes '92

Sandy Smolan
Rachel River '89

Phil Smoot
The Dark Power '85

Skott Snider
Miracle Beach '92

Michael Snyder
Caged in Paradiso '89

Michele (Michael) Soavi
The Church '90
The Devil's Daughter '91
Stagefright '87

Mark Sobel
Access Code '84
Sweet Revenge '87
Trial and Error '92

Steven Soderberg
Fallen Angels 2 '93
Kafka '91
King of the Hill '93
sex, lies and videotape '89

Hugo Sofovich
Departamento Compartido '85

Iain Softley
Backbeat '94

Joel Soisson
Maniac Cop 3 '93

Peter Solan
The Boxer and Death '63

Gilberto Martinez Solares
Face of the Screaming Werewolf '59

Russell Solberg
Forced to Kill '93
Payback '90

Alfred Sole
Alice Sweet Alice '76
Pandemonium '82
Tanya's Island '81

Sergio Sollima
The Family '73

Peter J. Solmo
Jack & the Beanstalk '76

Todd Solondz
Fear, Anxiety and Depression '89

Andrew Solt
This is Elvis '81

Ola Solum
The Polar Bear King '94
Turnaround '87

Paul Solvay
Devil's Wedding Night '73

Josef Sommer
Thoughts are Free '84

Stephen Sommers
The Adventures of Huck Finn '93
Catch Me...If You Can '89

Barry Sonnenfeld
The Addams Family '91
Addams Family Values '93
For Love or Money '93

Dror Soref
The Seventh Coin '92

Carlos Sorin
Eversmile New Jersey '89

Dimitri Sotirakis
Beverly Hills Brats '89

Jim Sotos
Forced Entry '75
Hot Moves '84
Sweet 16 '81

Colin South
In Too Deep '90

Larry Spangler
Joshua '76

Hans A. Spanuth
The Great Train Robbery: Cinema Begins '03

Teresa Sparks
Over the Summer '85

Robert Sparr
A Swingin' Summer '65

Shane Spaulding
Armed for Action '92

Martin Speer
The Hasty Heart '86

Michael Spence
Edge of Honor '91

Alan Spencer
Hexed '93

Benton Spencer
The Club '94

Jane Spencer
Little Noises '91

Josh Spencer
Easy Kill '89

Norman Spencer
Rainbow's End '35

Robert Spera
Witchcraft '88

Penelope Spheeris
The Beverly Hillbillies '93
The Boys Next Door '85
Decline of Western Civilization 1 '81
Decline of Western Civilization 2: The Metal Years '88
Dudes '87
Hollywood Vice Sqaud '86
The Little Rascals '93
Prison Stories: Women on the Inside '91
Suburbia '83
Thunder & Mud '89
Wayne's World '92

Larry Spiegel
Survival Run '80

Scott Spiegel
Intruder '88

Steven Spielberg
Always '89
Amazing Stories '85
Close Encounters of the Third Kind '77
The Color Purple '85
Columbo: Murder By the Book '71
Duel '71
Empire of the Sun '87
E.T.: The Extra-Terrestrial '82
Hook '91
Indiana Jones and the Last Crusade '89
Indiana Jones and the Temple of Doom '84
Jaws '75
Jurassic Park '93
Night Gallery '69
1941 '79
Raiders of the Lost Ark '81

Spielberg

Spielberg ►cont.

Schindler's List '93
The Sugarland Express '74
Twilight Zone: The Movie '83

Martin J. Spinelli
Sourdough '77

Alan Spires
Little Boy Lost '78

Murray Douglas Sporup
Rock, Baby, Rock It '57

Roger Spottiswoode
Air America '90
And the Band Played On '93
The Best of Times '86
The Last Innocent Man '87
The Pursuit of D.B. Cooper '81
Shoot to Kill '88
Stop! or My Mom Will Shoot '92
Terror Train '80
Third Degree Burn '89
Time Flies When You're Alive '89
Turner and Hooch '89
Under Fire '83

G.D. Spradlin
The Only Way Home '72

Tim Spring
Reason to Die '90

R.G. Springsteen
Apache Uprising '66
Arizona Cowboy '49
Hellfire '48
Hills of Oklahoma '50
Hostile Guns '67
Johnny Reno '66
Oklahoma Annie '51
The Red Menace '49
Stagecoach to Denver '46
Vigilantes of Boom Town '46
When Gangland Strikes '56

Robin Spry
A Cry in the Night '93
Drying Up the Streets '76
Keeping Track '86
Obsessed '88

Pasquale Squitieri
Blood Brothers '74
Corleone '79
Third Solution '89

Stephen Stafford
I Posed for Playboy '91

Juan Bautista Stagnaro
Under the Earth '86

Eric Steven Stahl
Final Approach '91

John M. Stahl
Immortal Sergeant '43
The Keys of the Kingdom '44
Letter of Introduction '38

Roy Stahl
Scarlet Spear '54

Sylvester Stallone
Paradise Alley '78
Rocky 2 '79
Rocky 3 '82
Rocky 4 '85
Staying Alive '83

John Stanley
Nightmare in Blood '75

Michael Stanley
Attack of the Beast Creatures '85

Paul Stanley
Cotter '72
The Ultimate Imposter '79

Richard Stanley
Dust Devil '93
Hardware '90

David L. Stanton
Chill Factor '90

Richard Stanton
American Pluck '25

Jeff Stanzler
Jumpin' at the Boneyard '92

George Stapleford
Mountain Charlie '80

Wladislaw Starewicz
Early Russian Cinema, Vol. 3: Starewicz's Fantasies '15

Bruce Starr
Boogey Man 2 '83

Ringo Starr
Born to Boogie '72

Steven Starr
Joey Breaker '93

Jack Starrett
Cleopatra Jones '73
Fatal Chase '77
Hollywood Man '76
Kiss My Grits '82
The Losers '70
Mr. Horn '79
On the Edge: The Survival of Dana '79
Race with the Devil '75
Run, Angel, Run! '69
Slaughter '72
A Small Town in Texas '76
Walking Tall: The Final Chapter '77

Ralph Staub
Country Gentlemen '36
Danger Ahead '40
Gene Autry Matinee Double Feature #3 '53
The Mandarin Mystery '37

Ray Dennis Steckler
Eegah! '62
The Hollywood Strangler Meets the Skid Row Slasher '79
Incredibly Strange Creatures Who Stopped Living and Became Mixed-Up Zombies '63
Rat Pfink a Boo-Boo '66
Sinthia: The Devil's Doll '70
The Thrill Killers '65
Wild Guitar '62

David Steensland
Escapes '86

Giorgio Stegani
Beyond the Law '68

Herbert Stein
Escape to Love '82

Ken Stein
Killer Instinct '92
The Rain Killer '90

Paul Stein
Black Limelight '38
Counterblast '48
Heart's Desire '37
Lottery Bride '30
Mimi '35
Sin Takes a Holiday '30

David Steinberg
Casey at the Bat '85
Going Berserk '83
Paternity '81

David Max Steinberg
Severance '88

Michael Steinberg
Bodies, Rest & Motion '93
The Waterdance '91

Ziggy Steinberg
The Boss' Wife '86

Danny Steinmann
Friday the 13th, Part 5: A New Beginning '85
Savage Streets '83

Jos Stelling
The Pointsman '86
Rembrandt—1669 '77

Steno
Flatfoot '78

Frederick Stephani
Flash Gordon: Rocketship '36

A.C. Stephen
Lady Godiva Rides '68
Orgy of the Dead '65
Saturday Night Sleazies, Vol. 1 '66

William Sterling
Alice's Adventures in Wonderland '72

Daniel Stern
Rookie of the Year '93

David Hillard Stern
Morning Glory '93

Noah Stern
Pyrates '91

Sandor Stern
Amityville 4 '89
Assassin '86
Dangerous Pursuit '89
Duplicates '92
Glitz '88
Jericho Fever '93
John & Yoko: A Love Story '85
Pin '88
Web of Deceit '90

Steven Hilliard Stern
The Ambush Murders '82
Anatomy of a Seduction '79
The Devil & Max Devlin '81
Draw! '81
Final Notice '89
Forbidden Love '82
Getting Physical '84
Harrad Summer '74
I Wonder Who's Killing Her Now? '76
Kill My Wife...Please!
Love & Murder '91
Mazes and Monsters '82
Miracle on Ice '81
Murder in Space '85
Not Quite Human '87
Obsessive Love '84
The Park is Mine '85
Personals '82
Portrait of a Showgirl '82
Rolling Vengeance '87
A Small Killing '81
Undergrads '85
Weekend War '88
Young Love, First Love '79

Tom Stern
Freaked '93

Andrew Stevens
Night Eyes 3 '93
Scorned '93
The Terror Within 2 '91

Arnold Stevens
Attack of the Swamp Creature '75

Art Stevens
The Fox and the Hound '81

David Stevens
Kansas '88
Roses Bloom Twice '77
A Town Like Alice '85

George Stevens
Alice Adams '35
Annie Oakley '35
A Damsel in Distress '37
The Diary of Anne Frank '59
Giant '56
The Greatest Story Ever Told '65
Gunga Din '39
I Remember Mama '48
Kentucky Kernels '34
The More the Merrier '43
Penny Serenade '41
A Place in the Sun '51
Quality Street '37
Separate But Equal '91
Shane '53
Swing Time '36
Talk of the Town '42
Vivacious Lady '38
Woman of the Year '42

Leslie Stevens
The Outer Limits: Galaxy Being '63
Three Kinds of Heat '87

Mark Stevens
Cry Vengeance '54

Robert Stevens
Never Love a Stranger '58

Stella Stevens
The Ranch '88

Robert Stevenson
The Absent-Minded Professor '61
Bedknobs and Broomsticks '71
Blackbeard's Ghost '67
Darby O'Gill & the Little People '59
Dishonored Lady '47
Forever and a Day '43
The Gnome-Mobile '67
Herbie Rides Again '74
In Search of the Castaways '62
The Island at the Top of the World '74
Jane Eyre '44
Joan of Paris '42
Johnny Tremain & the Sons of Liberty '58
Kidnapped '60
King Solomon's Mines '37
The Las Vegas Story '52
The Love Bug '68
The Man Who Lived Again '36
Mary Poppins '64
The Misadventures of Merlin Jones '63
Monkey's Uncle '65
My Dog, the Thief '69
My Forbidden Past '51
Nine Days a Queen '34
Non-Stop New York '37
Old Yeller '57
One of Our Dinosaurs Is Missing '75
The Shaggy D.A. '76
Son of Flubber '63
That Darn Cat '65
Tom Brown's School Days '40
Walk Softly, Stranger '50

Alan L. Stewart
Ghetto Blaster '89
Ghostriders '87

Douglas Day Stewart
Listen to Me '89
Thief of Hearts '84

John Stewart
Action U.S.A. '89
Hidden Obsession '92

Larry Stewart
The Initiation '84

Peter Stewart
Adventure Island '47
Arizona Gangbusters '40
Gun Code '40
State Department File 649 '49

Robert Stewart
Mark of the Beast
Rock & Roll Cowboys '92

Roger Stigliano
Fun Down There '88

Ben Stiller
Reality Bites '94

Mauritz Stiller
The Atonement of Gosta Berling '24
Hotel Imperial '27
Thomas Graal's Best Film '17
Thomas Graal's First Child '18
Treasure of Arne '19

Whit Stillman
Barcelona '94
Metropolitan '90

Alexander Stitt
Grendel, Grendel, Grendel '82

Mark Stock
Midnight Movie Massacre '88

John Stockwell
Undercover '87

Ben Stoloff
The Affairs of Annabel '38
It's a Joke, Son! '47
Night of Terror '33
Palooka '34
Sea Devils '37
Transatlantic Merry-Go-Round '34

Victor Stoloff
Washington Affair '77

Andrew L. Stone
The Girl Said No '37
Hell's Headquarters '32
Hi Diddle Diddle '43
The Last Voyage '60
Sensations of 1945 '44
Song of Norway '70
Stormy Weather '43

Norman Stone
Shadowlands '85
The Vision '87

Oliver Stone
Born on the Fourth of July '89
The Doors '91
The Hand '81
Heaven and Earth '93
JFK '91
Natural Born Killers '94
Platoon '86
Salvador '86
Seizure '74
Talk Radio '88
Wall Street '87

Virginia Lively Stone
Money to Burn '83
Run If You Can '87
The Treasure of Jamaica Reef '74

Tom Stoppard
Rosencrantz & Guildenstern Are Dead '90

Esben Storm
In Search of Anna '79

Howard Storm
Once Bitten '85
The Three Little Pigs '84

Jerome Storm
Courtin' Wildcats '29
Sweet Adeline '26

Mark Story
Odd Jobs '85

Thomas L. Story
Last Frontier '32

Larry N. Stouffer
Twisted Brain '74

Mark Stouffer
Man Outside '88

Louis Clyde Stouman
Operation Dames '59

Walter Strate
Violated '53**

Joe Straw
Kill or Be Killed '93

Frank Strayer
Blondie '38
Blondie Has Trouble '40
Blondie in Society '41
Blondie Takes a Vacation '39
Blondie's Blessed Event '42
Condemned to Live '35
Death from a Distance '36
Fugitive Road '34
The Ghost Walks '34
In the Money '34
It's a Great Life '43
The Monster Walks '32
Murder at Midnight '31
Tangled Destinies '32
The Vampire Bat '32

Barbra Streisand
The Prince of Tides '91
Yentl '83

Joseph Strick
The Balcony '63
Tropic of Cancer '70
Ulysses '67

John Strickland
Prime Suspect 2 '93

Herbert L. Strock
Blood of Dracula '57
The Crawling Hand '63
How to Make a Monster '58
Man on the Run '74
Monster '78
Teenage Frankenstein '58
Witches' Brew '79

William R. Stromberg
The Crater Lake Monster '77

Jonathan Stryker
Curtains '83

Brian Stuart
Sorceress '82

Mel Stuart
The Chisholms '79
Happy Anniversary 007: 25 Years of James Bond '87
I Love My...Wife '70
If It's Tuesday, This Must Be Belgium '69
Mean Dog Blues '78
Sophia Loren: Her Own Story '80
The Triangle Factory Fire Scandal '79
Willy Wonka & the Chocolate Factory '71

John Sturges
Bad Day at Black Rock '54
By Love Possessed '61
The Capture '50
Chino '75
The Eagle Has Landed '77
Escape from Fort Bravo '53
The Great Escape '63
Gunfight at the O.K. Corral '57
The Hallelujah Trail '65
Hour of the Gun '67
Ice Station Zebra '68
Joe Kidd '72
Last Train from Gun Hill '59
The Law and Jake Wade '58
The Magnificent Seven '60
The Magnificent Yankee '50
Marooned '69
McQ '74
Never So Few '59
Underwater '55

Preston Sturges
The Beautiful Blonde from Bashful Bend '49
Christmas in July '40
The Great McGinty '40
The Great Moment '44
Hail the Conquering Hero '44
The Lady Eve '41

Miracle of Morgan's Creek '44
The Palm Beach Story '42
The Sin of Harold Diddlebock '47
Sullivan's Travels '41
Unfaithfully Yours '48

Charles Sturridge
Aria '88
Brideshead Revisited '81
A Handful of Dust '88
Where Angels Fear to Tread '91

Richard Styles
Escape '90
Shallow Grave '87

Bobby Suarez
American Commandos '84
Pay or Die '83
Warriors of the Apocalypse '85

Eliseo Subiela
Man Facing Southeast '86

Arne Sucksdorff
The Great Adventure '53

L. Sudjio
Black Magic Terror '79

Andrew Sugarman
Basic Training '86

Toshio Sugie
Saga of the Vagabond '59

Terrence Sul
Wonsan Operation '78

Fred G. Sullivan
Cold River '81

Jack Sullivan
The Charge of the Light Brigade '36

Kevin Sullivan
Anne of Avonlea '87
Anne of Green Gables '85
Lantern Hill '90
Wild Pony '83

Dirk Summers
Survival of Spaceship Earth '90

Jeremy Summers
Five Golden Dragons '67
The House of 1000 Dolls '67

Walter Summers
House of Mystery '41
The Human Monster '39

Shirley Sun
Iron & Silk '91

Cedric Sundstrom
American Ninja 3: Blood Hunt '89
American Ninja 4: The Annihilation '91
Captive Rage '88
The Revenger '90

Neal Sundstrom
Howling 5: The Rebirth '89

Jack A. Sunseri
The Chilling '89

Fred Surin
The Bride Is Much Too Beautiful '58

Stephen Surjik
Wayne's World 2 '93

Henry Suso
Death Sport '78

Jean-Claude Sussfeld
Elle Voit des Nains Partout '83

Edward Sutherland
Behind the Front '26
Beyond Tomorrow '40
The Devil Thumbs a Ride/Having Wonderful Crime '47
Every Day's a Holiday '38

The Flying Deuces '39
Having Wonderful Crime '45
International House '33
The Invisible Woman '40
It's the Old Army Game '26
Mr. Robinson Crusoe '32
The Navy Comes Through '42
One Night in the Tropics '40
Sing Your Worries Away '42

Kiefer Sutherland
Last Light '93

Noribumi Suzuki
Shogun's Ninja '83

Jan Svankmajer
Alice '88

Peter Svatek
Mystery of the Million Dollar Hockey Puck '80s

E.W. Swackhamer
The Amazing Spider-Man '77
Are You Lonesome Tonight '92
The Dain Curse '78
Death at Love House '75
Death Sentence '74
Man & Boy '71
Night Terror '76
Perfect Family '92
The Rousters '90
The Secret Passion of Robert Clayton '92
Terror at London Bridge '85
The Winds of Kitty Hawk '78

Bob Swaim
Half Moon Street '86
Masquerade '88

Don Swan
Gore-Met Zombie Chef From Hell '87

Bob Sweeney
Return to Mayberry '85

Charles Swenson
Little Rascals Christmas Special '79

Arthur Swerdloff
Road Racers '59

Larry Swerdlove
The Skateboard Kid '93

David Swift
Good Neighbor Sam '64
How to Succeed in Business without Really Trying '67
The Interns '62
The Parent Trap '61
Pollyanna '60

Saul Swimmer
Mrs. Brown, You've Got a Lovely Daughter '68

Michael Switzer
Fergie & Andrew: Behind Palace Doors '93
The Lightning Incident '91
Nitti: The Enforcer '88

Ron Switzer
Science Crazed

Peter Sykes
Demons of the Mind '72
Jesus '79
Night of the Laughing Dead '75
To the Devil, A Daughter '76

Paul Sylbert
The Steagle '71

Istvan Szabo
Father '67
Hanussen '88
Love Film '70
Meeting Venus '91
Mephisto '81
25 Fireman's Street '73

Laszlo Szabo
Colonel Redl '84

William Szarka
Phantom Brother '88
South Bronx Heroes '85

Andras Szirtes
After the Revolution '90

Samy Szlingerbaum
Brussels Transit '80

Gyorgy Szomjas
Bad Guys '79

Reszo Szoreny
A Happy New Year! '79

Boris Szulzinger
Mama Dracula '80
Shame of the Jungle '90

Jeannot Szwarc
Bug '75
Code Name: Diamond Head '77
Enigma '82
Jaws 2 '78
The Murders in the Rue Morgue '86
Santa Claus: The Movie '85
Sex Through a Window '72
Somewhere in Time '80
Supergirl '84

Micheal Taav
The Paint Job '93

Sylvio Tabet
Beastmaster 2: Through the Portal of Time '91

Carlos Enrique Taboada
El Libro de Piedra '68

Jean-Charles Tacchella
Cousin, Cousine '76
The Last Winters '71

Gene Taft
Blame It on the Night '84

Kidlat Tahimik
Perfumed Nightmare '89
Turumba '84

Robert Taicher
Inside Out '91

Tibor Takacs
The Gate '87
Gate 2 '92
I, Madman '89
Red Shoe Diaries 2: Double Dare '92

Isao Takahata
Grave of the Fireflies '88

Glen Takakjian
Metamorphosis: The Alien Factor '93

Rachel Talalay
Freddy's Dead: The Final Nightmare '91
Ghost in the Machine '93

Igor Talankin
Tchaikovsky '71

Greg Tallas
Assignment Skybolt '80s
Cataclysm '81
Prehistoric Women '50

Richard Talmadge
Detour to Danger '45
Devil Horse '32
Project Moon Base '53

Harry Tampa
Fairytales '79
Nocturna '79

Shigeo Tanaka
Gamera vs. Barugon '66

Tokuzo Tanaka
Zatoichi: The Blind Swordsman's Vengeance '66

Senkichi Taniguhi
The Gambling Samurai '60
What's Up, Tiger Lily? '66

Terrell Tannen
A Minor Miracle '83
Shadows in the Storm '88

William Tannen
Deadly Illusion '87
Flashpoint '84
Hero and the Terror '88

Alain Tanner
In the White City '83
Jonah Who Will Be 25 in the Year 2000 '76

Robert Tanos
Fly with the Hawk

Robert Tansey
Arizona Roundup '42
Death Valley Rangers '44
The Driftin' Kid '41
Driftin' River '46
Dynamite Canyon '41
God's Country '46
Haunted Ranch '43
Lone Star Law Men '42
Outlaw Trail '44
Riding the Sunset Trail '41
Song of Old Wyoming '45
Sonora Stagecoach '44
Texas to Bataan '42
Western Mail '42
Where Trails End '42
Wild West '46
Wildfire '45

Daniel Taplitz
Black Magic '92
Nightlife '90

Michael Tarantini
Crimebusters '79

Quentin Tarantino
Pulp Fiction '94
Reservoir Dogs '92

Andrei Tarkovsky
Andrei Rublev '66
The Mirror '75
My Name is Ivan '62
The Sacrifice '86
Solaris '72
Stalker '79

Bela Tarr
Almanac of Fall

Max Tash
The Runnin' Kind '89

Frank Tashlin
The Alphabet Murders '65
Artists and Models '55
Cinderfella '60
Disorderly Orderly '64
Fuller Brush Man '48
The Geisha Boy '58
The Girl Can't Help It '56
The Glass Bottom Boat '66
Hollywood or Bust '56
Son of Paleface '52
Susan Slept Here '54

Nadia Tass
Malcolm '86
Pure Luck '91
Rikky and Pete '88

Jacques Tati
Jour de Fete '48
Mr. Hulot's Holiday '53
Mon Oncle '58
Parade '74
Playtime '67

John Tatoulis
The Silver Stallion: King of the Wild Brumbies '94

Norman Taurog
The Adventures of Tom Sawyer '38
Birds & the Bees '56
Blue Hawaii '62
Boys Town '38
Broadway Melody of 1940 '40
Bundle of Joy '56
The Caddy '53
Dr. Goldfoot and the Bikini
  Machine '66
Double Trouble '67
G.I. Blues '60
Girl Crazy '43
Girls! Girls! Girls! '62
Hold 'Em Jail '32
It Happened at the World's Fair
  '63
Jumping Jacks '52
Little Nellie Kelly '40
Live a Little, Love a Little '68
Men of Boys Town '41
Mrs. Wiggs of the Cabbage
  Patch '42
Palm Springs Weekend '63
Pardners '56
Presenting Lily Mars '43
Rich, Young and Pretty '51
Speedway '68
Spinout '66
The Stooge '51
Sunny Skies '30
That Midnight Kiss '49
Tickle Me '65
The Toast of New Orleans '50
Words and Music '48
Young Tom Edison '40

Bertrand Tavernier
Beatrice '88
The Clockmaker '76
Coup de Torchon '81
Daddy Nostalgia '90
Death Watch '80
The Judge and the Assassin
  '75
Life and Nothing But '89
Round Midnight '86
Spoiled Children '77
A Sunday in the Country '84

Paolo Taviani
Allonsanfan '73
Fiorile '93
Good Morning, Babylon '87
Kaos '85
The Night of the Shooting Stars
  '82
Padre Padrone '77

Vittorio Taviani
Fiorile '93
Good Morning, Babylon '87
Kaos '85
The Night of the Shooting Stars
  '82
Padre Padrone '77

Baz Taylor
Happy Since I Met You '89
Near Misses '91

Don Taylor
Damien: Omen 2 '78
The Diamond Trap '91
Escape from the Planet of the
  Apes '71
The Final Countdown '80
Going for the Gold: The Bill
  Johnson Story '85
Great Scout & Cathouse
  Thursday '76
Island of Dr. Moreau '77
Listen to Your Heart '83
My Wicked, Wicked Ways '84
Red Flag: The Ultimate Game
  '81
Ride the Wild Surf '64
Secret Weapons '85
September Gun '83
Tom Sawyer '73
Wild Women '70

Judd Taylor
The Christmas Coal Mine
  Miracle '77
Danielle Steel's Kaleidoscope
  '92
Foxfire '87
Future Cop '76
License to Kill '84
Lovey: A Circle of Children 2
  '82
Mary White '77
Out of the Darkness '85
Packin' It In '83
Question of Honor '80
Return to Earth '76
Say Goodbye, Maggie Cole '72
Search for the Gods '75

Ray Taylor
Adventures of Smilin' Jack '43
The Adventures of the Flying
  Cadets '44
Black Hills '48
Border Feud '47
Boss of Bullion City '41
Bury Me Not On the Lone
  Prairie '41
Check Your Guns '48
Cheyenne Takes Over '47
Dick Tracy: The Original Serial,
  Vol. 1 '37
Dick Tracy: The Original Serial,
  Vol. 2 '37
Don Winslow of the Coast
  Guard '43
Don Winslow of the Navy '43
Fighting Vigilantes '47
Flaming Frontiers '38
Ghost Town Renegades '47
Hawaiian Buckaroo '38
The Hawk of Powder River '48
Lost City of the Jungle '45
Master Key '44
Mystery of the Hooded
  Horseman '37
Mystery of the Riverboat '44
Outlaw Country '49
The Painted Stallion '37
Panamint's Bad Man '38
The Perils of Pauline '34
Phantom of the Air '33
Pony Post '40
Rawhide '38
Return of Chandu '34
Return of the Lash '47
Riders of Death Valley '41
Riders of Pasco Basin '40
Stage to Mesa City '48
The Throwback '35
The Tioga Kid '48
The Vigilantes are Coming '36
West to Glory '47
Wild Country '47
Winners of the West '40

Richard Taylor
Stingray '78

Robert Taylor
Nine Lives of Fritz the Cat '74

Roderick Taylor
Instant Karma '90

Sam Taylor
Ambassador Bill '31
Coquette '29
Dr. Jack/For Heaven's Sake '26
Dubarry '30
For Heaven's Sake '26
The Freshman '25
My Best Girl '27
Nothing But Trouble '44
The Taming of the Shrew '29
The Tempest '28
The Tempest/The Eagle '27

Ron Teachworth
Going Back '83

Lewis Teague
Alligator '80
Cat's Eye '85
Cujo '83
Deadlock '91

Fighting Back '82
The Jewel of the Nile '85
Lady in Red '79
Navy SEALS '90

Andre Techine
Rendez-vous '85
Scene of the Crime '87

Frank Telford
The Bamboo Saucer '68

Julien Temple
Absolute Beginners '86
Aria '88
Earth Girls are Easy '89
Running Out of Luck '86
The Secret Policeman's Other
  Ball '82

Andy Tennant
The Amy Fisher Story '93
Keep the Change '92

Del Tenney
Curse of the Living Corpse '64
Horror of Party Beach '64
I Eat Your Skin '64

Kevin S. Tenney
The Cellar '90
Night of the Demons '88
Peacemaker '90
Witchboard '87
Witchboard 2: The Devil's
  Doorway '93
WitchTrap '89

Pen Tennyson
Convoy '40

John Tenorio
Grad Night '81

George Terwilliger
Married? '26

Hiroshi Teshigahara
Face of Another '66
Rikyu '90
Woman in the Dunes '64

Duccio Tessari
Blood at Sundown '68

Ted Tetzlaff
Fighting Father Dunne '48
Riff-Raff '48
Son of Sinbad '55
The White Tower '50
The Window '49

Monica Teuber
Magdalene '88

Akiva Tevet
Atalia '85

Joan Tewkesbury
Acorn People '82
Cold Sassy Tree '89
Old Boyfriends '79
Strangers '91
Sudie & Simpson '90
Tenth Month '79

Peter Tewkesbury
Emil and the Detective '64
Stay Away, Joe '68
The Trouble with Girls (and
  How To Get Into It) '69

Leon Thau
Save the Lady '82

Otis Thayer
Riders of the Range '24

Groham Theakston
Tripods: The White Mountains
  '84

Harvey Thew
Confessions of a Vice Baron
  '42

Rolf Thiele
Tonio Kroger '65

Albie Thomas
Palm Beach '79

Antony Thomas
Code Name: Chaos '90

Dave Thomas
The Experts '89
Strange Brew '83

Gerald Thomas
The Cariboo Trail '50
Carry On at Your Convenience
  '71
Carry On Behind '75
Carry On Cleo '65
Carry On Cruising '62
Carry On Dick '75
Carry On Doctor '68
Carry On Emmanuelle '78
Carry On England '76
Carry On Nurse '59
Carry On 'Round the Bend '72
Carry On Screaming '66
Follow That Camel '67
Second Victory '87
Time Lock '57
The Vicious Circle '57

John G. Thomas
Arizona Heat '87
Banzai Runner '86
Tin Man '83

Ralph Thomas
Above Us the Waves '56
The Big Scam '79
Conspiracy of Hearts '60
Doctor at Large '57
Doctor at Sea '56
Doctor in Distress '63
Doctor in the House '53
It's Not the Size That Counts
  '74
No Love for Johnnie '60
Quest for Love '71
A Tale of Two Cities '58

Ralph L. Thomas
Apprentice to Murder '88
The Terry Fox Story '83
Ticket to Heaven '81

Scott Thomas
Silent Assassins '88

William C. Thomas
Big Town '47
Big Town After Dark '47
Dark Mountain '44
Navy Way '44

Harry Z. Thomason
The Day It Came to Earth '77
Encounter with the Unknown
  '75
Hootch Country Boys '75

Brett Thompson
Adventures in Dinosaur City '92

Caroline Thompson
Black Beauty '94

Don Thompson
Ugly Little Boy '77

**Donald W.
Thompson**
Blood on the Mountain '88
Heaven's Heroes '88
Mannikin '77
The Prodigal Planet '88

Ernest Thompson
1969 '89

J. Lee Thompson
The Ambassador '84
Battle for the Planet of the
  Apes '73
The Blue Knight '75
Cabo Blanco '81
Cape Fear '61
Conquest of the Planet of the
  Apes '72
Death Wish 4: The Crackdown
  '87
The Evil That Men Do '84
Firewalker '86

Flame Over India '60
The Greek Tycoon '78
The Guns of Navarone '61
Happy Birthday to Me '81
Huckleberry Finn '74
King Solomon's Mines '85
MacKenna's Gold '69
Messenger of Death '88
Murphy's Law '86
The Reincarnation of Peter
  Proud '75
St. Ives '76
Taras Bulba '62
Ten to Midnight '83
Tiger Bay '59
The White Buffalo '77
The Widow '76

Lee Thompson
Kinjite: Forbidden Subjects '89

Marcus Thompson
Adventures Beyond Belief '87

Peter Thompson
Films by Peter Thompson '87

Robert Thompson
Words by Heart '84

Robert C. Thompson
Bud and Lou '78

**Christian Braad
Thomsen**
Ladies on the Rocks '83

Chris Thomson
The Empty Beach '85
Swimsuit: The Movie '89
Three's Trouble '85
Waterfront '83

Michael Thornhill
Between Wars '74
The Everlasting Secret Family
  '88
Robbery '85

Dave Thorpe
Under Montana Skies '30

Jerry Thorpe
All God's Children '80
Kung Fu '72
The Possessed '77
A Question of Love '78
Smile, Jenny, You're Dead '74
Wonderland Cove '75

Richard Thorpe
Above Suspicion '43
The Adventures of Huckleberry
  Finn '39
After Midnight '33
All the Brothers Were Valiant
  '53
Athena '54
The Black Hand '50
Challenge to Lassie '49
A Date with Judy '48
Desert of the Lost '27
Double Wedding '37
Fiesta '47
Fun in Acapulco '63
The Girl Who Had Everything
  '53
The Great Caruso '51
Green Eyes '34
The Honeymoon Machine '61
The Horizontal Lieutenant '62
Ivanhoe '52
Jailhouse Rock '57
The King Murder Case '32
King of the Kongo '29
Knights of the Round Table '53
The Lone Defender '32
Malaya '49
On an Island with You '48
Prisoner of Zenda '52
Probation '32
The Prodigal '55
The Secrets of Wu Sin '32
The Student Prince '54
The Sun Comes Up '49
Tarzan Escapes '36

Tarzan Finds a Son '39
Tarzan's New York Adventure '42
Tarzan's Secret Treasure '41
The Thin Man Goes Home '44
Three Little Words '50
Thrill of a Romance '45
Two Girls and a Sailor '44
Vengeance Valley '51
White Cargo '42
Wild Horse '31

Alexis Thurn-Taxis
A Night for Crime '42

N.G. Tien Tsu
The Bloody Fight '70s

Eric Till
An American Christmas Carol '79
Bethune '77
Bridge to Terabithia '85
Buffalo Jump '90
A Case of Libel '83
Clarence '91
Glory Enough for All: The Discovery of Insulin '92
Hot Millions '68
If You Could See What I Hear '82
Improper Channels '82
Mary and Joseph: A Story of Faith '79
Oh, What a Night '92
To Catch a Killer '92
Wild Horse Hank '79

R.L. Tillmanns
Witchcraft 3: The Kiss of Death '90

Bruce W. Timm
Batman: Mask of the Phantasm '93

James Tinling
Tales of Robin Hood '52

George Tirl
Pay Off '89

James Toback
Exposed '83
Fingers '78
The Pick-Up Artist '87

Marice Tobias
Pulsebeat '85

Norman Tokar
The Apple Dumpling Gang '75
Big Red '62
The Boatniks '70
Candleshoe '78
The Cat from Outer Space '78
Follow Me, Boys! '66
The Happiest Millionaire '67
The Horse in the Gray Flannel Suit '68
No Deposit, No Return '76
Sammy, the Way-Out Seal '62
Savage Sam '63
Snowball Express '72
Those Calloways '65
A Tiger Walks '64
The Ugly Dachshund '65
Where the Red Fern Grows '74

Sergio Toledo
One Man's War '90

Michael Tolkin
The Rapture '91

Stephen Tolkin
Daybreak '93

Wilson Tong
Two Wondrous Tigers '79

Tom Topor
Judgment '90

Ralph Toporoff
American Blue Note '89

Burt Topper
Hell Squad '58

Soul Hustler '76
The Strangler '64
Suicide Battalion/Hell Squad '58
Tank Commando '59

Rip Torn
The Telephone '87

Giuseppe Tornatore
Cinema Paradiso '88
Everybody's Fine '90
Everybody's Fine '90

Joe Tornatore
Code Name: Zebra '84
Grotesque '87
Zebra Force '76

Robert Torrance
Mutant on the Bounty '89

Fina Torres
Oriane '85

Gabe Torres
December '91

Miguel Contreras Torres
Pancho Villa Returns '50

Cinzia Torrini
Hotel Colonial '88

Ivan Tors
Zebra in the Kitchen '65

Bruce Toscano
The Jar '84

Robert Totten
Dark Before Dawn '89
Huckleberry Finn '75
Pony Express Rider '76
The Red Pony '76
The Sacketts '79
The Wild Country '71

Mikhail Toumanichulli
Solo Voyage: The Revenge '90

Jacques Tourneur
Appointment in Honduras '53
Berlin Express '48
Cat People '42
The Comedy of Terrors '64
Curse of the Demon '57
Days of Glory '43
Easy Living '49
Experiment Perilous '45
The Flame & the Arrow '50
The Giant of Marathon '60
Great Day in the Morning '56
I Walked with a Zombie '43
The Leopard Man '43
Nightfall '56
Out of the Past '47
Stars in My Crown '50

Maurice Tourneur
A Girl's Folly '17
The Last of the Mohicans '20
Lorna Doone '22
A Poor Little Rich Girl '17
Pride of the Clan '18
Trilby '17
Volpone '39
The Wishing Ring '14

Robert Towne
Personal Best '82
Tequila Sunrise '88

Bud Townsend
Coach '78
Nightmare in Wax '69
Terror at Red Wolf Inn '72

Patrice Townsend
Beach Girls '82

Robert Townsend
Eddie Murphy: Raw '87
The Five Heartbeats '91
Hollywood Shuffle '87
The Meteor Man '93

Ian Toynton
The Maid '90

Shiro Toyoda
Mistress '53
Snow Country '57

Benno Trachtmann
The Jumper '85

Jean-Claude Tramont
All Night Long '81
As Summers Die '86

Alfred Travers
Dual Alibi '47

Bill Travers
Christian the Lion '76

Stephen Traxler
Slithis '78

Peter S. Traynor
Seducers '77

Norma Trelvar
A Nation Aflame '37

Brian Trenchard-Smith
BMX Bandits '83
Day of the Assassin '81
Day of the Panther '88
Dead End Drive-In '86
Deathcheaters '76
Escape 2000 '81
Fists of Blood '87
Night of the Demons 2 '94
Official Denial '93
Out of the Body '88
The Quest '86
The Siege of Firebase Gloria '89

John Trent
Best Revenge '83
The Bushbaby '70
Crossbar '79
Find the Lady '75
Middle Age Crazy '80
Vengeance Is Mine '84

Georg Tressier
Teenage Wolfpack '57

Monika Treut
My Father is Coming '91
Seduction: The Cruel Woman '89

Dale Trevillion
Las Vegas Weekend '85
One Man Force '89

Gus Trikonis
Dempsey '83
The Evil '78
First Affair '83
Jungle Heat '84
Love on the Run '85
Miss All-American Beauty '82
Moonshine County Express '77
Nashville Girl '76
The Rumor Mill '86
She's Dressed to Kill '79
Take This Job and Shove It '81
Touched by Love '80
Twirl '81

Nadine Trintignant
Next Summer '84

Victor Trivas
The Head '59

Jan Troell
The Emigrants '72
Flight of the Eagle '82
Hurricane '79
The New Land '73
Zandy's Bride '74

Tzipi Trope
Tell Me That You Love Me '84

Gary Trousdale
Beauty and the Beast '91

Gary A. Troy
Computer Beach Party '88

Fernando Trueba
Belle Epoque '92
Twisted Obsession '90

Francois Truffaut
The Bride Wore Black '68
Confidentially Yours '83
Day for Night '73
Fahrenheit 451 '66
The 400 Blows '59
Godard/Truffaut Shorts '58
The Green Room '78
Jules and Jim '62
The Last Metro '80
Les Mistons '57
Love on the Run '78
The Man Who Loved Women '77
Mississippi Mermaid '69
Shoot the Piano Player '62
Small Change '76
The Soft Skin '64
Stolen Kisses '68
Story of Adele H. '75
Two English Girls '72
The Wild Child '70
The Woman Next Door '81

Michael Truman
Koroshi '67

Dalton Trumbo
Johnny Got His Gun '71

Douglas Trumbull
Brainstorm '83
Silent Running '71

Glenn Tryon
Law West of Tombstone '38
Small Town Boy '37

Manolis Tsafos
Rip-Off '77

Chan Tsi-liang
Lai Shi: China's Last Eunuch '88

Shinya Tsukamoto
Tetsuo: The Iron Man '92

Slava Tsukerman
Liquid Sky '83

Michael Tuchner
Adam '83
Amos '85
The Hunchback of Notre Dame '82
The Misadventures of Mr. Wilt '90
Mistress '87
Not My Kid '85
The Old Curiosity Shop '75
The Summer of My German Soldier '78
Trapped in Silence '86
Trenchcoat '83

David Tucker
A Year in Provence '89

George Tucker
Traffic in Souls '13

James Tucker
Lunatic '91
Steps from Hell '92

Phil Tucker
Dance Hall Racket '58
Robot Monster '53

Roger Tucker
Deadly Recruits '86

Richard Tuggle
Out of Bounds '86
Tightrope '84

Montgomery Tully
Battle Beneath the Earth '68
Dead Lucky '60
The Electronic Monster '57
Glass Tomb '55

The House in Marsh Road '60
The Key Man '57
Paid to Kill '54
Strange Awakening '58
Terronauts '67
The Terronauts '67
The Way Out '56

Sandy Tung
Across the Tracks '89

Saul J. Turell
The Love Goddesses '65

Sophia Turkiewicz
Silver City '84

Rosemarie Turko
Dungeonmaster '85
Scarred '84

Zygmund Turkow
The Jolly Paupers '38

Lawrence Turman
Second Thoughts '83

Ann Turner
Celia: Child Of Terror '89

Chester Turner
Black Devil Doll from Hell '84

Jon Turteltaub
Cool Runnings '93
Driving Me Crazy '91
3 Ninjas '92

John Turturro
Mac '93

Frank Tuttle
Hell on Frisco Bay '55
Love 'Em and Leave 'Em '26
Lucky Devil '25
Roman Scandals '33
This Gun for Hire '42

Derek Twist
Green Grow the Rushes '51

David N. Twohy
Grand Tour: Disaster in Time '92

Tomu Uchida
Swords of Death '71

Seiichiro Uchikawa
One-Eyed Swordsman '63

Alan Uger
Blazing Saddles '74

Liv Ullmann
Sofie '92

Edgar G. Ulmer
The Amazing Transparent Man '60
Beyond the Time Barrier '60
The Black Cat '34
Bluebeard '44
Club Havana '46
The Daughter of Dr. Jekyll '57
Detour '46
Girls in Chains '43
Isle of Forgotten Sins '43
Jive Junction '43
Journey Beneath the Desert '61
The Light Ahead '39
Moon Over Harlem '39
Naked Venus '58
St. Benny the Dip '51
The Singing Blacksmith '38
Strange Illusion '45
The Strange Woman '46
Thunder Over Texas '34

Ron Underwood
City Slickers '91
Heart and Souls '93
Tremors '89

Lawrence Unger
Novel Desires '92

Michael Toshiyuki Uno
Blind Spot '93

Uno ▶*cont.*

The Wash '88
Without Warning: The James Brady Story '91

Rocco Urbisci
George Carlin: Doin' It Again '94

Jeff Ureles
Cheap Shots '91

Frank Urson
The Night Club '25

Chano Urueto
The Living Head '59
The Witch's Mirror '60

Peter Ustinov
Billy Budd '62
Hammersmith is Out '72
Lady L '65

Jamie Uys
Dingaka '65
The Gods Must Be Crazy '84
The Gods Must Be Crazy 2 '89

Jack Vacek
Rock House '92

Roger Vadim
And God Created Woman '57
And God Created Woman '88
Barbarella '68
Beauty and the Beast '83
Blood and Roses '61
Circle of Love '64
Dangerous Liaisons '60
The Game is Over '66
Game of Seduction '86
Le Repos du Guerrier '62
Night Games '80
Spirits of the Dead '68

Steve Vagnino
A Pleasure Doing Business '79

Ladislao Vajda
The Man Who Wagged His Tail '57

Luis Valdez
The Cisco Kid '94
La Bamba '87
La Pastorela '92
Zoot Suit '81

Frank Valenti
Delta Force Commando 2 '90
War Bus Commando '89

Jon Valentine
Night of the Living Babes '87

Jean Valere
Time Out for Love '61

Tonino Valerii
My Name is Nobody '74
A Reason to Live, A Reason to Die '73

Robert Van Ackeren
A Woman in Flames '84

Jaco Van Dormael
Toto le Heros '91

Bruce Van Dusen
Cold Feet '84

Woodbridge S. Van Dyke
After the Thin Man '36
Andy Hardy Gets Spring Fever '39
Another Thin Man '39
Bitter Sweet '40
Cairo '42
Forsaking All Others '35
Hide-Out '34
I Live My Life '35
I Love You Again '40
I Married an Angel '42
Journey for Margaret '42

Love on the Run '36
Manhattan Melodrama '34
Marie Antoinette '38
Naughty Marietta '35
Penthouse '33
Personal Property '37
The Prizefighter and the Lady '33
Rosalie '38
Rose Marie '36
San Francisco '36
Shadow of the Thin Man '41
Sweethearts '38
Tarzan, the Ape Man '32
The Thin Man '34
Trader Horn '31
White Shadows in the South Seas '28

Ruud Van Hemert
Army Brats '84

Buddy Van Horn
Any Which Way You Can '80
The Dead Pool '88
Pink Cadillac '89

Mario Van Peebles
New Jack City '91
Posse '93

Melvin Van Peebles
Identity Crisis '90
The Story of a Three Day Pass '68
Sweet Sweetback's Baadasssss Song '71
Watermelon Man '70

Gus Van Sant
Drugstore Cowboy '89
Even Cowgirls Get the Blues '94
My Own Private Idaho '91

Sterling Van Wagenen
Alan & Naomi '92

Joseph Van Winkle
The Woman Inside '83

Eric Van Zuylen
In for Treatment '82

Florestano Vancini
That Long Night in '43 '60

William Vanderkloot
Dead Aim '87

Norman Thaddeus Vane
The Black Room '82
Club Life '86
Frightmare '81
Midnight '89
Taxi Dancers '93

Carlo Vanzina
Dagger Eyes '80s
The Gamble '88
Millions '90
My Wonderful Life '90
Nothing Underneath '85

Agnes Varda
Cleo from 5 to 7 '61
Jacquot '91
Le Bonheur '65
Le Petit Amour '87
One Sings, the Other Doesn't '77
Vagabond '85

Marcel Varnel
Chandu the Magician '32
Oh, Mr. Porter '37

Henri Vart
Secret Obsession '88

Gregory Vasiliev
Chapayev '34

Sergei Vasiliev
Chapayev '34

Joseph P. Vasquez
The Bronx War '90
Hangin' with the Homeboys '91
Street Hitz '92

Bruno Ve Sota
The Brain Eaters '58
The Female Jungle '56

Francis Veber
La Chevre '81
Les Comperes '83
Out on a Limb '92
Three Fugitives '89

Pastor Vega
Portrait of Teresa '79

Carlos Velo
Torero '56

Itsvan Ventilla
Nicole '72

Ben Verbong
Lily was Here '89

Carlo Verdone
Acqua e Sapone '83

Enrique Vergara
The Snake People '68

Michael Verhoeven
Killing Cars '85
The Nasty Girl '90
The White Rose '83

Paul Verhoeven
Basic Instinct '92
The Eternal Waltz '54
Flesh and Blood '85
The 4th Man '79
Keetje Tippei '75
RoboCop '87
Soldier of Orange '78
Spetters '80
Total Recall '90
Turkish Delights '73

Henri Verneuil
The Big Grab '63
Just Another Pretty Face '58
Melodie en Sous-Sol '63
Night Flight from Moscow '73
The Sheep Has Five Legs '54
Un Singe en Hiver '62

Henry Vernon
Danger Zone '87

Richard Vernon
The Shadow Man '53

Stephen Verona
The Lords of Flatbush '74
Pipe Dreams '76
Talking Walls '85

Wim Verstappen
Fatal Error '83

Dziga Vertov
Kino Pravda/Enthusiasm '31
The Man with a Movie Camera '29

Robert Veze
Bikini Summer '91

Michael Vianey
Special Police '85

Marco Vicario
The Sensual Man '74
Wifemistress '79

Lindsey C. Vickers
The Appointment '82

Edward Victor
Alley Cat '84

Charles Vidor
Cover Girl '44
Gilda '46
Hans Christian Andersen '52
The Lady in Question '40
Love Me or Leave Me '55
The Loves of Carmen '48

Rhapsody '54
A Song to Remember '45
Song Without End '60
The Swan '56
The Tuttles of Tahiti '42

King Vidor
Beyond the Forest '49
The Big Parade '25
Bird of Paradise '32
The Champ '31
The Citadel '38
Comrade X '40
The Crowd '28
Duel in the Sun '46
The Fountainhead '49
Hallelujah! '29
The Jack Knife Man '20
Man Without a Star '55
Northwest Passage '40
Our Daily Bread '34
Peg O' My Heart '22
Ruby Gentry '52
Show People '28
The Sky Pilot '21
Solomon and Sheba '59
Stella Dallas '37
Street Scene '31
War and Peace '56

Berthold Viertel
The Passing of the Third Floor Back '36
Rhodes '36

Emilio Vieyra
The Curious Dr. Humpp '70

Daniel Vigne
One Woman or Two '85
The Return of Martin Guerre '83

Robert G. Vignola
The Scarlet Letter '34

Jean Vigo
L'Atalante '34
A Propos de Nice '29
Zero for Conduct '33

Camilo Vila
Options '88
The Unholy '88

Felix Vilars
Devil Woman '76

Reynaldo Villalobos
Conagher '91

Agustin Villaronga
In a Glass Cage '86

Christian Vincent
La Discrete '90

Chuck Vincent
American Tickler '76
Bedroom Eyes 2 '89
Cleo/Leo '89
C.O.D. '83
Deranged '87
Enrapture '90
Hollywood Hot Tubs '84
Hot T-Shirts '79
If Looks Could Kill '86
A Matter of Love '78
New York's Finest '87
Party Incorporated '89
Preppies '82
Sensations '87
Sexpot '88
Slammer Girls '87
Student Affairs '88
Thrilled to Death '88
Wildest Dreams '90
Wimps '87
A Woman Obsessed '88
Young Nurses in Love '89

Harry Vincent
She Came on the Bus '69

Jerry Vint
Another Chance '88

Will Vinton
The Adventures of Mark Twain '85

Joe Viola
Angels Hard as They Come '71
Hot Box '72

Luchino Visconti
Bellissima '51
Boccaccio '70 '62
Conversation Piece '75
The Damned '69
Death in Venice '71
The Innocent '76
La Terra Trema '48
Ossessione '42
Rocco and His Brothers '60
Senso '54
White Nights '57

Laszlo Vitezy
Red Earth

Piero Vivarelli
Satanik '69

Virgil W. Vogel
Beulah Land '80
Invasion of the Animal People '62
The Land Unknown '57
The Mole People '56
Portrait of a Rebel: Margaret Sanger '82
Walker: Texas Ranger: One Riot, One Ranger '93

Alfred Vohrer
Creature with the Blue Hand '70
Dead Eyes of London '61
Door with the Seven Locks '62
The Indian Scarf '63
Inn on the River '62
The Mysterious Magician '65
The Squeaker '65

Paul G. Volk
Sunset Strip '91

Josef von Baky
Baron Munchausen '43
The Strange Countess '61

Geza von Bolvary
Charm of La Boheme '36

Gunther Von Fristch
Curse of the Cat People '44

Veith von Furstenberg
Fire and Sword '82

Rosa von Praunheim
Anita, Dances of Vice '87

Geza von Radvanyi
Uncle Tom's Cabin '69

Akos Von Rathony
Cave of the Living Dead '65

Josef von Sternberg
Blonde Venus '32
The Blue Angel '30
Crime and Punishment '35
Dishonored '31
Docks of New York '28
Jet Pilot '57
Last Command '28
Macao '52
Morocco '30
Scarlet Empress '34
Shanghai Express '32
The Shanghai Gesture '42

Erich von Stroheim
Blind Husbands '19
Foolish Wives '22
Greed '24
Merry-Go-Round '23
Queen Kelly '29
The Wedding March '28
The Worst of Hollywood: Vol. 2 '90

Ernst R. von Theumer
Jungle Warriors '84

Lars von Trier
The Element of Crime '84
Zentropa '92

Margarethe von Trotta
The Lost Honor of Katharina Blum '75
Rosa Luxemburg '86
Sheer Madness '84

Bernard Vorhaus
The Amazing Mr. X '48
Broken Melody '34
Courageous Dr. Christian '40
Fisherman's Wharf '39
The Ghost Camera '33
Lady from Louisiana '42
Meet Dr. Christian '39
Three Faces West '40
Way Down South '39

Kurt Voss
Border Radio '88
Genuine Risk '89
Horseplayer '91

Otakar Votocek
Wings of Fame '93

Daniel Wachsmann
Hamsin '83

Jonathan Wacks
Ed and His Dead Mother '93
Mystery Date '91
Powwow Highway '89

Michael Wadleigh
Wolfen '81
Woodstock '70

George Waggner
The Commies are Coming, the Commies are Coming '57
The Fighting Kentuckian '49
Ghost Town Riders '38
Man Made Monster '41
Mystery Plane '39
Outlaw Express '38
Stunt Pilot '39
Western Trails '38
Wolf Call '39
The Wolf Man '41

Fernando Wagner
Virgin Sacrifice '59

Rupert Wainwright
Blank Check '93

Ralph Waite
On the Nickel '80

Andrzej Wajda
Ashes and Diamonds '58
The Conductor '80
Danton '82
Fury is a Woman '61
A Generation '54
Kanal '56
Korczak '90
Land of Promise '74
A Love in Germany '84
Maids of Wilko '79
Man of Iron '81
Man of Marble '76

Chris Walas
The Fly 2 '89
The Vagrant '92

Grant Austin Waldman
The Channeler '89
Teenage Exorcist '93

Mauricio Walerstein
Fin de Fiesta '71

Dorian Walker
Making the Grade '84
Teen Witch '89

Giles Walker
90 Days '86
Ordinary Magic '93
Princes in Exile '90

Hal Walker
At War with the Army '50
The Road to Bali '53
The Road to Utopia '46
The Stork Club '45

Nancy Walker
Can't Stop the Music '80

Pete Walker
The Big Switch '70
The Comeback '77
The Confessional '75
Die Screaming, Marianne '73
Flesh and Blood Show '73
Frightmare '74
Home Before Midnight '84
House of the Long Shadows '82
House of Whipcord '75
Man of Violence '71
Schizo '77
Tiffany Jones '75

Stuart Walker
Werewolf of London '35

Gary Walkow
The Trouble with Dick '88

Richard Wallace
Bombardier '43
Captain Caution '40
The Fallen Sparrow '43
A Girl, a Guy and a Gob '41
It's in the Bag '45
Little Minister '34
A Night to Remember '42
Sinbad the Sailor '47
Tycoon '47
The Young in Heart '38

Rick Wallace
Acceptable Risks '86
California Girls '84
A Time to Live '85

Stephen Wallace
For Love Alone '86
The Killing Beach '92
Prisoners of the Sun '91

Tommy Lee Wallace
Aloha Summer '88
The Comrades of Summer '92
Fright Night 2 '88
Halloween 3: Season of the Witch '82
Stephen King's It '90

Sigurd Wallen
The Count of the Old Town '34

Herb Wallerstein
Snowbeast '77

Hal B. Wallis
Anne of the Thousand Days '69

Raoul Walsh
Along the Great Divide '51
Band of Angels '57
Battle Cry '55
Big Trail '30
Blackbeard the Pirate '52
Captain Horatio Hornblower '51
College Swing '38
Dark Command '40
Desperate Journey '42
Distant Drums '51
The Enforcer '51
Gentleman Jim '42
Gun Fury '53
High Sierra '41
The Horn Blows at Midnight '45
The King and Four Queens '56
Klondike Annie '36
A Lion is in the Streets '53
The Man I Love '47
The Naked and the Dead '58
Northern Pursuit '43
Objective, Burma! '45

O.H.M.S. '37
Pursued '47
The Roaring Twenties '39
Sadie Thompson '28
Sea Devils '53
Silver River '48
Strawberry Blonde '41
The Tall Men '55
They Died with Their Boots On '41
They Drive by Night '40
The Thief of Baghdad '24
When Thief Meets Thief '37
White Heat '49

Walter Walsh
Going Hollywood '33

Charles Walters
Ask Any Girl '59
The Barkleys of Broadway '49
The Belle of New York '52
Billy Rose's Jumbo '62
Dangerous When Wet '53
Don't Go Near the Water '57
Easter Parade '48
Easy to Love '53
The Glass Slipper '55
Good News '47
High Society '56
Lili '53
Please Don't Eat the Daisies '60
Summer Stock '50
The Tender Trap '55
Texas Carnival '51
Three Guys Named Mike '51
Torch Song '53
The Unsinkable Molly Brown '64
Walk, Don't Run '66

Fred Walton
April Fool's Day '86
Hadley's Rebellion '84
Homewrecker '92
The Rosary Murders '87
Trapped '89
When a Stranger Calls '79
When a Stranger Calls Back '93

Sam Wanamaker
Catlow '71
The Executioner '70
Killing of Randy Webster '81
Sinbad and the Eye of the Tiger '77

Peter Wang
A Great Wall '86

Steve Wang
The Guyver '91

Wayne Wang
Chan is Missing '82
Dim Sum: A Little Bit of Heart '85
Eat a Bowl of Tea '89
The Joy Luck Club '93
A Man, a Woman and a Killer '75
Slamdance '87

Orville Wanzer
The Devil's Mistress '68

Grzegorz Warchol
I Like Bats '85

Bill Ward
Ballad of a Gunfighter '64

David S. Ward
Cannery Row '82
King Ralph '91
Major League '89
Major League 2 '94
The Program '93

Richard Ward
Sakura Killers '86

Vincent Ward
Map of the Human Heart '93
The Navigator '88
Vigil '84

Clyde Ware
Bad Jim '89
The Hatfields & the McCoys '75
No Drums, No Bugles '71

Chris Warfield
Little Miss Innocence '73

Regis Wargnier
Indochine '92

Ed Warnick
Manchurian Avenger '84

Charles Marquis Warren
Arrowhead '53
Charro! '69
Little Big Horn '51
Red Desert '50

Deryn Warren
Black Magic Woman '91
Bloodspell '87

Hal P. Warren
Manos, the Hands of Fate '66

Jerry Warren
Attack of the Mayan Mummy '63
Creature of the Walking Dead '60
Curse of the Stone Hand '64
Face of the Screaming Werewolf '58
Frankenstein Island '81
The Incredible Petrified World '58
Invasion of the Animal People '62
Man Beast '55
Teenage Zombies '58
Terror of the Bloodhunters '62
The Wild World of Batwoman '66

Joseph Warren
Urban Warriors '75

Norman J. Warren
Alien Prey '83
Bloody New Year '87
Horror Planet '80
Spaced Out '80
The Terror '79

Michal Waszynski
The Dybbuk '37

John Waters
Cry-Baby '90
Desperate Living '77
Divine '90
Female Trouble '74
Hairspray '88
Mondo Trasho '69
Multiple Maniacs '70
Pink Flamingos '72
Polyester '81
Serial Mom '94

Peter Watkins
Edvard Munch '74
The Gladiators '70

James C. Watson
Night of the Demon '80

John Watson
Deathstalker '83
The Zoo Gang '85

William Watson
Heroes in Blue '39

Harry Watt
Eureka Stockade '49
Overlanders '46

Nate Watt
Law of the Pampas '39
Rustler's Valley '37

Roy Watts
Hambone & Hillie '84

Al Waxman
Diamond Fleece '92

My Pleasure Is My Business '74
White Light '90

Keoni Waxman
Almost Blue '93

Ron Way
Frenchman's Farm '87

Keenan Ivory Wayans
I'm Gonna Git You Sucka '88
Low Down Dirty Shame '94

John Wayne
The Alamo '60
The Green Berets '68

Michael Weaver
Night Terror '89

Harry S. Webb
Laramie Kid '35
The Live Wire '34
Mesquite Buckaroo '39
Ridin' Thru '35
Riding On '37
Santa Fe Bound '37

Jack Webb
D.I. '57
Dragnet '54
Pete Kelly's Blues '55

Kenneth Webb
Just Suppose '26

Millard Webb
The Dropkick '27
Glorifying the American Girl '30

Peter Webb
Give My Regards to Broad Street '84

Robert D. Webb
Beneath the 12-Mile Reef '53
Love Me Tender '56
Seven Cities of Gold '55

William Webb
The Banker '89
Dirty Laundry '87
The Hit List '93
Party Line '88
Under Siege '92

Billy Weber
Josh and S.A.M. '93

Bruce Weber
Let's Get Lost '88

Lois Weber
The Blot '21
Chapter in Her Life '23
Discontent '16
Too Wise Wives '21

Christopher Webster
Demon Possessed '93

D.J. Webster
Dark Side of the Moon '90

Nicholas Webster
Gone are the Days '63
Mission Mars '67
Purlie Victorious '63
Santa Claus Conquers the Martians '64

David Wechter
Malibu Bikini Shop '86
Midnight Madness '80

Stephen Weeks
Madhouse Mansion '74
Sword of the Valiant '83

Paul Wegener
The Golem '20
Student of Prague '13

Lo Wei
Chinese Connection '73
Fists of Fury '73

Alfred Weidenmann
Adorable Julia '62

Ken Weiderhorn
Return of the Living Dead 2 '88

John Weidner
Private Wars '93

Paul Weiland
Bernard and the Genie '90s
City Slickers 2: The Legend of
Curly's Gold '94
Leonard Part 6 '87

Claudia Weill
Girlfriends '78
It's My Turn '80
Once a Hero '88

Chuck Wein
Rainbow Bridge '71

Bob Weinstein
Playing for Keeps '86

Harvey Weinstein
Light Years '88

Sandra Weintraub
The Deadliest Art: The Best of
the Martial Arts Films '90
Women's Club '87

Peter Weir
The Cars That Ate Paris '74
Dead Poets Society '89
Fearless '93
Gallipoli '81
Green Card '90
The Last Wave '77
The Mosquito Coast '86
Picnic at Hanging Rock '75
Plumber '79
Witness '85
The Year of Living Dangerously
'82

Bob Weis
The Wacky World of Wills &
Burke '85

Don Weis
The Affairs of Dobie Gillis '53
Billie '65
The Gene Krupa Story '59
I Love Melvin '53
Munster's Revenge '81
Pajama Party '64
Zero to Sixty '78

Gary Weis
All You Need Is Cash '78
Diary of a Young Comic '79
Wholly Moses! '80

Jack Weis
Crypt of Dark Secrets '76
Mardi Gras Massacre '78
Storyville '74

Sam Weisman
D2: The Mighty Ducks '94

Straw Weisman
Dead Mate '88

Adrian Weiss
The Bride & the Beast '58

Helmut Weiss
Tromba, the Tiger Man '52

Jiri Weiss
Sweet Light in a Dark Room '60

Rob Weiss
Amongst Friends '93

Robert Weiss
Amazon Women on the Moon
'87

Mel Welles
Lady Frankenstein '72

Orson Welles
Chimes at Midnight '67
Citizen Kane '41
It's All True '93
The Lady from Shanghai '48
Macbeth '48

The Magnificent Ambersons
'42
Mr. Arkadin '55
Othello '52
The Stranger '46
Touch of Evil '58
The Trial '63

David Wellington
The Carpenter '89

William A. Wellman
Across the Wide Missouri '51
Battleground '49
Beau Geste '39
Blood Alley '55
Buffalo Bill '44
Darby's Rangers '58
Goodbye, My Lady '56
Heroes for Sale '33
Lady of Burlesque '43
Lafayette Escadrille '58
Magic Town '47
The Next Voice You Hear '50
Night Nurse '31
Nothing Sacred '37
The Ox-Bow Incident '43
Public Enemy '31
The Purchase Price '32
A Star is Born '37
Till the Clouds Roll By/A Star Is
Born '46
Westward the Women '51
Wings '27

Simon Wells
An American Tail: Fievel Goes
West '91
We're Back! A Dinosaur's Story
'93

Li Wen-Hua
Breaking with Old Ideas '75

Wim Wenders
Alice in the Cities '74
The American Friend '77
Faraway, So Close! '93
The Goalie's Anxiety at the
Penalty Kick '71
Hammett '82
Kings of the Road—In the
Course of Time '76
Lightning Over Water '80
Paris, Texas '83
The Scarlet Letter '73
State of Things '82
Tokyo-Ga '85
Until The End of The World '91
Wings of Desire '88
The Wrong Move '78

Paul Wendkos
Angel Baby '61
Awakening of Candra '81
The Bad Seed '85
Betrayal '78
Blood Vows: The Story of a
Mafia Wife '87
Celebrity '85
Cocaine: One Man's Seduction
'83
A Cry for Love '80
Deadline Assault '90
The Death of Richie '76
The Execution '85
The Five of Me '81
The Flight '89
From the Dead of Night '89
Gidget '59
Gidget Goes Hawaiian '61
Gidget Goes to Rome '63
The Great Escape 2: The
Untold Story '88
Guns of the Magnificent Seven
'69
Haunts of the Very Rich '72
Honor Thy Father '73
Johnny Tiger '66
The Mephisto Waltz '71
The Ordeal of Dr. Mudd '80
Rage of Angels: The Story
Continues '86
Secrets '77

Special Delivery '76
The Taking of Flight 847: The
Uli Derickson Story '88
The Tattered Web '71
White Hot: The Mysterious
Murder of Thelma Todd '91
A Woman Called Moses '78

Richard Wenk
Vamp '86

Alfred Werker
The Adventures of Sherlock
Holmes '39
At Gunpoint '55
Devil's Canyon '53
He Walked by Night '48
It Could Happen to You '39
The Reluctant Dragon '41
Shock! '46

Jeff Werner
Cheerleaders' Wild Weekend
'85
Die Laughing '80

Peter Werner
The Alamo: Thirteen Days to
Glory '87
Don't Cry, It's Only Thunder '82
Hard Knox '83
Hiroshima: Out of the Ashes
'90
I Married a Centerfold '84
The Image '89
In the Region of Ice '76
LBJ: The Early Years '88
Lone Justice '93
No Man's Land '87

Lina Wertmuller
All Screwed Up '74
Belle Starr '79
Blood Feud '79
Camorra: The Naples
Connection '85
A Joke of Destiny, Lying in Wait
Around the Corner Like a
Bandit '84
Love and Anarchy '73
A Night Full of Rain '78
Seduction of Mimi '72
Seven Beauties '76
Sotto, Sotto '85
Summer Night '87
Summer Night with Greek
Profile, Almond Eyes &
Scent of Basil '87
Swept Away... '75

Jay Wertz
The Last Reunion '80

Roland West
The Bat '26
The Bat Whispers '30
Corsair '31
The Monster '25

William West
Flying Wild '41

Armand Weston
The Nesting '80

Eric Weston
Evilspeak '82
The Iron Triangle '89
Marvin & Tige '84
To Protect and Serve '92

Sam Weston
It's Called Murder, Baby '82

Fulvio Wetzl
Rorret '87

Haskell Wexler
Latino '85
Medium Cool '69

James Whale
The Bride of Frankenstein '35
Frankenstein '31
The Invisible Man '33
The Man in the Iron Mask '39
The Old Dark House '32
Show Boat '36

Sinners in Paradise '38
Wives Under Suspicion '38

George Whaley
Clowning Around 2 '93

Tom Wharmby
Bouquet of Barbed Wire '76

Tony Wharmby
The Equalizer: Memories of
Manon '88
The Kissing Place '90
Sorry, Wrong Number '89
Treacherous Crossing '92

Claude Whatham
All Creatures Great and Small
'74
Murder Elite '86
Sweet William '79
That'll Be the Day '73

Bob Whealing
What's Up Front '63

Jim Wheat
After Midnight '89
The Ewoks: Battle for Endor
'85
Lies '83

Ken Wheat
The Ewoks: Battle for Endor
'85
Lies '83

David Wheatley
Hostages '93

Anne Wheeler
Angel Square '92
Bye Bye Blues '89
Loyalties '86

Tim Whelan
Action for Slander '38
Badman's Territory '46
Clouds Over Europe '39
The Divorce of Lady X '38
Higher and Higher '44
The Mill on the Floss '37
Rage at Dawn '55
Seven Days' Leave '42
Sidewalks of London '40
Step Lively '44
Texas Lady '56

Forest Whitaker
Strapped '93

Jules White
Sidewalks of New York '31

Nathan J. White
The Carrier '87

Sam White
People Are Funny '46

Alexander Whitelaw
Lifespan '75

John Whitesell
Calendar Girl '93

Philip H. Whitman
Girl from Calgary '32
His Private Secretary '33

William Whitney
Arizona Raiders '65
Doctor Satan's Robot '40
Springtime in the Sierras '47

Richard Whorf
Champagne for Caesar '50
It Happened in Brooklyn '47
Love from a Stranger '47
Till the Clouds Roll By '46
Till the Clouds Roll By/A Star Is
Born '46

Michael Whyte
The Railway Station Man '92

William Wiard
Help Wanted: Male '82
Kicks '85
Snowblind '78

Tom Horn '80

David Wickes
Frankenstein '93
Jack the Ripper '88
Silver Dream Racer '83

Bernhard Wicki
Morituri '65

Bo Widerberg
Elvira Madigan '67

Ken Wiederhorn
Eyes of a Stranger '81
Meatballs 2 '84
Shock Waves '77

Robert Wiemer
Anna to the Infinite Power '84
The Night Train to Kathmandu
'88
Somewhere Tomorrow '85

Robert Wiene
The Cabinet of Dr. Caligari '19
The Hands of Orlac '25

Hal Wiener
Imagemaker '86

Crane Wilbur
The Bat '59
Tomorrow's Children '34
Yellow Cargo '36

Fred M. Wilcox
Courage of Lassie '46
Forbidden Planet '56
The Hills of Home '48
Lassie, Come Home '43
The Secret Garden '49
Three Daring Daughters '48

Herbert Wilcox
Bitter Sweet '33
The Courtney Affair '47
Elizabeth of Ladymead '48
Forever and a Day '43
I Live in Grosvenor Square '46
The King's Rhapsody '55
Let's Make Up '55
London Melody '37
Maytime in Mayfair '52
No, No Nanette '40
Nurse Edith Cavell '39
Sunny '41
Teenage Bad Girl '59
Trouble in the Glen '54

Cornel Wilde
The Naked Prey '66
Sharks' Treasure '75
Sword of Lancelot '63

Ted Wilde
The Kid Brother '27
Speedy '28

Billy Wilder
The Apartment '60
Avanti! '72
Buddy Buddy '81
Double Indemnity '44
The Fortune Cookie '66
The Front Page '74
Irma La Douce '63
Kiss Me, Stupid! '64
The Lost Weekend '45
Love in the Afternoon '57
One, Two, Three '61
The Private Life of Sherlock
Holmes '70
Sabrina '54
The Seven Year Itch '55
Some Like It Hot '59
Spirit of St. Louis '57
Stalag 17 '53
Sunset Boulevard '50
Witness for the Prosecution '57

Gene Wilder
The Adventures of Sherlock
Holmes' Smarter Brother '78
Haunted Honeymoon '86
The Woman in Red '84
World's Greatest Lover '77

Glenn Wilder
Master Blaster '85

John Wilder
Breaking Home Ties '87

W. Lee Wilder
Big Bluff '55
Fright '56
Killers from Space '54
Manfish '56
Phantom from Space '53
The Snow Creature '54
Woman in Brown '48

Gordon Wiles
Charlie Chan's Secret '35
The Gangster '47
Ginger in the Morning '73
Lady from Nowhere '36
Mr. Boggs Steps Out '38
Prison Train '38

Ethan Wiley
House 2: The Second Story '87

Charles Wilkinson
Blood Clan '91
Quarantine '89

Irwin Willat
The Michigan Kid '28

Anson Williams
All-American Murder '91
Dream Date '93
Little White Lies '89
A Perfect Little Murder '90

Douglas Williams
Overdrawn at the Memory
    Bank '83

Elmo Williams
Hell Ship Mutiny '57
Tall Texan '53

Emlyn Williams
The Last Days of Dolwyn '49

Oscar Williams
Death Drug '83
Final Comedown '72
Hot Potato '76

Paul Williams
Miss Right '81

Richard Williams
Raggedy Ann and Andy: A
    Musical Adventure '77

Spencer Williams, Jr.
Blood of Jesus '41
Go Down Death '41
Juke Joint '47

Tony Williams
Next of Kin '82
Solo '77

Fred Williamson
Adios Amigo '75
Big Score '83
Death Journey '76
Foxtrap '85
The Kill Reflex '89
The Last Fight '82
Mean Johnny Barrows '75
Mister Mean '77
No Way Back '74
One Down, Two to Go! '82
South Beach '92
Steele's Law '91
Three Days to a Kill '91

Gordon Willis
Windows '80

J. Elder Wills
Song of Freedom '38

Bruce Wilson
Bombs Away! '86

Dean Wilson
Blind Faith '89
Clayton County Line '80s
Free Amerika Broadcasting '89

Hugh Wilson
Burglar '87
Guarding Tess '94
Police Academy '84
Rustler's Rhapsody '85

Jim Wilson
Movie Maker '86
Stacy's Knights '83

John D. Wilson
Shinbone Alley '70

Richard Wilson
Al Capone '59
Invitation to a Gunfighter '64
It's All True '93
Three in the Attic '68

Sandy Wilson
American Boyfriends '89
My American Cousin '85

Yale Wilson
Truth or Dare? '86

Jim Winburn
The Death Merchant '91
Evil Altar '89

Simon Wincer
Dark Forces '83
D.A.R.Y.L. '85
Free Willy '93
The Girl Who Spelled Freedom
    '86
Harley Davidson and the
    Marlboro Man '91
The Lighthorsemen '87
Lightning Jack '94
Phar Lap '84
Quigley Down Under '90

Fred Windermere
The Taxi Mystery '26

Chris Windsor
Big Meat Eater '82

Simon Windsor
Lonesome Dove '89

Bretaigne Windust
The Enforcer '51
June Bride '48
Pied Piper of Hamelin '57
Winter Meeting '48

Harry Winer
JFK: Reckless Youth '93
Mirrors '78
Single Bars, Single Women '84
SpaceCamp '86

Lucy Winer
Rate It X '86

Gary Winick
Curfew '88
Out of the Rain '90

Charles Winkler
Disturbed '90
You Talkin' to Me? '87

Henry Winkler
Cop and a Half '93
Memories of Me '88
A Smoky Mountain Christmas
    '86

Irwin Winkler
Guilty by Suspicion '91
Night and the City '92

Terence H. Winkless
The Berlin Conspiracy '91
Bloodfist '89
Corporate Affairs '90
The Nest '88
Rage and Honor '92

Michael Winner
Appointment with Death '88
The Big Sleep '78
Bullseye! '90
Chato's Land '71
A Chorus of Disapproval '89
Cool Mikado '63

Death Wish '74
Death Wish 2 '82
Death Wish 3 '85
Firepower '79
Lawman '71
The Mechanic '72
Murder on the Campus '52
The Nightcomers '72
Scorpio '73
Scream for Help '86
The Sentinel '76
The Stone Killer '73
The Wicked Lady '83

David Winning
Killer Image '92
Storm '87

Peter Winograd
Flicks '85
One Last Run '89

Stan Winston
Pumpkinhead '88

Alex Winter
Freaked '93

John Wintergate
Boarding House '83

David Winters
Codename: Vengeance '87
Dr. Jekyll and Mr. Hyde '73
The Last Horror Film '82
Mission to Kill '85
Racquet '79
Rage to Kill '88
Space Mutiny '88
Thrashin' '86

Donovan Winters
The Seducer '82

Howard Winters
Dead Boyz Can't Fly '93

Paul Winters
The Freeway Maniac '88

Frank Wisbar
The Devil Bat's Daughter '46
Strangler of the Swamp '46

Herbert Wise
Alone Against Rome '62
Castle of the Living Dead '64
The Gathering Storm '74
I, Claudius, Vol. 1: A Touch of
    Murder/Family Affairs '91
I, Claudius, Vol. 2: Waiting in
    the Wings/What Shall We Do
    With Claudius? '80
I, Claudius, Vol. 3: Poison is
    Queen/Some Justice '80
I, Claudius, Vol. 5: Zeus, By
    Jove!/Hail Who? '80
I, Claudius, Vol. 6: Fool's Luck/
    A God in Colchester '80
I, Claudius, Vol. 7: Old King Log
    '80
Pope John Paul II '84
Strange Interlude '90
Woman in Black '93

Kirk Wise
Beauty and the Beast '91

Robert Wise
The Andromeda Strain '71
Audrey Rose '77
Blood on the Moon '48
The Body Snatcher '45
Born to Kill '47
Criminal Court '46
Curse of the Cat People '44
The Day the Earth Stood Still
    '51
The Desert Rats '53
Executive Suite '54
The Haunting '63
The Hindenburg '75
I Want to Live! '58
Mademoiselle Fifi '44
The Magnificent Ambersons
    '42
Rooftops '89

Run Silent, Run Deep '58
The Sand Pebbles '66
The Set-Up '49
Somebody Up There Likes Me
    '56
The Sound of Music '65
Star! '68
Star Trek: The Motion Picture
    '80
This Could Be the Night '57
Three Secrets '50
Tribute to a Bad Man '56
Two for the Seesaw '62
Until They Sail '57
West Side Story '61

Carol Wiseman
Does This Mean We're
    Married? '90
The Little Princess '87

Doris Wishman
The Amazing Transplant '70
Bad Girls Go to Hell '65
Deadly Weapons '70
Nude on the Moon '61

Grant Withers
Irish Luck '39
Mutiny in the Big House '39

Stephen Withrow
Friends, Lovers & Lunatics '89

William Witney
The Adventures of Captain
    Marvel '41
Adventures of Red Ryder '40
Apache Rose '47
Bells of Coronado '50
Bells of San Angelo '47
Colorado Sundown '52
Cyclotrode "X" '46
Daredevils of the Red Circle '38
Darktown Strutters '74
Dick Tracy Returns '38
Dick Tracy vs. Crime Inc. '41
Down Dakota Way '49
Drums of Fu Manchu '40
Eyes of Texas '48
Fighting Devil Dogs '38
G-Men vs. the Black Dragon
    '43
The Gay Ranchero '42
The Golden Stallion '49
Grand Canyon Trail '48
Hawk of the Wilderness '38
Heart of the Rockies '51
Helldorado '46
Home in Oklahoma '47
Jet Attack/Paratroop Command
    '58
King of the Texas Rangers '41
The Lone Ranger '38
Master of the World '61
Mysterious Doctor Satan '40
Night Time in Nevada '48
North of the Great Divide '50
Nyoka and the Tigermen '42
On the Old Spanish Trail '47
Outcast '54
The Painted Stallion '37
Roll on Texas Moon '46
Spy Smasher Returns '42
Susanna Pass '49
Trail of Robin Hood '50
Trigger, Jr. '50
The Trigger Trio '37
Twilight in the Sierras '50
Under California Stars '48
Western Double Feature 3:
    Rogers & Allen '50
Western Double Feature 6:
    Rogers & Trigger '50
Western Double Feature 10:
    Roy, Dale, & Trigger '80s
Western Double Feature 17
    '40s
Western Double Feature 18
    '40s
Western Double Feature 21
    '40s
Western Double Feature 22
    '40s

Western Double Feature 25
Zorro Rides Again '37
Zorro's Fighting Legion '39

Bill Wittliff
Red Headed Stranger '87

Peter Wittman
Ellie '84
Play Dead '81

Jay Woelfel
Beyond Dream's Door '88

Jerzy Wojcik
Karate Polish Style '82

James L. Wolcott
Wild Women of Wongo '59

Fred Wolf
Little Rascals, Book 16 '30s
Little Rascals Christmas
    Special '79
Mouse and His Child '77
The Point '71

Donald Wolfe
Savage Intruder '68

Art Wolff
Battling for Baby '92

Andy Wolk
Criminal Justice '90
Traces of Red '92

Dan Wolman
Hide and Seek '80
My Michael '75
Nana '82
Soldier of the Night '84

James Wolpaw
Complex World '92

John Woo
A Better Tomorrow '86
A Better Tomorrow, Part 2 '88
Hard-Boiled '92
Hard Target '93
The Killer '90

Raymond Woo
Ninja Brothers of Blood '89

Edward D. Wood, Jr.
Bride of the Monster '56
Glen or Glenda '53
Jail Bait '54
Night of the Ghouls '59
Plan 9 from Outer Space '56
The Sinister Urge '60
The Violent Years '56

James Wood
Dr. Jekyll's Dungeon of Death
    '82

Sam Wood
Casanova Brown '44
Command Decision '48
A Day at the Races '37
The Devil & Miss Jones '41
Goodbye, Mr. Chips '39
Guest Wife '45
Heartbeat '46
Hold Your Man '33
Kings Row '41
Kitty Foyle '40
Let 'Em Have It '35
Madame X '37
Navy Blue and Gold '37
A Night at the Opera '35
Our Town '40
Peck's Bad Boy '21
The Pride of the Yankees '42
The Stratton Story '49

Leslie Woodhead
Tragedy of Flight 103: The
    Inside Story '91

Frank Woodruff
Lady Scarface '41
Lady Scarface/The Threat '49

Jack Woods
Equinox '71

Mark Woods
Witchcraft 2: The Temptress '90

Joanne Woodward
Come Along with Me '84

Abbe Wool
Roadside Prophets '92

Gerry Woolery
Jokes My Folks Never Told Me '77

Carl Workman
The Money '75

Chuck Workman
Kill Castro '80
The Mercenaries '80
Stoogemania '85
Superstar: The Life and Times of Andy Warhol '90

Mary Woronov
Eating Raoul '82

Wallace Worsley
The Hunchback of Notre Dame '23

Clark Worswick
Agent on Ice '86

Aaron Worth
9 1/2 Ninjas '90

David Worth
Lady Dragon '92
Lady Dragon 2 '93
Warrior of the Lost World '84

William Worthington
The Tong Man '19

Martin Wragge
The Last Warrior '89

John Wray
Anna Christie '23
Beau Revel '21

Caspar Wrede
One Day in the Life of Ivan Denisovich '71
The Terrorists '74

Geoffrey Wright
Romper Stomper '92

Mack V. Wright
Big Show '37
Haunted Gold '32
Hit the Saddle '37
Man from Monterey '33
Riders of the Whistling Skull '37
Robinson Crusoe of Clipper Island '36
Robinson Crusoe of Mystery Island '36
Rootin' Tootin' Rhythm '38
Sea Hound '47
Somewhere in Sonora '33
The Vigilantes are Coming '36
Western Double Feature 3 '36
Winds of the Wasteland '36

Max Wright
Western Double Feature 5: Rogers & Autry '37

Patrick Wright
Hollywood High '77

Tenny Wright
The Big Stampede '32
Telegraph Trail '33

Thomas J. Wright
Chrome Soldiers '92
The Fatal Image '90
Highlander: The Gathering '93
No Holds Barred '89
Snow Kill '90
Torchlight '85

Tom Wright
Deadly Game '91

Donald Wrye
Born Innocent '74
Death Be Not Proud '75
Ice Castles '79

James Wu
Ninja Condors '87

Richard Wulicher
House of Shadows '83

William Wyler
Ben-Hur '59
The Best Years of Our Lives '46
Big Country '58
Carrie '52
The Children's Hour '61
The Collector '65
Come and Get It '36
Dead End '37
Desperate Hours '55
Detective Story '51
Dodsworth '36
Friendly Persuasion '56
Funny Girl '68
The Heiress '49
Jezebel '38
The Letter '40
The Liberation of L.B. Jones '70
The Little Foxes '41
Mrs. Miniver '42
Roman Holiday '53
These Three '36
War in the Sky '82
The Westerner '40
Wuthering Heights '39

Bob Wynn
Resurrection of Zachary Wheeler '71

Tracy Keenan Wynn
Hit Lady '74

Jim Wynorski
Big Bad Mama 2 '87
Body Chemistry 3: Point of Seduction '93
Chopping Mall '86
Deathstalker 2: Duel of the Titans '87
Dinosaur Island '93
Hard to Die '90
The Haunting of Morella '91
The Lost Empire '83
Munchie '92
976-EVIL 2: The Astral Factor '91
Not of This Earth '88
The Return of Swamp Thing '89
Sins of Desire '92
Sorority House Massacre 2: Nighty Nightmare '92
Transylvania Twist '89

Yabo Yablonsky
Manipulator '71

Michael Yakub
The Shaman '87

Mitsuo Yanagimachi
Himatsuri '85
Shadow of China '91

C.Y. Yang
Bruce Li in New Guinea '80

Jean Yarborough
The Brute Man '46
The Creeper '48
The Devil Bat '41
The Gang's All Here '41
Here Come the Co-Eds '45
Hillbillies in a Haunted House '67
Holiday in Havana '49
House of Horrors '46
In Society '44
Jack & the Beanstalk '52
King of the Zombies '41
Law of the Jungle '42
Let's Go Collegiate '41
Lost in Alaska '52

Lure of the Islands '42
Master Minds '49
Meet the Mob '42
The Naughty Nineties '45
Panama Menace '41
Under Western Stars '45

Bob Yari
Mind Games '89

Kimiyoshi Yasuda
Zatoichi, The Blind Swordsman and the Fugitives '68

Peter Yates
Breaking Away '79
Bullitt '68
The Deep '77
The Dresser '83
Eleni '85
Eyewitness '81
For Pete's Sake '74
The House on Carroll Street '88
An Innocent Man '89
Koroshi '67
Krull '83
Mother, Jugs and Speed '76
Murphy's War '71
Robbery '67
Suspect '87
Year of the Comet '92

Brook Yeaton
Ice '93

Irvin S. Yeaworth, Jr.
The Blob '58
Dinosaurus! '60
The Flaming Teen-Age '56
The 4D Man '59

Linda Yellen
Chantilly Lace '93

Isaac Yeshurun
Noa at Seventeen '82

Yevgeny Yevtushenko
Kindergarten '84

Zhang Yimou
Ju Dou '90
Raise the Red Lantern '91
Red Sorghum '84
The Story of Qui Ju '91

Edie Yolles
That's My Baby! '88

Jeff Yonis
Bloodfist 5: Human Target '93

Bud Yorkin
Arthur 2: On the Rocks '88
Come Blow Your Horn '63
Love Hurts '91
Start the Revolution Without Me '70
The Thief Who Came to Dinner '73
Twice in a Lifetime '85

Yaky Yosha
Sexual Response '92

Hiroaki Yoshida
Iron Maze '91
Twilight of the Cockroaches '90

Freddie Young
Arthur's Hallowed Ground '84

Harold Young
Dreaming Out Loud '40
Little Tough Guy '38
The Mummy's Tomb '42
The Scarlet Pimpernel '34

James Young
The Unchastened Woman '25

Karen Young
Deadly Darling '85

Robert Young
Romance with a Double Bass '74
Vampire Circus '71

The World is Full of Married Men '80
The Worst Witch '86

Robert M. Young
Ballad of Gregorio Cortez '83
Charlie Boy '81
Dominick & Eugene '88
Extremities '86
One Trick Pony '80
Rich Kids '79
Robin Hood...The Legend: Herne's Son '85
Robin Hood...The Legend: The Swords of Wayland '83
Saving Grace '86
Short Eyes '79
Splitting Heirs '93
Talent for the Game '91
Trauma '62
Triumph of the Spirit '89
We are the Children '87

Robert W. Young
Hostage '92
Scandalous '88

Roger Young
Bitter Harvest '81
The Bourne Identity '88
Geronimo '93
Gulag '85
Held Hostage '91
Into Thin Air '85
Lassiter '84
The Squeeze '87
Two of a Kind '82

Terence Young
The Amorous Adventures of Moll Flanders '65
Black Tights '60
Cold Sweat '74
Dr. No '62
From Russia with Love '63
The Jigsaw Man '84
The Klansman '74
The Poppy is also a Flower '66
Red Sun '71
Sidney Sheldon's Bloodline '79
Thunderball '65
Triple Cross '67
Valley of the Eagles '51
Wait Until Dark '67
When Wolves Cry '69

Gary Youngman
Dead as a Doorman '85

Robert Youngson
Days of Thrills and Laughter '61
When Comedy was King '59

Jerry Younkins
The Demon Lover '77

Albert Yu
Devil Woman '76

Ronny Yu
China White '91

Noriaki Yuasa
Gamera, the Invincible '66
Gamera vs. Gaos '67
Gamera vs. Guiron '69
Gamera vs. Zigra '71

Corey Yuen
No Retreat, No Surrender '86
No Retreat, No Surrender 2 '89

Johnny Yune
They Still Call Me Bruce '86

Larry Yust
Homebodies '74
Say Yes! '86

Peter Yuval
Dead End City '88
Firehead '90

Brian Yuzna
Bride of Re-Animator '89
Return of the Living Dead 3 '93

Silent Night, Deadly Night 4: Initiation '90
Society '92

Jose Maria Zabalza
The Fury of the Wolfman '70

Alfredo Zacharias
Bandits '73
The Bees '78
Crossfire '67
Demonoid, Messenger of Death '81

Michael Zachary
Sin of Adam & Eve '72

Robert Zagone
Stand-In '85

Raja Zahr
The Last Season '87

Steven Zaillian
Searching for Bobby Fischer '93

Nancy Zala
Round Numbers '91

Alain Zaloum
Canvas: The Fine Art of Crime '92

Luigi Zampa
Tigers in Lipstick '80
A Woman of Rome '56

Mario Zampi
The Naked Truth '58
Too Many Crooks '59

Susanne Zanke
The Scorpion Woman '89

Lili Fini Zanuck
Rush '91

Krzysztof Zanussi
The Catamount Killing '74
The Structure of Crystals '69
The Unapproachable '82
Year of the Quiet Sun '84

Janusz Zaorski
Baritone '85

Fabrice A. Zaphiratos
Bloodbeat '85

Frank Zappa
Baby Snakes: The Complete Version '79
200 Motels '71

Mier Zarchi
Don't Mess with My Sister! '85
I Spit on Your Grave '77

Tony Zarindast
The Guns and the Fury '83
Hardcase and Fist '89
Treasure of the Lost Desert '83

Cesare Zavattini
Love in the City '53

Edwin Zbonek
The Mad Executioners '65
The Monster of London City '64

Kristi Zea
Women & Men: In Love There Are No Rules '91

Nick Zedd
Geek Maggot Bingo '83

Franco Zeffirelli
Brother Sun, Sister Moon '73
The Champ '79
Endless Love '81
Hamlet '90
Jesus of Nazareth '77
Otello '86
Romeo and Juliet '68
The Taming of the Shrew '67

Primo Zeglio
Mission Stardust '68

Rafal Zeilinski
Ginger Ale Afternoon '89
Loose Screws '85
Recruits '86
Screwballs '83
Spellcaster '91

Alfred Zeisler
Amazing Adventure '37
Enemy of Women '44
Fear '46
Make-Up '37
Parole, Inc. '49

Yuri Zeltser
Eye of the Storm '91

Karel Zeman
Fabulous Adventures of Baron
 Munchausen '61
On the Comet '68
The Original Fabulous
 Adventures of Baron
 Munchausen '61

Robert Zemeckis
Back to the Future '85
Back to the Future, Part 2 '89
Back to the Future, Part 3 '90
Death Becomes Her '92
Forrest Gump '94
I Wanna Hold Your Hand '78
Romancing the Stone '84
Tales from the Crypt '89
Used Cars '80
Who Framed Roger Rabbit? '88

Will Zens
The Fix '84
Hell on Wheels '67
Hot Summer in Barefoot
 County '74
Trucker's Woman '83

Mai Zetterling
Scrubbers '82

V. Zhalakyavichus
Adomas Nori Buti Zmogumi '59

Arunas Zhebrunas
Grazuole '69

Yuri Zhelyabuzhsky
The Cigarette Girl of
 Mosselprom '24

Tian Zhuangzhuang
The Horse Thief '87

Claude Zidi
My New Partner '84
Stuntwoman '81

Howard Zieff
The Dream Team '89
Hearts of the West '75
House Calls '78
The Main Event '79
My Girl '91
My Girl 2 '94
Private Benjamin '80
Slither '73
Unfaithfully Yours '84

Rafal Zielinksi
Jailbait '93

Paul Ziller
Bloodfist 4: Die Trying '92
Deadly Surveillance '91

Vernon Zimmerman
Fade to Black '80
Unholy Rollers '72

Michael Zinberg
Accidental Meeting '93

Fred Zinneman
Behold a Pale Horse '64
The Day of the Jackal '73
Five Days One Summer '82
From Here to Eternity '53
High Noon '52
Julia '77
A Man for All Seasons '66

The Member of the Wedding
 '52
The Men '50
The Nun's Story '59
Oklahoma! '55
The Search '48
The Seventh Cross '44
The Sundowners '60

Peter Zinner
The Salamander '82

Joseph Zito
Abduction '75
Friday the 13th, Part 4: The
 Final Chapter '84
Invasion U.S.A. '85
Missing in Action '84
The Prowler '81
Red Scorpion '89

Dick Zondag
We're Back! A Dinosaur's Story
 '93

Ralph Zondag
We're Back! A Dinosaur's Story
 '93

Vilmos Zsigmond
The Two Jakes '90

David Zucker
Airplane! '80
The Naked Gun: From the Files
 of Police Squad '88
Naked Gun 2 1/2: The Smell of
 Fear '91
Police Squad! Help Wanted! '82
Ruthless People '86
Top Secret! '84

Jerry Zucker
Airplane! '80
Ghost '90
Police Squad! Help Wanted! '82
Ruthless People '86
Top Secret! '84

Ralph Zucker
Terror Creatures from the
 Grave '66

Andrzej Zulawski
Possession '81

Frank Zuniga
Fist Fighter '88
Further Adventures of the
 Wilderness Family, Part 2
 '77
The Golden Seal '83
Heartbreaker '83

Marcos Zurinaga
Tango Bar '88

Guido Zurli
Psychopath '68

John Zuru
The Mad Butcher '72

Martin Zweiback
Cactus in the Snow '72

Edward Zwick
About Last Night... '86
Glory '89
Having It All '82
Leaving Normal '92
Special Bulletin '83

Joel Zwick
Second Sight '89

Karl Zwicky
Contagion '87
Vicious '88

WRITER INDEX

The **WRITER INDEX** lists the video accomplishments of nearly 3,500 screenwriters and other masters of the script. Names are presented in a first name, last name format, and alphabetized by last name. The **Cast** and **Director Indexes** immediately precede this index; the **Composer Index** immediately follows.

Dough Aarniokoski
Puppet Master 4 '93

Anthony Able
Project: Alien '89

Jim Abrahams
Airplane! '80
Hot Shots! '91
Hot Shots! Part Deux '93
Kentucky Fried Movie '77
The Naked Gun: From the Files
   of Police Squad '88
Police Squad! Help Wanted! '82
Top Secret! '84

Celia Abrams
Easy Wheels '89

Ian Abrams
Undercover Blues '93

Jeffrey Abrams
Forever Young '92
Regarding Henry '91
Taking Care of Business '90

Jon Acevski
Freddie as F.R.O.7 '92

Rodney Ackland
The Forty-Ninth Parallel '41

Catlin Adams
Sticky Fingers '88

Daniel Adams
Primary Motive '92

Gilbert Adler
Children of the Corn 2: The
   Final Sacrifice '92

Percy Adlon
Bagdad Cafe '88
Celeste '81
Rosalie Goes Shopping '89
Sugarbaby '85

Nelly Adnil
Silent Victim '92

James Agee
The African Queen '51
The Night of the Hunter '55

Faruque Ahmed
Warlords 3000 '93

Chantal Akerman
The Eighties '83
Les Rendez-vous D'Anna '78
News from Home '76
Night and Day '91
Window Shopping '86

Andra Akers
Toute Une Nuit '82

William M. Akers
Ernest Rides Again '93

Marvin H. Albert
Rough Night in Jericho '67

Alan Alda
Betsy's Wedding '90
The Four Seasons '81
A New Life '88
The Seduction of Joe Tynan '79
Sweet Liberty '86

Will Aldis
Back to School '86
The Couch Trip '87
Stealing Home '88

Thomas Gutierrez Alea
Letters from the Park '88
Memories of
   Underdevelopment '68

Ronald Alexander
Billie '65

Scott Alexander
Ed Wood '94
Problem Child '90
Problem Child 2 '91

Richard Alferi
Children of Rage '75
Echoes '83
A Friendship in Vienna '88

Dan Algrant
Naked in New York '93

Ranald Allan
The Crossing '92

Ted Allan
Dr. Bethune '90
Falling in Love Again '80
Lies My Father Told Me '75
Love Streams '84

Pat Allee
Bums '93

Curt Allen
Blind Vengeance '90

Irwin Allen
Five Weeks in a Balloon '62
Voyage to the Bottom of the
   Sea '61

J.T. Allen
Geronimo '93

Jay Presson Allen
Cabaret '72
Deathtrap '82
Forty Carats '73
Funny Lady '75
Just Tell Me What You Want
   '80
Marnie '64
The Prime of Miss Jean Brodie
   '69
Prince of the City '81
Travels with My Aunt '72
Year of the Gun '91

Jim Allen
Hidden Agenda '90

Jordan Allen
Terminal Bliss '91

Woody Allen
Alice '90
Annie Hall '77
Another Woman '88
Bananas '71
Broadway Danny Rose '84
Crimes & Misdemeanors '89
Everything You Always Wanted
   to Know About Sex (But
   Were Afraid to Ask) '72
Hannah and Her Sisters '86
Husbands and Wives '92
Interiors '78
Love and Death '75
Manhattan '79
Manhattan Murder Mystery '93
A Midsummer Night's Sex
   Comedy '82
New York Stories '89
The Purple Rose of Cairo '85
Radio Days '87
September '88
Shadows and Fog '92
Sleeper '73
Stardust Memories '80
Take the Money and Run '69
What's New Pussycat? '65
Zelig '83

Pedro Almodovar
Dark Habits '84
High Heels '91
Labyrinth of Passion '82
Law of Desire '86
Matador '86
Pepi, Luci, Bom and Other Girls
   on the Heap '80
Tie Me Up! Tie Me Down! '90

What Have I Done to Deserve
   This? '85
Women on the Verge of a
   Nervous Breakdown '88

Paul Almond
The Dance Goes On '92

Emmett Alston
Nine Deaths of the Ninja '85

Robert Altman
Beyond Therapy '86
Buffalo Bill & the Indians '76
McCabe & Mrs. Miller '71
Quintet '79
Short Cuts '93
Thieves Like Us '74
A Wedding '78

Shelly Altman
Sweet Lorraine '87

Eric Ambler
Immortal Battalion '44
A Night to Remember '58

David Ambrose
Amityville 3: The Demon '83
Blackout '85
Dangerous Summer '82
D.A.R.Y.L. '85
The Fifth Musketeer '79
The Final Countdown '80
Survivor '80
Taffin '88
Year of the Gun '91

Sergio Amidei
Open City '45
Shoeshine '47

Morey Amsterdam
The Ghost and the Guest '43

Franco Amurri
Monkey Trouble '94

Allison Anders
Border Radio '88
Gas Food Lodging '92
Mi Vida Loca '94

Clyde Anderson
Troll 2 '92

Elizabeth Anderson
Lassie '94

Hesper Anderson
Children of a Lesser God '86
Grand Isle '92
Touched by Love '80

Jane Anderson
It Could Happen to You '94
The Positively True Adventures
   of the Alleged Texas
   Cheerleader-Murdering
   Mom '93

Robert Anderson
I Never Sang For My Father '70
The Nun's Story '59
The Sand Pebbles '66
Tea and Sympathy '56
Until They Sail '57

Steve Anderson
South Central '92

Lucette Andrei
My Father's Glory '91

Roger Andrieux
La Petite Sirene '80

Dan Angel
Body Bags '93

Michael Angeli
Conflict of Interest '92

Theo Angelopoulos
Landscape in the Mist '88

Maya Angelou
Georgia, Georgia '72

Gianfranco Angelucci
Intervista '87

Carole Angier
Wide Sargasso Sea '92

Edward Anhalt
Becket '64
Boeing Boeing '65
The Boston Strangler '68
Escape to Athena '79
Fatal Chase '77
Green Ice '81
The Holcroft Covenant '85
Jeremiah Johnson '72
Luther '74
The Madwoman of Chaillot '69
The Member of the Wedding
   '52
Not as a Stranger '55
Panic in the Streets '50
The Pride and the Passion '57
The Take '90
The Young Lions '58

Erik Anjou
The Cool Surface '92

Anjou ►cont.

976-EVIL 2: The Astral Factor '91
The Road to Ruin '28

Jean-Jacques Annaud
Black and White in Color '76
The Lover '92

Jean Anouilh
Circle of Love '64

Joseph Anthony
Crime and Punishment '35

Stuart Anthony
Arizona Mahoney '36
Border Law '31
Drift Fence '36
The Fighting Sheriff '31
The Monster and the Girl '41

Steve Antin
Inside Monkey Zetterland '93

Michelangelo Antonioni
Blow-Up '66
The Eclipse '66
Il Grido '57
L'Avventura '60
The Passenger '75
The Red Desert '64
Zabriskie Point '70

Bill Apablasa
Airborne '93

Max Apple
The Air Up There '94
Smokey Bites the Dust '81

Daniel Appleby
Bound and Gagged: A Love Story '93

A.L. Appling
Running Mates '92

Gregg Araki
The Living End '92

Denys Arcand
The Decline of the American Empire '86
Jesus of Montreal '89

Manuel Arce
Crossover Dreams '85
El Super '79

Jeffrey Arch
Iron Will '93
Sleepless in Seattle '93

Claudio Argento
Santa Sangre '90

Dario Argento
The Bird with the Crystal Plumage '70
The Cat o' Nine Tails '71
The Church '90
Creepers '85
Dario Argento's Trauma '93
Demons 2 '87
The Devil's Daughter '91
Once Upon a Time in the West '68
Suspiria '77
Terror at the Opera '88
Unsane '82

Alice Arlen
Alamo Bay '85
Cookie '89
Silkwood '83

George Armitage
Miami Blues '90
Private Duty Nurses '71

Carrie Armstrong
Ninja Vengeance '93

Karl Armstrong
Ninja Vengeance '93

David Arnott
The Adventures of Ford Fairlane '90
Last Action Hero '93

Alexandre Arnoux
Don Quixote '35

Antonin Artaud
Smiling Madame Beudet/The Seashell and the Clergyman '28

Art Arthur
Everything Happens at Night '39

Robert Arthur
Warlock '59

Victor Arthur
Hills of Oklahoma '50

William Asher
Bikini Beach '64
How to Stuff a Wild Bikini '65

Isaac Asimov
Light Years '88

Samson Aslanian
Torment '85

Peter Atkins
Hellbound: Hellraiser 2 '88
Hellraiser 3: Hell on Earth '92

Larry Atlas
Sleepless in Seattle '93

Paul Attanasio
Rapid Fire '92

Margaret Atwood
Heaven on Earth '89

Jacques Audiard
Barjo '92
Baxter '89

Bille August
The House of the Spirits '93
Pelle the Conqueror '88
Twist & Shout '84

Joe Augustyn
Night Angel '90
Night of the Demons '88
Night of the Demons 2 '94

Carlos Aured
Triumphs of a Man Called Horse '83

Carl Austin
Sexual Malice '93
Wild Cactus '92

Phillip Avalon
Fatal Bond '91

Roger Roberts Avary
Pulp Fiction '94

Antonio Avati
Bix '90

Pupi Avati
Bix '90
The Story of Boys & Girls '91

Howard (Hikmet) Avedis
The Fifth Floor '80
Scorchy '76

Robert J. Avereen
A Stranger Among Us '92

Barry Avrich
Scorned '93

George Axelrod
Breakfast at Tiffany's '61
Bus Stop '56
The Fourth Protocol '87
The Holcroft Covenant '85
How to Murder Your Wife '64
The Lady Vanishes '79

The Manchurian Candidate '62
Paris When It Sizzles '64
Phffft! '54
Secret Life of an American Wife '68
The Seven Year Itch '55

Dan Aykroyd
The Blues Brothers '80
Coneheads '93
Dragnet '87
Ghostbusters '84
Spies Like Us '85

Marcel Ayme
Crime and Punishment '35

Rafael Azcona
Ay, Carmela! '90
Belle Epoque '92

Beth B
Salvation! '87
Vortex '81

Scott B
Vortex '81

Hector Babenco
At Play in the Fields of the Lord '91
Pixote '81

Jimmy Santiago Baca
Blood In...Blood Out: Bound by Honor '93

Danilo Bach
April Fool's Day '86
Beverly Hills Cop '84

Michael Backes
Rising Sun '93

Peter Bacso
Oh, Bloody Life! '88

Randall Badat
Born to Run '93
Hear No Evil '93
Surf 2 '84

Giya Badridze
Ashik Kerib '88

Bill Baer
The Quiet Earth '85

Meredith Baer
The Magic Bubble '93

Fax Bahr
Hearts of Darkness: A Filmmaker's Apocalypse '91
In the Army Now '94
Son-in-Law '93

Frederick Bailey
Quick '93

John Baines
Dead of Night '45

Jon Robin Baitz
Fallen Angels 1 '93

Bart Baker
Baby of the Bride '91

Edwin Baker
Combination Platter '93

Michael Baker
Dead Ahead: The Exxon Valdez Disaster '92

John Balderston
Frankenstein '31
The Lives of a Bengal Lancer '35
Prisoner of Zenda '37
Red Planet Mars '52

James Baldwin
Malcolm X '72

Anne Bancroft
Fatso '80

Jack Baran
Band of the Hand '86
Great Balls of Fire '89

Dana Baratta
Andre '94

Franco Barbieri
Beyond the Door 2 '79

Ann Louise Bardach
Sorry, Wrong Number '89

Frank Barhydt
Short Cuts '93

Clive Barker
Hellraiser '87
Night Breed '90
Rawhead Rex '87
Transmutations '85

Peter Barnes
Enchanted April '92

Willie Baronet
Adventures in Dinosaur City '92

Douglas Barr
The Cover Girl Murders '93
Fade to Black '93

Jackson Barr
Bad Channels '92
Body Chemistry '90
800 Leagues Down the Amazon '90s
Mandroid '93
Seedpeople '92

James Lee Barrett
Angel City '80
Poker Alice '87

J.M. Barrie
As You Like It '36
Quality Street '37

Julian Barry
Lenny '74
Me, Myself & I '92
The River '84

Odile Barski
The Cry of the Owl '92

Hall Bartlett
All the Young Men '60
Children of Sanchez '79

Ronald Bass
Black Widow '87
Rain Man '88
Sleeping with the Enemy '91
When a Man Loves a Woman '94

William Bast
The Betsy '78
James Dean '76

Alan Bates
The Story of a Love Story '73

Joe Batteer
Blown Away '94
Chasers '94
Curiosity Kills '90

Bradley Battersby
Blue Desert '91

Lamberto Bava
Beyond the Door 2 '79
Demons 2 '87

John Baxter
The Time Guardian '87

Sergio Bazzini
Husbands and Lovers '91

David Beaird
My Chauffeur '86
Octavia '82
Party Animal '83
Scorchers '92

Henry Bean
Deep Cover '92

Richard Beattie
Cold Sweat '93

Warren Beatty
Heaven Can Wait '78
Reds '81
Reds '81
Shampoo '75

D.D. Beauchamp
Abbott and Costello Go to Mars '53

Josh Beck
Lunatics: A Love Story '92

Jacques Becker
Ali Baba and the 40 Thieves '54
Modigliani '58

Michael Frost Beckner
Sniper '92

Ford Beebe
Fighting Shadows '35
Riders of Pasco Basin '40

S.N. Behrman
Hallelujah, I'm a Bum '33
A Tale of Two Cities '35

Jean-Jacques Beineix
Betty Blue '86
Diva '82
Moon in the Gutter '83

Elisa Bell
Writer's Block '91

Ross Bell
To Die Standing '91

James Warner Bellah
Sergeant Rutledge '60

Marco Bellochio
Devil in the Flesh '87
The Eyes, the Mouth '83
Henry IV '85

Peter Bellwood
Highlander '86
Highlander 2: The Quickening '91
Phobia '80

Jerry Belson
Always '89
The End '78
Fun with Dick and Jane '77
How Sweet It Is! '68
Jekyll & Hyde...Together Again '82
Smile '75
Smokey and the Bandit, Part 2 '80
Surrender '87

James Belushi
Birthday Boy '85

Remy Belvaux
Man Bites Dog '92

Peter Benchley
The Deep '77
The Island '80
Jaws '75

Robert Benchley
Foreign Correspondent '40

Barbara Benedek
Immediate Family '89
Men Don't Leave '89

Tom Benedek
Cocoon '85

Glenn Benest
Deadly Blessing '81

Roberto Benigni
Johnny Stecchino '92

Richard Benner
Happy Birthday, Gemini '80

Alan Bennett
An Englishman Abroad '83
Prick Up Your Ears '87
A Private Function '84

A Question of Attribution '91

Bill Bennett
Backlash '86

Charles Bennett
Balalaika '39
Black Magic '49
Blackmail '29
Curse of the Demon '57
Dangerous Mission '54
The Evil Mind '34
Five Weeks in a Balloon '62
Foreign Correspondent '40
Forever and a Day '43
The Green Glove '52
The Man Who Knew Too Much '34
Sabotage '36
The Secret Agent '36
The 39 Steps '35
Voyage to the Bottom of the Sea '61

Parker Bennett
Super Mario Bros. '93

Wallace C. Bennett
George! '70

Robby Benson
Betrayal of the Dove '92
Die Laughing '80

Sally Benson
Anna and the King of Siam '46
Conspirator '49

Robert Benton
Bonnie & Clyde '67
Nadine '87
Places in the Heart '84
Superman: The Movie '78
There was a Crooked Man '70

Luc Beraud
This Sweet Sickness '77

Geza Beremenyi
The Midas Touch '89

Bruce Beresford
Barry McKenzie Holds His Own '74
Breaker Morant '80
The Fringe Dwellers '86
Mister Johnson '91
Money Movers '78

Rhoisin Beresford
The Fringe Dwellers '86

Pamela Berger
The Imported Bridegroom '89
Sorceress '88

Andrew Bergman
Big Trouble '86
Blazing Saddles '74
Fletch '85
The Freshman '90
Honeymoon in Vegas '92
The In-Laws '79
It Could Happen to You '94
Oh, God! You Devil '84
The Scout '94
So Fine '81
Soapdish '91

Ingmar Bergman
After the Rehearsal '84
Autumn Sonata '78
The Best Intentions '92
Cries and Whispers '72
The Devil's Eye '60
Devil's Wanton '49
Dreams '55
Face to Face '76
Fanny and Alexander '83
From the Life of the Marionettes '80
Hour of the Wolf '68
Lesson in Love '54
The Magician '58
Monika '52
The Passion of Anna '70
Persona '66
Sawdust & Tinsel '53

Scenes from a Marriage '73
Secrets of Women '52
The Serpent's Egg '78
The Seventh Seal '56
The Shame '68
The Silence '63
Smiles of a Summer Night '55
Summer Interlude '50
Through a Glass Darkly '61
Torment '44
The Touch '71
Wild Strawberries '57
The Winter Light '62

Martin Bergman
Peter's Friends '92

Robert Bergman
Skull: A Night of Terror '88
A Whisper to a Scream '88

Eric Bergren
The Elephant Man '80
Frances '82

Eleanor Bergstein
Dirty Dancing '87
It's My Turn '80

Martin Berkeley
The Deadly Mantis '57
Revenge of the Creature '55
Tarantula '55

Jeannie Berlin
In the Spirit '90

Barry Berman
Benny & Joon '93

Sam Bernard
Warlock: The Armageddon '93

Edward L. Bernds
Blondie Knows Best '46
Reform School Girl '57
Storm Rider '57

Peter Berneis
My Man Godfrey '57

Armyan Bernstein
One from the Heart '82

Jack Bernstein
Ace Ventura: Pet Detective '93

Nat Bernstein
Opportunity Knocks '90

Walter Bernstein
The Betsy '78
Heller in Pink Tights '60
The House on Carroll Street '88
Paris Blues '61
The Train '65
Yanks '79

Eric Bernt
Surviving the Game '94

Claude Berri
Jean de Florette '87
Manon of the Spring '87
One Wild Moment '78
Uranus '91

Michael Berry
Short Time '90

Tom Berry
Crazy Moon '87

Bernardo Bertolucci
Before the Revolution '65
The Conformist '71
The Last Emperor '87
Last Tango in Paris '73
Once Upon a Time in the West '68
The Sheltering Sky '90
The Spider's Stratagem '70
The Tragedy of a Ridiculous Man '81

Giuseppe Bertolucci
1900 '76

Luc Besson
The Big Blue '88

La Femme Nikita '91
Le Dernier Combat '84
Subway '85

Pete Best
Accidental Meeting '93

Eddie Beverly, Jr.
Ballbuster

Radha Bharadwaj
Closet Land '90

Grace Cary Bickley
The Gun in Betty Lou's Handbag '92

Kathryn Bigelow
Near Dark '87

Danny Bilson
Arena '88
The Eliminators '86
Future Cop '76
The Rocketeer '91
Trancers '85
The Wrong Guys '88
Zone Troopers '85

John Binder
Honeysuckle Rose '80

Mike Binder
Coupe de Ville '90
Crossing the Bridge '92
Indian Summer '93

William Bindley
Freeze Frame '92

Steve Bing
Every Breath '93
Missing in Action 2: The Beginning '85

Edfrid Bingham
Riders of the Purple Sage '25

Claude Binyon
Arizona '40

Dudley Birch
Flight from Singapore '62

Brad Bird
*batteries not included '87

Brian Bird
Bopha! '93

Sarah Bird
Don't Tell Her It's Me '90

Andrew Birkin
Burning Secret '89
The Final Conflict '81
King David '85
The Name of the Rose '86

Lajos Biro
The Private Life of Henry VIII '33

Louise Birt
The Three Weird Sisters '48

John Bishop
The Package '89

Shem Bitterman
Halloween 5: The Revenge of Michael Myers '89
Out of the Rain '90

Emerson Bixby
Bikini Island '91
Disturbed '90

David Black
Legacy of Lies '92

Shane Black
Last Action Hero '93
The Last Boy Scout '91
Lethal Weapon '87
The Monster Squad '87

Stephen Black
Eden '92
Eden 2 '93

Susan Black
State of Emergency '94

David Blair
Wax, or the Discovery of Television Among the Bees '93

Michael Blake
Dances with Wolves '90
Stacy's Knights '83

Dorothy Blank
Snow White and the Seven Dwarfs '37

Michael Blankfort
Tribute to a Bad Man '56

William Peter Blatty
Darling Lili '70
The Exorcist '73
The Exorcist 3 '90
Promise Her Anything '66
A Shot in the Dark '64
What Did You Do in the War, Daddy? '66

Barry W. Blaustein
Boomerang '92
Coming to America '88
Police Academy 2: Their First Assignment '85

Alan Bleasdale
No Surrender '86

Corey Blechman
Dominick & Eugene '88
Free Willy '93
Max and Helen '90

Lee Blessing
Cooperstown '93

Bertrand Bingham
Menage '86
My Best Friend's Girl '84
Too Beautiful for You '88

John W. Bloch
One Man's Way '63

Robert Bloch
The House that Dripped Blood '71
The Night Walker '64
Strait-Jacket '64
Torture Garden '67

Michael Blodgett
Turner and Hooch '89

Jeffrey Bloom
Dog Pound Shuffle '75
11 Harrowhouse '74
Flowers in the Attic '87
Nightmares '83
The Stick-Up '77
Swashbuckler '76

Len Blum
Beethoven's 2nd '93
Feds '88
Meatballs '79
Spacehunter: Adventures in the Forbidden Zone '83
Stripes '81

John Blumenthal
Short Time '90

Don Bluth
All Dogs Go to Heaven '89
The Secret of NIMH '82
Thumbelina '94

Jeffrey Boam
Dead Zone '83
Funny Farm '88
Indiana Jones and the Last Crusade '89
Innerspace '87
Lethal Weapon 2 '89
Lethal Weapon 3 '92
The Lost Boys '87
Straight Time '78

Al Boasberg
A Night at the Opera '35

Sam Bobrick
Jimmy the Kid '82
Norman, Is That You? '76

Steven Bochco
Columbo: Murder By the Book '71
Silent Running '71

Sally Bochner
Strangers in Good Company '91

Endre Boehm
Twenty Bucks '93

Leslie Boehm
The Horror Show '89
Nowhere to Run '93
Twenty Bucks '93

Sydney Boehm
Rough Night in Jericho '67

Michael Boekner
Psycho Girls '86

Peter Bogdanovich
The Last Picture Show '71
Saint Jack '79
Texasville '90
They All Laughed '81
The Wild Angels '66

Eric Bogosian
Sex, Drugs, Rock & Roll: Eric Bogosian '91
Talk Radio '88

Michael Derek Bohusz
Uninvited '93

Jerome Boivin
Barjo '93
Baxter '89

Heinrich Boll
Germany in Autumn '78

Joseph Bologna
Lovers and Other Strangers '70

Craig Bolotin
Black Rain '89
Straight Talk '92
That Night '93

Max Bolt
The Big Sweat '90

Robert Bolt
The Bounty '84
Doctor Zhivago '65
Lady Caroline Lamb '73
Lawrence of Arabia '62
A Man for All Seasons '66
The Mission '86
Ryan's Daughter '70
Without Warning: The James Brady Story '91

Guy Bolton
Weekend at the Waldorf '45

Julian Bond
Choice of Weapons '76
The Shooting Party '85
The Whistle Blower '87

Vittorio Bonicelli
Moses '76

Pascal Bonitzer
Night and Day '91

Andre Bonzel
Man Bites Dog '91

Connie Booth
Fawlty Towers '77

James Booth
American Ninja 2: The Confrontation '87
Pray for Death '85
Sunburn '79

Ethel B. Borden
I Live My Life '35

Herb Borkland
Honor and Glory '92

Michael Bortman
The Good Mother '88

Aida Bortnik
The Official Story '85
Old Gringo '89

Roselyne Bosch
1492: Conquest of Paradise '92

Jean Boudin
Being at Home with Claude '92

William Bowers
My Man Godfrey '57
Split Second '53
Support Your Local Sheriff '69

Alan Bowne
Spike of Bensonhurst '88

Daniel Boyd
Chillers '8
Invasion of the Space
   Preachers '90

Don Boyd
East of Elephant Rock '76
Twenty-One '91

William Boyd
Chaplin '92
Mister Johnson '91
Stars and Bars '88
Tune in Tomorrow '90

Bill Bozzone
Full Moon in Blue Water '88
Ivory Hunters '90

Gerard Brach
The Bear '89
Bitter Moon '92
Cul de Sac '66
Diary of Forbidden Dreams '73
The Fearless Vampire Killers
   '67
Frantic '88
I Sent a Letter to My Love '81
Jean de Florette '87
The Lover '92
Manon of the Spring '87
My Best Friend's Girl '84
The Name of the Rose '86
Pirates '86
Quest for Fire '82
Repulsion '65
Shy People '87
The Tenant '76

Charles Brackett
Ball of Fire '41
The Lost Weekend '45
Sunset Boulevard '50

Leigh Brackett
The Big Sleep '46
The Empire Strikes Back '80
The Long Goodbye '73

Jacob Brackman
The King of Marvin Gardens
   '72
Times Square '80

Malcolm Bradbury
The Green Man '91

Ray Bradbury
It Came From Outer Space '53
Moby Dick '56
Something Wicked This Way
   Comes '83

**Robert North
Bradbury**
The Gallant Fool '33
Texas Buddies '32
Valley of the Lawless '36

John Bradshaw
The Big Slice '90

Bill Brame
Miss Melody Jones '73

Kenneth Branagh
Henry V '89
Much Ado About Nothing '93

Larry Brand
Masque of the Red Death '89

Millen Brand
The Snake Pit '48

David Brandes
Dirt Bike Kid '86

Richard Brando
Martial Law 2: Undercover '91

Clark Brandon
Skeeter '93

Asher Brauner
Deadly Exposure '93

Irving Brecher
Ship Ahoy '42

Catherine Breillat
Police '85

**Frederick Hazlitt
Brennan**
Adventure '45

Richard Brennan
Bloodmoon '90

Lou Breslow
Merton of the Movies '47

Robert Bresson
Diary of a Country Priest '50
L'Argent '83

George Bricker
House of Horrors '46

Marshall Brickman
Annie Hall '77
For the Boys '91
Intersection '93
Lovesick '83
Manhattan '79
Manhattan Murder Mystery '93
The Manhattan Project '86
Simon '80
Sleeper '73

Paul Brickman
The Bad News Bears in
   Breaking Training '77
Citizens Band '77
Deal of the Century '83
Men Don't Leave '89
Risky Business '83

James Bridges
The Appaloosa '66
The Baby Maker '70
The China Syndrome '79
Colossus: The Forbin Project
   '70
Mike's Murder '84
The Paper Chase '73
Perfect '85
September 30, 1955 '77
Urban Cowboy '80
White Hunter, Black Heart '90

Matthew Bright
Forbidden Zone '80
Guncrazy '92

John Briley
Children of the Damned '63
Cry Freedom '87
Eagle's Wing '79
Enigma '82
Gandhi '82
Marie '85
Tai-Pan '86
That Lucky Touch '75

Steven Brill
D2: The Mighty Ducks '94
The Mighty Ducks '92

Deborah Brock
Rock 'n' Roll High School
   Forever '91
Slumber Party Massacre 2 '87

Oscar Brodney
Francis Goes to the Races '51
Ghost Fever '87
The Glenn Miller Story '54
Mexican Hayride '48
Tammy and the Doctor '63
When Hell Broke Loose '58

Larry Brody
The Night the City Screamed
   '80

Dan Bronson
The Last Innocent Man '87
A Taste for Killing '92

Peter Brook
Swann in Love '84

Ralph Brooke
Bloodlust '59

Howard Brookner
Bloodhounds of Broadway '89

Albert Brooks
Defending Your Life '91
Lost in America '85
Modern Romance '81
Real Life '79
The Scout '94

Halle Brooks
Who Shot Pat? '92

James L. Brooks
Broadcast News '87
I'll Do Anything '93
Starting Over '79
Terms of Endearment '83
Thursday's Game '74

Joseph Brooks
If Ever I See You Again '78
You Light Up My Life '77

Mel Brooks
Blazing Saddles '74
High Anxiety '77
History of the World: Part 1 '81
Life Stinks '91
The Producers '68
Robin Hood: Men in Tights '93
Silent Movie '76
Spaceballs '87
Twelve Chairs '70
Young Frankenstein '74

Richard Brooks
Any Number Can Play '49
Battle Circus '53
Bite the Bullet '75
Blackboard Jungle '55
The Brothers Karamazov '58
Cat on a Hot Tin Roof '58
Cobra Woman '44
Dollars '71
Elmer Gantry '60
Fever Pitch '85
The Happy Ending '69
In Cold Blood '67
Key Largo '48
The Last Hunt '56
The Last Time I Saw Paris '54
Looking for Mr. Goodbar '77
Lord Jim '65
The Professionals '66
Something of Value '57
Sweet Bird of Youth '62
Wrong is Right '82

Robert Brooks
Who Shot Pat? '92

Philip Brophy
Body Melt '93

Larry Brothers
An Innocent Man '89

Tamar Brott
The Linguini Incident '92

Barry Brown
Lonely in America '90

Billy Brown
Body Bags '93

Bruce Brown
The Endless Summer '66
The Endless Summer 2 '94

Dana Brown
The Endless Summer 2 '94

Gerard Brown
Juice '92

Harry Brown
All the Brothers Were Valiant
   '53
Arch of Triumph '48

Julie Brown
Earth Girls are Easy '89

Leigh Brown
A Christmas Story '83
It Runs In the Family '94

**Michael Henry
Brown**
Laurel Avenue '93

Rita Mae Brown
The Slumber Party Massacre
   '82

William O. Brown
The Witchmaker '69

Janet Brownell
The Amy Fisher Story '93
Sweet Revenge '90

Tod Browning
Devil Doll '36
Mystery of the Leaping Fish/
   Chess Fever '25

John Brownjohn
Bitter Moon '92

William Broyles, Jr.
JFK: Reckless Youth '93

George Bruce
Navy Blue and Gold '37

Glenn A. Bruce
Undercover Cop '94

Chris Bryant
Don't Look Now '73
Foreign Affairs '93
The Girl from Petrovka '74
Joseph Andrews '77
Man Who Had Power Over
   Women '70
Martin's Day '85
Stealing Heaven '88
Sword of Gideon '86
Young Catherine '91

John Bryant
Scanner Cop '94

**James David
Buchanan**
Brenda Starr '86
Deadly Currents '93

Larry Buchanan
It's Alive! '68
Mars Needs Women '66
Mistress of the Apes '79

Sidney Buchman
Here Comes Mr. Jordan '41
Holiday '38
Mr. Smith Goes to Washington
   '39

Andrea Buck
The Double O Kid '92

Robert Buckner
The Desert Song '53
Dive Bomber '41
Yankee Doodle Dandy '42

Adele Buffington
Bad Men of the Border '45
Haunted Gold '32

Takashi Bufford
House Party 3 '94

Charles Bukowski
Barfly '87

Alan Bunce
Babar: The Movie '88

Luis Bunuel
Diary of a Chambermaid '64
The Discreet Charm of the
   Bourgeoisie '72
L'Age D'Or '30
That Obscure Object of Desire
   '77
Tristana '70
Viridiana '61
The Young One '61

Anthony Burgess
Moses '76

Martyn Burke
Last Chase '81

Alan Burnett
Batman: Mask of the Phantasm
   '93
DuckTales the Movie: Treasure
   of the Lost Lamp '90

Charles Burnett
To Sleep with Anger '90

W.R. Burnett
Dangerous Mission '54
The Great Escape '63
High Sierra '41
I Died a Thousand Times '55
This Gun for Hire '42

Ken Burns
The Civil War, Episode 1: The
   Cause—1861 '90
The Civil War, Episode 2: A
   Very Bloody Affair—1862
   '90
The Civil War, Episode 3:
   Forever Free—1862 '90
The Civil War, Episode 4:
   Simply Murder—1863 '90
The Civil War, Episode 5: The
   Universe of Battle—1863 '90
The Civil War, Episode 6: Valley
   of the Shadow of Death—
   1864 '90
The Civil War, Episode 7: Most
   Hallowed Ground—1864 '90
The Civil War, Episode 8: War
   is All Hell—1865 '90
The Civil War, Episode 9: The
   Better Angels of Our
   Nature—1865 '90

Mark Burns
Married to the Mob '88
She-Devil '89

Tim Burns
Freaked '93

Jim Burnstein
Renaissance Man '94

Richard Burridge
Absolute Beginners '86
The Fourth Protocol '87

Abe Burrows
How to Succeed in Business
   without Really Trying '67

Tim Burstall
Alvin Purple '73
Alvin Rides Again '74

Michael Burton
Flight of the Navigator '86
Shoot to Kill '88

Tim Burton
Edward Scissorhands '90
Frankenweenie '84

Leszek Burzynski
Trapped Alive '93

Niven Busch
Scarlet Dawn '32

Frank Butler
Going My Way '44
Golden Earrings '47
My Favorite Blonde '42

Hugo Butler
The Southerner '45
Young Tom Edison '40

Michael Butler
Brannigan '75
Code of Silence '85
Fifty/Fifty '93
Flashpoint '84
The Gauntlet '77
Murder by Phone '82
Pale Rider '85

Floyd Byars
Mindwalk: A Film for Passionate Thinkers '91

David Byrne
True Stories '86

Jim Byrnes
Dead Man's Revenge '93

John Byrum
Scandalous '84
Sphinx '81

Cheri Caffaro
H.O.T.S. '79

Hy Cahl
Teenage Gang Debs '66

James Cameron
The Abyss '89
True Lies '94

Ken Cameron
Fast Talking '86
Monkey Grip '82

China Cammell
White of the Eye '88

Donald Cammell
Performance '70
Tilt '78
White of the Eye '88

Jane Campion
The Piano '93
Sweetie '89

Cuca Canals
Jamon, Jamon '93

Stephan J. Cannell
The Rousters '90

Dyan Cannon
The End of Innocence '90

Leon Capetanos
Down and Out in Beverly Hills '86
Fletch Lives '89
Greased Lightning '77
Gumball Rally '76
Moon Over Parador '88
Moscow on the Hudson '84
The Tempest '82

James Caplin
Transmutations '85

Truman Capote
Indiscretion of an American Wife '54

Frank Capra
Baby Face Harry Langdon '26
His First Flame '26

Fritjof Capra
Mindwalk: A Film for Passionate Thinkers '91

Jim Carabatsos
Hamburger Hill '87
Heartbreak Ridge '86

Heroes '77
No Mercy '86
Underground Aces '80

Frank Cardea
Dying to Remember '93

J.S. Cardone
A Climate for Killing '91
The Slayer '82
Thunder Alley '85

Mark Patrick Carducci
Buried Alive '90
Pumpkinhead '88

Topper Carew
D.C. Cab '84
Talkin' Dirty After Dark '91

Peter Carey
Bliss '85
Until The End of The World '91

Carlo Carlei
Flight of the Innocent '93

George Carlin
George Carlin: Doin' It Again '94

Matthew Carlson
Wagons East '94

Roy Carlson
China Moon '91
Stand Alone '85

Marcel Carne
La Merveilleuse Visite '74

Charles Robert Carner
Blind Fury '90

John Carpenter
Assault on Precinct 13 '76
Black Moon Rising '86
Dark Star '74
El Diablo '90
Escape from New York '81
Eyes of Laura Mars '78
The Fog '78
Halloween '78
Halloween 2: The Nightmare Isn't Over! '81
Prince of Darkness '87
They Live '88

Stephen Carpenter
The Kindred '87
The Power '80

Colby Carr
Blank Check '93

Richard Carr
Americana '81
Hell is for Heroes '62

Steven E. Carr
Puppet Master 4 '93

Keith Carradine
The Forgotten '89

Jim Carrey
Ace Ventura: Pet Detective '93

Jean-Claude Carriere
The Associate '82
At Play in the Fields of the Lord '91
Attack of the Robots '66
Borsalino '70
Cyrano de Bergerac '90
Danton '82
Diary of a Chambermaid '64
The Discreet Charm of the Bourgeoisie '72
Hotel Paradiso '66
The Mahabharata '89
Max, Mon Amour '86
May Fools '90
The Milky Way '68
The Return of Martin Guerre '83
Swann in Love '84

That Obscure Object of Desire '77
The Tin Drum '79
The Unbearable Lightness of Being '88
Valmont '89
Viva Maria! '65

L.M. Kit Carson
Breathless '83
David Holzman's Diary '67
The Last Word '80

Robert Carson
Just for You '52

Angela Carter
The Company of Wolves '85

Ruth Carter
Coming Up Roses '87

Sara Flanigan Carter
Sudie & Simpson '90

Richard Casey
Hellbent '90
Horror House on Highway 5 '86

Jim Cash
Dick Tracy '90
Legal Eagles '86
The Secret of My Success '87
Top Gun '86
Turner and Hooch '89

John Cassavetes
The Killing of a Chinese Bookie '76
Opening Night '77
A Woman Under the Influence '74

Shaun Cassidy
Strays '91

Alexander Cassini
Star Time '92

James C. Cassity
Man or Gun '58

Alien Castle
Desire and Hell at Sunset Motel '92
Jailbait '93

Nick Castle
The Boy Who Could Fly '86
Escape from New York '81
Hook '91
Kiss Me, Kill Me '69
Pray TV '80
Tap '89

Robert Caswell
A Cry in the Dark '88
The Doctor '91
A Far Off Place '93

Alain Cavalier
Therese '86

Frank Cavett
Going My Way '44

Vincenzo Cerami
Johnny Stecchino '92

Janus Cercone
Leap of Faith '92

Claude Chabrol
Blood Relatives '77
The Cousins '59
The Cry of the Owl '92
La Rupture '70
Le Beau Serge '58
Le Boucher '69
Les Biches '68
Madame Bovary '91
Six in Paris '68
The Story of Women '88

Kitty Chalmers
Cyborg '89
Deceit '93
Journey to the Center of the Earth '88

Tony Chan
Combination Platter '93

Harry Chandlee
The Adventures of Mark Twain '44

Harry Chandler
Sergeant York '41

Raymond Chandler
Double Indemnity '44
Strangers on a Train '51

Robert Chapin
Ring of Steel '94

Charlie Chaplin
Charlie Chaplin: Night at the Show '15
The Great Dictator '40
Modern Times '36
Monsieur Verdoux '47
Three Charlies and One Phoney! '18

Graham Chapman
And Now for Something Completely Different '72
Monty Python and the Holy Grail '75
Monty Python's Life of Brian '79
Monty Python's The Meaning of Life '83
Rentadick '72
Yellowbeard '83

John T. Chapman
Satan in High Heels '62

Leigh Chapman
Impulse '90

Matthew Chapman
Color of Night '94
Consenting Adults '92
Heart of Midnight '89
Hussy '80
Slow Burn '86
Strangers Kiss '83

Rebecca Charles
Nemesis '93

Borden Chase
Lone Star '52
Red River '48

David Chaskin
The Curse '87
I, Madman '89
Midnight's Child '93
A Nightmare on Elm Street 2: Freddy's Revenge '85

Etienne Chatiliez
Life Is a Long Quiet River '88
Tatie Danielle '90

Paddy Chayefsky
Altered States '80
The Americanization of Emily '64
As Young As You Feel '51
The Goddess '58
The Hospital '71
Marty '53
Marty '55
Network '76
Paint Your Wagon '69

Peter Chelsom
Hear My Song '91

Chenal
Crime and Punishment '35

John Cherry
Ernest Rides Again '93

Lionel Chetwynd
The Apprenticeship of Duddy Kravitz '74
Hanoi Hilton '87
The Heroes of Desert Storm '91
Quintet '79
To Heal a Nation '88

Deven Chierighino
The Wizard of Speed and Time '88

Helen Childress
Reality Bites '94

Charles Chiodo
Killer Klowns from Outer Space '88

Stephen Chiodo
Killer Klowns from Outer Space '88

David Chisholm
Dead Man's Revenge '93
The Wizard '89

Nathaniel Christian
California Casanova '89

Gene Church
Snapdragon '93

Gerard Ciccoritti
Psycho Girls '86
Skull: A Night of Terror '88
A Whisper to a Scream '88

Cynthia Cidre
Fires Within '91
In Country '89
The Mambo Kings '92

Michael Cimino
The Deer Hunter '78
Heaven's Gate '81
Magnum Force '73
Silent Running '71
Thunderbolt & Lightfoot '74
Year of the Dragon '85

Tony Cinciripini
Confessions of a Hit Man '94
The Lawless Land '88

Paul Ciotti
Ted & Venus '93

Cindy Cirile
Rapid Fire '92

Patrick Cirillo
Dangerous Heart '93
Homer and Eddie '89

Rene Clair
A Nous la Liberte '31

B.D. Clark
Galaxy of Terror '81

Bob (Benjamin) Clark
Children Shouldn't Play with Dead Things '72
A Christmas Story '83
From the Hip '86
It Runs In the Family '94
Loose Cannons '90
Porky's '
Porky's 2: The Next Day '83

Brian Clark
Whose Life Is It Anyway? '81

Bruce Clark
The Naked Angels '69

Duane Clark
Shaking the Tree '92

Greydon Clark
Angel's Brigade '79
Dance Macabre '91

Ron Clark
High Anxiety '77
Norman, Is That You? '76
Revenge of the Pink Panther '78
Silent Movie '76

Arthur C. Clarke
2001: A Space Odyssey '68

Frank Clarke
Letter to Brezhnev '86

Roy Clarke
Pictures '80s

T.E.B. Clarke
Dead of Night '45
The Lavender Hill Mob '51

James Clavell
The Fly '58
The Great Escape '63
The Last Valley '71
633 Squadron '64
To Sir, with Love '67

Thomas McKelvey Cleaver
Field of Fire '92
Heroes Stand Alone '89
The Terror Within '88

John Cleese
And Now for Something
   Completely Different '72
Fawlty Towers '77
A Fish Called Wanda '88
Monty Python and the Holy
   Grail '75
Monty Python Live at the
   Hollywood Bowl '82
Monty Python's Life of Brian
   '79
Monty Python's The Meaning
   of Life '83
Rentadick '72

Brian Clemens
And Soon the Darkness '70
Captain Kronos: Vampire
   Hunter '74
The Corrupt Ones '67
Dr. Jekyll and Sister Hyde '71
Golden Voyage of Sinbad '73
See No Evil '71
The Tell-Tale Heart '62
The Watcher in the Woods '81

Dick Clement
Catch Me a Spy '71
The Commitments '91
Prisoner of Zenda '79
Vice Versa '88
Water '85

Ron Clements
Aladdin '92

Laury Clemmons
The Fox and the Hound '81

Elmer Clifton
Captain America '44
Frontier Law '43
Gangsters of the Frontier '44
Guns of the Law '44
Lightning Raiders '45
Marked for Murder '45
Youth Aflame '59

Paul E. Clinco
Death Magic '92

Harry Clork
Broadway Rhythm '44
Ship Ahoy '42

Daniel Clough
Ninja, the Violent Sorcerer '86

Henri-Georges Clouzot
Wages of Fear '55

Rick Cluchey
The Cage '90

Craig Clyde
Little Heroes '91

Lewis (Luigi Cozzi) Coates
Alien Contamination '81
Black Cat '90
Hercules '83

Henry Cobbold
Lake Consequence '92

Arthur Coburn
Triumph of the Spirit '89

James Coburn
Circle of Iron '78

Stacy Cochran
My New Gun '92

Jay Cocks
The Age of Innocence '93

Jean Cocteau
Eternal Return '43

Fred Coe
This Property is Condemned
   '66

Wayne Coe
Grim Prairie Tales '89

Ethan Coen
Barton Fink '91
Blood Simple '85
Crimewave '85
The Hudsucker Proxy '93
Miller's Crossing '90
Raising Arizona '87

Joel Coen
Barton Fink '91
Blood Simple '85
Crimewave '85
The Hudsucker Proxy '93
Miller's Crossing '90
Raising Arizona '87

Lenore Coffee
Cash McCall '60
Evelyn Prentice '34
Young at Heart '54

Charlie Coffey
Earth Girls are Easy '89

Bennett Cohen
Come On Danger! '32
Melody of the Plains '37
Rainbow Drive '90
Sagebrush Law '43

Catherine Cohen
Indochine '92

Howard R. Cohen
Lords of the Deep '89

Joel Cohen
Pass the Ammo '88
Sister, Sister '87

Larry Cohen
The Ambulance '90
Best Seller '87
Daddy's Gone A-Hunting '69
Deadly Illusion '87
El Condor '70
God Told Me To '76
Guilty as Sin '93
Hell Up in Harlem '73
I, the Jury '82
Into Thin Air '85
It's Alive '74
It's Alive 3: Island of the Alive
   '87
Maniac Cop '88
Maniac Cop 2 '90
Maniac Cop 3 '93
Perfect Strangers '84
The Private Files of J. Edgar
   Hoover '77
Q (The Winged Serpent) '82
Return of the Seven '66
Return to Salem's Lot '87
Scandalous '84
Special Effects '85
The Stuff '85
Wicked Stepmother '89

Lawrence D. Cohen
Stephen King's The
   Tommyknockers '93

Neil Cohen
Pass the Ammo '88

Rob Cohen
Dragon: The Bruce Lee Story
   '93
Scandalous '84

Randolph Cohlan
Night Shadow '90

Art Cohn
The Seven Hills of Rome '58

Brandon Cole
Mac '93
Sons '91

Lester Cole
Objective, Burma! '45

Clifford Coleman
The Ice Runner '93

Christine Colfer
Double Exposure '93

Lewis Colick
Dirt Bike Kid '86
Judgment Night '93

Jeanne Collachia
Odd Birds '85

Cyril Collard
Les Nuits Fauves '92

John Collee
Paper Mask '91

Peter Colley
Illusions '91

John Collier
The War Lord '65

Boon Collins
Spirit of the Eagle '90

Jackie Collins
The Stud '78
The World is Full of Married
   Men '80
Yesterday's Hero '79

Arthur Collis
Blue Desert '91

Carl Colpaert
Delusion '91

Chris Columbus
The Goonies '85
Gremlins '84
Heartbreak Hotel '88
Little Nemo: Adventures in
   Slumberland '92
Only the Lonely '91
Reckless '84
Young Sherlock Holmes '85

Betty Comden
Auntie Mame '58
The Barkleys of Broadway '49
Bells are Ringing '60
It's Always Fair Weather '55
On the Town '49
Singin' in the Rain '52

Bob Comfort
Dogfight '91

George Conchon
Black and White in Color '76
The Elegant Criminal '92

Richard Condon
Prizzi's Honor '85

Heather Conkie
Beethoven Lives Upstairs '92

Nicole Conn
Claire of the Moon '92

Shane Connaughton
My Left Foot '89
The Playboys '92

Jon Connolly
The Dream Team '89

Steve Conrad
Wrestling Ernest Hemingway
   '93

Pat Conroy
The Prince of Tides '91

John Considine
A Wedding '78

Gary Conway
American Ninja 2: The
   Confrontation '87
American Ninja 3: Blood Hunt
   '89
Over the Top '86

Tim Conway
The Longshot '86
The Private Eyes '80
Prize Fighter '79
They Went That-a-Way & That-
   a-Way '78

Rif Coogan
The Invisible Maniac '90

Peter Cook
Bedazzled '67
The Hound of the Baskervilles
   '77
Yellowbeard '83

T.S. Cook
The China Syndrome '79
High Desert Kill '90
Nightbreaker '89
Out of the Darkness '85

Tony Cookson
And You Thought Your Parents
   Were Weird! '91

Barry Michael Cooper
Above the Rim '94
New Jack City '91
Sugar Hill '94

Dorothy Cooper
Rich, Young and Pretty '51

Merian C. Cooper
Chang: A Drama of the
   Wilderness '27

Natalie Cooper
Desert Hearts '86

Olive Cooper
Bandit King of Texas '49
The Border Legion '40
Hills of Oklahoma '50

Robert Cooper
The Club '94

Susan Cooper
George Balanchine's The
   Nutcracker '93
To Dance with the White Dog
   '93

Francis Ford Coppola
Apocalypse Now '79
The Bellboy and the Playgirls
   '62
The Conversation '74
The Cotton Club '84
Dementia 13 '63
The Godfather '72
The Godfather 1902-1959: The
   Complete Epic '81
The Godfather, Part 2 '74
The Godfather, Part 3 '90
The Great Gatsby '74
Is Paris Burning? '68
The Magic Voyage of Sinbad
   '52
New York Stories '89
One from the Heart '82
Patton '70
The Rain People '69
Rumble Fish '83
This Property is Condemned
   '66
Tonight for Sure '61
You're a Big Boy Now '66

Sofia Coppola
New York Stories '89

Jane Corbett
Tale of a Vampire '92

John Corcoran
American Samurai '92

Roger Corman
Frankenstein Unbound '90
The Skateboard Kid '93

Alain Corneau
Tous les Matins du Monde '92

Hubert Cornfield
The Night of the Following Day
   '69

Eugene Corr
Desert Bloom '86
Wildrose '85

Charles Correll
Fortune Dane '86

Bud Cort
Ted & Venus '93

Norman Corwin
The Naked Maja '59

Bill Cosby
Leonard Part 6 '87

Constantin Costa-Gavras
Missing '82
Z '69

Manny Coto
Dr. Giggles '92

Suzette Couture
Love and Hate: A Marriage
   Made in Hell '90

Michael Cove
Deathcheaters '76

Hil Covington
Adventures in Spying '92

Gil Cowan
Opposing Force '87

Noel Coward
Bitter Sweet '33
Bitter Sweet '40
Brief Encounter '46
In Which We Serve '43

Jim Cox
The Rescuers Down Under '90

Paul Cox
Cactus '86
Lonely Hearts '82
Man of Flowers '84
My First Wife '84
Vincent: The Life and Death of
   Vincent van Gogh '87
A Woman's Tale '92

Kerry Crabbe
The Playboys '92

Peter Crabbe
Car 54, Where Are You? '94

Wes Craven
Deadly Blessing '81
The Hills Have Eyes '77
The Hills Have Eyes, Part 2 '84
A Nightmare on Elm Street '84
A Nightmare on Elm Street 3:
   Dream Warriors '87
The People Under the Stairs
   '91
Shocker '89
Swamp Thing '82

Bobby Crawford
A Rage in Harlem '91

Joanna Crawford
The Birch Interval '78
Sophia Loren: Her Own Story
   '80

Richard Creedon
Snow White and the Seven Dwarfs '37

John Cresswell
Cast a Dark Shadow '55

Charles Crichton
A Fish Called Wanda '88

Michael Crichton
Coma '78
The Great Train Robbery '79
Jurassic Park '93
Looker '81
Rising Sun '93
Runaway '84
Sex Through a Window '72
Westworld '73

Michael Cristofer
The Bonfire of the Vanities '90
Falling in Love '84
Mr. Jones '93
The Witches of Eastwick '87

Keith Critchlow
New Jack City '91
Night Life '90

David Cronenberg
The Brood '79
Dead Ringers '88
Fast Company '78
The Fly '86
Naked Lunch '91
Rabid '77
Scanners '81
They Came from Within '75
Videodrome '83

Beverly Cross
Clash of the Titans '81
Half a Sixpence '67
Jason and the Argonauts '63
Sinbad and the Eye of the Tiger '77

Paul Cross
Ice Pawn '92

Cameron Crowe
Fast Times at Ridgemont High '82
Say Anything '89
Singles '92
The Wild Life '84

Christopher Crowe
Last Chase '81
The Last of the Mohicans '92
Mean Season '85
Nightmares '83
Off Limits '87
Whispers in the Dark '92

Jim Cruickshank
Mr. Destiny '90
Sister Act 2: Back in the Habit '93
Three Men and a Baby '87
Tough Guys '86

Tom Cruise
Days of Thunder '90

Robert Riley Crutcher
Key to the City '50

Billy Crystal
City Slickers 2: The Legend of Curly's Gold '94
Memories of Me '88
Mr. Saturday Night '92

Allan Cubitt
Prime Suspect 2 '93

Frank Cucci
Lily in Love '85

Alma Cullen
Intimate Contact '87

Robert Cullen
As You Like It '36

Hugh Cummings
Pardon My Gun '30

James Cummins
The Bone Yard '90

Rusty Cundieff
House Party 2: The Pajama Jam '91

Ray Cunneff
The Rain Killer '90

William Curran
Love, Cheat & Steal '94

Jean Curtelin
L'Addition '85

Valerie Curtin
And Justice for All '79
Best Friends '82
Inside Moves '80
Toys '92
Unfaithfully Yours '84

Richard Curtis
Four Weddings and a Funeral '93
The Tall Guy '89

Neil Cuthbert
Hocus Pocus '93

Bohdan Czeszko
A Generation '54

Renee Daalder
Massacre at Central High '76

John Dahl
Kill Me Again '89
Private Investigations '87
Red Rock West '93

Roald Dahl
Chitty Chitty Bang Bang '68

Salvador Dali
L'Age D'Or '30

Herbert Dalmas
The Last of the Redmen '47

Gerry Daly
Black Magic Woman '91

Suso Cecchi D'Amico
Bellissima '51

Herbert Danska
Sweet Love, Bitter '67

Frank Darabont
The Blob '88
The Fly 2 '89
A Nightmare on Elm Street 3: Dream Warriors '87

Istvan Darday
Red Earth

W. Scott Darling
The Ghost of Frankenstein '42
King of the Sierras '38

Julie Dash
Daughters of the Dust '92

Sean Dash
Ice '93

Jules Dassin
A Dream of Passion '78
Never on Sunday '60
Phaedra '61
Where the Hot Wind Blows '59

Delmer Daves
An Affair to Remember '57
Dames '34
Flirtation Walk '34
Hollywood Canteen '44
Love Affair '39
Parrish '61
Rome Adventure '62
Spencer's Mountain '63
Task Force '49

Marjorie David
Maria's Lovers '84

Shy People '87

Peter David
Trancers 4: Jack of Swords '93

Bill Davidson
The Art of Crime '75

Ronald Davidson
Range Renegades '48

Ray Davies
Return to Waterloo '85

Ron Davies
Blood Ring '93

Terence Davies
Distant Voices, Still Lives '88
The Long Day Closes '92

Valentine Davies
Bachelor in Paradise '69
It Happens Every Spring '49

William Davies
Ghost in the Machine '93
The Real McCoy '93
Twins '88

Fitzroy Davis
The Heat's On '43

Frank Davis
The Train '65

Jerry Davis
Cult of the Cobra '55
L.A. Goddess '92
Pardners '56

Stephen Davis
Ruby '92

Tom Davis
Coneheads '93

Valentine Davis
The Bridges at Toko-Ri '55

Norman Dawn
Orphans of the North '40

Anthony M. (Antonio Marghereti) Dawson
Invasion of the Flesh Hunters '82
Yor, the Hunter from the Future '83

Ennio de Concini
The Bachelor '93
Divorce—Italian Style '62
Il Grido '57

Frank de Felitta
Audrey Rose '77
The Entity '83
Scissors '91
Zero Population Growth '72

Merrill De Maris
Snow White and the Seven Dwarfs '37

Albert De Mond
Ridin' Down the Canyon '42

Giuliani G. De Negri
The Night of the Shooting Stars '82

Armando de Ossorio
Fangs of the Living Dead '68
Horror of the Zombies '74
People Who Own the Dark '75

Frank De Palma
Private War '90

Vittorio De Sica
The Children Are Watching Us '44
Two Women '61
Umberto D '55

Steven E. de Souza
Bad Dreams '88
Beverly Hills Cop 3 '94
Commando '85
Die Hard '88

Die Hard 2: Die Harder '90
The Flintstones '94
48 Hrs. '82
Hudson Hawk '91
Return of Captain Invincible '83
Ricochet '91
The Running Man '87
Seven Hours to Judgment '88

Gary De Vore
Back Roads '81
The Dogs of War '81
Raw Deal '86
Running Scared '86
Timecop '94
Traxx '87

Nicole De Wilde
The Raggedy Rawney '90

Karen De Wolf
Blondie in Society '41
Blondie's Blessed Event '42
It's a Great Life '43

Basil Dean
21 Days '37

Charles Deane
Blonde Blackmailer '58

William Dear
Harry and the Hendersons '87

James Dearden
Fatal Attraction '87
A Kiss Before Dying '91
Pascali's Island '88

Marge Decker
To Please a Lady '50

Denise DeClue
About Last Night... '86
For Keeps '88

Frank Deese
Josh and S.A.M. '93
The Principal '87

Christopher DeFaria
Amityville: A New Generation '93

Frank Deford
Trading Hearts '87

Allessandro DeGaetano
Bloodbath in Psycho Town '89

Steve DeJarnatt
Miracle Mile '89
Strange Brew '83

Colman DeKay
Bloodhounds of Broadway '89

Fred Dekker
If Looks Could Kill '91
The Monster Squad '87
Night of the Creeps '86
RoboCop 3 '91

Shelagh Delaney
Dance with a Stranger '85
The Railway Station Man '92
A Taste of Honey '61

Walter DeLeon
Little Giant '46
The Ruggles of Red Gap '35

Francis Delia
Freeway '88
Trouble Bound '92

William Delligan
Praying Mantis '93

Jeffrey Delman
Double Obsession '93
Voodoo Dawn '89

Vina Delmar
The Awful Truth '37

Rudy DeLuca
Caveman '81
High Anxiety '77
Life Stinks '91

Million Dollar Mystery '87
Silent Movie '76
Transylvania 6-5000 '85

John DeMarco
Impulse '90

Paul DeMeo
Arena '88
The Eliminators '86
Future Cop '76
The Rocketeer '91
The Wrong Guys '88
Zone Troopers '85

Gloria Demers
Strangers in Good Company '91

Paul DeMielche
American Ninja 3: Blood Hunt '89

Jonathan Demme
Angels Hard as They Come '71
Caged Heat '74
Fighting Mad '76
Hot Box '72

Jacques Demy
Umbrellas of Cherbourg '64

Claire Denis
Chocolat '88
No Fear, No Die '90

Pen Densham
Lifepod '93
Robin Hood: Prince of Thieves '91
The Zoo Gang '85

Alan Dent
Hamlet '48
Henry V '44

Brian DePalma
Blow Out '81
Body Double '84
Dressed to Kill '80
Greetings '68
Hi, Mom! '70
Home Movies '79
Phantom of the Paradise '74
Raising Cain '92
Sisters '73
The Wedding Party '69

Jacques Deray
Borsalino '70

John Derek
Bolero '84

Lorain Despres
Highlander: The Gathering '93

Helen Deutch
Valley of the Dolls '67

David Deutsch
A Day in the Death of Joe Egg '71

Helen Deutsch
Golden Earrings '47
National Velvet '44

Jacques Deval
Balalaika '39

Michel DeVille
La Lectrice '88
Peril '85

Rosalinde DeVille
La Lectrice '88

Christopher DeVore
The Elephant Man '80
Frances '82
Hamlet '90

Jack DeWitt
Bells of San Fernando '47
The Legend of the Sea Wolf '58
A Man Called Horse '70
Man in the Wilderness '71
Neptune Factor '73

DeWitt ▶cont.

The Return of a Man Called Horse '76
Sky Riders '76
Sky Riders '76
Triumphs of a Man Called Horse '83

Pete Dexter
Paris Trout '91
Rush '91

Gerald Di Pego
Keeper of the City '92

I.A.L. Diamond
The Apartment '60
Avanti! '72
Buddy Buddy '81
The Fortune Cookie '66
The Front Page '74
Irma La Douce '63
Kiss Me, Stupid! '64
Love in the Afternoon '57
Monkey Business '52
One, Two, Three '61
The Private Life of Sherlock Holmes '70

Tom DiCillo
Johnny Suede '92

Ernest R. Dickerson
Juice '92

Basil Dickey
Brand of Fear '49

James Dickey
Deliverance '72

Joan Didion
Panic in Needle Park '75
A Star is Born '76
True Confessions '81

Carlos Diegues
Bye Bye Brazil '79
Quilombo '84

John Dighton
The Happiest Days of Your Life '50

Eric Dignam
Denial: The Dark Side of Passion '91

Flint Dille
An American Tail: Fievel Goes West '91

Robert Dillon
Bikini Beach '64
Deception '92
Flight of the Intruder '90
French Connection 2 '75
The Last of the Mohicans '20
Muscle Beach Party '64
99 & 44/100 Dead '74
The Old Dark House '32
Prime Cut '72
Revolution '85
The River '84
The Survivalist '87
X: The Man with X-Ray Eyes '63

Greg Dinallo
Ladykillers '88

Pece Dingo
Midnight Cabaret '90

Paul Dini
Batman: Mask of the Phantasm '93

Mark DiSalle
Kickboxer '89

James Dixon
Return to Salem's Lot '87

Leslie Dixon
Look Who's Talking Now '93
Loverboy '89

Mrs. Doubtfire '93
Outrageous Fortune '87
Overboard '87

Peter Dixon
Down the Wyoming Trail '39

Lem Dobbs
The Hard Way '91
Kafka '91

Jacques Doillon
La Vengeance d'une Femme '89

Bob Dolman
Far and Away '92
Willow '88

Henry Dominick
Flight of Black Angel '91
Mindwarp '91

James Donadio
By the Sword '93

Tom Donnelly
Defiance '79
Quicksilver '86
Talent for the Game '91

Mary Agnes Donoghue
Beaches '88
The Buddy System '83
Deceived '91
Paradise '91

Martin Donovan
Apartment Zero '88
Death Becomes Her '92
Mad at the Moon '92

Anita Doohan
Whispers '89

Phoebe Dorin
Perfect Family '92

Shimon Dotan
The Finest Hour '91

Jean Douchet
Six in Paris '68

Joseph Dougherty
Attack of the 50 Ft. Woman '93
Cast a Deadly Spell '91
Steel and Lace '90

Nathan E. Douglas
The Defiant Ones '58

Lorenzo Doumani
Amore! '93

Sir Arthur Conan Doyle
Tales from the Darkside: The Movie '90

Roddy Doyle
The Commitments '91
The Snapper '93

Brian Doyle-Murray
Caddyshack '80
Club Paradise '86

Diane Drake
Only You '94

Oliver Drake
Fighting Valley '43

Tom Drake
Keeper '84

William A. Drake
The Three Musketeers '39

Peter Draper
Poldark '75

Tony Drazan
Zebrahead '92

Carl Theodor Dreyer
Day of Wrath '43
Gertrud '64
Vampyr '31

Jeremy Craig Dryden
Permissive

Lee Drysdale
Leather Jackets '90

Charles S. Dubin
The Meanest Men in the West '76

Charlotte Dubreuil
Spoiled Children '77

Warren Duff
Angels with Dirty Faces '38
Last Command '28

Jo Duffy
Puppet Master 4 '93

John Duigan
Flirting '89
Sirens '94
Wide Sargasso Sea '92
The Year My Voice Broke '87

Andrea Dunbar
Rita, Sue & Bob Too '87

David Duncan
The Leech Woman '59
Monster on the Campus '59

Patrick Duncan
84 Charlie Mopic '89
A Home of Our Own '93
Live! From Death Row '92

Winifred Dunn
The Dropkick '27

Gregory Dunne
Panic in Needle Park '75
A Star is Born '76
True Confessions '81

Philip Dunne
The Agony and the Ecstasy '65
David and Bathsheba '51
Demetrius and the Gladiators '54
The Egyptian '54
Forever Amber '47
The Ghost and Mrs. Muir '47
How Green was My Valley '41
Pinky '49
The Rains Came '39
Son of Fury '42
Ten North Frederick '58

John Dunning
SnakeEater 3: His Law '92

Rudy Durand
Tilt '78

Marguerite Duras
Hiroshima, Mon Amour '59

H. Kaye Dyal
Lone Wolf McQuade '83
Project: Eliminator '91

B. Reeves Eason
Roaring Ranch '30

Thom Eberhardt
All I Want for Christmas '91
Captain Ron '92
Honey, I Blew Up the Kid '92
The Night Before '88
Night of the Comet '84

Roger Ebert
Beneath the Valley of the Ultra-Vixens '79
Beyond the Valley of the Dolls '70

Nicolas Echevarria
Cabeza de Vaca '90

Patrick Edgeworth
BMX Bandits '83
Driving Force '88
Raw Deal '86

Dave Edison
Cast a Deadly Spell '91
Steel and Lace '90

Blake Edwards
The Atomic Kid '54
City Heat '84
Curse of the Pink Panther '83
Darling Lili '70
A Fine Mess '86
The Man Who Loved Women '83
My Sister Eileen '55
The Party '68
The Pink Panther '64
Return of the Pink Panther '74
Revenge of the Pink Panther '78
A Shot in the Dark '64
Skin Deep '89
S.O.B. '81
Soldier in the Rain '63
Son of the Pink Panther '93
Sunset '88
Switch '91
The Tamarind Seed '74
10 '79
That's Life! '86
This Happy Feeling '58
Trail of the Pink Panther '82
Victor/Victoria '82
What Did You Do in the War, Daddy? '66
Wild Rovers '71

Paul F. Edwards
Fire Birds '90
High Ballin' '78

Christine Edzard
Little Dorrit, Film 1: Nobody's Fault '88
Little Dorrit, Film 2: Little Dorrit's Story '88

Fred Eggers
Thunder Pass '54

Jan Egleson
The Tender Age '84

Atom Egoyan
The Adjuster '91
Family Viewing '88
Next of Kin '84
Speaking Parts '89

Max Ehrlich
The Reincarnation of Peter Proud '75
Zero Population Growth '72

Rosanne Ehrlich
Chantilly Lace '93

Sergei Eisenstein
Ivan the Terrible, Part 1 '44

Joe Eisinger
Crime of Passion '57
Night and the City '50

Kevin Elders
Iron Eagle '86
Iron Eagle 2 '88

Laurice Elehwany
My Girl '91

Richard Elfman
Forbidden Zone '80

Joyce Eliason
Small Sacrifices '89
Tell Me a Riddle '80

Irving Elinson
By the Light of the Silvery Moon '53

Mercer Ellington
Avenging Force '86

Ted Elliot
Aladdin '92
Little Monsters '89

B. Ron Elliott
The Acid Eaters '67

Anderson Ellis
The Mortal Storm '40

Bob Ellis
Cactus '86
Man of Flowers '84
My First Wife '84
Warm Nights on a Slow-Moving Train '87

Robert Ellis
Hello, Frisco, Hello '43
Iceland '42
Lucky Cisco Kid '40
Tin Pan Alley '40

Edward Emanuel
3 Ninjas '92

Jim Emerson
It's Pat '94

John Emerson
The Girl from Missouri '34
His Picture in the Papers '16

Robert Emmett
God's Country and the Man '37
Gun Packer '38
Riding the Sunset Trail '41

Clive Endersby
The Challengers '93

Otto Englander
Snow White and the Seven Dwarfs '37

John English
Dick Tracy vs. Crime Inc. '41

Nick Enright
Lorenzo's Oil '92

Ildiko Enyedi
My Twentieth Century '90

Delia Ephron
This is My Life '92

Henry Ephron
Look for the Silver Lining '49

Nora Ephron
Cookie '89
Heartburn '86
My Blue Heaven '90
Silkwood '83
Sleepless in Seattle '93
This is My Life '92
When Harry Met Sally '89

Phoebe Ephron
Look for the Silver Lining '49

Tom Epperson
One False Move '91

Jack Epps, Jr.
Dick Tracy '90
Legal Eagles '86
The Secret of My Success '87
Top Gun '86
Turner and Hooch '89

Julius J. Epstein
Any Wednesday '66
Arsenic and Old Lace '44
The Bride Came C.O.D. '41
Casablanca '42
Cross of Iron '76
Fanny '61
Forever Female '53
The Last Time I Saw Paris '54
The Man Who Came to Dinner '41
Once is Not Enough '75
Pete 'n' Tillie '72
Reuben, Reuben '83
Romance on the High Seas '48
Send Me No Flowers '64
Strawberry Blonde '41
Tall Story '60
The Tender Trap '55
Young at Heart '54

Philip G. Epstein
Any Wednesday '66
Arsenic and Old Lace '44
The Bride Came C.O.D. '41
Casablanca '42
Fanny '61

Forever Female '53
The Last Time I Saw Paris '54
The Man Who Came to Dinner
    '41
Once is Not Enough '75
Send Me No Flowers '64
Strawberry Blonde '41
Tall Story '60
Three of Hearts '93

John Eskow
Pink Cadillac '89

John Esposito
Graveyard Shift '90

Laura Esquivel
Like Water for Chocolate '93

Howard Estabrook
David Copperfield '35
Lone Star '52

Luis Esteban
Only the Strong '93

Emilio Estevez
Men at Work '90
That Was Then...This Is Now
    '85

Joe Eszterhas
Basic Instinct '92
Betrayed '88
Big Shots '87
Checking Out '89
Hearts of Fire '87
The Jagged Edge '85
Music Box '89
Nowhere to Run '93
Sliver '93

Ray Etheridge
The Vernonia Incident '89

**Corey Michael
Eubanks**
Forced to Kill '93

Bruce A. Evans
Kuffs '92
Made in Heaven '87
A Man, a Woman, and a Bank
    '79
Starman '84

David Mickey Evans
The Sandlot '93

Shelley Evans
Ladykiller '92

Gimel Everett
The Lawnmower Man '92

Roberto Faenza
The Bachelor '93

**Douglas Fairbanks,
Sr.**
Mr. Robinson Crusoe '32

**Douglas Fairbanks,
Jr.**
Scarlet Dawn '32

William Fairchild
Star! '68

Gerard Fairlie
Conspirator '49

Susanne Falck
House of Angels '92

David Fallon
Split Decisions '88
White Fang '91
White Fang 2: The Myth of the
    White Wolf '94

Kevin Falls
The Temp '93

Jamaa Fanaka
Black Sister's Revenge '76
Penitentiary '79
Penitentiary 2 '82
Penitentiary 3 '87
Soul Vengeance '75

Hampton Fancher
Blade Runner '82
The Mighty Quinn '89

John Fante
Maya '66

**Francis Edwards
Faragoh**
Frankenstein '31

Jean-Pol Fargeau
Chocolat '88
No Fear, No Die '90

Donald Farmer
Scream Dream '89

John Farrow
Around the World in 80 Days
    '56
John Paul Jones '59

Mike Farrow
Remote '93

**Rainer Werner
Fassbinder**
The American Soldier '70
Chinese Roulette '86
Effi Briest '74
The Marriage of Maria Braun
    '79
The Merchant of Four Seasons
    '71
Mother Kusters Goes to
    Heaven '76
The Stationmaster's Wife '77
Why Does Herr R. Run Amok?
    '69

William Faulkner
The Big Sleep '46
The Southerner '45
Today We Live '33

Jaqueline Feather
The Rumor Mill '86

F.X. Feeney
Frankenstein Unbound '90

Jarre Fees
Permanent Record '88

Jules Feiffer
Carnal Knowledge '71
Little Murders '71
Popeye '80

Steve Feinberg
Fortress '93

John Feldman
Alligator Eyes '90

**Jonathan Marc
Feldman**
Swing Kids '93

Randy Feldman
Hell Night '81
Nowhere to Run '93
Tango and Cash '89

Joao Felicio
Xica '76

Larry Feliz, Jr.
Shootfighter: Fight to the Death
    '93

Federico Fellini
Amarcord '74
And the Ship Sails On '83
Boccaccio '70 '62
City of Women '81
The Clowns '71
8 1/2 '63
Fellini Satyricon '69
Fellini's Roma '72
Ginger & Fred '86
I Vitelloni '53
Intervista '87
Juliet of the Spirits '65
La Dolce Vita '60
La Strada '54
Love in the City '53

Nights of Cabiria '57
Open City '45
Paisan '46
The Swindle '55
Variety Lights '51
The White Sheik '52

Andrew J. Fenady
Chisum '70
The Man with Bogart's Face
    '80
The Sea Wolf '93

Michael Fengler
Why Does Herr R. Run Amok?
    '69

Pablo F. Fenjves
A Case for Murder '93

Frank Fenton
Escape from Fort Bravo '53
Malaya '49

Claude Feraldo
Trade Secrets '90s

Larry Ferguson
Beverly Hills Cop 2 '87
Highlander '86
The Hunt for Red October '90
The Presidio '88
Talent for the Game '91

Peter Fernandez
Infra-Man '76

Abel Ferrara
Bad Lieutenant '92

Jesus Ferrere
Matador '86

Franco Ferrini
Creepers '85

Michael Fessier
Red Garters '54

Darrell Fetty
Freeway '88
Trouble Bound '92

Richard Fielder
George Washington '84

Herbert Fields
Honolulu '39

Sid Fields
In Society '44

W.C. Fields
The Bank Dick '40

Harvey Fierstein
Tidy Endings '88
Torch Song Trilogy '88

Jacques Fieschi
Un Coeur en Hiver '93

Mike Figgis
Liebestraum '91
Stormy Monday '88

Hal Fimberg
In Society '44

Scot Finch
Catlow '71

Yolande Finch
Bad Girls '94

Abe Finkel
Sergeant York '41

Fred Finklehoff
The Stooge '51

Melanie Finn
Lake Consequence '92

Alan Finney
Alvin Purple '73
Alvin Rides Again '74

Richard Fire
Henry: Portrait of a Serial Killer
    '90

Bob Fisher
A Global Affair '63
I'll Take Sweden '65

Carrie Fisher
Postcards from the Edge '90

Jim Fisher
The Beverly Hillbillies '93

Steve Fisher
Hostile Guns '67
Johnny Reno '66

Margaret Fitts
Stars in My Crown '50

Benedict Fitzgerald
Heart of Darkness '93

Edith Fitzgerald
Today We Live '33

F. Scott Fitzgerald
Marie Antoinette '38
Three Comrades '38

Jiles Fitzgerald
Martial Law 2: Undercover '91

Fannie Flagg
Fried Green Tomatoes '91

Ennio Flaino
8 1/2 '63
I Vitelloni '53
Juliet of the Spirits '65
La Dolce Vita '60
La Strada '54
Nights of Cabiria '57
The Swindle '55
Variety Lights '51
The White Sheik '52

Fionnula Flanagan
James Joyce's Women '85

Gregory Fleemand
F/X '86

Hugh Fleetwood
The Bachelor '93

A.S. Fleischman
Lafayette Escadrille '58

Andrew Fleming
Bad Dreams '88
Every Breath '93
Threesome '94

Bill Flemming
Northern Extremes '93

Rodman Flender
In the Heat of Passion '91

Theodore J. Flicker
The President's Analyst '67

Ruth Brooks Flippen
Love is Better Than Ever '52

Robert Florey
Frankenstein '31

Richard Flournoy
Blondie '38
Blondie Has Trouble '40
Blondie Takes a Vacation '39
Blondie's Blessed Event '42

Errol Flynn
Assault of the Rebel Girls '59

Tom Flynn
Watch It '93

Peter Foldy
Midnight Witness '93

James Foley
After Dark, My Sweet '90
S.F.W. '94

Naomi Foner
A Dangerous Woman '93
Running on Empty '88
Violets Are Blue '86

Leo Fong
Showdown '93

Randall Fontana
Bitter Harvest '93

Bradbury Foote
Of Human Hearts '38
Young Tom Edison '40

Horton Foote
The Chase '66
1918 '85
Of Mice and Men '92
On Valentine's Day '86
To Kill a Mockingbird '62
The Trip to Bountiful '85

Horton Foote, Jr.
Baby, the Rain Must Fall '64
Tender Mercies '83
Tomorrow '83

John Taintor Foote
The Mark of Zorro '40

Bryan Forbes
Chaplin '92
Of Human Bondage '64

Richard Ford
Bright Angel '91

Carl Foreman
The Bridge on the River Kwai
    '57
Cyrano de Bergerac '50
High Noon '52
The Key '58
Spooks Run Wild '41

Bengt Forslund
The Emigrants '72
The New Land '73

Bill Forsyth
Being Human '94
Gregory's Girl '80
Housekeeping '87
Local Hero '83
That Sinking Feeling '79

Frederick Forsyth
A Casualty of War '90
The Fourth Protocol '87

Garrett Fort
Dracula (Spanish Version) '31
Frankenstein '31

Robert Foster
Dead Bang '89

Tony Foster
The Sound and the Silence '93

Gene Fowler
Billy the Kid '41

Robbie Fox
So I Married an Axe Murderer
    '93

Terry Curtis Fox
Fortress '93

Michael France
Cliffhanger '93

Adolfe Franci
Shoeshine '47

Coleman Francis
The Beast of Yucca Flats '61

Bruno Frank
The Hunchback of Notre Dame
    '39

Harriet Frank, Jr.
Conrack '74
The Cowboys '72
Hombre '67
Home from the Hill '60
Hud '63
The Long, Hot Summer '58
Murphy's Romance '85
Norma Rae '79
The Reivers '69
Silver River '48
Stanley and Iris '90
Ten Wanted Men '54

Melvin Frank
Monsieur Beaucaire '46

Scott Frank
Dead Again '91
Fallen Angels 2 '93
Little Man Tate '91
Malice '93

David Frankel
Funny About Love '90
Nervous Ticks '93

Al Franken
One More Saturday Night '86
When a Man Loves a Woman '94

John Frankenheimer
The Manchurian Candidate '62

Carl Franklin
Eye of the Eagle 3 '91

Dean Franklin
The Fighting 69th '40

Howard Franklin
The Name of the Rose '86
The Public Eye '92
Quick Change '90
Someone to Watch Over Me '87

Jeff Franklin
Summer School '87

Paul Franklin
The Fighting Redhead '50

David Franzoni
Citizen Cohn '92
Jumpin' Jack Flash '86

George MacDonald Fraser
Casanova '87
The Return of the Musketeers '89

Harry Fraser
Galloping Romeo '33

Michael Frayn
Clockwise '86

Herb Freed
Beyond Evil '80

Robert Freedman
Taken Away '89

David Freeman
Street Smart '87

Everett Freeman
The Glass Bottom Boat '66
My Man Godfrey '57

Robert M. Fresco
The Monolith Monsters '57
Tarantula '55

Bill Freut
125 Rooms of Comfort '83

Fridrik Thor Fridriksson
Children of Nature '92

Randall Fried
Heaven is a Playground '91

Richard Friedenberg
Dying Young '91
A River Runs Through It '92

Bud Friedgen
That's Entertainment, Part 3 '93

William Friedkin
Cruising '80
The Guardian '90
Rampage '87
To Live & Die in L.A. '85

Ken Friedman
Bad Girls '94
Cadillac Man '90
Heart Like a Wheel '83
Johnny Handsome '89

Made in USA '88
Mr. Billion '77
White Line Fever '75

Richard S. Friedman
Scared Stiff '87

George Froeschel
The Miniver Story '50
Mrs. Miniver '42
The Mortal Storm '40
Never Let Me Go '53

Clayton Frohman
Under Fire '83

Seth Front
Nickel & Dime '87

Mark Frost
The Believers '87
Scared Stiff '87
Storyville '92

E. Max Frye
Amos and Andrew '93
Something Wild '86

Daniel Fuchs
Criss Cross '48

Lucio Fulci
The Black Cat '81

Samuel Fuller
Baron of Arizona '51
The Big Red One '80
China Gate '57
I Shot Jesse James '49
The Klansman '74
Let's Get Harry '87
Merrill's Marauders '62
Pickup on South Street '53
Run of the Arrow '56
Shark! '68
Shock Corridor '63
The Steel Helmet '51
Underworld, U.S.A. '60

Sidney J. Furie
The Boys in Company C '77
Iron Eagle '86
Iron Eagle 2 '88
Purple Hearts '84
The Taking of Beverly Hills '91

Jules Furthman
The Big Sleep '46
Mutiny on the Bounty '35
Only Angels Have Wings '39
Shanghai Express '32

John Fusco
The Babe '92
Crossroads '86
Thunderheart '92
Young Guns '88
Young Guns 2 '90

Richard Gabai
Virgin High '90

Bob Gale
Back to the Future '85
Back to the Future, Part 2 '89
Back to the Future, Part 3 '90
1941 '79
Trespass '92

Henrik Galeen
Waxworks '24

Chris Gallagher
White Phantom: Enemy of Darkness '87

Carlos Gallardo
El Mariachi '93

George Gallo
Midnight Run '88
29th Street '91

Kenneth Gamet
A Lawless Street '55
Pittsburgh '42

Abel Gance
Beethoven '36

Paul Gangelin
The Mad Ghoul '43

Lowell Ganz
City Slickers '91
City Slickers 2: The Legend of Curly's Gold '94
Greedy '94
Gung Ho '85
A League of Their Own '92
Mr. Saturday Night '92
Night Shift '82
Parenthood '89
Spies Like Us '85
Splash '84
Vibes '88

Louis Gardel
Indochine '92

Fred Gardner
Zabriskie Point '70

Herb Gardner
The Goodbye People '83
A Thousand Clowns '65

Leo Garen
Band of the Hand '86

Robert Garland
No Way Out '87

Helen Garner
The Last Days of Chez Nous '92

Tony Garnett
Deep in the Heart '83
Fat Man and Little Boy '89

Mick Garris
Critters 2: The Main Course '88
The Fly 2 '89
Hocus Pocus '93

Jacek Gasiorowski
Danton '82

Mark Gasper
An Empty Bed '90

Howard Gast
A Woman Called Golda '82

Ernesto Gastaldi
The Scorpion's Tail '71
Torso '73

Nate Gatzert
The Fiddlin' Buckaroo '33

Nils Gaup
Pathfinder '87
Shipwrecked '90

Eleanor Gaver
Dead in the Water '91

John Gay
The Courtship of Eddie's Father '62
Final Notice '89
The Four Horsemen of the Apocalypse '61
The Hallelujah Trail '65
Hennessy '75
The Last Safari '67
Manhunt for Claude Dallas '86
No Way to Treat a Lady '68
Run Silent, Run Deep '58
Separate Tables '58
Soldier Blue '70
Sometimes a Great Notion '71
A Tale of Two Cities '80
Windmills of the Gods '88

Armand Gazarian
Prison Planet '92

Glenn Gebhard
One Last Run '89

David Geeves
American Ninja 4: The Annihilation '91

Theodore (Dr. Seuss) Geisel
The 5000 Fingers of Dr. T '53

Larry Gelbart
Barbarians at the Gate '93
Blame It on Rio '84
Movie, Movie '78
Neighbors '81
Oh, God! '77
Rough Cut '80
Tootsie '82
The Wrong Box '66

Edwin Gelsey
Scarlet Dawn '32
The Strange Love of Molly Louvain '32

Jean Genet
Mademoiselle '66

Dr. Lance Gentile
State of Emergency '94

George S. George
The Heat's On '43

Nelson George
CB4: The Movie '93

Peter George
Dr. Strangelove, or: How I Learned to Stop Worrying and Love the Bomb '64

Terry George
In the Name of the Father '93

Gary Gerani
Pumpkinhead '88

Pietro Germi
Divorce—Italian Style '62

Chris Gerolmo
Miles from Home '88
Mississippi Burning '88

Vance Gerry
The Fox and the Hound '81

Robert Getchell
Alice Doesn't Live Here Anymore '74
Bound for Glory '76
The Client '94
Mommie Dearest '81
Point of No Return '93
Stella '89
Sweet Dreams '85
This Boy's Life '93

Steven Gethers
Jenny's War '85
A Woman Called Golda '82

Earl Ghaffari
The Kindred '87

Alfredo Giannetti
Divorce—Italian Style '62

Duncan Gibbins
A Case for Murder '93
Eve of Destruction '90

Tom Gibson
Covered Wagon Trails '40

Raynold Gideon
Kuffs '92
Made in Heaven '87
A Man, a Woman, and a Bank '79
Stand By Me '86
Starman '84

Barry Gifford
Hotel Room '93

David Giler
Fun with Dick and Jane '77
Southern Comfort '81

Stuart Gillard
Teenage Mutant Ninja Turtles 3 '93

Adrien Gilles
Delicatessen '92

Terry Gilliam
The Adventures of Baron Munchausen '89

And Now for Something Completely Different '72
Brazil '85
Jabberwocky '77
Monty Python and the Holy Grail '75
Monty Python Live at the Hollywood Bowl '82
Monty Python's Life of Brian '79
Monty Python's The Meaning of Life '83
Time Bandits '81

Vince Gilligan
Wilder Napalm '93

Dan Gilroy
Chasers '94
Freejack '92

Frank D. Gilroy
Desperate Characters '71
Fastest Gun Alive '56
From Noon Till Three '76
The Gallant Hours '60
The Gig '85
Jinxed '82
Once in Paris... '79

Tony Gilroy
The Cutting Edge '92

Steven Ginsburg
Family Prayers '91

George Gipp
The Man with Two Brains '83

Andre Girard
La Chienne '31

Francois Girard
32 Short Films About Glenn Gould '93

William Girdler
Asylum of Satan '72
Three on a Meathook '72

Gilbert Girion
American Blue Note '89

Francis Girod
The Elegant Criminal '92

Robert Glass
Death Dreams '92
Running Against Time '90

Handel Glassberg
The Take '90

Mitch Glazer
Mr. Mike's Mondo Video '79
Moon Over Miami '41
Scrooged '88

Russell Gleason
The Flying Fool '29

Peter Glenville
Hotel Paradiso '66

James Glickenhaus
McBain '91
Shakedown '88
Slaughter of the Innocents '93

Jean-Luc Godard
Alphaville '65
Band of Outsiders '64
Breathless '59
Contempt '64
Hail Mary '85
The Joy of Knowledge '65
A Married Woman '65
My Life to Live '62
Nouvelle Vague '90
Numero Deux '75
Oldest Profession '67
Six in Paris '68
Weekend '67

Peter Godfrey
Forever and a Day '43

Ivan Goff
Band of Angels '57
Captain Horatio Hornblower '51

Green Fire '55
Legend of the Lone Ranger '81
Man of a Thousand Faces '57
Midnight Lace '60
Shake Hands with the Devil '59

Menahem Golan
Hanna's War '88
What's Good for the Goose '93

Myron G. Gold
Frankenstein's Great Aunt Tillie '83

Willis Goldbeck
Sergeant Rutledge '60

Dan Goldberg
Feds '88

Gary David Goldberg
Dad '89

Michael Goldberg
Cool Runnings '93

John Golden
Samantha '92

Jorge Goldenberg
Eversmile New Jersey '89

Marilyn Goldin
Camille Claudel '89

Bo Goldman
Little Nikita '88
Melvin and Howard '80
One Flew Over the Cuckoo's Nest '75
Scent of a Woman '92
Shoot the Moon '82
Swing Shift '84

Gary Goldman
Big Trouble in Little China '86
Navy SEALS '90
Total Recall '90

James Goldman
Oliver Twist '82

Jim Goldman
Anastasia: The Mystery of Anna '86
The Lion in Winter '68

William Goldman
All the President's Men '76
A Bridge Too Far '77
Butch Cassidy and the Sundance Kid '69

William Goldman
Chaplin '92

William Goldman
The Great Waldo Pepper '75
Heat '87
Magic '78
Marathon Man '76
Maverick '94
Misery '90
The Princess Bride '87
Year of the Comet '92

Akiva Goldsman
The Client '94

Allan Goldstein
Death Wish 5: The Face of Death '94
Rooftops '89

Amy Goldstein
The Silencer '92

Josh Goldstein
18 Again! '88

Mark Goldstein
Prehysteria '93

Bob(cat) Goldthwait
Shakes the Clown '92

Nick Gomez
Laws of Gravity '92

William Goodhart
Cloud Dancer '80

Generation '69

David Zelag Goodman
Eyes of Laura Mars '78
Farewell, My Lovely '75
Fighting Back '82
Logan's Run '76
Lovers and Other Strangers '70
March or Die '77
Monte Walsh '70
Straw Dogs '72

Francis Goodrich
Father of the Bride '50
Father's Little Dividend '51
It's a Wonderful Life '46

Garry Goodrow
Honey, I Blew Up the Kid '92

Dan Gordon
Gotcha! '85
Highlander: The Gathering '93
Passenger 57 '92
Surf Ninjas '93
Taking the Heat '93
Wyatt Earp '94

Keith Gordon
The Chocolate War '88
A Midnight Clear '92
Static '87

Leon Gordon
Balalaika '39
They Met in Bombay '41
White Cargo '42

Ruth Gordon
Adam's Rib '50
A Double Life '47
Hardhat & Legs '80
It Should Happen to You '54
Pat and Mike '52

Stuart Gordon
Body Snatchers '93
Honey, I Shrunk the Kids '89
The Re-Animator '85
Robot Jox '89

Laszlo Gorog
The Land Unknown '57
The Mole People '56

Morleen Gorris
Broken Mirrors '85

Ron Gorton, Sr.
Whispers of White '93

Carl Gottlieb
Caveman '81
Doctor Detroit '83
Jaws '75
Jaws 2 '78
Jaws 3 '83
The Jerk '79
Which Way Is Up? '77

Michael Gottlieb
Mr. Nanny '93

Heywood Gould
The Boys from Brazil '78
Cocktail '88
Fort Apache, the Bronx '81
One Good Cop '91
Rolling Thunder '77
Streets of Gold '86

Edmund Goulding
Riptide '34
That Certain Woman '37

David S. Goyer
Arcade '93

Jean-Francois Goyet
La Vengeance d'une Femme '89

Todd Graff
Angie '94
Used People '92
The Vanishing '93

Norman Graham
Lost, Lonely, and Vicious '59

Ronny Graham
Finders Keepers '84
Spaceballs '87
To Be or Not to Be '83

Ruth Graham
Becoming Colette '92

Michael Grais
Death Hunt '81
Marked for Death '90
Poltergeist '82
Poltergeist 2: The Other Side '86

Derek Granger
A Handful of Dust '88

Percy Granger
My Brother's Wife '89

James Edward Grant
Angel and the Badman '47
Circus World '64
Johnny Eager '42
The Lady is Willing '42
McLintock! '63
Three Violent People '57

Joe Grant
Dumbo '41

John Grant
Abbott and Costello Go to Mars '53
Abbott and Costello in the Foreign Legion '50
Abbott and Costello Meet the Keystone Kops '54
Abbott & Costello Meet the Mummy '55
Comin' 'Round the Mountain '51
Here Come the Co-Eds '45
In Society '44
Ma and Pa Kettle at the Fair '52

Beverly Gray
Full Contact '93

John Gray
An American Story '92
Billy Galvin '86
The Lost Capone '90
Showdown at Williams Creek '91

Mike Gray
The China Syndrome '79
Code of Silence '85
Wavelength '83

Simon Gray
A Month in the Country '87

Spalding Gray
Monster in a Box '92

Charles Grayson
One Night in the Tropics '40

Brian Grazer
Armed and Dangerous '86
Housesitter '92

Kjell Grede
Good Evening, Mr. Wallenberg '93

Adolph Green
Auntie Mame '58
The Barkleys of Broadway '49
Bells are Ringing '60
It's Always Fair Weather '55
On the Town '49
Singin' in the Rain '52

Anthony Green
Ninja Fantasy '86

David S. Green
Out for Blood '93

Harry Green
Jude the Obscure '71

Howard J. Green
Blessed Event '32

Harmon of Michigan '41
I Am a Fugitive from a Chain Gang '32
They Call It Sin '32

Paul Green
The Cabin in the Cotton '32

Terry Green
Cold Justice '89

Walon Green
The Border '82
Brink's Job '78
Crusoe '89
RoboCop 2 '90
Solarbabies '86
Sorcerer '77
The Wild Bunch '69

Peter Greenaway
The Belly of an Architect '91
The Cook, the Thief, His Wife & Her Lover '90
The Draughtsman's Contract '82
Drowning by Numbers '87
Prospero's Books '91
A Zed & Two Noughts '88

Graham Greene
The Comedians '67
The Fallen Idol '49
The Third Man '49
21 Days '37

Harold Greene
Texas Across the River '66

Seth Greenland
Who's the Man? '93

Adam Greenman
Three of Hearts '93

Maggie Greenwald
The Ballad of Little Jo '93

William Grefe
The Checkered Flag '63

Richard Greggson
Eminent Domain '91

Sharon Greytak
Hearing Voices '90

Eleanore Griffin
One Man's Way '63

Charles B. Griffith
Atlas '60
The Beast from Haunted Cave '60
Creature from the Haunted Sea '60
Death Race 2000 '75
Devil's Angels '67
Dr. Heckyl and Mr. Hype '80
The Gunslinger '56
The Wild Angels '66

D.W. Griffith
Isn't Life Wonderful '24
Judith of Bethulia '14
The Love Flower '20

J.J. Griffith
Catlow '71

Thomas Ian Griffith
Excessive Force '93

Mark Griffiths
Running Hot '83

Trevor Griffiths
Singing the Blues in Red '87

Wallace Grissell
Zorro's Black Whip '44

Charles Grodin
Movers and Shakers '85

Ferde Grofe, Jr.
Warkill '65

Larry Grolin
Dead Connection '94

Jerry Gross
Girl on a Chain Gang '65

Joel Gross
Blind Man's Bluff '91
No Escape '94
No Escape '94

Larry Gross
Body Parts '91
48 Hrs. '82
Geronimo: An American Legend '93
Streets of Fire '84

Leonard Gross
Forbidden '85

Lynn Grossman
Tokyo Pop '88

Jean Gruault
The Eighties '83
Jules and Jim '62
Mon Oncle D'Amerique '80
The Mystery of Alexina '86
Paris Belongs to Us '60
Story of Adele H. '75
The Wild Child '70

David Grubin
LBJ: A Biography '91

Karl Grune
The Street '23

John Guare
Six Degrees of Separation '93

Paul Guay
The Little Rascals '94

Richard Guay
Household Saints '93
True Love '89

Mac Gudgeon
Wind '92

Einar Mar Gudmundsson
Children of Nature '92

Robert Guenette
Here's Looking at You, Warner Bros. '91

Andrew Guerdat
Fourth Story '90

Tonino Guerra
Amarcord '74
And the Ship Sails On '83
Blow-Up '66
Casanova '70 '65
Everybody's Fine '90
Ginger & Fred '86
Good Morning, Babylon '87
Henry IV '85
Kaos '85
Landscape in the Mist '88
L'Avventura '60
The Night of the Shooting Stars '82
The Red Desert '64
10th Victim '65
Zabriskie Point '70

Christopher Guest
The Big Picture '89
The Return of Spinal Tap '92
This is Spinal Tap '84

Judith Guest
Rachel River '89

Val Guest
Carry On Admiral '57
When Dinosaurs Ruled the Earth '70

Fred Guiol
Gunga Din '39

Yilmaz Guney
The Wall '83
Yol '82

Bill Gunn
Black Vampire '73

Robert Gunter
The Sandlot '93

Dan Gurskis
Body Language '92
The Stranger '87

Bart B. Gustis
The Bikini Car Wash Company 2 '93

Beth Gutcheon
The Good Fight '92

Richard Guttman
Ivory Hunters '90

Robert Guza, Jr.
Curtains '83

Stephen Gyllenhaal
The New Kids '85

Belinda Haas
The Music of Chance '93

Philip Haas
The Music of Chance '93

Albert Hacket
Father of the Bride '50
Father's Little Dividend '51
It's a Wonderful Life '46

George Hadjinassios
Shirley Valentine '89

Charles Haigh
In a Moment of Passion '93

Richard W. Haines
Alien Space Avenger '91

Mervyn Haisman
Jane & the Lost City '87

Sonnie Hale
Gangway '37

Julian Halevy
Circus World '64

Alex Haley
Superfly T.N.T. '73

Eyal Halfon
Cup Final '92

Karen Hall
The Women of Brewster Place '89

Kenneth J. Hall
Die Watching '93
Test Tube Teens from the Year 2000 '93

Norman S. Hall
The Topeka Terror '45

Peter Hall
Orpheus Descending '91

Craig Hamann
Dollman vs Demonic Toys '93

Pete Hamill
The Neon Empire '89

David Hamilton
White Phantom: Enemy of Darkness '87

Warren Hamilton
Kiss of the Tarantula '75

Sam Hamm
Batman '89
Never Cry Wolf '83

Oscar Hammerstein
Show Boat '36
State Fair '45

Dashiell Hammett
Watch on the Rhine '43

Christopher Hampton
Beyond the Limit '83
Dangerous Liaisons '88
A Doll's House '73
The Good Father '87

The Wolf at the Door '87

Blanche Hanalis
Where Angels Go, Trouble Follows '68

John Hancock
Weeds '87

John Lee Hancock
A Perfect World '93

Peter Handke
Wings of Desire '88

Daryl Haney
Crime Zone '88
Daddy's Boys '87
Friday the 13th, Part 7: The New Blood '88
Lords of the Deep '89
Masque of the Red Death '89
To Die Standing '91

William Hanley
The Attic: The Hiding of Anne Frank '88

Brian Hannant
The Time Guardian '87

Lorraine Hansberry
A Raisin in the Sun '61

Marion Hansel
Between Heaven and Earth '93
Dust '85

Erik Hansen
Heart and Souls '93

Gregory Hansen
Heart and Souls '93

Curtis Hanson
The Bedroom Window '87
The Dunwich Horror '70
Never Cry Wolf '83
The Silent Partner '78

John Hanson
Wildrose '85

Jonathon Hardy
Breaker Morant '80

David Hare
Damage '92
Plenty '85
Saigon: Year of the Cat '87
Strapless '90
Wetherby '85

Marion Hargrove
Cash McCall '60
The Music Man '62

Eric Harlacher
Homewrecker '92

Robert Harling
Soapdish '91
Steel Magnolias '89

John Harlow
Appointment with Crime '45
Meet Sexton Blake '44

Patricia Harper
The Topeka Terror '45

Sam Harper
Rookie of the Year '93

Damien Harris
The Rachel Papers '89

James B. Harris
Boiling Point '93
Cop '88

Leslie Harris
Just Another Girl on the I.R.T. '93

Owen Harris
Frontier Uprising '61

Richard Harris
Stepping Out '91

Steven Harris
At Gunpoint '90

Timothy Harris
Brewster's Millions '85
Cheaper to Keep Her '80
Kindergarten Cop '90
My Stepmother Is an Alien '88
Pure Luck '91
Trading Places '83
Twins '88

Trent Harris
Rubin & Ed '92

Wendell B. Harris, Jr.
Chameleon Street '89

Jim Harrison
Cold Feet '89
Revenge '90
Wolf '94

Joan Harrison
Foreign Correspondent '40
Rebecca '40

John Kent Harrison
Beautiful Dreamers '92
City Boy '93
Memories of Murder '90
Murder by Phone '82
The Sound and the Silence '93

Bruce Hart
Question of Faith '93

Jim V. Hart
Bram Stoker's Dracula '92

Moss Hart
Gentleman's Agreement '47
Hans Christian Andersen '52

Kenneth Hartford
Hell Squad '85

Hal Hartley
Simple Men '92
Trust '91
The Unbelievable Truth '90

Don Hartman
My Favorite Blonde '42

Phil Hartman
Pee Wee's Big Adventure '85

Edmund Hartmann
Ali Baba and the Forty Thieves '43
Casanova's Big Night '54
In Society '44
The Lemon Drop Kid '51

Anthony Harvey
The Disappearance of Aimee '76

Johanna Harwood
Call Me Bwana '63

Ronald Harwood
The Doctor and the Devils '85
A Fine Romance '92
One Day in the Life of Ivan Denisovich '71

Patrick Hasburgh
Aspen Extreme '93

Gustav Hasford
Full Metal Jacket '87

Shinobu Hashimoto
Throne of Blood '57
Yojimbo '61

Stephen Hawking
A Brief History of Time '92

Richard Hawley
Mother's Boys '94

Christopher Hawthorne
Parents '89

Clyde Allen Hayes
Rubdown '93

John Hayes
The Cut Throats '89
Pancho Barnes '88

John Michael Hayes
But Not for Me '59
Butterfield 8 '60
The Carpetbaggers '64
The Chalk Garden '64
The Dresser '83
Harlow '65
Iron Will '93
It's a Dog's Life '55
Peyton Place '57
Rear Window '54
The Rose Tattoo '55
Thunder Bay '53
To Catch a Thief '55
The Trouble with Harry '55
Where Love Has Gone '64

Joseph Hayes
Stolen Hours '63

Terry Hayes
Dead Calm '89
Mad Max: Beyond Thunderdome '85

Todd Haynes
Poison '91

Lillie Hayward
Lady Killer '33
They Call It Sin '32

Laurence Heath
Triumph of the Spirit '89

David Heavener
Eye of the Stranger '93
Killcrazy '89
Prime Target '91
Twisted Justice '89

Ben Hecht
Circus World '64
Comrade X '40
Hallelujah, I'm a Bum '33
The Indian Fighter '55
Let Freedom Ring '39
Monkey Business '52
Nothing Sacred '37
Notorious '46
Spectre of the Rose '46
Twentieth Century '34
Viva Villa! '34
Wuthering Heights '39

Amy Heckerling
Look Who's Talking '89

Rob Hedden
Friday the 13th, Part 8: Jason Takes Manhattan '89

Roger Hedden
Bodies, Rest & Motion '93

Peter Hedges
What's Eating Gilbert Grape '93

Victor Heerman
Golden Boy '39
Little Women '33

Carol Heikkinen
The Thing Called Love '93

Jo Heims
Double Trouble '67
Play Misty for Me '71

Mats Helge
The Russian Terminator '90

Brian Helgeland
A Nightmare on Elm Street 4: Dream Master '88

Lukas Heller
Blue City '86
Damnation Alley '77

Lillian Hellman
The Chase '66
Watch on the Rhine '43

Sam Hellman
The Three Musketeers '39

Frank Henenlotter
Basket Case 2 '90
Basket Case 3: The Progeny '92

James Henerson
The Fire Next Time '93

Liu Heng
The Story of Qui Ju '91

Paul Hengge
The Rose Garden '89

Kim Henkel
Last Night at the Alamo '83
The Texas Chainsaw Massacre '74

Hilary Henkin
Romeo Is Bleeding '93

Beth Henley
Crimes of the Heart '86
Miss Firecracker '89
Nobody's Fool '86
True Stories '86

Jack Henley
Blondie Hits the Jackpot '49
Ma and Pa Kettle Back On the Farm '51

Buck Henry
Catch-22 '70
The Day of the Dolphin '73
First Family '80
The Graduate '67
The Owl and the Pussycat '70
Protocol '84
What's Up, Doc? '72

Todd Henschell
Puppet Master 4 '93

Jonathan Hensleigh
A Far Off Place '93

J. Miyoko Hensley
Can You Feel Me Dancing? '85

Steven Hensley
Can You Feel Me Dancing? '85

Robert Herari
Everything Happens at Night '39

Hugh Herbert
Let's Make it Legal '51

John Herbert
Fortune and Men's Eyes '71

Ron Herbst
Deadly Diamonds '91
Warlords 3000 '93

Stephen Herek
Critters '86

Mark Herman
Blame It on the Bellboy '92

Gyula Hernadi
The Round Up '66

Michael Herr
Full Metal Jacket '87

Rowdy Herrington
Striking Distance '93

W. Blake Herron
Skin Art '93

Joel Hershman
Hold Me, Thrill Me, Kiss Me '93

Marshall Herskovitz
Special Bulletin '83

John Herzfeld
Casualties of Love: The "Long Island Lolita" Story '93

Werner Herzog
Aguirre, the Wrath of God '72
Every Man for Himself & God Against All '75
Fitzcarraldo '82
Woyzeck '78

Kit Hesketh-Harvey
Maurice '87

Fraser Heston
Treasure Island '89

Louis M. Heyward
Pajama Party '64

Stephen Hibbert
It's Pat '94

Jochen Hick
Via Appia '92

George Hickenlooper
Hearts of Darkness: A Filmmaker's Apocalypse '91

Seymour Hicks
Scrooge '35

Howard Higgin
Revolt of the Zombies '36

Colin Higgins
Harold and Maude '71
The Silver Streak '76

John C. Higgins
Robinson Crusoe on Mars '64

Lynn Rose Higgins
Mutator '90

David Hill
Promised a Miracle '88

Gladys Hill
The Man Who Would Be King '75

John Hill
Quigley Down Under '90

Walter Hill
Aliens '86
Blue City '86
The Driver '78
The Drowning Pool '75
48 Hrs. '82
The Getaway '72
The Getaway '93
Hard Times '75
Mackintosh Man '73
Red Heat '88
Southern Comfort '81
Streets of Fire '84
The Thief Who Came to Dinner '73
The Warriors '79

James Hilton
Foreign Correspondent '40
Mrs. Miniver '42

Lawrence Hilton-Jacobs
Angels of the City '89

David Himmelstein
Power '86
Talent for the Game '91

Alan Hines
Square Dance '87

Nigel Hinton
Buddy's Song '91

James G. Hirsch
Broken Badge '85

Roger O. Hirson
A Woman Named Jackie '91

Michael Hirst
The Ballad of the Sad Cafe '91
Fools of Fortune '90
Meeting Venus '91

Alfred Hitchcock
Blackmail '29
Champagne '28
The Farmer's Wife '28
Juno and the Paycock '30
The Lodger '26
Murder '30
No. 17 '32

Rich and Strange '32
The Ring '27
Saboteur '42
Skin Game '31

Michael Hitchcock
Where the Day Takes You '92

Ken Hixon
Caught in the Act '93

Godfrey Ho
Ninja Champion '80s
Ninja Destroyer '70s

Mike Hodges
Black Rainbow '91
Damien: Omen 2 '78
Pulp '72
The Terminal Man '74

Michael Hoey
Navy vs. the Night Monsters '66

Bridget Hoffman
Double Exposure '93

Charles Hoffman
The West Point Story '50

Michael Hoffman
Promised Land '88

Michael Hogan
Arabian Nights '42
Forever and a Day '43

Paul Hogan
Almost an Angel '90
Crocodile Dundee 2 '88
Lightning Jack '94

Brian Hohlfield
He Said, She Said '91
The Mighty Ducks '92

Agnieszka Holland
Angry Harvest '85
Anna '87
Danton '82
Europa, Europa '91
Korczak '90
A Love in Germany '84
Olivier, Olivier '92
To Kill a Priest '89

Steve Holland
Better Off Dead '85
One Crazy Summer '86

Tom Holland
The Beast Within '82
Child's Play '88
Class of 1984 '82
Cloak & Dagger '84
Fright Night '85
Psycho 2 '83
Scream for Help '86

Eli Hollander
Out '88

Don Holley
National Lampoon's Loaded Weapon 1 '93

Kari Holman
The Death Merchant '91

Brown Holmes
The Strange Love of Molly Louvain '32

Geoffrey Homes
Out of the Past '47

Kirk Honeycutt
Final Judgement '92

Harry Hook
The Kitchen Toto '87

Tobe Hooper
The Texas Chainsaw Massacre '74

Claudia Hoover
Double Exposure '93

Arthur Hopcraft
A Perfect Spy '88

Alan Hopgood
Alvin Purple '73
Alvin Rides Again '74

John Hopkins
Codename Kyril '91
The Holcroft Covenant '85
Murder by Decree '79
The Offence '73
Thunderball '65
Torment '85
The Virgin Soldiers '69

Robert Hopkins
Saratoga '37

Arthur T. Horman
Here Come the Co-Eds '45

Lanny Horn
Skeeter '93

Christopher Horner
Accidental Meeting '93

Israel Horovitz
Author! Author! '82
A Man in Love '87
The Strawberry Statement '70

Anthony Horowitz
Diamond's Edge '88

Ed Horowitz
On Deadly Ground '94

Jordan Horowitz
Alan & Naomi '92

Bob Hoskins
The Raggedy Rawney '90

Dan Hoskins
Chopper Chicks in Zombietown '91

John Houseman
Jane Eyre '44

Bobby Houston
Caged Fear '92

Clint Howard
Cotton Candy '82

Elizabeth Jane Howard
Getting It Right '89

Joseph Howard
Sister Act '92

Ron Howard
Cotton Candy '82
Grand Theft Auto '77
Parenthood '89

Sidney Howard
Gone with the Wind '39

Dorothy Howell
Platinum Blonde '31

Frank Howson
The Hunting '92

Perry Howze
Chances Are '89
Maid to Order '87
Mystic Pizza '88

Randy Howze
Chances Are '89

John Hubbard
Daniel Boone: Trail Blazer '56

Tom Hubbard
Thunder Pass '54

Jean-Loup Hubert
Le Grand Chemin '87

Tom Huckabee
Deathfight '93

Reginald Hudlin
Bebe's Kids '92
House Party '90

Dick Huemer
Dumbo '41

Chuck Hughes
Ed and His Dead Mother '93

John Hughes
Baby's Day Out '94
Beethoven '92
The Breakfast Club '85
Career Opportunities '91
Curly Sue '91
Dennis the Menace '93
Dutch '91
Ferris Bueller's Day Off '86
The Great Outdoors '88
Home Alone '90
Home Alone 2: Lost in New York '92
Mr. Mom '83
National Lampoon's Christmas Vacation '89
National Lampoon's Class Reunion '82
National Lampoon's European Vacation '85
National Lampoon's Vacation '83
Planes, Trains & Automobiles '87
Pretty in Pink '86
She's Having a Baby '88
Sixteen Candles '84
Some Kind of Wonderful '87
Uncle Buck '89
Weird Science '85

Ken Hughes
Arrivederci, Baby! '66
Chitty Chitty Bang Bang '68
Cromwell '70
Heat Wave '54
Oh, Alfie '75

Langston Hughes
Way Down South '39

Russell S. Hughes
Savage Wilderness '55

Jay Huguely-Cass
Jason Goes to Hell: The Final Friday '93

Steve Hulett
The Fox and the Hound '81

Ron Hulme
Fearless Tiger '94

Cyril Hume
The Invisible Boy '57
Trader Horn '31

Joel Don Humphreys
My Heroes Have Always Been Cowboys '91

Barry Humphries
Barry McKenzie Holds His Own '74

Tran Anh Hung
The Scent of Green Papaya '93

Jackson Hunsicker
Oddball Hall '91

Bob Hunt
The Hidden '87

Edward Hunt
Starship Invasions '77

Thomas Hunter
The Final Countdown '80

Lawrence Huntington
Man on the Run '49

Earl Hurd
Snow White and the Seven Dwarfs '37

Gladys Hurlbut
Love on the Run '36

Ben Hurst
Bums '93

Harry Hurwitz
Fleshtone '94
The Projectionist '71
That's Adequate '90
Under the Rainbow '81

John Huston
The African Queen '51
High Sierra '41
Key Largo '48
The Maltese Falcon '41
The Man Who Would Be King '75
Mr. North '88
Moby Dick '56
Sergeant York '41
Treasure of the Sierra Madre '48

Ron Hutchinson
Blue Ice '92

Aldous Huxley
Jane Eyre '44

Willard Huyck
American Graffiti '73
Best Defense '84
French Postcards '79
Howard the Duck '86
Indiana Jones and the Temple of Doom '84
Messiah of Evil '74

David Henry Hwang
Golden Gate '93
M. Butterfly '93

Peter Hyams
Busting '74
Capricorn One '78
Hanover Street '79
The Hunter '80
Narrow Margin '90
Outland '81
The Star Chamber '83
Telefon '77
2010: The Year We Make Contact '84

Chris Hyde
Chained Heat 2 '92

Jeremy Iacone
Blood In...Blood Out: Bound by Honor '93

Rustam Ibragimbekov
Close to Eden '90

Leon Ichaso
Crossover Dreams '85
El Super '79

Masato Ide
Ran '85

Eric Idle
Monty Python and the Holy Grail '75
Monty Python's Life of Brian '79
Monty Python's The Meaning of Life '83
National Lampoon's European Vacation '85
Splitting Heirs '93
The Tale of the Frog Prince '83

W. Peter Iliff
Patriot Games '92
Point Break '91

Lou Illar
Sidekicks '93

Shohei Imamura
The Ballad of Narayama '83

Thomas Ince
Disciple '15

William Inge
All Fall Down '62

Inge ▶cont.

Splendor in the Grass '61

Boris Ingster
Happy Landing '38
Thin Ice '37

J. Christian Ingvordsen
Comrades in Arms '91
The Outfit '93

Tino Insana
The Masters of Menace '90

Ronnie Isaacs
Warriors from Hell '90

Christopher Isherwood
Diane '55
Forever and a Day '43
The Loved One '65

Charles Israel
Arch of Triumph '85

Neal Israel
Police Academy '84
Real Genius '85

Juzo Itami
A Taxing Woman '87
A Taxing Woman's Return '88

Daisuke Ito
An Actor's Revenge '63

James Ivory
Maurice '87
Shakespeare Wallah '65

Bob Ivy
Dark Rider '91

David S. Jackson
Detonator '93

Donald G. Jackson
The Demon Lover '77

Felix Jackson
Destry Rides Again '39

Horace Jackson
The Animal Kingdom '32

Peter Jackson
Dead Alive '93

Philip Jackson
Project: Genesis '93

Lewis Jacobs
Sweet Love, Bitter '67

Matthew Jacobs
Lassie '94
Lorna Doone '90
Paperhouse '89

Nicholas A.E. Jacobs
The Refrigerator '93

Henry Jaglom
Always '85
Can She Bake a Cherry Pie? '83
Eating '90
New Year's Day '89
Sitting Ducks '80
Someone to Love '87
Tracks '76

Don Jakoby
Arachnophobia '90
Blue Thunder '83
Invaders from Mars '86
Lifeforce '85
The Philadelphia Experiment '84

Alan James
Dick Tracy: The Original Serial, Vol. 1 '37
Dick Tracy: The Original Serial, Vol. 2 '37

Polly James
Mrs. Parkington '44

Rian James
42nd Street '33

Tama Janowitz
Slaves of New York '89

Michael January
C.I.A. 2: Target Alexa '94
To Be the Best '93

Derek Jarman
Blue '93
Caravaggio '86
Edward II '92

Jim Jarmusch
Down by Law '86
Mystery Train '89
Night on Earth '91
Permanent Vacation '84
Stranger than Paradise '84

Kevin Jarre
Glory '89
Tombstone '93

Paul Jarrice
Messenger of Death '88

Charles Jarrott
Morning Glory '93

Griffin Jay
Captive Wild Woman '43
The Mummy's Ghost '44
The Mummy's Tomb '42

Henri Jeanson
Modigliani '58

Mahatma Kane Jeeves
The Bank Dick '40

Brian D. Jeffries
Hangfire '91

Herbert Jeffries
World of the Depraved '67

Dan Jenkins
Dead Solid Perfect '88

John Jenkins
Patti Rocks '88

Jim Jennewein
The Flintstones '94
Getting Even with Dad '94

Talbot Jennings
Anna and the King of Siam '46
Mutiny on the Bounty '35

Bill Jesse
Riff Raff '92

Anthony Jesu
Fist of Steel '93

Jack Jevne
Wintertime '43

Ruth Prawer Jhabvala
Autobiography of a Princess '75
Bombay Talkie '70
The Bostonians '84
The Europeans '79
Heat and Dust '82
The Householder '63
Howard's End '92
Hullabaloo Over Georgie & Bonnie's Pictures '78
Jane Austen in Manhattan '80
Madame Sousatzka '88
Mr. & Mrs. Bridge '91
Quartet '81
The Remains of the Day '93
A Room with a View '86
Roseland '77
Shakespeare Wallah '65

Neal Jimenez
For the Boys '91
River's Edge '87

The Waterdance '91

Mike Jittlov
The Wizard of Speed and Time '88

Alejandro Jodorowsky
Santa Sangre '90

Arthur Joffe
Alberto Express '92

Roland Joffe
Fat Man and Little Boy '89

Charles Eric Johnson
The George McKenna Story '86

George Clayton Johnson
The Twilight Zone '61

J. Randall Johnson
The Doors '91

Mark Steven Johnson
Grumpy Old Men '93

Monica Johnson
Americathon '79
Jekyll & Hyde...Together Again '82
Lost in America '85
Modern Romance '81
Real Life '79
The Scout '94

Nora Johnson
The World of Henry Orient '64

Nunnally Johnson
Along Came Jones '45
Casanova Brown '44
The Grapes of Wrath '40
How to Marry a Millionaire '53
The Keys of the Kingdom '44
Mr. Peabody & the Mermaid '48
Phone Call from a Stranger '52
Rose of Washington Square '39
We're Not Married '52
The World of Henry Orient '64

Randy Johnson
The Doors '91

Terry Johnson
Insignificance '85

Becky Johnston
The Prince of Tides '91

Norman Jolley
The Monolith Monsters '57

Amy Holden Jones
Beethoven '92
The Getaway '93
Indecency '92
Indecent Proposal '93
Mystic Pizza '88

Charles Reed Jones
The King Murder Case '32

Chuck Jones
Gay Purr-ee '62

Evan Jones
Champions '84
Funeral in Berlin '66
Kangaroo '86
Killing of Angel Street '81
Shadow of the Wolf '92
A Show of Force '90

Ian Jones
The Lighthorsemen '87
Ned Kelly '70

Laura Jones
An Angel at My Table '89
High Tide '87

Laurie Jones
In the Spirit '90

Mark Jones
Leprechaun '93

Robert C. Jones
Coming Home '78

Terry Jones
And Now for Something Completely Different '72
Erik the Viking '89
Labyrinth '86
Monty Python and the Holy Grail '75
Monty Python's Life of Brian '79
Monty Python's The Meaning of Life '83
Ripping Yarns '75

Glenn Jordan
O Pioneers! '91

Neil Jordan
The Company of Wolves '85
The Crying Game '92
Danny Boy '84
High Spirits '88
The Miracle '91
Mona Lisa '86

Robert L. Joseph
World War III '86

Julien Josephson
The Rains Came '39

Jon Jost
All the Vermeers in New York '91
Sure Fire '90

Adrien (Carole Eastman) Joyce
Five Easy Pieces '70
Man Trouble '92

C. Courtney Joyner
Catacombs '89
Class of 1999 '90
Desperate Motives '92
Lurking Fear '94
The Offspring '87
Prison '88
Trancers 3: Deth Lives '92
Vietnam, Texas '90

Aaron Julien
Dirty Work '92

Marcy Kahan
Antonia and Jane '91

Jeff Kahn
Revolution! A Red Comedy '91

Richard C. Kahn
Bronze Buckaroo '39

Tom Kalin
Swoon '91

Stanley Kalis
Road Racers '59

Bert Kalmar
Duck Soup '33
A Night at the Opera '35

Steven Kaman
The Outfit '93

Robert Mark Kamen
The Karate Kid '84
The Karate Kid: Part 2 '86
The Karate Kid: Part 3 '89
Lethal Weapon 3 '92
The Power of One '92
Split Image '82
Taps '81

Zbigniew Kaminski
Maids of Wilko '79

Stuart Kaminsky
Hidden Fears '93

Steven Kampmann
Back to School '86
Back to School '86
Clifford '92
The Couch Trip '87
Stealing Home '88

Aben Kandel
They Won't Forget '37

Michael Kane
All the Right Moves '83
The Bear '89
The Cisco Kid '94
Foolin' Around '80
Hard Country '81
Hot Stuff '79
Legend of the Lone Ranger '81
Smokey and the Bandit, Part 2 '80
Southern Comfort '81

Rolfe Kanefsky
There's Nothing Out There '90

Jeff Kanew
Natural Enemies '79

Charles Kanganis
Fist of Honor '92
No Escape, No Return '93
A Time to Die '91

Fay Kanin
The Opposite Sex '56
Rhapsody '54
Teacher's Pet '58

Garson Kanin
Adam's Rib '50
A Double Life '47
It Should Happen to You '54
Pat and Mike '52

Michael Kanin
How to Commit Marriage '69
The Opposite Sex '56
Rhapsody '54
Teacher's Pet '58
Woman of the Year '42

Hal Kanter
Bachelor in Paradise '69
Bachelor in Paradise '69
Blue Hawaii '62
Casanova's Big Night '54
Dear Brigitte '65
Here Come the Girls '53
Loving You '57
The Rose Tattoo '55

Jonathan Kaplan
Mr. Billion '77
White Line Fever '75

Marty Kaplan
The Distinguished Gentleman '92
Noises Off '92
Striking Distance '93

Larry Karaszewski
Ed Wood '94
Problem Child '90
Problem Child 2 '91

Tom Kartozian
Frozen Assets '92

Lawrence Kasdan
The Accidental Tourist '88
The Big Chill '83
Body Heat '81
The Bodyguard '92
Continental Divide '81
The Empire Strikes Back '80
Grand Canyon '91
Return of the Jedi '83
Silverado '85
Wyatt Earp '94

Meg Kasdan
Grand Canyon '91

Mitchel Katlin
Opportunity Knocks '90

A.L. Katz
Children of the Corn 2: The Final Sacrifice '92

Douglas Katz
Age Isn't Everything '91

Gloria Katz
American Graffiti '73

Best Defense '84
French Postcards '79
Howard the Duck '86
Indiana Jones and the Temple of Doom '84
Messiah of Evil '74

Lee Katz
Waterfront '39

Steven Katz
Fallen Angels 1 '93

Charles Kaufman
Mother's Day '80
Return to Paradise '53

George S. Kaufman
The Cocoanuts '29
A Night at the Opera '35

Ken Kaufman
In the Army Now '94

Lloyd Samuel Weil Kaufman
The Toxic Avenger, Part 2 '89
The Toxic Avenger, Part 3: The Last Temptation of Toxie '89

Millard Kaufman
The War Lord '65

Philip Kaufman
The Great Northfield Minnesota Raid '72
Henry & June '90
The Outlaw Josey Wales '76
Raiders of the Lost Ark '81
The Right Stuff '83
Rising Sun '93
The Unbearable Lightness of Being '88
Wanderers '79

Aki Kaurismaki
Ariel '89
La Vie de Boheme '93
Leningrad Cowboys Go America '89
The Match Factory Girl '90

Frances Kavanaugh
The Driftin' Kid '41
Driftin' River '46
Dynamite Canyon '41
Riding the Sunset Trail '41

Sandra Kay
Working Girls '87

Norman Kaye
Cactus '86

Richard Kaye
The Wizard of Speed and Time '88

Nicholas Kazan
At Close Range '86
Dream Lover '93
Frances '82
Mobsters '91
Patty Hearst '88
Reversal of Fortune '90

Fran Rubel Kazui
Tokyo Pop '93

Tim Kazurinsky
About Last Night... '86
For Keeps '88

James Keach
Armed and Dangerous '86
The Forgotten '89
Slashed Dreams '74

Robert Keats
The Closer '90

Peter Keglevic
Kill Cruise '90

Harvey Keith
Jezebel's Kiss '90

John Kelleher
Eat the Peach '86

George Keller
Six in Paris '68

Bob Kelljan
The Return of Count Yorga '71

Marjorie Kellogg
Rosebud '75

David Kelly
From the Hip '86

Mark Kelly
One in a Million '36

Kurt Kempler
The Big Stampede '32
Telegraph Trail '33

Anne Kennedy
Crush '93

Burt Kennedy
Dynamite and Gold '88
Hannie Caulder '72
Ride Lonesome '59
The Rounders '65
The Tall T '57
Train Robbers '73
The Trouble with Spies '87
White Hunter, Black Heart '90

Ken Kennedy
Iron Angel '64

Leon Isaac Kennedy
Knights of the City '85

Michael Kennedy
The Swordsman '92

William Kennedy
The Cotton Club '84
Ironweed '87

Doug Kenney
Caddyshack '80

Willis Kent
Mad Youth '40

Earl Kenton
Invisible: The Chronicles of Benjamin Knight '93
Mandroid '93

Sarah Kernochan
Impromptu '90
Sommersby '93

Claude Kerven
Mortal Thoughts '91

Emmanuel Kervyn
Rabid Grannies '89

Ken Kesey
One Flew Over the Cuckoo's Nest '75

Lyle Kessler
Orphans '87
The Saint of Fort Washington '93

Larry Ketron
Freeway '88
Permanent Record '88

Michael Keusch
Samurai Cowboy '93

Christopher Keyser
Benefit of the Doubt '93

Riffat A. Khan
Feelin' Screwy '90

Edward Khmara
Dragon: The Bruce Lee Story '93
Ladyhawke '85

Callie Khouri
Thelma & Louise '91

Krzysztof Kieslowski
The Double Life of Veronique '91
No End '84
Trois Couleurs: Bleu '93
Trois Couleurs: Rouge '94

Andrzej Kijowski
The Conductor '80

Riyuzo Kikushima
Throne of Blood '57

Jon Killough
Skinned Alive '89

Richard H. Kim
Kill Line '91

Tim Kincaid
Mutant Hunt '87
The Occultist '89
Robot Holocaust '87

Chloe King
Red Shoe Diaries 3: Another Woman's Lipstick '93

Rick King
Hard Choices '84

Robert King
Clean Slate '94
The Nest '88

Stephen King
Cat's Eye '85
Creepshow '82
Graveyard Shift '90
Maximum Overdrive '86
Pet Sematary '89
Silver Bullet '85
Sleepwalkers '92
Stephen King's It '90
Stephen King's The Stand '94
Tales from the Darkside: The Movie '90

Zalman King
Lake Consequence '92
9 1/2 Weeks '86
Red Shoe Diaries 3: Another Woman's Lipstick '93
Two Moon Junction '88
Wild Orchid '90
Wild Orchid 2: Two Shades of Blue '91
Wildfire '88

Dorothy Kingsley
Angels in the Outfield '51
Broadway Rhythm '44
Don't Go Near the Water '57
Green Mansions '59
Valley of the Dolls '67

Ernest Kinoy
Gore Vidal's Lincoln '88
Murrow '86
The Story of David '76
The Story of Jacob & Joseph '74

Teinosuke Kinugasa
An Actor's Revenge '63

Karey Kirkpatrick
The Rescuers Down Under '90

Leonard Kirtman
Carnival of Blood '71

Tim Kissell
In the Soup '92

Robert Klane
National Lampoon's European Vacation '85
Unfaithfully Yours '84
Weekend at Bernie's '89
Weekend at Bernie's 2 '93

Damian Klaus
Futurekick '91

Andrew Klavan
A Shock to the System '90

Dena Kleiman
Strapped '93

Dennis Klein
Family Dog: Complete Series '92

Don Klein
Frozen Assets '92

Ted Klein
Dario Argento's Trauma '93

Walter Klenhard
Dead in the Water '91
The Last Hit '93

Steven Kloves
The Fabulous Baker Boys '89
Flesh and Bone '93
Racing with the Moon '84

Nigel Kneale
First Men in the Moon '64

Andrew Knight
The Efficiency Expert '92

Patricia Louisianna Knop
9 1/2 Weeks '86
Siesta '87

Christopher Knopf
The King's Thief '55
Not My Kid '85

Bernard Knowles
Norman Conquest '53

Herman Koch
Wings of Fame '93

Howard Koch
Casablanca '42
The Letter '40
Rhapsody in Blue '45
The Sea Hawk '40
Sergeant York '41
War Lover '62

David Koepp
Apartment Zero '88
Carlito's Way '93
Death Becomes Her '92
Jurassic Park '93
The Paper '94
The Shadow '94

Steven Koepp
The Paper '94

Frederick Kohner
Three Daring Daughters '48

Kenneth Kolb
The Seventh Voyage of Sinbad '58

Emil Kolbe
American Kickboxer 1 '91

Amos Kollek
Crazy Streets '80s
Double Edge '92

Xavier Koller
Journey of Hope '90

Manuel Komroff
Scarlet Empress '34

Andrei Konchalovsky
The Inner Circle '91
Maria's Lovers '84
Runaway Train '85

Larry Konner
The Beverly Hillbillies '93
For Love or Money '93
The Jewel of the Nile '85

Arthur Kopit
Hands of a Stranger '87

Mari Kornhauser
Zandalee '91

Ken Koser
Sudie & Simpson '90

Ron Koslow
Into the Night '85

John Kostmayer
I Love You to Death '90

William Kotzwinkle
Book of Love '91

Jim Kouf
Another Stakeout '93
Stakeout '87

Janet Kovalcik
Married to It '93
My Girl 2 '94

Scott Kraft
The Silencer '92

Andrzej Krakowski
Eminent Domain '91
Triumph of the Spirit '89

Richard Kramer
All I Want for Christmas '91
Armistead Maupin's Tales of the City '93

Norman Krasna
The Ambassador's Daughter '56
The Big Hangover '50
It's a Date '40
Mr. & Mrs. Smith '41

Earl Kress
The Fox and the Hound '81

Marek Kreutz
Paper Marriage '93

Stu Krieger
In the Army Now '94
The Land Before Time '88
Monkey Trouble '94
A Troll in Central Park '94

Srinivas Krishna
Masala '91

Bill Krohn
It's All True '93

Frank Krom
To Play or To Die '91

Stanley Kubrick
A Clockwork Orange '71
Dr. Strangelove, or: How I Learned to Stop Worrying and Love the Bomb '64
Full Metal Jacket '87
Killer's Kiss '55
Paths of Glory '57
2001: A Space Odyssey '68

Lev Kulijanov
Crime and Punishment '70

Frank Kuntz
Harley '90

Sandy Kuntz
Harley '90

Hanif Kureishi
London Kills Me '91
My Beautiful Laundrette '85
Sammy & Rosie Get Laid '87

Harry Kurnitz
Ship Ahoy '42
Witness for the Prosecution '57

Akira Kurosawa
Akira Kurosawa's Dreams '90
Ran '85
Rashomon '51
Rhapsody in August '91
Seven Samurai '54
Throne of Blood '57
Yojimbo '61

Paul Kurta
Key Exchange '85

Andrew Kurtzman
Camp Nowhere '94

Diane Kurys
Entre-Nous '83
A Man in Love '87
Peppermint Soda '77

Gregory La Cava
My Man Godfrey '36

Celine La Freniere
Foreign Body '86

Lynda La Plante
Prime Suspect '92

Steven La Rocque
Samantha '92

Jeanne Labrune
Sand and Blood '87

Aldo Lado
Paralyzed '70s

John Lafia
Child's Play '88
Man's Best Friend '93

Ian LaFrenais
Catch Me a Spy '71
The Commitments '91
Prisoner of Zenda '79
Vice Versa '88
Water '85

Richard LaGravenese
The Fisher King '91
The Ref '93
Rude Awakening '89

Frank Laloggia
Fear No Evil '80
The Lady in White '88

John Lamb
The Mermaids of Tiburon '62

Gavin Lambert
Dead on the Money '91
I Never Promised You a Rose Garden '77
Inside Daisy Clover '65
Roman Spring of Mrs. Stone '61
Sweet Bird of Youth '89

Albert Lamorisse
Voyage en Balloon '59

Millard Lampell
Triumph of the Spirit '89

Ken Lamplugh
Midnight Kiss '93
Private Wars '93

James Landis
The Sadist '63
Stakeout '62

John Landis
An American Werewolf in London '81
The Blues Brothers '80
Clue '85
Schlock '73
Twilight Zone: The Movie '83

Joseph Landon
The Hoodlum Priest '61

Michael Landon
Killing Stone '78
Sam's Son '84

Karen Landry
Patti Rocks '88

I. Markie Lane
All Tied Up '92

Warren Lane
Happy New Year '87

Lanier Laney
Shag: The Movie '89

Fritz Lang
M '31

Krzysztof Lang
Paper Marriage '93

Perry Lang
Little Vegas '90

Harry Langdon
Road Show '41

Todd W. Langen
Teenage Mutant Ninja Turtles: The Movie '90

Noel Langley
The Adventures of Sadie '55
A Christmas Carol '51
Maytime '37
The Search for Bridey Murphy '56
Svengali '55
The Wizard of Oz '39

Kate Lanier
What's Love Got to Do With It? '93

Dale Lanner
Ruthless People '86

Ring Lardner, Jr.
The Cincinnati Kid '65
Cloak and Dagger '46
Forever Amber '47
The Greatest '77
M*A*S*H '70
Woman of the Year '42

Jeremy Larner
The Candidate '72

Pierre Laroche
Les Visiteurs du Soir '42

Keith Larsen
Whitewater Sam '78

Nancy Larson
The Wizard of Loneliness '88

Louis LaRusso, II
The Closer '91

Lawrence Lasker
Project X '87
Sneakers '92
WarGames '83

Ed Lasko
Road Racers '59

Jesse Lasky, Jr.
John Paul Jones '59

Louise Lasser
Just Me & You '78

Aaron Latham
Perfect '85
The Program '93
Urban Cowboy '80

Alberto Lattuada
Variety Lights '51

Lindy Laub
For the Boys '91

Tom Laughlin
Billy Jack '71
Born Losers '67

Frank Launder
The Happiest Days of Your Life '50
The Lady Vanishes '38

Dale Launer
Dirty Rotten Scoundrels '88
Love Potion #9 '92
My Cousin Vinny '92

S.K. Lauren
Crime and Punishment '35
When Ladies Meet '41

Michael Laurence
Which Way Home '90

Arthur Laurents
Anastasia '56
Bonjour Tristesse '57
Gypsy '93
Rope '48
The Turning Point '77
The Way We Were '73

Jean-Claude Lauzon
Leolo '92

Russell Lavalle
Secret Games 2: The Escort '93

Emmet Lavery
The Magnificent Yankee '50

Bruno Lawrence
The Quiet Earth '85
Smash Palace '82

Denny Lawrence
Warm Nights on a Slow-Moving Train '87

Marc Lawrence
Life with Mikey '93
Pigs '73

Vincent Lawrence
Adventure '45
Night After Night '32

John Howard Lawson
Smash-Up: The Story of a Woman '47

J.F. Lawton
Blankman '94
Cannibal Women in the Avocado Jungle of Death '89
Mistress '91
Pizza Man '91
Pretty Woman '90
Under Siege '92

Beirne Lay, Jr.
Above and Beyond '53

Paul Leadon
Around the World in 80 Ways '86

Larry Leahy
Confessions of a Hit Man '94
The Lawless Land '88

David Lean
Great Expectations '46
Oliver Twist '48
This Happy Breed '47

Norman Lear
Cold Turkey '71
Come Blow Your Horn '63
The Night They Raided Minsky's '69

George T. LeBrun
Death Ring '93

Patrice Leconte
The Hairdresser's Husband '92
Monsieur Hire '89

Jacques LeCotier
Teenage Zombies '58

Paul Leder
The Baby Doll Murders '92
Exiled in America '90
Killing Obsession '94
Murder by Numbers '89

Reuben Leder
Molly and Gina '94

Charles Lederer
Broadway Serenade '39
Comrade X '40
A Global Affair '63
His Girl Friday '40
I Was a Male War Bride '49
Monkey Business '52
The Thing '51

Ang Lee
The Wedding Banquet '93

Bruce Lee
Circle of Iron '78

Cinque Lee
Crooklyn '94

Gerard Lee
Sweetie '89

Joie Lee
Crooklyn '94

Lilian Lee
Farewell My Concubine '93

Mark Lee
The Next Karate Kid '94

Spike Lee
Do the Right Thing '89
Joe's Bed-Stuy Barbershop: We Cut Heads '83
Jungle Fever '91
Malcolm X '92
Mo' Better Blues '90
School Daze '88

Robert Lees
Comin' Round the Mountain '51
The Invisible Woman '40

Michael Leeson
Jekyll & Hyde...Together Again '82
Survivors '83
The War of the Roses '89

Peter Lefcourt
Fine Things '90

Adam Leff
P.C.U. '94

Ernest Lehman
Black Sunday '77
Executive Suite '54
Family Plot '76
From the Terrace '60
Hello, Dolly! '69
The King and I '56
North by Northwest '59
Portnoy's Complaint '72
The Prize '63
Sabrina '54
Somebody Up There Likes Me '56
The Sound of Music '65
Sweet Smell of Success '57
West Side Story '61
Who's Afraid of Virginia Woolf? '66

Lew Lehman
Phobia '80

Michael Lehmann
The Applegates '89

Peter Lehner
Megaville '91

Jerry Leichtling
Peggy Sue Got Married '86

Mike Leigh
Grown Ups '80
High Hopes '89
Life is Sweet '91
Naked '93
Who's Who '78

Warren Leight
Mother's Day '80
The Night We Never Met '93

David Leland
Personal Services '87
Wish You Were Here '87

Claude Lelouch
And Now My Love '74
Another Man, Another Chance '77
Bandits '86
Bolero '82
Happy New Year '74
A Man and a Woman '66
A Man and a Woman: 20 Years Later '86
Robert et Robert '79

Alan LeMay
The Adventures of Mark Twain '44
High Lonesome '50

James Lemmo
Relentless 3 '93
We're Talkin' Serious Money '92

Rusty Lemorande
Journey to the Center of the Earth '88

Peter M. Lenkov
Demolition Man '93

Isobel Lennart
Holiday in Mexico '46
Latin Lovers '53
A Life of Her Own '50
Meet Me in Las Vegas '56
Period of Adjustment '62
Two for the Seesaw '62

Robert W. Lenski
Who Is the Black Dahlia? '75

Connie Leo
Blondie's Blessed Event '42
It's a Great Life '43

Malcolm Leo
This is Elvis '81

Brett Leonard
The Lawnmower Man '92

Elmore Leonard
Cat Chaser '90
52 Pick-Up '86
Joe Kidd '72
Mr. Majestyk '74
The Rosary Murders '87
Stick '85

Hugh Leonard
Da '88
Widow's Peak '94

Sergio Leone
The Good, the Bad and the Ugly '67
The Last Days of Pompeii '60
Once Upon a Time in the West '68

Robert Leoni
Santa Sangre '90

Cory Lerios
Child's Play 3 '91

Alan Jay Lerner
An American in Paris '51
Gigi '58
The Little Prince '74
Royal Wedding '51

Michael Lessac
House of Cards '92

Mark L. Lester
Class of 1984 '82

Sheldon Lettich
Double Impact '91
Lionheart '90
Only the Strong '93

William A. Levey
Monaco Forever '83

Sonya Levien
The Hunchback of Notre Dame '39
In Old Chicago '38
Interrupted Melody '55
The Merry Widow '52
Oklahoma! '55
Three Daring Daughters '48
The Valley of Decision '45

Barry Levinson
And Justice for All '79
Avalon '90
Best Friends '82
High Anxiety '77
Inside Moves '80
Internecine Project '73
Jimmy Hollywood '94
Silent Movie '76
Tin Men '87
Toys '92
Unfaithfully Yours '84

Richard Levinson
The Execution of Private Slovik '74

Vanishing Act '88

Jefery Levy
S.F.W. '94

Louis Levy
The Lady Vanishes '38

Albert Lewin
The Private Affairs of Bel Ami '47

Ben Lewin
The Favor, the Watch, & the Very Big Fish '92

Al Lewis
Ma and Pa Kettle '49

Herschell Gordon Lewis
This Stuff'll Kill Ya! '71
2000 Maniacs '64

Jefferson Lewis
Ordinary Magic '93

Jerry Lewis
The Bellboy '60
Big Mouth '67
The Errand Boy '61
Family Jewels '65
Hardly Working '81
The Ladies' Man '61
The Nutty Professor '63
The Patsy '64

Michael Lewis
The Seventh Coin '92

Warren Lewis
Black Rain '89

Crash Leyland
Sniper '92

Peter Paul Liapis
Sins of Desire '93

Margarita Liberki
Phaedra '61

Carlo Liconti
Goodnight, Michelangelo '89

Alice Liddle
Permanent Record '88

Jeff Lieberman
Blue Sunshine '78
Squirm '76

Robert Lieberman
The Blue Angel '30

Walter Lima, Jr.
The Dolphin '87

Michael Lindsay-Hogg
The Object of Beauty '91

Jonnie Lindsell
I Don't Buy Kisses Anymore '92

William Link
The Execution of Private Slovik '74
Rollercoaster '77
Vanishing Act '88

Richard Linklater
Dazed and Confused '93
Slacker '91

Eugene Lipinski
Perfectly Normal '91

W.P. Lipscomb
Les Miserables '35
A Tale of Two Cities '35

Shelley List
And Baby Makes Six '79

Stephen Lister
Monolith '93

Ezra Litwack
The Butcher's Wife '91

William Lively
Range Renegades '48

Robert Locash
CB4: The Movie '93
Naked Gun 33 1/3: The Final Insult '94

Gene Lockhart
Forever and a Day '43

Walter Lockwood
Battling for Baby '92

Norman Loftis
Small Time '91

Bob Logan
Repossessed '90

Helen Logan
Hello, Frisco, Hello '43
Iceland '42
Lucky Cisco Kid '40
Tin Pan Alley '40

Joshua Logan
Mister Roberts '55

Tom Logan
Dream Trap '90

Christopher Logue
Crusoe '89
Savage Messiah '72

J. Anthony Loma
A Man of Passion '90s

Ulli Lommel
Brainwaves '82
Devonsville Terror '83
Strangers in Paradise '86
Warbirds '88

Robby London
Happily Ever After '93

Harry S. Longstreet
Sex, Love and Cold Hard Cash '93

Stephen Longstreet
Silver River '48

Anita Loos
The Girl from Missouri '34
His Picture in the Papers '16
Hold Your Man '33
I Married an Angel '42
San Francisco '36
Saratoga '37
Susan and God '40
They Met in Bombay '41
When Ladies Meet '41
The Women '39

Temistocles Lopez
Chain of Desire '93

Robert Lord
Big Business Girl '31
Heroes for Sale '33
The Purchase Price '32

Dean Lorey
Jason Goes to Hell: The Final Friday '93
My Boyfriend's Back '93

Eb Lottimer
Love Matters '93

Patrick Loubert
125 Rooms of Comfort '83

David Loucka
The Dream Team '89

David Loughery
Passenger 57 '92
The Three Musketeers '93

Pavel Lounguine
Taxi Blues '90

Michael James Love
Gaby: A True Story '87

Josephine Lovett
Our Modern Maidens '29

Steven Lovy
Circuitry Man '90

Edward T. Lowe
House of Dracula '45
Tangled Destinies '32

Sherman Lowe
Bury Me Not On the Lone Prairie '41
The Masked Rider '41
Pony Post '40

Richard Lowenstein
Dogs in Space '87

Nanni Loy
Head of the Family '71

George Lucas
American Graffiti '73
Raiders of the Lost Ark '81
Return of the Jedi '83
Star Wars '77
THX 1138 '71

William Luce
Lucy and Desi: Before the Laughter '91

William Ludwig
Athena '54
Gun Glory '57
The Hills of Home '48
Interrupted Melody '55
The Merry Widow '52
Oklahoma! '55
The Sun Comes Up '49

Kurt Luedtke
Absence of Malice '81
Out of Africa '85

Baz Luhrmann
Strictly Ballroom '92

Eric Luke
Explorers '85
Still Not Quite Human '92

Sidney Lumet
Prince of the City '81
Q & A '90

Bigas Luna
Anguish '88
Jamon, Jamon '93

Zoe Tamerlaine Lund
Bad Lieutenant '92

Semyon Lunghin
Rasputin '85

Ida Lupino
Private Hell 36 '54
Streets of Sin '49

Arnost Lustig
Diamonds of the Night '64

Jan Lustig
Homecoming '48
Young Bess '53

William Lustig
Maniac '80

Leslie Lyles
Me & Veronica '93

Brad Lynch
Mr. Frost '89

David Lynch
Blue Velvet '86
Dune '84
The Elephant Man '80
Eraserhead '78
Twin Peaks: Fire Walk with Me '92
Wild at Heart '90

Jennifer Lynch
Boxing Helena '93

Martin Lynch
Prayer for the Dying '87

Barre Lyndon
To Please a Lady '50

Jonathan Lynn
Clue '85
Nuns on the Run '90

Judd B. Lynn
Shootfighter: Fight to the Death '93

Charles MacArthur
Rasputin and the Empress '32
Twentieth Century '34
Wuthering Heights '39

Nino Maccari
Two Nights with Cleopatra '54

Ruggero Maccari
The Family '87

Kurt MacCarley
Sexual Intent '94

Ranald MacDougall
June Bride '48
Mildred Pierce '45
Objective, Burma! '45

Patricia MacLachlan
Skylark '93

Bernard MacLaverty
Cal '84
Hostages '93

Alison Maclean
Crush '93

Stephen MacLean
Around the World in 80 Ways '86

Matt MacManus
Flight of the Navigator '86

Angus MacPhail
Dead of Night '45

Don MacPherson
Absolute Beginners '86
The Big Man: Crossing the Line '91

Malcolm MacRury
The Man Without a Face '93

Guy Maddin
Careful '94

Brent Maddock
*batteries not included '87
Ghost Dad '90
Heart and Souls '93
Short Circuit '86
Short Circuit 2 '88
Tremors '89

Ben Maddow
The Asphalt Jungle '50

Robert Madero
All Tied Up '92

Doug Magee
Somebody Has to Shoot the Picture '90

Jeff Maguire
In the Line of Fire '93
Victory '81

Redge Mahaffey
Deadly Rivals '92

John Lee Mahin
Johnny Eager '42
Love on the Run '36

Anthony Mahon
The Premonition '75

Clelle Mahon
Pagan Island '60

Richard Maibaum
License to Kill '89
The Living Daylights '87
S*H*E '79
Thunderball '65

Norman Mailer
King Lear '87
Tough Guys Don't Dance '87

Dusan Makavejev
Innocence Unprotected '68
The Love Affair, or The Case of the Missing Switchboard Operator '67
Man is Not a Bird '65
Montenegro '81
Sweet Movie '75
WR: Mysteries of the Organism '71

Anne Makepeace
Thousand Pieces of Gold '91

Terence Malick
Badlands '74
Days of Heaven '78
Pocket Money '72

Louis Malle
Au Revoir Les Enfants '87
The Fire Within '64
The Lovers '59
May Fools '90
Murmur of the Heart '71
Viva Maria! '65
Zazie dans le Metro '61

Miles Malleson
Night Birds '31

Mark Malone
Dead of Winter '87
Signs of Life '89

Albert Maltz
Cloak and Dagger '46
This Gun for Hire '42
Two Mules for Sister Sara '70

David Mamet
Glengarry Glen Ross '92
Hoffa '92
Homicide '91
House of Games '87
A Life in the Theater '93
The Postman Always Rings Twice '81
Things Change '88
The Untouchables '87
The Verdict '82
We're No Angels '89

Don Mancini
Child's Play '88
Child's Play 2 '90
Child's Play 3 '91

Babaloo Mandel
City Slickers '91
City Slickers 2: The Legend of Curly's Gold '94
Greedy '94
Gung Ho '85
A League of Their Own '92
Mr. Saturday Night '92
Night Shift '82
Parenthood '89
Spies Like Us '85
Splash '84
Vibes '88

Dharan Mandrayar
Ele, My Friend '93

Herman J. Mankiewicz
Citizen Kane '41
Dinner at Eight '33
Pride of St. Louis '52
A Woman's Secret '49

Joseph L. Mankiewicz
All About Eve '50
The Barefoot Contessa '54
Cleopatra '63
Diplomaniacs '33
Forsaking All Others '35
Guys and Dolls '55
The Honey Pot '67
I Live My Life '35

Mankiewicz ►*cont.*

Julius Caesar '53
The Keys of the Kingdom '44
A Letter to Three Wives '49
Mannequin '37
People Will Talk '51

Tom Mankiewicz
The Cassandra Crossing '76
Diamonds are Forever '71
Dragnet '87
The Eagle Has Landed '77
Ladyhawke '85
Live and Let Die '73
The Man with the Golden Gun '74
Mother, Jugs and Speed '76

Abby Mann
A Child is Waiting '63
The Detective '68
Judgment at Nuremberg '61
King '78
Murderers Among Us: The Simon Wiesenthal Story '89
Report to the Commissioner '74
Ship of Fools '65

Edward Mann
Cauldron of Blood '67

Michael Mann
The Keep '83
The Last of the Mohicans '92
Manhunter '86
Thief '81
Vegas '78

K. Mannah
Bloodmatch '91

Albert Mannheimer
Three Daring Daughters '48

Guido Manuli
Volere Volare '92

Robert Marcarelli
Original Intent '91

David Marconi
The Harvest '92

Lawrence B. Marcus
Justine '69
Petulia '68
The Stunt Man '80

Andreas Marfori
Evil Clutch '89

Herbert Margolis
Ma and Pa Kettle '49

Francis Marion
The Big House '30
The Champ '31
Dinner at Eight '33
Tillie Wakes Up '17
The Wind '28

Chris Marker
Sans Soleil '82

Gene Markey
Female '33
On the Avenue '37

Goran Markovic
Tito and Me '92

Mitch Markowitz
Crazy People '90
Good Morning, Vietnam '87

Dennis Marks
Tom and Jerry: The Movie '93

Ben Markson
Lady Killer '33

Malia Scotch Marmo
Once Around '91

Malcolm Marmorstein
Dead Men Don't Die '91
Pete's Dragon '77
Return from Witch Mountain '78
S*P*Y*S '74
Whiffs '75

Gabriel Garcia Marquez
Letters from the Park '88
Miracle in Rome '88

Leon Marr
Dancing in the Dark '86

Andrew Marshall
Whoops Apocalypse '83

D.M. Marshman, Jr.
Sunset Boulevard '50

Al Martin
Blondie Knows Best '46
Prison Shadows '36

Charles Martin
My Dear Secretary '49

Denny Martin
Star Trek 6: The Undiscovered Country '91

Francis Martin
One Night in the Tropics '40

Mardik Martin
Mean Streets '73
New York, New York '77
Raging Bull '80
Valentino '77

Robert Martin
Basket Case 3: The Progeny '92

Steve Martin
Dead Men Don't Wear Plaid '82
The Jerk '79
L.A. Story '91
The Man with Two Brains '83
Roxanne '87
A Simple Twist of Fate '94
Three Amigos '86

William E. Martin
Harry and the Hendersons '87

Wyre Martin
The Unearthing '93

Raymond Martino
American Born '89
Angels of the City '89
DaVinci's War '92

Sergio Martino
Torso '73

Mike Marvin
Wishman '93

Arthur Marx
Cancel My Reservation '72
A Global Affair '63
I'll Take Sweden '65

R.J. Marx
C.O.D. '83
Dead Man Walking '88
Double Obsession '93
Dragonard '88
Gor '88
Master of Dragonard Hill '89
Outlaw of Gor '87
Platoon Leader '87

Judi Ann Mason
Sister Act 2: Back in the Habit '93

Lesley Mason
Man from Monterey '33

Sarah Y. Mason
Golden Boy '39
Little Women '33

Scott Mason
Ride Him, Cowboy '32

Nico Mastorakis
Blind Date '84
Blood Tide '82
Bloodstone '88
Glitch! '88
Hired to Kill '91

William Mastrosimone
The Beast '88
Extremities '86
Sinatra '92
With Honors '94

Eddy Matalon
Sweet Killing '93

Chris Matheson
Bill & Ted's Bogus Journey '91
Bill & Ted's Excellent Adventure '89

Richard Matheson
Burn Witch, Burn! '62
The Comedy of Terrors '64
Die! Die! My Darling! '65
Duel '71
Dying Room Only '73
The Fall of the House of Usher '60
The Incredible Shrinking Man '57
Jaws 3 '83
The Legend of Hell House '73
Loose Cannons '90
Master of the World '61
The Pit and the Pendulum '61
The Raven '63
Somewhere in Time '80
Tales of Terror '62
Trilogy of Terror '75
The Twilight Zone '61
Young Warriors '83

Richard Christian Matheson
Three O'Clock High '87

Melissa Mathison
The Black Stallion '79
The Escape Artist '82
E.T.: The Extra-Terrestrial '82

Hajime Matsumoto
Zeram '91

Burny Mattinson
The Fox and the Hound '81

Ned Mauldin
Renaissance Man '94

J. Stephen Maunder
Talons of the Eagle '92

Robert Mauri
The Slaughter of the Vampires '62

Richard Maxwell
The Challenge '82
The Serpent and the Rainbow '87
Shadow of China '91

Ronald Maxwell
Gettysburg '93

Elaine May
Heaven Can Wait '78
Ishtar '87
Mikey & Nicky '76
A New Leaf '71

Bernard Maybeck
The Cover Girl Murders '93

Carl Mayer
Shattered '21

Edwin Justus Mayer
They Met in Bombay '41

Wendell Mayes
Advise and Consent '62
Anatomy of a Murder '59

Bank Shot '74
Death Wish '74
Go Tell the Spartans '78
The Hanging Tree '59
Hotel '67
The Hunters '58
In Harm's Way '65
Love and Bullets '79
Monsignor '82
The Poseidon Adventure '72
Spirit of St. Louis '57
Von Ryan's Express '65

Melanie Mayron
Sticky Fingers '88

Steve Mazur
The Little Rascals '94

Paul Mazursky
Alex in Wonderland '70
Blume in Love '73
Bob & Carol & Ted & Alice '69
Down and Out in Beverly Hills '86
Enemies, a Love Story '89
Harry and Tonto '74
I Love You, Alice B. Toklas '68
Moon Over Parador '88
Moscow on the Hudson '84
Next Stop, Greenwich Village '76
The Pickle '93
Scenes from a Mall '91
The Tempest '82
An Unmarried Woman '78
Willie & Phil '80

Jim McBride
Breathless '83
David Holzman's Diary '67
Glen and Randa '71
Great Balls of Fire '89
Hot Times '74

Robert McCahon
Running Wild '73

Leo McCarey
An Affair to Remember '57
Going My Way '44
Love Affair '39
My Favorite Wife '40

Louise McCarn
Walker: Texas Ranger: One Riot, One Ranger '93

John P. McCarthy
Beyond the Rockies '32
Fighting Champ '33

Peter McCarthy
Car 54, Where Are You? '94

Todd McCarthy
Visions of Light: The Art of Cinematography '93

Nick McCarty
Merlin '93

John McClain
Cairo '42

Albert McCleery
The Lady is Willing '42

John McCormick
Living on Tokyo Time '87

Pat McCormick
Under the Rainbow '81

John McDonald
By the Sword '93

Kevin McDonough
I Was a Teenage TV Terrorist '87

Michael McDowell
Beetlejuice '88
Tales from the Darkside: The Movie '90

Maureen McElheron
The Tune '92

Alan B. McElroy
Rapid Fire '92

Ross McElwee
Sherman's March: An Improbable Search for Love '86
Time Indefinite '93

Ian McEwan
The Good Son '93
The Innocent '93

William F. McGaha
The Speed Lovers '68

Mark Thomas McGee
Bad Girls from Mars '90
Sins of Desire '92

Rex McGee
Pure Country '92

Josann McGibbon
The Favor '94
Three Men and a Little Lady '90
Worth Winning '89

Dorrell McGowan
The Showdown '50

Stuart E. McGowan
The Showdown '50

Douglas McGrath
Born Yesterday '93

John McGreevey
Consenting Adult '85
Hot Rod Girl '56
Night Crossing '81

Thomas McGuane
Cold Feet '89
Missouri Breaks '76
92 in the Shade '76
Rancho Deluxe '75
Tom Horn '80

Don McGuire
Artists and Models '55
The Delicate Delinquent '56
Meet Danny Wilson '52
Suppose They Gave a War and Nobody Came? '70
Tootsie '82

William Anthony McGuire
The Great Ziegfeld '36

Jay McInerney
Hotel Room '93

Douglas Lloyd McIntosh
Disaster at Silo 7 '88

Dennis McIntyre
State of Grace '90

Malcolm McKay
Maria's Child '93

Steven McKay
Diggstown '92

Michael McKean
The Big Picture '89
The Return of Spinal Tap '92

Don McKellar
Highway 61 '91
Roadkill '89
32 Short Films About Glenn Gould '93

Bernard McKenna
Yellowbeard '83

Duncan McLachlan
The Double O Kid '92

Victor McLeod
Boss of Bullion City '41
Bury Me Not On the Lone Prairie '41
The Masked Rider '41

Larry McMurtry
Falling from Grace '92
The Last Picture Show '71
Memphis '91
Montana '90

Terrance McNally
Earth Girls are Easy '89
Frankie and Johnny '91

John McNaughton
Henry: Portrait of a Serial Killer '90

James McTernan
Small Kill '93

John Meagher
Fantasy Man '84

Irene Mecchi
The Lion King '94

Mark Medoff
Apology '86
Children of a Lesser God '86
City of Joy '92
Clara's Heart '88
Good Guys Wear Black '78
Off Beat '86

John Meehan
Madame X '37
Three Daring Daughters '48
The Valley of Decision '45

Thomas Meehan
Spaceballs '87

Robert T. Megginson
F/X '86

Myron Meise
It's All True '93

Ib Melchoir
Robinson Crusoe on Mars '64

Ivan Menchell
The Cemetery Club '93

Ramon Menendez
Money for Nothing '93
Stand and Deliver '88

Nina Menkes
Queen of Diamonds '91

Tina "Tigr" Mennett
Kamikaze Hearts '91

Gian-Carlo Menotti
The Medium '51

Jiri Menzel
Larks on a String '68

Burgess Meredith
Yin & Yang of Mr. Go '71

Lawrence Merrick
Black Bikers from Hell '70

Monte Merrick
8 Seconds '94
Memphis Belle '90
Mr. Baseball '92

Norman Merrill
The Taking of Flight 847: The Uli Derickson Story '88

Roger Merton
Down the Wyoming Trail '39

Stephen Metcalfe
Cousins '89
Florida Straits '87
Jacknife '89

Tim Metcalfe
Fright Night 2 '88
Iron Maze '91
Kalifornia '93
Million Dollar Mystery '87
Revenge of the Nerds '84
Three for the Road '87

Andrew Meyer
Night of the Cobra Woman '72

Kevin Meyer
Invasion of Privacy '92
Under Investigation '93

Nancy Meyer
Father of the Bride '91

Nicholas Meyer
Company Business '91
Invasion of the Bee Girls '73
The Seven Percent Solution '76
Sommersby '93
Star Trek 4: The Voyage Home '86
Star Trek 6: The Undiscovered Country '91
Time After Time '79

Turi Meyer
Leprechaun 2 '94

Henry Meyers
Destry Rides Again '39
Diplomaniacs '33

Nancy Meyers
Baby Boom '87
Irreconcilable Differences '84
Private Benjamin '80

Patrick Meyers
K2: The Ultimate High '92

Lorne Michaels
Three Amigos '86

Boleslaw Michalek
Danton '82
A Love in Germany '84

Dave Michener
The Fox and the Hound '81
The Great Mouse Detective '86

Anne-Marie Mieville
Numero Deux '75

Ted V. Mikels
Assault of the Killer Bimbos '87
The Astro-Zombies '67
The Corpse Grinders '71

Elfi Mikesch
Seduction: The Cruel Woman '89

Andrej Mikhalkov-Kontchalovsky
Andrei Rublev '66

Lewis Milestone
Arch of Triumph '48

Djordje Milicevic
Iron Will '93
Runaway Train '85
Victory '81

John Milius
Apocalypse Now '79
Big Wednesday '78
Clear and Present Danger '94
Conan the Barbarian '82
Dillinger '73
Evel Knievel '72
Farewell to the King '89
Geronimo: An American Legend '93
Jeremiah Johnson '72
Life & Times of Judge Roy Bean '72
Magnum Force '73
Red Dawn '84
The Wind and the Lion '75

Ronald Millar
The Miniver Story '50
Never Let Me Go '53

Oscar Millard
The Conqueror '56

Annie Miller
The Little Thief '89

Arthur Miller
Everybody Wins '90
The Misfits '61

Claude Miller
The Little Thief '89
This Sweet Sickness '77

F.E. Miller
Harlem Rides the Range '39

Frank Miller
RoboCop 3 '91

George Miller
Lorenzo's Oil '92
Mad Max '80
Mad Max: Beyond Thunderdome '85
The Road Warrior '82

Gregory Miller
Conflict of Interest '92

Harvey Miller
Jekyll & Hyde...Together Again '82

Jennifer Miller
Family Pictures '93

Seton I. Miller
The Adventures of Robin Hood '38
Here Comes Mr. Jordan '41
Kid Galahad '37

Bertram Millhauser
The Invisible Man's Revenge '44

Andy Milligan
Man with Two Heads '72
The Rats are Coming! The Werewolves are Here! '72

Bill Milling
Body Trouble '92

Hugh Mills
Personal Property '37

Michael Miner
Deadly Weapon '88
RoboCop '87

Anthony Minghella
Truly, Madly, Deeply '91

Joe Minion
Motorama '91

Brad Mirman
Body of Evidence '92
Knight Moves '93

Yukio Mishima
Black Lizard '68

C. Gaby Mitchell
Fallen Angels 2 '93

Duke Mitchell
The Executioner '78

Robert Mitchum
Thunder Road '58

Robert Mittenthal
Hail Caesar '94

Hayao Miyazaki
My Neighbor Totoro '93

Wilson Mizner
Heroes for Sale '33

Moshe Mizrahi
Every Time We Say Goodbye '86
I Love You Rosa '72
I Sent a Letter to My Love '81

Peter Modos
A Happy New Year! '79

David Moessinger
Daddy-O '59

Clifford Mohr
Lady Dragon 2 '93

Edouard Molinaro
Pain in the A— '77

Paul Monash
Bail Out at 43,000 '57

Scarface Mob '62
Stalin '92

Nate Monaster
Call Me Bwana '63

Paul Mones
Fathers and Sons '92

Christopher Monger
Waiting for the Light '90

John Monks, Jr.
Knock on Any Door '49
The West Point Story '50

Carl Monson
The Acid Eaters '67

Eric Monte
Cooley High '75

Hugo Montenegro
Charro! '69

Eduardo Montes
Double Obsession '93

Mark Montgomery
South Beach '92

Brian Moore
Black Robe '91
The Blood of Others '84
Torn Curtain '66

Dudley Moore
The Hound of the Baskervilles '77
30 Is a Dangerous Age, Cynthia '68

Michael Moore
Canadian Bacon '94

Ronald W. Moore
Future Kill '85

Simon Moore
The Quick and the Dead '94
Under Suspicion '92

Wesley Moore
Are You Lonesome Tonight '92

Jocelyn Moorhouse
Proof '91

E. Edwin Moran
Wintertime '43

Jack Moran
Faster Pussycat! Kill! Kill! '66

Martha Moran
Happily Ever After '93

Patrick Moran
Dark Universe '93

Paul Morand
Don Quixote '35

Rick Moranis
Strange Brew '83

Miguel Morayta
Invasion of the Vampires '61

Larry Morey
Bambi '42

Denise Morgan
An Indecent Obsession '85

Glen Morgan
The Boys Next Door '85

Louis Morheim
Ma and Pa Kettle '49

Yoshimitsu Morita
The Family Game '83

Louis Morneau
Final Judgement '92

Tony Morphett
Sweet Talker '91

Michael Morpugo
When the Whales Came '89

David Burton Morris
Patti Rocks '88

Richard Morris
Ma and Pa Kettle at the Fair '52

Paul Morrissey
Andy Warhol's Dracula '74
Andy Warhol's Frankenstein '74
Beethoven's Nephew '88
The Hound of the Baskervilles '77
Mixed Blood '84
Spike of Bensonhurst '88

Douglas Morrow
The Stratton Story '49

John Mortimer
24 Hours in a Woman's Life '61

Penelope Mortimer
A Summer Story '88

Lisa Morton
Adventures in Dinosaur City '92

Ben Moses
Nickel & Dime '92

Harry Moses
Assault at West Point: The Court-Martial of Johnson Whittaker '77

D. Brent Mote
Deep Red '94

Marcel Moussey
The 400 Blows '59
Shoot the Piano Player '62

Allan Moyle
Pump Up the Volume '90
The Thing Called Love '93

Chris Mulkey
Patti Rocks '88

Ryu Murakami
Tokyo Decadence '91

John Murdy
Sorority House Party '92

Jane Murfin
The Shining Hour '38

Gary Murphy
Without a Clue '88

Geoff Murphy
Dark of the Night '85

Don Murray
Confessions of Tom Harris '72
The Hoodlum Priest '61

Michael J. Murray
Honor Thy Father and Mother: The True Story of the Menendez Brothers '94
The House of Usher '88
The Lightning Incident '91

Tom Musca
Money for Nothing '93
Stand and Deliver '88

Clarence Muse
Way Down South '39

John Musker
Aladdin '92

M.M. Musselman
The Three Musketeers '39

Floyd Mutrux
American Me '92
Blood In...Blood Out: Bound by Honor '93

Zion Myer
April Fool '26

Cindy Myers
Bed & Breakfast '92

Myers

Mike Myers
So I Married an Axe Murderer '93
Wayne's World '92
Wayne's World 2 '93

Nancy Myers
I Love Trouble '94

Scott Myers
K-9 '89

John Myhers
The Longshot '86
The Private Eyes '80
Terror in Beverly Hills '90

Troy Nabors
Fortress '93

Ed Naha
Dolls '87
Honey, I Shrunk the Kids '89

Suzanne Glazener Naha
Dragonworld '94

Kenji Nakagami
Himatsuri '85

Takehiro Nakajima
Okoge '93

Desmond Nakano
American Me '92

Michael Nankin
Gate 2 '92

Lisandro Duque Naranjo
Miracle in Rome '88

Paul Naschy
Curse of the Devil '73
Dracula vs. Frankenstein '69
The Fury of the Wolfman '70
House of Psychotic Women '73
Human Beasts '80
Inquisition '76
The Mummy's Revenge '73

N. Richard Nash
One Summer Love '76
The Rainmaker '56

Ogden Nash
The Shining Hour '38

Jack Natteford
The Crimson Trail '35

Gregory Nava
El Norte '83
End of August '82
A Time of Destiny '88

Jeff Neal
Virgin High '90

Hal Needham
Stroker Ace '83

William Neff
I Was a Male War Bride '49

B.J. Nelson
Scanners 2: The New Order '91

Jessie Nelson
Corrina, Corrina '94

John Allen Nelson
Best of the Best 2 '93

Judd Nelson
Every Breath '93

Peter Nelson
Getting Up and Going Home '92
The Lonely Passion of Judith Hearne '87

Richard Nelson
Ethan Frome '92

Dennis Nemec
God Bless the Child '88

Jan Nemec
Diamonds of the Night '64
The Report on the Party and the Guests '66

Avi Nesher
Doppelganger: The Evil Within '90
Timebomb '91

Edward Neumeier
RoboCop '87

John Thomas Neville
Trader Horn '31

Martin Newlin
The Crawlers '93

David Newman
Bad Company '72
Bonnie & Clyde '67
Jinxed '82
Santa Claus: The Movie '85
Sheena '84
Still of the Night '82
Superman: The Movie '78
Superman 2 '80
Superman 3 '83
There was a Crooked Man '70
What's Up, Doc? '72

Randy Newman
Three Amigos '86

Fred Newmeyer
The Freshman '25

Ted Newsom
Dracula: A Cinematic Scrapbook '91
Frankenstein: A Cinematic Scrapbook '91

Mbongeni Ngema
Sarafina! '92

Sloan Nibley
Hostile Guns '67

Fred Niblo
The Fighting 69th '40

Maurizio Nichetti
Volere Volare '92

Allan Nicholls
A Wedding '78

Dudley Nichols
Bringing Up Baby '38
The Fugitive '48
The Informer '35
Pinky '49
Prince Valiant '54

Jack Nicholson
Flight to Fury '66
Head '68
Ride in the Whirlwind '67
The Trip '67

William Nicholson
A Private Matter '92
Sarafina! '92
Shadowlands '93

Nicholas Niciphor
Fatal Charm '92

Daryl G. Nickens
House Party 2: The Pajama Jam '91

Ted Nicolaou
Bloodlust: Subspecies 3 '93
Bloodstone: Subspecies 2 '93
Dragonworld '94
Terrorvision '86

Rob Nilsson
Heat and Sunlight '87
Northern Lights '79
On the Edge '86
Signal 7 '83

Michael Norell
Diamond Fleece '92

Marc Norman
The Aviator '85
Bat 21 '88
The Killer Elite '75
Oklahoma Crude '73
Zandy's Bride '74

Marsha Norman
'night, Mother '86

Michael Normand
Leon the Pig Farmer '93

Chuck Norris
Braddock: Missing in Action 3 '88

Pamela Norris
Troop Beverly Hills '89

William J. Norris
The Re-Animator '85

Edmund H. North
Flamingo Road '49
Patton '70

William W. Norton, Sr.
Big Bad Mama '74
Brannigan '75
Day of the Animals '77
Dirty Tricks '81
Gator '76
McKenzie Break '70
Moving Violation '76
Night of the Juggler '80
The Scalphunters '68
A Small Town in Texas '76
White Lightning '73

Frank Norwood
Past Midnight '92

Blaine Novak
Strangers Kiss '83

Betriz Novaro
Danzon '91

Maria Novaro
Danzon '91

Louis Nowra
Map of the Human Heart '93

Simon Nuchtern
The Rejuvenator '88

Frank Nugent
Mister Roberts '55
The Quiet Man '52
The Searchers '56

Victor Nunez
A Flash of Green '85
Ruby in Paradise '93

Ilya Nusinov
Rasputin '85

Bruno Nuytten
Camille Claudel '89

Joseph Nuzzolo
Kill or Be Killed '93

Nelson Nye
Seven Sixgunners '87

Sven Nykvist
The Ox '91

Ron Nyswaner
Gross Anatomy '89
Love Hurts '91
Mrs. Soffel '84
Philadelphia '93
Prince of Pennsylvania '88
Purple Hearts '84
Smithereens '82
Swing Shift '84

Dan O'Bannon
Alien '79
Blue Thunder '83
Dark Star '74
Dead and Buried '81
Invaders from Mars '86
Lifeforce '85

Total Recall '90

Rockne S. O'Bannon
Alien Nation '88

Margaret Grieco Oberman
Troop Beverly Hills '89

Arch Oboler
One Plus One '61

Raymond Obon
Black Pit of Dr. M '47

Edna O'Brien
X, Y & Zee '72

Robert O'Brien
By the Light of the Silvery Moon '53
The Lemon Drop Kid '51

Jeffrey Obrow
The Kindred '87

Pat O'Connor
The January Man '89

Clifford Odets
Deadline at Dawn '46
The General Died at Dawn '36
None But the Lonely Heart '44
Sweet Smell of Success '57
Wild in the Country '61

Joseph O'Donnell
Border Caballero '36

Michael O'Donoghue
Scrooged '88

Hideo Oguni
Ran '85
Throne of Blood '57
Yojimbo '61

Colo Taverniev O'Hagan
Beatrice '88
Daddy Nostalgia '90
The Story of Women '88
A Sunday in the Country '84

Paul Ohl
Highlander 3: The Sorcerer '94

Kazuki Ohmori
Godzilla vs. Biollante '89

Steven Okazaki
Living on Tokyo Time '87

Joel Oliansky
Bird '88
The Todd Killings '71

David Oliver
Cave Girl '85

Ron Oliver
Hello Mary Lou: Prom Night 2 '87
Liar's Edge '92

Ruby L. Oliver
Love Your Mama '89

Laurence Olivier
Henry V '44

Ermanno Olmi
The Tree of Wooden Clogs '78

Arne Olsen
Cop and a Half '93
Final Round '93
Red Scorpion '89

David O'Malley
Easy Wheels '89
Edge of Honor '91
Fatal Instinct '93
Hangar 18 '80
Kid Colter '85
Mountain Man '77

Carlo Ombra
Dracula Blows His Cool '82

Szeto On
The Blazing Ninja

Robert Vincent O'Neil
The Baltimore Bullet '80
Deadly Force '83
Jailbait '93
Vice Squad '82

Eugene O'Neill
Long Day's Journey into Night '62

Max Ophuls
Lola Montes '55
Modigliani '58

Ron Ormond
Yes, Sir, Mr. Bones '51

Peter Ormrod
Eat the Peach '86

Alan Ormsby
Cat People '82
Children Shouldn't Play with Dead Things '72
Deathdream '72
Indecency '92
Little Dragons '80
My Bodyguard '80
Popcorn '89
Porky's 2: The Next Day '83
Touch & Go '80

James Orr
Breaking All the Rules '85
Mr. Destiny '90
Sister Act 2: Back in the Habit '93
Three Men and a Baby '87
Tough Guys '86

Erik Orsenna
Indochine '92

Paul Osborn
East of Eden '54
Homecoming '48

John Osborne
The Entertainer '60
Look Back in Anger '58
Tom Jones '63

Kent Osborne
Women Unchained '70s

William Osborne
Ghost in the Machine '93
The Real McCoy '93
Stop! or My Mom Will Shoot '92
Twins '88

Nagisa Oshima
The Cruel Story of Youth '60

Willem Jan Otten
Lily was Here '89

Richard Outten
Lionheart '87
Little Nemo: Adventures in Slumberland '92
Pet Sematary 2 '92

Reginald Owen
A Study in Scarlet '33

Jan Oxenberg
Thank You & Good Night '91

Yasujiro Ozu
An Autumn Afternoon '62
Tokyo Story '53

David Pabian
Puppet Master 2 '91

G.W. Pabst
Pandora's Box '28

Jo Pagano
The Man I Love '46

Marcel Pagnol
Cesar '36
Fanny '32
Harvest '37
Marius '31
Nais '45
Topaze '33

Nick Paine
Philadelphia Experiment 2 '93

Steve Pake
Provoked '89

Martin Pako
Batman: Mask of the Phantasm '93

Alan J. Pakula
The Pelican Brief '93
Presumed Innocent '90
See You in the Morning '89
Sophie's Choice '82

Euzhan Palcy
A Dry White Season '89
Sugar Cane Alley '83

Michael Palin
American Friends '91
And Now for Something Completely Different '72
Consuming Passions '88
The Missionary '82
Monty Python and the Holy Grail '75
Monty Python's Life of Brian '79
Monty Python's The Meaning of Life '83
Ripping Yarns '75
The Secret Policeman's Other Ball '82
Time Bandits '81

Satyajit Joy Palit
Lonely in America '90

Rospo Pallenberg
The Emerald Forest '85
Excalibur '81

Anders Palm
Dead Certain '92
Murder on Line One '90

Thomas Palmer, Jr.
Forever: A Ghost of a Love Story '92

Chazz Palminteri
A Bronx Tale '93

Frank Panama
Above and Beyond '53

Norman Panama
Above and Beyond '53
Court Jester '56
I Will, I Will for Now '76
Li'l Abner '59
Mr. Blandings Builds His Dream House '48
Monsieur Beaucaire '46
The Road to Hong Kong '62
The Road to Utopia '46
Thank Your Lucky Stars '43
The Trap '59
White Christmas '54

Dennis Paoli
Body Snatchers '93
From Beyond '86
Meridian: Kiss of the Beast '90
The Pit & the Pendulum '91
The Re-Animator '85

Sergei Paradjanov
The Color of Pomegranates '69

Edward Paramore
The Bitter Tea of General Yen '33
Three Comrades '38

Gail Parent
All I Want for Christmas '91

Alan Parker
Angel Heart '87
Bugsy Malone '76
Come See the Paradise '90
Melody '71

David Parker
Malcolm '86
Rikky and Pete '88

Dorothy Parker
A Star is Born '37

John Parker
Daughter of Horror '55

Scott Parker
Die Laughing '80
He Knows You're Alone '80

Tom S. Parker
The Flintstones '94
Getting Even with Dad '94
Stay Tuned '92

Walter F. Parkes
Sneakers '92
WarGames '83

Sara Parriott
The Favor '94
Three Men and a Little Lady '90
Worth Winning '89

Dolly Parton
A Smoky Mountain Christmas '86

Frank Partos
Honolulu '39
The Snake Pit '48

Christine Pascal
Spoiled Children '77

Pier Paolo Pasolini
The Gospel According to St. Matthew '64
The Grim Reaper '62
The Hawks & the Sparrows '67
Il Bell'Antonio '60
Porcile '69

Stuart Paton
20,000 Leagues Under the Sea '16

John Patrick
Daniel Boone: Trail Blazer '56

Vincent Patrick
Family Business '89
The Pope of Greenwich Village '84

Lino Patruno
Bix '90

Keith Payson
Puppet Master 4 '93

Craig Pearce
Strictly Ballroom '92

David Peckinpah
The Diamond Trap '91

Sam Peckinpah
Invasion of the Body Snatchers '56
Villa Rides '68
The Wild Bunch '69

Richard Pelusi
Mad at the Moon '92

Neil Peng
The Wedding Banquet '93

Sean Penn
The Indian Runner '91

Zak Penn
P.C.U. '94

John Penney
The Kindred '87
The Power '80
Return of the Living Dead 3 '93

Phil Penningroth
In the Line of Duty: Ambush in Waco '93
Silence of the Heart '84

David Peoples
Blade Runner '82
The Blood of Heroes '89
Deadfall '93
Hero '92
Leviathan '89

Unforgiven '92

Clare Peploe
High Season '88
Zabriskie Point '70

Mark Peploe
High Season '88
The Last Emperor '87
Little Buddha '93
The Passenger '75
The Sheltering Sky '90

S.J. Perelman
Around the World in 80 Days '56

Jack Perez
America's Deadliest Home Video '92

Frank Ray Perilli
Alligator '80
The Doberman Gang '72
Zoltan...Hound of Dracula '77

Anthony Perkins
The Last of Sheila '73

Arnold Perl
Malcolm X '92

Nat Perrin
Duck Soup '33
I'll Take Sweden '65
Whistling in Dixie '42

Bill Persky
Water '85

Charlie Peters
Blame It on Rio '84
Her Alibi '88
Hot to Trot! '88
Kiss Me Goodbye '82
My Father the Hero '93
Passed Away '92
Paternity '81
Three Men and a Little Lady '90

Wolfgang Petersen
Das Boot '81
The NeverEnding Story '84
Shattered '91

Daniel M. Peterson
Girlfriend from Hell '89

Patricia Petit
The Scent of Green Papaya '93

Sandro Petraglia
Fiorile '93
Forever Mary '89

Dan Petrie, Jr.
Beverly Hills Cop '84
The Big Easy '87
In the Army Now '94
Shoot to Kill '88
Toy Soldiers '91

Chuck Pfarrer
Hard Target '93

John B. Pfeifer
Illegal Entry: Formula for Fear '93

Anna Hamilton Phelan
Gorillas in the Mist '88
Mask '85

Bill Phillips
Christine '84
El Diablo '90
Fire with Fire '86
Physical Evidence '89
Rainbow Drive '90
Rising Son '90

Lou Diamond Phillips
Ambition '91

Maurice Phillips
Enid is Sleeping '90

Robert Phippeny
The Night of the Following Day '69

Maurice Pialat
Under Satan's Sun '87
Van Gogh '92

Astor Piazzolla
Henry IV '85

John Pielmeier
Agnes of God '85
The Shell Seekers '89

Charles B. Pierce
Boggy Creek II '83
The Evictors '79
Grayeagle '77
Legend of Boggy Creek '75
Norseman '78
Sacred Ground '83
Sudden Impact '83

Scott Pierce
A Nightmare on Elm Street 4: Dream Master '88

Frank Pierson
The Anderson Tapes '71
Cat Ballou '65
Cool Hand Luke '67
Dog Day Afternoon '75
In Country '89
King of the Gypsies '78
The Looking Glass War '69
Presumed Innocent '90
A Star is Born '76

Krzysztof Piesiewicz
The Double Life of Veronique '91
No End '84
Trois Couleurs: Blanc '94
Trois Couleurs: Bleu '93
Trois Couleurs: Rouge '94

Nicholas Pileggi
Goodfellas '90

Sam Pillsbury
The Quiet Earth '85

Gregory Pincus
Little Big League '94

Phillip Pine
Pot, Parents, and Police '71

Tullio Pinelli
8 1/2 '63
Ginger & Fred '86
Juliet of the Spirits '65
La Dolce Vita '60
La Strada '54
Nights of Cabiria '57
The Swindle '55
Variety Lights '51
The White Sheik '52

Sidney Pink
The Castilian '63

Seth Pinsker
The Hidden 2 '94

Harold Pinter
Accident '67
Betrayal '83
The Comfort of Strangers '91
Dumb Waiter '87
The French Lieutenant's Woman '81
The Go-Between '71
The Handmaid's Tale '90
The Heat of the Day '91
The Last Tycoon '76
The Quiller Memorandum '66
Reunion '88
The Room '87
The Servant '63
The Trial '93
Turtle Diary '86

Lucian Pintilie
The Oak '93

Robert Pirosh
Battleground '49
Hell is for Heroes '62

Mark Pirro
Buford's Beach Bunnies '92
Deathrow Gameshow '88
My Mom's a Werewolf '89

Glen Pitre
Belizaire the Cajun '86

C. William Pitt
Monaco Forever '83

Angelo Pizzo
Hoosiers '86
Rudy '93

Alan Plater
Coming Through '90
Fortunes of War '87
Priest of Love '81
The Virgin and the Gypsy '70

Jonathan Platnick
Silent Victim '92

Allen Plone
Sweet Justice '92

Bill Plympton
The Tune '92

George Plympton
Doomed at Sundown '37
Feud Maker '38

Rick Podell
Nothing in Common '86

Amos Poe
Alphabet City '84
The Foreigner '78
Rocket Gibraltar '88

James Poe
Around the World in 80 Days '56
Cat on a Hot Tin Roof '58
The Nightman '93
Riot '69
Toys in the Attic '63

Benoit Poelvoorde
Man Bites Dog '91

Charles Edward Pogue
D.O.A. '88
The Fly '86
Psycho 3 '86

Roman Polanski
Bitter Moon '92
Cul de Sac '66
Diary of Forbidden Dreams '73
The Fearless Vampire Killers '67
Frantic '88
Knife in the Water '62
Pirates '86
Repulsion '65
Rosemary's Baby '68
The Tenant '76
Tess '80

Jeff Pollack
Above the Rim '94

Jean-Daniel Pollet
Six in Paris '68

Jeffrey Polman
Benefit of the Doubt '93

Eddy Polon
Nickel & Dime '92

Vicki Polon
Girlfriends '78
Mr. Wonderful '93

Abraham Polonsky
Avalanche Express '79
Body and Soul '47
Force of Evil '49
Golden Earrings '47
Madigan '68
Monsignor '82

Polonsky ►*cont.*

Tell Them Willie Boy Is Here '69

Barry Poltermann
The Unearthing '93

Darryl Ponicsan
The Boost '88
Cinderella Liberty '73
Nuts '87
School Ties '92
Taps '81
Vision Quest '85

Gillo Pontecorvo
Kapo '59

Duane Poole
Praying Mantis '93
Sunstroke '92

Dennis Potter
Brimstone & Treacle '82
Christabel '89
Dreamchild '85
Gorky Park '83
Pennies From Heaven '81
Track 29 '88

Sally Potter
Orlando '92

Michael W. Potts
Night Eyes 3 '93
Tropical Heat '93

Peter Poulsen
Sofie '92

Michael Powell
Edge of the World '37
The Elusive Pimpernel '50
The Red Shoes '48

Tristam Powell
American Friends '91

Leonard Praskins
One in a Million '36

Burt Prelutsky
A Winner Never Quits '86

Eric Lee Preminger
Rosebud '75

Robert Presnell
Employees' Entrance '33

Emeric Pressburger
The Elusive Pimpernel '50
The Forty-Ninth Parallel '41
The Red Shoes '48

Steven Pressfield
Above the Law '88
Freejack '92
King Kong Lives '86

Kenneth Pressman
Diary of a Hitman '91

Gaylene Preston
Dark of the Night '85

Jacques Prevert
Children of Paradise '44
The Crime of Monsieur Lange
'36
Les Visiteurs du Soir '42

Dan Price
The Crawlers '93

Jeffrey Price
Doc Hollywood '91
Trenchcoat '83
Who Framed Roger Rabbit? '88

Richard Price
The Color of Money '86
Mad Dog and Glory '93
New York Stories '89
Night and the City '92
Sea of Love '89
Streets of Gold '86

Tim Rose Price
A Dangerous Man: Lawrence
after Arabia '91
Dark Obsession '90

James Prideaux
The Man Upstairs '93

J.B. Priestly
Last Holiday '50

Joseph Prieto
Savages from Hell '68

Barry Primus
Mistress '91

Prince
Graffiti Bridge '90

Jonathan Prince
18 Again! '88

Peter Prince
The Hit '85
Waterland '92

Allan Prior
The Charmer '89

David A. Prior
Deadly Dancer '90
Deadly Prey '87
Final Sanction '90
Hell on the Battleground '88
Mardi Gras for the Devil '93
Raw Justice '93
Raw Nerve '91

David Pritchard
Slashed Dreams '74
Violent Zone '89

Vincent J. Privitera
Witchfire '86

Leon Prochnik
Four Eyes and Six Guns '93

Pat Proft
Bachelor Party '84
Brain Donors '92
Hot Shots! '91
Hot Shots! Part Deux '93
Lucky Stiff '88
Moving Violations '85
The Naked Gun: From the Files
of Police Squad '88
Naked Gun 33 1/3: The Final
Insult '94
Naked Gun 2 1/2: The Smell of
Fear '91
Police Academy '84
Real Genius '85

Chip Proser
Iceman '84
Innerspace '87

Giorgio Prosperi
The Naked Maja '59
The Seven Hills of Rome '58

Richard Pryor
Blazing Saddles '74
Bustin' Loose '81
Jo Jo Dancer, Your Life is
Calling '86

Geof Pryssir
The Magic Bubble '93

Luis Puenzo
The Official Story '85
Old Gringo '89

Jack Pulman
Poldark '75

Gertrude Purcell
Destry Rides Again '39
The Invisible Woman '40
One Night in the Tropics '40

Charles Purpura
Heaven Help Us '85
Satisfaction '88

Mario Puzo
The Cotton Club '84

Earthquake '74
The Godfather '72
The Godfather 1902-1959: The
Complete Epic '81
The Godfather, Part 2 '74
The Godfather, Part 3 '90
Superman: The Movie '78
Superman 2 '80

Daniel Pyne
Doc Hollywood '91
The Hard Way '91
Pacific Heights '90
White Sands '92

Albert Pyun
Alien from L.A. '87
Down Twisted '89
Knights '93
Radioactive Dreams '86
Sword & the Sorcerer '82

Paris Qualles
The Inkwell '94

Paul Quarrington
Camilla '94
Perfectly Normal '91

Florence Quentin
Life Is a Long Quiet River '88

Pascal Quignard
Tous les Matins du Monde '92

Richard Quine
My Sister Eileen '55

Gene Quintano
Allan Quartermain and the Lost
City of Gold '86
Honeymoon Academy '90
King Solomon's Mines '85
Making the Grade '84
National Lampoon's Loaded
Weapon 1 '93
Police Academy 3: Back in
Training '86
Police Academy 4: Citizens on
Patrol '87

David Rabe
Casualties of War '89
I'm Dancing as Fast as I Can
'82
Streamers '83

Martin Rackin
The Enforcer '51
The Stooge '51

Bob Rafelson
Five Easy Pieces '70
Head '68
Mountains of the Moon '90
Stay Hungry '76

Stewart Raffill
Across the Great Divide '76
The Adventures of the
Wilderness Family '76
Ice Pirates '84
Mac and Me '88
Napoleon and Samantha '72
Sea Gypsies '78

Deborah Raffin
Morning Glory '93

John Raffo
Dragon: The Bruce Lee Story
'93

Martin Ragaway
Abbott and Costello in the
Foreign Legion '50
Lost in Alaska '52
Ma and Pa Kettle Go to Town
'50

Wess Rahn
Enemy Gold '93

Steve Railsback
The Forgotten '89

Ivan Raimi
Army of Darkness '92
Darkman '90

Easy Wheels '89

Sam Raimi
Army of Darkness '92
Crimewave '85
Darkman '90
Evil Dead '83
Evil Dead 2: Dead by Dawn '87
The Hudsucker Proxy '93

Norman Reilly Raine
The Fighting 69th '40

Yvonne Rainer
The Man Who Envied Women
'85

Harold Ramis
Armed and Dangerous '86
Back to School '86
Caddyshack '80
Caddyshack 2 '88
Club Paradise '86
Ghostbusters '84
Ghostbusters 2 '89
Groundhog Day '93
Meatballs '79
National Lampoon's Animal
House '78
National Lampoon's Vacation
'83
Rover Dangerfield '91
Stripes '81

Nick Randall
Chrome Soldiers '92

Joe Ranft
The Rescuers Down Under '90

Whitney Ransick
The Outfit '93

Peter Ransley
The Hawk '93

Frederic Raphael
Bachelor of Hearts '58
Daisy Miller '74
Darling '65
Far from the Madding Crowd
'67
The King's Whore '90
Richard's Things '80
Two for the Road '67

I.C. Rapoport
Jericho Fever '93

Ezra D. Rappaport
Deja Vu '84
Harry and the Hendersons '87

Mark Rappaport
Rock Hudson's Home Movies
'92

Elisabeth Rappeneau
One Woman or Two '85

**Jean-Paul
Rappeneau**
Cyrano de Bergerac '90
Lovers Like Us '75
That Man from Rio '64

Judith Rascoe
Eat a Bowl of Tea '89
Endless Love '81
Havana '90
Who'll Stop the Rain? '78

Tina Rathborne
Zelly & Me '88

Terence Rattigan
The Day Will Dawn '42
The V.I.P.'s '63
The Winslow Boy '48

Irving Ravetch
Conrack '74
The Cowboys '72
Hombre '67
Home from the Hill '60
Hud '63
The Long, Hot Summer '58
Murphy's Romance '85
Norma Rae '79

The Reivers '69
Stanley and Iris '90
Ten Wanted Men '54

Billy Ray
Color of Night '94

Satyajit Ray
The Adversary '71
Pather Panchali '54
Two Daughters '61
The World of Apu '59

David Rayfiel
Death Watch '80
The Firm '93
Havana '90
Intersection '93
Lipstick '76
Round Midnight '86
Three Days of the Condor '75
Valdez is Coming '71

Jan Read
First Men in the Moon '64
Jason and the Argonauts '63

Eric Red
Blue Steel '90
Body Parts '91
Cohen and Tate '88
Hitcher '86
The Last Outlaw '93
Near Dark '87

Robert Redlin
After Dark, My Sweet '90

Joel M. Reed
Night of the Zombies '81

Tom Reed
Pittsburgh '42

Michael Reeves
Batman: Mask of the Phantasm
'93

Theodore Reeves
National Velvet '44

Steven Reich
Rage and Honor 2: Hostile
Takeover '93

Norman Reilly
The Adventures of Robin Hood
'38

William Reilly
Men of Respect '91
Mortal Thoughts '91

Carl Reiner
Bert Rigby, You're a Fool '89
The Comic '69
Dead Men Don't Wear Plaid '82
Enter Laughing '67
The Man with Two Brains '83
The Thrill of It All! '63

Jeff Reiner
Blood & Concrete: A Love
Story '90

Lucas Reiner
Spirit of '76 '91

Gottfried Reinhardt
I Live My Life '35

Walter Reisch
Somewhere I'll Find You '42

Dean Reisner
Play Misty for Me '71

Richard Reitinger
Faraway, So Close! '93

Duncan Renaldo
Bells of San Fernando '47

Robert Reneau
Action Jackson '88
Demolition Man '93

Jean Renoir
La Chienne '31
La Marseillaise '37

The Little Theatre of Jean
   Renoir '71
The River '51
The Rules of the Game '39
The Southerner '45

David Renwick
Whoops Apocalypse '83

Ed Earl Repp
The Tioga Kid '48

David Reskin
Action U.S.A. '89
Hidden Obsession '92

Adam Resnick
Cabin Boy '94

Patricia Resnick
Maxie '85
9 to 5 '80
Quintet '79
Second Sight '89
Straight Talk '92
A Wedding '78

Robert Resnikoff
The First Power '89

**Paul (Pee Wee
Herman) Reubens**
Big Top Pee Wee '88
Pee Wee's Big Adventure '85

Alma Reville
The Lady Vanishes '38
The 39 Steps '35

Jonathan Reynolds
Leonard Part 6 '87
Micki & Maude '84
My Stepmother Is an Alien '88
Switching Channels '88

Kevin Reynolds
Fandango '85
Red Dawn '84

Lee Reynolds
Allan Quartermain and the Lost
   City of Gold '86
Delta Force 2: Operation
   Stranglehold '90
Storyville '92

Lynn F. Reynolds
Sky High '22

John Rice
Blown Away '94
Chasers '94
Curiosity Kills '90

Susan Rice
Animal Behavior '89
Something in Common '86

Matty Rich
Straight Out of Brooklyn '91

Dick Richard
Snow White and the Seven
   Dwarfs '37

Jean-Louis Richard
Day for Night '73

Pierre Richard
The Daydreamer '75

Doug Richardson
Die Hard 2: Die Harder '90

Scobie Richardson
Wildcard '92

Sy Richardson
Posse '93

Tony Richardson
The Hotel New Hampshire '84
Ned Kelly '70
A Taste of Honey '61

Mordecai Richler
The Apprenticeship of Duddy
   Kravitz '74
Fun with Dick and Jane '77
Joshua Then and Now '85
No Love for Johnnie '60

Young & Willing '42

W.D. Richter
All Night Long '81
Big Trouble in Little China '86
Brubaker '80
Dracula '79
Invasion of the Body Snatchers
   '78
Needful Things '93
Slither '73

Tom Ricostronza
The Inkwell '94

Philip Ridley
The Krays '90
The Reflecting Skin '91

Leni Riefenstahl
The Blue Light '32

J. Riffel
The House on Tombstone Hill
   '92

Adam Rifkin
The Chase '93
The Dark Backward '91
Never on Tuesday '88

Lawrence Riggins
Ironheart '92

Sharon Riis
Loyalties '86

Wolf Rilla
Roadhouse Girl '53

Fred Rinaldo
Comin' Round the Mountain '51
The Invisible Woman '40

David Rintel
Day One '89
World War II: When Lions
   Roared '94

Arthur Ripley
Baby Face Harry Langdon '26
Waterfront '39

Robert Riskin
It Happened One Night '34
Lost Horizon '37
Mr. Deeds Goes to Town '36
You Can't Take It with You '38

J. William Ritchie
George's Island '91

Joe Ritter
The Toxic Avenger '86

Thomas Ritz
Martial Outlaw '93

Jacques Rivette
Paris Belongs to Us '60

Janet Roach
Mr. North '88
Prizzi's Honor '85

Joe Roach
Somewhere in Sonora '33

M. Jay Roach
Lifepod '93

Matthew Robbins
*batteries not included '87
Bingo Long Traveling All-Stars
   & Motor Kings '76
Corvette Summer '78
Dragonslayer '81
MacArthur '77
The Sugarland Express '74
Warning Sign '85

Tim Robbins
Bob Roberts '92

Ben Roberts
Green Fire '55

Daryll Roberts
How U Like Me Now? '92

Jonathan Roberts
The Lion King '94

Once Bitten '85
The Sure Thing '85

June Roberts
Experience Preferred... But Not
   Essential '83
Mermaids '90

Marguerite Roberts
Somewhere I'll Find You '42

Scott Roberts
K2: The Ultimate High '92
Riders of the Storm '88

Stanley Roberts
The Caine Mutiny '54

William Roberts
The Bridge at Remagen '69
The Devil's Brigade '68
Easy to Love '53
The Last American Hero '73
Legend of the Lone Ranger '81
The Magnificent Seven '60
The Mating Game '59
Posse '75
Red Sun '71
Ten to Midnight '83
The Wonderful World of the
   Brothers Grimm '62

R.J. Robertson
Big Bad Mama 2 '87
Final Embrace '92
Forbidden World '82
The Haunting of Morella '91
Not of This Earth '88
Think Big '90
Transylvania Twist '89

Robbie Robertson
Carny '80

Herb Robins
The Worm Eaters '77

Bruce Robinson
Fat Man and Little Boy '89
How to Get Ahead in
   Advertising '89
Jennifer 8 '92
The Killing Fields '84
Withnail and I '87

Casey Robinson
The Egyptian '54
The Snows of Kilimanjaro '52

Phil Alden Robinson
All of Me '84
Field of Dreams '89
In the Mood '87
Rhinestone '84
Sneakers '92

Sally Robinson
A Far Off Place '93

Armando Robles
The Green Wall '70

Marc Rocco
Dream a Little Dream '89
Where the Day Takes You '92

Glauce Rocha
Antonio Das Mortes '68
Earth Entranced '66

Eric Rochant
The Fifth Monkey '90
Love Without Pity '91

Suzzy Roche
Crossing Delancey '88

Chris Rock
CB4: The Movie '93

Jay Dee Rock
Clifford '92

Kevin Rock
Philadelphia Experiment 2 '93
Warlock: The Armageddon '93

Alexandre Rockwell
In the Soup '92
Sons '91

Robert Rodat
The Comrades of Summer '92

Gene Roddenberry
Star Trek the Next Generation:
   Encounter at Farpoint '87

Howard A. Rodman
Fallen Angels 1 '93
Fallen Angels 2 '93

Serge Rodnunsky
Lovers' Lovers '94

Robert Rodriguez
El Mariachi '93

Michael Roemer
Nothing But a Man '64
The Plot Against Harry '69

**Howard Emmett
Rogers**
Hold Your Man '33

Ivan Rogers
Tigershark '87

Mary Rogers
A Billion for Boris '90

Steve Rogers
Triple Impact '92

Wayne Rogers
The Astro-Zombies '67

Will Rogers
Stand Up and Cheer '34

Eric Rohmer
Boyfriends & Girlfriends '88
Chloe in the Afternoon '72
Claire's Knee '71
Four Adventures of Reinette
   and Mirabelle '89
Full Moon in Paris '84
Le Beau Mariage '82
My Night at Maud's '69
Pauline at the Beach '83
Six in Paris '68
Summer '86
A Tale of Springtime '92

Bernie Rollins
Getting Over '81

Mark Romanek
Static '87

Eddie Romero
Cavalry Command '63

George A. Romero
The Crazies '73
Creepshow 2 '87
The Dark Half '91
Dawn of the Dead '78
Day of the Dead '85
Knightriders '81
Martin '77
Monkey Shines '88
Night of the Living Dead '90
Season of the Witch '73

Neil Ronco
Save Me '93

Brunello Rondi
8 1/2 '63
Juliet of the Spirits '65
La Dolce Vita '60
La Strada '54

Jean-Pierre Ronssin
La Discrete '90

Don Roos
Love Field '91
Single White Female '92

Wells Root
Texas Across the River '66

Wills Root
Prisoner of Zenda '37

Tom Ropelewski
The Kiss '88
Look Who's Talking Now '93

Loverboy '89
Madhouse '90

Bradford Ropes
Redwood Forest Trail '50

Bernard Rose
Candyman '92

Jack Rose
April In Paris '52
The Five Pennies '59
The Great Muppet Caper '81
Houseboat '58
I'll See You in My Dreams '51
It Started in Naples '60
Lost and Found '79
On Moonlight Bay '51
Papa's Delicate Condition '63
The Road to Rio '47
The Seven Little Foys '55
Sorrowful Jones '49
A Touch of Class '73
Trouble Along the Way '53
Who's Got the Action? '63

Reginald Rose
The Final Option '82
Man of the West '58
Sea Wolves '81
Twelve Angry Men '57
Whose Life Is It Anyway? '81
Whose Life Is It Anyway? '81
Wild Geese '78
Wild Geese 2 '85

William Rose
Guess Who's Coming to Dinner
   '67
Ladykillers '55

Gualtiero Rosella
Flight of the Innocent '93

Martin Rosen
The Plague Dogs '82
Watership Down '78

Jeanne Rosenberg
The Black Stallion '79
Heidi '93
The Journey of Natty Gann '85
White Fang '91

Mark Rosenthal
The Beverly Hillbillies '93
Desperate Hours '90
For Love or Money '93
The In Crowd '88
The Jewel of the Nile '85
Legend of Billie Jean '85
Superman 4: The Quest for
   Peace '87

Francesco Rosi
Bellissima '51
Christ Stopped at Eboli '79
Three Brothers '80

Arthur Ross
Brubaker '80
Creature from the Black
   Lagoon '54
The Creature Walks Among Us
   '56
The Three Worlds of Gulliver
   '59

Brian Ross
Body Language '92
The Secret Passion of Robert
   Clayton '92

Brian L. Ross
Dying to Remember '93

Gary Ross
Big '88
Dave '93
Lassie '94
Mr. Baseball '92

Roberto Rossellini
Era Notte a Roma '60
Paisan '46

Robert Rossen
All the King's Men '49

Rossen ►cont.

Billy Budd '62
Edge of Darkness '43
The Hustler '61
The Sea Wolf '41
They Won't Forget '37
A Walk in the Sun '46

Leo Rossi
We're Talkin' Serious Money '92

Terry Rossio
Aladdin '92
Little Monsters '89

Arthur Rosson
Boots of Destiny '37

Leo Rosten
Velvet Touch '48

Bobby Roth
Baja Oklahoma '87
Boss' Son '79
Dead Solid Perfect '88
Heartbreakers '84
The Man Inside '90

Cy Roth
Fire Maidens from Outer Space '56

Eric Roth
The Concorde: Airport '79 '79
Forrest Gump '94
Memories of Me '88
Mr. Jones '93
Suspect '87

Lynn Roth
The Portrait '93

Phillip J. Roth
A.P.E.X. '94
Ghostwriter '84

Stephanie Rothman
Starhops '78

Brigitte Rouan
Overseas: Three Women with Man Trouble '90

Jean Rouch
Six in Paris '68

Russel Rouse
Fastest Gun Alive '56

Kathleen Rowell
Hear No Evil '93
Joy of Sex '84
The Outsiders '83
Tainted Blood '93

Charles Francis Royal
Ridin' the Lone Trail '37

Fanchon Royer
Bell Ringer of Antigua '46

Michael Rubbo
The Peanut Butter Solution '85

Andy Ruben
Dance of the Damned '88
The Patriot '86
Poison Ivy '92
Streets '90
Stripped to Kill '87

Katt Shea Ruben
Dance of the Damned '88
The Patriot '86
Poison Ivy '92
Stripped to Kill '87
Stripped to Kill II: Live Girls '89

Bruce Joel Rubin
Brainstorm '83
Deadly Friend '86
Ghost '90
Jacob's Ladder '90
My Life '93

Daniel F. Rubin
Groundhog Day '93

Daniel N. Rubin
Dishonored '31

Sergio Rubini
The Station '92

George Rubio
Into Thin Air '85

Harry Ruby
Duck Soup '33
A Night at the Opera '35

Allen Rucker
Hometown Boy Makes Good '93

Rita Rudner
Peter's Friends '92

Paul Rudnick
Addams Family Values '93

Alan Rudolph
Buffalo Bill & the Indians '76
Choose Me '84
Endangered Species '82
Equinox '93
Love at Large '89
The Moderns '88
Premonition '71
Roadie '80
Trouble in Mind '86
Welcome to L.A. '77

Ed Rugoff
Mannequin '87
Mannequin 2: On the Move '91
Mr. Nanny '93

Raul Ruiz
The Hypothesis of the Stolen Painting '78

Terry Runte
Mystery Date '91
Super Mario Bros. '93

Richard Rush
Air America '90
Color of Night '94
Psych-Out '68
The Stunt Man '80

Lou Rusoff
Beach Party '63
Motorcycle Gang '57
Shake, Rattle and Rock '57

Chuck Russell
The Blob '88
Dreamscape '84
A Nightmare on Elm Street 3: Dream Warriors '87

Jack Russell
Poldark '75

Ken Russell
The Boy Friend '71
The Devils '71
The Lair of the White Worm '88
Lisztomania '75
Mahler '74
The Rainbow '89
Salome's Last Dance '88
Tommy '75
Valentino '77
Whore '91

Ray Russell
X: The Man with X-Ray Eyes '63
Zotz! '62

Vivian Russell
The Rainbow '89

Willy Russell
Educating Rita '83
Shirley Valentine '89

John Russo
Voodoo Dawn '89

Morrie Ryskind
Animal Crackers '30

The Cocoanuts '29
My Man Godfrey '36
A Night at the Opera '35

Michael Sadler
A Year in Provence '89

Arthur St. Claire
Boss of Bullion City '41

Nicholas St. John
Body Snatchers '93
China Girl '87
Dangerous Game '93
Fear City '85
King of New York '90

Alfredo Salazar
The Robot vs. the Aztec Mummy '59

Murray Salem
Kindergarten Cop '90

Martin Salinas
Gaby: A True Story '87

Waldo Salt
Midnight Cowboy '69
Shopworn Angel '38

Mark Saltzman
The Adventures of Milo & Otis '89
Iron & Silk '91
3 Ninjas Kick Back '94

Mark Salzman
Iron & Silk '91

Daniel S. Sample
Ex-Cop '93

Jon Robert Samsel
Carnal Crimes '91

Lesser Samuels
Bitter Sweet '40
Gangway '37

Duke Sandefur
Ghost Town '88

Barry Sandler
All-American Murder '91
Crimes of Passion '84
The Duchess and the Dirtwater Fox '76
Loners '72
Making Love '82
The Mirror Crack'd '80

Susan Sandler
Crossing Delancey '88

Anna Sandor
Miss Rose White '92

Jimmy Sangster
Blood of the Vampire '58
The Crawling Eye '58
The Curse of Frankenstein '57
The Devil & Max Devlin '81
Dynasty of Fear '72
The Hellfire Club '61
The Horror of Dracula '58
The Horror of Frankenstein '70
Hysteria '64
Maniac '63
The Mummy '59
Phobia '80
Scream of Fear '61

Alvin Sargent
Bobby Deerfield '77
Dominick & Eugene '88
Gambit '66
Julia '77
Nuts '87
Ordinary People '80
Other People's Money '91
Paper Moon '73
The Stalking Moon '69
The Sterile Cuckoo '69
Straight Time '78
What About Bob? '91
White Palace '90

Arlene Sarner
Peggy Sue Got Married '86

William Saroyan
The Human Comedy '43

Jean-Paul Sartre
The Respectful Prostitute '52

Oley Sassone
Wild Hearts Can't Be Broken '91

Shimako Sato
Tale of a Vampire '92

Stephen Saul
Ninja Hunt '80s

Derek Saunders
Deceived '91

George Saunders
Scanner Cop '94

Claude Sautet
Borsalino '70

Nancy Savoca
Household Saints '93
True Love '89

Jerry Sawyer
Empire of Spiritual Ninja

Linwood Sawyer
Alien Space Avenger '91

John Sayles
Alligator '80
Baby It's You '82
Battle Beyond the Stars '80
Breaking In '89
The Brother from Another Planet '84
The Challenge '82
City of Hope '91
The Clan of the Cave Bear '86
Eight Men Out '88
Enormous Changes '83
The Howling '81
Lady in Red '79
Lianna '83
Matewan '87
Passion Fish '92
Piranha '78
The Quick and the Dead '94
Return of the Secaucus 7 '80
Unnatural Causes '86
Wild Thing '87

George Wallace Sayre
Wings Over the Pacific '43

Joel Sayre
Gunga Din '39

Dario Scardapane
Posse '93

Furio Scarpelli
The Family '87
Time to Kill '89

Romano Scavolini
Nightmare '82

Sauro Scavolini
The Scorpion's Tail '71

James Schamus
The Wedding Banquet '93

Larry Schanker
American Blue Note '89

Dore Schary
Sunrise at Campobello '60
Young Tom Edison '40

Oliver Schatzky
A Man in Love '87

Richard Schayer
Trader Horn '31

Adam Scheinman
Little Big League '94

Andrew Scheinman
North '94

George Schenck
Dying to Remember '93
Escape 2000 '81
Futureworld '76

Fred Schepisi
A Cry in the Dark '88
The Devil's Playground '76

Shawn Schepps
Encino Man '92
Son-in-Law '93

Gregory Scherick
The Night Before '88

Roberto Scheuer
Eversmile New Jersey '89

Laura Schiff
800 Leagues Down the Amazon '90s

Robert Schiff
Swimsuit: The Movie '89

Michael Schiffer
Colors '88
Lean on Me '89

Karl Schiffman
Back in Action '94

Suzanne Schiffman
Confidentially Yours '83
Day for Night '73
The Last Metro '80
The Man Who Loved Women '77
Small Change '76
Sorceress '88
Story of Adele H. '75
The Woman Next Door '81

Lalo Schifrin
The Brotherhood '68

Fred Schiller
The Heat's On '43

Vivian Schilling
Soultaker '90

Murray Schisgal
All Over Town '37
Luv '67
Tootsie '82

George Schlatter
Fire and Ice '87
Norman, Is That You? '76

John Schlesinger
Madame Sousatzka '88

Volker Schlondorff
The Tin Drum '79
Voyager '91

Ronald Schmidt
A.P.E.X. '94

William Schmidt
The Sound and the Silence '93

David Schmoeller
The Arrival '90
Crawlspace '86
Day Time Ended '80
The Seduction '82
Tourist Trap '79

Charles Schnee
Butterfield 8 '60
Red River '48
Westward the Women '51

Barry Schneider
Deadly Force '83
Harper Valley P.T.A. '78
Mother's Boys '94
Roller Boogie '79
Ruby '77
Take This Job & Shove It '81

Peter Schneider
Knife in the Head '78

Ernest B. Schoedsack
Chang: A Drama of the
Wilderness '27

Pierre Schoendoerffer
The 317th Platoon '65

Amy Schor
Mr. Wonderful '93

David J. Schow
Critters 3 '91
Critters 4 '91
The Crow '93
Leatherface: The Texas
Chainsaw Massacre 3 '89

Leonard Schrader
Blue Collar '78
Kiss of the Spider Woman '85
Mishima: A Life in Four
Chapters '85
Old Boyfriends '79
The Yakuza '75

Paul Schrader
American Gigolo '79
Blue Collar '78
Hardcore '79
The Last Temptation of Christ
'88
Light of Day '87
Light Sleeper '92
Mishima: A Life in Four
Chapters '85
The Mosquito Coast '86
Obsession '76
Old Boyfriends '79
Raging Bull '80
Rolling Thunder '77
Taxi Driver '76
The Yakuza '75

Carol Schreder
In Love and War '91

David Schreiber
Body of Influence '93

Nevin Schreiner
The China Lake Murders '90
Linda '93
Memories of Murder '90

Doris Schroeder
Bullet Code '40

Budd Schulberg
A Face in the Crowd '57
On the Waterfront '54
Question of Honor '80

Arnold Schulman
And the Band Played On '93
A Chorus Line '85
Cimarron '60
Funny Lady '75
A Hole in the Head '59
Love with the Proper Stranger
'63
The Night They Raided
Minsky's '69
Players '79
Tucker: The Man and His
Dream '88

Tom Schulman
Dead Poets Society '89
Honey, I Shrunk the Kids '89
Second Sight '89
What About Bob? '91

Charles M. Schulz
Bon Voyage, Charlie Brown '80
A Boy Named Charlie Brown
'70
Race for Your Life, Charlie
Brown '77
Snoopy, Come Home '72

Douglas Schulze
Hellmaster '92

Joel Schumacher
Car Wash '76
D.C. Cab '84

St. Elmo's Fire '85
Sparkle '76
The Wiz '78

Marjorie Schwartz
The Butcher's Wife '91

Mark Evan Schwartz
Quake '92

S.S. Schweitzer
Hornet's Nest '70

Aleksander Scibor-Rylski
Man of Iron '81
Man of Marble '76

Ettore Scola
Down & Dirty '76
The Family '87
La Nuit de Varennes '82
Macaroni '85
Passion of Love '82
A Special Day '77
Two Nights with Cleopatra '54

Kathryn Scola
Alexander's Ragtime Band '38
Female '33
Night After Night '32
One Night in the Tropics '40

Martin Scorsese
The Age of Innocence '93
Goodfellas '90
Mean Streets '73

Allan Scott
Apprentice to Murder '88
The Awakening '80
Castaway '87
Cold Heaven '92
D.A.R.Y.L. '85
Don't Look Now '73
The 5000 Fingers of Dr. T '53
The Girl from Petrovka '74
Joseph Andrews '77
Man Who Had Power Over
Women '70
Martin's Day '85
Spiral Staircase '75
Top Hat '35
The Witches '90

Cynthia Scott
Strangers in Good Company
'91

George C. Scott
Descending Angel '90

Kevin Scott
Key Exchange '85

Sherman Scott
Bad Girls from Mars '90
Haunting Fear '91

Starr Emerald Catamas Scott
Men in Love '90

T.J. Scott
TC 2000 '93

Peter S. Seaman
Doc Hollywood '91
Trenchcoat '83
Who Framed Roger Rabbit? '88

Ted Sears
Snow White and the Seven
Dwarfs '37

George Seaton
Airport '70
The Counterfeit Traitor '62
Country Girl '54
Doctor Takes a Wife '40
Miracle on 34th Street '47

Beverly Sebastian
Gator Bait '73
Gator Bait 2: Cajun Justice '88
Running Cool '93

Ferd Sebastian
Gator Bait '73

Gator Bait 2: Cajun Justice '88
Running Cool '93

Manuel Seff
Love on the Run '36

Erich Segal
A Change of Seasons '80
Love Story '70
Man, Woman & Child '83
Oliver's Story '78
R.P.M. (*Revolutions Per
Minute) '70
Yellow Submarine '68

Harry Segall
Angel on My Shoulder '46

Robert Seidenberg
Dead in the Water '91

David Seidler
The Rumor Mill '86
Tucker: The Man and His
Dream '88

Shinichi Sekizawa
Dagora, the Space Monster '65

Jack M. Sell
Deadly Spygames '89

David Seltzer
Bird on a Wire '90
The Hellstrom Chronicle '71
King, Queen, Knave '72
Lucas '86
The Omen '76
The Other Side of the Mountain
'75
Prophecy '79
Punchline '88
Shining Through '92
Table for Five '83

Terrel Seltzer
Chan is Missing '82
Dim Sum: A Little Bit of Heart
'85
How I Got into College '89

David O. Selznick
Since You Went Away '44
A Star is Born '37

Ron Senkowski
Let's Kill All the Lawyers '93

Mack Sennett
Extra Girl '23

Al Septien
Leprechaun 2 '94

Yahoo Serious
Young Einstein '89

Rod Serling
Assault on a Queen '66
The Doomsday Flight '66
Patterns '56
Planet of the Apes '68
Requiem for a Heavyweight '56
Seven Days in May '64

Alexandra Seros
Point of No Return '93

Coline Serreau
Mama, There's a Man in Your
Bed '89
Three Men and a Cradle '85

Phillip Setbon
Honeymoon '87
Mr. Frost '90

Mark Sevi
Class of 1999 2: The Substitute
'93

Vernon Sewell
Frenzy '46
The World Owes Me a Living
'47

John Sexton
Wrangler '88

James Seymour
42nd Street '33

Samantha Shad
Class Action '91

Susan Shadburne
The Adventures of Mark Twain
'85
Shadow Play '86

Tom Shadyac
Ace Ventura: Pet Detective '93

Anthony Shaffer
Appointment with Death '88
Death on the Nile '78
Evil Under the Sun '82
Frenzy '72
Sleuth '72
Whodunit '82
The Wicker Man '75

Peter Shaffer
Amadeus '84
Equus '77

Josef Shaftel
Naked Hills '56

Peter Shaner
Shootfighter: Fight to the Death
'93

John Patrick Shanley
Alive '93
Five Corners '88
The January Man '89
Joe Versus the Volcano '90
Moonstruck '87
We're Back! A Dinosaur's Story
'93

Joy Shannon
Uptown Angel '90

Alan Shapiro
The Crush '93

J. David Shapiro
Robin Hood: Men in Tights '93

Paul Shapiro
Breaking the Rules '92
Calendar Girl '93

Richard Shapiro
Blood Ties '92

Stanley Shapiro
Carbon Copy '81
Dirty Rotten Scoundrels '88

Alan Sharp
Damnation Alley '77
The Last Hit '93
Little Treasure '85

Jan Sharp
Wide Sargasso Sea '92

William Shatner
Star Trek 5: The Final Frontier
'89

Melville Shavelson
April In Paris '52
Cast a Giant Shadow '66
Double Dynamite '51
The Five Pennies '59
Houseboat '58
I'll See You in My Dreams '51
It Started in Naples '60
A New Kind of Love '63
On Moonlight Bay '51
The Seven Little Foys '55
Sorrowful Jones '49
Trouble Along the Way '53
Yours, Mine & Ours '68

Irwin Shaw
Commandos Strike at Dawn '43

Philip Shaw
Tarzana, the Wild Girl '72

Harry Shearer
Real Life '79
The Return of Spinal Tap '92

Donald Shebib
The Climb '87

Arthur Sheekman
Duck Soup '33

David Sheffield
Boomerang '92
Coming to America '88

Sidney Sheldon
All in a Night's Work '61
The Bachelor and the Bobby-
Soxer '47
Billy Rose's Jumbo '62
Birds & the Bees '56
Easter Parade '48
Nancy Goes to Rio '50
Pardners '56
Rich, Young and Pretty '51
Three Guys Named Mike '51

Ron Shelton
The Best of Times '86
Blaze '89
Blue Chips '94
Bull Durham '88
Under Fire '83
White Men Can't Jump '92

Nina Shengold
Blind Spot '93

Richard Shepard
The Linguini Incident '92

Sam Shepard
Far North '88
Fool for Love '86
Paris, Texas '83
Silent Tongue '92
Zabriskie Point '70

Cybill Shepherd
Memphis '91

Jean Shepherd
A Christmas Story '83
It Runs In the Family '94

Jack Sher
Paris Blues '61
Shane '53
The Three Worlds of Gulliver
'59

Bob Sheridan
Dinosaur Island '93

Guillermo Sheridan
Cabeza de Vaca '90

Jim Sheridan
The Field '90
In the Name of the Father '93
Into the West '92
My Left Foot '89

Michael J. Sheridan
That's Entertainment, Part 3 '93

R.C. Sheriff
The Four Feathers '39
The Invisible Man '33

Gary Sherman
After the Shock '90
Fire and Rain '89
Phobia '80

Bill Sherwood
Parting Glances '86

Robert Sherwood
Abe Lincoln in Illinois '40
The Best Years of Our Lives
'46
The Ghost Goes West '36
Rebecca '40

John Shirley
The Crow '93

Mark Shmuger
Dead of Winter '87

Roger Sholes
The Tale of Ruby Rose '87

Del Shores
Daddy's Dyin'...Who's Got the
Will? '90

Dennis Shryack
Fifty/Fifty '93
Pale Rider '85

Bernard Shubert
The Mummy's Curse '44

Max Shulman
The Affairs of Dobie Gillis '53

Ronald Shusett
Freejack '92
Phobia '80

Charles Shyer
Baby Boom '87
Father of the Bride '91
Goin' South '78
House Calls '78
I Love Trouble '94
Irreconcilable Differences '84
Private Benjamin '80
Protocol '84
Smokey and the Bandit '77

Melville Shyer
Green Eyes '34

James Shyman
Slashdance '89

Mussef Sibay
A Woman, Her Men and Her
Futon '92

Andy Sidaris
Do or Die '91
Fit to Kill '93
Guns '90
Hard Hunted '92

Christian Sidaris
Enemy Gold '93

Lynn Siefert
Cool Runnings '93

Steven Siegel
K-9 '89

Mark Siegler
Galaxy of Terror '81

Tom Sierchio
Untamed Heart '93

Dai Sijie
China, My Sorrow '89

James R. Silke
Ninja 3: The Domination '84
Revenge of the Ninja '83
Sahara '83

Sterling Silliphant
Catch the Heat '87
Charly '68
Circle of Iron '78
Death Scream '75
The Enforcer '76
In the Heat of the Night '67
The Killer Elite '75
The Liberation of L.B. Jones
'70
Marlowe '69
Murphy's War '71
The New Centurions '72
Nightfall '56
Over the Top '86
The Poseidon Adventure '72
The Slender Thread '65
The Swarm '78
Telefon '77
The Towering Inferno '74
Village of the Damned '60
Walk in the Spring Rain '70
When Time Ran Out '80

Amanda Silver
Fallen Angels 1 '93
The Hand that Rocks the
Cradle '92

Joan Micklin Silver
Chilly Scenes of Winter '79

Marisa Silver
Old Enough '84

Stu Silver
Throw Momma from the Train
'87

Peter Silverman
American Heart '92

Nancy Silvers
Battling for Baby '92

Shel Silverstein
Things Change '88

Lawrence L. Simeone
Blindfold: Acts of Obsession
'94
Cop-Out '91
Eyes of the Beholder '92
Presumed Guilty '91

David Simkins
Adventures in Babysitting '87

Posy S. Simmonds
The French Lesson '86

Redbeard Simmons
The Applegates '89

Adam Simon
Carnosaur '93

J.P. Simon
Cthulhu Mansion '91

Neil Simon
After the Fox '66
Barefoot in the Park '67
Biloxi Blues '88
Brighton Beach Memoirs '86
Broadway Bound '92
California Suite '78
Chapter Two '79
The Cheap Detective '78
The Goodbye Girl '77
The Heartbreak Kid '72
I Ought to Be in Pictures '82
Last of the Red Hot Lovers '72
Lost in Yonkers '93
The Marrying Man '91
Max Dugan Returns '83
Murder by Death '76
The Odd Couple '68
Only When I Laugh '81
The Out-of-Towners '70
Plaza Suite '71
Prisoner of Second Avenue '74
Seems Like Old Times '80
The Slugger's Wife '85
Star Spangled Girl '71
The Sunshine Boys '75

Henri Simoun
Blind Vengeance '90

Byron Simpson
The Rescuers Down Under '90

Joshua Sinclair
Judgment in Berlin '88

Randi Mayem Singer
Mrs. Doubtfire '93

John Singleton
Boyz N the Hood '91
Poetic Justice '93

Gary Sinyor
Leon the Pig Farmer '93

Curtis Siodmak
Earth vs. the Flying Saucers '56
Invisible Agent '42

Robert Siodmak
Bride of the Gorilla '51

**Rosemary Anne
Sisson**
The Bretts '88

John Sjogren
Money to Burn '94

Victor Sjostrom
He Who Gets Slapped '24

Warren Skaaren
Batman '89

Beetlejuice '88
Beverly Hills Cop 2 '87

Vance Skarstedt
Man or Gun '58

Zachary Sklar
JFK '91

Jerzy Skolimowski
Knife in the Water '62

Jeremy Slate
Hell's Angels '69 '69

Damian F. Slattery
A Day in October '92

Holly Goldberg Sloan
Angels in the Outfield '94
Indecency '92
Made in America '93

Rick Sloane
Vice Academy 3 '91

Shawn Slovo
A World Apart '88

Adam Small
In the Army Now '94
Son-in-Law '93

Ebbe Roe Smith
Car 54, Where Are You? '94
Falling Down '93

Harold Jacob Smith
The Defiant Ones '58

Joshua Smith
Sun Ra & His Intergalactic
Solar Arkestra: Space is the
Place '74

Martin Smith
The Art of Crime '75
Under the Rainbow '81

Robert Smith
Girls' Town '59
Platinum High School '60

Webb Smith
Snow White and the Seven
Dwarfs '37

Stephen Smoke
Magic Kid '92
Street Crimes '92

Norman Snider
Body Parts '91
Dead Ringers '88

William Snowden, III
Primary Motive '92

Blake Snyder
Blank Check '93

Michael Snyder
Rescue Me '93

Carol Sobieski
The Bourne Identity '88
Fried Green Tomatoes '91
Honeysuckle Rose '80
Money for Nothing '93
Winter People '89

Steven Soderberg
King of the Hill '93
sex, lies and videotape '89

Gerard Soeteman
Flesh and Blood '85

Iain Softley
Backbeat '94

Rebecca Soladay
Shame '92

Franco Solinas
The Battle of Algiers '66

Peter J. Solmo
Jack & the Beanstalk '76

Edward Solomon
Bill & Ted's Bogus Journey '91

Bill & Ted's Excellent
Adventure '89
Leaving Normal '92
Super Mario Bros. '93

Todd Solondz
Fear, Anxiety and Depression
'89

Andrew Solt
For the First Time '59
In a Lonely Place '50
Little Women '33
This is Elvis '81

Bernie Somers
Cops and Robbersons '94

Edith Sommer
This Property is Condemned
'66

Stephen Sommers
The Adventures of Huck Finn
'93
Gunmen '93

Stephen Sondheim
The Last of Sheila '73

Dror Soref
The Seventh Coin '92

Carlos Sorin
Eversmile New Jersey '89

Aaron Sorkin
A Few Good Men '92
Malice '93

Terry Southern
Barbarella '68
The Cincinnati Kid '65
Dr. Strangelove, or: How I
Learned to Stop Worrying
and Love the Bomb '64
Easy Rider '69
End of the Road '70
The Loved One '65
The Magic Christian '69
The Telephone '87

Ralph Spence
Stand Up and Cheer '34

Alan Spencer
Hexed '93

Jane Spencer
Little Noises '91

Scott Spencer
Act of Vengeance '86
Father Hood '93

Milton Sperling
Happy Landing '38
Merrill's Marauders '62
Thin Ice '37

Bella Spewack
Boy Meets Girl '38
My Favorite Wife '40
Weekend at the Waldorf '45

Samuel Spewack
Boy Meets Girl '38
My Favorite Wife '40
Weekend at the Waldorf '45

Penelope Spheeris
The Little Rascals '94

Scott Spiegel
Evil Dead 2: Dead by Dawn '87

Kurt Spielberg
Clash of the Ninja '86

Steven Spielberg
Close Encounters of the Third
Kind '77
The Goonies '85
Poltergeist '82
The Sugarland Express '74

Adrian Spies
Dark of the Sun '68

Leonard Spigelgass
Athena '54

I Was a Male War Bride '49
The Perfect Marriage '46

Tony Spiridakis
Queens Logic '91

Marian Spitzer
Look for the Silver Lining '49

Roger Spottiswoode
48 Hrs. '82

Robin Spry
A Cry in the Night '93

Jim Staahl
The Beverly Hillbillies '93

Douglas Stalgren
The Deadly Secret '94

Joshua Stallings
The Ice Runner '93

Sylvester Stallone
Cliffhanger '93
Cobra '86
First Blood '82
F.I.S.T. '78
Over the Top '86
Paradise Alley '78
Rambo: First Blood, Part 2 '85
Rambo 3 '88
Rhinestone '84
Rocky '76
Rocky 2 '79
Rocky 3 '82
Rocky 4 '85
Rocky 5 '90
Staying Alive '83

Richard Stanley
Dust Devil '93

Jane C. Stanton
Our Time '74

Jeff Stanzler
Jumpin' at the Boneyard '92

Lynn Starling
Wintertime '43

Ben Starr
How to Commit Marriage '69
Texas Across the River '66

Steven Starr
Joey Breaker '93

Daniel Steel
Body Moves '90

Joseph Stefano
Black Orchid '59
Blackout '78
The Kindred '87
The Naked Edge '61
Psycho '60
Psycho 4: The Beginning '90

Mark Stein
Housesitter '92
A Perfect Little Murder '90

John Steinbeck
Viva Zapata! '52

Norman Steinberg
Blazing Saddles '74
Funny About Love '90
Johnny Dangerously '84
My Favorite Year '82
Yes, Giorgio '82

Reed Steiner
The Hit List '93

Christian Stengel
Crime and Punishment '35

A.C. Stephen
Saturday Night Sleazies, Vol. 1
'66

Jon Stephens
The Silver Stallion: King of the
Wild Brumbies '94

John Steppling
52 Pick-Up '86

William Sterling
Alice's Adventures in
  Wonderland '72

Henry Stern
Eden '92
Eden 2 '93

Leonard Stern
Abbott and Costello in the
  Foreign Legion '50
Lost in Alaska '52
Ma and Pa Kettle Go to Town
  '50

Noah Stern
The Opposite Sex and How to
  Live With Them '93

Sandor Stern
The Amityville Horror '79
Web of Deceit '90

Stewart Stern
The Last Movie '71
Rachel, Rachel '68
Rebel Without a Cause '55
Summer Wishes, Winter
  Dreams '73
The Ugly American '63

Tom Stern
Freaked '93
Hell's Angels '69 '69

Andrew Stevens
Night Eyes 3 '93

Art Stevens
The Fox and the Hound '81

Brinke Stevens
Teenage Exorcist '93

Dana Stevens
Blink '93

David Stevens
Breaker Morant '80

George Stevens
Separate But Equal '91

Gosta Stevens
The Count of the Old Town '34

Leslie Stevens
Probe '72

Louis Stevens
The Border Legion '40

Robert Stevenson
Jane Eyre '44

Donald Stewart
Clear and Present Danger '94
The Hunt for Red October '90
Jackson County Jail '76
Missing '82
Patriot Games '92

**Donald Ogden
Stewart**
Cass Timberlane '47
Dinner at Eight '33
Forever and a Day '43
Going Hollywood '33
Holiday '38
Love Affair '39
The Philadelphia Story '40
Prisoner of Zenda '37
Without Love '45

R.J. Stewart
Major League 2 '94

Roger Stigliano
Fun Down There '88

Whit Stillman
Barcelona '94
Metropolitan '90

Jerry Stoeffhaas
Cheap Shots '91

Christian Stoianovich
Perfect Family '92

Andrew L. Stone
The Girl Said No '37
The Last Voyage '60

Nick Stone
Bikini Summer '91

Oliver Stone
Born on the Fourth of July '89
Conan the Barbarian '82
The Doors '91
8 Million Ways to Die '85
The Hand '81
Heaven and Earth '93
JFK '91
Midnight Express '78
Platoon '86
Salvador '86
Scarface '83
Seizure '74
Talk Radio '88
Wall Street '87
Year of the Dragon '85

Peter Stone
Charade '63
Father Goose '64

Tom Stoppard
Billy Bathgate '91
Brazil '85
Despair '78
Empire of the Sun '87
The Human Factor '79
Romantic Englishwoman '75
Rosencrantz & Guildenstern
  Are Dead '90
The Russia House '90

David Storey
This Sporting Life '63

Jim Strain
Bingo '91

Larry Strawther
Without a Clue '88

Wesley Strick
Arachnophobia '90
Cape Fear '91
Final Analysis '92
True Believer '89
Wolf '94

Wladimir Strijewski
Crime and Punishment '35

Thomas Strittmatter
Drachenfutter '87

Max Strom
Best of the Best 2 '93

Fred Stroppel
Almost Pregnant '91

Jeffrey Strouth
American Fabulous '92

Barry Strugatz
Married to the Mob '88
She-Devil '89

Jeb Stuart
Another 48 Hrs. '90
Die Hard '88
The Fugitive '93
Leviathan '89
Lock Up '89
Vital Signs '90

**Christopher
Sturgeon**
Huck and the King of Hearts
  '93

Preston Sturges
The Great McGinty '40
The Lady Eve '41
Miracle of Morgan's Creek '44
Sullivan's Travels '41

Charles Sturridge
A Handful of Dust '88

Milton Subotsky
Vault of Horror '73

Henry Sucher
Captive Wild Woman '43
The Mummy's Ghost '44
The Mummy's Tomb '42

Arne Sucksdorff
The Great Adventure '53

Greg Suddeth
Prehysteria '93

Kevin Sullivan
Anne of Avonlea '87
Anne of Green Gables '85

Tim Sullivan
A Handful of Dust '88

Lasse Summanen
The Ox '91

Dirk Summers
Survival of Spaceship Earth '90

Walter Summers
Black Limelight '38
The Human Monster '39

Louis Sun
Rage and Honor 2: Hostile
  Takeover '93

Shirley Sun
A Great Wall '86
Iron & Silk '91

Joel Surnow
Ring of the Musketeers '93

E.W. Swackhamer
The Rousters '90

Julia Sweeney
It's Pat '94

Terry Sweeney
Shag: The Movie '89

Alfred Sweeny
Up from the Depths '79

Edithe Swensen
They Watch '93

Tommy Swerdlow
Cool Runnings '93

Jo Swerling
Blood and Sand '41
Crash Dive '43
Double Wedding '37
I Am the Law '38
It's a Wonderful Life '46
Lady by Choice '34
Platinum Blonde '31

Robin Swicord
Shag: The Movie '89

David Swift
How to Succeed in Business
  without Really Trying '67

Istvan Szabo
Father '67
Meeting Venus '91

Thomas Szollosi
Three O'Clock High '87

Reszo Szoreny
A Happy New Year! '79

Micheal Taav
The Paint Job '93

Jim Tabilio
Sweet Justice '92

Brian Taggert
Child of Darkness, Child of
  Light '91
The New Kids '85
Of Unknown Origin '83
Poltergeist 3 '88
Visiting Hours '82
Wanted Dead or Alive '86

Robert Taicher
Inside Out '91

Isao Takahata
Grave of the Fireflies '88

Ted Tally
The Silence of the Lambs '91
White Palace '90

Takeski Tamura
MacArthur's Children '85

Amy Tan
The Joy Luck Club '93

William Tannen
Inside Edge '92

Alain Tanner
Jonah Who Will Be 25 in the
  Year 2000 '76

Robert Tansey
The Driftin' Kid '41
Dynamite Canyon '41

Daniel Taplitz
Black Magic '92

Daniel Taradash
Bell, Book and Candle '58
Desiree '54
Doctors' Wives '70
Don't Bother to Knock '52
From Here to Eternity '53
Golden Boy '39
Hawaii '66
Knock on Any Door '49
Morituri '65
The Other Side of Midnight '77
Picnic '55
Rancho Notorious '52

Quentin Tarantino
Natural Born Killers '94
Pulp Fiction '94
Reservoir Dogs '92
True Romance '93

Sooni Taraporevala
Mississippi Masala '92
Salaam Bombay! '88

Andrei Tarkovsky
Andrei Rublev '66

Erik Tarloff
Car 54, Where Are You? '94

Frank Tarloff
Father Goose '64
A Guide for the Married Man
  '67

Bela Tarr
Almanac of Fall

Frank Tashlin
Cinderfella '60
The Fuller Brush Girl '50
The Lemon Drop Kid '51

Jacques Tati
Parade '74

John Tatoulis
The Silver Stallion: King of the
  Wild Brumbies '94

Catherine Tavel
Married People, Single Sex '93

Bertrand Tavernier
Coup de Torchon '81
Death Watch '80
The Judge and the Assassin
  '75
Life and Nothing But '89
Round Midnight '86
Spoiled Children '77
A Sunday in the Country '84

Paolo Taviani
Fiorile '93
Good Morning, Babylon '87
Kaos '85
The Night of the Shooting Stars
  '82
Padre Padrone '77

Vittorio Taviani
Fiorile '93

Good Morning, Babylon '87
Kaos '85
The Night of the Shooting Stars
  '82
Padre Padrone '77

Vincent Tavier
Man Bites Dog '91

Dwight Taylor
Today We Live '33
Top Hat '35
We're Not Married '52

Philip John Taylor
Lust in the Dust '85

Renee Taylor
Lovers and Other Strangers '70

Roderick Taylor
The Star Chamber '83

Sam Taylor
Girl Shy '24
Vertigo '58

Steve Taylor
Sorority House Party '92

Theodore Taylor
Showdown '73

Kevin S. Tenney
Peacemaker '90
Witchboard '87
Witchboard 2: The Devil's
  Doorway '93

**Gay Partington
Terry**
The Toxic Avenger, Part 2 '89
The Toxic Avenger, Part 3: The
  Last Temptation of Toxie '89

Steve Tesich
American Flyers '85
Breaking Away '79
Eleni '85
Eyewitness '81
Four Friends '81
The World According to Garp
  '82

Graham Tetley
Dark of the Night '85

Joan Tewkesbury
Cold Sassy Tree '89
Nashville '75
A Night in Heaven '83
Thieves Like Us '74

Harvey Thew
Illicit '31

Jack Thibeau
Off Limits '87

Nick Thiel
The Experts '89
Fire Birds '90
Shipwrecked '90
V.I. Warshawski '91
White Fang '91

Robert Thoeren
Mrs. Parkington '44

Robert Thom
Death Race 2000 '75

Anna Thomas
El Norte '83
End of August '82
A Time of Destiny '88

Dave Thomas
Strange Brew '83

Dylan Thomas
The Three Weird Sisters '48

Jerry Thomas
The Fighting Redhead '50

Jim Thomas
Predator '87
Predator 2 '90
The Rescue '88

John Thomas
Predator '87
Predator 2 '90
The Rescue '88

Michael Thomas
Backbeat '94
Burke & Wills '85
Deception '92
The Hunger '83
Ladyhawke '85
Scandal '89

Ralph Thomas
The Doors '91

Camille Thomasson
The Disappearance of Christina '93

Caroline Thompson
The Addams Family '91
Black Beauty '94
Edward Scissorhands '90
The Secret Garden '93

Carolyn Thompson
Homeward Bound: The Incredible Journey '93

Donald W. Thompson
Sidekicks '93

Ernest Thompson
On Golden Pond '81
Sweet Hearts Dance '88

Larry Thompson
The Addams Family '91

Rob Thompson
The Cowboy Way '94
Hearts of the West '75
Ratboy '86

Selma Thomson
Taken Away '89

Billy Bob Thornton
One False Move '91

Ralph Thornton
I Was a Teenage Werewolf '57

Roderick Thorp
Rainbow Drive '90

Ernest Tidyman
Shaft's Big Score '72
Stark '85

James Toback
Bugsy '91
Exposed '83
Fingers '78
The Gambler '74
The Pick-Up Artist '87

George Toles
Careful '94

John Toles-Bey
A Rage in Harlem '91

Michael Tolkin
Deep Cover '92
Gleaming the Cube '89
The Player '92
The Rapture '91

Stephen Tolkin
Captain America '89
Daybreak '93

Jerome Tonnerre
Un Coeur en Hiver '93

Tom Topor
The Accused '88
Judgment '90
Nuts '87

Burt Topper
Suicide Battalion/Hell Squad '58
Tank Commando '59

Tracy Torme
Fire in the Sky '93

The Spellbinder '88

Giuseppe Tornatore
Cinema Paradiso '88
Everybody's Fine '90

Antonio Toro
Amityville: A New Generation '93

Peter Torokvei
Armed and Dangerous '86
Back to School '86
Caddyshack 2 '88
Guarding Tess '94
Real Genius '85

Gabe Torres
December '91

Miguel Contreras Torres
Pancho Villa Returns '50

Robert Totten
Death of a Gunfighter '69

Maurice Tourneur
The Wishing Ring '14

Robert Towne
Chinatown '74
Days of Thunder '90
The Firm '93
The Last Detail '73
The Last Woman on Earth '61
Personal Best '82
Shampoo '75
Tequila Sunrise '88
Tomb of Ligeia '64
The Two Jakes '90
Villa Rides '68
The Yakuza '75

Leo Townsend
Beach Blanket Bingo '65
Bikini Beach '64
How to Stuff a Wild Bikini '65

Robert Townsend
The Five Heartbeats '91
Hollywood Shuffle '87
The Meteor Man '93

Sher Townsend
Beach Blanket Bingo '65

Stephen Traxler
Slithis '78

Monika Treut
My Father is Coming '91
Seduction: The Cruel Woman '89

Dale Trevillion
Las Vegas Weekend '85
One Man Force '89

Dorothy Tristan
Weeds '87

Victor Trivas
The Head '59

Jan Troell
The Emigrants '72
The New Land '73

Guy Trosper
Darby's Rangers '58
The Stratton Story '49

Lamar Trotti
Alexander's Ragtime Band '38
Immortal Sergeant '43
In Old Chicago '38
The Ox-Bow Incident '43
Wilson '44
Young Mr. Lincoln '39

Francois Truffaut
Day for Night '73
The 400 Blows '59
Mississippi Mermaid '69
Shoot the Piano Player '62

Dalton Trumbo
The Brave One '56
Exodus '60

The Fixer '68
A Guy Named Joe '44
Hawaii '66
The Horsemen '70
Our Vines Have Tender Grapes '45
Roman Holiday '53
Spartacus '60
Thirty Seconds Over Tokyo '44

Alan R. Trustman
The Arab Conspiracy '76
Bullitt '68
Hit! '73
Lady Ice '73
They Call Me Mr. Tibbs! '70
Thomas Crown Affair '68

Glenn Tryon
Small Town Boy '37

Dean Tschetter
Bloodsucking Pharoahs of Pittsburgh '90

Shinya Tsukamoto
Tetsuo: The Iron Man '92

Fred Tuch
The Speed Lovers '68

James Tucker
Lunatic '91
Steps from Hell '92

Larry Tucker
Alex in Wonderland '70
Bob & Carol & Ted & Alice '69

Harry Tugend
Caught in the Draft '41
My Lucky Star '38
Second Fiddle '39

Karl Tunberg
Beau Brummel '54
Week-End In Havana '41

Sandy Tung
Across the Tracks '89

Rosemarie Turko
Scarred '84

Ann Turner
The Killing Beach '92

Bonnie Turner
Coneheads '93
Wayne's World '92
Wayne's World 2 '93

Dennis Turner
Poor Little Rich Girl: The Barbara Hutton Story '87

Terry Turner
Coneheads '93
Wayne's World '92
Wayne's World 2 '93

Tyrin Turner
Menace II Society '93

Catherine Turney
The Man I Love '46

John Turturro
Mac '93

John Twist
Band of Angels '57
King Richard and the Crusaders '54
Pittsburgh '42

David N. Twohy
Critters 2: The Main Course '88
The Fugitive '93
Grand Tour: Disaster in Time '92
Terminal Velocity '94
Warlock '89

Nona Tyson
Hot Spot '90

Alan Uger
Blazing Saddles '74

Alfred Uhry
Driving Miss Daisy '89
Mystic Pizza '88
Rich in Love '93

Elwood Ullman
The Stooge '51

Liv Ullmann
Sofie '92

Yves Ulmann
Un Coeur en Hiver '93

Tara Untiedt
Provoked '89

John Updike
Pigeon Feathers '88

Rocco Urbisci
Jo Jo Dancer, Your Life is Calling '86

Jeff Ureles
Cheap Shots '91

Leon Uris
Gunfight at the O.K. Corral '57

Anatoli Usov
The Inner Circle '91

Peter Ustinov
Billy Budd '62
Hot Millions '68
Immortal Battalion '44
Lady L '65

Pierre Uytterhoeven
Bandits '86

Jack Vacek
Rock House '92

Roger Vadim
And God Created Woman '57
Blood and Roses '61
Dangerous Liaisons '60

Emilio Diaz Valcarcel
A Life of Sin '92

Luis Valdez
The Cisco Kid '94
La Bamba '87
La Pastorela '92
Zoot Suit '81

Thanassis Valtinos
Landscape in the Mist '88

Jean-Claude Van Damme
Double Impact '91
Kickboxer '89
Lionheart '90

Anne Van De Putte
To Play or To Die '91

Sytze Van Der Laan
Lily was Here '89

Keith Van Der Wat
Three Bullets for a Long Gun '73

Jaco Van Dormael
Toto le Heros '91

Dale Van Every
Trader Horn '31

Melvin Van Peebles
Greased Lightning '77
Sophisticated Gents '81
The Story of a Three Day Pass '68
Sweet Sweetback's Baadasssss Song '71

Gus Van Sant
Drugstore Cowboy '89
Even Cowgirls Get the Blues '94
My Own Private Idaho '91

Norman Thaddeus Vane
Taxi Dancers '93

Agnes Varda
Cleo from 5 to 7 '61
Jacquot '91
Le Bonheur '65
One Sings, the Other Doesn't '77
Vagabond '85

Michael Varhol
The Big Picture '89
The Last Word '80
Pee Wee's Big Adventure '85

John Varley
Millenium '89

Joseph P. Vasquez
Hangin' with the Homeboys '91

Francis Veber
Hothead '78
La Cage aux Folles '78
La Cage aux Folles 2 '81
Le Magnifique '76
Les Comperes '83
My Father the Hero '93
Pain in the A— '77
Partners '82
Return of the Tall Blond Man With One Black Shoe '74
The Tall Blond Man with One Black Shoe '72
Three Fugitives '89

Anthony Veiller
Red Planet Mars '52

Michael Ventura
Echo Park '86
Roadie '80

Ben Verbong
Lily was Here '89

Mark Verheiden
Timecop '94

Michael Verhoeven
The Nasty Girl '90

Paul Verhoeven
Flesh and Blood '85
Soldier of Orange '78

Cynthia Verlaine
The Substitute '93

Robert Veze
Bikini Summer '91

Michael Vianey
Special Police '85

Mark Victor
Death Hunt '81
Marked for Death '90
Poltergeist '82
Poltergeist 2: The Other Side '86

Gore Vidal
The Best Man '64
Caligula '80
The Catered Affair '56
Dress Gray '86
Is Paris Burning? '68
The Palermo Connection '91
Suddenly, Last Summer '59

King Vidor
The Jack Knife Man '20
Our Daily Bread '34

Peter Viertel
Saboteur '42
White Hunter, Black Heart '90

Daniel Vigne
The King's Whore '91
One Woman or Two '85
The Return of Martin Guerre '83

Jean Vigo
Zero for Conduct '33

Christian Vincent
La Discrete '90

Albert T. Viola
Mondo Balardo '64

C.G. Viola
Shoeshine '47

Joe Viola
Hot Box '72

Luchino Visconti
Bellissima '51

Gino Vissentini
Il Bell'Antonio '60

John Vlahos
Tonto Basin Outlaws '41

Stephen Volk
Gothic '87

Karl Vollmoller
The Blue Angel '30

Alexander Volodin
Autumn Marathon '79

Bobby Von Hayes
Clifford '92

Josef von Sternberg
Dishonored '31

Erich von Stroheim
Devil Doll '36

Lars von Trier
Zentropa '92

Margarethe von Trotta
Coup de Grace '78
Rosa Luxemburg '86
Sheer Madness '84

Niels Vorsel
Zentropa '92

Kurt Voss
Border Radio '88
Delusion '91
Genuine Risk '89
Where the Day Takes You '92

Otakar Votocek
Wings of Fame '93

Natto Wada
An Actor's Revenge '63

Kevin Wade
Mr. Baseball '92
Working Girl '88

Bruce Wagner
A Nightmare on Elm Street 3: Dream Warriors '87
Scenes from the Class Struggle in Beverly Hills '89
Wild Palms '93

Jane Wagner
The Incredible Shrinking Woman '81
Search for Signs of Intelligent Life in the Universe '91

Michael Waite
Fun Down There '88

Ralph Waite
On the Nickel '80

Andrzej Wajda
Danton '82
Land of Promise '74
A Love in Germany '84

Eliot Wald
Camp Nowhere '94

Edwards Waldman
The Pink Panther Strikes Again '76

Frank Waldman
The Pink Panther Strikes Again '76
Return of the Pink Panther '74

Revenge of the Pink Panther '78
Trail of the Pink Panther '82

Andrew Kevin Walker
Brainscan '94

Keith A. Walker
Free Willy '93

Earl W. Wallace
The Broken Chain '93

Irving Wallace
Sincerely Yours '56
Split Second '53
The West Point Story '50

Tommy Lee Wallace
Fright Night 2 '88

Ira Wallach
Boy's Night Out '62
Hot Millions '68

Hugh Walpole
David Copperfield '35

Fred Walton
Hadley's Rebellion '84
The Rosary Murders '87
Trapped '89
When a Stranger Calls Back '93

Peter Wang
A Great Wall '86

Orville Wanzer
The Devil's Mistress '68

David S. Ward
Cannery Row '82
King Ralph '91
Major League '89
The Milagro Beanfield War '88
The Program '93
Saving Grace '86
Sleepless in Seattle '93
Steelyard Blues '73
The Sting '73
The Sting 2 '83

Edmund Ward
Prayer for the Dying '87
Twinsanity '70

Kelly Ward
Once Upon a Forest '93

Stephen Ward
Backbeat '94

Vincent Ward
Map of the Human Heart '93
The Navigator '88
Vigil '84

David Warfield
Kill Me Again '89
Kiss of a Killer '93
Private Investigations '87

Regis Wargnier
Indochine '92

Hal P. Warren
Manos, the Hands of Fate '66

Jerry Warren
Terror of the Bloodhunters '62

John Warren
Naked in New York '93

Joyce Warren
The Ice Runner '93

Deric Washburn
The Border '82
The Deer Hunter '78
Extreme Prejudice '87
Silent Running '71

Daniel Waters
The Adventures of Ford Fairlane '90
Batman Returns '92
Demolition Man '93
Hudson Hawk '91

John Waters
Cry-Baby '90
Desperate Living '77
Female Trouble '74
Hairspray '88
Mondo Trasho '69
Pink Flamingos '72
Polyester '81
Serial Mom '94

Peter Watkins
Edvard Munch '74

John Watson
Robin Hood: Prince of Thieves '91
The Zoo Gang '85

Damon Wayans
Blankman '94
Mo' Money '92

Keenan Ivory Wayans
The Five Heartbeats '91
Hollywood Shuffle '87
I'm Gonna Git You Sucka '88
Low Down Dirty Shame '94

April Wayne
Dead On '93

Frank Wead
Ceiling Zero '35
Dive Bomber '41

Julian Weaver
Demon Possessed '93

James R. Webb
How the West was Won '63

Weaver Webb
Courage Mountain '89

David Wechter
Malibu Bikini Shop '86
Midnight Madness '80

Lu Wei
Farewell My Concubine '93

John Weidner
Midnight Kiss '93
Private Wars '93

Herschel Weingrod
Brewster's Millions '85
Cheaper to Keep Her '80
Kindergarten Cop '90
My Stepmother Is an Alien '88
Pure Luck '91
Trading Places '83
Twins '88

Sandra Weintraub
The Deadliest Art: The Best of the Martial Arts Films '90

Peter Weir
The Cars That Ate Paris '74
Gallipoli '81
Green Card '90
The Last Wave '77
Plumber '79
The Year of Living Dangerously '82

Brenda Weisberg
The Mad Ghoul '43
The Mummy's Ghost '44

Joe Weisenfeld
Anne of Green Gables '85

Stanley Weiser
Project X '87
Wall Street '87

David A. Weiss
All Dogs Go to Heaven '89
Rock-a-Doodle '92

Marie Weiss
The Ref '93

Rob Weiss
Amongst Friends '93

Colin Welland
Chariots of Fire '81
A Dry White Season '89
Twice in a Lifetime '85
Yanks '79

Michael Weller
Hair '79
Lost Angels '89
Ragtime '81

Halsted Welles
The Hanging Tree '59

Orson Welles
Chimes at Midnight '67
Citizen Kane '41
The Lady from Shanghai '48
The Magnificent Ambersons '42
Touch of Evil '58
Treasure Island '72

William A. Wellman
A Star is Born '37

George Wells
Angels in the Outfield '51
Designing Woman '57
Don't Go Near the Water '57
The Gazebo '59
The Horizontal Lieutenant '62
The Impossible Years '68
Merton of the Movies '47
The Show-Off '46

Wim Wenders
Alice in the Cities '74
The American Friend '77
Faraway, So Close! '93
Kings of the Road—In the Course of Time '76
Lightning Over Water '80
Tokyo-Ga '85
Until The End of The World '91
Wings of Desire '88

Gina Wendkos
Ginger Ale Afternoon '89
Jersey Girl '92

Mike Werb
Machine Gun Kelly '58
The Mask '94

Lina Wertmuller
All Screwed Up '74
Blood Feud '79
Camorra: The Naples Connection '85
A Joke of Destiny, Lying in Wait Around the Corner Like a Bandit '84
Love and Anarchy '73
A Night Full of Rain '78
Seduction of Mimi '72
Seven Beauties '76
Sotto, Sotto '85
Summer Night with Greek Profile, Almond Eyes & Scent of Basil '87
Swept Away... '75

Quentin Werty
Dark of the Sun '68

Richard Wesley
Fast Forward '84
Let's Do It Again '75
Native Son '86
Uptown Saturday Night '74

Claudine West
Mrs. Miniver '42
The Mortal Storm '40

Jessamyn West
Stolen Hours '63

Joseph West
Man Made Monster '41

Mae West
Belle of the Nineties '34
Every Day's a Holiday '38
Go West, Young Man '36
Goin' to Town '35
I'm No Angel '33

Klondike Annie '36
Night After Night '32

Roland West
The Bat '26
The Bat Whispers '30

Donald E. Westlake
Cops and Robbers '73
The Grifters '90
Hot Stuff '80
The Stepfather '87
Why Me? '90

Ellen Weston
Lies Before Kisses '92

Fulvio Wetzl
Rorret '87

Haskell Wexler
Latino '85
Medium Cool '69

John Wexley
Angels with Dirty Faces '38

James Whale
Hell's Angels '30

Jim Wheat
The Fly 2 '89

Ken Wheat
The Fly 2 '89

Joss Whedon
Buffy the Vampire Slayer '92

Anne Wheeler
Bye Bye Blues '89

Paul Wheeler
Poldark '75

Graeme Whifler
Dr. Giggles '92
Sonny Boy '87

Denis Whitburn
The Cursed Mountain Mystery '93

Garry Michael White
The Promise '78
Sky Riders '76

David Wickes
Frankenstein '93
Jack the Ripper '88

Bernhard Wicki
The Longest Day '62

Gregory Widen
Backdraft '91
Highlander '86

Bo Widerberg
Elvira Madigan '67

John Wierick
Bopha! '93

Crane Wilbur
Yellow Cargo '36

Billy Wilder
The Apartment '60
Avanti! '72
Ball of Fire '41
Buddy Buddy '81
Double Indemnity '44
The Fortune Cookie '66
The Front Page '74
Irma La Douce '63
Kiss Me, Stupid! '64
The Lost Weekend '45
Love in the Afternoon '57
Ninotchka '39
One, Two, Three '61
The Private Life of Sherlock Holmes '70
Sabrina '54
The Seven Year Itch '55
Some Like It Hot '59
Spirit of St. Louis '57
Stalag 17 '53
Sunset Boulevard '50
Witness for the Prosecution '57

Gene Wilder
The Adventures of Sherlock Holmes' Smarter Brother '78
Haunted Honeymoon '86
See No Evil, Hear No Evil '89
The Woman in Red '84
World's Greatest Lover '77
Young Frankenstein '74

John Wilder
Breaking Home Ties '87
Return to Lonesome Dove '93

Robert Wilder
Flamingo Road '49

Thorton Wilder
Shadow of a Doubt '43

Yvonne Wilder
The Return of Count Yorga '71

Ethan Wiley
House '86
House 2: The Second Story '87

Elaine Wilkerson
The Speed Lovers '68

Rich Wilkes
Airheads '94

Charles Wilkinson
Quarantine '89

Bob Williams
Silver City Bonanza '51

Charles Williams
Hot Spot '90

Chuck Williams
Dark Rider '91

Emlyn Williams
The Last Days of Dolwyn '49
The Man Who Knew Too Much '34

Samm-Art Williams
Charlotte Forten's Mission: Experiment in Freedom '85

Spencer Williams, Jr.
Blood of Jesus '41
Harlem Rides the Range '39
Son of Ingagi '40

Tennessee Williams
Baby Doll '56
The Glass Menagerie '87
Orpheus Descending '91
The Rose Tattoo '55
A Streetcar Named Desire '51

David Williamson
The Club '81
Dangerous Life '89
Don's Party '76
Gallipoli '81
Phar Lap '84
Travelling North '87
The Year of Living Dangerously '82

Fred Williamson
Adios Amigo '75
Boss '74

Thomas Williamson
Escape Me Never '47

Calder Willingham
The Graduate '67
Little Big Man '70
One-Eyed Jacks '61
Paths of Glory '57
Rambling Rose '91
Thieves Like Us '74
The Vikings '58

Constance Willis
A Man for All Seasons '66

Alice Wilson
I'm Dangerous Tonight '90

Carey Wilson
He Who Gets Slapped '24
Mutiny on the Bounty '35

David Wilson
The Perfect Weapon '91
Strangers in Good Company '91

Dean Wilson
Blind Faith '89

Gerald Wilson
Lawman '71

Hugh Wilson
Burglar '87
Guarding Tess '94
Police Academy '84
Rustler's Rhapsody '85
Stroker Ace '83

Michael Wilson
The Bridge on the River Kwai '57
Five Fingers '52

Michael G. Wilson
For Your Eyes Only '81
License to Kill '89
The Living Daylights '87
Octopussy '83
Planet of the Apes '68
A View to a Kill '85

Richard Wilson
It's All True '93

S.S. Wilson
*batteries not included '87
Ghost Dad '90
Heart and Souls '93
Short Circuit '86
Short Circuit 2 '88
Tremors '89

Sandy Wilson
American Boyfriends '89
My American Cousin '85

Snoo Wilson
Shadey '87

Kurt Wimmer
The Neighbor '93

Arthur Wimperis
Mrs. Miniver '42
The Private Life of Henry VIII '33
Young Bess '53

Charles Winkler
Disturbed '90
You Talkin' to Me? '87

Irwin Winkler
Guilty by Suspicion '91

Terence H. Winkless
Corporate Affairs '90
He's My Girl '87
The Howling '81
Rage and Honor '92

Michael Winner
Appointment with Death '88
The Big Sleep '78
Bullseye! '90
A Chorus of Disapproval '89
Firepower '79
Murder on the Campus '52
The Sentinel '76
The Wicked Lady '83

Peter Winograd
One Last Run '89

Alex Winter
Freaked '93

Norman Wisdom
What's Good for the Goose '93

Thomas Wiseman
Romantic Englishwoman '75

Doris Wishman
Bad Girls Go to Hell '65

Bill Wittliff
The Black Stallion '79
Country '84
The Cowboy Way '94

Honeysuckle Rose '80
Lone Justice '93
Lonesome Dove '89
Raggedy Man '81
Red Headed Stranger '87

Stefan Wodoslowsky
Crazy Moon '87

John Wohlbruck
End of the Line '88

David M. Wolf
Hit! '73

Dick Wolf
Gas '81
Masquerade '88
No Man's Land '87
School Ties '92
Skateboard '77

Andy Wolk
Criminal Justice '90

James Wolpaw
Complex World '92

Barry Wong
Hard-Boiled '92

James Wong
The Boys Next Door '85

John Woo
The Killer '90

Charles Wood
The Charge of the Light Brigade '68
Cuba '79
Help! '65
How I Won the War '67
The Knack '65

Edward D. Wood, Jr.
The Bride & the Beast '58
Orgy of the Dead '65
The Violent Years '56

Victoria Wood
Happy Since I Met You '89

Christopher Wooden
Dinosaur Island '93

Grahame Woods
Glory Enough for All: The Discovery of Insulin '92

Walter Woods
The Pony Express '25

Abbe Wool
Roadside Prophets '92

Linda Woolverton
Homeward Bound: The Incredible Journey '93

David Worth
Lady Dragon '92

Geoffrey Wright
Romper Stomper '92

Rudy Wurlitzer
Candy Mountain '87
Glen and Randa '71
Little Buddha '93
Pat Garrett & Billy the Kid '73
Shadow of the Wolf '92
Voyager '91
Walker '87
Wind '92

William Wyler
Detective Story '51

Philip Wylie
Island of Lost Souls '32

Ned Wynn
Don't Go to Sleep '82

Tracy Keenan Wynn
Carolina Skeletons '92
The Deep '77
The Drowning Pool '75
The FBI Murders '88
The Longest Yard '74

Jim Wynorski
Big Bad Mama 2 '87
Chopping Mall '86
Deathstalker 2: Duel of the Titans '87
Final Embrace '92
Forbidden World '82
The Haunting of Morella '91
The Lost Empire '83
Not of This Earth '88
Screwballs '83
Sorceress '82
Think Big '90

David Yallop
Beyond Reasonable Doubt '80

Mitsuo Yanagimachi
Shadow of China '91

Jack Yellen
My Lucky Star '38

Linda Yellen
Chantilly Lace '93

Rafael Yglesias
Fearless '93

Yoshikata Yoda
A Geisha '53
Sansho the Bailiff '54
Utamaro and His Five Women '46

Jeff Yonis
Bloodfist 5: Human Target '93
Firehawk '93

Philip Yordan
Bad Man's River '72
Battle of the Bulge '65
Big Combo '55
Bloody Wednesday '87
Blowing Wild '54
The Bramble Bush '60
The Bravados '58
Broken Lance '54
Captain Apache '71
The Chase '46
Day of the Triffids '63
Detective Story '51
Dillinger '45
Drums in the Deep South '51
El Cid '61
The Fall of the Roman Empire '64
55 Days at Peking '63
God's Little Acre '58
The Harder They Fall '56
Houdini '53
House of Strangers '49
Johnny Guitar '53
The King of Kings '61
The Man from Laramie '55
Men in War '57
Mutiny '52
Naked Jungle '54
Reign of Terror '49
Savage Wilderness '55
Studs Lonigan '60
The Unholy '88
Whistle Stop '46

Graham Yost
Speed '94

Robert Yost
Arizona Mahoney '36
Drift Fence '36

John Sacret Young
China Beach '88
Romero '89
Testament '83

Mark Young
Once Upon a Forest '93

Peter Young
The Fox and the Hound '81

Robert M. Young
Ballad of Gregorio Cortez '83
Triumph of the Spirit '89

Waldemar Young
Island of Lost Souls '32

The Lives of a Bengal Lancer '35

Jerry Younkins
The Demon Lover '77

Brian Yuzna
From Beyond '86

Bruce Zabel
Official Denial '93

Steven Zaillian
Awakenings '90
Clear and Present Danger '94
The Falcon and the Snowman '85
Jack the Bear '93
Schindler's List '93
Searching for Bobby Fischer '93

Nancy Zala
Round Numbers '91

Krzysztof Zanussi
The Structure of Crystals '69

Mier Zarchi
I Spit on Your Grave '77

Cesare Zavattini
Bellissima '51
The Bicycle Thief '48
The Children Are Watching Us '44
The Garden of the Finzi-Continis '71
Miracle in Milan '51
Shoeshine '47
Two Women '61
Umberto D '55

Edward Zebrowski
The Structure of Crystals '69

Franco Zeffirelli
Hamlet '90
The Taming of the Shrew '67

Alfred Zeisler
Enemy of Women '44

Robert Zemeckis
Back to the Future '85
Back to the Future, Part 2 '89
Back to the Future, Part 3 '90
I Wanna Hold Your Hand '78
1941 '79
Trespass '92
Used Cars '80

Michael Zettler
Sweet Lorraine '87

Shan Yuan Zhu
China, My Sorrow '89

Claude Zidi
My New Partner '84

Ulrich Zieger
Faraway, So Close! '93

Scott Ziehl
Money to Burn '94

Zhang Ziliang
Yellow Earth '89

Harv Zimmel
Shoot to Kill '88
Snow Kill '90

Stephen Zito
Diana: Her True Story '93
Full Exposure: The Sex Tape Scandals '89

David Zucker
Airplane! '80
Kentucky Fried Movie '77
The Naked Gun: From the Files of Police Squad '88
Naked Gun 33 1/3: The Final Insult '94
Naked Gun 2 1/2: The Smell of Fear '91
Police Squad! Help Wanted! '82
Top Secret! '84

Jerry Zucker
Airplane! *'80*
Kentucky Fried Movie *'77*
The Naked Gun: From the Files
  of Police Squad *'88*
Police Squad! Help Wanted! *'82*
Top Secret! *'84*

George Zuckerman
Written on the Wind *'56*

Carl Zuckmayer
The Blue Angel *'30*

Alan Zweibel
Dragnet *'87*
North *'94*

Edward Zwick
Special Bulletin *'83*

COMPOSER INDEX

The **COMPOSER INDEX** lists the video accomplishments of more than 800 notable composers, lyricists, and arrangers. Names are presented in a first name, last name format, while the arrangement is alphabetical by last name. **Cast**, **Director**, and **Writer Indexes** immediately precede this index.

AC/DC
Maximum Overdrive '86

Barry Adamson
Delusion '91

Richard Addinsell
A Christmas Carol '51

John Addison
The Amorous Adventures of Moll Flanders '65
The Bastard '78
A Bridge Too Far '77
Carlton Browne of the F.O. '59
The Charge of the Light Brigade '68
Code Name: Emerald '85
Eleanor: First Lady of the World '82
The Entertainer '60
A Fine Madness '66
Grace Quigley '84
Guns at Batasi '64
The Honey Pot '67
Joseph Andrews '77
The Loneliness of the Long Distance Runner '62
Look Back in Anger '58
The Loved One '65
Lucky Jim '58
Luther '74
Reach for the Sky '56
Ride a Wild Pony '75
The Seven Percent Solution '76
Sleuth '72
Something in Common '86
Start the Revolution Without Me '70
Swashbuckler '76
A Taste of Honey '61
Tom Jones '63
Torn Curtain '66

Larry Adler
A Cry from the Streets '57
Genevieve '53
Great Chase '63

Yashushi Akutagawa
An Actor's Revenge '63

Jeff Alexander
Gun Glory '57
Westward the Women '51

Cameron Allan
The Good Wife '86
Jericho Fever '93
Midnite Spares '85

Billy Allen
The Acid Eaters '67

Dave Allen
The Harvest '92

Woody Allen
Sleeper '73

Daniele Amfitheatrof
The Last Hunt '56

David Amram
The Arrangement '69
The Manchurian Candidate '62
Splendor in the Grass '61

Laurie Anderson
Monster in a Box '92
Swimming to Cambodia '87

Pete Anderson
Chasers '94

Pagan Angel
The Awful Dr. Orlof '62

Ramirez Angel
The Awful Dr. Orlof '62

Anthrax
Pledge Night '90

Philip Appleby
Maria's Child '93

Harold Arlen
Cabin in the Sky '43
Gay Purr-ee '62

Martin Armiger
The Crossing '92
Sweetie '89

Malcolm Arnold
Africa Texas Style '67
The Belles of St. Trinian's '53
Blue Murder at St. Trinian's '56
The Bridge on the River Kwai '57
Captain's Paradise '53
The Chalk Garden '64
Curtain Up '53
David Copperfield '70
Devil on Horseback '54
Four Sided Triangle '53
The Great St. Trinian's Train Robbery '66
Hobson's Choice '53
The Inn of the Sixth Happiness '58
Island in the Sun '57
The Key '58
No Love for Johnnie '60

The Pure Hell of St. Trinian's '61
The Sea Shall Not Have Them '55
The Sleeping Tiger '54
Solomon and Sheba '59
A Stolen Face '52
Suddenly, Last Summer '59
Trapeze '56
Tunes of Glory '60
Whistle Down the Wind '62
Wings of Danger '52

Bruce Arnston
Ernest Rides Again '93
Ernest Scared Stupid '91

Eduard Artemyev
Close to Eden '90
Homer and Eddie '89
The Inner Circle '91
A Slave of Love '78
Solaris '72
Stalker '79

Howard Ashman
Aladdin '92
Beauty and the Beast '91
The Little Mermaid '89
Little Shop of Horrors '86

Paul Aston
Joey Breaker '93

Michael Atkinson
Backlash '86

Georges Auric
Dead of Night '45
Gervaise '56
Lola Montes '55
Wages of Fear '55

Gene Austin
Follow the Leader '44

Burt Bacharach
After the Fox '66
Arthur '81
Arthur 2: On the Rocks '88
Butch Cassidy and the Sundance Kid '69
Casino Royale '67
Lost Horizon '37
Night Shift '82
The Sad Sack '57
Together? '79
What's New Pussycat? '65

Brian Backus
Young Guns '88

Angelo Badalamenti
Across the Great Divide '76
Blue Velvet '86
The Comfort of Strangers '91
Cousins '89
Gordon's War '73
Hotel Room '93
Law and Disorder '74
Naked in New York '93
National Lampoon's Christmas Vacation '89
A Nightmare on Elm Street 3: Dream Warriors '87
Parents '89
Tough Guys Don't Dance '87
Twin Peaks '90
Twin Peaks '90
Twin Peaks: Fire Walk with Me '92
Wait Until Spring, Bandini '90
Weeds '87
Wild at Heart '90

Wally Badarou
Kiss of the Spider Woman '85
The Lunatic '92

Tom Bahler
Cold Feet '89
Fast Forward '84
Mary, Mary, Bloody Mary '76
The Object of Beauty '91

Buddy Baker
The Apple Dumpling Gang '75
The Apple Dumpling Gang Rides Again '79
The Bears & I '74
The Devil & Max Devlin '81
The Fox and the Hound '81
The Gnome-Mobile '67
Hot Lead & Cold Feet '78
Million Dollar Duck '71
The Misadventures of Merlin Jones '63
Monkey's Uncle '65
Napoleon and Samantha '72
No Deposit, No Return '76
The Puppetoon Movie '87
The Shaggy D.A. '76
Summer Magic '63
Superdad '73
A Tiger Walks '64
The Treasure of Matecumbe '76

Michael Conway Baker
The Deserters '80s
The Grey Fox '83

Loyalties '86
One Magic Christmas '85
Showdown at Williams Creek '91
Silence of the North '81

Richard Band
The Alchemist '81
Arena '88
The Arrival '90
Bride of Re-Animator '89
The Caller '87
Crash and Burn '90
Day Time Ended '80
Dr. Heckyl and Mr. Hype '80
Doctor Mordrid: Master of the Unknown '92
Dollman vs Demonic Toys '93
Dolls '87
Dragonworld '93
Dungeonmaster '85
The Eliminators '86
From Beyond '86
Ghoulies '85
The House on Sorority Row '83
Laserblast '78
Metalstorm '83
Mutant '83
Parasite '81
The Pit & the Pendulum '91
Prison '88
Puppet Master '89
Puppet Master 2 '91
Puppet Master 3: Toulon's Revenge '91
Puppet Master 4 '93
The Re-Animator '85
Remote '93
The Resurrected '91
Terrorvision '86
Time Walker '82
Trancers 3: Deth Lives '92
Troll '85
Zone Troopers '85

Claus Bantzer
Drachenfutter '87

Jack Baran
Great Balls of Fire '89

Samuel Barber
The Elephant Man '80

John Barnes
Bebe's Kids '92
Daughters of the Dust '92

John Barry
Alice's Adventures in Wonderland '72
Beat Girl '60

▲ 1537 • COMPOSER INDEX

Barry ▶cont.

The Betsy '78
The Black Hole '79
Body Heat '81
Born Free '66
Chaplin '92
The Chase '66
The Cotton Club '84
Dances with Wolves '90
The Day of the Locust '75
Deception '92
The Deep '77
Diamonds are Forever '71
Dr. No '62
A Doll's House '73
The Dove '68
Dutchman '67
Eleanor & Franklin '76
First Love '77
Frances '82
From Russia with Love '63
Game of Death '79
The Gathering '77
The Golden Seal '83
Goldfinger '64
Hammett '82
Hanover Street '79
Hearts of Fire '87
High Road to China '83
Howard the Duck '86
Indecent Proposal '93
Inside Moves '80
The Ipcress File '65
The Jagged Edge '85
A Killing Affair '85
King Kong '76
King Rat '65
The Knack '65
The Last Valley '71
Legend of the Lone Ranger '81
The Lion in Winter '68
The Living Daylights '87
Love Among the Ruins '75
The Man with the Golden Gun '74
Masquerade '88
Midnight Cowboy '69
Mike's Murder '84
Monte Walsh '70
Moonraker '79
Murder by Phone '82
Murphy's War '71
My Life '93
Never Let Go '60
Night Games '80
Octopussy '83
On Her Majesty's Secret Service '69
Out of Africa '85
Peggy Sue Got Married '86
Petulia '68
The Public Eye '92
The Quiller Memorandum '66
Raise the Titanic '80
Robin and Marian '76
The Rocky Horror Picture Show '75
Seance on a Wet Afternoon '64
Shampoo '75
Somewhere in Time '80
Star Crash '78
Svengali '83
The Tamarind Seed '74
They Might Be Giants '71
Thunderball '65
Touched by Love '80
Until September '84
A View to a Kill '85
War Between the Tates '76
The White Buffalo '77
Willa '79
The Wrong Box '66
You Only Live Twice '67
Zulu '64

Steve Bartek
Cabin Boy '94
Guilty as Charged '92

Count Basie
Sex and the Single Girl '64

Richard Baskin
Buffalo Bill & the Indians '76
Honeysuckle Rose '80
Nashville '75
Uforia '81
Welcome to L.A. '77

Les Baxter
Battle Beyond the Sun '63
Battle Shock '56
Beach Blanket Bingo '65
Beach Party '63
The Beast Within '82
The Big Doll House '71
Bikini Beach '64
Born Again '78
The Bride & the Beast '58
The Comedy of Terrors '64
Cry of the Banshee '70
Devil & Leroy Basset '73
Dr. Goldfoot and the Bikini Machine '66
The Dunwich Horror '70
The Fall of the House of Usher '60
Frogs '72
Girl in Black Stockings '57
How to Stuff a Wild Bikini '65
The Invaders '63
The Invisible Boy '57
The Key Man '57
Lone Ranger and the Lost City of Gold '58
Master of the World '61
Monika '63
Muscle Beach Party '64
Pajama Party '64
Panic in the Year Zero! '62
The Pit and the Pendulum '61
The Raven '63
Samson and the 7 Miracles of the World '62
Storm Rider '57
Switchblade Sisters '75
Tales of Terror '62
Terror in the Jungle '68
Torture Chamber of Baron Blood '72
Wild in the Streets '68
X: The Man with X-Ray Eyes '63

Jeff Beal
Cheap Shots '91
Ring of Steel '94

The Beatles
Let It Be '70

Jeff Beck
Blue Chips '94
The Pope Must Diet '91

Frank Becker
American Kickboxer 1 '91
Terminal Bliss '91

Vassal Benford
Class Act '91
House Party 2: The Pajama Jam '91

James Bennett
Poison '91
Swoon '91

Richard Rodney Bennett
The Attic: The Hiding of Anne Frank '88
Billy Liar '63
Brink's Job '78
The Devil's Disciple '59
Ebony Tower '86
Enchanted April '92
Equus '77
Far from the Madding Crowd '67
Four Weddings and a Funeral '93
Heavens Above '63
Indiscreet '58

Lady Caroline Lamb '73
The Mark '61
Murder on the Orient Express '74
Nicholas and Alexandra '71
Only Two Can Play '62
Permission To Kill '75
Poor Little Rich Girl: The Barbara Hutton Story '87
Return of the Soldier '82
Secret Ceremony '69
The Wrong Arm of the Law '63
Yanks '79

Robby Benson
Die Laughing '80

Alan Bergman
Yentl '83

Marilyn Bergman
Yentl '83

Michael Berkeley
Twenty-One '91

Irving Berlin
Alexander's Ragtime Band '38
Carefree '38
The Cocoanuts '29
Easter Parade '48
Follow the Fleet '36
Hallelujah! '29
Le Bal '82
On the Avenue '37
Second Fiddle '39
Top Hat '35

Marie Bernard
Strangers in Good Company '91

Charles Bernstein
The Allnighter '87
April Fool's Day '86
Are You in the House Alone? '78
Bogie: The Last Hero '80
Caroline? '90
Chase '85
Coast to Coast '80
Cujo '83
Deadly Friend '86
Dudes '87
The Entity '83
Excessive Force '93
Foolin' Around '80
Gator '76
The House on Garibaldi Street '79
The Hunter '80
Independence Day '83
Invasion of the Bee Girls '73
Ivory Hunters '90
The Last Fling '86
The Long, Hot Summer '86
Love at First Bite '79
The Man Who Broke 1,000 Chains '87
Mr. Majestyk '74
Nightmare in Badham County '76
A Nightmare on Elm Street '84
Outlaw Blues '77
The Rumor Mill '86
Sadat '83
Scruples '80
Secret Weapons '85
The Shrieking '73
A Small Town in Texas '76
Steel Cowboy '78
Viva Knievel! '77
White Lightning '73
Wild & Wooly '78
The Winds of Kitty Hawk '78

Elmer Bernstein
The Age of Innocence '93
Airplane! '80
Airplane 2: The Sequel '82
Amazing Grace & Chuck '87
Amazing Mr. Blunden '72
An American Werewolf in London '81
The Babe '92

Baby, the Rain Must Fall '64
Big Jake '71
Birdman of Alcatraz '62
Bloodbrothers '78
Boots Malone '52
The Bridge at Remagen '69
The Buccaneer '58
By Love Possessed '61
Cahill: United States Marshal '73
Canadian Bacon '94
The Carpetbaggers '64
Cast a Giant Shadow '66
Cat Women of the Moon '53
The Cemetery Club '93
The Chisholms '79
Class '83
The Comancheros '61
Da '88
Desire Under the Elms '58
Doctors' Wives '71
The Ewok Adventure '84
Fallen Angels 1 '93
Fear Strikes Out '57
Five Days One Summer '82
From Noon Till Three '76
From the Terrace '60
Funny Farm '88
Ghostbusters '84
God's Little Acre '58
Going Ape! '81
The Good Mother '88
The Good Son '93
The Great Escape '63
The Great Santini '80
The Grifters '90
Gulag '85
Guns of the Magnificent Seven '69
The Guyana Tragedy: The Story of Jim Jones '80
The Hallelujah Trail '65
Hamburger...The Motion Picture '86
Hawaii '66
Hud '63
I Love You, Alice B. Toklas '68
The Incredible Sarah '76
It's a Dog's Life '55
Kings Go Forth '58
Legal Eagles '86
Leonard Part 6 '87
The Liberation of L.B. Jones '70
Little Women '78
Lost in Yonkers '93
Love with the Proper Stranger '63
The Magnificent Seven '60
Make Haste to Live '54
The Man with the Golden Arm '55
McQ '74
Meatballs '79
Men in War '57
My Left Foot '89
National Lampoon's Animal House '78
Never Wave at a WAC '52
A Night in the Life of Jimmy Reardon '88
The Old Curiosity Shop '75
Oscar '91
Prince Jack '83
A Rage in Harlem '91
Rambling Rose '91
The Rat Race '60
Report to the Commissioner '74
Return of the Seven '66
Robot Monster '53
Saturn 3 '80
The Scalphunters '68
See No Evil '71
The Shootist '76
Silent Raiders '54
Slap Shot '77
Slipstream '89
Some Came Running '58
Sons of Katie Elder '65
Spacehunter: Adventures in the Forbidden Zone '83

Spies Like Us '85
Stripes '81
Summer and Smoke '61
Sweet Smell of Success '57
The Ten Commandments '56
Thoroughly Modern Millie '67
Three Amigos '86
The Tin Star '57
To Kill a Mockingbird '62
Trading Places '83
The Trial of Billy Jack '74
True Grit '69
Walk in the Spring Rain '70
Walk on the Wild Side '62
Will Penny '67
The World of Henry Orient '64
Zulu Dawn '79

Leonard Bernstein
On the Town '49
On the Waterfront '54
West Side Story '61

Peter Bernstein
The Alamo: Thirteen Days to Glory '87
Bolero '84
Club Med '83
Fifty/Fifty '93
Hot Dog...The Movie! '83
Miracles '86
Morgan Stewart's Coming Home '87
My Science Project '85
National Lampoon's Class Reunion '82
Nightbreaker '89
Remote Control '88
Silent Rage '82
Summer Fantasy '84
Surf 2 '84

Nick Bicat
The Hawk '93
Oliver Twist '82
The Reflecting Skin '91
The Scarlet Pimpernel '82
Stealing Heaven '88
Strapless '90
To Catch a King '84
Wetherby '85

Arnold Bieber
Small Time '91

Ruben Blades
Q & A '90
The Story of Fausta '88

Howard Blake
Amityville 2: The Possession '82
Amityville 3: The Demon '83
Flash Gordon '80
The Lords of Discipline '83
A Month in the Country '87
The Odd Job '78
The Riddle of the Sands '79
S.O.S. Titanic '79

Terence Blanchard
Assault at West Point: The Court-Martial of Johnson Whittaker '94
Crooklyn '94
The Inkwell '94
Jungle Fever '91
Malcolm X '92
Sugar Hill '94

Ralph Blane
Athena '54

George Blondheim
Bye Bye Blues '89

Blue Oyster Cult
Bad Channels '92

Michael Boddicker
The Adventures of Buckaroo Banzai Across the Eighth Dimension '84
The Adventures of Milo & Otis '89
Get Crazy '83

White Water Summer '87

Todd Boekelheide
The Blood of Heroes '89
Dear America: Letters Home
    from Vietnam '88
Dim Sum: A Little Bit of Heart
    '85
Exposure '91

Claude Bolling
The Awakening '80
The Bay Boy '85
Borsalino '70
California Suite '78
Catch Me a Spy '71
The Day and the Hour '63
The Hands of Orlac '60
Le Magnifique '76
Lucky Luke: Daisy Town '71
The Passenger '75
Silver Bears '78
Willie & Phil '80

Bomb Squad
Juice '92

Bernardo Bonazzi
All Tied Up '92
Don Juan, My Love '90
Matador '86
Women on the Verge of a
    Nervous Breakdown '88

Luis Bonfa
Black Orpheus '58

Bono
In the Name of the Father '93

Rick Boston
The Harvest '92

Simon Boswell
Dangerous Obsession '88
Dust Devil '93
Hardware '90
Santa Sangre '90

Roger Bourland
New Jack City '91
Night Life '90
The Trouble with Dick '88
The Wolf at the Door '87

David Bowie
Christiane F. '82
Labyrinth '86
Party! Party! '83

Charles Bradshaw
Miracle of Morgan's Creek '44
The Stunt Man '80

Alan Brewer
Tokyo Pop '88

Peter Brewis
Morons from Outer Space '85
The Tall Guy '89

Leslie Bricusse
Babes in Toyland '86
Doctor Dolittle '67
Goodbye, Mr. Chips '69
Scrooge '70
Tom and Jerry: The Movie '93
Willy Wonka & the Chocolate
    Factory '71

David Brockman
Frankenstein '31

Nicholas Brodszky
Rich, Young and Pretty '51

Joseph Brooks
If Ever I See You Again '78
Invitation to the Wedding '73
The Lords of Flatbush '74
You Light Up My Life '77

Philip Brophy
Body Melt '93

Bruce Broughton
All I Want for Christmas '91
Baby's Day Out '94
Betsy's Wedding '90

Big Shots '87
The Blue and the Gray '85
The Boy Who Could Fly '86
The Cowboy & the Ballerina '84
Cross My Heart '88
Desperate Lives '82
The First Olympics: Athens
    1896 '84
For Love or Money '93
George Washington: The
    Forging of a Nation '86
Harry and the Hendersons '87
Homeward Bound: The
    Incredible Journey '93
Honey, I Blew Up the Kid '92
Ice Pirates '84
Jacknife '89
Killjoy '81
Last Rites '88
M.A.D.D.: Mothers Against
    Drunk Driving '83
The Monster Squad '87
One Shoe Makes It Murder '82
The Presidio '88
The Prodigal '83
The Rescue '88
The Rescuers Down Under '90
Return of Frank Cannon '80
Silverado '85
So I Married an Axe Murderer
    '93
Sorry, Wrong Number '89
Square Dance '87
Stay Tuned '92
Sweet Liberty '86
Tombstone '93
Young Sherlock Holmes '85

Leo Brower
Like Water for Chocolate '93

James Brown
Black Caesar '73

Nacio Herb Brown
Broadway Melody '29
Broadway Melody of 1936 '35
Broadway Melody of 1938 '37

Jackson Browne
Incident at Oglala: The Leonard
    Peltier Story '92

Jimmy Buffett
Rancho Deluxe '75

Sonny Burke
Lady and the Tramp '55

Ralph Burns
After the Promise '87
All Dogs Go to Heaven '89
All That Jazz '79
Annie '82
Bert Rigby, You're a Fool '89
Cabaret '72
A Chorus Line '85
Ernie Kovacs: Between the
    Laughter '84
First Family '80
In the Mood '87
The Josephine Baker Story '90
Kiss Me Goodbye '82
Lenny '74
Make Me an Offer '80
Movie, Movie '78
Moving Violations '85
The Muppets Take Manhattan
    '84
My Favorite Year '82
National Lampoon's Vacation
    '83
New York, New York '77
Penalty Phase '86
Pennies From Heaven '81
Perfect '85
Side Show '84
Star 80 '83
Sweet Bird of Youth '89
Urban Cowboy '80

George Burt
Fool for Love '86
Secret Honor '85

Carter Burwell
Airheads '94
And the Band Played On '93
Barton Fink '91
The Beat '88
Blood Simple '85
Buffy the Vampire Slayer '92
Checking Out '89
A Dangerous Woman '93
Doc Hollywood '91
The Hudsucker Proxy '93
It Takes Two '88
Pass the Ammo '88
Psycho 3 '86
Raising Arizona '87
Storyville '92
This Boy's Life '93
Waterland '92
Wayne's World 2 '93

Cobb Bussinger
I Don't Buy Kisses Anymore '92

David Buttolph
Crash Dive '43

David Byrne
The Last Emperor '87
Married to the Mob '88
True Stories '86

Sammy Cahn
Anchors Aweigh '45
Rich, Young and Pretty '51
The West Point Story '50

John Cale
Something Wild '86

Tony Carey
Lethal Obsession '87

Antonio Carlos
Gabriela '84

Larry Carlton
Against All Odds '84

Hoagy Carmichael
Hoppity Goes to Town '41

John Carpenter
Assault on Precinct 13 '76
Big Trouble in Little China '86
Body Bags '93
Christine '84
Dark Star '74
Escape from New York '81
The Fog '78
Halloween '78
Halloween 2: The Nightmare
    Isn't Over! '81
Halloween 3: Season of the
    Witch '82
Prince of Darkness '87
They Live '88

Gaylord Carter
Docks of New York '28
Last Command '28
My Best Girl '27
Old Ironsides '26
Rebecca of Sunnybrook Farm
    '17
Running Wild '27
Spiders '18
The Ten Commandments '23
The Wedding March '28

Del Casher
Tropical Heat '93

Matthieu Chabrol
The Cry of the Owl '92
Madame Bovary '91
The Story of Women '88

Gary Chang
The Breakfast Club '85
Dead Bang '89
52 Pick-Up '86
Firewalker '86
The House of Usher '88
Miami Blues '90
The Nightman '93
The Perfect Weapon '91
A Shock to the System '90

Sniper '92
Sticky Fingers '88
3:15—The Moment of Truth '86
Under Siege '92

Charlie Chaplin
Modern Times '36

John Charles
The Quiet Earth '85
A Soldier's Tale '91

Tom Chase
And God Created Woman '88
Catch the Heat '87
Creature '85
Little Nemo: Adventures in
    Slumberland '92
976-EVIL '88
Scared to Death '80
Syngenor '90

Cheap Trick
Rock & Rule '83

Frederick Chopin
Le Bal '82

Frank Churchill
Bambi '42
Dumbo '41
Snow White and the Seven
    Dwarfs '37

Eric Clapton
Communion '89
Edge of Darkness '86
The Hit '85
Homeboy '88
Lethal Weapon '87
Lethal Weapon 2 '89
Lethal Weapon 3 '92
Rush '91
Wonderwall: The Movie '69

Stanley Clarke
Book of Love '91
Boyz N the Hood '91
Cool As Ice '91
The Five Heartbeats '91
Passenger 57 '92
Poetic Justice '93
Watch It '93
What's Love Got to Do With It?
    '93

The Clash
Party! Party! '83

George S. Clinton
American Ninja '85
American Ninja 3: Blood Hunt
    '89
Avenging Force '86
The Boys Next Door '85
Brainscan '94
Cheech and Chong: Still
    Smokin' '83
Gotham '88
Hard Promises '92
Lake Consequence '92
The Lion of Africa '87
Mother's Boys '94
Platoon Leader '87
Wild Thing '87

Tom Cochrane
Skier's Dream '88

Harvey R. Cohen
Ghost Town '88

Leonard Cohen
McCabe & Mrs. Miller '71

Cy Coleman
Family Business '89
Father Goose '64
Garbo Talks '84
Power '86
Sweet Charity '69

Graeme Coleman
Common Bonds '91
Final Round '93

Jim Coleman
The Unbelievable Truth '90

Michel Colombier
Against All Odds '84
Backtrack '89
Buried Alive '90
Colossus: The Forbin Project
    '70
Cop '88
The Couch Trip '87
Deep Cover '92
Diary of a Hitman '92
Florida Straits '87
Folks! '92
The Golden Child '86
Impulse '90
Les Assassins de L'Ordre '71
Loverboy '89
Major League 2 '94
Midnight Cabaret '90
The Money Pit '86
New Jack City '91
Out Cold '89
Paul and Michelle '74
Posse '93
The Program '93
Purple Rain '84
Ruthless People '86
Satisfaction '88
Steel '80
Strictly Business '91
Surrender '87
White Nights '85
Who's Harry Crumb? '89
The Wizard of Loneliness '88

Betty Comden
It's Always Fair Weather '55
On the Town '91

Harry Connick, Jr.
When Harry Met Sally '89

Rick Conrad
Amityville 4 '89
Crime Zone '88
The Drifter '88
The Nest '88
The Terror Within '89
Watchers 2 '90

Jean Constantin
The 400 Blows '59

Bill Conti
The Adventures of Huck Finn
    '93
Baby Boom '87
Backstreet Dreams '90
Bad Boys '83
The Bear '89
Beer '85
The Big Blue '88
The Big Fix '78
Big Trouble '86
Blood In...Blood Out: Bound by
    Honor '93
Blume in Love '73
The Boss' Wife '86
Broadcast News '87
By the Sword '93
Carbon Copy '81
Citizens Band '77
Cohen and Tate '88
Dreamer '79
8 Seconds '94
F/X '86
F.I.S.T. '78
For Keeps '88
For Your Eyes Only '81
The Formula '80
The Fourth War '90
Gloria '80
Goldengirl '79
Gotcha! '85
Happy New Year '87
Harry and Tonto '74
I Love N.Y. '87
I, the Jury '82
The Karate Kid '84
The Karate Kid: Part 2 '86
The Karate Kid: Part 3 '89
Lean on Me '89
Lock Up '89
A Man, a Woman, and a Bank
    '79

Conti ▶*cont.*

Mass Appeal '84
Masters of the Universe '87
Murderers Among Us: The
  Simon Wiesenthal Story '89
Necessary Roughness '91
Neighbors '81
The Next Karate Kid '94
Next Stop, Greenwich Village
  '76
A Night in the Life of Jimmy
  Reardon '88
Nomads '86
North and South Book 1 '85
North and South Book 2 '86
Paradise Alley '78
Prayer for the Dying '87
Private Benjamin '80
The Right Stuff '83
Rocky '76
Rocky 2 '79
Rocky 3 '82
Rocky 5 '90
Rookie of the Year '93
The Scout '94
The Seduction of Joe Tynan '79
Split Image '82
The Terry Fox Story '83
That Championship Season '82
Unfaithfully Yours '84
An Unmarried Woman '78
Victory '81
Year of the Gun '91

Michael Convertino
Aspen Extreme '93
Bodies, Rest & Motion '93
Bull Durham '88
Children of a Lesser God '86
The Doctor '91
The End of Innocence '90
Guarding Tess '94
The Hidden '87
Hollywood Vice Sqaud '86
Mistress '91
Queen of Hearts '89
The Waterdance '91
Wrestling Ernest Hemingway
  '93

Ry Cooder
Alamo Bay '85
Blue City '86
The Border '82
Brewster's Millions '85
Crossroads '86
Geronimo: An American
  Legend '93
Johnny Handsome '89
The Long Riders '80
Paris, Texas '83
Southern Comfort '81
Streets of Fire '84
Tales from the Crypt '89
Trespass '92

David Cope
Out '88

Stewart Copeland
Airborne '93
The First Power '89
Hidden Agenda '90
Highlander 2: The Quickening
  '91
Out of Bounds '86
Riff Raff '91
Rumble Fish '83
See No Evil, Hear No Evil '89
She's Having a Baby '88
Surviving the Game '94
Talk Radio '88
Wall Street '87
Wide Sargasso Sea '92

Aaron Copland
The Heiress '49
The North Star '43
Of Mice and Men '39
Our Town '40
The Red Pony '49

Carmine Coppola
Apocalypse Now '79
The Black Stallion '79
Gardens of Stone '87
The Godfather, Part 2 '74
The Godfather, Part 3 '90
Napoleon '27
New York Stories '89
The Outsiders '83
The People '71
Tonight for Sure '61
Tucker: The Man and His
  Dream '88

Chick Corea
Cat Chaser '90

Vladimir Cosma
The Daydreamer '75
Diva '82
Dracula & Son '76
The Favor, the Watch, & the
  Very Big Fish '92
Just the Way You Are '84
La Boum '81
La Chevre '81
Le Bal '82
Les Comperes '83
Mistral's Daughter '84
My Father's Glory '91
My Mother's Castle '91
The Nightmare Years '89
Pardon Mon Affaire '76
Pardon Mon Affaire, Too! '77
Return of the Tall Blond Man
  With One Black Shoe '74
Salut l'Artiste '74
The Tall Blond Man with One
  Black Shoe '72

Elvis Costello
The Courier '88
Party! Party! '83

Wayne County
Jubilee '78

Noel Coward
In Which We Serve '43

Jonathan Crayford
Dark of the Night '85

Xavier Cugat
Bathing Beauty '44
The White Zombie '32

Carlos D'Alessi
Delicatessen '92

Roger Daltrey
Quicksilver '86

John D'Andrea
Body Slam '87
Boiling Point '93
Child's Play 3 '91
Grambling's White Tiger '81
Savage Streets '83
Swimsuit: The Movie '89

Charlie Daniels
Lone Star Kid '90s

Jeff Danna
The Big Slice '90

Mychael Danna
The Adjuster '91
The Big Slice '90
Family Viewing '88
Speaking Parts '89
Still Life '92
Termini Station '89

Mason Daring
The Brother from Another
  Planet '84
City of Hope '91
Day One '89
Eight Men Out '88
Fathers and Sons '92
Lianna '83
Little Vegas '90
Matewan '87
Osa '85
Passion Fish '92

Return of the Secaucus 7 '80
Wild Hearts Can't Be Broken
  '91

William Darling
Anna and the King of Siam '46

Hal David
The Sad Sack '57
What's New Pussycat? '65

Carl Davis
Catholics '73
Champions '84
The Eagle '25
The Far Pavilions '84
Frankenstein Unbound '90
The French Lieutenant's
  Woman '81
Hotel du Lac '86
King David '85
Man Friday '75
Murrow '86
The Naked Civil Servant '75
Naughty Knights '71
The Only Way '70
Praying Mantis '83
The Rainbow '89
Rentadick '72
Sakharov '84
Scandal '89
Silas Marner '85
The Thief of Baghdad '24
Weather in the Streets '84
Widow's Peak '94

Elsa Davis
Cactus '86

Miles Davis
Frantic '58
Siesta '87
Street Smart '87

Jean De Paul
Li'l Abner '59

Manuel De Sica
Bye Bye Baby '88
The Garden of the Finzi-
  Continis '71
Twist '76

John Debney
The Further Adventures of
  Tennessee Buck '88
Gunmen '93
Hocus Pocus '93
Jetsons: The Movie '90
Praying Mantis '93
Seven Hours to Judgment '88
White Fang 2: The Myth of the
  White Wolf '94
The Wild Pair '87

Marc David Deeker
Bikini Beach '91

Georges Delerue
Agnes of God '85
An Almost Perfect Affair '79
American Friends '91
Amos '85
Anne of the Thousand Days '69
Arch of Triumph '85
Beaches '88
Biloxi Blues '88
Black Robe '91
The Black Stallion Returns '83
The Brain '89
Cadence '89
Cartouche '62
Confidentially Yours '83
The Conformist '71
Contempt '64
Crimes of the Heart '86
Curly Sue '91
Dan Candy's Law '73
Day for Night '73
The Day of the Dolphin '73
The Day of the Jackal '73
Dear Detective '78
The Escape Artist '82
Escape from Sobibor '87
The Execution '85
Exposed '83

Get Out Your Handkerchiefs
  '78
Heartbreak Hotel '88
Her Alibi '88
Hiroshima, Mon Amour '59
The Horsemen '70
The House on Carroll Street '88
Joe Versus the Volcano '90
Jules and Jim '62
Julia '77
The King of Hearts '66
La Passante '83
La Vie Continue '82
The Last Metro '80
Le Cavaleur '78
A Little Romance '79
A Little Sex '82
The Lonely Passion of Judith
  Hearne '87
Love and the Frenchwoman '60
Love on the Run '79
Maid to Order '87
A Man for All Seasons '66
A Man in Love '87
Man Trouble '92
Man, Woman & Child '83
Maxie '85
Memories of Me '88
Mister Johnson '91
Muriel '63
One Deadly Summer '83
Partners '82
The Pick-Up Artist '87
Platoon '86
Queenie '87
Rich and Famous '81
Rich in Love '93
Richard's Things '80
Salvador '86
Shoot the Piano Player '62
A Show of Force '90
Silence of the Heart '84
Silkwood '83
The Slap '74
The Soft Skin '64
Steel Magnolias '89
A Summer Story '88
Sword of Gideon '86
That Man from Rio '64
Time Out for Love '61
A Time to Live '85
To Kill a Priest '89
True Confessions '81
Twins '88
Two English Girls '72
The Two of Us '68
Viva Maria! '65
The Woman Next Door '81
Women in Love '70
Women of Valor '86

Joe Delia
Bad Lieutenant '92
Body Snatchers '93
China Girl '87
Driller Killer '74
Freeway '88
King of New York '90

Adolph Deutsch
Little Women '33
The Maltese Falcon '41
Some Like It Hot '59
Stars in My Crown '50

Devo
Slaughterhouse Rock '88

Orlando Di Lasso
Every Man for Himself & God
  Against All '75

Neil Diamond
Jonathan Livingston Seagull
  '73

Andrew Dickson
Naked '93

Loek Dikker
Body Parts '91
The 4th Man '79
Pascali's Island '88
Slow Burn '86

Andrew Dixon
High Hopes '89

Willie Dixon
Ginger Ale Afternoon '89

Thomas Dolby
Fever Pitch '85
Gothic '87

Klaus Doldinger
Das Boot '81
A Father's Revenge '88
Me and Him '89
The NeverEnding Story '84

Pino Donaggio
Appointment with Death '88
The Assisi Underground '84
The Barbarians '87
The Berlin Affair '85
Beyond Evil '80
The Black Cat '81
Blow Out '81
Body Double '84
Carrie '76
Catacombs '89
Crawlspace '86
Dancers '87
Deja Vu '84
The Devil's Daughter '91
Don't Look Now '73
Dressed to Kill '80
The Fan '81
A Fine Romance '92
Gunfire '78
Haunts '77
Hercules '83
Hercules 2 '85
Home Movies '79
Hotel Colonial '88
The Howling '81
Indio 2: The Revolt '92
Kansas '88
Meridian: Kiss of the Beast '90
Night Game '89
Ordeal by Innocence '84
Over the Brooklyn Bridge '83
Phantom of Death '87
Piranha '78
Raising Cain '92
Tex '82
Tourist Trap '79
Two Evil Eyes '90
Zelly & Me '88

Mark Donohue
Murphy's Law '86
Opposing Force '87

Donovan
Brother Sun, Sister Moon '73
84 Charlie Mopic '89

Stephen Dorff
Back to the Beach '87
Bronco Billy '80
Cannonball Run 2 '84
Convicted '86
The Defiant Ones '58
Every Which Way But Loose
  '78
Honky Tonk Freeway '81
Honkytonk Man '82
Kiss Shot '89
Manhunt for Claude Dallas '86
My Best Friend Is a Vampire
  '88
Pink Cadillac '89
Pure Country '92
The Quick and the Dead '87
Ratboy '86
Rustler's Rhapsody '85
Stick '85
Waltz Across Texas '83

Michael Doucet
Belizaire the Cajun '86

Patrick Doyle
Carlito's Way '93
Dead Again '91
Henry V '89
Indochine '92
Into the West '92

Much Ado About Nothing '93
Needful Things '93
Shipwrecked '90

Daryl Dragon
Payback '90

George Dreyfus
The Fringe Dwellers '86
Tender Mercies '83

John Du Prez
Bullseye! '90
Bullshot '83
A Chorus of Disapproval '89
A Fish Called Wanda '88
Love with a Perfect Stranger '86
Monty Python Live at the Hollywood Bowl '82
Monty Python's The Meaning of Life '83
Mystery Date '91
Once Bitten '85
Oxford Blues '84
Personal Services '87
A Private Function '84
She'll Be Wearing Pink Pajamas '84
Teenage Mutant Ninja Turtles: The Movie '90
Teenage Mutant Ninja Turtles 3 '93
UHF '89

Al Dubin
42nd Street '33

Anne Dudley
Buster '88
The Crying Game '92
Disorderlies '87
Hiding Out '87
Knight Moves '93
The Mighty Quinn '89
The Miracle '91
The Misadventures of Mr. Wilt '90
The Pope Must Diet '91
Say Anything '89
Silence Like Glass '90

Antoine Duhamel
Daddy Nostalgia '90
Mississippi Mermaid '69
Pierrot le Fou '65
Stolen Kisses '68
Twisted Obsession '90
Weekend '67
The Wild Child '70

David Dundas
Freddie as F.R.O.7 '92
How to Get Ahead in Advertising '89
Withnail and I '87

George Duning
Abduction of St. Anne '75
Any Wednesday '66
Arnold '73
Bell, Book and Candle '58
The Dark Past '49
The Devil at 4 O'Clock '61
The Doolins of Oklahoma '49
Down to Earth '47
The Eddy Duchin Story '56
From Here to Eternity '53
Goliath Awaits '81
Her Husband's Affairs '47
Honor Thy Father '73
Houseboat '58
Jolson Sings Again '49
Lust for Gold '49
Man from Colorado '49
The Man with Bogart's Face '80
1001 Arabian Nights '59
Pat Garrett & Billy the Kid '73
Picnic '55
Salome '53
Terror in the Wax Museum '73
Yuma '70

Bob Dylan
The Situation '87

Charles Earland
The Dynamite Brothers

Earth Wind & Fire
Shining Star '75

Randy Edelman
Beethoven's 2nd '93
The Chipmunk Adventure '87
Come See the Paradise '90
The Distinguished Gentleman '92
Dragon: The Bruce Lee Story '93
Drop Dead Fred '91
Executive Action '73
Feds '88
Gettysburg '93
Ghostbusters 2 '89
Greedy '94
Kindergarten Cop '90
The Last of the Mohicans '92
My Cousin Vinny '92
Quick Change '90
Shout '91
Snatched '72
Troop Beverly Hills '89
Twins '88
V.I. Warshawski '91
When Your Lover Leaves '83

Cliff Eidelman
Animal Behavior '89
Christopher Columbus: The Discovery '92
Crazy People '90
Dead Man Out '89
Delirious '91
Leap of Faith '92
My Girl 2 '94
Star Trek 6: The Undiscovered Country '91
Strike It Rich '90
To Die for '89
Triumph of the Spirit '89
Untamed Heart '93

Richard Einhorn
Blood Rage '87
Closet Land '90
Dead of Winter '87
Don't Go in the House '80
Eyes of a Stranger '81
The Prowler '81
Shock Waves '77
Sister, Sister '87

Kahil El Zabar
How U Like Me Now? '92

Danny Elfman
Army of Darkness '92
Article 99 '92
Back to School '86
Batman '89
Batman Returns '92
Beetlejuice '88
Big Top Pee Wee '88
Darkman '90
Dick Tracy '90
Edward Scissorhands '90
The Flash '90
Forbidden Zone '80
Hot to Trot! '88
Midnight Run '88
The Nightmare Before Christmas '93
Pee Wee's Big Adventure '85
Scrooged '88
Sommersby '93
Summer School '87
Wisdom '87

Jonathan Elias
Almost You '85
Children of the Corn '84
Far from Home '89
Key Exchange '85
Leprechaun 2 '94
Morning Glory '93
Parents '89
Rude Awakening '89
Shakedown '88
Tuff Turf '85
Two Moon Junction '88

Vamp '86

Duke Ellington
Anatomy of a Murder '59
Cabin in the Sky '43
Paris Blues '61

Keith Emerson
Best Revenge '83
The Church '89
Inferno '78
Nighthawks '81

Charles Engstrom
A Flash of Green '85
Ruby in Paradise '93

Brian Eno
Dune '84
Land of the Minotaur '77
Sebastiane '79

Bengt Ernryd
The New Land '73

David Essex
Silver Dream Racer '83

Ray Evans
Red Garters '54

Sammy Fain
Calamity Jane '53

Harold Faltermeyer
Beverly Hills Cop '84
Beverly Hills Cop 2 '87
Fatal Beauty '87
Fire and Ice '87
Fletch '85
Fletch Lives '89
Kuffs '92
The Running Man '87
Tango and Cash '89
Thief of Hearts '84
Top Gun '86

Jim Farmer
Johnny Suede '92

Rikki Fataar
The Efficiency Expert '92
High Tide '87

Jack Feldman
Newsies '92
Thumbelina '94

Jose Feliciano
Aaron Loves Angela '75

Rick Fenn
White of the Eye '88

George Fenton
Born Yesterday '93
China Moon '91
Clockwise '86
The Company of Wolves '85
Cry Freedom '87
Dangerous Liaisons '88
The Dressmaker '89
84 Charing Cross Road '86
An Englishman Abroad '83
Final Analysis '92
Gandhi '82
Groundhog Day '93
A Handful of Dust '88
Hero '92
High Spirits '88
Hussy '80
The Jewel in the Crown '84
The Long Walk Home '89
Memphis Belle '90
Saigon: Year of the Cat '87
Shadowlands '93
We're No Angels '89
White Mischief '87
White of the Eye '88
White Palace '90

David Ferguson
Dead Ahead: The Exxon Valdez Disaster '91
Tailspin: Behind the Korean Airline Tragedy '89

Jay Michael Ferguson
Bad Dreams '88
Best Seller '87
Death of an Angel '86
Gleaming the Cube '89
Johnny Be Good '88
License to Drive '88
A Nightmare on Elm Street 5: Dream Child '89
The Patriot '86
Pulse '88
Quiet Cool '86
Race for Glory '89

Bryan Ferry
House of the Rising Sun '87

Brad Fiedel
The Accused '88
The Baron and the Kid '84
The Big Easy '87
Blink '93
Blue Steel '90
Bluffing It '87
Born Beautiful '82
Brotherhood of Justice '86
Calendar Girl Murders '84
Children in the Crossfire '84
Cocaine: One Man's Seduction '83
Cold Sassy Tree '89
Compromising Positions '85
The Day the Women Got Even '80
Deadly Hero '75
Desert Bloom '86
Eyes of Fire '84
Forgotten Prisoners '90
Fraternity Vacation '85
Fright Night '85
Fright Night 2 '88
Girls of the White Orchid '85
Hardhat & Legs '80
Hit & Run '82
Hostage '87
Immediate Family '89
Into Thin Air '85
Just Before Dawn '80
The Last Innocent Man '87
Let's Get Harry '87
Mae West '84
The Midnight Hour '86
Murder in Coweta County '83
My Mother's Secret Life '84
Night School '81
Nowhere to Hide '87
The People vs. Jean Harris '81
Perfect Witness '89
Playing for Time '80
Right of Way '84
The Serpent and the Rainbow '87
Straight Talk '92
Striking Distance '93
The Terminator '84
Terminator 2: Judgment Day '91
True Believer '89
Weekend War '88

Dorothy Fields
Joy of Living '38
Swing Time '36

Mike Figgis
Internal Affairs '90
Stormy Monday '88

Richard Fiocca
Alien Space Avenger '91

Jeff Fishman
Carnal Crimes '91

Robert Folk
Bachelor Party '84
Beastmaster 2: Through the Portal of Time '91
Can't Buy Me Love '87
A Climate for Killing '91
Happy Together '90
Honeymoon Academy '90
Miles from Home '88

NeverEnding Story 2: The Next Chapter '91
Odd Jobs '85
Police Academy '84
Police Academy 3: Back in Training '86
Police Academy 4: Citizens on Patrol '87
Police Academy 5: Assignment Miami Beach '88
Police Academy 6: City Under Siege '89
Prince of Bel Air '87
Purple Hearts '84
Rock-a-Doodle '92
The Slayer '82
Stewardess School '86
Toy Soldiers '91
A Troll in Central Park '94
Wicked Stepmother '89

Lou Forestieri
Crazy Moon '87

Keith Forsey
The Breakfast Club '85

David Foster
Fresh Horses '88
If Looks Could Kill '91
Listen to Me '89
The Little Rascals '94
St. Elmo's Fire '85
The Secret of My Success '87
Stealing Home '88

The Four Tunes
Harlem on the Prairie '38

Charles Fox
Barbarella '68
Better Late Than Never '79
The Broken Chain '93
Bug '75
Christmas Comes to Willow Creek '87
Doin' Time '85
The Drowning Pool '75
The Duchess and the Dirtwater Fox '76
Dying Room Only '73
False Witness '89
Foul Play '78
The Gods Must Be Crazy 2 '89
Goodbye Columbus '69
Hard to Kill '89
The Incident '67
The Last American Hero '73
The Last Married Couple in America '80
The Laughing Policeman '74
Little Darlings '80
The Longshot '86
Love at Stake '87
Love Child '82
National Lampoon's European Vacation '85
9 to 5 '80
Oh, God! Book 2 '80
One Man Force '89
One on One '77
The Other Side of the Mountain '75
Rainbow '78
Repossessed '90
A Separate Peace '73
Short Circuit 2 '88
Six Pack '82
Star Spangled Girl '71
Strange Brew '83
The Stranger Within '74
A Summer to Remember '84
Trenchcoat '83
Two Minute Warning '76
Unnatural Causes '86
Zapped! '82

David Michael Frank
Best of the Best 2 '93
I'm Gonna Git You Sucka '88
Linda '93

Michael Franks
Cockfighter '74
Zandy's Bride '74

Carlos Franzetti
The Mambo Kings '92

Arthur Freed
Broadway Melody '29
Broadway Melody of 1936 '35
Broadway Melody of 1938 '37
Yolanda and the Thief '45

Hugo Friedhofer
An Affair to Remember '57
Barbarian and the Geisha '58
The Best Years of Our Lives '46

Rudolf Friml
Rose Marie '36

Gary Fry
Cease Fire '85
Trancers 4: Jack of Swords '93

Lewis Furey
The Agency '81
American Dreamer '84
The Peanut Butter Solution '85

Giovanni Fusco
Hiroshima, Mon Amour '59
Il Grido '57

Peter Gabriel
Birdy '84
The Last Temptation of Christ '88

Serge Gainsbourg
The French Woman '79
Le Sex Shop '73
Menage '86
Too Pretty to Be Honest '72

Chen Qi Gang
China, My Sorrow '89

Ge Ganru
A Great Wall '86

Gato Garbieri
Notes for an African Orestes '70

Art Garfunkel
The Graduate '67

Robert Garrett
Eye of the Stranger '93

Raviv Gazil
Cup Final '92

Joseph Gershenson
Creature from the Black Lagoon '54

George Gershwin
An American in Paris '51
A Damsel in Distress '37
Funny Face '57
Girl Crazy '43
The Goldwyn Follies '38
Lady Be Good '41
Manhattan '79
Rhapsody in Blue '45
Shall We Dance '37

Ira Gershwin
An American in Paris '51
The Barkleys of Broadway '49
Cover Girl '44
A Damsel in Distress '37
Funny Face '57
Girl Crazy '43
The Goldwyn Follies '38
Lady Be Good '41
Rhapsody in Blue '45
Shall We Dance '37

Michael Gibbs
American Roulette '88
Being Human '94
Breaking In '89
Hard-Boiled '92
Heat '87
Housekeeping '87
Iron & Silk '91
Madame Sin '71
Secrets '71

Richard Gibbs
Amos and Andrew '93
Barbarians at the Gate '93
Bingo '91
The Chase '93
Clifford '93
Fatal Instinct '93
The Gun in Betty Lou's Handbag '92
A Killing in a Small Town '90
Ladybugs '92
Once Upon a Crime '92
Passed Away '92
Say Anything '89
Son-in-Law '93
Sweet Hearts Dance '88
Three of Hearts '93

Alan Gill
Letter to Brezhnev '86

Philip Glass
A Brief History of Time '92
Candyman '92
Hamburger Hill '87
Koyaanisqatsi '83
Mindwalk: A Film for Passionate Thinkers '91
Mishima: A Life in Four Chapters '85
Powaqqatsi: Life in Transformation '88
The Thin Blue Line '88

Patrick Gleeson
The Bedroom Window '87
The Children of Times Square '86
Deadly Illusion '87
The Plague Dogs '82
Stacking '87
The Zoo Gang '85

Ernest Gold
Betrayal '74
A Child is Waiting '63
Cross of Iron '76
Exodus '60
Fun with Dick and Jane '77
Gore Vidal's Lincoln '88
Inherit the Wind '60
It's a Mad, Mad, Mad, Mad World '63
Judgment at Nuremberg '61
Marciano '79
On the Beach '59
Pressure Point '62
The Runner Stumbles '79
Safari 3000 '82
The Screaming Skull '58
Ship of Fools '65
Tom Horn '80
Unknown World '51
The Young Philadelphians '59

Barry Goldberg
Beverly Hills Brats '89
Flashback '90
Hometown Boy Makes Good '93
Powwow Highway '89
Return of the Living Dead 3 '93
Thrashin' '86
Three for the Road '87
The Trip '67

Billy Goldenberg
All God's Children '80
The Best Little Girl in the World '81
Brand New Life '72
Busting '74
Callie and Son '81
Change of Habit '69
The Cracker Factory '79
Crisis at Central High '80
Dempsey '83
The Domino Principle '77
Dress Gray '86
Duel '71
18 Again! '88
The Family Man '79
Father Figure '80
For Love or Money '84

The Glass House '72
Helter Skelter '76
Jacqueline Bouvier Kennedy '81
James Dean '76
Johnnie Gibson F.B.I. '87
King '78
The Last of Sheila '73
The Lindbergh Kidnapping Case '76
Love on the Run '85
Memorial Day '83
The Miracle Worker '79
The Passing of Evil '70
Play It Again, Sam '72
Prototype '83
Queen of the Stardust Ballroom '75
A Question of Love '78
Rage of Angels '83
Rage of Angels: The Story Continues '86
Reflections of Murder '74
Rehearsal for Murder '82
Reuben, Reuben '83
Scavenger Hunt '79
Silent Night, Lonely Night '69
Up the Sandbox '72

Elliot Goldenthal
Alien 3 '92
Demolition Man '93
Drugstore Cowboy '89
Golden Gate '93
Pet Sematary '89

Peter Goldfoot
Judgment in Berlin '88

Jerry Goldsmith
The Agony and the Ecstasy '65
Alien '79
Babe! '75
Bad Girls '94
Ballad of Cable Hogue '70
Bandolero! '68
Basic Instinct '92
Blue Desert '91
The Blue Max '66
The Boys from Brazil '78
Breakheart Pass '76
Breakout '75
The 'Burbs '89
Cabo Blanco '81
Capricorn One '78
The Cassandra Crossing '76
The Challenge '82
Chinatown '74
Coma '78
Criminal Law '89
Culpepper Cattle Co. '72
Damien: Omen 2 '78
Damnation Alley '77
Dennis the Menace '93
The Detective '54
The Don is Dead '73
Escape from the Planet of the Apes '71
Explorers '85
Extreme Prejudice '87
The Final Conflict '81
First Blood '82
Flim-Flam Man '67
Forever Young '92
A Gathering of Eagles '63
The Great Train Robbery '79
Gremlins '84
Gremlins 2: The New Batch '90
High Velocity '76
Hoosiers '86
Hour of the Gun '67
The Illustrated Man '69
In Harm's Way '65
In Like Flint '67
Innerspace '87
Islands in the Stream '77
Justine '69
King Solomon's Mines '85
Legend '86
Leviathan '89
Lilies of the Field '63
Link '86
Lionheart '87

The List of Adrian Messenger '63
Logan's Run '76
Lonely are the Brave '62
The Lonely Guy '84
Love Field '91
MacArthur '77
Magic '78
Malice '93
Maniac Cop 3 '93
Masada '81
Matinee '92
Medicine Man '92
The Mephisto Waltz '71
Mr. Baseball '92
Mom and Dad Save the World '92
Morituri '65
Night Crossing '81
The Omen '76
100 Rifles '69
One Little Indian '73
The Other '72
Our Man Flint '66
Outland '81
Papillon '73
A Patch of Blue '65
Patton '70
Planet of the Apes '68
Players '79
Poltergeist '82
Poltergeist 2: The Other Side '86
The Prize '63
Psycho 2 '83
Pursuit '72
QB VII '74
Raggedy Man '81
Rambo: First Blood, Part 2 '85
Rambo 3 '89
The Reincarnation of Peter Proud '75
Rent-A-Cop '88
Rio Conchos '64
Rio Lobo '70
Rudy '93
Runaway '84
The Russia House '90
The Salamander '82
The Sand Pebbles '66
Sebastian '68
The Secret of NIMH '82
Seven Days in May '64
Shamus '73
Six Degrees of Separation '93
Sleeping with the Enemy '91
S*P*Y*S '74
Star Trek: The Motion Picture '80
Star Trek 5: The Final Frontier '89
The Stripper '63
Studs Lonigan '60
Supergirl '84
The Swarm '78
Take a Hard Ride '75
The Terrorists '74
Tora! Tora! Tora! '70
Total Recall '90
A Tree Grows in Brooklyn '45
The Trouble with Angels '66
Twilight Zone: The Movie '83
Twilight's Last Gleaming '77
Under Fire '83
The Vanishing '93
Von Ryan's Express '65
Warlock '91
Wild Rovers '71
The Wind and the Lion '75

Joel Goldsmith
Across the Tracks '89
Banzai Runner '86
Crystal Heart '87
Laserblast '78
The Man with Two Brains '83
Man's Best Friend '93
No Safe Haven '87
Ricky 1 '88
Watchers '88
A Woman, Her Men and Her Futon '92

William Goldstein
Aliens Are Coming '80
Bad Guys '86
Bingo Long Traveling All-Stars & Motor Kings '76
Blood Vows: The Story of a Mafia Wife '87
An Eye for an Eye '81
Force: Five '81
Forced Vengeance '82
Getting Physical '84
Hello Again '87
Holocaust Survivors...Remembrance of Love '83
A Long Way Home '81
Lots of Luck '85
Marilyn: The Untold Story '80
Norman, Is That You? '76
Saving Grace '86
Shocker '89
Terror Out of the Sky '78
Up the Creek '84

Vinnie Golia
Trouble Bound '92

John Gonzalez
Bikini Summer '91
Final Impact '91
Street Crimes '92
Sunset Strip '91

Jerry Goodman
Search for Signs of Intelligent Life in the Universe '91

Miles Goodman
About Last Night... '86
Blind Justice '86
Dirty Rotten Scoundrels '88
Footloose '84
Having It All '82
He Said, She Said '91
High School USA '84
Housesitter '92
Indian Summer '93
Jinxed '82
K-9 '89
La Bamba '87
Last Cry for Help '79
Like Father, Like Son '87
Little Shop of Horrors '86
Lookin' to Get Out '82
The Man Who Wasn't There '83
The Muppet Christmas Carol '92
Opportunity Knocks '90
Passion Flower '86
Poison Ivy '85
Problem Child '90
Real Men '87
Sister Act 2: Back in the Habit '93
Slumber Party '57 '76
The Squeeze '87
Staying Together '89
Table for Five '83
Teen Wolf '85
Thompson's Last Run '90
Traveling Man '89
Vital Signs '90
What About Bob? '91

Jim Goodwin
A.P.E.X. '94

Michael Gore
Broadcast News '87
The Butcher's Wife '91
Defending Your Life '91
Don't Tell Her It's Me '90
Fame '80
Mr. Wonderful '93
Pretty in Pink '86
Terms of Endearment '83

Jay Gottlieb
La Discrete '90

Gerald Gouriet
The Innocent '93
Madame Sousatzka '88
Philadelphia Experiment 2 '93
Rubdown '93

The Substitute '93
They Watch '93

Paul Grabowsky
The Last Days of Chez Nous '92

Georges Granier
Le Grand Chemin '87

Stephane Grappelli
May Fools '90

Adolph Green
It's Always Fair Weather '55
On the Town '91

Francis Gromon
Marius '31

Dave Grusin
Absence of Malice '81
And Justice for All '79
Author! Author! '82
Bobby Deerfield '77
The Bonfire of the Vanities '90
The Champ '79
Clara's Heart '88
A Dry White Season '89
The Electric Horseman '79
Eric '75
The Fabulous Baker Boys '89
Falling in Love '84
The Firm '93
For the Boys '91
The Front '76
Fuzz '72
Generation '69
The Goodbye Girl '77
The Goonies '85
The Graduate '67
The Great Northfield Minnesota Raid '72
Havana '90
The Heart is a Lonely Hunter '68
Heaven Can Wait '78
Ishtar '87
The Little Drummer Girl '84
Lucas '86
The Milagro Beanfield War '88
Mr. Billion '77
Murder by Death '76
My Bodyguard '80
On Golden Pond '81
The Pope of Greenwich Village '84
Racing with the Moon '84
Reds '81
Scandalous '84
Tell Them Willie Boy Is Here '69
Tequila Sunrise '88
Three Days of the Condor '75
Tootsie '82
Waterhole #3 '67
Winning '69
The Yakuza '75

Scott Grusin
We're Talkin' Serious Money '92

Jay Gruska
Mo' Money '92
The Principal '87
Shadow Dancing '88
Sing '89
Traxx '87
Wheels of Terror '90

Vince Guaraldi
A Boy Named Charlie Brown '70

Tonino Guerra
Henry IV '85

Christopher Gunning
Hands of the Ripper '71
Twinsanity '70
Under Suspicion '92
When the Whales Came '89

Jonas Gwangwa
Cry Freedom '87

Manos Hadjidakis
Blue '68
Never on Sunday '60
The Pedestrian '73
Stella '55
Sweet Movie '75
Topkapi '64

Jim Halfpenny
Bikini Summer 2 '92
Magic Kid '92
No Escape, No Return '93

Marvin Hamlisch
April Fools '69
Bananas '71
A Chorus Line '85
D.A.R.Y.L. '85
The Devil & Max Devlin '81
The Experts '89
Fat City '72
Frankie and Johnny '91
I Ought to Be in Pictures '82
Ice Castles '79
The January Man '89
Kotch '71
Little Nikita '88
Ordinary People '80
Pennies From Heaven '81
Prisoner of Second Avenue '74
Romantic Comedy '83
Same Time, Next Year '78
Save the Tiger '73
Seems Like Old Times '80
Sophie's Choice '82
The Spy Who Loved Me '77
Starting Over '79
The Sting '73
A Streetcar Named Desire '84
Swimmer '68
Take the Money and Run '69
Three Men and a Baby '87
The Way We Were '73
When the Time Comes '91
The World's Greatest Athlete '73

Jan Hammer
I Come in Peace '90
K-9000 '89

Oscar Hammerstein
Carousel '56
Cinderella '64
Flower Drum Song '61
The King and I '56
Lady Be Good '41
Oklahoma! '55
Show Boat '36
Show Boat '51
The Sound of Music '65
South Pacific '58
State Fair '45
Sweet Adeline '35

Herbie Hancock
Action Jackson '88
Blow-Up '66
Colors '88
Death Wish '74
The George McKenna Story '86
Harlem Nights '89
Jo Jo Dancer, Your Life is Calling '86
Livin' Large '91
Round Midnight '86
A Soldier's Story '84
The Spook Who Sat By the Door '73

Erik Hansen
The Deadly Secret '94

E.Y. Harburg
Cabin in the Sky '43

John Wesley Harding
The Paint Job '93

Hagood Hardy
An American Christmas Carol '79
Anatomy of a Seduction '79
Anne of Avonlea '87
Anne of Green Gables '85

Dirty Tricks '81
Forbidden Love '82
Home to Stay '79
Klondike Fever '79
Mazes and Monsters '82
Wild Pony '83

Leigh Harline
It Happens Every Spring '49
Savage Wilderness '55
Snow White and the Seven Dwarfs '37

Udi Harpaz
Hollywood Shuffle '87

Andre Harrell
Who's the Man? '93

Johnny Harris
Man in the Wilderness '71

Max Harris
Dreamchild '85

George Harrison
Shanghai Surprise '86
Wonderwall: The Movie '69

Michael Allen Harrison
Claire of the Moon '92

Deborah Harry
Polyester '81
Rock & Rule '83

Lorenz Hart
Babes in Arms '39
Evergreen '34
Hallelujah, I'm a Bum '33
I Married an Angel '42
The Merry Widow '34
Pal Joey '57
Too Many Girls '40
Words and Music '48

Hal Hartley
Simple Men '92

Richard Hartley
The Good Father '87

Richard Harvey
Paper Mask '91

Greg Hawkes
Anna '87

Fumio Hayasaka
Sansho the Bailiff '54
Seven Samurai '54

Isaac Hayes
Truck Turner '74

Randall Kent Heddon
Undercover Cop '94

Jimi Hendrix
Skier's Dream '88

Jerry Herman
Hello, Dolly! '69

Marc Herouet
Night and Day '91

Bernard Herrmann
The Bride Wore Black '68
Cape Fear '91
Citizen Kane '41
The Day the Earth Stood Still '51
Five Fingers '52
The Ghost and Mrs. Muir '47
Jane Eyre '44
The Magnificent Ambersons '42
Mysterious Island '61
North by Northwest '59
Obsession '76
On Dangerous Ground '51
Psycho '60
Psycho 4: The Beginning '90
The Seventh Voyage of Sinbad '58
Sisters '73

The Three Worlds of Gulliver '59
The Trouble with Harry '55
Vertigo '58

David Hershfelder
Strictly Ballroom '92

Marc Hillman
Baxter '89

Graydon Hillock
Midnight Witness '93

Hilmar Orn Hilmarsson
Children of Nature '92

Rupert Hine
Better Off Dead '85

Joel Hirschhorn
Rescue Me '93

Lee Holdridge
Heidi '93
Old Gringo '89

Deborah Holland
Circuitry Man '90

Rupert Holmes
No Small Affair '84

Nigel Holton
Bloodfist 3: Forced to Fight '92
Carnosaur '93
South of Reno '87

Arthur Honegger
Crime and Punishment '35
Harvest '37

James Horner
Aliens '86
An American Tail '86
An American Tail: Fievel Goes West '91
Another 48 Hrs. '90
*batteries not included '87
Battle Beyond the Stars '80
Between Friends '83
Bopha! '93
Brainstorm '83
Class Action '91
Cocoon '85
Cocoon: The Return '88
Commando '85
Dad '89
Deadly Blessing '81
The Dresser '83
A Far Off Place '93
Field of Dreams '89
48 Hrs. '82
Glory '89
Gorky Park '83
The Hand '81
Heaven Help Us '85
Honey, I Shrunk the Kids '89
Humanoids from the Deep '80
I Love You to Death '90
In Country '89
Jack the Bear '93
The Journey of Natty Gann '85
Krull '83
Lady in Red '79
The Land Before Time '88
The Man Without a Face '93
My Heroes Have Always Been Cowboys '91
The Name of the Rose '86
Off Beat '86
Once Around '91
Patriot Games '92
The Pelican Brief '93
A Piano for Mrs. Cimino '82
P.K. and the Kid '85
Project X '87
The Pursuit of D.B. Cooper '81
Red Heat '88
The Rocketeer '91
Searching for Bobby Fischer '93
Sneakers '92
Something Wicked This Way Comes '83

The Three Worlds of Gulliver '59

Star Trek 2: The Wrath of Khan '82
Star Trek 3: The Search for Spock '84
The Stone Boy '84
Swing Kids '93
Testament '83
Thunderheart '92
Uncommon Valor '83
Unlawful Entry '92
Up from the Depths '79
Vibes '88
Volunteers '85
Where the River Runs Black '86
Willow '88
Wolfen '81

Richard Horowitz
The Sheltering Sky '90

James Newton Howard
Alive '93
American Heart '92
Campus Man '87
Coupe de Ville '90
Dave '93
Diggstown '92
8 Million Ways to Die '85
Everybody's All American '88
Falling Down '93
Five Corners '88
Flatliners '90
The Fugitive '93
Glengarry Glen Ross '92
Grand Canyon '91
Guilty by Suspicion '91
Head Office '86
The Image '89
Intersection '93
King Ralph '91
Major League '89
My Girl '91
Never Too Young to Die '86
Night and the City '92
Nobody's Fool '86
Off Limits '87
The Package '89
Pretty Woman '90
The Prince of Tides '91
Promised Land '88
Russkies '87
The Saint of Fort Washington '93
Some Girls '88
Tap '89
Three Men and a Little Lady '90
Tough Guys '86
Wildcats '86
Wyatt Earp '94

Ken Howard
Foreign Body '86

Alan Howarth
Arcade '93
Big Trouble in Little China '86
Christine '84
They Live '88

Dick Hyman
Alan & Naomi '92
Leader of the Band '87
The Purple Rose of Cairo '85

Jacques Ibert
Don Quixote '35

Abdullah Ibrahim
No Fear, No Die '90

Ice-T
Return of Superfly '90

Shinichiro Ikebe
Akira Kurosawa's Dreams '90

Tassos Ioannides
The Silver Stallion: King of the Wild Brumbies '94

Ashley Irwin
Deadly Rivals '92
Secret Games 2: The Escort '93

Pat Irwin
My New Gun '92

Bjorn Isfalt
What's Eating Gilbert Grape '93

Mark Isham
The Beast '88
Billy Bathgate '91
Fire in the Sky '93
The Getaway '93
Hitcher '86
Little Man Tate '91
Made in America '93
Made in Heaven '87
A Midnight Clear '92
Mrs. Soffel '84
The Moderns '88
Mortal Thoughts '91
Nowhere to Run '93
Point Break '91
A River Runs Through It '92
Romeo Is Bleeding '93
Short Cuts '93

Neal Israel
All I Want for Christmas '91

Howard Jackson
Merrill's Marauders '62
Sergeant Rutledge '60

Joe Jackson
Party! Party! '83
Queens Logic '91
Tucker: The Man and His
  Dream '88

Chaz Jankel
D.O.A. '88
The Rachel Papers '89

Alaric Jans
House of Games '87
Things Change '88

Pierre Jansen
La Rupture '70

Maurice Jarre
After Dark, My Sweet '90
Apology '86
Ash Wednesday '73
Behold a Pale Horse '64
The Black Marble '79
The Bride '85
Chances Are '89
The Collector '65
Coming Out of the Ice '82
The Damned '69
Dead Poets Society '89
Distant Thunder '88
Doctor Zhivago '65
Don't Cry, It's Only Thunder '82
Dreamscape '84
El Condor '70
Enemies, a Love Story '89
Enemy Mine '85
Enola Gay: The Men, the
  Mission, the Atomic Bomb
  '80
Fatal Attraction '87
Fearless '93
Firefox '82
Five Card Stud '68
The Fixer '68
Gaby: A True Story '87
Gambit '66
Ghost '90
Gorillas in the Mist '88
Grand Prix '66
The Horror Chamber of Dr.
  Faustus '59
Is Paris Burning? '68
Isadora '68
The Island at the Top of the
  World '74
Jacob's Ladder '90
Jesus of Nazareth '77
Judex '64
Julia and Julia '87
The Last Flight of Noah's Ark
  '80
The Last Tycoon '76
Lawrence of Arabia '62

Life & Times of Judge Roy
  Bean '72
Lion of the Desert '81
The Longest Day '62
Mackintosh Man '73
Mad Max: Beyond
  Thunderdome '85
The Magician of Lublin '79
The Man Who Would Be King
  '75
Mandingo '75
March or Die '77
Mr. Jones '93
Mr. Sycamore '74
Mohammed: Messenger of God
  '77
Moon Over Parador '88
The Mosquito Coast '86
The Murder of Mary Phagan
  '87
Night of the Generals '67
No Way Out '87
Only the Lonely '91
A Passage to India '84
Plaza Suite '71
Posse '75
Prancer '89
The Prince and the Pauper '78
The Professionals '66
Red Sun '71
Resurrection '80
Ryan's Daughter '70
Samson and Delilah '84
School Ties '92
Shogun '80
Shout at the Devil '76
Solar Crisis '92
Solarbabies '86
Sundays & Cybele '62
Tai-Pan '86
Taps '81
The Tin Drum '79
Top Secret! '84
Topaz '69
The Train '65
Users '86
Villa Rides '68
Wildfire '88
Winter Kills '79
Witness '85
The Year of Living Dangerously
  '82
Young Doctors in Love '82

Jefferson Starship
Mannequin '87

Peter Jermyn
The Climb '87

Zhao Jiping
Farewell My Concubine '93

**Antonio Carlos
Jobim**
Black Orpheus '58

David Johansen
Mr. Nanny '93

Elton John
Friends '71
The Lion King '94

Laurie Johnson
Dr. Strangelove, or: How I
  Learned to Stop Worrying
  and Love the Bomb '64

Philip Johnston
The Music of Chance '93

David Allen Jones
House Party 3 '94

Mick Jones
Amongst Friends '93

Quincy Jones
The Anderson Tapes '71
Bob & Carol & Ted & Alice '69
Brother John '70
Cactus Flower '69
The Color Purple '85
Dandy in Aspic '68
Dollars '71

Enter Laughing '67
For Love of Ivy '68
The Getaway '72
Honky '71
The Hot Rock '70
In Cold Blood '67
In the Heat of the Night '67
The Italian Job '69
MacKenna's Gold '69
Man & Boy '71
Mirage '66
The New Centurions '72
The Pawnbroker '65
Roots '77
The Slender Thread '65
They Call Me Mr. Tibbs! '70
Walk, Don't Run '66
The Wiz '78

Trevor Jones
Angel Heart '87
Arachnophobia '90
Bad Influence '90
Blame It on the Bellboy '92
By Dawn's Early Light '89
Chains of Gold '92
Cliffhanger '93
Crisscross '92
The Dark Crystal '82
Defenseless '91
Diamond's Edge '88
Dominick & Eugene '88
Excalibur '81
Freejack '92
In the Name of the Father '93
Labyrinth '86
The Last of the Mohicans '92
Mississippi Burning '88
Murder by Moonlight '91
Nate and Hayes '83
Runaway Train '85
Sea of Love '89
The Sender '82
Sweet Lies '88
Those Glory, Glory Days '83

Alain Jonny
The Little Thief '86

Julian Joseph
Tale of a Vampire '92

Phil Judd
Rikky and Pete '88

Tom Judson
Barcelona '94

Larry Juris
The Rejuvenator '88

Bert Kalmar
Duck Soup '33

Michael Kamen
Action Jackson '88
Adventures in Babysitting '87
The Adventures of Baron
  Munchausen '89
Angelo My Love '83
The Arab Conspiracy '76
Between the Lines '77
Blue Ice '92
Brazil '85
Crusoe '89
Dead Bang '89
Dead Zone '83
Die Hard '88
Die Hard 2: Die Harder '90
Edge of Darkness '86
Highlander '86
Homeboy '88
The Krays '90
Last Action Hero '93
Lethal Weapon '87
Lethal Weapon 2 '89
Lethal Weapon 3 '92
License to Kill '89
Lifeforce '85
Mona Lisa '86
Pink Floyd: The Wall '82
Polyester '81
The Raggedy Rawney '90
Renegades '89
Rita, Sue & Bob Too '87

Road House '89
Robin Hood: Prince of Thieves
  '91
Rooftops '89
Shanghai Surprise '86
S*H*E '79
Shining Through '92
Someone to Watch Over Me
  '87
Splitting Heirs '93
Stunts '77
Suspect '87
The Three Musketeers '93
Venom '82
Wilder Napalm '93

Bronislau Kaper
Lili '53
Malaya '49
White Cargo '42

Dana Kaproff
Full Exposure: The Sex Tape
  Scandals '89

Al Kasha
The Closer '91
Rescue Me '93

Gerard Kawczynski
Life Is a Long Quiet River '88

Norman Kaye
Vincent: The Life and Death of
  Vincent van Gogh '87

John Keane
The Kitchen Toto '87

Rolfe Kent
Dead Connection '94

Jerome Kern
Cover Girl '44
Joy of Living '38
Lady Be Good '41
Lovely to Look At '52
Show Boat '36
Show Boat '51
Sweet Adeline '35
Swing Time '36
You Were Never Lovelier '42

**Kid Creole & the
Coconuts**
New York Stories '89

Wojciech Kilar
Land of Promise '74

Kevin Kiner
Freaked '93

Carole King
Murphy's Romance '85

Osamu Kitajima
Samurai Cowboy '93

Kitaro
Heaven and Earth '93

David Kitay
Breaking the Rules '92
Look Who's Talking '89
Surf Ninjas '93

Jurgen Knieper
River's Edge '87

Mark Knopfler
Cal '84
Comfort and Joy '84
Local Hero '83
The Princess Bride '87

Krzysztof Komeda
Rosemary's Baby '68

Brian Koonin
Mr. Nanny '93

Dave Kopplin
The Cool Surface '92

**Erich Wolfgang
Korngold**
The Adventures of Robin Hood
  '38
Kings Row '41

The Prince and the Pauper '37

Mark Korven
I've Heard the Mermaids
  Singing '87

Andrezej Korzynski
Man of Iron '81
Man of Marble '76

Joseph Kosma
Children of Paradise '44

Andre Kostelanetz
Music in My Heart '40

Robert Kraft
The Mambo Kings '92

Robby Krieger
The Freeway Maniac '88

Kris Kristofferson
The Last Movie '71

Djavashir Kuliev
Ashik Kerib '88

Francis Lai
Marie '85

Frankie Laine
3:10 to Yuma '57

Frank Laloggia
The Lady in White '88

Dennis Lambert
American Me '92

Jim Lang
Body Bags '93

k.d. lang
Even Cowgirls Get the Blues
  '94

Arthur Lange
Casanova Brown '44

Jeff Lass
DaVinci's War '92

**Angelo Francesco
Lavagnino**
Chimes at Midnight '67

Mario Lavista
Cabeza de Vaca '90

David Lawrence
Skeeter '93

Hughes LeBars
Barjo '93

Bill Lee
Mo' Better Blues '90
School Daze '88

Peggy Lee
Lady and the Tramp '55

Eric Leeds
Giant Steps

Michel Legrand
Ice Station Zebra '68
My Life to Live '62
The Pickle '93
Switching Channels '88
Umbrellas of Cherbourg '64
A Woman is a Woman '60
Yentl '83

Franz Lehar
The Merry Widow '34
The Merry Widow '52

Jed Leiber
Blue Chips '94

John Lennon
Le Bal '82

Patrick Leonard
At Close Range '86
Nothing in Common '86
Timebomb '91
With Honors '94

Cory Lerios
Boiling Point '93

One Crazy Summer '86

Alan Jay Lerner
Brigadoon '54
Camelot '67
The Little Prince '74
My Fair Lady '64
Paint Your Wagon '69

Oscar Levant
In Person '35
Nothing Sacred '37

Sylvester Levay
Courage Mountain '89
Hot Shots! '91
Howard the Duck '86

Louis Levy
The 39 Steps '35

Shuki Levy
Blindfold: Acts of Obsession '94

David Liang
A Great Wall '86

Daniel Licht
Final Embrace '92

Joseph J. Lilley
How to Commit Marriage '69

Jay Livingston
Red Garters '54

Joseph Lo Duca
Army of Darkness '92
Evil Dead 2: Dead by Dawn '87
Lunatics: A Love Story '92

Frank Loesser
Guys and Dolls '55
Hans Christian Andersen '52
Hoppity Goes to Town '41
How to Succeed in Business without Really Trying '67
The Perils of Pauline '47

Frederick Loewe
Brigadoon '54
Camelot '67
Gigi '58
The Little Prince '74
My Fair Lady '64
Paint Your Wagon '69

Nils Lofgren
Every Breath '93

Los Lobos
La Pastorela '92

Diane Louie
Latino '85

Jacques Loussier
Dark of the Sun '68

The Lovin' Spoonful
What's Up, Tiger Lily? '66

Donal Lunny
Eat the Peach '86

Evan Lurie
Johnny Stecchino '92
The Night We Never Met '93

John Lurie
Down by Law '86
Mystery Train '89
Permanent Vacation '84
Stranger than Paradise '84

Jens Lysdal
A Day in October '92

Mader
In the Soup '92

Gustav Mahler
Death in Venice '71

Gary Remal Malkin
Thousand Pieces of Gold '91

Mark Mancina
Monkey Trouble '94
Speed '94

Henry Mancini
Abbott and Costello Meet the Keystone Kops '54
Angela '77
Arabesque '66
Bachelor in Paradise '69
Back Roads '81
The Benny Goodman Story '55
Better Late Than Never '83
Blind Date '87
Breakfast at Tiffany's '61
A Change of Seasons '80
Charade '63
Condorman '81
Creature from the Black Lagoon '54
The Creature Walks Among Us '56
Curse of the Pink Panther '83
Darling Lili '70
Days of Wine and Roses '62
Experiment in Terror '62
Family Upside Down '78
Far Country '55
Fear '90
A Fine Mess '86
Ghost Dad '90
The Girl from Petrovka '74
The Glass Menagerie '87
The Glenn Miller Story '54
The Great Impostor '61
The Great Mouse Detective '86
Great Race '65
The Great Waldo Pepper '75
Harry & Son '84
Hatari '62
Horizons West '52
House Calls '78
It Came From Outer Space '53
The Land Unknown '57
Lifeforce '85
Little Miss Marker '80
Lost in Alaska '52
The Man Who Loved Women '83
Man's Favorite Sport? '63
Married to It '93
Mr. Hobbs Takes a Vacation '62
Molly Maguires '70
Mommie Dearest '81
The Monolith Monsters '57
Never Forget '91
Never Steal Anything Small '59
The Night Visitor '70
Nightwing '79
99 & 44/100 Dead '74
Oklahoma Crude '73
Once is Not Enough '75
The Party '68
Peter Gunn '89
Physical Evidence '89
The Pink Panther '64
The Pink Panther Strikes Again '76
Prisoner of Zenda '79
Return of the Pink Panther '74
Revenge of the Pink Panther '78
Rock, Pretty Baby '56
Santa Claus: The Movie '85
Second Thoughts '83
The Shadow Box '80
A Shot in the Dark '64
The Silver Streak '76
Skin Deep '89
S.O.B. '81
Soldier in the Rain '63
Sometimes a Great Notion '71
Son of the Pink Panther '93
Sunset '88
Switch '91
10 '79
That's Dancing! '85
That's Entertainment '74
That's Life! '86
The Thief Who Came to Dinner '73
This Island Earth '55
The Thorn Birds '83
Tom and Jerry: The Movie '93
Touch of Evil '58

Trail of the Pink Panther '82
Two for the Road '67
Victor/Victoria '82
Wait Until Dark '67
Welcome Home '89
What Did You Do in the War, Daddy? '66
The White Dawn '75
Who is Killing the Great Chefs of Europe? '78
Without a Clue '88

Johnny Mandel
I Want to Live! '58
The Last Detail '73
M*A*S*H '70

Harry Manfredini
House '86
Jason Goes to Hell: The Final Friday '93

Chuck Mangione
Children of Sanchez '79

Barry Manilow
Thumbelina '94

Hummie Mann
Benefit of the Doubt '93
In God We Trust '91
Robin Hood: Men in Tights '93
Stoogemania '85
Year of the Comet '92

Shelley Manne
T-Bird Gang '59

David Mansfield
The Ballad of Little Jo '93
Club Paradise '86
Me & Veronica '93
Miss Firecracker '89

Jim Manzie
Lurking Fear '94
Night of the Demons 2 '94

Anthony Marinelli
Young Guns '88

Yannis Markopolous
Cactus '86

Rick Marotta
The Cover Girl Murders '93

Branford Marsalis
Mo' Better Blues '90
Sneakers '92

Wynton Marsalis
Tune in Tomorrow '90

Phil Marshall
Full Moon in Blue Water '88
Noises Off '92

George Martin
Live and Let Die '73
Yellow Submarine '68

Hugh Martin
Athena '54

Cliff Martinez
King of the Hill '93
sex, lies and videotape '89

Rick Marvin
Save Me '93
3 Ninjas '92
3 Ninjas Kick Back '94

J. Mascis
Gas Food Lodging '92

Harvey W. Mason
Only the Strong '93

Nick Mason
White of the Eye '88

John Massari
The Big Sweat '90
Killer Klowns from Outer Space '88
The Wizard of Speed and Time '88

Greg Mathieson
American Flyers '85

Peter Matz
Lust in the Dust '85
Stepping Out '91
Torch Song Trilogy '88

Briany May
Bloodmoon '90

Curtis Mayfield
Piece of the Action '77
Return of Superfly '90
Sparkle '76
Superfly '72

Doug Maynard
Patti Rocks '88

Lyle Mays
The Falcon and the Snowman '85

Jim McBride
Great Balls of Fire '89

John McCallum
Little Heroes '91

Paul McCartney
Le Bal '82

John McCulloch
Careful '94

Garry McDonald
Official Denial '93

David McHugh
Daddy's Dyin'...Who's Got the Will? '90
The Dream Team '89
The Hidden 2 '94
Mr. North '88
Mystic Pizza '88

Rod McKuen
A Boy Named Charlie Brown '70

Joel McNeely
Iron Will '93

Andy McNeill
Project: Genesis '93

Meatloaf
Car Trouble '86

Peter Melnick
L.A. Story '91

Felix Mendelssohn
The Bedroom Window '87

Alan Menken
Aladdin '92
Beauty and the Beast '91
Life with Mikey '93
The Little Mermaid '89
Newsies '92

Johnny Mercer
Dangerous When Wet '53
Darling Lili '70
Days of Wine and Roses '62
The Harvey Girls '46
Li'l Abner '59
You Were Never Lovelier '42

Pat Metheny
The Falcon and the Snowman '85

Marcus Miller
Above the Rim '94
House Party '90
Siesta '87

Randall Miller
And You Thought Your Parents Were Weird! '91

Randy Miller
Black Magic Woman '91

Mario Millo
The Lighthorsemen '87
Wrangler '88

Ben Mink
Even Cowgirls Get the Blues '94

Jon Mirsalis
Grit of the Girl Telegrapher/In the Switch Tower '15

Boby Mithoff
Seedpeople '92

Egisto Mocchi
The Rose Garden '89

Cyril Mockridge
I Was a Male War Bride '49
Miracle on 34th Street '47
The Ox-Bow Incident '43

Mark Moffiatt
High Tide '87

Dudley Moore
Bedazzled '68
The Hound of the Baskervilles '77
Six Weeks '82
30 Is a Dangerous Age, Cynthia '68

Beo Morales
Wax, or the Discovery of Television Among the Bees '93

Patrick Moraz
The Stepfather '87

Larry Morey
Snow White and the Seven Dwarfs '37

Mark Morgan
Where the Day Takes You '92

Giorgio Moroder
Midnight Express '78
The NeverEnding Story '84

Ennio Morricone
Allonsanfan '73
Almost Human '79
Arabian Nights '74
Autopsy '78
The Bachelor '93
The Battle of Algiers '66
Before the Revolution '65
Beyond Justice '92
The Big Man: Crossing the Line '91
The Bird with the Crystal Plumage '70
Bluebeard '72
Bugsy '91
Burn! '70
Butterfly '82
Casualties of War '89
The Cat o' Nine Tails '71
The Chosen '77
Cinema Paradiso '88
City of Joy '92
Cold Eyes of Fear '70s
Corrupt '84
Danger: Diabolik '68
Days of Heaven '78
The Decameron '70
The Desert of the Tartars '76
Dirty Heroes '71
Divine Nymph '71
The Endless Game '89
Everybody's Fine '90
The Exorcist 2: The Heretic '77
Fat Man and Little Boy '89
Fatal Error '83
A Fistful of Dollars '64
A Fistful of Dynamite '72
For a Few Dollars More '65
Frantic '88
The Good, the Bad and the Ugly '67
Gun Fight at Red Sands '63
The Hawks & the Sparrows '67
Hellbenders '67
The Human Factor '75
Hundra '85
Husbands and Lovers '91

Morricone ►*cont.*

In the Line of Fire '93
The Inheritance '76
The Island '80
La Cage aux Folles '78
La Cage aux Folles 2 '81
La Cage aux Folles 3: The Wedding '86
La Grande Bourgeoise '74
Le Secret '74
Leonor '75
Lovers and Liars '81
Massacre in Rome '73
Master Touch '74
The Mission '86
Moses '76
My Name is Nobody '74
Nana '82
Navajo Joe '67
Night Flight from Moscow '73
Nightmare Castle '65
Once Upon a Time in America '84
Once Upon a Time in the West '68
Orca '77
Partner '68
Python Wolf '88
Rampage '87
Red Sonja '85
Red Tent '69
Sacco & Vanzetti '71
Sahara '83
Salo, or the 120 Days of Sodom '75
The Scarlet & the Black '83
Secret Agent 00 '67
Sidney Sheldon's Bloodline '79
So Fine '81
Sonny and Jed '73
Stalking Danger '86
State of Grace '90
The Tempter '74
Teorema '68
The Thing '82
Tie Me Up! Tie Me Down! '90
A Time of Destiny '88
A Time to Die '83
A Time to Die '91
Time to Kill '89
'Tis a Pity She's a Whore '73
The Tragedy of a Ridiculous Man '81
Treasure of the Four Crowns '82
Two Mules for Sister Sara '70
The Untouchables '87
When Women Had Tails '70
When Women Lost Their Tails '75
Windows '80
Wolf '94

John Morris
Blazing Saddles '74
Carolina Skeletons '92
Clue '85
Dirty Dancing '87
The Doctor and the Devils '85
The Elephant Man '80
The In-Laws '79
Ironweed '87
Spaceballs '87
Young Frankenstein '74

Tony Mottola
Running on Empty '88

Rob Mounsey
Working Girl '88

George Mouque
Children of Paradise '44

James Mtume
Native Son '86

Coati Munde
Spike of Bensonhurst '88

John Muri
College '27

Michael Martin Murphy
Hard Country '81

William Murphy
Bound and Gagged: A Love Story '93

Bill Murray
Polyester '81

Stanley Myers
Castaway '87
Dreamchild '85
Heart of Darkness '93
Paperhouse '89
Prick Up Your Ears '87
Sammy & Rosie Get Laid '87
Sarafina! '92
Scenes from the Class Struggle in Beverly Hills '89
Wish You Were Here '87
The Witches '90

Ogden Nash
One Touch of Venus '48

Chris Neal
Around the World in 80 Ways '86

Willie Nelson
Honeysuckle Rose '80
1918 '85
Stagecoach '86

John Neschling
Kiss of the Spider Woman '85
Pixote '81

Ira Newborn
Ace Ventura: Pet Detective '93
All Night Long '81
Amazon Women on the Moon '87
The Blues Brothers '80
Brain Donors '92
Caddyshack 2 '88
Cast the First Stone '89
Dragnet '87
Ferris Bueller's Day Off '86
Innocent Blood '92
Into the Night '85
My Blue Heaven '90
The Naked Gun: From the Files of Police Squad '88
Naked Gun 33 1/3: The Final Insult '94
Naked Gun 2 1/2: The Smell of Fear '91
The Opposite Sex and How to Live With Them '93
Planes, Trains & Automobiles '87
Short Time '90
Sixteen Candles '84
Uncle Buck '89
Weird Science '85
Wise Guys '86

Alfred Newman
Blood and Sand '41
Call Northside 777 '48
Foreign Correspondent '40
Gunga Din '39
How Green was My Valley '41
How to Marry a Millionaire '53
The Hunchback of Notre Dame '39
Les Miserables '35
A Letter to Three Wives '49
Love is a Many-Splendored Thing '55
The Mark of Zorro '40
Mr. Robinson Crusoe '32
Pinky '49
The Rains Came '39
The Snake Pit '48
Son of Fury '42
The Song of Bernadette '43
Stanley and Livingstone '39
Street Scene '31
Tin Pan Alley '40
Week-End In Havana '41
Wilson '44

David Newman
The Air Up There '94
Bill & Ted's Bogus Journey '91
Bill & Ted's Excellent Adventure '89
The Cowboy Way '94
Critters '86
Disorganized Crime '89
DuckTales the Movie: Treasure of the Lost Lamp '90
Fire Birds '90
The Flintstones '94
The Freshman '90
Gross Anatomy '89
Heathers '89
Hoffa '92
Honeymoon in Vegas '92
The Kindred '87
Little Monsters '89
Madhouse '90
Malone '87
The Marrying Man '91
The Mighty Ducks '92
My Demon Lover '87
My Father the Hero '93
Other People's Money '91
Paradise '91
Rover Dangerfield '91
The Runestone '91
The Sandlot '93
Talent for the Game '91
Throw Momma from the Train '87
Undercover Blues '93
Vendetta '85
The War of the Roses '89

Randy Newman
Avalon '90
Awakenings '90
Cold Turkey '71
Maverick '94
The Natural '84
The Paper '94
Parenthood '89
Ragtime '81

Thomas Newman
Career Opportunities '91
Cookie '89
Deceived '91
Desperately Seeking Susan '85
The Favor '94
Flesh and Bone '93
Fried Green Tomatoes '91
Girls Just Want to Have Fun '85
Grandview U.S.A. '84
The Great Outdoors '88
Gung Ho '85
Josh and S.A.M. '93
Jumpin' Jack Flash '86
Less Than Zero '87
Light of Day '87
The Linguini Incident '92
The Lost Boys '87
The Man with One Red Shoe '85
Men Don't Leave '89
The Player '92
Prince of Pennsylvania '88
Real Genius '85
Reckless '84
Revenge of the Nerds '84
Scent of a Woman '92
Threesome '94
Whispers in the Dark '92

David Nichtern
The Big Picture '89

Bruno Nicolai
The Scorpion's Tail '71

Lennie Niehaus
Bird '88
City Heat '84
Heartbreak Ridge '86
Never Too Young to Die '86
Pale Rider '85
A Perfect World '93
Ratboy '86

Sesame Street Presents: Follow That Bird '85
Tightrope '84
Unforgiven '92
White Hunter, Black Heart '90

Harry Nilsson
The Point '71
Popeye '80

Jack Nitzche
Blue Collar '78
Breathless '83
Cannery Row '82
Cruising '80
Cutter's Way '81
The Exorcist '73
Greaser's Palace '72
Hardcore '79
Heart Beat '80
Heroes '77
Hot Spot '90
The Jewel of the Nile '85
The Last of the Finest '90
Mermaids '90
Next of Kin '89
9 1/2 Weeks '86
An Officer and a Gentleman '82
One Flew Over the Cuckoo's Nest '75
Performance '70
Personal Best '82
The Razor's Edge '84
Revenge '90
The Seventh Sign '88
Stand By Me '86
Starman '84
Streets of Gold '86
Stripper '86
Village of the Giants '65
The Whoopee Boys '86
Windy City '84
Without a Trace '83

Erik Nordgren
The Emigrants '72
The Seventh Seal '56

Alex North
The Agony and the Ecstasy '65
All Fall Down '62
The Bad Seed '56
Bite the Bullet '75
Carny '80
Cheyenne Autumn '64
The Children's Hour '61
Cleopatra '63
Daddy Long Legs '55
The Dead '87
Death of a Salesman '86
Desiree '54
The Devil's Brigade '68
Dragonslayer '81
A Dream of Kings '69
Good Morning, Vietnam '87
Hot Spell '58
I'll Cry Tomorrow '55
Journey into Fear '74
The King and Four Queens '56
Les Miserables '52
The Long, Hot Summer '58
The Member of the Wedding '52
The Misfits '61
Once Upon a Scoundrel '73
The Passover Plot '75
The Penitent '88
Pocket Money '72
Prizzi's Honor '85
The Racers '55
The Rainmaker '56
Rich Man, Poor Man '76
The Rose Tattoo '55
The Shoes of the Fisherman '68
Spartacus '60
Stage Struck '57
A Streetcar Named Desire '51
Under the Volcano '84
Viva Zapata! '52
Who's Afraid of Virginia Woolf? '66
Willard '71
Wise Blood '79

The Word '78

Michael Nyman
Cold Room '84
The Cook, the Thief, His Wife & Her Lover '90
The Draughtsman's Contract '82
Drowning by Numbers '87
The Hairdresser's Husband '92
The Piano '93
Prospero's Books '91
A Zed & Two Noughts '88

Sinead O'Connor
In the Name of the Father '93

George Oddner
The New Land '73

Jacques Offenbach
Peter's Friends '92

Patrick O'Hearn
Silent Tongue '92

Patrick O'Hearn
White Sands '92

William Olvis
The Comrades of Summer '92
29th Street '91

Roy Orbison
Fastest Guitar Alive '68

Riz Ortolani
The Story of Boys & Girls '91

William Orvis
Red Rock West '93

Jason Osborn
High Season '88

Albinoni Pachelbel
Every Man for Himself & God Against All '75

J.M. Pagan
Anguish '88

Christopher Palmer
Valmont '89

Alan Parker
What's Eating Gilbert Grape '93

Ray Parker, Jr.
Quicksilver '86

Gordon Parks
Shaft's Big Score '72

Van Dyke Parks
Club Paradise '86
The Two Jakes '90

Arvo Part
Rachel River '89

Paul & Mary
The Situation '87

Rosemary Paul
Something Wild '86

Don Peake
The People Under the Stairs '91

Penguin Cafe Orchestra
Malcolm '86

Giovanni Pergolese
Cactus '86

William Perry
Sparrows '26

Peter, Paul & Mary
The Situation '87

Jean-Claude Petit
L'Addition '85
The Playboys '92
Uranus '91

Laurent Petitgand
Faraway, So Close! '93

Barry Phillips
Ele, My Friend '93

Stu Phillips
Jud '71

Nicholas Pike
Attack of the 50 Ft. Woman '93
Blank Check '93
Perfect Family '92

Pink Floyd
The Valley Obscured by the Clouds '72

Nicola Piovani
Fiorile '93
Ginger & Fred '86
Good Morning, Babylon '87
Intervista '87
Jamon, Jamon '93
The Night of the Shooting Stars '82

Edward Plumb
Bambi '42

Terry Plumer
Death Wish 5: The Face of Death '94

Basil Poledouris
Big Wednesday '78
The Blue Lagoon '80
Cherry 2000 '88
Conan the Barbarian '82
Conan the Destroyer '84
Defiance '79
Farewell to the King '89
Flesh and Blood '85
Flight of the Intruder '90
Free Willy '93
Hot Shots! Part Deux '93
The Hunt for Red October '90
Iron Eagle '86
Lone Justice '93
Lonesome Dove '89
Making the Grade '84
No Man's Land '87
On Deadly Ground '94
Protocol '84
Quigley Down Under '90
Red Dawn '84
RoboCop '87
RoboCop 3 '91
Serial Mom '94
Single Bars, Single Women '84
The Spellbinder '88
Split Decisions '88
Summer Lovers '82
Whale for the Killing '81
White Fang '91
Wind '92
Wired '89

Iggy Pop
Rock & Rule '83

Michel Portal
Max, Mon Amour '86

Cole Porter
Born to Dance '36
High Society '56
Panama Hattie '42
Rosalie '38

Rachel Portman
Antonia and Jane '91
Benny & Joon '93
Sharma & Beyond '84
Sirens '94
Used People '92
Where Angels Fear to Tread '91
Young Charlie Chaplin '88

Andrew Powell
Ladyhawke '85
Rocket Gibraltar '88

Reg Powell
Test Tube Teens from the Year 2000 '93

Pray For Rain
Car 54, Where Are You? '94

Zbigniew Preisner
At Play in the Fields of the Lord '91
Damage '92
Eminent Domain '91
The Secret Garden '93
Trois Couleurs: Rouge '94
When a Man Loves a Woman '94

The Pretenders
Fatal Fix '80s

Andre Previn
The Catered Affair '56
Cause for Alarm '51
Challenge to Lassie '49
Designing Woman '57
Elmer Gantry '60
Fastest Gun Alive '56
The Fortune Cookie '66
The Four Horsemen of the Apocalypse '62
The Girl Who Had Everything '53
Give a Girl a Break '53
Inside Daisy Clover '65
Irma La Douce '63
It's Always Fair Weather '55
Kim '50
Kismet '55
Kiss Me Kate '53
Kiss Me, Stupid! '64
Long Day's Journey into Night '62
One, Two, Three '61
Paint Your Wagon '69
Rollerball '75
Silk Stockings '57
Small Town Girl '53
The Sun Comes Up '49
Three Little Words '50
Two for the Seesaw '62

Alan Price
O Lucky Man! '73

Prince
Batman '89
J.D.'s Revenge '76

Sergei Prokofiev
Alexander Nevsky '38
Ivan the Terrible, Part 1 '44

Queen
Flash Gordon '80

Peer Raben
The American Soldier '70
Despair '78
The Marriage of Maria Braun '79
Querelle '83
The Stationmaster's Wife '77
Veronika Voss '82

Robert O. Ragland
Messenger of Death '88

Ralph Rainger
The Ruggles of Red Gap '35

Red Clay Ramblers
Far North '88

David Raskin
Forever Amber '47
Laura '44

J.A.C. Redford
D2: The Mighty Ducks '94

Lou Reed
Rock & Rule '83

Alan Reeves
Dr. Bethune '90

Ruth Rennie
When the Whales Came '89

Joe Renzetti
Basket Case 2 '90
Basket Case 3: The Progeny '92
The Buddy Holly Story '78
Child's Play '88

South Beach '92

Graeme Revell
Body of Evidence '92
Boxing Helena '93
Child's Play 2 '90
The Crow '93
The Crush '93
Dead Calm '89
Ghost in the Machine '93
The Hand that Rocks the Cradle '92
Hard Target '93
Hear No Evil '93
Love Crimes '92
No Escape '94
Spontaneous Combustion '89
Till There was You '91
Traces of Red '92
Until The End of The World '91

Tim Rice
Aladdin '92
The Lion King '94

Jason James Richter
The Band Wagon '53

David Rickets
Echo Park '86

Nelson Riddle
The Great Gatsby '74

Tony Riparetti
Bloodmatch '91

Lee Ritenour
American Flyers '85

David Robbins
Bob Roberts '92
Twenty Bucks '93

Richard Robbins
The Ballad of the Sad Cafe '91
Maurice '87
The Remains of the Day '93
Sweet Lorraine '87

Eric N. Robertson
Millenium '89

Harry Robertson
Jane & the Lost City '87

Robbie Robertson
Jimmy Hollywood '94

Leo Robin
Two Tickets to Broadway '51

J. Peter Robinson
The Believers '87
Blind Fury '90
Cocktail '88
Wayne's World '92

Milan Roder
The Lives of a Bengal Lancer '35

Nile Rodgers
Beverly Hills Cop 3 '94
Blue Chips '94
Coming to America '88
Earth Girls are Easy '89

Richard Rodgers
Babes in Arms '39
Carousel '56
Cinderella '64
Evergreen '34
Flower Drum Song '61
Hallelujah, I'm a Bum '33
I Married an Angel '42
The King and I '56
Oklahoma! '55
Pal Joey '57
The Sound of Music '65
South Pacific '58
State Fair '45
Too Many Girls '40
Words and Music '48

Pierre Rodnunsky
Lovers' Lovers '94

Patrick Roffe
Baxter '89

Joel Rosenbaum
Billy Galvin '86

Leonard Rosenman
Ambition '91
East of Eden '54
Lafayette Escadrille '58
Rebel Without a Cause '55

John Ross
Easy Wheels '89

Matthew Ross
Carnal Crimes '91

William Ross
Cops and Robbersons '94
Look Who's Talking Now '93
One Good Cop '91
Thumbelina '94

Nino Rota
The Clowns '71
8 1/2 '63
The Godfather '72
The Godfather 1902-1959: The Complete Epic '81
The Godfather, Part 2 '74
The Godfather, Part 3 '90
La Dolce Vita '60
La Strada '54
Romeo and Juliet '68
War and Peace '56

Bruce Rowland
Lightning Jack '94

Royal Philharmonic Orchestra
The Tales of Hoffmann '51

Miklos Rozsa
Adam's Rib '50
All the Brothers Were Valiant '53
The Asphalt Jungle '50
Ben-Hur '59
Bhowani Junction '56
Blood on the Sun '45
Command Decision '48
Criss Cross '48
Dark Waters '44
Dead Men Don't Wear Plaid '82
Diane '55
The Divorce of Lady X '38
Double Indemnity '44
A Double Life '47
East Side, West Side '49
El Cid '61
Eye of the Needle '81
The Four Feathers '39
Golden Voyage of Sinbad '73
The Green Berets '68
Green Fire '55
Ivanhoe '52
Jacare '42
Julius Caesar '53
The Jungle Book '42
The King of Kings '61
The King's Thief '55
Knight Without Armour '37
Knights of the Round Table '53
The Last Embrace '79
The Lost Weekend '45
Lust for Life '56
Lydia '41
Madame Bovary '49
Melody Master '41
Men of the Fighting Lady '54
The Miniver Story '50
Moonfleet '48
The Naked City '48
The Private Life of Sherlock Holmes '70
Providence '77
Quo Vadis '51
The Red House '47
Secret Beyond the Door '48
Sodom and Gomorrah '62
Something of Value '57
A Song to Remember '45
Spellbound '45

Spy in Black '39
The Squeaker '37
The Strange Love of Martha Ivers '46
Sundown '41
That Hamilton Woman '41
Thief of Baghdad '40
Thunder in the City '37
Time After Time '79
A Time to Love & a Time to Die '58
Tribute to a Bad Man '56
The V.I.P.'s '63
The Woman of the Town '44
Young Bess '53

Michael Rubini
Nemesis '93

Arthur B. Rubinstein
The Hard Way '91
Lost in America '85
Stakeout '87

Harry Ruby
Duck Soup '33

Steve Rucker
And God Created Woman '88
Catch the Heat '87
Creature '85
Little Nemo: Adventures in Slumberland '92
976-EVIL '88
Syngenor '90

Daryl Runswick
No Surrender '86

Patrice Rushen
Hollywood Shuffle '87

Willy Russell
Mr. Love '86
Shirley Valentine '89

David E. Russo
Shaking the Tree '92

Craig Safan
Money for Nothing '93
A Nightmare on Elm Street 4: Dream Master '88
Stand and Deliver '88
The Stranger '87

Martin St. Pierre
Dust '85

Camille Saint-Saens
Au Revoir Les Enfants '87

Ichiro Saito
A Geisha '53

Ryuichi Sakamoto
High Heels '91
The Last Emperor '87
Little Buddha '93
The Sheltering Sky '90
Tokyo Decadence '91
Wild Palms '93

David Sanborn
Lethal Weapon 2 '89
Lethal Weapon 3 '92

Carlos Santana
La Bamba '87

Chris Saranec
Huck and the King of Hearts '93

Philippe Sarde
Every Time We Say Goodbye '86
Joshua Then and Now '85
Lost Angels '89
Music Box '89
Spoiled Children '77

Erik Satie
Dancing in the Dark '86

Masaru Sato
The Silk Road '92
Throne of Blood '57
Yojimbo '61

Jordi Savall
Tous les Matins du Monde '92

Walter Scharf
Three Violent People '57

Prof. Peter Schickele
Silent Running '71

Poul Schierbeck
Day of Wrath '43

Lalo Schifrin
The Beverly Hillbillies '93
Boulevard Nights '79
The Fourth Protocol '87
Hit! '73

Franz Schubert
Au Revoir Les Enfants '87

Paul Schutze
The Tale of Ruby Rose '87

Arthur Schwartz
The Band Wagon '53
Dangerous When Wet '53

John Scott
Becoming Colette '92
Ruby '92
Shoot to Kill '88
The Whistle Blower '87
Winter People '89

Tom Scott
Final Notice '89

Vincent Scotto
Cesar '36
Fanny '32

Peter Sculthorpe
Burke & Wills '85

John Sebastian
The Act '82

Sholom Secunda
Eli Eli '40

Dov Seltzer
Hanna's War '88

Al Sendry
Bloody Wednesday '87

Eric Serra
La Femme Nikita '91

Patrick Seymour
Chantilly Lace '93

Marc Shaiman
The Addams Family '91
Addams Family Values '93
City Slickers '91
City Slickers 2: The Legend of Curly's Gold '94
A Few Good Men '92
Heart and Souls '93
Misery '90
Mr. Saturday Night '92
North '94
Sister Act '92
Sleepless in Seattle '93
That's Entertainment, Part 3 '93
When Harry Met Sally '89

Ravi Shankar
Pather Panchali '54
Wonderwall: The Movie '69
The World of Apu '59

Francis Shaw
The Fourth Protocol '87

Jonathan Sheffer
Bloodhounds of Broadway '89
On Valentine's Day '86

Kirby Shelstad
Ernest Rides Again '93

Robert Sherwood
The Adventures of Marco Polo '38

David Shire
All the President's Men '76
Backfire '88

Bed & Breakfast '92
The Big Bus '76
Class of '44 '73
The Conversation '74
Convicted: A Mother's Story '87
Farewell, My Lovely '75
Fast Break '79
God Bless the Child '88
Harry & Walter Go to New York '76
The Hindenburg '75
Jesse '88
Max Dugan Returns '83
Mayflower Madam '87
Monkey Shines '88

David Shire
'night, Mother '86

David Shire
The Night the Lights Went Out in Georgia '81
Norma Rae '79
Oh, God! You Devil '84
Old Boyfriends '79
Only When I Laugh '81
Paternity '81
The Promise '78
Raid on Entebbe '77
Return to Oz '85
Saturday Night Fever '77
Short Circuit '86
Showdown '73
Sidekicks '93
Skin Game '71
Steelyard Blues '73
Straight Time '78
Summertree '71
The Taking of Pelham One Two Three '74
Tell Me Where It Hurts '74
2010: The Year We Make Contact '84
Vice Versa '88
The Women of Brewster Place '89
The World According to Garp '82

Alfred Shnitke
Rasputin '85

Howard Shore
After Hours '85
Belizaire the Cajun '86
Big '88
The Brood '79
Dead Ringers '88
Fire with Fire '86
The Fly '86
Heaven '87
An Innocent Man '89
M. Butterfly '93
Mrs. Doubtfire '93
Moving '88
Nadine '87
Naked Lunch '91
Philadelphia '93
Places in the Heart '84
Prelude to a Kiss '92
Quick Change '90
Scanners '81
She-Devil '89
The Silence of the Lambs '91
Single White Female '92
Sliver '93
Videodrome '83

Dimitri Shostakovich
Ten Days That Shook the World '27

Michael Shrieve
The Bedroom Window '87

Leo Shuken
Miracle of Morgan's Creek '44
The Stunt Man '80

Sheila Silver
Alligator Eyes '90

Shel Silverstein
Ned Kelly '70

Alan Silvestri
The Abyss '89
The Amazing Dobermans '76
American Anthem '86
Back to the Future '85
Back to the Future, Part 2 '89
Back to the Future, Part 3 '90
The Bodyguard '92
Cat's Eye '85
The Clan of the Cave Bear '86
Clean Slate '94
Cop and a Half '93
Critical Condition '86
Death Becomes Her '92
Delta Force '86
Downtown '90
Fandango '85
Father of the Bride '91
Ferngully: The Last Rain Forest '92
Flight of the Navigator '86
Grumpy Old Men '93
Judgment Night '93
Las Vegas Lady '76
Mac and Me '88
My Stepmother Is an Alien '88
No Mercy '86
Outrageous Fortune '87
Overboard '87
Predator '87
Ricochet '91
Romancing the Stone '84
She's Out of Control '89
Sidekicks '93
Soapdish '91
Stop! or My Mom Will Shoot '92
Summer Rental '85
Super Mario Bros. '93
Tales from the Crypt '89
Who Framed Roger Rabbit? '88
Young Guns 2 '90

Carly Simon
Heartburn '86
Working Girl '88

Lucy Simon
The Positively True Adventures of the Alleged Texas Cheerleader-Murdering Mom '93

Marty Simon
George's Island '91
Scanners 2: The New Order '91

Paul Simon
The Graduate '67

Claudio Simonetti
Conquest '83

Frank Sinatra, Jr.
The Beach Girls and the Monster '65

Siouxsie & the Banshees
Jubilee '78

Sherrill Sisters
Follow the Leader '44

Frank Skinner
Destry Rides Again '39
Francis Goes to the Races '51
Francis the Talking Mule '49

Michael Small
Black Widow '87
Brighton Beach Memoirs '86
Orphans '87

Bruce Smeaton
Barbarosa '82
Circle of Iron '78
A Cry in the Dark '88
The Devil's Playground '76
Eleni '85
Grendel, Grendel, Grendel '82
Iceman '84
The Naked Country '85
Picnic at Hanging Rock '75
Plenty '85
Roxanne '87
Undercover '87

The Winds of Jarrah '83

Mauricio Smith
Crossover Dreams '85

Michael Smith
The Bikini Car Wash Company 2 '92

Paul Smith
Snow White and the Seven Dwarfs '37

David Snell
Billy the Kid '41

Curt Sobel
Alien Nation '88

George Solti
Wagner: The Complete Epic '85

Stephen Sondheim
Dick Tracy '90
Gypsy '93
Reds '81
Stavisky '74
Sunday in the Park with George '86
Sweeney Todd: The Demon Barber of Fleet Street '84
West Side Story '61

Michael Spicer
Backlash '86

Mischa Spoliansky
The Happiest Days of Your Life '50

Robert Springberry
Quick '93

Frank Stallone
Staying Alive '83

David Steele
Tin Men '87

Jule Stein
Two Tickets to Broadway '51

Ronald Stein
Invasion of the Saucer Men '57

Max Steiner
The Adventures of Tom Sawyer '38
All Mine to Give '56
Angels with Dirty Faces '38
Band of Angels '57
The Big Sleep '46
By the Light of the Silvery Moon '53
The Caine Mutiny '54
Casablanca '42
The Corn is Green '45
Darby's Rangers '58
The Desert Song '53
The Flame & the Arrow '50
Gone with the Wind '39
The Hanging Tree '59
Ice Palace '60
In This Our Life '42
The Informer '35
John Paul Jones '59
King Kong '33
Last Command '28
The Letter '40
Little Orphan Annie '32
The Lost Patrol '34
The McConnell Story '55
Now, Voyager '42
On Moonlight Bay '51
Rome Adventure '62
The Searchers '56
Sergeant York '41
Since You Went Away '44
Spencer's Mountain '63
A Summer Place '59
Treasure of the Sierra Madre '48

James Stemple
Adventures in Spying '92

Cat Stevens
Deep End '70
Harold and Maude '71

David A. Stewart
The Ref '93

Sting
Party! Party! '83

Georgie Stoll
Holiday in Mexico '46
The Seven Hills of Rome '58

Morris Stoloff
Here Comes Mr. Jordan '41
His Girl Friday '40
The Jolson Story '46
Song Without End '60

Howard Stone
Signs of Life '89

Laurie Stone
Official Denial '93

Richard Stone
Pumpkinhead '88

Michael Storey
Coming Up Roses '87

Herbert Stothart
Cairo '42
David Copperfield '35
Mrs. Miniver '42
Mutiny on the Bounty '35
National Velvet '44
A Night at the Opera '35
A Tale of Two Cities '35
The Wizard of Oz '39

Oscar Strauss
Make a Wish '37

Barbra Streisand
Nuts '87

William T. Stromberg
Silent Victim '92

Joe Strummer
Permanent Record '88
Walker '87

Jules Styne
Anchors Aweigh '45
Gypsy '93
My Sister Eileen '55
The West Point Story '50

L. Subramaniam
Mississippi Masala '92
Salaam Bombay! '88

Sparky Sugarman
Cinderella 2000 '78

Harry Sukman
Song Without End '60

Andy Summers
Down and Out in Beverly Hills '86
End of the Line '88
Motorama '91
Weekend at Bernie's '89

Mark Suozzi
Barcelona '94
Metropolitan '90

Bruce Sussman
Thumbelina '94

Stanislas Syrewicz
The Lair of the White Worm '88

Taj Mahal
Sounder '72
Zebrahead '92

Toru Takemitsu
Himatsuri '85
Kwaidan '64
Ran '85
Rising Sun '93
Woman in the Dunes '64

Billy Talbot
Confessions of a Hit Man '94

Roger Tallman
Hail Caesar '94

Tangerine Dream
City of Shadows '86
Heartbreakers '84
Kamikaze '89 '83
Miracle Mile '89
Near Dark '87
Rainbow Drive '90
Shy People '88
Three O'Clock High '87

John Tatgenhorst
Demon Possessed '93

Art Tatum
September '88

John Taylor
Mi Vida Loca '94

Piotr Ilich Tchaikovsky
George Balanchine's The Nutcracker '93

Fredric Teetsel
Adventures in Dinosaur City '92

Bob Telson
Bagdad Cafe '88
Rosalie Goes Shopping '89

Nicolaas Tenbroek
American Ninja 4: The Annihilation '91

Dennis Michael Tenney
Witchboard '87
Witchboard 2: The Devil's Doorway '93

Richard Termini
Mac '93

Vin Tese
Mac '93

Bush Tetras
Cave Girls '82

Mikis Theodorakis
Iphigenia '77
Phaedra '61

Maurice Thiriet
Children of Paradise '44

Linda Thompson
The Little Rascals '94

Richard Thompson
Sweet Talker '91

Virgil Thompson
Louisiana Story '48

Ken Thorne
A Funny Thing Happened on the Way to the Forum '66

Reg Tilsley
What's Good for the Goose '93

Dimitri Tiomkin
The Alamo '60
Cyrano de Bergerac '50
Dial "M" for Murder '54
D.O.A. '49
Friendly Persuasion '56
High Noon '52
It's a Wonderful Life '46
Lost Horizon '37
Mr. Smith Goes to Washington '39
Only Angels Have Wings '39
Red River '48
Shadow of a Doubt '43
Strangers on a Train '51
The Sundowners '60
The Thing '51

Ludus Tonalis
My Beautiful Laundrette '85

Gerard Torikian
Love Without Pity '91

Toto
Dune '84

Colin Towns
Bellman and True '88
Born of Fire '87
Fellow Traveler '89
Full Circle '77
Getting It Right '89
Knights & Emeralds '87
Rawhead Rex '87

Colin Towns
Shadey '87

Colin Towns
Slayground '84
Vampire's Kiss '88

Armando Trovajoli
The Family '87
Two Women '61

John Trudell
Incident at Oglala: The Leonard Peltier Story '92

Toshi Tsuchitori
The Mahabharata '89

Greg Turner
Eyes of the Beholder '92

Simon Fisher Turner
Blue '93
Edward II '92

Tina Turner
House of the Rising Sun '87

Joseph Turrin
A New Life '88

Steve Tyrell
Getting It Right '89

Steve Vai
P.C.U. '94

Nathan Van Cleave
Robinson Crusoe on Mars '64

David Van Tiegham
Working Girls '87

Vangelis
Antarctica '84
Bitter Moon '92
Chariots of Fire '81
1492: Conquest of Paradise '92
Third Solution '89

Richard Vanstone
White Hunter, Black Heart '90

Varouje
Fearless Tiger '94

Harley Venton
Presumed Innocent '90
Stanley and Iris '90

Giuseppe Verdi
Little Dorrit, Film 1: Nobody's Fault '88
Little Dorrit, Film 2: Little Dorrit's Story '88

Edith Vesperini
Van Gogh '92

The Vienna Philharmonic Orchestra
The Life and Loves of Mozart '59

The Vienna State Opera
The Life and Loves of Mozart '59

Karl Vollmoller
The Blue Angel '30

Vincent Vouman
Flying Down to Rio '33

Popul Vuh
Fitzcarraldo '82

Richard Wagner
Meeting Venus '91

Tom Waits
Down by Law '86
Night on Earth '91
On the Nickel '80
One from the Heart '82
Streetwise '85

Rick Wakeman
Crimes of Passion '84

Nathan Waks
Kangaroo '86

Dana Walden
Molly and Gina '94

W.G. Snuffy Walden
The Good Fight '92

Mal Waldron
Sweet Love, Bitter '67

Shirley Walker
Batman: Mask of the Phantasm '93

Oliver Wallace
Dumbo '41

Karl Wallinger
Reality Bites '94

Rob Walsh
Revenge of the Ninja '83

William Walton
Hamlet '48
Henry V '44
Spitfire '42

Edward Ward
Cheers for Miss Bishop '41

Harry Warren
The Barkleys of Broadway '49
42nd Street '33
The Harvey Girls '46
Yolanda and the Thief '45

Don Was
Backbeat '94

David Waters
Rescue Me '93

Franz Waxman
Cimarron '60
Honolulu '39
Mister Roberts '55
Night and the City '50
Objective, Burma! '45
The Philadelphia Story '40
A Place in the Sun '51
Rear Window '54
Rebecca '40
The Silver Chalice '54
Spirit of St. Louis '57
Stalag 17 '53
Three Comrades '38
Woman of the Year '42

Weather Report
Watched '73

Chuck Webb
How U Like Me Now? '92

Jim Webb
The Last Unicorn '82

Roy Webb
The Magnificent Ambersons '42

Andrew Lloyd Webber
Gumshoe '72
The Odessa File '74

Paul Francis Webster
Calamity Jane '53

Kurt Weill
One Touch of Venus '48

Eric Weissburg
Deliverance '72

Rick Wentworth
How to Get Ahead in Advertising '89

Jim West
Lady Dragon 2 '93

Paul Westerberg
Singles '92

Bernard Wheeler
Anna and the King of Siam '46

Scott Wilk
Plain Clothes '88

Brooks Williams
Wax, or the Discovery of Television Among the Bees '93

John Williams
The Accidental Tourist '88
Always '89
Black Sunday '77
Born on the Fourth of July '89
Cinderella Liberty '73
Close Encounters of the Third Kind '77
Conrack '74
The Cowboys '72
Daddy's Gone A-Hunting '69
The Deer Hunter '78
Diamond Head '62
Dracula '79
Earthquake '74
The Eiger Sanction '75
Empire of the Sun '87
The Empire Strikes Back '80
E.T.: The Extra-Terrestrial '82
Family Plot '76
Far and Away '92
Fiddler on the Roof '71
The Fury '78
Gidget Goes to Rome '63
Goodbye, Mr. Chips '69
A Guide for the Married Man '67
Heartbeeps '81
Heidi '67
Home Alone '90
Home Alone 2: Lost in New York '92
Hook '91
Indiana Jones and the Last Crusade '89
Indiana Jones and the Temple of Doom '84
Jaws '75
Jaws 2 '78
Jaws 3 '83
JFK '91
Jurassic Park '93
The Killers '64
The Long Goodbye '73
Man Who Loved Cat Dancing '73
Midway '76
Missouri Breaks '76
Monsignor '82
1941 '79
None But the Brave '65
The Paper Chase '73
Pete 'n' Tillie '72
The Plainsman '37
The Poseidon Adventure '72
Psychopath '73
Raiders of the Lost Ark '81
The Rare Breed '66
The Reivers '69
Return of the Jedi '83
The River '84
Schindler's List '93
Sergeant Ryker '68
SpaceCamp '86
Star Wars '77
The Sugarland Express '74
Superman: The Movie '78
Superman 2 '80
Superman 3 '83
Superman 4: The Quest for Peace '87
The Swarm '78
Tom Sawyer '73
The Towering Inferno '74
Valley of the Dolls '67
The Witches of Eastwick '87
Yes, Giorgio '82

Patrick Williams
Blind Spot '93
Cry-Baby '90
The Cutting Edge '92
Geronimo '93
In the Spirit '90
Violets Are Blue '86

Paul Williams
Bugsy Malone '76
The End '78
The Muppet Christmas Carol '92
The Muppet Movie '79
Phantom of the Paradise '74
A Star is Born '76

Meredith Wilson
The Unsinkable Molly Brown '64

Nancy Wilson
Say Anything '89

Edgar Winter
Netherworld '91

Peter Wolf
Weekend at Bernie's 2 '93

Stevie Wonder
The Woman in Red '84

Christine Woodruff
The Year My Voice Broke '87

Harry Woods
Evergreen '34

Bernie Worrell
Car 54, Where Are You? '94

Y Pants
Cave Girls '82

Yanni
Heart of Midnight '89

Gabriel Yared
Betty Blue '86
Camille Claudel '89
Light Years '88
Romero '89

Dwight Yoakam
Chasers '94

Vincent Youmans
Hit the Deck '55

Christopher Young
Bright Angel '91
The Dark Half '91
Dream Lover '93
Hellraiser '87
Rapid Fire '92

Neil Young
Where the Buffalo Roam '80

Victor Young
Arizona '40
Around the World in 80 Days '56
The Quiet Man '52
Shane '53

Paul Zaza
The Club '94

Wolfgang Zeller
Vampyr '31

Hans Zimmer
Backdraft '91
Black Rain '89
Calendar Girl '93
Cool Runnings '93
Dark Obsession '90
Days of Thunder '90
Driving Miss Daisy '89
Fools of Fortune '90
Green Card '90
The House of the Spirits '93
I'll Do Anything '93
Insignificance '85
A League of Their Own '92
The Lion King '94
Moonlighting '82
Pacific Heights '90

Zimmer

Zimmer ▶cont.

Paperhouse '89
Point of No Return '93
Prisoner of Rio '89
Rain Man '88
Regarding Henry '91
Renaissance Man '94
Success is the Best Revenge
  '84
Thelma & Louise '91
True Romance '93
Twister '89
Wonderland '88
A World Apart '88

MUSIC VIDEO GUIDE

The **MUSIC INDEX GUIDE** alphabetically lists the titles of more than 4,000 music videos and music performance recordings. These videos are typically prefaced by the name of the artist for quick identification. Due to space limitations and the remarkable sameness of most of the reviews (Music star sings, dances, songs include...), these videos are not covered elsewhere in the book. Three letter distributor codes immediately follow the video title. These codes refer to the distributors listed in the Distributor Guide at the back of the book. There, you'll find full contact information.

Music Video

ABBA: MVD, MON, TVC
ABBA: Again MVD, MON, TVC
ABBA Gold: Greatest Hits PGV, MVD
ABBA: In Concert MVD
ABBA: Story (1974-1982) MVD
ABBA: Waterloo MCA
Abbey Lincoln: You Gotta Pay the Band PGV, MVD
ABC: Absolutely ABC MVD, PGV
ABC: Mantrap MVD, COL
Abrasive Wheels MVD
AC/DC: Clipped AVE, FFF
AC/DC: Fly on the Wall MVD, AVE, FFF
AC/DC: Let There Be Rock MVD, WAR
AC/DC: Live at Donington MVD, AVE, FFF
AC/DC: The Interview Sessions MVD
AC/DC: Who Made Who MVD, AVE, FFF
A.C. Jobim/Gal Costa: Rio Revisited MVD
Acoustic Sounds from Africa
Adam and the Ants FOX
Adam and the Ants: Prince Charming Revue FOX
Adam Ant: Antics in the Forbidden Zone MVD, SMV
Aerosmith: The Making of "Pump" MVD, SMV, IME
Aerosmith: Things That Go Pump in the Night MVD
Aerosmith: 3 x 5 MVD
Aerosmith: Video Scrapbook MVD, FOX
Afrika Bambaataa & Family: Electric Dance Hop MVD, MPI
Agent Steel: Mad Locust Rising MVD
Agony MVD
A-Ha: The Hits MVD
Aida HMV, ING
Aim High America TGV
Air Supply: Live in Hawaii MVD
Al Green: Gospel According to Al Green MVD, IME, FCT
Al Green: On Fire in Tokyo MVD, XVC, FCT
Al Jarreau in London MVD, WRV, FCT
Al Jarreau: Tenderness WRV

Alabama: Greatest Hits Video MVD, COL, LTY
Alabama: Pass It on Down MVD, BMG
Alan Holdsworth: Tokyo Dream MVD
Alan Jackson: Livin', Lovin' and Rockin' That Jukebox MVD, PGV, SWH
Alan T.D. Wiggins & Band in Concert PRH, MVD
Alannah Myles MVD, AVE, FFF
The Alarm: Blaze of Glory— Greatest Hits Live in Concert SVI, MVD
Alarm: Spirit of '86 MCA, MVD
Alarm: Standards MVD
Alberta Hunter CMR
Alcatraz: Metallic Live '84 in Japan MVD
Alcatraz: Power Live MVD
Alejandra Guzman: La Diva del Rock MVD
Alejandra Guzman: Lo Mejor de Alejandra Guzman MVD
Alexander O'Neal: Live in London MVD, SMV
Alice Cooper & Friends MED
Alice Cooper: The Nightmare Returns MCA, MVD
Alice Cooper: Trash These Videos MVD, SMV
Alice Cooper Trashes the World MVD, SMV
Alice Cooper: Welcome to My Nightmare MVD, RHI
Alice in Chains: Live Facelift SMV
Alien Sex Fiend: A Purple Glistener MVD
Alien Sex Fiend: Edit MVD
Alien Sex Fiend: Overdose MVD
All Aboard: A Collection of Music Videos for Children
All Soul's Day Concert 1983 NO
All Soul's Day Concert 1985 NO
All-Star Country Music Fair BMG, MVD
All-Star Gospel Session MVD, AVE, HBO
The All-Star Reggae Session HBO, MVD, IME
All-Star Swing Festival MVD, VES
All Strings Attached MVD

The Allman Brothers Band: Brothers of the Road MVD, COL
Almighty: Soul Destruction Live MVD
Alyssa Milano: Look in My Heart MVD
Amazing Grace with Bill Moyers PBS, KAR, SIG
Amazon Dreams MTX, KAR
America Live in Central Park NO
American Patchwork: Land Where Blues Began PBS, TVC
American Suite KAR
America's Music, Vol. 2: Country & Western 2 MVD, CTY
America's Music, Vol. 3: Blues 1 CTY, MVD
America's Music, Vol. 4: Blues 2 CTY, MVD, FCT
America's Music, Vol. 5: Rhythm and Blues 1 CTY, MVD, FCT
America's Music, Vol. 6: Rhythm and Blues 2 CTY, MVD, FCT
America's Music, Vol. 7: Folk 1 MVD, CTY
America's Music, Vol. 8: Folk 2 MVD, CTY
America's Music, Vol. 9: Jazz Then Dixieland 1 MVD, CTY
America's Music, Vol. 10: Dixieland 2 CTY, MVD
America's Music, Vol. 11: Soul 1 CTY, MVD, FCT
America's Music, Vol. 12: Soul 2 CTY, MVD, FCT
America's Music, Vol. 13: Gospel 1 MVD, CTY, FCT
America's Music, Vol. 14: Gospel 2 MVD, CTY, FCT
America's Music, Vol. 15: Rock 'n Roll 1 MVD
America's Music, Vol. 16: Rock 'n Roll 2 MVD
Amy Grant: Age to Age MVD, A&M, COL
Amy Grant: Find a Way A&M, COL, MVD
Amy Grant: Heart in Motion A&M, MVD
Amy Grant's Old Fashioned Christmas PGV

Anasa Briggs: Gospel Festival NO
Anderson, Bruford, Wakeman and Howe: In the Big Dream MVD
Andre Walton: Arise Skates SPW
Andrew Lloyd Webber: Requiem HMV, KUL, MVD
Andrew Lloyd Webber: The Premiere Collection Encore PGV
Angelic Gospel Singers: Gospel in Motion MVD
Anima Mundi MIR
Animotion: Video EP MVD
Anita Baker: One Night of Rapture MVD
Anita O'Day: Live at Ronnie Scotts MVD
Anna Russell: The (First) Farewell Concert BFS, MVD, HMV
Anna Russell's Farewell Special MTP
Annie Lennox: Diva BMG, MVD
Anthrax: Attack of the Killer Videos PGV
Anthrax: Live Noize PGV, MVD
Anthrax: Oidivnikufesin (N.F.V.) NO
Anthrax: Through Time P.O.V. PGV, MVD
Any Child is My Child CIG
April Wine NO
April Wine: Live in London NO
Arabella MVD, PGV
Arcadia MVD
"Are My Ears on Wrong?"—A Profile of Charles Ives
Aretha Franklin: Greatest Hits (1980-1994)
Aretha Franklin: Ridin' on the Freeway MVD, COL
Aretha Franklin: The Queen of Soul AVE, MVD, IME
Arlen Roth Band: Live in England MVD
Armored Saint: A Trip Thru Red Times MVD, WRV
A.R.M.S. Concert: Complete MVD
A.R.M.S. Concert: Part 1 MVD, MED
A.R.M.S. Concert: Part 2 MVD, MED
Arrested Development: Home Video MVD

Art Blakey & The Jazz Messengers: Japan 1961 MVD
Art Blakey: The Jazz Life MVD
Art Ensemble of Chicago: Live from the Jazz Showcase MVD, RHP, KIV
The Art of Noise: In Visible Silence MVD
Artur Rubinstein KUL, MVD
Arvis Strickling Jones: From the Inside Out PRH, MVD
Ashford and Simpson NO
Asia in Asia MVD, VES
Asia: Live in Moscow MOV, RHI, MVD
Asia: Live in Moscow, 1990 MVD
Asia: Live in the UK, 1990 MVD
Aswad: Always Wicked MVD
Aswad & Pablo Moses: Reggae in the Hills MVD
Aswad: Distant Thunder Live MVD
Aswad: Live at Light House Studio MVD
Atlantic Starr: As the Band Turns...The Video A&M
Auf der schwaeb'sche Eise'bahne GLV
Aurex Jazz Festival Fusion Super Jam MVD
Australia Now MVD, MED
Avengers MVD
Average White Band Shine NO
B-52s: 1979-1989 MVD
Babalu Music! I Love Lucy's Greatest Hits FXV
Baby Snakes: The Complete Version MVD, MPI
Babyface: Tender Lover MVD, SMV
Bach: All That Bach—A Celebration MVD, VAI, VYG
Bach: Magnificat MVD
Bach: St. John Passion MVD, IME
Back to the 50's, Vol. 1 NO
Bad English MVD, SMV
Bad News Tour MVD, RHI
Bad Religion: Along the Way MVD
B.A.L.L. MVD
Bananarama: And That's Not All... MVD
Bananarama: The Greatest Hits Collection MVD, PGV
Bananarama: True Confessions MVD

The Band: Japan Tour '83 *MVD*
The Band Reunion *MED*
Band Together at CBGB's *MVD*
Banda Vallarta: Banda Vallarta Show *MVD*
Bangles Greatest Hits *MVD, SMV*
Banjo Feedback *WMM*
The Barber of Seville *HMV, MVD, STS*
Barbra Streisand: A Happening in Central Park *FOX, MVD*
Barbra Streisand: Color Me Barbra *MVD, FOX*
Barbra Streisand: My Name is Barbra *MVD, FOX*
Barbra Streisand: One Voice *FOX, MVD*
Barbra Streisand: Putting It Together *FOX, MVD*
Barnes and Barnes: Zabagabee *MVD, RHI*
Barney in Concert *NO*
Barrington Levy *MVD*
Barry Gibb: Now Voyager *MCA, MVD*
Barry Manilow: Because It's Christmas *BMG, SWH*
Barry Manilow: First Special *MGM*
Barry Manilow: Live at the Greek *NO*
Barry Manilow: Live on Broadway *MVD, BMG, SWH*
Barry Manilow: Making of 2 A.M. Paradise Cafe *MVD, COL, BMG*
Barry Manilow: The Concert at Blenheim Palace *MVD*
Barry Manilow: The Greatest Hits...And Then Some *BMG*
Baryshnikov: The Dancer and the Dance *MVD, HMV, PBC*
Basia: Prime Time TV *MVD, SMV*
Batouka: 1st International Festival of Percussion *RHP, FCT*
Bauhaus: Archive *MVD*
Bauhaus/Chrome: Compilation *MVD*
Bauhaus: Shadow of Light *MVD*
Bay City Rollers: Japan Tour, 1976 *MVD*
B.B. King and Friends: A Night of Red Hot Blues *HBO, AVE, MVD*
B.B. King: Blues Master #1 *MVD*
B.B. King: Live at Nick's *NO*
B.B. King: Live at the Apollo *GRP, MVD*
B.B. King: Live in Africa *HBO, MVD, FCT*
B.B. King: Memories of Greatness Live *MVD*
Beast of I.R.S., Vol. 1
The Beastie Boys *MVD, FOX*
The Beastie Boys: The Skills to Pay the Bills *EMI, MVD*
Beat of the Live Drum *COL*
Beatlemania! The Movie *IME*
The Beatles: Live at Budokan *MVD*
Beatles Live: Ready, Steady, Go *MVD, KAR*
The Beatles: The Mystery Trip *MVD*
Beats Go On: Percussion from Pleistocene to Paradiddle *CHI*
Bebe Cece Winans! *MVD*
The Bee Gees: Music Biography *MVD*
Bee Gees: One for All Tour, Vol. 1 *MVD, MPI*
Bee Gees: One for All Tour, Vol. 2 *MVD, MPI*
Beethoven *IFB*

Beethoven and His Music *MTI*
Beethoven Cycle *PRS*
Beethoven: Ordeal and Triumph *NO*
Beethoven Piano Concerti *MVD, HMV*
Beethoven: Piano Concerti 3 & 4 *MVD, PGV*
Beethoven: Piano Concerto No. 3 *MVD*
Beethoven: Piano Concerto No. 5 "Emperor" *MVD, PGV*
Beethoven: Symphony No. 5 *MVD*
Beethoven: Symphony No. 5—Concert *MVD, KUL*
Beethoven Symphony No. 6 "Pastoral" *VWW*
Beethoven: Symphony No. 9 *PGV, MVD*
Beethoven, the Cello, and Paul Tortelier
Beethoven: The Ninth Symphony *KUL*
Beggar's Opera *MVD, HMV, FCT*
Behind the Scenes *CMR, NYS*
Bela Fleck and the Flecktones: Flight of the Cosmic Hippo *WRV*
Belinda *MCA, MVD*
Belinda Carlisle: Belinda Live *MVD, MCG*
Belinda Carlisle: Runaway Live *MCA, MVD*
Belinda Carlisle: Runaway Videos *MVD, MCA*
Bell Biv Devoe: Mental Videos *MVD*
Bell Biv Devoe: Word to the Mutha! *MCA, MVD*
Bellini: La Sonnambula *MVD, VWW*
The Beloved: Happiness *MVD, AVE, FFF*
Ben Vereen: Sing Along Live with the Peter Pan Kids *PPI, MVD*
Ben Webster/Dexter Gordon: Top Tenors *MVD*
Benefit Concert 1
Benefit Concert 2
Benko of Hungary Jazz Band *NO*
Benny Golson/Tubby Hayes *MVD*
Benny Goodman: Adventures in the Kingdom of Swing *SMV*
Benny Goodman: At the Tivoli *KUL, FCT*
Benny Goodman: Live *MVD*
Benny Goodman: 1980 Aurex Jazz Festival *MVD*
Berlin *NO*
Berlin Dream *MVD*
Bernadette Peters in Concert *MCA*
Bernstein: Candide *MVD*
Bernstein Conducts Beethoven: Program 1 *FLI*
Bernstein Conducts Beethoven: Program 2 *FLI*
Bernstein Conducts Beethoven: Program 3 *FLI*
Bernstein Conducts Beethoven: Program 4 *FLI*
Bernstein Conducts Beethoven: Program 5 *FLI*
Bernstein Conducts Beethoven: Program 6 *FLI*
Bernstein Conducts Beethoven: Program 7 *FLI*
Bernstein Conducts Beethoven: Program 8 *FLI*
Bernstein Conducts Beethoven: Program 9 *FLI*
Bernstein Conducts Beethoven: Program 10 *FLI*
Bernstein In Berlin: Ode to Freedom, Beethoven's Symphony No. 9 *MVD*

Bernstein on Beethoven: A Tribute *BFA*
Bernstein on Beethoven: Fidelio *BFA*
Bernstein on Beethoven: Ode to Joy *BFA*
Bernstein: West Side Story *MVD*
Bessie Smith and Friends *MVD, AFR*
Best of Berlin Independence Days *MVD,*
Best of Blondie *MVD*
Best of Elvis Costello and the Attractions *MVD, FOX*
The Best of MTV's 120 Minutes *RHI*
The Best of New Faces *VDM*
The Best of New Orleans Live *MVD*
The Best of New Wave Theatre, Vol. 1 *MVD, RHI*
The Best of New Wave Theatre, Vol. 2 *MVD, RHI*
The Best of Perry Como *TVC*
The Best of Prince's Trust *MVD*
Best of Reggae Sunsplash, Part 1 *SMV, FCT*
Best of Reggae Sunsplash, Part 2 *MVD*
Best of Spike Jones, Vol. 1 *PAR*
Best of Spike Jones, Vol. 2 *PAR*
Best of the Cutting Edge, Vol. 1 *RHI, IME*
Best of the Cutting Edge, Vol. 2 *RHI, IME*
The Best of the Fest: New Orleans Jazz & Heritage Festival *MVD*
Best of Videophile *MVD*
Best of West Coast Rock, Vol. 1 *MVD*
Best of West Coast Rock, Vol. 2 *MVD*
Best of West Coast Rock, Vol. 3 *MVD*
Bette Midler: Art or Bust *VES, LIV*
Bette Midler: Mondo Beyondo *MVD, HBO*
Bette Midler Show *SUE, OM*
Beverly Sills in La Traviata
Big Audio Dynamite: BAD 1 & 2 *SMV, MVD*
Big Bands at Disneyland (3 volume set) *DIS, OM*
Big Bands, Vol. 101 *NO*
Big Bands, Vol. 102 *BAR*
Big Bands, Vol. 103 *BAR*
Big Bands, Vol. 104 *BAR*
Big Bands, Vol. 105 *BAR*
Big Bands, Vol. 106 *BAR*
Big Bands, Vol. 107 *MVD, BAR*
Big Bands, Vol. 108 *BAR*
Big Bands, Vol. 109 *BAR*
Big Bands, Vol. 110 *BAR*
Big Bands, Vol. 111 *BAR*
Big Black: Live Video *MVD*
Big Black: Pigpile *MVD*
Big Black: The Last Blast *MVD*
Big Brother and the Holding Company: Ball and Chain *MVD, RHI*
Big Country Live *MVD, MED*
Big Country: Live in New York *MVD*
Big Daddy Kane: Chocolate City *MVD, WRV*
Big Pig—Bonk: The Videos *A&M*
The Biggest Band Show in the World *TVC*
Bill Bruford: Bruford and the Beat *MVD,*
Bill Evans *CMR*
Bill Evans: Live at the Maintenance Shop, 1979 *MVD*

Bernstein on Beethoven: A
Bill Evans Trio *SHR*
Bill Evans: Universal Mind *FCT*
Bill Harley: Who Made this Mess *PGV, MVD*
Bill Watrous *NO*
Bill Wyman *NO*
Bill Wyman: Digital Dreams *MVD, MED*
Billy Bragg Goes to Moscow & Norton, Virginia Too *MVD*
Billy Dean: Video Hits *MVD*
Billy Eckstine/Dizzy Gillespie Be-Bop Big Bands *MVD*
Billy Idol: Shock to the System *MVD*
Billy Idol: The Charmed Life Videos *MVD*
Billy Idol: Vital Idol *MVD, VES, LIV*
Billy Joe Royal *MVD, AVE, FFF*
Billy Joel: Eye of the Storm *SMV*
Billy Joel Live at Yankee Stadium *MVD, SMV*
Billy Joel Live from Long Island *MVD, FOX*
Billy Joel: Shades of Grey *SMV, MVD*
Billy Joel: Stormfront *MVD*
Billy Joel: The Video Album, Vol. 1 *MVD, FOX*
Billy Joel: The Video Album, Vol. 2 *MVD, FOX*
Billy Ocean: In London *MVD, COL*
Billy Ocean: Tear Down These Hits *MVD, COL*
Billy Ray Cyrus *PGV, MVD*
Billy Ray Cyrus: Live *PGV*
Billy Ray Cyrus: The Video Collection *PGV, MVD*
Billy Squier *NO*
Bing Crosby: The Magic of Bing Crosby, Part 1 *AVE, MVD, FFF*
Bingoboys: How To Dance (The Extended Dance Version) *MVD, AVE, FFF*
Birthday Party: Pleasure Heads Must Burn *MVD*
Bizarre Music Television *MVD, RHI*
Black & Tan/St. Louis Blues *CCB*
Black Box: Video Dreams 1991 *BMG*
Black Crowes: Who Killed That Bird Out On Your Window Sill...The Movie *WRV*
Black Diamond Jazz Band *NO*
Black Eagle Jazz Band *NO*
Black Expo Gospel Explosion #4 *BMG, MVD*
Black Flag: Live in San Francisco *MVD*
Black Flag: Six Pack *MVD*
Black Flag: T.V. Party *NO*
Black Jazz & Blues *VYY, MVD, FCT*
Black Music in America: The Seventies *LCA*
Black Sabbath Live: Never Say Die *MVD*
Black Sabbath: Live 1978 *MVD*
Black Sabbath: The Black Sabbath Story, Vol. 1, 1970-1978 *WEA, MVD*
Black Sabbath: The Black Sabbath Story, Vol. 2, 1978-1992 *WRV, MVD*
Black Uhuru and Steel Pulse: Tribute to Bob Marley *MVD*
Black Uhuru: Tear It Up Live *PGV, MVD*
Blanche Thebom in Opera and Song *MVD, VAI, FCT*
Blancmange *NO*
Blondie: Eat to the Beat *MVD, WAR*
Blondie Live! *MCA, MVD*
Blood on the Cats III...For a Few Pussies More *MVD*

Blood Sweat and Tears: 1973 BST *MVD*
Blotto *NO*
Blow Monkeys: Digging Your Video *MVD, COL*
Blow Monkeys: Video LP *MVD*
Blue Note I *NO*
Blue Oyster Cult: Live '76 *MVD*
The Blue Sky Awards Music Videos: A Clean Air Celebration *MPI,*
Blue Suede Shoes: A Rockabilly Session with Carl Perkins and Friends *MVD, MCA*
Bluebeard's Castle *MVD, PGV, PME*
The Blues *MVD*
The Blues Accordin' to Lightnin' Hopkins *MVD, FFM, FCT*
Blues Alive *BMG, MVD, COL*
Blues Like Showers of Rain *MVD, RHP, FCT*
Blues Masters, Vol. 1 *FCT*
Blues Masters, Vol. 2 *FCT*
The Bluffers: Music Video *JFK, WTA*
Bo Diddley and the All Star Jam Show *PGV, MVD, FCT*
Bob Dylan: The 30th Anniversary Concert Celebration *COL*
Bob Dylan, Tom Petty & the Heartbreakers: Hard to Handle *FOX*
Bob James Live *VWW, MVD, MBP*
Bob Marley and the Wailers *COL*
Bob Marley and the Wailers: Live at the Rainbow *MVD, COL*
Bob Marley and the Wailers: Live from the Santa Barbara *NO*
Bob Marley: Legend *MVD, COL, FCT*
The Bob Marley Story: Caribbean Nights *FCT, MVD*
Bobby and the Midnites *VWW, FCT*
Bobby Brown: Bobby Bobby Bobby *MCA*
Bobby Brown: His Prerogative *MVD*
Bobby Brown: Humpin' Around *MCA, MVD*
Bobby Caldwell: Live in Tokyo 1991 *MVD*
Bobby Darin: The Darin Invasion *VWW, MVD, MBP*
Bobby McFerrin: Spontaneous Inventions *MVD, FFF*
Bobby Short & Friends *MVD, MGM*
Bobby Short at the Cafe Carlyle *MVD, VWW, MBP*
Bobby Vinton *RKO*
Body Music *NO*
Bolshoi Ballet: Les Sylphides *VWW, MBP, STS*
Bon Jovi: Access All Areas *MVD, PGV, BTV*
Bon Jovi: Breakout *MVD*
Bon Jovi: Keep the Faith, an Evening with Bon Jovi *PGV, MVD*
Bon Jovi: Keep the Faith—The Videos *PGV*
Bon Jovi: New Jersey—The Videos *MVD, PGV*
Bon Jovi: Slippery When Wet *MVD*
Bon Jovi: The Interview Sessions *MVD*
Bon Jovi: Tokyo Road *MVD*
Bones
Bonnie Raitt: The Video Collection *CAP, MVD*
Boogie-Doodle *IFB*

Boogie Down Productions: Edutainment *MVD*
Boogie Down Productions Live *MVD, BMG*
Born to Boogie *MPI, MVD*
Born to Rock: The T.A.M.I.-T.N.T. Show *MVD, MED, FCT*
Born to Swing: The Count Basie Alumni *MVD, KIV, FCT*
Boulez on Varese *CMR, NYS*
Boulez X 3 *CMR, NYS*
Boy George: Sold *MVD*
The Boys: Crazy *MVD*
The Boys: Video Messages *MVD*
Brahms and His Music *MTI*
Brahms: Concerto in "A" for Violin & Cello *MVD*
Brahms: Piano Concerto No. 1 *VWV*
Brahms: Symphonies 3 & 4 *MVD, PGV*
Brahms: Symphony No. 1 *VWV*
Branford Marsalis: Steep *MVD, FOX, FCT*
Branford Marsalis: The Music Tells You *SMV, MVD*
The Brass Menagerie *FVL*
Brazilian Knights & A Lady *MVD*
Breakin' Metal *MVD*
Breakin' Metal Special *MVD*
Breathe: All That Jazz *MVD*
Brecker Brothers: Return of the Brecker Brothers *GRP*
Brenda Lee: An Evening with Brenda Lee *MVD*
Brian Eno: Excerpt from the Khumba Nela *MVD*
Brian Eno: Imaginary Landscapes *MFV, FCT*
Brian Eno: Thursday Afternoon *MVD*
British Big Beat: The Invasion *MVD, RHI*
British Rock: The Legends of Punk & New Wave *MVD, VES, LIV*
Britny Fox: Year of the Fox *MVD, MVD*
Britten, the Voice, and Peter Pears
Broken Bones: Live at Leeds *MVD*
Brooks & Dunn: Pardners—The Brand New Man Videos *BMG*
Bruce Dickinson: Dive! Dive! Live *MVD, SMV*
Bruce Hornsby and the Range: A Night on the Town *MVD, COL, BMG*
Bruce Springsteen and Friends *MVD*
Bruce Springsteen in Concert: MTV Plugged *SMV, MVD*
Bruce Springsteen Video Anthology: 1978-88 *MVD, SMV*
Bruce Willis: Return of Bruno *MVD, HBO*
Bruckner: Symphony No. 7 *MVD, PGV*
Bryan Adams: Reckless *MVD, A&M, COL*
Bryan Adams: So Far, So Good *A&M*
Bryan Adams: Waking Up the Neighbors Videos *PGV*
Bryan Ferry: New Town *MVD*
Bubblegum Crisis Music Video: Hurricane Live 2032 *WTA*
Bubblegum Crisis Music Video: Hurricane Live 2033 *ANI*
Bubblegum Crisis Music Video: Tinsel City Rhapsody *WTA*
Buck Creek Jazz Band No. 1 *NO*
Buck Creek Jazz Band No. 2 *NO*

Buckwheat Zydeco: Taking it Home *MVD, PGV*
Bud Powell *MVD*
Buddy Barnes: Live from Studio B *MVD, FCT*
Buddy Rich *MVD*
Buddy Rich Memorial Scholarship Concert *MVD,*
Buffalo Jazz Fest *NO*
BulletBoys: Pigs in Mud *MVD, WRV*
Bunny Wailer in Concert *SHR*
Buried Treasures, Vol. 1: The Directors *MVD*
Buried Treasures, Vol. 2: Reggae Classics *PGV, MVD, FCT*
Burning Spear: Live in Paris *MVD*
Buzzcocks: Auf Wiedersehen *NO*
The Buzzcocks: Playback *MVD*
C/Z Records: We've Come For Your Daughters, Vol. 1 *MVD*
Cab Calloway and His Orchestra *MVD*
Cabaret Voltaire: Gasoline in Your Eye *NO*
The California Raisins 2: Raisins, Sold Out *TMG, WTA*
California to New York Island *CMR, NYS*
Camel: Pressure Points Live in Concert *MVD*
Cameo: Video EP *MVD*
Cameo: Word Up *PGV, MVD*
Canadian Brass: Home Movies *FCT*
Canadian Reggae Music Awards '88 *MVD, FCT*
Cancion Romantica *NJN*
Canciones de Mi Tierra *MVD*
C&C Music Factory: Everbody Dance Now *SMV*
Canned Heat: Boogie Assault *MVD,, MON*
Cannonball Adderly: 1983 Live *MVD*
Caribbean Music and Dance *MUS, FCT*
Carla Bley Band: Joyful Noise *MVD*
Carly Simon: Live from Martha's Vineyard *MVD, HBO, FFF*
Carly Simon: My Romance in Concert *MVD, BMG*
Carman: Coming on Strong (Live in Concert) *MVD, SMV*
Carmen *ING, COL, HMV*
Carmen McRae Live *MVD, HMV, FCT*
Carmina Burana *FCT, KUL*
Carnegie Hall at 100: A Place of Dreams *BMG, FCT*
Carnival of the Animals *CMR, NYS*
Carol Jo Brown: Turn It Up *NO*
Carole King: One to One *MVD, MGM*
Carols for Christmas *HMV, HBO*
Carreras, Domingo, Pavarotti: Three Tenors in Concert *MVD, PGV*
The Cars: Heartbeat City *MVD, WAR*
The Cars: 1984-1985—Live *MVD, VES*
Casey Kasem's Rock 'n Roll Goldmine: The San Francisco Sound *VES, MOV, MVD*
Casey Kasem's Rock 'n Roll Goldmine: The Sixties *VES, MOV, MVD*
Casey Kasem's Rock 'n Roll Goldmine: The Soul Years *VES, MOV, MVD*
Casiopea: Made in Melbourne *MVD*

Cassandra Wilson Live *PGV, MVD*
Catch a Rising Star's 10th Anniversary *COL*
Cathy Dennis: Touch Me *MVD*
Cavalcade of Stars, Vol. 2 *NOS*
Cavalleria Rusticana *MVD, VAI, FCT*
Cecil Taylor: Burning Poles *MFV, FCT*
A Celebration *MVD, MON*
Celine Dion: Unison *SMV*
Celtic Frost: Live at the Hammersmith Odeon *MVD*
Central Ohio Hot Jazz Fest *NO*
Chaconne for Traditional Japanese Instruments *NO*
Chaka Khan Live *NO*
Chaka Khan: My Night *NO*
Chamber Music: The String Quartet *NO*
The Chameleons: Live at Camden Palace *MVD*
Chant a Capella *EAI*
Charles Aznavour: Memories of Greatness Live *MVD*
Charles Haughey's Ireland *RGO*
Charles Johnson & the Revivers: One Night Revival *XVC*
Charles Mingus: Live in Norway, 1964 *MVD*
Charles Mingus Sextet *SHR*
Charles Trenet: Chansons *MVD*
Charley Pride: Live! *LTY, BMG*
Charlie Byrd: Live in New Orleans *MVD,*
The Charlie Daniels Band: Saratoga Concert *MVD, FOX*
Charlie Daniels: Homefolks and Highways *MVD, CAF*
Charlie Peacock
Charlie Pride: An Evening with Charlie Pride *MVD*
Chartbusters from Kids Incorporated *NO*
Chase the Devil: Religious Music of the Appalachians *MVD, FCT, SHR*
Cheap Trick: Every Trick in the Book *SMV, MVD, IME*
Cheech and Chong: Get Out of My Room *MCA*
Cheetachrome: M°S (Live) *MVD*
Chemical People: Live *MVD*
Chen and China's Symphony *CIG*
Cher: Extravaganza: Live at the Mirage *BMG, MVD*
Cherry Bombz *MVD*
Cheryl Ladd: Fascinated *NO*
Chess Moves *COL*
Chet Atkins and Friends: Music from the Heart *MVD, AVE, HBO*
Chet Baker: Candy *MVD*
Chet Baker/Elvis Costello: Live at Ronnie Scott's *MVD*
Chet Baker: My Funny Valentine *MVD*
Chicago: And the Band Played On *WRV, MVD*
Chicago Basketball: A Musical Celebration *MPI*
Chicago Bears: Super Bowl Shuffle *MPI*
Chicago Beat: Rock Lobster *MVD*
Chicago Blues *MVD, RHP, TLF*
Chicago: Chicago 17 *NO*
Chicago: In Concert at the Greek Theatre *WRV*
Chicago Rhythm *NO*
Chicago Six Jazz Band *NO*
Chick Corea *NO*
Chick Corea: A Very Special Concert *MVD*
Chick Corea & Gary Burton: Live in Tokyo *MVD*

Chick Corea Elektric Band: Inside Out *MVD*
Chick Corea: In Madrid *MVD*
Chico Hamilton: The Jazz Life *MVD, FCT*
The Chieftains: An Irish Evening *BMG, MVD*
The Chieftains: Another Country *BMG*
The Chieftains in China *SHR*
The Chieftains: The Bells of Dublin *BMG*
Children's Songs & Stories with the Muppets *FOX*
Children's Songs Around the World
Choices for the Future *NO*
Chopi Music of Mozambique/Banguza Timbila *FFM, ICA, FCT*
Chopin/Schubert Recital: Zimerman (laserdisc) *MVD, PGV*
Chris de Burgh: Live from Dublin *MVD*
Chris Isaak: Wicked Game *MVD, WRV*
Christian Death: The Heretics Alive *MVD*
Christians: The Collection *MVD*
Christine McVie: The Video Album *MVD, LIV, VES*
Christmas at Ripon Cathedral *HMV, VYG*
The Christmas Carol Video *NO*
Christmas Carols from England *KUL, FUS*
A Christmas Celebration *BTV, MPI*
Christmas Classics 3 *NO*
Christmas from St. Patrick's Cathedral *HMV*
The Christmas Oratorio *MVD, FHS*
Christmas Video Sing-Along *SMV, MVD*
Christmas with Eleanor Steber *VAI, FCT*
Christmas with Flicka *VWV, MVD, IME*
Christmas with Jose Carreras *KUL*
Christmas with Luciano Pavarotti *MVD, VTR, FUS*
Christmas with the Westminster Choir *NJN*
Christmastide with Jessye Norman
Christopher Tree *FFM*
Chronos *BMG, MVD, TVC*
Chrysanthemum Ragtime Band *NO*
Chuck Berry: Hail! Hail! Rock 'n' Roll *MCA, MVD, FCT*
Chuck Berry: Rock & Roll Music *WRV, MVD, FCT*
Chuck's Choice Cuts *AOV*
The Church: Goldfish (Jokes, Magic & Souvenirs) *BMG*
Cinderella: Heartbreak Station Video Collection *PGV*
Cinderella: Night Songs *MVD, PGV*
Cinderella: Tales from the Gypsy Road *MVD, PGV*
Circuit Rider With Noel Paul Stookey *TMP*
Cissy Houston: Sweet Inspiration *CIG*
Clancy Brothers and Tommy Makem: Reunion Concert *SHR*
Clannad: Pastpresent *MVD, BMG*
Clark Sisters in Concert *XVC, FCT*
The Clash: Rude Boy *MVD, FOX, SMV*
The Clash: This is Video Clash *MVD, FOX*
Classic Jazz *MVD*

Classic Performances *HBO*
A Classical Christmas *MVD*
Claude Bolling: Concerto for Classic Guitar & Jazz Piano *NO*
Claudio Abbado: Music for Europe *MVD*
Claudio Arrau Signature Performance Series *VAI*
Cliff Richard: Private Collection
Cliff Richard: The Event
Cliff Richard: The Video Connection
Cliff Richard: Together with Cliff Richard *MVD*
Clifton Chenier: The King of Zydeco *MVD, FFM*
Climax Blues Band: Live from London *COL*
Climie Fisher: The Best of Everything *MVD*
Clint Black: Put Yourself in My Shoes *MVD, BMG*
Clouds *NOR*
Club Date: Milt Jackson *NO*
Club MTV Party to Go *MVD*
Club MTV Party to Go, Vol. 2 *WEA, MVD*
Cobham Meets Bellson *VWV, MBP*
Cold Cut: Doctor in the Video *MVD*
Coleman Hawkins/Harry Edison Quintet *MVD*
Colombian Volcano Concert *MVD*
Color Me Badd: Video Scrapbook 1991 *WRV*
Coloratura Mad Scenes *CMR, NYS*
Combat Tour Live *MVD*
Comedy in Music *VYY*
Comedy Music Videos *VES*
Comedy Videos *VES*
Coming Home for Friends *MVD*
Commissioned in Concert *XVC, MVD*
Commissioned: Number 7 *PGV*
Communards: Live at Full House *MVD*
Community Three Records: Comm3TV, Vol. 1 *MVD*
The Compleat Beatles ▶*MVD, MGM*
The Complete Claudio Arrau Video Collection *NO*
Completely Country: Various Artists *MVD, WRV*
Concerning the French Horn *CMR, NYS*
Concert Aid *NO*
Concert for Bangladesh *PAR, MVD, FCT*
Concert for Planet Earth *SMV*
Concerto at Work *CIG*
Concerto! Claude Frank, Soloist
Concrete Blonde: 12/16/86 - 9/17/90 *MVD*
Concrete Blonde: Mid Life Crisis *EMI, MVD*
Coney Hatch *NO*
Conjunto Nuestro: Salsa *NJN*
Connie Francis: A Legend in Concert *MVD, MPI*
The Continuity of Tradition *UWA*
Contraband *MVD*
Contraband: All the Way from Memphis *MCA*
Conway Twitty: #1 Hits *SIM*
Conway Twitty: King of Hits *SIM*
Cool Cats: 25 Years of Rock 'n' Roll Style *MVD, MGM*
Cool Runnings: The Reggae Movie *MVD, TPV, FCT*
Coroner: No More Color Tour '90 *MVD, SVI*
Costume Party *FCT,*

Cottonmouth D'Arcy's Jazz Vipers *NO*
Count Basie & Friends *MVD*
Count Basie: In Concert *MVD*
Count Basie In England, 1965 *MVD*
Count Basie Live at the Hollywood Palladium *NO*
Count Basie: Live in Berlin, 1968 *MVD*
Countrified *MVD*
Country *MVD*
Country Christmas *BMG*
Country Comes Alive *MVD, COL, LTY*
Country Gold, Vol. 1 *UND, MVD*
Country Gold, Vol. 2 *RHI, MVD*
Country Ladies: Live *MVD*
Country Love Songs *MVD*
Country Music Classics *SHR*
Country Music Jamboree *NOS, DVT*
Country Music Video Magazine, Vol. 4 *BMG*
Country Music with the Muppets *FOX*
Country Outlaws: Live *MVD*
Country Stars: A New Tradition *MVD, AVE, HBO*
Country Video Hall of Fame, Vol. 1 *QVD, MVD*
Country Video Hall of Fame, Vol. 2 *QVD, MVD*
Country Video Hall of Fame, Vol. 3 *QVD, MVD*
Country Video Hall of Fame, Vol. 4 *QVD, MVD*
Country-Western All-Stars *NOS, DVT*
Country's Cutting Edge *BST*
Country's First Ladies *BST, FUS*
The Cramps: Live at Napa State Mental Hospital *MVD*
The Cranberries: Live *PGV*
Crash & Burn Rock! *MVD*
Cream Farewell Concert *NOS, DVT, MLB*
The Creation *NO*
Creation Compilation *MVD*
Creation Compilation, Vol. 1 *MVD*
Creation Compilation, Vol. 2 *MVD*
Critical Art Ensemble *MWF*
Crosby, Stills & Nash: Daylight Again *MVD, MCA*
Crosby, Stills & Nash: Long Time Comin' *MVD, MPI*
Crucifix & M.D.C.: Compilation *MVD*
Cruisin' *NO*
Cruisin' through the 50's *NO*
Cruisin' through the 50's, Vol. 2 *NO*
Cruisin' thru the 60's *NO*
The Crusaders: Live! Midnight Triangle *MCA, MVD*
The Crusaders: Live Tokyo Superjam *MVD*
Crystal Gayle Live *PSM*
Cuban Charanga Music *NJN*
Cuban Music: Marco Rizo *NJN*
Cubik Rave *MVD*
CUD: When at Home Film Me *MVD*
The Cult: Dream Time Live at the Lyceum *MVD*
The Cult: Electric Love *MVD*
The Cult: Sonic Ceremony *MVD*
Culture Club: Kiss Across the Ocean *FOX*
Culture Club: This Time *MVD*
The Cure: Live in Japan *MVD*
The Cure: Picture Show *MVD*
The Cure: Play Out *MVD*
The Cure: Show *MVD*
The Cure: Staring at the Sea—Images *MVD*
Curiosity Killed the Cat: Running the Distance *MVD*

A Currier & Ives Christmas *REP*
Curtain Call: USA *VCI*
Curtis Mayfield: Live at Ronnie Scott's *RHI, MVD*
Cutting Crew *MVD*
Cutting Crew: Live at Full House *MVD*
Cutting Edge *RHI*
Cyndi Lauper in Paris *MVD, FOX*
Czech Polkas
Czech Polkas and Songs
Czech Polkas and Waltzes
D-Mob: A Little Bit of This, a Little Bit of That *MVD, PGV*
Daily Intonalization Studies *NO*
Damn Yankees *WRV*
Damn Yankees: Uprising *WRV*
The Damned: Final Damnation *BMG, PGV, MVD*
The Damned: Live 79 *MVD*
Dan Fogelberg: Greetings from the West *MVD, PGV*
Dance Hall Report *MVD*
Dance Hall Sizzling in Tokyo *MVD*
Dance Hall Stage Show '86 *MVD, KRV*
Dance Now *MVD*
Dance Traxx *AVE*
Dance Traxx, Vol. 2 *WAR, OM*
Daniel Lanois: Rocky World *WRV, MVD*
Danspak *NO*
Danspak 2 *NO*
Danspak 3: Future Pop *NO*
Danzig *MVD, WRV*
Danzig 2: Lucifuge the Video *WRV, MVD*
Dark Ages: Video Collection *MVD, FCT*
Darwyn Apple: Darwyn Apple, Violinist *NET*
Daryl Coley: Live *MVD, SPW*
Daryl Hall and John Oates: Live at the Apollo *MVD, COL*
Daryl Hall and John Oates: Rhythm & Blues *MVD*
Daryl Hall and John Oates: Rock 'n Soul Live *MVD, COL*
Daryl Hall and John Oates: The Liberty Concert *MVD*
Daryl Hall and John Oates Video Collection: 7 Big Ones *MVD, COL, LTY*
Das EFX: Straight from da Sewer *MVD*
Das Konzert November 1989 *NO*
Das Rheingold *PGV, PME*
Date with Dizzy *FLI*
Dave Grusin and the New York/L.A. Dream Band *MVD, MCA*
Dave Holland Quintet: Freiburg Music Festival '85 *MVD*
Dave Koz & Phil Perry: Live at the Strand *EMI, MVD*
Dave Mason in Concert *MON, MVD*
Dave Mason: Live at Perkins Palace *NO*
Dave Stewart & the Spiritual Cowboys *MVD*
David Bowie *MVD*
David Bowie: Black Tie White Noise *BMG*
David Bowie: Day In Day Out *NO*
David Bowie: Jazzin for Blue Jean *NO*
David Bowie: Love You Till Tuesday *MVD, PGV*
David Bowie: Ricochet *MVD*
David Bowie: Serious Moonlight *MED*
David Bowie: The Glass Spider Tour *MVD, MPI*
David Bowie: The Video Collection

David Bowie: Ziggy Stardust & the Spiders from Mars *MVD, LTY*
David Byrne: Between the Teeth *MVD*
David Gilmour: In Concert *MVD, FOX*
David Jack Live! Makin' Music, Makin' Friends *NO*
David Lee Roth *MVD, WRV*
David Oistrakh: Remembering a Musician *MVD, KUL, ING*
David Sanborn: Love and Happiness *MVD, WRV*
David Stout: Lover's Cell *FCT*
David Sylvian: Special *MVD*
Dazzle Dancing: Let's Go Dancing *LIV*
Dead Kennedys: Documentary *MVD*
Dead Kennedys Live *RHI, MVD*
Dead Kennedys: Live 1978-1986 *MVD*
Dead Kennedys: Part 1 *NO*
Dead or Alive: Rip It Up *MVD*
Dead or Alive: Rip It Up Live! *MVD, SMV*
Death is Just the Beginning *MVD*
Debbie Gibson: Live Around the World *MVD, AVE, FFF*
Debbie Gibson: Live in Concert *MVD, AVE*
Debbie Gibson: Out of the Blue *MVD, AVE, FFF*
Debussy/Ravel *MVD, FCT*
Decline of Western Civilization 1 ▶*MVD, MED*
Decline of Western Civilization 2: The Metal Years *COL, MVD, FCT*
Decoder *MVD*
Deep Heat *MVD*
Deep Purple: Live at Budokan '75 *MVD*
Deep Purple: Machine Head Live 1972 *MVD*
Deep Purple: The Videosingles *MVD, PGV*
Def Hype Clips *MVD, MCA*
Def Jam Classics: Vols. 1 and 2 *MVD, SMV*
Def Leppard: Historia *MVD, PGV*
Def Leppard: In the Round - In Your Face - Live *PGV, MVD*
Def Leppard: Visualize *PGV, MVD*
Deja View *MVD, LHV, WAR*
Deleon Richards in Concert *MVD*
Dennis Brown: Superfest '89 *MVD*
Dennis Chambers: Serious Moves *MVD*
Dennis De Young: Three Piece Suite *A&M*
Depeche Mode: 101 *MVD, WRV*
Depeche Mode: Devotional *WRV, MVD*
Depeche Mode: Some Great Videos *WRV, MVD*
Depeche Mode: Songs of Faith and Devotion—Live *WRV*
Depeche Mode: Strange *MVD, WRV*
Depeche Mode: Strange Too *MVD, WRV*
Depeche Mode: The World We Live in and Live at Hamburg *MVD, WRV*
Der Rosenkavalier *HMV, MVD*
Derrick Harriott Live *KRV*
Desde Monterey con Sabor a Mexico *MVD*
Destination: Mozart: A Night at the Opera with Peter Sellars *KUL, FCT, MVD*
Destination: Universe *BMG, MVD, LUM*

Deutsche Weihnacht mit Heino *GLV*
Devo *NO*
Devo: The Men Who Make the Music *MVD, WAR*
Devo: We're All Devo *MVD*
Dexy's Midnight Runners: The Bridge *MVD, BMG, COL*
DFW Mass Choir: I Will Let Nothing Separate Me *MLC, MVD*
Dharma Bums: Live *MVD*
Diamanda Galas: Judgement Day *MVD*
Diamanda Galas: The Litanies of Satan *MVD*
Diana Ross in Concert *COL*
Diana Ross: The Lady Sings...Jazz & Blues *PGV, MVD*
Diana Ross: Visions of Diana Ross *MVD, COL*
Diane Reeves: The New Orleans Concert *MVD*
Diane Schuur and the Count Basie Orchestra *GRP*
Diane Schuur and the Count Basie Orchestra *MVD*
Diane Schuur: Live in Japan 1991 *MVD*
Dick Clark's Best of Bandstand *MVD, LIV, VES*
Dick Clark's Best of Bandstand: The Superstars *MVD, LIV, VES*
Dick Clark's Golden Greats *MPI*
The Dicks: Fun with Dick and Jane *MVD*
Didjits: Knocked Up *MVD*
Die Fledermaus, Vol. 1 & 2 *MVD, HMV*
Die Ganze Welt ist Himmelblau *GLV*
Die Musik kommt... *GLV*
Die Super Hit-Parade der Volksmusik *GLV*
Dino: "Dino" *MVD*
Dio: A Special from the Spectrum *MVD, WRV*
Dio: Diamonds—The Best of Dio *MVD*
Dio: Live Super Rock 1985 *MVD*
Dio: Sacred Heart Video *MVD, WRV*
Dio: Time Machine *MVD, WRV*
Dionne Warwick: In London *MVD, IME*
Dionne Warwick Live *MVD, PSM*
Dire Straits *WAR, OM*
Dire Straits: Alchemy Live *MED, MVD, IME*
Dire Straits: Brothers in Arms *MVD, WRV*
Dire Straits: On the Night *WAR, MVD*
Dire Straits: The Videos *WAR*
The Dirt Band Tonight *NO*
Dirty Dancing: Live in Concert *LIV, VES*
Divine Madness *WAR*
Dizzy Gillespie *NO*
Dizzy Gillespie: A Night in Chicago *VWV, FCT*
Dizzy Gillespie: A Night in Tunisia *VWV, MVD, KAR*
The Dizzy Gillespie Ages *MVD*
Dizzy Gillespie: Diz & Bird & Hawk *MVD*
Dizzy Gillespie: In Redondo Beach *MVD*
Dizzy Gillespie: Live in London *KUL, FCT*
Dizzy Gillespie's Dream Band *AFR*
DJ Jazzy Jeff & the Fresh Prince: Summertime (and Other Hits) *BMG*

Django Reinhardt: Gypsy Guitar—The Legacy of Django Reinhardt *MVD, SHR*
Do They Know It's Christmas? *VES, OM*
D.O.A.: A Night at the Assassination Club *MVD*
D.O.A.: A Right of Passage *VES, LIV, MVD*
D.O.A.: At the Stone *MVD*
D.O.A.: The End *MVD*
Doc & Merle Watson: Live Ramblin' *MVD, SHR, PMS*
Doc Mo She *MVD*
Doc Watson *MVD*
Dr. Demento's 20th Anniversary Collection *MVD, RHI, FCT*
Dr. Feelgood *MVD*
Dr. John & Friends: New Orleans Swamp *MVD*
Dr. John: Live at the Marquee *MVD*
Dr. Mattie Moss Clark and Friends *PRH, MVD*
Doggy Style: A Hard Dog's Night *MVD*
Dokken: Unchain the Night *MVD, CAN*
Dolly in London *COL*
Domingo/Pavarotti/Carreras: The Three Tenors—Encore *MVD, IME*
Don Carlo *HMV, PAR, MVD*
Don Giovanni *BFS, HMV, MVD*
Don Johnson: Heartbeat *MVD, FOX*
Don McLean: Live in Concert *MVD*
Don Menza: Live in New Orleans *MVD*
Don Williams Live! *MVD, BMG*
Donna Summer: A Hot Summer Night *MVD*
Donnie Harper & New Jersey Mass Choir: I'll Tell It *PRH, MVD*
Donnie Iris and the Cruisers *NO*
Don't Watch That, Watch This! *NO*
Don't Watch That, Watch This! Vol. 2 *NO*
Doobie Brothers: Cycle Tour in Hawaii '90 *MVD*
Doobie Brothers: Farewell Live '82 *MVD*
Doobie Brothers: Listen to the Music *MVD, LIV, VES*
Doomsday News: Cutting Edge Metal *MVD*
Doomsday News: More Cutting Edge Metal *MVD, SVI*
The Doors: A Tribute to Jim Morrison *MVD, WAR, FCT*
The Doors: Dance on Fire *MCA, MVD*
The Doors: Doors are Open *MVD, VMK*
The Doors: Light My Fire *MVD, AVE, FFF*
The Doors: Live at the Hollywood Bowl *MCA, MVD*
The Doors: Live in Europe, 1968 *MVD, AVE, HBO*
The Doors: Soft Parade, a Retrospective *MCA*
Dope, Guns & F——g in the Street *MVD*
Dope, Guns & F——g Up Your Videodeck, Vol. 2 *MVD*
Doug Stone: A Video Jukebox *SMV, MVD*
The Dream Academy *WRV*
The Dream Syndicate: Weathered and Torn *MVD*
Dream Theater: Images and Words—Live in Tokyo *AVE, MVD*
Dream Warriors *MVD*
D.R.I.: Live at the Ritz *PGV, MVD, IME*

The Drifters: There Goes My Baby *MVD*

Drivin N Cryin: Live On Fire *PGV, MVD*

Drums in the City *NJN*

DTV: Golden Oldies *DIS, OM*

DTV: Groovin' for a '60s Afternoon *DIS, OM*

DTV: Love Songs *DIS, OM*

DTV: Pop & Rock *DIS*

DTV: Rock, Rhythm and Blues *DIS, OM*

Dubliners Live *RGO, PPI*

Duets: Aaron Neville/Lou Reed *MVD, MPI*

Duke Ellington & His Orchestra: 1929-1952 *MVD, AFR*

Duke Ellington: In Europe, 1963-64 *MVD*

Duke Ellington: Memories of Duke *MVD, AFR*

Duke Ellington: 1962 *MVD*

Duke Ellington: Solitude *MVD*

Dukes of Dixieland and Friends *MVD,, FCT*

Dukes of Dixieland: Tribute to Jelly Roll Morton *MVD*

Duran Duran *NO*

Duran Duran: Arena *MVD*

Duran Duran: Dancing on the Valentine *NO*

Duran Duran: Decade *MVD*

Duran Duran: Girls on Film/Hungry Like the Wolf *MVD*

Duran Duran: Making of Arena *MVD*

Duran Duran: Sing Blue Silver *IME*

Duran Duran: Three to Get Ready *MVD*

Duran Duran: Working for the Skin Trade *MVD*

Dvorak: Symphony No. 8 *MVD, BMG*

Dvorak's Slavic Dance *NO*

Dwight Yoakam: Just Lookin' for a Hit *MVD, WRV*

Dynamite Chicken *NO*

Earl Hines & Coleman Hawkins: Jazz *MVD, KIV, RHP*

Earl Thomas Conley: Greatest Video Hits *MVD, COL, LTY*

Early American Song *CMR, NYS*

Early Elvis *NO*

Early Music from Chicago *NO*

Earth Dance: Nature in Motion *MVD, LUM, WSH*

Earth Dreaming *WSH, MVD, LUM*

Earth, Wind & Fire in Concert *MVD, VES*

Earth, Wind & Fire: The Eternal Vision *SMV*

Eartha Kitt: The Most Exciting Woman in the World *KUL*

Earthrise: The Rainforest Video *MVD*

Easter with Fred Waring *VAI, FCT*

EBN: Commercial Entertainment Product *MVD*

Echo & the Bunnymen: The Pictures on My Wall *MVD*

Echoes of Ellington, Vol. 1 *MVD, PGV*

Echoes of Ellington, Vol. 2 *MVD*

Eddie Jefferson: Live from the Jazz Showcase *MVD, RHP, KIV*

Eddie Money: Picture of Money *MVD, SMV*

Eddie "Son" House, Jr. & Buddy Guy *CMR*

Edinburgh Military Tattoo 1987 *PME, FUS*

Edinburgh Military Tattoo 1988 *HMV, PME*

Edith Piaf: Chansons *MVD*

Edith Piaf: La Vie en Rose *MVD, FHS, APD*

Edvard Grieg: The Man and His Music *AIM*

Edwyn Collins: Phantasmagoria *MVD*

Egberto Gismonti *MVD, PRS*

1812 Overture *BFA*

El Maestro: Primitivo Santos *NJN*

Eleanor Steber in Opera and Oratorio *VAI, FCT*

Eleanor Steber in Opera and Song *MVD, VAI, CTH*

Eleanor Steber in Opera and Song, Vol. 2 *MVD, VAI, FCT*

Electric Light Orchestra Live at Wembly *MVD, FOX*

Electric Light Orchestra Part 2: Live *BMG, MVD*

Elektra *PAR, FCT, MVD*

11th & B *MWF*

Ella Fitzgerald: J.A.T.P. *MVD*

Ella Jenkins: For the Family *MVD*

Ella Jenkins Live! at the Smithsonian *AFR*

Ellyn Rucker: Live in New Orleans *MVD*

Elton John *NO*

Elton John: Breaking Hearts Tour *MVD, LIV, VES*

Elton John: Live *MVD, AVE, FFF*

Elton John: Live in Australia *MVD, JTC*

Elton John: Live in Central Park *NO*

Elton John: Night & Day-The Nighttime Concert *MVD, LIV, VES*

Elton John: The Last Song *MCA, MVD*

Elton John: The Very Best *MVD*

Elton John: To Russia...With Elton *MVD, FOX*

Elton John: Visions *SUE, OM*

Elton John: World Tour 1992 *AVE*

Elvin Jones: A Different Drummer *MVD,*

Elvis *SIM, SPN*

Elvis: Aloha from Hawaii *BMG, MED, MVD*

Elvis Costello and The Brodsky Quartet: The Juliet Letters *WRV, MVD*

Elvis in Concert 1968 *NOS, DVT*

Elvis in the '50s *BTV, DVT*

Elvis on Television *DVT*

Elvis on Tour *MGM*

Elvis: One Night with You *MVD, MED, LTY*

Elvis Presley: 27 Songs That Shook the World *BVV*

Elvis: '68 Comeback Special *BMG, MED, MVD*

Elvis: That's the Way It Is *MGM, MVD*

Elvis: The Great Performances, Vol. 1: Center Stage *MVD, BVV, RDG*

Elvis: The Great Performances, Vol. 2: Man & His Music *MVD, BVV, RDG*

Elvis: The Lost Elvis *MVD*

Elvis: The Lost Performances *WAR, MGM*

Emerson, Lake and Palmer: Pictures at an Exhibition *MVD, IME*

Emerson, Lake & Palmer: Welcome Back *SVI, MVD*

EMF: Smoke the Banger *EMI, MVD*

EMI Video Series, Vol. 1: Between Us *MVD*

EMI Video Series, Vol. 2: Breakthrough Video *MVD*

Emmylou Harris and the Nash Ramblers at the Ryman *WRV, MVD*

An Emotional Fish *MVD, AVE, FFF*

An Emperor's Music *FVL*

En Vogue: Born to Sing *MVD, AVE,*

En Vogue: Funky Divas *AVE, MVD, FFF*

En Vogue: Runaway Love *AVE*

Engelbert Humperdinck in Concert *MVD, VES*

Engelbert Humperdinck Live *QVD, FUS*

The Enid *MVD*

Enigma: The Videos, Part 1 *WRV*

Enigma: Vision of Sadness *MVD*

Entertaining the Troops *COL*

Enuff Z'Nuff *MVD, AVE, FFF*

Enya: Moon Shadows *WRV, MVD*

Erasure: ABBA-Esque *MVD*

Erasure: Live—Wild *WRV, MVD, LUM*

Erasure: Pop—The First 20 Hits *WRV, MVD*

Eric B. & Rakim: Let the Rhythm Hit 'em *MVD, MCA*

Eric Burdon and the Animals: Finally *MVD, FFF*

Eric Clapton & Friends *MVD, LIV, VES*

Eric Clapton: Live '85 *VES, MVD*

Eric Clapton: On the Whistle Test *MVD*

Eric Clapton: The Cream of Eric Clapton *MVD, PGV*

Eric Clapton: 24 Nights *WRV*

Eric Clapton: Unplugged *WRV, MVD*

Erick Friedman Plays Fritz Kreisler *KUL*

Ernani *HMV, PAR, MVD*

Ernest Tubb: "Thanks Troubadour, Thanks" *CAF*

Erroll Garner: London/Copenhagen *MVD*

The Escape Club: Dollars, Sex & Wild, Wild West *AVE, FFF*

Essential Opera *MVD, PME*

Estrellas de la Cancion Nortena *MVD*

Eugene Onegin: Tchaikovsky *MVD, PME*

Europe in America #1 *MVD*

Europe in America #2 *MVD*

Europe: Live *MVD*

Europe: Live in Stockholm, 1986 *MVD*

Europe: The Final Countdown World Tour *MVD, SMV*

Eurythmics: Greatest Hits *MVD, SWH*

Eurythmics Live *MVD, PGV*

Eurythmics: Savage *MVD*

The Eurythmics: Sweet Dreams, the Video Album *MVD, COL, BMG*

Eurythmics: We Two Are One Too *MVD, SWH, BMG*

Eva Marton in Concert *HMV, FCT, PME*

The Eve *NO*

Evelyn Glennie *MVD*

An Evening with Danny Kaye *PAR, HMV, PME*

An Evening with Kiri Te Kanawa *MVD, HMV*

An Evening with Liza Minnelli *FOX*

An Evening with Marlene Dietrich *GLV*

An Evening with Paul Anka *NO*

An Evening with Ray Charles *MCA, MVD*

An Evening with Sammy Davis Jr. and Jerry Lewis *VES, LIV*

An Evening with Sister Sledge *VHE*

An Evening with the Kingston Trio *RHI*

Everly Brothers Album: Flash *NO*

The Everly Brothers Reunion Concert *MVD, MGM, FFF*

The Everly Brothers: Rock 'n' Roll Odyssey *AVE, MGM, MVD*

Evolutionary Spiral *NO*

Evviva Belcanto *MCA, ING*

Exile in Concert *MED*

Expanding Visions: An Introduction to the New Age *WSH*

The Exploited *MVD*

The Exploited: Live at Palm Grove *MVD*

The Exploited: Sexual Favours *MVD*

Expose: Video Exposure *MVD, BMG*

Extreme Art, Vol. 1 *MVD*

Extreme Art, Vol. 2 *MVD*

Extreme Noise Terror: From One Extreme to Another *MVD*

Extreme: Photograffiti *MVD*

Fabulous Thunderbirds: Hot Stuff—The Greatest Hits *MVD*

Fabulous Thunderbirds: Live from London *COL*

Fabulous Thunderbirds: Play It Tough & Play It Live *MVD*

Face/Other Titles

Fact Shorts *MVD*

A Factory Video *MVD*

Factrix: Night of the Succubus *MVD*

The Facts of Life

Fairport Convention: It All Comes Around Again *MVD, IME*

Faith No More: Live at the Brixton Academy *MVD, WRV*

Faith No More: Video Croissant *WRV, MVD*

Falco: Rock Me Falco *A&M, OM*

The Fall: Perverted by Language *MVD*

Falstaff *HMV, VAI, MVD*

Fantastic All-Electric Music Movie *GEM*

The Farm: Spartakus Live *MVD*

Fast Forward, Vol. 1 *MVD*

Fast Forward, Vol. 2 *MVD*

Faster than Lightning *MVD*

Fat Boys on Video: Brrr, Watch 'Em! *MCA, MVD*

Fat Boys: 3 x 3 *MVD*

Father M.C.: Quick Pix *MVD*

Fats Domino and Friends *MVD, AVE, HBO*

Fats Domino: 15 Greatest Hits Live *MVD*

Fats Domino Live! *MCA, MVD*

Fats Waller *CMR*

Fats Waller and Friends *MVD*

Fela: A Concert *MVD, VWV, MBP*

Fela Anikulapo Kuti: Teacher Don't Teach Me Nonsense *MVD*

Fela Live! *SHR*

Ferruccio Tagliavini in Opera and Song *VAI, FCT*

Fidelio *MVD, HMV, VAI*

Fields of the Nephilim *MVD*

Fields of the Nephilim: Morphic Fields *MVD*

The 5th Dimension Travelling Sunshine Show *VWV*

Fine Young Cannibals: Live at the Paramount *MVD, PGV*

The Firebirds: Rockin' at the Ritz *MVD*

Firehouse: Rock on the Road *SMV*

First Ladies of Opera *MVD, KAR*

The First World Festival of Negro Arts

The Fishbone: Reality of My Surroundings *SMV*

Five Star: Luxury of Life *MVD, COL*

The Fixx: Live in the USA *MCA, MVD*

Flamenco Greats *MVD*

Flaming Lips: Live *MVD*

Fleetwood Mac: Documentary & Live Concert *MCA*

Fleetwood Mac in Concert: Mirage Tour 1982 *MVD, COL*

Fleetwood Mac: Tango in the Night *MVD, WRV*

Flesh for Lulu: Live from London *MVD,*

Flipper *MVD*

Flipside Video, Vol. 1 *MVD*

Flipside Video, Vol. 2 *MVD*

Flipside Video, Vol. 3 *MVD*

Flipside Video, Vol. 5 *MVD*

Flipside Video, Vol. 6 *MVD*

Flipside Video, Vol. 7 *MVD*

Flipside Video, Vol. 8 *MVD*

Flipside Video, Vol. 9 *MVD*

Flipside Video, Vol. 10 *MVD*

The Floating World *LUM, BMG*

A Flock of Seagulls *NO*

Flora Purim & Airto: Latin Jazz All-Stars *VWV, MVD, MBP*

Florida Mass Choir: Higher Hope *MVD*

Florida Mass Choir: Now I Can See *MLC, MVD*

A Flower Out of Place *MED*

The Flying Dutchman *MVD*

Flying Nun: In Love with These Times *MVD*

Folk City 25th Anniversary *MVD, RHI, FCT*

The Folk Music Reunion *NO*

Fools: World Dance Party *NO*

For Our Children: The Concert *BVV*

Ford Star Jubilee Salute to Cole Porter *NOS, DVT*

Ford Star Jubilee: "Together with Music" *NOS, DVT*

The Foreigner Story: Feels Like the Very First Time *MVD, AVE, FFF*

Foreigner: Super Rock '85 *MVD*

The Forester Sisters: Talkin' 'Bout Men *MVD, WRV*

40 Pop Rock Video Hits *MVD*

Foster & Lloyd: Version of the Truth *MVD, BMG*

The Four Seasons *AIM*

The Four Tops Live *NO*

Framed! A Mammoth Video Thriller *MVD*

Frank Cappelli: All Aboard the Train and Other Favorites *A&M*

Frank, Liza and Sammy: The Ultimate Event *WKV*

Frank Patterson: Ireland's Golden Voice *RGO, PPI*

Frank Sinatra: A Man and His Music *WRV, MVD, RDG*

Frank Sinatra: A Man and His Music Ella Jobim *WRV, MVD, RDG*

Frank Sinatra: A Man and His Music, Part 2 *WRV, MVD*

Frank Sinatra: A Man and His Music with the Count Basie Orchestra *WRV, MVD*

Frank Sinatra: Francis Albert Sinatra Does His Thing *WRV, MVD*

Frank Sinatra in Concert at Royal Festival Hall *WRV*

Frank Sinatra: Ol' Blue Eyes Is Back *WRV, MVD, RDG*

Frank Sinatra: Reprise Collection, Vol. 1 *MVD, WRV*

Frank Sinatra: Reprise Collection, Vol. 2 *MVD, WRV*
Frank Sinatra: Reprise Collection, Vol. 3 *MVD, WRV*
Frank Sinatra Show *NOS, DVT*
Frank Sinatra: Sinatra *WRV*
Frank Sinatra: Sinatra, the Main Event *WRV*
Frank Zappa Presents: The Amazing Mr. Bickford *MVD, MPI*
Frank Zappa: Video from Hell *MVD, MPI*
Frank Zappa's Does Humor Belong in Music? *MVD, MPI*
Frankie Goes to Hollywood: Wasteland...Paradise *COL*
Frankie Valli: Hits From the 60's *MVD, PSM*
Freddie Hubbard *MVD*
Freddie Jackson: You Are My Lady *MVD*
Freddie King: Blues Band Live *MVD*
Freddie Mercury: Story *MVD*
The Freddie Mercury Tribute Concert *BVV, MVD*
Frederica von Stade: Christmas *MVD, PME*
Frederica von Stade: Christmas with Flicka *BTV, VWV*
Free for All *MVD*
Free: The Best of Free *MVD*
Freedom Beat: The Video *MVD, IME*
Frehley's Comet: Live 4 *MVD, AVE, FFF*
French Singers *ING, DVT, HEG*
Fresh 89, Part 1 *KRV, MVD, PPI*
Fresh 89, Part 2 *KRV, MVD, PPI*
Fresh 89, Part 2: Vol. 1 *KRV, MVD*
Fresh 89, Part 2: Vol. 2 *KRV, MVD*
Fresh 89, Part 3 *KRV, MVD*
Frightwig: Strip for Frightwig *MVD*
From Mao to Mozart: Isaac Stern in China *WAR, IME*
From the New World *NO*
Front Row with Charlie Peacock *SPW*
Front Row with Margaret Becker *SPW*
Front Row with Michael Card *SPW*
Front Row with Steve Curtis Chapman *SPW*
Front 242: Integration 8 X 10 *SMV, MVD*
Frontier Records' Picture Book *MVD*
Frontline Music Festival *WKV, MVD, KAR*
Frozen Ghosts *MVD*
Fullerton College Jazz Bands *NO*
Fulton Street #1 *NO*
Fulton Street #2 *NO*
Further on Down the Road *MVD*
Futurama 6 *MVD*
G. Lewis and D. Ewart Play Music by D. Ewart and G. Lewis
The Gadd Gang Live *MVD, HMV, MBP*
Gala Concert *NO*
Gala Lirica *BMG, MVD*
Gallon Drunk: One for the Ladies *MVD*
A Galway Christmas *HMV*
Gamma Ray: Heading For the East *MVD*
Gang Starr: Step in the Arena *EMI, MVD*
Gap Band Video Train *NO*
Garden Avenue Seven #2 *NO*
Garth Brooks: This is Garth Brooks *EMI, MVD*

Gary Glitter's Gangshow: The Gang, the Band, the Leader *MVD*
Gary Moore and the Midnight Blues Band: An Evening of the Blues *MVD, WEA*
Gary Moore and the Midnight Blues Band: Live Blues *AVE*
Gary Numan: Berserker *MVD*
Gary Numan: The Touring Principal '79 *WAR, OM*
Gatemouth Brown *BFA*
G.B.H.: Brit Boys Attacked by Rats *MVD*
G.B.H.: Live *MVD*
G.B.H.: Live in Japan, 1991 *MVD*
Genesis: Invisible Touch Tour *MVD*
Genesis Live: The Mama Tour *MVD, AVE, FFF*
Genesis: The Way We Walk in Concert *PGV, MVD*
Genesis: Three Sides Live *BMG*
Genesis: Videos, Vol. 1 *MVD, AVE, FFF*
Genesis: Videos, Vol. 2 *MVD, AVE, FFF*
Genesis: Visible Touch *MVD, AVE, FFF*
George Brassens Live *MVD*
George Clinton: Parliament/ Funkadelic *NO*
George Jones: Live in Tennessee *MVD*
George Jones: Living Legend in Concert *MED*
George Jones/Tammy Wynette: In Concert *MVD*
George Michael *SMV, MVD, IME*
George Michael: Faith *MVD, FOX, SMV*
George Shearing: Lullaby of Birdland *VWV*
George Strait Live! *MCA, MVD*
George Thorogood & the Destroyers: Live *NO*
George Thorogood: Born to Be Bad *MVD, EMI*
George Thorogood: On Tap *MVD*
Georgia Mass Choir: Hold On, Help is on the Way *MVD*
Gerardo: Behind the Scenes with the Latin King *AVE, MVD, FFF*
Gerardo: Rico Suave *MVD, AVE, FFF*
Gerry Mulligan *CMR*
Gerry Mulligan: Live at Eric's *MVD*
The Geto Boys: Uncut Dope *MVD*
Gibson Jazz Concert *KAR, COL*
Gil Bailey's 19th Anniversary Radio Show *MVD*
Gil Evans *MVD*
Gil Evans and His Orchestra *MVD, VWV, MBP*
Gil Scott-Heron: Black Wax *SMV, MVD, FCT*
Gil Scott-Heron: Tales of Gil *MVD*
Gilbert & Sullivan Present Their Greatest Hits *MVD, LIV, VES*
Gilbert and Sullivan: Their Greatest Hits *VWV, PBS*
Gilbert Becaud Live *MVD*
Gimme Shelter *COL, MVD*
Gino Vannelli *WAR, OM*
Giorno Video Pak 3 *MVD*
Gipsy Kings: Fuego! The Videos *MVD*
Gipsy Kings: Live at the Royal Albert Hall *BMG*
Girl Groups: The Story of a Sound *MVD, MGM*
Girls Bite Back *MVD*
Girlschool *NO*

Giulio Cesare *PGV, MVD, PME*
Give Peace a Chance *MVD*
Gladys Knight & the Pips & Ray Charles in Concert *VES*
Glam Rock *MVD*
Glam Rock, Vol. 2 *MVD*
Glen Campbell: Live in London *MVD, PSM*
Glenn Branca: Symphony No. 4 *MWF*
Glenn Frey: Strange Weather Live in Dublin *MCA, MVD*
Glenn Gould: A Portrait *KUL, MVD, HMV*
Glenn Medeiros, Vol. 1 *MVD, MCA*
Glenn Miller: A Moonlight Serenade *NO*
Gloria Estefan & the Miami Sound Machine: Evolution *MVD, SMV*
Gloria Estefan & the Miami Sound Machine: Homecoming *MVD, SMV*
Gloria Estefan: Coming Out of the Dark *SMV, MVD*
Gloria Estefan: Into the Light World Tour *SMV, MVD*
The Glory of Spain *MVD, VAI, APD*
The Go Betweens: That Way *MVD*
The Go-Betweens: Video Singles *MVD*
Go Go Big Beat *RHI*
Go-Go's: Live at the Capitol Center *MVD*
Go-Go's: Prime Time *MVD, BMG*
Go-Go's: Totally Go-Go's *NO*
Go-Go's: Wild at the Greek *MVD, COL*
God Bullies: Live *MVD*
Godley & Creme: History Mix *MVD, LIV, VES*
Golden Earring *NO*
Golden Earring: Live from the Twilight Zone *MVD, COL*
The Golden Ring: The Making of Solti's "Ring" *MVD, PGV, PME*
Gong Maison *MVD*
Good Mornin' Blues *SHR, PBS, MVD*
Goodtime Rock 'n' Roll *MCA*
Goodyear Jazz Concert with Bobby Hackett *MVD, VYY, DVT*
Goodyear Jazz Concert with Duke Ellington *VYY, DVT*
Goodyear Jazz Concert with Eddie Condon *MVD, VYY, DVT*
Goodyear Jazz Concert with Louis Armstrong *VYY, DVT*
Gospel *MVD, MON, FCT*
Gospel from the Holy Land *NO*
Gospel Keynotes: Live at Jackson State University *MVD*
Gotta Make This Journey: Sweet Honey in the Rock
Grace Jones: One Man Show *VES, MVD*
Grace Jones: State of Grace *COL*
Graham Parker *NO*
Grammy's Greatest Moments, Vol. 1 & 2 *AVE*
Gran Temas de la Fiesta Charra *MVD*
Grand Dominion Jazz Band *NO*
Grand Funk: The American Band Live *MVD*
Grand Ole Opry Country Music Celebration *MVD*
Grand Ole Opry Stars of the Fifties, Vol. 1 *MVD*
Grand Ole Opry Stars of the Fifties, Vol. 2 *MVD*

Grand Ole Opry Stars of the Fifties, Vol. 3 *MVD*
Grand Ole Opry Stars of the Fifties, Vol. 4 *MVD*
Grand Ole Opry Stars of the Fifties, Vol. 5 *MVD*
Grand Ole Opry Stars of the Fifties, Vol. 6 *MVD*
Grand Ole Opry Stars of the Fifties, Vol. 7 *MVD*
Grand Ole Opry Stars of the Fifties, Vol. 8 *MVD*
Grand Ole Opry Stars of the Fifties, Vol. 9 *MVD*
Grand Ole Opry Stars of the Fifties, Vol. 10 *MVD*
Grand Ole Opry Stars of the Fifties, Vol. 11 *MVD*
Grand Ole Opry Stars of the Fifties, Vol. 12 *MVD*
Grand Ole Opry Time *VDM*
Grand Ole Opry Time: Vol. 2 *VDM*
Grand Ole Opry's Classic Country Tributes *AMR*
Grapes of Wrath: Those Days *MVD*
The Grateful Dead: Backstage Pass—Access All Areas *MVD*
The Grateful Dead: Dead Ahead *NO*
The Grateful Dead: Making of the "Touch of Grey" Video *MVD, SWH, BMG*
The Grateful Dead Movie *MON, MVD, IME*
Grateful Dead: So Far *MVD, BMG*
Great American Gospel Sound, Vol. 1 *NO*
Great American Gospel Sound, Vol. 2 *NO*
Great American Gospel Sound, Vol. 3 *NO*
Great American Gospel Sound, Vol. 4 *NO*
Great American Jazz Band *NO*
Great Jazz Bands of the '30s *DVT*
Great Music from Chicago *VYY, FCT*
Great Video Hits, Vol. 1 *MVD, BMG*
Great Video Hits, Vol. 2 *MVD, BMG*
Great Video Hits, Vol. 3 *MVD, BMG*
Great White: My...My...My... *MVD*
Great White: Videos *MVD, LIV*
Greatest Rock n' Roll Hits of the '50s and '60s *RHI*
The Greatest Sound in Gospel: Vol. 1 - 4 *MVD*
The Greatest Week in Gospel *MVD, XVC, HHE*
Greatest Week in Gospel, Part 1 *MVD, XVC, HHE*
Greatest Week in Gospel, Part 2 *MVD, XVC, HHE*
Greatest Week in Gospel, Part 3 *MVD, XVC, HHE*
Greatest Week in Gospel, Part 4 *MVD, XVC, HHE*
The Greatest Years in Rock *MVD*
Green Jelly: Cereal Killer *BMG*
Greenpeace Non-Toxic Video Hits *MVD, VES*
Greg Giuffria: Live in Japan '85 *MVD*
Gregg Allman: One Way Out *MVD*
Gregory Isaacs: Maestro Meets the Cool Ruler *MVD*
Gregory Issacs Live *MVD, KRV*
Grim Tales *MVD*
Grok Gazer *LVI*
Grover Washington, Jr. in Concert *VWV*

GRP All-Star Big Band *UND, MVD, GRP*
GRP Christmas Collection *GRP, MVD*
GRP Live in Session *GRP*
GRP Superlive in Concert *GRP, MVD*
GRP Video Collection *GRP, MVD*
GTR: The Making of GTR *MVD, COL*
Guarneri String Quartet *NO*
The Guess Who Reunion *MVD, MED*
Guess Who: Together Again *NO*
Guitar from Three Centuries *CMR, NYS*
Guitar Men *MVD*
Gun: Taking on the World *MVD, A&M*
Guns & Roses: Use Your Illusion, Vol. 1 *MCA, MVD, PMS*
Guns & Roses: Use Your Illusion, Vol. 2 *MCA, MVD, PMS*
Guys Next Door *MVD*
GWAR: Live from Antarctica *MVD, WRV*
GWAR: Phallus in Wonderland *WRV, MVD*
GWAR: Tour De Scum *WRV*
Gypsy Kings: U.S. Tour '90 *MVD*
Haggadah: A Search for Freedom *NJN*
Hail to the Chieftains *CMR, NYS*
Hal Ketchum: Past the Point of Rescue *EMI, MVD*
Hal Smith Trio *NO*
Hal Smith's Rhythmakers *NO*
Hallelujah: A Gospel Celebration *XVC, FCT, MVD*
Hammer: Hammerin' Home the Legit Hits *MVD*
Hampton Hawes: All Stars *MVD, FCT*
Handel: Messiah Choruses *MVD, LUM*
Handel's Messiah
Hank Williams, Jr. *NO*
Hank Williams, Jr.: A Star-Spangled Country Party *MVD*
Hank Williams, Jr.: Full Access *MVD, CAF*
Hank Williams, Jr.: Greatest Video Hits *WRV, MVD*
Hank Williams, Jr.: Pure Hank *NO*
Hank Williams, Sr.: The Show He Never Gave *FFF, FCT*
Hanoi Rocks: The Nottingham Tapes *MVD*
Hanoi Rocks: Video LP *NO*
Hansel and Gretel *HMV, PAR, FCT*
Happy Hour with the Humans *NO*
Happy Mondays: Party Live at the G-Mex *MVD*
Happy Traum: Happy Traum in Concert *MVD, SHR*
Hard 'n Heavy: Grindcore Special *AVE, MVD, FFF*
Hard 'n' Heavy: Thrash Metal Speed *MPI*
Hard 'n' Heavy, Vol. 1 *MPI, MVD*
Hard 'n' Heavy, Vol. 2 *MPI, MVD*
Hard 'n' Heavy, Vol. 3 *MPI, MVD*
Hard 'n' Heavy, Vol. 4 *MPI, MVD*
Hard 'n' Heavy, Vol. 5 *MPI, MVD*
Hard 'n' Heavy, Vol. 6 *MPI, MVD*

Hard 'n' Heavy, Vol. 7 *MPI, MVD*
Hard 'n' Heavy, Vol. 8 *MPI, MVD*
Hard 'n' Heavy, Vol. 9 *MPI, MVD*
Hard 'n' Heavy, Vol. 10 *MPI, MVD*
Hard 'n' Heavy, Vol. 11 *MPI, MVD*
Hard 'n' Heavy, Vol. 12 *MPI, MVD*
Hard 'n' Heavy, Vol. 13 *AVE, MVD, FFF*
Hard 'n' Heavy, Vol. 14 *AVE, FFF*
Hard 'n' Heavy, Vol. 15 *MVD, FFF*
Hard 'n' Heavy, Vol. 16 *MVD*
Hard 'n' Heavy, Vol. 17 *MVD*
Hard 'n' Heavy, Vol. 18 *MVD*
Hard Time '77 *KRV*
Hardcore *MVD*
Hardcore, Vol. 1 *MVD*
Hardcore, Vol. 2 *MVD*
Hardcore, Vol. 3 *MVD*
Harlem Harmonies, Vol. 1 *MVD*
Harlem Harmonies, Vol. 2 *MVD*
Harlem Jazz Festival *VDM*
Harmony *PUL*
Harry Belafonte: Don't Stop the Carnival *FOX*
Harry Belafonte's Global Carnival *WKV, MVD, KAR*
Harry Chapin: The Final Concert *FOX*
Harry Connick, Jr.: Do You Know What It Means to Miss New Orleans? *KAR*
Harry Connick, Jr.: New York Big Band Concert *COL*
Harry Connick, Jr.: Singin' & Swingin' *SMV, IME, MVD*
Harry Connick, Jr.: Swingin' Out Live *SMV, IME, MVD*
Harry James: One Night Stand *MVD*
Harry Owens and His Royal Hawaiians *NO*
Harvest Jazz Series *NO*
Harvest Jazz Series: Alto Madness *FCT*
Hawkwind: Chronicle of the Black Sword *MVD*
Hawkwind: Live *MVD*
Hawkwind: Night of the Hawks *MVD*
Hawkwind: Solstice at Stonehedge 1984 *MVD*
Haydn: The Creation *MVD*
HBTV Music Videos *WOV*
H.E.A.L.: Heal Yourself *WEA, MVD*
Healing Yourself *WSH*
Heart & Soul *RHI*
Heart: If Looks Could Kill *MVD, MPI*
Heart of Rock *BHV, MVD*
Heart: Video 45 *MVD*
Heartstrings: Peter, Paul and Mary in Central America *ICA*
Heavenly Host and the Sons of Calvary *MVD*
Heavy D. & the Boyz: The Journey Continues *MCA, MVD*
Heavy D. & the Boyz: We Got Our Own Thang *MVD, MCA*
Heavy Metal *MVD*
Heifetz & Piatigorsky *MVD, HMV, KUL*
Heimat, deine Lieder 2 *GLV*
Helix *BAR*
Henry Mancini and Friends with Robert Goulet and Vicki Carr *MVD*
Herbie Hancock and the Rockit Band *MVD, FOX*
Herbie Hancock: Jazz Africa *PGV, MVD, FCT*
Herbie Hancock: Rockit Band Live in Tokyo *MVD*

Herbie Hancock Trio: Hurricane! *VWV, FCT*
Here it is, Burlesque *VES*
Heroes and Villains *MVD*
He's Right on Time - Live From Los Angeles *SPW*
Hi-Five: The Video Hits *BMG*
High Fidelity: The Adventures of the Guarneri String Quartet *NYF, FCT*
High School Yearbook: The '50s & the Early '60s *NO*
High Society Jazz Band #1 *NO*
High Society Jazz Band #2 *NO*
Highway 101: Greatest Hits (1987-1990) *WRV*
Highwaymen Live *MVD, SMV*
The Highwaymen: On the Road Again *WST, MVD*
Hijas #90: Un Videocassette Super Sexy *MVD*
His Legacy for Home Video Series *NO*
The Historic Debt *MVD*
History Never Repeats—The Best of Split Enz *A&M*
The History of Joan Jett & the Blackhearts *MVD*
History of Rock 1978 *MVD*
History of Rock 1979 *MVD*
History of Rock 1980 *MVD*
Hits Live from London *MVD*
The Hoffnung Festival Concert *MVD, PRS, HMV*
Holiday Sing Along With Mitch *MGM*
Holly Dunn: Milestones - Greatest Hits *WRV*
Hollywood Goes to War *NO*
Holst: The Planets *MVD, BMG*
Homage to Verdi *NO*
Homecoming *MLC, MVD*
Homemade American Music *NO*
Hooters: Nervous Night *MVD, FOX*
Horowitz in London *KAR, MVD*
Horowitz in Moscow *MVD, MGM, HMV*
Horowitz in Vienna *PGV, FCT, MVD*
Horse Guards Parade: The Light Division *FUS*
Hot Antic Jazz Band *NO*
Hot Frogs Jumping Jazz Band #1 *NO*
Hot Frogs Jumping Jazz Band #2 *NO*
Hot Guitarist Video Magazine, Vol. 1 *MVD*
Hot Guitarist Video Magazine, Vol. 2 *MVD*
Hot 'n' Heavy *MVD*
Hot Rock Videos, Vol. 1 *MVD, COL*
Hot Rock Videos, Vol. 2 *MVD, COL*
Hot Shop '89 *KRV, MVD*
Hot Shot '91, Vol. 1 *MVD, FCT*
Hot Summer Night...with Donna *COL*
Hothouse Flowers: Take a Last Look at the Sun *PGV, MVD*
How Many Fingers? *VDO*
Howard Jones: Last World Dream *MVD,*
Howard Jones: Like to Get to Know You Well *MVD, WAR*
Howard Jones: Live in Japan *MVD*
The Huberman Festival *KUL*
Huey Lewis & the News *FOX*
Huey Lewis & the News: All the Way Live *MVD*
Huey Lewis & the News: Fore and More *MVD, FOX*
Huey Lewis & the News: Live *MVD*
Huey Lewis & the News: The Heart of Rock n' Roll *NO*
Huey Lewis & the News: Video Hits *MVD, FOX*

Hugh Masekela: Notice to Quit (The Lion Never Sleeps) *MVD*
Hugh Shannon: Saloon Singer *MVD, VWV, MBP*
Hulk Hogan Real American *CSM*
Hullabaloo, Vol. 1 *NOS, DVT*
Human League: Greatest Hits *MVD*
Humans: Happy Hour *NO*
Hungry i Reunion *NO*
Hunks with Hats *BST*
Hurricane Irene *MVD, VMK*
Husker Du: Makes No Sense *MVD*
The Hutchinson Family Singers *CMR, NYS*
Hymn of the Nations *VYY, NOS, CCB*
I Lombardi Alla Prima Crociata *HMV, MVD*
Ian and Sylvia *CMR, NYS*
Ian Gillian: Live *MVD*
Ian Gillian: Live at the Rainbow *MVD*
Ian Hunter Rocks *MVD*
Iasos: Crystal Visa *MVD*
Ice Cube: True to the Game *MVD*
Ice-T: Iceberg *MVD*
Ice-T: O.G. The Original Gangster Video *WRV*
I.D.F.: Dark Arts (Live Treatment) *MVD*
Idomeneo *HMV, PAR, MVD*
Iggy Pop: Kiss My Blood *MVD*
Igor Gorin in Opera and Song *MVD*
Illumination *NEM, WSH*
Im Land der Lieder *GLV*
Imagine the Sound *FCT*
Immortal Canvas: Nettwerk Video Compilation #2 *MVD*
Impact Video Magazine *MVD, MPI*
Imperials: 20th Anniversary Concert *WRD*
The Impressions Series *WSH*
In a Dance All Style: New Yorker, New Yorker in Jamaica *KRV*
In Celebration of the Piano *MVD, VAI, FCT*
In Christ Alone: The Story Behind the Song *WEA*
In Concert *DCC*
In Love with These Times *MVD*
In mir klingt ein Lied *GLV*
In Our Hands▶ *NO*
In Performance: David Shifrin, Clarinet *FVL*
In the Country *BAR*
In the Hank Williams Tradition *KUL, FUS*
In the Silence of the Night *FCT*
Incantation: The Best of Incantation *NO*
Indecent Obsession *MVD*
The Indestructible Beat of Soweto *MVD*
Indie Top Video, Take 4 *MVD*
Indie Top Video, Take 5 *MVD*
Indigo Girls: Live at the Uptown Lounge *MVD, FOX, SMV*
Indoor Cycling
Industria del Amor: Des el Palace de Hollywood *MVD*
The Industrial Symphony No. 1: Dream of the Broken Hearted *MVD, WRV*
Infantasia *NO*
Infantastic Lullabies II *VWV, BTV*
Infantastic Lullabyes on Video *VWV, KAR, MBP*
Infrared Settings *MVD, IME*
Inside Country Music, Vol. 1: Edition 2 *MVD*
The International Choral Festival Film *BFA*
Invitation to Paris *NOS, DVT*

INXS: Greatest Video Hits (1980-1990) *MVD, AVE, FFF*
INXS: In Search of Excellence *MVD, PGV*
INXS: Kick the Video Flick *MVD, AVE, FFF*
INXS: Live Baby Live *AVE, FFF*
INXS: Living *MVD, MGM*
INXS: What You Need *MVD, AVE, FFF*
Irene Cara: Live in Japan *MVD*
Irish Magic, Irish Music *RGO*
Iron Maiden: Behind the Iron Curtain *MVD*
Iron Maiden: From There to Eternity *MVD*
Iron Maiden: Live After Death *MVD*
Iron Maiden: Live in London *MVD*
Iron Maiden: Maiden England *MVD, SMV*
Iron Maiden: Raising Hell *BMG*
Iron Maiden: 12 Wasted Years *MVD, MPI*
Iron Maiden: Video Pieces *NO*
Isaac Hayes: Black Moses of Soul *RHI, FCT, MVD*
Isaac Stern in Jerusalem: A Musical Celebration *MVD, HMV*
Isaac Stern, Itzhak Perlman, Pinchas Zukerman *HMV*
Island Reggae Greats *COL*
Israel in Dance: Shalom in Action *ERG*
Israel on Parade: A Variety Show *ERG*
Israel Philharmonic Orchestra Welcomes Berliner Philharmoniker *NO*
It's Clean, It Just Looks Dirty *FCT, TPV*
It's in Every One of Us *NEM, WSH*
Itzhak Perlman *KUL*
Itzhak Perlman, Pinchas Zukerman *MVD*
Ivo Perelman: Live in New York *MVD, VAI, FCT*
Ivo Pogorelich *NO*
Ivo Pogorelich in Villa Contarini *FCT*
J. Geils Band *NO*
Jack Jones: An Evening with Jack Jones *MVD*
Jack Ruby's 25th Anniversary Dance *MVD*
Jack Sheldon in New Orleans *MVD,*
Jackie McLean: Dynasty *MVD*
Jackie Patterson: Hip Hop Dance *MVD*
The Jackson Southernaires: Live at Jackson State University *MVD*
The Jacksons *MVD*
Jackyl *MVD*
Jacqueline Du Pre and the Elgar Cello Concerto (A Christopher Nupen Film) *NO*
J'ai Ete au Bal *MVD, FFM, BTV*
Jam: The Trans-Global Unity Express *MVD*
Jam: The Video Snap! *MVD, MED*
James Brown & Friends: Set Fire to the Soul *HBO, AVE, MVD*
James Brown and His Very Special Guest B.B. King *WST, MVD*
James Brown: Cold Sweat - In Japan *MVD*
James Brown Live in America *MVD, RHI, FCT*
James Brown Live in Berlin *MVD, PGV, WAX*
James Brown Live in Concert *MVD, MED, VTR*
James Brown Live in London *NO*

James Brown: Soulful Night in L.A. *MVD*
James Brown: Story 1956 - 1976 *MVD*
James Brown: The Lost James Brown Tapes *WRV, MVD, FCT*
James Cleveland & the Northern and Southern California Choirs: Breathe on Me *MVD*
James Cleveland: Down Memory Lane *MVD*
James Galway & the Chieftains in Ireland *MVD*
James Galway in Concert *MVD, PRS*
James Galway's Christmas Carol *BMG*
James Moore & the Mississippi Mass Choir *MVD*
The James: Seventh Live *MVD*
James Taylor in Concert *SMV, FOX, MVD*
James Taylor: Squibnocket *SMV, MVD*
Jan Peerce Anniversary *CMR, NYS*
Jan Peerce: If I Were a Rich Man *MVD, PRS*
Jan Pietrzak: Mr. Censor *FCT*
Jane's Addiction: The Fan's Video - Soul Kiss *MVD, WRV*
Janet Jackson: Control—The Videos *MVD, A&M*
Janet Jackson: Control—The Videos, Part II *MVD, A&M*
Janet Jackson: The Rhythm Nation Compilation *MVD, PGV, BTV*
Janet Jackson's Rhythm Nation *MVD, A&M*
Janis: A Film *MVD, MCA, FCT*
Janis Joplin: Comin' Home *MVD*
Jansen/Barbieri: The World's in a Small Room *MVD*
Japan: Instant Pictures *MVD*
Japan: Oil on Canvas *MVD*
Jaques Brel: Chansons *MVD*
Jason Donovan: The Videos, Vol. 2 *MVD*
Jazz at Ronnie's *MVD*
Jazz at the Smithsonian: Alberta Hunter *MVD, KUL, FCT*
Jazz at the Smithsonian: Bob Wilber *MVD, KUL*
Jazz at the Smithsonian: Joe Lewis *KUL*
Jazz at the Smithsonian: Joe Williams *MVD, KUL, FCT*
Jazz at the Smithsonian: Mel Lewis *MVD, KUL, FCT*
Jazz at the Smithsonian: Red Norvo *MVD, KUL*
Jazz from Studio 61 *MVD*
Jazz in America *COL, NLC, SUE*
Jazz in America: Dizzy Gillespie *NLC, MOV*
Jazz in America: Max Roach in Washington D.C. *NLC, MOV*
Jazz in America: Starring Gerry Mulligan *NLC, NLC, MOV*
Jazz Legends, Part 1 *MVD*
Jazz Legends, Part 2 *MVD*
Jazz Legends, Part 3 *MVD*
Jazz Legends, Part 4 *MVD*
Jazz on a Summer's Day *NYF, FCT, MVD*
Jazz Shorts *MVD, RHP, FCT*
Jazz Summit *ICA*
Jazz Vocal Special *MVD*
Jazzvisions: Implosions *PGV*
JB Horns with Fred Wesley & Maceo Parker *MVD*
Jeff Healey Band: See the Light *MVD, SWH*
Jefferson Starship: Live *MVD*
Jefferson Starship: The Definitive Concert *LTY, BMG*

Jellyfish: Gone Jellyfishin' *WEA, MOV*

Jermaine Jackson: Dynamite Videos *MVD, COL*

Jermaine Stewart: Frantic Romantic *MVD, COL*

Jerome Hines in Opera and Song *MVD, VAI*

Jerry Lee Lewis & Friends *MVD*

Jerry Lee Lewis: I Am What I Am *JTC, IME, MVD*

Jerry Lee Lewis: Live at the Arena *MVD*

Jerry Lee Lewis Live in London *MVD, FOX*

Jerry Lee Lewis: The Story of Rock and Roll *MVD*

Jerusalem: A Musical Celebration *HMV*

Jesse Rae: Rusha/ D.E.S.I.R.E. *NO*

Jessy Dixon: I Know What Prayer Can Do *BMG, MVD*

Jessye Norman at Notre Dame *MVD, PME*

Jessye Norman, Singer *FLL*

The Jesus and Mary Chain: Chain Reaction *MVD*

The Jesus and Mary Chain: Videos: (1985-1989) *MVD, WRV*

Jethro Tull: Slipstream *MVD*

Jethro Tull: The First Twenty Years *MVD*

The Jets: Airplay *MVD*

The Jickets: Direct Art *MWF*

Jim & Jesse: West Virginia Boys *MVD*

Jim Beard: Song of the Sun *MVD*

Jim McCann & the Morrisseys *RGO*

Jimi Hendrix: At the Isle of Wight *NO*

Jimi Hendrix: Atlanta Pop Festival *MVD*

Jimi Hendrix: Berkeley May 1970 *MVD, WRV, VES*

Jimi Hendrix Concerts Videogram *NO*

Jimi Hendrix: Experience *WRV, MVD, FCT*

Jimi Hendrix: Johnny B. Goode *NO*

Jimi Hendrix: Live in Monterey, 1967 *MVD*

Jimi Hendrix: Rainbow Bridge *MVD, RHI*

Jimi Hendrix: Rarities *MVD*

Jimi Hendrix: Story *MVD, WAR*

Jimmy Buffett: Live by the Bay *MCA, MVD*

Jimmy Cliff: Bongo Man *MVD*

Jimmy Smith: Midnight Special *MVD*

Jimmy Somerville: Video Collection 1984-90 *MVD, PGV*

Jive's Greatest Rap Hits *BMG, MVD*

Jivin' in Bebop *MVD, HHT, GVV*

J.J. Johnson & Kai Windig All Stars *MVD*

Joan Armatrading: Track Record *MVD, A&M*

Jodeci *MCA, MVD*

Jody Watley: Video Classics, Vol. 1 *MVD*

Joe Cocker: Live from Tokyo *TWE*

Jòe Cocker: Mad Dogs *NO*

Joe Cocker: Mad Dogs & Englishmen *COL*

Joe Cocker: Shelter Me *MVD*

Joe Cool Live *MVD, HMV*

Joe Ely: Live From Texas *MVD*

Joe Jackson: Laughter and Lust, Live *AVE, MVD, FFF*

Joe Jackson Live in Tokyo *MVD, A&M*

Joe Jackson: The Big World Sessions *MVD, A&M*

Joe Satriani: The Satch Tapes *MVD*

Joe Scruggs in Concert

Joe Williams: A Song is Born *VWV, FCT*

John Abercrombie: Live at the Village Vanguard *NO*

John Anderson: Seminole Wind *MVD, BMG*

John Cale & Brian Eno: Words for the Dying *MVD*

John Carter & Bobby Bradford: The New Music *MVD, KIV*

John Cougar Mellencamp: Ain't That America *MVD, COL*

John Hammond: Bessie Smith to Bruce Springsteen *MVD, SMV*

John Hartford: Learning to Smile All Over Again *MVD*

John Lee Hooker & Charlie Musselwhite *MVD, RHP*

John Lee Hooker: Blue Monday Party *KIV*

John Lennon: A Tribute *MVD*

John Lennon and the Plastic Ono Band: Live Peace in Toronto, 1969 *MVD, HBO*

John Lennon Live in New York City *MVD*

John Lennon: The John Lennon Video Collection *MVD*

John Lennon/Yoko Ono: Then and Now *MVD, MED*

John Pizzarelli: Live in Montreal *BMG, MVD*

John Renbourn: In Concert *MVD*

John Scofield Live *EMI*

John Scofield: Live Three Ways *MVD*

John Waite: No Brakes Live *MVD, COL*

Johnnie Taylor: Live in Dallas *MVD*

Johnny Cash: Live in London *NWV*

Johnny Cash: Ridin' the Rails *KAR*

Johnny Gill: Video Hits *MVD, MCA*

Johnny Griffin: The Jazz Life *MVD, FCT, AFR*

Johnny Maddox Plays Ragtime *BAR*

Johnny Mathis: Chances Are *MVD, SMV, RDG*

Johnny Mathis: Greatest Hits *PSM*

Johnny Mathis: Home for Christmas *SMV, MVD, IME*

Johnny Mathis: 25th Anniversary Concert *MVD, VES*

Johnny McEvoy: In Concert *RGO*

Johnny Thunders and the Heartbreakers: Dead or Alive *MVD*

Johnny Winter Live *MED*

Jonathan Butler: Heal Our Land *MVD, BMG*

Joni Mitchell *AIP*

Joni Mitchell: Refuge of Roads *MVD,*

Joni Mitchell: Shadows & Light *WAR, MVD*

Jose Carreras: A Life Story *PGV, MVD*

Jose Carreras & Friends: Charity Concert *MVD*

Jose Carreras: Montserrat Caballe and Jose Carreras in Moscow *KUL*

Jose Carreras: Silent Night *MVD, KUL, PME*

Jose Greco in Performance *MVD, VAI, FCT*

Jose' Jose' en Acapulco *MCA*

Jose Maria Napoleon: Aqui Entre Nous *MVD*

Jose Serebrier *NO*

Journey: Frontiers and Beyond *MED*

Joy Division: Here are the Young Men *MVD*

The Joy of Bach *IGP, GFV, KAR*

Joyful Gospel Christmas *MTP*

Joyous Sounds of Christmas *BUP*

'Ju Ju *MVD*

Juan Gabriel: Natural *MVD*

Juanita Hall *CMR*

Jubilee U.S.A. *NO*

Judas Priest: Fuel for Life *MVD, FOX*

Judas Priest Live *MVD, MED, FOX*

Judas Priest: Pain Killer *NO*

The Judds: Across the Heartland *MVD, KAR, MPI*

The Judds: Greatest Video Hits *MVD, BMG*

The Judds: Love Can Build a Bridge *MVD, MPI, RDG*

The Judds: Their Final Concert *MPI, MVD, TVC*

Judy Collins: Live *MVD*

Judy Garland (General Electric Theatre) *VYY*

Judy Garland in Concert, Vol. 1 *RKO*

Judy Garland in Concert, Vol. 2 *RKO*

Judy Garland: Judy Garland & Friends *WRV, MVD*

Judy Garland Scrapbook *DVT*

The Judy Garland Show *NO*

Judy Garland: The Golden Years at MGM *MGM*

Juju Music *RHP, FCT, KIV*

Juke Box Saturday Night: All Star Golden Classics *NO*

Julia Fordham: Porcelain *MVD*

Julian Cope: Copelation *MVD*

Julian Lennon: Live in Japan, 1986 *MVD*

Julian Lennon: Stand By Me *MCA, MVD*

Julie Andrews: In Concert *MVD*

Julie Andrews Sings Her Favorite Songs *QHV, TVC, MVD*

Julie London: In Japan 1964 *MVD*

Juliette Greco Live *MVD*

Julio Iglesias in Spain *MVD, FOX, SMV*

Julio Iglesias: Starry Night *MVD, MOV, SMV*

Jump the Blues Away *MVD, PGV*

Just Say Yes, the Video: Vol. 1 *WRV*

Just Say Yes, the Video: Vol. 2 *WRV*

Justice League: Hyp Existance *MVD*

The JVC Video Anthology of World Music and Dance *BTV*

Kajagoogoo *NO*

Kansas *NO*

Kansas City Jazz *NET*

KAOMA Worldbeat: The Lambada Videos *MVD, SMV*

Karajan Conducts *MVD*

Karajan: The Best on Video *PGV*

Karen Akers: On Stage at Wolf Trap *VWV, MVD, IME*

Karr Tunes

Kate Bush: Live at Hammersmith *MVD*

Kate Bush: Single File *MVD*

Kate Bush: The Sensual World (The Videos) *MVD, SMV*

Kate Bush: The Whole Story *MVD*

Kathleen Battle at the Metropolitan Museum *PME*

Kathleen Battle in The Magic Flute

Kathy Mattea: From the Heart Hits *MVD, PGV*

Katrina and the Waves *NO*

K.C. and the Sunshine Band in Concert *MVD, RHI*

k.d. lang: Harvest of Seven Years (Cropped and Chronicled) *WRV*

Kee Marcello: Guitar Instruction *MVD*

Keith Jarrett: Last Solo *HMV, MVD, FCT*

Keith Jarrett: Standards *MVD*

Keith Jarrett: Standards, Vol. 2 *MVD*

Keith Jarrett: Tokyo Live '85 *MVD, AVE, FFF*

Keith Richards & the X-Pensive Winos: Live at the Hollywood Palladium *NO*

Keith Whitley: I Wonder, Do You Think of Me? *MVD, BMG*

Kenny Drew: Live in Europe 1992 *MVD*

Kenny G Live *MVD, SWH, BMG*

Kenny Garrett: Computer G *MVD*

Kenny Loggins Alive *FOX*

Kenny Loggins: Live from the Grand Canyon *SMV*

Kenny Loggins: Outside: From the Redwoods *COL*

Kenny Rogers and the First Edition *VWV, MVD*

Kenny Rogers/Dolly Parton: Real Love *MVD, COL*

Kenny Rogers: Great Video Hits *MVD, BMG*

Kentucky Headhunters: Pickin' on Nashville *MVD, PGV*

Kerrang! *MVD*

Kid Creole & the Coconuts Live *SUE*

Kid Creole & the Coconuts: Live at the Ritz *MVD*

Kid Creole & the Coconuts: The Leisure Tour 1985 *NLC, COL, MVD*

Kid Creole & the Coconuts: The Lifeboat *MVD*

Kid 'n Play: The Video *MVD*

Kid Punch Miller: 'Til the Butcher Cuts Him Down *MVD, RHP*

The Kids are Alright *MVD*

Kids from Fame *MGM*

Killdozer *MVD*

Kim Carnes *NO*

Kim Wilde *NO*

Kim Wilde: You Keep Me Hangin' On *MVD*

King Crimson: The Noise *NO*

King Crimson: Three of a Perfect Pair *MVD*

King Sunny Ade: Authority of Your Ticket *MVD*

King Sunny Ade: Concert in the Park *MVD*

King Sunny Ade: Juju Music *FCT*

King Sunny Ade: Montreux '83 *MVD*

King Sunny Ade: With His African Beats *MVD*

King's Christmas *PRS, HMV*

Kings of Independence *MVD,*

The King's Singers Christmas *MVD*

The King's Singers in Concert *MVD, PRS*

King's X: Chronicles *MVD, AVE, FFF*

The Kingston Trio: An Evening with the Kingston Trio *MVD*

Kingston Trio & Friends: Reunion *CMR*

Kinks: Come Dancing *MVD, LTY, BMG*

Kinks: One for the Road *VES*

Kiri Te Kanawa at Christmas *VWV, MVD, IME*

Kiri Te Kanawa Sings Mozart *MVD*

Kirkpatrick Plays Bach *FHS*

KISS: Animalized Live & Uncensored *MVD, COL*

KISS: Crazy Nights *MVD, PGV*

KISS: Exposed *MVD, PGV*

KISS: Exposed 2 *PGV, PMS*

KISS: Konfidential *PGV*

KISS: The Interview Sessions *MVD*

KISS: X-Treme Close-Up *PGV*

Kitaro: Light of the Spirit *NO*

Kitaro: Live *MVD*

Kix: Blow My Fuse - The Videos *MVD, AVE, FFF*

KLF: The Stadium House Trilogy *NO*

K.M.C. Kru: Home Video *EMI, MVD*

KMFDM: Live *MVD*

Knack: Live at Carnegie Hall *NO*

Koko Taylor: Queen of the Blues *MPI, MVD, FCT*

Komm mit ins Land der Lieder *GLV*

Kool and the Gang in Concert *NO*

Kool & the Gang: Tonight! *MVD*

Kool Moe Dee: Funke, Funke Wisdom *MVD*

Kreator: Hallucinative Comas *MVD*

Krewmen: Live at Billy's *MVD*

Kriss Kross: A Totally Krossed Out World *SMV, MVD*

Kriss Kross: Jump Video Snapshot *SMV*

Krokus: Screaming in the Night *MVD, COL*

Krokus: The Video Blitz *MVD*

K.T. Oslin: Love in a Small Town *BMG, MVD*

Kylie Minogue: Live at Dublin *MVD*

Kylie Minogue: On the Go - Live in Japan *MVD*

Kylie Minogue: The Video *MVD*

Kyoto Vivaldi: The Four Seasons *KUL, IME*

L.A. All Stars: Big Joe Turner and Hampton Hawes *RHP*

La Bamba Party *GHV*

La Explosion del Video Musical

L.A. Guns: Love, Peace & Geese *MVD, PGV*

L.A. Guns: One More Reason *MVD*

La Scala di Seta *MVD, PME*

La Sombria: Concierto en Vivo!! *MVD*

La Toya Jackson *MVD, LIV*

La Traviata *MVD, PME*

Labor Songs *FVL*

The Ladies Sing the Blues *VWV, FUS, MVD*

Lady Day: The Many Faces of Billie Holiday *KUL, FCT, MVD*

Laibach: Live *MVD*

Lambada Dance Party *MVD, SMV*

Larry Carlton: Live *MVD*

Larry Coryell: Live from Bahia 1991 *MVD*

The LaSalle String Quartet *NET*

The Last of the Blue Devils *MVD, DCL, RHP*

The Last Polka ▶ *LIV, VES*

The Last Rally *EAI*

Last Romantic *MGM*

The Last Waltz *MVD, MGM*

Late Night Romantics *MVD*

Latina Familia *MVD*

Latino Sessions *RHI*

LaTour: People are Still Having Sex *NO*

Laura Branigan: Self Control *MVD*

Laurie Anderson: Collected Videos *MVD, WRV, FCT*

Laurie Anderson: Home of the Brave *MVD*

Lawrence Welk: America, What it Used to Be/Armed Forces Day *NO*

Lawrence Welk: Carnival/ Fashions & Hits Through the Years *NO*

Lawrence Welk: Country and Western Show/Salute to New York City *NO*

Lawrence Welk: Halloween Party/Thanksgiving *NO*

Lawrence Welk: Love Songs/ History of American Musical Entertainment *NO*

Lawrence Welk: 1985 Christmas Reunion Special/ New Year's Party

Lawrence Welk on Tour, Vol. 1 & 2 *NO*

Lawrence Welk: Riverboat Show/The Norma Zimmer Show *NO*

Lawrence Welk: St. Patrick's Day Show/Easter Show *NO*

Lawrence Welk: Salute to Swing Bands/Tribute to George Gershwin *NO*

Lawrence Welk: Salute to the Ladies/Spotlight on Our Musical Family *NO*

Lawrence Welk: Songs from the Movies/South of the Border *NO*

Lawrence Welk: Summer/ Vaudeville *NO*

Lawrence Welk: The Early Years Collector Series, Vol. 1 *NO*

Lawrence Welk: The Roaring Twenties/Sights and Sounds of L.A. *NO*

Le 'El Palm: Pull Back the Covers *NO*

Le Grandi Primadonne *MCA*

Le Nozze di Figaro *PGV, PME*

Le Piano Vivant *CMR, NYS*

The Leaders: Jazz in Paris 1988 *MVD, RHP, KIV*

Led Zeppelin: The Song Remains the Same *MVD, WAR*

Lee Aaron Live *NLC, MVD, SUE*

Lee Greenwood: God Bless the U.S.A. *MVD, MCA*

Lee Konitz: Portrait of the Artist as Saxophonist *MVD, RHP, KIV*

Lee Ritenour & Dave Grusin: Live from the Record Plant *MVD, HMV*

Lee Ritenour & Friends: Live from the Coconut Grove, Vol. 1 *HMV*

Lee Ritenour & Friends: Live from the Coconut Grove, Vol. 2 *HMV*

Lee Ritenour: Rit Special *MVD*

Lee Ritenour: Village, Live *NO*

Legendary Ladies of Rock & Roll *MVD, HBO, FFF*

Legendary Pink Dots: Live *MVD*

Legendary Voices: Cantors of Yesteryear *ERG*

Legends of Rock & Roll *MVD, HBO, FFF*

Legs Diamond *MVD*

Leise flehen meine Lieder *GLV*

L'Elisir d'Amore *PAR*

The Lemonheads: Two Weeks in Australia *AVE*

Lena Horne: The Lady & Her Music *RKO, IME*

Lennon: A Tribute *SMV*

Lenny Kravitz: Video Retrospective *AVE, MVD*

Leo Ferre: Chansons *MVD*

Leo Kottke: Home and Away *MVD, BMG*

Leo Sayer: The Very Best of Leo Sayer *PGV*

Leon Russell: Best of the Festivals Live *MVD*

Leon Russell/Edgar Winter: Main Street Cafe *MVD*

Leonard Bernstein: Berlioz Requiem *KUL*

Leonard Bernstein: Tchaikovsky *KUL*

Leonard Cohen: Songs from the Life of Leonard Cohen *MVD, KUL*

Leonid Kogan: Interpretations *MVD, KUL*

Les Blues de Balfa *FFM*

Les Contes D'Hoffman *PME*

Les McCann: Live in New Orleans *MVD*

Les McCann Trio *MVD, RHP, FCT*

Les Paul & Friends: He Changed the Music *MVD, HBO, BMG*

Les Paul: The Living Legend of the Electric Guitar *BMG*

Lester Young & Billie Holiday *MVD*

Leszek Dlugosz: It Can Be You *FCT*

Let the Good Times Roll *PGV, MVD*

Let's Cotton Together *FCT*

Let's Have an Irish Party *RGO, PPI*

Lettermen: Christmas Reflections *NO*

Level 42: Family of Five *MVD, PGV*

Level 42: Guaranteed Live *MVD*

Level 42: Level Best *MVD, PGV*

Level 42: Live and More *MVD*

Level 42: Live at Wembley *MVD, PGV*

Liberace *MPI, MVD, TVC*

Liberace in Las Vegas *WAR, OM*

Liberace Live *MVD, LIV, VES*

The Liberace Show *SHO, DVT*

Liberace Show Vol. 2 *MPI*

Lieder, die vom Herzen Kommen *GLV*

Lietuviskos Dainos Suente *IHF*

Lietuvos Dainu Svente *IHF*

Life, Sex & Death: The Invisible Majority *MVD*

Lifers Group: World Tour "Rahway Prison, That's It" *MVD*

Lifestreams Video *NO*

Light of the Spirit *WSH*

Lightnin' Hopkins: Live in the Late '60s *MVD*

Lightning Seeds *NO*

Lincoln Center's Mostly Mozart *PAR*

Linda Arnold's World of Make Believe *A&M*

Linda Ronstadt/Nelson Riddle "What's New" *MVD, LIV, VES*

Lindisfarne: Live *MVD*

Line Dancing With Christy Lane *BHV, MVD*

Lionel Hampton *FCT*

Lionel Hampton: Gypsy in My Soul *MVD*

Lionel Hampton's One Night Stand *NO*

Lionel Richie: All Night Long *MVD*

Lionel Richie: Making of Dancing on the Ceiling *MVD, LHV*

Lionel Richie: Super Live 1987 *MVD*

Lisa Stansfield: Real Life *SWH, BMG, MVD*

Liszt in Mid-Life at Mid-Century *CMR, NYS*

Lita Ford: A Midnight Snack *BMG, MVD*

Lita Ford: Dangerous Videos, Vol. 1 *MVD*

Lita Ford: Lita *MVD, BMG*

Lita Ford: Wembley *NO*

The Lithuanian Ethnographic Ensemble *IHF*

Little Richard: Keep on Rockin' *WRV, MVD, FCT*

Little River Band *NO*

Live & Red Hot *KRV*

Live at CBGB's *MVD*

Live at Target *MVD*

Live at the Biltmore Ballroom *MVD*

Live at the Village Vanguard, Vol. 1 *MVD, VAI*

Live at the Village Vanguard, Vol. 2 *MVD, VAI*

Live at the Village Vanguard, Vol. 3 *MVD, VAI*

Live at the Village Vanguard, Vol. 4 *MVD, VAI*

Live at the Village Vanguard, Vol. 5 *MVD, VAI*

Live at the Village Vanguard, Vol. 6 *MVD, VAI*

Live from New York City *MVD*

Live from the Met Highlights, Vol. 1 *MVD, HMV, PAR*

Live Skull: Live *MVD*

Live Skull: Live from Ohio *MVD*

Living Colour: Primer *MVD, SMV*

Living Colour: Time Tunnel *MVD, SMV*

Liza in Concert *NO*

Liza Minnelli: Live from Radio City Music Hall *SMV, PMS*

Liza Minnelli: Visible Results *MVD, SMV*

Lizzy Borden: Live Murderous Row Show *MVD*

L.L. Cool J: Future of the Funk *MVD, SMV*

Lo Mejor de Noches Tapatias I *MVD*

Lohengrin *PAR, FCT, MVD*

London Beat: Quick Pix *MOV*

London Rock and Roll Show *MVD*

Londonbeat: Quick Pix *MVD*

Lone Justice: Live *MVD*

Lonely is an Eyesore *MVD*

Lords of the New Church: Live from London *MVD, COL*

Loretta Lynn: An Evening with Loretta Lynn *MVD*

Loretta Lynn: Honky Tonk Girl *NO*

Loretta Lynn in Concert *MCA, MVD*

Lorrie Morgan: Great Video Hits *COL*

Los Angeles Raiders: The Silver & Black Attack *MPI*

Los Invasores de Nuevo Leon: The Video *MVD*

Los Joao *NO*

Los Yonics *MVD*

Lou Rawls: An Evening with Lou Rawls *MVD*

Lou Rawls with Duke Ellington *VWV, MVD, MBP*

Lou Reed: A Night with Lou Reed *MVD, COL, LTY*

Lou Reed & John Cale: Songs for Drella *MVD, WRV, LUM*

Lou Reed: Coney Island Baby *MVD, LIV, VES*

Lou Reed: Magic and Loss— Live in Concert *WEA, MVD*

Lou Reed: The New York Album *MVD, WRV*

Loudness: Eurobunds *MVD*

Loudness: In Tokyo *MVD*

Loudness: Live in Tokyo/ Lightning Strikes *MVD*

Loudness: Once for All *MVD*

Loudness: Thunder in the East (Complete Version) *MVD*

Loudness: Video Loudest *MVD*

Louie Bellson & His Big Band *VWV*

Louie Bluie *MVD, FCT*

Louis Armstrong & His Orchestra: 1942-1965 *MVD, AFR*

Louis Armstrong: Live in France, 1967 *MVD*

Louis Armstrong: 1963 *MVD*

Louis Armstrong: Satchmo *MVD, SMV, PTB*

Louis Bellson and His Big Band *MVD, MBP*

Louis Bellson Meets Billy Cobham *MVD, MBP*

Louis Jordan & Friends *MVD*

Louis Jordan and His Tympany Five *BMG, MVD*

Love & Napalm: The Video *MVD*

Love and Rockets: The Haunted Fish Tank *MVD, BMG*

Love Lion *MFV, FCT*

Love of Destiny *KUL, MVD*

Loverboy: Any Way You Look At It *MVD, FOX*

Loverboy: Rock & Roll *LIV, VES, MVD*

Love's Awakening

Lowell Fulsom/Percy Mayfield: Mark Naftalin's Blue Monday Party *MVD, KIV*

Lucia di Lammermoor *MVD, HMV, KUL*

Luciano Pavarotti: Christmas with Luciano Pavarotti *MVD*

Luciano Pavarotti Gala Concert *MVD, HMV, KUL*

Luciano Pavarotti: Pavarotti in Hyde Park *PGV, MVD*

Luciano Pavarotti: The Event *MCA, MVD, FCT*

Luciano Pavarotti: 30th Anniversary Gala Concert *MVD, PGV, PME*

Lucky Dube: Live in Concert *SHR*

Luis Miguel: Un Ano de Conciertos en Vivo *MVD*

The Lute and the Sword *CMR, NYS*

Luther Vandross: Live at Wembley *MVD, SMV*

Luther Vandross: The Best of Luther Vandross *SMV*

Lynyrd Skynyrd: Tribute Tour *MVD, CAF*

M/W/F Music Video One *NO*

Ma Vlast *NO*

Mabel Mercer *CMR, NYS, FCT*

Mabel Mercer: A Singer's Singer *MVD, VWV, MBP*

Mabel Mercer: Cabaret Artist "Forever and Always" *VWV, MVD, MBP*

Macbeth *HMV, VAI, MVD*

Madama Butterfly *HMV, MVD, PME*

Madonna and Dance Music *MVD*

Madonna: Blond Ambition *MVD*

Madonna: Ciao Italia *MVD, WRV*

Madonna: Erotica *MVD, WRV*

Madonna: Immaculate Collection *MVD, WRV*

Madonna: Justify My Love *MVD, WRV*

Madonna: Like a Virgin *MVD, WRV*

Madonna Live: The Virgin Tour *MVD, WRV*

Madonna Live: Who's That Girl? *MVD*

Madonna: The Girlie Show— Live Down Under *WRV*

The Maestro and the Diva *MVD*

Maestros in Moscow *WKV, KAR*

Maggie Staton Peebles: Born Again *MVD*

The Magic Flute *MVD, PGV, PME*

Magnolia Jazz Band *NO*

Magnum: Live *NLC, MVD, SUE*

Magnum: Live at Hammersmith Odeon, 1988 *MVD*

Mahalia Jackson: Give God the Glory *MVD, PTB*

Mahler: Song Cycles with Orchestra *MVD*

Mahler: Symphonies 1 & 4 *MVD*

Mahler: Symphony No. 1 *MVD, PGV*

Mahler: Symphony No. 7 *MVD*

Mahler: Symphony No. 9 *MVD*

Making Michael Jackson's Thriller *VES*

Making Music: The Symphony Orchestra *CAM*

Making of "Teenage Mutant Ninja Turtles: Coming Out of Their Shell Tour" *GKK*

The Making of "Will the Circle Be Unbroken," Vol. 2 *CAF, MVD*

Mal Waldron/Jackie MacLean: Left Alone '86 *WRV*

The Malady Lingers On *WRV*

Malcolm McLaren: Duck Rock *COL*

The Malibu Video Sampler *BMG*

Man: Bananas *MVD*

Manhattan Jazz Quartet *MVD*

Manhattan Jazz Quartet: Live in Japan *MVD*

Manhattan Project *MVD, CAP*

The Manhattan Transfer *CMR*

The Manhattan Transfer in Concert *NO*

The Manhattan Transfer: Vocalese *MVD, ATV, AVE*

The Manhattan Transfer: Vocalese Live 1986 *FFF*

Mannheim Steamroller: A Fresh Aire Christmas *BTV*

Mannheim Steamroller Video Sampler 1 & 2 *BTV*

Manon Lescaut *HMV, MVD, PME*

Manu Dibango: King Makossa *MVD, VWV, MBP*

Many Faces of Bird *MVD*

Marc Almond: 12 Years of Tears *LUM*

Marc Bolan: Story, Vol. 1 (1968-1973) *MVD*

Marc Bolan: Story, Vol. 2 (1973-1977) *MVD*

Marcia Griffiths/Yellowman: Caribbean Night *MVD*

Marcus Roberts: Deep in the Shed *MVD, BMG*

Margaret Becker

Maria Callas: Her Paris Debut *MVD*

Maria Callas 1962 Hamburg Concert *MVD, HMV, KUL*

Mariah Carey: Here is Mariah Carey *SMV*

Mariah Carey: The First Vision *MVD, SMV*

Mariah Carey: Unplugged 3 *SMV*

Marian Anderson *PBS, PTB*

Marianne Faithful: Blazing Away *MVD, PGV*

Marillion: From Stoke Row to Ipanema *MVD,*

Marillion: Live from Loreley *MVD*

Marillion: Six of One Half Dozen of the Other *EMI, MVD*

Marillion: The Videos 1982-1986 *MVD*

Mark Chesnutt: Almost Goodbye *MCA, MVD*

Mark Naftalin's Blue Monday Party: John Lee Hooker *RHP*

Mark Naftalin's Blue Monday Party: Lowell Fulson & Percy Mayfield *RHP*

Marky Mark & the Funky Bunch: Music for the People *WAR, MVD, FFF*

The Marriage of Figaro *BFS, MVD, HMV*

The Marshall Tucker Band: Live *PGV*

The Marshall Tucker Band: Then & Now *MVD*

Martin Briley: Dangerous Moments *NO*

Marvin Gaye *MVD, FRH*

Marvin Gaye: Greatest Hits Live *MVD, FRH, SMV*

Mary J. Blige: 411 Videos *MCA*

Mary Kate and Ashley Olsen: Our First Video *BMG, MVD*

Mary Lou's Mass *NJN*

Mary's Danish: Live Foxey Lady *MVD*

Massed Bands on Parade *FUS*

Maurice Bejart: Art of the Twentieth Century Ballet *MVD*

Maurice Jarre: Lean By Jarre *MVD, BMG*

Max Roach: In Concert/In Session *MVD*

Max Roach: In Washington D.C. *MVD*

Max Roach: Jazz in America - Video 45 *MVD, FCT*

Maxi Priest: Maxi *MVD*

Maynard Ferguson: Big, Bold, & Brassy *MVD, MCG*

Maze *NO*

Maze Featuring Frankie Beverly *NO*

M.C. Hammer: Addams Groove *MVD*

M.C. Hammer: Hammer Time *MVD, CAP*

M.C. Hammer: Here Comes the Hammer *MVD, CAP*

M.C. Hammer: Please Hammer Don't Hurt 'Em *MVD, CAP*

M.C. Hammer: 2 Legit 2 Quit *MVD*

M.C. Lyte: The Lyte Years *AVE, MVD, FFF*

McCoy Tyner *MVD*

The McDonald's Gospelfest: Vol. 1 *MVD, PRH*

The McDonald's Gospelfest: Vol. 2 *MVD, PRH*

Meat Loaf: Hits Out of Hell *SMV*

Meat Loaf Live! *VES, BMG, MVD*

Media: Zbig Rybczynski, a Collection *MVD*

Medieval Music Performed on Antique Instruments *CMR, NYS*

Mefistofele *FCT, HMV, PME*

Megadeth: Exposure of a Dream *MVD*

Megadeth: Rusted Pieces *MVD*

Mel Lewis & His Big Band *MVD, VWV, MBP*

Mel Torme *NO*

Mel Torme & Della Reese in Concert *MCA*

Mel Torme Special *MVD*

Melody Magic *GKK*

Melody Maker: MMV Vol. 1 *MVD*

The Melvins: Salad of a Thousand Delights *MVD*

The Memories: Music from the Yank Years, Vol. 1 *PPI*

The Memories: Music from the Yank Years, Vol. 2 *PPI*

Memphis Slim at Ronnie Scott's *MVD, PGV*

Men at Work: Live in San Francisco...or Was It Berkeley? *MVD, FOX*

The Men in the Blue Suits *IRP*

The Mentors: A Piece of Sinema *MVD*

The Mentors: Tour de Max *MVD*

Menudo: Live in Concert *COL*

Menudo: No Me Corten el Pelo *MVD*

Menudo: Video Explosion *MVD, BMG*

Meredith Monk *MVD*

Merengue: Music from the Dominican Republic *NJN*

Merle Haggard: Live in Concert *BHV, MVD*

Merle Haggard: Poet of the Common Man *MVD, BHV*

Messiah *NO*

The Messiah *HMV, MVD*

Messiah *MVD*

Messin' with the Blues *MVD, RHI, FCT*

Metal Edge: Heavy Metal Superstars *MVD*

Metal Hammer Video Magazine: Vol. 3 *MVD*

Metal Hammer Video Magazine: Vol. 5 *MVD*

Metal Hammer Video Magazine: Vol. 6 *MVD*

Metal Mania *MVD*

Metal Masters *MVD*

Metal Variations: Enigma Metal/Hard Rock Videos *MVD*

Metallica: A Year and a Half in the Life, Part 2 *MVD*

Metallica: Cliff 'em All *MVD, MVD*

Metallica: Two of One *MVD*

The Meteors: Attack of the Chainsaw Mutants *MVD*

The Meteors: Video Nasty *MVD*

Metro Media vs. Inna City, Part 1 *KRV*

Metro Media vs. Inna City, Part 2 *KRV*

The Metropolitan Opera Gala 1991 *SIG, PGV, TVC*

Mica Paris *PGV, MVD*

Michael Bolton: Soul and Passion *SMV, MVD*

Michael Bolton: Soul Provider *MVD, SMV*

Michael Bolton: This is Michael Bolton *SMV*

Michael Crawford: Touch of Music in the Night *AVE*

Michael Damian: Rock On *MVD, A&M*

Michael Feinstein & Friends *KUL, MVD*

Michael Jackson: Dangerous—The Short Films *EPC, MVD, SMV*

Michael Jackson: Moonwalker *MVD, SMV*

Michael Jackson's Thriller *MVD*

Michael LeGrand in Concert *SVI*

Michael Monroe: Rock Like XXXX-Live at the Whiskey A Go Go *MVD*

Michael Nesmith: Live at the Britt Festival *NO*

Michael Nesmith: Nesmith Live *MVD*

Michael Nesmith: Nezmuzic *MVD*

Michael Nesmith: Rio/Cruisin' *NO*

Michael Prophet *KRV*

Michael Schenker Group: Rock Will Never Die *MVD, VES*

Michael Stanley Band *NO*

Michael W. Smith: Big Picture Tour *MVD*

Michael W. Smith: Concert Video *MVD*

Michel Beroff Plays Olivier Messiaen *CMR, NYS*

Michel Petrucciani: Live at the Village Vanguard *NO*

Michel Petrucciani: Power of Three Video *MVD*

Michel'le *MVD, AVE, FFF*

Michelle Shocked: Captain Swing Revue *MVD, PGV*

Michelle Shocked: The Texas Campfire Video *MVD*

Michigan Nighthawks Jazz Band #1 *NO*

Michigan Nighthawks Jazz Band #2 *NO*

Michigan Nighthawks Jazz Band #3 *NO*

Midnight Oil: Black Rain Falls *MVD*

Midori: Live at Carnegie Hall *NO*

A Midsummer Night's Dream *HMV*

Mighty Clouds of Joy in Concert *MVD, XVC*

The Mighty Sparrow: Live *MVD*

The Mikado *HBO, MVD*

Mike & the Mechanics: A Closer Look *MVD, AVE, FFF*

Mike Mainieri: The Jazz Life *MVD*

Mike Oldfield: Essential *MVD*

Mike Oldfield: Tubular Bells 2 *MVD*

Mildred Dilling: Memoirs of a Harp Virtuoso

Miles Davis and Quincy Jones: Live at Montreux *WRV, RHP*

Miles Davis/John Coltrane: Miles & Trane *MVD*

Miles Davis: Live '85 *MVD*

Miles Davis: Live at Montreaux *WRV*

Miles Davis: The Sound of Miles Davis *MVD*

Milli Vanilli: In Motion *MVD, BMG*

The Mills Brothers Story *TVC, FCT, KUL*

Milton Berle, the Second Time Around: Legends *WKV, KAR*

Milton Brunson & the Thompson Community Singers: Rise Up and Walk *MVD, SMV*

Mingus: Charlie Mingus *MVD, KIV, FCT*

Ministry: In Case You Didn't Feel Like Showing Up *MVD, LUM, WRV*

Ministry: Live 1-28-90 *MVD*

Minor Detail *NO*

Minor Threat: Live *MVD*

Misbehavin' Jazz Band *NO*

Missa Luba *MVD, PGV, FCT*

Missing Persons *NO*

Mission: Crusade *MVD*

Mission: Dawn to Dusk *MVD*

Mission of Burma: Live at the Bradford *MVD, FCT*

The Mission U.K.: Waves Upon the Sand *MVD*

Mississippi Mass Choir: God Gets the Glory *MLC, MVD*

Mississippi Mass Choir: Live in Jackson, MS *MVD*

Mississippi Six Dixieland Band *NO*

Mr. Big *AVE*

Mr. Big: A Group Portrait *BHV*

Mr. Big: Lean to It *MVD, AVE, FFF*

Mr. Big: Live *AVE, MVD, FFF*

Mr. Charlie *JEF*

Mr. Mister: Videos from the Real World *COL*

Mit Musik durch Stadt und Land *GLV*

Mitch Ryder: Live in Ann Arbor *MVD*

Mitsou *MVD*

Modern British Live! *MVD*

The Modern Jazz Quartet *CMR, NYS*

Modern Jazz Quartet and the Juillard String Quartet *CMR, NYS*

The Moistro Meet the Cool Ruler *KRV*

Moliendo Vidrio *NJN*

Money Madness *FOX*

Monkees, Vol. 1 *MVD, COL*

Monkees, Vol. 2 *MVD, COL*

Monkees, Vol. 3 *MVD, COL*

Monkees, Vol. 4 *MVD, COL*

Monkees, Vol. 5 *MVD, COL*

Monkees, Vol. 6 *MVD, COL*

Monster TV Rap Hits *MVD*

Monterey Jazz Festival *SMV, MVD, FCT*

Monterey Pop▶*VYG, MVD, COL*

Moody Blues: A Night at Red Rocks with the Colorado Symphony Orchestra *PGV, MVD*

Mordred: In This Live Video *MVD*

More Baby Songs *MLT*

More of Jive's Greatest Rap Video Hits *MVD, BMG*

More Than the Music *CFV*

More Women in Rock *MVD*

The Mormon Tabernacle Choir Christmas Classics *LIV, VES*

The Mormon Tabernacle Choir Greatest Hits *MVD, VES*

Morrissey: Hulmerist *MVD, WRV*

Morrissey: Live in Dallas *WRV, MVD*

Morrissey: The Malady Lingers On *WRV*

Moscow Rock Laboratory *MVD*

The Moscow Sax Quintet: Jazznost Tour *VWV, MVD*

Motels: Shock *MVD*

Mother Mallard's Portable Masterpiece Company *EAI*

Motley Crue: Dr. Feelgood—The Videos *MVD*

Motley Crue: Uncensored *MVD, MVD*

Motorhead: Another Perfect Day *NO*

Motorhead: Deaf Not Blind *MVD*

Motorhead: 1916 Live...And It Serves You Right! *SMV*

Motorhead: The Best of Motorhead *MVD*

Motorhead: The Birthday Party *MVD*

Motown Returns to the Apollo *MVD*

Motown Sounds *MVD*

Motown Time Capsule: The '60s *MCA, MVD*

Motown Time Capsule: The '70s *MCA, MVD*

Motown 25: Yesterday, Today, Forever *MVD, MGM*

Moussorgsky: Pictures at an Exhibition *PGV*

Mouthful of Sweat Compilation *MVD*

Movie Memories Series *MVD*

Mozart *MVD*

Mozart/Barenboim Vol. 1 *NO*

Mozart/Barenboim Vol. 2 *NO*

Mozart: Flute Concerto/Andante/Piano Concerto K.271 *MVD*

Mozart No End and the Paradise Band *NO*

Mozart on Tour, Vol. 5 *MVD*

Mozart on Tour, Vol. 6: Munich a Staging Post *MVD, PGV*

Mozart on Tour, Vol. 7: Vienna, The Best City for My Metier *MVD, PGV*

Mozart/Smetana/Dvorak *KUL*

Mozart Under a Microscope *CMR, NYS*

Mozart's Requiem with Colin Davis *HMV, MVD*

MTV: Best of 120 Minutes *MVD*

MTV Closet Classics *MVD, LIV, VES*

MTV Collection: 3rd Annual Video Music Awards *MVD, WRV*

Muddy Waters & Friends: Blues Summit in Chicago *MVD*

Muse Concert: No Nukes▶ *FOX*

Music and Comedy Masters Series *DVT, FCT*

Music and Dance of Pakistan *CMR, NYS*

Music at Large—The Manhattan Percussion Ensemble *NYS*

Music Classics *MPI, MVD*

Music Court *MVD*

Music for Wilderness Lake *BUL*

Music in the Midnight Sun *BUL*

Music in the 12th Century *IFB*

Music in Time *FHS*

Music Maestro

The Music of Christmas *BTV, QHV*

The Music of Melissa Manchester *NO*

Music of the Baroque *CMR, NYS*

Music of the Night: Carreras Sings Andrew Lloyd Webber

Music? or Else *CMR, NYS*

Music Video From "Streets of Fire" *MCA*

Musica Latina: "Hot" *APD*

Musica Tipica *NJN*

Musical Personalities No. 1 *NO*

Musicourt *NO*

Musik aus allen Himmelsrichtungen *GLV*

Musik geht um die Welt, Part 1 *GLV*

Musik geht um die Welt, Part 2 *GLV*

Musik kennt keine Grenzen #1 *GLV*

Musik kennt keine Grenzen #2 *GLV*

Musik kennt keine Grenzen #3 *GLV*

Musik Laden, Part 1: Beat Club *MVD*

Musik Laden, Part 2: Beat Club *MVD*

Musik liegt in der Luft *GLV*

Mutabaruka: Live *MVD*

Mute Exhibit: Visible Evidence, Vol. 1 *MVD*

Mute Exhibit: Visible Evidence, Vol. 2 *MVD*

My Free Ukraine: Independence of Ukraine

My Generation: California Rock *RHI, MVD*

My Generation: Guitar Legends *RHI, MVD*

My Generation: Metal Roots *RHI, MVD*

My Ukraine 1: Ukraine Dancing Songs

My Ukraine 2: New Year in Kiev

My Ukraine 3: Folk Songs
My Ukraine 4: Most Popular Songs from the Ukraine
My Ukraine 5: Festival in Chernivce
My Ukraine 6: Ukraine Popular Songs
My Ukraine 7: Christmas Story
My Ukraine 8: Spring Dances
My Ukraine 9: New Years Eve in Kiev
My Ukraine 10: Childrens Stories
My Ukraine 11: Sokoly
My Ukraine 12: Songs of Sitch Riflemen
My Ukraine 14: Transcarpatian Dances
My Ukraine 15: Lvivski Muzyky
My Ukraine 16: Karpatski Akvareli
Mylene Farmer: Les Videos *MVD*
Mylon & Broken Heart: Crank It Up! *MVD*
Myrna Summers & the Myrna Summers Workshop Choir of Washington D.C. *MVD*
Myrna Summers: We're Going to Make It Live *MVD*
Nabucco *HMV, MVD*
Naked Eyes *NO*
The Naked Gershwin *NO*
Nana Mouskouri: Live at Herod Atticus *MVD*
Nanci Griffith: One Fair Summer Evening *MVD, MCA*
Nanci Griffith: Other Voices, Other Rooms *MVD*
Nancy Wilson *MVD*
Nancy Wilson at Carnegie Hall *VWV, MBP, KAR*
Napalm Death: Live Corruption *MVD, SVI*
Napoli *HMV, MVD*
Nashville Bluegrass Band *MVD*
Nashville Goes International *MVD, CAF*
Nashville Story *NO*
The Nat "King" Cole Story *KAR, AVD, FCT*
Nat "King" Cole: The Incomparable Nat "King" Cole *MVD*
Nat "King" Cole/The Mills Brothers/The Delta Rhythm *MVD, AFR*
Natalie Cole: Everlasting *MVD, EMI*
Natalie Cole: The Unforgettable Concert *WEA, MVD*
Natasha: A Dance Entertainment *MVD, PBC, KUL*
Natural Light: Windance *MVD, WSH, LUM*
Natural Selections *BMG*
Natural States *WSH*
Nazareth: Live! *MVD*
Ned's Atomic Dustbin: Nothing Is Cool *SMV, MVD*
Neil Diamond: Greatest Hits Live *MVD, SMV, RDG*
Neil Diamond: I'm Glad You're Here With Me Tonight *LIV, VES, MVD*
Neil Diamond: Love at the Greek *MVD, LIV, VES*
Neil Diamond: The Special Christmas *COL*
Neil Sedaka in Concert *MVD, MCA*
Neil Sedaka: Timeless In Concert *BMG*
Neil Young and Crazy Horse: Ragged Glory *MVD, WRV*
Neil Young and Crazy Horse: Rust Never Sleeps *WRV, MVD*
Neil Young: Freedom *MVD*
Neil Young in Berlin *MVD*

Neil Young: Solo Trans *NO*
Neil Young: Unplugged *WRV*
Neil Young: Weld *WRV, MVD*
Nelson Mandela 70th Birthday Tribute *MVD, SMV, FCT*
Neneh Cherry: The Rise of Neneh Cherry *MVD, BMG*
Neptune's Garden *MTX, KAR*
Nesmith Live *PBS*
Neville Brothers & Friends: Tell It Like It Is *MVD, HBO, FFF*
Neville Marriner *MVD, KUL*
New Born King *MVD, VAI*
New Edition: Past and Present *MVD*
New Fast Automatic Daffodils: Wake Up and Make Love Before 8:30 in the Morning *MVD*
New from London, Vol. 1 *MVD*
New Kids on the Block: Hangin' Tough *MVD, SMV*
New Kids on the Block: Hangin' Tough Live *MVD, SMV*
New Kids on the Block: Step by Step *MVD, SMV*
New Model Army: History—The Videos 1985-1990 *EMI, MVD*
New Order: Substance *MVD*
New Orleans Live: Cajun & Zydeco *MVD*
New Orleans Live: The Best of Blues *MVD*
New Orleans Live: The Best of Roots & Rock *MVD*
New Sousa Band: On Stage at Wolf Trap *MVD, PRS, HMV*
New Stars on Video *MVD, CAP*
New Year's Concert 1992 *MVD*
New York City: Performance *MVD*
New York Dolls: Live in a Doll's House *MVD*
New York Giants: We're the New York Giants *CSM*
New Yorker, New Yorker *MVD*
The Newborn King: A Festival of Carols from Westminster Cathedral *BTV*
NFL Country *PGV, MVD*
NFL Goes Motown: Songs From The Big Thrill *PGV*
NFL Rocks *PGV, MVD*
NFL Rocks: Extreme Football *PGV, MVD*
Nick Cave & the Bad Seeds: The Road to God Knows Where *MVD*
Nicko McBrain: Rhythms of the Beast *MVD*
Nico: An Underground Experience *MVD*
Nico: Velvet Memories—Tokyo 1986 *MVD*
Nicolai Ghiaurov: Tribute to the Great Basso *MVD, VWV, MBP*
Nigel Kennedy: The Four Seasons *EMI, MVD*
Night of the Guitar 2, Vol. 1 *MVD*
Night of the Guitar 2, Vol. 2 *MVD*
Night of the Guitar, Vol. 1 *MVD, A&M*
Night of the Guitar, Vol. 2 *MVD*
Night of the Long Knives *MVD*
Night Ranger: Japan in Motion *MVD*
Night Ranger: Japan Tour *MVD*
Night Ranger: 7 Wishes Tour *MCA, MVD*
Nightblooming Jazzmen 1 *NO*
Nightblooming Jazzmen 2 *NO*
Nightblooming Jazzmen 3 *NO*
Nina Simone *CMR*
Nina Simone: Live at Ronnie Scotts *MVD*
999: Feelin' Alright with the Crew *MVD*

1991: The Year Punk Broke *MOV*
Nitty Gritty Dirt Band: Twenty Years of Dirt *WRV, MVD*
No Alternative *PGV*
No More Disguises *ICA*
Nocturna *MED*
Nocturnal Emissions: Bleed *MVD*
Norman and Nancy Blake: Planet Riders *MVD*
Nostalgia for the '90s *NO*
Now That's What I Call Music *NO*
Nuclear Assault: Handle with Care *MVD*
Nugget Hotel Jazz Fest *NO*
Nugget Jazz Fest (Hymn-a-Long)▶ *NO*
N.W.A.: Niggaz4life *MVD*
Odyssey: Ron Hays' Music Image *FOX*
Of Men and Music *IVY*
Ofra Haza: From Dusk till Dawn *ERG*
Oh Happy Day *MVD, MON*
Oingo Boingo: Skeletons in the Closet *MVD, A&M*
Oktoberfest 1 - 2 - g'suffa *GLV*
Oktoberfest Stimmungsvideo *GLV*
Olatunji and His Drums of Passion *MVD*
Old-Fashioned Christmas *MVD, ING*
Oliver Samuels: Front Room *PPI*
Olivia *MCA*
Olivia in Concert *MCA, MVD*
Olivia: Physical *MCA, MVD*
Olivia: Soul Kiss *MCA, MVD*
Olivia: Twist of Fate *MVD, MCA*
On the Town *PGV, FCT*
One Last Time: The Beatles' Final Concert *TEL*
One Little Indian Compilation *MVD*
One Night With Blue Note Preserved *NO*
One Voice, One Guitar *NJN*
One World, One Voice *BMG, MVD*
Onegin *HMV*
Opening Concert Berlin: 750 Years *NO*
The Operas of Thomas Pasatieri *CMR, NYS*
Operation Rock 'n' Roll: The Home Video *SMV*
The Orb *MVD*
Orchestral Manoeuvres in the Dark: Crush, the Movie *NO*
An Orchestral Tribute to the Beatles *MVD, COL*
Oregon *MVD, PRS*
Oregon: Live at 87 Freiburg *NO*
Orfeo ed Euridice *MVD, HMV, PME*
Orleans: Live in Japan 1991 *MVD*
Ornette Coleman: Ornette Made in America *MVD*
Oscar Peterson: Quartet Live *MVD*
Osibisa: Warrior *MVD*
The Other Side of Nashville *MVD, MGM*
Otis Day and the Knights: Otis My Man! *MVD, MCA*
Otis Redding: Live in Monterey, 1967 *MVD, HBO*
Otis Redding: Ready, Steady, Go! *MVD*
Outlaws *NO*
Overkill: Videoscope *AVE, MVD, FFF*
Oyster Band *MVD*
Ozzy Osbourne: Bark at the Moon *MVD*
Ozzy Osbourne: Don't Blame Me *SMV*

Ozzy Osbourne: The Ultimate Ozzy *MVD, FOX*
Ozzy Osbourne: Wicked Videos *MVD, SMV*
Ozzy Ozbourne: Live and Loud *EPC*
Paddy Reilly Live *RGO, PPI*
Pain Teens: Live *MVD*
Palm Springs Yacht Club *NO*
Pantera: Cowboys from Hell *MVD, AVE, FFF*
Pantera: Vulgar Video *PAR, MVD, AVE*
The Paris Reunion Band *MVD, PRS*
Party Tillyadrop Tour Video *BVV*
Pat Benatar Hit Videos *MVD, COL*
Pat Benatar in Concert *MVD, COL*
Pat Benatar: The Visual Music Collection *MVD, VES*
Pat Metheny: At Cyclorama Hall *MVD*
Pat Travers: Boom Boom *MVD*
Pat Travers: Just Another Killer Day *MVD, COL*
Patrice Munsel in Opera and Song *MVD*
Patti La Belle: Live at the Apollo Theater *MCA, MVD*
Patti LaBelle: Look to the Rainbow Tour *MVD*
Patti Page Video Songbook *BAR, MVD, AVE*
Paul Brady: Echoes and Extracts *MVD*
Paul Dresher Ensemble: "Slowfire" *MVD*
Paul Dresher: Was Are/Will Be *MVD*
Paul McCartney: Liverpool Oratorio *EMI, MVD*
Paul McCartney: Once Upon a Video *MVD*
Paul McCartney: Paul is Live *PGV*
Paul McCartney: Put It There *MVD, PGV*
Paul McCartney: Rupert and the Frog Song *MVD*
Paul McCartney's Get Back *VES, LIV, MVD*
Paul Revere and the Raiders: The Last Mad Man of Rock and Roll *MCA, MVD*
Paul Simon: Born at the Right Time *WRV, MVD*
Paul Simon: Concert in Central Park *WRV, MVD*
Paul Simon: Graceland *MVD*
Paul Simon: Graceland, the African Concert *MVD, WRV*
Paul Simon in Concert *MVD, WAR*
Paul Simon Special *MVD*
Paul Taylor Dance Co.: Speaking in Tongues *MVD*
Paul Winter: Canyon Consort *MVD, A&M*
Paul Young: From Time to Time *MVD*
Paul Young: The Video Singles *MVD, FOX*
Paula Abdul: Captivated Video Collection '92 *AVE, MVD*
Paula Abdul: Straight Up *MVD, COL*
Paula Abdul: Under My Spell *PGV, MVD*
Pavarotti *TWE*
Pavarotti & Friends *PGV*
Pavarotti & Levine In Recital *MVD, FCT, HMV*
Pavarotti in London *COL*
P.D.Q. Bach: The Abduction of Figaro *BFS, VAI, MVD*
Peace/Allelujah *PUL*
The Peace Concert *NO*
Peace on Earth: A Bavarian Christmas *BMG, MVD*
The Peace Tapes *MPI, MVD*

Peerce, Anderson and Segovia *MVD, KUL, PME*
Peggy Lee: The Quintessential Peggy Lee *MVD*
Penelope Houston: Dash-30-Dash *MVD*
Pentecostal Community Choir with Minister Keith Pringle: No Greater Love *MVD*
Perfect Gentlemen: Rated PG *MVD, SMV*
Perfect Harmony: The Whiffenpoofs in China *DCL*
The Perfumed Handkerchief *KUL*
Personal Property *NO*
Pet Shop Boys: Actually *MVD*
Pet Shop Boys: Highlights *MVD*
Pet Shop Boys: Performance *MVD*
Pet Shop Boys: Television *MVD, LIV*
The Pet Shop Boys: Videography *EMI, MVD*
Pete Townshend *NO*
Pete Townshend: Deep End Live *MVD, FFF*
Pete Townshend: Live *PGV, MVD*
Pete Townshend: Video EP *MVD*
Peter Allen and the Rockettes *FOX*
Peter & the Test Tube Babies: Cattle and Bum *MVD*
Peter and the Wolf *PBS*
Peter and the Wolf: Natalia Sats *MVD, PRS, FCT*
Peter Gabriel: All About Us *MVD*
Peter Gabriel: Compilation Video *MVD*
Peter Gabriel: POV *MVD*
Peter Hammill: In the Passionskirche *MVD*
Peter Metro: Live & Hot *MVD*
Peter, Paul and Mary: Holiday Concert *MVD, RHI, FUS*
Peter, Paul and Mary: Peter, Paul and Mommy, Too *WRV, MVD, BTV*
Peter, Paul and Mary: 25th Anniversary Concert *MVD, RHI*
Peter Tosh Band with Andrew Tosh: Live *MVD*
Peter Tosh: Live *MVD*
Peter Tosh: Live in Africa *NO*
Petra: Backstage Pass *SMV, MVD*
Petra: Beyond Belief Video Album *MVD, SMV*
Phantom Empire *COL*
Phil Collins *NO*
Phil Collins: But Seriously...The Videos *AVE, MVD, FFF*
Phil Collins: Live at Perkins Palace *NO*
Phil Collins: No Jacket Required *MVD, AVE, FFF*
Phil Collins: No Ticket Required *MVD, FFF*
Phil Collins: Seriously Live *MVD, AVE, FFF*
Phil Collins: The Singles Collection *MVD, AVE, FFF*
Phil Coulter: A Touch of Tranquility *SHR*
Phil Woods in Concert *VWV, MVD, MBP*
Philip Glass *MVD*
Photonos *VCD*
Pia Zadora's American Songbook *MVD, FOX*
Piano Players Rarely Ever Play Together *SPI, MVD*
Picture Music *MVD, VES*
Pigface: Glitch *MVD*
P.I.L.: '83 *MVD*
P.I.L.: Live in 1985 - The Anarchy Tour *MVD*

Piledriver: The Wrestling Album 2 *COL*

Pilgrim Jubilees: Live in Jackson *MVD*

Pillows and Prayers *MVD*

Pinchers Live: Jumbo *KRV*

Pink Floyd at Pompeii *MVD, VES*

Pink Floyd in Concert: Delicate Sound of Thunder *MVD, SMV*

Pink Floyd: La Carrera Panamericana *SMV, MVD*

Pink Floyd's David Gilmour *FOX*

Pirates of Panasonic *MVD*

Pirates of the Mississippi *MVD*

Placido: A Year in the Life of Placido Domingo *MVD, HMV, KUL*

Placido Domingo: An Evening with Placido *MVD, HMV, KUL*

Placido Domingo: In Person *MVD*

Placido Domingo: Songs of Mexico, Vol. 1 *MVD, PPI*

The Platters/The Coasters: In Concert *MVD*

Playboy Jazz Festival, Vol. 1 *BMG, COL*

Playboy Jazz Festival, Vol. 2 *COL*

Playboy's Girls of Rock & Roll *FOX*

P.M. Dawn: Of the Heart, of the Soul and of the Cross *PGV*

The Pogues: Live at the Town and Country *MVD, PGV*

The Pogues: Poguevision *MVD*

Pointer Sisters: Live in Africa *MVD, HBO, FCT*

Pointer Sisters: So Excited *MVD, COL*

Poison: Flesh, Blood & Videotape *EMI, MVD*

Poison Idea: Mating Walruses *MVD*

Poison: Sight for Sore Ears *MVD, PGV*

Police: Around the World *MVD, A&M*

Police: Every Breath You Take (The Videos) *MVD, A&M*

The Police: Greatest Hits *MVD*

Police: The Synchronicity Concert *MVD, A&M, COL*

Polish Chamber Orchestra, Conducted by Jerzy Maksy *KUL*

Polish Christmas Carols *FCT*

A Portrait of Beverly Sills

Power Station: Video EP *MVD*

Praisin' His Name: The Gospel Soul Children of New Orleans *NO*

Prefab Sprout: The Best of Prefab Sprout—A Life of Surprises *SMV, MVD*

Presenting Joan Sutherland *CTH, FCT, MVD*

The Pretenders: The Singles *MVD, WRV*

Pretty Woman: The Music Videos *MVD, EMI*

Priest Live *FOX*

Primal Scream: Scremadelica *MVD*

Primal Sounds from N.Y.C. *MVD*

Prime Cuts *MVD, FOX*

Prime Cuts: Heavy Metal *MVD, FOX*

Prime Cuts: Jazz and Beyond *MVD, FOX*

Prime Cuts: Red Hots *MVD, FOX*

Primus: Cheesy Home Video *AVE, MVD, FFF*

Prince & the New Power Generation *MVD*

Prince & the New Power Generation: Diamonds & Pearls *WRV*

Prince & the New Power Generation: Sexy MF *WRV, MVD*

Prince and the Revolution: Live *MVD, WRV*

Prince Jammy *MVD, KRV*

Prince: Nothing Can Stop...Prince and the New Power Generation: Gett Off *WRV*

Prince: Sign O' the Times *MCA, MVD, FCT*

Prince: The Hits Collection *WRV, MVD*

Prince's Trust All-Star Rock Concert *MVD, MGM*

Prince's Trust Rock Gala *LIV*

Private Music Video Collection *MVD, NOR*

Professor Don Burns *NO*

Professor Plum's Jazz *NO*

Prokofiev: Classical Symphony *MVD*

Prokofiev: Romeo & Juliet Suite *MVD*

Propaganda Videozine, Vol. 2 *MVD*

Psychedelic Furs: All of This and Nothing *MVD, SMV*

Psychedelic High *RHI*

Psychedelic Rock *MVD*

Psychic T.V.: Black *MVD*

Psychic T.V.: 8Transmissions8 *MVD, FHS*

Psychic T.V.: Joy *MVD*

Psychic T.V.: Maple Syrup *MVD*

Public Enemy: Enemy Strikes...Live *SMV*

Public Enemy: The Fight Power—Live *MVD, SMV*

Public Enemy: Tour of a Black Planet *SMV, MVD*

Puerto Rican Danza *NJN*

Puerto Rican Plena *NJN*

Pulcinella Ballet/Histoire du Soldat *MVD*

Punk & Disorderly *MVD*

Punk and Its Aftershocks *MVD*

Punk in London *MVD*

Punk Pioneers *MVD*

Punk Rock Movie *MVD, SUN*

Punk Special *NO*

P.U.N.K.: Various Artists *MVD*

Puro Bronco: 12 Exitos en Video *MVD*

Pussy Galore: Live *MVD*

Pussy Galore: Maximum Penetration *MVD*

Queen: Classic Queen *MVD*

Queen: Greatest Hits *HHE, MVD*

Queen: Live at Budapest *MVD, MPI*

Queen: Live at Wembley '86 *MVD*

Queen: Live in Japan *MVD*

Queen: Live in Rio *MVD*

Queen of Spades: Bolshoi Opera *HMV, KUL, PME*

Queen: The Magic Years, Vol. 1 *MVD, MPI*

Queen: The Magic Years, Vol. 2 *MVD, MPI*

Queen: The Magic Years, Vol. 3 *MVD, MPI*

Queen: The Works *MVD*

Queen: We are the Champions *MVD*

Queen: We Will Rock You *MVD, VES, SVI*

Queensryche: Building Empires *MVD*

Queensryche: Live in Tokyo *MVD*

Queensryche: Operation Livecrime *EMI*

Queensryche: Videoo: Mindcrime *MVD, EMI*

Quiet Riot: Bang Thy Head *MVD, FOX*

Quiet Riot: Bang Thy Head (long play version) *NO*

Quincy Jones: A Celebration *VHE, HHE*

Quincy Jones: Live in Hawaii *MVD*

Quincy Jones: Reflections *MVD*

Raccoons: Let's Dance *SUE, NLC*

Radiance/Celebration *NEM, WSH*

Rafael en Raphael *NO*

Raffi in Concert with the Rise & Shine Band *MVD, PGV, A&M*

Raffi on Broadway *MCA*

Raffi: Young Children's Concert with Raffi *MVD, A&M, COL*

Raga with Ravi Shanker *WSH*

Raggamuffin Tek' Over *KRV*

Rahsaan Roland Kirk/John Cage: Music *MVD*

Rainbow Bridge *RHI, FCT*

Rainbow Goblins Story *PAR*

Rainbow: Japan Tour '84 *MVD*

Rainbow: Live Between the Eyes *MVD, COL*

Rainbow: Live '82 *MVD, COL*

Rainbow: The Final Cut *MVD, COL*

Rainier Jazz Band *NO*

The Rake's Progress *MVD, HMV, VAI*

Ralph Kirkpatrick Plays Bach *MVD, FHS*

Ralph Tresvant: Stone Cold *MVD*

Ramblin' Jack Elliot *MVD, SHR*

Ramblin' Video Series *SHR*

Ramones: Lifestyles of the Rich and Ramones *MVD, WRV*

Randy Newman Live at the Odeon *MVD*

Randy Stonehill: One Night in Twenty Years *MVD*

Randy Travis: Forever and Ever *WRV, FUS*

Randy Travis: This Is Me *WRV*

Rank & File: Live *MVD*

Rap Classics *MVD*

Rap from Atlantic Street *MVD, AVE, FFF*

Ratt: Detonator: Videoaction 1991 *MVD, AVE, FFF*

Ratt: The Video *MVD, AVE, FFF*

Ravi Shankar: Raga *MFV, FCT*

Raw and Rough Pinchers *KRV*

Raw Talent *AHV*

Ray Charles Live 1991: A Romantic Evening at the McCallum Theatre *MVD, AVE, FFF*

Ray Davies: Return to Waterloo *MVD, COL, LTY*

Ray Manzarek/Michael McClure: Love Lion *MFV, MVD*

RCA's All-Star Country Music Fair *COL*

Reader's Digest: Nature's Symphony *IVN, LUM*

Ready Steady Go, Vol. 2 *MVD*

Ready Steady Go, Vol. 3 *MVD*

Real Country *WRV, MVD*

Reba McEntire *NO*

Reba McEntire: For My Broken Heart *MCA, MVD*

Reba McEntire: Greatest Hits *MCA, MVD*

Red, Hot & Blue *MVD, SWH*

Red Hot & Dance *SMV, MVD*

Red Hot Chili Peppers: Funky Monks *WRV*

Red Hot Chili Peppers: Positive Mental Octopus *MVD, EMI*

Red Hot Chili Peppers: Psychedelic Sexfunk Live from Heaven *EMI, MVD*

Red Hot Chili Peppers: Red Hot Skate Rock *EMI*

Red Hot Chili Peppers: Various States of Undress *EMI, MVD*

Red Hot Rock *MVD, VES*

Red Rose Ragtime Band *NO*

Red Star Army Chorus and Dance Ensemble *MVD*

Red Star Red Army *AAE*

Reggae Dance Hall Clash Video *MVD*

Reggae Fest '90 *MVD*

Reggae in Babylon *MVD*

Reggae Music Awards *MVD*

Reggae Refreshers *MVD*

Reggae Stars in Concert *MVD*

Reggae Sting '85 *MVD, KRV*

Reggae Sting '89: Vol. 1 *MVD*

Reggae Sting '89: Vol. 2 *MVD*

Reggae Sting '89: Vol. 3 *MVD*

Reggae Sting '89: Vol. 4 *MVD*

Reggae Sting '91 *MVD*

Reggae Sunsplash *NO*

Reggae Sunsplash: Dance Hall 1987 *MVD*

Reggae Sunsplash: Dance Hall 1988 *MVD*

Reggae Sunsplash: Dance Hall 1989 *MVD*

Reggae Sunsplash: Dance Hall 1991 *AVE, MVD, FFF*

Reggae Sunsplash Music Festival Collector's Edition *AVE, MVD, FFF*

Reggae Sunsplash '90: Dance Hall Night *MVD*

Reggae Sunsplash '90: Singer's Night *MVD*

Reggae Sunsplash '90: Vintage Night *MVD*

Reggae Sunsplash '91: Best of Sunsplash *AVE, MVD, FFF*

Reggae Sunsplash: Variety Night *MVD*

Reggae Superstars in Concert *MVD*

Reggae Time *MVD, KRV*

Reggae Tribute: A Tribute to Bob Marley *MVD, FCT, COL*

Rehearsal *VYY*

Reinaldo Jorge: Parts 1 & 2 *NJN*

R.E.M.: Pop Screen *MVD, WRV*

R.E.M.: Selected Videos *NO*

R.E.M.: Succumbs *MVD, A&M*

R.E.M.: This Film Is On *WRV*

R.E.M.: Tourfilm *MVD, WRV*

The Ren & Stimpy Show: Have Yourself a Stinky Little Christmas *WTA*

Renata Scotto: Prima Donna in Recital *MVD, HMV, VAI*

Renee & Angela: The Video Singles *MVD, PGV*

Rent Party Revellers *NO*

REO Speedwagon: Live Infidelity *MVD, FOX*

REO Speedwagon: Video Anthology 1978-1990 *SMV, MVD*

REO Speedwagon: Wheels Are Turnin' *MVD, FOX*

Requiem *PGV, MVD, FCT*

The Residents: Moleshow/Whatever Happened to Vileness Fats *MVD*

The Residents: The Eyes Scream *MVD*

The Residents: Video Voodoo *MVD*

Restless Heart: Big Dreams in a Small Town *MVD*

Restless Heart: Fast Moving Train *BMG*

The Return of Ruben Blades *SMV, MVD, COL*

The Return of Spinal Tap *MPI, MVD*

Return of the Goddess for the New Millenium *MVD,, FCT*

Return of Ulysses *MVD*

Rev. James Cleveland and the L.A. Gospel Messengers *MLC, MVD*

Revival Temple Mass Choir *MVD*

Revolting Cocks: You Goddam Sonofabitch *MVD*

Rhythm & Blues Review *GVV*

Rhythms of the World Anthology *MVD*

Richard Clayderman: Live In Concert *QVD*

Richard Marx: Hold On to the Nights *MVD, MPI*

Richard Marx, Vol. 1 *MVD, EMI*

Richard Smallwood Singers: Video Celebration *MVD, PGV*

Richard Thompson *NO*

Rick Astley: Best Video Hits *MVD*

Rick Derringer *NO*

Rick Springfield: Platinum Videos *MVD*

Rick Springfield: The Beat of a Live Drum *MVD*

Rickie Lee Jones: Live at the Wiltern Theatre *NO*

The Ricky Grundy Chorale *MVD*

Ricky Lee Jones: Live 1992 *MVD*

Ricky Nelson in Concert *MCA, MVD*

Ricky Nelson: Special Memories *MVD*

Ricky Skaggs: Live in London *MVD, FOX*

Ricky van Shelton: RVS...To Be Continued *SMV, MVD*

Ride: Live at Brixton Academy, 1992 *MVD*

Ride: Today Forever *MVD*

Right On! The Original Last Poets *KIV*

The Right Stuff *MTX, KAR*

Rigoletto *HMV, HBO, MVD*

Ringo Starr and His All-Star Band *MVD, PGV, BTV*

Ringo Starr and His All Star Band: Live from Montreux *MPI*

Rio Revisited *PGV*

The Rippingtons: Live in L.A. *GRP*

Rise Stevens in Opera and Song, Vol. 2 *VAI, MVD, FCT*

Rita MacNeil in Concert *MVD*

Roadkill *AVE*

Rob McConnell & the Boss Brass *MVD*

Robert Cray: Collection *MVD*

Robert Fripp: Careful with that Axe *MVD*

Robert Fripp: Careful with that Axe, Vol. 2 *MVD*

Robert Lockwood, Jr.: Annie's Boogie *MVD*

Robert Palmer: Ridin' High *MVD*

Robert Palmer: Riptide *MVD, COL*

Robert Palmer: Super Nova *MVD, EMI*

Robert Palmer: Video Addictions *PGV, MVD*

Robert Plant: Mumbo Jumbo *MVD, AVE, FFF*

Robert (Ragtime Bob) Darch *NO*

Roberta Flack: An Evening with Roberta Flack *MVD*

Roberta Peters in Opera and Song, Vol. 2 *MVD*

Robyn Hitchcock: Brenda of the Lightbulb Eyes *MVD, A&M*

Robyn Hitchcock: Gotta Let this Hen Out *MVD*

The Roches: Live Nude Review *MCA*

Rocio Banquells, Video 1 *NO*

Rock Aid Armenia: The Earth Hour Video *MVD*

Rock Aid Armenia: The Making of "Smoke on the Water" *MVD*
Rock & Read *MCA*
Rock & Roll Call *MVD, LIV*
Rock & Roll Review *GVV*
Rock & Roll Wrestling Music Television *RHI*
Rock & Roll Wrestling Music Television: The Special Edition *RHI*
Rock Bottom Remainders *BMG, MVD*
Rock Classix *MVD*
Rock Classix: Heavy Metal *MVD*
Rock Encyclopedia: 1973 *MVD*
Rock Encyclopedia: 1974 *MVD*
Rock Encyclopedia: 1975 *MVD*
Rock Music with the Muppets *FOX*
Rock n' Roll #3: Sexy Girls & Sexy Guns *MOV*
Rock 'N Roll Classics, Vol. 1 *MVD*
Rock 'N Roll Classics, Vol. 2 *MVD*
Rock 'N Roll Classics, Vol. 3 *MVD*
Rock 'N Roll Classics, Vol. 4 *MVD*
Rock 'N Roll Classics, Vol. 5 *MVD*
Rock 'N Roll Classics, Vol. 6 *MVD*
Rock 'n' Roll Heaven *MGM*
Rock 'n' Roll History: American Rock, the '60s *MVD, GKK*
Rock 'n' Roll History: English Invasion, the '60s *MVD, GKK*
Rock 'n' Roll History: Fabulous Fifties *MVD, GKK*
Rock 'n' Roll History: Girls of Rock 'n' Roll *MVD, GKK*
Rock 'n' Roll History: Rock 'n' Soul Heaven *MVD, GKK*
Rock 'n' Roll History: Rockabilly Rockers *MVD, GKK*
Rock 'n' Roll History: Sixties Soul *MVD, GKK*
Rock 'n Roll Meltdown *MVD, PGV*
Rock 'n' Roll: The Early Days *MVD*
Rock 'n' Roll: The Greatest Years 1963 *SVI, MVD*
Rock 'n' Roll: The Greatest Years 1964 *SVI, MVD*
Rock 'n' Roll: The Greatest Years 1965 *SVI, MVD*
Rock 'n' Roll: The Greatest Years 1966 *SVI, MVD*
Rock Video Girls 2 *PGV, MVD*
Rock Video Girls 3 *PGV, MVD*
Rockcats: Raw in Japan 1992 *MVD*
Rockers *MVD*
Rockers '87 *KRV*
Rockin' Reindeer Christmas *GKK*
Rockin' the '50s *KAR*
Rockin' the Night Away *MVD*
Rock's Rebel Yell *BHV, MVD*
Rockshow *MVD*
Rod Stewart *NO*
Rod Stewart & the Faces: Videography 1969-1974 *MVD*
Rod Stewart Concert Video *MVD, LHV, WAR*
Rod Stewart Live at the L.A. Forum *WAR, OM*
Rod Stewart: Storyteller 1984-1991 *WRV*
Rod Stewart: Tonight He's Yours *SUE*
Rod Stewart: Vagabond Heart Tour *WEA, MVD*
Rodeo: The Music Video *CAF*
Roger Daltrey: Ride a Rock Horse *MVD*

Roger McGuinn/Nitty Gritty Dirt Band: Live! *MVD*
Roger Waters: Radio K.A.O.S. *MVD, SMV*
Roger Waters: What God Wants *MVD*
Roger Whittaker *MVD*
Roll Over Alice
Rolling Stone Presents Twenty Years of Rock & Roll *MVD, MGM*
The Rolling Stones: Let's Spend the Night Together *MVD, SUE, NLC*
The Rolling Stones: Live In Hyde Park *MVD*
The Rolling Stones: Rolling On *SIM*
The Rolling Stones: Video Rewind-Great Video Hits *MVD, VES*
Romeo and Juliet (Bolshoi Anniversary) *KUL*
Romeo and Juliet in Kansas City *PYR*
Ron Carter & Art Farmer: Live at Sweet Basil *VWV, FCT*
Ron Carter: Live Double Bass *HMV, MVD*
Ronnie Milsap: Golden Video Hits *MVD, VCI, LTY*
Ronnie Milsap: Greatest Video Hits *MVD*
The Roots of Gospel *XVC, HHE*
The Roots of Gospel: Part 2 *XVC, HHE*
Roots, Rock and Reggae: Inside the Jamaican Music Scene *MVD, SHR*
Roots/Salute the Saxophone *MVD, HMV*
Rosanne Cash: Retrospective *MVD, FOX, SMV*
Rosanne Cash: The Interiors Tour *MVD, SMV*
Roseanne Cash: Interiors Live *COL*
Rossini: Gala Concert *MVD*
Rossini/Strauss/Liszt *MVD, PGV*
Roxette: Live-ism *MVD*
Roxette: Look Sharp Live *MVD, EMI*
Roxette: The Video Hits *MVD*
Roxy Music: The High Road *MVD, COL*
Roxy Music: Total Recall *MVD*
Roy Acuff's Open House: Vol. 1 *NOS, DVT*
Roy Acuff's Open House: Vol. 2 *NOS, DVT*
Roy Ayers: In London 1992 *MVD*
Roy Ayers: Live at Ronnie Scott's *MVD*
Roy Brown: Aires Bucaneros *NJN*
Roy Orbison *MVD*
Roy Orbison & Friends: A Black and White Night *MVD, HBO, FFF*
Roy Orbison: I Drove All Night *UND, MVD*
Royal Society Jazz Orchestra *NO*
Royal Tournament Highlights: The Royal Air Force Years *TVC*
RRRecords Compilation Testament *MVD*
Rubber Rodeo *NO*
Rudolf Schock: Auf Schusters Rappen *GLV*
Ruff House Presents... *SMV, MVD*
Run D.M.C. *MVD*
Run D.M.C.: The Video *PFV*
Running Wild: Death or Glory Tour Live *MVD, SVI*
Rush: A Show of Hands *MVD, PGV*

Rush: Chronicles *MVD, PGV, BTV*
Rush: Exit...Stage Left *COL*
Rush: Grace Under Pressure Tour *MVD, COL*
Rush: Through the Camera Eye *MVD, BMG, COL*
Russ Carlyle: Story *MVD*
Russ Taff: A Christmas Song *SPW*
Russian Dances
Russian Fantasy: Songs and Dances
Russian Folk Song & Dance *KUL, APD*
Ryuichi Sakamoto: Beauty *MVD*
Ryuichi Sakamoto: Media Ban Live *MVD*
Ryuichi Sakamoto: Neo Geo *MVD*
Ryuichi Sakamoto: Tokyo Melody *MVD*
Sabbat: End of the Beginning *MVD*
The Sacred Music of Duke Ellington *MGM*
Sadao Watanabe: Mysha *MVD*
Sade: Diamond Life Video *MVD, FOX*
Sade: Life Promise Pride Love *EPC*
The St. John Passion *MVD, FHS*
St. Louis Blues *CIG, GVV*
St. Louis Ragtimers *NO*
St. Matthew Passion *MVD, FHS*
Salif Keita: Destiny of a Noble Outcast *PGV, FCT*
Salute to the Edinburgh Tattoo *PME, SIG, TVC*
Sam Kinison: Banned *MVD, WRV*
Samantha Fox: Just One Night *MVD, BMG*
Samantha Fox: Making Music *MVD*
Samantha Fox: The Music Video *MVD, BMG*
Sammy Kershaw: Cadillac Style *PGV, MVD*
San Francisco Blues Festival *MVD, FCT*
Sandi Patti: Let There Be Praise (Concert Video) *MVD, A&M*
Sandi Patti: Live *VBL*
Sandi Patti: The Making of Le Voyage *EPC*
Santana: Sacred Fire—Live in Mexico *PGV, MVD*
Santana: Viva Santana (A Conversation with Carlos) *MVD, SMV*
Sarah Vaughan: Live from Monterey *SMV, MVD, FCT*
Sarah Vaughan: Live in Tokyo *MVD*
Sarah Vaughan/Mel Torme: The Nearness of You *MVD*
Sass & Brass: A Jazz Session *MVD, HBO*
Savage Republic: Disarmament *MVD*
Sawyer Brown: Greatest Hits *MVD*
Sawyer Brown: Shakin' *MVD*
Saxon: Live *MVD*
Scarlatti/Debussy/Ravel *KUL*
Scenic Harvest from the Kingdom of Pain
Schubert: Piano Trio Op. 100, Piano Trio D. 897 *MVD, LUM*
Schubert: Schwanengesang *MVD*
Schubert: Symphony No. 9 *MVD*
Schubert: 3 Piano Sonatas *MVD, PGV*
Scorpions *NO*
Scorpions: Crazy World Tour Live - Berlin 1991 *PGV*

Scorpions: First Sting *MVD*
Scorpions: To Russia With Love *MVD, PGV*
Scorpions: World Wide Live *MVD, COL*
Scott Joplin, 1868-1917 *CMR, NYS*
Scott Joplin Ragtime Music *CMR*
Screamers: Live in San Francisco, 1978 *MVD*
Scritti Politti *MVD*
Scruggs *FOX*
The Sea: A Classical Music Video *BMV*
Seal *WRV, MVD*
Seal: Live at the Point *MVD*
Seascapes 2 *BMV*
The Secret Policeman's Other Ball▶ *MGM*
Secret Policeman's Private Parts *MED*
Sensational Nightingales: Ministry in Song *MVD*
Sepultura: Under Siege *MVD*
Serge Gainsbourg: Chansons *MVD*
Sermon on the Mount *VYY*
Seventeenth Annual Telluride Bluegrass Festival *MVD*
'70s Revival *NO*
Severed Heads: Overhead *MVD*
The Sex Pistols: Bollocks to Everyone *MVD*
Sex Pistols: Buried Alive *MVD*
Sex Pistols: Decade *MVD*
Sex Pistols: Filth & the Fury *MVD*
Sex Pistols: Last Winterland Concert *MVD*
Sex Pistols Live *NO*
Sex Pistols: The Great Rock & Roll Swindle *MVD, WRV*
Sha Na Na Rock 'n' Roll Concert and Party Video *MVD*
Shabba Ranks: Naked and Ready *SMV*
Shabba Ranks: Talk of the Town *SMV*
Shabba Ranks vs. Ninja Man: Super Clash Round *MVD*
Shadows on the Grass *NET*
Shai: Video Personification 1 *MCA*
Shakespear's Sister: Hormonally Yours *PGV, MVD*
Sham 69: Live in Japan '91 *MVD*
Shari Lewis: Lambchop's Play-Along *PGV, MLT*
Sharing...a Visual Musical Experience *VBL*
Sheena Easton *NO*
Sheena Easton: Act One *MVD, PSM*
Sheena Easton: Live at the Palace, Hollywood *NO*
Sheena Easton: Private Heaven *MVD*
Sheila E.: Live Romance 1600 *MVD, WRV*
Sheila Walsh: "Shadowlands" in Concert *MVD*
Shelley Duvall's Rock 'n' Rhymeland *MVD*
Shelly Manne Quartet *MVD, RHP*
Shenandoah: Greatest Video Hits *SMV*
Sherrill Milnes: Homage to Verdi *MVD, HMV, KUL*
Shimmy-Disc Compilation, Vol. 1 *MVD*
Shimmy-Disc Compilation, Vol. 2 *MVD*
Shimmy-Disc Compilation, Vol. 3 *MVD*
Shindig! Legends of Rock 'n' Roll *RHI*

Shindig! Presents British Invasion, Vol. 1 *MOV, RHI, MVD*
Shindig! Presents British Invasion, Vol. 2 *RHI, MVD*
Shindig! Presents Frat Party *RHI, FCT*
Shindig! Presents Groovy Gals *RHI, FCT*
Shindig! Presents Jackie Wilson *RHI, FCT*
Shindig! Presents Legends of Rock 'n Roll *RHI, MVD*
Shindig! Presents Motor City Magic *RHI, FCT*
Shindig! Presents Soul *RHI, FCT*
Shindig! Presents the Kinks *MOV, RHI, MVD*
Shindig! Presents the Righteous Brothers: Unchained Melody *RHI, MVD*
Shining Time Station: Singsongs, Vol. 1 *FFF, FFF*
Shirley Bassey: You Ain't Heard Nothin' Yet: Live *MVD*
Shirley Caesar: Hold My Mule (Live in Memphis) *MVD, AVE, SMV*
Shirley Caesar: I Remember Mama *MVD, WRD, SMV*
Shirley Horn Sings and Plays Here's to Life *PGV*
Shock Out With Metromedia *MVD, KRV*
Shockwave *MVD, LIV, VES*
Short Pieces *MWF*
Shorty Rogers: West Coast Giants *MVD*
Shout!: The Story of Johnny O'Keefe *FRH*
Show My People *BUP*
Showdown at the Hoedown
Showdown 1 *PPI*
Siam Odyssey *NO*
Silent Night with Jose Carreras
Simon and Garfunkel: The Concert in Central Park *MVD, FOX*
Simon Boccanegra *HMV, PAR*
Simon Phillips *MVD*
Simple Minds: Verona *MVD*
Simply Red: A Starry Night With Simply Red *MVD*
Simply Red: Let Me Take You Home *MVD*
Simply Red: Moving Picture Book *AVE, MVD, FFF*
Simultaneous *FCT*
Sinead O'Connor: Nothing Compares 2 U *MVD*
Sinead O'Connor: The Value of Ignorance *MVD, PGV*
Sinead O'Connor: Year of the Horse *MOV*
Sing Along with Israel *ERG*
Sing mir das Lied noch einmal *GLV*
Sing mit Heino *GLV*
Sing mit Mir, Tanz mit Mir *GLV*
Singer Presents "Elvis" (The 1968 Comeback Special) *NOS, DVT*
Singing French Songs for Children *MVD*
Siouxsie and the Banshees *NO*
Siouxsie and the Banshees: Nocturne *MVD, MED*
Siouxsie and the Banshees: Once Upon a Time *NO*
Sir George Solti Conducts the Chicago Symphony Orchestra in Tokyo, 1990 *NO*
Sir Mix-A-Lot: Baby Got Back *WRV, MVD*
Sir Mix-A-Lot: Maconomics *WRV*
Sisters of Mercy: Live *MVD*

Six Brandenburg Concertos *PGV*
Ska Beatz *MVD*
Ska Explosion *MVD*
Skid Row: No Frills *AVE, MVD*
Skid Row: Oh Say, Can You Scream? *MVD, AVE, FFF*
Skid Row: Roadkill *AVE, MVD*
Skin Deep: The Men *NO*
Skin Deep: The Women *NO*
Skinny Puppy: Ain't It Dead Yet? *MVD*
Sky Cries Mary: Until the Grinders Cease *MVD*
Slammin' Rap Video Magazine, Vol. 1 *MVD, GKK*
Slammin' Rap Video Magazine, Vol. 2 *MVD, BMG, BTV*
Slammin' Rap Video Magazine, Vol. 3 *MVD, BMG*
Slammin' Rap Video Magazine, Vol. 4 *BMG*
Slaughter: From the Beginning *MVD, CAP*
Slaughter: The Wild Life Home Video *EMI, MVD*
Slayer: Live at Wembley *MVD*
Slipping Through the Cracks *MVD*
Slovak Dancing Songs 1
Slovak Dancing Songs 2
Slovak Dancing Songs 3
Slovak Dancing Songs 4
Small Faces: Big Hits *MVD*
Smashin' the Palace '84 *NO*
Smithereens: Smithereens 10 *MVD, CAP*
The Smiths: The Complete Picture *MVD, WRV*
Snap: World Power—The Videos *MVD, BMG*
Snub TV, Vol. 2 *MVD*
So Proudly We Hail: A Salute to American Patriotism *FOX*
So Schoen wie Heut, so Muesst es Bleiben (Schlager, die Man nie Vergisst) *GLV*
S.O.D.: Live at Budokan, the Home Video *PGV, MVD*
Soft Cell *NO*
Soft Cell/Marc Almond: Memorabilia—Video Singles *PGV*
Soldiers of Music: Rostropovich Returns to Russia *NO*
Solo Tribute to Keith Jarrett *HMV, FCT*
Sondheim: A Celebration at Carnegie Hall *BMG*
A Song for Ireland *RGO*
Songs from Papua New Guinea
Songs from the Soul: The Negro Spiritual *FVL*
Sonic Youth: Goo *MOV*
Sonny & Cher Nitty Gritty Hour *VWV, MOV*
Sonny Rollins: Live *MVD, RHP, TLF*
Sonny Rollins: Montreux Jazz Festival *MVD*
Sonny Rollins: Saxophone Colossus *MVD*
Sonny Terry: Shoutin' the Blues *NO*
Sophisticated Ladies *JTC, FCT, MVD*
Soul Classix *MVD*
Soul Experience *NO*
The Soul of R & B *MVD, LIV*
Soul to Soul *NO*
Sound?? *RHP, FCT, KIV*
Sound of Jazz *MVD, GVV*
Soundgarden: Louder Than Live *MVD, A&M*
Soundgarden: Motorvision *PGV*
Soundies, Vol. 1: 1940's Music Machine *AHV*

Soundies, Vol. 2: Singing Stars of Swing Era *NO*
Soundies, Vol. 3: Big Band Swing *NO*
Soundies, Vol. 4: Harlem Highlights *NO*
Sounds of Motown *PTB*
Sounds of Scotland *TVC, FUS*
Soundstage: Aretha Franklin *RHI*
Soundstage: Blues Summit in Chicago *RHI*
Soundstage: Dr. John New Orleans Swamp *RHI*
Soundstage: Three Dog Night *RHI*
South Market Street Jazz Band: 1 *NO*
South Market Street Jazz Band: 2 *NO*
South Pacific: The London Sessions *FOX*
Southern Comfort Jazz Band #1 *NO*
Southern Comfort Jazz Band #2 *NO*
Southern Comfort Jazz Band #3 *NO*
Southside Johnny & the Asbury Jukes: Having a Party *MCA, UND, MVD*
Soviet Army Chorus, Band, and Dance Ensemble *KUL*
Space Dreaming *MVD, LUM*
Space Music *BMG, MVD*
Spandau Ballet: Live Hits *MVD*
Spandau Ballet: Over Britain *MVD, LIV, VES*
Spartacus (Bolshoi Ballet) *HMV, STS, CVC*
Spike Lee & Co.: Do It A Cappella *MVD*
Spinal Tap: Break Like the Wind the Videos *MCA, MVD*
The Spirit Travels: Immigrant Music in America *CIG*
Spirituals in Concert *PGV, FCT, MVD*
S.P.K.: Despair *MVD*
S.P.K.: 2 Autopsy Films *MVD*
Splashin' the Palace '84 *MVD,*
Split Enz: History Never Repeats—The Best of Split Enz *MVD*
Split Enz: Live *MVD*
Sprout Wings and Fly *FFM*
Spyro Gyra: War *WAR, OM*
Spyro Gyra: Graffiti *MVD, MCA*
Squeeze: A Round & a Bout *MVD, MCA*
Squeeze: Greatest Hits *MVD*
Squeeze Play: The Videos 1978-1987 *MVD, A&M*
Stage Show *VYY*
Stage Show with the Dorsey Brothers *VYY*
Stamping Ground *MVD*
Stan Getz with Richie Cole *MVD*
Stan Kenton & His Orchestra: London, 1970 *MVD*
Stan Kenton: Concert *MVD*
Stan Kenton: In the USA *MVD*
Stand and Be Proud: Voice of the City *BMG, MVD*
Stand By Me: AIDS Day Benefit Concert *MVD, LIV*
Standards II with Keith Jarrett, Gary Peacock and Jack DeJohnette *HMV, FCT*
Stanley Jordan: Cornucopia *MVD*
Stanley Jordan: Magic Touch *MVD, FCT*
Stanley Jordan: The Blue Note Concert *CAP*
Stanley Turrentine: In Concert *MVD, KUL, FCT*
Star Flight
Star Licks *NO*
Star Licks All-Star Bass Video Series *MVD*

Star Spangled Banner 1 *NO*
Star Spangled Video: Operation Desert Storm Welcome Home *TGV*
Stars on 45 *MCA*
Starship: Greatest Hits (Ten Years and Change 1979-1991) *MVD, BMG*
Starship: Video Hoopla *MVD, COL*
State of the Arts Performance Special: A Festival *NJN*
The Statler Brothers: Brothers in Song *MVD, COL*
Status Quo: Anniversary Waltz *MVD*
Status Quo: Rockin' All Over the Years *MVD*
Steel Pulse *MVD, IME*
Steeleye Span: A 20th Anniversary Celebration *SHR*
Steelheart: Quick Pix *MVD*
Stephan Kates, Cellist *CMR, NYS*
Stephane Grappelli in New Orleans *MVD*
Stephane Grappelli: Live in San Francisco *MVD, RHP, KIV*
Stephanie Mills: Home is Where the Heart is *MCA, MVD*
Stephanie Mills: Television Medicine *NO*
Steps Ahead: Live in Japan *MVD*
Steve and Annie Chapman: The Greatest Gift *NO*
Steve Gadd: In Session *MVD,*
Steve Green: Hymns—A Portrait of Christ *MVD, SPW*
Steve Hackett: Live '89 *MVD*
Steve Miller Band *MVD*
Steve Miller: Blues in the 20th Century *EMI, MVD*
Steve Taylor: Squint: Movies from the Soundtrack *WRV*
Steven Curtis Chapman: The Great Adventure Home Video *SPW, MVD*
Stevie Nicks & Friends *MVD*
Stevie Nicks: I Can't Wait *MVD, COL, LTY*
Stevie Nicks in Concert *FOX, MVD*
Stevie Nicks: Live at Red Rocks *SMV, MVD, COL*
Stevie Ray Vaughn and Double Trouble: Live at the El Mocombo 1983 *SMV*
Stevie Ray Vaughn and Double Trouble: Pride & Joy *MVD, SMV*
Stewart Copeland: Rhythmatist *COL*
Sting: Bring on the Night *MVD, LHV, WAR*
Sting: Nothing Like the Sun: The Videos *MVD, A&M*
Sting: Ten Summoner's Tales *PGV, MVD*
Sting: The Soul Cages Concert *A&M*
Sting: The Soul Cages Video *MVD, A&M*
Sting: The Videos Part 1 *MVD, PGV, BTV*
Sting: Unplugged *PGV*
The Stone Roses: Blackpool Live *MVD*
Stonehenge '84 *MVD*
Stop Making Sense▶*MVD, COL*
Stop Sellafield: The Concert *MCA, MVD*
Stop the Violence Movement: Self Destruction *BMG, MVD*
The Story of Creation *WRV, MVD*
Story of Hands Across America *LHV*

The Story of the Clancy Brothers and Tommy Makem *SHR*
Straight from the Hood *MVD*
The Stranglers *MVD*
Stratasphere: Portrait of Teresa Stratas *MVD, KUL, PME*
Stray Cats *NO*
Stray Cats: Bring It Back Again *MVD, EMI*
Stray Cats: Paris *MVD*
Stray Cats: Rock Detroit *MVD*
Stray Cats Rock Tokyo *BMG, MVD*
Streisand Collection *NO*
Strictly for the Beat *PGV, WAX, MVD*
String Trio of New York: Built by Hand *KIV*
Structures from Silence *NEM, WSH*
Stryper: Against the Law *MVD*
Stryper: In the Beginning *MVD, PGV*
Stryper: Live In Japan *MVD*
Style Council: Far East & Far Out *MED*
Style Council: Jerusalem *MVD, PGV*
Style Council: Live at Full House *MVD*
Style Council: Showbiz *MVD*
Style Council: What We Did On Our Holiday *MVD*
Styx: Caught in the Act *MVD, A&M, COL*
Subbulakshmi: Queen of Song *CMR, NYS*
The Sugar Cubes: Live Zabor *MVD*
Sugar Minott: Dance Hall Video *MVD*
Sugarcubes: Live Zabor *MVD, WAR*
Suicidal Tendencies: Lights...Camera...Suicidal *MVD, SMV*
Summerwind *WSH*
Sun City *LHV*
Sun, Moon & Feather *CIG*
Sun Ra: Mystery, Mr. Ra *MVD, RHP, KIV*
Sunday Mornin' Country *VBL*
Super Drumming *MVD*
Super Jam 3: Stone Love vs. Metromedia *KRV, MVD*
Super Jam '87 *KRV*
Super Rock '85 *MVD*
Superchunk: Take the Tube *MVD*
Superdrumming *MVD, PRS*
Supershow *MVD*
Superstars in Concert *MVD*
Supertramp: Brother Where You Bound *MVD, A&M, COL*
Supertramp: The Story So Far *MVD*
Surfing Beach Party *MED*
Survivor: Live in Japan *MVD*
Survivors: The Blues Today *MVD*
Suzanne Vega *MVD*
Suzuki Violin Concert Series *NO*
Sweet Baby: Live *MVD*
Sweet Home Chicago *BMG, MVD*
Sweet Sensation: Sweet Sensation *MVD, AVE, FFF*
Swing Out Sister: And Why Not? *MVD*
Swing Out Sister: Best Videos *MVD*
Swing Out Sister: Kaleidoscope World *MVD, PGV*
Swing: The Best of the Big Bands *MCA*
Swinging Singing Years *MVD, NOS, DVT*
Swinging U.K. *JEF*
The Swingle Singers in Concert *MVD, PRS, HMV*

Swingtime Video *MVD*
Sylvia Plath, Part 2: Getting There *CMR, NYS*
Sympathy for the Devil *FOX, OM*
Symphony for the Spire *COL, BTV, MVD*
Symphony of Swing *MVD*
T. Rex: Solid Gold *MVD*
T. Rex: T-Rexmas *MVD*
T. Rex: The Essential Video Collection *MVD*
Taj Mahal: Live at Ronnie Scott's *MVD*
Takanaka: World *PAR*
Take 6: All Access *WRV, MVD*
The Tales of Hoffmann *HMV, PME*
Talk Talk *NO*
Talk Talk: Natural History *MVD*
Talking Heads: Storytelling Giants *MVD, WRV*
Tam Tam: Do It Tam Tam *NO*
The T.A.M.I. Show *MED*
Tammy Wynette in Concert *MVD, LIV, VES*
Tangerine Dream: Three Phase *BMG*
Tanita Tikaram: Ancient Heart *MVD, WRV*
Tankard: Open All Night—Live at the Berlin Wall *MVD*
Tannhaeuser *HMV, PAR, MVD*
Tanya Tucker: Live *MVD*
Tanya Tucker: Video Hits *MVD*
Taylor Dayne: Twists of Fate *MVD, BMG*
Tchaikovsky Competition: Violin & Piano *MAS, MVD*
Tchaikovsky Gala in Leningrad *BMG*
Tchaikovsky: Piano Concerto #1 *MVD*
Tchaikovsky/Prokofiev Violin Concertos *BMG, MVD*
Tchaikovsky: Symphonies 4 & 5 *MVD*
Tear In My Beer & Other Great Country Videos *WRV, MVD*
Tears for Fears *MVD*
Tears for Fears: Going to California *MVD, PGV*
Tears for Fears: In My Mind's Eye *MVD, MED*
Tears for Fears: Live in London *MVD*
Tears for Fears: Scenes From the Big Chair *NO*
Tears for Fears: Sowing the Seeds *MVD, PGV*
Tears for Fears: Tears Roll Down (Greatest Hits 82-92) *PGV, MVD*
Teatro Alla Scala: Adrianna Lecouvrer *MVD*
Technotronic: Trip on This— The Videos *MVD*
Ted Nugent's New Year's Eve Whiplash Bash *MVD, AVE, FFF*
Teddy Pendergrass: Live in London *FOX*
Teenage Mutant Ninja Turtles: Coming Out of Their Shells Tour *GKK*
Teenage Mutant Ninja Turtles: Music Videos *MVD*
Teenage Mutant Ninja Turtles: The Gettin' Down in Your Town Tour *RAN*
TeenVid Video Magazine, Vol. 1 *MVD, BMG*
TeenVid Video Magazine, Vol. 2 *BMG*
TeenVid Video Magazine, Vol. 3 *BMG, MVD*
Telluride Bluegrass Festival *PBS*
The Temps and the Tops *FRH*
Temptations & Four Tops *MVD*
Temptations: Get Ready *MPI*

Temptations: Live in Concert *IME, FCT*
10,000 Maniacs: Time Capsule 1982-1990 *MVD*
Ten Years After: Going Home *MVD*
10CC: Changing Faces *MVD*
Terence Trent D'Arby: Introducing the Hardline... Live *SMV, MVD*
Tesla: Five Man Video Band *MVD, BTV*
Test Department: Program for Progress *MVD*
Testament: Seen Between the Lines *AVE, FFF*
Tex Wyndham's Red Lion Jazz Band *NO*
Texaco's Swing into Spring *NOS, DVT*
Texas: Southside *MVD*
Texas Style *NO*
Texas Tenor: The Illinois Jacquet Story *RHP, FCT, MVD, MED*
That Was Rock (The TAMI/TNT Show) *REP, CNG*
That'll Be the Day *REP, CNG*
The The: Infected *SMV, MVD*
The The: Versus the World *MVD, SMV*
Thelonious Monk: Monk in Europe *MVD*
Thelonious Monk: Music in Monk's Time *MVD*
Thelonious Monk: Portrait of... *MVD*
Thelonious Monk Quartet: Monk in Oslo *RHP, MVD*
Thelonious Monk: '63 in Japan *MVD*
Thelonious Monk: Straight, No Chaser *WAR, TTC*
Thelonious Sphere Monk: Celebrating a Jazz Master *NO*
There But For Fortune *NO*
There was No Room for You *FCT*
There's a Meetin' Here Tonight *NO*
They Might Be Giants: The Videos 1986-1989 *MVD, PGV*
They Might Be Giants: Video Compilation *BMG*
Thin Lizzy: Dedication *MVD, PGV*
Thin Lizzy: Live & Dangerous *MVD, AIP*
Thin White Rope: The Axis Calls *BMG*
3rd Bass: The Cactus Vidie/Yo *MVD, SMV*
Third World: Live in Japan '85 *MVD*
Third World: Prisoner in the Street *MVD*
38 Special: Wild Eyed and Live *MVD, A&M, COL*
Thomas Dolby: Live Wireless *NO*
Thomas Dolby: The Golden Age of Video *MVD, EMI*
Thomas Dolby: Video 45 *MVD*
Thomas Whitfield & The Whitfield Company Live *PGV*
Thompson Twins: Into the Gap Live *MVD, COL*
Thompson Twins: Live at Liverpool *NO*
Thompson Twins: Single Vision *MVD, COL*
Three Dog Night: Video Hits *MVD*
Three Tenors: Encore *NLC, COL, MVD*
3-Way Thrash *MVD*
The Thrill of the Orchestra
Throbbing Gristle: Destiny *MVD*

Throbbing Gristle: Live at Kezar *MVD*
Thunder: Backstreet Symphony *MVD*
Thunders, Kane, Nolan: Live on the Sunset Strip *MVD*
Tiffany: Live in Japan *MVD*
Tiger *KRV*
Tiger: Spectacular *MVD*
Tigertailz: Bezerk Live '90 *MVD*
'Til Tuesday *MVD, FOX*
Tim Blake *MVD*
Timbuk 3 *MVD, MCA*
Timbuk 3: Greetings from Eden Alley *MCA*
Time Groove *MVD, VAI, FCT*
Timeless *MVD, WSH*
Timex Watch Hour *VDM*
Timmy T. *QVD*
Tin Machine: Live in Hamburg 1991 *MVD*
Tina Turner: Break Every Rule *MVD, HBO*
Tina Turner: Do You Want Some Action! *MVD, PGV*
Tina Turner: Foreign Affair *EMI*
Tina Turner: Live in Rio *MVD, PGV*
Tina Turner: Live, Nice 'n' Rough *NO*
Tina Turner: Live, Private Dancer Tour *NO*
Tina Turner: Private Dancer *NO*
Tina Turner: Queen of Rock & Roll *NO*
Tina Turner: Simply the Best *MVD*
Tina Turner: The Girl from Nutbush *SVI, FCT*
Tino Rossi: Thanks to Dear Friends—Live *MVD*
Tiny and Ruby: Hell Divin' Women *CIG*
TLC: Oooooooohhh...on the TLC Video Tip *BMG, MVD*
Toad the Wet Sprocket: Seven Songs Seldom Seen *SMV, MVD*
Todd Rundgren: Grok Gazer, Visual Concert Hall *MVD*
Todd Rundgren: Live at the Riviera *RHI*
Todd Rundgren: Live in Japan *RHI*
Todd Rundgren: Nearly Human—Live in Japan *MVD, RHI*
Todd Rundgren: 2nd Wind Live Recording Sessions *RHI, FCT*
Todd Rundgren: The Desktop Collection *RHI, WEA*
Todd Rundgren: Videosyncracy *BMG*
Tom Chapin: This Pretty Planet *SMV, FFF*
Tom Jones: Live at This Moment *MVD,, AIP*
Tom Jones: Live in Las Vegas *FHE, OM*
Tom Paxton: In Concert *MVD, SHR*
Tom Petty: A Bunch of Videos & Some Other Stuff *MVD, MPI*
Tom Petty & the Heartbreakers: Pack Up the Plantation Live! *MVD, MCA*
Tom Petty: Full Moon Fever, the Videos *MVD, MPI*
Tom Petty: Take the Highway *MCA, MVD*
Tom Waits: Big Time *MVD, FRH*
Tommy *COL, MVD, WME*
Tommy Page: I'll Be Your Everything *MVD, WRV*
Tommy Puett: Heart Attack *MVD, BMG*

Tonadillas of Granados *CMR, NYS*
Toni Basil: Word of Mouth *MVD*
Toni Childs: The Videos *MVD, A&M*
Tony Bennett Live: Watch What Happens *SMV*
Tony Bennett Sings *MVD*
The Tony Marshall Show *GLV*
Tony Powers *NO*
Tony! Toni! Tone! *MVD, PGV*
Tony Williams: New York Live Video *MVD*
Too Short: Short Dog's in the House *MVD*
Too Short: Shorty the Pimp at the Player's Ball *BMG*
Toots and the Maytals Live from New Orleans *PGV*
Toots Thielemans in New Orleans *MVD,*
Tori Amos: Little Earthquakes *MVD, AVE, FFF*
Tori Amos: Tori Amos *AVE, FFF*
Tosca *HMV*
Toscanini: The Maestro/Hymn of the Nations *MVD, HMV*
Toscanini: The Television Concerts *BMG*
Toshiko Akiyoshi: Jazz is My Native Language *MVD*
Toto: Past to Present *MVD, SMV*
Tout Ecartille *NFB*
Toxic Reasons *MVD*
Toy Dolls *MVD*
Toy Dolls: Idle Gossip *MVD*
Toy Dolls: Live in Japan 1991 *MVD*
Traffic: Live at Santa Monica *MVD*
Tramaine Hawkins: Bring it Home, Live *MVD, SPW*
Transformation is Our Secret *MWF, FCT*
Travis Tritt: A Celebration: A Musical Tribute to the Spirit of the American Disabled Veteran *WRV, MVD*
Travis Tritt: It's All About to Change *WRV*
Tribal Area No. 1 *MVD*
Tribal Area No. 2 *MVD*
Tribal Area No. 3 *MVD*
Tribal Area No. 4 *MVD*
Tribal Area No. 5 *MVD*
A Tribe Called Quest: The Art of Moving Butts *MVD*
A Tribute to Bill Evans *MVD, HMV*
Tribute to John Coltrane *HMV, MVD*
Tribute to Ricky Nelson *RHI*
The Triplets: Video Triple Single *PGV*
Trisha Yearwood: The Song Remembers When *MCA*
Triumph: A Night of Triumph *MVD,, AIP*
Triumph: Live at the US Festival *MVD, MCA*
The Triumph of Charlie Parker: Celebrating Bird *KUL, FCT, MVD*
Trixter *MVD*
TROOP: Attitude *MVD, AVE, FFF*
The Tropicana Music Bowl 3 *NJN*
Troy Game *MVD, HMV*
True North *BMG, MIR, WSH*
True Story of 200 Motels *MVD, MPI*
Truth or Dare *LIV, FCT*
Tubes: Live at the Greek *MVD,, MON*
The Tubes Video *NO*
Turandot *HMV, MVD*
Turn Up the Volume, Vol. 1 & 2 *BHV*

Turn Up the Volume, Vol. 3 *BHV, MVD*
Turn Up the Volume, Vol. 4 *BHV, MVD*
Turn Up the Volume, Vol. 5 *BHV*
Turnpike Cruisers: Cable T.V. Show *MVD*
The Turtles: Happy Together *MVD, RHI*
Tuxedomoon: Four Major Events *MVD*
TV/ARM Video Magazine *MVD*
Twelve O'Clock High Video Compilation *MVD*
25 "Roots of Rap" Videos *MVD*
Twisted Sister: Come Out and Play *MVD, AVE, FFF*
Twisted Sister's Stay Hungry *MVD, SUE*
Two Fiddles, No Waiting *MVD*
200 Motels *MVD, MGM*
2-Kut: Rock That *MVD*
2 Live Crew: Banned in the USA *MVD, AVE, FFF*
2 Live Crew: Pop That Coochie *MVD, FFF, AVE*
2 Sound Clash Dance Hall *MVD, KRV*
Two X 4 *MVD*
UB40: CCCP (The Video Mix) *MVD, A&M*
UB40: Family Affair *MVD*
UB40: Labour of Love 2 *MVD, WAR*
UB40: The Best of UB40 *MVD*
U.F.O.: History of U.F.O. *MVD*
U.F.O. Live *NLC, MVD, SUE*
Ugly American Overkill *MVD*
Ugly Kid Joe: America's Least Wanted Tour '92 *MVD*
U.K./D.K. *MVD*
U.K. Subs: Down Amongst the Dead Men *MVD*
U.K. Subs: Grossout U.K. *MVD*
Ultimate Revenge 2 *MVD*
Ultimate Rock *MVD, SPW*
Ultravox: The Collection *MVD, LIV, VES*
Un Ballo in Maschera *MVD, PGV, EMI*
Una Aventura Llamada Menudo *SUE*
Uncle Floyd's Nostalgic Music Special *NJN*
Uncle Meat *MVD, MPI*
Und weiter geht's *GLV*
Underground Forces Volumes 1-8 *MVD*
Underground U.S.A. Vol. 1: Music Magazine *MVD*
Underground U.S.A. Vol. 2: Hardcore *MVD*
Underground U.S.A. Vol. 3: Heavy Metal *MVD*
Underground U.S.A. Vol. 4: New Music *MVD*
Underground U.S.A. Vol. 5: New Music *MVD*
Underground U.S.A. Vol. 6: Heavy Metal 2 *MVD*
Underground U.S.A. Vol. 7 *MVD*
Underground U.S.A. Vol. 8 *MVD*
Underground U.S.A. Vol. 9: Son of Heavy Metal *MVD*
Underground U.S.A. Vol. 10: Rap Rap Rap *MVD*
Underground U.S.A. Vol. 11: Rap Rap Rap *MVD*
Underground U.S.A. Vol. 12: Rap Rap Rap *MVD*
Underground U.S.A. Vol. 13: Heavy Metal *MVD*
Underground U.S.A. Vol. 14 *MVD*
Underground U.S.A. Vol. 15 *MVD*
Underground U.S.A. Vol. 16 *MVD*

Underground U.S.A. Vol. 17 *MVD*
Underground U.S.A. Vol. 18 *MVD*
Universal Congress Of: Live *MVD*
Unser kleines Platzkonzert 1 *GLV*
Unser kleines Platzkonzert 2 *GLV*
Unsere schoensten volkstuemlichen Lieder *GLV*
Upper Dallas Jazz Band *NO*
Uptown MTV Unplugged *MCA, MVD*
Urban Dance Squad: Mental Floss for the Globe *MVD*
URGH! A Music War *MVD, FOX*
Uriah Heep: Gypsy *MVD*
Ute Lemper: Illusions *PGV, PMS, PME*
Ute Lemper: Michael Nyman Songbook *FCT*
Utopia: A Retrospective 1977-1984 *BMG, MVD*
Utopia: An Evening with Utopia *MCA, MVD*
Utopia: Live at the Royal Oak *BMG, MVD*
Utopia Redux '92: Live in Japan *BMG, MVD*
The Utopia Sampler *NO*
U2: Achtung Baby *PGV*
U2: Live at Red Rocks "Under A Blood Red Sky" *COL, MVD*
U2: Numb *PGV*
U2: Rattle and Hum *MVD, PAR*
U2: The Unforgettable Fire Collection *PGV, COL, MVD*
U2 Zoo: Live from Sydney *PGV*
Van Halen: Live Right Here, Right Now *WRV, MVD*
Van Halen: Live Without a Net *MVD, WRV*
Van Morrison in Ireland *MVD*
Van Morrison: The Concert *MVD, PGV*
Vancouver New Music 1978-80 *VDO*
Vandenburg: Live in Japan *MVD*
Vanessa Williams: De Right Stuff Collection *MVD, PGV*
Vanessa Williams: The Comfort Zone Collection *PGV, MVD*
Vanilla Ice: Ninja Rap *MVD*
Vanilla Ice: Play That Funky Music, White Boy *MVD*
Vassar Clements: Dobro Summit *MVD*
Vassar Clements: The Fiddle According to Vassar *MVD*
The Velvet Underground: Velvet Redux, Live MCMXCIII *MVD, MVD*
Venom: Alive in '85! *NLC, SUE, MVD*
Venom: Live at Hammersmith Odeon *NO*
Venom: Live '90 *MVD, SVI*
The Ventures: Live in Japan '84 *MVD*
The Ventures: Live in Japan '90 *MVD*
The Ventures: Live in L.A. '81 *MVD*
Verdi Compilation *MVD*
Verdi: Requiem *HMV*
Vespers of the Blessed Virgin *FCT*
VH-1 '60s Music Video Album *WKV*
VH-1 '70s Music Video Album *WKV*
Vico Torriani's Internationale Schlager-Revue *GLV*
Victor Borge: 80th Birthday Gala *SIG, TVC*
Victor Borge in London *KUL, SIG, TVC*

Victor Borge: On Stage with Audience Favorites *SIG, TVC*

A Victorian Christmas in Song *FUS*

Victory Over the Sun: A Futuristic Opera *AAI*

Video a Go-Go: Vol. 1 *MVD, COL*

Video a Go-Go: Vol. 2 *MVD, COL*

Video Aid *MVD*

Video Band: War Dance *MWF*

A Video Christmas Card *NO*

Video Love Songs *MVD, COL*

Video Meltdown *BMG, MVD*

Video Rap Pack *MVD*

Video Sheet Metal *WRV*

Video Sheet Metal, Vol. 2 *WRV*

Video Void *MWF*

Videotomy, Vol. 1 *MVD*

Videotomy, Vol. 2 *MVD*

Vietnam Experience

Vince Gill: I Still Believe in You *MCA, MVD*

Virgin Prunes: The Sons Find Devils *MVD*

Vision Shared: A Tribute to Woody Guthrie & Leadbelly *MVD, SMV*

Vivaldi: The Four Seasons *MVD, PGV*

Vixen: Revved Up *MVD*

Vocomotion: Best of the '50s & '60s *NO*

Vocomotion: Classic Country *NO*

Vocomotion: Famous Star Classic Series *NO*

Vocomotion: Favorite Standards *NO*

Vocomotion: Holiday Favorites *NO*

Vocomotion: Spotlighting the '70s & '80s *NO*

A Voice from Soviet Russia *CMR, NYS*

Voice of the Whale *KIV*

Voices of Firestone Classic Performances *VAI, CTH, MVD*

Voices of Sarafina *NYF, FCT*

Voices that Care *MVD, WRV*

Volkstuemliches Europa *GLV*

Vow Now: Live *MVD*

The Voyager Odyssey *MVD*

Wagner: Concert in Leipzig *MVD, KUL*

Wagner: The Ring *SIG*

The Wall: Live in Berlin *MVD, PGV, BTV*

Walt Whitman & the Soul Children: Live and Blessed *MVD*

Walter Hawkins & the Love Alive Choir 4 *MVD*

Wanda Butler Nero: New Born Soul *PRH, MVD*

War Requiem *ING, MFV, MVD*

Warfare: A Concept of Hatred *MVD*

Warlock: Live from London *MVD, AIP,*

Warrant: Blood, Sweat & Beers *MVD*

Warrant: Cherry Pie *MVD, SMV*

Warrant: Dirty Rotten Filthy Stinking Rich Live *MVD, SMV*

Warren Zevon *NO*

W.A.S.P. *NO*

W.A.S.P.: Live at the Lyceum *MVD*

W.A.S.P.: Videos in the Raw *MVD, LIV*

Wax Trax: Video Compilation 1 in Stereo *MVD*

Waylon Jennings: America *MVD, COL, LTY*

Waylon Jennings: The Lost Outlaw Performance *NO*

Waylon Jennings: Waylon. Renegade. Outlaw. Legend. *NO*

Wayne Newton at the London Palladium *MGM*

We are the World: The Video Event *COL, OM*

We Like the Blues, Vol. 1 *MVD*

We Like the Blues, Vol. 2 *MVD*

Weather Report: Domino Theory *MVD*

Weavers: Wasn't That a Time! *WRV, MGM, MVD*

The Wedding Present: Punk *BMG*

Weird Al Yankovic: This is Life *MVD*

Weird Al Yankovic: Video Library *MVD*

Welcome Back, St. Petersburg *PGV*

Welt der Oper *GLV*

Wendy O. Williams: Live *NLC, SUE, MVD*

We're All Devo *RHI*

West End Jazz Band #1 *NO*

West End Jazz Band #2 *NO*

West End Jazz Band #3 *NO*

West End Jazz Band #4 *NO*

Wet, Wet, Wet *MVD*

Wha Dat Disco *MVD, KRV*

Whalesong *BUL*

Wham! in China: Foreign Skies *MVD, FOX*

Wham! The Final *MVD, FOX*

Wham! The Video *MVD, FOX*

What the F**k *MVD*

When the Music's Over *MVD*

White Lion: Escape from Brooklyn *AVE, MVD, FFF*

Whitesnake *NO*

Whitesnake: Live at Donnington *MVD*

Whitesnake: Live at the Monsters of Rock Festival *MVD*

Whitesnake: Live Commandos *MVD*

Whitesnake: Trilogy *MVD*

Whitney Houston: #1 Video Hits *MVD, COL*

Whitney Houston: The Star Spangled Banner *MVD, SWH, BMG*

Whitney Houston: Welcome Home Heroes *MVD, SWH*

The Who: Rocks America, 1982 American Tour *FOX*

The Who: The Kids are Alright *BMG*

The Who: The Who Live! Tommy *MVD, FOX, SMV*

The Who: Who's Better, Who's Best *MVD, PGV*

Whodini: Back in Black *MVD, COL*

Whodini: Greatest Rap Hits *MVD, BMG*

Widespread Panic: Live from the Georgia Theatre *WRV, MVD*

The Williams Brothers: I'm Just a Nobody *MVD*

Willie & the Poor Boys *NO*

Willie Banks & the Messengers: In Concert *MVD*

Willie N. Johnson & the New Gospel Keynotes *MVD, MLC*

Willie Nelson & Family in Concert *MVD, FOX*

Willie Nelson in Concert *SIM*

Willie Nelson: Live at Budokan *MVD*

Willie Nelson: On the Road Again *SIM*

Willie Nelson: Some Enchanted Evening *MVD, CAF*

Willie Nelson Special with Ray Charles *MVD, SUE*

Willie Nelson: The Big Six-O, An All-Star Birthday Celebration *FOX*

Willie Nelson's Greatest Hits: Live *MVD, LIV, VES*

Wilson Phillips *MVD*

Wilson Phillips: Shadows and Light *EMI, MVD*

The Winans: Live in Concert *MVD, XVC*

The Winans: Return *MVD, SPW*

Windham Hill in Concert *MVD, PAR*

Windham Hill Music Video Series *PAR, WSH*

Winger: In the Heart of the Young *MVD, AVE, FFF*

Winger: In the Heart of the Young, Part 2 *MVD, AVE, FFF*

Winger: Live in Tokyo *MVD*

Winger: The Videos, Vol. 1 *MVD, AVE, FFF*

Wir lassen uns das Singen nicht verbieten *GLV*

Wishbone Ash *MVD*

Wishbone Ash: Phoenix *MVD*

Wojceich Mlynarski: Lyrical Evening *FCT*

Wolf Trap Salutes Dizzy Gillespie: An All Star Tribute to the Jazz Master *MVD*

The Wolfe Tones: 25th Anniversary Concert *MVD*

Women in Rock *MCA, MVD, FFF*

Women in Rock: The Women of Heavy Metal *MVD*

The Wonder Stuff: Seven Appalling Promos *MVD*

The Wonder Stuff: Welcome to the Cheap Seats *PGV, MVD*

The Wonderful Planet *NO*

Woodstock *MVD, WAR*

Woodstock: The Lost Performances *WAR*

Woody Guthrie: Hard Travelin' *MVD, MGM, WOM*

Woody Herman: Live Thunder *MVD, MCG*

Woody Herman: 1982 Aurex Jazz Festival *MVD*

Word Rap Video Compilation, Vol. 1 *MVD, BMG*

Word Up: The Best *MVD*

The Work of Sefan Wolpe *CMR, NYS*

World Drums *BUL*

The World of Music *NYS*

World War II: The Music Video, Vol. 1 *CNG, KAR*

World War II: The Music Video, Vol. 2 *CNG, KAR*

The Worship of Music: The Dagar Singers of India *CMR, NYS*

Wozzeck *HMV, PME*

Wrathchild: Live from London *MVD, AIP*

Wreckx-N-Effect: Hard or Smooth Videos *MCA*

Wrestling Music Television: Born to Bleed *RHI*

Wynton Marsalis: Blues & Swing *MVD, FOX, FCT*

XL Recording: the Video Chaptor *MVD*

XTC: Look Look *MVD*

Y & T Live at the San Francisco Civic *MVD, A&M, COL*

Y & T: Summertime Girls & All American Boys - The Videos *MVD, A&M*

Yakety Yak: Take It Back *MVD, AVE, FFF*

Yankee Air Pirates *NO*

Yankee Doodle's Odyssey *NJN*

The Yardbirds: For Your Love *AVE, MVD*

Yehudi Menuhin: Brahms Violin Concerto in D, Opus 7 *KUL*

Yehudi Menuhin: Concert for the Pope *MVD, VWV, MBP*

Yehudi Menuhin: Tribute to J.S. Bach *VWV, MBP*

Yello: The Yello Video Show *MVD*

Yellow Magic Orchestra: Computer Game *MVD*

Yellow Magic Orchestra: Hurrah *MVD*

Yellow Magic Orchestra: Live '81 *MVD*

Yellow Magic Orchestra: Propaganda *MVD*

Yellow Magic Orchestra: YMO Live in L.A. *MVD*

Yellowman: Live at Woodbury *MVD*

Yellowman: Raw & Rough *MVD, KRV*

Yes *VDO*

Yes: Greatest Video Hits *AVE, MVD, FFF*

Yes: 9012 Live *MVD, AVE, FFF*

Yessongs *MVD*

The Yngwie Malmsteen Collection *PGV, MVD*

Yngwie Malmsteen: Rising Force - Live '85 *MVD, PGV*

Yngwie Malmsteen: Trial By Fire/Live in Leningrad *MVD, PGV*

Yo-Yo Ma: At Tanglewood *MVD*

A Young Children's Concert with Raffi *MLT, A&M*

The Young Composer *CMR, NYS*

Young Country *MVD, WAR*

Young M.C.: Bustin' Moves *MVD, PGV*

You're the Top: The Cole Porter Story *MVD, FCT*

Youri Vamos: Der Nussknacker - Eine Weihnachtsgeschichte *NO*

Yukihiro Takahashi: Boys Will Be Boys *MVD*

Yuletide TV Treats 2 *SHO*

Yumi Matsutoya: Train of Thought *COL*

Yves Montand Live *MVD*

Zbigniew Rybezynski: A Collection *NO*

Zenon Laskowik's Benefit: By the Back Door *FCT*

Zev: Six Examples *NO*

Ziggy Marley and the Melody Makers: Conscious Party Live at the Palladium *MVD*

Zildjian Day in New York *MVD, MVD*

Zoot Sims *MVD*

Zoot Sims Quartet *MVD, RHP*

Zydeco *FFM, MVD*

Zydeco Gumbo *RHP*

Zydeco: Night 'n' Day *PGV, MOV, FCT*

ZZ Top Greatest Hits: The Video Collection *WRV, MVD*

AAE-A & E Home Video
AAI-Arts America
ABC-ABC Video
ACA-Academy Entertainment
ACD-Academy Videos
ACE-Ace Video
ACN-Acorn Video
ADL-Anti-Defamation League of B'nai B'rith
AEV-Academic Entertainment Video
AFC-AEF/Capital Communications
AFF-American Film Foundation
AFR-Afro-Am Distributing Company
AHV-Active Home Video
AIM-AIMS Media
AIP-A.I.P. Home Video, Inc.
ALD-Alden Films
ALL-Allied Artists
AMB-Ambrose Video Publishing, Inc.
ANI-AnimEigo
AOV-Admit One Video
APD-Applause Productions, Inc.
APL-Appalshop Films
APP-Applause Theatre and Cinema
APX-A-Pix Entertainment Inc.
ART-Artec
ATL-Atlas Entertainment Corporation
ATM-Atomic Pictures
ATP-Apple Tree Productions
ATS-Atlas Video Inc.
ATV-Atlantic Video
ATU-Atlantic Video
AUD-Audio-Forum
AVC-Allied Video Corp.
AVE-A*Vision
AVL-American Video Library
AVT-American Video Tape
BAR-Barr Films
BBE-Blockbuster Entertainment Corporation
BBF-Bonnie Business Forms
BEI-Bandera Enterprises, Inc.
BFA-Phoenix/BFA Films
BFS-BFS Video
BFV-Best Film & Video Corporation
BIJ-Bijou Video
BMG-BMG
BMV-Bennett Marine Video
BOK-Bookpeople
BPG-Bridgestone Production Group

BRT-Britannica Films
BST-Best Video
BSV-Bosko Video
BTV-Baker & Taylor Video
BUL-Bullfrog Films, Inc.
BVG-Bennett Video Group
BVV-Buena Vista Home Video
CAB-Cable Films & Video
CAF-Cabin Fever Entertainment
CAL-California Newsreel
CAM-Cambridge International
CAN-Cannon Video
CAP-Capitol Video Communications, Inc.
CAR-Electronic Bookshelf
CCB-Critics' Choice Video, Inc.
CCC-Cyclops Communications Corporation
CCN-Cinevista
CCV-Concord Video
CEL-Celebrity Home Entertainment
CEN-Centre Communications
CFV-Carousel Film & Video
CGH-Cinema Group Home Video
CGV-Cineglobe Video Inc.
CHF-Churchill Media
CHI-Center for Humanities, Inc.
CHV-Coyote Home Video
CIC-Cinema International Canada
CIG-Cinema Guild
CMB-Columbia House Video Library
CMR-Camera Three Productions, Inc.
CNG-Congress Entertainment, Ltd.
CNM-Cinemacabre Video
COL-Columbia Tristar Home Video
CON-Continental Video
COV-Covenant Video
CPL-Cineplex, Inc.
CPM-Central Park Media/U.S. Manga Corps
CRC-Criterion Collection
CRV-Crown Video
CRY-Crystal Productions
CSM-Coliseum Video
CTC-Coast to Coast Video
CTD-Coast to Coast Home Video
CTH-Corinth Video
CTL-Capitol Home Video
CTP-Century Productions
CTY-Century Home Video, Inc.

CVC-Connoisseur Video Collection
CVD-Consumer Video Distributors
CVS-Condor Video
DCL-Direct Cinema Limited
DIS-Walt Disney Home Video
DMP-Donna Michelle Productions
DSN-Disney Educational Productions
DVT-Discount Video Tapes
DWE-Dusty Woods Entertainment
EAI-Electronic Arts Intermix
EAS-Easy Riders
ECU-EcuFilm
EDV-EDDE Entertainment
EHV-Enterprise Home Video
ELE-Electronic Products
ELV-Electronic Video
EMB-Embassy Home Entertainment
EMI-EMI Video
EPC-Epic Associated
ERG-Ergo Media Inc.
EVD-European Video Distributor
EXP-Expanded Entertainment
FCT-Facets Multimedia, Inc.
FFF-Fast Forward
FFM-Flower Films
FGF-Ferde Grofe Films
FHE-Family Home Entertainment
FHF-Finley-Holiday Film Corporation
FHS-Films for the Humanities & Sciences
FHV-Foothill Video
FLI-Films Inc. Video
FLL-Filmmakers Library, Inc.
FMT-Format International
FOC-Focus on Animals
FOX-CBS/Fox Video
FPE-Four Point Entertainment
FRA-Video France
FRG-Fright Video
FRH-Fries Home Video
FRV-First Run Video
FST-Festival Films
FUS-Fusion Video
FXL-Fox/Lorber Home Video
FXV-FoxVideo
GEM-Video Gems
GFV-Gateway Films/Vision Video
GHV-Genesis Home Video

GKK-Goodtimes/Kids Klassics Distribution Corporation
GLV-German Language Center
GNS-21st Genesis Home Video
GPV-Grapevine Video
GRG-Gorgon Video
GVV-Glenn Video Vistas, Ltd.
HBO-HBO Home Video
HCV-Henwood Cinema Video
HEG-Horizon Entertainment
HHE-Hollywood Home Entertainment
HHT-Hollywood Home Theatre
HMD-Hemdale Home Video
HMV-Home Vision Cinema
HPH-Hollywood Pictures Home Video
HSE-High/Scope Educational Research Foundation
HTV-Hen's Tooth Video
HVL-Home Video Library
ICA-First Run/Icarus Films
IFB-International Film Bureau, Inc.
IGP-Ignatius Press
IHF-International Historic Films, Inc. (IHF)
IME-Image Entertainment
IMP-Imperial Entertainment Corporation
INC-Increase/SilverMine Video
ING-Ingram Entertainment
INT-Interama, Inc.
ISS-Image Magnetic Associates
ITC-ITC
IUF-Interurban Films
IVE-International Video Entertainment (IVE)
IVY-Ivy Film/Video
JAF-James Agee Film Project
JCF-Judaica Captioned Film Center, Inc.
JEF-JEF Films, Inc.
JFK-Just for Kids Home Video
JHV-Jim Henson Video
JOU-Journal Films, Inc.
JPN-Japan Society, Inc.
JTC-J2 Communications
KAR-Karol Video
KBE-K-Beech Video, Inc.
KEP-Keep the Faith Inc.
KET-KET, The Kentucky Network Enterprise Division
KIT-Kit Parker Video
KIV-Kino on Video
KRT-Barr Entertainment
KUI-Knowledge Unlimited, Inc.
KUL-Kultur Video

LBD-LB Distributors, Inc.
LCA-Learning Corporation of America
LDV-LD Video
LHV-Lorimar Home Video
LIV-Live Home Video
LME-Lucerne Media
LOO-Loonic Video
LPC-Liberty Publishing Company, Inc.
LRP-Light Rain Productions
LSV-LSVideo, Inc.
LTG-Lightning Video
LTY-Lightyear Entertainment
LUM-Lumivision Corporation
MAD-Madera Cinevideo
MAS-Mastervision, Inc.
MAX-Miramax Pictures Home Video
MCA-MCA/Universal Home Video
MCG-Management Company Entertainment Group (MCEG), Inc.
MED-Media Home Entertainment
MFV-Mystic Fire Video
MGM-MGM/UA Home Video, Inc.
MGS-Magna Systems, Inc.
MHF-Magic Hour Films
MIL-Milestone Film & Video
MIV-Mark IV Pictures Film & Video
MLB-Mike Lebell's Video
MLT-Music for Little People
MNC-Monarch Home Video
MON-Monterey Home Video
MOR-Morris Video
MOV-Movies Unlimited
MPI-MPI Home Video
MRV-Moore Video
MSP-Modern Sound Pictures, Inc.
MTH-MTI Home Video
MTI-Coronet/MTI Film & Video
MTM-MTM Home Video
MTP-Maryland Public Television
MTT-MTI Teleprograms, Inc.
MTX-MNTEX Entertainment, Inc.
MVC-Moviecraft, Inc.
MVD-Music Video Distributors
MWF-Monday/Wednesday/Friday Video
MWP-Wade Williams Productions, Inc.
NBI-Newsbank, Inc.

NCJ-National Center for Jewish
Film
NEG-National Entertainment
Group, Inc.
NEW-New Video
NFC-National Film Board of
Canada
NHO-New Horizons Home
Video
NJN-New Jersey Network
NLC-New Line Home Video
NMD-Neville Meyer Distribution
(NMD)
NOS-Nostalgia Family Video
NWV-New World Entertainment
NYF-New Yorker Video
NYS-New York State Education
Department
OCE-Ocean Video
OHC-Ohlmeyer
Communications
ORI-Orion Home Video
PAR-Paramount Home Video
PAU-Paulist Productions
PAV-Pacific Arts Video
PBC-Princeton Book Company
Publishers
PBS-PBS Video
PCV-Pacific Coast Video
PEN-Pentrex Video
PEV-Palisades Entertainment
PGN-Paragon Video
Productions
PGV-Polygram Video (PV)
PHX-Phoenix Distributors
PIA-Pioneer Artists, Inc.
PIC-Picture Start
PII-Peerless Films, Inc.
PME-Public Media Video
PMH-PM Entertainment Group,
Inc.
PMR-Premiere Home Video
PMS-Professional Media
Service Corp.
PPI-Peter Pan Industries
PRD-Parade Video
Entertainment
PRV-Prime Video
PSM-Prism Entertainment
PSV-Power Sports Video
PTB-Proud to Be...A Black
Video Collection
PYR-Pyramid Film & Video
QHV-Questar Home Video
QNE-Quintex Entertainment
QVD-Quality Video
RAE-Raedon Entertainment
RAP-RAP Entertainment Inc.
RCA-RCA Video
RDG-Reader's Digest Home
Video
REP-Republic Pictures Home
Video
RHI-Rhino Home Video
RHP-Rhapsody Films
RHU-Random House Media
RHV-Regency Home Video
RIN-Rincon Children's
Entertainment
RKO-RKO Pictures
RME-RM Films International,
Inc.
RMF-FM Films, Inc.
RXM-Rex Miller
SAT-Saturn Productions, Inc.
SCH-Schoolmaster's Video
SFR-San Francisco Rush Video
SGE-SGE Home Video
SHO-Shokus Video
SHV-Snoopy's Home Video
Library
SIG-Signals
SIM-Simitar Entertainment
SMV-Sony Music Video
Enterprises
SMW-Something Weird Video
SNC-Sinister Cinema
SPW-Sparrow Distribution
SSI-Super Sitters, Inc.
STE-Starmaker Entertainment,
Inc.
STP-Streamline Pictures

STS-Stagestep
STV-Studio Video Productions
SUE-Sultan Entertainment
SUM-Summit Media Company
SUN-Sun Video
SUP-Super Source
SVE-Society for Visual
Education
SVI-Strand/VCI Entertainment
SVS-Sony Video Software
(SVS, Inc.)
SWC-Simon Wiesenthal Center
TAM-Ingram International Films
TCF-20th Century Fox Film
Corporation
TEM-Tempe Video
THA-3M Audio Visual Division
TIM-Timeless Video Inc.
TLF-Time-Life Video and
Television
TOU-Touchstone Home Video
TPI-Thomson Productions, Inc.
TPV-Tapeworm Video
Distributors
TRI-Triboro Entertainment
Group
TTC-Turner Home
Entertainment Company
TVC-The Video Catalog
TWE-Trans-World
Entertainment
UAV-UAV Corporation
UHV-Video Communications,
Inc.
UND-Uni Distribution
UNI-Unicorn Video, Inc.
UNT-Unity Productions
UWA-University of Washington
Instructional Media Services
VAI-Video Artists International,
Inc.
VAN-Vantage Communications,
Inc.
VBL-Video Bible Library, Inc.
VCD-Video City Productions
VCI-Video Communications,
Inc. (VCI)
VCN-Video Connection
VDA-Video Action
VDC-Vidcrest
VDE-Video Video
VDM-Video Dimensions
VEC-Valencia Entertainment
Corporation
VES-Vestron Video
VGD-Vanguard Video
VGR-Videograf
VHE-VCII Home Entertainment,
Inc.
VIC-Victory Video
VID-VidAmerica, Inc.
VIP-VIP Video
VIR-Virgin Vision
VIS-Vision Video
VMK-Vidmark Entertainment
VPL-Video Placement
International
VPR-DBA Hatzoff Productions
VRL-Video Rails
VRS-Video Resources
VSM-Video Search of Miami
VTK-Videotakes
VTR-Video Treasures
VVC-Video Visa
VVI-VideoVision, Inc.
VYG-Voyager Company
VYY-Video Yesteryear
WAC-World Artists Home Video
WAR-Warner Home Video
WAX-Waxworks
WBF-Water Bearer Films
WEA-Warner/Elektra/Atlantic
(WEA) Corporation
WEM-Worldwide Entertainment
Marketing, Inc.
WFV-Western Film & Video,
Inc.
WGE-Weiss Global Enterprises
WKV-Wood Knapp & Company,
Inc.
WLA-Western L.A. Film
Productions, Inc.

WLF-Wolfe Video
WME-Warren Miller
Entertainment
WNE-WNET/Thirteen Non-
Broadcast
WOM-Wombat Film and Video
WOV-Worldvision Home Video,
Inc.
WRV-Warner Reprise Video
WSH-Wishing Well Distributing
WST-White Star
WTA-Whole Toon Catalogue
WVE-World Video Enterprises,
Inc.
WWV-Westernworld Video, Inc.
XVC-Xenon
YOC-Yankee-Oriole Company

DISTRIBUTOR GUIDE

The **DISTRIBUTOR GUIDE** alphabetically lists the full address and phone, toll-free, and fax numbers of 340 distributors. Each video in the main section has at least one and as many as three distributor codes located immediately before the critical rating at the bottom of the review; the key to the codes precedes this guide. Those reviews with the code **OM** are on moratorium (distributed at one time, though not currently). Since a title enjoying such status was once distributed, it may well linger on your local video store shelf. When the distributor is not known, the code **NO** appears in the review. For new releases to the theater that have not yet made it to video (but likely will in the coming year), the code **NYR** (not yet released) appears. Canadian distributors are listed immediately following the **Distributor Guide.**

A-PIX ENTERTAINMENT INC.
(APX)
150 E. 52nd St., 14 West
New York, NY 10022
212-593-5100
Fax: 212-593-5456

A & E HOME VIDEO *(AAE)*
235 E. 45th St.
New York, NY 10017
212-210-1327

ABC VIDEO *(ABC)*
Capital Cities/ABC Video
  Enterprises
1200 High Ridge Rd.
Stamford, CT 06905
203-968-9100
Fax: 203-329-6464

ACADEMIC ENTERTAINMENT VIDEO *(AEV)*
155 W. 68th St., Ste. 25A
New York, NY 10023
212-877-3262
Fax: 212-877-4434

ACADEMY ENTERTAINMENT *(ACA)*
9250 Wilshire Blvd., Ste. 400
Beverly Hills, CA 90212
800-972-0001

ACADEMY VIDEOS *(ACD)*
Box 5224
Sherman Oaks, CA 91423-5224
818-788-6662
800-423-2397

ACE VIDEO *(ACE)*
19749 Dearborn St.
Chatsworth, CA 91311
818-718-1116
Fax: 818-718-9109

ACORN VIDEO *(ACN)*
c/o Academy Entertainment
9250 Wilshire Blvd., Ste. 400
Beverly Hills, CA 90212

ACTIVE HOME VIDEO *(AHV)*
12121 Wilshire Blvd., No. 401
Los Angeles, CA 90025
310-447-6131
800-824-6109
Fax: 310-207-0411

ADMIT ONE VIDEO *(AOV)*
PO Box 66, Sta. O
Toronto, ON, Canada M4A 2M8
416-463-5714

AEF/CAPITAL COMMUNICATIONS *(AFC)*
3807 Dickerson Rd.

Nashville, TN 37207
615-868-2040
800-522-5678
Fax: 615-868-5239

AFRO-AM DISTRIBUTING COMPANY *(AFR)*
407 E. 25th St., Ste. 600
Chicago, IL 60616
312-791-1611
Fax: 312-791-0921

AIMS MEDIA *(AIM)*
9710 DeSoto Ave.
Chatsworth, CA 91311-4409
818-773-4300
800-367-2467
Fax: 818-341-6700

A.I.P. HOME VIDEO, INC. *(AIP)*
10726 McCune Ave.
Los Angeles, CA 90034
800-456-2471
Fax: 213-559-8849

ALDEN FILMS *(ALD)*
PO Box 449
Clarksboro, NJ 08510
908-462-3522
Fax: 908-294-0330

ALLIED ARTISTS *(ALL)*
3415 S. Sepulveda Blvd., Ste. 630
Los Angeles, CA 90034
310-390-6161
Fax: 310-390-6031

ALLIED VIDEO CORP. *(AVC)*
PO Box 702618
Tulsa, OK 74170
918-496-3332
800-926-5892
Fax: 918-496-0292

AMBROSE VIDEO PUBLISHING, INC. *(AMB)*
1290 Avenue of the Americas, Ste. 2245
New York, NY 10104
212-265-7272
800-526-4663
Fax: 212-265-8088

ANIMEIGO INC. *(ANI)*
PO Box 989
Wilmington, NC 28402-0989
910-251-1850
Fax: 910-763-2376

ANTI-DEFAMATION LEAGUE OF B'NAI B'RITH *(ADL)*
Audio-Visual Dept.

823 United Nations Plaza
New York, NY 10017
212-490-2525
Fax: 212-867-0779

APPLAUSE PRODUCTIONS, INC. *(APD)*
85 Longview Rd.
Port Washington, NY 11050
516-883-2825
Fax: 516-883-7460

APPLAUSE THEATRE AND CINEMA *(APP)*
211 W. 71st St.
New York, NY 10023
212-496-7511
Fax: 212-721-2856

ARTEC *(ART)*
1 Pine Haven Shore Rd.
Shelburne, VT 05482
802-985-9411
800-451-5180
Fax: 802-985-3403

ATLANTIC VIDEO *(ATV)*
75 Rockefeller Plaza
New York, NY 10019
212-275-2000

ATLANTIC VIDEO *(ATV)*
150 S. Gordon St.
Alexandria, VA 22304
703-823-2800
Fax: 703-370-6748

ATLAS ENTERTAINMENT CORPORATION *(ATL)*
1 Jocama Blvd., Ste. 2E
Old Bridge, NJ 08857
908-591-1155
Fax: 908-591-0660

ATLAS VIDEO INC. *(ATL)*
4915 St. Elmo Ave., Ste. 305
Bethesda, MD 20814
301-907-0030
800-999-0212
Fax: 301-907-9049

ATOMIC PICTURES *(ATM)*
PO Box 15824
North Hollywood, CA 91615-5824

AUDIO-FORUM *(AUD)*
96 Broad St.
Guilford, CT 06437
203-453-9794
800-243-1234
Fax: 203-453-9774

A*VISION *(AVE)*
A Time Warner Company

75 Rockefeller Plaza
New York, NY 10019
212-275-2900
Fax: 212-765-0899

BAKER & TAYLOR VIDEO *(BTV)*
501 S. Gladiolus
Momence, IL 60954
800-775-2300
Fax: 800-775-3500

BANDERA ENTERPRISES, INC. *(BEI)*
Box 1107
Studio City, CA 91614
818-985-5050

BARR FILMS *(BAR)*
12801 Schabarum
Irwindale, CA 91706
818-338-7828
800-234-7878
Fax: 818-814-2672

BENNETT MARINE VIDEO *(BMV)*
730 Washington St.
Marina del Rey, CA 90292
213-821-3329
800-262-8862
Fax: 213-306-3162

BEST FILM & VIDEO CORPORATION *(BFV)*
108 New South Rd.
Hicksville, NY 11801-5223
516-931-6969

BEST VIDEO *(BST)*
10580 Newkirk, Ste. 100
Dallas, TX 75220
214-869-9641
800-541-1008
Fax: 214-556-1686

BIJOU VIDEO *(BIJ)*
1349 N. Wells
Chicago, IL 60610
312-943-5397

BLOCKBUSTER ENTERTAINMENT CORPORATION *(BBE)*
10540 Miller Rd.
Dallas, TX 75238
214-503-9222

BMG *(BMG)*
6363 Sunset Blvd., 6th Fl.
Hollywood, CA 90028-7318
213-468-4067

BONNIE BUSINESS FORMS *(BBF)*
2691 Freewood
Dallas, TX 75220
214-357-3956

BRIDGESTONE MULTIMEDIA *(BPG)*
1979 Palomar Oaks Way
Carlsbad, CA 92009
619-431-9888
800-523-0988
Fax: 619-431-0489

BRITANNICA FILMS *(BRT)*
310 S. Michigan Ave.
Chicago, IL 60604
312-347-7900
800-554-9862
Fax: 312-347-7966

BUENA VISTA HOME VIDEO *(BVV)*
500 S. Buena Vista St.
Burbank, CA 91521
818-562-3560
Fax: 818-567-6464

BULLFROG FILMS, INC. *(BUL)*
PO Box 149
Oley, PA 19547
610-779-8226
800-543-3764
Fax: 610-370-1978

CABIN FEVER ENTERTAINMENT *(CAF)*
100 W. Putnam Ave.
Greenwich, CT 06830
203-863-5200
Fax: 203-863-5258

CABLE FILMS & VIDEO *(CAB)*
Country Club Sta.
PO Box 7171
Kansas City, MO 64113
913-362-2804
Fax: 913-341-7365

CALIFORNIA NEWSREEL *(CAL)*
149 Ninth St., Ste. 420
San Francisco, CA 94103
415-621-6196
Fax: 415-621-6522

CAMBRIDGE EDUCATIONAL *(CAM)*
Box 2153
Charleston, WV 25328

304-744-9323
800-468-4227
Fax: 304-744-9351

CAMERA THREE PRODUCTIONS, INC. *(CMR)*
PO Box 994
Kent, CT 06757
203-868-1771
Fax: 203-868-9999

CANNON VIDEO *(CAN)*
8200 Wilshire Blvd., 3rd Fl.
Beverly Hills, CA 90211
213-966-5600
Fax: 213-653-5485

CAPITOL HOME VIDEO *(CTL)*
4818 Yuma St. NW
Washington, DC 20016
202-363-8800
Fax: 202-363-4680

CAPITOL VIDEO COMMUNICATIONS, INC. *(CAP)*
2121 Wisconsin Ave. NW
Washington, DC 20007
202-965-7800

CAROUSEL FILM & VIDEO *(CFV)*
260 5th Ave., Rm. 405
New York, NY 10001
212-683-1660
Fax: 212-683-1662

CBS/FOX VIDEO *(FOX)*
1330 Avenue of the Americas, 5th Fl.
New York, NY 10019
212-373-4800
800-800-2369
Fax: 212-373-4802

CELEBRITY HOME ENTERTAINMENT *(CEL)*
22025 Ventura Blvd.
PO Box 4112
Woodland Hills, CA 91365-4112
818-595-0666
Fax: 818-716-0168

CENTER FOR HUMANITIES, INC. *(CHI)*
Communications Park
Box 1000
Mount Kisco, NY 10549
914-666-4100
800-431-1242
Fax: 914-666-5319

CENTRAL PARK MEDIA/U.S. MANGA CORPS *(CPM)*
250 W. 57th St., Ste. 317
New York, NY 10107
212-977-7456
800-833-7456
Fax: 212-977-8709

CENTRE COMMUNICATIONS *(CEN)*
1800 30th St., Ste. 207
Boulder, CO 80301
303-444-1166
800-886-1166
Fax: 303-444-1168

CHURCHILL MEDIA *(CHF)*
12210 Nebraska Ave.
Los Angeles, CA 90025
310-207-6600
800-334-7830
Fax: 310-207-1330

THE CINEMA GUILD *(CIG)*
1697 Broadway, Ste. 506
New York, NY 10019
212-246-5522
800—723-5522
Fax: 212-246-5525

CINEMA INTERNATIONAL CANADA *(CIC)*
8275 Mayrand
Montreal, PQ, Canada H4P 2C8
514-342-2340
Fax: 514-342-1922

CINEMACABRE VIDEO *(CNM)*
PO Box 10005-D
Baltimore, MD 21285-0005

CINEVISTA *(CCN)*
560 W. 43rd, No. 8J
New York, NY 10036
212-947-4373
Fax: 212-947-0644

COAST TO COAST HOME VIDEO *(CTC)*
1919 N. Argyle Ave.
Hollywood, CA 90068
213-466-2252

COAST TO COAST VIDEO *(CTC)*
148 Lafayette St., 5th Fl.
New York, NY 10013
212-431-3890
800-221-3420

COLISEUM VIDEO *(CSM)*
430 W. 54th St.
New York, NY 10019
212-489-8130
800-288-8130
Fax: 212-582-5690

COLUMBIA HOUSE VIDEO LIBRARY *(CMB)*
1400 N. Fruitridge Ave.
Terre Haute, IN 47812-9701
800-538-7766

COLUMBIA TRISTAR HOME VIDEO *(COL)*
3400 Riverside Dr.
Burbank, CA 91505-4627
818-972-8193
Fax: 818-972-0937

CONCORD VIDEO *(CCV)*
7506 N. Broadway Ext., Ste. 505
Oklahoma City, OK 73116
405-840-6031
800-222-2811
Fax: 405-848-3960

CONDOR VIDEO *(CVS)*
c/o Jason Films
2825 Wilcrest, Ste. 670
Houston, TX 77042
713-266-3097

CONGRESS ENTERTAINMENT, LTD. *(CNG)*
Learn Plaza, Ste. 6
PO Box 845
Tannersville, PA 18372-0845
717-620-9001
800-847-8273
Fax: 717-620-9278

CONNOISSEUR VIDEO COLLECTION *(CVC)*
1543 7th St., Ste. 202
Santa Monica, CA 90401-2636
310-393-9000
Fax: 310-458-8881

CONSUMER VIDEO DISTRIBUTERS *(CVD)*
1427 Woodhurst St.
Bowling Green, KY 42104
502-843-8300

CORINTH VIDEO *(CTH)*
34 Gansevoort St.
New York, NY 10014
212-463-0305
800-221-4720

CORONET/MTI FILM & VIDEO *(MTI)*
108 Wilmot Rd.
Deerfield, IL 60015
708-940-1260
800-777-8100
Fax: 708-940-3640

COVENANT VIDEO *(COV)*
3200 W. Foster Ave.
Chicago, IL 60625

312-478-4676
800-621-1290
Fax: 312-478-2622

CRITERION COLLECTION *(CRC)*
c/o The Voyager Company
1 Bridge St.
Irvington, NY 10533-1543

CRITICS' CHOICE VIDEO, INC. *(CCB)*
PO Box 549
Elk Grove Village, IL 60009
800-367-7765
Fax: 800-544-9852

CROWN VIDEO *(CRV)*
225 Park Ave., S.
New York, NY 10003
212-254-1600

CRYSTAL PRODUCTIONS *(CRY)*
1812 Johns Dr.
Box 2159
Glenview, IL 60025
708-657-8144
800-255-8629
Fax: 708-657-8149

CYCLOPS COMMUNICATIONS CORPORATION *(CCC)*
44 Gibson Ave.
Toronto, ON, Canada M5R 1T5
416-926-8991
Fax: 416-926-9878

DBA HATZOFF PRODUCTIONS *(VPR)*
6th & Battery Bldg.
2326 6th Ave., Ste. 230
Seattle, WA 98121
206-728-9241
800-458-5335

DIRECT CINEMA LIMITED *(DCL)*
PO Box 10003
Santa Monica, CA 90410
310-396-4774
800-525-0000
Fax: 310-396-3233

DISCOUNT VIDEO TAPES, INC. *(DVT)*
PO Box 7122
Burbank, CA 91510
818-843-3366
Fax: 818-843-3821

DISNEY EDUCATIONAL PRODUCTIONS *(DSN)*
500 S. Buena Vista St.
Burbank, CA 91521
800-621-2131

DONNA MICHELLE PRODUCTIONS *(DMP)*
6253 Hollywood Blvd., Ste. 818
Hollywood, CA 90028
213-469-0672
800-356-4386

EASYRIDERS *(EAS)*
28210 Dorothy Dr.
Agoura Hills, CA 91301
818-889-8740
Fax: 818-889-4726

ECUFILM *(ECU)*
810 Twelfth Ave., S.
Nashville, TN 37203
615-242-6277
800-251-4091

EDDE ENTERTAINMENT *(EDV)*
19749 Dearborn St.
Chatsworth, CA 91311
800-727-2229

ELECTRIC PRODUCTIONS *(ELE)*
8700 Reseda Blvd.
Ste. 214
Northridge, CA 91325
818-993-1787

ELECTRIC VIDEO *(ELV)*
PO Box 784
Tiffin, OH 44883
419-447-0110

ELECTRONIC ARTS INTERMIX *(EAI)*
536 Broadway, 9th Fl.
New York, NY 10012
212-966-4605
Fax: 212-941-6118

EMI VIDEO *(EMI)*
1290 Ave. of the Americas, 42nd Fl.
New York, NY 10104
212-492-1200

ENTERPRISE HOME VIDEO *(EHV)*
12551 Cluster Pines Rd.
Garden Grove, CA 92645
800-553-5011
Fax: 714-895-5190

EPIC ASSOCIATED *(EPC)*
550 Madison Ave.
New York, NY 10022-3297
212-833-7442
Fax: 212-833-5719

ERGO MEDIA INC. *(ERG)*
668 Front St.
PO Box 2037
Teaneck, NJ 07666
201-692-0404
800-695-3746
Fax: 201-692-0663

EUROPEAN VIDEO DISTRIBUTOR *(EVD)*
2321 W. Olive Ave., Ste. A
Burbank, CA 91506
818-848-5902
800-423-6752
Fax: 818-848-1965

EXPANDED ENTERTAINMENT *(EXP)*
28024 Dorothy Dr.
Agoura Hills, CA 91301-2635
818-991-2884
800-996-TOON
Fax: 818-991-3773

FACETS MULTIMEDIA, INC. *(FCT)*
1517 W. Fullerton Ave.
Chicago, IL 60614
312-281-9075

FAMILY HOME ENTERTAINMENT *(FHE)*
c/o Live Home Video
15400 Sherman Way
PO Box 10124
Van Nuys, CA 91410-0124
818-499-5827

FAST FORWARD *(FFF)*
3420 Ocean Park Blvd., Ste. 3075
Santa Monica, CA 90405
310-396-4434
Fax: 310-396-2292

FERDE GROFE FILMS *(FGF)*
PO Box 399
Union Washington
Union, WA 98592
206-898-8080
Fax: 206-898-8081

FESTIVAL FILMS *(FST)*
6115 Chestnut Terrace
Excelsior, MN 55331-8107
612-470-2172
800-798-6083
Fax: 612-470-2172

FILMAKERS LIBRARY, INC. *(FLL)*
124 E. 40th
New York, NY 10016
212-808-4980
Fax: 212-808-4983

FILMS FOR THE HUMANITIES & SCIENCES *(FHS)*
PO Box 2053

Princeton, NJ 08543-2053
609-275-1400
800-257-5126
Fax: 609-275-3767

FILMS INC. VIDEO *(FLI)*
5547 N. Ravenswood Ave.
Chicago, IL 60640-1199
312-878-2600
800-323-4222

FIRST RUN/ICARUS FILMS *(ICA)*
153 Waverly Pl.
New York, NY 10014
212-727-1711
800-876-1710
Fax: 212-989-7649

FIRST RUN VIDEO *(FRV)*
3620 Overland Ave.
Los Angeles, CA 90034
310-202-8990
Fax: 310-838-5212

FLOWER FILMS *(FFM)*
10341 San Pablo Ave.
El Cerrito, CA 94530
510-525-0942
800-572-7618
Fax: 510-525-1204

FOCUS ON ANIMALS *(FOC)*
PO Box 150
Trumbull, CT 06611
203-377-1116

FOOTHILL VIDEO *(FHV)*
PO Box 547
Tujunga, CA 91043
818-353-8591

FORMAT INTERNATIONAL *(FMT)*
3921 N. Meridian St.
Indianapolis, IN 46208-4011
317-924-5163

FOUR POINT ENTERTAINMENT *(FPE)*
3575 Cahuenga Blvd., W., Ste. 600
Los Angeles, CA 90068
213-850-1600
Fax: 213-850-6709

FOX/LORBER HOME VIDEO *(FXL)*
419 Park Ave., S., 20th Fl.
New York, NY 10019
212-532-3392
800-229-9994
Fax: 212-685-2625

FOXVIDEO *(FXV)*
2121 Avenue of the Stars, 25th Fl.
Los Angeles, CA 90067
310-203-3900
800-800-2FOX
Fax: 310-774-5811

FRIES HOME VIDEO *(FRH)*
6922 Hollywood Blvd., 12th Fl.
Hollywood, CA 90028
213-466-2266
Fax: 213-466-2126

FRIGHT VIDEO *(FRG)*
PO Box 179
Billerica, MA 01821
508-663-2510

FUSION VIDEO *(FUS)*
100 Fusion Way
Country Club Hills, IL 60478
708-799-2073
800-338-7710
Fax: 708-799-8375

GENESIS HOME VIDEO *(GHV)*
15820 Arminta St.
Van Nuys, CA 91406
818-787-0660
800-344-1060

GERMAN LANGUAGE VIDEO CENTER *(GLV)*
7625 Pendleton Pike

Indianapolis, IN 46226-5298
317-547-1257
800-252-1957
Fax: 317-547-1263

GLENN VIDEO VISTAS, LTD.
(GVV)
6924 Canby Ave., Ste. 103
Reseda, CA 91335
818-881-8110
Fax: 818-981-5506

GOODTIMES
ENTERTAINMENT *(GKK)*
16 E. 40th St., 8th Fl.
New York, NY 10016-0113
212-951-3000
Fax: 212-481-9067

GORGON VIDEO *(GRG)*
5042 Wilshire Blvd., Ste. 465
Los Angeles, CA 90036-4305
213-505-1981
800-367-3845
Fax: 213-464-8920

GRAPEVINE VIDEO *(GPV)*
PO Box 46161
Phoenix, AZ 85063
602-973-3661
Fax: 602-973-0060

HBO HOME VIDEO *(HBO)*
1100 6th Ave.
New York, NY 10036
212-512-7400

HEMDALE HOME VIDEO
(HMD)
7966 Beverly Blvd.
Los Angeles, CA 90048
213-966-3758
Fax: 213-651-3107

HEN'S TOOTH VIDEO *(HTV)*
1124 S. Solano Dr.
Las Cruces, NM 88001
505-525-8233

HENWOOD CINEMA VIDEO
(HCV)
PO Box 376
Jamison, PA 18929-0376
215-552-8584
Fax: 215-788-7186

HIGH/SCOPE EDUCATIONAL
RESEARCH FOUNDATION
(HSE)
600 N. River St.
Ypsilanti, MI 48198-2898
313-485-2000
800-40-PRESS
Fax: 313-485-0704

HOLLYWOOD HOME
ENTERTAINMENT *(HHE)*
6165 Crooked Creek Rd., Ste.
B
Norcross, GA 30092-3105

HOLLYWOOD HOME
THEATRE *(HHT)*
1540 N. Highland Ave., Ste. 110
Hollywood, CA 90028
213-466-0127

HOLLYWOOD PICTURES
HOME VIDEO *(HPH)*
Fairmont Bldg. 526
500 S. Buena Vista St.
Burbank, CA 91505-9842

HOME VIDEO LIBRARY
(HVL)
Better Homes & Gardens
Books
PO Box 10670
Des Moines, IA 50381
800-678-2665

HOME VISION CINEMA
(HMV)
5547 N. Ravenswood Ave.
Chicago, IL 60640-1199
312-878-2600
800-826-3456
Fax: 312-878-8648

HORIZON ENTERTAINMENT
(HEG)
45030 Trevor Ave.
Lancaster, CA 93534
805-940-1040
800-323-2061
Fax: 805-940-8511

IGNATIUS PRESS *(IGP)*
15 Oakland Ave.
Harrison, NY 10528-9974
914-835-4216
Fax: 914-835-8406

IMAGE ENTERTAINMENT
(IME)
9333 Oso Ave.
Chatsworth, CA 91311
818-407-9100

IMPERIAL ENTERTAINMENT
CORPORATION *(IMP)*
4640 Lankershim Blvd., 4th Fl.
North Hollywood, CA 91602
818-762-0005

INCREASE/SILVERMINE
VIDEO *(INC)*
6860 Canby Ave., Ste. 118
Reseda, CA 91335
818-342-2880
800-233-2880
Fax: 818-342-4029

INGRAM ENTERTAINMENT
(ING)
1123 Heil Quaker Blvd.
La Vergne, TN 37086
615-793-5000
800-759-5000
Fax: 615-793-3875

INGRAM INTERNATIONAL
FILMS *(ING)*
10990 E. 55th Ave.
Denver, CO 80239
303-373-4583
800-356-3577

INTERAMA, INC. *(INT)*
301 W. 53rd St., Ste. 19E
New York, NY 10019
212-977-4830
Fax: 212-581-6582

INTERNATIONAL FILM
BUREAU, INC. *(IFB)*
332 S. Michigan Ave.
Chicago, IL 60604-4382
312-427-4545

INTERNATIONAL HISTORIC
FILMS, INC. (IHF) *(IHF)*
PO Box 29035
Chicago, IL 60629
312-927-2900
Fax: 312-927-9211

INTERURBAN FILMS *(IUF)*
PO Box 94911
Pasadena, CA 91109
818-793-3400
Fax: 818-793-3797

ITC *(ITC)*
13515 Dulles Technology Dr.
Herndon, VA 22071-3416
703-713-3335
800-638-3757
Fax: 703-713-0065

IVY FILM/VIDEO *(IVY)*
725 Providence Rd.
Charlotte, NC 28207
704-333-3991
Fax: 704-335-0672

J2 COMMUNICATIONS
(JTC)
10850 Wilshire Blvd., Ste. 1000
Los Angeles, CA 90024
310-474-5252
800-521-8273
Fax: 310-474-1219

JAMES AGEE FILM PROJECT
(JAF)
316 1/2 E. Main St.
Johnson City, TN 37601

615-926-8637
800-352-5111

JAPAN SOCIETY, INC. *(JPN)*
333 E. 47th St.
New York, NY 10017
212-715-1216
Fax: 212-755-6752

JEF FILMS, INC. *(JEF)*
Film House
143 Hickory Hill Circle
Osterville, MA 02655-1322
508-428-7198

JIM HENSON VIDEO *(JHV)*
500 S. Buena Vista St.
Burbank, CA 91521
818-562-3883
Fax: 818-567-6466

JOURNAL FILMS, INC.
(JOU)
1560 Sherman Ave., Ste. 100
Evanston, IL 60201
708-328-6700
800-323-9084
Fax: 708-328-6706

JUDAICA CAPTIONED FILM
CENTER, INC. *(JCF)*
PO Box 21439
Baltimore, MD 21208-0439
410-655-6767

JUST FOR KIDS HOME VIDEO
(JFK)
6320 Canoga Ave., Penthouse
Ste.
PO Box 4112
Woodland Hills, CA 91365-4112
818-715-1980
800-445-8210
Fax: 818-716-0168

K-BEECH VIDEO, INC. *(KBE)*
8841 Wilbur
Northridge, CA 91324
818-772-4201
800-255-5923
Fax: 818-772-4245

KAROL VIDEO *(KAR)*
PO Box 7600
Wilkes Barre, PA 18773
717-822-8899

KEEP THE FAITH INC. *(KEP)*
PO Box 1069
141 Main
Clifton, NJ 07014-1065
201-471-7494
800-221-1564
Fax: 201-471-7584

KET, THE KENTUCKY
NETWORK ENTERPRISE
DIVISION (KET)
560 Cooper Dr.
Lexington, KY 40502-2279
606-258-7225
800-354-9067
Fax: 606-258-7396

KINO ON VIDEO *(KIV)*
333 W. 39th St., Ste. 503
New York, NY 10018
212-629-0871
800-562-3330
Fax: 212-714-0871

KIT PARKER VIDEO *(KIT)*
c/o Central Park Media
250 W, 57th St., Ste. 317
New York, NY 10107
212-977-7456
Fax: 212-977-8709

KNOWLEDGE UNLIMITED,
INC. *(KUI)*
Box 52
Madison, WI 53701-0052
608-836-6660
800-356-2303
Fax: 608-831-1570

KULTUR VIDEO *(KUL)*
121 Hwy. No. 36
West Long Branch, NJ 07764

908-229-2343
800-458-5887
Fax: 908-229-0066

LB DISTRIBUTORS, INC.
(LBD)
3186 Doolittle Dr.
Northbrook, IL 60062
800-950-0255
Fax: 800-564-8656

LEARNING CORPORATION OF
AMERICA *(LCA)*
c/o Coronet/MTI
108 Wilmot Rd.
Deerfield, IL 60015
708-940-1260
800-621-2131
Fax: 708-940-3600

LIBERTY PUBLISHING
COMPANY, INC. *(LPC)*
440 S. Federal Hwy., Ste. 202
Deerfield Beach, FL 33441

LIGHT RAIN PRODUCTIONS
(LRP)
1927 NW Kearney
Portland, OR 97209
503-224-4080
Fax: 503-224-4180

LIGHTYEAR ENTERTAINMENT
(LTY)
350 5th Ave., Ste. 5101
New York, NY 10118
212-563-4610
800-229-7867
Fax: 212-563-1932

LIVE HOME VIDEO *(LIV)*
15400 Sherman Way
PO Box 10124
Van Nuys, CA 91410-0124
818-988-5060

LOONIC VIDEO *(LOO)*
2022 Taraval St., Ste. 6427
San Francisco, CA 94116
510-526-5681

LORIMAR HOME VIDEO
(LHV)
15838 N. 62nd St., Ste. 100
Scottsdale, AZ 85254
800-345-1441

LSVIDEO, INC. *(LSV)*
PO Box 415
Carmel, IN 46032

LUCERNE MEDIA *(LME)*
37 Ground Pine Rd.
Morris Plains, NJ 07950
201-538-1401
800-341-2293
Fax: 201-538-0855

LUMIVISION CORPORATION
(LUM)
1490 Lafayette St., Ste. 407
Denver, CO 80218
303-860-0400
800-776-5864
Fax: 303-860-0425

MADERA CINEVIDEO
(MAD)
525 E. Yosemite Ave.
Madera, CA 93638
209-661-6000
800-624-2204

MAGIC HOUR FILMS *(MHF)*
55 Bell St., Ste. 202
Seattle, WA 98121
206-443-9818

MANAGEMENT COMPANY
ENTERTAINMENT GROUP
(MCEG), INC. *(MCG)*
1888 Century Park, E., Ste.
1777
Los Angeles, CA 90067-1721
310-282-0871
Fax: 310-315-7850

MARK IV PICTURES FILM &
VIDEO *(MIV)*
5907 Meredith Dr.

Des Moines, IA 50322
515-278-4737
800-247-3456
Fax: 515-278-4738

MARYLAND PUBLIC
TELEVISION *(MTP)*
11767 Owings Mills Blvd.
Owings Mills, MD 21117-1499
410-356-5600
800-873-6154
Fax: 410-581-4338

MASTERVISION, INC.
(MAS)
969 Park Ave.
New York, NY 10028
212-879-0448
Fax: 212-744-3560

MCA/UNIVERSAL HOME
VIDEO *(MCA)*
70 Universal City Plaza
Universal City, CA 91608-9955
818-777-6419
Fax: 818-733-0226

MGM/UA HOME
ENTERTAINMENT *(MGM)*
10000 W. Washington Blvd.
Culver City, CA 90232
310-280-6212

MIKE LEBELL'S VIDEO
(MLB)
75 Freemont Pl.
Los Angeles, CA 90005
213-938-3333
Fax: 213-938-3334

MILESTONE FILM & VIDEO
(MIL)
275 W. 96th St., Ste 28C
New York, NY 10025
212-865-7449
Fax: 212-222-8952

MIRAMAX PICTURES HOME
VIDEO *(MAX)*
500 S. Buena Vista St.
Burbank, CA 91521

MNTEX ENTERTAINMENT,
INC. *(MTX)*
PO Box 667
Prior Lake, MN 55372-0667
612-440-6028
Fax: 612-447-8173

MODERN SOUND PICTURES,
INC. *(MSP)*
1402 Howard St.
Omaha, NE 68102
402-341-8476
800-228-9584
Fax: 402-341-8487

MONARCH HOME VIDEO
(MNC)
1123 Heil Quaker Blvd.
La Vergne, TN 37086-7006
615-793-5000
800-759-5000
Fax: 615-793-3875

MONARICH GROUP, INC.
(OCE)
2550 Corporate Pl., Ste. C103
Monterey Park, CA 91754
213-268-3733
800-700-8998
Fax: 213-268-3755

MONDAY/WEDNESDAY/
FRIDAY VIDEO *(MWF)*
c/o Moore
73 E. Houston St.
New York, NY 10012
212-219-0765
Fax: 212-966-6680

MONTEREY HOME VIDEO
(MON)
28038 Dorothy Dr., Ste. 1
Agoura Hills, CA 91301
818-597-0047
800-424-2593
Fax: 818-597-0105

MOORE VIDEO (MRV)
PO Box 5703
Richmond, VA 23220
804-745-9785
Fax: 804-745-9785

MORRIS VIDEO (MOR)
2730 Monterey St., No. 105
Monterey Business Park
Torrance, CA 90503
310-533-4800
800-843-3606

MOVIECRAFT, INC. (MVC)
PO Box 438
Orland Park, IL 60462
708-460-9082
Fax: 708-460-9099

MOVIES UNLIMITED (MOV)
6736 Castor Ave.
Philadelphia, PA 19149
215-722-8298
800-523-0823

MPI HOME VIDEO (MPI)
15825 Rob Roy Dr.
Oak Forest, IL 60452
708-687-7881
Fax: 708-687-3797

MTI HOME VIDEO (MTH)
14216 SW 136th St.
Miami, FL 33186
305-255-8684
800-821-7461
Fax: 305-233-6943

MTI TELEPROGRAMS, INC.
(MTT)
108 Wilmot Rd.
Deerfield, IL 60015-9990
708-940-1260
800-621-2131

MTM HOME VIDEO (MTM)
2100 Carolina Place
Fort Mill, SC 29715
803-548-7300
Fax: 803-548-3335

MUSIC FOR LITTLE PEOPLE
(MLT)
Box 1460
Redway, CA 95560
707-923-3991
800-727-2233
Fax: 707-923-3241

MUSIC VIDEO DISTRIBUTORS
(MVD)
O'Neill Industrial Center
1210 Standbridge St.
Norristown, PA 19403
215-272-7771
800-888-0486
Fax: 215-272-6074

MYSTIC FIRE VIDEO (MFV)
225 Lafayette St., Ste. 1206
New York, NY 10012
212-941-0999
Fax: 212-941-1443

NATIONAL CENTER FOR
JEWISH FILM (NCJ)
Brandeis University
Lown Bldg. 102
Waltham, MA 02254-9110
617-899-7044
Fax: 617-736-2070

NATIONAL FILM BOARD OF
CANADA (NFB)
1251 Avenue of the Americas,
16th Fl.
New York, NY 10020-1173
212-596-1770
800-542-2164

NEVILLE MEYER
DISTRIBUTION (NMD)
(NMD)
65 High Ridge Road, Ste. 304
Stamford, CT 06905
203-968-8905
Fax: 203-968-2953

NEW HORIZONS HOME VIDEO
(NHO)
2951 Flowers Rd., S., Ste. 237
Atlanta, GA 30341
404-458-3488
800-854-3323
Fax: 404-458-2679

NEW JERSEY NETWORK
(NJN)
CN-777
Trenton, NJ 08625-0777
609-777-5000
Fax: 609-633-2920

NEW LINE HOME VIDEO
(NLC)
116 N. Robertson Blvd.
Los Angeles, CA 90048
310-967-6670
Fax: 310-854-0602

NEW VIDEO (NEW)
250 Park Ave., S.
New York, NY 10003
212-982-9000
Fax: 212-982-0572

NEW WORLD
ENTERTAINMENT (NWV)
1440 S. Sepulveda Blvd.
Los Angeles, CA 90025
310-444-8100

NEW YORK STATE
EDUCATION DEPARTMENT
(NYS)
Bureau of Technology
Applications
Rm. C-7 - CEC
Empire State Plaza
Albany, NY 12230
518-474-3168

NEW YORKER VIDEO (NYF)
16 W. 61st St., 11th Fl.
New York, NY 10023
212-247-6110
800-447-0196
Fax: 212-307-7855

NEWSBANK, INC. (NBI)
58 Pine St.
New Canaan, CT 06840
203-966-1100
800-243-7694

NOSTALGIA FAMILY VIDEO
(NOS)
PO Box 606
Baker City, OR 97814
503-523-9034

ORION HOME VIDEO (ORI)
1888 Century Park E.
Los Angeles, CA 90067
310-282-0550

PACIFIC COAST VIDEO
(PCV)
635 1/2 Chapala St.
Santa Barbara, CA 93101
805-965-5015

PARADE VIDEO
ENTERTAINMENT (PRD)
88 St. Francis St.
Newark, NJ 07105
201-344-4214
Fax: 201-344-0465

PARAMOUNT HOME VIDEO
(PAR)
Bluhdorn Bldg, 1st Fl.
5555 Melrose Ave.
Los Angeles, CA 90038
213-956-8090
Fax: 213-956-1100

PAULIST PRODUCTIONS
(PAU)
PO Box 1057
Pacific Palisades, CA 90272
310-454-0688
800-624-8613
Fax: 310-459-6549

PBS VIDEO (PBS)
1320 Braddock Pl.
Alexandria, VA 22314-1698

703-739-5380
800-344-3337
Fax: 703-739-5269

PENTREX VIDEO (PEN)
PO Box 94911
Pasadena, CA 91109
818-793-3400
800-950-9333
Fax: 818-793-3797

PHOENIX/BFA FILMS (BFA)
PO Box 1850
New York, NY 10156-1850
212-684-5910
800-221-1274

PHOENIX DISTRIBUTERS
(PHX)
6253 Hollywood Blvd., No. 818
Hollywood, CA 90028
800-356-4386
Fax: 213-469-7041

PICTURE START (PIC)
1727 W. Catalpa
Chicago, IL 60640
312-769-2489
800-528-TAPE
Fax: 312-769-4467

PM ENTERTAINMENT GROUP,
INC. (PMH)
9450 Chivers Ave.
Sun Valley, CA 91352
818-504-6332
800-934-2111
Fax: 818-504-6380

POLYGRAM VIDEO (PV)
(PGV)
825 8th Ave.
New York, NY 10019
212-333-8000
800-825-7781
Fax: 212-603-7960

POWER SPORTS VIDEO
(PSV)
8444 Reseda Bvld., No. M
Northridge, CA 91324-4626
818-407-0590

PPI ENTERTAINMENT GROUP
(PPI)
88 Saint Frances St.
Newark, NJ 07105
201-344-4214
Fax: 201-344-0465

PREMIERE HOME VIDEO
(PMR)
755 N. Highland
Hollywood, CA 90038
213-934-8903
Fax: 213-934-8910

PRIME VIDEO (PRV)
19749 Dearborn St.
Chatsworth, CA 91311-6510
818-718-1116

PRINCETON BOOK COMPANY
PUBLISHERS (PBC)
PO Box 57
Pennington, NJ 08534
609-737-8177
800-326-7149
Fax: 609-737-1869

PRISM ENTERTAINMENT
(PSM)
1888 Century Park, E., Ste.
1000
Los Angeles, CA 90067
310-277-3270
Fax: 310-203-8036

PROFESSIONAL MEDIA
SERVICE CORP. (PMS)
19122 S. Vermont Ave.
Gardena, CA 90248
310-532-9024
800-223-7672
Fax: 800-253-8853

PROUD TO BE****A BLACK
VIDEO COLLECTION (PTB)
1235-E East Blvd., Ste. 209
Charlotte, NC 28203

704-523-2227

PUBLIC MEDIA VIDEO
(PME)
5547 N. Ravenswood Ave.
Chicago, IL 60640-1199
312-878-2600
800-826-3456
Fax: 312-878-8406

PYRAMID FILM & VIDEO
(PYR)
Box 1048
2801 Colorado Ave.
Santa Monica, CA 90406
310-828-7577
800-421-2304
Fax: 310-453-9083

QUALITY VIDEO (QVD)
7399 Bush Lake Rd.
Minneapolis, MN 55439-2027
612-893-0903
Fax: 612-893-1585

QUESTAR VIDEO, INC.
(QHV)
PO Box 11345
Chicago, IL 60611
312-266-9400
800-544-8422
Fax: 312-266-9523

RANDOM HOUSE MEDIA
(RHU)
400 Hahn Rd.
Westminster, MD 21157
410-848-1900
800-492-0782
Fax: 410-857-1948

RAP ENTERTAINMENT INC.
(RAP)
100-707 15th Ave. SW
Calgary, AB, Canada T2R 0R8
403-244-7000
800-565-7777
Fax: 403-245-0511

READER'S DIGEST HOME
VIDEO (RDG)
Reader's Digest Rd.
Pleasantville, NY 10570
800-776-6868

REGENCY HOME VIDEO
(RHV)
9911 W. Pico Blvd.
Los Angeles, CA 90035
310-552-2431
Fax: 310-552-9039

REPUBLIC PICTURES HOME
VIDEO (REP)
12636 Beatrice St.
Los Angeles, CA 90066-0930
310-306-4040

REX MILLER (RXM)
Rte. 1, Box 457-D
East Prairie, MO 63845
314-649-5048

RHAPSODY FILMS (RHP)
PO Box 179
New York, NY 10014
212-243-0152
Fax: 212-645-9250

RHINO HOME VIDEO (RHI)
10635 Santa Monica Blvd., 2nd
Fl.
Los Angeles, CA 90025-4900
310-828-1980
800-843-3670
Fax: 310-453-5529

RINCON CHILDREN'S
ENTERTAINMENT/BMG KIDZ
(RIN)
1525 Crossroads of the World
Hollywood, CA 90028

RKO PICTURES (RKO)
1801 Avenue of the Stars, Ste.
448
Los Angeles, CA 90067
310-277-0707

RM FILMS INTERNATIONAL,
INC. (RMF)
PO Box 3748
Los Angeles, CA 90078
213-466-7791
Fax: 213-461-4152

SAN FRANCISCO RUSH
VIDEO (SFR)
1576 Fell St., Ste. 1
San Francisco, CA 94117
415-921-8273
Fax: 415-921-8273

SCHOOLMASTERS VIDEO
(SCH)
745 State Circle
PO Box 1941
Ann Arbor, MI 48106
313-761-5175
800-521-2832
Fax: 313-761-8711

SGE HOME VIDEO (SGE)
Div. of Shapiro Glickenhaus
Entertainment
12001 Ventura Pl., 4th Fl.
Studio City, CA 91604
818-766-8500
Fax: 818-766-7873

SHOKUS VIDEO (SHO)
PO Box 3125
Chatsworth, CA 91313
818-704-0400
Fax: 818-701-0560

SIGNALS (SIG)
PO Box 64428
St. Paul, MN 55164-0428
800-669-5225
Fax: 612-659-4320

SIMITAR ENTERTAINMENT
(SIM)
3850 Annapolis Ln., Ste. 140
Plymouth, MN 55447
612-559-6660
800-486-TAPE
Fax: 612-559-0210

SIMON WIESENTHAL CENTER
(SWC)
9760 W. Pico Blvd.
Los Angeles, CA 90035-4792
310-553-9036
Fax: 310-553-8007

SINISTER CINEMA (SNC)
PO Box 4369
Medford, OR 97501-0168
503-773-6860

SNOOPY'S HOME VIDEO
LIBRARY (SHV)
c/o Media Home Entertainment
510 W. 6th St., Ste. 1032
Los Angeles, CA 90014-1311
213-236-1336

SOCIETY FOR VISUAL
EDUCATION, INC. (SVE)
55 E. Monroe, 34th Fl.
Chicago, IL 60603-5803
312-849-9100
800-829-1900
Fax: 312-849-9101

SOMETHING WEIRD VIDEO
(SMW)
c/o Mike Vraney
PO Box 33664
Seattle, WA 98133
206-361-3759
Fax: 206-364-7526

SONY MUSIC VIDEO
ENTERPRISES (SMV)
550 Madison Ave.
New York, NY 10022
212-833-7095
Fax: 212-833-8620

SPARROW DISTRIBUTION
(SPW)
101 Winners Circle
Brentwood, TN 37027

615-371-6800
800-877-4443
Fax: 615-371-6909

STAGESTEP *(STS)*
PO Box 328
Philadelphia, PA 19105
215-829-9800
800-523-0961
Fax: 215-829-0508

STARMAKER ENTERTAINMENT, INC. *(STE)*
151 Industrial Way, E.
Eatontown, NJ 07724
908-389-1020
800-233-3738
Fax: 908-389-1021

STRAND/VCI ENTERTAINMENT *(SVI)*
3350 Ocean Park Blvd., Ste. 205
Santa Monica, CA 90405
310-396-7011
Fax: 310-392-2472

STREAMLINE PICTURES *(STP)*
PO Box 691418
W. Hollywood, CA 90069
310-998-0070
Fax: 310-998-1145

STUDIO VIDEO PRODUCTIONS *(STV)*
793 Foothills Blvd., Ste. A
San Luis Obispo, CA 93405
805-543-0707
800-541-1843
Fax: 805-549-0352

SULTAN ENTERTAINMENT *(SUE)*
335 N. Maple Dr., Ste. 351
Beverly Hills, CA 90210-3899
310-285-6000

SUMMIT MEDIA COMPANY *(SUM)*
25510 Avenue Stanford, No. 101
Valencia, CA 91355
805-295-0675
800-777-8668
Fax: 805-295-0680

SUN VIDEO *(SUN)*
15 Donnybrook
Demarest, NJ 07627
201-784-0662
Fax: 201-784-0665

SUPER SITTERS, INC. *(SSI)*
10503 N. Cedarburg Rd.
PO Box 218
Mequon, WI 53092
800-323-3431

SUPER SOURCE *(SUP)*
PO Box 410777
San Francisco, CA 94141
415-777-1964
800-331-6304
Fax: 415-777-0187

TAPEWORM VIDEO DISTRIBUTORS *(TPV)*
12420 Montague St., Ste. B
Arleta, CA 91331
818-896-8899
800-367-8437
Fax: 818-896-3855

TEMPE VIDEO *(TEM)*
Box 6573
Akron, OH 44312
216-628-1950
Fax: 216-628-4316

THOMSON PRODUCTIONS, INC. *(TPI)*
PO Box 1225
Orem, UT 84059
801-226-0155
800-228-8491

3M AUDIO VISUAL DIVISION *(THA)*
Bldg. 223-15-02
St. Paul, MN 55144
612-736-2964
800-328-1371
Fax: 612-736-7479

TIME-LIFE VIDEO AND TELEVISION *(TLF)*
1450 E. Parham Rd.
Richmond, VA 23280
804-266-6330
800-621-7026

TIMELESS VIDEO INC. *(TIM)*
10010 Canoga Ave., Ste. B2
Chatsworth, CA 91311
818-773-0284
Fax: 818-773-0176

TOUCHSTONE HOME VIDEO *(TOU)*
500 S. Buena Vista St.
Burbank, CA 91521
818-562-3883

TRANS-WORLD ENTERTAINMENT *(TWE)*
8899 Beverly Blvd., 8th Fl.
Los Angeles, CA 90048-2412
213-969-2800

TRIBORO ENTERTAINMENT GROUP *(TRI)*
12 W. 27th St., 15th Fl.
New York, NY 10001
212-686-6116
Fax: 212-686-6178

TURNER HOME ENTERTAINMENT COMPANY *(TTC)*
1 CNN Center
N. Tower, 12th Fl.
Atlanta, GA 30348
404-827-2000

20TH CENTURY FOX FILM CORPORATION *(TCF)*
PO Box 900
Beverly Hills, CA 90213
310-277-2211

21ST GENESIS HOME VIDEO *(GNS)*
15820 Arminta St.
Van Nuys, CA 91406
818-787-0660
800-344-1060

UAV CORPORATION *(UAV)*
PO Box 7647
Charlotte, NC 28241
704-548-7300
Fax: 704-548-3335

UNI DISTRIBUTION *(UND)*
60 Universal City Plaza
Universal City, CA 91608
818-777-4400
Fax: 818-766-5740

UNICORN VIDEO, INC. *(UNI)*
9811 Independence Ave.
Chatsworth, CA 91311
818-407-1333
800-528-4336
Fax: 818-407-8246

UNITY PRODUCTIONS *(UNT)*
PO Box 31
Aberdeen, SD 57401-0031

UNIVERSITY OF WASHINGTON EDUCATIONAL MEDIA COLLECTION *(UWA)*
Kane Hall, DG-10
Seattle, WA 98195
206-543-9909
Fax: 206-685-7892

VALENCIA ENTERTAINMENT CORPORATION *(VEC)*
45030 Trevor Ave.
Lancaster, CA 93534-2648
805-940-1040
800-323-2061
Fax: 805-940-8511

VANGUARD VIDEO *(VGD)*
436 Creamery Way, Ste. D
Exton, PA 19341
800-323-7432

VANTAGE COMMUNICATIONS, INC. *(VAN)*
PO Box 546-G
Nyack, NY 10960
914-268-0715
800-872-0068
Fax: 914-268-3429

VCII HOME ENTERTAINMENT, INC. *(VHE)*
13418 Wyandotte St.
North Hollywood, CA 91605
818-764-1777
800-350-1931
Fax: 818-764-0231

VESTRON VIDEO *(VES)*
c/o Live Home Video
15400 Sherman Way
PO Box 10124
Van Nuys, CA 91410-0124
818-988-5060

VIDCREST *(VDC)*
PO Box 69642
Los Angeles, CA 90069
213-650-7310
Fax: 213-654-4810

VIDEO ACTION *(VDA)*
708 W. 1st St.
Los Angeles, CA 90012
213-687-8262
800-422-2241
Fax: 213-687-8425

VIDEO ARTISTS INTERNATIONAL, INC. *(VAI)*
158 Linwood Plaza, Ste. 301
Fort Lee, NJ 07024
201-944-0099
800-477-7146
Fax: 201-947-8850

VIDEO BIBLE LIBRARY, INC. *(VBL)*
Box 17515
Portland, OR 97217
503-892-7707
Fax: 503-254-8318

THE VIDEO CATALOG *(TVC)*
PO Box 64428
Saint Paul, MN 55164-0428
612-659-4312
800-733-6656
Fax: 612-659-4320

VIDEO CITY PRODUCTIONS *(VCD)*
4266 Broadway
Oakland, CA 94611
510-428-0202
800-847-8400
Fax: 510-654-7802

VIDEO COLLECTIBLES *(BFS)*
350 Newkirk Rd.
Richmond Hill, ON, Canada
L4C 3G7
905-884-1433
800-387-5758

VIDEO COMMUNICATIONS, INC. (VCI) *(VCI)*
6535 E. Skelley Dr.
Tulsa, OK 74145
918-622-6460
800-331-4077
Fax: 918-665-6256

VIDEO CONNECTION *(VCN)*
3123 W. Sylvania Ave.
Toledo, OH 43613
419-472-7727
800-365-0449

VIDEO DIMENSIONS *(VDM)*
322 8th Ave., 4th Fl.
New York, NY 10011
212-929-6135

VIDEO FRANCE *(FRA)*
4822 St. Elmo Ave.
Bethesda, MD 20814
301-654-2224
Fax: 301-229-0621

VIDEO GEMS *(GEM)*
12228 Venice Blvd., No. 504
Los Angeles, CA 90066

VIDEO PLACEMENT INTERNATIONAL *(VPL)*
240 E. 27th St., Ste. 81
New York, NY 10016
212-696-9207

VIDEO RAILS *(VRL)*
PO Box 80001
San Diego, CA 92138
619-581-6226
800-262-2776
Fax: 619-581-0131

VIDEO RESOURCES *(VRS)*
220 W. 71st St.
New York, NY 10023
212-724-7055
Fax: 212-595-0189

VIDEO SEARCH OF MIAMI *(VSM)*
PO Box 161917
Miami, FL 33116
305-387-6807

VIDEO TREASURES *(VTR)*
500 Kirts Blvd.
Troy, MI 48084
810-362-9660
800-786-8777
Fax: 810-362-4454

VIDEO VIDE *(VDE)*
1376 Soquel Ave.
Santa Cruz, CA 95062
408-427-2282

VIDEO VISA *(VVC)*
12901 Coral Tree Pl.
Los Angeles, CA 90066
310-827-7222

VIDEO YESTERYEAR *(VYY)*
Box C
Sandy Hook, CT 06482
203-426-2574
800-243-0987
Fax: 203-797-0819

VIDEOGRAF *(VGR)*
144 W. 27th St.
New York, NY 10001
212-242-7871

VIDMARK ENTERTAINMENT *(VMK)*
2644 30th St.
Santa Monica, CA 90405-3009
310-314-2000

VIP VIDEO *(VIP)*
c/o JEF Films
Film House
143 Hickory Hill Circle
Osterville, MA 02655-1322
508-428-7198

VISION VIDEO/GATEWAY FILMS *(GFV)*
2030 Wentz Church Rd.
Box 540
Worcester, PA 19490-0540
610-584-1893
800-523-0226
Fax: 610-584-4610

VOYAGER COMPANY *(VYG)*
1 Bridge St.
Irvington, NY 10533-1543

WADE WILLIAMS PRODUCTIONS, INC. *(MWP)*
9840 Wornall Rd.
Kansas City, MO 64114-3907
816-241-6684
Fax: 816-941-7055

WALT DISNEY HOME VIDEO *(DIS)*
500 S. Buena Vista St.
Burbank, CA 91521

818-562-3560

WARNER/ELEKTRA/ ATLANTIC (WEA) CORPORATION *(WEA)*
9451 LBJ Fwy., Ste. 107
Dallas, TX 75243
214-234-6200

WARNER HOME VIDEO, INC. *(WAR)*
4000 Warner Blvd.
Burbank, CA 91522
818-954-6000

WARNER REPRISE VIDEO *(WRV)*
3300 Warner Blvd.
Burbank, CA 91505-4694
818-846-9090
Fax: 818-953-3329

WARREN MILLER ENTERTAINMENT *(WME)*
505 Pier Ave.
Hermosa Beach, CA 90254
310-376-2494

WATER BEARER FILMS *(WBF)*
205 West End Ave., Ste. 24H
New York, NY 10023
212-580-8185
800-551-8304
Fax: 212-787-5455

WAXWORKS/VIDEOWORKS, INC. *(WAX)*
325 E. 3rd St.
Owensboro, KY 42303
502-926-0008
800-825-8558
Fax: 502-685-0563

WESTERN FILM & VIDEO, INC. *(WFV)*
30941 Agoura Rd., Ste. 302
Westlake Village, CA 91361
818-889-7350

WESTERN L.A. FILM PRODUCTIONS, INC. *(WLA)*
7425 Clinton St.
Los Angeles, CA 90036-5703

WHITE STAR *(WST)*
121 Hwy. 36
West Long Branch, NJ 07764
908-229-2343
800-458-5887
Fax: 908-229-0066

WHOLE TOON CATALOGUE *(WTA)*
PO Box 369
Issaquah, WA 98027-0369
206-391-8747
Fax: 206-391-9064

WISHING WELL DISTRIBUTING *(WSH)*
PO Box 1008
Silver Lake, WI 53170
414-889-8501
800-888-9355
Fax: 414-889-8591

WNET/THIRTEEN NON-BROADCAST *(WNE)*
356 W. 58th St.
New York, NY 10019
212-560-3045

WOLFE VIDEO *(WLF)*
PO Box 64
New Almaden, CA 95042
408-268-6782

WOMBAT FILM AND VIDEO *(WOM)*
1560 Sherman Ave., Ste. 100
Evanston, IL 60201
708-328-6700
800-323-9084
Fax: 708-328-6706

WOOD KNAPP & COMPANY, INC. *(WKV)*
Knapp Press
5900 Wilshire Blvd.

Los Angeles, CA 90036
213-965-3500
800-521-2666
Fax: 213-930-2742

**WORLD ARTISTS HOME
VIDEO** *(WAC)*
135 N. Detroit St.
PO Box 36788
Los Angeles, CA 90036
213-933-7057
800-821-1205
Fax: 213-933-2356

**WORLD VIDEO ENTERPRISES,
INC.** *(WVE)*
150 Executive Park Blvd., No.
1600
San Francisco, CA 94134-3303
415-468-6218
Fax: 415-468-1381

**WORLDVISION HOME VIDEO,
INC.** *(WOV)*
1700 Broadwaay
New York, NY 10019-5905
212-261-2700

XENON *(XVC)*
211 Arizona Ave.
Santa Monica, CA 90401
800-468-1913

YANKEE-ORIOLE COMPANY
(YOC)
398 Ogden Ave.
Jersey City, NJ 07307-1115
201-656-4348

**CANADIAN
DISTRIBUTORS**

**ASTRAL HOME
ENTERTAINMENT**
Toronto Branch
1185 Caledonia Rd.
North York, ON M6A 2X1
416-785-5580

**M.V. VIDEO
DISTRIBUTIONS INC.**
1955 Wylie St.
Vancouver, BC V5Y 3N7
604-874-2000

**PRESIDENTIAL VIDEO
DISTRIBUTOR**
101,6036 3rd St., SW
Calgary, AB T2H 0H9

**SHANNOCK
CORPORATION**
Mississauga Distribution
Centre
5582 Ambler Dr.
Mississauga, ON L4W 2K9
905-602-5922

**TED WHELBOURN
DISTRIBUTING LTD.**
347 Pido Rd., Unit 5
Peterborough, ON K9J 6X7
705-745-6200

TEVICA
614 Place Trans Canada
Longueuil, PQ J4G 1P1
514-651-4100

VIDEO L.P.S. INC.
8114 Trans Canadienne Rd.
Ville St. Laurent, PQ
H4S 1M5
514-956-7323

VIDEO ONE CANADA
Toronto Branch
105 Scarsdale Rd.
Don Mills, ON M3B 2R2
416-447-9600

VIDEO SOLUTIONS
54 Chamberlain Ave.,
Ste. 101
Ottawa, ON K1S 1V9
613-594-0024